Cookbook Writers

James Beard
Marian Burros
Julia Child
Craig Claiborne
M. F. K. Fisher
Pierre Franey
Jean D. Hewitt
Graham Kerr
Margaret Romagnoli
Raymond Sokolov
Jane Stern
. . . and more

Dance Critics

William Como
Arlene Croce
Edwin Denby
John Gruen
Deborah Jowitt
Marcia B. Siegel
Tobi Tobias
. . . and more

Dancers

George Balanchine
Christopher d'Amboise
Katherine Dunham
Margot Fonteyn
Jose Greco
Natalia Makarova
Peter Martins
Valery Panov
. . . and more

Diet Specialists

Stuart Berger
Jane Brody
Martin Katahn
Jean Nidetch
Nathan Pritikin
Lendon Smith
Herman Tarnower
Roy L. Walford
. . . and more

Drama Critics

Clive Barnes
Eric Bentley
Robert S. Brustein
Martin Esslin
Brendan Gill
Walter Kerr
Joseph Wood Krutch

John Simon
Stark Young
. . . and more

Economists

Alfred D. Chandler, Jr.
Martin S. Feldstein
Milton Friedman
John Kenneth Galbraith
L. St. Clare Grondona
Robert L. Heilbroner
Ursula Kathleen Hicks
Jean Monnet
Felix G. Rohatyn
Walt W. Rostow
Herbert A. Simon
Herbert Stein
James Tobin
Friedrich August von
  Hayek
Barbara Ward
. . . and more

Educators

J. D. Bernal
Joseph A. Califano, Jr.
Marva Collins
Robert Lyons Danly
Thomas Flanagan
Ronald Gross
Theodore M. Hesburgh
Jonathan Kozol
A. S. Neill
Neil Postman
Anne Rogovin
Richard B. Sewall
Norman R. Shapiro
Ellease Southerland
Daniel H. Yergin
. . . and more

Entrepreneurs

Walt Disney
Malcolm Forbes
J. Paul Getty
Mary Kay
Ray Kroc
Dan Lundberg
Ted Turner
. . . and more

Essayists

G. K. Chesterton
Bryan F. Griffin

Edward Hoagland
John McPhee
Joseph Mitchell
George Orwell
Calvin Trillin
E. B. White
Ellen Willis
Tom Wolfe
. . . and more

Explorers

Edwin E. Aldrin, Jr.
Michael Collins
Jacques Yves Cousteau
Thor Heyerdahl
Edmund Hillary
John Hunt
Peter Matthiessen
Alfred M. Worden
. . . and more

Feminists

Simone de Beauvoir
Susan Brownmiller
Andrea Dworkin
Barbara Ehrenreich
Betty Friedan
Germaine Greer
Kate Millet
Gloria Steinem
Rebecca West
. . . and more

Film Critics

Andre Bazin
Vincent Canby
Judith Crist
Roger Ebert
Pauline Kael
Stanley Kauffmann
Leonard Maltin
Harry Medved
Michael Medved
Rex Reed
Andrew Sarris
Richard Schickel
Gene Siskel
. . . and more

Folklorists

Roger Abrahams
Dan Ben-Amos

Jan Harold Brunvand
Richard M. Dorson
Da
Al
Ba

M
Al
Sti
. . . and more

Gossip Columnists

Rona Barrett
Sheilah Graham
Hedda Hopper
Diana McLellan
Louella Parsons
Liz Smith
. . . and more

Historians

Herbert Aptheker
Jacques Benoist-Mechin
Anthony Blunt (art)
Daniel J. Boorstin
Fernand Braudel
Arthur Bryant
Bruce Catton
Kenneth Clark
Alessandra Comini
Merle Eugene Curti
Robert Darnton
David Brion Davis
Bern Dibner
Ariel Durant
Will Durant
Antonia Fraser
Peter Gay
Eugene D. Genovese
Richard Hofstadter
Hugh Honour (art)
Paul Horgan
Rhys L. Isaac
Emmanuel Le Roy
  Ladurie
Golo Mann
Thomas K. McCraw
Edmund Morgan
Thomas Pakenham
Erwin Panofsky (art)
Meyer Schapiro
Arthur Schlesinger, Jr.
C. V. Wedgwood
Theodore H. White
C. Vann Woodward
Louis Booker Wright
. . . and more

Horror and

Writers

ey
r Blatty
ce

Richard Burton
Matheson
Ruth Shick
  Montgomery
Anne Rice
John Sand
John Saul
Jess Stearn
Whitley Strieber
. . . and more

Humorists

Roy Blount
Erma Bombeck
Art Buchwald
Peter De Vries
Ogden Nash
S. J. Perelman
James Stevenson
James Thurber
. . . and more

Jazz Artists

Louis Armstrong
Duke Ellington
Dizzy Gillespie
Benny Goodman
Charles Mingus
Art Taylor
Mel Torme
. . . and more

Lexicographers

Tana de Gamez
J. L. Dillard
Stuart Flexner
E. Arsenio Manuel
Leo C. Rosten
. . . and more

Literary Critics

M. H. Abrams
R. P. Blackmur

Literary Critics
(continued)

Harold Bloom
Cleanth Brooks
Malcolm Cowley
Jonathan Culler
David Daiches
Richard Ellmann
William Empson
Leslie A. Fiedler
Northrop Frye
Helen Gardner
Alfred Kazin
Frank Kermode
H. D. F. Kitto
F. R. Leavis
Q. D. Leavis
Percy Lubbock
John Crowe Ransom
I. A. Richards
Christopher Ricks
Lionel Trilling
Helen Hennessy Vendler
Rene Wellek
Edmund Wilson
W. K. Wimsatt, Jr.
. . . and more

Magazine and Journal Editors

Uri Avnery
Gray Davis Boone
Charles Brasch
Helen Gurley Brown
Tina Brown
Norman Cousins
Martha Foley
Tatyana Mamonova
Victoria Ocampo
William S. Schlamm
William Shawn
Jann S. Wenner
. . . and more

Media Figures and Celebrities

Alan Alda
Lauren Bacall

Joseph Bologna
Anita Bryant
George Burns
Rosalyn Carter
Dick Cavett
Charlie Chaplin
Sammy Davis, Jr.
Ruby Dee
Phil Donahue
Mike Douglas
Buddy Ebsen
Redd Foxx
Arlene Francis
David Frost
Chief Dan George
Julie Harris
Sterling Hayden
Charlton Heston
Bob Hope
Ann Jackson
Lady Bird Johnson
Angela Lansbury
Norman Lear
Shirley MacLaine
Mary Martin
Groucho Marx
Ed McMahon
Bette Midler
Roger George Moore
Nancy Davis Reagan
Robert Redford
Mister Rogers
Roy Rogers
Rosalind Russell
Margaret Truman
Liv Ullmann
Diana Dalziel Vreeland
John Wayne
Shelley Winters
. . . and more

Memoirists and Autobiographers

Quentin Crisp
Betty Ford
Helen Hanff
Billy Hayes
Nadezhda Mandelstam
Joyce Maynard

Veljko Micunovic
Richard Rodriguez
. . . and more

Military Scientists

Dwight D. Eisenhower
Basil Henry Liddell Hart
Daniel Lang
S. L. A. Marshall
John Cecil Masterman
C. Northcote Parkinson
William C. Westmoreland
Elmo Russell Zumwalt, Jr.
. . . and more

Music Critics

Lester Bangs
Robert Christgau
Jonathan Cott
Gary Giddins
Nat Hentoff
Greil Marcus
Dave Marsh
Hugues Panassie
Harold Schonberg
Nat Shapiro
Ritchie Yorke
. . . and more

Mystery and Suspense Writers

Edward S. Aarons
Eric Ambler
Gwendoline Williams Butler
James M. Cain
Agatha Christie
Mary Higgins Clark
Len Deighton
Ian Fleming
Ken Follet
Dick Francis

Sarah Gainham
Erle Stanley Gardner
John Edmund Gardner
Martha Grimes
Dashiell Hammett
Joseph Hansen
P. D. James
H. R. F. Keating
Harry Kemelman
William X. Kienzle
Emma Lathen
John le Carre
Elmore Leonard
Robert Ludlum
John D. MacDonald
Kenneth Millar
Margaret Millar
L. A. Morse
Bernard Newman
Ruth Rendell
Dorothy L. Sayers
Trevanian
. . . and more

Naturalists and Environmentalists

Cleveland Amory
Wendell Berry
Rachel Carson
Barry Commoner
Claude L. Fly
Euell Gibbons
Anne W. Simon
Victor Wolfgang Von Hagen
. . . and more

Novelists

Chinua Achebe
Alice Adams
Vassily Aksyonov
Jorge Amado
Kingsley Amis
Ivo Andric
Harriet Simpson Arnow
Miguel Angel Asturias
Margaret Atwood
James Baldwin

Djuna Barnes
John Barth
Donald Barthelme
Saul Bellow
Heinrich Boell
Jorge Luis Borges
Elizabeth Bowen
Anita Brookner
Pearl S. Buck
Anthony Burgess
Erskine Caldwell
Italo Calvino
Truman Capote
Angela Carter
Adolfo Bioy Casares
Louis-Ferdinand Celine
John Cheever
Julio Cortazar
Robertson Davies
Joan Didion
Isak Dinesen
Jose Donoso
John Dos Passos
Sergei Dovlatov
Margaret Drabble
Marguerite Duras
Lawrence Durrell
Ralph Ellison
William Faulkner
E. M. Forster
John Fowles
Ladislav Fuks
William Gaddis
Gabriel Garcia Marquez
Jean Genet
Jose Maria Gironella
Janusz Glowacki
Gail Godwin
William Golding
Nadine Gordimer
Mary Gordon
Guenter Grass
Shirley Ann Grau
Graham Greene
Jiri Grusa
Knut Hamsun
Peter Handke
Elizabeth Hardwick
John Hawkes
Joseph Heller
Ernest Hemingway

(continued on back endsheets)

**Check the *Contemporary Authors* Cumulative Index
to Locate Sketches on These and Thousands of Other Authors**

Contemporary Authors®

ISSN 0010-7468

Contemporary Authors®

A Bio-Bibliographical Guide to
Current Writers in Fiction, General Nonfiction,
Poetry, Journalism, Drama, Motion Pictures,
Television, and Other Fields

SUSAN M. TROSKY
Editor

LOUISE MOONEY
POLLY A. VEDDER
Associate Editors

LES STONE
Senior Writer

volume 126

Gale Research Inc. • Book Tower • Detroit, Michigan 48226

STAFF

Susan M. Trosky, *Editor, Original Volumes*

Louise Mooney and Polly A. Vedder, *Associate Editors*

Les Stone, *Senior Writer*

Christa Brelin and Elizabeth Thomas, *Senior Assistant Editors*

Thomas Kozikowski, Nancy Pear, and Joanne M. Peters, *Assistant Editors and Writers*

Barbara K. Carlisle, Emily J. Compagnone, Carol Lynn DeKane, Janice E. Drane,
and James F. Kamp, *Assistant Editors*

Arlene True, *Sketchwriter*

Peter Benjaminson, Jean W. Ross, and Walter W. Ross, *Interviewers*

Barbara A. Cicchetti, Michael Patrick Gillespie, and Curtis Skinner, *Contributing Editors*

James G. Lesniak, *Index Coordinator*

Linda Metzger, *Senior Editor, Contemporary Authors*

Mary Rose Bonk, *Research Supervisor*
Alysa I. Hunton, *Research Coordinator*
Jane Cousins-Clegg, *Assistant Research Coordinator*
Reginald A. Carlton, Andrew Guy Malonis, and Norma Sawaya, *Senior Research Assistants*
John P. Dodt, Shirley Gates, Clare Kinsman, Sharon McGilvray,
and Tracey Head Turbett, *Research Assistants*

Computerized photocomposition by
Typographics, Incorporated
Kansas City, Missouri

Contents

Authors and Media People
Featured in This Volume vii

Preface ix

Volume Update Chart xiii

Author Listings 1

Cumulative Index 485

Authors and Media People
Featured in This Volume

Warren Beatty (American film actor, producer, director, and screenwriter)—Considered one of Hollywood's most talented actors, Beatty has won accolades for his screenwriting credits, which include "Shampoo," "Heaven Can Wait," and the award-winning 1981 film "Reds" about Communist journalist John Reed.

Charlotte Bunch (American writer)—Since the 1960s Bunch has been an active feminist, gaining recognition as a representative of lesbian causes. She co-authored such works as *Lesbianism and the Women's Movement* and *International Feminism: Networking Against Female Sexual Slavery.*

Helene Cixous (French academician and author)—Founder of the feminist studies center at the University of Paris, Cixous is known for her personal, technically demanding fiction, including the novels *Inside* and *Angst,* and her feminist tract *The Newly Born Woman.*

Ethan and Joel Coen (American screenwriters and filmmakers)—Ethan Coen, as writer and producer, and his brother Joel, as writer and director, have earned substantial critical acclaim for their offbeat and eccentric film collaborations "Blood Simple" and "Raising Arizona."

John Darnton (American journalist)—As a foreign correspondent for the *New York Times,* Darnton received both a George Polk Award and a Pulitzer Prize in 1982 for his reports from Poland during the years of Solidarity activities. He earlier earned a George Polk Award for his correspondence from Africa. (Sketch contains interview.)

Elspeth Davie (Scottish fiction writer)—Davie is the author of fanciful stories and novels depicting bizarre, often macabre elements in otherwise ordinary lives. In 1978 she won the Katherine Mansfield Prize for her short story "The High Tide Talker." Her books include the story collection *The Night of the Funny Hats* and the novel *Climbers on a Stair.*

Zelda Fitzgerald (American author who died in 1948)—The wife of celebrated American writer F. Scott Fitzgerald, Zelda Fitzgerald was a peripheral figure in literary circles during the jazz age of the 1920s. She produced a novel, *Save Me the Waltz,* and collaborated with her husband on several short stories.

Elizabeth Frank (American biographer)—Frank's *Louise Bogan: A Portrait* won the 1986 Pulitzer Prize for biography. The book was commended in *Ms.* for its "sensitive narrative" and hailed in *New Republic* as a "finely shaded and impassioned" study of Bogan, an American poet and literary critic. (Sketch contains interview.)

Erich Fried (Austrian-born British author)—An acclaimed poet, novelist, and translator, Fried is particularly well known for his poetry, distinguished by its bluntness and concision. Among his works in English translation are the poetry collections *On Pain of Seeing* and *One Hundred Poems Without a Country.*

F. Gonzalez-Crussi (Mexican-born American physician and writer)—Gonzalez-Crussi has been praised for his scientific writings that neither confuse the layman nor patronize the specialist. His works include the essay collections *Notes of an Anatomist, Three Forms of Sudden Death,* and *On the Nature of Things Erotic.* (Sketch contains interview.)

Alasdair Gray (Scottish artist and author)—One of Scotland's most prominent contemporary novelists, Gray has written about the political concerns of many Scottish nationalists—alienation, powerlessness, and decline—in such works as *Lanark* and *1982 Janine.* A free-lance painter, Gray has also written plays for the stage, television, and radio. (Sketch contains interview.)

Brit Hume (American journalist and author)—Hume is a Washington correspondent and anchor for ABC-TV's "World News Tonight—The Weekend Report." He exposed union wrongdoings in his book *Death and the Mines: Rebellion and Murder in the United Mine Workers* and wrote the autobiographical *Inside Story.* (Sketch contains interview.)

Dan Jenkins (American author)—A longtime writer for *Sports Illustrated* and now *Playboy,* Jenkins is known for his irreverent and insightful perspectives on golf and football. Among his publications are the novels *Semi-Tough, Dead Solid Perfect,* and *Life Its Ownself: The Semi-Tougher Adventures of Billy Clyde Puckett and Them.*

James Joyce (Irish writer who died in 1941)—Joyce was probably the greatest experimentalist to write in English in the twentieth century, and his fiction reveals an acute awareness of linguistics, philosophy, mythology, and everyday life in Dublin. His principal works are the short story collection *Dubliners* and the novels *A Portrait of the Artist as a Young Man, Ulysses,* and *Finnegans Wake.*

Franz Kafka (Czechoslovakian author who died in 1924)—Considered one of the literary masters of the twentieth century, Kafka created a nightmarish world of alienation and frustration with his meticulous German prose. Among his best known works are the stories "In the Penal Colony" and "The Metamorphosis" and the novels *Amerika, The Trial,* and *The Castle.*

Perri Klass (American pediatrician and author)—Klass has published short stories, including two O. Henry Award-winners, and articles in various periodicals. Among her books are the novel *Recombinations* and the nonfiction *A Not Entirely Benign Procedure* about life in medical school. (Sketch contains interview.)

Larry Kramer (American film producer and writer)—Kramer is probably best known for his writings about homosexual life, such as the novel *Faggots* and the play "The Normal Heart." Kramer's screen adaptation of D. H. Lawrence's novel *Women in Love* was nominated for a 1970 Academy Award.

Shirley Mezvinsky Lauro (American playwright)—Lauro's "Open Admissions," a gripping indictment of discrimination in education, sparked controversy when it played Off-Broadway in the early 1980s. Her other works include "I Don't Know Where You're Coming From at All" and "The Coal Diamond." (Sketch contains interview.)

Joseph Lelyveld (American journalist)—A longtime correspondent for the *New York Times,* Lelyveld won a Pulitzer Prize in 1986 for *Move Your Shadow,* his account of life for both blacks and whites within South Africa's racist apartheid system. (Sketch contains interview.)

Walter A. McDougall (American historian)—McDougall wrote the Pulitzer Prize-winning *...the Heavens and the Earth,* a study of the American-Soviet space exploration race. In the *New York Times Book Review,* Alex Roland called McDougall's book "the most comprehensive history of space activity written to date." (Sketch contains interview.)

Henry Moore (British sculptor who died in 1986)—Regarded as one of the twentieth century's most radical artists, Moore produced abstract and distorted works that seemed to emphasize empty space as much as form and shape. He articulated his artistic concerns in *Henry Moore on Sculpture* and *Henry Moore: My Ideas, Inspiration, and Life as an Artist.*

Eilean Ni Chuilleanain (Irish poet)—Ni Chuilleanain is known for her vivid, mysterious poems ranging in subject from the loneliness of the mythological hero Odysseus to the plight of the contemporary poet. Among her verse collections are *Acts and Monuments, Site of Ambush,* and *The Rose-Geranium.*

Michael Parks (American journalist)—Parks, a correspondent for the *Los Angeles Times* since 1980, earned a Pulitzer Prize in 1986 for his coverage of social unrest stemming from racist policies in South Africa. He has also reported from China, the Soviet Union, and the Middle East.

Louis Poirier (French writer)—Under the pseudonym Julien Gracq, Poirier has written about the stability of nature and its dominance over humanity. His works, several of which have been translated into English, include the novels *Castle of Argol, The Opposing Shore,* and *Balcony in the Forest.*

Padgett Powell (American author)—Hailed as one of the most promising writers to appear from the American South in the 1980s, Powell earned great praise for his first novel, *Edisto,* about an adolescent boy's maturation in rural South Carolina. Powell's other writings include the book *A Woman Named Drown.*

John Rockwell (American writer)—Rockwell, a prominent critic of contemporary music for the *New York Times,* wrote the well-received *All American Music: Composition in the Late Twentieth Century* and *Sinatra: An American Classic.* (Sketch contains interview.)

Brian Ross (American broadcast journalist)—Ross has earned many awards, including two Emmys, for his work with NBC-TV and its affiliates. Among the controversial figures he has covered are fugitive financier Robert Vesco, labor leader Jackie Presser, and political candidate and convicted felon Lyndon LaRouche. (Sketch contains interview.)

Edmond Rostand (French playwright who died in 1918)—Rostand wrote the renowned play "Cyrano de Bergerac," in which a long-nosed swordsman and poet conceals his love for Roxane and helps another man win her heart. With its action, humor, and sentiment, "Cyrano" is a favorite throughout the world.

Norman Rush (American author)—Praised in *American Book Review* as "an extraordinary writer," Rush penned the prize-winning short story collection *Whites,* which depicts life among Caucasians in Africa's Botswana. (Sketch contains interview.)

Lisa St. Aubin de Teran (British author)—St. Aubin de Teran is considered one of England's important contemporary writers. She has published collections of poems and short stories, as well as such acclaimed novels as *The Long Way Home* and *The Tiger,* both of which concern bizarre events in South America. (Sketch contains interview.)

Robert J. Sternberg (American psychologist)—Named one of "America's Top 100 Young Scientists" by *Science Digest* in 1984, Sternberg is known for his expertise in the field of human intelligence. His writings include *Beyond IQ, Intelligence Applied,* and *The Psychologist's Companion.* (Sketch contains interview.)

Paul-Loup Sulitzer (French businessman and novelist)—Prominent entrepreneur Sulitzer drew on his business acumen to write the trilogy *Money, Cash!,* and *Fortune.* In another novel, *The Green King,* he tells the story of a Holocaust survivor who becomes the world's wealthiest man.

Margarethe von Trotta (West German filmmaker)—A key figure in the revitalized German film industry, von Trotta is acclaimed for her politico-feminist films such as "Sisters," the award-winning "Marianne and Juliane," and "Sheer Madness," all of which explore women's relationships.

George W. S. Trow (American writer)—Trow is a staff writer for *New Yorker* who has received substantial critical attention for his witty plays, essays, and fiction. His works include the novel *The City in the Mist,* the play "Elizabeth Dead," and the short story collection *Bullies.*

Preface

The nearly 900 entries in *Contemporary Authors* (*CA*), Volume 126, bring to more than 92,000 the number of authors now represented in the *Contemporary Authors* series. *CA* includes nontechnical writers in all genres—fiction, nonfiction, poetry, drama, etc.—whose books are issued by commercial, risk publishers or by university presses. Authors of books published only by known vanity or author-subsidized firms are ordinarily not included. Since native language and nationality have no bearing on inclusion in *CA*, authors who write in languages other than English are included in *CA* if their works have been published in the United States or translated into English.

Although *CA* focuses primarily on authors of published books, the series also encompasses prominent persons in communications: newspaper and television reporters and correspondents, columnists, newspaper and magazine editors, photojournalists, syndicated cartoonists, screenwriters, television scriptwriters, and other media people.

Starting with Volume 104, the editors of *CA* began to broaden the series' scope to encompass authors deceased since 1900 whose works are still of interest to today's readers. (Previously, *CA* covered only living writers and authors deceased 1960 or later.) Since the great poets, novelists, short story writers, and playwrights of the early twentieth century are popular writers for study in today's high school and college curriculums, and since their writings continue to be analyzed by literary critics, these writers are in many ways as contemporary as the authors *CA* has regularly featured.

Each volume of *CA*, therefore, includes a limited number of entries on authors deceased before 1960. Providing commentary about writers' lives and literary achievements, these sketches in addition offer both a historical and contemporary review of the authors' critical reputations. The entries in this volume on Zelda Fitzgerald, James Joyce, Franz Kafka, and Edmond Rostand reflect the variety of early twentieth-century authors to be featured in future *CA* volumes.

No charge or obligation is attached to a *CA* listing. Authors are included in the series solely on the basis of the above criteria and their interest to *CA* users.

Compilation Methods

The editors make every effort to secure information directly from the authors through questionnaires and personal correspondence. If writers of special interest to *CA* users are deceased or fail to reply to requests for information, material is gathered from other reliable sources. Biographical dictionaries are checked (a task made easier through the use of Gale's *Biography and Genealogy Master Index* and other volumes in the "Gale Biographical Index Series"), as are bibliographical sources such as *Cumulative Book Index* and *The National Union Catalog*. Published interviews, feature stories, and book reviews are examined, and often material is supplied by the authors' publishers. All sketches, whether prepared from questionnaires or through extensive research, are sent to the biographees for review prior to publication. Sketches on recently deceased authors are sent to family members, agents, etc., if possible, for a similar review.

Format

CA is designed to present, clearly and concisely, biographical and bibliographical information in three kinds of listings: sketches, brief entries, and obituary notices. The series' easy-to-use format ensures that a reader needing specific information can quickly focus on the pertinent portion of an entry. Sketches, for instance, contain individual paragraphs with rubrics identifying addresses, memberships, and awards and honors. Furthermore, in sketch sections headed "Writings," the title of each book, play, and other published or unpublished work appears on a separate line, clearly distinguishing one title from another. This same convenient bibliographical presentation is featured in the "Biographical/Critical Sources" sections of sketches and brief entries and in the "Obituaries and Other Sources" sections of obituary notices where individual book and periodical titles are also listed on separate lines. *CA* readers can therefore quickly scan these often-lengthy bibliographies to find the titles they need.

Informative Sidelights

Numerous *CA* sketches contain sidelights, which provide personal dimensions to the listings, supply information about the critical reception the authors' works have received, or both. Some authors presented in Volume 126 worked closely with *CA* editors to develop interesting, incisive sidelights. *Boston Globe* fashion editor Julie Hatfield, for example, tells *CA* that "if a dramatic photo and good fashion writing can draw a young person into the newspaper who would not otherwise be interested in reading, so much the better for this television age in which so few youngsters have been turned on to the written word and its joys."

CA's editors also compile sidelights when authors and media people of particular interest do not supply sidelights material or when demand for information about the critical reception accorded their writings is especially high. Volume 126, for instance, profiles Larry Kramer, a screenwriter, playwright, and novelist whose writings explore the day-to-day struggles of homosexual males. His subject matter, writes a *CA* editor, has "stirred strong reactions from audiences and critics whose adjectives describing Kramer's works range from 'sensitive' and 'intelligent,' 'seedy,' and 'grotesque,' to 'angry,' 'gripping,' and 'forceful.' " Also featured in this volume is Scottish novelist and short story writer Elspeth Davie, whose widely praised works, according to a *CA* editor, "often depict the profound influence that seemingly insignificant events have on a person's development."

We hope these sketches, as well as others with sidelights compiled by *CA*'s editors, provide informative and enjoyable reading.

Exclusive Interviews

CA provides exclusive, primary information on certain writers in the form of interviews. Prepared specifically for *CA,* the never-before-published conversations presented in the section of the sketch headed "*CA* Interview" give users the opportunity to learn the authors' thoughts, in depth, about their craft. Subjects chosen for interviews are, the editors feel, authors who hold special interest for *CA*'s readers.

Writers and journalists in this volume whose sketches include interviews are John Darnton, Elizabeth Frank, F. Gonzalez-Crussi, Alasdair Gray, Brit Hume, Perri Klass, Shirley Mezvinsky Lauro, Joseph Lelyveld, Walter A. McDougall, John Rockwell, Brian Ross, Norman Rush, Lisa St. Aubin de Teran, and Robert J. Sternberg.

Brief Entries

CA also includes short entries on authors of current popular appeal or literary stature whose full-length sketches are not yet ready for publication. Identified by the heading "Brief Entry," these short listings highlight the authors' careers and writings and often include a few sources where additional information may be found.

Obituary Notices Make *CA* Timely and Comprehensive

To be as timely and comprehensive as possible, *CA* publishes obituary notices on deceased authors within the scope of the series. These notices provide date and place of birth and death, highlight the author's career and writings, and list other sources where additional biographical information and obituaries may be found. To distinguish them from full-length sketches, obituaries are identified with the heading "Obituary Notice."

CA includes obituary notices for writers who already have full-length entries in earlier *CA* volumes—57 percent of the obituary notices in this volume are for such authors—as well as for authors who do not yet have sketches in the series. Deceased writers of special interest currently represented only by obituary notices will be scheduled for full-length sketch treatment in forthcoming *CA* volumes.

Contemporary Authors New Revision Series

A major change in the preparation of *CA* revision volumes began with the first volume of *Contemporary Authors New Revision Series*. No longer are all of the sketches in a given *CA* volume updated and published together as a revision volume. Instead, entries from a number of volumes are assessed, and only those sketches requiring *significant change* are revised and published in a *New Revision Series* volume. This enables us to provide *CA* users with updated information about active writers on a more timely basis and avoids printing entries in which there has been little or no change. As always, the most recent *CA* cumulative index continues to be the user's guide to the location of an individual author's revised listing.

Contemporary Authors Autobiography Series

Designed to complement the information in *CA* original and revision volumes, the *Contemporary Authors Autobiography Series* provides autobiographical essays written by important current authors. Each volume contains twenty to thirty specially commissioned autobiographies and is illustrated with numerous personal photographs supplied by the authors. The range of contemporary writers describing their lives and interests in the *Autobiography Series* encompasses authors such as Dannie Abse, Vance Bourjaily, Doris Grumbach, Elizabeth Forsythe Hailey, Marge Piercy, Frederik Pohl, Alan Sillitoe, William Stafford, Diane Wakoski, and Elie Wiesel. Though the information presented in the autobiographies is as varied and unique as the authors, common topics of discussion include their motivations for writing, the people and experiences that shaped their careers, the rewards they derive from their work, and their impressions of the current literary scene.

Autobiographies included in the *Contemporary Authors Autobiography Series* can be located through both the *CA* cumulative index and the *Contemporary Authors Autobiography Series* cumulative index, which lists not only personal names but also titles of works, geographical names, subjects, and schools of writing.

Contemporary Authors Bibliographical Series

The *Contemporary Authors Bibliographical Series* is a comprehensive survey of writings by and about the most important authors since World War II in the United States and abroad. Each volume concentrates on a specific genre and nationality and features approximately ten major writers. Volume 1, for instance, covers the American novelists James Baldwin, John Barth, Saul Bellow, John Cheever, Joseph Heller, Norman Mailer, Bernard Malamud, Carson McCullers, John Updike, and Eudora Welty. *Bibliographical Series* entries consist of three parts: a primary bibliography that lists works written by the author, a secondary bibliography that lists works about the author, and an analytical bibliographical essay that thoroughly discusses the merits and deficiencies of major critical and scholarly works. Complementing the information in other *CA* volumes, the *Bibliographical Series* is a new key to finding and evaluating information on the lives and writings of those authors who have attracted significant critical attention.

Each author's entry in the *Contemporary Authors Bibliographical Series* can be located through both the *CA* cumulative index and, beginning with Volume 2, the *Contemporary Authors Bibliographical Series* cumulative author index. A cumulative index to the critics discussed in the bibliographical essays also appears in each *Bibliographical Series* volume.

CA Numbering System

Occasionally questions arise about the *CA* numbering system. Despite numbers like "97-100" and "126," the entire *CA* series consists of only 91 physical volumes with the publication of Volume 126. The following information notes changes in the numbering system, as well as in cover design, to help users better understand the organization of the entire *CA* series.

CA First Revisions	• 1-4R through 41-44R (11 books) *Cover:* Brown with black and gold trim. There will be no further *First Revisions* because revised entries are now being handled exclusively through the more efficient *New Revision Series* mentioned below.
CA Original Volumes	• 45-48 through 97-100 (14 books) *Cover:* Brown with black and gold trim. • 101 through 126 (26 books) *Cover:* Blue and black with orange bands. The same as previous *CA* original volumes but with a new, simplified numbering system and new cover design.
CA New Revision Series	• *CANR*-1 through *CANR*-26 (26 books) *Cover:* Blue and black with green bands. Includes only sketches requiring extensive change; **sketches are taken from any previously published *CA* volume.**

***CA* Permanent Series**	• *CAP*-1 and *CAP*-2 (2 books) *Cover:* Brown with red and gold trim. There will be no further *Permanent Series* volumes because revised entries are now being handled exclusively through the more efficient *New Revision Series* mentioned above.
***CA* Autobiography Series**	• *CAAS*-1 through *CAAS*-9 (9 books) *Cover:* Blue and black with pink and purple bands. Presents specially commissioned autobiographies by leading contemporary writers.
***CA* Bibliographical Series**	• *CABS*-1 through *CABS*-3 (3 books) *Cover:* Blue and black with blue bands. Provides comprehensive bibliographical information on published works by and about major modern authors.

Retaining *CA* Volumes

As new volumes in the series are published, users often ask which *CA* volumes, if any, can be discarded. The Volume Update Chart on page xiii is designed to assist users in keeping their collections as complete as possible. All volumes in the left column of the chart should be retained to have the most complete, up-to-date coverage; volumes in the right column can be discarded if the appropriate replacements are held.

Cumulative Index Should Always Be Consulted

The key to locating an individual author's listing is the *CA* cumulative index bound into the back of alternate original volumes (and available separately as an offprint). Since the *CA* cumulative index provides access to *all* entries in the *CA* series, the latest cumulative index should always be consulted to find the specific volume containing an author's original or most recently revised sketch.

For the convenience of *CA* users, the *CA* cumulative index also includes references to all entries in these related Gale literary series: *Authors in the News, Children's Literature Review, Concise Dictionary of American Literary Biography, Contemporary Literary Criticism, Dictionary of Literary Biography, Short Story Criticism, Something About the Author, Something About the Author Autobiography Series, Twentieth-Century Literary Criticism,* and *Yesterday's Authors of Books for Children.*

Acknowledgments

The editors wish to thank Judith S. Baughman for her assistance with copy editing.

Suggestions Are Welcome

The editors welcome comments and suggestions from users on any aspects of the *CA* series. If readers would like to suggest authors whose entries should appear in future volumes of the series, they are cordially invited to write: The Editors, *Contemporary Authors,* Gale Research Inc., Book Tower, Detroit, MI 48226-1822; or call toll-free at 1-800-521-0707.

Volume Update Chart

IF YOU HAVE:	YOU MAY DISCARD:
1-4 First Revision (1967)	1 (1962) 2 (1963) 3 (1963) 4 (1963)
5-8 First Revision (1969)	5-6 (1963) 7-8 (1963)
Both 9-12 First Revision (1974) AND *Contemporary Authors Permanent Series,* Volume 1 (1975)	9-10 (1964) 11-12 (1965)
Both 13-16 First Revision (1975) AND *Contemporary Authors Permanent Series,* Volumes 1 and 2 (1975, 1978)	13-14 (1965) 15-16 (1966)
Both 17-20 First Revision (1976) AND *Contemporary Authors Permanent Series,* Volumes 1 and 2 (1975, 1978)	17-18 (1967) 19-20 (1968)
Both 21-24 First Revision (1977) AND *Contemporary Authors Permanent Series,* Volumes 1 and 2 (1975, 1978)	21-22 (1969) 23-24 (1970)
Both 25-28 First Revision (1977) AND *Contemporary Authors Permanent Series,* Volume 2 (1978)	25-28 (1971)
Both 29-32 First Revision (1978) AND *Contemporary Authors Permanent Series,* Volume 2 (1978)	29-32 (1972)
Both 33-36 First Revision (1978) AND *Contemporary Authors Permanent Series,* Volume 2 (1978)	33-36 (1973)
37-40 First Revision (1979)	37-40 (1973)
41-44 First Revision (1979)	41-44 (1974)
45-48 (1974) 49-52 (1975) ↓ ↓ 126 (1989)	NONE: These volumes will not be superseded by corresponding revised volumes. Individual entries from these and all other volumes appearing in the left column of this chart will be revised and included in the *New Revision Series.*
Volumes in the *Contemporary Authors New Revision Series*	NONE: The *New Revision Series* does not replace any single volume of *CA.* All volumes appearing in the left column of this chart must be retained to have information on all authors in the series.

Contemporary Authors

Indicates that a listing has been compiled from secondary sources believed to be reliable but has not been personally verified for this edition by the author sketched.

AARON, David (Laurence)   1938-

PERSONAL: Born August 21, 1938, in California; married Chloe Wellingham (a cultural television programming director); children: Tim. *Education:* Occidental College, B.A., 1960; Princeton University, M.A., 1962. *Politics:* Democrat.

ADDRESSES: Home—2525 Larkin, Penthouse North, San Francisco, Calif. 94109. *Agent:* The Lantz Office, 888 Seventh Ave., New York, N.Y. 10106.

CAREER: U.S. Foreign Service, diplomatic postings in South America, Washington, D.C., and the U.S. mission to the North Atlantic Treaty Organization in Paris, 1962-68; U.S. Arms Control and Disarmament Agency, Washington, D.C., served on the U.S. Delegation to the United Nations General Assembly, 1968, and on the U.S. Delegation to the first Strategic Arms Limitation Talks, 1969-72; National Security Council, Washington, D.C., senior member, 1972-74; U.S. Senate, Washington, D.C., task force director of Intelligence Committee, 1974-77; deputy national security adviser, 1977-81; Oppenheimer & Co. (investment banking firm), New York, N.Y., vice-president for mergers and acquisitions, beginning in 1981; president of D. L. Aaron & Co. (consulting firm); writer. Presidential emissary to Europe, Africa, and China, 1977-81; member of the board of directors of Oppenheimer International, beginning in 1981; director of Oppenheimer's mutual fund subsidiary.

WRITINGS:

State Scarlet (novel), Putnam, 1987.
Finance/Espionage (novel), Putnam, 1988.

Contributor of articles to periodicals and newspapers, including *Foreign Affairs, Foreign Policy,* the *New York Times,* and the *Los Angeles Times.*

WORK IN PROGRESS: A screenplay in collaboration with actor Paul Newman on scientists, ethics, and the defense program.

SIDELIGHTS: David Aaron, a diplomat turned author, drew upon his experience as a National Security Council adviser to write his first novel, a spy-thriller entitled *State Scarlet.* In the book, Aaron questions the U.S. Government's ability to handle a nuclear crisis when a weapon from its atomic stockpile falls into the wrong hands. The title, *State Scarlet,* refers to the stage of military alert in which the president's authority to initiate the use of nuclear weapons is diverted to the military.

Several critics have deemed Aaron's first novel a success. Rory Quirk, contributor to *Washington Post Book World,* called it "deftly plotted and thoroughly convincing." Douglas M. Hart, writing for the *Los Angeles Times Book Review,* commented that *State Scarlet* "is a well-crafted variation" on the popular doomsday theme.

When asked by Charles Trueheart of the *Washington Post* about a possible return to a career in Washington, Aaron replied, "I would love to have a small embassy in a country that was not endemically overrun by terrorists, where I could write in the morning and advance the national interest in the afternoon." Aaron has written a second novel, *Finance/Espionage,* based on his inside knowledge of Wall Street.

BIOGRAPHICAL/CRITICAL SOURCES:

PERIODICALS

Los Angeles Times, April 8, 1987.
Los Angeles Times Book Review, April 12, 1987.
Washington Post, April 5, 1987.
Washington Post Book World, May 10, 1987.

*   *   *

ABBOTT, Philip (R.)   1944-

PERSONAL: Born October 18, 1944, in Philadelphia, Pa.; married, 1967; children: two. *Education:* American University, B.A., 1966; Rutgers University, M.A., 1967, Ph.D., 1970.

ADDRESSES: Office—Department of Political Science, 856 MacKenzie Hall, Wayne State University, 5950 Cass Ave., Detroit, Mich. 48202.

CAREER: Wayne State University, Detroit, Mich., associate professor of political science, 1970—.

MEMBER: American Political Science Association.

AWARDS, HONORS: Fellow of Ford Foundation, 1972-73, and Earhart Foundation, 1977-78.

1

WRITINGS:

(Compiler with Michael P. Riccards) *Reflections in American Political Thought: Readings From Past and Present,* Chandler Publishing, 1973.
The Shotgun Behind the Door: Liberalism and the Problems of Political Obligation, University of Georgia Press, 1975.
Furious Fancies: American Political Thought in the Post-Liberal Era, Greenwood Press, 1980.
The Family on Trial: Special Relationships in Modern Political Thought, Pennsylvania State University Press, 1981.
(Editor with Michael B. Levy) *The Liberal Future in America: Essays in Renewal,* Greenwood Press, 1985.
States of Perfect Freedom: Autobiography and American Political Thought, University of Massachusetts Press, 1987.
Seeking Many Inventions: The Idea of Community in America, University of Tennessee Press, 1987.

BIOGRAPHICAL/CRITICAL SOURCES:

PERIODICALS

American Political Science Review, March, 1978.
Contemporary Sociology, May, 1986.
Virginia Quarterly Review, summer, 1976.*

*   *   *

ADAMS, Harold   1923-

PERSONAL: Born February 20, 1923, in Clark, S.D.; son of Lafayette Elihu (in sales) and Wilda (a homemaker; maiden name, Dickey) Adams; married Betty Skogsbergh, September 10, 1949 (divorced April 17, 1965); children: Wendy. *Education:* University of Minnesota, B.A., 1950.

ADDRESSES: Home—12916 Greenwood Rd., Minneapolis, Minn. 55343. *Agent*—Ivy Fischer Stone, Fifi Oscard Associates, Inc., 19 West 44th St., New York, N.Y. 10036.

CAREER: Better Business Bureau of Minneapolis, Minneapolis, Minn., assistant manager, 1956-65; Charities Review Council of Minnesota, Minneapolis, executive director, 1965-88; writer, 1981—. *Military service:* U.S. Army, 1943-46; became staff sergeant.

MEMBER: Author's Guild, Mystery Writers of America, National Society of Fund Raising Executives (honorary member), Minneapolis United Way Associates (secretary/treasurer, 1974-88).

WRITINGS:

Murder, Ace Books, 1981.
Paint the Town Red, Ace Books, 1982.
The Missing Moon, Ace Books, 1983.
The Naked Liar, Mysterious Press, 1985.
The Fourth Widow, Mysterious Press, 1986.
The Barbed Wire Noose, Mysterious Press, 1987.
When Rich Men Die, Doubleday, 1987.
The Man Who Met the Train, Mysterious Press, 1988.

WORK IN PROGRESS: A mystery novel for Mysterious Press entitled *Deep Enough to Kill;* another mystery, as yet untitled.

SIDELIGHTS: Harold Adams, author of eight mystery novels in as many years, is known for his stylistically sharp dialogue, complex characterizations, and wry humor.

Adams told *CA:* "I have been writing creatively in mornings between 5:00 and 7:00 for the past thirty years. After my retirement in February of 1988 from my post as executive

director of the Charities Review Council of Minnesota, I will be able to write full time. I plan to do some nonfiction about the world of charity in addition to continuing with mystery novels.

"I became a disciplined writer when I realized in middle age that nothing else I could do gave me true satisfaction. I became a published writer out of sheer persistence and application. The key for me was getting up so early no one else would bother me until I'd put in my hour or more every day. My advice to would-be writers is, don't ever say you'll write when you have the time. If you really want to write, you make the time. When asked how I sold my first book, I reply, 'It was easy; I just wrote the book and took ten years selling it. And between times wrote more books.' Three of my first books sold were rejected at least a dozen times each before acceptance of *Murder*.

"I believe there are an unconscionable number of capable writers in the mystery field and it makes the competition murder. I don't resent that, however, because I enjoy reading them."

AVOCATIONAL INTERESTS: "My interests include travel to England, Europe, Mexico, Puerto Rico, Colombia, and the Virgin Islands. I'm a compulsive letter writer, journal keeper, and a very amateur photographer."

BIOGRAPHICAL/CRITICAL SOURCES:

PERIODICALS

Minneapolis Star and Tribune, January 26, 1988.
Minneapolis-St. Paul Magazine, September, 1987.
Vinyl Arts, September, 1987.

*   *   *

ADAMS, Jay Edward   1929-

PERSONAL: Born January 30, 1929, in Baltimore, Md.; son of Joseph Edward and Anita Louise (Barnsley) Adams; married Betty Jane Whitlock, June 23, 1952; children: Holly, Todd, Clay, Heather. *Education:* Johns Hopkins University, A.B., 1952; Reformed Episcopal Seminary, B.D., 1952; Temple University, S.T.M., 1958; University of Missouri—Columbia, Ph.D., 1963.

ADDRESSES: Office—Department of Practical Theology, Westminster Theological Seminary, P.O. Box 2215, Escandido, Calif. 92025.

CAREER: Ordained United Presbyterian minister, 1952; pastor of Presbyterian church in Thomas, Pa., 1952-56, and Reformed Presbyterian church in Haddonfield, N.J., 1957-58; Reformed Presbyterian Church, St. Louis, Mo., secretary of home missions, 1958-59; Westminster Seminary, Philadelphia, Pa., professor of practical theology, 1963-76, visiting professor, 1976-88; Westminster Theological Seminary, Escandido, Calif., director of advanced studies, 1982—. Staley Lecturer at Cedarville College, 1975; lecturer at various colleges, including Grove City College and Southern College. Pastor of Orthodox Presbyterian church in Westfield, N.J., 1963-66; counselor and dean of Institute for Pastoral Studies at Christian Counseling and Educational Foundation, Philadelphia, 1975-88.

WRITINGS:

The Time Is at Hand, Presbyterian and Reformed, 1970.
Competent to Counsel: Introduction to Nouthetic Counseling, Baker Book, 1970.

Public Speech: A Textbook for Use in the Classroom or Study, Presbyterian and Reformed, 1971.

Christian Living in the Home, Baker Book, 1972.

The Big Umbrella: And Other Essays on Christian Counseling, Baker Book, 1972.

The Christian Counselor's Manual: The Practice of Nouthetic Counseling, Baker Book, 1973.

The Christian Counselor's Casebook, Presbyterian and Reformed, 1974.

Shepherding God's Flock: A Preacher's Handbook on Pastoral Ministry, Counseling, and Leadership, Baker Book, Volume I: *The Pastoral Life*, 1975, Volume II: *Pastoral Counseling*, 1975, Volume III: *Pastoral Leadership*, 1976, reprinted in one volume, 1979.

The Use of the Scriptures in Counseling, Baker Book, 1975.

Your Place in the Counseling Revolution, Baker Book, 1975.

Coping With Counseling Crises: First Aid for Christian Counselors, Baker Book, 1976.

The Meaning and Mode of Baptism, Presbyterian and Reformed, 1976.

Studies in Preaching, Volume I: *Sense Appeal in the Sermons of Charles Haddon Spurgeon*, Volume II: *Audience Adaptations in the Sermons and Speeches of Paul*, Volume III: *The Homiletical Innovations of Andrew W. Blackwood*, Baker Book, 1976.

What to Do About Worry, Baker Book, 1976.

The Christian Counselor's New Testament: A New Translation in Everyday English With Notations, Marginal References, and Supplemental Helps, Baker Book, 1977.

Godliness Through Discipline, Baker Book, 1977.

How to Overcome Evil, Presbyterian and Reformed, 1977.

What About Nouthetic Counseling? A Question and Answer Book With Historical Help and Hope for the Christian Counselor, Baker Book, 1977.

Four Weeks With God and Your Neighbor, Presbyterian and Reformed, 1978.

Lectures on Counseling (includes *The Student Pastor-Counselor Today, Your Place in the Counseling Revolution, Counseling and the Sovereignty of God, Coping With Counseling Crises*, and *The Use of the Scriptures in Counseling*), Baker Book, 1978.

God Has the Answer to Your Problems, Evangelical Press and Services, 1979.

Matters of Concern to Christian Counselors: A Potpourri of Principles and Practices, Baker Book, 1979.

More Than Redemption: A Theology of Christian Counseling, Baker Book, 1979, reprinted as *A Theology of Christian Counseling: More Than Redemption*, Ministry Resource Library, 1986.

(Translator) *The New Testament in Everyday English*, Baker Book, 1979.

Prayers for Troubled Times, Baker Book, 1979.

Trust and Obey: A Practical Commentary on First Peter, Baker Book, 1979.

Update on Christian Counseling, Baker Book, 1980.

Marriage, Divorce, and Remarriage in the Bible, Baker Book, 1980.

Helps for Counselors: A Mini-Manual for Christian Counseling, Baker Book, 1980.

Ready to Restore, Baker Book, 1981.

The Language of Counseling, Presbyterian and Reformed, 1981.

Counseling and the Five Points of Calvinism, Presbyterian and Reformed, 1981.

The Christian Counselor's Wordbook: A Primer of Nouthetic Counseling, Presbyterian and Reformed, 1981.

What to Do on Thursday: A Layman's Guide to the Practical Use of the Scriptures, Presbyterian and Reformed, 1982.

Truth Apparent: Essays on Biblical Preaching, Presbyterian and Reformed, 1982.

Preaching With Purpose: A Comprehensive Textbook on Biblical Preaching, Presbyterian and Reformed, 1982, reprinted as *Preaching With Purpose: The Urgent Task of Homiletics*, 1986.

Insight and Creativity in Christian Counseling: A Study of the Usual and the Unique, Presbyterian and Reformed, 1982, reprinted as *Insight and Creativity in Christian Counseling: An Antidote to Rigid and Mechanical Approaches*, Zondervan, 1986.

How to Handle Trouble God's Way, Presbyterian and Reformed, 1982.

Back to the Blackboard: Design for a Biblical Christian School; A Book for Parents, Teachers, and Administrators, Presbyterian and Reformed, 1982.

Solving Marriage Problems: Biblical Solutions for Christian Counselors, Presbyterian and Reformed, 1983.

Grist From Adam's Mill: Suggestions for Living the Christian Life, Presbyterian and Reformed, 1983.

The Biblical View of Self-Esteem, Self-Love, and Self-Image, Harvest House, 1986.

Essays on Biblical Preaching (includes *Truth Apparent* and *Preaching to the Heart*), Ministry Resources Library, 1986.

Essays on Counseling, Ministry Resources Library, 1986.

Handbook of Church Discipline, Ministry Resources Library, 1986.

How to Help People Change: The Four-Step Biblical Process, Ministry Resources Library, 1986.

Sermon Analysis, Accent Books, 1986.

A Call to Discernment, Harvest House, 1987.

A Thirst for Whatever, Victor Books, 1987.

Sibling Rivalry in the Church, Accent Books, 1988.

Also author of *Realized Millennialism: A Study in Biblical Eschatology*, 1959; *You Can Conquer Depression*, Baker Book; *You Can Defeat Anger*, Baker Book; *You Can Kick the Drug Habit*, Baker Book; *You Can Overcome Fear*, Baker Book; *You Can Stop Worrying*, Baker Book; and *You Can Sweeten a Sour Marriage*, Baker Book.

Editor of *Journal of Pastoral Practice*, 1977-82.

*   *   *

ADAMS, Samuel A.   1933(?)-1988

OBITUARY NOTICE: Born c. 1933 in Bridgeport, Conn.; died of a heart attack, October 10, 1988, in Strafford, Vt. Intelligence analyst and author. A Central Intelligence Agency analyst from 1963 to 1973 specializing for four years in Southeast Asia, Adams is best known for his theory that U.S. Army officials deliberately underestimated the strength of enemy troops during the Vietnam War, in order to make the American effort there appear successful. Adams related his ideas in the famed espionage trial of Daniel Ellsberg and Anthony J. Russo, in an article for *Harper's* magazine, and as a consultant to the 1982 CBS-TV documentary "The Uncounted Enemy: A Vietnam Deception," which implicated Army General William C. Westmoreland in the deceptive troop estimate conspiracy. Adams was one of several defendants in a libel case brought by Westmoreland that was settled out of court in 1985. At the time of his death, Adams was making final revisions on a book, *Who the Hell Are We Fighting Out There?*

OBITUARIES AND OTHER SOURCES:

PERIODICALS

Chicago Tribune, October 11, 1988.
Washington Post, October 11, 1988.

*   *   *

ADDAMS, Charles (Samuel) 1912-1988

OBITUARY NOTICE—See index for *CA* sketch: Born January 7, 1912, in Westfield, N.J.; died after a heart attack, September 29, 1988, in New York, N.Y. Cartoonist. Addams is best remembered for his macabre cartoons portraying monsters, ghosts, witches, and other ghouls in everyday settings, and for inspiring the spooky 1960s television comedy series "The Addams Family." Addams's cartoons appeared regularly in the *New Yorker* and other magazines beginning in the 1930s, and selections have been displayed at the Metropolitan Museum of Art, the Museum of the City of New York, and the Rhode Island School of Design. Addams's work is featured in several collections, including *Drawn and Quartered, Homebodies, Nightcrawlers, The Charles Addams Mother Goose, Charles Addams Favorite Haunts,* and *Creature Comforts: A New Collection of Classic Cartoons.*

OBITUARIES AND OTHER SOURCES:

BOOKS

Who's Who in American Art, 17th edition, Bowker, 1986.

PERIODICALS

Chicago Tribune, September 30, 1988.
Los Angeles Times, September 30, 1988.
New York Times, September 30, 1988, October 5, 1988.
Times (London), October 3, 1988.

*   *   *

ADELMAN, M(orris) A(lbert) 1917-

PERSONAL: Born May 31, 1917, in New York, N.Y.; son of David and Leah (Albert) Adelman; married Millicent Linsen, November 23, 1949; children: Lawrence, Barbara. *Education:* City College (now of the City University of New York), B.S.S., 1938; Harvard University, Ph.D., 1948.

ADDRESSES: Office—Department of Economics, E40-429, Massachusetts Institute of Technology, Cambridge, Mass. 02139.

CAREER: Economist for War Production Board, 1941-42, and Federal Reserve Board, 1946; Massachusetts Institute of Technology, Cambridge, assistant professor, 1948-53, associate professor, 1954-61, professor of economics, 1961—. *Military service:* U.S. Naval Reserve, active duty, 1942-45; served in the Pacific; became lieutenant.

MEMBER: American Economic Association, American Academy of Arts and Sciences.

AWARDS, HONORS: Fellow of Social Science Research Council, 1947-48; Ford Foundation fellow, 1962-63.

WRITINGS:

A & P: A Study in Price-Cost Behavior and Public Policy, Harvard University Press, 1959.
The Supply and Price of Natural Gas, Basil Blackwell, 1962.
(With Paul G. Bradley and Charles A. Norman) *Alaskan Oil: Cost and Supply,* Praeger, 1971.

The World Petroleum Market, Johns Hopkins University Press, 1972.
(Contributor) James M. Griffin and David J. Teece, editors, *OPEC Behavior and World Oil Prices,* Allen & Unwin, 1982.
(With John C. Houston, Gordon M. Kaufman, and Martin B. Zimmerman) *Energy Resources in an Uncertain Future: Coal, Gas, Oil, and Uranium Supply Forecasting,* Ballinger, 1982.

Contributor to economic and law journals.

WORK IN PROGRESS: A history of the world oil market from 1970 to the present, completion expected in 1989.

BIOGRAPHICAL/CRITICAL SOURCES:

BOOKS

Gordon, Richard L., Henry D. Jacoby, and Martin B. Zimmerman, editors, *Energy—Markets and Regulation: Essays in Honor of M. A. Adelman,* MIT Press, 1987.

PERIODICALS

Economist, May 13, 1972, June 2, 1973.

*   *   *

ADKINS, Patrick H. 1948-

PERSONAL: Born January 9, 1948, in New Orleans, La.; son of Albert Blackburn (a jeweler) and Grace (a secretary; maiden name, Viering) Adkins; married Dixie Wagoner, December 28, 1971; children: Alisha Beth, Alexander Lee, Adam Henry. *Education:* Attended University of New Orleans, 1966-70.

ADDRESSES: Home—Gretna, La. *Agent*—Ralph M. Vicinanza Ltd., 432 Park Ave. S., Suite 1205, New York, N.Y. 10016.

CAREER: P.D.A. Enterprises, New Orleans, La., mail order specialty bookseller, 1971-82; Midland, Inc., New Orleans, purchasing and inventory manager, 1983—. Security guard, 1976-83; editor and publisher of small press science fiction and fantasy books, 1977-80.

WRITINGS:

Lord of the Crooked Paths (novel), Ace Books, 1987.
Master of the Fearful Depths (novel), Ace Books, 1989.

Work represented in anthologies, including *Chrysalis 9*, edited by Roy Torgeson, Doubleday, 1981.

WORK IN PROGRESS: The Feasting Time, an "alternate world science fiction novel"; further volumes reconstructing the Ages of the Titans and the Olympians; research on Homeric Greece, Friedrich Nietzsche, and the radio comedy of the 1940s.

SIDELIGHTS: Patrick H. Adkins told *CA:* "*Lord of the Crooked Paths* and *Master of the Fearful Depths* began as a single manuscript. Over a period of three years, I was unable to find a firm that would issue the work in its original, complete length, and so was forced to divide the story into two separate books.

"These two volumes represent my initial attempt (in what I hope will be an ongoing cycle of stories) to apply the techniques of the old historical romance to the mythology of Greece: to produce accurately rendered mythology, conveyed through exciting tales of suspense, action, and amour. In an age when classical learning is rare indeed, I'll be satisfied if these books inspire a few readers to sample the cornucopia of Greek literature.

"My fiction, whether inspired by the ancients or not, belongs to the literature of the exotic. I'm interested in unusual characters in strange places and harrowing circumstances. If a smidgen of psychological or philosophical insight can be gained along the way (by author or reader), so much the better.

"I am an antiquarian by nature, instinctively reaching for the dusty tome instead of the bright, new paperback. My avocations include book collecting, particularly works of popular fiction from the nineteenth and early twentieth centuries. I collect recordings of radio shows from the 1930s through the 1950s, and, quite recently, I've developed an interest in the less technical aspects of computers."

*   *   *

ALDERSON, Michael (Rowland)   1931-1988

OBITUARY NOTICE: Born June 8, 1931, in Eastbourne, East Sussex, England; died July 1, 1988. Physician, medical statistician, educator, editor, and author. Alderson was noted for his investigation into the causes and treatments of cancer. A former professor of information science at Southampton University, he began examining statistical trends in the incidence of cancer in 1975 after becoming a professor of epidemiology at the Royal Marsden Hospital's Institute for Cancer Research. Later, as chief medical statistician at the Office of Population Censuses and Surveys, Alderson vastly improved the methods for measuring the health of England's population. He wrote a number of medical texts, including *An Introduction to Epidemiology* and *Occupational Cancer,* and edited *Prevention of Cancer,* a book in a series on malignant disease management.

OBITUARIES AND OTHER SOURCES:

BOOKS

Who's Who, 140th edition, St. Martin's, 1988.
The Writers Directory: 1988-1990, St. James Press, 1988.

PERIODICALS

Times (London), July 9, 1988.

*   *   *

ALLARDT, Linda   1926-

PERSONAL: Born June 9, 1926, in Brecksville, Ohio; daughter of Ernst W. (an engineer) and Lucile (a florist; maiden name, Clark) Allardt; married George A. Gallasch (an engineer), April 20, 1957 (died in 1987); children: Robert G., Margaret E. *Education:* Alfred University, B.A., 1948; Middlebury College, M.A., 1955; University of Rochester, Ph.D., 1977.

ADDRESSES: Home—2 Ann Lynn Rd., Pittsford, N.Y. 14534.

CAREER: University of Rochester, Rochester, N.Y., assistant professor of English, 1976-87.

MEMBER: Associated Writing Programs.

AWARDS, HONORS: Borestone Mountain Poetry Award, 1969, for "Singers," and 1975, for "The Names of the Survivors"; Hackney Literary Awards in Poetry from Birmingham Festival of Arts, 1973, for "In Recurrent Dream," 1974, for "Looking for Springs," 1980, for "Half a Recipe," and 1981, for "Fog"; Lillian Fairchild Award from the University of Rochester and

Elliston Special Distinction Citation from the George Elliston Poetry Foundation of the University of Cincinnati, both in 1980 for *The Names of the Survivors.*

WRITINGS:

(Editor) *The Journals and Miscellaneous Notebooks of Ralph Waldo Emerson,* Harvard University Press, Volume XII: *1835-1862,* 1976, Volume XV (with David W. Hill and Ruth H. Bennett): *1860-1866,* 1982.
The Names of the Survivors (poems), Ithaca House, 1979.
Seeing for You (poems), State Street Press, 1981.
(Editor with R. H. Orth, A. J. Von Frank, and D. W. Hill) *The Poetry Notebooks of Ralph Waldo Emerson,* University of Missouri Press, 1986.

Work represented in anthologies, including *Best Poems of 1975.* Contributor of poems to magazines, including *Poetry Northwest, Poetry Now, Hiram Poetry Review, Negative Capability,* and *Cincinnati Review.* Associate editor of State Street Press, 1982—.

WORK IN PROGRESS: Another book of poems, tentitively titled *Voice-Over.*

SIDELIGHTS: Linda Allardt told *CA:* "My poetry draws on my training in science and nature for its metaphor, but I don't consider myself a 'nature poet'—the poems are about people and have a strong sense of place."

*   *   *

ALLEN, Brian   1952-

PERSONAL: Born October 3, 1952, in Dublin, Ireland; son of Herbert Francis and Mary Patricia (Buckley) Allen; married Katina Michael, May 12, 1978; children: Andrew John, Nicholas Francis. *Education:* University of East Anglia, B.A., 1974; Courtauld Institute of Art, London, M.A., 1975, Ph.D., 1984.

ADDRESSES: Office—Paul Mellon Centre for Studies in British Art, 20 Bloomsbury Sq., London WC1A 2NP, England.

CAREER: Paul Mellon Centre for Studies in British Art, London, England, assistant director and librarian, 1977-87, deputy director of studies, 1987—.

MEMBER: Royal Society of Arts (fellow), Association of Art Historians, Association of Architectural Historians, Walpole Society, Georgian Group.

WRITINGS:

Francis Hayman, Yale University Press, 1987.

Contributor to history and art journals. Editor of *Journal of the Walpole Society,* 1977-85.

WORK IN PROGRESS: Editing the correspondence of Sir Joshua Reynolds, publication by Yale University Press expected c. 1991; a catalog of the works of William Hogarth, publication by Yale University Press expected c. 1994.

*   *   *

ALLEN, Oliver E.   1922-

PERSONAL: Born June 29, 1922, in Cambridge, Mass.; son of Frederick Lewis and Dorothy (a housewife; maiden name, Cobb) Allen; married Deborah Hutchison (a college administrator), May 8, 1948; children: Stephen, Frederick, Henry, Letitia, Jennie. *Education:* Harvard University, A.B., 1943. *Politics:* Democrat.

ADDRESSES: Home and office—42 Hudson St., New York, N.Y. 10013. *Agent*— Emilie Jacobson, Curtis Brown Ltd., 10 Astor Pl., New York, N.Y. 10003.

CAREER: Life, New York City, correspondent, writer, and editor, 1947-60; Time-Life Books, New York City, editor and planning director, 1960-76; free-lance writer, 1976—. *Military service:* U.S. Army, 1943-46; became first lieutenant.

WRITINGS:

(With James Underwood Crockett) *Wildflower Gardening,* Time-Life, 1977.
(With Crockett) *Decorating With Plants,* Time-Life, 1978.
Pruning and Grafting, Time-Life, 1978.
The Windjammers, Time-Life, 1978.
Shade Gardens, Time-Life, 1979.
Winter Gardens, Time-Life, 1979.
The Pacific Navigators, Time-Life, 1980.
Building Sound Bones and Muscles, Time-Life, 1981.
The Airline Builders, Time-Life, 1981.
Secrets of a Good Digestion, Time-Life, 1982.
The Atmosphere, Time-Life, 1983.
The Vegetable Gardener's Journal, Stewart, Tabori & Chang, 1985.
Gardening With the New, Small Plants: The Complete Guide to Growing Dwarf and Miniature Shrubs, Flowers, Trees, and Vegetables, Houghton, 1987.

WORK IN PROGRESS: A history of New York City, publication by Atheneum expected in 1990.

*   *   *

ALLEN, Pamela   1934-

PERSONAL: Born April 3, 1934, in Devonport, Auckland, New Zealand; daughter of William Ewart (a surveyor) and Esma (a homemaker; maiden name, Griffith) Griffiths; married William Robert Allen (head of an art school), December 12, 1964; children: Ben, Ruth. *Education:* Elam School of Art (now Auckland University), diploma of fine art, 1954; attended Auckland Teachers Training College, 1955-56.

ADDRESSES: Agent—Curtis Brown Ltd., 27 Union St., Paddington, Sydney, New South Wales 2021, Australia.

CAREER: Pio Pio District High School, New Zealand, art teacher, 1956; Rangitoto College, Auckland, New Zealand, art teacher, 1957-58, 1960-64; writer and illustrator, 1979—.

MEMBER: Australian Society of Authors, Children's Book Council of Australia.

AWARDS, HONORS: Picture Book of the Year commendation from Children's Book Council of Australia, and New South Wales Premier's Literary Award in children's book category, both 1981, and Book Design Award commendation from Australian Book Publishers Association, 1980-81, all for *Mr. Archimedes' Bath;* Children's Book of the Year Award from Children's Book Council of Australia, and New South Wales Premier's Literary Award in children's book category, both 1983, and honor diploma for illustration from International Board on Books for Young People, 1984, all for *Who Sank the Boat?;* Children's Book of the Year Award from Children's Book Council of Australia, 1984, for *Bertie and the Bear.*

WRITINGS:

SELF-ILLUSTRATED CHILDREN'S BOOKS

Mr. Archimedes' Bath, Lothrop, 1980.
Who Sank the Boat?, Thomas Nelson [Australia], 1982, Coward, 1983.
Bertie and the Bear (Junior Literary Guild selection), Thomas Nelson, 1983, Coward, 1984.
A Lion in the Night, Thomas Nelson, 1985, Putnam, 1986.
Simon Said, Thomas Nelson, 1985.
Watch Me, Thomas Nelson, 1985.
Herbert and Harry, Thomas Nelson, 1986.
Mr. McGee, Thomas Nelson, 1987.
Hidden Treasure, Putnam, 1987.
Fancy That!, Thomas Nelson, 1988.
Simon Did, Thomas Nelson, 1989.
Watch Me Now, Thomas Nelson, 1989.

Contributor to *School.*

ILLUSTRATOR

Jan Farr, *Mummy, Do Monsters Clean Their Teeth?* Heinemann [New Zealand], 1975.
Farr, *Mummy, How Cold Is a Witch's Nose?* Heinemann, 1976.
T. E. Wilson, *Three Cheers for McGinty,* Heinemann, 1976.
Wilson, *McGinty Goes to School,* Heinemann, 1976.
Wilson, *McGinty the Ghost,* Heinemann, 1976.
Wilson, *McGinty in Space,* Heinemann, 1976.
Farr, *Big Sloppy Dinosaur Socks,* Heinemann, 1977.
Farr, *Mummy, Are Monsters Too Big for Their Boots?* Heinemann, 1977.
N. L. Ray, *The Pow Toe,* Collins [Australia], 1979.
Sally Fitzpatrick, *A Tall Story,* Angus & Robertson [Australia], 1981.

WORK IN PROGRESS: I Wish I Had a Pirate Suit, Watch Me Now, and *Simon Did,* all for Penguin Books.

SIDELIGHTS: Pamela Allen told *CA:* "One does not go to school to learn to make a picture book. When I made the conscious decision to write and illustrate a picture book, I spent some time thinking about the order of my priorities. I put as my first priority the child. The child I had in mind was young and not yet able to read—a preschool child.

"Through my picture books I wanted to communicate with this young child. Young children gather meaning from many clues, language being only one possibility. I use pictures, sound, drama, and language. All of this only comes alive when it is shared. There is the adult, the child, and the book: the fun they have together is what it is all about."

BIOGRAPHICAL/CRITICAL SOURCES:

PERIODICALS

Reading Time, Number 5, 1983.
Review, December, 1984.

*   *   *

ALMQUIST, Gregg (Andrew)   1948-

PERSONAL: Born December 1, 1948, in Minneapolis, Minn.; son of Andrew Earl (a salesman) and Margaret (a teacher and housekeeper; maiden name, Yost) Almquist. *Education:* University of Minnesota—Twin Cities, B.A., c. 1971. *Politics:* "A sort of conservative liberal." *Religion:* "Indifferent agnostic."

ADDRESSES: Home—New York, N.Y. *Agent*—International Creative Management, 40 West 57th St., New York, N.Y. 10019.

CAREER: Actor and writer.

MEMBER: Players Club.

WRITINGS:

"Minnesota Gothic" (play), broadcast by KTCA-TV (Minneapolis, Minn.), 1969.
"The Eve of Saint Venus" (play; adapted from Anthony Burgess's novel), produced in Stratford, Conn., at American Shakespeare Theatre, July, 1973.
"The Duke" (one-act play), produced in Minneapolis at Walker Art Center, 1974.
Beast Rising (novel), Pocket Books, 1987.

WORK IN PROGRESS: A novel, tentatively titled *Infant Blood,* for Pocket Books; two other books.

SIDELIGHTS: Gregg Almquist told *CA:* "I have been involved with several careers. I started out in my early twenties as an actor, and for fifteen years I worked primarily in regional theaters around the country, doing classics, all the while writing plays, about half of which were produced by small theaters. In 1985, working a lot but never with any money, I began acting in commercials. Shortly after that I appeared on Broadway in the Tony Award-winning play 'I'm Not Rappaport.' My first novel, *Beast Rising,* was bought by Pocket Books. Subsequently I spent a good deal more time focusing on writing, while still doing some commercial work and appearing in the films *Heartburn* and *Radio Days* in very small roles. In the fall of 1988, I will be appearing on the television series 'Tattingers' as the bartender, Norris.

"An editor, in turning down a manuscript I had submitted, asked me why on earth, being an actor, I would pursue a second career even more difficult in which to make a living. I have been unable to answer the question satisfactorily, though I feel very fortunate indeed."

*   *   *

ALVAREZ, Luis W(alter)   1911-1988

OBITUARY NOTICE: Born June 13, 1911, in San Francisco, Calif.; died of cancer, August 31, 1988, in Berkeley, Calif. Physicist, educator, and author. A professor of physics at the Berkeley campus of the University of California for most of his five-decade-long career, Alvarez was a member of the team that developed the first atomic bomb. He received the Nobel Prize for physics in 1968 for his use of liquid hydrogen bubble chambers to detect new subatomic particles. Alvarez's diverse contributions to science also included the development of a radar-based approach system to aid in aircraft landings under limited visibility conditions, and a controversial theory on the extinction of dinosaurs. In addition, he assisted the Warren Commission in the investigation of the 1963 assassination of President John F. Kennedy. Alvarez was the author of an autobiography titled *Alvarez: Adventures of a Physicist.*

OBITUARIES AND OTHER SOURCES:

BOOKS

The International Who's Who, 51st edition, Europa, 1987.
Who's Who in America, 45th edition, Marquis, 1988.

PERIODICALS

Chicago Tribune, September 2, 1988.

Globe and Mail (Toronto), September 3, 1988.
New York Times, September 2, 1988.
Washington Post, September 3, 1988.

*   *   *

ALVERSON, Marianne   1942-

PERSONAL: Born October 11, 1942, in Shanghai, China; daughter of Otto Hans (a businessman) and Karin (a research analyst; maiden name, Lohman) Melchior; married Hoyt Sutliff Alverson (a professor of anthropology), June 6, 1964; children: Keith, Brian. *Education:* George Washington University, B.A., 1964.

ADDRESSES: Home—Freeman Rd., Hanover, N.H. 03755. *Office*—Asian Studies Program, Dartmouth College, Hanover, N.H. 03755.

CAREER: Dartmouth College, Hanover, N.H., administrative assistant in Asian Studies Program, 1980—. Volunteer for Head Start Association, 1968-70; public speaker on the women of Botswana, 1986—.

AWARDS, HONORS: Under African Sun was named to *Choice* magazine's Outstanding Academic List for 1988.

WRITINGS:

Under African Sun, University of Chicago Press, 1987.

Editor of *Orient Express,* a newsletter of Dartmouth College Asian Studies Program, 1981-86.

WORK IN PROGRESS: With Deborah Hodges, *The Civil War Letters of Watson Alverson,* a compilation of recently discovered Civil War correspondence between a Union soldier on the battlefield and his family in northern New York; a collection of short stories.

SIDELIGHTS: Under African Sun is an account of Marianne Alverson's settling in a Tswana tribe in Botswana, Africa, with her husband and two children. According to Adam Kuper, in the *Times Literary Supplement,* the book is "the first description by a woman of life with an anthropologist and his tribe." Using material from a journal she kept during her stay, Alverson describes her daily life with the Tswana—learning their customs and language, and teaching the local children in a small school—and its effects on her family relationships.

Alverson told *CA:* "While previous works on Africa (such as *Out of Africa, Under the Midday Sun,* and *West With the Night*) celebrate a certain nostalgia for the colonial past because the voices are those of expatriates, I felt compelled to write a book in which the expatriate narrator lives in an African society under its rules, with its language and its people. The voices in *Under African Sun* are those of the Batswana themselves."

AVOCATIONAL INTERESTS: Ceramics, classical music (violin), singing in the Handel Society Chorus.

BIOGRAPHICAL/CRITICAL SOURCES:

PERIODICALS

Chicago Tribune Book World, May 3, 1987.
Globe and Mail (Toronto), August 15, 1987.
Kansas City Star, September 13, 1987.
Man, March, 1988.
Richmond News Leader, July 8, 1987.
Times Literary Supplement, October 16, 1987.

ANDERSON, Leone Castell 1923-

PERSONAL: Born August 12, 1923, in Los Angeles, Calif.; daughter of Carl A. (a painter) and Elsa (a housewife; maiden name, Berggren) Castell; married J. Eric Anderson (an architect), August 17, 1946; children: Jon Scott, James Eric, Paul Lawrence. *Education:* Attended Austin Academy of Music, 1942-43.

ADDRESSES: Home—13115 East Chelsea Rd., Stockton, Ill. 61085. *Office*—Lee's Booklover's, 127 South Main, Stockton, Ill. 61085.

CAREER: Russell Seeds Advertising, Chicago, Ill., copywriter, 1944-46; free-lance writer, 1946-69; Elmhurst Public Library, Elmhurst, Ill., member of library staff, 1969-74; free-lance writer, 1974—. Owner and operator of Lee's Booklover's, 1979—.

MEMBER: Society of Children's Book Writers (Midwest representative, 1981-87), Children's Reading Round Table, Authors Guild, Off-Campus Writer's Workshop.

WRITINGS:

FOR CHILDREN

It's O.K. to Cry, Child's World, 1979.
The Wonderful Shrinking Shirt, Albert Whitman, 1983.
Learning About Towers and Dungeons, Childrens Press, 1983.
The Good-By Day, Golden Press, 1984, reprinted as *Moving Day,* 1987.
My Friend Next Door, Dandelion House, 1984.
(Contributor) *Christmas Handbook,* Child's World, 1984.
Surprise at Muddy Creek, Dandelion House, 1984.
How Come You're So Shy? Golden Press, 1987.
My Own Grandpa, Golden Press, 1987.

OTHER

"Glendenna's Dilemma" (readers' theater), first performed in Chicago, Illinois, at Performance Community, December 1, 1979.
"Come-Uppance" (readers' theater), first performed in Stockton, Illinois, at Stockton Unitarian-Universalist Church, February 23, 1986.

Author of columns in *Elmhurst Press* and *Stockton Herald News.* Contributor to magazines and newspapers.

WORK IN PROGRESS: Research on the Blackhawk War of 1832 and its impact on the people of Jo Daviess County, with a children's book expected to result.

SIDELIGHTS: Leone Castell Anderson told *CA:* "Why, after writing adult material (advertising copy, newspaper and magazine articles), did I turn to writing for children? I was prompted by memories of the pleasures of my own childhood reading, and the responsive chord struck by the books I read. I wanted to pass on to the children who follow after me the transport of books, like a heritage, like Emily Dickinson's 'bequest of wings.' With my writing, whether it is humorous or serious, fiction or nonfiction, and with my talks and workshops for children in their schools, I hope I am sharing this legacy."

*   *   *

ANDERSON, Nancy Fix 1941-

PERSONAL: Born August 23, 1941, in Dallas, Tex.; daughter of George J. (a mechanical engineer) and Frances (Bartlett) Fix; married Clifford H. Anderson; children: Michael T., Kathryn B. *Education:* Stanford University, B.A., 1965; University of California, Irvine, M.A., 1967; Tulane University, Ph.D., 1973.

ADDRESSES: Home—2031 Joseph St., New Orleans, La. 70115. *Office*—Department of History, Box 65, Loyola University of New Orleans, 6363 St. Charles Ave., New Orleans, La. 70118.

CAREER: University of New Orleans, New Orleans, La., assistant professor of history, 1969; Tulane University, New Orleans, instructor in history, 1972; instructor in history at Newman School, 1972-74; Loyola University of New Orleans, New Orleans, instructor in history, 1974-75; Tulane University, instructor in history, 1979; University of New Orleans, adjunct assistant professor of history, 1979-87; Loyola University of New Orleans, associate professor of history, 1987—. Instructor at Loyola University of New Orleans, 1982, 1986. Member of board of directors of Women's Studies Consortium of Louisiana, 1984—; public speaker on women's history.

MEMBER: American Historical Association, National Women's Studies Association, Southern Conference on British Studies.

AWARDS, HONORS: Scholar of English-Speaking Union at Oxford University, 1970; grant from National Endowment for the Humanities, 1976; William Langer Prize from *Pyschohistory Review,* 1983, for article "No Angel in the House: The Psychological Effects of Maternal Death."

WRITINGS:

Woman Against Women in Victorian England: A Life of Eliza Lynn Linton, Indiana University Press, 1987.

Contributor to *Victorian Britain: An Encyclopedia.* Contributor of articles and reviews to literature and history journals.

WORK IN PROGRESS: Research on psychodynamics of the Victorian family and on Annie Besent.

SIDELIGHTS: Nancy Fix Anderson told *CA:* "When I first began my research on Victorian England I was primarily concerned to write about women involved in the struggle for emancipation. The more I got into the research, however, the more interested and puzzled I was with women who opposed women's rights, especially women who were themselves emancipated. Deciding that the best way to understand the women's revolution was by studying the counter-revolution, I focused on Eliza Lynn Linton, the most intriguing and influential of the Victorian anti-feminists. Although Linton herself broke with the conventions of Victorian womanhood by living an independent self-supporting life, she nevertheless virulently opposed the emancipation of other women. I used psychoanalytic theory to explain her motivations, and concluded that, as an ambitious woman raised in a patriarchal society, she developed an unconscious sense of male identity which alienated her from her own sex. Linton was a fascinating person to study, but, after living with her in my head (and in my dreams) for four or five years, I, as an ardent feminist, am ready to move on to more congenial subjects.

"My new project is, however, as emotionally difficult as my work on anti-feminism. I am doing a study of the psychodynamics of the Victorian middle-class family in order to understand the formation of personality and social values. My focus is on the intensification of familial attachments, and on the psychological defenses against these unconscious incestuous feelings. Despite the many books on Victorian sex, there has been almost no work on incest and incestuous feelings, perhaps because the subject is so anxiety-provoking. Certainly many of my fellow historians seem very uncomfortable when I discuss this project with them. But the discomfort is worth it, in that I hope to show in my book how these feelings are of fundamental importance in shaping what we know as Victorianism.''

BIOGRAPHICAL/CRITICAL SOURCES:

PERIODICALS

Times Literary Supplement, January 1, 1988.

* * *

ANDERSON, Robert N(orris) 1944-

PERSONAL: Born March 27, 1944, in Alamosa, Colo.; married, 1962; children: two. *Education:* Adams State College, B.A., 1965, M.A., 1966; Colorado State University, Ph.D., 1969.

ADDRESSES: Office—Department of Agricultural and Resource Economics, University of Hawaii at Manoa, Honolulu, Hawaii 96821.

CAREER: University of Hawaii at Manoa, Honolulu, assistant agricultural economist, 1969—. Consultant to Water Resources Council, Western Region Area Developmental Research Center, and Hawaii State Department of Education.

MEMBER: American Agricultural Economics Association.

WRITINGS:

(With Richard Coller and Rebecca F. Pestano) *Filipinos in Rural Hawaii*, University of Hawaii Press, 1983.*

* * *

ANKERSON, Dudley (Charles) 1948-

PERSONAL: Born September 4, 1948, in Hereford, England; son of Richard and Norah Madeleine Ankerson; married Silvia Galicia (a teacher), December 8, 1973; children: Catherine, Richard. *Education:* Sidney Sussex College, Cambridge, M.A., 1971, D.Phil., 1981. *Politics:* Social Democrat. *Religion:* Church of England.

ADDRESSES: Home—12 Thurlby Rd., London SE27 0RL, England. *Office*—British Foreign and Commonwealth Office, 1 King Charles St., London SW1A 1AH, England.

CAREER: British Foreign and Commonwealth Office, London, England, 1976-84, held posts such as second secretary of embassy in Buenos Aires, Argentina, 1978-81, and first secretary of embassy in Mexico City, Mexico, 1985-88.

MEMBER: Marylebone Cricket Club.

WRITINGS:

(Contributor) D. A. Brading, editor, *Caudillo and Peasant in the Mexican Revolution*, Cambridge University Press, 1980.
Agrarian Warlord: Saturnino Cedillo and the Mexican Revolution in San Luis Potosi, Northern Illinois University Press, 1985.

WORK IN PROGRESS: Research on the politics of Central America since 1960.

SIDELIGHTS: ''Following a period of studying the history of Latin America at university,'' Dudley Ankerson wrote, ''I was drawn to look at the first major revolutionary upheaval of the twentieth century: the Mexican revolution. I decided to conduct a study of this movement on a regional basis, and selected as my field of study the state of San Luis Potosi. I was particularly interested in the career of the regional strongman who dominated local politics there for two decades—Saturnino Cedillo, a man whom the author Graham Greene had called upon when he visited Mexico in 1938 and who features in Greene's account of his journey, *The Lawless Roads*. I discussed with Greene his meeting with Cedillo and refer to it in my book.

''It seemed to me that Cedillo's career marked the passing of the old, rural-based system of Mexican politics and the transition to the new machine politics, which are a feature of contemporary Mexico. Like his better known counterpart, Emiliano Zapata, Cedillo was a small landholder, who joined the revolution in protest at the abuses of neighboring large landowners (*hacendados*). He later came to control the state and established a traditional form of *caudillo* rule there. This proved to be out of step with the more structured political system that emerged in Mexico in the 1930s. This fact led to Cedillo's overthrow by the central government in 1938, when he launched an abortive military uprising, the last such upheaval in Mexican history.''

Ankerson added: ''I have retained my interest in Latin America and have served with the British Foreign Office in both Argentina and Mexico, where I have been involved in reporting upon events in Central America. At some time in the future I would like to write a book about the history and contemporary politics of this last-mentioned region.

''Outside my work, I am interested in international affairs, classical music, sport, and religion. The first part of my undergraduate degree was in classical studies, and I retain an interest in Greek and Roman history and Greek and Latin literature. I speak fluent Spanish and can converse in French and Italian.''

* * *

ANSTRUTHER, Godfrey 1903-1988

OBITUARY NOTICE: Born March 5, 1903, in London, England; died July 23, 1988. Dominican friar, historiographer, translator, and author. Best known as an authority on Roman Catholic history, Anstruther entered the Dominican order at the age of seventeen and was ordained a priest in 1926. During the 1930s the self-taught historian translated the works of Italian philosopher and saint Thomas Aquinas and, twenty years later, began composing his own works. His first important book, *Vaux of Harrowden*, centered on a Roman Catholic family in the eastern midlands of England who refused to accept the Church of England as a religious authority. Anstruther was also the author of a monograph on post-Reformation English Dominicans titled *A Hundred Homeless Years* and *The Seminary Priests*, a highly regarded collection of biographical sketches on members of the English secular clergy that has become a standard reference work.

OBITUARIES AND OTHER SOURCES:

BOOKS

International Authors and Writers Who's Who, 7th edition, Melrose, 1976.

PERIODICALS

Times (London), July 28, 1988.

* * *

ANTONE, Evan Haywood 1922-

PERSONAL: Born December 12, 1922, in Clarksville, Tex.; son of Felix Arthur (a realtor and banker) and Eva (a housewife; maiden name, Goldberg) Antone; married Mary Ann Hamilton (a housewife), July 24, 1949; children: Leslie Ann Antone Wilder, Teri Gail Antone Paradiso. *Education:* University of Texas at El Paso, B.A., 1951, M.A., 1964; University of California, Los Angeles, Ph.D., 1971. *Politics:* Independent. *Religion:* Presbyterian.

ADDRESSES: Home—2401 Detroit Ave., El Paso, Tex. 79930. *Office*—Department of English, University of Texas at El Paso, El Paso, Tex. 79968.

CAREER: Times and Herald-Post, El Paso, Tex., retail advertising manager, 1947-65; University of California, Los Angeles, instructor in English, 1965-67; University of Texas at El Paso, associate professor of English, 1967—. Editor and member of board of directors of Texas Western Press, 1970-81.

MEMBER: Rocky Mountain Modern Language Association, El Paso County Historical Society (president, 1979-80).

WRITINGS:

William Farah, Industrialist, Carl Hertzog, 1969.
From Strength to Strength: A Centennial History of First Presbyterian Church of El Paso, Carl Hertzog, 1982.
Portals at the Pass, American Institute of Architects, 1984.
Tom Lea: His Life and Work, Texas Western Press, 1988.

WORK IN PROGRESS: Editing an anthology, *Texas Writers,* publication expected in 1990; writing "an updated survey of books by and about Texans such as Tom Lea, Larry McMurtry, William Humphrey, J. Frank Dobie, and Katherine Anne Porter."

SIDELIGHTS: Evan Haywood Antone told *CA* that his major interest is American literature.

* * *

APPLETON, George 1902-

PERSONAL: Born February 20, 1902, in Windsor, England; son of Thomas George and Lily Appleton; married Marjorie Alice Barrett, 1929 (died, 1980); children: one son, two daughters. *Education:* Selwyn College, Cambridge, B.A. (with first class honors), 1924, M.A., 1929; attended St. Augustine's College, Canterbury.

ADDRESSES: Home—112A St. Mary's Rd., Oxford OX4 1QF, England.

CAREER: Ordained priest of Church of England, 1926; curate of parish church in Stepney, England, 1925-27; Society for the Propagation of the Bible, missionary in charge in Irrawaddy Delta, 1927-33; College of the Holy Cross, Rangoon, Burma, warden, 1933-41; archdeacon of Rangoon, 1943-46; vicar of Headstone, 1947-50; Conference of British Missionary Societies, secretary, 1950-57; rector of Church of England in Aldgate, 1957-62; archdeacon of London and canon of St.

Paul's Cathedral, 1962-63; archbishop of Perth and metropolitan of Western Australia, 1963-69; archbishop and metropolitan of Jerusalem, Israel, 1969-74. Director of public relations for government of Burma, 1943-46.

AWARDS, HONORS: Member of Order of the British Empire, 1946; companion of Order of St. Michael and St. George, 1972; Buber-Rosenzweig Medal from Council of Christians and Jews, 1975.

WRITINGS:

(Editor) *Beginner's English-Burmese Dictionary,* C.L.S. Press, 1944.
Three Months' Hard Labour (Burmese grammar), B. R. Pearn, 1944.
John's Witness to Jesus, Association Press, 1955.
In His Name: Prayers for the World and the Church; A Discipline of Intercession Based on Biblical Insights, Edinburgh House Press, 1956, revised edition, Lutterworth, 1978.
The Christian Approach to the Buddhist, Edinburgh House Press, 1958.
Glad Encounter: Jesus Christ and the Living Faiths of Men, Edinburgh House Press, 1959, 2nd edition, S.P.C.K., 1978.
On the Eightfold Path: Christian Presence Amid Buddhism, Oxford University Press, 1961.
(Editor) *Daily Prayer and Praise: Morning and Evening Prayers for a Month,* Lutterworth, 1962, Association Press, 1963, revised edition, Westminster, 1978.
(Editor) *Acts of Devotion* (collection), 2nd edition (Appleton was not associated with earlier edition), John Knox Press, 1965.
One Man's Prayers, S.P.C.K., 1967, 2nd edition, 1977.
Journey for a Soul, Fontana, 1974.
Jerusalem Prayers for the World Today, S.P.C.K., 1974.
The Word Is the Seed: Meditations Starting From the Bible, S.P.C.K., 1976.
(With Teilhard de Chardin) *The Human Search,* Collins, 1979.
The Way of a Disciple, Collins, 1979.
The Practice of Prayer, Mowbray, 1979.
Praying With the Bible, Bible Reading Fellowship, 1981.
Glimpses of Faith: One Hundred Meditations for Today, Mowbray, 1982.
Prayers From a Troubled Heart, Fortress, 1983.
The Quiet Heart: Prayers and Meditations for Each Day of the Year, Collins, 1983, Fortress, 1984.
(General editor) *The Oxford Book of Prayer,* Oxford University Press, 1985.
Hour of Glory: Meditations on the Passion, Darton, Longman & Todd, 1985.
Entry Into Life: The Gospel of Death, Darton, Longman & Todd, 1985.
(Editor) *The Heart of the Bible,* Collins, 1986.
Understanding the Psalms, Mowbray, 1987.

BIOGRAPHICAL/CRITICAL SOURCES:

PERIODICALS

Christian Science Monitor, July 31, 1985.

* * *

ARMSTRONG, Henry
See JACKSON, Henry

ARON, Jean-Paul 1925(?)-1988

OBITUARY NOTICE: Born c. 1925 (some sources say 1926 or 1927); died of acquired immune deficiency syndrome (AIDS), August 20, 1988, in Paris, France. Philosopher, educator, and author. The first celebrity in France to publicly announce that he was suffering from AIDS, Aron, a homosexual, strove to eliminate the stigma associated with the disease. He was a professor of philosophy at the universities of Tourcoing and Lille in France and the author of a novel, plays, studies in nineteenth-century sociology, and newspaper articles for French newspapers, such as Le Matin and Le Monde. Aron was best known in literary circles, however, for his essays. His writings include Essais d'epistemologie biologique; a book on French dining available in English translation as The Art of Eating in France: Manners and Menus in the Nineteenth Century; a volume on sexual customs, deviations, and crimes, which he co-authored, titled Le penis et la demoralisation de l'Occident; and Les modernes.

OBITUARIES AND OTHER SOURCES:

PERIODICALS

Chicago Tribune, August 22, 1988.
Los Angeles Times, August 22, 1988.
New York Times, August 22, 1988.
Washington Post, August 22, 1988.

*   *   *

ARONSON, David 1894-1988

OBITUARY NOTICE: Born August 1, 1894, in Vitebsk, Russia (now U.S.S.R.); came to United States, 1906; naturalized citizen, 1918; died following a brief illness, October 20, 1988, in Los Angeles, Calif. Rabbi and author. Aronson was considered one of twentieth-century America's most prominent rabbis. Ordained in 1919, he spent most of his career serving the congregation of Beth El Synagogue in St. Louis Park, Minnesota, and was president of the Rabbinical Assembly of America from 1948 to 1950. Aronson's The Jewish Way of Life is considered a classic doctrine of the Jewish faith.

OBITUARIES AND OTHER SOURCES:

BOOKS

Who's Who in America, 45th edition, Marquis, 1988.
Who's Who in American Jewry, Standard Who's Who, 1980.

PERIODICALS

New York Times, October 24, 1988.

*   *   *

ARONSON, James (Allan) 1915-1988

OBITUARY NOTICE—See index for CA sketch: Born March 26, 1915, in Boston, Mass.; died of prostate cancer, October 21, 1988, in New York, N.Y. Educator, editor, journalist, and author. Aronson, who was an outspoken critic of the American media and an active supporter of left-wing causes, co-founded the leftist weekly National Guardian in 1948 and served as its editor from 1955 to 1967. He had previously worked on the editorial staffs of the Boston Evening Transcript, the New York Herald Tribune, the New York Post, and the New York Times, and from 1970 to 1975 he was editor of publications for the National Emergency Civil Liberties Committee. During that time Aronson also taught journalism at New York University and the New School for Social Research. In 1974 he became professor of communications at Hunter College of the City University of New York, a position he occupied until 1985. Aronson's writings include The Press and the Cold War, Packaging the News: A Critical Survey of Press, Radio, and Television, and Deadline for the Media.

OBITUARIES AND OTHER SOURCES:

BOOKS

The Encyclopedia of American Journalism, Facts on File, 1983.
Who's Who in the East, 15th edition, Marquis, 1975.

PERIODICALS

New York Times, October 22, 1988.

*   *   *

ATKINS, Gary 1949-

PERSONAL: Born August 22, 1949, in Terrell, Tex.; son of Leslie Roy and Adele (Koska) Atkins; married in 1974; children: Nathan S. R. Education: Loyola University, New Orleans, La., B.A., 1971; Stanford University, M.A., 1972. Religion: Society of Friends (Quakers).

ADDRESSES: Office—Department of Journalism, Seattle University, 900 12th and East Columbia, Seattle, Wash. 98122.

CAREER: Press-Enterprise, Riverside, Calif., reporter, 1972-78; Seattle University, Seattle, Wash., assistant professor, 1978-84, associate professor of journalism, 1984—.

MEMBER: Investigative Reporters and Editors, Association for Educators in Journalism and Mass Communications, Sigma Delta Chi.

WRITINGS:

Reporting With Understanding, Iowa State University Press, 1987.

Contributor to magazines and newspapers.

WORK IN PROGRESS: Communications Law, publication expected in 1989.

SIDELIGHTS: Gary Atkins told CA: "My motivation for writing is the enjoyment derived from the process of creating. I hope to assist the promotion of human rights, especially the fundamental right of a human being to expression—through speech and action. The purpose of my book Reporting With Understanding is to assist those journalists who will carry the profession into the twenty-first century, into a period of greater global emphasis. I try to include not only the 'how-to' advice on techniques that is common in such books but also to raise questions that can enable journalists to think about how they should report the events of the world. The book includes several chapters unique for such a text, including ones on reporting values and religion, and reporting minority affairs. Future editions will include chapters about reporting on foundations and philanthropic giving, on health, and on military/strategic arms issues."

*   *   *

AVERY, James S. 1923-

PERSONAL: Born March 24, 1923, in Cranford, N.J.; son of John H. and Martha Ann (Jones) Avery; married Joan Showers (an executive secretary), January 22, 1977; children: Sheryl

Avery Harris, James S., Jr. *Education:* Columbia University, B.A., 1948, M.A., 1949; also attended University of Southern California, 1971. *Religion:* Baptist.

ADDRESSES: Home—1949 Wood Rd., Scotch Plains, N.J. 07076.

CAREER: High school social studies teacher, department chairman, and assistant athletic coach in Cranford, N.J., 1949-56; Esso Standard Oil Co., New York, N. Y., public relations representative in charge of educational and minority-group relations programs, 1956-60; Humble Oil and Refining Co., Houston, Tex., community relations coordinator, 1960-68; Exxon Co., Houston, Tex., public relations manager for Northeastern Region, 1968-71, public affairs manager, 1971-81, executive vice-president attached to Council on Municipal Performance, 1981-82, senior public affairs consultant for Eastern States Public Affairs Area, 1983-86; retired, 1986. Chairman of Vice-President Hubert Humphrey's Task Force on Youth Motivation; past vice-chairman for public affairs of American Petroleum Institute's Committee on Exploration Affairs, Offshore Sub-Committee, and coordinator of Industry's Support Witness Program; national vice-chairman of annual United Negro College Fund campaigns; member of board of directors of Council on Municipal Performance. Chairman of executive committee of New York State Petroleum Council, 1978-79; vice-chairman of Energy Policy Committee of Associated Industries of New York State (now Business Council of New York State), 1976-80; past member of board of trustees of New York State Traffic Safety Council and New York State Council on Economic Education. Vice-chairman of board of directors of PRIME, Inc., 1985—; chairman of Union County (New Jersey) Coordinating Agency for Higher Education, 1968-80; past member of board of directors of Junior Achievement of Westchester County (New York) and Union County Psychiatric Clinic; past chairman of Plainfield (New Jersey) Local Assistance Board; charter member of Plainfield Human Relations Commission and past chairman of its Housing Committee; member of Plainfield Network of Adolescent Services, 1986. *Military service:* U.S. Army Air Forces, 1943-46.

MEMBER: National Association of Market Developers (past president; past chairman of board of directors), Omega Psi Phi (past national president).

AWARDS, HONORS: Named among the one hundred most influential blacks in America by publisher of *Ebony* and *Jet*, 1971-72.

WRITINGS:

The Book of American City Rankings, Facts on File, 1984.

Contributor to *Social Science Record*.

SIDELIGHTS: James S. Avery told *CA:* "I have lived and benefited from a strong belief that self-fulfillment comes from a life focused upon the reasonable use of one's human talent: directing the use of that talent outward particularly toward raising the knowledge and aspiration levels of the nation's youth."

B

BAILEY, J(ames) O(sler) 1903-1979

OBITUARY NOTICE—See index for CA sketch: Born August 12, 1903, in Raleigh, N.C.; died October 30, 1979. Educator and author. Bailey taught English at the University of North Carolina at Chapel Hill beginning in 1927 and retired as professor emeritus in 1971. Previously he had taught at Wofford College and at a North Carolina high school, and for two years he served as lecturer at Robert College and Istanbul University in Turkey. Bailey's writings include two textbooks, *Proper Words in Proper Places* and *Creative Exercises in College English*, and the books *Pilgrims Through Space and Time*, *Thomas Hardy and the Cosmic Mind*, *British Plays of the Nineteenth Century*, and *The Poetry of Thomas Hardy: A Handbook and Commentary*.

OBITUARIES AND OTHER SOURCES:

Date of death provided by wife, Mary M. Bailey.

BOOKS

Directory of American Scholars, Volume II: *English, Speech, and Drama*, 7th edition, Bowker, 1978.
Science Fiction and Fantasy Literature, Volume 2: *Contemporary Science Fiction Authors II*, Gale, 1979.

*   *   *

BAIRD, Jack
See BAIRD, John Charlton

*   *   *

BAIRD, John Charlton 1938-
(Jack Baird)

PERSONAL: Born June 24, 1938, in Pawtucket, R.I.; son of John A. (an engineer) and Marjorie (Charlton) Baird; married Margaret Wilck, May 12, 1959 (divorced, 1974); children: Audrey, Andrea. *Education:* Dartmouth College, A.B., 1960; University of Delaware, M.A., 1962; Princeton University, Ph.D., 1964.

ADDRESSES: Home—P.O. Box 549, Sunapee, N.H. 03782. *Office*—Department of Psychology, Dartmouth College, Hanover, N.H. 03755.

CAREER: Dartmouth College, Hanover, N.H., member of faculty beginning in 1967, professor of psychology, 1973—. Director of Sunapee Research Consultants. *Military service:* U.S. Army, 1964-66; became captain.

MEMBER: International Society of Psychophysics, Psychonomic Society.

AWARDS, HONORS: Fellow of National Institute of Mental Health in Stockholm, Sweden, 1966-67.

WRITINGS:

UNDER NAME JACK BAIRD

Psychophysical Analysis of Visual Space, Pergamon, 1970.
(With Anthony D. Lutkus) *Mind Child Architecture*, University Press of New England, 1982.
The Inner Limits of Outer Space, University Press of New England, 1987.
(Editor with W. T. Jackson) *Sick Plants and Buildings*, University Press of New England, 1988.

Also co-author of *Fundamentals of Scaling and Psychophysics*, Wiley, 1978.

WORK IN PROGRESS: *Pattern and Scale*, publication expected in 1990; *Everyday Perception*, with Birgitta Berglund, publication expected in 1990.

SIDELIGHTS: Jack Baird told CA: "I spend several months a year working in Sweden on applications of mathematics and psychology to environmental problems, including public health. My interests are broader than those of most experimental psychologists. At heart, I am a theoretician with a healthy respect for empirical facts gathered under reproducible conditions."

*   *   *

BALABAN, Nancy 1928-

PERSONAL: Born March 6, 1928, in New York, N.Y.; daughter of Louis (a lamp manufacturer) and Beatrice (a housewife; maiden name, Smith) Neuwirth; married second husband, Richard Crohn (a fundraiser), February 28, 1982; children: Richard, Nora, Joan. *Education:* Wellesley College, B.A., 1949; Bank Street College of Education, M.S., 1955; New York University, Ed.D., 1984.

ADDRESSES: Office—Graduate School of Education, Bank Street College of Education, 610 West 112th St., New York, N.Y. 10025.

CAREER: Nursery school teacher in New York, N.Y., 1956-65, and Yonkers, N.Y., 1967-71; Bank Street College of Education, New York City, director of infant and parent development program, 1971—, John H. Niemeyer fellow, 1987. Member of board of directors of Child Abuse Prevention Center of Westchester, Inc.

MEMBER: International Association for Infant Mental Health, Society for Research in Child Development, National Association for the Education of Young Children.

WRITINGS:

(With M. Cohen) *Primary School Potpourri,* Association for Childhood Education International, 1976.
(With W. H. Hooks, B. D. Boegehold, and S. V. Reit) *The Pleasure of Their Company: How to Have More Fun With Your Children,* Chilton, 1981.
(With Dorothy Cohen and Virginia Stern) *Observing and Recording the Behavior of Young Children,* 3rd edition (Balaban was not associated with earlier editions), Teachers College Press, 1983.
Starting School: From Separation to Independence; A Guide for Early Childhood Teachers (selection of Macmillan Early Learners Book Club and Instructor Magazine Preschool Book Club), Teachers College Press, 1985.
Learning to Say Goodbye: Starting School and Other Early Childhood Separations, New American Library, 1987.

Contributor to *Annual Editions: Early Childhood.* Contributor to magazines, including *Instructor, Three to Get Ready, Parents' Magazine,* and *Working Mother.*

SIDELIGHTS: Nancy Balaban told *CA:* "My books are unique because they're the only ones in print on the specific topic of school entry and separation. They can help because they inform teachers and parents about the nature of separation and how to use the event to encourage children's growth."

*   *   *

BALL, John (Dudley, Jr.)   1911-1988

OBITUARY NOTICE—See index for *CA* sketch: Born July 8, 1911, in Schenectady, N.Y.; died of colon cancer, October 15, 1988, in Encino, Calif. Amateur pilot, planetarium curator, public relations director, journalist, editor, and author. Ball won the 1965 Edgar Award from the Mystery Writers of America and the Golden Dagger from the British Crime Writers Association for his popular book *In the Heat of the Night.* The mystery novel, adapted into the 1967 Academy Award-winning motion picture starring Sidney Poitier, introduced the character of detective Virgil Tibbs, one of the first black protagonists in American fiction or film. Ball's varied career included stints as a commercial and Army pilot, music critic for the *Brooklyn Eagle* and the *New York World Telegram,* radio commentator, assistant curator of New York's Hayden Planetarium, public relations director for the Institute of Aerospace Sciences, and editor in chief of a Beverly Hills publishing company. He also helped found the Sherlock Holmes Society in Los Angeles, California, and served as vice-president of Mystery Writers of America. Ball wrote hundreds of stories and articles and more than thirty books, including *Johnny Get Your Gun, The First Team, Then Came Violence,* and *Singapore.* He edited *The Mystery Story.*

OBITUARIES AND OTHER SOURCES:

BOOKS

International Authors and Writers Who's Who, 10th edition, International Biographical Centre, 1986.

PERIODICALS

Chicago Tribune, October 19, 1988, October 23, 1988.
Los Angeles Times, October 18, 1988.
New York Times, October 18, 1988.
Times (London), October 22, 1988.
Washington Post, October 19, 1988.

*   *   *

BANE, Mary Jo   1942-

PERSONAL: Born February 24, 1942, in Princeville, Ill.; daughter of Fred Weller and Helen Catherine (Callery) Bane; married Kenneth I. Winston, May 31, 1975. *Education:* Georgetown University, B.S., 1963; Harvard University, M.A., 1966, Ed.D., 1972.

ADDRESSES: Office—Department of Public Policy, Harvard University, 79 John F. Kennedy St., Cambridge, Mass. 02138.

CAREER: Teacher at public schools in Brookline, Mass., 1968-71; Harvard University, Cambridge, Mass., lecturer in education, 1972-75; Wellesley College, Wellesley, Mass., assistant professor of education and associate director of Center for Research on Women, beginning in 1975; member of public policy faculty at Harvard University. Research associate at Center for the Study of Public Policy, Cambridge, 1971-75.

MEMBER: American Sociological Association, Population Association of America, National Council on Family Relations.

AWARDS, HONORS: Grant from National Endowment for the Humanities, 1975.

WRITINGS:

(With Donald M. Levine) *The "Inequality" Controversy: Schooling and Distributive Justice,* Basic Books, 1975.
Here to Stay: American Families in the Twentieth Century, Basic Books, 1978.
(With George Masrick, Neal Baer, and others) *The Nation's Families, 1960-1990,* Auburn House, 1980.
(Editor with Manuel Carballo, and contributor) *The State and the Poor in the 1990s* (foreword by Samuel H. Beer), Auburn House, 1984.

Contributor of articles and reviews to scholarly journals.

BIOGRAPHICAL/CRITICAL SOURCES:

PERIODICALS

Atlantic Monthly, December, 1976.
Contemporary Sociology, March, 1985.
New York Times, November 29, 1976.
New York Times Book Review, May 21, 1978.
Political Science Quarterly, winter, 1984-85.
Washington Post Book World, June 18, 1978.*

*   *   *

BANERJI, Sara   1932-

PERSONAL: Born June 6, 1932, in Stoke Poges, Buckinghamshire, England; daughter of Sir Basil (a tobacco planter) and Anita (a novelist; maiden name, Fielding) Mostyn; married

Ranjit Banerji (an economist), March 3, 1957; children: Bijoya Banerji Chisolm, Shobita, Juthika Banerji Slaughter. *Education:* Attended convent schools in Rhodesia (now Zimbabwe), Scotland, and England.

ADDRESSES: Home—7 London Pl., Oxford OX4 1BD, England. *Agent*—Gina Pollinger, 4 Garrick St., London WC2E 9BH, England.

CAREER: Worked as a waitress, courier for a travel agent, riding teacher, and gardener; exhibiting artist and lecturer on writing, cooking, and gardening.

WRITINGS:

Cobwebwalking (novel), Gollancz, 1984.
The Wedding of Jayanthi Mandel (novel), Gollancz, 1987.
The Tea Planter's Daughter (novel), Gollancz, 1988.
Shining Agnes (novel), Gollancz, 1989.

WORK IN PROGRESS: A novel, *Life of Lump,* for Gollancz.

SIDELIGHTS: Sara Banerji told *CA:* "I practice transcendental meditation and the 'flying' technique, and my experiences are central to my work. I have been an amateur jockey. My husband is Indian, and my first eighteen years of marriage were spent in India, where my children were born. I am an enthusiastic gardener and painter.

"I suppose the truest reason I can give for writing is that I can't help it! It is all stored up inside me and has to come out. I wrote five novels over a period of eighteen years before my first was accepted. No one but a fool or one who cannot do otherwise would have wasted so much time and effort.

"My Indian experience was fifteen years of being loved by my husband, Ranjit, and welcomed by his Brahmin family. There was also the joy of educating three daughters together with a husband with whom I get on frightfully well. He was an assistant general manager and very busy, yet he taught himself typing and then typed my books for me. He also acted as my agent during the Indian years. Probably the biggest reason for my continuing to write in spite of years of rejection was Ranjit, who encouraged me calmly, did everything he could to help me, and never lost faith.

"We employed servants who became beloved to us, and who write to me to this day asking me to name their grandbabies. One of my servants once put his body between mine and a murderous mob. The mobs themselves were a red, raw experience; we have been held with our children in our car all day, not knowing whether or not we were going to be killed. There were also years of flat racing, riding my own horses, one of which was the fastest in India over two furlongs. Once one horse reared backwards and took us both down a sheer hillside where our fall was broken thirty feet below by tea bushes and wild rhododendrons. We lived for thirteen years in spectacular hills and looked out onto breathtaking beauty; I woke to the sound of parakeets and myna birds. At night wild panthers used to groan under the bedroom window and wild elephants either demolished the swimming pool or tiptoed like ballet dancers among the lines of peas, and once, sitting on the roadside, we saw a wild tiger.

"*The Wedding of Jayanthi Mandel* is set in Calcutta during a period of near anarchy. My next, *The Tea Planter's Daughter,* is set in the beautiful tea estates and is about another India altogether, because between these two books I have become a meditator and had experience of the Absolute dimension. I never know where my ideas or my characters come from, and

I feel myself to be a sort of stainless steel, shining tube up which consciousness flows. The cleaner and the shinier I keep the tube, the purer is my work. I just feel so grateful to have had the honor of being allowed to write.

"I would like to say that no writers have influenced me, but those who I love must have. I'm sure the books one reads as a child are terribly influential. I adored Baroness Orzy's *The Scarlet Pimpernel,* and all those English Victorian writers like Mrs. Molesworthy, who wrote *The Cuckoo Clock.* I read ceaselessly, so the list is very long, but the strongest influences in my adult years have been Guenter Grass, who authored *The Tin Drum,* and Vladimir Nabakov, who authored *Lolita,* for their richness and rhythm and total immersion.

"I have very regular writing hours. I write every morning using a word processor from breakfast until lunch, five days a week. This is my basic schedule; then if I feel like it, I write all the rest of the day as well. I find I need a lot of physical exercise, so I jog four times a week, do two ten-minute yoga sessions a day, and work as a jobbing gardener three afternoons a week. At weekends I spend some time working in my own small flower and vegetable gardens. I also meditate for an hour in the morning and in the evening.

"The only advice I would offer to an aspiring author is to stick to the writing and let other people sell, publish, edit, and worry. I used to do lots of desperate things to get published. None of them worked. But when the moment came when it was meant to happen, a series of little miracles took place. My mother, also a novelist, found one of my manuscripts while tidying a drawer and read it. At a party that evening she told the assembled company of 'this marvelous book about India that my daughter has written.' One of the guests happened to be a literary agent, Gina Pollinger. She has been giving me the most excellent advice and the most soothing encouragement ever since. I have been extremely lucky to have Joanna Goldsworthy as my editor at Victor Gollancz; she has the most amazing wisdom, memory, and comprehension, and has helped me enormously in shaping my books."

BIOGRAPHICAL/CRITICAL SOURCES:

PERIODICALS

New York Times Book Review, October 18, 1987.
Times (London), September 17, 1987, September 20, 1987.
Times Literary Supplement, October 2-8, 1987.

*   *   *

BARBER, Noel (John Lysberg)   1909-1988

OBITUARY NOTICE: Born September 9, 1909; died July 10, 1988. Journalist and author. Barber is best remembered as the archetypal traveling newspaper correspondent, having reported from locales in Africa, the Far East, the U.S.S.R., and even the South Pole during his more than thirty years as a journalist. He began his career in the 1930s and was affiliated with several newspapers, including the Manchester *Daily Express,* the *Malaya Tribune,* and the Paris-based *Continental Daily Mail.* While a foreign correspondent for the *Daily Mail,* the journalist was twice wounded, first in a 1954 Moroccan battle of the French North African War and again in the Hungarian anti-Communist uprising two years later. Barber based many of his writings—especially his travelogues and historical accounts—on personal observations and recollections. His works include *The Black Hole of Calcutta: A Reconstruction; Sinister Twilight: The Fall and Rise Again of Singapore; The Fall of*

Shanghai; and an autobiography titled *The Natives Were Friendly, So We Stayed the Night.* His novels *Tanamera, A Farewell to France,* and *The Other Side of Paradise* were being adapted for television by Australian producer Red Grundy at the time of Barber's death.

OBITUARIES AND OTHER SOURCES:

BOOKS

Who's Who, 140th edition, St. Martin's, 1988.

PERIODICALS

Publishers Weekly, July 1, 1988.
Times (London), July 11, 1988.

* * *

BARNES, Lilly I. 1935-

PERSONAL: Born March 1, 1935, in Beresnicki, U.S.S.R.; daughter of Konrad (a mining engineer) and Mara (a pianist; maiden name, Skolnick) Grohspietsch; married Milton Barnes (a composer), June 24, 1956 (marriage ended); children: Micah, Daniel. *Education:* Attended University of Toronto, 1956-57, and University of Vienna, 1958-59. *Religion:* None.

ADDRESSES: Home and office—16 Washington Ave., Toronto, Ontario, Canada M5S 1L2.

CAREER: Canadian Broadcasting Corp., Toronto, Ontario, writer, interviewer, editor, and producer for children's television program "Mr. Dressup," 1961—. Radio journalist and broadcaster; writer. Social activist.

AWARDS, HONORS: Ohio Award; Genie Award for "Mr. Dressup."

WRITINGS:

A Hero Travels Light (story cycle), Oberon Press, 1986.

WORK IN PROGRESS: A novel about "a jazz pianist obsessed by a mysterious, older woman who has been accused of a crime."

SIDELIGHTS: Lilly I. Barnes told *CA:* "I am hooked on drama, and since other people will take only so much of that condition before calling it names, I write.

"In one way or another, all the stories in *A Hero Travels Light* break down stereotypes and prejudices. My work in progress juxtaposes and plays with appearance and realities."

* * *

BARNETT, Robert W(arren) 1911-

PERSONAL: Born November 6, 1911, in Shanghai, China, to American parents; son of Eugene Epperson (secretary general of the Young Men's Christian Association) and Bertha Mae (Smith) Barnett; married Patricia Glover (a research specialist on Asia), April 26, 1940 (divorced, 1977); married Joan Burrows (a foundation executive), December 10, 1983; children: (first marriage) Dickson, Robert Warren, Jr., Clare (deceased), Eugenia. *Education:* University of North Carolina at Chapel Hill, B.A. (Phi Beta Kappa), 1933, M.A., 1934; Oxford University, M.A., 1936, M.Litt., 1937; attended University of Michigan, 1938. *Politics:* Democrat. *Religion:* Protestant.

ADDRESSES: Home and office—5130 Chevy Chase Parkway N.W., Washington, D.C. 20008.

CAREER: University of North Carolina at Chapel Hill, lecturer in economics, 1932-34; Institute of Pacific Relations, New York, N.Y., research fellow, 1939-41; United China Relief, New York City, program executive officer, 1941-42; Institute of Pacific Relations, chief of Washington office, 1942; Far Eastern Commission for Occupation of Japan, U.S. member of economics and reparations committees, 1945-49; U.S. Department of State, Washington, D.C., officer in charge of China (mainland and Formosa) economic affairs, 1949-51, officer in charge of western European economic affairs, 1951-54, officer in charge of European economic organizations, 1954-56, counselor of embassy for economic affairs at U.S. Embassy in The Hague, Netherlands, 1956-59, counselor of mission for the European Economic Community (Common Market), U.S. Mission to the European Communities in Brussels, Belgium, 1960-61, deputy director of foreign economic advisory staff in office of the under-secretary of state, 1962-63, deputy assistant secretary of state for East Asian and Pacific affairs, 1963-70; Asia Society, New York City, vice-president and director of Washington Center, 1970-79; Carnegie Endowment for International Peace, Washington, D.C., resident associate, 1979-84. *Military service:* U.S. Army Air Forces, chief of combat intelligence, 1943-45; served in China; became major; received Bronze Star, Legion of Merit, and Order of Supreme Merit of Indonesia.

MEMBER: International Institute for Strategic Studies, Council on Foreign Relations, Association of Asian Studies, Washington Institute of Foreign Affairs, Phi Beta Kappa, Beta Theta Pi, Cosmos Club, Chevy Chase Club.

AWARDS, HONORS: Rhodes scholar at Oxford University, 1934-37; fellow of General Education Board at Yale University, 1937-39, and of Rockefeller Foundation, 1939-41; corporation fellow at Harvard University's Center for International Affairs, 1959-60.

WRITINGS:

The Industrial Revolution: China and Great Britain, U.N.C., 1934.
British Foreign Policy With Respect to the Russo-Japanese War, Oxford University Press, 1937.
Economic Shanghai: Hostage to Politics, Institute of Pacific Relations, 1941.
Quemoy: The Use and Consequences of Nuclear Deterrence, Harvard University Press, 1960.
The United States and China, Senate GPO Committee on Foreign Relations, 1976.
Pacific Region Interdependencies: A Compendium, U.S. Government Printing Office, 1981.
Beyond War: Japan's Concept of Comprehensive National Security, Pergamon, 1984.

Also author of *The Occupation of Japan: The Economic Aspect,* 1948; *Sino-American Detent and Its Policy Implications: A Future for Taiwan,* 1974; and *The New Political Economy of the Pacific: Conflict and Cooperation—Japan and America.* Contributor of articles and stories to economic and political science journals, popular magazines, including *Nation,* and newspapers.

WORK IN PROGRESS: Wandering Knights, a memoir of a great Chinese scholar and historian who headed China's Institute of History, publication expected in 1989.

BARROWS, Sydney (Biddle) 1952-

PERSONAL: Born January 14, 1952, in Long Branch, N. J.; daughter of Donald Barrows, Jr. (a publishing executive) and Jeannette (Ballantine) Molzer. *Education:* Graduated from Fashion Institution of Technology, 1973.

ADDRESSES: Home and office—210 West 70th St., New York, N. Y. 10023.

CAREER: Abraham & Strauss (department store), New York City, executive trainee, 1973-76; Young Innovators (boutique wholesaler), New York City, accessories buyer, 1978; proprietress of Cachet, Elan, and Finesse (three escort/call girl services), New York City, 1979-84; writer and television producer.

MEMBER: American Federation of Television and Radio Artists.

AWARDS, HONORS: Bergdorf Goodman Award, 1973, for academic excellence.

WRITINGS:

(With William Novak) *Mayflower Madam: The Secret Life of Sydney Biddle Barrows* (autobiography), Arbor House, 1986.

WORK IN PROGRESS: A book expected for publication in 1989.

SIDELIGHTS: In 1984 Sydney Biddle Barrows was arrested for promoting prostitution in New York City. As proprietress of the upscale escort services Cachet, Elan, and Finesse, Barrows (under the alias Sheila Devin) had a clientele that included some of society's most wealthy, powerful, and prominent figures—corporate executives, diplomats, and international businessmen. A well-connected but cash-poor young woman trained in fashion buying and merchandising, Barrows used her common sense and business acumen to make her agencies quite successful. Fined five thousand dollars, she has suffered few ill effects from her notoriety, becoming a media figure, writing an autobiography, and co-producing the television adaptation of her book. "If Sydney's 1984 bust was a shock, she has since come to see it as a blessing: How else might a businesswoman diversify with such dispatch?" contemplated Michelle Green in *People.* "Talk about a public-relations dream," noted Barrows. "I've just been so lucky. You can't buy this kind of luck."

When Barrows' clandestine activities were first exposed, New York City tabloids clamored for the tantalizing story of pedigree and prostitution; *Mayflower Madam: The Secret Life of Sydney Biddle Barrows* (written by Barrows with William Novak) subsequently sold impressively. Key to the book's appeal, according to Jonathan Yardley in the *Washington Post,* is its focus on business and sex—"two subjects Americans most love to read about." Talking to *Chicago Tribune* reporter Cheryl Levin, Barrows' manager Terry Whatley stated, "The hook is, first of all, that she comes from the equivalent of American royalty—the Mayflower descendents—and then that she ran something so slimy and dirty in a proper and dignified way." Other observers, such as *New York* writer Anthony Haden-Guest, found Barrows' arrest and conviction "at the edge of a hot issue"; questioning the illegality of this "victimless crime," a lawyer associated with her defense pointed out the incongruity of a state's right to prohibit prostitution but not abortion. "[Barrows is] certainly right," Yardley conceded, "that sex-for-sale is treated by respectable society with exquisite hypocrisy."

Seeing herself as a pragmatic businesswoman of high standards and integrity, Barrows does not "tell all" in *Mayflower Madam.* Anonymous anecdotes protect her list of illustrious clients; much of the book discusses her "excellence" theory of management, looking at marketing research, advertising, and employee relations. Barrows, who did not engage in prostitution, shares few personal details—"a reticence which," wrote Mim Udovitch in the *Village Voice,* "is a little out of place in an autobiography." "Miss Barrows repeatedly refers to her advice as her 'training program,' her 'marketing approach' and her 'management skills,' and bears down obsessively on the word 'entrepeneur' throughout the book so that yuppies can skip the sex and read the good parts," quipped *New York Times Book Review* critic Florence King. "But for the great unwashed and normally prurient rest of us, she offers a highly explicit but tastefully written view from the 50-yard line of what may well be the only lull in the battle of the sexes."

Expressing no remorse over her activities, Barrows maintains that she helped others obtain pleasure without bringing anyone pain. Myra MacPherson remarked in the *Washington Post* that such "rosy reminiscences overlook the nitty and the gritty"; "Barrows' approach is that if the snob appeal is high enough there should be no place for moral carping [but] . . . the bottom line was hiring young women to have sex for pay with strangers." Similarly, a reviewer for *Newsweek* suggested that the "real fascination [of *Mayflower Madam*] is the slippage of [Barrows'] moral cogs." And writing in the *Los Angeles Times Book Review,* John U. Loudon concluded: "Though she regards herself as a sophisticated martyr for sexual free choice, she emerges in these pages as a savvy manager. . . . who found profit in cleverly acquiescing to the male subjugation of women."

MEDIA ADAPTATIONS: Mayflower Madam was adapted as a television film featuring actress Candice Bergen and was broadcast by CBS-TV in 1987.

BIOGRAPHICAL/CRITICAL SOURCES:

BOOKS

Barrows, Sydney Biddle, and William Novak, *Mayflower Madam: The Secret Life of Sydney Biddle Barrows,* Arbor House, 1986.

PERIODICALS

Chicago Tribune, October 16, 1986.
Los Angeles Times Book Review, September 7, 1986.
Newsweek, October 27, 1986.
New York, December 10, 1984.
New York Times, October 6, 1986.
New York Times Book Review, October 5, 1986.
Parade, July 19, 1987.
People, September 22, 1986.
Time, October 29, 1984, September 1, 1986.
Times (London), November 19, 1986.
Village Voice, November 4, 1986.
Washington Post, September 3, 1986, September 9, 1986.

* * *

BARUCH, Grace K. 1936(?)-1988

OBITUARY NOTICE: Born c. 1936; died of cancer, October 3, 1988, in Newton Center, Mass. Researcher and author. Baruch, a specialist in women's studies, was associate director of the Wellesley Center for Research on Women. She participated with other researchers in a notable study that concluded that mature women in the 1980s had higher self-esteem than their predecessors. Baruch wrote several books, including *Gender and Stress, The Competent Woman,* and *Lifeprints: New Patterns of Love and Work for Today's Women.*

OBITUARIES AND OTHER SOURCES:

PERIODICALS

New York Times, October 4, 1988.

*   *   *

BASS, Altha Leah (Bierbower) 1892-1988
(Althea Bass)

OBITUARY NOTICE—See index for *CA* sketch: Born September 5, 1892, in Colfax, Ill.; died after a heart attack, July 11, 1988, in Potomac, Md. Educator, librarian, and author. Bass received her master's degree in English literature from the University of Oklahoma in 1921 and worked as a teacher and librarian in Oklahoma and Illinois. She wrote books, sometimes under the name Althea Bass, such as *Now That the Hawthorn Blossoms, Cherokee Messenger, A Cherokee Daughter of Mount Holyoke, The Thankful People, The Story of Tullahassee,* and *The Arapaho Way: A Memoir of an Indian Boyhood.*

OBITUARIES AND OTHER SOURCES:

PERIODICALS

Washington Post, July 14, 1988.

*   *   *

BASS, Althea
See BASS, Altha Leah (Bierbower)

*   *   *

BASS, Rick 1958-

PERSONAL: Born March 7, 1958, in Fort Worth, Tex.; son of C. R. (a geologist) and Lucy (a housewife; maiden name, Robson) Bass. *Education:* Utah State University, B.S., 1979.

ADDRESSES: Home—c/o Fix Ranch, Route 1, Troy, Mont. 59935. *Agent*—Timothy Schaffner, Schaffner Agency, 264 Fifth St., New York, N.Y. 10001. N.Y.

CAREER: Writer.

MEMBER: Outdoor Writers of America.

WRITINGS:

The Deer Pasture (natural history essays), Texas A&M University Press, 1985.
Wild to the Heart (wilderness essays), Stackpole, 1987.
Oil Notes (essays), Seymour Lawrence, 1988.
The Watch (stories), Norton, in press.

Work represented in anthologies, including *Tales From Gray's,* Gray's Sporting Journal Press; and *Best Stories From the South, 1988,* Algonquin Books. Contributor to periodicals.

WORK IN PROGRESS: Where the Sea Used to Be, a trilogy of novellas, publication expected in 1990; *Loon,* a novel; another novel.

SIDELIGHTS: Rick Bass has lived in Texas, Mississippi, Vermont, Utah, Arkansas, and Montana. He told *CA* that isolation is essential to his writing.

*   *   *

BASSETT, Lisa 1958-

PERSONAL: Born January 26, 1958, in Winter Park, Fla.; daughter of Samuel Taylor III and Barbara (an art teacher; maiden name, Crisler) Bassett. *Education:* Rollins College, B.A. (with honors), 1984; University of Texas at Austin, M.A., 1986, doctoral study, 1987—. *Religion:* Christian.

ADDRESSES: Home—Austin, Tex. *Office*—Department of English, 108 Parlin Hall, University of Texas at Austin, Austin, Tex. 78712-1164. *Agent*—Dilys Evans, P.O. Box 400, Norfolk, Conn. 06058.

CAREER: University of Texas at Austin, assistant instructor in English, 1986—.

MEMBER: Lewis Carroll Society of North America, Modern Language Association of America.

WRITINGS:

JUVENILE

A Clock for Beany (Junior Literary Guild selection), Dodd, 1985.
Beany and Scamp (Junior Literary Guild selection), Dodd, 1987.
Very Truly Yours, Charles L. Dodgson, Alias Lewis Carroll, Lothrop, 1987.
Beany Wakes Up for Christmas, Dodd, 1988.

WORK IN PROGRESS: Research on Shakespeare and Renaissance literature.

SIDELIGHTS: Lisa Bassett told *CA:* "I hope that in writing for children I can create the kind of world I always found in books. As a child I could enter the fantasy world of a book wholeheartedly, particularly the world of magical animals. My children's books are about animals, Beany bear and Scamp squirrel, and they are inspired by the whimsical drawings of my sister, Jeni Bassett. The friendship between Beany and Scamp is beautifully embodied in the warmth and charm of Jeni's illustrations. I write the stories with Jeni's pictures in mind.

"My biography of Lewis Carroll, *Very Truly Yours, Charles L. Dodgson, Alias Lewis Carroll,* is also about friendship. I wanted to introduce children to the Carroll who befriended hundreds of children in his lifetime. I want my readers to meet the man as he revealed himself to the actual children who knew him. Biographies for juvenile readers that are written like novels never appealed to me. I always had the feeling I was reading a fictional account rather than a realistic portrayal of the biographical subject. In my book, I want to let children meet Carroll and form their opinions about the man by reading his own words (in letters to children) and the words of the children who wrote about their relationships with him.

"My interest in Carroll began long ago when I read the Alice books to my sister. She had been ill for quite a while and to entertain her, I read about Alice's adventures. We laughed together, especially over Humpty Dumpty. Later as a college student, I read Carroll's letters and found the same hilarious nonsense in his epistles to children. I also found a man whom I thought children would like to know. I hope young people and adults finish my book about Carroll with a special sense of the man's love of childhood and children.''

* * *

BEARDMORE, Cedric
See BEARDMORE, George

* * *

BEARDMORE, George 1908-1979
(Cedric Beardmore, Cedric Stokes, George Wolfenden)

OBITUARY NOTICE—See index for *CA* sketch: Born May 18, 1908, in England; died in 1979. Writer. Beardmore, the nephew of English novelist and dramatist Arnold Bennett, wrote a biography of his uncle titled *Arnold Bennett in Love*. Beardmore's other writings include, under the pseudonym Cedric Beardmore, *Dodd the Potter;* under the pseudonym George Wolfenden, *The Little Doves of Destruction;* under the pseudonym Cedric Stokes, *All Space My Playground;* and, under his own name, *Civilians at War: Journals, 1938-46.* His writings for young adults, published under his own name, include *The Treasure of Spanish Bay.*

OBITUARIES AND OTHER SOURCES:

Year of death provided by Judy Carreck, publicity assistant at John Murray Ltd. (publisher).

PERIODICALS

Times Literary Supplement, November 9, 1984.

* * *

BEATTY, Warren
See BEATY, Warren

* * *

BEATY, Warren 1937(?)-
(Warren Beatty)

PERSONAL: Professionally known as Warren Beatty; born March 30, 1937 (some sources say 1938), in Richmond, Va.; son of Ira O. (a realtor) and Kathlyn (a drama coach; maiden name, MacLean) Beaty. *Education:* Attended Northwestern University, 1955-56, and Stella Adler Theatre School, 1957. *Politics:* Democrat.

ADDRESSES: Office—Traubner & Flynn, 1849 Sawtelle, Suite 500, Los Angeles, Calif. 90025.

CAREER: Actor, 1957—; film producer, 1967—; screenwriter, 1975—; film director, 1978—. Worked odd jobs in Washington, D.C., and New York, N.Y. Actor in stage plays, including ''A Hatful of Rain,'' ''The Happiest Millionaire,'' ''Visit to a Small Planet,'' ''The Boy Friend,'' and ''Compulsion'' during the late 1950s, and in the Broadway play ''A Loss of Roses,'' 1959; actor in television programs, including ''The Many Loves of Dobie Gillis,'' 1959-60, and ''Studio One,'' ''Playhouse 90,'' and ''Kraft Theatre'' during the late 1950s; actor in motion pictures, including ''Splendor in the Grass,'' 1961, ''The Roman Spring of Mrs. Stone,'' 1961, ''All Fall Down,'' 1962, ''Lilith,'' 1963, ''Mickey One,'' 1965, ''Promise Her Anything,'' 1966, ''Bonnie and Clyde,'' 1967, ''Kaleidoscope,'' 1968, ''The Only Game in Town,'' 1970, ''McCabe and Mrs. Miller,'' 1971, ''Dollars,'' 1971,

''The Parallax View,'' 1974, ''The Fortune,'' 1975, ''Shampoo,'' 1975, ''Heaven Can Wait,'' 1978, ''Reds,'' 1981, and ''Ishtar,'' 1987.

AWARDS, HONORS: Academy Award nominations from Academy of Motion Picture Arts and Sciences for best actor, 1967, for ''Bonnie and Clyde,'' for best actor, best director, best screenplay, and best film, 1978, for ''Heaven Can Wait,'' and for best actor, best screenplay, and best film, 1981, for ''Reds''; Academy Award for best director, 1981, for ''Reds.''

MEMBER: Writers Guild of America, Directors Guild of America, Screen Actors Guild.

WRITINGS:

SCREENPLAYS

(With Robert Towne) ''Shampoo,'' Columbia, 1975.
(With Elaine May; and co-director) ''Heaven Can Wait,'' Paramount, 1978.
(With Trevor Griffiths; and director) ''Reds,'' Paramount, 1981.

SIDELIGHTS: A major motion picture star since his first screen appearance in 1961's ''Splendor in the Grass,'' Warren Beatty has gone on to produce, direct, and write critically acclaimed films. His 1978 comedy ''Heaven Can Wait'' and his 1981 film epic ''Reds'' both earned him Oscar nominations in four categories: best actor, best director, best screenplay, and best picture. Beatty received the 1981 Academy Award for best director for ''Reds,'' which reviewer Vincent Canby applauded in the *New York Times* as ''a large, remarkably rich, romantic film.'' Critic Frank Rich praised Beatty in *Time:* ''No actor of his generation, not [Robert] Redford or [Jack] Nicholson, has been a star half as long as [he] has. . . . No one can do so many of the jobs required to create a successful film as he.''

The younger brother of actress Shirley MacLaine, Beatty was born in Richmond, Virginia, and grew up there and in Arlington. Though a quiet child fond of books, by the age of eight he had abandoned aspirations toward the presidency of the United States and the governorship of Georgia in favor of becoming an actor. Beatty's first job connected with the stage was in nearby Washington, D.C., at the National Theatre; he was hired when a teenager to stand outside the stage door and keep the rats in the alley from sneaking in. After graduating from high school Beatty studied drama at Northwestern University for a year before moving to New York City, where he enrolled in the Stella Adler Theatre School. He was soon making television appearances, including a stint as Milton Armitage in ''The Many Loves of Dobie Gillis'' and a starring role in the ''Kraft Theatre'' production of ''The Curly-Headed Kid.'' Beatty also did stock theater on Long Island, New York, and in Fort Lee, New Jersey, during the late 1950s, and it was in this setting that he attracted the attention of playwright William Inge and director Joshua Logan. Logan arranged a screen test for the young actor, and Inge decided to write a filmscript for him, to be directed by Elia Kazan. In the meantime they cast Beatty in Inge's 1960 Broadway play, ''A Loss of Roses.'' ''Roses'' was not well received by critics, but Beatty was, and many film offers were made to him.

First, however, Beatty played young Bud Stamper in Inge and Kazan's ''Splendor in the Grass.'' The story of two teenagers trying to come to terms with their sexuality in spite of the confusing effects of their parents' hypocrisy, the 1961 film was considered one of the year's most controversial. Many critics lauded ''Splendor,'' including Bosley Crowther, who hailed it as "a frank and ferocious social drama" in the *New York Times*. Crowther also thought well of Beatty's performance and cited the "amazing definition" with which he and co-star Natalie Wood portrayed their characters. "The authority and eloquence of the theme emerge in the honest, sensitive acting of Mr. Beatty and Miss Wood," Crowther asserted, further commenting that the young actor seemed "a striking individual."

Following his screen debut, Beatty acted in several more films, including 1961's "The Roman Spring of Mrs. Stone," in which he played an Italian gigolo, and 1966's "Promise Her Anything," which featured him as a small-time producer of pornographic movies. In 1967 Beatty made his first attempt at extending his involvement in motion pictures beyond acting when he produced "Bonnie and Clyde." Based on the lives of notorious 1930s bank robbers Bonnie Parker and Clyde Barrow, the film became a huge popular success after Beatty mounted an enormous publicity campaign to advertise it. Also starring in the film as Barrow, Beatty recounted to Rich that when he visited France after "Bonnie and Clyde" premiered he was surprised to find "people everywhere were dressed like Bonnie and Clyde; it was the pervasive theme." Critical response, however, was mixed. Some condemned the film for its combination of comedy and extremely graphic violence; others lauded that very combination as an important social commentary on both Parker and Barrow's era and the time of the film's release.

Always selective about his screen roles, Beatty acted in only a few films between "Bonnie and Clyde" and "Shampoo," his first attempt at screenwriting. Among these appearances were a part as a compulsive gambler in 1970's "Only Game in Town," a portrayal of a western frontier gambler and bordello owner up against the forces of big business and organized religion in 1971's "McCabe and Mrs. Miller," and a role as a reporter investigating a political assassination conspiracy in 1974's "The Parallax View." He also took a year and a half off from motion pictures to work for the campaign of 1972 Democratic presidential candidate George McGovern.

In 1975 Beatty brought "Shampoo" to the screen. A project he had long had in mind, the film details the escapades of a rakish hairdresser named George, played by Beatty, who has sex with his women customers. "Shampoo," which Beatty also produced, is set in Beverly Hills on election night, 1968. Against the backdrop of preparations for glamorous election parties and the parties themselves, George's carefully constructed life goes to pieces around him when all of his women find out about each other. "'Shampoo'... [is] the American film comedy of the year to date," proclaimed Vincent Canby, reviewing in the *New York Times*. Canby went on to praise the characterization of George and the film's debunking of the popular myth that all male hairdressers are homosexuals: "The fact that George isn't, and isn't in a quite spectacular way, may be one of the more revolutionary things in the film." Jay Cocks, critiquing the film in *Time*, lauded it as "crafty, funny and highspirited" and admitted that "much of the dialogue has a keen edge." He was troubled, however, by the reversal of the ending, in which George repents of his promiscuity and begs one of his lovers to marry him only to be refused, calling it "a betrayal of all that is best in the film." According to Canby, however, George's downfall helps reveal that "'Shampoo' is about a lot of quite nice, myopic people going to hell in a handcar and not noticing.... Thinking they're happy when they're miserable."

Beatty's next screen effort, which he produced, co-directed, and co-authored, was the 1978 smash "Heaven Can Wait." A remake of the 1941 motion picture "Here Comes Mr. Jordan," the film tells the story of Joe Pendleton, a professional football star portrayed by Beatty. Joe is cheated out of a chance to play in the Super Bowl by a mistake on the part of an overzealous heavenly messenger who removes his soul from his body before making sure a hit-and-run accident would have been fatal to him. As consolation, Joe is allowed to inhabit a new body, that of a multi-millionaire named Farnsworth who has just been murdered by his wife. "Heaven Can Wait" was praised by critics such as Canby and Rich for its witty dialogue, especially exchanges between Farnsworth's murderous wife and her lover. Canby, while regretting the film's close following of its 1941 basis, admitted that it has "a good deal of charm" and "a kind of earnest cheerfulness that is sometimes most winning." Rich concluded: "The movie has everything going for it: big laughs, populist politics, billowy sequences set in heaven, a murder plot, a climactic Super Bowl game ... and, best of all, a touching ... romance."

"Reds," the 1981 screen epic that Beatty produced, directed, co-wrote, and starred in, was applauded by critic Judith Crist in the *Saturday Review* for "its ambitious concept, its moments of brilliance, its texture, and its sincerity." The film, based on fact, is a historic account of the Bolshevik Revolution as seen through the eyes of American communist journalists John Reed, played by Beatty, and his wife, Louise Bryant, played by Diane Keaton. Some reviewers criticized "Reds" for trivializing history in order to focus on the romance between Reed and Bryant, but most critics had praise for the film's framing device of commentary by thirty-two contemporaries of the journalists, including author Henry Miller and entertainer George Jessel. "With closeups of their wonderfully aged faces," explains Crist, "they provide a magnificent temporal contrast to the youthful beauty of both Beatty and Diane Keaton as the couple in their prime." Citing the "great emotional impact" of "Reds," Canby avowed that "the film's scenes of epic events ... are stunning, but so are the more intimate moments, including a stuffy ... dinner party where Reed and Louise are formally introduced." Canby concluded that "Reds" "dramatizes—in a way that no other commercial movie in my memory has ever done—the excitement of being young, idealistic and foolish in a time when everything still seemed possible."

BIOGRAPHICAL/CRITICAL SOURCES:

PERIODICALS

Chicago Tribune, December 4, 1981.
Commonweal, February 12, 1982.
Esquire, January, 1982.
New Leader, December 28, 1981.
Newsweek, February 10, 1975.
New York Review, March 4, 1982.
New York Times, October 11, 1961, December 29, 1961, April 12, 1962, September 9, 1965, February 23, 1966, August 14, 1967, March 5, 1970, June 25, 1971, December 16, 1971, June 20, 1974, February 12, 1975, February 16, 1975, April 13, 1975, May 21, 1975, June 28, 1978, December 4, 1981.
People, April 2, 1979, July 9, 1979.
Saturday Review, January, 1982.
Time, February 24, 1975, July 3, 1978.
Washington Post, December 4, 1981.*

—*Sketch by Elizabeth Thomas*

BENEDICT, Elizabeth [a pseudonym]   1954-

BRIEF ENTRY: Born December 20, 1954, in Hartford, Conn. American educator and fiction writer. Benedict was an American Book Award finalist for her widely acclaimed first novel *Slow Dancing* (Knopf, 1985). Focusing on the conflict between personal and professional priorities, the work also garnered her a nomination for the *Los Angeles Times* Book Prize for fiction. Her second novel, *The Beginner's Book of Dreams* (Knopf, 1988), about a teenage girl coming to terms with her unsuccessful parents, elicited praise as well. After graduation from Barnard College in 1976, Benedict (the name is a pseudonym) became a speech and policy writer for a leading Mexican-American civil rights group in San Francisco, California, and later in Washington, D.C., where she began to pursue a writing career. She has also held part-time teaching positions at George Mason University and Swarthmore College. One of Benedict's stories was included in the 1983 O. Henry short story anthology, and in 1984 she won the National Magazine Award for fiction. The author has contributed articles and reviews to publications, including the *New York Times* and the *Washington Post. Addresses: Home*—Washington, D.C. *Agent*—Gail Hochman, Brandt & Brandt Literary Agents, Inc., 1501 Broadway, New York, N.Y. 10036.

BIOGRAPHICAL/CRITICAL SOURCES:

PERIODICALS

Los Angeles Times Book Review, April 24, 1988.
New York Times Book Review, March 3, 1985.
Washington Post, April 26, 1988.

*   *   *

BENJAMIN, Burton Richard   1917-1988

OBITUARY NOTICE—See index for *CA* sketch: Born October 9, 1917, in Cleveland, Ohio; died of a brain tumor, September 18, 1988, in Scarborough, N.Y. Television producer, journalist, lecturer, and author. Benjamin won a Peabody Award and eight Emmy awards during his twenty-nine-year career with the Columbia Broadcasting System (CBS). He began his news career in the late 1930s working for various print and television news agencies, including United Press (now United Press International). In 1957 he became executive producer of the CBS news series "The Twentieth Century" and, in 1967, of "The Twenty-first Century." Benjamin also produced numerous "CBS Reports" documentaries, and he helped develop the popular "CBS Sunday Morning." His various positions with the network included senior executive producer of CBS News, executive producer of "CBS Evening News With Walter Cronkite," and vice-president and director of CBS News.

During the early 1980s Benjamin led an internal investigation of the 1982 CBS documentary "The Uncounted Enemy: A Vietnam Deception." The investigation was prompted by a libel lawsuit filed against the network by General William C. Westmoreland, who later dropped the suit. Benjamin recounted the Westmoreland case and stressed the need for better standards in broadcasting in his book *Fair Play: CBS, General Westmoreland, and How a Television Documentary Went Wrong.* Upon his retirement in 1985 Benjamin was offered the presidency of CBS News, but he declined the position. In addition to his television work, Benjamin lectured at such institutions as Columbia University and University of Michigan.

OBITUARIES AND OTHER SOURCES:

BOOKS

Les Brown's Encyclopedia of Television, New York Zoetrope, 1982.
Who's Who in America, 42nd edition, Marquis, 1982.

PERIODICALS

Chicago Tribune, September 20, 1988.
Los Angeles Times, September 20, 1988.
New York Times, September 20, 1988.
Washington Post, September 20, 1988.

*   *   *

BENNET, Ruth
See STRAUBING, Harold (Elk)

*   *   *

BERGES, Marshall (William)   1921(?)-1988

OBITUARY NOTICE: Born c. 1921 in Chicago, Ill.; died in 1988 in Santa Monica, Calif. Journalist and author. A respected journalist whose career spanned more than four decades, Berges is best remembered as a writer of personality profiles for the *Los Angeles Times.* After graduating from Marquette University and serving in the U.S. Navy during World War II, Berges began working for *Time* in 1946. During his almost twenty-five-year affiliation with the publication he penned cover stories on such notable public figures as John F. Kennedy and Ronald Reagan and was eventually appointed the magazine's Los Angeles bureau chief. In 1970 Berges joined the *Los Angeles Times* as a staff writer and in 1984 published a historical account of the newspaper titled *The Life and Times of Los Angeles: A Newspaper, a Family, and a City.* His other writings include *Corporations and the Quality of Life.*

OBITUARIES AND OTHER SOURCES:

BOOKS

Who's Who in America, 45th edition, Marquis, 1988.

PERIODICALS

Los Angeles Times, September 21, 1988.

*   *   *

BERLIN, Ellin (Mackay)   1904(?)-1988

OBITUARY NOTICE—See index for *CA* sketch: Born March 22, 1904 (some sources say 1902 or 1903), in Roslyn, N.Y.; died after a series of strokes, July 29, 1988, in New York, N.Y. Writer. Ellin Berlin, the author of four novels, numerous short stories, and several articles denouncing the exclusive society of the wealthy, created a sensation in 1926 when she announced her intention to marry Irving Berlin, the famous immigrant Jewish songwriter, against the wishes of her multimillionaire Roman Catholic father, Clarence Mackay. Though he had threatened to disinherit her, Mackay and his daughter reconciled five years later. Ellin Berlin's novels, *Land I Have Chosen, Lace Curtain, Silver Platter,* and *The Best of Families,* were well received by critics and the public, as were her contributions to the *New Yorker, Saturday Evening Post,* and *Ladies' Home Journal.*

OBITUARIES AND OTHER SOURCES:

BOOKS

Current Biography, H. W. Wilson, 1988.

PERIODICALS

Chicago Tribune, July 30, 1988.
Los Angeles Times, July 30, 1988.
New York Times, July 30, 1988.
Times (London), August 4, 1988.
Washington Post, July 31, 1988.

*   *   *

BESSOM, Malcolm E(ugene)   1940-1988

OBITUARY NOTICE—See index for *CA* sketch: Born September 27, 1940, in Boston, Mass.; died of complications from liver and kidney failure, October 3, 1988, in Washington, D.C. Educator, editor, journalist, and author. Bessom was the winner of five distinguished achievement awards in journalism from the Educational Press Association of America, including one for his music column "Overtones," which appeared in the *Music Educators Journal.* He served as editor of that journal and director of publications for the Music Educators National Conference during the 1970s, after teaching music at public schools in Massachusetts and working on the editorial staff of the Boston publishing company Allyn & Bacon. From 1978 to 1981 he was president of David Allen Press in Washington, D.C. Bessom wrote textbooks on music and music education, including *Supervising the Successful School Music Program, How to Sell Your Songs Like Professionals Do,* and, with Alphonse M. Tatarunis and Samuel L. Forcucci, *Teaching Music in Today's Secondary Schools.* He edited *Music in Special Education, Music in World Cultures,* and *Careers and Music.*

OBITUARIES AND OTHER SOURCES:

BOOKS

Who's Who in America, 45th edition, Marquis, 1988.

PERIODICALS

Washington Post, October 8, 1988.

*   *   *

BINGHAM, (George) Barry   1906-1988

OBITUARY NOTICE: Born February 10, 1906, in Louisville, Ky.; died of complications from a brain tumor, August 15, 1988, in Louisville, Ky. Newspaper publisher and editor. Owner and editor, beginning in 1937, of Louisville, Kentucky, newspapers *Courier-Journal* and *Louisville Times,* Bingham was known for his business practice of placing editorial excellence above profit. Under Bingham's leadership the Pulitzer Prize-winning papers espoused a liberal doctrine, endorsed Democratic political candidates, and supported reforms in civil rights and the strip-mining industry. Bingham retired from active management of the newspapers in 1971, naming his son, Barry Bingham, Jr., editor and publisher. The family businesses, which also included Louisville television and radio stations and a printing company, were sold in 1986 following a bitter family power dispute.

OBITUARIES AND OTHER SOURCES:

BOOKS

Current Biography, H. W. Wilson, 1988.

The International Year Book and Statesmen's Who's Who, Thomas Skinner Directories, 1982.
Who's Who in America, Supplement to the 44th edition, Marquis, 1987.

PERIODICALS

Chicago Tribune, August 16, 1988.
Los Angeles Times, August 16, 1988.
New York Times, August 16, 1988.
Washington Post, August 16, 1988.

*   *   *

BINGHAM, John (Michael Ward)   1908-1988

OBITUARY NOTICE—See index for *CA* sketch: Listed in some sources under inherited title Baron John Michael Ward Bingham Clanmorris, or Lord Clanmorris; born November 3, 1908, in Yorkshire, England; died August 6, 1988. Civil servant, journalist, and writer. Bingham is best remembered as the author of numerous spy novels, including *My Name Is Michael Sibley* and *Deadly Picnic.* Early in his career Bingham worked as a journalist for the *Hull Daily Mail* and the London *Sunday Dispatch.* During the 1940s he served with the British Control Commission in Germany, and from 1950 to 1977 he was a civil servant for the Ministry of Defence in London. His knowledge of criminology and intelligence procedures added credibility to his fiction, which included short stories, a radio play titled "Not My Pigeon," and the novels *Fragment of Fear, I Love, I Kill,* and *Brock and the Defector.*

OBITUARIES AND OTHER SOURCES:

BOOKS

Twentieth-Century Crime and Mystery Writers, 2nd edition, St. Martin's, 1985.

PERIODICALS

Times (London), August 8, 1988.

*   *   *

BLAISDELL, Donald C(hristy)   1899-1988

OBITUARY NOTICE—See index for *CA* sketch: Born August 12, 1899, in Chautauqua, N.Y.; died of pneumonia, July 9, 1988, in Columbia, Md. Government official, educator, tree farmer, editor, and writer. Blaisdell served the U.S. government in various capacities from 1936 to 1953, working first for the Department of Agriculture and for Congress, then for the Department of State as a co-planner of the United Nations Charter and as a representative in Geneva, Switzerland. Prior to working for the government he taught engineering at Robert College in Istanbul, Turkey, then taught political science at Columbia University and Williams College. From 1955 to 1967 Blaisdell was a professor of political science at the College of the City of New York (now City College of the City University of New York). After retiring from teaching he started the Well House Certified Tree Farm with his wife, Dorothea. Blaisdell wrote such books as *European Financial Control in the Ottoman Empire, The Farmer's Stake in World Peace, American Democracy Under Pressure, International Organization,* and *Technology—The Key to Better Environment: Values, Profits, and Growth in Post-Industrial Society.* He also edited *The Riverside Democrats.*

OBITUARIES AND OTHER SOURCES:

PERIODICALS

Washington Post, July 12, 1988.

* * *

BLY, Amy Sprecher   1955-

PERSONAL: Born February 14, 1955, in Takoma Park, Md.; daughter of Thomas Barton (a manager of a book distribution business) and Patricia (a manager of a book distribution business; maiden name, Weigen) Sprecher; married Robert Wayne Bly (a copywriter and author), May 29, 1983. *Education:* University of Maine at Orono, B.A. (with high distinction), 1977; attended Katharine Gibbs School, 1977-78, and Fairleigh Dickinson University.

ADDRESSES: Home and office—174 Holland Ave., New Milford, N.J. 07646.

CAREER: Brigham and Women's Hospital, Boston, Mass., personnel secretary, 1979-80; American Broadcasting Companies, Inc., New York City, associate editor of *Wide World,* 1980-83; Muir Cornelius Moore, Inc. (advertising agency), New York City, assistant account executive, 1983-85; freelance writer, 1985—. Member of Friends of Wayne Animal Shelter.

MEMBER: Self-Employed Writers and Artists.

WRITINGS:

(With husband, Robert W. Bly) *Information Hotline USA,* New American Library, 1987.

Contributor to magazines, including *Business Marketing, Writer's Digest, Printing Manager,* and *Executive Business.*

WORK IN PROGRESS: A nonfiction book aimed at providing advice to homeowners.

SIDELIGHTS: Amy Sprecher Bly told *CA:* "The idea for *Information Hotline USA* was my husband's: while driving the car one day, he heard an advertisement for an auto safety hotline but couldn't write down the number. He realized there was no central source that both listed *and* described the many useful phone numbers he'd come across on radio, TV, or in magazines. So he decided we should compile a directory of numbers that provided helpful—and free—information, referrals, or literature.

"I think he had the easy part! As the primary researcher and writer of the book, I spent several months poring through stacks of magazines to collect as many hotline numbers as possible. Then I spent many more months calling, verifying, and collecting information on the more than five hundred numbers that ended up in the directory.

"Although health hotlines outnumber those in any another category, the book is geared to readers interested in a wide range of topics—everything from alcoholism and drug abuse to children's helplines to gardening and services for the disabled."

AVOCATIONAL INTERESTS: Travel (including the U.S.S.R.).

* * *

BOATWRIGHT, James III   1933-1988

OBITUARY NOTICE—See index for *CA* sketch: Born September 28, 1933, in Augusta, Ga.; died of acquired immune deficiency syndrome (AIDS), September 25, 1988, in Key West, Fla. Educator, editor, and writer. After teaching English briefly at the University of Georgia, Boatwright joined the faculty of Washington and Lee University in 1960, becoming a full professor of English in 1971. He was editor of the university's highly esteemed literary review *Shenandoah* beginning in 1962, for which he won an Editors' Award from the Coordinating Council of Literary Magazines. A frequent contributor to the *New York Times Book Review,* Boatwright also edited the 1986 *Shenandoah: An Anthology.*

OBITUARIES AND OTHER SOURCES:

BOOKS

Who's Who in America, 45th edition, Marquis, 1988.

PERIODICALS

New York Times, September 27, 1988.
Washington Post, September 27, 1988.

* * *

BODLEY, Hal
See BODLEY, Harley Ryan, Jr.

* * *

BODLEY, Harley Ryan, Jr.   1936-
(Hal Bodley)

PERSONAL: Born November 24, 1936, in Dover, Del.; son of Harley Ryan (a banker) and Mildred Olivia (a home economist; maiden name, Carver) Bodley; married Patricia Jean Hall (a secretary to a mayor), December 4, 1981. *Education:* University of Delaware, B.A., 1959; graduate study at American University, 1960. *Politics:* Republican. *Religion:* Episcopalian.

ADDRESSES: Home—978 Shallcross Lake Rd., Graylag, Middletown, Del. 19709. Office—USA Today, P.O. Box 500, Washington, D.C. 20044. Agent—Edward J. Acton, Inc., 928 Broadway, New York, N.Y. 10010.

CAREER: *Delaware State News,* Dover, sports editor, 1959-60; News-Journal Papers, Wilmington, Del., sports writer, 1960-63, night sports editor, 1963-67, assistant sports editor, 1967-71, sports editor, 1971-82; *USA Today,* Washington, D.C., baseball editor, 1982—. Sports director of WDOV-Radio, Dover, 1958-62; daily broadcaster of "USA Today Radio Report"; commentator for "NBC Sports." *Military service:* Army National Guard, 1956-64.

MEMBER: Associated Press Sports Editors (president, 1981-82), Baseball Writers Association of America (chairman of Philadelphia chapter, 1977-78), Wilmington Sportswriters and Broadcasters (president, 1963), Sigma Delta Chi.

AWARDS, HONORS: Twelve Sportswriter of the Year Awards from National Sportscasters and Sportswriters Association, 1961-79; Mark Twain Award from Associated Press, 1980, for superior coverage of college basketball; Best of Gannett Award from Gannett Co., Inc., 1981, for a collection of columns written throughout the year; Twenty-five-Year Award from the Commissioner of Baseball, 1983, for coverage of major league baseball on a regular basis for twenty-five years.

WRITINGS:

I Learned to Fly, So Can You, News-Journal Publishing, 1967.

The Team That Wouldn't Die, Serendipity Press, 1981.
Countdown to Cobb, Sporting News Publishing, 1985.

Writer for Gannett News Service. Author of regular column in *USA Today*.

WORK IN PROGRESS: Happily, but Not Forever, "a novel about the rise and fall both on and off the baseball field by a major leaguer"; co-writing baseball player Steve Carlton's autobiography.

SIDELIGHTS: Harley Bodley told *CA:* "At an early age I was taught that your world is whatever you want it to be. If you have an inner philosophy that gives you an impatience for excellence, this can provide the drive and motivation to pursue whatever goal appears. Throughout my writing career I have always felt the best compliment a writer can be paid is: 'He was very readable.' I am dedicated to making my work both easy and a delight for the reader—and at the same time inform and enlighten. If I am successful at that, I have done my job."

AVOCATIONAL INTERESTS: Flying (instrument-rated pilot), boating, golf.

*   *   *

BONAVIA, David Michael   1940-1988

OBITUARY NOTICE—See index for *CA* sketch: Born March 4, 1940, in Aberdeen, Scotland; died after a long illness, September 16, 1988. Journalist and author. After working briefly in Africa as a correspondent for the Reuters News Agency, Bonavia became a foreign correspondent for the London *Times* in 1967. He first served in Saigon, Vietnam, then from 1969 to 1972 reported from Moscow, U.S.S.R., where his interest in Soviet dissident activities led to his expulsion from the country. The *Times* then stationed the reporter in Peking, China. Bonavia's books, which are based on his reporting experiences, include *Fat Sasha and the Urban Guerilla: Protest and Conformism in the Soviet Union*, *Peking*, *The Chinese*, and *Verdict in Peking*.

OBITUARIES AND OTHER SOURCES:

PERIODICALS

Times (London), September 19, 1988.

*   *   *

BORMAN, William Alan   1948-

PERSONAL: Born September 18, 1948, in Brooklyn, N.Y.; son of Cornelius H. (a financial analyst) and Eleanor (Messener) Borman; married Suzanne Grams (a special education and elementary school teacher), August 5, 1967. *Education:* Attended Beloit College, 1966-67, and City College of the City University of New York, 1968; State University of New York College at Purchase, B.A., 1973; Graduate Center of the City University of New York, M.A., 1976, M.Phil., 1981, Ph.D., 1982.

ADDRESSES: Home—New York, N.Y.

CAREER: Worked various secretarial and administrative assistant positions in business and law firms in Los Angeles, Calif., and New York, N.Y.; writer. Instructor at various institutions, including Columbia University.

MEMBER: American Philosophical Association, Society for Philosophy and Current Affairs, Gandhi-King Society.

WRITINGS:

Gandhi and Non-Violence, State University of New York Press, 1986.
Metaphysics of Love and Its Application to Death and Dying, Foundation for Thanatology, in press.
(Contributor) A. H. Kutscher, editor, *Handbook of Thanatology*, Foundation of Thanatology, in press.
(Contributor) A. H. Kutscher, editor, *The Other Side of Death: Eschatology and Immortality in the Upanishads*, Foundation of Thanatology, in press.

Also contributor to *Metaphysics of Love and Its Application to Death and Dying*, edited by A. H. Kutscher.

WORK IN PROGRESS: A Manual of Obedience to Conscience.

SIDELIGHTS: William Alan Borman wrote: "In my study *Gandhi and Non-Violence*, I wanted to show academics and scholars the need to look seriously at the activists, and to show the activists the necessity of reflecting much more deeply on their ideals and methods. Also, I wanted to show that metaphysical and spiritual questions, and Indic philosophy, could be fruitfully examined with analytic and critical methods. My training is in analytic and critical Western philosophy, but I have always thought it scandalous that Eastern thought should be either ignored or looked down upon. Indic thought on these problems has developed for millennia more than in Western thought. Indic thought is highly analytical, highly experimental, and highly practical. Its analysis, experiments, and pragmatism have, however, an idealist or spiritual orientation, and they are used constructively, applying a deep phenomenological methodology from an existential standpoint, with a highly practical motivation. If the truth is truth, how can such a parochial dichotomy as East and West have anything to do with it? Gandhi provided an ideal subject. The West respects his moral and political greatness. He is a contemporary resource for both scholars and activists. His ideals, practical concepts, principles of action, and political methods, however, all derive from and are deeply rooted in the experimental spiritual idealism of the Upanishads, the Bhagavad Gita, and other classical Indic thought.

"In *Gandhi and Non-Violence*, I concluded that, though Gandhi immensely extended the domain of practical nonviolence, he fails to prove its perfect, practical infallibility and universal applicability. He fails to prove its absolute moral validity. The question then remains: if nonviolence is not invariably the correct practical and moral choice for political action, and if, therefore, violence may at some point be, not only admissible, but even morally required, then what is that point? What are the justifying criteria or circumstances? My present research is to find how that point, those justifying conditions, have in fact been determined by those who, having been deeply committed to nonviolence, find themselves in the political field, required by their own conscience to use force or even violence. President Kenneth Kaunda's book *The Riddle of Violence*, and the speeches of President Oliver Tambo, provide very deep resources in this area. On the other hand, Albert Schweitzer's efforts to propel the international community towards a test ban treaty and total disarmament provide a case study in the power of purest nonviolence in the political sphere. I feel that the problems of violence versus nonviolence, and of the use of reason versus force, are perhaps the preeminent moral and political questions for this nuclear age, as urged by such voices of collective conscience as Gandhi, Einstein, and Schweitzer.

"Other areas of current interest to me are the philosophy of self-examination of Socrates; the tyranny of moralism and pietism and the need for moral and political pluralism; the necessity for radical realism as a basis for practical idealism; the moral ascendancy and practical use of reason, i.e., the search for rational morality; 'humanity' as a deeper, fuller standard than 'morality'; the relation of individual to collective moral and political self-culture; poetry and imagination in politics and the relation of aesthetics and the arts to moral, political, and spiritual evolution. Underlying all of these is the problem of connecting the highest ideal with the smallest and most routine details and activities of everyday life, which is the quest for the beautiful through philosophy, and its translation to an art of living based on the scientific and philosophical understanding of life. I project writings on all these areas. Specific projects may include critical studies of A. J. Muste and Bayard Rustin, America's Gandhis, and a critical history of the future of the peace movement.

"Special influences have been Whitman, Pound, Ginsberg, Kathleen Reine, and Burroughs; Socrates, Spinoza, Kant, Russell, and Wittgenstein; Upanishads, Bhagavad Gita, Tulsi Ramayana, Ramakrishna, Rama Tirtha, Betty Heimann, S. K. Maitra, Sarama Dasgupta, Aurobindo, Krishna Prema, K. S. Kumar, and Ramananda; Muste, Rustin, King, and Gandhi (and the philosophical study of Gandhi by Arne Naess).''

*   *   *

BOURNE, Geoffrey Howard   1909-1988

OBITUARY NOTICE—See index for *CA* sketch: Born November 17, 1909, in Perth, Australia; immigrated to United States, 1957, naturalized citizen, 1962; died of heart failure, July 19, 1988, in New York, N.Y. Scientific researcher, educator, editor, and author. Bourne, who founded and edited the annual *World Review of Nutrition and Dietetics,* was internationally known for his research on nutrition and primates. He worked in Australia as a biologist and biochemist and in England as a research fellow at Oxford University, the Royal College of Physicians, and the Royal College of Surgeons of England. During World War II he was in charge of research and development for the British Army Special Forces in Southeast Asia, and from 1947 to 1957 taught histology at the University of London. Bourne then moved to Emory University in Atlanta, Georgia, where he was professor of anatomy and director of the university's prestigious Yerkes Regional Primate Research Center. He left the university in 1978, becoming vice-chancellor and professor of nutrition at St. George's University School of Medicine in Grenada. His numerous books include *Nutrition and the War, War-Time Food for Mother and Child, Starvation in Europe, The Ape People,* and *The Gentle Giants: The Gorilla Story,* which he wrote with Maury Cohen. He also edited several books, including the six-volume work *The Chimpanzee.*

OBITUARIES AND OTHER SOURCES:

BOOKS

International Who's Who, 51st edition, Europa, 1987.

PERIODICALS

Chicago Tribune, July 22, 1988.
Los Angeles Times, July 22, 1988.
New York Times, July 21, 1988.
Times (London), July 23, 1988.
Washington Post, July 22, 1988.

BOWERS, John M.   1949-

PERSONAL: Born April 7, 1949, in Richmond, Va.; son of Russell Vernon (a physician) and Jeanne (Mathews) Bowers. *Education:* Duke University, B.A., 1971; University of Virginia, M.A., 1973, Ph.D., 1978; Oxford University, M.Phil., 1975.

ADDRESSES: Office—Department of English, University of Nevada, Las Vegas, Nev. 89154.

CAREER: University of Virginia, Charlottesville, lecturer in English, 1978-80; Hamilton College, Clinton, N.Y., assistant professor of English, 1980-82; California Institute of Technology, Pasadena, Mellon fellow in humanities, 1982-84; Princeton University, Princeton, N.J., assistant professor of English, 1984-87; University of Nevada, Las Vegas, associate professor of English, 1987—.

MEMBER: International Courtly Literature Society, Mediaeval Academy of America, Modern Language Association of America, John Gower Society.

AWARDS, HONORS: Rhodes scholar, 1973-76; grants from National Endowment for the Humanities, 1985, 1986.

WRITINGS:

The Crisis of Will in "Piers Plowman," Catholic University of America Press, 1986.

Contributor to literary journals.

WORK IN PROGRESS: Chaucer in the House of Tidings.

SIDELIGHTS: John M. Bowers told *CA:* "Every literary gesture, even when it takes the form of scholarly writing, forms a fragment of an autobiography. It is most authentic, perhaps, when the author is at least self-conscious of those implications which his writings have in regard to his or her life's story. Though dealing with a fourteenth-century religious allegory called *Piers Plowman,* by interesting myself in 'the crisis of will' I was preparing myself for my own midlife crisis which now, on the other side, I can read in the pages of my academic books. Similarly, my training in the Japanese martial arts—Shotokan Karate under Tsutomu Ohshima and Ki-Aikido under Shuji Maruyama—have convinced me that the most worthwhile products of a culture are not, indeed cannot be, created by the individual in the sense understood by the West's Romantic ideology. Thus, I have come to study the products of the scribal communities of the fifteenth century as valid contributions inseparable from the achievement of English poet Geoffrey Chaucer—leading to my next book, *Chaucer in the House of Tidings.*''

*   *   *

BOXER, (Charles) Mark (Edward)   1931-1988
(Marc)

OBITUARY NOTICE: Born May 19, 1931; died of a brain tumor, July 20, 1988, in London, England. Cartoonist and editor. During the 1950s and 1960s Boxer served as art editor of the fashion magazine *Queen* and became founding editor of the color version of London's *Sunday Times* magazine. He was best known, however, for his cartoons, which he drew under the pen name Marc. Providing humorous, often biting commentary on England's social scene, they appeared in several publications, including the London *Times, Guardian, Observer,* and *Daily Telegraph Magazine.* The artist was credited with changing the face of periodical design and layout, and he assisted in the revamping of the financially ailing *Tatler*, a Conde Nast publication, beginning in 1983. He also served as editor in chief of *Vogue*, as well as editorial director of Conde Nast, both in 1987. His writings include *The Trendy Ape, The Times We Live In,* and *Marc Time.*

OBITUARIES AND OTHER SOURCES:

PERIODICALS

Los Angeles Times, July 24, 1988.
New York Times, July 23, 1988.
Times (London), July 21, 1988.

*   *   *

BOXILL, Roger   1928-

PERSONAL: Born March 27, 1928, in Sydney, Australia; son of William (an engineer) and Vera (a teacher; maiden name, Smith) Boxill; married Edith Hillman (a music therapist), 1965 (divorced, 1976). *Education:* Columbia University, A.B., 1953, Ph.D., 1966; Royal Academy of Dramatic Art, Certificate, 1954; Hunter College (now of the City University of New York), M.A., 1959.

ADDRESSES: Office—Department of English, City College of the City University of New York, Convent Avenue and 138th St., New York, N.Y. 10031.

CAREER: City College of the City University of New York, New York, N.Y., lecturer, 1965-66, instructor, 1966-67, assistant professor, 1967-72, associate professor, 1972-86, professor of English, 1986—. *Maitre de conferences* at University of Paris VII, 1985-86. Actor and director on Broadway and Off-Broadway, in repertory and films, and on more than one hundred television and radio programs. *Military service:* U.S. Air Force, 1946-48; became sergeant.

MEMBER: Modern Language Association of America, Actors' Equity Association, American Federation of Television and Radio Artists, Screen Actors Guild.

WRITINGS:

Shaw and the Doctors, Basic Books, 1969.
Tennessee Williams, St. Martin's, 1987.

New York theater critic for *Shakespeare Quarterly,* 1983-87.

SIDELIGHTS: Roger Boxill told *CA:* "Tennessee Williams was arguably the finest playwright in the history of the American theater. My book *Tennessee Williams* is the first comprehensive study of his work.

"The original productions of 'The Glass Menagerie,' 'A Streetcar Named Desire,' 'Summer and Smoke,' and 'Cat on a Hot Tin Roof' are described within full critical discussions of the scripts. Williams's writings, dramatic and non-dramatic, are examined for their themes, their patterns, and in particular for their archetypal characters—the wanderer and the faded belle. The remarkably prolific accomplishment of the dramatist's late period is assessed in a separate chapter. I conclude that Williams was essentially an elegiac writer whose lyric naturalism derived from the adaptation of the modern short story for the cinematic stage."

*   *   *

BOYD, (Charles) Malcolm   1932-

PERSONAL: Born May 24, 1932, in Newcastle-upon-Tyne,

England; son of Arthur Cecil and Elizabeth (Mahalski) Boyd; married Beryl Gowen, April 3, 1956; children: Paul Jeremy, Colin Alexander. *Education:* Royal College of Organists, A.R.C.O., 1950; University of Durham, B.A. (with honors), 1953, B.Mus., 1957, M.A., 1962.

ADDRESSES: Home—211 Fidlas Rd., Llanishen, Cardiff, Glamorganshire CF4 5NR, Wales. *Office*—Department of Music, University College, University of Wales, Cardiff, Glamorganshire CF1 1XL, Wales.

CAREER: Teacher and head of music department at grammar school in Hemsworth, Yorkshire, England, 1956-59; Welsh College of Music and Drama, Cardiff, Wales, lecturer, 1960-70, senior lecturer in music, 1970-73; University of Wales, University College, Cardiff, lecturer, 1973-85, senior lecturer in music, 1985—. *Military service:* British Army, 1953-55.

MEMBER: Royal Musical Association, Royal College of Organists.

AWARDS, HONORS: Literary award for music from *Yorkshire Post,* 1986, for *Domenico Scarlatti.*

WRITINGS:

Harmonizing "Bach" Chorales, Barrie & Rockliff, 1967, revised edition, 1967.
Bach's Instrumental Counterpoint, Barrie & Rockliff, 1967, revised edition, 1967.
(Editor) George Frederick Handel, *La Solitudine,* Baerenreiter, 1971.
(Editor) Alessandro Scarlatti, *Lontan dalla sua Clori,* Baerenreiter, 1972.
(Editor) Alessandro Scarlatti, *Io son pur solo,* Baerenreiter, 1972.
Palestrina's Style: A Practical Introduction, Oxford University Press, 1973.
William Mathias, University of Wales Press, 1978.
(Contributor) Meic Stephens, editor, *The Arts in Wales, 1950-1975,* Welsh Arts Council, 1979.
Grace Williams, University of Wales Press, 1980.
Bach, Dent, 1983.
Domenico Scarlatti: Master of Music, Weidenfeld & Nicolson, 1986.
(Editor) Alessandro Scarlatti, *The Italian Cantata in the Seventeenth Century,* Volume 14: *Cantatas,* Garland Publishing, 1987.

Contributor to *The New Grove Dictionary of Music and Musicians* and *The New Oxford Companion to Music.* Contributor of articles and reviews to music journals.

WORK IN PROGRESS: The Oratorio in Britain.

SIDELIGHTS: Malcolm Boyd's *Bach* was welcomed by *Times Literary Supplement* critic Stephen Daw as "probably the best, and without much doubt, the most constructive and fascinating book of this length on J. S. Bach that has yet been published in any language." The value of Boyd's study, Daw wrote, is that the author has made full use of the provocative and revealing scholarship that has appeared since the end of World War II "without losing a sense of proportion and of the value of it all." *Bach* is, first and foremost, a study of the music, blended with enough biographical and historical material to illuminate the composer's musical development. The book documents a wide variety of conflicting opinion, including the author's own analysis of the critical dissent. Stephen Daw informed his readers that Boyd's conclusions "cannot fail to stimulate and to delight the newcomer and the connoisseur alike.''

In *Domenico Scarlatti,* Boyd examined the mysterious life and music of the man *Times Literary Supplement* critic Winton Dean referred to as ''one of the most elusive of the great composers.'' The paucity of biographical material on Domenico Scarlatti has made critical study difficult indeed, for he did not spend his life in the public eye, and he left few hints that might illuminate his character. As Boyd pointed out in his book, the composer spent his early years in the heavy shadow of his musical father, Alessandro Scarlatti, and his later years in relative obscurity. Few of Domenico's original manuscripts have survived, and these have been the focus of Boyd's scholarship. The *Times Literary Supplement* critic found Boyd's analysis of Scarlatti's keyboard sonatas to be ''full of perceptive comment, well illustrated by quotation.'' Dean added that ''his analysis of the structure of the music is penetrating'' and ''there is an excellent chapter on Scarlatti's reputation and influence.''

Boyd told *CA:* ''My first three books, on J. S. Bach and Palestrina technique, were written because my experience as a school and college teacher suggested that there was a need for them. Since then, all my books (and most of my articles) have been commissioned, and these commissions have so far prevented my getting on with *The Oratorio in Britain,* though some progress has been made recently.''

BIOGRAPHICAL/CRITICAL SOURCES:

PERIODICALS

Times Literary Supplement, May 18, 1984, December 26, 1986.

* * *

BOYNTON, Sandra (Keith) 1953-

PERSONAL: Born April 3, 1953, in Orange, N.J.; daughter of Robert Whitney and Jeanne Carolyn (Ragsdale) Boynton; married James Patrick McEwan, October 18, 1978; children: Caitlin Boynton (daughter). *Education:* Yale University, B.A., 1974; graduate study at University of California, Berkeley, 1974-75, and Yale University, 1976-77. *Religion:* Society of Friends (Quakers).

CAREER: Author and illustrator of children's books. Recycled Paper Products, Inc., Chicago, Ill., designer of greeting cards, 1974—, vice-president, 1980—.

MEMBER: Cartoonists Guild.

AWARDS, HONORS: Irma Simonton Black Award, 1986, for *Chloe and Maude.*

WRITINGS:

SELF-ILLUSTRATED CHILDREN'S BOOKS

Hippos Go Berserk, Little, Brown, 1979.
Hester in the Wild, Harper, 1979.
If at First. . . , Little, Brown, 1980.
Body Parts, edited by Kate Klimo, Simon & Schuster, 1982.
But Not the Hippopotamus, edited by Klimo, Simon & Schuster, 1982.
The Going to Bed Book, edited by Klimo, Simon & Schuster, 1982.
Opposites, edited by Klimo, Simon & Schuster, 1982.
Sounds, edited by Klimo, Simon & Schuster, 1982.
A Is for Angry: An Adjective and Animal Alphabet, Workman Publishing, 1983.

Moo Baa La La La, edited by Klimo, Simon & Schuster, 1983.
Hey! What's That?, Random House, 1985.
Chloe and Maude, Little, Brown, 1985.
Good Night, Good Night, Random House, 1985.
Christmastime, Workman Publishing, 1987.

BOOKS OF CARTOONS

Gopher Baroque, and Other Beastly Conceits, Dutton, 1979.
The Compleat Turkey, Little, Brown, 1980, revised edition published as *Don't Let the Turkeys Get You Down,* Workman Publishing, 1986.
Chocolate: The Consuming Passion, Workman Publishing, 1982.

OTHER

Also author of *A to Z, Doggies, Horns to Toes,* and *Blue Hat Green Hat,* all published by Musson. Contributor to magazines, including *Redbook.*

SIDELIGHTS: Known for her best-selling greeting-card menagerie of whimsical animals displaying childlike behavior, Boynton is also an author who combines her talents as a cartoonist with clever and skillfully written texts. *Chocolate: The Consuming Passion,* for example, received much critical attention for its unique and sentimental look at chocolate. In her definitive guide to the popular confection Boynton profiles the numerous guises—from kisses to bunnies—of milk chocolate, offers proven methods for determining what's inside boxed candy, debunks such ''insidious'' myths as that chocolate is fattening or addictive, and even presents several recipes, all of which add up to what *Los Angeles Times Book Review* contributor Ben Reuven described as ''a delightful little bonbon of a book. Sometimes playful, sometimes perfectly serious, always displaying a rich sense of wit and style.''

Boynton has also written numerous books for younger children, including *Hippos Go Berserk,* in which she reveals her fine ear for nonsense rhyme. Not only a counting book but a visual tool as well, *Hippos Go Berserk* was described by *Wilson Library Bulletin* as ''a small, unpretentious book'' whose ''total effect is light, airy, and tender.'' The old adage of ''try, try again'' is spotlighted in *If at First . . . ,* a story that chronicles the desperate attempts of a little brown mouse to push a giant, disinteressed purple elephant up a hill. The mouse tries leading it, tempting it with a peanut, yelling, and pushing, but all tactics fail. Finally the mouse succeeds in startling the napping pachyderm awake and up the hill with the blast of a trumpet—only, however, to discover on the final page of text the word *again* and a view downhill of eight more purple elephants in line for the climb.

In *Chloe and Maude,* a 1985 Boynton publication, two cat friends star in a trio of brief stories, highlighting what *School Library Journal* called ''the vicissitudes of friendship.'' The two felines have minor disagreements, but their friendship endures as each learns how to be a better friend. Calling Chloe and Maude ''kissing cousins of the droll little animals in Boynton's greeting card line,'' the *Journal* reviewer complimented Boynton on ''mak[ing] the leap from card to book with considerable success.''

BIOGRAPHICAL/CRITICAL SOURCES:

PERIODICALS

Booklist, March 1, 1986.
Chicago Tribune Book World, May 23, 1982.

Christian Science Monitor, February 7, 1986.
Globe and Mail (Toronto), March 16, 1985.
Los Angeles Times Book Review, June 27, 1982, January 15, 1984.
New York Times Book Review, June 13, 1982.
School Library Journal, March, 1983, March, 1986.
Washington Post Book World, February 12, 1984.
Wilson Library Bulletin, March, 1980.

*   *   *

BRAM, Chris
  See BRAM, Christopher

*   *   *

BRAM, Christopher   1952-
  (Chris Bram; Thersites, a pseudonym)

PERSONAL: Born February 22, 1952, in Buffalo, N.Y. *Education:* College of William and Mary, B.A. (with honors), 1974.

ADDRESSES: Home—New York, N.Y. *Agent*—Eric Ashworth, 231 West 22nd St., New York, N.Y. 10011.

CAREER: Virginian-Pilot, Norfolk, Va., reporter, 1971; Social Security Administration, Flushing, N.Y., benefit authorizer, 1978-79; Scribner Bookstore, New York City, clerk, 1979-86; *New York Native*, New York City, typesetter, 1986-87; writer, 1987—.

MEMBER: Authors Guild, Omicron Delta Kappa.

WRITINGS:

Surprising Myself (novel), Donald I. Fine, 1987.
Hold Tight (novel), Donald I. Fine, 1988.

Also author, with Draper Shreeve, of screenplays for short films "George and Al" and "Business-like."

Work represented in anthologies, including *Aphrodisiac: Fiction From Christopher Street*, Coward, 1980. Contributor to magazines, including *Premiere, New York Times Book Review, New York Native* (under name Chris Bram), and *Night and Day* (under pseudonym Thersites). Editor of *William and Mary Review*, 1973-74; contributing editor of *Christopher Street*, 1979-82.

WORK IN PROGRESS: Another novel, set in the present day.

SIDELIGHTS: Christopher Bram wrote: "I am a gay novelist, but, like John Fox, Stephen McCauley, and other writers in my generation, I try to treat gayness as just one strand in a life that has more similarities with 'mainstream' life than dissimilarities, without denying the dissimilarities. We offer a different perspective on the world, as interesting, accessible, and valid to anyone as the perspectives offered by black, Jewish, or feminist writers. I am a reader, a cinephile, a comic realist, and a smoker."

*   *   *

BRASSAI
  See HALASZ, Gyula

*   *   *

BRAWLEY, Paul Holm
  See BRAWLEY, Paul L(eroy)

BRAWLEY, Paul L(eroy)   1942-1988

OBITUARY NOTICE—See index for *CA* sketch: Some sources cite name as Paul Holm Brawley; born September 27, 1942, in Granite City, Ill.; died October 2, 1988, in Chicago, Ill. Librarian and editor. During Brawley's fifteen-year term as editor in chief of *Booklist*, published by the American Library Association, the review bulletin doubled its annual number of reviews to more than six thousand. Brawley joined the *Booklist* staff in 1969 as its first editor of nonprint reviews, and he became editor in chief in 1973. Prior to his work with *Booklist* he worked as a librarian for the Boston Public Library.

OBITUARIES AND OTHER SOURCES:

BOOKS

Who's Who in Library and Information Services, American Library Association, 1982.

PERIODICALS

Chicago Tribune, October 6, 1988.

*   *   *

BRELIS, Matthew   1957-

BRIEF ENTRY: Born August 30, 1957, in Boston, Mass. American journalist. In 1987 Brelis won a Pulitzer Prize for his collaboration with Andrew Schneider on fourteen articles that probed the Federal Aviation Administration's screening of airline pilots for substance abuse and other medical problems, leading to important reforms in testing procedures. In the same year Brelis also received the Keystone Press and Roy W. Howard Newspaper awards. A 1980 graduate of Vassar College, Brelis began his career in journalism at the *Washington Star* and has been a reporter since 1981 for the *Pittsburgh Press*. *Addresses: Home*—Pittsburgh, Pa. *Office*—*Pittsburgh Press*, Box 566, Pittsburgh, Pa. 15230.

BIOGRAPHICAL/CRITICAL SOURCES:

PERIODICALS

New York Times, April 17, 1987.

*   *   *

BRENLOVE, Milovan S.   1948-

PERSONAL: Born December 6, 1948, in Pittsburgh, Pa.; son of R. Rhody (an attorney) and Diana (a teacher; maiden name, Vujnovic) Brenlove; married Barbara Caldarelli (an accountant), November 27, 1970; children: Rachael Morgan, Amanda Mildred. *Education:* Washington and Jefferson College, B.A., 1970.

ADDRESSES: Home—3 Orchard Hill Circle, Bedford, N.H. 03102.

CAREER: Air traffic controller in Pittsburgh, Pa., 1974-87; aviation writer, 1987—; Daniel Webster College, Nashua, N.H., faculty member, 1988—. Flight instructor, air traffic procedures designer, and pilot educator. *Military service:* U.S. Army, 1970-72.

MEMBER: Aviation/Space Writers Association.

WRITINGS:

The Air Traffic Control System: A Commonsense Guide, Iowa State University Press, 1987.

Author of columns in *Minnesota Flyer* and *Aviation USA*. Contributor to *Flying* and *Private Pilot*.

SIDELIGHTS: Milovan S. Brenlove told *CA:* "I began writing to fulfill a need which I believed the Federal Aviation Administration (FAA) had ignored. There was no material available that gave pilots access to a simple, easy-to-understand explanation of the air traffic control system. Pilots and controllers have specific roles and responsibilities that change greatly depending upon the circumstances.

"As I participated in safety seminars in which the same questions continued to be asked, and as I watched the same mistakes being made over and over within the system, I realized an area of pilot education that had been overlooked. I began writing about various topics for different aviation magazines. The response prompted me to write my first book. Although there are one or two other such books on the market, they were written from pilots' perspectives. Being both a pilot and a controller allowed me to approach the subject with a much better understanding of the problems that occur on both sides of the microphone. My main goal was to better educate pilots so that they too could safely enjoy a system that was supposed to have been designed for their benefit—a point many recent government bureaucrats seem to have missed.

"Probably the single most important way to achieve greater safety in the air traffic system is to remember that people are the reason for the tremendous safety record in the United States. Technology should be used to enhance human capabilities, not replace them. The other way to enhance safety it to provide a more in-depth education for pilots. As a faculty member at Daniel Webster College, a prominent aviation school, I hope to play a role in educating our future pilots."

*   *   *

BRICK, Howard   1953-

PERSONAL: Born December 6, 1953, in Amityville, N.Y.; son of Julius Herman (an engineer) and Janet (Frank) Brick; married Debra M. Schwartz (an editor), May 28, 1978; children: Michael Perry, Jessye Rose. *Education:* University of Michigan, A.B. (with high honors), 1975, A.M., 1976, Ph.D., 1983.

ADDRESSES: Office—Department of History, University of Oregon, 175 PLC Hall, Eugene, Ore. 97403.

CAREER: Free-lance writer, 1983-85; University of Chicago, Chicago, Ill., William R. Harper fellow in Social Science Division, 1985-87; University of Oregon, Eugene, assistant professor of history, 1987—. Mellon faculty fellow in American civilization at Harvard University, 1987-88. Member of Hyde Park Committee on Central America and Ann Arbor Committee on Human Rights in Latin America.

MEMBER: American Historical Association, Organization of American Historians, American Studies Association, Mid-Atlantic Radical Historians Organization, Phi Beta Kappa.

AWARDS, HONORS: Hopwood Award, Major Essay category, from University of Michigan, 1975, for "The Rosenbergs in Retrospect, and Other Essays."

WRITINGS:

Daniel Bell and the Decline of Intellectual Radicalism: Social Theory and Political Reconciliation in the 1940s, University of Wisconsin Press, 1986.

Contributor to history journals.

WORK IN PROGRESS: A study of Talcott Parsons and the making of his major work, *The Structure of Social Action,* completion expected in 1990.

BIOGRAPHICAL/CRITICAL SOURCES:

PERIODICALS

Times Literary Supplement, November 21, 1986.

*   *   *

BRITINDIAN
See SOLOMON, Samuel

*   *   *

BRITTON, John A(ndrew)   1943-

PERSONAL: Born August 15, 1943, in Jackson, N.C.; son of Guy (an employee of the U.S. Department of Agriculture) and Norma (a schoolteacher; maiden name, Brown) Britton; married Kathleen Smith (a college teacher), June 2, 1969; children: Jeanne MacDonald, Daniel Brown, Maria Henriquez. *Education:* University of North Carolina at Chapel Hill, B.A., 1965; Tulane University, M.A., 1967, Ph.D., 1971. *Politics:* Democrat. *Religion:* United Methodist.

ADDRESSES: Home—1364 Brookwood, Florence, S.C. 29501. *Office*—Department of History, Francis Marion College, Francis Marion Highway, Box F7500, Florence, S.C. 29501.

CAREER: Tulane University, New Orleans, La., instructor in history, 1970-72; Francis Marion College, Florence, S.C., assistant professor, 1972-79, associate professor, 1979-84, professor of history, 1984—.

MEMBER: Conference on Latin American History of the American Historical Association, Latin American Studies Association, Southeastern Conference on Latin American Studies.

WRITINGS:

Educacion y radicalismo en Mexico, 1931-1940 (title means "Education and Radicalism in Mexico, 1931-1940"), Sepsetentas, 1976.
Carleton Beals: A Radical Journalist in Latin America, University of New Mexico Press, 1987.

Contributor to history and Latin American studies journals.

WORK IN PROGRESS: The Influence of the Mexican Government in the Press of the United States, 1910-1940; The Mexican Revolution and United States Intellectuals, 1910-1950; a history of anti-imperialism in the western hemisphere in the twentieth century.

SIDELIGHTS: John A. Britton told *CA:* "While I was growing up during the Red Scare of the 1950s and the discordant radicalism of the 1960s, I became interested in the struggle of the left in its varied historical, political, and cultural manifestations, first in the United States, then in Mexico and Latin America in general. More a patient critic than an active participant, I focus my research and writing on the achievements and failures of the left in the recent past. Much of my work centers on the mass media as a field of conflict in the struggle involving leftists and their moderate and conservative opposition. I believe that the study of this ideological conflict offers valuable insights into the issues of revolution and imperialism—issues that have often dominated relations between the

United States and third world nations from the early twentieth century to the present. In my 'work in progress,' I intend to explore the themes discussed in the following paragraphs.

"Events in Mexico from 1910 to 1940 gave the United States its first intimate experience with a social revolution in a third world nation. The revolution first manifested itself in violence and civil strife from 1910 to 1920 which gave way to a series of stable governments that attempted to restructure the nation's economy and society. In 1914 and again in 1916 U.S. President Woodrow Wilson ordered military interventions in Mexico. The Mexican people deeply resented these interventions, and the nation's political leaders sought to avert their recurrence in part by shaping the image of the revolution in the U.S. print media. In order to persuade the American public and the policy makers in Washington, D.C., of its good intentions and thereby reduce the possibility of future interventions, the Mexican Government accorded special attention to well-known writers and editors such as Lincoln Steffins, William Randolph Hearst, John Dewey, and Ernest Gruening. In addition, Mexico found outlets in the *New York Times, Current History,* and other important media organs for its own version of controversies involving the United States. In 1938, however, Mexico's President Lazaro Cardenas confronted sharply negative commentary as a result of his radical policies and, in response to what he considered unjustified criticism, expelled *New York Times* correspondent Frank Kluckhohn. Clearly the print media of the United States was a significant factor in the Mexican revolution.

"The radical character of Mexico's government-directed economic and social program reached its peak under Cardenas when his administration engaged in extensive land reform, accepted socialism as the official doctrine in public education and supported the national labor organization led by a self-avowed Marxist and Communist sympathizer. For the U.S. Government and business interests, the most direct challenge came in the expropriation of extensive American-owned oil properties in 1938. Instead of resorting to the familiar device of military intervention or the more indirect techniques of manipulation and destabilization (to become components of U.S. policy after 1945), President Franklin Roosevelt's State Department chose to negotiate with Mexico. The peaceful diplomatic and financial settlement of this dispute and the subsequent improvement of relations between the two nations remains a highly unusual episode in the history of U.S. relations with left-wing governments in third world nations. Yet this accommodation with radicalism was quickly forgotten by U.S. political, diplomatic, and military leaders during World War II and the onset of the Cold War.

"A mixed and often divided group of U.S. leftist intellectuals disagreed about the ideological vascillations of the Mexican Government, accepted and/or rejected official efforts to gain favorable coverage in the print media, criticized the American Government's hostility to Mexico's social and economic programs, and generally applauded Washington's accommodation with Mexico's radicalism of the late 1930s. This body of information and analysis, unfortunately, fell outside the purview of U.S. policymakers during the Cold War. In 1954 President Dwight D. Eisenhower's administration overthrew a similar leftist government in Guatemala. The observations of these leftists on Mexico and its relations with the United States in the years from 1910 to 1950 constitute an insightful if sometimes overly enthusiastic portrayal of a lost legacy of reconciliation with radicalism, a forgotten chapter in the recent past of the western hemisphere that deserves a wider understanding in the current context of the hostile relations between the United States and left-wing movements in Latin America and throughout the third world."

AVOCATIONAL INTERESTS: Jogging, playing and watching sports, collecting books and videotapes of films from the period 1920 to 1960.

*   *   *

BROERMAN, Bruce M(artin)   1945-

PERSONAL: Born June 20, 1945, in Oskaloosa, Iowa; son of Frederic M. (a farmer) and Margaret (a secretary; maiden name, Scheuermann) Broerman; married Elisabeth Fruehauf, June 19, 1969 (divorced June 14, 1982); children: Stephanie, Martin. *Education:* University of Iowa, B.A., 1967; State University of New York at Albany, Ph.D., 1976.

ADDRESSES: Home—1043 South Harvey, Oak Park, Ill. 60304. *Office*—Institute of European Studies, 223 West Ohio St., Chicago, Ill. 60610.

CAREER: Bayerische-Julius-Maximilians-Universitaet, Wuerzburg, West Germany, lecturer in English, 1974-75; University of North Dakota, Grand Forks, assistant professor of German, 1976-77; University of Illinois at Chicago Circle, assistant professor of German, 1978-84, director of Austria-Illinois Exchange Program, 1982-84; Institute of European Studies, Chicago Ill., program officer, 1984—.

MEMBER: Modern Language Association of America, Fulbright Alumni Association, Gay and Lesbian Parents Group/Chicago (board of directors, co-chairperson, 1987-88), Phi Beta Kappa.

AWARDS, HONORS: Fulbright fellow at Philipps-Universitaet, Marburg/Lahn, 1967-68.

WRITINGS:

(Editor with John M. Spalek) *German Expressionism in the Fine Arts: A Bibliography,* Hennessey & Ingalls, 1977.
(Contributor) Donald G. Daviau and Lugwig M. Fischer, editors, *Das Exilerlebnis,* Camden House, 1982.
The German Historical Novel in Exile After 1933: Calliope Contra Clio, Pennsylvania State University Press, 1986.
(Contributor) John M. Spalek and Joseph P. Strelka, editors, *Deutsche Exilliteratur seit 1933; Band II: New York,* Francke, in press.

Contributor of articles to *Die deutsche Literatur: Biographisches und bibliographisches Lexikon: Reihe VI.* Contributor of articles and reviews to periodicals, including *Modern Austrian Literature, Colloquia Germanica,* and the *German Quarterly.*

SIDELIGHTS: Bruce M. Broerman told *CA:* "My major area of vocational interest is international/cross-cultural education with strong emphasis on the humanities."

AVOCATIONAL INTERESTS: "My avocational interests encompass all forms of artistic expression"; travel (United States and Europe); foreign languages (German, French).

*   *   *

BROWN, William Edward   1904-

PERSONAL: Born March 21, 1904, in Elbridge, N.Y.; son of Albert Edward (a grocer) and Adeline (a housewife; maiden name, Wall) Brown. *Education:* Syracuse University, A.B.,

1925, A.M., 1926; Yale University, Ph.D., 1941. *Politics:* Democrat.

ADDRESSES: Home—Route 3, Box 254, Grafton, Vt. 05146.

CAREER: Syracuse University, Syracuse, N.Y., instructor in Greek, 1926-27; Lafayette College, Easton, Pa., instructor, 1927-30, assistant professor, 1930-40, associate professor, 1940-47, professor of Greek, 1947-73, head of department of languages, 1947-58; writer, 1973—. *Military service:* U.S. Army, 1943-46; became major.

MEMBER: Modern Language Association of America, Chester Historical Society (president, 1986-88).

AWARDS, HONORS: Vucinich Prize from American Association for the Advancement of Slavic Studies, 1987, for *A History of Russian Literature in the Romantic Period.*

WRITINGS:

A History of Russian Seventeenth Century Literature, Ardis, 1980.
A History of Russian Eighteenth Century Literature, Ardis, 1980.
A History of Russian Literature in the Romantic Period, Ardis, 1986.
(Translator and author of commentary) Vladimir Sollogub, *Tarantas,* Ardis, 1988.

Contributor to classical periodicals.

WORK IN PROGRESS: Russian Romantic Poetry in the Realistic Period, 1840-1860.

SIDELIGHTS: William Edward Brown wrote: "My association with the late Professor Michael I. Rostovtseff of Yale University, with whom I wrote my doctoral dissertation, inspired me to learn Russian and led to my research on Russian literary history and my three published works in that area. I have taught comparative literature for many years and believe strongly in presenting all the European literatures as portions of the same whole, not in compartments. In fact, although my competence is mainly as a historian and literary critic, I have an avocational interest in art and music, which I consider equally with literature to be parts of an indivisible European whole.

"I have traveled extensively in Europe and the Near East, including Russia, and I have more or less competence in the major European languages."

AVOCATIONAL INTERESTS: Music, gardening, gourmet cooking.

*   *   *

BRUFORD, Walter Horace   1894-1988

OBITUARY NOTICE: Born in 1894 in Manchester, England; died June 28, 1988. Educator and author. Known for his innovative social interpretations of literature, Bruford was influential in the development of German studies in England. Beginning in the 1920s he was a professor of German at various British universities, including Edinburgh and Cambridge. Bruford helped found the International Association for Germanic Studies in 1955 and was credited with integrating historical, linguistic, and aesthetic aspects into the study of language. His writings include *Germany in the Eighteenth Century, Culture and Society in Classical Weimar,* and *The Organization and Rise of Prussia and German Constitutional and Social Development.* He also annotated and introduced an edition of

Johann Wolfgang von Goethe's *Faust* and published two studies on Russian writer Anton Chekhov.

OBITUARIES AND OTHER SOURCES:

BOOKS

Who's Who, 140th edition, St. Martin's, 1988.

PERIODICALS

Times (London), June 30, 1988.

*   *   *

BRUNETTE, Peter (Clark, Jr.)   1943-

PERSONAL: Born September 18, 1943, in Richwood, W.Va.; son of Peter Clark (a postal supervisor) and Mildred L. (a housewife; maiden name, Perkins) Brunette; married Lynne Ellen Johnson (a college teacher), August 10, 1974. *Education:* Duquesne University, B.A., 1965, M.A., 1967; University of Wisconsin—Madison, Ph.D., 1975.

ADDRESSES: Home—6540 North 27th St., Arlington, Va. 22213. *Office*—Department of English, George Mason University, Fairfax, Va. 22030.

CAREER: University of Paris, Paris, France, lecturer in English, 1970-72; University of Maryland at College Park, instructor in English in European Division, 1972-73; University of Maryland Eastern Shore, Princess Anne, instructor in English and director of Basic Skills Center, 1974-75; George Mason University, Fairfax, Va., assistant professor, 1975-79, associate professor, 1979-88, professor of English, 1988—.

MEMBER: Modern Language Association of America, Society for Cinema Studies.

AWARDS, HONORS: Fellow of National Endowment for the Humanities, 1981-82, 1987-88; associate fellow at Center for Advanced Study in the Visual Arts, National Gallery of Art, 1981-82; fellow at School of Criticism and Theory, Northwestern University, 1982.

WRITINGS:

(Contributor) Gerald Peary and Roger Shatzkin, editors, *The Classic American Novel and the Movies,* Ungar, 1977.
(Contributor) Gerald Peary and Roger Shatzkin, editors, *The Modern American Novel and the Movies,* Ungar, 1978.
(Contributor) Gerald Peary and Dannis Peary, editors, *American Cartoon Animation,* Dutton, 1978.
(Contributor) Andrew Horton and Joan Magretta, editors, *Modern European Filmmakers and the Art of Adaptation,* Ungar, 1980.
Roberto Rossellini, Oxford University Press, 1987.
(With David Wills) *Screen/Play: Derrida and Film Theory,* Princeton University Press, in press.

Contributor to magazines and newspapers, including *Cineaste, Film Quarterly, New Republic, Sight and Sound, Times Literary Supplement, New York Times Book Review,* and *American Film.*

WORK IN PROGRESS: A book on filmmaker Michelangelo Antonioni for Cambridge University Press; a book on filmmaker Luchino Visconti; contributing an article on the comedy team the Three Stooges to the book *Comedy/Cinema/Theory,* edited by Andrew Horton.

SIDELIGHTS: Peter Brunette told *CA:* "My work is rather schizophrenic, I'm afraid. On the one hand, I write book reviews for various newspapers like the *New York Times*, as well as do interviews with filmmakers for *Film Quarterly* and *Cineaste*. I do this because I think it is important to reach large audiences in order to have at least some tiny effect on contemporary culture. On the other hand, I find my own intellectual interests becoming increasingly theoretical. So much of what is printed in newspapers and magazines, after all, is forgotten in days or even hours. It also sometimes seems that most of that sort of writing is really a matter of recycling the obvious, and trying to find new ways to say the same old boring stuff. Writing more academic pieces, however, gives me the chance to exercise my intellectual capabilities to their maximum, even if those books and essays will never be read by more than a handful of people. Granted, the work that post-structuralist thinkers like Jacques Derrida are engaged in is often difficult and daunting. But it also seems to presage a revolution in the ways we currently think about things—everything, from love to politics to movies—and therefore more than worth the effort.''

BIOGRAPHICAL/CRITICAL SOURCES:

PERIODICALS

Film Criticism, fall, 1987.
New York Times Book Review, September 13, 1987.

* 		* 		*

BRUUN, (Arthur) Geoffrey 1898-1988

OBITUARY NOTICE—See index for *CA* sketch: Born October 20, 1898, in Montreal, Quebec, Canada; died of a kidney ailment, July 13, 1988, in Ithaca, N.Y. Educator and author. Bruun, a historian who specialized in European civilization, taught at New York University beginning in 1927, moved to Sarah Lawrence College in 1943, and served as professor of history at Columbia University from 1945 to 1947. He wrote such books as *The Enlightened Despots, Europe and the French Imperium, Clemenceau, Europe in Evolution, The World in the Twentieth Century*, and *Nineteenth-Century European Civilization*.

OBITUARIES AND OTHER SOURCES:

BOOKS

Directory of American Scholars, Volume I: *History*, 8th edition, Bowker, 1982.

PERIODICALS

New York Times, July 17, 1988.

* 		* 		*

BULMER, Ralph N(eville) H(ermon) 1928-1988

OBITUARY NOTICE: Born April 3, 1928, in Hereford, England; died July 18, 1988, in Auckland, New Zealand. Anthropologist, ethnobiologist, educator, and author. A highly respected anthropologist, Bulmer also made important contributions in the field of ethnobiology, the systematic study of the plant and animal lore of a race or people. Much of his work centered on folk classification of plants and animals, principally in the territory of what is now Papua New Guinea. Bulmer lectured at Auckland University in Australia and was the founding professor of social anthropology at the University of Papua New Guinea. He collaborated with Ian Saem Majnep, a Papua New Guinea tribesman, on two books titled *Birds of My Kalam Country* and *Animals Our Ancestors Hunted*.

OBITUARIES AND OTHER SOURCES:

BOOKS

Fifth International Directory of Anthropologists, University of Chicago Press, 1975.

PERIODICALS

Times (London), July 21, 1988.

* 		* 		*

BUNCH, Charlotte (Anne) 1944-
(Charlotte Bunch-Weeks)

PERSONAL: Born October 13, 1944, in West Jefferson, N.C.; daughter of Charles Pardue (a physician) and Marjorie (a social worker; maiden name, King) Bunch; married James L. Weeks, March 25, 1967 (divorced, 1971). *Education:* Attended University of California, Berkeley, 1965; Duke University, B.A. (magna cum laude), 1966; attended Institute for Policy Studies, 1967-68. *Politics:* ''Feminist.''

ADDRESSES: Home—392 Third St., No. 6, Brooklyn, N.Y. 11215. *Office*—Women's Studies, Voorhees Chapel, Douglass College, Rutgers University, New Brunswick, N.J. 08903.

CAREER: University Christian Movement, New York, N.Y., co-founder and national president, 1966-67, consultant to experimental education groups on fifty college campuses, 1967-68; Case Western Reserve University, Cleveland, Ohio, member of campus ministry staff, 1968-69; Institute for Policy Studies, Washington, D.C., visiting fellow, 1969-70, resident fellow, 1971-75, tenured fellow, 1975-77; Public Resource Center, Washington, D.C., founder and director, 1977-81; Interfem Consultants, New York City, founder, director, and consultant to various organizations, 1979-87; Douglass College, Rutgers University, New Brunswick, N.J., Laurie New Jersey chair in women's studies, 1987-89.

Guest lecturer at universities and colleges, including American University, Bowling Green State University, George Washington University, Graduate Theological Union, and University of Maryland. Organizer of or participant in numerous conferences, workshops, and seminars in several countries, including Australia, Canada, Chile, Denmark, Ethiopia, Finland, India, Japan, Kenya, Mexico, the Netherlands, New Zealand, Peru, the Philippines, Sri Lanka, Switzerland, Tanzania, Thailand, and the United States.

MEMBER: Isis International (associate, 1985—), National Organization for Women (NOW), National Gay and Lesbian Task Force (member of board of directors, 1974-81; member of executive committee, 1976-78), National Women's Studies Association, National Women's Conference Committee, American Friends Service Committee (member of National Women's Program Committee, 1980-83), Women's Liberation Movement (co-founder of Washington, D.C., group, 1968), Women's Institute for Freedom of the Press (associate, 1978-86), New York Feminist Art Institute (member of advisory board, 1979—), New York City Commission on the Status of Women (chair of United Nations Decade committee, 1982-86).

AWARDS, HONORS: Community service awards from Lambda Legal Defense Fund, 1982, and National Lesbian and Gay Health Foundation, 1986.

WRITINGS:

(Under name Charlotte Bunch-Weeks) *A Broom of One's Own*, Washington, D.C., Women's Liberation Movement, 1970.

Passionate Politics: Feminist Theory in Action—Essays, 1968-1986, St. Martin's, 1987.

EDITOR

(Under name Charlotte Bunch-Weeks; with Joanne Cooke and Robin Morgan) *The New Women: A Motive Anthology on Women's Liberation*, Bobbs-Merrill, 1970.

(With Nancy Myron) *Class and Feminism: A Collection of Essays From the Furies*, Diana Press, 1974.

(With Myron) *Women Remembered: A Collection of Biographies From the Furies*, Diana Press, 1974.

(With Myron) *Lesbianism and the Women's Movement*, Diana Press, 1975.

(With J. Flax, A. Freeman, N. Hartsock, and M. Mautner) *Building Feminist Theory: Essays From Quest*, Longman, 1981.

(With Sandra Pollack) *Learning Our Way: Essays in Feminist Education*, Crossing Press, 1983.

(With Kathleen Barry and Shirley Castley) *International Feminism: Networking Against Female Sexual Slavery*, International Women's Tribune Centre, 1984.

CONTRIBUTOR

Deborah Babcox and Madeline Belkin, editors, *Liberation NOW! Writings From the Women's Liberation Movement*, Dell, 1971.

Ginny Vida, editor, *Our Right to Love*, Prentice-Hall, 1978.

A. Jaggar and P. Struhl, *Feminist Frameworks*, McGraw, 1978.

Evelyn Shapiro and Barry M. Shapiro, *The Women Say, the Men Say*, Delacorte, 1979.

Caroline Bird, editor, *What Women Want: From the Report on International Women's Year in Houston*, Simon & Schuster, 1979.

Karla Jay and Allen Young, editors, *Lavender Culture*, Jove, 1979.

Sheila Ruth, editor, *Issues in Feminism: A First Course in Women's Studies*, Houghton, 1980.

Laura Lederer, editor, *Take Back the Night: Women on Pornography*, Morrow, 1980.

Edden Messer-Davidow, editor, *Women in Print II*, Modern Language Association of America, 1982.

William V. Burgess, editor, *Current Issues in Organizational Leadership*, Ginn Press, 1983.

John S. Friedman, editor, *First Harvest: Institute for Policy Studies, 1963-83*, Grove, 1983.

Diana Russell and Nicole Van de Ven, editors, *Crimes Against Women: Proceedings of the International Tribunal*, Frog in the Well, 1984.

Renate Duelli Klein, Candida Lacey, and Dale Spender, editors, *Women's Studies International Forum*, Pergamon, 1985.

OTHER

Author or co-author of pamphlets on feminist topics, including "Sweet Sixteen to Soggy Thirty-six: Saga of American Womanhood," "Facing Down the Right," "Going Public With Our Visions," "Bringing the Global Home," and "The Ferraro Factor: Symbolism or Substance?"

Contributor to numerous feminist, gay, and Christian periodicals, including *Broadsheet, Christianity and Crisis, Christopher Street, Heresies, IKON, Interact, Isis, Ms., Nouvelles Questions feministes, New Student, Response, Signs, Sinister Wisdom, Sojourner, Student World*, and *Women's World*.

Co-founder and editor of *The Furies*, 1972-73, and *Quest: A Feminist Quarterly*, 1974-81. Member of editorial board of *Motive*, 1967-73. Editor of special editions of *Motive* and *Off Our Backs*. Consultant to Daughters, Inc. (feminist publishing company), 1976-78.

WORK IN PROGRESS: Research on relationship of feminism and human rights.

SIDELIGHTS: "Within the Women's Movement, Charlotte Bunch is a touchstone," wrote former *Ms.* editor Gloria Steinem in 1977. "Sooner or later—and especially when any hard question of feminist theory or tactics comes up—one is likely to hear the question, 'But what does Charlotte think?'" Highly regarded in her field as a theorist, organizer, and consultant, Bunch became involved in feminism during the late 1960s and eventually devoted herself full-time to the movement. She is especially known for her ability to organize and motivate groups and for the timely insights she conveys in her many speeches. "She is often the first to articulate trends of thought as they percolate unevenly to the surface of various segments of the women's movement," observed interviewer Torie Osborn in *Commonground*, adding that Bunch "is one of the warmest and most accessible feminist leaders in the country, and she is a natural teacher."

Bunch became active in civil rights and student Christian organizations while an undergraduate at Duke University during the early 1960s. "The civil rights movement became my education," she told Osborn, and the campus ministry became her vocation for a time. After earning her bachelor's degree in 1966 Bunch helped found the University Christian Movement and became its national president, and she also joined the campus ministry staff of Case Western Reserve University. If there had been no women's movement, she reflected to Osborn, "I'm convinced I would have become one of those women who work in the Methodist Church bureaucracy for liberal causes. . . . I never was into the religion of Methodism; I was into the social action of it. I was into the notions of love and justice." Bunch, who was raised a Methodist, explained, "When I was a child, the only image I had of my life was that I would be a missionary. It was the only way I knew girls could travel around the world and do exciting things."

Bunch was married in 1967 to a man who had worked with her in civil rights projects, but they divorced in 1971 when Bunch discovered her lesbianism. Her family and friends, she told Steinem, had mixed reactions to this change in her life. "It was like coming out in a fishbowl," Bunch remarked. "Some friends were especially shocked because I had an 'ideal marriage' to a man who was very supportive of me and of feminism. How could I possibly leave? Other friends revealed to me that *they* were lesbians, and still others began to deal with lesbianism as at least a political possibility for other women, if not for themselves." That year, in 1971, Bunch helped found the Furies, a lesbian-feminist collective in Washington, D.C., that published a short-lived magazine by the same name. A few years later she helped found another magazine, *Quest: A Feminist Quarterly*. As a fellow of the Washington, D.C., Institute for Policy Studies from 1969 to 1977, a consultant to several international women's and human rights organizations through Interfem Consultants beginning in 1979, and a speaker and organizer for numerous conferences and seminars, Bunch gained the opportunity to voice her well-received opinions on feminism, lesbianism, and global concerns.

"Often called into some of the power struggles and debates that sporadically rend communities," observed Karla Dobinski in a 1983 *Feminist Connection* article, "Charlotte consistently emerges as a respected peacemaker and problem-solver, able to foster honest inquiry into the conflicts that arise." During the 1970s, differences between homosexual and heterosexual feminists, or separatist and non-separatist feminism, created a furor within the movement. Explaining the separatist point of view to Steinem in 1977, Bunch said, "Of course, nothing exists outside the system in the pure sense. We pay taxes, and obey certain rules. But the creation of institutions, projects, and movements that are essentially outside the system seems more important than ever now." She acknowledged the need to work occasionally within accepted social, political, and economic institutions to "see just how far we can make the system budge," but added that "we need to keep a base outside. We need a place to create ourselves."

Eventually, however, Bunch decided that feminism must move beyond mere separatism. "We saw separatism as a vehicle to bring attention to important issues being overlooked," Dobinski quoted her as saying. Once the problems were defined, however, "it [was] important to bring the issues into the perspective of a global picture" by applying feminist principles to non-feminist contexts. Bunch was one of the first to question separatism as an effective primary means of social change. "It was practically a national event in the women's liberation circles," declared Osborn, "when, in 1975 at a national conference, Charlotte declared herself no longer a separatist—that speech signaled the end to intense gay/straight and separatist/non-separatist splits which had swept through the movement." At another famous speech in Berkeley, California, in 1979, reported Osborn, Bunch called the lesbian-feminist subculture a "ghetto" and implored the group to "get out of the ghetto and into the mainstream."

"Feminists listened to Charlotte then," observed the interviewer, "and do now, because we *trust* her." Bunch notes that although women are beginning to apply what they've learned to areas outside the feminist movement, they tend to feel disloyal instead of adaptable when they take this approach. "Women are getting regular jobs for the first time in years," she explained to Osborn in their 1983 interview, "[but] they're still viewing it as the job they have INSTEAD of being a feminist. It's not being seen as valid political work." Emphasizing the importance of an inclusive feminist approach as opposed to the former separatist movement, Bunch declared, "We need to . . . let go of our possession of the past—not let go of what we learned from our past, but let go of our dependence on it. We must trust that our past will take us to our future."

As part of her feminist action, Bunch has co-edited a number of anthologies of women's writings, including *International Feminism: Networking Against Female Sexual Slavery, Learning Our Way: Essays in Feminist Education,* and *Lesbianism and the Women's Movement.* "To read *Learning Our Way* in the 1980s," commented Helene V. Wenzel in a *Women's Review of Books* article, "is to understand where feminist learning has come from and what it has been through. The editors [Bunch and Sandra Pollack] have been unusually conscientious in presenting the fullest political panorama of feminist education."

Bunch has also written numerous essays, many of which are included in her 1987 collection *Passionate Politics: Feminist Theory in Action—Essays, 1968-1986.* "My life as an activist

and organizer lies at the heart of this book," she writes, as quoted in the Toronto *Globe and Mail.* Naomi Black of the *Globe and Mail* asserted that "[Bunch's] voice, as it has been before, is the voice of the most innovative and important part of American feminism." Blanche Wiesen Cook in *Women's Review of Books* praised the essay collection as "a very personal theoretical odyssey which will serve as an organizing handbook far into the future." Noting Bunch's significant influence on the development of feminist ideology, Cook declared: "*Passionate Politics* is more than a collection of theoretical essays that touch on the most vital issues of our lives; it is a history of those issues as one feminist activist has lived through them, and vigorously helped to inform and to shape them."

"I see my own personal quest or search as very connected to the period of transition I see the women's movement to be in," she told Torie Osborn. Comparing the temporary stagnation of feminism during the late 1970s and early 1980s to her own "movement activist mid-life crisis" at that time, Bunch noted that both she and the movement seemed "discouraged and bored" and "stuck." She asserted: "I strongly believe that the primary way the movement in this country will get 'unstuck' will be by connecting with international feminism." Bunch's own worldwide activities involve consulting with a number of organizations, including the International Women's Tribune Centre, the Asian and Pacific Center for Women and Development, and the National Women's Studies Association; coordinating the "Global Feminist Workshop Against Trafficking in Women," held in the Netherlands in 1983; and organizing and participating in several other international workshops in Denmark, Ethiopia, Japan, Kenya, Mexico, Peru, Thailand, and other countries. "I see feminism as a movement of people working for a change across and despite national boundaries, not of representatives of nation-states or national governments," Dobinski quoted Bunch as saying. "We must be global, recognizing that the oppression of women in one part of the world is often affected by what happens in another, and that no woman is free until the conditions of oppression of women are eliminated everywhere."

BIOGRAPHICAL/CRITICAL SOURCES:

PERIODICALS

Commonground, April, 1983.
Feminist Connection, March, 1983.
Globe and Mail (Toronto), December 19, 1987.
Ms., July, 1977.
Signs, winter, 1987.
Women's Review of Books, October, 1984, November, 1987.

—*Sketch by Christa Brelin*

*   *   *

BUNCH-WEEKS, Charlotte
   See BUNCH, Charlotte (Anne)

*   *   *

BURSTEIN, Chaya M(alamud)   1923-

PERSONAL: Born October 9, 1923, in New York, N.Y., daughter of Benjamin (a grocer) and Rivka (a grocer; maiden name, Zeile) Malamud; married Murray Burstein (an engineer), April 7, 1946; children: Ranan, Dina, Beth. *Education:* Hofstra University, B.A., 1968; State University of New York at Stony Brook, M.A., 1983. *Religion:* Jewish.

ADDRESSES: Home—Mitzpeh Har Halutz, D.N. Maaleh haGalil 25129, Israel.

CAREER: U.S. Geological Survey, Rolla, Mo., draftsperson, 1950-54; mother and homemaker, 1954-70; writer and illustrator, 1970—. Volunteer teacher at Nassau County Jail, 1968-73.

MEMBER: American Association of University Women; Hadassah, The Women's Zionist Organization of America.

AWARDS, HONORS: National Jewish book awards from Jewish Book Council, 1976, for Rifka Grows Up, and 1983, for Jewish Kid's Catalogue.

WRITINGS:

Rifka Bangs the Teakettle (juvenile), Harcourt, 1970.
Rifka Grows Up (juvenile), Bonim Books, 1976.
A First Jewish Holiday Cookbook (juvenile), Bonim Books, 1979.
Jewish Kid's Catalogue (juvenile), Jewish Publication Society, 1983.
What's an Israel? (juvenile), Kar-Ben, 1983.
Joseph's and Anna's Time Capsule (juvenile), Summit Books, 1984.
Hebrew Alphabet Coloring Book (juvenile), Dover, 1986.
Kid's Catalogue of Israel (juvenile), Jewish Publication Society, 1988.
The Secret of the Coins (juvenile), Union of American Hebrew Congregations, 1988.
The Prophets (juvenile), Union of American Hebrew Congregations, 1989.

WORK IN PROGRESS: Juvenile Dictionary in Pictures for Jewish Publication Society, completion expected in 1989; Holiday Coloring Book for Dover, completion expected in 1989; a second holiday cookbook, completion expected in 1990.

SIDELIGHTS: Chaya M. Burstein told CA: "In my life and work I have struggled to balance my background of Jewish religion and culture with my American cultural environment. Jewish customs and holiday observances have always given me pleasure, so I have tried to impart a sense of fun as well as cultural richness in three juvenile 'how-to' books on Judaism. Because history fascinates me, I have chosen to write and illustrate stories and nonfiction about several historic periods. I hope that readers enjoy them, and at the same time gain a deeper understanding of their own origins. Three years ago my husband and I moved to Israel—perhaps searching for origins—and now live in a tiny settlement in the Galilee mountains. The site, layered with Hebrew and Arab antiquities, ancient cisterns, crumbled towers, and potsherds, is full of history and current, challenging problems and provides endless material for thinking, illustrating, and writing."

AVOCATIONAL INTERESTS: Gardening, hiking, writing letters, tutoring English.

*   *   *

BURTON, Orville Vernon 1947-

PERSONAL: Born April 15, 1947, in Royston, Ga.; son of Orville Verner (a marine) and Vera Beatrice (an insurance agent; maiden name, Human) Burton; married Georganne Butler (a teacher), November 6, 1980; children: Vera Joanna, Maya, Morgan, Beatrice, Alice-Anne. Education: Furman University, B.A. (summa cum laude), 1969; Princeton University, M.A., 1971, Ph.D., 1976. Politics: "Democrat/socialist." Religion: Baptist.

ADDRESSES: Home—605 West Washington, Urbana, Ill. 61801. Office—Woodrow Wilson International Center for Scholars, Smithsonian Institution Building, Washington, D.C. 20560.

CAREER: University of Illinois, Urbana, Ill., instructor, 1974-76, assistant professor, 1976-82, associate professor of history, 1982—. Consultant to educational bodies. Military service: U.S. Army, 1969 and 1974; became captain.

MEMBER: American History Association, Organization of American Historians, Southern Historical Society, South Carolina Historical Society, Faith and History Association, Society of Historians of the Early American Republic, Southern Regional Council, Edgefield Historical Society, Phi Beta Kappa.

AWARDS, HONORS: Grants from Andrew Carnegie Foundation, 1976, American Council of Learned Societies, 1977, University of Illinois, 1986-87; fellowships from Rockefeller Foundation for the Humanities, 1977-78, University of Illinois Center for Advanced Study, fall, 1982, National Endowment for the Humanities, summer, 1983, Woodrow Wilson International Center for Scholars, 1988-89; Pulitzer Prize nomination for history, 1985, for In My Father's House Are Many Mansions: Family and Community in Edgefield, South Carolina; Burlington-Northern faculty achievement award, 1986; named University Scholar by University of Illinois, 1988.

WRITINGS:

(Contributor) Edward Magdol and Jon L. Wakelyn, editors, The Southern Common People: Studies in Nineteenth Century Social History, Greenwood Press, 1980.
(Editor with Robert C. McMath, Jr.) Class, Conflict, and Consensus: Antebellum Southern Community Studies, Greenwood Press, 1982.
(Editor with McMath) Toward a New South? Studies in Post-Civil War Southern Communities, Greenwood Press, 1982.
In My Father's House Are Many Mansions: Family and Community in Edgefield, South Carolina, University of North Carolina Press, 1985.
(Contributor) Walter J. Fraser, Jr., Frank Saunders, and Wakelyn, editors, The Web of Southern Relations: Women, Family, and Education, University of Georgia Press, 1985.
(Author of foreword) Benjamin Elijah Mays, Born to Rebel: An Autobiography, University of Georgia Press, 1988.
(Contributor) Brett Williams, editor, The Carolina Connection, Smithsonian Institution Press, 1988.
(Contributor) David Chesnutt and Clyde Wilson, editors, The Meaning of South Carolina History: Essays in Honor of Dr. George C. Rogers, Jr., University of South Carolina Press, 1989.
(Contributor) Joanne L. Martin and Steve Lundstrom, editors, Supercomputer Applications, IEEE Computer Society Press, 1989.
(Contributor) David Bantz, editor, Technological Innovations in Computing and Instruction, in press.

Author of computer software packages for database use in history studies; contributor of articles and reviews to scholarly journals and reference books, including Dictionary of Afro-American Slavery, Dictionary of Twentieth Century Black Leaders, and The Encyclopedia of Southern Culture.

WORK IN PROGRESS: An essay on Frank Lawrence Owsley to be included in Historians of the American South, edited by

Rameth Owens and William Steirer, publication by Greenwood Press expected in 1991; a biography on Benjamin Ryan Tillman for the American History Biography series; a book on reconstruction for the "Fred W. Morrison Series in Southern Studies"; an introduction to a biography on Benjamin E. Mays.

SIDELIGHTS: Orville Vernon Burton's *In My Father's House Are Many Mansions* is a comprehensive study of family and community in his native county of Edgefield, South Carolina. A representative rural southern community save for the unusual violence and vengeance that has marked its politics and social relations, Edgefield "simply carried to extremes," described C. Vann Woodward in the *New York Review of Books*, "what was latent or prevalent elsewhere." Focusing on the period from 1850 to the early 1900s, Burton looked at family structure and character in all segments of society: free and slave, black and white, wealthy and poor; historical records reveal that male-headed, two-parent households prevailed throughout. Particularly damaging to the myth of black matriarchy, the book suggests that slavery reinforced—rather than weakened—family structures, that "family was the anchor of slave community and, along with religion, the main refuge and defense against slavery," Woodward remarked. Deeming *In My Father's House Are Many Mansions* a "highly quantified, computerized and methodologically sophisticated study," the critic concluded, "for thoroughness and comprehensiveness it rivals, if it does not exceed, any historical investigation of an American community of comparable scope."

Burton told *CA:* "My academic interests include Southern history, social history, family and community history, race relations, and quantitative techniques. These interests led to two edited books on southern communities, several articles, and a history of the southern family and community, *In My Father's House Are Many Mansions: Family and Community in Edgefield, South Carolina.* Briefly stated, my major intellectual interests include the influence of technology on culture and society especially in regard to computers and humanities and the dilemma of 'converging cultures.' Religion is both important to me personally as well as a major intellectual interest. I continue to study family, community, race relations, agrarian societies, and communication networks.

"Beyond academic scholarship and teaching, I am involved in church activities and take an activist role in race relations by being an expert witness in voting rights cases throughout the South, employing statistical and historical analyses to show how laws have been written and districts have been drawn so that blacks cannot be elected.

"Ironically, for someone who has studied patriarchy, I am the busy father of five daughters. My children, my wife, Georganne, and my mother, Vera, are the love and focus of my life."

BIOGRAPHICAL/CRITICAL SOURCES:

PERIODICALS

Chicago Tribune, June 17, 1988.
New York Review of Books, October 10, 1985.

* * *

BUSIA, Kofi Abrefa   1913-1978

OBITUARY NOTICE—See index for *CA* sketch: Born July 11,

1913, in Wenchi, Brongahafo District, Ghana; died following a heart attack, August 28, 1978, in London (one source says Oxford), England. Government official, educator, and author. Busia was prime minister of Ghana from 1969 to 1972, when a military coup ousted him from power while he was in England for medical treatment. Early in his career Busia taught sociology in Ghana at Wesley College, Achimota College, and University College of the Gold Coast (now University of Ghana). He also taught in the Netherlands at the Institute of Social Studies and University of Leiden and in Great Britain at Oxford University's St. Antony's College. In the late 1960s he served as vice-chairman and chairman of the National Liberation Advisory Council in Ghana, and in 1969 he founded the Progress Party, which he represented in his successful campaign that year for Ghanaian prime minister. Following his three-year term as such, Busia lectured at Oxford University. He wrote several books on sociology and politics, including *Africa in Transition: A Social and Anthropological Observation, Purposeful Education for Africa, The African Consciousness: Continuity and Change in Africa, The Way to Industrial Peace,* and *Apartheid and Its Elimination.*

OBITUARIES AND OTHER SOURCES:

BOOKS

Obituaries on File, Facts on File, 1979.

PERIODICALS

New York Times, November 6, 1978.

* * *

BUTEL, Jane
See de CALLES, Jane F. Butel

* * *

BUTTERICK, George F.   1942-1988

OBITUARY NOTICE—See index for *CA* sketch: Born October 7, 1942, in Yonkers, N.Y.; died of cancer, July 25, 1988, in Willimantic, Conn. Educator, library curator, editor, and author. Butterick was curator of the literary archives and a lecturer in English literature at the University of Connecticut beginning in 1972. Prior to that appointment he taught English at Wilson College in Pennsylvania. Butterick was highly regarded for his scholarship on the poetry of Charles Olson, winning an American Book Award for his 1987 edition *The Collected Poems of Charles Olson,* and the *Los Angeles Times* Book Award for poetry for his 1983 edition of Olson's *Maximus Poems.* Butterick also edited Olson's *Poetry and Truth: The Beloit Lectures and Poems* and *The Fiery Hunt and Other Plays.* Butterick's own poetry is presented in his collections *The Norse* and *Rune Power.*

OBITUARIES AND OTHER SOURCES:

BOOKS

International Authors and Writers Who's Who, 10th edition, International Biographical Centre, 1986.

PERIODICALS

Los Angeles Times, July 27, 1988.
New York Times, July 28, 1988.

C

CAHILL, Rick 1950-

PERSONAL: Born February 12, 1950, in Milwaukee, Wis.; son of Richard John (a business owner) and Elizabeth (a homemaker; maiden name, Garrett) Cahill. *Education:* University of Wisconsin—Madison, B.A., 1973. *Religion:* Roman Catholic.

ADDRESSES: Home—8550 East Speedway, No. 355, Tucson, Ariz. 85710.

CAREER: Shinners Publications, Brookfield, Wis., account executive, 1974-76; Post Newspapers, West Allis, Wis., promotion manager, 1976-79; *Los Angeles Herald Examiner,* Los Angeles, Calif., columnist, 1979-81; Tucson Newspapers, Inc., Tucson, Ariz., editor and copywriter, 1982—. President of Western Imports.

WRITINGS:

Colorado Hot Spring Guide, Pruett, 1983.
Border Towns of the Southwest: Shopping, Dining, Fun, and Adventure From Tijuana to Juarez, Pruett, 1987.
New Mexico Hot Spring Guide, Pruett, 1988.
The Mogollon Rim: A Pictorial, Pruett, in press.

Author of "Navajo Needlework," patterns and text. Travel correspondent for *Denver Post* and *Boulder Daily Camera.*

WORK IN PROGRESS: The Border Bum: A Travelogue, publication by Pruett expected in 1990.

SIDELIGHTS: Rick Cahill described himself to *CA* as "an editor, copywriter, graphic designer, and communications consultant, with experience in publication design and planning, writing, photography, and advertising layout." He added, "I began my career as an account executive for a chain of weekly newspapers in Milwaukee. There I learned how to operate typesetting equipment and prepare pasteups. Eventually I began planning brochure and publication layout for special sections. After a stint as an advertising account executive for a major rock music station, where I was responsible for writing, producing, and selling radio commercials, I decided it was time for a change.

"In search of a little adventure, I moved to Los Angeles. I worked as a reporter for an 'Answerline' column of the *Los Angeles Herald Examiner* and wrote feature stories for the entertainment sections. It was an interesting job, but the pay was lousy. It led me into restaurant management, which finally took me to San Francisco.

"Tired of big city life, I moved to Boulder, Colorado, to pursue a career as a free-lance writer. I used my travels, entrepreneurial spirit, and sense of design to establish a budding business: Western Imports. As the president of the company, I import quality Mexican art, and I have developed a needlecraft business, specializing in adapted Native American designs.

"Writing has always been an obsession. Finding subjects to write about has been a challenge. Discovering that I could indulge my personal interests to the limits has been the most rewarding part of my writing career. I have learned that I can take a little-known subject, research it, and enlighten myself, as well as my readers."

*   *   *

CALMAN, Mel 1931-

PERSONAL: Born May 19, 1931, in London, England; son of Clement and Anna Calman; married Pat McNeill, 1957 (divorced); married Karen Usborne (divorced, 1982); children: (first marriage) two daughters. *Education:* Received National Diploma in Design from St. Martin's School of Art, and Art Teachers Diploma from Goldsmiths College, London.

ADDRESSES: Office—83 Lambs Conduit St., London W.C.1, England.

CAREER: Daily Express, London, England, cartoonist, 1957-63; British Broadcasting Corp., London, cartoonist for "Tonight Programme," 1963-64; *Sunday Telegraph,* London, cartoonist, 1964-65; *Observer,* London, cartoonist, 1965-66; free-lance cartoonist for magazines and newspapers, 1966—. Designer of book jackets and advertising campaigns; illustrator for books; founder of Cartoon Gallery, 1970; producer of animated cartoon "The Arrow" and syndicated feature "Men and Women," 1976-82.

MEMBER: Alliance Graphique Internationale, Royal Society of Art (fellow), Society of Industrial Artists (fellow), Society of Artists and Designers (fellow), Garrick Club.

WRITINGS:

Bed-Sit, Cape, 1963.

Boxes, Cape, 1964.
The Penguin Calman, Penguin, 1968.
(Contributor) B. S. Johnson, editor, *The Evacuees,* Gollancz, 1968.
My God, Souvenir Press, 1970.
This Pestered Isle, Times Newspapers, 1973.
(Contributor) B. S. Johnson, editor, *All Bull: The National Servicemen,* Quartet Books, 1973.
The New Penguin Calman, Penguin, 1977.
Dr. Calman's Dictionary of Psychoanalysis, Allen & Co., 1979.
But It's My Turn to Leave You, Methuen, 1980.
How About a Little Quarrel Before Bed? Methuen, 1981.
Help! and Other Ruminations, Methuen, 1982.
Calman Revisited, Methuen, 1983.
The Big Novel (radio play; first broadcast by British Broadcasting Corp.), Methuen, 1983.
It's Only You That's Incompatible, Methuen, 1984.
What Else Do You Do?: Sketches From a Cartoonist's Life (biography), Methuen, 1986.
"Sweet Tooth" (radio play), first broadcast by British Broadcasting Corp., 1987.

Also author of *Through the Telephone Directory,* 1962, *Calman and Women,* 1967, and *Couples,* 1972.

*   *   *

CAMERON, Deborah   1958-

PERSONAL: Born November 10, 1958, in Glasgow, Scotland. *Education:* University of Newcastle upon Tyne, B.A. (with honors), 1980; Oxford University, M.Litt., 1985. *Politics:* "Feminist, socialist, and anti-racist." *Religion:* Atheist.

ADDRESSES: Home—London, England. *Office*—Digby Stuart College, Roehampton Lane, London SW15 5PH, England.

CAREER: Digby Stuart College, London, England, lecturer at Roehampton Institute of Higher Education, 1983—. Visiting professor at College of William and Mary, 1988-89. Worked as teacher of English as a foreign language; active in British women's movement for more than ten years.

WRITINGS:

Feminism and Linguistic Theory, St. Martin's, 1985.
(With T. J. Taylor) *Analysing Conversation,* Pergamon, 1987.
(With Elizabeth Frazer) *The Lust to Kill,* New York University Press, 1987.
(Editor) *The Feminist Critique of Language,* Routledge & Kegan Paul, 1989.
(Editor with Jennifer Coates) *Women in Their Speech Communities,* Longman, 1989.

Contributor of articles and reviews to magazines and newspapers, including *Language and Communication, City Limits,* and *Cosmopolitan.*

WORK IN PROGRESS: Research on language and gender.

SIDELIGHTS: Deborah Cameron told *CA:* "I write to entertain and to inform; the ideas which excite me intellectually I try to make accessible to people outside the charmed circle of professional academics. That is why I tend to write books for student and lay readers rather than publishing papers and monographs; it is also why I aim for a clear, plain style.

"The topics I choose to write about reflect a desire to make sense of my own experience as a Western woman—my own fear and fascination with sex murder, my sense of language as both restriction and liberation. This desire, I think, is common to all oppressed people as they come to political consciousness. It is fundamental to feminism: 'the personal is political.' For me, it transcends the boundaries of traditional academic disciplines and requires the writer instead to apply her intelligence and skill to whatever she feels strongly about."

BIOGRAPHICAL/CRITICAL SOURCES:

PERIODICALS

Times Literary Supplement, December 25, 1987.

*   *   *

CAMPBELL, Laurence R(andolph)   1903-1987

PERSONAL: Born March 11, 1903, in Batavia, Iowa; died March 16, 1987; son of Frank Thomas and Flora May (Harris) Campbell; married Katheryn Belle Gourley, June 9, 1942; children: Malcolm Randolph, Douglas Gourley, Laurence Barrett. *Education:* San Jose State Teachers College (now State University), A.B., 1926; Northwestern University, M.S., 1931, Ph.D., 1939; also attended University of Washington, Seattle, and University of Colorado.

CAREER: High school teacher in San Francisco, Calif., 1926-28, and Menlo, Calif., 1928-33; Yuba County Junior College (now Yuba Community College), Marysville, Calif., English teacher; *Rotarian,* editorial assistant, 1938-39; University of Illinois at Urbana-Champaign, Urbana, assistant professor of English, 1939-41; University of California, assistant professor of English, 1942-43; *Wall Street Journal,* New York, N.Y., news editor of San Francisco edition, 1943-44; Temple University, Philadelphia, Pa., associate professor of English, 1944-45; Syracuse University, Syracuse, N.Y., professor of English, 1945-47, acting dean of School of Journalism, 1945-46; University of Oregon, Eugene, professor of English, 1947-50; Florida State University, Tallahassee, professor of English, 1950-59, professor of education, 1960-61, professor of English education, 1963-73, dean of School of Journalism, 1950-59, head of department of educational foundations, 1961-63. U.S. State Department lecturer in Jordan, Egypt, and Syria, 1956; adjunct professor at Florida A & M University, c. 1977. Member of United Ministry Center and Christmas International House.

WRITINGS:

(Editor) *Careers in Journalism,* Quill and Scroll Foundation, 1946, revised edition, 1955.
(With John Paul Jones) *News Beat: A Workbook in Reporting,* Macmillan, 1949.
(With Roland E. Wolseley) *Newsmen at Work: Reporting and Writing the News,* Houghton, 1949.
(With Harry E. Heath, Jr. and Raymond V. Johnson) *A Guide to Radio-TV Writing,* Iowa State College Press, 1950.
(With Wolseley) *Exploring Journalism,* 3rd edition, Prentice-Hall, 1957.
(With Wolseley) *How to Report and Write the News,* Prentice-Hall, 1961.

Also editor of *The Social Basis for Education in Florida,* 1962. Associate editor of *Drug Progress,* 1942; book editor of *School Press Review;* contributing editor of *Quill and Scroll.*

OBITUARIES:

PERIODICALS

Tallahassee Democrat, March 17, 1987.*

CAMPBELL, Tom D.   1938-

PERSONAL: Born March 3, 1938, in Glasgow, Scotland; son of Sidney Thomson (a lawyer) and Bessie (a housewife; maiden name, Barrow) Campbell; children: Flora M., A. Magnus. *Education:* University of Glasgow, M.A., 1962, Ph.D., 1969; Oxford University, B.A., 1964.

ADDRESSES: Home—228 Nithsdale Rd., Glasgow G41 5PZ, Scotland. *Office*—Department of Law, University of Glasgow, Glasgow G12 8DD, Scotland.

CAREER: University of Glasgow, Glasgow, Scotland, lecturer in politics, 1964-69, and moral philosophy, 1970-73; University of Stirling, Stirling, Scotland, professor of philosophy, 1973-79; University of Glasgow, professor of jurisprudence, 1979—. *Military service:* British Army, 1956-58; became lieutenant.

MEMBER: United Kingdom Association of Legal and Social Philosophy (president, 1986—).

WRITINGS:

Adam Smith's Science of Morals, Allen & Unwin, 1971.
Seven Theories of Human Society, Oxford University Press, 1981.
The Left and Rights: Conceptual Analysis of the Idea of Socialist Rights, Routledge & Kegan Paul, 1983.
(Editor with David Goldberg, Sheila McLean, and Tom Mullen) *Human Rights: From Rhetoric to Reality,* Basil Blackwell, 1986.
Justice, Macmillan, 1988.
Mental Illness and Discrimination, Gower, 1989.

BIOGRAPHICAL/CRITICAL SOURCES:

PERIODICALS

Times Literary Supplement, August 22, 1986.

*   *   *

CANNING, Paul   1947-

PERSONAL: Born January 10, 1947, in Winston-Salem, N.C.; son of Thomas E. (a doctor) and Mary (a realtor; maiden name, Ralph) Canning; children: Justine. *Education:* University of Washington, Seattle, B.A., 1969, Ph.D., 1979; University of Connecticut at Storrs, M.A., 1971.

ADDRESSES: Home—185 Oxford, Hartford, Conn. 06105. *Office*—Department of History, University of Connecticut at Hartford, 85 Lawler Rd., West Hartford, Conn. 06117.

CAREER: Gonzaga University, Spokane, Wash., instructor, 1976-77, visiting assistant professor of history, 1982; professional travel and research, 1977-81; Marymount College, Tarrytown, N.Y., assistant professor of history, 1983-84; University of Connecticut at Hartford, assistant professor of history, 1985-88, associate professor of history, 1988—.

MEMBER: North American Conference on British Studies, American Historical Association, American Conference for Irish Studies, New England Historical Association.

WRITINGS:

British Policy Towards Ireland, 1921-1941, Oxford University

Press, 1985.

WORK IN PROGRESS: British Policy Towards Africa, 1945-1960, publication by Oxford University Press expected in 1993.

SIDELIGHTS: Paul Canning told *CA:* "I have always enjoyed reading, especially history and biography, and travel. At some point it occurred to me that I might like to try my hand at writing my own books. I think I gravitated towards a career in college teaching because it seemed to offer the best opportunity of pursuing all of these avocations while also making a living in the process. I was particularly gripped by European history, I think initially because of all the wars. English history offered the additional bonus that most of the material would be available in English, though my English and Irish background also inclined me in that direction. I did not really become interested in Irish history until I had a chance to teach a course in it. Since then I've been hooked. My interest in African history stemmed in part from a trip I made to Kenya in 1980. My favorite author is the English historian A. J. P. Taylor."

AVOCATIONAL INTERESTS: Travel ("I divide my time in the summer between England and the Pacific Northwest. I am an ardent Anglophile and Francophile."), reading, skiing, swimming, jogging, playing tennis.

*   *   *

CANNON, Bettie (Waddell)   1922-

PERSONAL: Born November 13, 1922, in Detroit, Mich.; daughter of William Ross (a businessman) and Willie Ruth (a homemaker; maiden name, Whitehead) Waddell; married Charles Joseph Cannon (a hydraulic engineer and business owner), July 22, 1944; children: Charles Joseph III, Sallie Jane Cannon Clover, Kathleen Laura Cannon Rafferty, Suzannah Whitehead Cannon Milling. *Education:* Attended Michigan State University, 1940-42, and Oakland University, 1972-74.

ADDRESSES: Agent—c/o Charles Scribner's, 866 Third Ave., New York, N.Y. 10022.

CAREER: Writer. Cannon Engineering and Equipment Co., Troy, Mich., vice-president and secretary, 1957-87; writer, 1987—. Conference coordinator at Oakland University, 1970-74; member of board of directors of Readings for the Blind, Southfield, Mich.

MEMBER: Authors Guild, Society of Children's Book Authors, Detroit Women Writers (president, 1975-77), Greater West Bloomfield Historical Society (member of board of directors).

AWARDS, HONORS: Award of merit from Historical Society of Michigan, 1980, for *All About Franklin.*

WRITINGS:

All About Franklin: From Pioneer to Preservation, Four Corners Press, 1980.
A Bellsong for Sarah Raines (young adult novel), Scribner, 1987.

Contributor of stories and articles to periodicals.

WORK IN PROGRESS: Writing and researching a novel about "teenagers who were brought up in communes and lived in the 'alternative culture' with hippies as their parents"; research for a novel on "the life of a young girl captured by Indians—a true story—in the 1850s and how she returned to her old life."

SIDELIGHTS: "On my mother's side of the family I am 'kin' to writers," Bettie Cannon informed *CA*, "and I always knew that writing was something I might do one day. On my father's side there were singers, and this was also important to me. I think, perhaps, these two parts of me were reconciled in the writing of *A Bellsong for Sarah Raines.* I used the music of my father's family and my own desire to be a singer and actress as a background while I wrote. In addition, the alcoholism and suicides in my family have motivated me to explore these themes."

Cannon's *A Bellsong for Sarah Raines* is the story of a young teenager and is set against the grim backdrop of the Depression. Upon the suicide of her alcoholic father, protagonist Sarah Raines leaves Detroit and travels with her mother to relatives in Kentucky, where Sarah must eventually come to terms with her father's death and her own feelings of grief and loss. Meg Wolitzer of the *Los Angeles Times* found the book to be "a finely wrought novel that never condescends to its audience." The critic particularly appreciated Cannon's realistic descriptions of city life during the Depression, as well as the author's handling of "such sophisticated issues as suicide, sexuality and grief." Wolitzer recommended *A Bellsong for Sarah Raines* as a "young adult novel of significance."

BIOGRAPHICAL/CRITICAL SOURCES:

PERIODICALS

Los Angeles Times, October 10, 1987.

* * *

CANTALUPO, Charles 1951-

PERSONAL: Surname is pronounced "*Cant*-uh-*loo*-poe"; born October 17, 1951, in Orange, N.J.; son of Charles Roger (an attorney) and Olga (a homemaker; maiden name, Skula) Cantalupo; married Catherine Musello (a poet), August 21, 1976 (died August 19, 1983); children: Pius. *Education:* Attended University of Kent at Canterbury, 1971-72; Washington University, B.A., 1973; Rutgers University, New Brunswick, M.A., 1978, Ph.D., 1980. *Religion:* Roman Catholic.

ADDRESSES: Home—R.D. #1, Box 237 B, Hecla, New Ringgold, Pa. 17960. *Office*—Department of English, Pennsylvania State University, Schuylkill Campus, Schuylkill Haven, Pa. 17972.

CAREER: Rutgers University, New Brunswick, N.J., teaching assistant, 1973-76, instructor in English, 1977-79; Pennsylvania State University, University Park, Pa., instructor, 1980, assistant professor of English, 1981—. Affiliated with a number of organizations at Pennsylvania State University, including faculty adviser of student newspaper *Collegian,* 1984, Literary Club, and student arts magazine *FISH,* both 1981—, and chairperson of Research Committee, 1983—. Chairperson and/ or speaker at scholarly conferences and conventions, including the Mid-Hudson Modern Language Association Conference, 1979-1984. Director and chairman of Catherine M. Cantalupo Scholarship Foundation at Rutgers University, 1984—. Eucharistic minister at Pottsville/Warne Hospital Clinic, Pottsville, Pa.

MEMBER: Modern Language Association, Mid-Hudson Modern Language Association, African Arts Center, Association for Hobbes Studies, Schuylkill Campus Faculty Organization, Phi Beta Kappa.

AWARDS, HONORS: American Academy of Poets Prize, 1976, for "The Death of Colin Clout"; Graduate School Bevier fellowship from Rutgers University, 1979; fellowships from Pennsylvania State University, 1981, 1982, 1984, 1986, and 1988; Faculty Organization Teaching Award, 1985-86; Student Government Association Faculty Student Service Award, 1987-88.

WRITINGS:

(Contributor) *Seabury in Memorium: A Bicentennial Anthology,* Foundation Press, 1983.
The Art of Hope (poetry), Erasmus Books of Notre Dame, 1983.
(Contributor) John H. Morgan, editor, *Fleet Street Poet: A Memorial Anthology to Samuel Johnson,* Foundation Press, 1984.
On Common Ground: An Anthology of Poems, Pennsylvania State University Press, 1985.
(Contributor) Thomas N. Corns, editor, *The Literature of Controversy,* Cass, 1986.
(Contributing editor) *Contemporary Authors,* Volume 120, Gale, 1987.

Contributor to *The Poetic Churchman: A Memorial Anthology to George Herbert,* edited by John H. Morgan, 1982, *Academic American Encyclopedia,* 1981, and *Dictionary of Literary Biography,* Volume 19: *British Poets, 1840-1914,* 1983. Contributor of poetry and essays to scholarly publications and periodicals, including *Journal of New Jersey Poets, The Cord, Wellspring, Christianity and Literature,* and *Studia Mystica.*

WORK IN PROGRESS: St. Orpheus, a book of poetry; *A Literary "Leviathan,"* "a scholarly book discussing Thomas Hobbes's *Leviathan* from a literary angle"; "The Beginning of Paradise" and "Religio Poetae," both essays; *ANIMA/L,* a book of poetry, and *ANIMA/L: Experimental Performance in Ten Movements,* a stage drama to be performed in Agadir, Morocco.

SIDELIGHTS: Charles Cantalupo told *CA:* "As a scholar I am interested in major writers such as Rudyard Kipling and Thomas Hobbes because they are, for the most part, excluded from contemporary literary study and education. Yet they are helpful in moving one's study beyond twentieth-century modernism and postmodernism.

"As a poet I am interested in religious and/or devotional content as it can be combined with nature, personal experience, and myth. Expert form or poetic technique (rhythm, rhyme, prosody in general) is a penultimate requirement—a necessary, clear, coherent message—for any poem I write.

"My last project is what I call 'performance poetry.' I have been performing, in a multi-media context, a poem that takes place in Africa titled *ANIMA/L: Experimental Performance in Ten Movements.* Such 'performance' takes lyric poetry to a much larger, more diversified audience than a publication in a journal, stresses cultural diversity and art's social function, and is indicative more of religious ritual than naturalistic 'western' traditions of theater."

AVOCATIONAL INTERESTS: Reading, swimming, travel, "the outdoors," and medieval, modern, and postmodern music.

* * *

CAPLAN, Frank 1911(?)-1988

OBITUARY NOTICE—See index for *CA* sketch: Born c. 1911

in Hull, England; died after a long illness, September 28, 1988, in Princeton, N.J. Toymaker, editor, and author. Caplan came to the United States with his family at the age of three from England, where his Russian parents had immigrated earlier. In the United States Caplan and his wife, Theresa Caplan, founded the educational toy company Creative Playthings and wrote *The Power of Play,* which suggests that play is an important part of child development. Frank Caplan also founded the Princeton Center for Infancy and Early Childhood, a research center that publishes child care information for parents. Using the center's research findings, Caplan edited the books *The First Twelve Months of Life: Your Baby's Growth Month by Month, The Parenting Advisor, Parents' Yellow Pages,* and *Growing-Up Years: Your Child's Record Keeping Book.* He also wrote *The Second Twelve Months of Life: A Kaleidoscope of Growth* with his wife.

OBITUARIES AND OTHER SOURCES:

PERIODICALS

Chicago Tribune, October 3, 1988.

*   *   *

CAREY EVANS, Olwen (Elizabeth)   1892-

PERSONAL: Born April 3, 1892, in Criccieth, Gwynedd, Wales; daughter of David (first Earl of Dwyfor; a statesman) and Margaret (Owen) Lloyd George; married Thomas John Carey Evans, 1917 (died, 1947); children: Margaret Carey Evans Barrett, Eluned Carey Evans Macmillan, Robin, David. *Education:* Educated in England, Germany, and France. *Politics:* Liberal. *Religion:* Baptist.

ADDRESSES: Home—Eisteddfa, Criccieth, Gwynedd, Wales. *Agent*—J. D. Lewis a'i Feibon Cyf., Argraffwyr a Chyhoeddwyr, Gwasg Gomer, Llandysul, Wales.

CAREER: Volunteer for such organizations as Young Women's Christian Association, Blind Association, Lifeboat Association, Society for the Prevention of Cruelty to Children, and Girl Guides.

AWARDS, HONORS: Dame Commander of Order of the British Empire, 1969.

WRITINGS:

Lloyd George Was My Father: The Autobiography of Lady Carey Evans as Told to Mary Garner, Gomer, 1985.

BIOGRAPHICAL/CRITICAL SOURCES:

PERIODICALS

Times Literary Supplement, July 26, 1985.

*   *   *

CARPENTER, Delores Bird   1942-

PERSONAL: Born December 6, 1942, in Chattanooga, Tenn.; daughter of Basil Ivan and Hazel (Hawkins) Bird; married Joe Keith Carpenter (a Methodist minister and elementary schoolteacher), December 27, 1959 (divorced July 21, 1987); children: Frederic Keith. *Education:* Attended University of Mississippi; Boston University, B.A. (summa cum laude), 1967; University of Hartford, M.A., 1974; University of Massachusetts at Amherst, Ph.D., 1978. *Politics:* Democrat. *Religion:* Methodist.

ADDRESSES: Home—3 South Sandwich Rd., Mashpee, Mass. 02649. *Office*— Department of English, Cape Cod Community College, Route 132, West Barnstable, Mass. 02668.

CAREER: Junior high school English teacher in Shrewsbury, Mass., 1967-70; University of Hartford, Hartford, Conn., member of adjunct faculty, 1971-73; Tunxis Community College, Farmington, Conn., member of adjunct faculty, 1973-74; Springfield College, Springfield, Mass., member of adjunct faculty, 1974; Suffield High School, Suffield, Conn., part-time teacher, 1974-75; Springfield Technical Community College, Springfield, member of adjunct faculty, 1975; University of Massachusetts at Amherst, member of adjunct faculty, 1976-77; Cape Cod Community College, West Barnstable, Mass., instructor, 1977-80, assistant professor, 1980-84, associate professor of English, 1984—. Southeastern Association for Cooperation in Higher Education Lecturer in southeastern Massachusetts, 1985-86.

MEMBER: Modern Language Association of America, Emily Dickinson Society, Thoreau Society, Phi Beta Kappa.

WRITINGS:

(Editor) Ellen Tucker Emerson, *The Life of Lidian Jackson Emerson,* G. K. Hall, 1980.
(Contributor) Joel Myerson, editor, *Studies in the American Renaissance,* G. K. Hall, 1980.
(Editor and author of introduction) *The Selected Letters of Lidian Jackson Emerson,* University of Missouri Press, 1987.

WORK IN PROGRESS: A paper on the friendship of Henry David Thoreau and Lidian Jackson Emerson; a paper on the structure of one or more of the fascicles of the poetry of Emily Dickinson; research for a composition textbook for college freshmen; research on Ruth Emerson, philosopher and author Ralph Waldo Emerson's mother; a short play on Lidian Jackson Emerson.

SIDELIGHTS: Delores Bird Carpenter told *CA:* "Lidian Jackson Emerson was the wife of Ralph Waldo Emerson for forty-six years, the mother of their four children, and the hostess to the Transcendentalist circle. She gave herself to at least four causes, including active membership in the Massachusetts Society for the Prevention of Cruelty to Animals, serving as its vice-president for Concord in 1872. She could conjure up in her mind's eye real or imagined sufferings of animals, making their agonies more intense than her own. Something as inconsequential as the sun in Bossy's eye might distress her. The sufferings of humans also touched both her heart and mind. She worked for the Anti-Slavery Society and got out of her sickbed to go to meetings in Boston. She worked on behalf of the Cherokee and Modoc Indians and was an ardent advocate of woman's suffrage. Locally, for forty years she received school children at New Year's with gifts and admonitions concerning her favorite causes.

"A well-rounded woman of the nineteenth century emerges from Lidian Emerson's letters. They trace the growth of her independent and incisive mind, reveal her active influence on her husband's thought, and present a domestic view of the lives of the Emersons, their children, and their friends, including such notable contemporaries as Henry David Thoreau, Margaret Fuller, Thomas Carlyle, Amos Bronson Alcott, Jones Very, and many others."

BIOGRAPHICAL/CRITICAL SOURCES:

PERIODICALS

New York Times Book Review, November 29, 1987.

*   *   *

CARPENTER, Lucas   1947-

PERSONAL: Born April 23, 1947, in Elberton, Ga.; son of Lucas Adams, Jr. (a U.S. civil servant) and Maria (Wasilenkov) Carpenter; married Judith Leidner (a counselor), September 2, 1972; children: Meredith Lauren. *Education:* College of Charleston, B.S., 1968; University of North Carolina at Chapel Hill, M.A., 1973; State University of New York at Stony Brook, Ph.D., 1982.

ADDRESSES: Home—2780 Club Forest Dr., Conyers, Ga. 30208. *Office*— Department of English, Oxford College, Emory University, Oxford, Ga. 30267.

CAREER: Suffolk Community College, Riverhead, N.Y., instructor, 1978-80, assistant professor of English, 1980-85, and editor of *Perspectives;* Emory University, Oxford College, Oxford, Ga., associate professor of English, 1984—. Judge of annual awards of Poetry Society of Georgia, 1979. *Military service:* U.S. Army, 1968-71; served in Vietnam; became sergeant; received Bronze Star.

MEMBER: Poetry Society of America, National Council of Teachers of English, Southeast Modern Language Association.

WRITINGS:

A Year for the Spider (poems), University of North Carolina YMCA Press, 1972.
(Editor with E. Leighton Rudolph, and co-author of introduction) *The Selected Poems of John Gould Fletcher,* University of Arkansas Press, 1988.
Slow Curves (poems), Linwood Publishers, 1988.
(Editor) *The Autobiography of John Gould Fletcher,* University of Arkansas Press, 1988.
(Editor) John Gould Fletcher, *Arkansas: A History,* University of Arkansas Press, in press.

Work represented in anthologies, including *New Writing in South Carolina,* edited by William Peden and George Garrett, University of South Carolina Press, 1970; *Carolina Sun,* edited by Billy Mishoe and Ronald C. Midkiff, American Literary Associates, 1973. Contributor of more than a hundredfifty poems, articles, and reviews to magazines and newspapers, including *Newsday, Kansas Quarterly, Sequoia, Poet Lore, Soundings,* and *Atlanta Review.*

WORK IN PROGRESS: Editing and writing introduction to *The Selected Essays of John Gould Fletcher* and editing with Ethel Simpson and co-authoring introduction to *The Selected Correspondence of John Gould Fletcher,* both to be published by University of Arkansas Press in 1990; editing and writing *John Gould Fletcher and Southern Modernism,* a six-volume series, publication by University of Arkansas Press expected in 1991.

SIDELIGHTS: Lucas Carpenter told *CA:* "My ongoing interest in John Gould Fletcher was prompted by my study of the Imagist movement while I was a graduate student at the State University of New York at Stony Brook. I was immediately attracted to Fletcher's boldly experimental poetry and to his enormously interesting and highly influential career as a writer. Among the very first of the so-called modern American literary expatriates, the native Arkansan left the United States in 1908 for what would become a twenty-four year period of self-imposed exile spent for the most part in England. Along with Ezra Pound, F. S. Flint, T. E. Hulme, and Richard Aldington, Fletcher was one of the founders of the Imagist movement and was an active participant in the intellectual ferment that produced literary Modernism. He was responsible for introducing Ezra Pound to French symbolism and Amy Lowell to 'polyphonic prose' and was friends with such luminaries as T. S. Eliot, D. H. Lawrence, Ford Madox Ford, and Robert Frost.

"In the second half of his career, Fletcher turned his interest to southern regionalism. After meeting John Crowe Ransom, Donald Davidson, and Allen Tate in Nashville during a lecture tour in 1927, Fletcher began his connection with the southern Fugitive-Agrarian movement and contributed an essay on education to the controversial manifest *I'll Take My Stand* in 1930. He returned to the United States for good in 1933, and in 1938 his *Selected Poems* won the Pulitzer Prize. However, by the time of his suicide in 1950, Fletcher had been largely forgotten as a literary figure.

"In addition to his poetry, Fletcher was a prodigious art and literary critic, contributing scores of essays to such influential periodicals as the *Dial,* the *Little Review, The Criterion,* and *Poetry.* I am collecting the best of these essays for *The Selected Essays of John Gould Fletcher.* His *Autobiography* (originally published in 1937 as *Life Is My Song*) is a crucial document in charting the history of literary Modernism. Also of significance to the literary historian will be *The Selected Correspondence of John Gould Fletcher.*

"My 'final say' on Fletcher will be in *John Gould Fletcher and Southern Modernism,* where I contend that Fletcher can be legitimately regarded as the first southern Modernist writer and as perhaps the most representative poet of the entire Modernist movement. However, my primary objective as general editor of and principal contributor to this six-volume series devoted to Fletcher's life and work is to reawaken and stimulate interest in a writer who has been unjustly forgotten and neglected.

"With regard to my own poetry, my chief concern is the transfiguration of the common moment, the breaking forth of the infinite from the daily. This is more evident in *Slow Curves,* my latest book of poems, than it is in my first publication, *A Year for the Spider,* which consists of poems coming out of my experience of the Vietnam War. I feel as if my writing has been influenced by virtually everything I've read, but I can identify William Wordsworth, William Butler Yeats, and Wallace Stevens as presences in my poetry. I believe that the role of the poet is to interpret reality, to read the world as a text of profound mystery presented through time, matter, space, energy, and, most importantly, imagination."

*   *   *

CARROLL, Raymond   1924-

PERSONAL: Born August 10, 1924, in Brooklyn, N.Y.; son of Raymond J. (a politician) and Margaret (a social worker; maiden name, McCarthy) Carroll; married Anne Starck, 1954 (divorced, 1979); children: Paul, Suzanne. *Education:* Hamilton College, B.A., 1948; graduate study at Johns Hopkins School of Advanced International Studies, 1949-51. *Politics:* "Usually Democrat." *Religion:* None.

ADDRESSES: Home—New York, N.Y.

CAREER: Cadmus Book Store, Washington, D.C., owner, 1953-55; Editors Press Service, New York, N.Y., designer of promotional material, translator from Spanish, and newspaper columnist, 1955-61; *Newsweek*, New York City, associate editor, 1961-69, general editor, 1969-81, also chief of United Nations Bureau; free-lance writer, 1981—. *Military service:* U.S. Army Air Forces, 1943-46.

MEMBER: English-Speaking Union, Amnesty International.

WRITINGS:

JUVENILE

Anwar Sadat, F. Watts, 1982.
The Palestine Question, F. Watts, 1983.
The Caribbean: Issues in U.S. Relations, F. Watts, 1984.
The Future of the United Nations, F. Watts, 1985.

CONTRIBUTOR

Family Encyclopedia of American History, Reader's Digest Association, 1975.
The Story of America, Reader's Digest Association, 1975.
America's Fascinating Indian Heritage, Reader's Digest Association, 1978.
Consumer Advisor: An Action Guide to Your Rights, Reader's Digest Association, 1984.

Contributor to *Funk and Wagnalls New Encyclopedia Yearbook*. Contributor to periodicals.

WORK IN PROGRESS: A book, tentatively titled *Morton of Merry Mount*, which is "a popular history focusing on some little-known yet extremely significant events in seventeenth-century Massachusetts," publication expected in 1990.

SIDELIGHTS: Raymond Carroll told *CA:* "In twenty years as a writer, reporter, and editor at *Newsweek* I learned to deal with an enormous variety of subject matter, to work quickly under pressure, and to tell a story accurately, clearly, and colorfully. Most of my assignments concerned foreign affairs, but from week to week I never knew what area of the world I would be covering. It might be Vietnam or South Africa one week, the Middle East or Northern Ireland the next. Then, on occasion, I would find myself assigned to such strange precincts as American politics or the world of international adventure.

"Covering the United Nations, which I did from time to time, was sometimes an exhilirating experience. Among the people I met and in some cases interviewed were such Middle East figures as Egypt's Anwar Sadat, Jordan's King Hussein, Israel's Golda Meir, and Palestine Liberation Organization chief Yasir Arafat, such diverse leaders as Sweden's Olaf Palme, Cambodia's Prince Sihanouk, and Uganda's infamous Idi Amin, and such varied American ambassadors as George Bush, Pat Moynihan, and Andy Young.

"How I became interested in foreign affairs is difficult to say. Spending time in the Pacific (Guam, Okinawa, and Japan) during my military service in World War II probably played a role. Then, at Hamilton College, a history professor named Graves (called 'Digger,' of course) steered me toward graduate studies at the School of Advanced International Studies of Johns Hopkins University, chiefly because an old friend of his was a leading professor there. As a result of this background, my writing has been concerned primarily with foreign affairs, but I have also written on subjects as diverse as America's pre-history, Eskimos, and consumer problems.

"The books I've written are meant for high-school readers, though some of the volumes find their way into general bookstores and college libraries. They are not in any sense textbooks; they are readable, concise supplementary reading. I must say I have been delighted to receive many letters from high-school students, teachers, and principals who have read my books and responded favorably."

* * *

CARRUTHERS, Peter 1952-

PERSONAL: Born June 16, 1952, in Manila, Philippines; son of Michael George (a banker) and Maureen (Booker) Carruthers; married Susan Levi (a teacher), October 21, 1978; children: Isaac. *Education:* University of Leeds, B.A., 1975, M.Phil., 1977; Oxford University, D.Phil., 1979. *Politics:* Labour. *Religion:* Atheist.

ADDRESSES: Home—48 Crowhurst Rd., Colchester, Essex CO3 3JN, England. *Office*—Department of Philosophy, University of Essex, Colchester, Essex CO4 3SQ, England.

CAREER: University of St. Andrews, St. Andrews, Scotland, lecturer in philosophy, 1979-81; Queen's University, Belfast, Northern Ireland, lecturer in philosophy, 1981-85; University of Essex, Colchester, England, lecturer in philosophy, 1985—.

WRITINGS:

Introducing Persons: Theories and Arguments in the Philosophy of Mind, State University of New York Press, 1986.
Sense and Sinn: Meaning and Metaphysics in Wittgenstein's Tractatus, Basil Blackwell, 1989.

Contributor to philosophy journals.

WORK IN PROGRESS: "What Is Empiricism?," a lecture series to be published in translation in China.

SIDELIGHTS: Peter Carruthers told *CA:* "*Introducing Persons* deals (in roughly equal measures) with the problem of other minds, dualism versus various forms of materialism, and the nature of personal identity and survival. The idea was to write a book which, while remaining an introduction, would be genuinely dialectical, both taking seriously the various theories in the field and arguing for views of my own.

"*Sense and Sinn* reflects my long-standing interest in Wittgenstein's *Tractatus Logico-Philosophicus* dating from my undergraduate studies at Leeds. It is an attempt to make sense of Wittgenstein's doctrines—extraordinary as some of them are—by presenting arguments in their support."

* * *

CARTER, Barbara (Ellen) 1925-1988

OBITUARY NOTICE—See index for *CA* sketch: Born August 7, 1925, in Detroit, Mich.; died of complications from amyotrophic lateral sclerosis (Lou Gehrig's disease), August 28, 1988, in Bronxville, N.Y. Journalist and author. After writing for *Reporter Magazine* from 1958 to 1964, Carter became a partner and vice-president of Free Lance Associates in Yonkers, New York. She was also a free-lance writer and editor for education, government, and civil rights organizations. In 1962 Carter received the National School Bell Award from the National Education Association for an article she wrote on integration. Carter was the author of *The Road to City Hall: How John V. Lindsay Became Mayor* and *Pickets, Parents, and Power: The Story Behind the New York Teachers' Strike.*

With Gloria Dapper she wrote *A Guide for School Board Members, School Volunteers: What They Do, How They Do It, Organizing School Volunteer Programs,* and *The War on Poverty: Newark's Story.*

OBITUARIES AND OTHER SOURCES:

PERIODICALS

New York Times, September 1, 1988.

*   *   *

CARTER, Sebastian 1941-

PERSONAL: Born February 20, 1941, in Cambridge, England; son of William N. (a printer) and Barbara (a singer; maiden name, Digby) Carter; married Penelope Ann Kerr (a book editor), October 29, 1966; children: Rebecca, Benjamin. *Education:* King's College, Cambridge, B.A., 1962, M.A., 1973.

ADDRESSES: Home—40 Oxford Rd., Cambridge CB4 3PW, England. *Office*—Rampant Lions Press, 12 Chesterton Rd., Cambridge CB4 3AB, England.

CAREER: John Murray Publishers Ltd., London, England, typographic designer, 1962-63; Trianon Press, Paris, France, typographic designer, 1963-65; Rampant Lions Press, Cambridge, England, typographic designer, 1966—.

MEMBER: Double Crown Club (president, 1983-84).

AWARDS, HONORS: Francis Minns Award for book design from London's National Book League, 1971, for David Piper's *Shades.*

WRITINGS:

Twentieth Century Type Designers, Trefoil Publications, 1987.

Contributor to magazines and newspapers, including *Matrix* and *Crafts.*

WORK IN PROGRESS: Editing the correspondence of Dutch type designer John van Krimpen and British typographical scholar Stanley Morison, publication by Matrix in four annual parts expected to begin in 1988.

SIDELIGHTS: Sebastian Carter told *CA:* "Although I am a working designer and printer by profession, I am naturally interested in the way a writer's thoughts are, or should be, given typographical form. Ultimately I should like to find time to examine if typographical styles and their evolution would be described in terms similar to those of art history. Meanwhile, type designs are the building bricks of typography, and so worth our attention. The survey of the van Krimpen/Morison correspondence grew out of *Twentieth Century Type Designers,* since it shows one of the greatest type designers of this century developing his ideas in consultation with one of the greatest critics and historians of the subject—and it was too long to be fitted in the book."

AVOCATIONAL INTERESTS: Music (especially chamber music and opera), vegetable gardening.

BIOGRAPHICAL/CRITICAL SOURCES:

PERIODICALS

Times Literary Supplement, August 28, 1987.

CARVER, Raymond 1938-1988

OBITUARY NOTICE—See index for *CA* sketch: Born May 25, 1938, in Clatskanie, Ore.; died of lung cancer, August 2, 1988, in Port Angeles, Wash. Educator and writer. Hailed in the *New York Times Book Review* as a writer who "stands squarely in the line of descent of American realism" and "should be famous for the conceptual beauty of his best stories," Carver will be best remembered for his portrayals of the working poor in both his short fiction and poetry. His writings garnered numerous honors, including three O. Henry awards, a 1979 National Endowment for the Arts Award, and nominations for a Pulitzer Prize for his short story collection *Cathedral,* a National Book Critics Circle Award, and a National Book Award in fiction for *Will You Please Be Quiet, Please?* For his poetry Carver won the National Endowment for the Arts Discovery Award in 1970. His poems are included in such volumes as *Winter Insomnia, Where Water Comes Together With Other Water,* and *Ultramarine.*

Married at age nineteen and shortly thereafter the father of two children, Carver worked a series of odd jobs during the 1960s. As his writing began to receive critical attention he started to lecture in English and creative writing at various institutions, including the University of California, the University of Iowa Writer's Workshop, and the University of Texas at El Paso. He also taught at Goddard College in Vermont and was a professor of English at Syracuse University from 1980 to 1983. Shortly before Carver's death his short story collection *Where I'm Calling From* was published, and the author was elected into the American Academy and Institute of Arts and Letters. Just prior to his death he completed a book of poems titled *A New Path to the Waterfall.*

OBITUARIES AND OTHER SOURCES:

BOOKS

Current Biography, H. W. Wilson, 1988.
International Authors and Writers Who's Who, 10th edition, International Biographical Centre, 1986.

PERIODICALS

Chicago Tribune, August 3, 1988.
Los Angeles Times, August 4, 1988.
New York Times, August 3, 1988.
New York Times Book Review, May 15, 1988.
Times (London), August 4, 1988.
Washington Post, August 4, 1988.

*   *   *

CATHCART, Noble Aydelotte 1898-1988

OBITUARY NOTICE: Born May 14, 1898, in Montgomery, Ala.; died July 27, 1988, in Summerville, S.C. Business executive and publisher. Cathcart was best known for his role as co-founder and publisher of *Saturday Review.* He began his career in publishing in the early 1920s as circulation manager of the *New York Evening Post.* After ending his fifteen-year affiliation with *Saturday Review* in 1939, Cathcart served as assistant to the president of Crowell-Collier Publishing Company for four years and then as assistant director of domestic operations for the Office of War Information during World War II.

OBITUARIES AND OTHER SOURCES:

BOOKS

American Authors and Books: 1640 to the Present Day, 3rd revised edition, Crown, 1972.

PERIODICALS

Chicago Tribune, July 28, 1988.
Los Angeles Times, July 28, 1988.
Washington Post, July 29, 1988.

*   *   *

CAYTON, Andrew R(obert) L(ee) 1954-

PERSONAL: Born May 9, 1954, in Cincinnati, Ohio; son of Robert Frank (a librarian) and Vivian (a high school teacher; maiden name, Pelley) Cayton; married Mary Kupiec (a college professor), August 23, 1975; children: Elizabeth Renanne. *Education:* University of Virginia, B.A. (with high honors), 1976; Brown University, M.A., 1977, Ph.D., 1981.

ADDRESSES: Home—Oxford, Ohio. *Office*—Department of History, Ball State University, Muncie, Ind. 47306.

CAREER: Harvard University, Cambridge, Mass., lecturer, 1980-81, instructor in history and literature, 1981-82; Ball State University, Muncie, Ind., assistant professor, 1982-86, associate professor of history, 1986—. Visiting assistant professor at Wellesley College, 1981-82.

MEMBER: American Historical Association, Organization of American Historians, Society for Historians of the Early American Republic, Indiana Historical Society, Ohio Historical Society.

AWARDS, HONORS: Ohioana Book Award for History, 1987, for *The Frontier Republic*.

WRITINGS:

The Frontier Republic: Ideology and Politics in the Ohio Country, 1780-1825, Kent State University Press, 1986.

Contributor to history journals. Co-editor of *Old Northwest: A Journal of Regional Life and Letters*.

WORK IN PROGRESS: A political and social history of the American Midwest from 1780 to 1880, publication by Indiana University Press expected in 1989.

SIDELIGHTS: Andrew R. L. Cayton told *CA:* "While my writing is primarily addressed to a scholarly audience, I undertook it for personal reasons. I grew up in the Ohio Valley and have always felt both fascinated and perplexed by its culture. I decided to study the early political history of the Midwest in order to get a fuller sense of where the region's political institutions came from. More broadly, I am interested in the question of midwestern regionalism.

"My academic research and publications are really nothing more than an effort to discover my own social and cultural origins. My maternal grandfather spent much of my childhood regaling me with long stories about his ancestors and the history of northern Kentucky. What I try to do is pretty much the same thing, although within the restrictions of an academic discipline."

*   *   *

CERAVOLO, Joseph 1934-1988

OBITUARY NOTICE—See index for *CA* sketch: Born April 22, 1934, in New York, N.Y.; died of cancer, September 4, 1988, in Belleville, N.J. Engineer and poet. Ceravolo became the first recipient, in 1968, of the Frank O'Hara Award in poetry from Columbia University Press, which published a collection of his poems that year titled *Spring in This World of Poor Mutts: The Frank O'Hara Award Series*. He also won four awards from the Poets Foundation and grants from the National Endowment for the Arts and the American Academy of Arts and Letters. Ceravolo worked as a design and hydraulic engineer for the New York State Department of Public Works and for companies in New Jersey, including Jersey Testing Laboratories, Purcell Associates, and Porter & Ripa Associates. His poems are collected in *Fits of Dawn, Wild Flowers Out of Gas, Transmigration Solo*, and *Inri*.

OBITUARIES AND OTHER SOURCES:

BOOKS

The Writers Directory: 1984-86, St. James Press, 1983.

PERIODICALS

New York Times, September 14, 1988.

*   *   *

CHACE, Isobel
See de GUISE, Elizabeth (Mary Teresa)

*   *   *

CHAMBERS, Anne 1949-

PERSONAL: Born August 3, 1949, in County Mayo, Ireland; daughter of John (an undertaker) and Margaret (a bookkeeper; maiden name, Cruise) Chambers. *Education:* National University of Ireland, University College, Cork, M.A., 1985.

ADDRESSES: Home—Dublin, Ireland. *Office*—c/o Wolfhound Press, 68 Mount Joy Sq., Dublin, Ireland.

CAREER: Central Bank of Ireland, Dublin, senior executive officer, 1969-88; writer, 1988—. Lecturer in the United States, for Irish American Cultural Institute, 1987; frequent lecturer in Ireland.

MEMBER: Writers Union of Ireland, Lansdowne Tennis Club (Dublin).

AWARDS, HONORS: Eleanor, Countess of Desmond was short listed for Irish Book Awards, 1987.

WRITINGS:

Granuaile: The Life and Times of Grace O'Malley, 1530-1605, Wolfhound Press, 1979.
Chieftain to Knight: Tibbott-ne-Long Bourke (1537-1629), First Viscount Mayo, Wolfhound Press, 1983.
Eleanor, Countess of Desmond (c. 1545-1636): A Heroine of Tudor Ireland, Wolfhound Press, 1986.

Author of television and radio scripts. Contributor of articles and reviews to periodicals.

WORK IN PROGRESS: A biography of Grace O'Malley, for young readers, and a biography of Irish-born international prima donna, Margaret Burke-Sheridan, 1889-1958, publication of both by Wolfhound Press expected in 1989; a historical novel set in eleventh-century Ireland and England, publication expected in 1990.

SIDELIGHTS: Anne Chambers told *CA:* "I find the sixteenth century very rich in people and events for both biographical and fictional writing. In fact the factual circumstances relating to people and events in this colorful and eventful age provide the imagery and adventure which fiction would find difficult to match. It is a century of exploration and discovery, of rebellions and intrigue, of armadas and invasions, of glorious empires at the pinnacles of their powers, of the demise and overthrow of entire civilizations and the birth of others, the age of transition and change. It is an era full of great and exotic characers: Henry VIII, Silken Thomas, Philip of Spain, Grace O'Malley, the Earl of Essex, the Earl of Leicester, Hugh O'Neill, Red Hugh O'Donnell, Elizabeth I, Sir Walter Raleigh, Sir Francis Drake, the Countess of Desmond, Edmund Spenser, William Shakespeare . . . The list is endless and impressive.

"My first venture into the swash-and-buckle of the sixteenth century was, I thought, to be a once-off crusade to release from the bondage of historical neglect and fictional misrepresentation an extraordinary woman of legend and lore, Grace O'Malley (or 'Granuaile,' as she is more familiarly known in Ireland). From the faded contemporary manuscripts of the time, their age-darkened, spider-like writing evidence of the passage of four hundred years since their authors first put quill to parchment, the facts about this remarkable woman leapt from the flourishes and swirls on the brittle parchment which had imprisoned her for four centuries. Soon the story of this unique woman—pirate, chieftain, mercenary, wife, mother, lover, politician, admiral of a fleet of ships, and leader of a private army—emerged to emphatically prove the adage of fact being stranger than fiction.

"My second venture back in time was to unearth the facts about Toby-of-the-Ships, the youngest son of the pirate queen. His life story proved to be a unique commentary on a crucial period of transition and political change in Ireland. His story was representative of the minor chieftains who occupied the middle ground between the fixed battle lines of two fundamentally incompatible protagonists—the old order of Gaelic Ireland and the incoming new system of England. Many became pawns in this momentous game of strategy and intrigue and were duly sacrificed. A few like Toby plotted their own moves and, in a game within a deadly game, became intrepid knights charting their own survival.

"The life of Eleanor, Countess of Desmond, is the story of a heroic and indomitable woman, set against the background of one of the stormiest periods of Irish history. She was an active participant and victim of the Elizabethan re-conquest and final subjugation of Gaelic Ireland. But through it all she rises phoenix-like, time after time, to bravely meet and contend with every personal and political challenge on the way."

*   *   *

CHAMBERS, Iain 1949-

PERSONAL: Born January 21, 1949, in Macclesfield, Cheshire, England; son of Lionel Wilfred (an accountant) and Elizabeth Marion (Innes) Chambers. *Education:* University of Keele, B.A., 1972; University of Birmingham, M.A., 1976. *Politics:* "Radical democrat." *Religion:* None.

ADDRESSES: Home—Via Egiziaca a Pizzofalcone 24, 80132 Naples, Italy.

CAREER: Istituto Universitario Navale, Naples, Italy, associate professor of English, 1977-87; Istituto Universitario Orientale, Naples, associate professor of English, 1987—.

WRITINGS:

Urban Rhythms: Pop Music and Popular Culture, St. Martin's, 1986.

Popular Culture: The Metropolitan Experience, Methuen, 1986.
In the Slipstream of the World, Routledge & Kegan Paul, 1989.

SIDELIGHTS: Iain Chambers told *CA:* "All my writings on contemporary culture are motivated by the desire to open up the sense of the possible in our daily lives and to contribute to an understanding of its further democratization."

The author described his book *In the Slipstream of the World* as "a series of essays on the contemporary critical condition, largely organized around the debate between modernism and postmodernism."

BIOGRAPHICAL/CRITICAL SOURCES:

PERIODICALS

Cultural Studies, January, 1987, January, 1988.
New Formations, summer, 1987.
Screen, summer, 1987.

*   *   *

CHANDLER, Lester Vernon 1905-1988

OBITUARY NOTICE: Born in 1905; died of leukemia, July 16, 1988, in Princeton, N.J. Economist, government adviser, and author. A respected monetary expert, Chandler perhaps is best remembered for his work as a fiscal adviser to the U.S. government. He served as price executive and economic adviser for the Office of Price Administration during World War II and, after the war, conducted research for a subcommittee of the U.S. House of Representatives Joint Economic Committee. Chandler taught at Dartmouth and Amherst colleges before becoming Princeton University's first Gordon S. Rentschler Memorial Professor of Economics in 1950. Three years later he was appointed public director and deputy chairman of the board of directors of the Federal Reserve Bank of Philadelphia, Pennsylvania. His writings include *A Preface to Economics, The Economics of Money and Banking,* and *An Introduction to Monetary Theory.*

OBITUARIES AND OTHER SOURCES:

PERIODICALS

New York Times, July 19, 1988.

*   *   *

CHAPPLE, Christopher 1954-

PERSONAL: Born September 4, 1954, in Medina, N.Y.; son of H. Edward (a horseman) and Julia (a librarian; maiden name, Peton) Chapple; married Maureen Shannon (a college instructor), August 10, 1974; children: Dylan Edward. *Education:* State University of New York at Stony Brook, B.A., 1976; Fordham University, M.A., 1978, Ph.D., 1980.

ADDRESSES: Home—22556 Guadilamar Dr., Santa Clarita, Calif. 91350. *Office*—Department of Theology, Loyola Marymount University, Los Angeles, Calif. 90045.

CAREER: State University of New York at Stony Brook, lecturer in religious studies, 1980-85; Loyola Marymount University, Los Angeles, Calif., assistant professor of theology, 1985—. Coordinator of Moksha Community Education Center, 1979-85; assistant director of Institute for Advanced Studies of World Religions, 1980-85; coordinator of Southern California Seminar on South Asia, 1986—.

MEMBER: American Academy of Religion, Society for Asian and Comparative Philosophy, College Theology Society.

WRITINGS:

(Editor) *Samkhya-Yoga* (proceedings of a conference), Institute for Advanced Studies of World Religions, 1982.

(Translator with Yogi Anand Viraj) *The Yoga Sutra of Patanjali,* Book I, Vajra Press, 1984.

(Editor) *Religious Experience and Scientific Paradigms,* Institute for Advanced Studies of World Religions, 1985.

Karma and Creativity, State University of New York Press, 1986.

Contributor to periodicals. Editor of *Hindu Text Information,* 1980-85, and *Sikh Religious Studies Information,* 1981-85.

WORK IN PROGRESS: Research on the origins, developments, and implications of Indian views toward nonviolence.

SIDELIGHTS: Christopher Chapple told *CA:* "*Karma and Creativity* explores the constructive side of Indian religious traditions, which too often are dismissed as fatalistic. Used properly, action can be seen as a means to bring one closer to liberation, rather than condemning one to continual rebirth. This book was written both for the scholar or student and for those with a personal interest in the applications of Eastern thought in a contemporary context."

*   *   *

CHASE, James Hadley
See RAYMOND, Rene (Brabazon)

*   *   *

CHODOROV, Edward   1904-1988

OBITUARY NOTICE—See index for *CA* sketch: Born April 17, 1904, in New York, N.Y.; died after a brief illness, October 9, 1988, in New York, N.Y. Filmmaker and playwright. Chodorov wrote Broadway plays and wrote or produced more than fifty motion pictures. His introduction to theatrical work came when his friend Moss Hart, who would later become a successful playwright, secured for Chodorov a job as stage manager in a 1922 production. Chodorov went on to write the Broadway plays "Those Endearing Young Charms," "Common Ground," and "Oh, Men! Oh, Women!" The motion pictures he wrote or produced include "The Story of Louis Pasteur," "The Hucksters," and "Road House."

OBITUARIES AND OTHER SOURCES:

BOOKS

The Oxford Companion to American Literature, 5th edition, Oxford University Press, 1983.

PERIODICALS

Chicago Tribune, October 15, 1988, October 16, 1988.
Los Angeles Times, October 14, 1988.
New York Times, October 12, 1988.
Washington Post, October 17, 1988.

*   *   *

CIXOUS, Helene   1937-

PERSONAL: Surname is pronounced "Siksu"; born June 5, 1937, in Oran, Algeria; daughter of Georges (a physician) and Eva (a midwife; maiden name, Klein) Cixous; married, 1955 (divorced, 1964); children: Anne Berger, Pierre-Francois Berger. *Education:* Received Agregation d'Anglais, 1959, and Docteur es Lettres, 1968. *Religion:* Jewish.

ADDRESSES: Home—38 bis, avenue Rene Coty, 75014 Paris, France. *Office*—Universite de Paris VIII, 2 rue de la Liberte, 93526 St. Denis, France.

CAREER: University of Bordeaux, Bordeaux, France, assistante, 1962-65; University of Paris (Sorbonne), Paris, France, maitre assistante, 1965-67; University of Paris X (Nanterre), Nanterre, France, maitre de conference, 1967-68; University of Paris VIII (Vincennes at St. Denis), St. Denis, France, helped found the university's experimental branch at St. Denis, 1968, professor of English literature, 1968—, founder and director of Centre de Recherches en Etudes Feminines, 1974—. Visiting professor and lecturer at several universities, including Columbia University, Cornell University, Dartmouth College, New York University, State University of New York at Binghampton and Buffalo, University of Wisconsin at Madison, Yale University, and universities in Austria, Canada, Denmark, England, and Spain.

AWARDS, HONORS: Prix Medici, 1969, for *Dedans.*

WRITINGS:

Le Prenom de Dieu (stories), Grasset et Fasquelle, 1967.
L'Exil de James Joyce; ou, L'Art du remplacement (doctoral thesis), Grasset et Fasquelle, 1968, translation by Sally A. J. Purcell published as *The Exile of James Joyce,* D. Lewis (New York), 1972.
Dedans (novel), Grasset et Fasquelle, 1969, translation by Carol Barko published as *Inside,* Schocken, 1986.
(Co-editor and co-author with Pierre Dommergues and Marianne Debouzy) *Les Etats-Unis d'aujourd'hui,* Colin, 1969.
Le Troisieme Corps (novel), Grasset et Fasquelle, 1970.
Les Commencements (novel), Grasset et Fasquelle, 1970.
Un Vrai Jardin (poetic short story), L'Herne, 1971.
Neutre (novel), Grasset et Fasquelle, 1972.
Portrait du soleil (novel), Denoel, 1973.
Tombe (novel), Seuil, 1973.
Prenoms de personne (essays), Seuil, 1974.
(With Catherine Clement) *La Jeune Nee* (essay), Union Generale d'Editions, 1975, translation by Betsy Wing published as *The Newly Born Woman,* with introduction by Sandra M. Gilbert, University of Minnesota Press, 1986.
Un K. incomprehensible: Pierre Goldman, Bourgois, 1975.
Revolutions pour plus d'un Faust (novel), Seuil, 1975.
Souffles (fiction), Femmes, 1975.
La (fiction), Gallimard, 1976.
Partie, Femmes, 1976.
Angst (fiction), Femmes, 1977, translation by Jo Levy published as *Angst,* Riverrun Press, 1985.
(With Madeleine Gagnon and Annie Leclerc) *La Venue a l'ecriture* (essay), Union Generale d'Editions, c. 1977.
Le Nom d'Oedipe: Chant du corps interdit (libretto), music by Andre Boucourechliev, Femmes, 1978.
Preparatifs de noces au dela de l'abime, Femmes, 1978.
Ananke, Femmes, c. 1979.
Vivre l'orange/To Live the Orange (fiction; bilingual edition), English translation by Ann Liddle and Sarah Cornell, Femmes, 1979.
Illa (fiction), Femmes, 1980.
With; ou, L'Art de l'innocence (fiction), Femmes, 1981.
Limonade tout etait si infini (fiction), Femmes, 1982.

Le Livre de Promethea (fiction), Gallimard, 1983, translation by Betsy Wing published by University of Nebraska Press, in press.

(With Madeleine Chapsal and Sonia Rykiel) Daniele Flis, editor, *Rykiel,* illustrations by Pascale Ogee, Herscher, c. 1985.

La Bataille d'Arcachon (tale), Trois, 1986.

Entre l'ecriture (essays), Femmes, c. 1986, translation by Deborah W. Carpenter, Sarah Cornell, and Suzan Sellers published by Femmes, 1988.

Author of manifesto "Le Rire de la Meduse" (title means "The Laugh of the Medusa"). Co-founder of *Revue de Theorie et d'Analyse Litteraire: Poetique* in 1969.

Work represented in anthologies, including *New French Feminisms,* edited by Elaine Marks and Isabelle de Courtivron, University of Massachusetts Press, 1980, and *The Future of Literary Theory,* edited by Ralph Cohen, 1987. Contributor to periodicals, including *Boundary, L'Herne, Le Monde, New Literary History, Poetique,* and *Signs.*

PLAYS

La Pupille, Gallimard, 1972.

Portrait de Dora, Femmes, 1976, translation by Anita Barros published as *Benmussa Directs: Portrait of Dora* [and] *The Singular Life of Albert Nobbs* (the latter adapted by Simone Benmussa from George Moore's short story "Albert Nobbs," and translated from the French by Barbara Wright), Riverrun Press, 1979.

"La Prise de l'Ecole de Madhubai," first produced at L'Avant-Scene Theatre, 1984.

"L'Histoire terrible mais inachevee de Norodom Sihanouk, Roi du Cambodge," first produced at Theatre du Soleil, 1985.

"L'Indiade; ou, L'Inde de mes reves," first produced at Theatre du Soleil, September, 1987.

SIDELIGHTS: Helene Cixous, a professor at the University of Paris and a founder and director of one of France's few centers for women's studies, was the winner of the 1969 Prix Medici for her first novel, *Dedans,* translated in 1986 as *Inside. La Jeune Nee,* which she wrote in 1976 with Catherine Clement and which was translated ten years later as *The Newly Born Woman,* was deemed a "ground-breaking feminist tract" by the *New York Times Book Review.* Cixous also received wide acclaim for her doctoral thesis, published in 1968 as *L'Exil de James Joyce; ou, L'Art de remplacement* and translated in 1972 as *The Exile of James Joyce.* Although she supports and writes women's literature, Cixous does not consider herself a feminist because of the political and masculine overtones she finds in the term. She is, however, one of the best known and most influential advocates of *ecriture feminine,* or feminine writing—a form that she stresses may include works by both male and female writers. "This writing is dedicated to exploding the binary oppositions on which Western thinking rests," explained Marianne Hirsch in the *New York Times Book Review,* "which relegate woman to the side of silence, of otherness."

Cixous, like other French feminist writers, emphasizes "the place of 'woman' in language and the question of a feminine relation to language that [has] relatively little currency within Anglophone feminist thought," explained translator Annette Kuhn in *Signs.* This concern is of particular importance to the French because their language, unlike English, is based upon distinctly "masculine" and "feminine" words and images.

Many of Cixous's writings attempt to negate the male/female distinction through puns and word manipulations. For this reason, Kuhn wrote, "it is very difficult for translation to do full justice to Cixous's writing, which is actually organized around a pervasive play with, and subversion of, linguistic signifiers."

The English translation of Cixous's award-winning first novel, *Dedans,* was published as *Inside* in 1986, seventeen years after the original French edition appeared. The highly metaphoric work is commonly regarded as an autobiography, although the author did not introduce the book as such. The main character, like Cixous, was born of a North African Jewish father and a German Jewish mother and was raised in Algeria. The novel depicts the daughter's intense love for her father and the grief she suffers when he dies young, as Cixous's father had. "It dwells on a sense of enclosure and entrapment," Marianne Hirsch described. "The nameless narrator . . . is inside a family romance where her father is God, the owner of all the words, and where her German-speaking mother offers no access to knowledge." After her father dies, the daughter imagines his death ceaselessly, trying to understand it. Finally, related Hirsch, "she gains the means to write from [her father's] overwhelming bodily closeness and from his empowering mental gifts in life."

Some feminists have decried the importance of the father's role in *Inside* as defeating the purpose of feminism, and a *Kirkus Review* critic deemed the "densely compact philosophical narrative" simply "intellectual passion from the school of radical French narrative, by turns brilliant and boring." Hirsch, however, offered high praise for the "series of reflections on identity, death and writing." The reviewer noted that *Inside* was timely as well as poignant, calling it a "moving and disturbing experimental work written at the moment of emergence of feminist consciousness—both for the author herself and for a broader intellectual and political movement whose important representative she would become."

Cixous maintains her "special and elusive style" in *Angst,* according to Lorna Sage in the *Observer.* The novel, first published in 1977, was translated into English in 1985. "The writing is dense, direct, often lurid with metaphor" as it records a woman's reflections on her life and her attempt to create mental order out of the chaos she finds, wrote Sage. Nicole Irving in *Times Literary Supplement* praised Cixous's innovative prose style as well as the "loving" translation by Jo Levy, despite calling much of the book "incomprehensible": "[Cixous's] text has a rhythmic pattern, moving from obscurity to relative clarity, from the bodily (erotic and otherwise) to the sometimes punning metaphysical, from violence to calm and occasional tenderness, and at the end, 'she' [the main character] reaches a wholeness." As Sage observed: "The writing is alive even at its oddest."

Most of Cixous's other works, like *Inside* and *Angst,* forsake a traditional literary plot in favor of a speculative or philosophical inner narrative. The works therefore contain elements of fiction, discourse, and poetry. "The categories are relative and deceptive," noted Judith Morganroth Schneider in *World Literature Today,* "for her texts . . . resolutely resist classification." Marianne Hirsch explained that the ambiguity arises because Cixous's "fiction is always based on literary, philosophical and psychoanalytic readings and her theory is written in a personal voice and metaphorical style." Schneider characterized Cixous's 1976 work, *La,* as "fiction and theory posing the question of the feminine text and the feminine unconscious." The reviewer commented that, in *La,* "rules of syntax, grammar, logic are incessantly, violently, exuberantly broken," expressing Cixous's interpretation of feminine writing, which Schneider described as "a passionate outpouring, indifferent to censorship, sensual, bisexually erotic, moving impetuously through disintegration and reintegration of language."

Like Hirsch and Schneider, Olga Prjevalinskaya Ferrer observed in her *World Literature Today* review of *Partie* that "Helene Cixous's works most certainly voice a protest against the very strict rules of French intellectual thought and its expression through speech and writing." Perhaps as a protest against even the traditional appearance of books, Ferrer speculated, Cixous presented the work as a wide book divided into two sections, each upside-down in relation to the other, with pages meeting in the middle of the volume. Commenting on the difficulty of classifying *Partie* in terms of genre, Ferrer stated: "Though [Cixous's] writings are, most of the time, poetic, her originality and freedom have surpassed any poetic thought, any poetic trends." The author's freedom of expression, the reviewer asserted, provides *Partie* "an enchanting depth."

The same freedom of thought and expression grants a "definite charm" to *Illa*, judged Ferrer in a later review. "From the first lines of *Illa*," the reviewer appraised, "we are fully immersed in a lyrical world of feminine self-awareness." The book—whose title is a Latin feminine pronoun and adjective—discusses the relationship between the various roles women fulfill in their lives. "Every passage, every syntagma, shows psycho-poetic mastery, creative uniqueness," lauded Ferrer. "No matter how unexpected Cixous's wording might seem, the reader feels at ease and allows himself to be carried away by the current of her suggestive prose, as by the rhythm of a musical composition."

With; ou, L'Art de l'innocence is likewise about woman's multiplicity. "Cixous's sinuous prose poem is a conversation between various aspects of her person," explained Rosette C. Lamont in *World Literature Today*. Although the author's various selves are disparate, Lamont observed, "the many voices of Cixous's novel-poem blend into a single interrogation about freedom, a multilingual existence in *l'ecriture* and the mystery of being woman."

Most of Cixous's critics, while echoing Judith Morganroth Schneider's assertion of being both "exhilarated and exasperated" by the author's unorthodox writing technique, praised Cixous's innovative theories of feminism and her unique manner of expressing them. "In her theoretical feminist writings, Cixous has called for a new language as the precondition of a new reality," observed Nicole Irving. The new language and syntax easily give rise to confusion and misinterpretation, but as Olga Prjevalinskaya Ferrer noted: "Despite the ambivalences and flagrant contradictions, truth and authentic logic always prevail." Rosette C. Lamont concluded in *World Literature Today*: "Helene Cixous is not moved by modest ambition; she would like to decipher the universe. Love of Woman, of women, of stars, words, languages, language allows her to rise from her finitude."

BIOGRAPHICAL/CRITICAL SOURCES:

BOOKS

Conley, Verena Andermatt, *Writing the Feminine*, University of Nebraska Press, 1984.
Gelfland, Elissa and Virginia Hules, editors, *French Feminist Criticism: Women, Language, and Literature*, Garland Publishing, 1985.

Marks, Elaine and Isabelle de Courtivron, editors, *New French Feminisms*, University of Massachusetts Press, 1980.
Moi, Toril, *Sexual/Textual Politics: Feminist Literary Theory*, Methuen, 1985.
Stambolian, George and Elaine Marks, editors, *Homosexuality and French Literature*, Cornell University Press, 1979.

PERIODICALS

Contemporary Literature, summer, 1983.
Kirkus Reviews, September 1, 1986.
Liberation, December 22, 1982, December 30, 1983.
Le Monde, July 28, 1977.
New York Times Book Review, February 11, 1973, August 24, 1986, December 7, 1986.
Observer, January 12, 1986.
Signs, autumn, 1981.
Substance, Volume X, number 3, 1981.
Times Literary Supplement, April 24, 1969, February 12, 1971, March 21, 1986.
Women's Review, May, 1985.
World Literature Today, winter, 1977, spring, 1977, summer, 1977, spring, 1981, summer, 1982, winter, 1984.

—*Sketch by Christa Brelin*

*   *   *

CLANCE, Pauline Rose   1938-

PERSONAL: Born October 19, 1938, in Welch, W.Va.; daughter of George W. (a businessman) and Gladys (a midwife; maiden name, Riley) Rose. *Education:* Lynchburg College, B.S. (cum laude), 1960; University of Kentucky, M.S., 1964, Ph.D., 1969; diplomate in clinical psychology, 1984.

ADDRESSES: Home—Atlanta, Ga. *Office*—Department of Psychology, Room 458, Sparks Hall, Georgia State University, University Plaza, Atlanta, Ga. 30303. *Agent*—Harvey Klinger, Harvey Klinger Inc., 301 West 53rd St., New York, N.Y. 10019.

CAREER: History teacher at high school in Amherst, Va., 1960-61; G. B. Dimmick Child Guidance Clinic, Lexington, Ky., clinical psychologist, 1965; University Hospital of Cleveland, Cleveland, Ohio, intern-psychologist, 1966-67, staff psychologist, 1967-71; Cleveland State University, Cleveland, lecturer in psychology, 1969-71; Oberlin College, Oberlin, Ohio, clinical psychologist in Psychological Services and assistant professor, 1971-74; Georgia State University, Atlanta, associate professor of psychology, 1974—, associate director of Psychotherapy and Behavior Therapy Clinic and chairperson of clinical committee. Ward psychologist for Brecksville Veterans Administration Hospital, Brecksville, Ohio, 1969-71; licensed clinical psychologist in Ohio, 1973-87, and Georgia, 1976—; faculty and board member and director of training of Atlanta Institute of Living-Learning, 1977—; member of advisory board of Odyssey Family Service, 1980-83; leader and participant in workshops and symposia; consultant.

MEMBER: American Psychological Association (chairperson of Task Force on Media Award for Division 35, 1977-78 and 1978-79; membership chairperson for Division 29, 1980; member of board of directors of Division 42, 1983-84; program chairperson for Division 42, 1984; fellow, 1988), American Association of University Professors, American Academy of Psychotherapy, Association of Women in Psychology, Southeastern Psychological Association (chairperson of Commission on the Status of Women, during 1970s; member of executive committee, 1978; president, 1982-83), Georgia Psychological Association (fellow).

AWARDS, HONORS: Grant from Urban Life Center, 1977.

WRITINGS:

(Contributor) Carolyn H. Rhodes, editor, *First Person Female American*, Volume II, Whitson, 1980.
(Editor with Mark Woodhouse, and contributor) *The Teaching Sourcebook*, Georgia State University, 1980.
(Contributor) Claire Brody, editor, *Women Therapists Working With Women: New Theory and Process of Feminist Therapy*, Springer Publishing, 1984.
The Impostor Phenomenon: Overcoming the Fear That Haunts Your Success, Peachtree Publishers, 1985.

Contributor of articles to professional journals, including *Journal of Clinical Child Psychology, Journal of Professional Psychology, Journal of Psychology, Journal of Psychosomatic Medicine and Dentistry, Perceptual and Motor Skills, Psychotherapy: Theory, Research, and Practice*, and *Sex Roles*. Member of editorial board of *Psychotherapy: Theory, Research, and Practice*, 1984-86.

WORK IN PROGRESS: An ongoing study of the impostor phenomenon, publication by Springer Publishing expected in 1989; research on the psychology of women, especially high achievers.

SIDELIGHTS: In *The Impostor Phenomenon: Overcoming the Fear That Haunts Your Success* Pauline Rose Clance describes the anxiety of successful people who believe they cannot maintain their status and may be found out. According to Clance, many professionals doubt they deserve their success, and their fear of being unmasked as less competent than others think can cause physical and emotional problems. Clance first isolated the phenomena in 1978 and deemed it a women's syndrome, but men proved equally susceptible to it in later studies. Reported *Time* writer Janice Castro: "Private feelings of fraudulence are shared by an estimated 70% of all successful individuals."

Clance told *CA:* "The impostor phenomenon (IP) is much more likely to be experienced by persons with very high grades or accomplishments than others. For example, honors students are more likely to experience these feelings than non-honor students. Professionals who are highly rated by peers and supervisors find numerous ways to discount the positive feedback they may receive.

"Although there is strong objective evidence that others perceive them as bright and successful, they have a terror of failure and think they may fail 'this time on this task.' My book indicates how this experience originates, what maintains the doubts, and how a person can overcome some of these doubts. I have also found that many persons who experience IP feelings may need the help of a qualified psychotherapist and that the behaviors that maintain the feelings can be changed.

"Out of my work in this area and my work as a psychotherapist, I find that people are searching for a meaning and purpose to life. They want to love and be loved but are not certain that either can occur in an in-depth way. They feel they may be judged or loved or not loved based on their external performance. They long for unconditional positive regard but cannot provide it for themselves and do not really expect to get this type of love from others. Yet external measures of success seem empty when compared to their longing. I think novelists often portray this psychological longing best, and I find novels

are a helpful adjunct to what I want to do. Pat Conroy's *Prince of Tides* is a recent novel that explores the psyche in a dramatic but truthful way."

BIOGRAPHICAL/CRITICAL SOURCES:

PERIODICALS

Time, August 12, 1985.

*   *   *

CLARK, Evert   1926(?)-1988

OBITUARY NOTICE: Born c. 1926 in Gainesville, Ga.; died of complications following surgery for an aneurysm, July 7, 1988, in Olney, Md. Reporter, editor, and author. Clark, a respected journalist for more than forty years, specialized in aviation, science, and space reporting. He began his career in 1947 as a reporter and editor for the Durham, North Carolina, *Morning Herald*. Clark later worked for various other publications, including *Aviation Week and Space Technology* magazine, the *New York Times*, and *Newsweek*, for which he covered the events following the 1972 break-in of the Democratic party headquarters in the Washington, D.C., Watergate Hotel—a scandal that involved Republican president Richard M. Nixon and led to his resignation in 1974. In 1969 Clark received an award for excellence in journalism from the National Space Club for his coverage of the U.S. space program. At the time of his death he was a senior staff writer for the Washington bureau of *Business Week* magazine. With Nicholas Horrock, Clark wrote two books, *Contrabandista!: The Busting of a Heroin Empire* and *The Corsican Contract*.

OBITUARIES AND OTHER SOURCES:

PERIODICALS

Chicago Tribune, July 11, 1988.
New York Times, July 9, 1988.
Washington Post, July 9, 1988.

*   *   *

CLARK, Robert P(hillips)   1921-

PERSONAL: Born December 3, 1921, in Randolph, Vt.; son of James S. (a clergyman) and Gladys M. (a teacher; maiden name, Phillips) Clark; married Jeanne Orr Rice, December 14, 1949; children: Patricia Orr Clark Blackstone, Elizabeth Phillips Clark Christiansen. *Education:* Tufts University, A.B., 1942; University of Missouri, M.A., 1948. *Politics:* Democrat. *Religion:* Presbyterian.

ADDRESSES: Home—3506 Elm Knoll, San Antonio, Tex. 78230.

CAREER: Owensboro Messenger and Inquirer, Owensboro, Ky., reporter, 1948-49; *Courier-Journal* and *Louisville Times* Co., Louisville, Ky., reporter and science writer for *Courier-Journal*, 1949-62, correspondent for *Courier-Journal* in Washington, D.C., 1958, managing editor of *Louisville Times*, 1962-71, executive editor of both newspapers, 1971-79; Florida Publishing Co., Jacksonville, Fla., editor of *Florida Times-Union* and *Jacksonville Journal*, 1979-82; Harte-Hanks Communications, Inc., San Antonio, Tex., vice-president for news, 1983-1986; news consultant, 1987—. Member of accrediting committee of Accrediting Council on Education in Journalism and Mass Communications. *Military service:* U.S. Army, 1942-46; became captain; received bronze star.

MEMBER: International Press Institute, American Society of Newspaper Editors (president, 1985-86), Associated Press Managing Editors Association (president, 1974-75), Association for Education in Journalism and Mass Communication, Sigma Delta Chi, Delta Tau Delta, River Club, Club Giraud.

AWARDS, HONORS: Nieman fellow at Harvard University, 1960-61; named editor of the year by National Press Photographers Association, 1967.

WRITINGS:

Success Stories: What Twenty-eight Newspapers Are Doing to Gain and Retain Readers, American Newspaper Publishers Association, 1988.

Contributor to periodicals, including *Associated Press Managing Editors News, Bulletin of the American Society of Newspaper Editors, Editor and Publisher, Nieman Reports,* and *Quill.*

BIOGRAPHICAL/CRITICAL SOURCES:

PERIODICALS

Courier-Journal (Louisville), July 8, 1979.
Editor and Publisher, December 21, 1974.

*   *   *

CLOSE, Frank (E.)   1945-

PERSONAL: Born July 24, 1945, in Peterborough, England; immigrated to United States, 1988. *Education:* University of St. Andrews, B.Sc., 1967; Oxford University, D.Phil., 1970.

ADDRESSES: Office—Department of Physics, University of Tennessee, Knoxville, Tenn. 37996-1200. *Agent*—Bolt & Watson, 26 Charing Cross Rd., London, England.

CAREER: Rutherford Appleton Laboratory, Oxfordshire, England, research theoretical physicist and senior principal scientist, 1975-87; University of Tennessee, Knoxville, Distinguished Professor of Physics, 1988—. Distinguished Scientist at Oak Ridge National Laboratory, 1988—.

MEMBER: British Association for the Advancement of Science (recorder of physics, 1984-88; member of general committee, 1985-88; member of council, 1986-88), Royal Institution of Great Britain.

WRITINGS:

Introduction to Quarks and Partons, Academic Press, 1979.
The Cosmic Onion: Quarks and the Nature of the Universe, Heinemann Educational, 1983, American Institute of Physics, 1987.
(With Michael Marten and Christine Sutton) *The Particle Explosion,* Oxford University Press, 1987.
End: Cosmic Catastrophe and the Fate of the Universe, Simon & Schuster, 1988.

Contributor of more than one hundred articles to scientific journals, including *New Scientist,* and newspapers.

WORK IN PROGRESS: Concentrating on research in particle physics, astrophysics, and nuclear physics; collecting material for a revised textbook; researching material for book about Lisa Meitner, *The Road to Manhattan,* adventure novelization about the discovery of atomic fission in fascist Germany and Italy in the 1930s.

SIDELIGHTS: Frank Close told *CA:* "I am researching a most exciting area of science. I want to communicate its wonder to the general reader. There are very few people who are both active writers and full-time professional research scientists of international stature. We swim in a small pond!"

AVOCATIONAL INTERESTS: Travel, squash, hiking.

*   *   *

COAKLEY, Michael   1947(?)-1988

OBITUARY NOTICE: Born c. 1947; died of acquired immune deficiency syndrome (AIDS), August 3, 1988, in Boston, Mass. Journalist. A respected newspaper reporter for two decades, Coakley was known in the industry for his versatility, fairness, accuracy, and eloquence as a writer. In 1968 he joined the staff of the Chicago, Illinois, *American* (which later became *Chicago Today),* covering civil rights protests and the famed "Conspiracy Seven" trial, in which the defendants in the case, dubbed "the Chicago Seven" by the media, were accused of inciting a riot at the 1968 Democratic National Convention. After moving to the *Chicago Tribune* he reported on the 1975 Joan Little murder case and the trial the following year of newspaper heiress Patty Hearst, in which Hearst was accused of aiding her Symbionese Liberation Army terrorist captors. Coakley served as the *Tribune's* Washington correspondent during U.S. president Jimmy Carter's administration and later reported for the newspaper's Los Angeles and New York City bureaus.

OBITUARIES AND OTHER SOURCES:

PERIODICALS

Chicago Tribune, August 4, 1988.

*   *   *

COEN, Ethan   1958-

PERSONAL: Born in 1958 in Minneapolis, Minn.; son of Edward (an economics professor) and Rena (an art historian) Coen; married wife, Hilary, in December, 1985. *Education:* Studied philosophy at Princeton University.

ADDRESSES: Home—New York, N.Y. *Office*—West 23rd St., New York, N.Y. *Agent*—c/o Leading Artists, 445 North Bedford Drive, Penthouse, Beverly Hills, Calif. 90210.

CAREER: Writer and producer of motion pictures, 1980—. Statistical typist at Macy's department store, New York, N.Y., 1979-80.

AWARDS, HONORS: Grand Jury Prize from the United States Film Festival, 1984, for "Blood Simple."

WRITINGS:

SCREENPLAYS

(With brother, Joel Coen) "Blood Simple," Circle Releasing Corporation, 1984.
(With J. Coen and Sam Raimi) "The XYZ Murders," Embassy, unreleased, limited release as "Crimewave," Columbia, 1986.
(With J. Coen) "Raising Arizona," Twentieth Century-Fox, 1987.

WORK IN PROGRESS: Another screenplay with brother, Joel Coen.

SIDELIGHTS: Producer-writer Ethan Coen has collaborated with his brother Joel to create films that have gained both critical and popular acclaim. The brothers' interest in movie-making dates back to the mid-1960s, when they filmed Super 8 remakes of vintage Hollywood B-movies, such as *Advise and Consent* and *The Naked Prey,* under Joel's direction. When the Coens left their hometown of Minneapolis to attend colleges in different states, they had no plans to resume their childhood partnership.

Ethan, the younger member of the filmmaking duo, majored in philosophy at Princeton University. He later moved to an apartment near his brother in New York and worked at a number of temporary office jobs. In his spare time Ethan began writing scripts with Joel, who had done some editing work for Sam Raimi, a director of low-budget horror films. The Coens wrote the thriller "Blood Simple" on nights and weekends over the course of six months in 1980 and spent the next year raising the 1.5 million dollars needed to film it. Ethan produced the movie and his brother directed it.

"Blood Simple" takes its title from the term that mystery writer Dashiell Hammett coined for the panic that an individual experiences after committing a murder. The film's plot spins the element of false perception into a web of adultery and murder reminiscent, say some critics, of the so-called *film noir* dramas of the 1940s. But Michael London of the *Los Angeles Times* wrote that "the brothers had never seen" much less been inspired by the old movies to which "Blood Simple" was compared. The Coens told Judy Klemesrud in an interview for the *New York Times* that they were greatly influenced by "the hard-boiled style" of James M. Cain's novels, such as *The Postman Always Rings Twice* and *Double Indemnity,* and wanted to capture their flavor in a modern movie.

Los Angeles Times staff writer Kevin Thomas's appraisal of "Blood Simple" suggests that the writers seem to make intangible human fears concrete by creating characters "with whom we'd be wiser to identify rather than patronize as they rush toward fates waiting to trip them up." Their film's characters are unable to perceive a reality to which the audience is privy. Thomas remarked that this aspect of the film allows its viewers to laugh at the players' folly from the safety of their seats in a curiously "gratifying" way. He called the movie "a dazzling *comedie noire,* a dynamic, virtuoso display" of filmmaking that is both "fresh and exhilarating."

"Blood Simple" was produced independently: "We made the movie because we wanted to make it," Ethan explained to Hal Hinson in a *Film Comment* interview. Major studios refused to distribute it because it was said to be too arty for the blood-and-gore crowd and too gory for the art audience. The movie was eventually released by the Circle Releasing Corporation in 1984 and has since attained cult status in cities throughout the United States. Critic Gene Siskel argued in the *Chicago Tribune* that "Blood Simple" would prove "too raw to win any awards in Hollywood." That did not stop the film from becoming a hit at the 1984 New York Film Festival or from bringing its writers a Grand Jury Prize at the United States Film Festival.

Coen and his brother next collaborated with Sam Raimi on a script originally entitled "The XYZ Murders." The farce about rat-exterminators-turned-people-exterminators achieved only limited release as "Crimewaves" and did not fare well with the few critics who reviewed it. It was not until Coen co-authored and produced "Raising Arizona" that he reached a mainstream American audience.

Critics agree that "Raising Arizona" represents a complete departure from the murderous cynicism that pervaded the

brothers' earlier works. The 1987 release details the courtship and marriage of Hi, a habitual but unarmed convenience store robber, and Edwina, the booking officer who takes Hi's mug shots each time he is jailed. When they can't have a baby of their own, they decide to kidnap one of unpainted-furniture king Nathan Arizona's quintuplets. Edwina tries to rationalize the couple's action: with five babies, the Arizonas "have more than they can handle, anyway."

While the majority of critics gave "Raising Arizona" rave reviews, a few were perturbed by what Sheila Benson of the *Los Angeles Times* called the "deeply condescending" attitude with which the Coens seemed to treat their subjects. In an article for *New York*, David Denby voiced the opinion of the numerous reviewers who countered this assessment. He argued that "the nihilistic Coens" are really "all heart." Hi and Edwina are dull witted but likeable, evoking affection from their audience. Denby considered it ironic that the law-breaking protagonists would actually make good parents: "That's why the comedy of their crime is also painful," he concluded. Rita Kempley, writing for the *Washington Post,* echoed Denby's sentiments, calling the Coens' unmistakable fondness for their characters "crucial to [the movie's] success." Ethan Coen himself answered the charge of snobbery in an interview for *American Film,* explaining that the Arizona depicted in the film is meant to represent a state of mind and is "not supposed to be" accurate.

The many critics who praised "Raising Arizona" were especially impressed by its script. Ethan and Joel wrote this screenplay together, smoking cigarettes and pacing their way through each scene as Ethan operated the typewriter. To avoid wasting time on the set, the writers engage in an unusually long pre-production period. Eric Pooley, writing for *New York,* observed that the brothers achieve stunning results by doing things "in the simplest, least expensive way." "Raising Arizona" was reportedly produced for only six million dollars, a fraction of an average Hollywood movie's budget.

It has been said that the brothers are surprised by their success and, consequently, can offer few comments on how they attained it. In the text accompanying an interview for *American Film,* David Edelstein called his formal consultations with the Coens "exercises in futility" and characterized Ethan as "the more silent and cryptic" of the two brothers. "Today" show co-host Jane Pauley reportedly told Ethan off camera that he should be spanked. One writer apparently even called the authors "space cadets," but readily acknowledged the team's talent. Observers say that the Coens see, think, and act as one: the artists combine their individual imaginative powers to realize a single vision—a new vision—that subverts the familiar and recasts it in a different light. Coen told Judy Klemesrud that he and his brother plan to collaborate for the rest of their careers because, as he is fond of saying, "two heads are better than one."

BIOGRAPHICAL/CRITICAL SOURCES:

PERIODICALS

American Film, May, 1985, April, 1987.
Chicago Tribune, March 1, 1985, March 25, 1987.
Film Comment, April, 1985, April, 1987.
Los Angeles Times, February 28, 1985, March 20, 1987.
New Republic, April 13, 1987.
Newsweek, January 21, 1985, March 16, 1987.
New York, March 16, 1987, March 23, 1987.
New Yorker, February 25, 1985, April 20, 1987.

New York Times, October 12, 1984, January 20, 1985, June 6, 1986, March 11, 1987.
Rolling Stone, May 21, 1987.
Time, January 28, 1985.
Times (London), February 1, 1985.
Village Voice, January 22, 1985.
Washington Post, February 10, 1985, March 20, 1987.*

—*Sketch by Barbara K. Carlisle*

*   *   *

COEN, Joel 1955-

PERSONAL: Born in 1955 in Minneapolis, Minn.; son of Edward (an economics professor) and Rena (an art historian) Coen; divorced, c. 1980. *Education:* Studied filmmaking at New York University.

ADDRESSES: Home—New York, N.Y. *Office*—West 23rd St., New York, N.Y. *Agent*—c/o Leading Artists, 445 North Bedford Drive, Penthouse, Beverly Hills, Calif. 90210.

CAREER: Writer and director of motion pictures, 1980—. Production assistant and assistant editor of low-budget horror films, including "The Evil Dead," in the late 1970s and early 1980s.

AWARDS, HONORS: Grand Jury Prize from the United States Film Festival, 1984, for "Blood Simple"; Independent Spirit Award for best director from Independent Film Project/West, 1986, for "Blood Simple."

WRITINGS:

SCREENPLAYS

(With brother, Ethan Coen; and director) "Blood Simple," Circle Releasing Corporation, 1984.
(With E. Coen and Sam Raimi) "The XYZ Murders," Embassy, unreleased, limited release as "Crimewave," Columbia, 1986.
(With E. Coen; and director) "Raising Arizona," Twentieth Century-Fox, 1987.

WORK IN PROGRESS: Another screenplay with brother, Ethan Coen.

SIDELIGHTS: Joel Coen, co-author and director of several screenplays with his brother, Ethan, has impressed critics with his technically adept and original independent films. Coen began making films at the age of eight, directing neighborhood youths in Super 8 remakes of Saturday afternoon matinees. David Denby wrote in *New York* that the young director has "the instincts" of a born moviemaker. More than one thousand of Coen's colleagues echoed that sentiment, naming him a 1986 winner of the Independent Spirit Award for best director of "Blood Simple," his official directorial debut.

Coen left his home state of Minnesota to attend New York University's film school, where, he explained to Judy Klemesrud for the *New York Times*, he "sat in the back of the room with an insane grin" on his face. He considers his work editing low-budget horror films for directors such as Sam Raimi more valuable to his screenwriting and directing career than his four years in college. When his brother Ethan moved to New York, the pair began collaborating on scripts. They wrote "Blood Simple" together in their spare time in 1980 and raised the money to produce it on their own.

Coen tells interviewers that he became the writing team's director because he is the older of the brothers. Theoretically, Joel directs and Ethan produces what they both write; but, as cinematographer Barry Sonnenfeld told Eric Pooley for *New York*, "they both do everything." Joel and Ethan talk out every scene of every script. Coen described the creative process to David Ansen for an article in *Newsweek:* "You paint yourself into a corner and then have to get out of it." The brothers make up their story lines as they go along, thus producing a script that will keep the audience guessing. Pooley wrote, "They pace the floor in step with each other, chain-smoke the same brand (Camel Lights), and share a telepathic sense of humor." Critics agree that the result of their almost ritualistic labor is a clean, concise script. Coen is adamant about following his polished script on the set to keep costs down and to assure that the finished film remains true to its authors' original conception.

Coen's first film, "Blood Simple," prompted critics to compare the young director to some of Hollywood's best known filmmakers, including Orson Welles, Alfred Hitchcock, and Brian DePalma. "Blood Simple," the story of a man who hires a detective to kill his adulterous wife and her lover, has been dubbed a throwback to the *film noir* genre of thrillers from the 1940s. In an interview with Hal Hinson for *Film Comment*, Coen explained that "'Blood Simple' utilizes movie conventions to tell the story. In a sense, it's about other movies—but no more so than any other film that uses the medium in a way that's aware that there's a history of movies behind it." In an article for *Newsweek*, Ansen called the film "the most inventive and original thriller in many a moon."

"Blood Simple" did not receive much exposure at the Los Angeles film festival, but after a well-received showing in Toronto, the movie went on to become a hit in New York and earned the Coens a Grand Jury Prize at the United States Film Festival. Critics throughout the country and as far away as England applauded its director's visual cleverness and ability to make even the bloodiest scenes humorous and beautiful in what Janet Maslin called a "bizarre" sort of way in an article for the *New York Times*. *Chicago Tribune* movie critic Gene Siskel explained "the look" of a Coen film: "If there is a more interesting way to look at a door, a bar, a drop of water, a soiled jacket, a plowed field, bullet holes, or even a bunch of dead fish, [Joel Coen] finds it."

After the limited release of gangster spoof "Crimewave," a collaboration with Sam Raimi that met with a less than enthusiastic reception, the Coens rebounded with the 1987 hit "Raising Arizona." The film centers on a nonviolent but recidivistic convenience store robber and his ex-police officer wife who kidnap a baby when they find that they cannot have one of their own. *Washington Post* staff writer Tom Shales commented that the Coens took a "truly risky premise" and turned it into "a prized package" that "puts a fresh, funny face on the American comedy movie." Inventive cinematic techniques, including crawling baby point of view shots, abstract illumination of a surrealistic character called the Lone Biker of the Apocalypse, and a shot of a car screaming to a halt within an inch of a baby on the road forced even *Los Angeles Times* film critic Sheila Benson, one of the few critics who disliked the movie, to admit that it was "miraculously technically adept."

A minority of reviewers felt that the Coens treated the characters in "Raising Arizona" with condescension, stereotyping them into hackneyed bumpkin roles. Joel countered the assumption in an interview with David Edelstein for *American Film:* "If the characters talk in cliches, it's because we *like* cliches. You start with things that are incredibly recognizable in one form and you play with them.'' In an article for *Film Comment,* Jack Barth expressed admiration for Coen's sight when he wrote that ''you can see things as they really are any time you like, but it takes a vision—by necessity self-conscious—to alter realities and suggest new ways of seeing.''

''Raising Arizona'' proved quite popular as an official entry at the Cannes Film Festival in 1987. Its resounding success reinforces the belief held by most critics: beyond producing a hilarious comedy, the Coens have called attention to the miraculous role that a child can play in the reformation of adults.

The Coen brothers plan to collaborate on scripts for the rest of their careers. They are presently writing another screenplay together, which Joel will direct and Ethan will produce.

BIOGRAPHICAL/CRITICAL SOURCES:

PERIODICALS

American Film, May, 1985, April, 1987.
Chicago Tribune, March 1, 1985, March 25, 1987.
Film Comment, April, 1985, April, 1987.
Los Angeles Times, February 28, 1985, March 20, 1987.
New Republic, April 13, 1987.
Newsweek, January 21, 1985, March 16, 1987.
New York, March 16, 1987, March 23, 1987.
New Yorker, February 25, 1985, April 20, 1987.
New York Times, October 12, 1984, January 20, 1985, June 6, 1986, March 11, 1987.
Rolling Stone, May 21, 1987.
Time, January 28, 1985.
Times (London), February 1, 1985.
Village Voice, January 22, 1985.
Washington Post, February 10, 1985, March 20, 1987.

—*Sketch by Barbara K. Carlisle*

* * *

COGGINS, Paul E. 1951-

PERSONAL: Born May 21, 1951, in Hugo, Okla.; son of Paul E., Sr. (a teacher) and Rebecca (a teacher; maiden name, Cates) Coggins; married Regina Montoya (an attorney), June 12, 1976; children: Jessica Chandler. *Education:* Yale University, B.A. (summa cum laude), 1973; Oxford University (first class honors), B.A., 1975, Diploma in Law, 1977; Harvard University, J.D. (cum laude), 1978.

ADDRESSES: Home—3202 Oakhurst St., Dallas, Tex. 75214. *Office*—Davis, Meadows, Owens, Collier & Zachry, 3700 First RepublicBank Plaza, 901 Main St., Dallas, Tex. 75202.

CAREER: Johnson & Swanson (law firm), Dallas, Tex., associate, 1979-80; U.S. Attorney's Office, Dallas, federal prosecutor, 1980-83; Johnson & Swanson, partner, 1983-86; Davis, Meadows, Owens, Collier & Zachry (law firm), Dallas, partner, 1986—. Taught in the New Mexico State Penitentiary. Member of Leadership Dallas, 1985-86, and Dallas mayor's Task Force on Criminal Justice, 1986-87.

MEMBER: Dallas Democratic Forum (member of board of directors, 1985—; president, 1986-87).

AWARDS, HONORS: Rhodes scholar, 1973-76.

WRITINGS:

The Lady Is the Tiger (mystery novel), Avon, 1987.

Contributor to periodicals, including *Southern* and *D Magazine.*

WORK IN PROGRESS: A sequel to *The Lady Is the Tiger.*

SIDELIGHTS: Paul E. Coggins told *CA:* ''My writing is an outgrowth of my fascination with crime and punishment, which motivated me to work for nine months as a teacher in the New Mexico State Penitentiary, tour European prisons, ride shotgun with the police at night, join the federal prosecutor's office in Dallas, become one of the few Harvard Law graduates to practice criminal law, and finally, to write crime novels. In the future I hope to continue writing mystery novels while branching out into crime nonfiction and screenplays.''

* * *

COHEN, Janet 1940-
(Janet Neel)

PERSONAL: Born July 4, 1940, in Oxford, England; daughter of George Edric (an architect) and Mary Isobel (a social worker) Neel; married James Lionel Cohen (a company director), December 18, 1971; children: Henry, Richard, Isobel. *Education:* Received degree from Newnham College, Cambridge (with honors), 1962. *Religion:* Church of England.

ADDRESSES: Home—50 Blenheim Ter., London NW8 0EH, England. *Office*—Charterhouse Bank Ltd., 1 Paternoster Row, London E.C.4, England.

CAREER: Department of Trade and Industry, London, England, assistant under-secretary of state, 1969-82; Charterhouse Bank Ltd., London, assistant director, 1982-88, director, 1988—. Director of Cape Pelican Ltd., 1983. Associate fellow of Newnham College, Cambridge, 1988.

MEMBER: Law Society.

WRITINGS:

UNDER NAME JANET NEEL

Death's Bright Angel (novel), Constable, 1988.
Death on Site (novel), Constable, 1989.

SIDELIGHTS: Janet Cohen told *CA:* ''The heroine of *Death's Bright Angel* is Francesca Wilson, a rising star at the Department of Trade and Industry and the leader of four younger brothers, one of whom is a pop music star. Francesca appears again in *Death on Site,* with the detective hero Chief Inspector John McLeish.

''Francesca Wilson is loosely based on my own career and family. She, like myself, is a well-educated middle class girl who in this generation is making a career in a man's world. Like many women rising to the top in their careers, she is an eldest child, fatherless from a relatively young age.

''I wrote my first detective novel some years ago but put it aside; *Death's Bright Angel* was written later, from real experience in a civil service and industrial world. Like author P. D. James, I had been waiting to write until I had more time; realizing this moment would never come, I wrote *Death's Bright Angel* between nine and eleven o'clock at night after the children were in bed and as opportunity offered over eighteen months. *Death on Site,* which is based on my experience as an industrial relations adviser to a construction company, is being written on the same principle.''

* * *

COLE, William Earle 1904-1979

OBITUARY NOTICE—See index for *CA* sketch: Born July 23,

1904, in Shady Valley, Tenn.; died March 14, 1979. Educator, editor, and author. Cole taught education and sociology at the University of Tennessee from 1930 to 1965. Associated with such organizations as the Tennessee Department of Welfare and the Tennessee Council for the Community Development Foundation, Cole was author and co-author of numerous books on education and sociology, including *Teaching of Biology, Urban Society, Introductory Sociology,* and *Social Foundations of Education.* He co-edited *Readings in Social Gerontology* and *Sociology of Aging.*

OBITUARIES AND OTHER SOURCES:

Date of death provided by wife, Beulah A. Cole.

*   *   *

COLLINS, Kathleen   1931-1988
(Kathleen Kranidas)

OBITUARY NOTICE—See index for *CA* sketch: Born January 30, 1931, in Seattle, Wash.; died of cancer, September 18, 1988, in New York, N.Y. Filmmaker, educator, and author. Collins, a professor of film history and production at the City College of New York, also wrote and directed plays for television and the stage. Among these are "The Brothers," "Losing Ground," and "The Cruz Brothers and Miss Molloy." Other writings include *One Year in Autumn,* a novel, and *The Mountain, the Stone,* a collection of short stories, both published under the name Kathleen Kranidas.

OBITUARIES AND OTHER SOURCES:

PERIODICALS

New York Times, September 24, 1988.

*   *   *

COLP, Ralph, Jr.   1924-

PERSONAL: Born October 12, 1924, in New York, N.Y.; son of Ralph (a surgeon) and Miriam (a housewife; maiden name, Mirsky) Colp; married Charlotte Rappaport (a physician), November 22, 1956; children: Ruth, Judith. *Education:* Columbia University, B.A., 1945, M.D., 1948; Tulane University, postdoctoral study, 1949-50. *Politics:* Liberal.

ADDRESSES: Home and office—301 East 79th St., Apt. 12A, New York, N.Y. 10021.

CAREER: Michael Reese Hospital, Chicago, Ill., intern, 1948-49; Tulane University, New Orleans, La., instructor in medicine, 1949-50; Mount Sinai Hospital, New York City, resident in surgery, 1950-53, surgeon, 1955-57; Massachusetts Mental Health Center (formerly Boston Psychopathic Hospital), Boston, resident in psychiatry, 1957-59; Harvard University, Boston, instructor in psychiatry, 1957-59; St. Luke's Hospital, New York City, resident in psychiatry, 1959-60, attending clinical psychiatrist, 1962-85, senior attending psychiatrist, 1985—; Columbia University Health Service, Mental Health Division, New York City, attending clinical psychiatrist, 1960-85, acting director, 1977-85, senior attending psychiatrist, 1985—; Columbia University, New York City, assistant professor of clinical psychiatry, 1977—; private practice in New York City, 1960—. *Military service:* U.S. Air Force Medical Corps, 1953-55; became captain.

MEMBER: International Psychohistorical Association, American Association of Sex Educators, Counselors, and Thera-

pists, American Psychiatric Association (fellow), Psychohistory Forum, Eastern Association of Sex Therapists.

WRITINGS:

To Be an Invalid: The Illness of Charles Darwin, University of Chicago Press, 1977.
(Contributor) Harold I. Kaplan and others, editors, *Comprehensive Textbook of Psychiatry,* Williams & Wilkins, 1980, fifth edition, 1988.
(Contributor) Zira DeFries and others, editors, *Sexuality: New Perspectives,* Greenwood Press, 1985.

Contributor of articles on Charles Darwin, psychohistory, the history of psychiatry and psychoanalysis, and sex in history to periodicals, including *Psychohistory Review, Journal of Psychohistory, Journal of the History of Medicine and Allied Sciences, Journal of the History of Biology, Journal of the History of Ideas, Isis,* and *Free Associations: Psychoanalysis, Politics, Groups, Culture.*

WORK IN PROGRESS: Editing *Darwin: The Critical Heritage,* Volume I: *Darwin the Man,* publication by Open University Press expected in 1990.

SIDELIGHTS: In *To Be an Invalid: The Illness of Charles Darwin* psychiatrist Ralph Colp, Jr., describes, analyzes, and offers a diagnosis of the chronic illnesses suffered by Charles Darwin, the noted nineteenth-century British naturalist who developed the theory of evolution by natural selection. Reviewing Colp's book for *New York Review of Books,* critic W. W. Bartley III included a description of Darwin's symptoms: "He suffered from 'fits of flatulence,' coughing up from his stomach acid, bitter, fetid odors. While this was happening, heavy pain would rack the lower parts of his chest. Many times each day he 'retched and vomited,' bringing up 'acid, slime, and clots of blood.' Accompanying these attacks were headaches, dizziness, giddiness, shivering, trembling of the hands, sinking sensations, palpitations of the heart. He was insomniac and 'chronically exhausted.' His skin erupted with boils, rashes, and eczema." Darwin sought relief for more than forty years, but successful diagnosis and treatment eluded his physicians, and he remained an invalid to the end of his life. He died in 1882 of a heart attack at the age of seventy-three.

Since then numerous theories have been offered to account for Darwin's illness, ranging from the strictly physical and medical to the psychoneurotic. In 1903, for instance, a doctor concluded that all of Darwin's symptoms arose from extreme eye strain. Other suggestions made over the ensuing years, according to the *New York Times,* include "Chagas' disease, arsenic poisoning, hypochondria or the stress caused by his wife's religious views." Bartley, in addition, listed "amoebiasis, gout, malaria, narcolepsy and diabetogenic hyperinsulinism syndrome, and acute inherited intermittent porphyria" and noted that the "Freudians have had a field day, agreeing among themselves only that Darwin must have had a repressed hostility to his father." Colp's interpretation, psychologically derived as well, results in a different diagnosis: Darwin's afflictions arose from stress due to anxieties induced by his theory of evolution.

As noted by the *New York Times,* Colp "drew on previously unpublished letters and manuscripts, a medical notebook and Darwin's own *Diary of Health*" and, according to Bartley, concluded that "[Darwin's] health started to deteriorate after he began his notebook on the transmutation of species in 1837. This was also the time when he began to give up his religious beliefs. One can trace a fairly close connection . . . between the times Darwin was working on evolutionary theory and the times when the illness was at its worst.'' Furthermore, since Darwin's theory of evolution provided "an alternative account of the creation . . . [it] was thus no minor 'scientific revolution,' but an ideological revolution of profound consequence, . . . [in effect] science and theology would never rest easily together again.'' To Colp this situation suggested that "the psychic consequences of slaying not his father . . . but his heavenly father . . . may well have gone underground, punishing him with all the sufferings of Job.''

Bartley pointed out in his review that though "Colp does not elaborate, and his argument remains vague,'' his explanation "does . . . serve to remind us of the immense pressures—personal, social, ideological—that [Darwin] would have had to face in the course of giving birth to the theory of natural selection.'' Bartley judged Colp's work "valuable in opening the way for a full-scale reconstruction of Darwin's probable emotional and intellectual situation,'' and concluded that *To Be an Invalid: The Illness of Charles Darwin* "can serve as a firm check on exclusively medical interpretations . . . which will henceforth have to be fully reconciled with the details adduced in Colp's text.''

Colp told *CA:* "When I was growing up in New York City, Darwin was a presence in my home: my father displayed the evolutionist's portrait in his office. When I was twelve years old, my mother purchased Darwin's *Life and Letters.* After reading parts of it, I came to view Darwin as a hero in science and a simple man who had achieved great success in an uncomplicated way. Later, my uncle Alfred Mirsky, a biochemist at the Rockefeller Institute, introduced me to the famous Russian geneticist Theodosius Dobzhansky, and I often listened to them talk about the controversy of the Darwinian theory. Since then, Darwin work has become part of my identity.

"While raising a family and learning how to be a psychoanalytically oriented psychotherapist, I tried to reconstruct how Darwin had experienced his undiagnosed illness in the context of his life. Peter Gautrey, librarian in charge of Darwin materials at the Cambridge University Library, Darwin scholar Paul Barrett, handwriting expert Karl Aschaffenburg, and analyst Dr. Max Schur all helped me to decipher the mystery surrounding Charles Darwin's illness.

"In 1977 I published *To Be an Invalid,* showing that Darwin's syndrome was mainly caused by mental conflicts—especially those connected with his transmutation theory. This meant that during most of his mature life, he experienced a cluster of emotions which were largely hidden from his colleagues and only expressed through his psychosomatic symptoms.''

AVOCATIONAL INTERESTS: Biography, psychobiography, and psychohistory.

BIOGRAPHICAL/CRITICAL SOURCES:

PERIODICALS

New York Review of Books, September 15, 1977.
New York Times, February 7, 1977.

*   *   *

CONARD, Robert C.   1933-

PERSONAL: Born August 10, 1933, in Cincinnati, Ohio; son of Robert G. (a pattern maker) and Antoinette Josephine (a homemaker; maiden name, Rielag) Conard; married Sheila

Hancock (a professor), July 24, 1957; children: Christopher, Anthony, Nicholas, Angela. *Education:* University of Cincinnati, B.B.A., 1956, M.A., 1964, Ph.D., 1969; attended University of Vienna, 1956-57; St. Xavier (now Xavier) University, Teaching Certificate, 1958.

ADDRESSES: Home—416 Irving Ave., Dayton, Ohio 45409. *Office*—Department of Languages, University of Dayton, Dayton, Ohio 45469.

CAREER: Teacher of English and German at primary and secondary schools in Cincinnati, Ohio, 1958-66; University of Dayton, Dayton, Ohio, instructor, 1967-68, assistant professor, 1968-71, associate professor, 1971-75, professor of German, 1975—.

MEMBER: International Brecht Society, German Studies Association, Modern Language Association of America, American Association of Teachers of German.

AWARDS, HONORS: Grants from National Endowment for the Humanities, 1978, 1986.

WRITINGS:

(Translator) Bero Rigauer, *Sport and Work,* New Critics Press, 1972.
(Contributor) Ralph Ley, editor, *Perspectives and Personalities: Studies in Modern German Literature Honoring Claude Hill,* C. Winter, 1978.
Heinrich Boell, G. K. Hall, 1981.
(Editor) Hermann Hesse, *Demian,* Edition Suhrkamp, 1985.
(Contributor) Gerhard Rademacher, editor, *Heinrich Boell als Lyriker* (title means "Heinrich Boell as Lyric Poet''), Verlag Peter Land, 1985.

Contributor of numerous articles and translations to literature and German studies periodicals.

WORK IN PROGRESS: Understanding Heinrich Boell, for University of South Carolina Press.

SIDELIGHTS: Robert C. Conrad told *CA:* "I became interested in German language and literature by accident. After graduating from college with a degree in business and a major in accounting and after practicing accounting for four years, I was appalled at my ignorance of things that really mattered: foreign languages, literature, culture in a broad sense. I concluded that learning a foreign language and studying in Europe were the only medicine for my miserable condition. The chance to study in Vienna was the first to come my way, and I jumped at it.

"Early in my reading of German literature, I realized that Heinrich Boell, because of his Catholic background and liberal, socialist, humanist commitment to society, was the writer who most interested me. Boell's main theme was simple and profound: only a collective moral memory can redeem a people. Boell's subject is always individual conscience placed in a dubious moral environment. Because he states over and over again in various ways the premise that Germany will never become a moral nation unless it deals individually and collectively with its recent history and converts the lessons of the Hitler years into a moral consciousness, his work creates a moral imperative for readers in all nations. Naturally, Boell's message is ultimately religious: but he is, because of the subtlety of his art, a religious writer in a nondidactic and unobtrusive manner.

"In general, Boell is easy to understand. His language, although poetically colloquial, deceptively refined, exact, and appropriate for each speaker and each occasion, is nonetheless accessible to the ordinary reader. In fact, his simple language is what gives his work its power. His concern for the right word and the correct tone for each voice, however, makes Boell's language difficult to translate, for the language that is correct in German often seems less natural in English. All translation has this problem, but it is more pronounced with Boell. It accounts, I believe, for the lack of success this Nobel laureate has had in English as compared to Russian, French, or Spanish. Additionally, his work may be received with some caution in the United States because of its apparent religious-moral commitment. The American reading public seems suspicious of religious ideas in fiction and of Boell's combination of piety and politics or the union of Christianity and socialism that has its home in his work. For this reason, interpreting Boell for the American reader is an extremely important task because his work has a message for twentieth century Americans from which we have much to learn.''

*   *   *

COOLEY, Denton A(rthur) 1920-

PERSONAL: Born August 22, 1920, in Houston, Tex.; son of Ralph C. (a dentist) and Mary (Fraley) Cooley; married Louise Goldsborough Thomas, January 15, 1949; children: Mary, Susan, Louise, Florence, Helen. *Education:* University of Texas at Austin, B.A., 1941; Johns Hopkins University, M.D., 1944.

ADDRESSES: Home—Houston, Tex. *Office*—Texas Heart Institute, P. O. Box 20345, Houston, Tex. 77030.

CAREER: Johns Hopkins University, Baltimore, Md., surgical intern at Johns Hopkins Hospital, 1944-45, resident in surgery, 1945-50; Brompton Hospital for Chest Diseases, London, England, senior surgical registrar in thoracic surgery, 1950-51; Baylor University, Houston, Tex., associate professor, 1954-62, professor of surgery, 1962-69; Texas Heart Institute, Houston, founder and chief surgeon, 1962—; University of Texas, Houston, clinical professor of surgery, 1975—. *Military service:* U.S. Army, Medical Corps, 1946-48; became captain.

MEMBER: International Cardiovascular Society, American College of Surgeons, American Surgical Association, American Association of Thoracic Surgery, Society of Thoracic Surgery, Society of University Surgeons, American College of Cardiology, American College of Chest Physicians, Society for Clinical Surgery, Society for Vascular Surgery, Western Surgical Association, Texas Surgical Society, Halsted Society.

AWARDS, HONORS: Named one of ten outstanding young men in the United States by U.S. Chamber of Commerce, 1955; man-of-the-year award from Kappa Sigma, 1964; Rene Leriche Prize from International Surgical Society, 1965-67; Billings Gold Medal from American Medical Association, 1967; Vishnevsky Medal from Vishnevsky Institute (Soviet Union), 1971; Theodore Roosevelt Award from National Collegiate Athletic Association, 1980; Presidential Medal of Freedom, 1984; gifted teacher award from American College of Cardiology, 1987. Honorary degrees from Hellenic College and Holy Cross Greek Orthodox School of Theology, Houston Baptist University, College of William and Mary, and United States Sports Academy.

WRITINGS:

Surgical Treatment of Congenital Heart Disease, Lea Febiger, 1966.

Techniques in Cardiac Surgery, Saunders, 1975, 2nd edition, 1984.
Techniques in Vascular Surgery, Saunders, 1979.
Essays of Denton A. Cooley, M.D.: Reflections and Observations, Eakin Press, 1984.
Surgical Treatment of Aortic Aneurysm, Saunders, 1986.
(With Carolyn E. Moore) *Eat Smart for a Healthy Heart Cookbook*, Barron's, 1987.

Contributor to numerous surgical texts. Author or co-author of more than one thousand scientific articles.

WORK IN PROGRESS: ''Ongoing research on all aspects of cardiovascular disease, with special interests in a total artificial heart and heart assist devices.''

SIDELIGHTS: Denton A. Cooley, one of the greatest heart surgeons, is probably best known for performing the first transplant of an artificial heart into a human being. But he has also contributed to development of the heart-lung bypass device and has pioneered such extraordinary surgical techniques as the replacing of diseased heart valves and the removal of aortic aneurysms. He has been particularly active in combating congenital heart diseases in infants. In addition, he helped establish the Texas Heart Institute at the Texas Medical Center in Houston.

Cooley told *CA:* ''During my medical career, I have played a role in the development of what was, when I began, an entirely new specialty—cardiovascular surgery. After I received my medical degree from Johns Hopkins University in 1944 and as a surgical intern at Johns Hopkins Hospital, I had the unique privilege of participating in the first operation for tetralogy of Fallot (the famous 'blue baby' operation) performed by my chief, Dr. Alfred Blalock. This deeply dramatic experience impressed me and first introduced me to the excitement and opportunity ahead in cardiovascular surgery.

''Upon leaving Baltimore, I joined Mr. Russell (subsequently Lord) Brock of London for a year (1950-51), another leader in the field, who was operating on heart valves raged with disease. When I returned to Houston, I continued to perfect techniques for treatment of infants with heart defects. After the introduction of the heart-lung machine in the late 1950s, 'open' heart surgery became a reality, and patients began to flock to physicians who would operate on the heart. Thus, my interest led me to believe that the time had come for an institution devoted to diseases of the heart and blood vessels, and, in 1962, the Texas Heart Institute was born. During the next twenty-five years, the institute would become the largest cardiovascular surgical center in the world, and its staff would perform more than seventy thousand open-heart operations, including the first 'successful' heart transplant in the United States and the first implantation in man of a total artificial heart.

''Although a certain number of patients have hereditary factors that predispose them to heart disease, in many others, disease could have been prevented or lessened through the appropriate combination of work, exercise, relaxation, and rest—all in practice with good nutrition and healthful eating habits. *Eat Smart for a Healthy Heart Cookbook* resulted from my desire to work toward preventing much of the heart disease I see daily in my practice. The cookbook offers gourmet menus from some of Houston's greatest chefs. The recipes, which have been modified to be 'heart healthy,' are low in sodium, fat, and cholesterol. A healthy and alert mind must be served by a fit and well-toned body. The incidence of heart disease, the major killer in our society, will be reduced by attention to such a balanced lifestyle.''

BIOGRAPHICAL/CRITICAL SOURCES:

BOOKS

Minetree, Harry, *Cooley: The Career of a Great Heart Surgeon*, Harper's Magazine Press, 1973.
Rapoport, Roger, *The Super-doctors*, Playboy Press, 1975.
Thompson, Thomas, *Hearts: Of Surgeons and Transplants; Miracles and Disasters Along the Cardiac Frontier*, McCall Publishing, 1971.

PERIODICALS

Esquire, December, 1969.
Life, August 2, 1968, April 10, 1970.
Time, October 25, 1971.

* * *

COOPER, (Fraser) Barry 1943-

PERSONAL: Born September 3, 1943, in Vancouver, British Columbia, Canada; son of Harry (a surgeon) and Helen (a teacher; maiden name, Legge) Cooper; married Denise Guichon (in business); children: Meghan, Brendan. *Education:* University of British Columbia, B.A. (with honors), 1965; Duke University, A.M., 1967, Ph.D., 1969. *Religion:* Anglican.

ADDRESSES: Office—Department of Political Science, University of Calgary, Calgary, Alberta, Canada T2N 1N4.

CAREER: Duke University, Durham, N.C., instructor in political science, 1967; Bishop's University, Lennoxville, Quebec, assistant professor of political science, 1969-70; McGill University, Montreal, Quebec, visiting assistant professor of political science, 1970; York University, Downsview, Ontario, assistant professor, 1970-76, associate professor of political science, 1976-81; University of Calgary, Calgary, Alberta, professor of political philosophy and Canadian political thought, 1981—. Guest on national radio programs.

MEMBER: American Political Science Association, Canadian Political Science Association, Phi Beta Kappa, Milk River Ridge Deer and Pheasant Association, Pennask Lake Fishing and Game Club.

AWARDS, HONORS: Canada Council grants, 1970-71, fellowship, 1980; Canada-France exchange fellow, 1975, 1978, 1980, and 1988; grant from Social Science and Humanities Research Council of Canada, 1983 and 1987-88; Alberta Manpower grants, 1984, 1984-85, 1985, and 1985-86; grant from Canada Employment and Immigration, 1985.

WRITINGS:

(Translator) Raymond Aron, *History and the Dialectic of Violence: An Analysis of Sartre's Critique de la raison dialectique*, Basil Blackwell, 1974.
(Translator) Jean Baechler, *The Origins of Capitalism*, Basil Blackwell, 1974.
(Translator) Jean Baechler, *Suicides*, Basic Books, 1979.
Merleau-Ponty and Marxism: From Terror to Reform, University of Toronto Press, 1979.
Michel Foucault: An Introduction to the Study of His Thought, Edwin Mellen Press, 1982.
The End of History: An Essay on Modern Hegelianism, University of Toronto Press, 1984.
The New Science: Essays on Eric Voegelin's Political Philosophy, Edwin Mellen Press, 1986.

Alexander Kennedy Isbister: A Respectable Critic of the Honourable Company, Carleton University Press, 1988.
(Editor with A. Kornberg and W. Mishler) *The Resurgence of Conservatism in the Anglo-American Democracies*, Duke University Press, 1988.
Action Into Nature: An Essay on the Meaning of Technology, Loyola University Press, in press.
(Editor with P. Emberley) *Reason and Revelation: The Strauss-Voegelin Correspondence*, University of Chicago, in press.

CONTRIBUTOR

David Shugarman, editor, *Thinking About Change*, University of Toronto Press, 1974.
John H. Hallowell, editor, *The Prospects for Constitutional Change: Festschrift for Taylor Cole*, Duke University Press, 1975.
Larry Schmidt, editor, *George Grant in Process: Essays and Conversations*, House of Anansi Press, 1978.
H. K. Betz, editor, *Recent Approaches to the Social Sciences*, University of Calgary, 1979.
Peter J. Opitz and Gregor Sebba, editors, *The Philosophy of Order: Essays on History, Consciousness, and Politics*, Klett-Cotta, 1981.
Frances Canavan, editor, *The Ethical Dimension of Political Life: Essays in Honor of John H. Hallowell*, Duke University Press, 1983.
Anthony J. Parel, editor, *Ideology*, Wilfrid Laurier University Press, 1983.
John Kirby and William M. Thompson, editors, *Voegelin the Theologian: Ten Studies in Interpretation*, Edwin Mellen Press, 1983.
Stephen Brooks, editor, *Political Thought in Canada*, Clarke, Irwin, 1984.
Neil Nevitte and Allan Kornberg, editors, *Minorities and the Canadian State*, Mosaic, 1985.
(Author of introduction) Eric Voegelin, *Political Religions*, Edwin Mellen Press, 1986.
Tom Darby, editor, *Sojourns in the New World: Reflections on Technology*, Carleton University Press, 1986.

Contributor of more than forty articles and reviews to philosophy and political science journals.

SIDELIGHTS: Barry Cooper told *CA:* "Like most people who write, I have tried to understand the world and express that understanding clearly. Like most academic scholars, this has taken the form of analysis and commentary on the work of others. There is a lot to learn before one ought be immodest enough to voice one's own opinion.''

* * *

COOPER, Kenneth H(ardy) 1931-

BRIEF ENTRY: Physician and author. Cooper, a specialist in preventive medicine, is known for promoting aerobic exercise as a deterrent to heart disease. He became interested in aerobics in the early 1960s when, despite seemingly good health, he became weak while attempting to ski after years of relative inactivity. Realizing that he generally felt sluggish and that his blood pressure was undesirably high, he adopted a vigorous exercise regime that included jogging. Soon Cooper was promoting aerobics, which exercise and strengthen the heart and lungs, as a form of preventive medicine. He developed programs for training astronauts and designed a regime for U.S. Air Force personnel. In 1970 he established the Aerobics Center in Dallas, Texas. The complex includes a clinic, an activities center, and a research institute. Among Cooper's writings are *Aerobics* (M. Evans, 1968), *The New Aerobics* (M. Evans, 1970), *The Aerobics Way: New Data on the World's Most Popular Exercise Program* (M. Evans, 1977), *The Aerobics Program for Total Well-Being: Exercise, Diet, Emotional Balance* (M. Evans, 1982), *Running Without Fear: How to Reduce the Risk of Heart Attack and Sudden Death During Aerobic Exercise* (M. Evans, 1985), and *Controlling Cholesterol: Dr. Kenneth H. Cooper's Preventive Medicine Program* (Bantam, 1988). *Addresses: Office*—Aerobics Center, Dallas, Tex.

BIOGRAPHICAL/CRITICAL SOURCES:

BOOKS

Hoffman, William, and Jerry Shields, *Doctors on the New Frontier*, Macmillan, 1981.

PERIODICALS

Chicago Tribune, June 19, 1985.
Los Angeles Times, August 15, 1985.
Publishers Weekly, March 25, 1988.

*   *   *

COUNSILMAN, James E(dward)   1920-

PERSONAL: Born December 28, 1920, in Birmingham, Ala.; son of Joseph Walter and Ottilia Lena (Schamburg) Counsilman; married Marjorie E. Scrafford, June 15, 1943; children: Cathy, James (deceased), Jill, Brian. *Education:* Ohio State University, B.S., 1947; University of Illinois at Urbana-Champaign, M.S., 1948; University of Iowa, Ph.D., 1951.

ADDRESSES: Home—3806 Cameron Ave., Bloomington, Ind. 47401. *Office*—Department of Physical Education, Indiana University—Bloomington, Bloomington, Ind. 47405.

CAREER: Cortland State Teachers College (now State University of New York College at Cortland), swim coach, 1952-57; Indiana University—Bloomington, swim coach, 1957—, professor of physical education, 1966—. President of Counsilman & Co., Inc. (film producers and publishers), 1971—, and Counsilman & Associates (swimming pool construction consultants), 1971—. Founding president of International Swimming Hall of Fame, 1963; coach of U.S. men's swimming team for Olympic Games of 1964 and 1976. *Military service:* U.S. Army Air Forces, bomber pilot, 1943-45; received Distinguished Flying Cross and Air Medal with cluster.

MEMBER: American College of Sports Medicine (fellow), American Association of Health, Physical Education, Recreation and Dance, American Swim Coaches Association (past president), College Swim Coaches Association, English Channel Swim Association.

WRITINGS:

The Science of Swimming, Prentice-Hall, 1969.
Competitive Swimming Manual for Coaches and Swimmers, Counsilman & Co., 1977.
The Complete Book of Swimming, Atheneum, 1977.

*   *   *

COURATIN, Arthur Hubert   1902-1988

OBITUARY NOTICE: Born in 1902; died July 9, 1988. Church historian, clergyman, educator, and author. Best known for his role in liturgical reform, Couratin was also a compelling and respected lecturer and teacher. Ordained in 1926, he served as vice-principal of Queen's College in Birmingham, England, before joining St. Stephen's House in Oxford, where he was first chaplain, then vice-principal, and later principal, holding the last post for twenty-six years. Couratin became a member of the Liturgical Commission of the Church of England at its inception in the 1950s and, after leaving St. Stephen's in 1962, was appointed canon and librarian at Durham Cathedral. His theological writings include a sermon on the holy spirit published in *Catholic Sermons*, an essay on sacramental grace in *Union of Christendom*, and a liturgical summary for *Pelican Guide to Modern Theology*. His unfinished work on eucharistic prayer was published in *The Sacrifice of Praise*.

OBITUARIES AND OTHER SOURCES:

BOOKS

Who's Who, 140th edition, St. Martin's, 1988.

PERIODICALS

Times (London), July 26, 1988.

*   *   *

COWAN, Paul   1940-1988

OBITUARY NOTICE: Born September 21, 1940; died of leukemia, September 25 (one source says September 26), 1988, in New York, N.Y. Journalist and author. A staff writer for the *Village Voice* for more than two decades, Cowan is perhaps best remembered for his 1982 book *An Orphan in History: Retrieving a Jewish Legacy*, which chronicles his rediscovery of his Jewish roots. He learned of his orthodox Jewish ancestry by accident, following the death of his parents in a New York City fire. This revelation prompted him to engage in a serious study of the faith and led to the founding, with his wife, Rachel, of a Hebrew school on Manhattan's West Side. He later participated in the revitalization of Ansche Chesed, a conservative synagogue. Cowan also wrote *The Making of an Un-American: A Dialogue With Experience* and, with his wife, *Mixed Blessings: Jews, Christians, and Intermarriage*. The journalist's articles for the *Village Voice* on the peace corps, the civil rights movement, and protests against the war in Vietnam were collected in a volume titled *The Tribes of America*.

OBITUARIES AND OTHER SOURCES:

PERIODICALS

Los Angeles Times, October 3, 1988.
New York Times, September 27, 1988.

*   *   *

COX, William R(obert)   1901-1988
(Willard d'Arcy, Mike Frederic, John Parkhill, Joel Reeve, Wayne Robbins, Roger G. Spellman, Jonas Ward)

OBITUARY NOTICE—See index for *CA* sketch: Born April 14, 1901, in Peapack, N.J.; died of congestive heart failure, August 7, 1988, in Los Angeles, Calif. Editor and author. In a writing career that spanned six decades, Cox produced more than eighty novels for adults and young adults and contributed more than one thousand stories to such magazines as *Saturday Evening Post*, *Collier's*, and *Cosmopolitan*. He specialized in sports stories, mysteries, and westerns, often writing under one of a number of pen names. Book titles include *Five Were Chosen: A Basketball Story*, *Comanche Moon*, *Death on Lo-*

cation, *The Sixth Horseman*, and *Cemetery Jones and the Maverick Kid*. In addition, Cox wrote several screenplays and scripts for more than one hundred television programs, among them "Fireside Theater," "Bonanza," "Zane Grey Theater," and "Route 66." Cox also edited *Rivers to Cross*, a collection of stories by members of the Western Writers of America, an organization of which he was onetime president.

OBITUARIES AND OTHER SOURCES:

BOOKS

The Writers Directory: 1988-1990, St. James Press, 1988.

PERIODICALS

Chicago Tribune, August 12, 1988.
Los Angeles Times, August 12, 1988.
New York Times, August 12, 1988.

* * *

CRIDDLE, Joan D(ewey) 1935-

PERSONAL: Born December 9, 1935, in Deweyville, Utah; daughter of Arlen G. (a salesman) and Fern (a homemaker; maiden name, Rainey) Dewey; married Richard Sheffield Criddle (a professor of biochemistry), June 1, 1956; children: Keith Richard, Laura Marie Criddle Brock, Linda Criddle Wathne, Karen Sheffield, Pamela Sue Criddle Hilton. *Education:* Attended Utah State University, 1954-55; Sacramento City College, A.A., 1978; attended California State University, Sacramento, 1979. *Religion:* Church of Jesus Christ of Latter-day Saints (Mormon).

ADDRESSES: Home and office—Davis, Calif. *Agent*—George Ziegler, 160 East 97th St., New York, N.Y. 10029.

CAREER: Utah State University, Logan, Utah, assistant manager of computer center, 1955-57; children's day care coordinator, 1957-67; homemaker and professional cake decorator, 1967-76; Davis Handbill Delivery Service (advertising distribution company), Davis, Calif., owner and manager, 1976-80; free-lance writer and editor, 1980—.

WRITINGS:

To Destroy You Is No Loss: The Odyssey of a Cambodian Family, Atlantic Monthly Press, 1987.

Contributor to magazines.

WORK IN PROGRESS: From Behind the Veil, a history of Kuwait, based on the experiences of three generations of Kuwaiti women: a grandmother, a mother, and an adult daughter; research on a sequel for *To Destroy You Is No Loss*.

SIDELIGHTS: Joan D. Criddle told *CA:* "I was born of Mormon pioneer ancestry in 1935, in Deweyville, Utah, a community founded by my great-grandfather. I grew up at the end of the Great Depression, a middle child in a family of six children. In Logan, Utah, I married my high school sweetheart while in college, then worked to put him through graduate school in Madison, Wisconsin. After his army stint in Lawton, Oklahoma, we settled in Davis, California.

"In connection with my husband's work, I have had opportunities to live in several countries: five months in Austria, seven months in England, one year in Australia, and eighteen months in Kuwait. I have also traveled extensively throughout the world. I traveled overland from Australia to France, using such local transportation as donkey cart, rickshaw, elephant,

and paddle wheel boat. I've visited East Germany, Hungary, Saudi Arabia, Abu Dhabi, Jordan, Egypt, and Israel. I have dived in the Red Sea, Belize, Fiji, New Caledonia, the New Hebrides, Bali, and Malaysia, and hiked in Tasmania, Nepal, the Alps, the Sierras, and through Thailand's primitive mountain villages. We camped in New Zealand, Kenya, and throughout Europe, Great Britain, the western United States, and Mexico. I have shopped at bazaars in Guatemala, India, Turkey, Sumatra, and Burma, and toured museums or attended theatrical productions all over the world. I even had my appendix removed in Afghanistan.

"In 1979, news reports told daily of the plight of Cambodian, Laotian, and Vietnamese refugees. My husband and I, along with four other couples, knew that we could do little to relieve the suffering of the thousands upon thousands of Southeast Asians seeking aid. But we could make a difference in the life of at least one refugee by becoming sponsors.

"Teeda But Mam and her family arrived in Davis, California, in March, 1980. In August, her family of thirteen moved into our home, while our family went on sabbatical leave to Kuwait for eighteen months. During the few months between Teeda's arrival in America and our departure, the Cambodians—in halting English—shared some of their shocking experiences under the Communists. I decided to spend my time abroad putting these stories into written form and doing the necessary background research to bring Teeda's story to the public's awareness.

"In 1975 and 1982 I spent time in Southeast Asia and learned to love the people and their lifestyle. A visit to Khao-I-Dong refugee camp on the Thai-Cambodian border validated what I had written about Teeda's camp experiences. A backpacking trip through colorful fields of opium poppies in northeastern Thailand took me to six remote, mountain tribal villages, which represented three different ethnic groups. This hike clarified facts and feelings about life in rural Southeast Asia. The culmination of seven years of research and writing is my book *To Destroy You Is No Loss*."

AVOCATIONAL INTERESTS: Scuba diving, snorkeling, camping, hiking, attending theatrical productions, visiting art museums, "building a cabin with our own hands on the north coast of California, where we retreat, as often as time permits, to build, chop firewood, clear timber, and cut trails," quilting, backpacking, painting, visiting archaeological sites, collecting miniature furniture and seashells, meeting people from other cultures.

BIOGRAPHICAL/CRITICAL SOURCES:

PERIODICALS

New York Times Book Review, August 2, 1987.

* * *

CROUCH, Bill, Jr.
See CROUCH, William Maxwell, Jr.

* * *

CROUCH, William Maxwell, Jr. 1945-
(Bill Crouch, Jr.)

PERSONAL: Born January 25, 1945, in Bridgeport, Conn.; son of William Maxwell (an executive of a paper and envelope company) and Dorothy (a professional Girl Scout executive;

maiden name, Miller) Crouch. *Education:* Columbia University, B.A., 1967; Pennsylvania State University, M.A., 1973. *Religion:* Episcopalian.

ADDRESSES: Home—Box 2311, Bridgeport, Conn. 06608. *Agent*—Dorothy Crouch, Crouch International, 1156 Avenue of the Americas, New York, N.Y. 10036.

CAREER: Equity Paper Co., Inc., Bridgeport, Conn., vice-president and general manager, 1974-81; General Business Envelope, Hartford, Conn., salesman, 1982—. Member of board of selection of Cartoon Hall of Fame, Museum of Cartoon Art. *Military service:* U.S. Air Force, 1968-72.

MEMBER: National Cartoonists Society, Sons of the American Revolution Rotary Club of Bridgeport.

WRITINGS:

UNDER NAME BILL CROUCH, JR.

(Editor with Mrs. Walt Kelly) *The Best of Pogo*, Simon & Schuster, 1982.
(Editor with Mrs. Walt Kelly) *Pogo Even Better*, Simon & Schuster, 1984.
(Editor with Mrs. Walt Kelly) *Outrageously Pogo*, Simon & Schuster, 1985.
(Editor with Mrs. Walt Kelly) *Pluperfect Pogo*, Simon & Schuster, 1987.
Dick Tracy: America's Most Famous Detective, Citadel, 1987.
(Editor with Mrs. Walt Kelly) *Phi Beta Pogo*, Simon & Schuster, 1989.

WORK IN PROGRESS: The Dragon Lady Scrapbook, compiled from the comic strip "Terry and the Pirates"; *Dick Tracy Scrapbook;* research on cartooning and the American military.

SIDELIGHTS: Bill Crouch, Jr. told *CA:* "I became interested in pop art while studying art history in college. Instead of drawing me further into 'fine art,' however, this led me to an interest in caricature and syndicated cartoons. My first writing course was at the Defense Information School at Fort Benjamin, in Harrison, Indiana, in 1968. After the Air Force, while I was at Penn State, I began interviewing cartoonists, initially for *Cartoonist Profiles* magazine of Westport, Connecticut."

*   *   *

CROWDER, Michael   1934-1988

OBITUARY NOTICE—See index for *CA* sketch: Born June 9, 1934, in London, England; died August 14, 1988. Historian, educator, editor, and author. A British writer and administrator who spent most of his adult life in Africa, Crowder served the University of Botswana and the Nigerian universities of Ibadan, Ife, Kano, Zaria, and Lagos, in both academic and executive capacities. He wrote prolifically on the social and political history of West Africa in such books as *A Short History of Nigeria, Senegal: A Study in French Assimilation Policy,* and *West Africa Under Colonial Rule.* Crowder was also editor of *West African Resistance: The Military Response to Colonial Occupation* and co-editor of several other African histories. He contributed articles on African affairs to periodicals and served as editor of *Nigeria* magazine, *History Today, Journal of African History,* and other publications.

OBITUARIES AND OTHER SOURCES:

BOOKS

Who's Who, 140th edition, St. Martin's, 1988.
The Writers Directory: 1988-1990, St. James Press, 1988.

PERIODICALS

Times (London), August 19, 1988.

*   *   *

CURTIS, Sharon   1951-
(Laura London, a joint pseudonym)

PERSONAL: Born March 6, 1951, in Dahran, Saudi Arabia; immigrated to the United States, naturalized citizen; married Thomas Dale Curtis (a writer), 1970; children: two. *Education:* Attended University of Wisconsin—Madison.

CAREER: Writer.

WRITINGS:

ROMANCE NOVELS; WITH HUSBAND, THOMAS DALE CURTIS, UNDER JOINT PSEUDONYM LAURA LONDON

A Heart Too Proud, Dell, 1978.
The Bad Baron's Daughter, Dell, 1978.
Moonlight Mist, Dell, 1979.
Love's a Stage, Dell, 1980.
The Gypsy Heiress, Dell, 1981.
The Windflower, Dell, 1984.

WITH THOMAS DALE CURTIS, UNDER NAME TOM CURTIS

Sunshine and Shadow, Bantam, 1986.
Keepsake, Jove, 1987.*

*   *   *

CURTIS, Thomas Dale   1952-
(Tom Curtis; Laura London, a joint pseudonym)

PERSONAL: Born November 11, 1952, in Antigo, Wis.; married wife, Sharon (a writer), 1970; children: two. *Education:* Attended University of Wisconsin—Madison.

CAREER: Writer. Worked as a professional musician and actor.

WRITINGS:

ROMANCE NOVELS; WITH WIFE, SHARON CURTIS, UNDER JOINT PSEUDONYM LAURA LONDON

A Heart Too Proud, Dell, 1978.
The Bad Baron's Daughter, Dell, 1978.
Moonlight Mist, Dell, 1979.
Love's a Stage, Dell, 1980.
The Gypsy Heiress, Dell, 1981.
The Windflower, Dell, 1984.

UNDER NAME TOM CURTIS; WITH SHARON CURTIS

Sunshine and Shadow, Bantam, 1986.
Keepsake, Jove, 1987.*

*   *   *

CURTIS, Tom
See CURTIS, Thomas Dale

D

DALE, Peter N(icholas) 1950-

PERSONAL: Born November 1, 1950, in Melbourne, Australia; son of Frank Melbourne (an architect) and Florence (a pharmacist; maiden name, Madden) Dale; married Angela Cubeddu (a teacher), August, 1982. *Education:* Attended University of Perugia, 1970, and Osaka Municipal University, 1975-76; University of Melbourne, B.A., 1973, graduate study, 1974, 1982-83.

ADDRESSES: Home—Via Prato Bini loc. Vascacce, Palestrina, Rome, Italy 00036; and 17 Newton St., Surrey Hills, Melbourne 3127, Australia.

CAREER: Farmer. Visiting lecturer at Australian National University, School of Pacific Studies, 1980, and at Oxford University, Nissan Institute of Japanese Studies, 1983 and 1988. Guest participant in the 1988 Japan Forum symposium in Tokyo, Japan.

WRITINGS:

The Myth of Japanese Uniqueness, St. Martin's, 1986.

WORK IN PROGRESS: Research on shamanism, myth, epic literature, the rise of children's literature, the comparative study of ideology, and the concept of the person.

SIDELIGHTS: Peter N. Dale told *CA* that his time is divided between study and farming.

*   *   *

DALEY, Brian 1947-

PERSONAL: Born December 22, 1947, in Englewood, N.J.; son of Charles J. and Myra A. (de la Cruz) Daley. *Education:* Jersey City State College, B.A., 1974.

ADDRESSES: c/o Box 327, Arnold, Md. 21012; c/o Ballantine/Del Rey Books, 201 East 50th St., New York, N.Y. 10022.

CAREER: Novelist. Worked as house painter, waiter, and county welfare case worker. *Military service:* U.S. Army, 1965-69; served in Vietnam and West Germany.

WRITINGS:

NOVELS

The Doomfarers of Coramonde, Ballantine, 1977.

The Starfollowers of Coramonde, Ballantine, 1979.
Han Solo at Stars' End, Ballantine, 1979.
Han Solo's Revenge, Ballantine, 1979.
Han Solo and the Lost Legacy, Ballantine, 1980.
The Exploits of Han Solo (contains *Han Solo at Stars' End, Han Solo's Revenge,* and *Han Solo and the Lost Legacy*), Ballantine, 1982.
Tron, Ballantine, 1982.
A Tapestry of Magics, Ballantine, 1983.
Requiem for a Ruler of Worlds, Ballantine, 1985.
Jinx on a Terran Inheritance, Ballantine, 1985.
Fall of the White Ship Avatar: A Hobart Floyt-Alacrity Fitzhugh Adventure, Ballantine, 1986.

OTHER

Scriptwriter for television series "Adventures of the Galaxy Rangers," 1986. Author of National Public Radio adaptations of "Star Wars" and "The Empire Strikes Back." Author of scripts for record albums "Wargames" and "Rebel Mission to Ord Mankell," both released by Disneyland/Buena Vista Records. Contributor to science fiction and fantasy periodicals.

WORK IN PROGRESS: Gamma Law, for Ballantine/Del Rey.

SIDELIGHTS: Brian Daley told *CA:* "The most horrible thing that can *possibly* happen to a novelist is to have Del Rey Books' senior editor and veteran science fiction/fantasy writer Lester Del Rey point to a plot device and sneer, 'How *convenient* for the author!' I recommend it, however, the earlier the better, for the breaking of certain bad habits. The phrase makes a great cautionary mantra."

*   *   *

DALY, Christopher B. 1954-

PERSONAL: Born July 7, 1954, in Boston, Mass.; son of John Edward III (an engineer) and Mary (Duggan) Daly; married Anne K. Fishel (a clinical psychologist), 1982; children: Gabriel Jackson. *Education:* Harvard University, B.A. (magna cum laude), 1976; University of North Carolina at Chapel Hill, M.A., 1982 . *Politics:* "Complicated." *Religion:* "Yes."

ADDRESSES: Home—134 Pleasant St., Brookline, Mass. 02146. *Office*—Associated Press, 184 High St., Boston, Mass. 02110.

CAREER: Associated Press, New York, N.Y., writer and editor, 1976-80; Associated Press, Boston, Mass., State House reporter, 1982-87, State House bureau chief, 1987—.

MEMBER: Wire Service Guild, American Federation of Labor-Congress of Industrial Organizations, Penultimate Society.

AWARDS, HONORS: Shared Merle Curti Prize from Organization of American Historians, 1988, for *Like a Family.*

WRITINGS:

(With Jacqueline D. Hall, Bob Korstad, Lu Ann Jones, and others) *Like a Family: The Making of a Southern Cotton Mill World,* University of North Carolina Press, 1987.

Author of a magazine column on politics, under a pseudonym.

WORK IN PROGRESS: A second book.

SIDELIGHTS: Christopher B. Daly informed *CA:* "My only hope is to write something that I feel sure will be read by strangers after I'm dead."

*   *   *

DANN, John C(hristie)   1944-

PERSONAL: Born May 3, 1944, in Wilmington, Del.; son of C. Marshall (a patent attorney) and Catharine (Christie) Dann; married Orelia Sparrow (a teacher) in 1970; children: Catharine, Orelia. *Education:* Dickinson College, B.A., 1966; College of William and Mary, M.A., 1970, Ph.D., 1975.

ADDRESSES: Home—7580 Fourth St., Dexter, Mich. 48130. *Office*—William L. Clements Library, University of Michigan, Ann Arbor, Mich. 48109.

CAREER: Christopher Newport College, Newport News, Va., instructor in American history, 1970-71; University of Michigan, Ann Arbor, curator of manuscripts, 1972-77, director of William L. Clements Library, 1977—. Member of National Historical Publications and Records Commission. Elected member of Dexter Village Council, 1980-84.

MEMBER: Organization of American Historians, American Antiquarian Society, Southern Historical Association, Cosmos Club, Rotary Club.

AWARDS, HONORS: Revolutionary Round Table named *The Revolution Remembered* best book on the American Revolution in 1980.

WRITINGS:

(Editor) *The Revolution Remembered: Eye-Witness Accounts of the War for Independence,* University of Chicago Press, 1980.

Also contributor of articles to periodicals; editor of *American Magazine and Historical Chronicle;* member of editorial board of "Great Lakes Books Series" for Wayne State University Press.

WORK IN PROGRESS: Editing the autobiography of Jacob Nagle, veteran of the American Revolution and the British Navy, and sailor to Australia, publication expected in 1989.

SIDELIGHTS: John C. Dann's *The Revolution Remembered* is a collection of seventy-nine personal accounts of service in the American Revolutionary War. Engendered by the comprehensive pension act passed by the United States Congress in 1832 that granted a yearly sum to every person who had served for at least six months in the American Revolution, the ac-

counts, primarily in the form of court depositions, are attempts on the part of their narrators to prove themselves eligible for pension. Selected from an even larger pool of such accounts existing in the National Archives, the narratives were chosen by Dann for qualities of historical importance, literary merit, and geographical variety.

In *The Revolution Remembered,* the stories of service include that of Jehu Grant, a black slave who ran away from his loyally British (Tory) master to fight in the Revolutionary War. Another interesting account belongs to Sarah Osborn, who followed her husband Aaron during his stint as a commissary sergeant. She cooked and did laundry for the troops, witnessed some of the war's most important events, and traded remarks with Commander in Chief General George Washington. In these testimonies and others, according to *Los Angeles Times* critic Robert Kirsch, "we have an extraordinary evocation of what it meant to be alive in those adrenal days, especially as an ordinary soldier. You can hear their voices." Also noting the historical value of seeing the American Revolution through the eyes of the average participant rather than those of famous generals, reviewer Edmund S. Morgan noted in the *New Republic* that "one gains from [*The Revolution Remembered*] a sense of immediacy that is lacking in more formal memoirs of the period."

Dann told *CA:* "I have a very strong commitment to preserving and making readable for a general audience primary historical source material. The country will be in poor shape if it forgets its historical perspective, the sources are inherently fascinating if properly served up to the public, and the schools are no longer teaching history as they did thirty and more years ago."

BIOGRAPHICAL/CRITICAL SOURCES:

PERIODICALS

Los Angeles Times, July 7, 1980.
New Republic, July 26, 1980.
New York Times, March 28, 1980.
New York Times Book Review, July 6, 1980.

*   *   *

d'ARCY, Willard
See COX, William R(obert)

*   *   *

DARNTON, John (Townsend)   1941-

PERSONAL: Born November 20, 1941, in New York, N.Y.; son of Byron (a newsman) and Eleanor (an editor; maiden name, Choate) Darnton; married Nina Lieberman, August 21, 1966; children: Kyra, Liza, James. *Education:* Attended University of Paris IV (Sorbonne) and Alliance Francaise, Paris, 1960-61; University of Wisconsin, B.A., 1966. *Politics:* Democrat.

ADDRESSES: Office—New York Times, City Desk, 229 West 43rd St., New York, N.Y. 10036.

CAREER/WRITINGS: New York Times, New York, N.Y., copy boy, news clerk, and news assistant, 1966-68, city reporter, 1968-69, Connecticut correspondent, 1969-70, chief suburban correspondent, 1970-71, night rewriter, 1971-72, reporter for New York City fiscal crisis, 1972-75, correspondent in Lagos, Nigeria, 1976-77, and Nairobi, Kenya, 1977-79, bureau chief in Warsaw, Poland, 1979-82, and Madrid, Spain, 1982-84, deputy foreign editor, 1984-86, metropolitan editor, 1987—. Correspondent and narrator for film, "Spain: Ten Years After." Member of board of directors, New York State Associated Press. Author of introduction to *A Day in the Life of Spain;* contributor to *Assignment America: A Collection of Outstanding Writing From the New York Times* and *About Men: Reflections on the Male Experience.* Contributor to periodicals, including *Readers Digest.*

MEMBER: French American Institute.

AWARDS, HONORS: George Polk Award from Long Island University, 1979 and 1982, for foreign reporting; Pulitzer Prize in international reporting from Columbia University Graduate School of Journalism, 1982, for dispatches from Poland.

WORK IN PROGRESS: A film script about the Polish underground, "The Fat Lady Sings."

SIDELIGHTS: An accomplished journalist who won a Pulitzer Prize and a George Polk Award in 1982 for his coverage of political turmoil in Poland and a Polk Award three years earlier for his reports from Africa, John Darnton has been with the *New York Times* for more than two decades. Joining the newspaper in 1966, he spent ten years assigned to positions in New York and Connecticut before becoming a foreign correspondent in Africa. He was subsequently sent to head the Warsaw, Poland, bureau in 1979, where he witnessed and wrote about the rise of the industrial trade union Solidarity, the wave of optimism that swept the country following a strike by the organized laborers, and the communist government's crushing response to the union activity.

Aside from the Pulitzer Prize-winning series of articles that appeared in the *New York Times* on the struggle for labor organization in Poland, Darnton has written hundreds of news reports as well as lengthy works for the journal's Sunday magazine. One piece, "Nigeria's Dissident Superstar," focuses on the extraordinarily popular and controversial Nigerian musician, Fela Anikulapo-Kuti, whom Darnton in the July, 1977, article describes as "a sort of African Bob Dylan." Because of the ruling military regime's annoyance with many of Fela's songs, which are critical of the inept governance of the country, the musician was severely beaten by soldiers and jailed in February of that year. Darnton's exposing this story embarrassed the government, and the journalist was expelled from the country without an explanation. He presumes that he was asked to leave for shining an unfavorable light on Nigeria's rulers in this and other articles, including one on the regime's attempt to alleviate traffic jams by stationing police officers on street corners with whips to use on motorists who violate traffic laws.

The first longer piece that Darnton wrote for the *New York Times*'s Sunday magazine after transferring to Poland, published in April, 1980, was "Eastern Europe After Tito," a look at Yugoslavia's leadership since the death of its dictator-president, Marshall Tito, earlier that year. He then commenced chronicling the struggle between Solidarity and the Polish Government over the next two years. "Sixty Days That Shook Poland," published in November, 1980, detailed the workers revolt that was prompted by a rise in meat prices on July 1. Laborers nationwide walked off their jobs in support of the strike incited by Solidarity union organizer Lech Walesa. Finally on August 30 the communist government signed a contract with Walesa, agreeing to meet the workers' demands, which included pay increases, the release of political pris-

oners, and freedom from oppression for the Roman Catholic Church.

Darnton's coverage of the events continued, and his June 14, 1981 *New York Times* magazine article "Polish Awakening" describes the intellectual, cultural, and spiritual renaissance that was the legacy of the Solidarity strike of the previous summer. The next longer piece that appeared in the magazine, "Poland: Still Defiant," was written more than one year later and is understandably less optimistic than his earlier reports from Poland, for it discusses the communist government's attempt to suppress the trade union movement by declaring martial law in December, 1981. The journalist left Eastern Europe the following year to become bureau chief in Madrid, Spain. Presently he is back in the United States and is the *New York Times*'s metropolitan editor.

CA INTERVIEW

CA interviewed John Darnton by telephone at his office in New York, N.Y., June 18, 1987.

CA: How did you come to study at the Sorbonne?

DARNTON: I didn't have any formal studies at the Sorbonne. I went to France in 1960 for a year, between high school and college. I took courses at Lycee Henri Quatre, a French high school, for a very short period, then went to the Alliance Francaise to learn French. I then audited courses at the Sorbonne. I went on to the University of Wisconsin after that.

CA: You majored in experimental psychology there. Has that been of any use in your subsequent career?

DARNTON: Life's sort of like running rats through mazes: a little cheese at one end, a shock at the other. It's the same thing.

CA: You're now Metropolitan Editor of the New York Times. *The* Times *used to be criticized for covering the world much better than it covered the metropolitan New York City area. Do you think the* Times *still has that problem?*

DARNTON: I don't. I think we cover New York very well now. We have a large staff. We deploy it now for the first time all over the city in all the boroughs full-time except in Staten Island, where we don't have a presence. And I think by and large we've increased the space devoted to metropolitan news. We've also improved the display of metropolitan stories. So I think we're doing much better by metropolitan news than we did whenever that statement was made.

CA: You've recently added a Metro Section to the Times's *format.*

DARNTON: Right. What happened essentially was that there was a shift of the index off the second front [the first page of the paper's second section] onto page two of the paper's second section. That freed up an entire front page as a display page for the metropolitan section.

CA: Some have suggested that that move might have been in response to Newsday's *New York edition, which features metropolitan as opposed to national and international news much of the time. Do you know if that is true?*

DARNTON: The change took place before I took over, but I never heard that.

CA: How would you improve the Times's *New York City area coverage now, if you think it needs improving?*

DARNTON: We're trying to do a number of things. We're covering areas we may not have covered in quite so much depth previously, such as the poor and middle classes, and we've embarked on a number of investigative projects. We also want to follow very closely the city corruption scandal and we've opened offices in all of the boroughs to give us a little more input from the field. We're also continuing coverage of police and courts out in the field rather than through centralized coverage out of the 43rd Street [Manhattan] office.

CA: Do you get a lot of reader complaints and/or suggestions for coverage?

DARNTON: Not as many as I would like, actually. A lot of people write letters to the editor, which is very healthy, and I'm sure that I see at least copies of all letters to the editor that involve metropolitan stories. I find that very helpful. I read them all, and I almost always reply to them.

CA: You were Connecticut correspondent and chief suburban correspondent for the Times *from 1969 through 1971. What did you think of the paper's suburban coverage at that time, as opposed to its city and international coverage?*

DARNTON: In those days it ranked very low indeed, at least judging by the manpower devoted to it. I was the only correspondent based in Connecticut, covering the entire state, which meant, essentially, a concentration on Fairfield County, since that's where the bulk of our readership was. I also covered the State Legislature at Hartford.

Obviously one person can't cover an entire state that's within the readership area. That has changed now. Among other things, we have a special weekly edition just for Connecticut, from Fairfield County. So on Sundays, Connecticut readers can get a heavy dose of news that is more localized. In addition, we now have people up in Hartford who specialize in coverage of the governor and the legislature. We also have offices in Stamford. It's a larger operation in general, and I think that's true of all the suburbs. The amount of staff in the suburbs has increased noticeably over the past ten to twenty years.

CA: After you were chief suburban correspondent, you were assigned to night rewrite in New York. What was the career development strategy involved in that move?

DARNTON: I think it was probably punishment. Well, not punishment, but the job of chief suburban correspondent, which was a new one, really hadn't worked out. So after six or eight months of that, I was brought back to night rewrite to sharpen my skills, to what I regarded as the onerous but essential duty of developing rewrite skills.

CA: What didn't work out about being chief suburban correspondent?

DARNTON: It was supposed to involve a lot of trend stories, a lot of wrap-up stories, and it meant intruding on other peoples' areas—someone in New Jersey, someone in Long Island—and it was not wholly worked out as a system so that there was sufficient cooperation all around or understanding of what we were trying to do. I think I probably was regarded as an interloper by the other suburban reporters.

CA: Is there a chief suburban correspondent now?

DARNTON: No. I'm not sure there has been one since, although I was away and can't be sure.

CA: Speaking of being away, did you ever have a say in which foreign bureau you'd be sent to?

DARNTON: No, not really. You of course have the option of refusing, and you can put in requests, but it all depends on whether or not that particular bureau falls vacant.

CA: Were you pleased with the bureaus you were sent to?

DARNTON: Some more than others, and in retrospect I was pleased, I think, by all of them. The one that I requested and got was Madrid.

CA: You were in Lagos, Nigeria, during its oil wealth days. That must have been interesting to cover.

DARNTON: It was. It was incredible, too, because the whole infrastructure was collapsing.

CA: You went from Lagos to Nairobi. Was that your last bureau in Africa?

DARNTON: Yes.

CA: Was there official censorship in Africa?

DARNTON: You mean prior censorship? Did I have to submit dispatches for clearance? Certainly not in Lagos and not in Nairobi.

CA: Did they try to interfere with your work in other ways?

DARNTON: Well, we covered fifty countries out of Africa. Working conditions were difficult in some of them. In what was then Rhodesia, because the war was on, and in Ethiopia, where there were two or three other wars on, working conditions were difficult, but I would not say that I fell into a system in which I had to formally submit everything I wrote to a censor.

CA: I didn't realize how many countries you were covering there.

DARNTON: We had essentially three people in Africa. One in South Africa, in Johannesburg, who just covered South Africa, and sometimes Rhodesia, one in West Africa, and one in East Africa. The two in black Africa were more or less interchangeable and were expected together to cover the entire rest of the continent. After I was expelled from Nigeria, and ended up in Kenya, I and my colleague there coordinated our coverage out of Nairobi for the rest of Africa.

CA: Why were you expelled from Nigeria?

DARNTON: No one ever actually formally told me. I did hear after the fact from the American Embassy that four stories I had written had angered the military government. This was out of dozens and dozens of stories. One of the stories that angered them was about infant mortality statistics; another was about piracy in Lagos Harbor. Men in dugout canoes would come up to ships and throw up grappling hooks and actually mount freighters in the harbor and in one case killed the captain. The piracy had become a major issue in shipping circles and the government was embarrassed by it. The third story was about Lagos traffic jams and the attempt to unsnarl them by using military police on the street corners with whips, who delivered summary punishment to motorists who committed minor infractions. So I wrote about the whipping campaign—which I almost favored, as a motorist myself—but I think they found the story, and the others, embarrassing. Lastly there was a story about a musician named Fela who was at that time a bit of a political dissident as well as a very charismatic musician in black Africa. And I think the sum total of these four stories made them feel that while there was no question about the veracity of any of it, it was not putting Nigeria in a good light.

All the other correspondents who had been in Nigeria had either already been expelled or were forced to close down their bureaus for financial reasons, except for Agence France Presse [AFP] and the AFP man's telex hadn't worked for months and months and months. I don't know how he got his stories out, actually. There were public telex systems, so maybe he used those. Sometimes his machine would come to life for a day or two and then give up the ghost. The Reuters man, who was expelled just two or three days after I arrived, was actually put in a little canoe and pushed across a river upcountry into Benin. He arrived in Benin with his wife and two- or three-year old daughter and without money or a passport and was thrown in jail in Benin as a spy. He eventually got out, though. I was arrested, stripped, thrown in a dungeon and interrogated, and finally given six hours to pack up my household and leave the country on the first plane out. My wife and two young daughters, aged three and six, were held in a separate detention area. We were all finally put on a plane to Nairobi.

CA: In Poland, all communications between the Times *and its Warsaw Bureau, in which you were serving, were cut off. What happened at that point?*

DARNTON: All communications between Poland and the outside world were severed. Everything was cut off within Poland also: telephones, telexes, nothing was functioning at all. After an initial period of total blackout, which lasted a week or two weeks, the government opened up three telexes, but instituted formal censorship. That is to say, each dispatch had to be submitted in English to a censor, but I didn't use that system. I pigeoned the copy out with people who were leaving.

CA: Were they searched when they left?

DARNTON: Some were, some weren't, but all the copy got through.

CA: If the copy had been discovered on those people, would you have been in trouble?

DARNTON: I don't know. I can only speculate: probably not. The government was so worried about so many other things at that point, such as keeping the public order, I'm not sure they would have taken the time to try and track down each of the correspondents who wrote a story that was not to their liking. On the other hand they might have used it as a pretext to expel someone from the country. After I left, a UPI [United

Press International] correspondent was expelled. And while I was there, after martial law was declared, my credentials were suspended for three or four days because they objected to a story I had written about meetings in an internment camp. But they returned the credentials to me. And my wife and I had trouble with our car—a lot of flat tires appeared just before curfew. They were caused by screws that had been filed to a sharp point and often happened while I was out interviewing someone, or my wife and I were dining with Polish friends at night. So I think my movements were watched fairly closely. But I was not expelled from the country.

CA: Was the idea behind flattening your tires to get you to violate curfew?

DARNTON: I'm not sure.

CA: Has Solidarity been completely destroyed?

DARNTON: For the moment, yes, but I don't think the idea has been destroyed. And I think ultimately there will be some other kind of situation in which there'll be some kind of massive reaction or rebellion against the government and it will take a new form. The postwar history of Poland shows these kind of cycles that seem to occur with the sort of regularity of the capitalist crises that Marx predicted for us. The contradictions of the country are such that they seem to be almost inevitable and inexorable. However, I doubt if they could take the same form again—a labor union—because both sides have learned too much.

CA: You said Madrid was your favorite posting.

DARNTON: It was the one I requested. Warsaw was also my favorite, but before I went there I knew very little about Eastern Europe and did not particularly think of it as a place that attracted me. But Warsaw did turn out to be my favorite posting, because of the Solidarity story.

CA: I notice you've had at least one article published in The New York Times Magazine. *Is writing an article for the* Times Magazine *considered a burden or an honor or neither?*

DARNTON: Neither. Most foreign correspondents are expected to write magazine articles, especially if they're on an important story, and most like to do it because it allows them to deal at length with a subject that sometimes they'd like to take a more personal view of.

CA: You did an article for Reader's Digest *on climbing Mount Kilimanjaro. Was there any particular reason for writing an article for that publication rather than for the* Times?

DARNTON: No. I think I was just asked to do it, so I did it. I don't recall offering it to the *Times*, but it wasn't really a competitive situation.

CA: Was your Polk Award for a specific story?

DARNTON: No, just the coverage. There were two awards. One was shared with my two colleagues in Africa. The other was for Poland. But I think they were for the year's work, not for specific stories.

CA: You became deputy foreign editor after Madrid. What does a deputy foreign editor do? Did you have administrative tasks as well as reportorial ones?

DARNTON: It was really basically helping the foreign editor run the desk and the correspondents and assemble the daily report and pretty much filling in for the foreign editor and becoming interchangeable. So it's functioning as an editor: talking to correspondents in the field; looking at and working with copy; ordering up stories; and sending correspondents to locations. Also dealing with other editors on the paper and recommending stories for Page One.

CA: Do you enjoy administrative tasks as much as or more than reporting?

DARNTON: That's very hard for me to answer. It really depends. I enjoy ordering up stories, having ideas for stories, and shaping the coverage, but I also miss writing.

CA: Is it your ambition to become executive editor eventually?

DARNTON: Well, I just don't know. It's very hard to say. On some days, perhaps, but on other days I could also imagine going back to writing, perhaps as a columnist.

BIOGRAPHICAL/CRITICAL SOURCES:

PERIODICALS

Detroit News, April 13, 1982.
New York Times, July 24, 1977, April 13, 1982.

—*Interview by Peter Benjaminson*

*   *   *

DAVEY, Thomas A.   1954-

PERSONAL: Born January 2, 1954, in Philadelphia, Pa.; son of Andrew D. (a business executive) and Adellaide (a nurse; maiden name, Schmitt) Davey. *Education:* Duke University, B.A., 1976; Harvard University, Ed.D., 1984.

ADDRESSES: Home—23 Bigelow St., No. 2, Boston, Mass. 02135.

CAREER: Worked as a child psychologist, 1977-88; was a teaching fellow at Harvard University, Cambridge, Mass.; conducts private practice in adult and child psychology, Cambridge. Works part time with MSPCC, Framingham, Mass.

MEMBER: American Psychological Association.

AWARDS, HONORS: Grants from German Academic Exchange Service, 1981-82 and 1988; Lyndhurst Foundation Prize, 1985, for pursuit of writing and research interests.

WRITINGS:

A Generation Divided: German Children and the Berlin Wall, Duke University Press, 1987.

Contributor of articles and reviews to magazines and newspapers, including *New Republic, Boston Review*, and *New Age Journal*.

WORK IN PROGRESS: "Follow-up work with the children (now adolescents) with whom I worked in East and West Berlin from 1981 to 1982."

SIDELIGHTS: Thomas A. Davey told *CA:* "I have traveled at great length—to South Africa, Northern Ireland, Poland, Israel, and East and West Berlin, for instance—in order to understand the moral and political life of children who grow up in politically volatile national circumstances. In all of these nations children made it quite clear that what happens to their nation is of great significance to them. Who they feel themselves to be and what matters to them—morally and politically—is ultimately bound up with their nation's life. I spent a year talking with children in East and West Berlin, and there I saw just how attentive even young children are to the vicissitudes of their national circumstances. They are inevitably torn between the demands of ideology and rhetoric, which insists that there is a critical difference between *East* and *West* Germans, and the fact that most of them have family on the 'other side'—a persuasive fact that challenges the polarity established by history and politics."

BIOGRAPHICAL/CRITICAL SOURCES:

PERIODICALS

Los Angeles Times Book Review, January 17, 1987.

*   *   *

DAVIE, Elspeth   1919-

PERSONAL: Born in 1919 in Kilmarnock, Scotland; married George Elder Davie (a philosopher). *Education:* Received D.A. from Edinburgh College of Art.

ADDRESSES: Agent—Anthony Sheil Associates Ltd., 2-3 Morwell St., London WC1B 3AR, England.

CAREER: Teacher, author.

AWARDS, HONORS: Scottish Arts Council grants, 1971, 1977, and 1979; Katherine Mansfield Prize from English Centre of International P.E.N., 1978, for short story "The High Tide Talker."

WRITINGS:

NOVELS

Providings, J. Calder, 1965.
Creating a Scene, Calder & Boyars, 1971, Riverrun Press, 1984.
Climbers on a Stair, Hamish Hamilton, 1978.

SHORT STORIES

The Spark, and Other Stories, Calder & Boyars, 1968, Riverrun Press, 1984.
The High Tide Talker, and Other Stories, Hamish Hamilton, 1976.
The Night of the Funny Hats, Hamish Hamilton, 1980.
A Traveller's Room, David & Charles, 1985.

SIDELIGHTS: "Elspeth Davie is expert at picking the sinister out of the ordinary," lauded a *Times Literary Supplement* reviewer, "and at heightening normal situations into something obsessive or macabre." Davie's short stories and novels often depict the profound influence that seemingly insignificant events have on a person's development. Admiring her ability to render trivial incidents extraordinary, critics such as Nicholas Shrimpton in *New Statesman* praised Davie's astute attention to detail and "her painterly sense of landscape."

Paul Bailey in *London Magazine* likewise noted that Davie "can 'place' a landscape, an eerie house, a seaside hotel with enviable accuracy." Although Bailey criticized the author's wordiness and the abundance of "Meaningful Conversations" among the characters in her first short story collection, he nonetheless lauded *The Spark, and Other Stories* as "very much a bloom from the literary hot-house.'' One notable story portrays a widow who decides to continue buying as many groceries as she had before her husband's death. Gradually she becomes obsessed with shopping and fills her apartment with food and household supplies.

Davie's focus on the trivial continues in her second collection. Each story in *The High Tide Talker* is a variation on the author's ''personal theory of relativity: one man's insignificant detail is another's obsession,'' wrote John Mellors in the *Listener*. For the title story, which concerns a preacher who avoids confronting God, Davie won the 1978 Katherine Mansfield Prize.

In the stories in *The Night of the Funny Hats*, wrote Jennifer Uglow in the *Times Literary Supplement*, Davie ''concentrates on moments when . . . people perceive order in random elements.'' The final tale ''reminds us of the dangers of too weighty interpretation, and [it] offers a delightful comic warning.'' In this story three sisters imagine that the letter ''B'' written in their late uncle's diary refers to a passionate affair, when in fact it refers to breadmaking. Upon learning the truth, explained Uglow, ''they attempt to appease the insulted spirit by a fury of baking.''

''The writing [in *The Night of the Funny Hats*] displays an acute observation of behaviour,'' noted the reviewer, ''especially of the way people reveal themselves in speech.'' Uglow added: ''Elspeth Davie sees language as pre-eminent, the cement which binds unrelated chunks of reality or personal history into structures with shape and meaning.'' But the author also recognizes the occasional inadequacy of language, she noted. In the title story, for example, travelers in Australia fail to articulate the beauty and expanse of the plains they are crossing. The characters' silence becomes Davie's means of describing the magnificence of the location. ''Many of the stories derive an unnerving strength and resonance from the intellectual toughness which underlies their elegant and suggestive surface,'' Uglow concluded. ''This is a most impressive collection.''

A Traveller's Room, like *The Night of the Funny Hats*, examines ''the idea of order—this unknown, perfect state of things that makes us feel askew,'' as Ann Hulbert quoted from one of Davie's tales. ''In studiously measured prose,'' Hulbert judged in the *New York Times Book Review*, ''the Scottish writer Elspeth Davie conveys a sense of the repressive power of that idea of order.'' In two stories, female characters abandon their inhibiting, structured lives, one to pursue a lover and the other to live alone at the sea. In other tales, characters find the security of apparent understanding proven false, as when a landlady and a tenant misinterpret each other's use of the word ''bulb,'' and when a young woman imagines that her boardinghouse room belongs to a dashing and mysterious explorer but later learns that it belongs to a nondescript traveling salesman. In one particularly absurd story, grass and flowers begin sprouting on a young man's head. ''Here the idea of order . . . is robust rather than repressive,'' Hulbert suggested, for as the young man attempts to make sense of the strange phenomenon, he begins to appreciate his unusual personal garden.

''The life of the herbaceously hirsute young man is full of incident,'' observed Toby Fitton in the *Times Literary Supplement*, ''making his story unusual in a series in which the point so often is that very little happens.'' Fitton remarked that Davie's emphasis on the trivial and her analysis of struc-

ture are at first intriguing, but eventually excessive and tedious. ''Most of the stories, taken individually, are excellent,'' the reviewer appraised. Nevertheless, he continued, ''the delicate incisiveness of Davie's refined technique seems somehow less impressive when its results are multiplied and gathered'' in one volume. In a London *Times* review, however, Andrew Sinclair complimented the ''scruple and judgement'' of Davie's writing in *A Traveller's Room* and admired the collection as a whole. ''A touch of the fey and a sense of the anarchy of things,'' he explained, ''provokes the reader into a fresh consciousness of an everyday society.''

Davie's longer works echo the themes and meticulous style of her short stories. Her first novel, *Providings*, is about an unexceptional young man, Peter Beck, who leaves his indulgent family to pursue life on his own. He cannot escape his childhood, however, which is symbolized in jars of jam sent unsolicited from home. ''The spirits of [absurdist playwrights] Ionesco, Beckett *et al* hover over the insane (and unseen) kitchen where the jams are prepared,'' noted a *Times Literary Supplement* critic. The author delineates the novel's ''painful absurdity with a sure sense of the dark comedy of Peter Beck's dilemma.''

Like Davie's other works, her second novel ''is calculatedly narrow,'' in the words of a *Times Literary Supplement* reviewer, ''engrossed in detail and in the slow, imperceptible growth of human beings—via small experience—into degrees of maturity and success.'' *Creating a Scene* depicts the relationship between an art teacher and two of his students, who are commissioned to paint a mural in a public building. ''The development of the painting, its sometimes subtle, sometimes radical (and once, significantly, forced) alternations,'' according to the reviewer, ''is an obvious parallel for the amorphous, though never strong, connexions between teacher and pupils.''

Davie's third novel, *Climbers on a Stair*, concerns neighbors whose tenement houses are connected by a common staircase. ''Holding her characters at an equal distance,'' explained Susannah Clapp in the *Times Literary Supplement*, ''[Davie] supplies brief glimpses not of daily habits but of different dominant passions''—a piano teacher's dislike for synthesized background music, for example, and a middle-aged widow's dreams of travel. Instead of a plot, Davie uses a series of conversations to develop the novel. ''The most intricate and widespread discussion,'' observed Clapp, ''is about ways of looking at the city . . . about the looming shadows of office blocks, the gleams of terraces at night, and about the bewildering quality of the tenement block itself.'' Davie masterfully reveals the different viewpoints, commended the reviewer, as she does the settings in her other writings: ''by a dazzle of physical description.''

BIOGRAPHICAL/CRITICAL SOURCES:

PERIODICALS

Listener, December 16, 1976.
London Magazine, May, 1969.
New Statesman, March 28, 1980.
New York Times Book Review, September 8, 1985.
Spectator, March 29, 1980.
Times (London), April 11, 1985.
Times Literary Supplement, December 2, 1965, February 13, 1969, September 17, 1971, August 4, 1978, April 18, 1980, April 19, 1985.*

—Sketch by Christa Brelin

DAVIES, Sumiko 1942-
(Sumiko)

PERSONAL: Born September 21, 1942, in Tokyo, Japan; daughter of Kunio (a doctor) and Kimiyo (Sato) Suzuki; married Derek Davies (a writer and editor), January 7, 1967; children: Ken, Hana. *Education:* Kuwazawa Design Institute, Diploma in Design and Illustration, 1966.

ADDRESSES: Home—17D Vienna Ct., Realty Gardens, 41 Conduit Rd., Hong Kong.

CAREER: Free-lance illustrator. Art director of Marklin Advertising Agency, in Thailand, 1966-67. Work exhibited at Pinky Gallery, Tokyo, Japan, 1979, and Museum of Modern Art, Oxford, England, 1984.

MEMBER: Foreign Correspondents Club of Hong Kong.

WRITINGS:

SELF-ILLUSTRATED BOOKS; UNDER NAME SUMIKO

The Cat Who Thought He Was a Mouse, Gakken, 1976.
Little Red Riding Hood, Shogakkan, 1977.
Kittymouse, Heinemann, 1978.
Hans Andersen's Fairy Tales, Ward Lock, 1979, Schocken, 1980.
My Baby Brother Ned, Heinemann, 1981.
My School, Heinemann, 1983.
A Kiss on the Nose, Heinemann, 1984.
My Holiday, Heinemann, 1987.
Peter and Cat, Heinemann, 1989.

SIDELIGHTS: Sumiko Davies told *CA:* "As a child I loved illustrated children's books, particularly the classics, such as stories by Hans Andersen and the brothers Grimm. I also loved to draw. So I suppose it was natural that I should one day become a children's illustrator. I would describe my style as somewhat orthodox and detailed and I particularly like to draw people. Some of my books, such as *Peter and Cat,* are probably reflections of myself and my character. Others, like *My School* and *My Holiday,* reflect my interest in the detail of everyday life and the experiences of childhood.

"Outside my work, my family is my chief activity. We travel a lot from our house in Hong Kong to other countries in Asia. We go to Japan twice a year, to England most years, and we once took a family holiday to the United States. I love mountains, and each summer we spend a month in the foothills of the Japan Alps."

BIOGRAPHICAL/CRITICAL SOURCES:

PERIODICALS

South China Morning Post, December 14, 1984.

*　　*　　*

DAVIS, Brian 1925-1988
(ffolkes, Michael Ffolkes)

OBITUARY NOTICE: Professionally known as Michael Ffolkes; born June 6, 1925, in London, England; died of complications from acute pancreatitis and cirrhosis of the liver, October 18, 1988, in London, England. Cartoonist, illustrator, and author. Davis, who signed his works "ffolkes" or "ff," was famous for his craggily drawn, wryly humorous cartoons. His satiric drawings—which appeared in *Punch* for more than four decades—often depicted figures from nineteenth-century litera-

ture, music, and history. Davis illustrated more than fifty books and his cartoons were featured in numerous American periodicals, such as the *New Yorker, Playboy,* and *Reader's Digest.* His writings include *ffanfare, ffolkes' fauna, ffolkes' Companion to Mythology,* and *ffundamental ffolkes.*

OBITUARIES AND OTHER SOURCES:

BOOKS

Who's Who, 140th edition, St. Martin's, 1988.
Who's Who in Art, 22nd edition, Art Trade Press, 1986.

PERIODICALS

New York Times, October 25, 1988, October 26, 1988.

*　　*　　*

DAVIS, Harold Eugene 1902-1988

OBITUARY NOTICE—See index for *CA* sketch: Born in 1902 in Girard, Ohio; died of cancer (one source says pneumonia), September 13, 1988, in Chevy Chase, Md. Educator and author. Davis, a member of the American University faculty from 1947 until his retirement as professor emeritus in 1973, served the university in a variety of posts, including professor in the schools of international studies and government and public administration, dean of the College of Arts and Sciences, and director of the university's language center. Prior to joining the American University staff, Davis taught at Hiram College, where he also served as chairman of the division of social studies and dean of administration. Among Davis's many publications are *The Americas in History; Latin American Social Thought; Revolutionaries, Traditionalists, and Dictators in Latin America;* and more than one hundred articles contributed to reference books and professional journals.

OBITUARIES AND OTHER SOURCES:

BOOKS

The Writers Directory: 1988-1990, St. James Press, 1988.

PERIODICALS

New York Times, September 18, 1988.
Washington Post, September 17, 1988.

*　　*　　*

de BROCA, Philippe (Claude Alex) 1933-

PERSONAL: Born March 15, 1933, in Paris, France; son of Yvor and Suzanne (Barrault) de Broca; married Michele Heurtaux, December 21, 1961 (marriage ended); married Valerie Rojan, July 7, 1987; children: Alexander. *Education:* Attended Ecole Nationale de Photographie et de Cinematographie.

ADDRESSES: Home—Vert, France. *Agent*—Artmedia, 10 avenue Georges V, 75008 Paris, France.

CAREER: Film producer and screenwriter, 1959—.

WRITINGS:

SCREENPLAYS

(With Michel Audiard) "Jupiter's Thigh," released by Quartet/Films, 1984.

Also author of "Dear Detective," 1978, "Psy," "The African," "Louisiana," "La Gitana," and "Chouans!"

OTHER

Producer of films, including "Cartouche," "The Man From Rio," "The Five Day Lover," "The Love Game," "Male Companion," and "La Poudre d'escampette."

* * *

de CALLES, Jane F. Butel   1938-
(Jane Butel)

PERSONAL: Born June 23, 1938, in Wamego, Kan.; daughter of Sidney L. (an agricultural economist) and Dorothy (an educator; maiden name, Krig) Franz; married Donald A. Butel (in food business), June 1, 1958 (divorced, April, 1973); married Brennan Reid de Calles (an executive designer), July 4, 1985; children: (first marriage) Amy E. *Education:* Kansas State University, B.S., 1959; attended University of New Mexico, Harvard University, and Columbia University. *Politics:* Republican. *Religion:* Methodist.

ADDRESSES: Home and office—Jane Butel Associates, 500 East 77th St., No. 2324, New York, N.Y. 10162. *Agent*—Sidney B. Kramer, Mews Books Ltd., 20 Bluewater Hill, Westport, Conn. 06880.

CAREER: Public Service Company of New Mexico, Albuquerque, director of Home Service, 1959-69; Con Edison, New York, N.Y., director of consumer affairs, 1969-73; General Electric Co., Louisville, Ky., manager of Consumer Institute, 1973-76; American Express, New York City, vice-president of consumer affairs, 1976-78; Jane Butel Associates (consulting firm), New York City, president, 1978—. Founder and president of Pecos Valley Spice Co., 1978—. Consultant on consumer marketing to major corporations, restaurants, and food manufacturers. Member of Chamber of Commerce; member of board of directors of Auburn University, American National Standards Institute, and Santa Fe Opera.

MEMBER: American Home Economics Association, Les Dames Escoffier, New York Home Economics Association (president).

AWARDS, HONORS: Awards from American Home Appliance Manufacturers, 1962, 1965, 1966, 1967, 1971, and 1972, all for outstanding education programs on equipment; Rose Award from *Seventeen*, 1966.

WRITINGS:

UNDER NAME JANE BUTEL

Favorite Mexican Foods, privately printed, 1968.
Jane Butel's Freezer Book, Coward, 1976.
Jane Butel's Tex-Mex Cookbook, Crown, 1980.
Chili Madness, Workman Publishing, 1980.
Finger Lickin', Rib Stickin', Great Tastin' Barbeque, Workman Publishing, 1982.
Tacos, Tortillas, and Tostados, Irena Chalmers, 1982.
The Woman's Day Book of New Mexico Cooking, Simon & Schuster, 1984.
Fiesta, Harper, 1987.
Hotter Than Hell, HP Books, 1987.

Contributor to magazines, including *Food and Wine, Woman's Day, Family Circle*, and *Southern Living*.

WORK IN PROGRESS: Research on the cuisine of the southwestern spa.

SIDELIGHTS: Jane F. Butel de Calles told *CA* that she truly loves the Southwest, especially the city of Santa Fe, New Mexico. "I decided to quit corporate work," she wrote, "to pursue my first love: the culture, especially the foods, of the Southwest. I loved the Southwest since childhood—the beauty of the mountains against the purple-blue skies and the fresh, dry, sunny air.

"New Mexican food is authentically native American with less Anglo influence yielding purer, higher taste levels. My cookbooks relate this tradition with a fun, easy-to-do approach. I've also tried to develop dry, flavorful foods that are creative and approachable—that is, easy for most any cook to prepare."

AVOCATIONAL INTERESTS: Travel, gardening, outdoor sports.

* * *

DEESE, Helen   1925-

PERSONAL: Born September 15, 1925, in San Diego, Calif.; daughter of Clyde T. (a military officer) and Ethel (a secretary and homemaker; maiden name, Findlay) Smith; married Rupert Julian Deese (a potter), March 4, 1951; children: Rupert T., Mary Ann Deese-Brow, Frank, R. Sam. *Education:* Attended University of California, Los Angeles, 1943-47; University of California, Riverside, B.A., 1968, M.A., 1970, Ph.D., 1977. *Politics:* Democrat. *Religion:* Unitarian-Universalist.

ADDRESSES: Home—601 East Baseline Rd., Claremont, Calif. 91711. *Office*—Department of English, Mount St. Mary's College, 12001 Chalon Rd., Los Angeles, Calif. 90049.

CAREER: Social worker for San Diego County Welfare Department in California, 1948-51; teacher and treasurer with Pomona Valley Cooperative Pre-School in California, 1953-65; University of California, Riverside, visiting lecturer, 1977-79; California State Polytechnic University, Pomona, Calif., lecturer, 1979-81; University of La Verne, La Verne, Calif., assistant professor, 1980-81; University of California, Riverside, visiting lecturer, 1981-83; Mount St. Mary's College, Los Angeles, Calif., associate professor of English, 1983—.

MEMBER: International Shakespeare Association, Modern Language Association of America, Shakespeare Association of America, Wallace Stevens Society.

WRITINGS:

(With Steven Gould Axelrod) *Robert Lowell: A Reference Guide*, G. K. Hall, 1982.
(Editor with Steven Gould Axelrod; and contributor) *Robert Lowell: Essays on the Poetry*, Cambridge University Press, 1987.
(Editor with Steven Gould Axelrod) *Critical Essays on Wallace Stevens*, G. K. Hall, 1988.
(Editor with Steven Gould Axelrod) *Critical Essays on William Carlos Williams*, G.K. Hall, in press.

WORK IN PROGRESS: A study of director Max Reinhardt's productions in California—Hollywood, San Francisco, Berkeley—in 1934 and his film of William Shakespeare's "A Midsummer Night's Dream," tentatively titled *Max Reinhardt's California "Dream."*

SIDELIGHTS: Helen Deese told *CA:* "In 1967, when I re-entered the University of California after a twenty-year absence in which I had done my best to promote the baby boom, I was one of the first 're-entries' or 'nontraditional students,' both rather inelegant labels. To my own mind I was then what

I think myself to be today—a student, still trying to understand what it's all about. And it—whatever 'it' refers to—seems to be about human achievement in art, about the creating human imagination, whether its material is the matter of science or of poetry.

"My own particular study of poetry and drama focuses on the visual images of these two arts—verbal or actual, concrete or metaphorical. That is why my study, editing, and writing have been on three twentieth-century American poets—William Carlos Williams, Wallace Stevens, and Robert Lowell—as well as on Shakespeare in production. The poetry of the three American writers is not only strongly visual, but is also a poetry that interacts consciously with the visual arts. In addition, each of these American poets has made serious contributions to the theatre, translating verbal visual images into the actually visual, each condition being signifying. The physical, intellectual, emotional impact, intended or unintended, of the visual image on the reader or viewer is the subject of my study."

*   *   *

de GUISE, Elizabeth (Mary Teresa)   1934-
(Elizabeth Hunter; Isobel Chace, a pseudonym)

PERSONAL: Surname is pronounced "de-*Geeze*"; born in 1934, in Nairobi, Kenya; daughter of Geoffrey Scott (a company director) and Edwyna (de Guise-Roussel-Cossy) Hunter. *Education:* Attended Open University. *Politics:* "Liberal/Labour." *Religion:* Roman Catholic.

ADDRESSES: Home and office—113 Nun St., St. David's Haverfordwest, Dyfed SA62 6BP, Wales. *Agent*—June Hall, 19 University Cross, London N.1, England.

CAREER: Landholder in Kent, England, 1952-58; English teacher to Arabic students in Folkestone, England, 1958-62; writer, 1960—.

MEMBER: Campaign for Nuclear Disarmament, Pax Christi.

WRITINGS:

ROMANCE NOVELS; UNDER NAME ELIZABETH HUNTER

Cherry-Blossom Clinic, Mills & Boon, 1961.
Spiced With Cloves, Mills & Boon, 1962.
Watch the Wall My Darling, Mills & Boon, 1963.
No Sooner Met, Mills & Boon, 1965.
There Were Nine Castles, Mills & Boon, 1967.
The Crescent Moon, Mills & Boon, 1973.
The Tree of Idleness, Mills & Boon, 1973.
The Tower of the Winds, Mills & Boon, 1973.
The Beads of Nemesis, Mills & Boon, 1974, J. Curley, 1985.
The Bride Price, Mills & Boon, 1974.
The Bonds of Matrimony, Mills & Boon, 1975, G. K. Hall, 1985.
The Spanish Inheritance, Mills & Boon, 1975, G. K. Hall, 1985.
The Voice in the Thunder, Mills & Boon, 1975.
The Sycamore Song, Mills & Boon, 1975.
The Realms of Gold, Mills & Boon, 1976, J. Curley, 1984.
Pride of Madeira, Harlequin, 1977.
Bride of the Sun, Silhouette, 1980.
The Lion's Shadow, Silhouette, 1980.
A Touch of Magic, Silhouette, 1981.
Written in the Stars, Silhouette, 1981.
One More Time, Silhouette, 1982.

Fountains of Paradise, Silhouette, 1983.
London Pride, Silhouette, 1983.
Shared Destiny, Silhouette, 1983.
A Silver Nutmeg, Silhouette, 1983.
Kiss of the Rising Sun, Silhouette, 1984.
Rain on the Wind, Silhouette, 1984.
Song of Surrender, Silhouette, 1984.
A Tower of Strength, Silhouette, 1984.
A Time to Wed, Silhouette, 1984.
Loving Relations, Silhouette, 1984.
Eye of the Wind, Silhouette, 1985.
Legend of the Sun, Silhouette, 1985.
The Painted Veil, Silhouette, 1986.
The Tides of Love, Silhouette, 1988.

ROMANCE NOVELS; UNDER PSEUDONYM ISOBEL CHACE

The African Mountain, Mills & Boon, 1960.
The Japanese Lantern, Mills & Boon, 1960.
Flamingoes on the Lake, Mills & Boon, 1961.
The Song and the Sea, Mills & Boon, 1962.
The Hospital of Fatima, Mills & Boon, 1963.
The Wild Land, Mills & Boon, 1963, J. Curley, 1985.
A House for Sharing, Mills & Boon, 1964.
The Rhythm of Flamenco, Mills & Boon, 1966.
The Spider's Web, Mills & Boon, 1966 (published in Canada as *The Secret Marriage*, 1966).
The Land of the Lotus-Eaters, Mills & Boon, 1966.
A Garland of Marigolds, Mills & Boon, 1967.
Brittany Blue, Mills & Boon, 1967.
Oranges and Lemons, Mills & Boon, 1967.
The Saffron Sky, Mills & Boon, 1968.
The Damask Rose, Mills & Boon, 1968.
A Handful of Silver, Mills & Boon, 1968.
The Legend of Katmandu, Mills & Boon, 1969.
Flower of Ethiopia, Mills & Boon, 1969.
Sugar in the Morning, Mills & Boon, 1969.
The Day That the Rain Came Down, Mills & Boon, 1970.
The Flowering Cactus, Mills & Boon, 1970.
To Marry a Tiger, Mills & Boon, 1971.
The Wealth of the Islands, Mills & Boon, 1971.
Home Is Goodbye, Mills & Boon, 1971.
The Flamboyant Tree, Mills & Boon, 1972, J. Curley, 1986.
The English Daughter, Mills & Boon, 1972.
Cadence of Portugal, Mills & Boon, 1972.
A Pride of Lions, Mills & Boon, 1972.
The Tartan Touch, Mills & Boon, 1972.
The House of Scissors, Mills & Boon, 1972.
The Dragon's Cave, Mills & Boon, 1972.
The Edge of Beyond, Mills & Boon, 1973.
A Man of Kent, Mills & Boon, 1973.
The Elban Adventure, Mills & Boon, 1974.
The Cornish Hearth, Mills & Boon, 1975.
A Canopy of Rose Leaves, Mills & Boon, 1976.
The Clouded Veil, Mills & Boon, 1976.
The Desert Castle, Harlequin, 1976.
Singing in the Wilderness, Mills & Boon, 1976.
The Whistling Thorn, Harlequin, 1977.
The Mouth of Truth, Harlequin, 1977.
Second Best Wife, Harlequin, 1978.
Undesirable Wife, Mills & Boon, 1978.

HISTORICAL NOVELS; UNDER NAME ELIZABETH DE GUISE

Dance of the Peacocks, Grafton, 1988.

Also author of *Puritan Wife*, Mills & Boon.

WORK IN PROGRESS: A novel, tentatively titled *Flight of the Dragonfly,* and a novel "set in Spain at the time of Isabel II, which will include the founding of a sherry bodega," tentatively titled *The Gate of Pardon,* both to be published by Grafton.

SIDELIGHTS: Elizabeth de Guise told *CA:* "As I come from a Commonwealth family—my mother was a fifth generation New Zealander, and I am myself the third generation to have lived in Kenya—my interests are more outside Europe than in the new European community. Thus, the first two stories I wrote for Grafton are set in India at the time of the early British Raj and in Malacca, Malaysia, also in Victorian times. For my third story, I am going to Spain—where I lived for more than a year back in the sixties—which is a country that I love and where I have many friends.

"I am now beginning to write historical novels, because I am particularly interested in the relationships between women of different races in the British Empire of Victorian times. My heroines are survivors, which is a quality I much admire in women of all ages. They love life and are blessed with a great curiosity about all the people they come in contact with. I suppose the great difference between my historical stories and the romances I wrote earlier is that it is the women, rather than the men, who take the center of the stage. In a romance, the heroine's reactions to the hero are all important; in these historical novels, it is the woman herself who is the main interest to me and, I hope, to the reader also.

"I wrote romance novels for years, first for Mills & Boon and then for Silhouette. My stories were sometimes serialized in women's magazines in England, the first being *The Song of the Sea* in the publication *Woman and Home,* when it was still being edited by the great Miss Johnson. She and Alan Boon between them practically invented the romance genre, and I count myself very fortunate to have known them both. Although things are greatly changed today, I can still admire the particular genius that first conceived the formula for the romance novel, which has given such pleasure to women of all kinds all over the world.

"My works have been translated into twenty-six different languages, and I have received letters ranging from university lecturers to women still in purdah in the Persian Gulf, all saying very much the same things about the stories they have read and enjoyed. There can't be many professions that can give one greater satisfaction than this one, which I fell into largely by chance, looking for something, *anything* that was easier than keeping hordes of hens in a fluctuating market! I have never regretted one moment of the change, and have yet to meet any writer who has.

"I have lived in five other countries and visited more than eighty, including the United States. I love living in Wales, in a city-village where both St. David (the patron of Wales) and St. Patrick (the patron of Ireland) were born and raised. Of course, I am not Welsh, but then nor am I English. The closest I come is some Irish and Scottish blood, mixed up with a lot of French and some from Jersey. Still, even mongrels have to live somewhere. The scenery is beautiful. The view from my windows is enough to make visitors catch their breath when they come into my living room—and I live with it all the time! Beat that for true good fortune!"

AVOCATIONAL INTERESTS: Pacifist activities.

DELANEY, Frank 1942-

PERSONAL: Born October 24, 1942, in Tipperary, Ireland (now Republic of Ireland); children: three sons.

ADDRESSES: Home and office—43 Old Town, London S.W.4, England. *Agent*—Curtis Brown, Curtis Brown Ltd., 162-168 Regent St., London W1R 5TB, England.

CAREER: British Broadcasting Corp., London, England, and Radio Telefis Eireann, Dublin, Ireland, broadcaster, 1966—.

WRITINGS:

James Joyce's Odyssey: A Guide to the Dublin of Ulysses, photographs by Jorge Lewinski, Holt, 1981.
Betjeman Country, photographs by James Ravilious, drawings by Leonora Ison, Hodder & Stoughton/John Murray, 1983.
The Celts (based on his script for the BBC-TV series of the same title), Harcourt, 1987.
Silver Apples, Golden Apples: Best-Loved Irish Verse, Blackstaff Press, 1987.

Also author of *Dust and Wind and Shadow* (travel/history), 1988, and a novella, *My Darn Rosaleen,* in press.

SIDELIGHTS: Frank Delaney illuminates James Joyce's classic novel *Ulysses* by emphasizing its most readily understood aspects in *James Joyce's Odyssey: A Guide to the Dublin of Ulysses.* Using maps and photographs to illustrate the physical territory covered by Joyce's story, the author presents what he described as "a plain man's guide to a novel, perhaps *the* novel, of the plain man." Delaney offers a common-sense discussion of the relationship of Joyce's book to Homer's *Odyssey,* biographical notes, and insight into Joyce's characters in what Christopher Lehmann-Haupt, writing for the *New York Times,* deemed "an enthusiast's commentary." The critic judged Delaney's work "handsome, . . . useful," and even, at times, "compelling."

The Celts is Delaney's examination of the history, literature, and art of the ancient residents of Britain, based on the British Broadcasting Corporation television series of the same title for which he also wrote the script. Delaney's cursory treatment of the origins and prehistory of the Celts disappointed critic M. T. Kelly, who reviewed the book for the Toronto *Globe and Mail,* but Kelly observed that "he does go on to do justice to the rest of Celtic history." The critic praised Delaney's insight and imagination, noting that he makes pertinent points about both the historical Celts and their modern-day descendants. "The discussions of Celtic literature and storytelling . . . are fascinating and moving," added Kelly, "and the discussion of the spirit in Celtic art is also deeply imaginative." Concluded the reviewer, "In the end [Delaney] serves well those magical people who 'believed in the suspension of reality. And . . . feared that the sky might fall.'"

BIOGRAPHICAL/CRITICAL SOURCES:

PERIODICALS

Globe and Mail (Toronto), March 7, 1987.
New York Times, February 2, 1982.

*   *   *

de LINT, Charles (Henri Diederick Hoefsmit) 1951-

PERSONAL: Born December 22, 1951, in Bussum, Netherlands; immigrated to Canada, 1952, naturalized citizen, 1961; son of Frederick Charles (a pilot and survey project manager)

Hoefsmit and Gerardina Margaretha (a high school teacher) Hoefsmit-de Lint; married MaryAnn Harris (an artist), September 15, 1980. *Education:* Attended Aylmer and Philemen Wright high schools.

ADDRESSES: Home—Ottawa, Ontario, Canada. *Office*—P.O. Box 9480, Ottawa, Ontario, Canada K1G 3V2. *Agent*—Richard Curtis, Richard Curtis Associates Inc., 164 East 64th St., Suite 1, New York, N.Y. 10021.

CAREER: Worked in various clerical and construction positions, 1967-71, and as retail clerk and manager of record stores, 1971-83; writer in Ottawa, Ontario, 1983—. Owner and editor of Triskell Press; juror for William L. Crawford Award, Canadian SF/Fantasy Award, World Fantasy Award, Theodore Sturgeon Memorial Short Fiction Award, Horror Writers of America Award, and Nebula Award; member of Wickentree, a traditional Celtic folk music band in Ottawa, 1972-85.

MEMBER: Science Fiction Writers of America, Horror Writers of America, Small Press Writers and Artists Organization.

AWARDS, HONORS: William L. Crawford Award for best new fantasy author from International Association for the Fantastic in the Arts, 1984; Canadian SF/Fantasy Award ("Casper") nominations, 1986, for *Mulengro*, and 1987, for *Yarrow*; Casper Award for best work in English, 1988, for *Jack the Giant-Killer*.

WRITINGS:

"The Fane of the Grey Rose" (novelette), published in *Swords Against Darkness IV*, edited by Andrew J. Offutt, Zebra, 1979.

De Grijze Roos (title means "The Grey Rose"; short stories), Een Exa Uitgave, 1983.

The Riddle of the Wren, Ace Books, 1984.

Moonheart: A Romance, Ace Books, 1984.

The Calendar of the Trees (poem), illustrations by Donna Gordon, Triskell Press, 1984.

"The Valley of the Troll" (short story), published in *Sword and Sorceress*, edited by Marion Zimmer Bradley, DAW, 1984.

The Harp of the Grey Rose, Starblaze, 1985.

Mulengro: A Romany Tale, Ace Books, 1985.

"Cold Blows the Wind" (short story), published in *Sword and Sorceress II*, edited by Bradley, DAW, 1985.

Yarrow: An Autumn Tale, Ace Books, 1986.

"Stick" (novella), published in *Borderland*, edited by Terri Windling and Mark Arnold, Signet, 1986.

"The Rat's Alley Shuffle" (short story), published in *Liavek: The Players of Luck*, edited by Will Shetterly and Emma Bull, Ace Books, 1986.

Ascian in Rose (novella), Axolotl Press, 1987.

Jack the Giant-Killer: A Novel of Urban Faerie, Armadillo-Ace, 1987.

"The Weeping Oak" (short story), published in *Sword and Sorceress IV*, edited by Bradley, DAW, 1987.

"The White Road" (short story), published in *Tales of the Witch World*, edited by Andre Norton, 1987.

Greenmantle, Ace Books, 1988.

Wolf Moon, New American Library, 1988.

Westlin Wind (novella), Axolotl Press, 1988.

(Contributor) *The Annual Review of Fantasy and Science Fiction*, Meckler Publishing, 1988.

Philip Jose Farmer's The Dungeon: Book Three, Byron Preiss/Bantam, 1988.

Philip Jose Farmer's The Dungeon: Book Five, Byron Preiss/Bantam, 1988.

The Killing Time, Ace Books, in press.

Svaha, Ace Books, in press.

Death Leaves an Echo, Tor Books, in press.

Also author of poetry. Work represented in anthologies, including *The Year's Best Fantasy Stories: 8*, edited by Arthur W. Saha, DAW, 1982; *Dragons and Dreams* and *Spaceships and Spells*, both edited by Jane Yolen, Martin H. Greenberg, and Charles G. Waugh, Harper, 1986 and 1987. Author of columns in horror and science fiction magazines, including "Urban Thrills: Reviews of Short Horror and Contemporary Fantasy Fiction," in *Short Form*, "Behind the Darkness: Profiles of the Writers of Horror Fiction," in *Horrorstruck*, "Scattered Gold," in *OtherRealms*, and "Night Journeys," in *Mystery Scene*. Contributor to periodicals, including *Isaac Asimov's Science Fiction Magazine*.

WORK IN PROGRESS: Drinking Down the Moon: A Novel of Urban Faerie, publication by Ace Books expected in 1990; a book, tentatively titled *The Little Country*, exploring the world of traditional music and folk tales, set in Cornwall, England, completion expected in 1989.

SIDELIGHTS: Known for his blend of the magical and the mundane, Charles de Lint has written a number of contemporary fantasy novels since publishing his first, *The Riddle of the Wren*, in 1984. Born in the Netherlands, he lives in Canada and features Canadian settings in books such as *Moonheart* and *Yarrow*. Reviewing *Moonheart* for the Toronto *Globe and Mail*, Douglas Hill described it as "an ambitious hybrid" that combines traditional fantasy elements with those of horror, suspense, and romance in a modern setting in Ottawa, Ontario. Strange events at an Ottawa mansion prove to be linked to a long-standing battle between good and evil forces, and modern weaponry and ancient spells come together in the climax. Observed the critic, "De Lint sustains his balance between ordinary reality and legend with skill." *Yarrow* concerns a modern-day vampire who feeds on others' dreams, particularly those of a Canadian writer whose dreams are the foundation of her books. Tom Easton described it in *Analog Science Fiction/Science Fact* as "a tasty item" and noted that the novel "is still more 'about' the wellsprings of fantasy, writing, and writer's block."

De Lint told *CA:* "Writing is, like all forms of creative endeavor, a form of communication, so I believe that it's the writer's job to make his work as accessible as possible to his or her readership—but not to the detraction of the work itself. In a world that's growing increasingly coldhearted and mechanical, I like to do what I can to remind my readers of the wonders that are still present and the need to preserve those wonders and mysteries, doing so through the exaggerated technique of fantasies set in the contemporary world. I'd like to add that I'm no Luddite—technological wonders are as magical as any to be found in nature."

BIOGRAPHICAL/CRITICAL SOURCES:

PERIODICALS

Analog Science Fiction/Science Fact, September, 1987.
Globe and Mail (Toronto), November 3, 1984.

* * *

de **MOURGUES, Odette (Marie Helene Louise)** 1914-1988

OBITUARY NOTICE—See index for *CA* sketch: Born May 14,

1914, in Le Puy, Haute Loire, France; died July 1, 1988. Educator and author. De Mourgues, who came from France to Cambridge University in 1946 as a British Council scholar and lecturer at Girton College, remained there for the rest of her academic career, advancing to professor of French in 1975. Her writings include *Metaphysical, Baroque and Precieux Poetry*, a comparative study of sixteenth- and seventeenth-century French and English poets that became a standard reference work; *Two French Moralists: La Rochefoucauld and La Bruyere;* the novels *Le Jugement avant-dernier* and *L'Hortensia bleu;* an anthology of seventeenth-century French poetry; and articles and reviews contributed to *French Studies* and other professional journals.

OBITUARIES AND OTHER SOURCES:

PERIODICALS

Times (London), July 6, 1988.

*   *   *

DESAI, Meghnad   1940-

PERSONAL: Born July 10, 1940, in Baroda, India; son of Jagdish Chandra (a civil servant) and Mandakini (a housewife; maiden name, Majmundar) Desai; married Gail Graham Wilson, June 27, 1970; children: Tanvi, Nuala, Sven. *Education:* University of Bombay, B.A., 1958, M.A., 1960; University of Pennsylvania, Ph.D., 1964. *Politics:* Socialist.

ADDRESSES: Home—51 Ellington St., London N7 8PN, England. *Office*—London School of Economics and Political Science, University of London, Houghton St., Aldwych, London W.C.2, England.

CAREER: University of California, Berkeley, associate specialist in agricultural economics, 1963-65; London School of Economics and Political Science, London, England, lecturer, 1965-76, senior lecturer, 1977-79, reader, 1980-82, professor of economics, 1983—, member of university senate. Past chairman of Holloway Labour Ward, Islington, London; consultant to United Nations Food and Agriculture Organization, World Bank, and University of Algeria.

MEMBER: Association of University Teachers in Economics, Royal Economic Society, Econometric Society, Economic History Society, Society for Economic Dynamics and Control, American Economic Association.

WRITINGS:

Marxian Economic Theory, Basil Blackwell, 1974.
Applied Econometrics, Philip Allan, 1976.
Marxian Economics, Rowman, 1979.
Testing Monetarism, Frances Pinter, 1981, St. Martin's, 1982.
(Editor with Dharma Kumar) *The Cambridge Economic History of India*, Volume II: *c. 1757-c. 1970*, Cambridge University Press, 1983.
(Editor) *Agrarian Power and Agricultural Productivity in South Asia*, University of California Press, 1985.
Hayek, Wheatsheaf Books, 1988.
(Editor and author of introduction) *Lenin's Economic Writings*, Lawrence & Wishart, 1988.
(Editor and author of introduction) *Denis Sargan: Lectures in Advanced Econometrics*, Blackwell, 1988.

Also author of *Leave All Things to Me*, 1989, and *Trahisons des Proletariat*, 1989. Contributor to economic journals.

WORK IN PROGRESS: Continuing research on Marxian economics and applied macroeconomics.

SIDELIGHTS: Meghnad Desai told *CA:* "I have always been interested in ideas. I hope ultimately to absorb in my work influences from a broad range of social sciences and history. In a sense, all social science provides a way to write history, if only in a more ugly and jargon-ridden way than historians manage. History is a key to change, and it is my wish to be able to harness ideas to changing society so that more people can indulge in the luxury of a concern with ideas."

BIOGRAPHICAL/CRITICAL SOURCES:

PERIODICALS

Times Literary Supplement, June 10, 1983.

*   *   *

DESOWITZ, Robert S.   1926-

PERSONAL: Born January 2, 1926, in New York, N.Y.; son of Charles (a contractor) and Bertha (Schaen) Desowitz; married Jeanette Gudgel, September 14, 1954 (divorced, 1968); married Carrolee Harned (a teacher), September 12, 1969; children: (first marriage) Duba, Gregory. *Education:* University of Buffalo, B.A., 1948; University of London, Ph.D., 1951, D.Sc., 1960.

ADDRESSES: Office—Department of Tropical Medicine, Leahi Hospital, University of Hawaii at Manoa, 2500 Campus Rd., Honolulu, Hawaii 96822.

CAREER: Colonial Medical Research Service, West African Institute for Trypanosomiasis Research, Vom, Nigeria, principal scientific officer, 1951-60; University of Singapore, Singapore, professor of parasitology and head of department, 1960-65; Southeast Atlantic Treaty Organization (SEATO) Medical Research Laboratory, Bangkok, Thailand, chief of department of parasitology, 1965-68; University of Hawaii at Manoa, Honolulu, professor of tropical medicine and public health at Leahi Hospital, 1968—. Member of World Health Organization expert committee on parasitic diseases, 1964—; consultant to governments of Burma, Fiji, Sri Lanka, Bangladesh, Thailand, India, and Tonga.

MEMBER: American Society of Parasitology, American Society of Tropical Medicine and Hygiene (fellow), Royal Society of Tropical Medicine and Hygiene (fellow), Malaysian Society of Tropical Medicine (honorary fellow).

WRITINGS:

Ova and Parasites, Harper, 1980.
New Guinea Tapeworms and Jewish Grandmothers: Tales of Parasites and People, Norton, 1981.
The Thorn in the Starfish: The Immune System and How It Works, Norton, 1987.

Contributor of nearly 150 articles to scientific journals.

SIDELIGHTS: Robert S. Desowitz told *CA:* "I am a working biomedical scientist, whose chief professional interests relate to the epidemiological, behavioral, and ecological aspects of parasitic diseases and their control. My laboratory research concerns the immune response to parasitic diseases. At present I am studying how the mother's immune status influences the immunity mounted by her embryo."

Desowitz's *New Guinea Tapeworms and Jewish Grandmothers* is a collection of true stories for the general reader. From prehistoric to modern times, parasites have been an integral part of human and animal life. As Desowitz implied in his book, parasites have even changed history: his collection includes the tale of a nineteenth-century Moslem invasion that was thwarted when a parasitic infection killed the cavalry's horses. Other stories point to the strong relationship between parasitic diseases and traditional religious practices and the ecological role that parasites play in the agricultural process. Critic J. F. Watkins, writing in the *Times Literary Supplement*, found the author's style to be "pleasantly hard-boiled, humane without sentimentality, and spiced with mild wisecracks and vernacular expressions." He recommended the book, not only to the curious general reader, but to medical students and social anthropologists as well.

BIOGRAPHICAL/CRITICAL SOURCES:

PERIODICALS

New York Review of Books, October 8, 1987.
New York Times, November 13, 1981.
Times Literary Supplement, September 24, 1982.

*   *   *

DESSI, Giuseppe   1909-1977

OBITUARY NOTICE—See index for *CA* sketch: Surname is accented on last syllable; born August 7, 1909, in Cagliari, Italy; died of cardiac arrest, July 6, 1977. Editor and author. Dessi was the author of plays, novels, and short stories—many of which were prizewinners—and the editor of several fiction collections. His works in English translation include *The House at San Silvano*, *The Deserter*, and *The Forests of Norbio*, all novels.

OBITUARIES AND OTHER SOURCES:

Date of death provided by wife, Luisa Dessi.

*   *   *

de TERAN, Lisa St. Aubin
See St. AUBIN de TERAN, Lisa

*   *   *

DEWEY, Jennifer (Owings)   1941-

PERSONAL: Born October 2, 1941, in Chicago, Ill.; daughter of Nathaniel Alexander (an architect) and Emily Webster (a housewife; maiden name, Otis) Owings; married Phelps Dewey (a newspaperman), June, 1955 (divorced); children: Tamar. *Education:* Attended Rhode Island School of Design, 1959-60, and University of New Mexico, 1960-62.

ADDRESSES: Home and office—607 Old Taos Highway, Santa Fe, N.Mex. 87501.

CAREER: Artist and writer, 1970—.

MEMBER: Society of Natural Science Illustrators, Science Fiction Society of Illustrators.

AWARDS, HONORS: Bookbinders West Award for illustration, 1980, for *Idle Weeds;* award for illustration from National Academy of Sciences, and Children's Science Book Award from New York Academy of Sciences, both 1984, for *The Secret Language of Snow;* grant for Antarctica from National Science Foundation, 1985-86; Outstanding Science Trade Book Award from Science Teachers of America 1986, for *Clem.*

WRITINGS:

SELF-ILLUSTRATED; JUVENILE

Clem, the Story of a Raven, Dodd, 1986.
At the Edge of the Pond, Little, Brown, 1987.
Animal Camouflage, Scholastic Inc., 1988.
Polar Light, Polar Darkness: A Penguin Year, Little, Brown, 1989.
The Village of Blue Stone, Macmillan, 1989.
The Wandering Albatross, Little, Brown, in press.
Desert: Night and Day, Little, Brown, in press.

ILLUSTRATOR

Harriett Weaver, *Frosty: A Raccoon to Remember*, Archway, 1977.
David Rains Wallace, *Idle Weeds*, Sierra Books, 1980.
Howard E. Smith, Jr., *Living Fossils*, Dodd, 1982.
Edith Thacher Hurd, *Song of the Sea Otter*, Sierra Books/Pantheon, 1983.
Terry Tempest Williams and Ted Major, *The Secret Language of Snow*, Sierra Books/Pantheon, 1984.
Lucia Anderson, *Mammals and Their Milk*, Dodd, 1985.
Joan Sugarman, *Snowflakes*, Little, Brown, 1985.
Louise B. Young, *The Blue Planet*, Little, Brown, 1985.
Robin Bates, *The Dinosaurs and the Dark Star*, Macmillan, 1985.
Fritz Ryser, *Birds of the Great Basin*, University of Nevada Press, 1986.
David Douglas, *Wilderness Sojourn*, Harper, 1987.
Millisent Selsam, *Strange Creatures That Really Lived*, Scholastic Inc., 1987.
Seymour Simon, *Questions and Answers About Dinosaurs*, Morrow, 1989.

WORK IN PROGRESS: A book about ice, for Little, Brown; a book about spiders.

SIDELIGHTS: Jennifer Owings Dewey told *CA:* "My primary interest is natural science for children, an aesthetic but realistic approach to understanding the natural world. I like writing about extreme environments—cold and hot, dry and wet. I like to write about boundaries or lines between one habitat and another, even to the extent of describing the boundary between water and air, water and pond bottoms, air and ice. I enjoy traveling to remote or wild places to do research—living and writing and drawing both in the wild place and when back at home. Writing about the world we live in prevents running out of ideas."

AVOCATIONAL INTERESTS: "I love to travel, especially out of doors, and explore the natural world."

*   *   *

DICKSON, Donald R(ichard)   1951-

PERSONAL: Born August 19, 1951, in Biloxi, Miss.; son of Vernon R. and Velma (Patton) Dickson. *Education:* University of Connecticut at Storrs, B.A., 1973; University of Illinois at Urbana-Champaign, A.M., 1976, Ph.D., 1981. *Politics:* Democrat.

ADDRESSES: Home—104 Lee Ave., College Station, Tex. 77840. *Office*—Department of English, Texas A&M University, College Station, Tex. 77843.

CAREER: Texas A&M University, College Station, assistant professor, 1981-87, associate professor of English, 1987—.

MEMBER: Modern Language Association of America, Milton Society, Renaissance Society, South Central Modern Language Association, South-Central Renaissance Conference (executive secretary, 1984-90), Phi Kappa Phi.

WRITINGS:

The Fountain of Living Waters, University of Missouri Press, 1987.
(Editor with Paul A. Parrish and Dennis A. Flynn) *The Variorum Edition of the Poetry of John Donne: The Anniversaries, Epicedes, and Obsequies,* University of Missouri Press, in press.

Assistant editor of *Seventeenth-Century News;* editor of newsletter of South-Central Renaissance Conference.

WORK IN PROGRESS: A study of the hermetic/literary relationship between Thomas and Henry Vaughan, publication expected in 1993.

*   *   *

DIGBY, Joan (Hildreth) 1942-

PERSONAL: Born November 16, 1942, in New York, N.Y.; daughter of Lovis (a high school principal) and Irma Evelyn (a professor of biochemistry; maiden name, Tuck) Weiss; married William Howard Owen, November 26, 1965 (divorced); married John Michael Digby (a collagist and poet), March 3, 1979. *Education:* New York University, B.A. (summa cum laude), 1963, Ph.D., 1969; University of Delaware, M.A., 1965.

ADDRESSES: Home—30 Kellogg St., Oyster Bay, N.Y. 11771. *Office*—Honors Program, C. W. Post Campus, Long Island University, Brookville, N.Y. 11548.

CAREER: Long Island University, C.W. Post Campus, Brookville, N.Y., assistant professor, 1969-73, associate professor, 1973-77, professor of English and director of Honors Program and Merit Fellowship, 1977—.

MEMBER: American Society for Eighteenth Century Studies, National Collegiate Honors Council, Phi Beta Kappa.

AWARDS, HONORS: Excellence in Teaching Award from New York State Council of English Teachers, 1987.

WRITINGS:

A Sound of Feathers (prose poems), collage illustrations by husband, John Digby, Red Ozier Press, 1982.
(With husband, John Digby) *The Collage Handbook,* Thames & Hudson, 1985.
(Editor with Bob Brier) *Permutations: Readings in Science and Literature,* Morrow, 1985.
(Editor with husband, John Digby) *Food for Thought,* Morrow, 1987.
(Editor with husband, John Digby) *Inspired by Drink,* Morrow, 1988.
Two Presses (nonfiction), Four Winds Press, 1988.
(With husband, John Digby) *The Wood Engravings of John de Pol,* Stone House Press, 1988.

BIOGRAPHICAL/CRITICAL SOURCES:

PERIODICALS

Chicago Tribune, June 16, 1987.
Los Angeles Times Book Review, July 28, 1985, August 11, 1985.

New York Times Book Review, September 22, 1985.
Washington Post Book World, June 28, 1987.

*   *   *

DIGBY, John (Michael) 1938-

PERSONAL: Born January 18, 1938, in London, England; immigrated to the United States, 1978; son of Joyce Beatrice Hilda Digby (a chef); married Erica Susan Christine Bewick-Stephens, 1963 (divorced); married Joan Hildreth Weiss (a professor of English and writer), March 3, 1979; children: (first marriage) Andrew Roland. *Education:* Attended school in London, England.

ADDRESSES: Home and office—30 Kellogg St., Oyster Bay, N.Y. 11771.

CAREER: Collagist and poet.

WRITINGS:

The Structure of Bifocal Distance (poems), Anvil Press, 1974.
Sailing Away From Night (poems and collages), Kayak Books, 1978.
To Amuse a Shrinking Sun (poems and collages), Anvil Press, 1985.
(With wife, Joan Digby) *The Collage Handbook,* Thames & Hudson, 1985.
Miss Liberty (collages), Thames & Hudson, 1986.
Incantation (poems and collages), Stone House Press, 1987.
(Editor with wife, Joan Dibgy) *Food for Thought,* Morrow, 1987.
(Editor with wife, Joan Digby) *Inspired by Drink,* Morrow, 1988.
(With wife, Joan Digby) *The Wood Engravings of John de Pol,* Stone House Press, 1988.
A Parliament of Owls (poems and collages), Anvil Press Poetry, 1989.

SIDELIGHTS: John Digby commented: "My interest in natural history (particularly birds) has been important from childhood. For six years I worked as a keeper at the London Zoo, leaving for the express purpose of becoming a poet. Since then my poetry and collages have been consistently tied to animal and bird imagery."

BIOGRAPHICAL/CRITICAL SOURCES:

PERIODICALS

Chicago Tribune, June 16, 1987.
Los Angeles Times Book Review, July 28, 1985, August 11, 1985.
Washington Post Book World, June 28, 1987.

*   *   *

DINAN, Carolyn

PERSONAL: Born in England. *Education:* Attended Chelsea School of Art; graduate study at Royal College of Art.

ADDRESSES: Home—Surrey, England. *Office*—Chelsea School of Art, Manresa Rd., London SW3 6LS, England.

CAREER: Writer and illustrator. Visiting lecturer in illustration at Chelsea School of Art, London, England.

WRITINGS:

SELF-ILLUSTRATED CHILDREN'S BOOKS

The Lunch Box Monster, Faber, 1983.

Skipper and Sam, Faber, 1984.
Say Cheese! Faber, 1985, Viking, 1986.
Ada and the Magic Basket, Hamish Hamilton, 1987.
Born Lucky, Hamish Hamilton, 1987.

ILLUSTRATOR

Charlotte Bronte, *The Search After Hapiness: A Tale* (reprint), Simon & Schuster, 1969.
Catherine Storr, *Puss and Cat,* Faber, 1969.
Janet McNeill, *Umbrella Thursday,* Hamish Hamilton, 1969.
Pamela Oldfield, *Melanie Brown Goes to School,* Faber, 1970.
Christobel Mattingley, *The Picnic Dog,* Hamish Hamilton, 1970.
Celia Turvey, *The Boy and the Donkey,* Longman, 1970.
Helen Cresswell, *At the Stroke of Midnight: Traditional Fairy Tales,* Collins, 1971.
Christobel Mattingley, *Worm Weather,* Hamish Hamilton, 1971.
Pamela Rogers, *The Magic Egg,* Lutterworth, 1971.
Gene Kemp, *The Prime of Tamworth Pig,* Faber, 1972.
Pamela Sykes, *The Birthday Glove,* Hamish Hamilton, 1972.
Zinnia Bryan, *Let's Talk to God Again,* Scripture Union, 1972.
Pamela Oldfield, *Melanie Brown Climbs a Tree,* Faber, 1972.
Ann Staden, *Pepper Face, and Other Stories,* Faber, 1972.
Gene Kemp, *Tamworth Pig Saves the Trees,* Faber, 1973.
Joan Tate, *Jock and the Rock Cakes,* Brockhampton Press, 1973, Childrens Press, 1976.
Geraldine Kaye, *Tim and the Red Indian Head-Dress,* Brockhampton Press, 1973, Childrens Press, 1976.
Pamela Oldfield, *The Adventures of Sarah and Theodore Bodgitt,* Brockhampton Press, 1974.
Pamela Oldfield, *Melanie Brown and the Jar of Sweets,* Faber, 1974.
George Patrick McCallum, *On Goes the River: An Intermediate Level Reader for Students of English as a Second Language,* Collier, 1974.
Christobel Mattingley, *The Surprise Mouse,* Hamish Hamilton, 1974.
Ivy Eastwick, *The Toyshop on the Avenue,* Lutterworth, 1974.
Rosemary Weir, *Uncle Barney and the Sleep-Destroyer,* Abelard, 1974.
Joyce Gard, *Handysides Shall Not Fall,* Kaye & Ward, 1975.
Boswell Taylor, *Little Donkey,* University of London Press, 1975.
James Thurber, *Many Moons* (reprint), Kaye & Ward, 1975.
Gene Kemp, *Tamworth Pig and the Litter,* Faber, 1975.
Joy Allen, *Boots for Charlie,* Hamish Hamilton, 1975.
Annie Maria Geertruida Schmidt, *Bob and Jilly,* Methuen, 1976.
Gene Kemp, *The Turbulent Term of Tyke Tiler,* Faber, 1977.
Gene Kemp, *Dog Days and Cat Naps,* Faber, 1980.
Robin Stemp, *Guy and the Flowering Plum Tree,* Faber, 1980, Atheneum, 1981.
Gene Kemp, editor, *Ducks and Dragons: Poems for Children,* Faber, 1980.
Gene Kemp, *The Clock Tower Ghost,* Faber, 1981.
Catherine Cookson, *Nancy Nutall and the Mongrel,* Macdonald & Co., 1982.
June Counsel, *But Martin!* Faber, 1984.
Martin Waddell, *Owl and Billy,* Methuen, 1986.
Dorothy Edwards, *Robert Goes to Fetch a Sister,* Methuen, 1986.

Also illustrator of *A Kingdom of Riches: Traditional Fairy Tales* by Helen Cresswell, 1971.*

DIXON, Laurinda S. 1948-

PERSONAL: Born September 4, 1948, in Toledo, Ohio; daughter of Joseph L. (an air force officer) and Margaret E. (an artist; maiden name, Pickering) Dixon; married Charles J. Klaus (a radio announcer and producer), October 31, 1986. *Education:* University of Cincinnati, B.A., 1970, M.A., 1972; Boston University, Ph.D., 1980.

ADDRESSES: Office—Department of Fine Arts, Syracuse University, Syracuse, N.Y. 13210.

CAREER: John Carroll University, Cleveland, Ohio, assistant professor of fine arts, 1981; Syracuse University, Syracuse, N.Y., associate professor of fine arts, 1982—.

MEMBER: College Art Association, Women's Caucus for Art, Historians of Netherlandish Art (vice-president, 1983-84; president, 1985-86), Midwest Art History Association.

AWARDS, HONORS: Grant from National Endowment for the Humanities, 1983; Getty grant in history of art and humanities, 1983; Mellon fellow in humanities, 1983; fellow at Woodrow Wilson International Center for Scholars, 1985-86.

WRITINGS:

Alchemical Imagery in Bosch's "Garden of Delights," UMI Research Press, 1981.
(With Gabriel P. Weisberg) *The Documented Image: Visions in Art History,* Syracuse University Press, 1987.

Contributor to art history journals.

WORK IN PROGRESS: A critical edition of *Hieroglyphica,* an early English hermetic text series by Nicolas Flamel, publication by Garland Press expected in 1990; a book on melancholia as it appeared in the art and medicine of the seventeenth century; a book on Hieronymus Bosch and early medical and pharmaceutical imagery, completion expected in 1991; interdisciplinary research on the relationship between early art and science in the Renaissance and the revival of the occult sciences in the nineteenth century.

SIDELIGHTS: Laurinda S. Dixon told *CA:* "My work links the visual arts with science. Often it has been the science of early eras—alchemy, astrology, humoral medicine—that reveals itself in paintings that we view today as enigmatic and mysterious. By uncovering the practical experience of early science and medicine, such works of art lose their mystery and become understandable in the context of medieval and Renaissance philosophy.

"I have always believed that scholars, especially art historians, should never ignore what is before their very eyes, nor should they confine themselves to the narrow boundaries of the purely visual. This is especially true in the case of Hieronymus Bosch, a painter whose life and works have been subject to volumes of idiosyncratic, esoteric interpretations. My attempts to cut through the miasma of legend and romance surrounding Bosch's most famous painting, the *Garden of Earthly Delights,* led me to alchemy, a philosophy that the pragmatic post-atomic era has labeled irrelevant. In Bosch's day, however, alchemy was chemistry—the means by which pharmacists made medicines and artists' colors. In the context of this science, which developed its own enigmatic pictorial symbolism, the strange hybrid forms and violent monsters in the *Garden of Earthly Delights* illustrate both the allegories of alchemy and its practical laboratory apparatus.

"Bosch's familiarity with alchemy is understandable in the context of his life and times. One of the few facts known about the painter is that he married a wealthy woman from a family of pharmacists. Furthermore, Bosch could have made his own paints by the process of alchemy, as did many artists. However, the case for Bosch's knowledge of early chemistry need not rest on either of these assumptions. Alchemy was part of the common wisdom of the pre-Enlightenment age, and its tenets were accepted without question by all literate persons. My study of the works of Bosch and others has shown me that, by looking at a work of art through the eyes of its intended audience, that audience lives again."

*   *   *

DOCHERTY, James L.
See RAYMOND, Rene (Brabazon)

*   *   *

DODD, David L(e Fevre)   1895-1988

OBITUARY NOTICE: Born August 23, 1895, in Berkeley County, W.Va.; died of respiratory failure, September 18, 1988, in Portland, Me. Financial analyst, educator, and author. A respected expert in the field of finance, Dodd taught business at Columbia University for almost forty years. He served as associate dean of the university's graduate school of business from 1948 to 1952 and retired from the Columbia faculty in 1961. He was co-author of *Security Analysis,* a book that was originally intended as a guide for the lay investor but became a standard college finance text.

OBITUARIES AND OTHER SOURCES:

BOOKS

Who's Who in America, 126th edition, St. Martin's, 1974.

PERIODICALS

New York Times, September 20, 1988.

*   *   *

DONNELLY, Esmond
See OBERDORF, Charles (Donnell)

*   *   *

DOUGHERTY, Philip H(ugh)   1923-1988

OBITUARY NOTICE: Born December 21, 1923, in New York, N.Y.; died of a heart attack, September 27, 1988, in Forest Hills, N.Y. Journalist and radio reporter. Best known for his humorous delivery of trade news items, Dougherty was an influential and respected figure in both the newspaper and the advertising businesses. He began his career in journalism in 1942 as a copy boy for the *New York Times.* Eight years later he became the paper's society reporter, and, in 1966, he advanced to advertising news columnist, a post he retained until his death. Dougherty also hosted a daily advertising news radio program for WQXR, a *New York Times*-owned radio station.

OBITUARIES AND OTHER SOURCES:

BOOKS

Who's Who in America, 45th edition, Marquis, 1988.

PERIODICALS

Chicago Tribune, September 29, 1988.

Los Angeles Times, September 28, 1988.
New York Times, September 28, 1988.

*   *   *

DUBOS, Jean (Porter)   1918(?)-1988

OBITUARY NOTICE: Born c. 1918 in Upper Sandusky, Ohio; died of ovarian cancer, August 6, 1988, in New York, N.Y. Microbiologist, researcher, and author. Dubos was famous for her biological and environmental research, carried out in collaboration with her husband, Rene Dubos. She was affiliated with the Dubos Laboratory at Harvard Medical School for two years before joining the staff of Rockefeller Institute (now Rockefeller University) in 1944. She and her husband worked together at the institute for decades, establishing a laboratory for the study of tuberculosis. Dubos was co-author of *The White Plague—Tuberculosis, Man, and Society,* a classic history of tuberculosis stressing the role of social reform in control of the disease. She also contributed to her husband's work, *So Human an Animal: How We Are Shaped by Surroundings and Events,* which won a Pulitzer Prize for nonfiction in 1969.

OBITUARIES AND OTHER SOURCES:

PERIODICALS

New York Times, August 10, 1988.
Washington Post, August 10, 1988.

*   *   *

DUCKHAM, A(lec) N(arraway)   1903-1988

*OBITUARY NOTICE—*See index for *CA* sketch: Born August 23, 1903, in London, England; died September 22, 1988. Government official, educator, editor, and author. A specialist in animal husbandry and agricultural administration, Duckham served both government and academia with distinction. During the first quarter century of his career Duckham held a number of posts with the British Ministry of Agriculture and Fisheries and the British Ministry of Food, spending the World War II years as chairman of home and overseas agricultural supplies committees and director of the Supply Plans Division, then several postwar years as an agricultural attache at the British embassy in Washington, D.C. In 1955 he was appointed professor of agriculture at the University of Reading, a position he held until his retirement in 1968. His publications include *Animal Industry in the British Empire, American Agriculture, The Fabric of Farming, Agricultural Synthesis: The Farming Year, Farming Systems of the World,* which he co-authored, and *Food Production and Consumption,* which he co-edited. Duckham also served as co-editor of the *Journal of Agricultural Administration.*

OBITUARIES AND OTHER SOURCES:

BOOKS

Who's Who, 140th edition, St. Martin's, 1988.

PERIODICALS

Times (London), September 27, 1988.

*   *   *

DUNLAP, Thomas R(ichard)   1943-

PERSONAL: Born September 9, 1943, in Appleton, Wis.; married, 1975. *Education:* Lawrence University, B.A., 1965;

University of Kansas, M.A., 1972; University of Wisconsin—Madison, Ph.D., 1975.

ADDRESSES: Office—Department of History, Virginia Polytechnic Institute and State University, Blacksburg, Va. 24061.

CAREER: Virginia Polytechnic Institute and State University, Blacksburg, assistant professor, 1975-81, associate professor of history, 1981—. *Military service:* U.S. Army, 1968-70.

MEMBER: Organization of American Historians, American Society for Environmental History, Agricultural History Society, Forest History Society.

AWARDS, HONORS: Theodore Blegan awards from Forest History Society, 1978, for article, "DDT on Trial: The Wisconsin DDT Hearing," 1984, for article "Values for Varmints: Predator Control and Environmental Ideas," and 1986, for article "American Wildlife Policy and Environmental Ideology: Poisoning Coyotes, 1939-1972"; grant from Canadian Studies Program of the Canadian Embassy.

WRITINGS:

DDT: Scientists, Citizens, and Public Policy, Princeton University Press, 1981.
Saving America's Wildlife, Princeton University Press, 1988.

Contributor to journals, including *Social Studies of Science*, *Journal of Canadian Studies*, and *Wisconsin Magazine of History*.

WORK IN PROGRESS: Work on cross-cultural studies.

SIDELIGHTS: In *DDT: Scientists, Citizens, and Public Policy*, Thomas R. Dunlap reveals how public involvement during the late 1960s and early 1970s led to the banning of the pesticide DDT for use in America. A history professor trained in chemistry, the author maintains that science is too crucial to be left to scientists and that the environment is best guarded by a watchful public. Reviewing the book for the *Times Literary Supplement*, British scientist Kenneth Mellanby commended its "useful account of the early history of DDT." The critic did, however, find Dunlap's vehement anti-DDT sentiments typical of the American "polarization of opinions" that precluded any "calm and fruitful" discussions about the pesticide's merits and dangers a decade ago; Mellanby also objected to the study's "out of date" scientific information. The reviewer concluded: "Since 1970 we have learnt . . . that DDT is still the most useful existing chemical in many situations, and we know how to use it safely."

Dunlap told *CA* that his primary interest is the effect of science on public ideas about nature in industrialized countries.

BIOGRAPHICAL/CRITICAL SOURCES:

PERIODICALS

Times Literary Supplement, August 21, 1981.

*   *   *

DYSON, George (Bernard)   1953-

PERSONAL: Born March 26, 1953, in Ithaca, N.Y.; dual citizen of United States and Canada; son of Freeman J. (a physicist and writer) and Verena E. (a mathematician; maiden name, Huber) Dyson; married Ann E. Yow (a photojournalist), September 21, 1985. *Education:* Educated in the United States.

ADDRESSES: Home and office—Box 18, Belcarra Park, R.R. 1, Port Moody, British Columbia, Canada V3H 3C8.

CAREER: Boatbuilder, designer, maritime historian, and author.

MEMBER: Baidarka Historical Society (founder; director, 1984—), Kodiak Historical Society, Oregon Historical Society, Hakluyt Society, Amateur Yacht Research Society.

WRITINGS:

Baidarka, Alaska Northwest Publishing, 1986.

Regular contributor to *Sea Kayaker*.

WORK IN PROGRESS: A chapter on the relation of fluid dynamics to Aleut kayak design, for a volume in the Canadian Museum of Civilization's *Mercury Series; Following the Fence*, a popular history of the Russian-American adventures of 1741-1867 from a maritime perspective.

SIDELIGHTS: In his introduction to George Dyson's *Baidarka*, writer Kenneth Brower described the book as "a history of a craft and of an obsession." For nearly two decades Dyson has researched, built, and sailed the small, decked, skin-covered and paddle-powered indigenous Aleut vessels, retracing the routes of the eighteenth-century fur hunters and explorers who adopted the baidarka for navigation of the Alaskan coast. An electric mix of travelogue, historical document, and personal reflection, *Baidarka* had difficulty finding a market and a publisher; Dyson told *CA* that at one point he "put the manuscript and book dummy in the back of a dark closet for more than a year." But, he continued, "I had accumulated such a wealth of historical documents and illustrations that I was determined, against all publishers' better judgment, to see the story of the Russian baidarka adventures told in pictures as well as words." Dyson recalled, "Eventually I found a publisher willing to put my obsession into print—and now, thank goodness, I have put the ordeal of publishing a book behind me and can return to my archival interests and to the task of building boats."

While Tom Carter, writing in the *Washington Times*, called *Baidarka* "the reassuring discourse of a man who knows what he is doing," Dyson maintains exactly the opposite. "Actually, my book is more the reassuring discourse of a young man who *didn't* know what he was doing," the adventurer reflected. "That's one of the elements that has led to my success, albeit in an otherwise obscure field. When I left home at age sixteen—with credentials as a juvenile deliquent and high school dropout, but little else—I had no idea where I was going. The prospects did not include pursuing, let alone publishing, scholarly research. As the son of [physicist] Freeman Dyson I well knew that I would be forever outshadowed in any intellectual field, and I set off, with only a knapsack, intending to leave all of academia behind. It is a credit to both my parents that they placed no additional obstacles in my way.

"After drifting around the mountains of Colorado and California, working occasionally as a potwasher and camp assistant for the Sierra Club (in the good old days when Sierra Club books weighed five to ten pounds, and the legendary Norman Clyde—who still wandered the Sierra Nevada—astonished us young backpackers by carrying a cast-iron skillet and an ax), I ended up at age seventeen in Vancouver, British Columbia, where a newspaper advertisement for unpaid crew aboard a small sailing vessel caught my eye. This ship, the *D'Sonoqua*, sat high and dry, and incomplete—except as a dream in the captain's imagination. But I signed on nevertheless, and the months ahead rekindled a deep, instinctive passion for building boats. After a couple of years on the *D'Sonoqua* delivering cargo up and down the British Columbia coast, I moved ashore, and, for reasons that remain obscure even to me, began to build canoes.''

George Dyson's passion for the eighteenth-century baidarka and his father's focus on futuristic space travel became the subject of a double biography published in 1978. Written by Brower, *The Starship and the Canoe* was perceived as an allegory for the twentieth century—our alliance with science and technology and the urgent need to reject them. Brower commented on his book, an excerpt of which appeared in *Atlantic Monthly:* "The book was an account of the vessels the two Dysons dreamed of building: Freeman's nuclear-powered spaceship, Orion, which in its most ambitious version was to be the size of Chicago and was destined for some nearby star; and George's canoe, a resurrection of the Aleut kayak that the Russian fur hunters named *baidarka*. It was the story of two men, two arks, two views of man's destiny.''

Dyson admitted to *CA* that "it is somewhat dangerous to see your own biography published when you are barely twenty-five, especially when your schemes had already tended toward the unrealistically grandiose. In a sense, my life since 1978 has unfolded as a sequel to Brower's book, though the ups and downs of reality have been harsher than the literary version would suggest. I owe Brower a great deal of credit for having bid my character such a favorable farewell at the end of his story ('George's dragon prow pranced onward into a sea of stars'); and the success of *The Starship and the Canoe* sparked the beginnings of my own. Brower's pioneering effort helped create the audience for *Baidarka*, which would otherwise have undoubtedly never made it into print.''

''I don't know why George Dyson builds baidarkas,'' contemplated Brower in his foreward to *Baidarka*, ''and I wonder whether he himself knows exactly. I imagine that from time to time his own persistence dismays him. I wrote half a book about the baidarka-builder without coming up with an answer, though I have vague ideas. How is it that a *vessel*, trim and gull-like though it may be, could so take up residence in one man's dreams, in his private iconography? What is it in the baidarka's simplicity, or swiftness, or silence; in its feather-lightness or taut-sidedness, or in the womblike way it embraces its paddler, that so resonated in a boy from Princeton, New Jersey? It is probably foolish to wonder. Why did Rembrandt [Harmensz van Rijn] fall in love with oils or [Ernest] Rutherford with electrons or [Gregor Johann] Mendel with peas?''

BIOGRAPHICAL/CRITICAL SOURCES:

BOOKS

Brower, Kenneth, *The Starship and the Canoe*, Holt, 1978.

PERIODICALS

Atlantic Monthly, May, 1978.
Canoe, August, 1985.
Country Journal, June, 1979.
New Age, August, 1980.
Omni, December, 1978.
Seattle Times, March 23, 1980.
Vancouver, April, 1980.
Washington Post Book World, August 10, 1986.
Washington Times, September 5, 1986.

E

EAKIN, Mary Mulford   1914-1980

PERSONAL: Born May 17, 1914, in Ithaca, N.Y.; died July 8, 1980, in Berkeley, Calif.; daughter of Walter and Vera (Wandling) Mulford; married Richard M. Eakin, August 8, 1935; children: David Marshall, Dorothy Alice. *Education:* University of California, A.B., 1935; Pacific School of Religion, M.A., 1957, B.D., 1966.

ADDRESSES: Home—1627 Spruce St., Berkeley, Calif. 94709. *Office*—First Congregational Church, 2345 Channing Way, Berkeley, Calif. 94704.

CAREER: Ordained minister of United Church of Christ, 1966; First Congregational Church, Berkeley, Calif., director of Christian education, 1954-66, associate minister, beginning in 1966.

WRITINGS:

Baptism: By Water and the Spirit, United Church Board for Homeland Ministries, 1966.
(With Browne Barr) *The Ministering Congregation*, United Church Press, 1972.
Scuffy Sandals: A Guide for Church Visitation in the Community, Pilgrim Press (New York, N.Y.), 1982.

Contributor to periodicals.*

[Date of death supplied by Cordelia M. Jacobs, administrative secretary at the First Congregational Church, Berkeley, California.]

*   *   *

EASTMAN, Lloyd E.   1929-

PERSONAL: Born April 16, 1929, in New Rockford, N.D.; son of Harry and Evelyn Eastman; married to wife, Margaret; children: Michael. *Education:* Pacific Lutheran College (now University), B.A., 1953; University of Washington, Seattle, M.A., 1957; Harvard University, Ph.D., 1963.

ADDRESSES: Office—Department of History, 429 Gregory Hall, University of Illinois at Urbana-Champaign, Urbana, Ill. 61801.

CAREER: Connecticut College for Women (now Connecticut College), New London, assistant professor of history, 1962-

66; Ohio State University, Columbus, associate professor of history, 1966-67; University of Illinois at Urbana-Champaign, Urbana, associate professor, 1967-71, professor of history, 1971—. *Military service:* U.S. Army, 1954-57.

MEMBER: Association for Asian Studies, Ch'ing Society.

AWARDS, HONORS: Grant from Commission for Exchanges With the Asian Institute, 1968-69; grant from East Asian Research Center for Harvard University, 1971-72; senior fellow of National Endowment for the Humanities, 1974-75.

WRITINGS:

Throne and Mandarins: China's Search for a Policy During the Sino-French Controversy, 1880-1885, Harvard University Press, 1967.
The Abortive Revolution: China Under Nationalist Rule, 1927-1937, Harvard University Press, 1974.
Seeds of Destruction: Nationalist China in War and Revolution, 1937-1949, Stanford University Press, 1984.
Family, Field, and Ancestors: Constancy and Change in China's Social and Economic History, 1550-1949, Oxford University Press, 1987.

Contributor to history and Chinese studies journals.

WORK IN PROGRESS: Chiang Kai-shek and Nationalist China: A History.

BIOGRAPHICAL/CRITICAL SOURCES:

PERIODICALS

Annals of the American Academy of Political and Social Sciences, September, 1975, January, 1985.
New York Times Book Review, June 15, 1975.

*   *   *

EATON, John P.

PERSONAL: Born in Easton, Pa.; son of Paul Burns (a teacher) and Hannah (Wilkins) Eaton. *Education:* Lafayette College, B.A., 1948. *Politics:* Republican. *Religion:* Episcopalian.

ADDRESSES: Home—53 Downing St., New York, N.Y. 10014. *Office*—Roosevelt Hospital, 428 West 59th St., New York, N.Y. 10019.

CAREER: Roosevelt Hospital, New York, N.Y., admitting clerk, 1958—. Guest lecturer at New School for Social Research, 1981; guest on radio and television programs, including "What's Up America?," "Canada Tonight," "The MacNeil-Lehrer Report," and "The Today Show"; consultant to National Geographic Society. *Military service:* U.S. Army, 1945-46.

MEMBER: Titanic Historical Society (co-founder; historian, 1963—), Steamship Historical Society of America.

WRITINGS

(Author of introduction) Lawrence Beesley, *The Loss of the SS Titanic,* 7C's Press, 1973.
(With Charles A. Haas) *Titanic: Triumph and Tragedy,* Norton, 1986.
(With Haas) *Titanic: Destination Disaster,* Norton, 1987.
Falling Star (history), Patrick Stephens Ltd., 1988.

Contributor to magazines.

WORK IN PROGRESS: Titanic: Profile of a Disaster, publication by Patrick Stephens Ltd. expected in 1991; *Titanic: Voices of Daring and Doom,* an oral history.

SIDELIGHTS: John P. Eaton told *CA:* "Relative to her short life, the ocean liner *Titanic* was among history's most photographed ships. She was also among the best-documented, with magazine and newspaper stories chronicling both her construction and maiden voyage; reports of official investigations concerning her loss; and court records regarding life and property insurance—a sea of paper on which the *Titanic*'s story floats.

"Yet during the turbulent decades following the disaster, these records were pushed further and further back on shelves to make room for new material about depressions, personalities, wars—the shaping of the twentieth century. The fascination with the *Titanic* is that, as one of history's most horrendous and dramatic disasters, the documentation of its demise exists in engrossing and almost infinite detail. But it must be searched out, tracked down—sometimes down many a dead end and blind alley—and then pieced together with other scraps of data. Finally, a fragment emerges, an element that must then be fitted to other elements until another piece of the picture is formed and fitted into the frame.

"The *Titanic* is a kaleidoscope. One studies the pattern, then gives the tube but a small turn. The entire design changes and must be restudied and appreciated anew. But the design's pieces remain the same: beauty, pride, disaster, heroism, man's vulnerability to nature's forces—the ever-changing, ever-constant . . . *Titanic.*"

BIOGRAPHICAL/CRITICAL SOURCES:

PERIODICALS

New York, January 14, 1980.
New York Times, May 30, 1987.

*   *   *

EBERSTADT, Isabel   1933-
(Isabel Nash)

PERSONAL: Born September 30, 1933, in Baltimore, Md.; daughter of Ogden (a poet) and Frances (Leonard) Nash; married Frederick Eberstadt (a photographer), November 12, 1954; children: Nicholas, Fernanda. *Education:* Attended Bryn Mawr College.

ADDRESSES: Home—791 Park Ave., New York, N.Y. 10021. *Agent*—Lynn Nesbit, International Creative Management, 40 West 57th St., New York, N.Y. 10019.

CAREER: Writer.

WRITINGS:

"Where Did Tuffy Hide?" series (for children), three books, Little, Brown, 1956.
(Under name Isabel Nash) *The Banquet Vanishes* (novel), Little, Brown, 1958.
(Editor with Linell Smith) Ogden Nash, *I Wouldn't Have Missed It: Selected Poems,* Little, Brown, 1975.
Natural Victims (novel), Knopf, 1983.

Contributor to periodicals.

SIDELIGHTS: In Isabel Eberstadt's novel *Natural Victims,* it is repeatedly stated that the visible rich are easy prey—natural victims. Their wealth alone attracts the envious and the acquisitive; gratification without responsibility shapes character and motivation. Sis Melmore, the socially prominent widow of an American businessman, is the exquisitely correct product of such staggering wealth, as is her deranged daughter Sarah. The novel shows one summer in the lives of these women, as Sis frantically searches for her estranged daughter among the artists and revolutionaries of Paris's underground.

Juxtaposed with this search for Sarah is Sis's long conversation with her sister Harriet, a Paris resident unfamiliar with her niece's troubled past. The American widow's retrospections give clues to Sarah's disintegration; they also give an intimate look at the woman behind the perfectly coiffed and manicured veneer. Sis "has a way of telling more than she knows, and it's this that makes the device worthwhile," decided novelist and critic Anne Tyler in the *New York Times Book Review.* "Mrs. Melmore unwittingly reveals her husband as a ruthless bully who crushed both his children. And she recalls her own tenuous position, forever teetering on the sharp edge of her husband's approval, stubbornly insisting on his basic goodness even when (as she will never consciously admit) the cost was her children's happiness."

Writing in the *Los Angeles Times,* reviewer Elizabeth Wheeler determined that "Eberstadt manages to make [mother and daughter] sympathetic even as she reveals their weaknesses." Sis "has a wry interior self that's unexpectedly sensible," Tyler agreed. The author "allows her a full measure of characterization, and the result is a portrait of a woman as delicate and enduring as piano wire." Tyler did, however, find the novel's plot too complicated, strained, and bewildering: *Natural Victims* "suffers from an overabundance of imagination," she related, "but . . . takes on power whenever it narrows in upon private lives." Wheeler likewise noted that "the plot sometimes seems out of control," but added, "The precision and insight Eberstadt brings to her characters makes up for those lapses." And deeming *Natural Victims* "exciting and serious," a writer for the *New Yorker* remarked: "The author is the daughter of Ogden Nash; much of his light verse was laced with dark and difficult ideas, and these aspects of his genius dominate in this novel."

I Wouldn't Have Missed It, edited by Eberstadt and Linell Smith, is a selection of poems by Ogden Nash, America's premier white-collar humorist. A creator of light verse notorious for its wordplay, the poet used devices like hyperpuns, archaisms, and elastic couplets called "Nash Ramblers" to examine the peculiarities of contemporary middle America.

"He wrote his verses about just those subjects that a well-behaved dinner guest might use for conversational fodder in mixed company," explained reviewer Tom Disch in the *Times Literary Supplement*. While no great admirer of the poet, Disch did express regret over the collection's exclusions and lack of variety, stating: "Time has not been kind to these jingles, since it is difficult to be at once pithy and innocuous, but even Nash's most skilful drolleries suffer from being heaped together into a *Selected Poems*."

BIOGRAPHICAL/CRITICAL SOURCES:

PERIODICALS

Chicago Tribune Book World, June 23, 1983.
Los Angeles Times, August 18, 1983.
New Yorker, May 9, 1983.
New York Times Book Review, April 24, 1983.
Times (London), January 26, 1984.
Times Literary Supplement, February 3, 1984.

*   *   *

EDELMAN, Bernard   1946-

PERSONAL: Born December 14, 1946, in Brooklyn, N.Y.; son of Sam (a textile worker) and Anne (a homemaker; maiden name, Greenberg) Edelman; married Ellen Leary (in video production), May 31, 1985. *Education:* Brooklyn College of the City University of New York, B.A., 1968; John Jay College of Criminal Justice of the City University of New York, M.A., 1983.

ADDRESSES: Home and office—340 East 57th St., New York, N.Y. 10022.

CAREER: Editor for chain of community-oriented weekly newspapers in New York, N.Y., 1972-78; free-lance photographer, editor, and journalist in New York City, 1978-87; director of veterans' affairs for the City of New York, 1987—. Curator of art exhibits showing works by Vietnam veteran artists, 1981, 1982, 1984, and 1985. Associate producer of film *Dear America: Letters Home From Vietnam,* 1988. *Military service:* U.S. Army, 1969-71.

MEMBER: New York City Vietnam Veterans Memorial Commission.

WRITINGS:

(Editor) *Dear America: Letters Home From Vietnam,* Norton, 1985.

Contributor of photographs and articles to periodicals, including *Police Magazine* and New York *Sunday News Magazine.*

WORK IN PROGRESS: Another book of letters.

SIDELIGHTS: Commemorating the dedication of a memorial to Vietnam veterans in New York City, Bernard Edelman's *Dear America: Letters Home From Vietnam* is a collection of correspondences from U.S. servicemen to their parents, lovers, and friends during the Vietnam war. The book begins with the testimony of soldiers fresh to the war, documents the terrors of combat, of loneliness and loss, and closes with soldiers' questions about America's place in this tragic foreign war. "The poignant letters collected here demonstrate that writers in America were not the only ones fighting a moral and emotional battle in the 1960s," wrote *Los Angeles Times Book Review* critic Alex Raksin. "They offer a picture of both confusion and bravery," reiterated a reviewer for the *Washington*

Post Book World, "confused feelings about what the war is all about, bravery in the face of certain danger." And finding "the book's strength . . . in its diversity," Myra MacPherson related in another *Washington Post Book World* critique: "This book tells of an ache as ancient as time—adolescents off to war with high expectations, who soon change greatly. Ambiguities abound—from pain, disillusionment and sorrow for dead comrades to hard-earned measure of individual strength and survival."

MEDIA ADAPTATIONS: Dear America was broadcast as a cable television special by Home Box Office (HBO) in April, 1988.

BIOGRAPHICAL/CRITICAL SOURCES:

PERIODICALS

Los Angeles Times Book Review, February 2, 1986.
Washington Post Book World, April 21, 1985, March 16, 1986.

*   *   *

EDMUNDSON, Bruce   1952-

PERSONAL: Born June 20, 1952, in Edmonton, Alberta, Canada; son of Samuel John and Joyce Catherine (Tebby) Edmundson. *Education:* University of Victoria, B.F.A., 1982; University of British Columbia, M.F.A., 1986.

ADDRESSES: Home—1240 South Dyke Rd., New Westminster, British Columbia, Canada V3M 5A2.

CAREER: Writer. Worked as a tree planter and carnival worker.

MEMBER: Amnesty International, Greenpeace, British Columbia Federation of Writers.

WRITINGS:

Two Voices (stories), Oberon Press, 1987.

Scriptwriter for Canadian Broadcasting Corp.

WORK IN PROGRESS: A short story collection.

*   *   *

EDSALL, Thomas Byrne   1941-

PERSONAL: Born August 22, 1941, in Cambridge, Mass.; son of Richard Linn (a market research executive) and Katharine (a museum administrator; maiden name, Byrne) Edsall; married Mary Deutsch (a housewife); children: Alexandra H. T. *Education:* Attended Brown University, 1959-61; Boston University, B.A., 1966. *Politics:* Independent.

ADDRESSES: Home—511 Fourth St. S.E., Washington, D.C. 20003. *Office*—*Washington Post,* 1150 15th St. N.W., Washington, D.C., 20071.

CAREER: Providence Journal, Providence, R.I., reporter, 1965; Volunteers in Service to America (VISTA), Baltimore, Md., volunteer worker, 1966-67; *Baltimore Sun,* Baltimore, reporter, 1967-81; *Washington Post,* Washington, D.C., reporter, 1981—. Chairman of Standing Committee of Correspondents at Congressional Press Gallery, 1981-83.

AWARDS, HONORS: Bill Pryor Memorial Award and Front Page Award from Washington-Baltimore Newspaper Guild, both 1981.

WRITINGS:

The New Politics of Inequality, Norton, 1984.

Power and Money, Norton, 1988.
(Editor with Sidney Blumenthal) *The Reagan Legacy,* Pantheon, 1988.
(Contributor) Gary Gerstle and Steven Fraser, editors, *The Rise and Fall of the New Deal Order,* Princeton University Press, 1989.

Contributor to magazines and newspapers, including *New York Review of Books, Atlantic, New Republic, Dissent, Washington Monthly, Nation,* and *Society.*

SIDELIGHTS: In *The New Politics of Inequality* Thomas Byrne Edsall takes a critical look at Ronald Reagan's presidential administration. The author states that the political activities of the 1980s have resulted in a redistribution of political control from the poor and the middle classes to society's elite. According to Robert Lekachman in a *Washington Post Book World* review, Edsall blames the erosion of New Deal social reform policy on many factors, including a decrease in tax resources, a decline in union membership (and concomitant political activity), and a realignment of the voting constituencies from the urban working class to the growing, upwardly mobile, suburban professional elite. Lekachman called the study "a first-class book—the best single explanation of Reagan's success that I have encountered."

BIOGRAPHICAL/CRITICAL SOURCES:

PERIODICALS

Washington Post Book World, June 10, 1984, August 14, 1988.

*   *   *

EDWARDS, David V(andeusen)   1941-

PERSONAL: Born May 25, 1941, in Chicago, Ill.; *Education:* Swarthmore College, B.A., 1962; Harvard University, M.A., 1964, Ph.D., 1966.

ADDRESSES: Office—Department of Government, University of Texas at Austin, Austin, Tex. 78712.

CAREER: Johns Hopkins University, Baltimore, Md., research associate at Washington Center for Policy Research, 1964-65, 1970-71; University of Texas at Austin, assistant professor, 1965-70, associate professor of government, 1970—. Consultant to Institute for Defense Analyses.

MEMBER: International Studies Association, American Association for the Advancement of Science, American Political Science Association, American Academy of Political and Social Science, Society for General Systems Research.

WRITINGS:

Arms Control in International Politics, Holt, 1969.
International Political Analysis, Holt, 1969.
(Editor with Roderick A. Bell and R. Harrison Wagner) *Political Power: A Reader in Theory and Research,* Free Press, 1969.
(Editor) *International Political Analysis: Readings,* Holt, 1970.
Creating a New World Politics: From Conflict to Cooperation, McKay, 1973.
(With Roderick A. Bell) *American Government: The Facts Reorganized,* General Learning Press, 1974.
The American Political Experience: An Introduction to Government, Prentice-Hall, 1979, 3rd edition, with learning guide, 1985.

**EDWARDS, James Keith O'Neill   1920-1988
(Jimmy Edwards)**

OBITUARY NOTICE: Born March 23, 1920; died July 7, 1988. Comedian and author. Best known for his huge mustache and wry wit, Edwards brought his unique brand of humor to British radio, television, and stage productions for more than forty years. As a pilot in the Royal Air Force during World War II, he suffered burns to his face when forced under enemy attack to crash-land his plane; he grew his famous mustache to hide the resulting scars. The comedian first became popular in the late 1940s for his role in the radio show "Take It From Here." Breaking into television a decade later, Edwards landed the role of the corpulent school headmaster in "Wacko" and continued his radio work with the panel game "Does the Team Think?" One of his many memorable stage roles was that of Sir Toby Belch in Peter Ustinov's "Halfway up the Tree." Edwards's writings include an autobiography titled *Take It From Me* and *Six of the Best,* a collection of memoirs.

OBITUARIES AND OTHER SOURCES:

BOOKS

Halliwell's Filmgoer's Companion, 7th edition, Granada, 1980.
Who's Who, 140th edition, St. Martin's, 1988.

PERIODICALS

Times (London), July 11, 1988.

*   *   *

**EDWARDS, Jimmy
See EDWARDS, James Keith O'Neill**

*   *   *

EDWARDS, Linda Strauss   1948-

PERSONAL: Born June 16, 1948, in White Plains, N.Y.; daughter of Arthur S. (a physician) and Joy (a homemaker; maiden name, Worth) Strauss; married Richard M. Edwards (a physician's assistant), September 12, 1970; children: Aaron Richard, Blythe Ellen. *Education:* Syracuse University, B.F.A., 1970.

ADDRESSES: Home and office—R.D.2, Box 218A, Lowville, N.Y. 13367.

CAREER: Jefferson-Lewis Board of Cooperative Educational Services, Glenfield, N.Y., graphic artist, 1973-74; Individualized Instruction, Inc., Oklahoma City, Okla., artist, 1974-75; South Oklahoma City Junior College, Oklahoma City, instructor, 1975-76; illustrator and author of children's books, 1978—. Lowville Free Library, member of Friends of the Library, 1982, member of board of trustees, 1983-85; panel member of Regional Decentralization Program, New York State Council of the Arts, 1979-81, 1984-86, panel chair, 1986-87; board member of Tri-County Arts Council.

WRITINGS:

The Downtown Day (self-illustrated children's book), Pantheon, 1983.

Contributor of children's stories to periodicals, including *Cricket.*

ILLUSTRATOR

Marguerita Rudolph, *The Sneaky Machine,* McGraw, 1974.
Barbara Williams, *So What If I'm a Sore Loser?* Harcourt, 1981.

Denise G. Orenstein, *When the Wind Blows Hard*, Addison-Wesley, 1982.

Jill Ross Klevin, *The Turtle Street Trading Company*, Delacorte, 1982.

Jill Ross Klevin, *Turtles Together Forever!* Delacorte, 1982.

Jamie Gilson, *Thirteen Ways to Sink a Sub*, Lothrop, 1982.

Betty Bates, *Call Me Friday the Thirteenth*, Holiday House, 1983.

Jamie Gilson, *4B Goes Wild*, Lothrop, 1983.

Alice Schertle, *Goodnight Hattie, My Dearie, My Dove*, Lothrop, 1985.

Betty Bates, *Thatcher Payne-in-the-Neck*, Holiday House, 1985.

Michele Granger, *Summer House Cat*, Dutton, 1989.

WORK IN PROGRESS: Bad Giggles and Angry Words, a self-illustrated children's book.

AVOCATIONAL INTERESTS: Photography, junk stores, window shopping, Sunday crossword puzzles, loud music, novels.

*   *   *

EFRON, Marshall   1938(?)-

PERSONAL: Born c. 1938. *Education:* Received B.A. from University of California, Los Angeles, and M.A. from University of California, Berkeley.

CAREER: Professional actor on stage, film, and television. Worked at Actor's Workshop, San Francisco, Calif., and Pittsburgh Playhouse; host of "A Satirical View," a weekly program on WBAI-Radio; appeared on "The Great American Dream Machine," a series on National Educational Television, 1971; films include "THX-1138."

WRITINGS:

(With Alfa-Betty Olsen) *Bible Stories You Can't Forget, No Matter How Hard You Try* (juvenile), Dutton, 1976.

(With Olsen) *Omnivores: They Said They Would Eat Anything, and They Did!* Viking, 1979.

(With Olsen) *Sin City Fables*, A & W Publishers, 1981.

BIOGRAPHICAL/CRITICAL SOURCES:

PERIODICALS

New York Times, March 28, 1971.
New York Times Book Review, November 14, 1976.
TV Guide, April 12, 1975.
Vogue, September 15, 1971.*

*   *   *

EICHENBAUM, Luise   1952-

PERSONAL: Born July 22, 1952, in New York, N.Y.; daughter of Bernard and Myrna (Peres) Eichenbaum; married Jeremy Pikser (a writer); children: Gina Eichenbaum-Pikser. *Education:* City University of New York, B.A. (with highest honors), 1973; State University of New York at Stony Brook, M.S.W., 1975.

ADDRESSES: Home—New York, N.Y. *Office*—Women's Therapy Centre Institute, 80 East 11th St., New York, N.Y. 10003.

CAREER: Women's Therapy Centre, London, England, co-founder and co-director, psychotherapist and lecturer, 1976-80; Women's Therapy Centre Institute, New York, N.Y., co-founder and co-director, psychotherapist and lecturer, 1980—.

WRITINGS:

(With Susie Orbach) *Outside In, Inside Out: Women's Psychology, A Feminist Psychoanalytic Approach*, Penguin Books, 1982.

(With Orbach) *Understanding Women*, Basic Books, 1983.

(With Orbach) *What Do Women Want?*, Coward-McCann, 1983.

(With Orbach) *Between Women: Love, Envy, and Competition in Women's Friendships*, Viking, 1987.

SIDELIGHTS: Founders of Women's Therapy Centres in London and New York City, Luise Eichenbaum and Susie Orbach have collaborated on a number of books about the female psyche, drawn from their years of experience as psychotherapists. Their first work, *Outside In, Inside Out*, presents their own developmental theory of gender identity, a synthesis of feminism and psychoanalysis that uncovers the misogyny hidden in much of traditional psychoanalytic thought. Reviewing the book for the *New Statesman*, Ann Shearer decided that "any serious attempt to bring nearer the outer and inner worlds of feminism and psychoanalysis is important." *Understanding Women*, another Eichenbaum-Orbach collaboration, explores how women's special therapy needs can be met with feminist-oriented psychoanalysis, counseling, and group treatment.

In *What Do Women Want?* Eichenbaum and Orbach look at challenges in the heterosexual relationship, complicated by the diametric way men and women are raised. Case vignettes illustrate how men are taught to expect gratification and to have their needs met while, conversely, women are taught to expect disappointment and to give rather than take, hence fostering resentment. The authors see a solution in the restructuring of domestic life, with both sexes equal nurturers. *Between Women: Love, Envy, and Competition in Women's Friendships* explores, with case examples, the emotional attachments as well as the difficult feelings that inform women's friendships. Because women are raised largely to see themselves in relation to others—connection is identity—their need for individuation and self-development vies with feminine capacities for empathy and emotional exchange. "The ideal for women, the authors say, is 'separated attachments and connected autonomy,'" remarked Nancy Goldberger in the *New York Times Book Review*. Deeming the study "touching and lively," the critic added, "As a well-written, easy-to-read account of the sticky dilemmas facing women today, 'Between Women' will undoubtedly be useful as a catalyst for discussion among women."

Eichenbaum told *CA* that her focus is "feminist theory and its contribution to the area of psychoanalytic thinking and practice."

BIOGRAPHICAL/CRITICAL SOURCES:

PERIODICALS

Los Angeles Times Book Review, July 24, 1983.
New Statesman, June 18, 1982, April 15, 1983.
New York Times Book Review, January 24, 1988.
Times Educational Supplement, September 24, 1982.

*   *   *

ELKINS, Aaron J.   1935-

PERSONAL: Born July 24, 1935, in Brooklyn, N.Y.; son of Irving Abraham (a machinist) and Jennie (Katz) Elkins; married Toby Siev, 1959 (divorced, 1972); married Charlotte Trangmar (a writer), 1972; children: (first marriage) Laurence, Robin. *Education:* Hunter College (now of the City University of New York), B.A., 1956; graduate study at University of Wisconsin—Madison, 1957-59; University of Arizona, M.A., 1960; California State University, Los Angeles, M.A., 1962; University of California, Berkeley, Ed.D., 1976.

ADDRESSES: Home—Bainbridge Island, Wash. *Agent*—Karpfinger Agency, 500 Fifth Ave., Suite 2800, New York, N.Y. 10110.

CAREER: Government of Los Angeles County, Calif., personnel analyst, 1960-66; Government of Orange County, Calif., training director, 1966-69; Santa Ana College, Santa Ana, Calif., instructor in anthropology and business, 1969-70; Ernst & Whinney, Chicago, Ill., management consultant, 1970-71; Government of Contra Costa County, Calif., director of management development, 1971-76; University of Maryland at College Park, European Division, lecturer in anthropology, psychology, and business, 1976-78; U.S. Office of Personnel Management, San Francisco, Calif., management analyst, 1979-80; Government of Contra Costa County, director of management development, 1980-83; University of Maryland at College Park, European Division, lecturer in business, 1984-85; writer, 1984—. Lecturer at California State University, Hayward and Fullerton, and at Golden Gate University. Member of Clallam County Civil Service Commission, 1987—.

MEMBER: Authors Guild, Mystery Writers of America.

AWARDS, HONORS: Edgar Allan Poe Award for best mystery novel from Mystery Writers of America, 1988, for *Old Bones.*

WRITINGS:

NOVELS

Fellowship of Fear, Walker & Co., 1982.
The Dark Place, Walker & Co., 1983.
Murder in the Queen's Armes, Walker & Co., 1985.
A Deceptive Clarity, Walker & Co., 1987.
Old Bones, Mysterious Press, 1987.
Curses! Mysterious Press, in press.

Contributor to personnel, education, and anthropology journals.

WORK IN PROGRESS: A Wicked Slice, with wife, Charlotte Elkins.

SIDELIGHTS: Aaron J. Elkins told *CA:* "I have been a voracious reader of fiction since I was eleven or twelve, but it never occurred to me that I could be a writer myself until a few years ago. Until then, I had classed novelists with opera singers, or baseball players, or movie stars—extraordinary people who inhabited some other world than mine.

"In 1978, at the age of forty-four, I returned from two years in Europe, with no likely job prospects in sight. I had been teaching anthropology for the University of Maryland's Overseas Division, on assignments that took me to NATO bases in England, Germany, Holland, Spain, Sicily, and Sardinia. I had kept a journal of my observations, and I thought I might be able to use it in writing a book. With considerable trepidation, I began a novel involving (of all things) an anthropology professor who moved through Europe, teaching at U.S. military bases."

BIOGRAPHICAL/CRITICAL SOURCES:

PERIODICALS

New York Times, February 6, 1983.
Seattle Times/Seattle Post-Intelligencer, July 3, 1988.
Washington Post Book World, June 19, 1988.

ELLIOT, John 1898-1988

OBITUARY NOTICE: Name originally John Elliot Blumenfeld; name legally changed, 1922; born May 6, 1898, in London, England; died September 18, 1988. Transport executive, journalist, and author. After fighting in World War I, Elliot spent four years as a journalist and then joined the public relations and advertising staff of the Southern Railway Company in 1925, with the initial assignment of handling public complaints during the disruption of service as the firm underwent modernization. Elliot developed a great interest in transportation itself and by 1947 had become general manager of Southern Railway's traffic operations. He went on to hold several important positions in the railroad industry, including chairman of the Railway Executive, and, later, of London Transport. He also served as vice-president of the International Union of Railways. In addition to numerous articles and book reviews, he wrote a book about the transportation industry entitled *On and Off the Rails.* In his spare time, Elliot studied historical events and wrote *The Way of the Tumbrils: Paris During the Revolution and Today,* about the French Revolution, and *Where Our Fathers Died,* a book discussing the famous World War I battle zone, the western front.

OBITUARIES AND OTHER SOURCES:

BOOKS

The International Who's Who, 51st edition, Europa, 1987.
Who's Who, 140th edition, St. Martin's, 1988.

PERIODICALS

Times (London), September 20, 1988.

*   *   *

ELLIOTT, John H(all) 1935-

PERSONAL: Born October 23, 1935, in New York, N.Y.; son of Charles E. and Nietta H. (Hall) Elliott; married Dietlinde M. Kattenstroth (a translator and musician), December 28, 1962; children: Mark G., Michael S. *Education:* Concordia Seminary, St. Louis, Mo., B.A., 1957, B.D., 1960; graduate study at Michigan State University, 1958-59; University of Munster, D.Th., 1963.

ADDRESSES: Home—819 Calmar Ave., Oakland, Calif. 94610. *Office*—Department of Theology, University of San Francisco, San Francisco, Calif. 94117.

CAREER: Ordained Lutheran minister, 1963; Concordia Seminary, St. Louis, Mo., assistant professor of theology, 1963-67; University of San Francisco, San Francisco, Calif., Honore F. Zabala Professor of Theology, 1967-68, associate professor, 1968-75, professor of theology, 1975—, National Endowment for the Humanities Professor of Humanities, 1986-88. Visiting professor at Webster College, St. Louis, 1965-67, Pontifical Biblical Institute, Rome, Italy, 1978, and University of Notre Dame, 1981; adjunct professor at Graduate Theological Union, Berkeley, Calif., 1977—; resident scholar at Disciples' Institute zur Erforschung des Uchristentums, Tuebingen, West Germany, 1977. Member of executive board of St. Louis Conference on Religion and Race, 1965-67.

MEMBER: Studiorum Novi Testamenti Societas, American Association of University Professors (president, 1972-73), Catholic Biblical Association of America (member of executive board, 1971-72 and 1986-88), Lutheran Human Relations Association of America, Franz Delitzsch Gesellschaft, Society of Biblical Literature (member of executive board of Pacific Coast region, 1975-77; vice-president, 1981-82; president, 1982-83).

AWARDS, HONORS: Grants from Lutheran World Federation Personnel Exchange Program, 1977-78, and American Council of Learned Societies, 1981; Distinguished Faculty Research Award from the University of San Francisco, 1982.

WRITINGS:

The Elect and the Holy: An Exegetical Examination. . ., E. J. Brill, 1966.
(With Bruce Vawter) *Pentecost Three*, Fortress, 1975.
1 Peter: Estrangement and Community, Franciscan Herald, 1979.
A Home for the Homeless: A Sociological Exegesis of 1 Peter, Its Situation and Strategy, Fortress, 1981.
(With R. A. Martin) *James, 1-2 Peter, Jude*, Augsburg, 1982.
(Editor) *Social-Scientific Criticism of the New Testament*, Scholars Press, 1986.

Contributor to scholarly journals, including *Forum*. Member of editorial board of Society of Biblical Literature, 1976-78, *Semeia*, 1983-87, and *Foundations and Facets*, 1983—.

WORK IN PROGRESS: Research on Christianity in Rome during the first two centuries.

SIDELIGHTS: John H. Elliott told *CA:* "The influential but mysterious book of the Bible is a prime focus of my research and writing. Reading and writing about the literature of cultures so far removed from the contemporary scene by history, geography, and social scripts is like visiting an alien planet, moving about as strangers in a strange land. As theological interpreter and tour guide, I aim at introducing contemporary readers to the language, customs, and society of the biblical natives, the social world from which the literature of the Bible derives its meaning and power. The topics which capture my interest and about which I write concern both the quirky and quintessential features of ancient life and thought which have struck modern readers as unexpected and strange, but which in reality reveal aspects of the heart and soul of biblical imagination and experience. Reconstructing the fragments of the biblical world and decoding its texts requires the nose of a detective, the eyes of a hawk, the imagination of a jigsaw puzzle-maker, and soul of a preacher—skills that make biblical interpretation for me a constant fascination and challenge."

AVOCATIONAL INTERESTS: Ancient numismatics, photography, sailing.

*   *   *

ELLIS, Roger (Melville)   1943-

PERSONAL: Born May 16, 1943, in Adelaide, Australia; son of Reginald Keith (a union official) and Yvonne Alice (a housewife; maiden name, Gumley) Ellis; married Lillian Veronica Horgan, August 23, 1969. *Education:* University of Adelaide, B.A. (with honors), 1964; Oxford University, B.Phil., 1966, D.Phil., 1974. *Religion:* Roman Catholic.

ADDRESSES: Home—52 Ninian Rd., Roath, Cardiff, South Glamorgan CF2 5EJ, Wales. *Office*—Department of English, University College, University of Wales, Cardiff, South Glamorgan CF1 1XL, Wales.

CAREER: Assistant master at secondary school in Adelaide, Australia, 1964; University of Wales, University College, Cardiff, lecturer in English, 1967-88, senior lecturer, 1988—.

MEMBER: New Chaucer Society, Early English Text Society.

WRITINGS:

Syon Abbey: The History of the English Bridgettines, Analecta Cartusiana [Salzburg], 1984.
Patterns of Religious Narrative in the "Canterbury Tales," Croom Helm, 1986.
The Liber Celestis of St. Bridget of Sweden, Volume I, Oxford University Press, 1987.
(Editor) *Acts of the Conference on the Theory and Practice of Translation in the Middle Ages*, Boydell & Brewer, 1989.
How to Study a Play, Methuen, in press.

Contributor to periodicals, including *Medium Aevum*, *Critical Quarterly*, *Notes and Queries*, and *Christian*.

WORK IN PROGRESS: The Liber Celestis of St. Bridget of Sweden, Volume II, publication by Oxford University Press expected in 1991; a novel on Australian mythological themes; contributions for a volume on "persona and voice in Chaucer," edited by David Lawton; a paper on St. Bridget of Sweden; research on medieval drama.

SIDELIGHTS: Roger Ellis told *CA:* "My critical writing has been largely but not solely concerned with religious literature, with the situation of whose writers—Greene, Hopkins, Herbert—I can readily identify. Latterly, especially when working on the *Canterbury Tales*, I have begun to appreciate how criticism is a particular kind of storytelling; consequently, I aim in my critical writing to tell a story that any reader will be able to understand. *How to Study a Play*, for example, is stylistically geared to students just beginning the serious study of literature. As for the novel in progress—which may turn out to be a collection of short stories—its heart is to be a collection of stories on the model of Ovid's *Metamorphosis*. In it I aim to take possession once more of a country in which I spent the first twenty years of my life, and to represent as much of my childhood experience as I can metaphorically. Fictional prose represents a new departure for me—hitherto, though I've not published any, I've written only poetry: I owe this new direction to a creative writing class I have taught and to the death of my mother."

*   *   *

ERICKSON, Peter (Brown)   1945-

PERSONAL: Born August 11, 1945, in Worcester, Mass.; son of Irving Peter (a public high school math teacher) and Elinor (a public high school English teacher; maiden name, Brown) Erickson; married Tay Gavin (an artist), June 30, 1968; children: Andrew Sven, Ingrid Adriana, Benjamin Peter. *Education:* Amherst College, B.A. (magna cum laude), 1967; graduate study at Center for Contemporary Cultural Studies, University of Birmingham, Birmingham, England, 1967-68; University of California at Santa Cruz, Ph.D., 1975; Simmons College, M.S.L.S., 1984.

ADDRESSES: Home—81 Buxton Hill Rd., Williamstown, Mass. 01267. *Office*—Clark Art Institute, P.O. Box 8, Williamstown, Mass. 01267.

CAREER: Williams College, Williamstown, Mass., assistant professor of English, 1976-81; Clark Art Institute, Williamstown, Mass., research librarian, 1985—. Kent fellow and visiting assistant professor at Wesleyan University, 1981-83.

MEMBER: Modern Language Association, Shakespeare Association of America, Renaissance Society of America.

WRITINGS:

Patriarchal Structures in Shakespeare's Drama, University of California Press, 1985.

(Editor with Coppelia Kahn, and contributor) *Shakespeare's "Rough Magic": Renaissance Essays in Honor of C. L. Barber*, University of Delaware Press, 1985.

(Contributor) Jean E. Howard and Marion F. O'Connor, editors, *Shakespeare Reproduced: The Text in History and Ideology*, Methuen, 1987.

(Contributor) Helen Tierney, editor, *The Study of Women: History, Religion, Literature, and the Arts*, Greenwood Press, 1988.

(Contributor) Marianne Novy, editor, *Women's (Re)Visions of Shakespeare*, University of Illinois Press, 1989.

Contributor of articles and reviews to literature journals.

WORK IN PROGRESS: "Gender and the Tragic Motif in *Venus and Adonis* and *The Rape of Lucrece*," to be included in *Shakespearean Tragedy and Gender*, edited by Shirley Nelson Garner and Madelon Sprengnether, completion expected in 1989; "The Political Effects of Gender and Class in *All's Well That Ends Well*," to be included in *Body and The Body Politic in Renaissance Drama*, edited by Carole Levin and Karen Robertson, completion expected in 1989; a book of commentary on seven of Shakespeare's works, completion expected in 1990.

SIDELIGHTS: Peter Erickson told *CA:* "Though I have published primarily as a Shakespearean, I have maintained the pattern of working in two different historical periods—in Renaissance literature and in contemporary twentieth-century literature, the latter exemplified by my essays on June Jordan, Toni Morrison, and Adrienne Rich. Because of my commitment to this second area, my investment in Shakespeare is not total; I see Shakespeare's work from outside as well as inside, and this double vision places his work in a qualified perspective. Full-strength feminist criticism of Shakespeare can be made to appear negative when is it cut off from its larger context, its contribution to the feminist revaluation of the tradition as a whole. The constructive spirit of the project of revision can emerge fully only if we reject narrow period specialization as the exclusive definition of what constitutes the professionally legitimate and instead acknowledge responsibility to the entire range of cultural heritage, including the present.

"My first book on Shakespeare was written almost entirely within the tradition of American feminist psychoanalytic criticism as it existed at the end of the 1970s. My second book is situated in a much wider theoretical frame of reference that takes into account both the changes within feminist Shakespeare criticism brought about by the entry of significant new critics such as Margaret Ferguson and Jean Howard, and the development outside of feminist criticism of the major critical currents of new historicism in the United States and cultural materialism in England. In particular I focus on the creative tensions between feminist criticism and new historicism. My goal is less to achieve an impossible, ideal synthesis or rec-

onciliation than to examine some of the conceptual elements necessary for a distinctively feminist historicism.

"A chief difference between feminist and new historicist approaches is that the critical spirit of the former is more conducive to the intellectual demands of political engagement, which the latter tends to suppress, shy away from, or leave less than fully developed. Two forms that this engagement takes in feminist criticism are canon revision and identity politics, and both involve alertness to the contemporary political implications of our scholarship. My new book will include a second part with chapters on the role of Shakespeare in the work of two twentieth-century authors, thus making possible a detailed analysis of how canon revision effects Shakespeare's status in the tradition and thereby enlarging the scope of the term historical.

"I pursue identity politics, a concept for which I am indebted to Adrienne Rich's foreword to *Blood, Bread, and Poetry* (1986), in order to extend the abstract notion of the 'critic in history' by giving it a high degree of specificity. Rather than treating contemporary critics as a unified collective body, I emphasize our differences and I consider my own situation with regard to gender, race, class, sexual orientation, and ethnic and national identity, as these multiple facets bear on literary interpretation. Placing my male gender in this larger context as one component in a whole set of specific cultural locations, I now address my role as a male feminist critic. While there are dangers in a male feminist position, I believe an even greater danger for male critics is the avoidance or abjuration of direct involvement with feminist issues. My goal is to explore the difficulties of male feminism while remaining committed to—rather than abandoning—my position as a male feminist critic."

*　　*　　*

ESTES, Eleanor   1906-1988

OBITUARY NOTICE—See index for *CA* sketch: Born May 9, 1906, in West Haven, Conn.; died of complications following a stroke, July 15, 1988, in Hamden, Conn. Librarian and author. A prolific author of books for children, Estes is best known for her earliest work, family stories based on the experiences of her own childhood. Included among her nineteen books for children are stories about the Moffat children, such as *The Moffats* and *Rufus M.*; her most popular book, *The Hundred Dresses*; her Newbery Award-winning novel *Ginger Pye*; and her last book, *The Curious Adventures of Jimmy McGee*. Estes also wrote an adult novel, *The Echoing Green*, and contributed to numerous magazines. Before pursuing a writing career full time, Estes worked as a children's librarian in New Haven, Connecticut, and in branches of the New York City Public Library system.

OBITUARIES AND OTHER SOURCES:

BOOKS

Current Biography, H. W. Wilson, 1988.
Who's Who of American Women, 15th edition, Marquis, 1986.
The Writers Directory: 1988-1990, St. James Press, 1988.

PERIODICALS

Chicago Tribune, July 20, 1988.
New York Times, July 19, 1988.
Publishers Weekly, August 26, 1988.
School Library Journal, September, 1988.

ESTES, Winston M(arvin)   1917-1982

OBITUARY NOTICE—See index for *CA* sketch: Born October 31, 1917, in Quanah, Tex.; died September 13, 1982, in Camden, South Carolina. Air force officer and author. A career officer for nearly thirty years in the U.S. Air Force, Estes was also the author of six novels and of military manuals, handbooks, and textbooks. His fiction titles are *Winston in Wonderland, Another Part of the House, A Streetful of People, A Simple Act of Kindness, Andy Jessup,* and *Homefront.*

OBITUARIES AND OTHER SOURCES:

Date of death provided by wife, Sarah S. Estes.

BOOKS

The Writers Directory: 1984-1986, St. James Press, 1983.

*   *   *

EULO, Ken   1939-

PERSONAL: Born November 17, 1939, in Newark, N.J.; son of Raymond and Therresa Eulo; married; children: Joey, Donald, Ken. *Education:* Attended University of Heidelberg, 1961-64.

ADDRESSES: Home and office—14633 Valley Vista Blvd., Sherman Oaks, Calif. 91403 *Agent*—Mitch Douglas, International Creative Management, 40 West 57th St., New York, N.Y. 10019.

CAREER: Playwright, director, and novelist. Director of Playwrights Forum and O'Neill Playwrights; artistic director of Courtyard Playhouse, New York, N.Y.; member of Actors Studio Playwriting Workshop; staff writer for Paramount, 1988—.

MEMBER: Italian Playwrights of America—The Forum, Writers Guild of America, Dramatists Guild.

AWARDS, HONORS: Prize from O'Neill Summer Conference, 1971, for "S.R.O."; grant from Howard P. Foster Memorial Fund, 1972; fellowship from Arken Industries and J. & L. Tanner, 1973-74; winner of children's theater contest sponsored by Children's Theatre of Richmond, 1974, for "Aladdin."

WRITINGS:

PLAYS

Bang? (one-act; first produced as "Bang? An Event in Boxes" in New York City at Courtyard Playhouse, March 19, 1969), published in periodical *Janus.*
"Zarf, I Love You" (two-act), first produced in New York City at Courtyard Playhouse, June 12, 1969.
"S.R.O." (two-act), first produced in Waterford, Conn., at O'Neill Theater Center, July 5, 1970.
"Puritan Night" (two-act), first produced in Hartford, Conn., March 11, 1971.
"Billy Hofer and the Quarterback Sneak" (two-act), first produced in New York City at Courtyard Playhouse, December 3, 1971.
"Black Jesus" (two-act), first produced in New York City at Lincoln Center, February 12, 1972.
"The Elevator" (one-act), first produced in New York City at Gate Theatre, March 11, 1972.
48 Spring Street (one-act; first produced in New Jersey at Ocean County College Theatre-in-the-Round, October 5, 1973), published in *Off-Off Broadway Theatre Collection,* Volume 1, Galaxie, 1977.

"Final Exams" (three-act), first produced in New York City at Courtyard Playhouse, November 17, 1975.
"The Frankenstein Affair" (three-act), first produced in New York City at Courtyard Playhouse, March 22, 1979.
"Say Hello to Daddy" (two-act), first produced in Chicago, Ill., at Pheasant Run Playhouse, June 1, 1979.

Also author of "That's the Way a Champ Should Go," 1971, "The Rise and Fall of Cris Cowlin" (three-act), and "Stationary Wave" (three-act).

NOVELS

Bloodstone, Pocket Books, 1982.
The Brownstone, Pocket Books, 1982.
The Deathstone, Pocket Books, 1982.
Nocturnal, Pocket Books, 1983.
The Ghost of Veronica Gray, Pocket Books, 1985.
The House of Caine, Tor Books, 1988.

OTHER

Script writer for television series, including "Small Wonder," "Benson," and "Marblehead Manor." Also contributor to magazines and newspapers, including *Back Stage, Janus, New York Post, New York Times, Off-Off Broadway, Show Business,* and *Village Voice.*

WORK IN PROGRESS: Two novels: *Manhattan Heat* and *Runner in the Dark.*

SIDELIGHTS: Ken Eulo told *CA:* "I believe very strongly in writing for all media and that the *story* is the most important aspect of writing. A good story with characters that people can care about is what good writing is all about."

AVOCATIONAL INTERESTS: Writing poetry.

*   *   *

EVANS, G. R.
See EVANS, Gillian (Rosemary)

*   *   *

EVANS, Gillian (Rosemary)   1944-
(G. R. Evans)

PERSONAL: Born October 26, 1944, in Birmingham, England; daughter of Arthur Raymond and Gertrude Elizabeth (Goodfellow) Evans. *Education:* St. Anne's College, Oxford, B.A., 1966, M.A., 1970, Ph.D., 1974, D.Litt., 1983, Litt.D., 1983.

ADDRESSES: Office—Fitzwilliam College, Cambridge University, Cambridge, England.

CAREER: Associated with Queen Anne's School, Caversham, Reading, Berkshire, England, 1967-72; associated with department of history at University of Reading, Reading, Berkshire, England, 1972-78; associated with department of theology at University of Bristol, Bristol, Gloucestershire, England, 1978-80; Cambridge University, Fitzwilliam College, Cambridge, England, lecturer in history, 1980—. Research reader in theology for British Academy, 1986-88.

MEMBER: Royal Historical Society (fellow).

WRITINGS:

(Under name Gillian Evans) *Chaucer,* Blackie & Son, 1977.
(Under name Gillian Evans) *The Age of the Metaphysicals,* Blackie & Son, 1978.

(With Alister E. McGrath and Allan D. Galloway) *The Science of Theology,* Eerdmans, c. 1986.

UNDER NAME G. R. EVANS

Anselm and Talking About God, Oxford University Press, 1978.
Anselm and a New Generation, Oxford University Press, 1980.
Old Arts and New Theology: The Beginnings of Theology as an Academic Discipline, Oxford University Press, 1980.
Augustine on Evil, Cambridge University Press, 1982.
Alan of Lille: The Frontiers of Theology in the Later Twelfth Century, Cambridge University Press, 1983.
(Editor with C. C. Singer) *The Church and the Sword,* 2nd edition, New Puritan Library, 1983.
The Mind of St. Bernard of Clairvaux, Oxford University Press, 1983.
A Concordance to the Works of St. Anselm, Kraus International, c. 1984.
The Language and Logic of the Bible: The Earlier Middle Ages, Cambridge University Press, 1984.
The Language and Logic of the Bible: The Road to Reformation, Cambridge University Press, 1985.
The Thought of Gregory the Great, Cambridge University Press, 1986.
(Editor with Anna S. Abulafia) Gilbert Crispin, *The Works of Gilbert Crispin,* Oxford University Press, 1986.
(Editor with Henry Chadwick) *Atlas of the Christian Church,* Facts on File, 1987.

WORK IN PROGRESS: The Keys and the Swords: The Theology of Authority in the Reformation Period.

*　　*　　*

EVANS, Harry   1896(?)-1988

OBITUARY NOTICE: Born c. 1896; died October 11, 1988, in St. Augustine, Fla. Entrepreneur and editor. In 1932 Evans founded *Family Circle* magazine, serving at the same time as its first editor. Initially offered free of charge in three chains of stores, *Family Circle*'s circulation grew within fourteen months to eighty thousand. Copies were no longer free beginning in 1946; the magazine, featuring subjects such as food, fashion, and entertainment, is now published by the New York Times Company and enjoys a circulation of nearly six million.

OBITUARIES AND OTHER SOURCES:

PERIODICALS

New York Times, October 26, 1988.

*　　*　　*

EVANS, Olwen (Elizabeth) Carey
See CAREY EVANS, Olwen (Elizabeth)

EVANS, William   1895-1988

OBITUARY NOTICE—See index for *CA* sketch: Born November 24, 1895, in Tregaron, Wales; died September 20, 1988. Physician, educator, and author. Evans, a distinguished cardiologist, won recognition for his contributions to the study of heart disease and for his success as a teacher of cardiology. During his long medical career Evans served in numerous posts, including consulting cardiologist for the London Hospital, the National Heart Hospital, the Institute of Cardiology, the Royal Navy, and the Royal Society of Musicians, and he earned many lectureships at home and abroad. Evans was the author of five books relating to cardiology, among them *Cardiography* and *Diseases of the Heart and Arteries,* and of two memoirs, *Journey to Harley Street* and *Diary of a Welsh Swagman.* He also contributed more than one hundred articles to British medical journals. His awards and honors included the 1954 Sydney Body Gold Medal and an honorary doctorate from the University of Wales in 1961.

OBITUARIES AND OTHER SOURCES:

BOOKS

Who's Who, 140th edition, St. Martin's, 1988.
The Writers Directory, 1988-1990, St. James Press, 1988.

PERIODICALS

Times (London), September 22, 1988.

*　　*　　*

EWEN, Frederic   1899-1988

OBITUARY NOTICE—See index for *CA* sketch: Born October 11, 1899, in Lemberg, Austria; immigrated to United States, 1912, naturalized citizen, 1912; died of a heart attack, October 18, 1988, in New York, N.Y. Educator and author. Ewen taught English at City College and Brooklyn College, now part of the City University of New York, for nearly thirty years. Following his retirement in 1952 he continued to lecture on literature and drama at various educational institutions. Ewen's writings include *The Prestige of Schiller in England, Bibliography of Eighteenth-Century English Literature, The Poetry and Prose of Heinrich Heine, Bertolt Brecht: His Life, His Art, and His Times,* and adaptations of literary classics for stage and television.

OBITUARIES AND OTHER SOURCES:

BOOKS

The Writers Directory, 1988-1990, St. James Press, 1988.

PERIODICALS

New York Times, October 19, 1988.

F

FAIRFIELD, James G(lencairn) T(homson) 1926-

PERSONAL: Born February 4, 1926, in Winnipeg, Manitoba, Canada; immigrated to the United States, 1963, naturalized citizen, 1971; son of Hugh Clarke and Eliza McNaught (Thomson) Fairfield; married Norma Basken, May 9, 1945; children: James, John, Deborah, Catherine. *Education:* Attended University of Manitoba, Ontario Mennonite Bible Institute, and Eastern Mennonite College; Eastern Mennonite Seminary, B.A., 1963, M.A., 1983. *Religion:* Roman Catholic, Mennonite.

ADDRESSES: Home and office—Route 2, Box 125A, Broadway, Va. 22815.

CAREER: Sales and advertising manager for a Canadian textile company from the 1950s to 1964; Mennonite Broadcasts, staff writer, 1964-70; Creative Counselors, Singers Glen, Va., public relations, marketing, and fundraising consultant, 1970—.

AWARDS, HONORS: Award of Merit from Religious Public Relations Council, 1965; Gold Award from International Film Festival of New York, 1970, for "Another Way"; Award of Merit from Levi-Strauss, Inc., 1974; Certificate of Merit from Southern Educational Communications Authority, 1976; Award of Merit from Golden Pyramid Competition, 1980.

WRITINGS:

(Editor) *Probe: Toward an Evangelism That Cares,* Herald Press, 1972.
(And producer) "The Middle East: Can There Be Peace?" (documentary film), released by Public Broadcasting System, 1974.
"If This Be Peace" (documentary film), released by the Mennonite Church, 1975.
When You Don't Agree, Herald Press, 1977.
All That We Are We Give, Herald Press, 1977.
(Author of revision) B. Charles Hostetter, *Living With No Regrets,* Choice Books, 1987.

Writer for series of six films on exemplary education in Virginia for WVPT-TV; for "Leighton Ford Presents," broadcast by Billy Graham Evangelistic Association, 1972-76; and for "CBS Mystery Theater," 1972. Author of weekly column for three daily newspapers and a syndicate of western Canadian weeklies. Contributor to periodicals, including *Mother Earth*

News. Editor of film and filmstrip series for Virginia Commonwealth University.

WORK IN PROGRESS: The Benign Groove (tentative title), a study of the impact of social environments on personal anxiety and stress, publication expected in 1989; a book of light essays on life along Joe's Creek in Frog Hollow (the author's home), publication expected in 1989.

*   *   *

FALCON, Walter P(hillip) 1936-

PERSONAL: Born September 28, 1936, in Cedar Rapids, Iowa; son of Norman and Esther (Hurwitz) Falcon; married Laura Hann, June, 1956; children: Lesley Diane, Phillip James, Andrew Robert. *Education:* Iowa State University, B.A., 1958; Harvard University, A.M., 1960, Ph.D., 1962.

ADDRESSES: Home—415 Gerona Rd., Stanford, Calif. 94305. *Office*—Food Research Institute, Stanford University, Stanford, Calif. 94305.

CAREER: Harvard University, Cambridge, Mass., instructor, 1962-63, assistant professor, 1963-66, lecturer and development adviser, 1966-72, general and agricultural economic adviser to Pakistan planning commission, 1964-65, director of research, 1966-70, and deputy director, 1970-72, of Development Advisory Service, research associate of Center for International Affairs, 1965-72; Stanford University, Stanford, Calif., professor of economics and director of Food Research Institute, 1972—, Helen C. Farnsworth Professor of International Agricultural Policy, 1976—, associate dean of humanities and sciences, 1985—.

Member of Presidential Commission on World Hunger, 1978—; member of board of trustees of Agricultural Development Council, 1979-84, International Maize and Wheat Improvement Center, 1980-87, Winrock International, 1984—, and International Rice Research Institute, 1987—; consultant to White House interior panel on Pakistan, 1962-63, U.S. Agency for International Development, 1963-67, government of Malaysia, 1967, government of Indonesia, 1968-72, U.S. Department of State, and World Bank.

MEMBER: American Economic Association, American Agricultural Economic Association, Western Agricultural Economic Association, Alpha Zeta, Cardinal Key, Omicron Chi Epsilon, Phi Eta Sigma, Phi Kappa Phi.

AWARDS, HONORS: Danforth fellowship, 1958-62, Fulbright scholar in Pakistan, 1961-62; research awards from American Agricultural Economic Association, 1971, for ''The Green Revolution: Generations of Problems,'' and 1984, for *Food Policy Analysis.*

WRITINGS:

(With Carl H. Gotsch) *Agricultural Development in Pakistan: Lessons From the Second-Plan Period,* Harvard University, Center for International Affairs, 1966.
(With Gotsch) *Agricultural Price Policy and the Development of West Pakistan,* Organization for Social and Technological Innovation, 1970.
(With Joseph J. Stern) *Growth and Development in Pakistan, 1955-1969,* Harvard University, Center for International Affairs, 1970.
(Editor with Gustav F. Papanek) *Development Policy II: The Pakistan Experience,* Harvard University Press, 1971.
(With Roger Revelle and others) *Research Issues Affecting Indus-Basin Agricultural Development Policy,* Pakistan Government Printing Office, 1978.
(With C. Peter Timmer and Scott R. Pearson) *Food Policy Analysis,* Johns Hopkins University Press, 1983.
(With William O. Jones and others) *The Cassava Economy of Java,* Stanford University Press, 1984.

CONTRIBUTOR

Irma Adelman and Erik Thorbecke, editors, *The Theory and Design of Economic Development,* Johns Hopkins Press, 1966.
Gustav F. Papanek, editor, *Development Policy: Theory and Practice,* Harvard University Press, 1968.
Lloyd G. Reynolds, editor, *Agriculture in Development Theory,* Yale University Press, 1975.
George S. Tolley, editor, *Agriculture, Trade, and Development,* Ballinger, 1975.
William F. Hueg, Jr., and Craig A. Gannon, editors, *Transforming Knowledge into Food in the Worldwide Context,* Miller Publishing Company, 1978.
Gustav F. Papanek, editor, *The Indonesia Economy,* Praeger, 1980.
Dale G. Anderson and Norman E. Tooker, editors, *Social, Cultural, Economic, and Political Dimensions of International Agricultural Development,* Lincoln, 1982.
H. O. Carter, editor, *Impact of U.S. Farm Policy and Technological Change on U.S. and California Agriculture,* California Agricultural Center, University of California, Davis, 1986.
D. J. McLaren and B. J. Skinner, editors, *Resources and World Development,* Springer-Verlag, 1986.
C. Peter Timmer, editor, *The Corn Economy of Indonesia,* Cornell University Press, 1987.

Also contributor of articles and reviews to periodicals, including *American Economic Review, American Journal of Agricultural Economics, Journal of Economic Literature, Journal of Farm Economics, Quarterly Journal of Economics, Science,* and *Stanford Magazine.*

OTHER

Associate editor of *Quarterly Journal of Economics,* 1963-72, member of editorial council of *American Journal of Agricul-*

tural Economics, 1968-72, editor of *Food Research Institute Studies,* 1977—.

SIDELIGHTS: Walter P. Falcon told *CA:* ''My interest in Asian agricultural development has its roots in my Iowa farm background. I was on the economics faculty at Harvard at the height of the development-economics era and served in Pakistan in the 1960s when that country was often referred to as a 'development miracle.' At Stanford since 1972, I have been outspoken about the need for food policy reform in developing countries, on the limitations of U.S. foreign aid, and on the urgency of building human capital in the Third World. For the last twenty years I have also been actively involved with teaching, research, and policy advice in Indonesia. In a series of published and unpublished papers, I have pressed for a broad set of economic policies that would permit Indonesian farmers to respond to economic incentives, thereby solving their own production and income problems.''

*   *   *

FEE, Elizabeth   1946-

PERSONAL: Born December 11, 1946, in Belfast, Northern Ireland; immigrated to the United States, 1968, naturalized citizen, 1978; daughter of John (a minister) and Deirdre (an artist) Fee. *Education:* Cambridge University, B.A. (with first class honors), 1968, M.A., 1975; Princeton University, M.A., 1971, Ph.D., 1978.

ADDRESSES: Home—4113 Westview Rd., Baltimore, Md. 21218. *Office*—Department of Health Policy and Management, Johns Hopkins University, 624 North Broadway, Baltimore, Md. 21205.

CAREER: State University of New York at Binghamton, instructor in history, 1972-74; Johns Hopkins University, Baltimore, Md., assistant professor, 1974-84, associate professor of health policy and management, 1984—, archivist of School of Health Services, 1974-78. Visiting assistant professor at Princeton University, 1984; Joseph S. Begando Lecturer at University of Illinois at Chicago, 1985.

MEMBER: International Association for the Political Economy of Health, International Group on Women and Health, American Public Health Association, American Association for the History of Medicine, History of Science Society, American Historical Association, Coordinating Committee on Women in the Historical Profession, Berkshire Conference on Women's History.

AWARDS, HONORS: Fulbright travel grant for England, 1968; Princeton University travel grant for France, 1971; grants from Rockefeller Archives Center, 1981 and 1984, National Science Foundation, 1981-84, New York Council for the Humanities, 1983 and 1984, and National Endowment for the Humanities, 1985-87; exchange scholar of Association for International Understanding of China, 1983; W. K. Kellogg Foundation National Fellowship, 1984-87.

WRITINGS:

(Contributor) Mary Hartman and Lois Banner, editors, *Clio's Consciousness Raised: New Perspectives on the History of Women,* Harper, 1974.
(Contributor) Michael Teitelbaum, editor, *Sex Differences: Social and Biological Perspectives,* Doubleday, 1976.
(Contributor) Claudia Dreifus, editor, *Seizing Our Bodies,* Random House, 1977.

(Contributor) Vicente Havarro, editor, *Health and Medical Care in the United States: A Critical Analysis*, Baywood, 1977.

(Editor with John Williamson and others) *Teaching Quality Assurance and Cost Containment in Health Care: A Faculty Guide*, Jossey-Bass, 1982.

(Editor) *Women and Health: The Politics of Sex in Medicine*, Baywood, 1983.

(Contributor) Marian Lowe and Ruth Hubbard, editors, *Women's Nature: Rationalizations of Inequality*, Pergamon, 1983.

(Contributor) Ruth Bleier, editor, *Feminist Approaches to Science*, Pergamon, 1986.

Disease and Discovery: A History of the Johns Hopkins School of Hygiene and Public Health, 1916-1939, Johns Hopkins University Press, 1987.

(Editor with Daniel Fox) *AIDS: The Burdens of History*, California University Press, 1988.

(Contributor) Andrew Wear, editor, *The History of Medicine in Society*, Cambridge University Press, 1988.

Life and Work in Baltimore: A Popular History, Temple University Press, in press.

Patterns of Health and Disease: A History of the Johns Hopkins School of Hygiene and Public Health, 1939-1967, Johns Hopkins University Press, in press.

(Editor with Roy M. Acheson) *A History of Public Education: Britain and the United States Contrasted*, Oxford University Press, in press.

Contributor to *Great Events From History*, Salem Press, 1982, and *Health Care Financing: The Next Fifty Years*, Rockefeller University Press, 1986. Contributor of articles and reviews to scholarly journals. Associate editor of *Feminist Studies*, 1977-81; editor of newsletter of International Association for the Political Economy of Health, 1979-80.

WORK IN PROGRESS: Politics and Health: A Social History of Public Health in Baltimore, 1910-1960.

*   *   *

FEINBERG, Beatrice Cynthia Freeman   1915(?)-1988
(Cynthia Freeman)

OBITUARY NOTICE—See index for *CA* sketch: Born c. 1915 in New York, N.Y.; died of cancer, October 22, 1988, in San Francisco, Calif. Interior decorator and author. Feinberg, who launched her writing career after she turned fifty, was the author of nine best-selling romance novels published under the name Cynthia Freeman. Titles include her first novel, *A World Full of Strangers*—the story of four generations in the life of an American Jewish family—*Fairytales*, *The Days of Winter*, *Come Pour the Wine*, *Seasons of the Heart*, and *The Last Princess*, her last book. Prior to her writing successes, Feinberg raised a family and worked many years as an interior decorator. Her books have been translated into thirty-three languages and have sold more than twenty million copies.

OBITUARIES AND OTHER SOURCES:

BOOKS

The Writers Directory: 1988-1990, St. James Press, 1988.

PERIODICALS

Chicago Tribune, October 27, 1988.
Los Angeles Times, October 27, 1988.
New York Times, October 26, 1988.

FERDINAND, Vallery III
See SALAAM, Kalamu ya

*   *   *

FERRARI, Enzo   1898-1988

OBITUARY NOTICE: Born February 18 (some sources say February 20), 1898, in Modena, Italy; died of a kidney ailment, August 14, 1988, in Modena, Italy; buried in San Cataldo, Italy. Automotive designer, engineer, and manufacturer, racing car driver and team manager, and author. Ferrari was known for the fast, fiery red sports cars he designed and built at his factory and racing headquarters in Maranello, Italy, for more than forty years. Beginning his career as a driver with the prestigious Italian Alfa Romeo racing team in 1920, he won thirteen of forty-seven races before he retired from the racing circuit in the early 1930s, remaining affiliated with Alfa Romeo as an engineer and administrator until 1939. The first Ferrari automobile was produced by his own company in 1946. Since then, Ferrari drivers have won more than four thousand victories and thirteen world titles, nine of them in the Formula One category. Ferrari's team racing successes, however, were marred on several occasions by serious accidents. One of these, which involved the deaths of a Spanish driver and several spectators, led to Ferrari's indictment for manslaughter in 1958. Although he was acquitted, the Italian press dubbed Ferrari a "Saturn," after the Greek god who devoured his children. Ferrari's 1962 autobiography, *Le Mie gioie terribili*, was later translated and published in the United States as *The Enzo Ferrari Story*.

OBITUARIES AND OTHER SOURCES:

BOOKS

Current Biography, H. W. Wilson, 1967, September, 1988.
Ferrari, Enzo, *Le Mie gioie terribili* (title means "My Terrible Joys"), Cappelli, 1962, translation by Ivan Scott published as *My Terrible Joys: The Enzo Ferrari Memoirs*, edited by Richard Hough, foreword by Stirling Moss, Hamish Hamilton, 1963, published as *The Enzo Ferrari Story*, Macmillan, 1964.

PERIODICALS

Chicago Tribune, August 16, 1988.
Los Angeles Times, August 16, 1988.
New York Times, August 16, 1988.
Times (London), August 16, 1988.
Washington Post, August 16, 1988.

*   *   *

FERRERI, Marco   1928-

PERSONAL: Born May 11, 1928, in Milan, Italy; married wife, Jacqueline. *Education:* Studied veterinary medicine in mid-1940s.

ADDRESSES: Home—Piazza Mattei 10, Rome, Italy.

CAREER: Screenwriter and director of motion pictures. Worked as liquor salesperson and advertising agent in late 1940s; founder and promoter of filmed periodical "Documento Mensile," 1950-51; actor and production assistant in Italian film industry in early 1950s; optical instruments salesperson in Spain in 1954.

AWARDS, HONORS: International Film Critics Award from Venice Film Festival, 1960, for "El cochecito"; International Critics Award from Cannes Film Festival, 1973, for "La Grande Bouffe."

WRITINGS:

SCREENPLAYS; AND DIRECTOR

(With Rafael Azcona; co-director, with Isidoro M. Ferry) "El pisito" (adapted from Azcona's short story), Documento Film, 1958.

(With Leonard Martin) "Los chicos," Epoca Films, 1959.

(With Azcona) "El cochecito" (title means "The Wheelchair"; adapted from Azcona's novel), Pedro Portabella, 1960.

"L'infidelita coniugale" (adapted from Gabriella Parca's book *Le Italian si confessano*), in collection "Le Italiane e l'amore," Magic Film, 1961.

(With Azcona, Pasquale Festa Campanile, Massimo Franciosa, and Diego Fabbri) "Una storia moderna: L'ape regina" (title means "A Modern Story: The Queen Bee"), Sancro Film/Fair Film/Marceau-Cocinor, 1963, released in the United States as "The Conjugal Bed," Embassy Pictures, 1963.

(With Azcona) "La donna scimmia," Compagnia Cinematografica Champion/Marceau-Cocinor, 1963, released in the United States as "The Ape Woman," Embassy Pictures, 1964.

(With Azcona) "Il professore" in collection "Controsesso," Carlo Ponti/C. C. Champion/Les Films Concordia, 1964.

(With Azcona) "L'uomo dei cinque palloni" in collection "Oggi, domani e dopodomani," Carlo Ponti/Compagnia Cinematografica Champion/Les Films Concordia, 1965; longer version released in the United States as "The Man With the Balloons," Carlo Ponti, 1968; revised version released as "Break-up," 1968.

(With Azcona and Diego Fabbri) "Marcia Nunziale" (short films; title means "Wedding March"; contains "Prima nozze," "Il dovere coniugale," "L'igiene coniugale," and "La famiglia felice"), Sancro Film/Transinter Film, 1966.

(With Azcona and Ugo Moretti) "L'harem," Alfonso Sansone/Enrico Chroschinski/Sancro Film, 1967.

(With Sergio Bazzini) "Dillinger e morto," Pegaso Film, 1969, released in England as "Dillinger Is Dead."

(With Bazzini) "Il seme dell'uomo" (title means "The Seed of Man"), Polifilm, 1969.

(With Azcona and Dante Matelli) "L'udienza," Franco Cristaldi/Vides Cinematografica, 1971.

(With Jean-Claude Carriere) "Liza" (adapted from Ennio Flaiano's story "Melampo"), Lira Film/Pegaso Film, 1972 (also released abroad as "La Cagna").

(With Azcona) "La Grande Bouffe" (title means "The Big Feast"), Mara Film/Les Films 66/Capitolina, 1973, released in the United States by ABKCO Films, 1973 (also released abroad as "Blow-out").

(With Azcona) "Touchez pas la Femme blanche," Mara Film/Les Films 66/PEA, 1974.

"L'ultima donna," Productions Jacques Roltfeld/Flaminia Produzioni, 1976, released in the United States as "The Last Woman," Columbia, 1976.

(Co-author) "Bye Bye Monkey," Fida, 1978.

"Chiedo asilo" (title means "My Asylum"), Gaumont, 1979.

(With Sergio Amidei and Anthony Foutz) "Tales of Ordinary Madness" (adapted from Charles Bukowski's short stories), Fred Baker Films, 1983.

(With Piera Degli Esposti and Dacia Maraini) "Storia di Piera," Faso Film/ S. R. L. T. Film/Sara Films/Ascot Film, 1983, released in the United States as "The Story of Piera," 1983.

(With Esposti and Maraini) "Il futuro e donna" (title means "The Future Is Woman"), Fasco Film/UGC/Ascot Film, 1984.

(With Didier Kaminka and Enrico Oldoini) "I Love You," 23 Giugno/A. F. C./U. G. C./Films A2/Top 1, 1988.

OTHER

Also co-author of screenplays for films "Donne e soldati," 1954, and "Mafioso," 1962; author of screenplay for film "El secreto de los hombres azules," 1960, and for television documentary "Perche pagare per essere felici!," 1970.

SIDELIGHTS: Marco Ferreri is a provocative figure in international cinema. In the United States, where only a few of his films have received substantial recognition, he is known for his frequently grotesque comedies, particularly "La Grand Bouffe," in which four men gorge themselves to death, and "The Last Woman," in which the protagonist gruesomely mutilates himself. In addition to these works, Ferreri has written and directed many others that are equally idiosyncratic in exploring the peculiarities of modern life. Among these lesser-known films are "The Conjugal Bed," a comedy about a husband's vain efforts to please his sexually insatiable bride, and "The Ape Woman," an alternately amusing and wrenching account of an unusually hairy woman. Still other works, many not yet shown widely in the United States, confirm Ferreri's status as an artist devoted to the unusual and the unsettling. As Vincent Canby noted in the *New York Times:* "The films of Marco Ferreri have a kind of aggressively grotesque intensity about them. . . . He delights in making audiences uncomfortable, which, given the nature of his subjects, isn't very difficult to do."

Ferreri entered the Italian film industry in the early 1950s as a production assistant for director Alberto Lattuada. Earlier, Ferreri had abandoned studies in veterinary medicine and worked in sales and advertising. In 1950, however, he developed "Documento Mensile," a magazine-style film—somewhat similar to newsreels—to be shown regularly in Italian cinemas. "Documento Mensile" featured contributions from Italy's leading filmmakers, including Michelangelo Antonioni, Luchino Visconti, and Vittorio De Sica, but it ended after only two editions, whereupon Ferreri secured a job in production. He obtained his first important screen credits in 1954 as co-writer of "Donne e soldati," in which he also acted. Unfortunately for Ferreri, the filming of "Donne e soldati" was consistently disrupted by personal and professional differences among various personnel. These conflicts, together with previous troubles on Lattuada's films, prompted Ferreri to leave the Italian film industry in 1954 and move to Spain, where he obtained work selling optical equipment.

In Spain, Ferreri soon befriended writer Rafael Azcona, and that friendship resulted in a partnership that, in turn, led to Ferreri's return to motion pictures. He first collaborated with Azcona on the 1958 film "El pisito," an adaptation of Azcona's tale about a young man who connives to inherit an old woman's fortune through marriage. "El pisito" marked Ferreri's debut as a director, though he shared responsibilities with Isidoro M. Ferry. The following year, Ferreri and Azcona completed a second collaboration, "Los chicos," about which there is little information, except that Azcona was denied screen credit by Spanish censors who considered him a corrupting influence. Instead, Ferreri was listed as co-writer with Leonardo Martin. In addition, Ferreri was sole director.

Despite interference from Spanish authorities, Ferreri and Azcona continued their partnership, and in 1960 they made "El cochecito," an adaptation of Azcona's novel about a deranged fellow who kills his relatives to obtain the family wheelchair. Strongly reminiscent of Luis Bunuel's surreal films, "El cochecito" proved a provocative blend of pessimism and understated humor, and it scored a surprising triumph at the 1960 Venice Film Festival, where it received the International Film Critics Award.

On the strength of his success in Venice, Ferreri resumed working in the Italian film industry. His first work there was "L'infedelta coniugale," an exploration on adultery in Italy's middle class. This short work, which Ferreri directed from his own adaptation of Gabriella Parca's book *Le Italiane si confessano,* was included in the 1961 collection "Le Italiane e l'amore."

Ferreri continued to explore aspects of sexuality with "The Conjugal Bed," which concerns a middle-aged husband's futile attempts to fulfill his young bride's voracious sexual appetite. The husband believes that he has accomplished an impressive feat in marrying an attractive younger woman, and he is initially delighted by her lusty compliance. Soon enough, however, he is exhausted and confused by her increasing determination to conceive a child. Her continuous and unreasonable demands eventually result in his death. "The Conjugal Bed," which Ferreri wrote with Azcona and others, became his first film released in the United States. The *New York Times*'s Bosley Crowther, in his 1963 review, called "The Conjugal Bed" a "completely candid job" and declared, "So much conjugal clattering about a boudoir has seldom been seen on the screen." Accordingly, he described Ferreri as "a close and amused observer of the Italian middle class."

With co-writer Azcona, Ferreri next completed "The Ape Woman," a quirky work of both humor and pathos. This work's title character is afflicted with a grotesquely hairy appearance. While working in a convent kitchen, she is discovered by a schemer who coerces her into publicly exhibiting herself, thus bringing her humiliation and abuse. The opportunist soon falls victim to his own devices, however, and is compelled by circumstance to marry the ape woman or risk losing her. Consistent with the film's offbeat perspective, the ending is a happy one, with the ape woman giving birth and consequently losing her hair. Crowther mocked this conclusion as "a hair-breadth escape" and condemned the entire film as "distasteful." He also rejected the work's humor as "more painful than amusing" and questioned Ferreri's artistic motivation. "Goodness knows why anybody could think he could make a humorous film out of a story of a poor young woman whose face and body are covered with hair," Crowther wrote. "Such a hideous physical affliction would hardly seem a matter for jokes, even among the fellows around the barbershop."

Following the release of "The Ape Woman," Ferreri wrote, with Azcona, and directed several shorter films featured in various Italian collections. Among these short works are "Il professore," which concerns a teacher whose impeccable reputation masks his phobias and perversions, and "La famiglia felice," in which a perfect couple of the future consists of a human being and a plastic doll. Like much of Ferreri's canon, these works have been either ignored or accorded only rare screenings in the United States.

But Ferreri's films have not always received proper distribution in Italy, either. His "L'uomo dei cinque palloni" showed there only after producer Carlo Ponti—ignoring Ferreri's protests—reduced it for inclusion in the collection "Oggi, domanti, dopodomanio." In the United States, however, Ferreri's restored version was released in 1968 as "The Man With the Balloons." This film depicts a fetishist candy manufacturer who grows increasingly obsessed with determining the volume capacity of balloons. To the dismay of his lover and friends, he relentlessly inflates balloons until, exhausted and mad, he kills himself. *New York Times* reviewer Renata Adler was unimpressed with the film, complaining that Ferreri "seems to have noticed one day that there is something very metaphorical-looking about a balloon . . . and gone on from this insight to make a film with no very clear idea beyond that." Adler also dismissed sequences parodying other films—such as Federico Fellini's "La dolce vita" and Michelangelo Antonioni's "Red Desert"—and seemed nonplussed by Ferreri's use of balloons to represent "youth, suspense, pregnancy, hope, potency, ambition, breasts, dreams, the Bomb, etc." She called "The Man With the Balloons" "a dreary, fizzled waste" of its actors.

From 1967 to 1972 Ferreri co-wrote and directed five films receiving only scant attention in American publications. Among these obscure works are "L'harem," a characteristically peculiar comedy in which a woman indulges herself with several lovers; "Il seme dell' uomo," a cynical account about two survivors of a nuclear holocaust; and "L'udienza," a Franz Kafka-like story of one man's futile efforts to convey information to the Pope. Better known, at least among some film scholars, is "Dillinger Is Dead," a study in alienation and despair. In this work, a bored man roams about his home, examining rooms and compartments before blandly shooting his sleeping wife. With its overwhelming monotony and dull domesticity, "Dillinger Is Dead" is considered an atypical work in Ferreri's canon. In addition, the film's studied pacing and extreme use of colors and dense imagery marked a stylistic deviation for Ferreri, who shared with Bunuel a disdain for obtrusive technical flourishes. The form of "Dillinger Is Dead," though, is hardly mere stylization. Instead, aspects such as pacing and framing serve a narrative purpose by emphasizing both the monotony and materialism plaguing the protagonist. As Dan Yakir noted in a 1983 *Film Comment,* "communication was smothered in stunning imagery" in "Dillinger Is Dead."

In 1973 Ferreri enjoyed his greatest recognition, if not acclaim, when he teamed again with co-writer Azcona for "La Grande Bouffe," a grotesque farce about four friends who gorge themselves until they die. This work, full of the sights and sounds of disgusting bodily functions, is considered an unforgettable depiction of bourgeois indulgence: The characters are so single-minded in their desire to eat that they eventually wallow in their own vomit and excrement.

Shown at the 1973 Cannes Film Festival, "La Grande Bouffe" provoked a wide range of responses. A few particularly disgusted Italians, hoping to avoid any association with Ferreri, claimed that his film—a French production—had been made by a Frenchman. Others hailed the work as a compelling metaphor for the wasteful ways of the bourgeoisie, and still others simply revelled in the work's vulgarity. The Cannes judges were especially impressed, according "La Grande Bouffe" the festival's International Critic's Award. Soon afterwards, the film was released in the United States, where it drew a range of reactions. *Nation*'s Robert Hatch deemed it both repulsive and juvenile, declaring that "anyone who could find this . . . comic would have been well entertained by an 18th-century sightseeing trip to a madhouse." Less negative was the *New York Times*'s Vincent Canby, who agreed that "La Grande Bouffe" is "not a successful film" but added that it nonetheless serves as "vulgar vaudeville on an epic scale" and that it is "sometimes very funny." Another *New York Times* writer, Foster Hirsch, expressed even greater enthusiasm, judging "La Grande Bouffe" as accomplished pornography and hailing it as "a porn epic in the grand manner, a mordant, chilling, hilarious dirty movie."

In 1976 Ferreri wrote and directed another grotesque comedy, "The Last Woman," which also shocked and disgusted some viewers. The film's protagonist is Gerard, a chauvinist engineer preoccupied with his job and his responsibilities as sole parent to his young son. Ever busy, Gerard only finds time for superficial sexual encounters with various women. One evening, however, Gerard encounters Valerie, a goodhearted and compassionate woman with whom he begins a more serious affair. Soon Gerard and Valerie become roommates, but as their relationship develops, so too does Gerard's uncertainty about his own manhood. When Valerie points out his ineffective lovemaking and his unaffectionate method of parenting, Gerard grows angry and confused. His insecurities intensify, and in a moment of desperation he emasculates himself with an electric carving knife. Canby, in his review for the *New York Times*, described "The Last Woman" as "an initially buoyant and erotic comedy that becomes . . . a satire of such literal brutality that most people may want to be warned." In addition, Canby declared that Ferreri "may be the most passionately wicked satirist since Jonathan Swift. His satire is an electric carving knife that cuts two ways at once."

Among Ferreri's next few films were "Bye Bye Monkey" and "Tales of Ordinary Madness," both in English. "Bye Bye Monkey" is a fairly obscure work about impending doom in rat-infested New York City. Better known is "Tales of Ordinary Madness," Ferreri's adaptation of various tales by Charles Bukowski. In this work Ferreri focuses on the day-to-day adventures of Charles Serking, an alcoholic poet (like Bukowski) who roams the seedier streets and bars of Los Angeles. Among Serking's more peculiar escapades are sexual encounters with an aggressively affectionate fat woman and her deranged neighbor, a bondage enthusiast who has Serking arrested for rape. Most of the film, though, centers on Serking's love for Cass, a beautiful, suicidal prostitute with whom he briefly shares living quarters. Weeks after Cass departs, Serkin learns from a bartender that she had recently killed herself. The film ends with the ever inebriated Serkin wandering along a beach in Venice, California.

"Tales of Ordinary Madness" generally fared poorly with American reviewers, who found it undermined by pretension and frequently awkward dialogue. Kevin Thomas, writing in the *Los Angeles Times*, described the film as "more often artifice than life" and added that "it's a great bad movie—but with the emphasis on bad." Janet Maslin was similarly harsh in the *New York Times*, where she wrote that "Tales of Ordinary Madness" is "strained, absurdly solemn, and full of inadvertent howlers." She also declared that Ferreri "invests this tale with such undue gravity that even its bawdiness becomes lifeless."

Upon completing "Tales of Ordinary Madness" Ferreri returned to Italy, where he has since co-written and directed three more films, including "The Story of Piera." This film concentrates on the intense, often sordid bond between a daughter and each of her parents. Here Ferreri depicts a family in which daughter and father kiss passionately and daughter and mother recline in what *New York Times* critic Vincent Canby described as "quasi-sexual positions." Canby appraised the entire film as a relatively slight work within Ferreri's canon. "'The Story of Piera,'" he wrote, "is a lunatic cartoon that isn't especially serious, at least in any consistent way."

Although "The Story of Piera" offers a provocative perspective on family life, Ferreri insisted—in 1983, the year of the film's release—that he no longer aspires to controversy. Interviewed by Dan Yakir in *Film Comment*, Ferreri conceded: "I used to make films to change society. . . . The explosions, the exaggerations, the black humor were meant to shock avant-garde audiences. But the young generation that now sees my films has already exploded." Ferreri added that he now strives for greater communication with filmgoers, and that since returning to Europe he has tried to reach a larger European audience. He told Yakir, "I make films to unify, bring people together, by using images that are common to all of Europe's new generation." Ferreri's most recent films, "Il futuro e donna" and "I Love You," still await American distribution.

BIOGRAPHICAL/CRITICAL SOURCES:

BOOKS

Bondanella, Peter, *Italian Cinema: From Neorealism to the Present*, Ungar, 1983.

PERIODICALS

Cinema Papers, July-August, 1975, September-October, 1976.
Film Comment, March, 1982, December, 1983.
Film Quarterly, winter, 1974-75.
Films and Filming, April, 1963, December, 1976, September, 1982.
Los Angeles Times, March 17, 1983.
Monthly Film Bulletin, April, 1983.
Nation, October 15, 1973.
New Republic, June 19, 1976.
Newsweek, March 21, 1983.
New York, June 21, 1976, March 21, 1983.
New Yorker, June 21, 1976, March 21, 1983.
New York Times, September 17, 1963, July 1, 1964, September 23, 1964, June 25, 1968, September 20, 1973, October 14, 1973, June 7, 1976, February 25, 1983, March 11, 1983, September 24, 1983.
Variety, September 5, 1984.
Village Voice, March 15, 1983.*

—*Sketch by Les Stone*

*　　*　　*

FERRO, Robert (Michael)　1941-1988

OBITUARY NOTICE—See index for *CA* sketch: Born October 21, 1941, in Cranford, N.J.; died of acquired immune deficiency syndrome (AIDS), July 11, 1988, in Ho-Ho-Kus, N.J. Educator and author. Ferro, a former teacher at Adelphi University, was the author or co-author of five books: *Atlantis: The Autobiography of a Search*, *The Others*, *The Family of Max Desir*, *The Blue Star*, and *Second Son*, his semi-autobiographical 1988 novel chronicling the love affair between two men suffering from AIDS.

OBITUARIES AND OTHER SOURCES:

BOOKS

The Writers Directory, 1988-1990, St. James Press, 1988.

PERIODICALS

Chicago Tribune, July 13, 1988.
New York Times, July 12, 1988.

*   *   *

FESSIER, Michael   1905(?)-1988

OBITUARY NOTICE: Born November 6, 1905 (one source says 1907), in Angel's Camp, Calif.; died September 20 (one source says September 19), 1988, in Northridge, Calif. Editor, short story writer, novelist, and screenwriter. Fessier was most noted for his collaborations with Ernest Pagano on the Columbia films "You Were Never Lovelier" and "You'll Never Get Rich," both starring Fred Astaire and Rita Hayworth. Fessier was also employed by Universal and Metro-Goldwyn-Mayer; his other movie credits include "Frontier Gal," "San Diego I Love You," and "It All Came True," starring Humphrey Bogart. In addition, he wrote scripts for the television shows "Bonanza," "Alfred Hitchcock Presents," and "The Thin Man." A former editor of the *San Rafael Independent Journal,* Fessier was also the author of the humorous novels *Fully Dressed and in His Right Mind* and *Clovis,* and of short stories for magazines. "That's What Happened to Me," his most acclaimed tale, was published in seventy anthologies.

OBITUARIES AND OTHER SOURCES:

BOOKS

American Authors and Books: 1640 to the Present Day, 3rd revised edition, Crown, 1972.
Science Fiction and Fantasy Literature, Volume 1: *Indexes to the Literature,* Gale, 1979.

PERIODICALS

Los Angeles Times, September 23, 1988.
New York Times, September 26, 1988.
Washington Post, September 27, 1988.

*   *   *

ffolkes
See DAVIS, Brian

*   *   *

FFOLKES, Michael
See DAVIS, Brian

*   *   *

FIDLER, James M.   1900-1988
(Jimmie Fidler)

OBITUARY NOTICE: Professionally known as Jimmie Fidler; born in 1900; died August 9, 1988, in Los Angeles, Calif. Public relations worker, radio personality, and columnist. At the peak of his popularity in 1950, Fidler's weekly program, "Jimmie Fidler in Hollywood," aired on 486 radio stations and his syndicated gossip column appeared in 360 newspapers across the country. After dropping out of high school, Fidler worked briefly as an extra, then as a film news editor, and

later as a public relations worker for Famous Players-Lasky (now Paramount), assigned to director Cecil B. DeMille's films. He attracted widespread notice (and larger profits for DeMille's movies) when he announced to national newspapers that the famous director had loaded a ship with rifles and planned to go cannibal hunting in Mexico. Fidler wrote his first gossip column in 1920 for the *Hollywood News;* he later claimed to be the first of such Hollywood writers. Having recruited a network of studio employee spies who supplied him with stories about the Hollywood elite, Fidler circulated timely entertainment gossip nationally, along with sharp commentary in the form of "open letters" to the movie stars and movie reviews conducted using a four-bell rating system. Although he prided himself on being the most disliked broadcaster in the business, he was popular with audiences and was reputed to have conducted the first radio interview with a movie star, to have written the first column to be syndicated, and to have obtained the only interview with reclusive actress Greta Garbo. He retired from radio broadcasting in 1983.

OBITUARIES AND OTHER SOURCES:

BOOKS

Who's Who in Hollywood, 1900-1976, Arlington House, 1976.

PERIODICALS

Chicago Tribune, August 11, 1988.
Collier's, May 29, 1948.
New York Times, August 12, 1988.
Washington Post, August 12, 1988.

*   *   *

FIDLER, Jimmie
See FIDLER, James M.

*   *   *

FILTZER, Donald   1948-

PERSONAL: Born January 8, 1948, in Baltimore, Md.; son of David L. (an orthopedic surgeon) and Frances (Sacks) Filtzer. *Education:* Wesleyan University, Middletown, Conn., B.A. (cum laude), 1969; University of Glasgow, Ph.D., 1976. *Politics:* Marxist.

ADDRESSES: Office—Center for Russian and East European Studies, University of Birmingham, P.O. Box 363, Birmingham, West Midlands B15 2TT, England.

CAREER: University of Birmingham, Birmingham, England, research fellow of Centre for Russian and East European studies, 1978—.

WRITINGS:

(Editor and author of introduction) E. A. Preobrazhensky, *The Crisis of Soviet Industrialization,* M. E. Sharpe, 1979.
(Editor and translator) I. I. Rubin, *A History of Economic Thought,* Ink Links, 1979.
Soviet Workers and Stalinist Industrialization: The Formation of Modern Soviet Production Relations, 1928-41, Pluto Press, 1986.

WORK IN PROGRESS: Research on the position of the Soviet work force during the Khrushchev period and the impact of "de-Stalinization" on Soviet production relations.

SIDELIGHTS: In the *Times Literary Supplement,* reviewer Geoffrey Hosking hailed *Soviet Workers and Stalinist Indus-*

trialization as "one of the most important contributions of recent years to Soviet social history." Author Donald Filtzer asserted that, in the 1930s, Soviet workers assumed enough control over production to undermine every authoritarian attempt to govern them. The production demands of the young Soviet regime required an enormous work force, and this in itself forced planners to make concessions to the working class. Laziness, theft, and slipshod work habits had to be tolerated. Incentive programs to reward good workers were resented by other members of the work force. Treatment of work infringements as criminal offenses only encouraged middle-level management to cover up for fellow workers. Filtzer concluded that the stalemate created by Soviet workers more than fifty years ago has not abated. It contributes to the Soviet Union's present reputation for waste and corruption in the workplace, poor quality of production, and an ongoing shortage of manual laborers. Hosking told his readers that Filtzer's "account of how the situation has arisen is vivid and instructive." He concluded: "This is a book which should be pondered by anyone who wants to understand the state of the Soviet Union today. '

BIOGRAPHICAL/CRITICAL SOURCES:

PERIODICALS

Times Literary Supplement, May 27, 1987.

*   *   *

FISHBEIN, Harold D(ennis)   1938-

PERSONAL: Born May 13, 1938, in Milwaukee, Wis.; married, 1962; children: two. *Education:* University of Illinois at Urbana-Champaign, B.A., 1959; University of Pennsylvania, M.A., 1961, Ph.D., 1963.

ADDRESSES: Office—Department of Psychology, McMicken College of Arts and Sciences, University of Cincinnati, Cincinnati, Ohio 45221.

CAREER: Indiana University—Bloomington, research fellow in psychology, 1963-64; University of Cincinnati, Cincinnati, Ohio, assistant professor, 1964-68, associate professor of psychology, 1968—, associate dean of McMicken College of Arts and Sciences, 1971—. Member of staff at Laboratory of Human Development, Harvard University, 1970-71; consultant to Veterans Administration.

MEMBER: American Psychological Association, Psychonomic Society.

AWARDS, HONORS: Grants from National Institutes of Health, 1965-66 and 1970-71, National Science Foundation, 1966-68, and U.S. Office of Education, 1972-73.

WRITINGS:

Evolution, Development, and Children's Learning, Goodyear Publishing, 1976.
The Psychology of Infancy and Childhood: Evolutionary and Cross-Cultural Perspectives, Lawrence Erlbaum, 1984.

Author of text for sound recordings on auditory perception.*

*   *   *

FISHER, James (Maxwell McConnell)   1912-1970

PERSONAL: Born September 3, 1912, in Clifton, Bristol, England; died from injuries sustained in an automobile accident, September 25 (some sources say 29), 1970, in London, England; son of Kenneth (a headmaster) and Constance Isabel

(Boyd) Fisher; married Margery Lilian Edith Turner (a novelist and historian), September 16, 1936; children: Edmund Boyd, Crispin James, Selina Toussaint (Mrs. Randal Charlton), Adam J. Kenneth, Anstice Rosina, Clemency Thorne. *Education:* Graduated from Eton College, 1931; Magdalen College, Oxford, M.A. (second class honors), 1935.

ADDRESSES: Home—1 Ashton Manor, Northampton NN7 2JL, England.

CAREER: Assistant master at Bishop's Stortford College, 1935-36; Zoological Society of London, London, England, assistant curator, 1936-39; affiliated with Bureau of Animal Population, Oxford University, Oxford, England, 1940-43; affiliated with Edward Grey Institute of Field Ornithology, Oxford, 1944-46; natural history editor at William Collins Sons & Co., 1946-56; director and chief editor at Rathbone Books Ltd., 1956-64; director and chief editor at Aldus Books Ltd., 1962-64. Broadcaster with the British Broadcasting Corporation, 1933-70; nature writer, 1939-70. Chairman of Northamptonshire Naturalists Trust; deputy chairman of Natural Parks Commission (now Countryside Commission), 1968-70.

MEMBER: International Union for Conservation of Nature and Natural Resources (member Survival Service Commission), British Ornithologists' Union (council member), British Trust for Ornithology (founder; honorary secretary, 1938-44; past treasurer; past vice-chairman), British Ornithologists' Club, Royal Society for the Protection of Birds (council member), Royal Geographical Society, American Ornithologists' Union (corresponding fellow), National Audubon Society, Canadian Audubon Society, Danish Ornithological Society (honorary member), Northeastern Bird Banding Association, Wildfowl Trust (council member), Geological Society, Zoological Society, Arctic Club (now Explorers Club; past president), Cooper Ornithological Society, Wilson Ornithological Society, Linnean Society of London (council member).

AWARDS, HONORS: Gold medal from Royal Society for the Protection of Birds, 1961; Bernard Tucker medal from British Trust for Ornithology, 1966; Arthur A. Allen award from Cornell University, 1968; silver medal from Zoological Society of London, 1969; Union medal from British Ornithologist's Union.

WRITINGS:

Birds as Animals, Heinemann, 1939, completely revised and rewritten edition, Hutchinson University Library, 1954.
(Editor with Julian Huxley) Charles Darwin, *The Living Thoughts of Darwin,* Longmans, Green, 1939.
(With Margaret Shaw) *Animals as Friends and How to Keep Them,* foreword by Huxley, Dent, 1939, revised edition, 1952.
Watching Birds, Penguin, 1940, revised edition, Collins, 1953, revised by Jim Flegg with illustrations by Fisher's son, Crispin Fisher, Poyser, 1974.
(Editor and author of preface and notes) Gilbert White, *The Natural History of Selborne,* Penguin, 1941.
The Birds of Britain (picture book), Collins, 1942.
Birds of the Village (picture book), illustrations by P. F. Millard, Penguin, 1944.
Bird Recognition, illustrations by David K. Wolfe Murray and map compilation by W. B. Alexander, Penguin, 1947, new and revised edition, three volumes, 1951-55.
The Fulmar, illustrations by Peter Scott, Collins, 1952, reprinted, 1984.

(With Sacheverell Sitwell and Handasyde Buchanan) *Fine Bird Books: 1700-1900* (bibliography), Van Nostrand, 1953.

(With Scott) *A Thousand Geese,* Collins, 1953, Houghton, 1954.

A History of Birds, Houghton, 1954.

(With R. M. Lockley) *Sea-birds: An Introduction to the Natural History of the Sea-birds of the North Atlantic,* Houghton, 1954.

(With Roger Tory Peterson) *Wild America: The Record of a Thirty-Thousand-Mile Journey Around the Continent by a Distinguished Naturalist and His British Colleague,* illustrations by Peterson, Houghton, 1955 (published in England as *Wild America: The Record of a Thirty-Thousand-Mile Journey Around the North American Continent by an American Naturalist and His British Colleague,* Collins, 1956).

Rockall, Bles, 1956.

(With wife, Margery Fisher) *Shackleton,* illustrations by W. E. How, Barrie & Rockliff, 1957, published as *Shackleton and the Antarctic,* Houghton, 1958.

(Editor with Huxley, Gerald Barry, and J. Bronowski) *Nature: Earth, Plants, Animals,* illustrations by Hans Erni, Doubleday, 1960, published as *The Doubleday Pictorial Library of Nature: Earth, Plants, Animals,* 1961.

(With Peterson) *The World of Birds,* illustrations by Peterson, Doubleday, 1964 (published in England as *The World of Birds: A Comprehensive Guide to General Ornithology,* Macmillan, 1964), new and revised edition, Crescent Books, 1971 (published in England as *Birds: An Introduction to General Ornithology,* Aldus, 1971), new and revised edition published as *James Fisher and Roger Tory Peterson's World of Birds,* c. 1977.

(With Geoffrey Grigson) *The Shell Nature Book: Containing Flowers of the Countryside, Trees and Shrubs, Birds and Beasts, Fossils, Insects and Reptiles, Wild Life,* Phoenix House, 1964.

The Shell Bird Book, Ebury Press, 1966.

Shell Nature Lovers' Atlas of England, Scotland, and Wales, illustrations by John R. Flower, Ebury Press, 1966.

Zoos of the World, edited by M. H. Chandler and Vernon Reynolds, Aldus, 1966, published as *Zoos of the World: The Story of Animals in Captivity,* Natural History Press, 1967.

(Editor and author of introduction and new text) Archibald Thorburn, *Thorburn's Birds,* Ebury Press, 1967, revised by John Parslow, Overlook Press, 1976, revised edition, Mermaid Books, 1982.

(With Noel Simon, Jack Vincent, and members and correspondents of the Survival Service Commission of the International Union for Conservation of Nature and Natural Resources) *Wildlife in Danger,* foreword by Harold J. Coolidge and Scott, preface by Joseph Wood Krutch, Viking, 1969 (published in England as *The Red Book: Wildlife in Danger,* Collins, 1969).

(With L. Dudley Stamp) *Nature Conservation in Britain,* Collins, 1969.

(With Philip, Duke of Edinburgh) *Wildlife Crisis,* forewords by Bernard, Prince of the Netherlands, and Scott, epilogue by Stewart L. Udall, Cowles, 1970.

JUVENILE

(Editor) *Nature Parliament: A Book of the Broadcasts by L. Hugh Newman, Peter Scott, and James Fisher,* introduction by Derek McCulloch, Dent, 1952.

The Wonderful World: The Adventure of the Earth We Live On, art edited by F. H. K. Henrion, Hanover House, 1954 (published in England as *Adventure of the World,* Rathbone, 1954).

Adventure of the Sea, Rathbone, 1956, published as *The Wonderful World of the Sea,* Garden City Books, 1957, new edition, revised and enlarged, Doubleday, 1970.

Adventure of the Air, illustrations by Isotype Institute, Bernard Myers, G. Leigh Davies, and others, Rathbone, 1958, published as *The Wonderful World of the Air,* Garden City Books, 1959, new edition, revised and enlarged, Macdonald, 1970.

The Migration of Birds (picture book), illustrations by Crispin Fisher, Bodley Head, 1966.

OTHER

Also author of pamphlets, including *Natural History of the Kite,* Royal Society for the Protection of Birds, 1949; *Bird Preservation,* Royal Society for the Protection of Birds, 1951; *Birds of the Field,* illustrated by Eric Hosking and others, Collins, 1952; and *Hemel Hempstead, Hertsfordshire, Rural District,* Century Publications, 2nd edition, 1952, 5th edition, 1959. Editor of pamphlet *Birds and Beasts,* illustrated by Maurice Wilson and Rowland Hilder, Phoenix House, 1956.

Contributor of articles to periodicals, including *Animal Behaviour, British Birds, Guardian* (London), *Ibis, Life, Observer* (London), and *Sunday Times* (London).

SIDELIGHTS: A leading authority on birds and nature conservation in England, James Fisher made more than one thousand radio and television broadcasts and wrote numerous best-selling books on subjects ranging from the care of common and exotic household pets to plants and animals facing extinction. His works are popular with the general reader as well as the scholar because they offer a wealth of information in a straightforward manner. Largely responsible for the popularity of bird-watching in Britain, at the time of his death in 1970 Fisher had sold an estimated two million volumes. During the early stages of his career he concentrated primarily on the seabirds of England and northern Europe, then turned his attention to the plight of endangered species and promoting wildlife conservation worldwide.

Pursuing an early interest in ornithology, Fisher studied zoology at Eton College and at Magdalen College, Oxford. After graduation he worked as an assistant curator at the London Zoo, and at that time he helped found the British Trust for Ornithology. He and biologist Julian Huxley organized that association's Hatching and Fledgling Enquiry, a body that engaged the assistance of professional and amateur ornithologists to record nest findings in England. Fisher also surveyed the population of the North American gannet, analyzed the rook's diet, and observed the habits of the fulmar, a bird that originally occupied areas of the Arctic and the islands of the North Atlantic Ocean but began colonizing Great Britain extensively during the nineteenth century. Fisher published the detailed records of his studies—complete with maps and diagrams—in *The Fulmar,* a work that ornithologists found invaluable. Two years later, in 1941, he wrote *Sea-birds: An Introduction to the Natural History of the Sea-birds of the North Atlantic* with fellow ornithologist R. M. Lockley, an in-depth look at other species of northern European birds. Like *The Fulmar, Sea-birds* was popular with professional bird-watchers, yet the 1954 work also found an audience in amateurs who appreciated its clarity and brevity.

With American author, artist, and ornithologist Roger Tory Peterson, Fisher set off from Newfoundland, Canada, in April, 1953, on a three-month tour of the North American continent in search of birds. They traveled down the Atlantic coast to the Florida Keys, across the Gulf States to Mexico, and up the Pacific coast to the Bering Sea. The result of their tour was *Wild America: The Record of a Thirty-Thousand-Mile Journey Around the Continent by a Distinguished Naturalist and His British Colleague,* which was enthusiastically received by critics and commended for its fascinating observations and Peterson's beautiful drawings. With Peterson Fisher also wrote *The World of Birds,* which David Bannerman in the *New York Review of Books* deemed "a mine of information" on the eighty-six hundred species of birds that the authors discuss. They outline each species's biology, evolution, migratory patterns, and the impact of man on them, focusing on the 143 types of endangered birds.

Perhaps Fisher's most important work is *Wildlife in Danger,* an encyclopedia of animals and plants that are threatened by extinction, which he authored with Noel Simon and Jack Vincent under the auspices of the Survival Service Commission of the International Union for Conservation of Nature and Natural Resources, which publishes the *Red Data Book.* Extrapolating on the information gathered for the *Red Data Book* by scientists, zoologists, ecologists, and other conservationists located worldwide for the *Red Data Book,* Fisher and his co-authors present the data in a less scholarly language that is more understandable to the layman. They list facts on each species, including the ideal conditions of their natural habitat, their range and history, and their present status, then offer realistic proposals on how they might be saved—for example, by establishing nature reserves and by prohibiting hunting. *Wildlife in Danger* has become a standard reference on threatened animals such as the blue whale, the Indian rhinoceros, the Mikado pheasant, and the gorilla and is praised for its objective and unsentimental view of conservation.

With Prince Philip, consort of Queen Elizabeth II of Great Britain, Fisher wrote *Wildlife Crisis,* published in 1970 after Fisher's death. A comprehensive study of man's effect on nature, *Wildlife Crisis* lists the more than 350 kinds of mammals and birds that have become extinct since 1600, when man introduced modern industrial machinery, and the eight hundred that are threatened today. The work also outlines the history and growth of the nature conservation movement, beginning in eighteenth-century Britain and in nineteenth-century America, to the establishment of nature reserves and national parks worldwide in the twentieth century.

Fisher also wrote books on science and nature for juvenile readers that critics consistently lauded for presenting a wealth of scientific information in an interesting and imaginative way and for their colorful illustrations, diagrams, and maps. One reviewer judged the works "absorbing," claiming that many adults find the books as fascinating as children do. In *The Wonderful World: The Adventure of the Earth We Live On* Fisher simplifies the big bang theory of the creation of the universe and offers his view of cities of tomorrow. *Adventure of the Sea* discusses the origins of the ocean and the life it supports, as well as present-day explorations of the sea, while *Adventure of the Air* explains the relationship between the earth and its atmosphere, outlines the evolution of birds and the development of aircraft, and introduces young readers to astronomy, aerodynamics, physics, and mechanics in what one critic called a "painless manner."

AVOCATIONAL INTERESTS: Music; reading literature, especially poetry.

BIOGRAPHICAL/CRITICAL SOURCES:

PERIODICALS

New Statesman, December 4, 1970.
New York Review of Books, August 5, 1965.
New York Times, April 25, 1969, December 22, 1970.
New York Times Book Review, August 10, 1969.
Spectator, June 21, 1969.
Times Literary Supplement, January 14, 1965, February 2, 1967, April 9, 1969, May 6, 1983.

OBITUARIES:

PERIODICALS

New York Times, September 30, 1970.
Publishers Weekly, October 26, 1970.
Time, October 12, 1970.
Times (London), September 28, 1970.*

—*Sketch by Carol Lynn DeKane*

*   *   *

FITZGERALD, John D(ennis)   1907(?)-1988

OBITUARY NOTICE—See index for *CA* sketch: Born in 1907 (one source says 1906) in Utah; died following a long illness, May 21 (one source says May 20), 1988, in Titusville, Fla. Musician, agent, educator, journalist, and author. Fitzgerald was best known for his books about growing up in Utah when it was still a territory and, in particular, for his "Great Brain" juvenile series based on adventures with his brother Tom. His memoirs include *Papa Married a Mormon, Mamma's Boarding House, Uncle Will and the Fitzgerald Curse,* and seven titles in the "Great Brain" series. In addition, Fitzgerald co-authored two volumes about his craft, *The Professional Story Writer and His Art* and *Structuring Your Novel: From Basic Idea to Finished Manuscript,* and contributed more than five hundred short stories and articles to various periodicals. At times he also worked as a jazz drummer, a publicity agent for Metro-Goldwyn-Mayer, a foreign feature editor for United Press in Europe, Asia, and Australia, and a teacher of creative writing.

OBITUARIES AND OTHER SOURCES:

BOOKS

Twentieth-Century Children's Writers, 2nd edition, St. Martin's, 1983.

PERIODICALS

Publishers Weekly, August 26, 1988.
School Library Journal, September, 1988.

*   *   *

FITZGERALD, Zelda (Sayre)   1900-1948

PERSONAL: Born July 24, 1900, in Montgomery, Ala.; died in a fire, March 10 (some sources say March 11), 1948, in Asheville, N.C.; daughter of Anthony Dickinson (a legislator and Alabama Supreme Court judge) and Minnie (a homemaker; maiden name, Machen) Sayre; married F(rancis) Scott (Key) Fitzgerald (a writer), April 3, 1920; children: Frances Scott (Scottie) Fitzgerald Smith. *Education:* Attended schools in Montgomery, Ala.

CAREER: Writer, painter. Paintings exhibited at the New York Gallery, 1934; in a retrospective at the Montgomery Museum of Fine Arts, Montgomery, Ala., 1974; and in small showings in Montgomery and in Asheville, N.C., prior to Fitzgerald's death.

WRITINGS:

Save Me the Waltz (novel), Scribner, 1932, reprinted with preface by Harry T. Moore and notes by Matthew J. Bruccoli, J. Cape, 1968.

(With husband, F. Scott Fitzgerald) Bits of Paradise: Twenty-one Uncollected Stories (contains "The Popular Girl," "Love in the Night," "Our Own Movie Queen," "A Penny Spent," "The Dance," "Jacob's Ladder," "The Swimmers," "The Original Follies Girl," "The Southern Girl," "The Girl the Prince Liked," "The Girl With Talent," "A Millionaire's Girl," "Poor Working Girl," "The Hotel Child," "A New Leaf," "Miss Ella," "The Continental Angle," "A Couple of Nuts," "What a Handsome Pair," "Last Kiss," and "Dearly Beloved"), selected by daughter, Scottie Fitzgerald Smith, and Matthew J. Bruccoli, foreword by Smith, Bodley Head, 1973, Scribner, c. 1973 (foreword by Smith does not appear in American edition).

Scandalabra (play; first produced in Baltimore, Md., by Junior Vagabond Players, June 26, 1933), Bruccoli Clark, 1980.

Also author of Caesar's Things, a novel combining elements of romance and betrayal with religious allegory, left uncompleted at time of death.

Contributor of essays and short stories to newspapers and periodicals, including College Humor, Esquire, Harper's Bazaar, McCall's, New Yorker, Saturday Evening Post, and Scribner's.

SIDELIGHTS: Zelda Fitzgerald is best remembered as the eccentric wife of American writer F. Scott Fitzgerald. Together they came to embody the jazz age, an era of confidence, prosperity, and flamboyance that existed in the United States from the end of World War I until the stock market crash of 1929. According to Nancy Milford in her biography Zelda, humorist Ring Lardner dubbed the couple "Cinderella and the Prince" of their generation. A creative painter, promising ballet dancer, and author, Zelda Fitzgerald lived her life in the shadow of her husband's fame. Not until twenty years after her death in a 1948 fire did she begin to receive serious critical attention as a perceptive and impassioned writer.

Born in Montgomery, Alabama, at the dawn of the twentieth century, Fitzgerald was an exuberant and mischievous Southern beauty who rejected the conventions represented by her father, a distinguished Alabama judge, and rebelled against the entire Southern establishment. In an article for Harper's, Milford related the recollections of Zelda's contemporaries. Former schoolmates described her as a daring and theatrical teenager who tantalized the boys with her "one-piece flesh-colored swimming suit," danced on the tops of tables, and showed up to a commencement exercise at school with her stockings rolled to her knees, "a racy thing to do in 1918." She met the aspiring writer Scott Fitzgerald after her high school graduation at a summer dance and, dazzled by his romantic dreams, married him two years later.

Scott gained popularity during the early years of their marriage with the release of his novels This Side of Paradise and The Beautiful and the Damned in the early 1920s. But tensions grew and the marriage slowly disintegrated over the next decade. Unsatisfied with his literary progress, a temperamental Scott turned to alcohol for solace. Several critics note that his fits of temper, bouts of depression, and obsessive drive to create a perfect work of fiction—he was working on The Great Gatsby and Tender Is the Night, both widely regarded as his best novels, during this time—paralleled Zelda's growing restlessness. Seeking her own identity and a sense of accomplishment, she turned to writing as a creative and emotional outlet.

Zelda began writing under her husband's tutelage with short stories published in periodicals under Scott's name or a joint Fitzgerald byline. W. R. Anderson wrote in the Fitzgerald/Hemingway Annual, 1977 that Scott's interest in the "potential marketability" of his wife's 1923 story "Our Own Movie Queen" led him to sell the piece to the Chicago Sunday Tribune under his sole byline. According to Anderson, the surviving typescript of the story confirms that although Scott Fitzgerald revised the work, Zelda was its principal author. "Despite its rudimentary characterization, trick ending, and overall slickness," Anderson noted, Fitzgerald "was not ashamed to claim ['Our Own Movie Queen'] as his own creation, at least for the sake of selling it." But what Scott viewed as trite literary dabblings would become, theorized Milford, Zelda's "work," an all-embracing search for meaning in her life.

For the next few years Zelda Fitzgerald continued to write occasional magazine pieces—thought to be primarily Scott's work at the time they were published—that centered on youth and the jazz age. As a result College Humor commissioned Scott in 1928 to write a series of sketches on different types of girls. Anderson assessed that Scott Fitzgerald bore little respect for the "youth-cult-oriented" magazine, considering it a low-paying "market for hastily written or second-rate material." But Scott did not discount the offer entirely; instead he saw the project as a diversion for his wife that would provide a vent for her creative tensions and subsidize the couple's income while he struggled to write the preliminary version of what eventually became Tender Is the Night. Zelda agreed to write the articles, allowing Scott to revise them, and signed them jointly in order to command a higher price from the magazine.

Between April of 1929 and March of 1930, while living with Scott in Paris, Zelda composed "The Original Follies Girl," "Poor Working Girl," "The Southern Girl," "The Girl the Prince Liked," "The Girl With Talent," and "A Millionaire's Girl." The first five stories were published in College Humor beginning in July of 1929. The last of the series, "A Millionaire's Girl," was so well written that it was sold to the Saturday Evening Post for four thousand dollars and published under Scott's name alone. Critics agree that the stories evolved from undeveloped character sketches to impressive, concretely detailed short fiction pieces written from a sympathetic but objective narrative perspective. Anderson contended that these writings, as a group, "are a record of Zelda Fitzgerald's struggle toward seriousness of expression, of her growth toward competence in literary technique, and of her husband's continuing but increasingly sparing and wary guidance."

Milford suggested that the prevailing public image of the Fitzgeralds as a happy couple sharply contrasted the turmoil of their private lives. Anderson seconded Milford's appraisal, indicating that by early 1930 an "ominous tinge of rivalry" surfaced between the two Fitzgeralds as Zelda "came closer to writing good, serious fiction." Scott, failing to make headway on his novel, began drinking, and Zelda worked herself to physical and psychological exhaustion in pursuit of artistic achievement on her own. She combined writing with a serious, almost obsessive devotion to ballet dancing, her girlhood passion. Even her artwork—expressionistic paintings of the human form with oversized limbs and musculature—revealed what several critics interpret as her strained and distorted view of the world. On April 23, 1930, only one month after finishing her last article in the girls series, Zelda suffered a nervous collapse and entered a hospital located on the outskirts of Paris. A diagnosed schizophrenic, she would spend the rest of her life in and out of sanatoriums both abroad and in the United States.

Characterized as an "intuitive" and "brilliant" individual by her doctors, Zelda Fitzgerald was able to face her illness: according to Milford, she turned to writing in an effort to understand her condition. Besides composing letters to Scott that chronicled their life together, Zelda also wrote works of fiction while institutionalized, including the short stories "Miss Ella" and "A Couple of Nuts" and her only novel, *Save Me the Waltz.*

More than any of her previous work, "Miss Ella" appears to be Zelda's first independent creation from its initial draft to final revision. Published in the December 1931 issue of *Scribner's,* "Miss Ella" is the story of a spinster haunted by the memory of her rejected suitor who committed suicide on the day that she was to marry his rival. Several critics see the piece as an outgrowth of the author's earlier writings, having achieved a higher degree of maturity and depth than the sketches in the girls series. Utilizing a technique that Anderson termed "narrator-protagonist fusion," Fitzgerald imbued her story with suspense, sympathy, and psychological tension. Anderson proclaimed that the narrator, in effect, "*becomes* Miss Ella, leading the reader into a mind and soul rigidly bound in guilty self-denial." He further asserted that through her writing, Fitzgerald seemed to "explore the complexities of the feminine psyche struggling unsuccessfully for mature fulfillment. . . . [making] art of her [own] internal conflicts."

The author's last published short fiction, "A Couple of Nuts," appeared in *Scribner's* in August of 1932. Widely regarded as her most accomplished short work, the story, assessed Milford, is testament to Zelda "in control of her talent." "A Couple of Nuts" centers around a young couple's metamorphosis from innocent romantic adventurers exposed to the decadent circles of European cafe society to victims of emotional and moral disintegration. The action is precipitated by a third character, Jeff Daugherty, the personification of ruin. Commenting on the story Anderson wrote, "Zelda Fitzgerald called on all her practice to suffuse the story with a sustained tone, ominous and sinister, of loss and destruction." *Scribner's* acceptance of "A Couple of Nuts" and its predecessor, "Miss Ella," seems to have endowed Zelda with the confidence to attempt more challenging fiction.

Just as she was beginning her novel in early 1932, Zelda Fitzgerald experienced another major psychological collapse. Her doctors encouraged her to write, and, in a short time, she had completed a typescript of her novel which she submitted for publication without Scott's review.

According to Milford, Zelda patterned *Save Me the Waltz* "closely upon her own life." The book details the life of Alabama Beggs, a girl who grows up prior to World War I in a strict, traditional Southern household, marries successful artist David Knight, and, with him, mingles in the fast and flashy social circles of the elite in New York, Paris, and the Riviera.

Eventually seeking self-sufficiency and an identity separate from her husband, Alabama embarks on a career in dance and accepts an offer for a solo debut with a dance company in Naples, Italy. She learns that her father is dying at the same time that she falls ill in Naples with blood poisoning from a foot infection. Alabama recovers but, her tendons severed, will never dance again. By the book's end, the Knights are reunited and Alabama returns to the states to make final peace with her father.

Critical reaction to *Save Me the Waltz* was mixed upon its publication in 1932. Most reviewers faulted the book for its excessively elaborate and obscure prose and numerous grammatical errors—it does not appear to have been copyedited—but conceded that its author evoked both the mood and texture of an era with striking realism. Milford reported that Zelda was especially fond of a review by William McFee written for the *New York Sun.* McFee called the author "a peculiar talent" and said of her writing, "With all its crudity of conception . . . and its pathetic striving after psychological profundity, there is the promise of a new and vigorous personality in fiction." Fitzgerald's unusual use of "fantastic metaphors" produced, in McFee's opinion, "a kind of dizzy delight" and "an almost alcoholic vitality." Only 1,392 copies of *Save Me the Waltz* were sold, however, and because of extensive revisions of galleys, Zelda earned a mere $120.73.

Thirty-five years after its initial publication, the novel was reissued and reevaluated. Richard Aldington agreed in the *Times Literary Supplement* with Scott Fitzgerald's assessment of the work as "a bad book," but admitted that "both Zelda and her novel needed" to be saved "from the status of [a] footnote" to Scott's body of literature. In an article for the *New York Times Book Review,* Arthur Mizener proclaimed *Save Me the Waltz,* "despite some serious flaws, a remarkable book." Deeming the original reviews of the book "not very perceptive," Mizener countered accusations that the plot—especially Alabama's joining the European ballet circuit—was implausible by selecting passages from the text that reveal what the fulfillment of the protagonist's dream represented to the author. Zelda wrote in her book: "In proving herself [as a dancer], [Alabama] would achieve that peace which she imagined went only in the surety of one's self." Mizener pointed out, "Zelda Fitzgerald worked like a slave for three years to be a dancer"—to find that peace—and was finally destroyed by the "conflict between the uncompromising romantic and the irrepressible realist within her."

Anderson theorized that "by 1932, the quality of Zelda Fitzgerald's writing had truly improved to a point at which she must have seemed to her husband a kind of ungrateful rival." Milford's documentation of Scott's correspondence with his publisher, with the clinic doctors, and with Zelda following the completion of *Save Me the Waltz* supports this assumption. He wrote to one of Zelda's doctors that for four years he had been "unable to proceed" with his own novel "*because* of the necessity of keeping Zelda in sanitariums." Scott accused his wife of imitating "literally one whole section" of his uncompleted novel in both "rhythm" and "materials." The "materials" of Scott's book were drawn from the Fitzgeralds' marriage. Indeed, Scott readily admitted that Zelda's illness served as the model for his character Nicole Diver's psychic disintegration in *Tender Is the Night.* As Anderson put it, in seriously fictionalizing her life with Scott in *Save Me the Waltz,* Zelda "inevitably infringe[d] on a reservoir of deeply-felt personal experience [Scott] insisted was 'his' material." In a letter to Scott, as cited by Milford, Zelda tried to explain why she had submitted her manuscript without showing it to him. She wrote: "I [feared] we might have touched the same [themes]. Also, feeling it to be a dubious production due to my own instability I did not want a scathing criticism such as you have mercilessly—if for my own good given my last stories, poor things. I have had enough discouragement, generally, and could scream with that sense of inertia that hovers over my life and everything I do. . . . Life is very confusing—but I love you."

Recent studies, especially those conducted by Milford and Anderson, have "quashe[d] the simplistic myth that Zelda ruined Scott's career, an albatross pulling the mercurial mariner down into a sea of gin," wrote Paul D. Zimmerman in *Newsweek*. In an undated letter to Zelda uncovered by Milford, Scott chronicled their marriage and concluded, "We ruined ourselves—I have never honestly thought that we ruined each other." That they seemed to thrive on their destructive relationship is evidenced by Scott's words, again quoted by Milford: "I cherish her most extravagant hallucinations."

Zelda Fitzgerald died in a fire at Highland Hospital in Asheville, North Carolina, in 1948, eight years after her husband's death. Having been sedated on the night of the blaze, she was unable to escape from her room on the top floor of the hospital's main building. Zelda's body was identified by dental records and a charred slipper found beneath her body. She was buried next to Scott in a plot in Maryland on St. Patrick's Day of 1948.

BIOGRAPHICAL/CRITICAL SOURCES:

BOOKS

Authors in the News, Volume 1, Gale, 1976.
Dictionary of Literary Biography Yearbook: 1984, Gale, 1985.
Hemingway/Fitzgerald Annual, Bruccoli Clark/Gale, *1977*, 1977, *1979*, 1980.
Milford, Nancy, *Zelda: A Biography*, Harper, 1970.

PERIODICALS

Harper's Magazine, January, 1969.
New Leader, May 19, 1980.
Newsweek, June 15, 1970.
New York Times Book Review, October 16, 1932, August 13, 1967.
Saturday Review, October 22, 1932.
Times Literary Supplement, October 5, 1967.

OBITUARIES:

PERIODICALS

Newsweek, March 22, 1948.
Time, March 22, 1948.*

—*Sketch by Barbara K. Carlisle*

* * *

FLOURNOY, Don Michael 1937-

PERSONAL: Born October 20, 1937, in Shawnee Prairie, Tex.; son of Morgan Mitchell and Ruby May (Pitre) Flournoy; married Mary Anne Boone, July 27, 1963; children: Hylie Michelle, Elihu Daniel. *Education:* Southern Methodist University, B.A., 1959; attended National University of Mexico, 1958, University of London, 1960-61, and Boston University, 1962-63; University of Texas at Austin, M.A., 1964, Ph.D., 1965.

ADDRESSES: Home—6675 Baker Rd., Athens, Ohio 45701. *Office*—School of Telecommunications, Ohio University, Athens, Ohio 45701.

CAREER: Case Institute of Technology (now Case Western Reserve University), Cleveland, Ohio, assistant director of research administration and assistant dean of Case Institute, 1965-69; State University of New York at Buffalo, associate dean of Division of Undergraduate Studies, 1969-71; Ohio University, Athens, dean of University College, 1971-81, director of Center for International Studies, 1981-83, associate professor of telecommunications, 1983—. Professional photographer; farmer and rancher. Founder of Ohio Consortium for Individualized Degrees, 1972; chairman of Special Degree Programs Workshops, 1972-73 and 1975.

MEMBER: International Interactive Communications Society, International Television Association, International Association of Mass Communications Research, Ohio Association of Broadcasters.

WRITINGS:

The New Teachers, Jossey-Bass, 1972.
The Rationing of American Higher Education, Schenkman, 1982.

Contributor to education, communications, and scientific journals.

WORK IN PROGRESS: A textbook on satellite communications; research on new technologies in telecommunications research and on telecommunications in Asia and the Pacific.

* * *

FOLDESSY, Edward P(atrick) 1941-

PERSONAL: Born September 20, 1941, in New York, N.Y.; son of Joseph and Elizabeth (Holmoker) Foldessy; married Andrea I. Vescia (an artist), August 21, 1965; children: Jennifer J., Heather L. *Education:* Iona College, B.S., 1963.

ADDRESSES: Home—Allendale, N.J. *Office*—*Wall Street Journal*, 200 Liberty St., New York, N.Y. 10281.

CAREER: Wall Street Journal, New York, N.Y., assistant on national news desk and for "What's News," 1963-64, news assistant for columns "Bond Markets" and "Financing Business," 1964-68, reporter and special writer, 1966—, author of column "Credit Markets," 1980—.

WRITINGS:

(Co-author with others) *Crime and Business*, Dow Jones-Irwin, 1968.

Editor, *News Systems*.

SIDELIGHTS: Edward P. Foldessy told *CA:* "A structured background in natural sciences has been a major asset in preparing clear and organized writing. Highlights of my career include covering the decline and fall of Franklin National Bank in New York in a long series of investigative pieces. Also, I created my "Credit Markets" column in 1980, focusing heavily on the interaction of the economy, international developments, and the financial markets. As such, the column, which closely monitors monetary and fiscal policy, provides an economic diary of the events and principles of the massive money and bonds markets."

* * *

FOLEY, Richard 1947-

PERSONAL: Born February 12, 1947, in South Bend, Ind.;

son of William and Gladys (Hass) Foley; married Holly Bocker (a banker), January 10, 1976. *Education:* Miami University, Oxford, Ohio, B.A., 1969, M.A., 1971; Brown University, Ph.D., 1976.

ADDRESSES: Home—1512 East Wayne, South Bend, Ind. 46615. *Office*—Department of Philosophy, University of Notre Dame, Notre Dame, Ind. 46556.

CAREER: University of Notre Dame, Notre Dame, Ind., assistant professor, 1976-81, associate professor, 1981-85, professor of philosophy, 1985—, became chairman of department.

WRITINGS:

The Theory of Epistemic Rationality, Harvard University Press, 1987.

WORK IN PROGRESS: A book on different conceptions of rationality, publication expected in 1990.

* * *

FOOTMAN, Robert 1916-

PERSONAL: Born April 26, 1916, in Oakland, Calif.; son of Henry Edward (in insurance) and Clara Winifred (Wilson) Footman; married Ella Hedrick, June 21, 1937 (divorced, 1951); married Margaret Conha, September 26, 1952 (died July 21, 1987); children: Duncan, Farel, Courtenay, Peter. *Education:* Yale University, B.A., 1937. *Politics:* Independent. *Religion:* Protestant.

ADDRESSES: Home—465 Boynton, Berkeley, Calif. 94707. *Agent*—Bonnie Nadell, Frederick Hill Associates, 2237 Union St., San Francisco, Calif. 94123.

CAREER: Middlebury College, Middlebury, Vt., instructor in English, 1937-38; Marot Junior College, Thompson, Conn., instructor in English, 1938-41; worked for advertising agencies, including McCann Erickson, 1946-54, Guild Bascom Bonfigli, 1954-59, D'Arcy, 1959-66, Foote Cone Belding, 1966-70, Honis-Cooper, 1970-72, and M. Arnold, 1972-78; free-lance writer, 1978—.

MEMBER: California Tennis Club.

WRITINGS:

Once a Spy (novel), Dodd, 1978.
Always a Spy (novel), Dodd, 1986.
China Spy (novel), Dodd, 1987.

WORK IN PROGRESS: A suspense novel set in Southeast Asia.

SIDELIGHTS: Robert Footman told *CA:* "I left teaching and began working in advertising because I suspected I would be good at it. There is nothing wrong with teaching, but that world—academic—seemed too easy. I wanted the real world. I don't know if advertising was real, but it wasn't easy. Some of the highlights of my advertising career include creating a campaign for Lucky Lager Beer, helping rescue Bankamericard from its disastrous introduction, and naming and guiding Master Card from birth to worldwide success.

"I first decided to write novels when I was fourteen. Over the years, at four o'clock in the morning or thereabouts, I wrote four or five novels. Two were not all bad; the others were horrible. I retired at eleven o'clock in the morning on February 23, 1978, and started writing *Once a Spy* at ten minutes after twelve. After that I fussed around with an autobiographical

novel and a historical novel. The first was an abomination. The second was a good story but not a commercial one. The next two spy novels followed in quick order.

"I began writing spy novels because I like the discipline of the genre. I like to write and tell stories, and I still have something of the teacher in me. Spy stories enable me to sneak in a thought or two."

* * *

FORD, Peter 1936-

PERSONAL: Born June 3, 1936, in Harpenden, Hertfordshire, England; son of Fletcher Calvert (an accounts clerk) and Muriel (a housewife; maiden name, Mayo-Smith) Ford; married Laura Geeve (a teacher), August 28, 1960 (separated); children: Piers, Julian, Isabel. *Education:* Attended school in Harpenden, England.

ADDRESSES: Home—42 Friars St., Sudbury, Suffolk CO10 6AG, England. *Agent*—David Grossman, 110-114 Clerkenwell Rd., London EC1M 5SA, England.

CAREER: Cassell & Co., London, England, assistant editor, 1957-61; Penguin Books, Harmondsworth, England, senior copy editor, 1961-65; Nelson & Co., London, senior editor, 1965-71; free-lance writer and editor, 1971—. Consultant to publishing companies. *Military service:* British Army, lance bombardier in Royal Artillery, 1955-56; served in Malaya.

MEMBER: Society of Authors, Royal Commonwealth Society, Folklore Society, Eastern Arts Association.

WRITINGS:

(With Franz Bergel and D. R. A. Davies) *All About Drugs,* Thomas Nelson, 1970.
(With Max Wall) *The Fool on the Hill,* Quartet, 1975.
(With Feliks Topolski) *Topolski's Buckingham Palace Panoramas,* Quartet, 1977.
(With Anthony Feldman) *Scientists and Inventors,* Aldus Books, 1979.
(Translator with Kenneth Mitchell) Julius Braunthal, *History of the International: World Socialism, 1943-1968,* Gollancz, 1980.
(With Michael Howell) *The True History of the Elephant Man,* Penguin, 1980, revised edition published as *The Illustrated True History of the Elephant Man,* Penguin, 1983.
The Elephant Man (juvenile), Allison & Busby, 1983.
(With Michael Howell) *The Beetle of Aphrodite and Other Medical Mysteries,* Random House, 1985, reprinted as *The Ghost Disease and Twelve Other Stories of Detective Work in the Medical Field,* Penguin, 1986 (published in England as *Medical Mysteries,* Viking, 1985).
(With John Fisher) *The Picture Buyer's Handbook,* Harrap, 1988.

WORK IN PROGRESS: A "history of future history," publication by Boydell & Brewer expected c. 1990; research for a book about the late Tommy Cooper, a British conjurer and comedian.

SIDELIGHTS: "Since becoming a full-time free-lancer in 1971," Peter Ford wrote, "I have tended to specialize in co-authorship and to use my editorial skills in assignments on texts that need a degree of special attention or that require a sensitive application of the invisible editorial hand to make them publishable. Over the years, I have therefore worked on several hundred books, with a wide range of London publishers and with authors or would-be authors from a great variety of backgrounds. I have never had a specialist subject *per se*. I have also, through our local regional arts association, Eastern Arts, presented talks and creative writing workshops in schools and other institutions. I am now at the difficult transitional stage where I want to devote more time and energy to my own writing, which means, in turn, some acts of faith and a certain amount of disentangling from the guarantees of fee-paying commissions. We shall see.''

* * *

FOSTER, John (Andrew)   1941-

PERSONAL: Born May 5, 1941, in Enfield, Middlesex, England; son of Leonard Purkiss (a bank manager) and Stella Emma (a nurse and housewife; maiden name, Williams) Foster; married Helen Patricia Munns (a teacher), August 5, 1967; children: Rachel Caroline, Gerard Sebastian, Richard Gervase, Alice Elizabeth. *Education:* Lincoln College, Oxford, B.A. (with first class honors), 1964, M.A., 1966. *Religion:* Anglican.

ADDRESSES: Home—14 Quarry High St., Headington, Oxford, England. *Office*—Brasenose College, Oxford University, Oxford, England.

CAREER: Oxford University, Oxford, England, lecturer in philosophy, fellow and tutor at Brasenose College, 1966—.

MEMBER: Aristotelian Society, LIFE.

WRITINGS:

(Contributor) Gareth Evans and John McDowell, editors, *Truth and Meaning,* Oxford University Press, 1976.
(Contributor) G. F. Macdonald, editor, *Perception and Identity,* Macmillan, 1979.
The Case for Idealism, Routledge & Kegan Paul, 1982.
A. J. Ayer, Routledge & Kegan Paul, 1985.
(Editor with Howard Robinson) *Essays on Berkeley: A Tercentennial Celebration,* Oxford University Press, 1985.
(Contributor) J. H. Channer, editor, *Abortion and the Sanctity of Human Life,* Paternoster Press, 1985.

Contributor to philosophy journals.

WORK IN PROGRESS: Cartesian Dualism.

SIDELIGHTS: John Foster told *CA:* ''My main interest as a philosopher is in the relationship between the mental and the physical. There are two distinct issues here. First, there is the issue of how, for each human person, his mind is related to his body, and, in particular, of whether we should think of a person's mentality as separate from or as part of his corporeal nature. Secondly, there is the issue of how the physical world as a whole is related to the human mind, and, in particular, of whether we should think of the world as something whose existence depends on or is independent of human experience and thought. The first issue arises in the philosophy of mind, and the position I take on it is radically dualist: like Descartes, I think of the mind as a nonphysical substance, wholly distinct from the body and without location in physical space. The second issue arises in the philosophy of the physical world, and the position I take on it is idealist: like Berkeley, I think of the physical world as something which exists in virtue of, and is nothing over and above, the thematic character of human experience and the law-like constraints (ultimately the product of divine volition) which are imposed on it.

''I am a Christian. This interacts with my philosophy in a number of ways—most conspiciously, in my commitment to the sanctity of human life and my consequent opposition to such practices as abortion, euthanasia, and experimentation on the human embryo. Although I am not a 'fundamentalist,' my Christian beliefs are of a fairly conservative kind: I have no sympathy with the modern attempts to demythologize (desupernaturalize) Christian doctrine—such as those which diminish the transcendent reality of God or deny the full deity of Christ or cast doubt on the literal truth of the Virgin Birth and Resurrection.''

AVOCATIONAL INTERESTS: ''I enjoy playing chess (mainly nowadays with my computer), watching professional football, and drinking red wine—sometimes all three together!''

BIOGRAPHICAL/CRITICAL SOURCES:

PERIODICALS

Times Literary Supplement, March 7, 1986, April 25, 1986.

* * *

FOX, Harrison W(illiam), Jr.   1944-

PERSONAL: Born January 24, 1944, in Minneapolis, Minn.; son of Harrison William (a business executive) and Ruth (Pirtle) Fox; married Lynn Hussey (a professor of education); children: Harrison William III, Thomas Randolph, Leigh Lynn. *Education:* University of South Florida, B.A., 1965; American University, M.A., 1969, Ph.D., 1972. *Religion:* Presbyterian.

ADDRESSES: Home—217 41st Ave. N.E., St. Petersburg, Fla. 33703.

CAREER: American University, Washington, D.C., lecturer in political science, 1970-75; U.S. Civil Service Commission, General Management Training Center, lecturer, 1975-78; realtor, 1978-79; CUMC Mortgage Corp., currently general manager and vice-president. Chairman of board of directors of Harrison Group, Inc. (financial services firm). Fellow at Institute of Politics, John F. Kennedy School of Government, Harvard University, 1977; fellow at Dalhousie University; adjunct professor at Eckerd College; lecturer at Federal Executive Institute, 1977; lecturer at National War College, American Enterprise Institute for Public Policy Research, Harvard University, Catholic University of America, and Boston University. Minority counsel to Budgeting Management and Expenditures Subcommittee, U.S. Senate Government Operations Committee, 1973-74, and U.S. Senate Governmental Affairs Committee, 1977-78; counsel to co-chairman of Committee to Study the Senate Committee System, 1976-77.

WRITINGS:

Improving Congressional Control Over the Budget, U.S. Government Printing Office, 1973.
It's Your Government, Too!, Dow Chemical, 1975.
(Contributor) *Readings in Citizen Education,* U.S. Office of Education, 1976.
Congressional Staff, Free Press, 1977.
Doing Business in Washington, Free Press, 1981.

Also author of U.S. Senate publications *Leglislative Oversight* and *Program Evaluation.* Contributor to periodicals.

AVOCATIONAL INTERESTS: Squash, carpentry, backpacking, tennis, Disraeli, pottery.

FOX, Matthew (Timothy) 1940-

PERSONAL: Born December 21, 1940, in Madison, Wis.; son of George Thomas and Beatrice (Sill) Fox. *Education:* Aquinas Institute of Philosophy, Dominican College of St. Rose of Lima, River Forest, Ill. (now Aquinas Institute, St. Louis, Mo.), M.A., 1964; Aquinas Institute of Philosophy and Theology, Dubuque, Iowa (now Aquinas Institute, St. Louis, Mo.), M.A., 1967; Institut Catholique de Paris, S.T.D. (summa cum laude), 1970; postdoctoral study at University of Muenster, 1970. *Politics:* Independent.

ADDRESSES: Office—Department of Religious Education, University of St. Thomas, 3812 Montrose Blvd., Houston, Tex. 77006.

CAREER: Entered Ordo Praedicatorum (Order of Preachers; Dominicans; O.P.), 1960, ordained Roman Catholic priest, 1967; Aquinas Institute of Philosophy and Theology, Dubuque, Iowa (now Aquinas Institute, St. Louis, Mo.), assistant professor of theology, 1970-71; Emmanuel College, Boston, Mass., assistant professor of theology, 1971-72; Loyola University of Chicago, Chicago, Ill., assistant professor of theology, 1972-73; Barat College, Lake Forest, Ill., professor of religious studies and chairman of department, beginning in 1973; professor of religious education at University of St. Thomas, Houston, Tex. Lecturer for Thomas More Association, 1973—; member of secretariat of Lorscheid International Movement of Dominicans, 1969.

MEMBER: Catholic Theological Association.

WRITINGS:

Religion USA: An Inquiry Into Religion and Culture by Way of Time Magazine, Listening Press, 1971.
On Becoming a Musical, Mystical Bear: Spirituality American Style, Harper, 1972.
Whee! We, Wee, All the Way Home: A Guide to the New Sensual Spirituality, Consortium, 1976.
A Spirituality Named Compassion and the Healing of the Global Village, Humpty Dumpty, and Us, Winston Press, 1979.
(Editor) *Western Spirituality: Historical Roots, Ecumenical Routes*, Fides/Claretian, 1979.
(Author of introduction and commentary) Meister Eckhart, *Breakthrough: Meister Eckhart's Creation Spirituality in New Translation*, Doubleday, 1980.
(With Brian Swimme) *Manifesto for a Global Civilization*, Bear & Co., 1982.
(Author of introduction) *Meditations With Meister Eckhart*, Bear & Co., 1982.
Original Blessing, Bear & Co., 1983.
(Author of commentary) *Illuminations of Hildegard of Bingen*, Bear & Co., 1985.
(Editor) *The Hildegard Reader: Operatione Dei and Letters by Hildegarde of Bingen*, Bear & Co., 1986.

Founding editor of *Listening*, 1964-67.*

*   *   *

FRANCIS, Frank Chalton 1901-1988

OBITUARY NOTICE—See index for *CA* sketch: Born October 5, 1901, in Liverpool, England; died September 15, 1988. Librarian, lecturer, editor, and author. Francis spent most of his career serving the British Museum in London, England, beginning as an assistant keeper in the department of printed books in 1926. He advanced to secretary of the museum in 1946, returned to the department of printed books as keeper in 1948, and was appointed director and principal librarian in 1959, a post he held until his retirement in 1968. Francis was also a frequent lecturer in bibliography at London University and elsewhere. Among his publications on various aspects of bibliography were the books *The Shakespeare Collection in the British Museum, Oriental Printed Books and Manuscripts, Many Cultures: One World, A Bibliographic Ghost Revisits His Old Haunts,* and articles and reviews contributed to library journals and newspapers. Francis also served as editor of *Library* from 1936 to 1953, as joint editor of *Journal of Documentation* from 1947 to 1968, as associate editor of *Libri,* and as advisory editor of *Library Quarterly.* Furthermore, he wrote the historical bibliography sections that appeared in *The Year's Work in Librarianship* from 1929 through 1938. The recipient of numerous honorary degrees, Francis was knighted in 1960.

OBITUARIES AND OTHER SOURCES:

BOOKS

Who's Who, 140th edition, St. Martin's, 1988.
The Writers Directory: 1988-1990, St. James Press, 1988.

PERIODICALS

Times (London), September 16, 1988.

*   *   *

FRANK, Elizabeth 1945-

PERSONAL: Born September 14, 1945, in Los Angeles, Calif.; daughter of Melvin G. (a screenwriter) and Anne (a radio writer; maiden name, Ray) Frank; married Howard Buchwald (a painter), August 3, 1984; children: Anne Louise. *Education:* Attended Bennington College, 1963-65; University of California, Berkeley, B.A., 1967, M.A., 1969, Ph.D., 1973.

ADDRESSES: Office—Department of English, Bard College, Annandale on Hudson, N.Y. 12504. *Agent*—Joy Harris, Lantz Office, 888 7th Ave., New York, N.Y. 10106.

PERSONAL: Writer. Teacher of English literature at various institutions, including Mills College, 1971-73, Williams College, 1973-75, University of California, Irvine, 1975-76, Temple University, 1976-77, and Bard College, 1982—. Story editor for Connaught Films, 1979-82.

AWARDS, HONORS: Pulitzer Prize for biography and nomination for best biography from National Book Critics Circle, both 1986, both for *Louise Bogan: A Portrait.*

WRITINGS:

Jackson Pollock, Abbeville Press, 1984.
Louise Bogan: A Portrait (biography), Knopf, 1985.

Contributor to periodicals, including *Art in America, Nation, New York Times Book Review,* and *Artnews.*

WORK IN PROGRESS: A biographical essay on painter Esteban Vicente; a novel, *Cheat and Charmer,* publication by Morrow expected in the early 1990s.

SIDELIGHTS: Elizabeth Frank is best known as the author of *Louise Bogan: A Portrait,* her Pulitzer Prize biography of the contemporary American poet and literary critic. Bogan was a particularly prominent poet from the 1930s to the 1950s, a period when her poetry and criticism appeared regularly in the *New Yorker.* Occasionally unstable, Bogan twice committed herself to mental institutions, and in her early romantic affairs she endured considerable disappointment and frustration. In her verse, however, she exhibits discipline and precision. By adhering to traditional metric structures while exploring her often turbulent life, Bogan produced poems that were at once classical and contemporary. In her lifetime she published only a few collections, but those volumes—notably *Dark Summer* and *The Sleeping Fury*—established her as an important artist, and she received praise from such revered peers as Theodore Roethke and W. H. Auden. After publishing *The Sleeping Fury* in 1937 Bogan slowed her production of poetry, but she continued contributing literary criticism to the *New Yorker,* and before retiring in 1969 she was probably America's most respected poetry reviewer. Bogan suffered a fatal heart attack after her retirement.

In tracing Bogan's life, Frank conducted extensive interviewing and studied the poet's letters and incomplete memoirs. In addition, Frank analyzed Bogan's poetry, which often proves disturbingly realistic, particularly when Bogan writes of the problems that necessitated her stays in mental institutions. The often trying task of compiling, sorting, and analyzing information on Bogan preoccupied Frank for more than ten years while she taught English at various American colleges. But her endeavors proved richly rewarding, for with *Louise Bogan: A Portrait* Frank was recognized as an accomplished biographer.

Upon publication in 1985, *Louise Bogan: A Portrait* earned Frank widespread praise from reviewers. *Ms.* critic Marion Meade noted Frank's "sensitive narrative," and Elizabeth Wheeler wrote in the *Los Angeles Times Book Review* that Frank's book was "a fine biography" and "almost a classic." Among Frank's most enthusiastic reviewers was Richard Howard, who wrote in *New Republic* that *Louise Bogan: A Portrait* was "finely shaded and impassioned" and that Frank proved "astonishing" in her ability to fathom the complexities of Bogan's life and work. Similarly, *New York Times* reviewer John Gross wrote that Frank's book was an extremely impressive achievement. Gross contended that Bogan, in her poetry, had sought to objectify her personal feelings, thus rendering difficult any attempts to interpret her own life. "To reconstruct such a life is a difficult task," Gross declared. "It calls for exceptional empathy and insight, and for the ability to set imaginative work in its biographical context without reducing it to mere documentation. Fortunately, Elizabeth Frank . . . has risen to the challenge." Gross called the Bogan biography "a model of its kind, and one that does full justice to a remarkable woman."

Reviewers of *Louise Bogan: A Portrait* accorded special recognition to Frank's skills in researching, organizing, and analyzing her materials. Richard Howard wrote in *New Republic* that Frank was "scholarly and even scrupulous in her sleuthing," while Bogan's friend and fellow writer William Maxwell wrote in the *New Yorker* of Frank's "secure . . . exegesis" and of her interpretations suggesting "many years of thoughtful reading" of Bogan's writings. Wheeler also noted Frank's "impressively thorough job" and commended her "patient, perceptive and level-headed manner." And Bodine Williams, in his assessment for the Toronto *Globe and Mail,* acknowledged the biography as "well researched and presented with care." Williams especially appreciated Frank's use of Bogan's own accounts, contending that her memoirs are the most interesting parts of the book. "Bogan may not have been a major poet," he wrote, "but she showed herself to be an articulate thinker." The *New York Times*'s John Gross found that Frank used Bogan's poems to similar effect. "Above all, of course, there is the poetry," he wrote, "which Miss

Frank analyzes at length, and with considerable skill." According to Gross, *Louise Bogan: A Portrait* was "a biography of the caliber [Bogan] deserves."

Also impressive to many critics was Frank's ability to interpret Bogan's work within the context of her life. Wheeler wrote, "Frank uses Bogan's work to find her ideas, and she uses the ideas to theorize intelligently about those events in Bogan's life that can be documented." Similarly, Alicia Ostriker wrote in the *New York Times Book Review* that Frank "plainly admires both the poet's art and her life, and enables us to see how they illuminate each other, triumphantly and tragically." Ostriker also commended Frank for not "reducing her subject to a titillating love life or a neurosis, though the material for that kind of treatment is not lacking in Bogan's life." For Ostriker, *Louise Bogan: A Portrait* was a "thoughtful biography" of particular interest to Bogan's own readers. And *New Republic* reviewer Richard Howard declared that Frank's elucidation of Bogan's writings resulted in compelling insights into the poet's often tragic life. "This is not a work of literary criticism only, or of biographical exposure merely," Howard contended. "It is a meditation on how to live, traced through the agon of a difficult woman's art."

In her other book, *Jackson Pollock,* Frank surveys the life and work of the abstract American painter whose dense, chaotic works sparked immense controversy in the 1940s and 1950s. Pollock pioneered a form of abstraction known as drip painting, in which colors were splashed and scattered onto vast canvases, and Frank traces the development of his technique within the context of twentieth-century art movements. In arguing that Pollock is "the greatest . . . American painter" of the twentieth century, Frank notes his significance in extending and re-working aspects of the visual arts, and she offers detailed analysis of specific works. Sarah McFadden, reviewing *Jackson Pollock* in *Art in America,* reported that Frank's book would prove "invaluable" to "future students of Pollock's work." McFadden also noted that "Frank provides a distillation of virtually everything that has been published about [Pollock]," and she concluded that Frank had written a nearly "essential Pollock."

Frank told *CA*: "*Louise Bogan: A Portrait* was written out of personal necessity. That is the only way I can write. Biography, it seems me, is a very impure art, and biographical truth perhaps the most elusive of all. More than this I cannot say, except that I continue in current projects to be driven by necessity, and surprised, always, by the uncertainty of everything."

CA INTERVIEW

CA interviewed Elizabeth Frank by telephone on April 1, 1987, at her home in New York City.

CA: Your Pulitzer Prize-winning Louise Bogan: A Portrait *is, as several critics noted, a real "life and works" biography. Did you come to Bogan through an admiration for her writing?*

FRANK: Absolutely. I had admired her works for many years.

CA: Did you ever meet her?

FRANK: No, I didn't. She died three years before I started the project.

CA: As you said in your foreword to the biography, Bogan was "a woman whose passion for reticence bordered on ob-

session," so you had very little to go on. Was this daunting when you set out to research the book?

FRANK: That's why it took me so long to do it. Her papers were housed at the Amherst College Library. There was a great deal in them, but putting the pieces together, finding out where the emphases should be, was a much harder task than I thought it would be. It took a great deal of time and a great deal of research finding what things to follow, what things were more or less important.

CA: You had to become a sort of detective, then.

FRANK: Certainly. And I think any biographer does who doesn't have an authorized relationship to the subject of the book.

CA: Were you ever tempted not to go ahead with it? Was it that frustrating at any point?

FRANK: No, I was never tempted to give it up, but it never occurred to me that this was going to lead to such a large book, and certainly not to a book that would ever enter the Pulitzer ranks or anything like that. I just kept going. And I had to do so many other things while I was writing it—I had to teach, to make a living—that it seemed to me I would never be finished.

CA: What other problems did Bogan present as a subject?

FRANK: Oddly enough, she knew herself so well that it was very difficult to come up with a view of her that wasn't merely a kind of parroting of her own insight about herself. And I'm not sure I actually succeeded in seeing her in a way that's all that different from the way she saw herself. She was so very wise about the patterns in her life that every time I'd formulate a real insight about her, I would find that in many ways she had anticipated me. In fact, I even had to learn how to not use her language. Very few people know themselves as well as this woman knew herself.

CA: That must be related, rather paradoxically perhaps, to her detachment about things.

FRANK: It often meant that there were things I never found out about. Certain events in her childhood I don't think anybody will ever know about; I think they're simply lost forever—certain aspects of her relationship with her mother and her brother and her father that she hinted at but never went into in full. I have come to know her daughter, Maidie Alexander Scannell, quite well, and she doesn't know them either. So I think there were aspects of Bogan's life that were so painful that one simply cannot find out what they are as facts. You can find out what the meaning was in a certain sense, but not the actual content of the events or developments.

CA: In your comments to Contemporary Authors *before this interview, you said that "biography . . . is a very impure art, and biographical truth perhaps the most elusive of all." Is this problem with Bogan the sort of thing you were referring to?*

FRANK: Yes. When you write biography, any shape you put on the subject's life has to be in some way a kind of arbitrary one. You cannot account for every minute and every second. The kind of biography that tries to do that, the huge documentary biography, I usually find unreadable and a terrible bore. You simply can't stuff everything between the covers of a book, and therefore what you select has to be governed by your interest in the subject and not necessarily by how that subject saw herself or lived her life. You don't lie; you don't change the facts. But you always know at the same time that there's an elusive relationship between what you know and what the person's life was really like.

CA: Which may be one of the best reasons for having several biographies of an important figure.

FRANK: I would think so. Certainly if it comes to a diplomat or a president, a statesman, this is true. And I think it's probably true with a literary person as well.

CA: Maidie Alexander Scannell comes across as a very loving and understanding daughter.

FRANK: Yes.

CA: She was away from her mother a great deal, and that must have been hard on her.

FRANK: I think so, but the women in the Bogan line—that is to say, not Bogans but Murphys—are not self-pitiers; they have tremendous energy and gumption, and are very tolerant of one another. Certainly I have found that true of Miss Bogan's daughter.

CA: Did you get very emotionally involved with Louise Bogan along the way?

FRANK: I think I must have. I always knew that I was not she and she was not I; I did not identify with her. I always felt that I was watching and observing someone else. But I cared and still do care very greatly for her, and admired her enormously, and wished very deeply that she had been saved some of the worst of her suffering.

CA: Has the book brought Bogan's poetry more recognition?

FRANK: I don't really think so. I wish it had, but I don't believe that it has brought about more sales of her books. I occasionally hear from this person or that person that reading my book has brought him back to the poetry, and he has realized what a wonderful poet Bogan was. But I'm afraid this is a culture in which poetry is one of the very last of the spiritual necessities. My book has received a wonderful critical reception; I couldn't complain about that at all. But commercially it's a story I'd rather not go into. Neither my biography nor her poetry has really helped one another all that much. I wish the opposite were true.

CA: I suspect that, of the relatively few people who are interested in poetry now, many of them read confessional poetry rather than the kind of poetry they'd need more background for.

FRANK: I think this is true. I'm not a poet, and I don't want to issue wholesale judgments about poetry in this country, especially since right now there are some wonderful poets—among them, women—who are working. But certainly what Louise Bogan herself referred to as formal verse, that is to say poetry written out of a sense of the challenges and the difficulties and the history of the forms of poetry itself, is very rare and is only done well by a small number of people in any generation.

CA: Jackson Pollock, one of the Abbeville Press's Modern Masters Series books, was published in 1984, just a year before Louise Bogan. How did you come to do the Pollock book?

FRANK: The Pollock book, which was of course a very different kind of book from the Bogan, came about because I had been writing about art for many years, mostly in the form of exhibition reviews. I happened to get to know the editor of the Abbeville series, who was looking for people who like to write about art and who are not necessarily involved in a specialized language, in the profession of art history. She listed the titles that were going to appear in the proposed series and asked if I was interested in anybody. As soon as she said Pollock, I absolutely jumped. I said, "I'd love to do that." I'd been an admirer of Pollock's for years, and I also knew that this was not the kind of book that involved original research; it was really a synthesis of available material. It would give me a chance to spend a year or so with Pollock without investing myself in another ten-year job. The Bogan book at that time was in final revision stages. So I was able to do a lot of the work on Pollock and know that I could get the book in. Frankly, after working on one book for ten years and thinking, My God, this will never get done, it was delicious to be able to write a book in a matter of months and see it come out within a year. The Pollock book was written and published long before the Bogan came out.

CA: Have art and literature been equally strong passions for most of your life?

FRANK: Yes. I grew up in the movie industry, and words and images seem to me utterly intertwined parts of the way I think. I'm married to a painter, Howard Buchwald, who is wonderfully visual *and* verbal. I can't imagine an involvement in one aspect of the arts without an involvement in the other. I don't know anything about music, although I have a brother who is a composer and another who is a songwriter. I don't know anything about dance. So my interests don't fan out over all the arts; I wish they did. But certainly words and pictures seem to me two parts of the same language.

CA: Are you a painter or collector?

FRANK: I'm a minor, minor collector. I painted in high school, but that's not where the necessity lay for me.

CA: In writing about someone who has lived in our time, one has the obvious advantage of being able to talk with relatives and friends of the subject, as you did. Are there disadvantages?

FRANK: Sure. This is where one of the impurities of the art of biography most decidedly asserts itself. One has to be very, very careful how one manages information one receives from people who may have less than wholly generous impulses toward the subject. Though I have to say that one of the pleasures of doing the Bogan book was to meet people who knew her and cared about her. My favorite in this group would be the American novelist William Maxwell, who is a fine writer and an extraordinary man. He was a loyal and tender and understanding friend of Louise Bogan's.

Beyond the problem of unfriendly sources, there are always questions of diplomacy and tact. Certain anecdotes which can be highly amusing simply violate the really private life of your subject. And we live in a time in which there tends to be no discrimination about more or less private kinds of information. On the one hand, any biographer who's going to do a good job has to violate the restrictions that the subject places on his or her privacy. That's necessary, because you have to get inside. On the other hand, you have to use your judgment about what constitutes a really and truly revealing piece of information. I think it's not just a question of tact, but of the related word *taste*. If you hear stories about somebody's bedroom life, you have to decide whether they make a true contribution to the story that you want to tell.

I think this is particularly true in the case of people who have died recently, who may have enemies as well as friends. Not everybody adored Louise Bogan. One of the things you have to do when you're a biographer is try not to believe that you are simply a medium for the recording of information. Everything you put down on paper, you are responsible for, even if you got it from somebody else. If you hear a story that you know might entertain a popular kind of audience, but that you feel really violates the dignity of your subject, and if it's not a piece of information that is absolutely essential to your profile, then you don't put it in. On the other hand, you cannot overprotect your subject. That's where biography is an art. It's involved with selection and decision. It's a tremendous responsibility. You are the one who is writing the epitaph.

CA: Are there biographers and biographies that you consider inspirations?

FRANK: This is a terrible thing to say: One, I never thought I would be a biographer—I always thought I was going to write fiction; and two, I've read very few biographies in my life. Certainly the biographies I've read are mostly literary biographies. When I was a child, I read all sorts of biographies for children, oddly enough, and I loved them. But it never occurred to me that I would write biography. There's a wonderful book, out of print, by Geoffrey Scott, an English writer who died. It's called *Portrait of Zelide*. It's a biographical essay about a very obscure late eighteenth-century Dutch bluestocking who lived in Switzerland. It's an interior portrait which is really an imaginative reconstruction, every word of which you believe; you don't think you're reading fiction, and you're not. But it's from the inside, and yet it's based upon the writer's utter mastery of the external facts about this woman's life. Zelide had a very close relationship—one cannot say one way or the other whether it was a love affair—with the young writer Benjamin Constant. It's a lovely book, and it had a great influence on me. It may have been a book that Bogan herself loved; here my memory fails me. Certainly people who knew her and loved her told me to read it.

CA: You were story editor at Connaught Films from 1979 to 1982. Could you tell me something about your work there?

FRANK: That was my father's film company. I read scripts for him and we wrote two scripts together, which I am sad to say have not been made into movies.

CA: You divide your time between teaching and writing, between Bard College and New York City. Is the combination a good one for you?

FRANK: I suppose it is; I don't have much of a choice about it at this point in my life. I teach to make a living. Perhaps, as the years go by and other things happen, I will teach a little bit less. Certainly, since I must teach, I'm fortunate to teach at a wonderful institution with terrific students and colleagues. That part is great. But I make no secret of the fact that I wish I had more time to write.

CA: I know you don't talk about work in progress. Can you at least say if there's going to be another biography?

FRANK: I swore I'd never do another biography, but in fact I'm working on a biographical essay about the painter Esteban Vicente, who is one of the last first-generation New York School artists, a man who came to this country from Spain in 1936. The profile is shorter than the Bogan book, but still long. I work on that when I'm not working on the novel which I have in progress.

BIOGRAPHICAL/CRITICAL SOURCES:

PERIODICALS

Art in America, April, 1984.
Globe and Mail (Toronto), March 30, 1985.
Los Angeles Times Book Review, March 31, 1985.
Ms., December, 1984.
Nation, February 23, 1985.
New Republic, March 25, 1985.
New Yorker, July 29, 1985.
New York Times, February 15, 1985.
New York Times Book Review, March 3, 1985, November 30, 1986.
Washington Post Book World, February 24, 1985.

—Sketch by Les Stone

—Interview by Jean W. Ross

* * *

FRANK, Melvin   1913(?)-1988

OBITUARY NOTICE: Born August 13, 1913 (one source says 1917), in Chicago, Ill.; died of complications from open-heart surgery, October 13, 1988, in Los Angeles, Calif. Film producer and director, radio scriptwriter, and screenwriter. From 1938 until 1960, Frank collaborated with Norman Panama on the writing, production, or direction of many films, including the 1954 box-office hit "White Christmas." After they met in the early 1930s as students at the University of Chicago, the duo moved to Hollywood to write for comedian Bob Hope's radio show, beginning an association that would last for years. Hope went on to star in several movies that Frank and Panama wrote, including "My Favorite Blonde" and "The Road to Hong Kong." The pair was nominated for Academy awards for their work on "The Road to Utopia," "Knock on Wood," and "The Facts of Life." In addition, the partners wrote a Broadway musical based on Al Capp's comic strip "Li'l Abner," which they later made into a movie. After 1960, Frank produced several movies on his own, notably "The Prisoner of Second Avenue" and "Lost and Found." He received Academy Award nominations for producing and for writing, with Jack Rose, the 1973 film "A Touch of Class," for which he is perhaps best remembered. In 1987 he directed "Walk Like a Man," his last film.

OBITUARIES AND OTHER SOURCES:

BOOKS

Halliwell's Filmgoer's Companion, 7th edition, Granada, 1980.

International Motion Picture Almanac, Quigley, 1988.

PERIODICALS

Chicago Tribune, October 16, 1988.
Los Angeles Times, October 15, 1988.
New York Times, October 15, 1988.
Times (London), October 26, 1988.
Washington Post, October 17, 1988.

* * *

FRANKLIN, Jimmie Lewis   1939-

PERSONAL: Born April 10, 1939, in Moscow, Miss.; married, 1961; children: one. *Education:* Jackson State College (now University), B.A., 1961; University of Oklahoma, M.A., 1964, Ph.D., 1968.

ADDRESSES: Office—Department of History, Eastern Illinois University, Charleston, Ill. 61920.

CAREER: University of Wisconsin—Stevens Point, assistant professor of history, 1966-69; University of Washington, Seattle, assistant professor of history, 1969-70; Eastern Illinois University, Charleston, associate professor of history, 1970—. Visiting professor at American Studies Center, Hyderabad, India, 1970.

MEMBER: Organization of American Historians, Association for the Study of Negro Life and History, Southern Historical Association.

WRITINGS:

Born Sober: A History of Prohibition in Oklahoma, 1907-1959, University of Oklahoma Press, 1971.
The Blacks in Oklahoma, University of Oklahoma Press, 1980.
Journey Toward Hope: A History of Blacks in Oklahoma, University of Oklahoma Press, 1982.*

* * *

FRANTZ, Douglas   1949-

PERSONAL: Born September 29, 1949, in North Manchester, Ind.; son of Donald E. (a builder) and Jo Joyce (a golfer; maiden name, Urschel) Frantz; married Catherine Ann Collins (a writer), October 15, 1983; children: Elizabeth, Nicholas, Rebecca. *Education:* DePauw University, B.A., 1971; Columbia University, M.S., 1975.

ADDRESSES: Home—San Pedro, Calif. *Office*—*Los Angeles Times,* Times Mirror Sq., Los Angeles, Calif. 90053. *Agent*—Dominick Abel, 498 West End Ave., New York, N.Y. 10024.

CAREER: Albuquerque Tribune, Albuquerque, N.M., city editor, 1975-78; *Chicago Tribune,* Chicago, Ill., reporter, 1978-87; *Los Angeles Times,* Los Angeles, Calif., reporter, 1987—.

AWARDS, HONORS: Sigma Delta Chi Award, 1985, for financial reporting; Associated Press-Illinois Award, 1986, and Raymond Clapper Award, 1987, both for investigative reporting; *Business Week* named *Levine & Co.* one of the best books in 1987.

WRITINGS:

Levine & Co.: The Story of Wall Street's Insider Trading Scandal, Holt, 1987.

Contributor to magazines, including *Esquire.*

WORK IN PROGRESS: A nonfiction book, with wife, Catherine Collins.

SIDELIGHTS: In 1978, investor Dennis Levine entered Wall Street with a modest investment of forty thousand dollars. His goal was to become rich as quickly as possible, regardless of the means employed. Within five years his fortune, stored in a Swiss bank located in the Bahamas, had grown to twelve million dollars. In 1986 Levine was arrested and pleaded guilty to the felony of insider trading. He was sentenced to spend two years in a federal prison in Pennsylvania.

In his book *Levine & Co.*, investigative reporter Douglas Frantz traces the felon's career from Baruch College in New York where, by his own admission, Levine learned the philosophy of greed through the prestigious investment houses of Smith Barney, Harris Upham and Company, Lehman Brothers Kuhn Loeb, Inc., and Drexel Burnham Lambert, Inc. Levine's phenomenal success was based largely on illegal inside tips from lawyers and bankers who informed him of potential corporate takeovers in time to profit from them. The investor's relationships with these informants and with the foreign bankers who accepted his money are the focus of Frantz's book. The author emphasizes that most of the participants in Wall Street's insider trading scandal were by no means innocent victims of Levine's trading scheme. They were knowledgeable bankers who were willing to turn a blind eye to his illegal activities and reap their share of the profits. The scheme was only uncovered, related Bernie Shellum in the *Detroit Free Press*, "because of a seemingly rare expression of ethical concern; an anonymous note from someone in Caracas to Merrill Lynch's New York headquarters." Patricia O'Toole of the *New York Times Book Review* found *Levine & Co.* to be "a taut and admirably clear reconstruction of one of the biggest scandals in Wall Street history." She recommended the book as "a lucid and compelling introduction to the arcane world of corporate finance."

Frantz told *CA:* "I started work on *Levine & Co.* for a selfish reason: After nearly fifteen years on newspapers, mostly as an investigative reporter, I thought this was the most compelling story I had ever come across. Greed, ambition, and betrayal were set on Wall Street, Park Avenue, and Nassau. There were bags stuffed with cash, code names, and a red Ferrari. The scandal also symbolized the 1980s pursuit of money by a new generation. As a participant in the protest movement of the 1960s and early 1970s, I had difficulty understanding the attitude of these young people. And along the way I discovered that I was writing a cautionary tale. The story of Dennis Levine is not only about shattered lives and stolen millions. It is a warning that Wall Street is out of control, its culture nourishing a dozen Dennis Levines and Ivan Boeskys whose only crime seems to be that they got caught. Without abandoning my role as a fact-gatherer and storyteller and donning a preacher's robe, I think the book conveys this message in terms that anyone can understand."

BIOGRAPHICAL/CRITICAL SOURCES:

PERIODICALS

Detroit Free Press, October 14, 1987.
New York Times Book Review, October 25, 1987.

*   *   *

FRAZE, Candida (Merrill)   1945-

PERSONAL: Born March 25, 1945, in Washington, D.C.; daughter of France and Kathleen (a translator; maiden name, Dillon) Fraze; married Peter Moskovitz (an orthopedic surgeon), August 25, 1967; children: David, Zoe. *Education:* Swarthmore College, B.A., 1967; attended Columbia University, 1968-69, and George Washington University, 1969-71.

ADDRESSES: Home—Washington, D.C. *Agent*—John Ware, 392 Central Park W., New York, N.Y. 10025.

CAREER: Urban planner, 1971-73; writer, 1980—. Member of board of directors and faculty of Writer's Center, Bethesda, Md.; member of board of Watershed Foundation; member of Poetry Committee, Folger Library.

MEMBER: Authors Guild.

WRITINGS:

Renifleur's Daughter (novel), Holt, 1987.

Contributor of poems to magazines, including *Poet Lore* and *Centennial*.

WORK IN PROGRESS: Another novel.

SIDELIGHTS: Candida Fraze told *CA:* "I began writing as a poet, and that impulse informs all my work. Poetry is where it all begins, but I am equally devoted to the idea of story or narrative. I expect my writing life to be occupied with fiction, primarily in the form of the novel."

AVOCATIONAL INTERESTS: Looking at art, listening to vocal music.

BIOGRAPHICAL/CRITICAL SOURCES:

PERIODICALS

Los Angeles Times, July 24, 1987.

*   *   *

FREDERIC, Mike
See COX, William R(obert)

*   *   *

FREEDMAN, Dan   1952-

PERSONAL: Born October 27, 1952, in New York, N.Y.; son of Alfred M. (a physician) and Marcia (an economist; maiden name, Kohl) Freedman; married Mary Anne Hess (a homemaker), July 26, 1981; children: Aleksandra Johnson, Jacob, Andrew. *Education:* Rutgers University, B.A., 1974; Columbia University, M.S., 1977.

ADDRESSES: Office—Hearst Newspapers, 1701 Pennsylvania Ave. N.W., Washington, D.C. 20006.

CAREER: Camden-Cherry Hill Courier-Post, Cherry Hill, N.J., reporter, 1978-80; free-lance journalist in Guatemala, El Salvador, and Honduras, 1980-81; *Philadelphia Bulletin*, Philadelphia, Pa., reporter, 1981-82; *San Antonio Light*, San Antonio, Tex., reporter and editor, 1982-87; Hearst Newspapers, Washington Bureau, Washington, D.C., legal affairs correspondent, 1987—.

AWARDS, HONORS: State awards for editorial writing from Associated Press and United Press International of Texas; awards for reporting from Hearst Corporation and San Antonio chapter of Sigma Delta Chi Society of Professional Journalists.

WRITINGS:

(Editor with Jacqueline Rhoads) *Nurses in Vietnam: The Forgotten Veterans,* Texas Monthly, 1987.

WORK IN PROGRESS: Research for a historical novel set in Mexico and Central America.

SIDELIGHTS: Dan Freedman told *CA:* "*Nurses in Vietnam: The Forgotten Veterans* began as a Sunday newspaper magazine article; I was working for the *San Antonio Light* at the time. I discovered that there was a significant population of nurses who served in Vietnam now living in San Antonio. The idea that women had served in Vietnam struck me as news, and as I learned more about what these women went through, I realized that their experiences transcended the formats of both the newspaper and the Sunday magazine. With one of the nurses who formed the basis of the original magazine article, I gathered together nine nurses whose memories represented the broadest range of experiences of nurses who were in Vietnam.

"There was one slightly odd personal twist to this. In high school in New York in the late 1960s, I was an activist against the war in Vietnam. I was the kind of person these women and their male colleagues in uniform loathed: one who marched in parades and shouted protest epithets. Having transformed myself at some point in the 1970s into an objective journalist, I found it possible to empathize with these women and relate their stories honestly, and also to maintain my conviction that our protests against the Vietnam War were correct. In one way, their recounting of the horror and brutality of working in field hospitals trying to save young soldiers helped reconfirm that conviction. But in another way, I came to admire the heroism and sacrifice of these women—qualities I don't think I would have recognized back in 1968.

"Since the publication of *Nurses in Vietnam,* my focus has returned to journalism, this time in Washington, D.C., as a correspondent covering the Supreme Court and the Department of Justice. In time, I hope to embark on another project, a work of fiction that traces the crisis of Central America in the 1970s and 1980s back to the individual experiences in the 1920s and 1930s of revolutionaries like Augusto Cesar Sandino of Nicaragua and Farabundo Marti of El Salvador."

*   *   *

FREEMAN, Cynthia
See FEINBERG, Beatrice Cynthia Freeman

*   *   *

FREI, Hans W(ilhelm)   1922-1988

OBITUARY NOTICE: Born April 29, 1922, in Breslau, Germany (now East Germany); immigrated to United States, 1938, naturalized citizen, 1945; died of a stroke, September 13 (one source says September 12), 1988, in New Haven, Conn. Theologian, educator, and author. After teaching at Wabash College and at the Episcopal Theological Seminary Southwest, Frei joined the Yale University faculty in 1957 and went on to become John A. Hoober Professor of Religious Studies there. His best-known work was the influential *Eclipse of Biblical Narrative: A Study in Eighteenth and Nineteenth Century Hermeneutics,* in which he suggested that modern theology had neglected to study the Bible's narrative form. His *Identity of Jesus Christ: The Hermeneutical Bases of Dogmatic Theology*

offered an interpretation of Jesus's life and teachings based on a study of the Scripture's narrative features, making popular the use of literary criticism's methods for biblical analysis. Frei, an Episcopal priest, also wrote several essays on prominent twentieth-century theologians.

OBITUARIES AND OTHER SOURCES:

BOOKS

Directory of American Scholars, Volume IV: *Philosophy, Religion, and Law,* 8th edition, Bowker, 1982.
Who's Who in Religion, Marquis, 1975.

PERIODICALS

New York Times, September 14, 1988.
Washington Post, September 16, 1988.

*   *   *

FRENAY, Henri   1905-1988

OBITUARY NOTICE: Born November 19, 1905, in Lyons, France; died August 6, 1988, in Paris, France. Soldier, political leader, publisher, manufacturing executive, and author. A career soldier in the French army, Frenay became an important resistance leader during the World War II Nazi occupation of France. He organized a liberation movement called Combat in 1941 and became the publisher of its underground newspaper of the same name. After escaping the Nazi secret police several times, Frenay joined his forces with the Secret Army led by future president Charles de Gaulle, and he served for nearly two years as political adviser in the organization. Rivalries within the French resistance, however, prevented Frenay from ever gaining much political power in the newly formed provisional government, and in 1944 he worked in Algeria as minister for prisoners and refugees. For his efforts in liberating the country, Frenay was made a grand officer of the French Legion of Honor. Retiring from political life in 1946, Frenay became an executive for a toy manufacturing firm and wrote several books about his wartime experiences, including *La Nuit finira: Memoires de Resistance,* translated as *The Night Will End,* its sequel, *Volontaires de la nuit,* and *L'Enigme Jean Moulin.*

OBITUARIES AND OTHER SOURCES:

BOOKS

The Historical Encyclopedia of World War II, Facts on File, 1980.
Who's Who in France, 18th edition, Lafitte, 1985.

PERIODICALS

Los Angeles Times, August 9, 1988.
Times (London), August 9, 1988.

*   *   *

FREY, Richard L(incoln)   1905-1988

OBITUARY NOTICE—See index for *CA* sketch: Born February 12, 1905, in New York, N.Y.; died of cancer, October 17, 1988, in New York, N.Y. Cardplaying expert, business manager, editor, and author. During his career as a contract bridge player Frey won six national bridge tournaments and was a runner-up in seven. He was nominated a life master in 1936, the year the rank was introduced. Frey also served as writer, editor, and business manager of Kem Cards, an early manufacturer of plastic playing cards, and as editor and public relations director for the American Contract Bridge League. After his retirement in 1970 from League duties Frey became president of the International Bridge Press Association, a post he held until 1981, when he was appointed president emeritus. Frey wrote or edited numerous books on bridge and other card games, including *How to Win at Contract Bridge in Ten Easy Lessons, The Official Encyclopedia of Bridge,* and *According to Hoyle—Rules of Games: Official Rules of More Than 300 Popular Games of Skill and Chance, With Expert Advice on Winning Play.* Frey also collaborated on a syndicated daily bridge column and contributed articles to *Cosmopolitan, McCall's, Reader's Digest, Sports Illustrated,* and other periodicals.

OBITUARIES AND OTHER SOURCES:

BOOKS

Who's Who in America, 43rd edition, Marquis, 1984.

PERIODICALS

Chicago Tribune, October 20, 1988, October 23, 1988.
New York Times, October 19, 1988.

*   *   *

FREYRE, Gilberto (de Mello)   1900-1987

PERSONAL: Born March 15, 1900, in Recife, Brazil; died of a stroke, July 18, 1987, in Recife, Brazil; son of Alfredo (a teacher and judge) and Francisca (de Mello) Freyre; married Magdalena Guedes Pereira, 1941; children: one son, one daughter. *Education:* Baylor University, B.A., 1920; Columbia University, M.A.; graduate study at several universities in Europe and the United States.

ADDRESSES: Home—Rua Dois Irmaos, 320, Apipucos, 50000 Recife, Brazil.

CAREER: Pernambuco State Normal School, Recife, Brazil, teacher of sociology, 1928-30; University of Sao Paolo, Sao Paolo, Brazil, professor of sociology and founding professor of social anthropology, 1935-38; member of the Brazilian Chamber of Deputies, Rio de Janeiro, Brazil, 1946-51; Joaquim Nambuco Institute for Research in the Social Sciences, Recife, founder, 1949; Brazilian ambassador to the United Nations, 1949 and 1964; North-East Brazil Social and Educational Research Center, Recife, supervisor, 1957-87. Visiting professor and lecturer at numerous universities in Brazil, Europe, and the United States; organized first Afro-Brazilian Congress, 1934; adviser to the Brazilian government on the preservation of historical documents and monuments; member of the Federal Council of Culture of Brazil, the Ibero-American Council of Cultural Affairs, and the United Nations Committee on Race Relations in South Africa, 1954; director of scholarly journals *Diogene* and *Cahiers Internationaux de Sociologie.*

MEMBER: American Anthropological Association, American Philosophical Association, Lisbon Geographical Society, Portuguese Academy of Sciences, Real Academia of Spain, Hispanic Society of America, numerous historical societies.

AWARDS, HONORS: Filipe d'Oliveira Award for *The Masters and the Slaves,* 1934, Amsfield-Wolf Award from Princeton University, 1957; Brazilian Academy of Letters Award for high literary merit, 1959; Great Cross of Military Merit (Brazil), 1960; Great Cross of the Brazilian Order of Baron of Rio Branco for diplomacy, 1966; Aspen Award from the Aspen

Institute for Humanistic Studies, 1967, for contribution to the advancement of the humanities; knighted by Queen Elizabeth II, 1971; twice nominated for the Nobel Prize in literature.

WRITINGS:

Casa-grande e senzala, Schmidt, 1933, 20th edition published by J. Olympio, 1980, translation by Samuel Putnam published as *The Masters and the Slaves,* Knopf, 1946, University of California Press, 1986.
Guia pratico, historico e sentimental de cidade do Recife, J. Olympio, 1934, 4th revised edition, 1968.
(Contributor) *Estudos afro-brasileiros,* Ariel, 1935-37.
Artigos de jornal, Edicoes Mozart, 1935, revised and expanded edition published as *Retalhos de jornais velhos,* J. Olympio, 1964.
Sobrados e mucambos, Editora Nacional, 1936, 4th edition, J. Olympio, 1968, translation by Harriet de Onis published as *The Mansions and the Shanties,* Knopf, 1963, University of California Press, 1986.
Nordeste, aspectos de influencia da canna sobre a vide e a paizagem do nordeste do Brasil, J. Olympio, 1937, 2nd revised edition, 1951.
Conferencias na Europa, lidas nas universidades de Coimbra, Lisboa e Porto e no King's College, Servico Grafico, 1938.
Olinda, 2do guia pratico historico e sentimental de cidade brasileira, Drechsler, 1939, 5th revised edition, J. Olympio, 1980.
O mundo que o portugues criou: Aspectos das relacoes sociaes e de cultura do Brasil com Portugal e as colonias portuguesas, J. Olympio, 1940.
Uma cultura ameacada: A luso-brasileira, Casa do Estudante do Brasil, 1940.
Um engenheiro frances no Brasil, J. Olympio, 1940.
Regiao e tradicao, J. Olympio, 1941.
Ingleses, J. Olympio, 1942.
Problemas brasileiros de antropologia, Casa do Estudante do Brasil, 1943.
Na Bahia em 1943, Companhia Brasileira de Artes Graficas, 1944.
Perfil de Euclydes e outros perfis, J. Olympio, 1944.
Sociologia, J. Olympio, 1945, 5th revised edition, 1973.
Brazil: An Interpretation, Knopf, 1945, revised and expanded edition published as *New World in the Tropics: The Culture of Modern Brazil,* 1959, reprinted, Greenwood, 1980.
Ingleses no Brasil: Aspectos da influencia britanica sobre a vida, a paisagem e a cultura do Brasil, J. Olympio, 1948, 2nd edition, 1977.
Quase politica, J. Olympio, 1950.
Aventura e rotina, J. Olympio, 1953, 2nd revised edition, 1980.
Um brasileiro em terras portuguesas, J. Olympio, 1953.
Assombrancoes do Recife velho, Conde, 1955.
Manifesto regionalista de 1926, Ministerio da Educacao e Cultura, 1955.
Integracao portuguesa nos tropicos/Portuguese Integration in the Tropics (text in both Portuguese and English), Minerva (Lisbon), 1958.
A proposito de frades, Livraria Progresso, 1959.
Ordem e progresso, J. Olympio, 1959, translation by Rod W. Horton published as *Order and Progress: Brazil From Monarchy to Republic,* Knopf, 1970, University of California Press, 1986.
Brasis, Brasil, e Brasilia, Edicao Livros do Brasil (Lisbon), 1960.

Uma politica transnacional de cultura para o Brasil do hoje, Faculdade de Direito da Universidade de Minas Gerais, 1960.

O luso e o tropico, [Lisbon], 1961.

Sugestoes de um novo contacto com universidades europeias, Imprensa Universitaria, 1961.

Arte, ciencia e tropico: Em torno de alguns problemas de sociologia da arte, Martins, 1962, 2nd revised edition, DIFEL, 1980.

Talvez poesia (poetry), J. Olympio, 1962.

Homem, cultura e tropico, Imprensa Universitaria, 1962.

Brazil, Pan American Union, 1963.

O escravo nos anuncios de jornais brasileiros do seculo XIX, Imprensa Universitaria, 1963, 2nd revised edition, Editora Nacional, 1979.

Dona Sinha e o filho padre: Seminovela (novel), J. Olympio, 1964, translation by Barbara Shelby published as *Mother and Son: A Brazilian Tale,* Knopf, 1967.

Seis conferencias em busca de un leitor, J. Olympio, 1965.

The Racial Factor in Contemporary Politics, MacGibbon & Kee, 1966.

Sociologia da medicina, Fundacao Calouste Gulbenkian (Lisbon), 1967.

Oliveira Lima, Don Quixote gordo, Universidade Federal de Pernambuco, 1968.

Como e porque sou e nao sou sociologo, Editora da Universidade, 1968.

Acucar: Em torno da etnografia da historia e da sociologia da doce Nordeste canaveiro do Brasil, Ministerio da Industria e do Comercio, 1969.

(Contributor) *Cana e reforma agraria,* Instituto Joaquim Nambuco de Pesquisas Sociais, 1970.

Nos e a Europa germanica, Grifo Edicoes, 1971.

Seleta para jovens, J. Olympio, 1971, translation by Barbara Shelby published as *The Gilberto Freyre Reader,* Knopf, 1974.

Sociologia do acucar, Museu do Acucar, 1971.

Pernambuco, sim, Agencia Jornalistica Image, 1972.

A condicao humana e outras temas, Grifo Edicoes, 1972.

Alem do apenas moderno, J. Olympio, 1975.

O brasileiro entre os outros hispanos, J. Olympio, 1975.

A presenca do acucar na formacao brasileira, Ministerio da Industria e do Comercio, 1975.

Tempo morto e outros tempos: Trechos de um diario de adolescencia e primeira mocidade, 1915-1930, J. Olympio, 1975.

Obra escolhida (selected works; contains *Casa-grande e senzala, Nordeste,* and *Novo Mundo nos tropicos,* biographical notes, and bibliography), Editora Nova Aguilar, 1977.

O outro amor do Dr. Paulo: Seminovela (novel), J. Olympio, 1977.

Prefacios desgarrados, Editora Catedra, 1978.

Alhos e bugalhos (literary criticism), Editora Nova Fronteira, 1978.

Cartas do proprio punho sobre pessoas e coisas do Brasil e do estrangeiro, Conselho Federal de Cultura e Departamento de Assuntos Culturais, 1978.

Contribuicao para uma sociologia da biografia: O exemplo de Luiz de Albuquerque, governador de Mato Grosso no fim do seculo XVIII, Fundacao Cultural de Mato Grosso, 1978.

Recife e Olinda, Editora Nacional, 1978.

Tempo de aprendiz: Artigos publicados em jornais na adolescencia e na primeira mocidade do autor, 1918-1926, Instituicao Brasileira de Difusao Cultural, 1979.

Oh de casa! Em torno da casa brasileira e de sua projecao sobre um tipo nacional de homem, Editora Artenova, 1979.

Herois e viloes no romance brasileiro, Editor Cultrix, 1979.

Pessoas, coisas e animais, MPM Propaganda, 1979.

Poesia reunida (poetry), Edicoes Pirata, 1980.

Author of numerous short scholarly works; contributor of articles to newspapers and magazines.

SIDELIGHTS: The Brazilian social anthropologist Gilberto Freyre won international renown for his studies tracing the evolution of modern Brazilian society from its roots in the paternalistic slaveholding culture of past centuries. Although he produced more than one hundred books during his long career, Freyre's first major work, *The Masters and the Slaves,* is regarded as his masterpiece. Freyre wrote the outlines of this work as his master's thesis under the aegis of the celebrated American anthropologist Franz Boas at Columbia University, and critic H. L. Mencken later encouraged him to expand the published paper into a full-fledged study. The resulting book has been hailed as one of the outstanding works of Latin American scholarship and a brilliant analysis of the origin of Brazilian cultural mores and racial attitudes.

A principal—and controversial—argument that Freyre advanced in *The Masters and the Slaves* to explain Brazil's relatively harmonious race relations is that the country's Portuguese colonizers from the sixteenth to the nineteenth centuries were more tolerant about race-mixing than were their Anglo-Saxon counterparts in North America. Freyre asserts that many early Portuguese settlers were of a rather liberal disposition, their Catholicism tempered by Moorish and Jewish influences, which led them to take somewhat more human attitudes towards the native Amerindians and the African slaves they imported to work on the colony's vast sugar plantations. Unlike the Puritans, who usually brought their European wives with them to North America, the Brazilian colonizers tended to be single men who took black concubines and recognized and supported their mixed-race offspring.

This widespread race-mixing and cultural cross-fertilization created, according to Freyre, a population with a vibrant and distinctive civilization uniquely suited to the conditions of life in tropical Brazil. African religion and music, Amerindian knowledge of the land and natural resources, and Portuguese technical and commercial skills combined agreeably to make the modern Brazilian a triumph of natural selection. Freyre's thesis clashed head-on with the prevailing sociological opinion of the day, which regarded the mixed-race *mestizo* as degenerate and held that miscegenation was a principal cause of Brazil's social and economic backwardness. Ridiculing this racist theory based on nineteenth-century pseudoscience, Freyre pointed to the legacy of slavery and other social and cultural factors in explaining Brazil's failure to overcome endemic poverty and develop into an advanced industrial society.

Freyre also broke new ground with his discursive and multidisciplinary approach to history, which emphasized the minutiae of everyday social life to concretely illustrate the broader sweep of historical events and give an accurate flavor of the time. Combining the tools and insights of sociology, anthropology, psychology, philosophy, and art criticism, Freyre offered colorful details about colonial diets, speech, architecture, furniture, and countless other particularities that made up the typical lifestyles of the various social classes. In keeping with this conception, the author adopted a vivid and spontaneous writing style that the Latin Americanist Frank Tannenbaum likened to "a flowing stream after a storm; it is full, deep, and sparkling."

Though usually hailed as a most impressive work of literature and scholarship, *The Masters and the Slaves* has seen its share of detractors over the years. Freyre in particular has come under criticism for his insistence that the Brazilian slaveholding system was relatively benign and for generalizing about social behavior in Brazil as a whole on the basis of a study that focuses exclusively on the north-eastern region of the country. Freyre has also been accused of exaggerating the degree of "racial democracy" in contemporary Brazil and for ignoring widespread and longstanding discrimination against dark-skinned Brazilians. Some academics, moreover, find fault with the author's multidisciplinary approach and broad subject range and question the study's scientific rigor. Finally, Freyre's unorthodox style and organization irritate readers accustomed to linear and thematic history.

Few of Freyre's critics dispute the profound effect that this work of social anthropology has had on contemporary Brazilian society, however. Freyre's demolition of old racist myths and insistence on the benefits of mestizism revolutionized Brazilians' self-image, encouraging a new sense of pride in cultural diversity and an identity as a mixed-race nation. As Tannenbaum remarked, *The Masters and the Slaves* succeeded in "changing Brazil's image of itself. . . . The only other country in Latin America where a similar development has taken place is Mexico. But there it required a bloody revolution, untold suffering, and the loss of a million lives. In Brazil it was accomplished by one man and one book."

Freyre wrote two subsequent companion volumes to *The Masters and the Slaves* that describe the evolution of Brazilian society and culture to the present century. *The Mansions and the Shanties* analyzes the gradual disintegration of the patriarchal plantation system in the nineteenth century and the development of urban society in Brazil. The author particularly noted the rise of a new *mestizo* political and economic elite. In *Order and Progress* Freyre discussed the circumstances surrounding the overthrow of the Brazilian monarchy in 1889 and the foundation of a conservative republic that presided over the transition from a slave- to a wage-labor economy. Freyre's trilogy has been published in numerous languages and in 1986 was reissued in English by the University of California Press.

Among Freyre's many other works on Brazilian social history, *Brazil: An Interpretation*, published in 1945, holds special interest as a guide to the author's key historiographical ideas. Written in English, the book is based on a lecture series Freyre delivered at Indiana University in 1944 and discusses the problem of racial integration, the political and social role of the *mestizo* in modern Brazil, and the challenge of creating political unity while respecting regional diversity. One of Freyre's most popular works, *Brazil: An Interpretation* was also well-received critically, although the Brazilian scholar Afranio Coutinho objected to what he regarded as the author's overemphasis on social phenomena to interpret national life.

While pursuing his writing and academic work, Freyre was also active in Brazilian political and artistic circles during much of his life. In the 1920s he became a principal leader of the regionalist movement in the northeast, the first and most important of several such movements that were organized around the country beginning in those years. The northeast movement helped inspire a number of outstanding local writers and artists, including the well-known novelist Jorge Amado. This new pride in regional culture and social traditions also helped forge an incipient nationalist consciousness in Brazil and stimulated Freyre's interest in politics. He worked for four years in the 1920s as secretary to the governor of his native state of Pernambuco and was briefly imprisoned by dictatorial governments in 1930 and 1934 as a "leftist agitator." Freyre later shifted his political views to the right and served as a conservative federal congressman from 1946 to 1951 and then as Brazil's ambassador to the United Nations.

Late in life the renowned social historian decided to try his hand at writing a historical novel, or a "semi-novel," as he put it, constructed with an original technique that combined slices of actual history with a fictional narrative. Set during a period of great political and religious ferment in nineteenth-century Brazil, *Mother and Son* is the story of a young man pushed into the priesthood and into homosexuality by an overprotective mother. *New York Review of Books* critic John Wain judged *Mother and Son* a failure in novelistic terms but added that Freyre's historical passion still made it "a charming book, capable of giving much pleasure and illumination." Alexander Coleman of the *New York Times Book Review* called the novel "delicate, immensely touching, generous in its comprehension of sexual ambivalence. Just as Freyre's earlier work elevated the mulatto of mixed race from the realm of supposed cultural inferiority, so 'Mother and Son' brings about a greater historical understanding of bisexuality in a matriarchal culture."

BIOGRAPHICAL/CRITICAL SOURCES:

BOOKS

Coutinho, Afranio, *An Introduction to Literature in Brazil*, translated from the Portuguese by Gregory Rabassa, Columbia University Press, 1969.

Freyre, Gilberto, *Tempo morto e outros tempos: Trechos de um diario de adolescencia e primeira mocidade, 1915-1930*, J. Olympio, 1975.

Freyre, Gilberto, *The Mansions and the Shanties*, introduction by Frank Tannenbaum, Knopf, 1963.

Meneses, Diogo de Melo, *Gilberto Freyre: Notas biograficas com ilustraciones*, [Rio de Janeiro], 1944.

PERIODICALS

Americas, May, 1949, January/February, 1984.
National Review, October 6, 1970.
New York Review of Books, May 4, 1967.
New York Times, May 2, 1967, June 2, 1980.
New York Times Book Review, May 7, 1967.

OBITUARIES:

PERIODICALS

Los Angeles Times, July 20, 1987.
New York Times, July 19, 1987.
Times (London), July 20, 1987.*

—*Sketch by Curtis Skinner*

*   *   *

FRIED, Erich   1921-

PERSONAL: Born May 6, 1921, in Vienna, Austria; immigrated to England, 1938; son of Hugo (a haulage contractor and hypnotist) and Nellie (a fashion designer; maiden name, Stein) Fried; married Maria Marburg, 1944 (marriage ended); married Nan Spence, 1951 (marriage ended); married Katherine Boswell, 1965 (marriage ended); children: two sons, two daughters. *Education:* Attended state schools in Vienna, Austria. *Politics:* Socialist. *Religion:* Jewish.

CAREER: Writer and translator, 1938—. Child actor in Vienna, Austria, c. 1926-27; chemist analyzing milk for United Dairies, librarian, and glass-factory worker in London, England, 1938-46; joint editor of *Blick in die Welt* (a periodical), London, 1950-52; translator in German language division, British Broadcasting Corporation, London, 1952-68.

MEMBER: Gruppe 47 (a German writers' association).

AWARDS, HONORS: Co-recipient of Schiller-Gedaechtnispreises des Landes Baden-Wuerttemberg, 1967; Oesterreichischer Wuerdigungspreis fuer Literatur, 1972; International Publishers' Prize, 1977, for *Hundert Gedichte ohne Vaterland;* Preis der Stadt Wien fuer Literatur, 1980; Bremer Literaturpreis, 1983.

WRITINGS:

POETRY IN ENGLISH

Last Honors (dual language edition), translation by Georg Rapp, Turret, 1968.
On Pain of Seeing, translation by Rapp, Swallow Press, 1969.
Hundert Gedichte ohne Vaterland, Wagenbach, 1978, translation by Stuart Hood published as *One Hundred Poems Without a Country,* J. Calder, 1978, Red Dust, 1980.

POETRY IN GERMAN

Deutschland (title means "Germany"), Austrian P.E.N., 1944.
Oesterreich (title means "Austria"), Atrium, 1945.
Gedichte, Claassen, 1958.
Reich der Steine (title means "Realm of Stones"), Claassen, 1963.
Ueberlegungen (title means "Reflections"), Hanser, 1964.
Warngedichte (title means "Poems of Warning"), Hanser, 1964.
Und Vietnam und . . . (title means "And Vietnam and . . ."), Wagenbach, 1966.
Anfechtungen (title means "Arguments"), Wagenbach, 1967.
Zeitfragen, Hanser, 1968.
Befreiung von der Flucht (title means "Deliverance from Flight"), Claassen, 1968, enlarged edition, 1983.
Die Beine der groesseren Luegen (title means "The Legs of the Bigger Lies"), Wagenbach, 1969.
Unter Nebenfeinden, Wagenbach, 1970.
Aufforderung zur Unruhe, Deutscher Taschenbuch, 1972.
Die Freiheit den Mund aufzumachen, Wagenbach, 1972.
Gegengift, Wagenbach, 1974.
Hoere, Israel! Verlag Association (Hamburg), 1974, expanded edition, Syndikat, 1983.
Kampf ohne Engel, Volk und Welt, 1976.
Die bunten Getueme, Wagenbach, 1977.
So kam ich unter die Deutschen, Verlag Association, 1977.
Liebesgedichte (title means "Love Poetry"), Wagenbach, 1979.
Lebensschatten, Wagenbach, 1981.
Zur Zeit und zur Unzeit, Bund-Verlag, 1981.
(Contributor) Stephanie Vernholz, editor, *Ganz oben leichte Voegel,* Flieter Verlag, 1982.
Das Missverstaendnis, Alibaba, 1982.
Das Nahe suchen, Wagenbach, 1982.
Es ist was es ist: Liebesgedichte, Angstgedichte, Zorngedichte, Wagenbach, 1983.
Beunruhigungen, Wagenbach, 1984.
Verstandsaufnahme, Wagenbach, 1984.
Um Klarheit, Wagenbach, 1985.
In die Sinne einradiert, Bund, 1985.

Von Bis nach Seit: Gedichte aus den Jahren 1945-1958, Promedia, 1985.
Fruehe Gedichte, Claassen, 1986.
(With Claudia Hahm and David Fried) *Waechst das Rettende auch? Gedichte fuer den Frieden,* Bund-Verlag, 1986.

FICTION

Ein Soldat und ein Maedchen (novel; title means "A Soldier and a Girl"), Claassen, 1960.
Kinder und Narren (title means "Children and Fools"), Hanser, 1965.
Fast alles Moegliche (collection of stories), Wagenbach, 1975.
Das Unmass aller Dinge (collection of stories), Wagenbach, 1982.

RADIO PLAYS

"Izanagi und Izanami," Norddeutscher Rundfunk, 1960.
"Die Expedition," Norddeutscher Rundfunk, 1962.
"Indizienbeweise," Norddeutscher Rundfunk/Sueddeutscher Rundfunk, 1966.
"Welch' Licht scheint dort," Radio DRS, 1980.

VOLUMES TRANSLATED BY FRIED

Dylan Thomas, *Am fruehen Morgen: Autobiographisches, Radio-Essays, Gedichte und Prosa,* Drei Bruecken Verlag, 1957.
Dylan Thomas, *Unter dem Milchwald,* Rowohlt, 1958.
Thomas Stearns Eliot, *Ein verdienter Staatsmann,* Suhrkamp, 1959.
Graham Greene, *Der verbindliche Liebhaber,* Zsolnay, 1960.
Euripides, *Die Bacchantinnen,* Bloch, 1960.
William Shakespeare, *Ein Sommernachtstraum,* Fischer, 1964.
(And compiler) *Der Stern, der tat sie lenken* (carols), Hanser, 1966.
Aristophanes, *Lysistrata,* Wagenbach, 1985.

Translator of numerous works into German, including many of William Shakespeare's plays.

OTHER

(Author of text with Ernst Koeller) *Wesen und Entwicklung des Malers,* G. Grasl, 1964.
(Author of libretto) Alexander Goehr, *Arden muss sterben* (opera), translation by Geoffrey Skelton published as *Arden Must Die,* Schott, Associated Music Publishers, 1967.
(With Paul A. Baran and Gaston Salvatore) *Intellektuelle und Sozialismus* (essays and lectures), Wagenbach, 1968.
(Editor with Helga M. Novak and Peter-Paul Zahl) *Am Beispiel Peter-Paul Zahl* (politico-social document), Sozialistische Verlagsauslieferung, 1976.
Angst und Trost: Erzaehlungen und Gedichte ueber Juden und Nazis (stories and poems), Alibaba, 1983.
Ich grenz noch an ein Wort und an ein andres Land: Ueber Ingeborg Bachmann; Erinnerung, einige Anmerkungen zu ihrem Gedicht "Boehmen liegt am Meer" und ein Nachruf, Friedenauer Presse, 1984.
(With Peter Schneider) *Immendorf: Neue Bilder und Skulpturer* (exhibition catalog), Galerie Ascan Crone, 1984.
—und alle seine Moerder— (play), Promedia, 1984.
Und nicht taub und stumpf werden: Unrecht, Widerstand, und Protest, Multi Media Verlag, 1984.
(With Alfred Hrdlicka and Erwin Ringel) Alexander Klauser, Judith Klauser, and Michael Lewin, editors, *Die da reden gegen Vernichtung: Psychologie, bildende Kunst und Dichtung gegen den Krieg,* Europaverlag, 1986.

Mitunter sogar Lachen: Zwischenfaelle und Erinnerungen, Wagenbach, 1986.

Reteller of stories from the English appearing in *Theater haute,* including "Kesselflickers Hochzeit" (title means "The Tinker's Wedding"), "Die Kueche" (title means "The Kitchen"), and "Die Teufel" (title means "The Devils").

Fried's works have been collected into a number of omnibus volumes, including *Die Beine der grosseren Luegen; Unter Nebenfeinden; Gegengift: drei Gedichtsammlungen,* Wagenbach, 1974, and *Zeitfragen und Ueberlegungen: Achtzig Gedichte, sowie ein Zyklus,* Wagenbach, 1984.

SIDELIGHTS: Highly regarded as a poet, novelist, and translator, Austrian author Erich Fried is particularly known for his linguistically blunt and concise poetry that addresses important political and social issues. Fried showed his first signs of political activism in 1921 at the age of six: after witnessing the slaughter of eighty-three people by police during his native Vienna's "Bloody Friday," he refused to recite poetry at school, stating it was wrong to waste time with meaningless recitation in the face of social unrest and injustice.

As Jews in Vienna during the 1930s, Fried and his family faced the growing threat of Nazi anti-Semitism. Their fears were not unfounded: in 1938, Erich's father was arrested and sent to a prison camp, where he remained until the day of his death. Erich and his mother fled to London, England, that same year, and assisted other Jews in their escape from Europe throughout the remaining years of World War II.

Fried first took an interest in writing in the 1930s while still in Austria recuperating from the effects of a failed business venture and a lost love. A girl he met by chance in a mountain sanitorium converted him to socialism and showed him the value of the written word. Consequently, after settling in London where he worked at odd jobs, Fried wrote in his spare time. His first collection of poems, entitled *Deutschland,* was published in 1944. The publication of subsequent verse collections, including *Gedichte* in 1958 and *Reich der Steine* in 1963, captured the attention of the critics. These works were rich in aphorisms and epigrams and appealed to the reader's intellect with what have been called "linguistic experiments." A critic suggested in the *Times Literary Supplement* that Fried manipulated words in the hope that their very arrangement would yield its own profound meaning.

In addition to his verbal powers, critics praised the humanity evident in Fried's first novel, *Ein Soldat und ein Maedchen,* which was published in 1960. The book tells the story of a girl awaiting execution at Nuremburg who falls in love with her prison guard. One critic has contended that the short volume is "in form and content one of the weightiest works of modern German literature." Fried's subsequent prose release, *Kinder und Narren,* was considered equally impressive in its mastery of the language: it was described as an exploration into "the hidden implications of words" in a review for the *Times Literary Supplement.* Even more than Fried's previous work, this prose collection marked an increasing intensity and urgency in its author's message. Reviewers noted that the fictional conventions of plot, setting, and character were unimportant to Fried in *Kinder und Narren.* Through generic characters in generic places, Fried expressed his moral commitment in a plea for modern man to be more humane. The book's title, which means "Children and Fools" in English, alludes to the clarity of vision that the innocent possess and the malignant state of human affairs that they witness.

Following *Kinder und Narren,* Fried returned to writing verse as an outlet for his political and social concerns. The forty-one poems in *Und Vietnam und . . .* contain the verbal inventiveness that is Fried's signature. Beyond that, however, critics admired the timeless quality of the collection. At the height of the Vietnam War, a reviewer for the *Times Literary Supplement* predicted that the poems would "remain valid" long after the fighting had ceased "both because of their poetic quality and because the moral issues with which they [were] concerned" were likely to "remain acute." *Und Vietnam und . . .* won critical acclaim in America despite its harsh criticism of American involvement in the Asian civil war. It has been suggested that Fried's words echoed the doubts of the very nation he was condemning.

The desolation of spirit that permeated Fried's war poems is also evident in the collection *On Pain of Seeing.* Once again, the verses convey the author's anger over the irreparable damage brought about by armed conflict. But Fried's is not a voice of despair. In a preface to the collection, he establishes art as a weapon in the fight against alienation and sets out to awaken his readers to mankind's impending devolution. In a poem entitled "Answer," Fried—as the translation was presented in *Library Journal*—wrote: "Someone/came to the stones/and said:/ Be human/The stones/replied:/ We are not/hard enough/ yet."

Critics have reflected on Fried's use of fear and doubt as sources of inspiration in his poetry. One reviewer writing for the *Times Literary Supplement* theorized that the author views "fear as a positive force in the perception of artistic responsibility" and doubt as the vehicle for "a radical change in human, not merely political attitudes." Fried's own words confirm this evaluation. In the translated version of the poem "Angst und Zweifel" (which means "Fear and Doubt"), cited in a 1974 *Times Literary Supplement* article, he states: "Don't doubt/ the man/who tells you/he's afraid/but be afraid/of him/who tells you/he doesn't know doubt."

In an effort to make Fried's insights available to an English-speaking audience, three of his verse collections have been translated: two of these volumes, *On Pain of Seeing* and the award-winning *One Hundred Poems Without a Country,* were translated by Stuart Hood. Rex Last spoke for most critics when he asserted in the *Times Literary Supplement* that "Hood's sensitive translation accurately captures Fried's style, his incisive, constant questioning, and his refusal to shy away from any issue."

Perhaps nothing better captures the intensity of Fried the man than the words he spoke in his last broadcast to his East German listeners from London in 1968, the text of which was printed the *Listener* that same year. After working for fifteen years in the German language division of the British Broadcasting Corporation (BBC), an institution that had afforded him considerable freedom to express his views without censorship, Fried felt compelled to resign his post. Fried told his listeners that he would not burden them with all of his "reflections about whether and how far it made—or still makes— sense for a socialist to apply constructively meant criticism from *outside,* from London." He explained that in spite of the BBC's tolerance of his opinions, the fact that most of its other broadcasters held different views, especially concerning the war in Vietnam, seemed to diminish the credibility of his convictions. The writer concluded his resignation speech with the hope that his listeners would "in the future read, or hear, or see on stage" some of his works.

For more than forty years, Fried has been inspiring readers of all ages with his prose and verse centered around injustice and oppression. A reviewer for the *Times Literary Supplement* summarized the elements of the author's appeal when he portrayed Fried as "one of the few contemporary German poets to have mastered the art of public poetry, of putting across a political statement without succumbing to the twin pitfalls of bombast and naively overstating the obvious." Each of Fried's books finds a larger audience than the last and his frequent appearances in German-speaking countries have attracted a new generation of readers to his work. His tone has changed somewhat in the recent past: Della Couling noted in a review of *Liebesgedichte* for the *Times Literary Supplement* that "we hear now the voice of [an older man] who fears age, death, and the loss of the beloved." Fried's bare and basic style, however, remains the same. He is still, concluded Couling, "a poet who not only knows what he wants to say, but how to say it."

BIOGRAPHICAL/CRITICAL SOURCES:

PERIODICALS

Library Journal, April 15, 1970.
Listener, January 25, 1968.
Times Literary Supplement, January 7, 1965, November 4, 1965, January 19, 1967, April 20, 1967, January 4, 1968, February 27, 1969, March 23, 1973, October 4, 1974, October 13, 1978, October 10, 1980.*

—*Sketch by Barbara K. Carlisle*

*   *   *

FRIEDMAN, Josh(ua M.) 1941-

BRIEF ENTRY: Born December 22, 1941, in Roosevelt, N.J. American journalist. Friedman won a Pulitzer Prize for international reporting in 1985 for his coverage of the African famine. He began his journalism career in 1972 as statehouse bureau chief for the *New York Post*, then worked in the late 1970s for the *Philadelphia Inquirer*, where he shared a Pulitzer for reporting on the 1979 mishap at the Three Mile Island nuclear power plant in Pennsylvania. In 1980, after joining the *Soho Weekly News* as editor in chief, Friedman was also a Pulitzer finalist for his series of articles on toxic waste. He became a bureau chief for *Newsday* in 1982. Among his other honors for reporting are the Thomas L. Stokes Award from the Washington Journalism Center and a Page One Award from the New York Newspaper Guild. *Addresses: Office—Newsday*, 780 Third Ave., New York, N.Y. 10017.

BIOGRAPHICAL/CRITICAL SOURCES:

BOOKS

Who's Who in America, 44th edition, Marquis, 1986.

*   *   *

FRISCH, Michael H(erbert) 1942-

PERSONAL: Born April 18, 1942, in Brooklyn, N.Y.; son of Emanuel X. (in movie theater business) and Pearl (Schor) Frisch; married Maria Boynton (a folklorist), July 17, 1983. *Education:* Tufts University, B.A., 1963; Princeton University, M.A., 1965, Ph.D., 1967.

ADDRESSES: Office—Department of History, Park Hall, Amherst Campus, State University of New York at Buffalo, Buffalo, N.Y. 14260.

CAREER: Princeton University, Princeton, N.J., 1967-69, began as instructor, became assistant professor of history; State University of New York at Buffalo, assistant professor, 1969-72, associate professor, 1971-79, professor of history and American studies, 1979—, chairman of department of American studies, 1984-87, 1988—. Fulbright senior lecturer at Seoul National University, 1973-74; visiting research professor at University of Pennsylvania, 1979-81.

MEMBER: American Studies Association (member of national executive council, 1985-89), American Historical Association, Organization of American Historians, Oral History Association.

AWARDS, HONORS: Fulbright scholar, 1973-74; grant from National Endowment for the Humanities, 1981-82.

WRITINGS:

Town Into City, Harvard University Press, 1972.
(Editor with Daniel J. Walkowitz) *Working Class America: Essays on Labor, Community, and American Society*, University of Illinois Press, 1983.
A Shared Authority: Essays on Oral and Public History, State University of New York Press, 1989.
Portraits in Steel: American Workers and the Dream Deferred, with photographs by Milton Pogovin, Cornell University Press, 1989.

Editor of *Oral History Review*, 1986-89.

SIDELIGHTS: Michael H. Frisch told *CA:* "In recent years, I have been broadening my initial focus on issues in urban and social/labor history to include a major involvement in oral and public history. In this work, collected in *A Shared Authority*, I have been especially interested in the relationship between historical interpretation and the broader dynamics of public discourse. I argue that oral and public history are most important not so much as either new sources of evidence or as alternatives to interpretation, though both of these frequently cited dimensions are important. Rather, what is most significant is the capacity of these approaches to democratize the process of interpretation itself—to involve a broader public in the process of thinking critically about the meaning of the past, and its relevance to the present. Both the explicit oral history interview and the implicit discussion with the public in a documentary or museum exhibit, I argue, invite an active dialogue about history, in which the authority for interpretation—literally the author-ing-of—history is sharable. Hence the title of my book and, I believe, the significance of these new approaches."

BIOGRAPHICAL/CRITICAL SOURCES:

PERIODICALS

American Historical Review, June, 1973.
Annals of the American Academy of Political and Social Science, May, 1973.
Nation, April 2, 1983.

*   *   *

FROST, Roon 1943-

PERSONAL: Born February 6, 1943, in Richmond, Va.; daughter of William White (an insurance executive) and Josephine (a housewife; maiden name, Luck) Ray; married Edmund L. Frost, Jr. (a publisher), February 18, 1967; children: Ned. *Education:* Attended Randolph-Macon Women's College and Columbia University, 1961-64; George Washington University, B.A., 1974.

ADDRESSES: Office—P.O. Box 1602, Portsmouth, N.H. 03801. *Agent*—Raphael Sagalyn, 2813 Bellevue Ter., N.W., Washington, D.C. 20007.

CAREER: International Voluntary Services, Washington, D.C., assistant to program officer, 1965-68; Thomson McKinnon Auchincloss, Inc., Washington, D.C., sales assistant, 1968-72; assistant recruiting officer for International Voluntary Services, 1972-73; writer, 1973-82; Waterford Foundation, Waterford, Va., publicity director, 1982-83; writer. Secretary-treasurer of Frost Productions, Inc., 1967-76, and Glove Compartment Books, 1987—. Producer of audio-visual presentations for Piedmont Environmental Council, 1972-73; writing instructor and lecturer, 1980—. Founding director of Loudoun Nutrition Council, 1980-85.

MEMBER: Seacoast Writers Association, York Writers.

AWARDS, HONORS: First prize in adult fiction from State of Maine Writers Conference, 1986, for "Winter Trees."

WRITINGS:

(With Sheila Moore) *The Little Boy Book: A Guide to the First Eight Years,* Crown, 1986.
(With husband, Ed Frost) *Coast Guide: Seabrook, New Hampshire to Freeport, Maine,* Glove Compartment Books, 1987.
Mountain Guide: The White Mountains of Maine and New Hampshire, Glove Compartment Books, 1988.
Island Guide: Block Island, Martha's Vineyard, Nantucket, Vinalhaven, Acadia National Park, Glove Compartment Books, 1989.

Work represented in anthologies, including *A Christmas Treasury,* York Writers Club, 1968. Contributor of stories and articles to magazines and newspapers, including *Early American Life, Better Homes and Gardens, Commonwealth, Discovery, Gourmet,* and *Country.* Editor of *Loudoun County Cooks;* past restaurant critic of *Virginia Country.*

WORK IN PROGRESS: The Only Child, a nonfiction "look at single-child families of the future"; *The Middle Years,* the journal of a marriage; *Scrapbook,* the fictional saga of a twentieth-century family.

SIDELIGHTS: Roon Frost told *CA:* "Writing, fiction and nonfiction, has allowed me to explore the human condition and to continue learning about the world as it was and will be. Human sciences (biology, sociology, psychology), history (particularly of a social nature), the environment and the human role in its interactions have been important areas of interest. In addition, I've been able to follow my hobbies (photography, cooking, and travel) through my work. In return for the pleasure writing has given me, I have tried to be as honest and as clear as possible in my work, whether I am explaining complicated scientific theories or creating memorable characters and scenes."

BIOGRAPHICAL/CRITICAL SOURCES:

PERIODICALS

Hartford Courant, May 31, 1986.
Philadelphia Daily News, June 9, 1986.
San Jose Mercury, June 6, 1986.
Seattle Post-Intelligencer, June 12, 1986.
USA Today, June 9, 1986.

FRYKLUND, Verne C(harles)   1896-1980

OBITUARY NOTICE—See index for *CA* sketch: Born January 4, 1896, in Prentice, Wis.; died November 15, 1980. University administrator, educator, editor, and author. During his long academic career Fryklund taught at public schools in Arizona, Michigan, Colorado, and Texas, and at schools of higher education in Nebraska, Minnesota, and Michigan. He capped his career as president of Stout Institute, now known as the University of Wisconsin at Stout. Fryklund was the author and editor of numerous textbooks and bulletins, including nine military training bulletins, and more than seventy articles, mainly on aspects of industrial arts and vocational education. His book titles include *Industrial Arts Teacher Education in the United States, Trade and Job Analysis,* and *Repair and Overhaul of Light Tanks.*

OBITUARIES AND OTHER SOURCES:

Date of death provided by son, Verne C. Fryklund, Jr.

* * *

FULLER, Thomas C(harles)   1918-

PERSONAL: Born August 2, 1918, in Evanston, Ill.; son of Leslie Elmer (a theologian) and Mabel (an artist and pianist; maiden name, Gore) Fuller; married Mary Smiles (a registered nurse and health counselor), December 22, 1945; children: Nicholas R., Kenneth W. *Education:* Northwestern University, B.S., 1940; University of New Mexico, M.S., 1942; University of Chicago, Ph.D., 1947. *Religion:* Greek Orthodox.

ADDRESSES: Home—171 Westcott Way, Sacramento, Calif. 95864.

CAREER: Rhode Island State College (now University of Rhode Island), Kingston, instructor in botany, 1946-48; Hanover College, Hanover, Ind., professor of botany, 1948-49; University of Southern California, Los Angeles, assistant professor of botany, 1949-53; California Department of Food and Agriculture, Sacramento, junior plant pathologist, 1953-54, assistant plant pathologist, 1954-57, botanist, 1957-81; writer and weed specialist, 1981—. Research associate of California Academy of Sciences. *Military service:* U.S. Army, Medical Administration Corps, 1942-45; became first lieutenant.

MEMBER: Asian-Pacific Weed Science Society, California Botanical Society.

WRITINGS:

(With Elizabeth McClintock) *Poisonous Plants of California,* University of California Press, 1987.

WORK IN PROGRESS: Weeds of California: An Illustrated Manual.

* * *

FYE, W(allace) Bruce (III)   1946-

PERSONAL: Born September 25, 1946, in Meadville, Pa.; son of Wallace Bruce, Jr. (a banker) and Anne (a music instructor; maiden name, Schreck) Fye; married Lois Baker (a nurse), May 10, 1969; children: Katherine Anne, Elizabeth Jane. *Education:* Johns Hopkins University, B.A. (with honors), 1968, M.D., 1972, M.A., 1978.

ADDRESSES: Home—1607 North Wood Ave., Marshfield, Wis. 54449. *Office*— Department of Cardiology, Marshfield Clinic, 1000 North Oak Ave., Marshfield, Wis. 54449.

CAREER: New York Hospital-Cornell Medical Center, New York, N.Y., intern, 1972-73, assistant resident, 1973-74, senior assistant resident in cardiology, 1974-75; Johns Hopkins University, School of Medicine, Baltimore, Md., fellow in cardiology, 1975-77, postdoctoral fellow in history of medicine, 1976-78, Robert Wood Johnson clinical scholar, 1976-78; Marshfield Clinic, Marshfield, Wis., cardiologist and director of Cardiographics Laboratory, 1978—, chairman of department of cardiology, 1981—. Diplomate of American Board of Internal Medicine. University of Wisconsin—Madison, adjunct assistant professor of history of medicine, 1978-85, adjunct associate professor, 1985—, clinical assistant professor of medicine, 1980-85, clinical associate professor, 1985—; clinical assistant professor at Medical College of Wisconsin, 1982—. St. Joseph's Hospital, Marshfield, physician, 1978—, member of medical staff executive committee, 1981—; member of research committee of Marshfield Medical Foundation, 1980-84; consultant to National Endowment for the Humanities and National Science Foundation.

MEMBER: International Society for the History of Medicine, American College of Physicians (fellow), American Association for the History of Medicine (member of council, 1981-84), American Heart Association (delegate to Council of Clinical Cardiology, 1987—), American Society of Echocardiography, History of Science Society, Medical Library Association, American College of Cardiology (fellow), American Medical Association, American Osler Society (member of board of governors, 1980-84, 1986—; second vice-president, 1986-87; first vice-president, 1987-88; president, 1988-89), American Institute of the History of Pharmacy, New York Academy of Sciences, Wisconsin State Medical Society, Aesculapian Society of Wisconsin, Wood County Medical Society, Osler Club of London, Johns Hopkins Medical and Surgical Association, Phi Beta Kappa, Alpha Omega Alpha, Alpha Epsilon Delta (president, 1967-68), Delta Phi Alpha.

WRITINGS:

(Editor and author of introduction) *William Osler's Collected Papers on the Cardiovascular System*, Gryphon Editions, 1985.

The Development of American Physiology: American Medicine in the Nineteenth Century, Johns Hopkins University Press, 1987.

(Contributor) Gerald L. Geison, editor, *Physiology in the American Context, 1850-1940*, American Physiological Society, 1987.

Editor in chief of "Classics of Cardiology Library," Gryphon Editions. Editor of "Preludes and Progress," a regular feature in *Circulation*. Contributor of nearly one hundred articles and reviews to history and medical journals. Member of editorial board of *Journal of the History of Medicine and Allied Sciences*, 1984—, and *Marshfield Medical Bulletin*, 1985—.

WORK IN PROGRESS: Several projects relating to the history of American medical education, medical research, and the history of cardiology.

SIDELIGHTS: W. Bruce Fye told *CA:* "My interest in medical history can be traced to a passion for collecting books. When I was fourteen I began collecting books dealing with Abraham Lincoln, the Civil War, African exploration, and American literature. Once I entered the Johns Hopkins Medical School in 1968, it seemed logical that I shift my collecting interests to medical books. Two individuals in Baltimore, one a medical librarian and the other an antiquarian bookseller, encouraged this shift in focus.

"Johns Hopkins has a rich tradition in medical history—America's first full-time department devoted to this subject was established there in 1929. As a medical student I became interested in the origins of the structure and philosophy of modern medical education. An opportunity arose during postgraduate training in cardiology that enabled me to enroll in a master's program in medical history at Hopkins. It was then that I inaugurated my formal research into the history of American medical science and education that culminated in the publication of *The Development of American Physiology: American Medicine in the Nineteenth Century* in 1987.

"William Osler was the first professor of medicine at Johns Hopkins, America's most prominent internist at the turn of the century, an avid book collector, and a prolific author. About one-third of his medical papers dealt with the cardiovascular system. As a cardiologist and ardent Oslerian, I welcomed the opportunity to publish a volume in which his most important writings on the heart were assembled for the first time. This work, *William Osler's Collected Papers on the Cardiovascular System*, appeared in 1985 as the first volume in a series published by the 'Classics of Cardiology Library,' which I edit.

"My historical activities are undertaken in the context of a full-time medical practice. There are ten cardiologists in the department I have chaired at Marshfield Clinic since 1981. This permits cross-coverage that enables me to devote most nights and weekends to reading and writing medical history. There are relatively few physician-historians who can find the time to pursue serious research in the history of medicine, a field that has become rapidly professionalized over the past two decades. I am pleased that I have been able to combine my interests in medicine and history. A structured medical practice, a small town with few distractions, a large personal reference collection of medical history titles, and a supportive family have made this possible."

AVOCATIONAL INTERESTS: Bibliophile, seller of antiquarian medical books.

G

GABBARD, Glen O(wens) 1949-

PERSONAL: Born August 8, 1949, in Charleston, Ill.; son of E. G. (an actor) and Lucina (an actress; maiden name, Paquet) Gabbard; married Joyce Davidson (a psychiatrist), June 14, 1985; children: Matthew, Abigail, Amanda, Allison. *Education:* Eastern Illinois University, B.S., 1972; Rush Medical College, M.D., 1975; postdoctoral study at Karl Menninger School of Psychiatry, 1975-78, and Topeka Institute of Psychoanalysis, 1977-84.

ADDRESSES: Home—5410 Southwest Mission, Topeka, Kan. 66610. *Office*—Menninger Foundation, C. F. Menninger Memorial Hospital, Box 829, Topeka, Kan. 66601.

CAREER: C. F. Menninger Memorial Hospital, Topeka, staff psychiatrist, 1978-83, section chief, 1984—. J. Cotter Hirschberg Professor of Clinical Psychology at Karl Menninger School of Psychiatry, 1986-87; instructor at Topeka Institute for Psychoanalysis, 1981—. President of board of directors of Topeka Civic Theater, 1982-83.

MEMBER: American Psychiatric Association, American Psychoanalytic Association, American Association for the Advancement of Science, Society for Psychotherapy Research, Forum for the Psychoanalytic Study of Film, Sigma Xi, Alpha Omega Alpha.

AWARDS, HONORS: Falk fellow of American Psychiatric Association, 1976; Edward Hoedemaker Award from Seattle Psychoanalytic Society, 1986, for article ''The Treatment of the 'Special' Patient in a Psychoanalytic Hospital.''

WRITINGS:

(Contributor) Robert Morgan, editor, *The Iatrogenics Handbook: A Critical Look at Research and Practice in the Helping Professions,* IPI Publications, 1983.
(With Stuart W. Twemlow) *With the Eyes of the Mind: An Empirical Analysis of Out-of-Body States,* Praeger, 1984.
(With brother, Krin Gabbard) *Psychiatry and the Cinema,* University of Chicago Press, 1987.
(Contributor) Maurice Charney and Joseph Reppen, editors, *Psychoanalytic Approaches to Literature and Film,* Associated University Presses, 1987.
(Editor with Roy W. Menninger, and contributor) *Medical Marriages,* American Psychiatric Press, 1988.

(Editor) *Professional Incest: Sexual Exploitation Within Professional Relationships,* American Psychiatric Press, in press.

Contributor of about seventy articles and reviews to periodicals. Member of editorial board of *Bulletin of the Menninger Clinic* and *Journal of Near-Death Studies.*

WORK IN PROGRESS: A Handbook of Psychodynamic Psychiatry, publication by American Psychiatric Press expected in 1990.

SIDELIGHTS: Glen O. Gabbard told *CA:* ''I grew up in a theatrical family and majored in drama as an undergraduate. At some ill-defined point in my college career, I became more interested in analyzing the psychology of the characters I was playing than in performing on stage. I switched to a premedical emphasis, but I was rejected by a registration computer because premedical studies and a drama major were deemed incompatible. I persevered nonetheless and eventually combined my interests in my writings on stage fright and the interface between psychiatry and movies. My interest in film culminated in *Psychiatry and the Cinema,* which I wrote in collaboration with my brother and fellow film buff, Krin Gabbard. This book will require frequent updates to keep abreast of current developments in film, so I anticipate work on future editions for the rest of my professional career.''

BIOGRAPHICAL/CRITICAL SOURCES:

PERIODICALS

New York Times, July 24, 1987.
San Francisco Chronicle, August 9, 1987.

*   *   *

GABBARD, Krin 1948-

PERSONAL: Born January 29, 1948, in Illinois; son of Glendon (an actor) and Lucina (an actress; maiden name, Paquet) Gabbard; married Paula Beversdorf (a librarian), July 31, 1973. *Education:* University of Chicago, A.B., 1970; Indiana University—Bloomington, Ph.D., 1978.

ADDRESSES: Home—505 Court St., Apt. 4B, Brooklyn, N.Y. 11236. *Office*—Department of Comparative Literature, State University of New York at Stony Brook, Stony Brook, N.Y. 11794.

CAREER: University of South Dakota, Vermillion, assistant professor of comparative literature, 1977-79; Stephens College, Columbia, Mo., assistant professor of comparative literature, 1979-81; member of faculty in comparative literature, State University of New York at Stony Brook. Producer and announcer of "Jazz on the Air," on WUSB-FM Radio.

MEMBER: Modern Language Association of America, American Comparative Literature Association (chairman of Student Affairs Committee, 1987—), Society for Cinema Studies.

WRITINGS:

(With Glen O. Gabbard) *Psychiatry and the Cinema*, University of Chicago Press, 1987.

Contributor to magazines, including *Helios, Bucknell Review, Literature/Film Quarterly,* and *Psychoanalytic Review.*

WORK IN PROGRESS: Low and High: The Cultural History of Jazz, 1945-1980.

BIOGRAPHICAL/CRITICAL SOURCES:

PERIODICALS

New York Times, July 24, 1987.

*　　*　　*

GAGNIER, Regenia (A.)   1953-

PERSONAL: Born June 24, 1953; daughter of Clenton J. (an industrial machinist) and Jean (a painter; maiden name, Young) Gagnier. *Education:* University of California, Berkeley, Ph.D., 1981. *Politics:* "Socialist-feminist." *Religion:* "Lapsed Roman Catholic."

ADDRESSES: Home—860 San Jude Ave., Palo Alto, Calif. 94305. *Office*—Department of English, Stanford University, Stanford, Calif. 94305.

CAREER: Stanford University, Stanford, Calif., assistant professor of English, 1981—.

MEMBER: Modern Language Association of America.

AWARDS, HONORS: Fellow of Humanities Center at Stanford University, 1985-86; grant from Pew Memorial Foundation, 1986.

WRITINGS:

Idylls of the Marketplace: Oscar Wilde and the Victorian Public, Stanford University Press, 1986.

Contributor to literature and women's studies journals.

WORK IN PROGRESS: The Social Pleasures of the Text: A Cross-Class and Gendered Analysis of the Writing Subject.

BIOGRAPHICAL/CRITICAL SOURCES:

PERIODICALS

Times Literary Supplement, June 19, 1987.

*　　*　　*

GALLAHER, John G(erard)   1928-

PERSONAL: Born December 28, 1928, in St. Louis, Mo.; son of James E. and Bess Gallaher; married C. Maia Hofacker, 1956; children: Patricia, Michael, Jennifer. *Education:* Washington University, St. Louis, Mo., A.B., 1954; St. Louis University, A.M., 1957, Ph.D., 1960.

ADDRESSES: Office—Department of Historical Studies, Southern Illinois University, Edwardsville, Ill. 62026.

CAREER: Manhattanville College of the Sacred Heart (now Manhattanville College), Purchase, N.Y., instructor, 1960-62, assistant professor of history, 1962-64; Southern Illinois University, Edwardsville, associate professor, 1964-71, professor of history, 1971—.

MEMBER: American Historical Association, American Catholic Historical Association, American Military Institute, Society for French Historical Studies.

AWARDS, HONORS: Fulbright scholar, 1959-60; grant from American Philosophical Society, 1965, 1986.

WRITINGS:

The Iron Marshal: A Biography of Louis N. Davout, Southern Illinois University Press, 1976.
The Students of Paris and the Revolution of 1848, Southern Illinois University Press, 1980.

Contributor to history journals, including *French Historical Studies, The Irish Sword,* and *Military Affairs.*

WORK IN PROGRESS: Napoleon's Irish Legion, completion expected in 1988.

BIOGRAPHICAL/CRITICAL SOURCES:

PERIODICALS

American Historical Review, February, 1977, October, 1981.
Times Literary Supplement, March 11, 1977.

*　　*　　*

GALLIGAN, Edward L(awrence)   1926-

PERSONAL: Born January 14, 1926, in Taunton, Mass.; son of Joseph E. and Monica L. (Lawlor) Galligan; married Isabel M. Brown, January 1, 1949; children: Joseph E., James M. *Education:* Swarthmore College, B.A., 1948; Columbia University, A.M., 1949; University of Pennsylvania, Ph.D., 1958. *Politics:* Democrat.

ADDRESSES: Home—152 Millview Ave., Kalamazoo, Mich. 49001. *Office*—Department of English, Western Michigan University, Kalamazoo, Mich. 49008.

CAREER: DePauw University, Greencastle, Ind., began as instructor, became assistant professor of English, 1949-58; Western Michigan University, Kalamazoo, began as assistant professor, became professor of English, 1958—, chairman of department, 1985—. *Military service:* U.S. Navy, 1943-46; became seaman first class.

MEMBER: Mark Twain Society, P. G. Wodehouse Society, American Civil Liberties Union.

WRITINGS:

(Editor) H. L. Mencken, *A Choice of Days*, Knopf, 1981.
The Comic Vision in Literature, University of Georgia Press, 1984.

Contributor of articles and reviews to literary journals, including *Sewanee Review, South Atlantic Quarterly,* and *Midwest Quarterly,* and newspapers.

WORK IN PROGRESS: Research on American humor, especially that of Mark Twain, the history of American newspaper columns, prose style, and the theory and practice of satire.

SIDELIGHTS: Edward L. Galligan told *CA:* "About thirty years ago I became interested in a subject, comedy and humor, and a form, the essay; I am still busy with both. My motives for writing are the standard ones—curiosity and vanity."

*   *   *

GALSTER, George C(harles) 1948-

PERSONAL: Born April 10, 1948, in Toledo, Ohio; son of George M. (an executive) and Helen M. (Schmuck) Galster; married Patricia A. Higgins (a registered nurse), July 12, 1969; children: G. Geoffrey, Joshua C. *Education:* Wittenberg University, B.A. (summa cum laude), 1970; Case Western Reserve University, B.S., 1971; Massachusetts Institute of Technology, Ph.D., 1974.

ADDRESSES: Office—Department of Economics, College of Wooster, Wooster, Ohio 44691.

CAREER: Mathematics and science tutor, 1968-69; high school mathematics teacher in Cleveland, Ohio, 1969-70; analyst and programmer of industrial systems, 1970; College of Wooster, Wooster, Ohio, assistant professor, 1974-80, associate professor, 1980-86, professor of economics, 1986—, chairperson of urban studies, 1975-77, 1982-86. Visiting scholar at Harvard University, 1981-82, and University of California, Berkeley, 1986-87; director of Comparative European Urban Team for Great Lakes College Association, 1977; member of Joint Center for Political Studies; workshop leader; consultant to U.S. Department of Housing and Urban Development, National Committee Against Housing Discrimination, and National Association of Realtors. Chairperson of City of Wooster Economic Task Force, 1975, and Housing Task Force, 1978; Wayne County Community Action Commission, member of board of directors, 1976-81, president of board, 1978-80; member of governing board of Wooster Interfaith Housing Commission, 1984-86.

MEMBER: American Economic Association, Association for Social Economics, American Real Estate and Urban Economics Association, Urban Affairs Association, Eastern Economic Association.

AWARDS, HONORS: Grants from Ohio Real Estate Research Foundation, 1975, 1980, U.S. Department of Housing and Urban Development, 1978, and Ford Foundation, 1981; Luce grant, 1985-86.

WRITINGS:

Information Nexus and Neighborhood Change (monograph), Department of City Planning, Kennedy School of Government, Harvard University, 1982.
Homeowners and Neighborhood Reinvestment, Duke University Press, 1987.
(With William Grigsby, Duncan Maclennan, and Morton Baratz) *The Dynamics of Neighborhood Change and Decline,* Pergamon, 1987.

Also contributor to *Housing Desegregation and Federal Policy,* University of North Carolina Press, 1986. Contributor to economic and urban studies journals.

WORK IN PROGRESS: More Than Skin Deep (tentative title), a study of racial segregation in America; research on national fair housing policy.

SIDELIGHTS: George C. Galster told *CA:* "My continuing writing on urban, racial, and housing issues stems from my underlying concern to create the social circumstances in which all people have the opportunity to become fully realized human beings."

AVOCATIONAL INTERESTS: Sports, novels, artist (watercolor, charcoal, ink).

*   *   *

GANNON, Frank 1952-

PERSONAL: Born August 30, 1952, in Camden, N.J.; son of Bernard (a bar owner) and Anne (a housewife; maiden name, Forde) Gannon; married Paulette Piquet (a teacher), April 2, 1971; children: Aimee, Anne, Frank. *Education:* University of Georgia, B.A. (magna cum laude), 1974, M.A., 1977. *Politics:* Democrat. *Religion:* Roman Catholic.

ADDRESSES: Home and office—P. O. Box 547, Demorest, Ga. 30535. *Agent*—Kristine Dahl, 137 Fifth Ave., New York, N.Y. 10010.

CAREER: Writer.

WRITINGS:

Yo, Poe (humor), Viking, 1987.
Vanna Karenina (humor), Viking, 1988.

Contributor to magazines, including *New Yorker, Atlantic, Harper's,* and *Gentleman's Quarterly.* Contributing editor of *Southern.*

WORK IN PROGRESS: Another book.

SIDELIGHTS: Frank Gannon told *CA:* "I'm a humorist. I'm not a very talented writer, but I do what I can. I would rather be one of these guys on the Left Bank looking out into the Parisian night and having profound thoughts, but I'm not smart enough to do that. I started out to be a serious artist person but it didn't work out because I don't have anything to say. I lack depth, like the serving dishes in certain Chinese restaurants, but, like those dishes, I try my best to give the illusion of depth. I like what Joe Orton said about all this: 'I was born without a soul, but I've tried to develop very good manners to compensate.'

"I guess that my two books, and the one I'm writing now, are about my hopeless inability to have values, thoughts, and beliefs like other writers. I had a very happy childhood, and I've had a very nice life, so I can't really blame anybody. But, given enough time, I probably will."

*   *   *

GARAGIOLA, Joe
See GARAGIOLA, Joseph Henry

*   *   *

GARAGIOLA, Joseph Henry 1926-
(Joe Garagiola)

PERSONAL: Born February 12, 1926, in St. Louis, Mo.; son of John and Angelina (Garavaglia) Garagiola; married Audrie Dianne Ross, November 5, 1949; children: Joseph, Jr., Stephen, Gina. *Education:* Attended parochial schools in St. Louis, Mo.

ADDRESSES: Office—c/o FSM, Inc., One Rockefeller Plaza, New York, N.Y. 10020.

CAREER: Professional baseball player with St. Louis Cardinals, 1946-51, Pittsburgh Pirates, 1951-53, Chicago Cubs, 1953-54, New York Giants, 1954; radio and television broadcaster, 1955—; writer, 1960—. Sports broadcaster covering St. Louis Cardinal games, beginning in 1955, "Game of the Week," beginning in 1960, and World Series clips on "Today" show, 1960-61, all for National Broadcasting Company, Inc. (NBC-TV); provided play-by-play coverage of the World Series, 1963-64; announced New York Yankee games, beginning in 1965, and All-Star Baseball games. Regular cast member of "Today" show in the early 1970s; host for "Monitor" programs, syndicated game shows, 1969-77, own radio program, 1963—, and television show; public speaker, 1960—. *Military service:* U.S. Army, 1944-46; became sergeant.

MEMBER: UNICO National, Ad Club.

AWARDS, HONORS: Made honorary governor's colonel; named "Man of the Year," 1959, by UNICO; George Foster Peabody Award, 1974, for television show "The Baseball World of Joe Garagiola"; named honorary member of Arkansas Hall of Fame.

WRITINGS:

UNDER NAME JOE GARAGIOLA

Baseball Is a Funny Game, Lippincott, 1960.
It's Anybody's Ballgame, Contemporary Books, 1988.

SIDELIGHTS: Former professional baseball player Joe Garagiola has made a name for himself on the radio and television broadcasting circuit. Born and raised in St. Louis, Missouri, the catcher joined the St. Louis Cardinals in 1946, helping the team to a World Series win over the Boston Red Sox that same year. He began his career in sportscasting in 1954 when the effects of an injury sustained three years earlier curtailed his performance as a ball player.

Garagiola's inside knowledge of baseball is humorously chronicled in his first book, *Baseball Is a Funny Game.* Critics praised the book for its readability and entertaining anecdotes.

Garagiola, who is also a respected public speaker and master of ceremonies, has appeared on the "Jack Parr," "Ed Sullivan," and "Johnny Carson" shows. His second book, *It's Anybody's Ballgame,* was published in 1988.

*   *   *

GATTEGNO, Caleb   1911-1988

OBITUARY NOTICE: Born November 11, 1911, in Alexandria, Egypt; died after surgery for cancer, July 28, 1988, in Paris, France. Educator and writer. Author of more than fifty books on the learning process, Gattegno argued that modern teaching practices do more to hinder learning than to encourage and assist it. Gattegno proposed that since children learn such fundamental functions as walking and speaking primarily by themselves, the teaching process should be geared toward developing their ability to solve problems on their own through the use of instructional devices and games. After he earned doctorates in mathematics and psychology, Gattegno directed the Institute of Higher Scientific Studies in Cairo, Egypt, from 1937 to 1945. He taught at universities in England for the next twelve years, then accepted a position in Ethiopia for the United Nations, in which he produced textbooks and developed new instruction methods. Beginning in 1966 Gattegno directed the New York City research organization Schools for the Future, and in 1969 he became head of Educational Solutions, a publisher of teaching materials and a training institute for teachers.

Gattegno's works include *The Common Sense of Teaching Mathematics, Teaching Reading With Words in Color: A Scientific Study of the Problems of Reading, Towards a Visual Culture: Educating Through Television,* and *What We Owe Children: The Subordination of Teaching to Learning.*

OBITUARIES AND OTHER SOURCES:

BOOKS

Leaders in Education, 5th edition, Bowker, 1974.

PERIODICALS

Los Angeles Times, August 13, 1988.
New York Times, August 4, 1988.

*   *   *

GELB, Alan
See GELB, Alan Lloyd

*   *   *

GELB, Alan Lloyd   1950-
(Alan Gelb; Adrien Lloyd, a pseudonym)

PERSONAL: Born June 15, 1950, in New York, N.Y.; son of Harold S. (a certified public accountant) and Sylvia (a housewife; maiden name, Miller) Gelb; married Karen Levine (a writer), 1975; children: Noah, Nathaniel. *Education:* Johns Hopkins University, B.A., 1972, M.A., 1973. *Religion:* Jewish.

ADDRESSES: Home and office—East Chatham, N.Y. *Agent*—Ellen Levine, Ellen Levine Literary Agency, Inc., 432 Park Ave. S., Suite 1205, New York, N.Y. 10016.

CAREER: Highgate Pictures (television producers), New York City, director of creative affairs, 1979-80; Entertainment Partners, Inc. (television producers), New York City, director of development, 1984, consultant, 1985-86; *New York Times,* New York City, book reviewer, 1986—. Adjunct lecturer at Queens College of the City University of New York, 1985-86.

AWARDS, HONORS: Grant from Creative Artists Program Service, 1983.

WRITINGS:

NOVELS

The Janissary, Rawson, Wade, 1978.
(Under pseudonym Adrien Lloyd) *Fever on the Wind,* Dell, 1979.
(Under name Alan Gelb) *Columbus Avenue,* St. Martin's, 1984.
(Under name Alan Gelb) *Mussolini* (adapted from the television mini-series), Pocket Books, 1986.
(Under pseudonym Adrien Lloyd) *Acres in the Sky,* Pocket Books, 1986.
(Under name Alan Gelb) *Playgrounds,* Putnam, 1987.

OTHER

Most Likely to Succeed (nonfiction), Dutton, 1989.

Also author of "Did Katharine Hepburn's Mother Cook Kumquats?" (television script), for Multimedia.

SIDELIGHTS: Alan Lloyd Gelb's writings include the suspense novel *The Janissary* and, under the pseudonym Adrien Lloyd, the historical novel *Fever on the Wind.* He has also written *Most Likely to Succeed,* which he described to *CA* as "a nonfiction account of the quadruple murder of four family members by Wyley Gates, salutatorian of the Chatham, New York, high school and a neighbor of the author."

Alan Gelb informed *CA:* "I have been interested in exploring the subject of the modern family, how it holds together or doesn't hold together in the face of the stresses of contemporary society. My novel *Playgrounds* explores a number of families who are connected by the fact that their children go to the same day care center. *Most Likely to Succeed* analyzes an endemic alienation that resulted in a conspiracy and murder in a small, upstate New York town."

BIOGRAPHICAL/CRITICAL SOURCES:

PERIODICALS

Philadelphia Inquirer, August 23, 1987.

*   *   *

GEORGE, Hermon, Jr.   1945-

PERSONAL: Born November 22, 1945, in Tampa, Fla.; son of Hermon (a carpenter) and Henrene (a personnel manager; maiden name, Smith) George; married Susan McIntosh (a homemaker), August 24, 1968; children: Dahren Malcolm, Melissa Niani. *Education:* Wilkes College, B.A., 1967; Middlebury College, M.A., 1968; University of California, Irvine, Ph.D., 1979.

ADDRESSES: Office—Black Studies Program, University of Northern Colorado, Greeley, Colo. 80631.

CAREER: Wartburg College, Waverly, Iowa, instructor in Spanish, 1968-70; Fisk University, Nashville, Tenn., instructor in Spanish, 1970-71; Spelman College, Atlanta, Ga., instructor in Spanish, 1971-73; California State University, Fresno, assistant professor of ethnic studies, 1978-81; State University of New York College at New Paltz, assistant professor of black studies, 1981-85; University of Northern Colorado, Greeley, associate professor of black studies and coordinator of Black Studies Program, 1985—. Member at large of executive board of National Council for Black Studies, 1980-87.

AWARDS, HONORS: Fellow of National Endowment for the Humanities at Institute on African-American Culture, 1987.

WRITINGS:

American Race Relations Theory: A Review of Four Models, University Press of America, 1984.

Contributor of reviews to *Social Science Journal,* 1980-81 and 1985—; contributor of articles and reviews to social science and ethnic studies journals.

WORK IN PROGRESS: A sequel to *American Race Relations Theory,* dealing with the theory of Afro-American culture and with a comparative, sociological investigation of South Africa and the United States; research on Afro-Latin America.

SIDELIGHTS: Hermon George, Jr., told *CA:* "My work is an attempt to grapple with the dynamics of race and class, as they occur in a capitalist political economy. The four models described in my book are the ethnic group, caste, colonial, and Marxist models. Since the study of American racism is a deeply fragmented field, I do not think that a general consensus will be reached. However, I am convinced that only a synthesis of the last two named perspectives can hope to render an historically accurate, politically astute, and conceptually authentic representation of the Afro-American experience."

GEVIRTZ, Stanley   1929-1988

OBITUARY NOTICE: Born January 27, 1929, in Brooklyn, N.Y.; died of cancer, July 29, 1988. Biblical scholar, educator, and author. A history professor at the University of Chicago from 1958 until 1972, Gevirtz was internationally known for his instruction of American rabbis. In 1972 he accepted a position as professor of the Bible and ancient Near Eastern civilization at the Hebrew Union College and Jewish Institute of Religion in Los Angeles, California, where he remained a professor until his death. Gevirtz contributed many articles to scholarly journals and wrote a book, *Patterns in the Early Poetry of Israel,* which was published in 1973.

OBITUARIES AND OTHER SOURCES:

BOOKS

Directory of American Scholars, Volume IV: *Philosophy, Religion, and Law,* 7th edition, Bowker, 1978.

PERIODICALS

Los Angeles Times, August 2, 1988.

*   *   *

GIBSON, William (Ford)   1948-

BRIEF ENTRY: Born March 17, 1948, in Conway, S.C. American author. Gibson is an acclaimed science-fiction writer whose first novel, *Neuromancer* (Ace Books, 1984), won several prizes the year it was published—a Hugo Award from the World Science Fiction Society, a Nebula Award from the Science Fiction Writers of America, and a Philip K. Dick Memorial Award. In his books Gibson brings scientific sophistication to the grim, tough view of life projected by crime novels: criminal gangs use advanced technology to destroy their victims, and computers have become so complex that their intellectual power and self-awareness rival that of human beings. Gibson also wrote the novels *Count Zero* (Arbor House, 1986) and *Mona Lisa Overdrive* (Bantam, 1988). His short stories have appeared in magazines and in the collection *Burning Chrome* (Arbor House, 1986). *Addresses: Agent*—Martha Millard, 24 Rosedale Ave., Madison, N.J. 07940.

BIOGRAPHICAL/CRITICAL SOURCES:

BOOKS

Contemporary Literary Criticism, Volume 39, Gale, 1986.
Twentieth-Century Science Fiction Writers, 2nd edition, St. James, 1986.
The Writers Directory: 1986-88, St. James Press, 1988.

PERIODICALS

Rolling Stone, December 4, 1986.
Times Literary Supplement, June 20, 1986.
Village Voice, May 6, 1986.

*   *   *

GILES, Molly   1942-

PERSONAL: Born March 12, 1942, in California; daughter of John Daniel (in business) and Doris (a writer; maiden name, McConnell) Murphy; married Daniel Giles, September 29, 1961 (divorced, 1974); married Richard King (in business), July 22, 1976; children: Gretchen, Rachel, Devon. *Education:* Attended University of California, Berkeley, 1960-61; San Francisco State University, B.A., 1978, M.A., 1980.

ADDRESSES: Home—234 Railroad Ave., Woodacre, Calif. 94973. *Agent*—Ellen Levine, Blassingame, McCauley & Wood, 432 Park Ave. S., New York, N.Y. 10016.

CAREER: San Francisco State University, San Francisco, Calif., lecturer in creative writing, 1980-86; writer.

AWARDS, HONORS: Herbert Wilner Prize, 1979; Henfield Prize, 1981; Flannery O'Connor Award for Short Fiction, 1984, for *Rough Translations.*

WRITINGS:

Rough Translations (short stories), University of Georgia Press, 1985.

Contributor of short stories to periodicals, including *North American Review, New England Review, Ascent, Redbook,* and *Playgirl.*

WORK IN PROGRESS: A second collection of short stories, entitled *Talking to Strangers.*

SIDELIGHTS: Molly Giles's first collection of short stories, *Rough Translations,* touches on issues of loneliness, fear, and despair. The stories of this award-winning collection, told mainly from a woman's point of view, are woven together with recurring characters who experience impediments to communication, warmth, and intimacy. Giles's women attempt to translate their dreams and ideas into reality only to find that the reality they have created is an imperfect representation of their vision.

Called an "accomplished" writer by Roberta Grant in an article for the *New York Times Book Review,* Giles reveals a unique insight into the human condition through her direct and unsentimental approach to highly emotional situations. Through Ramona, for example, one of the characters from *Rough Translations,* Giles evokes "social panic": Ramona defines such panic as the way she used to feel when her husband wanted her "to give a dinner party for his clients and the guests would arrive and [she'd] still be in [her] slip clutching a bucket of live lobsters." Commenting on the author's realistic character portrayals, Michael J. Carroll wrote in a review for the *Los Angeles Times Book Review* that Giles is "a perceptive writer with a fine ear for the psyche's voice." Keith Cushman, writing for *Studies in Short Fiction,* observed that *Rough Translations* exhibits the universal nature of its author's perspective and "offers an effective, absorbing vision of the perils that are part of being alive."

BIOGRAPHICAL/CRITICAL SOURCES:

BOOKS

Contemporary Literary Criticism, Volume 39, Gale, 1985.

PERIODICALS

Los Angeles Times Book Review, August 11, 1985.
New York Times Book Review, May 12, 1985.
Studies in Short Fiction, summer, 1986.
Voice Literary Supplement, June, 1985.

*   *   *

GILLON, Werner 1905-

PERSONAL: Surname originally Goldmann; name changed c. 1948; born July 30, 1905, in Berlin, Germany; son of David

(a merchant) and Jenny (Gusdorf) Goldmann; married Sarah Golt, December 10, 1937; children: Dan. *Education:* Attended Technische Hochschule, Berlin, Germany, and University of Berlin (now Humboldt University), 1922-25. *Religion:* Jewish.

ADDRESSES: Home—101 Century Court, Grove End Rd., London NW8 9LD, England. *Agent*—Deborah Rogers Ltd., 49 Blenheim Cres., London W11 2EF, England.

CAREER: Sela Quarries, Jerusalem, Palestine (now Israel), company secretary, 1925-27; Bank der Templegesellschaft, Jerusalem, chief of correspondence and chief accountant, 1927-29; Anglo Palestine Bank, Jerusalem, trustee of A. Salzman Ltd., 1929-31; Lawrence T. Beck and Co. (contractors), Jerusalem, commercial manager, 1931-33; J. W. Goldman and Co. Ltd., Tel Aviv, Palestine (now Israel), managing director, 1933-40; Adam & Harvey Ltd., London, England, joint managing director, 1951-63; Status Shoe Corp., New York, N.Y., and Montreal, Quebec, president, 1963-73; free-lance writer in New York City, 1973-76; writer and lecturer on African art, 1976—. Lecturer at Tel-Aviv University. *Military service:* British Army, Royal Engineers, 1940-45; received Africa Star. Israel Defense Force, Army Corps of Engineers, 1948-51; became staff major; received War of Independence Medal and Volunteers Medal.

MEMBER: Royal Anthropological Institute (fellow), Association of Art Historians.

WRITINGS:

Collecting African Art, Rizzoli International, 1979.
Studio Vista, Cassel, 1979.
A Short History of African Art, Facts on File, 1984.

WORK IN PROGRESS: Memoirs, 1917-51, publication expected in 1990.

SIDELIGHTS: Werner Gillon told *CA:* "We had built up a collection of modern paintings and African sculpture and this led to research on the tribes and their art. The first book, *Collecting African Art,* was meant to be a guide for other collectors. My advice to them is: when you start a collection always buy from the best and most reliable dealers; buy only what you really like and do not be guided by fashion. Buy only the best quality objects in your chosen subject; it is better to own one very good piece than twenty mediocre ones.

"*A Short History of African Art* was undertaken because I felt that an attempt should be made to write such a history, knowing full well that a lot of further fieldwork and digging is needed before the writing of a comprehensive history can be attempted."

AVOCATIONAL INTERESTS: Collecting African art, international travel.

BIOGRAPHICAL/CRITICAL SOURCES:

PERIODICALS

American Ethnography, August, 1987.
Apollo, June, 1980.
Art and Artist, November, 1986.
Daily Telegraph, November 29, 1979, November 23, 1984, March 8, 1985.
Ebony, June, 1980.
Essence, July, 1980.
International Journal of African Historical Studies, Volume XX, number 1, 1987.
Jewish Chronicle, June 20, 1980.

Oxford Times, December 28, 1979.
Philadelphia Daily News, February 26, 1985.
Primitive Arts Newsletter, February, 1979, June, 1980.
Washington Post Book World, February 22, 1987.
West Africa, October 29, 1979, September 16, 1985.
World of Interiors, March, 1985.

*   *   *

GILMORE, Daniel F(rancis)   1922-1988

OBITUARY NOTICE—See index for *CA* sketch: Born March 24, 1922, in New York; died after suffering from emphysema, August 7, 1988, in Falls Church, Va. Journalist. During an association with United Press International (UPI) that spanned four decades, Gilmore reported stories from around the world. For the first twenty-five years of that affiliation, assignments as foreign correspondent and bureau manager took him to Asia, Europe, the Middle East, Africa, and Indochina. He then served as European news editor based in London and as Asian news editor based in Hong Kong until 1973, when he was transferred to Washington and named editor of national security affairs, the post from which he retired in 1987. Stories Gilmore covered include the aftermath of the Arab-Israeli war in 1949, conflicts in Cyprus in 1950, American intervention in Lebanon in 1958, the Iraqi revolt in Baghdad in 1958, the erection of the Berlin Wall in 1961, and activities in Moscow, Vietnam, and Cambodia.

OBITUARIES AND OTHER SOURCES:

PERIODICALS

Washington Post, August 9, 1988.

*   *   *

GLOER, (William) Hulitt   1950-

PERSONAL: Born December 23, 1950 in Atlanta, Ga.; son of William Talmadge (a retailer) and Francis (Lancaster) Gloer; married Sheila Katherine Rogers (a teacher), December 29, 1972; children: Jeremy Hulitt, Joshua William. *Education:* Baylor University, B.A., 1972; Pittsburgh Theological Seminary, M.Div., 1975; Southern Baptist Theological Seminary, Ph.D., 1981; post-graduate study at the University of Tuebingen, 1987-88. *Religion:* Baptist.

ADDRESSES: Home—616 Northeast 98th Terrace, Kansas City, Mo. 64155. *Office*—Department of the New Testament, Midwestern Baptist Theological Seminary, 5001 North Oak St., Kansas City, Mo. 64118.

CAREER: Southern Baptist Theological Seminary, Louisville, Ky., instructor, 1979-81; North American Baptist Seminary, Sioux Falls, S.D., assistant professor, 1981-83; Midwestern Baptist Theological Seminary, Kansas City, Mo., associate professor, 1983—. Adjunct faculty member of Shalom-Ecumenical Center for Continuing Education, Augustana College, Sioux Falls, S.D., 1982-83; participant in the National Endowment for the Humanities summer seminar series, 1986.

MEMBER: National Association of Baptist Professors of Religion, Society of Biblical Literature, Catholic Biblical Association, Institute for Biblical Research.

AWARDS, HONORS: Michael Wilson Keith Prize in Homiletics, 1975, from Pittsburgh Theological Seminary.

WRITINGS:

(Editor) *Jesus Christ: The Man From Nazareth and the Exalted Lord,* Mercer University Press, 1987.
(Editor) *Eschatology and the Kingdom of God,* Hendrikson, in press.

Contributor to *Layman's Bible* and the *Mercer Dictionary of the Bible.*

Contributor of articles to periodicals including the *Baptist Peacemaker, Biblical Illustrator, Biblical Theology Bulletin, Perspectives in Religious Studies,* and *Review and Expositor.*

WORK IN PROGRESS: Articles for the *International Standard Bible Encyclopedia;* an article for *Biblical Illustrator.*

SIDELIGHTS: Hulitt Gloer told *CA:* "I have a special interest in the theme of discipleship in the New Testament and church history and the history and practice of Christian spirituality."

AVOCATIONAL INTERESTS: Peacemaking activities, travel.

*   *   *

GLUCK, Carol   1941-

PERSONAL: Born November 12, 1941, in Newark, N.J.; married Peter L. Gluck (an architect), 1966; children: Thomas, William. *Education:* Attended University of Munich, 1960-61; Wellesley College, B.A. (with special honors), 1962; Columbia University, M.A. and Certificate in East Asian Studies, 1970, Ph.D., 1977; attended Tokyo University, 1972-74.

ADDRESSES: Home—440 Riverside Dr., New York, N.Y. 10027. *Office*—912 International Affairs Building, East Asian Institute, Columbia University, New York, N.Y. 10027.

CAREER: Columbia University, New York, N.Y., assistant professor, 1975-83, associate professor, 1983-86, professor of Japanese history, 1986-88, George Sansom Professor of History, 1988—, chairman of Undergraduate Program in East Asian Studies, 1977-87. Visiting research associate in law at Tokyo University, 1978-79 and 1985-86. Member of advisory committee for Senior Fulbright Awards Program, Council for the International Exchange of Scholars, 1981-84; member of American Council of Learned Societies and Social Science Research Council Joint Committee on Japanese Studies, 1984—; member of American advisory committee of Japan Foundation, 1986—; co-director of National Endowment for the Humanities seminar "Asia in the Core Curriculum," 1987—; member of committee on research libraries at New York Public Library, 1987—.

MEMBER: International Commission for the History of Historiography, American Historical Association (member of council, 1987—), Association for Asian Studies (member of Northeast Area council, 1981-84), Society for Historians of American Foreign Relations, Phi Beta Kappa.

AWARDS, HONORS: Woodrow Wilson fellow, 1963-64; Social Science Research Council foreign area fellow in Japan, 1972-74; grants from Council for Research in the Social Sciences, 1978, 1980, 1982, and American Council of Learned Societies and Social Science Research Council, 1978-79; Japan Foundation fellow, 1978-79; Mark Van Doren Award for teaching from Columbia College, 1982; Fulbright grant, 1985-86; John King Fairbank Prize in East Asian History from American Historical Association, 1986, and Lionel Trilling Award from Columbia University, 1987, both for *Japan's Modern Myths.*

WRITINGS:

Japan's Modern Myths: Ideology in the Late Meiji Period, Princeton University Press, 1985.

Co-editor of series "The United States and Pacific Asia: Studies in Social, Economic, and Political Interaction," Columbia University Press, 1987—.

CONTRIBUTOR

Warren Cohen, editor, *New Frontiers in American-East Asian Relations,* Columbia University Press, 1983.
Thomas Burkman, editor, *The Occupation of Japan: Arts and Culture,* MacArthur Memorial, 1988.
M. Takebatake and A. Igarashi, editors, *Sengo Nihon seishinshi no saikento* (title means "Reevaluations of Postwar Japanese Intellectual History"), Iwanami shoten, 1988.

Contributor to *Encyclopedia of Asian History.* Contributor of articles and reviews to scholarly journals and Japanese newspapers.

WORK IN PROGRESS: Versions of the Past: The Japanese and Their Modern History, on historical consciousness in twentieth-century Japan, publication by Princeton University Press expected in 1990; editing *The Media in Contemporary Japan,* with Michael Reich and Eleanor Westney; editing *Varieties of Japanese History,* translations from the Japanese.

SIDELIGHTS: Carol Gluck told *CA* that she has focused her attention on the intellectual and social history of nineteenth- and twentieth-century Japan. She also expressed an interest in the history of international relations and comparative (European, American, and Japanese) historiography. The author's languages include Japanese, German, Spanish, and French.

* * *

GODFREY, Martyn N. 1949-

PERSONAL: Born April 17, 1949, in Birmingham, England; immigrated to Canada, 1957, naturalized citizen; son of Sidney (an engineer) and Helen (a secretary; maiden name, Brown) Godfrey; married Carolyn Boswell, 1973 (divorced, 1985); children: Marcus, Selby. *Education:* University of Toronto, B.A. (with honors), 1973, B.Ed., 1974.

ADDRESSES: Agent—Nancy Colbert, Colbert Agency, 303 Davenport Rd., Toronto, Ontario, Canada M5R 1R4.

CAREER: Teacher at elementary schools in Kitchener and Waterloo, Ontario, 1974-77, Mississauga, Ontario, 1977-80, and Assumption, Alberta, 1980-82; junior high school teacher in Edson, Alberta, 1983-85; writer, 1985—.

MEMBER: Writers Union of Canada, Canadian Authors Association, Canadian Society of Children's Authors, Illustrators, and Performers, Writers Guild of Alberta (vice-president, 1986; president, 1987).

AWARDS, HONORS: Award for best children's short story from Canadian Authors Association, 1985, and award for best children's book from University of Lethbridge, 1987, both for *Here She Is, Ms. Teeny-Wonderful.*

WRITINGS:

FOR CHILDREN

The Vandarian Incident, Scholastic-TAB, 1981.
Alien Wargames, Scholastic-TAB, 1984.
The Beast, EMC Publishing, 1984.

Spin Out, EMC Publishing, 1984.
Here She Is, Ms. Teeny-Wonderful, Scholastic-TAB, 1985.
Ice Hawk, EMC Publishing, 1985.
Fire! Fire!, EMC Publishing, 1985.
Plan B Is Total Panic, Lorimer, 1986.
The Last War, Macmillan, 1986.
It Isn't Easy Being Ms. Teeny-Wonderful, Scholastic-TAB, 1987.
Wild Night, EMC Publishing, 1987.
More Than Weird, Macmillan, 1987.
Rebel Yell, EMC Publishing, 1987.
It Seemed Like a Good Idea at the Time, Tree Frog Press, 1987.
Baseball Crazy, Lorimer, 1987.
Sweat Hog, EMC Publishing, 1988.
Send for Ms. Teeny-Wonderful, Scholastic-TAB, 1988.
In the Time of the Monsters, Macmillan, 1988.

WORK IN PROGRESS: Mystery in the Frozen Lands, a young adult novel; *Teach Me How to Pick My Nose* and *There Are No Pine Trees at Pine Grove School,* both juvenile novels.

SIDELIGHTS: Martyn N. Godfrey told *CA:* "I flunked grade three and I hated writing then because I couldn't spell. I couldn't understand why the teacher was so worried about it. So what if I wrote 'ship' like 'sihp'; the letters are the same, aren't they? By grade five I was actually enjoying school, especially creative writing. It felt good to tell things in an interesting way. By grade seven I had created my first *real* character, Benny Bernhart Bortorowski, a thinly disguised self-image. Every week when the creative writing lesson was assigned, I'd sit and wonder how I could work my character into 'descriptive paragraphs of a winter's morning.' Finally, my language arts teacher complained, 'Drop this guy, Godfrey.' I couldn't. Benny was part of me. I couldn't throw him away, just like I can't throw my arm away. He was attached.

"That happens when you write. The characters you create become living parts of you, parts that—unlike an arm—have their own lives to live. Carol Weatherspoon in my Ms. Teeny-Wonderful stories is part of me as well. So is Dwayne in *Rebel Yell,* Nicholas Hughes in *Plan B Is Total Panic,* Deea in *Fire! Fire!,* and so on. It's interesting to have so many friends sharing your life, sort of like having a split personality but enjoying it.

"I always enjoyed writing and playing with words, but I didn't view it as a possible occupation. In fact, I can truthfully say that I wouldn't have become an author of books for young people, if it wasn't for a twelve-year-old student of mine named Tom. A science fiction fan who hated school, he challenged: 'I think that if I'm writing a story for you, then you should write a story for me. Why don't you write a space story for me?'

"By recess, I'd finished a page and a half of foolscap about a boy who went to school on another planet. I didn't get finished and Tom suggested the same deal for the next week. I agreed. After all, Tom, who was a 'reluctant learner,' was showing an interest in something that went on in school. We continued our mutual efforts for a third week as well. My finished story was seven pages long, and Tom 'filed' it in his desk.

"A few days later, Tom sauntered up to my desk with the idea that I send my story to a book club for publication. Well, seven pages is hardly a book, but my teacher brain saw this as a way to get Tom to do some more work. We sent those seven pages to Scholastic along with a letter that Tom and I had carefully drafted for the editor. To shorten the story, Scholastic asked me to turn the story into a book; it became *The Vandarian Incident.*

"It took me three years to write my second novel, another space story titled *Alien Wargames,* because I knew very little about science fiction. What I did know was schools and kids.

"In the spring of 1984, my grade seven homeroom class began jumping their BMX bikes over side-by-side garbage cans at the bottom of a hill near the schoolyard. The first student to clear four cans was one of the girls in my class. About the same time, I saw a beauty contest on television. Considering that they have beauty contests for ladies and teenagers, but not for younger girls, I decided to invent one and make my BMX jumper one of the contestants. That's how *Here She Is, Ms. Teeny-Wonderful* was created.

"Now I only write about what I know. In my books you'll find incidents about a flouride rinse disaster, a student with a raisin caught in his nose, a bear attack, spiders in a cheeseburger, and so on. They're all true. I just twist reality a little on my computer screen to make them more interesting. Writers have to grab their readers in the first few sentences. You know, the last thing I ever write in a novel is the first paragraph. Hook the reader as fast as possible, and then don't let go."

BIOGRAPHICAL/CRITICAL SOURCES:

PERIODICALS

Quill and Quire, October, 1986.
Zoot, September, 1987.

* * *

GOFF, James R., Jr. 1957-

PERSONAL: Born January 9, 1957, in Goldsboro, N.C.; son of James R. (a grocer) and Kathryn (a substitute teacher; maiden name, Forehand) Goff; married Connie W. Crawford (an elementary school teacher), December 22, 1978; children: Gideon, Kacy. *Education:* Emmanuel College, Franklin Springs, Ga., A.A., 1976; Wake Forest University, B.A., 1978; Duke University, M.Div., 1981; University of Arkansas, Ph.D., 1987.

ADDRESSES: Home—Route 1, Box 472, Deep Gap, N.C. 28618. *Office*—Department of History, Appalachian State University, Boone, N.C. 28608.

CAREER: Ordained minister of Pentecostal Holiness Church, 1976; Pentecostal Holiness Church, Cary, N.C., associate pastor, 1980-82; Appalachian State University, Boone, N.C., lecturer, 1986-87, assistant professor of history, 1988—; Watauga High School, Boone, teacher of social studies, 1987-88.

MEMBER: American Historical Association, Organization of American Historians, Society for Pentecostal Studies, Southern Historical Association.

WRITINGS:

Fields White Unto Harvest: Charles F. Parham and the Missionary Origins of Pentecostalism, University of Arkansas Press, 1988.

Contributor to religious dictionaries and to history and religion journals.

WORK IN PROGRESS: Research on the history of southern gospel music.

SIDELIGHTS: James R. Goff, Jr., told *CA:* "My general interest is American religious history, which I approach from a socio-cultural point of view. I was reared in the Pentecostal Holiness Church and served for several years as a minister in the denomination.

"Charles F. Parham, the subject of my book, was a Kansas evangelist who secured a substantial following in the Midwest during the first decade of the twentieth century. His theological speculations led directly to the eruption of the Pentecostal movement, today a worldwide phenomenon of more than fifty-one million persons. Parham's ministry was rocked by personal scandal in 1907, and he was never able to secure control of the rapidly growing revival. As a result, his importance and prominence in founding the movement was lost among later generations of Pentecostals.

"I enjoy researching and writing American religious history. For most people, religion is an emotional issue that reflects their deepest beliefs and convictions. Studying the American people and their religious culture objectively can help reveal where we have been and why we think and believe like we do.

"I believe history unfolds largely from the opportunities given to us by our social and cultural environment. We cannot become something we have no contact with or knowledge of. Yet history is not determined for us; within the range of opportunities that come our way, we make choices. The diversity of choices offered and decisions made is what makes studying history so much fun.

"My interest in Southern gospel music stems from my childhood experience attending rural gospel sings; the phenomenon remains widespread among much of rural America. Southern gospel music contributed to the roots of both rock and roll and rhythm and blues and is felt today in the popularity of much of contemporary country-western music."

* * *

GOGGIN, Dan 1943-

PERSONAL: Born May 31, 1943, in Alma, Mich.; son of Edward Ralph (a lawyer) and Gretchen Hassig (a teacher; maiden name, Wilson) Goggin. *Education:* Attended Manhattan School of Music and University of Michigan. *Religion:* Roman Catholic.

ADDRESSES: Agent—Mitch Douglas, International Creative Management, 40 West 57th St., New York, N.Y. 10019.

CAREER: Singer, composer, playwright, and stage director. Performed as lead singer for the musical "Luther," first produced on Broadway at St. James Theater, New York, N.Y., in 1963. Toured for five years with the folk singing duo, The Saxons. Creator, with Marilyn Farina, of Nunsense greeting cards.

MEMBER: Dramatists Guild.

AWARDS, HONORS: Best Musical, Best Book, and Best Music awards from the Outer Critics Circle, 1986, all for "Nunsense."

WRITINGS:

(And director) "Nunsense" (musical), first produced off-Broadway at Cherry Lane Theater, New York City, 1985.

Contributor of musical scores for Broadway and off-Broadway productions, including "Hark," "Legend," and "Seven," and for the revues "Because We're Decadent" and "Something for Everybody's Mother."

WORK IN PROGRESS: "A One-Way Ticket to Broadway," a musical.

SIDELIGHTS: With his first musical, "Nunsense," Dan Goggin received both popular and critical acclaim, garnering three Outer Critics Circle awards for the production. The parody on Roman Catholicism concerns a group of nuns—the Little Sisters of Hoboken—who put on a vaudevillian musical in a parochial school gym to raise money. "The show is milked for every nun sequitur (it's catching) in the book," remarked Herbert Mitgang in the *New York Times,* "including a few that never should have made it to the convent," such as references to the sisters' resemblance to penguins and other predictable puns on nuns. Still, the reviewer admitted, "after a while it becomes habit-forming." Even an unimpressed reviewer, Jeremy Kingston of the London *Times,* was unable to resist quipping that the show was "a conception that should have been dispatched before birth." Mitgang assured potential theatergoers that the play, despite its parodies on religious themes, is not offensive. "Dan Goggin's Little Sisters of Hoboken are all to the good," he wrote. "Nobody need worry about picketing 'Nunsense.'"

BIOGRAPHICAL/CRITICAL SOURCES:

PERIODICALS

New York Times, December 15, 1985.
Times (London), March 25, 1987.

* * *

GOLDBERG, Lester 1924-

PERSONAL: Born February 3, 1924, in Brooklyn, N.Y.; son of Jacob and Fanny (Joseph) Goldberg; married Dorothy Weinstein (a professor of mathematics), June, 1947; children: Jean, Judith, Larry and Barbara (twins). *Education:* City College (now of the City University of New York), B.S., 1946. *Religion:* Jewish.

ADDRESSES: Home—18 Woods Hole Rd., Cranford, N.J. 07016.

CAREER: Worked in real estate; affiliated with the State Division of Housing, 1988—. Writer.

MEMBER: Poets and Writers, Metropolitan Association of Housing and Redevelopment Officials.

AWARDS, HONORS: Fellow of National Endowment for the Arts, 1979; grants from New Jersey Arts Council, 1982 and 1986; award from International P.E.N. Syndicated Fiction Project, 1984, for short story "Hardware."

WRITINGS:

One More River (stories), University of Illinois Press, 1978.
In Siberia It Is Very Cold (novel), Dembner, 1987.

Work represented in anthologies, including *Best American Short Stories,* edited by Martha Foley, 1974-77, and *O. Henry Prize Stories,* edited by William Abrahams, 1979. Contributor of more than fifty stories to magazines, including *Cimarron Review, Sou'Wester, Mid-American Review, Kansas Quarterly, National Jewish Monthly,* and *Transatlantic Review.*

WORK IN PROGRESS: A collection of short stories.

SIDELIGHTS: Lester Goldberg told *CA:* "I started writing at the age of forty-five, which is considered quite late. Writing simply enhances my life, and I feel most alive when I am writing, rewriting, or generating a story by listening or notetaking."

BIOGRAPHICAL/CRITICAL SOURCES:

PERIODICALS

New York Times Book Review, August 2, 1987.

* * *

GOLDSMITH, Raymond W(illiam) 1904-1988

OBITUARY NOTICE—See index for *CA* sketch: Surname originally Goldschmidt; born December 23, 1904, in Brussels, Belgium; immigrated to United States, 1934 (one source says 1930), naturalized citizen, 1939; died of heart failure, July 12, 1988, in Hamden (one source says New Haven), Conn. Economist, educator, and author. During his long career Goldsmith served governmental agencies and the academic community with distinction. Goldsmith joined the U.S. Securities and Exchange Commission in its earliest days in the 1930s, leaving his post there in 1941 to serve the War Production Board. After World War II he taught economics at American University and at the graduate business school of New York University. In 1962 he joined the economics faculty at Yale University, where he served until his retirement as professor emeritus. Goldsmith was also a longtime member of the research staff of the National Bureau of Economic Research and served on several key committees for the Federal Reserve Board and other national and international government agencies. Notable among his published works are *The Changing Structure of American Banking; The National Balance Sheet of the United States, 1953-1980; The Financial Development of India, 1860-1977; The Financial Development of Japan, 1868-1977;* and the three-volume *A Study of Savings in the United States,* a standard reference tool on the role of savings in the national economy.

OBITUARIES AND OTHER SOURCES:

BOOKS

Who's Who in Economics: A Biographical Dictionary of Major Economists, 1700-1986, 2nd edition, MIT Press, 1986.

PERIODICALS

New York Times, July 15, 1988.
Washington Post, July 15, 1988.

* * *

GOLDTHORPE, Rhiannon 1934-

PERSONAL: Born June 16, 1934, in Neath, Wales; daughter of Daniel (a lecturer) and Hannah (Davies) Harry; married John H. Goldthorpe (a sociologist); children: Sian, David. *Education:* University of Wales, B.A., 1954, M.A., 1956; attended Royal Academy of Music, 1958-59.

ADDRESSES: Home—32 Leckford Rd., Oxford OX2 6HX, England. *Office*—St. Anne's College, Oxford University, Oxford OX2 6HS, England.

CAREER: University of Wales, University College of North Wales, Bangor, fellow in French, 1956-58; University of Glasgow, Glasgow, Scotland, assistant lecturer in French, 1959-61; Cambridge University, Newnham College, Cambridge,

England, lecturer in French, 1961-69; Oxford University, St. Anne's College, Oxford, England, fellow, tutor, and lecturer in French, 1971—.

MEMBER: Society for French Studies, British Society for Phenomenology.

WRITINGS:

Sartre: Literature and Theory, Cambridge University Press, 1984.

Contributor to literature journals. Co-editor of *French Studies.*

WORK IN PROGRESS: Sartre: La Nausee, for Unwin Hyman.

* * *

GONZALEZ-CRUSSI, F(rank)   1936-

PERSONAL: Born October 4, 1936, in Mexico City, Mexico; immigrated to United States, 1973, naturalized citizen, 1987; son of Pablo (a pharmacist) and Maria (a pharmacist; maiden name, Crussi) Gonzalez; married Ana Luz, December 22, 1961 (divorced, 1974); married Wei Hsueh (a research pathologist), October 7, 1978; children: (first marriage) Daniel, Francis Xavier, Juliana. *Education:* Universidad Nacional Autonoma de Mexico, B.A., 1954, M.D., 1961.

ADDRESSES: Home—2626 North Lakeview Ave., Chicago, Ill. 60614. *Office*—Department of Pathology, Children's Memorial Hospital, 2300 Children's Plaza, Chicago, Ill. 60614.

CAREER: Licensed to practice medicine in Indiana, Illinois, and Ontario; certified by American Board of Pathology, 1967, Canada Register, Ontario, 1970. Penrose Hospital, Colorado Springs, Colo., intern, 1962; St. Lawrence Hospital, Lansing, Mich. and Shands Teaching Hospital at the University of Florida, Gainesville, Fla., resident in pathology, 1963-67; Queen's University, Kingston, Ontario, assistant professor of pathology, 1967-73; Indiana University-Purdue University at Indianapolis, Ind., associate professor of pathology, 1973-78; Northwestern University, Chicago, Ill., professor of pathology, 1978—; writer. Head of laboratories at Children's Memorial Hospital, Chicago.

MEMBER: International Academy of Pathology, Society for Pediatric Pathology, American Society of Clinical Pathologists, Royal College of Physicians and Surgeons of Canada, Chicago Pathology Society, Authors Guild, Society of Midland Authors.

AWARDS, HONORS: Best Nonfiction award from the Society of Midland Authors, 1985, for *Notes of an Anatomist.*

WRITINGS:

Notes of an Anatomist (essays), Harcourt, 1985.
Three Forms of Sudden Death; and Other Reflections on the Grandeur and Misery of the Body (essays; includes "Some Expressions of the Body [in Four Movements]"), Harper, 1986.
On the Nature of Things Erotic (essays), Harcourt, 1988.

Also author of a medical book entitled *Extragonadal Teratomas;* editor of *Wilm's Tumor and Related Renal Neoplasms of Childhood,* a book for specialists on a malignancy of the kidney that appears in children.

Contributor to numerous specialized medical journals.

SIDELIGHTS: Pathologist F. Gonzalez-Crussi established himself as a noteworthy author with the publication of three nontechnical essay collections. Described as "witty" and "well-read" by Brett Singer in the *Los Angeles Times Book Review,* Gonzalez-Crussi colors his informal writings with the insight he has gained from an almost three-decade career in medicine. Critics credit him with renewing the essay as a viable literary form in the twentieth century and liken his style to that of classic writers, such as Herman Melville, Michel Eyquem Montaigne, and Charles Lamb.

Gonzalez-Crussi's first collection of essays, entitled *Notes of an Anatomist,* deals with a vast array of subjects, including corpses, ancient embalming techniques, the phemonenon of multiple births, bodily appendages, and natural monstrosities from a pathologist's perspective. The volume is considered to be an unusually rich and thought-provoking first effort that artfully blends the author's personal experience and wry humor with mythic and literary references. Gonzalez-Crussi spices his essays with fascinating asides: his use of allusions ranging from mention of sixteenth-century French king Henry IV's venereal diseases and Greek painter El Greco's astigmatism to the look of a Federico Fellini film prompted critic Dennis Drabelle to call him a "skilled wielder of literary references" in a review for *Washington Post Book World.*

John Gross, writing for the *New York Times,* suggested that *Notes of an Anatomist* "could also have been entitled 'A Pathologist's Apology,'" as it attempts to purge doctors who perform autopsies of their presumed callousness. Gonzalez-Crussi asserted the nobility of pathologists in "The Dead as a Living," an essay from the volume that was cited in part in *Washington Post Book World:* physicians who search for the cause of their patients' deaths, explained the author, are unequaled in their "interest in the dead as dead persons, rather than abstractions." In the same excerpt, the doctor went on to argue that pathologists regard a corpse as a unique repository of clues capable of disclosing the cause of an individual human being's death. Ironically, however, the highly personal postmortem examination also reveals man's sameness in what Gonzalez-Crussi, quoted by Edward Schneidman for the *Los Angeles Times Book Review,* calls "a most brutal way." The author reminds us, wrote Bruce Hepburn in an article for *New Statesman,* of the disturbing but undeniable fact that "decomposition of one sort or other is our universal fate and that it is salutary for us all to keep our latter end in mind."

Critics applauded Gonzalez-Crussi's literary debut for both its form and content. D. J. Enright wrote in the *New York Times Book Review* that the essays "mix fact with speculation and gravity with humor, are rich in apposite and astounding anecdote and are elegant in expression." Schneidman echoed Enright's praise and expressed the consensus of the critics when he called the essays the "marvelously original and provocative" products of a "gifted" writer. *Notes of an Anatomist* earned Gonzalez-Crussi the Best Nonfiction Award from the Society of Midland Authors in 1985.

The author's follow-up volume of essays, *Three Forms of Sudden Death; and Other Reflections on the Grandeur and Misery of the Body,* centers on issues of aging and death. Allan J. Tobin, commenting on the doctor's unconventional treatment of a seemingly somber topic, wrote in the *Los Angeles Times Book Review:* "Gonzalez-Crussi deals less with the gloom of death than with the joy of life, especially of a life devoted to inquiry." Tobin suggested that just as the doctor examines physiological abnormalities in an effort to better understand normal life processes, he writes his essays in an attempt to explore timeless human mysteries: "There are only two themes worth writing . . . about,'' Gonzalez-Crussi stated according to Tobin, ''love and death, *eros* and *thanatos*.''

Three Forms of Sudden Death, which refers to death by lightning, asphyxiation, or unknown causes, intersperses thoughts on cannibalism and the female breast with a philosophical view of the human emotions in what several critics have referred to as ''pithy'' and ''engaging'' essays. While the collection was hailed as both cogent and well worth reading, it did not enjoy the exposure or popularity of its predecessor.

Gonzalez-Crussi's third publication, *On the Nature of Things Erotic*, marks a departure from the scientifically inspired writings that dominated the doctor's earlier collections. The essays deal with love, desire, and seduction, achieving ''something that it is not too much to call wisdom,'' stated John Gross, writing for the *New York Times*. Reviewers expressed a desire for the author to offer his own theories on the subjects he addresses, rather than a compilation of the thoughts of others, but were content to enjoy his intriguing accounts of ancient Greek love diagnoses, medieval Chinese seduction, and the classical view of homosexuality as a sign of high culture.

While Gonzalez-Crussi has gained both critical and popular success for his reflections on human nature, he continues an active career in medicine, teaching pathology at Northwestern University in Chicago, Illinois. As an author, he is the practitioner of a long-ignored art, ''a true essayist,'' wrote Gross in an article for the *New York Times*. By following the paths of his imagination, Gonzalez-Crussi has touched upon what critics consider to be universal themes in essays of universal appeal.

Gonzalez-Crussi told *CA:* ''In my books, I have attempted to join science and the humanities. I would like to produce works of literature inspired on medical and biological subjects—not scientific divulgation. *Notes of an Anatomist* originated from a desire to reflect on the personal experience of a pathologist. *Three Forms of Sudden Death* attempts to be a personal statement of perplexity at the limitations and strengths of the human body.''

CA INTERVIEW

CA interviewed F. Gonzalez-Crussi by telephone on April 23, 1987, at his office in Chicago, Illinois.

CA: Both your mother and father were pharmacists. Did their work have some bearing on your decision to go into medicine?

GONZALEZ-CRUSSI: Probably so. I had no pressure from my parents to go into any special branch of work, but it is likely that I was influenced by contact with the medical milieu.

CA: Since 1983 you've had four books published, one a year, first two technical books and then the essay collections Notes of an Anatomist *and* Three Forms of Sudden Death. *Was writing a long-standing ambition also?*

GONZALEZ-CRUSSI: Yes. Ever since I was young, I had wanted to do some literary production, but various circumstances determined that I would go into medicine rather than into literature, not the least of which was the fact that the future of a writer, the ability of a writer to provide for a family and so forth, was uncertain to say the least. I was always interested in biology as well, so I thought that I would go into medicine.

All these things are obscure; I never gave too much thought to these various circumstances and the way they converge to orient a person in one way or another. But as it turned out, I think it was a good result because there is a place for the physician-writer. Physicians have a certain viewpoint that people who are not used to confronting birth and death in a frequent way do not have.

CA: Your essays are packed with references to mythology, the classics, religious writings, and contemporary books—the kind of background that's usually neglected in a medical education. Did you acquire these interests early on?

GONZALEZ-CRUSSI: Yes, in my adolescence. I think I was especially fortunate in one experience, which I consider important in my formation. That was the fact that I came under the sphere of French influence. The French spend a great amount of effort and money to promote French culture and civilization in Latin America. At that time they organized a yearly contest among people who were just about to go to college, and the first prize was a trip to Paris to spend a few months in a school annexed to the Sorbonne. I was fortunate enough the year I graduated from high school to be the winner. So, even though my background is humble and my family would never have been able to afford to send me to Europe, I won the first prize in that competition and got to go to Paris for a few months, and I became progressively more immersed in the culture.

I think the French have a great literature. Somerset Maugham said, I believe it was in his book *Summing Up*, that other countries have great writers, but only France has a great literature. I think that was a bit of a hyperbolic statement, but he meant that it's a continuous production over many centuries in different areas of literature, and not isolated in drama or one such field.

Having been born and raised in a Latin country and then gone to France, I always felt this tendency to study and read in the humanities. Then I became a physician, but as I say, it behooves the physician at least now and then to step back and contemplate his activities from a broader perspective. I don't know if it's fortunate or unfortunate, but medicine is an extremely demanding field, and one has to keep up with the journals and the specialized literature. That leaves very little time for sallies into the field of the humanities. I don't think it's an unfair comment to say that this is why physicians—in North America, especially—are extremely competent, very proficient in their fields of interest, but often have a very narrow approach to the broader humanistic outlook.

CA: Yes. And a great deal has been written about that lately. Do you feel that affects their medical practice in some way?

GONZALEZ-CRUSSI: In some way, yes. But one should not be too glib in passing judgment on these matters. When a patient has an intense pain and wants somebody who knows how to alleviate it, it would not be relevant in certain situations for the physician to be a wise counselor. There are many, many situations in which the important thing is to get rid of the malaise. Medicine is vast, and all I can say is that frequently the situation arises in which the patient would rather have an expert technician to take care of the immediate physical problem, and later see about consulting someone on the broader problems or emotional impact or whatever. If the person who's going to approach the problem is a specialized and glorified technician, it doesn't matter; the pressing concern is to cure the patient.

CA: Your work as a pathologist and some of the work you describe in your essays is very much that of a detective. Does each new case you take on seem exciting to you on some level?

GONZALEZ-CRUSSI: Yes. There are too many areas of obscurity now, and every case seems to be telling something. Sometimes the message is overt; often it is obscure. But there is always something to spur one's detective instinct, if you want to call it that. I confine myself to the examination and investigation of tissues in cases of disease, and I confine my practice to pediatrics, because I work in a pediatric hospital. I am generally averse to the more spectacular part of the job of a pathologist, or at least the one that gets more in the news, the forensic field. The medical-legal complications and all the entanglements that go with them are not to my liking. I have now and then been obligated to appear as an expert witness in cases involving crime or at least suspicion of foul play, but if I can avoid it, I avoid it. My work is more retiring, quieter, and I hope more academic rather than being in the limelight. I of course read some forensic pathology, but I do not like it.

CA: In any one of your essays there's an amazing variety of facts and observations from a wide range of sources. How does the process of collection work? Do you make notes of interesting things from routine reading and then find at some point that you have an essay's worth of material on a given topic?

GONZALEZ-CRUSSI: I think my collection of material is very imperfect. There ought to be a better way, especially now with the technology that's available with computers. One could make files and store information and retrieve it just by pushing buttons. I am a little familiar, of course, with computers, but I don't do that. I work in an atavistic way, a really old-fashioned way. I do routinely read things that interest me, and sometimes I take notes. Often I do not. When I want to recall where things were, I hardly ever find them again. I even write down the notes with a fountain pen—not a ballpoint, but a real fountain pen—because I like the physical sensation; it's a little bit like drawing. So my notes are in notebooks, difficult to retrieve. There's a lot of material that I would have liked to use in the books but never could come up with again. I think writers would benefit from becoming a little bit more attuned to the advances in technology, and I certainly am not an exception to that. I do use an IBM word processor, but that is at the end, when my notes are almost in the final stage.

CA: Have Notes of an Anatomist *and* Three Forms of Sudden Death *attracted readers that you might not have expected?*

GONZALEZ-CRUSSI: Yes, but it's a peculiar thing to me. I'm relatively new in the literary field and came late to it, so I don't know how these things work, but I was astounded to see there's a trace of one book at the library, and none of the other one. It is interesting to observe the fate of these two productions, two books which are basically of the same type. *Notes of an Anatomist* caught the attention of the readers and the critics. It was highly praised in the *New York Times*. It has already been translated into six languages, and there's an offer for a seventh one. It met with considerable success, although it's not the type of book that would be snatched up in supermarkets. It appeals to the educated reader and would not have a mass audience anyway. But *Three Forms of Sudden Death*, for reasons that are completely unknown to me, was not reviewed. There was a minor comment in the *New York Times*, but more like a summary of content; it certainly did not say whether the book was good, bad, or mediocre. A friend of mine sent me a small comment from someone in a North Carolina newspaper. But the national newspapers and magazines did not comment on it. So I think the diffusion of the second book was limited very severely. I went from very high notoriety to complete obscurity!

But that doesn't worry me. I do the writing because I feel that I have to do it, and I like to do it. Everything worked well in that respect, even though I would have liked to write earlier. When I was younger, many things deterred me. Also, one of the felicitous by-products of all this is that I don't depend on writing for a living. My profession is satisfactorily remunerated. I write because I like to, and that's how these last two books evolved.

CA: Notes of an Anatomist *won the Society of Midland Authors Best Nonfiction award for a 1985 book. Do you see much of other writers through such organizations?*

GONZALEZ-CRUSSI: They issue newsletters and tell members of activities they are organizing, so the opportunities for meeting other writers are there through the society. But I don't avail myself of every opportunity. I'm leading this double life, and it really takes very much of my time. I would like to very much, and in the future I will try to whenever possible.

CA: Are your fellow doctors aware of you as a writer also?

GONZALEZ-CRUSSI: Yes. Locally, I perceived some misgivings. I was afraid some of my colleagues might think it inappropriate for a member of a conservative profession to indulge in the uninhibited exercise of the imagination and of free association. I was careful not to use the "M.D." after my name in my books. I thought people used to scientific writing, which is like the gymnastics of a disciplined mind, would not take kindly to one of their number going into purely literary writing, which is like the tickling of the imagination, much more unrestrained, and at times wild. I now realize I did not give my colleagues due credit. They have been quite supportive. They acknowledge the need for the physician-writer, which is for them a viable entity. They have even invited me as a speaker, devoting the same respectful attention to my rambling thoughts as they would to a clinical talk.

CA: Music is your metaphor in the essay "Some Expressions of the Body (in Four Movements)." Is music a special interest of yours?

GONZALEZ-CRUSSI: I like music very much, but I don't have a strong musical background. I cannot say that I am a music connoisseur by any means; I simply enjoy it. I have tried learning the concert guitar, but I think it was too late in the game. The problem is that to perform on an instrument at a level of proficiency I would find pleasurable would take so many hours of practice and study. You can't have everything. You can't do pathology, write, and be a soloist virtuoso. So in the end I decided that I would have to forego something.

CA: What about the interest in art? There are references to works of art throughout your writing.

GONZALEZ-CRUSSI: It's the same as with the music. Although I enjoy some artistic manifestations and I read about art, I don't have any special expertise. I am a lay person in that regard, no more.

CA: *You've said that your wife's being Chinese has given you access to literature that would have been inaccessible otherwise. Would you tell me more about that?*

GONZALEZ-CRUSSI: Yes. She is a doctor, also a pathologist; in fact, she works with me in the same department, although she does mostly basic research and I am more concerned with diagnostic aspects of the practice of pathology. Through her I have learned a little Chinese, not enough to read the classics, but just for very simple texts. When I have an interest in something, I ask my wife to translate from the Chinese, then I take notes. So she is a source of access to material that is not readily available in the West.

Although there are a great many translations of the Oriental languages—in this particular case, Chinese—often they must be regarded with a lot of caution. A great deal of background is needed to do an acceptable translation from Chinese. Often people translate from translations. There are some very abstract things, particularly in philosophical writing, which are quite difficult to render properly from the original. Of course I don't take up very abstract writing, but stories, legends, history—especially chroniclers of past dynasties. And my wife is very helpful in that respect.

CA: *Does she also read your essays in progress?*

GONZALEZ-CRUSSI: Yes. She is a good critic for the general flavor—whether it is getting a little bit too big or too boring, whether her attention can still be held to the text. In terms of the language itself, I think going from an Oriental background to a Western language is very difficult unless one does it young or is especially gifted. My wife does not have a good ear for the musicality of the language, but for the general appeal of the text she's a very good judge.

CA: *How do you manage to combine the medical practice and teaching with writing and all the reading you obviously do?*

GONZALEZ-CRUSSI: As I said, I had to abandon other things that I would have liked very much to pursue, such as playing the classical guitar. Also, I really don't do anything else except the work and writing. My wife complains that I don't fix anything in the house that needs repairing. I don't cut the lawn. I go home and I read and write, and that's all. That's how it is.

CA: *Would you care to comment on your latest work,* On the Nature of Things Erotic?

GONZALEZ-CRUSSI: I see I cannot do away with the fact that I am a pathologist, and I will keep coming back to biomedical themes as a source of inspiration. I wanted to do a book that would have very little connection with medicine. I've been frustrated by seeing my books in the bookstores sometimes in the science and technology section. Many booksellers put them there despite the fact that they are a literary effort, not scientific. But because I'm a physician, it's difficult to place myself in a special category. So I wanted to do something that would be purely literary, and I tried to do a small collection of essays on love. My preferred title was *On Love and Related Maladies*. Sometimes the title is the most difficult part of the book. But my publisher wanted something that would catch the eye; he wanted the word *erotic* in it. So he has suggested the name *On the Nature of Things Erotic*. I don't know if that is a reference to *On the Nature of Things* by Lucretius or just something that occurred to him.

BIOGRAPHICAL/CRITICAL SOURCES:

PERIODICALS

Los Angeles Times Book Review, July 7, 1985, December 7, 1986, March 27, 1988.
New Statesman, April 11, 1986.
New York Times, May 14, 1985, April 15, 1988.
New York Times Book Review, July 7, 1985.
Observer (London), April 13, 1986.
Washington Post, July 5, 1985.

—*Sketch by Barbara K. Carlisle*

—*Interview by Jean W. Ross*

*   *   *

GOOCH, John   1945-

PERSONAL: Born August 25, 1945, in Weston Favell, England; married Catherine Ann Staley. *Education:* King's College, London, B.A. (with first class honors), 1966, Ph.D., 1969.

ADDRESSES: *Office*—Department of History, University of Lancaster, Lancaster LA1 4YW, England.

CAREER: U.S. Naval War College, Washington Navy Yard, Washington, D.C., Secretary of the Navy senior research fellow, 1985-86; University of Lancaster, Lancaster, England, reader in history, 1986—. Visiting professor at Yale University, 1988.

MEMBER: Royal Historical Society (fellow), Army Records Society (chairman).

AWARDS, HONORS: Premio internazionale di cultura from Citta di Anghiari, 1983, for *Soldati e Borghesi nell' Europa moderna*.

WRITINGS:

Armies in Europe, Routledge & Kegan Paul, 1980.
The Prospect of War: Studies in British Defence Policy, 1847-1942, Frank Cass, 1981.
Strategy and the Social Sciences, Frank Cass, 1981.
(Editor with Ian F. W. Beckett) *Politicians and Defence: Studies in the Formulation of British Defence Policy*, Manchester University Press, 1982.
Military Deception and Strategic Surprise, Frank Cass, 1982.
Soldati e Borghesi nell' Europa moderna, Laterza, 1982.
Army, State, and Society in Italy, 1870-1915, Macmillan, 1988.
Military Misfortune, Free Press, 1988.

Contributor to history journals.

SIDELIGHTS: John Gooch's *The Prospect of War* contains a selection of the author's previously published articles. According to Brian Bond in the *Times Literary Supplement*, the thread that binds the articles together is Gooch's concern with "the transition in foreign policy and strategy from preoccupation with the defence of a scattered empire . . . to the acceptance of a Continental commitment against Germany." It is the author's contention that this transition was neither sudden nor traumatic, but that it evolved over a twenty-year period, beginning during the 1890s. Gooch's book also reveals a concern about the lack of understanding between the politicians who determine bureaucratic policy in times of war and the military generals who must implement that policy in the field. Concluding that "all serious students of this subject will be glad to have these scattered articles available in one volume,"

Bond judged *The Prospect of War* "a stimulating book with a considerable revisionist thesis regarding the relationship between soldiers and statesmen."

In the 1982 *Politicians and Defence*, Gooch and his co-editor, Ian F. W. Beckett, present selections by other authors on a similar topic. The theme of this collection, according to Michael Howard in the *Times Literary Supplement*, derives from the fact that generally "ministers responsible for managing the economy and those responsible for maintenance of defense forces have . . . found themselves natural adversaries." Commending the skill and care with which the book was assembled and subsequently presented, Howard praised Gooch and Beckett for their "good, clear introduction [that] pulls all the threads together."

BIOGRAPHICAL/CRITICAL SOURCES:

PERIODICALS

Times Literary Supplement, May 16, 1980, July 10, 1981, September 4, 1981.

* * *

GOODMAN, Joan Elizabeth   1950-

PERSONAL: Born June 18, 1950, in Fairfield, Conn.; daughter of Milton Joel (an architectural engineer) and Fayalene (a psychiatric social worker; maiden name, Decker) Goodman; married Keith A. Goldsmith, September 12, 1987. *Education:* Attended L'Accademia de Belle Arti, Rome, Italy, 1969-70; Pratt Institute, B.F.A., 1973.

ADDRESSES: Home—684 Washington St., No. 1-B, New York, N.Y. 10014. *Agent*—Paige Gillies, Publisher's Graphics, 251 Greenwood Ave., Bethel, Conn. 06801.

CAREER: Village Voice, New York, N.Y., type specker, 1968-69; Hallmark Cards, Kansas City, Mo., greeting card artist, 1974-76; free-lance writer and illustrator, 1976—.

WRITINGS:

SELF-ILLUSTRATED CHILDREN'S BOOKS

Teddy Bear, Teddy Bear, Grosset, 1979.
Bear and His Book, Simon & Schuster, 1982.
Right's Animal Farm, Western Publishing, 1983.
Amanda's First Day of School, Western Publishing, 1985.
The Secret Life of Walter Kitty, Western Publishing, 1986.
Good Night, Pippin, Western Publishing, 1986.
The Bunnies' Get Well Soup, Western Publishing, 1987.
Edward Hopper's Great Find, Western Publishing, 1987.
Hillary Squeak's Dreadful Dragon, Western Publishing, 1987.
The Bear's New Baby, Western Publishing, 1988.
Time for Bed, Western Publishing, 1989.

ILLUSTRATOR

David Cutts, *The Gingerbread Boy*, Troll, 1979.
Olive Blake, *The Grape Jelly Mystery*, Troll, 1979.
Ruben Tanner, *The Teddy Bear's Picnic: A Counting Book*, Dutton, 1979.
Carol Beach York, *Johnny Appleseed*, Troll, 1980.
Judith Grey, *Yummy, Yummy*, Troll, 1981.
Rose Greydanus, *Hocus Pocus, Magic Show!* Troll, 1981.
Robyn Supraner, *The Case of the Missing Rattles*, Troll, 1982.
Eileen Curran, *Easter Parade*, Troll, 1985.
Robyn Supraner, *The Cat Who Wanted to Fly*, Troll, 1986.

WORK IN PROGRESS: Happy Birthday, Walter Kitty!, a sequel to *The Secret Life of Walter Kitty; Max and Lulu*, a story about two contentious cats; *Bunnies by the Sea*, "about six bunnies who spend a lovely day at the beach"; and *Our Town*, "about going shopping with mother"—all picture books; *Grace*, "a novel about the adventures of a young bunny in the wide world."

SIDELIGHTS: Joan Elizabeth Goodman told *CA:* "I think that people who write children's books have special kinds of memories. I don't particularly remember details about the past. Neither do I always remember the sense of a past situation. My past, my childhood, is a jumble of oddly assorted sounds, scents, and images sometimes vague and sometimes crystal clear. What I *do* remember with extreme clarity are the feelings of childhood.

"When I write a picture book text or a 'young' novel, I reach back into that emotional grab bag for my material. My aim is to convey that emotional truth whether I'm writing about bunnies, duckies, or bears."

AVOCATIONAL INTERESTS: Tennis, bridge, medieval history.

* * *

GOODMAN, Mark   1939-

PERSONAL: Born May 5, 1939, in Dallas, Tex., son of Jason J. (an executive) and Ellen (an interior designer; maiden name, McGrath) Goodman; married Sherida Shepherd, September 14, 1968 (divorced, 1972); married Esther Nichol (a housewife), December 19, 1981; children: (first marriage) Elizabeth, (second marriage) Meade. *Education:* Cornell University, B.A., 1961. *Religion:* Episcopalian.

ADDRESSES: Home—2411 Old Stone Mill Dr., Cranbury, N.J. 08512. *Agent*—Owen Laster, William Morris Agency, 1350 6th Ave., New York, N.Y. 10019.

CAREER: Bartender in San Francisco, Calif., Fort Lauderdale, Fla., and Hyannis, Mass., 1961-63; United Press International, New York, N.Y., reporter, 1965-66; *Time* magazine, New York City, film critic, 1967-72; writer, 1972—. *Military service:* U.S. Army, 1963-65.

AWARDS, HONORS: U.S. Army in Europe award, 1964, for "outstanding journalism."

WRITINGS:

Hurrah for the Next Man Who Dies (novel), Atheneum, 1985.
(With Kenneth Blanchard) *Funny Business*, Simon & Schuster, in press.

Author of "Final Tribute" column in *New Times*. Contributor to *Esquire, Gentlemen's Quarterly, New York Times* Sunday magazine, *Playboy, Reader's Digest*, and *Time*.

WORK IN PROGRESS: "A novel set in Hollywood in the twenties, at the end of the silent film era," tentatively titled *Silent Dreams*, publication expected in 1990.

SIDELIGHTS: Mark Goodman told *CA:* "The 'Final Tribute' columns I wrote for *New Times* showed me that my best work lay in the arena of American mythology. I want to pursue this and the underlying theme of my first book—the destructiveness of American narcissism—into the subsequent decade and beyond. My overall plan is to set a novel in each decade of the twentieth century."

In his book *Hurrah for the Next Man Who Dies*, Goodman attempts to analyze how, in an effort to create representatives who validate its values and perceptions of itself, American society attempts to "mythologize" its heroes. By choosing to write about a real person—Hobey Baker, a graduate of Princeton and inductee of both the football and hockey halls of fame—and a specific historical time period—the early years of World War I—Goodman addresses the complex interrelationships between a heroic figure and the society that adored and respected him. The result, wrote Carolyn See in the *Los Angeles Times Book Review*, is "a . . . meticulous, even luminous evocation of those times . . . [when] . . . America [was] still young, still gullible and eternally narcissistic."

Goodman's *Hurrah for the Next Man Who Dies* has been described by several critics as a "docu-novel," a detailed portrayal of American society unfolding through the rise and tragic fall of one of its heroes, Hobey Baker. From the playing fields and parties of Princeton to the celebrated Lafayette Escadrille, an elite World War I air force squadron where, to no one's surprise, he becomes an ace fighter pilot and national war hero, Baker leads his squadron with the passion and bravado he had earlier exhibited on the sports field. He accepts the war in the spirit of "the game" and never fully examines what it stood for or his own motives for fighting in it. The latter tasks are reserved for Jeb Runcible, Baker's closest friend and the book's narrator. In a role many critics have likened to that of Nick Carraway in F. Scott Fitzgerald's *The Great Gatsby*, it is Runcible whose vision reveals the disappearance of American prewar innocence and suggests that Baker's heroism has become displaced and desperate. A *Time* reviewer noted, "as Jeb becomes progressively disenchanted, the golden pilot [Baker] goes into a nose dive, changing from superhero in goggles to another classic American archetype: the perennial juvenile."

The theme of Baker's inability to cope with a rapidly changing world, a world for which his education left him underprepared, is central to *Hurrah*. Early on, as See recorded, Baker reflected at his graduation that he "never imagined Princeton going on without me." By Armistice Day, some four years later, "Baker himself seems to realize that there will be no place for his individualistic heroics in adult civilian life," as Carol Ames in the *Los Angeles Times Book Review* observed, and effectively commits suicide by test flying an airplane he knows to be faulty. By retelling the decline of the heroic Baker, Ames continued, "Goodman shows us the limitation of the ideal," when events supersede an individual's, or society's, ability to change and adjust.

A few critics, including Richard Smith of the *New York Times Book Review*, found the ending of Goodman's novel anachronistic. "I couldn't crank out much sympathy for Hobey, who 'dies by the rules that the rest of the world has buried beneath tramping boots forever,'" Smith wrote, objecting to the "fake lyricism" of parts of Goodman's writing style. Ames, too, deemed the style "overwrought"—the result, she remarked, of Goodman's "homage" to the "aristocratic milieu" of Fitzgerald's style—but agreed with many other critics, such as See, who found Goodman's "evocation of Europe and New York just before the war—the pleasures laced with the intolerable boredom . . . particularly fine."

BIOGRAPHICAL/CRITICAL SOURCES:

PERIODICALS

Atlantic Monthly, April, 1985.

Los Angeles Times Book Review, March 25, 1985, April 7, 1985.
New York Times Book Review, May 19, 1985.
Time, March 25, 1985.

*   *   *

GOODMAN, Steven M(ichael)   1957-

PERSONAL: Born August 3, 1957, in Detroit, Mich. *Education:* University of Michigan, B.S., 1981.

ADDRESSES: Office—Museum of Zoology, University of Michigan, Ann Arbor, Mich. 48109.

CAREER: University of Michigan, Ann Arbor, research associate at Museum of Zoology, 1983—.

WRITINGS:

(With Patrick F. Houlihan) *The Birds of Ancient Egypt*, Bolchazy-Carducci, 1985.
(With P. L. Meininger and W. C. Mullie) *The Birds of the Egyptian Western Desert*, Museum of Zoology, University of Michigan, 1986.
(Editor with P. L. Meininger) *The Birds of Egypt*, Oxford University Press, in press.

WORK IN PROGRESS: The Reptiles and Amphibians of Egypt; Rock Paintings in the Egyptian Eastern Desert; and *The Wildlife of Egypt*, a picture book.

*   *   *

GOODSELL, Jane Neuberger   1921(?)-1988

OBITUARY NOTICE: Born c. 1921 in Portland, Ore.; died of cancer, September 7, 1988, in Portland, Ore. Journalist and author. Primarily known as the author of biographies for children, Goodsell wrote about the lives of such notable Americans as former First Lady Eleanor Roosevelt and Hawaiian Senator Daniel Inouye. Goodsell had also worked as a weekly columnist for the *Astorian Budget* and was the author of the syndicated column "From Soup to Nonsense" for Press Associates of Washington, D.C. She contributed articles to *Ladies' Home Journal*, *McCall's*, *Reader's Digest*, and *Redbook*, among other publications. Her books include *Katy's Magic Glasses*, *I've Only Got Two Hands and I'm Busy Wringing Them*, and *Not A Good Word About Anybody*, an assortment of anecdotes about the errors and accidents of famous historical personalities.

OBITUARIES AND OTHER SOURCES:

BOOKS

Who's Who Among Pacific Northwest Authors, 2nd edition, Pacific Northwest Library Association, 1969.

PERIODICALS

Washington Post, September 12, 1988.

*   *   *

GOODWIN, H(arry) Eugene   1922-

PERSONAL: Born December 19, 1922, in Council Bluffs, Iowa; son of Harry Lars (a labor organizer) and Mary Ellen (a homemaker; maiden name, James) Goodwin; married Frances Jean Prudhon (a cartoonist), July 3, 1943; children: Geri Goodwin Huey, Gibson Eugene, Susan Goodwin Havens, Michael Jay. *Education:* University of Iowa, B.A., 1946, M.A., 1947. *Politics:* Liberal. *Religion:* Unitarian-Universalist.

ADDRESSES: Home—119 Bathgate Dr., State College, Pa. 16801.

CAREER: Daily Iowan, Iowa City, Iowa, editor, 1946-47; *Sun,* Baltimore, Md., copy editor, 1947-48; Associated Press, Baltimore, writer, 1948-50; *Washington Star,* Washington, D.C., reporter and columnist, 1950-57; Pennsylvania State University, University Park, professor of journalism, 1957-85, professor emeritus, 1985—, director of School of Journalism, 1957-69. Mellet Fund for a Free and Responsible Press, member of board of directors, 1967-84, president of board, 1976-84; member of admissions committee at Washington Journalism Center, 1968—; lecturer and consultant on the ethics of journalism. *Military service:* U.S. Army Air Forces; became first lieutenant.

MEMBER: Association for Education in Journalism and Mass Communications (chairman of Division of Mass Communications and Society, 1966-67), Society of Professional Journalists, Omicron Delta Kappa.

AWARDS, HONORS: Outstanding teacher award from Amoco Foundation, 1980; Frank Luther Mott-Kappa Tau Alpha Research Award in Journalism, 1983, for *Groping for Ethics in Journalism.*

WRITINGS:

Groping for Ethics in Journalism, Iowa State University Press, 1983, 2nd edition, 1987.

Member of editorial board of *Mass Communications Review,* 1978—, and *Journal of Mass Media Ethics,* 1985—.

SIDELIGHTS: H. Eugene Goodwin told *CA:* "I continue to teach and do research in journalism ethics, but my writing is turning to essays on more personal subjects, such as travel, growing old, and relationships. I have not yet offered these essays for publication."

*   *   *

GORAK, Jan   1952-

PERSONAL: Born October 12, 1952, in Blackburn, England; son of Jozef (a road mender) and Mary (a nurse; maiden name, Niland) Gorak; married Irene Elizabeth Mannion, November 17, 1984. *Education:* University of Warwick, B.A., 1975; attended University of Leeds, 1975-77; University of Southern California, M.A., 1981, Ph.D., 1983. *Politics:* "Disillusioned independent."

ADDRESSES: Office—Department of English, University of Denver, University Park, Denver, Colo. 80208.

CAREER: University of the Witwatersrand, Johannesburg, South Africa, lecturer in English, 1984-87, senior lecturer in English, 1987-88; University of Denver, Colorado, visiting associate professor, 1988-89; writer.

MEMBER: Modern Language Association of America.

AWARDS, HONORS: Pringle Prize from English Academy of Southern Africa, 1986, for article "*Deus Artifex:* Transformations of a *Topos.*"

WRITINGS:

God the Artist: American Novelists in a Post-Realist Age, University of Illinois Press, 1987.

Critic of Crisis: A Study of Frank Kermode, University of Missouri Press, 1987.

The Alien Mind of Raymond Williams, University of Missouri Press, 1988.

Contributor to *English Studies in Africa.*

WORK IN PROGRESS: Charismatic Critics: Four Makers of the Postwar Canon, publication expected in 1990.

SIDELIGHTS: Jan Gorak told *CA:* "I am one of a number of displaced academic personnel trekking the five continents after the breakup of the British university system. Not surprisingly, my books reflect the darker areas of interest of the scholar in exile. In *God the Artist* I examined the effect of the destructive creator-god on modern literary culture. In *Critic of Crisis* and *The Alien Mind of Raymond Williams* I showed how that culture induces a sense of crisis and alienation in its strongest critical exponents. Future projects will no doubt have a similar emphasis on the skeptical, restless, deracinated intelligence induced by an intellectual life of perpetual motion."

AVOCATIONAL INTERESTS: Film, music (especially rock music).

*   *   *

GOSSET, W(illiam) P(atrick)   1946-

PERSONAL: Born October 24, 1946, in Salisbury, England; son of Isaac Henry (a doctor) and Margery Eve (Clarke) Gosset; married Wendy Elizabeth Sutton (a teacher); children: Matthew, Sarah. *Education:* Bristol Polytechnic, A.R.I.C.S.

CAREER: Chartered surveyor; District Valuer's Office, Kettering, England, valuer, 1969-78; District Valuer's Office, London, England, valuer, 1978-85; senior estate surveyor for Commission for the New Towns in England, 1985—.

MEMBER: Royal Institution of Chartered Surveyors (associate), British Sub-Aqua Club.

WRITINGS:

The Lost Ships of the Royal Navy, 1792-1900, Mansell, 1986.

WORK IN PROGRESS: The Lost Ships of the Royal Navy, 1680-1792; research on the loss of H.M.S. *Victory* in 1744.

SIDELIGHTS: W. P. Gosset told *CA:* "I've been an active member of the British Sub-Aqua Club since 1965. I am an enthusiastic wreck diver, mainly (but not exclusively) in British waters. My diving experiences led to an interest in nautical archaeology, and this led directly to my book."

*   *   *

GOTTLIEB, Alex   1906-1988

OBITUARY NOTICE: Born December 21, 1906, in Russia (now U.S.S.R.); died of a cerebral hemorrhage, October 9, 1988, in Woodland Hills, Calif. Advertising manager, film and television producer, and writer. During a career lasting more than forty years, Gottlieb was a producer and writer for radio, television, film, and theater. From 1930 to 1937 he worked as an advertising manager for United Artists and Columbia, and he served New York's Paramount theater as publicity director at one time. Having written for radio personalities Al Jolson, Eddie Cantor, Edgar Bergen, and George Jessel, Gottlieb went on to produce more than fifty television programs, including "The Bob Hope Chrysler Theater" and "The Donna Reed Show," for which he was perhaps most noted.

He wrote, among others, the films "Susan Slept Here," which he later adapted for stage, and "I'll Take Sweden." Gottlieb also penned several Broadway plays, including "Separate Rooms," "Two for the Money," and "Your Place or Mine?" His one-act plays were published in the *Best Short Plays* anthologies of 1969, 1976, and 1985.

OBITUARIES AND OTHER SOURCES:

BOOKS

International Motion Picture Almanac, Quigley, 1988.

PERIODICALS

Chicago Tribune, October 11, 1988.

* * *

GOUDGE, Eileen   1950-
(Elizabeth Merrit, Marian Woodruff)

PERSONAL: Born July 4, 1950, in San Mateo, Calif.; daughter of Robert James (an insurance executive) and Mary Louise (a housewife; maiden name, Woodruff) Goudge; married Roy Bailey, July 4, 1974 (divorced); married Albert J. Zuckerman (a literary agent), April 28, 1985; children: Michael James, Mary Rose. *Education:* Attended San Diego State College (now University). *Politics:* Democrat. *Religion:* Jewish.

ADDRESSES: Home—234 West 22nd St., New York, N.Y. 10011. *Agent*—Albert J. Zuckerman, Writers House, 21 West 26th St., New York, N.Y. 10016.

CAREER: Worked as secretary; Spin Physics, San Diego, Calif., micro-electronics assembler, 1971-76; writer, 1976—.

WRITINGS:

YOUNG ADULT ROMANCE NOVELS

(Under pseudonym Marian Woodruff) *It Must Be Magic,* Bantam, 1982.
(Under pseudonym Marian Woodruff) *Kiss Me Creep,* Bantam, 1984.
Winner All the Way, Dell, 1984.
Smart Enough to Know, Dell, 1984.
(Under pseudonym Elizabeth Merrit) *'Till We Meet Again,* Silhouette, 1984.
Too Much Too Soon, Dell, 1984.
Afraid to Love, Dell, 1984.
Bad Girl, Dell, 1985.
Before It's Too Late, Dell, 1985.
Don't Say Goodbye, Dell, 1985.
Forbidden Kisses, Dell, 1985.
Hands Off, He's Mine, Dell, 1985.
Presenting Superhunk, Dell, 1985.
A Touch of Ginger, Dell, 1985.
Against the Rules, Dell, 1986.
Eileen Goudge's Swept Away Number One: Gone With the Wish, Avon, 1986.
Hawaiian Christmas, Dell, 1986.
Heart for Sale, Dell, 1986.
Kiss and Make Up, Dell, 1986.
Life of the Party, Dell, 1986.
Looking for Love, Dell, 1986.
Night After Night, Dell, 1986.
Old Enough: Super Seniors Number One, Dell, 1986.
Sweet Talk, Dell, 1986.
Treat Me Right, Dell, 1986.
(With Fran Lantz) *Woodstock Magic,* Avon, 1986.

Something Borrowed, Something Blue, Dell, 1988.

Also author of *Too Hot to Handle,* Dell; and—under pseudonym Marian Woodruff—*Forbidden Love,* Bantam, and *Dial L for Love,* Bantam.

Contributor to magazines, including *Highlights for Children.*

FOR ADULTS

Garden of Lies (novel), Viking, 1989.

Contributor of stories and articles to magazines, including *McCall's* and *Good Housekeeping.*

WORK IN PROGRESS: A novel for Viking.

SIDELIGHTS: Eileen Goudge told *CA:* "Writing for children has been the greatest 'university' for me in terms of seasoning my craft. I never write down to my teen audience, because they are the most discriminating of all readers. If a book doesn't grab their interest by page three, they'll put it down (unless it is assigned reading in school, in which case they'll either suffer through till the end or try to sneak by on Cliff Notes). But if the magic clicks, they'll devour the book, and everything else that author has written, inside a matter of weeks—sometimes days. Teens are passionate in their appetites. An author must be unstinting when it comes to filling their hunger for pathos, romance, fun. When you've learned how to do this, and do it successfully, you can move on to any audience, as I have. In writing for adults, I've deployed those same passions on the same grand scale, with one difference—I've graduated from shorter scenes and proscribed page counts. *Garden of Lies* is a grand opera without music, the story of a mother who switches her own newborn for another woman's baby and spends a lifetime regretting her terrible choice. The book will be published at a time, I hope, when many of my teen readers have also 'graduated' to adult fiction."

* * *

GRACE, J. Peter   1913-

PERSONAL: Born May 25, 1913, in Manhasset, N.Y.; son of Joseph P. and Janet (Macdonald) Grace; married Margaret Fennelly, May 24, 1941. *Education:* Yale University, B.A., 1936. *Religion:* Roman Catholic.

ADDRESSES: Office—W. R. Grace & Co., Grace Plaza, 1114 Avenue of the Americas, New York, N.Y. 10036-7794.

CAREER: W. R. Grace & Co., New York, N.Y., member of staff, 1936-42, secretary, 1942-43, member of board of directors, 1943—, vice-president, 1945, chief executive officer, 1945—, president, 1945-81, chairman, 1981-86, chairman, president, and chief executive officer, 1986—. Member of board of directors of Atlantic Reinsurance Co., Centennial Insurance Co., Milliken & Co., Omnicare, Inc., Restaurant Enterprises Group, Inc., Roto-Rooter, Inc., Stone & Webster, Inc., and Universal Furniture Ltd.; past member of board of directors of Ingersoll-Rand Co.; honorary member of board of directors of Brascan Ltd.; chairman of board and director of Chemed Corp. and Taco Villa, Inc.; member of board of trustees of Atlantic Mutual Insurance Co. Chairman of President Reagan's Private Sector Survey on Cost Control in the Federal Government (Grace Commission), 1982-84; founding member of Emergency Committee for American Trade; member of development committee of National Bureau of Economic Research; trustee of U.S. Council for International Business; chairman of Radio Free Europe/Radio Liberty Fund, Inc. President and trustee of Grace Institute; chairman of council of national trustees of National Jewish Center for Immunology and Respiratory Medicine; member of the corporate grants committee, President's Committee of Greater New York, and Emeritus Trustee Committee of University of Notre Dame; member of National Advisory Board of Boys Clubs of America.

MEMBER: Council on Foreign Relations, Newcomen Society, American Association of the Sovereign Military Order of Malta (president; member of board of counselors), Madison Square Garden Club (member of board of governors), Everglades Club, Pacific-Union Club, Links, Lotos Club, Lost Tree Club, Meadow Brook Club, River Club.

AWARDS, HONORS: Nearly twenty honorary degrees, including LL.D. from Mount St. Mary's College, Manhattan College, Fordham University, Boston College, University of Notre Dame, Belmont Abbey, Stonehill College, Christian Brothers College, Fairleigh Dickinson University, and Adelphi University; D.Latin American Relations from St. Joseph's College; D.C.S. from St. John's University, Jamaica, N.Y.; D.Sc. from Clarkson College; Cardinal Gibbons Medal from Catholic University of America; outstanding achievement award from University of Southern California; decorated by governments of Colombia, Chile, Ecuador, Panama, and Peru; Captain Robert Dollar Memorial Award from National Foreign Trade Council; Palladium Medal from France's Societe de Chimie Industrielle; Dodge Medallion from Young Men's Christian Association; Jefferson Award from American Institute for Public Service; James J. Kilpatrick Award from International Platform Association; Laetare Medal from University of Notre Dame; named churchman of the year by Religious Heritage of America; Knight Grand Cross of Equestrian Order of the Holy Sepulchre of Jerusalem.

WRITINGS:

Burning Money: The Waste of Your Tax Dollars, Macmillan, 1984.

*   *   *

GRACQ, Julien
See POIRIER, Louis

*   *   *

GRAFTON, David   1930-

PERSONAL: Born November 13, 1930, in Brockport, N.Y.; son of Joseph (a "gentleman farmer") and Molly (Collins-Lynch) Grafton. *Education:* Attended Columbia University, 1950-52. *Politics:* Democrat.

ADDRESSES: Home—707 Woodland Ave., No. 404, Chicago, Ill. 60613. *Agent*—Bleecker Street Associates, Inc., 88 Bleecker St., New York, N.Y. 10012.

CAREER: Assistant director of public relations for Ferre Industries, 1959-61; editor and publisher of *Top of the Town* magazine (Puerto Rico), 1961-67; Contact US (performing arts management company), Chicago, Ill., president, 1971-82; Triad Consulting Services, Chicago, consultant, 1982—. Lecturer on Cole Porter and the Cafe Society.

MEMBER: Authors Guild.

AWARDS, HONORS: Award from Illinois Humanities Council, 1987, and from Friends of Literature, 1988.

WRITINGS:

Red, Hot, and Rich: An Oral History of Cole Porter, Stein & Day, 1987.

Contributor to *Interview, Photo,* and European edition of *Life*.

WORK IN PROGRESS: Cafe Society, with photographs by Jerome Zerbe; *The Sisters*, a biography of the Cushing sisters—Mrs. William S. (Barbara) Paley, Mrs. Vincent (Mary) Astor, and Mrs. Jock (Betsey) Whitney; research for a biography of jazz entrepreneur John Hammond.

SIDELIGHTS: David Grafton told *CA* that his motivation springs from "a love of music, especially the music of Cole Porter." He continued: "My introduction to the world of Cole Porter and Cafe Society had its beginning at the feet of a dazzling flapper-era mother. Thus I became an instant devotee of Cole Porter's music and that carefree world between the two world wars. As a result Cole Porter's name and the Cafe Society period that gave birth to his music were all part of a certain mystique associated with a time, and a frame of mind associated with a devil-may-care attitude in a world with far simpler values.

"Years later, my first meeting with the legendary composer was wonderfully serendipitous. I was a guest at a dinner party held in the now-extinct Colony Restaurant in New York. As we finished dinner Rosie Dolly, my dinner hostess, received a note from Cole Porter inviting Miss Dolly and her guests to join him and his guests at his table for coffee and after-dinner drinks. That evening was to make a very lasting impression upon my young self; I would later be fortunate to visit him in his New England country home.

"When decades after I had an irresistible desire to write a book about the fascinating playboys and playgirls of the 1930s, I was advised by a friend in publishing to select one subject from that period. Since I had met Cole Porter on a number of occasions and the music and the man's lifestyle stayed with me all those years, my multi-subject project evolved into a select and unique one.

"It was in early adulthood that I experienced firsthand the world of Cafe Society during its final days in the mid-to late 1950s. Nightclubbing and wonderfully inventive parties defined this very 'new' order. It was a screwball world of international nomads who made the great cities and most fashionable resorts of the world their campgrounds. If you had great wealth you gained immediate entrance. Without money it was beauty, wit, charm, or a creative profession—one was also most welcome. Gossip and small talk were the common denominator that assured your continued membership in this select group. I found it an amusing world and one that I remember well."

BIOGRAPHICAL/CRITICAL SOURCES:

PERIODICALS

Avenue M, April, 1987.
Chicago Tribune, December 20, 1987.
New York Times Book Review, June 21, 1987.
Skyline, July 16, 1987.
Sun-Times (Chicago), May 11, 1988.

*   *   *

GRAHAM, Gerald (Sandford)   1903-1988

OBITUARY NOTICE—See index for *CA* sketch: Born April

27, 1903, in Sudbury, Ontario, Canada; died July 5, 1988. Historian, educator, editor, and author. Graham was a highly regarded teacher and scholar of Canadian history, maritime history, and British imperial history. Though born and raised in Canada, Graham spent most of his professional career in England at London University. There he served first on the faculty of Birkbeck College and then at King's College, where he was appointed Rhodes Professor of Imperial History in 1949, a post he retained until his retirement in 1970 as professor emeritus. Among his publications are *Empire of the North Atlantic: The Maritime Struggle for North America; A Concise History of Canada; Great Britain in the Indian Ocean: A Study of Maritime Enterprise, 1810-1850; The China Station: War and Diplomacy, 1830-1860;* and *The Hamlyn History of the World in Colour,* Volume XII: *New Worlds to Conquer,* which he edited. Graham also served as editor of "Imperial Studies Series," commissioned by the Royal Commonwealth Society, and as general editor of "West Africa History Series," for Oxford University Press.

OBITUARIES AND OTHER SOURCES:

BOOKS

Who's Who, 140th edition, St. Martin's, 1988.
The Writers Directory: 1988-1990, St. James Press, 1988.

PERIODICALS

Times (London), July 7, 1988.

*　　*　　*

GRAHAM, Sonia
See SINCLAIR, Sonia

*　　*　　*

GRANT, Ambrose
See RAYMOND, Rene (Brabazon)

*　　*　　*

GRANT, George (Parkin)   1918-1988

OBITUARY NOTICE: Born November 13, 1918, in Toronto, Ontario, Canada; died of pancreatic cancer, September 27, 1988, in Halifax, Nova Scotia, Canada. Educator, social commentator, and author. Grant, who earned his doctorate at Oxford University, was professor of philosophy at Dalhousie University from 1947 to 1960 and of religion at McMaster University from 1961 to 1980, after which he returned to Dalhousie to teach political science in 1980. He was best known for his influential nationalistic criticism of Canadian-American relations, featured in his 1965 book *Lament for a Nation: The Defeat of Canadian Nationalism.* Grant argued that the liberal party under Canadian Prime Minister Lester Pearson allowed the United States to dominate Canadian affairs by accepting American nuclear weapons for the nation's defense. The book helped solidify a growing opinion in the country that Canada's survival depended on its becoming more independent in economic and foreign policy matters, a mood that resulted in the nationalization of U.S.-controlled companies in Canada and opposition to America's participation in the Vietnam War. Grant voiced his concern about the conflicts of technological growth and Western values in his book *Technology and Empire: Perspectives on North America.* He also wrote *Philosophy in the Mass Age.*

OBITUARIES AND OTHER SOURCES:

BOOKS

Directory of American Scholars, Volume IV: *Philosophy, Religion, and Law,* 8th edition, Bowker, 1982.

PERIODICALS

Times (London), September 29, 1988.
Washington Post, September 30, 1988.

*　　*　　*

GRAY, Alasdair   1934-

PERSONAL: Born December 28, 1934, in Glasgow, Scotland; son of Alex (a machine operator) and Amy (a homemaker; maiden name, Fleming) Gray; children: Andrew. *Education:* Glasgow Art School, received diploma, 1957. *Politics:* "Devolutionary Scottish C.N.D. [Campaign for Nuclear Disarmament] Socialist." *Religion:* None.

ADDRESSES: Home—39 Kersland St., Glasgow G12 8BP, Scotland.

CAREER: Part-time art teacher in area of Glasgow, Scotland, 1958-62; theatrical scene painter in Glasgow, 1962-63; freelance playwright and painter in Glasgow, 1963-75; People's Palace (local history museum), Glasgow, artist-recorder, 1976-77; University of Glasgow, Glasgow, writer in residence, 1977-79; free-lance painter and maker of books in Glasgow, 1979—.

MEMBER: Scottish Society of Playwrights, Glasgow Print Workshop, various organizations supporting coal miners and nuclear disarmament.

AWARDS, HONORS: Three grants from Scottish Arts Council, between 1968 and 1981; award from Saltire Society, 1982, for *Lanark: A Life in Four Books;* award from Cheltenham Literary Festival, 1983, for *Unlikely Stories, Mostly;* award from Scottish branch of P.E.N., 1986.

WRITINGS:

Lanark: A Life in Four Books (novel), author-illustrated, Harper, 1981, revised, Braziller, 1985.
Unlikely Stories, Mostly (short stories), author-illustrated, Canongate, 1983, revised, Penguin, 1984.
1982 Janine (novel), Viking, 1984, revised, Penguin, 1985.
The Fall of Kelvin Walker: A Fable of the Sixties (novel; adapted from his television play of the same title; also see below), Canongate, 1985, Braziller, 1986.
(With James Kelman and Agnes Owens) *Lean Tales* (short story anthology), author-illustrated, J. Cape, 1985.
Saltire Self-Portrait 4, Saltire Society Publications, 1988.
Old Negatives (poems), author-illustrated, J. Cape, 1989.
The Anthology of Prefaces, Canongate, 1989.
McGrotty and Ludmilla; or, The Harbinger Report: A Romance of the Eighties, White Leaf, 1989.

Contributor to periodicals, including *Chapman* and *The Edinburgh Review.*

PLAYS FOR THE STAGE

"Dialogue" (one-act), first produced in Edinburgh at Gateway Theatre, 1971.
"The Fall of Kelvin Walker" (two-act; adapted from his television play of the same title; also see below), first produced in Stirling at McRoberts Centre, University of Stirling, 1972.

"The Loss of the Golden Silence" (one-act), first produced in Edinburgh at Pool Theatre, 1973.

"Homeward Bound" (one-act), first produced in Edinburgh at Pool Theatre, 1973.

(With Tom Leonard and Liz Lochhead) "Tickly Mince" (two-act), first produced in Glasgow at Tron Theatre, 1982.

(With Liz Lochhead, Tom Leonard and James Kelman) "The Pie of Damocles" (two-act), first produced in Glasgow at Tron Theatre, 1983.

RADIO PLAYS

"Quiet People," British Broadcasting Corporation (BBC), 1968.

"The Night Off," BBC, 1969.

"Thomas Muir of Huntershill," BBC, 1970.

"The Loss of the Golden Silence," BBC, 1974.

"McGrotty and Ludmilla," BBC, 1976.

"The Vital Witness," BBC, 1979.

"Near the Driver," translation into German by Berndt Rull-kotter broadcast by Westdeutsche Rundfunk, 1983, original text broadcast by BBC, 1988.

TELEVISION PLAYS

"The Fall of Kelvin Walker," BBC, 1968.

"Dialogue," BBC, 1972.

"Triangles," Granada, 1972.

"The Man Who Knew About Electricity," BBC, 1973.

"Honesty," BBC, 1974.

"Today and Yesterday" (series of three 20-minute educational documentaries), BBC, 1975.

"Beloved," Granada, 1976.

"The Gadfly," Granada, 1977.

"The Story of a Recluse," BBC, 1987.

SIDELIGHTS: After more than twenty years as a painter and a scriptwriter for radio and television, Alasdair Gray rose to literary prominence with the publication of several of his books in the 1980s. His works have been noted for their mixture of realistic social commentary and vivid fantasy, augmented by the author's own evocative illustrations. Jonathan Baumbach wrote in the *New York Times Book Review* that Gray's work "has a verbal energy, an intensity of vision, that has been mostly missing from the English novel since D. H. Lawrence." And David Lodge of *New Republic* said that Gray "is that rather rare bird among contemporary British writers—a genuine experimentalist, transgressing the rules of formal English prose . . . boldly and imaginatively."

In his writing Gray often draws upon his Scottish background, and he is regarded as a major force in the literature of his homeland. Author Anthony Burgess, for instance, said in the *Observer* that he considered Gray the best Scottish novelist since Walter Scott became popular in the early nineteenth century. Unlike Scott, who made his country a setting for historical romance, Gray focuses on contemporary Scotland, where the industrial economy deteriorates and many citizens fear that their social and economic destiny has been surrendered to England. Critics praised Gray, however, for putting such themes as decline and powerlessness into a larger context that any reader can appreciate. "Using Glasgow as his undeniable starting point," Douglas Gifford wrote in *Studies in Scottish Literature*, "Gray . . . transforms local and hitherto restricting images, which limited [other] novelists of real ability, . . . into symbols of universal prophetic relevance."

Gray's first novel, *Lanark,* is a long and complex work that some reviewers considered partly autobiographical. It opens in Unthank, an ugly, declining city explained in reviews as a comment on Glasgow and other Western industrial centers. As in George Orwell's *Nineteen Eighty-four,* citizens of Unthank are ruled by a domineering and intrusive bureaucracy. Lanark is a lonely young man unable to remember his past. Along with many of his fellow-citizens, he is plagued with "dragonhide," an insidious, scaly skin infection seen as symbolic of his emotional isolation. Cured of his affliction by doctors at a scientific institute below the surface of the earth, Lanark realizes to his disgust that the staff is as arrogant and manipulative as the ruling elite on the surface. Before escaping from this underworld, Lanark has a vision in which he sees the life story of a young man who mysteriously resembles him—Duncan Thaw, an aspiring artist who lives in twentieth-century Glasgow.

Thaw's story, which comprises nearly half the book, is virtually a novel within a novel. It echoes the story of Lanark while displaying a markedly different literary technique. As William Boyd explained in the *Times Literary Supplement,* "the narration of Thaw's life turns out to be a brilliant and moving evocation of a talented and imaginative child growing up in working-class Glasgow. The style is limpid and classically elegant, the detail solidly documentary and in marked contrast to the fantastical and surrealistic accoutrements of the first 100 pages." Like Gray, Thaw attends art school in Glasgow, and as with Lanark, Thaw's loneliness and isolation are expressed outwardly in a skin disease, eczema. With increasing desperation Thaw seeks fulfillment in love and art, and his disappointment culminates in a violent outburst in which he kills—or at least thinks he kills—a young woman who had abandoned him. Bewildered and hopeless, he commits suicide. Boyd considered Thaw's story "a minor classic of the literature of adolescence," and Gifford likened it to James Joyce's novel *A Portrait of the Artist as a Young Man.* The last part of Gray's book focuses once more on Lanark, depicting his futile struggle to improve the world around him.

Critics have generally lauded *Lanark,* although some expressed concern that it was hampered by its size and intricacy. Boyd, for instance, felt that the parallel narratives of Thaw and Lanark "do not happily cohere." *Washington Post Book World*'s Michael Dirda said that *Lanark* was "too baggy and bloated," but he stressed that "there are such good things in it that one hardly knows where it could be cut." Many critics echoed Boyd's overall assessment that "*Lanark* is a work of loving and vivid imagination, yielding copious riches." Moreover, Burgess featured *Lanark* in his book *Ninety-nine Novels: The Best in English Since 1939,* declaring, "It was time Scotland produced a shattering work of fiction in the modern idiom. This is it."

Although *Lanark* rapidly achieved critical recognition in Britain, Gray's second novel, *1982 Janine,* was the first to be widely known in the United States. The novel records the thoughts of Jock McLeish, a disappointed, middle-aged Scottish businessman, during a long night of heavy drinking. In his mind Jock plays and replays fantasies in which he sexually tortures helpless women, and he gives names and identities to his victims, including the Janine of the title. Burgess spoke for several reviewers when he wrote in the *Observer* that such material was offensive and unneeded. But admirers of the novel, such as Richard Eder of the *Los Angeles Times,* felt that Jock's sexual fantasies were a valid metaphor for the character's own sense of helplessness. Jock, who rose to a managerial post from a working-class background, now hates himself because he is financially dependent on the ruling classes he once hoped to change.

As Eder observed, Jock's powerlessness is in its turn a metaphor for the subjugation of Scotland. Jock expounds on the sorry state of his homeland in the course of his drunken railings. Scotland's economy, he charges, has been starved in order to strengthen the country's political master, England; what is more, if war with the Soviet Union breaks out, Jock expects the English to use Scotland as a nuclear battlefield. As the novel ends, Jock resolves to quit his job and change his life for the better. Eder commended Gray for conveying a portrait of helplessness and the search for self-realization "in a flamboyantly comic narrator whose verbal blue streak is given depth by a winning impulse to self-discovery, and some alarming insight."

Gray's short story collection, *Unlikely Stories, Mostly*, is "if anything more idiosyncratic" than *1982 Janine*, according to Jonathan Baumbach of the *New York Times Book Review*. Many reviewers praised the imaginativeness of the stories while acknowledging that the collection, which includes work dating back to Gray's teenage years, is uneven in quality. As Gary Marmorstein observed in the *Los Angeles Times Book Review*, some of the stories are "slight but fun," including "The Star," in which a boy catches a star and swallows it, and "The Spread of Ian Nicol," in which a man slowly splits in two like a microbe reproducing itself. By contrast, "Five Letters From an Eastern Empire" is one of several more complex tales that received special praise. Set in the capital of a powerful empire, the story focuses on a talented poet. Gradually readers learn the source of the poet's artistic inspiration: the emperor murdered the poet's parents by razing the city in which they lived, then ordered him to write about the destruction. "The tone of the story remains under perfect control as it darkens and deepens," Adam Mars-Jones noted in the *Times Literary Supplement*, "until an apparently reckless comedy has become a cruel parable about power and meaning."

Gray's third novel, *The Fall of Kelvin Walker*, was inspired by personal experience. Still struggling to establish his career several years after his graduation from art school, Gray was tapped as the subject of a documentary by a successful friend at the British Broadcasting Corporation (BBC). Gray, who had been living on welfare, suddenly found himself treated to airline flights and limousine rides at the BBC's expense. In *Kelvin Walker* the title character, a young Scotsman with a burning desire for power, has a similar chance to use the communications media to fulfill his wildest fantasies. Though Walker arrives in London with few assets but self-confidence and a fast-talking manner, his persistence and good luck soon win him a national following as an interviewer on a television show. But in his pride and ambition Walker forgets that he exercises such influence only at the whims of his corporate bosses, and when he displeases them his fall from grace is as abrupt as his rise.

Kelvin Walker, which Gray adapted from his 1968 teleplay of the same title, is shorter and less surrealistic than his previous novels. The *Observer*'s Hermione Lee, though she stressed that Gray "is always worth attending to," felt that this novel "doesn't allow him the big scope he thrives on." By contrast, Larry McCaffery of *New York Times Book Review* praised *Kelvin Walker* for its "economy of means and exquisite control of detail." Gray "is now fully in command of his virtuoso abilities as a stylist and storyteller," McCaffery said, asserting that Gray's first four books—"each of which impresses in very different ways—indicate that he is emerging as the most vibrant and original new voice in English fiction."

Gray told *CA:* "I write to extend an excitement by giving it to others. I get ideas by conversing with others or by reading them. I have been influenced by most of the usual books, frequently in translation; by some very fine films; and by several kinds of popular and commercial rubbish."

CA INTERVIEW

Alasdair Gray answered *CA*'s questions in writing from Glasgow, Scotland, in March, 1987.

CA: How early did you begin to think of yourself as "an artist in words and pictures," to consider the possibility of having a career that encompassed both interests? Was there ever a feeling of having to choose between?

GRAY: No. As soon as I could draw and tell stories, which was around the age of four or five, I spent a lot of time doing these or planning to do them. My parents were friendly to my childish efforts, as were most of my teachers, though they also told me I was unlikely to make a living by either of these jobs for a long long time. So there was obviously no need to choose between them. I was delighted to go to art school, because I was a maturer draftsman and painter than writer. My writings while at art school were attempts to prepare something I knew would take long to finish: though I didn't know how long. I was an art teacher for four years, then wrote and sold a TV play.

CA: You told Scott L. Malcomson of the Voice Literary Supplement *that you had "worked out the essential line of* Lanark*" by the time you were eighteen. Was it already in essence the two interwoven stories it ended up being?*

GRAY: Yes, but the Thaw part was more completely imagined than the Lanark part, which I intended to be a flash-*forward* inside the short life of suicidal Thaw. Ten years later the story of Lanark got so big that I made Thaw's life a flashback inside it, instead.

CA: What other kinds of changes did it go through over the years before it was finished and published?

GRAY: Too many for me to recapitulate without a lot of research into old manuscripts.

CA: The characters in Lanark's *Unthank setting suffer from certain diseases: dragonhide, mouths, twittering rigor, softs. Do the diseases have allegorical significance?*

GRAY: Probably, but I came to that conclusion after, not before, I imagined and described them. And it would limit the reader's enjoyment and understanding of my stories to fix on one "allegorical significance" and say "This is it." (Example: I wrote "Five Letters From an Eastern Empire" when writer-in-residence at Glasgow University. When I finished, it occurred to me that the Eastern empire was an allegory of modern Britain viewed from Glasgow University by a writer-in-residence. A year ago I met someone just returned from Tokyo, who said he had heard a Chinese and a Japanese academic having an argument about my Eastern empire story. The Chinese was sure the empire was meant to be China, the Japanese that it was Japan. My only knowledge of these lands is from a few color prints, Arthur Waley's translations of the novel *Monkey* [by Wu Ch'eng-en] and some translated poems.)

CA: The Fall of Kelvin Walker, *which later became your third novel, was the first produced play, done on television by the British Broadcasting Corporation (BBC) in 1968 and staged in 1972. How did* Kelvin Walker *catch the eye of the BBC and make you an official playwright?*

GRAY: I sent it to the BBC in London by way of a director I know. He gave it to a producer who liked it. This made me a free-lance playwright, not an official one.

CA: You have a long list of credits for radio, television, and stage plays, going back at least to 1968. Were they your primary support before the publication of the books began in 1981?

GRAY: They were half my primary support. The other half was portrait and mural commissions, or the sale of a landscape. For half a year in 1978 I was artist-recorder for the Glasgow local history museum, painting cityscapes and portraits for a civic collection.

CA: In both Lanark *and* 1982 Janine *you give copious notes about literary influences and references, some of them very funny. What are some of the films and "popular and commercial rubbish" you've also cited as influences?*

GRAY: Walt Disney cartoons, Tarzan films, Bob Hope and Bing Crosby "Road" films, British comics (all printed in Dundee, between 1940 and 1957, with more words than illustrations), gruesome gaudy American comics of the fifties (when they first came to Britain), lots of science fiction, legend, and tales of magic (before these became commonplace), cheap pornography of the sort that videos have ousted.

CA: The illustrations in your books and on their covers, along with typographical arrangements in the texts for literary effects, are visible evidence of the mutually enriching relationship of your art and writing. Do they help each other along or intermingle on a subtler level?

GRAY: The illustrations and cover designs of my books are not essential to them, being thought of after the text is complete. I add them because they make the book more enjoyable. The queer typography, in the three stories which use it, was devised in the act of writing, not added after, like sugar to porridge.

CA: Tell me about the typographical eccentricities in your work with regard to their journey from first draft—or first vision, maybe—to final print. Is there a direct collaboration between you and the typesetter to get them to come out right?

GRAY: The typescript given to the publisher incorporated all that I wanted the typographer to set—my typist typed single or no spacing for small or very small type, double or treble spacing for large, and I drew columns, wedges, et cetera for him (or her sometimes) to type inside. Four or five proofreadings were required to get *almost* exactly what I wanted. I was never given the chance to overlook the typographer while he worked, alas.

CA: Lanark *really does seem to be in part a celebration of Glasgow, as almost all the reviewers noted. William Boyd, in the* Times Literary Supplement, *wrote, "Not the least of Alasdair Gray's achievements in* Lanark *will be to put the city decisively on the literary map." Has Glasgow figured largely in your painting as well?*

GRAY: Yes, but my paintings, like my books, show people and things which also exist in other places. I don't think I celebrate my city. I use the bits of it I know. In *1982 Janine* I use the mining town of Stonehouse, in Lanarkshire, and the city of Edinburgh, rather more than I use Glasgow.

CA: Is being in the city a necessary stimulus to your work?

GRAY: I don't know, because I have never worked outside cities. But I think I could work wherever I had an enjoyable job, and the means of doing it, and a climate that didn't damage my health.

CA: Do you see much of other writers and artists?

GRAY: Yes. A lot of good ones live within a ten-minute walk of my home, and we've been friends for fifteen years or more.

CA: You're known for your views on the coalminers' situation and nuclear disarmament, among other issues, and there's a very strong political voice in Lanark *and* 1982 Janine. *Is social concern one of the compelling reasons you write?*

GRAY: Yes, which makes me ordinary. All but the cheaply escapist writers care for their own people if they live among them. Social concern is not separate from other concerns. Even hatred and exasperation are forms of it.

CA: How have we been fortunate enough to get most of your books here in U.S. editions? Was Lanark *responsible for that?*

GRAY: Lanark *was the first novel I had published in the U.S.A., by Harper & Row in 1981. It was speedily remaindered, because Harper & Row classified it as science fiction, only sent it to sci-fi magazines for review, and the sci-fi reviewers were not amused. My first good American reviews were for* Unlikely Stories *and* 1982 Janine, *which led George Braziller to reprint* Lanark *in 1985. I suppose my books have been published in the States because they sold well in Britain, and were praised by authors of* A Clockwork Orange *[Anthony Burgess] and* The History Man *[Malcolm Bradbury].*

CA: How do you feel about the critical treatment of Scottish literature? Should there be a better balance between its consideration as Scottish, as representative of the country's history and traditions and current concerns, and its place in the broader context of literature?

GRAY: Critics of literature will understand the prose and poetry of modern Scotland better if they have read enough Barber / Dunbar / Lindsay / folk ballads / Burns / Smollet / Scott / Galt / Hogg / Carlyle / Ruskin / Brown / McDiarmid to see that our literary tradition is as unlike the English as is the Irish and American. But few critics understand their own traditions, so we must not expect them to grasp foreign ones.

CA: Are there Scottish review publications that you consider especially good—academic journals, newspapers, literary magazines?

GRAY: There are three small literary magazines, published in Edinburgh, which I enjoy (*Edinburgh Review, Cenerastus, Chapman*) because they are trying to recreate a Scottish culture which is not merely provincial (i.e. chip-on-shoulder vehemence or smug ignorance) and they sometimes manage this.

CA: Are you generally pleased with the critical attention given your books?

GRAY: Yes.

CA: Somewhere I've read that you're working on some poems now. Do you find that form particularly challenging as compared to the plays and novels, or requiring a different frame of mind to approach?

GRAY: I have a sequence of poems, written between 1951 and 1982, called *Old Negatives*. The work I must do to finish it is purely illustrative. I mostly wrote these poems in a state of loss which struck me as almost (but not quite) unbearable. Writing the poems made the loss easily bearable, for a while. I have written no poems after 1982, because I've lost nobody since then.

BIOGRAPHICAL/CRITICAL SOURCES:

BOOKS

Burgess, Anthony, *Ninety-nine Novels: The Best in English Since 1939—A Personal Choice*, Allison & Busby, 1984.
Contemporary Literary Criticism, Volume 41, Gale, 1987.

PERIODICALS

Christian Science Monitor, October 5, 1984.
Los Angeles Times, November 21, 1984.
Los Angeles Times Book Review, December 9, 1984.
New Republic, November 12, 1984.
New York Times Book Review, October 28, 1984, May 5, 1985, December 21, 1986.
Observer (London), April 15, 1984, March 31, 1985.
Spectator, February 28, 1981.
Stage, November 30, 1972.
Studies in Scottish Literature, Volume 18, 1983.
Times (London), April 1, 1986.
Times Literary Supplement, February 27, 1981, March 18, 1983, April 13, 1984, March 29, 1985, May 10, 1985.
Voice Literary Supplement, December, 1984.
Washington Post Book World, December 16, 1984, August 31, 1986.

—*Sketch by Thomas Kozikowski*

—*Interview by Jean W. Ross*

*   *   *

GREANIAS, George C. 1948-

PERSONAL: Surname is pronounced "*Grenn*-ee-us"; born April 20, 1948, in Decatur, Ill.; son of Gus George and Katherine (Pappas) Greanias. *Education:* Rice University, B.A. (magna cum laude), 1970; Harvard University, J.D., 1973. *Politics:* Independent. *Religion:* Eastern Orthodox.

ADDRESSES: Home—1744 Harold, Houston, Tex. 77098. *Office*—City of Houston, P.O. Box 1562, Houston, Tex. 77251.

CAREER: Liddell, Sapp & Zivley, Houston, Tex., associate attorney, 1973-74; Singer, Hutner, Levine & Seeman, New York, N.Y., associate attorney, 1975-77; Rice University, Houston, assistant professor, 1977-83, associate professor of

administrative science, 1983-86; Wood, Lucksinger & Epstein, Houston, attorney, 1986—. City of Houston, council member, 1981-87, controller, 1987—; member of steering committee of Houston/Harris County Sports and Health Association; advisory director of Reading, Education, and Development Council; member of board of directors of Aid to Victims of Domestic Abuse, Older American Services, Westbury Hospital, Young Audiences of Houston, and Midtown Art Center; member of advisory board of Girls Club of Houston, Houston Action for Soviet Jewry, Houston Symphony Orchestra, and Alley Theatre; trustee of Annunciation Church School, Lighthouse for the Blind, and Houston Museum of Fine Arts.

MEMBER: American Bar Association, Texas Bar Association, Houston World Trade Association (director), Art League of Houston (director), Harvard Law School Association.

WRITINGS:

"Hello Hamlet!" (two-act play), first produced in Houston, Tex., at Weiss College, Rice University, October, 1967.
"Wilson" (two-act play), first produced in Miami, Fla., at Players Repertory Theater, August, 1973.
(With Duane Windsor) *The Changing Boardroom: Making Policy and Profits in an Age of Corporate Citizenship*, Gulf Publishing, 1982.
(With Windsor) *The Foreign Corrupt Practices Act: Anatomy of a Statute*, Lexington Books, 1982.
(Contributor) Lee E. Preston, editor, *Research in Corporate Social Performance and Policy: A Research Annual*, Volume IV, Jai Press, 1982.
(Contributor) James M. Higgins, editor, *Organizational Policy and Strategic Management: Text and Cases*, 2nd edition, Dryden, 1983.
(Contributor) K. Mark Weaver and other editors, *Cases in Business Strategy and Policy*, South-Western Publishing, 1983.

Contributor of articles and reviews to newspapers and communication and law journals.

SIDELIGHTS: George C. Greanias told *CA:* "I wrote *The Changing Boardroom* with Duane Windsor, a colleague at the Jesse H. Jones Graduate School of Administration. Both of us had become aware through our teaching and research of substantial changes that were taking place in expectations placed upon corporations, their management, and their boards of directors.

"We called the increasingly complex world in which corporations must now operate the 'New Corporate Environment.' This phrase was meant to reflect both the much more intricate corporate world of the 1980s as well as the need for more complex, yet increasingly flexible responses required to survive and prosper in that environment.

"To survive in the 1980s, corporate managers need to know that management styles have changed. Managers today are less autocratic and more like cheerleaders. They must cope with increased democracy inside and outside the firm, make decisions in a complex socio-political environment where number-crunching calculations will not necessarily lead to the best answers, and be willing to change patterns of thought acceptable not that long ago. The world of management may seem chaotic, but it is up to today's managers to discern a real corporate rationale."

GREEN, John F. 1943-

PERSONAL: Born June 5, 1943, in Saskatoon, Saskatchewan, Canada; son of Fred (a dentist) and Lillian (a music teacher; maiden name, Kirton) Green; married Maureen Anne Horne, February 1, 1969; children: Scott, Stuart, Geoffrey, Kristen. *Education:* Attended Ryerson Institute, 1964-67; Red River Community College, teacher's certificate, 1976.

ADDRESSES: Home—966 Adelaide St. E., No. 70, Oshawa, Ontario, Canada L1K 1L2. *Office*—Durham College, 2000 Simcoe St. N., Oshawa, Ontario, Canada L1H 7L7.

CAREER: Durham College, Oshawa, Ontario, teaching master of arts and science, 1976—. Writer and producer for western Canadian broadcasting companies.

WRITINGS:

There Are Trolls (juvenile), Peguis Publishing, 1974.
"The Bargain" (one-act play), first produced by Winnipeg Chancel Players, 1974.
"The House on Geoffrey Street" (one-act play), first produced by Durham Shoestring Performers, 1981.
"The Gadfly" (one-act play), first produced by Whitby Theatre Co., 1983.
There's a Dragon in My Closet (juvenile), Scholastic Book Service, 1986.
The House That Max Built (juvenile), Prairie Publishing, 1988.
There's a One-Eyed Giant in Alice's Room, Scholastic Inc., 1989.

SIDELIGHTS: John F. Green told *CA:* "I write for children because they are the most demanding of all readers. They are completely honest. An adult will read a bad book thinking that something good will come of it if he persists with it long enough. But a writer of juvenile fiction must have a child's attention by the second page: that's the challenge.

"The first job of the children's writer is to entertain. If something else happens in the process, so be it. But to begin with any hidden agenda is wrong. Children must be allowed to fantasize; the real world comes along soon enough.

"Many of my story ideas come from people and things in my immediate environment. When I see or hear something that gets my interest, I spend a lot of time thinking about the idea. When I'm ready to write, I tend to dump the whole thing out at once in one or two sittings."

*   *   *

GREENE, Sara
See STRONG, June

*   *   *

GREENOUGH, Sarah 1951-

PERSONAL: Born May 25, 1951, in Boston, Mass.; daughter of Malcolm (an author) and Sarah (Browne) Greenough; married Nicolai Cikovsky, Jr. (an art historian and curator) June 17, 1978; children: Sophia Greenough. *Education:* University of Pennsylvania, B.A., 1972; University of New Mexico, M.A., 1976, Ph.D., 1984.

ADDRESSES: Office—Department of Graphic Arts, National Gallery of Art, Washington, D.C. 20565.

CAREER: Metropolitan Museum of Art, New York, N.Y., researcher in department of prints and photographs, summers,

1976-77; University of New Mexico, Albuquerque, instructor in history of photography, 1977; National Gallery of Art, Washington, guest curator, 1979-84, guest scholar at Alfred Stieglitz Collection of Photographs, 1984-86, research curator, 1987—. Instructor at University of New Mexico, 1980.

AWARDS, HONORS: Fellowship from National Gallery of Art, 1978-79; award from Samuel H. Kress Foundation, 1983; American Book Award, 1983, for *Alfred Stieglitz.*

WRITINGS:

(With Juan Hamilton) *Alfred Stieglitz: Photographs and Writings,* National Gallery of Art/Callaway Editions, 1983.
(Contributor) *Essays in Honor of Beaumont Newhall,* University of New Mexico Press, 1986.
(With Jack Cowart and Juan Hamilton) *Georgia O'Keefe: Art and Letters,* National Gallery of Art/Little, Brown, 1987.
(With David Travis, Joel Snyder, and Colin Westerbeck) *On the Art of Fixing a Shadow: 150 Years of Photography,* National Gallery of Art, 1989.

Contributor to magazines and newspapers.

*   *   *

GRIFFITH-JONES, Stephany 1947-

PERSONAL: Born June 5, 1947, in Prague, Czechoslovakia; daughter of Francisco (a factory owner) and Clara (a housewife; maiden name, Kafka) Novy; married Robert Griffith-Jones (an educator), April 23, 1977; children: Edward, David. *Education:* University of Chile, B.A. (with distinction), 1969; Cambridge University, Ph.D., 1981.

ADDRESSES: Home—12 Lenham Rd. E., Brighton, Sussex, England. *Office*—Institute of Development Studies, University of Sussex, Brighton, Sussex BN1 9RE, England.

CAREER: Corporacion de Fomento, Santiago de Chile, research officer in Division of Industrial Planning, 1969-70; Central Bank of Chile, Santiago de Chile, member of section of credit and savings policy, 1970-72, head of department of credit for public enterprise, 1972; University of Sussex, Brighton, England, research officer at Institute for Development Studies, 1978-81, research fellow, 1982—. Professor of economic analysis at Inter-American Center of Statistics, 1971; has lectured at Cambridge University, London School of Economics and Political Science, London, University of Warwick, and University of Birmingham; interviewed on British and Scottish radio programs. Member of board of directors of Banco O'Higgins, 1971-72; adviser to Barclays Bank International, 1977; consultant to World Bank, UNICEF, UNCTAD, UNIDO, and European Economic Community.

MEMBER: Society for International Development (member of executive committee).

AWARDS, HONORS: Alide Prize from Association of Latin American Financial Institutions, 1983, for essay "International Finance and Latin America."

WRITINGS:

The Role of Finance in the Transition to Socialism, Allanheld, Osmun, 1981.
(Contributor) Diane Tussie, editor, *Latin America in the World Economy,* Gower, 1983.
(Contributor) R. Cruise O'Brien, editor, *Information, Economics, and Power,* Hodder & Stoughton, 1984.
International Finance and Latin America, Croom Helm, 1984.

(Editor with Charles Harvey) *World Prices and Development*, Gower, 1985.

(With Osvaldo Sunkel) *The Crisis of International Debt and National Development*, Oxford University Press, 1986.

(Contributor) Altaf Gauhar, editor, *Third World Affairs 1985*, Third World Foundation, 1986.

Managing World Debt, St. Martin's, 1987.

Chile to 1991, Economist Intelligence Unit, 1987.

Contributor to magazines, including *Banker* and *South*, and newspapers, including *Guardian*.

WORK IN PROGRESS: Research on "cross-conditionality" and its impact on developing countries, with a book expected to result.

SIDELIGHTS: Stephany Griffith-Jones told *CA:* "My area of interest in writing and research is the impact of international finance and external debt, and the impact of adjustment policies on the development of poorer countries, with a view to defining better alternatives to those currently in operation. I also write stories for children; some were published in the main Chilean newspaper in the sixties. I have traveled to Latin America, the United States, and Europe to exchange ideas and to learn from policymakers and other academics.

"The debt crises in Latin America and Africa have caused profound damage to these continents. Though the international banking system's stability has been maintained, international debt management has caused the interruption of development in Latin America. In my writing I have analyzed this and explored alternative ways of dealing with the international debt problem which would still safeguard the stability of the international banks, but would also allow for growth in the highly indebted countries. I emphasize, particularly in *Managing World Debt*, bargaining tactics which, if pursued by debtor governments, would help them obtain better outcomes. In Latin America there is a movement towards more understanding and collaboration between countries. I see my work as part of that process."

BIOGRAPHICAL/CRITICAL SOURCES:

PERIODICALS

Times Literary Supplement, October 9, 1984.

*   *   *

GRIGOROVICH, Yuri Nikolayevich   1927-

PERSONAL: Born January 2, 1927, in Leningrad, U.S.S.R.; son of M. G. and K. A. (Rosai) Grigorovich; married Natalia Igorevna Bessmertnova (a ballerina), August 30, 1968. *Education:* Leningrad Choreographic School, graduated, 1946; Lunarcharski Institute of Theatrical Art (now National Institute for the Performing Arts), graduated, 1959.

ADDRESSES: Office—State Academic Bolshoi Theater, 1 Ploshchad Sverdlova, Moscow, U.S.S.R.

CAREER: Kirov Opera and Ballet Theater, U.S.S.R., soloist, 1946-64, ballet master, 1962-64; State Academic Bolshoi Theater, Moscow, U.S.S.R., artistic director and chief choreographer, 1964—. Professor at Leningrad Rimsky-Korsakov Conservatory; president of dance committee of UNESCO's International Theatre Institute, 1973—; chairman and member of juries of international ballet competitions in the U.S.S.R., Finland, Bulgaria, the United States, France, and Japan.

AWARDS, HONORS: Named People's Artist of the U.S.S.R., 1973; Lenin Prize from the Committee on Lenin and U.S.S.R. State Prizes, 1970; State Prize, 1977; Order of Lenin, 1976, and Hero of Socialist Labour with the Order of Lenin, 1987, both from the Presidium of the Supreme Soviet of the U.S.S.R.

WRITINGS:

(With Boris Alexandrovich Pokrovsky) *The Bolshoi*, Morrow, 1979.

SIDELIGHTS: For nearly twenty years Yuri Nikolayevich Grigorovich was the leading grotesque dancer of the Kirov Ballet, where he performed such parts as Polovchanin in "Prince Igor" and Nurali in "The Fountain of Bakhchisarai." He also created dances for operas and staged ballets for amateur companies. The dancer's first work as a choreographer was "Baby Stork," which was first produced at a children's ballet studio.

Since 1964 Grigorovich has been the artistic director and chief choreographer of the Bolshoi Ballet. Among the works he has staged are "Sleeping Beauty," "Swan Lake," "The Nutcracker," "Spartacus," "Ivan the Terrible," "Romeo and Juliet," "The Golden Age," and "Raymonda," and his ballets have been performed by leading Soviet dancers. His works have also been performed in Stockholm, Prague, Sofia, Vienna, Rome, Paris, Ankara, Copenhagen, and Helsinki. Grigorovich's impact on the development of Soviet ballet art was extended when he was appointed to train a new ballet generation at the Leningrad Rimsky-Korsakov Conservatory.

*   *   *

GROSSBART, Ted A.   1946-

PERSONAL: Born June 3, 1946, in Detroit, Mich.; son of Samuel A. (a real estate developer) and Mary (a teacher; maiden name, Spilkin) Grossbart; married Rosely Traube (a clinical psychologist), February 9, 1974; children: Zachary, Matthew. *Education:* University of Michigan, A.B. (with high honors), 1967; Boston University, M.A., 1971, Ph.D., 1971.

ADDRESSES: Home—Goodwin's Landing, Marblehead, Mass. 01945. *Office*—466 Commonwealth Ave., No. 201, Boston, Mass. 02215. *Agent*—Gloria Stern Agency, 1230 Park Ave., New York, N.Y. 10028.

CAREER: Private practice of clinical psychology in Boston, Mass., 1970—. Instructor at Harvard Medical School and senior associate at Beth Israel Hospital, both 1975—; member of board of advisers of American Board of Medical Psychotherapists.

MEMBER: American Psychological Association, Society for Clinical and Experimental Hypnosis.

WRITINGS:

(With Carl Sherman) *Skin Deep: A Mind/Body Program for Healthy Skin*, Morrow, 1986.

WORK IN PROGRESS: A mind/body approach to medical problems, focused on sexually transmitted diseases.

SIDELIGHTS: Ted A. Grossbart told *CA:* "My book was designed to give to a wider group of people who suffer from skin problems access to the techniques that are so helpful in my office practice. Hypnosis, relaxation, and psychotherapy, to the surprise of many, can cure or substantially improve conditions like eczema, hives, itching and scratching, psoriasis, acne, herpes, and warts."

BIOGRAPHICAL/CRITICAL SOURCES:

PERIODICALS

American Health, January/February, 1986.
Psychology Today, February, 1982.
Self, December, 1985.

*   *   *

GUNLICKS, Arthur B.   1936-

PERSONAL: Born July 7, 1936, in North Platte, Neb.; son of Anfin B. and Verna M. (Waltemath) Gunlicks; married Regine J. Sattler (a teacher), July 19, 1962; children: Michael, Lars. *Education:* University of Denver, B.A., 1958; attended University of Freiburg, 1958-59, and University of Goettingen, 1964-66; Georgetown University, Ph.D., 1967. *Religion:* Lutheran.

ADDRESSES: Home—602 Ridge Top Rd., Richmond, Va. 23229. *Office*—Department of Political Science, University of Richmond, Richmond, Va. 23173.

CAREER: East Tennessee State University, Johnson City, Tenn., assistant professor of political science, 1966-68; University of Richmond, Richmond, Va., assistant professor, 1968-71, associate professor, 1971-81, professor of political science, 1981—. Visiting professor in West Germany, 1980, 1982-83. President of College Hills Neighborhood Association, 1981-82, 1985-86, and Ridgetop Recreation Association, 1985-86. *Military service:* U.S. Army, 1959-61; became first lieutenant.

MEMBER: American Political Science Association, American Association of University Professors, Council of European Studies, German Studies Association, Conference Group on German Politics, Fulbright Alumni Association, Deutsche Vereinigung fuer Parlamentsfragen, Southern Political Science Association, Virginia Social Science Association.

AWARDS, HONORS: Scholarship from the German Academic Exchange Service, 1958-59; Fulbright scholar, 1964-66 and 1975-76; scholar of Virginia Social Science Association, 1987.

WRITINGS:

(Editor and contributor) *Local Government Reform and Reorganization: An International Perspective,* Kennikat, 1981.
Local Government in the German Federal System, Duke University Press, 1986.
(Editor with John D. Treadway) *The Soviet Union Under Gorbachev: Assessing the First Year,* Praeger, 1987.

Editor of *Publius: Journal of Federalism.*

WORK IN PROGRESS: A special *Publius* issue on German federalization for winter of 1989.

*   *   *

GURKO, Miriam   1910(?)-1988

OBITUARY NOTICE—See index for *CA* sketch: Born c. 1910 in Union City, N.J.; died of pneumonia, July 3, 1988, in Peekskill, N.Y. Editor and author. A chronicler for young adults of the accomplishments of individuals who have shaped history, Gurko wrote *The Lives and Times of Peter Cooper, Restless Spirit: The Life of Edna St. Vincent Millay, Clarence Darrow, Indian America: The Black Hawk War, The Ladies of Seneca Falls: The Birth of the Woman's Rights Movement,* and *Theodor Herzl: The Road to Israel.* As a young woman Gurko also pursued editorial work, publicity, and research in New York City.

OBITUARIES AND OTHER SOURCES:

BOOKS

The Writers Directory: 1988-1990, St. James Press, 1988.

PERIODICALS

New York Times, July 21, 1988.
School Library Journal, September, 1988.

H

HABERMAN, David A. 1928-

PERSONAL: Born May 29, 1928, in Milwaukee, Wis.; son of Frederick A. and Cora (a homemaker; maiden name, Miller) Haberman; married Joan E. Beltz (an elementary school teacher), November 25, 1954; children: Robert J., Michael F., Margaret R., Mary Sarah, Helen A. *Education:* Marquette University, A.B. (cum laude), 1950; University of Wisconsin—Madison, M.A., 1955; Creighton University, J.D., 1964. *Religion:* Roman Catholic.

ADDRESSES: Home—3512 North 58th St., Omaha, Neb. 68104. *Office*—Department of Journalism and Mass Communications, Creighton University, California at 24th St., Omaha, Neb. 68178-0119.

CAREER: Creighton University, Omaha, Neb., instructor, 1955-57, assistant professor, 1957-64, associate professor, 1964-85, professor of journalism and mass communications, 1985—, Jacobson Professor of Communications, 1982-83. Attorney in private practice. Past president of board of directors of St. Vincent de Paul Store, Inc., Omaha; trustee of OPC Journalism Education, Inc. *Military service:* U.S. Army, 1950-52.

MEMBER: Association for Education in Journalism and Mass Communications, Nebraska State Bar Association, Omaha Press Club (member of board of directors), Society of Professional Journalists/Sigma Delta Chi.

WRITINGS:

Public Relations: The Necessary Art, Iowa State University Press, 1988.

* * *

HACKWELL, W. John 1942-

PERSONAL: Born July 19, 1942, in Melbourne, Australia; son of Richard Neville (a clerk) and Hilda Ruth (Smith) Hackwell; married Yvonne Joan Popple (a researcher); children: Allison, Natalie, Bronwyn, Andrew. *Education:* Received B.A., Avondale College; received M.A., doctoral study, Andrews University. *Religion:* Christian.

ADDRESSES: Home—Coila Creek Rd., Coila, New South Wales 2537, Australia.

CAREER: View Street Gallery, Dunedin, New Zealand, administrative director, 1980-84; director at South Pacific Archaeological Institute, 1984—. Worked as a tour guide in the Middle East, 1975-86; administrative director of Institute of Archaeology at Andrews University, Berrien Springs, Mich., 1984-85.

MEMBER: American Schools of Oriental Research.

WRITINGS:

Digging to the Past, Scribner, 1986.
Signs, Letters, Words, Scribner, 1987.
Diving to the Past, Scribner, 1988.

WORK IN PROGRESS: Exploring Antarctica; Great Architects and Their Finds.

SIDELIGHTS: W. John Hackwell told *CA* that he is motivated by a desire to contribute toward human knowledge and learning. As well as working as a tour guide in the Middle East for more than ten years, he lived among headhunters in Papua New Guinea from 1977 to 1979 and led the first Papua New Guinea World Tour. Hackwell is interested in ancient languages, including Greek, Hebrew, and hieroglyphics.

* * *

HADLEY CHASE, James
See RAYMOND, Rene (Brabazon)

* * *

HAGER, Thomas Arthur 1953-

PERSONAL: Born April 18, 1953, in Portland, Ore.; son of Donald Preston (a dentist) and Betty Jean (a homemaker; maiden name, Buehner) Hager; married Lauren Jeanne Kessler (a writer and university professor), July 7, 1984; children: Jackson Kessler, Zane Kessler. *Education:* Portland State University, B.S., 1975; Oregon Health Sciences University, M.S. (microbiology and immunity; with honors), 1978; University of Oregon, M.S. (journalism; with honors), 1982.

ADDRESSES: Home—3015 Friendly St., Eugene, Ore. 97405. *Office*—*Old Oregon,* 101 Chapman Hall, University of Oregon, Eugene, Ore. 97403. *Agent*—Dominick Abel Literary Agency, Inc., 498 West End Ave., New York, N.Y. 10024.

CAREER: National Cancer Institute, Bethesda, Md., science writer, 1981; Aster Publishing, Eugene, Ore., editor, 1982-83; University of Oregon, Eugene, adjunct professor, 1983—, director of university relations, 1985—, assistant professor of journalism, 1987—.

MEMBER: Council for the Advancement of Secondary Education, University of Oregon Alumni Association (ex-officio member of board of directors).

AWARDS, HONORS: First place award in magazine publishing from Council for the Advancement of Secondary Education, 1986, for *Old Oregon*.

WRITINGS:

(With wife, Lauren J. Kessler) *Staying Young: The Whole Truth About Aging and What You Can Do to Slow Its Progress*, Facts on File, 1987.

Contributor to magazines, including *Reader's Digest, Self, American Health, New Body, Microcomputing,* and *New Physician.* Editor of *LC,* 1982-83, and *Old Oregon,* 1985—.

WORK IN PROGRESS: Continuing research on the human aging process, with a book expected to result.

SIDELIGHTS: Thomas Arthur Hager told *CA:* "Scientific and medical research are commonly misunderstood by the public and misused by journalists and quacks eager to make a buck. My goal is to use my skills accurately and clearly to demystify these areas in books and articles geared for general consumption.

"In *Staying Young* my wife, Lauren, and I explode a number of popular myths about aging and convey a wealth of solid, simple advice about how to stay healthier longer. By approaching the topic as journalists looking for facts rather than doctors with a pet therapy or health gurus with a line of vitamins to sell, we discovered that there is an enormous amount we can all do to improve our lives. For example: If there's one key to aging well, its simple aerobic exercise three or four times each week for one half of one hour. The benefits cut across all body systems from heart, lungs, and muscle to the immune system and sexual response. Yet people would rather hear about a magic pill or potion—something that doesn't require any work or change in a more sedentary lifestyle. That longing for a simple answer to aging will, unfortunately, continue to fund a number of unscrupulous 'aging experts' as our population's average age moves up."

BIOGRAPHICAL/CRITICAL SOURCES:

PERIODICALS

Chicago Tribune, October 14, 1987.

*   *   *

HAGUE, Richard   1947-

PERSONAL: Born August 7, 1947, in Steubenville, Ohio; son of James R. (an engineer) and Ruth (a homemaker; maiden name, Heights) Hague; married Pamela Korte (a potter), June 24, 1980; children: Patrick, Brendan. *Education:* Xavier University, B.S., 1969, M.A., 1971. *Religion:* Roman Catholic.

ADDRESSES: Home—6203 Erie Ave., Cincinnati, Ohio 45227. *Office*—Purcell Marian High School, 1935 Hackberry, Cincinnati, Ohio 45206.

CAREER: Purcell Marian High School, Cincinnati, Ohio, teacher and chairman of English department, 1969—. Adjunct lecturer at Xavier University; co-coordinator of Southern Appalachian Writers Cooperative, 1982; literary artist at Kentucky Institute for Arts in Education, University of Louisville, 1984; member of literary panel of Ohio Arts Council, 1984-87; member of poetry staff of Appalachian Writers Workshop, 1988. Gives writing workshops and lectures on poetry. Site manager of Madisonville Community Garden, 1987.

AWARDS, HONORS: President's Award in Poetry from *Ohio Journal,* 1979, for "An Unsent Letter of Darwin's," and 1981, for "Moose Ridge Apple Wine"; Post-Corbett Award in Literary Arts from *Cincinnati Post,* 1982, for a continuing contribution to the arts in Cincinnati; grant from Greater Cincinnati Foundation, 1984; first prize in professional prose category from Ohio Educational and Library Media Association, 1985, for story "Whistling Woman and the Man of Light"; named co-poet of the year in Ohio by Ohio Poetry Day Association, 1985, for *Ripening;* runner-up for Poetry Center Prize from Cleveland State University, 1987, for *Possible Debris.*

WRITINGS:

Crossings (poems), Cincinnati Area Poetry Press, 1979.
A Week of Nights Down River (poems), privately printed, 1981.
Ripening (poems), Ohio State University Press, 1984.
Possible Debris (poems), Poetry Center, Cleveland State University, 1988.

Work represented in anthologies, including *I Have a Place,* edited by Jim Wayne Miller, Alice Lloyd College, 1981; *Footsteps on the Mountain,* Appalachian Consortium Press, 1987; *Oyo: An Ohio River Anthology,* Volume II, Oyo Press, 1988. Contributor to periodicals, including *Appalachian Heritage, Country Journal, Gambit, Laurel Review, Open Places,* and *Wooster Review.* Poetry editor of *Pine Mountain Sand and Gravel.*

WORK IN PROGRESS: Lives of the Poem, poems; *Public Hearings: Satires, Diatribes, Monologues, and Rants,* poems; *Shitepokes, Night Fish, and the Jumping Buckeyes,* essays; *Learning How,* stories, completion expected in 1989; *Ruined Choirs,* stories, completion expected in 1990.

SIDELIGHTS: Richard Hague told *CA* that one of the most important events of his career "was the growing realization that I came from a specific and interesting place, that I was an Ohioan, a border Appalachian, and that these places had value and significance. Becoming aware of my own roots, I lived alone on Greenbrier Ridge in southeastern Ohio for several summers, and it was these stays, and their attendant lessons, that shaped me early in my career, and continue to do so now. Recently, I have centered even more: now I am a resident of Madisonville, an old neighborhood in Cincinnati, and I am a husband and father and gardener there. These, too, shape my work more and more. I try to celebrate the local; I try to find in the commonly overlooked or misapprehended detail some significance that may allow me to speak to people elsewhere, to reach them where they live.

"My major areas of vocational interest are the teaching of writing, both prose and poetry; studying and teaching the literature of place, so-called regional literature, discovering in it the universal."

AVOCATIONAL INTERESTS: "Science, in particular local geology and archaeology, and the powers and functions of the brain and memory; gardening, which I practice compulsively and yet with great enjoyment."

BIOGRAPHICAL/CRITICAL SOURCES:

PERIODICALS

Appalachian Journal, summer, 1985.
Ohioana Quarterly, spring, 1986.
Western Ohio Journal, spring, 1988.

*   *   *

HAIGH, Christopher 1944-

PERSONAL: Born August 28, 1944, in Birkenhead, England; son of Ernest (an engineer) and Ethel (Griffiths) Haigh; married Clare Irene Martin, August 26, 1967 (divorced, 1986); children: Lucy Victoria Clare, Emily Louisa. *Education:* Cambridge University, B.A., 1966; Victoria University of Manchester, Ph.D., 1969. *Politics:* Labour. *Religion:* None.

ADDRESSES: Office—Christ Church, Oxford University, Oxford OX1 1DP, England.

CAREER: Victoria University of Manchester, Manchester, England, lecturer in history, 1969-79; Oxford University, Christ Church, Oxford, England, lecturer in modern history, 1979—.

MEMBER: Royal Historical Society (fellow).

WRITINGS:

The Last Days of the Lancashire Monasteries, Manchester University Press, 1969.
Reformation and Resistance in Tudor Lancashire, Cambridge University Press, 1975.
(Editor) *The Cambridge Historical Encyclopedia of Great Britain and Ireland,* Cambridge University Press, 1984.
(Editor) *The Reign of Elizabeth I,* Macmillan, 1985.
(Editor) *The English Reformation Revised,* Cambridge University Press, 1987.
Elizabeth I: A Profile in Power, Longman, 1988.

WORK IN PROGRESS: A general survey of the English Reformation, publication by Oxford University Press expected in 1989; *The Church of England and Its People, 1559-1642,* publication by Longman expected in 1990.

*   *   *

HAIMSON, Leopold Henri 1917-

PERSONAL: Born April 28, 1917, in Brussels, Belgium; immigrated to the United States, naturalized citizen; married wife in 1951; children: two. *Education:* Harvard University, B.A., 1945, A.M., 1947, Ph.D., 1952.

ADDRESSES: Office—Department of History, Columbia University, Broadway and West 116th St., New York, N.Y. 10027.

CAREER: Columbia University, New York, N.Y., research associate, beginning in 1952; research associate at the American Museum of Natural History; Harvard University, Cambridge, Mass., lecturer in history, 1955-56; University of Chicago, Chicago, Ill., 1956-66, began as assistant professor, became associate professor of history; Columbia University, professor of history, 1966—. Visiting research scholar at Princeton University, 1952-53; postdoctoral research fellow at Harvard University, 1953-56.

WRITINGS:

The Russian Marxists and the Origins of Bolshevism, Harvard University Press, 1955.

(Editor) *The Mensheviks: From the Revolution of 1917 to the Second World War,* University of Chicago Press, 1974.
(Editor) *The Politics of Rural Russia, 1905-1914,* Indiana University Press, 1979.
(With Petr Garvi) *Zapiski Sotsial Demokrate, 1906-1921,* Oriental Research Partners, 1982.
(With Ziva Galili y Garcia and Richard Wortman) *The Making of Three Russian Revolutionaries: Voices From the Menshevik Past,* Cambridge University Press, 1987.

Contributor to *Soviet Attitudes Toward Authority.* General editor of "History of Menshevism," University of Chicago Press and Hoover Institution on War, Revolution, and Peace, 1967—. Contributor to Slavic studies journals.

BIOGRAPHICAL/CRITICAL SOURCES:

PERIODICALS

American Historical Review, October, 1976, April, 1980.
Library Quarterly, October, 1958.
Virginia Quarterly Review, winter, 1980.*

*   *   *

HALASZ, Gyula 1899-1984
(Brassai)

PERSONAL: Known professionally as Brassai; born September 9, 1899, in Brasso, Austro-Hungarian Empire (now Brasov, Romania); immigrated to France, 1924, naturalized citizen, 1948; died of a heart attack, July 8, 1984, in Nice (one source says Eze sur Mer), France; buried in Montparnasse Cemetery in Paris, France; son of Gyula (a teacher of French literature) and Matilda (Verzar) Halasz; married Gilberte-Mercedes Boyer, July 18, 1948. *Education:* Attended Academy of Fine Arts, Budapest, Hungary, 1918-19; Akademische Hochschule, Berlin-Charlottenburg, Germany, B.A., 1922.

CAREER: Photographer, painter, sculptor, illustrator, and writer, working principally in Paris, France, beginning in 1924. Set designer for theater and ballet productions, including "Rendez-vous," 1945, and "D'Amour et d'eau fraiche," 1949; creator of film "Tant qu'il y aura des betes" (title means "As Long as There Are Animals"), 1955. Exhibitions of photographs held in numerous cities, including Paris, New York City, Chicago, and London. Works represented in permanent collections, including Bibliotheque Nationale, Paris; Victoria and Albert Museum, London; and Museum of Modern Art, New York City. *Military service:* Austro-Hungarian Army, 1917-18.

MEMBER: P.E.N. Club Francais.

AWARDS, HONORS: Emerson Medal from photographer Peter Henry Emerson, 1934, for *Paris de nuit;* medal from Daguerre Centennial Exposition (Budapest), 1937; prize from Cannes Film Festival, 1956, for "Tant qu'il y aura des betes"; gold medal from Biennale de Fotografia (Venice), 1957; Obelisk of Honor from Photokina (Cologne), 1963; award from American Society of Magazine Photographers, 1966; medal from city of Arles, France, 1974; Chevalier des Arts et des Lettres, 1974; Chevalier de la Legion d'Honneur, 1976; Grand Prix National de la Photographie, 1978.

WRITINGS—UNDER NAME BRASSAI:

WITH OWN PHOTOGRAPHS

Camera in Paris, Focal Press, 1949.

(With others) *Seville en fete*, Edition Neuf, 1954, translation by Eric Earnshaw Smith published as *Fiesta in Seville*, Studio Publications, 1956.

Graffiti, Editions du Temps, 1960.

Conversations avec Picasso, Gallimard, 1964, translation by Francis Price published as *Picasso and Company*, preface by Henry Miller, introduction by Roland Penrose, Doubleday, 1966.

(Author of introduction) *Portfolio Brassai*, Witkin-Berley, 1973.

Henry Miller, grandeur nature (title means "Henry Miller, Life Size"), Gallimard, 1975.

Le Paris secret des annees trente, Gallimard, 1976, translation by Richard Miller published as *The Secret Paris of the Thirties*, Pantheon, 1976.

Henry Miller, rocher heureux, Gallimard, 1978.

(Contributor) Bryn Campbell, editor, *World Photography*, Ziff-Davis Books, 1981.

Les Artistes de ma vie, Denoel, 1982, translation by Richard Miller published as *The Artists of My Life*, Viking, 1982.

Photographs represented in numerous books, including *Paris de Nuit*, Edition Arts et Metiers Graphiques, 1933, and *Les Sculptures de Picasso*, Editions du Chene, 1948. Contributor of photographs to periodicals, including *Coronet, Harper's Bazaar, Labyrinthe, Lilliput, Minotaure, Picture Post, Realites, Verve,* and *Weekly Illustrated*.

OTHER

Histoire de Marie (novel), introduction by Henry Miller, Editions du Point du Jour, 1949.

(Author of introduction) *Images de Camera*, Hachette, 1964.

Paroles en l'air, J.-C. Simoen, 1977.

Elohivas: Levelek, 1920-1940 (letters), Kriterion (Bucharest, Romania), 1980.

Contributor of articles to periodicals, including *Camera* and *L'Intransigeant*.

SIDELIGHTS: Celebrated in the London *Times* as "one of the greatest photographers of the twentieth century," Brassai was renowned for his pioneering photographs of the nightlife of Paris in the 1930s. At a time when many in his field were tied to their studios by the bulky and awkward equipment of the day, he helped change the nature of photography by taking pictures in darkened streets and in the studios of artists at work. Although his work shows an underlying preference for strong lines of composition, Brassai tried to limit the effect of personal style on his pictures, wishing his subjects to be the center of attention. "I do not look for exceptional subjects, I avoid them," he said, quoted by Jacob Deschin in the *New York Times*. "It is daily life which is the great event, the true reality."

Brassai was of Hungarian ancestry, born Gyula Halasz in the Transylvania region of present-day Romania. He adopted his professional name, meaning "from the town of Brasso," after he moved to Paris as a young man in 1924. With a fine arts education, he originally intended to be a painter in the city, and he supported himself by writing for Hungarian and German periodicals. But journalism introduced him to photographers, one of whom—fellow Hungarian Andre Kertesz—encouraged him to work with a camera.

Brassai, who already spent hours walking the streets of nighttime Paris, fascinated by its mix of criminals, drifters, nightshift workers, and partygoers, realized that he could use film to portray his vision of the city. With forthright curiosity he photographed pimps, prostitutes, tramps, cesspool cleaners, and sometimes lovers. A selection of these pictures, published in 1933 as *Paris de nuit* ("Paris by Night"), established Brassai's reputation as a talented photographer; the acclaim re-echoed in the 1970s when Brassai produced an enlarged volume, *Le Paris secret des annees trente (The Secret Paris of the Thirties)*, that included his own text. "Brassai's photographs," wrote Eve Auchincloss in the *Washington Post Book World*, "look at all these nocturnal underdogs without sentimentality or sensation. His understatement, his respect for form, his unmanipulative curiosity and sympathy, make his work original, beautiful, and moving." The author's prose, Auchincloss continued, was a fit accompaniment to his pictures, and she praised the evocative detail of his reminiscences.

In the text of *Secret Paris* Brassai describes the work habits of the cesspool cleaners, who ate their late supper without washing their hands; the frenzy of fine arts students as they took to the streets for their annual obscene parade; and the voluminous slang of the city's petty criminals. The criminals, he reminds readers, disliked publicity and were difficult and dangerous to photograph. To shoot in a disreputable dance hall, for instance, Brassai first had to gain the acceptance of a friend of the owner, then the owner himself, then the customers; even so, his subjects could become hostile at any moment. One morning the photographer was awakened by a man who was furious because Brassai's picture of him had been published with a caption identifying him as a murderer. The police also distrusted Brassai, hauling him off the dark streets several times for questioning. As he surmises, they simply could not believe that an honest man would be out beside a Paris canal at three o'clock in the morning. He began carrying copies of his pictures in order to make his intentions clear.

Brassai's new career brought him prominent, lifelong friends in the artistic community of Paris, including American expatriate author Henry Miller, who sometimes accompanied him on nighttime expeditions. Miller praised Brassai's work and made him a character in the autobiographical novel *Tropic of Cancer*. Later Brassai reciprocated by writing two lengthy tributes, *Henry Miller, grandeur nature* and *Henry Miller, rocher heureux*. In 1932 the French periodical *Minotaure* sent Brassai to photograph sculptures by Pablo Picasso, a founder of modern art who was perhaps the most influential artist in Paris. The two men became close friends, and Brassai continued to photograph the artist and his work for decades. Brassai also had photo sessions with such major artists as painters Henri Matisse and Oskar Kokoschka and sculptor Aristide Maillol.

Later in life Brassai produced two volumes that combine his photographs of artists with personal recollections about his encounters with them. In the first book, *Conversations avec Picasso (Picasso and Company)*, "Brassai shows himself to be observant, cultivated and shrewd as he talks to Picasso and looks around the studio," said a writer for the *Times Literary Supplement,* adding that "unlike so much which is written about Picasso today it is neither adulatory nor malicious." Filmmaker Jean Renoir told readers of the *New York Times Book Review* that the text provides "invaluable knowledge of the real preoccupations, not only of Picasso but of a group of artists and writers representing the genuine spirit of Paris." In the subsequent volume, *Les Artistes de ma vie (The Artists of My Life)*, Brassai placed increased emphasis on Picasso's contemporaries. Susan Grace Glassi of *Nation* praised Brassai's skill at suiting his photos to the personality of each individual artist. As with other reviewers, she was particularly charmed by a shot of Henri Matisse at work on a sketch, casting a clinical eye on his nude model. Moreover, as Rhoda Koenig and Edith Milton declared in *New York*, "Brassai's recollections of his subjects and friends are often as vivid and revealing as his pictures."

Much of Brassai's work with artists resulted from decades of association with the magazine *Harper's Bazaar*, where staff members such as Carmel Snow encouraged him to create his own assignments. After Snow's death in 1962 Brassai largely retired from photography, concentrating instead on the artwork and writing that had been his first career. By the time he died in 1984, observers generally agreed that his enduring legacy would be the photographs he took of Paris by night. As Deschin wrote, such work embodies "the lively response of a complete human being in love with life and accepting people for what they are."

BIOGRAPHICAL/CRITICAL SOURCES:

BOOKS

Brassai, *The Secret Paris of the Thirties,* translation by Richard Miller, Pantheon, 1976.
Campbell, Bryn, editor, *World Photography,* Ziff-Davis Books, 1981.
Hill, Paul and Thomas Cooper, editors, *Dialogue With Photography,* Thames & Hudson, 1979.

PERIODICALS

Camera, May, 1975.
Nation, May 29, 1967, December 18, 1982.
New Republic, November 6, 1976.
Newsweek, October 18, 1976.
New York, November 8, 1982.
New York Review of Books, April 6, 1967.
New York Times, November 3, 1968, November 17, 1968, July 22, 1984, September 23, 1984.
New York Times Book Review, November 20, 1966, December 5, 1982.
Spectator, November 24, 1979, November 13, 1982, July 23, 1983.
Times Literary Supplement, May 18, 1967.
Village Voice, December 6, 1976, December 21, 1982.
Washington Post Book World, October 3, 1976.

OBITUARIES:

PERIODICALS

Chicago Tribune, July 13, 1984.
Los Angeles Times, July 14, 1984.
Newsweek, July 23, 1984.
New York Times, July 12, 1984.
Time, July 23, 1984.
Times (London), July 12, 1984.*

—Sketch by Thomas Kozikowski

*   *   *

HALE, Keith   1955-

PERSONAL: Born July 3, 1955, in Little Rock, Ark.; son of Billy Charles (a minister) and Carolyn Jean (Harrell) Hale. *Education:* Attended University of Arkansas at Little Rock, 1973, McLennan Community College, 1974-75, and University of Oklahoma, 1975, 1977; University of Texas at Austin, B.S.E., 1980. *Religion:* "None in particular."

ADDRESSES: Home—4801 Hillcrest, Little Rock, Ark. 72205.

CAREER: Schoolteacher in Austin, Tex., 1981-82; University of Texas at Austin, Performing Arts Center, worked in pub-

licity office, 1982-84; English Language Book Editors, Amsterdam, Netherlands, editor, 1984; Arkansas Writers' Project, Little Rock, editor, 1984-87; *Arkansas Gazette,* Little Rock, copy editor, 1987—.

WRITINGS:

Clicking Beat on the Brink of Nada (novel), Spartacus [Amsterdam], 1983.
Cody (novel), Alyson, 1987.

WORK IN PROGRESS: What Daniel Did With His Life.

SIDELIGHTS: Keith Hale told *CA* that among his influences are Michael Campbell's *Lord, Dismiss Us,* Paul Covert's *Cages,* Andre Gide's *The Counterfeiters,* Vladimir Nabokov's *Pale Fire,* "as well as the work of A. E. Housman, Joan Didion, David Malouf, S. E. Hinton, and, especially, Hermann Hesse."

*   *   *

HALE, Nancy   1908-1988

OBITUARY NOTICE—See index for *CA* sketch: Born May 6, 1908, in Boston, Mass.; died after suffering a stroke, September 24, 1988, in Charlottesville, Va. Painter, journalist, and author. During the five decades of her writing career Hale produced nineteen volumes of fiction, biography, and memoirs and numerous short stories documenting changing American upper-class manners. Educated in Boston art schools, Hale worked briefly as a painter before moving to New York City, where she worked as an assistant editor, first at *Vogue* and later at *Vanity Fair.* In 1935 she held the distinction of being the *New York Times*'s first woman reporter. Her publications include the novels *The Young Die Good, The Prodigal Women,* and *Heaven and Hardpan Farm;* autobiographical essays *A New England Girlhood* and *The Life in the Studio,* recollections of her painter mother; short story collections *The Earliest Dreams, Between the Dark and the Daylight* and *The Empress's Ring;* a children's book, *The Night of the Hurricane;* a biography of the American painter Mary Cassatt; two plays; and *The Realities of Fiction: A Book About Writing.* Hale also edited *Discovery,* an anthology of three hundred years of New England writing, and contributed short stories to more than thirty anthologies and to magazines such as *American Mercury, Harper's, Harper's Bazaar, McCall's,* and *New Yorker.* She received the O. Henry Prize in 1933, the Benjamin Franklin Special Citation for short story writers in 1958, and the Henry H. Bellamann Award for literature in 1969.

OBITUARIES AND OTHER SOURCES:

BOOKS

Contemporary Novelists, 4th edition, St. Martin's, 1986.
Dictionary of Literary Biography Yearbook: 1980, Gale, 1981.

PERIODICALS

New York Times, September 26, 1988.
Washington Post, September 27, 1988.

*   *   *

HALL, Leslie   1948-
   (Leslie Hall Pinder)

PERSONAL: Born September 21, 1948, in Elrose, Saskatchewan, Canada; daughter of Raymond Leslie (a doctor) and Margaret (a nurse; maiden name, Rathwell) Hall. *Education:*

Attended University of Saskatchewan; Dalhousie University, B.A., 1968; University of British Columbia, LL.B., 1977.

ADDRESSES: Home—3569 West 12th Ave., Vancouver, British Columbia, Canada V6R 2N3. *Office*—310-111 Water St., Vancouver, British Columbia, Canada V6R 1A7. *Agent*—Anthony Sheil Associates Ltd., 43 Doughty St., London WC1N 2LF, England.

CAREER: Barrister and solicitor in Vancouver, British Columbia, 1978—.

MEMBER: Law Society of British Columbia, British Columbia Federation of Writers, Authors League of America, Authors Guild.

WRITINGS:

(Under pseudonym Leslie Hall Pinder) *Under the House* (novel), Talonbooks, 1986, Random House, 1988.

WORK IN PROGRESS: A novel, tentatively titled *Selbie*, publication expected in 1989.

SIDELIGHTS: Leslie Hall told *CA:* "I started out to become a writer and ended up working at the police department, then became a lawyer. My field of legal work is Indian land claims. I wrote mainly journals, then from 1984 to 1986 a short story that I was writing became the novel *Under the House*. My inspiration for the novel came from a story I heard of two women, raised as sisters, who were in fact mother and daughter. The unravelling and understanding of such a relationship led to the book. My second novel will be about the relationship between an old man and a young woman. It explores the idea that there was no death until the first killing."

*   *   *

HALLIDAY, M(ichael) A(lexander) K(irkwood) 1925-

PERSONAL: Born April 13, 1925; son of Wilfrid J. and Winifred (Kirkwood) Halliday. *Education:* Received B.A. from University of London; received M.A. and Ph.D. from Cambridge University.

ADDRESSES: Office—Department of Linguistics, University of Sydney, Sydney, New South Wales 2006, Australia.

CAREER: Cambridge University, Cambridge, England, assistant lecturer in Chinese, 1954-58; University of Edinburgh, Edinburgh, Scotland, lecturer, 1958-60, reader in general linguistics, 1960-63; University of London, London, England, director of Communication Research Centre at University College, 1963-65, professor of general linguistics, 1965-71; Center for Advanced Study in the Behavioral Sciences, Palo Alto, Calif., research fellow, 1972-73; University of Illinois at Urbana-Champaign, Urbana, professor of linguistics, 1973-74; University of Essex, Colchester, England, professor of language and linguistics, 1974-75; University of Sydney, Sydney, Australia, professor of linguistics, 1976—. Linguistic Society of America Professor at Indiana University—Bloomington, 1964; visiting professor at Yale University, 1967, Brown University, 1971, and University of Nairobi, 1972. *Military service:* British Army, 1944-47.

MEMBER: American Historical Association (fellow).

AWARDS, HONORS: D.H.C. from University of Nancy.

WRITINGS:

The Language of the Chinese: The Secret History of the Mongols, Basil Blackwell, 1959.
(With Angus McIntosh and Peter Strevens) *The Linguistics Sciences and Language Teaching,* Indiana University Press, 1964.
(With McIntosh) *Patterns of Language: Papers in General, Descriptive, and Applied Linguistics,* Indiana University Press, 1967.
Intonation and Grammar in British English, Mouton, 1967.
A Course in Spoken English: Intonation, Oxford University Press, 1970.
(With McIntosh and Strevens) *Linguistik, Phonetik und Sprachunterricht,* Quelle & Meyer, 1972.
Explorations in the Functions of Language, Edward Arnold, 1973.
Language and Social Man, Longman, 1974.
Learning How to Mean: Explorations in the Development of Language, Edward Arnold, 1975.
Halliday: System and Function in Language; Selected Papers, Oxford University Press, 1976.
(With Ruqaiya Hasan) *Cohesion in English,* Longman, 1976.
Language as a Social Semiotic: The Social Interpretation of Language and Meaning, University Park Press, 1978.
(Editor with J. R. Martin) *Readings in Systemic Linguistics,* Batsford, 1981.
An Introduction to Functional Grammar, Edward Arnold, 1985.
(Editor with Robin P. Fawcett) *New Developments in Systemic Linguistics,* Volume I: *Theory and Description,* Pinter, 1987.

Also author of *Spoken and Written Language,* 1985. Contributor to linguistic and philology journals.

BIOGRAPHICAL/CRITICAL SOURCES:

BOOKS

de Joia, Alex and Adrian Stenton, *Terms in Systemic Linguistics: A Guide to Halliday,* Batsford, 1980.

PERIODICALS

Modern Language Journal, March, 1972, September, 1978.
Times Literary Supplement, April 29, 1975.*

*   *   *

HAMILTON, David   1939-

PERSONAL: Born June 30, 1939, in Rothesay Bute, England; son of James Hay and Olive Hamilton; married Jean Duncan, 1982; children: Duncan. *Education:* University of Glasgow, B.Sc., 1960, M.B., Ch.B., 1963, Ph.D., 1963, F.R.C.S., 1966. *Politics:* Labour.

ADDRESSES: Agent—David Fletcher, 58 John St., Penicuik, Midlothian, Scotland.

CAREER: Western Infirmary, Glasgow, Scotland, surgeon, 1963-84; Partick Press, owner, 1984—.

WRITINGS:

The Healers: A History of Scottish Medicine, Canongate, 1981, 2nd edition, 1987.
A Good Golf Guide to Scotland, Canongate, 1985.
Early Golf: Glasgow, Partick Press, 1985.
Early Golf: Aberdeen, Partick Press, 1986.
The Monkey Gland Affair, Chatto & Windus, 1986.

Early Golf: St. Andrews, Partick Press, 1987.

WORK IN PROGRESS: History of Surgery, publication expected in 1989.

SIDELIGHTS: David Hamilton told *CA:* "I try to bring serious-minded scholarship to the history of Scotland, notably in the areas of medicine and golf. My Partick Press books contain new material on the history of golf printed by letterpress in limited editions."

BIOGRAPHICAL/CRITICAL SOURCES:

PERIODICALS

Times (London), December 11, 1986.
Times Literary Supplement, September 19, 1986.

*   *   *

HAMMICK, Georgina   1939-

PERSONAL: Born May 24, 1939, in Hampshire, England; daughter of George Douglas (an army officer) and Patricia (a housewife; maiden name, Marsh) Heyman; married Charles C. W. Hammick, October 24, 1961 (divorced, 1983); children: Thomas, Kate, Rose. *Education:* Attended Academie Julian, Paris, 1956-57; attended Salisburg School of Art, 1957-58. *Politics:* Social democrat. *Religion:* Anglican.

ADDRESSES: Home—Bridgewalk House, Brixton Deverill, Warminster, Wiltshire BA12 7EJ, England. *Agent*—Rachel Calder, Curtis Brown, 162-168 Regent St., London W1R 5TB, England.

CAREER: Teacher of English and art, 1959-61; worked at Hammicks Bookshops Ltd., beginning in 1968, served as director, 1970-80; tutor in creative writing and writer-in-school, 1980—.

MEMBER: Writers Guild of Great Britain, Authors Lending and Copyright Society, National Trust, Southern Arts Association (member of literature panel).

WRITINGS:

(With Angus Nicolson, Valerie Owen, and others) *A Poetry Quintet*, Gollancz, 1976.
People for Lunch (short stories), Methuen, 1987.

Contributor of short stories to anthologies, including *Best of Fiction Magazine*, *Best Short Stories, 1987*, *Best Short Stories, 1988*, and *Best Short Stories From Stand*, and to magazines, including *Fiction*, *Stand*, *Listener*, *Critical Quarterly*, and *Woman's Journal*. Author of garden column in *Books*.

WORK IN PROGRESS: Short stories.

SIDELIGHTS: Georgina Hammick told *CA:* "Authors who have influenced my writing include George Eliot, Virginia Woolf, Katherine Mansfield, Anton Chekhov, Elizabeth Bowen, Elizabeth Bishop, Elizabeth Taylor (the writer, not the actress!), Raymond Carver, Alice Munro, Ellen Gilchrist, and John Cheever. My working habits are slow. I am constantly revising drafts—five or six for each story—but my aim is to get it right. My advice to students is to read and to keep reading."

*   *   *

HANCOCK, Keith
See HANCOCK, W(illiam) K(eith)

HANCOCK, W(illiam) K(eith)   1898-1988
(Keith Hancock)

OBITUARY NOTICE—See index for *CA* sketch: Born June 26, 1898, in Melbourne, Victoria, Australia; died August 13, 1988. Historian, educator, and author. Widely recognized for his scholarship in the humanities, Hancock spent most of his career as a university professor of history in England and Australia. His affiliations included posts at the University of Adelaide, the University of Birmingham, Oxford University, London University, and the Australian National University at Canberra, from which he retired in 1968 as professor emeritus. During World War II Hancock worked in the British War Cabinet Office supervising the writing of the civil history of the war, a thirty-volume achievement. As part of that monumental collection he co-authored the highly regarded *British War Economy*. Hancock's prodigious writing output also included the seminal work *Australia;* the three-volume *Survey of British Commonwealth Affairs;* the two-volume *Smuts: The Sanguine Years* [and] *The Fields of Force*, a biography of South African statesman Jan Smuts; *Discovering Monaro: A Study of Man's Impact on His Environment*, a pioneering study in environmental history; *Economists, Ecologists, and Historians*, one of several books he wrote under the name Keith Hancock; and *Country and Calling*, an autobiographical work. The recipient of numerous honorary doctorates, Hancock was knighted in 1965.

OBITUARIES AND OTHER SOURCES:

BOOKS

The International Who's Who, 51st edition, Europa, 1987.

PERIODICALS

Times (London), August 16, 1988.

*   *   *

HANNA, S(uhail) S(alim)   1943-

PERSONAL: Born October 10, 1943, in Jerusalem, Palestine (now Israel); son of Salim and Nabiha Hanna; married Mahera Awwad (a registered nurse), August 26, 1975; children: Rita, Sal, Paul, Sami. *Education:* University of Wisconsin—Madison, B.A., 1966; Indiana University—Bloomington, M.A., 1970, Ph.D., 1973. *Politics:* Independent. *Religion:* Christian.

ADDRESSES: Home—3223 Fifth Ave., Beaver Falls, Pa. 15010. *Office*—Department of English, Geneva College, Beaver Falls, Pa. 15010-3599.

CAREER: Kickapoo Spur Press, Shawnee, Okla., founder and editor of *Bananas: A Thatch of Creativity* (magazine), 1974-75; Sterling College, Sterling, Kan., teacher of English, 1976-79, assistant football coach, 1976, 1977, 1979; Geneva College, Beaver, Pa., professor of English, 1982—, head women's soccer coach, 1985. Teacher of English at small colleges in Oklahoma in the early 1970s, and Virginia, 1979-82. Vice-president of St. Philomena Boosters Club, 1987-88.

WRITINGS:

Albino Cockroaches (poetry chapbook), Woodhix Press, 1979.
The Gypsy Scholar: A Writer's Comic Search for a Publisher, Iowa State University Press, 1987.

Contributor to *Collier's Encyclopedia*. Contributor to magazines, including *Saturday Review*, *Literature East and West*, and *Cimarron Review*.

WORK IN PROGRESS: Lady Princeton Kicks, "a clean comic novel about a filthy rich old lady."

SIDELIGHTS: S. S. Hanna told *CA:* "While in Pennsylvania, I wrote about my academic, literary, and coaching experiences, but no publisher expressed interest in me, in a man who was as unknown as television personality Vanna White was known. My inability to locate a publisher for my autobiography led me to abridge that work and to add three chapters to it on the frolics and frustrations that I had encountered in trying to market my life's story. The result is *The Gypsy Scholar.*"

* * *

HANS, Valerie P(atricia) 1951-

PERSONAL: Born January 24, 1951, in South Bend, Ind.; daughter of John Julius (in sales) and Mary Frances (an office manager; maiden name, Roberts) Hans. *Education:* University of California, San Diego, B.A. (with highest honors), 1973; University of Toronto, M.A., 1974, Ph.D., 1978.

ADDRESSES: Office—Division of Criminal Justice and Psychology, University of Delaware, Newark, Del. 19711.

CAREER: Lecturer at University of Toronto, Toronto, Ontario, 1976-78; visiting assistant professor at Arizona State University, Tempe, 1978-79, and at Simon Fraser University, Burnaby, British Columbia, 1979-80; University of Delaware, Newark, assistant professor of criminal justice and psychology, 1980—. Visiting scholar at Stanford University, 1986-87. Member of jury advisory board of Law Reform Commission of Canada, 1977-78.

MEMBER: American Psychological Association, American Psychology-Law Society, Law and Society Association, Society of Personality and Social Psychology.

AWARDS, HONORS: Grants from Law Reform Commission of Canada and British Columbia Ministry of Justice.

WRITINGS:

(With Neil Vidmar) *Judging the Jury,* Plenum, 1986.

WORK IN PROGRESS: Research on the civil jury, and on public views of law and legal institutions.

SIDELIGHTS: In *Judging the Jury,* Valerie P. Hans and Neil Vidmar cover the history of the jury from its origin in medieval England to the present-day. They analyze historical, psychological, and social data in an effort to pinpoint the ways in which the typical jury has changed over the centuries. The authors conclude that, on the whole, juries perform well and make fair decisions. According to Lee Dembart of the *Los Angeles Times,* "the authors consider, examine and reject the claims that juries are incompetent . . . that their decisions are swayed by prejudice or sympathy, and that they disregard the law when it goes against their own sense of justice." Hans and Vidmar emphasize that "American democracy is founded on the belief that truth resides in the collective wisdom of the people," added the reviewer. Similarly, Toronto *Globe and Mail* critic Allan C. Hutchinson observed that the jury functions as "a partial antidote to the false cult of the expert. . . . It is one of the few opportunities for meaningful popular participation in government. . . . the paradigm of participatory self-government."

BIOGRAPHICAL/CRITICAL SOURCES:

PERIODICALS

Globe and Mail (Toronto), May 24, 1986.
Los Angeles Times, July 22, 1986.

* * *

HARDEN, Ian (John) 1954-

PERSONAL: Born March 22, 1954, in Norwich, England; son of Arthur Eric (an administrator) and Mary (a nurse; maiden name, Newson) Harden; married Susan Stephens (an administrator), March 28, 1987. *Education:* Churchill College, Cambridge, B.A., 1975, M.A., 1979, LL.B., 1976.

ADDRESSES: Home—36 Oakhill Rd., Sheffield S7 ISH, England. *Office*—Centre for Criminological and Socio-Legal Studies, University of Sheffield, 430-2 Crookesmoor Rd., Sheffield, England.

CAREER: University of Sheffield, Sheffield, England, lecturer in criminological and socio-legal studies, 1976—. Member of Constitutional Reform Centre.

MEMBER: Society of Public Teachers of Law.

WRITINGS:

(With Norman Lewis) *The Noble Lie: The British Constitution and the Rule of Law,* Hutchinson, 1986.

WORK IN PROGRESS: Corporatism and Accountability: The Democratic Dilemma, with Norman Lewis and Patrick Birkinshaw, publication expected in 1989; work on the public law framework of budgetary processes.

SIDELIGHTS: In *The Noble Lie,* Ian Harden and Norman Lewis propose that the government of England is not, as comfortable tradition would have it, accountable to the people it governs, and that the administration of government does not operate under an efficient system of checks and balances. Effective judicial review is limited. The people do not have access to information about public decision-making, even in the sensitive area of human rights and, therefore, cannot challenge the decisions of their elected officials.

The authors have compared British law to that of continental Europe and the United States and have presented alternatives that could work in England. In particular they have challenged the secrecy that has consistently surrounded British public life and policy. Harden and Lewis recommend change that some critics have called too moderate, but which they believe could be enacted without a complete upheaval of the status quo.

BIOGRAPHICAL/CRITICAL SOURCES:

PERIODICALS

Times Literary Supplement, April 24, 1987.

* * *

HARDESTY, Sarah 1951-

PERSONAL: Born January 12, 1951, in Fairmont, W.Va.; daughter of C. Howard (an executive) and Doris (a homemaker; maiden name, Wilson) Hardesty. *Education:* Attended Duke University, 1972, and Northwestern University, 1973; graduate study at New York University.

ADDRESSES: Home—3033 Cambridge Place N.W., Washington, D.C. 20007. *Office*—Council for the Advancement and Support of Education, 11 Dupont Circle, Washington, D.C. 20036.

CAREER: J. Walter Thompson Advertising, Chicago, Ill., copywriter, 1973-75; *Forbes* Magazine, New York, N.Y., reporter/researcher, 1976-78; Hill & Knowlton Inc., New York City, vice-president, 1978-80 and 1981-87; Mobil Corp., New York City, senior staff member, 1980-81; Council for Advancement and Support of Education, Washington, D.C., director of communications, 1987—. Member of board of directors of Horizons Theatre, 1988—, of the Foundation for Modern Dance, 1983—, and of Literacy Volunteers of New York City, 1981-87; member of advisory board of *Duke* magazine, 1988—.

MEMBER: Overseas Press Club, National Council on Women's Studies, Arts and Business Council, Museum of Modern Art.

WRITINGS:

(With Nehama Jacobs) *Success and Betrayal: The Crisis of Women in Corporate America*, F. Watts, 1986.

Contributor of articles to *Family Weekly*.

SIDELIGHTS: Sarah Hardesty, a corporate manager herself, had a wealth of personal experience from which to draw in co-authoring *Success and Betrayal: The Crisis of Women in Corporate America*, a book which relates the frustrating plight of women with limited opportunities in the business world.

Hardesty and co-author Nehama Jacobs argue that the idealized visions women hold of corporate opportunities clash with the realities of the working world and lead, ultimately, to widespread disillusionment among females in management positions. Besides identifying a series of unfulfilled myths that contribute to women's sense of "loss and betrayal," Jewelle W. Bickford contended in the *Washington Post* that the authors also offer "some practical ways for women to reconcile differences between what exists in the corporate experience and what they wish existed." Bickford asserted, "The book does the best job I've seen yet documenting the crisis for women in American corporations today."

Even the few critics who point to the extensive amount of quoted material in the book as a source of fragmentation and vagueness admit that its authors have reached valid conclusions and have addressed a problem which merits further investigation. The women who succeed in business, according to Hardesty and Jacobs in an excerpt of *Success and Betrayal* that appeared in the *Boston Globe*, are those who "quickly see that politics and timing play a much larger role in corporate advancement than merit."

Hardesty told *CA:* "When Nehama Jacobs and I began writing *Success and Betrayal*, most of the information about women's relatively new experience in the male-dominated corporate world was limited to 'how-to' manuals and profiles of a few exceptional 'superwomen.'

"The purpose of our book was to give a wider range of women an opportunity to talk honestly and openly about their corporate experiences and to share the lessons they had learned with others. Women in all different industries, of all different ages, in all parts of the country, in all levels of jobs, have told us that after reading the book, they have realized they are not alone in their views and experiences.

"One of the most rewarding aspects of reporting and writing the book has been the gratitude so many women have expressed to us for 'telling the truth.' We are especially pleased the book has occasioned more discussion and a greater sharing of ideas between corporate women—and sometimes men. A search for solutions to common problems will benefit not only women, but men and the corporate world in general."

BIOGRAPHICAL/CRITICAL SOURCES:

PERIODICALS

Boston Globe, November 10, 1986.
Los Angeles Times, January 8, 1987.
Philadelphia Inquirer, January 4, 1987.
Savvy, April, 1988.
USA Today, April 30, 1987.
Wall Street Journal, December 23, 1986.

                              *   *   *

HARDING, Susan Friend   1946-

PERSONAL: Born September 2, 1946, in Columbus, Ohio; daughter of Harold Friend (a professor) and Elizabeth (a nutritionist; maiden name, Reeves) Harding. *Education:* University of Michigan, B.A., 1968, M.A., 1971, Ph.D., 1977; Columbia University, Certificate in Anthropology, 1969.

ADDRESSES: Office—Department of Anthropology, University of Michigan, Ann Arbor, Mich. 48109. *Agent*—Charlotte Sheedy Literary Agency, Inc., 145 West 86th St., New York, N.Y. 10024.

CAREER: University of Michigan, Ann Arbor, lecturer, 1974-77, assistant professor, 1977-84, associate professor of anthropology, 1984—.

WRITINGS:

Remaking Ibieca: Rural Life in Aragon Under Franco, University of North Carolina Press, 1984.
(Editor with Charles Bright) *Statemaking and Social Movements*, University of Michigan Press, 1984.

WORK IN PROGRESS: A book on fundamental Baptists and the congregation of Jerry Falwell, tentatively titled *And the Word Was God*.

SIDELIGHTS: Anthropologist Susan Friend Harding explores the ramifications of social, political, and cultural changes on a small village's people in her book, *Remaking Ibieca: Rural Life in Aragon Under Franco*. For many years, relates Harding, the village of Ibieca, located near the border of France and Spain, was a peasant community run by local masters. Spanish dictator Francisco Franco's regime pushed the village into the twentieth century. Mechanized agriculture and large landowners gradually replaced traditional farming methods and small peasant landholdings. Landless workers and many young people left Ibieca to work in the city. The village population declined by 50 percent, and the family unit deteriorated. The farmer who formerly worked the land in an intimate relationship with local ecology was displaced by the farming businessman whose success was bound to the market economy and a centralized government administration.

According to Jeremy MacClancy, writing in the *Times Literary Supplement*, Harding postulates in her book that "the agrarian programmes of the Francoist state did not directly determine change. Rather, they set the direction and pace of people's choices." MacClancy called *Remaking Ibieca* a "carefully written, sensitive ethnography," that balanced statistical data with personal life histories of Ibieca's villagers. The critic continued: "The book is a valuable contribution to a previously neglected topic in Mediterranean anthropology: how villagers make economic decisions when the State controls the market and how those economic choices transform the nature of their lives."

BIOGRAPHICAL/CRITICAL SOURCES:

PERIODICALS

Times Literary Supplement, June 7, 1985.

*   *   *

HARGREAVES, (Charles) Roger   1935-1988

OBITUARY NOTICE: Born in 1935; died of a heart attack, September 12, 1988, in Kent, England. Advertising executive, illustrator, and author. Hargreaves was the creator, illustrator, and author of the "Mister Men" children's book series. Conceived in a moment of boredom at his job as creative director for a London advertising firm in 1972, Hargreaves's cast of characters, such as Mister Tickle, Mister Greedy, and Mister Silly, became an immediate international success. Selling more than eighty-five million copies worldwide, his books have been translated in twenty languages, and hundreds of products decorated with Mister Men have been marketed, including mugs, T-shirts, and stationery. Hargreaves also wrote and illustrated a set of stories about "Timbuctoo" animals, including *Neigh, Oink, Snap,* and *Roar,* in 1979, and later augmented his "Mister Men" series with the similar "Little Miss" series.

OBITUARIES AND OTHER SOURCES:

PERIODICALS

Chicago Tribune, September 14, 1988.
Times (London), September 13, 1988.
Washington Post, September 16, 1988.

*   *   *

HARMAN, Barbara Leah   1946-

PERSONAL: Born December 14, 1946, in Jamaica, N.Y.; married; children: one. *Education:* Tufts University, B.A., 1968; Brandeis University, M.A., 1969, Ph.D., 1974.

ADDRESSES: Office—Department of English, Wellesley College, Wellesley, Mass. 02181.

CAREER: University of California, Santa Barbara, lecturer, 1974-75; Temple University, Philadelphia, Pa., assistant professor of English, 1976-77; Wellesley College, Wellesley, Mass., assistant professor, 1977-83, associate professor of English, 1983—.

WRITINGS:

Costly Monuments: Representatives of the Self in George Herbert's Poetry, Harvard University Press, 1982.

WORK IN PROGRESS: In Promiscuous Company: Female Public Appearance and the Nineteenth-Century English Novel.

SIDELIGHTS: Barbara Leah Harman told *CA:* "My first book, *Costly Monuments,* is a study of how a seventeenth-century poet managed to 'represent' himself in a religious universe where sanctions against self-representation were clear. My current project has to do with nineteenth-century women, and though I am obviously dealing with material that differs in

dramatic ways from my earlier work, there are some surprising continuities. My new work in women's studies combines an analysis of social and historical documents with a study of the nineteenth-century women's movement. My intention is to explain why women's public appearances in the Victorian novel are so fraught with tension, so mired in complication, so charged with a sense of danger. In a sense, I am still interested in the problem of representation—in the question of how people seek to appear and how they structure their appearances, even in the midst of efforts to suppress and constrain them.

"The nineteenth-century women's movement is an important context for my investigation because it sought to transform women's access to the public sphere—to education, to the professions, to the right to vote—in the midst of powerful efforts to maintain the status quo. In doing so it raised crucial questions, and stirred agonizing debate, about the meaning of what I call 'female public appearance.' The vexed portrayal of public women in the nineteenth-century novel is a manifestation of this crucial nineteenth-century debate about the position and status of women.

"My interest in the means and forms of 'representation' has thus taken a new turn—and taken me, I confess, into a century that seems more immediately and personally compelling. Studying the meanings of 'private' and 'public' for nineteenth-century women helps me to think more clearly about their contemporary meanings, and helps to clarify pressing contemporary questions about women's roles."

*   *   *

HARRIS, Ann Sutherland   1937-

PERSONAL: Born November 4, 1937, in Cambridge, England; immigrated to United States, 1965; daughter of Gordon (a physicist) and Gunborg (an artist; maiden name, Wahlstrom) Sutherland; married William V. Harris (a historian), July 13, 1965; children: Neil W. O. Sutherland Harris. *Education:* Courtauld Institute of Art, London, B.A. (with first class honors), 1961, Ph.D., 1965. *Politics:* "Somewhere left of most Democrats." *Religion:* None.

ADDRESSES: Home—1315 Denniston Ave., Pittsburgh, Pa. 15217. *Office*—Frick Fine Arts Building, University of Pittsburgh, Pittsburgh, Pa. 15260.

CAREER: Columbia University, New York, N.Y., assistant professor, 1966-71; Hunter College of the City University of New York, assistant professor, 1971-73; State University of New York at Albany, associate professor, 1973-77; Juilliard School, New York City, adjunct professor, 1978-84; University of Pittsburgh, Pittsburgh, Pa., professor of art history, 1984—. Visiting professor at Columbia, Yale, and New York universities and University of Texas at Arlington. Member of advisory board of National Museum of Women in the Arts, Washington, D.C.

MEMBER: College Art Association of America (member of board of directors, 1975-79), Women's Caucus for Art (president and founding member, 1971-74; member of executive advisory board, 1974).

AWARDS, HONORS: D.A. from Eastern Michigan University, 1981.

WRITINGS:

(With Linda Nochlin) *Women Artists: 1550-1950,* Knopf, 1977.

Andrea Sacchi: Complete Edition of the Paintings, Phaidon, 1977.

(Editor) *Selected Drawings of Gian Lorenzo Bernini,* Dover, 1977.

Landscape Painting in Rome: 1595-1675, R. L. Feigen, 1985.

The Drawings and Paintings of G. L. Bernini, Gruyter, in press.

Contributor of articles, reviews, and essays to periodicals and catalogues.

SIDELIGHTS: In *Women Artists: 1550-1950,* Ann Sutherland Harris and co-author Linda Nochlin make a "serious attempt," noted reviewer Grace Glueck in the *New York Times,* to answer the question, "Why have there been no great women artists?" The work, continued Glueck, reasons that "the nature of social institutions and what they denied to women" have kept females in the background of Western European art history. Confined, for example, to the home after marriage, shunned from serious art training opportunities in the fifteenth and sixteenth centuries, and denied access to nude models until the end of the nineteenth century, women artists struggled for prominence.

In the first half of the book, Harris traces the role of female painters from the Middle Ages to the time of the 1789 French Revolution. She attests that it was not until the end of the Renaissance—a Western art movement spanning the thirteenth through sixteenth centuries—that the artwork of women was preserved and their accomplishments chronicled. Nochlin, in the second half of the book, outlines women artists from the end of the French Revolution to the present. She reports that although women eventually made progress in a male-ordered art world, they were still only permitted second-class art training, restricted to painting sentimental subjects, and continually denied membership to established art institutions. The twentieth century finally brought positive changes for female artists, who are now able to enjoy equal opportunities in art education, training, and career pursuits. But, as *Women Artists* documents, some discrimination against exhibiting the work of women by museums and dealers still exists.

Harris and Nochlin's book was hailed for its excellence of style and format and its extensive scholarly examination. Glueck deemed the work "a richly researched and highly readable book." Although she regretted that it excluded the documentation of female sculptors, photographers, and craftswomen, as well as women painters born after 1910, the reviewer concluded that *Women Artists* is "a very useful book, one that makes plain as the nose on a man's face" why women have been so lightly regarded in the history of art.

Harris told *CA:* "I am motivated by my interest in all forms of visual art, past and present. I collect art by twentieth-century women. My politics are feminist, and this influences my teaching and provides the main focus of my writings on twentieth-century art. My aims as a writer are modest—to convey my ideas as lucidly and vividly as possible, and thus to make others understand and appreciate a visual work of art, whether of the past or the present."

AVOCATIONAL INTERESTS: Playing and listening to classical keyboard music, gardening.

BIOGRAPHICAL/CRITICAL SOURCES:

PERIODICALS

New York Times, April 27, 1977.

HARRIS, Donald   1931-

PERSONAL: Born April 7, 1931, in St. Paul, Minn.; son of Barney William (a businessman) and Hattie (a housewife; maiden name, Paper) Harris; married first wife, Nadine, 1959 (divorced, 1983); married Marilyn Hackett (a housewife), 1983; children: Daniel, Jeremy. *Education:* University of Michigan, Mus.B., 1952, Mus.M., 1954; studied privately with Paul Wilkinson, Ross Lee Finney at University of Michigan, Nadia Boulanger, Andre Jolivet, and Max Deutsch.

ADDRESSES: Office—College of the Arts, Ohio State University, 304 Mershon Auditorium, 30 West 15th Ave., Columbus, Ohio 43210-1393.

CAREER: U.S. Information Service, Paris, France, music consultant at American Cultural Center, 1965-67; New England Conservatory of Music, Boston, Mass., assistant to president for academic affairs, 1967-71, vice-president, 1971-74, executive vice-president, 1974-77, member of teaching faculty in departments of composition and music literature, 1967-77; University of Hartford, Hartford, Conn., composer in residence, professor of music, and chairman of composition and theory, 1977-80, dean of Hartt School of Music, 1981-88; Ohio State University, Columbus, professor of music composition and dean of College of the Arts, 1988—. Lecturer at Schoenberg Institute, 1974. Compositions commissioned by Serge Koussevitzky Music Foundation, Elizabeth Sprague Coolidge Foundation, Goethe Institute, Connecticut Commission on the Arts, French National Radio, Festival of Contemporary American Music at Tanglewood, Boston Musica Viva, Cleveland Orchestra, and Arnold Schoenberg Institute; music recorded by CRI, Delos, and Golden Crest Records.

MEMBER: International Alban Berg Society, American Society of Composers, Authors, and Publishers.

AWARDS, HONORS: Award from Louisville Orchestra, 1954; Fulbright scholar, 1956; Prince Rainier of Monaco Composition Prize, 1960; Guggenheim fellow, 1965; grants from Rockefeller Foundation, 1969, and Chapelbrook Foundation, 1970; awards from American Society of Composers, Authors, and Publishers, 1973—; fellow of National Endowment for the Arts, 1974.

WRITINGS:

(Editor with Juliane Brand and Christopher Hailey) *The Berg-Schoenberg Correspondence: Selected Letters,* Norton, 1987.

Contributor to music journals.

MUSICAL COMPOSITIONS

"Piano Sonata," Jobert, 1956.
"Fantasy for Violin and Piano," Jobert, 1957.
"Symphony in Two Movements," Jobert, 1961.
"String Quartet," Jobert, 1965.
"Ludus for Ten Instruments," Jobert, 1966.
"Ludus II for Five Instruments," Jobert, 1973.
"On Variations," Jobert, 1978.
"For the Night to Wear," Theodore Presser, 1978.
"Balladen," Theodore Presser, 1979.
"Of Hartford in a Purple Light," Theodore Presser, 1979.
"Les Mains," Theodore Presser, 1983.

Also composer of "Charmes for Voice and Orchestra," (1977), "Prelude to a Concert in Connecticut" (1981), "Meditations for Solo Organ'' (1984), "Three Fanfares for Four Horns" (1984), and "Pierrot Lieder" (1988).

WORK IN PROGRESS: Music for a three-act opera, "The Little Mermaid," from a libretto by Marguerite Yourcenar adapted from the Hans Christian Andersen fairy tale; a biography of Alban Berg for Editions du Seuil.

SIDELIGHTS: Donald Harris told *CA:* "*The Berg-Schoenberg Correspondence: Selected Letters* came about through my interest in the music of Alban Berg. I had initially begun a biography of Berg, in French, at the request of the Editions du Seuil, to whom I was under contract. This biography is two-thirds complete. It was interrupted by my work on the Berg-Schoenberg correspondence, of which I was the senior editor. This project has taken me twenty years, however, and the biography remains incomplete.

"In the meantime I have divided my time between administration and composing. Through the years I developed a very close relationship with Marguerite Yourcenar, who provided the libretto for the opera 'The Little Mermaid,' on which I have been working these past five years. Her influence on my thought has been decisive. I published one song, 'Les Mains,' based on a text she adapted, and consider the opera to be the quintessential project of my creative career. It will continue to be my first and foremost compositional project as I now leave for a position of greater educational advocacy in the arts at Ohio State."

BIOGRAPHICAL/CRITICAL SOURCES:

PERIODICALS

Los Angeles Times, January 31, 1988.
Washington Post Book World, November 22, 1987.

*   *   *

HARRIS, Jacqueline L.   1929-

PERSONAL: Born April 6, 1929, in Columbus, Ohio; daughter of Booker W. (a dentist) and Alberta (a teacher; maiden name, Adams) Harris. *Education:* Ohio State University, B.Sc., 1951, B.A., 1966. *Religion:* Roman Catholic.

ADDRESSES: Home—118 Westwood Dr., Wethersfield, Conn. 06109. *Office*—Northeast Utilities, P.O. Box 270, Hartford, Conn. 06141.

CAREER: Ohio State University, Medical Center, Columbus, supervisor of main chemistry laboratory, 1952-54; Providence Hospital, Detroit, Mich., medical technologist, 1954-55; medical technologist at Princeton Hospital, 1955-57; certified medical technologist aboard the hospital ship S.S. *Hope*, 1962-64; Xerox Education Publications, Middletown, Conn., writer, 1966-78; Grolier Publishing, Danbury, Conn., science editor of *The New Book of Knowledge*, 1978-79; Purdue-Frederick Co. (pharmaceutical firm), Norwalk, Conn., medical writer, 1980-81; Northeast Utilities, Berlin, Conn., senior corporate news representative, 1981—.

MEMBER: Women in Communications.

AWARDS, HONORS: Nine Black American Doctors was named one of "one hundred best science books for children" by National Science Teachers Association, 1976.

WRITINGS:

JUVENILE

(With Joseph Marfuggi) *Martin Luther King, Jr.: Marching to Freedom*, Xerox Education Publications, 1968.
(With Robert Hayden) *Nine Black American Doctors*, Addison-Wesley, 1976.
(With others) *Basic Science Readers*, seven volumes, McGraw, 1979.
Martin Luther King, Jr., F. Watts, 1982.
Henry Ford, F. Watts, 1983.
Science in Ancient Rome, F. Watts, 1988.

Contributor to *Current Science*.

SIDELIGHTS: Jacqueline L. Harris told *CA:* "I enjoy writing for children. Much of my writing has focused on explaining science concepts in the context of science news. No one subject, however, has been more satisfying than Martin Luther King, Jr. He was, in my opinion, the greatest man the twentieth century has produced. To explain his complex philosophy to young people has been the high point of my writing career."

AVOCATIONAL INTERESTS: Travel (Europe, South America, the Galapagos, the Caribbean), bowling, cooking, dogs, American history, leaded glass.

*   *   *

HARRIS, James E(dward)   1928-

PERSONAL: Born August 25, 1928, in Ann Arbor, Mich. *Education:* University of Michigan, A.B., 1950, D.D.S., 1954, M.S., 1960 and 1963.

ADDRESSES: Office—Department of Orthodontics, University of Michigan, Ann Arbor, Mich. 48104.

CAREER: University of Michigan, Ann Arbor, research associate, 1963-64, became assistant professor and associate professor, professor of orthodontics, 1970—, chairman of department, 1969—, associate professor of human genetics until 1970. Consultant to Plymouth State Hospital.

MEMBER: American Association for the Advancement of Science, American Dental Association, American Association of Physical Anthropology, American Society of Human Genetics.

AWARDS, HONORS: Grant from National Institutes of Health, 1964.

WRITINGS:

(With Kent R. Weeks) *X-Raying the Pharaohs*, Scribner, 1973.
(Editor with Edward F. Wente) *An X-Ray Atlas of the Royal Mummies*, University of Chicago Press, 1980.

BIOGRAPHICAL/CRITICAL SOURCES:

PERIODICALS

Atlantic Monthly, April, 1973.
Saturday Review/World, April, 1973.
Times Literary Supplement, December 21, 1973.*

*   *   *

HARRIS, Richard   1955-

PERSONAL: Born October 2, 1955, in Sutton Coldfield, England; son of Worman (an accountant) and Mary (a homemaker; maiden name, Rudge) Harris; married Carol Town (an organizer), May 18, 1978; children: Alexandra, Peter. *Edu-*

cation: Cambridge University, B.A., 1974; Ohio State University, M.A., 1976; Queen's University, Kingston, Ontario, Ph.D., 1981. *Politics:* Social Democrat. *Religion:* "No affiliation."

ADDRESSES: Office—Department of Geography, McMaster University, 1280 Main St. W., Hamilton, Ontario, Canada L8S 4K1.

CAREER: University of British Columbia, Vancouver, assistant professor of geography, 1981-83; University of Toronto, Toronto, Ontario, assistant professor of geography, 1983-88; McMaster University, Hamilton, Ontario, associate professor of geography, 1988—.

MEMBER: Canadian Association of Geographers, Institute of British Geographers, Association of American Geographers.

AWARDS, HONORS: Fulbright scholar, 1974-76; Canada Research fellow, 1988-91.

WRITINGS:

Democracy in Kingston, McGill-Queen's University Press, 1988.

Contributor to scholarly journals.

WORK IN PROGRESS: Housing in Toronto and Montreal Since the Mid-Nineteenth Century; research on the social geography of North American cities, 1900-1940.

SIDELIGHTS: Richard Harris told *CA:* "I am interested in the recent past. A past that yet lies within living memory is in many ways strange—a past that historians neglect because it is too recent and that social scientists ignore because it is not current. At the same time I try to combine the techniques of the social scientist with those of the historian and novelist: statistics and data samples of the one, the synthetic interpretation and narrative technique of the other. I don't view my work as being technically innovative, though I don't find many people trying to do the same thing.

"My special angle of vision is geographical. I believe that geographical patterns not only reflect the social world, but they also help to shape it. For example, where people choose to live within a city is an expression of who they are and, at the same time, helps to shape who they become. In my research and writing on the recent past—whether it be on housing, residential segregation, or local politics—I aim to elucidate the complex interrelation of society and space."

*   *   *

HARRIS, William McKinley, Sr.   1941-

PERSONAL: Born October 29, 1941, in Richmond, Va.; son of Rosa (a seamstress; maiden name, Minor) Harris; divorced; children: Rolisa, Dana D. *Education:* Howard University, B.S., 1964; University of Washington, Seattle, M.U.P., 1972, Ph.D., 1974.

ADDRESSES: Home—485 14th St. N.W., Charlottesville, Va. 22903. *Office*—Division of Urban and Environmental Planning, School of Architecture, 138 Campbell, University of Virginia, Charlottesville, Va. 22903.

CAREER: Affiliated with U.S. Atomic Energy Commission, Richland, Wash., 1966-68; Battelle Northwest, Richland, research physicist, 1968-70; Battelle Research Center, Richland, experimental physicist, 1970-71, visiting student, 1971-73; Portland State University, Portland, Ore., assistant professor

of urban studies and coordinator of Black Studies Center, 1974-76; University of Virginia, Charlottesville, 1976—, began as associate professor, became professor of city planning, 1986—, dean of Office of Afro-American Affairs and assistant provost, 1976-81. President of Harris Engineering and Planning, Inc. Director of Center for Urban Studies at Western Washington State College, 1973-74; chairman of board of directors of Charlottesville Industrial Development Authority, 1981-85; member of board of directors of Rural Virginia, 1984-85; member of local planning commission, 1986—.

MEMBER: American Planning Association, National Association for the Advancement of Colored People, Community Development Society, Charlottesville Anglers Club, Masons, Danforth Associates.

AWARDS, HONORS: Outstanding service award from Community Development Society, 1984.

WRITINGS:

Black Community Development, R & E Research Associates, 1976.
"Freedom Frontier" (television documentary), Oregon Educational and Public Broadcasting Service, 1976.
(With Darrell Millner) *Perspectives of Black Studies*, University Press of America, 1977.
Conceptual Model for Analysis of Social Planning, J. Community Development Society, 1987.
Public Housing Tenant Training, Western J. Black Studies, 1989.

Contributor to periodicals.

SIDELIGHTS: William McKinley Harris, Sr., told *CA:* "Excellent writing is not a function of intelligence but of practice. Quality writing requires constant effort. My writing practice is driven by the need to fulfill the goal of self-determination by my people—African Americans."

*   *   *

HARRISON, Michael A.   1936-

PERSONAL: Born April 11, 1936, in Philadelphia, Pa.; son of Milton and Mamie May (Gross) Harrison; married first wife, Evalee, August 23, 1959 (divorced, July, 1971); married Susan Graham (a professor), October 16, 1971; children: Craig. *Education:* Case Institute of Technology (now Case Western Reserve University), B.S. (with honors), 1958, M.S., 1959; University of Michigan, Ph.D., 1963. *Politics:* Republican.

ADDRESSES: Office—Department of Computer Science, University of California, Berkeley, Calif. 94720.

CAREER: University of Michigan, Ann Arbor, instructor in computer science, 1963; University of California, Berkeley, assistant professor, 1963-66, associate professor, 1966-71, professor of computer science, 1971—. National lecturer for Association for Computing Machinery, 1969-70; distinguished visitor of Institute of Electrical and Electronics Engineers Computer Society, 1978; member of executive committee of University Consortium in Atmospheric Research, 1983-85; conferant at Vrije Universiteit, 1980. National Research Council, member of Computer Science and Technology Board, 1980-84, chairman of Panel on International Developments in Microelectronics and Computer Science, 1983—; director and member of executive committee of American Federation of Information Processing Societies, 1982-86; member of Japanese Technology Assessment Panel of U.S. Department of

Commerce, 1983-85; member of Afips Government Affairs Committee, 1986—. Director of Charles Babbage Institute and trustee of Charles Babbage Foundation, 1984—.

MEMBER: Association for Computing Machinery (chairman of special interest group on automata and computability theory, 1973-77; member of council, 1978—; chairman of SIG board, 1978-80; chairman of Turing Award committee, 1980; vice-president, 1980-82; chairman of external activities board, 1986—), American Association for the Advancement of Science (fellow), Institute of Electrical and Electronics Engineers (senior member), Sigma Xi, Tau Beta Pi, Eta Kappa Nu.

AWARDS, HONORS: Guggenheim fellow, 1969-70; University Medal from University of Helsinki, 1980.

WRITINGS:

Introduction to Switching and Automata Theory, McGraw, 1965.
Lectures on Linear Sequential Machines, Academic Press, 1969.
Introduction to Formal Language Theory, Addison-Wesley, 1978.
Formal Languages, Fernuniversitaet-Gesamathochschule, 1981.
(With Richard A. DeMillo, George I. Davida, and others) *Applied Cryptology, Cryptographic Protocols, and Computer Security,* American Mathematical Society, 1983.
(With David H. Brandin) *The Technology War,* Wiley, 1987.

Editor of *Discrete Mathematics,* 1970—, *Theoretical Computer Science* and *Journal of Computer and System Sciences,* 1974—, *Journal of the Association for Computing Machinery,* 1975-81, *Annals of Discrete Mathematics,* 1978—, *Information Processing Letters,* 1980-86, and *Future Generation Computer Systems,* 1983—.

CONTRIBUTOR

Amar Mukhopadhyay, editor, *Recent Developments in Switching Theory,* Academic Press, 1961.
J. T. Tou, editor, *Advances in Information Systems Science,* Plenum, 1972.
Wilfred Brauer, editor, *Lecture Notes in Computer Science,* Springer Verlag, 1973.
J. Becvar, editor, *Mathematical Foundations of Computer Science 75,* Springer Verlag, 1975.
Morris Rubinoff and M. C. Yovits, editors, *Advances in Computers,* Academic Press, 1976.
Richard A. DeMillo and other editors, *Foundations of Secure Computation,* Academic Press, 1978.
M. C. Yovits, editor, *Advances in Computers,* Academic Press, 1985.

Contributor of about one hundred articles to scientific journals.

WORK IN PROGRESS: Research on software engineering and electronic publishing.

SIDELIGHTS: Michael A. Harrison told *CA:* "Most of my books have been devoted to research issues in computing. As such the books have been quite specialized and technical. Someone once wrote that scientists are like turtles in that they are of interest only to other turtles. So the early books were for 'turtles.'

"The book *The Technology War,* written with David H. Brandin, is different. Both David and I have been involved in a number of studies regarding the competition between the United States and Japan in high technology. I had chaired a National Research Council panel on international developments in microelectronics and computer science while David chaired a Department of Commerce assessment of Japanese and American activities in computer science. This book was an attempt to convey the importance of this race to the general public because of its impact on the global economy and on the future of the United States. We outlined a strategy for America to become more competitive."

AVOCATIONAL INTERESTS: Running and other sports, photography, travel.

*   *   *

HARRISON, Ray(mond Vincent) 1928-

PERSONAL: Born October 26, 1928, in Chorley, Lancashire, England; son of William (a farmer) and Hilda (Marsden) Harrison; married Gwyneth Margaret Hughes (an insurance underwriter for Lloyd's of London). *Education:* Magdalene College, Cambridge, B.A. (with honors), 1951, M.A., 1952.

ADDRESSES: Home—11 Fife Way, Great Bookham, Surrey KT23 3PH, England. *Agent*—Curtis Brown Ltd., 575 Madison Ave., New York, N.Y. 10022.

CAREER: Department of Inland Revenue, London, England, inspector of taxes, 1952-76, member of fraud squad, 1962-70, principal inspector, 1970-76; Alexander Howden Group (insurance group), London, managing director, 1977-80; Abbey Financial Services Ltd. (financial consultants), London, director, 1980-83; writer, 1983—.

AWARDS, HONORS: Named Freeman of the City of London, 1964.

WRITINGS:

NOVELS

French Ordinary Murder, Quartet, 1983, published as *Why Kill Arthur Potter?,* Scribner, 1984.
Death of an Honourable Member: A Sergeant Bragg-Constable Morton Mystery, Scribner, 1984.
Deathwatch, Scribner, 1985.
Death of a Dancing Lady, Scribner, 1985.
Counterfeit of Murder, St. Martin's, 1986.
A Season for Death, St. Martin's, 1988.

SIDELIGHTS: Ray Harrison's series of detective thrillers featuring turn-of-the-century London sleuths Detective-Sergeant Joseph Bragg of the City Police and his newly installed Constable James Morton, a young aristocrat, have earned both popular and critical recognition. Variously described as witty, fast-paced, and fascinating, they have drawn praise particularly for their lively evocation of period atmosphere, their convincing characterizations, and their rich and varied plots.

Harrison told *CA:* "My novels are set in London in the 1890s. That was a transitional period of great color and excitement. If you look back twenty years from there, you see the world of Dickens; yet the motor car has been invented, and the airplane is just around the corner. My hope is to give the reader some of the flavor of those rumbustious years.

"Placing a story in a different historical context from our own adds an additional dimension to it. At the same time, an author should not do so purely for reasons of embellishment. In my view, a period setting should be used to add to our understanding of society as it was then, and perhaps help us to evaluate our own attitudes. The written histories of Victorian times are concerned with the rich and powerful, with the burgeoning of empire, and the extension of the Anglo-Saxon ethic throughout the world. Yet these very people were imprisoned in a caste system that kept women in aimless subordination and that was subject to an evangelical moral code of stultifying rigidity. The vast majority of the population, however, lived a very different life—insecure, often at subsistence level, where getting a living absorbed all their time and energy and where pleasures were savoured all the more because they were few.

"My novels are written in response to 'tell me a story' rather than 'set me a puzzle.' I want my characters to be recognizable as real people, not just lay figures to hang a convoluted plot on. Sergeant Bragg comes from the bottom of the pile. He is a countryman, with only basic formal education. He has developed a view of right and wrong that only loosely accords with justice under the law, and a cynical attitude to the upper-class society it is his function to protect. Constable Morton, on the other hand, is a young man from a wealthy and influential family. He has a university degree and a conviction that he ought to do something useful with his life. From their differing viewpoints, I hope the reader will get a fresh insight into one of the most exciting periods in our history."

*   *   *

HART, Benjamin   1958-

PERSONAL: Born February 18, 1958, in New York, N.Y.; son of Jeffrey Peter (a professor of English) and Stephanie (Woods) Hart. *Education:* Dartmouth College, B.A., 1982. *Politics:* Conservative/Republican. *Religion:* Roman Catholic.

ADDRESSES: Home—W-339, 1111 Arlington Blvd., Arlington, Va. 22209. *Office*—Heritage Foundation, 214 Massachusetts Ave. N.E., Washington, D.C. 20002.

CAREER: Heritage Foundation (public policy research group), Washington, D.C., political analyst, beginning in 1983; writer.

WRITINGS:

Poisoned Ivy (nonfiction), Stein & Day, 1984.

Contributor of articles to newspapers and magazines, including *National Review, Policy Review, Detroit News, Washington Post,* and *USA Today.*

SIDELIGHTS: A founder of the controversial right-wing student newspaper *Dartmouth Review,* Benjamin Hart recounts his experiences as a conservative undergraduate on the campus of Dartmouth College during the early 1980s in his book *Poisoned Ivy.* The volume centers on his work with the *Review,* which he and other conservative students began publishing in 1980 to oppose what they saw as a prevailing liberal "ethos" among the Dartmouth faculty and administration. Funded with large grants from rightist alumni and foundations and advised by Hart's father Jeffrey, a Dartmouth professor and columnist for the conservative *National Review,* the weekly newspaper quickly inflamed tempers with its acerbic diatribes denouncing student sexual "deviancy" (homosexuality), college affirmative action programs, and elective courses on women's studies and black history. The *Dartmouth Review* also stirred controversy by charging certain black and women faculty members (the latter dubbed "professorettes") with incompetence, among other things. Perhaps the most notorious incident involving the *Review* occurred in May, 1982, when a black college administrator scuffled with Hart and bit him in the ribs while attempting to prevent the student publisher from distributing his paper. Hart describes the altercation in *Poisoned Ivy,* but, critics noted, omits the fact that it followed a provocative *Review*

article that mocked black students in exaggerated dialect and characterized them as freeloading underachievers and struck many members of the Dartmouth community as blatantly racist.

From the controversial birth of the *Dartmouth Review* Hart broadens his focus in *Poisoned Ivy* to lament the decline of social and academic traditions at Dartmouth, arguing that a new liberal-left "Establishment" with little tolerance for opposing views has usurped control of the college and other elite Ivy League institutions. The author advocates a return to a core curriculum, reflects on the character-building aspects of football, and waxes nostalgic about the partying life with his conservative fraternity brothers, among them an Evelyn Waugh devotee who carried a foam rubber shark named Chesterton on a leash. According to Hart, growing numbers of collegians nationwide share his conservative values, representing a new, right-leaning student movement. "In my view," the author writes, "there is a counter-revolution brewing on campus, and it is going to roll back much of what we are left with from the Sixties. The weapons employed by the new revolutionaries will not be pot, placards, riots, and a sloppy physical appearance, but ideas, wit, and creativity."

Hart finds liberalism unappealing to college students in the Ronald Reagan era in part because they identify it with social criticism and personal self-questioning. "It's all somehow connected: feminism, atheism, Marxism, liberalism, and unattractiveness," he states in *Poisoned Ivy.* In an interview with Lloyd Grove of the *Washington Post,* the author elaborated, "Liberals are always in self-analysis. It's constant self-evaluation. You know, am I really a sexist? Should my entire generation be forced to live out in a desert until we all die off, because there's no other way we can get rid of the sexist attitudes in society? I think constant self-evaluation and self-psychoanalysis is kind of damaging—and really inhibiting."

Poisoned Ivy is indeed "devoid of the neurotic self-absorption of so many college writers," *Christian Science Monitor* reviewer Jim Bencivenga observed. "If nothing else, the college can use it as evidence that someone knows how to teach writing at Dartmouth. Readers not directly connected with this campus may not be so keenly interested in the institutional self-analysis. But they will find the liberal and conservative biases pinpointed by Hart more than entertaining." *New Republic*'s Chuck Lane also judged *Poisoned Ivy* "a lively read" although "its prose is straight out of freshman English. Moreover, its thesis—that Dartmouth's administration was 'openly hostile toward American values' and persecuted the *Review* because it dared to stand up for Western culture and patriotism—is barely credible." Diane Saenz of *Washington Post Book World* concurred that Hart "does not construct a watertight case" for liberal intolerance at Dartmouth, but added that his descriptions of "colorful characters" and his "philosophical, albeit often sarcastic asides" make the book "very entertaining to read, no matter what your political persuasion."

Events on campuses in the years since *Poisoned Ivy* was published have failed to bear out Hart's prediction of a conservative counterrevolution in the making. Although the *Dartmouth Review* inspired a number of similar conservative student newspapers, liberal and leftist students also took a high profile in the latter years of the Reagan administration, launching numerous actions on campuses across the country to protest apartheid in South Africa and the United States's intervention in Central America. Hart himself, though, remains a conservative stalwart who now works as a political analyst for the right-wing Heritage Foundation think tank in Washington, D.C.

In addition to his research project work, he contributes to the foundation's quarterly journal *Policy Review* and organizes lectures and discussions for a group of young conservatives called the Third Generation.

Hart told *CA:* "I consider myself an ardent defender of the free market and of individual liberty generally. I am skeptical of all government intervention, while recognizing the need to protect our national security from the greatest evil of the century, namely the Soviet empire. I am a believing Christian and a strong proponent of religious freedom, including the right to express one's religious beliefs in public institutions, now prohibited by the Supreme Court's interpretation of the Constitution."

BIOGRAPHICAL/CRITICAL SOURCES:

PERIODICALS

Christian Science Monitor, December 24, 1984.
Commentary, April, 1985.
Detroit Free Press, January 7, 1985.
Los Angeles Times Book Review, December 23, 1984.
National Review, December 14, 1984.
New Republic, February 11, 1985.
New York Times, December 12, 1984.
Washington Post, November 13, 1984.
Washington Post Book World, March 8, 1985.

—Sketch by Curtis Skinner

*   *   *

HARTMANN, Betsy
See HARTMANN, Elizabeth

*   *   *

HARTMANN, Elizabeth 1951-
(Betsy Hartmann)

PERSONAL: Born July 20, 1951, in Princeton, N.J.; daughter of Thomas B. (a professor) and Martha (an activist; maiden name, Bothfeld) Hartmann; married James Kenneth Boyce (an economist), November 17, 1976; children: Jamie, Thomas. *Education:* Yale University, B.A. (magna cum laude), 1974. *Politics:* "Progressive."

CAREER: Writer, 1980—. Project manager at Economic Development Bureau, New Haven, Conn.; visiting lecturer in economics at Yale University; public speaker on issues of international development and reproductive rights. Fellow of Institute for Food and Development Policy, 1978-79.

MEMBER: Women's Global Network on Reproductive Rights, Bangladesh International Action Group, National Women's Health Network, National Writers Union, New England Women and Development Group.

AWARDS, HONORS: Howland fellowship, 1974.

WRITINGS:

UNDER NAME BETSY HARTMANN

(With husband, James Boyce) *Needless Hunger: Voices From a Bangladesh Village*, Institute for Food and Development Policy, 1979.
(With Boyce) *A Quiet Violence: View From a Bangladesh Village*, Institute for Food and Development Policy, 1983.

(With Hilary Standing) *Food, Saris, and Sterilization: Population Control in Bangladesh*, Bangladesh International Action Group, 1985.
Reproductive Rights and Wrongs: The Global Politics of Population Control and Contraceptive Choice, Harper, 1987.

Contributor to magazines and newspapers in the United States and abroad, including *Nation*, *New Internationalist*, and *South*.

WORK IN PROGRESS: A novel.

SIDELIGHTS: Elizabeth Hartmann told *CA:* "I became interested in international development issues by virtue of living and working in India and Bangladesh. I first went to India in 1968 as an exchange student and then returned in 1971 as a volunteer. In 1974 I went to Bangladesh with the goal of learning Bengali, living in a village and getting to know the people, and writing a book about the experience. While there I became interested in how aid from the United States and the World Bank was essentially benefitting the rich and how the philosophy of population control was hindering the development of family planning and health services.

"My writing to date has been an attempt to present these issues in a readable, comprehensive way to the general public and to initiate debate over relevant aspects of U.S. foreign policy. In *Reproductive Rights and Wrongs*, I bring a feminist perspective to the population problem. I argue that rapid population growth is not the *cause* of poverty in the third world, but rather a reflection of people's—and especially women's—lack of basic rights, notably the right to food, employment, education, and health care. Ironically, population control does little to improve this situation and often makes matters worse. The narrow goal of reducing birth rates as fast as possible has distorted the process of contraceptive development in the West and undermined many health and family planning programs in the third world, so that they do not meet women's needs. I believe there should be a fundamental shift in population policy away from the obsession with population reduction towards the expansion of basic rights and individual reproductive choice.

"I am currently writing a novel, but intend to stay active, both through writing and campaigning, in the international development field, as well as in the women's health movement."

*   *   *

HARVEY, Andrew 1952-

BRIEF ENTRY: Born in 1952 in India. English educator, translator, poet, and author. Harvey, who spent much of his childhood in India, was educated in England, became a fellow of Oxford University's All Souls College, and taught at Hobart and William Smith Colleges in the United States. Since early in his career critics have praised his poetry, which has appeared in several collections, including *Masks and Faces* (Deutsch, 1978) and *No Diamonds, No Hat, No Honey* (Houghton, 1984). In 1981 Harvey made a pilgrimage to the Himalayan district of Ladakh, India, in search of spiritual enlightenment from Buddhist teachers. He recounted the experience in *A Journey in Ladakh* (Houghton, 1983) and used similar material in such novels as *One Last Mirror* (Houghton, 1985) and *The Web* (Houghton, 1987). With Anne Pennington he translated three works from Yugoslavian languages, including Vasko Popa's compilation of Serbian folk literature, *The Golden Apple: A Round of Stories, Songs, Spells, Proverbs, and Riddles* (Rex Collings, 1980).

BIOGRAPHICAL/CRITICAL SOURCES:

BOOKS

Harvey, Andrew, *A Journey in Ladakh*, Houghton, 1983.

PERIODICALS

Atlantic Monthly, July, 1983.
Los Angeles Times Book Review, August 18, 1985.
Times Literary Supplement, December 11, 1987.

*   *   *

HARVEY, Brett   1936-

PERSONAL: Born April 28, 1936, in New York, N.Y.; daughter of Robert (a stockbroker) and Marjorie (a writer; maiden name, Abbott) Harvey; married Louis Vuolo, 1960 (divorced, 1971); children: Robert, Katherine. *Education:* Attended Northwestern University, 1956-59.

ADDRESSES: Home—305 8th Ave., Brooklyn, N.Y. 11215.

CAREER: WBAI-FM, New York, N.Y., drama and literature director, 1971-74; *The Feminist Press*, Old Westbury, N.Y., publicity and promotion director, 1974-80; free-lance journalist, book critic, and children's book author, 1980—.

MEMBER: Authors Guild, National Writers' Union (co-chair of New York local).

AWARDS, HONORS: My Prairie Year was named a notable children's book by the American Library Association, 1986, and was named to the William Allen White Award Master List for 1988-89; award from Philadelphia Children's Reading Round Table, 1986, and Golden Sower Award nomination from Nebraska Library Association, 1988, both for *My Prairie Year.*

WRITINGS:

My Prairie Year (juvenile), Holiday House, 1986.
Immigrant Girl (juvenile), Holiday House, 1987.
Cassie's Journey (juvenile), Holiday House, 1988.
(Editor) *Various Gifts: Brooklyn Fiction*, Fund for Borough of Brooklyn, 1988.

Contributor of articles to periodicals, including *Village Voice, New York Times Book Review, Psychology Today, Voice Literary Supplement*, and *Mademoiselle.*

WORK IN PROGRESS: A book about American women in the 1950s for Harper & Row.

SIDELIGHTS: Brett Harvey told *CA:* "An incorrigible activist, the moment I became a freelancer in 1981 I realized that isolation and low pay were my deadly enemies, and joined the then-fledgling National Writers' Union (NWU) to remedy both. I now juggle my writing with union organizing—sometimes one takes precedence, sometimes the other. I'm co-chief-steward of the NWU's campaign to get a contract for *Village Voice* freelancers, and serve as co-chair of the New York local. Also, now that I'm working on a book for a major publisher, I've become keenly aware of the importance of the NWU's 'fair pay and fair treatment' campaign for book authors. Our initial goals include timely payments, comprehensible royalty statements, and non-returnable advances—surely all authors deserve these as a minimum!"

BIOGRAPHICAL/CRITICAL SOURCES:

PERIODICALS

New York Times Book Review, September 13, 1987.

HARVEY, Geoffrey   1943-

PERSONAL: Born October 25, 1943, in Bournemouth, England; son of Cyril Alfred (a printer) and Joan (a housewife; maiden name, Allen) Harvey; married Lynne Dodsworth (a librarian), August 29, 1970; children: Nicholas Peter, Michael Richard. *Education:* University of Hull, B.A., 1966, Ph.D., 1972. *Politics:* Social Democrat. *Religion:* Christian.

ADDRESSES: Home—4 Kirkwood Cres., Burghfield Common, Reading RG7 3LL, England. *Office*—Bulmershe College of Higher Education, Woodlands Ave., Earley, Reading RG6 1HY, England.

CAREER: Dalhousie University, Halifax, Nova Scotia, assistant professor of English, 1970-74; Bulmershe College of Higher Education, Reading, England, principal lecturer in English, 1975—.

WRITINGS:

The Art of Anthony Trollope, Weidenfeld & Nicolson, 1980.
The Romantic Tradition in Modern English Poetry: Rhetoric and Experience, Macmillan, 1986.
D. H. Lawrence: "Sons and Lovers"; The Critics' Debate, Macmillan, 1987.
(Editor) Anthony Trollope, *Mr. Scarborough's Family*, Oxford University Press, 1988.

Contributor to literature journals.

SIDELIGHTS: Geoffrey Harvey told *CA:* "I am particularly interested in literature of the nineteenth and twentieth centuries. In my literary criticism I adopt a broadly formalist approach."

BIOGRAPHICAL/CRITICAL SOURCES:

PERIODICALS

Times Literary Supplement, April 17, 1987, July 3, 1987.

*   *   *

HASSALL, Anthony J.   1939-

PERSONAL: Born June 1, 1939, in Young, New South Wales, Australia; son of D. J. and L. C. Hassall; married Loretta M. McMahon, May 22, 1955; children: Marcus, Bartley, Sophia. *Education:* University of New South Wales, B.A. (with honors), 1964; Monash University, Ph.D., 1970.

ADDRESSES: Office—Department of English, James Cook University, Townsville, Queensland 4811, Australia.

CAREER: University of Newcastle, Newcastle, Australia, lecturer, 1968-74, senior lecturer in English, 1975-82; James Cook University, Townsville, Australia, professor of English, 1983—. Executive director of Foundation for Australian Literary Studies, 1983—.

WRITINGS:

Henry Fielding's "Tom Jones," Sydney University Press, 1979.
Strange Country: A Study of Randolph Stow, University of Queensland Press, 1986.

WORK IN PROGRESS: A book on the fiction of Peter Carey.

SIDELIGHTS: Anthony J. Hassall told *CA:* "I am currently particularly interested in recent Australian fiction, especially the writing of Randolph Stow, Patrick White, and Peter Carey, and the ways in which they explore the European experience of the strange country of the Australian continent.''

* * *

HATFIELD, Julie (Stockwell) 1940-

PERSONAL: Born March 22, 1940, in Detroit, Mich.; daughter of William Hume and Ruth Reed (Palmer) Stockwell; married Philip Mitchell Hatfield, August 1, 1964 (divorced, 1979); married Timothy Leland, November 23, 1984; children: (first marriage) Christian Andrew, Juliana, Jason David; (second marriage; stepchildren) Christian Bourso, London Chamberlain. *Education:* University of Michigan, B.A., 1962. *Religion:* Episcopalian.

ADDRESSES: Office—Boston Globe, Boston, Mass. 02107.

CAREER: Women's Wear Daily, New York, N.Y., staff writer, 1962-64; *Bath-Brunswick Times,* Brunswick, Me., feature writer, 1964-68; *Wisconsin State Journal,* Madison, feature writer, 1964-68; *Quincy Patriot Ledger,* Quincy, Mass., feature writer, 1968-77; *Boston Herald,* Boston, Mass., music critic and fashion editor, 1977-79; *Boston Globe,* Boston, fashion editor, 1979—.

AWARDS, HONORS: Grant from National Endowment for the Arts, 1973; Lulu Award from Men's Fashion Association, 1985; Atrium Award from the University of Georgia, 1987.

WRITINGS:

(With Ruth Weinstein and Lois Diefendorf) *Guide to the Recommended Thrift Shops of New England: Financial Survival in the Eighties,* Globe Pequot, 1982.

Contributor to travel magazines.

WORK IN PROGRESS: More travel relating to fashion writing for the *Boston Globe.*

SIDELIGHTS: Some of Julie Hatfield's travel articles are based on her own experiences, including bicycling in France and northern Italy, skiing with a family in France, and visiting a French chef.

Hatfield told *CA:* ''A very personal effect of my travel has been the benefits to my children, each of whom I have taken with me separately on my various travels to international fashion shows. For me, the travel changes my narrow midwestern and Boston viewpoint on what is beautiful and what is atrocious; it opens my mind to accept looks and styles that I never would have dreamed were valid before the travel. My writing on fashion I hope expresses my personal view that fashion is not so much an activity of snobbism and 'one-up-manship,' but an expression of an artistic and creative mind that simply appears on some people as clothing and a way of putting themselves together. It is something fun in an often too-serious world—in the same way as are concerts, artist's shows, and poetry readings: they're not necessary but they're a delightful addition to one's life.

''If a dramatic photo and good fashion writing can draw a young person into the newspaper who would not otherwise be interested in reading, so much the better for this television age in which so few youngsters have been turned on to the written work and its joys. I would do almost anything for shock value, as far as photography and layout, to entice a young reader into reading more and using the language.

''*Guide to the Recommended Thrift Shops of New England* was written because of the tremendous interest I saw among New Englanders in getting a fashion bargain. They are obsessive about finding something for almost nothing when it comes to wearing apparel! It's as much of a game for the true Yankee as is the stock market.''

* * *

HAWKING, S. W.
See HAWKING, Stephen W(illiam)

* * *

HAWKING, Stephen W(illiam) 1942-
(S. W. Hawking)

BRIEF ENTRY: Born January 8, 1942, in Oxford, England. British physicist, educator, editor, and author. Frequently compared with such important theoretical physicists as Galileo and Albert Einstein, Hawking has developed significant theories on gravity, the origin of the universe, and previously undetected emissions, now known as ''Hawking radiation,'' from so-called black holes. The physicist, who is almost completely paralyzed from a neuromuscular disorder commonly known as Lou Gehrig's disease, holds Cambridge University's Lucasian Chair in mathematics—a post formerly held by Isaac Newton, the British natural philosopher who conceived the idea of universal gravitation. Among Hawking's numerous awards for achievement in mathematics and physics are the 1975 Pius XI Gold Medal from the Pontifical Academy of Sciences, the 1976 Dannie Heineman Prize for Mathematical Physics from the American Physical Society and the American Institute of Physics, the 1985 Royal Astronomical Society Gold Medal, and the 1987 Paul Dirac Medal and Prize from the Institute of Physics.

Hawking is the editor and author, under different variations of his name, of numerous works for both scientists and lay readers, including his best-selling book *A Brief History of Time: From the Big Bang to Black Holes* (Bantam, 1988). He has also written *Is the End in Sight for Theoretical Physics? An Inaugural Lecture* (Cambridge University Press, 1980); co-authored *The Large Scale Structure of Space-time* (Cambridge University Press, 1973); and co-edited *Superspace and Supergravity: Proceedings of the Nuffield Workshop* (Cambridge University Press, 1981), *The Very Early Universe: Proceedings of the Nuffield Workshop* (Cambridge University Press, 1983), and *Three Hundred Years of Gravitation* (Cambridge University Press, 1987). *Addresses: Home*—5 West Rd., Cambridge, England.

BIOGRAPHICAL/CRITICAL SOURCES:

BOOKS

Current Biography Yearbook, H. W. Wilson, 1984.
Who's Who, 140th edition, St. Martin's, 1988.

PERIODICALS

Newsweek, June 13, 1988.
New York Times Book Review, April 3, 1988.
Washington Post Book World, April 3, 1988.

* * *

HAWKINS, Angus 1953-

PERSONAL: Born April 12, 1953, in Portsmouth, England; immigrated to United States, 1982; son of Brian (a banker) and Janette (Thomson) Hawkins; married Esther Hawkins, May

24, 1980; children: Emma Victoria. *Education:* University of Reading, B.A. (with honors), 1975; London School of Economics and Political Science, London, Ph.D., 1979.

ADDRESSES: Office—Department of History, Loyola Marymount University, Loyola Blvd. West 80th St., Los Angeles, Calif. 90045.

CAREER: Harlaxton College, Grantham, England, professor of history, 1979-82; Loyola Marymount University, Los Angeles, assistant professor, 1982-86, associate professor of modern British history, 1986—, T. H. Chilton Professor of Research in the Humanities, 1987. Academic visitor at London School of Economics and Political Science, London, 1983 and 1987.

MEMBER: American Historical Association, Institute of Historical Research.

WRITINGS:

Parliament, Party, and the Art of Politics in Britain, 1855-1859, Stanford University Press, 1987.

Contributor to *Victorian Studies, Parliamentary History*, and *Journal of British Studies*.

WORK IN PROGRESS: A political biography of the fourteenth Earl of Derby (1799-1869); an edition of the journal of Sir Charles Wood, First Viscount Halifax.

SIDELIGHTS: Angus Hawkins told *CA:* "My major intellectual interests are political theory and the relationship between doctrine, language, and policy. Investigations of this relationship have focused on the transition to democracy and the attendant constitutional and parliamentary issues that accompanied this change in Victorian England. These specific concerns are framed within a broader interest in the experience of modern British society over the past three hundred years, and the opportunities and dilemmas facing Britain today.

"I was drawn to a study of the years 1855 to 1859 because it was a curiously neglected period of obvious significance, given the fact that the British Liberal party was formulated, in a Parliamentary sense, in 1859. The question therefore arose, what occurred and how did events develop so as to lead to that momentous outcome? *Parliament, Party, and the Art of Politics* is an attempt to answer that question.

"Lord Derby is worthy of a full-scale biography for a number of reasons. First, he is the first British statesman to have become prime minister on three occasions. Second, he remains the longest-serving party leader in modern British politics. Finally, for a variety of reasons, no full-scale study of his career, based upon his own papers and correspondence, has ever been written. This glaring gap in historical literature requires filling."

AVOCATIONAL INTERESTS: Music, the theater, modern literature.

*   *   *

HAZEN, Margaret Hindle   1948-

PERSONAL: Born May 14, 1948, in Philadelphia, Pa.; daughter of Brooke (a historian) and Helen (a psychologist; maiden name, Morris) Hindle; married Robert M. Hazen (a scientist), August 9, 1969; children: Benjamin, Elizabeth. *Education:* Wellesley College, B.A., 1970; Simmons College, M.L.S., 1971; Boston University, M.A., 1974.

ADDRESSES: Home—Bethesda, Md. *Office*—9105 East Parkhill Dr., Bethesda, Md. 20814. *Agent*—Gabriele Pantucci, 92 Chilton Court, Baker St., London NW1 5TE, England.

CAREER: Boston University, Boston, Mass., cataloger at Mugar Memorial Library, 1971-73; New England Historic Genealogical Society, Boston, manuscript and rare book librarian, 1974-75; raising children and reading at home, 1975-87; Archives Center, National Museum of American History, Smithsonian Institution, Washington, D.C., consultant, 1987—.

MEMBER: American Library Association, Organization of American Historians, Sonneck Society, Beta Phi Mu.

WRITINGS:

(With husband, Robert M. Hazen) *American Geological Literature, 1669-1850*, Dowden, Hutchinson/Ross, 1980.
(With Robert M. Hazen) *Wealth Inexhaustible: A History of America's Mineral Industries to 1850*, Van Nostrand, 1985.
(With Robert M. Hazen) *The Music Men: An Illustrated History of Brass Bands in America, 1800-1920*, Smithsonian Institution Press, 1987.

WORK IN PROGRESS: A book on the cultural history of fire in America, with Robert M. Hazen, publication by Princeton University Press expected in 1990.

SIDELIGHTS: According to critic Esmond Wright of the *New York Times Book Review, The Music Men* is a tribute to the way of life which featured band concerts in the town square. In this book, Margaret Hindle Hazen and her husband have provided a lavishly illustrated history of the brass band movement of nineteenth-century America. They have related the presence of the brass band to a fervid community spirit, one which suffered a rapid decline after the turn of the century. The authors concentrated on the variety of music performed and the wide range of community functions the bands fulfilled. To Wright, these bands were a symbol of "a unique and thoroughly democratic movement," and the Hazens' book is "a stunning account," a "compelling testimony to the important cultural elements of the American brass band movement."

Margaret Hindle Hazen told *CA:* "My attitude toward writing is similar to that of Peter De Vries: I like being a writer but I don't care for the paperwork! Nevertheless, one book seems inevitably to lead to another. In an age of specialization I'm an incurable generalist and, with my husband as collaborator, have spent the last ten years reading and writing about various aspects of nineteenth-century American history."

BIOGRAPHICAL/CRITICAL SOURCES:

PERIODICALS

New York Times Book Review, July 5, 1987.
Washington Post Book World, November 29, 1987, December 6, 1987.

*   *   *

HAZLETON, Lesley   1945-

BRIEF ENTRY: Born September 20, 1945, in England; immigrated to United States, 1979. Psychologist, educator, journalist, and writer. Hazleton is consistently praised for her writings on psychology and on Israeli concerns. Three of her books, *Israeli Women: The Reality Behind the Myth* (Simon & Schuster, 1978), *Where Mountains Roar: A Personal Report From the Sinai and Negev Desert* (Holt, 1980), and *Jerusalem, Jerusalem: A Memoir of War and Peace, Passion and Politics*

(Atlantic Monthly Press, 1986), are based on her observations and experiences in Jerusalem, where she lived from 1966 to 1979. *Israeli Women* was named best book of the year for current affairs by the *New York Times,* and *Jerusalem, Jerusalem* won the Present Tense/Joel H. Cavior Literary Award from the American Jewish Committee. Hazleton, a psychologist, also wrote *The Right to Feel Bad: Coming to Terms With Normal Depression* (Doubleday, 1984), which received an award for medical self-care. She is a visiting professor of creative writing at Pennsylvania State University, and she has lectured in writing and psychology at several other American universities and colleges since moving to the United States in 1979. During the late 1960s and 1970s she was a features writer for the *Jerusalem Post* and a reporter for the Jerusalem bureau of *Time-Life.* Hazleton has also contributed articles to numerous magazines and newspapers. *Addresses: Agent*—Watkins, Loomis Agency, Inc., 150 East 35th St., New York, N.Y. 10016.

BIOGRAPHICAL/CRITICAL SOURCES:

PERIODICALS

Nation, June 21, 1986.
New York Times Book Review, February 26, 1978.
Time, June 18, 1984.

*   *   *

HEATH, Robert L.   1941-

PERSONAL: Born November 3, 1941, in Hotchkiss, Colo.; son of James L. (a farmer) and Mary A. (a housewife; maiden name, Houseweart) Heath; married Mary V. Bradley (an expediter), September 11, 1965; children: Janna Marie. *Education:* Western State College of Colorado, B.A., 1963; University of New Mexico, M.A., 1965; University of Illinois at Urbana-Champaign, Ph.D., 1971.

ADDRESSES: Home—11815 South Nottingham, Houston, Tex. 77071. *Office*—School of Communication, University of Houston Central Campus, University Park, 4800 Calhoun Rd., Houston, Tex. 77004.

CAREER: University of New Mexico, Albuquerque, instructor in communication, 1965-66; Purdue University, Fort Wayne Campus (now Indiana University—Purdue University at Fort Wayne), Fort Wayne, Ind., instructor in communication and director of forensics, 1966-68; University of Houston Central Campus, Houston, Tex., assistant professor, 1971-75, associate professor, 1975-87, professor of communication, 1987—, founding director of the Institute for the Study of Issues Management, associate director of graduate studies and curriculum development, 1983-86, director of graduate studies, 1977-86. Principal and consultant with Communication Management. Chairman of Planning Commission of Missouri City, Tex., 1977—.

MEMBER: International Communication Association, Speech Communication Association, Modern Language Association of America, Issues Management Association, Southern Speech Communication Association.

AWARDS, HONORS: Grant from Edison Electric Institute, 1987.

WRITINGS:

(With Richard Alan Nelson) *Issues Management: Corporate Public Policymaking in an Information Society,* Sage Publications, 1986.

Realism and Relativism: A Perspective on Kenneth Burke, Mercer University Press, 1986.
Strategic Issues Management, Jossey-Bass, 1988.
(With Jennings Bryant) *Human Communication Theories and Research: Concepts, Contexts, and Challenges,* Erlbaum Publications, 1989.

Contributor of more than thirty articles, reviews, and editorials to communication journals and newspapers.

SIDELIGHTS: Robert L. Heath told *CA:* "Three writers have been extraordinarily influential upon my work. Aristotle offered sage advice upon the tactics of rhetoric and the role of rhetoric in society. Kenneth Burke provided insight into how motivation is tied to language. He argued that people are best understood by examining their unique ability to use words. James Madison's writings on government laid out a solid rationale justifying the importance of public discussion of controversial issues."

*   *   *

HECK, Frank H(opkins)   1904-1983

OBITUARY NOTICE—See index for *CA* sketch: Born October 18, 1904, in Racine, Wis.; died March 30, 1983; buried in Bellevue Cemetery, Danville, Ky. Educator and author. Heck was a history professor for most of his career, teaching at Nebraska State Teachers College from 1929 to 1938, at Miami University of Ohio from 1938 to 1948, and at Centre College from 1948 to 1974. He wrote *The Civil War Veteran in Minnesota Life and Politics; Proud Kentuckian: John C. Breckinridge, 1821-1875;* and *A Century and a Half on Main Street: Trinity Episcopal Church, 1829-1979.* He also contributed to history journals.

OBITUARIES AND OTHER SOURCES:

BOOKS

Directory of American Scholars, Volume I: *History,* 8th edition, Bowker, 1982.
Who Was Who in America, With World Notables, Volume VIII: *1982-1985,* Marquis, 1985.

*   *   *

HEISS, Jerold (Sheldon)   1930-

PERSONAL: Born March 4, 1930, in Brooklyn, N.Y.; children: two. *Education:* New York University, B.A., 1951, M.A., 1953; Indiana University—Bloomington, Ph.D., 1958.

ADDRESSES: Office—Department of Sociology, University of Connecticut, Storrs, Conn. 06268.

CAREER: Cornell University, Ithaca, N.Y., assistant statistician at medical college, 1955-56; University of Connecticut, Storrs, instructor, 1958-60, assistant professor, 1960-64, associate professor, 1964-68, professor of sociology, 1968—. Research specialist for Middlesex County Heart Study, 1959; visiting research fellow in Western Australia, 1962-63.

MEMBER: American Sociological Association.

WRITINGS:

(Editor) *Family Roles and Interaction: An Anthology,* Rand McNally, 1968, 2nd edition, 1976.
(Editor) *Readings on the Sociology of the Caribbean,* MSS Educational Publishing, 1970.

The Case of the Black Family: A Sociological Inquiry, Columbia University Press, 1975.
The Social Psychology of Interaction, Prentice-Hall, 1981.
(Contributor) Morris Rosenberg and Ralph H. Turner, editors, *Social Psychology: Sociological Perspectives*, Basic Books, 1981.
(Contributor) Harriet McAdoo, editor, *The Black Family*, Sage Publications, 1981.
(Contributor) Frances A. Boudreau, Roger W. Sennott, and Michele Wilson, editors, *Sex Roles and Social Patterns*, Praeger, 1985.

Contributor to sociology journals, including *American Sociological Review, Marriage and Family Living, Sociometry, Human Relations, Journal of Marriage and the Family, International Migration, Human Organization, Sociological Quarterly, Social Forces, American Journal of Sociology*, and *Sociology and Social Research.*

*   *   *

HELMINIAK, Daniel A.   1942-

PERSONAL: Surname is pronounced "Hel-*min*-i-ak"; born November 20, 1942, in Pittsburgh, Pa.; son of Albert F. (a bricklayer) and Cecelia (a housewife; maiden name, Ziolkowski) Helminiak. *Education:* St. Vincent College, B.A., 1964; Gregorian University, Rome, S.T.B., 1966, S.T.L., 1968; Boston College, Ph.D., 1979; Boston University, M.A., 1983; doctoral study at University of Texas at Austin.

ADDRESSES: Home—P.O. Box 13527, Austin, Tex. 78711.

CAREER: Ordained Roman Catholic priest, 1967; associate pastor of Roman Catholic church in Pittsburgh, Pa., 1968-72; Paulist Leadership Project, Boston, Mass., coordinator, 1979-81; Oblate School of Theology, San Antonio, Tex., assistant professor of theology, 1981-85; writer. Mental health worker at McLean Hospital, Boston, 1980-81; chaplain to Dignity/Boston, 1976-81, Dignity/San Antonio, 1982-85, Dignity/Austin, 1985-88.

MEMBER: American Academy of Religion, American Association of Pastoral Counselors, American Psychological Association, Catholic Theological Society of America, Society for the Scientific Study of Religion.

AWARDS, HONORS: Honorable mention from *Catholic Journalist*, 1987, for *The Same Jesus: A Contemporary Christology.*

WRITINGS:

The Same Jesus: A Contemporary Christology, Loyola University Press, 1986.
Spiritual Development: An Interdisciplinary Study, Loyola University Press, 1987.

Contributor to magazines, including *Heythrop Journal, Journal of Pastoral Care, New Blackfriars, Spiritual Life, Journal of Religion and Health*, and *Spirituality Today.*

WORK IN PROGRESS: Research on a psychological (nontheist) treatment of spirituality; research on human sexuality and spirituality.

SIDELIGHTS: Daniel A. Helminiak told *CA:* "*The Same Jesus* clarifies the essence of Christianity and contrasts it with other religions. *Spiritual Development* distinguishes and relates Christianity, theism, and authentic humanism. My current work is to fill out the meaning and implications of authentic humanism for psychology. This project will challenge psychology to expand its horizons to address human spiritual issues adequately and will challenge theology to cede to psychology treatment of many religious—but actually human—issues that cut across all religions. The plan is to integrate the thought of Bernard Lonergan with that of humanistic and developmental psychologists. To this end, I am presently working on a doctorate in psychology, human development, and personality, to be completed by 1991."

Helminiak's languages include French, German, Italian, Greek, Latin, and Spanish.

*   *   *

HELWEG, Hans H.   1917-

PERSONAL: Born February 21, 1917, in Denmark; immigrated to United States, 1939; married Jane Barrett (an actress). *Education:* Attended Hornsey Art School, Heatherley School of Art, and Royal Academy of Art, Oslo, Norway.

CAREER: Author and illustrator of children's books. *Military service:* U.S. Army Air Forces, war artist, 1942-46; served in Europe.

AWARDS, HONORS: The Tales of Olga da Polga was named one of the Children's Books of the Year of the Child Study Association of America, 1973, and a Notable Book of the American Library Association.

WRITINGS:

FOR CHILDREN

Farm Animals, Random House, 1978.
Animal Babies, Collins, 1981.
Caring for Your Pet, Collins, 1981.
Dogs and Puppies, Collins, 1981.
Animals on the Farm, Collins, 1981.

ILLUSTRATOR OF CHILDREN'S BOOKS

A. N. Bedford (pseudonym of Jane Werner Watson), *Roy Rogers and the New Cowboy*, Simon & Schuster, 1953.
Eric M. Knight, *Lassie Come-Home*, abridged edition by Felix Sutton, Grosset, 1954.
Mark Twain (pseudonym of Samuel L. Clemens), *The Adventures of Tom Sawyer*, abridged edition by Anne Terry White, Simon & Schuster, 1956.
Frank Sayers, *Cowboys*, Simon & Schuster, 1956.
M. A. Jagendorf and C. H. Tillhagen, *The Gypsies' Fiddle, and Other Gypsy Tales*, Vanguard, 1956.
Borghild M. Dahl, *The Daughter*, Dutton, 1956.
John M. Schealer, *Zip-Zip and His Flying Saucer*, Dutton, 1956.
Philip D. Jordan, *Fiddlefoot Jones of the North Woods*, Vanguard, 1957.
Borghild M. Dahl, *The Cloud Shoes*, Dutton, 1957.
John M. Schealer, *Zip-Zip Goes to Venus*, Dutton, 1958.
Bryna Untermeyer and Louis Untermeyer, editors, *Unfamiliar Marvels*, Golden Press, 1962.
Charles Dickens, *A Christmas Carol*, Golden Press, 1969.
Hans Christian Andersen, *The Emperor's New Clothes*, Golden Press, 1970.
L. A. Hill, *The Old Woman and Her Pig*, Oxford University Press, 1971.
Michael Bond, *The Tales of Olga da Polga*, Penguin, 1971, reprinted as *Olga da Polga*, Volume I: *Olga Makes a Wish*, Volume II: *Olga's New Home*, Volume III: *Olga Counts Her Blessings*, Volume IV: *Olga Makes Her Mark*,

Volume V: *Olga Takes a Bite,* Volume VI: *Olga's Second House,* Volume VII: *Olga Makes a Friend,* Volume VII: *Olga's Special Day,* Puffin, 1975, published in the United States as separate volumes, EMC Corp., 1977, reprinted as *The First Olga da Polga Book,* Longman, 1983, and *The Second Big Olga da Polga Book,* Longman, 1983.

Bond, *Olga Meets Her Match,* Longman Young Books, 1973, Hastings House, 1975.

Ann Lawrence, *The Travels of Oggy,* Gollancz, 1973.

Bond, *Olga Carries On,* Kestrel Books, 1976, Hastings House, 1977.

Lawrence, *Oggy at Home,* Gollancz, 1977.

Lawrence, *Oggy and the Holiday,* Gollancz, 1979.

Bond, *Olga Takes Charge,* Kestrel Books, 1982.

Bond, *The Complete Adventures of Olga da Polga* (contains *The Tales of Olga da Polga, Olga Meets Her Match, Olga Carries On,* and *Olga Takes Charge*), Delacorte, 1983.*

*　　　*　　　*

HENDERSON, Algo D(onmyer)   1897-1988

OBITUARY NOTICE—See index for *CA* sketch: Born April 26, 1897, in Solomon, Kan.; died of cancer, October 20, 1988, in San Francisco, Calif. Educator, administrator, editor, and author. For much of his career Henderson was concerned with the administration of colleges and universities. He joined Antioch College as a professor of business administration in 1925, also serving as dean from 1930 to 1936 and president from 1936 to 1948. After leaving Antioch in the late 1940s, he spent two years helping to organize and administer the system of colleges known collectively as the State University of New York. From 1950 to 1967 he was a professor of higher education at the University of Michigan, where he created the first doctoral program for college administrators in the United States. Retiring as professor emeritus in 1967, he remained active as a research educator at the Center for Research and Development in Higher Education at the University of California, Berkeley. Henderson's books include *Vitalizing Liberal Education, Antioch College: Its Design for Liberal Education, Policies and Practices in Higher Education, The Innovative Spirit,* and *Ms. Goes to College,* which he wrote with his wife, Jean G. Henderson.

OBITUARIES AND OTHER SOURCES:

PERIODICALS

New York Times, October 24, 1988.

*　　　*　　　*

HENDERSON, Katherine Usher   1937-

PERSONAL: Born June 9, 1937, in Fall River, Mass.; daughter of Munroe M. and Mabel Margaret (Reagan) Usher; married Francis T. Henderson, Jr., June 27, 1959; children: Ellen Elizabeth, Matthew Munroe, Geoffrey Francis. *Education:* Connecticut College for Women (now Connecticut College), A.B., 1959; Radcliffe College, M.A.T., 1960; New York University, M.A., 1964; Columbia University, Ph.D., 1969.

ADDRESSES: Home—75 Columbia Heights, Brooklyn Heights, N.Y. 11201. *Office*—Department of English, College of New Rochelle, New Rochelle, N.Y. 10801.

CAREER: City College of the City University of New York, New York, N.Y., lecturer in English, 1966-67; College of New Rochelle, New Rochelle, N.Y., instructor, 1968-70, as-sistant professor, 1970-73, associate professor, 1973-82, professor of English, 1982—, director of women's studies, 1972-73, dean of School of Arts and Sciences, 1973-78.

MEMBER: Modern Language Association of America, American Association of University Professors, Northeast Modern Language Association.

WRITINGS:

Joan Didion, Ungar, 1980.

(With Barbara F. McManus) *Half Humankind: Contexts and Texts of the Controversy About Women in England, 1540-1640,* University of Illinois Press, 1985.

WORK IN PROGRESS: Research on three modern American women novelists who took literary traditions created by men and redefined them to celebrate the experience of women.

SIDELIGHTS: Katherine Usher Henderson told *CA:* "My writing and teaching have always been linked and even interdependent. I discovered the documents of the controversy about women when my women students in English Renaissance literature asked me whether Renaissance women had ever published their writings.

"In the microfilm holdings of Columbia University I discovered that women had written on many topics, but their writings had never been republished. In addition to the religious topics that one might expect, they had written pamphlets defending the virtue and intelligence of women against men who attacked and satirized women in misogynistic treatises. Their pamphlets are lively, clever, and often learned, although not feminist in the modern sense—that is, they argued not for social change but simply affirmed the worth and dignity of women. I asked my colleague, Barbara McManus, to edit these pamphlets with me both because it was a major task (the book includes a long introduction that places them in both a social and literary context) and because, as a classicist, she was able to translate the Latin passages and annotate the classical allusions.

"I became fascinated by Joan Didion when I taught *Play It As It Lays* in a course on contemporary women novelists. At the time, feminists were highly critical of Didion because her heroines were passive and helpless, but I felt that, through her sympathy with her female characters, she was in fact portraying the problems of women today."

*　　　*　　　*

HENDRICKSON, David C.   1953-

PERSONAL: Born March 22, 1953, in Oklahoma City, Okla.; son of Calvin W. (a lawyer) and Frances (Hewitt) Hendrickson; married Clelia deMoraes (an editor), June 30, 1979. *Education:* Colorado College, B.A., 1976; Johns Hopkins University, Ph.D., 1982.

ADDRESSES: Office—Department of Political Science, Colorado College, Colorado Springs, Colo. 80903.

CAREER: Colorado College, Colorado Springs, assistant professor of political science, 1983—.

WRITINGS:

(With Robert W. Tucker) *The Fall of the First British Empire: The Origins of the War of American Independence,* Johns Hopkins University Press, 1982.

The Future of American Strategy, Holmes & Meier, 1987.

Reforming Defense: The State of American Civil Military Relations, Johns Hopkins University Press, 1988.

WORK IN PROGRESS: The Influence of History Upon Strategy; The Statecraft of Thomas Jefferson, with Tucker.

SIDELIGHTS: The prevailing view among twentieth-century social historians is that the American Revolution was precipitated by misrule of British ministers following the Seven Years War. David C. Hendrickson and his co-author Robert W. Tucker dismiss this explanation, insisting in *The Fall of the British Empire: The Origins of the War of American Independence* that the Americans themselves assisted in creating the problems that led to the revolution. Paul Langford, writing for the *English Historical Review,* praised the authors for displaying "a marked readiness to accept the intractability of the American problem from the British standpoint," and for placing "emphasis . . . on the imperial dilemma, rather than the colonial predicament." Ian R. Christie in the *Times Higher Education Supplement* called *The Fall of the British Empire* "an intellectually enjoyable work, lively and provoking in its critical judgments, and an admirable example of the stiffening which can be given to historical discussion by the skills of the political scientist."

The Future of American Strategy, Hendrickson's 1987 work, discusses American economic policies concerning Western Europe, the Middle East, and "the maintenance of strategic nuclear stability," according to Michael Howard in the *Times Literary Supplement.* The critic praised the author, judging that "On all of these [strategies] he has wise things to say, and he says them in a language which is not only intelligible to the layman, but a pleasure to read." Hendrickson's third book, *Reforming Defense: The State of American Military Relations,* defines and analyzes the three major military reform movements that have arisen in the 1980s. The "organizational reformers" hope for change in the military as an institution; the "administrative reformers" look for change in the vast military bureaucracy; and the "military reformers" claim basic military theories must be overhauled in order to suit the government's changing military strategies.

BIOGRAPHICAL/CRITICAL SOURCES:

PERIODICALS

English Historical Review, fall, 1985.
Times Higher Education Supplement, June 3, 1983.
Times Literary Supplement, October 14, 1983, September 18-24, 1987.

*   *   *

HERMAN, William 1926-

PERSONAL: Born October 19, 1926, in New York, N.Y.; son of Abraham (a carpenter) and Yetta (a housewife; maiden name, Jackson) Herman; married Joanna Clapps (an administrator), December 18, 1976; children: Donna Ann, Lisa Jane, James Paul. *Education:* City College (now of the City University of New York), B.S., 1948; Fordham University, M.F.A., 1949, Ph.D., 1969.

ADDRESSES: Home—370 Riverside Dr., New York, N.Y. 10025. *Office*—Department of English, City College of the City University of New York, New York, N.Y. 10031.

CAREER: City College of the City University of New York, New York, N.Y., lecturer, 1967-69, assistant professor, 1969-74, associate professor, 1974-86, professor of English, 1986—. Visiting professor at New York University, 1981-82; exchange professor at University of Paris VIII, 1982-83.

WRITINGS:

(Contributor) Glauco Cambon, editor, *Pirandello: A Collection of Critical Essays,* Prentice-Hall, 1967.
(With Dennis DeNitto) *Film and the Critical Eye,* Macmillan, 1975.
(Editor and contributor) *Reading, Writing, and Rhetoric,* Holt, 1977.
The Portable English Handbook, Holt, 1978.
(With Jeffrey M. Young) *Troubleshooting: Basic Writing Skills,* Holt, 1978.
Understanding Contemporary American Drama, University of South Carolina Press, 1987.
Basic Writer's Rhetoric, Holt, 1987.

*   *   *

HERR, Pamela (Staley) 1939-

PERSONAL: Born July 24, 1939, in Cambridge, Mass.; daughter of A. Eugene (an economist) and Phyllis (Parker) Staley; children: Christianna, Robin Elizabeth. *Education:* Harvard University, B.A. (magna cum laude), 1961; George Washington University, M.A., 1971.

ADDRESSES: Home and office—2300 Hanover St., Palo Alto, Calif. 94306. *Agent*—Frederick Hill, 2237 Union St., San Francisco, Calif. 94125.

CAREER: Field Educational Publications, Palo Alto, Calif., writer and editor, 1973; Sullivan Associates, Palo Alto, editor, 1973-74; Sanford Associates, Educational Development Corp., Menlo Park, Calif., project manager, 1974-76; *American West,* Cupertino, Calif., managing editor, 1976-79; historian and writer, 1980—.

MEMBER: Coalition for Western Women's History, Western Writers of America, Western History Association, Western Association of Women Historians, Phi Beta Kappa.

AWARDS, HONORS: Grant from National Historical Publications and Records Commission, 1987-88; Western Writers of America Spur Award for best Western nonfiction book, 1987, for *Jesse Benton Fremont: A Biography.*

WRITINGS:

(Contributor) *The Women Who Made the West,* Doubleday, 1980.
Jessie Benton Fremont: A Biography, F. Watts, 1987.
(With Mary Lee Spence) *Selected Letters of Jessie Benton Fremont,* University of Illinois Press, in press.

Contributor of articles and reviews to magazines and newspapers, including *Californians, American West, California History,* and *Western Historical Quarterly.*

*   *   *

HERTZ, Leah 1937-1988

OBITUARY NOTICE: Name originally Leah Treiser; born in 1937 in what is now Israel; naturalized British citizen; died in an accident, September 22, 1988, in Mexico. Scholar, feminist, civic and business leader, tapestry maker, and author. Holder of doctorate degrees from Cambridge University's Darwin College and London City University, Hertz spent much time promoting feminist causes in England, most notably the Women Into Public Life Campaign. In addition, she was founder and managing director of an international association of businesses which included firms in the real estate, clothing, construction, and textile industries. Her commitment to business and women's causes led her to write *In Search of a Small Business Definition* and *The Business Amazons,* the latter becoming a best-seller in both the United States and Great Britain. She was a borough councillor in London and the first woman vice-president of England's Small Business Bureau. Her tapestries have been exhibited in Britain and America.

OBITUARIES AND OTHER SOURCES:

PERIODICALS

Times (London), September 27, 1988.

* * *

HERTZBERG, Hazel W(hitman)   1918-1988

OBITUARY NOTICE—See index for *CA* sketch: Born September 16, 1918, in Brooklyn, N.Y.; died October 19, 1988, in Rome, Italy. Educator and author. Hertzberg spent much of her career teaching history and was considered an expert on the history of native Americans. She was a high school teacher before she joined the faculty of the Teachers College of Columbia University in 1963, beginning as instructor and rising to the rank of associate professor of history and education in 1970. Hertzberg wrote *Anthropological Contribution to the Teaching of State History, Teaching the Age of Homespun, Teaching a Pre-Columbian Culture: The Iroquois, The Great Tree and the Long House: The Culture of the Iroquois,* and *The Search for an American Indian Identity: Modern Pan-Indian Movements.*

OBITUARIES AND OTHER SOURCES:

BOOKS

Directory of American Scholars, Volume I: *History,* 8th edition, Bowker, 1982.

PERIODICALS

New York Times, October 21, 1988.
Washington Post, October 22, 1988.

* * *

HERTZBERG, Hendrik   1943-

PERSONAL: Born July 23, 1943, in New York, N.Y.; son of Sidney (a journalist) and Hazel (a historian; maiden name, Whitman) Hertzberg. *Education:* Harvard University, B.A., 1965. *Politics:* Democrat.

ADDRESSES: Home—1808 Kilbourne Pl., Washington, D.C. 20010. *Office—New Republic,* 1220 Nineteenth St. N.W., Washington, D.C. 20036.

CAREER: U.S. National Student Association, Washington, D.C., editorial director, 1965-66; *Newsweek,* San Francisco, Calif., correspondent, 1966-67; *New Yorker,* New York, N.Y., staff writer, 1969-77; the White House, Washington, D.C., speechwriter, 1977-79, chief speechwriter, 1979-81; *New Republic,* Washington, D.C., editor, 1981-85, contributing editor, 1985-87, correspondent, 1988—. Harvard University, John Fitzgerald Kennedy School of Government, fellow at Institute of Politics, 1985-86, senior associate at Joan Shorenstein Barone Center on the Press, Politics, and Public Policy, 1987-88. *Military service:* U.S. Naval Reserve, active duty, 1967-69; became lieutenant junior grade.

MEMBER: National Press Club, Harvard Club of New York City.

WRITINGS:

One Million (nonfiction), Simon & Schuster, 1970.
(With Marvin Kalb) *Candidates '88* (nonfiction), Auburn House, 1988.

Contributor to magazines and newspapers, including *Dissent, Esquire,* and *New York Times Book Review.*

* * *

HETHERINGTON, Norriss Swigart   1942-

PERSONAL: Born January 30, 1942, in Berkeley, Calif.; son of Norriss Wilburn (a mathematician) and Edith Lorene (Swigart) Hetherington; married Edith Wiley White (a litigation analyst), December 10, 1966; children: Elizabeth Lorene, Robert Norriss. *Education:* University of California, Berkeley, B.A., 1963, M.A., 1965, M.A., 1967; Indiana University—Bloomington, Ph.D., 1970.

ADDRESSES: Home—1742 Spruce, Apt. 201, Berkeley, Calif. 94709. *Office*—Office for History of Science and Technology, 470 Stephens Hall, University of California, Berkeley, Calif. 94720.

CAREER: Agnes Scott College, Decatur, Ga., lecturer in physics and astronomy, 1967-68; York University, Toronto, Ontario, assistant professor of mathematics and science, 1970-72; National Aeronautics and Space Administration, Washington, D.C., administrative specialist in History Office, 1972; University of Kansas, Lawrence, assistant professor of history, 1972-76, chairman of program in history and philosophy of science, 1973-74; Razi University, Samandaj, Iran, assistant professor of science, technology, and society, 1976-77; Cambridge University, Cambridge, England, visiting scholar, 1977-78; Oklahoma University, Norman, associate professor of history of science, 1981; University of California, Berkeley, research associate at Office for History of Science and Technology, 1981—. Founder and managing partner of Berkeley Investments (specializing in merger arbitrage), 1981—. Visiting fellow at Henry E. Huntington Library, 1973; conducted research at Lick Observatory, University of California Space Science Laboratory and Forest Products Laboratory, Cambridge Observatories, and in Iran. Program director of Boys Club of El Cerrito, 1959-64; treasurer of El Cerrito Junior Chamber of Commerce, 1963-64. Member of program management committee of Chabot Observatory and Science Center, 1987.

MEMBER: International Astronomical Union, American Association for the Advancement of Science, Berkeley Science Historians (chief financial officer, 1984—), Sigma Xi.

AWARDS, HONORS: Robert H. Goddard Historical Essay Award from National Space Club, 1974, for "Winning the Initiative: NASA and the U.S. Space Science Program"; fellow of National Endowment for the Humanities, 1974-75, American Historical Association, 1986-87, and National Science Foundation, 1988; Dudley Award, 1984 and 1988, for research in the history of astronomy.

WRITINGS:

Ancient Astronomy and Civilization, Pachart Publishing House, 1987.
Science and Objectivity: Episodes in the History of Astronomy, Iowa State University Press, 1988.

Public Perception, Politics, and War: Three Factors in U.S. Aeronautical Research, University of California Press, 1989.

Contributor to magazines and newspapers, including *Journal of the History of Ideas, Annals of Science, Middle East Journal, Journal of Portfolio Management, Bay Area Business, American Scientist, Nature,* and *Science.*

WORK IN PROGRESS: Editing Edwin Hubble's previously unpublished scientific manuscripts on the extra-galactic nature of spiral nebulae, publication by Pachart Publishing House expected in 1989.

SIDELIGHTS: Norriss Swigart Hetherington told *CA* that he traveled overland across Central Asia with his wife and four-year-old daughter shortly before the revolutions in Iran and Afghanistan. "My most memorable birthday," Hetherington added, "was spent at Persepolis, the royal Iranian palace built by Darius around 500 B.C. and conquered by Alexander the Great in 330 B.C. And my best summer vacation was two months in Turkey and Greece on our way back from Iran, exploring ancient ruins and sampling local wines. The trip inspired a book examining science in ancient civilizations and a journal article on interrelationships between science, technology, and society leading up to the Iranian revolution.

"I am interested in corporate takeovers and merger arbitrage investments because—to quote bank robber Willie Sutton when he was asked why he picked on banks—'that's where the money is.' Also, research and analysis skills honed in the academic world were easily transferred to the world of investments.

"In addition to the pleasure of matching wits with Wall Street's best and winning more times than not, profits from investments funded research for a book on science and objectivity. Hailed as a model of the sophistication of current research in the history of science and as a revelation to readers, the book has also raised a storm of controversy among scientists.

"I am supportive of science, though, and am participating in the American Association for the Advancement of Science project to improve liberal education and the sciences. Other projects include a book on the unpublished manuscripts of astronomer Edwin Hubble—which are so controversial that their publication was suppressed—and a book examining the impact of public perception, politics, and war on the progress of science and technology in the United States, the course of which has often been a roller-coaster ride between heights of technical supremacy and bottoms of near obsolescence, a series of schizophrenic swings between the roles of world leader and world laggard.

"What's next? Physical and intellectual rambling until another idea grows to the stage that it demands birth in another book or in another business."

*   *   *

HEWTON, Eric 1934-

PERSONAL: Born October 28, 1934, in Liverpool, England; son of William Edward (a port labor officer) and Gladys (Brennan) Hewton; married Jeanne Dameral (a music therapist), April 1, 1973; children: Joseph. *Education:* Garnett College, teachers certificate, 1962; Brunel University, B.Tech., 1967, Ph.D., 1970.

ADDRESSES: Home—Hurstpierpoint, Sussex, England. *Office*—Department of Education, University of Sussex, Falmer, Brighton, Sussex, England.

CAREER: Insurance loss adjuster in Cardiff, Wales, 1958-62; Nuffield Foundation, London, England, research fellow, 1968-73; University of Sussex, Brighton, England, lecturer, 1973-84, reader in education, 1984—.

MEMBER: Chartered Insurance Institute (associate).

WRITINGS:

Rethinking Educational Change, Society for Research in Higher Education, 1982.
Education in Recession, Allen & Unwin, 1986.
School-Focused Staff Development, Falmer Press, 1988.
The Appraisal Interview, Open University Press, 1988.

SIDELIGHTS: Eric Hewton told *CA:* "I work with teachers in all sectors of education. I attempt to encourage them to think about educational issues which I see as important. These teachers are my audience. The theme which runs through my writing is one of change: how it originates, how it might be implemented more effectively, and how to evaluate it. I make every effort to write simply and clearly. Clarity of message, for me, overrides the need for complex academic discourse. I evaluate my work according to the extent to which people read and act upon the ideas which I put forward. There has probably been more change in the British educational system in the 1980s than in any previous period, and teachers welcome literature which helps them to see these changes in perspective and adjust their skills and attitudes accordingly."

*   *   *

HICKMAN, Tracy Raye 1955-

PERSONAL: Born November 26, 1955, in Salt Lake City, Utah; son of Harold R. (a professor) and Joan P. (a receptionist; maiden name, Parkinson) Hickman; married Laura Curtis (an author), June 17, 1977; children: Angel Dawn, Curtis Raye. *Education:* Attended Brigham Young University. *Religion:* Church of Jesus Christ of Latter-day Saints (Mormons).

ADDRESSES: Home—P.O. Box 96, Springfield, Wis. 53176. *Office*—TSR, Inc., P.O. Box 756, Lake Geneva, Wis. 53147. *Agent*—Ray Peekner, 3210 South Seventh St., Milwaukee, Wis. 53215.

CAREER: Mann Theatres, Provo, Utah, projectionist, 1974-78, theater manager in Provo and Logan, Utah, 1978-81; TSR, Inc., Lake Geneva, Wis., game designer, 1981-86, consultant, 1986—. Assistant director of KBYU-TV, Provo, 1976-77; missionary in Java and Indonesia.

WRITINGS:

"DRAGONLANCE CHRONICLES"; WITH MARGARET WEIS

Dragons of Autumn Twilight, TSR, 1984.
Dragons of Winter Night, TSR, 1985.
Dragons of Spring Dawning, TSR, 1985.

"DRAGONLANCE LEGENDS"; WITH MARGARET WEIS

Time of the Twins, TSR, 1986.
War of the Twins, TSR, 1986.
Test of the Twins, TSR, 1986.

"DRAGONLANCE TALES"; WITH MARGARET WEIS

Magic of Krynn, TSR, 1986.
Kender, Gnomes, and Gully Dwarves, TSR, 1987.
Love and War, TSR, 1987.

"DARKSWORD" SERIES

Forging the Darksword, Bantam, 1988.
Doom of the Darksword, Bantam, 1988.
Triumph of the Darksword, Bantam, 1988.

OTHER

Rose of the Prophet (trilogy), Bantam, in press.

Creator of adventure games "Pharaoh," "Lost Tomb of Martek," "Oasis of the White Palm," "Ravenloft" and "Ravenloft II," and seven versions of "Dragonlance."

SIDELIGHTS: Tracy Raye Hickman told *CA:* "The heart of any writing is the story. While technique and discipline are essential to a writer, these elements are without substance unless, at the base, there is the simple tale. Nothing can compensate for a lack of plot.

"I am an active member of the Church of Jesus Christ of Latter-day Saints, where I conduct the congregational hymns and teach the Elders Quorum in my local ward. It is this moral foundation which is reflected most strongly in my work.

"I still retain my interest in all forms of creative entertainment. Videotape production and postproduction still interest me, as do the newer fields of computer music composition and computer games. I play the guitar and piano and enjoy folk singing from time to time. I was once a private pilot of sail planes (gliders) but have not flown for quite some time now for a variety of excuses. Games of all kinds (excluding gambling) were my hobby before they became my vocation. They are now coming back as a hobby. Manned space exploration remains my greatest dream.

"I would describe myself as an incurable romantic in the classic sense."

AVOCATIONAL INTERESTS: Video, music.

*   *   *

HIGGINS, Colin   1941-1988

OBITUARY NOTICE—See index for *CA* sketch: Born July 28, 1941, in Noumea, New Caledonia; died of complications of acquired immune deficiency syndrome (AIDS), August 5, 1988, in Los Angeles, Calif. Director, producer, playwright, and screenwriter. Higgins wrote the screenplay of "Harold and Maude," the 1971 comedy about a young man who is saved from suicide through his love affair with an old woman. The film slowly emerged as one of the most notable cult movies of its decade and is viewed repeatedly by fans worldwide. Eventually Higgins adapted the work as a novel and a play. From the late 1970s to the early 1980s he wrote and directed several major Hollywood comedies, including "Foul Play," "Nine to Five," and "The Best Little Whorehouse in Texas," which he helped to adapt from a popular Broadway musical. Higgins was co-producer and co-author of the 1987 television miniseries "Out On a Limb," which recounted the spiritual odyssey of actress Shirley MacLaine.

OBITUARIES AND OTHER SOURCES:

BOOKS

Contemporary Theatre, Film, and Television, Volume 1, Gale, 1984.
Who's Who in America, 45th edition, Marquis, 1988.

PERIODICALS

Chicago Tribune, August 7, 1988.

Detroit Free Press, August 7, 1988.
Los Angeles Times, August 6, 1988.
New York Times, August 7, 1988.
Times (London), August 10, 1988.
Washington Post, August 7, 1988.

*   *   *

HIGHAM, David (Michael)   1949-

PERSONAL: Born August 16, 1949, in Barking, Essex, England; son of Robert Walter (a handyman) and Heather (a homemaker; maiden name, Garmen) Higham; married Viktoria Johnson (a graphic designer), August 13, 1979; children: Ignatz. *Education:* Attended Thurrock Technical College, 1965-67, and Central School of Art, London, 1967-70.

ADDRESSES: 27 Ryedale, East Dulwich, London SE22 0QW, England. *Agent*—Margaret Hanbury, 27 Walcot Sq., London SE11 4UB, England.

CAREER: Carpenter, 1972-82; free-lance illustrator, 1976—.

WRITINGS:

G. Was a Giant (self-illustrated children's book), Methuen, 1981.

ILLUSTRATOR

Dorothy Edwards, *Here's Sam*, Methuen, 1979.
Rayner Sussex, *The Magic Apple*, Methuen, 1979.
Ian Fennell, *Robottom the Robot*, Methuen, 1980.
Olive Jones, *The Tom and Sandy Book* (four volumes), Methuen, 1980.
Rayner Sussex, *King Otto's Apprentice*, Methuen, 1983.
Carol Watson, *Opposites*, Usborne, 1983.
Watson, *Shapes*, EDC, 1983.
Watson, *Sizes*, EDC, 1983.
Watson, *Simple Sums*, Usborne, 1984.
Watson, *1.2.3.*, Usborne, 1984.
Watson, *Colours*, Usborne, 1984.
Watson, *Telling the Time*, Usborne, 1984.
Lee Pressman, *Muckfield's Midnight Monster Match*, Deutsch, 1985.
Alison Prince, *A Job for Merv*, Belitha Press, 1986.
Pressman, *Muckfield and the Muckold Menace*, Deutsch, 1987.
Pressman, *Muckfield Marooned on Muckatoa*, Deutsch, 1988.
Anne Fine, *Crummy Mummy and Me*, Deutsch, 1988.
Michael Rosen, *Norma and the Washing Machine*, Deutsch, 1988.

Illustrator of "Rainbow" programs for Thames Television. Contributor of illustrations to periodicals, including *Home Computer Course*.

WORK IN PROGRESS: Illustrations for Lee Pressman's *Mucky IV;* illustrations for the animated sections of an interactive video series for the British Sugar Corporation.

*   *   *

HIJIRIDA, Kyoko   1937-

PERSONAL: Born October 20, 1937, in Hanechi, Okinawa, Japan; immigrated to United States, 1968, naturalized citizen, 1975; daughter of Eisho and Shizuko Oshiro; married Henry T. Hijirida, July, 1969; children: David. *Education:* Keio University, B.A., 1963; University of Hawaii at Manoa, M.A., 1970, Ed.D., 1980.

ADDRESSES: Home—1105 Palekaiko St., Pearl City, Hawaii 96782. *Office*—Department of Japanese, University of Hawaii at Manoa, Dole St., Honolulu, Hawaii 96822.

CAREER: High school teacher in Naha, Japan, 1963-66, and Chuba, Japan, 1966-68; University of Hawaii at Manoa, Honolulu, education associate, 1970, instructor, 1971-81, assistant professor, 1981-86, associate professor of Japanese, 1986—.

MEMBER: National Association of Teachers of Japanese, Hawaii Association of Teachers of Japanese (president, 1985-87), Pi Lambda Theta.

WRITINGS:

(With Muneo Yoshikawa) *Japanese Language and Culture for Business and Travel,* University of Hawaii Press, 1987.

Contributor to professional journals.

WORK IN PROGRESS: Japanese Language and Culture for Business and Travel, Part 2.

SIDELIGHTS: Kyoko Hijirida told *CA:* "As language study becomes widespread, the goals and motivation of people who study the Japanese language changes. Recently Hawaii has experienced a great increase in the number of people who come from Japan to either visit or work in the islands. The goals of our students have changed in response to this. No longer is language just a research tool, but it has become a necessary skill in career development. As a result of this, curriculum developers like myself have had to identify these changes and develop materials accordingly. *Japanese Language and Culture for Business and Travel* was written in response to this need. Not only does this book contain information about such subjects as hotels, restaurants, souvenirs, etc., it also contains cultural notes not usually found in a textbook."

* * *

HILL, Jane Bowers   1950-

PERSONAL: Born October 17, 1950, in Seneca, S.C.; daughter of James Harrison (a physician) and Alberta (a nurse; maiden name, Ramey) Bowers; married Lon Bolt Martin, December 27, 1969 (divorced, January 4, 1977); married Robert White Hill (a professor of English), August 16, 1980; children: (first marriage) Elizabeth Bolt. *Education:* Clemson University, B.A., 1972, M.A., 1978; University of Illinois at Urbana-Champaign, Ph.D., 1985. *Politics:* Democrat. *Religion:* Episcopalian.

ADDRESSES: Home—1419 Arden Dr., Marietta, Ga. 30060. *Office*—Longstreet Press, 2150 Newmarket Parkway, Suite 102, Marietta, Ga. 30067.

CAREER: High school English teacher in Beaufort, S.C., 1973-76; Clemson University, Clemson, S.C., instructor in English, 1978-79; high school English teacher and department chairman in Westminster, S.C., 1981-83; University of Georgia, Athens, instructor in English, 1983-85; Kennesaw College, Marietta, Ga., assistant professor of English, 1985-86; Peachtree Publishers, Atlanta, Ga., assistant editor, 1986-88; Longstreet Press, Atlanta, associate editor, 1988—. Volunteer hotline counselor for Cobb County Young Women's Christian Association (YWCA) Battered Women's Hotline, 1985—.

WRITINGS:

(Editor) *An American Christmas: A Sampler of Contemporary Stories and Poems,* Peachtree, 1986.
(Editor with Emily Ellison) *Our Mutual Room: Modern Literary Portraits of the Opposite Sex,* Peachtree, 1987.

Gail Godwin, G. K. Hall, 1989.

Contributor of articles, poems, stories, and reviews to literary magazines and newspapers.

WORK IN PROGRESS: Ila, a collection of related stories; *Getting Naked,* a novel.

SIDELIGHTS: Jane Bowers Hill told *CA:* "The motivational circumstances of my career have depended in large measure on family and financial considerations. I have done what I have done and worked where I have worked in order to live with and contribute to the support of my family. As a result, I have enjoyed enormous variety in the teaching and the writing that I have done. I've edited the autobiography of a stripper and a reference book that was on *Library Journal*'s best of 1987 list. I've written short stories, poems, literary criticism, and reviews of network television shows. I've taught gifted seventh-graders, remedial college students, creative writers, and technical writers. I hope the end result of this history is that I have remained a 'normal' person, aware of the way life works for most people, and that my awareness is evidenced in my work, both writing and teaching."

* * *

HINDING, Andrea   1942-

PERSONAL: Surname is pronounced "*Hin*-ding"; born July 15, 1942, in St. Paul, Minn.; daughter of Haakon and Isabelle Marie (a homemaker; maiden name, Supan) Hinding; married William R. Van Essendelft, April 25, 1970 (divorced, 1976). *Education:* Attended Marquette University, 1960-62; University of Minnesota—Twin Cities, B.A. (magna cum laude), 1966, M.A., 1973.

ADDRESSES: Home—909 East Magnolia, St. Paul, Minn. 55106. *Office*—107 Walter Library, University of Minnesota—Twin Cities, Minneapolis, Minn. 55455.

CAREER: University of Minnesota—Twin Cities, Minneapolis, library assistant, 1964-66, research assistant, 1966-67, curator of manuscripts, 1967-78, director of Walter Libraries, 1978-84, archivist, 1985—, assistant professor, until 1978, associate professor, 1978-86, professor of library science, 1986—. Director of Women's History Sources Survey, 1975-79, and Minnesota Welfare Records Survey, 1976-77; member of National Archives advisory council, 1977-80, and Joint Committee of Historians and Archivists, 1980-82.

MEMBER: Society of American Archivists (fellow; member of executive council, 1975-79; vice-president, 1983-84; president, 1984-85), Organization of American Historians (member of executive council, 1977-80), American Association of University Professors.

WRITINGS:

(Editor) *Women's History Sources: A Guide to Archives and Manuscript Collections in the United States,* two volumes, Bowker, 1979.
(Editor) *Feminism: Opposing Viewpoints,* Greenhaven Press, 1986.
Proud Heritage: A Pictorial History of the YMCA, Donning, 1988.

SIDELIGHTS: Andrea Hinding told *CA:* "My feminism is central to my identity and work. I define a feminist as one who believes, and acts on the belief, that women are fully human and therefore entitled to direct their lives as talents and preferences indicate. Feminists may be homemakers or neurosurgeons; what is essential is that women choose, rather than have identity and work imposed on them by family, church, and society. Extending this freedom to choose to women who lack middle- and upper-middle-class advantages implies addressing race, class, and other conditions that limit choice.''

* * *

HIRSH, Marilyn   1944-1988

OBITUARY NOTICE—See index for *CA* sketch: Born January 1, 1944, in Chicago, Ill.; died of cancer, October 18, 1988. Educator, illustrator, and author. Hirsh's career spanned both Jewish and Indian culture. She was known for writing and illustrating children's books on Jewish themes, sometimes inspired by the recollections of her older relatives. She was exposed to the art of India while working there for the Peace Corps during the 1960s, and her first children's works were on Indian subjects. Later Hirsh specialized in Indian and Buddhist art history, teaching at New York University's Institute of Fine Arts and at the Cooper Union School for the Advancement of Science and Art. Her works include *The Elephants and the Mice: A Panchatantra Story, Where Is Yonkela?, How the World Got Its Color, Deborah the Dybbick: A Ghost Story, Potato Pancakes All Around,* and *I Love Hanukkah.*

OBITUARIES AND OTHER SOURCES:

PERIODICALS

New York Times, October 22, 1988.

* * *

HOBHOUSE, Penelope
See MALINS, Penelope

* * *

HODGKINSON, Anthony   1916-1983

PERSONAL: Born December 29, 1916, in London, England; immigrated to United States, 1963, naturalized citizen, c. 1979; died December 26, 1983, in Sturbridge, Mass.; married Phyllis Beagley, December 22, 1947. *Education:* Gaddesden Training College, Teachers Certificate, 1948.

CAREER: Law clerk in London, England, 1933-40; British Broadcasting Corp., London, news secretary for European News Service, 1946; high-school teacher in London, 1949-53; British Film Institute, London, education officer, 1953-57; high-school teacher in London, 1957-63; Boston University, Boston, Mass., visiting professor, 1963, assistant professor of film, 1964-65, head of department, 1966-70; Clark University, Worcester, Mass., associate professor of film study, 1970-81, director of Screen Studies Program, 1972-81. Visitor at School of the Boston Museum of Fine Arts, 1968-73; teacher and adviser to Worcester Consortium for Higher Education, 1970-72. British Council lecturer in Finland, 1963; British Embassy lecturer in Mexico, 1964; guest lecturer at Sinking Creek Film Celebration, 1975, 1980; guest on local television programs. Founder of New England Center of Films for Children, 1966; co-founder of New England Screen Education Association, 1967; member of media advisory panel of New York State Council on the Arts, 1967-72; founder of Worcester Area Media Council and its Media Festival, 1971. Voluntary observer with the British social survey organization Mass-Observation,

1938-57; organizer of British Film Institute's Summer Schools of Film, 1953-77; member of British Television Viewers' Council, 1960-63; member of advisory board of Prix Jeunesse Seminar, Munich, West Germany, 1969-79; special consultant-delegate to UNESCO Australian Seminar on Screen Education, 1970. Founder of Society of Film Teachers (now Society for Education in Film and Television), 1950; chairman of board of directors of American Federation of Film Societies, 1966; consultant to UNESCO, American Film Institute, World Law Fund, and Fund for Media Research. *Military service:* British Army, Royal Artillery, 1940-46; became sergeant.

AWARDS, HONORS: Grant from Mellon Foundation, 1979.

WRITINGS:

Screen Education: Teaching a Critical Approach to Cinema and Television, UNESCO, 1964.
(Co-author) *The American Film Heritage,* Screen Studies, 1969.
(Contributor) *Developing in Schools a Critical Study of Film and Television,* Australian Government Publishing Service, 1971.
(Contributor) *A Common Wealth,* Massachusetts Council of Teachers of English, 1972.
(Contributor) *Cultural Pluralism in Education,* Appleton, 1973.
Teaching the Screen Language: A Basic Method, New England Screen Education Association, 1976.
(With Rodney E. Sheratsky) *Humphrey Jennings: More Than a Maker of Films,* University Press of New England, 1983.

Contributor to *Screen Education Yearbook.* Contributor to periodicals. Editor of *Teenscreen,* 1952, and *Film Guide,* 1953-57; guest editor of *Media and Methods,* 1967.

* * *

HOGUE, W. Lawrence   1951-

PERSONAL: Born August 30, 1951, in Yazoo City, Miss.; son of Wilkerson and Katie (Taylor) Hogue. *Education:* Attended University of Ife, 1971-72; University of Minnesota—Twin Cities, B.A. (cum laude), 1973; University of Chicago, M.A., 1974; Stanford University, Ph.D., 1980.

ADDRESSES: Home—6401 Warner Ave., No. 314, Huntington Beach, Calif. 92647. *Office*—Department of English, University of California, Irvine, Calif. 92717.

CAREER: Tougaloo College, Tougaloo, Miss., instructor in English, 1974-75; Jackson Community College, Jackson, Mich., assistant professor of English, 1975-76; University of California, Irvine, assistant professor of English and comparative literature, 1980—. Consultant.

MEMBER: Modern Language Association of America, Philological Association of the Pacific Coast.

AWARDS, HONORS: Fellow of National Research Council and Ford Foundation, 1982-83; visiting research scholar at Center for Afro-American Studies, University of California, Los Angeles, 1982-83.

WRITINGS:

(Contributor) Joe Weixlmann and Houston A. Baker, editors, *Belief vs. Theory in Black American Literary Criticism,* Volume II: *Studies in Black American Literature,* Penkevill, 1986.
Discourse and the Other: The Production of the Afro-American Text, Duke University Press, 1986.

(Contributor) Harold Bloom, editor, *Modern Critical Views: Alice Walker*, Chelsea House, 1987.

Contributor of articles to literature and black studies journals.

WORK IN PROGRESS: Ethnicity, Modernism, Post-Modernism: A Critique of the Grand Narrative, publication expected in 1989; a novel, tentatively titled *The Noise of the Whirlwind;* a collection of political essays.

SIDELIGHTS: W. Lawrence Hogue told *CA:* "My intellectual and research focus has shifted to modernism and post-modernism. I am concerned with identifying relevant rituals that can accommodate the predicament of post-modern life. My first book, *Discourse and the Other,* is unique because it is the first in Afro-American critical practices to examine thoroughly the literary and ideological forces that produce Afro-American literature.

"In my next book, *Ethnicity, Modernism, Post-Modernism,* I hope to show how, as ethnic American minorities—Asian-Americans, Afro-Americans, Native-Americans, and Chicanos—move into America's post-industrial, modern, and post-modern society where partiality, fragmentation, and alienation are the norm, it becomes difficult for members of these non-white ethnic groups to use grand narratives—conceptualized world views—to make sense out of their lives. Modern and post-modern society will force them to come up with their own narratives and rituals to make sense out of their lives and their existences.

"In my novel, tentatively titled *The Noise of the Whirlwind,* I try to work out this same phenomenon in fiction. I am producing a character who realizes that he now lives in a world where traditional notions of community and wholeness and grand narrative have become obsolete. His existence—his awareness of the reality of his existence—forces him to gradually begin to answer larger metaphysical questions—Who am I? Why am I here? What am I suppose to do here?—within the context of this modern and post-modern existence. Unlike existential novels, he does not bemoan the loss of the grand narrative. He, instead, begins to develop his own small narratives and rituals that will allow him to make sense out of his existence and to go on with his life.

"The personal views, values, and experiences that are reflected in both my non-fiction and fiction are the notions that we economically have entered a modern and post-modern American society where traditional values such as wholeness, community, and some kind of metaphysical unity have made it increasingly difficult to explain our lived experiences. Those traditional values were produced by and belong to a pre-industrial, pre-modern society. Therefore, they are not effective in explaining our modern, and post-modern lived experiences. We must examine our lives today and come up with new narratives and new rituals that are in harmony with our lived experiences."

*   *   *

HOLLAND, Gail Bernice   1940-

PERSONAL: Born April 13, 1940, in London, England; immigrated to United States, 1963, naturalized citizen, 1984; daughter of Bernard and Dorothy (McLeod) Peters; married Peter Holland; children: Anya. *Education:* Attended collegiate school in Toronto, Ontario.

ADDRESSES: Home—P.O. Box 370971, Montara, Calif. 94037-0971.

CAREER: Modern Woman, London, England, staff writer, 1957-59; *Home*, London, staff writer, 1959-61; Sears-Golick Fabrics, Montreal, Quebec, staff writer, 1962; Gumps, San Francisco, Calif., staff writer, 1963-65; Joseph Magnin, San Francisco, staff writer, 1965-67; free-lance writer, 1967-69; *Peninsula Living*, Palo Alto, Calif., staff writer, 1969; free-lance writer, 1969-74; Cinema Financial of America, Inc., San Francisco, staff writer, 1974; *San Francisco Examiner*, San Francisco, staff writer, 1975-78; free-lance writer, 1978—.

AWARDS, HONORS: Award of Merit from Valley Writers Council, 1969, for a humorous article; top award from Sigma Delta Chi and California State Bar, 1972, for "outstanding achievement by an editorial worker in reporting and interpreting the administration of justice in California."

WRITINGS:

(Contributor) Marian May, editor, *Weekend Guide to San Francisco*, Gousha Publications, 1972.
For Sasha, With Love: An Alzheimer's Crusade, Dembner, 1985.

Contributor to magazines and newspapers, including *Mademoiselle, Saturday Review, Science Digest, California Living, Harley Davidson, Family, Women's Sports*, and *San Francisco Magazine.*

WORK IN PROGRESS: Another book.

SIDELIGHTS: Gail Bernice Holland told *CA:* "We only have to look at our newspapers or watch television to know that writers keep us informed about all the critical problems in the world. Yet I feel that the writer also has a responsibility to focus on solutions. It's the writer who can offer hope and shed apathy by highlighting ideas that will enhance the quality of all our lives.

"During the thirty years that I have been interviewing people, I have found it's not difficult to find inspiring stories, and if a writer looks long enough and listens with the heart as well as the ears, it's not even difficult to find wisdom. When writers take the time to communicate these stories, then they are playing a significant role in society by revealing what is possible, not what might be considered inevitable. In other words—by our words—we have the choice of whether to merely report the present, or ultimately influence the future."

*   *   *

HOLLAND, Tom   1947-

PERSONAL: Born July 11, 1947, in Poughkeepsie, N.Y.; son of Franklin Thomas and Helena (a clerk; maiden name, Schoomaker) Holland. *Education:* University of California, Los Angeles, B.A. (summa cum laude), 1970, J.D., 1973. *Religion:* Methodist.

ADDRESSES: Office—Columbia Pictures, Producers Eight, Room 247, Burbank, Calif. 91505. *Agent*—Joel Gotter, The Agency, 10351 Santa Monica Blvd., Los Angeles, Calif. 90025.

CAREER: Screenwriter. Actor in plays and motion pictures, director of plays, and director of motion pictures, including "Fright Night," 1985.

MEMBER: Phi Beta Kappa.

AWARDS, HONORS: Nominated for Edgar Allan Poe Award from Mystery Writers of America for "Psycho II."

WRITINGS:

SCREENPLAYS

"The Beast Within," United Artists, 1981.
"Psycho II," Universal Pictures, 1983.
"Class of 1984," United Artists, 1984.
"Scream for Help," Lorimar, 1984.
"Cloak and Dagger," Universal Pictures, 1984.
(And director) "Fright Night," Columbia Pictures, 1985.

SIDELIGHTS: Screenwriter Tom Holland is most noted for his thriller films "Psycho II," "Cloak and Dagger," and "Fright Night." The works, containing what critics noted as clever twists and unconventional genre deviations, often pay homage to the chilling psycho-dramas of the deceased master filmmaker, Alfred Hitchcock. Reviewing "Fright Night," for example, Richard Harrington of the *Washington Post* commented that Holland "obviously intended [it] as a redemptive film for a genre for which he has genuine affection."

Perhaps most exemplary of his tribute to Hitchcock is Holland's 1983 "Psycho II," a sequel to the famed director's 1960 film, "Psycho." In Hitchcock's black and white original, a nervous Norman Bates—played by actor Anthony Perkins—runs the mostly vacant Bates Motel while living in the Victorian mansion that looms behind it. Visitors of the motel are gruesomely murdered seemingly by Norman's crazy and jealous mother. At the end of the film it is revealed that the murderer is actually Norman himself, whose split personality causes him to dress up and become the mother he killed years ago and whose body he has preserved in the house. Radically deviating from traditional movie conventions and breaking taboos—introducing, for example, nudity, bloody murders, and necrophilia—"Psycho" not only unnerved moviegoers of that time but drastically changed Hollywood's perception of the horror film.

"'Psycho II' . . . has all of the characteristics of a conventional sequel to Hitchcock's 1960 classic," declared Vincent Canby of the *New York Times*. Borrowing techniques from the late filmmaker, Holland and director Richard Franklin "haven't robbed the grave," explained Canby, "They've opened it up to have some fun." "Psycho II" opens with the most famous, and the most shocking, scene from "Psycho," the stabbing murder in the shower. Dissolving from black and white to color, Norman Bates, again played by Perkins, is shown returning to the mansion after spending twenty-two years in an asylum. He obtains a job at a diner but soon quits to resume managing the old Bates Motel. A woman, Lila, and her daughter Mary are opposed to Norman's return, and, in an effort to have him recommitted, they vengefully plot to drive Norman crazy, leaving him notes and making telephone calls from "Mother." Again, murders are committed, seemingly by an old woman. Moviegoers are led to believe the killer is Lila dressed as the late Mrs. Bates, but she, too, is killed. In the end, an elderly woman approaches Norman, saying that she is his mother. She explains that shortly after his birth she was committed to a mental institution and subsequently gave Norman to her sister (the long-dead Mrs. Bates) to raise. Recently released from confinement, the woman heard of Lila's plot to drive Norman crazy and proceeded to kill those involved. Upon hearing this explanation, Norman, in keeping with Hitchcock's murder-mother theme, hits her over the head with a shovel, killing her.

Reviewers criticized the film for the excessive gore accompanying the many murders: "We are . . . wading in explicit effects," lamented a writer in the *Los Angeles Times*. Additionally, "Psycho II" was faulted for overly imitating the camera angles, lighting, and composition of the original. The *Los Angeles Times* critic, however, found the film enjoyable because of this. The reviewer recounted a scene of Norman in the kitchen after being suspected of wrongdoing: "Close up of Norman's hand and a knife, chopping a head of lettuce. Chop. Chop. Chop. . . . This is the sort of noose-tightening you expect in a Hitchcock film or one taking off from his material. So are some of the twists the story takes."

Holland's next feature film to meet with popular acception is his 1984 "Cloak and Dagger." The story depicts a young computer-game aficionado, Davey, and his flamboyant imaginary hero, Jack Flack. "Flack is not just one character," proclaimed Sheila Benson in the *Los Angeles Times*, "but a never-ending succession of imaginary playmates who must someday be put aside, along with other childish things. It's this idea that gives the film its distinction." Running an errand for the owner of a video-game store, Davey witnesses a murder. Before the murder victim dies, however, he hands Davey a sought-after video-game tape. No one believes Davey's account of what happened, including his subtly heroic father, played by the same actor who portrays Jack Flack. The killers pursue Davey for the tape, resulting in an adventuresome and suspenseful chase.

Again collaborating with director Franklin on "Cloak and Dagger," Holland looks to the mastery of Hitchcock to evoke suspense. One critic labeled the film "an anthology of Hitchcock twists." Benson observed that "homage can be felt through [the] staging, as well as in the borrowing of Hitchcock story elements." Benson also noted, however, that Holland and Franklin were not as meticulous about details as the master. "Still and all," she concluded, "when it deals with the realms of childhood and imagination, 'Cloak and Dagger' becomes something out of the ordinary." Concurring, *New York Times* reviewer Janet Maslin called the film "clever and enjoyable."

Marking his debut as a director as well as his third commercially successful screenplay is Holland's "Fright Night." A modern-day vampire tale, the film was praised by Maslin for having "a lot more personality than the usual horror film." The movie portrays a teenaged vampire-film cultist, Charlie, who suspects that his new neighbor, Jerry, is a vampire. When his friends and family do not believe him, Charlie enlists the help of a washed up horror-movie actor, Peter Vincent, who now hosts a television show running old monster movies. Vincent, upon a visit to Jerry's house, discovers that Jerry is indeed a vampire and cowardly flees. After Jerry turns Charlie's friend and girlfriend into ghouls, Charlie begs Vincent to help him, and the fearful film host reluctantly agrees. The two succeed in killing Jerry by exposing him to the light.

Critics lauded Holland for creating a work that demonstrates a fondness of classic horror films, hence deviating from the popular "slasher" horror movies of the 1980s. Richard Harrington pointed out how Holland cleverly incorporated his sentiment into "Fright Night": "In one sly aside, he has [Vincent] complaining after his show has been canceled for low ratings: 'Nobody wants to see vampires anymore. All they want to see is some demented madman running around in a ski mask hacking up young virgins.'" Harrington remarked that the director nonetheless falls back on grisly special effects at the end of the film. He maintained, however, that "there are some cute twists on genre convention." Maslin reported that Holland's "material . . . is uneven and often flat" but conceded that his "handling of his stars is successful enough to establish him as a newcomer with promise."

Less popular were Holland's other horror films, including "The Class of 1984," a film about a high school terrorized by a gang of punk-rock hoodlums; "The Beast Within"; and "Scream for Help." The latter two motion pictures Holland told *CA* are "bad movies produced from my screenplays."

BIOGRAPHICAL/CRITICAL SOURCES:

PERIODICALS

Los Angeles Times, June 3, 1983, August 10, 1984.
New York Times, June 3, 1983, August 10, 1984, August 2, 1985.
Washington Post, June 7, 1983, August 5, 1985.

—Sketch by Janice E. Drane

*   *   *

HOLMES, Richard   1945-

BRIEF ENTRY: Born November 5, 1945, in London, England. British poet and biographer. Holmes received England's 1974 Somerset Maugham Award for his monumental biography, *Shelley: The Pursuit* (Weidenfeld & Nicolson, 1974, Dutton, 1975). The book is described by Morris Dickstein in *The New York Times Book Review* as "lively and eloquent," advancing "our understanding of Shelley's poetry by giving us in certain key details a truer picture of Shelley's life and character than any we've yet had." Holmes's subsequent books include *Coleridge* (Oxford University Press, 1982) and *Footsteps: Adventures of a Romantic Biographer* (Viking, 1985). He also wrote a volume of poems, *One for Sorrow, Two for Joy* (Cafe Books, 1970), and "Inside the Tower," a 1977 BBC-Radio play about nineteenth-century French writer Gerard de Nerval. He edited *Shelley on Love: An Anthology* (University of California Press, 1980). *Addresses: Agent*—Peter Janson-Smith, 31 Newington Green, London N16 9PU, England.

BIOGRAPHICAL/CRITICAL SOURCES:

PERIODICALS

New York Times Book Review, June 22, 1975, October 20, 1985.
Spectator, August 3, 1974, July 6, 1985.
Washington Post Book World, January 5, 1986.

*   *   *

HOLZEL, Thomas Martin   1940-
(Tom Holzel)

PERSONAL: Surname is pronounced "*Hoe*-zel"; born October 26, 1940, in Berlin, Germany; immigrated to United States, 1946; son of Erhard Holzel and Margaret (Martin) Holzel; married Dianne Wave, September 27, 1968; children: Peter, Maggie. *Education:* Dartmouth College, A.B., 1963.

ADDRESSES: Home—Concord, Mass. *Office*—c/o Raytheon Co., 465 Centre St., Quincy, Mass.

CAREER: Advent Corp., Cambridge, Mass., manager of industrial video division, 1976-81; Arcturus, Inc. (electronics manufacturing firm), Acton, Mass., president, 1981-88; Raytheon Co., Quincy, Mass., marketing manager for industrial components operations, 1988—. *Military service:* U.S. Army Reserve, 1964-70; became first sergeant.

MEMBER: Society for Information Display, American Alpine Club, Atlantic Alpine Club.

WRITINGS:

(Under name Tom Holzel; with Audrey Salkeld) *The Mystery of Mallory and Irvine*, J. Cape, 1986, published in the United States as *First to the Top: The Mystery of Mallory and Irvine*, Holt, 1987.

Contributor of articles and reviews to magazines, including *Mountain*, *Summit*, and *American Alpine Journal*.

WORK IN PROGRESS: Organizing a second Mount Everest expedition.

SIDELIGHTS: Tom Holzel told *CA:* "I have been in sales and marketing of audio-visual products for my entire career, and now I am a marketing manager of military flight displays for Raytheon Co. I possess an inventive streak and am an inveterate writer of letters to the editor. I believe I have nearly perfected the five-paragraph essay form of writing that was drummed into me in college, which is the essence of a good, one-page letter.

"My book *First to the Top: The Mystery of Mallory and Irvine* was the outcome of a spare-time investigation that lasted fifteen years: research on the disappearance of George Mallory and Andrew Irvine. Through a break in the clouds, these two climbers were last seen three hours from the top of Mount Everest in 1924, 'going strong for the top.' Did they make it before perishing? Although much has been written about this famous episode, practically no scientific investigation had been conducted. Other writers merely assembled various opinions and quotations of the time, arranging them to suit one preconceived notion or another. The nearly unanimous opinion was that Mallory and Irvine could not have reached the summit.

"What made my research so interesting was that there was so much information about the climb. There was enough, it seemed to me, that one might still be able to prove the issue one way or another. Casting this romantic, almost nineteenth-century episode under the sharp glare of scientific inquiry in the 1970s brought a number of elements into sharp focus. First, the older British types were outraged that a foreigner should tread so profanely on their hallowed ground. As I started reporting my findings and theories, the newspapers and climbing journals resounded with angry complaints. Second, I learned you *can* examine old facts carefully and squeeze out an enormous amount of previously invisible information. For example, by analyzing their oxygen use, I was able to discover the climbers' exact climbing speed: a crucial fact not previously recognized. From my analysis I became convinced that Mallory, at least, had made it to the top.

"After writing the book, and becoming certain that one could solve the mystery—but only on the mountain—I organized an expedition to climb Mount Everest to search for the body of one of the two climbers, who I had predicted would be lying on a snow terrace at 26,700 feet. Each climber had a camera, and Eastman Kodak scientists believe that if it were undamaged, the 64-year-old film would yield 'printable images.' Imagine if they showed the view from the top of the world!

"Our expedition met with terrible weather, and we got only to 25,500 feet. Yet, Mount Everest is such a magnificent place that I hope to try again. Then I shall write the sequel, *The Search for Mallory and Irvine*."

BIOGRAPHICAL/CRITICAL SOURCES:

PERIODICALS

Climbing, February, 1987.

*　　*　　*

HOLZEL, Tom
　See HOLZEL, Thomas Martin

*　　*　　*

HOMEL, Michael W.　1944-

PERSONAL: Born February 10, 1944, in Chicago, Ill.; son of Irving and Bernice Homel; married Nina Berger (a teacher), August 29, 1965. *Education:* Grinnell College, B.A., 1965; University of Chicago, M.A., 1966, Ph.D., 1972.

ADDRESSES: Home—1357 Huron River Dr., Ypsilanti, Mich. 48197. *Office*—Department of History and Philosophy, Eastern Michigan University, Ypsilanti, Mich. 48197.

CAREER: Eastern Michigan University, Ypsilanti, assistant professor, 1970-75, associate professor, 1975-81, professor of U.S. history, 1981—. Member of Ypsilanti City Council, 1983-87, Ypsilanti Historic District Commission, 1983, Ypsilanti Public Housing Commission, 1984-85.

MEMBER: Organization of American Historians, American Historical Association, American Association of University Professors, Chicago Historical Society, Ypsilanti Historical Society, Ypsilanti Heritage Foundation.

WRITINGS:

(Contributor) Melvin G. Holli and Peter d'A. Jones, editors, *Biographical Dictionary of American Mayors, 1820-1980,* Greenwood Press, 1981.
Down From Equality: Black Chicagoans and Public Schools, 1920-41, University of Illinois Press, 1984.
(Contributor) David Plank and Rick Ginsburg, editors, *Southern Cities, Southern Schools,* Greenwood Press, in press.

Contributor to history journals.

WORK IN PROGRESS: A history of the Chicago branch of the National Association for the Advancement of Colored People, 1909-1940.

SIDELIGHTS: Michael W. Homel told *CA:* "*Down From Equality* details the transition of black education in one major city from equal distribution of resources and substantial integration of black students and teachers before World War I to a segregated, unequal school system by the 1930s. Though Chicago blacks have more power now than they did in the 1920s and 1930s, the patterns emerging during those decades still shape the city's schools today."

BIOGRAPHICAL/CRITICAL SOURCES:

PERIODICALS

American Historical Review, April, 1985.

*　　*　　*

HORNSBY-SMITH, Michael P(eter)　1932-
　(Michael Peters)

PERSONAL: Born November 30, 1932, in Southsea, England; son of Frederick Charles (a Royal Air Force officer) and Edith (a homemaker; maiden name, Harrison) Hornsby-Smith; married Margaret Mary Leonide Early (a teacher), December 29, 1960; children: Andrew, Gillian Mary Barnes, Stephen Paul, Richard Thomas. *Education:* University of Sheffield, B.Sc.Tech., 1954, Ph.D, 1958; University of London, B.Sc.(Soc.), 1968. *Politics:* Labour. *Religion:* Roman Catholic.

ADDRESSES: Home—13 Cunningham Ave., Merrow, Guildford, Surrey GU1 2PE, England. *Office*—Department of Sociology, University of Surrey, Guildford GU2 5XH, England.

CAREER: Battersea College of Technology, London, England, lecturer in metallurgy, 1959-65, lecturer in humanities and social science, 1965-68; University of Surrey, Guildford, England, lecturer in sociology, 1968-82, senior lecturer in sociology, 1982—. Member of Catholic Education Council, 1970-80; member of council and issues committee, Catholic Union of Great Britain, 1977-85; chairman of Arundel and Brighton Justice and Peace Commission, 1979-85; member of executive committee, Catholic Institute of International Relations, 1981-87.

MEMBER: International Conference of Sociology of Religion (council member, 1987—), Association for the Sociology of Religion, Religious Research Association, Society for the Scientific Study of Religion, British Sociological Association (treasurer or convener, Sociology of Religion study group, 1979-85 and 1987-88).

WRITINGS:

Catholic Education, the Unobtrusive Partner: Sociological Studies of the Catholic School System in England and Wales, Sheed & Ward, 1978.
(With Raymond M. Lee) *Roman Catholic Opinion,* Department of Sociology, University of Surrey, 1979.
Roman Catholics in England, Cambridge University Press, 1987.
Parishes, Priests and Parishioners, Routledge & Kegan Paul, 1989.
Roman Catholic Beliefs, Cambridge University Press, in press.

Contributor of articles to more than one hundred sociology journals and Catholic periodicals, including *Tablet, Month, New Blackfriars, America,* and, under name Michael Peters, *A&B News.*

WORK IN PROGRESS: Research on black Catholics, the changing nature of Roman Catholicism, justice and the peace movement, and the application of 'preferential option for poor' in Britain.

SIDELIGHTS: Michael P. Hornsby-Smith told *CA:* "A visit to the Philippines in 1984 stimulated my interest in development processes. I fantasize about writing a novel illustrating social and religious changes in Catholicism and preparing an autobiography of 'The Mediocre Man; or, The Man With Two Talents.' I keep a diary with the purpose of providing data for future historians on the everyday lives of Catholics in the last quarter of the twentieth century."

BIOGRAPHICAL/CRITICAL SOURCES:

PERIODICALS

Times Literary Supplement, October 23, 1987.

*　　*　　*

HOROWITZ, Donald L(eonard)　1939-

PERSONAL: Born June 27, 1939, in New York, N.Y.; son of

Morris (an attorney) and Yetta (Hibscher) Horowitz; married Judith Anne Present (a university administrator), September 4, 1960; children: Marshall, Karen, Bruce. *Education:* Syracuse University, A.B., 1959, LL.B., 1961; Harvard University, LL.M., 1962, M.A., 1965, Ph.D., 1967.

ADDRESSES: Home—2501 Wrightwood Ave., Durham, N.C. 27705. *Office*—School of Law, Duke University, Durham, N.C. 27706.

CAREER: Harvard University, Center for International Affairs, Cambridge, Mass., research associate, 1967-69; U.S. Department of Justice, Washington, D.C., attorney, 1969-71; Woodrow Wilson Foundation, Washington, D.C., fellow, 1971-72; Brookings Institution, Washington, D.C., research associate, 1972-75; senior fellow of Research Institute for Immigration and Ethnic Studies, 1975-81; Duke University, Durham, N.C., professor of law, public policy studies, and political science, 1980—. Consultant to Ford Foundation, 1977-81; member of Council on the Role of the Courts, 1979-83; member of panel of arbitrators for American Arbitration Association; chairman of North Carolina Advisory Committee to U.S. Commission on Civil Rights, 1985—.

AWARDS, HONORS: Louis Brownlow Prize from National Academy of Public Administration, 1977, for *The Courts and Social Policy;* Guggenheim fellowship, 1980-81; National Humanities Center fellowship, 1984.

WRITINGS:

(Contributor) Nathan Glazer and Daniel P. Moynihan, editors, *Ethnicity: Theory and Experience,* Harvard University Press, 1975.
The Courts and Social Policy, Brookings Institution, 1977.
The Jurocracy: Government Lawyers, Agency Programs, and Judicial Decisions, Lexington Books, 1977.
Coup Theories and Officers' Motives: Sri Lanka in Comparative Perspective, Princeton University Press, 1980.
(Contributor) Glazer and Ken Young, editors, *Ethnic Pluralism and Public Policy,* Heinemann, 1983.
Ethnic Groups in Conflict, University of California Press, 1985.

Member of editorial board, *Ethnicity,* 1974-82, *Law and Society Review,* 1979-82, and *Law and Contemporary Problems,* 1983-84.

WORK IN PROGRESS: Research on ethnic group violence, Malaysian ethnic politics and policy, and U.S. labor relations law.

SIDELIGHTS: Donald L. Horowitz told *CA:* "I have spent most of my career writing in two fields—comparative ethnic group relations, with an emphasis on ethnic conflict and politics in Asia and Africa, and American law and the legal system. There are several ways in which these two subjects play point-counterpoint with each other. The United States is a large but still idiosyncratic, even parochial, country. Studying Asia and Africa sweeps the mind clean and puts America in what I generally find to be a revealing contrast. American law is beautifully documented; the problem is not finding it but rather figuring out what it means, imparting significance to it. In Asia and Africa the facts about most things are not so clear, so it becomes necessary to dig them out. One needs to start with a pretty good sense of meaning to know what to ask and to interpret what one hears.

"The contrast between the figuring and the digging, between sitting in the study and scratching around in the field, is what most invigorates me. It reminds me of British philosopher-economist John Stuart Mill's advice that a satisfied life consists of a balance between activity and inactivity. Almost by inadvertence, I have achieved that balance.

"My interest in Asia and Africa grew from what probably should be called a general internationalism (developed as a child following the progress of the Korean War on a map in a fourth-grade classroom); a taste for the exotic—by which I mean not a desire to sample the exotic, but to delve into it; sheer fortuity in the combination of teachers and research topics in graduate school; and a spouse who is engrossed in similar geographic interests. My wife and I read many of the same British colonial novels, eat the same Malay curries, and quiver with pleasure when a plane ticket arrives.

"What I feel best about is that I seem to have been able to juggle these disparate subject interests without doing too much damage to either. I am particularly pleased by critical references to a felicitous style in my writing because the materials with which I characteristically work are murky, intractable, and amorphous, and it is no small challenge to shape them into something that is at once coherent and interesting.

"While my interest in comparative ethnicity has led me to look at American ethnicity, via articles on the racial violence of the 1960s and on Mexican-Americans, down the road I want to work on putting the U.S. legal system into a new comparative perspective."

In his 1985 book, *Ethnic Groups in Conflict,* Horowitz examines how democracy and peace are undermined by the ever-increasing dissention among various ethnic circles. His discussion extends to eighty nations around the globe and includes more than 150 different peoples. Arend Lijphart in the *New York Times Book Review* commended Horowitz on this "admirable" study that, unlike similar works, has "the ambition and courage" to address the topic from its proper perspective as a widespread, rather than a limited, occurrence. The author is especially skilled at "dissecting and differentiating," noted the reviewer, and the volume's "most important part . . . deals with the wide range of practical policies that can be used to resolve or manage ethnic conflicts." While ethnic conflict is a pervasive and persistent circumstance, there are numerous alternatives to brutality and force. According to Lijphart, Horowitz "offers a great deal of constructive advice," maintaining that "ethnic violence is by no means inevitable" and blaming the lack of "political will" for continued violent recourse in countries such as Northern Ireland, Lebanon, and South Africa.

BIOGRAPHICAL/CRITICAL SOURCES:

PERIODICALS

America, May 14, 1977.
Commentary, October, 1979.
Kansas City Star, March 13, 1977.
New York Times Book Review, November 10, 1985.
Times Literary Supplement, April 3, 1981, March 18, 1986.
Washington Post, February 25, 1977.

*   *   *

HOSTETLER, Beulah Stauffer   1926-

PERSONAL: Born July 8, 1926, in Tofield, Alberta, Canada; immigrated to United States, 1943; daughter of Ezra (a farmer and teacher) and Irene (a homemaker; maiden name, Lehamn) Stauffer; married John A. Hostetler (a writer and professor),

February 14, 1953; children: Ann Hostetler Smucker, Mary Hostetler Hoyt, Laura Hostetler Liechty. *Education:* Goshen College, B.A., 1947; attended Pennsylvania Academy of Fine Arts, 1949-50; University of Pennsylvania, M.A., 1975, Ph.D., 1977. *Religion:* Mennonite.

ADDRESSES: Home—2550 Ball Rd., Willow Grove, Pa. 19090. *Office*—Center for Anabaptist and Pietist Studies, Elizabethtown College, Elizabethtown, Pa. 17022.

CAREER: Mennonite Central Committee, Akron, Pa., administrator of summer service programs, 1947-50; Herald Press, Scottdale, Pa., book editor and designer, 1950-54, free-lancer, 1954-59; Johns Hopkins University, Baltimore, Md., part-time research director of Genealogical Research Project for School of Medicine, 1964-68; independent writer and researcher, 1975-87; Elizabethtown College, Elizabethtown, Pa., assistant professor of sociology, 1986-89, associate director of Center for Anabaptist and Pietist Studies, 1987-89. Teacher at Keystone Bible Institute, 1988 and 1989; workshop leader; public speaker. Past member of Mennonite Council on Faith, Life, and Strategy, and Task Force on Principles of Biblical Interpretation; past member of board of trustees of Christopher Dock Mennonite High School and Eastern Mennonite College.

MEMBER: American Academy of Religion, American Society of Church History, Mennonite Historians of Eastern Pennsylvania, Lancaster Mennonite Historical Society.

AWARDS, HONORS: Portraiture awards from Edmonton Exhibition; grants from National Endowment for the Humanities and Lancaster Mennonite Historical Society, both 1981; fellow of National Endowment for the Humanities, 1984.

WRITINGS:

American Mennonites and Protestant Movements: A Community Paradigm, Herald Press, 1987.

Also editor of *The Complete Writings of Menno Simons.* Contributor to Mennonite and history journals. Member of editorial council of *Mennonite Encyclopedia V.*

WORK IN PROGRESS: Research on the role of confessions in the Mennonite church; "Mennonites and the 'Mainline Peace Emphasis,' 1950-80"; a chronicle of Amish and Mennonite flight, migration, and acculturation.

SIDELIGHTS: Beulah Stauffer Hostetler told *CA:* "During the 1953-54 school year my husband and I had a residence in Heidelberg, Germany, and from there we visited more than one hundred South-German estate-farms (hofs) managed by Mennonites who were Amish descendants. My husband had a Fulbright scholarship and during this time I edited *The Complete Writings of Menno Simons,* an early leader of the Dutch Mennonites. From 1970 to 1971 we were again in Europe, this time in Vienna, Austria, and the subject of research was the early communities of the Hutterites. As a family we travelled extensively in both Eastern and Western Europe. In the fall of 1977 we were again in Europe, this time researching Alsatian origins of the Amish. These experiences will provide vital background for my next project—a saga of Amish and Mennonite flight, migration, and acculturation.

"I was basically a homemaker from 1954 to 1968, doing free-lance jobs that could be done on the side. In 1968 I began graduate studies on a half-time basis at the University of Pennsylvania. Beginning my formal study of religious thought at mid-life and with a family, I recognized it was important to take advantage of what I already knew something about, which

was Mennonites, and a place that was geographically accessible, which became my community model or paradigm. While the study has broad application to Mennonites, the selection of one settlement as the primary focus enabled me to illustrate abstract concepts with particular examples. I was interested in outside influences on Mennonite thought, and of course the main outside influences were dominant American Protestant movements—revivalism (and peitism), fundamentalism, and institutionalization. In order to assess the interaction of Mennonites with these movements it was necessary to establish the core values of the community. In contrast to the prevailing interpretation that these communities were 'dead,' 'ignorant,' and 'petrified' during the nineteenth century, I found they had core religious values that undergirded both their continuity and their resistance to change. From their beginning the Mennonites have in a sense been a counterculture, representing an alternative value orientation. My research is directed toward understanding the deeper spiritual values of Mennonite groups and toward clarifying some of the longstanding ambiguities about the Mennonites."

*   *   *

HOUSEHOLD, Geoffrey (Edward West)   1900-1988

OBITUARY NOTICE—See index for *CA* sketch: Born November 30, 1900, in Bristol, England; died October 4, 1988, near Banbury, England. Businessman, intelligence officer, and author. Household was an adventure novelist best known for the 1939 thriller *Rogue Male.* Inspired by the author's own wish to eliminate the threat of Nazi leader Adolf Hitler, the book depicts an English big-game hunter who tries to stalk and kill an unnamed European dictator. Household gleaned material for his stories from his own extensive travels. During the 1920s he was a confidential secretary for a bank in Romania, then joined United Fruit Company to market bananas in Spain. In 1929 he moved to New York City, where he worked briefly as a writer for an encyclopedia and composed children's radio plays for the Columbia Broadcasting System. He soon became a salesman for an English ink manufacturer, traveling throughout Europe, the Middle East, and South America. As an English intelligence officer from 1939 to 1945 he served in Romania, Greece, Palestine, Syria, and Iraq. Household's other novels include *The Third Hour, A Rough Shoot, Arrows of Desire,* and *Rogue Justice,* the 1982 sequel to *Rogue Male.* His autobiography, *Against the Wind,* was published in 1958.

OBITUARIES AND OTHER SOURCES:

BOOKS

Who's Who, 140th edition, St. Martin's, 1988.

PERIODICALS

Chicago Tribune, October 7, 1988, October 9, 1988.
Los Angeles Times, October 7, 1988.
New York Times, October 7, 1988.
Times (London), October 6, 1988.
Washington Post, October 7, 1988.

*   *   *

HUBKA, Thomas C.   1946-

PERSONAL: Born April 9, 1946, in Danville, Pa.; son of Eugene Louis (a history teacher) and Martha Jane (Reed) Hubka. *Education:* Carnegie-Mellon University, B.Arch., 1969; University of Oregon, M.Arch., 1972.

ADDRESSES: Office—Department of Architecture, University of Wisconsin—Milwaukee, Milwaukee, Wis. 53211.

CAREER: University of Oregon, Eugene, assistant professor, 1972-80, associate professor of architecture, 1980-84; architectural practice with Portland & Kennebunk in Maine, 1984-87; University of Wisconsin—Milwaukee, associate professor of architecture, 1987—.

AWARDS, HONORS: Abbott Lowell Cummings Award from Vernacular Architecture Forum, 1984, for *Big House, Little House, Back House, Barn.*

WRITINGS:

Big House, Little House, Back House, Barn, University Press of New England, 1984.

WORK IN PROGRESS: Research on H. H. Richardson and John Ruskin, Polish wooden synagogues, and Wisconsin farm architecture.

*   *   *

HUEBNER, Klaus H(ermann)   1916-

PERSONAL: Born April 28, 1916, in Thansau, Bavaria, Germany; immigrated to United States, 1926, naturalized citizen, 1935; son of Richard H. (a chemist) and Amalie (a housewife; maiden name, Mueller) Huebner; married Margaret Nuber (a housewife), April 25, 1946; children: Karl. *Education:* University of Pennsylvania, B.A., 1938, M.D., 1942. *Religion:* Lutheran.

ADDRESSES: Home—65 Hillcrest Lane, North East, Md. 21901. *Agent*—Ted Bellmont, 2001 Kirby, Suite 900, Houston, Tex. 77019.

CAREER: Lankenau Hospital, Philadelphia, Pa., intern, 1942-43; private practice of medicine in North East, Md., 1946-63; Hospital of American Samoa, Pago Pago, chief of outpatient department, 1963-65; private practice of medicine in North East, Md., 1965-68; Coco-Solo Hospital, Cristobal, Canal Zone, staff physician at Family Practice Clinic, 1968-70; Veterans Administration Medical Center, Perry Point, Md., staff physician, 1970-86; writer. *Military service:* U.S. Army, Medical Corps, 1943-46; became captain; received Bronze Star.

MEMBER: Southern Medical Association, Medical and Chirurgical Faculty of the State of Maryland, Cecil County Medical Society, Phi Beta Kappa.

WRITINGS:

Long Walk Through War: A Combat Doctor's Diary, Texas A & M University Press, 1987.

SIDELIGHTS: Klaus H. Huebner told *CA:* "I accepted positions to practice medicine in Pago Pago and the Canal Zone because tropical medicine was one of my favorite subjects in medical school. These positions were a change of pace from a country practice and also gave me an opportunity to observe and appreciate the skills of native physicians.

"I wrote my combat memoirs in 1947 from notes I had scribbled on scraps of paper during lulls in the front lines in Italy during World War II. I had stored the finished manuscript in a foot locker in my attic, where it stayed until 1986 when a war buddy (now my agent) asked me to resurrect it and have it published.

"My book deals with my experiences as a physician who joined the 88th Infantry Division in San Antonio, Texas, in Septem-

ber of 1943, trained with it in the Atlas mountains in northern Africa, and then *walked* with it from Naples, Italy to the Brenner Pass in Austria, a walk of about five hundred miles lasting approximately one and a half years.

"In writing this book, my purpose was to show that all a physician walking with a combat infantry battalion could do was learn to survive, render first aid, and boost morale by his presence. I learned more military tactics than medicine during the war and will never again be shocked by the appearance of any casualty, no matter how severe. My experience also made me realize that the valor of our draftees and of the well-trained German soldiers was the same."

AVOCATIONAL INTERESTS: Golf, fishing, travel.

*   *   *

HUGGETT, Joyce   1937-

PERSONAL: Born September 16, 1937, in Exeter, England; daughter of Sidney Ernest (a baker) and Winifred Lilian (a waitress; maiden name, Parkhouse) Duguid; married David John Huggett (a priest), July 16, 1960; children: Kevin John, Christina Joy. *Education:* Attended University of Southampton, 1956-59, and Victoria University of Manchester, 1959-60.

ADDRESSES: Home—18 Lenton Rd., The Park, Nottingham NG7 1DU, England.

CAREER: Nutfield Priory School, Redhill, England, teacher of the deaf, 1960-62; Health Centre, peripatetic teacher of the deaf in Croydon, England, 1963-65, and in Cambridge, England, 1971-73; St. Nicholas Church, Nottingham, England, director of pastoral care and counselor, 1973—. Regular broadcaster on television and radio in England.

WRITINGS:

Two Into One: Relating in Christian Marriage, Inter-Varsity Press, 1981.
Growing Into Love, Inter-Varsity Press, 1982.
(Editor) *We Believe in Marriage,* Marshalls, 1982.
Growing Into Freedom, Inter-Varsity Press, 1984, published as *Living Free,* Inter-Varsity Press, 1986.
Creative Conflict, Inter-Varsity Press, 1984 (published in England as *Conflict: Friend or Foe?* Kingsway, 1984).
Dating, Sex, and Friendship, Inter-Varsity Press, 1985 (published in England as *Just Good Friends?* Inter-Varsity Press, 1985).
The Joy of Listening to God, Inter-Varsity Press, 1986, published as *Listening to God,* Hodder & Stoughton, 1986.
Approaching Easter, Lion, 1987.
Marriage on the Mend, Kingsway, 1987.
Approaching Christmas, Lion, 1987.
Listening to Others, Hodder & Stoughton, 1988.
Life in a Sex-Mad Society, Inter-Varsity Press, 1988.

Also writer of scripture union notes. Contributor to magazines and newspapers, including *Decision, Christian Family, Today,* and *Home and Family.*

WORK IN PROGRESS: A continuation of *Listening to Others,* as yet untitled, publication by Hodder and Stoughton expected in 1989.

SIDELIGHTS: Joyce Huggett told *CA:* "*Listening to God* is autobiographical. It is an account of my own prayer pilgrimage, and I wrote it to show that prayer is not man presenting a list of requests to God, but rather man and God enjoying a relationship with each other. The book also shows how Christians from a variety of backgrounds can learn from one another's prayer practices.

"*Approaching Easter* and *Approaching Christmas* are illustrated meditations. I wrote these because busy people ask me how they can keep Christ central to Christmas and how they can observe Lent, the six-week buildup to Easter. These meditations provide seasonal food for thought, which is intended to nourish the reader spiritually.

"*Just Good Friends?* was written with young people in mind, particularly students. Over the years many young people have asked me questions about the dating process: Is it permissible for Christians to have premarital sex? If not, how far is too far? How do you cope with the breakup of a relationship? Why do I feel lonely without a partner? Is masturbation a sin? What about homosexuality? I have attempted to answer these questions and many more, because I believe that we owe it to our young people to give them clear guidelines on such subjects.

"*Growing Into Love* speaks to another set of people: those who have fallen in love and are wondering whether to marry each other. Some of the material is the teaching we give to engaged couples when we prepare them for marriage.

"*Two Into One* was intended for newlyweds, but it seems to be appreciated by the middle-aged, too. It attempts to spell out some of the Bible's teachings on marriage and provides couples with questions which they can use as starters for in-depth sharing.

"*Marriage on the Mend* continues to explain the Bible's teaching on marriage, but it also bears a message of hope to those whose marriage is in a bad state of repair. Such marriages can be and are being mended. I have seen this modern miracle take place many times, and in this book I share that piece of good news.

"*Conflict: Friend or Foe?* underlines the fact that, when conflict erupts between husband and wife, parent and child, or two friends, it need not spell disaster. Conflict can become a counselor or a wise friend.

"My next book, *Listening to Others*, shows that we can help our neighbors, relatives, friends, and fellow Christians simply by listening to them. It shows how to listen to the bereaved, the depressed, the anxious—and the successful.

"My husband and I conduct Marriage Refreshment Weekends and conferences for lay people and for clergy couples. We have done these, not only in various corners of England, but in Poland, France, Singapore, Malaysia, Australia, and New Zealand. We have also addressed student and young peoples' groups in those countries and in Holland, and we have spoken to groups of clergy in Kenya and Tanzania."

AVOCATIONAL INTERESTS: Walking, reading, travel, dressmaking, music.

*   *   *

HUGHES, (John) Cledwyn   1920-1978

OBITUARY NOTICE—See index for *CA* sketch: Born May 21, 1920, in Llansantffraid, Wales; died of a brain tumor, January 23, 1978. Pharmacist and author. After serving briefly as a hospital pharmacist during the 1940s, Hughes became a full-time writer. His works include *He Dared Not Look Be-*

hind, *Poaching Down the Dee, The King Who Lived on Jelly, Portrait of Snowdonia,* and *The Colour Book of Wales.* He received short story awards from the now-defunct *New York Herald Tribune.*

OBITUARIES AND OTHER SOURCES:

Date of death provided by wife, Alyna Hughes.

*   *   *

HUGHES, William W(auters)   1918-

PERSONAL: Born June 3, 1918, in David City, Neb.; son of William Wauters (an actor and promoter) and Elzada (a housewife; maiden name, Albritton) Hughes; married Winifred Bruce, June 29, 1941 (deceased); married LaVerne Anderson (a retail store manager), March 13, 1980; children: Kathryn Ann, Holly Hughes Weiland, Mary Laurel, Virginia Hughes Coats. *Education:* University of Nebraska, B.A., 1946. *Politics:* Democrat. *Religion:* Presbyterian.

ADDRESSES: Home—3806 Harrison, Oakland, Calif. 94611.

CAREER: United Press (now United Press International), Little Rock, Ark., began as assistant bureau manager, became bureau manager, 1948-56; *Arkansas Gazette,* Little Rock, general assignment writer, 1956-57; University of Arkansas, Fayetteville, director of public information, 1957-86; writer, 1986—. Member of public relations committee of Southern Regional Education Board, 1960-75; member of steering committee of Arkansas Community Development Program, 1960-85. *Military service:* U.S. Army, 1941-46; became first lieutenant; received China War Memorial Medal from government of China.

MEMBER: American College Public Relations Association (member of board of trustees, 1965-68 and 1969-70), American Association of State Universities and Land Grant Colleges (member of national information committee, 1965-1975).

WRITINGS:

Archibald Yell, University of Arkansas Press, 1988.

WORK IN PROGRESS: Research for a book on duelling in the American Southwest during the early 1800s.

SIDELIGHTS: William W. Hughes told *CA:* "I am motivated primarily toward writing and publishing information which will fill significant gaps in the historical record of the United States. This is why my first published work is a biography of an unsung hero, who was one of the most colorful pre-Civil War figures in American political and military activity.

"Archibald Yell probably fought in more wars than any other soldier in the nation's history. He certainly was the only one who fought British, Spanish, Mexican, and American Indian adversaries in four different conflicts during the expansionist period, when the nation was reaching for Manifest Destiny. (He fought the Spanish in the Battle of Pensacola during the Creek War.) Yell was elected by his men to be the captain of his company when he was only seventeen years of age, and he died a hero in the Mexican War at the age of fifty. He was President James K. Polk's closest personal friend and political ally, serving as Polk's principal agent in negotiations with Sam Houston for the annexation of the Republic of Texas. Yell was a strong force in carrying Jacksonian dynamics westward in the political development of the nation, and he served as the first congressman and the second governor of the state of Arkansas.

"Yet Archibald Yell has been virtually unknown to posterity, and it is to help amend such inequities in the historical record that I wish to devote my literary efforts. This applies to the elements of history, as well as to its personalities. I am now at work on a manuscript which is focused on the importance of nineteenth-century duelling to the social, economic, and political development of the old Southwest, including the impacts which the outcomes of specific duels exerted on this development. Like my first book, this work will synthesize historical events that have been inadequately recorded."

Hughes added: "If there is validity to the term 'bleeding-heart liberal,' I am then a left-leaning (but anti-Communist) hemophiliac. Ironically, my first published work is the biography of an avid right-winger who regarded anti-slavery abolitionists as loathsome creatures."

AVOCATIONAL INTERESTS: Travel, hiking, bicycling, chess, bridge, pocket billiards, fishing, ping pong, tennis.

*   *   *

HULL, Lynda   1954-

PERSONAL: Born December 5, 1954, in Newark, N.J. *Education:* University of Arkansas at Little Rock, B.A., 1983; Johns Hopkins University, M.A., 1985.

ADDRESSES: Home—401 Eastside Dr., Bloomington, Ind. 47405. *Office*—Department of English, BH-442, Indiana University—Bloomington, Bloomington, Ind. 47405.

CAREER: Indiana University—Bloomington, instructor in English, 1985-87; Vermont College, Montpelier, member of field faculty, 1987—.

MEMBER: Associated Writing Programs, Academy of American Poets, Poetry Society of America.

AWARDS, HONORS: Pushcart Prize, 1985, for poem "Tide of Voices"; Juniper Prize from University of Massachusetts Press, 1986, for *Ghost Money*.

WRITINGS:

Ghost Money (poems), University of Massachusetts Press, 1986.

Poetry editor of *Crazyhorse*.

WORK IN PROGRESS: Another collection of poems.

*   *   *

HUME, Basil
See HUME, George Haliburton

*   *   *

HUME, (Alexander) Brit(ton)   1943-

PERSONAL: Born June 22, 1943, in Washington, D.C.; son of George (in business and an inventor) and Virginia Powell (a housewife; maiden name, Minnigerode) Hume; married Clare Jacobs Stoner (a student nurse), February 10, 1965; children: Louis, Virginia, Alexander, Jr. *Education:* University of Virginia, B.A., 1965. *Religion:* Episcopalian.

ADDRESSES: Home—5409 Blackistone Rd., Bethesda, Md. 20816. *Office*—1717 DeSales St., Washington, D.C. 20036.

CAREER: Hartford Times, Hartford, Conn., reporter, 1965-66; United Press International (UPI), Washington, D.C., reporter in Connecticut, 1967; *Evening Sun,* Baltimore, Md.,

reporter, 1968; free-lance reporter in Washington, D.C., 1969; investigative reporter for Jack Anderson's syndicated column "Washington Merry-Go-Round," 1970-72; *MORE* magazine, Washington, D.C., Washington editor, 1973-75; American Broadcasting Co., Inc. (ABC-TV), Washington, D.C., consultant to the "ABC News Closeup" documentary series, 1973-79, general correspondent, 1976-77, principal correspondent to the U.S. House of Representatives, 1977-80, chief Senate correspondent, 1981—, anchor of "World News Tonight—The Weekend Report," 1985—. Author, with T. R. Reid, of column "The Computer Report," distributed by the Washington Post Writers Group Syndicate; host of "Brit Hume: On Line," a weekly radio commentary on computers for ABC News.

MEMBER: Radio-Television Correspondents Association.

AWARDS, HONORS: Washington Journalism Center fellow, 1969.

WRITINGS:

Death and the Mines: Rebellion and Murder in the United Mine Workers, Grossman, 1971.
Inside Story, Doubleday, 1974.
St. A.: An Illustrated History of St. Alban's School, Glastonbury Press, 1981.

Co-author and narrator of documentaries for "ABC News Close-Up," including "Arson: Fire for Hire," 1978; "The Killing Ground," 1979; "Nobody's Children," 1979; and "Battleground Washington: The Politics of Pressure," 1979.

Contributor of articles to periodicals, including *New York Times Magazine, Harper's, Atlantic Monthly,* and *New Republic.*

SIDELIGHTS: Washington correspondent and ABC news anchor Brit Hume began his career in journalism as a reporter for the *Hartford Times,* a Connecticut daily newspaper, in 1965. After writing for United Press International (UPI) and the Baltimore *Evening Sun* and free-lancing in Washington, Hume landed a position as investigative reporter for Jack Anderson, author of the syndicated column "Washington Merry-Go-Round," in 1970. Hume's first book, *Death and the Mines: Rebellion and Murder in the United Mine Workers,* was published in 1971 while he was still affiliated with Anderson.

In *Death and the Mines* Hume documents the historic plight of the American coal miner and reveals the corruption that swelled within the ranks of the United Mine Workers union under the leadership of William Anthony Boyle (better known as Tony) in the 1960s and 1970s. The author illustrates the perilous conditions that routinely existed in mines throughout Kentucky, West Virginia, Pennsylvania, Alabama, and Illinois by focusing on the tragedy that struck the Consolidation Coal Company's Number 9 mine in Farmington, West Virginia, in 1968. Hume's investigation, the results of which were recounted by Harry M. Caudill in the *New York Review of Books,* showed that despite repeated violations of federal anti-explosive measures, the Number 9 mine remained in operation until a series of blasts claimed the lives of seventy-eight men. *Death and the Mines* calls into question the effectiveness of the mine safety act which Congress reluctantly passed in 1952 at the insistence of early union leader John L. Lewis after a mining explosion in West Frankfort, Illinois, the year before. As Caudill remarked, at a time when "an average of 119 men—the death total at West Frankfort—had died every seventeen days since 1900," the inspections mandated under the 1952 law seemed to guarantee "that labor peace and a benign prosperity" would reign in the coalfields. But Hume contends that when Tony Boyle succeeded Lewis as president of the United Mine Workers, union leaders developed alliances with industry mine owners that compromised the interests of the miners they were elected to protect.

Death and the Mines reveals the self-interested motivations and negligent actions of what Thomas Bethell, writing in the *Nation,* termed "a union gone wrong." And according to Caudill, Hume found that the United Mine Workers safety committee consisted of only one employee, and mining and safety laws and regulations went unenforced by both the union and the federal government. In addition, the union's welfare fund never sponsored any research into the prevention and treatment of black lung disease, which, caused by the habitual inhalation of coal dust, debilitated thousands of miners. Instead, chronicled Hume, almost one million dollars of the same welfare fund was set aside to finance the retirement of Boyle and his aides while miners drew pensions of only $115 each month.

Excerpts of *Death and the Mines* appearing in a *Saturday Review* article by Thomas Goldwasser indicate that the Consolidation Coal Company mining disaster resulted from an "excessive accumulation of flammable gas" that had caused the mine to shut down for several hours the night before the blasts: in that time, Hume implies, the situation was not rectified. The author quoted West Virginia governor Hulett Smith's reaction to the tragedy: "We must remember," Smith said, "that this is a hazardous business and what has occurred here is one of the hazards of mining." According to the same excerpt, Tony Boyle made no commitment to reform after the explosions, stating only that "as long as we mine coal, there is always this inherent danger." The union president went on to call Consolidation "one of the best companies to work with as far as cooperation and safety are concerned." But as Hume discovered, reported Goldwasser, three weeks before the West Virginia explosions, a federal jury found that the United Mine Workers had conspired with Consolidation and other mining companies for two decades to create an industrial monopoly. Furthermore, the Number 9 mine that had been declared "safe" by a Consolidation vice-president prior to the accident was, according to a surviving miner interviewed by Hume, actually "filled with gas."

Response to the West Virginia mining accident developed into what Caudill termed "outrage against government, the coal industry, and the union." A movement for reform within the union became a coal miners' revolt in 1969; the revolt continued until legislation was passed providing compensation to workers with black lung and until Boyle and his men were indicted for fraud.

Hume ends *Death and the Mines* with an account of an attempt by Joseph Yablonski (better known as Jock) to replace Boyle as president of the United Mine Workers. Yablonski exposed the corruption that existed within the union and lost to Boyle in a questionable 1969 election: three months later, Yablonski, his wife, and their daughter were killed by assassins who, Caudill wrote, "said they did the job for a mysterious 'Tony' who promised them $5200."

Critics found Hume's *Death and the Mines* an impressive piece of investigatory work. Goldwasser called the book a "brilliant account of the perils of mining," and Bethell asserted that "it needs to be read, for its heroes are ordinary, battered people who, having taken it as long as they could, decided not to take it any longer."

In his second book, *Inside Story,* Hume chronicles his experiences as a reporter for Jack Anderson's Washington column from 1970 to 1972. Published in 1974, *Inside Story* details the events surrounding the famed ITT (International Telephone and Telegraph Corporation)-Dita Beard case, a story that Hume broke in 1972. The first in a series of scandals that befell the administration of United States President Richard Nixon, the ITT affair grew out of allegations that Nixon allowed the company to settle its antitrust suits out of court in return for a pledge by the conglomerate of four hundred thousand dollars to subsidize the cost of the 1972 Republican Convention. Commenting on the implications of the case in *Washington Post Book World* Anthony Marro concluded "that the administration had been more sensitive to the needs of bloated and powerful corporations than to the needs of the urban poor, and that the custodians of our government apparently had no qualms about lying blatantly and repeatedly under oath."

Hume became involved with the antitrust case when an incriminating memo concerning a deal with the Nixon administration from Dita Beard, ITT's Washington lobbyist, came into his possession. His coverage of the scandal earned him considerable acclaim as an investigative reporter. In a quote from *Inside Story* printed in the *New York Times Book Review,* Hume claims that "the ITT affair was the best thing that ever happened to [his] career," making him "well known throughout the news business and even known to some outside it." This remark prompted critic Steven R. Weisman to comment in the *New York Times Book Review* that the book's revelations "are hardly flattering to the [journalistic] profession." Weisman implied that journalists who seek and enjoy celebrity status compromise their own integrity, remarking, "Fame is the painted lady journalists pretend not to lust after . . . not many people in the newspaper business will be happy that Hume can be so openly delighted with the . . . ways he has profited from the country's misfortunes." But Marro defended Hume's book as "not just a gratuitous bit of self-promotion." "At its best," Marro wrote, *Inside Story* "is a sensitive accounting of the pressures and fears that beset a reporter whose stories have set in motion events he can no longer control, and whose reputation, and perhaps his future, ride on the outcome."

Since resigning from his reporting position with Anderson in late 1972, Hume has become a widely recognized broadcast journalist. He serves as ABC-TV's chief Senate correspondent and anchors the network's Saturday edition of "World News Tonight—The Weekend Report."

CA INTERVIEW

CA interviewed Brit Hume by telephone at his office in Washington, D.C., on October 13, 1987.

CA: You became a free-lance writer in 1969. What inspired you to take that step?

HUME: Well, I had a passion at that point in my life to become an investigative reporter. I had been working for some mainstream wire services and newspapers—I worked for UPI [United Press International] and then the *Evening Sun* in Baltimore—but in my heart what I wanted most to do was to work as an investigative reporter in Washington and I was searching for a way to do that. I got a semester-long fellowship at the Washington Journalism Center in the spring term of 1969. Part of my schedule was set aside to do a research or reporting project. I devoted my time to research and inquiry into the United Mine

Workers of America labor union at the suggestion of [consumer advocate] Ralph Nader, who said there was a great story to be had about the deterioration, decline, and corruption of that union. He suggested that I could do a book on the subject. I had never done a magazine article of any consequence before that time and I didn't have any certainty that I could do a book. But I was willing to try if, as he insisted, he could arrange the contract. Well, he did. He got me a contract with Grossman Publishers, which was a subsidiary of Viking Press and was his publisher. It was a small advance, but enough so that between the time the fellowship ended and about the end of the year, I could get by. So I became a free lance, trying to finish in book form the work I had begun while a research fellow at the Washington Journalism Center. At the end of the year, most of the work was done and I had begun writing, but I hadn't gotten very far, and I had to take it from there.

CA: Let me ask you about the book that eventually resulted, Death in the Mines. *Were you pleased with the critical reaction to it?*

HUME: I thought it had pretty good critical reaction. I was disappointed that it didn't get reviewed in the *New York Times,* and I was disappointed in a couple of the reviews, but in the main—remember, I was only twenty-eight years old—I was pleased that it got reviewed as much as it did, as favorably as it did, by as many publications as was the case. As I recall, *Newsweek* [January 3, 1972] gave it a pretty good review, and there were a number of others. But the thing I was most pleased about was the book itself. I'll never forget coming back from New York on the train after the first copies had come in. I'd gone and picked them up, and I had them in a briefcase, just a couple of them, and all the way back to Washington on the train I kept taking the briefcase out and opening it up and taking the book out and just kind of staring at it. It's one of those things that you never believe is really going to happen to you; you never believe you're really going to see it in your hand. That was the day I did and it was a big day for me.

CA: One of [United Mine Workers President Tony] *Boyle's men filed suit against you over that book, didn't he?*

HUME: It wasn't over the book; it was over an item I subsequently did for [investigative reporter and newspaper columnist] Jack Anderson's column that actually was published before the book came out. The suit dragged on for five years. It was a very painful and worrisome circumstance because it involved a news source who did not want to be identified, and it also involved a court order that I identify the source. We fought it all the way to the Supreme Court and ultimately lost, but by the time that case was decided—actually, the Supreme Court didn't decide the case, they decided not to hear it and refused to grant a stay of the lower court's order—by that time a lot had happened. Most of the offending characters in the mine workers' union were either out of office or in jail and many of the original reasons for confidentiality of the source had evaporated. Ultimately the source herself came forward and voluntarily identified herself to the court, which got me off the hook, and a year later enabled the case to go to trial. We won it at trial.

CA: You mean the plaintiff wanted money, too?

HUME: His original goal in filing the suit was to identify the source, but as time went by and the officers of that union fell on more and more difficult times, I think his ambitions for the

case changed. He finally, I think, believed that he could possibly win the trial and some money, but he failed. It was a long process, though. Having a suit pending with the possibility of a court order that you might be forced to defy hanging over you is no fun. I wouldn't want to go through that again.

CA: Has the situation in the mines or with the United Mine Workers union improved at all since your book came out?

HUME: Yes, I think it has, though not necessarily as a result of the book. The old crowd got ousted and a new group of officers came in. The newcomers were not really experienced in managing a major labor union. They were essentially coal miners who had defied their organization and because no dissent was tolerated in the union hierarchy, there was nobody—except the murdered [Jock] Yablonski—of any standing who could have stepped into the job. So the first group who came in was relatively inexperienced, but they've since given way to a better group of officers. I think that the union is on a better footing now than it was then, although to a great extent, the union's fortunes ebb and flow with the fortunes of the coal industry. That situation was really malignant at the time that I first started looking into it, but I think it's much better now.

CA: What did you do after you finished the book?

HUME: I went to work for Jack Anderson in early 1970. I finished writing the book while working for Anderson, and it was published while I was still there. In late 1972, after almost three years with him, I resigned and went back to work as a free lance. I had a contract for a book about my experiences with him: a memoir of my days there. I sort of set myself up as a journalist in private practice. I had an office downtown, I was the Washington editor of *MORE* [a journal of press criticism], I did some lecturing—quite a lot of lecturing for a couple of years—and I worked on that book and wrote magazine articles. I was a fairly busy guy there for a couple of years as a free lance. Eventually, in late 1973, I signed on as a consultant to ABC News and over a period of several years thereafter, that consumed more and more of my time.

CA: Why did you move from MORE *to* ABC?

HUME: Increasingly my time was devoted to ABC and I became less active with *MORE.* Eventually I talked it over [with the editors of *MORE*] and they felt they wanted to get somebody who could be more active. I certainly didn't have any problem with that so I dropped out of the picture there. But my time as Washington editor of *MORE* was important for me; I really enjoyed it.

CA: What do you think of press criticism in the country these days?

HUME: I'm not very impressed with what's being done these days. I think that press criticism has become pretty tame. I think we in the media have gotten awfully self-righteous about what we do and awfully willing to excuse our own excesses on the grounds that we're doing God's work. I think sometimes we are, but I wonder if we recognize that those whom we inconvenience or offend may also be doing what they consider to be God's work. We're on thin ice when we're so pompous and self-righteous about ourselves.

CA: As you indicated, you worked with Jack Anderson for several years. How much of the work that appeared in that column was done by you and Anderson's other employees and how much did he do himself?

HUME: He had a team of reporters who worked for him as do the reporters who work for any other publication. He called them his associates. The way he gave credit to those who had done a particular piece was to mention that staff member in the column. Somewhere in the body of the story, he would write, "As X told my associate Brit Hume" or whoever it was, which would be a signal to the column's readers that the person mentioned had covered the case. Jack was really quite generous with credit of that kind, although everything went under his by-line. Those of us who worked for him submitted stories not as memos or as rough drafts; we actually wrote what were intended to be, if he so chose to use them, columns, or portions of columns, and he would use them if he liked them, or he would rewrite or edit them. His hands were on everything that ever went out and things that were submitted to him would be changed to one degree or another depending upon what he thought of them. Frequently he would rewrite things and then let us check them to make sure that in rewriting he hadn't distorted anything.

CA: Would you run the operation the same way if you were to be Anderson's successor?

HUME: I don't know whether I would or not. The reason I say that is I can't tell what it's like over there anymore. It's been fourteen or fifteen years since I was there. I left with a feeling of disappointment that a lot of what he had worked for had unfortunately been lost in one single incident: that was the famous Eagleton affair [Anderson alleged that the 1972 democratic vice-presidential candidate, Senator Thomas Eagleton, was guilty of driving while intoxicated, although the accusation had no basis in fact], in which he [Anderson]—not in the column but on the radio—went with a story that was really not ready to be broadcast. He was a little slow in coming off of it and the result was a great embarrassment which cost him dearly—much more than it would have cost anyone else because Jack was always a maverick in the eyes of his colleagues. It's hard for a maverick journalist to have an impact as an investigative reporter because an investigative reporter uniquely depends on the acceptance of his work by his colleagues for its impact. If the story can run, no matter how devastating, and never be heard of again after the day it appears—then its impact, obviously, is greatly diminished. But if the story runs and is seized upon by others and becomes widely reported. . . .

Drew Pearson, Jack's predecessor and the founder of the column, had a reputation as a maverick and his work was always looked at with some skepticism. Other journalists were slow to pick up on what he reported. Jack was much more of a pure reporter than he was a political crusader in Pearson's mold. He felt that his own strength was in investigative reporting and wanted to establish that what he reported, while it might have been phrased in a less dignified and more racy and colloquial style than the *New York Times* or the *Washington Post* would have put it, was nonetheless as reliable as anything that appeared anywhere else. And over a period of several years in the early going when he first took over the column, he did. He won the Pulitzer Prize in 1972 for his expose of the India-Pakistan papers, documents of the highest security classification which established beyond a doubt that Henry Kissinger and the Nixon Administration had been lying about where we stood in the war between India and Pakistan, that their assur-

ances to Congress had been false, and so forth. Then came the ITT-Dita Beard affair [allegations that the Nixon administration dropped an antitrust suit against International Telephone and Telegraph (ITT) after the corporation granted a four hundred thousand dollar subsidy to the 1972 Republican national convention], which was my story, and there were other stories done by others on the staff as well as stories Jack himself acquired. Jack had a terrific year in 1972, and it reached the point where the *Washington Post*, the *New York Times*, and the wire services were hanging on his every word, recognizing that what he published was often new, frequently terribly newsworthy, and nearly always reliable. And that impression, which I think was by and large the correct impression, was shattered by the Eagleton case and I'm not quite sure that he has ever been able to recover. His column remains popular, he remains a wonderful after-dinner speaker, and a commanding kind of presence in our business, but I'm not sure that he's ever recovered at the level of impact that he had before.

As one who participated and did what little I could to help him develop the credibility that he had, it was painful to see it disappear so quickly. Not out of any outrage with him but just out of disappointment that it had turned out the way it did, I moved on at the end of that period and I don't know what it's like over there now. But it seems to me the way he runs it is sensible. You can't do a column that appears seven days a week and all the other things that he does and not rely heavily on your staff. There's no way around it that I can see.

CA: In the reviews of the memoir you wrote about your work there, entitled Inside Story, *there was one particularly interesting comment. A New York Times Book Review critic said that for you and Anderson, "the bare facts almost never speak loud enough. With gusto, therefore, the two of them unabashedly seek publicity by plunging into press conferences, issuing public denunciations, and even testifying before Congress—things most reporters would shrink from—with their eyes focused constantly on the promotion of the column as an influential, even commercial enterprise." Do you think that was a fair comment?*

HUME: I think that's a fair comment to some extent. Jack always used to say that the column business, as Drew Pearson had taught it to him, was three parts journalism and one part show business. There was no question that Jack was seeking recognition for the column when he was participating, in a sense, in cases like the ITT case. But mind you this: Jack Anderson was not supported by a large media enterprise like the Times-Mirror Company or the Washington Post Company or the New York Times Company. He was a guy alone, with no real net under him if he fell. As a member of his staff, I was in the same situation. For example, in the ITT-Dita Beard case, my credibility and the credibility of my work were at stake. I testified under oath in that case before the Senate Judiciary Committee and there was really no way around doing that. The committee wanted to hear from us and my testimony had been challenged by perjured testimony given by Dita Beard. We had a lot at stake. We were in a situation where there was a kind of political-public relations contest going on in which we didn't really have any choice but to participate, to defend our own work. You have to defend yourself. I certainly benefited from the experience of doing the Dita Beard story, but because I was the only one who had talked to her [Dita Beard], I became the sole source of knowledge and information about what happened. I suppose I could have said "no comment" to everybody, but that would have been an odd thing to do when what I was saying was in fact the truth.

It seems to me that we're entitled to go around and answer questions and be heard on the subject of our work. It can be charged that this is a naked commercial enterprise if that's the way someone is determined to see it and to some extent perhaps it is. But there's more to it than that: there's the question of how we did our work and our accountability for it. Mind you, a lot of the questions I found myself answering were questions that I would rather not have had to deal with. I was asked on network television if I was lying and so forth. It wasn't all a press agent's dream, I assure you.

CA: After working for Anderson, as you indicated, you went on to work as a consultant to ABC News. About what were you being consulted?

HUME: ABC had started a documentary series called "Close-Up," which had an investigative purpose. The series didn't have anybody on its staff who was really an investigative reporter by specialty. The network was looking for someone who could help in that department. And it also happened that the first subject being addressed was the coal industry in West Virginia. I was, in their eyes, a natural choice and I was also available, so ABC hired me on and I worked on a whole series of documentaries. They hired me for thirteen weeks, then they signed me on for another year after that, and it just sort of kept going for several years, until I finally decided that I would take them up on their suggestion that I try being a correspondent, which I've been ever since.

CA: You hadn't been on the air previously?

HUME: Only as an interviewer of people; I had done no live on-air reporting.

CA: Have you found being a correspondent as satisfying as you perhaps thought it might be?

HUME: Well, I've found it to be very challenging. It's very different from print journalism. It has a number of obvious shortcomings as a journalistic form. You tend to find yourself cruising along the surface of stories that you were able to penetrate more deeply as a member of the writing press but you also find that you have to be fast, calm, poised, and able to respond on very short notice to breaking developments in a way that places far more pressure on you than it does on a print journalist. I find it enormously challenging. Of course the need to develop broadcast skills and what's called 'air presence' is an additional challenge. So I found it not at all easy to do. I find that the work we do on the evening news night after night is valid and useful and hard to do well and I certainly feel that I've had my hands full with it from the very first day.

CA: You're covering the U.S. Senate now. Is that what you had originally planned to do?

HUME: I'm not sure that when I started on this I had any clear plans. I knew that I was an awfully raw piece of material as far as broadcasting was concerned, that I had a lot to learn, and a lot of skills to try to develop. I think my original hope was that I'd just be able to become a competent correspondent, which, as I say, has been a difficult challenge. I was hoping to be able to develop a full range of skills, so if they wanted

me to sit in an anchor chair, I'd be okay doing that; if they wanted me to go live from some remote location, I could do that; if they wanted me to do a light feature piece that people would be amused by, I could do that; if they wanted me to do a very serious examination of some weighty issue, I could do that as well. I was just hoping to become sort of a full-service correspondent. But soon after I started I gravitated toward the idea of having a regular beat. You live a better life when you have a regular beat. You get on the air more, you're used more often, you have a greater standing, and you're not at the mercy of the nervous whim of a show producer or an assignment editor who is simply trying to make sure that he or she has all the bases covered. So it's a more comfortable existence, although I can't say over the past year that there's been anything terribly comfortable about it. It certainly wasn't comfortable in 1984 when I was on [Democratic Presidential Candidate] Walter Mondale's plane virtually from January through November. That was a murderous marathon, as were the Iran-*contra* hearings and many other stories here.

CA: Are you still anchoring?

HUME: I do a late show on Saturday nights and I occasionally sit in for Ted Koppel [on ABC's "Nightline"]. So I have that regular show and I do some other substitute anchor duty as well.

CA: Isn't that an overload, having the beat, the anchor job, and the substitution?

HUME: Well, it would be if I had to do that all the time. I know I'm going to get an extra day off during the week as compensation for my Saturday night work. I work a four-day week in the Senate, and then the Saturdays become less burdensome.

CA: You also write magazine articles, some of them published fairly recently.

HUME: Yes, I started writing magazine articles again about a year and a half ago, the reason being that I had bought a personal computer and gotten interested in figuring out how to use it. I realized as countless others before me had realized that the computer makes writing a lot less of a chore and a lot less painful. I enjoyed it so much that I went back to writing magazine articles.

CA: Is that the only reason, or does your return to magazine article writing indicate that you're dissatisfied somehow with what you can get across on television?

HUME: Well, it may. I haven't really searched myself on that. But understand that I've always thought of myself as a writer, or at least as a print journalist, first. I'm a little bit like [President Ronald] Reagan. Reagan's an actor who became a politician and I'm a print journalist who went into broadcasting. And while I hope that I've developed a full set of skills, I'm pleased to be included in something like *Contemporary Authors* because it's a reminder that I have some standing as a member of the writing craft. Also, I get a lot of satisfaction out of magazine pieces, and I always have. It's just an entirely different endeavor, and one for which I have a particular regard.

CA: It may be an unfair question to ask you considering everything else that you're doing, but are you planning another book?

HUME: I'm not planning on any book in particular. I find books hard work, grueling work, in fact, and I think they're kind of daunting, but I certainly don't feel I've written the last book I'll ever write. I don't have any ideas for a book in mind right now, but I've developed a total fascination with computers, and I know that using one will make the next book I write a much less painful undertaking. In fact, I'm so interested in personal computers that I've been doing a weekly radio commentary for ABC News and a column in the *Washington Post* every other week on the subject. The column, in fact, is syndicated: it goes out to most papers every week under a double by-line with T. R. Reid. We write on alternate weeks: he writes one week and I write the next. The column appears in the *Post* under the single by-line of whoever wrote it, but it's sent to about thirty other newspapers—some of them pretty big papers in Philadelphia, Houston, Atlanta, Indianapolis, Seattle—where it appears as a double by-line on a weekly basis.

BIOGRAPHICAL/CRITICAL SOURCES:

PERIODICALS

Nation, January 10, 1972.
Newsweek, January 3, 1972.
New York Review of Books, December 2, 1971.
New York Times Book Review, August 11, 1974.
Saturday Review, April 1, 1972.
Washington Post Book World, September 8, 1974.

—*Sketch by Barbara K. Carlisle*

—*Interview by Peter Benjaminson*

*   *   *

HUME, George Haliburton   1923-
(Basil Hume)

PERSONAL: Name in religion, Basil Hume; born March 2, 1923, in Newcastle upon Tyne, England; son of Sir William Errington (a physician and educator) and Lady Marie Elisabeth (Tisseyre) Hume. *Education:* St. Benet's Hall, Oxford, M.A., 1947; University of Fribourg, S.T.L., 1951.

ADDRESSES: Home—Archbishop's House, Ambrosden Ave., Westminster, London SW1P 1QJ, England.

CAREER: Entered Ordo Sancti Benedicti (Order of St. Benedict; Benedictines; O.S.B.), 1934, made the vows of a monk, 1945, ordained Roman Catholic priest, 1950; Ampleforth Abbey, Ampleforth, England, monk, 1942-50, assistant priest at village church and teacher at monastery's secondary school for boys, 1950-63, rugby coach, 1951-63, head of modern languages department, 1952-63, abbot, 1963-76; archbishop of Westminster, London, England, 1976—, created cardinal, 1976. Delegate to General Chapter of English Benedictine Congregation, 1957, elected *magister scholarum,* 1957, 1961; president of Bishops' Conference of England and Wales, 1979—. Chairman of Benedictine Ecumenical Commission, 1972-76; president of Council of European Episcopal Conferences, 1978-87; member of Vatican Secretariat for Christian Unity and Council of Synod on the Family; member of Sacred Congregation for Religious and Secular Institutes, Pontifical Commission for the Revision of the Canon Law, and Joint Commission of the Holy See and Orthodox Church to promote theological discussion between the churches, 1980—; vice-president of Council of Christians and Jews; president of Catholic Institute for International Relations and European Committee of Bishops' Conferences, 1979-87. Co-founder of Benedictine monastery in St. Louis, Mo. Guest on television and radio programs.

AWARDS, HONORS: Honorary degrees include D.D. from University of Newcastle upon Tyne and Cambridge University, 1979, University of London, 1980, Oxford University, 1981, University of York, 1982, University of Durham and Benedictine International Athenaeum of St. Anselm, Rome, 1987, and D.H.L. from Manhattan College and Catholic University of America, both 1980; Honorary Bencher of Inner Temple, 1976; Honorary Freeman of London and Newcastle upon Tyne, 1980.

WRITINGS:

UNDER NAME BASIL HUME

Searching for God, Hodder & Stoughton, 1977.
In Praise of Benedict, Hodder & Stoughton, 1981.
To Be a Pilgrim: A Spiritual Notebook, Harper, 1984.

Contributor to British periodicals.

SIDELIGHTS: Since his ordination as the Archbishop of Westminster in 1976, Cardinal Basil Hume has remained vigorously active in both spiritual and secular matters. As archbishop, he established regular team ministries in Westminster, as well as special apostolates to deal with the needs of young people, the handicapped, ethnic minorities, and other special groups. He has remained accessible, not only to his priests, but to his congregations, and particularly to groups of young people. Hume has promoted actively the theological dialogue between the Roman Catholic and Orthodox churches, and he himself has traveled widely to encourage this spirit of cooperation. His travels have taken him to the West Indies, Ethiopia, Canada, and the United States, as well as the countries of western Europe.

On the secular front, the Cardinal has tackled his country's housing problem, and he works with Anglican clergy to improve the social welfare of the poor. In the area of human rights, Hume has supported racial justice in London, opposed the sale of arms to El Salvador, and worked strenuously toward peace in Northern Ireland. He visited Ethiopia in 1984 and coordinated projects to increase aid to the country's famine victims.

Hume's first book, *Searching for God,* is a selection of the talks he gave to monks as the abbot of Ampleforth. It has been translated into many European languages.

To Be a Pilgrim is a collection of addresses, speeches, and sermons. "These notes come from the heart," wrote Alan Webster in the *Times Literary Supplement,* "not from the scriptwriter or the ecclesiastical diplomatist. Here is a pastor with a wise and intelligent concern." The book is intended for Catholic and Protestant readers alike, and stresses, according to Webster, "the teaching of the scriptures" rather than "the dogmas of infallibility." It treats honestly the problems now facing the Roman Catholic church and addresses such secular issues as employment and nuclear war. In *To Be a Pilgrim,* the cardinal stresses the need for a universal priesthood and for increased effort at the community and local level. To his reviewer, "This pilgrim at Westminster . . . has given a sense of hope and integrity to English Churches just when it is most needed."

BIOGRAPHICAL/CRITICAL SOURCES:

PERIODICALS

Times Literary Supplement, February 24, 1984.

HUMPHREYS, A(rthur) R(aleigh)   1911-1988

OBITUARY NOTICE: Born March 28, 1911, in Wallasey, England; died August 9, 1988. Scholar, educator, editor, and author. Professor of English and chairman of the English department at Leicester University from 1947 until his retirement in 1976, Humphreys was recognized both at home and abroad as a leading Shakespearean scholar. During his long career, he taught in Turkey, Austria, Denmark, India, and Pakistan. He also served as a research fellow at the Folger Shakespeare Library in Washington, D.C., from 1960 to 1962 and in 1964. He was perhaps best known for his authoritative annotated editions of Shakespeare's plays, including *Henry V, Henry VIII, Much Ado About Nothing,* and *Julius Caesar,* but he also produced editions of works by Henry Fielding and Herman Melville. In addition, Humphreys wrote several books of his own, including *William Shenstone, The Augustan World, From Dryden to Johnson, Melville, Shakespeare's "Richard II,"* and *Shakespeare's "Merchant of Venice."*

OBITUARIES AND OTHER SOURCES:

BOOKS

Who's Who in the World, 4th edition, Marquis, 1978.

PERIODICALS

Times (London), August 11, 1988.
Times Literary Supplement, November 19, 1982.

*   *   *

HUMPHREYS, (Robert Allan) Laud   1930-1988

OBITUARY NOTICE—See index for *CA* sketch: Born October 16, 1930, in Chickasha, Okla.; died of lung cancer, August 23, 1988, in Van Nuys, Calif. Clergyman, educator, sociologist, psychotherapist, and author. Humphreys was known for his studies of homosexuality, including the books *Tearoom Trade: Impersonal Sex in Public Places* and *Out of the Closets: Homosexual Liberation.* In 1975 he produced a study of more than one hundred gay murder victims, alleging that their attackers were typically heterosexuals who were hostile to gays. Ordained an Episcopal priest in 1955, Humphreys served for the next ten years in parishes in Oklahoma, Colorado, and Kansas. He then taught sociology and criminal justice at various colleges and universities, including Southern Illinois University, the State University of New York at Albany, Pitzer College, and Claremont Graduate School. Humphreys became chairman of the Institute for the Study of Human Resources in 1978 and began private practice of psychotherapy two years later. He was a member of the editorial boards of *Archives of Sexual Behavior* and *Journal of Homosexuality.*

OBITUARIES AND OTHER SOURCES:

BOOKS

The Writers Directory: 1988-1990, St. James Press, 1988.

PERIODICALS

Los Angeles Times, August 26, 1988.

*   *   *

HUMPHREYS, Susan L.
See LOWELL, Susan

HUNTER, Elizabeth
See de GUISE, Elizabeth (Mary Teresa)

*   *   *

HUNTINGTON, Madge   1937-

PERSONAL: Born July 9, 1937, in Port Jefferson, N.Y.; daughter of William Reed and Katrina (Roelker) Huntington; married Sergio A. Truini, April 3, 1960 (divorced, 1970); married Arnold M. Cooper (a physician), June 28, 1973; children: (first marriage) Margot, Stefano, William, Adrian. *Education:* Radcliffe College, B.A., 1958; Adelphi University, M.A., 1970.

ADDRESSES: Agent—Russell & Volkening, 50 West 29th St., New York, N.Y. 10024.

CAREER: Fiber artist, 1964-86; writer, 1986—.

WRITINGS:

The Traveler's Guide to Chinese History, Holt, 1986.

WORK IN PROGRESS: Family history, 1800-1865.

SIDELIGHTS: Madge Huntington told *CA:* "Chinese history is very confusing and spans four thousand years. *The Traveler's Guide to Chinese History* was an act of self-education written after a first trip to China when I couldn't find anything like it. It provides a concise but anecdotal overview of key figures and events in Chinese history for those who, whether traveling or simply curious, want to begin somewhere in grasping this complex topic. It is intended as a first run-through, with appendices on art, geography, and places to visit, to which one can add and add, as interest grows."

*   *   *

HUTCHINGS, Edward, Jr.   1912-

PERSONAL: Born August 25, 1912, in Brooklyn, N.Y.; son of Edward and Marjorie (McCann) Hutchings; married Martha Elizabeth Kelly, June 28, 1941; children: Alison, David. *Education:* Dartmouth College, B.A., 1933.

ADDRESSES: Home—2231 Midlothian Dr., Altadena, Calif. 91001. *Office*—Division of Humanities and Social Science, California Institute of Technology, 1201 East California Blvd., Pasadena, Calif. 91125.

CAREER: Worked as reporter for *Literary Digest,* 1934, and for *Tide,* 1935-37; news editor of *Business Week,* 1937-40; *Look,* New York, N.Y., associate editor, 1941; executive editor of *Liberty,* 1941-46; managing editor of *Science Illustrated,* 1946-48; *Engineering and Science,* Pasadena, Calif., editor, 1948-79; writer, 1979—. California Institute of Technology, lecturer in journalism, 1952—, director of publications, 1964-79.

WRITINGS:

(Editor) *Frontiers in Science: A Survey,* Basic Books, 1958.
(Editor) *Scientific Progress and Human Values,* Elsevier, 1967.
(Editor with Harrison Brown) *Are Our Descendants Doomed? Technological Change and Population Growth,* Viking, 1972.
(Editor with Norman H. Horowitz) *Genes, Cells, and Behavior: A View of Biology Fifty Years Ago,* W. H. Freeman, 1980.

(Editor) Richard P. Feynman, *"Surely You're Joking, Mr. Feynman": Adventures of a Curious Character,* Norton, 1985.

*   *   *

HUY, Nguyen Ngoc
See NGUYEN Ngoc Huy

*   *   *

HYBELS, Bill 1951-

PERSONAL: Surname sounds like "*High*-bulls"; born December 12, 1951, in Kalamazoo, Mich.; son of Harold (a business owner) and Gertrude (a homemaker; maiden name, VeldKamp) Hybels; married Lynne Barry (an author and speaker), May 18, 1974; children: Shauna, Todd. *Education:* Attended Dordt College, 1970-72; Trinity College, Deerfield, Ill., B.A., 1975.

ADDRESSES: Home—Barrington, Ill. 60010. *Office*—Willow Creek Community Church, 67 East Algonquin, South Barrington, Ill. 60010.

CAREER: Ordained interdenominational minister, 1975; youth minister at church in Park Ridge, Ill., 1973-75; Willow Creek Community Church, South Barrington, Ill., senior pastor, 1975—. Chaplain for Chicago Bears, 1982-87. International conference speaker and church consultant.

WRITINGS:

Caution: Christians Under Construction, Victor Books, 1978.
Christians in the Marketplace, Victor Books, 1982.
Laws That Liberate, Victor Books, 1985.
One Church's Answer to Abortion, Moody, 1986.

Who You Are When No One's Looking, Inter-Varsity Press, 1987.
Too Busy Not to Pray, Inter-Varsity Press, 1988.
Seven Wonders of the Spiritual World, Word Books, 1988.
Christians in a Sex-Crazed World, Victor Books, 1988.
Authentic Christianity, Moondy Press, 1989.

SIDELIGHTS: Bill Hybels told *CA:* "Willow Creek Community Church, which I and a team of Christian leaders founded in 1975, was specifically designed to reach the unchurched people of our community. My personal passion is to communicate the traditional truths of the Christian faith in a contemporary manner. That passion is reflected in our church, which uses contemporary music, drama, multi-media slide presentations, and dance, in addition to more traditional spoken messages, to communicate biblical principles.

"In my speaking and writing, I make every attempt to be true to my primary passion. I try to avoid religious cliches and 'churchy' terminology, and to offer practical, up-to-date guidelines for living out the Christian faith in the twentieth century.

"Before entering the ministry, I spent a number of years in the marketplace. My genuine love for business and my kinship with businessmen has motivated me to develop a style of communication that relates well to the 'real world.' I have done my best to reflect that style in my writing."

AVOCATIONAL INTERESTS: Travel (Mexico, South America, India, Europe), bare-boat sailing in the Virgin Islands.

BIOGRAPHICAL/CRITICAL SOURCES:

PERIODICALS

Moody Monthly, October, 1988.

I

ICHIKAWA, Satomi 1949-

PERSONAL: Born January 15, 1949, in Gifu, Japan.

CAREER: Author and illustrator of books for children, 1974—. Work exhibited at Gallery Printemps Ginza, 1984.

AWARDS, HONORS: Special mention for Prix Critici in Erba, Bologna Children's Book Fair, 1978, for *Suzette et Nicolas au marche.*

WRITINGS:

SELF-ILLUSTRATED CHILDREN'S BOOKS

A Child's Book of Seasons (poems), Heinemann, 1975, Parents Magazine Press, 1976.

Friends, Heinemann, 1976, Parents Magazine Press, 1977.

Suzette et Nicolas dans leur jardin, Gautier-Languereau, 1976, translation by Denise Sheldon published as *Suzette and Nicholas at the Market,* F. Watts, 1977, adaptation by Robina Beckles Willson published as *Sophie and Nicky Go to Market,* Heinemann, 1984.

Let's Play, Philomel, 1981.

Children Through Four Seasons, Kaiseisha, 1981.

Angels Descending From the Sky, Kaiseisha, 1983.

Children in Paris, two volumes, Kaiseisha, 1984.

Nora's Castle, Kaiseisha, 1984, Philomel, 1986.

Happy Birthday! A Book of Birthday Celebrations, Putnam, 1988.

ILLUSTRATOR OF CHILDREN'S BOOKS

Elaine Moss, compiler, *From Morn to Midnight* (poems), Crowell, 1977.

Clyde R. Bulla, *Keep Running, Allen!* Crowell, 1978.

Marie-France Mangin, *Suzette et Nicolas et l'horloge des 4 saisons,* Gautier-Languereau, 1978, translation published as *Suzanne and Nicholas and the Four Seasons,* F. Watts, 1978, translation by Joan Chevalier published as *Suzette and Nicholas and the Seasons Clock,* Philomel, 1982, adaptation by Robin Beckles Willson published as *Sophie and Nicky and the Four Seasons,* Heinemann, c. 1985.

Cynthia Mitchell, *Playtime* (poems), Heinemann, 1978.

Cynthia Mitchell, compiler, *Under the Cherry Tree* (poems), Collins, 1979.

Michele Lochak and Marie-France Mangin, *Suzette et Nicolas et le cirque des enfants,* Gautier-Languereau, 1979, trans-

lation by Joan Chevalier published as *Suzette and Nicholas and the Sunijudi Circus,* Philomel, 1980.

Suzette et Nicolas au Zoo, Gautier-Languereau, 1980.

Robin Beckles Willson, *Sun Through Small Leaves: Poems of Spring,* Collins, 1980.

Martine Jaureguiberry, *La Joyeuse Semaine de Suzette et Nicolas,* Gautier-Languereau, 1980, translation by Joan Chevalier published as *The Wonderful Rainy Week: A Book of Indoor Games,* Philomel, 1983.

Resie Pouyanne, *Suzette et Nicolas: L'Annee en fetes,* Gautier-Languereau, 1982.

Robin Beckles Willson, *Merry Christmas! Children at Christmastime Around the World,* Philomel, 1983.

Suzette et Nicolas font le tour du monde, Gautier-Languereau, 1984.

Cynthia Mitchell, editor, *Here a Little Child I Stand: Poems of Prayer and Praise for Children,* Putnam, 1985.

WORK IN PROGRESS: Writing and illustrating *Dolls;* illustrations for *Sophie, bout de chou,* a book about birthdays.

AVOCATIONAL INTERESTS: Collecting dolls.*

* * *

IMAMURA, Anne E(lizabeth Sommers) 1946-

PERSONAL: Born April 17, 1946, in Fort Wayne, Ind.; daughter of Robert H. (a watchmaker) and Irena E. (a secretary; maiden name, Schlegel) Sommers; married Katsuyuki Imamura (a consultant), June 13, 1970; children: Haruto Robert, Alysia Julia. *Education:* Ohio Dominican College, B.A. (cum laude), 1968; University of Hawaii at Manoa, M.A. (Asian studies), 1969; Columbia University, M.A. (sociology), 1976, Certificate from East Asian Institute and M.Phil., both 1977, Ph.D., 1980. *Religion:* Roman Catholic.

ADDRESSES: Home—1907 Amberstone Court, Silver Spring, Md. 20904. *Office*—Department of Sociology, University of Maryland at College Park, College Park, Md. 20742.

CAREER: Conducted field study in Tokyo, Japan, 1969-70; Sophia University, Tokyo, lecturer in religions and Japanese society, 1970-71; University of Malaya, Kuala Lumpur, lecturer in history, 1972-74; University of Tokyo, Tokyo, foreign research fellow in sociology, 1977-79; University of Maryland at College Park, assistant professor of sociology, 1981—. Lecturer at Sophia University, 1978-79. Director of Mid-Atlantic Region Clearinghouse for Japan-Related Instructional Material, Japan in the Schools Program, 1987—. Guest on Japanese television and National Public Radio; consultant to National Geographic Society.

MEMBER: American Sociological Association, Association of Asian Studies, Sociologists for Women in Society, Fulbright Alumni Association, East-West Center Association.

AWARDS, HONORS: Fellow of Japan Foundation, 1977-78; Fulbright fellow, 1978, 1983-84.

WRITINGS:

Urban Japanese Housewives: At Home and in the Community, University of Hawaii Press, 1987.

Contributor of articles and reviews to sociology and Asian studies journals.

WORK IN PROGRESS: A book on socioeconomic change in a small town in Hokkaido.

SIDELIGHTS: Anne E. Imamura told CA: "My interest in Japan developed out of the junior year program of the East-West Center at the University of Hawaii. I applied for the program out of an interest in seeing the world and future hopes to enter the Foreign Service. To make a long story short, I received the scholarship and spent a year in Hawaii doing intensive language study in Japanese and studying East Asian history, culture, and so forth. In the summer of 1967 I first visited Japan as part of that program. I lived with a host family and our group had regular classes and tours to orient us to Japan.

"After this my appetite was sufficiently whetted and I went on to pursue an academic rather than a foreign service career. In twenty years I have seen Japan grow and develop, and the present is a very exciting time to be a Japanologist.

"I am currently working on a new book. Its subject is socioeconomic change in a small town in Hokkaido, and focuses specifically on a town once composed of small family businesses now incorporated into the bedtown of a large metropolis. In particular, I aim to uncover and analyze the plans of the current generation of heads of family businesses. Many of these people are eldest sons, who inherited the business from their fathers. Many of the fathers or mothers of these men are still alive. I hope to catch the town poised for and planning to cope with socioeconomic change that is not springing from unemployment, but rather from increased and new economic options."

*   *   *

INCE, W(alter) N(ewcombe)   1927(?)-1988

OBITUARY NOTICE: Born c. 1927; died c. March, 1988. Educator, editor, and author. A graduate of Cambridge University's Selwyn College, Ince was chairman of the department of French at the University of Southampton from 1970 to 1985 and dean of the faculty of arts there from 1980 to 1983. He began his career teaching at the University of London's King's College and became senior lecturer at Leicester University before joining the faculty at Southampton. Interested primarily in French poetry of the nineteenth and twentieth centuries, Ince wrote an influential book entitled The Poetic Theory of Paul Valery: Inspiration and Technique. He later edited a volume of poetry by Jose-Maria de Heredia called Les Trophees and wrote a book that offers critical interpretation of Heredia's work.

OBITUARIES AND OTHER SOURCES:

PERIODICALS

Times (London), March 22, 1988.

*   *   *

ISHERWOOD, Robert M.   1935-

PERSONAL: Born April 18, 1935, in Waynesburg, Pa.; married, 1959; children: two. Education: Allegheny College, B.A., 1957; University of Chicago, M.A., 1959, Ph.D., 1964.

ADDRESSES: Home—109 Stokeswood Pl., Nashville, Tenn. 37215. Office—Department of History, Vanderbilt University, Nashville, Tenn. 37235.

CAREER: University of New Hampshire, Durham, assistant professor of history, 1964-67; Vanderbilt University, Nashville, Tenn., assistant professor, 1967-71, associate professor, 1971-86, professor of history, 1986—.

MEMBER: American Historical Association, American Society for Eighteenth-Century Studies, Society for French Historical Studies, Societe Francais Etude XVIII Siecle.

AWARDS, HONORS: Fellow of American Council of Learned Societies, National Endowment for the Humanities, and Camargo Foundation.

WRITINGS:

Music in the Service of the King: France in the Seventeenth Century, Cornell University Press, 1973.
(Contributor) The Third War of the Musical Enlightenment, University of Wisconsin Press, 1975.
Farce and Fantasy: Popular Entertainment in Eighteenth-Century Paris, Oxford University Press, 1986.

Contributor to history journals. Member of board of editors of French Historical Studies.

WORK IN PROGRESS: The Critics of Culture: The Philosophers and Musical Controversy in Eighteenth-Century France, completion expected in 1990.

AVOCATIONAL INTERESTS: French women, food, and wine.

BIOGRAPHICAL/CRITICAL SOURCES:

PERIODICALS

New York Times Book Review, June 15, 1986.

J

JACKSON, Charles O. 1935-

PERSONAL: Born August 22, 1935, in Orlando, Fla.; married wife in 1954; children: two. *Education:* Oglethorpe University, A.B., 1960; Emory University, M.A., 1962, Ph.D., 1967.

ADDRESSES: Office—Department of History, University of Tennessee, Knoxville, Tenn. 37996.

CAREER: Reinhardt College, Waleska, Ga., instructor in history, 1960-61; Women's College of Georgia (now Georgia College), Milledgeville, instructor, 1962-65, assistant professor of history, 1966-69; University of Tennessee, Knoxville, associate professor, 1969-75, professor of history, 1975—, associate dean of College of Liberal Arts, 1977—.

MEMBER: American Historical Association, American Association for the History of Medicine, American Studies Association, Southern Historical Association.

WRITINGS:

Food and Drug Legislation in the New Deal, Princeton University Press, 1970.
(Editor and contributor) *Passing: The Vision of Death in America,* Greenwood Press, 1977.
(With Charles W. Johnson) *City Behind a Fence: Oak Ridge, Tennessee, 1942-1946,* University of Tennessee Press, 1981.

Contributor to history and American studies journals.

BIOGRAPHICAL/CRITICAL SOURCES:

PERIODICALS

American Historical Review, March, 1971, April, 1979, April, 1982.
Annals of the American Academy of Political and Social Sciences, March, 1971.
Virginia Quarterly Review, winter, 1971.*

*   *   *

JACKSON, Henry 1912-1988
(Henry Armstrong)

OBITUARY NOTICE: Professionally known as Henry Armstrong; born December 12, 1912, in Columbus, Miss. (one source says Jackson, Miss.); died of heart failure, October 22 (one source says October 24), 1988, in Los Angeles, Calif. Professional boxer, evangelist, and author. The only man in boxing history to win and then defend three titles simultaneously, Jackson, along with Joe Louis and Jack Dempsey, was inducted into the boxing Hall of Fame in 1954. Raised in St. Louis, Missouri, Jackson graduated from high school, changed his name to Armstrong, and made his way to California, where he began his boxing career. In 1931 he turned professional, fighting steadily until 1937, when he won twenty-seven consecutive matches by knockout during a forty-six-bout winning streak. Publicity from his success sent him to New York City in search of a championship. Between October 29, 1937, and August 17, 1938, Jackson won the world featherweight, welterweight, and lightweight titles, earning the nicknames "Homicide Hank" and "Hammerin' Henry." Although he had lost all three titles by October of 1940, Jackson was and is considered a great champion, fighting for four more years before he retired from the ring. In 1947 he was ordained as a Baptist minister and in the 1950s founded and directed the Henry Armstrong Youth Foundation, an organization he hoped would help prevent juvenile delinquency. Jackson's health deteriorated steadily in the year before he died, probably the result, his doctors speculated, of the punishment his body suffered during his career as a boxer. Jackson was the author, under his professional name, of *Gloves, Glory, and God: An Autobiography,* published in 1956.

OBITUARIES AND OTHER SOURCES:

BOOKS

Armstrong, Henry, *Gloves, Glory, and God: An Autobiography,* Fleming Revell, 1956.
In Black and White, 3rd edition, Gale, 1980.
Who's Who in Boxing, Arlington House, 1974.

PERIODICALS

Los Angeles Times, October 24, 1988.
New York Times, November 13, 1982, October 25, 1988.
Times (London), October 25, 1988.

*   *   *

JACOB, John 1950-

PERSONAL: Born August 27, 1950, in Chicago, Ill.; son of

Bertram Frank (an insurance agent) and Eleanor (Addy) Jacob; children: Lucas John, Kathleen Rebecca. *Education:* University of Michigan, A.B., 1972; University of Illinois at Urbana-Champaign, M.A., 1973, Ph.D., 1989.

ADDRESSES: Home—527 Lyman St., Oak Park, Ill. 60304. *Office*—Department of English, North Central College, 30 North Brainard, Naperville, Ill. 60566. *Agent*—Nat Sobel, Nat Sobel Associates, Inc., 146 East 19th St., New York, N.Y. 10003.

CAREER: Northwestern University, Evanston, Ill., instructor in English, 1974-79; Illinois Legislative Investigating Commission, Chicago, chief writer, 1979-82; Northwestern University, instructor in English, 1984—. Development director for Community Advancement Programs, Chicago, 1973-77. Lecturer at Roosevelt University, 1975—; assistant professor at North Central College, Naperville, Ill., 1987—. Member of board of directors of domestic violence support group, Sarah's Inn. Consultant to Illinois Arts Council.

MEMBER: International P.E.N., Modern Language Association of America, Associated Writing Programs, Authors Guild, Multi-Ethnic Literature Society of the United States.

AWARDS, HONORS: Carl Sandburg Award from Friends of Chicago Public Library, 1980, for *Scatter;* grants from Illinois Arts Council, 1985 and 1987.

WRITINGS:

Scatter: Selected Poems, Wine Press, 1979.
Hawk Spin (poems), Pentagram Press, 1983.
Summerbook (poems), Spoon River Poetry Press, 1983.
Wooden Indian (poems), Kestrel Editions, 1987.
Long Ride Back (novel), Thunder's Mouth Press, 1988.

Also author of story collection, *The Light Fandango,* 1988. Columnist for *Margins.* Reviewer for *ALA Booklist,* 1976-86.

WORK IN PROGRESS: A second novel, publication by Another Chicago Press expected in 1988; research on the poetry of Charles Olson.

SIDELIGHTS: John Jacob told *CA:* "I've been interested in subjects from a 'non-literary' point of view: anthropology, social work, philosophy, psychology, and psychiatry. Urban scenes and life interest me a great deal, and so does the American Indian.

"Most of my poetry is concerned with concrete ways of looking at abstract concepts. My recent work is more narrative. Some of the work has the urban experience as a theme.

"My novel, *Long Ride Back,* ostensibly is about the war in Vietnam, the antiwar movement, and a particular man's involvement in both and his life in the 1980s. I consider it a personal rather than a universal statement. My personal view in my fiction is that random activity governs the 'order' we try to create in our worlds. Obviously, we do not always succeed. My second novel will attempt to trace this theme or point of view in a smaller, less obvious, and shorter format."

BIOGRAPHICAL/CRITICAL SOURCES:

PERIODICALS

Chicago Tribune, June 28, 1988.

*   *   *

JACOBS, Nehama 1951-

PERSONAL: Given name is pronounced like "Bahama"; born

December 9, 1951, in Chicago, Ill.; daughter of Sidney J. (a rabbi, writer, and publisher) and Helen (maiden name, Rosenzweig) Jacobs. *Education:* Harvard University, B.A., (cum laude), 1974.

ADDRESSES: Home—50 Riverside Dr., New York, N.Y. 10024. *Office*—Tucker, Anthony & R. L. Day, Inc., 120 Broadway, Suite 3146, New York, N.Y. 10271.

CAREER: Young & Rubicam (advertising agency), New York, N.Y., copywriter and creative supervisor, 1973-74, vice-president, 1978-86; Tucker, Anthony & R. L. Day, Inc. (investment bankers), New York City, investment banker, 1986—. Marketing, organizational, and media consultant on the status of women in corporate America.

MEMBER: Council on Foreign Relations (1984—), Young Professional Group of the Foreign Policy Association of New York (founding chairperson), Harvard Club of New York City (member of executive committee; member of board of managers, 1988—).

WRITINGS:

(With Sarah Hardesty) *Success and Betrayal: The Crisis of Women in Corporate America,* F. Watts, 1986.

Contributor to periodicals, including *Plain Dealer* (Cleveland), *Savvy, Management Journal, Careers, Across the Board,* and *New Woman.*

WORK IN PROGRESS: Research and writing on management and corporate culture issues of critical interest; exploring women's issues.

SIDELIGHTS: A former advertising vice-president turned investment banker, Nehama Jacobs has lived through the curious cycle of disappointment which many women in corporate management positions experience. In *Success and Betrayal: The Crisis of Women in Corporate America,* Jacobs and co-author Sarah Hardesty examine the possible causes of disillusionment among today's working women.

A study by the recruitment firm Korn Ferry, as quoted in the *Boston Globe,* indicates that while one-third of all corporate managers are female, only 2 percent of the top management positions are held by women. Jacobs addresses this incongruity in what Linda Palmarozza, writing for the *Philadelphia Inquirer,* called an "intense, well-researched" study of the factors contributing to women's frustration and dissatisfaction in the workplace.

Success and Betrayal shatters the myths that Jacobs claims women hold about the business world, including the belief that corporations recognize the achievements of individual workers and reward those workers on the basis of merit. The book's authors maintain that most women reach a plateau after achieving a certain degree of success. The few women who advance to the highest echelons of corporate management feel a "sense of loss and betrayal," wrote Jacobs and Hardesty in an excerpt quoted by the *Boston Globe,* "when the corporate mystique fails to live up to its billing."

Although several critics felt that the quotes and excerpts which make up a large portion of the book were presented in a fragmented fashion, Jewelle Bickford commended the authors on their balanced, analytical method of documentation in a review for the *Wall Street Journal.* She wrote that Jacobs and Hardesty suggest some changes in corporate operations, "but only in ways that would benefit men, women, and the company alike.'' An approach that ''urges women to be more realistic when they enter the workforce,'' according to Bickford and other critics, makes *Success and Betrayal* a credible exploration into an important issue.

Jacobs told *CA:* ''To quote Elizabeth Janeway, 'American women are not the only people in the world who manage to lose track of themselves, but we do seem to mislay the past in a singularly absent-minded fashion.' In the course of researching and writing *Success and Betrayal* with Sarah Hardesty, I discovered an urgent truth I shared with many other women: we had all mislaid our pasts, or at best, diverted those early hopes and expectations of success to fit a corporate world.

''*Success and Betrayal* was written on weekends when everyone else at the advertising agency [Young and Rubicam] was at the beach. Ironically, in exploring the myths and expectations that collectively shaped women's careers in the 1970s and 1980s, the book has shattered many myths about the making of first successful books and their authors: you *can* write a book in what is laughably termed your 'spare time'; you *can* develop a daring and controversial thesis about corporate America and be heard; you *can* write powerfully and persuasively about women and have that scholarship be accepted— if not embraced—by men.

''Hardesty and I set out to write the first book by women managers *for* women managers. This book is only the beginning of what I hope will be an ongoing exploration into how— and why—men and women work in business.''

BIOGRAPHICAL/CRITICAL SOURCES:

BOOKS

Success and Betrayal: The Crisis of Women in Corporate America, F. Watts, 1986.

PERIODICALS

Boston Globe, November 10, 1986.
Los Angeles Times, January 8, 1987.
Philadelphia Inquirer, January 4, 1987.
Savvy, April, 1988.
USA Today, April 30, 1987.
Wall Street Journal, December 23, 1986.

*   *   *

JAMES, Robin (Irene)   1953-

PERSONAL: Born September 24, 1953, in Seattle, Wash.; daughter of Robert Leroy (an artist) and Irene Elizabeth (an artist; maiden name, Weinberger) James; married Michael George Cosgrove (a heavy equipment surveyor), July 1, 1980. *Education:* Graduated from Shorecrest High School, Seattle, Wash.

ADDRESSES: Snohomish, Wash.

CAREER: Free-lance artist, 1971—.

MEMBER: International Wildlife Federation, American Humane Association, Animal Protection Institute, Humane Society of the United States, National Wildlife Federation, People for the Ethical Treatment of Animals, Delta Society.

WRITINGS:

SELF-ILLUSTRATED CHILDREN'S BOOKS; PUBLISHED BY PRICE, STERN

Baby Pets, 1984.

Baby Forest Animals, 1984.
Baby Zoo Animals, 1984.
Baby Farm Animals, 1984.
Baby Puppies, 1985.
Baby Kittens, 1985.
Baby Horses, 1986.
Baby Unicorns, 1986.

ILLUSTRATOR OF BOOKS BY STEPHEN COSGROVE; PUBLISHED BY PRICE, STERN

Tale of Three Tails, 1974.
Wheedle on the Needle, 1974.
Serendipity, 1974.
Muffin Muncher, 1974.
The Dream Tree, 1974.
Little Mouse on the Prairie, 1975.
Cap'n Smudge, 1975.
The Gnome From Nome, 1975.
In Search of the Saveopotomas, 1975.
Morgan and Me, 1975.
Bangalee, 1976.
Creole, 1976.
Kartusch, 1976.
Jake O'Shawnasey, 1976.
Hucklebug, 1976.
Gabby, 1977.
Leo the Lop, 1977.
Leo the Lop: Tail Two, 1977.
Leo the Lop: Tail Three, 1977.
Snaffles, 1978.
Flutterby, 1978.
Catundra, 1978.
Feather Fin, 1978.
Grampa-Lop, 1979.
Nitter Pitter, 1980.
Raz-Ma-Taz, 1980.
Trafalgar True, 1980.
Trapper, 1980.
Maui-Maui, 1981.
Ming Ling, 1981.
Tee-Tee, 1981.
Morgan and Yew, 1982.
Morgan Mine, 1982.
Morgan Morning, 1983.
Flutterby Fly, 1983.
Kiyomi, 1983.
Minikin, 1984.
Dragolin, 1984.
Shimmeree, 1984.
Squeakers, 1985.
Glitterby Baby, 1985.
Jingle Bear, 1985.
Crabby Gabby, 1985.
Buttermilk, 1986.
Fanny, 1986.
Pish Posh, 1986.
Mumkin, 1986.
Misty Morgan, 1987.
Buttermilk-Bear, 1987.
Memily, 1987.
Crickle-Crack, 1987.
Persnickity, 1988.
Sassafras, 1988.
Sniffles, 1988.
Rhubarb, 1988.

Gigglesnitcher, 1989.

ILLUSTRATOR OF BOOKS BY KITTY HIGGINS; PUBLISHED BY PRICE, STERN

Tippy Potter the Otter, 1989.
Polly LaPush the Platypus, 1989.
Perry P. Plum the Possum, 1989.
Andy McClark the Aardvark, 1989.

SIDELIGHTS: Robin James told *CA:* "I've been drawing since I could hold a pencil, and after fifteen years of illustrating children's books, I am still in awe of being able to make a living doing what I love to do. I've been told my work reflects my love of animals and nature, and living on a horse farm gives me an opportunity to help many animals in need. I also believe strongly in fantasy, and that it plays an important part in keeping our imaginations alive. This in turn will always keep life full of beauty and intrigue."

*   *   *

JAMES, William C(losson)   1943-

PERSONAL: Born May 20, 1943, in Sudbury, Ontario, Canada; son of Frederick Stanley (an accountant) and Kathryn (a librarian; maiden name, Closson) James; married Elizabeth Ann Maclellan (a secretary), December 31, 1964 (divorced November 19, 1987); children: Matthew, Andrew, Caroline. *Education:* Queen's University, Kingston, Ontario, B.A., 1965, B.D., 1968; University of Chicago, M.A., 1970, Ph.D., 1974.

ADDRESSES: Home—169 Casterton Ave., Kingston, Ontario, Canada K7M 1R9. *Office*—Department of Religion, Queen's University, Kingston, Ontario, Canada K7L 3N6.

CAREER: Queen's University, Kingston, Ontario, lecturer, 1973-75, assistant professor, 1975-80, associate professor, 1980-85, professor of religion and literature, 1985—, chairman of undergraduate studies in religion, 1978-81. Member of board of directors, Canadian Corp. for Studies in Religion, 1978-79.

MEMBER: Canadian Society for the Study of Religion (member of executive board, 1975-78; publications officer, 1986—), Canadian Theological Society, American Academy of Religion (president of Eastern International Region, 1987-88).

AWARDS, HONORS: Grants from Ontario Arts Council, 1981-82.

WRITINGS:

(Contributor) Peter Slator, editor, *Religion and Culture in Canada*, Wilfrid Laurier University Press, 1977.
(Editor) Arthur C. Twomey, *Needle to the North*, Oberon Press, 1982.
A. A. Chesterfield: Ungava Portraits, 1902-04, Agnes Etherington Art Centre, 1983.
A Fur Trader's Photographs: A. A. Chesterfield in the District of Ungava, 1901-1904, McGill-Queen's University Press, 1985.
(Editor) *AIDS in Religious Perspective: Three Essays*, Queen's Theological College, 1987.
(With Daniel Fraiken and Harold Remus) *Religious Studies in Ontario: A State-of-the-Art Review*, Canadian Corporation for Studies in Religion, 1989.

Contributor to periodicals. Book review editor of *Studies in Religion*, 1979-86.

WORK IN PROGRESS: The Religious Dimensions of Canadian Fiction.

SIDELIGHTS: William C. James told *CA:* "My already active general interest in the Canadian north, native peoples, the wilderness, and the fur trade was activated further by the 1974 discovery of an important body of photography by a fur trader and photographer, A. A. Chesterfield. This finally culminated in the publication of *A Fur Trader's Photographs*. A seminal essay, 'The Canoe Trip as Religious Quest,' has been reprinted and led to an invitation to lecture at a conference on the canoe. Other interests include 'Inuit Art and the Sacred,' the hero and the quest theme in literature, the Canadian imagination, and nature mysticism."

In an article in Toronto's *Globe and Mail*, reviewer Thomas York described the discovery of Chesterfield's photographs as "a fascinating tale of treasure in your own back yard." James found the photographs in an office at Queen's University and began a quest to trace them to the original photographer. This led the author to an even larger collection of Chesterfield's work and, eventually, to his book *A Fur Trader's Photographs*. York reported that this book reveals not only the work of the photographer, but the "Inuit and Cree cultures of northern Labrador . . . at the cusp of their turning from their autonomous, open-faced ways into the disastrous twentieth century." The critic called the book "a unique document, carefully researched and written with concern. . . . There is not an unnecessary word in the text and the pictures, while they do not speak for themselves, are presented in such a way as to make a reader see."

AVOCATIONAL INTERESTS: Canoeing, sailing, woodworking, restoring and maintaining a twenty-six-foot classic Danish folkboat.

BIOGRAPHICAL/CRITICAL SOURCES:

PERIODICALS

Globe and Mail (Toronto), November 30, 1985.

*   *   *

JASON, Kathrine   1953-

PERSONAL: Born February 9, 1953, in New York, N.Y.; daughter of Leon (a toy designer) and Lucille Lee (an interior designer; maiden name, Kramer) Jason; married Peter Rondinone (a professor and writer), April 23, 1984. *Education:* Bard College, A.B., 1975; Columbia University, M.F.A., 1978; doctoral study at Graduate Center of the City University of New York, 1980-81.

ADDRESSES: Home—348 West 11th St., No. 3B, New York, N.Y. 10014. *Office*—International English Language Institute, Hunter College of the City University of New York, 695 Park Ave., New York, N.Y. 10021.

CAREER: Hunter College of the City University of New York, New York, N.Y., instructor in writing and literature, 1981—.

AWARDS, HONORS: Grant from National Endowment for the Arts, 1985; Fulbright fellow, 1978-79; finalist for Renato Poggioli Award from PEN for translation, 1984; finalist for the Discovery/Nation Award for *Unstringing*, 1985.

WRITINGS:

(Translator) Enzo Ferrari, *Piloti, che gente* (autobiography; title means "Racers, What People!"), Ferrari, 1984.

(Editor and translator) Tommaso Landolfi, *Words in Commotion and Other Stories*, Viking, 1986.

Work represented in anthologies, including *Italian Poetry Today*, New Rivers Press, 1979; *Armenian Poetry Through the Ages*, University of Illinois Press, 1980; *The New Directions Anthology 45*, New Directions, 1982. Contributor of poems and translations to periodicals, including *Omni, New Yorker, City, Lampeter Muse, Fiction, Il progresso,* and *Translation*.

WORK IN PROGRESS: Editing an anthology of contemporary Italian fiction, publication by Graywolf expected in 1989; *Unstringing,* a collection of poems; *Excavations and Other Poems.*

SIDELIGHTS: Kathrine Jason told *CA:* "My experience in Italy was not only the foundation for my professional development as a translator, but was seminal for my own work as well. I'd often been drawn in my work to 'otherness,' to the distant and foreign; perhaps the fact that I was adopted put the spirit of the seeker in me, as if through the imagination, I might locate some lost fragment of origin and self. In Italy, I was captivated, as so many writers and artists have been, as much by the landscapes and contemporary culture as by the spectacle of history and continuum. My Italian experience became a context, an 'objective correlative' for many of the ideas and impulses I was exploring in my poems. James Wright, whose Italian poems I think capture the essence of those landscapes, was a teacher and inspiration for my work of that period. Thus my work over the past ten years has been an exploration of Italian places and their meaning for me; half the material in *Unstringing* reflects that interest.

"Returning to Italy year after year, gradually another door opened for me: antiquity. Like most of my subjects, this one came serendipitously and unexpectedly, though in retrospect I can see how it evolved out of my continuing involvement with things Italian. Over the past year, I have been reading widely about the Greco-Roman world, particularly about daily life and the lives of women. My most recent work, *Excavations and Other Poems,* explores events, personae, and art of the ancient world."

*   *   *

JENKINS, Dan (Thomas B.)   1929-

PERSONAL: Born December 2, 1929, in Fort Worth, Tex.; son of a salesman and an antiques dealer; married third wife, June Burrage (a restaurant owner); children: Sally, Marty, Danny. *Education:* Attended Texas Christian University.

CAREER: Affiliated with *Fort Worth Press*, Fort Worth, Tex., 1948-60; affiliated with *Dallas Times Herald*, Dallas, Tex., 1960-62; affiliated with *Sports Illustrated*, New York, N.Y., 1962-84; affiliated with *Playboy*, Chicago, Ill., beginning in 1985; writer.

WRITINGS:

Sports Illustrated's The Best Eighteen Golf Holes in America, foreword by Ben Hogan, Delacorte, 1966.
The Dogged Victims of Inexorable Fate, Little, Brown, 1970.
Saturday's America, Little, Brown, 1970.
Semi-Tough (novel), Atheneum, 1972.
Dead Solid Perfect (novel), Atheneum, 1974.
(With Edwin Shrake) *Limo* (novel), Atheneum, 1976.
Baja Oklahoma (novel), Atheneum, 1981.
Life Its Ownself: The Semi-Tougher Adventures of Billy Clyde Puckett and Them (novel), Simon & Schuster, 1984.

Football, photographs by Walter Iooss, Jr., Abrams, 1986.
Fast Copy, Simon & Schuster, 1988.

Also author of film and television screenplays.

SIDELIGHTS: A popular golf and football writer at *Sports Illustrated* for more than two decades, Dan Jenkins was hailed as possibly "the best sportswriter in America" by Larry L. King in *Harper's*. His books include the football best-seller *Semi-Tough,* which *Chicago Tribune* columnist Bob Greene called "the best novel of the '70s." Widely appreciated for his sense of humor and strongly expressed personal opinions, Jenkins has been compared to such noted American humorists and satirists as H. L. Mencken and Mark Twain. "I always thought it takes tremendous ego to be a writer," Jenkins told Stephanie Mansfield of the *Washington Post*. "To sit down and put your name on it and presume to tell people. But I enjoy it. Because I . . . *do* know more about it than they do and I want to inform them."

According to Sarah Ballard of *People* magazine, Jenkins has "two artistic premises—that sport is primarily a laughing matter and that life is best viewed from the back table of a friendly joint, preferably late at night." Though based in New York City for much of his career, Jenkins is proud of his Texas roots and often prefers the company of friends from his home state to people Greene says he calls the "New York killer elite." Admirers say he loves to sit around and talk, and they suggest that his conversation is as funny and outspoken as his writing. But as Jenkins reminded Mansfield, laughter is a tactic for survival. In life, he observed, "most of what's going to happen is bad. You know that going in. You got to learn to laugh."

Jenkins was "the quintessential Sports Illustrated writer" according to Roy Blount, Jr., a co-worker who spoke to Mansfield. "He knew everything and everybody," Blount said, and he could report on a golf tournament by sitting at a nearby bar, where the contestants talked to him about the day's play. One of Jenkins's first books, *The Dogged Victims of Inexorable Fate,* is a collection of *Sports Illustrated* articles surveying golf tournaments and golf history. Jenkins evokes the early days of the professional tour in the 1930s, when the prizes were small and players compensated with a wild sense of fun. He proceeds to the more careerist atmosphere of contemporary tours, where successful golfers operate like businessmen and the lesser players await their chance at riches. According to Rex Lardner of the *New York Times Book Review,* "Jenkins dissects golfing . . . but does it so good-naturedly that the reader must marvel at the knowledge displayed while trying not to fall out of his hammock laughing."

Saturday's America is a similar collection, but about college football. Jenkins comments on the famous personalities, teams, and rivalries, questioning such mainstays of football lore as the football movie and the Heisman Trophy. The people he meets range from a high school prospect harassed by college recruiters to a group of dedicated Texans for whom a "football weekend" means driving hundreds of miles to attend four different games. In King's opinion Jenkins offers his readers more than great sportswriting. "There is social commentary in Jenkins' work," King said, "delightful airings of the latest cultural absurdities, and some of the funniest one-liners since [comedians] Mel Brooks or Woody Allen sat down to tickle the typewriter."

With no commitment from an agent or a publisher, Jenkins wrote his first novel, *Semi-Tough*. "It was the first raunchy sports book,'' in Blount's words, and its success rocketed Jenkins to fame and fortune. Set during the week before a Super Bowl game, the novel parodies a popular commodity in sportswriting, the athlete's diary. The narrator is Billy Clyde Puckett, a football star from Texas who plays for the New York Giants. Billy Clyde and his teammates are uninhibited and unrefined, and they spend their time drinking, chasing women, and making racist jokes about black football players. But Billy Clyde is more than just a wild country boy, as David Halberstam pointed out in the *New York Times Book Review*—he is a "country slicker," whose glamorous, well-paid job gives him unusual access to the social elites of both Texas and New York City. By viewing life through Billy Clyde's eyes, Jenkins can mock Texas oil millionaires, homecoming queens, and trendy New York restaurants. Not much happens in *Semi-Tough*, but everyone talks a great deal—including Billy Clyde, who speaks his diary into a tape recorder. "The style throughout is essentially black-white-rural-Southern, our richest national language," Halberstam observed, and "Jenkins has a marvelous command of it." "Even veteran Jenkins readers will be amazed at the achievement of his first novel," sportswriter Pete Axthelm wrote in *Newsweek,* and King said in *Life* that "if you have the stomach for belly laughs, semi-tough language and spoofing just about everything in modern America, this book should be your stick of tea."

The freewheeling comedy continues in Jenkins's later novels. *Dead Solid Perfect* views professional golf through the eyes of Billy Clyde's uncle, Kenny Puckett. *Limo,* written with a friend from Texas, Edwin Shrake, records the misadventures of a television network program director. *Baja Oklahoma* (meaning "Lower Oklahoma," that is, Texas) focuses on a small-town waitress who fulfills her dream of becoming a country music star.

Reviewers often say that Jenkins bases his writing on vivid language: Texas slang, colorful insults, and, most notably, the comic one-liner. He concentrates on language so much, some suggest, that his books are episodic and lack the plot and character development many readers expect in a novel. To Jonathan Yardley of *Washington Post Book World,* "locker-room lingo hardly compensates" for such deficits as "slipshod plotting" and "cliched characterizations." Jenkins fans, however, do not consider his idiosyncrasies to be flaws. "Jenkins loves a good line so much that he'll work it in whether it fits or not," wrote Wyatt Wyatt in the *Detroit News,* "but who's going to complain?" Citing the author's caricature of the Super Bowl in *Semi-Tough,* King asked readers of *Life* magazine, "In all these exaggerations, who does not recognize huge lumps of truth?" Asked about his prose style, Jenkins told Mansfield: "I'm not committed to boring people. I'm not committed to long, drawn-out boring soliloquies. I basically write books that I want to read."

A number of reviewers have been offended by the rough manner of Jenkins's characters, particularly the disrespect they show toward blacks and women. In *New Statesman,* for instance, Brian Glanville suggested that Jenkins identifies personally with Billy Clyde and that he holds up the players' bigotry and crudeness for admiration rather than ridicule. But Jenkins's many defenders suggest that humor is irreverent by its very nature, and so cannot respect anyone's sensibilities. As Axthelm explained, *Semi-Tough* "treats blacks no more disrespectfully than it treats women, Texans, businessmen, coaches, referees . . . and anyone else who happens to take the game of pro football too seriously." In *Modern Fiction Studies,* David L. Vanderwerken compared Jenkins to such

renowned comic writers as Mark Twain, Jonathan Swift, and Lenny Bruce, all of whom, he noted, "have been accused of grossness and viciousness." He reminded readers that "the voice of American satire is a voice of outrage expressed outrageously."

Won over by the liveliness of Jenkins's humor, some reviewers admitted to liking his work despite their better judgment. "I am living proof," wrote Carolyn Banks in *Washington Post Book World,* "that even a feminist can love Billy Clyde, who, if he were real, would have to be served with an apple in his mouth." Similarly, *New Republic*'s William C. Woods read *Dead Solid Perfect* with "grudging delight." He commented: "The people are so weird, the jokes so vile, the dialogue so infected with vindictive humor, and the whole mood of the book so animated by feverish indifference to the 'rules' of storytelling that . . . you wonder whether Dan Jenkins' casual and contemptuous way of writing fiction isn't a valid new voice, so reactionary as to be truly avant-garde."

In 1977 *Semi-Tough* was adapted for a major motion picture (in *People,* Jenkins called the result "semi-okay"). Shortly thereafter the book became the basis of a television series, and Jenkins, to his great frustration, was invited to participate. He wrote six scripts, none of which were produced, and the program was canceled after less than one month on the air. The experience encouraged Jenkins to write *Life Its Ownself,* a sequel to *Semi-Tough* that adds extensive lampoons of the media world to the targets of its predecessor. Billy Clyde Puckett, sidelined by a knee injury, quits professional football to become a television sports commentator. He endures the jargon of network executives and sports celebrities while his wife stars in a situation comedy about a woman who bravely runs a restaurant while succumbing to an unspecified illness. Meanwhile professional football disintegrates as players strike for free agency by making their game as inept and boring as possible. The book, which returned Jenkins to the best-seller lists, was praised by Christopher Lehmann-Haupt of the *New York Times* for its "outrageous inventiveness." *Life Its Ownself* "needs no more life pumped into it," the critic asserted, because "it's got a superabundance."

In 1984, after twenty-two years and more than five hundred articles for *Sports Illustrated,* Jenkins angrily left the magazine. As he told Mansfield, he and the managing editor "had a big difference about the quality of my golf writing." Jenkins continued: "Since I knew a whole lot more about it than he did and since I had as much journalistic experience as he did . . . I didn't think I oughta take that." Instead he became a monthly columnist for *Playboy,* where, in Vanderwerken's opinion, Jenkins's bosses put him on "a very loose editorial leash" and Jenkins "certainly has unleashed himself." He attacked such social ills as the affectations of 1980s cuisine, but he reserved special venom for two of the biggest institutions in American football, the National Football League (NFL) and the National Collegiate Athletic Association (NCAA). He lambasted the NFL's version of the professional game, contending that the play is brutal and ridiculous at the same time, greatly inferior to college football. On the other hand, he repeatedly criticized the NCAA, college football's governing body, for its hypocrisy. Jenkins was outraged that the NCAA would penalize college athletes, many of whom grew up in poverty, for surreptitiously accepting money while the colleges openly make multimillion-dollar profits from the athletes' work. In such columns, Vanderwerken said, Jenkins is "outrageously and unabashedly prejudiced, jaundiced, eccentric, ornery, taking well-aimed slapshots at all sorts of tomfoolery across the spectrum of contemporary sport.'' As with any satirist, the critic suggested, Jenkins speaks to the world's ''good people''—whoever finds pretension the most unforgivable human failing.

MEDIA ADAPTATIONS: Semi-Tough was adapted by Walter Bernstein for a film of the same title, United Artists, 1977; and for a television series of the same title, American Broadcasting Companies, Inc. (ABC), 1980.

BIOGRAPHICAL/CRITICAL SOURCES:

PERIODICALS

Chicago Tribune, October 28, 1981, November 3, 1988.
Chicago Tribune Book World, October 4, 1981.
Detroit News, November 8, 1981, November 4, 1984.
Harper's, January, 1971.
Life, September 29, 1972.
Modern Fiction Studies, spring, 1987.
National Observer, November 16, 1974.
New Republic, September 16, 1972, December 28, 1974.
New Statesman, November 29, 1974.
Newsweek, September 18, 1972, November 11, 1974, October 22, 1984.
New York Review of Books, January 25, 1973.
New York Times, October 6, 1972, October 18, 1984, October 27, 1988.
New York Times Book Review, June 7, 1970, September 17, 1972, November 3, 1974, October 24, 1976, October 21, 1984, November 13, 1988.
People, December 3, 1984.
Publishers Weekly, October 23, 1972.
Saturday Review, October 14, 1972.
Sports Illustrated, February 15, 1982.
Washington Post, November 10, 1981, November 10, 1984, November 4, 1988.
Washington Post Book World, May 31, 1970, September 17, 1972, October 7, 1984.*

—*Sketch by Thomas Kozikowski*

*   *   *

JENNINGS, Phillip C.   1946-

PERSONAL: Born March 5, 1946, in Seattle, Wash.; son of Charles Phillip (a barber) and Hazel Audrey (a postal clerk; maiden name, Haarsager) Jennings; married Deborah Louise McCarl (an obstetrician and gynecologist), September 6, 1969; children: Mary McCarl, Benjamin. *Education:* Macalester College, B.A., 1968; attended Duke University, 1969. *Politics:* ''Enlightened Liberal.'' *Religion:* Episcopalian.

ADDRESSES: Home and office—32130 County Road 1, St. Cloud, Minn. 56303.

CAREER: State of Minnesota, St. Paul, programmer and analyst, 1969-78; Control Data Corp., Arden Hills, Minn., programmer and analyst, 1978-79; United Information Services, Kansas City, Mo., programmer and analyst, 1979-83; writer, 1983—. Member of St. John's Episcopal Church Choir.

MEMBER: Science Fiction Writers of America, Planetary Society, National Organization for Women.

WRITINGS:

Tower to the Sky (novel), Baen Books, 1988.
The Bug-Life Chronicles (stories), Baen Books, 1989.

Work represented in anthologies, including *There Will Be War.* Contributor of stories to magazines, including *Amazing Stories, Isaac Asimov's Science Fiction, Argos Fantasy and Science Fiction, New Destinies, Tales of the Unanticipated,* and *Far Frontiers.*

WORK IN PROGRESS: Two works of science fiction entitled *DownUp* and *Earwig.*

SIDELIGHTS: Phillip C. Jennings told *CA:* ''I became a science fiction writer after realizing that all my personal heroes were science fiction writers. Two things that cleared the way for me were word processors (I loathe typewriters) and the fact that my wife could and does support me during the long, lean period while I'm teaching myself how to write. Readers will discover my interest in religion, immortality, and feminism, as well as a quirkish obsession with obesity and the vertical dimension.''

*   *   *

JERINA, Carol   1947-

PERSONAL: Surname is pronounced ''Jereena''; born September 2, 1947, in Dallas, Tex.; daughter of Cecil Anthony (a street maintenance foreman) and Ida Elizabeth (a bank bookkeeper; maiden name, Cook) Davis; married Drew Jerina (a materials control manager), December 20, 1968; children: Patrick Anthony, Matthew Jason, Daniel Adam, Michael Andrew. *Education:* Attended Dallas Baptist College. *Politics:* Republican. *Religion:* Southern Baptist.

ADDRESSES: Home and office—3109 Bluffview Dr., Garland, Tex. 75043. *Agent*—Eileen Fallon, Lowenstein Associates, Inc., 121 West 27th St., Suite 601, New York, N.Y. 10001.

CAREER: Sanger-Harris (retail store), Dallas, Tex., sales clerk, 1964-66; City of Dallas, Dallas, Tex., tax and data processing clerk, 1966-68; homemaker, 1968—; writer.

MEMBER: Romance Writers of America, Greater Dallas Writers' Association.

AWARDS, HONORS: Reviewer's Choice awards from *Romantic Times* for best humorous historical romance, 1985, for *Fox Hunt,* and nomination for best post-Civil War romance, 1987, for *Embrace An Angel.*

WRITINGS:

NOVELS

Lady Raine (historical romance), Pocket Books, 1984.
Gallagher's Lady (historical romance), Pocket Books, 1984.
Fox Hunt (historical romance), Pocket Books, 1985.
Brighter Than Gold (historical romance), Pocket Books, 1987.
Embrace An Angel (historical romance), Pocket Books, 1987.
Tropic Gold (contemporary romance), Pocket Books, 1988.
The Tall Dark Alibi (contemporary romance), Berkley Publishing, 1988.
Sweet Jeopardy (contemporary romance), Berkley Publishing, 1988.

WORK IN PROGRESS: ''An action adventure/romance revolving around two rival reporters based in Washington, D.C., who discover bribery, blackmail, and murder within the System itself.''

SIDELIGHTS: Carol Jerina told *CA:* ''As the mother of four sons, my writing time is more than valuable—it's rare. But thanks to my word processor, I can successfully combine writing, mothering, and, occasionally, homemaking. Despite my *Romantic Times* award, my greatest achievement came when I received a favorable review of *The Tall Dark Alibi* in the *New York Times Book Review*. In my opinion, the review underscored the fact that I am no longer 'just a housewife,' but that I have an honest-to-goodness place in contemporary literature.''

BIOGRAPHICAL/CRITICAL SOURCES:

PERIODICALS

New York Times Book Review, April 17, 1988.

*   *   *

JOFFE, Josef   1944-

PERSONAL: Born March 15, 1944, in Lodz, Poland; married Christine Brinck; children: Jessica, Janina. *Education:* Swarthmore College, B.A., 1965; Johns Hopkins University, M.A., 1967; Harvard University, Ph.D., 1975.

ADDRESSES: Office—Sueddeutsche Zeitung, Sendlingerstrasse 80, 8 Munich 2, West Germany.

CAREER: Harvard University, Cambridge, Mass., research associate for Center for International Affairs, 1975-76; *Die Zeit,* Hamburg, West Germany, senior editor, 1976-82; fellow at Woodrow Wilson Center for Scholars, 1982-83; Carnegie Endowment for International Peace, Washington, D.C., senior associate, 1983-84; Johns Hopkins University, Baltimore, Md., professorial lecturer for School of Advanced International Studies, 1983-84; *Sueddeutsche Zeitung,* Munich, West Germany, foreign editor, 1985—.

MEMBER: International Institute for Strategic Studies.

WRITINGS:

The Limited Partnership: Europe, the United States, and the Burdens of Alliance, Ballinger, 1987.
(With Lincoln Gordon and others) *Eroding Empire: Western Relations With Eastern Europe,* Brookings Institution, 1987.

Contributor of opinions, analysis, and book reviews to periodicals, including *New York Times, Wall Street Journal, Los Angeles Times, New Republic, U.S. News and World Report,* London *Times, New York Times Book Review,* and *Los Angeles Times Book Review.* Contributing editor of *U.S. News and World Report.*

WORK IN PROGRESS: A book on the history of West German foreign policy since World War II, tentatively titled *Society and Foreign Policy in the Federal Republic,* publication expected in 1990.

SIDELIGHTS: Josef Joffe told *CA:* ''Born in Europe but trained in the United States, I was always fascinated by America's postwar role in Europe—at first reluctantly undertaken and then gestating into a 'permanently entangling alliance.' A kind of 'benign empire,' that entanglement is the greatest postwar success of American foreign policy, and it has accomplished more than the obvious, which has been to hold the balance against Soviet power. America's lasting intrusion has also transformed the international relations *within* Europe—to the point where the traditional fountainhead of international conflict (for example, two world wars) has become an island of ultra-stable peace. Hence, I wrote *The Limited Partnership,*

which analyzes the new European state system at a time when the old signposts are vanishing and the distances between the two shores of the Atlantic are growing.

''Evidently, Germany—at once divided and *the* critical mass in Europe—plays a key role in the postwar drama; I focus on this in my work in progress, tentatively titled *Society and Foreign Policy in the Federal Republic.*''

*   *   *

JOHN, Errol   1924-1988

OBITUARY NOTICE: Born in 1924 in Port of Spain, Trinidad; died July 10, 1988, in London, England. Actor and playwright. An actor in Britain during the 1950s and 1960s, John is best remembered for writing the play *Moon on a Rainbow Shawl,* published in 1958. Set in his native Trinidad, it concerns the poverty-stricken and oppressed lives of the country's inhabitants; the play won the London *Observer* play writing competition in 1957. John began his stage career in Port of Spain with the Whitehall Players amateur theater group, designing sets, acting, directing, and writing several one-act plays. Increasingly frustrated by the lack of opportunity in Trinidad to develop his professional and artistic skills, John went to England in 1950. Although he landed some major roles there, such as the lead in Shakespeare's ''Othello,'' John was often forced to accept minor background parts for dark-skinned characters on the basis of his race, rather than his ability. It was this circumstance that led him to compose more of his own plays. In 1966 John wrote *The Tout,* and in 1967 he published *Force Majeure, The Dispossessed, Hasta Luego: Three Screenplays.* He was also the author of several television plays, including ''The Emperor Jones,'' ''Teleclub,'' ''Dawn,'' and ''The Exiles.''

OBITUARIES AND OTHER SOURCES:

BOOKS

The Concise Encyclopedia of Modern Drama, Horizon Press, 1964.
Contemporary Dramatists, 4th edition, St. James Press, 1988.

PERIODICALS

Times (London), July 16, 1988.

*   *   *

JOHNSON, Fridolf (Lester)   1905-1988

*OBITUARY NOTICE—*See index for *CA* sketch: Born February 24, 1905, in Chicago, Ill.; died of a heart attack, July 19, 1988, in Kingston, N.Y. Artist, administrator, editor, and author. Johnson was executive editor of *American Artist* from 1962 to 1970. In a varied career he twice headed his own firms—Contempo Art Service in the late 1940s and Mermaid Press beginning in 1958—and regularly worked as a free-lance artist and designer. Johnson was also art director of Frankel-Rose Advertising Agency from 1925 to 1934, publicity designer for Universal-International in the mid-1940s, and planning director for Norcross Company from 1952 to 1962. Actively interested in calligraphy and the history of book publishing, he helped to found the Society of Graphic Arts in San Francisco, the Society of Calligraphers in Los Angeles, and the New York Chappell of Private Presses. His books include *Two Hundred Years of American Graphic Art, American Illustrators in Line, Mythical Beasts Coloring Book,* which he illustrated himself, *Treasury of American Pen-and-Ink Il-*

lustration, 1881-1938, and *Rockwell Kent: An Anthology of His Works.*

OBITUARIES AND OTHER SOURCES:

BOOKS

Who's Who in American Art, 17th edition, Bowker, 1986.

PERIODICALS

New York Times, July 27, 1988.

*   *   *

JOHNSON, (Hettie) Jean   1937-

PERSONAL: Born January 16, 1937, in Fort Collins, Colo.; daughter of Ezra Myron and Clara E. (Adams) Hornibrook; married LeRoy C. Johnson (a forester and writer), October 22, 1959; children: Eric Lee, Mark Leigh. *Education:* Mills College, B.S., 1959.

ADDRESSES: Home—2595 Cohansey St., Roseville, Minn. 55113.

CAREER: Portland Symphony, Portland, Ore., second chair cellist, 1960-63; Sacramento Symphony, Sacramento, Calif., first chair cellist, 1964-77; New Mexico Symphony, Albuquerque, cellist, 1978-81; free-lance writer and scientific editor, 1981—. Elementary school music teacher; cello teacher at Willamette University; volunteer teacher of non-readers. Member of National Ski Patrol.

MEMBER: American Association of University Women, Musicians Union (Albuquerque, N.M.), Professional Editors' Network (Twin Cities, Minn.), Death Valley '49ers.

WRITINGS:

(With husband, LeRoy C. Johnson) *Julia: Death Valley's Youngest Victim* (history), privately printed, 1981.
(With L. C. Johnson) *Escape From Death Valley: As Told by William Lewis Manly and Other '49ers* (history), University of Nevada Press, 1987.

Contributor to scientific journals.

Editor and author of introduction, with L. C. Johnson, of historical monograph *Route of the Manly Party of 1849 to 1850 in Leaving Death Valley for the Coast,* by John E. Wolff, 1988.

WORK IN PROGRESS: With husband, LeRoy C. Johnson: *Corruption, Camels, and Confusion,* a book on the boundary survey of California, for University of Nevada Press; a hiking guide to historic trails in Death Valley.

SIDELIGHTS: In their book *Escape From Death Valley,* Jean Johnson and her husband, LeRoy, relate the story of two families who set out by wagon train in the winter of 1849 to reach the gold fields of California. Trapped by winter weather in the hostile interior of California's Death Valley, the Bennetts and Arcans would have perished without the heroic efforts of William Lewis Manly and his companion John Haney Rogers. These two adventurers walked frozen and half-starved across nearly three hundred miles of desert to lead a rescue team back to the stranded wagon train. The weakened families were saved, and Manly told their story in letters, journals, and memoirs.

For the Johnsons *Escape From Death Valley* represents the culmination of thirteen years of scholarly research in libraries and archives throughout the United States. Additionally, the

authors traced the route of the Bennett-Arcan wagon train from Cobble Creek, Utah, through Nevada to Los Angeles, California, and traveled on foot across the same stretch of desert where the pioneers had faced their life-threatening ordeal. The narrative, culled from Manly's own writings on the rescue, "is vastly enriched," wrote Jonathan Kirsch in the *Los Angeles Times,* "by the meticulous and lengthy annotations provided by the Johnsons."

AVOCATIONAL INTERESTS: Hiking, stained glass, cast jewelry.

BIOGRAPHICAL/CRITICAL SOURCES:

PERIODICALS

Los Angeles Times, April 16, 1987.

*   *   *

JOHNSON, LeRoy C.   1937-

PERSONAL: Born October 13, 1937, in Little Falls, Minn.; son of Curtis James and Pearl (an artist; maiden name, Bjornoos) Johnson; married Jean Hornibrook (a musician, teacher, and writer), October 22, 1959; children: Eric Lee, Mark Leigh. *Education:* Oregon State University, B.S., 1962, M.S., 1965.

ADDRESSES: Home—2595 Cohansey St., Roseville, Minn. 55113.

CAREER: U.S. Department of Agriculture, Washington, D.C., assistant regional geneticist in California, 1963-66, director of Institute of Forest Genetics in Placerville, Calif., 1966-77, research forester in Berkeley, Calif., 1977-78, regional geneticist in Albuquerque, N.M., 1978-81, field representative in St. Paul, Minn., 1981—. Member of National Ski Patrol. *Military service:* U.S. Air Force, pilot, 1958-60.

MEMBER: Society of American Foresters, Western History Association, Professional Editors' Network (Twin Cities, Minn.), Death Valley 49'ers.

WRITINGS:

(With wife, Jean Johnson) *Julia: Death Valley's Youngest Victim* (history), privately printed, 1981.
(With J. Johnson) *Escape From Death Valley: As Told by William Lewis Manly and Other '49ers* (history), University of Nevada Press, 1987.

Contributor of about thirty articles to scientific journals.

Editor and author of introduction, with J. Johnson, of historical monograph *Route of the Manly Party of 1849 to 1850 in Leaving Death Valley for the Coast,* by John E. Wolff, 1988.

WORK IN PROGRESS: With wife, Jean Johnson: *Corruption, Camels, and Confusion,* a book on the boundary survey of California, for University of Nevada Press; a hiking guide to historic trails in Death Valley.

SIDELIGHTS: For more than a decade, LeRoy C. Johnson and his wife, Jean, researched the adventures of the men and women who trekked to California during the Gold Rush of 1849 and who gave Death Valley its name. Avid hikers themselves, the Johnsons traversed on foot the same routes traveled by some of these intrepid, but forgotten, pioneers. The authors' book *Escape From Death Valley* recounts the story of two families, the Bennetts and Arcans, whose small wagon train bound for the gold fields of California met with disaster in the winter of 1849. Primarily a compilation from the memoirs of William Lewis Manly and John Haney Rogers, this historical saga details how the two would-be prospectors befriended and eventually rescued the stranded families from their near demise in Death Valley. According to Jonathan Kirsch in the *Los Angeles Times,* the volume serves as "a field guide to the deserts of Nevada and California, as well as a tale of heroism in the Old West." In Kirsch's opinion, *Escape From Death Valley* "is one of the most stirring (if seldom-told) stories in the history of the West and the literature of survival."

Johnson told *CA:* "Jean and I spent thirteen years researching and writing *Escape From Death Valley.* Our efforts paid off because the book is now considered the definitive work on the subject. We were introduced to Death Valley through scouting; my first trip there was in 1951, and Jean's was in 1953. We involved our two boys in our trips and research, too, and it wasn't until they had their own cars that they knew one could vacation somewhere other than Death Valley. Jean and I work closely as a team: Jean does much of the writing, and I do most of the technical footnotes and hiking (though Jean and the boys have done their share) and all of the library and archive work. We've rewritten some of the notes more than twenty-five times. Our strength comes from coupling *extensive* field work with extensive literature review. We love the desert and have several ideas for additional books dealing with the Southwest.

"*Julia* relates the previously untold story of Mrs. Arcan, one of the '49ers, who was five-months pregnant when she walked from Death Valley to Los Angeles—some 250 miles. She subsequently carried her child, Julia, full term only to have the infant die when she was nineteen days old.

"Our forthcoming book, *Corruption, Camels, and Confusion,* covers some of the same ground as *Escape From Death Valley.* Last year we flew to California (from Minnesota) five times to do field work on the subject. Since the bibliography exceeds eighty typewritten pages, we will include an index for it, something that probably has not been done before. We firmly believe that historical works must be clearly written and properly documented. As an outgrowth of our research, and at our doing, the National Park Service holds an annual conference on 'History and Prehistory.'"

AVOCATIONAL INTERESTS: Mountain climbing, rock climbing, photography, public speaking.

BIOGRAPHICAL/CRITICAL SOURCES:

PERIODICALS

Los Angeles Times, April 16, 1987.

*   *   *

JOHNSON, Phyllis (Anne)   1937-1985

PERSONAL: Born May 7, 1937, in Grantsburg, Wis.; died April 12, 1985, in Fontana, Calif. *Education:* Pomona College, B.A., 1959; University of California, Los Angeles, M.A., 1963, Ph.D., 1967.

ADDRESSES: Office—Department of Modern European Languages, Pomona College, Claremont, Calif. 91711.

CAREER: Pomona College, Claremont, Calif., 1963-85, began as instructor, became assistant professor, associate professor, 1974-81, professor of French, 1981-85.

MEMBER: Modern Language Association of America, Mediaeval Academy of America, Philological Association of the Pacific Coast, Medieval Association of the Pacific.

WRITINGS:

(With Brigitte Cazelles) *Le Vain Siecle guerpir: A Literary Approach to Sainthood Through French Hagiography of the Twelfth Century,* Department of Romance Languages, University of North Carolina at Chapel Hill, 1979.

Contributor to philology journals.

[Date of death provided by Howard Young, acting chair of department of modern languages and literatures at Pomona College.]*

*   *   *

JOHNSON, Ronald M(aberry)   1936-

PERSONAL: Born October 15, 1936, in Kansas City, Mo.; married, 1965; children: one. *Education:* Kansas State Teachers College (now Emporia State University), B.A., 1961; University of Kansas, M.A., 1965; University of Illinois at Urbana-Champaign, Ph.D., 1970.

ADDRESSES: Office—Department of History, 610 ICC, Georgetown University, 37th and O Sts. N.W., Washington, D.C. 20057.

CAREER: Cleveland State University, Cleveland, Ohio, assistant professor of Afro-American history, 1969-72; Georgetown University, Washington, D.C., assistant professor, 1972-76, associate professor of American history, 1976—, director of American studies, 1979—.

MEMBER: American Historical Association, Organization of American Historians.

WRITINGS:

(With Abby Arthur Johnson) *Propaganda and Aesthetics: The Literary Politics of Afro-American Magazines in the Twentieth Century,* University of Massachusetts Press, 1979.

Contributor to history, American studies, and black studies journals.*

*   *   *

JOYCE, James (Augustine Aloysius)   1882-1941

PERSONAL: Born February 2, 1882, in Dublin, Ireland; died following surgery for a perforated ulcer, January 13, 1941, in Zurich, Switzerland; son of John Stanislaus (a tax collector) and Mary Jane (a pianist; maiden name, Murray) Joyce; married Nora Barnacle, July 4, 1931; children: Giorgio, Lucia. *Education:* University College, Dublin, B.A., 1902.

ADDRESSES: Home—Zurich, Switzerland.

CAREER: Novelist, short story writer, poet, and dramatist. Clifton School, Dalkey, Ireland, teacher, 1904; Berlitz School in Pola, Austria-Hungary (now Yugoslavia), and in Trieste, Austria-Hungary (now Italy), language instructor, 1904-06 and 1907; private language instructor in Trieste, 1907-1915, and sporadically in Zurich, Switzerland, 1915-19; Scuola Superiore di Commericio Revoltella, Trieste, language instructor, 1913-15 and 1919-20.

AWARDS, HONORS: Grants from the Royal Literary Fund, 1915, and the Civil List and the Society of Authors, both 1916.

WRITINGS:

NOVELS

A *Portrait of the Artist as a Young Man* (first published serially in *Egoist*, February 2, 1914-September 1, 1915), B. W. Huebsch, 1916, definitive edition, corrected by Chester G. Anderson, edited by Richard Ellmann, Viking, 1964, reprinted, 1982.

Ulysses (some chapters first published serially in *Little Review*, March, 1918-September/December, 1920, and in *Egoist*, January/February, 1919-December, 1919), Shakespeare and Company (Paris), 1922, Random House, 1934, reprinted, with a foreword by Morris L. Ernst and the decision of the U.S. District court rendered by Judge John M. Woolsey, Modern Library, 1942; published as *Ulysses: The Corrected Text*, edited by Hans Walter Gabler with Wolfhard Steppe and Claus Melchoir, Random House, 1986.

Finnegans Wake (excerpts first published as fragments of "Work in Progress" [also see below]; portions also published in journals and anthologies, 1928-38), Viking, 1939, reprinted, 1967, recent edition, 1982.

Stephen Hero: A Part of the First Draft of "A Portrait of the Artist as a Young Man," edited with an introduction by Theodore Spencer, New Directions, 1944, revised edition with additional material published as *Stephen Hero*, edited by John J. Slocum and Herbert Cahoon, 1963.

SHORT FICTION

Dubliners (short story collection; three stories first published in *Irish Homestead*, 1904; contains "The Sisters," "An Encounter" [also see below], "Araby," "Eveline," "After the Race," "Two Gallants," "The Boarding House" [also see below], "A Little Cloud," "Counterparts," "Clay," "A Painful Case," "Ivy Day in the Committee Room," "A Mother," "Grace," and "The Dead" [also see below]), Grant Richards, 1914, B. W. Huebsch, 1916, reprinted, edited by Robert Scholes and A. Walton Litz, Viking, 1969, recent edition, 1982.

Anna Livia Plurabelle (later published in *Finnegans Wake* [also see above]), preface by Padraic Colum, Crosby Gaige, 1928 (published in England as *Anna Livia Plurabelle: Fragment of "Work in Progress,"* Faber, 1932); published as *Anna Livia Plurabelle: The Making of a Chapter*, edited with an introduction by Fred H. Higginson, University of Minnesota Press, 1960.

Tales Told of Shem and Shaun: Three Fragments From "Work in Progress" (later published in *Finnegans Wake* [also see above]; contains "The Mookse and the Gripes," "The Muddest Thick That Was Ever Heard Dump," and "The Ondt and the Gracehoper"), Black Sun Press (Paris), 1929.

Haveth Childers Everywhere: Fragment of "Work in Progress" (later published in *Finnegans Wake* [also see above]), Fountain Press, 1930, reprinted, Richard West, 1980.

The Mime of Mick, Nick, and the Maggies: A Fragment From "Work in Progress" (later published in *Finnegans Wake* [also see above]), Servire Press, 1934.

Storiella as She is Syung (fragment of "Work in Progress"; later published in *Finnegans Wake* [also see above]), Corvinus Press, 1937.

The Dead, edited by William T. Moynihan, Allyn & Bacon, 1965 (also see above).

An Encounter, illustrations by Sandra Higashi, Creative Education, 1982 (also see above).

Boarding House, illustrations by Sandra Higashi, Creative Education, 1982 (also see above).

POETRY

Chamber Music, Elkin Mathews, 1907, authorized edition, B. W. Huebsch, 1918, reprinted, edited with an introduction by William York Tindall, Columbia University Press, 1954, recent edition, Hippocrene Books, 1982 (also see below).

Pomes Penyeach, Shakespeare and Company, 1927, Walton Press, 1971, recent edition, Bern Porter, 1986 (also see below).

Collected Poems of James Joyce (contains "Chamber Music" [also see above], "Pomes Penyeach" [also see above], and "Ecce Puer"), Black Sun Press (New York), 1936; published as *Collected Poems*, Viking, 1937, reprinted, 1974, recent edition, Penguin Books, 1986.

Also author of "The Holy Office," c. 1904.

CRITICAL WRITINGS

(With F. J. C. Skeffington) "The Day of the Rabblement" [and] "A Forgotten Aspect of the University Question" (the former by Joyce, the latter by Skeffington), Gerrard Brothers (Dublin), 1901, Folcroft, 1970.

The Early Joyce: The Book Reviews, 1902-1903, edited with an introduction by Stanislaus Joyce and Ellsworth Mason, Mamalujo Press, 1955, reprinted, Richard West, 1978.

The Critical Writings of James Joyce, edited by Ellsworth Mason and Richard Ellmann, Viking, 1959.

Also author of "Ibsen's New Drama," published in *Fortnightly Review*, April, 1900.

CORRESPONDENCE

Letters of James Joyce (includes *The Cat and the Devil* [also see below]), Viking, Volume I, edited by Stuart Gilbert, 1957, reissued with corrections, 1966, Volumes II and III, edited by Richard Ellmann, 1966.

The Cat and the Devil, illustrations by Richard Erdoes, Dodd, 1964, recent edition, with illustrations by Blachon, Schocken, 1981 (also see above).

Selected Letters of James Joyce, edited by Richard Ellmann, Viking, 1975.

James Joyce's Letters to Sylvia Beach, 1921-1940, edited by Melissa Banta and Oscar A. Silverman, Indiana University Press, 1987.

OTHER

Exiles (three-act play; German language version first produced in Munich, August 7, 1919; English language version first produced in New York at Neighborhood Playhouse, February 19, 1925), B. W. Huebsch, 1918, reprinted, with the author's own notes and an introduction by Padraic Colum, Viking, 1951, revised edition, 1965.

Epiphanies, introduction and notes by O. A. Silverman, Lockwood Memorial Library, 1956, reprinted, Richard West, 1979.

Scribbledehobble: The Ur-workbook for "Finnegans Wake," edited with an introduction by Thomas E. Connolly, Northwestern University Press, 1961.

A *First-Draft Version of "Finnegans Wake,"* edited by David Hayman, University of Texas Press, 1963.

The Workshop of Daedalus: James Joyce and the Raw Materials for "A Portrait of the Artist as a Young Man," collected and edited by Robert Scholes and Richard M. Kain, Northwestern University Press, 1965.

A *Shorter "Finnegans Wake,"* edited by Anthony Burgess, Viking, 1967.

Giacomo Joyce (memoir), introduction and notes by Richard Ellmann, Viking, 1968.

Joyce's "Ulysses" Notesheets in the British Museum, edited by Phillip F. Herring, University Press of Virginia, 1972.

Ulysses: The Manuscript and First Printings Compared, annotated by Clive Driver, and *Ulysses: A Facsimile of the Manuscript,* introduction by Harry Levin, bibliographical preface by Driver, Octagon Books, 1975.

James Joyce in Padua, edited, translated, and with an introduction by Louis Berrone, Random House, 1977.

Joyce's Notes and Early Drafts for "Ulysses": Selections From the Buffalo Collection, edited by Phillip F. Herring, University Press of Virginia, 1977.

The James Joyce Archive (facsimiles of surviving manuscripts), sixty-three volumes, edited by Michael Groden, Hans Walter Gabler, David Hayman, A. Walton Litz, and Danis Rose, Garland Publishing, 1977-79.

OMNIBUS EDITIONS

The Portable James Joyce, introduction and notes by Harry Levin, Viking, 1947, reprinted, 1986.

The Essential James Joyce (contains *Dubliners, A Portrait of the Artist as a Young Man, Exiles, Collected Poems,* and selections from *Ulysses* and *Finnegans Wake*), introduction and notes by Harry Levin, J. Cape, 1948, reprinted, Panther, 1977.

A James Joyce Selection: A Selection of His Early Prose and Poetry With a Sequence of Photographs Showing James Joyce's Dublin, edited with an introduction by Richard Adams, Longman, 1977.

SIDELIGHTS: Richard Ellmann in the opening passage of his monumental biography, *James Joyce,* aptly summarized the writer's impact on twentieth-century letters: "We are still learning to be James Joyce's contemporaries, to understand our interpreter." Since the publication of *Finnegans Wake,* a critical commonplace has held that no author now writing in English can attempt to create a work of prose fiction without contending with the force of Joyce's reconstitution of the genre; but, as Ellmann's statement implies, such a presumption projects only a small measure of Joyce's intellectual and artistic achievement.

Contemporary readers can hardly take up a work of fiction without falling under the influence of the conventions that Joyce established for experiencing a text. Many feel his influence directly; editors regularly anthologize short stories from his 1914 *Dubliners* collection, and Joyce's first published novel, *A Portrait of the Artist as a Young Man* (1916), has become a popular text in high school and college literature courses. His last two books, *Ulysses* (1922) and *Finnegans Wake* (1939), though not as widely read as *Dubliners* or *A Portrait,* stand as paradigms of aesthetic achievement: often quoted, paraphrased, alluded to, or simply invoked in the name of artistic excellence. Those who do not encounter the influence of Joyce's consciousness through direct exposure to his works most likely absorb it from the writings of one or more of his literary heirs. Elements within the styles of authors as different from one another as Irish novelist and playwright Samuel Beckett, modern American novelist William Faulkner, English fiction writers Malcolm Lowry and John Fowles, and contemporary American novelists Thomas Pynchon and John Irving identify them as some of those most overtly shaped by Joyce's canon. But no author today can begin to compose without confronting

in some way the impact on modern literature brought about by Joyce's new methods of composition, and, consequently, no reader can today take up a work of modern fiction without feeling the repercussions of Joyce's influence.

Although critics have argued over the precise elements that give Joyce his prominence, most would agree that the power within his writings comes not so much from the topics that they explore as from their complex formal structures. The fascination he had for the form of his work is very neatly illustrated in an anecdote recorded by Frank Budgen in *James Joyce and the Making of Ulysses.* Budgen tells of meeting Joyce one night on the Bahnhofstrasse in Zurich:

> "I've been working hard on [*Ulysses*]all day," said Joyce.
>
> "Does that mean that you have written a great deal?" I said.
>
> "Two sentences," said Joyce.
>
> I looked sideways but Joyce was not smiling. I thought of [French novelist Gustave] Flaubert.
>
> "You've been seeking the *mot juste?*" I said.
>
> "No," said Joyce. "I have the words already. What I am seeking is the perfect order of words in the sentence."

Throughout his canon the style of Joyce's prose commands immediate attention and involvement because it disrupts traditional assumptions about the role and the perceptual abilities of readers while engaging those readers in the attempt to discover alternative methods for experiencing the text. In *Dubliners* Joyce subtly mitigates condemnations of the suffocating atmosphere of society with evocative portrayals of the humanity of its victims. While descriptions in his stories often seem to reflect the detachment characteristic of late nineteenth-century naturalistic fiction, they also introduce descriptive techniques able to draw from readers empathetic responses to the suffering that characters undergo.

A Portrait of the Artist as a Young Man continues to develop methods of rendering alternating points of view and to enhance reader awareness of the limitations in the credibility of the narrative voice within the text. It presents a highly personal depiction of the childhood, the adolescence, and the emergence into maturity of the novel's central character, Stephen Dedalus, who moves from a bright, pious, confused child into a fiercely independent, strong-minded, irreverent young man and fledgling artist. At the same time, Joyce's depiction of his central character retains an ironic detachment that highlights the supercilious points of Stephen's rebellion and compels readers to reconstruct their impressions of his nature as it evolves over each chapter.

In *Ulysses* a deluge of precise and variegated details recreates for readers the tempo of a single Dublin day, but rapidly fluctuating perspectives inhibit full comprehension of the impressions created by Joyce's montage-like construction. Interior monologue makes one intimately aware of the needs, the aspirations, the strengths, and the failings of the major characters—Stephen Dedalus, Leopold Bloom, and Bloom's wife, Molly—but at the same time a protean succession of styles impedes the emergence of a dominant attitude that would serve as a standard for measuring the actions of any individual in the work.

Finally, *Finnegans Wake*, Joyce's last work, displaces all previous stylistic patterns in his canon as it presents a dream vision of Dublin that amalgamates the particular and the universal, the subjective and the objective. Its digressive form overturns the reader's sense of the primacy of a single attitude and instead gives legitimacy to a wide range of impressions and perceptions. Its sardonic yet sensitive presentations of characters, events, issues, and ideas representing the central features of Western culture survey modern society without clearly idealizing or denigrating it. If Joyce shows a reluctance in his writing to interpret, to lecture, or to make pronouncements, he imposes no such restraints upon his readers. Quite the contrary, in each work and with increasing power, Joyce calls upon his audience to impose meaning on the text rather than to embrace an interpretation dictated by the work itself; he thus inverts conventional assumptions of the reader as a docile and pliant individual approaching a piece of literature like a jigsaw puzzler searching for the pattern hidden by the author under its formal layers.

Joyce's education began in 1888 at Clongowes Wood College, a Jesuit school located about twenty miles west of Dublin. The Jesuit influence permeated every aspect of Joyce's early intellectual growth. With this instruction came a moral imperative to excel to the limits of one's ability that directly underscored the value of the personal acquisition of knowledge. As Stanislaus Joyce put it in his memoir *My Brother's Keeper:* "In the Jesuit schools [Joyce] attended, the masters used to dwell rather heavily on the dangers of 'human respect,' by which they meant doing something or leaving it undone against one's conscience for fear of what people might say or think of you.... They desired to put their pupils on guard against a certain inferiority complex that might invade them when, in the little world of Dublin, they came in contact with a dominant Protestant class. In my brother they found an apter pupil than they expected, or, indeed, wished for.'' Erosion of the family finances forced Joyce's withdrawal from the college in 1891. (Around the same time when he was nine years old, he wrote "Et Tu, Healy!", probably his first poem but no longer extant, memorializing the betrayal and death of Irish nationalist Charles Stewart Parnell.) After a brief time at a Christian Brothers' school in North Richmond Street, Joyce entered the Jesuit's Belvedere College as a scholarship boy in 1893. At Belvedere Joyce gained academic distinctions, wavered on the brink of agnosticism, and undertook incipient artistic efforts (most of which are now lost). In 1898 he enrolled at University College, Dublin, and quickly earned a reputation as a brilliant if idiosyncratic student.

In 1902 Joyce graduated from University College with a degree in modern languages and left Dublin for Paris with the idea of studying medicine there. His mother's illness brought him back to Ireland in April of 1903, and by this time he had committed himself to becoming an artist. He found, however, the Dublin literati antipathetic to his efforts. Despite Joyce's considerable achievement of publishing at the age of eighteen an essay on Norwegian dramatist Henrik Ibsen in the *Fortnightly Review*, Irish editors seemed to take little interest in his work. Robert Scholes and Richard M. Kain in *The Workshop of Daedalus* record that one such editor, William Magee, refusing an essay Joyce submitted to the journal *Dana*, declared an unwillingness "to publish what was to myself incomprehensible." In 1904, at the invitation of poet and editor George Russell, Joyce did succeed in placing three stories, later to appear in the *Dubliners*, in the *Irish Homestead;* but the parochial intellectual atmosphere of Dublin was becoming

too much for him. In June of the same year Joyce had met Nora Barnacle, the woman with whom he would spend the remainder of his life, and he began to form plans for escaping the suffocating intellectual atmosphere of his native city.

Joyce was opposed to the idea of marriage. Writing to Nora Barnacle in an August, 1904, letter collected in *Letters of James Joyce*, he declared: "My mind quite rejects the whole present social order and Christianity—home, the recognized virtues, classes of life, and religious doctrines. How could I like the idea of home? My home was simply a middle-class affair ruined by spendthrift habits which I have inherited." But he was also painfully aware that he could not live openly with Nora in Dublin outside the sanction of the Church. Joyce was determined to leave Ireland and seek a more tolerant moral and intellectual climate. (The Joyces were, in fact, married on July 4, 1931, in order to safeguard their children's rights of inheritance.) In October, 1904, on the promise of a position as a language instructor for a Berlitz School, Joyce and Nora left for the continent. After a brief period in Pola, Joyce and Nora settled in Trieste where he gave language lessons and worked on his short stories and a novel. In July of 1905 the Joyces' first child, Giorgio, was born. Although Joyce would return to Ireland briefly in 1909 and again in 1912, for the rest of his life he lived abroad while keeping Dublin before him in his writing.

Dubliners grew out of the core of stories that Joyce began before he left Ireland. Each piece depicts some aspect of middle- and lower middle-class urban life in Dublin. According to Marvin Magalaner's *Time of Apprenticeship*, Joyce explained his choice of setting to his friend, Arthur Power: "For myself, I always write about Dublin, because if I can get to the heart of Dublin I can get to the heart of all the cities of the world. In the particular is contained the universal." The stories in *Dubliners* emphasize the circumscription of the individual consciousness by the social institutions of family, church, and state. The collection divides itself into narratives of childhood ("The Sisters," "An Encounter," "Araby"), adolescence ("Eveline," "After the Race," "Two Gallants," "The Boarding House"), adult life ("A Little Cloud," "Counterparts," "Clay," "A Painful Case"), and public experiences (politics, "Ivy Day in the Committee Room"; the family, "A Mother"; religion, "Grace"), with the final story ("The Dead") acting as a coda.

In many ways the collection is an indictment of the paralysis that Joyce felt gripped his city. As he told his at first reluctant publisher Grant Richards in a June, 1906, letter collected in *Letters of James Joyce:* "It is not my fault that the odour of ashpits and old weeds and offal hangs round my stories. I seriously believe that you will retard the course of civilisation in Ireland by preventing the Irish people from having one good look at themselves in my nicely polished looking-glass." At the same time, the stories reflect a sense of the humanity of Dubliners caught in situations that they cannot fully comprehend or overcome. "The Dead," with its ambiguous ending, leaves open the possibility of some sort of salvation for the central character, Gabriel Conroy, projecting most overtly Joyce's sympathy for his fellow citizens, but even in stories with protagonists who are clearly doomed—"Eveline," "Clay," "A Painful Case" are all examples—his depictions retain an empathy for the hopelessness and the apparent inevitability of their condition.

Throughout the collection Joyce's subtle narrative manipulation balances feelings of understanding and detachment. Probing the consciousness of his characters, Joyce forces the reader to share the sense of desolation of these figures, yet he maintains a narrative distance that allows a clear perception of the flaws and the weaknesses in their natures. A passage from "Counterparts" describing a man's reaction to the sudden realization of the sorry state of his finances exemplifies this balance in Joyce's art: "He cursed his want of money and cursed all the rounds he had stood, particularly all the whiskies and Apollinaris which he had stood to Weathers. If there was one thing that he hated it was a sponge." The words, while echoing the feelings of the protagonist of the story, belong to its unnamed narrator. Experiencing the sharp disappointment that the character Farrington feels, the reader also retains enough detachment to see the full irony of the situation Farrington has brought upon himself. This same pattern, combining association and disengagement, repeats itself throughout the book. In each story Joyce delves into his characters' minds while maintaining a sense of distance, bringing to readers a clear rendition of the anxiety and suffering that individuals endure without absolving them of the venality or the complicity that contributed to their condition.

In May of 1907, two months before the birth of Joyce's second child, Lucia, Stanley Elkins published a collection of poems, *Chamber Music,* that Joyce had written before he left Dublin. Beautiful in its own right, the poetry has an atavistic relation to the work Joyce was doing at the time the volume appeared. It relies on symbolist techniques that he had already largely abandoned by the time he left Dublin. He would continue throughout his life to write poetry, but he would make little effort to develop his technique beyond the form of these early poems. With each succeeding year his prose fiction claimed more of his time and his creative energy.

While composing and refining the short stories that would make up *Dubliners,* Joyce was also writing a novel, *Stephen Hero.* It traces the childhood and early adult life of a middle-class Dublin boy, Stephen Daedalus, from precocious intellectualism to the stirrings of an artistic vocation. Joyce's work, a fragment of which survived and was published posthumously in 1944, follows the linear, cause-and-effect pattern of a conventional nineteenth-century novel. Structured around the commonplace frame of self-effacing, third person narrative, it examines the features of Stephen's intellectual and physical maturation with minute attention to detail. Late in 1907, around the same time that he completed the first version of "The Dead," Joyce radically revised his novelistic approach. He decided to abandon his manuscript, at this point over nine hundred pages long and by Joyce's own calculation approximately half completed, and to begin the process again, this time following a much less orthodox method of composition.

In his new novel, *A Portrait of the Artist as a Young Man,* Joyce retained the basic plot and themes of *Stephen Hero.* Even specific scenes like Stephen's discussion of aesthetics with the dean of studies reappeared, though Joyce reconstructed these scenes to suit the emphasis of his new work. At the same time he introduced fundamental changes in the narrative form and structure. Joyce drastically cut the work, dropping the number of chapters from the proposed fifty to five. To accomplish this formidable task of condensation, Joyce eschewed presentation of linked chronological events, depicting instead a series of lyrical episodes illustrating the developing consciousness of the artist. The changes produced an intimate knowledge of the character of Stephen Dedalus (whose surname too goes through a minor condensation with a single vowel replacing its initial diphthong) while preventing the reader's close association with Stephen's attitudes. This process also further distanced the novel from Joyce's own experiences in Dublin, and, although Ireland and Irish life had a profound effect upon Joyce's art, it is a mistake to read *A Portrait* as if it were his autobiography.

To heighten sensitivity to the stages of Stephen's maturation, each episode unfolds in a style that approximates the intellectual level of the protagonist at the time. Every chapter has its unique tone and cadence, but the novel's opening lines provide perhaps the most familiar and accessible example of this technique: "Once upon a time and a very good time it was there was a moocow coming down along the road and this moocow that was coming down along the road met a nicens little boy named baby tuckoo." The story is one that Stephen's father has told him, and the words are those that he, baby tuckoo, could understand, although they are a bit beyond his own ability to form, as the passage of his speech that immediately follows this section demonstrates; for *"O, the wild rose blossoms/On the little green place,"* he sings, *"O, the green wothe botheth."* The narrative thus presents an evolving perspective parallel to but independent from Stephen's own nature. This emphasis on a fluctuating point of view within the narrative stands as the central feature of Joyce's new approach in *A Portrait.* It gives the reader a strong sense of Stephen's maturing consciousness, yet it allows one to maintain a detached and at times ironic perspective on his nature.

This method for establishing the tone of the work also influences the formal design of Joyce's chapters. Each is organized around a series of "epiphanies"—moments of lyrical insight derived from the seemingly banal occurrences of daily life leading towards an event at the close of the chapter which marks a turning point in Stephen's emotional, intellectual, and spiritual growth. To balance these euphoric moments Joyce introduces throughout each chapter a series of "anti-epiphanies"—instances underscoring the misperceptions resulting from certain elevated attitudes. Moreover, he begins chapters two through five with "anti-epiphanies" aimed at directly undercutting the triumphs of the scenes immediately preceding them in the conclusions of chapters one through four.

The path of alternating feelings traced by these epiphanies and anti-epiphanies follows the thematic development of the novel. Chapter one ends with Stephen on the shoulders of his classmates at Clongowes Wood College celebrating his apparent triumph over Father Dolan's unjust punishment, yet the second chapter begins with an account of how the sinking fortunes of his family have forced Stephen to leave the college. The final scene of the second chapter, his encounter with a prostitute, marks the triumph of Stephen's erotic and romantic passion over what he perceives as hypocritical social repression, but the opening of the next chapter shows Stephen's current sense of the tawdriness of these pleasures. The third chapter, with its famous retreat sermon, ends with Stephen's reception of the Eucharist and his temporary, but at the time quite sincere, reconciliation with the forces of conformity. The first scene opening chapter four, however, shows that his religious practices have lost their efficacy; the aesthetic revelation of his vision on the beach of the birdgirl, which closes the chapter, redirects his psychological development by replacing religion with art as the moral center of his life. The shabby circumstances of the Dedalus household at the opening of chapter five seems to belie this sense of liberation, but the novel ends with a final moment of transcendence, Stephen's articulation of his motives behind his decision to leave Ireland: "I go to encounter for the millionth time the reality of experience and to forge in the smithy of my soul the uncreated conscience of my race." The statement summarizes the thematic paradoxes upon which the novel rests, for it marks both Stephen's break with the constraints of the Irish world in which he grew up and his commitment to reform that world through his artistic powers. Stylistic distinction and multiple perspective function in an efficient but muted manner in *A Portrait;* but in mastering their manipulation and in introducing the reader to the demands made by subtle shifts in tone and point of view, Joyce prepared for the more rigorous presentation of the same techniques in *Ulysses.*

In 1914, as Joyce was finishing *Portrait,* he began to receive the public notice that he had been striving to gain for a decade. Grant Richards, who had proposed in 1906 to publish *Dubliners* and who had subsequently abrogated the agreement after a prolonged conflict with Joyce over cuts in particular stories, renewed his offer. (The collection appeared in June of 1914.) American poet and editor Ezra Pound, put in touch with Joyce by Irish poet William Butler Yeats, took an interest in *A Portrait,* and through his influence the *Egoist* began serial publication of the novel in February. Two more years would pass before Joyce found a publisher, B. W. Huebsch, to bring out the novel in book form, but the increased interest in his work reinforced Joyce's determination to continue his writing.

During 1914, as work on *A Portrait* was coming to a close and planning for *Ulysses* had already begun, Joyce abruptly took up a new project, the composition of his play *Exiles* (1918). The drama focuses on the return to Ireland of Richard Rowan, a successful, middle-aged author, after years of self-imposed exile on the continent. *Exiles* highlights the inevitable clash between an individual who values personal freedom above all else and a society whose central concerns are conformity and superficial appearances. Joyce presents Rowan as a man who has defied convention by eloping rather than marrying and who feels repulsed by the idea of pretending that he and Bertha are husband and wife and that their child, Archie, was not born out of wedlock. In contrast to Rowan stands Robert Hand, an old friend who has remained in Ireland and who has grown accustomed to using superficial acquiescence as a cover for his own depravity. While urging Rowan not to contradict impressions that he is now married, Hand attempts to seduce Bertha. Rowan is aware of Hand's efforts, but he refuses to tamper with individual freedom by intervening. The action of the work is played out through the struggle of wills between Rowan, Hand, and Bertha. Ponderous dialogue and stereotypical characterization hamper the play itself. Its 1919 premier in Munich was described by Joyce as "A flop!," according to Ellmann's biography, and subsequent performances have met with mixed success at best. Its composition, however, proved an important stage in Joyce's artistic development, for it enabled him to examine questions of fidelity, loyalty, and control that would stand at the center of the action of *Ulysses.*

Shortly after the completion of the play, Joyce again became an exile himself. With the onset of World War I his British passport made him a hostile alien in Trieste, a city at that time part of the Austro-Hungarian Empire, and he was forced in 1915 to move with his family to neutral Switzerland. From 1915 to 1919 Joyce lived in Zurich, where he completed drafts of the first twelve episodes of *Ulysses.* After the war he returned briefly to Trieste, and in 1920, at the urging of Pound, he went to Paris where he hoped to find accommodations less chaotic than those in postwar Trieste. Joyce intended the move only as a temporary displacement, meant to last no longer than the few months he judged necessary to finish *Ulysses,* but life

in Paris proved more congenial than expected. Among the friends whom Joyce made early in his stay was a young American, Sylvia Beach, owner of the book shop Shakespeare and Company, who agreed to bring out *Ulysses* under her own imprint. By the time the book appeared on February 2, 1922, Joyce and his family were firmly established in Paris and would remain in the city for the next twenty years.

Using the *Odyssey* of Homer as a frame, Joyce depicts in *Ulysses* the events of a single day in Dublin—June 16, 1904. Attention settles on three individuals. Stephen Dedalus, a bit older and more disillusioned than he was as the protagonist of *A Portrait,* spends the day seeking recognition from his fellow Dubliners for his artistic talent while drinking up the salary he has just received for teaching duties at Garret Deasy's school in Dalkey. Leopold Bloom, a middle-aged, Jewish advertising canvaser for a Dublin newspaper, wanders around the city intent upon driving from his mind feelings of guilt over his father's death, remorse for the loss, eleven years earlier, of his infant son, apprehension over the maturity of his daughter Milly, and despair over his wife's impending infidelity. Molly Bloom, the wife of Leopold and the only one of the three not to spend her day crisscrossing Dublin, passes her time preparing for and conducting her first act of adultery. Joyce overlays this interaction with a masterful depiction of minor characters and a Rabelaisian delight in the seedy details of urban living. (Such details caused the novel to be banned from the United States until December, 1933, when Judge John M. Woolsey delivered the legal verdict that *Ulysses* was not obscene; it was published in America by Random House in early 1934, twelve years after Sylvia Beach's Paris edition appeared.) Despite the banality surrounding the lives of Bloom, Molly, Stephen, and the other Dubliners, Joyce gives each a dignity and fallibility that makes his or her experiences important to the reader.

As in Joyce's earlier works, style endows *Ulysses* with kinetic force. Its evolving form supplies narration with the power to make mundane characters and events interesting while constraining the reader to participate in the creation of the text by attempting to bring meaning (though not certitude) to it. The novel's introductory chapters establish its tone in a fairly conventional, if sometimes baroque, manner; its first lines read, "Stately, plump Buck Mulligan came from the stairhead, bearing a bowl of lather on which a mirror and a razor lay crossed. A yellow dressinggown, ungirdled, was sustained gently behind him by the mild morning air." After progressing through the first third of the work, Joyce begins to vary the form of succeeding episodes, continually shifting narrative perspective and compelling his audience to reconstruct standards for interpretation: for example, the first line of the "Sirens" episode reads, "Bronze by gold heard the hoofirons, steelyringing imperthnthn thnthnthn." Within chapters Joyce confronts readers with the disjointed impressions of the central characters through various forms of interior monologue, as in the following example of Leopold Bloom's ruminations on the household cat: "Cruel. Her nature. Curious mice never squeal. Seem to like it." (This passage, of course, in a rather prosaic way also illustrates how Joyce conditions his readers to impose meaning, since few will read the passage without inserting a comma after Bloom's "Curious.") The interspersion of more straightforward narration produces tension through overlapping depictions of the action, and perhaps most significantly, Joyce alternately presents a range of perspectives throughout the text, giving no voice primacy. As a consequence the reader must establish, without the intervention or guidance of the author, a personal system of values for weighing the significance of events.

Ulysses stands as a vigorous but logical extension of the stylistic innovation begun in Joyce's earlier works. The diffusion of narrative discourse in *Dubliners* and *A Portrait* manifests itself in every facet of *Ulysses*'s textual structure, and the 1922 novel signals the continuing formal experimentation of *Finnegans Wake*. On a broader level, the publication of *Ulysses* also marks the high point of the dominant literary impulse of its time. Critics have come to see the year 1922, with the appearance of *Ulysses*, of T. S. Eliot's *The Waste Land*, and of German poet Rainer Maria Rilke's *Duino Elegies* and *Sonnets to Orpheus*, as the culmination of modernism. Although Joyce avoided association with artistic groups or literary movements, the characteristics distinguishing his novel—antipathy towards the institutions devoted to preserving the status quo, faith in the humanity of individuals, and a deep interest in stylistic experimentation—reflect the concerns animating the works of the major artists of the period.

Almost immediately after the publication of *Ulysses*, Joyce began the project that would occupy him for the remainder of his life, *Finnegans Wake*. As Ellmann recorded in his biography, from the start the nature of this new work puzzled and disturbed many of Joyce's old friends. Early in the process of his writing, he sent a draft of the opening passage to Harriet Shaw Weaver, who had provided financial and moral support since Joyce's Zurich days. She wrote to him, noted Ellmann, that "the poor hapless reader loses a very great deal of your intention; flounders, helplessly, is in imminent danger, in fact, of being as totally lost to view as that illfated vegetation [the shamrock] you mentioned." Ellmann related that Ezra Pound was left equally nonplussed by his encounter with a selection from the manuscript: "I will have another go at it, but up to present I make nothing of it whatever. Nothing so far as I make out, nothing short of divine vision or a new cure for the clapp [sic] can possibly be worth all the circumambient peripherization." Conditions surrounding its composition were as unsettling as the text itself. Financial troubles continued to plague Joyce at sporadic intervals. Problems with his vision that had begun while he was writing *Ulysses* proved steadily debilitating, and his daughter Lucia came increasingly under the influence of the mental disorder that would eventually institutionalize her. Through it all, Joyce proceeded with an unwavering faith in his "Work in Progress" (the name he used to designate *Finnegans Wake*, refusing to divulge its true title until its publication), and the book appeared, after seventeen years of planning, writing, and revising, on May 4, 1939.

As *Ulysses* examines the culture and society of Ireland by recording the events surrounding a single Dublin day, *Finnegans Wake* traces the prominent features of Western culture through its account of the activities of one Dublin night. Putatively the book concerns itself with the family of a Protestant Dublin pub-keeper living near Phoenix Park on the western border of the city: Humphrey Chimpden Earwicker (commonly referred to in the text as HCE), the father; Anna Livia Plurabelle (ALP), his wife; Shem and Shaun, their twin sons; and Issy, their daughter. In fact, from the opening pages Joyce extends the topical limits of the text by using HCE and his family to serve as representative manifestations of a range of psychological, theological, political, and sociological questions. Episodes in the book operate on both the microcosmic and the macrocosmic levels. They present archetypal views of the institutions and of the attitudes that have traditionally shaped the evolution of European society; simultaneously they offer a sensitive rendition of the complex relations that characterize the makeup of the modern family. Earwicker and others in the family assume a variety of transparent roles—historical and mythological—giving a local habitation to Joyce's ideas while at the same time recalling figures and events from history, mythology, and folklore already well known to the reader. By incorporating both the particular and the universal in his depictions of the major themes of the text, Joyce insures that his work will simultaneously appeal to a range of individuals on a variety of levels.

Joyce intended *Finnegans Wake* less as a critique of Western society than as a reflection of its cyclical nature that acted, as the work itself notes, as "one continuous present tense integument [that] slowly unfolded all marryvoising moodmoulded cyclewheeling history." Its sardonic humor and multiplicity of allusions can, however, create the impression that the text aims at censure. By their very nature the central concerns of *Finnegans Wake* lend themselves to clashes between the spectacular and the absurd, and the figurative language that Joyce employs in his descriptions accentuates the reader's sense of the ridiculous elements in the human condition.

As part of Joyce's efforts to encompass in his work as much of Western civilization as possible, the narration makes repeated reference to cataclysmic events, both historical and mythological, that shaped the evolution of our culture—the Stock Market Crash of 1929, the Battle of Waterloo, the Medieval Irish Battle of Clontarf, the resurrection of Jesus, the murder of Abel by Cain. At the same time it defamiliarizes conventional associations with these events through comical distortion: the Duke of Wellington becomes "Sraughter Willingdone"; Napoleon Bonaparte, Wellington's opponent at Waterloo, is now "Lipoleum"; Joyce rechristens Saint Patrick, the patron saint of Ireland, "flop hattrick"; and its last king, Brian Boru, has his name transformed into "Brewinbaroon." The text also explores more personal elements of society—the rise and fall of the father figure; the bitter struggles of sibling rivalry; the impulses, at times conflicting and at times complementary, of sensual love and sexual depravity; and the perceptions of woman as matriarch and concubine—with the same wry tone with which the novel describes public characters and events. If the juxtaposition of these impressions and observations seems haphazard or contradictory, it is because Joyce repeatedly refused to oversimplify the world as he saw it or to take a polemical position regarding the way one should spend one's life.

In *Finnegans Wake* form does not simply follow content; it enhances and, to a large degree, defines it. The syntactical structure of the text adheres to a circular rather than a linear configuration. The final sentence breaks off at its midpoint to be completed by the fragment opening the text. This pattern is repeated on the thematic level by progressively extravagant re-introductions of dominant issues and by the analogies created between individual experience and cultural events. In one instance, for example, Joyce examines the ramifications of the figurative and literal fall of the father by connecting it with the fall of the Roman Empire, the fall of Adam, and the fall of Humpty-Dumpty, and throughout the entire passage the dissolution of its descriptive language both records and parodies the events it depicts.

In an effort to break the dominance of rigid linguistic codes, Joyce gives words in *Finnegans Wake* a sensuous, organic quality of their own. To emphasize the range of perceptions and feelings conveyed by what passes for straightforward communication, he twists, stretches, supplements, and reshapes ordinary conversations and descriptions to reform them into multilayered statements. Topical puns on the names of psychologists Carl Jung and Sigmund Freud emerge in a sentence expressing concern for preadolescent girls who "were yung and easily freudened." A familiar scriptural passage suffers the variations of etymology and entomology: "In the buginning is the woid." And in a sentence asking how a man was hurt the words rearrange themselves to extend their range by combining commentary with inquiry: "What then agentlike brought about that tragoady thundersday this municipal sin business?" Through it all Joyce remains aware of the interpretive demands that his methods place on his readers, but even when he offers a bit of comfort he cannot resist the freeplay of language. "You is feeling like you was lost in the bush, boy? You says: It is a puling sample jungle of woods. You most shouts out: Bethicket me for a stump of beech if I have the poultriest notions what the farest he all means."

On first encounter the virtuosity of *Finnegans Wake* can move a reader to perceive it and Joyce as his or her adversaries, sardonically mocking any attempt to bring comprehension to a conglomeration of unfamiliar or newly created words and disconnected imagery. Such a response is understandable and, to some extent, accurate. While Joyce did not write *Finnegans Wake* out of a perverse wish to destroy language or to render meaning superfluous, he did intend to overthrow the notion that a single interpretation of a work of art could enjoy primacy over all others. To achieve this end he attempted to draw the reader into active, creative reconstruction of the text, not the physical artifact but the metaphysical concept: the product of the imagination responding to words on a page. The digressions, the redundancies, the non sequitors of his book are not meant to impede understanding but rather to enlarge it. Joyce refuses in *Finnegans Wake* to dictate a single, inclusive meaning informed by a faith in the authority of cause-and-effect logic. He aims, instead, as he says in the novel, at "that ideal reader suffering from an ideal insomnia." He wishes to inspire an intense involvement with the work that will reveal the opportunities of interpretation implicit in the ranges of responses that one can make to his polymorphous material. To label this intention as perverse, however, does an injustice to Joyce, for it demands that he conform to the standards set by the tradition of the nineteenth-century English novel. Judged along those lines, *Finnegans Wake* is a hopeless failure, but such methods deny the very imaginative impulse that art is meant to celebrate, for, as the work itself declares, "the unfacts, did we possess them, are too imprecisely few to warrant our certitude." Joyce would rather have readers trust in their instincts and in the text itself, which at one point asserts: "He is cured of faith who is sick of fate."

The advent of World War II quickly followed the publication of *Finnegans Wake*, and Joyce sardonically expressed the opinion that the war was a plot to undermine interest in his book. Late in 1940, after the German Army had occupied Paris, Joyce and his family left France to return again to neutral Switzerland. In Zurich Joyce became ill; Ellmann in his biography noted that the writer suffered a perforated duodenal ulcer. After an apparently successful operation, Joyce lapsed into a coma, and at 2:15 on the morning of January 13, 1941, he died. The final lines of *Finnegans Wake* may provide a fitting epitaph: "We pass through grass behush the bush to.

Whish! A gull. Gulls. Far calls. Coming, far! End here. Us then. Finn, again! Take. Bussoftlhee, mememormee! Till thousendsthee. Lps. The keys to. Given! A way a lone a last a love a long the"

MEDIA ADAPTATIONS: Finnegans Wake was adapted for a film by Expanding Cinema, 1965; *A Portrait of the Artist as a Young Man* was adapted for a film by Ulysses/Howard Mahler, 1979; "The Dead" was adapted for a film by Vestron Pictures, 1987.

BIOGRAPHICAL/CRITICAL SOURCES:

BOOKS

Adams, Robert M., *Surface and Symbol: The Consistency of James Joyce's "Ulysses,"* Oxford University Press, 1962.

Adams, Robert M., *James Joyce: Common Sense and Beyond,* Random House, 1966.

Anderson, Chester G., *James Joyce and His World,* Thames & Hudson, 1967.

Atherton, James S., *The Books at the Wake: A Study of Literary Allusions in James Joyce's "Finnegans Wake,"* Viking, 1960.

Bowen, Zack and James Carens, editors, *A Companion to Joyce Studies,* Greenwood Press, 1984.

Boyle, Robert, *James Joyce's Pauline Vision: A Catholic Exposition,* Southern Illinois University Press, 1978.

Bradley, Bruce, *James Joyce's Schooldays,* St. Martin's, 1982.

Brivic, Sheldon, *Joyce Between Freud and Jung,* Kennikat, 1980.

Budgen, Frank, *James Joyce and the Making of "Ulysses,"* University of Indiana Press, 1960.

Campbell, Joseph and Henry Morton Robinson, *A Skeleton Key to "Finnegans Wake,"* Viking, 1961.

Connolly, Thomas E., editor, *Joyce's Portrait: Criticisms and Critiques,* Appleton-Century-Crofts, 1962.

Curran, C. P., *James Joyce Remembered,* Oxford University Press, 1968.

Dictionary of Literary Biography, Gale, Volume 10: *Modern British Dramatists, 1940-1945,* 1982, Volume 19: *British Poets, 1840-1914,* 1983, Volume 36: *British Novelists, 1890-1929: Modernists,* 1985.

Ellmann, Richard, *James Joyce,* Oxford University Press, 1959, revised edition, 1984.

Ellmann, Richard, *The Consciousness of James Joyce,* Oxford University Press, 1977.

Epstein, E. L., *The Ordeal of Stephen Dedalus,* Arcturus, 1973.

Feehan, Joseph, editor, *Dedalus on Crete,* Saint Thomas More Guild of Immaculate Heart College, 1956.

Gifford, Don, *Notes for Joyce,* Dutton, 1967.

Gifford, Don, *Notes for Joyce: An Annotation of James Joyce's "Ulysses,"* Dutton, 1974.

Gilbert, Stuart, *James Joyce's "Ulysses,"* Random House, 1952.

Gillespie, Michael Patrick, *Inverted Volumes Improperly Arranged: James Joyce and His Trieste Library,* UMI Research Press, 1983.

Glasheen, Adaline, *A Third Census of "Finnegans Wake,"* University of California Press, 1977.

Goldman, Arnold, *The Joyce Paradox: Form and Freedom in His Fiction,* Northwestern University Press, 1966.

Gorman, Herbert, *James Joyce: A Definitive Biography,* Lane, 1941.

Hart, Clive, *Structure and Motif in "Finnegans Wake,"* Faber, 1962.

Hart, Clive, editor, *James Joyce's "Dubliners": Critical Essays,* Faber, 1969.

Hart, Clive and David Hayman, *James Joyce's "Ulysses": Critical Essays,* University of California Press, 1974.

Hayman, David, *"Ulysses": The Mechanics of Meaning,* Prentice-Hall, 1970.

Joyce, James, *Letters of James Joyce,* Viking, Volume I, edited by Stuart Gilbert, 1957, reissued with corrections, 1966, Volumes II and III, edited by Richard Ellmann, 1966.

Joyce, James, *A Portrait of the Artist as a Young Man,* Viking, 1964.

Joyce, James, *Dubliners,* Viking, 1969.

Joyce, James, *Finnegans Wake,* Viking, 1969.

Joyce, James, *Ulysses,* Random House, 1986.

Joyce, Stanislaus, *My Brother's Keeper,* Faber, 1958.

Kenner, Hugh, *Dublin's Joyce,* Chatto & Windus, 1955.

Kenner, Hugh, *Ulysses,* Allen & Unwin, 1980.

Lawrence, Karen, *The Odyssey of Style in "Ulysses,"* Princeton University Press, 1981.

Litz, A. Walton, *James Joyce,* Twayne, 1966.

Magalaner, Marvin, *Time of Apprenticeship: The Fiction of Young James Joyce,* Abelard-Schuman, 1959.

McHugh, Roland, *The Sigla of "Finnegans Wake,"* Arnold, 1976.

Morris, William E. and Clifford A. Nault, Jr., editors, *Portraits of an Artist: A Casebook on James Joyce's "A Portrait of the Artist as a Young Man,"* Odyssey Press, 1962.

Noon, William T., *Joyce and Aquinas: A Study of Religious Elements in the Writings of James Joyce,* Yale University Press, 1957.

Norris, Margot, *The Decentered Universe of "Finnegans Wake": A Structuralist Approach,* Johns Hopkins University Press, 1976.

Peake, Charles H., *James Joyce: The Citizen and the Artist,* Arnold, 1977.

Ryf, Robert S., *A New Approach to Joyce: The Portrait of the Artist as a Guidebook,* University of California Press, 1962.

Scholes, Robert and Richard M. Kain, *The Workshop of Daedalus,* Northwestern University Press, 1965.

Staley, Thomas F. and Bernard Benstock, editors, *Approaches to Joyce's Portrait,* University of Pittsburgh Press, 1976.

Sullivan, Kevin, *Joyce Among the Jesuits,* Columbia University Press, 1958.

Thornton, Weldon, *Allusion in "Ulysses": An Annotated List,* University of North Carolina Press, 1968.

Tindall, William York, *A Reader's Guide to "Finnegans Wake,"* Barrar, Straus, 1959.

Tindall, William York, *A Reader's Guide to James Joyce,* Noonday Press, 1959.

Twentieth-Century Literary Criticism, Gale, Volume 3, 1980, Volume 8, 1982, Volume 16, 1985.

PERIODICALS

Accent, winter, 1952.

Atlantic Monthly, March, 1958.

James Joyce Quarterly, fall, 1968.

Los Angeles Times Book Review, July 20, 1986.

New Republic, February 17, 1982.

New York Times Book Review, December 31, 1944.

Partisan Review, summer, 1939.

Poetry, July, 1930.

Times Literary Supplement, February 10, 1984.*

—*Sidelights by Michael Patrick Gillespie*

K

KAFKA, Franz   1883-1924

PERSONAL: Born July 3, 1883, in Prague, Bohemia (now Czechoslovakia); died of tuberculosis of the larynx, June 3, 1924, in Kierling, Klosterneuburg, Austria; buried in Jewish cemetery in Prague-Straschnitz, Czechoslovakia; son of Hermann (a merchant and manufacturer) and Julie (Loewy) Kafka; children: one son. *Education:* Ferdinand-Karls University (Prague), earned doctorate in law, 1906; also attended technical institute in Prague.

ADDRESSES: Home—Prague, Czechoslovakia.

CAREER: Worked for attorney Richard Loewy drafting legal notices, Prague, Bohemia (now Czechoslovakia), 1906; intern in law courts, Prague, 1906-07; staff member of insurance company Assicurazioni Generali, Prague, 1907-08; specialist in accident prevention and work-place safety for Workers' Accident Insurance Institute for the Kingdom of Bohemia, Prague, 1908-22; writer. Worked at Prague Asbestos Works Hermann & Co. (manufacturers), Zizkov, Bohemia (now Czechoslovakia), 1911-17.

WRITINGS:

SHORT FICTION IN GERMAN

Betrachtung (title means "Meditations"; includes stories later published in English translation as "Children on a Country Road," "Unmasking a Confidence Trickster," "Excursion into the Mountains," and "The Street Window"; see below), Rowohlt Verlag, 1913.

In der Strafkolonie (includes story published in English translation as "In the Penal Colony"; see below), Kurt Wolff Verlag, 1919.

Ein Landzart, Kleine Erzaehlungen (includes story published in English translation as "A Country Doctor"; see below), Kurt Wolff Verlag, 1919.

Ein Hungerkunstler, Vier Geschichten (includes stories published in English translation as "A Hunger Artist," "A Little Woman," "First Sorrow," and "Josephine the Singer; or, the Mouse Folk"; see below), Verlag Die Schmiede, 1924.

Beim Bau der Chinesischen Mauer, Ungedruckte Erzaehlungen und Prosa aus dem Nachlass (includes stories published in English translation as "The Great Wall of China," "The Village Schoolmaster [The Giant Mole]," "The Hunter Gracchus," "Investigations of a Dog," and "The Burrow"; see below), edited by Max Brod and Hans Joachim Schoeps, Gustav Kiepenheuer Verlag, 1931.

SHORT FICTION IN ENGLISH TRANSLATION

The Complete Stories (includes "Description of a Struggle," "Wedding Preparations in the Country," "The Judgment," "The Metamorphosis," "In the Penal Colony," "The Village Schoolmaster [The Giant Mole]," "Blumfeld, an Elderly Bachelor," "The Warden of the Tomb," "A Country Doctor," "The Hunter Gracchus," "The Great Wall of China," "A Report to an Academy," "The Refusal," "A Hunger Artist," "Investigations of a Dog," "A Little Woman," "The Burrow," "Josephine the Singer; or, The Mouse Folk," "Children on a Country Road," "Excursion Into the Mountains," "The Street Window," and "Unmasking a Confidence Trickster"), translations by Willa Muir and Edwin Muir, Tania Stern and James Stern, and Ernst Kaiser and Eithne Wilkins, postscript by Nahum N. Glatzer, Schocken, 1971.

Stories also published in English translation independently and in additional collections and anthologies.

NOVELS

Der Prozess, edited by Max Brod, Verlag Die Schmiede, 1925, translation by Willa Muir and Edwin Muir published as *The Trial,* Gollancz, 1935, Knopf, 1937; revised edition with additional chapters in English translation by E. M. Butler, Secker & Warburg, 1956; definitive edition, with illustrations by George Salter, Knopf, 1957, with drawings by Kafka, Schocken, 1968.

Das Schloss, edited by Max Brod, Kurt Wolff Verlag, 1927, translation by Willa Muir and Edwin Muir published as *The Castle,* Knopf, 1930; new edition with introduction by Thomas Mann, Knopf, 1941; definitive edition with additional material translated by Eithne Wilkins and Ernst Kaiser and with introduction by Thomas Mann, Secker & Warburg, 1953, Knopf, 1954, revised edition reprinted, Schocken, 1974.

Amerika, edited by Max Brod, Kurt Wolff Verlag, 1927, translation by Willa Muir and Edwin Muir published under same title, with preface by Thomas Mann, afterword by Brod, and illustrations by Emlen Etting, Routledge & Kegan Paul, 1938, New Directions, 1946, reprinted,

Schocken, 1962, reprinted with foreword by John Updike, Schocken, 1983.

Novels also collected in single-volume editions.

NONFICTION

The Diaries of Franz Kafka, edited by Max Brod, Volume 1: *1910-1913*, translation by Joseph Kresh from German manuscripts, Schocken, 1948, Volume 2: *1914-1923*, translation by Martin Greenberg with Hannah Arendt from German manuscripts, Schocken, 1949.

Briefe an Milena (correspondence), edited and ·with epilogue by Willy Haas, Schocken, 1952, translation by Tania Stern and James Stern published as *Letters to Milena*, Schocken, 1953.

Briefe an den Vater, S. Fischer Verlag, 1953, translation by Ernst Kaiser and Eithne Wilkins published as *Letter to His Father* in bilingual edition, *Letter to His Father/Briefe an den Vater*, Schocken, 1966.

Briefe an Felice und andere Korrespondenz aus der Verlobungszeit, edited by Erich Heller and Juergen Born, introduction by Heller, S. Fischer Verlag, 1967, translation by James Stern and Elizabeth Duckworth published as *Letters to Felice*, Schocken, 1973.

Briefe an Ottla und die Familie, S. Fischer Verlag, 1974, translation by Richard Winston and Clara Winston published as *Letters to Ottla and the Family*, Schocken, 1982.

OMNIBUS VOLUMES

Hochzeitvorbereitungen auf dem Lande und andere Prosa aus dem Nachlass, Schocken, 1953, translation by Ernst Kaiser and Eithne Wilkins published as *Dearest Father: Stories and Other Writings*, notes by Max Brod, Schocken, 1954.

I Am a Memory Come Alive: Autobiographical Writings, edited by Nahum N. Glatzer from previous translations, Schocken, 1976.

The Basic Kafka, edited by Erich Heller, Pocket Books, 1983.

Fiction and nonfiction also published together in other collections.

OTHER

Contributor to periodicals, including *Arkadia*, *Bohemia*, and *Hyperion*.

COLLECTED WORKS

German editions include *Gesammelte Schriften*, edited by Max Brod with Heinz Politzer, Volumes 1-4, Schocken, 1935, Volumes 5-6, Verlag Heinrich Mercy Sohn, 1936-37; *Gesammelte Schriften*, edited by Brod, five volumes, Schocken, 1946; *Gesammelte Werke*, edited by Brod, ten volumes, S. Fischer Verlag, 1950-67.

SIDELIGHTS: Franz Kafka, a Jewish Czechoslovakian who wrote in German, ranks among the twentieth century's most acclaimed writers. He is often cited as the author whose works best evoke the bewildering oppressiveness of modern life, and though his writings accommodate a vast range of interpretations, his general perspective is inevitably one of anxiety and alienation. His characters constantly face failure and futility, and they struggle to survive in a world that is largely unfeeling and unfamiliar. This world, rendered with great detachment and detail, is one in which the fantastic is entirely normal, the irrational is rational, and the unreasonable seems reasonable. It is a bizarre, senselessly oppressive world in which characters endure between madness and despair, and between defeat and mere failure. Kafka's protagonists subject themselves to extraordinary torture contraptions, negotiate unfathomable bureaucratic mazes, and execute astounding transformations. It is a world in which a man becomes an insect and an ape becomes a sophisticate. Today, with genocide, madness, and even impending doom seen as everyday possibilities, Kafka's voice sounds vital and prophetic. As Ernst Pawel wrote in *The Nightmare of Reason: A Biography of Franz Kafka*, Kafka articulates "the anguish of being human."

Kafka was born in Prague in 1883, a time when that city was still part of Bohemia within the Austro-Hungarian Empire. Anti-Semitism was rife throughout eastern Europe, and in Prague, as in many European cities, Jews were reduced by economic and social disadvantage to congregating in ghettos. Within Prague's Jewish ghetto, Kafka's father, Hermann, owned and operated a dry-goods wholesale store. Hermann Kafka was an uneducated but extremely industrious Czech who had married Julie Loewy, an urbane, German-speaking Jew from a slightly higher social class. Although her husband's superior within Prague's Jewish society, Julie Kafka subordinated herself to him helping in the store most days and joining him at card games most evenings.

Hermann Kafka's domineering manner greatly distressed young Kafka, who found his father loud, impatient, unsympathetic, and, consequently, overwhelming and intimidating. Particularly vivid to Kafka was his childhood memory of an incident in which he repeatedly cried from his bed for water, whereupon his father removed him to a balcony and locked him out of the house. Years later, at age thirty-six, the event still powerfully haunted Kafka, and in a missive later published as *Letter to His Father* he reproached Hermann Kafka for his crude methods. "For years thereafter," Kafka wrote, "I kept being haunted by fantasies of this giant of a man, my father, the ultimate judge, coming to get me in the middle of the night, and for almost no reason at all dragging me out of bed onto the *pavlatch*—in other words, that as far as he was concerned, I was an absolute Nothing."

With Kafka's parents devoting their time and energy to the dry-goods store, his upbringing was left largely to maids and governesses. He found himself further separated from his parents when he finally began his education, for Prague's schools, known as gymnasiums, operated ten months each year and assigned extensive homework. Student life proved arduous and trying for Kafka, who was a minority as both a German-speaker and a Jew; and the school, which was designed to shape children into functionaries for the empire's ever-flourishing bureaucracy, offered little of insight or interest to him. Kafka coped with this unappealing and even alienating approach to education by daydreaming and, in adolescence, by reading extensively, with a preference for the works of evolutionist Charles Darwin and philosophers Benedict Spinoza and Friedrich Nietzsche.

In adolescence Kafka also dwelled obsessively on his own self-perceived inadequacy, rejecting his intellect as inferior and his body as loathsome. As his self-perception degenerated, his grades suffered accordingly, and only with a great deal of relentless studying, and some cheating, did he survive his school's hellish period of rigorous final examinations and thereby complete his studies.

For a graduation present, Kafka's parents financed his vacation to a town near the North Sea. The vacation was his first venture from Prague and was intended, at least by his father, as his respite before entering the family business. Kafka, however, had already decided to enter Ferdinand-Karls University, a German school where he intended to study philosophy. Upon returning home, Kafka announced his scholastic intentions and met with powerful disapproval from his father. Despite the parent's objections and harangues, Kafka entered the university in 1901, and soon afterwards he decided to pursue a law degree.

At Ferdinand-Karls University, Kafka became acquainted with intellectuals and aspiring artists. Like many German-speaking students, he joined the Hall of Lecture and Discourse for German Studies, an organization widely recognized as Prague's leading institution for German culture. The Hall had been conceived as an anti-Semitic organization, but the steady influx of German-speaking Jews gradually transformed it into a predominantly Judaic body. Through this group Kafka met his closest friends, including Max Brod, a sickly, hunchbacked student who played and composed music and wrote poetry. While delivering a lecture on philosopher Arthur Schopenhauer, Brod had denounced Nietzsche as a fraud, and when Kafka vehemently protested afterwards, their friendship began.

With Brod, Kafka began sampling Prague's cultural offerings, which included theatrical productions and more esoteric events such as theosophic and anthroposophic lectures and spiritualist seances. In addition, Kafka and Brod frequented Prague's cafes, which numbered more than two hundred, and visited the city's brothels, which also numbered in the hundreds. As a result of his carousing and extra-curricular studies, Kafka's grades suffered. The insufferable boredom of the gymnasium had been replaced by the equally lethal monotony of law school, in which information was inevitably conveyed by such dull lecturers that it was rendered appallingly useless to Kafka and his fellow students. Briefly, Kafka abandoned law studies for chemistry, then returned to law before leaving it again for German studies and art history. He then returned once more to law and continued in that field throughout the remainder of his education.

In 1905, one year before finishing his studies, Kafka's hectic and demanding life finally affected his health and compelled him to recover at a sanatorium. There he enjoyed one of his rare pleasurable relationships with a woman. Although his lover was considerably older, Kafka apparently toyed with the notion of marriage. Once back in Prague, however, he abandoned the affair and resumed his association with Jewish intellectuals and artists. At night he frequented theaters, bordellos, and cafes, and listened as his friends and acquaintances discussed politics, art, and their own writings. Unlike his peers, though, Kafka showed little interest in politics or political concepts such as socialism, choosing instead to continue reading works by masters such as Goethe, Kleist, Kierkegaard, Flaubert, Dickens, and Dostoyevsky.

Unbeknownst to his friends, Kafka had also begun writing his own novel, one referred to now as "Beschreibung eines Kampfes" ("Description of a Struggle"). This work—eventually abandoned by Kafka and given incomplete to Brod, who later provided the title—is a funny and fantastic account of a nameless narrator's adventures on a winter's evening. Among the notable episodes in the story is "Gespraech mit dem Beter" ("Conversation With the Supplicant"), an unsettling church encounter recalled by a grotesque fat man as four nude servants carry him across a river. Upon reading "Description of a Struggle," Brod immediately recognized that Kafka had already surpassed his peers as a writer, and in an essay for a

local journal he placed Kafka in the "sainted company" of German literature's elite. Kafka received Brod's praise with humility and, characteristically, apprehension. He expressed concern that any writings he published henceforth might disappoint readers aware of his allegedly unmerited stature. To Brod, Kafka confessed that he could never "hope to produce an effect to rival that with which your sentence has endowed my name."

Aside from reading and writing, Kafka also devoted considerable time to preparing for his grueling, extensive final examinations. Upon successfully completing his first two tests, Kafka qualified for work in his prospective field, and in the spring of 1906 he began drafting legal notices for a local attorney. In addition, he also assisted his parents at the family store whenever such involvement was required. His jobs, together with his literary pursuits and his ongoing, seemingly endless studies, considerably diminished his other extra-curricular activities, though he managed to continue indulging in one of his rare athletic interests, swimming.

Strained by constant pressure to fulfill familial, professional, and scholastic obligations and expectations, Kafka again succumbed to exhaustion after earning his law doctorate in June, 1906. Shortly thereafter he re-entered the sanatorium, where he briefly revived his affair with the mysterious older woman. But as before, upon returning home he promptly discontinued the relationship and resumed his relatively carefree social life with Brod and other friends.

Back in Prague Kafka also began writing another story, one now known as "Hochzeitsvorbereitungen auf dem Lande" ("Wedding Preparations in the Country"). This tale—left incomplete by Kafka and consequently titled by Brod—recounts a bridegroom's dread as he travels to meet his beloved. Unlike "Description of a Struggle," which only superficially explores alienation, "Wedding Preparations in the Country" offers a disturbing evocation of apprehension in its all-encompassing banality. The protagonist, Raban, even resorts to childlike optimism by imagining that his two-weeks stay in the countryside will actually be the predicament of someone other than himself. Biographer Ronald Hayman, in *Kafka*, asserted that Kafka used this strategy in his own personal life and added that the tale itself served as a vehicle for Kafka's displacement. Hayman wrote: "Raban's belief that everything could be explained is a projection of Kafka's need to explain everything, by means of a story about an *alter ego*."

Upon returning to Prague Kafka also began one year's unpaid apprenticeship in the city's court system. His position, while apparently a career necessity, afforded him little opportunity to free himself from his father's household and authority. This continued dependence resulted in increased anxiety for Kafka in mid-1907 when his father decided to move the family into a new building, one recently constructed on a razed portion of the ghetto. To Kafka's utter dismay, the new dwelling afforded him only minimal privacy, for his bedroom was situated between the living room and his parents' bedroom, thus serving as a nerve-racking vantage point from which could be heard all noises and conversations occurring within the home. Also distressing to Kafka were his father's seemingly constant interruptions and his parents' ineffective discretion within their own room. Relaxing, much less writing, proved extremely difficult for the already hypersensitive Kafka.

Fortunately for Kafka, his social activities afforded him substantial distraction from his tense home life. After graduating, he devoted more time to recreation, including motorcycling, swimming, sunbathing, and billiards. He also entered into his first sustained love affair, though it is unclear whether this romance inhibited his enthusiasm for prostitutes. He had, by this time, also revealed serious literary aspirations to Brod and others. But with typically curious reasoning, he maintained that his income should derive from an occupation quite dissimilar from his literary pursuits, and he therefore sought an undistracting, undemanding position, preferably one abroad.

The job that Kafka eventually obtained, though, was a tedious post at an Italian insurance company with a Prague office. Offering low pay and long hours, the post was immensely unappealing, and Kafka almost immediately began hoping for a transfer. But such wishes were futile, and Kafka, sensing unending and unendurable boredom and poverty, contemplated suicide. In the throes of anguish, he abandoned writing and became a more frequent patron of bordellos and low-life cafes. In addition, he entered into relations with a Jewish student. But, realizing that he was psychologically incapable of reciprocating a woman's love, he confessed to Brod that, conversely, he could only love women unlikely to share his feelings. Thus his relationships with women were, understandably, impaired by his neurotic perspective.

In 1908 Kafka's fortunes improved when a friend's father, responding to Kafka's pleas for help, secured him a post at the Workmen's Accident Insurance Institute for the Kingdom of Bohemia. Although the firm was steadfastly anti-Semitic—Kafka became only the second Jew of two hundred and fifty employees—he was nonetheless offered a promising job, one with regular hours and with greater pay than was accorded him by the Italian company. Seizing the opportunity, Kafka hastily obtained a medical report certifying him as prone to nervousness and agitation. This certificate assured his departure from the Assicurazioni, and in late July he assumed the post that he would hold until his death sixteen years later.

At the Workmen's Institute Kafka rapidly attained a level of substantial responsibility. Despite only limited seniority, he was selected to formally introduce new administrator Robert Marschner at a company gathering, and in the ensuing years he contributed segments on work-place safety to Marschner's annual report of 1910, and produced press releases. In *The Nightmare of Reason,* Pawel reports that Kafka's work-related writings, including more technical articles on accident prevention, contradict his image as an incompetent and show him, instead, as a serious, forthright employee. Pawel relates that Kafka's articles "combine an astonishing grasp of abstruse detail with a lucidity of presentation seldom encountered in writings of this sort," and he adds that the technical writings "quite incisively refute the caricature of Kafka as a bumbling fool forever sleepwalking in broad daylight and incapable of tying his shoelaces."

Although the change in employment lessened Kafka's anxieties, its increased responsibilities left him little time for writing and carousing. In March, 1908, Kafka had collected eight brief prose pieces under the title "Betrachtung" ("Meditations") and published them in the Franz Blei's journal *Hyperion.* But these works brought him little recognition, and some readers even mistook them for those of another writer, Robert Walser. Kafka consequently held little enthusiasm for the distractions of writing, and it was only through Brod's own efforts and encouragement that he agreed to produce a review of one of Blei's books. This enterprize, however, only exposed Kafka's ambivalence to writing, for he produced a twisted, tentative report. He later apologized to Blei, and along with that written apology he enclosed several pages containing his contributions to a company report.

As an alternative to the constant demands of the Workmen's Institute, Kafka renewed his interest in boating and swimming. But these activities offered only minimal respite from the company, and in late summer, 1909—several months after the Jewish student had ended their largely epistolary relationship—Kafka finally took a brief vacation with Brod. Earlier that summer, he had published excerpts from his abandoned novel *Description of a Struggle* in *Hyperion,* but that publication, like his earlier work in *Hyperion,* apparently gained him little attention. The vacation, however, sufficiently inspired him to engage in a writing contest with Brod, and in early autumn his piece, a description of airplanes, appeared in the publication *Bohemia.*

Invigorated by the vacation, Kafka returned to Prague with renewed interest in writing. In January, 1910, he published a book review in *Bohemia;* in March he produced five prose works for the same periodical; and soon afterwards, he also began a diary. Aside from writing, Kafka improved his physical fitness with daily calisthenics, horseback riding and—in summer—swimming and rowing. These activities, however, failed to ease his increasing digestive distress, and he therefore adopted a vegetarian diet. While converting to vegetarianism, Kafka became preoccupied with his bowel regularity, and he maintained both the vegetarian diet and a bowel obsession throughout his life.

1910 is also the year that Kafka began his interest in Yiddish theater. In May, Brod took him to a performance at a Prague cafe, and Kafka responded enthusiastically. The following autumn—1911—Kafka befriended members of a troupe and even arranged a performance. For Kafka, the Yiddish theater was appealing for various reasons: Its coarse melodramas afforded him insights into his ancestry and allowed him to explore aspects of race and nationality detested and ignored by his father, who considered the ethnic tradition a vulgar reminder of the ghetto. Inspired by the troupe and its performances, Kafka began studying Yiddish literature and Judaism and even attended a musical presentation arranged by Zionists. He also fell in love with actress Mania Tschissik, but his affections were not reciprocated, and when the troupe finally left Prague Kafka turned to Brod for solace.

This period was one of almost constant personal turmoil for Kafka. In October, 1911, his brother-in-law, Karl Hermann, founded Prague's first asbestos factory at the behest of Kafka's father. Kafka offered his assistance, assuming that such involvement would be only occasional and menial. His father, however, perceived the factory as an opportunity for his son to redeem his wasted life through application to a family business. Since Karl Hermann was often traveling to promote business, Kafka soon found himself constantly working at the factory after leaving his insurance post each afternoon. The factory's noise and filth immensely disturbed Kafka's already sensitive disposition, and endless confrontations with his father, who demanded greater commitment from him, further exacerbated his anxiety. Even in his room Kafka was hardly free of unnerving distractions, for his father's apparently constant shouting rang throughout the home, and barely muffled sounds from the parents' bedroom continually undermined the son's sense of privacy and decency.

Perhaps as a result of living in a state of nearly unending anxiety, Kafka soon suffered declining health, including weak breathing, migraine headache, and more stomach distress. In

June, 1912, he obtained one week's sick leave from the insurance company, and in July he spent three more weeks in a German sanatorium. His stay at the sanatorium, however, was motivated largely by recreational considerations, for he longed to swim and languish in the summer sun. Evenings at the sanatorium he devoted to writing a novel that he referred to as "Der Verschollene" (which means "the missing one"). But this work, later developed into *Amerika,* came slowly to Kafka, and by autumn, when he had already returned to Prague, he was still at work on the first chapter.

Once back in Prague, Kafka also occupied himself by collecting several prose works for publication as the volume *Betrachtung.* While compiling that work, he realized a sudden burst of creativity, and within three months he produced two of his greatest stories, "Das Urteil" ("The Judgment") and "Die Verwandlung" ("The Metamorphosis"), and completed the first chapter of *Amerika.* "The Judgment" is certainly a key work in Kafka's canon, for it constitutes one of his most incisive renderings of the father-son conflict that so devastated his personal life. In the tale, protagonist Georg Bendemann suffers from total subordination to his totalitarian father, a domineering widower. One afternoon, Georg nervously considers his wedding engagement while alone with his father. He tells his father of a friend in St. Petersburg. His father doubts the existence of such a friend and criticizes his son for besmirching the memory of his mother by succumbing to his fiancee's sexual advances. Upon shaming his son, the father then reveals that he actually knows of the St. Petersburg friend and has actually kept him abreast of Georg's engagement. Gleefully proclaiming his deception, the father mocks his son's naivete and condemns him to drown himself. The son complies by dropping himself from a bridge, pausing beforehand only to say, "Dear parents, I have always loved you, all the same."

"The Judgment" is hailed as a masterful articulation of a father-son conflict and an extraordinary expression of oppression and anxiety. "The Metamorphosis" is acclaimed for the same qualities, and is prized additionally for its fantastic premise. In perhaps his most memorable and well-known tale, Kafka wrote of Gregor Samsa, a traveling salesman who awakens at home one morning to find that he has become an enormous insect. Like "The Judgment," "The Metamorphosis" is often interpreted as a reflection of Kafka's own anxieties, for like Kafka, protagonist Samsa is repulsed by his physical existence and is overwhelmed with guilt for his very presence. Samsa's father, in turn, is both angered and disgusted by his son's transformation, which he considers a personal effrontery. Eventually, the father arms himself with fruit and bombards the hideous insect, sinking one apple deep into his back. For more than one month Samsa lives on while the apple rots and inflames his back. His parents and sister try to ignore him, and he usually remains in his room, where he had taken to crawling on the ceiling before the apple incident somewhat incapacitated him. One evening, however, his parents and recent lodgers are enjoying music when Samsa suddenly appears and repulses everyone. The family then decides that the gigantic insect that is Gregor Samsa must be destroyed. Sensing his inconvenient presence within the otherwise harmonious household, Samsa retreats to his room and thinks of his family with "tenderness and love." The next morning, a cleaning woman discovers his already dried corpse.

Both "The Judgment" and "The Metamorphosis," like most of Kafka's subsequent writings, have inspired a wide range of interpretations, and both works have been categorized in often contrasting terms. "The Judgment" has been appraised as both realistic and absurd, while "The Metamorphosis," though more consistently considered a fantastic allegory, is nonetheless perceived by some critics as comedy and by others as tragedy. Despite making these diverging assessments, many critics agree that the tales are dream-like masochistic fantasies reflecting Kafka's father-son conflict and his own traumas and insecurities. Ronald Hayman, for instance, notes in his biography *Kafka* that "Kafka draws on his flow of anxieties" in writing "The Metamorphosis" and adds that even the tale's "root idea . . . was a gift from his father—an invitation to think of himself as verminous."

In 1912, aside from writing "The Judgment" and "The Metamorphosis," Kafka also completed "Der Heizer" ("The Stoker"), the first chapter of his novel *Amerika.* Kafka apparently delighted in reading aloud from this novel, which concerns the odd adventures of a naive young man sent to the United States after having seduced a maid. Upon publication in May, 1913, this chapter drew impressive praise from prominent novelist Robert Musil and received comparisons with the work of Heinrich von Kleist, whom Kafka had long admired as an artist. The next month, "The Judgment" appeared in Brod's periodical *Arkadia,* earning Kafka further recognition as a prominent new writer.

But Kafka was not immediately able to enjoy his newfound celebrity, for as early as 1912 the family factory began amassing imposing debts. The factory's problems were hardly Kafka's fault, for he worked regular hours at the insurance company and devoted only afternoons and some weekends to the plant's operations. But as Karl Hermann was constantly away on business, Kafka had been presumed responsible for the factory by his father, who claimed that various employees were swindling funds. Enduring the harangues of his desperate and incompetent parent, Kafka suffered migraine headaches and further stomach pains, and he once again considered suicide. He expressed such thoughts in a letter to Brod, who consequently wrote to Kafka's mother and urged her to intercede on her son's behalf. She responded by secretly hiring Karl Hermann's brother to fulfill Kafka's management duties. The plan ensued without Hermann Kafka's knowledge, and until the outbreak of World War I it enabled Kafka to live his already traumatic life free of the troublesome family business.

Once freed from his duties at the factory, Kafka devoted greater energy to his budding romance with Felice Bauer, an independent woman he met through Brod. Confident and extroverted, Bauer was the opposite of the insecure and inhibited Kafka in temperament, and biographer Pawel notes in *The Nightmare of Reason* that Kafka was attracted to precisely those qualities that he lacked. With Bauer he quickly established a close, and often confused, relationship, soliciting her opinions on his soon-to-be-published short prose works. Their communication was largely epistolary, with Kafka re-introducing himself to her through a missive on which he labored intermittently for ten days. Pawel calls this first letter "a masterpiece . . . of cunning and dissimulation," one designed by Kafka to present an acceptable image of himself as earnest, educated, and fairly sophisticated.

In his first several letters to Bauer, Kafka obsessively pursued her as a correspondent, writing daily and vigorously encouraging her to reciprocate. In *Kafka's Other Trial: The Letters to Felice,* Elias Canetti notes the almost parasitic nature of these initial missives. Kafka, Canetti writes, "was establishing a connection, a channel of communication, between [Bauer's] efficiency and health and his own indecisiveness and weakness.'' Canetti adds that Kafka derived a great deal of strength from these letters, and that strength, in turn, led to a great increase in his self-assurance as a writer. Shortly after writing his first letter to Bauer, Kafka felt sufficiently invigorated to produce ''The Judgment'' in one evening-long burst of creativity, and upon completing the tale he was still so euphoric with thoughts of Bauer that he dedicated the story to her.

Initially, Bauer did not share Kafka's obsession for letter writing. Kafka's extraordinary intimacy and sheer volume of correspondence, however, eventually convinced her of his passionate sincerity and prompted her to begin writing on a daily basis too. Increasingly, Kafka used his correspondence with Bauer as a forum for explaining his phobias, fears, and failures. He also began subordinating himself to her, describing himself as unworthy of her affection. Though more worshipful than reasonable, Kafka proposed marriage in the summer of 1913. Bauer accepted, and the couple's largely epistolary relationship—though they lived only six hours apart by train—seemed destined to result in matrimony.

Soon after becoming engaged, though, Kafka questioned the appeal of marriage. He feared the loss of the very solitude that seemed to him so integral to his recent fortunes as a writer, and in his diary he expressed extreme reservations about his suitability as a spouse. His anxieties led to physical distress, including heart pains. Upon soliciting his father's counsel, he was criticized as an unsuitable marriage prospect. Although Kafka had repeatedly tried to persuade Bauer of their folly, his father's words proved disheartening and unsettling.

In the autumn of 1913, seeking a respite from his traumatic personal life, Kafka entered a sanatorium, where he had a brief, inconsequential affair with a young Swiss woman. After returning to Prague he met with Bauer's friend Grete Bloch, who had agreed to help reconcile differences between the engaged couple. Bloch recounted Bauer's own personal difficulties, including dental decay, which Kafka found particularly repellant. Unable to articulate his objections to the impending marriage, Kafka spontaneously departed for Bauer's home in Berlin. But they met there only briefly before Bauer left to fulfill personal obligations, and so Kafka returned home full of doubt and uncertainty about the status of his engagement.

When Bauer failed to write to him after his brief visit to Berlin, Kafka decided that he could not live without her. In his biography *Kafka*, Hayman recounts a letter to Bauer in which Kafka both confessed his recent infidelity and stressed his love as nonetheless strong: ''I love you, Felice, with everything in me that's humanly good, everything that makes me worthy of staying among the living.'' Instead of responding to Kafka, Bauer once again appealed to her friend Bloch, who reacted by disclosing to Kafka the contents of Bauer's letters to her. Soon Kafka and Bloch had developed their own correspondence, and though by mid-1914 he and Bauer had renewed their engagement, shortly thereafter he and Bloch began their own affair.

Bloch, though sexually involved with Kafka, nonetheless continued advocating Bauer as his wife. Kafka, once again confronted with the likelihood of marriage, responded by pursuing Bloch instead of his fiancee. Events culminated in a confrontation between Kafka and both Bloch and Bauer in a hotel room, where Bauer berated him for his infidelity and indecisiveness. She ended their engagement and departed with Bloch, who, unbeknownst to Kafka, was pregnant with his child. Seemingly free of romantic ties, Kafka then vacationed with friends at a Danish seaside resort. Around this time, the Archduke Ferdinand, heir to the kingdom of Austro-Hungary, was assassinated. His death sparked World War I.

With Karl Hermann and his brother fighting in the war, Kafka once again entered the family's asbestos factory. He also continued working at the insurance company, where he had earlier been promoted to deputy secretary. Though working these two jobs, Kafka still found time for his writing. By July he had begun another novel, *Der Prozess* (*The Trial*), and in November he wrote ''In der Strafkolonie'' (''In the Penal Colony''). The latter work, largely viewed as one of Kafka's most disturbing, concerns an interrogating officer who becomes so proud of his mechanistic torture device—which involves long needles writing a proclamation onto victims' flesh—that he voluntarily submits himself to its deathly function. Like most of Kafka's fiction, ''In the Penal Colony'' has prompted a vast array of interpretations and has consequently been described in terms ranging from realism to absurdity and from comedy to tragedy. Critics analyzing from a psychological perspective see the tale as an expression of Kafka's own susceptibility for self punishment, while Hayman speculates in his biography that the story may have been influenced by accounts of World War I trench fighting.

After completing ''In the Penal Colony'' in late 1914, Kafka returned to several others stories in various stages of completion. Believing that he could easily lose inspiration, he often worked on his tales long into the night. His concentration, however, was disrupted by his responsibilities at both the insurance company and the family factory. In addition, he experienced continued poor health, including headaches, exhaustion from insomnia, and severe chest pain, though an earlier doctor's examination disclosed no indication of physical abnormality.

As a result of both business obligations and health problems, Kafka completed few works between the winters of 1914, when he produced ''In the Penal Colony,'' and of 1916, when he wrote ''Ein Landarzt'' (''A Country Doctor''). During that two-year interim he experienced various changes in his personal life. Most significant was his departure from his parents' household: When one of his sisters returned with her children for the duration of her husband's military service, Kafka moved to another sister's apartment, one vacated when she moved in with her in-laws, and he stayed there more than a year before renting an entire flat in March, 1917, around the same time that the factory finally closed. By that time he and Felice Bauer had once again renewed their courtship. Nearly five months later, he again suffered severe stomach pains, and in August, 1917, two months after he and Bauer announced their second official engagement, Kafka experienced his first tubercular hemorrhage.

By the time of his renewed engagement to Bauer, Kafka was once again writing regularly. ''A Country Doctor,'' his first sustained effort since ''In the Penal Colony,'' recounts a doctor's gruesome, surreal experience on a snowy evening. Summoned to a village, the doctor rides through a blizzard until he arrives at a farmhouse in which a young boy is apparently dying. The doctor initially pronounces the boy healthy, though the lad pleads for death. Upon closer examination, the doctor discovers, near the youth's right hip, a gaping hole in which worms wriggle through clotted blood. After noting the source of the boy's distress, the doctor is inexplicably stripped of his clothing and left alone with the youth, who proclaims that his repulsive hole is his "sole endowment" in the world. The doctor reassures the boy that the wound is relatively slight, whereupon the boy falls silent. The doctor then flees and rides home naked, seemingly unable to either retrieve his clothing or return home in time to salvage his medical practice.

Kafka followed "A Country Doctor" with "A Report to an Academy," in which a socially integrated ape recounts his experiences as a wild animal, and "The Great Wall of China," an ultimately uncompleted account of the wall's construction and its suitability as a defense measure. These works signaled the end of Kafka's very brief period of renewed creativity, for by the end of summer his health had declined seriously and his personal life had once again degenerated into despair and confusion. Following his first sign of internal bleeding, Kafka proceeded to the insurance company and only consulted a physician after having worked that day. His ailment was misdiagnosed as bronchial catarrh, and though he bled again that evening, he waited nearly one month before seeing a specialist. By that time he had also experienced fever, particular during evenings, and shortness of breath. His first doctor, however, had assured him that tuberculosis was unlikely.

With his health uncertain, Kafka returned to his parents' residence, and in September, at Brod's behest, he consulted a specialist and learned that both lungs were congested. He appealed to his employers for a leave of absence and received three months leave. Inexplicably, Kafka disregarded sanatoriums and stayed instead with his sister Ottla in the Bohemian countryside. There he met with Bauer, to whom he was once again engaged, and at that meeting he was fairly unresponsive to her presence. He subsequently neglected her correspondence, then wrote to her that death was preferable to their troubling relationship. In December Kafka returned to Prague, and at Christmas he met with Bauer at the home of Brod, who had earlier interceded on Bauer's behalf. Soon afterwards Kafka and Bauer parted at the train station, whereupon Kafka visited Brod and told him that the engagement was ended. Brod later recalled the occasion as the only one at which he saw Kafka weep.

In explaining to Brod the engagement's demise, Kafka declared that, as a Western Jew, he was unsuited for marriage. But in January, 1919, he entered into a romance with Julie Wohryzek at the Pension Stuedl, where he had begun a four-month convalescence in December. Kafka had entered the Pension Stuedl weak from his tuberculosis and a recent bout of Spanish influenza. His relationship with Wohryzek was initially frivolous, but when the couple rejoined in Prague in March, he found himself once again drawn to marriage. He announced their engagement that summer, much to the disapproval of his father, who implied that Wohryzek was merely a Jewish seductress. Though burdened by poor health and the strain of personal obligations and familial conflict, Kafka pursued the engagement and even found a desirable flat in Prague-Wrschowitz. When the flat proved unattainable, however, Kafka abruptly withdrew from the marriage plans and proposed instead that Wohryzek live with him in Munich, where he hoped to work for publisher Kurt Wolff. Plans for that job failed, though, and both Kafka and Wohryzek remained, separately, in Prague.

During the period of his involvement with Julie Wohryzek, Kafka's relations with his father strained further. In May, 1919, Kafka presented Hermann Kafka with a copy of *In der Strafkolonie* upon its publication by Kurt Wolff. His father paid scant attention to the book, telling Kafka to place it on the bedside table. Kafka was deeply offended by what he perceived as his father's deliberate disregard for the book. Soon afterwards, Kafka's sensitivity was further violated when his father reacted to the engagement announcement by questioning his son's maturity and Wohryzek's integrity. Kafka vented his frustration by writing the missive posthumously published as *Letter to His Father*, in which he tirelessly examined and analyzed the failings of their relationship. In the letter, which Kafka never delivered, he decried his father as grossly inconsiderate and condemned his behavior as dictatorial. But Kafka, inevitably susceptible to self-doubt, also filled the work with recriminations against his own worthiness and dwelled on his own inadequacies and insecurities. Ultimately, Kafka refrained from attributing his shortcomings to his traumatic childhood, and the entire letter is, perhaps, best seen today as an insightful document into Kafka's ambivalence about himself and others. Erich Heller, in his book *Franz Kafka*, notes as much when writing that Kafka "was unable to sustain any particular indictments against anyone except himself—and even not quite against himself."

Though still ill in December, 1919, Kafka returned to the insurance company, and in early 1920 he received a promotion and a salary increase. By April, however, he was once again weak and in need of another leave from work. After failing to secure occupancy at a sanatorium, he stayed briefly at a hotel, then moved to a pension. At this time he began corresponding regularly with Milena Jesenska-Polak, who had earlier written him seeking permission to translate his tales into Czech. Kafka's first letters were cordial and even kindly, with Kafka sympathizing with Jesenska-Polak's own lung disease and warning her not to squander unnecessary energy on translations of his modest works.

After exhausting his sick-leave, Kafka used his vacation time to remain at the pension, from which he soon adopted a more intimate tone in his correspondence with his translator. Undaunted by Jesenska-Polak's marriage, Kafka wrote to her that through their literary relationship he already possessed her and that, though unworthy of her love, he nonetheless demanded it. He felt that Jesenska-Polak understood him more profoundly than had any other woman, and he courted her accordingly. He disclosed as much to Julie Wohryzek, who tearfully withdrew from his life, whereupon Kafka immediately began doubting Jesenska-Polak's sincerity.

Such suspicions were nearly accurate, for Jesenska-Polak refused to leave her husband. She did, however, comply with Kafka's wish that they meet, and in August they shared a weekend. At this time Kafka renewed his interest in writing, producing preliminary drafts for the novel *Das Schloss (The Castle)*. But his health proved consistently tenuous, and by autumn he was frequently feverish and suffering labored breathing. After a medical examination disclosed further infection in both his lungs, Kafka entered a clinic in the nearby mountains. He intended to leave after three months, but when that time elapsed he was still weak with coughing spasms and breathing difficulties. Deciding to remain through the winter, Kafka grew increasingly lethargic and spent most days reclining and reading. He socialized rarely, as he was easily repulsed by the often advanced state of other patients' physical deterioration, and he wrote not at all, for at the sanatorium—despite his grave state—he was free of the tension and emotional anxiety that was apparently necessary to his creativity. When spring came, Kafka finally began taking walks in the sanatorium's wooded countryside, and by August he recovered sufficiently to leave the institution and return to work in Prague.

Almost immediately upon resuming his insurance work, though, Kafka ran a constant fever. By September, a cold, and consequent cough, had ravaged him still further, and by autumn, doctors once again urged him to enter a sanatorium. But Kafka did not heed his medical counsel, choosing instead to remain in Prague and endure further physical and emotional distress. Now obsessed with his own demise, Kafka was unable to relax or overcome his overwhelming anxiety. In early 1922, despite securing yet another sick leave from the insurance company, he suffered three weeks of only minimal sleep. As that insomnia threatened to undermine his already tenuous mental and emotional equilibrium, he finally left Prague.

In late January, 1922, Kafka arrived at a mountain resort, where he showed surprising enthusiasm and energy for outdoor activities, including mountain climbing. Within a few days, however, he collapsed while outside, and pneumonia seemed inevitable. Though hardly undaunted by his illness, he showed little of the anxiety that normally characterized his reaction to adversity. Instead, he anticipated emancipation from the trials of life, though such emancipation might bring sorrow, at least temporarily, to his loved ones. But he avoided exacerbating his already serious condition, and by February he was back in Prague, though he still had several weeks left of his sick leave.

To distract himself from anxiety and despair, Kafka turned once more to writing, and in February he completed his celebrated tale "Ein Hungerkuenstler" ("A Hunger Artist"), about a man whose celebrity derives from his refusal to eat. This tale, at once both tragic and comedic, and both absurd and disturbingly realistic, culminates in grim humor when the hunger artist explains his motivation. Diminished to a nearly skeletal state, the dying hunger artist reveals that he had refrained from eating simply because he could not obtain palatable food. "If I had found it," he tells an inquisitive fellow, "believe me, I should have made no fuss and stuffed myself like you or anyone else." Like much of Kafka's fiction, "A Hunger Artist" is often perceived by critics as an absurdist perspective on his condition. Kafka's own wasting away from tuberculosis lends credibility to this interpretation of the tale, though other approaches—including allegorical and even literal interpretations—may seem equally valid.

In early 1922 Kafka also wrote both "Forschungen eines Hundes" ("Investigations of a Dog"), an ultimately unfinished tale about a dog's recollections of life in the "canine community," and most of *The Castle*, his account—also unfinished—of a land surveyor's desperate attempt to secure an audience with obscure and distant higher authorities. By this time Kafka, having obtained his employer's permission for temporary retirement, lay bedridden with near-constant fever and exhaustion. Believing that death was near, he wrote to Brod requesting that he destroy any manuscripts left incomplete, including "Investigations of a Dog" and the novels-in-progress *Amerika*, *The Trial*, and *The Castle*.

By summer, having once again avoided pneumonia, Kafka left Prague to live with his sister Ellie in the German seaside town Mueritz. There he befriended Dora Dymant, a volunteer worker at a nearby camp for Jewish children. Though weak from fever and chronic coughing, Kafka mustered enough energy to enjoy Dymant's company, and by September he was living with her in Berlin-Steglitz. This residence was intended as temporary, for both Kafka and Dymant, who shared his recent interest in Hebrew studies, planned on immigrating to Palestine.

In Berlin-Steglitz, Kafka and Dymant continued their Hebrew readings, and Kafka, despite his frail condition, even attended lectures at the nearby Academy of Hebrew Studies. He also wrote, but only when rare bursts of energy enabled him to produce an entire work in one sitting. Such was the case in November when he produced "Der Bau" ("The Burrow"), his story about an animal and its obsession with its burrow. Initially, the animal is quite confident of its security within its well hidden, expertly organized domain. So proud is the creature—presumably, a mole—that it even conceals itself outside the burrow and marvels at its concealment. But, as one would expect in a Kafka tale, anxiety and suspicion slowly undermine the animal's confidence, and the creature imagines that the burrow is actually part of a much larger one built by a creature that will soon discover the vulnerable intruder. Eventually, the animal discerns whistling from within the burrow and suspects an unwelcome presence. Though Kafka provided an ending for the tale, it was either destroyed or lost, and the story stops with the creature determined to move from the whistle's direction.

Kafka wrote "The Burrow" in November, 1923, after moving with Dymant into two rooms of a home also occupied by a physician. He saw little of his parents, for they disapproved of Dymant and her background of traditional Judaism, and they condemned the couple's living arrangement. Despite these objections, the parents did supply him with occasional funds, which were useful supplements to his own modest pension. But by early 1924, when digestive troubles joined Kafka's continual fever, even the two rooms proved too costly, and in February he and Dymant moved into one inexpensive room. There he continued to study Hebrew on a daily basis, but his health severely diminished his energy for any sustained activity.

In March, when Brod visited him, Kafka suffered from constant fever and bouts of racking coughing. Dying he traveled back to Prague and once again stayed at his parents' home. There he produced his final tale, "Josefine die Saengerin oder Das Voelk der Mauese" ("Josephine the Singer; or, The Mouse Folk"), about a singing mouse and her effect on others in her community. Josephine is prized by other mice for her beautiful singing voice, but when she argues that her talent should exempt her from more menial tasks, she is denied the privilege. She then refrains from singing and withdraws from the community, which, it is expected, will soon forget her.

Soon after completing "Josephine," Kafka experienced extreme swelling in his tubercular larynx. Swallowing became painful and difficult, and eating became impossible. He was moved to a sanatorium, and Dora Dymant was told that Kafka would probably die within three to four months. When a subsequent diagnosis revealed an improved condition, Kafka was so overwhelmed with happiness that he proposed marriage to Dymant. But within two weeks he suffered great pain and pleaded for his physician to administer morphine. Injections were given, and an ice pack was set on Kafka's throat. On June 3, he awoke and threw the ice pack from himself, then lapsed again into unconsciousness and death.

To his credit, Brod ignored Kafka's will and salvaged the incomplete tales and novels. During the next few years he organized and edited these works, occasionally shaping various drafts into coherent texts and even supplying titles and chapter headings. In the mid-1920s Kafka's three incomplete novels were published, and in 1931 a collection of his incomplete tales—including "The Great Wall of China"—was also printed. Additionally, Brod organized editions of Kafka's complete works and edited collections of his diaries and letters. These posthumous volumes, as much as Kafka's previous publications, established Kafka as one of the twentieth century's major literary figures, a master writer whose works, perhaps more than those of any other artist, reflect the alienation and frustration of modern life.

Critically, Kafka's works have prompted a vast and varied array of interpretations. He has been hailed as a realist, an absurdist, a sociologist, and even, by Thomas Mann, as a comedic theologian. Some writers have emphasized the psychological in analyzing his works, others have concentrated on the Judaic aspects; some have traced his fiction as thinly disguised autobiography, and others have noted the same works as full-fledged fantasies. Consistent in these divergent interpretations is the respect accorded Kafka's works as unique and compelling, and the regard for Kafka as a literary master. More than a few critics share the opinion of Vladimir Nabokov, himself a highly regarded writer, who called Kafka, in *Lecturers on Literature*, "the greatest German writer of our time."

MEDIA ADAPTATIONS: The Trial was adapted by writer-director Orson Welles as a film of the same title in 1963; *Amerika* was adapted by writer-directors Jean-Marie Straub and Daniele Huillet for a film released in the United States as "Class Relations" in 1984; works adapted for the stage include "The Metamorphosis" and "The Hunger Artist."

BIOGRAPHICAL/CRITICAL SOURCES:

BOOKS

Anders, Gunther, *Franz Kafka*, translated by A. Steer and A. K. Thorlby, Bowes & Bowes, 1960.
Bauer, Johann, *Kafka and Prague*, Praeger, 1971.
Brod, Max, *Franz Kafka*, translated by G. Humphreys Roberts and Richard Winston, Schocken, 1960.
Buber-Neumann, Margarete, *Mistress to Kafka*, Secker & Warburg, 1966.
Camus, Albert, *The Myth of Sisyphus, and Other Essays*, translated by Justin O'Brien, Knopf, 1955.
Canetti, Elias, *Kafka's Other Trial: The Letters to Felice*, translated by Christopher Middleton, Schocken, 1982.
Carrouges, Michel, *Kafka Versus Kafka*, translated by Emmet Parker, University of Alabama Press, 1968.
Eisner, Pavel, *Franz Kafka and Prague*, Arts, Inc., 1950.
Emrich, Wilhelm, *Franz Kafka*, Ungar, 1968.
Flores, Angel, editor, *The Kafka Problem*, New Directions, 1946.
Flores, Angel, and Homer Swander, editors, *Franz Kafka Today*, University of Wisconsin Press, 1958.
Flores, Angel, editor, *The Kafka Debate: New Perspectives for Our Time*, Gordonian Press, 1977.
Frynta, Emanuel, *Kafka and Prague*, Batchworth Press, 1960.
Goodman, Paul, *Kafka's Prayer*, Vanguard, 1947.
Gray, Ronald, *Kafka: A Collection of Critical Essays*, Prentice-Hall, 1962.
Gray, Ronald, *Franz Kafka*, Cambridge University Press, 1973.
Greenberg, Martin, *The Terror of Art: Kafka and Modern Literature*, Basic Books, 1968.
Hall, Calvin S., and Richard E. Lind, *Dreams, Life, and Literature: A Study of Franz Kafka*, University of North Carolina Press, 1970.
Hayman, Ronald, *Kafka*, Oxford University Press, 1982.
Heller, Erich, *Franz Kafka*, edited by Frank Kermode, Viking, 1974.
Heller, Erich, *The Disinherited Mind*, Harcourt, 1975.

Howe, Irving, *Modern Literary Criticism: An Anthology*, Beacon Press, 1958.
Hughes, Kenneth, *Franz Kafka: An Anthology of Marxist Criticism*, New England University Press, 1981.
Janouch, Gustav, *Conversations With Kafka*, translated by Goronwy Rees, New Directions, 1971.
Kazin, Alfred, *The Inmost Leaf: A Selection of Essays*, Harcourt, 1955.
Kuna, Franz, editor, *On Kafka: Semi-Centenary Perspectives*, Harper, 1976.
Nabokov, Vladimir, *Lectures on Literature*, edited by Fredson Bowers, Harcourt, 1980.
Nagel, Bert, *Franz Kafka*, Schmidt, 1974.
Pascal, Roy, *Kafka's Narrators: A Study of His Stories and Sketches*, Cambridge University Press, 1982.
Pawel, Ernst, *The Nightmare of Reason: A Life of Franz Kafka*, Farrar, Straus, 1984.
Politzer, Heinz, *Franz Kafka: Parable and Paradox*, Cornell University Press, 1966.
Robert, Marthe, *Kafka*, Gallimard, 1968.
Robert, Marthe, *The Old and the New: From Kafka to Don Quixote*, University of California Press, 1977.
Robert, Marthe, *As Lonely as Franz Kafka*, Harcourt, 1982.
Rolleston, James, *Kafka's Negative Theater*, Pennsylvania State University Press, 1974.
Seltzer, Alvin J., *Chaos in the Novel, the Novel in Chaos*, Schocken, 1974.
Sokel, Walter H., *Franz Kafka*, Columbia University Press, 1966.
Spann, Meno, *Franz Kafka*, Twayne, 1976.
Spilka, Mark, *Dickens and Kafka: A Mutual Interpretation*, Indiana University Press, 1963.
Stern, J. P., *The World of Franz Kafka*, Holt, 1980.
Sussman, Henry, *Franz Kafka: Geometrician of Metaphor*, Coda Press, 1979.
Tauber, Herbert, *Franz Kafka: An Interpretation of His Works*, Kennikat, 1968.
Thorlby, Anthony, *Kafka: A Study*, Heinemann, 1972.
Tiefenbrun, Ruth, *Moment of Torment: An Interpretation of Franz Kafka's Short Stories*, Southern Illinois University Press, 1973.
Twentieth-Century Literary Criticism, Gale, Volume 2, 1979, Volume 6, 1982, Volume 13, 1984.
Urzidil, Johannes, *There Goes Kafka*, Wayne State University, 1968.
West, Rebecca, *The Court and the Castle: Some Treatments of a Recurrent Theme*, Yale University Press, 1957.
Ziolkowski, Theodore, *Dimensions of the Novel: German Texts and European Contexts*, Princeton University Press, 1969.

PERIODICALS

Approach, fall, 1963.
Bookman, November, 1930.
Commonweal, September 4, 1964.
Comparative Literature, fall, 1959.
Criterion, April, 1938.
German Life and Letters, January, 1953.
Jewish Heritage, summer, 1964.
Journal of English and Germanic Philology, January, 1954.
Journal of Modern Literature, September, 1977.
Kenyon Review, winter, 1939.
Literary Review, summer, 1983.
Literature and Psychology, Volume XXVII, no. 4, 1977.
Modern Fiction Studies, summer, 1958.
Modern Language Notes, October, 1970.

Mosaic, spring, 1972.
Nation, December 7, 1946.
New Republic, October 27, 1937.
New Yorker, May 9, 1983.
Quarterly Review of Literature, Volume II, no. 3, 1945, Volume XX, nos. 1-2, 1976.
Reconstructionist, April 3, 1959.
Studies in Short Fiction, summer, 1965, spring, 1973.
Symposium, fall, 1961.
Thought, summer, 1951.
TriQuarterly, spring, 1966.*

—*Sketch by Les Stone*

* * *

KAGAN, Robert A.   1938-

PERSONAL: Born June 13, 1938, in Newark, N.J.; son of George M. and Sylvia (Gurkin) Kagan; married Elizabeth Keller (a dance teacher), July 30, 1967; children: Elsie. *Education:* Harvard University, A.B., 1959; Columbia University, LL.B., 1962; Yale University, Ph.D., 1974. *Religion:* Jewish.

ADDRESSES: Home—68 Plaza Dr., Berkeley, Calif. 94705. *Office*—Department of Political Science, University of California, Berkeley, Calif. 94720.

CAREER: University of California, Berkeley, professor of political science, 1974—.

WRITINGS:

Regulatory Justice: Implementing a Wage Price Freeze, Russell Sage Foundation, 1978.
(With Eugene Bardach) *Going by the Book: The Problem of Regulatory Unreasonableness*, Temple University Press, 1982.
(Editor with Eugene Bardach) *Social Regulation: Strategies for Reform*, Institute for Contemporary Studies [San Francisco, Calif.], 1982.

Contributor to scholarly journals.

* * *

KAGANOFF, Nathan M.   1926-

PERSONAL: Born April 8, 1926, in Gaisin, U.S.S.R.; immigrated to United States, 1932, naturalized citizen, 1937; son of David and Miriam (Drazhner) Kaganoff; married Baila Wolk, 1950 (deceased); married Rosalyn Winchester, April, 1970; children: (first marriage) Joshua, Jeremy, Abigail, David. *Education:* Northwestern University, B.A., 1947; Hebrew Theological College, Chicago, Ill., Rabbi, 1948; American University, M.A., 1956, Ph.D., 1961.

ADDRESSES: Office—American Jewish Historical Society, Waltham, Mass. 02154.

CAREER: Library of Congress, Washington, D.C., librarian specializing in religion and Judaica, 1950-62; American Jewish Historical Society, Waltham, Mass., librarian, 1962—, editor, 1969—. Lecturer at College of Jewish Studies, Washington, D.C., 1955-56; principal of Midrasha Community Hebrew High School, 1960-62; member of board of directors of Hebrew Academy, Washington, D.C., 1952-62. Visiting professor at Brandeis University, 1969—. *Military service:* U.S. Army, chaplain, 1951-56.

MEMBER: Religious Zionists of America (president, 1960-62; member of national executive council, 1962-66), Association of Jewish Libraries (chairman of Technical Processes Committee, 1966-72; president of Research and Special Library Division, 1968-70; president, 1970-72), American Historical Association, American Library Association, Association of College and Research Libraries, Institute for Early New York History, Phi Beta Kappa, Phi Eta Sigma, Pi Mu Epsilon.

AWARDS, HONORS: America-Holy Land scholar at Hebrew University of Jerusalem, 1973-74.

WRITINGS:

(Contributor) Charles Berlin, editor, *Studies in Jewish Bibliography, History, and Literature in Honor of I. Edward Kiev*, Ktav, 1971.
(Editor with Melvin I. Urofsky) *"Turn to the South": Essays on Southern Jewry*, University Press of Virginia, 1979.
(Editor) *Solidarity and Kinship: Essays on American Zionism; in Memory of Dewey David Stone*, American Jewish Historical Society, 1980.
(Editor) *Guide to America-Holy Land Studies, 1620-1948*, Arno, Volume I: *American Presence*, 1980, Volume II: *Political Relations and American Zionism*, 1982, Volume III: *Economic Relations and Philanthropy*, 1983, Volume IV: *Resource Material in British, Israeli, and Turkish Repositories*, 1984.

Also author of *The Occident Reader*.

Editor of "Haym Salomon Papers," National Historic Publications and Records Commission. Contributor to periodicals.*

* * *

KAHANE, Claire   1935-

PERSONAL: Surname originally Katz; name legally changed in 1974; born February 18, 1935, in New York, N.Y.; daughter of Max (a retailer) and Diana (a housewife; maiden name, Rubinstein) Katz; married Ronald Hauser (a professor), February 14, 1976; children: Lukas. *Education:* City College (now of the City University of New York), B.A. (cum laude), 1956; University of California, Berkeley, M.A., 1963, Ph.D., 1975.

ADDRESSES: Home—98 Woodward Ave., Buffalo, N.Y. 14214. *Office*—Department of English, State University of New York at Buffalo, Buffalo, N.Y. 14260.

CAREER: Queens College of the City University of New York, Flushing, N.Y., lecturer in English, 1963-64; Brooklyn College of the City University of New York, Brooklyn, N.Y., lecturer in English, 1964-66; University of San Francisco, San Francisco, Calif., lecturer in English, 1969-71, 1972-73; University of California, Berkeley, associate lecturer, 1971-73; State University of New York at Buffalo, assistant professor, 1974-81, associate professor of English, 1981—.

MEMBER: Modern Language Association of America.

WRITINGS:

(Editor, contributor, and author of introduction) *Psychoanalyse und das Unheimliche: Essays aus der amerikanischen Literaturkritik*, Bouvier Press, 1981.
(Contributor) Juliann Fleenor, editor, *The Female Gothic*, Eden Press, 1983.
(Editor with Charles Bernheimer) *In Dora's Case: Freud, Hysteria, Feminism*, Columbia University Press, 1985.
(Contributor) Beverly Lyon Clark and Melvin J. Friedman, editors, *Critical Essays on Flannery O'Connor*, G. K. Hall, 1985.

(Editor with Shirley Nelson Garner and Madelon Spreng-nether; and contributor) *The M/Other Tongue: Essays in Feminist Psychoanalytic Interpretation*, Cornell University Press, 1985.
(Contributor) Richard Feldstein and Judith Roof, editors, *Feminism and Psychoanalysis*, Cornell University Press, in press.
(Contributor) Dianne Hunter, editor, *Seduction and Theory*, University of Illinois Press, in press.

Contributor of articles and reviews to periodicals, including *Studies in American Fiction, Literature and Psychology, Centennial Review, Massachusetts Review, American Literature,* and *Journal of English and German Philology.*

WORK IN PROGRESS: Hysteria, Feminism, and the Emergence of Modernist Narrative, publication expected in 1989 or 1990.

SIDELIGHTS: Claire Kahane told *CA:* "Both feminism and psychoanalysis were empowering systems of thought in my life. They also became the means by which I engage literary texts."

*   *   *

KAISER, Daniel H. 1945-

PERSONAL: Born July 20, 1945, in Philadelphia, Pa.; son of Walter Christian (a farmer and carpenter) and Estelle Evelyn (a homemaker; maiden name, Jaworsky) Kaiser; married Jonelle Marie Marwin, August 10, 1968; children: Nina Marie, Andrew Eliot. *Education:* Wheaton College, Wheaton, Ill., A.B., 1967; University of Chicago, A.M., 1970, Ph.D., 1977; also attended Moscow State University, 1974. *Religion:* Presbyterian.

ADDRESSES: Home—1433 Main St., Grinnell, Iowa 50112. *Office*—Department of History, Grinnell College, P.O. Box 805, Grinnell, Iowa 50112-0806.

CAREER: King's College, Briarcliff Manor, N.Y., instructor in history, 1968-71; Trinity College, Deerfield, Ill., assistant professor of history, 1971-73; University of Chicago, Chicago, Ill., visiting assistant professor of history, 1977-78; Grinnell College, Grinnell, Iowa, assistant professor, 1979-84, associate professor, 1984-87, professor of history, 1987—, Joseph F. Rosenfield Professor of Social Studies, 1984—.

MEMBER: American Historical Association, American Association for the Advancement of Slavic Studies.

AWARDS, HONORS: John Nicholas Brown Prize from Medieval Academy of America, 1984, for *The Growth of the Law in Medieval Russia.*

WRITINGS:

The Growth of the Law in Medieval Russia, Princeton University Press, 1980.
(Editor) *The Workers' Revolution in Russia,* Cambridge University Press, 1987.

WORK IN PROGRESS: Family Life in Early Modern Russia, publication expected in 1990.

SIDELIGHTS: Daniel H. Kaiser told *CA:* "*The Workers' Revolution in Russia* differs from most such books by emphasizing the social legitimacy of Bolshevik political success in the cities of Russia. As such, the book corrects the image dominant in both American scholarly and popular opinion that in some fundamental way the Bolsheviks usurped power. Certainly there were many places in the Russian Empire where Bolshevism was unwelcome, but it is equally true—and less well known— that there were many places where Bolsheviks were very welcome, and this book attempts to tell that story for the general reader.

"My chief interest, however, continues to be in early Russia, to which I was drawn long ago. My present work on family life derives from my first book in which I discovered a legal system suitable for a social system quite different from that normally depicted in the histories of Russia. There was, for example, almost no trace of a 'court' in the sense in which we normally understand that term; most justice depended exclusively upon the initiative of the aggrieved parties. In cases of homicide, they could practice revenge or exact compensation; in cases of property loss, the victims sought compensation directly from the responsible party. But the available materials say very little about the social structure that undergirded this legal system, although historians have fashioned some very detailed descriptions of early Russian society. The available materials do not permit, however, a serious examination of any of the fundamental social units of early Russia, so I turned my attention to the sixteenth and seventeenth centuries, employing methodologies developed for family history in early modern Europe. In many respects the sources are still wanting (in comparison with French and English parish registers, for example), but I have been able to collect a substantial body of testaments and dowry contracts together with other related materials in order to write a history of family life in this period.

"Of course, these themes are by their very nature of interest whether the time is the sixteenth or twentieth century, and I continue to spend considerable time reading not only about family life in other parts of the world but especially about family life in the contemporary U.S.S.R. One of the chief concerns of family historians has been to determine whether and when a significant change in family life took place. In Russia this issue becomes especially important immediately on the heels of the 1917 Revolution, so that a historian can follow the development of this issue all the way through the historical process. As a result, we learn a good deal not only about Russian family life, but about the way that family life affects each of us."

*   *   *

KAPLAN, Jim 1944-

PERSONAL: Born March 6, 1944, in Washington, D.C.; son of Benjamin (a judge) and Felicia (a poet; maiden name, Lamport) Kaplan; divorced; children: Benjamin, Matthew. *Education:* Yale University, B.A., 1966; Northwestern University, M.J., 1967.

ADDRESSES: Home and office—125 Warner St., Northampton, Mass. 01060. *Agent*—Dominick Abel, Dominick Abel Literary Agency, Inc., 498 West End Ave., New York, N.Y. 10024.

CAREER: Minneapolis Star, Minneapolis, Minn., staff writer, 1967-70; *Sports Illustrated,* New York, N.Y., reporter, 1970-73, writer-reporter, 1973-80, staff writer, 1980-86; free-lance writer and editor, 1986—. Baseball consultant to National Public Radio. Sustaining member of Democratic National Committee; Democratic precinct captain, 1968-70; member of Kings County Democratic Central Committee, 1977-81. Chairman of Yale Alumni Schools Committee, Brooklyn, N.Y., 1979-87.

MEMBER: Society for American Baseball Research, Bay State Authors Guild, Yale Club of New York City.

AWARDS, HONORS: Sportswriting awards from Minnesota Associated Press, 1969.

WRITINGS:

Pine-Tarred and Feathered: A Year on the Baseball Beat, Algonquin Books, 1985.
Playing the Field: Why Defense Is the Most Fascinating Art in Major League Baseball, Algonquin Books, 1987.

Contributor to magazines and newspapers, including *Esquire, New York Times, Sport, TV Guide,* and *Village Voice.* Editor of *Baseball Research Journal.*

WORK IN PROGRESS: A book about the Hall of Fame, publication by Baseball Ink expected in 1989.

SIDELIGHTS: Jim Kaplan told *CA:* "The story that gave me the most pleasure was called 'Italians and Jews: That Special Relationship' and ran in the *New York News Magazine* in 1974. It was nice to write about two ethnic groups who actually get along, and the piece touched a lot of people deeply. I like to take little-noted subjects and bring them alive; that's why the baseball stories I did for *Sport* on triples and right fielders were so much fun.

"People are always asking me about the appeal of baseball. Baseball is the *Wizard of Oz* of sport, because it focuses on the most precious idea in all the world: going home. Everything about the game is familial and familiar—the smell of hot dogs and popcorn, the guarding of home base, the sight of an individual in a sea of green. Baseball is a perfect combination of individual and team play, sudden action followed by long periods to reflect, violence and gentleness. There's no time clocks or artificial boundaries: in theory, fair territory extends forever. Most of all, baseball is freedom and imagination. Anything can and does happen when a ball is put in play—kind of like my golf game. The possibilities are endless. The three aspects of baseball that interest me most are its press coverage, fielding, and spring training. I've handled the first two in my books."

AVOCATIONAL INTERESTS: Race-walking, paddle tennis, golf, skiing, cross-country skiing, tennis.

*   *   *

KAPLAN, William   1957-

PERSONAL: Born May 24, 1957, in Toronto, Ontario, Canada; son of Igor (a lawyer) and Cara (Cherniak) Kaplan; married Susan Mardane Krever (an editor), July 8, 1985. *Education:* University of Toronto, B.A. (with honors), 1980, M.A., 1985; Osgoode Hall Law School, LL.B., 1983. *Religion:* Jewish.

ADDRESSES: Office—Faculty of Law, University of Ottawa, 550 Cumberland St., Ottawa, Ontario, Canada K1N 6N5. *Agent*—Stanley Colbert, Colbert Agency, 303 Davenport, Toronto, Ontario, Canada.

CAREER: University of Ottawa, Ottawa, Ontario, assistant professor of law, 1986—, faculty editor of *Ottawa Law Review,* 1987—. Barrister and solicitor.

MEMBER: Canadian Bar Association, Canadian Civil Liberties Association, Law Society of Upper Canada.

WRITINGS:

Everything That Floats: Pat Sullivan, Hal Banks, and the Seamen's Unions of Canada, University of Toronto Press, 1987.
(Editor with Dean Beeby) *Moscow Despatches: Inside Cold War Russia,* Lorimer, 1987.

WORK IN PROGRESS: An *Outrageous Quid to a Doubtful Quo: The World War II Ban of the Jehovah's Witnesses in Canada,* publication expected in 1989 or 1990.

BIOGRAPHICAL/CRITICAL SOURCES:

PERIODICALS

Globe and Mail (Toronto), February 15, 1988.

*   *   *

KARAMANSKI, Theodore J.   1953-

PERSONAL: Born August 1, 1953, in Chicago, Ill. *Education:* Loyola University, B.A., 1975, M.A., 1978, Ph.D., 1980.

ADDRESSES: Home—3603 West 64th, Chicago, Ill. 60629. *Office*—Mid-American Research Center, Loyola University, Chicago, Ill. 60611.

CAREER: Historian at Fischer-Stein Association, 1978-79; Loyola University, Chicago, Ill., assistant professor of history and director of historical preservation at Mid-American Research Center, 1979—, research director at center.

MEMBER: American Historical Association, Organization of American Historians, National Council for Public History, National Trust for Historic Preservation, Society for the History of Archaeology.

WRITINGS:

Fur Trade and Exploration: Opening the Far Northwest, 1821-1852, University of Oklahoma Press, 1983.
Deep Woods Frontier: A History of Logging in Northern Michigan, Wayne State University Press, 1988.

Contributor to history journals.

WORK IN PROGRESS: Rally 'Round the Flag: Chicago in the Civil War Era.

*   *   *

KARAS, Jim   1949-1981

PERSONAL: Born November 16, 1949, in Hartford, Conn.; died of cancer, April 18, 1981; son of James (in business) and Helen (a secretary; maiden name, Gabriel) Karas. *Education:* Central Connecticut State College, B.S., 1971; University of Connecticut, M.A., 1972; Nova University, M.S., 1974.

CAREER: Elementary schoolteacher in Simsbury, Conn., 1971-72, and Fort Lauderdale, Fla., 1972-74; Advertising Concepts of America, Fort Lauderdale, writer of commercials, 1974-75; Broward County Schools, Fort Lauderdale, kindergarten teacher, 1976-79, education specialist, 1979. Teacher in Oxford and Norwich, England. Rock musician.

AWARDS, HONORS: Certificate of Recognition from State of Florida.

WRITINGS:

(With Carolyn Griesse) *The Raw Foods Diet: The Vital Gift of Enzymes,* New Century Publishers, 1981.

Contributor to *Cancer News Journal.*

UNPUBLISHED

Doctors Please! Treat All of Me.
The Songs of My Life.
Mr. Turtle (juvenile).
Mothers Are Great (juvenile).
A Spooky Song (juvenile).

SIDELIGHTS: Before his death in 1981, Jim Karas wrote: "I have always . . . envisioned myself as a singer-songwriter, backed up by a full orchestra, doing what I've always loved best in life. God has always been good to me and gave me a life full of new and challenging experiences. Travel, education, and opportunity always seemed available to me. And of course, I always took full advantage of them.

"I am and always will remain a dreamer, someone who foresees the future as positive and life a challenge. Nothing appears impossible to a dreamer, and my songwriting is an expression of those dreams. My lyrics are a true expression of how I perceive the people, places, and things that influence my world.

"On April 27, 1977, I was diagnosed as having multiple myeloma, a cancer of the blood. Life suddenly turned sour and was slipping from my grip. Never before had my body, mind, or spirit comprehended such an experience. Only those who have been through cancer can truly understand."

After unsuccessful chemotherapy and radiation treatments, Karas joined a local self-help group of cancer patients. There he learned about alternate, non-invasive methods of treatment. He wrote: "The program I chose was known as metabolic therapy. It involved adjusting the metabolism of the body to its full strength through nontoxic measures. It involved a diet high in raw fruits, vegetables, and grains, supplemental enzymes, vitamins, and minerals, and the use of laetrile. The therapy is designed to increase the strength of one's own immune system so it becomes the key to the whole program. All of the other parts have their value, but they revolve around the special diet."

Karas died shortly before his book was published, but he and his co-author believed that the raw foods diet gave him the last three years of his life.

[Date of death provided by Carolyn Griesse.]

*   *   *

KARIN, Sidney   1943-

PERSONAL: Born July 8, 1943, in Baltimore, Md.; son of Norman and Lillian (Zarlad) Karin. *Education:* City College of the City University of New York, B.E., 1966; University of Michigan, M.S.E., 1967, Ph.D., 1973.

ADDRESSES: Home—Del Mar, Calif. *Office*—San Diego Supercomputer Center, GA Technologies, Inc., P.O. Box 85608, San Diego, Calif. 92138-5608.

CAREER: ESZ Associates, Inc., Ann Arbor, Mich., computer programmer and nuclear engineer, 1968-72; GA Technologies, Inc. (became General Atomics for Advanced Computing), San Diego, Calif., senior engineer and section leader in

high temperature gas-cooled reactor program, 1973-75, manager of fusion division computer center, 1975-82, director of information systems division, 1982-85, director of San Diego Supercomputer Center, 1985—, vice-president for advanced computing, 1987—. Adjunct professor of electrical engineering and computer sciences at University of California, San Diego, 1986—; member of Industrial Liaison Council, Department of Nuclear Engineering and Engineering Physics, University of Wisconsin—Madison, 1987—. Member of Oak Ridge National Laboratory Fusion Energy Division Computing Review Panel, 1980; member of Princeton Plasma Physics Laboratory Computing Review Panel, 1983-85; member of National Science Foundation Technical Advisory Group for Centers, 1984-85, and Scientific Computer Systems Technical Advisory Panel, 1984—; National Research Council, member of Panel for National Bureau of Standards Computing, 1985, chairman of Panel for National Bureau of Computing, 1986—, member of NASA Computer Science Research Program Review Panel, 1987; member of Lawrence Livermore National Laboratory Computer Center Annual Review Panel, 1986.

MEMBER: American Association for the Advancement of Science, Association for Computing Machinery, Institute of Electrical and Electronics Engineers, American Nuclear Society.

AWARDS, HONORS: Atomic Energy Commission special fellowship in nuclear science and engineering and National Defense Education Act fellowship.

WRITINGS:

(With Norris Parker Smith) *The Supercomputer Era,* Harcourt, 1987.

Contributor to *SuperComputing.*

WORK IN PROGRESS: A book on the air-traffic control system.

AVOCATIONAL INTERESTS: Flying (certified flight instructor for multi-engine and instruments, with commercial pilot's license), rock climbing, motorcycle riding, Alpine skiing, reading.

BIOGRAPHICAL/CRITICAL SOURCES:

PERIODICALS

Los Angeles Times Book Review, July 26, 1987.

*   *   *

KARMAN, James W.   1947-

PERSONAL: Born August 12, 1947, in Moline, Ill.; son of Chris J. (a foundry executive) and Roberta (a company president; maiden name, Alexander) Karman; married Paula Marie Anderson (a university admissions coordinator for graduate students), November 30, 1968. *Education:* Augustana College, Rock Island, Ill., A.B., 1969; University of Iowa, M.A., 1971; Syracuse University, Ph.D., 1976.

ADDRESSES: Office—Department of English, California State University, Chico, Calif. 95929.

CAREER: Syracuse University, Syracuse, N.Y., postdoctoral fellow in religion, 1976-77; California State University, Chico, assistant professor of religion, 1977-84, associate professor of English, 1984—, co-director of summer study program in Florence, Italy. Member of bioethics committee of M. T. Enloe and Chico Community Hospitals.

MEMBER: Modern Language Association of America.

AWARDS, HONORS: Scholar in residence of Tor House Foundation, 1982-84.

WRITINGS:

Robinson Jeffers: Poet of California, Chronicle Books, 1987.
Critical Essays on Robinson Jeffers, G. K. Hall, in press.

WORK IN PROGRESS: Research on the poetry of T. S. Eliot, Robinson Jeffers, and Wallace Stevens.

SIDELIGHTS: James W. Karman told *CA:* "Most broadly, my research and teaching interests embrace the artistic, religious, and literary traditions of western civilization. My principle concern is modern thought, especially as it is revealed through poetry. I am particularly interested in Robinson Jeffers, whom I regard as one of this century's most important authors."

*   *   *

KASTNER, Patricia Wilson
See WILSON-KASTNER, Patricia

*   *   *

KATO, Tsuyoski   1943-

PERSONAL: Born January 21, 1943, in Tokyo, Japan; son of Tamotsu (an engineer) and Fuji (a restaurant owner) Kato; married Nakayama Hiroko, February 25, 1983. *Education:* Hitotsubachi University, B.A., 1966, M.A., 1968; Cornell University, Ph.D., 1977.

ADDRESSES: Home—641 Higashi-Godo, Taichoro, Momoyama, Fushimi, Kyoto, Japan. *Office*—Center for Southeast Asian Studies, Kyoto University, Yoshida, Sakyo-ku, Kyoto, Japan.

CAREER: Sophia University, Tokyo, Japan, lecturer in sociology, 1977-79; Kyoto University, Kyoto, Japan, associate professor of sociology, 1979—.

MEMBER: Japanese Sociological Association, Japanese Association of Social Psychology, Japan Society for Southeast Asian History.

WRITINGS:

Matriliny and Migration: Evolving Minangkabau Traditions in Indonesia, Cornell University Press, 1982.
(Editor with Muchtar Lutfi and Narifumi Maeda) *Environment, Agriculture, and Society in the Malay World,* Center for Southeast Asian Studies, Kyoto University, 1986.

Editor of *Southeast Asian Studies.*

WORK IN PROGRESS: A Social History of a Sumatran Village, publication expected in 1988; research on socio-economic change and cultural transformation in rural Malaysia.

SIDELIGHTS: Tsuyoski Kato told *CA:* "I have been studying the Minangkabau of West Sumatra, Indonesia, for more than fifteen years. The Minangkabau have long been a tangle of paradoxes to the outsider. While they are ardent believers in Islam—a patrilineally oriented religion—they are also one of the few remaining matrilineal groups in the world. A well-educated and enterprising people, they continue to uphold a seemingly archaic kinship system. They have always been highly mobile, yet their strong sense of ethnic identity is rooted in their homeland. My first book, *Matriliny and Migration,* was essentially an attempt to untangle these paradoxes, focusing on Minangkabau matriliny and its relation to migration. Since its publication, my interest shifted to Minangkabau 'colonies,' which were established outside their homeland—that is, the western part of Riau (central Sumatra) and Negeri Sembilan in the western part of the Malay Peninsula. Ultimately, I want to find out how the different Minangkabau societies have adjusted to the penetration of capitalism."

*   *   *

KATROVAS, Richard   1953-

PERSONAL: Born November 4, 1953, in Norfolk, Va.; married wife, Elizabeth (a ballet instructor), March 17, 1980. *Education:* San Diego State University, B.A., 1976; graduate study at University of Virginia, 1979-80, and University of Arkansas, 1980-82; University of Iowa, M.F.A., 1983. *Politics:* Socialist. *Religion:* None.

ADDRESSES: Office—Department of English, University of New Orleans, New Orleans, La. 70148.

CAREER: University of New Orleans, New Orleans, La., instructor, 1983-85, assistant professor of English, 1986—.

MEMBER: Associated Writing Programs, Poetry Society of America.

WRITINGS:

Green Dragons (poems), Wesleyan University Press, 1983.
Snug Harbor (poems), Wesleyan University Press, 1986.

Author of essays and a novel.

WORK IN PROGRESS: The Public Mirror, poems, publication by Wesleyan University Press expected in 1989 or 1990; *Willy's Constant,* a novel; a book of essays, as yet untitled.

SIDELIGHTS: Richard Katrovas told *CA:* "My writing, verse and prose, is concerned with social engagement. Accepting that private troubles depend upon public issues, I center my writing upon the belief that the goal of humankind should be the achievement of maximum individuality within maximum community.

"I write anecdotal and dramatic lyrics set in southern urban landscapes; I'd like to be known as an urban poet of the New South. As a critic, I try to bring a celebratory Marxist-humanist perspective to bear upon post-Modern American poetry. Put simply, my task is to reconcile my love for America with my loathing for it, as a poet and as a critic.

"More and more I am writing about my fellow citizens who are black; I wish to understand better the genius of black America, how I can authentically feel it to be a legacy that I—as a white American—may have purchase on. Among other things, I wish to celebrate the genius and courage of the Southern urban black without television sentimentality."

*   *   *

KATZ, Michael M.   1956(?)-1988

OBITUARY NOTICE: Born c. 1956; died of complications from acquired immune deficiency syndrome (AIDS), September 14, 1988, in Century City, Calif. Actor and playwright. Katz acted in repertory theater and films and participated in acting workshops before he began writing and staging plays dealing with the social, physical, and emotional problems of AIDS. His first production was entitled "AIDS/US: Portraits in Personal Courage" and was performed in 1986 in Hollywood, California, at the Skylight Theater. The play featured cast members describing their battles with AIDS or telling of how they coped with the sickness of a loved one. In 1988 Katz produced a musical entitled "Taking Care," in which teens explored their concerns about the fatal disease and about other aspects of growing up. He also took part in the Names Project AIDS Quilt celebration at the University of California at Los Angeles, held in April of 1988 to publicize a memorial quilt sewn by the relatives and friends of AIDS victims.

OBITUARIES AND OTHER SOURCES:

PERIODICALS

Los Angeles Times, September 22, 1988.

* * *

KAUFMAN, Paula T. 1946-

PERSONAL: Born July 26, 1946, in Perth Amboy, N.J.; daughter of Harry (in business) and Clara (Katz) Kaufman. *Education:* Smith College, A.B., 1968; Columbia University, M.S.L.S., 1969; University of New Haven, M.B.A., 1978.

ADDRESSES: Office—313 Butler Library, Columbia University, New York, N.Y. 10027.

CAREER: Columbia University, New York, N.Y., reference librarian, 1969-70; McKinsey & Co., New York City, information specialist, 1970-73; Information for Business, New York City, partner, 1973-76; Yale University, New Haven, Conn., principal reference librarian, 1976-79; Columbia University, business librarian, 1979-82, acting East Asian librarian, 1982, director of Library Services Group, 1982-86, director of Academic Information Services, 1986-87, acting university librarian and acting vice-president for information services, 1987—. Consultant to Council on Library Resources.

MEMBER: American Library Association, Association of College and Research Librarians, Society for Scholarly Publishing.

WRITINGS:

(Editor) *The Reader's Adviser: A Layman's Guide to Literature,* Volume III, Bowker, 1986.

Contributor to library journals. Member of editorial board of *Journal of Academic Librarianship.*

WORK IN PROGRESS: Three books, *Scholarly Communications, The Library of the Future,* and *The Coming Crisis in Higher Education: The Costs of Scholarly Information.*

* * *

KAVANAGH, James H. 1948-

PERSONAL: Born March 5, 1948, in New York, N.Y.; son of Charles Murray (a lawyer) and Mary (an actress and homemaker; maiden name, Howard) Kavanagh; married, wife's name Eileen (divorced); children: Ian. *Education:* Fordham University, B.A., 1970; University of California, San Diego, Ph.D., 1971, D.Phil., 1977.

ADDRESSES: Home—5800 Walnut St., Pittsburgh, Pa. 15232. *Office*—Department of English, Carnegie-Mellon University, Pittsburgh, Pa. 15213.

CAREER: San Diego State University, San Diego, Calif., lecturer in English, 1976-77; University of California, San Diego, La Jolla, visiting assistant professor of English, 1978; Wesleyan University, Middletown, Conn., Andrew W. Mellon,

Jr., postdoctoral fellow at Center for the Humanities, 1978-79; Princeton University, Princeton, N.J., assistant professor of English, 1979-85; Carnegie-Mellon University, Pittsburgh, Pa., associate professor of literary and cultural studies, 1985—. Lecturer at Northwestern University, University of Iowa, and University of Pennsylvania, 1981-82; visiting associate professor at Graduate Center of the City University of New York, 1986. Principal organizer of Marxist Literary Group Summer Institute on Culture and Society, 1986.

MEMBER: Modern Language Association of America, Marxist Literary Group.

AWARDS, HONORS: Grant from Surdna Foundation, summer, 1980.

WRITINGS:

(Contributor) Bertell Ollman and Edward Vernoff, editors, *The Left Academy,* Volume II, Praeger, 1984.
(Contributor) John Drakakis, editor, *Alternative Shakespeares,* Methuen, 1985.
(Contributor) Sacvan Bercovitch and Myra Jehlen, editors, *Ideology and Emily Bronte,* Basil Blackwell, 1985.
Classic American Literature, Cambridge University Press, 1986.

Contributor of articles and reviews to literary journals, including *Bucknell Review, Diacritics, Praxis: A Journal of Cultural Criticism, Alien,* and *Jump Cut: A Review of Contemporary Cinema.*

WORK IN PROGRESS: Contemporary Cultural Theory and Theories of Ideology, with special reference to "the new pragmatism and conventionalism"; editing a volume of previously untranslated writings of Louis Althusser for New Left Books; a chapter to be included in *Critical Terms,* edited by Frank Lentricchia and Tom McLaughlin, for University of Chicago Press; a book "on some of the more critical versions of the American popular suspense film"; research on modern American film.

SIDELIGHTS: James H. Kavanagh told *CA* that his research is motivated by a "desire to revise and promote the Marxist theory of ideology in contemporary cultural and literary studies."

AVOCATIONAL INTERESTS: Travel, politics.

* * *

KAYE, Howard L. 1951-

PERSONAL: Born July 5, 1951, in Washington, D.C.; son of Murray (a waste paper dealer) and Nettie (Aronowitz) Kaye; married Barbara Shickman, December 26, 1976; children: Hannah Bess, Eleanor Miriam. *Education:* University of Pennsylvania, B.A., 1974, M.A., 1976, Ph.D., 1981; University of Chicago, M.A., 1975.

ADDRESSES: Home—809 Tarpley Dr., Lancaster, Pa. 17601. *Office*—Department of Sociology, Franklin and Marshall College, Box 3003, Lancaster, Pa. 17604.

CAREER: Franklin and Marshall College, Lancaster, Pa., assistant professor of sociology, 1982—.

MEMBER: American Sociological Association.

WRITINGS:

The Social Meaning of Modern Biology, Yale University Press, 1986.

WORK IN PROGRESS: Freud and Social Theory, publication expected in 1989.

SIDELIGHTS: Howard L. Kaye told *CA:* "Although the subject matter of *The Social Meaning of Modern Biology* is the various attempts by prominent biologists and theoreticians since the time of Darwin to articulate the social implications of their scientific work, the title has another meaning as well. It is one of the principal aims of the book to show how particular aspects of modern biology do indeed have a 'social meaning' in that they have been profoundly influenced by the social concerns, philosophical presuppositions, and moral commitments of the scientists themselves.

"*The Social Meaning of Modern Biology* grew out of my interest in the controversies surrounding the development and popularization of sociobiology and out of my belief that most accounts of sociobiological writings were historically inadequate and overlooked what was most significant about them culturally: that here were distinguished scientists ready at last to fulfill the positivist dream of becoming our spiritual guides to a no longer Christian culture.

"My work on Freud is in part a continuation of *The Social Meaning of Modern Biology* in that it too examines a powerful and, I believe, a more successful attempt to analyze the complexities of human nature in order to deepen our understanding of social and cultural life. The question of human nature has, regrettably, been largely ignored in the social sciences for nearly a century, on the assumption that nature is mere clay molded into whatever shape social and cultural structures predetermine. To challenge this assumption and to revive sociological interest in Freudian theory will be the major goals of my work."

*   *   *

KEARNS, Michael S.   1947-

PERSONAL: Born November 13, 1947, in Barnesville, Ohio; son of William S. and Evalyn V. (Tamplen) Kearns; married Ulrike B. Kalt (an English teacher), in 1983; children: Monica Leah, Shannon Alexandra. *Education:* Massachusetts Institute of Technology, S.B., 1971; University of California, Davis, M.A., 1975, Ph.D., 1980.

ADDRESSES: Office—Department of English, Ohio Wesleyan University, Delaware, Ohio 43015.

CAREER: Ohio Wesleyan University, Delaware, assistant professor of English, 1980—. Senior Fulbright professor at Mainz University, West Germany, 1984-85.

MEMBER: Midwest Modern Language Association, Midwest Victorian Studies Association, Society for the Study of Literature, Dickens Society.

AWARDS, HONORS: Grant from National Endowment for the Humanities, 1984; first book award from Midwest Modern Language Association, 1987, for *Metaphors of Mind in Fiction and Psychology.*

WRITINGS:

Metaphors of Mind in Fiction and Psychology, University Press of Kentucky, 1987.

Contributor to journals, including *College English, Journal of Teaching Writing*, and *Dickens Quarterly.*

WORK IN PROGRESS: Research on "the experiencing of time in fictional works of the nineteenth and twentieth centuries.

I'm particularly interested in identifying how nineteenth-century readers differ from contemporary readers in terms of their expectations about the flow of time in fiction, the meaning of time, and the possible kinds of time that might be presented."

SIDELIGHTS: Michael S. Kearns told *CA:* "I've found endurance sports an excellent preparation for maintaining a sane family life and for keeping alive a scholarly career while working in an institution that does not particularly reward scholarship. Included here are running, swimming, mountain climbing, and parenting—the latter probably is the best overall preparation for learning patience and pragmatics.

"*Metaphors of Mind in Fiction and Psychology* would probably fall within the 'new historicism' camp, because one of the book's main goals is to make more accessible to contemporary readers the ways earlier centuries represented mind and mental activities in figurative language. One of the more interesting discoveries I made is that during the latter half of the nineteenth century the language used by novelists to describe mental activity was actually closer to representing the developing theories of the organic relationship between mind and the external world than was the language used by psychologists to present these theories. This difference reflects the psychologists' greater reliance on the older metaphor of mind as a relatively passive, tangible, localized entity—a metaphor that such novelists as George Eliot and Henry James recognized as inadequate to represent the variety of mental experiences they wanted to treat in their works."

*   *   *

KEEFE, Susan E.   1947-

PERSONAL: Born December 1, 1947, in Spokane, Wash.; daughter of Ivan T. (a corporate contractor) and Palma T. (a realtor; maiden name, Plett) Emley; married Thomas K. Keefe (a college professor), September 3, 1970; children: Megan M. E. *Education:* University of California, Santa Barbara, B.A., 1969, M.A., 1971, Ph.D., 1974. *Politics:* Democrat.

ADDRESSES: Home—P.O. Box 949, Blowing Rock, N.C. 28605. *Office*—Department of Anthropology, Appalachian State University, Boone, N.C. 28608.

CAREER: University of California, Santa Barbara, postdoctoral research assistant at Social Process Research Institute, 1974-78; Appalachian State University, Boone, N.C., assistant professor, 1978-82, associate professor, 1982-87, professor of anthropology, 1987—. Member of board of directors of Blue Ridge Mountain Crafts Educational Fund, 1982-87; consultant to mental health and social services.

MEMBER: American Association for the Advancement of Science, American Anthropological Association (fellow), Society for Applied Anthropology (fellow), Society for Urban Anthropology, Society for Medical Anthropology, League of Women Voters, Southern Anthropological Society.

AWARDS, HONORS: Woodrow Wilson fellow, 1972-73; grants from National Institute of Mental Health, 1974-79, and National Science Foundation, 1983-84.

WRITINGS:

(With Amado M. Padilla) *Chicano Ethnicity*, University of New Mexico Press, 1987.
(Editor) *Appalachian Mental Health*, University Press of Kentucky, 1988.

Contributor to ethnology and anthropology journals.

SIDELIGHTS: Susan E. Keefe told *CA:* "My continuing interest has been in ethnicity and inequality. My most recent research has dealt with the concept of ethnicity as it might be applied to Appalachian people, thus clarifying our understanding of their unequal access to education and mental health services."

*   *   *

KEENY, S. M.
See KEENY, Spurgeon Milton

*   *   *

KEENY, Spurgeon Milton   1893-1988
(S. M. Keeny)

OBITUARY NOTICE: Born July 16, 1893, in Shrewsbury, Pa.; died of a stroke, October 20, 1988, in Washington, D.C. Administrator, consultant, and author. Keeny spent much of his career involved in the administration of relief programs to people in underdeveloped or war-ravaged parts of the world. He began his relief work during World War I, when he traveled to Europe and assisted, until 1922, Siberian, Estonian, Polish, and Czechoslovakian prisoners of war as a volunteer for the Young Men's Christian Association (YMCA). After spending two years with the American Relief Administration, Keeny rejoined the YMCA, this time reporting to its national council, where he held various positions, including director of its association press, until 1942. Keeny worked for the U.S. Government during the remainder of World War II as a supply consultant and coordinator, directing plans for civilian relief after the Allied invasions of Africa and Italy. Near the end of the war, he joined the staff of the United Nations Relief and Rehabilitation Administration as chief of operations in Italy. In 1948 Keeny served UNICEF as head of UNICEF's European supply office, and became director of the organization's Asian region in 1950. Based in Bangkok, Thailand, he held that post until he retired in 1963. Keeny then worked as a consultant for the Population Council in Asia until 1976. He described the humanitarian benefits of his relief programs in his 1957 book, *Half the World's Children: A Diary of UNICEF at Work in Asia.* He also wrote *Organizing National Family Planning Programs: Some Current Problems in Asia,* under his name S. M. Keeny, and made a sound recording entitled "Wanted: Fewer, Better Babies," in which he outlined a birth control plan for Asian families.

OBITUARIES AND OTHER SOURCES:

BOOKS

Current Biography, H. W. Wilson, 1958.

PERIODICALS

Washington Post, October 23, 1988.

*   *   *

KEITH, Stuart   1931-

PERSONAL: Born September 4, 1931, in Bacdock, England; immigrated to United States, 1958; son of William G. (an architect) and Cornelia (a horse breeder; maiden name, Stuart) Keith; married Ronalda Whitman, June 20, 1958 (divorced, 1968); married Sallyann Burgess (a teacher and writer), March 22, 1975. *Education:* Oxford University, M.A. (with honors), 1955. *Politics:* Conservative. *Religion:* Presbyterian.

ADDRESSES: Home—344 Grove St., Ramsey, N.J. 07446. *Office*—American Museum of Natural History, Central Park W., New York, N.Y. 10024.

CAREER: American Museum of Natural History, New York, N.Y., research associate in department of ornithology, 1958—. *Military service:* British Army, King's Own Scottish Borderers, 1950-51; served in Korea; became lieutenant.

MEMBER: American Ornithologists Union, Wilson Ornithological Society, American Birding Association (president, 1970-77), British Ornithologists Union, British Ornithologists Club.

WRITINGS:

(With C. W. Benson and M. P. S. Irwin) *The Genus Sarothrura (Aves, Rallidae),* American Museum of Natural History, 1970.
(With John Gooders) *Collins Bird Guide,* Collins, 1980.
(With C. Hilary Fry and Emil K. Urban) *The Birds of Africa,* Academic Press, Volume II, 1986, Volume III, 1988.

Contributor of articles to scientific journals and popular magazines.

WORK IN PROGRESS: Four more volumes of *The Birds of Africa,* with C. Hilary Fry and Emil K. Urban, publication by Academic Press expected in 1990-96.

SIDELIGHTS: Stuart Keith is listed in the *Guinness Book of World Records* as a champion bird watcher. He told *CA:* "Birds have always been both an avocation and a vocation. I have studied them on every continent except Antarctica, and I've led bird watching tours in Africa, Europe, and Madagascar.

"*The Birds of Africa* will consist of seven volumes of approximately five hundred pages each and will contain everything that has ever been known about the birds of the continent. It is a scientific handbook, not a coffee-table book, but it does have paintings of every species in color, for identification, many of them painted for the first time. An eighth volume is contemplated on the birds of the Malagasy region. This is essentially the 'bible' on the birds of Africa, and, since I started work on it in 1981 and will continue to 1990 and beyond, I regard this as my major life's work or magnum opus. I am proud and pleased to be part of the project."

BIOGRAPHICAL/CRITICAL SOURCES:

PERIODICALS

Times Literary Supplement, December 5, 1986.

*   *   *

KELLEHER, Victor (Michael Kitchener)   1939-

PERSONAL: Born July 19, 1939, in London, England; son of Joseph (a builder) and Matilda (a dressmaker; maiden name, Newman) Kelleher; married Alison Lyle (a potter and sculptor), January 2, 1962; children: Jason, Leila. *Education:* University of Natal, B.A., 1961; University of St. Andrews, Diploma in Education, 1963; University of the Witwatersrand, B.A. (with honors), 1969; University of South Africa, M.A., 1970, D.Litt. et Phil., 1973. *Religion:* Atheist.

ADDRESSES: Home—149 Wigram Rd., Glebe, New South Wales 2037, Australia.

CAREER: University of the Witwatersrand, Johannesburg, South Africa, junior lecturer in English, 1969; University of South Africa, Pretoria, lecturer, 1970-71, senior lecturer in English,

1972-73; Massey University, Palmerston North, New Zealand, lecturer in English, 1973-76; University of New England, Armidale, Australia, lecturer, 1976-79, senior lecturer, 1980-83, associate professor of English, 1984-87; writer.

AWARDS, HONORS: Patricia Hackett Prize from *Westerly* magazine, 1978, for story "The Traveller"; senior writer's fellowship from the Literature Board of the Australia Council, 1982; West Australian Young Readers' Book Award from the West Australian Library Association, 1982, for *Forbidden Paths of Thual;* West Australian Young Readers' Special Award from the West Australian Library Association, 1983, for *The Hunting of Shadroth;* Australian Children's Book of the Year Award from the Children's Book Council of Australia, 1983, for *Master of the Grove;* Australian Science Fiction Achievement Award from the National Science Fiction Association, 1984, for *The Beast of Heaven;* Honour Award from the Children's Book Council of Australia, 1987, for *Taronga.*

WRITINGS:

Voices From the River (novel), Heinemann, 1979.
Africa and After (stories), University of Queensland Press, 1983, published as *The Traveller: Stories of Two Continents,* University of Queensland Press, 1987.
The Beast of Heaven (novel), University of Queensland Press, 1984.

Work represented in anthologies, including *Introduction 6,* Faber, 1977. Contributor of articles and stories to magazines.

FOR YOUNG ADULTS

Forbidden Paths of Thual, Penguin Books, 1979.
The Hunting of Shadroth, Penguin Books, 1981.
Master of the Grove, Penguin Books, 1982.
Papio: A Novel of Adventure, Penguin Books, 1984.
The Green Piper, Penguin Books, 1984.
Taronga, Penguin Books, 1986.
The Makers, Penguin Books, 1986.
Em's Story, University of Queensland Press, 1988.

SIDELIGHTS: Victor Kelleher told *CA:* "I began writing after I left Africa in 1973. At first it was merely therapy—an attempt to assuage feelings of nostalgia, but the writing soon became an end in itself. Before I started to write, I spent most of my time studying or traveling, mainly in Africa.

"I divide my time about equally between writing for adults and for the adolescent age group. I find that the work in one genre tends to generate ideas for the other. The major literary influence on my work is undoubtedly the writing of Joseph Conrad."

Kelleher's first novel, *Voices From the River,* is an ironic treatment of the detective story set in the 1950s. It reflects the author's observations of life in colonial Central Africa and the cross-cultural conflicts bred there. His writing for young people includes *Forbidden Paths of Thual,* which traces the harrowing quest of a young boy through a fantasy world fraught with pitfalls and danger. *The Hunting of Shadroth* is another fantasy, in which the hero must pit himself against not only the violence of his mythological world but the violence within his own nature. *Master of the Grove* is a deliberate twining of the fantasy and mystery traditions.

Not all of Kelleher's juvenile novels, however, are dark fantasies. *Papio* is the story of two teenagers in contemporary Africa who take pity on a pair of laboratory baboons and set them free in the wild. Their resultant adventures take the children deep into the Zambezi, where they must assume responsibility for the welfare of the tamed animals. *The Green Piper* is a "modern, science fiction interpretation of the Pied Piper legend," according to the author. "In this very different version of the legend, a realistic, contemporary setting is disrupted by an eerie, alien music that proves to be inimical to all animal life. Out of a whole village, only two teenagers and Mad Jack, a local tramp, realize what is happening."

Keller continued: "*Taronga* is set in the near future, during a period of chaos. Sydney's Taronga Zoo has become a sinister mixture of farm and fortress, defended during the day by armed guards and at night by the big cats that are released to roam the grounds. Two young people, whose dangerous task it is to re-cage the cats each dawn, decide to destroy Taronga and all it stands for.

"*The Makers* is a blend of fantasy and futuristic fiction. Within a strange warrior culture presided over by the unseen Makers, two young warriors are unjustly treated. Outraged and frustrated, they turn their backs on their society and set out not only to unmask the Makers, but also to challenge their authority.

"My children's fiction, which is aimed primarily at the young adult group of readers, ranges from realism to fantasy. Regardless of the type of novel I'm writing, I always try to create a fast pace and strong story line. Equally important to me is the idea of a serious subtext which raises issues that are, I hope, both challenging and pertinent to all my readers, irrespective of their age."

AVOCATIONAL INTERESTS: Running, making pottery, working with silver, travel.

BIOGRAPHICAL/CRITICAL SOURCES:

PERIODICALS

Times Literary Supplement, January 1-7, 1988.

*   *   *

KENNEDY, Dane K(eith) 1951-

PERSONAL: Born May 30, 1951, in Bonne Terre, Mo.; son of William J. (a politician) and Helen (a postmaster; maiden name, Mueller) Kennedy; married Martha Hoeprich (a librarian), June 16, 1974; children: Alene Elizabeth. *Education:* University of California, Berkeley, B.A., 1973, M.A., 1975, Ph.D., 1981. *Politics:* Social Democrat. *Religion:* None.

ADDRESSES: Home—3001 South 44th St., Lincoln, Neb. 68506. *Office*—Department of History, University of Nebraska, Lincoln, Neb. 68588.

CAREER: University of Nebraska, Lincoln, assistant professor, 1981-87, associate professor of history, 1987—.

MEMBER: North American Conference on British Studies, American Historical Association, African Studies Association.

WRITINGS:

Islands of White, Duke University Press, 1987.

Contributor to history journals and *Nation.*

WORK IN PROGRESS: Research on issues in colonial culture, the collapse of settler regimes in Africa, and the relationship between literature and history in the colonial world.

SIDELIGHTS: Dane K. Kennedy told *CA:* "The lively nostalgia in recent years for British colonial life—evoked so shrewdly in 'Out of Africa,' 'A Passage to India,' and other popular entertainments—taps the seminal experience of the encounter between the West and the 'other.' Of course, it does so in a highly sanitized and mythologized form, clearing it of all violence, bewilderment, anxiety, guilt, desire, and fear. My own work attempts to retrieve that experience as it was felt, understood, and articulated by white settlers in colonial Africa. How did these representatives of the West respond to the alien environment and people they encountered? How far was their response mediated by the cultural baggage they brought with them? How did they incorporate their experience into a comprehensible pattern of meaning? These are the questions that give my book, *Islands of White,* its shape and purpose.

"My current research extends these questions geographically and temporally. I want to explore the circumstances that gave British colonial communities throughout the world a distinctively hermetic, defensive character. I also want to examine how these closed societies disintegrated under the pressures of nationalism and decolonization. All my work is preoccupied by the clash of cultures and, more broadly, by culture itself— 'the webs of significance' as Clifford Geertz calls it. The colonial encounter is marvelously suited for exposing how a people give meaning and order to their world, defining it in terms of race or class or gender or some other network of abstractions. One can trace in the experiences of British settlers in Africa and other European colonists abroad the process by which a society comes into being as a self-conscious entity, a culture, shaping experience to serve its needs."

BIOGRAPHICAL/CRITICAL SOURCES:

PERIODICALS

Sunday Journal Star (Lincoln, Neb.), May 3, 1987.

*   *   *

KENT, Allegra   1938(?)-

PERSONAL: Born August 11, 1938 (some sources say 1937), in Los Angeles (some sources say Santa Monica), Calif.; married Bert Stern (a photographer), February 28, 1959; children: Tristiana, Susannah, Bret. *Education:* Studied dance with Bronislava Nijinska; attended School of American Ballet and University of California, Los Angeles.

ADDRESSES: Office—c/o New York City Ballet Company, Lincoln Center Plaza, New York, N.Y. 10023.

CAREER: New York City Ballet Company, New York, N.Y., principal dancer, 1953—.

WRITINGS:

Allegra Kent's Water Beauty Book, St. Martin's, 1976.
(With James Camner and Constance Camner) *The Dancer's Body Book,* Morrow, 1984.*

*   *   *

KENZER, Robert C.   1955-

PERSONAL: Born February 11, 1955, in Chicago, Ill.; son of Sidney and Frances (Shanies) Kenzer; married Carol Bleise (a teacher), August 7, 1976. *Education:* University of California, Santa Barbara, B.A., 1976; Harvard University, M.A., 1977, Ph.D., 1982.

ADDRESSES: Office—Department of History, Brigham Young University, Provo, Utah 84602.

CAREER: Brigham Young University, Provo, Utah, assistant professor of history, 1982—.

MEMBER: American Historical Association, Organization of American Historians, Southern Historical Association.

WRITINGS:

Kinship and Neighborhood in a Southern Community: Orange County, North Carolina, 1849-1881, University of Tennessee Press, 1987.

WORK IN PROGRESS: Research on southern blacks who experienced economic and social success after the Civil War.

SIDELIGHTS: Robert C. Kenzer told *CA:* "*Kinship and Neighborhood in a Southern Community* draws on a wealth of sources, including genealogies, letters, diaries, marriage records, wills, mercantile ledgers, church minutes, and military records. The book examines the roles that family, kinship, and neighborhood played in the structure of a southern county during the antebellum, Civil War, and postwar years. By focusing on a basic unit of southern society—the rural neighborhood— I have advanced a new framework for addressing the central issues of nineteenth-century southern history. I find that the self-contained, tightly knit, geographically isolated neighborhoods, bound by kinship ties, served as the basis of social existence and the fundamental units of political activity. Politicians exerted their efforts to serve their kin networks, and ideology took a backseat to kinship ties in the evolution of Orange County. The impact of the neighborhood was so profound that it crossed racial lines and had a parallel influence on blacks and whites. Disrupted by the war, the structures of the rural neighborhoods were revived a few years after the conflict and continued to shape the lives and outlooks of the county's residents."

*   *   *

KEOGH, Dermot (Francis)   1945-

PERSONAL: Born May 12, 1945, in Dublin, Ireland; son of Bill (a receptionist) and Maureen (a civil servant; maiden name, O'Sullivan) Keogh; married Ann Brigid Grainger (a teacher), June 11, 1949; children: Eoin, Niall, Aoife, Clare. *Education:* National University of Ireland, University College, Dublin, B.A. (honors), 1970, M.A. (first class honors), 1974; European University Institute, Ph.D., 1980. *Religion:* Roman Catholic.

ADDRESSES: Home—9 Tara Ct., Glasheen Rd., Cork, Ireland. *Office*—Department of Modern History, University College, National University of Ireland, Cork, Ireland.

CAREER: Irish Press, Dublin, Ireland, journalist, 1970-76; television and radio journalist, 1979-80; National University of Ireland, University College, Cork, lecturer in modern history, 1980—. Fulbright professor at San Jose State University, 1983. Irish representative on the liaison group of Contemporary European Historians and for the Institute for European-Latin American Relations. Director of National Working Group for Church-State Studies. Historical adviser for the "Age of de Valera" television series, 1982.

MEMBER: Association of Europeans for Research on the Caribbean and Central America (executive committee member), Irish Association for European Studies (treasurer and member of academic committee), Irish Council of the European Movement (academic committee member).

AWARDS, HONORS: Irish government doctoral scholarship, 1976-79; Robert Schuman award for research, 1983; Woodrow Wilson Fellowship, 1988.

WRITINGS:

Romero: Church and State in El Salvador, Dominican Publications (Dublin), 1981.
The Rise of the Irish Working Class: The Dublin Trade Union Movement and Labour Leadership, 1890-1914, Appletree Press, 1982.
(Editor) Central America: Human Rights and U.S. Foreign Policy, Cork University Press, 1985.
The Vatican, the Bishops, and Irish Politics, 1919-1939, Cambridge University Press, 1986.
External Affairs: Ireland and Europe, 1919-1948, Gill & Macmillan, 1987.
(Editor) Vatican and Political Conflict in Latin America, Macmillan, 1988.

Work represented in anthologies, including Sources for the Study of European Integration, 1945-1955, edited by Walter Lipgens, 1980; The Times Survey of Foreign Ministries of the World, edited by Zara Steiner, 1982; and Britain and Argentina, edited by Alistair Hennesy, 1988.

Contributor to periodicals, including Soathar, Capuchin Annual, Doctrine and Life, Historia, Irish Studies in International Affairs, and Millenium Journal of International Studies. Editor of anthology Religion and Political Conflict in Nineteenth and Twentieth Century Europe, 1987, and Latin America, a research review, 1988—.

WORK IN PROGRESS: Essays in Church and State.

SIDELIGHTS: The Vatican, the Bishops, and Irish Politics proposes, according to critic Brendan Bradshaw of the Times Literary Supplement, that the "Irish addiction to religion" is the result of the Catholic church's close, official connection with the forces of social and political change in nineteenth-century Ireland. Bradshaw asserted that "Keogh's major achievement is to dispel the impression of the Church as a monolith . . . that is, an institution possessed of total unity of purpose and of action." Rather, the author focuses on the individual personalities and events that had the greatest impact on Irish society and politics.

BIOGRAPHICAL/CRITICAL SOURCES:

PERIODICALS

Times Literary Supplement, June 20, 1986.

*   *   *

KERCHEVAL, Jesse Lee   1956-

PERSONAL: Born July 27, 1956, in Fontainebleau, France; daughter of Edwin Gregory (an American army officer) and Mary (an American army officer; maiden name, Boggess) Beggs; married Dan Hughes Fuller (a photographer), June, 1984. Education: Florida State University, B.A., 1983, graduate study, 1983-84; University of Iowa, M.F.A., 1986.

ADDRESSES: Home—Madison, Wis. Office—Department of English, White Building, University of Wisconsin—Madison, Madison, Wis. 53706. Agent—Gail Hochman, Brandt & Brandt, 1501 Broadway, New York, N.Y. 10036.

CAREER: DePauw University, Greencastle, Ind., assistant professor of English, 1986-87; University of Wisconsin—Madison, assistant professor of English, 1987—.

MEMBER: Modern Language Association of America, Associated Writing Programs, Greenpeace.

AWARDS, HONORS: Exxon fellow at Iowa Writer's Workshop, 1985; literary award from Iowa Arts Council, 1986; short fiction award from Associated Writing Programs, 1986, for The Dogeater; Granville Hicks fellow at Yaddo Colony, 1987; James A. Michener fellow of Copernicus Society, 1987.

WRITINGS:

(Contributor) Janet Burroway, editor, Writing Fiction: A Guide to Narrative Craft, 2nd edition, Little, Brown, 1986.
The Dogeater (stories), University of Missouri Press, 1987.

Work represented in anthologies, including Twenty Under Thirty: Best Stories by America's New Young Writers, edited by Debra Spark, Scribner, 1986. Contributor of stories and poems to magazines in the United States and abroad, including London, Southern Review, Redbook, Ohio Review, Carolina Quarterly, and Poetry Wales.

WORK IN PROGRESS: The Museum of Happiness, a novel set in Paris and Alsace in 1929; research for a novel on American-born religions, based on the author's short story "The History of the Church in America."

*   *   *

KEYES, Claire J.   1938-

PERSONAL: Born November 2, 1938, in Boston, Mass.; daughter of James J. (a motorman) and Mary (a housewife; maiden name, Reilly) Keyes; married Johnes K. Moore (a professor of biology), March 7, 1987. Education: Boston State College, B.S., 1960; Boston College, M.A., 1963; University of Massachusetts at Amherst, Ph.D., 1980.

ADDRESSES: Home—12 Higgins Rd., Marblehead, Mass. 01945. Office—Department of English, Salem State College, 352 Lafayette St., Salem, Mass. 01970.

CAREER: Salem State College, Salem, Mass., instructor, 1966-70, assistant professor, 1970-80, associate professor, 1981-87, professor of English, 1987—, and arts coordinator. Writer-in-residence at Helene Wurlitzer Foundation, 1983. Director of Eastern Writers' Conference; member of board of directors of North Shore Women's School.

MEMBER: Poetry Society of America, New England Women's Studies Association.

WRITINGS:

The Aesthetics of Power: The Poetry of Adrienne Rich, University of Georgia Press, 1986.

Contributor to magazines, including Kalliope, Passages North, Tendril, Crescent Review, Bennington Review, and Embers. Advisory editor of Soundings East.

WORK IN PROGRESS: Woman as Hero in the Novels of Nadine Gordimer; In Her Image, poems; research on Ralph Waldo Emerson and women.

SIDELIGHTS: Claire J. Keyes told CA: "Without the women's movement, I would not have become a writer. My study of Adrienne Rich's poetry has emboldened me both to deal with my male literary heroes (Ralph Waldo Emerson, for example) and to discover in the works of women writers I admire (Nadine Gordimer, Doris Lessing) forms of female heroism and creative power that I can use to enrich my life, my teaching, and my writing."

"In the late 1960s Anne Sexton came to my campus to read her poetry. She was dynamic and exciting. I decided I wanted to read more and know more about women poets: Sexton, Sylvia Plath, Denise Levertov, Adrienne Rich. It was an easy jump to teach a course called 'American Women Poets.' In my reading and teaching, I grew convinced that Adrienne Rich was 'healthier' than Plath or Sexton; at least it seemed unlikely that she would commit suicide. In addition, I found her poetry intellectually and emotionally strong. She demanded my utmost involvement as a reader. What scorn Rich felt for passive 'pretty' pleasing! Since I had been active in a local way with women's rights and also with the Women's School, I was a good audience for the feminist poetry Rich was writing in the 1970s. My receptivity to her work led in a natural way to my writing about her poetry.

"In my study of Rich's poetry, I also become aware of the importance of female literary predecessors and of a woman's literary tradition. Without Emily Dickinson we would not have the strong, versatile, abundant women's poetry of today. I saw my role as a critic in pointing out the links in that tradition. The more I read and analyzed the literature of women, the more convinced I became of the value of my endeavors to other women. I knew what the women's movement had meant to me and I wanted to make a contribution to that movement so that other women could advance the cause. If I sound 'political,' that is my intent.

"For the same reason, I turned with interest and admiration to the novels of Nadine Gordimer. She was a woman, a writer, a critic of her own South African society. My university training had given me the tools to examine the mythology of heroism. With my sensibilities as a feminist critic, I, of course, looked for female heroes. Gordimer gave them to me.

"I began taking myself seriously as a poet around the same time I began writing my book on Rich's poetry. The subject of my poetry is an excuse to find out what really matters and how I feel about it. I discover new needs as I go along. A present need is to write poems that are truly lyrical: poems that sing. I'm finally getting the hang of meter and my rhythms are growing more musical. When I read my poems in public, people always tell me they love my voice. I think I have the power to entrance by my sounds and this makes me feel that perhaps the power of the bard is within my grasp. This excites me."

*　　*　　*

KINZER, Nora Scott 1936-

PERSONAL: Born December 12, 1936, in Toronto, Ontario, Canada; American citizen; daughter of Eugene Wilfred Victor and Margaret (Campbell) Scott; married Donald Edward James Stewart, 1977; children: Andrew, Peter, John, Patrick. *Education:* University of Toronto, B.A., 1958; Middlebury College, M.A., 1959; Purdue University, Ph.D., 1971. *Religion:* Episcopalian.

ADDRESSES: 1609 North Kirkwood Dr., Arlington, Va. 22201.

CAREER: Earlham College, Richmond, Ind., instructor in Spanish, 1959-60; Purdue University, West Lafayette, Ind., instructor, 1960-67, assistant professor of sociology, 1968-74; senior research scientist at U.S. Army Research Institute for Behavioral Sciences, 1975-78; National Defense University, Industrial College of the Armed Forces, Washington, D.C., visiting professor of human resource management, 1978-81;

U.S. Department of the Army, Washington, D.C., deputy assistant secretary of human resource management for Army Manpower and Research Affairs, 1981-83; Veterans Administration, Washington, D.C., special assistant to the administrator, 1983—. Visiting professor at University of El Salvador, Buenos Aires, Argentina, 1967, Georgetown University, 1977, and University of Maryland at College Park, 1977-78; guest lecturer at U.S. Foreign Service Institute, 1974-77. Visiting research associate at Instituto Torcuato di Tella, Buenos Aires, 1967-68; co-director of Project Athena, U.S. Military Academy, West Point, N.Y., 1976-78. Member of Presidential Task Force on Legal Equity for Women, 1984—.

MEMBER: American Sociological Association, American News and Women's Club, Latin American Studies Association (member of executive board, 1974-75), Military Operations Society (chairman of Human Resource Management Section, 1976-77), Executive Women in Government, Inter-University Seminar on the Armed Forces and Society, Inter-Agency Seminar Group of Brookings Institution, Alpha Kappa Delta, Sigma Delta Pi.

AWARDS, HONORS: Fellow of Tufts University School of Law and Diplomacy, 1967; Commander Award for Civilian Service, 1981; Administrative Commendation from Veterans Administration, 1983.

WRITINGS:

(With Alan G. Vitters) *Report of the Admission of Women to the U.S. Military Academy: Project Athena,* Department of Behavioral Sciences and Leadership, U.S. Military Academy, 1977.
Put Down and Ripped Off: The American Woman and the Beauty Cult, Crowell, 1977.
(Editor with Richard P. Schaedel and Jorge E. Hardoy) *Urbanization in the Americas From Its Beginnings to the Present,* Mouton, 1978.
Stress and the American Woman, Doubleday, 1979.*

*　　*　　*

KLAITS, Joseph (Aaron) 1942-

PERSONAL: Born September 23, 1942, in New York, N.Y.; son of Julius (a business executive) and Beatrice (a business executive; maiden name, Kossey) Klaits; married Barrie Gelbhaus (a social worker), September 5, 1965; children: Frederick, Alexander. *Education:* Columbia University, A.B., 1964; University of Minnesota—Twin Cities, M.A., 1966, Ph.D., 1970.

ADDRESSES: Home—Columbia, Md. *Office*—Department of History, Oakland University, Rochester, Mich. 48063.

CAREER: Oakland University, Rochester, Mich., 1969—, began as instructor, became assistant professor, associate professor, 1975-87, professor of history, 1987—. Visiting associate professor at Catholic University of America, 1982-83; academic adviser to European Fulbright Program, U.S. Information Agency, 1983-86.

MEMBER: American Historical Association, Society for French Historical Studies, American Society for Eighteenth-Century Studies, Western Society for French History (member of governing council, 1980-83).

AWARDS, HONORS: Fellow of Folger Shakespeare Library, 1974, National Endowment for the Humanities, 1981-82, and American Council of Learned Societies, 1986-87.

WRITINGS:

(Editor with Barrie Klaits) *Animals and Man in Historical Perspective,* Harper, 1974.
Printed Propaganda Under Louis XIV: Absolute Monarchy and Public Opinion, Princeton University Press, 1976.
(Contributor) F. E. Weaver and Richard M. Golden, *Church, State, and Society Under the Bourbon Kings of France,* Coronado Press, 1982.
Servants of Satan: The Age of the Witch Hunts, Indiana University Press, 1986.

Contributor to history journals.

WORK IN PROGRESS: Cultural Change in Alsace During the Eighteenth Century; research on witchcraft trials and misogyny in Europe.

*   *   *

KLASS, Perri 1958-

PERSONAL: Born April 29, 1958, in Tuna-puna, Trinidad; American citizen born abroad; daughter of Morton (an anthropologist) and Sheila (a writer and English professor; maiden name, Solomon) Klass; living with Larry Wolff (a writer and history professor); children: Benjamin Orlando Klass. *Education:* Harvard University, A.B., 1979, M.D., 1986; attended University of California, Berkeley, 1979-81.

ADDRESSES: Home—Cambridge, Mass. *Office*—Children's Hospital, 300 Longwood Ave., Boston, Mass. 02115. *Agent*—Maxine Groffsky, 2 Fifth Ave., New York, N.Y. 10011.

CAREER: Boston's Children's Hospital, Boston, Mass., resident in pediatrics, 1986—.

MEMBER: American Medical Women's Association, Massachusetts Medical Society.

AWARDS, HONORS: Le Baron Russell Briggs Prize from Harvard University, 1978, for "Two New Jersey Stories"; Elizabeth Mills Crothers Awards from the University of California, Berkeley, 1980, for "Style and Substance," and 1981, for "A Gift of Sweet Mustard"; O. Henry Award from Doubleday & Company, 1983, for "The Secret Lives of Dieters," and 1984, for "Not a Good Girl."

WRITINGS:

Recombinations (novel), Putnam, 1985.
I Am Having an Adventure (short stories; includes "I Am Having an Adventure," "How Big the World Is," "Clytemnestra in the Suburbs," "Gringo City," "The Almond Torte Equilibrium," "Cowboy Time," "Television Will Betray Us All," and "Officemate With Pink Feathers"), Putnam, 1986.
A Not Entirely Benign Procedure: Four Years as a Medical Student (nonfiction), Putnam, 1987.

Author of "Hers" column for the *New York Times,* 1984; author of monthly "Vital Signs" column in *Discover* magazine. Contributor to *Encyclopaedia Britannica.* Contributor of articles and short stories to periodicals, including *Boston Globe, New York Times, Vogue, Esquire, Ms., Massachusetts Medicine, Self, Mademoiselle, Antioch Review, Christopher Street,* and *Berkeley Fiction Review.*

SIDELIGHTS: Pediatrician, columnist, essayist, fiction writer, and mother, Perri Klass has inspired several articles on her ability to juggle her various careers. She "can make a mere hard worker feel downright inadequate," according to *People* magazine's Cable Neuhaus. A member of a family of writers that includes her mother, novelist Sheila Solomon Klass, and her brother, David Klass, who has published four adolescent novels, Klass was penning short stories before she decided to become a physician. She has also recorded her experiences as a student of medicine and as a resident in columns for the *New York Times* and *Discover* and in her 1987 book, *A Not Entirely Benign Procedure: Four Years as a Medical Student.* Klass won two O. Henry awards for her stories, and her 1985 first novel *Recombinations* elicited warm praise from many critics, as did her later volume of short fiction, *I Am Having an Adventure.*

"*Recombinations* makes tantalizing reading," according to reviewer BettyAnn Kevles in the *Los Angeles Times.* "Klass writes of a generation of scientists," explained Dinitia Smith in a *New York* article, "who have never known a scientific universe without [James D.] Watson and [Francis] Crick's discovery of the double helix." Indeed, many critics have noted the modernity of *Recombinations*'s heroine, Anne Montgomery. A deoxyribonucleic acid (DNA) researcher in Manhattan, New York, Anne, unlike the women scientists of Watson and Crick's era, experiences little if any sexual discrimination in her field. "Not only is she not downtrodden," reported critic Caroline Seebohm in the *New York Times Book Review,* but "she's considered a rising star and given all sorts of plum projects." Like other Klass heroines, Smith pointed out, Anne is also "confident and easygoing" in her sex life. Anne begins a casual affair with Jason, a lab technician with a terrific body that almost all of *Recombinations*'s reviewers noticed includes a twenty-nine-inch waist, innocently believing that it will not affect her relationship with her long-time live-in lover, Kent. When she tells Kent, however, he is furious and Anne moves out, first to live with her cousin Louisa and another woman, then to live with Jason (whose ex-girlfriend lives next door to them), and finally into an apartment of her own. *Recombinations* "succeeds primarily as [a] . . . *Bildungsroman,* a novel of development in which the protagonist overcomes a series of obstacles to attain freedom and selfhood," opined critic Joseph Coates in the *Chicago Tribune.* He added that Klass's "wit and observation are so lethal we want more." Klass "has a flair for capturing contemporary foibles," agreed reviewer Ellen Lesser in the *Village Voice.* Coates concluded that *Recombinations* was "an impressive debut."

I Am Having an Adventure contains "portraits of young Americans in the throes of interesting crises," as Marta Tarbel put it, critiquing the short story collection in the *Los Angeles Times Book Review.* The title piece concerns Pammy, bored by her French civilization class in Paris, who runs off to Egypt with a male stranger. Similarly, Michele in "How Big the World Is" is addicted to traveling; her biggest fear is that she will run out of unknown places to visit. "The Almond Torte Equilibrium" features two lesbians who run a catering business; their relationship is strained when one of the women becomes pregnant by a former lover. "Gringo City" depicts another pair of women, each deserted by her husband, who move to Guatemala. In "Clytemnestra in the Suburbs," lauded as "subtly astonishing and very funny" by reviewer Mark Childress in the *New York Times Book Review,* the title character lives with her boyfriend Guy in a New Jersey suburb, sharpening her shoplifting skills. "Television Will Betray Us All" recounts the seduction of a television interviewer with a somewhat artificial personality by what Tarbel labeled "an emotionally unstable heroine." Tarbel had high praise for the collection's "imaginative, sharply focused plots" and "disarming" characters. Childress commented that "Klass writes stories that sound true," and concluded: "She has plenty to say about love in a science-drunk world, how the brain works, and the heart. And how sparks fly when the two collide."

Klass's nonfiction work, *A Not Entirely Benign Procedure: Four Years as a Medical Student,* is primarily composed of articles she had previously published in periodicals. Labeled a "fascinating account" by critic Ina Yalof in the *New York Times Book Review,* the book details Klass's grueling journey toward becoming a doctor, from the early years of lectures, lab classes, and practicing on cadavers to learning procedures with live patients. "Klass writes in a smooth, easy-to-read style that sounds like a letter to her best friend," reported Robin Marantz Henig, reviewing the volume for the *Washington Post.* The pediatrician's other nonfiction efforts include a 1984 stint as the "Hers" columnist for the *New York Times* in which she described how she planned her pregnancy to fit in with the schedule of her second year of medical school. Klass's "Vital Signs" columns for *Discover* have tackled such subjects as the confidence gained and lessons learned by the end of the first year of medical internship, and the dangers of becoming an impersonal physician.

AVOCATIONAL INTERESTS: Reading, cooking, knitting.

CA INTERVIEW

CA interviewed Perri Klass by telephone on April 13, 1987, at her home in Boston.

CA: Your third book has recently been published, A Not Entirely Benign Procedure: Four Years as a Medical Student. *To write the essays about your training that have now been collected in that book, you had to "hear and see things not only as a doctor . . . but also as a nondoctor," to retain some of the "greenness" of the new medical student. Was it hard to hold the perspective of both sides as you came closer and closer to being a doctor?*

KLASS: I think it was counter-intuitive, or at least it went against the grain, because it's so horribly frightening to be a nondoctor in the hospital trying to function as a doctor. Those first few months, you don't know how to do anything. Even drawing blood is frightening. Everything is frightening. You really want to forget that time. You want to lose that perspective as quickly as you can, and I felt that as much as anyone. So it was kind of fighting against myself to try to remember that these things were all scary, that it all looked new and strange.

CA: One of the most talked-about problems in medicine is that the education of doctors neglects the humanities. You were lucky enough to grow up in a family of writers, and to become a writer before you became a medical student. Do you see the educational system trying harder to give medical students a more rounded education?

KLASS: I think people are trying, but I think it's a very hard thing to do by decree. If people aren't interested in a subject, or they don't see why they should be studying it, or people they admire who are a little further down the line don't use and respect and discuss that subject, it's hard to make them believe that that's what they should be thinking about. I think society probably is becoming more and more divided: non-

doctors and nonscientists are more and more afraid or confused or unwilling to delve into the sciences, and it works both ways. It's very hard to legislate, to say, "You will become literate in the sciences," or, "You will become literate in the humanities." It doesn't actually accomplish anything.

CA: There's a tone of genuine humility in your writing about being a doctor. How do so many doctors lose that?

KLASS: I think almost everybody at the beginning of the training would have that tone of genuine humility. As you go on, you have to find a way to deal with the fact that you're given the responsibility for human lives and that frequently there's nothing you can do, that people come to you with their children's illnesses and frequently you fail them. That's an impossible thing to live with day after day, and I think one of the defenses is a kind of arrogance. You can tell yourself, I'm the best these people can do; and that may well be true. There are an awful lot of people to whom medical science has nothing to offer. You tell yourself: whatever happens, at least I'm the best for them; they're doing the best thing they can do in coming to me. And I think sometimes the arrogance is just a very simple defense against the fact that you're going to fail them, that you're not going to be able to stop the pain or prolong the life. I also think that for me, as a medical student writing about medical school, it was very important to avoid a tone of *I'm-the-sensitive-one-and-all-the-people-around-me-aren't.*

CA: One thing everybody wonders about you is how you manage to do everything you do: study medicine, write fiction and nonfiction, be a mother, have a good relationship with your man, even cook and have hobbies. You seem relatively unharried about it all. How do you keep from going crazy?

KLASS: If I thought I was going to live like this forever, I *would* go crazy. This is *not* a way to live. I'm always tired, always hurried. I don't have enough time for the things that matter to me. I think that ultimately there ought to be a life with a balance, but internship is wildly unbalanced—not just for me, but for everyone I know who's doing it. Everyone I know, male or female, who's an intern and has small children feels deprived of time with the children. I'm not doing a lot of writing this year, and I'm not writing any fiction. I don't feel like it's unharried. But I feel that ultimately there ought to be a way to do it, a few years down the line when I've completed my training and I have some say in what my schedule is and what kind of job I'm to have.

CA: Obviously you have to work everything else around your hospital hours. Do you set specific times for things like the writing?

KLASS: Not really. Like any intern with a family, I try to go on the assumption that all my time outside the hospital does belong to my family, because they have so little of my time to begin with since my work hours are so ridiculous. Then time to do anything beyond that—to write, for example—is squeezed out of corners. If I'm home for Saturday and my son is going to take his nap, I'll use those two hours. Or I'll stay up at night after he goes to sleep. But I don't have any kind of set schedule.

CA: Are there tricks to keeping the energy level high?

KLASS: The drama and the melodrama of the hospital keep your adrenaline high when you're there, the knowledge that you're responsible, the fear of something going wrong. And maybe out of the hospital there's a kind of energetic pleasure in the freedom from that life-and-death responsibility. Also, I nap a lot—usually without meaning to.

CA: Your fiction, the novel Recombinations *and the stories collected in* I Am Having an Adventure, *has been well received critically. Does the fiction require a different kind of energy and effort from the nonfiction?*

KLASS: Yes. I can't do the fiction in these one-and two-hour blocks around the edges the way I can the nonfiction. I can't plan the fiction out in my head during the day in odd minutes in the hospital the way I can the nonfiction. I need a little more time. There isn't really any escaping the hospital the way I'm living now, and to write fiction I would need to feel I was escaping the hospital.

CA: One thing reviewers like to do is connect fiction writers with other fiction writers, to place people in schools, as it were. Do you give any thought to current modes of fiction and where your work may fit into them?

KLASS: I can't read my work objectively enough to know. There are lots of people I read and I like to read, but because I read them, I don't really compare myself to them. It's probably a better thing for other people to say about you than to say about yourself.

CA: You've named Jane Austen, the Bronte sisters, Charlotte, Emily, and Anne, George Eliot, and the Bloomsbury group, including novelist Virginia Woolf and literary figures Harold Nicolson and Vita Sackville-West, among others, as writers who are important to you. Do you consider any of them direct influences on your writing?

KLASS: It's so hard to say. The books I love are probably direct influences on me, but I wouldn't be so arrogant as to say that any of those people had actually influenced me in a way that you can see in my writing. It would be wonderful to think so, but I'm not sure it would be true. It would also be true to say that Louisa May Alcott [author of *Little Women*] and [Louise Fitzhugh's] *Harriet the Spy* and books that I read obsessively when I was very young had a lot to do with my writing, but again I don't know if I can discern specific influences. It's possible that someone else can do that with my work, but I don't think I can.

CA: In both Recombinations *and some of your short stories, such as "The Almond Torte Equilibrium," there's a consideration of the concept of family, which can take many shapes. Would you comment on your feelings about the importance of family?*

KLASS: I'm very close to my own immediate family and to my parents. And there have been a number of other people in my life at times who either have been family to me or to whom I've been family. I think I see that in other people I know, especially nowadays when many people don't grow up and get married and form their own families, or live close to their own parents, or remain connected in the way that one used to as a matter of course. There are different kinds of families, sometimes temporary and sometimes permanent, connections beyond just friendships, which form an arrangement. In my life

certainly there have been times when *a family* has meant people whom I saw frequently, on whom I depended, or who depended on me, to whom I felt almost related, and who helped me get through the year.

CA: Many writers in big cities like New York and Boston see a great deal of other writers. Assuming you don't have time for that in your life, do you find it a loss in any way?

KLASS: I know some other writers in the area just from events or through common acquaintances, but I probably see less of them than many writers see of each other. Where I work, in the hospital, there's a tremendous luxury in knowing that when you get a bad review, you walk in the next day and nobody's seen it, nobody's heard about it, nobody gives a damn. People aren't caught up in that world. If you get a good review, people aren't jealous. It's an escape. Most people in the hospital know that I write. I get razzed about being a "celebrity." But there is still a certain kind of anonymity. People generally don't know what questions to ask there, whereas if I worked somewhere else, people might ask questions about my agent or how many copies of something I sold or who bought the rights for that or that. In the hospital, the questions tend to be less close to the bone. I like that.

CA: Do you think we're getting close to a time when the distinction "woman doctor" won't be made?

KLASS: Well, they're still making it for writers, and you'd think we'd be past that. Nobody ever says "one of the best male writers of our age," but people frequently say "one of the best female writers" despite the long tradition of female novelists and poets. All those nineteenth-century writers I've mentioned, you'd think that would be enough. So people may go on making the distinction with doctors too. Certainly in pediatrics we're close to a time when people don't take for granted that doctors are male, but I think people will continue to be amazed to find that surgeons are female.

CA: You've written about how people—including medical students—get their ideas of practicing medicine from television shows like "General Hospital." How do you feel about the impact of such shows on the general viewer? Are they better, for example, than no idea at all of what it would be like to be in a hospital with a serious disease?

KLASS: That's probably true, but I think the media in general, not just doctor shows but also news shows and science shows, have a lot to answer for in that they give people a false sense of hope. People believe, "If my child is sick and I get the best doctor, the best hospital, the best medicine, then my child will get well." People believe, "If I go to the right obstetrician, do all the right things, follow all the right rules, I'll have a perfect, healthy baby." The fact is that, no matter what you do, there's no guarantee that your child will get well or that you'll have a perfect baby. There's no guarantee that *you'll* get well. Some of that is due to the medical profession's own arrogance, but I think a lot of it too is the way that every discovery has to be presented as a great leap forward, in the way that cures for cancer are constantly being announced in the press, the way that doctor shows present doctors who cure things no cure has been found for. I think this is part of why there are so many malpractice suits, part of why there's so much dissonance between doctors and the public.

CA: How would you like to see the "not entirely benign procedure" of medical school changed?

KLASS: I'd like them to make it a requirement for medical school admission that people take several years off after college, and preferably not work in medicine during that time. It's such a long tunnel. Part of admission to medical school should be the requirement that you look around and live on your own, travel, do something, but live for a while, not just go right back into school. I'd like to see some of the financial aspects altered so that you don't have to go so deeply into debt that it's prohibitive for people from less fortunate backgrounds. You could perhaps generate some kind of trade-off with service to subsidize a medical education. That used to exist on a limited scale, but this administration has done away with it, such as it was. Everyone would like to see less emphasis on memorization, but that's not going to happen. And ultimately I'd like to see, as other people would, a less grueling scheduling.

CA: You've dedicated a book to your father, one to your mother, and one to Larry Wolff. Can you envision a book, when you're not so busy, for your son Benjamin?

KLASS: Oh, sure. It will either be the next one, or maybe there'll be one in the works then that's more appropriate. But I'm sure he's going to get one.

BIOGRAPHICAL/CRITICAL SOURCES:

PERIODICALS

Chicago Tribune, March 26, 1985, September 22, 1985.
Discover, October, 1986, August, 1987.
Esquire, July, 1986.
Los Angeles Times, December 13, 1985.
Los Angeles Times Book Review, October 26, 1986.
Ms., November, 1985, July/August, 1987.
Newsweek, November 11, 1985.
New York, October 14, 1985.
New York Times Book Review, September 29, 1985, July 13, 1986, May 10, 1987.
People, November 18, 1985.
Village Voice, October 22, 1985.
Washington Post, November 15, 1985, April 1, 1987, May 25, 1987.

—*Sketch by Elizabeth Thomas*

—*Interview by Jean W. Ross*

* * *

KLEIN, Gene 1921-

PERSONAL: Born January 29, 1921, in New York; son of Benjamin and Sadie (Olson) Klein; married Frances Lillian Fisher, June 20, 1943 (died March 21, 1973); married Joyce Fay Finberg (a homemaker), February 10, 1976; children: (first marriage) Randee, Michael. *Education:* Attended New York University. *Religion:* Jewish.

ADDRESSES: Home—P.O. Box 2468, Rancho Santa Fe, Calif. 92067. *Office*—Del Rayo Racing Stables, P.O. Box 8382, Rancho Santa Fe, Calif. 92067. *Agent*—Henry Morrison, Inc., 320 McLain St., Bedford Hills, N.Y. 10507.

CAREER: Owner of an automobile dealership in Los Angeles, Calif., 1946—. President and chairman of board of directors of National General Corp., Los Angeles, 1961; general partner

and president of San Diego Chargers football team, 1965; owner of Del Rayo Racing Stables, 1982; associated with Columbia Savings and Loan Association and San Fernando Valley Bank; director of Zenith National Insurance Co. Member of board of trustees of City of Hope, Scripps Memorial Hospital, Eisenhower Medical Center, San Diego Museum of Art, and Palm Springs Museum of Art; member of board of governors of Cedars-Sinai Medical Center. *Military service:* U.S. Army Air Forces, 1941-46; became captain.

AWARDS, HONORS: Medal of Honor from State of Israel, 1969.

WRITINGS:

(With David Fisher) *First Down and a Billion: The Funny Business of Pro Football* (memoir), Morrow, 1986.

SIDELIGHTS: In 1966 Gene Klein bought the San Diego Padres for the sum of ten million dollars. Nearly twenty years later he sold the team for eight times as much. Klein's book is the story of his life in football. The author comments on the personalities with whom he was involved in a style that *New York Times* reviewer Christopher Lehmann-Haupt has described as "breezy" and "often funny if relentless with its wisecracks." The reviewer appreciated the humor and perspective that Klein and his co-author added to the world of professional football.

BIOGRAPHICAL/CRITICAL SOURCES:

PERIODICALS

New York Times, January 15, 1987.

* * *

KLINE, Linda 1940-

PERSONAL: Born August 8, 1940, in Boston, Mass.; daughter of George and Eva (Wiener) Kline. *Education:* Boston University, B.A., 1962. *Politics:* Democrat.

ADDRESSES: Office—3 East 48th St., New York, N.Y. 10017.

CAREER: Block Engineering, Inc., Cambridge, Mass., director of personnel, 1964-66; Eastern Life Insurance Co. of New York, Boston, Mass., brokerage manager, 1966-68; Lendman Associates, Norfolk, Va., and New York, N.Y., manager of direct placement, between 1968 and 1972; Roberts-Lund Ltd., New York City, director of Women in Management Division, 1972-77; Genesis Management Corp., New York City, vice-president of executive search, 1977-78; Maximus Consulting, Inc., New York City, president, 1978—. Executive director of Majority Money (women's network), 1976-79; president of Kline-McKay, Inc., 1978—. Instructor at Marymount Manhattan College, 1977; lecturer at colleges and universities. Vice-president of Co-op Board; director of Women Business Owners Education Fund; member of community board of directors of Mount Sinai Medical Center, 1984—, and Moms Amazing, 1985—.

MEMBER: Women Business Owners of New York (director, 1978-81).

WRITINGS:

(With Lloyd L. Feinstein) *Career Changing: The Worry-Free Guide,* Little, Brown, 1982.

WORK IN PROGRESS: Producing a series of audio tapes for people who have been fired from a job.

AVOCATIONAL INTERESTS: American antiques and folk art.

KNUTSON, Roger M.   1933-

PERSONAL: Born January 3, 1933, in Montevideo, Minn.; son of Melvin A. (a farmer) and Lydia (a homemaker; maiden name, Hanson) Knutson; married Sharon Belding (a homemaker), August 31, 1957; children: Karin, Anne, Benjamin, Steven, Samuel. *Education:* St. Olaf College, B.A., 1957; Michigan State University, M.S., 1961, Ph.D., 1965.

ADDRESSES: Home—807 Maple Ave., Decorah, Iowa 52101. *Office*—Department of Biology, Luther College, Decorah, Iowa 52101. *Agent*—Jeanne K. Hanson, 5111 Woodale, Minneapolis, Minn. 55424.

CAREER: Luther College, Decorah, Iowa, assistant professor, 1964-70, associate professor, 1971-74, professor of biology, 1974—. Science faculty fellow at University of Georgia, 1971-72. *Military service:* U.S. Navy, 1953-55.

MEMBER: American Association for the Advancement of Science, American Institute of Biological Sciences.

AWARDS, HONORS: Fellow of National Science Foundation, 1971-72.

WRITINGS:

Flattened Fauna, Ten Speed Press, 1987.

Contributor to *Natural History*.

WORK IN PROGRESS: Ecology for Congressmen and Other Ill-informed Citizens.

SIDELIGHTS: Roger M. Knutson told *CA:* "*Flattened Fauna* was written as an educational effort. No one is going to read about dead animals on the road unless it is approached with humor. A similar approach characterizes my classroom teaching. The book has a bibliography that serves to set it among the serious works of science."

BIOGRAPHICAL/CRITICAL SOURCES:

PERIODICALS

Chicago Tribune, June 4, 1987.
Washington Post, June 15, 1987.

*   *   *

KOGAN, Judith   1956-

PERSONAL: Born May 9, 1956, in Newark, N.J.; daughter of Edgar (a physician) and Leanore (Radack) Kogan. *Education:* Harvard University, B.A. (magna cum laude), 1978; Royal Academy of Music, recital diploma, 1979; Juilliard School, M.M., 1980; New York University, J.D., 1983.

ADDRESSES: Agent—Amanda Urban, International Creative Management, 40 West 57th St., New York, N.Y. 10019.

CAREER: Professional harpist.

WRITINGS:

Nothing But the Best: The Struggle for Perfection at the Juilliard School, Random House, 1987.

BIOGRAPHICAL/CRITICAL SOURCES:

PERIODICALS

Chicago Tribune, November 22, 1987.

KOHL, Benjamin G.   1938-

PERSONAL: Born October 26, 1938, in Middletown, Del.; son of Victor P. (a farmer) and Catherine B. (a housewife; maiden name, Carpenter) Kohl; married Judith Ann Cleek (a professor), January 2, 1961; children: Benjamin G., Jr., Laura Ann. *Education:* Bowdoin College, A.B. (cum laude), 1960; University of Delaware, M.A., 1962; Johns Hopkins University, Ph.D., 1968. *Politics:* Democrat. *Religion:* Episcopalian.

ADDRESSES: Home—59 South Grand Ave., Poughkeepsie, N.Y. 12603. *Office*—Department of History and Program in Medieval and Renaissance Studies, Vassar College, Poughkeepsie, N.Y. 12601.

CAREER: Vassar College, Poughkeepsie, N.Y., instructor, 1966-68, assistant professor, 1968-74, associate professor, 1974-81, professor of history, 1981—, coordinator of Program in Medieval and Renaissance Studies, 1983—. Lecturer at American and European universities. City historian of Poughkeepsie, 1971-78.

MEMBER: American Historical Association, Mediaeval Academy of America, Renaissance Society of America, American Association of University Professors (president of Vassar chapter, 1987—), Society of Fellows of the American Academy in Rome (member of council, 1984—), Royal Historical Society (fellow), Columbia University Renaissance Colloquium (associate), Amrita Club.

AWARDS, HONORS: Fulbright fellow in Italy, 1964-65; fellow in postclassical humanistic studies at American Academy in Rome, 1970-71; Delmas fellow in Venice, 1978; fellow of Folger Shakespeare Library, 1980.

WRITINGS:

(Contributor) A. Scaglione, editor, *Francis Petrarch: Six Centuries Later*, University of North Carolina Press, 1975.
(Editor with Ronald G. Witt) *The Earthly Republic: Italian Humanists on Government and Society*, University of Pennsylvania Press, 1978.
Renaissance Humanism, 1300-1550: A Bibliography of Materials in English, Garland Publishing, 1985.
(Editor and translator with James Day) Giovanni Conversini da Ravenna, *Two Court Treatises*, Fink Verlag, 1987.
(Editor with R. C. Mueller) F. C. Lane, *Studies in Venetian Social and Economic History*, Variorum Reprints, 1987.
(Contributor) A. Rabil, editor, *Renaissance Humanism, Foundations, Forms, and Legacy*, University of Pennsylvania Press, 1988.

Contributor of more than fifty articles and reviews to history journals.

WORK IN PROGRESS: Padua Under the Carrara, 1337-1405, publication expected in 1990; with Gherardo Ortalli, editing *Codex Statutorum Carrariensis*, on the fourteenth-century Latin statues of Padua, Italy, completion expected in 1989; a new scholarly synthesis of the Italian Renaissance.

AVOCATIONAL INTERESTS: Farming in Delaware, fishing and swimming in the Chesapeake Bay.

*   *   *

KOHLS, R. L.
See KOHLS, Richard L(ouis)

KOHLS, Richard L(ouis) 1921-
(R. L. Kohls)

PERSONAL: Born April 19, 1921, in Kentland, Ind.; son of Clarence E. and Helen (Littlejohn) Kohls; married Irene Elizabeth Shuster, April 20, 1944; children: Michael E., Kathryn Ann. Education: Purdue University, B.S., 1942, Ph.D., 1950; University of Missouri—Columbia, M.A., 1947. Religion: Christian Church.

ADDRESSES: Home—1520 Woodland St., West Lafayette, Ind. 47906. Office—Department of Agricultural Economics, Purdue University, West Lafayette, Ind. 47907.

CAREER: University of Missouri—Columbia, instructor in marketing and prices, 1946-48; Purdue University, West Lafayette, Ind., instructor, 1948-50, assistant professor, 1950-52, associate professor, 1952-54, professor of agricultural economics, 1954—, Hovde Distinguished Professor, 1981—, dean of School of Agriculture, 1968—, assistant vice-president for academic affairs, 1966-68. Special lecturer for Clergy Economic Education Foundation, 1955—; visiting professor at University of Exeter, 1964. Member of Indiana Health Facilities Planning Council, 1968-77; member of public advisory board of Chicago Mercantile Exchange, 1968-77; member of board of directors of Purdue Research Foundation; consultant to U.S. Department of Agriculture. Member of board of directors of Indiana 4H Foundation, Lafayette Symphony Society, and West Lafayette Library. Military service: U.S. Army, Military Intelligence, 1942-46; became captain.

MEMBER: International Agricultural Economics Association, American Agricultural Economics Association (vice-president, 1965-66), American Marketing Association, American Association for Higher Education, Purdue Agricultural Alumni Association (member of board of directors), Sigma Xi, Alpha Gamma Rho, Gamma Sigma Delta, Alpha Zeta, Greater Lafayette Chamber of Commerce.

AWARDS, HONORS: Outstanding Teacher Award from American Agricultural Economics Association, 1966.

WRITINGS:

Marketing of Agricultural Products, Macmillan, 1955, 4th edition (with W. David Downey), 1972, 6th edition (with Joseph N. Uhl), 1985.
(Contributor) Disparities in the Pace and Form of Agricultural and Rural Development: Proceedings of the International Conference of Agricultural Economics, Oxford University Press, 1966.
(Contributor) Marketing and Economic Development, University of Nebraska Press, 1967.

Also author of bulletins for Indiana Agricultural Experiment Station, under name R. L. Kohls.*

* * *

KOONZ, Claudia

BRIEF ENTRY: American feminist, educator, and author. Koonz received both widespread critical acclaim and a nomination for the 1987 National Book Award with her book Mothers in the Fatherland: Women, the Family, and Nazi Politics (St. Martin's, 1987), a comprehensive account of women's roles in Nazi Germany. Robert J. Lifton, writing in the New York Times Book Review, complimented Koonz for tackling "an extremely difficult issue—that of gender responses to situations of potential and actual evil" and judged Mothers in the

Fatherland "a book of great historical and moral importance." Koonz, a professor of history at College of the Holy Cross in Worcester, Massachusetts, also co-edited Becoming Visible: Women in European History (Houghton, 1977). Addresses: Office—Department of History, College of the Holy Cross, College St., Worcester, Mass. 01610.

BIOGRAPHICAL/CRITICAL SOURCES:

PERIODICALS

Nation, April 18, 1987.
New York Review of Books, July 16, 1987.
New York Times Book Review, January 3, 1988.

* * *

KOOP, Theodore Frederick 1907(?)-1988

OBITUARY NOTICE: Born c. 1907 in Monticello, Iowa; died of complications following surgery (one source says cancer), July 7, 1988, in Washington, D.C. Administrator, editor, journalist, and author. A graduate of the University of Iowa School of Journalism, Koop began his career as a reporter and editor for the Associated Press, working in Des Moines, Iowa, and New Haven, Connecticut, before arriving in Washington, D.C., in 1932. He accepted a job as head of the National Geographic Society's news service in 1941 and spent World War II working at the Washington Office of Censorship, monitoring and advising the press on its coverage of wartime news events that might have endangered national security. His book Weapon of Silence was based on his experiences in the program. In 1948 Koop became Washington bureau manager for the Columbia Broadcasting System (CBS), where he was responsible for news coverage and where he created and helped develop the news program "Face the Nation." Koop was promoted in 1961 to vice-president in charge of the company's relations with the government, including Congress and the Federal Communications Commission. In this position Koop acted as standby censor, ready to prohibit the spread of information that the government felt might aid the enemy, throughout the presidencies of John F. Kennedy, Richard M. Nixon, and Lyndon B. Johnson. He retired in 1971.

OBITUARIES AND OTHER SOURCES:

BOOKS

Les Brown's Encyclopedia of Television, New York Zoetrope, 1982.
New York Times Encyclopedia of Television, Times Books, 1977.

PERIODICALS

Chicago Tribune, July 9, 1988.
New York Times, July 9, 1988.
Washington Post, July 9, 1988.

* * *

KOUHI, Elizabeth 1917-

PERSONAL: Born November 11, 1917, in Lappe, Ontario, Canada; daughter of Antti (a farmer) and Aliina (a housewife and farmer; maiden name, Keisteri) Kaija; married George A. Kouhi, July 1, 1951; children: Christine Kouhi Hallemeier, Aline Kouhi Klemencic, Philip, Emily Kouhi Lavender. Education: McGill University, B.A., 1949; Ontario College of Education, Teaching Certificate, 1964. Politics: New Democrat. Religion: Lutheran.

ADDRESSES: Home—224 North Norah St., Thunder Bay, Ontario, Canada P7C 4H2.

CAREER: Schoolteacher in Raith, Ontario, 1950-52; homemaker and mother, 1952-63; Lakehead Board of Education, Thunder Bay, Ontario, teacher, 1963-82; writer, 1982—.

MEMBER: League of Canadian Poets, Writers Union of Canada, Canadian Society of Children's Authors, Illustrators, and Performers, Lakehead Association for the Mentally Retarded (member of board of directors).

WRITINGS:

Jamie of Thunder Bay (juvenile novel), Borealis Press, 1977.
North Country Spring (juvenile poetry), Penumbra Press, 1980.
The Story of Philip (juvenile), Queenston House, 1982.
Sarah Jane of Silver Islet (juvenile novel), Queenston House, 1983.
Round Trip Home (adult poetry), Penumbra Press, 1983.

Contributor of poetry to anthologies for children. Editor of newsletter of Lakehead Association for the Mentally Retarded.

WORK IN PROGRESS: A children's novel; a book of poems.

SIDELIGHTS: Elizabeth Kouhi told *CA:* "I have always wanted to write. Since retiring from teaching I have had more time to concentrate on writing, and I now consider it my full-time profession. I started writing children's novels when my children were young, using local historical material. Both *Jamie of Thunder Bay* and *Sarah Jane of Silver Islet* are set here in the last century, the first about the fur trade and the second set in a mining town. *The Story of Philip* is a picture book about our developmentally handicapped son. *North Country Spring* and *Round Trip Home* are books of poetry. Although the books are not autobiographical, they do perhaps reflect the ambitions of the country kid that I was. Indirectly my poetry reflects my ideas on social justice and basic spiritual values, as well as the wonder at the riches of this world in nature, arts, literature, and so on.

"The local school board, the Lakehead Board of Education, has constructed learning kits around my two novels, and I often get into the schools to talk to the children. I have also visited other towns in Ontario through the Writers Union of Canada and the League of Canadian Poets."

AVOCATIONAL INTERESTS: Travel to Europe and the South Pacific; a wilderness cabin on the Canadian Shield.

*   *   *

KOZAK, Roman   1948(?)-1988

OBITUARY NOTICE: Born c. 1948 in Germany; died of heart failure following a stroke, October 13, 1988, in Las Vegas, Nev. Journalist and author. Kozak became a correspondent for *Billboard* magazine while living in Rome, Italy, and working as a sports editor for the *Daily American* newspaper there. *Billboard* later assigned him to New York City as a reporter, where he wrote a series of articles on rock and roll music. From the late 1970s to 1984, Kozak served as the publication's first rock and roll editor. Kozak was the author of a book about the history of New York City's rock club "CBGB" titled *This Ain't No Disco.*

OBITUARIES AND OTHER SOURCES:

PERIODICALS

New York Times, October 20, 1988.

KRAMER, Larry   1935-

PERSONAL: Born June 25, 1935, in Bridgeport, Conn.; son of George L. (an attorney) and Rea W. (a social worker; maiden name, Wishengrad). *Education:* Yale University, B.A., 1957.

ADDRESSES: Home and office—New York, N.Y.

CAREER: Screenwriter, playwright, and novelist. Associated with training programs in New York, N.Y., for William Morris Agency, 1958, and for Columbia Pictures, 1958-59; Columbia Pictures, assistant story editor in New York City, 1960-61, and production executive in London, England, 1961-65; assistant to the president of United Artists, 1965; associate producer of motion picture "Here We Go Round the Mulberry Bush," 1967; producer of motion picture "Women in Love," 1969. Co-founder of Gay Men's Health Crisis in New York City, 1981; founder of ACT UP (AIDS Coalition to Unleash Power), 1988. *Military service:* U.S. Army, 1957.

AWARDS, HONORS: Academy Award nomination for best screenplay from the Academy of Motion Picture Arts and Sciences and nomination from the British Film Academy for best screenplay, both 1970, both for "Women in Love"; Dramatists Guild Marton Award, City Lights Award for best play of the year, Sarah Siddons Award for best play of the year, and nomination for Olivier Award for best play, all 1986, all for "The Normal Heart"; Arts and Communication Award from the Human Rights Campaign Fund, 1987.

WRITINGS:

(And producer) "Women in Love" (screenplay; adapted from the novel by D. H. Lawrence), United Artists, 1969.
Faggots (novel), Random House, 1978.
The Normal Heart (two-act play; first produced Off-Broadway at Public Theater, April, 1985), introduction by Andrew Holleran and foreword by Joseph Papp, New American Library, c. 1985.
"Just Say No" (play), first produced Off-Broadway at WPA Theater, October 16, 1988.
Reports From the holocaust: The Making of an AIDS Activist (non-fiction), St. Martin's, 1989.

Also author of Off-Off-Broadway play "Sissies' Scrapbook" and two-act play "The Furniture of Home," 1989.

Contributor of political writings to periodicals, including *New York Times* and *Village Voice.*

WORK IN PROGRESS: Another novel.

SIDELIGHTS: Larry Kramer is most known for his controversial works dealing with the difficulties homosexual males face in their everyday lives. Containing subject matter derived from his own experiences, his writings address such topics as the lifestyle of New York City's gay community and the tragic, fast-spreading epidemic of acquired immune deficiency syndrome, or AIDS, among homosexuals. Kramer's screenplay "Women in Love," his novel *Faggots,* and his stage play "The Normal Heart" have stirred strong reactions from audiences and critics whose adjectives describing Kramer's works range from "sensitive" and "intelligent," "seedy" and "grotesque," to "angry," "gripping," and "forceful."

Kramer's first work to confront the complexities of homosexuality is the 1969 "Women in Love," a film based on D. H. Lawrence's 1921 novel of the same title. Some forty years after a film adaptation of the book was proposed but never fulfilled, Kramer obtained the rights to the novel and was urged by United Artists to enlist Ken Russell as the film's director. Critiquing the film for the *New York Times,* one reviewer observed that much of the film was taken directly from Lawrence's work: "Ken Russell, the director, and Larry Kramer, the screenwriter, seem almost to have used the novel as a screenplay." The critic praised this tactic, declaring that it "results in a very 'literary' movie." Timothy M. Johnson, in *Magill's Survey of Cinema,* agreed, remarking that Russell and Kramer's "sensitive interpretation" is a "splendid cinematic equivalent of Lawrence's writing, and the necessary condensation of the book is well done. The result is a dense but not overburdened example of film art on many levels."

Like the novel, the film depicts "an intensely romantic love story about four people and their curiously desperate struggles for sexual power," wrote Vincent Canby of the *New York Times.* In England around the time of World War I, two sisters, Ursula and Gudren Brangwen, develop relationships with Rupert Birkin and Gerald Crich respectively. Rupert, noted Canby, seeks "'pure' relationships both with woman and man." He thus directs his conventional love towards Ursula while advocating the virtues and importance of spiritual intimacy between males to Gerald. Accordingly, the film reproduces a scene in the novel where Rupert and Gerald engage in a nude wrestling match, physically demonstrating their male compatibility. Rupert and Ursula eventually marry, and the film's focus switches to the tumultuous relationship of Gudren and Gerald. The two couples decide to take a ski vacation in the Alps, where Gudren proceeds to deride Gerald for his possessive—hence destructive—nature in love. She then purposely irritates him by sparking an affair with Loerke, a bisexual German artist. Tormented, angry, and jealous, Gerald attempts to strangle Gudren before he wanders off into the mountains and dies. "The film ends," Johnson, related "with Ursula and Rupert in their cottage in England discussing love: 'You can't have two kinds of love. Why should you?' Ursula says. 'It seems as if I can't,' Rupert responds. 'Yet I wanted it.'"

Kramer's "Women in Love" was well-received by critics. Judging the film "a loving, faithful, intelligent, visual representation" of the novel, Canby observed that "the movie . . . capture[s] a feeling of nature and of physical contact between people, and between people and nature, that is about as sensuous as anything you've probably ever seen in a film." He further praised the film for picking up on Lawrence's underlying theme of homosexual love: "Also faithful . . . is the feeling that the relationship between the two men, who though unfulfilled, is somehow cleaner, less messy, than the relationships of the men with their women." Canby proclaimed the wrestling scene between Gerald and Rupert "the movie's loveliest sequence—there is a sense of positive grace in the eroticism."

Arthur Schlesinger, Jr., in his review of "Women in Love" for *Vogue,* however, disagreed on the mastery with which Kramer and Russell handled Lawrence's intentions. "This sharper homosexual emphasis . . . seems an obvious response to the preoccupations of our own time," claimed the critic. He further noted that the film "can not be claimed as a success" but conceded that "it is a fascinating and intelligent try." Johnson was more enthusiastic about the film, affirming that it "is not only a masterpiece of visual stylization but also a fully realized dramatic narrative."

Less subtle in its portrayal of homosexuality is Kramer's first novel, *Faggots.* Set in the 1970s, the book delineates the lifestyle of the male gay community on New York's Fire Island, known for promiscuous sex and frequent drug use among its members. Specifically, the book follows the escapades of a forty-year-old homosexual, Fred Lemish. He regularly visits discotheques and bathhouses, witnessing much hedonistic behavior, while at the same time searching for some kind of love and stability in his life. Barbara G. Harrison in the *Washington Post Book World* explained that Lemish considers himself part of a privileged elite but is also looking for someone to blame for his "condition"; he, like the other "faggots" in the novel, is both narcissistic and self-loathing.

Deeming *Faggots* an "extraordinary new novel," Samuel McCracken of *Commentary* interpreted the work as a satire, "written like all good ones, from the inside." Many critics, however, were less favorable in their assessment of Kramer's novel. Martin Duberman in the *New Republic* reported that although the book was "announced as a searing indictment of the giddy Fire Island set" and is supposedly chiding gays for confusing promiscuity with liberation, *Faggots* is "foolish, even stupid" in that it merely exemplifies the lifestyle. He concluded that the book is a "plastic, trashy artifact of the worst aspects of [the] scene." Harrison found the book "revolting," noting that its graphic descriptions leave "nothing to the imagination." She voiced the opinion of a number of reviewers who believed the book to be "the work of a cynic who has done the homosexual community an enormous disservice." Kramer, the critic added, "is in fact writing about a peculiarly ugly . . . subculture in which love does not exist —a culture that homosexuals have been at pains to say is not representative of homosexual life."

Despite its poor reception initially, *Faggots* remained in print over the next decade, eventually becoming a best-seller. Upon its republication in 1987, the book was hailed as a work of historical importance, significant for its unsparingly honest portrayal of gay life. This candid depiction was, as Kramer explained to Richard Christiansen in the *Chicago Tribune,* the purpose behind writing the novel: "I never read a book that reflected homosexuality as I was living it. The novel became a personal odyssey for me." "I purposely made the chief characters in my book intelligent, educated, and affluent men who should be role-models for the rest of us," explained Kramer. "Instead they're cowardly and self-pitying persons who retreat into their own ghetto because they feel the world doesn't want them. . . . Most of these men have everything to live for, yet they spend much of their life saying, 'Poor me! Nobody loves me! The world hates me!' It just seems that we should be angry at our own cowardice instead of the world's cruelty. We should be examining what we're doing and why we're doing it. We should be coming to terms with ourselves.'"

In his next work, the 1985 drama "The Normal Heart," Kramer not only expresses anger about gays' inability to deal with their sexuality, but, as Frank Rich of the *New York Times* conveyed, "the playwright starts off angry, soon gets furious and then skyrockets into sheer rage." Through his work concerning the presently incurable disease, AIDS—a malady that destroys the body's natural immunity to infection and is most prevalent among homosexual males—the author directs his rage at several sources. "What gets Mr. Kramer mad," stated Rich, "is his conviction that neither the hetero- nor homosexual community has fully met the ever-expanding crisis posed by [AIDS]. He accuses the Governmental, medical and press establishments of foot-dragging in combating the disease—especially in the early days of its outbreak, when much of the play is set—and he is even tougher on homosexual leaders who, in his view, were either too cowardly or too mesmerized by the ideology of sexual liberation to get the story out.''

"The Normal Heart" is one of the first stage productions to deal with AIDS. It relates the struggle of activist Ned Weeks, a homosexual who embarks on a campaign to arouse public concern for AIDS sufferers and to curb further spread of the disease. He reprimands his fellow gays for being unnecessarily promiscuous, and he develops an organization designed to help the victims of AIDS as well as to promote safe sex among gays. Abrasive and fanatical in his preaching, though, Weeks is expelled from the group. Soon thereafter, his lover dies from the disease. Emotionally motivated to investigate the causes of the harmful spread of AIDS, Weeks verbally lashes out at the *New York Times* for not taking advantage of their media power to alert the public of the disease when it was first documented; he accuses New York Mayor Ed Koch of being indifferent to the suffering of AIDS patients; and he scolds the gay community for not coming to terms with the disease—or their sexuality—and organizing politically to make the government accountable.

The actions of the fictional Ned Weeks closely parallel those of Kramer, who in addition to ardently campaigning to control the spread of AIDS, was a founder of the Gay Men's Health Crisis. Writing "The Normal Heart" as an autobiographical account, Kramer, moreover, wrote the drama as a message play. Samuel G. Freedman quoted the author in his *Chicago Tribune* critique: "I got involved in the AIDS mess early on—I lost two friends and someone I was in love with—and I knew it was the saddest thing I'd ever know. And it was obscenely difficult to get anyone to pay attention to AIDS. There's a line in the play in which the young man who's dying says, 'There's not a good word to be said for anybody in this entire mess.' It seems to me that was what had to be said."

Considered Kramer's most successful work, "The Normal Heart" has been staged worldwide and is generally considered a forceful and deeply felt political document; upon its release, Rich deemed it "the most outspoken play around." But "is it a good [play]?" asked Dan Sullivan in the *Los Angeles Times.* "No. It almost doesn't have time to be one, so intent is it on imparting its rage at the Establishment and in inspiring gays in the audience to stop playing victim—and to stop killing themselves." Because of the extensive scientific, political, and sociological information included in the drama, some reviewers found it exhausting and repetitive. Furthermore, "some of the author's specific accusations are questionable, and, needless to say, we often hear only one side of inflammatory debates," noted Rich. But "there are also occasions," he continued, "when the stage seethes with the conflict of impassioned, literally life-and-death argument." In his review of the play for the *Chicago Tribune,* Christiansen added: "The anger . . . produces eloquence; the confrontations are truly dramatic; the battles produce light as well as heat. . . . There are many stirring moments in this play." Kramer's work was hailed not only for its intensity but for its timeliness in confronting a presently fast-spreading disease. Mel Gussow in the *New York Times* called the play a "rarity" for its "immediate and responsive stand on issues of great . . . consequence." Sullivan concluded: "As an AIDS documentary, ['The Normal Heart'] is . . . already something of a period piece, thank God: The causes of the disease have been more clearly pinpointed now."

Kramer told *CA:* "All of my concerns and writings now are devoted to fighting the AIDS epidemic, which has taken so many of my friends and acquaintances from me. Starting with 'The Normal Heart' and continuing with *Reports From the holocaust*—a collection of all my political writings that have appeared over the past ten years, mostly in the gay press around the world but also in the *New York Times* and the *Village Voice*—all of my energies are focused here. My new play, 'The Furniture of Home,' is a companion play to 'The Normal Heart.' I have already begun work on a very long novel that starts where *Faggots* left off. The interesting thing about *Faggots* has been that, although it was excoriated in some quarters, it was also a best-seller and has remained in print continuously since its first publication in 1978; it is now considered an important book and still continues to sell well. This has, of course, been gratifying to me. It's not often in a writer's lifetime that the pendulum swings so markedly.

"But with *Faggots,* my political journalism, and my writing about gay issues, I've discovered it's difficult not to say things that aren't considered controversial by someone. Even harder has been to learn to somehow find the tenacity to carry on saying what I want to say in the face of criticism and opposition. That's why the lesson I learned from the reception of *Faggots* was so important to me: the original anger turned into supportive acceptance. It's a good lesson for writers to learn: say what you must say and hope that the world will eventually come around to your way of thinking, but try not to be defeated while waiting for it to do so.

"My play 'Just Say No' is a farce about sexual hypocrisy in high places—about people who make the rules that they insist the rest of us live by, and then don't live by these rules themselves. It takes place in the capital city, Georgetown, of the mythical country of New Columbia. The leading characters, among others, are Mrs. Potentate, the wife of the Potentate in Chief, their gay son, Junior, and the gay Mayor of Appleberg, which is New Columbia's largest northeastern city. The play is by far the most controversial thing I have ever written; I have no idea if the play will or will not be a success, but it is going to attract attention."

BIOGRAPHICAL/CRITICAL SOURCES:

BOOKS

Contemporary Literary Criticism, Volume 42, Gale, 1987.
Magill's Survey of Cinema, Volume VI, Salem Press, 1981.

PERIODICALS

Chicago Tribune, January 15, 1979, April 11, 1985, May 6, 1985.
Commentary, January, 1979.
Daily News, April 22, 1985.
Los Angeles Times, December 5, 1985, December 13, 1985.
New Republic, January 6, 1979.
New York Post, May 4, 1985.
New York Times, March 26, 1970, March 29, 1970, April 22, 1985, April 28, 1985, October 21, 1988.
Times (London), March 27, 1986.
Vogue, March 1, 1970.
Washington Post Book World, December 17, 1978.

                                                        —*Sketch by Janice E. Drane*

*   *   *

KRANIDAS, Kathleen
See COLLINS, Kathleen

KRESS, Nancy 1948-

PERSONAL: Born January 20, 1948, in Buffalo, N.Y.; daughter of Henry Francis (a businessman) and Angelina (a housewife; maiden name, Canale) Koningisor; married Michael J. Kress, July 14, 1973 (divorced, 1984); married Mark P. Donnelly, August 19, 1988; children: (first marriage) Kevin Michael, Brian Stephen. *Education:* State University of New York College at Plattsburgh, B.S., 1969; State University of New York College at Brockport, M.S. (education), 1978, M.A. (English), 1979.

ADDRESSES: Home—50 Sweden Hill Rd., Brockport, N.Y. 14420. *Office*—Stanton & Hucko, 555 West Main St., Palmyra, N.Y. 14522. *Agent*—Writers House, 21 West 26th St., New York, N.Y. 10010.

CAREER: Elementary school teacher in Penn Yan, N.Y., 1970-73; Stanton & Hucko, Palmyra, N.Y., senior copywriter, 1984—. Adjunct instructor at State University of New York College at Brockport, 1980—.

MEMBER: Science Fiction Writers of America (director of Speakers Bureau).

AWARDS, HONORS: Nebula Award from Science Fiction Writers of America, 1985, for story "Out of All Them Bright Stars."

WRITINGS:

The Prince of Morning Bells (novel), Pocket Books, 1981.
The Golden Grove (novel), Bluejay, 1984.
The White Pipes (novel), Bluejay, 1985.
Trinity and Other Stories, Bluejay, 1985.
An Alien Light (novel), Arbor House, 1988.

Work represented in anthologies, including *The Best Science Fiction of the Year 12*, edited by Terry Carr, Timescape; *Universe 12*, edited by Terry Carr, Doubleday, 1982; *Full Spectrum*, edited by Shawna McCarthy, Bantam, 1988. Contributor of stories to periodicals, including *Isaac Asimov's Science Fiction, Omni, Fantasy and Science Fiction*, and *Twilight Zone*.

WORK IN PROGRESS: Another science fiction novel.

SIDELIGHTS: Nancy Kress told *CA:* "My first three novels are fantasy; the last two are science fiction. The shift is important to me—it represents an attempt to move from setting as a determiner of character and motivation. Science fiction provides an ideal genre for such an exploration because the setting can be specifically chosen to throw into sharp relief those aspects of human nature which concern the writer. For me, the central aspect has always been: How do human beings attempt to make sense of the world around them? In the absence of a central societal religion, what becomes the faith, the god, the point outside oneself worth building a life on? There can be more than one right answer."

*　　　*　　　*

KRIMS, Milton Robert 1904(?)-1988

OBITUARY NOTICE: Born c. 1904; died of pneumonia while suffering from Parkinson's disease, July 11, 1988, in Woodland Hills, Calif. Actor, journalist, novelist, and screenwriter. A writer with more than twenty-five films to his credit, Krims began his career as a Broadway actor and journalist, writing for the *Brooklyn Eagle* in the late 1920s and utilizing these skills again as a war reporter for an Air Force magazine during his World War II service with the Army Air Corps. Krims also wrote several novels; his popular *Dude Ranch* was made into a movie in 1931. Employed by major studios such as Warner Bros., Twentieth Century-Fox, and Universal during the 1930s and 1940s, he wrote screenplays for movies including "The Great O'Malley," "The Iron Curtain," "Confessions of a Nazi Spy," "Green Light," and "Anthony Adverse." Throughout the next two decades Krims wrote mainly for television, producing scripts for the "Perry Mason" series and other programs. He worked as a film editor for *Holiday* and *Saturday Evening Post* magazines during the 1970s.

OBITUARIES AND OTHER SOURCES:

PERIODICALS

Chicago Tribune, July 21, 1988.
Los Angeles Times, July 16, 1988.
New York Times, July 20, 1988.

*　　　*　　　*

KRISTOF, Nicholas D(onabet) 1959-

PERSONAL: Born April 27, 1959, in Chicago, Ill.; son of Ladis K. D. (a professor) and Jane (a professor; maiden name, McWilliams) Kristof. *Education:* Harvard University, B.A., 1981; Oxford University, Law Degree, 1983; American University in Cairo, Arabic Language Diploma, 1984.

ADDRESSES: Office—New York Times, 229 West 43rd St., New York, N.Y. 10036.

CAREER: New York Times, New York, N.Y., economics reporter, 1984-85, Los Angeles correspondent, 1985-86, foreign correspondent, 1986—.

WRITINGS:

Freedom of the High School Press, University Press of America, 1983.

WORK IN PROGRESS: A children's book about two escaped slaves, set in the year 1858; research on China.

SIDELIGHTS: Nicholas D. Kristof told *CA:* "Since my student days, when I began to travel with a backpack around Africa and Asia, I have had a fascination with foreign lands, cultures, and languages. In Cairo I studied Arabic and exulted in meeting Bedouin camel herders. At the moment, the *New York Times* is sending me to Taiwan to study Chinese language and culture."

*　　　*　　　*

KRUPAT, Arnold 1941-

PERSONAL: Surname is pronounced "*Crew*-pat"; born October 22, 1941, in New York, N.Y.; son of Milton and Ruth (Haberfeld) Krupat; married Cynthia Muser (a book designer), September 14, 1968; children: Tanya, Jeremy. *Education:* New York University, B.A., 1962; graduate study at University of Strasbourg, 1962-63; Columbia University, M.A., 1965, Ph.D., 1967. *Politics:* Socialist. *Religion:* "Anti-religion."

ADDRESSES: Home—305 East 10th St., New York, N.Y. 10009. *Office*—American Studies, Sarah Lawrence College, Bronxville, N.Y. 10708.

CAREER: Rutgers University, New Brunswick, N.J., instructor, 1966-67, assistant professor of English, 1967-68; on staff of Sarah Lawrence College, Bronxville, N.Y., 1968—, tenured member of faculty, director of American Studies program.

MEMBER: Modern Language Association of America, National Indian Youth Council, Western Literature Association, Southern Poverty Leadership Conference, Amnesty International, American Civil Liberties Union.

AWARDS, HONORS: Woodrow Wilson fellow, 1962; Fulbright fellow, 1962; grants from National Endowment for the Humanities, 1970 and 1987; Leopold Schepp fellow, 1979; Mellon Foundation fellow, 1987.

WRITINGS:

Woodsmen; or, Thoreau and the Indians (novel), Letter Press, 1979.
For Those Who Come After: A Study of Native American Autobiography, University of California Press, 1985.
(Editor with Brian Swann) *Recovering the Word,* University of California Press, 1987.
(Editor with Brian Swann) *I Tell You Now: Autobiographical Essays by Native American Writers,* University of Nebraska Press, 1987.

Contributor to magazines, including *Georgia Review, Diacritics, American Literature, Critical Inquiry, American Indian Culture and Research Journal,* and *Nation.*

WORK IN PROGRESS: From Here to Eternity: Native American Literature and the Canon; a critical study; essays on anthropology and modernism, and on American autobiography.

SIDELIGHTS: Arnold Krupat told *CA:* "My aim has been to raise the theoretical sophistication of criticism of Native American literature, and to achieve a deeper understanding of the cultural contribution of Native Americans to American culture in general. I see myself as a cultural critic, working to produce knowledge in the interest of social justice and human freedom."

BIOGRAPHICAL/CRITICAL SOURCES:

PERIODICALS

Los Angeles Times Book Review, September 13, 1987.
Washington Post Book World, February 7, 1988.

*   *   *

KUBIE, Eleanor Gottheil   1899-1988
(Nora Benjamin Kubie)

OBITUARY NOTICE: Born January 4, 1899, in New York, N.Y.; died of acute leukemia, September 4, 1988, in Westport, Conn. Artist and author. Kubie, who used the pseudonym Nora Benjamin Kubie, wrote and illustrated several fiction and nonfiction books for juveniles, including *Roving All Day, The First Book of Israel, The First Book of Archaeology,* and *King Solomon's Navy,* which won the 1955 Isaac Siegel Award for best book. She was considered an amateur archaeologist and wrote *Road to Nineveh,* a biography of archaeologist Austin Henry Layard. Kubie was a member of the Author's League of America, Artists Equity, Art Students League of America, and Artists Village of Ein Hod, and served as chairman of the juvenile book commission of the Writers War Board from 1942 to 1943. Her other books include *Fathom Five: A Story of Bermuda, Remember the Valley,* and *The Jews of Israel: History and Sources.*

OBITUARIES AND OTHER SOURCES:

BOOKS

Who's Who in World Jewry: A Biographical Dictionary of Outstanding Jews, Olive Books of Israel, 1978.

PERIODICALS

New York Times, September 8, 1988.

*   *   *

KUBIE, Nora Benjamin
See KUBIE, Eleanor Gottheil

*   *   *

KUHN, Bowie (Kent)   1926-

PERSONAL: Name is pronounced "*Boo*-ee Kewn"; born October 28, 1926, in Takoma Park, Md.; son of Louis (an oil executive) and Alice (a housewife; maiden name, Roberts) Kuhn; married Louise Hegeler (a housewife), October 20, 1956; children: George Ludwig, Paul Hartley, Alix Roberts, Stephen Bowie. *Education:* Attended Franklin and Marshall College, 1944-45; Princeton University, B.A. (cum laude), 1947; University of Virginia, J.D., 1950. *Politics:* Republican. *Religion:* Roman Catholic.

ADDRESSES: Home—320 North Murray Ave., Ridgewood, N.J. 07450. *Office*—Myerson & Kuhn, 237 Park Ave., New York, N.Y. 10017.

CAREER: Willkie Farr & Gallagher (law firm), New York, N.Y., associate, 1950-61, partner, 1961-69, counsel, 1984-87; Commissioner of Baseball, 1969-84; Myerson & Kuhn (law firm), New York City, senior partner, 1988—. Senior member of advisory board of Burson-Marsteller, 1984—; director of Better Business Bureau, 1984—, and Northern Telecom Ltd., 1985—; Center for Public Resources, member of judicial panel, 1985—, member of executive committee, 1986—. Member of board of directors and advisory committee of International Tennis Hall of Fame, 1984—; member of board of directors of Baseball Hall of Fame and Museum, 1969—, Jackie Robinson Foundation, 1985—, and Layman's National Bible Association. Member of Cardinal's Committee of the Laity for the Archdiocese of New York, 1972—; knight of American Association of the Order of Malta, 1975—, member of board of councillors and hospitaller, 1987; member of board of directors of Catholic Youth Organization, 1985—. Chairman of Greenwood Foundation, 1985—; member of advisory board of Arthritis Foundation, 1986—; president of TARGET (a function of the National Federation of High School Associations to help students cope with drug abuse), 1986—; chairman of Task Force Committee on Drugs of New York County Lawyers Association, 1986—. Member of executive committee of American Friends of Hebrew University of Jerusalem, 1982—; member of board of trustees of College of Mount St. Vincent and Franklin and Marshall College, both 1985—. *Military service:* U.S. Navy, 1944-46.

MEMBER: Laymen's National Bible Association (member of board of directors, 1976—), Fellowship of Christian Athletes (member of board of directors).

AWARDS, HONORS: Ph.D. from Greenville College, 1982, and St. John's University, Jamaica, N.Y., 1983; Golden Medal of Honor from Dutch baseball organization, 1983; Diamonte del Oro from Italian baseball organization, 1983; Imperial Order of the Sacred Treasure of Japan, 1984.

WRITINGS:

Hardball: The Education of a Baseball Commissioner, Times Books, 1987.

SIDELIGHTS: "My sixteen years as the Commissioner of Baseball marked a great watershed period in the history of America's national game," Bowie Kuhn told *CA*. "Given the formidable impact of baseball on our national culture, I thought that period merited a definitive treatment by the man who was professional baseball's chief executive officer during those years."

Kuhn's admirers and critics agree on one thing: for more than fifteen years the world of professional baseball was governed by a man of integrity and moral determination. The commissioner's critics claimed that his actions were biased in favor of the club owners who hired, and eventually fired, him. His admirers urged the public to believe that Kuhn's commitment was neither to the owners nor the players themselves but to the game of baseball as the American national pastime.

In a very personal way, *Hardball* reflects the highlights of baseball history from 1969 to 1984 and Kuhn's role in the development of the sport to its present form. Daniel Okrent wrote in the *New York Times Book Review* that Kuhn "never took his eye off his main public task: the marketing of his product." Kuhn dealt with reversing the decline of baseball as a spectator sport in the face of the increasing popularity of professional football. He faced the conflict between the obvious appeal of television and live broadcasting of night games and the equally apparent desire of baseball's most dedicated fans to preserve the traditional simplicity of the game. Kuhn also had to reconcile the issues of players' rights, weighing their demands for extensive freedom and astronomical salaries against the interests of the wealthy, powerful, and sometimes obstreperous men who paid his own salary. The commissioner's decisions were often controversial, and Kuhn himself was frequently the subject of sportswriters' wrath.

His memoirs, however, met with critical approval. Okrent called *Hardball* "a much worthier, more interesting and better-written book than the autobiographies we're used to getting." The reviewer added: "It is in many ways a remarkable book, by a man who deserved better than the hand that most baseball writers—myself included—dealt to Bowie Kuhn during his tenure." Jonathan Yardley reported in the *Washington Post Book World:* "Kuhn's account . . . is livelier and more pungent than might be expected. . . . Kuhn is a person of decided opinions, and he expresses them here [in *Hardball*] with a candor that baseball fans will find quite winning." He con-

cluded that the commissioner's "fierce integrity will be remembered long after the stuffed shirt has been forgotten."

BIOGRAPHICAL/CRITICAL SOURCES:

PERIODICALS

New York Times, February 18, 1987.
New York Times Book Review, March 8, 1987.
Washington Post, February 8, 1987, March 6, 1987.
Washington Post Book World, February 15, 1987.

*   *   *

KURTZ, Lester R. 1949-

PERSONAL: Born April 11, 1949, in York, Neb.; son of Merwin R. (a Methodist minister) and Jeannie B. (Anderson) Kurtz. *Education:* Westmar College, B.A., 1972; Yale University, M.A.R., 1974; University of Chicago, Ph.D., 1980. *Religion:* United Methodist.

ADDRESSES: Office—Department of Sociology, University of Texas at Austin, Austin, Tex. 78712.

CAREER: Illinois Institute of Technology, Chicago, visiting lecturer in sociology, 1979-80; University of Texas at Austin, assistant professor, 1980-86, associate professor of sociology and director of religious studies, 1986—. National co-chairman of United Campuses to Prevent Nuclear War, 1986—.

MEMBER: International Peace Research Association, American Sociological Association, Society for the Scientific Study of Religion, Association for the Sociology of Religion, Society for Values in Higher Education, Southwestern Social Science Association.

AWARDS, HONORS: Distinguished Book Award from Society for the Scientific Study of Religion, 1987, for *The Politics of Heresy*.

WRITINGS:

Evaluating Chicago Sociology: A Guide to the Literature, With an Annotated Bibliography, University of Chicago Press, 1984.
The Politics of Heresy: The Modernist Crisis in Roman Catholicism, University of California Press, 1986.
The Nuclear Cage: A Sociology of the Arms Race, Prentice-Hall, 1988.

Contributor to sociology journals. Book review editor of *American Journal of Sociology*, 1978-80.

WORK IN PROGRESS: Bibles and Bombs: The Rhetoric and Structure of Violence.

L

LACKEY, Mercedes R. 1950-

PERSONAL: Born June 24, 1950, in Chicago, Ill.; daughter of Edward George and Joyce (a housewife; maiden name, Anderson) Ritche; married Anthony Lackey, June 10, 1972. *Education:* Purdue University, B.S., 1972. *Politics:* "Esoteric." *Religion:* "Nontraditional."

ADDRESSES: Home and office—207 South Harvard, Tulsa, Okla. 74112. *Agent*—Russell Galen, 845 Third Ave., New York, N.Y. 10022.

CAREER: Artist's model in and near South Bend, Ind., 1975-81; Associates Data Processing, South Bend, computer programmer, 1979-82; CAIRS (survey and data processing firm), South Bend, surveyor, layout designer, and analyst, 1981-82; American Airlines, Tulsa, Okla., computer programmer, 1982—.

MEMBER: Science Fiction Writers of America.

WRITINGS:

FANTASY NOVELS

Arrows of the Queen, DAW Books, 1987.
Arrow's Flight, DAW Books, 1987.
Arrow's Fall, DAW Books, 1988.
Oathbound, DAW Books, 1988.
Oathbreakers, DAW Books, 1989.
Reap the Whirlwind, Baen, 1989.
Magic's Pawn, DAW Books, 1989.
Magic's Promise, DAW Books, in press.

OTHER

Burning Water (horror novel), Tor Books, 1989.

Has written lyrics for and recorded nearly fifty songs for Off-Centaur, a small recording company specializing in science fiction folk music.

SIDELIGHTS: Mercedes R. Lackey told *CA:* "I'm a storyteller; that's what I see as 'my job.' My stories come out of my characters; how those characters would react to the given situation. Maybe that's why I get letters from readers as young as thirteen and as old as sixty-odd. One of the reasons I write song lyrics is because I see songs as a kind of 'story pill'—they reduce a story to the barest essentials or encapsulate a particular crucial moment in time. I frequently will write a lyric when I am attempting to get to the heart of a crucial scene; I find that when I have done so, the scene has become absolutely clear in my mind, and I can write exactly what I wanted to say. Another reason is because of the kind of novels I am writing: that is, fantasy, set in an other-world semi-medieval atmosphere. Music is very important to medieval peoples; bards are the chief newsbringers. When I write the 'folk music' of these peoples, I am enriching my whole world, whether I actually use the song in the text or not.

"I began writing out of boredom; I continue out of addiction. I can't 'not' write, and as a result I have no social life! I began writing fantasy because I love it, but I try to construct my fantasy worlds with all the care of a 'high-tech' science fiction writer. I apply the principle of TANSTAFL ('There ain't no such thing as free lunch') to magic, for instance; in my worlds, magic is paid for, and the cost to the magician is frequently a high one. I try to keep my world as solid and real as possible; people deal with stubborn pumps, bugs in the porridge, and love-lives that refuse to become untangled, right along with invading armies and evil magicians. And I try to make all of my characters, even the 'evil magicians,' something more than flat stereotypes. Even evil magicians get up in the night and look for cookies, sometimes.

"I suppose that in everything I write I try to expound the creed I gave my character Di Tregarde in *Burning Water*—there's no such thing as 'one, true way'; the only answers worth having are the ones you find for yourself; leave the world better than you found it. Love, freedom, and the chance to do some good—they're the things worth living and dying for, and if you aren't willing to die for the things worth living for, you might as well turn in your membership in the human race."

AVOCATIONAL INTERESTS: Scuba diving.

*　　*　　*

LAMB, Patricia Frazer 1931-

PERSONAL: Born January 15, 1931, in Long Beach, Calif.; daughter of Richard B. (a car dealer) and Georgia King (a homemaker; maiden name, Lucas) Lamb; married John Millard Jones (a mechanic), 1951 (divorced, 1953; died, 1965); married second husband, 1953 (divorced, 1974); children: (second marriage) two sons. *Education:* Boston University,

B.A. (cum laude with distinction), 1966; Brandeis University, M.A., 1968; Cornell University, Ph.D., 1977.

ADDRESSES: Home—New Wilmington, Pa. *Office*—Department of English, Westminster College, New Wilmington, Pa. 16172. *Agent*—Martha Casselman, 1263 12th Ave., San Francisco, Calif. 94122.

CAREER: University of Kentucky, assistant professor of English, 1974-76; University of Nevada at Las Vegas, lecturer in English, 1977-78; Westminster College, New Wilmington, Pa., professor of English, 1978—.

MEMBER: International Association of Fantasy in the Arts, National Organization for Women, Popular Culture Association.

AWARDS, HONORS: Bunting fellowship from Radcliffe College, 1984-85; Jane Bakerman Award for excellence in feminist writing in a published article, 1986.

WRITINGS:

(With Richard L. Sprow) *Write This Way: A Manual of Rhetoric and Composition,* Westminster College, 1980.
(With Kathryn Joyce Hohlwein) *Touchstones: Letters Between Two Women, 1953-1964,* Harper, 1983.
(Contributor) Donald Palumbo, editor, *Erotic Universe: Sexuality and Fantastic Literature,* Greenwood Press, 1986.
Wayfaring Strangers: An Annotated Bibliography of Women Travelers in Africa, G. K. Hall, 1989.

SIDELIGHTS: An eleven-year correspondence between two college friends of the prefeminist era, *Touchstones: Letters Between Two Women: 1953-1964,* according to Ruth Ikerman in the *Los Angeles Times,* "speak[s] for many women of their generation." Patricia Frazer Lamb and Kathryn Joyce Hohlwein began exchanging letters after they married foreign men and moved away from each other. Postmarked from England, Germany, Lebanon, Tanganyika, and the United States, the letters illustrate the authors' growth from naive conformity to mature independence as they coped with unsatisfying marriages, childbirth, and the guilt that resulted from their attempts to balance family relationships with personal fulfillment. *Nation* reviewer Elizabeth Royte noted that although by the end of the book both women decided to divorce their husbands (Lamb becoming a feminist and Hohlwein a poet), each experienced a "moving awakening to self-knowledge and strength."

Lamb told *CA:* "*Touchstones* was the turning point in my writing life, and I am working on a second volume of letters written between 1964 and 1979. I have written all my life—letters and journals, especially—simply because I was impelled to do so. Now the Schlesinger Library at Radcliffe has requested the donation of all these papers (after my death), and I feel good about that. I now address some of my journal entries to 'F.P.' (Future Person), and we have long one-sided conversations as I imagine her sifting through the mound of papers looking for dissertation material a century hence."

AVOCATIONAL INTERESTS: Music, the nineteenth century, travel, travel literature, friendship, science fiction, movies, and television.

BIOGRAPHICAL/CRITICAL SOURCES:

PERIODICALS

Los Angeles Times, March 30, 1983.

Ms., July, 1983.
Nation, April 16, 1983.
New York Times Book Review, March 20, 1983.

*   *   *

LANDIS, J(ames) D(avid)   1942-

PERSONAL: Born June 30, 1942, in Springfield, Mass.; son of Edward (a lawyer) and Eve (a painter and teacher; maiden name, Saltman) Landis; married Patricia Lawrence Straus, August 15, 1964 (divorced); married Denise Evelyn Tiller (a writer), July 20, 1983; children: (first marriage) Sara Cass; (second marriage) Jacob Dean, Benjamin Nicholas. *Education:* Yale University, B.A. (magna cum laude), 1964.

ADDRESSES: Home—New York, N.Y. *Office*—William Morrow and Co., Inc., 105 Madison Ave., New York, N.Y. 10025. *Agent*—Kathy Robbins, The Robbins Office, 2 Dag Hammarskjold Plaza, New York, N.Y. 10017.

CAREER: Abelard-Schuman, New York, N.Y., assistant editor, 1966-67; William Morrow and Co., Inc., New York City, editor, beginning in 1967, later served as senior editor, until 1980, editorial director, senior vice-president, and publisher of Quill trade paperbacks, 1980-85, senior vice-president of company, and publisher and editor in chief of Beech Tree Books, all 1985—.

MEMBER: Phi Beta Kappa.

AWARDS, HONORS: Roger Klein Award for Editing, 1973; named Advocate Humanitarian, 1977.

WRITINGS:

FOR YOUNG PEOPLE

The Sisters Impossible, Knopf, 1979.
Love's Detective, Bantam, 1984.
Daddy's Girl, Morrow, 1984.
Joey and the Girls, Bantam, 1987.
Judy the Obscure, Harper, in press.

WORK IN PROGRESS: A novel, publication by Bantam expected in 1990.

*   *   *

LANDSMAN, Ned C.   1951-

PERSONAL: Born September 30, 1951, in New York, N.Y.; son of Donald (an engineer) and Shirley (a civil servant; maiden name, Kriploe) Landsman; married Alison Hubbard (a writer and musician), January, 1982; children: Emily. *Education:* Columbia University, B.A., 1973; University of Pennsylvania, Ph.D., 1979.

ADDRESSES: Office—Department of History, State University of New York at Stony Brook, Stony Brook, N.Y. 11794.

CAREER: State University of New York at Stony Brook, assistant professor, 1979-86, associate professor of history, 1986—.

MEMBER: Organization of American Historians, Columbia University Faculty Seminar on Early American History (program chairman, 1987-88).

AWARDS, HONORS: Richard McCormick Prize from New Jersey Historical Commission, 1986, for *Scotland and Its First American Colony.*

WRITINGS:

(Contributor) Michael Zuckerman, editor, *Friends and Neighbors: America's First Plural Society*, Temple University Press, 1982.
(Editor with Mary Maples Duan and Richard S. Dunn), *The Papers of William Penn*, Volume II, University of Pennsylvania Press, 1982.
Scotland and Its First American Colony, 1683-1765, Princeton University Press, 1986.

Contributor to history journals.

WORK IN PROGRESS: Research on evangelical religion in eighteenth-century Scotland.

SIDELIGHTS: Ned C. Landsman told *CA:* "Having long had an interest in the history of religion in early America, and undertaking graduate work at the University of Pennsylvania, I decided to undertake a doctoral thesis on the history of religion in the relatively neglected mid-Atlantic region of early America. This led me to Presbyterian immigrants and eventually to the Scottish colony in East New Jersey, founded in 1683, which became the focal point of Scottish settlement in the New York to Philadelphia corridor throughout the colonial period. That became the subject of my book, *Scotland and Its First American Colony.*

"My current research pursues the topic of evangelical culture in eighteenth-century Scotland and the trans-Atlantic world. There is at present an extraordinary surge of interest in eighteenth-century Scotland, most of it focused on the Scottish enlightenment. For American historians, at least as significant was a very different side of Scottish culture, that connected with the evangelical movement of mid-century, closely connected to the evangelical movement in America and of fundamental importance in shaping Scotland's provincial identity and America's growing identity as a British province within the larger provincial world."

*   *   *

LANE, Ann J(udith)   1931-

PERSONAL: Born July 27, 1931, in New York, N.Y.; daughter of Harry and Elizabeth (Brown) Lane; divorced; children: Leslie Patricia, Joni Alexandra. *Education:* Brooklyn College (now of the City University of New York), B.A., 1952; New York University, M.A., 1958; Columbia University, Ph.D., 1968.

ADDRESSES: *Office*—Department of History, Colgate University, Hamilton, N.Y. 13346.

CAREER: Sarah Lawrence College, Bronxville, N.Y., visiting instructor in history, 1965-66; Rutgers University, New Brunswick, N.J., assistant professor of history, 1968-71; John Jay College of Criminal Justice of the City University of New York, New York, N.Y., associate professor, 1971-80, professor of history, 1980-83; Colgate University, Hamilton, N.Y., professor of history, 1983—, director of women's studies, 1983—. Visiting professor at Sarah Lawrence College, 1975; research associate in women's history at Radcliffe College, 1977-79; founder and member of executive board of Columbia University's Women and Society, 1974. Member of board of directors of Louis M. Rabinowitz Foundation, 1972-76; consultant to Children's Television Workshop.

MEMBER: Women in the Historical Profession (member of executive board, 1971-74).

AWARDS, HONORS: Grant from American Council of Learned Societies, 1974.

WRITINGS:

(Editor) *The Debate Over Slavery: Stanley Elkins and His Critics*, University of Illinois Press, 1971.
The Bronxville Affair: National Outrage and Black Reaction, Kennikat, 1971.
(Contributor) Berenice Carroll, editor, *Liberating Women's History: Theoretical and Critical Essays*, University of Illinois Press, 1976.
(Editor) *Mary Ritter Beard: A Sourcebook*, Schocken, 1977.
(Editor and author of introduction) *The Charlotte Perkins Gilman Reader: The Yellow Wallpaper and Other Fiction*, Pantheon, 1980.

Also contributor to *The Age of Industrialization in America: Essays in Social Structure and Cultural Values*, Free Press, 1968, and *Failure of a Dream: Essays in the History of American Socialism*, Doubleday, 1974.

WORK IN PROGRESS: *Women's History in the Courtroom: The EEOC vs. Sears, Roebuck, and Company.*

SIDELIGHTS: Ann J. Lane told *CA:* "'What would happen if one woman told the truth about her life? The world would split open.' These words, written by the poet Muriel Rukeyser, embody the spirit of feminist scholarship, and reflect my personal and intellectual goals as a writer and a teacher."

BIOGRAPHICAL/CRITICAL SOURCES:

PERIODICALS

Times Literary Supplement, March 17, 1972.

*   *   *

LANE, Harlan (Lawson)   1936-

PERSONAL: Born August 19, 1936, in Brooklyn, N.Y.; son of Benjamin and Del Lane. *Education:* Columbia University, B.A. and M.A., both 1958; Harvard University, Ph.D., 1960; Sorbonne, University of Paris, Doc. es lettres, 1973.

ADDRESSES: *Office*—Department of Psychology, 133 NI, Northeastern University, 360 Huntington Ave., Boston, Mass. 02115.

CAREER: University of Michigan, Ann Arbor, assistant professor, 1960-64, associate professor, 1964-67, professor of psychology, 1967-71, founder and director of Center for Research on Language and Language Behavior, 1965-69; University of Paris, Sorbonne, Paris, France, professor of linguistics, 1969-73; University of California, San Diego, La Jolla, visiting professor of linguistics, 1973-74; Northeastern University, Boston, Mass., professor of psychology, 1974—, distinguished professor, 1985-87, chairman of department, 1974-79, founder of Center for Research in Hearing, Speech, and Language, 1986. Research associate at Centre National de la Recherche Scientifique, 1985—; investigator for Massachusetts Eye and Ear Infirmary, 1985—; research affiliate of Research Laboratory of Electronics at Massachusetts Institute of Technology, 1986—; visiting fellow at Japan Society for the Promotion of Science, 1986.

MEMBER: American Psychological Association (fellow), Psychonomic Society, American Association of Phonetic Science, Registry of Interpreters for the Deaf (honorary member).

AWARDS, HONORS: Award from American Speech and Hearing Association, 1969, for best article; Thomas J. Wilson Memorial Prize from Harvard University, 1976, for *The Wild Boy of Aveyron;* Robert D. Klein Memorial Award from Northeastern University, 1984, for distinguished research; officier de l'Ordre des Palmes Academiques, 1985—; Book Award from President's Commission on the Handicapped, 1986, for *When the Mind Hears: A History of the Deaf;* Thomas Hopkins Gallaudet Award from Massachusetts State Association of the Deaf, 1987, for distinguished service; Frederick C. Schreiber Distinguished Service Award from National Association of the Deaf, 1987. Grants from U.S. Office of Education, 1962-65 and 1965-69, National Science Foundation, 1963-64, 1977-81, 1979, and 1982-85, Rockefeller Foundation and National Library of Medicine, 1966-71, National Endowment for the Humanities, 1978-80 and 1981-83, North Atlantic Treaty Organization's Advanced Study Institute, 1979, National Institutes of Health, 1980-83 and 1986-91, and Sloan Foundation, 1983.

WRITINGS:

(With Daryl Bem) *A Laboratory Manual for the Control and Analysis of Behavior,* Brooks/Cole, 1964.
(With Guy Capelle) *The World's Research in Language Learning,* Volume I: *Europe,* UNESCO, 1969.
(With Francois Grosjean and others) *Introduction a l'etude du langage* (title means ''An Introduction to the Study of Language''), University of Paris-Vincennes, 1972.
The Wild Boy of Aveyron: A History of the Education of Retarded, Deaf, and Hearing Children, Harvard University Press, 1976.
The Wild Boy of Burundi: Psychological Catastrophes of Childhood, Random House, 1979.
(Editor with Grosjean) *Current Perspectives on American Sign Language,* Lawrence Erlbaum Associates, 1980.
(Translator with Franklin Philip) *Major Philosophical Works of Etienne Bonnot de Condillac,* Lawrence Erlbaum Associates, 1982.
(Editor with Philip) *The Deaf Experience: Classics in Language and Education,* Harvard University Press, 1984.
When the Mind Hears: A History of the Deaf, Random House, 1984.
(Contributor) Roselyn Rosen, editor, *NAD Forum '86: Life and Work in the Twenty-First Century; The Deaf Person of Tomorrow,* National Association of the Deaf, 1986.
(Contributor) Marina McIntire, editor, *Interpreting: The Art of Cross-Cultural Mediation,* Registry of Interpreters for the Deaf, 1986.

Contributor to *Encyclopedia of Deaf People and Deafness.* Contributor to scholarly journals. Founder and editor of *Language and Language Behavior Abstracts.*

WORK IN PROGRESS: Research on bilingual education and the deaf, psychology and deafness, and speech deterioration in deafened adults.

BIOGRAPHICAL/CRITICAL SOURCES:

PERIODICALS

Atlantic Monthly, February, 1979.
New York Times Book Review, February 4, 1979, October 21, 1984.
Times Literary Supplement, May 29, 1987.

LANG, Mabel L(ouise)   1917-

PERSONAL: Born November 12, 1917, in Utica, N.Y.; daughter of Louis Bernard and Katherine (Werdge) Lang. *Education:* Cornell University, B.A., 1939; Bryn Mawr College, M.A., 1940, Ph.D., 1943.

ADDRESSES: Home—905 New Gulph Rd., Bryn Mawr, Pa. 19010. *Office*—Department of Greek, Bryn Mawr College, Bryn Mawr, Pa. 19010.

CAREER: Bryn Mawr College, Bryn Mawr, Pa., instructor, 1943-46, assistant professor, 1946-50, associate professor of classical philology, 1950-59, professor of Greek, 1959-88, chairman of department, 1960-88. American School of Classical Studies at Athens, chairman of admissions and fellowships committee, 1966-72, chairman of managing committee, 1975-80. Blegen Distinguished Research Professor at Vassar College, 1976-77; Martin Classical Lecturer at Oberlin College, 1982. Summer archaeological fieldwork at Gordion, 1952-56, and Pylos, 1957-64.

MEMBER: American Philosophical Society, American Academy of Arts and Sciences, American Philological Association, Archaeological Institute of America, Society for the Promotion of Hellenistic Studies (England), Classical Association (England), German Archaeological Institute.

AWARDS, HONORS: Guggenheim fellow, 1953-54; Fulbright fellow in Greece, 1959-60; Litt.D. from College of the Holy Cross, 1975, and Colgate University, 1978.

WRITINGS:

(With Margaret Crosby) *Weights, Measures, and Tokens,* American School of Classical Studies at Athens, 1964.
The Palace of Nestor at Pylos in Western Messenia, Volume II: *The Frescoes,* Princeton University Press, 1969.
Graffiti and Dipinti, American School of Classical Studies at Athens, 1976.
Herodotean Narrative and Discourse, Harvard University Press, 1984.

Contributor to scholarly journals.

WORK IN PROGRESS: Ostraka in the Athenian Agora, for American School of Classical Studies at Athens.

BIOGRAPHICAL/CRITICAL SOURCES:

PERIODICALS

Classical World, March/April, 1986.
Virginia Quarterly Review, summer, 1985.

*   *   *

LANGDALE, Cecily   1939-

PERSONAL: Born July 27, 1939, in New York, N.Y.; daughter of A. Barnett (an educator) and Elizabeth (a teacher and librarian; maiden name, Armstrong) Langdale; married Roy Davis (an art dealer), July 24, 1972. *Education:* Swarthmore College, B.A., 1961.

ADDRESSES: Home and office—231 East 60th St., New York, N.Y. 10022.

CAREER: Davis Galleries, New York, N.Y., gallery assistant, 1961-63, 1964-67; Hirschl & Adler Galleries, New York City, assistant director of American Department, 1967-73; Davis & Long Co. (art gallery), New York City, associate director,

1973-80; Davis & Langdale Co. (art gallery), New York City, partner, 1980—.

MEMBER: Art Dealers Association of America, Cosmopolitan Club.

WRITINGS:

(With Betsy G. Fryberger) *Gwen John: Paintings and Drawings From the Collection of John Quinn and Others*, Stanford University Press, 1982.
Monotypes by Maurice Prendergast in the Terra Museum of American Art, Terra Museum, 1984.
(With David Fraser Jenkins) *Gwen John: An Interior Life*, Phaidon, 1985, Rizzoli International, 1986.
Gwen John: With a Catalogue Raisonne of the Paintings and a Selection of the Drawings, Yale University Press, 1987.

WORK IN PROGRESS: Research on the monotypes of Maurice Prendergast.

BIOGRAPHICAL/CRITICAL SOURCES:

PERIODICALS

Times Literary Supplement, December 18, 1987.

*   *   *

LAPPE, Marc   1943-

PERSONAL: Surname is pronounced "Lah-pay"; born January 14, 1943, in Irvington, N.J.; son of Paul and Jeanette (Baum) Lappe; married Nichol Lovera, November 5, 1977; children: Anthony, Anna, Matthew, Martine, Gina. *Education:* Wesleyan University, B.A., 1964; University of Pennsylvania, Ph.D., 1968.

ADDRESSES: Office—University of Illinois at Chicago, Department of Medical Education, 9th Floor, 808 S. Wood St., Chicago, Ill. 60612.

CAREER: State University of New York College at Purchase, acting assistant professor of biology, 1975-76; Institute of Society, Ethics, and Life Sciences, Hastings-on-Hudson, N.Y., associate for biological sciences, 1971-76; affiliated with California Department of Health Services, as chief of office of Health, Law, and Values, 1976-77, as chief of office of planning and evaluation, 1977-79, and as chief of hazard evaluation system, 1979-81; University of California at Berkeley, adjunct associate professor of health policy, 1981-86; University of Illinois at Chicago, director of humanistic studies program, 1986-88, professor of ethics and health policy, 1988—. Fellow of Hastings Center.

MEMBER: American Public Health Association.

AWARDS, HONORS: Warner-Chilcott Award; Anna Fuller Fund fellow; honorary post-doctoral fellow of University of California, Berkeley.

WRITINGS:

Genetic Politics: The Limits of Biological Control, Simon & Schuster, 1980.
Germs That Won't Die: Medical Consequences of the Misuse of Antibiotics, Doubleday, 1982.
Broken Code: The Exploitation of DNA, Siérra Books, 1985.

WORK IN PROGRESS: A revised edition of *Germs That Won't Die*, titled *When Antibiotics Fail: Restoration of the Ecology of the Body; Fooling Mother Nature: Health Consequences of* *Disturbing the Internal and External Environment*, for North Atlantic Books.

SIDELIGHTS: In *Broken Code: The Exploitation of DNA* Marc Lappe discusses industry's use of gene-splicing to increase profits as well as its tendency to dominate a science originally developed by public institutions. Fierce competition among corporations marketing genetically produced goods has encouraged talented scientists to leave universities for the private sector and withhold knowledge from each other. "A respected critic of the health and genetic sciences," according to *Los Angeles Times Book Review* contributor David Graber, Lappe advocates using the technology for the public good and criticizes the private sector for stifling scientific exchange. Observed Graber, Lappe's "concern for the social responsibility of science and scientists, and his socialist ideology, are openly, objectively and dispassionately presented." The reviewer found the detailed and scholarly account "excessively daunting" at times, but he praised it, in the end, as "a real book, by a scientist-author who knows what he's talking about."

AVOCATIONAL INTERESTS: Skin diving, reading Franz Kafka, and swimming.

BIOGRAPHICAL/CRITICAL SOURCES:

PERIODICALS

Los Angeles Times Book Review, August 18, 1985.

*   *   *

LARSEN, Jack Lenor   1927-

PERSONAL: Born August 5, 1927, in Seattle, Wash.; son of Elmer Lenor and Mabel Larsen. *Education:* Graduated from University of Washington, Seattle; Cranbrook Academy of Art, M.F.A., 1951. *Politics:* Liberal. *Religion:* Protestant.

ADDRESSES: Office—Jack Lenor Larsen, Inc., 41 East 11th St., New York, N.Y. 10003. *Agent*—Charlotte Sheedy Literary Agency, Inc., 145 West 86th St., New York, N.Y. 10024.

CAREER: Jack Lenor Larsen, Inc., New York, N.Y., owner and design director, 1951—. Owner of Larsen Design Studio, 1958, Jack Lenor Larsen International (Zurich, Switzerland), 1963, Thaibok Fabrics Ltd., 1972—, Larsen Carpet and Larsen Leather, 1973—, and Larsen Furniture Division, 1976—. Co-director of fabric design department at Philadelphia College of Art, 1959-61; artist in residence at Royal College of Art, 1975; chairman of Haystack Mountain School of Crafts, 1976-81, then appointed honorary chairman; affiliate professor at University of Washington, Seattle; associate of Cranbrook Academy of Art. Designer and director of traveling exhibitions; design director and member of United States commission of XIII Trienale di Milano, 1964; curator of exhibitions at Museum of Modern Art; fabric designs represented in permanent collections at Museum of Modern Art, Victoria and Albert Museum, Metropolitan Museum of Art, Art Institute of Chicago, Archives of American Art, Cooper-Hewitt Museum, Fashion Institute of Technology, and Royal Scottish Museum. Overseer of Parsons School of Design; member of international advisory council of Pilchuck Glass Center; life member of Surface Design; member of board of trustees of Textile Museum, Washington, D.C., and Arango Design Foundation; member of advisory board of Fiberworks; member of council of advisers of Golden Eye Foundation; consultant to U.S. Department of State.

MEMBER: World Craft Council (past president in United States), Centre International de la Tapisserie Ancienne et Moderne, American Crafts Council (fellow; member of board of trustees; president, 1981—), American National Color Association (member of advisory board), Contemporary Craft Association (member of board of advisers), American Society of Interior Designers (associate; fellow), Decorative Arts Association (member of advisory committee and governing committee), Home Fashions League, Society of Arts and Crafts (member of board of trustees), Royal Society of Art (fellow), Royal Horticultural Society, Pierre Pauli Association (member of executive committee), Architectural League of New York (vice-president, 1966-67), Municipal Art Society of New York (life member), Arts Club of Chicago, Brooklyn Botanical Garden, Metropolitan Museum of Art, Metropolitan Opera Guild (fellow), Crescent Spa of Dallas (life member; member of board of governors), Omicron Nu.

AWARDS, HONORS: Design awards include Gold Medals from XIII Trienale di Milano, 1964, and American Institute of Architects, 1968, Elsie De Wolfe Award from American Institute of Interior Designers, 1971, Tommy, the American Print Designer Award, 1971, Pace Setter Award from *House Beautiful,* 1973, Nieman-Marcus Award for Distinguished Service in the Field of Fashion, 1984, and Wise Owl Award from National Home Furnishings League, 1985; Elliot Noyes fellow at Aspen International Design Conference, 1978; fellow of American Craft Council, 1978; D.F.A. from Parsons School of Design, 1981, Rhode Island School of Design, 1982, and Philadelphia College of Art, 1982; named Royal Designer for Industry by Royal Society of Arts, 1983.

WRITINGS:

(With Azalea Thorpe) *Elements of Weaving,* Doubleday, 1967.
(With Alfred Buehler, Bronwen Solyom, and Garrett Solyom) *The Dyer's Art: Ikat, Batik, Plangi,* Van Nostrand, 1971.
(With Mildred Constantine) *Beyond Craft: The Art Fabric,* Van Nostrand, 1972.
(With Jeanne Weeks) *Fabric for Interiors,* Van Nostrand, 1975.
(With Constantine) *The Art Fabric: Mainstream,* Van Nostrand, 1981.
(With Betty Freudenheim) *Interlacing: The Elemental Fabric,* Kodansha International, 1986.

Editor of *Design Since 1945,* 1983-84.

WORK IN PROGRESS: Interior Fabrics Today.

SIDELIGHTS: Jack Lenor Larsen told *CA:* "Jack Lenor Larsen, Inc., is today a dominant force in international fabrics and a major influence on environmental design. Mentors of the Larsen Design Studio include both masters of old (William Morris, Mariano Fortuny, and Louis C. Tiffany), as well as the weavers of ancient and tribal cultures. The Larsen look began with the power weaving of 'hand-woven' fabrics of varied yarns and random repeats. The Larsen team looks to evolving needs, creates within new and old technologies, and sustains quality and style. Our prints are not applied graphics, but a handicraft expressing the marriage of the thirsty cloth and the liquid dye.

"Many of our collections derive from a culture or a people. Others have grown out of involvement with new technologies. These new techniques are landmarked by many developments over the years, including the first printed velvet upholsteries in 1959 and the first stretch upholsteries in 1961. I stress the need for a brave new vision, and a new kind of environmental design team, in which all of the design disciplines will contribute as a unit.

"As part of a logical growth process, I acquired Thaibok Fabrics in 1972, established Larsen Carpet and Larsen Leather in 1973, and Larsen Furniture in 1976. Today the Larsen organization is international, with production centers in thirty countries and Larsen showrooms in as many major cities around the world."

*   *   *

LARSEN, Jens Peter   1902-1988

OBITUARY NOTICE: Born June 14, 1902, in Copenhagen, Denmark; died of complications from gallbladder surgery, August 22, 1988, in Copenhagen, Denmark. Musicologist, educator, and author. Larsen published books and articles on Austrian composer Franz Joseph Haydn, including *The New Grove Haydn,* and was working on a study of Haydn's musical predecessors at the time of his death. He had a distinguished academic career as a musicologist that included teaching positions at Copenhagen University and visiting lectureships at the universities of California, Berkeley, and of Wisconsin. He was also musicologist-in-residence at the John F. Kennedy Center in Washington, D.C. Larsen belonged to the Royal Danish Academy of Science and Letters and served as chairman of the Danish Society for Musicology from 1959 to 1963. Awarded Austria's Grand Golden Cross of Honor, Larsen was also noted for his study of composer George Frederick Handel, publishing *Handel's Messiah* in 1957 and *Handel Studies* in 1972.

OBITUARIES AND OTHER SOURCES:

BOOKS

International Who's Who in Music and Musicians' Directory, 9th edition, Melrose, 1980.

PERIODICALS

Chicago Tribune, August 28, 1988.

*   *   *

La SALLE, Dorothy (Marguerite)   1895-1980

OBITUARY NOTICE—See index for *CA* sketch: Born June 2, 1895, in Lake Geneva, Wis.; died October 6, 1980, in Sharon, Conn. Educator, administrator, and author. A specialist in physical education and public health, La Salle worked in public service from the 1920s to the end of World War II, employed by the U.S. Office of Education, the White House Conference on Child Health and Protection, and the public schools of Detroit, Michigan, and East Orange, New Jersey. She was a professor of health and physical education at Wayne State University from 1946 until she retired in 1965. La Salle's books include *Play Activities for Elementary Schools, Physical Education for the Classroom Teacher, Guidance of Children Through Physical Education,* and, with Gladys Geer, *Health Instruction for Today's Schools.*

OBITUARIES AND OTHER SOURCES:

Date of death provided by Wayne State University.

BOOKS

International Authors and Writers Who's Who, 8th edition, Melrose, 1977.

LAURIE, Michael M. 1932-

PERSONAL: Born January 19, 1932, in Dundee, Scotland; immigrated to United States, naturalized citizen. *Education:* University of Reading, Diploma in Library Administration, 1956; University of Pennsylvania, M.L.A., 1962.

ADDRESSES: Office—Department of Landscape Architecture, University of California, Berkeley, Calif. 94720.

CAREER: Affiliated with the office of Sylvia Crowe, London, England, 1956-58, and the Department of Landscape Architecture at University of California, Berkeley, 1962—.

MEMBER: American Society of Landscape Architects (fellow), Landscape Institute (England; associate).

WRITINGS:

An Introduction to Landscape Architecture, Elsevier, 1975, 2nd edition, 1986.
(With Thomas D. Church and Grace Hall) *Gardens Are for People*, McGraw, 1983.

WORK IN PROGRESS: Urban Parks and Open Spaces.

*   *   *

LAURO, Shirley (Shapiro) Mezvinsky 1933-
(Shirley Mezvinsky)

PERSONAL: Born November 18, 1933, in Des Moines, Iowa; daughter of Phillip (in business) and Helen Frances (a secretary; maiden name, Davidson) Shapiro; married Norton Mezvinsky (a professor), July 22, 1956 (divorced in 1966); married Louis Paul Lauro (a psychoanalyst), August 18, 1973; children: (first marriage) Andrea Lynn. *Education:* Northwestern University, B.S. (cum laude), 1955; University of Wisconsin—Madison, M.S., 1957, graduate study, 1958-59; graduate study at Columbia University, 1963 and 1970-73, and at City University of New York. *Politics:* Democrat. *Religion:* Jewish.

ADDRESSES: Home—275 Central Park W., New York, N.Y. 10024. *Agent*—Gilbert Parker, William Morris Agency, 1350 Ave. of the Americas, New York, N.Y. 10019.

CAREER: University of Wisconsin—Madison, instructor in drama and literature, 1959; professional film, television, and stage actress in New York, N.Y., Boston, Mass., Detroit, Mich., Chicago, Ill., and Wisconsin, beginning in 1959; writer, beginning in 1961; City College of the City University of New York, New York City, instructor in speech and theater, 1967-71; Yeshiva University, New York City, instructor in speech, theater, and playwriting, 1971-76; Ensemble Studio Theater, New York City, literary consultant, 1975-80, production critic, 1975—, member's council, 1975—, resident playwright, 1976—; Manhattan Community College, New York City, instructor in speech, 1978; Marymount Manhattan College, New York City, instructor in English and creative writing, 1978-79. Resident playwright at Alley Theater, Houston, Tex., 1987; actress and free-lance editor; affiliated with American Place Theater Women's Project.

MEMBER: Writers Guild of America, P.E.N., League of Professional Theater Women (vice-president), Authors League, Authors Guild, Dramatists Guild.

AWARDS, HONORS: Residency at Edna St. Vincent Millay Colony, 1977; New York State Council on the Arts Program alternate, 1977; Samuel French Short Play Awards, 1979, for "Nothing Immediate" and "Open Admissions"; Heidemann Prize for best one-act play from Actors' Theater of Louisville in Great American Play Contest, 1980, for "The Coal Diamond" and "Nothing Immediate"; Off-Off Broadway Playwright's Residency Award, 1980; Susan Blackburn Prize for best English-language play by a woman finalist, 1980, for "Margaret and Kit"; award for best play on a Jewish theme from National Foundation for Jewish Culture, 1981, for "The Contest"; Elizabeth Hull-Kate Warriner Award for best play on a controversial theme from New York Dramatists Guild, 1981, for "Open Admissions"; Universal Pictures Playwright's Commission, 1982; playwrights commission from Actors Theater of Louisville, 1982; residency grant from National Conference on Jewish Playwriting, 1983; playwrights fellowship from New York Foundation for the Arts, 1984-85; John Simon Guggenheim playwrights fellowship, 1985-86; playwrights fellowship from National Endowment for the Arts, 1986-87; finalist in Maude Adams Playwriting Competition, 1988, for "Pearls on the Moon."

WRITINGS:

(Under name Shirley Mezvinsky) *The Edge* (novel), Doubleday, 1965.

PLAYS

(Under name Shirley Lauro) "The Contest" (three-act), first produced in Houston, Tex., at Alley Theater, May, 1975; produced Off-Broadway at Ensemble Studio Theater, October 21, 1976.
(Under name Shirley Lauro) *Open Admissions* (one-act; first produced Off-Broadway at Ensemble Studio Theater, April, 1979; revised version produced in two acts in New Haven, Conn., at Long Wharf Theater, October, 1982; produced on Broadway at Music Box, January 29, 1984), one-act version published in *An Empty Space* [and] *Open Admissions* [and] *Nothing Immediate*, Samuel French, 1980, two-act version, Samuel French, 1984.
"Nothing Immediate" (one-act), first produced Off-Broadway at Double Image Theater, June, 1979, published in *An Empty Space* [and] *Open Admissions* [and] *Nothing Immediate*, Samuel French, 1980.
(Under name Shirley Lauro) *I Don't Know Where You're Coming From at All!* (one-act; first produced Off-Broadway at Ensemble Studio Theater, April, 1979), Samuel French, 1981.
(Under name Shirley Lauro) *The Coal Diamond* (one-act; first produced Off-Broadway at Ensemble Studio Theater, June, 1979), Dramatists Play Service, 1979.
"In the Garden of Eden" (one-act), first produced in Malvern, Pa., at People's Light and Theater Company, July, 1982; produced as "Set-Up" in Malvern, Pa., at People's Light and Theater Company, July, 1982; produced Off-Broadway at Ensemble Studio Theater, October, 1986.
"Sunday Go to Meetin'" (one-act), first produced in Louisville, Ky., at Actor's Theater, June, 1986; produced in New York at League of Professional Theater Women, May, 1988.
"Margaret and Kit" (two-act), first produced as a staged reading in Amenia, N.Y., at Ensemble Studio Theater Summer Conference, July, 1979; produced Off-Broadway at Playwrights Horizons, December, 1982.
"Pearls on the Moon" (two-act), first produced in Houston, Tex., at Alley Theater, December, 1987.

OTHER

Contributor of short stories to periodicals, including *Jewish Horizon* and *New Idea*.

WORK IN PROGRESS: A film adaptation of "Open Admissions"; "A Piece of My Heart," a full-length play adapted from Keith Walker's novel of the same title.

SIDELIGHTS: Shirley Mezvinsky Lauro, who became a playwright after publishing a novel, has won acclaim for plays such as "The Contest," "The Coal Diamond," and the Tony Award-nominee "Open Admissions." Her plays impress reviewers with their sincerity, freshness, and ability to evoke time, place, and character. *New York Times* theater critic Mel Gussow, reviewing her first play, praised Lauro's "natural talent for the theater" and described her as "a playwright to be encouraged."

Lauro's first written work, the novel *The Edge*, displays many of the virtues later praised in her plays. Reviewing the book in *Saturday Review*, Daniel Stern commended Lauro's "piece of genuine, artfully created experience . . . written with the assurance of an artist and with great (and, for the most part, unsentimental) sensibility." Lauro examines the plight of a young, intelligent modern woman who is an unfulfilled and unchallenged housewife, involving the reader in a potentially humdrum tale by relating the woman's thoughts and experiences during a typical day. According to Stern, the story works because of the character's "almost involuntary, bitter charm" and the "absolute authenticity of most of the inner exploration." Faulting Lauro for introducing a dominating mother as an apparent explanation for the protagonist's problems when "the rest of the novel suggests [that] the tragedy of the Lois Markses is a general one today," Stern nonetheless characterized the work as an "excellent literary debut."

In 1975 Lauro received favorable reviews for her first play, "The Contest," in which a poor, musically talented girl tries to cope with her mother's addiction to contests and disregard for her family. Describing it as "an old-fashioned, naturalistic slice-of-life," Gussow asserted that the play "rises far above its genre." Lauro's own experiences growing up in a midwestern Jewish family informed the work, which Patricia O'Haire of the *New York Daily News* deemed "a pot of gold." Noted Gussow, "Lauro is dealing with familiar material in a traditional manner, but the characters are freshly observed, the situation richly specific, and the play has a dramatic impact."

Lauro's understatement and affection for her characters impressed critics, including Gussow, when "The Coal Diamond," a one-act play, opened in 1979. The work explores the relationships among four women who work at an insurance firm and drew Gussow's compliments for effectively evoking time, place, and community. Playing bridge on their lunch break, the women gossip until their card game becomes a vicious struggle for pride and position. Reviewing the play for the *New York Post*, Marilyn Stasio judged it "an unflawed gem."

In 1981 Lauro struck nerves when "Open Admissions," her hard-hitting study of discrimination and education, opened Off-Broadway. The play focuses on the conflict between Calvin Jefferson, a black student who desperately wants to improve himself, and Alice Miller, the overworked and underinspired white teacher who fails to provide the education Calvin demands. Praised for illuminating the flaws of an open-admissions college, the one-act play "is a small powerhouse," wrote Gussow. Observed the critic, Lauro "needs less than 30 min-

utes to give us a comprehensive picture of a crucial emotional conflict as well as perceptive investigation of the limits of an educational system." The play sent teachers out of the theater searching their consciences, some weeping in self-recognition, and arguing the question of who was at fault, recounted actress Marilyn Rockafellow in a 1984 *New York Times* article.

Lauro expanded "Open Admissions" for Broadway in 1984, garnering mixed reviews yet prompting *New York Times* reviewer Frank Rich to admit, "there's no denying [the play's] power to shake an audience." Whereas the earlier production featured only the student and the teacher, for Broadway Lauro added an entire classroom of students, another teacher, and members of the principal characters' families. Several writers criticized the additions. Rich, for example, lamented that many of the new scenes and characters contributed little more than running time, but he concluded that they "do not rob the play's central conflict of its force." In another *New York Times* article Benedict Nightingale asserted, "Amplification has muffled and muted the sum impact" of the play, an opinion Catharine Hughes echoed in *America*. Nevertheless, each critic qualified his complaints, confirming the play's power. Assessed Rich, "['Open Admissions'] is a rarity for Broadway these days: It thrusts us onto the front line of an agonizing contemporary social crisis and refuses to show us the easy way out."

MEDIA ADAPTATIONS: "Open Admissions" was adapted for television by Columbia Broadcasting System (CBS-TV) in 1987.

CA INTERVIEW

CA interviewed Shirley Mezvinsky Lauro by telephone on June 12, 1987, at her home in New York City.

CA: Though you're better known as a playwright and were a professional actress, your first major publication was a novel, The Edge, *in 1965. Did you come to writing through wanting to have a career in theater?*

LAURO: I think I was on a double track at the beginning. I was always interested in theater, but in those years, if you were a woman, you were destined either to act, do costume design, or teach. So my theater interest manifested itself at first through acting. Parallel to this theater interest was a writing interest, but when I started out, the only woman playwright was Lillian Hellman—or at least she was the only one I had heard of. There were no role models. It wasn't considered a field for a woman to enter. Women writers were poets or fiction writers. So I turned to fiction, writing short stories and then my novel, *The Edge*. And while all of this was going on I was also acting in regional theater companies and stock and educational TV.

With the publication of *The Edge* I stopped acting and began to devote full time to writing and teaching. I started a second novel and was in a creative writers seminar at Columbia University and would bring in chapters every week. This was the late sixties and a lot of barriers for women were breaking down then. Richard Ellmann taught the seminar and I remember everybody thinking the novel I was working on had so much dialogue in it that it sounded like a play. Someone suggested I should try it as a play. I dropped out of the seminar and a year later rewrote the material in dramatic form. It became my first play, "The Contest."

CA: You were already acting in college, weren't you?

LAURO: I was actually a child actress appearing in all kinds of theatrical events in Iowa from the time I was three or four. I sang and danced and recited "pieces" my mother or elocution teacher made up. My mother had named me after [child actress] Shirley Temple and I think her dream was that I would become her successor. By the time I was in college I was very seriously interested in acting and was very active both at Northwestern and in grad school at Wisconsin.

CA: When did you actually begin writing?

LAURO: I began writing also at a very young age—third or fourth grade. I was editor of my high school paper and all that sort of thing. But it was in grad school at Wisconsin that I came in contact with [Irish author] Elizabeth Bowen, who was very influential in my life. She was writer in residence at Wisconsin and I took a creative writing seminar with her and she became very interested in my work. She submitted my short stories to her own agent, who took me on, and when I wrote *The Edge* she read the manuscript for me and served as critic and editor before I ever submitted it to a publisher. Through the years she remained a wonderful mentor and friend to me, and I am deeply indebted to her.

CA: "Open Admissions" was a one-act play produced first in 1979 at the Ensemble Studio Theater, then enlarged and produced on Broadway in 1984. The conflict of the play centers around the practice of passing minority students through school and college without educating them. Did the idea grow out of your own teaching?

LAURO: Yes, it did. I was a full-time college instructor here for ten years, and it certainly grew out of my own experience with teaching in the inner city. There wasn't one student who became the character of Calvin, the young protagonist; he was based on many young men and women that I came in contact with in my teaching.

CA: Your topic is still a very timely one.

LAURO: The play has just been made into a television special for CBS, to be aired this fall. Yes, it couldn't be more timely. I think the problem is even worse now than it was at the time I was teaching.

CA: Your characters are often frustrated by the limitations that arise from their upbringing or their place in society. Do your plays usually begin with the idea of such a character in a difficult situation?

LAURO: In retrospect I would say yes, that seems to be what I'm interested in and what I'm drawn to. I think on a subjective level I just move into a story and it feels comfortable to me if I feel any emotion toward the characters. If I think back on it, it seems that almost all of the characters in my stories have been people who can be described by what you've just said. The novel *The Edge*, which was kind of a pre-women's lib novel—it came out around the same time as Betty Friedan's *Feminine Mystique*, we were handled by the same agent, and it had the same kind of response—was about a young married woman who had wanted to be an actress but gave up the career and was living in a very small town in the Midwest and having a nervous breakdown. She kills herself at the end of the book. That was 1965, before there was such a thing as women's lib.

Starting with that character, I have certainly been drawn to people coming out of circumstances in which they've been frustrated, pushed down, not allowed to experience life at the level at which they might if they had been born at a different place or time or circumstance. I am drawn to people forced to buck tremendous odds in order to find any measure of happiness or fulfillment.

CA: I thought The Edge *was a very powerful novel, by the way. And it was interesting that Martha Foley had a comment on the dust jacket about how strongly men responded to it.*

LAURO: Their reaction was quite extraordinary at that time. One of the most perceptive reviews I got on the novel was from the *Saturday Review* by a man who is still reviewing and writing, Daniel Stern. I remember that we went to lunch, and he was very taken with the book and felt I had identified something under the surface and pervasive among American women. He was extremely interested in the topic and very sympathetic. There were a great many men at that time, more than there are not, who were troubled by the condition of women in society, and were in fact more sympathetic and more open about identifying with the situation.

CA: Your midwestern background is very important to your writing. New York seems to sharpen the midwestern sensibility in its transplanted writers.

LAURO: Yes. I think I continue to draw on my midwestern roots in my work. In fact, though I live here in New York, I've found that my work more and more seems to reflect where I came from. My new play, "Pearls on the Moon," is set in a mental sanitarium in a tiny town in Iowa and deals with midwestern people. People always say that Iowa is a good place to come *from*. I think I do carry that sensibility with me, and it does become sharpened. Rural things continue to obsess me as a writer, even though I am living in an urban setting. In "Open Admissions," the teacher is a transplanted woman from Iowa coming to grips with urban education. And I have found quite a large reception for my work in the Midwest.

CA: Do you write every day?

LAURO: I write every day when I'm writing. If I am on a project, I work seven days a week. I can't take a day or two off and come back to it; I feel like I've lost a week. I used to be a night writer until I was a mother, and after that I turned into a dawn writer, so that I'm prone to get up at four-thirty or five in the morning and work through until twelve or one in the afternoon. I'll put in those six or seven hours seven days a week while I'm on something. But I can go for as long as seven or eight months without putting pen to paper if I don't have a project. It's sort of an agony-ecstasy thing for me. I work at home; I'm very much a family person. For many years I looked for just the right place to work. I moved from room to room in the house, I rented rooms in hotels, I rented rooms in offices—I did a whole bunch of things. And finally I settled down and was able to make a very comfortable work room at home. It made a lot of difference.

CA: Could you tell me about your connection with the Ensemble Studio Theater [E.S.T.], where you've been a playwright in residence?

LAURO: The first play I ever wrote, "The Contest," which I mentioned, was first produced in New York by E.S.T. in

1977. It got quite a nice reception. The production really sent me on my way. It did very well for me and for E.S.T. At that time E.S.T. was a very small, low-budget theater operating out of a loft—which it still is—over on 11th Avenue. They were just getting going; they had started in 1971. They took me in and I became a member playwright. I have continued an affiliation with them since that time. I served on their executive committee for quite a number of years and I'm still a member of their playwrights' unit. "Open Admissions" began there, and another play of mine, "The Coal Diamond," that then was taken to the Actors Theater of Louisville, won one of the prizes in their Humana Festival of New American Plays and then was chosen for *Best Short Plays of 1980*. Another play called "Nothing Immediate," which also won some awards, was developed at E.S.T. They have a situation in which you can workshop a play. Members are entitled to put their work up on its feet to get a look at it. In addition to resident playwrights, they have resident actors that you can use. It's particularly good, I think, for beginning playwrights, when you're just starting and you need something like a family around you, a group of people to use as sounding boards. Now that isn't always necessary for me—but when you're just starting, it's particularly important.

CA: In the Christian Science Monitor *Hilary DeVries wrote about the Actors Theater of Louisville Humana Festival as a "cultural sounding board." Last year the Festival had decided not to limit productions to new works because of the difficulty of finding good ones, according to Actors Theater. Do you see that as a major concern now in American theater?*

LAURO: I don't see *that* as a major concern, but I see it as a major concern that Louisville has made that decision. I think there are as many if not more brilliant plays being written right now, and I think it's a shame that Louisville has chosen to do that. I don't know why they have since they have been for years one of the few places for developing new material. Maybe they're tired—because it does take a lot of work to bring a new play into production. But I'm sorry to hear that statement because the American playwright is in terrible straits today. The chances and possibilities for getting his work up on the stage are dwindling alarmingly. The government has cut back tremendously in terms of the National Endowment's funding of institutional theaters, and the commercial theater in New York, both Broadway and Off-Broadway, is in very bad economic straits because of the soaring costs of mounting a show in New York and because of the financial situation caused by the tax reform which now has totally destroyed the idea of venture investment for backers of Broadway shows. There are no more write-offs. That no longer exists. I've got a play in the offing that's supposed to come Off-Broadway next season, and several of my producer's investors are pulling out because of the new tax reform. And my story is very much like a number of others.

So the American playwright becomes more and more dependent on regional theaters and/or the institutional theaters in New York; and if, as they say, Louisville is going to do less and less new work, it becomes devastating—particularly for very young people starting out now. They are snatched away by television and by the movies, because there's an outlet for their work. They might develop into very strong stage talents otherwise. But they will do maybe one thing in the theater, and by the age of twenty-five they've got a chance to write films. They take it, and they do not have mastery of their craft in the theater to such a degree that they can come back to it.

It's very different if you've mastered your craft and then go off and work in another form. But these are fledgling dramatic writers who are siphoned off so quickly into film writing that they're lost; they never come back. The fewer chances there are either to get work on stage or to make a living or to make their name as a playwright, the more people are lost. So I'm very sorry that Louisville is doing that; I think it's too bad.

CA: Some of your plays have been produced in regional theaters in Canada and Europe. Have you worked enough with theater abroad to compare regional theater in Europe with our own regional theater?

LAURO: I can't do that, but I know that the attitude is different. I feel that the playwright is held in much higher respect in Ireland and England and Italy, but particularly in Ireland and England, where the theater always has had such a distinguished tradition. I remember going to see something at the Abbey Theater a couple of years ago. In the lobby I looked around me, and there were framed photographs of all the playwrights through the ages, including O'Casey and Shaw, but right down to a very young playwright whose works they were doing that summer. I was really taken aback by it, because you would never see that in American theater anywhere.

CA: No. It's even hard to find the writer's name on a play ad in the New York Times.

LAURO: That's right. In New York, you might find an oil painting of Mr. Shubert at the Shubert Theater and in the regional theaters you will find the playbill framed, and you might find the leading actress or the local actress framed. But it's true that you will rarely find the playwright's name on the bill unless his agent has fought to get it there. There is that difference that I know of between European theater and ours.

CA: Do you envision new approaches to funding for theater in this country?

LAURO: I think it will have to come from foundations. I think it's going to have to come from the corporate world, from business, from individual patrons of the art, which we have always had. The public funding is just not there; it has increasingly dried up. I have a National Endowment for the Arts Fellowship this year; I think I was one of ten playwrights to get one in the United States. Eight or ten years ago there must have been twenty-five or thirty. What happens is that if you've only got ten grants to give, you have to give them to known quantities so that among the ten writers you know you're going to get something back. I don't mean to look a gift horse in the mouth—I was very fortunate to get one—but it makes it rough for a young person starting out.

CA: In the past few years there have been programs to help women who want to produce and direct theater and movies. How well do you think they're working to bring in talented women who have in the past found it hard to break the barriers against them?

LAURO: I think they're working relatively well. I belong to two groups here in New York. I was just elected vice-president of the League of Professional Theater Women of New York. The other group that I'm involved with is the Women's Project at the American Place Theater. I think these particular groups have helped women in the theater. It's a little hard to give examples, but I think that some of it has to do with consciousness-raising; some of it has to do with helping women in the theater gain a kind of self-dignity. It's a very difficult field in terms of the assertiveness needed, as opposed to writing fiction. In theater, your work only begins once the play is written. You have to come into the theater in person in a very assertive way and get your work up on the stage to the best of your creative ability, and collaborate in a very intensive artistic collaboration. It isn't always easy for women to do that, for a number of reasons. There's a business side to the theater: you are selling a product to be marketed in a very competitive field. I know that happens with a novel too, but in that case the publishing company takes over in a way that doesn't happen with playwrights. A play is published at the end of its success, not at the beginning. So the kinds of things that women need are helped by these groups. I think that breaking the psychological barrier that makes us passive, that keeps us from coming forward, is what these groups do in addition to trying to get specific plays placed or specific directors into jobs, though that happens too.

CA: Have you directed your own work?

LAURO: Only to a point. I usually invite people to a public reading when a play is in the first or second draft, because I want to get criticism of the material in advance. I direct those because I'm not really willing to let another artistic sensibility come in then, another director. I have never directed a full production of my plays. On one production the director got sick halfway through and I had to jump in and take over, but that was not by choice. By and large, I don't think playwrights are good directors. The joke is that if you get a playwright directing his own play, all he'll really want to do is line the actors up across the stage and have them say their words in very loud voices, so the playwright can hear what he's written over and over again—which isn't very interesting to the audience.

CA: How responsibly do you think play reviewing is done?

LAURO: Not very responsibly at all. There are no more Harold Clurmans around, I'm afraid. I believe that good criticism allows the playwright and the audience to learn something— it educates in the best sense of the word. I think that most critics working today tend to be narcissistic, overwhelmed by their own needs—not the least of which is advancing their own careers—and that they have very little sense of what good, constructive criticism is. I also think the power of one or two critics in the country to arbitrate taste for the whole country in terms of what plays will be successes and thus go out to the regionals and be turned into movies, etc., and then be seen around the world, is not good. I wish we had more critics and that the power was spread around as it was in the heyday of Broadway when there were—what?—ten or eleven critics of power covering every opening night.

CA: Beyond the play you've mentioned hoping to get produced in New York, and the televised production of "Open Admissions," is there work in progress that you'd like to talk about?

LAURO: I've gotten a residency at the Alley Theater in Houston for "Pearls on the Moon" for next December. We are going to do a staged reading followed by rewrites followed by a workshop production of the play there to which their subscription audience will come, probably with an audience-participation discussion afterwards. So I can get this play ready then to go into full production, and I'm very excited about that.

BIOGRAPHICAL/CRITICAL SOURCES:

PERIODICALS

America, March 24, 1984.
Christian Science Monitor, February 9, 1984, April 2, 1987.
New York Daily News, November 1, 1976.
New York Post, June 18, 1979.
New York Times, October 27, 1976, June 8, 1979, June 15, 1979, February 15, 1981, June 14, 1981, November 7, 1982, January 22, 1984, January 30, 1984, February 5, 1984.
New York Times Book Review, March 21, 1965.
Saturday Review, March 20, 1965.
Time, February 13, 1984.
Times Literary Supplement, October 14, 1965.
Variety, February 1, 1984.
Village Voice, February 14, 1984.
Wall Street Journal, February 10, 1984.

—*Interview by Jean W. Ross*

*   *   *

LAWLER, Ronald (David) 1926-

PERSONAL: Born July 29, 1926, in Cumberland, Md.; son of Leo and Lillian (Laing) Lawler. *Education:* St. Fidelis College, B.A., 1948; St. Louis University, M.A., 1957, Ph.D., 1959.

ADDRESSES: Office—Department of Theology, St. Joseph's Seminary, Yonkers, N.Y. 10704.

CAREER: Entered Order of Friars Minor Capuchin (Capuchins; O.F.M.Cap.), 1946, ordained Roman Catholic priest, 1951; assistant professor of philosophy at St. Fidelis College, 1958-59; Capuchin College, Washington, D.C., assistant professor of philosophy, 1959-60; associated with St. Fidelis College, 1960-72, began as assistant professor, became associate professor of philosophy, dean of students, 1961-64, president of college, 1964-69; Capuchin College, associate professor of philosophy, 1972-75; director of Center for Thomistic Studies at Pontifical College Josephinum, beginning in 1980; associated with theology faculty of St. Joseph's Seminary, Yonkers, N.Y. Instructor at Oblate College, Washington, D.C., and Oxford University, 1973-74; visiting professor at Catholic University of America, 1971-72.

MEMBER: American Philosophical Association, Metaphysical Society of America, American Catholic Philosophical Association (member of executive board), Catholic Theological Society of America, Fellowship of Catholic Scholars (president, 1977-79), Society for Christian Ethics.

WRITINGS:

Philosophical Analysis and Ethics, Bruce, 1968.
(Editor with Donald W. Wuerl and Thomas Comerford Lawler) *The Teaching of Christ: A Catholic Catechism for Adults*, Our Sunday Visitor, 1976, abridged edition, 1979, 2nd edition, 1983.
(Editor and contributor) *Philosophy in Priestly Formation*, Catholic University of America Press, 1978.
The Christian Personalism of John Paul II, Franciscan Herald, 1982.
(With William E. May) *Perspectives in Bioethics*, Pope John Paul II Bioethics Center, 1983.

(With Joseph M. Boyle, Jr., and William E. May) *Catholic Sexual Ethics: A Summary, Explanation, and Defense,* Our Sunday Visitor, 1985.

(With Thomas Comerford Lawler and Donald W. Wuerl) *The Catholic Catechism,* Our Sunday Visitor, 1986.

Light From Light: What Catholics Believe About Jesus, Our Sunday Visitor, 1988.

Contributor to *Curriculum for Renewal,* 1966, and to theology and philosophy journals.*

*   *   *

LAWLESS, Elaine J. 1947-

PERSONAL: Born September 29, 1947, in Poplar Bluff, Mo.; daughter of James (a farmer) and Angie Mae (a housewife; maiden name, Dunlap) Lawless; married James Rikoon (a folklorist); children: Alexander Keller, Jesse. *Education:* Attended Southeast Missouri State College (now University), 1965-69, University of Illinois at Urbana-Champaign, 1971-75, and Indiana University—Bloomington, 1977-82.

ADDRESSES: Office—Department of English, 231 Arts and Sciences Building, University of Missouri—Columbia, Columbia, Mo. 65211.

CAREER: University of Missouri—Columbia, assistant professor of English, 1983—. Co-producer of television documentary "Joy Unspeakable," for Indiana University—Bloomington, 1981.

WRITINGS:

God's Peculiar People: Women's Voices and Folk Tradition in a Pentecostal Church, University Press of Kentucky, 1987.

Handmaidens of the Lord: Pentecostal Women Preachers and Traditional Religion, American Folklore Society and University of Pennsylvania Press, 1988.

Contributor to folklore journals.

*   *   *

LAWRENCE, Gale 1941-

PERSONAL: Born September 6, 1941, in Springfield, Vt.; daughter of John (an executive) and Janet (Beal) Lawrence. *Education:* Attended Wellesley College, 1959-60, and University of Vienna, 1963; Earlham College, A.B., 1966; Emory University, M.A., 1968. *Religion:* Society of Friends (Quakers).

ADDRESSES: Home—Huntington, Vt.

CAREER: Schoolteacher in Washington, D.C., 1968-70; instructor at Montgomery College, Roseville, Md., 1971-74; lecturer at American University, Washington, D.C., 1974-75, and at University of Vermont, Burlington, 1976—. Member of board of directors of Vermont Institute of Natural Science, 1983-86, Vermont Ecology Course, 1985—, Vermont Green Up, 1986—, and Birds of Vermont Museum, 1986—.

MEMBER: Authors Guild, League of Women Voters.

AWARDS, HONORS: First prize from Vermont Sportswriters and Sportscasters Association, 1978, for column in *Rutland Herald-Times Argus.*

WRITINGS:

The Beginning Naturalist, New England Press, 1979.
Vermont Life's Guide to Fall Foliage, Vermont Life, 1984.

A Field Guide to the Familiar, Prentice-Hall, 1984.
The Indoor Naturalist: Observing the World of Nature Inside Your Home, Prentice-Hall, 1986.

Author of a weekly natural history column in *Rutland Herald-Times Argus,* 1977-86.

WORK IN PROGRESS: Continuing research on natural history.

SIDELIGHTS: Gale Lawrence told *CA:* "I have taken it as a personal mission to combat 'outdoor illiteracy,' a condition I discovered in myself in midlife. Though I am still in the process of educating myself, I write about common plants and animals—the species most likely to engage the interest of outdoor illiterates. By combining humor and autobiography with scientific information, I want to invite readers to rediscover their lost connections with the natural world."

*   *   *

LAWRENCE, Joseph D(ouglas) 1895-

PERSONAL: Born January 10, 1895, in Roanoke, Va.; son of Joseph Henry (a physician) and Mary Lucy (a housewife; maiden name, Jones) Lawrence; married Mary Roberson (a registered nurse), November 25, 1971; children: Joseph D., Jr., Anna Marie Lawrence Glenn. *Education:* Attended University of Virginia. *Politics:* None. *Religion:* Baptist.

ADDRESSES: Home—25 Downs Loop, Clemson, S.C. 29631.

CAREER: Accountant and farmer; employed by Farm Credit banks in Columbia, S.C., and Washington, D.C., for nearly fifty years. *Military service:* U.S. Army, 1918-19; served in Belgium and France; received Croix de Guerre.

WRITINGS:

Fighting Soldier: AEF, 1918 (autobiography), Colorado Associated Universities Press, 1986.

SIDELIGHTS: Joseph D. Lawrence told *CA:* "I decided to write *Fighting Soldier: AEF, 1918* to make a record of my war experiences for my children and grandchildren. At the outbreak of World War I the American people were very patriotic and those eligible for service were enlisting in large numbers. One of the objectives in writing this book was to tell how the individual soldier behaved in combat. Most war books write about generals and other high-ranking officers and the movement of the troops. There is not much in such narrative that showed the performance of the American soldier in 1918. In writing this book I reported on the actions of the privates, corporals, sergeants, and first and second lieutenants. They were the men in the mud and in the poison gas, who encountered the enemy and attacked the enemy's strongholds and who were subjected to the never-ending murderous shell fire. Most of the captains took part in movements and directed subordinates from, usually, concrete dugouts."

*   *   *

LAWRENCE, Karen 1949-

PERSONAL: Born March 18, 1949, in New York, N.Y.; daughter of Mel (a doll manufacturer) and Rosalie (Roth) Rosenblum; married Peter F. Lawrence (a vascular surgeon), June 27, 1971; children: Andrew Michael, Jeffrey Taylor. *Education:* Attended Smith College, 1967-69; Yale University, B.A., 1971; Tufts University, M.A., 1973; Columbia University, Ph.D., 1978.

ADDRESSES: *Office*—Department of English, University of Utah, Salt Lake City, Utah 84112.

CAREER: University of Utah, Salt Lake City, assistant professor, 1978-82, associate professor of English, 1982—, chairperson of department, 1984—. Member of board of trustees of James Joyce Foundation; member of executive committee of Association of Departments of English.

MEMBER: Modern Language Association of America, James Joyce Society, Society for the Study of Narrative, Utah Women's Forum.

WRITINGS:

The Odyssey of Style in Ulysses, Princeton University Press, 1981.
(With Betsy Seifter and Lois Ratner) *The McGraw-Hill Guide to English Literature,* two volumes, McGraw, 1985.

Contributor to *The Cambridge Companion to Joyce Studies,* edited by Derek Attridge, Cambridge University Press, in press. Contributor to literature journals, including *English Literary History* and *Nineteenth-Century Literature.*

Advisory editor of *James Joyce Quarterly;* on editorial board of *Western Humanities Review.*

WORK IN PROGRESS: A study of nineteenth- and twentieth-century British travel novels and narratives involving women travelers; editing *Canonical Reconsiderations of Twentieth-Century British Literature.*

SIDELIGHTS: Karen Lawrence told *CA* that her special interests include twentieth-century British literature, the novel, nineteenth- and twentieth-century women writers, and feminist theory and criticism.

BIOGRAPHICAL/CRITICAL SOURCES:

PERIODICALS

Times Literary Supplement, August 20, 1982.

* * *

LAWRENCE, Karen   1951-

PERSONAL: Born February 5, 1951, in Windsor, Ontario, Canada; immigrated to United States, 1979; daughter of Kenneth W. and Wanda Mary Lawrence; married Robert O. Gabhart. *Education:* University of Windsor, B.A. (with honors), 1973; University of Alberta, M.A., 1977.

ADDRESSES: *Home*—San Diego, Calif. *Agent*—Esther Newberg, International Creative Management, 40 West 50th St., New York, N.Y. 10019.

CAREER: University of Alberta, Edmonton, instructor in English, 1974-75; Notre Dame University of Nelson, Nelson, B.C., instructor in English, 1975; *Branching Out,* Edmonton, member of editorial staff, 1976-79; writer, 1976—.

MEMBER: Authors Guild, Writers Union of Canada, Association of Canadian Television and Radio Artists.

AWARDS, HONORS: Canada Council grant, 1973; W. H. Smith Award from *Books in Canada* and Literary Award from Los Angeles Center of International P.E.N., both 1987, both for *The Life of Helen Alone.*

WRITINGS:

At the Doll Hospital (poems), Black Moss Press, 1973.

Nekuia: The Inanna Poems, Longspoon Press, 1980.
The Life of Helen Alone (novel), Villard Books, 1986, Ballantine, 1987.

Contributor to periodicals, including *Canadian Forum, Quarry, Event, America,* and *Pacific Review.*

WORK IN PROGRESS: A novel, publication by Random House expected in 1989; screenplay, based on *The Life of Helen Alone,* for Norstar Entertainment, 1987.

BIOGRAPHICAL/CRITICAL SOURCES:

PERIODICALS

Books in Canada, April, 1987.
Globe and Mail (Toronto), March 7, 1987, April 18, 1987.
New York Times Book Review, October 12, 1986.

* * *

LAWRENCE, Mary
See YOUNG, Mary Lou Daves

* * *

LAWSON, Ronald (Lynton)   1940-

PERSONAL: Born January 6, 1940, in Sydney, Australia; immigrated to the United States, 1970; son of Harold James (a printer) and Ruby (a teacher; maiden name, Fraser) Lawson. *Education:* University of Queensland, B.A., 1963, Ph.D., 1970. *Religion:* Seventh-day Adventist.

ADDRESSES: *Home*—39-28 45th St., Sunnyside, N.Y. 11104. *Office*—Department of Urban Studies, Queens College of the City University of New York, Flushing, N.Y. 11367.

CAREER: Hunter College of the City University of New York, New York, N.Y., assistant professor of sociology, 1973-77; Queens College of the City University of New York, Flushing, N.Y., associate professor, 1977-83, professor of urban studies, 1984—. Senior research associate at Center for Policy Research, 1973-77. President of New York Adventist Forum, 1975-84, 1986—; church liaison, Seventh-day Adventist Kinship, 1980—.

MEMBER: American Sociological Association, Organization of American Historians, Society for the Scientific Study of Religion, Society for the Study of Social Problems, Sociologists' Gay Caucus (president, 1974-78), Eastern Sociological Society.

AWARDS, HONORS: Fulbright scholar, 1970-71; postdoctoral visiting scholar at Columbia University, 1971-73; Australian and New Zealand Bank Prize, 1973, for *Brisbane in the 1890s: An Australian Urban Society;* Ford Foundation fellow, 1975; grants from National Institute of Mental Health, 1973-76, New York Community Trust, 1977, and U.S. Department of Housing and Urban Development, 1978-80; National Endowment for the Humanities fellow, 1984.

WRITINGS:

Brisbane in the 1890s: An Australian Urban Society, University of Queensland Press, 1973.
Owners of the Last Resort, New York City Department of Housing Preservation and Development, 1984.
(Editor with Mark Naison, and contributor) *The Tenant Movement in New York City, 1904-1984,* Rutgers University Press, 1986.

Contributor to sociology, history, and religious studies journals.

WORK IN PROGRESS: A broad, sociological study of Seventh-day Adventism around the world, with Maren Lockwood Carden, publication by Rutgers University Press expected in 1991.

SIDELIGHTS: Ronald Lawson told *CA:* "A deep concern for social justice, akin to theology of liberation, motivates my concern for underdogs such as tenants and gays. My study of Seventh-day Adventism in crisis and conflict is partly motivated by my wish to explore the pros and cons of my roots in a system that produces both saints and bigots in abundance.

"Up until the 1890s there had been very little attention paid to Australian cities, even though Australia was, in terms of percentage of population in cities, the most urbanized of all the continents by 1900. *Brisbane in the 1890s* was new in the sense that it was historical sociology.

"*The Tenant Movement in New York* was the first major study of the development—over a lengthy period—of a consumers' movement dominated largely by women, members of the political left, and religiously motivated activists. The Jews who began the movement were joined by blacks in the 1930s and Hispanics in the 1970s. No issue could have been closer to home as I live in New York City, but the project proved very difficult to organize.

"Regarding religion, the gay wing of Seventh-day Adventists has put some strain on the church, leaving leaders confused about where to go from here. I plan to examine the sociological aspects of the religion in my forthcoming book."

*   *   *

LAZARUS, Paul N.   1913-

PERSONAL: Born March 31, 1913, in Brooklyn, N.Y.; son of Paul N. (a motion picture executive) and Hattie W. (a housewife) Lazarus; married Elinor Tolins, April 23, 1936; children: Paul N. III, John T., Thomas L. *Education:* Cornell University, B.A., 1933.

ADDRESSES: Home—4895 La Gama Way, Santa Barbara, Calif. 93111. *Office*—Film Studies Department, University of California, Santa Barbara, Calif. 93106.

CAREER: General assistant in press book department at Warner Brothers, beginning in 1933; motion picture account executive at Buchanan and Co., 1942-43; affiliated with United Artists Corp., as director of advertising and publicity, 1943-48, and assistant to the president, 1948-50; Columbia Pictures, New York, N.Y., member of executive staff, 1950-54, vice-president, 1954-62; executive vice-president at Samuel Bronston Productions, 1962-64; vice-president in charge of motion pictures at Subscription Television, Inc., 1964; executive officer and partner at Landau Releasing Organization, 1964-65; executive vice-president and member of board of directors at National Screen Service Corp., 1965-75; University of California, Santa Barbara, lecturer in film studies and consultant, 1975—. Vice-chairman of Recording for the Blind, Inc.; member of board of directors of Santa Barbara Film Festival; consultant to Kenya Film Corp. *Military service:* U.S. Army.

MEMBER: Santa Barbara Writers Conference (chief of staff), Sigma Delta Chi.

WRITINGS:

(Contributor) Jason E. Squire, editor, *The Movie Business Book*, Prentice-Hall, 1983.

The Movie Producer: A Handbook for Producing and Picture-Making, Harper, 1986.

Contributor to *Screen Producers Guild Journal*. Associate editor of *Film Bulletin*, 1975-80.

BIOGRAPHICAL/CRITICAL SOURCES:

PERIODICALS

Los Angeles Times Book Review, November 17, 1985.

*   *   *

LEARY, James F.   1942-

PERSONAL: Born May 23, 1942, in Waterbury, Conn.; son of James F. and Myrtle M. (Burr) Leary. *Education:* St. Thomas Seminary, Bloomfield, Conn., A.A., 1962; St. John Seminary, Boston, Mass., B.A., 1964, M.A., 1968.

ADDRESSES: Office—St. Joseph Church, 37 Queen St., Bristol, Conn. 06010.

CAREER: Ordained Roman Catholic priest, 1968; affiliated with St. Lawrence O'Toole Church, Hartford, Conn., 1968-72; St. Thomas Seminary, Bloomfield, Conn., dean of students, 1972-81; affiliated with St. Timothy Church, West Hartford, Conn., 1981-86; St. Joseph College, West Hartford, lecturer in religious studies, 1971—. Co-pastor of St. Joseph Church, Bristol, Conn., 1986—.

MEMBER: Catholic Biblical Association.

WRITINGS:

Hear, O Israel: A Guide to the Old Testament, Christian Classics, 1986.
A Light to the Nations: A Guide to the New Testament, Christian Classics, 1986.

*   *   *

LEBEDOFF, David (Michael)   1938-

PERSONAL: Born April 29, 1938, in Minneapolis, Minn.; son of Martin (a businessman) and Mary (a housewife; maiden name, Galanter) Lebedoff; married Randy Miller (an attorney), February 7, 1981; children: Caroline, Jonathan, Nicholas. *Education:* University of Minnesota—Twin Cities, B.A. (magna cum laude), 1960; Harvard University, LL.B., 1963.

ADDRESSES: Office—Lindquist & Vennum, IDS Center Building, 80 Eighth St. S., Minneapolis, Minn. 55402.

CAREER: Admitted to the Bar in 1963. Lindquist & Vennum (law firm), Minneapolis, Minn., partner, 1982—. Member of Higher Education Coordinating Committee of Minnesota, 1975-77. University of Minnesota—Twin Cities, member of board of regents, 1977—, chairman of board, 1987—.

MEMBER: Minnesota Society for Fine Arts (member of board of trustees, 1976—), Phi Beta Kappa (president of Minnesota chapter, 1975).

WRITINGS:

The Twenty-first Ballot, University of Minnesota Press, 1969.
Ward Number Six, Scribner, 1972.
The New Elite: Death of Democracy, F. Watts, 1981.

BIOGRAPHICAL/CRITICAL SOURCES:

PERIODICALS

Annals of the American Academy of Political and Social Science, January, 1970, September, 1973, November, 1982.

*   *   *

LEE, C(live) H(oward)   1942-

PERSONAL: Born April 21, 1942, in Leeds, England; son of Denis and Rose Lee; married Chris Jones (a schoolteacher). Education: Fitzwilliam College, Cambridge, M.A. and M.Litt., 1966.

ADDRESSES: Home—169 Forest Ave., Aberdeen AB1 6UU, Scotland. Office—Department of Economic History, University of Aberdeen, Aberdeen AB9 1TY, Scotland.

CAREER: University of Aberdeen, Aberdeen, Scotland, lecturer, 1966-77, senior lecturer, 1977-84, reader in economic history, 1984—.

WRITINGS:

Regional Economic Growth in the United Kingdom Since the 1880s, McGraw, 1971.
A Cotton Enterprise: A History of M'Connel & Kennedy, Fine Cotton Spinners, 1795-1840, Manchester University Press, 1972.
The Quantitative Approach to Economic History, Martin Robertson, 1977.
British Regional Employment Statistics, 1841-1971, Cambridge University Press, 1979.
The British Economy Since 1700: A Macroeconomic Perspective, Cambridge University Press, 1986.

WORK IN PROGRESS: A history of world economic development from the middle of the nineteenth century to the present day, publication expected in 1992.

SIDELIGHTS: C. H. Lee told CA: "My interest in economic development in general and the British economy in particular stemmed from a fascination with the notion of an 'industrial revolution' transforming Britain and then the world and from an inability to make sense of this thesis. I explored this in a variety of ways, and my recent book, The British Economy Since 1700, represents the conclusion of that work and the development of an explanatory thesis which I find satisfactory. This thesis refutes the traditional notion of industrial revolution either as the beginning of British or world development. British growth was found to be very slow and change extremely gradual. Far from being transformed by industrialization, the British economy, reflecting an extremely conservative society, prospered through international trade and investment and manufacturing played a much more modest role than conventional wisdom suggested.

"In The British Economy Since 1700 I trace the effects of this in the long run, in the importance of the city and its international perspective, in the slow and reluctant adjustment to modern technology oriented industry. Britain's main role in the world economy has been as a trader and financier throughout the past three hundred years. Modern industrialization really has its beginnings in the late nineteenth century American and German manufacturing. The British Economy Since 1700 represents the end of a long phase of my work. The next phase, upon which I am now embarked, consists of the study of international growth from the mid-nineteenth century to the pre-

sent. I am currently working on the advanced economies in that period and the links between structural change, productivity, and growth."

*   *   *

LEE, James A(lvin)   1922-

PERSONAL: Born August 7, 1922, in Breckenridge, Tex.; son of James Arlington (an oil field superintendent) and Aultna Lee; married Frances Irene Smith (a linguist), in 1949; children: five. Education: Trinity College of Music, London, Diploma in Composition, 1946; Fresno State College (now California State University, Fresno), A.B., 1950; University of Utah, M.S., 1951; Harvard University, D.B.A., 1968.

ADDRESSES: Home—92 North Congress, Athens, Ohio 45701. Office—Department of Management Systems, Ohio University, Athens, Ohio 45701.

CAREER: Douglas Aircraft, Long Beach, Calif., and Oklahoma City, Okla., tool designer, 1941-43; North American Aviation, Inglewood, Calif., tool designer, 1943-44; Kennecott Copper Corp., Arizona Division, Ray, Ariz., director of industrial relations, 1951-55; O. S. Stapley Co., Phoenix, Ariz., personnel director, 1955-56; Sperry Rand, Flight Systems Division, Phoenix, personnel director, 1956-60; University of Wisconsin—Madison, Madison, associate professor of industrial relations, 1960-61; University of Southern California, Los Angeles, associate professor of management, attached to University of Karachi, 1961-64; Harvard University, Cambridge, Mass., research associate in personnel administration, 1965-66; Haile Selassie I University, Addis Ababa, Ethiopia, professor of business and dean of College of Business, 1966-69; Ohio University, Athens, professor of management, 1969—, chairman of department of organizational science, 1969-72, chairman of graduate programs, 1976-78 and 1981-83, director of Ohio Programs in Malaysia, 1983-85. Professor, chairman of department of industrial management, and founding dean of College of Industrial Management at Saudi Arabia's University of Petroleum and Minerals, Dhahran, 1974-76. International Management Development Institute, Inc., co-founder, vice-president, academic head, and member of board of directors, 1970—; consultant to Kinetics Technology International, U.S. Civil Service Commission, and Shell Oil Co. Military service: U.S. Army Air Forces, 1944-46; served in Europe.

MEMBER: Academy of Management.

WRITINGS:

The Gold and Garbage in Management Theories and Prescriptions, Ohio University Press, 1980.

Contributor to business and management journals.

WORK IN PROGRESS: A book on "our destruction of the mechanisms for solving our societal problems such as our intractable high crime rate, choking litigiousness, homelessness and unemployment rates, deterioration of our physical infrastructures such as roads, bridges, harbors, subways, railways, water, and waste disposal systems."

SIDELIGHTS: James A. Lee told CA: "The Gold and Garbage in Management Theories and Prescriptions was prompted by my astonishment at the proliferation of theories about how to manage that had little or no scientific support. The book is the result of about two thousand hours of research looking for such support. Little was found."

AVOCATIONAL INTERESTS: Squash racquets, music, antique British sports cars.

*   *   *

LEED, Theodore W(illiam) 1927-

PERSONAL: Born February 11, 1927, in Canton, Ohio; son of William H. and Myrtle (Harman) Leed; married Doris Renner, 1949; children: Sheryl, Lisa, Brian. *Education:* Ohio State University, B.Sc., 1950, M.Sc., 1951, Ph.D., 1957.

ADDRESSES: Office—Leed Marketing, 108 Rolling Ridge Rd., Amherst, Mass. 01002.

CAREER: Ohio State University, Columbus, assistant professor of agricultural economics, 1954-57; University of Massachusetts at Amherst, professor of agricultural economics, 1957-83, professor emeritus, 1983—; affiliated with Leed Marketing, Amherst.

MEMBER: Food Distribution Research Society (president, 1968-69).

WRITINGS:

(Editor with Donald M. Marion) *Research Papers in Food Distribution*, Department of Agricultural and Food Economics, University of Massachusetts at Amherst, 1965.
(With Howard C. Jensen) *An Economic Analysis of Competitive Strategy and Sales in the Supermarket Industry*, Department of Agricultural and Food Economics, University of Massachusetts at Amherst, 1966.
(With Gene A. German) *Food and Merchandising: Principles and Practices*, Chain Store Age Books, 1973, 3rd edition, Lebhar-Friedman Books, 1985.
Convenience Store Merchandising: For the People Who Make It Work, Cornell University, 1983.

WORK IN PROGRESS: A revision of *Convenience Store Merchandising*.

*   *   *

LEGG, (Francis) Stuart 1910-1988

OBITUARY NOTICE: Born August 31, 1910, in London, England; died July 23, 1988. Documentary film producer, director, and author. Legg, who "brought film compilation to a high art," according to a London *Times* writer, was perhaps best known for his "World in Action" documentary series on global struggles for food, oil, and manpower—a cooperative effort with John Grierson and the National Film Board of Canada. Legg's work in Canada between 1939 and 1948 was highlighted by the Oscar-winning "Churchill's Island." His additional screen credits include "BBC: The Voice of Britain," "The Rival World," a study of the threat insects pose to food supply in third world countries, "A Light in Nature," a survey of world science from the seventeenth century to modern day, and "Powered Flight," an examination of aeronautical development during the first half of the twentieth century. He turned to historical writing in his later career, publishing *Jutland*, *Trafalgar*, *The Heartland*, and *From Suez to Khartoum* between 1966 and 1972.

OBITUARIES AND OTHER SOURCES:

BOOKS

International Motion Picture Almanac, Quigley, 1988.
The Oxford Companion to Film, Oxford University Press, 1976.

PERIODICALS

Times (London), July 27, 1988.

*   *   *

LEGRAND, Catherine Carlisle 1947-

PERSONAL: Born November 4, 1947, in Baltimore, Md. *Education:* Reed College, B.A., 1970; Stanford University, M.A., 1973, M.A., 1974, Ph.D., 1980.

ADDRESSES: Office—Department of History, Queen's University, Kingston, Ontario, Canada K7L 3N6.

CAREER: University of British Columbia, Vancouver, assistant professor of history, 1980-86; Queen's University, Kingston, Ontario, associate professor of history, 1986—.

MEMBER: Latin American Studies Association, Canadian Association of Latin and Caribbean Studies.

WRITINGS:

Frontier Expansion and Peasant Protest in Colombia, 1850-1936, University of New Mexico Press, 1986.

Contributor to Latin American studies journals.

WORK IN PROGRESS: Research on "New Perspectives on Politics and La Violencia in Colombia."

*   *   *

LEITES, Edmund 1939-

PERSONAL: Surname is pronounced "*Lie*-tess"; born November 24, 1939, in Chicago, Ill.; son of Nathan (a political scientist) and Wilma (a piano teacher; maiden name, Weyns) Leites; married Susan Miller, February 3, 1963 (divorced, 1985); children: Justin. *Education:* Yale University, A.B., 1959; Harvard University, A.M., 1965, Ph.D., 1972.

ADDRESSES: Home—333 Central Park W., New York, N.Y. 10025. *Office*—Department of Philosophy, Queens College of the City University of New York, 65-30 Kissena Blvd., Flushing, N.Y. 11367.

CAREER: Vassar College, Poughkeepsie, N.Y., lecturer in philosophy, 1966-69; Queens College of the City University of New York, Flushing, N.Y., lecturer, 1969-72, assistant professor, 1972-79, associate professor, 1980-85, professor of philosophy, 1986—, Mellon scholar, 1977. *Directeur d'etudes associe* at Ecole des Hautes Etudes en Sciences Sociales, Paris, France, 1981-82 and 1983-84.

MEMBER: International Society for the Comparative Study of Civilizations.

AWARDS, HONORS: Fellow of American Council of Learned Societies, 1978; Mellon fellow at William Andrews Clark Memorial Library, University of California, Los Angeles, 1978; fellow of National Endowment for the Humanities at the Institute for Advanced Study, Princeton, N.J., 1979-80.

WRITINGS:

The Puritan Conscience and Modern Sexuality, Yale University Press, 1986.
(Editor) *Conscience and Casuistry in Early Modern Europe*, Cambridge University Press, 1988.

Co-editor of *Comparative Civilizations Review*, 1978—.

LEITES, Nathan Constantin   1912-1987

PERSONAL: Born in 1912 in St. Petersburg, Russia (now Leningrad, U.S.S.R.); immigrated to United States, 1936; died of pulmonary complications from Parkinson's disease, June 5, 1987, in Avignon, France; cremated. *Education:* Educated in Denmark and Germany.

CAREER: Member of faculty of University of Chicago, before World War II; worked with Office of War Information and Foreign Broadcast Intelligence Service, during World War II; Rand Corp., Santa Monica, Calif., research scientist, c. 1947-62, consultant, 1962-86. Member of faculty of University of Chicago, 1962-74.

WRITINGS:

(With Harold D. Lasswell) *The Language of Politics: Studies in Quantitative Semantics*, G. W. Stewart, 1949.
(With Martha Wolfenstein) *Movies: A Psychological Study*, Free Press, 1950.
The Operational Code of the Politburo, McGraw, 1951.
A Study of Bolshevism, Free Press, 1953.
(With Elsa Bernaut) *Ritual of Liquidation: The Case of the Moscow Trials*, Free Press, 1954.
(With Christian de la Malene) *Paris From EDC to WEU*, Rand Corp., 1956.
Du malaise politique en France, Plon, 1958, translation published as *On the Game of Politics in France*, Stanford University Press, 1959.
(With Constantin Melnik) *The House Without Windows: France Selects a President*, Harper, 1958.
La Regle du jeu a Paris, Mouton, 1966, translation published as *The Rules of the Game in Paris*, University of Chicago Press, 1969.
(With Charles Wolf, Jr.) *Rebellion and Authority: An Analytic Essay on Insurgent Conflicts*, Markham, 1970.
The New Ego: Pitfalls in Current Thinking About Patients in Psychoanalysis, Science House, 1971.
Psychopolitical Analysis: Selected Writings of Nathan Leites, Sage Publications, 1977.
Interpreting Transference, Norton, 1979.
Depression and Masochism: An Account of Mechanisms, Norton, 1979.
The Soviet Style in War, Crane, Russak, 1982.
Le Muerte de Jesus moyen de salut? Embarras des theologiens et deplacements de la question, Editions du Cerf, 1982.
The Soviet Style in Management, Crane, Russak, 1985.
Art and Life: Aspects of Michelangelo, New York University Press, 1986.

BIOGRAPHICAL/CRITICAL SOURCES:

PERIODICALS

Annals of the American Academy of Political and Social Science, November, 1970.
Carleton Miscellany, spring, 1970.
Los Angeles Times, December 17, 1982, June 11, 1987.
New York Times, June 10, 1987.
Washington Post, June 13, 1987.*

*   *   *

LELYVELD, Joseph (Salem)   1937-

PERSONAL: Born April 5, 1937, in Cincinnati, Ohio; son of Arthur Joseph (a rabbi) and Toby (a teacher; maiden name, Bookholtz) Lelyveld; married Carolyn Fox (a teacher), June 14, 1959; children: Amy, Nita. *Education:* Harvard University, A.B. (summa cum laude), 1958, M.A., 1959; Columbia University, M.S., 1960.

ADDRESSES: Home—London, England. *Office*—c/o *New York Times*, 229 West 43rd St., New York, N.Y. 10036. *Agent*—Carl D. Brandt, 1501 Broadway, New York, N.Y. 10036.

CAREER: New York Times, New York, N.Y., staff member, 1962—, correspondent in the Congo and South Africa, 1965-66, in London, England, 1966, in India and Pakistan, 1966-69, in Hong Kong, 1973-75, in South Africa, 1980-83, deputy foreign editor, 1978-80, staff writer for *New York Times Magazine*, 1984-85, London bureau chief, 1985-86, foreign editor, 1987—. *Military service:* U.S. Army Reserves, 1961-67.

AWARDS, HONORS: Fulbright fellowship to Burma, 1960; Page One Award, 1970, for article on death of twelve-year-old heroin user in Harlem; George Polk Memorial Award, 1972, for series of articles on a fourth-grade class and, 1984, for coverage of South Africa; John Simon Guggenheim fellowship, 1984; Pulitzer Prize and *Los Angeles Times* Book Award, both 1986, both for *Move Your Shadow: South Africa Black and White*.

WRITINGS:

(Contributor) Roger Klein, editor, *Young Americans Abroad*, Harper, 1963.
(Author of introduction) *House of Bondage*, photographs by Ernest Cole, Random House, 1967.
Calcutta, photographs by Raghubir Singh, Paragon Press, 1974.
Move Your Shadow: South Africa Black and White, Times Books, 1985.

Author of "In America," a weekly column for *New York Times Magazine*, 1977. Contributor of articles and reviews to *New York Times* and other periodicals.

SIDELIGHTS: Joseph Lelyveld's Pulitzer Prize-winning *Move Your Shadow* is based on two reporting tours in South Africa—a one-year stint ending in 1966 when Lelyveld was expelled for being too critical of the government and a return in 1980 that lasted three years. Lelyveld makes the long hiatus between his journeys a strength of the book. "I long had a weakness amounting to a craving for going back," he writes. "There was something irresistible about returning to a story you had once covered; it was like a trip in a time machine, one of the few ways a newspaperman could inject a little coherence and resonance into a vagabond life."

Consequently, unlike many newcomers to the South African scene, Lelyveld was able to compare current events with what was going on nearly two decades earlier. In 1966 the "grand-apartheid" policy of setting aside "independent homelands" for each ethnic subdivision of the black population, and removing blacks from the "white areas" to these poverty-stricken and desolate pseudo-nations, was in its early stages of implementation, and there were doubts about how far it could be carried. When he returned in 1980, he was shocked to observe that apartheid was more entrenched than ever and an education system was established so that "there would be no place for [blacks] in the European community above the level of certain forms of labor." The only changes he could see were cosmetic ones, such as Pretoria's repealing the Prohibition of Marriages Act and opening industrial jobs to blacks. Whites persistently asked him if he could see the reforms. His answer, which he hedged for months, eventually came out in Cape Town at lunch with an Afrikaner: "Yes," he answered, "I never imagined they would be able to carry apartheid so far."

Lelyveld begins his book with two epigraphs. The first is the translation of a phrasebook command helpful to a white golfer instructing his black caddy or, by analogy, to white rulers addressing the troublesome black majority, and gives *Move Your Shadow* its title. The second, from Herman Charles Bosman's *Mafeking Road,* reflects the purpose, technique, and vision of the book: "I can tell you the things that happened as I saw them, and what the rest were about only Africa knows."

In carrying out this commitment to describe "the things that happened as I saw them," Lelyveld ignores the news items, statements, speeches, analyses—the stock of his journalistic trade—and instead concentrates on the ordinary details of ordinary South African lives. He attends the university seminars, political meetings, and private parties of the English and the Afrikaners. He makes friends with revolutionaries and poets as well as workers. He travels with black commuters. As noted by George Packer, in his review of *Move Your Shadow* for *Nation,* "[Lelyveld] writes not of famous people like Steve Biko or Nelson Mandela, whom he couldn't know, but of the people he came to know well: an Afrikaner farmer in Zimbabwe trying to accept the fact of black power; a black activist troubled by the problem of evil and 'the role of God in this situation.'"

Lelyveld explains Afrikaners as very religious and deeply moral people who have consequently developed many laws and euphemisms to rationalize their abuses. He also points out that their patronizing depictions of blacks as backward and ignorant and shiftless unconsciously echo prejudices that the former British rulers of South Africa had about the Boers. He reveals a deep appreciation as well of the thinking and the fear of whites at many levels of society, and he underscores their capacity to convince themselves that their country is actually evolving toward multiracial harmony, simply because—as *Newsweek* contributor Mark Whitaker mused—"they run ads featuring black models in South African *Vogue* and allow Stevie Wonder songs to be played on the airwaves."

However, Lelyveld has far more empathy for the blacks than for the white community. Not content to see black reality through the eyes of a handful of black leaders, he seeks out common black folk—befriending his housekeeper and the watchman in his office building and asking to visit their homes as well. He goes to see for himself what living in a resettlement camp is like. He arrives by commuter bus, experiencing the long, bumpy ride undertaken daily by many thousands of "homeland" dwellers who work in white cities hours away. He writes, "I thought I understood, but I was not prepared for the visual shock of what Kwaggerfontien had become in two and a half years. It was no longer just a rash of 'closer settlements.' Now it was part of a nearly continuous resettlement belt . . . a serpentine stream of shanties and mud houses." Such sights, he observed, "can be seen in other countries, usually as a result of famine or wars. I don't know where else they have been achieved as a result of planning." Additionally, Lelyveld describes the courage of black families who risk jail and worse to avoid being separated by the homelands policy, and the dignity of black prisoners who fail to succumb to detention and torture.

Lelyveld left South Africa in 1983, and his conclusions as of that point are gloomy. Twenty-five years after Hendrik Verwoerd began to modernize the apartheid system, he sees President P.W. Botha's reforms as amounting to no more than "the old Verwoerdian trick of changing attitudes without changing practices, of annihilating white supremacy in theory without losing its advantages." He also finds that the "earnest but inconsistent dabbling" of U.S. policymakers on both the left and the right has not been helpful. As for the blacks, he concludes that after twenty years of exile, the outlawed African National Congress has become militarily ineffective and spiritually exhausted. Skeptical about the prospects for change, Lelyveld maintains, "The question, it seemed to me, was not whether there would be violence in South Africa but whether there would ever be an end to it."

Move Your Shadow won the attention and praise of many critics. In *Newsweek* Mark Whitaker commented, "For anyone trying to make sense of the complexities of South Africa, Joseph Lelyveld's superb new book is must reading. . . . Coming to the story with prior knowledge, Lelyveld manages to avoid the naivete of many first-impression reports from South Africa. With a prose style of engaging elegance and a novelist's eye for detail, he delves beneath the surface of apartheid— exploring its subtleties as well as its savagery, its inanities as well as its injustices." Charles T. Powers, writing in the *Los Angeles Times,* began his review by declaring *Move Your Shadow* "not an easy read" but a book "that will be well read in Washington, in academia and among those people seriously interested in the unfolding cataclysm of South Africa." Jonathan Kapstein, reviewing Lelyveld's book in *Business Week,* commended his achieving "a fine level of eloquence in his personal narrative, combining a journalist's eye for making sense out of the chaos of daily events with a full grasp of their longer-term implications."

New York Times Book Review contributor Anthony Sampson was particularly enthusiastic in his praise of *Move Your Shadow,* which he dubbed an "extraordinary feat of reporting . . . unlike any other book about South Africa." Sampson continued, "It provides the kind of authentic evidence of the ordeals of black life that few white South Africans themselves discover. And it is superbly written, presenting characters and dialogue with the vividness of the great Russian novels, with a sense of careful observation." Lelyveld, assessed Sampson, "has not only limitless curiosity that never seems to flag, but a novelist's eye for detail and dialogue. His blacks talk realistically, their gusto and emphasis bursting through the pages. . . . His grass-roots reporting, with his procession of little-known heroes or villains, has a powerful cumulative effect; and his wide reading and experience enable him to compare South African events with other nations and eras." Similarly, veteran reporter Ted Morgan, writing in review in the *New York Times,* called *Move Your Shadow* a "tale . . . based on personal experience and observations, laced with history," adding that "it was only when I read Lelyveld's book that I understood the true meaning of apartheid: that is, bending the entire weight and power of government to the single purpose of maintaining the dominance of a white minority over a black majority."

In his review of *Move Your Shadow* for the Toronto *Globe and Mail,* Robin Breon applauded Lelyveld for "paint[ing] a sweeping portrait of South Africa." Moreover, noted Breon, "Lelyveld makes passing allusions to classical Russian literature and they seem appropriate. The worlds of Nicolai Gogol and Leo Tolstoy are often suggested," continued Breon, "and, indeed, South Africa can almost be seen as a modern Chekhovian drama in which the white minority stubbornly ignores the historical inevitability that is knocking at their doors."

Yale Review contributor Janet Devine made a different—though likewise complimentary—analogy by declaring that "Lelyveld does for South Africa today what Dickens did for nineteenth century London. His eye for the small, personal dramas of everyday South African life makes the inhumanity of the apartheid society vivid and real." Devine described Lelyveld's tone as "controlled," explaining that his anger at the white regime "emerges in his choice of material rather than in any polemic of his own." Furthermore, posited Devine, "in simple, concise language he describes the life circumstances of the various workers who ride with him, slowly building a documentary of deprivation, grinding poverty, and the greed of the white 'master' race. His odyssey on the commuter bus becomes a journey into the hellish interior of South Africa's labyrinthine political, sociological, and economic landscape." In the same way, according to the critic, the stories told by numerous political prisoners of their torture in detention "build on one another to produce a shattering picture of the cruel repression of the apartheid state."

Still other reviewers expressed similar opinions of *Move Your Shadow*. *Washington Post Book World* contributor Vincent Crapanzano averred that Lelyveld, as a foreign journalist, "came to know South Africa the way no South African, white or black, can know it," adding that "within limits he could cross the psychological and legal barriers of apartheid and see the contrasting worlds of whites and blacks." Donald Woods, a former newspaper editor in South Africa who was banned by the government in 1977, wrote in review of Lelyveld's book for *Books and Bookmen*: "*Move Your Shadow* is the best book I've read about South Africa by a writer who isn't from the country. Joseph Lelyveld is an American. Yet his is not a 'foreign look' at the country, and his are not the perspectives of the bystander or outsider. In fact the book is so informed and perceptive that on completing the last page I was left with the conviction that Lelyveld knows more about the essence of South Africa than most South Africans do."

R. W. Johnson, writing in *London Review of Books*, concurred, commenting that "this montage of interviews, reflections and rapportage conveys the texture of South African life at every level with a sensitivity and honesty not often found." Johnson explained further: "The characters do not quite talk for themselves. They are the people Lelyveld has chosen to interview and we always get his sensitive, wry, humane asides about them. Since it is these which thread the book together, it is difficult in the end not to feel that Lelyveld, for all his self-effacement, emerges as the hero of his own book." Additionally, Steven F. McDonald remarked in *New Leader*: "Lelyveld brings the whole country to life. In the process, he dispels the myths and irrelevant analogies whites use to defend their actions. . . . It is precisely the personal character of the narrative, the contact with the apartheid world Lelyveld affords us, that is the real strength of *Move Your Shadow*. Although a great deal has been written about South Africa, little focuses as sharply on the people, on their humanity and the truth of their daily existence." McDonald concluded: "Whether or not you agree, you will be touched—and troubled—by *Move Your Shadow*. Joseph Lelyveld is a talented, insightful writer, and his journal is marked by a rare sensitivity to the suffering in South Africa." Ronald Segal's tribute to *Move Your Shadow*, in his review for *Spectator*, was the declaration that "once in a while there comes a book on South Africa that hurtles its way into the heart. *Move Your Shadow* is such a book."

The only negative criticism of *Move Your Shadow* that appeared at all regularly in reviews was that Lelyveld offered no clear-cut predictions on the future of South Africa, nor did he suggest what the rest of the world should do, if anything, to hasten change there. "He does not address the question of sanctions against South Africa, which seems odd," noted *Los Angeles Times* foreign correspondent Charles T. Powers in his review for the *Los Angeles Times Book Review*. "There are cogent arguments on both sides of the debate," asserted Powers, "and it seems a deficiency of this book that Lelyveld, clearly a journalist of keen analytical abilities, does not discuss them, let alone recommend an answer." Similarly, George M. Fredrickson, writing in *New Republic*, had mixed feelings about the book: on the one hand, he announced that "for anyone who wants to comprehend the human meaning of apartheid his book is indispensable," and called Lelyveld "an extraordinarily perceptive and sensitive observer"; on the other hand he qualified his praise by adding, "But if we ask of the book what is likely to happen, or where do we go from here, is to invite disappointment." Shortly after Lelyveld left South Africa in 1983, the cultural and political situation worsened into a volatile pattern of protest and government reaction, and several critics faulted him for his lack of prescience. A writer in *Nation*, for example, made the point that "for all his keenness of vision, [Lelyveld] doesn't prepare us for the South Africa we read about today." The critic does, however, note that there are "a number of possible explanations for this short-sightedness, if that's what it is," and he suggested the possibilities that "the distortion is ours: restricted to newspaper and television accounts, we get only the flashpoints" or even that "no one could have predicted the magnitude of the current upheaval."

Conversely, a number of reviewers defended Lelyveld's abstention from the role of prognosticator. Among them was McDonald, who asserted, "Lelyveld does not indulge in the growth industry of predicting future scenarios for South Africa, nor does he spell out specific policy recommendations on such questions as divestment or constructive engagement. Instead, he leaves us with a statement of faith in South Africa's evolution: He believes the human animal has a will to survive."

Lelyveld himself, near the end of his book, made his position in resisting the seer's role explicit when he wrote, "Beyond all the fatuous theorizing and scenarios, there is the reality of what actually happens, day after day. Those I admired most, blacks and whites, were those who really looked." And, according to George Packer, in his *Nation* commentary, "if 'really looking' at South Africa means anything, it means looking at the things that don't fit our ideas. A first step is to remember that South Africa is more a part of Africa than a part of us, to concede its reality apart from our obsessions, to begin to fill in our ignorance about its continent. Really looking may be as simple as forcing ourselves to assume that we don't understand South Africa. *Move Your Shadow* contributes very little to the theoretical discussion; it doesn't advocate an American position or point a way out; and part of it has already been outdated by events. But in its insight and sensitivity to 'the reality of what actually happens, day after day,' Joseph Lelyveld's book is the best place I know of to begin to look."

CA INTERVIEW

CA interviewed Joseph Lelyveld by telephone on May 28, 1986, at the London Bureau of the *New York Times*.

CA: You've just been awarded a Pulitzer Prize, which was announced in April, 1986, for Move Your Shadow: South

Africa Black and White. *The book was described at my bookstore a couple of months before the announcement as a "steady seller." Has the Pulitzer raised attention and sales even more?*

LELYVELD: I think my publisher hopes it will. I don't stay in touch with that side of things on a very close basis. They made a small third printing as a result of the Pulitzer, and they're putting stickers on the covers. But it has been quite remarkable; it's sold at almost the same rate ever since it came out—never very sensationally, but quite steadily, across the country.

CA: Move Your Shadow *grew out of your two stints in South Africa as a* New York Times *correspondent, the first ending in 1966 when you were declared "one of South Africa's most notorious enemies in the world" and "out-kicked," and the second lasting from 1980 to 1983. Did you know when you returned that you'd be writing a book about apartheid?*

LELYVELD: I had in the back of my mind that, if the experience were as interesting and as rich as I hoped it would be, I might attempt to do that. I hadn't made any commitments or signed any contracts, but I'd thought about it as a possibility and kept it in mind while I was there. So I guess in some sense the idea of the book incubated all the time I was there, and I was looking at things both from the perspective of a newspaper correspondent and that of somebody who might want to sum up his experiences in a book.

CA: It must have been good having that opportunity to write about the experience both ways. There's so much you can't say in a news story, especially if it's very personal.

LELYVELD: There's so much you don't want to say in a news story. As a correspondent, I don't exactly try to conceal my feelings, but it's a matter of great importance to me that everyone I cover feels he's gotten a fair hearing and has been accurately and fairly represented. I think I had that reputation in South Africa the second time and had very good access to the government. Although the *New York Times* was not considered a friendly newspaper and in some respects I was not considered a friendly correspondent, they trusted me at some level and talked to me. I was grateful for that kind of relationship as a newspaper correspondent. When it came to writing my book, I felt that I could be personal and that I could be polemical to a degree. I didn't think of it as the work of a newspaper correspondent.

CA: Your mother is a scholar of English literature, and I noticed that you did your Harvard honors thesis on the poet William Butler Yeats. Were you an aspiring poet at that time, or was journalism already your chosen career?

LELYVELD: I wasn't an aspiring poet, but I wasn't interested in journalism either at that stage. I don't know quite what I was interested in; I was very confused about what I was going to do with my life. I really didn't think about journalism until after I'd graduated from Harvard.

CA: How did you get into journalism, then, and how did you happen to start at the New York Times?

LELYVELD: I went to the Columbia Journalism School after I left Harvard, really just hoping I would find some path there. Even then I believe I was probably thinking of something more like literary criticism than reporting. While I was there, I worked

for the first time for the *Times* as a copyboy. At the end of that year, I got a Fulbright fellowship to go to Burma. I'd left the *Times* before I got the Fulbright, but while I was in Burma I was a stringer for the *Times*. I wasn't on a retainer, but they did take a lot of articles from me, maybe twenty stories or so in the course of that year. That created a certain interest in me.

I then had to go in the army, and when I came out of the army I went back to the *Times* and was taken on again as a copyboy, but with what quickly became a kind of understanding that they would move me through to a staff position very rapidly, which they did in less than a year. And in less than three years after I came back as a copyboy, I was on my way to Africa as a foreign correspondent.

CA: Besides South Africa, you've written on a diversity of topics, including, for the New York Times Magazine *for January 20, 1985, CIA director William J. Casey. Do you usually choose your own topics for special pieces like that one, or are they suggested to you?*

LELYVELD: I suggested that one. I've done many pieces for the magazine. At that time I was a staff correspondent for the magazine and writing for no other part of the paper, so there was a feeling that I had to write on major subjects and themes. I would say that I suggested the great majority of them.

CA: At the beginning of Move Your Shadow *you said, "I had long had a weakness, amounting to a craving, for going back not only to South Africa but practically anywhere I had worked as a reporter"; that it was "one of the few ways a newspaperman could inject a little coherence and resonance into a vagabond life." Did the stays in New York between foreign posts lend a kind of perspective to what you'd seen and done while you were abroad?*

LELYVELD: Actually, when I first joined the *Times*, the thing I wanted to do most of all was to be a correspondent in India, where I had traveled on my way back from Burma. I thought that was the best assignment you could have on the *Times*. Luckily or unluckily, I got it very early. My life's ambition was fulfilled before I was thirty. I went to India. I found that very satisfying, but by the end of it, I no longer wanted to be a foreign correspondent; I came back to New York with the intention of never being a foreign correspondent again. As it happens, I've gone abroad three more times since then. But each time I've come back, it's been with the intention of never doing it again. In some ways, I'm not enthralled with the life of a foreign correspondent, although I always seem to be drawn into it.

CA: Your family must be very supportive. Has there been a place you've worried about taking them?

LELYVELD: The Congo—but they came.

CA: You said in the "Author's Note" in Move Your Shadow *that your wife, Carolyn, "discovered the book's title and much else," and that she'd seen the country from a perspective you hadn't. Would you tell me more about that?*

LELYVELD: She was working in two hospitals while she was there, a black hospital and a white hospital, doing play therapy programs for very sick kids. She was experiencing the society at a much more intimate level than I was, because she was dealing with moments of crisis in both black and white families whose children suffered from the same illnesses—largely leukemia, as it happens. She got to know a lot about the society and how people feel about things. One of the odd things was that whites tend to assume that blacks don't have the same feelings they do, when of course the reactions to such things as the imminent death of a child are not culturally determined. As far as I can see, they're very much the same.

CA: You described in Move Your Shadow *how jargon like "segmental autonomy" was used heavily in official circles to make the workings of apartheid seem more palatable morally. Did such deliberate linguistic muddling ever make it hard for you to discern and report the news?*

LELYVELD: I don't think so. To me, that was just another intriguing part of the country, the way people shielded themselves from the harsh realities that were really quite visible all around them. I liked the linguistic games in a way; I enjoyed keeping track of them. The people whose job it is to see what's going on there, if they're any good at all, aren't going to be misled by that sort of thing.

CA: Are the written histories of South Africa as skewed as one would expect them to be? Is the tribal history scantily treated?

LELYVELD: There are some very good histories of South Africa and of the various African peoples. There's a two-volume Oxford University history of South Africa that includes essays by scholars, and there's an awful lot of good social history by white and black scholars.

CA: One of the many interesting observations in the book—and one I hadn't read anywhere else—was that "for a people obsessed with their cultural identity, Afrikaners have surprisingly few cultural artifacts they can call their own." Do you attribute that to a lack of imagination?

LELYVELD: I think it's partly Calvinist culture. If you think of people like the Puritans and the various American Protestants that have descended from them, you realize that they did not normally (except in furniture, to some degree) express themselves through the visual arts.

CA: Has Move Your Shadow *drawn a large response from other people who've written about South Africa?*

LELYVELD: Many South African writers and foreigners who have written about South Africa have had a crack at reviewing the book—people like Nadine Gordimer, Anthony Sampson, and Conor Cruise O'Brien, to mention a few. Out of fifty or sixty reviews in the United States and Britain that I've seen, only two have been negative—a rather sneering one by an American academic and a very hurt one, I'm saddened to say, by Alan Paton.

CA: Do you read South African fiction?

LELYVELD: Yes, quite a lot. I read Nadine Gordimer, J. M. Coetzee, and many others. Among the black writers of the current generation, I just dip into their work for the flavor and the kinds of preoccupations; I don't think there's anyone in that group doing outstanding writing from a serious literary point of view. It's as if there is a feeling at large that you can only write about the struggle, and you can only write about the struggle from a heroic standpoint that will give people the

courage to go on. That's all very understandable, but it has a certain tendency to create propaganda. There are lots of other interesting writers. Among the mystery writers there's one named Wessel Ebersohn who's done some very clever, interesting, and in their way quite serious books.

CA: For the reporter living outside of South Africa—in London, for example—and trying to get that country's news, what are the best sources?

LELYVELD: You can't really do it from London unless you're dealing with the exiled groups. But I don't report South Africa from London.

CA: There are still plenty of correspondents there?

LELYVELD: Yes. And I think you have to be there now to get the news. The situation is so complex, and changing so fast.

CA: Is the conflict as far along as you might have predicted when you finished writing your book?

LELYVELD: I really steeled myself—maybe I went too far in this direction—not to put down what was going to happen. I think the whole drift of the book, from the title right on down, is that something big is going to happen, and probably soon. But I certainly didn't predict what has happened in the last two years. I can't exactly say I'm surprised by it, either. I just had the feeling that something has to break, that the iceberg is breaking up and there's going to be a lot of crashing.

CA: You moved to London in the fall of 1985 to become New York Times *bureau chief there. How are your working patterns different from what they've been before?*

LELYVELD: Not very. The story is very different, and I'm working in a bigger office, supervising other people as well as doing my own work. But I'm an old dog in this business, and I go about things the way I've always gone about them, which tends to be spending a little less time worrying about the higher politics of a place and a little more time trying to understand the society.

CA: What besides the wire services and the New York Times *do you read regularly for news or for perspective on current events?*

LELYVELD: I read the British press a lot now, five British papers every morning and three or four British weeklies. It's a very literate, well-informed perspective. I do that also for obvious occupational reasons.

CA: Do you have specific goals in your writing and reporting, or completely new interests you'd like to pursue?

LELYVELD: I have some projects in the back of my mind that I'd like to get to someday, but they're mostly things that I couldn't do and do the job I now have at the same time. And I'm quite happy in the job I have, so they're on the back burner.

CA: Then there isn't another book in the making?

LELYVELD: Not at this time. I hope there will be.

CA: What about the possibility of a collection of some of your past writing?

LELYVELD: I've toyed with that idea, because I have done some things that might lend themselves to a collection. In 1977 I had a weekly column in the *New York Times Magazine*. I did a long series once on a grade-school class. I've done things that had a certain continuity and are maybe a little less perishable than the daily news report from Washington. I've thought a bit about wanting to think it all out someday and see if a coherent collection could be shaped, but at the moment it's all in a warehouse. I don't know when I'll do that. Maybe after the movers come—we're not really settled into London yet.

BIOGRAPHICAL/CRITICAL SOURCES:

BOOKS

Move Your Shadow: South Africa Black and White, Times Books, 1985.

PERIODICALS

America, May 31, 1986.
Best Sellers, January, 1986.
Booklist, September 15, 1985.
Books and Bookmen, February, 1986.
Business Week, December 30, 1985.
Economist, April 12, 1986.
Globe and Mail (Toronto), May 3, 1986.
Kliatt, winter, 1987.
London Review of Books, July 3, 1986.
Los Angeles Times, November 8, 1986.
Los Angeles Times Book Review, December 8, 1985, November 2, 1986.
Mother Jones, November/December, 1985.
Nation, January 25, 1986.
New Leader, February 24, 1986.
New Republic, December 23, 1985.
New Statesman, March 13, 1987.
Newsweek, November 4, 1985.
New Yorker, November 24, 1986.
New York Review of Books, November 7, 1985.
New York Times, October 8, 1985, April 18, 1986.
New York Times Book Review, October 13, 1985, December 8, 1985, October 19, 1986.
Observer, December 1. 1985, February 9, 1986, July 20, 1986, February 15, 1987.
Spectator, February 22, 1986.
Washington Post Book World, November 3, 1985.
Yale Review, summer, 1986.

—Sketch by Joanne M. Peters
—Interview by Jean W. Ross

*   *   *

LESCHAK, Peter M.   1951-

PERSONAL: Born May 11, 1951, in Chisholm, Minn.; son of Peter (a miner) and Agnes (in retail sales; maiden name, Pavelich) Leschak; married Pamela Cope (a writer), May, 1974. *Education:* Attended College of St. Thomas, St. Paul, Minn., 1969-70; Ambassador College, B.A., 1974.

ADDRESSES: Home—Box 51, Side Lake, Minn. 55781.

CAREER: Lumberjack in Roseburg, Ore., 1973; printer in Baton Rouge, La., 1974; water plant operator in Chisolm, Minn., 1975-79; City of Hibbing, Hibbing, Minn., operator of waste water plant, 1979-84; writer, 1984—. Fire chief of French, Minn., volunteer fire department.

MEMBER: Authors Guild, Minnesota Fire Chiefs Association.

WRITINGS:

Letters From Side Lake: A Chronicle of Life in the North Woods, Harper, 1987.

Author of regular column in *TWA Ambassador*, 1985-86. Contributor to magazines. Contributing editor of *Twin Cities*, 1984-86, and *Minnesota Monthly*, 1984—.

WORK IN PROGRESS: The Bear Guardian: Northwoods Tales and Reflections and *Bumming With the Furies*, both collections of essays, and *Antelucan*, a novel.

SIDELIGHTS: Peter M. Leschak grew up in a small mining town in northern Minnesota. In 1969 he left the Mesabi Iron Range to attend college in the city of St. Paul. The author never felt comfortable with city life, however, so, after earning his college degree, Leschak returned to rural Minnesota. He and his wife settled near Side Lake, where they built a log home and began to explore the wilderness around them. Their experiences form the core of *Letters From Side Lake*.

"Mr. Leschak is an acute observer with genuine affection for his material," wrote John Tallmadge in the *New York Times Book Review*. His book is a collection of "dozens of stories told in a breezy, journalistic style." *Washington Post Book World* critic Vic Sussman agreed that Leschak is "a fine writer with an eye both for natural wonder and for irony . . . [and with a] great sense of humor that carries this lively book along." He added: "Leschak's engaging essays are happily free of bile, evangelism, and Thoreauvian moralizing on the evils of modern life." Sussman saw *Letters From Side Lake* as a celebration of "the beauty and adventure of the north woods . . . and the simplicity of small-town life."

Leschak told *CA:* "I agree with novelist Philip Roth that 'We writers are lucky: nothing truly bad can happen to us. It's all material.' One of the goals of a writer is to weave his own life into the tapestry of the culture. We're entertainers as well as reporters and teachers, and if we wish to reach others, we must be willing to offer a piece of ourselves. If you can tell a story (and all writing boils down to that) in such a way that the reader feels he knows you, then you are successful. In the terms of our ancient forebears, we are closer to the shaman than the scribe. It's just too bad it doesn't pay better."

BIOGRAPHICAL/CRITICAL SOURCES:

PERIODICALS

New York Times Book Review, June 28, 1987.
Washington Post Book World, July 12, 1987.

*   *   *

LESLIE, Phil   1909(?)-1988

OBITUARY NOTICE: Born c. 1909; died of cancer, September 23, 1988, in San Fernando (one source says Tarzana), Calif. Radio and television scriptwriter. Leslie, after being a Hollywood free-lance writer who wrote for such stars as Bob Hope and Roy Rogers, was hired as a radio scriptwriter for the popular "Fibber McGee and Molly" after its creator, Don Quinn, left in 1943. Calling the subsequent thirteen years the happiest of his writing life, Leslie went on to create radio favorites "Beulah" and "Major Hoople" after "Fibber" went off the air in the late fifties. Leslie successfully made the transition into television scriptwriting by contributing to such shows as "Dennis the Menace," "Hazel," "The Farmer's Daughter," "The Lucy Show," and "The Brady Bunch."

OBITUARIES AND OTHER SOURCES:

PERIODICALS

Los Angeles Times, September 24, 1988.
New York Times, September 26, 1988.
Washington Post, September 27, 1988.

* * *

LEVANT, Victor 1947-

PERSONAL: Born November 26, 1947, in Winnipeg, Manitoba, Canada; son of Edgar (a fur cutter) and Sarah (Blackerman) Levant. *Education:* Attended Sorbonne, University of Paris, 1968-69; McGill University, B.A. (with distinction), 1969, M.A. (with distinction), 1973, Ph.D., 1981.

ADDRESSES: *Home*—3490 Dorion, Montreal, Quebec, Canada H2K 4B6. *Office*—Department of Social Science, John Abbott College, Box 2000, de Bellevue, Quebec, Canada H9X 3L9.

CAREER: Lecturer in sociology at Dawson College, 1971-72; lecturer in political science at Concordia University, 1972-74; John Abbott College, de Bellevue, Quebec, professor of humanities, 1972—. Lecturer at University of Quebec, summers, 1976 and 1977; lecturer at international conferences; interviewed on Canadian television and radio programs; political commentator for Radio-Canada. Director of research for Via le Monde Film Productions, 1982-84; film and television consultant; consultant to National Film Board of Canada.

WRITINGS:

Capital and Labor: Partners?, Steel Rail Press, 1966.
(Co-author) *How to Make a Killing: Canadian Military Involvement in the Indo-China War*, Presse Solidaire, 1972.
(Co-editor) *How to Buy a Country: Research Monograph on Pentagon Contracts*, Presse Solidaire, 1973.
Quiet Complicity: Canada and the Vietnam War, Between the Lines, 1987.
The Restaurant Guide of Montreal, Hurtubise, 1988.

Contributor to magazines and newspapers.

WORK IN PROGRESS: *A Personal Guide to Health*, publication expected in 1990.

AVOCATIONAL INTERESTS: Gestalt therapy training, international travel (Europe, China, Japan, Pakistan, Algeria, the Caribbean).

BIOGRAPHICAL/CRITICAL SOURCES:

PERIODICALS

Globe and Mail (Toronto), February 21, 1987.

* * *

LEVINE, Abby 1943-

PERSONAL: Born September 27, 1943, in New York, N.Y.; daughter of Charles A. (in business) and Edna (a librarian; maiden name, Deshel) Bernstein; married Jonathan Levine (a human relations executive), June 13, 1965; children: Sarah, Susannah. *Education:* Cornell University, B.A., 1964, M.Ed., 1966.

ADDRESSES: *Home*—9509 Ridgeway Ave., Evanston, Ill. 60203. *Office*—Albert Whitman and Co., 5747 West Howard, Niles, Ill. 60648.

CAREER: Free-lance editor, 1970-80; University of Pittsburgh Press, Pittsburgh, Pa., editor, 1980-81; free-lance editor, 1981-83; Albert Whitman and Co., Niles, Ill., editor, 1983—. Writer.

MEMBER: Children's Reading Round Table.

WRITINGS:

FOR CHILDREN

(With daughter, Sarah Levine) *Sometimes I Wish I Were Mindy*, Albert Whitman, 1986.
What Did Mommy Do Before You?, Albert Whitman, 1987.

WORK IN PROGRESS: A third children's book, for Albert Whitman.

* * *

LEVINE, Charles H(oward) 1939-1988

OBITUARY NOTICE—See index for *CA* sketch: Born July 13, 1939, in Hartford, Conn.; died of a heart attack, September 23, 1988. Educator, editor, and author. A specialist in the study of public administration, Levine spoke out in favor of the civil service and warned against too great a reliance on political appointees. Beginning in the mid-1960s he taught business, government, and urban studies at a succession of universities, including Michigan State, Maryland, Syracuse, Kansas, and American. During the 1980s he held senior posts at the Brookings Institution, the Library of Congress, and the National Commission on the Public Service. Levine wrote *Racial Conflict and the American Mayor: Power, Polarization, and Performance; Managing Fiscal Stress;* and, with Irene S. Rubin and George G. Wolohojian, *The Politics of Retrenchment: How Local Governments Manage Fiscal Stress.* He helped to edit publications such as the book *Urban Politics: Past, Present, and Future* and the periodical *Administration and Society.*

OBITUARIES AND OTHER SOURCES:

BOOKS

Who's Who in America, 45th edition, Marquis, 1988.

PERIODICALS

New York Times, September 25, 1988.
Washington Post, September 25, 1988.

* * *

LEVINE, Peter D. 1944-

PERSONAL: Born June 23, 1944, in Brooklyn, N.Y.; son of Sam (a teacher) and Pearl (a teacher) Levine; married Gale Auerbach (an artist), June 19, 1965; children: Ruth. *Education:* Columbia University, B.A., 1965, M.A., 1966; Rutgers University, Ph.D., 1971. *Religion:* Jewish.

ADDRESSES: *Home*—1895 Melrose, East Lansing, Mich. 48823. *Office*—Department of History, 336 Morrill Hall, Michigan State University, East Lansing, Mich. 48824.

CAREER: Michigan State University, East Lansing, instructor, 1969-70, assistant professor, 1970-71, associate professor, 1971-82, professor of American history and associate chairman of department of history, 1982—.

WRITINGS:

State Legislative Parties in the Jacksonian Era: New Jersey, 1829-1844, Fairleigh Dickinson University Press, 1977.

A. G. Spalding and the Rise of Baseball, Oxford University Press, 1985.

Editor of series on sport and history for Oxford University Press. Contributor to history journals. Editor of *Journal of Baseball History*.

WORK IN PROGRESS: Jewish Experience in American Sport, 1881-1980, completion expected in 1989; *A Documentary History of Sport in America*.

*   *   *

LINDEY, Christine   1947-

PERSONAL: Born in 1947 in England; daughter of J. C. A. and M. M. (Taichardat) Chaimowicz; married Raymond Lindey (a caretaker), 1967. *Education:* Courtauld Institute of Art, London, B.A., 1973.

ADDRESSES: Home—London, England. *Office*—Watford School of Art, Hertfordshire, England.

CAREER: Part-time lecturer in art history at art schools in and around London, England, 1973—. Lecturer at Watford School of Art, 1976—.

WRITINGS:

Surrealist Painting and Sculpture, Morrow, 1980.
Twentieth Century Painting: Bonnard to Rothko, F. Warne, 1981.

WORK IN PROGRESS: A comparative study of Soviet and Western art during the Cold War; a film about popular Western art in the 1950s.

SIDELIGHTS: Christine Lindey told *CA:* "My current area of interest is art since World War II. I aim to write in a manner which is accessible to the non-specialist, and I try to avoid unnecessarily obtuse terms. My concern is with public response and the context within which art operates, as well as the aims of the artists themselves."

*   *   *

LINN, Allen   1955-

PERSONAL: Born September 3, 1955, in Callah, Mich.; son of Hollis B. (a teacher) and Nora A. (a nurse; maiden name, Weidermann) Linn; married Vanessa Tailler (a writer), December 28, 1986; children: Joseph. *Education:* Attended Vishing Community College, 1973-75, and Wharfside State University, 1981; Southeastern Michigan University, B.S., 1984. *Politics:* "Libertarian/anarchist." *Religion:* "Undecided."

ADDRESSES: Home—8330 Lochdale Ave., Dearborn Heights, Mich. 48127.

CAREER: Worked odd jobs, including pizza delivery, 1973-75; Monolith Electronics, Satenee, Mich., radio repairman, 1976-84; Western Electronics, Detroit, Mich., engineer, 1985—. Columnist for *Monitor-Leader*, 1986—.

WRITINGS:

Lawyers: How to Eliminate Them From Your Life, LeMans, 1985.
Fundamentalists: The Threat to Our Constitution, Archangel, 1986.
Higher Ground; or, How to Arrive at the Truth, Archangel, 1987.
The Beginner's Guide to Anarchy, LeMans, 1988.

WORK IN PROGRESS: Ninja Driving, "a spoof on books relating Zen practices to everyday tasks"; *I've Heard That*, "a guide to twisting ordinary conversation into double-entendre."

AVOCATIONAL INTERESTS: Computers, cats, science fiction, cooking, coffee, and beer.

*   *   *

LIPSCOMB, Commander F. W.
See LIPSCOMB, F(rank) W(oodgate)

*   *   *

LIPSCOMB, F(rank) W(oodgate)   1903-1983
(Commander F. W. Lipscomb)

OBITUARY NOTICE—See index for *CA* sketch: Born August 27, 1903, in Monmouth, England; died January 3, 1983. Naval officer and author. Lipscomb was an officer in the Royal Navy who spent part of his career in submarine service, receiving the Order of the British Empire in 1930 for heroism during a submarine accident. He rose to the rank of commander, under which title he wrote several books. His first, *The British Submarine*, was considered a standard work on the subject and was issued by the Board of Admiralty to ships and to shore installations. Lipscomb also wrote *The D-Day Story*, *Historic Submarines*, *One Hundred Years of the America's Cup*, and, with John Davies, *"Up She Rises": The Story of Naval Salvage*. He also contributed to naval journals.

OBITUARIES AND OTHER SOURCES:

Date of death provided by wife, Theodora Lipscomb.

*   *   *

LIZOTTE, Ken   1948-

PERSONAL: Surname is pronounced "Liz-ott"; born June 26, 1948, in Framingham, Mass.; son of Harold Ernest (a machinist) and Virginia (Walsh) Lizotte. *Education:* Stonehill College, B.A., 1970.

ADDRESSES: Home and office—99 Oxford St., Arlington, Mass. 02174.

CAREER: Free-lance writer. Has worked as an educational writer for American Management Association, New York, N.Y., as a public relations writer for Public Broadcasting Service (PBS), and as a technical and promotional writer for Polaroid Corporation, Parker Brothers, and Lalama Advertising; has taught writing and visual imagery courses at Boston Architectural Center and Cambridge Center for Adult Education. Founder of CareerScape (a career strategies firm). Public relations director of Cambridge Family Young Men's Christian Association (YMCA), 1980-87.

MEMBER: National Writers Union.

WRITINGS:

(With Danielle Gagnon Torrez) *High Inside: Memoirs of a Baseball Wife*, Putnam, 1983.
(With Manfred F. R. Kets de Vries and Danny Miller) *Unstable at the Top: Inside the Troubled Corporation*, New American Library, 1988.

Contributor of articles to periodicals, including the *Boston Herald, Boston Globe, Boston Phoenix, San Francisco Ex-*

aminer, Las Vegas Journal, New Age, Real Paper, Nevada, Gloucester, Cosmopolitan, Hustler, Business Today, Basketball Digest, and *New York Post.* Business columnist for *Boston* magazine.

WORK IN PROGRESS: Executive Funhouse, a book about humor in the American workplace.

SIDELIGHTS: Ken Lizotte told *CA* that he is "interested in causing people to debate issues" and to explore the importance of controversial subjects. He is also interested in "catalyzing new ways of thinking and interpersonal interaction."

BIOGRAPHICAL/CRITICAL SOURCES:

PERIODICALS

Los Angeles Times, August 11, 1983.
Middlesex News, November 3, 1985.

*   *   *

LLOYD, Adrien
    See GELB, Alan Lloyd

*   *   *

LOCK, Margaret M.   1936-

PERSONAL: Born February 26, 1936, in Bromley, Kent, England; daughter of Albert and Anne (Forrester) Foreman; married Richard Lock (a professor), May 2, 1965; children: Adam, Gudrun. *Education:* University of Leeds, B.Sc., 1961; Stanford Inter-University Center, Tokyo, Japan, Japanese Language Diploma, 1973; University of California, Berkeley, Ph.D., 1976.

ADDRESSES: Home—356 Landsdowne Ave., Westmount, Quebec, Canada H3Z 2L4. *Office*—Department of Humanities and Social Studies in Medicine, McIntyre Medical Sciences Bldg., 3655 Drummond St., Montreal, Quebec, Canada H3G 1Y6.

CAREER: McGill University, Montreal, Quebec, assistant professor, 1977-81, associate professor, 1981-86, professor of anthropology, 1987—.

MEMBER: International Association for the Study of Traditional Asian Medicine, American Anthropological Association (fellow), Canadian Sociological and Anthropological Association (fellow), Canadian Asian Studies Association, Association for Asian Studies (fellow), Society for Medical Anthropology, Groupe Inter-Universitaire de Recherche en Anthropologie Medicale et en Ethnopsychiatrie, Sigma Xi (national lecturer, 1988-90).

WRITINGS:

East Asian Medicine, University of California Press, 1980, revised edition, 1984.
(Editor with Edward Norbeck) *Health, Illness, and Medical Care in Japan: Cultural and Social Dimensions,* University of Hawaii Press, 1987.
(Editor with Deborah Gordon) *Biomedicine Examined,* D. Reidel (Holland), 1988.

Contributor to academic journals. Editor of series "Culture, Illness, and Healing," published by D. Reidel.

WORK IN PROGRESS: Aging in Japan: Modernization, Mid-Life, and Menopause, publication expected in 1990.

SIDELIGHTS: Margaret M. Lock told *CA:* "I have been visiting and doing research in Japan since 1965. My original interest was prompted by exposure to Japanese literature, film, and the martial arts. As an anthropologist, I am interested in the way in which ideas about health and illness, including those of modern medicine, are products of a particular historical and cultural milieu. At present, for example, I am studying the way in which Japanese ideas about death are different from those generally accepted in the West. Brain death is not acceptable in Japan, hence heart transplants cannot be performed there despite the availability of the necessary technology."

Lock added that she is fluent in Japanese and French and that her travels have taken her throughout Europe, Africa, South and Southeast Asia, and the Far East. Her motivation for writing is to promote cross-cultural understanding and an awareness of the limitations of current approaches to modernization.

AVOCATIONAL INTERESTS: Tennis, skiing, gardening.

*   *   *

LOERTSCHER, David V.   1940-

PERSONAL: Born August 22, 1940, in Park City, Utah; son of David W. and Maurine (Vickers) Loertscher; married Sandra Despain; children: Paul, Landon, Nathan, Mark, Noal, Dion, Phyllis, Darin, Rebecca. *Education:* University of Utah, B.S., 1964; University of Washington, Seattle, M.L., 1967; Indiana University—Bloomington, Ph.D., 1973.

ADDRESSES: Home—P.O. Box 266, Castle Rock, Colo. 80104. *Office*—Libraries Unlimited, Inc., P.O. Box 3988, Englewood, Colo. 80112.

CAREER: Purdue University, West Lafayette, Ind., assistant professor of library science, 1973-76; University of Arkansas, Fayetteville, professor of library science, 1978-85; University of Oklahoma, Norman, professor of library science, 1986; Libraries Unlimited, Inc., Englewood, Colo., senior acquisitions editor, 1987—.

MEMBER: American Library Association, Association for Educational Communications and Technology.

WRITINGS:

A Nonbook Cataloging Sampler, Armadillo Press, 1975.
(With Janet G. Stroud) *PSES: Purdue Self-Evaluation System for School Media Centers,* Volume I: *Elementary Catalog,* Volume II: *Junior Senior High Catalog,* Hi Willow Research and Publishing, 1976.
(With Blanche Woolls and Donald Shirey) *Evaluation Techniques for School Library/Media Programs: A Work Shop Outline,* Graduate School of Library and Information Sciences, University of Pittsburgh, 1977.
School Library Media Centers, ERIC Clearinghouse on Information Resources, Syracuse University, 1980.
(With Paul M. Roper) *Modular Computer Lesson Design,* Hi Willow Research and Publishing, 1982, 2nd edition, 1985.
(With Blanche Woolls) *The Use of Technology in the Administrative Function of School Library Media Programs,* Hi Willow Research and Publishing, 1983.
(With May L. Ho) *Computerized Collection for School Library Media Centers,* Hi Willow Research and Publishing, 1986.
(Editor with Blanche Woolls) *The Microcomputer Facility and the School Library Media Specialist,* American Library Association, 1986.
(Editor) *Measures of Excellence for School Library Media Centers,* Libraries Unlimited, 1987.

Taxonomies of the School Library Media Program, Libraries Unlimited, 1988.
(With William Studwell) *Cataloging Books: A Workbook of Examples,* Libraries Unlimited, 1989.

SIDELIGHTS: David V. Loertscher told *CA:* "The aim of all my research and writing has been to point the school library media program toward having a substantial impact on the curriculum of the school as opposed to a peripheral one. After lecturing in twenty-nine states, I am impressed that school library service in the nation's schools is unbalanced and spotty, in spite of considerable spending by the federal government in the 1960s. My research has shown that school libraries, where they are staffed properly, do have a considerable impact on how much and what young people read. More and more, library media specialists are trying to assist teachers to exploit the vast resources of the library media center in learning activities.

"As a sideline, and in view of having seven sons, I have had considerable experience in Boy and Explorer Scouting, the aim of which has been not only to have many young men achieve the rank of Eagle Scout, but to build strong moral character and leadership skills. To help build young men who can contribute to the solution of societal problems rather than be a problem has been one of my most rewarding experiences."

*   *   *

LOGAN, Joshua (Lockwood)   1908-1988

OBITUARY NOTICE—See index for *CA* sketch: Born October 5, 1908, in Texarkana, Tex.; died of supranuclear palsy, July 12, 1988, in New York, N.Y. Director, producer, actor, and author. In the late 1940s Logan directed and co-authored two of Broadway's most popular productions—"Mister Roberts," written with Thomas Heggen, and "South Pacific," for which he shared a Pulitzer Prize in drama with Richard Rodgers and Oscar Hammerstein. His many other director's credits include the Broadway shows "Annie Get Your Gun" and "The World of Suzie Wong" and the films "Bus Stop" and "Camelot." Logan worked in theater and film throughout his career, showing talent from the time he was a young student at Princeton University. He acted on stage before achieving his first major success as a director with "I Married an Angel," in 1938; he also produced several shows. For many years Logan struggled with manic-depressive illness, and late in life he toured the country to offer encouragement to fellow sufferers. In addition to plays, his writings include the screen adaptation of "Mister Roberts"; its sequel, "Ensign Pulver"; and the autobiographies *Josh: My Up and Down, In and Out Life* and *Movie Stars, Real People, and Me.*

OBITUARIES AND OTHER SOURCES:

BOOKS

Contemporary Theatre, Film, and Television, Volume 4, Gale, 1987.
Current Biography, H. W. Wilson, 1988.

PERIODICALS

Chicago Tribune, July 13, 1988.
Los Angeles Times, July 13, 1988.
New York Times, July 13, 1988.
Times (London), July 14, 1988.

LOGUE, John   1933-

PERSONAL: Born July 7, 1933, in Bay Minette, Ala.; son of Hanchey E. (a 4-H leader) and Pauline (a homemaker and musician; maiden name, McLoed) Logue; married Helen Roberts (a technical writer and computer expert), August 15, 1959; children: John, Jr., Mac, Joey. *Education:* Auburn University, B.A., 1955. *Religion:* Episcopalian.

ADDRESSES: Home—2737 11th Ave. S., Birmingham, Ala. 35205. *Office*—Southern Progress Corp., P.O. Box 523, Birmingham, Ala. 35201. *Agent*—Frederick Hill Assoc., 2237 Union St., San Francisco, Calif. 94123.

CAREER: Montgomery Adviser, Montgomery, Ala., police reporter, 1955; reporter for United Press (UP; now United Press International), 1957; *Atlanta Journal,* Atlanta, Ga., sportswriter, 1957-67; Southern Progress Corp., Birmingham, Ala., feature writer, 1967-68, managing editor, 1968-73, and creative director, 1988—, for *Southern Living* magazine. Editor in chief of Oxmoor House, 1973—. *Military service:* U.S. Air Force, 1955-57; became first lieutenant.

MEMBER: P.E.N., Mystery Writers of America.

AWARDS, HONORS: Edgar Allen Poe Award nomination for best first novel from Mystery Writers of America, 1979, for *Follow the Leader.*

WRITINGS:

Follow the Leader (mystery novel), Crown, 1979.
Replay: Murder (mystery novel), Ballantine, 1983.
Flawless Execution (mystery novel), Ballantine, 1986.
Boats Against the Current (novel), Little, Brown, 1987.

WORK IN PROGRESS: A World War II novel.

SIDELIGHTS: Atlanta's U.S. Open golf tournament is the setting of John Logue's murder mystery *Follow the Leader.* Two tournament leaders are killed and clues point to a member of the Tour; Associated Press sportswriter John Morris and a local detective pursue the investigation. "Mr. Logue, himself a former sportswriter familiar with the Tour, gives us good golf, good suspense, and an interesting look at the golf professional and his life," wrote a *New Yorker* critic. "'Follow the Leader' brings us the talk, tensions and hangups of the pros," concurred Newgate Callendar in the *New York Times Book Review.* "Mr. Logue writes very well. His dialogue is crisp and unsentimental, his knowledge of the subject is all-encompassing. Not only golfers will be delighted with this book." In *Replay: Murder,* another Logue mystery novel, sportswriter Morris reappears, investigating a case that involves Georgia A & M's football organization and includes scandal, drugs, and murder.

Logue's novel *Boats Against the Current*—set in Montgomery, Alabama, in 1967—tells of a black woman intent on burying her son, killed in Vietnam, in a whites-only cemetery. Newsman Jack Harris covers the provocative story; in the course of his reporting he uncovers an even more incendiary situation that involves the state governor's peddling of criminal pardons. Writing in the *New York Times Book Review,* Henry Mayer commented that "Mr. Logue . . . nicely catches the inky ambiance of the newsroom . . . and he has created a persuasive narrative voice for Jack Harris." The critic did feel, however, that Logue's "shifting in and out of third-person narration . . . sever[s] the dramatic links his complicated tale requires"; Mayer also pointed out that, at times, "violent action substitutes for acuity in characterization" and "the mood of the novel seems distinctly late 1970's." Yet the reviewer concluded: "Despite the historical discontinuities of the mood, Mr. Logue has written a powerful epitaph for the social conflict that still gripped Alabama in 1967."

Logue told *CA* that he has "an abiding interest in the roles of journalists in the interpretation of their own times, and in their own impact upon those times."

BIOGRAPHICAL/CRITICAL SOURCES:

PERIODICALS

Los Angeles Times Book Review, September 4, 1983.
New Yorker, September 10, 1979.
New York Times Book Review, June 24, 1979, April 26, 1987.

*   *   *

LOMPERIS, Timothy J.   1947-

PERSONAL: Born March 6, 1947, in Guntur, India; son of Clarence G. (an American missionary) and Marjorie (an American missionary; maiden name, Larsen) Lomperis; married Ana Maria Turner (a university professor), May 15, 1976; children: Kristina Maria, John Scott Anders. *Education:* Augustana College, Rock Island, Ill., A.B., 1969; Johns Hopkins School of Advanced International Studies, M.A., 1975; Duke University, M.A., 1978, Ph.D., 1981. *Religion:* Lutheran.

ADDRESSES: Home—105 Autumn Dr., Chapel Hill, N.C. 27514. Office—Department of Political Science, 214 Perkins Library, Duke University, Durham, N.C. 27706.

CAREER: Lutheran Immigration and Refugee Service, New York, N.Y., special assistant to the director and head of Lao program, 1975-76; Louisiana State University, Baton Rouge, assistant professor of political science, 1980-83; Duke University, Durham, N.C., assistant professor of political science, 1983—. *Military service:* U.S. Army, 1969-73; served in Vietnam; became first lieutenant; received Bronze Star and Vietnam Army Staff Medal first class.

MEMBER: International Studies Association, American Political Science Association, American Studies Association.

AWARDS, HONORS: Helen Dwight Reid Award from American Political Science Association, 1981, for dissertation in international relations, "A Conceptual Framework for Deriving the Lessons of History: The U.S. Involvement in Vietnam as a Case Study"; Olin fellow at Harvard University's Center for International Affairs, 1985-86.

WRITINGS:

Hindu Influence on Greek Philosophy: The Odyssey of the Soul From the Upanishads to Plato, Minerva Associates, 1984.
The War Everyone Lost—and Won: America's Intervention in Vietnam's Twin Struggles, Louisiana State University Press, 1984.
Reading the Wind: The Literature of the Vietnam War, Duke University Press, 1987.

WORK IN PROGRESS: *Through a Prism: The Lessons of Vietnam in Comparative Context*, publication expected in 1989.

SIDELIGHTS: Timothy J. Lomperis told *CA:* "My interest in Vietnam was sparked by the two tours of duty I served there, during which time a fear gnawed at me: we Americans didn't seem to know what we were doing in Indochina. Since I had invested too much of myself in this war, I was determined, for myself at least, to plumb the depths of this experience.

This 'plumbing' is continuing, but one of the first things to strike me was that after 1968 the communists had lost their direction as well. It is from this perspective on mutual ignorance that I developed the thesis for *The War That Everyone Lost—And Won*, that victory and defeat were shared by both sides. Obviously, then, when the subject turns to lessons, I have come to strongly believe that the Vietnam War is too complicated for easy historical lessons.

"In my next book, *Through a Prism*, I will explore the quest for lessons from the vantage point that whatever lessons there are will have to be teased out from the political setting of each historical case. There is an enormous amount of literature on Vietnam, both nonfiction and fiction. It was the weighing of the relative contributions of each against an overall understanding of the war that I sought to analyze in my recent *Reading the Wind*."

*   *   *

LONDON, Jack   1915-1988

OBITUARY NOTICE—See index for *CA* sketch: Born October 10, 1915, in Duluth, Minn.; died of cancer complicated by Parkinson's disease, January 18, 1988. Educator, lithographer, and author. London worked in industry, chiefly lithography, until he turned to academia in the late 1940s. He was an assistant professor and researcher at the University of Chicago between 1948 and 1953, specializing in industrial relations. He then taught adult education at the University of California, Berkeley, beginning as assistant professor, rising to full professor in 1964, and retiring in 1983. London was co-author of several works, including *The Worker Views His Union*, *Some Reflections on Defining Adult Education*, *Adult Education and Social Class*, and *Learning Opportunities for Adults*, Volume III: *The Non-Participation Issue: Case Study, United States*. With Jeanne Ewing he wrote *Societal Factors Affecting Education: Cultural and Social Foundations*. He also contributed to numerous scholarly studies and periodicals.

OBITUARIES AND OTHER SOURCES:

Date of death provided by Jeanne B. Ewing.

*   *   *

LONDON, Laura
   See CURTIS, Sharon and
   CURTIS, Thomas Dale

*   *   *

LONG, Cynthia   1956-

PERSONAL: Born October 9, 1956, in Toronto, Ontario, Canada; daughter of Robert G. (an engineer) and Vivien (Wearne) Long; married Michael Waldin (a publisher), July 29, 1984; children: Robert Mikael. *Education:* Trent University, B.A. (with honors), 1978.

ADDRESSES: Home—2 Chicora Ave., No. 2, Toronto, Ontario, Canada M5R 1T6. *Agent*—Harold Ober Associates, 40 East 49th St., New York, N.Y. 10017.

CAREER: Writer.

AWARDS, HONORS: Grants from Canada Council and Ontario Arts Council.

WRITINGS:

Wishbones (novel), McClelland & Stewart, 1985.

Also author of play "Monroe."

WORK IN PROGRESS: A collection of children's stories and fairytales.

SIDELIGHTS: Cynthia Long told *CA:* "I received warm support and inspiration from the late Margaret Lawrence. At the moment I am very much a mother and only somewhat a writer, but my life is so full that I believe there will be much to write about, and soon."

*   *   *

LONG, Earlene (Roberta)   1938-

PERSONAL: Born October 4, 1938, in Ford County, Ill.; daughter of Earl Robert (a farmer) and Estella Mary (a director of Christian education; maiden name, Rollins) Ketchum; married Richard Guy Long, Jr. (a parts counterman), September 3, 1965; children: Mary Catherine, Richard Vincent. *Education:* Purdue University, B.S., 1963.

ADDRESSES: Home—P.O. Box 1712, Cheyenne, Wyo. 82003. *Office*—Needs, Inc., P.O. Box 404, Cheyenne, Wyo. 82003.

CAREER: Writer, 1954—. Director of Needs, Inc., a non-profit, short-term emergency help agency, 1982—.

WRITINGS:

CHILDREN'S PICTURE BOOKS

Johnny's Egg, Addison-Wesley, 1980.
Gone Fishing, Houghton, 1984.

Contributor to magazines, including *Family Circle, Woman's Day,* and *Good Housekeeping.*

WORK IN PROGRESS: Several children's books; an adult horror novel; a nonfiction book on "how to make it on almost nothing."

SIDELIGHTS: Earlene Long told *CA:* "I write because I must. A story just screams to come out. The fact that it is published is very nice and I do enjoy seeing my work in print. But published or not, I must write. Sometimes it is to make a special point in a new way as in *Johnny's Egg* (if at first you don't succeed, try, try again). Sometimes the story is to show relationships as in *Gone Fishing.* All of it is meant to show at least one particular 'slice of life,' to hopefully 'be there' for someone who really needs it at the proper time."

AVOCATIONAL INTERESTS: Reading, quilting, knitting, land reclamation, earthworms, organic gardening.

*   *   *

LONG, Theodore E(dward)   1944-

PERSONAL: Born September 7, 1944, in Steubenville, Ohio; son of Edward Victor (a Lutheran pastor) and Christine (a librarian; maiden name, Hecht) Long; married Betty Grube (a health administrator), August 20, 1965; children: Edward Andrew, Rachel Elizabeth. *Education:* Capital University, B.A., 1965; Duke University, M.A., 1968; University of Virginia, Ph.D., 1979. *Religion:* Lutheran.

ADDRESSES: Home—Washington, Pa. *Office*—Department of Sociology, Washington and Jefferson College, Washington, Pa. 15301.

CAREER: George Washington University, Washington, D.C., visiting assistant professor of sociology, 1969-70; Hollins College, Roanoke, Va., 1970-80, began as instructor, became assistant professor of sociology, chairman of department, 1974-75; Washington and Jefferson College, Washington, Pa., associate professor of sociology and chairman of department, 1980—. Guest lecturer at Hollins College, 1984. Member of advisory board of Clinical Pastoral Education Center, Mental Health Services, Roanoke, 1974-75; member of board of directors of Citizen's Association for Justice in Virginia, 1974-75, and Offender Aid and Restoration of Roanoke, 1975-76; member of council of Southwestern Pennsylvania Synod, Evangelical Lutheran Church in America, 1987-91.

MEMBER: American Sociological Association, Association for the Sociology of Religion (member of executive council, 1981-83; executive officer, 1983-87), Society for the Study of Social Problems, Society for the Scientific Study of Religion, Religious Research Association (member of board of directors, 1984-86 and 1987-89), Southern Sociological Society, Eastern Sociological Society, North Central Sociological Society, Pennsylvania Sociological Society.

AWARDS, HONORS: Grant from Society for the Scientific Study of Religion, 1985-86.

WRITINGS:

(Editor with Jeffrey K. Hadden, and contributor) *Religion and Religiosity in America: Studies in Honor of Joseph H. Fichter,* Crossroad/Continuum, 1983.
(Contributor) *Prophetic Religion and Politics,* Paragon House, 1986.
(Contributor) *Religion and the Political Order,* Paragon House, 1987.

Contributor to sociology journals. Associate editor of *Sociological Analysis,* 1979-81, and *Review of Religious Research,* 1980-83.

WORK IN PROGRESS: Smokestacks and Steeples, "a study of a church-labor coalition's challenge to Pittsburgh banks, industrial corporations, and church denominations, on the issue of unemployment."

*   *   *

LOSEV, S(ergei) A(ndreevich)   1927-1988

OBITUARY NOTICE: Born September 22, 1927, in Yurino, U.S.S.R.; died of a heart attack, October 3, 1988, in Moscow, U.S.S.R. Administrator, journalist and author. Losev, an influential member of the Communist party, was director general of the official Soviet news agency, Tass. He wrote a number of books in Russian on such subjects as American crime and criminals, President Richard M. Nixon and the Watergate affair, and assassinations of the 1960s (including those of John F. Kennedy, Martin Luther King, Jr., Robert F. Kennedy, and Malcolm X). His only book translated into English is *The Middle East—Oil and Oil Policy,* which discusses the petroleum industry and world politics from 1945 to the 1980s. Losev was a member of the Communist party's Central Auditing Commission, a delegate to two Communist party congresses, the president of the European Alliance of News Agencies, and the deputy chairman of the U.S.S.R. Union of Journalists.

OBITUARIES AND OTHER SOURCES:

BOOKS

The International Who's Who, 50th edition, Europa, 1986.

PERIODICALS

Chicago Tribune, October 5, 1988.
Washington Post, October 5, 1988.

* * *

LOTHSTEIN, Leslie Martin 1942-

PERSONAL: Born October 20, 1942, in New York, N.Y.; son of Marvin Louis (a lawyer) and Rose (an entertainer; maiden name, Matler) Lothstein; married Mary Anne Williams (a clinical psychologist), December 24, 1971; children: Ted, Dan, Jessica. *Education:* Attended Johns Hopkins University, 1960-61; Queens College of the City University of New York, B.A., 1964; Columbia University, M.A., 1967; Duke University, Ph.D., 1971; postdoctoral study at Harvard University, 1971-73.

ADDRESSES: Office—Department of Psychology, Case Western Reserve University, University Circle, Cleveland, Ohio 44106.

CAREER: Director of psychology at the Institute of Living, Hartford, Conn.; associate professor of psychology at Case Western Reserve University, Cleveland, Ohio. Member of advisory board of Whiting Forensic Institute.

MEMBER: American Psychological Association (fellow), American Group Psychology Association, Harry Benjamin Gender Dysphoria Association, Connecticut Psychological Association.

WRITINGS:

Female-to-Male Transsexualism: Historical, Clinical, and Theoretical Issues, Routledge & Kegan Paul, 1983.

WORK IN PROGRESS: Theoretical Aspects of Sexual Deviations: An Annotated Bibliography of Transsexualism; research on gender identity in adolescence.

SIDELIGHTS: Leslie Martin Lothstein informed *CA* that he is interested in "the origins of self identity and the treatment of borderline and narcissistic disorders."

* * *

LOTT, Bret 1958-

PERSONAL: Born October 8, 1958, in Los Angeles, Calif., son of Wilman Sequoia (a corporative executive) and Barbara (a banker; maiden name, Holmes) Lott; married Melanie Kai Swank (an office manager), June 28, 1980; children: Zebulun Holmes, Jacob Daynes. *Education:* California State University, Long Beach, B.A., 1981; University of Massachusetts—Amherst, M.F.A., 1984. *Religion:* Christian.

ADDRESSES: Home—1215-A Meadow Park Ln., Mt. Pleasant, S. C. 29464. *Office*—Department of English, College of Charleston, Charleston, S. C. 29424. *Agent*—Marian Young, Young Agency, 812 West 181 St., New York, N. Y. 10033.

CAREER: Big Yellow House, Inc., Santa Barbara, Calif., cook's trainer, 1977-79; RC Cola, Los Angeles, Calif., salesman, 1979-80; *Daily Commercial News*, Los Angeles, reporter, 1980-81; Ohio State University, Columbus, instructor in remedial English, 1984-86; College of Charleston, Charleston, S. C., assistant professor of English, 1986—.

MEMBER: Associated Writing Programs, Poets and Writers, Inc.

AWARDS, HONORS: Syndicated fiction project award from PEN/National Endowment for the Arts, for "I Owned Vermont"; Ohio Arts Council fellowship in literature, 1986; South Carolina Arts Commission fellowship in literature, 1987-88; South Carolina syndicated fiction project award, 1987, for "Lights."

WRITINGS:

The Man Who Owned Vermont (novel), Viking, 1987.
A Stranger's House (novel), Viking, 1988.
A Dream of Old Leaves (short stories), Viking, 1989.

Short stories represented in anthology *Twenty Under Thirty*, Scribner, 1986. Contributor of fiction to periodicals, including *Missouri Review, Michigan Quarterly Review, Iowa Review, Yale Review, Yankee, Seattle Review, Redbook,* and *Confrontation;* contributor of literary reviews to periodicals, including *New York Review of Books, Los Angeles Times,* and *Michigan Quarterly Review.*

SIDELIGHTS: Rick Wheeler, a Massachusetts soft drink salesman who both knowingly and unknowingly sabotages his marriage, is the protagonist of Bret Lott's first novel, *The Man Who Owned Vermont*. With an existence and marriage that fall short of expectations, Rick is often sullen and self-defeating; on one occasion he refuses to stop the car to let his pregnant wife find a bathroom, and her subsequent miscarriage—along with the guilt and blame—trigger a growing breach that culminates in separation. Only then, as Rick tries to connect with others in order to fill the emptiness, does he recognize his complicity in the gradual disintegration of the relationship. "It is the story of the unwitting betrayals that slowly erode his marriage . . . that eventually leads him to greater self-knowledge—and back to his wife," detailed Lori B. Miller in the *New York Times Book Review*. "Mr. Lott knows how ordinary people work and love (or try to love), and knows how intractable, even perverse, human feelings can be," wrote the *New York Times*'s Michiko Kakutani. "He shows us how small lies and resentments can fester into something ugly and irrevocable, and he shows us, as well, the redemptive powers of love."

Writing in *Time* magazine, one critic perceived Wheeler's story as a tale of ordinary human courage. "Given every reason to surrender, he struggles on," the reviewer reflected. "*The Man Who Owned Vermont* is a vivid example of mind and spirit grappling with oppressive fates." "What makes this narrative so engrossing is the pure familiarity of it," agreed Carolyn See in the *Los Angeles Times*. "If Brett Lott isn't lying, this is one of the most interesting stories on the sadness of American men that's out there in our world." Yet discussing *The Man Who Owned Vermont* in the *Washington Post*, Dennis Drabelle found in the "unrelieved dreariness" of Wheeler's world "surprising vividness, even a kind of stark beauty"; "Lott lets Rick work his way out of his predicament with commendable restraint," the reviewer continued, and "the book bears an unforced shapeliness to it that augurs the development of a talented novelist." "This novel manages to capture ordinary life's poetic—and tragic—moments," Miller similarly observed. "Mr. Lott's . . . storytelling . . . is subtle but powerful; his prose, uncluttered and simple. Yet the story he chooses to tell demonstrates a profound understanding of human interaction and the precarious condition called marriage."

Lott told *CA:* "Though I'd always enjoyed writing—whether letters, or essays for school—the idea of being a writer never really occurred to me until I was a senior in college, after first having been a forestry major, then a marine biology major, then quitting school to work as a salesman, then coming back to school with the notion of teaching high school. But finally, in my senior year, my teacher John Herman suggested I go on for a master's degree, which I did. At the University of Massachusetts—Amherst I studied under Jay Neugeboren and James Baldwin, and my first stories started appearing in *Writer's Forum*, the *Yale Review*, and the *Iowa Review*. After graduation I got a job teaching five sections of remedial English each quarter at Ohio State University. Even though we had our first child then, and even though I was teaching so much, I managed to sneak down to the basement of our apartment each morning at about 4:30 to write for a couple of hours before my wife, Melanie, and Zeb woke up. In that way I was able to complete *The Man Who Owned Vermont*.

"All my writings, whether short stories or novels, are about working people—people who have to sort through their personal lives and problems while working to pay bills and put food in the refrigerator. I think this comes from the fact that my family is a working one (I was the first person to go to college in the Lott family in three generations). My brothers and sister and wife and in-laws and most friends all work forty hours a week; that seems real to me—not a professor's life or a writer's life that so many people imagine is glamorous and full of interesting activities. And so writing is for me my own work, my job, what I do. And though it is work, I still have a blast every time I sit down at my desk, imagining the lives of other people and putting them down on paper."

BIOGRAPHICAL/CRITICAL SOURCES:

PERIODICALS

Los Angeles Times, July 6, 1987.
New York Times, June 6, 1987, August 18, 1988.
New York Times Book Review, July 12, 1987.
Time, July 27, 1987.
Tribune Books, August 7, 1988.
Washington Post, August 14, 1987.

*   *   *

LOUDON, Irvine   1924-

PERSONAL: Born August 1, 1924, in Cardiff, Wales; son of Andrew and Morag (Lees) Loudon; married Jean Norman; children: Andrew, Michael, Catherine, Elizabeth, Mary. *Education:* Oxford University, B.A., 1948, B.M., B.Ch., 1951, D.M., 1973; Royal College of Obstetrics and Gynecology, D.Obst., 1961. *Politics:* Neutral. *Religion:* None.

ADDRESSES: Home—Mill House, Wantage, Oxfordshire OX12 9EH, England. *Office*—Wellcome Unit, History of Medicine, Oxford University, 45-47 Banbury St., Oxford OX2 6PE, England.

CAREER: General medical practitioner in Wantage, England, 1952-81; Oxford University, Oxford, England, medical historian at Wellcome Unit, 1981—. Member of Green College, Oxford. *Military service:* Royal Air Force, pilot, 1942-45; became flying officer.

MEMBER: Royal Society of Medicine, British Medical Association, Royal College of General Practitioners (fellow).

WRITINGS:

The Demand for Hospital Care, United Oxford Hospitals, 1970.
Medical Care and the General Practitioner, 1750-1850, Oxford University Press, 1986.

Contributor to periodicals.

WORK IN PROGRESS: Obstetric Care and Maternal Mortality, 1750-1950, publication by Oxford University Press expected in 1991.

SIDELIGHTS: Irvine Loudon told *CA:* "I became seriously interested in research into medical history as a result of undertaking an analysis of hospital care and primary care in Oxfordshire in 1970. This analysis was the subject of my first book, *The Demand for Hospital Care*. It became clear to me that one could not understand the organization of medical care today except in a historical context. This led me to undertake a series of investigations into the history of hospitals and dispensaries, most of which were undertaken on a part-time basis while I was still in clinical practice. Historical research came to dominate my life to such an extent that I took the opportunity, as a result of being awarded a Wellcome Research Fellowship in 1981, to resign from general practice after thirty years as a clinician and devote my time totally to historical research.

"My present research into the history of obstetric care and maternal mortality from 1750 to 1950 is a large and ambitious project since it is based not only on data from Britain but also on data from the continent of Europe, including Scandinavia, Australasia, and especially North America. The findings are not solely of academic and historical interest. Many of the conclusions have a direct bearing on obstetric care in the third world today where the levels of maternal mortality that prevail resemble those seen in Europe in the eighteenth and nineteenth centuries. But the primary reason for undertaking this and previous research projects is simply curiosity about people, health, sickness and medical care in the past, and the challenge of trying to find answers which inspire confidence."

*   *   *

LOUGHLIN, Caroline   1940-

PERSONAL: Born October 18, 1940, in New Orleans, La.; daughter of Charles, Jr. (an engineer) and Rosa (Freeman) Keller; married Philip H. Loughlin III (a professor), June 8, 1962; children: Philip H. IV, Thomas K. *Education:* Cornell University, B.A., 1961.

ADDRESSES: Home—800 Kent Rd., St. Louis, Mo. 63124.

CAREER: International Business Machines (IBM) Corp., computer programmer and systems analyst in Portland, Ore., and Syracuse, N.Y., 1961-62; State of Florida, Jacksonville, computer programmer and systems analyst, 1962-65; writer. Volunteer worker at St. Louis Zoo, 1972—; member of advisory task force of St. Louis mayor's Forest Park Master Plan, 1978—; Junior League of St. Louis, member of board of directors, 1978-83, vice-president, 1981-82; member of board of directors of St. Louis Zoo Friends Association, 1980-85.

WRITINGS:

(With Catherine Anderson) *Forest Park*, University of Missouri Press, 1986.

*   *   *

LOUIS, Murray   1926-

PERSONAL: Surname originally Fuchs; name legally changed in 1965; born November 4, 1926, in New York, N.Y.; son of Aaron and Rose (Mintzer) Fuchs. *Education:* New York University, B.S., 1951.

ADDRESSES: Home—New York, N.Y. Office—33 East 18th St., New York, N.Y. 10003.

CAREER: Murray Louis Dance Company, New York, N.Y., artistic director, 1953—. Principal dancer with Nikolais Dance Theatre, 1950-59; associate director of Dance Division at Henry Street Playhouse, 1953-70; artistic director of Nikolais/Louis Foundation for Dance and Chimera Foundation for Dance, both 1970—; co-director of Choreoarts, 1973—. Choreographer for films and television, including "Hoopla," "Index," "Scheherezade," "Geometrics," "Porcelain Dialogues," "Moments," "Catalogue," "Cleopatra," "Ceremony," "Deja Vu," "Glances," "Schubert," "The Canarsie Venus," "Figura," "A Suite for Erik," "Afternoon," "The City," "November Dances," "Aperitif," "A Stravinsky Montage," "Frail Demons," "Four Brubeck Pieces," "The Station," "Revels," "The Disenchantment of Pierrot," "Black and White," "Return to Go," "By George," "Asides," and "Bach II." Military service: U.S. Naval Reserve, active duty, 1945-46.

MEMBER: American Guild of Musical Artists, Association of American Dance Choreographers, Association Council Arts, Dance Notation Bureau, New York Dance Alliance.

AWARDS, HONORS: Grants from National Endowment for the Arts, 1968, 1970, 1972, and 1974-76, Rockefeller Foundation, 1974, and Mellon Foundation, 1976; Guggenheim fellow, 1969 and 1973; critics' award from International Festival in Weisbaden, West Germany, 1972; award from Dance, 1977; Grand Medaille de la Ville de Paris, 1979; knight of French Order of Arts and Letters, 1984.

WRITINGS:

Inside Dance, St. Martin's, 1980.

WORK IN PROGRESS: They Saw America Dancing.

SIDELIGHTS: Murray Louis told CA: "I think that it is essential for the creative artist to discover the intuitive force within oneself and then learn how to utilize and trust its judgment. My aesthetics were achieved by this intuitive judgment."

*   *   *

LOVELAND, Anne C(arol)   1938-

PERSONAL: Born December 23, 1938, in Jamaica, N.Y.; daughter of John Wayne and Edith Ellen (Anderson) Loveland. Education: University of Rochester, B.A., 1960; Cornell University, M.A., 1963, Ph.D., 1968.

ADDRESSES: Office—Department of History, Louisiana State University, Baton Rouge, La. 70803.

CAREER: Louisiana State University, Baton Rouge, instructor, 1964-68, assistant professor, 1968-72, associate professor, 1972-80, professor of history, 1980—.

MEMBER: American Historical Association, Organization of American Historians, American Studies Association, Southern Historical Association.

AWARDS, HONORS: Younger humanist fellow of National Endowment for the Humanities, 1973-74; Francis Mackemie Award from Historical Foundation of the Presbyterian and Reformed Churches, 1980-82, for Southern Evangelicals and the Social Order; Willie Lee Rose Publication Prize from Southern Association for Women Historians, 1987, for Lillian Smith.

WRITINGS:

Emblem of Liberty: The Image of Lafayette in the American Mind, Louisiana State University Press, 1971.
Southern Evangelicals and the Social Order, 1800-1860, Louisiana State University Press, 1980.
Lillian Smith: A Southerner Confronting the South, Louisiana State University Press, 1986.

Contributor to history journals.

WORK IN PROGRESS: Morale in the U.S. Military, 1940-1985.

BIOGRAPHICAL/CRITICAL SOURCES:

PERIODICALS

American Historical Review, June, 1974.

*   *   *

LOWELL, Susan   1950-
(Susan L. Humphreys)

PERSONAL: U.S. citizen born abroad; born October 27, 1950, in Chihuahua, Mexico; daughter of James David (a geologist and rancher) and Edith (a rancher; maiden name, Sykes) Lowell; married William Ross Humphreys (an executive), March 31, 1975; children: Anna, Mary. Education: Stanford University, B.A. (with honors), 1972, M.A., 1974; Princeton University, M.A., 1979, Ph.D., 1979.

ADDRESSES: Home and office—332 East Rudasill Rd., Tucson, Ariz. 85704.

CAREER: Daily Citizen, Tucson, Ariz., reporter, 1968-70; University of Arizona, Tucson, instructor in creative writing and English, 1974-76; University of Texas at Dallas, Richardson, visiting assistant professor of language and literature, 1979-80; free-lance writer, 1980—.

MEMBER: Associated Writing Programs, Phi Beta Kappa.

AWARDS, HONORS: Danforth fellow, 1972-79; National Fiction Prize from Milkweed Editions, 1988, for Ganado Red.

WRITINGS:

Ganado Red (stories), Milkweed Editions, 1988.

Contributor, under name Susan L. Humphreys, of scholarly articles to literature journals.

WORK IN PROGRESS: We'll Dance the Wild West Waltz (tentative title), a "biography-autobiography project," depicting a family of Western women over the last century; Growth (tentative title), a novel about contemporary life in a Southwestern city.

SIDELIGHTS: Susan Lowell told CA: "I find myself working from short stories toward larger structures and drawing on my experience both as a scholar and a fourth-generation Arizonian. My debts as a reader and writer range from Anthony Trollope to Colette, Gabriel Garcia Marquez to Janet Lewis Winters, Jane Austen to Raymond Carver. My career, like many women's, started late. But those were rewarding years, seed time, spent first as a student then as a mother of small children. I hope now to watch my garden grow."

*   *   *

LOWRY, S(tanley) Todd   1927-

PERSONAL: Born June 26, 1927, in Laredo, Tex.; son of

Willis Edwards (a physician) and Ruby (a physician; maiden name, South) Lowry; married Faye Cole, July 9, 1948; children: Lynn Lowry Williams, Timothy Cole. *Education:* University of Texas at Austin, B.A., 1945, LL.B., 1951; Louisiana State University, M.A., 1956, Ph.D., 1958. *Religion:* None.

ADDRESSES: Home—Route 1, P.O. Box 52, Rockbridge Baths, Va. 24473. *Office*—Department of Economics, Washington and Lee University, Lexington, Va. 24450.

CAREER: East Carolina College (now University), Greenville, N.C., assistant professor of economics, 1958-59; Washington and Lee University, Lexington, Va., assistant professor, 1959-65, associate professor, 1965-74, professor of economics, 1974—.

MEMBER: American Economic Association, Association for Evolutionary Economics, History of Economics Society (member of executive committee, 1984-86), Southern Economic Association.

WRITINGS:

(Editor) *Pre-Classical Economic Thought: From the Greeks to the Scottish Enlightenment,* Kluwer Academic Publishers, 1987.
The Archaeology of Economic Ideas: The Classical Greek Tradition, Duke University Press, 1988.

Book review editor of *History of Political Economy.*

WORK IN PROGRESS: A History of Law and Economics.

*   *   *

LUBRANO, Linda L.   1943-

PERSONAL: Born January 29, 1943, in New York, N.Y.; daughter of Joseph (an artist) and Lucia (an interior designer; maiden name, Colonna) Lubrano; married Randall Slate (a computer technician), 1986. *Education:* Hunter College of the City University of New York, B.A., (cum laude), 1963; Indiana University—Bloomington, Russian Area Certificate, 1966, M.A., 1966, Ph.D., 1969.

ADDRESSES: Office—School of International Service, American University, 4400 Massachusetts Ave. N.W., Washington, D.C. 20016.

CAREER: American University, Washington, D.C., instructor, 1968-69, assistant professor, 1969-72, associate professor, 1973-81, professor of political science, 1981—.

MEMBER: American Association for the Advancement of Slavic Studies, American Association for the Advancement of Science, International Studies Association, Society for Social Studies of Science, Phi Beta Kappa, Phi Kappa Phi.

AWARDS, HONORS: Fellowships and grants from the Ford Foundation, 1964-68, National Science Foundation, 1974-76, American Council of Learned Societies, 1975, the Hoover Institution, 1981-82, and the Woodrow Wilson International Center for Scholars, 1988; distinguished teaching award, 1972-73.

WRITINGS:

Soviet Sociology of Science, American Association for the Advancement of Slavic Studies, 1976.
(With Susan Gross Solomon) *The Social Context of Soviet Science,* Westview, 1980.

Contributor of chapters to books and articles to periodicals on Soviet science policy, American-Soviet scientific cooperation, and survey research in the Soviet Union.

WORK IN PROGRESS: A book on the U.S.S.R. Academy of Sciences.

SIDELIGHTS: Linda L. Lubrano told *CA:* "I became interested in Soviet sociology of science through my research on the scientific community in the U.S.S.R. Academy of Sciences. Surveys conducted by Soviet scholars provide a useful insight into the social and psychological conditions of work in Soviet scientific collectives. Soviet sociology of science tends to be much more policy oriented than American sociology of science, and in that sense it is helpful for our understanding of Soviet science policy.

"The social context of scientific research is very important in understanding the impact of institutional constraints on science and the informal behavioral environment for scientific communication. One of the key objectives in my research is to see the extent to which scientific activity in the U.S.S.R. is similar to the conduct of science in other countries and the extent to which it is culturally and historically unique."

BIOGRAPHICAL/CRITICAL SOURCES:

PERIODICALS

American Inquiry, 1983-84.
Problems of Communism, July-August, 1977.
Science, August 26, 1977, June 19, 1981.

*   *   *

LUND, Robert T.   1924-

PERSONAL: Born September 30, 1924, in Minnesota; son of Robert J. (in insurance) and E. Luella (a homemaker; maiden name, Tosdal) Lund; married Marilyn J. Spoehr (an educator and homemaker), July 1, 1950; children: Elizabeth R. Lund Zahniser, Kathryn K. Lund-Wilde, Eric R. *Education:* Harvard University, B.A. (with honors), 1949, M.B.A., 1951.

ADDRESSES: Home—134 Worthen Rd., Lexington, Mass. 02173. *Office*—Center for Technology and Policy, Boston University, 100 Cummington St., Boston, Mass. 02215.

CAREER: Raytheon Co., Waltham, Mass., in contract administration, cost control, shop supervision, personnel administration, and procurement, 1951-56, manager of engineering services department at Airborne Electronics Operations in Sudbury and Maynard, Mass., 1956-60; Polaroid Corp., Cambridge, Mass., assistant to general manager and vice-president for manufacturing, 1960-61, manager of services department in Film Division, Waltham, 1961-67, materials manager in Film Division, 1967-68, corporate materials coordinator in Cambridge, Mass., 1968-70, consultant in new product development and manufacturing, 1970-72; Massachusetts Institute of Technology, Cambridge, assistant director and senior research associate at Center for Policy Alternatives, 1972-83, lecturer, 1972-81, senior lecturer in mechanical engineering, 1981-83; Boston University, Boston, Mass., professor of manufacturing engineering and research professor at Center for Technology and Policy, 1983—, member of Manufacturing Roundtable and Human Resources Policy Institute.

Lecturer at Harvard University's Graduate School of Business Administration, 1970-72. Director of Simaco. Member of International Federation of Automatic Control; organizer and chairman of National Conference on Manufacturing Technology and Productivity, 1973, International Workshop and Government Briefing on Computer-Managed Manufacturing, 1974, National Conference on Consumer Research for Consumer Policy, 1977, and National Remanufacturing Conference on "Remanufacturing in the 1980s," 1981; member of Manufacturing Studies Board panel to evaluate the DOD Manufacturing Technology Program, National Research Council, 1986-87; consultant to government and industry. *Military service:* U.S. Army, light mortar gunner, 1943-45; served in France and Germany; received Silver Star and four battle stars.

MEMBER: American Association for the Advancement of Science, American Society for Engineering Education, Society of Manufacturing Engineers.

AWARDS, HONORS: Grants from International Business Machines Co., U.S. Department of Energy, World Bank, National Science Foundation, Federal Trade Commission, and U.S. Army.

WRITINGS:

(With Marvin A. Sirbu, Jr., and James M. Utterback) *Microprocessor Applications: Cases and Observations,* H.M.S.O., 1980.
(Contributor) Richard L. Rowan, editor, *Readings in Labor Economics and Labor Relations,* Irwin, 1984.
(With John A. Hansen) *Keeping America at Work: Strategies for Employing the New Technologies,* Wiley, 1985.
(With Stephen R. Rosenthal and Tom Wachtell) *The Manufacturing Executive for the 1990's,* Center for Technology and Policy, Boston University, 1986.

Contributor to business and engineering journals and popular magazines, including *Harvard Business Review, Technology Review,* and *Computerworld.*

WORK IN PROGRESS: Research on principles for machine-human compatibility.

SIDELIGHTS: Robert T. Lund told *CA:* "My main areas of professional interest at this time are manufacturing policy and technology strategy. Of particular concern are strategies for using technology effectively to enhance U.S. competitiveness and the quality of working life in manufacturing. Another interest is remanufacturing. I have conducted the only systematic investigation of this resource: conserving industrial activity."

AVOCATIONAL INTERESTS: Woodworking, tennis, swimming, skiing, hunting mushrooms, photography, community affairs.

*   *   *

LUNDSTROM, David E.   1929-

PERSONAL: Born March 5, 1929, in Minneapolis, Minn.; son of Arvid Elliot (a wholesale grocery executive) and Lenore (a schoolteacher; maiden name, Hatlestad) Lundstrom. *Education:* University of Minnesota—Twin Cities, B.S. (with high distinction) and B.E.E. (with high distinction), both 1951. *Politics:* Republican. *Religion:* Protestant.

ADDRESSES: Home—4912 Ridge Pl., Minneapolis, Minn. 55424.

CAREER: Western Union Telegraph Co., Minneapolis, Minn., field engineer, 1951-52; Sperry Rand (now Unisys), Univac Division, St. Paul, Minn., product design engineer, 1955-63; Control Data Corp., Minneapolis, product manager, 1963-68,

systems manager, 1968-70, marketing manager, 1970-85; writer, 1985—. Registered professional engineer in state of Minnesota. *Military service:* U.S. Naval Reserve, active duty as shipboard electronics officer, 1952-55; served in Korea; became lieutenant senior grade.

MEMBER: Institute of Electrical and Electronics Engineers, IEEE Computer Society, Computer Museum of Boston, Decathlon Athletic Club of Bloomington (Minnesota), Tau Beta Pi.

WRITINGS:

A Few Good Men From Univac, MIT Press, 1987.

Contributor to magazines, including *Aviation Week and Space Technology* and *Data Communications User.*

WORK IN PROGRESS: "Exploring further the causes of the decline in engineering productivity in the United States, with particular emphasis on the demise of the consumer electronics business and its effect on the computer business."

SIDELIGHTS: David E. Lundstrom told *CA:* "I wrote *A Few Good Men From Univac* in an attempt to address three failures of understanding, which I believe have an impact on the technological leadership of the United States. First, almost no one outside the engineering profession, including students of engineering, understands what development engineers actually *do* on a day-to-day basis. Second, even people who have long been in the computer business do not understand how a computer (or any high-tech product, for that matter) actually gets designed and built, what mix of talents is required, and how important is the close physical and emotional proximity of the team members. Finally, and most important, even experienced engineering executives seldom realize just how critical to the success of an engineering development is the single, brilliant individual who can envision and keep in focus all aspects of the project.

"Using my own thirty-year career in the computer business as a thread, I tell a number of true stories of advanced development projects which took the industry from the huge vacuum-tube computers of the 1950s to the latest supercomputers of today, and of the dozen or so key individuals I knew who provided the technical leadership, the 'few good men' of the title. The best known of these is Seymour R. Cray, founder of Cray Research, unquestionably the most innovative computer designer in the world. These individuals are invariably driven by a desire to design the product which is the very best technically, and they are relatively unmotivated by money and titles. Thus a conflict with certain middle and upper managers (who are primarily interested in furthering their personal careers) is almost inevitable. All too often, the politicized atmosphere of the larger companies eventually causes the very best designers to become disillusioned, to resign, and to form new companies. Some of these have become the industry leaders; many more have failed because of inadequate financing or marketing.

"The interpersonal relationships in a high-tech company I find fascinating. The same mistakes in development group organization and leadership are repeated year after year, and the U.S. leadership in computer technology, which was unquestioned in the fifties, sixties, and seventies, diminishes steadily today. I would hope that *A Few Good Men From Univac* stimulates some thought and discussion about how to make more effective use of our finest, most dedicated engineers and programmers."

LYDON, James G(avin)   1927-

PERSONAL: Born September 23, 1927, in Boston, Mass; married, 1958; children: one. *Education:* Harvard University, B.A., 1949; Boston University, M.A., 1950; Columbia University, M.A., 1951, Ph.D., 1956.

ADDRESSES: Office—Department of History, Duquesne University, Pittsburgh, Pa. 15219.

CAREER: Lewis College (now University), Romeoville, Ill., 1956-60, began as assistant professor, became associate professor of history; Duquesne University, Pittsburgh, Pa., associate professor, 1960-65, professor of history, 1965—, director of History Forum, 1969-72.

MEMBER: North American Society for Oceanic History, American Historical Association, Organization of American Historians, Economic History Society.

AWARDS, HONORS: Fulbright fellow in Spain, 1967-68.

WRITINGS:

Pirates, Privateers, and Profits, Gregg, 1970.
Struggle for Empire: A Bibliography of the French and Indian Wars, Garland Publishing, 1985.

Contributor to history journals.

BIOGRAPHICAL/CRITICAL SOURCES:

PERIODICALS

American Historical Review, June, 1975.

*   *   *

LYON, Bryce Dale   1920-

PERSONAL: Born April 22, 1920, in Bellevue, Ohio; son of E. Paul and Florence (Gundrum) Lyon; married Mary Elizabeth Lewis, June 3, 1944; children: Geoffrey P., Jacqueline M. *Education:* Baldwin-Wallace College, A.B., 1942; Cornell University, Ph.D., 1949.

ADDRESSES: Home—41 Laurel Ave., Providence, R.I. 02912. *Office*—Department of History, Brown University, Brown Station, Providence, R.I. 02912.

CAREER: University of Colorado, Boulder, assistant professor of history, 1949-51; Harvard University, Cambridge, Mass., assistant professor of history, 1951-56; University of Illinois at Urbana-Champaign, associate professor of history, 1956-59; University of California, Berkeley, professor of history, 1959-65; Brown University, Providence, R.I., Barnaby and Mary Critchfield Keeney Professor of History, 1965—, chairman of department, 1968—. *Military service:* U.S. Army Air Forces, 1942-46.

MEMBER: American Academy of Arts and Sciences (fellow), Mediaeval Academy of America (fellow), American Historical Association, Economic History Association, Conference on British Studies, Royal Historical Society (fellow), Belgian Royal Academy (fellow).

AWARDS, HONORS: Fellow of Belgian American Educational Foundation, 1951-52, American Council of Learned Societies, 1962-63, and National Endowment for the Humanities, 1973-74; Guggenheim fellow, 1954-55 and 1972-73; Ph.D.

from Baldwin-Wallace College, 1972; honorary degree in letters and philosophy from University of Ghent, 1988.

WRITINGS:

(Editor) Carl Stephenson, *Medieval Institutions: Selected Essays,* Cornell University Press, 1954.
From Fief to Indenture: The Transition From Feudal to Non-Feudal Contract in Western Europe, Harvard University Press, 1957.
A Constitutional and Legal History of Medieval England, Harper, 1960, 2nd edition, Norton, 1980.
(With others) *A History of the World,* Rand McNally, 1960.
(With Stephenson) *Mediaeval History,* 4th edition, Harper, 1962.
(Editor) *The High Middle Ages, 1000-1013,* Free Press of Glencoe, 1964.
(With A. E. Verhulst) *Medieval Finance: A Comparison of Financial Institutions in Northwestern Europe,* Brown University Press, 1967.
(Translator with wife, Mary Lyon) Francois L. Ganshof, *Frankish Institutions Under Charlemagne,* University Press of New England, 1968.
(With Herbert H. Rowen and Theodore S. Hamerow) *A History of the Western World,* Rand McNally, 1969, 2nd edition, 1974.
The Origins of the Middle Ages: Pirenne's Challenge to Gibbon, Norton, 1972.
Henri Pirenne: A Biographical and Intellectual Study, E. Story-Scientia, 1974.
(Editor with M. Lyon) *The Journal de Guerre of Henri Pirenne,* North-Holland Publishing, 1976.
Studies of West European and Medieval Institutions, Variorum Reprints, 1978.
Magna Carta, the Common Law, and Parliament in Medieval England, Forum Press, 1980.
(With Henry S. Lucas and M. Lyon) *The Wardrobe Book of William de Norwell: 12 July 1338 to 27 May 1340,* Palais de Academies (Brussels), 1983.

Contributor to history journals.

WORK IN PROGRESS: The Riviera and its Perched Villages; The Letters of Marc Bloch and Lucien Febvre to Henri Pirenne; The Methodology of Marc Bloch and Jules Romains.

BIOGRAPHICAL/CRITICAL SOURCES:

PERIODICALS

American Historical Review, June, 1968, October, 1975.
Times Literary Supplement, October 3, 1975.

*   *   *

LYONS, Albert S.   1912-

PERSONAL: Born May 28, 1912, in New York, N.Y.; son of Richard H. and Isabelle (Lieberthal) Lyons; married Shirley Coles, June 20, 1941 (divorced, 1968); married Barbara Moldauer (a publishing photo editor), February 2, 1972; children: Lenore Lyons Robinson, Terry Teresa Lyons Thielen. *Education:* New York University, B.S., 1932; Columbia University, M.D., 1936.

ADDRESSES: Home—88 Central Park W., New York, N.Y. 10023. *Office*—Mount Sinai School of Medicine, 1 Gustave Levy Pl., New York, N.Y. 10029.

CAREER: Cornell University, teaching assistant in pathology at Medical College, New York, N.Y., 1936-37; Beth Israel

Hospital, New York City, surgical intern, 1937-39; Mount Sinai Hospital, New York City, resident, 1940-42; New York Hospital, New York City, intern in pathology, 1941; Park City Hospital, Bridgeport, Conn., director of surgery, 1957-58; Elmhurst City Hospital, Queens, N.Y., attending surgeon, 1966-82; Mount Sinai School of Medicine, New York City, archivist and coordinator of history of medicine department, 1967-87, clinical professor of surgery, 1970-82. Kate Hurd Mead Lecturer at College of Physicians of Philadelphia, 1972. Chairman of American Cancer Society service and rehabilitation committee, 1981-83.

MEMBER: History of Science Society, American Association for the History of Medicine, Oral History Association (founding member; chairman, 1966), Society for Surgery of the Alimentary Tract (founding member), United Ostomy Association (honorary medical adviser), New York Surgical Society, Medical Archivists of New York (president, 1977-79), Colostomy Society of New York (founder), New York Ileostomy Society (founder), Medical Society of the County of New York (secretary, 1973-78), Friends of the Rare Book Room at New York Academy of Medicine (president, 1970-72), Phi Beta Kappa.

AWARDS, HONORS: Wortis Biological Prize from New York University, 1932, for highest standing in biology; Jacobi Medal from Mount Sinai Alumni Association, 1960, for contributions to medicine; distinguished service award from American Cancer Society, 1982; citations from local, national, and international Ostomy Associations.

WRITINGS:

(With R. Joseph Petrucelli II) *Medicine: An Illustrated History*, Abrams, 1978.

Contributor to medical journals, including *Sciences* and *Medical Tribune*. Co-editor of *Critical Summaries From the U.S.A.*, 1945-49; medical editor of *United Ostomy Quarterly*, 1960—; member of editorial board of *Medical Heritage*, c. 1986-87.

WORK IN PROGRESS: The history of prediction, publication expected in 1990; the history of prognosis; inflammatory diseases of the intestinal tract.

SIDELIGHTS: Medicine: An Illustrated History is a comprehensive look at the healing arts from prehistory to the present day. Written by physician Albert S. Lyons and R. Joseph Petrucelli II (and containing the contributions of more than one dozen specialists), the volume weighs nearly eight pounds, contains more than one thousand illustrations, and possesses, according to John Leonard in the *New York Times,* "a surprisingly agreeable text." "Medicine, from its dim beginnings in herbalism and sorcery to the modern lucidity of its electron microscopes, is allowed to swim in the sea of the culture around it," praised the critic, declaring the book's "clutter of information and anecdotes" about medical drugs, devices, practices, and beliefs "wonderful." And while disappointed with the volume's account of psychiatry and non-Western modern medicine, Leonard nonetheless concluded: "[Medicine] satisfies what I take to be its two principal intentions—to acquaint us with the healing arts as liberal arts, and to be gorgeous."

Lyons told *CA:* "I am an author, not a professional writer, a term I reserve for creative writers, journalist, essayists, and poets."

BIOGRAPHICAL/CRITICAL SOURCES:

PERIODICALS

New York Times, December 29, 1978.

*   *   *

LYONS, Gene   1943-

PERSONAL: Born September 20, 1943, in Elizabeth, N.J.; son of Eugene Aloysius III (a clerk) and Helen (a typist; maiden name, Sheedy) Lyons; married Diane Haynie (a hospital administrator), June 10, 1967; children: Gavin David, Douglas Eugene. *Education:* Rutgers University, B.A., 1965; University of Virginia, M.A., 1966, Ph.D., 1969.

ADDRESSES: Home and office—204 Crystal Court, Little Rock, Ark. 72205. *Agent*—Esther Newberg, International Creative Management, 40 West 57th St., New York, N.Y. 10022.

CAREER: University of Massachusetts at Amherst, assistant professor of English, 1969-72; University of Arkansas—Little Rock, associate professor of English, 1972-75; University of Texas at Austin, visiting associate professor of English, 1975-76; free-lance magazine writer, 1976-80; *Texas Monthly,* Austin, associate editor, 1980; *Newsweek,* New York, N.Y., general editor, 1981-86; free-lance writer and television commentator, 1986—.

MEMBER: International P.E.N., American Civil Liberties Union.

AWARDS, HONORS: National Magazine Award from Graduate School of Journalism at Columbia University and Clarion Award from Women in Communications, both 1980, both for article "Why Teachers Can't Teach."

WRITINGS:

The Higher Illiteracy, University of Arkansas Press, 1988.
Rough Justice: Little Rock's Orsini-McArthur Murders, Simon & Schuster, in press.

Author of monthly column in *Arkansas Times* and weekly news contribution to KATV-TV. Contributor of articles and reviews to magazines and newspapers, including *Harper's, Newsweek, Nation, Esquire, Inside Sports,* and *Inquiry.*

SIDELIGHTS: Gene Lyons told *CA:* "I'm an essayist, reviewer, and nonfiction writer. I write for fun and profit, and in the anticipation of giving the world a passing kick whenever I can. My literary heroes are writers like Jonathan Swift, George Orwell, H. L. Mencken, and Anthony Powell—by which I mean to cite antecedents, rather than to invite comparison. I value clarity, independence, moral courage, a certain playfulness, and a degree of impudence.

"*Rough Justice* is a nonfiction book about two related killings that turned the state of Arkansas on its collective ear from 1981 to 1983. Besides investigating the crimes themselves—in which a woman murdered her husband in his sleep, escaped prosecution, then hired two 'hit men' to kill her defense lawyer's wife—it is an evocation of a place and time. It is also a story of ambition and political opportunism, as a bitter personal tragedy metamorphosed into a public soap opera in utter disregard for the facts of the case. It also caused a near breakdown in three of the most important civilizing entities in a contemporary American city: the police, the courts, and the press.

"Like any sensible person who lives in a place as determinedly provincial as Arkansas, I like to travel when I can afford to. I'm virtually blind to art, and theater people make me uneasy. My musical tastes are as proletarian as my origins and run in the direction of Anglo-rock: the Rolling Stones, the Who, Eric Clapton, and Dire Straits. My pastimes are tennis and outdoor activities, including hunting, fishing, and camping. I also raise beagles."

BIOGRAPHICAL/CRITICAL SOURCES:

PERIODICALS

Esquire, January, 1983.

       *   *   *

LYONS, Phyllis I. 1942-

PERSONAL: Born July 4, 1942, in New York, N.Y.; daughter of Maurice R. and Martha Lyons. *Education:* University of Rochester, B.A., 1964; University of Chicago, M.A., 1967, Ph.D., 1975; attended Keio University, 1968-70.

ADDRESSES: Home—548 Sheridan, No. 2N, Evanston, Ill. 60202. *Office*—Program of African and Asian Languages, Northwestern University, 2010 Sheridan Rd., Evanston, Ill. 60208.

CAREER: University of Washington, Seattle, assistant professor of Japanese, 1975-78; Northwestern University, Evanston, Ill., assistant professor, 1978-84, associate professor of Japanese, 1984—.

MEMBER: Association for Asian Studies (member of board of Northeast Asia Council, 1987—), Association of Teachers of Japanese (member of board of directors, 1987—), Phi Beta Kappa.

AWARDS, HONORS: Grants from Social Science Research Council, 1977, and National Endowment for the Humanities, 1981 and 1987; Japanese Literature Translation Prize from Japan-United States Friendship Fund, 1983, for five short stories contained in *The Saga of Dazai Osamu;* grant from Japan Foundation, 1986.

WRITINGS:

The Saga of Dazai Osamu: A Critical Study With Translations, Stanford University Press, 1985.

Author of fiction review column in *Journal of the Association of Teachers of Japanese,* 1986—.

WORK IN PROGRESS: Discontinuous Dialogue: Contemporary Japanese Women Writers and the Modern Literary Tradition, a study of Kono Taeko, Kurahashi Yumiko, Tomioka Taeko, and Tsushima Yuko.

SIDELIGHTS: Phyllis I. Lyons told *CA:* "The study of Japanese writers by Western critics tends to be strongly canonical. Therefore my first book, *The Saga of Dazai Osamu*, is devoted to one of the key canonical figures in mid-twentieth-century Japanese literature. I describe Osamu, who committed suicide in 1948, as "the poet of adolescence"; his popularity continues undiminished today, although a large part of his works continue to be read by eighteen-year-olds to twenty-four-year-olds.

"The work I am now doing on women writers is undecidedly uncanonical. Although these are some of the most exciting voices in the contemporary scene, their reception in Japan offers interesting problems: while they are all multiple prize winners, they are seldom considered for critical study by the still largely male critical establishment. That is, while prizes are awarded gender-blind, critical study tends yet to follow traditional gender lines. Therefore, the work that I (with other Western critics) am doing is likely to be challenging to accepted Japanese attitudes. In the process of discussing these writers, I am having to consider issues in the usefulness (or non-utility) of the central critical term used by Japanese critics to subsume these writers: *joryu sakka* ('women writers')."

M

MAAKESTAD, William J(ohn) 1951-

PERSONAL: Born February 5, 1951, in Aurora, Ill.; son of Jacob M. and Justine A. Maakestad. *Education:* Monmouth College, A.B., 1973; Valparaiso University, J.D., 1977.

ADDRESSES: Home—608 East Carroll St., Macomb, Ill. 61455. *Office*—414K Stipes Hall, Western Illinois University, Macomb, Ill. 61455.

CAREER: Intern with governor of Illinois, in Springfield, 1972; James E. Daugherty, Merrillville, Ind., legal researcher, 1975-77; Ferris State College, Big Rapids, Mich., instructor in business law, 1977-78; Western Illinois University, Macomb, assistant professor, 1978-83, associate professor of law, 1983—. Member of board of directors of National Safe Workplace Institute and local Young Men's Christian Association (YMCA).

MEMBER: American Bar Association, American Judicature Society, American Civil Liberties Union, Illinois State Bar Association, Blue Key.

AWARDS, HONORS: Grants from National Endowment for the Humanities, 1981 and 1984.

WRITINGS:

(With Francis T. Cullen and Gray Cavender) *Corporate Crime Under Attack: The Ford Pinto Case and Beyond*, Anderson Publishing, 1987.

Member of editorial advisory board of *Corporate Criminal Liability Reporter*.

WORK IN PROGRESS: Research on corporate crime.

*   *   *

MacANDREW, Elizabeth 1924-1983(?)

PERSONAL: Born May 21, 1924, in Tonbridge, England; U.S. citizen; died c. 1983. *Education:* Columbia University, B.S., 1966, M.A., 1967, Ph.D., 1970.

CAREER: Cleveland State University, Cleveland, Ohio, assistant professor, 1970-73, associate professor, 1973-80, professor of English and director of Extended Campus College, beginning in 1980.

MEMBER: Modern Language Association of America, American Society for Eighteenth Century Studies, Midwest Modern Language Association.

WRITINGS:

(Contributor) Harold E. Pagliaro, editor, *Studies in Eighteenth-Century Culture*, Volume 4, University of Wisconsin Press, 1975.
The Gothic Tradition in Fiction, Columbia University Press, 1979.

Contributor to journals, including *College English, Journal of Popular Culture,* and *Essays in Literature.*

BIOGRAPHICAL/CRITICAL SOURCES:

PERIODICALS

Times Literary Supplement, March 14, 1980.*

*   *   *

MacAVOY, Paul W(ebster) 1934-

PERSONAL: Born April 21, 1934, in Haverhill, Mass.; son of Paul Everett and Louise Madeline (Webster) MacAvoy; married Katherine Ann Manning, June 13, 1955; children: Libby, Matthew. *Education:* Bates College, A.B., 1955; Yale University, M.A., 1956, Ph.D., 1960.

ADDRESSES: Home—3333 Elmwood Ave., Rochester, N.Y. 14610. *Office*—William E. Simon Graduate School of Business Administration, University of Rochester, Wilson Blvd., Rochester, N.Y. 14627.

CAREER: Yale University, New Haven, Conn., instructor in economics, 1960; University of Chicago, Chicago, Ill., assistant professor of management, 1961-63; Massachusetts Institute of Technology, Cambridge, assistant professor, 1963-65, professor of management, 1966-74, Henry R. Luce Professor of Public Policy, 1974-75; Yale University, professor of economics and management, 1976-81, Milton Steinbach Professor of Organization and Management, 1978-81, Frederick William Beinecke Professor of Economics, 1981-83; University of Rochester, William E. Simon Graduate School of Business Administration, Rochester, N.Y., dean, 1983—, John M. Olin Professor of Government Policy and Business, 1987—. President's Council of Economic Advisers, senior staff economist,

1965-66, member of council, 1975-76; member of New York State Council of Economic Advisers, 1969-73. Member of board of directors of Amax Corp., Colt Industries, Combustion Engineering Corp., American Cyanamid Corp., and Gleason Corp.; past member of board of directors of Columbia Gas System; past member of board of trustees of Bates College.

AWARDS, HONORS: Ford Foundation fellow, 1961-62; fellow of Brookings Institution, 1968-69; grants from National Science Foundation, 1972-75; LL.D. from Bates College, 1976.

WRITINGS:

Price Formation in Natural Gas Fields: A Study of Competition, Monopsony, and Regulation, Yale University Press, 1962.
The Economic Effects of Regulation: The Trunk-Line Railroad Cartels and the Interstate Commerce Commission 1870-1900, MIT Press, 1965.
(With James Sloss) *Regulation of Transport Innovation: The Case of Unit Trains of Coal to the Eastern Seaboard*, Random House, 1967.
Economic Strategy for Developing Nuclear Breeder Reactors, MIT Press, 1969.
(With Dean F. Peterson) *Large-Scale Desalting: A Study in the Engineering Economics of Regional Development*, Praeger, 1969.
(Editor and contributor) *The Crisis of the Regulatory Commissions*, Norton, 1970.
(With Robert S. Pindyck) *Price Controls and the Natural Gas Shortage*, American Enterprise Institute for Public Policy Research, 1975.
(With Robert S. Pindyck) *The Economics of Natural Gas Shortage, 1960-1980*, North-Holland, 1975.
The Regulated Industries and the Economy, Norton, 1979.
(With D. Tella) *Government Regulation of Business: Its Growth, Impact, and Future*, Council on Trends and Perspectives, Chamber of Commerce of the United States, 1979.
(With Andrew S. Carron) *The Decline of Service in the Regulated Industries*, American Enterprise Institute for Public Policy Research, 1981.
Crude Oil Prices, as Determined by OPEC and Market Fundamentals, Ballinger, 1982.
Energy Policy: An Economic Analysis, Norton, 1983.

EDITOR OF "FORD ADMINISTRATION PAPERS ON REGULATORY REFORM"

The Deregulation of Cable Television, American Enterprise Institute for Public Policy Research, 1977.
Federal-State Regulation of the Pricing and Marketing of Insurance, American Enterprise Institute for Public Policy Research, 1977.
(With John W. Snow) *Regulation of Passenger Fares and Competition Among Airlines*, American Enterprise Institute for Public Policy Research, 1977.
OSHA Safety Regulation: Report of the Presidential Task Force, American Enterprise Institute for Public Policy Research, 1977.
Federal Energy Administration Regulation: Report of the Presidential Task Force, American Enterprise Institute for Public Policy Research, 1977.
(With John W. Snow) *Railroad Revitalization and Regulatory Reform*, American Enterprise Institute for Public Policy Research, 1977.
(With John W. Snow) *Regulation of Entry and Pricing in Truck Transportation*, American Enterprise Institute for Public Policy Research, 1977.

Federal Milk Marketing Orders and Price Supports, American Enterprise Institute for Public Policy Research, 1977.

OTHER

Editor of *Bell Journal of Economics and Management Science*, 1970-75.

WORK IN PROGRESS: The Collapse of Metals Prices; The Record of the United States Federal Government Enterprises, with George McIsaac; *Telecommunications Policy After the AT&T Divestiture*, with Kenneth Robinson.

BIOGRAPHICAL/CRITICAL SOURCES:

PERIODICALS

Time, July 15, 1974.

*   *   *

MacDONALD, Jake (M.)   1949-

PERSONAL: Born April 6, 1949, in Winnipeg, Manitoba, Canada; son of Donald Ian (in civic politics) and Peggy (a homemaker; maiden name, Monahan) MacDonald; married Carolyn MacKinnon (a nurse), June 18, 1983; children: Caitlin (daughter). *Education:* University of Manitoba, B.A., 1971. *Religion:* Roman Catholic ("lapsed").

ADDRESSES: Home—950 McMillan Ave., Winnipeg, Manitoba, Canada R3M OV6. *Agent*—Sarah Parker & Associates, 108 Withrow, Toronto, Ontario, Canada.

CAREER: Writer. Fishing guide in northern Ontario, summers, 1969—.

MEMBER: Writers Union of Canada, Manitoba Writers Guild, Ducks Unlimited.

WRITINGS:

NOVELS

Indian River, Queenston House, 1981.

Also author of *Stonehouse*.

RADIO PLAYS

"Becoming," CBC Winnipeg, 1982.
"The Man From the Boy," CBC Winnipeg, 1983.
"Men Who Say No," CBC Winnipeg, 1984.
"The Highway Is for Gamblers," CBC Winnipeg, 1985.
"The Longest Night of the Year," CBC, 1986.
"Tax Dodge Lodge," Real Special Productions, 1986.

SHORT STORIES

The Bridge Out of Town (collection), Oberon Press, 1986.

Short stories represented in anthologies *Manitoba Stories*, Queenston House, 1981; and *West of Fiction*, NeWest Press, 1984. Contributor of fiction to *Descant, Heartland Magazine, NeWest Review, Big Fin, Winnipeg, Arts Manitoba, Prairie Fire*, and *Western Living*. Short Stories broadcast by CBC-Radio Thunder Bay and Winnipeg.

OTHER

Contributor of articles to periodicals.

SIDELIGHTS: Jake MacDonald's *The Bridge Out of Town* is a collection of eleven short stories connected by recurring characters and places, the small northern Ontario fishing village of Keewuttunnee their shared setting. "The name means 'dead end,' and few characters manage to take the bridge out of town unless they are tourists going home,'' wrote Antanas Sileika in the Toronto *Globe and Mail*. "The squalor of the town limits their potential for love and redemption; victories are small and accidental death is easy to come by." Still, despite the gritty surroundings, MacDonald offers "a good variety of well-defined characters, all of them likeable," related *Winnepeg Free Press* critic David Williamson, who added, "linear in development [and] . . . presented in a clear, straightforward style" the stories show how "a good plot and some fascinating characters can still provide a rewarding reading experience." "There is a lack of pretension about Mac-Donald's work that keeps it both entertaining and meaningful," agreed John Danakas in a review for the *Winnepeg Sun*. "He deals with real people in real situations, with compassion, humour, and perceptiveness."

Williamson commented that in these days of literary "postmodernism and deconstructionism and dirty realism" it is a bold writer who deals with plots and people, creating the kind of stories the public likes to read. In MacDonald's case—Sileika regretted—this talent is attended by a measure of predictability and "a tendency to say just a little too much"; Danakas also noted a few instances where "plotting and characterization come off a might contrived." Nonetheless, the *Sun* reviewer applauded MacDonald's "uncanny powers of insight" and his "impressive . . . ability to tell the stories from different points of view"—an American tourist, the waitress at the Bay Inn, a native fishing guide. Adding that "The writing here is often sublime," Danakas called the author "a people's writer . . . the best kind of writer to be." "These efforts . . . prove what's possible when a writer is brave enough to risk the ordinary," Williamson concurred. "*The Bridge Out of Town* is storytelling at its best, comic and tragic, appealing to all our emotions, while applying gentle satire to many recognizable aspects of everyday life, yet still evoking the distinctive quality of the specific northern Ontario setting."

BIOGRAPHICAL/CRITICAL SOURCES:

PERIODICALS

Globe and Mail (Toronto), August 23, 1986.
Winnepeg Free Press, June 21, 1986.
Winnepeg Sun, June 15, 1986.

*   *   *

MACDONALD, Nancy (Gardiner Rodman)   1910-

PERSONAL: Born May 24, 1910, in New York, N.Y.; daughter of Cary Selden and Nannie (Marvin) Rodman; married Dwight Macdonald, November 16, 1934 (divorced, June, 1954); children: Michael Dwight, Nicolas Gardiner. *Education:* Vassar College, B.A., 1932.

ADDRESSES: Home—117 East 10th St., New York, N.Y. 10003.

CAREER: Member of staff of Institute of Persian Art and Archaeology, 1932-33, and *Common Sense* magazine, 1932-35; business manager of *Partisan Review*, 1937-43, and *Politics* magazine, 1943-47; director of Political Packages Abroad, 1945-1950; member of staff of International Rescue Committee, 1951-52; Spanish Refugee Aid, New York, N.Y., co-founder, director, executive secretary, and chairman of advisory committee, 1953-84; writer, 1984—.

MEMBER: Phi Beta Kappa.

AWARDS, HONORS: Dama de la Orden de la Liberacion de Espana from the Republican Government of Spain in Exile, 1956; El Lazo de Dama de la Orden de Isabel la Catolica from the king of Spain, 1982.

WRITINGS:

(Translator from French) Abel Paz, *Buenaventura Durruti: The People Armed*, Black Rose Press, 1977.
Homage to the Spanish Exiles: Voices From the Spanish Civil War, introduction by Mary McCarthy, Human Sciences, 1987.

Contributor to *Politics*.

WORK IN PROGRESS: Family memoirs.

SIDELIGHTS: After the Spanish Civil War of the 1930s ended with the overthrow of the Republican government by fascists led by General Francisco Franco, many veterans of the Republican forces, impoverished and in ill health, lived as exiles in France and throughout Europe. Nancy Macdonald became known in American intellectual circles for her relief efforts on behalf of these refugees, and in 1952 she helped found the Spanish Refugee Aid to coordinate her efforts. *Homage to the Spanish Exiles* combines Macdonald's own story with first-person accounts by some of the veterans she met in the course of her work. In the *New York Review of Books*, novelist Mary McCarthy wrote that the book "constitutes a remarkable history of the Spanish civil war." Moreover, she declared, Macdonald's own experiences make the work "the story of a vocation—a calling, such as came to figures in religious history."

BIOGRAPHICAL/CRITICAL SOURCES:

PERIODICALS

Chicago Tribune, March 11, 1987.
New Leader, March 9, 1987.
New York Review of Books, February 12, 1987.
New York Times, April 18, 1987.

*   *   *

MacGREGOR, Loren J.   1950-

PERSONAL: Born July 12, 1950, in Seattle, Wash.; son of Gerard Donald (a "jack-of-all-trades") and Marietta (a cook and dietician; maiden name, Wright) MacGregor. *Education:* Central Seattle Community College, A.A., c. 1979. *Politics:* "Liberal curmudgeon." *Religion:* Roman Catholic.

ADDRESSES: Home—134 Freelon St., San Francisco, Calif. 94107-1625. *Agent*—Jane Butler, Virginia Kidd Literary Agents, Box 278, 538 East Harford St., Milford, Pa. 18337.

CAREER: Respiratory therapist and cardiopulmonary technician at Doctors Hospital, Swedish Hospital, Virginia Mason Medical Center, Maynard General Hospital, Northgate Medical Center, and Evergreen General Hospital, in Seattle, Wash.; secretary, word processor, and legal assistant at Graham & James, Lasky, Haas, Cohler & Munter, and Heller, Ehrman, White & McAuliffe, in San Francisco, Calif; carpenter; projectionist; stock clerk; actor; publisher's representative; typesetter; graphic designer; book store clerk at Fantasy, Etc., in San Francisco; temporary office worker, including work as secretary, system analyst, time and motion specialist, and programmer. Volunteer worker for Seattle Human Rights Commission.

MEMBER: National Association of Cardiopulmonary Technicians.

WRITINGS:

The Net (novel), Ace Books, 1987.
Strands (science-fiction novel), Ace Books, in press.

Contributor to *New York Review of Science Fiction;* also contributor of articles and columns to newspapers. Founder, publisher, and editor of *Pacific Northwest Review of Books,* 1978-79, *Churn Works,* 1978—, and *Ed's Veto Kit;* editor of *Arterial Line;* copy editor of *Gnosis.*

WORK IN PROGRESS: A book, tentatively titled *Fighting for the Right: The Propaganda Art of Steve Ditko;* research on Greek mythology, San Francisco in 1929, space flight (especially independent groups engaged in space research), genetic research and experimentation, and nuclear winter.

SIDELIGHTS: Loren J. MacGregor told *CA:* "When I first discovered John Gardner's book *On Moral Fiction,* it set a template for feelings which I hadn't codified until then. I think the concept of 'moral fiction'—fiction which poses moral dilemmas and clearly shows when characters have chosen good or evil—is absolutely necessary. I am an entertainer, and that is how I see the writer's role, but that entertainment *must* be bound with concepts of right and wrong. The moral issue may be complex, and its presentation subtle, but the choice must be present, and it must be clear eventually that to choose the proper path will ennoble oneself and aid others. Sounds pretentious, doesn't it? But fiction has for centuries been entertaining without sacrificing this ideal.

"I have a long-standing admiration for ancient Greek moral drama and for medieval morality plays, both of which carried the charm of inevitability and familiarity. Even when such fiction was designed as a lesson in the hierarchy of society (as, for example, in *Piers Plowman*), teaching people 'their place,' it taught that each had a responsibility to every other, that the magistrate owed to the esne the guaranty of a harsh but equable life.

"My fiction supports honor, duty, and responsibility. Good is triumphant and evil is cast down—but often it takes time, effort, intelligence, and skill. Working out the details is fun for me and, I hope, for my readers. (I enjoy keeping people guessing, because you often can't believe what my characters *say,* only what they do.)"

MacGregor also wrote: "Richard Haas, a senior partner at Lasky, Haas and one of the finest lawyers and gentlemen I have ever known, taught me more about writing than any seminar or writing course of which I have heard."

*   *   *

MACK, Charles R. 1940-

PERSONAL: Born May 23, 1940, in Baltimore, Md.; son of Mary Catherine (a U.S. foreign service officer; maiden name, Dirnberger) Mack; married Ilona Schulze (a secretary), July 1, 1965; children: Katrina Anne. *Education:* University of North Carolina at Chapel Hill, A.B., 1962, Ph.D., 1972. *Politics:* Democrat.

ADDRESSES: Home—122 Woodrow St., Columbia, S.C. 29205. *Agent*—Department of Art, University of South Carolina—Columbia, Columbia, S.C. 29208.

CAREER: University of South Carolina—Columbia, instructor, 1970-73, assistant professor, 1973-75, associate professor, 1975-85, professor of art, 1985—. *Military service:* U.S. Army, Intelligence Corps, 1962-65; became sergeant.

MEMBER: College Art Association of America, Renaissance Society of America, Southeastern Renaissance Conference, Southeastern College Art Conference (president, 1975-76; member of board of directors, 1984—), Southeastern Society of Architectural Historians (member of board of directors, 1984—).

AWARDS, HONORS: Grants from Samuel H. Kress Foundation, 1982 and 1984, American Council of Learned Societies, 1982, and National Endowment for the Humanities, 1984.

WRITINGS:

Pienza: The Creation of a Renaissance City, Cornell University Press, 1987.

Contributor to *Macmillan Encyclopedia of Architects.* Contributor to art journals. Editor of *Southeastern College Art Conference Review,* 1973-75.

WORK IN PROGRESS: Thermal Spa Architecture of the Italian Renaissance.

SIDELIGHTS: Charles R. Mack told *CA:* "I am an art historian, teacher, and researcher, whose principal areas of concentration are fifteenth-century art and architecture in Italy and Etruscan and Roman art. I am also interested in the traditional folk pottery of the American Southeast. My primary research and publication efforts have been devoted to central Italian architecture and urbanistic studies centering around the work of Filippo Brunelleschi, L. B. Alberti, and Bernardo Rossellino. Articles have dealt with several Florentine palaces and monastic building programs and with the urban renewal of Renaissance Rome and Pienza.

"My research approach has made extensive use of Renaissance tax records and other archival documentation. I helped to formulate a new investigative technique involving analysis of area property statements, site plans, and building dates (these were applied to the Rucellai Palace in 1974 and the Spinelli Palace in 1983, both in Florence). My research has taken me to Italy as well as to Germany, and I am competent in both Italian and German.

"I have curated museum exhibits dealing with ancient art (1974 and 1977), the paintings of contemporary German artist Robert Bonsack (1975, 1979, and 1981), and currently I have a traveling photographic exhibit of Renaissance Pienza. I am organizing a show of Southeastern folk pottery and an exhibit of ancient coinage. I believe in a broad, interdisciplinary approach to the study of art history and in defining the cultural links of a period."

BIOGRAPHICAL/CRITICAL SOURCES:

PERIODICALS

Times Literary Supplement, May 6, 1988.

*   *   *

MacLEOD, Jay 1961-

PERSONAL: Surname is pronounced "Mac-*Cloud*"; born September 12, 1961, in Stoughton, Mass.; son of John Malcolm (a school counselor) and Nancy (a school counselor; maiden name, Ela) MacLeod. *Education:* Harvard University, B.A. (social studies; magna cum laude), 1984; Pembroke College, Oxford, B.A. (theology), 1987. *Politics:* "Well to the left." *Religion:* Christian.

ADDRESSES: Home—Kings Hollow, North Sutton, N.H. 03260. *Office*—Rural Organizing and Cultural Center of Holmes County, Route 4, Box 18, Lexington, Miss. 39095.

CAREER: Rural Organizing and Cultural Center of Holmes County, Lexington, Miss., community organizer, 1987—.

AWARDS, HONORS: Rhodes scholar, 1987.

WRITINGS:

Ain't No Makin' It: Leveled Aspirations in a Low-Income Neighborhood, Westview, 1987.

SIDELIGHTS: Jay MacLeod told *CA:* "I am a political and social activist before I am an author. *Ain't No Makin' It* grew directly out of my experience of running a youth program in a public housing project. Although it is an academic book, the work is permeated by my indignation that those who are born into our nation's underclass (whether they are black or white) are dealt a hand that makes a mockery of the United States as a land of opportunity. My current work in rural Mississippi may or may not lead to another book."

The author plans eventually to continue his community work through the ministry.

BIOGRAPHICAL/CRITICAL SOURCES:

PERIODICALS

Washington Post Book World, August 30, 1987.

* * *

MADDEN, Tara Roth   1942-

PERSONAL: Born November 16, 1942, in Pittsburgh, Pa.; daughter of Leo (a small business owner) and Charlotte (a homemaker; maiden name, Taras) Roth; married Edward E. Madden (a public relations executive), May 24, 1980. *Education:* Kent State University, B.A., 1970; Walsh College, M.B.O., 1975; also attended Miami College, Oxford, Ohio, Glassboro State College, and University of Seattle.

ADDRESSES: Home—2 Serena Ct., Newport Beach, Calif. 92663.

CAREER: Communications specialist for public schools in Cuyahoga Falls, Ohio, 1970; American Red Cross, Northern Ohio Blood Services, Cleveland, communications specialist, 1978-79; Ohio Edison Electric Co., Akron, communications specialist, 1979; Laser Images, Inc., Van Nuys, Calif., manager of publicity and public relations, 1980; Marketing Association Services, Los Angeles, Calif., promotion manager and assistant production director, 1980; Pertec Computer Corp., Los Angeles, editor of marketing communications, 1980-81; Microdata Computer Corp., Newport Beach, Calif., manager of Marketing Communications Services, 1981-83. Director of development for Laguna Art Museum. Lecturer at colleges, corporations, and management seminars.

WRITINGS:

Women vs. Women: The Uncivil War, AMACOM, 1987.

WORK IN PROGRESS: A screenplay based on *Women vs. Women;* a book on women's new career goals.

SIDELIGHTS: Tara Roth Madden described herself as a woman who has been involved in business management since 1970. As such, she told *CA,* she became aware that women have (still) not been absorbed into senior management in large num-

bers. The author believes that women themselves are to blame for this, because of their fear of failure and their combative attitude toward each other in the workplace. That is the thesis of Madden's book *Women vs. Women.*

"Grab the basic good sense of this book," Ivan Strenski urged readers of the *Los Angeles Times Book Review*. He described the book as "a battle manual for an entire social class of women in business and management." Madden's advice, according to Strenski, is to learn to trust other women, to share the hard-won top rungs of the corporate ladder. The author emphasizes that the increasing numbers of women in the workplace will aid the struggle, but only if women encourage and support each other, instead of destroying their own opportunities for success.

Madden added: "From the beginning—as a woman in middle management—I saw infighting among women right under the friendly surface. Women like one another socially. The problem is that they bring rules of social behavior into the workplace and this has held women from top-level positions.

"I wrote *Women vs. Women* to pinpoint the danger zones for women in the office. As I've been lecturing around the world discussing the issue, I always include myself in 'sometime' lists of offenders. It's easy to err if we don't know, or don't follow, business rules. My table of contents gives categories of behavior—improper attire, won't work for one another although all want to be 'boss,' bringing home problems to work, violating business-social borders, method of leave-taking, giving away power by confiding in co-workers, not respecting one another's work efforts, and more. I have observed all of these at work—as have the women who responded to my survey and the women who responded from audiences during my 110 talk show appearances. Many were at home traumatized by their work experiences.

"I'm not at all optimistic about women's potential for senior management unless they 'wake up and smell the coffee.' Women are still—in a government-released study for 1987-88—earning the same wages as in 1978. A fifty-five-year-old woman is earning the same as a twenty-five-year-old and the population is aging. We really must reverse the trend to survive independently. Many are giving up. I am optimistic that this can change if women want to change."

BIOGRAPHICAL/CRITICAL SOURCES:

PERIODICALS

Los Angeles Times Book Review, September 6, 1987.

* * *

MADER, Katherine   1948-

PERSONAL: Born August 2, 1948, in Los Angeles, Calif.; daughter of Paul Pinkas (a chemist) and Ruth Maria (a nurse; maiden name, Muller) Mader; married Norman Stanley Kulla (an attorney), December 27, 1967; children: Julia, David Paul. *Education:* University of California, Los Angeles, A.B., 1969; University of California, Davis, J.D., 1972.

ADDRESSES: Office—Los Angeles County District Attorney's Office, 210 West Temple, Los Angeles, Calif. 90012. *Agent*—Michael Hamilburg, Mitchell J. Hamilburg Agency, 292 South La Cienega Blvd., Suite 212, Beverly Hills, Calif. 90211.

CAREER: Criminal defense attorney, 1973-85; Los Angeles County District Attorney's Office, Los Angeles, Calif., deputy district attorney, 1985—.

WRITINGS:

(With Marvin J. Wolf) *Fallen Angels: Chronicles of L.A. Crime and Mystery,* Facts on File, 1986.
The Story of Santa Monica, Windsor Publications, in press.

Contributor to *Los Angeles.*

WORK IN PROGRESS: "Justice Denied: The Story of the Delia Case," for *California.*

SIDELIGHTS: Katherine Mader told *CA:* "I've always enjoyed, as a hobby, nonfiction crime stories. I've worked as a criminal lawyer, both defense and prosecution, for fifteen years. Writing about crime and mysteries and working in the same field provides a way to integrate my professional and personal lives. While defending Angelo Buono, who was charged with ten murders in the 'Hillside Strangler' case, I noticed how fascinated people were with the locations of the crime scenes that the jurors visited on six successive nights. It occurred to me that many scenes of interesting crimes in Los Angeles's past were being driven by every day without being recognized by motorists. Thus evolved the idea for a book telling the stories of some of the more notorious Los Angeles crimes and including directions to visit the sites."

*   *   *

MAJA-PEARCE, Adewale   1953-

PERSONAL: Born June 3, 1953, in London, England; son of Jameson Akintola (a doctor) and Marion Donalda (Cameron) Pearce. *Education:* University of Wales, University College of Swansea, B.A., 1975; School of Oriental and African Studies, London, M.A., 1986.

ADDRESSES: Home—33 St. George's Rd., Hastings, Sussex TN34 3NH, England. *Office*—Index on Censorship, 39c Highbury Pl., London N5 1QP, England. *Agent*—Shelley Power, International Public Relations Association, P.O. Box 149a, Surbiton, Surrey KT6 5JH, England.

CAREER: Index on Censorship, London, England, researcher, 1986—; Heinemann Educational Books, Oxford, England, consultant, 1986—.

MEMBER: International P.E.N.

WRITINGS:

(Editor) Christopher Okigbo, *Collected Poems,* Heinemann, 1986.
In My Father's Country: A Nigerian Journey (nonfiction), Heinemann, 1987.
Loyalties (stories), Longman, 1987.
How Many Miles to Babylon? (nonfiction), Heinemann, 1989.

Contributor to periodicals.

SIDELIGHTS: Adewale Maja-Pearce told *CA:* "Both *In My Father's Country* and *How Many Miles to Babylon?* explore the nature of my double inheritance, Nigeria and Great Britain. They are both extended essays in form, and I have come to believe that it is the essay and not the novel that is best suited to an examination in prose of the modern experience. Some of the questions I want to ask are: What do we mean by race? How does it differ from culture? What is the nature of our allegiances to either or both? Who determines that allegiance?"

BIOGRAPHICAL/CRITICAL SOURCES:

PERIODICALS

Times Literary Supplement, August 14, 1987.

MALINS, Penelope   1929-
(Penelope Hobhouse)

PERSONAL: Born October 20, 1929, in Castledawson, Northern Ireland; daughter of James J. L. G. (a naval officer) and Marion Caroline (Dehra Chichester) Chichester Clark; married first husband, surname Hobhouse, May, 1952 (divorced, 1984); married John Malins (a professor of medicine), November 1, 1984; children: (first marriage) Georgina Dehra Catherine, Neil Alexander, David Paul. *Education:* Received degree from Cambridge University, 1951. *Politics:* Liberal. *Religion:* Church of England.

ADDRESSES: Home and office—Tintinhull House, Yeovil, Somerset BA22 8PZ, England. *Agent*—Felicity Bryan, Curtis Brown Ltd., 162-168 Regent St., London W1R 5TB, England.

CAREER: Writer, 1976—. Runs National Trust garden at Tintinhull House; garden restorer, historian, and consultant.

MEMBER: International Dendrology Society, Royal Horticultural Society, Garden History Society (member of council, 1976-84), National Council for the Conservation of Plants and Gardens.

WRITINGS:

UNDER NAME PENELOPE HOBHOUSE

The Country Gardener, Phaidon, 1976.
The Smaller Garden: Planning and Planting, Collins, 1981.
Gertrude Jekyll on Gardening, Collins, 1985.
Color in Your Garden, Collins, 1985.
Private Gardens of England, Weidenfeld & Nicolson, 1985.
The National Trust: A Book of Gardening, Pavilion, 1986.
Garden Style, Windward, 1988.
Painted Gardens: Watercolours, 1850-1920, Pavilion, 1988.
(Editor) *Guide to the Gardens of Europe,* George Philip & Son, 1989.

Editor of series "The National Trust Gardening Guide." Contributor to newspapers and gardening journals, including *Englishwoman's Garden.*

WORK IN PROGRESS: The Border, publication expected in 1989; *American Gardening.*

*   *   *

MALKIN, Lawrence   1930-

PERSONAL: Born July 30, 1930, in Richmond Hill, N.Y.; son of David and Jennie (Temko) Malkin; married Edith Stark, 1960; children: Elisabeth, Victoria. *Education:* University of Chicago, A.B., 1949; Columbia University, A.B. (honors), 1951.

ADDRESSES: Agent—Wallace & Shiel, 170 East 77th St., New York, N.Y. 10021.

CAREER: Associated Press, United Nations bureau, London, England, correspondent, 1954-69; *Time,* national economics correspondent in Washington, D.C., European cultural correspondent in London, bureau chief in New Delhi, India, European correspondent in Paris, France, and correspondent in Boston, Mass., 1969-88. *Military service:* U.S. Army, Combat Infantry, 1952-54.

MEMBER: Phi Beta Kappa, St. Botolph's Club (Boston), Reform Club (London).

AWARDS, HONORS: E. W. Fairchild Award for foreign financial reporting from Overseas Press Club of America, 1967.

WRITINGS:

The National Debt, Holt, 1987.

Contributor to magazines and newspapers, including *Horizon, Commentary, Times Literary Supplement,* and *Atlantic Monthly.*

WORK IN PROGRESS: A major study of the politics of the American economy, both domestic and international, publication expected by 1990, work to be performed at the Brookings Institution in Washington, D.C.

SIDELIGHTS: Lawrence Malkin told *CA:* "Our economic destiny is now an inseparable part of our political future and our relations with the rest of the world. As an author, I am dedicated to explaining this in plain language that ordinary people, often desperate to understand, will be able to follow and actually enjoy reading. I write by describing events in terms of the people who make them happen, with some wit and irony, because things never happen in quite the way people foresee. Therein lies the drama of this subject."

*   *   *

MANN, Chris(topher Michael Zithulele)   1948-

PERSONAL: Born April 6, 1948, in Port Elizabeth, South Africa; son of Norman (a wool broker) and Daphne (an actress; maiden name, Martin) Mann; married Julia G. St. John Skeen (a painter), 1982; children: Amy Honor, Luke Fleetwood. *Education:* University of the Witwatersrand, B.A., 1970; Oxford University, B.A. (honors), 1973; University of London, M.A., 1975.

ADDRESSES: Home—Box 444, Botha's Hill, Natal 3660, South Africa.

CAREER: High school teacher in Nhlangano, Swaziland, 1976-78; Rhodes University, Grahamstown, South Africa, lecturer in English literature, 1979-81; director of Valley Trust, outside Durban, South Africa, 1982—. Co-founder and musician for the band "Zabalaza" during 1980s.

AWARDS, HONORS: Rhodes scholar, 1971; Olive Schreiner Prize from English Academy of Southern Africa, 1983, for *New Shades.*

WRITINGS:

First Poems, Bateleur Press, 1977.
(Editor with Guy Butler) *A New Book of South African Verse in English,* Oxford University Press (Cape Town), 1979.
"The Sand Labyrinth" (play), first produced in Grahamstown, South Africa, at Box Theatre, July 7, 1980.
New Shades (poems), David Philip, 1982.

Contributor to poetry journals.

SIDELIGHTS: Chris Mann told *CA:* "The Valley Trust where I work takes a holistic approach to the problems of underdevelopment. We are based in a large Zulu community on the peri-urban and rural fringe of Durban and share our adaptations of Western disciplines such as agriculture, health, education, and engineering with the larger Southern African community by means of publications and trainee and visitor programs. We believe our work would expand greatly in a just post-apartheid society. While poetry is my chief literary love I see it at one pole of a continuum with all the writing that goes into my daily work, the mundane but essential prose that is an expres-sion of a political commitment and a Christian faith in practice, compromised though these are in a violent society.

"Influenced by African oral literature I write poems for the ear as well as the eye. This led to using music as a vehicle to deliver the work and the composition of Zulu and English songs for as Afro-Western fusion band, "Zabalaza," that I helped found in the mid-1980s. We played round Durban, won a competition on television, and folded when the increasing pressure of work at Valley Trust and a first child brought a delayed adolescence to an undemonstrative close."

*   *   *

MANNING-SANDERS, Ruth   1895(?)-1988

OBITUARY NOTICE—See index for *CA* sketch: Born in 1895 (one source says c. 1888) in Swansea, Wales; died October 12, 1988, in Penzance, Cornwall, England. Editor and author. Manning-Sanders was best known for regional folk and fairy tales that she retold for children, including the Cornish collection *Peter and the Piskies* and the French collection *Jonnikin and the Flying Basket.* She also wrote original works for young people such as *Mystery at Penmarth* and *Hedgehog and Puppy Dog Tales* and edited a number of anthologies. Before concentrating on children's books in the late 1930s, Manning-Sanders wrote several books for adults, including *The Pedlar and Other Poems* and the novel *The Twelve Saints.* The two years she spent with a traveling carnival inspired her study *The English Circus.* Her last book, *A Cauldron of Witches,* was published in 1988.

OBITUARIES AND OTHER SOURCES:

BOOKS

Twentieth-Century Children's Writers, 2nd edition, St. Martin's, 1983.

PERIODICALS

Times (London), October 13, 1988.

*   *   *

MANOFF, Robert Karl   1944-

PERSONAL: Born April 23, 1944, in New York, N.Y.; son of Richard K. (in advertising) and Lucy (an administrator; maiden name, Deutscher) Manoff; married Katherine DeSaulles Ellis (a physician assistant), November 3, 1979; children: Alexandra, Morgan; stepchildren: Katherine, David. *Education:* Haverford College, B.A., 1968; Massachusetts Institute of Technology, M.C.P., 1973.

ADDRESSES: Office—Center for War, Peace, and the News Media, New York University, 10 Washington Pl., New York, N.Y. 10003. *Agent*—Diane Cleaver, Inc./Sanford J. Greenburger Associates, 55 Fifth Ave., New York, N.Y. 10003.

CAREER: More (magazine), New York, N.Y., senior editor, 1977-78; *Columbia Journalism Review,* New York City, editor, 1978-80; *Soho News,* New York City, managing editor, 1980-82; *Harper's,* New York City, managing editor, 1983-84; Center for War, Peace, and the News Media, New York City, director, 1984—. Member of steering committee of Alerdinck Foundation, The Hague, Netherlands, 1986—; member of board of directors of Council on Nuclear Affairs, 1988—.

MEMBER: International Communications Association, American Association for the Advancement of Slavic Studies, Association for Education in Journalism and Mass Communication.

AWARDS, HONORS: Olive Branch Award for outstanding coverage of the nuclear arms issue from Editor's Organizing Committee, 1984, for article "The Silencer"; Lowell Mellett Award (special citation) for Improving Journalism Through Critical Evaluation from Pennsylvania State University School of Communications, 1987, for the work of New York University's Center for War, Peace, and the News Media.

WRITINGS:

(Editor with Michael Schudson) *Reading the News* (essays), Pantheon, 1987.

Author of "Media," a column for *Progressive*, 1985-87. Contributor of articles to periodicals, including *Bulletin of the Atomic Scientists, Harper's, International Herald Tribune, Nation, New York Times,* and *Quill.*

WORK IN PROGRESS: The Press and the Bomb, "a study of media coverage of nuclear issues, arms control, and the Soviet Union since 1945," publication by Harper expected in 1991.

SIDELIGHTS: Reading the News, edited by Robert Karl Manoff and Michael Schudson, is a collection of critical essays directed toward readers of contemporary American newspapers. According to reviewer Douglas Balz in the *Chicago Tribune,* the intention of this book is "to help a nation of newspaper readers to better understand their daily paper" through an "examination of the press as an institution." Balz explains further that if citizens more fully comprehend what is published by the American press, "they will be better able to exercise their rightful role in a democratic society."

BIOGRAPHICAL/CRITICAL SOURCES:

PERIODICALS

Chicago Tribune, May 8, 1987.
Des Moines Sunday Register, April 26, 1987.
Newsday, February 22, 1987.
New York Times Book Review, May 3, 1987.
Washington Times, February 16, 1987.

* * *

MANSFIELD, Irving   1908(?)-1988

OBITUARY NOTICE: Born c. 1908 in Brooklyn, N.Y.; died of a heart attack, August 25, 1988, in Manhattan, N.Y. Television producer, publicity agent, and author. Mansfield, one of the first publicists to make use of the mass media in his profession, promoted the best-selling novels of his wife, Jacqueline Susann, including her 1966 *Valley of the Dolls.* Selling nearly twenty-nine million copies by mid-1987, the novel earned a spot in the *Guinness Book of World Records* as the novel with the highest sales. Susann was also the subject of *Life with Jackie,* a book Mansfield wrote with Jean Libman Block in 1983. Before becoming a publicist and author, he produced such television programs as "Arthur Godfrey's Talent Scouts," "Your Show of Shows," and "The Jane Froman Show," and later produced movie versions of his wife's novels, including "Valley of the Dolls" and "Once Is Not Enough."

OBITUARIES AND OTHER SOURCES:

BOOKS

Les Brown's Encyclopedia of Television, New York Zoetrope, 1982.

PERIODICALS

New York Times, August 26, 1988.
Publishers Weekly, September 9, 1988.

* * *

MARC
See BOXER, (Charles) Mark (Edward)

* * *

MAREK, Richard (William)   1933-

PERSONAL: Born June 14, 1933, in New York, N.Y.; son of George and Muriel (a housewife; maiden name, Hepner) Marek; married Margot Lynn Ravage, June 17, 1954 (died September 29, 1987); children: Elizabeth, Alexander. *Education:* Haverford College, B.A., 1955; Columbia University, M.A., 1956. *Politics:* Democrat. *Religion:* Jewish.

ADDRESSES: Home—12 West 96th St., New York, N.Y. 10025. *Office*—E. P. Dutton, 2 Park Ave., New York, N.Y. 10016.

CAREER: McCall's, New York, N.Y., editor, 1958-64; Macmillan Publishing Co., New York City, senior editor, 1964-69; World Publishing, New York City, associate director, 1969-72; Dial Press, New York City, editor in chief, 1972-76; Richard Marek Books, New York City, publisher, 1977-81; St. Martin's Press/Marek, New York City, publisher, 1981-85; E. P. Dutton, New York City, president, 1985—. *Military service:* U.S. Army, 1956-57; served in Japan.

MEMBER: Phi Beta Kappa.

WRITINGS:

Works of Genius, Atheneum, 1987.

Contributor to periodicals.

SIDELIGHTS: Editor and publisher Richard Marek won acclaim for his first novel, *Works of Genius.* The book concerns the publishing industry—in particular the "strange, sick symbiosis between Eric Meredith, bestselling novelist, megalomaniac enigma and (let's face it) galactic-class swine," wrote Curt Suplee in the *Washington Post,* "and Tony Silver, literary agent, reluctant stooge and the novel's first-person narrator." Meredith, an insecure, little known writer when he meets Silver, becomes conceited and unreasonably demanding after the literary agent succeeds in publishing the author's novels. "He's touchy about his work," explained Elaine Kendall in the *Los Angeles Times Book Review,* "convinced he's a genius and therefore exempt from the rules governing the conduct of more ordinary mortals." Silver, while recognizing his unappreciated role as "nursemaid and valet to his client," the reviewer continued, recognizes Meredith's talent and feels that "he can't afford to lose his star author." The men's personal as well as professional lives are strained by their destructive relationship.

"The pacing is splendid, the scenes well conceived," lauded Suplee in his review. "[*Works of Genius*] is an extraordinary achievement for a man in Marek's position, and a courageous one as well." Kendall likewise praised the publisher's fictional interpretation of the publishing industry. "There's hilarity, pathos and suspense in this book," she wrote, calling *Works of Genius* "an exceptionally original take on an enduring theme."

AVOCATIONAL INTERESTS: Tennis, bridge.

BIOGRAPHICAL/CRITICAL SOURCES:

PERIODICALS

Los Angeles Times Book Review, August 2, 1987.
People, July 20, 1987.
Publishers Weekly, July 17, 1987.
Washington Post Book World, September 17, 1987.

*   *   *

MARQUESS, William Henry   1954-

PERSONAL: Born June 14, 1954, in Atlanta, Ga.; son of John Rogers and Jane Anne (Newton) Marquess. *Education:* Duke University, B.A., 1976; Harvard University, Ph.D., 1983. *Politics:* "Progressive." *Religion:* None.

ADDRESSES: Home—28 Converse Ct., No. 6, Burlington, Vt. 05401. *Office*—Department of English, St. Michael's College, Winooski, Vt. 05404.

CAREER: St. Michael's College, Winooski, Vt., assistant professor of English literature, 1984—.

WRITINGS:

Lives of the Poet: The First Century of Keats Biography, Pennsylvania State University Press, 1985.

WORK IN PROGRESS: Short fiction.

SIDELIGHTS: "I am primarily a teacher of literature and writing," William Henry Marquess told *CA.* "*Lives of the Poet* grew out of my doctoral dissertation, which was largely inspired by the work of Walter Jackson Bate and the generous guidance of Jerome Hamilton Buckley."

Lives of the Poet provides the reader with a brief history of early English biography. The author then considers the original sources of biographical material on Keats: his own letters and poems. Marquess analyzes the biographies of Keats which appeared in the first one hundred years after the poet's death, paying particular attention to the critical styles of the times. In the *Times Literary Supplement,* Emma Crichton-Miller described the book as "a story with the narrative suspense and character interest of a novel. The book has verve," she added, "as well as scholarship."

BIOGRAPHICAL/CRITICAL SOURCES:

PERIODICALS

Times Literary Supplement, January 9, 1987.

*   *   *

MARSHALL, Raymond
See RAYMOND, Rene (Brabazon)

*   *   *

MARTIN, Chryssee (MacCasler) Perry   1940-

PERSONAL: Born December 21, 1940, in Tulsa, Okla.; daughter of Louis MacCasler (an interior designer) and Betty (Baber) Perry; married Esmond Bradley Martin (a geographer), October 22, 1966. *Education:* Bennett College, A.A., 1960; University of Arizona, B.A. (with distinction), 1962, M.A., 1966, Ph.D., 1974.

ADDRESSES: Home and office—P.O. Box 15510, Mbagathi, Nairobi, Kenya.

CAREER: Writer. Kenya National Parks, Nairobi, honorary warden, 1970-76.

MEMBER: Lamu Society, Horse Association of Kenya (life member), Kenya Society for the Protection and Care of Animals (member of administrative staff, 1977—).

AWARDS, HONORS: Medal from French Government, 1962.

WRITINGS:

Quest for the Past: An Historical Guide to the Lamu Archipelago, Marketing and Publishing (Nairobi, Kenya), 1973.
(With husband, Esmond Bradley Martin) *Cargoes of the East: The Ports, Trade, and Culture of the Arabian Seas and Western Indian Ocean,* Hamish Hamilton, 1978.
(With husband, Esmond Bradley Martin) *Run, Rhino, Run,* Chatto & Windus, 1982.

Contributor to *Swara* and *Oryx.* Editor of *Kenya Past and Present,* 1975—.

WORK IN PROGRESS: Russelas the Rhinoceros, a tale about a rhino from Kenya who searches the world markets for rhino horn; continuing research on the international trade in rhinoceros products.

SIDELIGHTS: Chryssee Perry Martin told *CA:* "As an American who has lived in Kenya for most of her adult life, I am particularly concerned with wildlife programs. I have traveled extensively in Africa and Asia, surveying and monitoring the elephant ivory and rhino horn trade. I have also become interested in the historical geography of the Kenya coast, and I have written several articles in this field."

*   *   *

MARTIN, Don W.   1934-

PERSONAL: Born April 22, 1934, in Grants Pass, Ore.; son of George E. (a dairyman) and Irma Ann (Dallas) Martin; married Kathleen Elizabeth Murphy, 1969 (divorced, 1981); married Betty Woo (a pharmacist, realtor, and writer), March 18, 1985; children: Kimberly Ann, Daniel Clayton. *Education:* Attended high school in Wilder, Idaho. *Politics:* Liberal Republican. *Religion:* Protestant ("not active").

ADDRESSES: Home and office—P.O. Box 1494, 11362 Jackson St., Columbia, Calif. 95310. *Agent*—Scott Meredith Literary Agency, Inc., 845 Third Ave., New York, N.Y. 10022.

CAREER: Blade-Tribune, Oceanside, Calif., member of editorial staff, 1960-64; *Press-Courier,* Oxnard, Calif., entertainment and feature editor, 1964-69; *Argus-Courier,* Petaluma, Calif., managing editor, 1969-70; *Motorland* (travel magazine), San Francisco, Calif., associate editor, 1970-88; free-lance writer and photographer, 1988—. *Military service:* U.S. Marine Corps, correspondent, 1952-58; became staff sergeant.

WRITINGS:

WITH WIFE, BETTY WOO MARTIN: GUIDEBOOKS

The Best of San Francisco, Chronicle Books, 1986, revised, 1989.
The Best of the Gold Country, Pine Cone Press, 1987.
San Francisco's Ultimate Dining Guide, Pine Cone Press, 1988.

OTHER

The Best of the Wine Country (guidebook), Pine Cone Press, 1989.

Contributor of travel articles and photographs to magazines and newspapers.

WORK IN PROGRESS: Endangered Species, a fictional animal fantasy.

SIDELIGHTS: Don W. Martin told *CA:* "Inside every employed journalist is an author struggling to escape into the sunlight. Now that I've set mine free, I've never been happier—even though mortgage payments can be something of a challenge.

"I was moved to begin writing guidebooks because I felt that most of the ones on the market were dry and bland. The guidebooks I wrote with my wife are highly opinionated, yet written in a light and humorous style. They are intended to entertain the armchair traveler, as well as the functioning tourist. The books reflect our personal tastes, but then, our tastes are closer to middle-of-the-road than to lunatic fringe. Hopefully, our writings chart for the traveler a useful course through the good, the bad, and the awful.

"*Endangered Species* will reflect my deep concern for threatened wildlife as population growth continues to destroy natural habitats. The book will suggest that the real threat to our environment is not greed, but indifference and carelessness. We must convince ourselves that, in our enviable position as the most intelligent of mammals, we have a responsibility to nurture our environment, not trample it underfoot."

*   *   *

MARTIN, Eva M.   1939-

PERSONAL: Born April 24, 1939, in Woodstock, Ontario, Canada; daughter of Harvey A. and Daisybelle (Blake) Martin. *Education:* University of Toronto, B.A., 1960, B.L.S., 1961, M.L.S., 1972.

ADDRESSES: Office—Scarborough Public Library, 1076 Ellesmere Rd., Scarborough, Ontario, Canada M1P 4P4.

CAREER: Toronto Public Library, Toronto, Ontario, children's librarian, 1961-63, head of children's department, 1963-71, head of Community Branch, 1971-77; Scarborough Public Library, Scarborough, Ontario, coordinator of services for children and young adults, 1977—. Lecturer at University of Toronto, 1975-76. Chairman of Canadian section of International Board on Books, 1984-86; member of Storytellers School of Toronto.

MEMBER: Canadian Library Association, Canadian Association of Children's Librarians, Book Publishers Professional Association, American Library Association, Ontario Library Association (chairman of Children's Services Guild, 1979-80; vice-president, 1981-83; chairman of Teen Services Guild, 1986-87), Ontario Puppetry Association, Ontario Association for Children With Learning Disabilities.

WRITINGS:

Tales of the Far North, Methuen, 1987.

Contributor to periodicals.

WORK IN PROGRESS: Another collection of fairy tales; a novel for children.

SIDELIGHTS: Eva M. Martin wrote: "At present I live in a house, more than one hundred years old, in downtown Toronto, with two cats who are my alter egos, and where I grow roses, vegetables, and herbs in my garden. My home is the sanctuary where I write and learn stories to tell in workshops at schools and libraries.

"I love to travel, and I have spent time in Ireland, England, Austria, Italy, and Japan. I have always been fascinated by what motivates writers to write, and so I read literary biography with a passion. I also enjoy perusing the work of women writers, particularly Canadian ones. Canadian women are the major force behind contemporary Canadian literature."

AVOCATIONAL INTERESTS: Music (singing in a choir which specializes in liturgical music).

*   *   *

MARTIN, Reginald   1956-

PERSONAL: Born May 15, 1956, in Memphis, Tenn.; son of Lester (a janitor) and Carrie Lee (a maid; maiden name, Jones) Jackson. *Education:* Boston University, B.S., 1977; Memphis State University, M.A., 1979; University of Tulsa, Ph.D., 1985.

ADDRESSES: Home—P.O. Box 111306, Memphis, Tenn. 38111-1306.

CAREER: News, Boston, Mass., feature editor and reporter, 1974-77; Memphis State University, Memphis, Tenn., instructor in English, 1979-80; Tulsa Center for the Study of Women's Literature, Tulsa, Okla., research fellow, 1980-81; Tulsa Junior College, Tulsa, instructor in English, 1982; University of Tulsa, Tulsa, assistant instructor in English, 1982-83; Memphis State University, assistant professor, 1983-87, associate professor of composition, 1988—. Visiting lecturer at Mary Washington College, 1984; lecturer in literary criticism at University of Wisconsin—Eau Claire, 1988. Filer and clerk at Boston Public Library, 1976-77; editor at Continental Heritage Press, 1981; director of professional writing programs, 1987—.

MEMBER: National Council of Teachers of English, National Council of Black Studies, National Honors Association, Modern Language Association, Popular Culture Association, Philological Association (Tennessee, Arkansas, Mississippi, and Louisiana), Society for Technical Communicators, Southeastern Society for Nineteenth-Century Studies, Conference on College Composition and Communication, Southern Conference on Afro-American Studies.

AWARDS, HONORS: Mark Allen Everett Poetry Contest winner, 1981; Friends of the Library Contest winner in fiction, 1982, and in poetry, 1983; Award in Service for Education from Alpha Kappa, 1984; award for best novel from Deep South Writers Competition, 1987; award for best critical article from South Atlantic Modern Language Association, 1987.

WRITINGS:

Ntozake Shange's First Novel: In the Beginning Was the Word, Mary Washington College Press, 1984.
Ishmael Reed and the New Black Aesthetic Critics, Macmillan, 1985.
The Failure to Interface: "Mainstream" Criticism and Black Aesthetic Criticism, St. Martin's, in press.
The Writing Circle (rhetorical reader), Macmillan, in press.

Contributor of stories, poems, articles, and reviews to anthologies, including *HomeSpun Images,* and to periodicals, including *Calamus, Callaloo, Explicator, Griot, Obsidian, South Atlantic Review, South Central Review,* and *Yellow Silk.* Contributing editor of *Next Move,* 1977; editor of *Phoenix,* 1978, and *Interpretations,* 1980.

WORK IN PROGRESS: Secrets, a book of poems, to be published in 1990; *Technical Exchanges,* a book on intra-company business and technical writing texts, to be published in 1990; *Everybody Knows What Time It Is,* a novel.

SIDELIGHTS: Reginald Martin told *CA:* "I write because I must, to get it out. While I do enjoy writing, it has to be done even when I don't feel like it, otherwise I'll explode—like the singers who must sing because it's in them and has to get out, whether they have an audience or not. In my personal life, singing, weightlifting, and running seem to help round out and make pleasant the awesome and unspeakable things I encounter each day.

"My desire to study Ishmael Reed came from my initial and still debilitatingly persistent weakness for reading criticism. It became apparent to my nineteen-year-old lizard brain that I had better start reading this guy who seemed to both fascinate and repel so many people. I believe I read his poetry first, and it both intrigued and clued me to the fact that I should read the fiction also. Usually, I try to encounter an author's works chronologically, but the first novel of Reed's that I read (luckily for me) was his 1972 *Mumbo Jumbo.* I have yet to recover from the cleansing and mind-expanding experience, and the book opened up my knowledge of my and my family's past and our relationship to Voodoo.

"Doing research on Reed introduced me to the new black aesthetic critics, a powerful group of academics in the late 1960s and early 1970s who had concrete notions on what writing by black authors should and should not do. Their movement fascinated me so much that they are currently the subjects of my second literary-critical book, which will principally concern Amiri Baraka, Houston Baker, and Addison Gayle.

"As is true of Reed's work, I find that all of my writings turn back upon themselves to explain themselves and make a part of 'the big picture.' My poetry is, I think, especially relevant in this respect as I think it is the most concise and clear of my works, completely unencumbered by publishing houses who think that my novels, short stories, and scholarly books must be of a certain length to fit in a genre. Sometimes, when you change the length of a work just to fit into an arbitrary genre, you hurt the force of the work immensely. Brevity, excitement, and clarity are the three gods I constantly seek to evoke when I write."

BIOGRAPHICAL/CRITICAL SOURCES:

PERIODICALS

Times Literary Supplement, July 15-21, 1988.

*   *   *

MARTYN, J(ames) Louis 1925-

PERSONAL: Born October 11, 1925, in Dallas, Tex.; son of William Pitt and Ruby (Bettis) Martyn; married Dorothy Lee Watkins, June 10, 1950; children: Timothy, Peter C., David P. *Education:* Texas Agricultural and Mechanical College (now Texas A & M University), B.S.E.E., 1946; Andover Newton Theological School, B.D., 1953; Yale University, M.A., 1956, Ph.D., 1957.

ADDRESSES: Home—606 West 122nd St., New York, N.Y. 10027. *Office*—Union Theological Seminary, 3041 Broadway, New York, N.Y. 10027.

CAREER: Wellesley College, Wellesley, Mass., instructor in biblical history, 1958-59; Union Theological Seminary, New York, N.Y., assistant professor, 1959-63, associate professor, 1963-67, Edward Robinson Professor of Biblical Theology, 1967-87, Robinson Professor Emeritus, 1987—. Columbia University, chairman of New Testament seminar, 1965-67, adjunct professor of religion, 1970-87; seminar director for Ecumenical Institute for Advanced Theological Studies, Jerusalem, Israel, 1974-75; visiting professor at Yale University, 1982 and 1988.

MEMBER: Society of Biblical Literature (past president of mid-Atlantic section), Studiorum Novi Testamenti Societas.

AWARDS, HONORS: Fulbright fellow at University of Goettingen, 1957-58; Guggenheim fellow, 1963-64.

WRITINGS:

(Contributor) W. R. Farmer, C. F. D. Moule, and R. R. Niebuhr, editors, *Christian History and Interpretation: Studies Presented to John Knox,* Cambridge University Press, 1967.
History and Theology in the Fourth Gospel, Harper, 1968, 2nd edition, Abingdon, 1979.
(With Charles Rice) *Easter,* Fortress, 1975.
The Gospel of John in Christian History: Essays for Interpreters, Paulist Press, 1978.
(Editor with Leander E. Keck) *Studies in Luke-Acts: Essays Presented in Honor of Paul Schubert,* Fortress, 1980.

Contributor to journals.

WORK IN PROGRESS: Anchor Bible commentary on Paul's Letter to the Galatians.

*   *   *

MARX, Leo 1919-

PERSONAL: Born November 15, 1919, in New York, N.Y.; married, 1943; children: Stephen, Andrew, Lucy. *Education:* Harvard University, S.B., 1941, Ph.D., 1950.

ADDRESSES: Home—19 Joy St., Boston, Mass. 02114. *Office*—Massachusetts Institute of Technology, Cambridge, Mass. 02139.

CAREER: University of Minnesota—Twin Cities, Minneapolis, began as assistant professor, became associate professor of English, 1949-58; Amherst College, Amherst, Mass., professor of English and American studies, 1958-71, Kenan Professor, 1971-77; Massachusetts Institute of Technology, Cambridge, W. R. Kenan, Jr., Professor of American Cultural History, 1977—. Fulbright lecturer at University of Nottingham, 1956-57, and University of Rennes, 1965-66; visiting professor at Brandeis University, 1969-70; member of National Humanities Faculty, 1971-73.

MEMBER: American Academy of Arts and Sciences (fellow), American Studies Association (president, 1976-78), Modern Language Association of America.

AWARDS, HONORS: Guggenheim fellow, 1961-62; bicentennial fellow of Phi Beta Kappa, 1974-75.

WRITINGS:

The Machine in the Garden, Oxford University Press, 1964.
(Editor) Mark Twain, *The Adventures of Huckleberry Finn,* Bobbs-Merrill, 1967.
(Editor with Saul Friedlaender and Eugene Skolnikoff) *The End of the World: Images of Apocalypse in Western Civilization,* Holmes & Meier, 1982.

The Pilot and the Passenger: Essays on Literature, Technology, and Culture in the United States, Oxford University Press, 1987.

(Editor) *The Railroad in American Art,* MIT Press, 1987.

Also editor of *Anthology of American Literature,* 1974.

BIOGRAPHICAL/CRITICAL SOURCES:

PERIODICALS

Los Angeles Times, December 24, 1987.

* * *

MASER, Edward A(ndrew)   1923-1988

OBITUARY NOTICE—See index for *CA* sketch: Born December 23, 1923, in Detroit, Mich.; died October 7, 1988, in Chicago, Ill. Educator, administrator, translator, editor, and author. Maser was considered an authority on Central European art of the seventeenth and eighteenth centuries. In 1953 he began working as both art history teacher and art museum director at the University of Kansas. He transferred in 1961 to the University of Chicago, where he was professor of art history, chairman of his department for three years, and, beginning in 1972, founding director of the Smart Gallery of Art. He left the museum post in 1983. Maser wrote the exhibit catalog *Il Museo del opificio delle pietre dure* with Lando Bartoli and also penned *Gian Domenico Ferretti* and *Disegni inediti di Johann Michael Rottmayr.* He was translator, editor, and commentator for Cesare Ripa's *Baroque and Rococo Pictorial Imagery* and was editor of the *Register of University of Kansas Museum of Art.*

OBITUARIES AND OTHER SOURCES:

BOOKS

Who's Who in American Art, 17th edition, Bowker, 1986.

PERIODICALS

Chicago Tribune, October 8, 1988, October 9, 1988.

* * *

MASLOW, Jonathan Evan   1948-

PERSONAL: Born August 4, 1948, in Long Branch, N.J.; son of Bernard (an engineer) and Clara (a teacher; maiden name, Rosenberg) Maslow; married Sarah Lazin, March 2, 1984 (divorced September 8, 1987). *Education:* Attended Wesleyan University, Middletown, Conn., 1966-70; Marlboro College, B.A., 1971; Columbia University, M.S., 1974.

ADDRESSES: Home—Dennisville, Cape May County, N.J. *Office*—R.D.3, Woodbine, N.J. 08270. *Agent*—Kathy P. Robbins, Robbins Office, Inc., 2 Dag Hammarskjold Plaza, 866 Second Ave., 12th Floor, New York, N.Y. 10017.

CAREER: Writer. Columbia University, New York, N.Y., adjunct at graduate school of journalism, 1977-80.

MEMBER: Amnesty International, Greenpeace, National Writers Union, Authors Guild, Nature Conservancy, New Jersey Audubon Society, Cape May Geographic Society, Cape May Bird Observatory.

WRITINGS:

The Owl Papers, Dutton, 1983.
Bird of Life, Bird of Death: A Naturalist's Journey Through a Land of Political Turmoil, Simon & Schuster, 1986.

WORK IN PROGRESS: Torrid Zone, about the Gulf Coast and Caribbean Rim; *Guanacaste Grows a Tropical Forest,* a children's book.

SIDELIGHTS: For his first book, *The Owl Papers,* author Jonathan Evan Maslow collected numerous facts and fables about the owl from history and legend. Then he turned to scientific investigation and his own field experiences, which ranged from Connecticut to Cape May. Maslow's adventures and those of other owl fanciers provided, according to one reviewer, an enjoyable and delightful account for the general reader. The book also entreats the nonspecialist to consider the dangers of modern land development and other traumatic threats to the environment of these creatures of the night. His message to the naturalist reader is that preservation is as necessary to scientific endeavor as is discovery itself.

In *Bird of Life, Bird of Death,* Maslow recounts his adventures in Guatemala, where he engaged himself in a search for the mystical and endangered quetzal bird. The book reflects more than a naturalist's journey, however. Maslow relates the history of Guatemala and the effect of historical and political events upon the natural world of Central America. The author found his colorful quetzal, at last, in the threatened "cloud forests" of the highlands. His relief and joy allowed him to put behind him, for a time, the oppressive atmosphere he had encountered in the Guatemalan lowlands. Maslow's message, however, remains as strong as it was in his first book: the natural world is in great peril, most often at human hands, and the scientist and amateur alike must work for preservation before it is too late. Graeme Gibson wrote in the *New York Times Book Review:* "Among the great pleasures afforded by this book . . . is the detail and control of Mr. Maslow's information . . . His touch is sure and his control admirable." The critic concluded: "*Bird of Life, Bird of Death* is a wonderful book." John A. C. Greppin reported in the *Times Literary Supplement* that Maslow is "a truly powerful writer and an original. This is his second book . . . and I look forward to more."

BIOGRAPHICAL/CRITICAL SOURCES:

PERIODICALS

Globe and Mail (Toronto), February 25, 1984, July 26, 1986.
New Yorker, December 26, 1983.
New York Times Book Review, March 9, 1986.
Times Literary Supplement, August 15, 1986.
Washington Post, February 28, 1986.

* * *

MASON, Ellsworth (Goodwin)   1917-

PERSONAL: Born August 25, 1917, in Waterbury, Conn.; son of Frederick William (an enamelist) and Kathryn Loretta (Watkins) Mason; married Rose Ellen Maloy, May 13, 1951 (divorced October, 1961); married Joan Lou Shinew, August 16, 1964; children: (first marriage) Kay Iris Morice, Joyce Iris Lande; (second marriage) Sean David. *Education:* Yale University, B.A., 1938, M.A., 1942, Ph.D., 1948. *Politics:* "I vote for conservatives." *Religion:* Presbyterian.

ADDRESSES: Home and office—756 6th St., Boulder, Colo. 80302.

CAREER: Williams College, Williamstown, Mass., instructor in English, 1948-50; Marlboro College, Marlboro, Vt., instructor in English, 1951-52, librarian, 1951-52; University of Wyoming, Laramie, serials librarian, 1952-54; Colorado College, Colorado Springs, lecturer in English, 1954-63, reference librarian, 1954-58, librarian, 1958-63; Hofstra University, Hempstead, N.Y., director of library services and professor, 1963-72; University of Colorado, Boulder, director of libraries and professor, 1972-76, head of special collections department, 1976-82, consultant to the library, 1982—. Director of theses and member of dissertation committees at Colorado College, Hofstra University, and the University of Colorado, 1965-79; adjunct professor at the Graduate School of Library Science at the University of Illinois, 1968; member of the Chancellor's Council of the University of Texas; consultant to numerous school and university libraries. *Military service:* U.S. Navy, 1943-46; served as mechanic in Constructions Battalions.

MEMBER: American Library Association, Association of College and Research Libraries, Library Association (London), New Zealand Library Association, Bibliographic Center for Research (Denver; vice-president, 1961-63), Mountain-Plains Library Association, New York Library Association, Colorado Library Association, Colorado Council for Library Development (chairman, 1962-63, 1976-80), Long Island Library Resources Council, Nassau County Library Association, Alpha Sigma Lambda, Sigma Kappa Alpha (vice-president, 1967-68; president, 1969-70), Mason Associates Ltd. (president, 1976—), Ghost Town Club (Colorado Springs).

AWARDS, HONORS: Council on Library Resources fellow, 1969-70; Long Island Librarians Roundtable Service Award, 1972; L.H.D. from Hofstra University, 1973; design award from the New York State Association of Architects/American Institute of Architects, 1974, for consulting on the Sarah Lawrence College Library; Progressive Architecture Award, 1975, for consulting on the Ohio State University Library addition; Harry Bailly Speaker's Award, 1975; designated honorary librarian by the University of Lethbridge, 1977.

WRITINGS:

(Editor and author of introduction; with Stanislaus Joyce) *The Early Joyce: The Book Reviews, 1902-1903*, Mamalujo Press, 1955, reprinted, Richard West, 1978.
(Editor with Richard Ellmann) *The Critical Writings of James Joyce*, Viking, 1959.
(Author of historical background and chapter commentaries) *A Portrait of the Artist as a Young Man: A Critical Commentary*, American R.D.M. Corporation, 1966.
James Joyce's "Ulysses" and Vico's Cycle, Yale University Library Publications, 1973.
Mason on Library Buildings, Scarecrow, 1980.

Translator, from the Italian, of a memoir on James Joyce by his brother. Contributor of more than one hundred articles to periodicals, including *Modern Language Review*, *Italica*, *Twentieth Century Literature*, *Criticism*, *ALA Bulletin*, *Library Journal*, *James Joyce Quarterly*, and the *Explicator*.

Member of editorial board, *Serials Librarian*.

WORK IN PROGRESS: A book entitled *The University of Colorado Library and Its Makers*, for Scarecrow; a revision of *The Critical Writings of James Joyce*, publication by Faber & Faber expected in 1990.

SIDELIGHTS: Esteemed as an editor, writer, educator, and librarian, Ellsworth Mason is particularly known for collecting rare books, including the works of authors such as Robert Graves, Laura Riding, Louis Auchincloss, Roy Campbell, and John D. MacDonald. In an interview with Margaret Carlin of the *Rocky Mountain News*, Mason commented, "My mind is

an all-embracing room into which I can put many books and characters." His four decades of involvement in various aspects of the literary field are a testament to his love for the written word.

Mason told *CA:* "My school years from 1922 to 1948 came at the only time in our history when education was solid from first grade through graduate school. There were almost no hazards. Automobile traffic was very light, ecological poisons almost unknown, and personal security was nearly absolute. Children were not torn apart by conflicting values because personal values in the home, the school, the churches, and in government were sound and nearly identical. Rules were clear and reasonable and discipline was expected. If you got out of line and got clobbered, that seemed fair. In the 1920s and 1930s the entire country was poor, but it didn't hurt because we didn't know we were poor: everyone was like us. It was a stable world.

"When the stock market crashed in 1929, I was twelve years old; my father was out of work all four of my high school years. But through a remarkable series of coincidences, I was able to earn every cent of my way through three degrees at Yale University. I have subsequently contributed to four fields: English literature, book collecting, librarianship, and library building planning.

"Of all my activities as an educator and a librarian, I feel that the book collections I have formed are the most enduring. All are of research strength and are in research libraries where they will continue passing on useful information to younger generations."

AVOCATIONAL INTERESTS: Tramping, reading, translating New Testament Greek.

BIOGRAPHICAL/CRITICAL SOURCES:

PERIODICALS

Catholic Library World, November, 1982.
College and Research Libraries, September, 1958, September, 1982.
Rocky Mountain News, February 7, 1982.

*   *   *

MASON, Mike   1952-

PERSONAL: Born February 3, 1952, in Peterboro, Ontario, Canada; son of Frank Lindsay (an officer of a trust company) and Mary Margaret (a housewife; maiden name, Calder) Mason; married Karen Elizabeth McRuer (a physician in general practice), August 7, 1982; children: Heather Lynne. *Education:* University of Manitoba, B.A. (with honors), 1974, M.A., 1975; further graduate study at Regent College, Vancouver, British Columbia, 1982-83. *Religion:* Christian.

ADDRESSES: Home—Box 427, Hope, British Columbia, Canada V0X 1L0.

CAREER: Valley Leader, Carman, Manitoba, reporter and feature writer, 1975-76; part-time journalist, cook, farm worker, garbage collector, store clerk, and carpenter, 1976-78; Morden Elementary School, Morden, Manitoba, library clerk, 1979-80; Pembina Valley Public Library, Morden, part-time library clerk, 1980-82; part-time caseworker for Morden-Winkler Big Brothers Association, 1980-82; full-time writer, 1983—.

AWARDS, HONORS: Gold Medallion Award in marriage and family category from Evangelical Christian Publishers Association, and Book Award in religious inspirational category from Logos Bookstores, both 1986, for *The Mystery of Marriage*.

WRITINGS:

The Mystery of Marriage: As Iron Sharpens Iron, Multnomah, 1985.
The Mystery of the Word: Parables of Everyday Faith (stories and reflections), Harper, 1988.
The Furniture of Heaven, and Other Parables for Pilgrims (short stories), Harold Shaw, 1989.

Contributor to periodicals.

WORK IN PROGRESS: The Gospel According to Job, a devotional commentary; a novel; a book of essays.

SIDELIGHTS: Mike Mason told *CA:* "I grew up in Eastern Canada but later spent ten years living on the prairies, and in 1975 I graduated from the University of Manitoba with a master's degree in contemporary American prose. I wrote a thesis on Thomas Wolfe, and several years later scribbled in the front of it a quotation from W. H. Auden: 'A false conception of human nature led Thomas Wolfe to write the grandiose rubbish he mistook for great prose.'

"I wasted my twenties knocking around the country, living hand to mouth, drinking, pretending to write fiction, publishing in little magazines, and getting nowhere. At about the age of thirty, I was converted to Christianity, and only after that, gradually, did I begin to hear my own voice as a writer. My conversion came through reading Thomas Merton, and ever since then I've been much influenced by Roman Catholic spirituality and the monastic tradition, as well as by Protestant evangelical theology. As a Christian writer I see my aim or calling as being threefold: literary evangelism, the deepening of evangelical spirituality, and the raising of literary standards in Christian publishing.

"I pursue these goals through the writing of both fiction and nonfiction. However, I feel my primary vocation is the communication of the gospel through fiction, and I see no real contradiction in trying to write good literature with a Christian message. In fact, I maintain that there is no such thing as 'pure' literature, for all the world's greatest writing is deeply informed by ideology, whether it be Marxist, existentialist, nihilist, humanist, or religious."

*   *   *

MAST, Gerald   1940-1988

OBITUARY NOTICE—See index for *CA* sketch: Born May 13, 1940, in Los Angeles, Calif.; died from complications of acquired immune deficiency syndrome (AIDS), September 1, 1988, in Chicago, Ill. Educator, editor, and author. Mast pioneered the academic study of film history, contending that film had replaced the novel as the leading art form of its time. He was associate professor of performing and creative arts at the College of Staten Island of the City University of New York from 1967 until 1978, when he joined the University of Chicago as professor of English and humanities. Later he founded Chicago's Film Archive and Study Center. Mast wrote the texts *The Comic Mind: Comedy and the Movies, Film/Cinema/Movie: A Theory of Experience*, and *Can't Help Singin': The American Musical on Stage and Screen*. His editing credits include the anthologies *Movies in Our Midst: Documents in the Cultural History of Film in America* and *Film Theory and Criticism: Introductory Readings*.

OBITUARIES AND OTHER SOURCES:

BOOKS

Who's Who in America, 45th edition, Marquis, 1988.

PERIODICALS

Chicago Tribune, September 2, 1988.
Los Angeles Times, September 3, 1988.
New York Times, September 2, 1988.

*   *   *

MATHESON, Don(ald S.)   1948-

PERSONAL: Born February 17, 1948, in Charlotte, N.C.; son of Gordon Graham (a textile executive) and Martha (a housewife; maiden name, Withers) Matheson; married Vickie Diaz (an estate manager), December 12, 1981. *Education:* Vanderbilt University, B.A., 1972; graduate study at Purdue University, 1972.

ADDRESSES: Home—P.O. Box 174, East Hampton, N.Y. 11937. *Agent*—Liz Darhansoff, 1220 Park Ave., New York, N.Y. 10128.

CAREER: Kendall Co., began as salesman in hospital products division in Atlanta, Ga., 1973, district manager in Dallas, Tex., beginning in 1978, and Kansas City, Mo., beginning in 1979, regional manager in Boston, Mass., beginning in 1980, strategic planning manager, beginning in 1982, leaving company as national accounts manager, 1983; writer and estate manager, 1983—.

MEMBER: International Association of Crime Writers, Ashawagh Hall Writers Workshop.

WRITINGS:

"CHARLIE GAMBLE" NOVELS

Stray Cat, Summit Books, 1987.
Ninth Life, Summit Books, 1989.

OTHER

Contributor to local newspapers.

WORK IN PROGRESS: A third "Charlie Gamble" book, for Summit Books.

SIDELIGHTS: Don Matheson told *CA:* "I came to writing in a circuitous fashion. While I received encouragement from high school and college teachers, I did not see writing as a career choice, probably in part because my early career planning had been preempted by parental direction. ('Donald, you like to argue so much; you oughta be a lawyer.') Lest that give the impression of the classic cop-out of blaming one's parents for what one is, I should add that their efforts were very well-intended, and they were fast fans when, years later, I announced that I would try writing.

"As a fan of Perry Mason, I planned to be a lawyer until the summer between my junior and senior years of college. I worked in a law firm, and realized that I would hate being a lawyer. From there, it took about twelve more years for me to realize that what I had liked about Perry Mason wasn't lawyering, but storytelling.

"The dormant writing seed that I carried through the years of my business career came mostly from courses in fiction writing under Walter Sullivan at Vanderbilt, courses I had taken as enjoyable electives. Mr. Sullivan praised my work and encouraged me to embrace writing as a career. When I dig those stories out and read them now, I think he was very generous to find potential in them, but he taught me some things about writing that stuck in my mind and serve me well in my efforts today.

"I did not have the requisite courage to follow Mr. Sullivan's advice into a profession for which there was no surety of a paycheck, but his comments stayed in the back of my mind. Only after some years of experiencing just how inadequate a good paycheck could be in providing a satisfactory life was I driven back to the idea of writing. My wife, Vickie, was courageous enough to encourage me to quit my well-paying job and give writing a shot, no matter what it took to do that.

"The skill I had to fall back on to support my writing was carpentry and a general handiness with fixing things. I had spent two years of my spare time building a house from scratch, and I had bought, renovated, and sold two older houses. I knew that there were many writers and many large estates that might need a resident couple in East Hampton, New York. Our advertisement in the local newspaper ran something like 'Writer and spouse seek permanent live-in situation, to trade part-time handyman and housekeeper services for free living space and salary. Capable but not proud, we'll do anything that's legal.'

"The first position, which we took in mid-1983, was trying emotionally because of a personality conflict, but it did enable me to write forty to fifty hours per week, and I found writing every bit as challenging and exciting as I had hoped it would be. In November of 1984, Vickie and I found a new situation as estate couple, which continues to serve our purposes. We get along very well with our employers, have a lovely place to live and a situation in which I continue to work full-time at becoming a writer. The success of *Stray Cat* has punctured my lugubrious attitude and allowed a bit of hope to leak in: that just maybe, if I work hard enough and stay lucky, I can make a living at this thing I enjoy."

Matheson added: "*Stray Cat* is a mystery/suspense novel. It draws on my business background and my long-term hobby of ocean sailing, through the main character, Charlie Gamble. Charlie is a burned-out salesman from the computer industry, a boat bum who lives aboard his sailboat in Boston Harbor."

*   *   *

MATTHEWS, Glenna C.   1938-

PERSONAL: Born November 7, 1938, in Los Angeles, Calif.; daughter of Glen (an editor) and Alberta (Nicolais) Ingles; divorced; children: Karen, David. *Education:* San Jose State University, B.A., 1969; Stanford University, M.A., 1971, Ph.D., 1977.

ADDRESSES: 2112 C. McKinley Ave., Berkeley, Calif. 94703.

CAREER: University of California, Davis, lecturer in American history, 1975-76; Oklahoma State University, Stillwater, assistant professor of American history, 1978-86; visiting associate professor at various University of California campuses, 1986—.

MEMBER: American Historical Association, Organization of American Historians.

AWARDS, HONORS: Grant from American Council of Learned Societies, 1982-83.

WRITINGS:

"Just a Housewife": The Rise and Fall of Domesticity in America, Oxford University Press, 1987.
The Rise of Public Woman: Woman's Power and Woman's Place From the Colonial Period to the Present, Oxford University Press, in press.

Contributor to magazines, including *Nation*.

SIDELIGHTS: Glenna C. Matthews told *CA:* "As a 're-entry' woman who went back to school, I was angered by the low esteem in which housewives were held, both in graduate-student circles and in the larger society. For me, the final straw was the publication of a book, *The Feminization of American Culture* by Ann Douglas, which blamed women for sapping the virility from American culture. I vowed to write what I thought of as the housewife's response to that book, and *"Just a Housewife": The Rise and Fall of Domesticity in America* is the result. In doing the research, I concluded that the virtual worship of scientific expertise in the late nineteenth and early twentieth century had a particularly negative impact on the status of housewifely expertise.

"While finishing the housewife book, I had the opportunity to teach a course on women and politics at Berkeley. I argued to my students that there is a strong relationship between respect for female experience in the culture and women's access to political influence. That is the germ of my book in press, *The Rise of Public Woman*."

BIOGRAPHICAL/CRITICAL SOURCES:

PERIODICALS

Globe and Mail (Toronto), February 6, 1988.
Washington Post Book World, November 1, 1987.

*   *   *

McADAM, Doug   1951-

PERSONAL: Born August 31, 1951, in Pasadena, Calif.; son of Donald Neer (a civil engineer) and Patricia (a librarian; maiden name, Tapscott) McAdam. *Education:* Occidental College, B.A., 1973; State University of New York at Stony Brook, M.A., 1977, Ph.D., 1979.

ADDRESSES: Office—Department of Sociology, University of Arizona, Tucson, Ariz. 85721.

CAREER: George Mason University, Fairfax, Va., assistant professor of sociology, 1979-82; University of Arizona, Tucson, associate professor of sociology, 1983—.

MEMBER: American Sociological Association.

AWARDS, HONORS: Guggenheim fellow, 1985.

WRITINGS:

(With James Rule, Linda Stearns, and David Uglow) *The Politics of Privacy*, Elsevier, 1980.
Political Process and the Development of Black Insurgency, 1930-1970, University of Chicago Press, 1982.
Freedom Summer, Oxford University Press, 1988.

WORK IN PROGRESS: Collective Behavior and Social Movements, with Gary Marx, for Prentice-Hall.

McCLANE, A(lbert) J(ules) 1922-

PERSONAL: Born January 26, 1922, in New York, N.Y.; son of Benjamin and Ann (Conklin) McClane; married Patricia Murphy, February 19, 1952; children: Susan. *Education:* Attended Pratt Institute, 1936, and Cornell University, 1939.

ADDRESSES: Home—200 Queens Lane, Palm Beach, Fla. 33480. *Office*—383 Madison Ave., New York, N.Y. 10017.

CAREER: Registered fisheries research technician, 1940-41; *Field and Stream*, New York, N.Y., fishing editor, 1947-72, executive editor, 1972-77, editor at large, 1977—. Technical adviser to RKO Pathe Sportscope films (also actor) and National Film Board of Canada, 1947-50; New York state publicity director for Izaac Walton League of America, 1948; chairman of board of directors of McClane Fishing Schools and Food/Telesis, Inc., both 1977—; consultant to government of Venezuela. *Military service:* U.S. Army, 1942-46.

MEMBER: American Fisheries Society, Outdoor Writers of America, Confrerie des Chevaliers du Tastevin (grand officer), Lotos Club, Tuscarora Club, Fario Club, Chub Cay.

WRITINGS:

(Editor) *The Wise Fishermen's Encyclopedia: An Encyclopedic Handbook for Fishermen Covering the Game Fish of the World and How to Catch Them*, William Wise, 1951.
One Hundred of the World's Best Fishing Spots, United Aircraft Corp., 1952.
Spinning for Fresh and Salt Water Fish of North America, Prentice-Hall, 1952.
The Practical Fly Fisherman, Prentice-Hall, 1953.
The American Angler, Holt, 1954.
(Editor) *McClane's Standard Fishing Encyclopedia and International Angling Guide*, Holt, 1965, 2nd edition published as *McClane's New Standard Fishing Encyclopedia and International Angling Guide*, 1974, 3rd edition, 1976.
The Field and Stream International Fishing Guide, Holt, 1971, revised edition published as *The Field and Stream International Fishing Guide: The First Fishing Guide Ever Published for Globe-Trotting Anglers*, Scribner, 1973.
Fishing With McClane: Thirty Years of Angling With America's Foremost Fisherman, Prentice-Hall, 1975.
The Encyclopedia of Fish Cookery, Holt, 1977.
(Editor) *McClane's Field Guide to Saltwater Fishes of North America: A Project of the Gamefish Research Association*, Holt, 1978.
(Editor) *McClane's Field Guide to Freshwater Fishes of North America*, Holt, 1978.
McClane's Secrets of Successful Fishing, Holt, 1980.
McClane's North American Fish Cookery, Holt, 1981.
(Editor and author of introduction) *McClane's Great Fishing and Hunting Lodges of North America*, Holt, 1984.
(With Keith Gardner) *McClane's Game Fish of North America: The Best Fishing in the United States, Canada, Mexico, and the Bahamas*, Times Books, 1984.
McClane's Angling World: Al McClane's Greatest Adventures; Game Fishing Across America, Truman Talley Books, 1986, reprinted as *McClane's Angling World: Great Fishing Adventures With Al McClane All Across America*, Dutton, 1986.

Also author of *Pan American World Airways International Fishing Guide*, 1971.

Radio writer for Hunting and Fishing Club of the Air, 1950. Author of syndicated column distributed by NEA Service, Inc., 1952-60. Editor of "TV Travelogues," 1950—.

BIOGRAPHICAL/CRITICAL SOURCES:

PERIODICALS

Esquire, May, 1987, August, 1987.*

*   *   *

McCRACKEN, James (Eugene) 1926-1988

OBITUARY NOTICE: Born December 16, 1926, in Gary, Ind.; died following a stroke, April 30, 1988, in Manhattan, N.Y. Dramatic tenor and author. McCracken, hailed as "the most successful dramatic tenor yet produced by the United States and pillar of the Metropolitan Opera" by Will Crutchfield of the *New York Times*, was best known for his stormy but prosperous association with the Met. Frustrated in his minor roles during his first years at the Met during the 1950s, McCracken left for Europe where he built up a strong reputation playing such roles as Manrico in "Il Trovatore," Samson in "Samson et Delilah," and Canio in "Pagliacci." He also had success playing the lead in "Otello"—first for the Washington, D.C., Opera Society and later for the Zurich Municipal Theater, Switzerland's leading opera house. The role proved especially beneficial to McCracken and led to his return to the Met on March 10, 1963, when he became the first American-born singer in the history of the Metropolitan Opera to play Otello. Proclaiming that night to be the high point of his career, McCracken went on to star in such operas as "Carmen" and "Tannhauser." He left the Met again in 1978 because of unfulfilled promises of a television debut, but he was eventually wooed back in 1983, when the Met management asked him to play Radames in a televised version of "Aida," which was billed as the farewell opera of soprano Leontyne Price. After this second return, McCracken remained with the Met until the time of his death. In 1971 McCracken published *A Star in the Family*, a book he wrote with his wife, opera singer Sandra Warfield.

OBITUARIES AND OTHER SOURCES:

BOOKS

Current Biography, H. W. Wilson, 1963, June, 1988.
The International Who's Who, 51st edition, 1987.

PERIODICALS

New York Times, May 1, 1988.

*   *   *

McDOUGALL, Walter A(llan) 1946-

PERSONAL: Born December 3, 1946, in Washington, D.C.; son of Dugald Stewart (a patent attorney) and Carol (Brueggeman) McDougall; married Elizabeth Swoope, August 8, 1970 (divorced, 1979). *Education:* Amherst College, B.A. (cum laude), 1968; University of Chicago, M.A., 1971, Ph.D., 1974. *Religion:* "Continuing Anglican."

ADDRESSES: Office—Department of History, University of California, Berkeley, Calif. 94720.

CAREER: University of California, Berkeley, assistant professor, 1975-83, associate professor, 1983-87, professor of history, 1987—. Vestryman at St. Peter's Episcopal Church. *Military service:* U.S. Army, 1968-70; served with artillery in Vietnam.

MEMBER: American Church Union, Pumpkin Papers Irregulars, Delta Kappa Epsilon.

AWARDS, HONORS: Fellow of Smithsonian Institution at Woodrow Wilson International Center for Scholars, 1981-82, and National Air and Space Museum, 1982; selected by *Esquire* as one of the "men and women under 40 who are changing America," 1984; finalist for American Book Award for nonfiction from Association of American Publishers, 1985, and winner of Pulitzer Prize in history from Columbia University Graduate School of Journalism, 1986, both for . . . *the Heavens and the Earth;* visiting scholar at Hoover Institution, 1986; selected by *Insight* as one of America's ten best college professors, 1987; Dexter Prize for best book from the Society for the History of Technology, 1987.

WRITINGS:

France's Rhineland Diplomacy, 1914-1924: The Last Bid for a Balance of Power in Europe (adaptation of Ph.D. thesis), Princeton University Press, 1978.
(Editor with Paul Seabury) *The Grenada Papers*, foreword by Sidney Hook, Institute for Contemporary Studies, 1984.
(Contributor) T. Stephen Cheston, Charles M. Chafer, and Sallie Birket Chafer, editors, *Social Sciences and Space Exploration: New Directions for University Instruction*, National Aeronautics and Space Administration, 1984.
. . . *the Heavens and the Earth: A Political History of the Space Age*, Basic Books, 1985.

Contributor of numerous articles and reviews to periodicals, including *American Historical Review, Bulletin of the Atomic Scientists, Business History Review, Discover, The Final Frontier, Journal of Modern History, Los Angeles Times, National Review, New Oxford Review, Reviews in American History, Society, Technology and Culture, Wilson Quarterly*, and *The World and I.*

WORK IN PROGRESS: "A 132,000-word article on international relations in the twentieth century," for inclusion in a new edition of the *Encyclopaedia Britannica;* "a major monograph on the colonization of the Pacific Ocean from the Spaniards to the twentieth century."

SIDELIGHTS: In October of 1957 the Soviet Union placed in orbit the earth's first artificial satellite, *Sputnik I.* The launch occurred at the height of the cold war, a competition between the Soviet Union and the United States for worldwide political dominance. The Sputnik project was widely seen in both countries as a sign of emerging Soviet superiority, and the United States reacted with a massive effort to surpass its rival. The ensuing "space race" culminated when Americans became the first to land on the moon in 1969. In his Pulitzer Prize-winning study . . . *the Heavens and the Earth: A Political History of the Space Age*, historian Walter A. McDougall focuses on America and the Soviet Union in the years immediately preceding and following Sputnik. Asserting that the cold war made technology an indispensable part of a nation's political might, he charts the development of both superpowers into technocracies—governments, in his view, that control the work of science in order to increase their own power. In the United States, he warns, technocracy threatens many traditional freedoms.

According to McDougall the Soviet Union is a technocracy by nature because of its Marxist ideology. Since a Marxist state controls industry, it must also control the scientists whose discoveries make modern industry possible. McDougall recounts the harsh subordination of Soviet scientists to their government: under dictator Joseph Stalin the Academy of Sciences lost its independence, and eventually many scientists conducted their research as inmates of Soviet prison camps.

In contrast, McDougall believes, for many years the development of American technology reflected such American cultural virtues as individual initiative, free enterprise, and limited government intervention. Technology developed in response to the needs and desires of private citizens. Thus in the years before World War II, some of the most notable American research on space flight was conducted by Robert Goddard, an individualistic genius whose development of increasingly powerful rockets was largely ignored by the U.S. Government (and his fellow citizens). Meanwhile state-funded rocket research was already in progress in the Soviet Union and Nazi Germany.

With the advent of the cold war at the end of World War II, many political and military leaders thought the United States could only survive the Soviet challenge by pursuing science in a centralized, systematic fashion. McDougall, in accord with many historians in the 1980s, applauds U.S. President Dwight Eisenhower for retaining a common-sense belief in government restraint. He argues that Eisenhower, though a longtime military man, believed strongly that scientific research should remain in private hands because the growth of government power diminishes the personal freedom of American citizens. Expanding on the president's fears, McDougall stresses that the greatest danger to liberty is not from scientists who seek to control society but from politicians who would exploit the power of science to control society.

Unfortunately, in McDougall's view, Americans ignored Eisenhower's insights because of international tensions engendered by Soviet leader Nikita Khrushchev. Flamboyant and outspoken, Khrushchev tried to use advances in technology to increase his country's international prestige. After the success of Sputnik he led a public relations campaign that boasted of high Soviet achievements in military and space technology—claims, McDougall emphasizes, that later turned out to be greatly overstated. But in America the result was a national panic, which the author believes was fanned by the communications media and by Democratic politicians eager to gain a political advantage on Eisenhower's Republicans. And so during the presidencies of Democrats John Kennedy and Lyndon Johnson in the 1960s, McDougall says, technocracy became an accepted part of American life. Heavy spending for complex weaponry and space vehicles became difficult to question. Moreover, American leaders began to believe that central planning and technical expertise could solve the country's social problems, an idea the author considers grievously mistaken.

In the closing chapters of . . . *the Heavens and the Earth* McDougall puts his fear of technocracy in philosophical terms. Technical experts, McDougall suggests, should never be the final authority in a society because science is only a tool, devoid of any sense of right and wrong. Unfortunately, he believes, while technology "might have nothing to say to us about the timeless concerns of culture—love, death, justice," it "inevitably attract[s] people's attention away from those concerns." For McDougall, the answer is to look beyond technology and believe in a supreme being in order to preserve one's humility and one's sense of ethics. As Naomi Bliven summarized his message in the *New Yorker*, "we cannot expect expertise to do the work of wisdom."

Reviewers generally lauded . . . *the Heavens and the Earth* while taking issue with some of its author's conclusions. Many disputed McDougall's contention that America had been largely free of technocracy until the era of the space race, arguing that the successive crises of the Great Depression and World War II had already led the American people to accept the notions of centralized planning and rule by trained experts. In the *Bulletin of the Atomic Scientists,* David Holloway wondered if technocracy were really more a reflection of Soviet, rather than American, values. "Technocracy had American roots too," Holloway observed, citing both a tradition of corporate planning and the work of Frederick Winslow Taylor, who told Americans before World War I that scientific principles could be used to manage business and industry. In *Science* Robert Griffith questioned McDougall's "idiosyncratically conservative premises," including "occasionally strident anticommunism" and faith in pure free-market economics. The critic was moved to ask, "Did the appropriation of science and technology by large corporations, about which McDougall is curiously silent, also imperil liberty and democracy?" Several reviewers were skeptical of McDougall's appeal for religious values. *Newsweek*'s Gene Lyons, for instance, wrote that "this solution has its charm. But exactly how the world's technocratic heathens will be converted McDougall doesn't say."

There was general admiration, however, for McDougall's exhaustive research, which included interviews with many of the major figures in his account and documents from presidential archives and the National Aeronautics and Space Administration (NASA). Alex Roland, who worked at NASA as a historian, declared in the *New York Times Book Review* that . . . *the Heavens and the Earth* "is the most comprehensive history of space activity written to date, the most thorough analysis of the political and social forces at work." Even reviewers who disagreed with McDougall on specific issues praised his overall achievement as a scholar. Astronaut Michael Collins, who reviewed the book for *Washington Post Book World,* said he was "more bullish" on space flight than the author but still found the book "a superb piece of work." Griffith asserted that his questions about . . . *the Heavens and the Earth* "are themselves testament to the power of McDougall's provocative book." "Indeed," the reviewer concluded, McDougall "has raised the history of the space age to a new high ground on which the triumphs and failures of our recent past will henceforth be debated."

In 1986, the year after . . . *the Heavens and the Earth* was published, the American space program suffered an unprecedented disaster when the space shuttle *Challenger* exploded in mid-flight with the loss of all its crew. Writing in *Discover,* McDougall rejected the view of some observers that the explosion proved there was no justification for manned space flight. Astronauts must continue to explore space, he argued, because they embody America's belief that human beings are as important as machines. If Americans believe they are aided by machines, not controlled by them, they can aspire to new levels of individual achievement—new heroism. "The cult of hero and machine that makes us . . . ecstatic at the moon landing and sick at the loss of *Challenger,* is no mere romanticism," he wrote. "It's our admiration for heroism that ensures our sovereignty over machines and makes our love for technology a healthy one."

McDougall told *CA:* "I became a historian because I never decided to do anything else. I remained a historian by dint of hard work and good luck. Gradually, I came to the conclusion that writing and teaching history was my calling. My role model was William H. McNeill of the University of Chicago. Hence I am something of a generalist in an age of rampant specialization. I believe, like [sociologist] Max Weber, that

the purpose of scholarship and teaching is to communicate our cultural values stemming (ultimately) from Athens and Jerusalem."

AVOCATIONAL INTERESTS: Baseball, "music of all kinds from [Johann Sebastian] Bach to Bob Dylan, wine and spirits, a sense of humor, and British writer C. S. Lewis."

CA INTERVIEW

CA interviewed Walter A. McDougall by telephone on June 22, 1987, at his home in Oakland, California.

CA: When your department chairman and colleagues at Berkeley didn't like your future research plans, you said—in the preface to your book . . . the Heavens and the Earth—"with the boldness that sometimes crystallizes out of confusion, I determined to please myself, to follow my own curiosity no matter how academically outrageous its direction." How did your curiosity lead you to write this Pulitzer Prize-winning work?

McDOUGALL: The statement is true about departmental disapproval. I originally planned to do a second book on a subject similar in theme to my first book, but instead I got a cryptic response from the chairman suggesting that he and others in the department thought this was rather pedestrian. Needless to say, this was rather dismaying, since they had hired me on the basis of my first book! So, in a strange way, I rebelled in my confusion over this indication of disapproval and decided—since playing the game had not done the trick—to just work on any topic that was intellectually interesting to me personally and let the chips fall where they may.

I don't know what it was that the chairman wanted me to do, but outer space certainly wasn't it. Both the way-out nature of the topic and the fact that it dealt with a period of history so recent made most of my colleagues think I'd gone completely nuts. But I had always been interested in the problem of international competition in technology and the way that rivalries among states drove technology forward. Warfare is the most obvious example, but economic competition and, in our own time, competition for prestige also have played this role.

I was especially interested in the international aspects of technological competition because of a historical dispute in my field of diplomatic history about the relative importance of the balance of power as the primary motivator for a nation's foreign policy versus domestic social or economic factors as the primary determinant of foreign policy. Very often this breaks down on a political spectrum, with more conservative historians giving greater weight to international competition and balance of power while more liberal or leftist historians tend to stress such things as social conflict or corporate interests as the major factors in the formation of foreign policy. When I began to investigate this problem of international competition in technology and struck upon Sputnik and the space race as one primary example, I also came to realize that this would be a wonderful test for these two broad views on how foreign policy is formed.

Finally, my curiosity was served because I had previously worked in the 1920s, which had become a very hot field among diplomatic historians. Many people were writing books about the 1920s and interpreting the history of that decade, and I frankly felt a bit claustrophobic in the field. There were numerous petty disputes and the typical rivalries among historians all working in the same field, all of which disgusted me. I wanted to find a new problem area or time period that hadn't really been explored. The period after World War II, and particularly the early years of the Space Age, had not been subject to any serious historical treatment at all. I felt I could plow new earth and be the person who did the exploration rather than just arguing about the crossing of *t*s and dotting of *i*s.

CA: Writing about . . . the Heavens and the Earth *in the* New York Times Book Review, *Alex Roland called it "the most comprehensive history of space activity written to date, the most thorough analysis of the political and social forces at work." He concluded, "With this book, the history of space activity has come of age." Did you envision a book of such scope when you started out?*

McDOUGALL: It's interesting that you should preface that question with a quote from Alex Roland. When I first started to research the topic, Alex Roland was the assistant historian of NASA [National Aeronautics and Space Administration]. The first place I went to do my research, of course, was the NASA history office. Roland and his boss, the NASA chief historian, were very skeptical of what I was doing. They were delighted to have a serious scholar from a major university come to work in their office, but they would ask me, "What's your topic?" "What's your interpretation?" I would tell them I didn't know, that I didn't have any, that I was simply trying to study the political and domestic politics of the early years of the Space Age. So they kept trying to get me to limit my view, and I kept resisting and telling them that I didn't know yet. I did know that I didn't want to do anything very narrow, that there were great themes here, great dilemmas of modern international affairs and maybe even of modern culture involved in Space Age technology. I didn't know how to define them yet, but that was what I wanted to write about. So in a way you could say that I did envision a book of great scope, but I didn't know what the scope was.

CA: What were the biggest research headaches? Maybe what you've just been talking about was one of them.

McDOUGALL: Yes, not knowing what you're doing is certainly one headache, but in a way I think it's an advantage. One of the great problems we have in the history profession nowadays is what I believe to be the excessive concentration, especially by young historians, on a certain methodological or ideological approach. Historians today, in part because they usually work on such narrow topics, bring to their research a kind of ideological or methodological baggage; they're trying to prove or disprove something. They already have their basic thesis in mind, and they go to the empirical research and gather their evidence to prove or disprove it. I don't think this is historically sound; in fact, I think it's very dangerous. The problem of selection for the historian is already immense, and subjective factors that enter when you already know what you're trying to prove or disprove magnify the problem of objectivity that all historians have automatically since we're fallible, limited human beings. But if you come to the topic fresh, with an open mind—not because you are more virtuous than the other guy, but because you are ignorant—then the evidence itself can help to form your own thesis or conclusion over the course of time.

Not only do I think this open-minded empiricism is a more functional way of doing history, I also think it makes it a lot

more adventuresome. If I look back on my own short life—compared to the lives of more senior historians—I can already see how my research has helped to shape my political and philosophical views, rather than my political and philosophical views determining my history.

There are some big research headaches involved in doing any topic on international affairs in the post-World War II period. Number one is the sheer volume of information. Some historians say that you can't really write good history about recent events because, among other reasons, you don't have access to all the sources; some of them are still classified. Well, the fact is that you have too many sources. The world produces so much more paper now than it did fifty years ago or five hundred years ago that the sheer scale of source material—government reports, congressional testimony, archival documents, books, articles, newspapers, technical information—on a subject like the space program is so huge that at some point you have to learn, not to limit your coverage, because you don't want arbitrarily not to look at some whole body of sources, but to sift through them and learn to identify quickly the most rewarding data. You have to learn to read for main points and content, and for the facts you don't know and are trying to fill in.

Another problem has to do with declassification. I had declassified, under the Freedom of Information Act, a large number of documents on American space policies including some secret National Security Council reports and policy statements. By and large, the National Archives people who do this are very efficient and friendly, but the process can sometimes take six months to eighteen months. You locate a hot document you want declassified, you put in your request, and then it disappears into a time warp. Twelve or eighteen months later, long after you've forgotten about having put in this request, all of a sudden the document will appear in the mail. It's aggravating, needless to say, to have to go through that kind of wait.

The third problem, and the biggest one of all, is the problem of the Soviet Union. It's a closed society. We do not have access to any of their government documents, and of course what's written in journals and books in the Soviet Union has to be scrutinized with great care. As a result, there is a terrible asymmetry between what we know about the United States and other open societies and what we know about the Soviet Union and other closed societies. All of our dirty linen is washed in public, as we are seeing today. Not even the Soviet *clean* linen is. This creates a great problem. I'm not defensive about this, though obviously what I said about the Soviet space program had to be tentative in many areas. This problem is not limited to my study; it exists for every scholar in the world who wants to write anything about the Soviet Union. But we can scarcely give up trying to understand the Soviet Union just because they don't make life easy for empirical scholars.

CA: . . . the Heavens and the Earth *is a philosophical treatment of space technology as well as a history. In your introduction to the book, you pose the question that we've lived with since the first atomic explosions: "whether we can mate our tools with our dreams, but not with our nightmares." Did your philosophy, like the rest of your conclusions, grow largely out of your work on the book?*

McDOUGALL: When I started the book, I was pretty much a fan of the space program and of big technology. I didn't have a thought-out philosophical position about it all, and I was not a space buff, but I was essentially a strong supporter of the idea of space exploration and the NASA program in space. This is one of the things that did change. I'm by no means antispace or antitechnology now, but my views have grown extremely complicated. I learned that the tremendous explosion in the creation of new technology in our century, particularly since Sputnik, and the very heavy government involvement in the creation of new technology, not only in the United States but even more so in countries with more centrally directed economies, tend to create great tensions and dilemmas for government and for humanity.

My philosophy, such as it is, did indeed grow out of my work on the book. What that philosophy may be is another question. Various reviewers and other people who have written to me privately about the book have drawn an incredible spectrum of conclusions. I've been accused of being everything from a scientific positivist to a religious mystic. I suppose I should be flattered by that; obviously the book does cover the range of viewpoints about the technological revolution of our time and must do a pretty good job of expressing the tensions and dilemmas we face if people could draw such a wide spectrum of views about the book. I'd hate to have to pin *myself* down about what my views are right now.

CA: In the overall picture of the space program, how would you assess the significance of the 1986 Challenger *disaster?*

McDOUGALL: Historians don't like to predict the future, and I am uncomfortable doing it because it depends so much on what decisions our government makes over the next one to ten years. First, a great disaster with loss of life was inevitable someday. Space exploration is just about the riskiest thing imaginable. There was no question that one day a shuttle was going to blow up or crash-land or get marooned. Those things will probably continue to happen in the future. Everybody knew that. All the engineers would probably have told you if you had asked them professionally that someday something like that would happen, but after twenty-four successful flights, people quit asking the question.

The *Challenger* disaster is forcing the United States to reexamine everything about the space program—not only the technical features of the shuttle system and the decision-making process about launches, but also the entire bureaucratic organization of NASA, the entire space strategy, such as it is, of the United States government in concentrating on the shuttle rather than on other types of launch vehicles, reevaluation of what other countries have been doing in space while we've been obsessed with the shuttle, reevaluation of private versus public enterprise in space.

Because all of these major policy areas are being reexamined as a result of the *Challenger* disaster, it is very important in the short run. Whether it will be important in the long run will depend on what is done about those different policy areas. There are signs so far, frankly, of business as usual; signs that NASA is going to continue basically along the way they have previously, selling perhaps overambitious programs to the president and the Congress, supported by strong public relations; signs that the government will continue to dominate the field of space enterprise, and that we may be in for no major changes in our space policy. If that's the case, the *Challenger* disaster will have been a missed opportunity.

CA: You've spoken of the historian William H. McNeill as model for your own career. In what ways do you find his work and his outlook exemplary?

McDOUGALL: McNeill is an extraordinary man. He was inspired to a large degree by [English sociologist and economist] Arnold J. Toynbee. McNeill is a self-described world historian, one of the last of the great generalists, somebody who not only looks at the big picture but actually *sees* the big picture. He is, furthermore, a historian who writes literature; he doesn't write ''academese'' or social science gobbledygook. He is a humanist, not a social scientist, and yet he is committed to historical standards and his own historical works are based on demonstrable, arguable large patterns of human development. He proceeds in what you might call the old-fashioned, rigorous way and lets his mind do the work rather than some social science theory that somebody dreamed up.

I don't always agree with McNeill. (I hope it's a sign of maturity when you begin to disagree with your mentor!) But in terms of his role as a model, I have infinite respect for him. He's not just exemplary as a writer and as the generalist historian; he's also exemplary as a teacher and a leader. I've never known any other professor who works so efficiently, with such self-discipline, for extremely long hours, but isn't a workaholic. He seems so relaxed that he doesn't give the appearance of working all that hard. He's tremendously productive, turns out a new book every year, and in addition sits on many different committees and publishing boards. On top of all that, he never, to my knowledge, has turned a student away from his door.

CA: Your interests extend beyond history into literature and music. Was it hard for you to make a decision about what kind of career to pursue?

McDOUGALL: Yes, it was very difficult, so difficult that I never made one. I thought when I was in college about going into political science, economics, or law. But I ended up taking more history courses and, after the army, going to graduate school in history and then staying in the profession, not because I decided I wanted to be a historian, but because I never decided to do anything else.

CA: Your first book, France's Rhineland Diplomacy, 1914-1924, *grew out of the dissertation you wrote at the University of Chicago. What attracted you to your topic?*

McDOUGALL: I had studied diplomatic history at Chicago under a fine professor named Greg Campbell. Most of my work had been in German history, but when it came time for me to do a dissertation, we learned that the French foreign ministry had just opened up all of its documents for the 1920s. This provided a great opportunity for original research on a period that I was interested in, but previously mostly from the German side. I worked up a topic and my advisors approved it. But I went through an identity crisis. I was nervous about going to Paris and researching French foreign policy when my previous work had been primarily in Germany. I went through a period in which I almost backed out. I've since learned that many graduate students get cold feet at the last minute before going off to do their dissertations. But my advisors helped pull me through. What attracted me to it was solely this opportunity to get in on the ground floor of a large new body of documentation. As it turned out—as I said—lots of other historians had the same idea.

CA: Have those documents shed much new light on the thinking about World War I and its aftermath?

McDOUGALL: Yes, very much indeed. The prevailing views up until that time were oversimplified, certainly, and did not take into account the political, military, financial, and economic problems that France faced coming out of the First World War. The usual story had been that the French imposed this very harsh treaty on Germany—the Treaty of Versailles—and then tried to execute every clause of it, that they had been stupidly stubborn in their treatment of the Germans and that this helped to undermine German democracy and create the great inflation in Germany, and therefore helped set the stage for the Nazi takeover ten years down the road. That was the traditional view, an unsympathetic, liberal Anglo-American view of French policy.

I went to Paris with this viewpoint, with a personal history of studying German affairs. I was prepared at that point to be very unsympathetic with French policy. And yet, reading through the French documents, I became more and more aware of the real problems the French faced, and how much the British and the Americans, not to mention the Germans, were refusing to meet France's reconstruction needs after the war. Even though I had the usual American's distaste for the Parisians—particularly the French librarians—and I had all the insecurities of the Yankee in Paris and came away with no great love for the French, I nevertheless became quite sympathetic with the French diplomatic position.

CA: In your article "Mais ce n'est pas l'histoire!" in the Journal of Modern History, *you point out that the idea of progress working through civilization is on the defensive. Does this seem to have left many contemporary historians wondering what history really is?*

McDOUGALL: I think thoughtful historians in every era have wondered what history is. Whether or not you believe there is meaning to history, whether or not you believe that history has an internal logic and is tending toward some natural conclusion either by providence or by evolution is less important for the *doing* of history than the methodological questions involved. Is history a science? Some people would say it's a social science. Others of us would say "social science" is a contradiction in terms: human behavior is just not susceptible to scientific testing or to scientific laws the way a chemical or an amoeba is. If history isn't a science, then what is it? Is it fiction? Certainly we hope not; we try our best not to make our history fiction. It's somewhere in between. Historians down through the ages have preferred not to define history, but rather just to do it.

The real crisis in history in our own age has to do in part with the crack-up with the old liberal view that history is the story of progress, the unfolding of freedom. But the real crisis, I think, is between the people who are essentially empiricists, who start with the facts and then try to work to limited conclusions about limited questions, and the theoreticians, who want, in a sense, to use history as a kind of grab bag of facts in order to prove their own theory about human life, be it Marxist or any other ideology. But then the question is asked, if we can understand the origins of the French Revolution empirically but the origins of the French Revolution have no significance for anything else, who cares? So you go around in a circle between the theoreticians and the empiricists.

The theoreticians have had the upper hand for the last twenty or thirty years, not so much because of the influence of Marxism, although that is important, but because of the influence of the French structuralists. But now that people are getting away from that and beginning to critique these rigid structuralists, and the empiricists are rising again, we're in another state of flux about whether there is any legitimate purpose in history, whether you can put any credence in a work of history. Are we really only saying something about ourselves when we write a book of history? And does that in turn have any importance for the present?

These are timeless questions that have troubled historians since Thucydides. I think that over the past couple of hundred years, maybe since the Enlightenment, Western historians have tended to downplay these philosophical questions perhaps because of the belief in progress—not only the progress of mankind generally, but also the progress of scholarship. But now I think we're entering another era of great self-examination. And that's all to the good. I think history as a subject in the humanities benefits by humility. If it's due to confusion and disruption and lack of self-confidence—fine. The profession of history will end up benefiting as a result.

CA: You've said your literary heroes are Walker Percy, Robertson Davies, C. S. Lewis, and Tom Wolfe. Wolfe seems distinctly unrelated to the other three. Is there a connection, or do you admire him for entirely separate qualities from those you see in the other writers?

McDOUGALL: I'd like to ask all four of them if *they* see any connection. Maybe the connection is that Percy, Davies, Lewis, and Wolfe are people who do not suffer hypocrisy gladly, who are all in their own ways good-natured hole-punchers. I wouldn't say they're satirists; none of them have that style. But they are all truth-tellers. Wolfe is a tremendous stylist. He may be the most distinctive and the best American stylist today. And even though he writes primarily nonfiction, he has that same truth-telling quality that we usually find only in fiction. That may sound like an anomaly, but I tend to agree with [English writer] Malcolm Muggeridge that myth is truer than history. Every historian is a frustrated novelist. To the extent that we do grasp pearls of truth when we study the human past, I think many historians believe that we could better express or polish those pearls through the medium of fiction rather than of history. Unfortunately, either we don't have the skill or the courage, or we're professionally bound to write nonfiction.

CA: What's in progress that you'd like to talk about?

McDOUGALL: I was asked about two years ago to write an extremely long article for the new edition of the *Encyclopaedia Britannica* on the history of international relations in the twentieth century. I took last year off on sabbatical to write most of it, and I'm currently up to 1972. I have one more chapter to do, and then I have to go back and revise the whole thing and cut substantially. I hope, after it appears in the encyclopedia, to publish a book version, an extended essay on world politics in the twentieth century. That's something I could use in my classes.

I'm also editing a book of sermons. A friend of mine is an Anglican clergyman and a prize-winner in homiletics, the art of preaching. I got a bee in my bonnet to take a collection of his best sermons and try to get them published in book form. That's kind of a sidelight, of course, but something I consider important. Finally, I have in mind a new project for another space-type book, but not on space—a big history book on the scale of . . . *the Heavens and the Earth*. But I'll keep you guessing about that for awhile.

BIOGRAPHICAL/CRITICAL SOURCES:

BOOKS

McDougall, Walter A., . . . *the Heavens and the Earth: A Political History of the Space Age*, Basic Books, 1985.

PERIODICALS

American Heritage of Invention and Technology, fall, 1987.
American Historical Review, June, 1979, April, 1986.
Bulletin of the Atomic Scientists, January, 1986.
Discover, April, 1986.
Esquire, December, 1984.
Insight, May 11, 1987.
Journal of American History, June, 1986.
Journal of Modern History, December, 1979, March, 1986.
Los Angeles Times, May 21, 1985.
New Republic, June 3, 1985.
Newsweek, May 27, 1985.
New Yorker, April 21, 1986.
New York Times Book Review, April 7, 1985.
Science, December 6, 1985.
Washington Post Book World, April 7, 1985.
The World and I, May, 1988.

—Sketch by Thomas Kozikowski

—Interview by Jean W. Ross and Walter W. Ross

* * *

McGARRY, Jean 1952-

PERSONAL: Born June 18, 1952, in Providence, R.I.; daughter of Frank and Deborah (Sklover) McGarry. *Education:* Harvard University, A.B., 1970; Johns Hopkins University, M.A., 1983.

ADDRESSES: Home—100 West University Parkway, Baltimore, Md. 21210. *Office*—The Writing Seminars, Johns Hopkins University, Baltimore, Md. 21210. *Agent*—Helen Brann, 157 West 57th St., New York, N.Y. 10019.

CAREER: Johns Hopkins University, Baltimore, Md., lecturer in English, 1983-85; University of Missouri—Columbia, assistant professor of English, 1985-86; George Washington University, Washington, D.C., associate professor of English, 1986-87; Johns Hopkins University, Baltimore, affiliated with writing seminars, 1988—.

AWARDS, HONORS: Short Fiction Prize from *Southern Review*, 1985, for *Airs of Providence;* Pushcart Prize, 1987, for "World With a Hard K"; grants from National Endowment for the Arts, 1987.

WRITINGS:

Airs of Providence (short stories), Johns Hopkins University Press, 1985.
The Very Rich Hours (novel), Johns Hopkins University Press, 1987.

WORK IN PROGRESS: The Courage of Girls, a novel.

* * *

McGINN, Richard 1939-

PERSONAL: Born December 23, 1939, in Spokane, Wash.; son of Richard, Sr., and Cathrine (Murphy) McGinn; married Judy Brooks (a librarian), January 10, 1970; children: Colleen, Andrew. *Education:* Gonzaga University, M.A., 1966; University of Hawaii at Manoa, Ph.D., 1979.

ADDRESSES: Home—67 Franklin, Athens, Ohio 45701. *Office*—Department of Linguistics, Ohio University, Athens, Ohio 45701.

CAREER: U.S. Peace Corps, Washington, D.C., volunteer in the Philippines, 1963-66; Ohio University, Athens, director of Southeast Asia Center, 1984—. President of Consortium of Teachers of Southeast Asian Languages, 1985-87.

MEMBER: Association for Asian Studies, Linguistic Society of America.

WRITINGS:

Outline of Rejang Syntax (monograph), Universitas Atma Jaya Press, 1982.
(Editor) *Studies in Austronesian Linguistics*, Ohio University Press, 1988.

SIDELIGHTS: Richard McGinn told *CA:* "Language acquisition by children is a miracle and is the best evidence available that the spirit of man—like his physical nature—is one species that has filled the earth. This is linguist Noam Chomsky's thesis, and I agree."

* * *

McGREEVY, Susan Brown 1934-

PERSONAL: Born January 28, 1934, in Chicago, Ill.; daughter of Irving Leslie and Edna (Joselit) Colby; married Thomas J. McGreevy, June 16, 1973; children: Patricia Leigh Brown, Lori Alyn Brown, Cynthia Diane Brown. *Education:* Attended Mount Holyoke College, 1951-53; Roosevelt University, B.A. (with honors), 1969; Northwestern University, M.A., 1971.

ADDRESSES: Home—Route 7, Box 129-E, Santa Fe, N.M. 87505. *Office*—704 Camino Lejo, Box 5153, Santa Fe, N.M. 87502.

CAREER: Heart of America Indian Center, Kansas City, Mo., staff consultant, 1973-75; Kansas City Museum of History and Science, Kansas City, curator of North American ethnology, 1975-77; Wheelwright Museum of the American Indian, Santa Fe, N.M., director, 1978-82, research associate, 1983—, member of board of trustees, 1987. Adjunct professor at Ottowa University, Kansas City campus, 1976-77; guest lecturer at colleges and museums, 1978—; member of faculty at Northwestern University, Gallina, N.M., 1980—. Conducted field work on Navajo reservation, 1970, 1971, and 1978—; member of board of directors of Morning Star Lodge Indian Halfway House, 1974-77, and Santa Fe Mountain Center, 1983—. Member of board of trustees of Kansas City Symphony, 1974-77.

MEMBER: American Anthropological Association, American Association of Museums, American Ethnological Society, American Society for Ethnohistory, Council for Museum Anthropology, Society for Applied Anthropology, Native American Art Studies Association, Mountain-Plains Museum Association, New Mexico Museum Association.

AWARDS, HONORS: Grants from National Historic Publications and Records Commission, 1980, National Endowment for the Humanities, 1981, and National Endowment for the Arts, 1985.

WRITINGS:

(Editor) *Woven Holy People: Navajo Sandpainting Textiles,* Wheelwright Museum, 1983.
(With Andrew Hunter Whitleford) *Translating Tradition: Basketry Arts of the San Juan Paiutes* (catalogue), Wheelwright Museum, 1985.
(With Katherine Spencer Halpern) *Guide to the Microfilm Edition of the Washington Matthews Papers,* University of New Mexico Press, 1985.

Contributor to art journals.

WORK IN PROGRESS: Journey Towards Understanding, a biography of Mary Cabot Wheelwright, for University of New Mexico Press; ''Daughters of the Desert,'' to be included in *Good Housekeeping: A Ladies' Home Journal of Southwestern Institutions,* edited by Barbara A. Babcock and Nancy J. Parezo; further research on art and culture change as it relates to Navajo basket making.

SIDELIGHTS: Susan Brown McGreevy told *CA:* "My first summer on the Navajo reservation in 1970 (Shonto area) irrevocably changed my life. During that time I was conducting research for my M.A. thesis for the department of anthropology at Northwestern University. For the first time everything I had read previously concerning differences in cultural world views became a reality. I developed a profound respect for the Navajos and continue to visit the reservation whenever I can. The current focus of my research is art and culture change, specifically as it relates to Navajo basket making (to be the subject of my next book after completion of Mary Cabot Wheelwright's biography). The exhibit and catalogue on San Juan Paiute basketry was related to this ongoing research as these people live on the western Navajo reservation.

"My interest in Mary Cabot Wheelwright developed while I was director of the museum she founded. The legend of the Wheelwright Museum involves the adventures of two remarkable individuals from dramatically different worlds: a wealthy Bostonian intellectual, Mary Cabot Wheelwright, and an esteemed Navajo intellectual and ceremonial practitioner, Hastiin Klah. For fifteen years they worked together to create a unique and important record of Navajo culture, a record that was to culminate in the founding of an equally unique and important institution. Writing Wheelwright's biography unites three subjects that are of great interest to me: women's studies, Navajo studies, and the history of Southwestern anthropology.

"'Daughters of the Desert,' my chapter on women and southwestern museums for Barbara A. Babcock and Nancy J. Parezo's book, is a further expression of these interests. I am particularly impressed with the number of women from the East who founded or nurtured southwestern museums during the first half of this century. These 'strangers in a strange land' found emotional emancipation in the vast desert landscapes and intellectual stimulation in the cultures of the indigenous people. The museums they founded were idiosyncratic and highly personal reflections of their individual and collective responses to the people and terrain of the Southwest."

* * *

McGURN, William 1958-

PERSONAL: Born in 1958, in Oceanside, Calif.; son of William A. (an agent of the Federal Bureau of Investigation) and Mary S. (a housewife; maiden name, Gormley) McGurn. *Ed-*

ucation: University of Notre Dame, B.A., 1980; Boston University, M.S., 1981.

ADDRESSES: Home—84 Pokfulam Rd., F-1 Hong Kong. *Office*—c/o *Wall Street Journal,* 200 Liberty St., New York, N.Y. 10281. *Agent*—L. A. Sabatier, P.O. Box 10448, Arlington, Va. 22210.

CAREER: American Spectator, Bloomington, Ind., assistant managing editor, 1981-83; *This World,* New York City, managing editor, 1983-84; *Wall Street Journal,* New York City, editorial features editor for European edition in Brussels, Belgium, 1984-86, editorial page editor for Asian edition in Hong Kong, 1987—.

WRITINGS:

Terrorist or Freedom Fighter? The Cost of Confusion (monograph), Institute for European Defense and Strategic Studies, 1987.
(Editor) *Basic Law, Basic Questions: The Debate Continues,* Review Publishing (Hong Kong), 1988.

Contributor to magazines, including *National Catholic Register, Crisis, New Republic,* and *Spectator.*

WORK IN PROGRESS: Research for a book on terrorism and a book on the moral dimensions of capitalism.

* * *

McKEON, Zahava Karl 1927-

PERSONAL: Born March 11, 1927, in Chicago, Ill.; daughter of Meyer (a businessman) and Bertha (a housewife; maiden name, Freeman) Karl; married second husband, Richard P. McKeon (a philosopher, educator, and author), March 11, 1979 (deceased); children: (first marriage) Karl M. Dorinson, Alexandra Dorinson Slade. *Education:* Roosevelt University, A.B., 1952, A.M., 1963; University of Chicago, Ph.D., 1974.

ADDRESSES: Home and office—5632 South Blackstone Ave., Chicago, Ill. 60637.

CAREER: University of Chicago, Chicago, Ill., secretary to dean of students, humanities, 1952-55; homemaker, 1955-63; De Paul University, Chicago, Ill., instructor, 1963-c. 1974, assistant professor, c. 1974-82, associate professor of English, c. 1982-1985; writer and editor, 1985—.

MEMBER: Modern Language Association of America.

AWARDS, HONORS: Danforth fellow, c. 1970-72.

WRITINGS:

Novels and Arguments: Inventing Rhetorical Criticism, University of Chicago Press, 1982.

WORK IN PROGRESS: Editing *Collected Works of Richard McKeon,* eight or nine volumes, publication by University of Chicago Press expected by 1992.

SIDELIGHTS: Zahava Karl McKeon told *CA:* "I have always been interested in literary criticism and philosophy. Following the death of my husband, I retired from teaching to edit his published work. When that task is completed, I hope to write his biography and edit his correspondence. I consider these projects to be an important contribution to the history of higher education in the twentieth century."

McMAHON, Edwin Mansfield 1930-

PERSONAL: Born May 28, 1930, in Sonora, Calif.; son of Edwin Fremont (a rancher) and Anna Mae (a homemaker and teacher; maiden name, Bromley) McMahon. *Education:* University of Santa Clara, B.S., 1952, M.A., 1966; graduate study at University of San Francisco, 1953; Gonzaga University, M.Ed., 1958; University of Ottawa, Ph.D., 1971. *Politics:* Democrat.

ADDRESSES: Home and office—Institute for Research in Spirituality, 6305 Greeley Hill Rd., Coulterville, Calif. 95311.

CAREER: Entered Society of Jesus (Jesuits), 1953 (resigned, 1973), ordained Roman Catholic priest, 1965; high school teacher and counselor, 1959-62; St. Paul's University, Ottawa, Ontario, lecturer in psychology of religion, 1968-75; University of Ottawa, Ottawa, lecturer in psychology of religion, 1968-75; Institute for Research in Spirituality, Coulterville, Calif., co-director, 1975—. Leader of workshops and retreats in United States and Canada.

WRITINGS:

Becoming a Person in the Whole Christ, Sheed, 1967.
The Inbetween: Evolution in Christian Faith, Sheed, 1969.
Please Touch, Sheed, 1969.
Bio-Spirituality: Focusing as a Way to Grow, Loyola University Press, 1985.

Also author of more than twenty pamphlets for Institute for Research in Spirituality. Contributor to journals. Co-editor of *Kairos.*

WORK IN PROGRESS: Research for a book on "addictive religion."

SIDELIGHTS: Edwin Mansfield McMahon told *CA:* "The main thrust of my research and writing is in the area of what is healthy and what is pathological in religion. I also try to connect, develop new syntheses, practical approaches, and so on, joining together healthy, sound psychology with what is healthy in the tradition of Christian spirituality. I have always felt that all religions need careful psychological evaluation after centuries of uncritical accumulations. This would help preserve what is supportive of human growth, as well as clarify what is destructive of human wholeness.

"After being primarily a healer and therapist for more than thirty years, I write today to teach people to be gentle with what they fear most in themselves. I have found over the years that people don't know how to treat themselves when they experience feelings of terror, confusion, pain, shame—anything that is negative. Without being taught how to own in their bodies whatever they experience as real, the story that is in these feelings can't express itself. They don't grow emotionally, spiritually, socially, even in physical wellness. I strongly suspected years ago that all this is what the 'spiritual life' is about. God-consciousness and self-consciousness are one and the same, and the basic truths of the Christian tradition now have to be 'reinvented' for this age. This time in history demands that Christians look to the carefully researched efforts of science in order to take the Incarnation literally and put Humpty Dumpty together again. Most of my writing therefore explores Dr. Eugene Gendlin's 'focusing' as an intrinsically unifying and spiritual process.

"While leading workshops and retreats I began to realize that very often the way people practiced their religion blocked their spiritual growth. So frequently their religious practice was ad-dictive, in the sense that they used religion as a substitute for a growing truthful relationship with themselves, others, the world around them, and God. Each day as I research and experience how much organized religion naively 'sets people up' for addictive behavior, new writing is taking shape.''

*   *   *

McMILLIN, (Harvey) Scott 1934-

PERSONAL: Born June 29, 1934, in Pittsburgh, Pa.; son of Harvey Scott (a businessman) and Elizabeth (Bradley) McMillin; married Sally Hyde, May 11, 1957; children: David, Paul, Andrew. *Education:* Princeton University, B.A., 1956; George Washington University, M.A., 1960; Stanford University, Ph.D., 1965.

ADDRESSES: Office—Department of English, Cornell University, Ithaca, N.Y. 14850.

CAREER: Cornell University, Ithaca, N.Y., instructor, 1964-66, assistant professor, 1966-72, associate professor, 1972-78, professor of English, 1978—. Member of editorial board of Cornell University Press, 1981-85 and 1987—. *Military service:* U.S. Navy, 1957-60; became lieutenant junior grade.

MEMBER: Modern Language Association of America, Shakespeare Association of America (chairman of Theatre History Seminar, 1987-88, trustee, 1988—), American Society for Theater Research, Medieval and Renaissance Drama Association.

AWARDS, HONORS: Leverhulme fellow, 1963-64; grants from National Endowment for the Humanities, 1968 and 1986; fellow of American Philosophical Society, 1972-73.

WRITINGS:

(Editor and author of commentary) *The Norton Critical Edition of Restoration and Eighteenth-Century Comedy,* Norton, 1973.
(Contributor) Harold Bloom, editor, *Modern Critical Views: Elizabethan Dramatists,* Chelsea House, 1986.
The Elizabethan Theatre and the Book of Thomas More, Cornell University Press, 1987.
(Contributor) T. H. Howard-Hill, editor, *Shakespeare and the Book of Sir Thomas More,* Cambridge University Press, 1988.
(Contributor) James Bulman and Herbert Courson, editors, *Shakespeare on Television,* University Press of New England, 1988.
(Contributor) John Astington, editor, *The Development of Shakespeare's Theatre,* AMS Press, in press.

Contributor to literature and theater journals.

WORK IN PROGRESS: The Queen's Men, 1583-1600, including related studies of other Elizabethan acting companies; *Shakespeare: The Theory of Acting;* a book on modern productions of William Shakespeare's "Henry IV, Part I," for Manchester University Press; a computerized study of Elizabethan play texts.

*   *   *

McQUOWN, Norman A(nthony) 1914-

PERSONAL: Born January 30, 1914, in Peoria, Ill.; son of George McKinsey and Frieda (Campen) McQuown; married Dolores Milleville (a dietician), November 7, 1942; children: Kathryn Ann (Mrs. David W. Connell), Patricia Ellen (Mrs.

Elton Wildermuth). *Education:* University of Illinois at Urbana-Champaign, B.A., 1935, M.A., 1936; attended Brown University, 1936-37, and University of Michigan, 1937; Yale University, Ph.D., 1940.

ADDRESSES: Home—5708 South Drexel Ave., Chicago, Ill. 60637. *Office*—1126 East 59th St., Chicago, Ill. 60637.

CAREER: National School of Anthropology, Mexico City, Mexico, lecturer in linguistics, 1939-42; Indiana University—Bloomington, lecturer in Turkish, 1942-43; Hunter College (now of the City University of New York), New York, N.Y., lecturer in linguistics and Russian, 1945-46; University of Chicago, Chicago, Ill., assistant professor, 1946-51, associate professor, 1951-58, professor of anthropology, 1958-79, professor emeritus, 1979—, chairman of department, 1958-61. Research associate in Totonac with Mexican Department of Indian Affairs, 1939-40; research associate in Turkish with American Council of Learned Societies, 1941-43; research associate in Maya with Carnegie Institute, Washington, D.C., 1946-47. Visiting professor at University of Seville, 1962-63, University of Uruguay, 1966, University of Mexico, 1967-68 and 1982-86, and University of Hamburg, 1971-72. U.S. delegate to UNESCO seminar in Ceylon, 1953; Center for Applied Linguistics, member of advisory board, 1959-64, trustee, 1965-70; Inter-American Program on Linguistics and Language Teaching, member of executive committee, 1963—, president, 1965-71, chairman, 1973-77. *Wartime service:* Army Service Forces, 1943-45; language technician in Washington, D.C. and New York, N.Y.

MEMBER: Linguistic Society of America (vice-president, 1968), American Anthropological Association, American Association for the Advancement of Science, American Council of Learned Societies (chairman of committee on language programs, 1952-54), Mexican Council on Indigenous Languages, Cosmopolitan Club of University of Illinois (president, 1935-36).

AWARDS, HONORS: Senior fellow of National Science Foundation in Europe, 1962-63, and National Endowment for the Humanities, 1971-72; Fulbright fellow in Guatemala, 1981; Alexander von Humboldt Research Prize, 1988.

WRITINGS:

Spoken Turkish: Basic Course, two volumes, Linguistic Society of America and Intensive Language Program of the American Council of Learned Societies, 1944-45, reprinted, Spoken Language Service, 1971.
Handbook of Middle American Indians, Volume V: *Linguistics*, University of Texas Press, 1967.
(Editor with Julian Pitt-Rivers, and contributor) *Ensayos de antropologia en la zona central de Chiapas* (title means "Essays on the Anthropology of the Central Zone of Chiapas"), Instituto Nacional Indigenista (Mexico), 1970.
American Indian Linguistics in New Spain, Peter de Ridder Press, 1976.
Language, Culture, and Education: Essays, Stanford University Press, 1982.
(Editor) *Arte de la lengua totonaca* (facsimile of sixteenth-century manuscript; title means "A Grammar of the Totonac Language"), Press of the Mexican National University, 1988.
Gramatica de la lengua totonaca (title means "Grammar of the Totonac Language"), Press of the Mexican National University, 1988.

Contributor to scholarly journals.

WORK IN PROGRESS: Inventory of books and manuscripts on or in Middle American languages in the libraries and archives of Western Europe.

*   *   *

MEAD, Taylor   1931(?)-

PERSONAL: Born December 31, c. 1931, in Detroit, Mich.; son of Harry (a politician, attorney, and chemical company owner) and Priscilla Mead. *Education:* Studied acting at the Pasadena Playhouse and Herbert Berghof Studio.

CAREER: Office worker, sometimes employed at Merrill Lynch Securities Investment Co., in Detroit, Mich.; actor and writer. Actor in films, including "The Flower Thief" (1960), "Hallelujah the Hills" (1962), "Queen of Sheba Meets the Atom Man" (1963), "Babo 73" (1964), "Lonesome Cowboys" (1968), "Brand X" (1969), "Cleopatra," "Detective," "The Hobo and the Circus," "The Illiac Passion," "Imitation of Christ," "Lemon Hearts," "The Nude Restaurant," "Open the Door and See All the People," "Passion in a Seaside Slum," "San Diego Surfer," "Tarzan and Jane Regained . . . Sort Of," "Taylor Mead Dances," "Taylor Mead's Ass," "To L.A. . . . With Lust," and "Too Young, Too Immoral." Actor in plays, including "The General Returns From One Place to Another" and "The Baptism" Off-Off Broadway, and in "Le Desir attrape par la queue" in St. Tropez, France.

AWARDS, HONORS: Obie Award from *Village Voice*, 1963, for performance in "The General Returns From One Place to Another."

WRITINGS:

Excerpts From the Anonymous Diary of a New York Youth, privately printed, 1961.
Second Excerpts From the Anonymous Diary of a New York Youth, privately printed, 1962.
On Amphetamine and in Europe: Excerpts From the Anonymous Diary of a New York Youth, Volume III, Boss Books, 1968.
Son of Andy Warhol, Hanuman Books, c. 1987.

Contributor to periodicals.

SIDELIGHTS: "Before World War II you could sleep in Central Park or on the beach or anywhere you wanted to—since World War II the enemy has moved in—you can't sleep anywhere or do anything—in other words we lost the war." In these words, Taylor Mead lamented the loss of personal liberty in the United States in his *On Amphetamine and in Europe: Excerpts From the Anonymous Diary of a New York Youth*, quoted by Gordon Ball in a *Dictionary of Literary Biography* article. A product of the unconventional and rebellious "Beat Generation" of literary artists active from the late 1940s through the 1960s who were often at odds with authority, Mead wrote three volumes of the autobiographical *Excerpts From the Anonymous Diary of a New York Youth* and appeared in scores of avant-garde films during the 1960s and 1970s, including Bob Downey's "Babo 73" and Andy Warhol's "Lonesome Cowboys." "I started acting in the fifth grade," Mead was quoted in *Mug Shots* in 1972. "And I played the lead in all the high school plays. I guess I'm still doing high-school plays."

After graduation from a prep school in Connecticut, Mead wandered around the country and held a variety of jobs, including working at an investment company in Detroit. In California he studied acting at the Pasadena Playhouse, appeared in "The Flower Thief," a silent film directed by Ron Rice, and was run out of San Francisco's North Beach area by a policeman who did not like beatniks. He was arrested more than a dozen times while on the road, once in Columbia, South Carolina, for playing a piano in a church and in another incident by an incognito police officer for being homosexual. After years of drifting and run-ins with the police Mead arrived in New York City and welcomed the privacy it afforded. Introverted and shy, he thought that in the bustling, unconventional atmosphere of Lower Manhattan in the late 1950s he would be anonymous.

But "The Flower Thief" was released in 1960 and it was enthusiastically received by New York's Beat circles. Mead, thrust into the limelight, lost much of his privacy so he began to keep journals, "really to keep from masturbating, because I was so totally self-absorbed," he was quoted by Ball. In his diaries Mead composed poetry and recorded his private thoughts and comments on current affairs and social injustice, and his reflections on filmmaking, authors, and musicians. Urged by friends to share these intimations with his public, he gave readings from his journals in coffeehouses, and his work was so well accepted that in 1961 he mimeographed the pamphlet-sized *Excerpts From the Anonymous Diary of a New York Youth* at his own expense. The following year he printed *More Excerpts From the Anonymous Diary of a New York Youth*, which was twice as long as the first volume.

Mead also gained notoriety by continuing to play in more avant-garde films, not performing or acting in the strictest sense, according to *Mug Shots*, but offering "a portrait of Taylor Mead in whatever situation the director sets up." He worked with Adolfas Mekas in "Hallelujah the Hills" and for Win Chamberlain in "Brand X," with Rice again in "The Queen of Sheba Meets the Atom Man," and in "Lonesome Cowboys" with Andy Warhol, who, Mead reflected in *Mug Shots*, did not pay his actors well: "For all his revolutionary art, he's absolutely nineteenth century about money." Mead also appeared on stage in Off-Off Broadway and experimental theater productions. At the height of his career he starred in LeRoi Jones's "Baptism," playing a homosexual cavorting in a church during services, and in Frank O'Hara's "The General Returns From One Place to Another," for which he won an Obie. Critics were enchanted by his stage presence and comic ability. Susan Sontag remarked in *Partisan Review* that she was awed by Mead's extraordinary talent: "The source of his art is the deepest and purest of all: he just gives himself, wholly and without reserve, to some bizarre autistic fantasy. Nothing is more attractive in a person, but it is extremely rare after the age of four."

From 1962 to 1964, at the height of his fame, Mead wrote the journals that would be published in 1968 in the third, and longest, volume of *Excerpts From an Anonymous Diary of a New York Youth, On Amphetamine and in Europe.* As in his earlier contributions, Mead's wit is obvious by the comments that Ball cited from *On Amphetamine and in Europe.* Exemplary are Mead's views on politics: "Oh for Christ's sake, United States and Russia—get it over with"; his impressions of writers, including Jack Kerouac, who, Mead concluded after a futile attempt at seducing him, "was kind of square"; and his verse about a fellow actor and a hero of the Beat generation: "Was I the first Beatnick? / No, Marlon Brando was the first beatnick and / he married me and / we had children."

In volume three Mead also addresses a theme explored by many of the Beat writers: creativity versus authority. Incensed

by his harassment in San Francisco and angered by the courts' attempts to ban and censor films and writings, including a poem of his own that was considered obscene because it depicted President John Kennedy having sex with his daughter Caroline, Mead was prompted to write: "the police have / appointed / themselves music / critics / art critics / literary critics / movie critics / burlesque critics / pornography critics / critic critics . . . / they do everything / but blood stop shed / and they are / paid for it," quoted Ball. More recently Mead wrote another small volume, *Son of Andy Warhol*, which C. Carr in the *Village Voice* compared to Mead's youthful notebooks: full of outrage, lament, and his "grocery list."

BIOGRAPHICAL/CRITICAL SOURCES:

BOOKS

Dictionary of Literary Biography, Volume 16: *The Beats: Literary Bohemians in Postwar America*, Gale, 1983.
Mead, Taylor, *On Amphetamine and in Europe: Excerpts From the Anonymous Diary of a New York Youth*, Volume III, Boss Books, 1968.
Mug Shots: Who's Who in the New Earth, World Publishing, 1972.

PERIODICALS

Partisan Review, summer, 1964.
Village Voice, December 22, 1987.

—Sketch by Carol Lynn DeKane

*   *   *

MEHTA, J. L.   1912(?)-1988

OBITUARY NOTICE: Born c. 1912; died of a heart attack, July 11, 1988, in Cambridge, Mass.; cremated. Philosopher, educator, and author. Mehta was an expert on the existentialist philosophy of Germany's Martin Heidegger and was a scholar of both Western and Eastern philosophies. A retired professor at Banaras Hindu University, Mehta also taught courses in Indian philosophy at Harvard Divinity School between 1968 and 1978. *The Philosophy of Martin Heidegger* is considered his major work, though he also wrote *India and the West: The Problem of Understanding* and *Advanced Study in the History of Medieval India.* Mehta lived in Jabalpur, India, and was visiting the United States at the time of his death.

OBITUARIES AND OTHER SOURCES:

PERIODICALS

Chicago Tribune, July 13, 1988.
New York Times, July 12, 1988.
Times (London), July 16, 1988.

*   *   *

MEINE, Curt   1958-

PERSONAL: Surname is pronounced "*My*-nee"; born November 29, 1958, in New Castle, Pa.; son of Kenneth and Evelyn (DeVivo) Meine. *Education:* DePaul University, B.A., 1980; University of Wisconsin—Madison, M.S., 1983, Ph.D., 1988. *Politics:* Independent. *Religion:* "Unaffiliated."

ADDRESSES: Home—Madison, Wis. *Office*—Institute for Environmental Studies, University of Wisconsin—Madison, Madison, Wis. 53705.

CAREER: Writer, 1984-86; University of Wisconsin—Madison, teaching assistant, project assistant, and research assistant at Institute for Environmental Studies, 1985—.

WRITINGS:

Aldo Leopold: His Life and Work, University of Wisconsin Press, 1988.

CONTRIBUTOR

J. Baird Callicott, editor, *Companion to a Sand County Almanac,* University of Wisconsin Press, 1987.
Thomas Tanner, editor, *Aldo Leopold: The Man and His Legacy,* Soil Conservation Society of America, 1987.

Contributor to magazines, including *Journal of Soil and Water Conservation, Wilderness,* and *Wisconsin Academy Review.*

SIDELIGHTS: Curt Meine told *CA:* "Aldo Leopold was a widely influential figure in forestry, soil conservation, wilderness preservation, wildlife ecology and management, and conservation education. At the University of Wisconsin Leopold was the nation's first professor of game (later wildlife) management, and through his writing and teaching he became one of the conservation movement's most important figures. He also led efforts to establish wilderness areas in the national forests of the Southwest. In the last years of his life Leopold put together the collection of essays that would be published posthumously as *A Sand County Almanac,* a principal document in the rising environmental movement. It remains a seminal piece of nature writing and environmental philosophy, and it has secured Leopold a position, along with Henry David Thoreau and John Muir, as a leading environmental voice.

"*Aldo Leopold: His Life and Work* is the first comprehensive biography of Leopold. Undertaken in conjunction with the centenary of Leopold's birth, it presents a detailed record of Leopold's activities, interests, influences, and thought, and endeavors to place Leopold in the broader context of environmental history. I have made an effort in this book to present a picture of Leopold that is fair and accurate, and that highlights the relevancy of his work to today's environmental situations. Until now, Leopold has been interpreted rather narrowly, if at all; this biography was written to flesh out the personality, to present Leopold in all his facets, to place him in his geographical and historical settings, and to lay out his many contributions, many of them heretofore overlooked, to the practice and philosophy of conservation."

BIOGRAPHICAL/CRITICAL SOURCES:

PERIODICALS

Bloomsbury Review, July-August, 1988.
New York Times Book Review, February 28, 1988.
Science, September 2, 1988.
Wilderness, spring, 1988.

* * *

MELCHETT, Sonia
See SINCLAIR, Sonia

* * *

MENARD, Russell   1942-

PERSONAL: Born March 20, 1942, in Taunton, Mass. *Education:* University of Delaware, B.A., 1965; University of Iowa, M.A., 1967, Ph.D., 1974.

ADDRESSES: Office—Department of History, University of Minnesota—Twin Cities, Minneapolis, Minn. 55455.

CAREER: Affiliated with history department of University of Minnesota—Twin Cities, Minneapolis.

WRITINGS:

(With John J. McCusker) *The Economy of British America, 1607-1789,* University of North Carolina Press, 1985.

* * *

MENDELSON, Sara Heller   1947-

PERSONAL: Born April 24, 1947, in Philadelphia, Pa.; daughter of David (a proofreader) and Miriam (an artist; maiden name, Moskowitz) Heller; married Alan Mendelson (a university professor), January 24, 1971; children: David, Daniel. *Education:* Attended University of Pennsylvania, 1965-66; University of Chicago, B.A., 1970; Oxford University, D.Phil., 1982. *Religion:* Jewish.

ADDRESSES: Home—Hamilton, Ontario, Canada. *Office*—Department of History, University of Toronto, Toronto, Ontario, Canada M5S 1A1.

CAREER: Hebrew University of Jerusalem, Jerusalem, Israel, research assistant in history, 1971-73; University of Toronto, Toronto, Ontario, visiting assistant professor of history, 1984—.

AWARDS, HONORS: Grants from Social Science and Humanities Research Council of Canada, 1984-85 and 1986-87; Canada Research fellowship, 1988-92.

WRITINGS:

(Contributor) Mary Prior, editor, *Women in English Society,* Methuen, 1985.
The Mental World of Stuart Women: Three Studies, University of Massachusetts Press, 1987.
Testaments of Women, 1350-1914, Volume III: *1660-1720,* Oxford University Press, in press.

Contributor to history journals.

WORK IN PROGRESS: Tudor and Stuart Women: A Social History, with P. M. Crawford, publication by Oxford University Press expected in 1991.

BIOGRAPHICAL/CRITICAL SOURCES:

PERIODICALS

Times Literary Supplement, April 1-7, 1988.

* * *

MEREDITH, Christopher (Laurence)   1954-

PERSONAL: Surname is accented on middle syllable; born December 15, 1954, in Tredegar, South Wales; son of Emrys H. (a steelworker) and Joyce (Roberts) Meredith; married Valerie A. Smythe (a schoolteacher), August 1, 1981; children: Rhodri, Steffan. *Education:* University of Wales, University College of Wales, Aberystwyth, B.A. (with honors), 1976; University of Wales, University College, Swansea, postgraduate certificate of education, 1978.

ADDRESSES: Home—9 Lon Slwch, Aberhonddu/Brecon, Powys, Wales. *Office*—Brecon High School, Cerrig Cochion, Aberhonddu/Brecon, Powys, Wales.

CAREER: British Steel Corp., Glyn Ebwy, Wales, steelworker, 1977; Brecon High School, Aberhonddu/Brecon, Wales, English teacher, 1978—.

MEMBER: Yr Academi Gymreig (executive member of English language section), Association of Writers in Wales.

AWARDS, HONORS: Eric Gregory Award from Society of Authors, 1984, for a selection of poems; Young Writer's Prize from Welsh Arts Council, 1985, for *This.*

WRITINGS:

This (poems), Poetry Wales Press, 1984.
"The Carved Chair" (one-act play), first produced in Cardiff,
    Wales, at Sherman Theatre, May, 1986.
Shifts (novel), Seren, 1988.

Work represented in anthologies, including *The Gregory Poems 1983-84*, Salamander Press, 1985; *Poets Against Apartheid*, Wales Anti-Apartheid Movement, 1986; and *Picture: Welsh Poets*, Seren, 1987.

Contributor of stories, poems, articles, and reviews to magazines, including *Anglo-Welsh Review, Arcade, Planet, Poetry Wales, Outposts*, and *New Welsh Review.*

WORK IN PROGRESS: A novel; poems and prose.

SIDELIGHTS: Christopher Meredith told *CA:* "My poetry, so far, has mainly concerned itself with inner and family experience, though I hope it's remained accessible. I hope to touch the larger themes through particular experience. My part of Wales is one of the oldest heavy industrial regions on earth, and in my novel I've found myself dealing with the relationship between the individual consciousness of ordinary people and the industrial experience. Like most Welsh writers in English, I feel the tension between being Welsh and, perforce, writing in English. (I speak and read Welsh quite fluently, but not confidently enough to use it in my own creative writing.) It is a difficult, complex situation, but potentially a fruitful one."

*　　*　　*

MERRIT, Elizabeth
  See GOUDGE, Eileen

*　　*　　*

MEZVINSKY, Shirley
  See LAURO, Shirley (Shapiro) Mezvinsky

*　　*　　*

MIDDLETON, Roger   1955-

PERSONAL: Born May 19, 1955, in England. *Education:* Victoria University of Manchester, B.A. (with first class honors), 1976; Cambridge University, Ph.D., 1981. *Politics:* Socialist.

ADDRESSES: Office—Department of Economic and Social History, University of Bristol, Bristol BS1 1TB, England.

CAREER: University of Durham, Durham, England, lecturer in economic history, 1979-87; University of Bristol, Bristol, England, lecturer in economic history, 1987—.

MEMBER: Royal Economic Society, Economic History Society, Conference of Socialist Economists, Institute of Fiscal Studies.

AWARDS, HONORS: T. S. Ashton Prize from Economic History Society, 1980, for best paper of the year by a young scholar in the society's journal, *Economic History Review.*

WRITINGS:

Towards the Managed Economy, Methuen, 1985.

Contributor to economic and history journals.

WORK IN PROGRESS: The Economic Management of Britain in the Twentieth Century, for Edward Elgar, completion expected about 1992.

SIDELIGHTS: Roger Middleton's *Towards the Managed Economy* was labeled "one of the best studies of economic policy-making in the inter-war years to have appeared" by Robert Skidelsky in the *Times Literary Supplement.* Examined in Middleton's book are the British budget balances of the 1930s, which he asserts to be highly deflationary. Middleton arrives at this conclusion by removing the effects of factors such as falling tax receipts and rising unemployment payments to determine cyclically adjusted budgets. The process revises the earlier belief "that budgetary policy was slightly reflationary between 1929 and 1931 . . . but then became deflationary from 1931 to 1937, when the budget was balanced," according to Skidelsky, who praised Middleton as "the best kind of modern economic historian."

BIOGRAPHICAL/CRITICAL SOURCES:

PERIODICALS

Times Literary Supplement, June 20, 1986.

*　　*　　*

MILLER, Danny   1947-

PERSONAL: Born November 15, 1947, in Montreal, Quebec, Canada; son of Morris and Maria (Verbruggen) Miller. *Education:* Sir George Williams University, B.Com. (with distinction), 1968; University of Toronto, M.B.A., 1970; McGill University, Ph.D., 1976.

ADDRESSES: Office—Faculty of Management, McGill University, 1001 Sherbrooke St. W., Montreal, Quebec, Canada H3A 1G5.

CAREER: Bank of Montreal, Montreal, Quebec, administrative manager, 1968-69, senior project analyst, 1970-72; McGill University, Montreal, Quebec, postdoctoral research associate, 1976-82, associate professor of management, 1982—. University of Montreal, associate professor, 1980-86, professor, 1986—. Consultant to public and private organizations and foundations.

MEMBER: Macro-Organizational Behavior Society.

AWARDS, HONORS: Grants from Canada Council, Social Science and Humanities Research Council of Canada, Government of Quebec, Federal Department of Industry, Trade, and Commerce, and private industry.

WRITINGS:

(With Lawrence Gordon and Henry Mintzberg) *Normative Models of Managerial Decision Making*, National Association of Accountants, 1975.
(With Lawrence Gordon, Robert Cooper, and Haim Falk) *The Pricing Decision*, National Association of Accountants, 1980.

(Contributor) Gareth Morgan, editor, *Beyond Method*, Sage Publications, 1983.
(With Peter H. Friesen and Henry Mintzberg) *Organizations: A Quantum View*, Prentice-Hall, 1984.
(With Manfred F. R. Kets de Vries) *The Neurotic Organization: Diagnosing and Changing Counterproductive Styles of Management*, Jossey-Bass, 1984.
(Contributor) Kim Cameron and other editors, *Organizational Decline: Frameworks, Research, and Perspectives*, Ballinger, 1988.
(Contributor) Robert Lamb, editor, *Advances in Applied Business Strategy*, JAI Press, 1988.
(With Manfred F. R. Kets de Vries) *Unstable at the Top*, New American Library, 1988.

Contributor to *Contemporary Issues in Cost and Managerial Accounting*, 1978. Contributor of about fifty articles and reviews to journals, including *Psychology Today*, *Harper's*, *Administrative Science Quarterly*, *Management Science*, *Academy of Management Journal*, and *Academy of Management Review*. Member of editorial board of *Journal of Management*, 1983-86, *Academy of Management Journal*, 1986—, *Strategic Management Journal*, 1986—, *Administrative Science Quarterly*, 1987—, and *Industrial Crisis Quarterly*, 1987—.

WORK IN PROGRESS: Research topics include organizational strategy and change; the relationships among executive personality, strategy, decision making, and administrative structure; the differential applicability of paradigms of organizational theory to common types of organizations; patterns of strategic behavior in the international oil industry; precursors to serious industrial accidents; and mathematical game theoretic models of the firm.

SIDELIGHTS: Danny Miller told *CA:* "The work closest to my heart is *Organizations: A Quantum View*. Its themes are simple, although their articulation in the book is somewhat abstract and technical. First, organizational reality is too complex to be described by generalizing across all organizations. Distinctions must be made and the only way to discover those that are most important is through taxonomy. Second, the variety of organizations is limited by internally reinforcing complementarities among a multitude of managerial, strategic, and structural factors. These form common configurations or gestalts that allow for a better understanding and more accurate prediction of organizational behavior. Finally, since configurations resist change, firms undergo long periods of stability punctuated by brief intervals of revolutionary change as they move quickly to a different configuration.

"Subsequent work with psychoanalyst Manfred Kets de Vries probed into pathological configurations and found that in many cases, their roots could be traced to the personalities of top executives. *The Neurotic Organization* lays out the theoretical and conceptual basis for failing, personality-driven firms, and *Unstable at the Top* presents examples of the common failure configurations. These configurations include the bold *dramatic* firms run by impulsive and narcissistic managers who expand operations too rapidly and recklessly; *detached* firms that are really fragmented fiefdoms beset by political infighting; as well as organizations that are *compulsive, suspicious,* or *depressive*. Organizational problems are very deeply embedded in the culture, structure, strategy, and executive personality of organizations, all of which are in varying degrees mutually reinforcing. Change is rarely possible without extensive administrative overhauls, which almost never take place until performance declines manifestly and until top managers depart."

BIOGRAPHICAL/CRITICAL SOURCES:

PERIODICALS

Academy of Management Journal, October, 1984.
Globe and Mail (Toronto), February 27, 1988.
Maclean's, July 15, 1985.
Montreal Gazette, March 27, 1987.
Ottawa Citizen, July 14, 1987.

*   *   *

MILLER, Jake C.   1929-

PERSONAL: Born December 28, 1929, in Hobe Sound, Fla.; son of Jake (a gardener) and Augustine (White) Miller; married Nellie Carrol (a teacher), December 22, 1956; children: Charles, Wayne, Warren. *Education:* Bethune-Cookman College, B.S., 1947; University of Illinois at Urbana-Champaign, M.A., 1957; University of North Carolina at Chapel Hill, Ph.D., 1967. *Religion:* United Methodist.

ADDRESSES: Home—1103 Lakewood Park Dr., Daytona Beach, Fla. 32010. *Office*—Department of Political Science, Bethune-Cookman College, 640 Second Ave., Daytona Beach, Fla. 32015.

CAREER: Teacher at public schools in Martin County, Fla., 1954-59; Bethune-Cookman College, Daytona Beach, Fla., assistant professor of political science, 1959-64; Fisk University, Nashville, Tenn., associate professor of political science and director of international studies, 1967-76; Bethune-Cookman College, professor of political science, 1976—. *Military service:* U.S. Marine Corps, 1951-53.

MEMBER: International Studies Association, American Political Science Association, Caribbean Studies Association, Transafrica, Alpha Kappa Mu.

AWARDS, HONORS: Outstanding achievement award from Danforth Foundation, 1970; fellow of National Endowment for the Humanities, 1981-82; distinguished scholar of United Negro College Fund, 1986-87; distinguished alumni citation from National Association for Equal Opportunity in Higher Education, 1988.

WRITINGS:

The Black Presence in American Foreign Affairs, University Press of America, 1978.
The Plight of Haitian Refugees, Praeger, 1984.

Contributor to political science journals.

WORK IN PROGRESS: Prophets of a Just Society, publication expected in 1988.

SIDELIGHTS: Jake C. Miller told *CA:* "For the last twenty years my teaching has focused upon oppressed people. It has been my belief that problems of oppression in the United States are related to those throughout the world.

"My first book was written as a result of not being able to provide a young student with information on the role of blacks in American foreign affairs. My first thought was that someone should write a book on the subject. It then occurred to me that that someone should be me. On that day I began the project which four years later resulted in the publication of *The Black Presence in American Foreign Affairs*.

"For several years we have conducted a model United Nations project at Bethune-Cookman College. Refugeeism, hunger, and racism were constant themes of these conferences. Simultaneously we were coming in constant contact with Haitians, who had fled their dictatorial governments, but were not accorded treatment similar to others defined as refugees. I was encouraged to conduct research on their plight—their economic, social, and legal predicament.

"My fascination with the nonviolent approach to conflict resolution led me to write *Prophets of a Just Society*, which analyzes the philosophies and works of Mohandas Gandhi, Martin Luther King, Jr., Albert Luthuli, and Desmond Tutu. Although progress seems slow in the obtaining of a just society, I continue to have faith in the nonviolent approach."

*   *   *

MILLER, James A. 1957-

PERSONAL: Born June 25, 1957; son of Mark A. and Leatrice Miller. *Education:* Occidental College, A.B., 1979; Oxford University, M.Litt., 1984; Harvard University, M.B.A., 1988.

ADDRESSES: Office—CBS News, 2020 M St. N.W., Washington, D.C. 20036.

CAREER: U.S. Senate, Washington, D.C., aide to Senator Howard Baker, 1981-83; producer for CBS News in Washington, D.C.

WRITINGS:

Running in Place: Life Inside the Modern Senate, Simon & Schuster, 1986.

BIOGRAPHICAL/CRITICAL SOURCES:

PERIODICALS

Washington Post Book World, April 20, 1986.

*   *   *

MILLER, Lily Poritz 1938-
(Lily Poritz)

PERSONAL: Born June 7, 1938, in Cape Town, South Africa; daughter of Joseph (an engineer) and Sarah (a singer and stockbroker; maiden name, Shapiro) Poritz; married Stephen Miller, 1966 (divorced). *Education:* Attended American Academy of Dramatic Arts, 1957-59, and New School for Social Research, 1959-61.

ADDRESSES: Home—17 Lascelles Blvd., Apt. 1105, Toronto, Ontario, Canada M4V 2B6. *Office*—McClelland and Stewart Ltd., 481 University Ave., Toronto, Ontario, Canada M5G 2E9. *Agent*—Bertha Klausner, International Literary Agency, 71 Park Ave., New York, N.Y. 10016.

CAREER: Collier-Macmillan (publisher), New York, N.Y., editor, 1961-65; McGraw-Hill (publisher), New York City, editor, 1965-67; Lothrop, Lee & Shepard, New York City, editor, 1967-69; consulting editor in New York City, 1969-71; City University of New York, New York City, instructor of creative writing, 1971; McClelland & Stewart (publisher), Toronto, Ontario, Canada, senior editor, 1972—.

MEMBER: International P.E.N., Playwrights Union of Canada, Dramatists Guild (New York).

AWARDS, HONORS: Samuel French publishers award, 1974, for *The Proud One*.

WRITINGS:

"My Star of Hope" (three-act play), first produced in New York at New School for Social Research, 1962.
The Proud One (three-act play; first produced at Backdoor Theatre, Toronto, Ontario, March, 1974), Playwrights Canada, 1973.
(Adapter of translation) Vladimir Jovicic, *Once There Was a Man*, translation by Vida Jankovic, McClelland & Stewart, 1987.

Works represented in anthologies, sometimes under the name Lily Poritz, including *American Scene: New Voices*, edited by Don Marion Wolfe, Lyle Stuart, 1963.

WORK IN PROGRESS: The Empty Rooms, a novel set in Cape Town, South Africa; *The Stroke of Nine*, a three-act play.

SIDELIGHTS: Lily Poritz Miller told *CA:* "As a writer, my best material was born of tragedy and pain—my father's death when I was a child and my inability to follow in the footsteps of most young girls when I was growing up. I did not consciously know the form these experiences were taking until my early twenties when in creative writing workshops in New York I was asked to search into myself and recreate indelible moments. After sitting one night before the blank page, knowing an assignment was due the next day, there suddenly blossomed a voice that came from deep within me, a voice I had never before heard, and I became only the vehicle who delivered the tale. This was the story of my father's death—'Where Is My Father?'—my first published work. A three-act play I wrote soon after—'In Place of Love'—was again born in a single weekend. It released the loneliness and pain I experienced because my life was not following the prescribed route.

"Now that I am older and have worked for many years as an editor developing other writers, I know my craft better, but I have mellowed and am more conscious of form and technique. Has this helped me in my own writing? Sadly, my work has become too self-conscious and I yearn for the day when I can once again lose myself in the world of my characters and let them guide me."

*   *   *

MILLER, Orson K., Jr. 1930-

PERSONAL: Born December 19, 1930, in Cambridge, Mass.; son of Orson K. Miller; married wife in 1954; children: three. *Education:* University of Massachusetts at Amherst, B.Sc., 1952; University of Michigan, M.F., 1957, Ph.D., 1963.

ADDRESSES: Office—Department of Biology, Virginia Polytechnic Institute and State University, Blacksburg, Va. 24061.

CAREER: U.S. Department of Agriculture, Washington, D.C., research forester at Northeastern Forest Experiment Station, 1956-57, plant pathologist at Intermountain Forest and Range Experiment Station, 1961-65, and at forest laboratory, 1965-70; Virginia Polytechnic Institute and State University, Blacksburg, associate professor, 1970-73, professor of botany, 1973—, curator of fungi, 1974—.

MEMBER: Arctic Institute of North America, American Association for the Advancement of Science, Mycological Society of America, Botanical Society of America, American Society of Plant Taxonomists.

WRITINGS:

Mushrooms of North America, Dutton, 1972, revised edition, 1979.
(With David F. Farr) *An Index of the Common Fungi of North America: Synonomy and Common Names*, J. Cramer, 1975.
(With Hope H. Miller) *Mushrooms in Color*, Dutton, 1980.
(With Miller) *Gasteromycetes: Morphological and Developmental Features*, Mad River, 1987.

BIOGRAPHICAL/CRITICAL SOURCES:

PERIODICALS

Christian Science Monitor, November 22, 1972.
New York Times Book Review, June 10, 1973.
Washington Post Book World, August 29, 1976.*

*   *   *

MILLER, Timothy (Alan)   1944-

PERSONAL: Born August 23, 1944, in Wichita, Kan.; son of Paul A. (an engineer) and Margaret J. (a teacher and activist; maiden name, Thompson) Miller; married Tamara Lea Dutton (a bookstore manager), August 11, 1982; children: Jesse, Abraham. *Education:* University of Kansas, A.B., 1966, M.A., 1969, Ph.D., 1973; Crozer Theological Seminary, M.Div., 1968.

ADDRESSES: Home—Lawrence, Kan. *Office*—Department of Religious Studies, 12 Smith Hall, University of Kansas, Lawrence, Kan. 66045.

CAREER: University of Kansas, Lawrence, lecturer, 1969-88, assistant professor of religious studies, 1988—. Lawrence Traffic Safety Commission, member, 1982-88, chairman, 1985-88; consultant to U.S. Department of Labor.

MEMBER: American Academy of Religion (chairman of New Religious Movements Group, 1983—), National Historic Communal Societies Association, Mid-America American Studies Association.

WRITINGS:

(With Tom Johnson) *The Sauna Book*, Harper, 1977.
Following in His Steps: A Biography of Charles M. Sheldon, University of Tennessee Press, 1987.
American Communalism, 1860-1960: An Annotated Bibliography, Garland Publishing, 1988.

Editor of *Plumber's Friend*, 1981—; associate editor of *American Studies*, 1982-86.

SIDELIGHTS: Timothy Miller told *CA:* "The biography of Charles M. Sheldon was a piece of salvage archaeology. Sheldon was an important figure in his day, but he was disappearing from public memory. I wanted to compile biographical materials while some of the people who had known him were still alive. Sheldon wrote what may be the best-selling novel of all time, *In His Steps*, and lived the life of a caring pastor who was also a committed social reformer. He worked hard for civil rights for blacks and women many decades before those causes developed large followings. He helped bring about national prohibition. A pacifist, he tirelessly campaigned against war. His simple creed was living in imitation of the example of Jesus, and he spent his life trying to inject his understanding of the Christian principles into the larger society. Sheldon's was a story worth preserving.

"*The Sauna Book* was written when Tom Johnson and I wanted to build a sauna. We couldn't find much information on the subject, so we decided to write a book."

*   *   *

MINHINNICK, Robert   1952-

PERSONAL: Born August 12, 1952, in Neath, Glamorganshire, Wales; son of Albert and Decima (a housewife) Minhinnick; married Margaret Bates (an environmentalist), November 19, 1977; children: one daughter. *Education:* University of Wales, University College, Cardiff, B.A., 1981, M.A., 1982.

ADDRESSES: Home—11 Park Ave., Porthcawl, Mid-Glamorgan, Wales. *Office*—Friends of the Earth, 3A Lias Rd., Porthcawl, Mid-Glamorgan, Wales.

CAREER: Worked as clerk, postman, salvage worker, and teacher, 1971-84; manager of an environmental program, 1984-85; writer in residence, 1985-86; Friends of the Earth, Porthcawl, Wales, environmental education worker, 1986—. Visited the United States and Canada on poetry reading tours in 1982 and 1985.

MEMBER: Yr Academi Gymreig (Welsh Academy; member of executive committee, 1983—).

AWARDS, HONORS: Eric Gregory Award from Society of Authors, 1980; awards from Welsh Arts Council, 1980 and 1984.

WRITINGS:

A Thread in the Maze (poems), Christopher Davies, 1978.
Native Ground (poems), Christopher Davies, 1979.
Life Sentences (poems), Poetry Wales Press, 1983.
The Dinosaur Book (poems), Poetry Wales Press, 1985.

Author of a regular column in *Planet*.

*   *   *

MINICHIELLO, Sharon

PERSONAL: Born in Lynn, Mass.; daughter of Philip L. (an engineer) and Margaret M. (Corcoran) Minichiello. *Education:* Attended University of New Hampshire; Salem State College, B.A. (summa cum laude), 1968; University of Hawaii at Manoa, M.A., 1970, Ph.D., 1975.

ADDRESSES: Home—2987 Kalakaua Ave., No. 603, Honolulu, Hawaii 96815. *Office*—Department of History, University of Hawaii at Manoa, Sakamaki Hall, 2530 Dole St., Honolulu, Hawaii 96822.

CAREER: Asahi shimbun, Tokyo, Japan, editorial assistant, 1972-75; translator of Japanese academic materials, 1972-75; International House of Japan, Tokyo, editorial assistant, 1973-74; Loyola Marymount University, Los Angeles, Calif., assistant professor, 1975-82, associate professor of history, 1982-85; University of Hawaii at Manoa, Honolulu, assistant professor of history, 1985—. Visiting research scholar at University of Tokyo, summers, 1977, 1979, 1980, and 1986; visiting scholar at Harvard University, 1980-81; visiting professor at University of Hawaii, summers, 1984 and 1985.

MEMBER: American Historical Association, Association for Asian Studies, Alpha Sigma Nu, Phi Alpha Theta, International House of Japan.

AWARDS, HONORS: Grants for Japan from Yoshida International Education Foundation and Hatakeyama Cultural Foundation, 1973-74; fellow of American Council of Learned Societies, 1977, Japan Foundation, 1978-79, American Philosophical Society, 1980, and Japan-U.S. Friendship Commission, 1986; grant from Association for Asian Studies, 1986.

WRITINGS:

Retreat From Reform: Patterns of Political Behavior in Interwar Japan, University of Hawaii Press, 1984.

Contributor to a commemorative volume in honor of Professor Masumi Junnosuke, University of Tokyo Press, 1988, and *Kodansha Encyclopedia of Japan.*

Contributor of articles and book reviews to periodicals, including *American Historical Review, Bulletin of the Center for American Studies of the University of Tokyo, Japan Interpreter, Journal of Asian Studies, Monumenta Nipponica, Nempo-kindai nihon kenkyu.*

WORK IN PROGRESS: The Founding of American Studies in Japan, a study of Takagi Yasaka, who was chosen by the Japanese government to create and help direct a national American studies program; a monograph, *Changing Japanese Perceptions of Democracy;* translating Mitani Taichiro's *Taisho demokurashii ron* (title means "Taisho Democracy").

*   *   *

MINTZ, Lannon W.   1938-1988

PERSONAL: Born May 10, 1938, in St. Paul, Minn.; died August 5, 1988; son of William and Ruth Mintz; married Linda Wille, November 23, 1974. *Education:* Attended University of Minnesota—Twin Cities, 1957-59, and University of New Mexico, 1968-85.

CAREER: KQEO-Radio, Albuquerque, N.Mex., announcer, 1962-69, sales manager, 1969-78; KABQ-Radio, Albuquerque, sales manager, 1978-83; KOAT-TV, Albuquerque, account executive, beginning in 1983.

MEMBER: Albuquerque Westerners.

WRITINGS:

Cookes Peak, privately printed, 1975.
The Trail, University of New Mexico Press, 1987.

SIDELIGHTS: Lannon W. Mintz described himself as an amateur historian and a western traveler, explorer, and adventurer.

[Date of death provided by Linda W. Mintz.]

*   *   *

MOERK, Ernst L(orenz)   1937-

PERSONAL: Surname rhymes with "work"; born March 10, 1937, in Gallbrunn, Austria; son of Georg (a farmer) and Magdalena (a housewife; maiden name, Geistler) Moerk; divorced; children: Kirstin. *Education:* Attended University of Vienna, 1956-61; University of Innsbruck, M.A., 1962, Ph.D., 1964; attended University of Zurich, 1962-63.

ADDRESSES: Home—4178 West San Jose, Fresno, Calif. 93722. *Office*—Department of Psychology, California State University, 6241 North Maple, Fresno, Calif. 93740.

CAREER: Affiliated with Infratest, Munich, West Germany, 1964-65; affiliated with Landeskrankenhaus, Heiligenhafen, West Germany, 1965-66; affiliated with Mount Sinai Hospital, Los Angeles, Calif., 1966-67; affiliated with psychology department of California State University, Fresno, 1967—.

MEMBER: International Society for the Study of Behavioral Development, Society for Research in Child Development, Psychologists for Social Responsibility.

WRITINGS:

Pragmatic and Semantic Aspects of Early Language Development, University Park Press, 1977.
The Mother of Eve: As a First Language Teacher, Ablex Publishing, 1983.

Contributor of about fifty articles to professional journals.

WORK IN PROGRESS: A book on teaching and learning a first language in the home; research on societal learning: attitude change from war-prone to preserving the peace, with special application to the history of Sweden.

SIDELIGHTS: Ernst L. Moerk told *CA:* "My past research and writing resulted from the combination of language studies (Greek and Latin, as well as my reading competence in about ten living languages) and my specialization in psychology. Now I plan to expand into 'culture learning' and especially the variables that influence change toward the peaceful orientation of societies. This contribution of psychology to the prevention of wars and the survival of mankind appears to me most needed."

*   *   *

MONAGAN, John S(tephen)   1911-

PERSONAL: Surname is pronounced with a hard "g"; born December 23, 1911, in Waterbury, Conn.; son of Charles Andrew (a physician) and Margaret (a housewife; maiden name, Mulry) Monagan; married Rosemary Anne Brady (a housewife), May 23, 1949; children: Charles, Michael, Parthenia, Laura Susan. *Education:* Dartmouth College, A.B., 1933; Harvard University, J.D., 1937. *Religion:* Roman Catholic.

ADDRESSES: Home—3043 West Lane Keys N.W., Washington, D.C. 20007.

CAREER: Private practice of law in Waterbury, Conn., 1938-40; alderman and finance commissioner of city of Waterbury, 1940-43, mayor, 1942-48; private practice of law, 1948-59; U.S. House of Representatives, Washington, D.C., Democratic representative from Fifth District of Connecticut, 1959-73, member of Committee on Finance Affairs and Committee on Government Operations, chairman of Subcommittee on Special Studies and Legal and Monetary Affairs, chairman of special study missions to Venezuela, Peru, Chile, Argentina, and Brazil, 1961, 1963, and to Moscow, Prague, Budapest, and Warsaw, 1962, 1964, chairman of Hearings on Central Europe, 1965-66, member of Joint Parliamentary Discussion Group at the Kremlin, 1969, official observer at disarmament conference in Geneva, 1962, and ECOSAC conference in Trinidad, 1969; Whitman & Ransom (law firm), New York, N.Y., senior resident partner, 1973-80; writer, 1980—. Visiting lecturer at U.S. Naval Academy, 1980, and College of William and Mary, 1982; Interparliamentary Union, member of U.S. Group, 1965-73, member of council, 1972, member of executive committee, 1970-73; conducted personal mission to the Middle East, 1970.

MEMBER: Association of Former Members of Congress (president, 1981-82), American Bar Association, Connecticut Bar

Association, District of Columbia Bar Association, Washington Institute of Foreign Affairs, American Council on Germany, Alpha Delta Phi, Cosmos Club.

WRITINGS:

Horace, Priest of the Poor (biography), Georgetown University Press, 1985.
The Grand Panjandrum: The Mellow Days of Justice Holmes, University Press of America, 1988.

Contributor of articles and reviews to law journals and newspapers.

WORK IN PROGRESS: A series of vignettes of Washington political figures (congressional and presidential); a "Washington novel."

SIDELIGHTS: John S. Monagan told *CA:* "I wrote *Horace* because I felt that the career of Reverend Horace McKenna provided a needed lesson of sacrifice in today's materialistic world. I met Father McKenna when I went to him to make a contribution in support of his charitable work. I was impressed by his simplicity, his complete dedication to his vocation, his lack of interest in possessions, his humor, his personal interest in his clients, and their obvious affection for him. Later I became aware of his sanctity and his dogged independence of thought which impelled him to pursue his ministry as he saw fit in spite of the opposition of constituted authority. I was particularly struck by the realization that he was carrying on his ambitious program in the face of severe and increasing blindness.

"His life provides a lesson in today's world because he recognized early the needs of our misfits and cast-offs, and in a society which places such a premium upon luxury and wealth he spurned these and gave his energy and imagination to helping the helpless and deprived.

"I wrote *The Grand Panjandrum* to add proportion to the reverential or inhuman existing studies of Justice Holmes. His 'mellow years' were his later decades when life had become quieter and he could devote time to his friends, his books, his correspondence, and his cogitation. It is interesting to note that he was the complete opposite of Horace McKenna in philosophy and way of life. Skeptical, self-centered, reclusive, and caste-conscious, he was not an ideal figure for today's concerned activists.

"I developed my perspective over many years by reading his own opinions, writings, and letters, and reading books, plays, and articles about him and, finally, by interviewing a whole series of people who knew him, including former secretaries, women friends, family connections, his housekeeper, and legal scholars. I also examined pictures and other artifacts at Harvard University and visited areas where he lived and worked in Boston, Cambridge, Beverly Farms, and Washington.

"Holmes is one of the major figures in American law. He changed the way we look at legal problems and he provided much of the rationale for the modern approach of the Supreme Court to constitutional interpretation. A great master of the English language, he has left us a body of powerful and moving opinions and provocative essays couched in brilliant language and studded with memorable aphorisms and stirring phrases. He remains an influence in legal thought more than half a century after his death."

AVOCATIONAL INTERESTS: Swimming (former captain of the Dartmouth swimming team), musician (plays piano and sings in choruses, choirs, and groups; supports the Washington Bach Consort).

BIOGRAPHICAL/CRITICAL SOURCES:

PERIODICALS

Washington Post, November 4, 1985.

*   *   *

MONROE, Jonathan B(eck)   1954-

PERSONAL: Born August 23, 1954, in Newberry, S.C.; son of Paul Eugene (a Lutheran minister) and Josephine (a teacher; maiden name, Beck) Monroe; married Mary Josephine Lash (an exhibits coordinator for a university publishing company), August 5, 1979; children: Gabriel, Holly. *Education:* Attended University of Montpellier, 1974-75; Davidson College, B.A. (cum laude), 1976; attended University of Constance, 1980-82; University of Oregon, M.A., 1980, Ph.D., 1983.

ADDRESSES: Home—426 Winthrop Dr., No. 10, Ithaca, N.Y. 14850. *Office*—Department of Comparative Literature, Cornell University, Ithaca, N.Y. 14853.

CAREER: Library of Congress, Congressional Research Service, Washington, D.C., editorial and research assistant, 1977; ERIC Clearinghouse on Educational Management, Eugene, Ore., document analyst, 1983-84; Cornell University, Ithaca, N.Y., assistant professor of comparative literature, 1984—. Lecturer at University of Oregon, 1984.

MEMBER: Modern Language Association of America, Phi Beta Kappa.

AWARDS, HONORS: Fellow of German Academic Exchange, 1980-82.

WRITINGS:

A Poverty of Objects: The Prose Poem and the Politics of Genre, Cornell University Press, 1987.

*   *   *

MOOLSON, Melusa
See SOLOMON, Samuel

*   *   *

MOORE, Daniel G(eorge)   1899-1977

OBITUARY NOTICE—See index for *CA* sketch: Born March 5, 1899, in Springfield, Mo.; died December 22, 1977. Cowboy, prison guard, livestock inspector, and author. Moore was a self-proclaimed cowboy until 1938 and spent the following ten years as a state prison guard in Florence, Arizona. From 1949 to 1965 he was an Arizona livestock inspector. He wrote *Log of a Twentieth Century Cowboy; Shoot Me a Biscuit: Stories of Yesteryear's Roundup Cooks;* and *Enter Without Knocking.*

OBITUARIES AND OTHER SOURCES:

Date of death provided by wife, Jean C. Moore.

*   *   *

MOORE, Henry (Spencer)   1898-1986

PERSONAL: Born July 30, 1898, in Castleford, Yorkshire, England; died August 31, 1986, in Much Hadham, Hertfordshire, England; son of Raymond Spencer (a coal miner) and Mary (Baker) Moore; married Irina Radetzky (a painter), July 27, 1929; children: Mary Spencer Moore Danovsky. *Education:* Attended Leeds School of Art, 1919-21, and Royal College of Art, 1921-1925.

ADDRESSES: Home—Hoglands, Perry Green, Much Hadham, Hertfordshire, England.

CAREER: Sculptor, 1922-86; Royal College of Art, London, England, instructor in sculpture, 1925-32; Chelsea School of Art, London, instructor in sculpture, 1932-39. Established department of sculpture at the Chelsea School of Art, 1932; served as official war artist in London, 1940-45; trustee of the Tate Gallery, London, 1941-48, 1949-56, and of the National Gallery, London, 1955-63, 1964-74; member of the Art Panel of the British Council, 1945, of the Royal Fine Art Commission, 1947-71, and of the Arts Council of Great Britain, 1963-67; formed Henry Moore Foundation, 1977. *Military Service:* British Army, Civil Service Rifles, 1917-19; bayonet instructor.

First solo show at the Warren Gallery, London, 1928; first American museum show at the Museum of Modern Art, New York, N.Y., 1946. Major works include the *Reclining Figure,* 1929, *Mother and Child,* 1931, *Three Standing Figures,* 1947-48, the bronze *Draped Reclining Figure* for the *Time-Life* building in London, 1952-53, and *King and Queen,* 1952-53. Exhibitions of sculptures and drawings have been held in the galleries of numerous cities throughout the world, including London, Paris, Geneva, Munich, Berlin, Warsaw, Florence, Jerusalem, Tokyo, Sao Paulo, Toronto, and New York City. Permanent collections housed in numerous museums, including Musee Nationale d'Art Moderne, Paris; Leeds City Art Gallery, West Yorkshire, Leeds; Tate Gallery, London; Stadtische Galerie, Munich; National Gallery of Canada, Ottawa; Museum of Modern Art, New York; Art Institute of Chicago; Cranbrook Academy of Art, Bloomfield Hills, Michigan.

MEMBER: British Academy (fellow), American Academy of Arts and Sciences (foreign honorary member), Akademie der Kunste (Berlin; foreign honorary member), Swedish Royal Academy of Fine Arts (foreign member), Academie des Beaux-Arts (Paris; foreign corresponding member), Academie des Lettres et Beaux-Arts (Belgium; foreign corresponding member), Academie Flamande des Sciences (foreign corresponding member), Weiner Secession (Vienna; honorary member), Royal Institute of British Architects (honorary associate), Churchill College, Cambridge (honorary fellow).

AWARDS, HONORS: International Prize for Sculpture from the twenty-fourth Venice Biennale, 1948; International Sculpture Prize from the second Biennale of Sao Paulo, 1953; named Companion of Honour, 1955; Stefan Lochner Medal from the city of Cologne, 1957; second prize for sculpture from the Carnegie International, Pittsburgh, Penn., 1958; International Sculpture Prize from the Feltrinelli Foundation, Milan, Italy, 1963; named to British Order of Merit, 1963; Gold Medal from the city of Florence, 1967; Erasmus Prize, 1968; Einstein Prize, 1968; Commemorative Award for the Arts from Yeshiva University, New York, 1968; named to Order of Merit (Federal Republic of Germany, Bonn), 1968, (Italy), 1972; medal from the Royal Canadian Academy of Arts, 1972; named Commandeur de l'Ordre des Arts et des Lettres (France), 1973; Biancoumano Prize, 1973; Goslar Prize, 1975; Decoration of Honour for Science and Art (Austria), 1978; Grand Cross of the Order of Merit (Federal Republic of Germany), 1980; Order of the Aztec Eagle (Mexico), 1984. Twenty honorary degrees from colleges and universities in United States, England,

Canada, and Germany, including Leeds University, London University, University of Oxford, Royal College of Art, Harvard University, Yale University, University of Toronto, and Technische Hochschule, Berlin; honorary professor emeritus of sculpture, Carrara Academy of Fine Arts.

WRITINGS:

Shelter Sketch Book, Editions Poetry London, c. 1940, Marlborough Fine Art, 1967.

Heads, Figures, and Ideas, with comment by Geoffrey Grigson, New York Graphic Society, 1958.

Henry Moore on Sculpture: A Collection of the Sculptor's Writings and Spoken Words, edited with an introduction by Philip James, MacDonald & Co., 1966, Viking, 1967, revised and expanded edition, Viking, 1971.

Henry Spencer Moore, edited and photographed by John Hedgecoe, Simon & Schuster, 1968.

(Author of introduction and collaborator on photographs with Ilario Bessi) Michael Ayrton, *Giovanni Pisano: Sculptor,* Thames & Hudson, 1969.

(Illustrator) Constantine Fitz Gibbon, *The Blitz,* MacDonald & Co., 1970.

Energy in Space (text in English, French, and German), photographs by Hedgecoe, German translation by Renate Zauscher, French translation by Emmanuela de Nora, New York Graphic Society, 1973.

(Illustrator) *Auden Poems, Moore Lithographs,* British Museum Publications, 1974.

(Author of commentaries) David Finn, *Henry Moore: Sculpture and Environment,* Abrams, 1976.

(Author of introduction) Stephen Spender, *Sculptures in Landscape,* photographs and forward by Geoffrey Shakerley, Studio Vista, 1978, C. N. Potter, 1979.

(With Kenneth Clark) *Henry Moore's Sheep Sketch Book,* Thames & Hudson, 1980.

(Author of comments) David Mitchinson, editor, *Henry Moore Sculpture,* Rizzoli, 1981.

Large Two Forms: A Sculpture, preface by Clark, introduction by William T. Ylvisaker, photographs by Finn, Abbeville Press, 1981.

Henry Moore at the British Museum, photographs by Finn, British Museum Publications, 1981, Abrams, 1982.

(Author of commentary) *Henry Moore: Wood Sculpture,* photographs by Gemma Levine, Universe Books, 1983.

(With Hedgecoe) *Henry Moore: My Ideas, Inspiration, and Life as an Artist,* edited by Suzanne Webber, photographs by Hedgecoe, Chronicle Books, 1986.

Photographs and reproductions of exhibited art works have been collected and published in several volumes, including, *Henry Moore: Mother and Child, As the Eye Moves: A Sculpture by Henry Moore, Catalogue of Graphic Work,* and *Henry Moore: The Reclining Figure.*

Contributor of articles to periodicals, including *Architectural Association Journal, Listener, Transformation, Ark,* and *Art News.*

SIDELIGHTS: Englishman Henry Moore is widely regarded as the most famous and controversial sculptor of the twentieth century. His practice of radicalizing traditional art themes and expressing them in abstract, often distorted figures has been both misunderstood and ridiculed in the past. Derisive critics dubbed him "the sculptor of the hole" for his unusual use of hollowed space to disrupt the volume of his often mammoth wood, stone, and metal sculptures. Art historians agree that it was not until Moore won the Venice Biennale international prize for sculpture in 1948, the first of numerous awards the artist would receive, that he gained acclaim as an innovative sculptor of unequaled talent and diversity.

Moore became interested in art at the age of eleven when he heard his Sunday school teacher describe the esteemed Renaissance artist Michelangelo Buonarroti as the greatest sculptor who ever lived. Moore told Carll Tucker in an interview for *Saturday Review* that he was moved "then and there to decide to become a sculptor" himself, even though he "had never done any sculpture at that time."

Encouraged by his grammar school's headmaster and art instructor to nurture his artistic aspirations, Moore attended the Leeds School of Art and later, the Royal College of Art. He was first exposed to the power of primitive art, a power that his figures would come to embody, when he discovered critic Roger Frye's *Vision and Design,* a study of African art and the principles of three dimensionality in sculpture, at Leeds's library. While living in London in the early 1920s, Moore frequented the British Museum, which housed pre-Columbian, Egyptian, and African sculptures. The artist's work reflects the primitive beauty of these pieces, which intrigued him in a way that classical Greek and Renaissance sculpture did not.

In an article for *Newsweek,* John Ashbery wrote that prior to World War II, Moore's "work was dismissed as 'rubbish'— or worse—by the English art establishment." His experimental primeval carved-stone figures of the 1920s and surrealistic bronzeworks of the 1930s afforded him little acclaim. Ironically, it was Moore's sketches and not his sculptures that first turned the heads of critics. The sight of Londoners seeking refuge from German air raids in underground shelters inspired a series of famous drawings that were later published in the *Shelter Sketch Book.* According to Ashbery, these drawings "fired the imagination of a war-weary world" and captured a post-war audience that was willing to accept Moore's subsequent sculptures.

Alan Bowness, a longtime student of the Moore technique and editor of several volumes of *Henry Moore: Sculpture and Drawings,* wrote of the "timeless, universal quality" of Moore's figures in the London *Times.* He considered the sculptor a humanist, that is, a proponent of the philosophy that asserts man's dignity, worth, and inherent capacity for self-realization through reason. "In the language of sculpture," Bowness explained, Moore "was expressing his faith in the continuity of life and in the strength of the bonds that tied man to woman, child to mother, mother to child."

The impression of a human figure imbues and tempers even the most abstract of Moore's figures. Bowness suggested that Moore used distortion to achieve greater expressiveness and monumental power in his pieces. Many art historians believe that the fundamentally organic and human forms which dominate Moore's work make both the artist and his art accessible to the public. Commenting on his reclining forms in an excerpt from *Sculptures and Drawings* appearing in *Times Literary Supplement,* Moore asserted that "even the untrained eye is more critical of a human figure—because it is ourselves."

Recurrent themes of the female and reclining figures, the mother and child, and the form within a form, all Moore trademarks, are generally considered to be manifestations of the sculptor's childhood experiences. The craggy faces and jaggedly etched bodies of many of Moore's reclining figures are said to reflect the bold and rugged landscape of the artist's native Yorkshire. His preoccupation with the female form and the long smooth lines of his sculpted figures' backs are attributed to his early relationship with his mother: as a boy, Moore frequently rubbed his mother's back with liniment to relieve the pain of her rheumatism. Moore's vision of his mother and love of the land are fused into each of his reclining forms, the poses of which were patterned after a statue of the pre-Columbian rain god *Chacmool. Chicago Tribune* art critic William Wilson called Moore's interpretation "a true Earth Mother figure." Another critic echoed Wilson's appraisal, calling his "sensitive but nonsentimental portrayals of feminine procreativity and protectiveness" suggestive of "both the power and lyricism of nature."

Some critics suggest that the attitudes Moore held toward sculpture were not radical in nature, but rather inspired by the same traditional spirit that produced Stonehenge, a mysterious rock formation with origins dating back to prehistoric times. In an article for *Time* magazine, Robert Hughes commented on Moore's use of open landscape as a setting for his sculptures. The critic alluded to Moore's 1952-53 form, *King and Queen,* which, "gazing out over the stony ocean of Scottish moors" offers proof that its creator "did more than any other artist of his time" to recover sculpture's "archaic roots" and rightful, free-standing place in the environment. Hughes further contended that Moore's recognition of tactile as well as visual elements contributing to a full experience of his figures ran counter to the twentieth-century view of sculpture as something to be seen from afar. Moore believed that artwork created by touch should be appreciated by touch, and according to William Lieberman, an art chairman at the Metropolitan Museum quoted in the *New York Times,* the artist "really liked the idea" of children "[climbing] all over his sculpture."

Prints and photographs of Moore's pieces have been compiled into numerous collections, among them the five volume work, *Henry Moore: Sculpture and Drawings.* Moore usually took his own sculpture photographs or personally supervised and approved photo sessions with selected photographers as a means of "self defense," according to a quote cited in an article for *Saturday Review.* In the same article, Moore explained that in order to satisfy him, the pictures appearing in his collections had to complement one another and adequately reproduce the detail, texture, and overall effect of his works "so that anyone who studied all the photographs together might learn how the various forms of a piece of sculpture can fit together" into a coherent whole. Moore's penchant for a three-dimensional representation of his figures stemmed from his desire to simulate for his vicarious viewers the experience of actually seeing his pieces in person. The artist maintained that a figure must be studied from all sides and angles for the subtleties of its form and construction to be fully realized.

Moore reflected on his development as an artist and on art in general in several texts, including *Henry Moore on Sculpture* and *Henry Moore: My Ideas, Inspiration, and Life as an Artist.* The latter bears an imprint on its title page that reads: "I would like my work to be thought of as a celebration of life and nature." Moore consistently refrained from analyzing his art in lengthy, philosophical terms: he only acknowledged his belief that abstraction and nature could exist simultaneously. *Saturday Review* cited a statement that the artist made about his art in 1962: "I'd like to be able to carry the form as far as possible, without having to define the significance. And there *are* one or two of my recent pieces that I simply can't explain. I don't know what they are. They just came about."

The unpretentious Moore, as quoted in the *Chicago Tribune*, said that he repeatedly refused offers of knighthood because "titles change one's name and one's opinion of oneself." He continued to sketch from his bed and wheelchair during his last years for as long as his physical condition allowed. Moore died on August 31, 1986, from the debilitating effects of arthritis and diabetes which worsened with age. Alan Bowness, paying tribute to the artist on the occasion of his death wrote, "In the death of Henry Moore, we have lost one of the greatest Englishmen of our time." Moore's legacy of sculptures and drawings continue to gain critical and popular praise as the works of one of the twentieth century's most gifted sculptors.

BIOGRAPHICAL/CRITICAL SOURCES:

BOOKS

Bowness, Alan, editor, *Henry Moore: Sculpture and Drawings,* five volumes, Lund, Humphries, 1977.
Clark, Kenneth, *Henry Moore Drawings,* Harper, 1974.
Hall, Donald, *Henry Moore: The Life and Work of a Great Sculptor,* Harper, 1966.
Levine, Gemma, *With Henry Moore: The Artist at Work,* Sidgwick & Jackson, 1978.
Mitchinson, David, *Henry Moore: Unpublished Drawings,* Abrams, 1972.
Moore, Henry, *Henry Moore on Sculpture: A Collection of the Sculptor's Writings and Spoken Words,* edited with an introduction by Philip James, MacDonald & Co., 1966.
Moore, Henry and John Hedgecoe, *Henry Moore: My Ideas, Inspiration, and Life as an Artist,* Chronicle Books, 1986.
Read, Herbert, *Henry Moore: A Study of His Life and Work,* Praeger, 1966.
Teague, Edward H., *Henry Moore Bibliography and Reproductions Index,* McFarland & Co., 1981.
Wilkinson, Alan G., *The Drawings of Henry Moore,* Borden Publishing, 1970.

PERIODICALS

Contemporary Review, November, 1983.
Newsweek, May 23, 1983.
New York, June 6, 1983.
New York Times Book Review, July 23, 1967.
Saturday Review, November 25, 1967, April 3, 1971, March, 1981.
Spectator, April 12, 1986.
Times Literary Supplement, July 29, 1965, November 24, 1966, December 16, 1977, August 5, 1988.

OBITUARIES:

PERIODICALS

Chicago Tribune, September 1, 1986.
New York Times, September 1, 1986, September 3, 1986, September 14, 1986.
Time, September 15, 1986.
Times (London), September 1, 1986, September 2, 1986.
Washington Post, September 1, 1986.*

—*Sketch by Barbara K. Carlisle*

*   *   *

MORELLO, Karen Berger   1949-

PERSONAL: Born February 11, 1949, in New York, N.Y.; daughter of Irving (a musician) and Norma (Nadel) Berger; married Joseph V. Morello (an attorney), September 17, 1978. *Education:* Queens College of the City University of New York, B.A., 1969; New York Law School, J.D., 1972.

ADDRESSES: Home—704 Patrick St., Westhampton, N.Y. 11978. *Office*—Metropolitan Assistance Corp., 2 Lafayette St., New York, N.Y. 10007. *Agent*—Sterling Lord Literistic, 1 Madison Ave., New York, N.Y. 10010.

CAREER: Senior attorney at Community Action Legal Services, 1972-79; Metropolitan Assistance Corp., New York, N.Y., general counsel, 1979-88. Member of New York City Community Planning Board 2.

MEMBER: American Bar Association, Women's Bar Association of the State of New York (historian), New York County Lawyers Association, Queens County Women's Bar Association, Association of the Bar of the City of New York.

AWARDS, HONORS: Gavel Award from American Bar Association and special achievement award from National Conference of Women's Bar Associations, both 1987, for *The Invisible Bar.*

WRITINGS:

(Editor and contributor) *Gerry! Biography of Geraldine Ferraro,* Pinnacle Books, 1984.
The Invisible Bar: The Woman Lawyer in America, 1638 to the Present, Random House, 1986.

Contributor to law journals.

SIDELIGHTS: At about the same time that Sandra Day O'Connor became the first woman to sit on the U.S. Supreme Court, Karen Berger Morello was researching the history of American women in the law profession. The chronicle begins in the year 1638, when Margaret Brent practiced law in the colony of Maryland, to the present day, when nearly 40 percent of America's law students are women. In *The Invisible Bar,* Morello follows women attorneys through the 1870s, when the few who were allowed to practice law had to overcome rigorous social and political bias, to the 1950s, when women were finally admitted to the Harvard Law School. The author emphasizes, however, that, while women may have been allowed to study law at Harvard in 1950, even honors graduates like Justice O'Connor were considered fit for no more strenuous work than that of a legal stenographer. In the 1970s it became easier for women to work in prestigious law firms and to choose their specialties within the field, but even today, Morello writes, very few women occupy the higher levels of the profession. The author believes the struggle to achieve this higher goal will be the crusade of the 1990s.

In a *Chicago Tribune* review of *The Invisible Bar,* Charlotte Adelman wrote: "The short profiles presented are tantalizing: They are so absorbing that one wishes there were more." Carol E. Rinzler told readers of the *Washington Post Book World:* "Perhaps what is most remarkable about the story is how long things stayed virtually the same." Rinzler recommended the book to the more than one hundred thousand women who now practice law in the United States. "I can't think of one," she commented, "who won't enjoy reading this book, and who won't frequently have springing to her lips that odd, rueful smile women smile when confronted with the similarities between their past situation and their present."

BIOGRAPHICAL/CRITICAL SOURCES:

PERIODICALS

Chicago Tribune, February 6, 1987, July 19, 1987.
Washington Post Book World, November 23, 1986.

*   *   *

MORLEY, John(athan) David   1948-

PERSONAL: Born January 21, 1948, in Singapore; son of John Arthur Elwell (a civil servant) and Patricia (a housewife; maiden name, Booth) Morley. *Education:* Merton College, Oxford, B.A. (with first class honors), 1969; Waseda University, Diploma from Language Research Institute, 1975.

ADDRESSES: Home—An der Dornwiese 5, D-8032 Lochman, West Germany. *Agent*—A. P. Watt, 26-28 Bedford Row, London WC1R 4HL, England.

CAREER: Japan Broadcasting Corp., free-lance interpreter, translator, researcher, and general coordinator in Western Europe, 1976—.

AWARDS, HONORS: Pictures From the Water Trade won an award for best first work from *Yorkshire Post,* and was nominated by *Time* magazine as one of the five best nonfiction books of the year, both 1985.

WRITINGS:

Pictures From the Water Trade: Adventures of a Westerner in Japan (autobiographical novel), Atlantic Monthly Press, 1985.
In the Labyrinth, Atlantic Monthly Press, 1986.
The Case of Thomas N. (novel), Atlantic Monthly Press, 1987.

Contributor to newspapers and magazines in the United States, Australia, West Germany, and Denmark, including the *New York Times* and *Vanity Fair.*

SIDELIGHTS: Since 1985 John David Morley has published three critically acclaimed books addressing the "mysteries of identity," in the words of *New York Times Book Review* critic Ann Hulbert. In his first two works, *Pictures From the Water Trade* and *In the Labyrinth,* Morley created a potent mix of real life and fiction, but in *The Case of Thomas N.,* the author relied entirely upon his own imagination and invention. Informing his writings are various personal experiences, cultural and historical facts, and what a number of critics described as an engaging array of details. According to Kendall Mitchell in the *Tribune Books,* the results of Morley's efforts prove both "subtle and surprising."

In his autobiographical novel, *Pictures From the Water Trade,* Morley offers an inside look at Japan—a country the author writes is noted for its contradictory and elusive nature, where confused foreigners are deliberately kept at a distance. While a student at Waseda University in Tokyo during the 1970s, Morley learned much about the Japanese language and culture. Moreover, he witnessed firsthand the social indulgences not usually observed by foreigners or "outsiders." In area bars, baths, and brothels collectively known as the "water trade," myriads of businessmen routinely engage in uninhibited drinking and sexual encounters at the end of their work day. This unbridled revelry counterposes the Western image of Japanese society as particularly formal and proper, thus lending itself to curious speculation and interpretation.

Morley relates his limited understanding of Japanese mores through the experiences of his main character, Boon. Originally content to observe his subjects from afar and to perfect their language through solitary studies, Boon embarks upon a "revealing binge," wrote David Remnick in the *Washington Post Book World,* guided by a local man he meets in a Japanese tavern. A night of alcohol-induced camaraderie and carousing follows, in which Boon discovers many secrets about the dual personalities of the Japanese.

Especially revealing are the vignettes involving male-female relationships. Describing a visit to one of the popular "pink cabarets," Boon relates "how his friends 'sat down with the hostesses . . . and almost at once reached out for their breasts as nonchalantly as they helped themselves to the fruit on the table,'" reported Ian Buruma in the *New York Review of Books.* Boon analyzes this behavior as "the gropings of a spent animal towards a haven of safety" rather than an indecent act, informing readers that the pleasure derived from the water trade serves as a pressure valve to release the stress of daily living in Japan. In another episode a barmaid submits to dancing naked in front of Boon and his male companion. Astonishing to Boon at first, the woman's provocative display is also rationalized if not fully vindicated. It is Buruma's opinion that "the best part" of *Pictures From the Water Trade* is the portrayal of Mariko, Boon's mysterious and elusive lover. "In a way Mariko symbolizes Japan" with her obvious detachment, lack of direction, and seemingly "infinite capacity . . . to live with contradictions."

Discussing the water trade itself in the *Times Literary Supplement,* Jonathan Burnham commented that it "provides an image of a deeply rooted Japanese spirit that coexists with the grimmer world of the factory and office." Opined Buruma, *Pictures From the Water Trade* gives "a unique view of . . . the inside of a nation few outsiders ever get close to." But Boon—having surmounted otherwise restrictive barriers such as the complex language—"is learning all the time," commented Burnham, and as "a disenchanted but sympathetic Westerner," his findings provide a "stimulating account" of life in Japan. Expressing a similar view in *Time,* Paul Gray wrote that Boon's "attempt . . . to merge with an alien culture constitutes an intriguing psychodrama." Likewise, Toronto *Globe and Mail* critic Jay Scott described *Pictures From the Water Trade* as a "compelling introduction" to Japanese culture.

Morley's second book, *In the Labyrinth,* recounts the postwar, real-life incarceration of German businessman Joseph Pallehner. Part fact and part "imaginative elaboration," remarked *New York Times Book Review* critic Ann Hulbert, the story details the horrific treatment and conditions typically endured by political prisoners in the aftermath of World War II. Pallehner, who was arrested in 1946, served six years in a Czechoslovakian prison for his alleged collaboration with the Nazi regime. Disavowing any crimes aimed at furthering the fascist cause in Germany, he is portrayed in Morley's book as essentially victimized by the political chaos that pervaded Eastern Europe following the collapse of Hitler's Third Reich. According to Carolyn See in the *Los Angeles Times,* Pallehner "gets gobbled up in the great Mouli Grinder of Life" with an assortment of "'politicians, generals, administrators, currency smugglers and black marketeers,' . . . all of them washed into this jail like flotsam left over from the shipwreck of the war." Comparing Morley's account of Pallehner's real-life ordeal to the short story "In the Penal Colony" by Franz Kafka and the novel *The Enormous Room* by E. E. Cummings, the reviewer decided that in keeping with the traditions set by "those two classics, [Morley's volume] states the horrors, but cannot begin to explain them." In conclusion, See judged that *In the Labyrinth* "is marked by great elegance of style."

The Case of Thomas N., Morley's third book, was described as "a sort of existential whodunnit" by London *Times* critic Gillian Greenwood. Again echoing the works of Kafka and also novelist Fedor Dostoevski, the bizarre tale chronicles the "philosophical, even metaphysical" experiences of a teenage amnesiac with no recollection of his past sixteen years of life, related Mitchell. Dispassionately shuffled from the police to numerous hospitals and later boarding houses while specialists probe for the cause of his affliction, Thomas ultimately entangles himself with a drug user and is soon implicated as the girl's murderer. His unexplained memory loss, together with his seeming reluctance to acknowledge his own existence, prompt authorities to speculate on Thomas's identity and guilt. The youth cannot be sure of his innocence since he is incapable of remembering his actions during the past night's hallucination-filled dope spree. Finally, having awakened liberally splattered with blood to the sight of Nancy's severed head perched on a chair before him, Thomas succumbs to a dubious confession.

Alluding to the literary techniques used in *Pictures From the Water Trade* and *In the Labyrinth*, Hulbert noted that in *The Case of Thomas N.* Morley deviates from the "cultural, social and historical texture" that marked those previous works. Instead, the author concentrates on "the most alien condition of all" in which the "mysteries of identity [are presented] in extreme form." Mitchell concluded that the strength of *The Case of Thomas N.* derives from the "brilliant psychological detailing" of the main character and two other major figures and deemed Morley's writing "bloodless, manipulative and dazzling." "This is Kafka land," summed up Campbell Geeslin in *People* magazine, adding that surrealism pervades every hollow of Morley's "darkly dazzling, suspenseful jewel of a novel."

BIOGRAPHICAL/CRITICAL SOURCES:

PERIODICALS

Globe and Mail (Toronto), November 16, 1985.
Los Angeles Times, July 14, 1986.
New York Review of Books, July 18, 1985.
New York Times Book Review, September 13, 1987.
People, August 24, 1987.
Time, August 19, 1985.
Times (London), October 16, 1986, September 3, 1987.
Times Literary Supplement, January 3, 1986.
Tribune Books, August 30, 1987.
Washington Post Book World, June 16, 1985.

—*Sidelights by Barbara A. Cicchetti*

*   *   *

MUELLER-VOLLMER, Kurt   1928-

PERSONAL: Born June 28, 1928, in Hamburg, Germany (now West Germany); immigrated to the United States, naturalized citizen; married Patricia Ann Bialecki; children: two. *Education:* University of Cologne, Philosophicum, 1953; attended University of Bonn and University of Paris; Brown University, M.A., 1956; Stanford University, Ph.D., 1962.

ADDRESSES: Home—774 Seneca St., Palo Alto, Calif. 94301. *Office*—Department of German Studies, Stanford University, Stanford, Calif. 94305.

CAREER: Stanford University, Stanford, Calif., instructor, 1958-61, assistant professor, 1962-64, associate professor, 1964-67, professor of German, 1967-76, professor of German studies and humanities, 1976—, visiting professor at Overseas Study Center in West Berlin, 1985. Bicentennial research professor at University of Bonn, spring-summer, 1976; visiting professor at University of Washington, Seattle, spring, 1983; guest professor at Institute for Germanic Philology, Jagiellonian University, summer, 1986.

MEMBER: International Herder Society, Modern Language Association of America, American Association of Teachers of German, Schiller Gesellschaft, Societe des Etudes Staeliennes, Humboldt-Gesellschaft (life member of board of counselors, 1975—).

AWARDS, HONORS: Grants from American Philosophical Society, 1965-66 and 1975; National Endowment for the Humanities, junior fellow, 1968, senior fellow, 1972-73 and 1979-80.

WRITINGS:

Towards a Phenomenological Theory of Literature: A Study of Wilhelm Dilthey's Poetics, Mouton, 1963.
Poesie und Einbildungskraft: Zur Dichtungstheorie Wilhelm von Humboldts, Metzler, 1967.
(Editor and author of preface, introduction, and commentary) *Humboldt Studienausgabe*, Fischer Verlag, Volume I: *Asthetik und Literatur*, 1970, Volume II: *Politik und Geschichte*, 1971.
(Editor and author of notes and commentary) *Return From Italy: Goethe's Notebook, 1788* (bilingual edition), Guido Press, 1970.
Wilhelm von Humboldt und der Anfang der amerikanischen Sprachwissenschaft: Der Briefe an John Pickering, Klostermann, 1976.
(Editor and author of introduction and notes) *The Hermeneutics Reader: Texts of the German Tradition From the Enlightenment to the Present*, Continuum/Crossroad, 1985.

Contributor to *Literary Theory and Criticism: Festschrift in Honor of Rene Wellek*, 1985, to *Grolier's Encyclopedia International*, and of articles and reviews to literature and German studies journals. Co-editor of "Stanford German Studies," a series published by P. Lang.

WORK IN PROGRESS: Editing *Grundzuege des Allgemeinen Sprachtypus* by Wilhelm von Humboldt, for Schoeningh Verlag; a repertory of von Humboldt's (mostly unpublished) linguistic, anthropological, and literary manuscripts; a monograph, *Otherness: The Hermeneutics of Language and Culture*, based on von Humboldt's unpublished studies of non-Indoeuropean languages and cultures; a historical and critical edition of correspondence between von Humboldt and Madame de Stael; a monograph, *How a Discipline Is Born: The Origin and Formation of American Linguistics as a Human Science, 1790-1850; Discourse Theory: From a Hermeneutical-Phenomenological Point of View; The Reception of German Culture in the Early American Republic, 1812-1835; Vico's Hermeneutics of the Human Sciences*.

*   *   *

MULLINS, June B(onner)   1927-

PERSONAL: Born June 13, 1927, in Chicago, Ill.; daughter of Gordon Wilson and Agnes (Russell) Bonner; married William W. Mullins (a university professor), June 26, 1948; children: William W., Oliver, Timothy, Garrick. *Education:* University of Chicago, B.S., 1948; University of Pittsburgh, M.Ed., 1958, Ph.D., 1968.

ADDRESSES: Office—School of Education, 4F29 Forbes Quadrangle, University of Pittsburgh, Pittsburgh, Pa. 19260.

CAREER: University of Chicago, Chicago, Ill., counselor of emotionally disturbed children at Orthogenic School, 1946-48; Western Psychiatric Institute, Pittsburgh, Pa., teacher of severely disturbed and brain damaged children, 1958-61; Home for Crippled Children, Pittsburgh, teacher, 1963-66; Point Park College, Pittsburgh, demonstration preschool teacher and director of research at Laboratory School, 1966-67; University of Pittsburgh, Pittsburgh, assistant professor, 1967-74, associate professor of special education, 1974-88. National lecturer at Nova University, 1984-85. Board member of United Cerebral Palsy of Pittsburgh, 1980—; member of national professional services committee of United Cerebral Palsy, Inc., 1984-87; member of board of directors of Generations Together, 1987—.

MEMBER: American Psychological Association, American Association for Adult and Continuing Education, Council for Exceptional Children (president of Division of the Physically Handicapped, 1985-86; historian, 1988—), League of Women Voters, Pittsburgh Doctoral Association, Phi Delta Kappa.

AWARDS, HONORS: Accept Me As I Am was named one of the best reference books of 1985 by the American Library Association.

WRITINGS:

(With Suzaane Wolfe) *Special People Behind the Eight-Ball: An Annotated Bibliography of Literature by Handicapping Conditions,* Mafex, 1975.
(With Kirsti Hammermeister) *Hospital,* Western Pennsylvania School for the Deaf, 1978.
A Teacher's Guide to Management of Physically Handicapped Students, C.C. Thomas, 1979.
(Contributor) Milton Seligman, editor, *Supporting Families With Handicapped Children,* Grune, 1982.
(Editor with J. Brest Friedberg and A. Weir Sukiennik) *Accept Me As I Am: Best Books of Juvenile Nonfiction on Impairments and Disabilities,* Bowker, 1985.

Contributor to education journals. Associate editor of *Exceptional Children,* 1983-85.

WORK IN PROGRESS: Revising *Accept Me As I Am,* publication expected in 1989; a survey of educational and vocational barriers and opportunities for vocational rehabilitation clients who matriculated in higher education programs.

*   *   *

MULVANEY, Robert J(oseph)   1937-

PERSONAL: Born March 24, 1937, in Brooklyn, N.Y.; son of Joseph Patrick (a systems supervisor) and Alice (a homemaker; maiden name, Waite) Mulvaney; married Jayne Ford (a professor), May 5, 1962; children: Norah, Evan, Kieran. *Education:* College of the Holy Cross, A.B., 1958; University of Toronto, M.A., 1961; Emory University, Ph.D., 1965.

ADDRESSES: Home—2705 Duncan St., Columbia, S.C. 29205. *Office*—Department of Philosophy, University of South Carolina—Columbia, Columbia, S.C. 29208.

CAREER: Fordham University, Bronx, N.Y., instructor, 1963-65, assistant professor of philosophy, 1965-70; University of South Carolina—Columbia, assistant professor, 1970-72, associate professor of philosophy, 1972—. Visiting associate professor at Catholic University of America, 1973-74.

MEMBER: American Philosophical Association, American Society for Eighteenth Century Studies, American Association of University Professors, Gottfried Wilhelm Leibniz Gesellschaft.

AWARDS, HONORS: Fellow of American Council of Education at University of Michigan, 1968-69.

WRITINGS:

(Editor with Philip M. Zeltner) *Pragmatism: Its Sources and Prospects,* University of South Carolina Press, 1986.

Contributor to periodicals, including *Journal of the History of Ideas, Mediaeval Studies, Educational Theory,* and *Thinking, the Journal of Philosophy for Children.*

WORK IN PROGRESS: Translating and writing notes and commentary for *Confessio Philosophi,* by Gottfried Wilhelm Leibniz; research on critical thinking and philosophy of children.

SIDELIGHTS: Robert J. Mulvaney told *CA:* "My research and scholarly interests range from the history of thought (particularly in early modern Europe) to the extension of philosophical education to elementary and high schools. *Pragmatism: Its Sources and Prospects* was first of all a contribution to the nation's bicentenary celebration, but it stands as well as a touchstone for my other interests. American pragmatism is heir to Europe's thought, despite its peculiarly new-world flavor. And 'philosophy of children' is an expression of democracy in education, the inclusion of philosophy within the program of study of one of our largest neglected minorities, young children!"

*   *   *

MUMFORD, Erika   1935(?)-1988

OBITUARY NOTICE: Born c. 1935 in Geneva, Switzerland; immigrated to United States, 1946; died of breast cancer, July 30, 1988, in Cambridge, Mass. Poet. Mumford, whose poetry won prizes from the Poetry Society of America and *Poet Lore,* published three volumes of her poetry: *The Door in the Forest, Willow Water,* and *The Karma Bazaar.* Her work was also featured in such publications as the *Hudson Review, Poetry,* and *Prairie Schooner.*

OBITUARIES AND OTHER SOURCES:

BOOKS

Directory of American Poets & Fiction Writers, 1987-1988 Edition, Poets & Writers, 1987.

PERIODICALS

Chicago Tribune, August 3, 1988.
New York Times, August 4, 1988.

*   *   *

MURRAY, Ken   1903-1988

OBITUARY NOTICE: Name originally Don Court; born July

14, 1903, in New York, N.Y.; died August 10, 1988, in Burbank, Calif. Stage and screen producer, director, actor, and author. Murray, who worked in vaudeville, movies, and television, became famous with his "Ken Murray Blackouts," a bawdy World War II stage review with Marie Wilson playing the so-called classic "dumb blonde." His motion picture career spanned five decades and included "Half Marriage," "A Night at Earl Carroll's," "The Man Who Shot Liberty Valance," "Son of Flubber," and "Bill and Coo," which won an Academy Award in 1947. He produced, directed, and starred in his own television show, "The Ken Murray Show," and contributed to such television programs as "Where Were You?" and "El Coyote." Murray also compiled his own footage of Hollywood celebrities and released it for television as "Hollywood: My Home Town," and later as a motion picture entitled "Ken Murray's Shooting Stars." Murray wrote his autobiography in 1960, *Life on a Pogo Stick,* as well as other books including *The Golden Days of San Simeon* and *The Body Merchant.*

OBITUARIES AND OTHER SOURCES:

BOOKS

Halliwell's Filmgoer's Companion, 8th edition, Scribner, 1984.
International Motion Picture Almanac, Quigley, 1988.

PERIODICALS

Chicago Tribune, October 14, 1988.
Los Angeles Times, October 13, 1988.

* * *

MURRAY, Robin 1940-

PERSONAL: Born in September, 1940; married; children: two. *Education:* Attended Balliol College, Oxford, and London School of Economics.

ADDRESSES: Office—Institute for Development Studies, University of Sussex, Falmer, Brighton, Sussex BN1 9RH, England.

CAREER: University of Sussex, Brighton, England, fellow at Institute for Development Studies, 1970—.

WRITINGS:

UCS: The Anatomy of Bankruptcy, Spokesman Books, 1972.
Multinational Companies and Nations States, Spokesman Books, 1975.
(Editor) *Multinationals Beyond the Market,* Harvester, 1981.
(Editor with Gordon White and Christine White) *Revolutionary Socialist Development in the Third World,* University Press of Kentucky, 1983.

N

NASH, Isabel
   See EBERSTADT, Isabel

*   *   *

NEEL, Janet
   See COHEN, Janet

*   *   *

NEHAMAS, Alexander   1946-

PERSONAL: Born March 22, 1946, in Athens, Greece; son of Albert (a banker) and Christine (maiden name, Yannuli) Nehamas; married Susan Glimcher (an attorney), June 22, 1983. *Education:* Swarthmore College, B.A., 1967; Princeton University, Ph.D., 1971.

ADDRESSES: Home—2128 Delancey Place, Philadelphia, Pa. 19103. *Office*—Department of Philosophy, University of Pennsylvania, Philadelphia, Pa. 19104.

CAREER: University of Pittsburgh, assistant professor, 1971-76, associate professor, 1976-81, professor of philosophy, 1981-86; University of Pennsylvania, professor of philosophy, 1986—. Visiting professor at University of California at Berkeley, 1983, and at Princeton University, 1988.

MEMBER: American Philosophical Association (program chairman, 1982-83), American Society for Aesthetics, Modern Language Association, Society for Ancient Greek Philosophy, Modern Greek Studies Association, North America Nietzsche Society.

AWARDS, HONORS: Grant from National Endowment for the Humanities, 1978-79; Guggenheim fellowship, 1983-84.

WRITINGS:

Nietzsche: Life as Literature, Harvard University Press, 1986.
(Translator, with Paul Woodruff, and author of introduction and notes) Plato, *Symposium,* Hackett, 1989.

WORK IN PROGRESS: Research on Plato and aesthetics, "particularly issues raised by television."

SIDELIGHTS: Times Literary Supplement reviewer Michael Tanner proclaimed Alexander Nehamas's *Nietzsche: Life as Literature* to be "the best and most important book on Nietzsche in English." In this scholarly critical work, Nehamas offers a post-structuralist analysis of Frederick Wilhelm Nietzsche's philosophy. Writing in the *New York Times Book Review,* Karsten Harries deemed the volume an "elegant and challenging interpretation" unified by the related themes of Nietzsche's perspectivism and Nietzsche's aestheticism, i.e., the philosopher's theory that one can view the world as one would a literary text, wherein "persons and things," according to Harries, are "characters or entities in some work of fiction, [and] our relationship to the world . . . [is] textual interpretation."

Nehamas told *CA:* "It is extremely difficult to write philosophical works that meet the high standards of rigor and detailed discussion necessary to deal with abstract problems and also focus on issues that a broad public will find engaging and important. To be able to do so has been an important concern of mine in recent years. Plato and Nietzsche, the two philosophers I most admire, and the most different thinkers one can imagine, were masters of this. I continue studying them in the hope that I can learn from them a little about their art."

AVOCATIONAL INTERESTS: Opera, film.

BIOGRAPHICAL/CRITICAL SOURCES:

PERIODICALS

New York Times Book Review, January 19, 1986.
Times Literary Supplement, May 16, 1986.

*   *   *

NEWBERRY
   See VELLACOTT, Jo

*   *   *

NEWBERRY, Vellacott
   See VELLACOTT, Jo

*   *   *

NEWMAN, Leslea   1955-

PERSONAL: Given name is pronounced "Les-*lee*-a"; born November 5, 1955, in Brooklyn, N.Y.; daughter of Edward (an attorney) and Florence (a housewife; maiden name, Levin)

Newman. *Education:* University of Vermont, B.S., 1977; Naropa Institute, certificate in poetics, 1980. *Religion:* Jewish.

ADDRESSES: Home—50 Hawley St., Northampton, Mass. 01060.

CAREER: Mademoiselle and *Redbook,* New York, N.Y., manuscript reader, 1982; *Valley Advocate,* Hatfield, Mass., book reviewer and writer, 1983-87; Mt. Holyoke College summer program, South Hadley, Mass., director and teacher of creative writing for high school women, 1986-88; Write From the Heart: Writing Workshops for Women, Northampton, Mass., director and teacher, 1987—. Lectures and conducts writing workshops at educational institutions, including Yale University and Amherst, Smith, Swarthmore, and Trinity colleges.

MEMBER: Poets and Writers, Feminist Writers Guild.

WRITINGS:

Good Enough to Eat (novel), Firebrand Books, 1986.
Love Me Like You Mean It (poetry), Her Books, 1987.
A Letter to Harvey Milk and Other Stories, Firebrand Books, 1988.

Contributor to magazines, including *Conditions, Heresies, Common Lives, Backbone, Sinister Wisdom,* and *Sojourner.*

WORK IN PROGRESS: A collection of short stories, a children's book, and a play.

SIDELIGHTS: Leslea Newman told *CA:* "I write because I'm good at it and because it brings me a tremendous amount of pleasure. Writing continues to teach me, surprise me, and inform me in new and exciting ways. I have learned to expect the unexpected, and to push harder just when I am ready to give up. The sources that continue to feed my life and writing are my Jewish heritage and feminist values. They help me to continue to be myself, to take risks, and to explore uncharted territory. I am motivated to learn the truth about my own life, and the learning is in the telling."

*   *   *

NEWTON, Maxwell 1929-

PERSONAL: Born April 28, 1929, in Perth, Australia; immigrated to United States, 1980; son of George William and Norah (Christian) Newton; married Anne Kirby Robertson, 1952 (divorced, 1974); married Diane Austin, April 28, 1975 (divorced, June, 1979); married Valerie Olivia Waldron, November 14, 1981; children: (first marriage) Sarah Jane, Anthony James, Penelope Anne; (second marriage) Natasha, Sally, Emma Jane. *Education:* University of Western Australia, B.A., 1951; Cambridge University, B.A., 1953.

ADDRESSES: Home—89 Old Belden Hill Rd., Wilton, Conn. 06897. *Office*—*New York Post,* 210 South St., New York, N.Y. 10002.

CAREER: Sydney Morning Herald, Sydney, Australia, political correspondent, 1957-60; John Fairfax Ltd., Sydney, foundation editor of *Australian Financial Review,* 1960-64, and *Australian,* 1964-65; Maxwell Newton Publications, Melbourne, Australia, managing director, 1966-79; *New York Post,* New York, N.Y., financial columnist, 1980—. Financial columnist for *Australian,* London *Times, Boston Herald, Chicago Sun-Times,* and *South China Morning Post,* 1980—; president of Max News Financial Network, Wilton, Conn., 1983-85; publisher and editor in chief of *Fed Fortnightly;* associate of Lehrman Institute; consultant to banks and securities firms in

Australia, England, the United States, Singapore, Hong Kong, and Japan.

AWARDS, HONORS: Honorary scholar of Clare College, Cambridge; French Medal for most outstanding French student from Alliance Francaise of Western Australia, 1946.

WRITINGS:

The Fed: Inside the Federal Reserve, the Secret Power Center That Controls the American Economy, Times Books, 1983.

SIDELIGHTS: Maxwell Newton told *CA* that his application for U.S. naturalization was submitted in April, 1988. Explaining his reasons for immigrating to the United States from Australia, Newton wrote: "I was asked by [newspaper publisher] Rupert Murdoch, an old friend, to come to New York to write some speeches for him in June of 1980. I was supposed to stay for two weeks. He asked me to stay on to write a daily column for the *New York Post,* which I am still doing six times weekly. Since coming to the United States, I have written about 2,500 columns for the *Post.* I usually write those columns at about six o'clock each morning. Then I write my New York money market report, which is about nine hundred words and is sent by radio facsimile to clients worldwide each evening. Weekends, I write my columns for various newspapers, and I also write two special reports on economic affairs.

"I wrote my book *The Fed: Inside the Federal Reserve* because I had become keenly interested in the U.S. bond market. These days, I am putting most of my energies into clients' consulting and building up my own publishing business."

BIOGRAPHICAL/CRITICAL SOURCES:

BOOKS

Packer, Clyde, *No Return Passport,* Angus & Robertson, 1983.

PERIODICALS

Times (London), January 31, 1988.

*   *   *

NEYREY, Jerome H(enry) 1940-

PERSONAL: Born January 5, 1940, in New Orleans, La.; son of Henry Gabriel and Marie Olga (Lux) Neyrey. *Education:* St. Louis University, B.A., 1963, M.A., 1964; Regis College Seminary, M.Div., 1970, Th.M., 1971; Yale University, Ph.D., 1977; Weston School of Theology, S.T.L., 1987. *Politics:* Democrat.

ADDRESSES: Office—Department of New Testament, Weston School of Theology, 3 Phillips Pl., Cambridge, Mass. 02138.

CAREER: Entered Societas Jesu (Society of Jesus; Jesuits; S.J.), 1957, ordained Roman Catholic priest, 1970; Weston School of Theology, Cambridge, Mass., assistant professor, 1977-83; associate professor of New Testament, 1983—.

MEMBER: Society of Biblical Literature, Catholic Biblical Association.

AWARDS, HONORS: Young scholar grant from Associated Theological Schools, 1983; Bannan fellow at Santa Clara University, 1984-85.

WRITINGS:

First Timothy, Second Timothy, Titus, James, First Peter, Second Peter, Jude, Liturgical Press, 1983.

Christ Is Community, Michael Glazier, 1985.
The Passion According to Luke, Paulist Press, 1985.
(With Bruce Malina) *Calling Jesus Names,* Polebridge, 1988.
An Ideology Revolt: John's Christology in Social Science Perspective, Fortress, 1988.
Resurrection Stories, Michael Glazier, 1988.

Also contributor to periodicals, including *Semeia.* Associate editor of *Biblical Theology Bulletin* and *Catholic Biblical Quarterly.*

WORK IN PROGRESS: A social science handbook for reading Luke and Acts, publication by Polebridge expected in 1989.

SIDELIGHTS: Jerome H. Neyrey told *CA:* "I was trained early in the classics and literature. When I began my divinity studies, I realized that I could employ those skills and interests apropos the Bible. Most recently I have read in the social sciences, in particular cultural anthropology, as a way of imagining the first-century Semitic world. That interest in anthropology matured first in *Calling Jesus Names,* in which I assessed the accusation that Jesus was a 'witch' (Matthew 12:24); then, in regard to John's christology, the use of anthropology led me to see how the high christology serves as an ideology of revolt. Other creative use of anthropology for New Testament interpretation would include my work on 'Body Language in 1 Corinthians' in *Semeia* and on concepts of purity."

*   *   *

NGOC, Nguyen Huy
   See NGUYEN Ngoc Huy

*   *   *

NGUYEN Ngoc Huy   1924-

PERSONAL: Born November 2, 1924, in Cholon, Vietnam; immigrated to the United States, 1975; son of Hua Ngoc and Huan Thi (Tran) Nguyen; married Thu Thi Duong, 1952 (died, 1974); children: Quoc Thuy Ngoc (son), Thuy Tan Ngoc (daughter; now Tanette Nguyen McCarty). *Education:* University of Paris, graduate of Institute of Political Studies, 1958, Licence en Droit, 1959, D.E.S. en Science Politique, 1960, Doctorat en Science Politique, 1963.

ADDRESSES: Home—72-74 Shirley Ave., Revere, Mass. 02151. *Office*—Law School, Harvard University, Cambridge, Mass. 02138.

CAREER: Member of central executive committee of Vietnam's Dai Viet Nationalist Party (Dai Viet Quoc Dan Dang), 1945-64; founder and general secretary of Vietnam's Neo Dai Viet Party (Tan Dai Viet), 1964-75; Harvard University, Cambridge, Mass., research associate at Harvard Law School, 1976—.

General secretary of Nationalist Progressive Movement (Phong Trao Quoc Gia Cap Tien), 1969-75; co-chairman of National Social Democratic Alliance, 1973-75; chairman of central executive committee of Alliance for Democracy in Vietnam (Lien Minh Dan Chu Viet Nam), 1981. Director of cabinet for Vietnam's deputy prime minister for pacification, 1964; member of People and Army Council of South Vietnam, 1967; member of South Vietnamese delegation to Paris Peace Talks, 1968-70, and delegate to La Celle St. Cloud discussions with the communists, 1973. From 1965-75 served as professor of political science and constitutional law at Saigon's National Institute of Administration, University of Cantho, University of Saigon, University of Hue, and Universities of Dalat, Van Hanh, and Minh Duc; also lecturer at National Defense College, Command and General Staff College, and College of the Staff for Political and Psychological Warfare; dean of faculty of law and social science at University of Cantho, 1967-68.

WRITINGS:

Hon Viet (poems; title means "The Vietnamese Soul"), Duoc Viet, 1950, 2nd edition, [Paris], 1984, 3rd edition, [San Jose, Calif.], 1985.
Dan toc sinh ton (title means "The Doctrine of the Nation's Survival"), two volumes, Dai Viet Party, 1964.
De tai nguoi uu tu trong chanh tri Trung Quoc co thoi (title means "Elite Notions in Traditional Chinese Political Thought"), Cap Tien, 1969.
Lich su cac hoc thuyet chanh tri (title means "A History of Political Theories"), two volumes, Cap Tien, 1970-71.
(Translator from Chinese into Vietnamese) Han Fei, *Han Phi Tu* (title means "Master Han Fei"), two volumes, Lua Thieng, 1974.
(With Stephen B. Young) *Understanding Vietnam,* Displaced Persons Center Information Service [Bussum, Netherlands], 1982.
A New Strategy to Defend the Free World Against Communist Expansion, Alliance for Democracy in Vietnam, 1985.
Pour une strategie de defense du monde libre contre l'expansion communiste (title means "A New Strategy to Defend the Free World Against Communist Expansion"), Alliance Pour la Democratie au Vietnam, 1985.
Cac an so chanh tri trong tieu thuyet vo hiep Kim Dung (title means "The Hidden Political Thoughts in Jin Yung's Martial-Arts Fiction Novels"), Thanh Phuong Thu Quan, 1986.
(With Ta Van Tai and Tran Van Liem) *The Le Code: Law in Traditional Vietnam: A Comparative Sino-Vietnamese Legal Study With Historical-Juridicial Analysis and Annotations,* Ohio University Press, 1987.
(With Stephen B. Young) *Virtue and Law: Human Rights in Traditional China and Vietnam,* Yale Southeast Asian Studies, 1988.

Contributor of poems to periodicals.

WORK IN PROGRESS: Ho va ten cua nguoi Viet Nam (title means "The Vietnamese Names and Surnames"); *History of Vietnam From 1939 to 1975.*

SIDELIGHTS: Nguyen Ngoc Huy told *CA:* "I have participated in the struggle for an independent and free Vietnam since 1945 and continue to fight for this ideal. I began to write poems to celebrate Vietnamese history and heroes and to arouse Vietnamese patriotic feelings in order to mobilize them for the struggle for independence. These poems were published first in my party's newspapers and were later gathered in a book entitled *Hon Viet* ('The Vietnamese Soul'). But because I was in charge of my party's department of political training and propaganda, I also did research on law, political doctrines, and political institutions. I later became a professor of constitutional law and political science in various universities in South Vietnam. Thus, I wrote books essentially for the cadres of my party and for my students. My researches led me to a better knowledge of Vietnamese traditional society. I was pleased to find that despite a strong Chinese influence, the Vietnamese culture had original features, and that in our traditional society, considered as authoritarian, the respect for laws and consideration for human rights were higher than in modern totalitarian regimes. My views about the problem are presented in *The Le Code* and *Virtue and Law.*"

* * *

NICHOLS, K(enneth) D(avid)   1907-

PERSONAL: Born November 13, 1907, in Cleveland, Ohio; son of Wilbur L. (a construction contractor) and M. May (Colbrunn) Nichols; married Jacqueline Darriculat, December 15, 1932; children: Jacqueline A. Nichols Thompson, Kenneth David, Jr. *Education:* U.S. Military Academy, B.S., 1929; Cornell University, C.E., 1932, M.C.E., 1933; University of Iowa, Ph.D., 1937. *Politics:* Republican. *Religion:* Protestant.

ADDRESSES: Home and office—16715 Thurston Rd., Dickerson, Md. 10842.

CAREER: U.S. Army, career officer, 1929-53: affiliated with U.S. Army engineer battalion in Nicaragua, 1929-31; affiliated with Cornell University, 1931-33; assistant director of U.S. Waterways Experiment Station in Mississippi, 1933-34; research fellow at Technische Hochschule, Charlottenburg (now West Berlin), Germany, 1934-35; assistant director of U.S. Waterways Experiment Station in Mississippi, 1935-36; affiliated with Student Corps of Engineers Officer School in Fort Belvoir, Va., 1936-37; instructor in civil and military engineering at U.S. Military Academy in West Point, N.Y., 1937-41, professor of mechanics, 1947-48; area construction engineer for Rome Air Depot in New York and for Pennsylvania Ordnance Works, 1941-42; deputy district engineer for Manhattan Engineer District in New York, 1942-43, district engineer, 1943-47; chief of armed forces special weapons project and Army member of military liaison committee to U.S. Atomic Energy Commission, 1948-50; deputy director of guided missiles for Office of the Secretary of Defense, 1950-53; chief of research and development for U.S. Army, 1952-53, retiring as major general. General manager of U.S. Atomic Energy Commission, Washington, D.C., 1953-55; consulting engineer, 1955-87. Member at large of Engineering and Industrial Research Division of National Research Council, 1954-58; member of Army Scientific Advisory Panel, 1956-65; chairman of Westinghouse International Atomic Power Co., 1958-71; member of board of directors of Detroit Edison Co., 1962-80, and Fruehauf Corp., 1964-72; trustee of Thomas Alva Edison Foundation, 1963-76; director of Atomic Industry Forum, 1964-70.

MEMBER: National Academy of Engineers, American Nuclear Society (fellow), American Society of Mechanical Engineers (honorary member).

AWARDS, HONORS: Nicaraguan Medal of Merit, 1932, for emergency relief work after Managua earthquake; Sigma Xi award, 1933; Collinwood Prize from American Society of Civil Engineers, 1938, for Ph.D. thesis "Observed Effects of Geometric Distortion in Hydraulic Models"; Distinguished Service Medal with oak leaf cluster, 1943-45 and 1948-53; honorary commander of Order of the British Empire, 1946, for responsibilities in development and production of atomic bombs; Distinguished Service Award from Atomic Energy Commission, 1953-55.

WRITINGS:

The Road to Trinity (memoir), Morrow, 1987.

SIDELIGHTS: K. D. Nichols told *CA:* "*The Road to Trinity* is a personal account of how America's nuclear policies were made. In June, 1942, our leading atomic scientists assured President Franklin Delano Roosevelt that atomic research looked promising and that it was time to construct plants to produce fissionable materials. A new organization, the Manhattan Engineer District, was created within the U.S. Army Corps of Engineers and assigned the initial construction mission and other related missions. In June, 1942, I was fortunate in being assigned as deputy district engineer and after a year was promoted to district engineer. I thus had responsibilities for many of the functions pertaining to the research, development, design, construction, and operation of production plants for plutonium, enriched uranium, feed materials, and heavy water. From this position and by frequently participating with the policy committee I was generally informed of policy.

"Eventually, as some writers, scientists, media representatives, and activists concentrated on turning public opinions for or against nuclear weapons and nuclear electric power, it seemed to me that some historic events and technical facts had been distorted. So I have given my account of the way many controversial decisions were made.

"Most of the scientists involved in the project supported the development of the atomic weapons, and a majority supported the military use of the atomic weapons against Japan in 1945. The president's decision to use them was based on the recommendation of top scientists and policy individuals. After the war the United States proposed an international agreement to control atomic energy and weapons. The president's decision for development of the hydrogen weapons was made only after full discussion by the key participants. Development of nuclear energy for commercial use was approved in 1954. After a hydrogen test irradiated a Japanese fishing boat, radiation became a key issue. Comparison of nuclear and fossil electric plants for safety, economy, and environmental concerns became increasingly important issues. The United States' Three Mile Island nuclear power plant accident, followed by the Chernobyl accident in the Soviet Union, became media extravaganzas toward the end of the twentieth century.

"In spite of the controversies, I believe we will absolutely need nuclear power and I expect that for many areas nuclear energy will prove to be the least expensive, least dangerous, and least damaging to our environment among the major sources for providing adequate electricity needs. I am still an optimist for nuclear energy."

* * *

NICHTERN, Sol   1920-1988

OBITUARY NOTICE—See index for *CA* sketch: Born January 4, 1920, in New York, N.Y.; died of an apparent suicide, c. June 6, 1988, in New York, N.Y. Psychiatrist, administrator, educator, editor, and author. Nichtern was a specialist in child psychiatry. Beginning in the late 1950s he directed psychiatric services at such institutions as West Nassau Mental Health Center, League School, Hillside and Elmhurst hospitals, and the Jewish Child Care Association. He also taught at New York University and New York Medical College. Nichtern wrote *Helping the Retarded Child,* and with George T. Donahue he authored *Education and Rehabilitation of Childhood Schizophrenics* and *Teaching the Troubled Child.* He was editor of *Mental Health Services for Adolescents.*

OBITUARIES AND OTHER SOURCES:

BOOKS

Biographical Directory of the Fellows and Members of the American Psychiatric Association, Bowker, 1977.

PERIODICALS

New York Times, June 12, 1988.

* * *

NI CHUILLEANAIN, Eilean 1942-

PERSONAL: Surname is pronounced "Nee-Quillenoin"; born November 28, 1942, in Cork, Ireland; daughter of Cormac (a university professor) and Eilis (a writer; maiden name, Dillon) O'Cuilleanain; married Macdara Woods (a poet and editor), June 27, 1978; children: Niall. *Education:* University College, National University of Ireland, B.A., 1962, M.A., 1964; Lady Margaret Hall, Oxford, B.Litt., 1968.

ADDRESSES: Office—Department of English, University of Dublin Trinity College, Dublin 2, Ireland.

CAREER: University of Dublin Trinity College, Dublin, Ireland, lecturer, beginning in 1966, senior lecturer in English, 1984—. Founder of *Cyphers* literary magazine, 1975.

AWARDS, HONORS: Irish Times Poetry Award, 1966, for poems including "Ars Poetica"; Patrick Kavanagh Award for Poetry, 1973, for *Acts and Monuments;* Books Ireland Publishers' Award, 1975, for *Site of Ambush.*

WRITINGS:

Acts and Monuments (poetry; includes "Acts and Monuments," "Death and Engines," "Evidence," "Exhumation," and "Family"), Gallery Books, 1972.
(Contributor) Sean Lucy, editor, *Irish Poets in English*, Mercier Press, 1973.
Site of Ambush (poetry; includes "The Lady's Tower," "The Ropesellers," and "Site of Ambush"), Gallery Books, 1975.
The Second Voyage (poetry; includes "Barrack Street," "A Gentleman's Bedroom," "Night Journeys," and "Seamus Murphy, Died 2nd October, 1975"), Wake Forest University Press, 1977.
(With Brian Lalor) *Cork* (poetry; includes "Barrack Street," "Gearsmacht na mBradan" [title means "The Harsh Discipline of the Salmon"], and "A Gentleman's Bedroom"), illustrations by Lalor, Gallery Books, 1977.
The Rose-Geranium (poetry; includes "Barrack Street," "A Gentleman's Bedroom," "He Hangs in Shades the Orange Bright," "The Last Glimpse of Erin," "March 18th 1977," "Night Journeys," "The Rose Geranium," and "Seamus Murphy, Died 2nd October, 1975"), Gallery Books, 1981.
(Contributor) Sean Mac Reamoinn, editor, *The Pleasures of Gaelic Poetry,* Allen Lane, 1982.
(Editor) *Irish Women: Image and Achievement*, Arlen House, 1985.

Poems represented in anthologies, including *Choice,* edited by Desmond Egan and Michael Hartnett, Goldsmith Press, 1973. Contributor to periodicals, including *Aquarius, Broadsheet, Irish Press, Irish Times,* and *Ploughshares.* Co-editor of *Cyphers,* 1975—.

WORK IN PROGRESS: Research on religious poetry of the English Renaissance; a new edition of poems.

SIDELIGHTS: Eilean Ni Chuilleanain, who helped found the distinguished Irish literary magazine *Cyphers,* has become known for her own "intensely imagined, private, and frequently mysterious" poetry, asserted Joseph Browne in the

Dictionary of Literary Biography. A sense of connection between past and present characterizes her work, which draws on legend and mythology in its examination of being and death and the poet's struggle to reveal her self. Ni Chuilleanain's distant style has drawn criticism from some reviewers, but in Browne's opinion, "Her poetry's creative vigor, thematic depth, and technical range are consistently and sufficiently evident to authenticate its artistic worth. . . . In her more than one hundred published poems, . . . [Ni Chuilleanain] has, like the Gaelic poetry she so admires, provided us with a body of work 'full of suggestions and fascinating patterns.'"

In early poems such as "The Second Voyage" Ni Chuilleanain's awareness of history and isolation figure strongly. Her choice of the Greek hero Odysseus as a protagonist—a persona which can safely shield her own—demonstrates her historical orientation; Odysseus's isolation, as a traveler at sea, expresses one of her common themes. As Ni Chuilleanain identifies memory and connection with the earth, in her early poems the sea becomes a symbol of separation and forgetting. "The Second Voyage" bears this out through Odysseus's yearning to leave the lonely sea for a settled home on land. Remarked Browne, "Odysseus is so thoroughly realized as a human being that the poem becomes brilliantly immediate and harmonious in the poet's blending of subject, theme, language, structure, and personal vision."

The problem of self has dominated Ni Chuilleanain's writing and criticism of it. Her unwillingness to identify herself with female characters or even to write in an intimate, personal voice leads some reviewers to judge her poems unemotional, asexual, and elusive. Yet in Browne's opinion, "what has been misconstrued as 'paralytic politeness' may actually be a unique blend of intentional and unintentional mystery, anonymity, and reticence." In her essays Ni Chuilleanain has expressed support for the poet's right to reveal only what she chooses in order to deal with the corresponding mystery of life. Thus, suggested Browne, the important question is whether the reader is "convinced that a poem's specific mystery reflects the general mystery of humanity."

In poems such as "The Lady's Tower," from Ni Chuilleanain's second volume, *Site of Ambush,* the poet reveals herself more fully in a feminine persona isolated from, yet caught up in, the world around her. Observed Browne, "Unlike earlier poems, which were often obscured by a vague or incompletely realized persona that excluded the reader, 'The Lady's Tower' is an entirety because its persona and her world complement and complete one another, thereby engaging the reader in their existence." Ni Chuilleanain's use of a female protagonist is considered significant; Browne quoted the poet as saying she believed she had succeeded in "partly solving the female 'I' problem" with this poem.

The collections *Cork* and *The Rose-Geranium* present Ni Chuilleanain's different responses to natural and human subjects, the first resulting from a commission and the second from her own musings. Written to accompany Brian Lalor's drawings, the poems in *Cork* sometimes seem uninspired to reviewers, lacking the originality and vigor of Ni Chuilleanain's independent writings about humanity. "Ironically," reported Browne, "it is when she deals with the natural world in her personal, imaginative fashion that Ni Chuilleanain is at her best" in this collection. *The Rose-Geranium,* in contrast, offers a vivid and personal perspective on human concerns and relationships. "The themes of time, change, aging, and death which previously had been simply characteristics of mythology, legend, history, and the natural world, that is, of the world outside her, are now observed as an intimate part of her own being and of her relations with others," Browne averred.

Ni Chuilleanain told *CA:* "My motivation is obscure, connected with the stimulus of mythology, folklore, and religious writing (which is also an academic interest). The problem of addressing the special (Irish) audience in a special (female) voice remains unsolved and many of my poems are attempts to solve it.

"I have traveled and lived at various times in Italy, with shorter expeditions elsewhere in Europe and Morocco. All are important to my writing. I speak Irish, Italian, and French, read Latin, and hope to learn Arabic."

BIOGRAPHICAL/CRITICAL SOURCES:

BOOKS

Dictionary of Literary Biography, Volume 40: *Poets of Great Britain and Ireland Since 1960,* Gale, 1985.

PERIODICALS

Times Literary Supplement, July 27, 1973, December 25-31, 1987.

*   *   *

NIXON, K.
See NIXON, Kathleen Irene (Blundell)

*   *   *

NIXON, Kathleen Irene (Blundell)   1894-1988(?)
(K. Nixon)

OBITUARY NOTICE—See index for *CA* sketch: Born in 1894 in London, England; died c. 1988. Illustrator and author. Nixon became a commercial artist in the early 1900s and in 1928 moved to India where she continued her career on behalf of the Times of India Press and the Indian State Railways. She is best known for the numerous children's books that she wrote and illustrated under the name K. Nixon beginning in the 1950s, after she had returned to England. These works include *Pushti* and *Pindi Poo,* inspired by her pets; *The Bushy Tail Family; Animal Legends;* and *Strange Animal Friendships.*

OBITUARIES AND OTHER SOURCES:

PERIODICALS

Times (London), October 6, 1988.

*   *   *

NOLAN, Michael   1940-

PERSONAL: Born January 15, 1940, in Ottawa, Ontario, Canada; son of Michael Joseph and Gertrude Mary (Smyth) Nolan; married Carole Tucker, August 14, 1976. *Education:* University of Ottawa, B.A., 1961; University of Western Ontario, M.A., 1976, Ph.D., 1983. *Religion:* Roman Catholic.

ADDRESSES: Home—380 King St., Apt. S14-7, London, Ontario, Canada N6B 3L6. *Office*—Department of Journalism, Middlesex College, University of Western Ontario, London, Ontario, Canada N6A 5B7.

CAREER: CKOX-Radio, Woodstock, Ontario, newscaster and editor, 1961-62; CKOC-Radio, Hamilton, Ontario, news director, 1962-63; CKCO-Television and CKKW-Radio, Kitch-

ener, Ontario, newscaster-editor, reporter, television news anchorman, 1963-65; CKEY-Radio, Toronto, Ontario, newscaster, editor, and political reporter, 1965-66; CTV Radio Network, network news anchorman and parliamentary correspondent in Toronto and Ottawa, Ontario, 1966-70; CFPL-Radio, London, Ontario, political editor, 1970-76; University of Windsor, Windsor, Ontario, associate professor of communication studies, 1976-77; University of Western Ontario, London, assistant professor, 1977-88, associate professor of journalism, 1988—. Owner of Michael Nolan Productions: Public History Research, which is involved in preparing corporate histories and research relating to public histories.

MEMBER: Canadian Historical Association, Canadian Communications Association, Association for the Study of Canadian Radio and Television, Broadcast Education Association.

WRITINGS:

Joe Clark: The Emerging Leader, Fitzhenry & Whiteside, 1978.
Foundations: Alan Plaunt and the Early Days of CBC Radio, CBC Enterprises, 1986.

Contributor to scholarly journals and newspapers.

WORK IN PROGRESS: A Man of All Media: Walter J. Blackburn and the Family Dynasty; a book about Canadian politicians and the media.

SIDELIGHTS: Michael Nolan told *CA:* "I entered the academic arena after fifteen years of broadcasting because I found that broadcasting, including television, could really only be superficial media at best. The time constraints of network television were a continuing frustration. Basically I wanted to explore issues in more depth, and academic life allows one to do more thorough writing. In general, the history of the media has been my main interest, because it blends both my academic work and past, practical experience.

"*Foundations* is the story of Alan Plaunt, the leading architect of the present-day Canadian Broadcasting Corporation (CBC). Plaunt saw the CBC as a bulwark against Americanization; he argued that a properly led public broadcasting network would be a cultural showpiece for Canada and allow Canadian talent and Canadian programming to be nurtured. *A Man of All Media* is a biography of Walter J. Blackburn, the third-generation publisher of London's *Free Press* and owner of CFPL Broadcasting, who controlled a regional media monopoly in London, Ontario, for almost fifty years. My book on Canadian politicians and the media will provide a broad sweep of federal elections in Canada from 1867 to the present day, showing the way in which politicians have utilized the mass media in their campaigning.

"I am not overly optimistic about the political use of the electronic media. All politicians want exposure. But they also want to control their campaign environment. Therefore it is difficult for the electronic media to be useful vehicles if politicians, with the help of advertising agencies, continue to present themselves in a superficial way. I would like to see more debates among leaders and candidates and longer periods on television where voters could analyze the depth of politicians and their grasp of the issues."

*   *   *

NORDSTROM, Ursula   1910-1988

OBITUARY NOTICE—See index for *CA* sketch: Born February 1, 1910, in New York, N.Y.; died of ovarian cancer,

October 11, 1988, in New Milford, Conn. Publisher, editor, and author. Nordstrom was an editor and executive at Harper & Row publishing company for most of her life, specializing in children's books. Hailed as an innovator in young people's literature, she spurned the didacticism of earlier works in favor of characters and situations that reflected the experiences of her young audience. Nordstrom joined Harper & Row in 1936 and became director of children's books during the 1940s. In 1960 she became the company's first female vice-president, rising to senior vice-president and publisher seven years later. Though withdrawing from the publisher's post in 1973, she remained associated with Harper until 1979 as a senior editor in charge of her own line of books. Nordstrom aided the publication of such classics as E. B. White's *Charlotte's Web* and Maurice Sendak's *Where the Wild Things Are*. She wrote the children's book *The Secret Language*, believed to have been based on her own experiences at boarding school.

OBITUARIES AND OTHER SOURCES:

PERIODICALS

Chicago Tribune, October 16, 1988.
Los Angeles Times, October 14, 1988.
New York Times, October 12, 1988.
Publishers Weekly, October 28, 1988.
School Library Journal, November, 1988.
Washington Post, October 14, 1988.

*　　*　　*

NORMAN, Hilary

PERSONAL: Born in London, England. *Education:* Attended Queen's College, London.

ADDRESSES: Agent—John Hawkins Associates, 71 West 23rd St., New York, N.Y. 10010.

CAREER: Henry Norman (textile manufacturing and retail firm), London, England, director, 1971-79; Capital Radio, London,

production assistant, 1980-82; British Broadcasting Corp., London, production assistant, 1982-85; writer, 1985—.

WRITINGS:

In Love and Friendship (novel), Hodder & Stoughton, 1986, Delacorte, 1987.
Chateau Ella (novel), Delacorte, 1988.

Contributor of stories to *Woman's Own*.

SIDELIGHTS: In Love and Friendship has been translated into French, Italian, Finnish, Swedish, Norwegian, Hebrew, Portuguese, and Dutch.

*　　*　　*

NYREN, Karl　1922(?)-1988

OBITUARY NOTICE: Born c. 1922; died of cancer, August 13, 1988 (one source says August 12), in Beacon, N.Y. Educator, library director, film narrator, editor, scriptwriter, and poet. Highlighting Nyren's list of career distinctions was his twenty years of service as senior editor for the *Library Journal*, during which time he founded and edited the *Library Hotline*. His career in librarianship also included serving as director of two Massachusetts libraries, the Peabody Institute and the Cary Memorial Library, and writing and narrating the library film *Fifth Freedom*. He was co-founder and editor of *The Volusia Review*, a Florida literary magazine, and taught courses in art history, literature, and creative writing at Boston University and other small colleges. As a writer, he published a limited edition of his poetry, and won the Cahners Medal of Excellence in 1986.

OBITUARIES AND OTHER SOURCES:

PERIODICALS

Library Journal, September 15, 1988.
Publishers Weekly, August 26, 1988.

O

OAKLEY, Allen 1943-

PERSONAL: Born July 22, 1943, in Adelaide, Australia; married Renate Rosenauer (a language teacher), February 1, 1982; children: Tania. *Education:* University of Adelaide, B.Ec. (with first class honors), 1972, Ph.D., 1980. *Politics:* "Democratic Socialist."

ADDRESSES: Office—Department of Economics, University of Newcastle, Newcastle, New South Wales 2308, Australia.

CAREER: Adelaide College of Advanced Education, Adelaide, Australia, lecturer in economics, 1973-77; University of Newcastle, Newcastle, Australia, senior lecturer in economics, 1977—.

MEMBER: International Joseph A. Schumpeter Society, Association for Evolutionary Economics, History of Economic Thought Society (Australia), History of Economics Society (United States).

WRITINGS:

The Making of Marx's Critical Theory: A Bibliographical Analysis, Routledge & Kegan Paul, 1983.
Marx's Critique of Political Economy: Intellectual Sources and Evolution, two volumes, Routledge & Kegan Paul, 1984-85.
(Editor) Adolph Lowe, *Essays in Political Economics: Public Control in a Democratic Society,* New York University Press, 1987.

Contributor to economic journals.

WORK IN PROGRESS: A monograph, *Schumpeter's Theory of Capitalist Motion: A Critical Exposition and Reassessment,* for Edward Elgar Publishing.

*   *   *

OBERDORF, Charles (Donnell) 1941-
(Esmond Donnelly)

PERSONAL: Born February 25, 1941, in Sunbury, Pa.; son of Charles Donnell, Jr. (in sales) and Helen (a teacher; maiden name, Potteiger) Oberdorf; married Mechtild Hoppenrath (a journalist/consultant), October 25, 1977; children: Anya. *Education:* Carnegie Institute of Technology (now Carnegie-Mellon University), B.F.A., 1963.

ADDRESSES: Home—Toronto, Canada. *Office*—Magazine Division, Maclean Hunter Ltd., 777 Bay St., Toronto, Ontario, Canada M5W 1A7.

CAREER: WCAU-TV, Philadelphia, Pa., story editor, 1963-66; Canadian Broadcasting Corp., Toronto, Ontario, writer/interviewer, 1966-69; *Weekend Magazine,* Toronto, editor, 1977-78; *Maclean Hunter,* Toronto, editor in magazine division, 1983—. Producer and consultant on multi-media presentations to the National Film Board of Canada and private production houses; free-lance journalist in all media, 1968—. *Military service:* Pennsylvania National Guard, 1961-63.

MEMBER: Society of American Travel Writers, Association of Canadian Television and Radio Artists, Periodical Writers Association of Canada.

AWARDS, HONORS: Canadian National Magazine Award, 1979, 1980, and 1984, for magazine articles about travel and food; La Pluma de Plata from the Mexican Government, 1977 and 1984, for magazine articles about Mexico.

WRITINGS:

(Associate editor) *Between Friends/Entre amis,* National Film Board of Canada/McClelland & Stewart, 1976.
(With Mechtild Hoppenrath and others) *Fodor's Toronto,* Fodor Guides, 1984.
(With Hoppenrath) *First-Class Canada,* William Collins (Canada), 1987.

Contributor of articles and reviews, some under pseudonym Esmond Donnelly, to periodicals, including the *Financial Post Magazine, Toronto Life,* and the *Toronto Star;* travel editor of *Saturday Night,* 1974-77; senior editor of *City and Country Home,* 1984—.

SIDELIGHTS: Charles Oberdorf told *CA:* "I feel very fortunate that for fifteen years my journalism allowed me a continuing education on subjects about which I am passionately interested: architecture and design, food and drink, and, especially, other cultures. I believe that travel, and the best travel journalism, has an important political component, in that it can lead to an understanding and respect between peoples and an unwillingness to go to war.

"Now that I stay closer to home to enjoy my daughter's childhood, I am doubly blessed to be able to commission others' stories in these areas, further enlarging my knowledge and staying in touch.''

AVOCATIONAL INTERESTS: ''Baseball as a game of strategy, all aspects of turn-of-the-century life in Europe and North America, novel-length nonfiction of all sorts, what used to be called 'documentaries,' gardening, urban street life and street culture.''

* * *

O'BRIEN, Michael 1943-

PERSONAL: Born August 22, 1943, in Green Bay, Wis.; married Sally Pratsch (a corporate nurse), August 20, 1966; children: Timothy, Sean, Jeremy, Carey. *Education:* University of Notre Dame, B.A., 1965; University of Wisconsin—Madison, M.A., 1966, Ph.D., 1971.

ADDRESSES: Office—Department of History, University of Wisconsin, Center Fox Valley, 1478 Midway Rd., Menasha, Wis. 54952.

CAREER: Teacher of history at the University of Wisconsin, Menasha, Wis.

WRITINGS:

McCarthy and McCarthyism in Wisconsin, University of Missouri Press, 1981.
Vince: A Personal Biography of Vince Lombardi, Morrow, 1987.

WORK IN PROGRESS: Portraits of Excellence, ''a book stressing the achievements and character of three excellent individuals: Reverend Theodore Hesburgh, Joe Paterno, and former Michigan senator Philip Hart.''

* * *

O'CONNOR, James I(gnatius) 1910-1988

OBITUARY NOTICE—See index for *CA* sketch: Born July 30, 1910, in Chicago, Ill.; died July 9, 1988, in Chicago, Ill. Clergyman, educator, and author. O'Connor was considered an authority on the law of the Roman Catholic church, known as canon law. After entering the Jesuit religious order in 1930, he was ordained a priest in 1943. O'Connor was a professor of canon law at West Baden College from 1948 until 1964, when he transferred to Bellarmine School of Theology. He stayed with the school when it relocated to Chicago and was renamed the Jesuit School of Theology, and retired as professor emeritus in 1975. Thereafter he was associated with St. Mary of the Lake Seminary. O'Connor wrote *Dispensation From Irregularities to Holy Orders* and *An Introduction to the Divine Office.* With T. Lincoln Bouscaren he prepared several volumes of *Canon Law Digest* and *Canon Law Digest for Religious.*

OBITUARIES AND OTHER SOURCES:

BOOKS

The Writers Directory: 1988-1990, St. James Press, 1988.

PERIODICALS

Chicago Tribune, July 13, 1988.

* * *

O'HARA, Georgina 1956-

PERSONAL: Born March 13, 1956, in Surrey, England;

daughter of Norman G. and Patricia (Imrie) O'Hara; married A. Stevens Callan, September 7, 1985.

ADDRESSES: Office—1209 Joseph St., New Orleans, La. 70115. *Agent*—June Hall, 19 College Cross, London N1 1PT, England.

CAREER: Woman's Journal, England, associate editor, 1978-82; free-lance writer, 1983—. Associated with Callan Publishing, Inc.

WRITINGS:

Moneywoman, Sphere Books, 1983.
The Encyclopedia of Fashion, Abrams, 1986.
The World of the Baby, M. Joseph, 1988.

WORK IN PROGRESS: The World of the Bride, publication by M. Joseph expected in 1991; a biography of Captain Edward Molyneux, to be completed in 1989.

SIDELIGHTS: Georgina O'Hara told *CA:* ''I am interested in social history, especially relating to fashion, the arts, and daily life. It fascinates me to consider what it was like to live at different times in the past. I enjoy research and it is a great challenge to me to present history in a manner to which people are able to relate today.

''My books take accepted ideas and traditions and explore them further. *The Encyclopedia of Fashion* is an A-Z reference book on the fashion world from about the 1840s to the 1980s. It covers not only the fashions during this period but those people who helped create a particular look: designers, artists, photographers, models, hairdressers, and magazine editors. Also included are important styles and cuts of garments and fabrics. *The World of the Baby* is not a 'how to' book but one that looks at the social history of babies in our society and how our ideas about infancy have changed over the years. *The World of the Bride* will deal with engagements, marriages, and weddings in a similar manner.''

* * *

OLIN, John C(harles) 1915-

PERSONAL: Born October 7, 1915, in Buffalo, N.Y.; son of Newell and Dorothy (Britt) Olin; married Marian Gouse, January 10, 1943; children: Marybeth Olin Deambrosis, Margaret Olin Santos, John Charles, Jr., Thomas. *Education:* Canisius College, B.A., 1937; Fordham University, M.A., 1941; Columbia University, Ph.D., 1960. *Religion:* Roman Catholic.

ADDRESSES: Home—150 Van Houten Fields, West Nyack, N.Y. 10994.

CAREER: Fordham University, Bronx, N.Y., instructor, 1946-52, assistant professor, 1952-62, professor of history, 1962-86, professor emeritus, 1986—. *Military service:* U.S. Navy, 1942-46; became lieutenant senior grade.

MEMBER: Renaissance Society of America, American Catholic Historical Association, Neo-Latin Studies Association, Erasmus of Rotterdam Society, Amici Thomae Mori.

WRITINGS:

Christian Humanism and the Reformation, Harper, 1965, revised, Fordham University Press, 1987.
(Editor) *A Reformation Debate,* Harper, 1966.
The Catholic Reformation: Savonarola to Ignatius Loyola, Harper, 1969.

(Editor) *The Autobiography of St. Ignatius Loyola,* Harper, 1974.
Six Essays on Erasmus, Fordham University Press, 1979.

WORK IN PROGRESS: Two books on the patristic editions of Erasmus, publication by University of Toronto Press expected in 1989.

SIDELIGHTS: John C. Olin told *CA:* "My field of study and teaching as a historian has been the Renaissance and the Reformation, and I have worked extensively on Erasmus. I have also been interested in Catholic reform (as contrasted with Protestant reform) in the sixteenth century. My interest in Erasmus has been both because of his views and his pivotal role in his own times and because of the relevance of his ideas in ours. My concern with Catholic reform has been personal, but it is also part and parcel of an attempt to broaden out the story of the Reformation and to see and evaluate it in a much fuller context."

* * *

OLSON, (Elizabeth) Ann 1953-

PERSONAL: Born June 2, 1953, in New Haven, Conn.; daughter of William Clinton (a professor) and Mary (an artist; maiden name, Matthews) Olson; married Christopher Laxton (an editor), May 17, 1977; children: Sarah Lindsay. *Education:* Attended Colorado College, 1972-73; McGill University, B.A. (with honors), 1977; attended Clark University, 1977-80.

ADDRESSES: Home—626 North Nelson St., Arlington, Va. 22203.

CAREER: Free-lance geography editor for textbook publisher, 1976-77; United Nations University, Katmandu, Nepal, ethnographer, 1979-80; U.S. Geological Survey, Reston, Va., cartographer, 1980—. Fellow of Institute for Policy Studies and Wellesley College's Center for Research on Women, both 1985. Member of board of directors of Capitol Area Map Alliance, 1984-85, and Infant and Child Development Center of Arlington, Inc., 1986-87; volunteer worker in health and the arts.

MEMBER: North American Cartographic Information Society, American Congress on Surveying and Mapping, American Association of Geographers.

AWARDS, HONORS: Grants from Rockefeller Foundation and Ford Foundation, 1985; publication award from Chicago Geographic Society, 1986, for *Women in the World.*

WRITINGS:

(With Joni Seager) *Women in the World: An International Atlas,* Simon & Schuster, 1986.

Contributor of articles and reviews to scholarly journals.

WORK IN PROGRESS: Research on demographic mapping of specific reference to women.

SIDELIGHTS: The book *Women in the World* emphasizes the fact that, behind all historical events and sociological statistics, there are female perspectives which have generally been ignored by other researchers. Though the data are presently inadequate for an exhaustive examination, Ann Olson and her co-author have gathered all the information they could find on the female experience in various parts of the world. They investigated education, health, employment, political power, and many other aspects of human existence, comparing women against men and country against country. Their comparison is rigorous, and the statistics, in some cases, reflect appalling inequities. Olson's interest in mapping and geography is reflected in numerous maps and charts, which illustrate the facts in ways that one reviewer found to be ingenious. Laurien Alexander wrote in the *Los Angeles Times Book Review:* "This concise atlas is an invaluable reference that reminds the reader of that 'invisible' woman's story. The bleakness of its message—that in the world of women, there are few 'developed' countries—is only tempered by realizing that that story now no longer remains invisible."

BIOGRAPHICAL/CRITICAL SOURCES:

PERIODICALS

Los Angeles Times Book Review, December 14, 1986.

* * *

OMAN, Julia Trevelyan 1930-

PERSONAL: Born July 11, 1930, in Kensington, England; daughter of Charles Chichele and Joan (Trevelyan) Oman; married Roy C. Strong, 1971. *Education:* Attended Royal College of Art.

ADDRESSES: Agent—Curtis Brown Ltd., 162-168 Regent St., London W1R 5TA, England.

CAREER: British Broadcasting Corporation (BBC-TV), England, designer, 1955-67; designer for theatrical productions, ballets, operas, and exhibitions in New York City, London, and Europe, 1967—. Director of Oman Productions Ltd.

AWARDS, HONORS: Designer of the Year Award, 1967; D.Litt from University of Bristol, 1987; commander of Order of the British Empire; Silver Medal from Royal College of Art; named royal scholar, royal designer for industry, and designer by Royal College of Art.

WRITINGS:

(Photographer) B. S. Johnson, *Street Children,* Hodder & Stoughton, 1964.
(With husband, Roy C. Strong) *Elizabeth R,* Stein & Day, 1971.
(With Strong) *Mary Queen of Scots,* Stein & Day, 1972.
(With Strong) *The English Year: A Personal Selection From Chambers' Book of Days,* Ticknor & Fields, 1982.

* * *

ONSTOTT, Kyle 1887-1966

OBITUARY NOTICE—See index for *CA* sketch: Born January 12, 1887, in DuQuoin, Ill.; died of heart failure brought on by bronchial pneumonia, June 3, 1966, in San Francisco, Calif.; cremated. Dog show judge and author. Onstott will be best remembered as the pulp novelist who scored his greatest success with the "Falconhurst" series of books, most of which he wrote with Lance Horner, and the novels *Mandingo* and its sequel *Drum.* Focusing on the effect of slavery on both master and slave in the eight "Falconhurst" books—including *Master of Falconhurst, Heir to Falconhurst,* and *Falconhurst Fancy*—the dramatic tension in the works is generally supplied by interracial sexual relationships and the violence they engender. Onstott's other books with Horner include *Child of the Sun, Street of the Sun,* and *The Black Sun.* The author was also an all-breeds dog show judge licensed in 1921 by the American

Kennel Club, and he wrote *Your Dog as a Hobby,* with Irving C. Ackerman, *Beekeeping as a Hobby,* and *The Art of Breeding Better Dogs.*

OBITUARIES AND OTHER SOURCES:

Date of death provided by Martin Praul.

BOOKS

Twentieth-Century Romance and Gothic Writers, Gale, 1982.

PERIODICALS

San Francisco Chronicle, June 24, 1966.

*   *   *

OPPENHEIMER, Joel (Lester)   1930-1988

OBITUARY NOTICE—See index for *CA* sketch: Born February 18, 1930, in Yonkers, N.Y.; died of lung cancer, October 11, 1988, in Henniker, N.H. Educator, administrator, typographer, editor, journalist, and author. Oppenheimer will be best remembered as one of the foremost Black Mountain Poets, a literary group centered at North Carolina's Black Mountain College, where he studied from 1950 to 1953. In addition to his more than one dozen poetry collections, including *names, dates, and places, Why Not,* and *Names and Local Habitations,* Oppenheimer wrote a book of short stories, *Pan's Eyes;* a collection of plays titled *The Great American Desert;* and two nonfiction works, one on the 1972 New York Mets baseball team, *The Wrong Season,* and one on actress Marilyn Monroe, *Marilyn Lives!* He worked as a typographer before joining the faculty of the City College of the City University of New York as a poet-in-residence in 1969. He stayed there until 1982, when he became an associate professor of communications and writer-in-residence at New England College. For six years, beginning in 1966, Oppenheimer was director of the Poetry Project at New York City's St. Mark's Church and from 1969 until 1984 he was a contributing editor for the *Village Voice.* He also edited *Kulchur 5* and *The Genre of Silence.*

OBITUARIES AND OTHER SOURCES:

PERIODICALS

New York Times, October 13, 1988.

*   *   *

ORELLANA, Sandra L.   1941-

PERSONAL: Surname is pronounced "Or-e-*ya*-na"; born March 6, 1941, in Fredericksburg, Va.; daughter of Melvin H. (in U.S. Navy) and Margaret (a beautician; maiden name, Alexander) Davey; married Carlos Orellana (divorced). *Education:* University of California, Los Angeles, B.A., 1963, M.A. (political science), 1965, M.A. (Latin American studies), 1968, Ph.D., 1976.

ADDRESSES: Office—Department of Anthropology, California State University, Dominguez Hills, 1000 East Victoria St., Carson, Calif. 90747.

CAREER: Instituto Brasil-Estados Unidos, Fortaleza, Ceara, Brazil, English teacher and librarian, 1965-66; California State University, Dominguez Hills, Carson, assistant professor, 1973-78, associate professor, 1979-82, professor of anthropology, 1982—. University of California, Los Angeles, extension instructor, 1974—, visiting scholar in international business, 1984-

86. Member of archaeological excavation at Rancho La Brea Tar Pits, 1971; conducted archaeological survey in Santiago Atitlan, Guatemala, 1971; conducted ethnological research on the Indian art of Vancouver Island and the Gitskan Indians of British Columbia; consultant to RAND Corp. and Systems Research Analysis.

MEMBER: Academy of International Business, United States Space Foundation, American Institute of Archaeology, American Society for Ethnohistory, National Space Society, Society of Manufacturing Engineers, League of Women Voters, Southwestern Anthropological Association, Beverly Hills Chamber of Commerce.

AWARDS, HONORS: Grant for Guatemala from Cora Black Fund, 1971; fellowship for Spain from Del Amo Foundation, 1977; grants from American Philosophical Society, 1979, U.S. Department of Health, Education and Welfare, 1980, and California State University Dominguez Hills Foundation, 1987.

WRITINGS:

The Tzutujil Mayas: Continuity and Change, 1250-1630, University of Oklahoma Press, 1984.
Indian Medicine in Highland Guatemala, University of New Mexico Press, 1987.
The Ethnohistory of the Abaj Takalik Region, University of California, Berkeley, 1988.

Contributor to *Inside Kung Fu Yearbook.* Contributor to anthropology journals and martial arts magazines.

SIDELIGHTS: Sandra L. Orellana told *CA:* "I have spent several summers living in Santiago Atitlan, learning as much as I can about contemporary people. This has helped me a great deal in reconstructing their ancient culture. I have also written on Atiteco folktales. I am basically interested in ancient highland Maya culture, whether it focuses on sociopolitical behavior or medical.

"My recent work looks at the Pacific coastal region from about 1250 to 1800. The Pacific coastal region is relatively unknown but figured prominently in prehispanic and colonial history. The region is not well explored archaeologically, and many areas have not even been properly surveyed. This work is an extension of my work on the Tzutujil, one of the important aboriginal Guatemalan peoples. Their kingdom also included lands in the Pacific coast. Cacao was mainly grown there, and the coast was the source of wealth for highland peoples.

"My basic findings about the Indian medical system, primarily herbal, was that much of it worked. I analyzed around one hundred plants and showed how they actually alleviated the illnesses mentioned. Prehispanic medicine was fairly sophisticated, and much of the knowledge remains in the highlands today.

"I have always believed that good research and writing are essential to good teaching. I enjoy sharing anecdotes about my work with my students."

*   *   *

ORLANDO, Guido   1908(?)-1988

OBITUARY NOTICE: Born c. 1908 (one source says 1906) in Barisciano, Italy; immigrated to United States, 1917; died after suffering a heart attack, May 22, 1988, in Hollywood, Calif. Publicist, actor, and author. Famous for his manipulative though good-natured distortions of the truth, Orlando was the flamboyant press agent for dozens of people desiring fame. One of his better-known antics occurred when he was hired by the Millinery Institute of America to increase hat sales. Orlando invented a fictitious research institute that released a "survey" revealing millions of women were going to church every Sunday without hats; then, through a friend at the Vatican in Rome, he obtained a statement from Pope Pius XII expressing the propriety of wearing hats in church. Hat sales soared. Other publicity stunts included the fabrication of a romance between Egyptian King Farouk and a young American client of Orlando's so that she could obtain a movie contract. Before becoming a press agent, Orlando worked as an errand boy for a film company, as an actor, and as a man-in-waiting for silent-screen star Rudolph Valentino. He outlined his early exploits in a 1954 book, *Confessions of a Scoundrel* and, before his death, was compiling his memoirs.

OBITUARIES AND OTHER SOURCES:

PERIODICALS

Los Angeles Times, May 26, 1988.
New York Times, May 28, 1988.

*   *   *

O'ROURKE, Andrew P(atrick) 1933-

PERSONAL: Born October 26, 1933, in Plainfield, N.J.; son of Andrew Patrick and Helen (Anderson) O'Rourke; married Alice McKenna, April 19, 1954; children: Alice T., Andrew Jr., Aileen B. *Education:* Fordham University, B.S., 1954, J.D., 1962; New York University, LL.M., 1965.

ADDRESSES: Home—25 Martine Ave., White Plains, N.Y. 10606. *Office*—148 Martine Ave., White Plains, N.Y., 10601.

CAREER: Lee & O'Rourke (law firm), Bronxville, N.Y., partner, 1968-74; O'Rourke & LoCascio (law firm), White Plains, N.Y., partner, 1975-82; executive of Westchester County, N.Y., 1983—. Member of Yonkers City Council, 1965-73; member of Westchester County legislature, 1973-82. *Military service:* U.S. Air Force, 1955-63; became captain. U.S. Naval Reserve, 1964—; present rank, captain.

MEMBER: Member of various bar associations, civic organizations, and arts groups.

AWARDS, HONORS: Honorary doctorates from Mercy College, 1985, and Manhattanville College, 1986.

WRITINGS:

The Red Banner Mutiny (novel), Bantam, 1986.
Hawkwood (novel), Bantam, 1988.

WORK IN PROGRESS: A second *Hawkwood* novel.

BIOGRAPHICAL/CRITICAL SOURCES:

PERIODICALS

New York Times, April 21, 1986.

*   *   *

OSLER, Margaret Jo 1942-

PERSONAL: Born November 27, 1942, in New York, N.Y.; daughter of Abraham George (a professor) and Sonia (a professor; maiden name, Fellner) Osler. *Education:* Swarthmore College, B.A., 1963; Indiana University—Bloomington, M.A., 1966, Ph.D., 1968.

ADDRESSES: Office—Department of History, University of Calgary, 2500 University Dr. N.W., Calgary, Alberta, Canada T2N 1N4.

CAREER: Oregon State University, Corvallis, assistant professor of history of science, 1968-70; Harvey Mudd College, Claremont, Calif., assistant professor of history, 1970-74; Wake Forest University, Winston-Salem, N.C., assistant professor of history, 1974-75; University of Calgary, Calgary, Alberta, assistant professor, 1975-77, associate professor of history, 1977—.

MEMBER: Canadian Society for the History and Philosophy of Science (president, 1987—), History of Science Society, West Coast History of Science Society.

WRITINGS:

(Contributor) Paula R. Backscheider, editor, *Probability, Time, and Space in Eighteenth-Century Literature*, AMS Press, 1978.
(Editor with M. P. Hanen and R. G. Weyant) *Science, Pseudo-Science, and Society*, Wilfrid Laurier University Press, 1980.
(Editor with P. L. Farber) *Religion, Science, and Worldview: Essays in Honour of Richard S. Westfall*, Cambridge University Press, 1986.

Contributor to *Encyclopaedia Britannica*. Contributor to philosophy journals.

WORK IN PROGRESS: Research on mechanical philosophy in the seventeenth century, Pierre Gassendi, Rene Descartes, and science and religion.

BIOGRAPHICAL/CRITICAL SOURCES:

PERIODICALS

Times Literary Supplement, August 1, 1986.

*   *   *

O'TOOLE, James (Joseph) 1945-

PERSONAL: Born April 15, 1945, in San Francisco, Calif.; son of James Joseph (a laborer) and Irene (a secretary; maiden name, Nagy) O'Toole; married Mairlyn Louise Burrill (a lawyer), June 17, 1967; children: Erin Kathleen, Kerry Louise. *Education:* University of Southern California, B.A. (magna cum laude), 1966; Oxford University, D.Phil., 1970.

ADDRESSES: Home—422 South Las Palmas Ave., Los Angeles, Calif. 90020. *Office*—Graduate School of Business, University of Southern California, Los Angeles, Calif. 90089.

CAREER: Time-Life News Service, Los Angeles, Calif., and Nairobi, Kenya, correspondent, 1967-68; McKinsey and Co., San Francisco, Calif., management consultant, 1969-70; U.S. Department of Health, Education and Welfare, Washington, D.C., special assistant to secretary, 1970-73, chairman of Secretary's Committee on Work in America, 1971-72; University of Southern California, Los Angeles, assistant professor, 1973-77, associate professor, 1977-79, professor of management, 1980—, University Associates' chair of management, 1982—, director of Twenty Year Forecast Project for Center for Futures Research, 1973-81. Coordinator of general field investigations for President's Commission on Campus Unrest, 1970; director of Aspen Institute Project on Education, Work, and the Quality of Life, 1973-74; executive director of Town Hall of California Study of Los Angeles Public Pension Plans, 1978-79. Host of

"Why in the World," a television series broadcast by Public Broadcasting System, 1981, 1983. Speaker for U.S. Information Agency in Italy and West Germany, 1976.

MEMBER: American Association for Higher Education (member of board of directors, 1977-79), Phi Beta Kappa.

AWARDS, HONORS: Rhodes scholar, 1966-69; George and Cynthia Mitchell Prize, 1979, for a paper on sustained growth; *Vanguard Management* was named "one of the ten best business and economics books of 1985" by *Business Week*.

WRITINGS:

Watts and Woodstock: Identity and Culture in the United States and South Africa, Holt, 1973.
Work in America: Report of a Special Task Force to the Secretary of Health, Education, and Welfare, MIT Press, 1973.
(Editor) *Work and the Quality of Life*, MIT Press, 1974.
Energy and Social Change, MIT Press, 1976.
Work, Learning, and the American Future, Jossey-Bass, 1977.
(With others) *Tenure*, Change Magazine Press, 1979.
Making America Work, Continuum, 1981.
(Editor) *Working: Changes and Choices*, Human Sciences, 1981.
Vanguard Management: Redesigning the Corporate Future, Doubleday, 1985.

Contributor to journals, including *Annals of the American Academy of Political and Social Science, Change*, and *Worklife*. Editor of *New Management*, 1983—; member of board of editors of *Encyclopaedia Britannica*, 1983-87.

SIDELIGHTS: Making America Work is a study of the work force and the culture of American management. In his book, James O'Toole compares the new values of young workers to the attitudes of the generation that produced them. He points out that declining productivity and the apparent selfishness of the work force is a direct product of management policies that have depersonalized the workplace, and that have emphasized material benefits like pension funds and monetary rewards over intangible benefits that result from worker responsibility and participation. Furthermore, O'Toole suggests that American management's insistence on total authority and total control has undermined workers' incentives to make meaningful contributions to the production process. According to Milton Moskowitz of the *Los Angeles Times Book Review*, O'Toole's prescription for improving productivity includes an increase in worker-owned companies and a working pattern that is "designed around such criteria as diversity, choice, flexibility, mobility and participation rather than the old criteria of mindless efficiency and managerial authority." Moskowitz described *Making America Work* as a "book rich in insights as well as stories" and O'Toole as an author who "writes clearly and . . . tells good stories."

BIOGRAPHICAL/CRITICAL SOURCES:

PERIODICALS

Los Angeles Times Book Review, October 18, 1981.
Washington Post Book World, December 27, 1981.

*   *   *

OWEN, Norman G.   1944-

PERSONAL: Born January 23, 1944, in Los Angeles, Calif.; son of Henry (a missionary) and Marguerite (a missionary; maiden name, Goodner) Owen; married Roberta Yule (an actress), October 4, 1969; children: Robert Henry. *Education:* Occidental College, A.B., 1964; University of London, B.A. (with honors), 1967; University of Michigan, M.A., 1971, Ph.D., 1976.

ADDRESSES: Home—Block 1, Flat B15, 23 Sha Wan Dr., Pokfulam, Hong Kong. *Office*—Department of History, University of Hong Kong, Hong Kong.

CAREER: University of Michigan, Ann Arbor, lecturer, 1974, instructor, 1974-76, assistant professor of history, 1976-81; Australian National University, Canberra, research fellow, 1982-85, senior research fellow in history, 1985-86; University of Hong Kong, Hong Kong, lecturer in history, 1986—. *Military service:* U.S. Army, 1967-69.

MEMBER: American Historical Association, Asian Studies Association of Australia, Royal Asiatic Society (Hong Kong and Malaysian branches), Association for Asian Studies, Hong Kong Welsh Male Voice Choir.

AWARDS, HONORS: Marshall scholar, 1964-67; Foreign Area fellow, 1971-73; fellow of National Endowment for the Humanities at Newberry Library, 1981-82.

WRITINGS:

(Editor and contributor) *Compadre Colonialism*, Center for South and Southeast Asian Studies, University of Michigan, 1971.
(Editor and contributor) *The Philippine Economy and the United States*, Center for South and Southeast Asian Studies, University of Michigan, 1983.
Prosperity Without Progress: Manila Hemp and Material Life in the Colonial Philippines, University of California Press, 1986.
(Editor and contributor) *Death and Disease in Southeast Asia*, Oxford University Press, 1987.

Contributor to Asian studies journals.

WORK IN PROGRESS: Research on the social and economic history of Southeast Asia and on Philippine historical demography.

SIDELIGHTS: Norman G. Owen told *CA:* "A quarter of a century ago I decided to specialize in the history of modern Southeast Asia. It seemed as if it might be significant, yet very little was known about it at the time, which meant that I would not always be retracing others' footsteps. Everything else—travel, writing, etc.—follows from that decision. Although I would like to believe that from my years of studying and teaching abroad I have developed a greater understanding of human—not just American—society, I have only written on topics on which I possess particular scholarly expertise. I admire, and often envy, more creative writers, but my own gift is for expository prose."

*   *   *

OZBUDUN, Ergun   1937-

PERSONAL: Born July 1, 1937, in Ankara, Turkey; son of Fahri (a judge) and Sefika (a homemaker; maiden name, Sezen) Ozbudun; married Umay (a homemaker), March 17, 1961; children: Ipek, Yasemin. *Education:* Ankara University, Li.B., 1959, Ph.D., 1962.

ADDRESSES: Home—Kader 1/8 G.O.P., Ankara, Turkey. *Office*—Faculty of Law, Ankara University, Tandogan, Ankara, Turkey.

CAREER: Ankara University, Ankara, Turkey, professor of constitutional law and comparative politics, 1975—. *Military service:* Turkish Armed Forces, 1969-70.

MEMBER: International Political Science Association, Turkish Political Science Association (president, 1984—), Turkish Democracy Foundation (vice-president, 1987—).

WRITINGS:

NONFICTION

Party Cohesion in Western Democracies, Sage Publications, 1970.
Social Change and Political Participation in Turkey, Princeton University Press, 1976.

Ataturk: Founder of a Modern State, Croom Helm, 1981.
(Co-author and co-editor) *Competitive Elections in Developing Countries,* Duke University Press, 1987.

WORK IN PROGRESS: Further research on political changes in Turkey and on the state of the Middle East.

SIDELIGHTS: Ergun Ozbudun told *CA:* "In addition to being a student of politics, I have been active in promoting democratic values and institutions in Turkey through my writings, my lectures, and my work at the Turkish Democracy Foundation. I am a strong believer in the virtues of international cooperation. Throughout my years at the International Political Science Association, as a member and officer, I tried to promote the international cooperation of political scientists."

P

PAGE, Diana (Preuthun) 1946-

PERSONAL: Born August 17, 1946, in Detroit, Mich.; daughter of Edward Lupton (a professor of engineering) and Carla (an anthropologist; maiden name, Preuthun) Page; married Horacio Villalobos, February 21, 1973 (marriage ended April 12, 1980). *Education:* University of Michigan, B.A., 1968; Johns Hopkins School of Advanced International Studies, M.A., 1982.

ADDRESSES: Office—International Institute for Environment and Development, 1717 Massachusetts Ave. N.W., Washington, D.C. 20036. *Agent*—Elizabeth Grossman, Literistic Ltd., 1 Madison Ave., New York, N.Y. 10010.

CAREER: U.S. Peace Corps, Washington, D.C., volunteer worker in Bahia, Brazil, 1968-70; United Press International, correspondent from Rio de Janeiro, Brazil, 1970-72, and Buenos Aires, Argentina, 1972-79; *El Dia/Noticias Argentinos,* Washington, D.C., correspondent, 1980-83; *St. Petersburg Times,* St. Petersburg, Fla., correspondent, 1984-85; International Institute for Environment and Development, Washington, D.C., director of public affairs, 1986—.

WRITINGS:

(With Jose Napoleon Duarte) *Duarte: My Story,* Putnam, 1986.

SIDELIGHTS: Diana Page told *CA:* "I covered the president of El Salvador, Jose Napoleon Duarte, while working as a journalist. His publisher, Putnam, was looking for a journalist familiar with El Salvador and contacted me about the book. Duarte gave me full access to his papers, his family, and his colleagues. I conducted thirty hours of interviews and was given an office in the presidential palace. Afterwards, I wrote the book at home in Maine, then returned to El Salvador twice to go over the manuscript and update it. We built a good collaborative relationship based on mutual trust and respect."

BIOGRAPHICAL/CRITICAL SOURCES:

PERIODICALS

New York Times Book Review, November 2, 1986.
Washington Post Book World, January 18, 1987.

PAGELS, Heinz R(udolf) 1939-1988

OBITUARY NOTICE—See index for *CA* sketch: One source spells middle name Rudolph; born February 19, 1939, in New York, N.Y.; died in a mountaineering accident, July 23 (some sources say July 24), 1988, on Pyramid Peak, near Aspen, Colo. Physicist, human rights activist, administrator, educator, editor, and author. "Heinz Pagels is one of less than a handful of active scientists who can write excellent prose about the scientific frontier for a general audience," cosmologist David Schramm, as quoted in the *Chicago Tribune,* remarked in a review of Pagels's 1985 work, *Perfect Symmetry: The Search for the Beginning of Time.* Pagels became a member of the physics faculty of Rockefeller University in 1966, and in 1981 he also assumed the duties of executive director of the New York Academy of Sciences. In addition, he was president of the International League for Human Rights and a fellow of the New York Institute of the Humanities. His analysis of the effects of computers on society, *The Dreams of Reason: The Computer and the Rise of the Sciences of Complexity,* was published in 1988. His other works include *The Cosmic Code: Quantum Physics as the Language of Nature,* which won an American Book Award nomination in 1983, and he edited *Computer Culture: The Scientific, Intellectual, and Social Impact of the Computer.*

OBITUARIES AND OTHER SOURCES:

PERIODICALS

Aspen Times, July 28, 1988.
Chicago Tribune, July 27, 1988.
New York Times, July 26, 1988.

*   *   *

PAIGE, Richard E(aton) 1904-1988

OBITUARY NOTICE—See index for *CA* sketch: Born December 30, 1904, in New York, N.Y.; died of leukemia, August 15, 1988, in New York, N.Y. Inventor, entrepreneur, musician and composer, lecturer, and author. Paige is best remembered as an inventor who held more than 170 patents, most of them in consumer packaging. He gave up a musical career—he was an orchestra leader for a New York radio station, a vaudeville performer, and a composer of radio theme songs and commercials during the 1920s—to virtually found the field of cardboard engineering. Paige was granted all of the basic patents for paper manufacture, with his inventions (such as folding boxes and cardboard display stands) commissioned by companies including General Electric, Colgate, Seagram, Hallmark Cards, and General Foods. In 1940 he established his own business in New York City, and later he was a guest lecturer at the New School for Social Research and at Pratt Institute. Paige was named to the Packaging Hall of Fame in 1975. His writings include *Complete Guide to Making Money With Your Ideas and Inventions, The Science of Creating Ideas for Industry,* and *Lines to Remember.*

OBITUARIES AND OTHER SOURCES:

BOOKS

Who's Who in the World, 9th edition, Marquis, 1988.

PERIODICALS

New York Times, August 19, 1988.

* * *

PALMER, Winthrop Bushnell   1899-1988

OBITUARY NOTICE—See index for *CA* sketch: Born September 14, 1899, in New York, N.Y.; died August 8, 1988, in Centre Island, N.Y. Educator, editor, and author. Palmer and her husband, Carleton Humphreys Palmer, founded the Palmer School of Library and Information Science at Long Island University's C. W. Post College. In 1974 she became the first woman to serve as chair of the board of trustees of that university, where she was also professor of literature and fine arts. Among her writings are the poetry collections *The Invisible Wife and Other Poems, The New Barbarian, Fables and Ceremonies,* and *Like a Passing Shadow;* plays, including "Rosemary and the Planet" and "Beat the Wind"; a ballet libretto, "The Man From Midian"; and the nonfiction work *Theatrical Dancing in America.* Palmer, a member of such literary societies as the American Academy of Poets and P.E.N., was also associate editor of *Dance News* from 1935 to 1950 and of *Confrontation,* beginning in the early 1970s.

OBITUARIES AND OTHER SOURCES:

BOOKS

Directory of American Scholars, Volume II: *English, Speech, and Drama,* 8th edition, Bowker, 1982.
International Authors and Writers Who's Who, 9th edition, [and] *International Who's Who in Poetry,* 6th edition, Melrose, 1982.

PERIODICALS

New York Times, August 11, 1988.

* * *

PAPAZOGLOU, Orania   1951-

PERSONAL: Name is pronounced "O-rah-*nee*-ah Pa-pa-*zog*-lou"; born July 13, 1951, in Bethel, Conn.; daughter of George Sotirios (a lawyer) and Ann (a painter; maiden name, Paris) Papazoglou; married William L. DeAndrea (a writer), January 1, 1984; children: Matthew William. *Education:* Vassar College, A.B., 1973; University of Connecticut, A.M., 1975; doctoral study at Michigan State University, 1975-80. *Politics:* "Pessimist/anarchist." *Religion:* Greek Orthodox.

ADDRESSES: *Home and office*—41 Roberts St., Watertown, Conn. 06795. *Agent*—Meredith Bernstein, 470 West End Ave., New York, N.Y. 10024.

CAREER: *Greek Accent* (magazine), assistant to the editor, 1980-81, executive editor, 1981-83; full-time writer, 1983—.

WRITINGS:

Sweet, Savage Death (novel), Doubleday, 1984.
Wicked Loving Murder (novel), Doubleday, 1985.
Death's Savage Passion (novel), Doubleday, 1986.
Sanctity (novel), Crown, 1986.
Rich, Radiant Slaughter, Doubleday, 1988.

Columnist for *Mystery Scene.* Contributor to magazines, including *Working Woman, Mother,* and *Intro.*

SIDELIGHTS: Orania Papazoglou told *CA:* "I was christened Eastern Orthodox and educated Roman Catholic when Roman Catholics were what most people still think they are. In other words, I was brought up in two traditions, in which man's ability to choose evil as well as good was a given. Oh, there were people who were mentally ill, and people who were victims of circumstances, but mostly there were people who could and did control their actions. (In Orthodox Christianity, nobody controls his own destiny.) I suppose I'm still there, in a way.

"My longer books, like *Sanctity,* are mostly about choice. *Sanctity* has a religious setting, but my new book will not. I don't think I'll ever use a religious setting again. That is limiting, too. Many of us, myself included, haven't been to church in years. We manage to make our decisions on questions of good and evil in other than religious terms. The only thing I've really decided is that evil—especially physical violence—should not be portrayed as attractive or 'entertaining' in the conventional sense. *Sanctity* was, I think, in many ways an ugly book, but then a lot of it was about an extreme case of child abuse. I got a certain amount of criticism about the book not being for 'weak stomachs,' but I still think I was correct to write it the way I did.

"On the other hand, if I wrote that sort of thing all the time, I would go nuts. I do lighter writing to keep my mind from disintegrating into paranoia.

"As for motivations—well, I started trying to write when I was six. If I had a day off from school, I went and pounded away on a little manual typewriter my grandmother gave me for Christmas. Given a choice, this is still what I'd rather be doing—next to anything. It would be nice to have a mission. It would be even nicer to have a 'purpose in life.' Unfortunately, as far as I can tell, I write because I write."

Sweet Savage Death is a mystery novel about a writer of romance novels, who is accused of murdering a literary agent. The heroine is intelligent, independent, and courageous, surrounded by the seemingly frivolous participants in a romance writers' convention. The book is, according to critic Claire Harrison of the *Washington Post,* a satire of the world in which romance novelists work. Harrison called the novel "fast-paced, fun and successful." She added: "I certainly never figured out who had done it."

BIOGRAPHICAL/CRITICAL SOURCES:

PERIODICALS

Washington Post, April 28, 1984.

PARKER, Kristy 1957-

PERSONAL: Born May 3, 1957, in Decatur, Ill.; daughter of James F. (a university dean of admissions) and Emily (a teacher; maiden name, Siegrist) Kettelkamp; married Thomas E. Parker (an engineer), August 19, 1978; children: Erin, Andy, Sara. *Education:* Attended Millikin University, 1975-77; University of Illinois at Urbana-Champaign, B.S., 1979. *Religion:* Presbyterian.

ADDRESSES: Home—4897 Chimney Springs Dr., Greensboro, N.C.

CAREER: Teacher's aide in Dubuque, Iowa, 1979-80; North Scott Community School System, Scott County, Iowa, substitute teacher, 1980-81; writer, 1982—.

MEMBER: National League of American Pen Women, Juvenile Forum Writers Group.

AWARDS, HONORS: First prize in beginner's category for essay "Lookout Superman" and honorable mention in religious category for "The One Who Suffered First," both from Mississippi Valley Writer's Conference, both 1985; honorable mention in National League of American Pen Women's contest, 1986, for essay "Tender Moments."

WRITINGS:

"I Talked With God" (choral arrangement), Alfred Publishing, 1979.
My Dad, the Magnificent (juvenile), Dutton, 1987.

WORK IN PROGRESS: Picture books for children.

SIDELIGHTS: Kristy Parker told *CA:* "My children provide me with a wealth of ideas for picture stories. I care about providing quality literature for 'little people' and their parents to share. Hopefully I will touch their hearts in the process."

*   *   *

PARKHILL, John
See COX, William R(obert)

*   *   *

PARKS, Michael 1943-

PERSONAL: Born November 17, 1943, in Detroit, Mich.; son of Robert J. (a teacher) and Rosalind (Smith) Parks; married Linda K. Durocher (a librarian), December 26, 1964; children: Danielle, Christopher, Matthew. *Education:* University of Windsor, A.B., 1964.

ADDRESSES: Home—P. O. Box 5660, Johannesburg, South Africa. *Office—Los Angeles Times,* Times Mirror Square, Box 387, Los Angeles, Calif. 90012.

CAREER/WRITINGS: Detroit News, Detroit, Mich., reporter, 1962-65; Time-Life News Service, New York, N.Y., correspondent, 1965-66; *Suffolk Sun,* Deer Park, N.Y., assistant city editor, 1966-68; *Sun* (Baltimore), Baltimore, Md., political reporter, 1968-70, southeast Asia correspondent, 1970-72, Moscow correspondent, 1972-75, Mideast correspondent, 1975-78, Peking correspondent, 1978-80; *Los Angeles Times,* Los Angeles, Calif., Peking correspondent, 1980-84, southern Africa correspondent, 1984-88, Moscow correspondent, 1988—.

MEMBER: Hong Kong Foreign Correspondents Club.

AWARDS, HONORS: Pulitzer Prize, 1987, for international reporting.

SIDELIGHTS: Foreign correspondent Michael Parks began his award-winning career in journalism more than twenty-five years ago as a reporter for the *Detroit News.* As a correspondent in southeast Asia in the early 1970s, Parks covered the Vietnam war for the Baltimore *Sun.* He also reported from Moscow, Cairo, and Peking before moving to the *Los Angeles Times* in 1980. Parks continued his correspondence from Peking for the *Los Angeles Times* and went on to become the paper's southern Africa bureau chief four years later.

In December of 1986, the South African government refused to extend Parks's visa and ordered him to leave the country. This official ordinance was made in a move to curb news coverage of the political and social unrest brewing in South Africa over apartheid, the republic's systemized policy of segregation and discrimination against black and mulatto people. Parks's editors appealed to the South African government on the basis of the writer's reputation for fair and impartial reporting. Because they were unable to find a single inaccuracy in any of the 265 stories Parks had filed in 1986, officials repealed the order and allowed the correspondent to stay.

Los Angeles Times staff writer John J. Goldman reported that a panel of judges named Parks the winner of the Pulitzer Prize for international reporting in 1987 for his "balanced and comprehensive coverage of South Africa."

BIOGRAPHICAL/CRITICAL SOURCES:

PERIODICALS

Los Angeles Times, April 17, 1987.

*   *   *

PARKS, Tim(othy Harold) 1954-

BRIEF ENTRY: Born December 19, 1954, in Manchester, England. British educator, translator, and author. Park's first novel, *Tongues of Flame,* focusing on the disruption in a minister's family after his parish is agitated to religious hysteria, was rejected by twenty publishing houses before he entered it in the competition for the Sinclair Prize, awarded for an outstanding unpublished novel. It placed as a runner-up, and after Heinemann—one of the twenty original rejecters—published the book in 1985, it went on to win the prestigious Somerset Maugham and Betty Trask awards. Parks also won the John Llewellyn Rhys Memorial Prize for his second novel, *Loving Roger* (Heinemann, 1986), involving a clandestine and eventually violent love affair between Anna, a passive typist, and Roger, a typesetter and an aspiring but untalented writer. His third work, *Home Thoughts* (Collins, 1987), is written in epistolary form and centers on an English woman studying in Verona, Italy, and her relationships with other expatriates there. In addition to writing fiction, Parks translated two of Alberto Moravia's books from Italian, *Erotic Tales* (Farrar, Straus, 1986) and *The Voyeur* (Farrar, Straus, 1987), and teaches English in Verona. *Addresses: Home*—Via Casaletto 10, Montorio 37033, Verona, Italy. *Agent*—Watson, Little Ltd., 26 Charing Cross Rd., Suite 8, London WC2H 0DG, England.

BIOGRAPHICAL/CRITICAL SOURCES:

PERIODICALS

Los Angeles Times Book Review, January 30, 1987, January 24, 1988.
New York Times Book Review, January 4, 1987, January 10, 1988.

Times Literary Supplement, September 13, 1985, October 17, 1986, September 25, 1987.

* * *

PAROT, Joseph (John) 1940-

PERSONAL: Born June 4, 1940, in Hammond, Ind.; son of John and Louise Parot; married Barbara Przybysz, 1962; children: Mary Elizabeth, John Joseph. *Education:* St. Joseph's College, Rensselaer, Ind., B.A., 1963; DePaul University, M.A., 1967; Northern Illinois University, Ph.D., 1971.

ADDRESSES: Office—Department of History and Department of Social Science, Founders Library, Northern Illinois University, Dekalb, Ill. 60115.

CAREER: High school history teacher in Chicago, Ill., 1963-67; Northern Illinois University, Dekalb, 1967—, began as instructor, became assistant professor, associate professor, 1975-82, professor of history, 1982—, and head of department of social science. Instructor with Chicago Community Urban Opportunity Program, 1966-67; visiting professor at George Williams College, 1972-73.

MEMBER: American Historical Association, Polish American Historical Association, American Association of University Professors, Pi Gamma Mu.

AWARDS, HONORS: Oskar Halecki Award from Polish American Historical Association, 1983.

WRITINGS:

Polish Catholics in Chicago, 1850-1920: A Religious History, Northern Illinois University Press, 1981.

Contributor to *Dictionary of American Biography.* Contributor of articles and reviews to periodicals, including *Catholic Historical Review, Ethnicity, Illinois Historical Journal, Indiana Magazine of History, International Migration Review,* and *Polish American Studies.* Associate editor of *Polish-American Studies,* 1975—.

WORK IN PROGRESS: Assistant editor of *Historya Polska w Ameryce* (title means "Polish History in America"), two volumes, for Polish American Historical Association and Catholic University Press.

* * *

PASTOS, Spero 1940-

PERSONAL: Born February 18, 1940, in Chicago, Ill.; son of Vasillios (a candy maker) and Gregoria (Malanos) Pastos. *Education:* Northwestern University, B.S., 1962; University of California, Los Angeles, M.A., 1973. *Religion:* Greek Orthodox.

ADDRESSES: Agent—Ray Powers, 417 East 72nd St., New York, N.Y. 10036.

CAREER: Professional actor and singer, 1959-70; Los Angeles Board of Education, Los Angeles, Calif., special education teacher, 1970—.

WRITINGS:

Pin-Up: The Tragedy of Betty Grable, Putnam, 1986.

WORK IN PROGRESS: Liberace.

SIDELIGHTS: Spero Pastos's book *Pin-Up* is currently being adapted for a feature film on the life of actress Betty Grable.

Pastos told *CA:* "The reading of biographies, all kinds, have always been of great interest to me. Therefore the research involved in developing the life story of a celebrity was a challenge that put to the test all my skills of understanding and perceptions for human behavior. Initially I chose to write about Betty Grable because of the World War II era she personified. In recalling the 1940s, images of President Franklin Roosevelt, Iwo Jima, and Betty Grable interchangeably come to mind. What then were the social, political, and economic forces that led to the creation of a Grable pin-up?

"Grable, as I discovered, was a tragic person in that she was a victim of terrible circumstances which, when added to all her flaws of character, led to a life filled with bitterness, anger, and contempt. As an actress she appeared to be straightforward, independent, and a liberated woman of her times. She was all those things. But she was also an abused child, an abusive parent, and despairingly insecure despite her enormous success.

"My book on Liberace will also examine the life of the man from a sociopolitical point of view. Like Grable, his success was built on the results of conditions that helped shape his flamboyant image for illusion."

AVOCATIONAL INTERESTS: Collecting contemporary art.

* * *

PATEL, I(ndraprasad) G(ordhanbhai) 1924-

PERSONAL: Born November 11, 1924, in Sunav, India; son of Gordhanbhai and Kashiben Patel; married Alaknanda Dasgupta, 1958; children: Rehana. *Education:* Attended Baroda College; Bombay University, B.A. (with honors), 1944; King's College, Cambridge, B.A., 1946, Ph.D., 1949; also attended Harvard University, 1947-48.

ADDRESSES: Home—The Anchorage, 9 Clements Inn Passage, London WC2A 2HB, England. *Office*—Office of the Director, London School of Economics and Political Science, University of London, Houghton St., London WC2A 2AE, England.

CAREER: Maharaja Sayajirao University, Baroda, India, professor of economics and principal of Baroda College, 1949-50; International Monetary Fund, Washington, D.C., economist and assistant chief of Financial Problems and Policies Division, 1950-54, alternate executive director for India, 1958-61; Indian Ministry of Finance, New Delhi, deputy economic adviser, 1954-58, chief economic adviser, 1961-63, chief economic adviser, 1965-67, special secretary, 1968-69, secretary, 1970-72; United Nations Development Program, New York, N.Y., deputy administrator, 1972-77; Government Reserve Bank of India, Bombay, governor, 1977-82; Indian Institute of Man, Ahmedabad, director, 1982-84; University of London, London, England, director of London School of Economics and Political Science, 1984—. Economic adviser to Indian Planning Commission, 1961-63; visiting professor at Delhi School of Economics, 1964; member of board of directors of World Institute for Development Economics Research, Helsinki, Finland; member of council of Overseas Development Institute, London.

MEMBER: Royal Economic Society (member of council), Group of Thirty.

AWARDS, HONORS: D.Litt. from Sardar Patel University, 1979; honorary fellow of King's College, Cambridge, 1986.

WRITINGS:

Inflation—Should It Be Cured or Endured?, Gokhale Institute of Politics and Economics, 1983.
Essays on Economic Progress and Welfare, Oxford University Press, 1986.
Essays in Economic Policy and Economic Growth, St. Martin's, 1986.

Contributor to economic journals.

SIDELIGHTS: I. G. Patel told *CA:* "It is my conviction that recent changes in economic policy, particularly in relation to macroeconomic management and economic development, are to some extent justified as a corrective to earlier treatment, but have gone too far in the opposite direction. A new consensus is both necessary and feasible. My attempt generally is to try and develop such a consensus, not so much by research of my own, but by analyzing the results of current research and publications."

BIOGRAPHICAL/CRITICAL SOURCES:

PERIODICALS

Times Literary Supplement, July 31, 1987.

*   *   *

PATTERSON, June (Marie)   1924-

PERSONAL: Born June 8, 1924, in Elaine, Ark.; daughter of Ben F. (a farmer) and Jettie (Sparks) Patterson. *Education:* Texas State College for Women (now Texas Woman's University), B.S., 1946; Pennsylvania State University, M.A., 1950.

ADDRESSES: Home—10 Point Comfort, Waterford, Conn. 06385. *Office*—Department of Child Development, Connecticut College, New London, Conn. 06320.

CAREER: University of California, Los Angeles, clinical educationist, 1957-67; Yale University, New Haven, Conn., educational director of Child Study Center, 1967-71; Connecticut College, New London, professor of child development, 1970-86, professor emeritus, 1986—. Member of local Child and Family Board, 1980-85; Headstart consultant, 1972-86.

MEMBER: National Association for the Education of Young Children (member of board of directors, 1958-60), American Association of University Women.

WRITINGS:

(With Katherine Read Baker) *The Nursery School and Kindergarten: Human Relationships and Learning,* 7th edition, Holt, 1980.
(With Sally Provence and Audrey Naylor) *The Challenge of Daycare,* Yale University Press, 1982.

*   *   *

PATTERSON, Kevin   1956(?)-1988

OBITUARY NOTICE: Born c. 1956; died of complications from acquired immune deficiency syndrome (AIDS), March 18, 1988, in New York, N.Y. Theater press representative and playwright. Patterson represented many Broadway and Off-Broadway theater productions before becoming a press representative on the staff of the New York Shakespeare Festival. A graduate of Duke University who held a Master of Fine Arts degree from Rutgers University, Patterson also wrote plays,

including "A Most Secret War," "A Safe Harbor," and "Fascination Cha-Cha."

OBITUARIES AND OTHER SOURCES:

PERIODICALS

New York Times, March 22, 1988.

*   *   *

PEARCE, David (Robert)   1937-

PERSONAL: Born September 11, 1937, in Harrow, England; son of Percy Orlando (a musician) and Thurza (a housewife; maiden name, Thorne) Pearce. *Education:* Architectural Association School, Diploma, 1962. *Politics:* Conservative.

ADDRESSES: Home and office—109E Richmond Ave., London N1 0LR, England.

CAREER: Chartered architect in London, England, 1963-70; *Architects' Journal,* London, journalist, 1970; architect in government research with University Grants Committee, 1970-72; Builder Group (publishers), London, assistant editor of *Building* magazine, 1971, editor of *Built Environment* magazine, 1972-75, director of George Godwin Books, 1974-78; public relations officer of National Building Agency, 1975-78; Society for the Protection of Ancient Buildings, London, secretary, 1978-83; *Architect* magazine, London, editor, 1986-87; writer.

MEMBER: Save Britain's Heritage (founding committee member; vice-chairman, 1975-80).

AWARDS, HONORS: Leverhulme scholar, 1957.

WRITINGS:

(Editor with Marcus Binney, and contributor) *Railway Architecture,* Orbis, 1979.
The Great Houses of London, Vendome, 1986 (published in England as *London's Mansions: The Palatial Houses of the Nobility,* Batsford, 1986).
London: Capital City, photographs by Derek Forss, Batsford, 1988.

Also author and illustrator of short guidebooks for teenagers, for the National Trust for England. Contributor of about five hundred articles and reviews to architecture and design journals, including *Building Design.*

WORK IN PROGRESS: A book on conservation, its origins, the motivation for conservation, and its recent history, publication by Routledge & Kegan Paul expected in 1989.

SIDELIGHTS: David Pearce told *CA:* "I set out to be a 'modern architect.' About 1970 I returned to a teenage passion for history, and I became chiefly interested in architectural conservation. Why, at the end of the twentieth century, is there an intense interest in 'heritage?' As usual, I am seeking to clarify my thoughts by writing about the subject."

BIOGRAPHICAL/CRITICAL SOURCES:

PERIODICALS

Spectator, November 1, 1986.
Times Literary Supplement, October 31, 1986.

PEARSALL, (F.) Paul

PERSONAL: Education—University of Michigan, B.A., 1963; Wayne State University, received M.A., Ph.D., 1968.

ADDRESSES: Office—Department of Psychology, Henry Ford Community College, 5101 Evergreen Rd., Dearborn, Mich. 48128.

CAREER: Sinai Hospital of Detroit, Detroit, Mich., director of Problems of Daily Living Clinic. Lecturer at Henry Ford Community College and Wayne State University; director of Kinsey Summer Institute.

WRITINGS:

Superimmunity: Master Your Emotions and Improve Your Health, McGraw, 1986.
Super Marital Sex: Loving for Life, McGraw, 1987.
Super Joy: Delight in Daily Living, Doubleday, 1988.

BIOGRAPHICAL/CRITICAL SOURCES:

PERIODICALS

Times (London), October 29, 1987.

*   *   *

PEARSON, Lionel (Ignatius Cusack)   1908-1988

OBITUARY NOTICE—See index for *CA* sketch: Some sources spell middle name Cussack; born January 30, 1908, in London, England; died of pancreatic cancer, September 18, 1988, in Menlo Park (one source says Stanford), Calif. Classical scholar, educator, translator, editor, and author. Pearson was a professor of classics at Stanford University from 1940 to 1973 except for three years during World War II, when he served with the British Army Intelligence Corps. Previously he taught such subjects as Greek, Latin, and classics at the universities of Glasgow and Sydney, Dalhousie and Yale universities, and the New York State College of Teachers. He was awarded a Guggenheim fellowship in 1957. Pearson's writings include *The Art of Demosthenes, The Commentary of Didymus on Demosthenes, The Greek Historians of the West: Timaeus and His Predecessors, Selected Papers,* and *Aristoxenus: The Elements of Harmony,* completed just prior to his death. He also translated and edited, with F. Sandbach, Plutarch's *On the Malice of Herodotus,* edited, with S. A. Stephens, *Didymus, in Demosthenem Commenta,* and edited *Demosthenes: Six Private Orations, Text and Commentary.*

OBITUARIES AND OTHER SOURCES:

BOOKS

Directory of American Scholars, Volume III: *Foreign Languages, Linguistics, and Philology,* 8th edition, Bowker, 1982.
The Writer's Directory: 1988-1990, St. James Press, 1988.

PERIODICALS

Chicago Tribune, September 23, 1988.
New York Times, September 22, 1988.
Washington Post, September 22, 1988.

*   *   *

PERL, William R.   1906-

PERSONAL: Born in 1906 in Prague, Czechoslovakia; immigrated to United States, 1941, naturalized citizen, 1943; son of Rudolf and Camilla (Fischer) Perl; married Lore Rollig (a housewife), April 17, 1938. *Education:* College of Economics, Vienna, Austria, M.A., 1928; University of Vienna, Ph.D., 1931; Columbia University, M.A. (psychology), 1950.

ADDRESSES: Home—3901 Harrison Rd., Beltsville, Md. 20705. *Agent*—William Morris Agency, 1350 Avenue of the Americas, New York, N.Y. 10019.

CAREER: Practiced law in Vienna, Austria, 1930-38; organized the release of Jews incarcerated by the Nazi Party and the immigration of 40,000 Jews to Palestine, 1938-41; self-employed, 1946-50; Department of Welfare, Washington, D.C., chief psychologist, 1958-68; retired from civil service, 1968. Professorial lecturer in psychology at George Washington University, 1958-68; lecturer at American University; consultant to Walter Reed Medical Center; consultant to Nebraska Legislature for Crime and Delinquency. Chairman of Jewish Defense League of Greater Washington, 1970-73, and of Jewish Defense League of America, 1973-75. *Military service:* U.S. Army, active duty, 1942-46 and 1950-58; became lieutenant colonel; received Commendation Ribbon with four battle stars.

MEMBER: American Psychological Association, New York Academy of Sciences.

AWARDS, HONORS: Medal from State of Israel, 1980; Book of the Month award from Young Leadership Board of United Jewish Appeal, 1981, for *The Four Front War;* Scroll of Honor from State of Israel, 1983, for "exceptional leadership and dedication on behalf of the economy of the State of Israel"; Commendation from California Senate, 1984, for "his illustrious record of professional and civic accomplishments"; Distinguished Service Award from the Simon Wiesenthal Center of Yeshiva University, 1984, "for his decades of service to the Jewish people and humanity."

WRITINGS:

The Four Front War: From the Holocaust to the Promised Land, Crown, 1979, revised and expanded edition published as *Operation Action,* Ungar, 1981.
The Holocaust Conspiracy, Shapolsky, 1988.

Contributor to professional and military journals, including *American Journal of Psychiatry, International Journal of Social Psychiatry, Journal of Group Psychotherapy,* and *Psychiatric Archives.*

SIDELIGHTS: William R. Perl told *CA:* "*The Holocaust Conspiracy* refutes the general assumption that the nations of the world stood idly by while the Germans committed mass murders. It was not inaction but deliberate action in support of the German plan that contributed to the unfortunate effect of the Holocaust. The Germans set the house aflame and the 'free nations' blocked the escape gates, doing that in collaboration with each other."

*   *   *

PERRY, Regenia (Alfreda)   1941-

PERSONAL: Born March 30, 1941, in Virgilina, Va. *Education:* Virginia State College (now University), B.S., 1961; Western (now Case Western) Reserve University, M.A., 1962, Ph.D., 1966; further graduate study at University of Pennsylvania, 1963-64; postdoctoral study at Yale University, 1970-71.

ADDRESSES: Home—2200 West Grace St., Richmond, Va. 23220. *Office*—Department of Art, Virginia Commonwealth University, 922 West Franklin St., Richmond, Va. 23284.

CAREER: Howard University, Washington, D.C., assistant professor of art history, 1965-66; Indiana State University, Terre Haute, assistant professor of art history, 1966-67; Virginia Commonwealth University, Richmond, professor of art history, 1967—. Visiting lecturer at University of Maryland at College Park, summers, 1965-66, Georgetown University, summers, 1966-67, and Harvard University, spring, 1976; visiting scholar at Piedmont University Center, 1971-72. Metropolitan Museum of Art, guest curator of American Wing, 1975-76, organizer of exhibition "Selections of Nineteenth-Century Afro-American Art," 1976; member of board of directors of Federated Arts Council, 1981—; member of Richmond Mayor's Economics of Amenity Committee, 1981—.

MEMBER: College Art Association of America, Society of Architectural Historians, American Museum Association, American Association of University Professors, African-American Museum Association, Studio Museum (New York, N.Y.), James Van Der Zee Institute (member of board of directors).

AWARDS, HONORS: Danforth fellow at Yale University, 1969-70; grant from Eastern Virginia International Studies Consortium, 1974; Andrew W. Mellon fellow at Metropolitan Museum of Art, 1975-76; fellow of Ford Foundation, 1984-85.

WRITINGS:

James Van Der Zee, Photographer (monograph), Morgan & Morgan, 1973.
The Folk Tradition in Black American Art, University Press of Mississippi, 1975.
(With John Beardsley) *Black Folk Art in America, 1930-1980,* University Press of Mississippi, 1982.

Also author of *A History of Black-American Art, 1619-1983.*

Contributor of articles and reviews to magazines and newspapers.

* * *

PETERS, Michael
    See HORNSBY-SMITH, Michael P(eter)

* * *

PETERSON, A(lexander) D(uncan) C(ampbell) 1908-1988

OBITUARY NOTICE—See index for *CA* sketch: Born September 13, 1908, in Edinburgh, Scotland; died October 17, 1988. Educator, administrator, intelligence officer, editor, and author. Peterson will be best remembered for his influential role in international education. He began his forty-year career in the field as an assistant schoolmaster at a private boys' school and went on to become headmaster of a number of other secondary schools in England before joining Oxford University, where he served for fifteen years as director of the university's department of education. He later headed the fledgling International Baccalaureate Office until his retirement in 1977, and was subsequently appointed vice-president of the International Council of the United World Colleges. In addition, Peterson helped found the United World College of the Atlantic. Made an officer of the Order of the British Empire in 1946, he served with the propaganda branch of the Special Operations Exec-

utive during World War II. In the postwar years Peterson headed the information services of the Federation of Malaya, and was chairman of the Army Education Board from 1959 until 1966. His writings include *The Far East, The Future of Education,* and *Schools Across Frontiers.* He also edited the three-volume *Techniques of Teaching* and was editor in chief of the journal *Comparative Education* from 1964 until 1977.

OBITUARIES AND OTHER SOURCES:

BOOKS

Who's Who, 140th edition, St. Martin's, 1988.

PERIODICALS

Times (London), October 19, 1988.

* * *

PHILLIPS, David Atlee 1922-1988 (George Spelvin)

OBITUARY NOTICE—See index for *CA* sketch: Born October 31, 1922, in Fort Worth, Tex.; died of cancer, July 7, 1988, in Bethesda, Md.; buried in Arlington National Cemetery, Arlington, Va. Actor, intelligence officer, lecturer, publisher, editor, and author. In 1975, when he was chief of the Western Hemisphere Division of the Central Intelligence Agency (CIA), Phillips retired, ending his more than twenty-five-year career with the agency. Prompted by the revelation the year before that the CIA was illegally spying on American citizens, Phillips left government employment to establish the Association of Former Intelligence Officers, an organization devoted to explaining to the public the nature of the CIA and to defending its actions.

Phillips was an actor in New York City prior to serving with the U.S. Army Air Force during World War II. After the war he studied in Chile, where he published and edited the *South Pacific Mail,* an English-language newspaper. There he was recruited by the CIA, and went on to participate in clandestine operations in the Dominican Republic, Cuba, and Chile from the 1950s to the early 1970s. His writings include an account of his career with the CIA, *The Night Watch: Twenty-five Years of Peculiar Service,* two novels, *The Carlos Contract* and *The Great Texas Murder Trials,* the children's play "Meet Romeo Morgan," *Careers in Secret Operations,* and *Counterterrorist.* Beginning in 1986 he served as editor of *International Journal of Intelligence and Counterintelligence,* and, under the pseudonym George Spelvin, he edited *Periscope,* a quarterly magazine for intelligence professionals. In 1984 he founded Stone Trail Press.

OBITUARIES AND OTHER SOURCES:

BOOKS

Who's Who in America, 45th edition, Marquis, 1988.
The Writers Directory: 1986-1988, St. James Press, 1986.

PERIODICALS

Chicago Tribune, July 11, 1988.
New York Times, July 11, 1988.

* * *

PIERSEN, William D. 1942-

PERSONAL: Born April 15, 1942, in Highland Park, Ill.; son of Benjamin G. (a real estate broker) and Katherine A. (a housewife; maiden name, Dillon) Piersen; married Charlotte L. Graham (a librarian), August 3, 1968; children: Katherine L. *Education:* Grinnell College, B.A., 1964; Indiana University—Bloomington, M.A., 1967, M.A., 1968, Ph.D., 1975.

ADDRESSES: Home—405 Arrowwood Dr., Nashville, Tenn. 37211. *Office*—Department of History, Fisk University, 17th Ave. N., Nashville, Tenn. 37208.

CAREER: Purdue University, Calumet Campus, Hammond, Ind., instructor in history, 1971-73; Springfield College, Springfield, Mass., instructor in history, 1974-75; Texas Tech University, Lubbock, visiting assistant professor of history, 1976-77; Fisk University, Nashville, Tenn., assistant professor, 1977-84, associate professor, 1985-88, professor of history, 1988—, chairman of department, 1980-87.

MEMBER: American Historical Association, Organization of American Historians, African Studies Association, Association for the Study of Afro-American Life and History, Tennessee Conference of Historians, Tennessee Folklore Society.

WRITINGS:

Black Yankees: The Development of an Afro-American Subculture in Eighteenth-Century New England, University of Massachusetts Press, 1988.

Contributor of more than 370 articles and abstracts to history journals.

WORK IN PROGRESS: A study of African cultural influence in America, publication expected in 1990; a monograph on African and Afro-American royalty in the Americas; a brief introductory world history textbook.

SIDELIGHTS: William D. Piersen told *CA:* "Most of my writings argue that the history of the Americas cannot be understood without knowledge of the African cultural legacy. So it has been with *Black Yankees: The Development of an Afro-American Subculture in Eighteenth-Century New England,* which began as a doctoral dissertation combining my interests in African and American studies with my background in folklore. I picked New England to study because that region was home to a number of festivals honoring black kings and governors elected by the local population. Soon I discovered that New England's town histories were also rife with remembrances of black folk life and humor taken from local traditions. The region's historians had used this folklore for local color, but, at the same time, they were leaving sketches of early yankee life drawn from a long-neglected perspective. The view from New England's black subculture suggests that political power is vastly overrated in historical importance and that common people are ultimately wiser, and surely funnier, than the hypocritical 'great men' who seek to rule over them."

*   *   *

PINDER, Leslie Hall
   See HALL, Leslie

*   *   *

PINKA, Patricia G(arland)   1935-

PERSONAL: Born February 27, 1935, in Pittsburgh, Pa.; daughter of Edward S. (a lawyer) and R. Isabelle (a secretary; maiden name, Mathias) Garland; married Donald A. Nicolson, July 23, 1957 (divorced); married John B. Pinka (a social work administrator), May 21, 1966; children: (second marriage) Grant Garland. *Education:* University of Pittsburgh, B.A., 1956, Ph.D., 1969; San Francisco State College (now University), M.A., 1964.

ADDRESSES: Home—5476 Leather Stocking Lane, Stone Mountain, Ga. 30087. *Office*—Department of English, Agnes Scott College, Decatur, Ga. 30030.

CAREER: Valley Daily News, Tarentum, Pa., reporter, 1956-57; *Alameda Times Star,* Alameda, Calif., reporter, 1959-60; high school English teacher in Alameda, 1960-64; Point Park College, Pittsburgh, Pa., instructor in English, 1966-67; Agnes Scott College, Decatur, Ga., assistant professor, 1969-76, associate professor, 1976-82, professor of English, 1982—.

MEMBER: Modern Language Association of America, American Association of University Women (past vice-president), South Atlantic Modern Language Association, John Donne Society, Milton Society.

AWARDS, HONORS: Andrew Mellon fellow, 1968-69; grants from National Endowment for the Humanities, 1976 and 1985.

WRITINGS:

(Contributor) Margaret W. Pepperdene, editor, *That Subtile Wreath,* Agnes Scott College, 1976.
This Dialogue of One: The Songs and Sonnets of John Donne, University of Alabama Press, 1983.
(Contributor) Claude Summers and Ted-Larry Pebworth, editors, *Bright Shootes of Everlastingnesse,* University of Missouri Press, 1987.

WORK IN PROGRESS: Research on the relationship between meditation and the essays of Francis Bacon.

SIDELIGHTS: Patricia G. Pinka told *CA:* "My favorite professor, the late Charles Crow, sparked my interest in John Donne, indeed in seventeenth-century literature. Donne first appealed to me because he combines the language of science and mathematics with the emotions of love and Christian devotion and doubt. I had always liked mathematics and especially chemistry as a young woman. Donne was a poet who shared my interests—modified, of course, by four hundred years of scientific knowledge."

*   *   *

PITT, David G(eorge)   1921-

PERSONAL: Born December 12, 1921, in Musgravetown, Newfoundland, Canada; son of Thomas J. (a clergyman) and Edith F. (a teacher; maiden name, Way) Pitt; married Marion Woolfrey (a teacher), June 5, 1946; children: Ruth Pitt Francis, Robert. *Education:* Mount Allison University, B.A., 1946; University of Toronto, M.A., 1948, Ph.D., 1960. *Politics:* Independent. *Religion:* United Church of Canada.

ADDRESSES: Home—7 Chestnut Pl., St. John's, Newfoundland, Canada A1B 2T1. *Office*—Department of English, Memorial University of Newfoundland, St. John's, Newfoundland, Canada A1C 5S7.

CAREER: Memorial University of Newfoundland, St. John's, associate professor, 1949-60, professor, 1960-83, professor emeritus of English, 1983—, head of department, 1970-82.

MEMBER: Humanities Association of Canada, Association of Canadian University Teachers of English.

AWARDS, HONORS: Medal for biography from University of British Columbia, 1984, for *E. J. Pratt: The Truant Years.*

WRITINGS:

Windows of Agates (history), Jesperson Press, 1966.
On E. J. Pratt (critical essays), Ryerson Press, 1969.
Goodly Heritage (history), Jesperson Press, 1984.
E. J. Pratt: The Truant Years (biography), University of Toronto Press, 1984.
E. J. Pratt: The Master Years (biography), University of Toronto Press, 1987.
Towards the First Spike: The Evolution of a Poet (bio-criticism), Memorial University of Newfoundland, 1987.

WORK IN PROGRESS: The Collected Letters of E. J. Pratt, for University of Toronto Press.

SIDELIGHTS: David G. Pitt told *CA:* ''Having tried writing both fiction and history, I find biography the most satisfying genre in which to work, combining as it does the techniques of the fiction writer with the skills of the historian. For the same reason, biography is my favorite reading matter.''

Much of Pitt's work examines the life of E. J. Pratt, one of Canada's most widely known poets and author of the epic poems ''Brebeuf and his Brethren,'' ''Towards the Last Spike,'' and ''The Titanic.'' The two-volume biography *E. J. Pratt: The Truant Years* and *E. J. Pratt: The Master Years* was described by William French in the *Globe and Mail* as ''judicious, sympathetic yet clear-eyed, elegantly written and exhaustively researched'' in its portrayal of Pratt as family man, professor, editor of *Canadian Poetry Magazine,* popular public figure, and poet.

AVOCATIONAL INTERESTS: Music and reading.

BIOGRAPHICAL/CRITICAL SOURCES:

BOOKS

de Leon, Lisa, *Writers of Newfoundland and Labrador,* Jesperson Press, 1984.

PERIODICALS

American Review of Canadian Studies, summer, 1985.
Canadian Literature, autumn, 1985.
English Studies in Canada, December, 1986.
Globe and Mail (Toronto), December 1, 1984, December 5, 1987.
Quill and Quire, August, 1987.
Toronto Star, November 10, 1984, December 19, 1987.
University of Toronto Quarterly, summer, 1985.

* * *

PLASKOW, Judith (Ellen) 1947-

PERSONAL: Born March 14, 1947, in Brooklyn, N.Y.; married, 1969; children: one. *Education:* Clark University, A.B., 1968; Yale University, M.Phil., 1971, Ph.D., 1975.

ADDRESSES: Home—64-53 Bell Blvd., Bayside, N.Y. 11364. *Office*—Department of Religious Studies, Manhattan College, College Parkway, Riverdale, N.Y. 10471.

CAREER: New York University, New York, N.Y., assistant professor of religion, 1974-75; Wichita State University, Wichita, Kan., assistant professor of religion, 1976-79; Manhattan College, Riverdale, N.Y., assistant professor of religion, 1979—.

MEMBER: American Academy of Religion, Society for Values in Higher Education, Women's Caucus for Religious Studies.

WRITINGS:

(Editor with Joan Arnold Romero) *Women and Religion: Papers of the Working Group on Women and Religion, 1972-1973,* revised edition, American Academy of Religion, 1974.
(Contributor) Rita M. Gross, editor, *Beyond Androcentrism: New Essays on Women and Religion,* Scholars Press, 1977.
(Editor with Carol P. Christ) *Womanspirit Rising: A Feminist Reader in Religion,* Harper, 1979.
Sex, Sin, and Grace: Women's Experience and the Theologies of Reinhold Niebuhr and Paul Tillich, University Press of America, 1980.

Contributor to journals, including *Response.*

BIOGRAPHICAL/CRITICAL SOURCES:

PERIODICALS

New York Times Book Review, July 29, 1979.*

* * *

POIRIER, Louis 1910-
(Julien Gracq)

PERSONAL: Born July 27, 1910, in St. Florent le Vieil, Maine-et-Loire, France; son of Emmanuel (a merchant) and Alice (a merchant; maiden name, Belliard) Poirier. *Education:* Ecole des Sciences Politiques, diplome, 1933; Ecole Normale Superieure, agregation d'histoire, 1934.

ADDRESSES: Home—61 rue de Grenelle, 75007 Paris, France.

CAREER: Professor of history at numerous public schools in French cities, including Nantes, Quimper, Amiens, and Angers, and assistant to the faculty of Caen University, Normandy, France, 1935-47; Lycee Claude Bernard, Paris, France, professor of history, 1947-70. Guest professor of literature at the University of Wisconsin, Madison, 1970. Writer, 1939—. *Military service:* French Army, infantry, 1939-40; became lieutenant; taken prisoner during defense of the port of Dunkerque; repatriated to France, 1941.

AWARDS, HONORS: Prix Goncourt, 1951, for *Le Rivage des Syrtes* (refused by author).

WRITINGS:

UNDER PSEUDONYM JULIEN GRACQ

Au chateau d'Argol, Corti, c. 1938, translation by Louise Varese published as *The Castle of Argol,* J. Laughlin, c. 1951.
Un Beau tenebreux, Corti, 1945, translation by W. J. Strachan published as *A Dark Stranger,* New Directions, c. 1950.
Liberte grande (prose poems), Corti, 1946.
Andre Breton: Quelques aspects de l'ecrivain, Corti, 1948.
Le Roi pecheur (three-act play; first produced in Paris at Theatre Montparnasse, 1949), Corti, 1948, translation by Rollo H. Myers and E. J. King Bull issued on microfilm as ''The Fisher King,'' Columbia University, 1957.
La Litterature a l'estomac (nonfiction), Corti, 1950.
Le Rivage des Syrtes (novel; title means ''The Bay of Syrtes''), Corti, 1951, translation by Richard Howard published as *The Opposing Shore,* Columbia University Press, 1986.

Un Balcon en foret, Corti, 1958, translation by Howard published as *Balcony in the Forest,* Braziller, 1959, reprinted, Columbia University Press, 1987.

Preferences, Corti, 1961, new enlarged edition, 1969.

(Translator) Heinrich von Kleist, *Penthesilee,* Corti, 1966.

Lettrines, Corti, 1967.

La Presqu'ile (contains *La Presqu'ile, La Route* [also see below], and *Le Roi Cophetua*), Corti, 1970.

Lettrines 2, Corti, 1974.

Les Eaux etroites, Corti, 1976.

En lisant, en ecrivant, Corti, 1981.

La Route (novella), illustrations by Jean Solombre, Broutta, 1981 (also see above).

La Forme d'une ville, Corti, 1985.

SIDELIGHTS: French novelist, playwright, and poet Louis Poirier is famous for weaving elements of history, myth, and allegory into his work. A former teacher of history, Poirier writes under the pseudonym Julien Gracq, a name that hearkens back to the age of the ancient Roman orator and reformer, Gracchus. Critics agree that through his writings, Poirier asserts the superiority of a stable, natural universe—one that exists independent of man—over the impermanence and transiency of all that is human.

Poirier made his literary debut with *Au chateau d'Argol* during the 1930s, when the literary and artistic movement known as surrealism was fashionable. According to Elisabeth Cardonne-Arlyck in an article for the *New York Times Book Review,* Andre Breton, the French writer, critic, and founder of the surrealistic movement in France, considered *Au chateau d'Argol* to be the first truly surrealistic novel. Much debate exists, however, as to whether or not Poirier should be thought of as a surrealist. Proponents of the movement were dedicated to the free and dreamlike expression of the imagination. Although critics saw a seed of surrealism in Poirier's works that reflected a faith in the potential of the human mind, Cardonne-Arlyck argued that *Au chateau d'Argol* was "in fact, a departure from [surrealism]." Since surrealistic writers emphasize the associations and implications of words rather than their literal meanings, writings produced during the movement are considered to be obscure. Poirier, Cardonne-Arlyck asserted, diverged from the surrealistic style with "an idiosyncratic blend of linear storytelling and poetic reliance on language." Alluding to statements the author had made concerning the debate, Cardonne-Arlyck concluded that Poirier admired the movement, but "never joined" it.

Poirier first became well known outside of France in 1951 when he was awarded the Prix Goncourt for his novel *Le Rivage des Syrtes,* the story of two imaginary countries engaged in a three-century-long war. Designed to honor a prose work that exhibits originality of form and spirit, the Prix Goncourt is the highest literary prize offered in France. Poirier, who censured writers for accepting literary awards in his essay *La Litterature a l'estomac,* refused the laurel. His fourteen-dollar cash prize was donated to a fund for disadvantaged writers.

Le Rivage des Syrtes was not published in English until thirty-five years after its first release in France. The critically acclaimed translation by Richard Howard, entitled *The Opposing Shore,* is said to retain the semantic and imaginative brilliance of the original French version. Its plot centers on two fictitious countries, Orsenna and Farghestan, whose failure to communicate has perpetuated a state of war for three hundred years. Aldo, Poirier's protagonist and narrator, is an Orsennian eager to cross the line that divides the countries. In a review for the *Los Angeles Times,* Francis McConnel theorized that "Aldo's obsession with the mysterious Farghestan and his longings to break through and to make contact represent Orsenna's desire to embrace the void, to invite disaster, and with it, destiny." Several critics also point to blatant sexual overtones in the text, symbolic of what reviewer Cardonne-Arlyck called Poirier's "acute delight in the physical world."

Poirier admitted in an interview with Richard Bernstein for the *New York Times Book Review* that the ideas for his novels, though veiled in myth and allegory, grow out of a concern for particular historical circumstances. Fascism, a totalitarian political philosophy that holds the concerns of the state above those of the individual and strictly controls all aspects of its citizens' lives, was on the rise in Germany shortly before Poirier began writing. The eventual German occupation of France during World War II is thought to have moved the author to write *Le Rivage des Syrtes.*

The 1970 publication of three novellas under the title *La Presqu'ile* preserved Poirier's reputation as an accomplished and sensitive writer and supported an evaluation of the author that appeared in an article for the *Times Literary Supplement* almost two decades earlier. In the article, Poirier was described as a writer who believes "that the business of novelists is to give new meanings to old myths and not to describe and judge the world which surrounds them." It is Poirier's trademark to offer only a concrete description of his characters' thoughts and encounters in his writings, leaving an interpretation of those descriptions to his reader. The protagonists in each of the three stories contained in *La Presqu'ile* are isolated and detached, unable to relate to the world around them. In a review of the collection written for the *Times Literary Supplement,* Poirier was praised for his "intense, absorbing descriptions," his ability to "exteriorize the inner world of characters," and his "superbly sustained evocative writing."

In his last novel, *La Forme d'une ville,* Poirier conjures up images of the French town of Nantes where he was a boarder at the *lycee Clemenceau* in the 1920s. The author "makes clear," wrote Philip Thody in the *Times Literary Supplement,* that "this is a fragment of autobiography presented as a portrait of the town." Richard Cobb, writing for the *Spectator,* characterized the book as "the vague muffled perception of a city, its movements, its noises, the clatter of its cream-coloured trams, its lowering or brilliant skies, its mists and fogs, as filtered through the high barrack-like walls and the closed iron gates of the grim *lycee.*" Critics applauded the rich and visually lustrous prose Poirier used to convey his impressions of the city from behind the school's walls.

In his interview with Bernstein for the *New York Times Book Review,* Poirier claimed that his writings are "based on elements furnished by the memory" and function "to give form, stability, and precision to things that are vague in the mind." Finding the work of a novelist too draining after the age of seventy-five, the author brought his fiction-writing career to a close with the publication of *La Forme d'une ville* in 1985.

AVOCATIONAL INTERESTS: Chess.

BIOGRAPHICAL/CRITICAL SOURCES:

BOOKS

Contemporary Literary Criticism, Volume 48, Gale, 1988.

Denis, Ariel, *Julien Gracq,* Seghers, 1978.

Hoy, Peter, *Essai de bibliographie sur Julien Gracq: 1938-1972*, Grant & Cutler, 1973.

PERIODICALS

Los Angeles Times, July 3, 1986.
New Yorker, December 15, 1951.
New York Times Book Review, June 22, 1986.
Spectator, December 7, 1985.
Times Literary Supplement, August 29, 1952, July 16, 1970, August 30, 1985.
Washington Post Book World, July 27, 1986.

—*Sketch by Barbara K. Carlisle*

* * *

PONGE, Francis (Jean Gaston Alfred) 1899-1988

OBITUARY NOTICE—See index for *CA* sketch: Born March 27, 1899, in Montpellier, France; died August 6 (one source says August 7), 1988, in Le Bar-sur-Loup, Maritime Alps, France. Secretary, educator, editor, and author. Ponge's surrealist poetry was considered by philosopher Jean-Paul Sartre, quoted in the *Chicago Tribune,* to be "the most curious and perhaps the most important of the age." Ponge is best known for his "thing-poetry," characteristic of which was extensive and exhaustive description of a simple object such as a stone, a cigarette, or a plant. Although his first poetry collection, *Douze Petits Ecrits,* was published in 1926, he only began to receive wide acclaim in 1942 when his second book, *The Voice of Things,* was issued. His most famous work is his long poem of 1967 titled *Soap.*

A secretary for Parisian publishing houses briefly in the early 1920s and again during the 1930s, Ponge became a professor at Paris's Alliance Francaise in 1952, a position he held for twelve years. Later he was a visiting professor of French at Barnard College and Columbia University. He explained his poetic philosophy in a 1961 book of essays, *The Grand Collection.* His other works include *Rain: A Prose Poem, The Sun Placed in the Abyss and Other Texts, The Power of Language: Texts and Translations,* and *Georges Braque,* a biography of the painter. A member of the French Resistance during World War II, Ponge also edited one of its newspapers, *Progres de Lyon.* He won numerous national and international literary awards, including the grand prize for poetry from the French Academy in 1972.

OBITUARIES AND OTHER SOURCES:

BOOKS

Contemporary Foreign Language Writers, St. Martin's, 1984.
The International Who's Who, 51st edition, Europa, 1987.

PERIODICALS

Chicago Tribune, August 10, 1988.
New York Times, August 9, 1988.
Times (London), August 11, 1988.
Washington Post, August 10, 1988.

* * *

POPE, Generoso Paul, Jr. 1927-1988

OBITUARY NOTICE: Born January 13, 1927, in New York, N.Y.; died after suffering a heart attack, October 2, 1988, in Atlantis (some sources say West Palm Beach), Fla. Publisher and editor. Pope will be remembered for his longtime ownership of the *National Enquirer,* a supermarket tabloid known for sensational headlines and fantastic stories. Scorned by more conventional newspapers despite its success, the *Enquirer* has also been the object of many highly publicized lawsuits, including those filed by entertainers Carol Burnett, Frank Sinatra, and Cary Grant. Pope graduated from the Massachusetts Institute of Technology at the age of nineteen and began a four-year stint as editor of his father's newspaper, the Italian-language *Il Progresso,* in 1947. In 1952 he bought the *New York Enquirer,* which then featured pieces on politics, sports, and theater. Detecting the mass appeal of gore, Pope gave the newspaper a new focus on mutilation, murder, and bizarre accidents and renamed it. In the late 1960s the publisher targeted the *Enquirer* toward housewives, changing its style again to include stories on consumerism, entertainment, and inspiration. The paper has since flourished, achieving a circulation of more than four million and helping build Pope's personal fortune to an estimated 150 million dollars.

OBITUARIES AND OTHER SOURCES:

PERIODICALS

Chicago Tribune, October 3, 1988.
Los Angeles Times, October 3, 1988.
New York Times, October 3, 1988.
Washington Post, October 3, 1988.

* * *

PORITZ, Lily
See MILLER, Lily Poritz

* * *

POWELL, Padgett 1952-

PERSONAL: Born April 25, 1952, in Gainesville, Fla.; son of Albine Batts (a brewmaster) and Bettyre (a teacher; maiden name, Palmer) Powell; married Sidney Wade (a poet), May 22, 1984; children: Amanda Dahl. *Education:* College of Charleston, B.A., 1975; University of Houston, M.A., 1982.

ADDRESSES: Home—Gainesville, Fla. *Office*—Department of English, University of Florida, Gainesville, Fla. 32611. *Agent*—Lynn Nesbit, International Creative Management, 40 West 57th St., New York, N.Y. 10019.

CAREER: Freight handler, household mover, and orthodontic technician in the southern United States, including Jacksonville, Fla., Florence, S.C., and Charleston, S.C., 1968-75; day laborer in Houston, Tex., 1975; roofer in Texas, 1975-82; writer, 1983—; University of Florida, Gainesville, assistant professor in creative writing, 1984—.

MEMBER: Authors Guild, Writers Guild of America, East.

AWARDS, HONORS: Edisto named one of the year's five best books, 1984, by *Time;* American Book Award nominee for first fiction, 1984, and Whiting Foundation Writers' Award, 1986, both for *Edisto;* American Academy and Institute of Arts and Letters Rome Fellowship in Literature, 1986 and 1988.

WRITINGS:

Edisto (novel), Farrar, Straus, 1984.
"Edisto" (screenplay; adapted by Powell from his own novel), Metro-Goldwyn-Mayer/United Artists, 1985.
A Woman Named Drown (novel), Farrar, Straus, 1987.

(Contributor) Alex Harris, editor, *A World Unsuspected: Portraits of Southern Childhood,* University of North Carolina Press, 1987.

Contributor of stories to periodicals, including *Esquire* and *Grand Street.*

WORK IN PROGRESS: Of Chiropractors, Come-back Boxers, and Other Human Dainties, a nonfiction collection, publication expected in 1988; *Letter from a Dogfighter's Aunt, Deceased,* a novel, for Farrar, Straus; *Mr. Irony,* a novel, publication by Farrar, Straus expected in 1990.

SIDELIGHTS: Padgett Powell burst onto the literary scene in 1984 with his first novel, entitled *Edisto.* A college chemistry major turned day-laborer and roofer, Powell nurtured his literary aspirations by reading American novelist William Faulkner's works in his spare time and eventually enrolled in the University of Houston's creative writing graduate program. In the words of *Time* columnist R. Z. Sheppard, *Edisto,* which was Powell's master's thesis, showed that its author had "all the literary equipment for a new career: a peeled eye, a tuning-fork ear, and an innovative way with local color and regional dialect."

Critics have compared Powell's technique to that of the great American regional writers, including Mark Twain, Tennessee Williams, J. D. Salinger, Flannery O'Connor, and Faulkner. Although he has been influenced by the styles of past writers, Powell's mode of expression remains distinctive. Reviewing *Edisto* for the *Washington Post Book World,* Jonathan Yardley commented that much of the book is "so fresh and original; Padgett Powell clearly knows what he is doing, and he does it very well." And in a piece for the *New York Times Book Review,* Ron Loewinsohn similarly praised Powell, calling him "an extravagantly talented writer."

Named for the predominantly black, rural, backwater section of undeveloped South Carolina coastline near what the narrator calls the "architect-conceived, Arab-financed" Hilton Head, *Edisto* is a young man's episodic account of his unusual coming of age. Simons (pronounced Simmons) Manigault, the book's narrator, is a precocious, prepubescent twelve-year-old trapped in an incomprehensible world of adults. Simons's parents are separated and his college-professor mother, known among the local blacks as "the Duchess," has decided that her only son should be a writer. Simons is no ordinary child. He is, assessed R. Z. Sheppard of *Time,* "one of the most engaging fictional small fry ever to cry thief: sly, pungent, lyric, funny, and unlikely to be forgotten." In a review for *Newsweek,* Peter Prescott pointed to the "great comic effect" the author manages in his treatment of Simons: Powell endows his protagonist with a sophisticated sort of innocence that is at once poignant and amusing.

In return for his pursuit of literary knowledge, Simons' mother gives him free reign to do virtually anything he pleases. Simons frequents the Baby Grand, a predominantly black local bar whose clientele has dubbed the youth something of a folk hero. Simons explains, "I am a celebrity because I'm white, not even teenage yet, and possess the partial aura of the Duchess." The Duchess's aura, however, is informed by her drinking and promiscuity, both of which figure in her son's development.

It is not until Taurus, the Duchess's mysterious lover and Simons's substitute father, enters the story that the child, in a sense, becomes a man. Sybil Estess, writing for the *Southwest Review,* dubbed Taurus a "blessed intruder into [the] story"

who teaches Simons how to live fully in the present. Taurus inspires in Simons the courage to move on without knowing what might happen in the future. "Something is happening, happening all the time," Simons learns, and a life in Edisto is not what lies ahead for the boy. Taurus's influence allows Simons to willingly accept the changes he is about to encounter: by the end of the novel, Simons's parents reunite and the family moves to the cardboard world of Hilton Head. Taurus, having fulfilled his role as teacher in the story, exits Simons's life as unexpectedly as he had entered it.

Powell's pages are filled with the symbolism, colorful characters, and precise vernacular of past regionalist giants, but the young writer, as pointed out by Jonathan Yardley in his review for *Washington Post Book World,* has added "a new twist, and a most agreeable one." Avoiding the trap of sentimentality, Powell addresses the highly developed and commercial "new" South of the 1980s, "finds it imperfect—but accepts it anyway." An air of honesty permeates the author's advice to readers living on the brink of the twenty-first century: the "best thing to do," Powell tells us through Simons, "is to get on with it."

Edisto is ironic in its implication that one must learn the ways of the world in spite of one's parents. But more than an examination of a youth's rite of passage, the book, explained Peter Ross, writing for the *Detroit News,* is "a masterwork of invention, and even more of intelligent feeling, of emotion tempered by sound thinking." Robert Towers' evaluation of *Edisto* echoed Ross's enthusiastic response to Powell's first effort. Towers wrote in the *New York Times Review of Books* that he was "charmed by the book's wit and impressed by its originality. Some turn of phrase, some flash of humor, some freshly observed detail, some acutely rendered perception of a child's pain or a child's amazement transfigures nearly every page."

Powell's follow-up to *Edisto,* a novel entitled *A Woman Named Drown,* also fared well among the critics. Like its predecessor, Powell's second book explores conventional occurrences in unconventional terms.

Al, the narrator of *A Woman Named Drown,* has been called a grown-up version of *Edisto's* Simons Manigault. Al is working on his Ph.D. in inorganic chemistry when he receives a surprising good-bye letter from his girlfriend of six years. In reaction, he quickly moves in with a woman whom he hardly knows—an aging actress named Mary Constance Baker whose last role was the lead in a play entitled *A Woman Named Drown.* Mary uses Al as a substitute for her late husband, and after they roam around Florida together for a while, she leaves him in a motel to continue, in Powell's words, his "little downside sabbatical"—alone. Paul Gray of *Time* suggested that the book's hero "arrives back where he started a mildly wiser fellow."

A Woman Named Drown, as T. Coraghessan Boyle evaluated in the *New York Times Book Review,* recreates "the distinctive, understated humor that is Mr. Powell's signature. He presents a terrific, hyper-real dialogue in quick, bludgeoned pieces, and his narrator's phrasing and dialect are always surprising and inventive."

Critics suggest that part of Powell's appeal as a writer lies in his honest treatment of universal themes. His rare ability to attach an intangible moment of insight to a single, concrete experience adds intimacy and credence to his words. In "Hitting Back," an essay the author contributed to *A World Un-*

suspected, a collection of childhood memoirs edited by Alex Harris, Powell recalls an incident that sparked a transformation in the way he looked at the world: disapproving little Don, a so-called "friend," put dog excrement on the author's Sunday best. As Powell puts it, "I recall this as my very first instance of moral outrage."

In the same essay, Powell mourns the tainting of his southern junior-high-school innocence by the mindset of ignorant whites in positions of power. He and his friend were punished for breaking their school's segregated-sex rule on the bus, considered an indirect but effective way of keeping black boys away from white girls. Powell recollects with a sense of loss the naivete that inspired his befuddlement when asked if he knew why this rule existed. "That was precisely it," he recalls. "We couldn't begin to know."

In a phone interview with Andrea Stevens for the *New York Times Book Review,* Powell reflected upon himself, "I couldn't fit in ten years ago. I couldn't fit in twenty years ago. My interest remains with those who fail deliberately and those who can't help it." His third novel, entitled *Mr. Irony,* appears to be populated by the same odd personalities and inspired by the same preoccupation with the absurd that made this writer's past works so appealing.

Powell told *CA:* "Bad luck at fishing and worse with women made me what little writer I am. Had things turned out a bit differently, I'd be Doug Flutie. Reading William Faulkner's *Absalom! Absalom!* did it."

AVOCATIONAL INTERESTS: "My early interest in dog-fighting has swelled, you might say, since my stay in Turkey, to an interest in camel-wrestling. I will fish and drink beer, also."

BIOGRAPHICAL/CRITICAL SOURCES:

BOOKS

Contemporary Literary Criticism, Volume 34, Gale, 1984.
Harris, Alex, editor, *A World Unsuspected: Portraits of Southern Childhood,* University of North Carolina Press, 1987.
Powell, Padgett, *Edisto,* Farrar, Straus, 1984.
Powell, *A Woman Named Drown,* Farrar, Straus, 1987.

PERIODICALS

Books and Bookmen, October, 1984.
Detroit News, July 22, 1984.
Harper's, August, 1987.
Los Angeles Times, April 22, 1984.
New Republic, April 30, 1984.
Newsweek, April 16, 1984.
New York Review of Books, May 31, 1984.
New York Times, May 4, 1984, May 6, 1987.
New York Times Book Review, April 15, 1984, June 7, 1987.
Southwest Review, autumn, 1984.
Time, April 2, 1984, May 18, 1987.
Times (London), December 27, 1984.
Times Literary Supplement, August 31, 1984.
Washington Post Book World, March 28, 1984.

—*Sketch by Barbara K. Carlisle*

*　　　*　　　*

PRANTERA, Amanda 1942-

BRIEF ENTRY: Born April 23, 1942, in England. British author. Many critics consider Prantera a master of the modern gothic tale. Her first novel, *Strange Loop* (Dutton, 1984), cen-

ters on Ludwig, an aged Austrian philosopher who revisits an English convent where in his youth he had an affair with a woman who thought herself to be a werewolf. Prantera's subsequent work, *The Cabalist* (J. Cape, 1985), an account of the last days of a dying sorcerer in Italy, was judged "an impressive blend of acute characterization, occult mysteries, and cool, detached humour" by Miranda Seymour in the *Times Literary Supplement.* Prantera mixes fact with fiction in her 1987 novel, *Conversations With Lord Byron on Perversion, 163 Years After His Lordship's Death* (Atheneum). After technicians feed a computer the poet Byron's complete works and all of the biographical information available on him in an attempt to emulate his thinking, a young student tries to identify the mysterious Thyrza, to whom Byron wrote love poetry. The computer eventually develops an exact replica of Byron's ego, complete with the poet's legendary sex drive and preoccupations with weight, and ultimately is able to compose Byronic verse. *Conversations* "is good fun," wrote Carolly Erickson in the *Los Angeles Times Book Review,* "and a caveat to investigators into Cognitive Emulation." *Addresses: Agent*—Jane Conway-Gordon, c/o Clarke Conway-Gordon, 213 Westbourne Grove, London W11 2SG, England.

BIOGRAPHICAL/CRITICAL SOURCES:

PERIODICALS

Los Angeles Times Book Review, August 24, 1986, August 30, 1987.
New York Times Book Review, September 7, 1986.
Times Literary Supplement, June 29, 1984, November 8, 1985.

*　　　*　　　*

PREMACK, David 1925-

PERSONAL: Born October 26, 1925, in Aberdeen, S.D.; son of Leonard B. and Sonja (Liese) Premack; married Ann M. James (a writer), October 26, 1951; children: Ben, Lisa, Timothy. *Education:* University of Minnesota, B.A., 1949, M.A., 1951, Ph.D., 1955.

ADDRESSES: Office—Department of Psychology, University of Pennsylvania, 3813-15 Walnut St., Philadelphia, Pa. 19104-6196.

CAREER: Yerkes Laboratories of Primate Biology, Orange Park, Fla., research associate, 1955; University of Missouri—Columbia, began as research associate, became professor of psychology, 1956-64; University of California, Santa Barbara, professor of psychology, 1965-75, research lecturer, 1974; University of Pennsylvania, Philadelphia, professor of psychology, 1975—. Visiting professor at Harvard University, 1970-71; fellow at Center for Advanced Study in the Behavioral Sciences, Palo Alto, Calif., 1972-73; fellow at Van Leer Jerusalem Institute, 1980; visiting scientist of Japan Society for the Promotion of Science, 1980; fellow at Wissenschafts Kollege, Berlin, 1985-86. *Military service:* U.S. Army, 1943-46.

MEMBER: American Association for the Advancement of Science (fellow), Society of Experimental Psychologists.

AWARDS, HONORS: Fellow of U.S. Public Health Service, 1956-59, and Social Science Research Council, 1963; grants from U.S. Public Health Service, 1960-80, and National Science Foundation, 1961-83; Guggenheim fellow, 1979-80; Kenneth Kraik Research Award from Cambridge University, 1987; International Research Prize from Fyssen Foundation, Paris, 1987.

WRITINGS:

Intelligence in Ape and Man, Wiley, 1976.
(With wife, Ann James Premack) *The Mind of an Ape*, Norton, 1983.
Gavagai! or, The Future of the Animal Language Controversy, MIT Press, 1986.

Member of editorial board of *Journal of Experimental Psychology: Animal Processes*, 1976—, *Cognition*, 1977—, *Journal of Human Evolution*, 1977—, and *Brain and Behavior Science*, 1978—.

WORK IN PROGRESS: A book, tentatively titled *Pedagogy: How Humans Teach Humans to Be Human*, for MIT Press.

BIOGRAPHICAL/CRITICAL SOURCES:

PERIODICALS

Times Literary Supplement, June 29, 1984.

*   *   *

PRESTON, Michael B.   1933-

PERSONAL: Born August 20, 1933, in Tyler, Tex.; son of Dwight M. (a plumber) and Marie B. (a housewife) Preston; married Mary Metters (a real estate broker); children: Sherry, Sonja, Adrienne, Rymicha. *Education:* Wiley College, B.A., 1954; University of California, Berkeley, M.A., 1971, Ph.D., 1974.

ADDRESSES: Home—6454 Laurelwood Dr., Inglewood, Calif. 90302. *Office*—Department of Political Science, University of Southern California, Los Angeles, Calif. 90007.

CAREER: Teacher at public schools in Oakland, Calif., 1964-68; affiliated with School of Education at University of California, Berkeley, 1968-73; University of Illinois at Urbana-Champaign, Urbana, assistant professor, 1973-80, associate professor, 1980-85, professor of political science, 1986; University of Southern California, Los Angeles, professor of political science, 1986—. *Military service:* U.S. Army, 1955-57.

MEMBER: American Political Science Association, American Society for Public Administration, National Conference of Black Political Scientists, Midwestern Political Science Association, Western Political Science Association.

WRITINGS:

Race, Sex, and Public Policy, Lexington Books, 1979.
(With others) *The New Black Politics*, Longman, 1981, 2nd edition, revised, 1987.
The Politics of Bureaucratic Reform: The Case of the California State Employment Service, University of Illinois Press, 1984.

Contributor of about twenty articles to political science journals.

WORK IN PROGRESS: From Daley to Washington: Chicago Politics in Transition, publication expected in 1990; *Ethnic Politics in California: 1973-1988*.

SIDELIGHTS: Michael B. Preston told *CA:* "I enjoy traveling to different cities to study political systems and the different groups that inhabit them. Most of my writings, whether they deal with race or gender, all center around one basic question—how to achieve equality in a political system that has been structured to favor the majority. Since I started writing

on these subjects in 1973, small yet significant changes have taken place in politics. Both blacks and women have become significant players in American politics, but neither has achieved as yet the status they deserve in the American political system. Yet, as slow as progress is, it is significant to note that a female was selected as a Democratic vice-presidential candidate in 1984 and a black male made a serious bid for the Democratic presidential nomination in 1988. Thus there is hope that American society will become more egalitarian as we move in to the twenty-first century."

AVOCATIONAL INTERESTS: Tennis, football.

*   *   *

PRITCHARD, John Paul   1902-1976

OBITUARY NOTICE—See index for *CA* sketch: Born February 8, 1902, in White Lake, N.Y.; died in 1976. Educator, translator, editor, and author. Pritchard will be best remembered as the author of *Return to the Fountains: Some Classical Sources of American Criticism*. He began his long academic career in 1925 as a professor of ancient languages at Catawba College. He then taught classics at Washington and Jefferson College for sixteen years and, in 1944, became professor of English at the University of Oklahoma, where he served until 1972. His other writings include *Criticism in America, The Literary Wise Men of Gotham: Criticism in New York, 1815-1860*, and *A Literary Approach to the New Testament*. He also edited and translated Auguste Boeckh's *On Interpretation and Criticism*.

OBITUARIES AND OTHER SOURCES:

Date of death provided by wife, Ruth Belle Pritchard.

BOOKS

Who's Who in America, 39th edition, Marquis, 1976.

*   *   *

PROSTANO, Joyce S.

PERSONAL: Married Emanuel Theodore Prostano, Jr. (a professor of library science), November 27, 1952; children: Stephen, Loren Joy. *Education:* Southern Connecticut State College, B.S., 1969, M.S., 1970; Nova University, Ed.D., 1975.

ADDRESSES: Home—2415 Shepard Ave., No. 81, Hamden, Conn. 06518. *Office*—Humanities Division, South Central Community College, 60 Sargent Dr., New Haven, Conn. 06511.

CAREER: Library media specialist at school in Orange, Conn., 1969-70; Southern Connecticut State University, New Haven, director of Independent Learning Center, 1970-74; South Central Community College, New Haven, director of Division of Library and Media Services, 1974—.

WRITINGS:

(With husband, Emanuel T. Prostano) *The School Library Media Center*, Libraries Unlimited, 1971, 4th edition, 1987.
(Editor with E. T. Prostano) *Case Studies in Library-Media Management*, Libraries Unlimited, 1982.

*   *   *

PYM, Peter and Delores
See SANDLIN, Tim

R

RABINOWITZ, Isaac   1909-1988

OBITUARY NOTICE: Born July 3, 1909, in Brooklyn, N.Y.; died after a brief illness, September 11, 1988, in Ithaca, N.Y. Educator, administrator, translator, and author. A professor at Cornell University for more than thirty years, Rabinowitz was known for his expertise on the Dead Sea Scrolls, which include copies of Old Testament writings more ancient than any previously known. After receiving a Ph.D. from Yale University in 1932, Rabinowitz directed several youth and biblical organizations, including the B'nai B'rith Hillel foundations at various universities and the Young Men's and Young Women's Hebrew associations in New York City. He joined the Cornell University faculty in 1957, beginning as a professor of biblical and Semitic studies and becoming professor emeritus of Near Eastern language and literature in 1975. Author of more than forty articles on the Dead Sea Scrolls, ancient Semitic inscriptions, and medieval and Arabic manuscripts, Rabinowitz wrote and translated *The Book of the Honeycomb's Flow.*

OBITUARIES AND OTHER SOURCES:

BOOKS

The Blue Book: Leaders of the English-Speaking World, St. Martin's, 1976.
Directory of American Scholars, Volume III: *Foreign Languages, Linguistics, and Philology,* 8th edition, Bowker, 1982.

PERIODICALS

New York Times, September 20, 1988.

*   *   *

RADLEY, Sheila
See ROBINSON, Sheila Mary

*   *   *

RAHMAN, F.
See RAHMAN, Fazlur

RAHMAN, Fazlur   1919-1988
(F. Rahman)

OBITUARY NOTICE: Born in 1919; died of complications related to heart surgery, July 26, 1988, in Chicago, Ill. Educator, administrator, and author. An expert on Islamic law with a doctorate from Oxford University, Rahman achieved international recognition for his liberal interpretation of Muslim faith. Directly opposed to the religious beliefs of Islamic fundamentalists such as Ayatollah Khomeini, the scholar believed that the Koran—the sacred book of Islam—gave moral prescriptions that were broad and that its religious tenets should adapt to changing social conditions. Such radical ideas led to Rahman's move to the West in the late 1940s, where his philosophy found support at several universities. Rahman also served the U.S. State Department as an adviser in negotiating with Arab nations, and he directed Pakistan's Central Institute of Islamic Research from 1962 to 1968. Beginning in 1969 he worked at the University of Chicago as Harold K. Swift Distinguished Service Professor. Rahman's books, published under variations of his name, include the acclaimed *Avicenna's Psychology,* which he edited and translated, as well as *The Philosophy of Mulla Sadra Shirazi, Islam and Modernity: Transformation of an Intellectual Tradition, Islam,* and *Health and Medicine in the Islamic Tradition.*

OBITUARIES AND OTHER SOURCES:

PERIODICALS

Chicago Tribune, July 27, 1988.
Los Angeles Times, July 30, 1988.
New York Times, July 28, 1988.

*   *   *

RANKIN, Robert   1915-

PERSONAL: Born September 14, 1915, in Des Moines, Iowa; son of Wiley Strange and Estelle Blanche (Renne) Rankin; married Martha Jean Roberts, September 7, 1940; children: Mary Renne (Mrs. Robert M. Dawson), Margaret Lloyd, Wiley Robert, William Roberts. *Education:* University of Iowa, B.A., 1937; Yale University, B.D., 1940, M.A., 1942.

ADDRESSES: Home—737 Alden Rd., Claremont, Calif. 91711.

CAREER: Ordained minister of the Methodist Church, 1944, and United Church of Christ, 1960; Yale University, New Haven, Conn., vocational counselor, 1939-42; minister in Sunnyvale, Calif., 1942-44; Oberlin College, Oberlin, Ohio, campus minister and director of Young Men's Christian Association, 1946-51, lecturer in religion, 1948-51; Claremont Colleges, Claremont, Calif., chaplain and associate professor of religion, 1951-58; Danforth Foundation, St. Louis, Mo., associate director, 1958-66, vice-president, 1966-80, director of campus ministry programs, 1958-80, program associate, 1958-75; writer, 1975—.

Member of board of directors of White House Conference on Education, St. Louis, 1959-65; member of St. Louis region selection panel of White House Fellows, 1975 and 1977, chairman, 1978; member of board of directors of St. Louis United Nations Conference on Food and Population, 1975, and National Task Force for Disability and the Arts, 1978-81; member of National Commission on Higher Education of the United Methodist Church, 1975-77, and National Committee for Persons With Disability, United Church of Christ; fellow of Wilton Park Conference, Sussex, England; vice-president and member of board of directors of American Friends of Wilton Park; chairman of executive committee of American Wilton Park Conference at Wingspread, 1969-73. Executive director of Rockefeller Brothers Theological Fellowship Program, Princeton, N.J., 1954-55. Chairman of St. Louis Metropolitan Conference on Education of the Culturally Disadvantaged, 1962; member of board of directors of Health Care Center of St. Louis, 1975, Healing Community of St. Louis, 1976-81, Therapy Consulting Associates, St. Louis, 1976-81, Radio Information Service, 1978-81, Campus Young Men's-Young Women's Christian Association of Washington University, St. Louis, 1980-81, Pomona Valley Community Services, Family Service of Pomona Valley, Claremont Senior Center Task Force, Evangelicals for Social Action, and Service Center for Independent Living; member of Claremont Committee on Disability. Member of board of campus ministry at California Polytechnic University. Member of board of directors of Loretto Hilton Repertory Theatre, 1971-73. Consultant to Fund for Theological Education, Lilly Endowment, and President's Commission on Campus Unrest. *Military service:* U.S. Army Air Forces, chaplain, 1944-46; became captain.

MEMBER: American Academy of Religion, Association of American Colleges, American Association for Higher Education, American Friends Service Committee, National Association of College and University Chaplains, National Campus Ministry Association, National Association of College Ministers, Association for the Coordination of University Religious Affairs, Christian Society for College Work (member of board of directors, 1970-75), Society for Values in Higher Education (fellow), American Association of the United Nations, American Civil Liberties Union, National Association for the Advancement of Colored People, Common Cause, Sigma Chi, Friends of the St. Louis City Museum, University of Claremont Club.

AWARDS, HONORS: D.D. from Lindenwood College (now Colleges), 1964, and Northland College, Ashland, Wis., 1981; Leadership Citation from Iowa Wesleyan College, 1965, and Therapy Consulting Associates, 1981; D.H.L. from University of Southern California, 1967; E. Harris Harbison Award from Danforth Foundation, 1970.

WRITINGS:

(Editor with Myron B. Bloy, Jr., David A. Hubbard, and Parker J. Palmer) *The Recovery of Spirit in Higher Edu-*

cation: Christian and Jewish Ministries in Campus Life, Seabury, 1980.

Contributor to theology journals and religious magazines, including *Christian Century.**

*   *   *

RASKIN, Barbara   1935-

BRIEF ENTRY: Born August 25, 1935, in Minneapolis, Minn. American novelist. Raskin is the author of feminist fiction that revolves around daughters of the Depression who are rapidly approaching middle age. A former flight attendant, Raskin sold her first short story to *Seventeen* when she was only twelve years old. Her best-selling fourth novel *Hot Flashes* (St. Martin's, 1987), dubbed "a menopausal version of 'The Big Chill'" by Karen Stabiner in the *Los Angeles Times Book Review,* focuses on three women in their forties who gather together for the funeral of their eccentric writer friend, Sukie. Several critics contend that Raskin—whose characters in *Hot Flashes* discuss the 1960s, sex, marriage, divorce, and the onset of menopause—is forging a path toward a new subgenre of literature. She has written three additional novels, *Loose Ends* (Bantam, 1973), *The National Anthem* (Dutton, 1977), and *Out of Order* (Simon & Schuster, 1979), before achieving best-seller status. *Addresses: Home*—Washington, D.C. *Agent*—Charlotte Sheedy, 145 West 86th St., New York, N.Y.

BIOGRAPHICAL/CRITICAL SOURCES:

PERIODICALS

Los Angeles Times, September 6, 1987.
New York Times Book Review, September 27, 1987.
Village Voice Literary Supplement, September, 1987.

*   *   *

RAUDIVE, Konstantin   1909-1974

OBITUARY NOTICE—See index for *CA* sketch: Born April 30, 1909, in Uppsala, Sweden; died September 2, 1974. Psychologist, parapsychological experimenter, and author. Raudive was a psychologist who will be best remembered for his extensive experimentation with electronic tape recordings, which he performed with Friedrich Jurgenson, of voices allegedly of dead individuals. In the field of parapsychology, such utterances became known as "Raudive Voices." His analysis of his more than 100,000 recordings was published in 1971 in *Break-through: An Amazing Experiment in Electronic Communication With the Dead.* His other writings include the philosophical treatise *The Chaosman and His Subdual,* the novel trilogy *The Memoirs of Sylvester Perkons,* the novels *The Invisible Light* and *The Damned Souls,* and *Dreams and Reality: Meditations on Cervantes' "Don Quixote."*

OBITUARIES AND OTHER SOURCES:

BOOKS

Encyclopedia of Occultism and Parapsychology, 2nd edition, Gale, 1984-85.

*   *   *

RAY, Robert J.   1935-

PERSONAL: Born May 15, 1935, in Amarillo, Tex.; son of George B. (a newspaper editor) and Lillian M. (an artist and housewife; maiden name, Duncan) Ray; married Ann Allen (a university editor; divorced); married Margot M. Waale (a university personnel manager), July, 1983. *Education:* University of Texas at Austin, B.A., 1957, M.A., 1959, Ph.D., 1962. *Politics:* "Texas Democrat."

ADDRESSES: Home—Irvine, Calif. *Agent*—Ben Kamsler, H. N. Swanson, Inc., 8523 Sunset Blvd., Los Angeles, Calif. 90069.

CAREER: Beloit College, Beloit, Wis., instructor, 1963-65, assistant professor, 1965-68, associate professor, 1968-75, professor of English, 1976; certified tennis instructor in San Diego, Calif., 1976-81; free-lance writer, 1981—. Partner of Owning the Store, 1983-88; writing teacher at Valley College, 1984-88, and at University of California—Irvine, 1985-88; adjunct professor at Chapman College, 1988—.

MEMBER: Mystery Writers of America, Fictionaires.

WRITINGS:

(With Ann Ray) *The Art of Reading: A Handbook on Writing,* Ginn, 1968.
The Heart of the Game (novel), Berkley Publishing, 1975.
Cage of Mirrors (novel), Harper, 1980.
(With L. A. Eckert and J. D. Ryan) *Small Business: An Entrepreneur's Plan,* Harcourt, 1985.
Bloody Murdock (novel), St. Martin's, 1986.
Murdock for Hire (novel), St. Martin's, 1987.
The Hitman Cometh (novel), St. Martin's, 1988.
Dial "M" for Murdock (novel), St. Martin's, 1988.
Murdock in Xanadu (novel), Delacorte, 1989.

WORK IN PROGRESS: The Elements of Fiction: Exercises for Fiction Writers, to be completed in 1989; a book of short stories, titled *First Love: The Education of Jacob Hollanbeck;* a large novel "about passion and gridlock, California style, snazzy heroine, no title."

SIDELIGHTS: Robert J. Ray told *CA:* "Words buzz. They hum, sing, ring, smell, taste, reach, teach. Words are a writer's best friends, and when the writing is going well it's better than sex. With the right words you can put your arms around the cosmos, which is why I work every day, seven days a week. I do charts first—bubble charts, mind-maps—I plot diagrams, reaching down into my subconscious to see what's there, what needs to come to light today. I speedwrite—ignoring grammar, spelling, caps, meaning, information—and then I lift off from there and plunge into the word processor. Before you can be an American writer, you need to study these works: *Moby Dick* by Herman Melville, *The Education of Henry Adams* by Henry Adams, *The Waste Land* by T. S. Eliot, and *All the King's Men* by Robert Penn Warren.

"Advice to a young writer: One, master your craft. Two, focus on your own power, what you do best, what gives you unending joy. Three, scope the marketplace, walk the labyrinth of publishing, and do not enter the writing game blindfolded, your heart on your sleeve. Four, before you cast your words into concrete, make sure you prepare, prepare, prepare. A work of writing is a house of words. Before you cut and hammer and paint and shingle and wallpaper and lay carpet, you'd better plan. Shifting the blueprint is faster (cheaper, easier, less heartbreaking) than shifting the finished building. Dig your foundation deep—all the way to China."

RAYMOND, Rene (Brabazon)   1906-1985
(James Hadley Chase, James L. Docherty, Ambrose Grant, Raymond Marshall)

PERSONAL: Born December 24, 1906, in London, England; died February 6, 1985, in Corseaux-sur-Vevey, Switzerland; married Sylvia Ray; children: one son. *Education:* Attended schools in Rochester, Kent, England.

ADDRESSES: Home—Villa Helias, Fonatanivent, Vaud, Switzerland. *Office*—Robert Hale Ltd., 45-47 Clerkenwell Green, London EC1R 0HT, England. *Agent*—David Higham Associates Ltd., 5-8 Lower John St., Golden Square, London W1R 4HA, England.

CAREER: Writer. Door-to-door encyclopedia salesman in Hastings, England, in the mid 1920s; associated with Simkin Marshall (wholesale bookselling firm), London, England, in the late 1920s; editor of *RAF Journal. Military service:* Royal Air Force; became squadron leader.

WRITINGS:

(Under pseudonym James L. Docherty) *He Won't Need It Now,* Rich and Cowan, 1939, (under pseudonym James Hadley Chase) Panther, 1975.
(Editor with David Langdon) *Slipstream: A Royal Air Force Anthology,* Eyre & Spottiswoode, 1946.
I'll Get You for This (novel), Jarrolds, 1946, R. Hale, 1980, (under Chase pseudonym) Jarrolds, 1947, Avon, 1951.
(Under pseudonym Ambrose Grant) *More Deadly Than the Male,* Eyre & Spottiswoode, 1946, (under Chase pseudonym) Hamilton, 1960.

NOVELS; UNDER PSEUDONYM JAMES HADLEY CHASE

No Orchids for Miss Blandish, Jarrolds, 1939, Howell, Soskin, 1942, revised edition, Hamilton, 1961; published as *The Villain and the Virgin,* Avon, 1948.
The Dead Stay Dumb, Jarrolds, 1939, Panther, 1971; published as *Kiss My Fist,* Eton, 1952.
Twelve Chinks and a Woman, Jarrolds, 1940, Howell, Soskin, 1941, revised edition published as *Twelve Chinamen and a Woman,* Novel Library, 1950, published as *The Doll's Bad News,* Panther, 1970.
Miss Callaghan Comes to Grief, Jarrolds, 1941.
Miss Shumway Waves a Wand, Jarrolds, 1944, Corgi, 1977.
Eve, Jarrolds, 1945, Corgi, 1975.
I'll Get You for This, Jarrolds, 1947, Avon, 1951 (see also above).
The Flesh of the Orchid, Jarrolds, 1948, Pocket Books, 1972.
You Never Know With Women, Jarrolds, 1949, Pocket Books, 1972.
You're Lonely When You're Dead, R. Hale, 1949, reprinted, 1973, Duell, Sloan & Pearce, 1950.
Figure It Out for Yourself, R. Hale, 1950, reprinted, 1981, Duell, Sloan & Pearce, 1951; published as *The Marijuana Mob,* Eton, 1952.
Lay Her Among the Lilies, R. Hale, 1950, Corgi, 1974; published as *Too Dangerous to Be Free,* Duell, Sloan & Pearce, 1951.
Strictly for Cash, R. Hale, 1951, reprinted, 1972, Pocket Books, 1973.
The Fast Buck, R. Hale, 1952, reprinted, 1972.
The Double Shuffle, R. Hale, 1952, Dutton, 1953, Corgi, 1974.
This Way for a Shroud, R. Hale, 1953.
I'll Bury My Dead, R. Hale, 1953, Dutton, 1954, Corgi, 1980.
Tiger by the Tail, R. Hale, 1954.

Safer Dead, R. Hale, 1954, published as *Dead Ringer*, Ace Books, 1955.

You've Got It Coming, R. Hale, 1955, revised edition, 1975.

There's Always a Price Tag, R. Hale, 1956, Pocket Books, 1973.

The Guilty Are Afraid, R. Hale, 1957, New American Library, 1959.

The Case of the Strangled Starlet, New American Library, 1958 (published in England as *Not Safe to Be Free*, R. Hale, 1958, reprinted, 1979).

Shock Treatment, New American Library, 1959.

The World in My Pocket, R. Hale, 1959, Popular Library, 1962.

More Deadly Than the Male, Hamilton, 1960 (see also above).

What's Better Than Money?, R. Hale, 1960, Pocket Books, 1972.

Come Easy—Go Easy, R. Hale, 1960, Pocket Books, 1974.

A Lotus for Miss Quon, R. Hale, 1961.

Just Another Sucker, R. Hale, 1961, Pocket Books, 1974.

I Would Rather Stay Poor, R. Hale, 1962, Pocket Books, 1974.

A Coffin From Hong Kong, R. Hale, 1962.

Tell It to the Birds, R. Hale, 1963, Pocket Books, 1974.

One Bright Summer Morning, R. Hale, 1963, Pocket Books, 1974.

The Soft Centre, R. Hale, 1964.

This Is for Real, R. Hale, 1965, Walker & Co., 1967.

The Way the Cookie Crumbles, R. Hale, 1965, Pocket Books, 1974.

You Have Yourself a Deal, R. Hale, 1966, Walker & Co., 1968.

Cade, R. Hale, 1966.

Well Now, My Pretty—, R. Hale, 1967.

Have This One on Me, R. Hale, 1967.

An Ear to the Ground, R. Hale, 1968.

Believed Violent, R. Hale, 1968.

The Violent Is a Patient Bird, R. Hale, 1969.

The Whiff of Money, R. Hale, 1969.

There's a Hippie on the Highway, R. Hale, 1970.

Like a Hole in the Head, R. Hale, 1970.

Want to Stay Alive?, R. Hale, 1971.

An Ace up My Sleeve, R. Hale, 1971.

Just a Matter of Time, R. Hale, 1972.

You're Dead Without Money, R. Hale, 1972.

Knock! Knock! Who's There?, R. Hale, 1973.

Have a Change of Scene, R. Hale, 1973.

Three of Spades, R. Hale, 1974.

Goldfish Have No Hiding Place, R. Hale, 1974.

So What Happens to Me?, R. Hale, 1974.

Believe This, You'll Believe Anything, R. Hale, 1975.

He Won't Need It Now, Panther, 1975 (see also above).

The Joker in the Pack, R. Hale, 1976.

Do Me a Favour—Drop Dead, R. Hale, 1976.

I Hold the Four Aces, R. Hale, 1977.

Meet Mark Girland, R. Hale, 1977.

My Laugh Comes Last, R. Hale, 1977.

Consider Yourself Dead, R. Hale, 1978.

You Must Be Kidding, R. Hale, 1979.

Can of Worms, R. Hale, 1979.

You Can Say That Again, R. Hale, 1980.

Try This One for Size, R. Hale, 1980.

Hand Me a Fig Leaf, R. Hale, 1981.

Have a Nice Night, R. Hale, 1982.

We'll Share a Double Funeral, R. Hale, 1982.

Not My Thing, R. Hale, 1983.

Hit Them Where It Hurts, R. Hale, 1984.

Meet Helga Rolfe, R. Hale, 1984.

NOVELS; UNDER PSEUDONYM RAYMOND MARSHALL

Blondes' Requiem, Jarrolds, 1945, Crown, 1946.

No Business of Mine, Jarrolds, 1947, R. Hale, 1976.

In a Vain Shadow, Jarrolds, 1951, Panther, 1965, R. Hale, 1977.

NOVELS; ORIGINALLY UNDER PSEUDONYM RAYMOND MARSHALL, SUBSEQUENTLY UNDER PSEUDONYM JAMES HADLEY CHASE

Lady—Here's Your Wreath, Jarrolds, 1940, (under Chase pseudonym) Hamilton, 1961.

Just the Way It Is, Jarrolds, 1944, (under Chase pseudonym) Panther, 1976.

Make the Corpse Walk, Jarrolds, 1946, (under Chase pseudonym) Hamilton, 1964.

Trusted Like the Fox, Jarrolds, 1948, (under Chase pseudonym) Hamilton, 1964.

The Paw in the Bottle, Jarrolds, 1949, (under Chase pseudonym) Hamilton, 1961.

Mallory, Jarrolds, 1950, (under Chase pseudonym) Hamilton, 1964.

But a Short Time to Live, Jarrolds, 1951, (under Chase pseudonym) Hamilton, 1960.

Why Pick on Me?, Jarrolds, 1951, (under Chase pseudonym) Hamilton, 1961.

The Wary Transgressor, Jarrolds, 1952, (under Chase pseudonym) Hamilton, 1963.

The Things Men Do, Jarrolds, 1953, (under Chase pseudonym) Hamilton, 1962.

Mission to Venice, R. Hale, 1954, (under Chase pseudonym) Panther, 1973.

The Sucker Punch, Jarrolds, 1954, (under Chase pseudonym) Hamilton, 1963.

Mission to Siena, R. Hale, 1955, (under Chase pseudonym) Panther, 1966.

You Find Him—I'll Fix Him, R. Hale, 1956, (under Chase pseudonym) Panther, 1966.

Hit and Run, R. Hale, 1958, (under Chase pseudonym) R. Hale, 1978.

PLAYS; UNDER PSEUDONYM JAMES HADLEY CHASE

(With Arthur Macrea) ''Get a Load of This,'' produced in London, 1941.

(With Robert Nesbitt) ''No Orchids for Miss Blandish'' (adapted from Chase's novel of the same name), produced in London, 1942.

Last Page, S. French, 1947.

SIDELIGHTS: Rene Raymond, British author of approximately one hundred suspense novels, revolutionized the spy thriller genre with a style considered shocking in the 1930s and 1940s. Raymond reacted to England's changing taste in crime fiction with what has been called a ''hard-boiled'' detective story formula that incorporates speed, sex, and violence into its American-set plots.

Raymond is most widely known for his first novel, *No Orchids for Miss Blandish*, the best-seller written under the pseudonym James Hadley Chase, which sold more than one million copies in its first five years of publication. His subsequent books followed the same sensational formula that made *No Orchids* famous and gave Raymond world-wide notoriety as a master storyteller. In sharp contrast to his flashy characters, Raymond was described by a London *Times* reporter as "a typical quiet Englishman" who did not like to talk about his work. In a rare interview cited in *Twentieth Century Crime and Mystery Writers*, Raymond conceded that outside of his fiction, his audience probably would not be interested in what he had to say. The author felt that all his readers wanted from him was "a good read" which, he stated, "is what I try to give them."

"A good read," according to Raymond, blends bizarre plot elements such as a cobra-kissing exotic dancer, an amnesiac with a tattooed derriere, or an array of prostitutes and transvestites into a circa 1940 American atmosphere of spies, mystery, and suspense. Although Raymond's settings are almost exclusively American, his knowledge of the States was limited to the information he could glean from U.S. maps, police reports, and slang dictionaries. While critics contend that his plots and characters are both unbelievable and amoral, readers throughout the world find the author's distinctive brand of suspense appealing enough to keep even his earliest works in print. His last books, including *Not My Thing, Hit Them Where It Hurts,* and *Meet Helga Rolfe* were published shortly before his death at age seventy-eight in 1985.

MEDIA ADAPTATIONS: Raymond was especially popular in France and Italy, where more than twenty of his novels were made into films. On the American film scene, Robert Aldrich produced "The Grissom Gang" in 1971, a Cinerama film release of writer Leon Griffith's screenplay, which was based on Raymond's *No Orchids for Miss Blandish.* Raymond wrote his own adaptation of the novel for the stage in 1942 and has two other play credits to his name in addition to his almost one hundred novels.

BIOGRAPHICAL/CRITICAL SOURCES:

BOOKS

Twentieth Century Crime and Mystery Writers, St. Martin's, 1985.

OBITUARIES:

PERIODICALS

Times (London), February 7, 1985.*

* * *

REEVE, Joel
    See COX, William R(obert)

* * *

REEVES, Patricia Houts   1947-
    (Trish Reeves)

PERSONAL: Born November 8, 1947, in Columbia, Mo.; daughter of Joseph Kinyoun (an attorney) and Patricia (a housewife; maiden name, Collins) Houts; married Jerry E. K. Reeves, June 28, 1969; children: Caroline Houts, Jeremiah Krug. *Education:* University of Missouri—Columbia, B.J., 1969; Warren Wilson College, M.F.A., 1983.

ADDRESSES: Home—6231 Glenfield Dr., Shawnee Mission, Kan. 66205.

CAREER: Missouri Western State College, St. Joseph, adjunct teacher of English composition and leader of poetry workshop, 1985; University of Missouri—Kansas City, editor of *New Letters Review of Books,* 1986—. Poetry workshop leader at Central Missouri State University, 1980-82; poetry reader.

AWARDS, HONORS: Yaddo fellow, 1987; Poetry Center Prize from Cleveland State University, 1988, for *Returning the Question;* fellow of National Endowment for the Humanities, 1988.

WRITINGS:

UNDER NAME TRISH REEVES

Returning the Question (poems), Cleveland State University Press, 1988.

Work represented in anthologies, including *Missouri Poets: An Anthology,* 1982, and *Ploughshares Poetry Reader,* 1986. Contributor of about thirty poems to magazines, including *Passages North, Poet and Critic, Quarterly West, Ironwood, Prairie Schooner,* and *Seneca Review.*

* * *

REEVES, Trish
    See REEVES, Patricia Houts

* * *

REGISTER, Cheri
    See REGISTER, Cheryl Lynn

* * *

REGISTER, Cheryl Lynn   1945-
    (Cheri Register)

PERSONAL: Born April 30, 1945, in Albert Lea, Minn.; daughter of Gordon L. (a packing house worker) and Ardis Valborg (a sales clerk; maiden name, Petersen) Register; married, 1966-85; children: Grace Keun Young De Jong, Maria Eun Sook De Jong. *Education:* University of Chicago, B.A. (with honors), 1967, M.A. (with honors), 1968, Ph.D. (with honors), 1973. *Politics:* Democrat. *Religion:* Presbyterian.

ADDRESSES: Home and office—4226 Washburn Ave. S., Minneapolis, Minn. 55410.

CAREER: Emma Willard Task Force on Education, Minneapolis, Minn., co-founder, organizer, and workshop leader, 1970-73; University of Idaho, Moscow, coordinator of Women's Center, 1973-74; University of Minnesota—Twin Cities, Minneapolis, assistant professor of women's studies and Scandinavian languages and literatures, 1974-80; writer and academic consultant in women's studies, 1980—.

WRITINGS:

UNDER NAME CHERI REGISTER

(Co-author) *Sexism in Education,* Emma Willard Task Force on Education, 1971.
Kvinnokamp och litteratur i USA och Sverige (title means "Women's Liberation and Literature in the United States and Sweden"), Raben & Sjoegren, 1977.
(Editor and contributor) *A Telling Presence: Westminster Presbyterian Church, 1857-1982,* Westminster Presbyterian Church, 1982.
Mothers, Saviours, Peacemakers: Swedish Women Writers in the Twentieth Century, University of Uppsala, 1983.
Living With Chronic Illness: Days of Patience and Passion, Free Press, 1987.
Are Those Kids Yours? American Families With Internationally Adopted Children, Free Press, in press.

Josephine Donovan, editor, *Feminist Literary Criticism: Explorations in Theory,* University Press of Kentucky, 1975.

Karin Westman Berg, editor, *Textanalys fraan Koensrollssynpunkt* (title means "Textual Analysis From a Sex-Role Perspective"), Prisma, 1976.

Mildred Joel, editor, *The Evolving Status of Women in Scandinavian and American Society,* Augsburg College, 1980.

Anne R. Clauss, editor, *Contemporary Women in Life and Literature,* University of Copenhagen and Danish Research Council, 1981.

Renate Duelli-Klein and other editors, *Feministische Wissenschaft und Frauenstudium* (title means "Feminist Scholarship and Women's Studies"), Arbeitsgemeinschaft fuer Hochschuldidaktik, 1982.

Ingrid Holmquist and Ebba Witt-Brattstroem, editors, *Kvinnornas litteraturhistoria* (title means "Women's Literary History"), Foerfattarfoerlaget, 1983.

Contributor to *Dictionary of Scandinavian Literature.* Contributor to magazines, including *Hurricane Alice: A Feminist Review, Women's Studies International Forum, Signs: Journal of Women in Culture and Society, Edda, Ord och Bild, Scandinavian Review, Image,* and *Synod News.*

WORK IN PROGRESS: Biographical research on Ellen Key, a turn-of-the-century Swedish social reformer.

SIDELIGHTS: Cheryl Register told *CA:* "For the first fifteen years of my career, I was caught up in my chosen academic specialty, Scandinavian women's history and literature. The topic fascinates me still, but it is of little interest to potential readers. With the publication of *Living With Chronic Illness,* I shifted into a new vocation, as an interpreter of life experiences that I know firsthand, but that are not uniquely mine. The book on chronic illness is my attempt to come to terms with a congenital liver disease and to take issue with the dominant messages in the health literature: the military victories over acute illness and the advice to cure yourself with wishful thinking. I think of this book as a collective autobiography because it also features the voices of twenty-five other people who have invisible, incurable illnesses. It examines the impact that being unhealthy in a culture that expects perfection has on self-image, social behavior, friendship, family relationships, vocation, daily habits, emotional well-being, religious faith, and general outlook on life. Its tone is optimistic, though it avoids glossy cliches and does not deny the significance of pain and suffering. Lifelong illness requires BOTH patience and passion. The best reward the book has brought is hearing from chronically ill readers that what I have written is true to their experience, yet has helped them to reinterpret it and find value in a life of limitations.

"My next book, *Are Those Kids Yours? American Families With Internationally Adopted Children,* grows out of my minute-by-minute experience as the mother of two daughters born to young, unmarried women in Korea who saw no better choice than to place them for adoption wherever a home could be found. International adoption raises ethical questions that parents must address in very immediate, practical ways. For example, am I benefiting from another person's poverty or oppression? How do I interpret that to my children when I tell them about their birthparents? Is it fair to remove children from the culture of their birth and make them racial minorities in a white-dominated society? How do I help them deal with racism? In recounting my family's experience and that of the people I interview, I hope to show how these issues are resolved in raising children to be responsible adults of dual heritage. Concern for the welfare of children and the women who bear them makes me an enthusiastic advocate of international adoption who nevertheless will not disregard its complexities. I guess living with paradox is the underlying theme in my writing.

"Writing is my one consistent, lifelong 'calling.' I'm not sure where it came from. I had a great-grandfather who wrote Tennyson-style poetry in celebration of Minnesota's moratorium on farm mortgage foreclosures in the 1930s. All I know is that the words were always there, pressing to be written down. Like many essay writers, I see fiction as the supreme form of written expression. I would like to become good enough at it to put my fascination for Scandinavian feminism into a novel of consequence. My favorite period of Scandinavian history is 1880 to 1920, a time of social upheaval in which nostalgia for the pre-industrial past co-existed with unbounded hope for a progressively just and egalitarian society. Women began writing in greater numbers than before and used the novel to express both social criticism and vision. Some of these novelists were also active feminists and pacifists who worked on an international scale. World War I seems to have dimmed their optimism and directed their feminist and pacifist sympathies into a kind of literary escapism. It is that evolution I would like to trace in a novel, in part because it is my legacy as a Scandinavian-American feminist and in part because the tendency toward romantic escapism is a constant risk for people who seek fundamental social change. Curiously enough, the characters who have 'peopled' my imagination include an adoptive mother and the woman who gave birth to her child. I don't think either of them is chronically ill."

BIOGRAPHICAL/CRITICAL SOURCES:

PERIODICALS

New York Times Book Review, October 4, 1987.
Psychology Today, September, 1987.

*   *   *

REICH, Nancy B(assen)

PERSONAL: Born in New York, N.Y.; daughter of Hyman (a furrier) and Ida (Orland); married Haskell A. Reich (a physicist), June 25, 1945 (died October 11, 1983); children: Matthew, Susanna. *Education:* Queens College (now of the City University of New York), B.A., 1945; Columbia University, M.A., 1947; New York University, Ph.D., 1972.

ADDRESSES: Home and office—121 Lincoln Ave., Hastings-on-Hudson, N.Y. 10706.

CAREER: New York University, New York, N.Y., adjunct assistant professor of music, 1972-74; Manhattanville College, Purchase, N.Y., assistant professor of music, 1975-81; Stanford University, Stanford, Calif., visiting scholar at Center for Research on Women, 1982-83; free-lance writer and lecturer in history of music, 1983—. Rubin Academy of Music, Jerusalem, Israel, assistant professor of music, summer, 1976; College Music Association, member of council, 1977-80, chairperson for committee on status of women, 1984—.

MEMBER: International Musicological Society, American Musicological Society, Music Library Association (chairperson of greater New York chapter, 1975-77).

AWARDS, HONORS: Penrose grant from the American Philosophical Society, 1978, for research on Clara Schumann; grant from German Academic Exchange Service, 1978, for travel and research on Louise Reichardt and Clara Schumann; fellowship from the National Endowment for the Humanities, 1982, for biography on Clara Schumann; second place Pauline Alderman Prize for new scholarship on women in music from International Congress on Women in Music, 1986, ASCAP-Deems Taylor Award, 1986, runner-up Washington Irving Book Award for nonfiction from Westchester Library Association, 1987, all for *Clara Schumann: The Artist and the Woman*.

WRITINGS:

(Compiler) *A Catalog of the Works of William Sydeman: A Machine-Readable Pilot Project in Information Retrieval*, 2nd edition, Division of Music Education, New York University, 1968.

(Contributor) *Ars Musica Scientia: Festschrift Heinrich Hueschen*, Gitarre & Laute Verlag (Cologne), 1980.

(Editor, compiler, and author of introduction) *Selected Songs of Louise Reichardt*, Da Capo Press, 1981.

(Author of introduction) Friedrich Wieck, *Piano and Song*, reprinted, Da Capo Press, 1982.

(Contributor) Jane Bowers and Judith Tick, editors, *Women Making Music: Studies in the Social History of Women Musicians and Composers*, University of Illinois Press, 1985.

Clara Schumann: The Artist and the Woman, Cornell University Press, 1985.

Also author of *Resources in Music*, 1975. Contributor to *The New Grove Dictionary of Music and Musicians*, 1980, and to music and other publications, including *Music Educators Journal, Notes of the Music Library Association, Fontes Artis Musicae, Journal of the American Liszt Society, College Music Symposium, Musical Quarterly, TV Guide, Keyboard Classics*, and *Nineteenth-Century Music*.

WORK IN PROGRESS: A thematic catalog of the works of Clara Schumann; a project on women and music.

SIDELIGHTS: In her 1985 biography, *Clara Schumann: The Artist and the Woman*, musicologist Nancy B. Reich provides a substantial amount of new material concerning the life and work of the German musician. A child prodigy whose talent was exploited by her ambitious father, Schumann distinguished herself mainly as a pianist and was celebrated for her skillful interpretations of pieces by composers such as Frederic Chopin, Franz Liszt, and her husband, Robert Schumann. According to a *Washington Post Book World* article by Richard Freed, Reich claims that "no other woman achieved the eminence [Schumann] did on the concert stage, nor did any other pianist, male or female, maintain a like position for so long." Her success was accompanied by a cataclysm of personal hardships and disasters, however, among them a bitter emotional and legal struggle to break from her manipulative father's domination. Also chronicled in Reich's book are the subsequent physical, emotional, and financial burdens imposed on Schumann by her husband's mental instability and early death. At the age of thirty-six the musician became the sole support of her seven children, and later of six grandchildren and the widow of a deceased son. Reich utilizes previously untapped sources—family diaries, letters, and papers—to examine Schumann's personal relationships with her divorced parents, her composer husband, and various music associates, including her close friend Johannes Brahms. The biographer discusses the alleged romantic involvement between Schumann and Brahms, but she focuses primarily on Schumann's musical aspirations as a talented pianist and experienced composer.

Despite a few complaints that Reich downplayed the romance in Schumann's life, critics hailed *Clara Schumann* for its scholarship and documentation. A noted feature of Reich's biography is a comprehensive list of Schumann's works, some of which were previously undiscovered. "One can only admire the research that has gone into" the volume, opined Judith Chernaik in the *Times Literary Supplement*. In Freed's opinion, *Clara Schumann* is a "remarkably thorough" work that serves as a "convenient factual reference" for the general reader. Likewise, Harold C. Schonberg called Reich's biography "the best modern study of [the celebrated pianist] available in English," and Alan Walker in *Music and Letters* declared that "there is a verve and spirit to Nancy Reich's book that will ensure for it a long life and an important place in the vast literature on the Schumanns. No one who is interested in the music of the nineteenth century can afford to overlook it."

Reich told *CA:* "My writing has evolved from my work as a musician, teacher, and wife and mother. I am particularly interested in the choices facing women in our society, and I believe we can learn from a study of the past. Because I read and speak German, I have looked first at German women musicians, but I will not necessarily limit my work to that topic in the future. In addition to writing and translating, I hope to lecture here and abroad, especially since travel and seeing friends in other states and lands are two great delights."

AVOCATIONAL INTERESTS: Travel and gardening.

BIOGRAPHICAL/CRITICAL SOURCES:

PERIODICALS

Chicago Tribune Book World, October 27, 1985.
Christian Science Monitor, August 4, 1985.
Classical Music Weekly, November 23, 1985.
Los Angeles Times Book Review, September 8, 1985.
Music and Letters, October, 1986.
New York Times Book Review, August 11, 1985.
Times Literary Supplement, November 22, 1985.
Washington Post Book World, June 16, 1985.
Women's Review of Books, October, 1985.
Women's Studies Review, March/April, 1986.

*   *   *

REICHERT, Edwin C(lark)   1909-1988

OBITUARY NOTICE: Born April 6, 1909, in Duluth, Minn.; died July 7, 1988, in Lake Forest, Ill. Educator, administrator, consultant, and author. A specialist in educational administration and psychology, Reichert was the author of popular children's books featured in the "Book Elf" and "Time to Read" series. Reichert held various teaching and supervisory posts in Minnesota and Wisconsin school districts before becoming superintendent of schools in Highland Park, Illinois, in 1944. In 1946 he became head of the education department at Lake Forest College, remaining there until his retirement in 1974. Additionally, Reichert was a consultant to a children's program on WBBM-TV during the 1960s. Among Reichert's books are *My Truck Book, Space Ship to the Moon, Freight Train*, and *Bucky's Friends*.

OBITUARIES AND OTHER SOURCES:

BOOKS

Leaders in Education, 5th edition, Bowker, 1974.

PERIODICALS

Chicago Tribune, July 14, 1988.

*   *   *

RELLA, Ettore   1907(?)-1988

OBITUARY NOTICE: Born c. 1907 in Telluride, Colo.; died of a stroke, October 16, 1988, in Hudson, N.Y. Educator, poet, and playwright. Rella will be remembered for his Off-Broadway plays written in verse. After studying in Rome, Italy, the writer moved to New York, where his dramas, which include "Communicate Please," "Ten Star General," "Making Change," "Stars for a Dark Cave," and "Sign of Winter," were produced in the 1940s and 1950s. Rella received grants from various foundations and taught at Bennington College. His 1981 poetry collection is titled *The Scenery for a Play.*

OBITUARIES AND OTHER SOURCES:

PERIODICALS

New York Times, October 21, 1988.

*   *   *

REVELEY, W(alter) Taylor III   1943-

PERSONAL: Born January 6, 1943, in Churchville, Va.; son of Walter Taylor and Marie (Eason) Reveley; married Helen Bond, December 18, 1971; children: Walter Taylor IV, George Everett Bond, Nelson Martin Eason. *Education:* Princeton University, A.B., 1965; University of Virginia, J.D., 1968. *Religion:* Presbyterian.

ADDRESSES: Home—2314 Monument Ave., Richmond, Va. 23220. *Office*—Hunton & Williams, 707 East Main St., Richmond, Va. 23212.

CAREER: Admitted to the Bar of the Commonwealth of Virginia and the Bar of the District of Columbia; University of Alabama, Tuscaloosa, assistant professor of law, 1968-69; U.S. Supreme Court, Washington, D.C., law clerk, 1969-70; Hunton & Williams (law firm), Richmond, Va., associate, 1970-76, partner, 1976—, managing partner, 1982—. Lecturer at College of William and Mary, 1978-80. Fan District Association, member of board of directors, 1976-80, president, 1979-80; Richmond Symphony, member of board of directors, 1980—, executive vice-president, 1986—; member of board of directors of Presbyterian Outlook Foundation and Book Service, 1985—, and Downtown Present, 1987—; member of board of trustees of Princeton University, 1986—.

MEMBER: Various bar associations, Phi Beta Kappa, Omicron Delta Kappa, Coif, Raven Society, Knickerbocker Club, Country Club of Virginia, Downtown Club.

AWARDS, HONORS: Fellow at Woodrow Wilson International Center for Scholars, 1972-73; International Affairs fellowship from Council on Foreign Relations, 1972-73.

WRITINGS:

(Contributor) John Norton Moore, editor, *Law and Civil War in the Modern World,* Johns Hopkins University Press, 1974.
(Contributor) Francis O. Wilcox and Richard A. Frank, editors, *The Constitution and the Conduct of Foreign Policy: An Inquiry by a Panel of the American Society of International Law,* Praeger, 1976.

War Powers of the President and Congress: Who Holds the Arrows and Olive Branch, University Press of Virginia, 1981.
(Contributor) John Rourke, editor, *Congress and the Presidency in U.S. Foreign Policymaking: A Study of Interaction and Influence, 1945-1982,* Westview, 1983.

Contributor to periodicals, including *American Political Science Review, Columbia Law Review, This Constitution,* and *Virginia Journal of International Law.* Member of editorial and managing boards of *Virginia Law Review,* 1966-68.

*   *   *

RICHARD-AMATO, Patricia (Abbott)   1940-

PERSONAL: Born May 29, 1940, in Erskine, Minn.; daughter of Wallace M. (an employment counselor) and Myrtle L. (a housewife) Abbott; married Kenyon E. Richard, Jr., August 24, 1964 (divorced February 14, 1979); married James J. Amato (a physicist and software engineer), May 16, 1983. *Education:* University of Minnesota—Duluth, B.S., 1962; University of Arizona, M.Ed., 1965; University of New Mexico, Ph.D., 1984.

ADDRESSES: Home—1435 26th St., No. 6, Santa Monica, Calif. 90404. *Office*—Division of Curriculum and Instruction, California State University, Los Angeles, 5151 State University Dr., Los Angeles, Calif. 90032.

CAREER: Teacher of English as a second language and language arts at public schools in Tucson, Ariz., 1962-68, and Lakewood, Colo., 1968-78; English as a Second Language Intensive Center, Lakewood, director, 1978-81; California State University, Los Angeles, assistant professor, 1984-87, associate professor of education, 1987—.

MEMBER: Teachers of English to Speakers of Other Languages, American Association for Applied Linguistics, California Association of Teachers of English to Speakers of Other Languages, California Association for Bilingual Education, Amnesty International, Society for the Prevention of Cruelty to Animals, Westside Nuclear Arms Freeze.

AWARDS, HONORS: Kenneth W. Mildenberger Medal from Modern Language Association of America, 1983, for *Methods That Work.*

WRITINGS:

(Editor with John W. Oller, Jr.) *Methods That Work: A Smorgasbord of Ideas for Language Teachers,* Newbury House, 1983.
Making It Happen: Interaction in the Second Language Classroom, Longman, 1988.

Contributor to education journals.

WORK IN PROGRESS: Academic Readings for ESL Students, for Longman.

SIDELIGHTS: Patricia Richard-Amato told *CA:* "My book *Making It Happen: Interaction in the Second Language Classroom* is intended to be a practical sourcebook for pre- and in-service teachers. It explores ways to create optimal classroom settings which promote second language acquisition through interaction. The book also offers a look at real programs in action and includes a section of related readings highlighting the seminal ideas of Noam Chomsky, Lev Vygotsky, Henry Widdowson, Michael Breen, Christopher Candlin, Stephen

Krashen, Rod Ellis, H. D. Brown, John Oller, Jr., and Jim Cummins.

"I am currently writing a textbook on English as a second language for academic purposes. The book will include a collection of readings and activities for students of English as a second language who are preparing for the university academic mainstream."

BIOGRAPHICAL/CRITICAL SOURCES:

PERIODICALS

Modern Language Association Newsletter, spring, 1985.
Modern Language Journal, summer, 1985.
Teachers of English to Speakers of Other Languages Newsletter, April, 1985.

*   *   *

RICHTER, William L.   1942-

PERSONAL: Surname is pronounced "*Rick*-ter"; born January 20, 1942, in Fort Madison, Iowa; son of Gerard R. (a professor of international trade) and Lillian (a housewife; maiden name, Werner) Richter; married Lynne Chalmers (a medical technologist), August 26, 1967. *Education:* Arizona State University, B.A., 1964, M.A., 1965; Louisiana State University, Ph.D., 1970; postdoctoral study at Kentucky State College (now University), 1971; University of Arizona, M.L.S., 1980.

ADDRESSES: Home—2917 East Elm St., Tucson, Ariz. 85716.

CAREER: U.S. National Park Service, Grand Canyon, Ariz., laborer, 1961-67; Louisiana State University, Baton Rouge, visiting instructor in history, 1970; Cameron University, Lawton, Okla., assistant professor of history, 1970-75; Bill's Farrier Service, Tucson, Ariz., owner and operator, 1975—.

MEMBER: American Historical Association, Organization of American Historians, American Farriers Association, Southern Historical Association, Texas State Historical Association, Missouri State Historical Association, Association of Oklahoma College History Professors.

WRITINGS:

(Contributor) Elinor Miller and Eugene D. Genovese, editors, *Plantation, Town, and Country: Essays on the Local History of American Slave Society,* University of Illinois Press, 1974.
(Contributor) Frank N. Magill and John L. Loos, editors, *Great Events in American History: American Series,* three volumes, Salem Press, 1975.
The Army in Texas During Reconstruction, 1865-1870, Texas A&M University Press, 1987.

Contributor of more than twenty articles and reviews to history journals.

WORK IN PROGRESS: A study of relations between the U.S. Army and the Freedmen's Bureau in Texas.

SIDELIGHTS: William L. Richter told *CA:* "The study of the reconstructing of the United States after the Civil War is an important lesson of how well-intended reforms often go awry in a democratic society. Reconstruction was designed to bring the former Confederate states into the Union with new loyal governments that recognized the freedom and citizenship of the recently freed blacks through the administration of the U.S. Army. Compromised and eventually abandoned through the ebb and flow of national politics, the refusal of many northern states to voluntarily treat their own black populations as they compelled the South to do by force, and the desire of most Americans to forget the war and get on with the settlement of the West and the industrializatin of the East, Reconstruction failed to achieve its potential.

"By deploying the Army against the South as an occupation force with the mission to oversee Reconstruction, the Congress gave Southerners and ultimately all white Americans a convenient scapegoat that allowed them to oppose Reconstruction as as un-American attempt at 'military rule,' without facing up to the racism that really made the process unpalatable. In Texas, the Army guaranteed the success of Reconstruction's opponents by crassly manipulating the voting process to subvert the electoral results on behalf of the local Republicans.

"In addition to the soldiers, and controlled by the War Department, the Bureau of Refugees, Freedmen, and Abandoned Lands (commonly known as the Freedmen's Bureau), sought to guarantee the rights of the blacks as freedpersons in the South. The agents of the Bureau came into conflict, not only with the former slaveholders, but with the more conservative Army command structure. In addition, the Bureau itself was shot through with nineteenth-century upperclass prejudices against the working poor. The result was that the Bureau's effectiveness in dealing with the problems the blacks faced as free laborers was crippled. In the end, the Army and the Bureau unwittingly helped establish the pseudo-slavery of peonage (characterized by tenancy, sharecropping, and the lien) that endured into the twentieth century."

*   *   *

RICKFORD, John R(ussell)   1949-

PERSONAL: Born September 16, 1949, in Georgetown, Guyana; son of Russell H. (an accountant) and Eula (a housewife; maiden name, Wade) Rickford; married Angela E. Marshall (a day-care proprietor), June 19, 1971; children: Shiyama, Russell, Anakela, Luke. *Education:* University of California, Santa Cruz, B.A. (with highest honors), 1971; University of Pennsylvania, M.A., 1973, Ph.D., 1979. *Religion:* Christian.

ADDRESSES: Home—745 Kendall Ave., Palo Alto, Calif. 94306. *Office*—Department of Linguistics, Stanford University, Stanford, Calif. 94305.

CAREER: Sunday Graphic, Georgetown, Guyana, features reporter, 1967; junior English master at high school in Georgetown, 1967-68; University of Guyana, Georgetown, lecturer and reader in English, 1974-80; Stanford University, Stanford, Calif., visiting professor, 1980-81, assistant professor, 1981-87, associate professor of linguistics, 1987—. Visiting assistant professor at Johns Hopkins University, 1977; member of National Science Foundation Linguistics Panel, 1986-89; conference coordinator. Member of editorial board of Camden House, 1982-86, and Foris Publications, 1983-86.

MEMBER: International Sociolinguistics Association, American Dialect Society, Linguistic Society of America, Society for Caribbean Linguistics (member of executive committee, 1974-80), Bay Area Sociolinguistics Association (co-founder; co-chairman), Toastmasters International (educational vice-president, 1982).

AWARDS, HONORS: Fulbright grant for the United States, 1968; Danforth fellow, 1971; grants from Stanford University's Center for Research on International Studies, 1982, and

Center for Research on Language and Information, 1984; Rockefeller Foundation fellow, 1984; grant from Pew Foundation, 1985; fellow of Center for Urban Studies, 1986.

WRITINGS:

(Editor and contributor) *A Festival of Guyanese Words*, University of Guyana, 1976, 2nd edition, 1978.
Dimensions of a Creole Continuum, Stanford University Press, 1987.
Linguistic Variation and the Social Order, Academic Press, 1988.

Editor of *Carrier Pidgin*, 1982-86, and *International Journal of the Sociology of Language*, 1988; member of editorial board of *American Speech*, 1986, *Journal of Pidgin and Creole Languages*, 1986, and *Papers in Pragmatics*, 1987.

CONTRIBUTOR

D. DeCamp and I. Hancock, editors, *Pidgins and Creoles: Current Trends and Prospects*, Georgetown University Press, 1974.
R. Fasold and R. Shuy, editors, *Analyzing Variation in Language*, Georgetown University Press, 1975.
G. Cave, editor, *New Directions in Creole Studies*, Society for Caribbean Linguistics, 1976.
J. H. Brunvand, editor, *Readings in American Folklore*, Norton, 1976.
A. Valdman, editor, *Pidgin and Creole Linguistics*, Indiana University Press, 1977.
R. Day, editor, *Issues in English Creoles: Papers From the 1975 Hawaii Conference*, Julius Groos, 1980.
Valdman and A. Highfield, editors, *Theoretical Orientations in Creole Studies*, Academic Press, 1980.
R. Andersen, editor, *Pidginization and Creolization as Language Acquisition*, Newbury House, 1983.
N. Wolfson and J. Manes, editors, *The Language of Inequality*, Mouton, 1985.
M. Montgomery and G. Bailey, editors, *Language Variety in the South: Perspectives in Black and White*, University of Alabama Press, 1985.
J. A. Fishman, editor, *The Fergusonian Impact*, Volume II, Mouton, 1986.
U. Ammon, N. Dittmar, and K. J. Mattheier, editors, *Sociolinguistics: An International Handbook of the Science of Language and Society*, de Gruyter, 1987.
G. Gilbert, editor, *Pidgin and Creole Languages: Essays in Honor of John E. Reinecke*, University Press of Hawaii, 1987.
J. Cheshire, editor, *English Around the World: Sociolinguistic Perspectives*, Cambridge University Press, 1988.
Bailey, N. Maynor, and P. Cukor-Avila, editors, *The Emergence of Black English: Texts and Commentary*, John Benjamins, 1988.

Contributor to *Theoretical and Descriptive Issues in Creole and Black Linguistics*, edited by W. Edwards, A. Spears, and D. Winford; also contributor of articles and reviews to scholarly journals.

WORK IN PROGRESS: Research on linguistic convergence and divergence in black English vernacular in East Palo, California; research on the social and linguistic aspects of language variation in Guyana, in Gullah off the South Carolina coast, and in theories of pidginization, creolization, and decreolization generally, especially in relation to sociolinguistics.

RIPPON, Angela   1944-

PERSONAL: Born October 12, 1944, in Plymouth, England; daughter of John and Edna Rippon; married Christopher Dare, 1967. *Education:* Attended grammar school in Plymouth, England.

ADDRESSES: Agent—International Management Group, Pier House, Strand on the Green, London W4 3NN, England.

CAREER: British Broadcasting Corp. (BBC-TV), Plymouth, England, presenter and reporter, 1966-69; Westward Television, Plymouth, England, editor, producer, and presenter, 1967-73; BBC-TV, London, reporter for "National News," 1973-75, newsreader, 1975-81; WNEV-TV, Boston, Mass., arts and entertainment correspondent, 1984-85; television and radio presenter for BBC, 1985—.

MEMBER: International Club for Women in Television (vice-president, 1979—).

AWARDS, HONORS: Radio and Television Industries awards for newsreader of the year, 1975, 1976, and 1977, and for television personality of the year, 1977.

WRITINGS:

Riding, Sidgwick & Jackson, 1980.
Victoria's Plum (children's stories), Purnell, 1981.
In the Country, BBC Publications, 1980.
Angela Rippon's West Country, M. Joseph, 1982.
Mark Phillips: The Man and His Horses, David & Charles, 1982.
Badminton: A Celebration, Pavilion Books, 1987.

*   *   *

ROBBINS, Anthony J.   1960-

PERSONAL: Born February 29, 1960, in California; son of Jim and Niki (Shows) Robbins; married Rebecca Biggerstaff (an executive), November 16, 1985; children: Tyler Jenkins, Jolie Jenkins, Joshua Jenkins, Jairek. *Education:* Attended University of California, Los Angeles, 1974.

ADDRESSES: Home—544 Avenida Primavera, Del Mar, Calif. 92014. *Office*—Robbins Research Institute, Inc., 3366 North Torrey Pines Court, Suite 100, La Jolla, Calif. 92037. *Agent*—Jan Miller, 5518 Dyer St., Suites 3, 4, 4A, Dallas, Tex. 75206.

CAREER: Achievement Enterprises, Los Angeles, Calif., president, 1979-81; Diamond Method, Los Angeles, president, 1981-83; Robbins Research Institute, Inc., La Jolla, Calif., president, 1984—. Spokesperson for Missing Children's Foundation; consultant to U.S. Army, Record Bar Corp., and Olympic athletes.

MEMBER: Young Entrepreneurs Association.

WRITINGS:

Unlimited Power: Strategies for Personal Excellence, Premier Publishing, 1984.
Unlimited Power: The Way to Peak Personal Achievement, Simon & Schuster, 1986.

WORK IN PROGRESS: Unlimited Passion: The Power of Human Values; Unlimited Success.

SIDELIGHTS: Anthony J. Robbins told *CA:* "My life is committed to discovering and developing ideas and strategies that increase the quality of life for all people. To live and give passionately is my motto in life."

ROBBINS, Wayne
    See COX, William R(obert)

*   *   *

ROBERTS, Elliott B.   1899-1988

OBITUARY NOTICE—See index for *CA* sketch: Born August 9, 1899, in Boston, Mass.; died of cancer and pneumonia, July 15, 1988, in Alexandria, Va. Geophysicist, administrator, inventor, editor, and author. During his more than forty-year career with the U.S. Coast and Geodetic Survey, Roberts surveyed in Alaska and the Philippine Islands, headed the geophysics division for thirteen years, and remained as assistant director of the Survey for three years after he retired in 1959. He invented various oceanographic instruments and co-authored a number of books, including *Triangulation in the Philippine Islands* and *The Coast and Geodetic Survey, 1807-1957*. Roberts also wrote two science books for children, *Deep Sea, High Mountain* and *Our Quaking Earth*, and was editor of *Explorers Journal* beginning in 1962.

OBITUARIES AND OTHER SOURCES:

BOOKS

The Writers Directory: 1984-1986, St. James Press, 1983.

PERIODICALS

Washington Post, July 30, 1988.

*   *   *

ROBINSON, Kim Stanley   1952-

PERSONAL: Born March 23, 1952, in Waukegan, Ill.; married Lisa Howland Nowell, 1982. *Education:* University of California, San Diego, B.A., 1974, Ph.D., 1982; Boston University, M.A., 1975.

ADDRESSES: Home—17811 Romelle Ave., Santa Ana, Calif. 92705. *Agent*—Patrick Delahunt, John Schaffner Associates Inc., 114 East 28th St., New York, N.Y. 10016.

CAREER: Visiting lecturer at University of California at San Diego, 1982 and 1985, and University of California, Davis, 1982-84 and 1985.

AWARDS, HONORS: Nebula Award nomination from Science Fiction Writers of America, 1981, for "Venice Drowned"; Science Fiction Achievement Award ("Hugo") from World Science Fiction Society, 1982, for "To Leave a Mark," and nomination for "Black Air"; World Fantasy Award for best novella from World Fantasy Convention, 1983, and Nebula Award, both for "Black Air"; Locus Award for best first novel from *Locus* magazine, 1985, for *The Wild Shore*.

WRITINGS:

The Wild Shore (science fiction novel), Ace Books, 1984.
Icehenge (science fiction novel), Ace Books, 1984.
The Novels of Philip K. Dick (criticism), UMI Research Press, 1984.
The Memory of Whiteness: A Scientific Romance (science fiction novel), Tor Books, 1985.
"Green Mars" (science fiction short story), published in *Isaac Asimov's Science Fiction Magazine*, September, 1985.
The Blind Geometer, illustrations by Judy King-Rieniets, Cheap Street, 1986.

The Planet on the Table (science fiction short stories; includes "Venice Drowned," "Mercurial," "Ridge Running," "The Disguise" "The Lucky Strike," and "Black Air"), Tor Books, 1986.
The Gold Coast, Tor Books, 1988.

Stories represented in anthologies, including *Orbit 18* and *Orbit 19*, both edited by Damon Knight, Harper, 1975 and 1977; *Clarion SF*, edited by Kate Wilhelm, Berkley, 1977; *Universe 11, Universe 12, Universe 13, Universe 14*, and *Universe 15*, all edited by Terry Carr, Doubleday, 1981-85; and *The Year's Best Science Fiction 1*, edited by Gardner Dozois and Jim Frenkel, Bluejay Books, 1984.

SIDELIGHTS: Kim Stanley Robinson's first novel, *The Wild Shore*, was the eagerly awaited vanguard of a new line of science fiction from Ace Books. With a reputation for discovering excellent little-known authors, the Ace Specials were first published in the 1960s and were eventually discontinued, to be resurrected by their former editor, Terry Carr, with Robinson's novel in 1984. *The Wild Shore* depicts the United States in the aftermath of a nuclear holocaust of mysterious origin, a country reduced to primitive technology and quarantined by an unknown outside force. Assessed Algis Budrys in the *Magazine of Fantasy and Science Fiction*, "what [Robinson] has here is a Class A science fiction idea . . . a future which is both clearly possible and yet has not hitherto been notably proposed."

Throughout the novel Robinson concentrates on his protagonists, residents of a southern California town who generally know little and care less about their history and about the world beyond them. According to Budrys, the regional flavor and strong characterization of Robinson's book recall the writings of John Steinbeck and Mark Twain; "Robinson has brought an American culture to life as surely as was ever done by anyone who had a real American culture to research," judged the critic. Writing in the *Washington Post Book World*, Stephen P. Brown concurred, praising the "vivid depth" of characterization "rarely encountered in science fiction."

In *The Memory of Whiteness*, published the following year, music is the universal language of a space-faring civilization. With access to free energy, humanity has colonized all the sun's planets and developed a "rich mixture of cultures, based on divergent notions of political order, but unified by an appreciation of music," noted Gerald Jonas in the *New York Times Book Review*. A genius, Johannes Wright, attempts to use the language of music to express universal truths in his compositions for a computer-enhanced instrument known as the Orchestra, but enemies seek to destroy him and the Orchestra. Jonas expressed disappointment in being unable to identify with Wright, whose genius places him beyond the reader, but appreciated Robinson's variations on the theme of music's power. The critic judged the end, in which Wright lands on Mercury after performing on various other planets, "most spectacular."

A number of Robinson's short stories, originally published in the late 1970s and early 1980s, appear in his 1986 collection *The Planet on the Table*. Exploring future societies or alternate histories, Robinson "invests his flights of imagination with a palpable sense of place," asserted Jonas in another *New York Times Book Review* article. The stories earned praise for their merits as straight fiction as well as for their science fiction content and prompted Jonas's commendation of Robinson's "powerful and consistent science fiction voice."

Depicting another future society is Robinson's 1988 novel, *The Gold Coast*. Set in twenty-first century Orange County, California, the book portrays a populace inundated by freeways, shopping malls, and apartment complexes, where the "people are as frantic as the landscape is dense, and there's a deadness in the soul of most," noted T. Jefferson Parker in the *Los Angeles Times Book Review*. The protagonist of the story, twenty-seven-year-old poet Jim McPherson, joins a terrorist group that sabotages national defense plants. Jim's father, however, works for such a defense contractor, and Jim finds himself caught between his own idealist views condemning military buildup and his father's values. Parker commended *The Gold Coast* for the ideas that Robinson addresses, noting that the author has "extrapolated a future . . . that feels accurate, arresting and frightening. . . . Who among us, watching a wasteful defense industry that helps to drain an already overspent economy . . . doesn't share Jim's outrage and disgust?" In what the reviewer deemed an "ambitious, angry, eccentric" book, Robinson exhibits "breathless, headlong prose" and some "beautifully written rhapsodies." More important, concluded Parker, "Robinson has succeeded at a novelist's toughest challenge: He's made us look at the world around us. This isn't escapist stuff—it sends you straight into a confrontation with yourself."

BIOGRAPHICAL/CRITICAL SOURCES:

BOOKS

Contemporary Literary Criticism, Volume 34, Gale, 1985.

PERIODICALS

Los Angeles Times Book Review, March 13, 1988.
Magazine of Fantasy and Science Fiction, May, 1984.
New York Times Book Review, October 20, 1985, September 21, 1986.
Washington Post Book World, April 22, 1984, August 25, 1985.*

*   *   *

ROBINSON, Sheila Mary 1928-
(Sheila Radley, Hester Rowan)

BRIEF ENTRY: Born November 18, 1928, in Cogenhoe, Northamptonshire, England. British author. Although Robinson has penned romance novels, including *Overture in Venice* (Collins, 1976) and *Snowfall* (Collins, 1978), under the pseudonym Hester Rowan, she is best known for her series of crime novels written under the name Sheila Radley. Critics have praised these mystery stories—which feature recurring character Chief Inspector Douglas Quantrill—for their well-drawn characters, stylish prose, and entertaining use of irony. Robinson garnered considerable acclaim for the first novel in the series, *Death in the Morning* (Scribner, 1979), in which the circumstances surrounding a girl's drowning death in England's East Anglia river bear a startling resemblance to the death of Ophelia in William Shakespeare's *Hamlet*. The author followed *Death in the Morning* with *The Chief Inspector's Daughter* (Constable, 1981), about the mutilation murder of a gothic romance writer. Other books in the series include *A Talent for Destruction* (Scribner, 1982), *The Quiet Road to Death* (Scribner, 1984), and *Who Saw Him Die?* (Scribner, 1988). *Addresses: Agent*—Curtis Brown, Curtis Brown Ltd., 162-168 Regent St., London W1R 5TB, England.

BIOGRAPHICAL/CRITICAL SOURCES:

BOOKS

International Authors and Writers Who's Who, 10th edition, International Biographical Centre, 1986.
The Writers Directory: 1986-1988, St. James Press, 1986.

PERIODICALS

New Yorker, August 6, 1979.
New York Times Book Review, May 20, 1984.

*   *   *

ROBINSON, W. Stitt
See ROBINSON, W(alter) Stitt, Jr.

*   *   *

ROBINSON, W(alter) Stitt, Jr. 1917-
(W. Stitt Robinson)

PERSONAL: Born August 28, 1917, in Matthews, N.C.; son of Walter Stitt and Mary Irene (Jamison) Robinson; married Constance Lee Mock, March 18, 1944; children: Ethel Barry, Walter Lee. *Education:* Davidson College, B.A. (summa cum laude), 1939; University of Virginia, M.A., 1941, Ph.D., 1950. *Religion:* Methodist.

ADDRESSES: Home—801 Broadview Dr., Lawrence, Kan. 66044. *Office*—Department of History, 3032 Wescoe, University of Kansas, Lawrence, Kan. 66045.

CAREER: Florence State Teachers College (now University of North Alabama), Florence, assistant professor, 1946-47, associate professor of history, 1947-48; University of Kansas, Lawrence, assistant professor, 1950-54, associate professor, 1954-59, professor of history, 1959—, chairman of department, 1968-73. Member of National Civil War Centennial Commission, 1961-65; Kansas Committee on the Humanities, member of committee, 1971-78, chairman, 1975-77; Kansas School of Religion, president, 1983-86, member of executive committee and board of directors. *Military service:* U.S. Army, 1941-45; became captain; received Bronze Star.

MEMBER: American Historical Association, Organization of American Historians, Southern Historical Association, Kansas Historical Society (member of board of directors), Douglas County Historical Society (president, 1979-81), Raven Society, Phi Beta Kappa, Phi Alpha Theta (member of international council, 1978-80; president, 1984-85).

AWARDS, HONORS: Grants from Social Science Research Council, 1959-60, and American Philosophical Society, 1967 and 1983; Distinguished Scholarship Award from University of Kansas, 1976.

WRITINGS:

(Editor and contributor) Richard Oswald, *Memorandum on the Folly of Invading Virginia, the Strategic Importance of Portsmouth, and the Need for Civilian Control of the Military: Written in 1781 by the British Negotiator of the First American Treaty of Peace*, University Press of Virginia, 1953.
Mother Earth: Land Grants in Virginia, 1607-1699, University Press of Virginia, 1957.
(Contributor) D. B. Rutman, editor, *The Old Dominion*, University Press of Virginia, 1964.

(Under name W. Stitt Robinson) *The Southern Colonial Frontier, 1607-1763,* University of New Mexico Press, 1979.

Also editor of *Indian Treaties of Colonial Virginia* (two volumes) and *Indian Treaties of Colonial Maryland,* and contributor to history journals. Member of editorial board of *Philosophical Quarterly,* 1975-78.*

* * *

ROCKWELL, John (Sargent) 1940-

PERSONAL: Born September 16, 1940, in Washington, D.C.; son of Alvin John (an attorney) and Anne Sargent (Hayward) Rockwell. *Education:* Harvard University, B.A., 1962; graduate study at University of Munich, 1962-63; University of California, M.A., 1964, Ph.D., 1972.

ADDRESSES: Home—New York, N.Y. *Office*—New York Times, 229 West 43rd St., New York, N.Y. 10036. *Agent*—Robert Cornfield, 145 West 79th St., New York, N.Y. 10024.

CAREER: Music critic and writer. Worked in radio and on television on opera programs and miscellaneous free-lance jobs for stations such as WHRB-Radio, Cambridge, Mass., KPFA-Radio, Berkeley, Calif., and KPED-TV, San Francisco, Calif., 1965-69; *Opera News,* New York, N.Y., West Coast correspondent, 1968-72; *Tribune,* Oakland, Calif., music and dance critic, 1969; *Los Angeles Times,* Los Angeles, Calif., assistant music and dance critic, 1970-72; *New York Times,* New York City, free-lance music critic, 1972-74, staff music critic, 1974—. Lecturer in cultural history at Princeton University, 1977-79; lecturer in music at Brooklyn College of the City University of New York, 1980.

MEMBER: Music Critics Association (treasurer, 1977-81), Phi Beta Kappa.

AWARDS, HONORS: German academic exchange fellowship, 1962-63; Woodrow Wilson fellowship from Woodrow Wilson National Fellowship Foundation, 1963-64; *All American Music: Composition in the Late Twentieth Century* was nominated for a 1983 National Book Critics Circle Award.

WRITINGS:

(Contributor) Jim Miller, editor, *The Rolling Stone Illustrated History of Rock and Roll,* Rolling Stone Press, 1976.
(With Robert Stearns) *Robert Wilson: A Theater of Images,* Contemporary Arts Center, 1980.
All American Music: Composition in the Late Twentieth Century, Knopf, 1983.
Sinatra: An American Classic (contains photographs), Random House/Rolling Stone Press, 1984.
(Contributor and editorial adviser) Stanley Sadie and H. Wiley Hitchcock, editors, *New Grove Dictionary of American Music,* Macmillan, 1986.

Also author of book introductions for publications such as *A Virgil Thomson Reader* and *The Compleat Beatles.* Contributor of essays to works on Laurie Anderson, John Lennon, and the cultural history of New York. Contributor to periodicals, including *Rolling Stone, Esquire, Opera News, High Fidelity, Saturday Review,* and *Keynote.*

WORK IN PROGRESS: A book on the state of music today, publication expected in 1989; a monograph on the history and ideology of rock criticism, publication by the Institute for Studies in American Music expected in 1989; a book on opera and music theater.

SIDELIGHTS: As a music critic for the *New York Times* since 1972, John Rockwell "has spent years listening to string quartets, violin recitals, squeaks, squonks, tape hisses, thunder rolls, and drips of notes from the ceiling," wrote James Wolcott in *Harper's.* Assessing a wide range of both established and experimental music that spans from classical to jazz to rock, he has given audience to musicians as varied as composer Leos Janacek and rock poet Patti Smith. No stranger to public opinion, Rockwell has weathered a fair amount of criticism for his musical observations, but a number of critics agree that over the years he has performed this task with unflagging enthusiasm and considerable insight. Musically, Rockwell regards the 1980s as a time of "quite remarkable excitement," quoted Wolcott, and in the reviewer's words, he predicts that this fervor will inevitably "prove world-contagious."

All American Music: Composition in the Late Twentieth Century reflects Rockwell's appreciation for a variety of musical styles. In an excerpt from the volume's introduction, Wolcott cited Rockwell's motivation: "I write about all kinds of music because I now love all kinds . . . and want to share that love as best I can." To that end *All American Music* profiles such diverse talents as serialist Milton Babbitt, Broadway composer Stephen Sondheim, and the new wave rock group Talking Heads. Rockwell addresses a melange of "contemporary tendencies in classical music, jazz, rock and various in-between genres that defy easy labeling," observed *Washington Post Book World* critic Joseph McLellan, in his attempt both to show how these seemingly incongruous musical categories interact and to defend the aesthetic merit of each. Examining the traditions of classical music, for instance, alongside representative modern and popular influences such as jazz, Latin American salsa, and experimentation with electronically synthesized sound, Rockwell provides a cross section of the cultural and historical elements contributing to the total experience of music in the United States. Through "spirited" argument that blends "judicious evaluation with slam-bang wit," averred Langdon Winner in the *New York Times Book Review,* Rockwell celebrates the multitude of innovations shaping contemporary composition and expands the definition of composer in a "most liberal way." The result, as judged by *Times Literary Supplement* critic Wilfrid Mellers, is a "brilliant, lucidly written book [that] helps us to understand not merely music but also the world we live in."

While some critics were encouraged by the originality of the concept presented in *All American Music,* a few questioned Rockwell's criteria for inclusion into the volume. *New Republic* reviewer Jeffrey Pundyk, for example, wondered why a book on American music excludes both blues and country artists along with legendary music figures—such as Duke Ellington, Miles Davis, and Leonard Bernstein—while featuring foreign composers such as Austrian-born Ernst Krenek and Canadian rock star Neil Young. On the other hand, Pundyk resolved that some prime examples of American music "are written and performed" by non-native American musicians who imitate styles that "originated in the United States." In particular, Pundyk cited British groups such as the Rolling Stones, whose songs derive from the country and rock music of various American artists.

Linda Sanders, reviewing in the *New York Times,* attributed the book's curious assortment of composers to Rockwell's preoccupation with what he terms "a special kind of outsider"—rebel composers who variously earned reputations as individualists, pioneers, and iconoclasts. By virtue of association with such "classic American character," explained Sanders, these composers have distinguished themselves as representative of the "experimental tradition" in American music, despite their national origins. According to Jim Miller in *Newsweek*, the "engaging, warmly partisan style" of *All American Music* contributes to its "impassioned and highly provocative" nature. And in Sanders's opinion, Rockwell's book "is probably unique" among sources of its kind. Gregory Sandow, writing in the *Village Voice*, ventured further that this "epoch-making" volume is "already defining the future shape of contemporary serious music."

Like *All American Music*, Rockwell's 1984 *Sinatra: An American Classic* received mixed reviews yet nonetheless proved an innovative study. Described by *New Statesman* critic David Lancaster as the "first intelligent" analysis of singer Frank Sinatra's stature as an artist, *Sinatra* combines biography with critical commentary and chronicles the singer's career from his beginnings in New Jersey nightclubs during the 1930s to his latter-day performances in stadiums, concert halls, and Las Vegas, Nevada, casinos. While the more sensational aspects of Sinatra's personal life—such as troubled marriages and alleged links to organized crime—are duly noted, they are not the focus of this volume. Instead, with "lively" narrative, opined Michael Lydon in the *New York Times Book Review*, Rockwell establishes the singer's place in popular American music history and confirms his greatness through "acute musical insight and thorough knowledge" of the Tin Pan Alley tradition that influenced Sinatra's musical development. In another *New York Times* review, Sanders assessed that *Sinatra* captures the vocalist's "unique pizazz" while discussing his talent from a "historical and stylistic perspective" that transcends Rockwell's personal bias and enthusiasm. Similarly, Lancaster deemed the book "excellent . . . well-written and full of original thinking," adding that "it will appeal to many . . . who have never taken Sinatra seriously before."

CA INTERVIEW

CA interviewed John Rockwell by telephone on September 12, 1985, at his home in New York City.

CA: You've said you were an avid "Hit Parade" listener as a boy and then got hooked on classical music by a Columbia record sampler called Meet Andre Kostelanetz.

ROCKWELL: I had had piano lessons before that, and had also listened to classical music with my parents at home. It just became an obsession when I happened to get that record.

CA: When did you know that you wanted to write about music for other people?

ROCKWELL: Pretty early on. I remember at the age of fifteen going to see Alfred Frankenstein, who at that time was the music critic of the *San Francisco Chronicle*, to ask him how I could become a music critic. He was very kind; he said many are called, few are chosen, et cetera, but he did spend a lot of time with a fifteen-year-old kid he didn't know. But the visit to Frankenstein indicates that I had a real interest in being a music critic that early. I had ascertained that I was not a child prodigy; even though I had taken piano lessons, I had not manifested any Horowitzean talent, so I figured that I wasn't going to be able to make a career as a composer or a performer. But I loved music, so I thought that since I could write and loved to read and was interested in words, writing about music was a reasonable way to go.

When I got to Harvard, I toyed for a while with majoring in music, presumably with the idea of becoming a musicologist. I took the preliminary harmony course to qualify to take actual serious music courses, as opposed to layman's music appreciation courses. I did take a number of those, but at that time especially, the Harvard music department was particularly past-oriented. Transcribing Renaissance music was the center of the profession, as far as they were concerned, and I was interested in more contemporary stuff. So I wound up concentrating in a program called "History and Literature," which is sort of like the German *Kulturgeschichte*, or cultural history. Instead of doing history and literature, though, I did mostly history and music; in other words, I wrote about music, but from a historian's humanist, generalist perspective. I wrote my senior honors thesis on Richard Strauss's opera *Arabella*, in part because all of Hugo von Hofmannsthal's papers—he was the librettist—were at Harvard.

Majoring in history and literature, I realize in retrospect, was terrific training for becoming a music critic. It's funny, because musicology now has changed. A lot of attention is being paid to the nineteenth century, which was very declasse in the early 1960s. A good deal of attention is even being paid to the twentieth century now. But I was interested in music from the present looking backwards rather than from the past looking forward or from the past staring right at itself.

CA: Criticism must be one of the hardest kinds of writing to get established in.

ROCKWELL: The mechanisms by which music critics are chosen are erratic at best.

CA: Where did you get your first break?

ROCKWELL: After college I went to Munich for a year, and then in 1963 I began graduate school at Berkeley, just in time for all the amusements of the 1960s. I stayed there through the 1960s; I eventually got a Ph.D. in 1972, but I had completed my course work there by 1967 or 1968. I started teaching and working on my dissertation in the late 1960s. This was in cultural history, once again, and the subject was the politics of opera in Berlin in the 1920s. I'd also written a seminar paper on [German composer Richard] Wagner and the symbolists—I was still very much concerned with musical stuff. I was doing free-lance things all during this period, but didn't see any obvious way to make it my career, and so was proceeding with no great enthusiasm toward the prospect of being a professor of history somewhere.

When I was at Harvard, I had started doing radio work—opera programs, mostly—at WHRB, the Harvard radio station. I continued that out in Berkeley at KPFA, which is the Pacifica Station, part of a network of listener-supported, left-wing stations, including WBAI in New York and several others. I did programs there and started writing program notes for the San Francisco Opera and doing miscellaneous free-lance jobs. By 1968 I had become the West Coast correspondent of *Opera News*, which meant basically covering San Francisco, but also whatever else was going on on the West Coast—which wasn't much.

Through that, I was called up one day in late 1968 and asked if I would be interested in filling in during the first six months of 1969 for the classical music and dance critic of the Oakland [California] *Tribune*, who was going on a six-month leave. I said, sure. But even before I'd begun, I'd been contacted by

Martin Bernheimer at the *Los Angeles Times*, who was looking for an assistant. He held off a decision until he actually saw what I wrote for the Oakland *Tribune*. In the middle of the spring of 1969 I was offered a job teaching history at Mills College in Oakland. So it came down to a choice, and Bernheimer came through with a real job offer and I didn't have a second thought. But I asked to begin at the beginning of 1970, because I wanted to finish the first draft of my Ph.D. dissertation. Then I went down to Los Angeles at the very beginning of 1970, the first work day of the new year, and stayed there for two-and-a-half years before I came to New York.

CA: Your writing is very lucid, directed to the general reader without being condescending. Is that something you work especially hard at?

ROCKWELL: Some people think that I'm too intellectualized or Germanically complicated for the general reader. In my opinion, an intellectual (which I flatter myself to be) who chooses to work in journalism is making, whether he knows it or not—and I know it—a populist statement: we live in a democracy, and to write journalism means to make a deliberate attempt to purge oneself of obscurantism. I think journalism at its best is a very healthy way of doing that: it's a way of purging yourself of writer's block, because there are deadlines, and it's a way of purging yourself of prolixity, because there are space limitations. On the other hand, there are definite limitations; you can't always go as far as you want. But the *New York Times*, for all its stress on bright writings, tolerates and encourages a more sophisticated level of writing than any other newspaper in the country. So in that sense it poses fewer limitations than other newspapers might.

CA: In All American Music, *which is certainly a celebration of our musical diversity, you said, "my writing in recent years has reflected a deliberate attempt to open myself up to all forms of musical expression." Are there forms that you've found difficult to learn to enjoy?*

ROCKWELL: I did have the early interest in pop music, but then I got tied up with classical music. I got back into pop when I went out to Berkeley, really. In Berkeley during the 1960s, one was surrounded by the whole counterculture, and that got me interested in it again. But I still didn't write about it with any regularity. When I got to the *Los Angeles Times*, there was a strict jurisdictional division between pop and classical. Also, Bernheimer wanted me to be his person and write about his stuff rather than pop. A lot of classical people, Bernheimer included, have real prejudices against popular music. But when I came to the *New York Times*, it was a kind of accident in the bureaucracy; it turned out that they needed people to do pop criticism, and I was eager to do it and they said OK. I became the chief pop critic in 1974 but continued writing about classical. Then I sort of retired from the regular coverage of the beat of popular music in 1980 because I didn't want to spend a disproportionate amount of time on it. But I still keep doing it.

In answer to your question, I've always loved mainstream classical music; contemporary music, which many people now see as my specialty, came later. I only started getting interested in contemporary music in the 1960s, but I was interested in opera and standard symphonic music in the 1950s. I then got involved with ethnic music—Indian music, Japanese music, Chinese music, African music, and so on. I'd always had a latent interest in rock 'n' roll. Jazz is something that I came

into later. One of the reasons I wrote the [Frank] Sinatra book was that I was very interested in addressing directly a style of music that I didn't have a natural affinity for—I'd always loved Sinatra's own singing, but the big-band era as a whole was not something that I was particularly close to. I have no great interest in easy-listening, Muzak-y kind of stuff, although I find it interesting from a sociological standpoint. And I'm not madly interested in the more ornate and campy forms of cabaret music.

CA: Do you have any sense of how good a musical audience Americans are generally, how open to musical variety, as compared to people in other countries?

ROCKWELL: I think Americans are probably more open than people in other countries. A lot of modernist composers argue that it's cultural prejudices that cause people to be narrow in their views, and therefore, if you take a really unwashed audience, it will be more open than a supposedly sophisticated audience. I've definitely found, for example, that New York, which has in some ways the most sophisticated of American audiences, is in other ways the most conservative of American cities. They're not really willing to accept radical production styles in opera or radical new music because there's so much of everything in New York. If you're an opera buff, you could spend your life just going to opera, whereas if you live in a smaller city and aren't told that you're supposed to hate modern music, you might go to a modern music concert, just because that was the only thing in town that night, and rather enjoy it. I don't think Americans are more prejudiced, certainly, and they may be less prejudiced. Certainly they are assaulted, both in terms of concerts and in terms of recordings and radio, with a greater variety of music than any other culture in the world.

CA: Does knowing you're going to be writing about a performance or a piece of music ever detract from your enjoyment in hearing it?

ROCKWELL: Not at all; quite the reverse. I find at this point that if I go to a concert just because I'm interested in going, but I'm not writing about it, the experience seems incomplete. To formulate an opinion in my own mind and then to articulate it in the course of actually writing out the review is to me the fulfillment of the experience of going to the concert. Therefore, just to go on my own—although I do fairly often—is sort of a strange half-experience.

CA: Do you often hear from readers who disagree vehemently with some assessment you've made?

ROCKWELL: I hear from them, but not often. As Martin Bernheimer used to say, you don't go into this business to be loved. There are people out there in readerland who think I am (a) a total fraud, or (b) a vicious demonic figure bent on destroying the music they love. Every once in a while, of course, you make a really dumb mistake. And when you make a really dumb mistake, people are eager to tell you about it. But I wouldn't say that I'm bombarded with hostile mail. I get a lot of fan letters, too.

CA: What other critics do you read and enjoy?

ROCKWELL: I am a deliberate generalist, yet my pure faith in generalism is undercut by the fact that I enjoy reading specialist critics. It's nice to read someone who can make connections between different kinds of music, but it's also nice to read someone who really knows what the hell he or she is writing about—I don't mean total obscurantism or lists of collectible records, but somebody who really brings an impact to the act of criticism. I enjoy reading several writers on opera: Conrad Osborne, David Hamilton, Peter Davis, Will Crutchfield of the *Times*. I enjoy reading Greg Sandow on experimental music, and Greil Marcus, Bob Christgau, and Dave Marsh on rock; I even enjoy reading Gary Giddins on jazz, even though Gary Giddins has a real animus towards me. I enjoy reading anybody who can write lucidly and with obvious expertise. I also enjoy reading a lot of critics outside of music, like Andrew Sarris and J. Hoberman on movies and Arlene Croce on dance.

CA: Have you still not heard from Frank Sinatra in response to Sinatra: An American Classic?

ROCKWELL: No, but that's not his thing, and I'm not particularly miffed by it. I've never met the man, I never talked to him on the telephone, and I don't imagine I ever will. I wrote that book as a study of his recordings, really, with commentary on his life. And given his reputation as a kind of gnarled and weird character, I'm quite content not to have met him.

CA: How did you manage to round up the photos and get permission to use them?

ROCKWELL: That really wasn't my doing. Rolling Stone Press has put out a series of these coffee table books in conjunction with other publishers. Basically the other publishers function as the publisher and Rolling Stone Press functions as the editor. They had a whole lot of practice in putting out these big picture books, so they had a staff of picture editors. The deal with the Sinatra book was that I would provide the text and advice about the pictures, but wouldn't be responsible for organizing the pictures. So their people pulled them all in and then I went through them and suggested that they get pictures in other areas and helped them identify some of the people they didn't know and that kind of thing. When you put out a cattle call for Sinatra pictures, what you get is endless film stills and pictures of him in nightclubs. What you don't necessarily get right away are pictures of him in recording sessions and with his musical collaborators. That was what I was constantly pushing for. My role in the picture selection was to redress the balance and get more musical pictures into the book.

CA: In All American Music *you commented on John Cage's allowing "an indigenously American sense of humor . . . to flower." Do you see a lot of humor in the music that's being made today?*

ROCKWELL: Some. You'll note also that in *All American Music* I take a swipe at the whole idea of musical humor. I don't think that abstract music independent of words is often successfully funny. You have Mozart's "Musical Joke," the end of Beethoven's Eighth Symphony, and a few other obvious jokes in music, but as a general rule—in my perhaps Germanically serious view—music is a romantic, impassioned, intensely profound art. Sure, there are all kinds of cute novelties—Cyndi Lauper is cute and there's some cute experimental stuff. But I don't think there's any more humor in music now than there ever was, and there's plenty of deep seriousness too. People who don't necessarily like avant-garde music, or aren't familiar with a composer, are prone to assume that the composer is trying to play a joke on them. As a general rule, he isn't.

CA: You've described the difference between "uptown music" and "downtown music" in New York. How much downtown music is being done now?

ROCKWELL: In Manhattan, the downtown scene is in a lull, which has largely to do with real estate. The developers have priced artists out of SoHo and Tribeca and forced them into the East Village, Brooklyn, Hoboken, or wherever, and that's diffused the scene somewhat. So has the general conservative climate of the times. But downtown music, so-called, is the same as California music or experimental music in general, and there's plenty of that going on, especially in California. So I don't think we've lost the experimental spirit, compared with the more gnomic and mandarin-like aspects of uptown music—which also exists in places other than middle and upper Manhattan, too; it's all over the country. The basic polarity between romanticism and classicism, emotionalism and intellectualism, the feminine and masculine principles—whatever you want to call it—still exists and there's plenty of action on both sides, with something of a swing of the pendulum, I think, towards the romantic, feminine, and emotional.

CA: How early do you think music should be taught in some form in the schools, and how do you think it should be approached?

ROCKWELL: I'm all for the people who bemoan the decline of musical literacy. It's unfair, but if you compare the whole sweep of American culture today with only the upper-middle classes of Europe a hundred years ago, there's obviously less literacy today. But even if you compare the upper-middle classes of today with the upper-middle classes a hundred years ago, there's still less musical literacy now. On the other hand, there are plenty of people playing instruments and doing a hands-on approach to music; it's just that most of them are playing a kind of music that classical-music educators don't recognize as music, that is, rock 'n' roll.

I think the Orff and Kodaly methods, with real hands-on or voice-on involvement of kids, are terrific. In a rational culture, we'd spend less on bombs and more on humanistic education, and the humanistic education would include some form of musical literacy and the demystifying of music at an early age. And I think the earlier the better; I like the idea of these little babies being thrown into swimming pools at the age of two months, and starting to sing little songs at two or three years old. There's no reason that when you learn to write words, you couldn't also learn to write and sing and play music.

CA: Do you foresee anything new in music in the next few years, or are we likely to stay in what you've described as a time of synthesizing the existing forms?

ROCKWELL: The future's hard to predict. I think all sorts of interesting things are happening in the electronic and computer areas. Bear in mind that there are fashions of the moment that will be viewed differently in the twenty-second century. People will look back and see grand, simple lines defining late twentieth-century music, generalizations that will weed out stuff that's important to us now. Connections will be made between things that seem divided today—for example, Cage's irrationalism versus Babbitt's rationalism: the music sounds similar sometimes, and I think people two hundred years from now will concentrate more on the fact that it sounds similar than on the fact that they were polemical opposites at this point. I think the vernacularization of cultivated music will continue, that the trend towards accessibility will continue, that musical theater will continue, and that electronic and computer experiments will continue. Music theater and electronic music seem to me to be two obvious areas for development.

CA: What's in the works for you? Are there more books you'd like to do?

ROCKWELL: I've been bogged down the last couple of years by the forthcoming *New Grove Dictionary of Music in the United States,* plus a monograph I've owed Brooklyn College for years. But I'm trying to gear up now to do a book on opera and music theater.

BIOGRAPHICAL/CRITICAL SOURCES:

PERIODICALS

Best Sellers, February, 1985.
Harper's, April, 1983.
Nation, November 17, 1984.
National Review, April 11, 1986.
New Republic, July 11, 1983.
New Statesman, May 24, 1985.
Newsweek, April 18, 1983.
New York Review of Books, July 21, 1983.
New York Times, March 19, 1983, November 8, 1984.
New York Times Book Review, April 17, 1983, November 11, 1984.
Times Literary Supplement, October 28, 1983.
Village Voice, May 3, 1983.
Washington Post Book World, April 10, 1983.

—Sketch by Barbara A. Cicchetti

—Interview by Jean W. Ross

*   *   *

ROOKE, Constance 1942-

PERSONAL: Born November 14, 1942, in New York, N.Y.; daughter of Charles M. (a publisher) and Hilary (Fitch) Raymond; married Leon Rooke (a writer), May 25, 1969; children: Jonathan Blue. *Education:* Smith College, B.A., 1964; Tulane University, M.A., 1966; University of North Carolina at Chapel Hill, Ph.D., 1973.

ADDRESSES: Home—1019 Terrace Ave., Victoria, British Columbia, Canada V8S 3V2. *Office*—*Malahat Review,* University of Victoria, Victoria, British Columbia, Canada V8W 2Y2.

CAREER: University of Victoria, Victoria, British Columbia, lecturer, 1969-73, assistant professor, 1973-77, associate professor, 1977-88, professor of English, 1988—, director of Learning and Teaching Centre. Member of Canada Council's Advisory Panel on Writing and Publication.

MEMBER: Canadian Periodical Publishers Association (member of board of directors, 1986—).

WRITINGS:

Reynolds Price, Twayne, 1983.
(Editor) *Night Light: Stories of Aging,* Oxford University Press, 1986.

Editor of *Malahat Review,* 1983—.

WORK IN PROGRESS: Home Movies, a collection of short stories, publication expected in 1989; a critical work on old age and contemporary fiction, completion expected in 1990.

*   *   *

ROOTS, John McCook 1904(?)-1988

OBITUARY NOTICE: Born c. 1904 in Hankou, China; died July 26, 1988, in St. Ignace, Mich. Journalist and author. Roots was a foreign correspondent who covered events in more than ninety countries. Specializing in East Asian affairs, the journalist wrote for such newspapers as the *New York Times, Wall Street Journal,* and *Los Angeles Times.* Roots was also the author of the 1978 book *Chou: An Informal Biography of China's Legendary Chou En-lai.*

OBITUARIES AND OTHER SOURCES:

PERIODICALS

New York Times, July 29, 1988.

*   *   *

ROSEN, Charles (Welles) 1927-

PERSONAL: Born May 5, 1927, in New York, N. Y.; son of Irwin and Anita (Gerber) Rosen. *Education:* Attended Juilliard School of Music, 1933-1938; Princeton University, B.A. (summa cum laude), 1947, M.A., 1949, Ph.D., 1951.

ADDRESSES: Home—New York, N. Y. *Office*—Department of Music, State University of New York at Stony Brook, Stony Brook, N. Y. 11790.

CAREER: Concert pianist, 1951—; Massachusetts Institute of Technology, Cambridge, Mass., assistant professor of modern languages, 1953-55; State University of New York at Stony Brook, Stony Brook, N. Y., professor of music, 1971—; writer. Messenger Lecturer at Cornell University, 1975; Ernest Bloch Professor at University of California, Berkeley, 1977; Charles Eliot Norton Professor of Poetry at Harvard University, 1980-81; professor of music and social thought at University of Chicago, 1986; George Eastman Professor at Oxford University, 1987-88. Pianist in solo recitals and with numerous orchestras in both concert performances and recordings.

MEMBER: National Academy of Arts and Sciences.

AWARDS, HONORS: Fulbright fellowship, 1951-53; Deems Taylor Award from American Society of Composers, Authors, and Publishers and National Book Award in arts and letters, both 1972, both for *The Classical Style: Haydn, Mozart, Beethoven;* Guggenheim fellowship, 1973; Edison Prize, 1974; D.Mus. from Trinity College (Dublin), 1976, University of Leeds, 1978, and Durham University, 1980.

WRITINGS:

The Classical Style: Haydn, Mozart, Beethoven, Viking, 1971.
Arnold Schoenberg (monograph), Viking, 1975 (published in England as *Schoenberg,* Calder & Boyars, 1975).
Sonata Forms, Norton, 1982.
(With Henri Zerner) *Romanticism and Realism: The Mythology of Nineteenth-Century Art* (essays), Viking, 1984.

Contributor to periodicals, including *New York Review of Books.*

SIDELIGHTS: Charles Rosen has distinguished himself as both a concert pianist and a scholar. In childhood he attended the Juilliard School of Music, and in adolescence he studied piano under the celebrated instructor Moritz Rosenthal, a former pupil of Franz Liszt. Rosen continued his musical training while at Princeton University, where he earned a doctorate in French literature in 1951. That same year he made his professional debut as a concert pianist. Since that time, Rosen has gained recognition as a pianist of commanding technique and sensitivity. He has also earned respect for his wide-ranging repertoire, which stretches from works of Baroque master Johann Sebastian Bach to those of modern composers such as Pierre Boulez. In addition, Rosen has assayed the staples of piano literature—compositions by Ludwig van Beethoven and those of Romantics such as Robert Schumann—and has thus proved himself an artist of great versatility as well as one of great technical and interpretative mastery.

Though probably best known as a performer, Rosen has also gained substantial recognition as a critic. His first book, 1971's *The Classical Style: Haydn, Mozart, Beethoven*, is a complex and demanding analysis of musical language as developed by three great composers. He argues that the development of each artist's musical language was predicated on the "symmetrical resolution of opposing forces," and he illustrates his thesis through detailed analysis of examples from genres such as symphonies, string quartets, and even operas. Alan Tyson, writing in the *New York Review of Books*, deemed Rosen's effort "a formidable task: first to describe and then to explain and trace the development and maturation of what has so far proved the richest stylistic achievement in Western music."

Critics were generally enthusiastic in assessing *The Classical Style*. Tyson wrote that the book succeeds "in such a way and on such a scale as to make it hard for anyone who cares about the music characterized here to remain without illumination." Similarly, E. T. Cone reported in the *New York Times Book Review* that *The Classical Style* is a "thoughtful and illuminating study." And even *Nation* reviewer Robert Lilienfeld, who complained that Rosen's rhetoric was "elusive and allusive," nonetheless conceded that the book contains "brilliant observations on particular works." Lilienfeld added that *The Classical Style* is "genuinely valuable for its details, for its incidental insights."

In 1975 Rosen completed the monograph *Arnold Schoenberg*, which he wrote for Viking's "Modern Masters" series. In this short book, Rosen considered Schoenberg's development from expressionism to atonality and from serialism to neoclassicism, and he assessed the composer's entire career within the context of European musical history. Reviewers of *Arnold Schoenberg* agreed that the book offered an incisive analysis of the composer and his work. Donal Henahan affirmed in the *New York Times Book Review*, "What Mr. Rosen does, far better than one could reasonably expect in so concise a book, is not only to elucidate Schoenberg's composing techniques and artistic philosophy but to place them in history." Robert Craft, in his commentary for the *New York Review of Books*, noted that *Arnold Schoenberg* would prove most useful to musicians and musicologists, but he praised Rosen's exposition as "admirably lucid" and commended his "directness in identifying and confronting central issues." Craft ultimately commended *Arnold Schoenberg* as "one of the most brilliant monographs ever to be published on any composer."

In Rosen's third book, *Sonata Forms*, he traces the development of the sonata structure. He notes that the nineteenth-century definition of the sonata is woefully imprecise and establishes that a proper definition of the term encompasses several interdependent forms. In addition, he analyzes stylistic differences, illustrating how the first movements from different sonatas may differ substantially. As with Rosen's previous works, *Sonata Forms* was praised as a provocative and compelling volume. "After studying such analyses," wrote Edward Rothstein in the *New York Times Book Review*, "one's ears return to the music more educated, more aware of the life behind the forms." Joseph Kerman, writing in the *New York Review of Books*, was even more enthusiastic, contending that "to familiar and unfamiliar music alike Rosen brings not only an uncommonly refined ear and sensibility but also . . . unerring insight into just the features that make the music special and fine."

Romanticism and Realism: The Mythology of Nineteenth-Century Art, Rosen's following work, presents a wide-ranging assessment of artistic schools leading to the present avant-garde. With collaborator Henri Zerner, a museum curator, Rosen explores the development of nineteenth-century art—music, painting and sculpture, and literature—as the result of artists' continual effort to avoid convention. This pursuit of the unknown and socially unacceptable is traced from romanticism to realism to today's avant-garde art. Marina Vaizey, writing in the *New York Times Book Review*, described Rosen and Zerner's volume as a collection of "audacious, ambitious essays." *Spectator* reviewer Marc Jordan found the volume appealing and refreshing, observing that "what is most impressive about the articles which make up *Romanticism and Realism* is their sense of engagement." Jordan added, "At a time when art criticism and art history seem to have drawn away in to opposite corners, it is healthy to be reminded that serious writing about the art of the past can be in the best sense 'partial, passionate, and political.'"

Despite enjoying great prominence as a critic, Rosen insists that he is primarily a pianist. Interviewed by the *New York Times* in 1977, Rosen referred to writing as "a sort of hobby." He explained: "At the piano, if you practice 10 hours a day, then you have no time to write. I really can't practice more than about four to five. I can play the piano for eight to 10 hours a day, but I can't practice for that long. So I have to do something with my time."

BIOGRAPHICAL/CRITICAL SOURCES:

BOOKS

Dubal, David, *Reflections From the Keyboard: The World of the Concert Pianists*, Summit Books, 1984.

PERIODICALS

Christian Century, October 22, 1975, May 30, 1984.
Christian Science Monitor, May 24, 1976.
Clavier, March, 1984.
Nation, December 6, 1971.
Newsweek, May 3, 1971.
New York Review of Books, June 15, 1972, September 18, 1975, October 23, 1980.
New York Times, October 16, 1977.
New York Times Book Review, May 23, 1971, December 28, 1975, December 21, 1980, April 1, 1984.
Observer, May 23, 1976.
Spectator, May 26, 1984.
Time, December 29, 1952.
Times Literary Supplement, April 16, 1971, June 10, 1977.
Village Voice, January 4, 1983.

—*Sketch by Les Stone*

ROSS, Brian (Elliot) 1948-

PERSONAL: Born October 23, 1948, in Chicago, Ill.; son of Kenneth Earl (in business) and Shirley Louise (an artist; maiden name, Johnston) Ross; married Lucinda Sanman (a photographer), May, 1985. *Education:* University of Iowa, B.A., 1971.

ADDRESSES: Office—NBC News, 30 Rockefeller Plaza, New York, N.Y. 10020.

CAREER/WRITINGS: National Broadcasting Company (NBC), news correspondent for affiliates KWWL-TV in Waterloo, Iowa, 1971, and WCKT-TV in Miami, Fla., 1972-74, and for NBC News in Cleveland, Ohio, 1974-76, and New York, N.Y., 1976—.

AWARDS, HONORS: George Foster Peabody Broadcasting Award from the University of Georgia Henry W. Grady School of Journalism and Mass Communication, 1974; Alfred I. duPont-Columbia University awards from Columbia University Graduate School of Journalism, 1975, 1985, and 1986; Sigma Delta Chi Award, 1976; National Broadcasters awards, 1976, 1978, 1980, and 1987; Robert F. Kennedy Journalism Award from Robert F. Kennedy Memorial, 1979; National Emmy awards from the National Academy of Television Arts and Sciences, 1980 and 1986; award from Overseas Press Club, 1988.

CA INTERVIEW

CA interviewed Brian Ross by telephone on June 29, 1987, at his office in New York, N.Y.

CA: What attracted you to television news in the first place? How did you break into it?

ROSS: I was attracted to journalism in general back in my high school days. I had a wonderful high school journalism newspaper adviser, and, as a student, I worked on our town's local newspaper—the *Highland Park Star* in Highland Park, Illinois—which had a crusading editor. I then started doing some broadcast work, and it turned out that I enjoyed not only the journalism part but the camera work, the editing, putting things together.

CA: Since you've become a professional, you have never worked for a medium other than radio and television. Do you think newspapers have a future?

ROSS: I think so. I find if I haven't read a number of newspapers each day I don't know all of what's going on. There are real limitations to television news, but there are also wonderful advantages, such as the ability to convey feelings.

CA: You've been at NBC or with its affiliates for your entire career. Was that a plan?

ROSS: It wasn't a plan, although I grew up in a household where we always watched NBC.

CA: Corporate loyalty aside, do you think NBC network news is superior to the other networks' news operations?

ROSS: They're all very, very good. Some are stronger in some areas than in others. I think we now have the strongest staff of any evening news program, and we have the strongest commitment to tough enterprise reporting.

CA: It's said that competition among the networks causes them to do silly things they wouldn't do in the absence of competition. What do you think?

ROSS: Competition means you're doing something to attract viewers or readers, and there you have a judgment about whether what you do is going to be silly or whether it's going to be serious. NBC has always favored more and tougher reporting, more effort on the substantive side. There's never been a time when anyone at NBC has said to me, "This is ratings week. Can you put in something peppier or jazzier?"

CA: What problems did you have moving from Cleveland to New York City in terms of the kind of reporting you were doing in both towns?

ROSS: None, really. I've done the same kind of reporting in both places. The only difference is that in writing for a national audience you have to adopt a different style. People in Cleveland know very well who their local officials are, and you can use a kind of shorthand; in national reporting you can't.

CA: You're a network correspondent. How is it decided when the network is going to send you to cover a story rather than use footage from a local affiliate?

ROSS: For the most part, my producer at the network, Ira Silverman, and I come up with our own story ideas, get them by our producers, and venture out on our own. In almost all cases we do our own shooting. Sometimes if some event is happening, a local station will cover it if we can't get there; or if something happened a year ago that a local station covered that now has significance for a national story, we'll use the local station's footage.

CA: People in print journalism say it's much more difficult to do investigative reporting for television than for the print media.

ROSS: That's true. In most instances, at the time we begin shooting, we could at that point sit down and write the story for print. We have the bulk of the facts and information. But then we have to track down the people we need to interview, arrange the shoots, and get them on screen. For instance, we did a story on [fugitive financier] Robert Vesco hiding out in Cuba. We went down to Cuba under the guise of covering a Third World economic conference and spent two days following the rough directions we had to Vesco's hideaway. Then we hid in the bushes across from his house from early one morning to late that day and finally got footage of him. We aired it the following day. That story could have appeared in print before we flew off to Cuba, but to get that footage took a week of hard, long hours. We also put ourselves in quite a bit of personal jeopardy. Castro announced that we were CIA agents and that if we came back we would be arrested as spies.

CA: Have you been back to Cuba since?

ROSS: No, although NBC was allowed back in in February of 1988.

CA: Didn't you also do a major story about Vesco's activities in the Bahamas?

ROSS: Yes, it was a story about a major drug operation at an island in the Bahamas called Norman's Cay, which became the stronghold of a major Colombian drug dealer who, by his own admission, was in partnership with Vesco. They claimed they were paying off members of the Bahamian Government. It was a very strong story and had a lot to do with some steps being taken toward ending corruption in the Bahamas.

CA: What were those steps? Were they taken by the Bahamian Government?

ROSS: Well, they were sort of compelled to be more cooperative with the American authorities. There's still a serious, serious problem there. It's far from resolved. However, for the most part we don't really expect to see any particular result from the stories we do. It's our job to report it; it's the job of others to act on that information.

CA: There was some speculation that the story might affect [Bahamian Prime Minister Lynden Oscar] Pindling's reelection chances.

ROSS: He was reelected easily. By picturing the story as American intervention, he turned the issue around so it weighed in his favor.

CA: Speaking of controversial stories, entertainer Wayne Newton sued you and your producer for a story you did about him.

ROSS: And the jury found against us. That verdict has not yet been certified by the judge and will be appealed.

CA: What did that story say?

ROSS: It reported that organized crime figures from New York had a relationship with Wayne Newton. What we said is that Newton did not tell the whole story of that relationship in his public testimony.

CA: Have you been sued often, successfully?

ROSS: Never before successfully. We were sued by [perennial political candidate and cult leader] Lyndon LaRouche in 1984. We did the first national story on him and his cult, and he sued. We went to trial on that, and not only did he lose the suit, but the jury awarded NBC two million dollars in damages. And Prime Minister Pindling has sued us in Canada where journalists do not have any first amendment protections.

CA: So NBC stood behind you in these suits?

ROSS: Yes. They've been terrific about it.

CA: Some newspapers have tried to cut themselves loose from their reporters when those reporters are sued.

ROSS: That could be terribly discouraging. However, NBC's been nothing but terrific.

CA: Didn't you once overcome a hijacker?

ROSS: Yes. I was returning from an assignment as one of the first reporters, if not the first, to cover the Nicaraguan *contras* in their Honduran base camps just over the Nicaraguan border. The Honduran Airlines commercial flight I was on was hijacked by four Honduran guerillas trained in Cuba. They held us for three days and nights on the plane, parked at the airport at Tegucigalpa, the capital of Honduras. In the end we escaped from the plane while they were preparing to blow it up with dynamite charges.

CA: How did you escape?

ROSS: A number of efforts at negotiation had failed. So, as a last ditch effort, I suggested that they take me to Cuba and let everybody else go. They went to the back of the plane to discuss it. It was the first time they had left us unguarded the entire time. At that point, I and two others pulled the exit releases, and we dived out through the windows. I got badly hurt, cut up in the fall. But it could have been worse; the hijackers shot at us as we ran across the airport tarmac. They didn't hit us, though.

CA: You also investigated Teamster leader Jackie Presser, didn't you?

ROSS: I did a five-part series on Presser when I was in local television; that's what catapulted me to the network. The series reported that the Cleveland Teamsters played a key role in a national scheme of corruption and that Presser and his father had close ties to certain Cleveland organized crime figures and were involved in the robbery of the union pension and welfare funds.

CA: What was the local reaction?

ROSS: A lot of it was very negative. That sort of story had not been done before in Cleveland. One newspaper fellow was about to do a story like that and was told by an editor, "You know who distributes our newspaper every day? Teamsters."

CA: Of the stories you've done, what's your favorite?

ROSS: The story I'm working on at the moment is always my favorite.

CA: Do you call your stories documentaries when they're aired?

ROSS: Well, rather than be broadcast separately, most of my stories are broadcast on the evening news, so I'm not sure if you'd call them documentaries per se. Sometimes they take up as much as one-third of the program, though.

CA: Some say the Golden Age of television documentaries has passed; do you think that statement's true?

ROSS: I don't know, but I've always worked in this format, and I find it particularly effective. It has a lot of impact to be on the "NBC Evening News With Tom Brokaw" three or four nights in a row with a hard-hitting report.

CA: Does being on the Brokaw show give you a larger audience share?

ROSS: I don't know. Those documentaries have overall low ratings, a small percentage of the audience, but the pie is so much bigger at night. I don't know. I have no complaints.

CA: Do you have any desire to work out of Washington, D.C., rather than New York?

ROSS: I travel so much it doesn't really matter where I work from.

CA: What's your eventual professional goal? Do you want to be a news anchorman or stay where you are?

ROSS: If I could just keep doing what I'm doing and do it better, that would be fine with me.

—*Interview by Peter Benjaminson*

*   *   *

ROSTAND, Edmond (Eugene Alexis) 1868-1918

PERSONAL: Born April 1, 1868, in Marseilles, France; died December 2 (one source says December 22), 1918, in Paris, France; son of Eugene (a journalist, poet, and economist) Rostand; married Rosemonde Gerard (a poet) April 8, 1890; children: Maurice, Jean. *Education:* Attended the College Stanislas in Paris, beginning in 1884; briefly studied law.

CAREER: Poet and playwright.

MEMBER: Academie Francaise.

AWARDS, HONORS: Marseilles Academy prize, 1887, for "Deux Romanciers de Provence: Honore d'Urfe et Emile Zola"; Toirac prize from the Academie Francaise, 1894, for "Les Romanesques"; Ordre de Legion d'Honneur, 1900.

WRITINGS:

PLAYS

(With Henry Lee) "Le Gant rouge" (title means "The Red Glove"), first produced at the Cluny Theater, 1888.

Les Romanesques (three-act; first produced in Paris at the Comedie-Francaise, May 21, 1894), Charpentier et Fasquelle, 1900; translation by Mary Hendee published as *The Romancers,* Doubleday, 1899; translation by George Fleming published as *The Fantasticks,* R. H. Russell, 1900, reprinted, Fertig, 1987; edited by Henry Le Daum with preface, introduction, and notes, Ginn & Co., 1903, with vocabulary by Noelia Dubrule, 1924; translation by Barrett H. Clark published as *The Romancers,* Samuel French, 1915.

La Princesse lointaine (four-act; first produced in Paris at the Theatre de la Renaissance, April 5, 1895), edited by J. L. Borgerhoff with introduction and notes, Heath, 1909; translation and preface by Charles Renauld, F. A. Stokes, 1899; translation by Anna Emilia Bagstad published as *The Princess Far-away,* R. G. Badger, 1921; translation by John Heard, Jr., with introduction by Stark Young, published as *The Far Princess,* Holt, 1925, reprinted, Fertig, 1987; published by French & European Publications, 1947.

La Samaritaine (title means "The Woman of Samaria"; three-act; first produced in Paris at the Theatre de la Renaissance, April 14, 1897), Fasquelle, 1897; published by French & European Publications, 1953.

Cyrano de Bergerac (five-act; first produced in Paris at the Theatre de la Porte-Saint-Martin, December 28, 1897), Fasquelle, 1898; translation by Howard Thayer Kingsbury, Lamson, Wolfe & Co., 1898, edited and modernized by Oscar H. Fidell, Washington Square Press, 1966; translation by Gertrude Hall, Doubleday, 1898; translation by Gladys Thomas and Mary F. Guillemard, G. Munro's Sons, 1898; translation by Helen B. Dole with introduction by William P. Trent, Crowell, 1899, with illustrations by Nino Carbe, 1931; translation by Charles Renauld with introduction by Adolphe Cohn, F. A. Stokes, 1899; with introduction and notes by Oscar Kuhns, Holt, 1899; with introduction and notes by Reed Paige Clark, W. R. Jenkins, 1902; with introduction, notes, and vocabulary by Kuhns and Henry Ward Church, Holt, 1920;

edited by A. G. H. Speirs with introduction, notes, and list of proper names and vocabulary, Oxford University Press, 1921, 2nd edition, 1938; translation by Brian Hooker with preface by Clayton Hamilton, Holt, 1923, with introduction by Hooker and illustrations by Sylvain Sauvage, Limited Editions, 1936, with introduction and notes by Elisabeth Hooker, Holt, 1937; adaptation by Erna Kruckemeyer, S. French, 1934; edited by Leslie Ross Meras, Harper, 1936; translation by Humbert Wolfe, Hutchinson & Co., 1937; edited by H. Aston, Blackwell, 1942; translation by Louis Untermeyer with illustrations by Pierre Brissaud, Limited Editions, 1954; translation by James Forsyth, Dramatic Publishing, 1968; edited by Edward A. Bird, Methuen, 1968; translation and adaptation by Anthony Burgess, Knopf, 1971; translation by Lowell Bair with an afterword by Henry Hanes, New American Library, 1972; translation by Christopher Fry, Oxford University Press, 1975; annotated by Patrick Besnier, Gallimard, 1983; edition with commentary by Jacques Truchet and illustrations by Jean-Denis Malcles, Imprimerie National, 1983.

L'Aiglon (title means "The Eaglet"; six-act; first produced in Paris at the Theatre Sarah-Bernhardt, March 15, 1900), Brentano's, 1900; translation by Louis N. Parker, R. H. Russell, 1900; translation by Basil Davenport, Yale University Press, 1927; translation and adaptation by Clemence Dane and Richard Addinsell published as *Edmond Rostand's L'Aiglon,* Doubleday, 1934; published as *Aiglon,* French & European Publications, 1964.

Chantecler (four-act; first produced in Paris at the Theatre de la Porte-Saint-Martin, February 7, 1910), Fasquelle, 1910; translation by Hall, Duffield & Co., 1910; translation by John Strong Newberry, Duffield & Co., 1911, translation by Kay Nolte Smith with drawings from original French edition adapted by Joan Mitchell Blumenthal, University Press of America, 1987.

La Derniere Nuit de don Juan (two-act; first produced in 1922), Charpentier et Fasquelle, 1921; translation by T. Lawrason Riggs with introduction by William Lyon Phelps published as *The Last Night of Don Juan,* Kahoe & Co., 1929.

Also author of play *Les Deux Pierrots; ou, Le Souper blanc* (title means "The Two Pierrots; or, The White Supper"), 1891, and of the unfinished, unpublished plays "Yorick" and "Les Petites Manies."

POETRY

Les Musardises (includes "Les Deux Cavaliers," "Nos Rires," "Le Cauchemar," "Le Contrebandier," "Priere d'un matin bleu," "La Fleur," "Le Mendiant fleuri," "Tout d'un coup," "Les Boeufs," "L'If," "La Brouette," "L'Eau," and "Ombres et fumees"), 1890, revised edition, Fasquelle, 1911, French & European Publications, 1955.

Le Vol de la Marseillaise (title means "The Flight of the Marseillaise"; includes "L'Etoile entre les peupliers"), Charpentier et Fasquelle, 1919.

Also author of *Le Cantique de l'aile* (title means "The Canticle of the Wing"; includes "Le Cantique de l'aile," "Un Soir a Hernani," "Les Mots," and "Le Bois Sacre"), 1910. Contributor of poetry to periodicals, including *Mireille.*

COLLECTED WORKS

Oevres completes illustrees de Edmond Rostand (contains "L'Aiglon," "Cyrano de Bergerac," "Les Romanesques," "La Samaritaine," "Chantecler," "La Princesse lointaine," "Les Musardises," and "Le Bois sacre"), seven volumes, P. Lafitte, 1910-11.

Plays of Edmond Rostand (contains "Romantics," "The Princess Far Away," "The Woman of Samaria," "Cyrano de Bergerac," "The Eaglet," "Chanticleer"), two volumes, translation by Henderson Daingerfield Norman, illustrations by Ivan Glidden, Macmillan, 1921.

Cyrano de Bergerac [and] *Chanticleer*, translation by Clifford Hershey Bissell and William Van Wyck, Ritchie, 1947.

OTHER

Also author of essay *Deux Romanciers de Provence: Honore d'Urfe et Emile Zola: Le Roman sentimental et le roman naturaliste*, E. Champion, 1921.

SIDELIGHTS: Edmond Rostand penned many plays and three volumes of poetry, but he is best remembered today for creating the romantic "Cyrano de Bergerac." The play, which combines comedy and heroic tragedy, has been continually revived since its first performance in Paris in 1897 and has been translated from its original French into many languages, including English, Spanish, Russian, and Hebrew, making its long-nosed title character beloved worldwide. In writing the role of Cyrano, Rostand provided a showcase for many great actors, starting with French theater star Constant Coquelin and including noted thespians Ralph Richardson, Jose Ferrer, and Christopher Plummer. Especially with "Cyrano de Bergerac," but also with his dramas "The Far Princess," "The Eaglet," and "Chantecler," Rostand is credited with briefly reviving the popularity of romance and heroism on a turn-of-the-century French stage dominated by realism. Rostand is also known for his early comedic success "The Romancers," which continues to be performed in its 1960 adaptation as a popular Off-Broadway musical "The Fantasticks."

Rostand was born in 1868 in Marseilles, France, to wealthy parents. His father was the prominent economist Eugene Rostand, a member of the Academy of Moral and Political Sciences of Marseilles and the Institut de France, who wrote poems and translated the works of the ancient Roman lyric poet Gaius Valerius Catullus. One of Rostand's aunts, Victorine Rostand, was also a poet, and his uncle Alexis Rostand was a well-known composer of oratorios, pieces for piano, and an opera. As Alba della Fazia Amoia pointed out in her 1978 biography of the author, *Edmond Rostand*, "the cult of the arts was in the family tradition." Rostand's childhood in Marseilles also contains clues to his future career: his favorite activity was designing stage sets and costumes for his puppet theater, and one of his boyhood heroes was French emperor Napoleon Bonaparte, whose son Francois he would later bring to the stage as the subject of his "Eaglet." By his adolescence, according to Amoia, Rostand had been proclaimed the "school poet" of the Marseilles Lycee, and he had begun to publish his poetry in *Mireille* magazine.

After finishing secondary school in 1884, Rostand left Marseilles for Paris to attend classes at the College Stanislas. While studying law to please his father, he spent more of his concentration penning plays and poems, including the unfinished efforts "Yorick" and "Les Petites Manies." In 1888 Rostand's first play, "Le Gant rouge" (title means "The Red Glove"), written in collaboration with Henry Lee, was performed at the Cluny Theater, but it did not meet with much success. Though he won the Marseilles Academy prize in 1887 for his essay *Deux Romanciers de Provence* (title means "Two Provencal Novelists"), the French public was not aware of

Rostand until 1890, the year in which he married poet Rosemonde Gerard, when his first volume of poems, *Les Musardises,* appeared.

Though *Musardises* was not critically acclaimed at its publication, Amoia asserted that the volume holds "a certain fascination." Dedicated to Rostand's wife, *Musardises* is divided into three sections: "La Chambre d'etudiant" (title means "The Student's Room"), "Incertitudes" (title means "Uncertainties"), and "La Maison des Pyrenees" (title means "Home in the Pyrenees"). Another section, criticized as "overly lyric and personal," according to Amoia, was taken out in the revised version of 1911. Besides containing some meritorious pieces, such as "Le Cauchemar" (title means "Nightmare"), which Amoia lauded as "an extremely well-constructed poem, vibrant with scorn," *Musardises* is interesting because many of the trademarks of Rostand's more famous works are already apparent in it. "The dedicatory poem which opens *Les Musardises,*" explained Amoia, "is, in fact, Rostand's declaration of love for 'les rates' (failures in life), whom the public scorns and insults because it cannot understand the dreams and ideals of the great poet's struggle for beauty and perfection." She continued: "To all Bohemian artists, painters, musicians—the lost children of society whose symphonies remain forever unfinished—Rostand declares his fraternity and friendship, joining with the outcast knights-errant to go out in search of Art." One of the poems in "Home in the Pyrenees," the section of *Musardises* inspired by the Rostand family vacation home in Cambo near the French-Spanish border, deals with Spanish author Miguel de Cervantes Saavedra's famous character Don Quixote and laments the fact that France no longer admires the spirit of the knight. This theme is picked up again in Rostand's *Cyrano de Bergerac.* Cyrano has often been compared to Don Quixote, and in a confrontational scene between Cyrano and the Comte de Guiche, de Guiche asks, "Have you read *Don Quixote?*" Cyrano returns, "I have—and found myself the hero."

Rostand's first taste of popular success came with the 1894 production of "The Romancers." Declared by novelist Henry James in *The Critic* "as charming an examination of the nature of the romantic, [and] as pleasant a contribution to any discussion, as can be imagined," the play concerns Sylvette and Percinet, a pair of young lovers who think they are comparable to playwright William Shakespeare's Romeo and Juliet in defying their mutually hostile fathers to become betrothed. In actuality, though, they have been tricked into falling in love. Their fathers, in reality the best of friends, have been feigning hostility and separating their adjoining properties by a stone wall because they believe their children will only marry each other if forbidden to do so. The fathers hire a group of men to stage a fake abduction of Sylvette so that Percinet can rescue her and thus provide an excuse for the pretended enemies' subsequent "reconciliation." When Sylvette and Percinet discover their respective danger and heroism were only contrived, they become disillusioned with their love, and separately seek true adventure. The lovers reunite, however, when they find that real adventure is not as appealing as their familiar, comfortable relationship.

James commented that in "The Romancers," the "action takes place in that happy land of nowhere—the land of poetry, comedy, drollery, delicacy, profuse literary association . . . and if the whole thing is the frankest of fantasies . . . it is the work of a man already conscious of all the values involved." Though he complained that "The Romancers" is "really too much made up of ribbons and flowers," James concluded that "we note as its especial charm the ease with which the author's fancy moves in his rococo world." Similarly, in the *Fortnightly Review*, G. Jean-Aubry saw "The Romancers" as a balanced example of both Rostand's writing talents and his deficiencies. There is in the play, he claimed, "the germ of all that is best and least good in Rostand; a very great technical cleverness, a facility for making his personages live and move, a tendency to complicate the simplest situations by play of words, and a real charm . . . in making his rhymes 'sing'. . . . Already he writes verses that are supple, natural, unforced, and others that are tortured and wrung out with difficulty." While most critics have concluded that "The Romancers," as a comedic satire on love, is lighter than Rostand's later plays, Amoia asserted that it "contain[s] a moral also: we must have faith in what we are doing and we must remain faithful to love." Rostand received the Toirac prize from the Academie Francaise for the play.

Encouraged by the success of "The Romancers," Rostand penned a more serious work, "The Far Princess," designed to showcase the talents of the famed French actress Sarah Bernhardt. Based on the medieval legend of troubadour prince Joffroy Rudel and Melissinde, princess of Tripoli, the play was produced in 1895. The action takes place on Rudel's ship—as he lies dying, his shipmates, inspired by the purity of his passion, row on in spite of hunger, thirst, and sickness in order that he might see before his death the princess he has long worshipped from afar—and in Melissinde's palace, where tales of Rudel's fervent love for her have kindled reciprocal feelings in the princess. Mistaking Bertrand, Rudel's faithful friend and messenger, for Rudel himself, Melissinde falls in love with him. Bertrand falls in love with the princess also, and the two of them almost ignore Rudel's dying request that Melissinde come to his deathbed. The force of Melissinde's idealized love for Rudel, however, proves stronger than her more earthly attraction to Bertrand, and she reaches Rudel's ship in time for him to die in her arms, his vision realized.

Though "The Far Princess" was judged by author Stark Young in his preface to John Heard's translation of the play "the most completely achieved of Rostand's works" with the exception of "Cyrano de Bergerac," and even "the most perfect" and "the high-water mark of [Rostand's] literary achievement" by a critic for the *Edinburgh Review*, most others did not share this enthusiasm. Rostand's contemporary, playwright and critic George Bernard Shaw, commenting on the seriousness with which "The Far Princess" treats an unrealistic, ideal love, complained: "When the woman appears and plays up to the height of [Rudel and his companions'] folly, intoning her speeches to an accompaniment of harps and horns . . . always in the character which their ravings have ascribed to her, what can one feel except that an excellent opportunity for a good comedy is being thrown away?" Virginia M. Crawford in her 1899 *Studies in Foreign Literature* declared that "there is not a line that will live" in "The Far Princess." But while recognizing the unrealistic nature of the play, James announced that "the finest thing [in 'The Far Princess'] is the author's gallantry under fire of the extravagance involved in his subject; as to which . . . we can easily see that it would have been fatal to him to be timid." Amoia found the idealism of "The Far Princess" significant in its relation to the body of Rostand's work. "The reality of life for Rostand, the poet, is the dream," she asserted. "The dream in ['The Far Princess'] is incarnated in Melissinde, who symbolizes love." She concluded, however, that "the literary and

artistic value" of the play "falls short of" Rostand's earlier "Romancers."

Regardless of its literary merit, "The Far Princess" was not very popular with Parisian theatergoers. This lack of public response disappointed Rostand and he went into a period of seclusion until he was inspired to write "La Samaritaine" (title means "The Woman of Samaria"). Another vehicle for Bernhardt, the play is based on a story from the Gospel of John, and was presented during the week before Easter of 1897. Rostand dramatizes the encounter between Jesus and the Samaritan woman he asks for a drink from her well. "La Samaritaine" depicts the transformation of the woman, Photine, from a devotee of sensual pleasure to a spiritually fulfilled follower of Christ who persuades her fellow Samaritans to listen to Jesus. Though "La Samaritaine" stresses the superiority of spiritual satisfaction over physical, like "The Far Princess," it also glorifies earthly love. Echoing the statement of Brother Trophimus, Joffroy Rudel's confessor, that "Love / is sanctified, and God hath willed it thus," and therefore that Rudel needs to make no last confession to gain heaven after death, Rostand's Jesus accepts Photine's erotic love song—the only kind she knows how to sing—as a sincere form of prayer. He even tells her, "The love of Me comes always to a heart / Where lesser, human loves have had a part."

"La Samaritaine" won high praise from an *Edinburgh Review* critic, who exclaimed, "With what precision is the situation put before us . . . with how few words, and yet how definitely, is the characterisation of the individual disciples . . . how swiftly and unconsciously we find ourselves informed of the political situation, the warring interests, all the complicated policy of the little inconspicuous mountain town!" Amoia, by contrast, lamented "the absence of a truly mystic sense," complaining that "the language and style of the play are too refined and . . . too affected." Though she felt that "La Samaritaine" lacked dramatic action, noting that Jesus remains seated throughout, Amoia conceded the beauty of the work, saying "as a gospel in painting it is a composition worthy of admiration."

By the end of 1897, however, the curtain had risen on the drama that most critics agree eclipses the rest of Rostand's oeuvre: "Cyrano de Bergerac." Loosely based on the life of seventeenth-century French author and soldier Savinien de Cyrano de Bergerac, the play opens, significantly, in a theater. By threatening to display his fighting prowess, Cyrano, from the audience, stops the performance of Montfleury, a bad actor with an unsavory reputation who has dared to look amorously upon Cyrano's cousin and secret object of adoration, Roxane. When another spectator protests the closing, Cyrano challenges him to a duel. To emphasize his superior swordsmanship and demonstrate his proficiency at creating impromptu verse, Cyrano composes a ballad while fencing with his opponent, proposing to time his victory to coincide with the end of his poetic creation: "Then, as I end the refrain, thrust home!"

After wounding his adversary to end the duel, Cyrano confesses his love for Roxane to his friend Le Bret, explaining that his nose "that marches on / before me by a quarter of an hour" keeps him silent about his feelings: "I follow with my eyes / Where some boy, with a girl upon his arm / Passes a patch of silver . . . and I feel / Somehow, I wish I had a woman too, / Walking with little steps under the moon, / And holding my arm so, and smiling. Then / I dream—and I forget. . . . / And then I see / The shadow of my profile on the wall!" Le Bret tries to encourage Cyrano, pointing out that some women seem to overlook his oversized nose, and that Roxane herself seemed pale while watching his duel. Punctuating Le Bret's enthusiasm, Roxane's chaperone enters the scene to tell Cyrano that his cousin wishes to speak to him. Hopeful, Cyrano arranges for Roxane to meet him at his friend Ragueneau's pastry shop the next morning.

Roxane, however, has requested a meeting with Cyrano not to tell him that she loves him, but to ask her cousin to befriend the man she does love, the handsome Baron Christian de Neuvillette. Christian has just joined the same regiment that Cyrano serves in, and Roxane fears that as a Norman in a group of men predominantly Gascon he may be subject to bullying. Hiding his disappointment, Cyrano agrees to look out for Christian.

Cyrano continues to contain his feelings when the members of his regiment descend on the pastry shop demanding his account of his feat the night previous—in the height of his hope for Roxane's love, Cyrano had defeated a gang of one hundred men hired to ambush a fellow poet who had angered the Comte de Guiche. As he begins narrating, he is frequently interrupted by Christian, who turns each of Cyrano's phrases into a remark about his nose in order to prove to the Gascons that they do not have a monopoly on bravery. Cyrano is incensed until he learns the identity of his tormentor and remembers Roxane's request. Congratulating Christian on his courage, he tells him of his cousin's love for him. Christian has fallen in love with Roxane also, but he tells Cyrano that his love is hopeless because he does not have the gift of speaking or writing eloquently enough to a woman he loves, and he fears ridicule. Seeing an opportunity to express his fervent emotions without exposing himself to Roxane's indifference, Cyrano offers to coach Christian's speeches and write his letters to her for him.

Their scheme works well, and Roxane is greatly pleased at Christian's supposedly poetic nature, until Christian thinks Roxane loves him enough so that he no longer needs Cyrano's help. Alone with her without Cyrano's words, Christian fails utterly when Roxane asks him to rhapsodize upon the theme of his love for her—he can only extend his "I love you" to "I love you so!" Angered at Christian's sudden lack of eloquence, Roxane retreats into her house, and Christian begs Cyrano for assistance. Initially Christian speaks to Roxane from beneath her balcony while Cyrano feeds him his lines, but the slowness of this process leads Cyrano to speak the words himself in a disguised voice, shadowed so that Roxane cannot see him. Intoxicated by the chance to tell Roxane of his love for her, Cyrano proclaims: "Love, I love beyond / Breath, beyond reason, beyond love's own power / Of loving! Your name is like a golden bell / Hung in my heart; and when I think of you, / I tremble, and the bell swings and rings— *Roxane!* . . . / *Roxane!* . . . along my veins, *Roxane!*" Knowing he has won her for Christian, Cyrano nevertheless is happy at the part he has played. "In my most sweet unreasonable dreams," he tells Roxane, "I have not hoped for this! . . . / . . . It is my voice . . . / That makes you tremble there in the green gloom / Above me—for you do tremble . . . / . . . and I can feel, / All the way down along these jasmine branches, / . . . the passion of you / Trembling. . . ." Christian demands that Cyrano ask Roxane for a kiss, and Cyrano, though disliking the idea, consents, saying to himself "Since it must be, I had rather be myself / The cause of . . . what must be."

After Christian obtains Roxane's kiss, a monk comes by her house with a message from the Comte de Guiche, who has been trying to force himself on Roxane despite the fact that

he is married. Roxane intentionally misreads the message, which was to notify her that de Guiche would meet her that night, to the monk, tricking him into performing a marriage between herself and Christian. Meanwhile at Roxane's request, Cyrano—whom she assumes has just appeared on the scene—wrapped in his cloak and shading his face with his hat, distracts de Guiche by pretending to have fallen from the moon. When Cyrano gives up his charade and de Guiche finds that Roxane has married Christian, he sends Cyrano and Christian, with the rest of their regiment, to fight the Spanish at Arras. De Guiche, also going to fight, gloats, "The bridal night is not so near!" and Cyrano says to himself: "Somehow that news fails to disquiet me."

The fourth act opens on the siege of Arras. The Gascon regiment is hungry, their supplies having been cut off by the Spanish. Cyrano has been slipping through the enemy forces twice daily to carry his letters to Roxane, ostensibly written by Christian. After Cyrano casts aspersions on de Guiche's courage, de Guiche decides to use the Gascon regiment as a sacrifice; the men are almost certain to be killed. As they prepare for battle, Christian tells Cyrano that he wishes he could write Roxane a farewell letter; Cyrano has already composed one for him. In perusing it, Christian finds the water spots of Cyrano's tears, and finally realizes that Cyrano has loved Roxane all along.

Soon afterwards, Roxane arrives in her carriage, having smuggled food for the regiment through enemy territory. The Spanish, she claimed, because they were romantic, let her go through when she told them she was going to meet her lover. Refusing to leave when warned of the imminent battle, she tells Christian that she came because of his letters, which made her love him so much that she could not bear to be away from him. She begs his forgiveness for first loving him for his appearance, and says that because his letters have revealed his soul to her she would now love him even if he were ugly. Christian tells Cyrano about this and demands that he tell Roxane the truth so that she may choose between them. Cyrano is about to do this when Christian is mortally wounded by enemy fire. Feeling that he must now never reveal his secret because to do so would destroy Roxane's belief in Christian's perfect love for her, Cyrano comforts the dying Christian with a lie—that he has told Roxane, and that she still loves Christian.

In the fifth act, fifteen years have gone by. Both Cyrano and Roxane have survived Arras; Roxane lives among the nuns of a convent, still wearing mourning for Christian and keeping what she believes is his last letter over her heart. Cyrano, because of his proud refusal to submit to any rich man's patronage for his plays, has grown steadily poorer and made more enemies. He has visited Roxane at the convent every Saturday to give her the latest news of Paris, but this Saturday Cyrano is a few moments late for the first time. Giving his usual report, he struggles to hide from Roxane the fact that he has been severely hurt in an ambush prepared by his foes. Feeling his death approaching, Cyrano reminds Roxane that she once said he could read Christian's letter, and asks to do so. He reads it to her aloud, though the sky grows dark with the oncoming night. Roxane realizes that Cyrano could not possibly be reading it and that he must have it memorized; she also realizes that he is using the same voice that she remembered hearing beneath her window before her marriage to Christian. When Le Bret and Ragueneau rush in to exclaim over his foolhardiness in leaving his bed, Cyrano tells Roxane of the assault upon him. Roxane tells him that she loves him, lamenting, "I never loved but one man in my life, / And I have lost him—twice.'' Cyrano rises to face death on his feet, taking pride in the fact that he has remained true to his ideals throughout his life, symbolized by the white plume in his hat, or, in the original French, his ''panache.'' His last words are: ''There is one crown I bear away with me... / ... One thing without stain, / Unspotted from the world, in spite of doom / Mine own! ... / ... My white plume.''

Though ''Cyrano de Bergerac'' was to be Rostand's greatest success and was to win him lasting fame, before its debut the theater community had serious doubts about its value. Rostand had to pay for the play's costumes himself, and a few minutes before the curtain rose on ''Cyrano'' for the first time, he was begging forgiveness of its star, Constant Coquelin, for having involved him in such a fiasco. But when the curtain had fallen, Amoia reported, there was ''overwhelming applause ... for the poet who finally had dissipated the atmosphere of sadness and futility with which young Frenchmen had lived for so long.... *Cyrano* marked a complete reaction against the Realism of the problem plays then in vogue. It was a new and fresh Romantic poem, with a folk hero ... whose identity was shared by all.''

Not all critics agreed, however, on the importance or even on the theme of ''Cyrano.'' Crawford felt that while nothing ''could be more noble and beautiful ... than Cyrano's love for his cousin Roxane ... the whole *motif* of the play is ... radically false, and consequently lacking in any permanent interest.'' A contemporary *Poet Lore* reviewer did not take the play's idealism seriously and saw it as a ''satirical extravaganza,'' saying that it would be ''naive ... to take such double-edged fooling as all this for unvarnished tenderness and fresh-born romance.'' The critic also claimed that to do so would leave the work ''bare of any literary distinction worth mentioning. If it is to be considered as a serious dramatic or poetic work, it must be perceived that its structure is of the slightest and most casual.'' But Hugh Allison Smith in his 1925 *Main Currents of Modern French Drama* pointed out that ''Cyrano'' should not ''be judged ... by realistic criterions. It is more proper to ask if it is artistic, beautiful, noble or poetic than it is to determine if it is practical, probable, typical or informative.'' Similarly, an *Edinburgh Review* critic found the play large enough to successfully explore many themes, declaring that to ''say of 'Cyrano' that it is too elaborate is like objecting to some vigorous forest tree that its leafage is confusing. And the comparison holds good on this point—that 'Cyrano de Bergerac' is as structural and organic as a noble tree.'' He concluded: ''In France, it is necessary to go back to Moliere and to [Pierre Augustin Caron de] Beaumarchais to find anything of equal dramatic fulness of conception, of equal reach and lightness of touch.'' Though many modern critics relegate Rostand to the position of minor literary figure, most would agree with Amoia's insistence that ''*Cyrano* [*de*] *Bergerac* will continue to have meaning throughout the ages, will continue to move audiences everywhere, and probably will remain identified with the name of Edmond Rostand long after his other works have sunk into complete oblivion.''

The success of ''Cyrano'' solidified Rostand's position in Parisian social circles, and he counted Bernhardt and Coquelin among his close friends. Like many other intellectuals of his time, Rostand risked his newfound status to become involved in the controversy surrounding the imprisonment for treason of French army captain Alfred Dreyfus, staunchly defending him as an innocent victim of anti-Semitism when new evidence suggested someone else had been responsible for giving secret documents to Germany. Dreyfus was eventually pardoned.

Rostand followed ''Cyrano'' with ''L'Aiglon,'' or ''The Eaglet,'' the story of Napoleon Bonaparte's son Francois and his vain efforts to win his rightful title of Emperor of France. Amoia posited that Rostand used this historical episode because in it ''he found inspiration for the negative counterpart of the swashbuckling hero.... since no figure could possibly outdo Cyrano.'' Also, when Rostand was a child, a portrait of Francois, often called the Duke of Reichstadt or the King of Rome, hung over the author's bed. Haunted by the poignancy of the youth dying without realizing his dreams, Rostand found the sickly Francois, kept a virtual prisoner by his royal Austrian relatives because they feared he had inherited the ruthless strategical abilities of his father, a fit subject for tragedy. Rostand's version pits Francois (first played by Bernhardt) and his allies, including Seraphin Flambeau, a flamboyant old soldier of his father's who invites comparisons with Cyrano, against Prince Metternich, who as an Austrian administrator-spy must foil the young man's plots to return to France in triumph. Francois's daring plans, however, fail predominantly because of his own nature—a bold move on his part is too often followed by indecision or hesitation, and ''The Eaglet'' ends with Francois's deathbed scene. Despite being a failure, the twenty-year-old would-be emperor dies with royal dignity.

Edward Everett Hale, Jr., in his 1911 *Dramatists of Today* judged ''The Eaglet'' to be superior to ''Cyrano,'' announcing, ''This tragedy, with its poor, weak little hero ... made a stronger effect than its wonderful predecessor—stronger, if less obvious.'' Not many agreed with his assessment; Jean-Aubry complained that ''there is little action'' in the play, though he felt that the third act—containing confrontations between Francois and his maternal grandfather the Austrian emperor, Flambeau and Metternich, and Metternich and Francois—''is amongst the best that Rostand ever wrote.'' Critic Max Beerbohm in his *Around Theaters* condemned ''The Eaglet'' for its length, saying that it ''wearies us beyond measure'' and should have been cut in half. Amoia saw the play in a more balanced light. Though she praised it as a ''masterpiece,'' she labeled it a ''defective'' one, flawed by ''too many details and excessive refinements, ... too many superfluous literary allusions weighed down with alliterations.'' She also noted, however, that ''*The Eaglet* contains the great qualities of Rostand's art: lyricism and sincerity.'' The play was popular with French audiences, who shared Francois's reverence for his father, Napoleon.

In 1900, the same year that ''The Eaglet'' saw its first performance, Rostand began suffering from the lung problems that would plague him for the rest of his life; pulmonary congestion forced him to retire to his family home in the Pyranees Mountains. He was elected to the Academie Francaise in 1901, the youngest writer to be so honored, but the formal reception celebrating the occasion had to be postponed until 1903 because of his ill health. Rostand's father died in 1907; setbacks such as these are probably a factor in the ten-year period between the premiere of ''The Eaglet'' and Rostand's next play, ''Chantecler.'' An allegory about the pretentiousness of contemporary society and of the era's literary circles, ''Chantecler'' uses farm animals and creatures of the woods to make its statements. After the success of ''Cyrano'' and ''The Eaglet,'' the play was eagerly awaited by Parisian theatergoers; according to translator Kay Nolte Smith in her preface to the work, the anticipation included ''Chantecler fashions, toys, [and] floats.'' Smith reported further: ''The advance [ticket] sale was an extraordinary (for the time) $200,000;

people traveled from as far as America to attend; diplomats prolonged their stay to see it, making the French foreign minister complain that 'diplomatic relations between France and many a foreign power are being interrupted all because of a cock and a hen pheasant.'" A South American journalist attempted to steal part of the manuscript and was caught at Rostand's home.

Ironically, after all the prefatory excitement, "Chantecler" was something of a disappointment to audiences. Most critics now feel that while it is quality reading, "Chantecler" is not well-suited to performance; possibly the fact that the characters are animals makes it more difficult for the audience to identify with them. Chantecler, the rooster, believes that it is his pre-dawn song that brings the sun up, though he tells no one of this belief until he falls in love with a beautiful pheasant hen. The night animals—owls, cats, moles, etc.—know his secret anyway and plot to kill Chantecler so that the sun will not rise again, making night eternal. Aided by the faithful farm dog Patou, and mocked by the sarcastic caged blackbird, Chantecler nevertheless manages to defeat the vicious steel-spurred white pile rooster that allied itself with the forces of night and laid in wait for him at the pretentious gathering of the Guinea Hen. The conflict leaves the hero disillusioned and exhausted, and he seeks refuge in the forest with the Pheasant Hen. She is jealous of Chantecler's love for the dawn, and tricks him into not singing, proving to him that the morning will come without him. Chantecler is only temporarily daunted, however, and concludes that his song is still important because it wakes the other animals. He triumphs and follows his own ideal in spite of the cynicism, affectation, and pettiness of those around him.

Though "the play is too contrived, too far-fetched . . . and the language and style are too exaggerated," according to Amoia, "the invocation to the Sun, the ballads, and the dramatic, fast-paced dialogue of the Night Birds constitute examples of outstanding verse." Jean-Aubry felt "Chantecler" was evidence that Rostand's genius had run dry, noting that "one is conscious of the despairing efforts of an inspiration which seeks to keep itself alive, but no longer succeeds," and lamenting that Rostand had "no longer the strength to do justice to" his subject. By contrast, though admitting the difficulties in staging an animal allegory, Hale lauded "Chantecler" as "a play of very great beauty," and questioned "whether the judgment of time will not pronounce it Rostand's greatest."

In the same year that "Chantecler" was first performed, Rostand published a volume of twenty-four poems, *Le Cantique de l'aile* (title means "The Canticle of the Wing"). The first seven, reported Amoia, "reflecting the composite elements of the title, abound in personifications of song, winged images, expressions of flight, and a highly ethereal vocabulary." The title poem celebrates France's heroes and urges all people to help praise them. Another, perhaps the best known of Rostand's poems, "Les Mots" (title means "Words"), depicts a closet containing all the French words ever printed. The words protest at the way they are being mutilated by grammarians and bad writers. Amoia explained: "Rostand was in love with words, with each letter in each word. On them, he performed delicate vivesections to know and love them better." "Un Soir a Hernani" (title means "An Evening at Hernani") recognizes the centenary of the birth of French author Victor Hugo and takes its name from his drama "Hernani." The collection also contains "Le Bois Sacre," labeled by Amoia "a delightful blend of ancient mythology and modern tech-

nology" which concerns a young couple whose car is repaired by the Greek gods on Mount Olympus.

Rostand published a third volume of poems, *Le Vol de la Marseillaise* (title means "The Flight of the Marseillaise"), in 1914, but the work has been dismissed by most as unredeemed sentimental patriotism. Rostand probably saw writing these poems as his duty, since his health prevented him from serving France in World War I. He reportedly often visited the trenches, however, wanting to see the suffering and devastation even though it distressed him greatly and added to his decline in health. He died shortly after the war ended in 1918, leaving the unfinished play "The Last Night of Don Juan" to be published and performed posthumously.

"Don Juan" portrays the legendary lover conversing with the Devil before being dragged down to Hell. The Devil shows Don Juan the ghosts of all the women he has ever seduced—one thousand and three in number—and defies him to assign the correct name to any of them. He fails, and he also learns that he has had no real impact on the hearts of these women; the tears they have shed for him were all false. The White Ghost, though, has produced a sincere tear, but when she tells Don Juan her name, he does not remember her because he has not seduced her. Because of the White Ghost's tear Don Juan has an opportunity to save himself from Hell if he can learn to love, but he refuses to repent. The Devil traps him in the wooden body of a puppet—the appropriate version of Hell for a man who cannot love. Though Amoia claimed that "The Last Night of Don Juan" was a "complete fiasco" when it was first produced in 1922, other critics felt that the play showed a new direction in Rostand's creative thinking that would have brought forth even greater works if the playwright had lived longer.

MEDIA ADAPTATIONS: The Hooker translation of *Cyrano de Bergerac* was adapted for film and released, starring Jose Ferrer, Mala Powers, and William Prince, by United Artists in 1950; *The Romancers* was adapted as a musical titled "The Fantasticks," with book and lyrics by Tom Jones and music by Harvey Schmidt, in 1960; a loose, modern adaptation of *Cyrano de Bergerac,* titled "Roxanne" and starring Steve Martin, Daryl Hannah, and Rick Rossovich, was released by Columbia Pictures in 1987.

BIOGRAPHICAL/CRITICAL SOURCES:

BOOKS

Amoia, Alba della Fazia, *Edmond Rostand*, Twayne, 1978.
Beerbohm, Max, *Around Theatres*, Hart-Davis, 1953.
Chesterton, G. K., *Twelve Types*, Arthur L. Humphreys, 1906.
Chiari, Joseph, *The Contemporary French Theatre: The Flight From Naturalism*, Rockliff, 1958.
Clark, Barrett H., *Contemporary French Dramatists*, Stewart & Kidd Co., 1915.
Crawford, Virginia M., *Studies in Foreign Literature*, Duckworth, 1899.
Gerard, Rosemonde, *Edmond Rostand*, Fasquelle, 1935.
Hale, Edward Everett, Jr., *Dramatists of Today: Rostand, Hauptmann, Sudermann, Piner, Shaw, Phillips, Maeterlinck*, revised edition, Holt, 1911.
Hapgood, Norman, *The Stage in America 1897-1900*, Macmillan, 1901.
Rostand, Edmond, *Plays of Edmond Rostand*, translation by Henderson Daingerfield Norman, Macmillan, 1921.
Rostand, Edmond, *Cyrano de Bergerac*, translation by Brian Hooker, Holt, 1923.

Rostand, Edmond, *The Far Princess*, translation by John Heard, Jr., with introduction by Stark Young, Fertig, 1987.

Rostand, Edmond, *Chantecler*, translation and preface by Kay Nolte Smith, University Press of America, 1987.

Smith, Hugh Allison, *Main Currents of Modern French Drama*, Holt, 1925.

Twentieth Century Literary Criticism, Volume 6, Gale, 1982.

PERIODICALS

Arena, September, 1905.
Athenaeum, July 25, 1919.
Atlantic, January, 1972.
Chicago Tribune, June 19, 1987.
Critic, November, 1901.
Edinburgh Review, October, 1900.
Fortnightly Review, January 1, 1919.
New York Times, November 17, 1950, June 19, 1987.
New York Times Book Review, December 26, 1971.
Nineteenth-Century French Studies, February, 1973.
Poet Lore, winter, 1899.
Saturday Review, June 22, 1895.
Studies in Philology, October, 1949.
Times Literary Supplement, January 16, 1976.
Washington Post, February 1, 1985, February 10, 1985.*

—*Sketch by Elizabeth Thomas*

* * *

ROSTAND, J.
See ROSTAND, Jean

* * *

ROSTAND, Jean   1894-1977
(J. Rostand)

PERSONAL: Born October 30, 1894, in Paris, France; died September 3, 1977; son of Edmond (a poet and playwright) and Rosemonde (a poet and playwright; maiden name, Gerard) Rostand; married Andree Mante (a sculptor), April 10, 1920; children: Francois. *Education:* Attended Sorbonne University, 1913-18.

ADDRESSES: Home—29 rue Pradier, Ville d'Avray, Paris, France.

CAREER: Biologist and writer. University of Paris, Paris, France, member of biology section of Palace of the Discovery, beginning in 1939. Director of "Avenir de la science" (title means "Future of Science"), "Histoire naturelle" (title means "Natural History"), and "Grandes Pages de la science" collections of writings for Editions Gallimard, Paris. *Military service:* Served with French Army, 1915-18, in anti-typhoid vaccination laboratory.

MEMBER: Academie Francaise (elected in 1959), Societe de Biologie, Academie Internationale d'Histoire des Sciences.

AWARDS, HONORS: Grand Prix Litteraire de la Ville de Paris, 1951; Prix Singer-Polignac, 1955; Kalinga Prize from UNESCO, 1959, for popularizing science; Prix de l'Academie des Sciences; Prix du Palais de la Decouverte; recognized for contributions in France for peace and free expression.

WRITINGS:

La Loi des riches (satire), Grasset & Fasquelle, 1920.
Pendant qu'on souffre encore (novel), Grasset & Fasquelle, 1921.

Ignace; ou, L'Ecrivain (novel), [Paris], 1923.
Deux Angoisses: La Mort-l'amour (two essays), Grasset & Fasquelle, 1924.
Les Familiotes et autres essais de mystique bourgeois (essays), [Paris], 1924.
L'Homme: Introduction a l'etude de la biologie humaine, Gallimard, 1926, reprinted, 1956.
Valere; ou, L'Exaspere (novel), Grasset & Fasquelle, 1927.
Le Mariage (essays), Hachette, 1927, reprinted, 1964.
Julien; ou, Une Conscience (novel), Grasset & Fasquelle, 1928.
Les Chromosomes: Artisans de l'heredite et du sexe, Hachette, c. 1928.
De la mouche a l'homme, [Paris], 1930.
La Formation de l'etre: Histoire des idees sur la generation, Hachette, c. 1930.
L'Etat present du transformisme, Stock, 1931.
Journal d'un caractere (essays), Charpentier, c. 1931.
L'Evolution des especes: Histoire des idees transformistes, Hachette, c. 1932.
Les Problemes de l'heredite et du sexe, Rieder (Paris), 1933.
La Vie des crapauds, Stock, 1933, revised edition published with *La Vie des libellules* (see below) as *La Vie des crapauds* [and] *La Vie des libellules*, Club des Libraires de France, 1963; translation by Joan Fletcher published as *Toads and Toad Life*, Methuen, 1934.
L'Aventure humaine, Grasset & Fasquelle, Volume I: *Du germe au nouveau-ne*, c. 1933, published as *L'Aventure avant la naissance*, Gonthier, 1966, translation by Joseph Needham published as *Adventures Before Birth*, Gollancz, 1936; Volume II: *Du nouveau-ne a l'adulte*, c. 1934; Volume III: *De l'adulte au vieillard*, 1935; revised edition published as *L'Aventure humaine: Du germe au nouveau-ne; du nouveau-ne a l'adulte; de l'adulte au vieillard*, one volume, 1947.
La Vie des libellules, Stock, 1935, revised edition published with *La Vie des crapauds* (see above) as *La Vie des crapauds* [and] *La Vie des libellules*, Club des Libraires de France, 1963.
(With Lucien Claude Marie Julien Cuenot) *Introduction a la genetique*, [Paris], 1936.
Insectes, Flammarion, c. 1936.
La Nouvelle Biologie, Grasset & Fasquelle, 1937.
La Parthenogenese des vertebres, Hermann, 1938.
La Vie et ses problemes, Flammarion, 1939.
Pensees d'un biologiste (essays; title means "A Biologist's Thoughts"), Stock, 1939, revised edition, 1978; translation by Irma Brandeis published with *Carnet d'un biologist* (see below) in *The Substance of Man*, Doubleday, 1962.
Heredite et racisme, Gallimard, 1939.
Biologie et medecine, [Paris], 1939.
Science et generation, Grasset & Fasquelle, c. 1940.
Les Idees nouvelles de la genetique, Presses Universitaires de France, 1941.
La Genese de la vie: Histoire des idees sur la generation spontanee, Hachette, 1943.
Hommes de verite: Pasteur, Claude Bernard, Gontenelle, La Rochefoucauld, Stock, 1943.
(Under name J. Rostand) *La Vie des vers a soie*, Gallimard, 1943.
Esquisse d'une histoire de la biologie, Gallimard, 1945.
L'Avenir de la biologie, Sablon (Brussels), 1946.
Charles Darwin, Gallimard, 1947.
Nouvelles Pensees d'un biologiste (essays), Stock, 1947.

(With others) *Journees medicales de la Clinique propedeutique de Broussais*, Flammarion, 1947.

Hommes de verite, deuxieme serie: Lamarck, Davaine, Mendel, Fabre, et Barbellion, Stock, 1948.

La Parthenogenese Animale, Presses Universitaires de France, 1950.

(Translator from English) Thomas Hunt Morgan, *Embryologie et genetique*, [Paris], 1950.

La Genetique des batraciens, Hermann, 1951.

Les Grands Courants de la biologie, Gallimard, 1951.

Les Origines de la biologie experimentale et l'abbe Spallanzani, Grasset & Fasquelle, 1951.

L'Heredite humaine, Presses Universitaires de France, 1952, revised edition, 1965; translation by Wade Baskin published as *Human Heredity*, Philosophical Library, 1961.

Pages d'un moraliste, Grasset & Fasquelle, 1952.

Instruire sur l'homme (essays), [Nice], 1953.

Ce que je crois, Grasset & Fasquelle, 1953, revised edition, 1963; translation by D. R. Newth published as *A Biologist's View*, Heinemann, 1956.

(With Andree Tetry) *Atlas de genetique humaine*, Societe d'Edition d'Enseignement Superieur, 1955, translation by Kennedy McWhirter published as *An Atlas of Human Genetics*, Hutchinson, 1965.

(With Paul Bodin) *Life, the Great Adventure: Discussions With Paul Bodin* (translation of original French text, *La Vie, cette aventure*), translation by Alan Houghton Brodrick, Century Hutchinson, 1955, published as *Life, the Great Adventure*, with foreword by Marston Bates, Scribner, 1956.

Les Crapauds, les grenouilles, et quelques grands problemes biologiques, [Paris], 1955.

Peut-on modifier l'homme?, Gallimard, 1956, translation by Jonathan Griffin published as *Can Man Be Modified?*, Basic Books, 1959.

L'Atomisme en biologie, Gallimard, 1956.

Aux sources de la biologie, Gallimard, 1958.

Les Anomalies des amphibiens anoures, Societe d'Edition d'Enseignement Superieur, 1958.

Bestiaire d'amour, illustrations by Pierre-Yves Tremois, Laffont, 1958, translation by Cornelia Schaeffer published as *Bestiaire d'amour*, Doubleday, 1961 (published in England as *Bestiaire d'amour: Love and Courtship Among the Animals*, Routledge & Kegan Paul, 1961).

Science fausse et fausses sciences, Gallimard, 1958, translation by A. J. Pomerans published as *Error and Deception in Science: Essays on Biological Aspects of Life*, Basic Books, 1960.

Carnet d'un biologiste (title means "A Biologist's Notebook"), Stock, 1959, translation by Irma Brandeis published with *Pensees d'un biologiste* (see above) in *The Substance of Man*, Doubleday, 1962.

La Biologie et les problemes humains, Cercle Parisien de la Lingue Francaise de l'Enseignement, 1960.

Discours de reception a l'Academie Francaise et reponse de Jules Romains, Gallimard, 1960.

L'Evolution, Robert Delpire (Paris), 1960, translation by Rebecca Abramson published as *The Orion Book of Evolution*, Orion Press, 1961, translation published as *Evolution*, Prentice-Hall International, 1962.

(With Oscar Forel) *Synchromies*, Editions du Temps (Paris), 1961.

La Biologie inventrice, Palais de la Decouverte, 1961.

Aux frontieres du surhumain, Union Generale d'Editions, 1962.

(With Andree Tetry) *La Vie*, Larousse, 1962, translation by Delano Ames published as *Larousse Science of Life: A Study of Biology, Sex, Genetics, Heredity, and Evolution*, Hamlyn, 1971.

L'Homme, Gallimard, 1962.

Il faut reinventer l'amour, Fayard, 1963.

Le Droit d'etre naturaliste, Stock, 1963.

Biologie et humanisme, Gallimard, 1964.

(Contributor) *Ecrits sur l'heredite*, Seghers, 1964.

(Contributor of response) Louis Armand, *Discours de reception de M. Louis Armand a l'Academie Francaise*, Calmann-Levy, 1964.

(With Andree Tetry) *Biologie*, Gallimard, 1965.

(With others) *Hommage au crapouillot: Histoire d'un journal libre et de son directeur*, [Paris], 1965.

Un Grand Biologiste: Charles Bonnet, experimentateur et theoricien, Palais de la Decouverte, 1966.

Hommes d'autrefois et d'aujourd'hui, Gallimard, 1966.

(Editor) *Le Bouton du mandarin: L'Ecole face a notre avenir*, Casterman, 1966.

Maternite et biologie, Gallimard, 1966.

(Editor with Albert Delaunay) *Man of Tomorrow*, Doubleday, 1966.

(With Claude-Maxime Bertrand, Pierre Fouquet, and Pierre Quillet) *Biologie et alcool; Dix Ans d'action contre l'alcoolisme; L'Homme et l'alcool;* [and] *Dix ans au service des buveurs*, Comite Departemental de Defense Contre l'Alcoolisme (Versailles), 1966.

Discours prononce le 22 octobre, 1966, pour l'inauguration de la place Edouard-Herriot, Firmin-Didot, 1966.

Espoirs et inquietudes de l'homme, Estienne, 1966.

Inquietudes d'un biologiste, Stock, 1967.

Le Patrimoine hereditaire de l'homme est-il menace?, Palais de la Decouverte, 1967.

(Contributor) *Contre la peine de mort: Reunion d'information organisee par l'Association francaise contre la peine de mort, le 10 mai, 1966, au Palais de justice de Paris*, L'Association Francaise contre la Peine de Mort (Paris), c. 1967.

Hommes de verite, preface by Albert Delaunay, Stock, 1968.

Pensee scientifique et oeuvre litteraire: Choix de textes, notes by Pierre-Christian Blin, Larousse, 1968.

La Parthenogenese (ou reproduction virginale) des vertebres, Palais de la Decouverte, 1969.

Le Courrier d'un biologiste (essays), Gallimard, 1970, translation by Lowell Bair published as *Humanly Possible: A Biologist's Notes on the Future of Mankind*, Saturday Review Press, 1973.

Quelques Discours, 1964-1968, Club Humaniste (Paris), 1970.

Les Etangs a monstres: Histoire d'une recherche, 1947-1970, Stock, 1971.

(With Henry de Montherlant) *Pierre-Yves Tremois: Gravures, monotypes*, foreword by Louis Pauwels, Jacques Frapier, 1971.

(Author of introduction) Georges Louis Leclerc Buffon, *De l'homme: Histoire naturelle*, Vialetay (Paris), 1971.

(With Andree Tetry) *L'Homme: Initiation a la biologie*, Larousse, 1972.

Contributor to numerous scientific and literary journals, including *Bulletin de la Societe entomologique*, *Comptes rendus de la Societe de biologie*, and *Annales politiques et litteraires*.

SIDELIGHTS: French biologist Jean Rostand, called "the venerable dean of biological generalists" by Theodosius Dobzhansky in the *New York Times Book Review*, has been recognized for popularizing such scientific disciplines as evolutionary theory, genetics, entomology, and herpetology. The son of French poet and playwright Edmond Rostand, who is probably best known for his play "Cyrano de Bergerac," Jean Rostand incorporates literary and philosophical techniques into his scientific essays. The biologist has written more than ninety books, including novels such as *La Loi des riches, Pendant qu'on souffre encore,* and *Julien; ou, Une Conscience,* as well as his better-known scientific writings such as *Pensees d'un biologiste* and *Carnet d'un biologiste* (translated together as *The Substance of Man*), *L'Evolution* (translated as *The Orion Book of Evolution*), *Peut-on modifier l'homme?* (translated as *Can Man Be Modified?*), and *Le Courrier d'un biologiste* (translated as *Humanly Possible: A Biologist's Notes on the Future of Mankind*).

Likened to the famous *Pensees* of mathematician and philosopher Blaise Pascal, Rostand's essays in *The Substance of Man* and *The Orion Book of Evolution* describe not only science but also art, religion, and philosophy with "the frank and forthright speculation for which the author has a notable fondness and well as a felicitous gift," lauded renowned anthropologist Loren Eiseley, reviewing the 1961 *Orion Book of Evolution* in the *New York Times Book Review*. In addition to defining and outlining the evolutionary process, Eiseley explained, *The Orion Book of Evolution* features the author's opinions and personal conjectures on evolution—"unlike those frequent and stiff textbooks that express with undeviating formalism" only the most popular scientific theories. Rostand is distinguished from his fellow scientists, Eiseley asserted, by "his capacity for doubt—not doubt about the reality of that great enigma we call evolution but doubt that we have sufficiently mastered its secrets."

In other works, Rostand considers the moral implications of such modern scientific procedures as *in vitro* or "test tube" fertilization, the genetic alteration of embryos, and cloning. *Can Man Be Modified?*, for instance, "has some good points to make, and a subject—the biological control of man by man—which urgently needs public discussion," declared Anthony Barnett in a *New Statesman* review. "This lively little work, written with a truly Gallic logic and wit against a lifetime of biological research," explained a *Times Literary Supplement* critic, ponders the imminence of the *Brave New World* predicted in 1932 by novelist Aldous Huxley. Commenting in *Can Man Be Modified?* that brain size originally distinguished humans from other animals, Rostand wonders whether computers and other instruments that simulate thinking can be considered "extensions of the brain," or even whether, by genetic manipulation, "the functioning of the brain or its conformation could be altered so as to give a race of supermen," wrote the reviewer. "It is a bewildering prospect."

Also formidable, according to Dobzhansky, are "the problems posed by the progress of medical arts, which permit maintenance of vegetative life that persists for days and even years in the absence of all human attributes." Questions can arise, for example, on how long to allow respiratory and circulatory machines to sustain the life of a person who remains unconscious and non-functional, and whether or not the life-supporting machines should be used at all. In some essays in *Humanly Possible: A Biologist's Notes on the Future of Mankind*, Rostand attempts to reconcile his aversion to this artificial sustenance of human life with his equally strong desire to overcome death. In other chapters, Rostand speculates on the origin of life—the process that produced living matter on earth from nonliving matter—and he wonders whether the same process has occurred elsewhere in the universe. "It is a pleasure to read these essays, with their unfailingly urbane, slightly old-fashioned style and their admirable sense of moderation and good taste," lauded Dobzhansky. "Rostand knows how to instruct, without being either boring, or condescending, or showing off his remarkable erudition."

BIOGRAPHICAL/CRITICAL SOURCES:

PERIODICALS

New Statesman, March 14, 1959.
New York Times Book Review, June 25, 1961, March 11, 1973.
Times Literary Supplement, March 20, 1959.*

*   *   *

ROTA, Gian-Carlo   1932-

PERSONAL: Born April 27, 1932, in Vigevano, Italy; immigrated to the United States, 1950, naturalized citizen, 1961; son of Giovanni (an architect) and Gina (a housewife; maiden name, Facsetti) Rota; married Teresa Rondon, June 23, 1956 (divorced, 1979). *Education:* Princeton University, B.A. (summa cum laude), 1953; Yale University, M.A., 1954, Ph.D., 1956.

ADDRESSES: Home—Boston, Mass. *Office*—Department of Mathematics, Massachusetts Institute of Technology, 77 Massachusetts Ave., Cambridge, Mass. 02139.

CAREER: New York University, New York, N.Y., fellow at Courant Institute of Mathematical Sciences, 1956-57; Harvard University, Cambridge, Mass., Benjamin Pierce Instructor in Mathematics, 1957-59; Massachusetts Institute of Technology, Cambridge, assistant professor, 1959-62, associate professor of mathematics, 1962-65; Rockefeller University, New York City, professor of mathematics, 1965-67; Massachusetts Institute of Technology, professor of mathematics, 1967—, professor of applied mathematics and philosophy, 1974—. Hedrick Lecturer of American Mathematical Association, 1967; visiting professor at University of Colorado, 1969-80; Andre Aisenstadt Visiting Professor at University of Montreal, 1971; Taft Lecturer at University of Cincinnati, 1971; Hardy Lecturer at London Mathematical Society, 1973. Member of committee of mathematics advisers of Office of Naval Research, 1963-67; consultant to Rand Corp, 1965-74; fellow at Los Alamos Scientific Laboratory, 1971—; trustee of Scuola Normale Superiore di Pisa, 1988—.

MEMBER: National Academy of Sciences, American Mathematical Society, Society of Industrial and Applied Mathematics (vice-president, 1975), Institute of Mathematical Statistics (fellow; chairman of mathematics section, 1988), American Association for the Advancement of Science (fellow), American Academy of Arts and Sciences (fellow), Academia Argentina de Ciencias (fellow).

AWARDS, HONORS: Honorary doctorate from University of Strasbourg, 1984.

WRITINGS:

(With Henry Crapo) *On the Foundations of Combinatorial Theory: Combinatorial Geometries,* MIT Press, 1970.
Science and Computers: A Volume Dedicated to Nicholas Metropolis, Academic Press, 1986.
(With M. Kac and J. T. Schwartz) *Discrete Thoughts,* Birkhauser Boston, 1986.

(With Garrett Birkhoff) *Ordinary Differential Equations*, 4th edition, Wiley, 1988.

EDITOR

Studies in Foundations and Combinations: Advances in Mathematics Supplementary Studies, Academic Press, 1978.
Studies in Probability and Ergodic Theory: Advances in Mathematics Supplementary Studies, Academic Press, 1978.
Studies in Algebra and Number Theory, Academic Press, 1979.
Studies in Algebraic Topology, Academic Press, 1979.
(With Joseph Hersch) George Polya, *Collected Papers*, MIT Press, Volume III: *Analysis*, 1984, Volume IV: *Probability; Combinatories; Teaching and Learning in Mathematics*, 1984.
(With Mark Reynolds) *Science, Computers, and People: From the Tree of Mathematics, Stanislaw Ulam*, Birkhauser Boston, 1986.

Editor in chief of *Encyclopedia of Mathematics*. Editor in chief of "Advances in Mathematics," Academic Press, 1968—, and "Advances in Applied Mathematics," Academic Press, 1979—. Editor of *Studies in Applied Mathematics*, 1970—, and *Journal of Mathematical Analysis and Applications*.

WORK IN PROGRESS: An autobiography, publication expected in 1992.

SIDELIGHTS: Gian-Carlo Rota told *CA:* "I am interested in combinatories, probability, and mathematical logic. I am also interested in phenomenology and existential philosophy, especially of German philosophers Edmund Husserl and Martin Heidegger."

*   *   *

ROWAN, Hester
    See ROBINSON, Sheila Mary

*   *   *

ROWATT, G(eorge) Wade, Jr.   1943-

PERSONAL: Born March 7, 1943, in Herrin, Ill.; son of George Wade (a professor) and Genevieve Ellen (a homemaker; maiden name, Hogg) Rowatt; married Mary Jo Brock (a music teacher), September 3, 1965; children: John Brock and Wade Clinton (twins), Ashley. *Education:* Southern Illinois University, B.S., 1964; Southern Baptist Theological Seminary, M.Div., 1968, Th.M., 1971, Th.D., 1974.

ADDRESSES: Home—3511 Forest Brook Dr., Louisville, Ky. 40207. *Office*—Department of Psychology of Religion, Southern Baptist Theological Seminary, 2825 Lexington Rd., Louisville, Ky. 40206.

CAREER: Ordained Southern Baptist minister, 1965; associate pastor of Baptist church in Lakeland, Fla., 1968-70; Kentucky Baptist Hospital, Louisville, staff chaplain, 1970-72; Southern Baptist Theological Seminary, Louisville, instructor, 1972-74, professor of psychology of religion and chairman of department, 1974—. Pastoral counseling practice, 1971—; co-founder of Youth Opportunities Unlimited.

MEMBER: American Association of Pastoral Counselors, American Association for Clinical Pastoral Education, Kentucky Hospital Chaplains Association, Kentucky Chaplains Association.

WRITINGS:

(With Wayne Oates) *Before You Marry Them*, Broadman, 1975.

(With wife, Mary Jo Brock Rowatt) *The Two-Career Marriage*, Westminster, 1980.
(With Richard Ross) *Ministry With Youth and Their Families*, Convention Press, 1987.

WORK IN PROGRESS: Counseling Teenagers in Crises, publication expected in 1989.

SIDELIGHTS: G. Wade Rowatt, Jr., told *CA:* "Because I am a professor of psychology of religion, the impact of faith systems upon family life and the human developmental cycle interest me. While I am concerned with counseling dysfunctional persons, my primary interest is in providing environments in which normal growth can take place. Healthy families produce functional offspring!"

*   *   *

RUNNELS, Curtis   1950-

PERSONAL: Born May 24, 1950, in Lawrence, Kan.; son of Russell (a geochemist) and Jean (a music teacher; maiden name, Moffit) Runnels; married Priscilla Murray (an archaeologist). *Education:* University of Kansas, B.A., 1972; Indiana University—Bloomington, M.A., 1976, Ph.D., 1981.

ADDRESSES: Office—Department of Archaeology, Boston University, 675 Commonwealth Ave., Boston, Mass. 02215.

CAREER: Stanford University, Stanford, Calif., lecturer in archaeology, 1981-87; Boston University, Boston, Mass., assistant professor of archaeology, 1987—.

MEMBER: Archaeological Institute of America, Society for American Archaeology, Prehistoric Society of England.

WRITINGS:

(With Tjeerd J. van Andel) *Beyond the Acropolis: A Rural Greek Past*, Stanford University Press, 1987.
(With van Andel and Michael Jameson) *A Greek Countryside: The Southern Argolid From Prehistory to the Present Day*, Stanford University Press, in press.

Contributor of more than thirty articles to professional journals.

WORK IN PROGRESS: A Prehistory of Greece, publication by Stanford University Press expected in 1991.

SIDELIGHTS: Curtis Runnels told *CA:* "I have committed my life to the archaeological exploration of the prehistoric world, especially in Greece and other Mediterranean lands. I have a deep sense of obligation to communicate the research results of modern archaeologists to the general public by means of the written word.

"I have a fascination with deep time, the prehistory of the human race that goes back three million years. My research in Greece has been directed toward the remains of the earliest Stone Age inhabitants of the land and the first farmers, who appeared in Greece from the Near East about nine thousand years ago. No novelist, no imagination, can capture the depth and complexity of the mystery of our early ancestors. Although my research is a matter of searching for and analyzing rather mundane artifacts, like simple stone tools or pottery shards, my interest remains in the people who made and discarded these artifacts. Turning the raw data of modern scientific archaeology into a readable account, a history, of the doings of early human beings is an even greater challenge. Yet I am sustained by the human interest that is ever present.

"The story of early humankind leaving Africa and colonizing new continents where human beings had never before set foot is a story unsurpassed in interest, drama, and importance. The migrations and the diffusion of ideas, people, and technology that followed have made the world of today what it is. Greece is a good place to conduct this research, for the earlier prehistory—overshadowed as it is by the well-known glories of the Classical period—remains relatively unknown. Yet Greece then as now has served as a land bridge between Asia and Europe, and the human story can be read from her archaeological record.

"My books, *Beyond the Acropolis, A Greek Countryside,* and *A Prehistory of Greece,* offer more than an archaeologist's view of the past in Greece. They stress also the other side of the story, the relationship of human settlement and landscape. I and my colleagues have shown that humans and their environment have been closely linked in Greece, as elsewhere, for nine thousand years or more. This relationship has not always been a happy one, for it is clear that humans have more than once had devastating impacts upon their immediate environs, destroying their own land even as they depended upon it for their needs. More than once, the rise and fall of prehistoric and later societies in Greece coincides with catastrophic degradation of the land."

BIOGRAPHICAL/CRITICAL SOURCES:

PERIODICALS

Antiquity, June, 1988.
New York Times, January 13, 1987.
Times Literary Supplement, February 19-25, 1988.

*   *   *

RUSH, Norman   1933-

PERSONAL: Born October 24, 1933, in San Francisco, Calif.; son of Roger (a trainer of salesmen) and Leslie (Chesse) Rush; married Elsa (a teacher and weaver), July 10, 1955; children: Jason, Liza. *Education:* Swarthmore College, B.A., 1956.

ADDRESSES: Home and office—10 High Tor Rd., New City, N.Y. 10956. *Agent*—Wylie, Aitken & Stone, Inc., 250 West 57th St., Suite 2106, New York, N.Y. 10107.

CAREER: Part-time writer and self-employed as a dealer of antiquarian books, 1958-73; Rockland Community College, Suffern, N.Y., instructor in English and history and co-director of College A, 1973-78; U.S. Peace Corps, Botswana, Africa, co-director, 1978-83; full-time writer, 1983—.

MEMBER: American Economic Association.

AWARDS, HONORS: Short fiction selected for *Best American Short Stories,* 1971, 1984, and 1985; *Paris Review* Aga Khan Award, 1985, for "Instruments of Seduction"; New York Foundation for the Arts fellowship, 1985; grant from National Endowment for the Arts and finalist for American Book Award, both 1986, nominated for Pulitzer Prize and recipient of annual literary award from the Academy and Institute of Arts and Letters, both 1987, all for *Whites;* Guggenheim fellowship, 1987.

WRITINGS:

Whites: Stories, Knopf, 1986.
Mating (novel), Knopf, 1989.

Contributor of short stories to anthologies, including *Best American Short Stories,* and to periodicals, including *New York, Paris Review, Grand Street,* and *Massachusetts Review.* Contributor of poetry and journalism to periodicals, including *Folio, Minnesota Review, Jeopardy, Poetry Bag, Village Voice, Grand Street,* and *Gentleman's Quarterly.*

WORK IN PROGRESS: A book, tentatively titled *Kerekang the Incendiary,* publication by Knopf expected in 1992; a second story collection on American themes.

SIDELIGHTS: In his highly acclaimed collection of six short stories, *Whites,* Norman Rush explores what *Nation's* reviewer George Packer described as the "moral and spiritual quandaries of middle-class foreigners who happen to be stuck out in [the African country of] Botswana." While living in Botswana for five years as co-director of the Peace Corps, the author became familiar with the political and racial difficulties existing in a country bordering the controversial apartheid nation of South Africa. Herbert Mitgang quoted Rush in the *New York Times:* "'In these stories I concentrate on whites, especially American whites, as they define themselves against the contours of African life and encounter the limits and contradictions of the Western undertaking in that part of the world.'" The characters in Rush's "low-keyed yet forceful" stories exist under unique circumstances, explained Jonathan Yardley in the *Los Angeles Times Book Review* (review also published in *Washington Post Book World*), because for them "Africa is a place where the ordinary rules do not apply. They are in a country that is not their own, in a civilization they do not understand, cannot really connect to, and feel no obligation toward." As missionaries in a country plagued by drought and poverty, "they are at a distance . . . because they are white and because, of course, they can always go home."

With what Packer labeled "intricate structures and ironic themes," Rush presents a variety of situations involving sexual and power struggles, inequity, disillusionment, and political apathy. A story in the collection illustrating some responses of whites to the plight of Africans is "Near Pala." Two white couples driving through the desert discuss race; one of the women, Nan, is sensitive to racial injustice, the other is oblivious to it, and the men are obviously impatient with the issue. In a heated part of the conversation and in a particularly rough part of the journey, the group passes three African women and an infant pleading for water. Nan begs her husband Gareth to stop. When he doesn't, she frantically, though too late, throws their water bottle from the vehicle. Relating the author's message in this story, Yardley commented that "Rush has presented in Nan and Gareth opposing white attitudes toward Africa, and by placing them inside a single marriage has shown how intimately connected they are."

Another story—"Instruments of Seduction," which received the Aga Khan Fiction Prize after its original appearance in the *Paris Review*—depicts a middle-aged American dentist's wife, Ione, in one episode of her secret career of seducing men. Ione believes that skillfully manipulated allusions to death and danger are erotic, and she finds the atmosphere of expatriate life in Botswana conducive to satisfying her desires. Assessing Ione's acclimation to Botswana's climate, Leslie Marmon Silko of the *New York Times Book Review* remarked that ironically Ione is one of few foreigners able "to grasp the possibilities for personal salvation Africa offers them despite all its contradictions and ugly colonial legacies. . . . She not only fashions a sense of self and identity that keeps her humanity intact, she also manages to realize how the terrifying atmosphere of Botswana can actually be used to deliver her from isolation and loneliness."

Ione also appears in the stories "Official Americans" and "Alone in Africa." In the former she persuades an American agency bureaucrat, Carl, to seek a local medicine man to cure him of insomnia caused by a neighbor's barking dog. When the prescribed witchcraft results in permanent injury to Carl, he is nevertheless overjoyed, believing that the price of white life in black Africa make any cost a bargain. In "Alone in Africa" Ione's husband, Frank, is visited by the seductive young daughter of a neighbor's maid. Described by Christopher Lehmann-Haupt in the *New York Times* as "a perfect little sexual psychodrama," the story reveals Frank's weakness and propensity for self-delusion and delineates the girl's victory, achieved by her drive and cunning, as well as by her youth, strength, and poverty.

The remaining stories in the collection—"Bruns" and "Thieving"—render, according to Packer, a vision of political futility: "Simply put, any effort at change does more harm than good, though vanity and naivete will delude us into trying." In "Bruns" a Dutch pacifist volunteer is unable to free a tribe from its violent injustices and ends up killing himself out of revenge. And in "Thieving" a christianized African boy, Paul Ojang, interprets the various injustices and temptations to which he is subjected as comprehensible only if God desires that he, an honest boy, become a thief. Paul's effort to retain his personal integrity while satisfying God's injunction to steal is doomed to tragic failure.

Asserting that Rush is "a master at plot," Packer observed that "his stories often end with an ironic inversion on a nearly farcical chain of events that exposes the self-deception his characters use to detach themselves from any meaningful connection to other lives. . . . Their lack of conviction haunts them without initiating deep change." Critic Silko concurred: "The failure of American idealism and technical resources that Mr. Rush describes in these stories, and the subsequent disillusionment—both national and personal—are second only to the Vietnam War in their continuing impact on the direction of American foreign and domestic policy today."

Rush, in *Whites,* has been further hailed for not offering simplistic analyses of the political and economic crises in southern Africa. Silko, for example, stated that "Mr. Rush attempts to articulate what Americans or whites in general may be able to salvage where the legacies of apartheid and colonialism make it almost impossible to live and remain decent human beings." The author seems to be saying, she suggested, that "it isn't just whites who must face up to moral and political failures in the third world today." Deeming Rush "an effective political writer," Steve Katz of *The American Book Review* noted that the author "has the experience and talent to give us the political forces operating in the lives of ordinary, imperfect people." "If we are honest with ourselves," added the reviewer, "we have no trouble isolating the contradictions and ironies in the attitudes of Carl, Ione, Frank, etc., in our own hearts. We can be grateful to Norman Rush for identifying them with so much wit and compassion, so that the healing might begin."

Reviewer Lehmann-Haupt noted minor difficulties in the conceptions and structures of Rush's stories, criticizing that "here and there, [Rush's] endings are a trifle abrupt or heavy-handed" and that "there are passages where the characters' behavior is psychologically fuzzy." He qualified those remarks, however, with the observation that the author may be doing this intentionally in order to heighten the unreal and hallucinatory feel of some of the stories. Comments like Katz's, though, were more common: "*Whites* is a terrific book, important for our

understanding of white people in the world, particularly of the roles of whites in Botswana. Everyone should read it. . . . Norman Rush is an extraordinary writer." Proclaiming *Whites* "one of the richest books of the last ten years. Twenty years?," Katz concluded: "I wish there were more books in print by Norman Rush. I would read them now."

CA INTERVIEW

CA interviewed Norman Rush by telephone on July 27, 1987, at his home in New City, New York.

CA: Before you went with the Peace Corps to Botswana, which provided the setting for your stories in Whites, *you were a dealer in antiquarian books and a teacher of history and English. Have books and literature always been important to you?*

RUSH: Yes. I've always been obsessed with writing and reading.

CA: Were you writing, in some form, from early on?

RUSH: I was writing as a child. When I was in junior high school, I put out a neighborhood paper called the *Town Crier.* I went through the usual adolescent attempts to write detective stories and adventure stories and that sort of thing.

CA: With lots of early encouragement?

RUSH: Yes. My father was a failed writer, and I guess I picked up part of my impulse from him.

CA: How did you and your wife decide to join the Peace Corps, and how did you choose Botswana?

RUSH: We didn't join the Peace Corps as volunteers. We were staff people, co-directors of the Peace Corps Program in Botswana. We got into it through a combination of circumstances. Sam Brown had just taken over at Action, the umbrella organization that Vista and the Peace Corps were then part of. He came in with the [U.S. President Jimmy] Carter administration. They wanted to make some changes; they had an innovation in mind. In the past, Peace Corps country directors had gone overseas with their spouses, and the spouses had frequently performed as actively as the actual directors had, but without getting any credit for it—so they wanted to try the concept of a co-directorship, whereby a husband and wife would split the position and the salary. They had some rather difficult requirements. Since this would be the first of these appointments, they were looking for a couple who had been married for at least twenty years—they didn't want people working out their marital problems in a foreign setting. And they wanted people who had a history of work-sharing.

We met Sam Brown socially and got into a heated political argument with him. The subject was what we felt was the inadequacy of the amnesty plank in the Democratic platform. The upshot of this, for some reason, was that he thought we make a good co-director pair. We were then approached by the talent search department at the Peace Corps and went through the whole interviewing and screening process. We were extremely skeptical about the whole proposal and were originally more curious than enthusiastic about it. But ultimately we went.

As to our choice of Botswana, it happened by accident and rather comically. We both have French in our backgrounds and the original idea was to brush up our French at the Foreign Service Institute, after which we would be sent to Francophone Africa. We had turned down Zaire, where we thought we would be unhappy because of the political situation, and were being considered as country directors for Benin, another post in Francophone Africa. But when we were taken down for a final round of interviews, we were deposited entirely by mistake at the Botswana desk—evidently a mix-up of countries beginning with *B*. Botswana interested us, and we took advantage of the opportunity to talk, at some length, to that desk officer. As it happened, the Botswana country director position was soon to be open. The desk officer decided to bring pressure to bear to have us sent to "her" (Anglophone) country, a development we encouraged. Botswana is a fascinating country, and a front-line state, and a political democracy.

CA: You've said in previous interviews that you collected many ideas and notes while you were in Botswana, but it wasn't until after you came back to the States that you began writing the African stories that make up Whites. *Was that partly a matter of needing time and distance to shape the material?*

RUSH: It was mainly the pressure of work while we were there. Directing that program meant being responsible for anywhere from 90 to 120 people spread out over a country the size of Texas. The pressure was great. It was possible to get a little bit of preliminary work done on weekends, but not much. I wrote one short story in the five years I lived in Africa.

CA: When you began later to look at the material and start the writing, did you find that your perceptions of the experiences in Africa had shifted in any way?

RUSH: It was when I began writing that I learned what my perceptions were. The mechanics of doing the job itself, as I said, kept me so flush with events that it was hard to think in a political aesthetic sense about things for very long at a time.

CA: The reviewer for Time *noted about the events of your stories in* Whites *that "what passes for daily routine on the continent may strike outsiders as magical or malign." Is the somewhat sinister feeling of everyday events in Africa something you particularly wanted to convey?*

RUSH: "Sinister" is probably putting it a little strongly. It would be more accurate to call it a sense of disjunction, of things not conforming to the paradigm that you carry with you. You develop a sense that it's important to get the paradigm right, a sense of its being dangerous not to understand. That is clearly something that I wanted to convey.

CA: Some of the misunderstandings you write about between whites and blacks arise from the whites' neglect of local custom, such as the business of greeting the black person properly before beginning to talk to him or her. Do the various branches of the foreign service provide adequate instruction in such matters?

RUSH: The Peace Corps is very good about that. In each country there is a mechanism that exists for acculturating you rapidly to the situation you're entering. You're encouraged to learn the language and so on. That intense preparation is not characteristic of the regular foreign service. In the Peace Corps, of course, there's a variation in the degree to which staff embraces those opportunities. But in general, both in the preparation of volunteers and in the preparation of the staff, the

Peace Corps, as you might expect, goes out of its way to see that people are ready.

CA: You dedicated Whites *to your wife, Elsa. Did she act as a first reader for all the stories in the book?*

RUSH: Yes. She's an active first reader and an active editor for everything I write.

CA: Two of the stories in Whites, *"Bruns" and "Thieving," are told by first-person narrators, and both voices seem to me amazing achievements, in different ways. Where those voices hard to find?*

RUSH: They're both based on individuals that I knew in Africa. Writing the second story, "Thieving," felt like a case of possession. It took a great deal out of me to will myself into that persona and to think and express myself in African English. As to the narrator of "Bruns," I'm using that persona for *Mating*, the novel I'm currently writing, and am still in the grip of it.

CA: I'm sorry that "Thieving" didn't get more treatment in the reviews, and I wonder why.

RUSH: Some people found it difficult. I got a lot of letters from people about that story. Many people understand it immediately—this is especially true of people who've either been in Africa or had some contact with African English—but a number found it hard to follow, for the first few pages at least. Some people—Ben Sonnenberg, the editor of *Grand Street*, for instance—think it's the best thing I've ever done. Sonnenberg actually said he thought it might be the best short story ever written—we may assume complimentary hyperbole—but it does show what vastly differing reactions a particular story can evoke.

CA: Whites *drew high praise from African writers Nadine Gordimer and J. R. Coetzee. Have you heard widely, on a more personal level, from readers who aren't professional writers but have lived in Africa in circumstances similar to your own there?*

RUSH: I've had a surprising amount of mail. It's still coming in, in fact. I'd say 10 or 15 percent of the writers are people who've been in Africa. The rest are general readers who liked the book.

CA: Were you generally pleased with the reviewers' perceptions?

RUSH: Yes, with the single exception of a lack of attention to the style and the literary characteristics of the work. It did bother me that many of the reviews—more, I think, than with other short-story collections I've seen reviewed—tended simply to tell the stories. They were positive in their assessments of the work, so I certainly have no complaint about that. But I have a slight feeling that the endings were being tipped, and I wasn't too happy with that. And there was not much concentration on the actual writing.

CA: Do you read the work of African writers?

RUSH: I do, although right now I'm reading almost nothing except African ethnography, in an attempt to remain within the persona that's the center of my novel. I like Ngugi wa Thiongo, and I'm an admirer of Chinua Achebe's work.

CA: Was your work in Botswana affected by the situation in South Africa?

RUSH: Yes, of course. The country of Botswana is deeply affected by, and menaced by, South Africa. This is a situation of which one is never unaware, and that caused problems on a number of levels. Also, we were there during the final phase of the independence struggle in Zimbabwe. At one point we had Peace Corps volunteers posted along the Botswana-Zimbabwe border, and there were military actions taking place in that vicinity. It was and is a tense part of the world.

CA: Would you like to go back to Africa?

RUSH: I have been back once, in the fall of 1985, and I'm going back in the spring of 1988.

CA: Since the publication of Whites, *are you writing full-time?*

RUSH: Yes. And I now have a Guggenheim fellowship, which is an enormous help.

CA: You'd written stories before the African ones. Did you deliberately set out to write short stories first, or did the short story form choose you?

RUSH: I've always written short stories, except for an early five-year period when I worked on a novel. That novel was never published. Maybe I'll go back to that book now that I have the leisure to do it. I'd also like to gather the uncollected short stories on American themes and add a couple more to make a book of them.

CA: That seems a timely idea, so that people will be aware that you've written stories in both settings.

RUSH: Yes. There is a danger of being cast as someone who is claiming a patch of literary-geographical territory or of being cast in topical terms.

CA: Is that collection a possibility?

RUSH: Yes. But I'm pressing very hard now on the novel, and it's turning out to be quite long, so the second story collection will have to wait.

CA: Have you found it hard going from stories to this big novel?

RUSH: No. What I'm writing is a kind of triptych, really. The stories in *Whites* are sort of a tour d'horizon of some of the themes I'm interested in. The second book, *Mating*, is about Americans and other whites in Africa under the aspect of benevolence; that is to say, the main setting is a model development project in the Kalahari. Then I have planned, beyond that, a final Africa book, tentatively called *Kerekang the Incendiary*, which is about Americans and other whites in Africa under the aspect of violence—its characters are associated with an insurrectionary movement.

BIOGRAPHICAL/CRITICAL SOURCES:

BOOKS

Contemporary Literary Criticism, Volume 44, Gale, 1986.

PERIODICALS

American Book Review, March-April, 1987.

Los Angeles Times Book Review, March 9, 1986.
Nation, May 24, 1986.
New York Times, February 27, 1986, April 19, 1986.
New York Times Book Review, March 23, 1986.
Time, July 7, 1986.
Washington Post Book World, March 23, 1986.

—Sketch by Janice E. Drane

—Interview by Jean W. Ross

* * *

RUSSELL, Frank D. 1923-

PERSONAL: Born July 4, 1923, in Paris, France; son of Edward H. (a writer) and Rose (a teacher; maiden name, Gutterman) Russell. *Education:* Columbia University, B.A., 1946; Temple University, M.F.A., 1950; New York University, M.A., 1956.

ADDRESSES: Home—Ardnageehy, Banton, County Cork, Ireland. *Office*—Department of Art History, Maryland Institute, 1300 Mount Royal Ave., Baltimore, Md. 21217. *Agent*—Jacques de Spoelberch, 1 Wilson Point, South Norwalk, Conn.

CAREER: Affiliated with Maryland Institute, Baltimore; affiliated with Rutgers University, New Brunswick, N.J. *Military service:* U.S. Army, 1942-45.

WRITINGS:

Picasso's Guernica: The Labyrinth of Narrative and Vision, Allanheld & Schram, 1980.

* * *

RUSSELL, William F(rank) 1945-

PERSONAL: Born November 4, 1945, in Oak Park, Ill.; son of Harley Spencer (a purchasing agent) and Eleanor (a teacher; maiden name, Johnson) Russell. *Education:* Ohio Wesleyan University, B.A., 1967; Northern Illinois University, M.S.Ed., 1981, Ed.D., 1984.

ADDRESSES: Home—356 Waverley St., Menlo Park, Calif. 94025. *Agent*—Mark L. Levine, 58 East 83rd St., New York, N.Y. 10028.

CAREER: High school English teacher in Oswego, Ill., 1967-72; Harcourt Brace Jovanovich, Inc., New York, N.Y., editor, 1974-79; educational consultant and lecturer, 1985—.

MEMBER: Authors Guild, American Association for Adult and Continuing Education.

WRITINGS:

(Editor) John Warriner, *English Grammar and Composition*, Harcourt, 1978.
The Parents' Handbook of Grammar and Usage, Stein & Day, 1980.
Classics to Read Aloud to Your Children, Crown, 1984.
More Classics to Read Aloud to Your Children, Crown, 1986.
Classic Myths to Read Aloud, Crown, 1988.
Families in the Wild (tentative title; animal stories), illustrated by John Butler, Crown, 1989.

SIDELIGHTS: William F. Russell told *CA:* "The idea for the 'Read-Aloud Classics' books grew out of my doctoral studies in adult education, which focused on the profound influences that parents have on the educational achievement of their children. My experience, both as a teacher and as a textbook editor, had shown me that the great literary works of the Western world were being removed from the curriculum in many public schools, and so children were not being introduced to the authors, characters, and scenes that had become fixtures in our common culture.

"By putting excerpts of these works in books that encouraged parents to read to their children, I felt that not only would I be helping children become familiar with some literary masterpieces, but I would also be providing a non-threatening way for parents to introduce themselves to authors, stories, and poems that, for whatever reason, they had not encountered previously. In addition, these classics would allow parents and children to become accustomed to the sound of standard English usage and to the artful use of precise vocabulary. At the same time, they would stimulate the imagination and help bond the parent and child together in their sharing of a most enjoyable time together.

"The idea of compiling such a collection was a good one, and I was quite surprised to find that it had not been seized upon by others before me. (I did find a few collections that had a similar intent, but none gave any attention to anticipating the problems that adults might encounter in reading aloud to their children, or to the almost limitless possibilities for incorporating various learnings into the telling of the tales.) But the success of the series will, for me, be determined by whether it actually does help achieve the lofty educational and social goals that I have for my life's work: the advancement of lifelong learning in our society and the encouragement of stable and happy families."

*   *   *

RYBAKOV, Anatoli (Naumovich)   1911-

BRIEF ENTRY: Given name sometimes transliterated Anatoly; born January 1 (one source says January 14), 1911, in Chernigov, Russia (now U.S.S.R.). Russian author. Best known in the West for his novels *Heavy Sand* (Viking, 1981) and *Children of the Arbat* (Little, Brown, 1988), Rybakov, a Soviet Jew, is one of Russia's most popular and controversial novelists. His works are widely praised for their important political content, as well as for their accurate and long-suppressed depictions of Russian history. After graduating from the Moscow Institute of Railroad Engineers in 1934, Rybakov served in the Soviet army for five years before becoming a full-time writer. His early adventure fiction, which includes *The Dirk* (Foreign Languages Publishing House, 1956) and *The Bronze Bird* (Foreign Languages Publishing House, 1958), garnered considerable critical approval, but it was not until the publication of *Heavy Sand* that Rybakov established himself as a major novelist. An epic-style narrative, the book relates the struggle of a Jewish family living in the Nazi-occupied Ukraine during World War II and condemns Russian actions toward its Jewish population during the Holocaust.

Further criticizing past Soviet policy is Rybakov's *Children of the Arbat*. The semi-autobiographical novel examines the events of the 1930s that led to Russian leader Joseph Stalin's purge of Jewish citizens. Because Soviet officials considered the book's contents subversive, *Children of the Arbat*, though written in the 1960s, was denied publication in the Soviet Union until

the late 1980s. Immensely popular with both Russian and American readers, the book was widely hailed for its strong and candid depictions of the terror experienced under the Stalin regime. Rybakov's works have been translated into many languages, and most have been adapted for film and television.

BIOGRAPHICAL/CRITICAL SOURCES:

BOOKS

Contemporary Literary Criticism, Volume 23, Gale, 1983.
Who's Who in the Soviet Union, K. G. Saur, 1984.

PERIODICALS

New York Times, April 26, 1986.
New York Times Book Review, May 22, 1988.
Washington Post Book World, April 26, 1981.

*   *   *

RYDELL, Robert W(illiam)   1952-

PERSONAL: Born May 23, 1952, in Evanston, Ill.; son of Robert and Cristol Rydell; married Kiki Leigh. *Education:* University of California, Berkeley, A.B., 1974; University of California, Los Angeles, M.A., 1975, C.Phil., 1977, Ph.D., 1980.

ADDRESSES: Office—Department of History and Philosophy, Montana State University, Bozeman, Mont. 59717.

CAREER: Montana State University, Bozeman, assistant professor, 1980-84, associate professor of history, 1984—. Visiting assistant professor at University of California, Los Angeles, summer, 1981; John Adams Professor at University of Amsterdam, 1985-86; visiting associate professor at University of Michigan, 1987. Fellow at Smithsonian Institution, 1982-83.

MEMBER: American Historical Association, American Studies Association.

AWARDS, HONORS: Alan Nevins Prize from Society of American Historians, 1981, for Ph. D. dissertation "All the World's a Fair: American International Expositions, 1876-1916."

WRITINGS:

All the World's a Fair: Visions of Empire at American International Expositions, 1876-1916, University of Chicago Press, 1985.

Contributor to history journals.

WORK IN PROGRESS: Books of the Fairs, publication by Smithsonian Institution Libraries expected in 1990; *A Century of Progress Expositions*, completion expected in 1990.

SIDELIGHTS: Robert W. Rydell told *CA:* "I became interested in world's fairs as vehicles for transmitting scientific ideas about race when I learned of the presence of 'living ethnological villages' at the fairs. I then tried to determine the function of the exhibits within the fairs and within American society as a whole. My current work seeks to expand these interests to include twentieth-century expositions and expositions held around the world."

S

SAATKAMP, Herman J(oseph), Jr. 1942-

PERSONAL: Born September 29, 1942, in Knoxville, Tenn.; son of Herman Joseph (a pharmacist) and Geneva May (a housewife) Saatkamp; married Dorothy Tyre (a teacher), June 13, 1964; children: Barbara, Joseph. *Education:* Carson-Newman College, B.A., 1964; Southern Seminary, M.Div., 1967; Vanderbilt University, M.A., 1970, Ph.D., 1972.

ADDRESSES: Home—1203 Merry Oaks Dr., College Station, Tex. 77840. *Office*—Department of Philosophy and Humanities, Texas A & M University, College Station, Tex. 77843-4237.

CAREER: University of Tampa, Tampa, Fla., assistant professor, 1970-73, associate professor, 1973-78, professor of philosophy, 1978-80, Dana Professor of Philosophy, 1981-85, chairman of Philosophy/Religion Area, 1975-83, and Humanities Division, 1983-85; Texas A & M University, College Station, professor of philosophy and head of department, 1985—, chairman of University Chamber Music Series, 1985—. Adjunct lecturer at University of South Florida, 1971-72. Brazos Valley Symphony Society, first vice-president, 1987-88; chairman of finance committee, 1986—.

MEMBER: American Philosophical Association, Association of Documentary Editing, Modern Language Association of America, Opera and Performing Arts Society, Santayana Society, Society for the Advancement of American Philosophy, Society for Computers and the Humanities, Society for Textual Scholarship, Word-Processors Topical Study Group (chairman, 1985-87), Bibliographical Society of the University of Virginia, Alpha Chi (honorary member), Omicron Delta Kappa.

AWARDS, HONORS: Grants from National Endowment for the Humanities, 1975-89, General Electric Co., 1976, Council for Philosophical Studies, 1976, Penrose Fund of the American Philosophical Society, 1977, and Conn Foundation, 1982.

WRITINGS:

(Contributor) Peter Caws, editor, *Two Centuries of Philosophy,* Littlefield, Adams, 1980.
(With John Jones) *George Santayana: A Bibliographical Checklist, 1880-1980,* Philosophy Documentation Center, Bowling Green State University, 1982.
(Editor with William G. Holzberger) *The Works of George Santayana,* MIT Press, Volume I: *Persons and Places,*

1987, Volume II: *The Sense of Beauty,* 1988, Volume III: *The Interpretations of Poetry and Religion,* in press.

Contributor to philosophy journals. General editor of "The Works of George Santayana," MIT Press. Co-editor of *Overhead in Seville: Bulletin of the Santayana Society.*

WORK IN PROGRESS: Editing *The Works of George Santayana,* Volume IV: *The Last Puritan,* Volume V: *The Letters of George Santayana,* publication by MIT Press expected in 1991-92; editing *Don't Forget Your Loving Father: Agustin to George Santayana,* letters from father to son; *George Santayana,* a monograph on his philosophy.

*   *   *

St. AUBIN de TERAN, Lisa 1953-

PERSONAL: Born October 2, 1953, in London, England; daughter of Jan Rynveld (a professor) and Joan (a teacher; maiden name, St. Aubin) Carew; married Jaime Teran (a farmer), October, 1970 (divorced January, 1981); married George MacBeth (a poet), March, 1981 (divorced, 1986); children: (first marriage) Iseult Joanna Teran St. Aubin; (second marriage) Alexander Morton George MacBeth. *Education:* Attended school in London. *Politics:* "Tolerant." *Religion:* "Nominally Church of England."

ADDRESSES: Home and office—5437 Castello, Venezia, Italy; and 7 Canynge Square, Clifton, Bristol, England. *Agent*—A. M. Heath, 79 St. Martins Lane, London WC2N 4AA, England.

CAREER: Farmer of sugar cane, avocados, pears, and sheep in Venezuela, 1972-78; writer, 1972—.

MEMBER: Royal Society of Literature (fellow).

AWARDS, HONORS: Somerset Maugham Award from the Society of Authors for *The Long Way Home,* John Llewellyn Rhys Memorial Prize from the Book Trust for *Slow Train to Milan,* and Eric Gregory Award from the Society of Authors for poetry, all 1983.

WRITINGS:

The Streak (poetry), Martin Booth, 1980.
Keepers of the House (novel), J. Cape, 1982, published as *The Long Way Home,* Harper, 1983.

The Slow Train to Milan (novel), Harper, 1983.
The Tiger (novel), J. Cape, 1984, F. Watts, 1985.
The High Place (poems), J. Cape, 1985.
The Bay of Silence (novel), F. Watts, 1986.
Black Idol (novel), J. Cape, 1987.
Off the Rails (memoir), Bloomsbury, 1989.
The Marble Mountain and Other Stories, J. Cape, 1989.

WORK IN PROGRESS: Joanna, "a novel in three voices."

SIDELIGHTS: Lisa St. Aubin de Teran was named one of Britain's twenty best young novelists by the London *Times* in 1983. At the time, she had only published her first novel, *The Long Way Home*. Most critics hailed the book as a remarkable debut, and St. Aubin de Teran was compared to many American literary greats, including Willa Cather and William Faulkner. Because of the South American setting for much of her work, however, she became most often classed with the "magical realism" literary school predominantly associated with South American writers such as Gabriel Garcia Marquez. St. Aubin de Teran has won the Somerset Maugham Award and the John Llewelyn Rhys Memorial Prize for her novels and the Eric Gregory Award for her poetry.

The Long Way Home, lauded for its "charm and verve" by Hermione Lee reviewing in the London *Observer*, is narrated by Lydia Beltran. Somewhat comparable to St. Aubin de Teran herself, Lydia at the age of sixteen marries a South American, Diego Beltran, and returns with him to his ancestral farm in the Andes mountains. At first her new surroundings seem paradisiacal, but the quality of Lydia's life worsens as she is drawn into the aura of doom and decay that pervades her husband's family. The sheep she imports die of anthrax, her husband spends his days quietly reading while suffering from kidney disease and what St. Aubin de Teran describes as "a sleeping sickness of the heart," and her newborn baby dies.

Lydia's stories of the Beltran ancestors—told to her by Benito, a longtime family servant—stretch back two hundred years and are the true focal point of *The Long Way Home*. They feature such characters as mass-murderer Arturo Lino; General Mario, who contracts leprosy from eating cheese, isolates himself, and becomes a village oracle; and Sara and Rosa, two sisters who spend their entire lives playing cards and waiting to be rescued from spinsterhood as the de Labastida sisters were rescued by the first Beltrans to settle in the area, Rodrigo and Sancho. The accounts of these and other characters are filled with events as strange and macabre as those that happen to Lydia, adding to the novel's dark tone. As Lee pointed out, "Locusts, maggots, weevils, running sores, goitres, amputated limbs, rotting avocados, litter the book with an almost boisterous abandon." Coinciding with Lydia's realization that she is pregnant again, Diego has a stroke that leaves him paralyzed. After old Benito dies, Lydia decides to leave the Beltran farm, taking with her a helpless husband, their unborn child, and the tales of Beltran history.

Citing the combination of poetic imagery in *The Long Way Home* with its somewhat bizarre story content, Ben Pleasants, critiquing in the *Los Angeles Times Book Review*, declared "there is a curious, haunting quality to this book; it is the smell of heliotrope carried across the slave quarters of a rotting plantation. There is an essence here as well as a stench." Pleasants also praised St. Aubin de Teran's "desire to expand myths and textures, to explore events until they reveal specific rather than generic characters." On the subject of the chaotic, surreal events of the narrative, critic Douglas Hill of the Toronto *Globe and Mail* judged, "What is exemplary is the con-

trol the author maintains over her unruly materials; the novel is both expansive and tight." Concluded reviewer Holly Eley in the *Times Literary Supplement*, *The Long Way Home* is "particularly gripping because of the quality of the writing and the esoteric setting."

St. Aubin de Teran's second novel, *Slow Train to Milan*, was also seen by many critics as autobiographical. Again, the story is told by a young girl, this time named Lisaveta, who in her teens marries a Venezuelan. In *The Long Way Home*, Lydia's past included travel in Europe with her husband before settling on his farm; at the end of *Slow Train to Milan*, which focuses on European travel, the reader is informed that Lisaveta and her husband Cesar have decided to go to Venezuela to raise avocados. Thus the events of the second book may be seen as a prelude to those of the first, though the names of the characters differ.

During much of *Slow Train*, Lisaveta, Cesar, and his friends Elias and Otto ride trains, most often between Milan, Italy, and Paris, France, because the three men are wanted by the International Criminal Police Organization (Interpol) for bank robbery and must keep moving. They are also small-scale political terrorists, but as Marion Glastonbury observed reviewing for the *New Statesman*, "their political commitment" seems "manifested only in peremptory scorn for democracy, communism, religion, clerks, waiters and the unemployed." The men are drawn in St. Aubin de Teran's prose as eccentrics, particularly Cesar—a member of the nobility in his own country, he expects to be catered to wherever he goes. His greatest diversion, reported Anatole Broyard in the *New York Times*, "is to seek the perfect strap for his wrist watch." Philip Horne, critiquing in the *London Review of Books*, commented "Lisa St. Aubin de Teran is a fine writer, and her subtle prose looks best when it looks, unblinking, at the oddity of the dealings of out-manoeuvred men so courageous and ridiculous." Lisaveta, on the other hand, is seen by many critics as an impassive observer. Madison Bell complained in the *New York Times Book Review* that "Lisaveta's lack of curiosity . . . at first astounds and finally irritates." Reviewer Isabel Raphael disagreed in the London *Times*, finding the narrator's impassivity an asset. According to Raphael, "once committed to life with Cesar, [Lisaveta] becomes indifferent to anything else, accepting each turn of fortune with what seems like apathy. But in this novel Lisa St. Aubin de Teran manages to give aimlessness a kind of purpose and lassitude a kind of power."

Critical reception of *The Slow Train to Milan* was more mixed than that of *The Long Way Home*. Nicholas Shakespeare of the *Times Literary Supplement* opined that *Slow Train* "is an altogether tamer novel, without the wars and pestilence, the madness and legends which made [*Long Way Home*] such a success." He had praise, however, for "the vividness and consistency of the writing," though he felt that the book lacked substance. "Nothing much happens in *The Slow Train to Milan*," Shakespeare lamented. Glastonbury, on the other hand, concluded that the novel's style is "so fluent, merry and felicitous that even the most reluctant and charm-resistant reader is, finally, glad to have gone along for the ride."

Called her "most ambitious and most imaginative" by critic Laurel Graeber in the *New York Times Book Review*, St. Aubin de Teran's third novel, *The Tiger*, departs from autobiography to focus on Lucien, a Venezuelan of German descent. Though Lucien is *The Tiger*'s protagonist, the entire novel is deeply infused with the presence of Lucien's grandmother, Misia

Schmutter. Lucien spends his childhood in Misia Schmutter's house, along with his brothers and sisters. His father, El Patron, lives there, too, but Misia Schmutter controls them all, ruling the family's feudal estate like a dictator. Being his grandmother's favorite and her heir does not allow Lucien to escape her cruelty. Like his siblings, he is beaten for minute mistakes in manners at the dinner table. He is, however, more fortunate than many other characters in *The Tiger* who meet death and torture at his grandmother's hands. Servants are punished by being thrown into lime pits, and pregnant peasants seduced by El Patron are given often fatal abortions. For all of her viciousness, however, Misia Schmutter has great skills with herbal medicines and effects many miraculous cures. This, in combination with her harsh domination of all around her, leads to popular belief that she is a witch.

Even after Misia Schmutter dies of a cancerous tumor Lucien continues to feel her presence. By playing roulette, which he learned from his grandmother, Lucien manages to build a fortune. Eventually, at what he perceives as Misia's urging, he also builds a magnificent house in Caracas, Venezuela's capital city, where he entertains and gambles. Lucien's luck runs out, however. After a bad run at the roulette wheel reduces his riches considerably, he tours his ancestral Germany, which is then under the grip of Nazi rule. Shortly after he returns he is imprisoned for a crime he did not commit—cannibalism. Twenty-five years later he is released from prison. Lucien is by this time an old man, but he has acquired his grandmother's almost mystic healing abilities.

Most reviewers responded favorably to *The Tiger*. Some, however, like Jonathan Loake in *Books and Bookmen*, had doubts about the depth of characterization. "In this department," he opined, "[St. Aubin de Teran] shows her limitations. Her characters seem distant, the subjects of a tale handed down and exaggerated in the retelling." Valentine Cunningham, on the other hand, declared in the *Observer* that *The Tiger* "makes extraordinary headway against the perennial difficulty of providing would-be mythic characters like these with a presence awesome enough for the reputations which their author seeks to assign them." About the novel's tone and atmosphere there was little argument. Francis King proclaimed in the *Spectator*: "There is no doubt of the depth and range of this author's talent. The book contains innumerable haunting descriptions of human folly, cruelty and degradation, and it evokes with extraordinary clarity its desolate landscapes of dust, sun and cactus." Philip Howard concluded in the London *Times* that *The Tiger* "is always interesting, beautifully written, with the delicacy and intelligence of a great cat; perhaps a literary tiger."

St. Aubin de Teran's fourth novel, *The Bay of Silence*, concerns William and Rosalind, a married couple with children. Each narrates part of the book. Rosalind, however, is a schizophrenic whose mental illness is at least in part responsible for the death of her young son. *Black Idol*, the author's fifth novel, is a fictionalized account of poet and publisher Harry Crosby who killed his mistress Josephine Bigelow in a murder-suicide pact in a New York City hotel.

MEDIA ADAPTATIONS: Screenplays of *The Slow Train to Milan*, release expected in May, 1989, and *The Bay of Silence*, an Anglo-Dutch production, release expected in May, 1990, adapted by the author.

AVOCATIONAL INTERESTS: Travel, Italian and Spanish language, botany, herbal medicine, Victoriana, restoring country houses, reading.

CA INTERVIEW

CA interviewed Lisa St. Aubin de Teran by telephone on January 23, 1987, at her home in Bristol, England.

CA: Your first two novels, The Long Way Home *and* The Slow Train to Milan, *have strong autobiographical elements and have been called by reviewers a blend of autobiography and fiction. When you set out to write them, did you have any concern about blending the two?*

St. AUBIN de TERAN: Not really. *The Long Way Home* was originally written as a series of short stories which were entirely about that hacienda in the Andes, and there was no autobiography at all. It was just about those characters. Then it was suggested to me by another writer that I should put in an autobiographical link to make the material more accessible to a public who had never been to that part of the world and wouldn't really understand the culture at first go. So the autobiographical links were added in to existing material, and the book was rewritten with that in mind.

CA: Was there really a Benito, as in the book, a person who knew the history of the Beltran family and passed the stories on so that they could be recorded?

St. AUBIN de TERAN: Yes, there was. He was a sort of family retainer. Just as in the book, he started off working for the character Arturo Lino as a boy and kept on working for the family. At the point where I went out, he was very old, and alcoholic, but with a very good memory for the family history. It was as is written.

CA: Did you keep a kind of notebook in which you recorded events and stories that later became part of your books?

St. AUBIN de TERAN: No. I never keep notes, ever, for anything. I don't keep a diary and I don't write anything down until I come to write an actual story or novel. I have what they call total recall.

CA: When did you begin to write, or to think about writing, for publication?

St. AUBIN de TERAN: I didn't think of writing for publication as such, but I began to write when I was twelve years old. By the time I was sixteen, I decided that that was really what I was going to do; I was going to be a writer. I chose that profession, as it were. But then I went out to Italy and Venezuela and I was farming for years and years. And I think partly because the language around me was Spanish and I was always writing in English, there didn't seem any point in even trying to publish, because nobody could read what I was writing. But I just kept on writing. All the time that I lived abroad, those ten years, I wrote pretty consistently. In fact, the material from *The Long Way Home* was all written while I was living in Venezuela, in the Andes, and was selected from a much larger body of work. I had probably five or six times as much material as I included in the book, written up as short stories.

CA: Reviewers often mention Gabriel Garcia Marquez and magical realism when they deal with your work. Have the South American writers been a conscious influence?

St. AUBIN de TERAN: I think the South American writers have been an influence, but the biggest influence has been

South America, which I suppose is the influence that there is on those South American writers—the fact of having lived there for a long time and been, as it were, a part of the society. Magical realism is something that comes out of South American culture and is reflected in the literature. The culture was the greatest influence. Many of the writers I didn't actually have access to while I was there, because I was out of contact with book shops or libraries. I just read what was there, which was often predating any contemporary writers. I'd read Garcia Marquez and always greatly admired him and still do. I suppose there must be some influence from him. But I think, for me, the greatest influence has come through poets rather than prose writers—South American poets like Vicente Huidobro.

CA: You won an Eric Gregory Award for poetry in 1983 and had a book of poems published in 1985, The High Place. *Have you been writing poetry as long as you have fiction?*

St. AUBIN de TERAN: Much longer. I started writing poetry first and moved into fiction when I was about twenty-two, with short stories, and into novels when I was about twenty-six. But I've been writing poetry since I was a girl, and I still write poetry. For me, poetry has always been very important and I think always will be. I don't publish a lot of poetry, but I write a lot of poetry.

CA: You would have approached the South American culture from a different sensibility from that of the writers who grew up there, so it is interesting that much of the same kind of feeling comes out of it in your work.

St. AUBIN de TERAN: I find it very hard in my own case to know to what extent South America has influenced my work—whether because I lived there, or in fact because I am half South American. My father is South American, but not Latin American; he's from British Guiana [now Guyana]. I was born here in England and brought up here. But I'm not entirely English, so there's always been an influence of something foreign. Maybe when I went to Latin America, the reason why I felt so at home there was because I'd always felt a bit of an alien in England.

CA: In the third novel, The Tiger, *you seemed to be getting away from autobiography. How did that feel?*

St. AUBIN de TERAN: It felt very good. It was never my intention to write an autobiographical novel. I wrote *The Long Way Home* first with no autobiography, as I said, and put the autobiography in to try to make it more accessible. With *The Slow Train to Milan*, although it's called autobiographical, I'm not really writing about myself; I'm writing about the men in the book. I'm not very interested in the autobiographical side of my work. It's really an endeavor to represent other people. So with *The Tiger* it was very easy to just write about other people, and I particularly wanted to do that. I didn't want to be there again, although I made a brief appearance at the end of the book. I didn't point that out very clearly. I'm not really interested in writing about myself. I'd rather write about other people.

CA: Can you tell me anything about the inspiration for the dreadful grandmother in The Tiger, *Misia Schmutter?*

St. AUBIN de TERAN: There is a basis of truth through the whole of *The Tiger* in that it's a fantasized story of an actual event. The character Lucien existed and was somebody I met

in his later years, after he'd come out of prison. He told me about his growing up and about his grandmother, but I never met the grandmother. I knew one anecdote about her, and from that anecdote I built up the character. What he told me was that when he was a little boy, nobody would come and eat at their house because they were all terrified of Misia Schmutter, who came from Prussia and had very, very exact table manners. Eating was agony for the family because they always used to make mistakes, and then there were these terrible punishments. But one day a stranger came who'd never been there before, and he didn't know that nobody visited this household for this reason. He arrived and sat down for a meal and he slurped his food. The children were sitting there dying because they thought something terrible would happen. The grandmother apparently made no murmur or gesture, and the visitor went on slurping through his meal. At the end of the meal, the grandmother stood up and left the table and then called for this man to come out to the yard. The children didn't see what happened. They heard one shot, and the man was never seen again. That was the one story I heard about her, and I heard that she was a botanist. Her great love in life had been botany. She had been the daughter of a famous botanist in Germany, and she had been penalized for being a woman by not being allowed to pursue her natural bent for botany. The twisting of her character from having been thwarted, and then coming to this new place where anything was allowed to happen—my character just grew up from that. But I should say that my own second biggest interest, after writing, is botany and herbal medicines, so the character wasn't just somebody who was very cruel, but also my idea of somebody who was good at something that I was interested in, and had her whole life ruined by not being allowed to pursue it.

CA: So you could approach her with at least a grain of sympathy because of those common interests?

St. AUBIN de TERAN: Yes, there was a grain of sympathy. And there was another grain of sympathy because my own grandmother, whom I never met, was a very cruel, vicious personality and made my mother suffer to a tremendous degree. Although I never met her, I heard stories constantly when I was a child of how my mother had had a terrible childhood at the hands of this very tyrannical woman. So the idea of a tyrannical woman who also had something good inside of her that few people could see has interested me from the time I was young.

CA: The Bay of Silence *is very unlike the first three novels, a story that unfolds as a kind of mystery and gradually develops its characters. It also seems to me a love story. Can you tell something about how the idea for the book was conceived?*

St. AUBIN de TERAN: The Bay of Silence originally was written as a story, just the middle sequence about the child on the beach. That grew out of a family trip; I took my own children and nanny and a sort of human zoo of people off to France. We went to this very desolate area. It was meant to be a holiday. I'd been under a lot of strain, and I wanted to go somewhere where I could just relax and get back my health. It turned out to be a sort of nightmarish place. There was a nuclear reactor just a little way away, which made the people in the village very strange; they were all superstitious about this reactor. While we were there, a very unpleasant incident occurred with my children, and one of them was hurt. Out of that a kind of nightmare grew, so that I became obsessed by the idea of losing them. The boy character Amadeus was based on my own son, who was at that time two years old and resembled very much the description of the character in the book. I became very paranoid that something would happen to my son because something had already happened, and one of the children had been hurt. So I went away to Italy, trying to calm myself down. When I arrived in Italy, I went to live in the place I describe in the book, by the Bay of Silence in Sestri Levante. The book grew out of being in a very strange, sort of schizophrenic place where the people are weird, and feeling very schizophrenic myself at the time and having these children who were behaving strangely, having this fear that something would happen. So it became a kind of study in the responsibility of people to each other—a mother to her children, a woman to her lover, a woman to herself, in a way. Although it doesn't seem autobiographical, it's probably got more genuine autobiography in it than any of the other books.

CA: It must have been difficult to develop the character Rosalind, approaching her mental illness in a roundabout way as you did.

St. AUBIN de TERAN: It wasn't. At the time I wrote *The Bay of Silence,* I had actually intended to write another book. I had started another novel, in fact, and I literally just sat down one day and the whole book came to me and I started writing it. I'd never done that before, but it was easy to write because I had it in my mind, and the character of Rosalind was very clearly in my mind. It was never difficult at any time. When I write any piece of prose, I don't actually sit down and try to think up a character. I never start writing until I've got it all in my head. So I start, I think, at the point where other people finish, because I get an entire novel in my head and then I sit down and dictate it to myself. I never start writing until I know exactly, word-for-word, what I'm going to say.

CA: Do you go back then and polish?

St. AUBIN de TERAN: I do go back and do some polishing, but only after the whole book is there. I go straight through one draft, which will be very nearly the way it will be published, but then I get a bit obsessive about tuning it up. When I write, I sit down and literally say it out loud, and I just type at the pace I can speak at.

CA: Being married to the poet George MacBeth, do you find it helpful to read your work in progress to him?

St. AUBIN de TERAN: I've actually been separated from George for some time, but we still read each other's work and have a very close working relationship. There's a mutual exchange of ideas before stuff gets to the publisher. We criticize each other's work, and I put a lot of stock by his opinion. He's a very good critic.

CA: You said in the British magazine She *that you still hadn't gone to a computer for the writing. Do you think you'll stick with a typewriter forever?*

St. AUBIN de TERAN: For my novels, I will always stick with a typewriter. The fact that a computer can do lots of different things doesn't interest me for writing a novel. For me, the only interesting thing is the sound. When I say it out loud, every sentence has to sound right. Nothing can help that more than hearing it and writing it down. Somebody else always types it up for me again and makes it clean. But I've been

writing films, and I can see that for films a computer is very useful. It's such a different technique, with going over and changing things. A director will come along and say, "What about this?" and then there's a change. A computer is very useful for that. I've been doing two screenplays for books that I've written, and in doing those, I now think a computer is pretty useful.

CA: One of the screenplays is for The Slow Train to Milan?

St. AUBIN de TERAN: I've done a screenplay for *The Slow Train to Milan,* which will be shot later this year by an English director called Michael Radford. My new novel, which will be published in September, is again very different. It's called *Black Idol,* and it's based on the life of Harry Crosby, the American poet and diarist and publisher. That will be made into a film this summer.

CA: How did you happen to become interested in Harry Crosby?

St. AUBIN de TERAN: I was spending a couple of months in New York City, and I was staying in the Hotel des Artistes, where he and Josephine Bigelow killed themselves. I'd heard the story about eight years ago and found it very fascinating. Since then I've been collecting stuff about Crosby. So a few years ago I wrote a novel based very much on the real events of his life. There was a two-hour time gap between the time he shot himself and the time Josephine died. My novel occurs during that time gap, on the idea that as a man drowns, his life flashes before him. In those two hours, the whole of Harry Crosby's life flashes before him.

CA: Will that book be published here in the States right away?

St. AUBIN de TERAN: It's just gone off to America, so hopefully there will be a joint publication. With the film coming up as well, I think that's quite likely.

CA: We've been lucky in getting your books quickly, which often doesn't happen with British writers. Do you hear from a lot of readers here in the States?

St. AUBIN de TERAN: I hear from quite a lot of readers, yes. I get very interesting mail, actually, from there. My books are published in a lot of different languages, and so I get mail in from different places. But my letters from America are often very detailed; there's a level of interest that is surprising in a way, in that it's hard to think that somebody from a different culture will be so interested. When they come, I carry them around with me for a while and look at them, they make such an impact.

CA: Travel obviously is very important to you personally and figures highly in your work. Can you write anywhere?

St. AUBIN de TERAN: Yes, I can. And I do like to travel; I find it very therapeutic. I have a lot of manic energy, and I like traveling partly because I find it physically calming. Now I have a solution, which is not to live in any one place. I spend a few months somewhere and then go somewhere else. I divide my time now permanently between Italy and England, and so I live at least half the year in Italy. I also go to Scotland. So I get the sense of traveling, but of still being at home. And because I have children, that's feasible. It's not possible to be a gypsy now.

BIOGRAPHICAL/CRITICAL SOURCES:

BOOKS

St. Aubin de Teran, Lisa, *The Long Way Home*, Harper, 1983.

PERIODICALS

Books and Bookmen, September, 1984.
Globe and Mail (Toronto), May 12, 1984.
London Review of Books, April 1-20, 1983.
Los Angeles Times, October 24, 1985.
Los Angeles Times Book Review, April 10, 1983.
New Statesman, March 11, 1983.
New York Times, April 25, 1984.
New York Times Book Review, October 13, 1985.
Observer (London), July 11, 1982, September 16, 1984.
She, May, 1986.
Spectator, March 19, 1983, September 29, 1984.
Times (London), February 28, 1983, March 3, 1983, September 13, 1984, May 1, 1986, October 1, 1987.
Times Literary Supplement, July 9, 1982, March 11, 1983, September 21, 1984.
Washington Post Book World, September 16, 1985.

—Sketch by Elizabeth Thomas

—Interview by Jean W. Ross

*   *   *

St. JOHNS, Adela Rogers   1894-1988

OBITUARY NOTICE—See index for *CA* sketch: Born May 20, 1894, in Los Angeles, Calif.; died August 10, 1988, in Arroyo Grande, Calif. Minister, educator, journalist, and author. St. Johns earned the sobriquet "the world's greatest girl reporter" with her controversial sixteen-part expose she wrote in 1931 for the *Los Angeles Herald* (now the *Herald Examiner*) on the treatment of the city's indigent. She began her long journalism career in 1913, when newspaper magnate William Randolph Hearst hired her as a reporter for the *San Francisco Examiner*. She subsequently joined the fledgling *Photoplay* fan magazine in the early 1920s, for which she interviewed many prominent entertainers, including Greta Garbo, Mary Pickford, and Rudolph Valentino. She later returned to the newsroom, reporting on such national and international events as the Lindbergh baby kidnapping and the abdication of King Edward VIII.

St. Johns retired in 1948 but resumed working in 1976, at the age of eighty-two, to cover the bank robbery and conspiracy trial of Hearst's granddaughter, Patricia Hearst, for the *Examiner*. In 1970 she was awarded the Medal of Freedom—the highest civilian honor in the United States—by President Richard M. Nixon in recognition of her years devoted to the free press. St. Johns's other writings include the novels *The Skyrocket*, *A Free Soul*, and *Tell No Man;* the biographies *First Step Up Toward Heaven: Hubert Eaton and Forest Lawn* and *Some Are Born Great;* the screenplays "Broken Laws," "The Arizona Wildcat," and "The Heart of a Follies Girl"; and two best-selling autobiographies, *The Honeycomb* and *Love, Laughter, and Tears: My Hollywood Story*. In addition, St. Johns taught journalism at the University of California at Los Angeles, and at Stanford, Loyola, and Pepperdine universities. Also a minister in the Church of Religious Science, she was writing *The Missing Years of Jesus* at the time of her death.

OBITUARIES AND OTHER SOURCES:

BOOKS

Current Biography, H. W. Wilson, September, 1988.
Dictionary of Literary Biography, Volume 29: *American Newspaper Journalists, 1926-1950*, Gale, 1984.

PERIODICALS

Chicago Tribune, August 11, 1988.
Los Angeles Times, August 11, 1988.
New York Times, August 11, 1988.

*   *   *

SALAAM, Kalamu ya   1947-
(Vallery Ferdinand III)

PERSONAL: Name originally Vallery Ferdinand III; name legally changed, c. 1971; born March 24, 1947, in New Orleans, La.; son of Vallery and Inola (Copelin) Ferdinand; married Tayari kwa Salaam; children: five. *Education:* Attended Carlton College, 1964-65, and Southern University, 1968-69; received A.A. from Delgado Junior College.

ADDRESSES: Home—1708 Tennessee, New Orleans, La. 70117.

CAREER: Free Southern Theater, New Orleans, La., artist, writer, and actor, 1968-71, director of BLKARTSOUTH (performing ensemble); *Black Collegian*, New Orleans, founding member, 1970—, began as managing editor, became editor at large, 1983—. Director of New Orleans Jazz and Heritage Foundation, New Orleans; co-founder of Ahidiana, New Orleans, 1973; Southern delegate to Sixth Pan-African Conference in Tanzania, 1974. *Military service:* U.S. Army, 1965-68.

MEMBER: Afrikan Liberation Support Committee, People Defense Coalition (New Orleans-based chairman).

AWARDS, HONORS: Richard Wright award from *Black World* (now *First World*), 1971, for literary criticism; Deems Taylor award from American Society of Composers, Authors, and Publishers (ASCAP), 1981, for excellence in writing about music; two first place Unity awards in Media from Lincoln University of Missouri; George Washington award from Freedom's Foundation at Valley Forge, "for an outstanding individual contribution reflecting the ideals of human dignity and the principles of a free society."

WRITINGS:

(Under name Vallery Ferdinand III) *The Blues Merchant: Songs for Blkfolk* (poetry), BLKARTSOUTH (New Orleans), 1969.
Hofu ni kwenu: My Fear Is for You (poetry and essays), Ahidiana (New Orleans), 1973.
Pamoja tutashinda: Together We Will Win (poetry), Ahidiana, 1973.
Ibura (poetry and fiction), illustrations by Arthrello Beck, Jr., Ahidiana, 1976.
Tearing the Roof off the Sucker: The Fall of South Afrika (treatise), Ahidiana, 1977.
South African Showdown: Divestment Now (treatise), Ahidiana, 1978.

Nuclear Power and the Black Liberation Struggle (pamphlet), Ahidiana, 1978.

Revolutionary Love (poetry and essays), drawings by Douglas Redd, photographs by Kwadwo Oluwale Akpan, Ahidiana-Habari, 1978.

(With wife, Tayari kwa Salaam) *Who Will Speak for Us? New Afrikan Folk Tales* (juvenile), Ahidiana, 1978.

Herufi: An Alphabet Reader (juvenile), Ahidiana, 1978.

Iron Flowers: A Poetic Report on a Visit to Haiti (poetry), Ahidiana, 1979.

Our Women Keep Our Skies From Falling: Six Essays in Support of the Struggle to Smash Sexism and Develop Women (essays), Nkombo (New Orleans), 1980.

Work represented in anthologies, including *What We Must See: Young Black Storytellers*, edited by Orde Coombs, Dodd & Mead, 1971, and *We Be Word Sorcerers: Twenty-five Short Stories by Black Americans*, edited by Sonia Sanchez, Bantam Books, 1973. Contributor to periodicals, including *Black Scholar, Callaloo, Encore, Journal of Black Poetry*, and *Nimrod*.

Editor and publisher of *Expressions;* co-editor and publisher of *Nkombo;* contributing editor of *Culture;* advisory editor of *First World*.

PLAYS

"Cop Killer" (one-act), first produced in 1968.

"The Picket" (one-act), first produced in New Orleans at Free Southern Theater, 1968.

"Mama" (one-act), first produced in New Orleans at Free Southern Theater, 1969.

"Happy Birthday, Jesus" (one-act), first produced in New Orleans at Free Southern Theater, 1969.

"Black Liberation Army" (one-act), first produced in New Orleans at Free Southern Theater, 1969.

(With Tom Dent) "Song of Survival" (one-act), first produced in 1969.

"Homecoming" (one-act), first produced in New Orleans at Free Southern Theater, 1970, published in *Nkombo*, August, 1972.

"Black Love Song #1" (one-act), first produced in New Orleans at Free Southern Theater, 1971, published in *Black Theater, U.S.A.*, edited by James V. Hatch and Ted Shine, Free Press, 1974.

"The Quest" (one-act), first produced in New Orleans at BLKARTSOUTH, 1972.

"Somewhere in the World (Long Live Asatta)," first produced in New Orleans at Art for Life Theater Company, 1982.

WORK IN PROGRESS: *Banana Republic*, on black life and culture in New Orleans.

SIDELIGHTS: Kalamu ya Salaam, a writer, editor, artist, and actor, devotes his talents to supporting minority and women's rights. In addition to his involvement with such organizations as the Afrikan Liberation Support Committee and New Orleans' Free Southern Theater, Salaam helped found Ahidiana, a Pan-African nationalist organization that remained active from 1973 to 1984. The group, based in New Orleans, ran an independent school for children aged three to five, promoted the arts with its "Essence of Life" poetry and music ensemble—directed for a time by Salaam—and published books on topics concerning human rights, including several by Salaam. A founding member of *Black Collegian* in 1970, the writer later

served as the journal's managing editor and became its editor at large in 1983. Salaam is recognized for his expertise in critiquing music, and he serves as executive director of the New Orleans Jazz and Heritage Foundation.

Salaam's writings—which include poetry, fiction, essays, plays, and music criticism—are as varied as his activities. His first books, including *The Blues Merchant: Songs for Blkfolk, Hofu ni kwenu: My Fear Is for You, Pamoja tutashinda: Together We Will Win*, and *Ibura*, consist of poetry and prose intended to inspire black people to create their own cultural identity in America. Believing that art is valuable only if it conveys a social or political message, Salaam imbues these writings with the theories of Pan-African nationalism, urging men and women to remember their heritage and to create a balanced society by reconciling their past with their present.

In *Revolutionary Love*, a volume of poems and essays, and in the essay collection *Our Women Keep Our Skies From Falling*, Salaam argues for the social and political rights of women. *Revolutionary Love*, Salaam's best selling book, encourages men and women to strive for political unity through family love. The essays in *Our Women Keep Our Skies From Falling* favor social revolution through the education and liberation of all women, who have traditionally been "subjected to the exploitation that is an integral part of every social system," as Arthenia J. Bates Millican quoted in *Dictionary of Literary Biography*.

During the late 1970s Salaam published treatises denouncing South Africa's policy of apartheid and the support the United States gives to the South African Government. Urging the United States to cease investing money in South African companies, wrote Millican, Salaam declared in *South African Showdown: Divestment Now:* "Investment in South Africa, like apartheid, like segregation, like colonialism makes no sense at all and faces the anger and opposition of the majority of the peoples of the world. . . . In the face of this reality, divestment is the natural choice of U.S. companies."

Salaam deplores the oppressive conditions in Haiti through his 1979 work, *Iron Flowers: A Poetic Report on a Visit to Haiti*. Exhibiting the poet's desire for harmony between various forms of artistic expression, *Iron Flowers* "speaks in its physical dimensions (color, photographs, design) as well as in its poems," observed Alvin Aubert in the *Small Press Review*. Describing how the intricate "black lacework" that borders the book's pages recalls the Iron Market of Haiti's Port au Prince, Aubert explained that the poems are equally "finely wrought, as fine ironwork should be, and their forms are appropriate to the urgency of their messages." The title poem, which refers to Haitian funeral flowers that are made of iron, describes the permanence of death. Another poem laments the inability of Haitian citizens to attain refuge in the United States from economic and political oppression. Aubert praised "this book of mourning" as "so deftly, so poignantly and urgently written."

BIOGRAPHICAL/CRITICAL SOURCES:

BOOKS

Dictionary of Literary Biography, Volume 38: *Afro-American Writers After 1955: Dramatists and Prose Writers*, Gale, 1985.

PERIODICALS

Small Press Review, August, 1980.

SALEMSON, Harold J(ason) 1910-1988

OBITUARY NOTICE—See index for *CA* sketch: Born September 30, 1910, in Chicago, Ill.; died of a heart attack, August 25, 1988, in Glen Cove, N.Y. Film industry employee, publisher, editor, translator, film and literary critic, and author. Salemson will be best remembered as the editor of *Tambour*, a French-English literary magazine he published in Paris between 1929 and 1931. Born in Chicago, Salemson moved with his family to France in 1922 and became active on the French literary scene in the late 1920s, writing film criticism for *Le Monde* and founding *Tambour*, which featured writings by such authors as Theodore Dreiser, William Carlos Williams, Andre Gide, and Jean Cocteau. When Salemson returned to the United States in 1931 he settled in Hollywood, California, where he worked as a film critic and subsequently in other capacities related to the movie industry: as a bit actor, a technical adviser, a publicist, a film executive and distributor, and as a foreign film subtitler. In 1966 he became a book reviewer for *Newsday* magazine and began translating writings. The more than twenty works he translated include Pierre Cabanne's *Pablo Picasso: His Life and Times*, Cheikh A. Diop's *Black Africa: Economic and Cultural Basis for a Federated State*, the autobiography *The Unspeakable Confessions of Salvador Dali*, and *Sayings of the Ayatollah Khomeini*. Additionally, Salemson taught film history at Long Island University from 1975 to 1977 and edited *Thought Control in the U.S.*, Beverly Hills, California.

OBITUARIES AND OTHER SOURCES:

PERIODICALS

New York Times, August 28, 1988.

* * *

SALTMAN, Judith 1947-

PERSONAL: Born May 11, 1947, in Vancouver, British Columbia, Canada; daughter of Harry and Ruth (Berezovsky) Saltman; married Bill Barringer (a journalist); children: Anne. *Education:* University of British Columbia, B.A., 1969, B.L.S., 1970; Simmons College, M.A., 1982. *Politics:* Social Democrat.

ADDRESSES: Home—129 West 11th Ave., Vancouver, British Columbia, Canada V5Y 1S8. *Office*—School of Library, Archival, and Information Studies, University of British Columbia, 831-1956 Main Mall, Vancouver, British Columbia, Canada V6T 1Y3.

CAREER: Toronto Public Library, Toronto, Ontario, children's librarian, 1970-72; West Vancouver Memorial Library, West Vancouver, British Columbia, children's librarian, 1973-79; Vancouver Public Library, Vancouver, British Columbia, children's librarian, 1980-83; University of British Columbia, Vancouver, assistant professor, 1983-88, associate professor of children's literature and librarianship, 1988—. Member of International Board on Books for Young People.

MEMBER: Canadian Library Association, American Library Association, Children's Literature Association, Association for Library and Information Science Education, British Columbia Library Association.

AWARDS, HONORS: Howard V. Phalin-World Book scholar of Canadian Library Association, 1981; Frances E. Russell Memorial Award from Canadian section of International Board on Books for Young People, 1986.

WRITINGS:

(Editor) *Riverside Anthology of Children's Literature*, 6th edition, Houghton, 1985.
Goldie and the Sea (juvenile), Groundwood Books, 1987.
Modern Canadian Children's Books, Oxford University Press, 1987.

WORK IN PROGRESS: An edition of *The Republic of Childhood: A Critical Guide to Canadian Children's Literature in English*, with Sheila Egoff, for Oxford University Press.

SIDELIGHTS: Judith Saltman told *CA:* "All my work as a writer, teacher, and librarian has been devoted to the creation of quality children's literature and the promotion and mediation of literature with children. This is a very exciting time to be working in this field in Canada. Canadian authors and illustrators are interpreting Canadian life and values, telling our children about our culture, history, and ourselves as members of the human community."

* * *

SALUSINSZKY, Imre 1955-

PERSONAL: Born April 5, 1955, in Budapest, Hungary; son of Andor Laszlo (an engineer) and Livia (Szalkai) Salusinszky; married Karen Barrett (an editor), December 8, 1984. *Education:* University of Melbourne, B.A., 1977; Oxford University, D.Phil., 1983.

ADDRESSES: Home—108 Mitchell St., Stockton, New South Wales 2295, Australia. *Office*—Department of English, University of Newcastle, Newcastle, New South Wales 2308, Australia.

CAREER: Age, Melbourne, Australia, journalist, 1978; Yale University, New Haven, Conn., lecturer in English, 1985-86; University of Melbourne, Melbourne, tutor in English, 1986-87; University of Newcastle, Newcastle, Australia, lecturer in English, 1987—.

AWARDS, HONORS: Fulbright fellow, 1985-86; Violet Vaughan Morgan Commonwealth fellow, 1979-82.

WRITINGS:

Criticism in Society, Methuen, 1987.

Contributor of articles and reviews to magazines and newspapers in England, Australia, and the United States.

WORK IN PROGRESS: A book on Northrop Frye, publication by Routledge & Kegan Paul expected in 1989.

SIDELIGHTS: Imre Salusinszky told *CA:* "I have come to the view that literary criticism participates, along with philosophy, in the exploration of a space which is unique and rather personal: the space in which consciousness, or being, ventures forth to engage with a 'world' that is partly itself and partly some Other. Critics should explore this area of literature in favor of alternative terrains like social preaching or historical illumination. That criticism is best which makes the literature it deals with seem most humanly imperative, where we witness a real dialogue proceeding between critic and text. The fact that this kind of literary criticism has been rare in Australia serves to make Australia a more exciting place to work for contemporary poets and novelists."

SAMEK, Hana 1953-

PERSONAL: Surname is pronounced "*Sah*-mek"; born September 23, 1953, in Nachod, Czechoslovakia; immigrated to Canada, 1968, naturalized citizen; immigrated to United States, 1979; daughter of Vladimir and Marie (Sekmiler) Samek; married Harry Patrick S. Norton, September 27, 1986. *Education:* University of Western Ontario, B.A., 1977, M.A., 1979; University of New Mexico, Ph.D., 1986.

CAREER: Forensic historian in Albuquerque, N.M.

MEMBER: Association for Canadian Studies in the United States, Western History Association, New Mexico Historical Society.

WRITINGS:

The Blackfoot Confederacy, 1880-1920: A Comparative Study of Canada and U.S. Indian Policy, University of New Mexico Press, 1987.

WORK IN PROGRESS: Research on western American, southwestern, and Indian history.

SIDELIGHTS: Hana Samek told *CA:* "As a historian, I specialize in research on Indian land and water rights in support of litigation."

* * *

SANDLIN, Tim 1950-
(Peter and Delores Pym)

PERSONAL: Born August 10, 1950, in Duncan, Okla.; son of Hoyt Nick (a school administrator) and Elizabeth (a writer and journalist; maiden name, Bernard) Sandlin; married Emily West (a waitress), September 13, 1986. *Education:* University of Oklahoma, B.A., 1974; University of North Carolina at Greensboro, M.F.A., 1986. *Politics:* "Environmental anarchist." *Religion:* "Militant pantheism."

ADDRESSES: Home—Box 1974, Jackson, Wyo. 83001. *Agent*—Phillipa Brody, Sterling Lord Literistic, 1 Madison Ave., New York, N.Y. 10010.

CAREER: Rocky Mountain Big Game, Jackson, Wyo., elk skinner, 1974-76; Bridger Teton National Forest, Jackson, conducted trail inventory, 1976-77; Lame Duck Chinese Restaurant, Jackson, cook, 1982-87; writer, 1987—.

MEMBER: Associated Writing Programs, Poets and Writers, Enoch Emery Society, Earth First!

AWARDS, HONORS: Fellow of Wyoming Council for the Humanities, 1988.

WRITINGS:

Sex and Sunsets (novel), Holt, 1987.
Western Swing (novel), Holt, 1988.

Author of "As the Hole Deepens," a column in *Jackson Hole News,* under pseudonym Peter and Delores Pym.

WORK IN PROGRESS: The Yeast Infection, publication by Holt expected in 1990.

SIDELIGHTS: Tim Sandlin told *CA:* "I write because one life is not enough. My work does not always turn out artistically neat: my characters tend to live in chaos, and from that, I find a quiet joy and peace. There aren't any real people around the Gros Ventre Mountains where I live, so my created characters give me someone interesting to talk to."

AVOCATIONAL INTERESTS: Environmental action, country western music, college basketball, his cats.

* * *

SAPIA, Yvonne (V.) 1946-

PERSONAL: Born April 10, 1946, in New York, N.Y.; daughter of Facundo Pedro (a barber) and Antonia (a housewife; maiden name, Segarra) Sapia. *Education:* Miami-Dade Community College, A.A., 1967; Florida Atlantic University, B.A., 1970; University of Florida, M.A., 1976; doctoral study at Florida State University. *Politics:* Democrat. *Religion:* Roman Catholic.

ADDRESSES: Home—702 South Marsh St., Lake City, Fla. 32055. *Office*—Department of English, Lake City Community College, Route 3, P. O. Box 7, Lake City, Fla. 32055.

CAREER: Village Post, Miami, Fla., reporter, 1971-73; University of Florida, Gainesville, editorial assistant in department of ornamental horticulture, 1974-76; Lake City Community College, Lake City, Fla., instructor in English and resident poet, 1976—, publications editor, 1976—, chairperson of fine arts committee, 1980-86. Member of Fine Arts Council of Lake City, 1986—. Editorial supervisor of educational programs for Florida Horticultural Industries, 1975-76; teacher at Florida state prisons, 1977-78; poetry teacher at workshops for the elderly and for gifted children, 1980-82; member of editorial advisory board of Roxbury Publishing Co.; gives poetry readings.

MEMBER: Academy of American Poets.

AWARDS, HONORS: Fellow of Department of State's Division of Cultural Affairs and Florida Fine Arts Council, 1981-82 and 1987-88, and National Endowment for the Arts, 1986-87; Poetry Chapbook Award from Florida State University, 1983, for *The Fertile Crescent;* Samuel French Morse Poetry Prize from Northeastern University Press, 1987, for *Valentino's Hair.*

WRITINGS:

(Editor with Dennis McConnell) *The Nurseryman's Retail Sales Handbook,* University of Florida, 1974.
(Editor with McConnell) *The Landscape Installation Handbook,* University of Florida, 1975.
(Editor with McConnell) *The Landscape Maintenance Handbook,* University of Florida, 1976.
The Fertile Crescent (poems), Anhinga, 1983.
Valentino's Hair (poems), Northeastern University Press, 1987.

Work represented in anthologies, including *Anthology of Magazine Verse and 1985 Yearbook of American Poetry,* Monitor Book, 1985. Contributor of about seventy poems, articles, and reviews to magazines, including *Pacific Review, Kalliope, Panhandler, Partisan Review, Prairie Schooner,* and *Americas Review.* Editor of *Woodrider.*

WORK IN PROGRESS: Valentino's Hair: A Novel, about the barber who cut Rudolph Valentino's hair and uses the hair in magical ways; *The Mythology of Hair and Other Poems.*

SIDELIGHTS: Yvonne Sapia told *CA:* "My work explores relationships through the reconstruction of memories, dreams, and reflections of each poem's persona. In order to understand what is happening to all of us in a world we have become too busy to observe significantly, I try to convey the intense emotion of illuminating experience with sparse and carefully chosen language."

BIOGRAPHICAL/CRITICAL SOURCES:

PERIODICALS

Albatross, Volume II, number 1, 1987.
Florida Times-Union, December 16, 1986.
Kalliope, Volume X, numbers 1 and 2, 1988.

* * *

SAPIRO, Virginia 1951-

PERSONAL: Born February 28, 1951, in East Orange, N.J.; daughter of William H. (a scriptwriter) and Florence (an educator; maiden name, Michaels) Sapiro; married Graham K. Wilson (a professor), 1981; children: Adam. *Education:* Clark University, B.A. (with high honors), 1972; University of Michigan, M.A. and Ph.D., both 1976.

ADDRESSES: *Office*—Department of Political Science, University of Wisconsin—Madison, Madison, Wis. 53706.

CAREER: Clark University, Worcester, Mass., instructor in political science, summer, 1974; University of Michigan, Ann Arbor, instructor in political science, summer, 1975; University of Wisconsin—Madison, assistant professor, 1976-81, associate professor, 1981-86, professor of political science and women's studies, 1986—, member of executive committee of Institute for Legal Studies, 1986—, chairperson of Women's Studies Program, 1986—.

MEMBER: International Society for Political Psychology, American Political Science Association (chairperson of Committee on the Status of Women, 1985-86; founding president of Organized Section on Women and Politics, 1986), Women's Caucus in Political Science, Inter-University Consortium for Political and Social Research, Midwest Political Science Association (member of executive council, 1984-86), Michigan Political Science Association (member of board of directors, 1975-76), Michigan Women's Caucus in Political Science (chairperson, 1974-75), Phi Beta Kappa.

AWARDS, HONORS: Chastain Award from Southern Political Science Association, 1975, for paper "New Pride, Old Prejudice: Political Ambition and Role Orientations Among Female Partisan Elites"; award from Western Political Science Association's Committee on the Status of Women, 1978, for article "News From the Front: Inter-Sex and Intergenerational Conflict Over the Status of Women"; Sophinisba Breckinridge Award from Midwest Political Science Association, 1983, for paper "Women, Citizenship, and Immigration Policy in the United States"; Erik Erikson Award for Early Career Contribution to Political Psychology from International Society for Political Psychology, 1986.

WRITINGS:

The Political Integration of Women: Roles, Socialization, and Politics, University of Illinois Press, 1983.
Women, Political Action, and Political Participation, American Political Science Association, 1983.
(Editor and contributor) *Women, Biology, and Public Policy,* Sage Publications, 1985.
Women in American Society: An Introduction to Women's Studies, Mayfield Publishing, 1986.

Member of editorial board of *American Journal of Political Science,* 1979-82, *Woman and Politics,* 1980—, *Political Psychology,* 1981—, *Youth and Society,* 1982—, and *Political Science Quarterly,* 1984—.

CONTRIBUTOR

D. McGuigan, editor, *New Research on Women and Sex Roles,* Center for Continuing Education, University of Michigan, 1976.
J. Sherman and E. Beck, editors, *The Prism of Sex: Essays in the Sociology of Knowledge,* University of Wisconsin Press, 1979.
Drude Dahlerup, editor, *The New Women's Movement,* Sage Publications, 1986.

Also contributor to *Transforming the Consciousness of the Academy,* for Indiana University Press. Contributor of articles and reviews to political science and women's studies journals.

WORK IN PROGRESS: *The Political Theory of Mary Wollstonecraft,* completion expected in 1991; a study of the political significance of "life course development."

SIDELIGHTS: Virginia Sapiro told *CA:* "My primary concern is a feminist analysis of the relationship of women to the political world. Although my work is scholarly and employs the methods of contemporary social science, my view is that writing in the social sciences should be intelligible and even enjoyable to read."

* * *

SATIR, Virginia (Mildred) 1916-1988

OBITUARY NOTICE: Born June 26, 1916, in Neillsville, Wis.; died of pancreatic cancer, September 10, 1988, in Menlo Park, Calif. Social worker, therapist, educator, and author. For the techniques she created to treat troubled families, Satir was known worldwide as a pioneer in the development of family therapy. After earning a bachelor's degree from Wisconsin State University in 1936, Satir taught for six years at schools in Wisconsin, Michigan, and Louisiana. She became interested in the relationship between dysfunctional individuals and their families, and, deciding to specialize in family analysis, went back to school to earn a master's degree in 1948 at the University of Chicago. Satir subsequently worked as a therapist and social worker at mental hospitals and public welfare programs and conducted more than four hundred workshops for the government, hospitals, and universities throughout the United States. In addition, Satir helped found the Mental Research Institute in 1959 and, twenty years later, established the International Human Learning Resource Network. A leader in developing the concept of self-worth, Satir conveyed her psychological philosophies in such books as *Conjoint Family Therapy: A Guide to Theory and Technique, Peoplemaking, Self Esteem, Helping Families to Change,* and *Making Contact.*

OBITUARIES AND OTHER SOURCES:

BOOKS

American Women Writers: A Critical Reference Guide From Colonial Times to the Present, Volume I, Ungar, 1979.

PERIODICALS

Chicago Tribune, September 12, 1988.
Los Angeles Times, September 12, 1988.
Washington Post, September 16, 1988.

* * *

SATTIN, Anthony (Neil) 1956-

PERSONAL: Born June 28, 1956, in London, England; son

of Gerald (an antiques dealer) and Mona (Maer) Sattin. *Education:* University of Warwick, B.A. (with honors), 1979; University of East Anglia, M.A., 1984.

ADDRESSES: Home—London, England. *Agent*—Curtis Brown Ltd., 162-168 Regent St., London W1R 5TB, England.

WRITINGS:

(Editor) *An Englishwoman in India: The Memoirs of Harriet Tytler, 1828-1858,* Oxford University Press, 1986.
(Editor) Florence Nightingale, *Letters From Egypt,* Barrie & Jenkins, 1987.
The British in Egypt: A Social View of Britons in Egypt, 1801-1956 (tentative title), Dent, 1988.

Contributor of articles and stories to magazines, including *Times Literary Supplement, Fiction, Punch,* and *Literary Review.*

WORK IN PROGRESS: A novel.

*   *   *

SAVAGE, Thomas   1915-

BRIEF ENTRY: Born April 25, 1915, in Salt Lake City, Utah. American ranch hand, educator, and novelist. A critically acclaimed though relatively little-known author, Savage is recognized for his novels set in the American West. Largely concerned with characters' responses to pressures created by familial and societal expectations, his works are consistently praised for their sincerity, skillful characterization, and sensitive observations. Savage was raised on a ranch in southwestern Montana and later spent two years at the University of Montana, where he studied writing. After receiving a B.A. in 1940 from Colby College, Savage held various jobs, including that of a wrangler at a dude ranch. Among Savage's novels set in the West are *The Pass* (Doubleday, 1944) and *Lona Hanson* (Simon & Schuster, 1948), both of which deal with the hardships faced by frontiersmen in the early 1900s. Another work, *The Power of the Dog* (Little, Brown, 1967), concerns the tragic relationship between two brothers during the 1920s. Additional works sharing Savage's recurring theme of pained family relations are *The Liar* (Little, Brown, 1969) and *I Heard My Sister Speak My Name* (Little, Brown, 1977). A more recent novel, *For Mary, With Love* (Little, Brown, 1983), explores the crises involved in the life of a beautiful but selfish and destructive adventuress. The author has taught at various academic institutions, including Brandeis University and Franconia College.

BIOGRAPHICAL/CRITICAL SOURCES:

BOOKS

Contemporary Literary Criticism, Volume 40, Gale, 1986.
Who's Who Among Pacific Northwest Authors, 2nd edition, Pacific Northwest Library Association, 1969.

PERIODICALS

New York Times Book Review, April 27, 1969.
Publishers Weekly, July 15, 1988.
Washington Post Book World, September 18, 1983.

*   *   *

SCALES, Junius Irving   1920-

PERSONAL: Born March 26, 1920, in Greensboro, N.C.; son of Alfred Moore (a lawyer) and Mary Leigh (Pell) Scales; married Gladys Meyer (a teacher), February 25, 1950 (died,

1981); children: Barbara Arline. *Education:* University of North Carolina at Chapel Hill, B.A., 1940, graduate study, 1946-48. *Politics:* Democratic Socialist. *Religion:* "Presbyterian family."

ADDRESSES: Home—90 La Salle St., No. 11-D, New York, N.Y. 10027.

CAREER: Trade union organizer in High Point, N.C., 1940-42; Communist party organizer and spokesman (chairman, district organizer, and southern regional leader), 1946-56; proofreader for a printer in New York, N.Y., 1957-61; *New York Times,* New York City, proofreader, 1963-83.

WRITINGS:

(With Richard Nickson) *Cause at Heart: A Former Communist Remembers,* University of Georgia Press, 1987.

SIDELIGHTS: Junius Irving Scales told *CA:* "Growing up in an impoverished, oppressive, racist South, I became a Communist in 1939. The Communist party opposed fascism, organized workers, projected a Socialist future, and, alone, stood for the full, economic, political, and social equality of blacks. I stayed in the party for eighteen years and became a leader and spokesman. I left it in 1957, still proud of its pioneering struggle for civil rights, its opposition to war and McCarthyism, and its support of the workers. I was, however, profoundly disgusted with its subservience to the Soviet Union, its sectarianism, its grandiosity, its ambivalence on democratic issues. The revelations of Soviet leader Nikita Khrushchev about his predecessor Joseph Stalin and the Soviet suppression of the Hungarian Revolution completed my disillusionment. Nearly five years later, I began serving a six-year sentence (under the Smith Act) for having been a member of the Communist party. After fifteen months in close confinement at a maximum-security federal penitentiary in Lewisburg, Pennsylvania, my sentence was commuted by President John Kennedy."

BIOGRAPHICAL/CRITICAL SOURCES:

PERIODICALS

New York Times Book Review, July 12, 1987.

*   *   *

SCARR(-SALAPATEK), Sandra (Wood)   1936-

PERSONAL: Born August 8, 1936, in Washington, D.C.; daughter of John Ruxton (a research scientist) and Jane (Powell) Wood; married Harry Alan Scarr, 1961 (marriage ended); married Philip H. Salapatek, 1971; children: Phillip, Karen, Rebecca, Stephanie. *Education:* Vassar College, A.B. (with honors), 1958; Harvard University, A.M. (with distinction), 1963, Ph.D., 1965.

ADDRESSES: Office—Department of Psychology, University of Virginia, Charlottesville, Va. 22903.

CAREER: Family and Child Service of Omaha, Nebraska, case aide, 1958-59; National Institute of Mental Health, Bethesda, Md., research assistant at Laboratory of Socio-Environmental Studies, 1959-60; University of Maryland at College Park, instructor, 1964-65, assistant professor of child studies, 1965-66; University of Pennsylvania, Philadelphia, visiting lecturer, 1966-67, lecturer, 1967-68, assistant professor, 1968-70, associate professor of educational psychology, 1970-71, acting director of William T. Carter Foundation for Child Development, 1967-70; University of Minnesota—Twin Cities, Minneapolis, associate professor, 1971-74, professor of child development, 1974-77; Yale University, New Haven, Conn., professor of psychology, 1977-83; University of Virginia, Charlottesville, Commonwealth Professor of Psychology, 1983—, chairman of department, 1984-87, fellow at Center for Advanced Study, 1983-84. Visiting associate professor at Bryn Mawr College, 1969; fellow at Center for Advanced Studies in the Behavioral Sciences, Stanford, Calif., 1976-77.

Member of board of directors of Model Cities Mini-School, 1973-74; member of executive committee and board of directors of Minnesota Program for the Victims of Sexual Assault, 1975-76. Member of national advisory committee of John F. Kennedy Center at Peabody College, Vanderbilt University, 1982—; member of Environmental Protection Agency's Expert Committee on the Neurobehavioral Effects of Lead Exposure on Children, 1983-84; member of G. D. Searle Committee on the Evaluation of Nutra-Sweet, 1984; member of Advisory Committee on the College for Human Development, at Pennsylvania State University, 1985—; member of National Advisory Board on Infant Studies, Robert Wood Johnson Foundation, 1986—; consultant to government of Bermuda, National Science Foundation, and Office of Child Development.

MEMBER: International Society for the Study of Behavioral Development, American Psychological Association (fellow; member of executive committee, 1972-75, 1981-83, and 1985-88; member of board of scientific affairs, 1975-77; chairman of Committee on the Protection of Human Subjects in Psychological Research, 1977-80; divisional president, 1981-83; member of council of editors, 1981-86, chairman of council, 1982-83; chairman of Task Force on Accreditation, 1985-88; member of council, 1985-88), Society for Research in Child Development (member of governing council, 1976-83), Behavior Genetics Association (member of board of directors, 1973-75 and 1984-87; president, 1985-86), American Association for the Advancement of Science (fellow), Society for the Study of Social Biology (member of board of directors, 1971-83), Society for Life History Research in Psychopathology, American Civil Liberties Union.

AWARDS, HONORS: National Book Award from American Psychological Association, 1985, for *Mother Care/Other Care.*

WRITINGS:

(With husband, Philip H. Salapatek) *Socialization,* C. E. Merrill, 1973.
(Editor with F. D. Horowitz, E. M. Hetherington, and G. Siegel, and contributor) *Review of Child Development Research,* Volume IV, University of Chicago Press, 1975.
Race, Social Class, and Individual Differences in IQ: New Studies of Old Issues, Lawrence Erlbaum Associates, 1981.
Child Care, Federation of Behavioral, Psychological, and Cognitive Sciences, 1984.
Mother Care/Other Care, Basic Books, 1984, revised edition, Warner Books, 1985.
(With James Vander Zanden) *Understanding Psychology,* Random House, 4th edition, 1984, 5th edition, 1987.
(With Ann Levine and R. A. Weinberg) *Understanding Development,* Harcourt, 1986.
(With Judy Dunn) *Mother Care/Other Care: Dilemma in Britain,* Penguin, 1987.

Editor of *Developmental Psychology,* 1981-86; special editor of *Behavior Genetics,* 1981; *American Psychologist,* associate editor, 1976-80, guest editor, 1979; member of editorial board of *Social Biology,* 1972-78, *Monographs of the Society for*

Research in Child Development, 1973, *Review of Child Development Research,* 1974, *Child Development,* 1974-76, *Intelligence,* 1976-81, and series "Advances in Psychology," 1981-84.

CONTRIBUTOR

H. V. Perkins, editor, *Human Development and Learning,* Wadsworth, 1970.
Saul Sells, editor, *Prospects for Psychology and Education,* Institute for Behavioral Research, Texas Christian University, 1972.
Gardner Lindzey, Calvin Hall, and Richard Thompson, editors, *Psychology: An Introduction,* Worth Publishers, 1975.
Elizabeth Hall, editor, *Developmental Psychology Today,* 2nd edition, CRM Books, 1975.
Michael Lewis, editor, *Origins of Intelligence: Infancy and Early Childhood,* Plenum, 1976.
Lewis Lipsett, editor, *Developmental Psychobiology: The Significance of Infancy,* Lawrence Erlbaum Associates, 1976.
M. H. Marx and M. E. Bunch, editors, *Fundamentals of Learning: A Survey,* Macmillan, 1977.
R. M. Bossone and M. Weiner, editors, *Proceedings of the National Conference on Testing: Major Issues,* Center for Advanced Study in Education, 1977.
M. S. Collins, I. W. Wainer, and T. A. Brenmer, editors, *Science and the Question of Human Equality,* Westview, 1981.
Michael J. Begab, H. C. Haywood, and Howard J. Garber, editors, *Psychosocial Influences in Retarded Performance: Strategies for Improving Competence,* Volume II, University Park Press, 1981.
Marvin Friedman, J. P. Das, and Neil O'Connor, editors, *Intelligence and Learning,* Plenum, 1981.
R. A. Kasschau and Charles Coffer, editors, *Psychology's Second Century: Enduring Issues,* Praeger, 1981.
Edward F. Zigler and Edmund W. Gordon, editors, *Day Care: Scientific and Social Policy Issues,* Auburn House, 1981.
L. A. Bond and J. M. Joffee, editors, *Facilitating Infant and Early Childhood Development,* University Press of New England, 1982.
D. A. Wilkerson, editor, *Human Diversity and the Assessment of Intellectual Development,* Mediax, 1982.
Michael Lamb and Brian Sutton-Smith, editors, *Sibling Relationships,* Lawrence Erlbaum Associates, 1982.
John L. Fuller and Edward C. Simmel, editors, *Behavior Genetics: Principles and Applications,* Lawrence Erlbaum Associates, 1983.
Marshall Haith and Joseph Campos, editors, *Manual of Child Psychology: Infancy and the Biology of Development,* Volume II, Wiley, 1983.
L. F. Cofer and Charles Cofer, editors, *Women, Children, and Social Policy,* Lawrence Erlbaum Associates, 1986.
R. J. Linn, editor, *Intelligence: Measurement, Theory, and Public Policy,* University of Illinois Press, 1986.
R. J. Sternbert and D. K. Ketterman, editors, *What Is Intelligence?,* Ablex Publishing, 1986.
J. J. Gallagher, editor, *The Malleability of Children,* Brooke, 1986.
Joel Aronoff, A. L. Robin, and R. A. Zucker, editors, *The Emergence of Personality,* Springer, 1987.
Irving Sigel and Gene Brody, editors, *Family Research,* Volume I, Lawrence Erlbaum Associates, 1987.
Stuart Oskamp and Steven Spacapan, editors, *Interpersonal Processes: The Claremont Symposium on Applied Social Psychology,* Sage Publications, 1987.

(Author of foreword) Rogers Elliott, *Litigating Intelligence,* Auburn House, 1987.

Also contributor to *At Risk Children,* edited by Robert Emde and William Frankenberg, and to *Encyclopedia of Education* and *Handbook of Intelligence.* Contributor of about 150 articles and reviews to academic journals.

* * *

SCHAEFER, John   1958-

PERSONAL: Born December 17, 1958, in New York, N.Y.; son of Jack Peter (a building manager) and Lorraine (Hussey) Schaefer; married Ellen Shea (a writer), October 16, 1982. *Education:* Fordham University, B.A. (summa cum laude), 1980.

ADDRESSES: Home—Brooklyn, N.Y. *Office*—WNYC-Radio, 1 Centre St., New York, N.Y. 10007. *Agent*—Writer's House, 21 West 26th St., New York, N.Y. 10010.

CAREER: WFUV-Radio, Bronx, N.Y., announcer, 1976-80; WDCS-Radio, Portland, Maine, announcer, 1981; WNYC-Radio, New York, N.Y., producer of "New Sounds" series, 1981—. Announcer for WFAS-Radio, White Plains, N.Y., 1979-80.

WRITINGS:

New Sounds: A Listener's Guide to Music, Harper, 1987.

Author of liner notes for sound recordings. Contributor to magazines, including *Video Review, In Fashion, Performance Today,* and *Future Forward.*

WORK IN PROGRESS: Research on the musical movement known as minimalism.

SIDELIGHTS: John Schaefer told *CA:* "Contemporary music is still an area that has been largely unexplored. Much has been written about 'mainstream' forms, like classical, jazz, and pop, but the spectrum of modern music is quite broad. It encompasses a lot of music many people never get to hear, or even hear about. The 'New Sounds' series was conceived as a means of introducing people to music that is unusual, original, weird perhaps, but also entertaining and communicative. The response of listeners ranged from bemused curiosity to active enjoyment, and this prompted me to write my book. *New Sounds* is a kind of central reference source for background, current state, and available recordings of this music."

BIOGRAPHICAL/CRITICAL SOURCES:

PERIODICALS

Billboard, December 26, 1987.
Ear, December, 1987.
New York Newsday, July 8, 1987.
Wall Street Journal, October 23, 1986.
Wavelength, July, 1987.

* * *

SCHALLER, Michael   1947-

PERSONAL: Born June 2, 1947, in New York, N.Y. *Education:* State University of New York at Binghamton, B.A., 1968; University of Michigan, M.A., 1969, Ph.D., 1974.

ADDRESSES: Office—Department of History, University of Arizona, Tucson, Ariz. 85721.

CAREER: University of Arizona, Tucson, assistant professor, 1974-79, associate professor of history, 1979—.

MEMBER: Organization of American Historians, Society of Historians of American Foreign Relations.

AWARDS, HONORS: Bernath Book Prize from Society of Historians of American Foreign Relations, 1980; fellow of National Endowment for the Humanities, 1980-81; Guggenheim fellow, 1981-82.

WRITINGS:

The U.S. Crusade in China, 1938-1945, Columbia University Press, 1979.
The United States and China in the Twentieth Century, Oxford University Press, 1979.
The American Occupation of Japan: The Origins of the Cold War in Asia, Oxford University Press, 1985.

Contributor to history journals.

BIOGRAPHICAL/CRITICAL SOURCES:

PERIODICALS

American Historical Review, December, 1979.
Journal of American History, June, 1986.
New Republic, December 29, 1979, December 30, 1985.
New Yorker, April 9, 1979.
New York Review of Books, May 17, 1979.
New York Times Book Review, January 14, 1979, October 27, 1985.
Virginia Quarterly Review, summer, 1979.*

* * *

SCHIER, Flint   1954(?)-1988

OBITUARY NOTICE: Born c. 1954; died May 28, 1988. Educator and author. A philosophy and aesthetics instructor at Glasgow University, Schier wrote the 1986 study *Deeper Into Pictures: An Essay on Pictorial Representation.* In the book Schier analyzed the nature of depiction by expounding on various philosophers' points of view. Schier was a Rhodes scholar and winner of the John Locke Prize.

OBITUARIES AND OTHER SOURCES:

PERIODICALS

Choice, June, 1987.
Times (London), June 9, 1988.

* * *

SCHLESINGER, Leonard A.   1952-

PERSONAL: Born July 31, 1952, in Brooklyn, N.Y.; son of Joe (an upholsterer) and Edith (a housewife; maiden name, Smukles) Schlesinger; married Phyllis Fineman (a professor), December 23, 1973; children: Rebecca, Emily, Katharine. *Education:* Brown University, A.B., 1972; Columbia University, M.B.A., 1973; Harvard University, D.B.A., 1978.

ADDRESSES: Home—78 Leeson Lane, Newton Centre, Mass. 02159. *Office*—Au Bon Pain Co., Inc., 19 Fid Kennedy Ave., Boston, Mass. 02210. *Agent*—Michael Cohn, 420 Lexington Ave., New York, N.Y. 10017.

CAREER: Brown Student Agencies, Providence, R.I., president, 1971-72; Proctor & Gamble Paper Products Co., Green Bay, Wis., team manager, 1973-74, organizational development specialist, 1974-75; Bentley College, Waltham, Mass., lecturer in business and management, 1976; Harvard University, Graduate School of Business Administration, Boston, Mass., instructor, 1978-79, assistant professor, 1979-82, associate professor of business administration, 1983—. Executive vice-president, treasurer, and director of Au Bon Pain Co., 1985—. Associate coordinator of Rhode Island governor's Council on Youth Opportunities, 1971-72; lecturer at University of Wisconsin—Green Bay, 1974-75; associate of MAC Group.

MEMBER: Academy of Management, Organizational Behavior Teaching Society (member of board of directors).

WRITINGS:

(With John P. Kotter and Vijay Sathe) *Organization: Text, Cases, and Readings on the Management of Organization Design and Change,* Irwin, 1979, 2nd edition, 1985.
(Editor with Tom Chase) *The Ecology of Work: Readings on Employee Productivity and Quality of Work Life,* NTL Institute, 1981.
Quality of Work Life and the Supervisor, Praeger, 1982.
(With John J. Gabarro and Robert G. Eccles) *Managing Behavior in Organizations,* McGraw, 1983.
(Contributor) Jay W. Lorsch, editor, *Handbook of Organizational Behavior,* Prentice-Hall, 1986.
(With Davis Dyer, Thomas Clough, and Dianne Landau) *Chronicles of Corporate Change: Lessons for American Managers From AT&T and Its Offspring,* Lexington Books, 1987.
(With Ardis Burst) *The Management Game,* Viking/Penguin, 1987.

Contributor to business and management journals. Member of editorial board of *Exchange: Organizational Behavior Teaching Journal, Academy of Management Executive, Academy of Management Review,* and *Human Resource Management.*

WORK IN PROGRESS: Research on management of service organizations, employee productivity and quality of work life, organization design and development, organization change and adaptation in deregulated industries, organizational culture, and human resource management.

BIOGRAPHICAL/CRITICAL SOURCES:

PERIODICALS

Globe and Mail (Toronto), October 3, 1987.

*   *   *

SCHLESINGER, Roger   1943-

PERSONAL: Born December 23, 1943, in London, England; American citizen born abroad; son of Edward (a businessman) and Pauline (a housewife; maiden name, Glickman) Schlesinger; married Margaret A. Grimaldi, September 16, 1978 (divorced, 1985). *Education:* Hofstra University, B.A., 1964; University of Illinois at Urbana-Champaign, M.A., 1965, Ph.D., 1970.

ADDRESSES: Home—Northwest 1220 State St., No. 49, Pullman, Wash. 99163. *Office*—Department of History, Washington State University, Pullman, Wash. 99164-4030.

CAREER: Washington State University, Pullman, assistant professor, 1968-75, associate professor of history, 1975—.

MEMBER: American Historical Association, Society for the History of Discoveries, French Colonial Historical Association.

AWARDS, HONORS: Grant from National Endowment for the Humanities, 1980; Columbian Quincentennial fellow at Newberry Library, 1987.

WRITINGS:

(Editor and translator, with Arthur P. Stabler) *Andre Thevet's North America: A Sixteenth-Century View,* McGill-Queen's University Press, 1986.

WORK IN PROGRESS: Research on sixteenth-century biographies of explorers and American natives written by Andre Thevet.

SIDELIGHTS: Roger Schlesinger told *CA:* "My interest in travel influenced me to take up the Age of Exploration as a subject for investigation. I became interested in Andre Thevet after reading the favorable assessment of his work contained in W. F. Ganong's 1964 book *Crucial Maps in the Early Cartography and Place-Nomenclature of the Atlantic Coast of Canada.* Thevet was one of the most widely traveled of all sixteenth-century French figures, having been to various places in Western Europe, as well as the Middle East, Brazil, and North America. In the second half of the sixteenth century Thevet served four French kings as royal cosmographer.

"I am especially interested in the consequences of cultural interactions; for some time Thevet has been considered a valuable and authentic source of information on the Tupinamba peoples of Brazil. His work on North America, though, has not enjoyed a good reputation. Despite the fact that the firsthand experiences he claims to have had in North America are either fabricated or much exaggerated, there are items of real worth contained in his work. Tracking down the sources of his information—which he took considerable pains to conceal—proved to me that the task of the historian is very similar to that of the detective."

*   *   *

SCHMIDT, Michael Jack   1949-
(Mike Schmidt)

PERSONAL: Born September 27, 1949, in Dayton, Ohio. *Education:* Received B.S. from Ohio University.

ADDRESSES: Office—Philadelphia Phillies, P.O. Box 2575, Philadelphia, Pa. 19101.

CAREER: Philadelphia Phillies, Philadelphia, Pa., professional baseball player, 1972—; writer.

AWARDS, HONORS: Member of eleven National League All-Star Teams, 1974-87; named most valuable player in the National League, 1980, 1981, and 1986, and most valuable player in the 1980 World Series.

WRITINGS:

(Under name Mike Schmidt; with Barbara Walder) *Always on the Offense,* Atheneum, 1982.*

*   *   *

SCHMIDT, Mike
See SCHMIDT, Michael Jack

*   *   *

SCHMIECHEN, James A.   1940-

PERSONAL: Born January 23, 1940, in Washington, Tex.;

son of Kurt and Charlotte Schmiechen. *Education:* Elmhurst College, B.A., 1962; Illinois State University, M.A., 1967; University of Illinois at Urbana-Champaign, Ph.D., 1974.

ADDRESSES: Office—Department of History, Central Michigan University, Mount Pleasant, Mich. 48858.

CAREER: Central Michigan University, Mount Pleasant, assistant professor, 1978-81, associate professor of history, 1981—.

WRITINGS:

Sweated Industries and Sweated Labor: The London Clothing Trades, 1867-1914, University of Illinois Press, 1984.

Contributor to economic and history journals, including *American Historical Review.*

WORK IN PROGRESS: A book on Victorian architecture and design; a book on nineteenth-century British markets, completion expected in 1989.

SIDELIGHTS: James Schmiechen told *CA:* "The two books in progress are in the area of 'social architecture'—that is, the study of architecture within its social and economic context."

BIOGRAPHICAL/CRITICAL SOURCES:

PERIODICALS

Times Literary Supplement, August 31, 1984.

*   *   *

SCHOENBERG, Ronald 1942-

PERSONAL: Born April 25, 1942, in Spokane, Wash.; son of James and Lyla (Thompson) Schoenberg; married Janis Howell, September 7, 1965; children: Lisa, Joel, Jennifer. *Education:* University of Washington, Seattle, B.A., 1970, M.A., 1972, Ph.D., 1974.

ADDRESSES: Home—3304 Ferndale St., Kensington, Md. 20895. *Office*—National Institute of Mental Health, 9000 Rockville Pike, Bethesda, Md. 20014.

CAREER: University of Arizona, Tucson, assistant professor of sociology, 1974-78; National Institute of Mental Health, Bethesda, Md., research sociologist, 1979—.

MEMBER: American Sociological Association, American Statistical Association.

WRITINGS:

(With Melvin L. Kohn and Carmi Schooler) *Work and Personality: An Inquiry Into the Impact of Social Stratification,* Ablex Publishing, 1982.

Contributor to sociology journals. Member of editorial board of *Sociological Methodology* and *Sociological Research and Methods.*

*   *   *

SCHOENBERGER, Nancy 1950-

PERSONAL: Born December 3, 1950, in Oakland, Calif.; daughter of Sigmund Bernard (a test pilot and aeronautical engineer) and Betty (a housewife; maiden name, Beydler) Schoenberger. *Education:* Louisiana State University, B.A., 1972, M.A., 1974; Columbia University, M.F.A., 1981.

ADDRESSES: Home—406 East 83rd St., No. 4B, New York, N.Y. 10028. *Office*—Academy of American Poets, 177 East 87th St., New York, N.Y. 10128.

CAREER: Academy of American Poets, New York, N.Y., program director and workshop instructor, 1983—. Associate professor in School of the Arts at Columbia University, spring, 1988.

MEMBER: Poetry Society of America.

AWARDS, HONORS: Resident at Centrum, 1984, Rockefeller Conference and Study Center, Bellagio, Italy, 1985, and MacDowell Colony, 1987; Mary Carolyn Davies Memorial Prize from Poetry Society of America, 1984, for a lyric poem; grant from National Endowment for the Arts, 1984; Editor's Choice Award from *Columbia,* 1985, for the poem "Easy the Life of the Mouth"; Richard Hugo Memorial Award from *Cutbank,* 1985, for the poem "Girl on a White Porch"; Devins Award from University of Missouri Press, 1987, for the book *Girl on a White Porch.*

WRITINGS:

The Taxidermist's Daughter (poems), Calliopea Press, 1979.
Girl on a White Porch (poems), University of Missouri Press, 1987.

Contributor of poems to magazines, including *New Yorker, Antaeus, Antioch Review, Columbia, Southern Review,* and *Poetry.*

*   *   *

SCHOTT, Jeffrey J. 1949-

PERSONAL: Born April 19, 1949, in Newark, N.J. *Education:* Washington University, St. Louis, Mo., B.A. (magna cum laude), 1971; Johns Hopkins School of Advanced International Studies, M.A. (with distinction), 1973; further graduate study at Georgetown University.

ADDRESSES: Home—2344 Nebraska Ave. N.W., Washington, D.C. 20016. *Office*—Institute for International Economics, 11 Dupont Circle N.W., Washington, D.C. 20036.

CAREER: Brookings Institution, Washington, D.C., research assistant in foreign policy studies, 1971-73, and economic studies, 1973-74; U.S. Treasury Department, Washington, D.C., staff official in Office of International Trade, responsible for trade relations with Japan, 1974-77, member of delegation to negotiate multilateral trade, 1977-80, deputy director of Office of International Energy Policy, 1981-82; Carnegie Endowment for International Peace, New York, N.Y., senior associate, 1982-83; Institute for International Economics, Washington, D.C., visiting fellow, 1983-84, research associate, 1984-87, research fellow, 1987—. Adjunct professor at Georgetown University, 1986-88.

MEMBER: Phi Beta Kappa.

AWARDS, HONORS: Certificate of merit from U.S. Treasury Department, 1977 and 1979.

WRITINGS:

(Co-author) *Economic Sanctions in Support of Foreign Policy Goals,* Institute for International Economics, 1983.
The Trade Policy Debate: A Discussion of the Issues, Council on U.S. International Trade Policy, 1984.
(With Gary Clyde Hufbauer) *Economic Sanctions Reconsidered: History and Current Policy,* MIT Press, 1984.

(Contributor) David W. Conklin and Thomas J. Courchene, editors, *Canadian Trade at a Crossroads: Options for New International Agreements*, Ontario Economic Council, 1985.

(Contributor) Theodore H. Moran, editor, *Multinational Corporations*, Heath, 1985.

(Co-author) *Trading for Growth: The Next Round of Trade Negotiations*, Institute for International Economics, 1985.

(Co-author) *Auction Quotas and U.S. Trade Policy*, Institute for International Economics, 1987.

Contributor to *New Technologies and World Trade*, 1984, and *Economic Cooperation in the Middle East*, edited by Leonardo Leiderman, 1987. Also contributor to journals, including *Challenge, World Economy, PS*, and *Journal of World Trade Law*.

*   *   *

SCHRIBER, Mary Suzanne 1938-

PERSONAL: Born September 22, 1938, in Muskegon, Mich.; daughter of Francis C. (a pharmacist) and A. Marie (a teacher; maiden name, Jeannot) Schriber; married Anthony E. Scaperlanda (a professor of economics), September 12, 1986. *Education:* Michigan State University, B.A., 1960, M.A., 1963, Ph.D., 1967.

ADDRESSES: Home—317 Fairmont, DeKalb, Ill. 60115. *Office*—Department of English, Northern Illinois University, DeKalb, Ill. 60115.

CAREER: Michigan State University, East Lansing, lecturer in English, 1966-67; Northern Illinois University, DeKalb, assistant professor, 1967-72, associate professor, 1972-87, professor of English, 1987—. Visiting professor at Xian Foreign Languages Institute, 1982.

MEMBER: Modern Language Association of America, Edith Wharton Society, Midwest Modern Language Association.

WRITINGS:

(Contributor) P. A. Dionisopolous, editor, *Racism in America: An Interdisciplinary Analysis*, Northern Illinois University Press, 1971.

Gender and the Writer's Imagination: From Cooper to Wharton, University Press of Kentucky, 1987.

Contributor of articles and reviews to literature journals.

WORK IN PROGRESS: A study of nineteenth-century American travel books "by women who show an awareness of themselves as *women* travelers"; research on the travel book as a literary genre, concentrating on nineteenth-century American books about travel in Europe.

SIDELIGHTS: Mary Suzanne Schriber told *CA:* "My work on the writing of Edith Wharton, and within that, on Wharton's travel books, has led to my interest in travel books, their conventions, and their strategies. Having determined that Wharton finds the travel book and its conventions to be freeing, an arena in which to revel in her intellect, I now am concerned to test the general proposition that genre and gender are related, that the conventions of given genres, such as the travel book, may bear differently on men and women writers."

*   *   *

SCHRIFTGIESSER, Karl (John) 1903-1988

OBITUARY NOTICE—See index for *CA* sketch: Born November 12, 1903, in Boston, Mass.; died August 19, 1988, in Ludlow, Vt. Administrator, editor, journalist, and author. For thirty years Schriftgiesser was a member of the editorial staffs of numerous publications, including the *Boston Post, Boston Evening Transcript, Washington Post, New York Post, New York Times*, and *Newsweek* magazine. He also served as editor and assistant information director for the Committee for Economic Development in both New York City and Washington, D.C., from 1956 until his retirement in 1969. His writings include *The Amazing Roosevelt Family, 1613-1942; The Gentleman From Massachusetts: Henry Cabot Lodge; The Lobbyists: The Art and Business of Influencing Lawmakers; Business and the American Government;* and *CMC: An Adventure in Policy Making.*

OBITUARIES AND OTHER SOURCES:

BOOKS

Who's Who in the East, 17th edition, Marquis, 1979.

PERIODICALS

New York Times, August 20, 1988.

*   *   *

SCHUBEL, J(erry) R(obert) 1936-

PERSONAL: Born January 26, 1936, in Bad Axe, Mich.; son of Ted H. and Alberta (Gobel) Schubel; married Margaret Ann Hostetler (a teacher), June 14, 1958; children: Susan E., Kathryn A. *Education:* Alma College, B.S., 1957; Harvard University, M.A.T., 1959; Johns Hopkins University, Ph.D., 1968.

ADDRESSES: Home—4 Hiawatha Lane, Setauket, N.Y. 11733. *Office*—Office of the Provost, State University of New York at Stony Brook, Stony Brook, N.Y. 11794.

CAREER: Johns Hopkins University, Bethesda, Md., assistant research scientist at Chesapeake Bay Institute, 1967-68, associate research scientist, 1968-69, research scientist, 1969-74, adjunct research professor of marine geology and associate director of institute, 1973-74; State University of New York at Stony Brook, professor of marine science, 1974—, dean and director of Marine Science Research Center, 1974—, leading professor, 1983—, provost of university, 1986—. Visiting associate professor at University of Delaware, 1969; lecturer at University of Maryland at College Park, 1969-71; visiting professor at Franklin and Marshall College, 1970-71. Scientific director and vice-president of Hydrocom, Inc., 1971-74; University-National Oceanography Laboratory System, member of advisory council, 1977-80, vice-chairman, 1980; workshop chairman for Scientific Committee for Ocean Research, Intergovernmental Oceanography Commission, 1980; member of scientific working group of National Aeronautics and Space Administration's National Oceanic Satellite System, 1980—; Member of board of trustees of Stony Brook Foundation, 1978—. Chairman of board of directors of Marine Division of National Association of State Universities and Land Grant Colleges, 1986-88.

MEMBER: American Society of Limnology and Oceanography, American Association for the Advancement of Science, National Association of Geology Teachers, New York Academy of Sciences, Estuarine Research Federation (vice-president, 1981-83, president, 1985-87).

WRITINGS:

The Living Chesapeake, Johns Hopkins University Press, 1981.

(With Homer A. Neal) *Solid Waste Management and the Environment*, Prentice-Hall, 1987.

WORK IN PROGRESS: The World of the Estuary; The Chesapeake Revisited.

SIDELIGHTS: J. R. Schubel told *CA:* "*The Living Chesapeake* was my first attempt at writing for a non-technical audience. There were two important reasons why I chose to write about Chesapeake Bay. First, it was the estuary that I knew most about. Second, it is an estuary for which there is a rich scientific literature and a rich popular literature that deals with the watermen and other sociocultural aspects. It also was an estuary for which the popular scientific literature was impoverished. Writing *The Living Chesapeake* was far more difficult than writing any of the more than one hundred papers I had published for specialists in my field, but I enjoyed the challenge and have begun a sequel, *The Chesapeake Revisited.* I also have begun work on another popular book about estuaries, *The World of the Estuary.*

"Estuaries are semi-enclosed bodies of water along marine coasts. They are freely connected to the ocean and within them salt water is mixed with and measurable diluted by fresh water from runoff. Estuaries are the most productive segments of the world ocean and the most troubled.

"It is in the estuary where society has its most intimate contact with the world ocean and its greatest impact on it. We use estuaries for recreation, for fishing, and for aesthetic enjoyment. We also use them for shipping and transportation, for cooling water for power plants and for the disposal of society's waste products. The pressures on estuaries by society are enormous and growing. Most stresses are related to increases in population in the drainage basins of estuaries. It has been predicted that by the year 2000, approximately 75 percent of the total U.S. population will live withing fifty miles of the coast. Most will live around our estuaries. The stresses from society have resulted in declines of fisheries, loss of wetlands and other important habitats, and degradation of water quality. Fish kills and the closing of fisheries because of pollution have increased in frequency. All of these events are fodder for environmental 'doom-sayers.'

"Non-technical writing is one of my avocations. It must be done on evenings and weekends, during brief periods stolen on trips aboard planes and in airports. I always write with pen and paper and prepare numerous drafts. My writing has been influenced by Lewis Thomas, Stephen Jay Gould, and John McPhee. I admire all of them."

*   *   *

SCHURKE, Paul   1955-

PERSONAL: Surname sounds like "sure key"; born July 18, 1955, in Minneapolis, Minn.; son of G. Roger (a carpenter) and Lois (a homemaker; maiden name, Knutson) Schurke; married Susan Hendrickson (a seamstress), October 10, 1981; children: Bria. *Education:* St. John's University, Collegeville, Minn., B.A., 1977; graduate study at University of Minnesota—Twin Cities, 1977-81.

ADDRESSES: Office—Wintergreen Dogsled Treks, 1708 Savoy, Ely, Minn. 55731. *Agent*—Carl Brandt, Brandt & Brandt Literary Agents, Inc., 1501 Broadway, New York, N.Y. 10036.

CAREER: Wilderness Inquiry, Minneapolis, Minn., program director, 1977-85; Wintergreen Dogsled Treks, Ely, Minn.,

proprietor, 1986—. Science feature writer for University News Service, Minneapolis, 1978-80; news editor for *Pergamon Press,* Minneapolis, 1980-81. Expedition leader for Steger Polar Expedition, Ely, 1984-86; member of board of directors of International Wolf Center, 1986—.

MEMBER: Physicians for Social Responsibility (associate member), Explorers Club.

AWARDS, HONORS: Explorers Club Award, 1986, for accomplishments in polar navigation; Outsider of the Year Award from *Outsider,* 1986, for contributions to outdoor program development and environmental education.

WRITINGS:

(With Will Steger) *North to the Pole,* Times Books, 1986.
Adventure Diplomacy, Times Books, in press.

Editor of *Underground Space Journal.*

SIDELIGHTS: Paul Schurke told *CA:* "I have long been interested in using the outdoors and outdoor adventure as a meeting ground for persons with cultural differences. My activities and my writing focus on adventure as a means of bringing people together to share goals that transcend ideological obstacles. I have worked with and helped establish a number of outdoor adventure recreation programs. In recent years my focus has been on opening winter wilderness recreation opportunities, ski camping and dogsled treks in particular, to a wide variety of people. My own skill-building experiences with winter camping culminated in a dogsled expedition to the North Pole that I and a partner, Will Steger, led in 1986. Our expedition was distinguished as the first one to reach the Pole since Admiral Robert Peary's 1909 trek without resupply or outside assistance.

"My next expedition project is slated for March-April, 1990, and involves a one-thousand-dogsled and skin-boat trek by a group of Soviets and Americans along a route that will link the principal native settlements of eastern Siberia and western Alaska. The "Bering Bridge" trek is sponsored by the International Physicians for the Prevention of Nuclear War and is intended to help open new lines of communication between our two countries and reduce Cold War tensions in the Arctic. The beauty of outdoor adventures shared by people of diverse backgrounds is that the journeys underscore the fact that the importance of human needs that people share far outweighs the importance of cultural or ideological issues on which they differ or conflict."

*   *   *

SCHUYLER, David   1950-

PERSONAL: Born April 9, 1950, in Albany, N.Y.; son of Ruth C. Schuyler Cote; married Marsha Sener, September 6, 1985; children: Nancy. *Education:* University of North Carolina, M.A., 1976; University of Delaware, M.A., 1976; Columbia University, Ph.D., 1979.

ADDRESSES: Home—519 West James St., Lancaster, Pa. 17603. *Office*—Department of American Studies, Franklin and Marshall College, Box 3003, Lancaster, Pa. 17604.

CAREER: Franklin and Marshall College, Lancaster, Pa., assistant professor, 1979-86, associate professor of American Studies, 1986—, chairman of department of American Studies, 1988—.

MEMBER: Organization of American Historians, American Studies Association, Society of Architectural Historians, Society of Winterthur Fellows, Athenaeum of Philadelphia.

WRITINGS:

(Editor with Charles E. Beveridge and Charles C. McLaughlin) *The Papers of Frederick Law Olmsted,* Volume 2: *Slavery and the South, 1852-1857,* Johns Hopkins University Press, 1981.

(Editor with Beveridge) *The Papers of Frederick Law Olmsted,* Volume 3: *Creating Central Park, 1857-1861,* Johns Hopkins University Press, 1983.

The New Urban Landscape: The Redefinition of City Form in Nineteenth-Century America, Johns Hopkins University Press, 1986.

(Editor) *The Papers of Frederick Law Olmsted,* Volume 6, Johns Hopkins University Press, 1989.

Associate editor of "The Frederick Law Olmsted Papers," 1982—.

SIDELIGHTS: David Schuyler told *CA:* "As a boy I played in a park in Newburgh, New York, designed by Frederick Law Olmsted and Calvert Vaux. Perhaps as a result of what Olmsted termed 'unconscious influence,' I became interested in studying how and why nineteenth-century Americans created openly-built recreational and domestic areas. After more than a decade of research I still find Olmsted a fascinating subject and the Olmsted papers the single best resource for understanding the development of American culture in the nineteenth century. I should probably spend less time studying, though, and more time relaxing with my family in parks."

*   *   *

SCHWALLER, John Frederick 1948-

PERSONAL: Born July 2, 1948, in Hays, Kan.; son of Henry (a businessman) and Juliette (a housewife; maiden name, Trembly) Schwaller; married Anne Cardot Taylor (a housewife), August 15, 1970; children: Robert Clemens, William Henry. *Education:* Grinnell College, A.B., 1969; University of Kansas, M.A., 1971; Indiana University—Bloomington, Ph.D., 1978. *Religion:* Episcopalian.

ADDRESSES: Home—Boca Raton, Fla. *Office*—Department of History, Florida Atlantic University, Boca Raton, Fla. 33431.

CAREER: Worked with Mexican Government, 1971; radio announcer for English language radio station in Mexico City, Mexico, 1974-76; Instituto Audio Activo de Lenguas, Mexico City, teacher of English as a second language, 1975-76; Fort Hays State University, Fort Hays, Kan., assistant professor of history, 1978-79; Florida Atlantic University, Boca Raton, assistant professor, 1979-82, associate professor, 1982-86, professor of history, languages, and linguistics, 1986—, coordinator of Curriculum in Latin American Studies, 1979—. Instructor at Indiana University—Bloomington, 1974, 1977; visiting professor at Instituto Nacional de Antropologia e Historia, 1985-86.

MEMBER: American Historical Association, Latin American Studies Association, Conference on Latin American History, Historians of Early Modern Europe, South Eastern Council of Latin American Studies, Sigma Delta Pi, Phi Alpha Theta, Phi Kappa Phi.

AWARDS, HONORS: Fellow of Mexican Highway Association and Secretaria de Obras Publicas, 1971; Benito Juarez-

Abraham Lincoln fellow of Mexican Secretaria de Relaciones Exteriores, 1974-75; Fulbright fellow, 1976-77, 1982-83; grants from National Endowment for the Humanities, 1980, 1984, American Philosophical Society, 1982, and Center for Latin American Studies, University of Florida, 1984; fellow at Newberry Library, 1982, and Tinker Foundation, 1984-86; Andrew W. Mellon fellow at Tulane University, 1983.

WRITINGS:

A Kansan Looks at the Mexican Highway Association, Kansas State Highway Commission, 1971.

Partidos y parrocos bajo la real corona en la Nueva Espana, siglo XVI (title means "Parishes and Curates Under the Royal Crown in New Spain, Sixteenth Century"), Instituto Nacional de Antropologia e Historia, 1981.

(Contributor) Jeffery Cole, editor, *Church and Society in Latin America,* Tulane University, 1984.

Origins of Church Wealth in Mexico: Ecclesiastical Finances and Church Revenues, 1523-1600, University of New Mexico Press, 1985.

(Contributor) Jack Hopkins, editor, *Latin America: Perspectives on a Region,* Holmes & Meier, 1987.

The Church and Clergy in Sixteenth-Century Mexico, University of New Mexico Press, 1987.

(Contributor) Melvyn C. Resnick, editor, *Studies in Caribbean Spanish Dialectology,* Georgetown University Press, 1987.

Contributor to history and Latin American studies journals. Editor of *Latin American Historical Statistics Newsletter,* 1982—.

WORK IN PROGRESS: Mexico in 1600, publication expected in 1990; a biography of Don Luis de Velasco, 1539-1617, publication expected in 1991.

SIDELIGHTS: John Frederick Schwaller told *CA:* "I first travelled to Mexico as a small child with my parents for Christmas vacations. For nearly twenty years I would spend a month or so in Mexico with my family. In 1971 I worked with the Mexican government on a project to construct farm-to-market roads. Then from 1974 to 1976 my wife and I lived in Mexico City. At that point, in addition to doing research in public and church archives, I was a radio announcer for the English language radio station.

"In the past eight years my wife and sons and I have lived in Mexico, Spain, and Peru. This included many adventures such as the devastating Mexico City earthquake, political terrorism in Lima, attempted coups d'etat in Ecuador, earthquakes in Cuzco, and the derailment of the Machu Picchu train."

*   *   *

SCHWANDT, Stephen (William) 1947-

PERSONAL: Born April 5, 1947, in Chippewa Falls, Wis.; son of Roland Lawrence (a minister) and Mildred (a homemaker; maiden name, Ulvestad) Schwandt; married Karen Sambo (a teacher), June 13, 1970; children: Reed, Andrew. *Education:* Valparaiso University, B.A., 1969; St. Cloud State University, B.S., 1972; University of Minnesota—Twin Cities, M.A., 1972. *Religion:* Lutheran.

ADDRESSES: Home and office—2941 Orchard Ave. N., Minneapolis, Minn. 55422. *Agent*—Marilyn Marlow, Curtis Brown Ltd., 10 Astor Pl., New York, N.Y. 10003.

CAREER: Irondale High School, New Brighton, Minn., teacher of composition and American literature, 1974—. Instructor at

Concordia College, St. Paul, Minn., 1975-80, and Normandale Community College, 1983—.

MEMBER: National Education Association, Authors Guild, Book Critics Circle, National Council of Teachers of English, The Loft.

WRITINGS:

YOUNG ADULT NOVELS

The Last Goodie, Holt, 1985.
A Risky Game, Holt, 1986.
Holding Steady, Holt, 1988.

Contributor to newspapers.

WORK IN PROGRESS: Two novels; a screenplay; a collection of short stories.

SIDELIGHTS: Stephen Schwandt told *CA:* "During the middle 1960s I participated in basketball and track at a north suburban high school near Milwaukee. I held a state high jump record for a year or two and still hold (I think) the career scoring mark in basketball at my old high school. Back then I showed absolutely no literary promise.

"I attended Valparaiso University on a basketball scholarship and started for the 1966-67 team that appeared in the NCAA (National Collegiate Athletic Association) College Division Finals. The next year I played against the great Elvin 'Big E' Hayes (then of the University of Houston, now recently retired from the Houston Rockets) and, with the help of several teammates, held him to sixty-two points in thirty-eight minutes. The final score, 158 to 81, is still the NCAA record for the most points scored in a major college game. It also marked the end of my basketball career.

"For the last few years I've come to enjoy more diverse activities, including sailing and fishing, reading and writing. All of these bring my family to our log home on Washington Island, the setting of my novel *Holding Steady.*

"That book, like my others, attempts to explore the themes of freedom and confinement, particularly the limitations people impose on themselves by addictive dependence on certain roles or perspectives and the empowerment that can accompany the shedding of such dependencies. My lead characters, then, don't experience much success until they decide to *do* something, take an active role in winning the freedom to invent their own lives and see with their own eyes.

"In all of my books it is my primary assumption that young adult (and adult) readers are genuinely interested in puzzling, even troubling explorations of significant subjects. Such readers are looking for workable definitions of merit regarding values and behavior.

"I place a great deal of emphasis on voice in my writing, and I work hard to create believable, energetic dialogue. When one reviewer called me a 'master of conversation,' I took it as a supreme compliment."

*   *   *

SCHWARTZ, Stuart B.   1940-

PERSONAL: Born September 4, 1940, in Springfield, Mass. *Education:* Middlebury College, A.B., 1962; Columbia University, M.A., 1963, Ph.D., 1968.

ADDRESSES: Office—Department of History, 727 Social Science Building, University of Minnesota—Twin Cities, Minneapolis, Minn. 55455.

CAREER: University of Minnesota—Twin Cities, Minneapolis, 1967—, began as instructor, professor of history, 1973—, chairman of department, 1976-79. Visiting assistant professor at University of California, Berkeley, 1969-70; visiting professor at Brazil's Federal University of Bahia, 1974; adviser to Mexican Conference on Latin American Social Sciences, 1972—.

MEMBER: American Historical Association, Conference on Latin American History, Latin American Studies Association.

AWARDS, HONORS: Fellow of American Council of Learned Societies, 1974-75; Guggenheim fellow, 1978-79.

WRITINGS:

(Contributor) *Colonial Roots of Modern English,* University of California Press, 1973.
Sovereignty and Society in Colonial Brazil: The High Court of Bahia and Its Judges, 1609-1751, University of California Press, 1973.
(Editor) Juan Lopes Sierra, *A Governor and His Image in Baroque Brazil: The Funereal Eulogy of Alfonso Furtado de Castro do Rio de Mendoca,* University of Minnesota Press, 1979.
(With James Lockhart) *Early Latin America: A History of Colonial Spanish America and Brazil,* Cambridge University Press, 1983.
Sugar Plantations in the Formation of Brazilian Society: Bahia, 1550-1835, Cambridge University Press, 1986.

Contributor to history journals.

BIOGRAPHICAL/CRITICAL SOURCES:

PERIODICALS

American Historical Review, April, 1975.
Annals of the American Academy of Political and Social Sciences, May, 1974.*

*   *   *

SCOTT, Joanna   1960-

PERSONAL: Born June 22, 1960, in Greenwich, Conn.; daughter of Walter Lee and Yvonne (a psychologist; maiden name, DePotter) Scott. *Education:* Trinity College, Hartford, Conn., B.A., 1982; Brown University, M.A., 1985.

ADDRESSES: Home—1600 East-West Highway, Silver Spring, Md. 20110. *Agent*—Elaine Markson Literary Agency, Inc., 44 Greenwich Ave., New York, N.Y. 10011.

CAREER: Elaine Markson Literary Agency, Inc., New York, N.Y., assistant, 1984-85; Brown University, Providence, R.I., adjunct lecturer in English, 1985-86; University of Maryland at College Park, assistant professor of English, 1986-88; University of Rochester, Rochester, N.Y., assistant professor, 1988—.

AWARDS, HONORS: Guggenheim fellowship, 1988-89.

WRITINGS:

Fading, My Parmacheene Belle (novel), Ticknor & Fields, 1987.
The Closest Possible Union (novel), Ticknor & Fields, 1988.

BIOGRAPHICAL/CRITICAL SOURCES:

PERIODICALS

New York Times Book Review, August 14, 1988.

* * *

SCOTT, John (Peter) 1949-

PERSONAL: Born April 8, 1949, in London, England; son of Philip Charles (a manager) and Phyllis (Bridges) Scott; married Jill Wheatley (a school assistant), September 4, 1971; children: Michael, Susan. *Education:* Attended Kingston College of Technology, 1968-71; London School of Economics and Political Science, London, B.Sc., 1972; University of Strathclyde, Ph.D., 1976.

ADDRESSES: Office—Department of Sociology, University of Leicester, University Rd., Leicester LE1 7RH, England.

CAREER: University of Strathclyde, Glasgow, Scotland, lecturer in sociology, 1972-76; University of Leicester, Leicester, England, lecturer, 1976-87, reader in sociology, 1987—.

MEMBER: British Sociological Association.

WRITINGS:

Corporations, Classes, and Capitalism, Hutchinson, 1979, 2nd edition, 1985.
(With Michael D. Hughes) *The Anatomy of Scottish Capital*, Croom Helm, 1980.
The Upper Classes! Property and Privilege in Britain, Macmillan, 1982.
(With Catherine Griff) *Directors of Industry*, Polity Press, 1984.
(Editor with Frans Stokman and Rolf Ziegler) *Networks of Corporate Power*, Polity Press, 1985.
Capitalist Property and Financial Power: A Comparative Study of Britain, the United States, and Japan, Wheatsheaf, 1986.

Editor of *Network* (newsletter of the British Sociological Association); co-editor of *Social Studies Review*.

WORK IN PROGRESS: Research on property ownership, social research, and social history.

* * *

SCOTT, Sheila (Christine) 1927-1988

OBITUARY NOTICE—See index for *CA* sketch: Surname originally Hopkins; born April 27 (one source says April 29), 1927, in Worcester, England; died of lung cancer, October 20, 1988, in London, England. Airplane pilot, actress, lecturer, and author. Scott, Britain's foremost female aviator, learned to fly in 1959 at age thirty-two. From then until she retired in 1971 she set more than one hundred flying records, won more than fifty racing trophies, and flew three solo flights around the world. In 1966 she became the first Briton to make a solo global flight in a light plane, and with that same flight she set the record for the longest voyage ever undertaken: thirty-one thousand miles in thirty-three days. In addition, her round-the-world flight of 1971 made Scott the first person to fly solo across the North Pole. Originally a repertory actress who subsequently played minor roles on television and in films, Scott also modeled and designed clothes before becoming a pilot. In addition to lecturing on aviation in Europe and in America, she wrote two books on her flying experiences, *I Must Fly* and *Barefoot in the Sky*, and was working on a third at the time

of her death. She founded the British Balloon and Airships Club and was made an officer of the Order of the British Empire in 1968.

OBITUARIES AND OTHER SOURCES:

BOOKS

Who's Who, 140th edition, St. Martin's, 1988.

PERIODICALS

Chicago Tribune, October 21, 1988.
Los Angeles Times, October 22, 1988.
New York Times, October 21, 1988.
Times (London), October 21, 1988.
Washington Post, October 22, 1988.

* * *

SCOTT, William B(utler) 1945-

PERSONAL: Born February 27, 1945, in Charleston, S.C.; son of Fred G. (a farmer) and Charlotte H. (a farmer) Scott; married Donna Hurt (a college administrator), August 6, 1966; children: Fred Scott Allsbook, Ansley, Laine. *Education:* Presbyterian College, B.A., 1967; Wake Forest University, M.A., 1968; University of Wisconsin—Madison, Ph.D., 1973. *Politics:* Democrat. *Religion:* Presbyterian.

ADDRESSES: Home—301 East Brooklyn, Gambier, Ohio 43022. *Office*—Department of History, Kenyon College, Gambier, Ohio 43022.

CAREER: Kenyon College, Gambier, Ohio, assistant professor, 1973-80, associate professor, 1980-87, professor of history, 1987—.

MEMBER: American Historical Association, Organization of American Historians, Ohio Academy of History.

AWARDS, HONORS: Fellowship from American Council of Learned Societies, 1980-81; grant from the National Endowment for the Humanities, 1987-88.

WRITINGS

In Pursuit of Happiness: American Conceptions of Property, Indiana University Press, 1977.
(Editor with Peter M. Rutkoff) Han Staudinged, *Inner Nazi*, Louisiana State University Press, 1982.
(With Rutkoff) *New School: A History of the New School for Social Research*, Free Press, 1986.

WORK IN PROGRESS: New York Modern: Modernist Moment in the Arts in New York City, 1890-1970, with Rutkoff, publication by Johns Hopkins University Press expected in 1992.

SIDELIGHTS: William B. Scott's *New School: A History of the New School for Social Research* chronicles the founding and growth of New York City's New School for Social Research, which was created in 1919 to provide what was then a revolutionary alternative to traditional higher education. The institution was intended by its founders to provide lectures and research facilities to mature adults who had no need for grades, degrees, and stifling academic hierarchies. Among its early faculty members were such academic scholars as Charles A. Beard, James Harvey Robinson, Thorstein Veblen, John Dewey, and Lewis Mumford. In 1922 the school entered a period of growth and expansion which would last for more than forty years. During World War II the New School became a haven for Jewish professors fleeing the horrors of Nazi Germany, and their continental philosophy added a new dimension to the institution, which had been guided for many years by the philosophical spirit of John Dewey. "It is a remarkably rich story," commented Nathan Glazer in the *New York Times Book Review*. Its authors, the critic pointed out, "uncovered a great deal that is interesting and surprising," and presented the reader with an intellectual history, as well as an institutional one.

William B. Scott told *CA:* "The history of the New School was the beginning of my interest in twentieth-century New York City and its role as incubator of American culture, an interest now being pursued in my present work, *New York Modern: Modernist Moment in the Arts, 1875-1970.*"

BIOGRAPHICAL/CRITICAL SOURCES:

PERIODICALS

New York Times Book Review, August 31, 1986.

* * *

SCRIBNER, Charles III 1951-

PERSONAL: Born May 24, 1951, in Washington, D.C.; son of Charles (a book publisher) and Joan (a figure skater; maiden name, Sunderland) Scribner; married Ritchie Harrison Markoe (an artist and teacher), August 4, 1979; children: Charles IV, Christopher Markoe. *Education:* Princeton University, A.B., M.F.A., 1975, Ph.D., 1977. *Religion:* Roman Catholic.

ADDRESSES: Home—655 Park Ave., New York, N.Y. 10021. *Office*—Macmillan Publishing Co., 866 Third Ave., New York, N.Y. 10022.

CAREER: Charles Scribner's Sons, New York City, editor, 1975-78, director of subsidiary rights, 1978-82, publisher of paperback division, 1982-83, executive vice-president, 1983-84; Macmillan Publishing Co., New York City, vice-president for special projects, 1984—. Princeton University, instructor, 1976-77, member of advisory council of university library, 1981—, and department of art and archaeology, 1983—; member of board of trustees of Princeton University Press, 1984—; adviser to Wethersfield Institute, 1985—.

MEMBER: College Art Association of America, Phi Beta Kappa, River Club, Ivy Club, Racquet and Tennis Club, Piping Rock Club.

WRITINGS:

The Triumph of the Eucharist: Tapestries Designed by Rubens, UMI Research Press, 1982.
(Contributor) Diane Apostolos-Cappadona, editor, *Art, Creativity, and the Sacred,* Crossroad Publishing, 1984.
(Contributor) Ingrid H. Shafer, editor, *The Incarnate Imagination: Essays in Theology, the Arts, and Social Sciences in Honor of Andrew Greeley,* Popular Press, 1988.
Rubens, Abrams, 1989.

Also author of introductions to reprinted editions of F. Scott Fitzgerald's *The Great Gatsby* and *Tender Is the Night.* Contributor of articles and reviews to art journals, including *Art Bulletin* and *Burlington.*

WORK IN PROGRESS: Books on "The Garden of Love" in baroque and rococo painting and on illusionistic ceiling paintings; research on baroque art, especially that of Rubens and Bernini.

SIDELIGHTS: Charles Scribner III told *CA:* "I fell into publishing as an act of birth—into a highly unoriginal family of five generations of book publishers. I have happily stayed through the choice: it is one of the few professions that may legitimately embrace a wide spectrum of intellectual and cultural pursuits.

"As an art historian, I continue to focus my research, writing, and lecturing on the Baroque—the art of the seventeenth to eighteenth centuries—for similar reasons. The age of Galilei Galileo and Sir Isaac Newton, as well as of Peter Paul Rubens, Rembrandt van Rijn, and Giovanni Bernini, the Baroque encompassed the rise of the modern nation-states, of opera, of science, and of an artistic impulse and aesthetic that strove to reconcile and unify naturalism with classicism, mysticism with realism, and different media (painting, sculpture, and architecture). An expansive world view was combined with an unabashed appeal to the emotions and a probing of psychological depths. At the same time, artists, as well as writers and philosophers, breathed new life into the dual western heritage of Christian spirituality and Graeco-Roman classicism. A triumph of synthesis and wholeness, Baroque art provides an effective antidote to the fragmentation of our own times."

AVOCATIONAL INTERESTS: Opera, classical music, theology, English and American literature.

* * *

SCUDDER, Thayer 1930-

PERSONAL: Born August 4, 1930, in New Haven, Conn.; son of Townsend III and Virginia (Boody) Scudder; married Mary Eliza Drinker, August 26, 1950; children: Mary Eliza, Alice Thayer. *Education:* Harvard University, A.B., 1952, Ph.D., 1960; attended Yale University, 1953-54, and London School of Economics and Political Science, London, 1960-61.

ADDRESSES: Office—Department of Anthropology, California Institute of Technology, 1201 East California Blvd., Pasadena, Calif. 91125.

CAREER: U.S. Climatic Research Laboratory, technologist in environmental physiology, 1953; Rhodes-Livingstone Institute, Lusaka, Northern Rhodesia (now Zambia), research officer, 1956-57; American University of Cairo, Cairo, Egypt, assistant professor of social anthropology, 1961-62; Rhodes-Livingstone Institute, senior research officer, 1962-63; Harvard University, Cambridge, Mass., fellow at Center for Middle Eastern Studies, 1963-64; California Institute of Technology, Pasadena, assistant professor, 1964-66, associate professor, 1966-69, professor of anthropology, 1969—. Director of Institute for Developmental Anthropology, Binghamton, N.Y., 1976—; consultant to International Bank for Reconstruction and Development, World Health Organization, and U.S. Agency for International Development.

MEMBER: American Anthropological Association, Society for Applied Anthropology, American Alpine Club.

AWARDS, HONORS: Fellow of Social Science Research Council in London, England, 1960-61; Guggenheim fellow, 1975-76.

WRITINGS:

The Ecology of the Gwembe Tonga, Manchester University Press, 1962.
Gathering Among African Woodlands Savannah Cultivators: A Case Study—The Gwembe Tonga, Manchester University Press, 1971.

(With David F. Aberle) *Expected Impacts of Compulsory Relocation on Navajos, With Special Emphasis on Relocation From the Former Joint Use Area Required by Public Law 93-531,* Institute for Developmental Anthropology, 1979.

(With Elizabeth Colson) *Secondary Education and the Formation of an Elite: The Impact of Education on Gwembe District, Zambia,* Academic Press, 1980.

(With Aberle) *No Place to Go: The Effects of Compulsory Relocation on Navajos,* Institute for the Study of Human Issues (Philadelphia), 1982.

(With Thomas Conelly) *Management Systems for Riverine Fisheries,* Food and Agriculture Organization of the United Nations, 1985.

Also co-editor of *Long-Term Field Research in Social Anthropology,* 1979.*

*   *   *

SCUDDER, Townsend (III)   1900-1988

OBITUARY NOTICE: Born August 27, 1900, in Glenwood, N.Y.; died of heart failure, October 7, 1988, in Southbury, Conn. Educator, administrator, editor, and author. A professor of English at Swarthmore College for more than twenty years, Scudder will be remembered as a founder and longtime president of the Center for Information on America. He received a B.A. and a Ph.D. from Yale University and, in the early 1920s, did editorial work for Doubleday publishers and the Rockefeller Foundation. After teaching English at Yale from 1924 to 1931, Scudder joined the staff of Swarthmore College as an assistant professor, eventually becoming a full professor in 1943. In 1950 Scudder helped establish the Center for Information on America, which publishes non-partisan pamphlets discussing U.S. issues. He was the organization's executive director beginning in 1951 and served as its president from 1956 until his retirement in 1980. Among Scudder's books are *The Lonely Wayfaring Man: Emerson and Some Englishmen, Jane Welsh Carlyle,* and *Concord: American Town.* In addition, he edited *Letters of Jane Welsh Carlyle to Joseph Neuberg.*

OBITUARIES AND OTHER SOURCES:

BOOKS

Directory of American Scholars, Volume I: *History,* 8th edition, Bowker, 1982.
Who's Who in America, 44th edition, Marquis, 1986.

PERIODICALS

New York Times, October 11, 1988.

*   *   *

SEYMOUR, William Kean   1887-1975

OBITUARY NOTICE—See index for *CA* sketch: Born September 27, 1887, in London, England; died January 21, 1975. Bank employee, lecturer, editor, journalist, and writer. A prolific author and editor, Seymour wrote in various genres, including poetry, fiction, biography, and criticism. For nearly forty years he worked in the British banking business. His diverse writings include the poetry collections *The Street of Dreams* and *Caesar Remembers, and Other Poems;* the parody volumes *A Jackdaw in Georgia: A Book of Polite Parodies and Imitations of Contemporaries and Others* and *Captain Gunn;* the novels *The Little Cages, Friends of the Swallow* and *The*

Secret Kingdom; and the verse play *The First Childermas.* He also authored *Burns Into English: Renderings of Selected Dialect Poems of Robert Burns* and the biographical pamphlet *Jonathan Swift: The Enigma of a Genius.* In addition, Seymour edited, with Cecil Palmer, *Air Pie: The Royal Air Force Annual* and the two-volume *A Miscellany of British Poetry, 1919.* A lecturer and an active member of the Poetry Society of England, he and John Smith edited *The Pattern of Poetry: The Poetry Society Verse-Speaking Anthology.*

OBITUARIES AND OTHER SOURCES:

Date of death provided by wife, Rosalind Wade.

BOOKS

International Who's Who in Poetry, 5th edition, Melrose, 1977.

*   *   *

SHANKS, Hershel   1930-

PERSONAL: Born March 8, 1930, in Sharon, Pa.; son of A. Martin and Mildred (Freedman) Shanks; married Judith Alexander Weil, February 20, 1966; children: Elizabeth Jean, Julia Emily. *Education:* Haverford College, B.A., 1952; Columbia University, M.A., 1953; Harvard University, LL.B., 1956.

ADDRESSES: Home and office—5208 38th St. N.W., Washington, D.C. 20015.

CAREER: U.S. Department of Justice, Washington, D.C., trial attorney in Civil Division, 1956-59; private practice of law in Washington, D.C., 1959-64; Glassie, Pewett, Dudley, Beebe & Shanks (law firm), Washington, D.C., partner, 1964-88. President of Jewish Educational Ventures, Inc., 1987—.

MEMBER: American Bar Association, Federal Bar Association, American Judicature Society, Biblical Archaeology Society (president, 1975—), American Schools of Oriental Research, National Press Club, District of Columbia Bar Association, Lawyers Committee on Civil Rights, Phi Beta Kappa, National Lawyers Club.

WRITINGS:

(Editor and author of introduction and annotations) *The Art and Craft of Judging: The Decisions of Judge Learned Hand,* Macmillan, 1968.
The City of David: A Guide to Biblical Jerusalem, Biblical Archaeology Society, 1973.
Judaism in Stone: The Archaeology of Ancient Synagogues, Harper, 1979.
(Editor with Benjamin Mazar) *Recent Archaeology in the Land of Israel,* Biblical Archaeology Society, 1984.
(Editor) *Ancient Israel: A Short History From Abraham to the Roman Destruction of the Temple,* Prentice-Hall, 1988.

Contributor to law books. Also contributor of articles and reviews to periodicals. Editor of *Biblical Archaeology Review,* 1975—, *Bible Review,* 1985—, and *Moment* magazine, 1988—.

SIDELIGHTS: Hershel Shanks told *CA:* "We should think more and write less. Mea culpa."

*   *   *

SHANNON, William V(incent)   1927-1988

OBITUARY NOTICE—See index for *CA* sketch: Born August 24, 1927, in Worcester, Mass.; died of lymphoma, September

27, 1988, in Boston, Mass. Politician, educator, journalist, and author. Shannon was a journalist for twenty-five years before he was appointed U.S. ambassador to Ireland by President Jimmy Carter in 1977. Previously he served as Washington correspondent for the *New York Post*, beginning in 1951, but left that newspaper in 1964 to write editorials for the *New York Times*. When he returned to the United States from Ireland in 1981, he joined the faculty of Boston University and wrote for the *Boston Globe*. His other writings include *The Truman Merry-Go-Round*, with Robert S. Allen; *The American Irish;* the biography *The Heir Apparent: Robert Kennedy and the Struggle for Power;* and *They Could Not Trust the King: Nixon, Watergate and the American People*. When writing for the *New York Post* Shannon won a Page One Award from the New York Newspaper Guild for his coverage of national affairs and, while working for the *New York Times*, won two Edward J. Meeman awards from the Scripps-Howard Foundation for conservation writings.

OBITUARIES AND OTHER SOURCES:

BOOKS

The International Who's Who, 50th edition, Europa, 1986.

PERIODICALS

Chicago Tribune, September 29, 1988.
Los Angeles Times, October 1, 1988.
New York Times, September 29, 1988.
Times (London), September 29, 1988.
Washington Post, September 28, 1988.

*   *   *

SHAPARD, Robert (Perry)   1942-

PERSONAL: Surname is pronounced "*Shap*-ard"; born June 13, 1942, in New York, N.Y.; son of William and Betsy (Bentley) Shapard; married Reve French, June 5, 1976; children: Gwen Celeste. *Education:* Southern Methodist University, B.B.A., 1966, B.A., 1970, M.A., 1972; University of North Carolina at Greensboro, M.F.A., 1978; University of Utah, Ph.D., 1986.

ADDRESSES: Home—Honolulu, Hawaii. *Office*—Department of English, University of Hawaii at Manoa, 1733 Donaghho Rd., Honolulu, Hawaii 96822. *Agent*—Nat Sobel, Nat Sobel Associates, Inc., 146 East 19th St., New York, N.Y. 10003.

CAREER: Worked as night watchman, real estate agent, life insurance salesman, stockbroker, manufacturing supervisor, construction worker, automobile repossesser, and traveling auditor; editor of *Quarterly West*, 1981-83; *Western Humanities Review*, Salt Lake City, Utah, managing editor, 1981-86; University of Hawaii at Manoa, Honolulu, assistant professor of English, 1986—. *Military service:* U.S. Marine Corps Reserve, 1961-67; became sergeant.

AWARDS, HONORS: Award for younger writers from General Electric Co. and Coordinating Council of Literary Magazines, 1983, for short story "Tosteson's Dome"; fellow at Yaddo Colony, 1983, and Fine Arts Work Center, Provincetown, Mass., 1983-84; grant from National Endowment for the Arts, 1987-88.

WRITINGS:

(Editor with James Thomas) *Sudden Fiction: American Short-Short Stories*, Peregrine Smith, 1986.

(Editor) *World Sudden Fiction*, Norton, in press.

Contributor of articles, stories, and reviews to magazines, including *Greensboro Review, Mid-American Review, Studies in Short Fiction, Literary Magazine Review, Cimarron Review, Literary Review, Cosmopolitan, Prism International, Fiction Network*, and *Short Story Review*.

WORK IN PROGRESS: A novel; short stories; research toward establishing a new journal of American poetry, fiction, criticism, and reviews, as well as translations of similar contemporary works from Asia and the Pacific.

*   *   *

SHAWCHUCK, Norman   1935-

PERSONAL: Surname is pronounced "*Shav*-chuck"; born May 13, 1935, in Elgin, N.D.; son of Aleck (a farmer) and Ava (a housewife; maiden name, Brown) Shawchuck; married Verna Dalin (a marketing executive), January 19, 1956; children: Carita Renee, Melody Kim, Kay Marie. *Education:* Jamestown College, B.A., 1968; Garrett Theological Seminary, M.Div., 1969; Northwestern University, Ph.D., 1974.

ADDRESSES: Home—214 Barker Rd., Michigan City, Ind. 46360. *Office*—United Methodist Church, 121 East Seventh St., Michigan City, Ind. 46360.

CAREER: Ordained United Methodist minister, 1961; United Methodist Church, Dakotas Area Program, associate director of staff, 1974-80, Indiana area director of spiritual formation, 1981-85, pastor in Michigan City, Ind., 1985-88. Member of adjunct faculty at McCormick Theological Seminary, 1975—, and Trinity Evangelical Divinity School, 1980—. President of Shawchuck & Associates Ltd., 1974—; consultant to religious organizations in the United States, the Far East, and the Middle East. Member of board of directors of American Indian Brotherhood, 1974-80, Leadership Network, 1984-87, and Michigan City Young Men's Christian Association (YMCA), 1985-87.

MEMBER: Religious Research Association.

WRITINGS:

Merging Two Seminaries, Garrett Theological Seminary, 1974.
Taking a Look at Your Leadership Styles, Organization Resources Press, 1975, reprinted as *How to Be a More Effective Church Leader: A Special Edition for Pastors and Other Church Leaders*, Spiritual Growth Resources, 1981.
(Contributor) Gustave Rath, editor, *Fundamentals of Evaluation*, Organization Resources Press, 1976.
(Contributor) Gustave Rath, editor, *The Systems Approach*, Organization Resources Press, 1976.
(With Alvin J. Lindgren) *Management for Your Church: How to Realize Your Church's Potential Through a Systems Approach*, Abingdon, 1977.
(With Lindgren) *Let My People Go: Empowering Laity for Ministry*, Abingdon, 1979.
How to Manage Conflict in the Church, Volume I: *Understanding and Managing Conflict*, Volume II: *Conflict Interventions and Resources*, Spiritual Growth Resources, 1982.
(With Lloyd Perry) *Revitalizing the Twentieth Century Church*, Moody, 1983.
(With Reuben Job) *A Guide to Prayer for Ministers and Other Servants*, Upper Room, 1984.
What It Means to Be a Church Leader: A Biblical Point of View, Spiritual Growth Resources, 1985.

(With Job) *How to Conduct a Spiritual Life Retreat*, Upper Room, 1986.

Also author, with Robert Worley, Doug Lewis, and Rhea Grey, of *Experiences in Activating Congregations*, 1976.

Contributing editor of *Leadership*. Contributor of about forty articles to religious journals.

WORK IN PROGRESS: A Guide to Prayer for All God's People, with Reuben Job, publication by Upper Room expected in 1990; *A Theology of Protestant Spirituality*, Abingdon Press, 1991; a marketing book for religious organizations, with Philip Kotler and Gustave Rath, 1991.

SIDELIGHTS: Norman Shawchuck told *CA:* "Shawchuck & Associates is a management consulting organization serving religious organizations, offering consultation in the full range of management problems.

"My research and writing interests are in the management of religious organizations and in spiritual formation. I was prompted to write my books in order to provide church leaders with practical concepts and tools for managing church agencies and ministries. In writing on marketing for religious organizations, I am interested in helping persons utilize a systems marketing approach in the church; analyzing opportunities, segmenting the market, targeting selected markets, etc.

"I view conflict in the church as a normal phenomenon which, if managed properly, can strengthen the church. Church leadership must be based upon sound theology and modern management theory and practice. Leadership is learned; it is not a function of personality or a bestowed gift."

Shawchuck's books have been translated into Korean and Spanish.

*   *   *

SHELLEY, Mack Clayton II   1950-

PERSONAL: Born June 21, 1950, in Fort Campbell, Ky.; son of Mack Clayton and Sarah (Flanagan) Shelley; married Kathleen Diane Rogers (in statistical computing); children: Anne Elizabeth, William Ryan. *Education:* American University, B.A., 1972; University of Wisconsin—Madison, M.S., 1973, Ph.D., 1977.

ADDRESSES: Home—3454 Southdale Dr., Ames, Iowa 50010. *Office*—Department of Political Science, 543 Ross Hall (and Department of Statistics, 210-B Snedecor Hall), Iowa State University, Ames, Iowa 50011.

CAREER: Mississippi State University, Starkville, assistant professor of political science, 1977-79; Iowa State University, Ames, assistant professor, 1979-83, associate professor of political science and statistics, 1983—. Guest on radio and television programs.

MEMBER: American Political Science Association, American Statistical Association, Midwest Political Science Association, Southern Political Science Association, Phi Kappa Phi, Pi Gamma Mu, Omicron Delta Kappa, Pi Sigma Alpha, Mu Sigma Rho.

AWARDS, HONORS: Grant from U.S. Department of Health, Education, and Welfare, 1977-79.

WRITINGS:

The Permanent Majority: The Conservative Coalition in the United States Congress, University of Alabama Press, 1983.

(Editor with Steffen W. Schmidt) *Readings and Discussion Exercises in American Government and Politics*, Ginn, 1984.

(With Schmidt and Barbara A. Bardes) *American Government and Politics Today*, West Publishing, 1985, 2nd edition, 1987.

(With Schmidt and Bardes) *American Government and Politics Today: The Essentials*, West Publishing, 1986, 2nd edition, 1988.

(With Robert Krause and Dinker Patel) *Transportation Policy in the States: Current and Future Trends*, Council of State Governments, 1987.

(With William F. Woodman and Brian J. Reichel) *Biotechnology and the Research Enterprise: A Guide to the Literature*, Iowa State University Press, 1988.

Contributor of articles and reviews to political science and statistics journals.

WORK IN PROGRESS: Research on elections, urban migration, and biotechnology.

SIDELIGHTS: Mack Clayton Shelley II told *CA:* "The study of public policy takes many different forms. I have approached this by examining a factor that often dictates the outcomes of votes in Congress—the "conservative coalition" of Republicans and conservative, mostly southern, Democrats which wins about two out of every three times it appears. My studies of public policy have also included state transportation policy, urban migration, and biotechnology. The impact of biotechnology research is dramatic on university research agendas, on corporate funding policy and economic development, and on people's hopes and fears about the future. Together with other high technology initiatives, biotechnology will very likely change how we work, how we live, and what we know about ourselves and the world in which we have evolved."

*   *   *

SHEN, James C. H.   1909-

PERSONAL: Born June 15, 1909, in Shanghai, China; son of Shen Yung-tang and Yen Ching-feng; married Winifred Wei, January 22, 1939; children: Joyce Shen Hsu, Cynthia Shen Rastogi, Carl. *Education:* Yenching University, B.A., 1932; University of Missouri—Columbia, M.A., 1935.

ADDRESSES: Office—c/o Ministry of Foreign Affairs, Taipei, Taiwan.

CAREER: China Press, Shanghai, reporter, 1932-34; Central News Agency, Nanking, China, editor, 1936-37; Ministry of Information, Chongqing, China, chief of editorial section in International Department, 1938-43, director of Pacific Coast Bureau in San Francisco, Calif., 1943-47; director of international development for Government Information Office, 1947-48; *China Mail*, Hong Kong, night editor, 1949; Rediffusion Broadcasting Co., Hong Kong, Chinese program director, 1949-55; secretary to the president of the Republic of China, in Taipei, 1956-59; Ministry of Foreign Affairs, Taipei, director of Information Department, 1959-61; director general of Government Information Office, 1961-66; Republic of China, ambassador to Australia, 1966-68, vice-minister of foreign affairs, 1968-71, ambassador to the United States, 1971-79; writer, 1979—.

AWARDS, HONORS: Faculty-Alumni Gold Medal from University of Missouri—Columbia, 1972.

WRITINGS:

The U.S. and Free China: How the U.S. Sold Out Its Ally; A View From the Former Ambassador of Free China, Acropolis Books, 1983.

*   *   *

SHER, Jack   1913-1988

OBITUARY NOTICE: Born in 1913 in Minneapolis, Minn.; died of respiratory and heart problems, August 23, 1988, in Beverly Hills, Calif. Film producer and director, playwright, screenwriter, columnist, and author. With dozens of writing, directing, and producing credits to his name, Sher will be remembered for writing such popular productions as "Paris Blues," starring Paul Newman and Joanne Woodward, and contributing dialogue to the 1953 classic Western "Shane." His 1971-72 television play, "Goodbye, Raggedy Ann," was nominated for an Emmy Award. In addition to writing columns, which have been syndicated in more than forty newspapers, Sher was the author of *The Cold Companion, Twelve Sports Immortals,* and *Twelve More Sports Immortals.* He also wrote the 1962 Broadway play "The Perfect Setup."

OBITUARIES AND OTHER SOURCES:

BOOKS

The Filmgoer's Companion, 4th edition, Hill & Wang, 1974.
International Motion Picture Almanac, Quigley, 1988.

PERIODICALS

Los Angeles Times, August 25, 1988.
New York Times, October 25, 1962, August 24, 1988.

*   *   *

SHERATON, Mimi   1926-

PERSONAL: Born February 10, 1926, in Brooklyn, N.Y.; daughter of Joseph H. and Beatrice R. (Breit) Solomon; married William Sheraton, August 20, 1945 (divorced, 1954); married Richard Falcone, July 30, 1955; children: Marc Christopher. *Education:* New York University, B.S., 1947.

ADDRESSES: Home—New York, N.Y. *Office*—P.O. Box 1396, Old Chelsea Station, New York, N.Y. 10011.

CAREER: Seventeen, New York, N.Y., food and home furnishing editor, 1947-53; *House Beautiful,* New York City, managing editor of supplement division, 1954-56; free-lance writer, 1956-69; *New York,* New York City, food critic, 1969-75; *New York Times,* New York City, food critic, 1975-83; *Time,* New York City, food critic, 1984—. Publisher of newsletter *Mimi Sheraton's Taste;* consultant on folk art exhibitions.

AWARDS, HONORS: Penney Missouri Award from School of Journalism at University of Missouri—Columbia, 1974, for articles in *New York* magazine; Front Page Award from Newswomen's Club of New York, 1977, for *New York Times* article on nitrites in meats.

WRITINGS:

Visions of Sugar Plums, Harper, 1968.

From My Mother's Kitchen, Harper, 1979.
Mimi Sheraton's New York Times Guide to New Restaurants, Times Books, 1983.
(With Alan King) *Is Salami and Eggs Better Than Sex?,* Little, Brown, 1985.
Mimi Sheraton's Favorite New York Restaurants, Simon & Schuster, 1986, revised, Weidenfeld & Nicholson, 1989.

Also author of *The Seducer's Cookbook,* 1962; *City Portraits,* 1963; *The German Cookbook,* 1965.

Contributor to magazines, including *Conde Nast Traveler* and *Town and Country.*

BIOGRAPHICAL/CRITICAL SOURCES:

PERIODICALS

New York Times Book Review, December 2, 1979, October 6, 1985.
Time, November 11, 1985.

*   *   *

SHERIF, Muzafer   1906-1988

OBITUARY NOTICE—See index for *CA* sketch: Born July 29, 1906, in Odemis, Izmir, Turkey; died of a heart attack, October 16, 1988, in Fairbanks, Alaska. Social psychologist, educator, and author. Sherif will be best remembered as a social psychologist who was an expert on group interaction and hostility. After attending graduate school at Harvard and Columbia universities, Sherif ventured to his native Turkey to teach, but returned to the United States in 1945. He joined the faculty of Princeton University that year, and subsequently taught at Yale University and the University of Oklahoma before joining the University of Pennsylvania as a professor of sociology in 1966. He conducted the influential "Robber's Cave" study, in which he observed the hostility arising from competitiveness and team loyalty of two groups of boys at a summer camp, and their apparent lack of hostility when the groups came together to work on a common project. Sherif published his findings in *Intergroup Conflict and Cooperation: The Robber's Cave Experiment.* His additional writings include *The Psychology of Social Norms* and *In Common Predicament: Social Psychology of Intergroup Conflict and Cooperation.* He also edited a number of volumes, including *Social Psychology at the Crossroads, Group Relations at the Crossroads,* and *Intergroup Relations and Leadership.*

OBITUARIES AND OTHER SOURCES:

BOOKS

International Encyclopedia of the Social Sciences, Volume 18: *Biographical Supplement,* Free Press, 1979.

PERIODICALS

New York Times, October 27, 1988.

*   *   *

SHERLOCK, Richard   1947-

PERSONAL: Born February 22, 1947, in Salt Lake City, Utah; son of Howard James and Ione (Frankland) Sherlock; married Margaret Louise Hansen (a teacher), August 31, 1973; children: Thomas, Alexandra. *Education:* University of Utah, B.A. (magna cum laude), 1973; Harvard University, M.T.S. and Ph.D., both 1972.

ADDRESSES: Home—1680 East 1400 N., Logan, Utah 84321. *Office*—Department of Languages and Philosophy, Utah State University, Logan, Utah 84322.

CAREER: Harvard University, Cambridge, Mass., research fellow in medical ethics, 1973-75; Northeastern University, Boston, Mass., instructor in philosophy and religion, 1976-78; University of Tennessee, Center for Health Sciences, Memphis, assistant professor of human values and ethics, 1978-83; Fordham University, Bronx, N.Y., assistant professor of theology, 1983-85; Utah State University, Logan, assistant professor of theology, 1985—.

MEMBER: Society for Health and Human Values, American Academy of Religion, American Political Science Association, Utah Academy of Sciences, Arts, and Letters.

AWARDS, HONORS: Grants from Earhart Foundation, 1987 and 1988, and from National Endowment for the Humanities, 1988.

WRITINGS:

Preserving Life: Public Policy and the Life Not Worth Having, Loyola University Press, 1987.
(With Mary Dingus) *Families and the Gravely Ill: Roles, Rules, and Rights,* Greenwood Press, 1987.
(Editor with Dawson Schultz) *Rethinking the Clinical Relationship,* Indiana University Press, 1989.

WORK IN PROGRESS: Taming the Whirlwind: Politics and Theology in John Locke.

* * *

SHIRLEY, John 1953-

PERSONAL: Born February 10, 1953, in Houston, Tex.; son of John Edward (an automotive parts manager) and Ruth (a teacher of the blind and deaf; maiden name, Thomson; present surname, Mace) Shirley; married first wife, Alexandra Allinne (divorced, 1985); married second wife, Kathy Woods, April 18, 1986; children: (first marriage) Byron and Perry (twins); (second marriage) Julian. *Education:* "Self-educated." *Politics:* Democrat. *Religion:* "Methodist (agnostic)."

ADDRESSES: Home—1217 Park Ave., Alameda, Calif. 94501. *Agent*—Martha Millard, 21 Kilsyth Rd., Brookline, Mass. 02146.

CAREER: Self-employed.

WRITINGS:

City Come A-Walkin' (fantasy novel), Dell, 1980.
The Brigade (suspense thriller), Avon, 1981.
Cellars (horror), Avon, 1982.
Eclipse (political science fiction thriller), Popular Library, 1987.
A Splendid Chaos (science fiction allegory), F. Watts, 1988.
Heat Seeker (stories), Scream Press, 1988.
In Darkness Waiting, Signet, 1988.
Eclipse Penumbra (science fiction thriller), Popular Library, 1988.
Eclipse Shattered, Popular Library, 1989.

WORK IN PROGRESS: Research on the connections between the Central Intelligence Agency and cocaine smugglers.

SIDELIGHTS: John Shirley told *CA:* "I have published in the science fiction and horror fields because they have provided a way to get unconventional notions on the nature of social and objective reality into print. This has also given me a way to

publish surrealism—meaningful surrealism—in a marketable guise. Meaningful surrealism is allegorical and explores the crises of the collective unconscious through the medium of individual unconscious.

"Any given reality is subjective or consensual, never absolute. It is shaded, edged, distortionally defined by cultural icons, advertising logos, and shared assumptions; all of these exert a kind of neurological gravitational pull on the perceptions (in a metaphorical sense). I explore alternative pre-structural identities in *A Splendid Chaos,* an entertaining (I trust) interplanetary fantasy novel. In the book the other planet is a convenient stage for critiquing the hideous, piquant, nightmarish, glorious, exquisite, erotic, elemental dynamics of 'Being' itself.

"*In Darkness Waiting* is about the human capacity for the suppression of empathy; it is my protest of the sociological applications of dehumanization. In *The Brigade* I strive for an Elmore Leonard quality in texture and characterization (but that's hard to achieve). I'm thinking of writing a horror novel about Los Angeles called *The Users.* I'm also planning a 'mainstream' novel about the roots of street violence in California."

* * *

SHIRLEY, John William 1908-

PERSONAL: Born September 27, 1908, in Swea City, Iowa; son of William and Grace (Barger) Shirley; married Geraldine E. Lewis, June 6, 1932; children: Jean Ann Shirley Frohlicher, Linda Carol Shirley Neuse (deceased). *Education:* Attended University of Nebraska, 1932-33; Iowa State University, A.B. (with honors), 1932, Ph.D. (with distinction), 1937.

ADDRESSES: Home—31 Bridle Brook Lane, Newark, Del. 19711. *Office*—402 Morris Library, University of Delaware, Newark, Del. 19711.

CAREER: Michigan State College (now University), East Lansing, instructor, 1937-42, assistant professor of English, 1942-48, assistant professor of physics, 1942-46, associate professor, 1946-49; California Institute of Technology, Pasadena, visiting lecturer in history of science, 1946-47; North Carolina College of Agriculture and Engineering (now North Carolina State University), Raleigh, professor of English, 1949-62, dean of liberal arts, 1949-55, dean of faculty, 1955-62; University of Delaware, Newark, provost and vice-president for academic affairs, 1962-72, acting president, 1967-68, professor of English, 1962-72, H. Fletcher Brown Professor of History of Science, 1972-74, professor of history of science and provost emeritus, 1974—. Member of educational exchange with the U.S.S.R., 1958; president of North Carolina College Conference, 1961; College Entrance Examinations Board, member of examinations committee, 1961-65, chairman of committee, 1963-65, member of board of trustees, 1964-70, national chairman, 1965-66, member of executive committee, 1965-70.

MEMBER: American Society for Engineering Education (chairman of Humanities Division; member of executive committee), Association of Land Grant Colleges (chairman of liberal arts, 1955).

AWARDS, HONORS: Guggenheim fellow in England, 1947-48; L.H.D. from St. Lawrence University, 1978; Litt.D. from University of Durham, 1983; Medal of Distinction from University of Delaware, 1983.

WRITINGS:

Soviet Education and Its Challenge, North Carolina State Press, 1959.
(Editor) *Thomas Harriot, Renaissance Scientist*, Clarendon Press, 1974.
A Source Book for the Study of Thomas Harriot, Arno, 1981.
Thomas Harriot: A Biography, Clarendon Press, 1983.
(With F. David Hoeniger) *Science and the Arts in the Renaissance*, Folger Library Press, 1985.
Sir Walter Raleigh and the New World, North Carolina Division of Archives and History, 1985.

Contributor of about fifty articles to education and history journals.

*   *   *

SHOR, Ira 1945-

PERSONAL: Born June 2, 1945, in New York, N.Y.; son of Eli Ruben (a metalworker) and Ruth (a bookkeeper; maiden name, Mathross) Shor. *Education:* University of Michigan, B.A., 1966; University of Wisconsin—Madison, M.A., 1968, Ph.D., 1971.

ADDRESSES: Office—Department of English, College of Staten Island, Staten Island, N.Y. 10301.

CAREER: College of Staten Island, Staten Island, N.Y., professor of English. Member of core faculty at Union Graduate School, Cincinnati, Ohio, 1977-80.

MEMBER: National Writers Union.

AWARDS, HONORS: Woodrow Wilson fellow, 1966; Carnegie-Mellon fellow, 1982; Guggenheim fellow, 1983; chancellor's scholar in research at City University of New York, 1985.

WRITINGS:

Culture Wars: School and Society in the Conservative Restoration, 1969-1984, Methuen, 1986.
(With Paulo Freire) *A Pedagogy for Liberation: Dialogues on Transforming Education*, Bergin & Garvey, 1987.
(Editor) *Freire for the Classroom: A Sourcebook for Liberatory Teaching*, Boynton Cook, 1987.

Also author of the book *Critical Teaching and Everyday Life*, and of screenplays. Contributor to education journals.

WORK IN PROGRESS: Cultural Power: Learning and Transformation, a Paulo Freire model for teaching the theory and practice of "empowering pedagogy."

SIDELIGHTS: Ira Shor told *CA:* "I am very interested in critical learning and cultural democracy."

*   *   *

SHULMAN, Max 1919-1988

OBITUARY NOTICE—See index for *CA* sketch: Born March 14, 1919, in St. Paul, Minn.; died of bone cancer, August 28, 1988, in Hollywood (one source says Los Angeles), Calif. Humorist and author. Shulman will be best remembered as the creator of the television and film character Dobie Gillis, a girl-crazy adolescent. A Doubleday book editor who had read Shulman's humor columns in the University of Minnesota student paper urged him to write his first novel, *Barefoot Boy With Cheek;* the book became a best-seller when it was issued

in 1943. While in the Army Air Corps during World War II, Shulman wrote two more novels, *The Feather Merchants* and *The Zebra Derby*, both published after the war. In 1951 his next novel, *The Many Loves of Dobie Gillis*, received rave reviews. It spawned a prime-time television series of the same name and a motion picture titled "The Affairs of Dobie Gillis," both of which Shulman scripted. He next won acclaim with the Broadway play "The Tender Trap" (written with Robert Paul Smith and later made into the film starring Frank Sinatra and Debbie Reynolds), and in the late 1970s he collaborated with Julius Epstein on the screenplay for "House Calls," the comedy featuring Walter Matthau and Glenda Jackson. Shulman's other writings include the novels *Rally Round the Flag, Boys, Sleep Till Noon*, and *I Was a Teenage Dwarf*.

OBITUARIES AND OTHER SOURCES:

BOOKS

Dictionary of Literary Biography, Volume 11: *American Humorists, 1800-1950*, Gale, 1982.
International Motion Picture Almanac, Quigley, 1986.

PERIODICALS

Chicago Tribune, August 29, 1988.
Los Angeles Times, August 29, 1988.
New York Times, August 29, 1988.
Washington Post, August 31, 1988.

*   *   *

SIEGEL, Lee 1945-

PERSONAL: Born July 22, 1945, in Los Angeles, Calif.; son of Lee E. and Noreen (Roth) Siegel; children: Dmitri, Sebastian. *Education:* University of California, Berkeley, B.A., 1967; Columbia University, M.F.A., 1969; Oxford University, D.Phil., 1975.

ADDRESSES: Office—Department of Religion, University of Hawaii at Manoa, 2500 Campus Rd., Honolulu, Hawaii 96822.

CAREER: Western Washington University, Bellingham, instructor in English, 1969-72; University of Hawaii at Manoa, Honolulu, professor of English, 1976—, chairman of graduate program. Guest lecturer at Oriental Institute, Oxford University, 1985, and College de France, 1985.

MEMBER: International Brotherhood of Magicians, Society of American Magicians, Society of Indian Magicians.

AWARDS, HONORS: Senior fellow of American Institute of Indian Studies and Smithsonian Institution, 1979, 1983, and 1987; grants from Center for Asian and Pacific Studies, 1981, and American Council of Learned Societies and Social Science Research Council, 1982, 1985, and 1987; presidential award for excellence in teaching from the University of Hawaii, 1986.

WRITINGS:

Vivisections (drawings and poems), Goliards Press, 1973.
Sacred and Profane Love in Indian Traditions, Oxford University Press, 1979.
(With Jagdish Sharma) *Dreams in the Sramanic Traditions*, Firma KLM, 1980.
Fires of Love, Waters of Peace: Passion and Renunciation in Indian Culture, University of Hawaii Press, 1983.
Laughing Matters: Satire and Humor in India, University of Chicago Press, 1987.

Sweet Nothings (translation of the *Amarusataka*), Ravi Dayal Publishing, 1988.

Author and director of "Mask and Mystery," a television series produced at Media Center, University of Hawaii at Manoa, 1978. Contributor to *Encyclopedia of Religion*. Contributor of articles and reviews to history, religion, and philosophy journals and to newspapers.

WORK IN PROGRESS: Indra's Net: Magic and Conjuring in Indian Traditions.

SIDELIGHTS: Lee Siegel told *CA:* "India is a metaphor. Writing is what interests me—writing and magic. They are the same. And scholarship is a literary genre; I am exploring the poetics of scholarship."

* * *

SILVER, James W(esley) 1907-1988

OBITUARY NOTICE—See index for *CA* sketch: Born June 28, 1907, in Rochester, N.Y.; died of complications from emphysema, July 25, 1988, in Tampa, Fla.; cremated. Civil rights activist, historian, educator, editor, and author. Silver will be best remembered as the civil rights activist who wrote the controversial 1964 work *Mississippi: The Closed Society*, a condemnation of white supremacist attitudes then prevalent throughout the southern state. A member of the American history faculty at the University of Mississippi beginning in 1936, he left in 1965 to teach at Notre Dame University. In 1969 he joined the University of South Florida at Tampa, where he was a professor of history until his retirement ten years later. Silver's other writings include *Confederate Morale and Church Propaganda* and *Mississippi in the Confederacy: As Seen in Retrospect*. He also penned an account of the hostility he faced after publishing *Mississippi: The Closed Society* titled *Running Scared: Silver in Mississippi*. He edited *A Life For the Confederacy* and *The Confederate Soldier*, and was a member of the editorial boards of *Journal of Mississippi History, Journal of Southern History*, and *Mississippi Valley Historical Review*.

OBITUARIES AND OTHER SOURCES:

BOOKS

Directory of American Scholars, Volume I: *History*, 8th edition, Bowker, 1982.

PERIODICALS

Chicago Tribune, July 27, 1988.
Los Angeles Times, July 28, 1988.
New York Times, July 26, 1988.
Washington Post, July 27, 1988.

* * *

SINCLAIR, Bruce A. 1929-

PERSONAL: Born April 30, 1929, in Artesia, N.Mex.; son of Bert Thomas and Helen Evelyn (Cleveland) Sinclair; married Christine E. Roen, June 17, 1956 (divorced, January, 1968); married Mary P. Winsor, February 15, 1975; children: (first marriage) Alan Douglas (deceased), Margaret Elizabeth. *Education:* University of California, Berkeley, B.A., 1956; New Mexico Highlands University, M.A., 1959; University of Delaware, M.A., 1959; Case Institute of Technology (now Case Western Reserve University), Ph.D., 1966.

ADDRESSES: Home—550 Spadina Cres., Toronto, Ontario, Canada M5S 2J9. *Office*—Institute of History and Philosophy

of Science and Technology, University of Toronto, Toronto, Ontario, Canada M5S 1A1.

CAREER: Merrimack Valley Textile Museum, North Andover, Mass., director, 1959-64; Kansas State University, Manhattan, 1966-69, began as assistant professor, became associate professor of history; University of Toronto, Toronto, Ontario, associate professor, 1969-80, professor of history, 1981—, director of Institute of History and Philosophy of Science and Technology, 1975-81. *Military service:* U.S. Air Force, 1950-54.

MEMBER: Canadian Historical Association, Canadian Society for the History and Philosophy of Science, Organization of American Historians, Society for the History of Technology.

AWARDS, HONORS: Grants from American Philosophical Society, 1967-68, National Science Foundation, and Canada Council; Dexter Prize from Society for the History of Technology, 1975.

WRITINGS:

(Contributor) Nathan Reingold, editor, *Science in Nineteenth-Century America: A Documentary History*, Hill & Wang, 1964.
Philadelphia's Philosopher Mechanics: A History of the Franklin Institute, 1824-1865, Johns Hopkins University Press, 1974.
(Editor with Norman R. Ball and James O. Peterson) *Let Us Be Honest and Modest: Technology and Society in Canadian History*, Oxford University Press, 1974.
(With James P. Hull) *A Centennial History of the American Society of Mechanical Engineers, 1880-1980*, University of Toronto Press, 1980.

Contributor to scholarly journals.

BIOGRAPHICAL/CRITICAL SOURCES:

PERIODICALS

American Historical Review, June, 1976, June, 1981.*

* * *

SINCLAIR, Sonia 1928-
(Sonia Graham, Sonia Melchett)

PERSONAL: Born September 6, 1928, in Nainital, India; daughter of Roland Harris (a doctor) and Kathleen (Dunbar) Graham; married Julian Mond, Lord Melchett (a steel magnate; died, June, 1973); married Andrew Sinclair (a historian and writer); children: (first marriage) Peter, Lord Melchett, Kerena Mond Boulton, Pandora Mond. *Education:* Attended Royal School, Bath, and Queen's Secretarial College, Windsor, England. *Politics:* "Alliance." *Religion:* Church of England.

ADDRESSES: Home—16 Tite St., London SW3 4HZ, England.

CAREER: Writer. Member of board of directors of English Stage Company and National Theatre, 1974-87; magistrate in Marylebone, London, 1974-81.

WRITINGS:

(Under name Sonia Graham) *Tell Me Honestly* (nonfiction), Weidenfeld & Nicolson, 1964.
(Under name Sonia Melchett) *Someone Is Missing* (nonfiction), Weidenfeld & Nicolson, 1987.
Intrepid Women: Modern Travellers Across the World, William Heinemann, 1989.

Contributor to periodicals, including *Vogue, Harper's,* and *Portraits.*

SIDELIGHTS: Sonia Sinclair told *CA:* "My first book was motivated by my disillusionment with so-called London society, and my second book by the death of my first husband, my years alone, and my happy re-marriage.

"After reading many fascinating books about Victorian lady travelers, I feel the challenge of present-day women more than ever is to explore the untrampled parts of the globe, to scale mountains, and to sail the ocean. One of my aims in my third book is to discover whether the intrepid and unusual lifestyles of adventuresome women have given them a deeper understanding of everyday life denied to mortals who take fewer risks."

AVOCATIONAL INTERESTS: "Traveling, reading, long-distance swimming, and walking."

* * *

SINOFSKY, Esther R. 1951-

PERSONAL: Born June 11, 1951, in Chicago, Ill., daughter of Boris (a teacher) and Faye (a librarian and archivist) Sinofsky. *Education:* University of California, Los Angeles, B.A. (cum laude), 1973; University of Southern California, M.S.L.S., 1974, Ph.D., 1982.

ADDRESSES: Home—Los Angeles, Calif. *Office*—Robert Frost Junior High School, 12314 Bradford Pl., Granada Hills, Calif. 91344.

CAREER: University of Southern California, Los Angeles, instructional designer, 1982-84; Los Angeles Unified School District, Los Angeles, librarian, 1985—. Instructional design consultant, 1982-86; adjunct lecturer at University of Southern California, 1985—.

MEMBER: Association for Educational Communication and Technology, American Library Association, California Media and Library Educators Association, Phi Delta Kappa, Beta Phi Mu.

WRITINGS:

Off-Air Videotaping in Education: Copyright Issues, Decisions, Implications, Bowker, 1984.
A Copyright Primer for Educational and Industrial Media Procedures, Copyright Information Services, 1988.
A Copyright for Computer-Using Educators (tentative title), Copyright Information Services, 1989.

Contributor to education journals, *TechTrends,* and *PC Week.*

SIDELIGHTS: Esther R. Sinofsky told *CA:* "I feel that educators must be knowledgeable about the legal implications of their actions; hence my interest in copyright as it is applied to education. My book *A Copyright Primer for Educational and Industrial Media Producers* addresses in plain language some of the key legal and production issues which media producers who do not have an in-house attorney should know about. I especially try to focus my discussion on education-related incidents or how law suits might hold implications in the educational setting.

"I am always amazed by the range of questions I receive at conference sessions on copyright. We are slowly developing a better communication system among educators. Producers are also taking note of the questions and contributing to a growing dialogue. The trick is to prevent a reoccurence of the producer-educator impasse of the late 1970s."

* * *

SITWELL, Sacheverell 1897-1988

OBITUARY NOTICE—See index for *CA* sketch: Born November 15, 1897, in Scarborough, England; died October 1, 1988, near Towcester, Northamptonshire, England. Art critic, public servant, publisher, journalist, and author. Sitwell was the last of the famous writing Sitwell siblings who electrified the British literary and art scenes in the 1920s and 1930s. Along with his sister Edith and brother Osbert, Sitwell published the poetry magazine *Wing,* in addition to organizing art exhibitions, the most controversial of which was the 1919 Exhibition of Modern French Art introducing Pablo Picasso and Amedeo Modigliani to the British public. Although Sitwell received modest praise for his third poetry collection, the 1922 *Hundred and One Harlequins,* he sealed his reputation with his prose work *Southern Baroque Art,* published two years later. *German Baroque Art* and *British Architects and Craftsmen* followed. His other writings include the *Canons of Giant Art;* the biographies *Mozart* and *Life of Liszt; Far From My Home, Stories: Long and Short; The Homing of the Winds, and Other Passages in Prose; For Want of the Golden City; Sacheverell Sitwell's England;* and *An Indian Summer: One Hundred Recent Poems.* In addition, Sitwell wrote a column for the London *Sunday Times* in 1950 and served as a justice of the peace and as high sheriff of Northamptonshire.

OBITUARIES AND OTHER SOURCES:

BOOKS

Who's Who, 140th edition, St. Martin's, 1988.

PERIODICALS

Chicago Tribune, October 3, 1988.
Los Angeles Times, October 3, 1988.
New York Times, October 3, 1988.
Times (London), October 3, 1988.
Washington Post, October 6, 1988.

* * *

SKINNER, Jeffrey 1949-

PERSONAL: Born December 8, 1949, in Buffalo, N.Y.; son of Thomas F. (a businessman) and Doris Ann (Donhauser) Skinner; married Sarah Gorham (a poet), May 8, 1982; children: Laura Katherine, Bonnie Anne. *Education:* Rollins College, B.A., 1971; graduate study at University of Bridgeport, 1973-74; Columbia University, M.F.A., 1978.

ADDRESSES: Home—1637 Rosewood Ave., Louisville, Ky. 40204. *Office*—Department of English, University of Louisville, Louisville, Ky. 40292.

CAREER: University of Bridgeport, Bridgeport, Conn., lecturer in English, 1978-86; Salisbury State College, Salisbury, Md., assistant professor of English, 1986-88; University of Louisville, Louisville, Ky., assistant professor of English and creative writing, 1988—. Vice-president and general manager of Gleason Plant Security, Inc., 1978-86. Lecturer at Norwalk Community College, 1982; creative writing teacher to young people at Liberation House, 1982-83, and Center for Creative Youth, Wesleyan University, Middletown, Conn., 1986-88.

Adviser to World Prison Poetry Center, 1984-86; gives poetry readings at colleges and other institutions.

AWARDS, HONORS: Fellow at Indiana University Writers Conference, 1973, Colorado Writers Conference, 1975, and Provincetown Fine Arts Center, 1981-82; guest of MacDowell Colony and Yaddo, 1981; grants from Connecticut Commission on the Arts, 1983, Ingram Merrill Foundation, 1985, and Delaware State Arts Council; fellow of National Endowment for the Arts, 1987; Book Award from National Poetry Series, 1987, for *A Guide to Forgetting*.

WRITINGS:

Late Stars (poems), Wesleyan University Press, 1985.
A Guide to Forgetting (poems), Graywolf Press, 1988.

Also author of two-act play "The Last Time I Saw Richard." Work represented in anthologies, including *Anthology of Magazine Verse and Yearbook of American Poetry*, 1981 and 1984, and *Anthology of New England Poetry*. Contributor of more than fifty poems and reviews to magazines, including *Atlantic Monthly, Commonweal, Iowa Review, Nation, New Yorker, Paris Review*, and *Poetry*. Literary editor of *Small Press Book Review*.

WORK IN PROGRESS: The Company of Heaven; a novel; a high school creative writing textbook.

SIDELIGHTS: Jeffrey Skinner told *CA:* "I was a businessman for ten years, and I like to include that experience in my writing when possible; it's a way of life lived by many millions of people, but rarely addressed in our literature. I also write 'form' poetry—sonnets, sestinas, villanelles, etc.—and I find the effort to simultaneously satisfy the demands of form while still speaking in a twentieth-century voice challenging and, oddly, liberating.

"I want, at bottom, to address directly and without sentimentality the issues that have always been most important to us as humans—love, death, family, and the dimensions of our spiritual selves, an area sadly ignored or treated by our culture as yet another commodity to be acquired and flaunted."

*   *   *

SKUTSCH, Otto   1906-

PERSONAL: Born December 6, 1906, in Breslau, Germany; son of Franz (a professor of Latin) and Selma (Dorff) Skutsch; married Gillian Mary Stewart, December 19, 1938; children: John Charles, Elizabeth, Margaret, Ann Catharine. *Education:* Attended University of Breslau, University of Kiel, University of Berlin, and University of Goettingen, 1925-32, D.Phil., 1934. *Religion:* Protestant.

ADDRESSES: Home—3 Wild Hatch, London NW11 7LD, England.

CAREER: Thesaurus Linguae Latinae, Munich, Germany, assistant, 1932; Queen's University, Belfast, Northern Ireland, senior assistant in Latin, 1938; Victoria University of Manchester, Manchester, England, assistant lecturer, 1939-46, lecturer in classics, 1946-49, senior lecturer in Latin, 1949-51; University of London, University College London, London, England, professor of Latin, 1951-72, professor emeritus, 1972—. Guest professor at Harvard University, 1958; guest member of Institute for Advanced Study, Princeton, N.J., 1963, 1968, and 1974; Mellon visiting professor at University of Pittsburgh, 1972-73 and 1981.

MEMBER: British Academy (honorary fellow), Society for the Promotion of Roman Studies (vice-president), Kungliga Vetenskaps-och Vitterhets-Samhaellet i Goeteborg (foreign member).

AWARDS, HONORS: Loeb fellow at Harvard University, 1973; D.Litt. from University of Padua, 1986, and University of St. Andrews, 1987.

WRITINGS:

Prosodische und metrische Gesetze der Iambenkuerzung (title means "Prosodic and Metrical Laws of Iamb Shortening"), Vandenhoeck & Ruprecht, 1934.
Alfred Edward Housman, 1859-1936, Athlone Press, 1959.
Studia Enniana (title means "Studies in Ennius"), Athlone Press, 1968.
(Editor) *The Annals of Q. Ennius: Text and Commentary*, Clarendon Press, 1985, corrected edition, 1986.

Contributor to classical journals in the United States, Denmark, England, France, Germany, Holland, and Italy.

WORK IN PROGRESS: "Bits and pieces."

SIDELIGHTS: Otto Skutsch told *CA:* "I publish the highly specialized results of research for the benefit of other scholars in my field. When Clarendon Press wanted an edition of and commentary on Ennius's *Annals*, I gladly accepted their offer, mainly because I knew that the task would be fascinating, but also because my father had done important work on Ennius. Born in 239 B.C., Ennius, known as 'the father of Latin poetry,' was the most important of the Latin poets. His *Annals* is an epic poem telling the history of Rome from its mythical beginnings to his own day. To write it, he adopted the Greek dactylic hexameter and adapted it to the requirements of the Latin language. The work survives in minute fragments, and their interpretation and arrangement pose many problems."

*   *   *

SLATER, Niall W.   1954-

PERSONAL: Born August 19, 1954, in Massillon, Ohio; son of John Eick (a teacher) and Thelma (a teacher; maiden name, Tourney) Slater. *Education:* College of Wooster, B.A. (with honors), 1976; Princeton University, M.A., 1978, Ph.D., 1981; graduate study at American School of Classical Studies at Athens, 1979-80. *Religion:* Lutheran.

ADDRESSES: Office—Department of Classics, University of Southern California, Los Angeles, Calif. 90089-0352.

CAREER: Concordia College, Moorhead, Minn., assistant professor of classics, 1981-82; University of Southern California, Los Angeles, assistant professor, 1982-87, associate professor of classics, 1987—.

MEMBER: Archaeological Institute of America, American Philological Association, Petronian Society, Women's Classical Caucus, Phi Beta Kappa.

AWARDS, HONORS: Fellow of American Council of Learned Societies, 1984-85; junior fellow at Center for Hellenic Studies, 1987-88; Alexander von Humboldt fellow at University of Konstanz, 1988-89.

WRITINGS:

Plautus in Performance: The Theatre of the Mind, Princeton University Press, 1985.

Contributor to classical studies and philology journals.

WORK IN PROGRESS: Reading Petronius, a book about Roman author Gaius Petronius's *Satyricon.*

SIDELIGHTS: Niall W. Slater told *CA:* "My principal interest is in performance criticism of ancient drama. I have also excavated at Pella, Jordan, with the Wooster/Sydney expedition."

BIOGRAPHICAL/CRITICAL SOURCES:

PERIODICALS

Times Literary Supplement, July 12, 1985.

*　　*　　*

SLATIN, John M.   1952-

PERSONAL: Born December 9, 1952, in Buffalo, N.Y.; son of Myles (a professor of English) and Diana (an artist; maiden name, Bluestein) Slatin; married Deborah Anne Carroll (a management consultant), March, 1984; children: Ledia, Mason. *Education:* University of Michigan, B.A., 1973; Johns Hopkins University, M.A., 1976, Ph.D., 1979.

ADDRESSES: Home—Austin, Tex. *Office*—Department of English, University of Texas at Austin, Austin, Tex. 78712.

CAREER: University of Texas at Austin, associate professor of English, 1979—.

WRITINGS:

The Savage's Romance: The Poetry of Marianne Moore, Pennsylvania State University Press, 1986.
(Contributor) Helen Vendler, editor, *Voices and Visions: The Poet in America,* Random House, 1987.
(Contributor) Patricia C. Willis, editor, *Marianne Moore: Woman and Poet,* National Poetry Foundation, 1987.
(Contributor) Ed Barrett, editor, *Text, Context, and Hypertext,* MIT Press, 1988.

Contributor to literature journals and literary magazines, including *William Carlos Williams Review.*

WORK IN PROGRESS: The Imagination of Blindness: Essays on Blindness in Literature and Society; a book on computers, literature, and the humanities.

*　　*　　*

SLOCUM, Milton Jonathan   1905-

PERSONAL: Surname originally Rosenberg; surname legally changed c. 1929; born November 7, 1905, in Clifton Forge, Va.; son of Joseph LaBau-Slochum (an entrepreneur) and Effie Helen (a homemaker; maiden name, Kanter) Rosenberg; married Belle Gibralter (a weaver, rug maker, and homemaker), November 29, 1929; children: Susan Hope Slocum Hinerfeld. *Education:* New York University, B.S., 1928; New York Medical College, M.D., 1932. *Politics:* Independent. *Religion:* Hebrew.

ADDRESSES: Home and office—371 24th St., Santa Monica, Calif. 90402. *Agent*—Susan Slocum Hinerfeld, 131 Cliffwood Ave., Los Angeles, Calif. 90049.

CAREER: Licensed to practice medicine in New York, 1932, in Nevada, 1946, and in California, 1966; general practice of medicine in New York, N.Y., 1934-68, and in Santa Monica, Calif., 1968-82; writer. Reporter for the *Brooklyn Daily Ea-*

gle, Brooklyn, N.Y., 1924-28, and the *Jersey Journal,* Jersey City, N.J., 1928-30; free-lance correspondent for Paris edition of the *New York Herald* and other New York newspapers; clinical instructor in medicine at New York Medical College, 1938-1962; consultant to Southern California Research Laboratory, 1986. *Military service:* U.S. Naval Reserve, 1943-46; served as lieutenant commander on active duty; became commander on inactive duty.

MEMBER: New York County Medical Society, Plato Society of University of California at Los Angeles (life member), Phi Delta Epsilon (life member).

WRITINGS:

Manhattan Country Doctor, Scribner, 1986.

Contributor of poetry and articles to periodicals, including *Omni.*

WORK IN PROGRESS: Two books, titled *Growing Up in Virginia* and *Invasion Physician.*

SIDELIGHTS: In his book *Manhattan Country Doctor,* Milton Jonathan Slocum offers his readers a glimpse into the world of his general medical practice in Hell's Kitchen, one of the poorest, most notorious sections of Manhattan, from 1934 to 1968. With limited resources and technology, the doctor faced a bizarre cast of characters ranging from mobsters and prostitutes to the mentally ill. Several critics note that Slocum's clear and direct writing style make his autobiographical work read like fiction. Irvin Faust, writer for the *New York Times Book Review,* commented that "the doctor has a deadpan humanism that allows the story to tell itself, no small achievement for the first-time author."

Slocum told *CA:* "Everybody is and has a story. I write only about people, what happens to them, and what they cause to happen to one another."

BIOGRAPHICAL/CRITICAL SOURCES:

PERIODICALS

Los Angeles Times Book Review, March 1, 1987.
Newsday, November 30, 1986.
New York Times Book Review, December 7, 1986.
Washington Post, December 17, 1986.

[Sketch verified by daughter, Susan Hope Slocum Hinerfeld.]

*　　*　　*

SMEETON, Miles (Richard)   1906-1988

OBITUARY NOTICE—See index for *CA* sketch: Born March 5, 1906, in North Yorkshire, England; died September 23, 1988. Military serviceman, conservationist, farmer, yachtsman, and author. Smeeton enlisted in the British Army in 1925 and served in India and Egypt during World War II. When he retired in 1947 Smeeton and his wife, Beryl, purchased a farm in Canada, but they later returned to England, bought a boat, and devoted the next twenty years to sailing around the world. Their journeys included voyages from England to Vancouver via the Panama Canal; from Vancouver to Australia; from Australia to Chile; up the American Pacific coast to the Arctic Circle; and a 3,774-mile trip from Singapore to Japan. In addition to writing numerous 1960s travelogues based on his voyages, Smeeton described his sailing adventures in *Once is Enough, Sunrise to Windward,* and *Because the Horn is There.* His other works include *A Taste of the Hills, A Change of*

Jungles, and The Misty Islands. In 1968 he bought land in Calgary, Alberta, and founded the Wild Life Reserve of Western Canada.

OBITUARIES AND OTHER SOURCES:

BOOKS

The Oxford Companion to Ships and the Sea, Oxford University Press, 1976.

PERIODICALS

Times (London), September 30, 1988.

*   *   *

SMITH, C. Ray   1929-1988

OBITUARY NOTICE—See index for CA sketch: Born March 3, 1929, in Birmingham, Ala.; died of a heart attack, August 18, 1988, in New York, N.Y. Educator, arts patron, editor, and author. Smith was an authority on architecture and design. His career included stints as editor of the publications Theatre Crafts and Interiors and as teacher at schools such as the Parsons Institute and the Fashion Institute of Technology. He was also an arts devotee, and in the mid-1970s he served as managing editor of the Aston Magna Foundation for Music. Among his writings are Supermannerism: New Attitudes in Post-Modern Architecture, The Wood Chair in America, Interior Design in the Twentieth Century, and Interior Design in Twentieth-Century America: A History. In addition, Smith edited several volumes on theater crafts.

OBITUARIES AND OTHER SOURCES:

BOOKS

Who's Who in America, 45th edition, Marquis, 1988.

PERIODICALS

New York Times, August 20, 1988.

*   *   *

SMITH, Mary Ann   1934-

PERSONAL: Born August 4, 1934, in Charlotte, N.C.; daughter of Charles S. (a textile executive) and Elma (a housewife; maiden name, Parrish) Clegg; divorced; children: Stephen L. Smith, David W. Smith. Education: Attended Duke University, 1951-53; Rhode Island School of Design, B.F.A., 1956; University of North Carolina at Chapel Hill, M.A., 1968; Pennsylvania State University, Ph.D., 1974.

ADDRESSES: Home—Fayetteville, N.Y. Office—School of Architecture, 103 Slocum Hall, Syracuse University, Syracuse, N.Y. 13244.

CAREER: University of South Carolina, Columbia, instructor in art history, 1968-70; Syracuse University, Syracuse, N.Y., assistant professor, 1974-78, associate professor, 1978-82, professor of architectural history and preservation, 1982—. Member of board of directors of Syracuse Preservation Board, 1981-84; chairman of Fayetteville Historical Review Commission, 1987-88.

MEMBER: Society of Architectural Historians, National Trust for Historic Preservation, Preservation League of New York State, Preservation Association of Central New York, Landmarks Association of Central New York (member of board of directors, 1980-84).

AWARDS, HONORS: John Ben Snow Prize from Syracuse University Press, 1983, and certificate of merit from Regional Council of Historical Agencies, both for Gustav Stickley, the Craftsman.

WRITINGS:

Gustav Stickley, the Craftsman, Syracuse University Press, 1983.

Contributor to art, craft, and preservation journals.

WORK IN PROGRESS: James Street, Syracuse, a book on the houses and social history of Syracuse from 1830 to 1930, completion expected in 1989.

SIDELIGHTS: Mary Ann Smith told CA: "I began the research that resulted in Gustav Stickley, the Craftsman because I wanted to learn more about him. I admired the simple, wholesome lifestyle he advocated and the physical environment in which it would take place. Since Stickley started out in Syracuse, I was also on the spot where his ideas evolved.

"My research on James Street and Syracuse architecture will culminate in a complete history of nineteenth-century architecture as the development of the city took place. I am interested in the connections between society and its architecture. I am also involved in preservation and have recently rehabilitated a local historic property."

*   *   *

SMOLUCHOWSKI, Louise   1922-

PERSONAL: Surname sounds like "small house key"; born September 25, 1922, in Washington, D.C.; daughter of Charles Edward (in U.S. Navy Medical Corps) and Louise (Pugh) Riggs; married Roman Smoluchowski (a professor of astronomy), February 3, 1951; children: Peter, Irena. Education: Attended private high school for girls in Washington, D.C. Politics: Democrat. Religion: "Nothing formal."

ADDRESSES: Home—1401 Ethridge St., Austin, Tex. 78703.

CAREER: Club worker for American Red Cross, 1945-46; Museum of Modern Art, New York, N.Y., in public relations department, 1946-47; volunteer for presidential candidate Adlai Stevenson, 1951-60; mathematics teacher in Miss Mason's preschool and primary school, 1961-67; homemaker, 1967-78; writer, 1978—.

WRITINGS:

Lev and Sonya: The Story of the Tolstoy Marriage, Putnam, 1987.

WORK IN PROGRESS: Research for another biography.

SIDELIGHTS: Louise Smoluchowski told CA: "My interests are British literature, particularly of the nineteenth and twentieth centuries, and nineteenth-century Russian literature. The motivation to write my one book was to give a fairer view of the Tolstoys' marriage. The most popular biographies of Tolstoy pictured him as an extremely difficult husband and his wife as hysterical and shrewish. These opinions were largely based on the books by the Tolstoys' youngest daughter, Aleksandra, who resented her mother and left an unkind portrait of her. I began translating the Tolstoys' diaries when I moved to Texas in 1978 as a present for a friend, but when I discovered from the diaries such a different and more positive view of the marriage I felt impelled to write a book to correct the popular impression."

BIOGRAPHICAL/CRITICAL SOURCES:

PERIODICALS

New York Times, July 4, 1987.

*   *   *

SNYDER, Don J.   1950-

PERSONAL: Born August 11, 1950, in Lansdale, Pa.; son of Richard (a pastor) and Peggy (Schwartz) Snyder; married Colleen McQuinn, December 14, 1985; children: Erin, Nell. *Education:* Colby College, B.A., 1972; University of Iowa, M.F.A., 1986.

ADDRESSES: Home—Hancock Point, Maine 04640. *Agent*—Victoria Pryor, 221 West 82nd St., New York, N.Y. 10024.

CAREER: Free-lance writer, 1972—. Writer in residence at Colby College, 1986; president, principal fundraiser, and planner for Maine Charitable Foundation (organization for improving quality of life of families with terminally ill children).

AWARDS, HONORS: James A. Michener fellowship from the Copernicus Society of America and James A. Michener, 1986.

WRITINGS:

Veterans Park (novel), F. Watts, 1987.
A Soldier's Disgrace (nonfiction), Yankee Books, 1987.
From the Point (novel), F. Watts, 1988.

Contributor of articles and stories to magazines and newspapers, including *Yankee, Reader's Digest, Saturday Evening Post,* and *NorthEast.* Editor of *Bar Harbor Times,* 1978.

WORK IN PROGRESS: Eventide, a novel "dealing with acts of betrayal among friends and family," publication by F. Watts expected in 1991.

SIDELIGHTS: Don Snyder's book *A Soldier's Disgrace* is the story of Ronald Alley, a U.S. Army major who was captured in Korea in 1950. Alley survived three years as a prisoner of war, then returned to the United States, only to be court-martialed and convicted of collaboration with the enemy. He became the only American military officer to be imprisoned for such a crime in this century, even though hundreds of other military personnel conducted themselves as he did, trading bits of noncrucial intelligence information for the lives of other prisoners. According to reporter Patrick Reardon in the *Chicago Tribune,* Alley approached journalist Don Snyder for help in clearing his name of the charges but died of a heart attack before any action could be taken. Reardon wrote: "Almost against his will, Snyder took up the search for truth that, for four years, became the obsession of his life." With the assistance of Alley's widow, Snyder tried to have the major's conviction overturned; *A Soldier's Disgrace* describes Alley's ordeal as well as Snyder's efforts on his behalf.

Snyder told *CA:* "My only aspiration as a writer is to drive a wedge against the world's greed and indifference. All of my novels and my nonfiction book are about people who try to live decent lives, believe in good things, and then wake up one morning to discover that *nothing* is the way they thought it was.

"My only interests beyond my world of fiction are the Maine Charitable Foundation, my wife and daughters, and sailing. I want my books to provide me with a way to take care of people less fortunate than I."

BIOGRAPHICAL/CRITICAL SOURCES:

PERIODICALS

Chicago Tribune, September 29, 1987.
Los Angeles Times Book Review, September 27, 1987.

*   *   *

SOBOSAN, Jeffrey G.   1946-

PERSONAL: Born March 30, 1946, in Chicago, Ill.; son of John (an executive) and Louise (a housewife; maiden name, Maurier) Sobosan. *Education:* University of Notre Dame, A.B., 1969, M.Th., 1972; Graduate Theological Union, Berkeley, Calif., Th.D., 1977.

ADDRESSES: Office—Department of Theology, University of Portland, 5000 North Willamette Blvd., Portland, Ore. 97203.

CAREER: Entered Congregatio a Sancta Cruce (Fathers and Brothers of the Holy Cross; C.S.C.), 1962, ordained Roman Catholic priest, 1973; University of Portland, Portland, Ore., assistant professor, 1978-84, associate professor of theology, 1984—.

WRITINGS:

The Tapestry of Faith, Alba House, 1976.
Act of Contrition, Ave Maria Press, 1979.
The Ascent to God: Faith as Art, Risk, and Humor, Thomas More Press, 1981.
Guilt and the Christian: A New Perspective, Thomas More Press, 1982.
Christian Commitment and Prophetic Living, Twenty-Third, 1986.

Contributor of approximately ninety articles to scholarly journals and popular magazines.

*   *   *

SOLOMON, Samuel   1904-1988
(Britindian, Melusa Moolson)

OBITUARY NOTICE—See index for *CA* sketch: Born September 20, 1904, in Calcutta, India; died July 2, 1988. Civil servant, political candidate, lecturer, translator, editor, and author. Solomon was involved in a wide variety of endeavors throughout his life. After studying at Cambridge University in the 1920s, he returned to his native India and held various judicial posts within the Indian Civil Service, including judge and magistrate. In 1947, after twenty years of civil work, he began devoting himself more fully to literature by both translating and writing. He also ran for Parliament in 1959 and 1964. Solomon's books include *Poems From East and West, The Saint and Satan,* which he wrote under the pseudonym Melusa Moolson, *The Dying Rajput and Other Poems, The Causes and Solution of India's Communal Problem,* which he wrote under the pseudonym Britindian, and *Garden at Hazaribagh.* He also translated and edited collections of works by many European masters, including Jean Racine, Heinrich Heine, and Franz Grillparzer.

OBITUARIES AND OTHER SOURCES:

BOOKS

International Authors and Writers Who's Who, 10th edition, International Biographical Centre, 1986.
Who's Who in the World, 5th edition, Marquis, 1980.

The Writers Directory: 1988-1990, St. James Press, 1988.

PERIODICALS

Times (London), July 9, 1988.

*   *   *

SOMMERS, Lawrence M(elvin)   1919-

PERSONAL: Born April 17, 1919, in Clinton, Wis.; son of Emil L. (a farmer) and Inga (a homemaker; maiden name, Anderson) Sommers; married Marjorie Smith (a geographer), April 26, 1948; children: Laurie Kay. *Education:* University of Wisconson, B.S., 1942, Ph.M., 1946; Northwestern University, Ph.D., 1950.

ADDRESSES: Home—4292 Tacoma Blvd., Okemos, Mich. 48864. *Office*—Department of Geography, Michigan State University, East Lansing, Mich. 48824.

CAREER: Michigan State University, East Lansing, began as instructor, became associate professor, 1949-55, professor of geography, 1955—, chairman of department, 1955-79, assistant dean of International Programs, 1983-85, acting assistant provost, 1987-88. Chairman of steering committee, Michigan State University Academic Council, 1981-84; member of Michigan State University Graduate council. *Military service:* U.S. Army, 1942-45.

MEMBER: American Geographical Society, Association of American Geographers (executive council, 1967-70; chairman, constitution service, 1970-77), National Council for Geographic Education (executive board, 1967-70), American Scandinavian Foundation, Scandinavian Studies Association, Michigan Academy of Science, Arts and Letters, Phi Kappa Phi (president, Michigan State University chapter, 1980-82, vice-president, north-central region, 1986-89), Sigma Xi (president, Michigan State University chapter, 1959-60).

AWARDS, HONORS: Grants for research in Norway from Social Science Research Council and American-Scandinavian Foundation, 1948, and in Denmark from Office of Naval Research, 1953; travel grants to Europe, 1960, 1982, 1984, 1986.

WRITINGS:

(Editor with Fred E. Dohrs) *Outside Readings in Geography*, T. Y. Crowell, 1955.
(Editor with Dohrs) *Introduction to Geography*, T. Y. Crowell, 1967.
(Compiler with Dohrs) *Physical Geography*, T. Y. Crowell, 1967.
(Compiler with Dohrs) *Cultural Geography*, T. Y. Crowell, 1967.
(Compiler with Dohrs) *Economic Geography*, T. Y. Crowell, 1970.
(With Dohrs) *World Regional Geography: A Problem Approach*, West Publishing, 1976.
(Editor) *Atlas of Michigan*, Michigan State University Press, 1977.
(With others) *Energy and the Adaptation of Human Settlements*, Michigan State University Press, 1980.
(Editor with John F. Lounsbury and Edward A. Fernald) *Land Use: A Spatial Approach*, Kendall/Hunt, 1981.
Michigan: A Geography, Westview, 1984.

WORK IN PROGRESS: Regional Development Issues in Norway, Spatial Impacts of Norwegian Oil and Gas Exploitation, and *The World Is Not Like Us*.

SIDELIGHTS: Lawrence M. Sommers told *CA:* "My writing is based on the conviction that there is a great need to eliminate geographical ignorance among young people in the United States. This nation and its people must be able to compete in an increasingly independent world."

AVOCATIONAL INTERESTS: The geography of Norway, gardening, bulb growing.

*   *   *

SORIA, Regina   1911-

PERSONAL: Born March 17, 1911, in Rome, Italy; immigrated to United States, 1940, naturalized citizen, 1946; daughter of Angelo Levi Bianchini (a naval commander) and Marcella Levi; married Dino Charles Philip Soria, January 12, 1936 (deceased). *Education:* University of Rome, Litt.D., 1933; University of London, English proficiency certificate, 1933.

ADDRESSES: Home—4000 North Charles St., Apt. 805, Baltimore, Md. 21218.

CAREER: College of Notre Dame, Baltimore, Md., instructor, 1942-50, assistant professor, 1950-61, professor of foreign languages, 1961-76, professor emeritus, 1976—. Instructor at McCoy College, 1950-52; Archives of American Art, field researcher, 1960-63, archivist in Rome, Italy, 1963-64.

MEMBER: Modern Language Association of America, American Association of Teachers of Italian, American Italian Historical Association.

AWARDS, HONORS: Cavaliere al merito della Repubblica Italiana, 1986.

WRITINGS:

Elihu Vedder: American Visionary Artist in Rome, 1836-1923, with catalogue raisonne, Fairleigh Dickinson University Press, 1970.
(Author of introduction) Joshua C. Taylor, Jane Dillenberger, and Richard Murray, editors, *Perceptions and Evocations: The Art of Elihu Vedder*, Smithsonian Institution Press, 1979.
The Dictionary of Nineteenth-Century American Artists in Italy, 1760-1914, Fairleigh Dickinson University Press, 1982.

Contributor to periodicals, including *Journal of Aesthetics and Art Criticism*, *Art Quarterly*, and *American Quarterly*.

WORK IN PROGRESS: Dictionary of American Artists of Italian Heritage, 1776-1945, publication expected in 1991.

SIDELIGHTS: Regina Soria told *CA:* "I am interested in the relationship between Italy and the United States, the influence of Italy on American art, and the history of the Italian immigrant artists and their fortunes before World War II. These subjects have gained in popularity since I started studying them about thirty years ago, and my research on American artists in Italy in the nineteenth century has evinced a gratifying interest in younger scholars and museums."

BIOGRAPHICAL/CRITICAL SOURCES:

PERIODICALS

Italica, autumn, 1983.
Times Literary Supplement, November 12, 1982.

SPELLMAN, Roger G.
  See COX, William R(obert)

*   *   *

SPELVIN, George
  See PHILLIPS, David Atlee

*   *   *

SPERBER, A(nn) M.

PERSONAL: Born in Vienna, Austria; daughter of Fred (a lawyer) and Liselotte (an actress; maiden name, Suess) Sperber. *Education:* Attended Julliard School of Music, 1947-52; Barnard College, B.A., 1956.

ADDRESSES: Home—New York, N.Y. *Agent*—William Morris Agency, 1350 Avenue of the Americas, New York, N.Y. 10019.

CAREER: G. P. Putnam's Sons, New York, N.Y., senior editor, 1963-68; McGraw-Hill Book Co., New York, N.Y., senior editor, 1968-70; writer, c. 1974—. Consultant to Alfred A. Knopf, Inc.; member of the executive council of the New York City Opera Guild (past president), and of the board of managers of the Women's National Book Association, 1969.

MEMBER: Authors Guild.

AWARDS, HONORS: Fulbright fellow at Freie Universitaet Berlin, West Berlin, 1956-57; *Murrow: His Life and Times* was named a 1986 Notable Book of the Year by the *New York Times*.

WRITINGS:

Murrow: His Life and Times (Book-of-the-Month Club selection), Freundlich Books, 1986.

Contributor of articles and reviews to newspapers and periodicals, including *New York Newsday, New York Times Book Review, Opera News,* and the *American Record Guide.*

WORK IN PROGRESS: A biography, as yet untitled.

SIDELIGHTS: A former editor of children's books, A. M. Sperber originally planned to write a biography of Edward R. Murrow, the broadcast journalism pioneer, for the children's literary market. Her initial draft of the book grew into almost eight hundred pages of adult prose, however, and took thirteen years to complete.

Sperber's fascination with Murrow began in 1954 when she first saw the now infamous showing of his documentary "See It Now," which marked the ruin of Joseph R. McCarthy, the U.S. senator known for his excessive anticommunist activities during the 1950s. She was captivated by Murrow's distinctive personality, presence, and the artful power of manipulation which he displayed in allowing Joseph McCarthy to condemn himself with his own obsessive words on the live broadcast of "See It Now." Sperber told *New York Times Book Review* writer George Stevens, Jr., that seeing a broadcast of Murrow's program again in 1971 made her want "all of a sudden to know all about [Murrow]."

Sperber's undertaking reveals a deep sense of dedication to her subject with the finished work resembling nothing less than what Stevens called a glimpse "into [Murrow's] soul." Utilizing previously untapped resources, including files from the Columbia Broadcasting System, the Federal Bureau of Inves-

tigation, the British Broadcasting Corporation, the U.S. Information Agency, the White House, Murrow's widow, Janet Brewster Murrow, and over 150 interviews, Sperber created *Murrow: His Life and Times,* a biography that Stevens described as "a delicately shaded portrait of a man, not a saint." In it, she explores the public and private triumphs and disappointments of "a conservative farm boy with a sense of justice."

While some critics felt that the author sacrificed an analysis of pertinent issues for an exhaustive enumeration of extraneous details, others suggested that Sperber's approach was, in fact, a stylistic mirror reflecting the intangibility of Murrow's character. Jack Lessenberry of the *Detroit News* contended that "the book succeeds in part by failing" and added that Murrow "would have liked the idea of remaining something of an enigma." The book-buying public seemed pleased with Sperber's account, keeping *Murrow* on the *New York Times* bestseller list for ten weeks. Even those critics who thought that the book was inordinately long and circumstantial admit that its author has rendered an honest and compelling portrait of the man. Those who gave it rave reviews, however, went so far as to call it a biography truly worthy of both Murrow and his time.

Sperber told *CA:* "Writing *Murrow: His Life and Times* brought all of my interests together: history, the mass media, specifically journalism, a chance to look backstage, deep into the doings of the generation that shaped my generation, and a chance to read up on my idol. Murrow was the leader of the great reporting team that we remembered as our heroes in the great days of radio and television. It took almost thirteen years to write the book and was worth every minute."

BIOGRAPHICAL/CRITICAL SOURCES:

PERIODICALS

Detroit News, July 6, 1986.
Newsweek, June 23, 1986.
New York Times, July 2, 1986.
New York Times Book Review, July 6, 1986.
Time, June 9, 1986.

*   *   *

SPERLING, Milton M.   1912-1988

OBITUARY NOTICE: Born July 6, 1912, in New York, N.Y.; died after a long illness, August 26, 1988, in Beverly Hills, Calif. Film producer and screenwriter. Active in the American film industry for more than fifty years, Sperling was known for his writing and producing contributions to such films as "The Bramble Bush" and "Battle of the Bulge." Beginning his career as a messenger boy and shipping clerk for Paramount in Long Island, New York, the fledgling producer later moved to Hollywood and worked as a secretary to prominent producers at Twentieth Century-Fox. He became an associate producer for Edward Small Productions before collaborating on his first screenplay, "Sing Baby Sing," at the age of twenty-four. Sperling went on to produce such films as "Distant Drums" and "Captain Apache," and in 1955 the screenplay for "The Court Martial of Billy Mitchell," which he coauthored, was nominated for an Academy Award. In addition, Sperling was a founding member of the Writers Guild of America and the founder of United States Pictures, an independent production company.

OBITUARIES AND OTHER SOURCES:

BOOKS

International Motion Picture Almanac, Quigley, 1988.
Who's Who in World Jewry: A Biographical Dictionary of Outstanding Jews, Olive Books of Israel, 1978.
The World Encyclopedia of Film, A. & W. Visual Library, 1972.

PERIODICALS

Chicago Tribune, August 29, 1988.
Los Angeles Times, August 30, 1988.

*   *   *

STAMEY, Sara (Lucinda)   1953-

PERSONAL: Born January 23, 1953, in Bellingham, Wash.; daughter of H. Neil (a machinist) and Helen (a nurse; maiden name, Weihe) Stamey; married Jesse Berst, February, 1976 (divorced, 1979). *Education:* Attended University of Puget Sound, 1971-73; Western Washington University, B.A. (magna cum laude), 1981, graduate study, 1988—.

ADDRESSES: Home and office—324 North State St., No. 1, Bellingham, Wash. 98225. *Agent*—Merilee Heifetz, Writer's House, 21 West 26th St., New York, N.Y. 10010.

CAREER: Nuclear reactor control operator in Hanford, Wash., and San Onofre, Calif., 1974-78; scuba diving instructor in the Mediterranean, the Virgin Islands, and Honduras, 1982-87; writer, 1987—. Teacher of English composition.

MEMBER: Science Fiction Writers of America, Pacific Northwest Writers Conference.

WRITINGS:

Wild Card Run (science fiction novel), Berkley Publishing, 1987.
Win, Lose, Draw (science fiction novel), Berkley Publishing, 1988.
Double Blind (science fiction novel), Berkley Publishing, 1989.

WORK IN PROGRESS: Krysta, a science fiction novel set in the Mediterranean of the twenty-first century; *Islands,* a mainstream novel set in the Caribbean.

SIDELIGHTS: Sara Stamey told *CA:* "My work with nuclear engineers and other scientists stimulated my latent interest in writing science fiction. My more recent travels to teach scuba diving have provided the inspiration for stories and research on such diverse topics as Mayan history, the Vaudun, geology, and lasers. At present, I am completing the graduate program in professional writing at Western Washington University and teaching English composition.

"My books generally reflect an interest in balance—balancing an active lifestyle with intellectual interests, balancing demands of heart and mind, and balancing technological advance with quality of life. My "Ruth" science fiction series transforms into fictional conflicts such experiences as my work in the exciting but daunting nuclear industry, my concern about the logging of old-growth timber in the Northwest, and the magic of diving on the beautiful, fragile coral reefs of the Caribbean."

AVOCATIONAL INTERESTS: Hiking, bicycling, tennis, playing classical piano.

STAMP, Robert M(iles)   1937-

PERSONAL: Born February 11, 1937, in Toronto, Ontario, Canada. *Education:* University of Western Ontario, B.A., 1959, Ph.D., 1970; University of Toronto, M.A., 1962.

ADDRESSES: Home—Toronto, Ontario, Canada. *Office*—Heritage Books, 866 Palmerston Ave., Toronto, Ontario, Canada. *Agent*—c/o Publicity Director, Fitzhenry & Whiteside, Ltd., 195 Allstate Pkwy., Markham, Ontario L3R 4T8, Canada.

CAREER: University of Western Ontario, London, Ontario, assistant professor of history of education, 1965-69; University of Calgary, Calgary, Alberta, professor of educational foundations and Canadian studies, 1969-83; Heritage Books, Toronto, Ontario, proprietor, 1983—.

WRITINGS:

NONFICTION

School Days: A Century of Memories, McClelland & Stewart, 1975.
About Schools: What Every Canadian Parent Should Know, New Press, 1975.
(Editor with David C. Jones and Nancy M. Sheehan) *Shaping the Schools of the Canadian West,* Detselig, 1979.
The Schools of Ontario, 1876-1976, University of Toronto Press, 1982.
The World of Tomorrow: A View of Canada in 1939, Fitzhenry & Whiteside, 1985.
Kings, Queens, and Canadians, Fitzhenry & Whiteside, 1987.
The Queen Elizabeth Way: Canada's First Superhighway, Boston Mills Press, 1987.
Royal Rebels: Princess Louise and the Marquis of Lorne, Dundurn Press, 1988.
Riding the Radials: Toronto's Suburban Streetcar Lines, Boston Mills Press, 1989.
The Canadian Obituary Record for 1988, Dundurn Press, 1989.

BIOGRAPHICAL/CRITICAL SOURCES:

PERIODICALS

Globe and Mail (Toronto), April 16, 1988.

*   *   *

STERN, Steve   1947-

BRIEF ENTRY: Born December 21, 1947, in Memphis, Tenn. American educator and author. Stern is known primarily as a Southern Jewish writer, but told Bruce Weber of the *New York Times Book Review* that he dislikes that label. Nonetheless, he added, "if there's anything that made my being Southern and Jewish necessary and important to my fiction, it's that the combination of the two serves to provide a sense of community." Judged a "prodigiously talented writer" by *New York Times Book Review* contributor Morris Dickstein, Stern is best known for his two prize-winning collections of short stories. Winner of the 1983 Pushcart Writer's Choice award, *Isaac and the Undertaker's Daughter* (Lost Roads, 1983) is a collection featuring his 1981 O. Henry award-winning short story of the same name. His next volume, *Lazar Malkin Enters Heaven* (Viking, 1986), won the 1987 Edward Lewis Wallant award. Stern also wrote a novel, *The Moon and Ruben Shein* (August House, 1984). He was a visiting lecturer at Memphis College of Art and at the University of Wisconsin, and is a lecturer at Skidmore College. His more recent works have been for children and include *Mickey and the Golem* (St. Luke's

Press, 1986) and *Hershel and the Beast* (Ion Books, 1987). *Addresses: Home*—13 1/2 Jumel Place, Saratoga Springs, N.Y. 12866. *Office*—Skidmore College, Saratoga Springs, N.Y. 12866. *Agent*—Liz Darhansoff, 1220 Park Ave., New York, N.Y. 10028.

BIOGRAPHICAL/CRITICAL SOURCES:

PERIODICALS

Los Angeles Times Book Review, May 24, 1987.
New York Times Book Review, February 10, 1985, March 1, 1987.

*   *   *

STERNBERG, Robert J(effrey)   1949-

PERSONAL: Born December 8, 1949, in Newark, N.J.; son of Joseph and Lillian (Politzer) Sternberg; married; children: Seth, Sara. *Education:* Yale University, B.A. (summa cum laude, with exceptional distinction in psychology), 1972; Stanford University, Ph.D., 1975.

ADDRESSES: Home—105 Spruce Bank Rd., Hamden, Conn. 06518. *Office*—Department of Psychology, Yale University, Box 11A Yale Station, New Haven, Conn. 06520. *Agent*— John Brockman, 2307 Broadway, New York, N.Y. 10024.

CAREER: Yale University, Department of Psychology, New Haven, Conn., assistant professor, 1975-80, associate professor, 1980-83, professor of psychology and education, 1983-86, IBM Professor of Psychology and Education, 1986—. Has done research for the Office of Naval Research, the Army Research Institute, the National Institute of Education, and the Venezuelan Ministry for the Development of Intelligence. Member of Educational Testing Service Board of Visitors and of Social Science Research Council on Cognitive Development and Giftedness, both 1984—. Chairman of Selection Committee for American Psychological Association Early Career Award in Cognition, 1984. Guest on television program "Today Show."

MEMBER: National Association for Gifted Children, American Association for the Advancement of Science, American Educational Research Association, American Psychological Association (fellow), Society for Mathematical Psychology, Society for Philosophy and Psychology, Society for Research in Child Development, Merrill-Palmer Society, Society of Multivariate Experimental Psychology, Eastern Psychological Association, Sigma Xi, Phi Beta Kappa.

AWARDS, HONORS: Sidney Siegel Memorial Award from Stanford University, 1975; grants from the National Science Foundation, 1976-78, for "The Componential Analysis of Human Intelligence," and from the Spencer Foundation, 1982-84, for "Insight in the Gifted"; Distinguished Scientific Award for an Early Career Contribution to Psychology from the American Psychological Association, 1981; Boyd R. Mc-Candless Young Scientist Award from the American Psychological Association Division of Developmental Psychology, and Cattell Award from the Society of Multivariate Experimental Psychology, both 1982; named by *Science Digest* as one of "America's Top 100 Young Scientists," 1984; included in *Esquire* Register of Outstanding Young Men and Women, 1985; Research Review Award, 1986, and Distinguished Book Award, 1987, both from American Educational Research Association.

WRITINGS:

Barron's How to Prepare for the Miller Analogies Test (MAT), Barron's, 1974, 3rd and 4th editions published as *Barron's How to Prepare for the MAT Miller Analogies Test*, 1981 and 1986.
Intelligence, Information Processing, and Analogical Reasoning: The Componential Analysis of Human Abilities, Lawrence Erlbaum, 1977.
Beyond IQ: A Triarchic Theory of Human Intelligence, Cambridge University Press, 1985.
Intelligence Applied: Understanding and Increasing Your Intellectual Skills, Harcourt, 1986.
The Psychologist's Companion, 2nd edition, Cambridge University Press, 1988.
The Triarchic Mind, Viking, 1988.
The Triangle of Love, Basic Books, 1988.

EDITOR

(With Douglas K. Detterman) *Human Intelligence: Perspectives on Its Theory and Measurement*, Ablex Publishing, 1979.
(And contributor) *Advances in the Psychology of Human Intelligence*, four volumes, Lawrence Erlbaum, 1982-88.
(With Detterman; and contributor) *How and How Much Can Intelligence Be Increased*, Ablex Publishing, 1982.
(And contributor) *Handbook of Human Intelligence*, Cambridge University Press, 1982.
(And contributor) *Mechanisms of Cognitive Development*, W. H. Freeman, 1984.
(And contributor) *Human Abilities: An Information-Processing Approach*, W. H. Freeman, 1985.
(With Janet E. Davidson; and contributor) *Conceptions of Giftedness*, Cambridge University Press, 1986.
(With Detterman) *What Is Intelligence? Contemporary Viewpoints on Its Nature and Definition*, Ablex Publishing, 1986.
(With Richard K. Wagner) *Practical Intelligence: Nature and Origins of Competence in the Everyday World*, Cambridge University Press, 1986.
(With Ronna F. Dillon) *Cognition and Instruction*, Academic Press, 1986.
(With Joan Boykoff Baron) *Teaching Thinking Skills: Theory and Practice*, W. H. Freeman, 1987.
(And contributor) *The Nature of Creativity*, Cambridge University Press, 1988.
(With Michael L. Barnes) *The Psychology of Love*, Yale University Press, 1988.
(With Edward Smith) *The Psychology of Human Thought*, Cambridge University Press, 1988.

CONTRIBUTOR

Contributor to more than forty volumes, including *A Model for Intelligence*, edited by H. J. Eysenck; *Classroom Computers and Cognitive Science*, edited by A. C. Wilkinson; *The Development and Assessment of Human Competence*, edited by D. A. Wilkerson and E. W. Gordon; *Current Topics in Human Intelligence*, Volume I, edited by D. K. Detterman; *Arthur Jensen: Consensus and Controversy*, edited by Sohan and Celia Modgil; and *Test Design: Contributions From Psychology, Education, and Psychometrics*, edited by S. E. Embretson. Also contributor of hundreds of articles to numerous science and psychology journals, including *American Scientist, Psychology Today, Behavioral and Brain Sciences, Journal of Experimental Child Psychology*, and *Phi Delta Kappan*.

WORK IN PROGRESS: Research on "the nature of practical intelligence, the nature of love, creativity, teaching intelligence."

SIDELIGHTS: An award-winning professor of psychology and education at Yale University, Robert J. Sternberg is renowned for his pioneering work in the study of human intelligence. With the publication of his book *Beyond IQ* in 1985, he established an innovative three-part system for defining and measuring mental ability. The combined impact of his "triarchic theory of human intelligence" and Sternberg's related discoveries advanced the field of cognitive science and called for a re-evaluation of traditional methods, such as standardized tests, used in determining an individual's aptitude or intelligence quotient (IQ). Similarly, Sternberg developed a three-dimensional theory for analyzing human love, which he terms the "love triangle." His diligent research and writings in these areas of human development earned the psychologist widespread professional acclaim and public recognition, and in 1984 *Science Digest* included him among the top one hundred young scientists in the United States.

Sternberg's preoccupation with intelligence dates back to his childhood. Reminiscing about his performance in elementary school, he recalled to Robert J. Trotter in *Psychology Today:* "I really stunk on IQ tests. . . . I had severe test anxiety." A turning point came in the sixth grade when Sternberg had to retake the IQ exam for fifth-graders. Experiencing more confidence and less stress in the company of a "bunch of babies" who were a year younger than he, the twelve-year-old outperformed his initial testing. Commenting in a 1985 *Science Digest* article written by Signe Hammer, Sternberg reflected that "the absurdity of that situation helped me get over the test anxiety." Inspired by his breakthrough, the precocious student subsequently fashioned his own "Sternberg Test of Mental Ability," which he administered to classmates as part of a science project; in high school, he examined how various distractions affect individual performance on intelligence tests.

Sternberg continued to study intelligence after completing his secondary education. As a research assistant at the Psychological Corporation in New York and later at the Educational Testing Service in New Jersey, he spent his summers working alongside major designers of formal testing materials. In fact, Sternberg himself devised a system for categorizing the test items that appear on the Miller Analogies Test (MAT) while employed at the Psychological Corporation, which publishes the MAT. Later, as a graduate student at Stanford University, he was prompted by Barron's Educational Publishing Company to write a book on how to prepare for the test. Discouraged by the halt in progressive research on intelligence and yet eager for the opportunity to further his own study in that area, Sternberg agreed and wrote a doctoral dissertation that formed the basis of his first book, the 1974 *Barron's How to Prepare for the Miller Analogies Test (MAT)*.

Throughout the 1970s Sternberg's research focused on the analytical processes involved in taking intelligence tests. Consequently, his work included critical examinations of the kinds of mental exercises typically featured on such tests. Relating Sternberg's observations on his efforts, Trotter wrote, "His research gave a good account of what people did in their heads" to solve the problems "and also seemed to account for individual differences in IQ test performance." Encouraged by the results of these early studies, Sternberg established a "componential" theory of intelligence, in which he associates the various stages of information processing with specific func-

tions of the brain. At that point "I thought I knew what was going on," the psychologist revealed to Trotter, "but that was just a delusion on my part." It became increasingly apparent to Sternberg that there was more to intelligence than just thinking analytically.

Further research and examination of existing theories suggested to the psychologist that there were probably three main aspects or subtheories of intelligence. In addition to the componential aspect, from which he derived his original theory of intelligence, Sternberg formulated two others which he identified as experiential and contextual (or external). Through their interaction with one another, the psychologist alleges, these subtheories govern and determine the range of cognitive mental ability, thus corroborating Sternberg's triarchic theory of intelligence. Providing Trotter with an example of the individual characteristics dominating each subtheory, Sternberg described three students: one who excelled in academic or "test smarts" (componential); another who was especially creative and insightful and could formulate original ideas from dissimilar experiences (experiential); and a third whose "street-smart" intelligence enabled her to adapt to, or to manipulate, the environment to her advantage (contextual). In varying degrees each of them possessed "all three of the intellectual abilities" determined by Sternberg, wrote Trotter, "but each was especially good in one aspect." As Hammer pointed out, standard IQ tests ignore such capabilities as insight and adaptability, evaluating only those mental skills used in taking the tests. Sternberg consequently maintains that the results calculated from the intelligence tests say nothing "about why my best student is the one with the relatively low GRE [Graduate Record Examination] scores," or why other students with exceptionally high test ratings "sometimes come to Yale and flop."

Historically, intelligence testing began in France more than eighty years ago. Commissioned by their country's government, psychologists Alfred Binet and Theodosius Simon invented a series of tests initially intended as a means for identifying the special needs of schoolchildren. The Binet-Simon scale—as it was called—subsequently underwent a number of revisions, which were variously implemented not only in schools but in industry and the military as well. Since its inception, this prototype for IQ tests has evolved into what most people generally accept as "a measure of something real—something fixed, innate and inheritable—that was, in fact, intelligence," recorded Hammer, and traditionally intelligence has been collectively interpreted as a strictly academic achievement.

Sternberg redefines the nature of intelligence to include practical knowledge. Insisting that "real life is where intelligence operates" and not the classroom, reported Hammer, the psychologist points out that the true measure of success is not how well one does in school, but how well one does in life. In everyday situations on the job or in person-to-person contact, "people no more go around solving testlike analogies . . . than they go around pressing buttons in response to lights or sounds," Hammer quoted from Sternberg's book *Beyond IQ*. Moreover, what's important and necessary to succeed in the real world generally comes from individual experience rather than a textbook. Described as practical or tacit knowledge, these abilities include such things as "knowing how to prioritize tasks and allocate your time and other resources," Hammer noted, "and how to establish and enhance your reputation in your career, by convincing your boss of the value of your work." In effect, "Sternberg aims to change the way we think about intelligence'' by putting it into perspective within the context of real-life situations.

In his ground-breaking *Beyond IQ*, Sternberg expounds on the nature and origin of his triarchic theory of human intelligence. While much of the volume focuses on his early work on the componential aspect of the theory—including research and data on mental skills such as inductive and deductive reasoning, verbal comprehension, and information processing—the overall message in *Beyond IQ* conveys "that a broader view must be taken" to more accurately assess and measure the range of intellectual capabilities, observed Robert Glaser in *Science* magazine. In that respect "Sternberg carries us over the threshold from old to modern thought," but he "separates content and process too much" to achieve a truly integrated theory on the subject, argued Glaser. In Hammer's opinion, however, Sternberg "aims at nothing less than a kind of grand synthesis of ideas that for others are mutually contradictory. . . . And, like the physicist who is comfortable with the knowledge that light is both a particle and a wave," he accepts that intelligence is "a wide array of cognitive and other skills" that are simultaneously unified by their direct interaction with one another. Acknowledging the significance of Sternberg's research, Glaser resolved that *Beyond IQ* serves as a "challenge to further experiment and theory" as well as an indicator of the direction in which scientific study is advancing toward understanding and enhancing intellectual proficiency.

Having established that the range of intelligence is directly influenced by individual skills, Sternberg set to work discovering ways that people could best utilize their practical abilities. In the psychologist's opinion, related Hammer, "most people, including himself, don't work anywhere near their potential." On the other hand, the reviewer added, they "can learn to be smarter." Expanding on that idea, Sternberg wrote *Intelligence Applied: Understanding and Increasing Your Intellectual Skills*. Described by Hammer as a "'how to' version" of Sternberg's triarchic theory of intelligence, the book offers various exercises that serve to hone a person's mental capabilities, to make the most of what he or she does best. "And that's what I think practical intelligence is about," Sternberg reported to Trotter, "capitalizing on your strengths and minimizing your weaknesses. It's sort of mental self-management," whereby an individual tailors the environment to accommodate his or her particular talents. Claiming that "the ultimate test" is whether our abilities can improve the quality of our lives, Sternberg also intends "to revise intelligence testing to take practical intelligence into account," wrote Hammer. In fact, he has rejoined the Psychological Corporation—now located in Texas—for the purpose of developing the Sternberg Multidimensional Abilities Test, an IQ test based on his triarchic theory of human intelligence.

Sternberg originated a similar theory explaining the intricacies of love. In an article for *Psychology Today*, Robert J. Trotter explained how the psychologist at first concluded "that love, as different as it feels from situation to situation, is actually a common entity." When questions concerning sex were raised, however, Sternberg "had to rethink his position" in order to distinguish between such phenomena as the physical loving of one's lover and the platonic loving of one's child. According to Trotter, the psychologist's "research generated a lot of publicity in 1984 . . . and earned Sternberg the appellation 'love professor.'"

Like his triarchic theory of intelligence, Sternberg's "love triangle" derives from the interaction of three primary compo-

nents or subtheories. Specifically, the psychologist defines these as emotional, motivational, and cognitive—or more commonly, intimacy, passion, and commitment. Applying some basic principles of mathematics, Sternberg determined that there are eight possible combinations in which the components may occur. From this information he further concluded that there are also eight different kinds of interpersonal relationships: Nonlove, Liking, Infatuation, Empty Love, Romantic Love, Fatuous Love, Companionate Love, and Consummate Love. Only with consummate, or complete, love are all three subtheories present. Conversely, Nonlove represents the absence of all three.

In addition to naming the peculiarities of the different types of love, Sternberg suggests ways to improve or sustain a particular relationship. Foremost among them are a "willingness to change . . . to tolerate each other's imperfections" and "the sharing of values, especially religious values," noted Trotter. Advising people to maintain "realistic expectations for . . . what is going to be important in a relationship," Sternberg further discusses the contradiction that frequently exists between the way we feel and the way we act. He recommends learning how to recognize "just what actions are associated with each component of love" and then conforming our actions to appropriately reflect our feelings. Emphasizing how important it is to understand the various ways in which people express love, Sternberg cautions that in the absence of expression "even the greatest of loves can die."

AVOCATIONAL INTERESTS: Playing with his children, reading (especially science fiction), hiking, investing.

CA INTERVIEW

CA interviewed Robert J. Sternberg by telephone on June 30, 1986, at his office at Yale University.

CA: How did you get interested in the field of intelligence?

STERNBERG: When I was a kid, I did poorly on IQ tests. That made me interested in the whole issue. I was test-anxious, and I got over it.

CA: How did you get over it?

STERNBERG: It happened in the sixth grade, when I was sent back to retake an IQ test for fifth-graders. When you're in sixth grade, fifth-graders seem like babies, so I didn't feel anxious taking a test with them. And after that, I wasn't anxious ever again.

CA: Are there signs that any efforts are being made to alleviate stressful conditions during tests?

STERNBERG: No. I don't think much effort is being made in that direction.

CA: In the preface to Intelligence, Information Processing, and Analogical Reasoning, *you acknowledged your gratitude to a Mr. Adams, who stood up for you at a crucial time.*

STERNBERG: Yes. He was my seventh-grade science teacher. When I was in seventh grade, I did a project on mental testing, and one part of it was giving the Stanford-Binet, which I found in the adult section of the Maplewood Memorial Library, to classmates. I got into trouble because the mother of one of the kids finked to the school district. The head school psychologist threatened to burn the book if I ever brought it back into school and wanted me to work on rats. Adams encouraged me to stay with people and do everything else I was doing with the project, except give the test to kids.

CA: You've written a book on writing the psychology paper. Do you feel that jargon is too much used in writing about psychology, or is it largely necessary?

STERNBERG: The important thing is to know your audience. One person's jargon is another person's basic vocabulary. You have to know for whom you're writing.

CA: In your book Advances in the Psychology of Human Intelligence *you say that late in the 1960s research in the field of intelligence had gone into remission. But then in the 1970s there was a renewed interest. How do you explain this?*

STERNBERG: I think it was largely a result of work being done by a few people who started saying that maybe instead of just giving IQ tests and doing factor analyses, we could do a little bit better and try to understand the mental processes underlying intelligent performance. So I, and Earl Hunt and Jack Carroll and some others, started doing something which was relatively new—which was mental process analysis of intelligence. I think that woke people up and started a whole new wave of research.

CA: How does mental process analysis work?

STERNBERG: You take a person's performance on a cognitive test, solving analogies or reading a book or something, and you ask the question: What are the mental processes or mental steps the person goes through? The reason that's important to do is to eliminate confounding. For example, if someone takes a difficult verbal analogies test and gets a low score, is it because he can't reason or because he doesn't know the meanings of the words? The goal of this kind of research is in part to distinguish between those two kinds of explanations. It could be that the person is a good reasoner but doesn't know the meanings of the words.

CA: You shifted away from mental process analysis in the 1980s and started to develop what you call the triarchic theory. Could you explain that?

STERNBERG: The triarchic theory has three basic parts. One is that we're talking about the relation of intelligence to the internal world of the individual; in other words, what goes on inside a person's head when the person thinks intelligently? That's the kind of stuff we're talking about in the mental process analysis. But I decided that's not enough. We also have to look at the relation of intelligence to the external world. There are several reasons you have to look at the external world. One is that what is considered intelligence differs from one culture to another, from one place to another, from one time to another. You can't just look at mental processing to understand what's considered intelligent in a given setting. For example, suppose you're a professor. In some settings, the smart thing is to be a really good teacher. In others, it's to be a really good researcher. There are different values as to what's intelligence. The second thing is that there are lots of people who are IQ-test smart, but when it comes to their everyday lives, they do a lot of dumb things. There are some people who are IQ-test dumb, but who are very savvy in a practical way—they're street smart.

CA: As in the business world?

STERNBERG: Certainly in the business world, but in other fields, too. They may not have the highest IQs, but they're very practically sharp. No matter how much process analysis you do, if you're only process analyzing their IQ tests, you won't find that out. The third thing is the relation of intelligence to experience and particularly how a person copes with new situations. In other words, if you woke up in Morocco tomorrow morning and didn't know the language, how well would you be able to handle that? Or if things start to change in your life, how well can you cope with it? Ability to cope with a new situation requires a kind of intelligence, synthetic thinking, thinking in more creative ways, which is not measured well by the tests.

CA: Does research on intelligence go back a long way?

STERNBERG: Yes, certainly to the beginning of the century, and even to the late 1800s. The early people in the field were Sir Francis Carlton and Alfred Binet. They're usually the two who are given the most credit for starting the business.

CA: Is the Stanford-Binet test still commonly used in schools?

STERNBERG: Yes. That says something about how fast the field is moving.

CA: There is an organization called MENSA. Is that a reputable organization, do you think?

STERNBERG: It's an organization for people of IQs in the top two percentile of the general public. I think people should join whatever organizations they want, within reason, but I don't tend to associate with people just on the basis of their IQs. I look for more than that. But on the other hand, I'm at Yale, and most of the people at Yale would meet that criterion. Maybe if everyone I dealt with was an absolute dummy, I would have to start looking for better company and would be interested in that kind of group. It's not the kind of organization that would appeal to me, but I'm not one to speak for other people.

CA: Does the general public have a lot of fanciful ideas about intelligence?

STERNBERG: Generally their ideas are not fanciful. I think the worst idea is that it's fixed, that it's something you're born with and it's unchangeable. That seems to be a pretty common belief, and I think some psychologists have fostered it. And I think it's wrong. There's enough research showing that there are things you can do to increase your intelligence.

CA: What can be done?

STERNBERG: There are different programs. I have a program called ''Intelligence Applied,'' which is based on my triarchic theory and is a program for increasing intellectual skills. It is a yearly program. The idea there is that people do not utilize what they have as well as they could. Sure, there are some genetic limits. If you've got a person with average intelligence, you're not going to turn him into a genius. However, virtually everyone can make better use of his intelligence, and the goal of the program is to help people do just that.

CA: Let's say I took an IQ test and scored 110. Could I raise it thirty points if I worked at it?

STERNBERG: I think a thirty-point increase would be pretty rare. But a ten-to-fifteen-point increase would not be out of the question. Another thing to remember—misconception number two—is that IQ is not intelligence. IQ to me and to many other people is just a small part of intelligence. For example, IQ tests don't measure street-smarts, practical intelligence, your ability to use your intellect in everyday kinds of events. Common sense. That's a part of intelligence the tests don't measure. They're not very good at measuring synthetic thinking, or going beyond the information given, seeing things in novel ways, seeing new problems in old ways and old problems in new ways. They don't really measure insight very well. They don't measure very well what we call executive processes—planning, monitoring, evaluating. It's not that the tests measure nothing, but if you were to define intelligence just in terms of IQ, that would be a pretty narrow definition.

CA: You've written articles for the Phi Delta Kappan *on teaching critical thinking and how so little of that is done adequately in our schools now. Do you think some of your ideas are finding their way into the classroom?*

STERNBERG: Yes. But not everywhere. It's very slow.

CA: Intelligence can be defined in so many different ways. Doesn't that make it difficult to talk about?

STERNBERG: Yes. People have different conceptions about what intelligence is. But I think there's some overlap. A critical commodity is the notion that intelligence involves purposive adaptation to the environment.

CA: One of the things the average person on the street is interested in is how much intelligence we get from our ancestry and how much from growing up—the old "nature versus nurture" question. Is that still discussed quite a bit?

STERNBERG: It's discussed some, but less than it used to be because it's turned out not to be a particularly good way of formulating the question. There's some genetic rough upper bound; you're not going to make a genius out of a retarded kid, probably. But within the genetic boundaries, there's a lot of room for change. Percentages don't show that. People often don't realize that H2 [H square], the heritability coefficient, is dependent on population, place, time—a lot of things. It's not a fixed number.

CA: Do you think intelligence declines with age?

STERNBERG: Certain aspects of intellectual functioning decline with age. For example, mental speed generally declines with age. Fluid reasoning abilities, like abstract reasoning, decline with age. Other aspects of intelligence don't decline with age, like many practical skills. Certain crystallized abilities, like vocabulary, go up.

CA: You don't think speed is always a measure of intelligence, do you?

STERNBERG: No, I don't. It's part of it, but certainly not the whole thing. Sometimes it's smart to do things slowly, as when one has an important decision to make.

CA: A lot of people who don't do very well on math tests think that they're not very bright. Is there any justification in that belief?

STERNBERG: People overinterpret test scores. I was just reading in the *Chronicle of Higher Education* this morning an article about the colloquium the college board had on the use of tests and admissions. The biggest problem, for most people, is overinterpreting tests, thinking they mean more than they mean.

CA: What can be learned about intelligence from studying the mentally handicapped, the retarded?

STERNBERG: We get a sense of the necessary ingredients for adaptation. Retarded people tend to be weakest on the executive processes of intelligence: defining problems, setting up strategies for solving the problems, monitoring their solutions, and so on.

CA: How much research is being done on racial intelligence?

STERNBERG: Not much. A few people are doing it, but it's not popular.

CA: One thinks of psychologist Arthur Jensen, who has concluded on the basis of intelligence test results that blacks as a race are less intelligent than whites.

STERNBERG: I would say that he's preoccupied with racial intelligence. He reacts very strongly to where the public pushes him, and it's almost as if he had this ax to grind to show that there are racial differences. Yet he shows courage in trying to attack an unpopular problem scientifically. There *is* a difference in IQ scores between blacks and whites. Where I would disagree with him is in the interpretation. I've never found the racial question that interesting, because it tends to give numbers without explanations. I have felt that much of the work in this area has not been very enlightening in terms of why you get the differences. I have felt that environmental variables, and particularly early socialization, are very important.

CA: Aside from intelligence, you've written a lot about love and interpersonal relations. Is that more or less a side interest?

STERNBERG: It's becoming half and half. My interest now is about equally divided between the two.

CA: Did that interest grow out of your work on intelligence in some way?

STERNBERG: In fact, it did. I saw certain structural parallels between models of intelligence and models of love—not in the context, but in the structure. For example, balance is important in both. To succeed, relationships need to be balanced, as does the use of one's abilities.

CA: What are some of the current developments in research on intelligence?

STERNBERG: I would say the two main theories of the 1980s are my own triarchic theory and Howard Gardner's theory of multiple intelligences. My book on the triarchic theory is *Beyond IQ*, and Gardner wrote *Frames of Mind*.

CA: You and Gardner seem to be the principal researchers in intelligence at this time. What are the similarities and differences in your ideas?

STERNBERG: To start with, we both believe that the concept of intelligence ought to be extended beyond where it has been. Where we disagree, I would say, is in two main areas. One is that he extends intelligence further than I do. For example, he would call musical talent an intelligence. I wouldn't. I think there's a test you can apply. If you take away from someone all of the abilities of the triarchic theory, the person couldn't survive in the world. He'd just have to be institutionalized. Take someone who utterly can't plan, or who is completely unable to cope with novelties, or who is entirely unable to adapt to the environment. It's hard to imagine such a person, but if there were one, he certainly couldn't survive. Now take someone with no musical ability. He'd be fine. He'd better not be a musician, but there are lots of things he could do. Someone who is tone-deaf or has very little pitch discrimination is not going to have to be institutionalized. He's not going to be unable to adapt. There are lots of things he could do. So, to me, the difference between intelligence and specialized talent is this necessary test: If you had none of the ability, could you cope? In the case of the musical ability, you could. Or if you take Gardner's bodily kinesthetic ability, it would label someone who is spastic—say, as a klutz—as unintelligent or retarded. Someone may be klutzy, but most people would not view that as mental retardation because there are lots of things that person can do to cope, even though he probably won't be a basketball player. So I think Gardner carries his theory too far.

A second difference between us is that he believes that each of the so-called intelligences is independent, whereas I believe that they are interactive—not that they are unitary, but that they interact. And the bulk of the literature shows that that's true.

CA: Do other researchers in intelligence usually go along with your interpretation of it?

STERNBERG: You would have to ask them. Scientists try to convince other scientists that they are right about something; but what others think, I'm not able to say.

CA: In the years ahead, will you be focusing more and more on studies of practical intelligence?

STERNBERG: Yes. It seems to me that the most important question about intelligence is that of how we use it in our lives.

BIOGRAPHICAL/CRITICAL SOURCES:

BOOKS

Gardner, Howard, *Frames of Mind: The Theory of Multiple Intelligences,* Basic Books, 1983.

PERIODICALS

New York Times Book Review, June 26, 1988.
Psychology Today, April, 1982, June, 1982, August, 1986, September, 1986.
Science, October, 1985.
Science Digest, June, 1985.

—*Sketch by Barbara A. Cicchetti*

—*Interview by Walter W. Ross*

STEYERMARK, Julian A(lfred) 1909-1988

OBITUARY NOTICE—See index for *CA* sketch: Born January 27, 1909, in St. Louis, Mo.; died of complications from throat cancer, October 15, 1988, in St. Louis, Mo. Botanist, curator, educator, and author. Steyermark was a renowned authority on plants. He spent much of his career with Venezuela's Ministry of Agriculture, where he was a botanist at an institute in Caracas from 1959 to 1980 and an assessor to the director there from 1981 to 1984. He also conducted expeditions in South America in the 1940s and 1950s and taught at Southern Illinois University in 1958. During his long career Steyermark amassed more than 137,000 plant collections, an apparently unmatched quantity that gained him recognition in the *Guiness Book of World Records.* His writings include *Vegetational History of the Ozark Forest, Flora of Missouri,* the three-volume *Rubiaceae of Venezuela,* and *Flora of the Venezuelan Guayana.* He also produced approximately three hundred articles for various publications.

OBITUARIES AND OTHER SOURCES:

PERIODICALS

Chicago Tribune, October 20, 1988.

*　　*　　*

STILLWELL, Paul (Lewis) 1944-

PERSONAL: Born April 22, 1944, in Dayton, Ohio; son of Carl Neller (a minister) and Vera Pauline (a homemaker; maiden name, Limper) Stillwell; married Karen Lee McKenzie (a homemaker), August 12, 1970; children: Joseph Paul, Robert Carl, James Lee. *Education:* Drury College, A.B., 1966; University of Missouri—Columbia, M.A., 1978. *Religion:* United Church of Christ.

ADDRESSES: Home—262 Waycross Way, Arnold, Md. 21021. *Office*—U.S. Naval Institute, Annapolis, Md. 21402.

CAREER: St. Louis Cardinals (professional baseball team), St. Louis, Mo., assistant public relations director, 1972; St. Louis Cardinals (professional football team), St. Louis, assistant public relations director, 1972-74; U.S. Naval Institute, Annapolis, Md., member of editorial staff of *Proceedings,* 1974-81, editor of *Naval Review,* 1981-87, director of oral history, 1982—, editor in chief of *Naval History,* 1987—. *Military service:* U.S. Navy, 1966-69; served in Pacific theater; received Navy Commendation Medal with combat "V." U.S. Naval Reserve, 1962-66, 1969—; present rank, commander.

MEMBER: Naval Reserve Association.

WRITINGS:

(Editor) *Air Raid: Pearl Harbor! Recollections of a Day of Infamy,* Naval Institute Press, 1981.
Battleship New Jersey: An Illustrated History, Naval Institute Press, 1986.

Contributor to *Encyclopedia Americana.* Contributor to periodicals, including *Sea Power* and *Marine Corps Gazette.*

WORK IN PROGRESS: Battleship Arizona: An Illustrated History, publication by the Naval Institute Press expected in 1991.

SIDELIGHTS: Paul Stillwell's *Air Raid: Pearl Harbor!* is a collection of forty-seven memoirs. The book includes an article by the Japanese pilot who led the attack in 1945. Other contributors are American and Japanese officers and enlisted personnel, civilians, both men and women, and professional journalists. The work is heavily illustrated with photographs, which were described thus in the *Washington Post Book World* by Roger Pineau: "some [are] familiar, some rare, but all well chosen and arranged. Finding Pearl Harbor-vintage photographs of all forty-seven authors was a nice touch and no mean task." Clay Blair of the *Chicago Tribune* found *Air Raid: Pearl Harbor!* to be "provocative, informative, nicely balanced between Big and Little Picture. In its own highly personal and subjective way it gives a full account of what happened."

Stillwell told *CA:* "My service in the crew of the USS *New Jersey* in 1969 led to an interest in battleships and their history. This was reflected in *Battleship New Jersey: An Illustrated History*. I did a great deal of documentary research to form the factual skeleton for the story, but the real flesh and blood came in the words of other former crew members. I conducted oral history interviews with more than one hundred of them and thus was able to tell the human side of the story of this great ship. I plan a similar approach in writing about the battleship *Arizona*. Because of her loss at the hands of the Japanese on December 7, 1941, she became one of the most famous U.S. Navy ships. Curiously, though, little has been written about her twenty-five years of active service prior to World War II. By interviewing former *Arizona* men, I want to bring her story to life, as I did with the *New Jersey*."

BIOGRAPHICAL/CRITICAL SOURCES:

PERIODICALS

Chicago Tribune, December 6, 1981.
Washington Post Book World, November 22, 1981.

*   *   *

STIMSON, Dorothy 1890-1988

OBITUARY NOTICE: Born October 10, 1890, in St. Louis, Mo.; died of arterial sclerosis, September 19, 1988, in Owls Head, Me. Educator, editor, and author. Stimson will be remembered for her long association with Maryland's Goucher College. Beginning her academic career at Transylvania College in Lexington, Kentucky, she was dean of women and professor of history from 1917 to 1921. Stimson then joined Goucher, serving as dean and a member of the history faculty until 1947 and as chairman of the department from 1948 to 1955. Later she was a visiting professor of history at Vassar, Sweet Briar, and Mt. Holyoke colleges and, in 1958, became John Hay Whitney Professor at Sarah Lawrence College. Her books include *The Gradual Acceptance of the Copernican Theory of the Universe* and *Scientists and Amateurs: A History of the Royal Society*. In 1962 she edited *Sarton on the History of Science*.

OBITUARIES AND OTHER SOURCES:

BOOKS

Who's Who of American Women, 3rd edition, Marquis, 1964.

PERIODICALS

New York Times, September 24, 1988.

*   *   *

STOCK, A(my) G(eraldine) 1902-1988

OBITUARY NOTICE: Born in 1902; died July 13, 1988, in Chippenham, England. Educator, editor, and author. A professor of English literature, Stock will be remembered for her many travels and teachings in such countries as Uganda and Bangladesh. After attending Oxford University's Somerville College, Stock began her teaching career, first at Bingley Training College and later at Uganda's Makerere College (now University). She subsequently became chair of English at the University of Dacca in Bangladesh. After retiring, Stock took a visiting post at Cambridge University and, when Bangladesh gained its independence in 1971 at the end of the Indo-Pakistan war, she returned to Bangladesh to work again at Dacca. She wrote *W. B. Yeats: His Poetry and Thought* and edited *Prison Anthology* with Reginald Reynolds.

OBITUARIES AND OTHER SOURCES:

PERIODICALS

Times (London), July 25, 1988.

*   *   *

STOKES, Cedric
  See BEARDMORE, George

*   *   *

STORER, Tracy I(rwin) 1889-1973

OBITUARY NOTICE—See index for *CA* sketch: Born August 17, 1889, in San Francisco, Calif.; died June 25, 1973. Zoologist, educator, curator, editor, and author. Storer taught at the University of California at Davis from 1923 to 1956, when he retired after fourteen years as professor of zoology. Prior to teaching, Storer worked as a museum curator for the University of California at Berkeley. Among his writings are *General Zoology*, *Elements of Zoology*, and *Sierra Nevada Natural History: An Illustrated Handbook*, all written with Robert Usinger. Storer edited the *Journal of Wildlife Management* from 1942 to 1946.

OBITUARIES AND OTHER SOURCES:

Date of death provided by wife, Ruth R. Storer.

*   *   *

STOUT, William 1949-

PERSONAL: Born September 18, 1949, in Salt Lake City, Utah; son of William (a farmer) and Joyce (an insurance adjuster; maiden name, Newirth) Stout; married Mary Kent Wilson (an actress), June 21, 1982; children: Andrew William Dragon, James Dylan Wolf. *Education:* Chouinard Art Institute (now California Institute of the Arts), B.A., 1971. *Politics:* "Extreme environmentalist."

ADDRESSES: Home—1468 Loma Vista St., Pasadena, Calif. 91104. *Office*—812 South La Brea, Los Angeles, Calif. 90036.

CAREER: Artist and writer. Art director of *Bomp*, 1976-77, and Varese-Sarabande Records, 1978—.

MEMBER: Comic Art Professional Society (founding member of board of directors, 1977-81; president, 1986-87), American Film Institute, National Geographic Society, Audubon Society, Oceanic Society, Sierra Club, Smithsonian Institution, American Museum of Natural History, Greater Los Angeles Zoo Association.

AWARDS, HONORS: Inkpot Award, 1978; Children's Choice Award, 1985, for *The Little Blue Brontosaurus*.

WRITINGS:

The Dinosaurs: A Fantastic New View of a Lost Era, Bantam, 1981.

The Little Blue Brontosaurus (children's book), self-illustrated, Caedman, 1983.

(Illustrator) Ray Bradbury, *Dinosaur Tales*, Bantam, 1983.

Also author of screenplays, including "The Warrior and the Sorceress" (1984), re-released as "Kain of Dark Planet"; "Conan the Buccaneer"; "Spawn of the Dead"; and "Natural History Project."

WORK IN PROGRESS: A sequel to *The Little Blue Brontosaurus;* a book on his work as a film artist; a sequel to "Raiders of the Lost Ark"; a low-budget horror film.

SIDELIGHTS: "My first professional work came in 1968," William Stout told *CA*, "when I did the cover for the first issue of the pulp magazine *Coven 13.* I continued making illustrations for a variety of clients and contributed to Petersen Publications' *Cycle-Toons.* In 1971 I began to assist Russ Manning on the 'Tarzan' syndicated comic strips. I worked with Harvey Kurtzman and Will Elder on the 'Little Annie Fanny' strip for *Playboy* in 1972. In Paris the following year, I was offered work by the European magazine *Pilote.* From 1973 to 1974 I produced more than thirty-five 'bootleg' record album covers, which earned me international recognition and a recent retrospective in the French magazine *Metal Hurlant.* I also worked with the Firesign Theatre to create the graphics for their film 'Everything You Know Is Wrong' and the cover for their album *In the Next World, You're on Your Own.*

"From 1976 to 1977 I was the art director for the rock magazine *Bomp.* I also made my first movie poster for 'Wizards.' Dozens more followed, including posters for 'Monty Python's Life of Brian,' 'More American Graffiti,' 'Allegro non Troppo,' and 'Rock 'n' Roll High School.' The same year my first one-man show, 'The Prehistoric World of William Stout,' attracted paleontologists and fantasy lovers alike.

"I worked as a production artist for Buck Rogers in 1978. This led to more film work, including a large series of paintings and designs for the 'Amber' epic based on the popular science-fantasy series written by Roger Zelazny. This finally culminated with my work with Ron Cobb as the production artist on John Milius's 'Conan.' It was also at this time that my work came to the attention of Steven Spielberg. I storyboarded the stunt sequences for 'First Blood' and was the co-author of the film 'Kain of Dark Planet.'

"Since then I designed the monsters on 'Monster in the Closet,' then worked for five months in Mexico as the concept artist for 'Conan the Destroyer.' While in Mexico, I dubbed the voice of a robot in 'Dune.' A series of paintings and drawings for 'The Clan of the Cave Bear' and 'Red Sonja' followed. Then I worked as the production designer for Steve Miner's 'Godzilla, King of the Monsters' and Dan O'Bannon's 'Return of the Living Dead.'

"My screenwriting began as a painful, but quick, path to my goal of becoming a film director. The writing eventually became fun and fulfilling in itself. Whether I am working as an artist or writer, I strive for specific standards. I will not relinquish a piece until the problems I have set for myself are completely solved. They may not be solved in the way I imagined at the beginning of the project, but they will be solved in a way that is not ordinary, that is stimulating, positive, and/or funny. I never do less than my best on any given project.

I also feel it is crucial to give back to the community that gives to me. Hence, I do community service work and head community groups in an effort to make life better for other people.

"I speak passable Spanish and crummy French, Serbo-Croatian, and Italian due to my film travels. I have traveled extensively through Canada, Czechoslovakia, Belgium, Germany, the Galapagos, Ecuador, Peru, Tanzania, Kenya, Ethiopia, and Colombia. I have lived for extended periods of time in Mexico, Spain, Italy, Yugoslavia, and France."

Since 1978 Stout has been the art director for Varese-Sarabande Records. He has continued to produce covers for other companies and recording artists such as Rhino Records and the Beach Boys. His work appears in the form of prints, television commercials, T-shirt designs, comic books, murals, and even toy box covers. It has been published in Australia, England, France, Germany, Italy, Spain, and Japan.

BIOGRAPHICAL/CRITICAL SOURCES:

PERIODICALS

Comics Feature, September, 1984.
Life, November, 1981.
Metal Hurlant, January, 1981.
Starlog, May, 1987.
Starlog (Japan), April, 1982.

*   *   *

STRAUB, Gerard Thomas 1947-

PERSONAL: Born March 31, 1947, in Brooklyn, N.Y.; son of William V. (a business executive) and Frances (Croake) Straub; married second wife, Kathleen Grosso (a television and film production assistant), July 11, 1986; children: Adrienne Frances.

ADDRESSES: Home and office—P. O. Box 1342, Carmel-by-the-Sea, Calif. 93921. *Agent*—Jay Garon, Jay Garon-Brooke Associates, Inc., 415 Central Park W., New York, N.Y. 10025.

CAREER: Columbia Broadcasting System, Inc., New York, N.Y., executive, 1964-78; Christian Broadcasting Network, Virginia Beach, Va., producer of "The 700 Club" and creator of soap opera "Another Life," 1978-80; American Broadcasting Companies, Inc., Hollywood, Calif., associate producer of "General Hospital," 1980-81; National Broadcasting Company, Inc., New York City, executive producer of "The Doctors," 1982; Dick Clark Productions, Burbank, Calif., producer of "You Are the Jury," 1983; independent television director and free-lance writer, San Francisco, Calif., and New York City, 1983-86; John Conboy Productions, Hollywood, supervising producer of "Capitol," 1986-87; free-lance writer, 1987—.

WRITINGS:

Salvation for Sale: An Insider's View of Pat Robertson's Ministry, Prometheus Books, 1986, revised paperback edition, 1988.

God Said What?, Prometheus Books, in press.

WORK IN PROGRESS: Other Voices, quotations and commentary; *At Odds With Myself*, a novel "exploring the social and spiritual shifts of the last twenty-five years"; "Molly and the Monk," "Mac the Maid," and "Dog Days," all screenplays.

SIDELIGHTS: Gerard Thomas Straub told *CA:* "My writing mirrors my life's two main interests: show biz and spirituality. As a young teenager, I dreamed of becoming a missionary priest, yet, in an ironic twist of fate, I wound up producing soap operas for all three television networks. However, my two interests merged for two-and-a-half years during the late seventies, when I abandoned my network television career in order to join forces with television evangelist Pat Robertson. During my time at Christian Broadcasting System, I produced 'The 700 Club,' created 'Another Life'—the first internationally syndicated Christian soap opera—and wrote and produced many variety and dramatic specials.

"*Salvation for Sale* is the story of my own spiritual odyssey, played against the fascinating backdrop of fundamentalist Christian television. *God Said What?* is a less personal and more hard-hitting book that examines not only the emotionalism of faith and the nature of religious beliefs, but also the power and dangers of the fundamentalist dark side of Christianity as it is reflected in the presidential campaign of preacher-turned-politician Pat Robertson.

"With these two serious books under my belt, my goal is to move into more fictional and entertaining writing, especially in the field of films. I want to write work that will be funny and dramatic, yet still touch upon the important philosophical issues that confront our changing society. In that vein, I have just completed a treatment for a television situation comedy, entitled 'You Gotta Be Kidding,' that portrays the inner conflict of a television talk show host with lofty ideals who toils in the bottom-line business of ratings, where quality has no value and success is guaranteed with sleaze. On the literary horizon is a book that takes a behind-the-scenes look at the wacky world of soap operas."

BIOGRAPHICAL/CRITICAL SOURCES:

PERIODICALS

Los Angeles Times, August 23, 1986, June 12, 1987, June 15, 1987.
Los Angeles Times Book Review, May 3, 1987.
New York Review of Books, August 13, 1987.
New York Times, December 27, 1987.
Toronto Star, May 2, 1987.
USA Today, March 5, 1987.

*   *   *

STRAUBING, Harold (Elk)   1918-
(Ruth Bennet, Ann Tower)

PERSONAL: First syllable of surname rhymes with "cow"; born February 19, 1918, in New York, N.Y.; son of Jack (a milliner) and Mollie (an accountant; maiden name, Begun) Straubing; married Helen Mozlin (a stage manager), March 13, 1943; children: Michelle. *Education:* Long Island University, B.A., 1940.

ADDRESSES: Home—11911 Magnolia Ave., No. 14, North Hollywood, Calif. 91607-4406. *Agent*—Florence Feiler, 1524 Sunset Plaza Dr., Los Angeles, Calif. 90069.

CAREER: Fleischer Studios, Miami, Fla., artist and writer, 1940-42; Goodman Publications, comics editor, 1945-47; *New York Herald Tribune,* New York, N.Y., comics editor of the newspaper and its syndicate, 1947-51; Associated Press Newsfeatures, comics editor, 1951-52; Lev Gleason Publications, editor, 1952-54; Crestwood Publishing Company, New York,

N.Y., magazine editor, 1954-61; American Art Enterprises, Inc., North Hollywood, Calif., executive editor, general manager, 1961-75; Chatsworth Enterprises, Inc., Chatsworth, Calif., executive editor, 1975-82; writer, 1982—. Producer and director of radio dramas, chairman of board of directors of Oceanside Community Theater, Oceanside, N.Y. *Military service:* U.S. Army, 1942-45.

MEMBER: Writers Guild of America West, Mystery Writers of America.

AWARDS, HONORS: Fletcher Pratt Award nomination from Civil War Round Table of New York, 1985, for *Civil War: Eyewitness Reports.*

WRITINGS:

"Little Girl With Red Nails" (3-act play), readings of script first given in New York City, 1961.
Target Number One (novel), Pinnacle Books, 1983.
Civil War: Eyewitness Reports, Archon Books, 1985, reprinted as *The Fateful Lightning,* Paragon House, 1987.
The Last Magnificent War, Paragon House, 1988.

Also author of advice columns for romance magazines, under pseudonyms Ann Tower and Ruth Bennet; contributor to magazines and newspapers, including *Saturday Evening Post;* former editor of men's adventure magazines *Man's Life* and *True Men's Stories;* food editor of *Chelsea Clinton News.*

WORK IN PROGRESS: Bandages, Bullets, and Beans, a book about the medical treatment afforded the troops during the Civil War; *Window on the Storm,* "a record of World War II—its background, the insecurity of the times, and its emotional conclusion."

SIDELIGHTS: Harold Straubing told *CA:* "I have had a checkered literary career, interspersed with editorial positions. I have written for diverse publications, from comic books to the *Saturday Evening Post,* as well as for animated cartoons such as 'Popeye' and 'Betty Boop,' and animated shorts for *Snafu.* As a member of the *Tribune*'s lecture bureau, I gave many talks on the history and evolution of the comic strip. I have held several editorial positions in newspaper, magazine, and book publishing. As executive editor for Chatsworth Enterprises, I was responsible for the production of over four thousand titles in fiction and in non-fiction.

"My interest in the Civil War in the United States began when I took my basic training in the army on the same ground where the Blue and the Gray shed their blood in battle. We also tumbled in and out of the World War I trenches dug by doughboys long gone to their glory. I became curious about the people of those eras, how they lived, what they thought, how they suffered. I read some of the books on these periods but found them less than satisfying. I found that writers researched their books, digested the information, and regurgitated a story that contained their own shaded inferences and prejudices.

"To get closer to the material I began to explore old letters, diaries, and essays written by people who helped form this country by word and deed. This has led me unwittingly into a third career in my lifetime: writing history books. I trust my fascination with the past is contagious. The courage, fortitude, and bravery of our ordinary citizens in crisis is as amazing as it is heart-warming. I guess I am just hooked on people, their outlooks, their emotions."

STRAWSON, Galen   1952-

PERSONAL: Born February 5, 1952, in Oxford, England; son of Peter Frederick (a professor of philosophy) and Ann (a teacher; maiden name, Martin) Strawson; married Jose Said (a university teacher), July 20, 1974; children: Emilie, Thomas. *Education:* Trinity Hall, Cambridge, M.A., 1973; Wolfson College, Oxford, B.Phil., 1977, D.Phil., 1983; attended Ecole Normale Superieure (Paris), 1977-78.

ADDRESSES: Home—16 Polstead Rd., Oxford, Oxfordshire OX2 6TN, England. *Office*—Jesus College, Oxford University, Oxford, Oxfordshire OX1 3DW, England.

CAREER: Oxford University, Oxford, England, lecturer in philosophy at University College, 1979-80, at Exeter College, 1980-83, at St. Hugh's College, 1983-85, at New College, 1985-86, and at St. Hilda's College, 1986-87, fellow and tutor in philosophy at Jesus College, 1987—. *Times Literary Supplement*, assistant editor, 1978-88, consultant editor, 1988—.

MEMBER: Mind Association, Aristotelian Society.

AWARDS, HONORS: French Government scholar, 1977-78; T. H. Green Prize for Moral Philosophy from Oxford University, 1983.

WRITINGS:

Freedom and Belief, Oxford University Press, 1986.
Realism and Causation: A Study of Hume, Oxford University Press, 1989.

Contributor of articles and reviews to philosophy journals and newspapers.

WORK IN PROGRESS: Research on the nature of mind.

SIDELIGHTS: Galen Strawson told *CA:* "I do philosophy because it is so intensely interesting. Perhaps this has to be experienced to be understood; I don't know. In *Freedom and Belief* I argue that we have a certain image of ourselves that cannot be correct—an image of ourselves as moral agents who are ultimately and absolutely responsible for our actions. I suggest that although this image of ourselves is provably false, it may be that we cannot help believing it is true. One way of conveying the image is this: We think of ourselves as ultimately responsible for our actions in such a way that the idea that it might be fair to punish us for them with eternal damnation (or reward us for them with eternal bliss) makes perfect and clear sense, at least, even if it is in fact part of a highly extravagant myth.

"In the book about David Hume I attack the idea—extraordinary but orthodox in Western philosophy—that causation is never a matter of one thing producing or bringing about another, but is merely a matter of things 'just happening' one after another in a regular way. I also attack the idea, equally orthodox in Western philosophy, that this weird view is David Hume's view.

"In the work on the nature of mind I hope to argue that behaviorism is still distorting our views about the mind, despite all the denials and rebuttals."

*   *   *

STRONG, June   1928-
(Sara Greene)

PERSONAL: Born March 17, 1928, in Vermont; daughter of Max Wright and Alice (Greene) Kimball; married Donald W. Strong (a president of a manufacturing firm), September 14, 1947; children: Kimball, Lori Strong Sands, Jeffrey, Mitchell, Amy Strong De Lillo. *Education:* Attended Atlantic Union College, 1945-46, and Burlington Business College, 1946-47.

ADDRESSES: Home—8507 Prole Rd., Batavia, N.Y. 14020.

CAREER: Secretary in Batavia, N.Y., 1947-49 and 1950-52; writer.

MEMBER: Writers Workshop.

WRITINGS:

Journal of a Happy Woman, Southern Publishing Association, 1973.
Mindy, Southern Publishing Association, 1977.
Project Sunlight, Southern Publishing Association, 1980.
A Little Journey, Review and Herald, 1984.
Song of Eve, Review and Herald, 1987.

Also author of *Why Are We Running?* Author of monthly column in *Signs of the Times,* 1974-87. Contributor to magazines, sometimes under pseudonym Sara Greene.

WORK IN PROGRESS: Research for a book on Susannah Wesley.

*   *   *

STUCKENSCHMIDT, H(ans) H(einz)   1901-1988

OBITUARY NOTICE—See index for *CA* sketch: Born November 1, 1901, in Strasbourg, Alsace, Germany (now Alsace, France); died August 15, 1988. Musicologist, educator, editor, and author. Stuckenschmidt was known for his expertise in twentieth-century classical music. Long considered a major figure in German music criticism, he wrote for many periodicals, including the *Frankfurter Allgemeine Zeitung* from 1956 until his death. In addition, he was professor of music at the Technical University of Berlin from 1948 to 1966. His translated writings include *Arnold Schoenberg, Maurice Ravel: Variations on His Life and Work, Ferruccio Busoni: Chronicle of a European, Twentieth-Century Music,* and *Schoenberg: His Life, World, and Work.* Stuckenschmidt also wrote an autobiography, *Zum Hoeren geboren,* and edited several books.

OBITUARIES AND OTHER SOURCES:

PERIODICALS

Times (London), August 20, 1988.

*   *   *

STUCKEY, Elma   1907(?)-1988

OBITUARY NOTICE: Born c. 1907; died of a heart attack, September 23 (one source says September 25), 1988, in Washington, D.C. Educator, supervisor, and poet. Although her first book was not published until she was sixty-nine years old, Stuckey was highly regarded for her poems about black Americans. After obtaining a teaching certificate from Lane College in Jackson, Tennessee, Stuckey became a teacher in that state and ran a nursery school. She moved to Chicago in 1945 and later began working for the Illinois Department of Labor, where she became a supervisor. Interested in poetry for most of her life, Stuckey was first recognized for her literary talents when she read her work on a radio program hosted by historian and writer Studs Terkel. She went on to recite her poems at various universities, including Harvard, Cornell, and Stanford, and her widest acclaim came with the 1976 publication of *The Big Gate*. Stuckey followed that with a second volume, *The Collected Poems of Elma Stuckey*, published when she was eighty years old. Her poetry deals with blacks from the time of slavery to the present.

OBITUARIES AND OTHER SOURCES:

BOOKS

In Black and White, 3rd edition, Gale, 1980.

PERIODICALS

Chicago Tribune, September 30, 1988.
New York Times, September 30, 1988.

*   *   *

SUKIENNIK, Adelaide Weir   1938-

PERSONAL: Born August 16, 1938, in Pittsburgh, Pa.; daughter of John C. and Esther (Lee) Weir; married Leopold J. Sukiennik (an engineer), September 20, 1970; children: Esther Olga, Lana Rachel. *Education:* Otterbein College, B.A., 1961; University of Pittsburgh, M.L.S., 1965, Ph.D., 1978. *Politics:* Democrat. *Religion:* Jewish.

ADDRESSES: Home—5885 Bartlett St., Pittsburgh, Pa. 15217. *Office*—207 Hillman Library, University of Pittsburgh, Pittsburgh, Pa. 15260.

CAREER: High school English teacher in Pittsburgh, Pa., 1961-64, assistant librarian, 1964-66; Ohio State University, Columbus, humanities bibliographer, 1966-68; University of Pittsburgh, Pittsburgh, instructor in library and information science, 1970-72, bibliographer at Hillman Library, 1972—.

MEMBER: American Library Association, Pennsylvania Library Association, Beta Phi Mu.

WRITINGS:

(Contributor) Kathleen M. Hein, editor, *The Status of Women in Librarianship*, Neal-Schuman, 1983.
(With Joan Brest Friedberg and June B. Mullins) *Accept Me as I Am: Best Juvenile Books of Nonfiction on Impairments and Disabilities*, Bowker, 1985.

Contributor to *Encyclopedia of Library and Information Science*.

WORK IN PROGRESS: A sequel to *Accept Me as I Am*, with Friedberg and Mullins, publication by Bowker expected in 1989.

SIDELIGHTS: Adelaide Weir Sukiennik told *CA:* "I believe that the vital issue, overriding all others, is still the vast amount of inequality in American society, despite all the advances that have purportedly been made in the last thirty years.

"*Accept Me as I Am: Best Juvenile Books of Nonfiction on Impairments and Disabilities* reviews approximately three hundred nonfiction book titles suitable for young people from kindergarten to high school age. These books deal with the lives of persons who are physically challenged in some way—deafness, blindness, mobility impairments, etc. Introductory chapters set these books in a historical context and review the present-day status of rights for children and adults whose lives have been challenged by physical or mental impairments or disabilities."

SULITZER, Paul-Loup   1946-

PERSONAL: Born July 22, 1946, in Paris, France; son of Jules (in business) and Cecile Sulitzer; married Lyne Chardonnet (an actress), 1968 (divorced, 1970); married Magali Colcanap, March 24, 1973 (divorced); children: (second marriage) Olivia Marie. *Education:* Attended schools in Paris, France.

ADDRESSES: Home—5 Square des Ecrivains Combattants, F-75116 Paris, France.

CAREER: Laborer in Spain, kibbutz worker in Israel, and movie assistant, 1959-64; founder and chief executive officer of a key ring collectors' club in France, 1965-67; designer of novelties and founder of a French company that imported gadgets from Hong Kong, 1967-68; investor, financial counselor, and international consultant, early 1970s—; writer, 1979—.

MEMBER: International Safari Club and Hunting Association.

WRITINGS:

NOVELS; IN FRENCH

Money, Denoel, 1980, translation by Susan Wald published as *Money*, Lyle Stuart, 1985.
Cash!, Denoel, 1981, translation by Susan Wald published as *Cash*, Lyle Stuart, 1986.
Fortune, Denoel, 1982, translation published as *Fortune*, Lyle Stuart, 1986.
Le Roi vert, Edition No 1/Stock, 1983, translation by Denise Roab Jacobs published as *The Green King* (Literary Guild alternate selection), Lyle Stuart, 1984.
Popov, Edition No 1/Orban, 1984.
Hannah, Edition No 1/Stock, 1984.
Duel a Dallas, Edition No 1, 1984.

WORK IN PROGRESS: Three short novels on the continuing adventures of protagonist Franz Cimballi.

SIDELIGHTS: Entrepreneur and financial consultant Paul-Loup Sulitzer, dubbed "France's hottest author" in the mid-1980s, began his writing career by chance. At the age of twenty-five, Sulitzer had become France's youngest company president and was one of twelve individuals whose achievements were detailed in a book about succeeding in business. A publisher soon approached him for the rights to his autobiography, but Sulitzer believed that publishing his memoirs would jeopardize his clients' professional secrets and his own reputation as a highly esteemed financial consultant. However, Sulitzer felt that he could safely relate his insights if they were hidden under the veil of fiction. He turned out a novel entitled *Money*, the first in a string of international best-sellers for the new author.

Before Sulitzer attained his celebrity status, he experienced a series of personal calamities. While he had been born into relative affluence, when Sulitzer was only ten years old, his father died without leaving a will. The boy and his mother were left with only a pittance of their rightful inheritance. Sulitzer left school at the age of fifteen, quite "literally," as Thomas A. Sancton wrote from France in an article for *Time*, "to make his fortune." The ambitious youth worked at a series of odd jobs for a few years, then he had the brainstorm that would make him rich. Playing upon a French fad in the mid-1960s, Sulitzer organized a key ring collectors' club with a loan from his father's former chauffeur and was soon making more money than he could spend. He sold the business in 1967 before the collecting craze ended, earning more than half a million dollars before he turned twenty. Shortly thereafter,

Sulitzer started his next venture, the importation of novelties from Hong Kong, and sold the company the next year while it was thriving, this time making $600,000.

The Frenchman encountered setbacks in both his personal and professional life by 1970: his first marriage failed and his trendy marketing ideas were rejected. Sulitzer then worked to establish himself as a successful financial counselor. He had made a name for himself in the international world of finance when the French publisher Denoel asked him to write the book that made him a best-selling author.

Sulitzer uses his own knowledge of corporate dealings to offer his readers an insider's view of the world of money and power. He chose the English word as the French title of his novel *Money*, a semi-autobiographical account of a young fictional entrepreneur named Franz Cimballi. "My real hero was money," the author told Herbert R. Lottman in an interview for *Publishers Weekly*, "but that was a sin in France, where in good company you don't use the word." Sulitzer, who fell in love with the United States after touring the country in his twenties, told Sancton of *Time*, "Americans understand everything about making money." He continued, "All of my books are set in the U.S.—it's the greatest country in the world." Sulitzer's publisher, Denoel, went so far as to promote *Money* as "the first financial Western." Sulitzer captured the interest of what he calls "the rising generation" of entrepreneurs who are willing to take risks for their gains. "They are the real adventurers of today," he contends.

Those "adventurers" helped *Money* and its two sequels, *Cash!* and *Fortune*, sell more than one hundred thousand copies apiece. Sulitzer now spends more than half of each business day writing. For his fourth book, *Le Roi vert*, published in the United States as *The Green King*, he departed somewhat from his trilogy's formula to create a larger-than-life hero named Reb Michael Klimrod. In the book, Klimrod, taken for dead, emerges from a pile of strewn bodies in a Nazi death camp to become the richest man in the world. Sulitzer told Lottman that he put a lifetime's worth of personal experience into *The Green King*. Klimrod is what Sulitzer calls "a mosaic" of real people. Lottman wrote, "Klimrod's camp experience owes something to the death of the author's uncle, a resistance activist, at Buchenwald, and to other family stories." Sulitzer himself admits that a "shock" occurring early in an individual's life can push that person "to achieve great things."

The Green King fared well with French and American critics. A few reviewers were distressed by what they saw as an exploitive use of the Nazi prison camp horrors in fiction; others felt that Sulitzer failed to explain his most interesting ideas. Many critics, however, were impressed. One French critic compared Sulitzer to Alexandre Dumas, the famous French novelist and playwright who wrote *The Three Musketeers*. Roy Katz, writing for the *Los Angeles Times Book Review*, summed up the favorable reviews when he called *The Green King* "a fast-paced, literate novel" with "sizzling action."

Sulitzer writes about what he knows best: his two follow-up novels to *The Green King* are variations on the corporate theme. *Popov*, the story of a Soviet banker intent upon furthering Moscow's interests, sold 165,000 copies during its first six weeks in print. *Hannah* is the story of a woman in business. When asked to comment on what he thought was the reason for his books' popularity for *Time*, Sulitzer said, "People say my books energize them and make them want to do great things." The author's own climb to the top, built on the prem-

ise that money buys freedom, is inspiring his readers around the world.

AVOCATIONAL INTERESTS: Skiing, going on African safaris, canoeing.

MEDIA ADAPTATIONS: A film based on Sulitzer's novel *Money* is planned.

BIOGRAPHICAL/CRITICAL SOURCES:

PERIODICALS

Los Angeles Times Book Review, August 12, 1984.
New York Times Book Review, July 22, 1984.
Publishers Weekly, July 6, 1984.
Time, August 27, 1984.

—*Sketch by Barbara K. Carlisle*

*   *   *

SUMIKO
  See DAVIES, Sumiko

*   *   *

SUTTON, Remar   1941-

PERSONAL: Born May 11, 1941, in Swainsboro, Ga.; son of Remar M. (a contractor) and Mildred (a teacher; maiden name, George) Sutton. *Education:* Attended University of the Seven Seas, 1962-64, Emory University, 1965-67.

ADDRESSES: Home and office—603 West Sandtown Rd. S.W., Marietta, Ga. 30064. *Agent*—Reid Boates, 44 Mountain Ridge Dr., Wayne, N.J. 07470.

CAREER: Young & Rubicam Advertising, Inc., New York, N.Y., account executive, 1968-69; Richard K. Manoff Advertising, New York City, vice-president, 1970-72; writer, 1980—. Guest on television and radio programs, including "Good Morning, America," "Today," "Nightline," "Donahue," "Oprah Winfrey," and "Sonya Live"; originator and promoter of public service events benefiting American Hospital in Paris and National Public Radio.

MEMBER: Underwater Explorers Society.

WRITINGS:

Don't Get Taken Every Time, Viking, 1982.
Body Worry, Viking, 1987.
Long Lines (novel; Book-of-the-Month Club selection), Weidenfeld & Nicolson, 1987.
Ebola (novel), Weidenfeld & Nicolson, 1988.
Like New, Viking, 1988.
Selling Without Selling Out: Marketing in the New Age, Viking, 1989.

Author of columns "Body Worry," and "Fitness File," syndicated by United Features, and of *Washington Post* column "Remar Sutton's Journal." Contributor to magazines and newspapers, including *Sports Illustrated, Reader's Digest,* and *Family Weekly*. Editor of *American Health* magazine.

WORK IN PROGRESS: A book based on the author's work with dolphins.

SIDELIGHTS: Publicity from Remar Sutton's popular syndicated column "Body Worry" led the author to write a book of the same name, an account of his nine-and-a-half-month eating and exercise program that resulted in Sutton's trimming more than ten inches from his waistline, losing more than thirty-five pounds, and improving his health significantly. The former advertising executive and author of the successful car shopping guide *Don't Get Taken Every Time* left business and moved to Grand Bahama Island to write the story of his own physical improvement in early 1986. After spending $100,000 on consultations, travel, and a personal trainer, Sutton began an exercise regimen consisting of aerobics, cycling, jogging, and weight lifting. Once a three-pack-a-day smoker with mild heart disease and impaired lungs, the forty-five year old decreased his biological age, estimated his doctor, from fifty-five to forty years. "The key is [moderation]," Sutton told Bill Barol in a *Newsweek* interview. "I've made modest eating changes and undertaken a modest exercise program. This isn't a diet book. . . . Diets are deprivation. The rest of your life's not going to be worth living if you have to be miserable."

BIOGRAPHICAL/CRITICAL SOURCES:

BOOKS

Plimpton, George, *One More July*, Harper, 1977.
Plimpton, George, *Fireworks*, Doubleday, 1984.

PERIODICALS

Newsweek, April 27, 1987.
Time, April 6, 1987.
U.S. News and World Report, October 5, 1987.

* * *

SWEENY, Mary K. 1923-

PERSONAL: Born December 4, 1923, in Cleveland, Ohio; daughter of James M. (a physician) and Fredericka (a housewife; maiden name, Kline) Seliskar; married John T. Sweeny, April 23, 1949; children: Paul, Mary Sweeny Hornung. *Education:* Notre Dame College of Ohio, A.B., 1944; Western Reserve (now Case Western Reserve) University, M.S. in L.S., 1966; John Carroll University, M.A., 1984. *Religion:* Roman Catholic.

ADDRESSES: Home—2865 Clarkson Rd., Cleveland Heights, Ohio 44118. *Office*—Library, John Carroll University, Cleveland, Ohio 44118.

CAREER: Catholic Universe Bulletin, Cleveland, Ohio, reporter, 1944-49; John Carroll University, Cleveland, reference head at university library, 1966—.

MEMBER: Catholic Library Association, Academic Library Association of Ohio.

WRITINGS:

Walker Percy and the Postmodern World, Loyola University Press, 1987.

Author of radio scripts for WCLV-FM Radio program "Library Spectrum." Contributor to *America* and *Critic*.

WORK IN PROGRESS: A collection of poetry.

* * *

SYMEONOGLOU, Sarantis 1937-

PERSONAL: Born February 14, 1937, in Athens, Greece; immigrated to United States, 1966, naturalized citizen, 1976; son of Miltiades and Olga (Souvatzoglou) Symeonoglou; married, 1965 (divorced). *Education:* University of Athens, B.A., 1961; Columbia University, Ph.D., 1971. *Religion:* Greek Orthodox.

ADDRESSES: Home—3615 Flora Pl., St. Louis, Mo. 63110. *Office*—Department of Art and Archaeology, Washington University, Lindell-Skinner Blvd., St. Louis, Mo. 63130.

CAREER: Greek Archaeological Service, Delphi, Athens, and Thebes, Greece, assistant curator of archaeology, 1963-66; Washington University, St. Louis, Mo., assistant professor, 1969-76, associate professor, 1977-85, professor of archaeology, 1985—, research fellow, 1973-74. Field director of excavations for Columbia University Archaeological Expedition, 1970-74; founder and director of Odyssey Project, 1984—. *Military service:* Greek Army, 1961-62.

MEMBER: Archaeological Institute of America, Association of Field Archaeologists, American Oriental Society, Archaeological Society of Athens, Explorers Club.

AWARDS, HONORS: Fellow of American Philosophical Society, 1976; grants from National Geographic Society, 1984 and 1985.

WRITINGS:

The Topography of Thebes: From the Bronze Age to Modern Times, Princeton University Press, 1985.

Also author of *Kadmeia 1: Mycenaean Finds From Thebes, Greece: Excavations at 14 Oedipus St.*, P. Astrom (Sweden), 1973, and contributor of articles and reviews to archaeological and anthropological journals.

WORK IN PROGRESS: A book on Odysseus, publication expected in 1990; excavations of Ithaca, Greece, related to Homer's *Odyssey;* research on classical sculpture, particularly the temple of Zeus at Olympia.

SIDELIGHTS: Sarantis Symeonoglou told *CA* that his current research is intended to examine "the connection between the oral tradition of Homer's *Odyssey* and the archaeological finds on the island of Ithaca. I am interested in the nature of 'oral literature,' with an emphasis on identifying historical and cultural truths in the work of Homer.

"Ancient Thebes has occupied much of my career. I spent twenty years trying to interpret its jumbled archaeological remains most of which appeared in small fragments while digging foundations for the modern town. I also tried in vain to excite Greek and international support for its salvation and preservation. Unfortunately, modern construction has destroyed or covered up most of the remains and there is little hope for future archaeological work there. I wrote the book on Thebes as my epitaph to a glorious archaeological site and a world-class center of culture destroyed by human indifference. Frustration over the problem of Thebes was also the main reason for leaving the Greek Archaeological Service and seeking an academic career. When my book on Thebes was completed, I had to turn away from this city. I chose to focus on a major achaeological problem: whether or not the city of Ithaca, the center of the action in the *Odyssey* of Homer, really existed. After five years of research, I am convinced that it did; the evidence I accumulated is fairly strong. I found a city in the exact spot specified in the *Odyssey;* this city was occupied during the crucial centuries before Homer—at least as early as the thirteenth century B.C. and continuously thereafter until the time of Homer, the eighth century B.C. This is the only such city on the island and in the region; a specific monument referred to in the *Odyssey* has also been identified, the shrine of Apollo. I expect that more evidence will be produced when systematic excavations resume."

The tragedy of Thebes has its origin in the political events of the Persian Wars, and it continues to the present day, which reveals an archaeological mecca virtually smothered by modern apartment buildings. Existing archaeological sites in the city of Thebes number nearly three hundred, but many consist of tiny fragments of land, looted of artifacts and difficult to excavate. "The great achievement of *The Topography of Thebes*," reported A. M. Snodgrass in the *Times Literary Supplement*, "is to preserve almost everything that can be salvaged from this unhappy history." Symeonoglou's book itemizes all known evidence of archaeological discovery in and near the ancient city, and it summarizes, according to Snodgrass, "the implications of these disoveries," in such a way that the critic calls the work "an unqualified success." He added that *The Topography of Thebes* also contains the most current hypotheses about the history of Thebes, which, though not yet proven, "add to the readability of a text which is already exemplary in its clarity." The author, Snodgrass commented, "writes with the ideal mixture of firsthand experience . . . and discreet distance from recent activity." The book, he concluded, "will be the first place to which future scholars will turn."

AVOCATIONAL INTERESTS: Music, performing *lieder*, wine, food.

BIOGRAPHICAL/CRITICAL SOURCES:

PERIODICALS

Times Literary Supplement, December 27, 1985.

*   *   *

SYMONDS, Craig L.   1946-

PERSONAL: Born December 31, 1946, in Long Beach, Calif.; son of Lee and Virginia (Garrison) Symonds; married Marylou Hayden (in development), January 17, 1969; children: Jeffrey K. *Education:* University of California, Los Angeles, B.A., 1967; University of Florida, M.A., 1969, Ph.D., 1976.

ADDRESSES: Office—Department of History, U.S. Naval Academy, Annapolis, Md. 21402.

CAREER: U.S. Naval War College, Washington, D.C., assistant professor of strategy, 1973-74; U.S. Naval Academy, Annapolis, Md., assistant professor, 1976-80, associate professor, 1980-85; professor of history, 1985—, chairman of department, 1988—. *Military service:* U.S. Navy, 1971-74; became lieutenant.

MEMBER: American Military Institute, Southern Historical Association.

WRITINGS:

Navalists and Antinavalists: The Naval Policy Debate in the United States, 1785-1827, University of Delaware Press, 1980.

A Battlefield Atlas of the Civil War (Book-of-the-Month Club selection), Nautical and Aviation Press, 1983.
A Battlefield Atlas of the American Revolution (Book-of-the-Month Club selection), Nautical and Aviation Press, 1986.

EDITOR

John B. Marchand, *Charleston Blockade: The Journals of John B. Marchand, USN*, Naval War College Press, 1976.
New Aspects of Naval History, Naval Institute Press, 1981.
William H. Parker, *Recollections of a Naval Officer, 1841-1865*, Naval Institute Press, 1985.
Alvah F. Hunter, *A Year on a Monitor*, University of South Caroloina Press, 1987.

CONTRIBUTOR

Robert W. Love, Jr., editor, *The Chiefs of Naval Operations*, Naval Institute Press, 1980.
James Bradford, editor, *Command Under Sail*, Naval Institute Press, 1985.
Kenneth J. Hagan and William R. Roberts, editors, *Against All Enemies: Interpretations of American Military History From Colonial Times to the Present*, Greenwood Press, 1986.

WORK IN PROGRESS: A biography of Confederate general Joseph E. Johnston, publication by Norton expected in 1991.

*   *   *

SYSYN, Frank E.   1946-

PERSONAL: Born December 27, 1946, in Passaic, N.J.; son of Frank and Hattie (Miller) Sysyn. *Education:* Princeton University, B.A., 1968; London School of Slavonic and East European Studies, London, M.A., 1969; Harvard University, Ph.D., 1976.

ADDRESSES: Office—Ukrainian Research Institute, 1583 Massachusetts Ave., Cambridge, Mass. 02138.

CAREER: Harvard University, Cambridge, Mass., lecturer, 1976-77, assistant professor, 1977-80, associate professor of history, 1980-85, associate director of Ukrainian Research Institute, 1985—.

WRITINGS:

(Editor with Andrei J. Markovits) *Nationbuilding and the Politics of Nationalism: Essays on Austrian Galicia*, Harvard University Press, 1982.
Between Poland and the Ukraine: The Dilemma of Adam Kysil, 1600-1653, Harvard University Press, 1985.

Associate editor of *Harvard Ukrainian Studies*.

WORK IN PROGRESS: The Great Ukrainian Revolt: An Examination of the Khmel'nyts'kyi Uprising, 1648-1659, publication expected in 1989.

T

TAKTSIS, Costas 1927-1988

OBITUARY NOTICE—See index for *CA* sketch: Born October 8, 1927, in Salonika, Greece; died of strangulation, c. August 25, 1988, in Athens, Greece. Author. Known for his novel *The Third Wedding Wreath,* Taktsis received little attention in his native Greece after financing the book's publication in 1962. Six years later, however, when the work appeared in English translation, he earned substantial acclaim for his humorous account of one woman's experiences through both World War II and the Greek civil war. Taktsis also wrote *Grandmother Athina,* a collection of various accounts inspired by his grandmother. Despite his success, Taktsis resided in a rundown district in Athens. His corpse was found at his home there on August 28, 1988, at least two days after his murder.

OBITUARIES AND OTHER SOURCES:

PERIODICALS

Chicago Tribune, August 29, 1988.
Washington Post, August 29, 1988.

*   *   *

TALAMINI, John T(homas) 1940-

PERSONAL: Born April 25, 1940, in Philadelphia, Pa.; *Education:* St. Joseph's College (now University), Philadelphia, Pa., B.S., 1962; attended Temple University, 1962-63; Fordham University, M.A., 1964; Rutgers University, Ph.D., 1971.

ADDRESSES: Home—7277 Bradford Rd., Upper Darby, Pa. *Office*—Department of Sociology, University of Scranton, Scranton, Pa. 18510.

CAREER: Opinion Research Corp., N.J., research assistant in mass media, public opinion, and consumer behavior research, 1965-66; Rutgers University, New Brunswick, N.J., instructor in sociology, 1966-69; Newark State College, Union, N.J., lecturer in sociology, 1969-70; University of Bridgeport, Bridgeport, Conn., assistant professor of sociology, 1970-74; Albertus Magnus College, New Haven, Conn., assistant professor of sociology, 1974-77; University of Scranton, Scranton, Pa., associate professor, 1977-82, professor of sociology, 1982—.

MEMBER: International Sociological Association, International Society of Law Enforcement and Criminal Justice Educators, Academy of Criminal Justice Sciences, Sex Information and Education Council of the United States, Society for the Scientific Study of Sex, American Academy of Political and Social Sciences, American Sociological Association, Industrial Relations Research Association, Society for the Study of Social Problems.

AWARDS, HONORS: Grant from National Endowment for the Humanities, 1980.

WRITINGS:

(Editor with Charles H. Page) *Sport and Society: An Anthology,* Little, Brown, 1973.
Boys Will Be Girls: The Hidden World of the Heterosexual Male Transvestite, University Press of America, 1982.

BIOGRAPHICAL/CRITICAL SOURCES:

PERIODICALS

New York Times Book Review, December 2, 1973.
Washington Post Book World, December 9, 1973.*

*   *   *

TARNAWSKI, Wit(old) 1894-1988

OBITUARY NOTICE: Born July 6, 1894, in Kosow, Galicia, Austria-Hungary (now U.S.S.R.); died August 4, 1988. Physician and author. Tarnawski was known as an authority on the life and works of twentieth-century writer Joseph Conrad. After military service in World War I and in the Polish-Soviet war of 1919 to 1920, Tarnawski obtained a medical doctorate in 1926 and helped his father run a sanatorium until the outbreak of World War II. In 1940 and 1941 he chaired the Polish National committees in Romania and Cyprus and, beginning in 1942, was chief medical officer of cadet schools with the Polish Armed Forces of the Middle East. Moving to England in the late 1940s, Tarnawski worked in a Polish hospital from 1950 to 1954, later serving as a consultant at the Mount Pleasant Geriatric Hospital. He wrote novels and nonfiction books in Polish, of which *Conrad: The Man, the Writer, the Pole,* published in 1972 and translated in 1984, is among the best known.

OBITUARIES AND OTHER SOURCES:

PERIODICALS

Times (London), August 13, 1988.

TAYLOR, Andrew   1944-1988

PERSONAL: Born October 12, 1944, in Scotland; died March, 1988; son of John (a member of Parliament) and Olive (a teacher; maiden name, Fox) Taylor; married Rosalind Marie (a consultant), September, 1969; children: Alex Claire, Tom Bryden. *Education:* University of Bristol, B.Sc. (with honors), 1967.

ADDRESSES: Home and office—5 Maple Ave., Gilesgate, Durham DH1 2HB, England. *Agent*—David Higham Associates Ltd., 5/8 Lower John St., Golden Sq., London W1R 2HA, England.

CAREER: Copywriter, television and radio producer, and creative director for advertising agencies in London, England, 1966-81; free-lance writer, 1981-88. Scriptwriter in Hollywood, Calif.; creative and marketing consultant; cathedral chorister; school governor.

AWARDS, HONORS: Whitbread Award for juvenile fiction, 1986, for *The Coal House*.

WRITINGS:

"The Sniffer and the Pug" (television script), first broadcast by British Broadcasting Corporation (BBC), 1975.
"Even Solomon" (television script), first broadcast by BBC, 1977.
"The First Time I Saw Britain" (radio script), first broadcast by BBC, 1980.
"Passing Place" (radio script), first broadcast by BBC, 1987.
The Coal House (juvenile novel), Collins, 1987.

WORK IN PROGRESS: Novels for young people, including *The Boat House, Sasha's Harvest,* and *Witch Riding a Pig,* completed but unpublished at the time of death.

SIDELIGHTS: A radio and television scriptwriter for over a decade, Andrew Taylor wrote his first novel for children in 1987. Titled *The Coal House,* the book was named for the Durham countryside coal house where thirteen-year-old protagonist Alison Lucas and her father moved after the death of Alison's mother. The girl was reluctant to leave her friends and relatives in Hertfordshire, and she resisted adjustment to her new surroundings. Gradually, though, the coal country, its simple lifestyle, and its people drew Alison into a local miners' strike and awakened a new understanding and level of maturity. Joanna Motion wrote in the *Times Literary Supplement,* "Andrew Taylor handles serious and sombre material without overloading the book."

Taylor told *CA:* "I want my writing to bridge the gap between kids' books and adult writing."

AVOCATIONAL INTERESTS: The natural world (the country), European travel.

BIOGRAPHICAL/CRITICAL SOURCES:

PERIODICALS

Times Literary Supplement, March 20, 1987.

*   *   *

TAYLOR, William Ewart, Jr.   1927-

PERSONAL: Born November 21, 1927, in Toronto, Ontario, Canada; son of William Ewart and Margaret (Patrick) Taylor; married Joan Elliott, September 12, 1952; children: Alison, Beth, William. *Education:* University of Toronto, B.A. (with honors), 1951; University of Illinois at Urbana-Champaign, A.M., 1952; University of Michigan, Ph.D., 1965.

ADDRESSES: Home—509 Piccadilly Ave., Ottawa, Ontario, Canada K1Y 0H7. *Office*—Social Science and Humanities Research Council of Canada, 255 Albert St., P.O. Box 1610, Ottawa, Ontario, Canada K1P 6G4.

CAREER: National Museums of Canada, Ottawa, Ontario, arctic archaeologist, 1956-60, chief of Archaeology Division, 1960-67, director of Human History Branch, 1967-68; National Museum of Man, Ottawa, director, 1967-83; Social Science and Humanities Research Council of Canada, Ottawa, president, 1982-87; writer. Conducted arctic field research, 1950-65; visiting professor at University of Alaska, 1966.

MEMBER: International Union of Anthropological and Ethnological Sciences, International Union of Prehistoric and Protohistoric Sciences (permanent council), Arctic Institute of North America (fellow), Royal Society of Canada (fellow), American Anthropological Association (fellow), American Association for the Advancement of Science, National Press Club, Royal Anthropological Institute (fellow), Royal Geographical Society (fellow), Society of Antiquaries of Scotland (honorary fellow), Sigma Xi.

AWARDS, HONORS: LL.D. from University of Calgary, 1975; Centennial Medal from Royal Society of Canada, 1982; D.Litt. from University of Newfoundland, 1983; Fiftieth Anniversary award from Society for American Archaeology, 1985; Queen's Jubilee Medal; Bicentennial Medal from Society of Antiquaries of Scotland.

WRITINGS:

(General editor) *The Arctic World,* Sierra Books, 1985.

Author of four books in arctic prehistory. Contributor of nearly one hundred articles to archaeology, native art, and museology journals.

WORK IN PROGRESS: Research on Canadian arctic archaeology.

AVOCATIONAL INTERESTS: Roses, skiing, bicycling, history (social, military, and medieval), classical music, Dixieland jazz.

*   *   *

THEMERSON, Stefan   1910-1988

OBITUARY NOTICE—See index for *CA* sketch: Born January 25, 1910, in Plock, Poland; died September 6, 1988, in London, England. Filmmaker, publisher, and author. Themerson distinguished himself in a variety of career endeavors. As a filmmaker, he collaborated in Poland with his wife, the painter Franciszka Weinles, on several experimental works in the 1930s and 1940s. When Poland fell to the Germans in 1939, Themerson lived briefly in France and then moved to London, his home throughout the remainder of his life. After World War II he and Weinles established the Gaberbocchus Press and published editions of works such as Alfred Jarry's *Ubu Roi* and Christian-Dietrich Grabbe's *Comedy, Satire, Irony, and Meaning.* Themerson's own writings include the novels *Bayamus, Professor Mmaa's Lecture,* and *Cardinal Polatuo,* and the essay collections "*Factor T*" and "*Semantic Sonata*" and *Kurt Schwitters in England.* Only one of his experimental films,

"The Adventures of a Good Citizen," survived World War II.

OBITUARIES AND OTHER SOURCES:

BOOKS

International Authors and Writers Who's Who, 10th edition, International Biographical Centre, 1986.

PERIODICALS

Times (London), September 8, 1988.

*   *   *

THERSITES
    See BRAM, Christopher

*   *   *

THOMAS, (Thomas) George   1909-

PERSONAL: Born January 29, 1909, in Rhondda, Wales; son of Zacharia and Emma Jane Thomas. *Education:* Attended University of Southampton.

ADDRESSES: *Home*—Tilbury, 173 King George V Dr. E., Cardiff, Mid-Glamorgan, Wales.

CAREER: British Parliament, London, England, member of House of Commons for Central Cardiff, 1945-50, and West Cardiff, 1950-83, parliamentary under-secretary of state at Home Office, 1964-66, minister of state at Welsh Office, 1966-67, and Commonwealth Office, 1967-68, secretary of state for Wales, 1968-70, deputy speaker and chairman of Ways and Means Committee, 1974-76, speaker, 1976-83, member of House of Lords, 1983—. Chairman of Bank of Wales, 1984—. Vice-president of Methodist Conference, 1960-61; president of Community Projects Foundation, 1981—; chairman of Joint Commonwealth Society Council, 1984-87. Freeman of Borough of Rhondda, 1970, City of Cardiff, 1975, and London, 1980.

AWARDS, HONORS: Dato Setia Negara of Brunei, 1971; honorary fellow of University of Wales, University College, Cardiff, 1972—; LL.D. from Asbury College, Wilmore, Ky., 1976, University of Southampton, 1977, University of Birmingham, 1978, and University of Leeds, 1982; honorary member of the Livery of the Worshipful Company of Blacksmiths, 1980; honorary Master of the Bench of Gray's Inn, 1982—; created first Viscount Tonypandy, 1983; D.C.L. from Oxford University, 1983.

WRITINGS:

The Christian Heritage in Politics, Epworth, 1959.
Mr. Speaker (autobiography), Century Press, 1985.
My Wales, Century Press, 1986.

WORK IN PROGRESS: A book entitled *My Faith*.

BIOGRAPHICAL/CRITICAL SOURCES:

PERIODICALS

Times (London), February 21, 1985.

*   *   *

THOMAS, Rosie

BRIEF ENTRY: British novelist. Thomas is known primarily for her Romantic Novel of the Year award-winner, *Sunrise*

(Fontana, 1984), and her best-seller, *The White Dove* (Viking, 1986). *Sunrise* heroine Angharad Owain finds herself in a lovers' triangle with an incestuous sister-brother pair. Set against the backdrop of the Spanish Civil War, Literary Guild dual main selection *The White Dove* is a melodrama involving lovers from different social classes. Thomas's strong showing in these two novels, coupled with her work in *Strangers* (Simon & Schuster, 1987), a romance of a mildly discontented housewife and a cynical advertising executive who discover each other in the aftermath of a department-store bombing, caused *Washington Post Book World* editor Brigitte Weeks to call Thomas "a gifted British writer . . . [whose strength lies in] catching the ordinary while avoiding the banal." Thomas has also written *Celebration* (Fontana, 1982), *Love's Choice* (Avon, 1982) and *Follies* (Fontana, 1983).

BIOGRAPHICAL/CRITICAL SOURCES:

PERIODICALS

New York Times Book Review, July 12, 1987.
Washington Post Book World, February 14, 1984, June 29, 1984, July 28, 1987.

*   *   *

THOMIS, Wayne   1907-1988

OBITUARY NOTICE: Born in 1907 in Cairo, Ill.; died September 28, 1988, in Fort Lauderdale, Fla. Pilot and journalist. A writer for the *Chicago Tribune* for forty years, Thomis was well known for his coverage of aviation events and was respected for his versatility. He joined Chicago's City News Bureau in 1925 and began writing for the *Tribune* in 1932, reporting on topics from aviation to murder and political corruption. In 1934 he became the paper's aviation writer. Himself a pilot, Thomis often transported *Tribune* publisher Robert R. McCormick to his destinations, and during World War II he enlisted in the U.S. Navy to be a combat pilot. Disqualified because he was overweight, he tested Navy planes and ferried them to combat areas instead. Thomis covered the first commercial flight across the Atlantic Ocean in 1939, the battle of Midway, General Douglas MacArthur's surprise attack at Inchon, South Korea, and the 1963 assassination of U.S. President John F. Kennedy; he was also a war correspondent in Vietnam. After retiring from the *Tribune* in 1972 Thomis wrote for the *Fort Lauderdale News*.

OBITUARIES AND OTHER SOURCES:

PERIODICALS

Chicago Tribune, September 29, 1988.

*   *   *

THURSTON, Carol (M.)

PERSONAL: Born in Chicago, Ill.; daughter of Cecil E. and Vera B. McWharter; married George B. Thurston (a professor); children: John Douglas, Mary Elizabeth. *Education:* University of Texas at Austin, M.A., 1977, Ph.D., 1979.

ADDRESSES: *Home*—1000 Madrone Rd., Austin, Tex. 78746. *Agent*—Robin Rue, Anita Diamant, Writers Workshop, Inc., 310 Madison Ave., New York, N.Y. 10017.

CAREER: University of Houston, Houston, Tex., assistant professor, 1979-82; press aide and speech writer for Senator Lloyd Doggett, Austin, Tex., 1983-84; writer.

WRITINGS:

(With Robert F. Schenkkan) *Case Studies in Institutional Licensee Management* (monograph), National Association of Educational Broadcasters, 1980.
Flair (novel), Pocket Books, 1987.
The Romance Revolution: Erotic Novels for Women and the Quest for a New Sexual Identity, University of Illinois Press, 1987.
Sins of Our Mothers (novel), Pocket Books, 1989.

WORK IN PROGRESS: A third novel, tentatively titled *The Chosen Few.*

SIDELIGHTS: Carol Thurston told *CA:* "For me the bridge between nonfiction and fiction was speech writing, a liberating experience in the sense of freeing the imagination after years of expository writing, and entering into thinking in dialogue."

BIOGRAPHICAL/CRITICAL SOURCES:

PERIODICALS

Globe and Mail (Toronto), October 17, 1987.
Psychology Today, October, 1987.
Times Literary Supplement, March 11-17, 1988.

*   *   *

TILLER, Ted
See TILLER, Theodore II

*   *   *

TILLER, Theodore II   1913(?)-1988
(Ted Tiller)

OBITUARY NOTICE: Known professionally as Ted Tiller; born c. 1913; died of complications following brain surgery, September 24, 1988, in Manhattan, N.Y. Radio broadcaster, actor, director, and playwright. For nearly half a century Tiller directed and performed on Broadway, in regional theater, and on television. Beginning his career as a radio broadcaster, he first appeared on Broadway in the 1944 play "Sing Out, Sweet Land!" and later held roles in such productions as "No, No, Nanette" and "Witness for the Prosecution." Tiller was a performer and director with the Valley Players in Holyoke, Massachusetts, for eleven seasons, and he often took parts in Off-Broadway shows. A scriptwriter and actor for television programs such as "Omnibus" and "Mr. I. Imagination," Tiller also wrote the 1971 play *Count Dracula,* which was published by Samuel French the following year.

OBITUARIES AND OTHER SOURCES:

PERIODICALS

New York Times, October 1, 1988.

*   *   *

TILLOTSON, G(iles) H(enry) R(upert)   1960-

PERSONAL: Born July 25, 1960, in Tidworth, England; son of Henry Michael (an army officer) and Angela (Shaw) Tillotson; married Sarah Glynn (an architect), September 16, 1984. *Education:* Trinity College, Cambridge, B.A., 1982, Ph.D., 1986.

ADDRESSES: Office—Peterhouse, Cambridge CB2 1RD, England.

CAREER: Schoolmaster in Darjeeling, India, 1979; Cambridge University, Cambridge, England, fellow of Peterhouse, 1986—.

WRITINGS:

The Rajput Palaces: The Development of an Architectural Style, 1450-1750, Yale University Press, 1987.
Fan Kwae Pictures: Paintings and Drawings by George Chinnery and Other Artists in the Collection of the Hongkong and Shanghai Banking Corporation, Spink and Son, 1987.

Contributor to scholarly journals.

WORK IN PROGRESS: A study of changes in Indian architecture since 1850, and of the controversies arising from them.

SIDELIGHTS: G. H. R. Tillotson told *CA:* "I have been visiting India since 1979. I have traveled extensively within the country, but especially in the Northwest. My doctoral thesis described the palace architecture of Rajasthan. I now have two principal research interests: the later architectural history of India, and Western art relating to India and the colonial East. The motivation for this research is, of course, the joy of traveling in these countries."

BIOGRAPHICAL/CRITICAL SOURCES:

PERIODICALS

Architects Journal, September 16, 1987.
Artention (Hong Kong), July-August, 1988.
Spectator, July 25, 1987.
Times Literary Supplement, October 23, 1987.

*   *   *

TITUNIK, Irwin R(obert)   1929-

PERSONAL: Born June 8, 1929, in New York, N.Y.; son of Samuel and Regina (Terner) Titunik; divorced; children: Regina Titunik-Yoshikawa, Deborah Titunik Wilcox, Vera. *Education:* Attended University of Chicago, 1947-48, and City College (now of the City University of New York), 1949-50; University of California, Berkeley, B.A. (with highest honors), 1951, M.A., 1956, Ph.D., 1963; attended London School of Slavonic and East European Studies, London, 1956-57, and University of Moscow, 1964-65.

ADDRESSES: Office—Department of Slavic Languages and Literatures, University of Michigan, Ann Arbor, Mich. 48109.

CAREER: University of Michigan, Ann Arbor, instructor, 1959-63, assistant professor, 1963-68, associate professor, 1968-74, professor of Slavic languages and literatures, 1974—. Visiting assistant professor at University of California, Berkeley, 1966-67, and University of Texas at Austin, 1978.

MEMBER: American Association for the Advancement of Slavic Studies, Phi Beta Kappa.

AWARDS, HONORS: Grant for studying in the U.S.S.R. from University of Michigan, 1964-65; grants from U.S. Office of Education, 1970, and Kenan Institute for Advanced Russian Studies, 1987.

WRITINGS:

(Translator) B. M. Ejxenbaum, *O. Henry and the Theory of the Short Story,* Michigan Slavic Contributions, 1968.
(Translator) P. V. Annenkov, *The Extraordinary Decade: Political Memoirs of Pavel Nikolaevich Miliukov, 1905-1917,*

edited by Arthur P. Mendel, University of Michigan Press, 1968.

(Editor and translator with Ladislav Matejka) V. N. Volosinov, *Marxism and the Philosophy of Language*, Seminar Press, 1973.

(Editor with Matejka, and contributor) *Semiotics of Art*, MIT Press, 1976.

(Editor with N. Bruss, and translator) Volosinov, *Freudianism: A Marxist Critique*, Academic Press, 1976, published as *Freudianism: A Critical Sketch*, Indiana University Press, 1987.

(Editor with Matejka, M. Suino, and S. Shishkoff) *Readings in Soviet Semiotics*, Michigan Slavic Publications, 1977.

Associate editor of *Cross-Currents*, 1986.

CONTRIBUTOR

Matejka and K. Pomorska, editors, *Readings in Russian Poetics*, MIT Press, 1971.

Morris Halle and other editors, *Semiosis: Semiotics and the History of Culture*, Michigan Slavic Contributions, 1984.

Contributor to *Language and Literary Theory*, edited by B. Stolz and others; *Russian Literature and American Critics*, edited by K. Brostrom; *Handbook of Russian Literature;* and *The Modern Encyclopedia of Russian and Soviet Literatures*. Also contributor of articles, translations, and reviews to scholarly journals.

WORK IN PROGRESS: "A study on the incomparable *Dushen'ka*, I. F. Bogdanovich's masterpiece, against the background of the versions of the Cupid and Psyche tale by second-century philosopher Lucius Apuleius and seventeenth-century French fabulist Jean de LaFontaine and their eighteenth-century Russian translators."

*   *   *

TOLES, Thomas G.   1951-
(Tom Toles)

PERSONAL: Born October 10, 1951, in Buffalo, N.Y.; son of George E. (a free-lance writer) and Rose (Riehle) Toles; married Gretchen Saarnijoki (a parks preservationist), May 26, 1973. *Education:* State University of New York at Buffalo, B.A., 1973.

ADDRESSES: Home—Hamburg, N.Y. *Office*—*Buffalo News*, 1 News Plaza, Buffalo, N.Y. 14240. *Agent*—Universal Press Syndicate, 4400 Johnson Dr., Fairway, Kan. 66205.

CAREER: Buffalo Courier-Express, Buffalo, N.Y., staff artist, 1973-80, graphics designer, 1980, editorial cartoonist, 1980-82; *Buffalo News*, Buffalo, editorial cartoonist, 1982—.

MEMBER: Association of American Editorial Cartoonists.

AWARDS, HONORS: Twenty Page One Awards from Buffalo Newspaper Guild, 1973-82; George W. Thorn Award from University of Buffalo Alumni Association, 1983; first place award in John Fischetti Editorial Cartoonist Competition, 1984; Golden Apple Award for Excellence in Educational Journalism from New York State United Teachers, 1984; New York State Historic Preservation Award, 1985; Pulitzer Prize nomination, 1985.

WRITINGS:

UNDER NAME TOM TOLES

The Taxpayer's New Clothes (editorial cartoons), foreword by Jeff Macnelly, Andrews, McMeel & Parker, 1985.

Mr. Gazoo: A Cartoon History of the Reagan Era, Pantheon, 1987.

Cartoons distributed by Universal Press Syndicate, 1982—.

*   *   *

TOLES, Tom
See TOLES, Thomas G.

*   *   *

TOWER, Ann
See STRAUBING, Harold (Elk)

*   *   *

TREVELYAN, Julian O(tto)   1910-1988

OBITUARY NOTICE—See index for CA sketch: Born February 20, 1910, in Dorking, England; died July 12, 1988. Artist, educator, and author. Trevelyan was known for his achievements in art styles such as surrealism and expressionism. In his first one-person exhibition—held in London in 1935—he presented paintings indicating his interests in fantasy and humor. Soon afterward he began associating with surrealists. By the 1940s, however, Trevelyan had broken from surrealism to develop a relatively primitive style marked by brightness and simplicity. Trevelyan taught at the Royal College of Art in the 1950s and 1960s. He wrote such works as *Indigo Days*, *The Artist and His World*, *Etching*, and *A Place, a State*.

OBITUARIES AND OTHER SOURCES:

BOOKS

Who's Who, 140th edition, St. Martin's, 1988.

PERIODICALS

Times (London), July 14, 1988.

*   *   *

TRIFONOV, Yuri (Valentinovich)   1925-1981

PERSONAL: Given name sometimes transliterated as Yury, Iurii, or Uri; born August 28, 1925, in Moscow, U.S.S.R.; died after surgery, March 28, 1981, in Moscow, U.S.S.R.; son of Valentin A. Trifonov; children: Valentin. *Education:* Graduated from Gorky Institute of Literature, 1949.

CAREER: Writer, 1947-81.

AWARDS, HONORS: Received Stalin Prize, 1951, for *Students*.

WRITINGS:

NOVELS IN ENGLISH TRANSLATION

Students, translation from the Russian by Ivy Litvinova and Margaret Wettlin, Foreign Languages Publishing House (Moscow), 1953.

The Impatient Ones, translation from the Russian by Robert Daglish, Progress Publishers (Moscow), 1978.

The Long Goodbye: Three Novellas (contains *The Exchange*, *Taking Stock*, and *The Long Goodbye*), translation from the Russian by Helen P. Burlingame and Ellendea Proffer, Harper, 1978.

Another Life [and] *The House on the Embankment*, translation from the Russian by Michael Glenny, Simon & Schuster, 1983.

The Old Man, translation from the Russian by Jacqueline Edwards and Mitchell Schneider, Simon & Schuster, 1984.

OTHER

Also author of a posthumously published novel, *Vremia i mesto* (title means ''Place and Time'').

SIDELIGHTS: Often called ''the Soviet Anton Chekhov,'' Yuri Trifonov chronicled the everyday lives and aspirations of the new Russian middle class in a series of novellas that earned him acclaim in the Soviet Union and abroad. The son of a Bolshevik revolutionary who was executed during Communist dictator Joseph Stalin's political purges of the 1930s, Trifonov used his work to subtly explore the ways in which the fear and betrayals of the Stalinist past had helped shape the values and morality of contemporary Soviet society. In so doing, he rejected broad political and ideological themes to focus on personal moral conflicts that reflect both Soviet history and the universal human dilemma. Trifonov, who died in 1981 at the age of fifty-five, was highly regarded for his stylistic artistry as well as his thematic originality.

Trifonov enjoyed success and official recognition early in his career, winning the prestigious Stalin Prize in 1951 at age twenty-six for his first book, *Students,* a novel of university life in the post-World War II years. When the Stalinist era drew to a close not long afterward, he began writing novellas that dealt candidly with the often petty, materialist ambitions and careerist rivalries common among the intelligentsia in a supposedly socialist society. Never a political dissident, Trifonov did not criticize the Soviet system as such but rather the obstinate human reality that gave the lie to official propaganda declaring the end of class divisions and egotistical behavior. Indeed, the novelist depicted unscrupulous self-seeking as usually the best way to ''get ahead'' in the official bureaucracy and secure scarce living space and consumer luxuries. Trifonov's moralistic rather than political approach allowed him to accommodate the Soviet censor and publish freely in his own country. His low political profile, however, contributed to his relative obscurity in the West during his lifetime.

The three novellas published in the United States under the title *The Long Goodbye* typify Trifonov's themes of moral choice, family conflicts, and career dilemmas among Moscow's petty bourgeoisie and his Chekhovian attention to the emotional nuances of everyday life. *The Exchange* describes a couple who attempt to secure a roomier apartment for themselves by having the husband's dying mother move in with them, thus appearing to deserve more living space. *Taking Stock* compares the petty passions of a quarreling family with the exhausted vigor of old religious icons, now collected by the middle class as decorative objects. The title work, finally, recounts the loves, triumphs, and disappointments of a Moscow actress. In a later novella, *Another Life,* Trifonov offered perhaps his most artfully realized portrait of a couple's failed marriage and frustrated careers, showing their personal and professional fates joined by character and history. *New York Times Book Review* critic Richard Lourie judged the work ''nearly flawless,'' remarking that the author moves ''from the errands and arguments of daily existence to memory and then back again with perfect ease. . . . By placing his story far in the background and by allowing himself to be absorbed in minutiae, Trifonov seems to say that our lives are made of small enduring traces, and all the rest, no matter how much harm it does us, really doesn't matter in the end.''

In *The House on the Embankment,* published in the Soviet Union in 1976, Trifonov adds a more direct historical and autobiographical context to his familiar themes of professional rivalry and personal opportunism. Glebov, the novella's anti-hero, is an ambitious young literature student whose tenuous moral sense fails him when his favorite professor and prospective father-in-law is falsely accused of disseminating counterrevolutionary ideology during the Stalinist era. Returning later in life to the large riverside apartment house where the professor and other prominent thinkers and revolutionaries had once lived, Glebov finds the building shabby and dilapidated, a mirror of the talent and ideals lost to the bureaucratic purges to which he owed his own career. Trifonov modeled the novella's apartment house on the Moscow building in which he lived as a boy with his grandmother after his parents were imprisoned in the 1930s. The building housed high government officials and the families of revolutionary heroes, and Trifonov later recalled witnessing numerous midnight arrests as Stalin consolidated his regime during that decade of terror.

Appearing during the conservative years of Soviet leader Leonid Brezhnev's administration, *The House on the Embankment* caused a stir with its clear evocation of the suppressed Stalinist past. But the novella, Trifonov's most popular work in the Soviet Union, also owed its success to its many literary merits. Trifonov tempered his somber historical narrative with subtly satirical jabs at the intelligentsia and the new managerial class, and his study of human values and motivations transcended the Soviet setting. ''The tortuous and dismal light in which Trifonov observes Russian character has changed very little, ironically, since the time of [writer Fedor] Dostoevski,'' Martin Lebowitz observed in a review for the *Chicago Tribune Book World.* ''Indeed he is a critic not of Russia but of human nature. His unusual talent may be unique among current Russian writers.''

Trifonov brought the Soviet Union's tumultuous early history more fully into focus in *The Old Man,* one of the last works he completed before his death. In fact, as *New York Times Book Review* critic Harlow Robinson remarked, the terrible years of civil war following the 1917 revolution are ''the protean and elusive protagonist'' of this work, which is considered unique to the author's *oeuvre.* The old man of the title is Pavel Evgrafovich Letunov, a civil war veteran driven by the need to make moral sense of his past and the chaotic events in which he played a part. His particular preoccupation is his conduct toward the cossack Migulin, a Bolshevik military commander and later a suspected counterrevolutionary who had married Letunov's youthful love, Asya. After lengthy research through the historical archives, Letunov writes an article urging that Migulin be politically ''rehabilitated,'' i.e., restored his status as a member of the Communist party. Letunov receives a letter in response from Asya that he hopes will shed light on his personal role in Migulin's tragedy. Throughout the novella Trifonov contrasts Letunov's ethical and historical concerns with his children's petty bickering over the use of a summerhouse, suggesting ironically that the moral failure of the earlier generation may have sown the barrenness and frivolity of the latter.

Stylistically, the author underscores his theme of moral ambiguity and shifting history with a fragmented and disjointed narrative that makes use of flashbacks, interior monologues, and passages from real and fictitious war documents. Dubbing *The Old Man* Trifonov's most ambitious effort, *New York Times* critic Walter Goodman noted that the novella also refers autobiographically to Trifonov's years of effort to rehabilitate his father's name. ''In its evocation of the intoxicating civil war years,'' the reviewer surmised, ''this novel is a considerable feat of imagination, bringing alive the unremitting threats and improvised responses, the daily bursts of panic, the chronic power struggles and the rough-and-ready justice.'' Trifonov died shortly after completing his final novel, *Place and Time,* a semi-autobiographical account of the life of a Soviet novelist.

BIOGRAPHICAL/CRITICAL SOURCES:

BOOKS

Contemporary Literary Criticism, Volume 45, Gale, 1987.

PERIODICALS

Chicago Tribune Book World, February 19, 1984.
Los Angeles Times, December 22, 1983.
Nation, September 9, 1978.
New Leader, September 10, 1979.
New York Times, October 2, 1984.
New York Times Book Review, March 18, 1984, February 3, 1985.
Washington Post Book World, November 11, 1978.

OBITUARIES:

PERIODICALS

New York Times, March 29, 1981.
Washington Post, March 29, 1981.*

—*Sketch by Curtis Skinner*

*   *   *

TROTTER, Patrick C.   1935-

PERSONAL: Born January 26, 1935, in Longview, Wash.; son of Clarence A. (a television repairman) and Maurine (a housewife; maiden name, Fugitt) Trotter; married Rena Rebecca Langille (a photographer), January 6, 1984; children: Scott, Diana; (stepchildren) Diana Davis, Benjamin Barrett, Adam Barrett. *Education:* Attended Lower Columbia College, 1953-55; Oregon State College (now University), B.S., 1957; Lawrence University, M.S., 1959, Ph.D., 1961.

ADDRESSES: Home—4926 26th Ave. S., Seattle, Wash. 98108. *Office*—Weyerhaeuser Technology Center, WTC 2H2, Tacoma, Wash. 98477.

CAREER: Weyerhaeuser Co., Tacoma, Wash., research scientist in pulp and paperboard division, 1961-68, department manager of fiber sciences in pulp and paperboard division, 1968-81, biotechnology department manager in corporate R. & D. division, 1981-86, biotechnology awareness project leader in strategic biological sciences division, 1986—.

MEMBER: American Fisheries Society, American Chemical Society, Technical Association of the Pulp and Paper Industry, Federation of Flyfishers, Trout Unlimited (chairman of Washington Council Trout Committee).

WRITINGS:

(With Bruce Ferguson and Les Johnson) *Flyfishing for Pacific Salmon,* Frank Amato Publications, 1985.
Cutthroat: Native Trout of the West, Colorado Associated University Press, 1987.

Author of ''From the Fly Book,'' a regular feature in *Salmon-Trout-Steelheader.* Contributor to national flyfishing magazines.

WORK IN PROGRESS: Research on the science behind the issues in fishery management.

SIDELIGHTS: Patrick C. Trotter told *CA:* ''I am a scientist with a deep interest in trout biology. In my writings I attempt to translate the technical complexities into language a layperson can understand. Most of my current projects have this as an underlying goal. I am also an avid fly fisherman and fly tier, and I enjoy writing about those subjects as well.''

*   *   *

TROW, George W. S.   1943-

PERSONAL: Surname rhymes with ''throw''; born September 28, 1943, in Greenwich, Conn.; son of George Swift (in the newspaper business) and Anne (a housewife; maiden name, Carter) Trow. *Education:* Harvard University, A.B., 1965. *Religion:* Episcopalian.

ADDRESSES: Office—c/o *New Yorker,* 25 West 43rd St., New York, N.Y. 10036.

CAREER: New Yorker, New York City, staff writer, 1966—.

AWARDS, HONORS: Jean Stein Award from the American Academy and Institute of Arts and Letters, 1986, for essays ''Within the Context of No Context'' and ''The Harvard Black Rock Forest'' and for novel *The City in the Mist.*

WRITINGS:

''Prairie Avenue'' (three-act play), first produced Off-Broadway at the South Street Theater, April, 1979.
The Tennis Game (three-act play; first produced Off-Broadway at the Theater of the Open Eye, February, 1978), Dramatists Play Service, 1979.
''Elizabeth Dead'' (one-act play), first produced in New York City at the Cubiculo Theater, November, 1980.
Bullies (collection of stories), Little, Brown, 1980.
Within the Context of No Context (nonfiction essays; contains ''Within the Context of No Context'' and ''Within That Context, One Style''), Boston, 1981.
The City in the Mist (novel), Little, Brown, 1984.

Contributor to periodicals, including *New Yorker* and *Harper's.*

WORK IN PROGRESS: One School, ''a novel about wild, unhappy young boys at the Phillips Exeter Academy.''

SIDELIGHTS: A longtime contributor to the *New Yorker,* George W. S. Trow is widely regarded as an innovator in the school of fiction. Trow's plays, short stories, and novel evidence what Roger Dionne, writing for the *Los Angeles Times,* called ''a truly new way of perceiving the world.'' The author's writings, likened by critics to the works of controversial American writer Gertrude Stein for their anti-establishment themes and abstract style, take a satiric look at a vapid and pretentious society.

Two of Trow's plays enjoyed Off-Broadway runs and brought the young author critical attention. ''The Tennis Game,'' staged in 1978, used tennis as a metaphor for society, evolving from a genteel nineteenth-century sport to a contemporary display of frenzied competition. The play was hailed as a ''clever'' work of ''literate as well as literary quality'' by Mel Gussow in the *New York Times.* Similarly, the 1980 production ''Elizabeth Dead''—consisting solely of a seventy-five minute soliloquy spoken by a dying Queen Elizabeth—was considered an imaginative effort. Jennifer Dunning noted in the *New York Times* that the played contained ''some touching, deft conceits.'' Dunning and Gussow suggested, however, that each stage work was obscured by an overly self-conscious posture.

In 1980, the same year in which "Elizabeth Dead" was staged, a collection of the author's short fiction pieces for the *New Yorker* were published in a volume entitled *Bullies*. According to Trow on the book's jacket copy, "The stories in *Bullies* take place in a landscape rather like history with the tide out." The writings are populated by a wide array of personalities, including an Upper East Side divorcee who likes to throw dinner parties, members of the rock critic establishment, aging stars, and faded royalty: in short, both the bullies who set the fashion and the bullied who feel compelled to follow it. Eve Babitz, writing for the *New York Times Book Review*, lauded *Bullies* as "a victory for things exactly as they are" and proof "that style, taste, those little refinements used in everyday life to separate the elegant and delightful from the rest of us, are nothing more than 'specifics.'"

In an article for the *Village Voice*, however, Eve Ottenberg accused Trow of creating "an in-joke," thereby falling victim to the same pretentious vice that he purports to expose. Ottenberg argued that many readers would miss the significance of Trow's recurring Alani Beach setting. "The spirit of the gossip column haunts these stories," she wrote, and those "who are expected to know what [the Hotel Reine American] is without being told, will probably not be amused." But in a review for *Harper's*, Jeffrey Burke viewed the "crumbling resort" of Alani Beach as a source of illumination in the stories rather than obscurity or condescension: Trow created an appropriate backdrop for his dark satire by shifting to a "surreal" context colored with "malevolence," assessed Burke.

Trow offered more observations on the state of contemporary American society in his 1981 essay collection *Within the Context of No Context*. The volume consists of two nonfiction pieces that originally appeared in the *New Yorker*. Several critics considered the title essay more relevant and insightful than its companion. "Within the Context of No Context" presents a generation without a past, a generation raised on television, whose members lack a sense of history beyond their own personal recollections. Eva Hoffman explained in the *New York Times Book Review* that Trow has diagnosed an "elusive middle-class malaise" as a chronic case of "reality anemia." The second essay, "Within That Context, One Style," profiles Turkish-born Atlantic Records president Ahmet Ertegun as an individual embedded within Trow's "context of no context." While pointing out that the author "sometimes risks glibness" in his essays, Hoffman appraised *Within the Context of No Context* as a "penetrating" and "convincing" work of criticism that is "diametrically opposed to the myth . . . of America the raw, America the energetic."

In 1984 Trow published his first novel, a short volume titled *The City in the Mist*. It chronicles a century in the lives of the Coonlons and the Aspairs, two wealthy New York families. The central figure is sixty-year-old bachelor Edward Coonlon Jones, grandson of the Coonlon patriarch. Schooled from an early age in the art of materialism, the unemployed Edward's main occupation involves looking after his legacy, especially his mother's precious Adam-Sheraton chairs. Although several critics faulted the book for its self-contained chapters, confusing myriad of characters, and general lack of direction, Richard Eder, writing for the *Los Angeles Times Book Review*, judged *The City in the Mist* "a witty and powerful vision of our contemporary disarray." He went on to say that "it devises a golden and magical legend for New York's rackety energy and confusion; and seeks in that legend the means to restore to us our sense of who we might really be."

Some critics contend that Trow's black humor, deadpan style, and often harsh evaluation of society at large can only appeal to a limited audience. But Joseph McLellan of *Washington Post Book World* ventured that "in the rarefied, eccentric field he cultivates, his writing is consistently good and sometimes brilliant." Commenting on the author's ability to unearth the "mold, rot, [and] terror" that exist beneath elitist pretensions, Dionne asserted, "The measure of Trow's achievement is that such chilling themes as his become in his stories so damnably amusing."

Trow told *CA*: "I was brought up in the shadow of the Victorian world. In all my work, I am thinking about how we got from that world to the one we live in."

BIOGRAPHICAL/CRITICAL SOURCES:

PERIODICALS

Atlantic Monthly, June, 1984.
Detroit News, October 4, 1981.
Harper's, May, 1980.
Los Angeles Times, June 3, 1980.
Los Angeles Times Book Review, February 12, 1984.
New York Times, February 15, 1978, April 26, 1980, November 27, 1980.
New York Times Book Review, April 20, 1980, October 11, 1981, February 5, 1984.
Saturday Review, September, 1981.
Village Voice, July 9-15, 1980, December 23-29, 1981.
Washington Post, June 12, 1980.
Washington Post Book World, March 25, 1984.

—*Sketch by Barbara K. Carlisle*

* * *

TRUMP, Richard F. 1912-

PERSONAL: Born March 19, 1912, in Kahoka, Mo.; son of Karl R. (a shoe salesman) and Elizabeth (Feigel) Trump; married Lorene Elizabeth Weiser (a travel agent, homemaker, and silversmith), June 17, 1937; children: David M., Richard F., Jr., Bruce C. *Education:* Iowa State College (now University), B.S., 1936, M.S., 1943. *Religion:* Presbyterian.

ADDRESSES: Home—1511 13th St., Ames, Iowa 50010.

CAREER: High school biology teacher in Keokuk, Iowa, 1936-43, and Ames, Iowa, 1943-77; Iowa State University, Ames, part-time teacher of beekeeping courses, 1977-87; writer, 1987—. *Military service:* U.S. Naval Reserve, active duty, 1944-45; served in Pacific theater; became lieutenant junior grade.

MEMBER: National Audubon Society (president of Ames chapter, 1972), Nature Conservancy, Iowa Natural Heritage.

AWARDS, HONORS: Award from Chi Delta Phi Inkhorn Literary Contest, 1935, for story "When Winter Comes."

WRITINGS:

(With David Fagle) *Design for Life*, Holt, 1963.
(With Roger Volker) *Foundations of Life Science*, Holt, 1971.
Bees and Their Keepers, Iowa State University Press, 1987.

Contributor of more than forty articles to magazines, including *American Bee Journal*, *Popular Science*, and *Natural History*.

WORK IN PROGRESS: A light-hearted journal of the author's years as a biology teacher, tentatively titled *Fall Fever;* a popular account of the ecology of the woodchuck.

SIDELIGHTS: Richard F. Trump told *CA:* "When I began writing articles in the late thirties, I found that I must learn photography in order to sell my work. I spent much time with cameras and then decided I must learn to write better in order to sell pictures. When I retired from Ames High School at the mandatory retirement age in 1977, I was offered a half-time appointment in the entomology department at Iowa State University. This led me to write *Bees and Their Keepers.* Now I have retired again and have many ideas for magazine articles in the hopper."

*   *   *

TUSHNET, Mark V. 1945-

PERSONAL: Born November 18, 1945, in Newark, N.J.; son of Leonard (a physician and author) and Fannie (a social worker; maiden name, Brandchaft) Tushnet; married Elizabeth Alexander (an attorney), August 23, 1969; children: Rebecca Leah, Laura Eve. *Education:* Harvard University, A.B. (magna cum laude), 1967; Yale University, M.A. and J.D., both 1971.

ADDRESSES: Home—1416 Holly St. N.W., Washington, D.C. 20012. *Office*—Law Center, Georgetown University, 600 New Jersey Ave. N.W., Washington, D.C. 20001.

CAREER: U.S. Court of Appeals for the Sixth Circuit, Detroit, Mich., law clerk to Judge George Edwards, 1971-72; U.S. Supreme Court, Washington, D.C., law clerk to Justice Thurgood Marshall, 1972-73; University of Wisconsin—Madison, assistant professor, 1973-76, associate professor, 1976-79, professor of law, 1979-81; Georgetown University, Washington, D.C., professor of law, 1981—. Dolan Lecturer at University of Delaware, 1983; Donley Lecturer at West Virginia University, 1983; Brendan Brown Lecturer at Loyola University, New Orleans, La., 1986; Cleveland-Marshall Fund Lecturer, 1987.

MEMBER: Organization of American Historians, American Historical Association, American Society for Legal History, Conference on Critical Legal Studies (secretary), 1976-85.

AWARDS, HONORS: Fellow of Rockefeller Foundation, 1979-80.

WRITINGS:

The American Law of Slavery, 1810-1860: Considerations of Humanity and Interest, Princeton University Press, 1981.
(With Howard Fink) *Federal Courts: Practice and Policy,* Michie Co., 1984.
(With Geoffrey Stone, L. Michael Seidman, and Cass Sunstein) *Constitutional Law: Cases, Texts, Materials,* Little, Brown, 1986.
The NAACP's Legal Strategy Against Segregated Schools, 1925-1950, University of North Carolina Press, 1987.
Red, White, and Blue: A Critical Analysis of Constitutional Law, Harvard University Press, 1988.

CONTRIBUTOR

M. May, J. Foster, and R. Gambitta, editors, *Governing Through Courts,* Sage Publications, 1981.
David Kairys, editor, *The Politics of Law,* Pantheon, 1982.
B. Ollman and E. Vernon, editors, *The Left Academy,* Volume II, 1984.
David Bodenhamer and James Ely, editors, *Ambivalent Legacy: A Legal History of the South,* University of Mississippi Press, 1984.
Guide to American Law, West, 1984.

Charles Eagles, editor, *The Civil Rights Movement in America,* University of Mississippi Press, 1986.
Burke Marshall, editor, *A Workable Government: The Constitution After Two Hundred Years,* Norton, 1987.

Contributor of articles and reviews to law journals.

WORK IN PROGRESS: Thurgood Marshall: A Biography, publication by Basic Books expected in 1993.

SIDELIGHTS: Mark V. Tushnet told *CA:* "My work on Justice Marshall's biography combines my interest in black legal history with my specialization in constitutional law. Justice Marshall's career is fascinating, and my clerkship with him led me to appreciate, and to try to capture in the biography, the complexity of the man and his career. In addition, my work in constitutional law has involved what has been called 'the critique of rights,' expressing skepticism about the ability of legal rights to secure a just society. Justice Marshall's career, and the civil rights movement more generally, is a key testing ground for the critique of rights."

BIOGRAPHICAL/CRITICAL SOURCES:

PERIODICALS

American Historical Review, June, 1982.

*   *   *

TUTTLE, Lisa 1952-

PERSONAL: Born September 16, 1952, in Houston, Tex.; daughter of R. E. and Elizabeth Tuttle. *Education:* Syracuse University, B.A., 1973.

ADDRESSES: Home—1 Ortygia House, 6 Lower Rd., Harrow, Middlesex HAZ ODA, England. *Agent*—Howard Marhaim, 175 Fifth Ave., Room 709, New York, N.Y. 10010.

CAREER: American Statesman, Austin, Tex., columnist, 1976-79; University of London, London, England, teacher of courses in science fiction for extramural department, 1984-88; freelance journalist in London, England, 1985—; writer. Editor of *Mathom* (a fan magazine), 1968-70; editor for the Women's Press, 1987—.

MEMBER: Science Fiction Writers of America, Women in Publishing.

AWARDS, HONORS: John W. Campbell Memorial Award for Best New Writer from World Science Fiction Society, 1974.

WRITINGS:

(With George R. R. Martin) *Windhaven,* Simon & Schuster, 1980.
Familiar Spirit, Berkley Publishing, 1983.
(Author of text) *Catwitch* (for children), idea and illustrations by Una Woodruff, Doubleday, 1983.
(With Rosalind Ashe) *Children's Literary Houses,* Facts on File, 1984.
Encyclopedia of Feminism, Facts on File, 1986.
A Nest of Nightmares, Sphere Books, 1986.
A Spaceship Built of Stone and Other Stories, Women's Press, 1987.
Gabriel, Tor Books, 1988.
Heroines: Women Inspired by Women, Harrap, 1988.

Work represented in anthologies, including *Clarion II* and *Clarion III,* both edited by Robin Scott Wilson, New American Library, 1972 and 1973; *Survival From Infinity,* edited by

Roger Elwood, Watts, 1974; *Best SF 75*, edited by Harry Harrison and Brian Aldiss, Bobbs Merrill, 1976; *Lone Star Universe*, edited by George W. Proctor and Steven Utley, Heidelberg, 1976; *Ascents of Wonder*, edited by David Gerrold and Stephen Goldin, Popular Library, 1977; *New Voices in Science Fiction*, edited by George R. R. Martin, Macmillan, 1977; *SF Choice 77*, edited by Mike Ashley, Quartet, 1977; and *New Voices 2*, edited by Martin, Harcourt, 1979. Contributor of stories to periodicals, including *Amazing, Analog, Fantastic, Galaxy, Interzone, Twilight Zone, Isaac Asimov's Science Fiction Magazine*, and *Magazine of Fantasy and Science Fiction*.

WORK IN PROGRESS: A new novel.

BIOGRAPHICAL/CRITICAL SOURCES:

PERIODICALS

Times Literary Supplement, June 3-9, 1988.

U

UNGAR, Steven (Ronald) 1945-

PERSONAL: Born September 8, 1945, in Chicago, Ill.; son of Egon and Lisbeth (Feigel) Ungar; married Roberta Lee Hoffmann, March 2, 1968; children: Anna-Marie, Shira Claire. *Education:* University of Wisconsin—Madison, B.A., 1966, M.A., 1968; Cornell University, Ph.D., 1973.

ADDRESSES: Office—Department of French and Italian, University of Iowa, Iowa City, Iowa 52242.

CAREER: Case Western Reserve University, Cleveland, Ohio, assistant professor of French, 1972-76; University of Iowa, Iowa City, assistant professor, 1976-79, associate professor, 1979-85, professor of French, 1985—. Lecturer in English at Lycee Technique d'Etat, Rennes, France, 1968-69; research fellow at Camargo Foundation, Cassis, France, 1981.

MEMBER: Modern Language Association of America, Association for the Study of Dada and Surrealism.

WRITINGS:

Roland Barthes: Professor of Desire, University of Nebraska Press, 1984.

Contributor to literature journals.

WORK IN PROGRESS: Research on interwar French culture and on Maurice Blanchot.

SIDELIGHTS: Steven Ungar told *CA:* "My writings on Roland Barthes grew from my sense that his critical and theoretical activities were part of a more basic project of writing that came through with increasing force after the appearance of his *S/Z* in 1970. His writing was a profession in a number of senses; an expression of intelligence as well as one of a *desire* to writie that takes full form in his last major text, *Camera Incida.*

"My interest in Maurice Blanchot and the 1930s follows up my work on Barthes by setting the urge to write in a specific set of historical and theoretical problems. It also inscribes the figure of the individual writer within historical and institutional contexts that I had only begun to explore in tracing Barthes's evolution beyond the 1960s period of structural analysis."

UNGER, J(ames) Marshall 1947-

PERSONAL: Born May 28, 1947, in Cleveland, Ohio; son of Roy Brown (an executive in the bedding industry) and Grace (a housewife; maiden name, Friedman) Unger; married Mutsuyo Okumura (an administrative assistant), October 18, 1976. *Education:* University of Chicago, A.B., 1969, A.M., 1971; Yale University, M.A., 1973, Ph.D., 1975.

ADDRESSES: Home—Honolulu, Hawaii. *Office*—Department of East Asian Languages and Literatures, Moore Hall, University of Hawaii at Manoa, 1890 East West Rd., Honolulu, Hawaii 96822.

CAREER: University of Canterbury, Canterbury, New Zealand, senior lecturer in Japanese, 1975-76; University of Hawaii at Manoa, Honolulu, assistant professor, 1977-82, associate professor, 1982-87, professor of Japanese, 1987—, department chairman, 1988—.

MEMBER: Linguistic Society of America, Association for Asian Studies, Association of Teachers of Japanese (member of board of directors, 1985-88), American Oriental Society, Kokugo Gakkai (Japan), International House (Tokyo).

WRITINGS:

Studies in Early Japanese Morphophonemics, Linguistics Club, Indiana University—Bloomington, 1977.
(Contributor) Ronald A. Morse and Richard J. Samuels, editors, *Getting America Ready for Japanese Science and Technology,* Asian Program, Woodrow Wilson Center for International Scholars, 1986.
The Fifth Generation Fallacy: Why Japan Is Betting Its Future on Artificial Intelligence, Oxford University Press, 1987.

Contributor to *Kodansha Encyclopedia of Japan.* Contributor of articles and reviews to scholarly journals.

WORK IN PROGRESS: Research on writing systems, literacy, and computer software development; research on Japanese, Korean, and Tungusic languages.

SIDELIGHTS: J. Marshall Unger told *CA:* "Well in excess of one thousand undergraduates from every conceivable background take Japanese at the main campus of the University of Hawaii every semester. Because of this extraordinary demand, I began developing instructional computer software for Japanese as a second language shortly after arriving in Hawaii in

1977—quite a change from historical linguistics. Personal computers lay in the future, so I did all my programming on large Control Data PLATO networks, developing my own Japanese word processing utility around the time Toshiba began marketing its first commercial systems.

"My book *The Fifth Generation Fallacy* documents the connection between Japanese word-processing software and the Fifth Generation project launched in 1982. In a nutshell, the fallacy is the belief that artificial intelligence machines can somehow rescue Japan from the inefficiencies of its highly complex writing system."

AVOCATIONAL INTERESTS: "I played chamber music throughout college and graduate school; accompanied, ar-

ranged, and composed for the Chicago Children's Choir; and sang in the Bach Society and the Russian Chorus at Yale. In 1982 I recorded a performance of 'Sonata for Viola and Piano' by the modern American composer Nancy Van de Vate, with violist Maxine-Karen Johnson, for Orion Records. I am also an amateur 2-*dan* at the Japanese game of *go*."

BIOGRAPHICAL/CRITICAL SOURCES:

PERIODICALS

AI Journal, April, 1986.
Congress and Convention, autumn, 1985.
Globe and Mail (Toronto), October 24, 1987.
Technical Japanese Translation, April, 1984.

V

VALENTINE, James W(illiam) 1926-

PERSONAL: Born November 10, 1926, in Los Angeles, Calif.; son of Adelbert C. (a carpenter) and Isabel (a housewife; maiden name, Davis) Valentine; married Diane Mondragon, 1987; children: three. *Education:* Phillips University, B.A., 1951; University of California, Los Angeles, M.A., 1954, Ph.D., 1958.

ADDRESSES: Home—Goleta, Calif. *Office*—Department of Geology, University of California, Santa Barbara, Calif. 93106.

CAREER: University of Missouri—Columbia, assistant professor, 1958-62, associate professor of geology, 1962-64; University of California, Davis, associate professor, 1964-68, professor of geology, 1968-78; University of California, Santa Barbara, professor of geological sciences, 1978—. *Military service:* U.S. Naval Reserve, active duty, 1944-45.

MEMBER: National Academy of Science, American Academy of Arts and Sciences (fellow), American Association for the Advancement of Science (fellow), American Society of Naturalists, Geological Society of America (fellow), Ecological Society of America, Paleontological Society (president, 1974-75), Society for Paleontology and Mineralogy, Palaeontological Association, Society for the Study of Evolution, California Academy of Sciences (fellow).

AWARDS, HONORS: Fulbright scholar in Australia, 1962-63; Guggenheim fellow, 1969-70.

WRITINGS:

Evolutionary Paleoecology of the Marine Biosphere, Prentice-Hall, 1972.
(With Theodore Dobzhansky, G. L. Stebbins, and F. J. Ayala) *Evolution*, W. H. Freeman, 1977.
(With Ayala) *Evolving*, Benjamin-Cummings, 1979.
(Editor) *Phanerozoic Diversity Patterns*, Princeton University Press, 1985.

Contributor of more than two hundred articles to scientific journals. Associate editor of *Paleobiology, Geological Society of America Bulletin,* and *Palaeogeography, Palaeoclimatology, Palaeoecology.*

WORK IN PROGRESS: Macroevolution, publication expected in 1990; research on the origin of phyla.

SIDELIGHTS: James W. Valentine told *CA:* "Traditionally, microevolution deals with processes that produce and regulate heritable change within lineages that can lead to the origin of new species. Macroevolution deals with the origin of novel branches of the tree of life, and with the processes involved as these branches wax or wane through geological time."

AVOCATIONAL INTERESTS: Collecting the writings of Charles Darwin (all issues in all languages).

BIOGRAPHICAL/CRITICAL SOURCES:

PERIODICALS

Times Literary Supplement, May 22, 1987.

*   *   *

VANCE, Eugene 1934-

PERSONAL: Born April 14, 1934, in Cambridge, Mass.; son of Robert (a physician) and Anna Mary (Blount) Vance; married Christie McDonald, June 11, 1965 (divorced, June, 1985); children: Adam, Jacob. *Education:* Dartmouth College, B.A., 1957; Cornell University, M.A., 1958, Ph.D., 1964.

ADDRESSES: Home—447 Emory Dr., Atlanta, Ga. 30307. *Office*—Department of French and Italian, Emory University, Atlanta, Ga. 30322.

CAREER: Yale University, New Haven, Conn., instructor, 1962-66, assistant professor of English and French, 1966-69; Universite de Montreal, Montreal, Quebec, associate professor, 1969-75, professor of comparative literature, 1975-84, chairperson of Program of Comparative Literature, 1969-74; Emory University, Atlanta, Ga., professor of French and comparative literature, 1984—, director of Program of Comparative Literature, 1985—, member of Classical Studies Program and Literature and Religion Program. Visiting professor at University of Toronto, 1973, 1982, Johns Hopkins University and Hebrew University of Jerusalem, 1981, Centro Internazionale di Semiotica e Linguistica (Urbino, Italy), 1982, Duke University, 1985, and University of California, Berkeley, 1986; visiting lecturer at University of Abidjan, Brown University, University of California at Davis, Irvine, La Jolla, Los Angeles, and Santa Barbara, University of Cape Town, Columbia University, Dartmouth College, University of Durban, University of Fez, University of Geneva, Hiram College, University of Lausanne, Louisiana State University, McGill University, Miami University (Oxford, Ohio), Mohammed V University in Rabat, New York University, Oberlin College, Ohio State University, University of Ottawa, Paul Valery University in Toulouse, University of Pennsylvania, University of Rochester, University of Southern California, Southern Methodist University, Stanford University, State University of New York at Binghamton and Buffalo, Tel Aviv University, University of Texas at Austin, University of the South, University of Tunis, University of Urbino, University of Utrecht, University of Wisconsin, and University of the Witwatersrand.

MEMBER: Modern Language Association of America, Medieval Academy, Canadian Association of Comparative Literature, Societe Rencesvals.

AWARDS, HONORS: Morse fellow at Yale University, 1966-67; fellow of Canada Council at Oxford University, 1974-75; fellow of Social Science and Humanities Research Council of Canada, 1981-82; research fellow, Newberry Library, 1989.

WRITINGS:

Reading the Song of Roland, Prentice-Hall, 1970.
(Editor) *Language as Action*, Yale University Press, 1970.
(Editor with Lucie Brind'Amour) *Archeologie du signe* (title means "The Archeology of the Sign"), Pontifical Institute of Mediaeval Studies [Toronto, Ontario], 1983.
Mervelous Signals: Poetics and Sign Theory in the Middle Ages, University of Nebraska Press, 1986.
From Topic to Tale: Logic and Narrativity in the Middle Ages, University of Minnesota Press, 1987.

Principal editor of monograph series "Regents' Studies in Medieval Culture," University of Nebraska Press. Member of founding editorial board of *Canadian Review of Comparative Literature*, 1973-86; member of editorial board of *Quaderni urbinati di cultura classica, French Forum, Exemplaria, Olifant, Assays: Critical Approaches to Medieval and Renaissance Texts*, and *Recherches semiotiques/Semiotic Inquiries*.

CONTRIBUTOR

Mario Valdes and Martin Mueller, editors, *The Interpretation of Narrative*, University of Toronto Press, 1978.
Josue Harari, editor, *Textual Strategies: Perspectives in Post Structural Criticism*, Cornell University Press, 1979.
Minnette Gaudet and Robin F. Jones, editors, *The Nature of Medieval Narrative*, French Forum, 1980.
Claude Levesque and Christie McDonald, editors, *L'oreille de l'autre: Texte et debats avec Jacques Derrida* (title means "The Ear of the Other: Text and Discussions With Jacques Derrida"), VLB Editions, 1982.
Stephen G. Nichols, Jr. and John Lyons, editors, *Mimesis: From Mirror to Method*, New England University Press, 1983.
Patricia Parker and Chaviva Hosek, editors, *Lyric Poetry: Beyond the New Criticism*, Cornell University Press, 1985.
(Author of introduction) Paul Zumthor, *Speaking of the Middle Ages*, University of Nebraska Press, 1986.
Christiane Marchello-Nizia and Emmanuelle Baumgartner, editors, *Le nombre du temps* (title means "The Number of Time"), Champion, 1988.

Contributor to *Encyclopedic Dictionary of Semiotics* and *The Harvard History of French Literature*. Contributor of articles and reviews to literature journals.

WORK IN PROGRESS: A book on icons, relics, and poetics in the middle ages, publication by University of Nebraska Press

expected in 1990; a book on paternity, rhetoric, and theology in St. Augustine, publication expected in 1992.

SIDELIGHTS: Eugene Vance told *CA:* "My principal wish is to study medieval literature and art in relationship to the semiotic and semantic theories of their time."

BIOGRAPHICAL/CRITICAL SOURCES:

PERIODICALS

Times Literary Supplement, August 14, 1987.

*   *   *

VAUGHN, Sally N(orthrop)   1939-

PERSONAL: Born November 23, 1939, in San Diego, Calif.; daughter of Arnold E. and Marie (Carney) Northrop; married William E. Vaughn, November 2, 1965 (died, March, 1970); married Loyd S. Swenson, Jr. (a professor of history), July 17, 1986; children: Jerry A. Simmons, Jr., David N. Simmons, John M. Vaughn. *Education:* California State University, Fullerton, B.A., 1972; University of California, Santa Barbara, Ph.D., 1978.

ADDRESSES: Home—1948 North MacGregor Way, Houston, Tex. 77023. *Office*—Department of History, University of Houston, Central Campus, Houston, Tex. 77004.

CAREER: Rider College, Lawrenceville, N.J., adjunct assistant professor of medieval history, 1978-79; St. Lawrence University, Canton, N.Y., assistant professor of history, 1979-81; University of Houston, Central Campus, Houston, Tex., assistant professor of medieval history, 1981—.

MEMBER: American Historical Association, Mediaeval Academy of America, Haskins Society for Viking, Anglo-Saxon, Anglo-Norman, and Angevin History (conference director).

AWARDS, HONORS: Bethell Prize from Haskins Society for Viking, Anglo-Saxon, Anglo-Norman, and Angevin History, 1985.

WRITINGS:

The Abbey of Bec and the Anglo-Norman State, 1034-1136, Boydell, 1981.
Anselm of Bec and Robert of Meulan: The Innocence of the Dove and the Wisdom of the Serpent, University of California Press, 1987.

Contributor to history journals.

WORK IN PROGRESS: Women in Anselm's World: Spiritual Daughters, Aristocratic Allies, and Handmaidens of God, completion expected in 1988; *Charles Homer Haskins: A Biography*, completion expected in 1990; *Prudent Pilots and Spiritual Charioteers: The Students of Bec, 1040-1160*, completion expected in 1995.

BIOGRAPHICAL/CRITICAL SOURCES:

PERIODICALS

Times Literary Supplement, July 3, 1981, March 11-17, 1988.

*   *   *

VEHR, Bill   1940(?)-1988

OBITUARY NOTICE: Born c. 1940 in Green Hills, Ohio; died of acquired immune deficiency syndrome (AIDS), August 2, 1988, in New York, N.Y. Actor, filmmaker, and playwright.

Although he had no formal training in theater, Vehr earned a following as an actor and cult filmmaker during the late 1960s and 1970s. Among the motion pictures he created and directed are "Avocada," "Brothel," and "The Mystery of the Spanish Lady," all of which star actor Mario Montez and are regarded as underground classics. Vehr was also an original member of Charles Ludlam's Ridiculous Theater Company; he wrote "Whores of Babylon" for the company in the late 1960s and starred in their productions of "Bluebeard" and "Camille," among others. An acclaimed performer, Vehr was generally respected for his strong stage presence and classical voice.

OBITUARIES AND OTHER SOURCES:

PERIODICALS

New York Times, August 5, 1988.

*   *   *

VELLACOTT, Jo 1922-
(Newberry, Vellacott Newberry)

PERSONAL: Born April 20, 1922, in Plymouth, England; daughter of Harold Fitz (a surgeon) and Josephine (a nurse; maiden name, Sempill) Vellacott; divorced; children: Douglas John Newberry, Mary Newberry, Susan Newberry. *Education:* Somerville College, Oxford, B.A. (with honors), 1943, M.A., 1947; University of Toronto, M.A., 1965; McMaster University, Ph.D., 1975. *Religion:* Society of Friends (Quakers).

ADDRESSES: Office—Simone de Beauvoir Institute, Concordia University, 1455 Blvd. de Maisonneuve W., Montreal, Quebec, Canada H3G 1M8.

CAREER: Queen's University, Kingston, Ontario, assistant to dean of women, 1978-80; Concordia University, Montreal, Quebec, teacher of women's studies at Simone de Beauvoir Institute, 1982—. Consultant to Bertrand Russell Editorial Project. *Military service:* Women's Royal Naval Service (WRENS), air mechanic and air engineer officer, 1943-45.

MEMBER: Canadian Historical Association, Canadian Research Institute for the Advancement of Women, Council on Peace Research in History, Voice of Women, American Historical Association.

AWARDS, HONORS: Canada Council grant, 1975; Calouste Gulbenkian fellow at Lucy Cavendish College, Cambridge, 1976-78; fellow at Institute for Advanced Studies in the Humanities, University of Edinburgh, 1976; grant from Social Science and Humanities Research Council of Canada, 1987-88.

WRITINGS:

Bertrand Russell and the Pacifists in the First World War, Harvester, 1980.
(Editor with Margaret Kamester) Mary Sargent Florence, Catherine Marshall, and C. K. Ogden, *Militarism Versus Feminism,* Virago, 1987.

Contributor to *Women and Peace,* edited by Ruth Roach Pierson. Contributor to history journals, sometimes under name Vellacott Newberry or simply Newberry.

WORK IN PROGRESS: A biography of Catherine E. Marshall, a British feminist, pacifist, and internationalist (1880-1961).

SIDELIGHTS: During World War I, though he was not an absolute pacifist, Bertrand Russell became involved with England's No-Conscription Fellowship (NCF). When conscrip-

tion finally became a fact of British life, the fellowship became a welfare organization for conscientious objectors. After the leaders of the NCF were imprisoned, Russell, by default, became the organizer and propagandist of the fellowship. His role cost the philosopher his job at Trinity College, Cambridge, and he was imprisoned for a while in 1917.

Jo Vellacott's book *Bertrand Russell and the Pacifists in the First World War* was described in the *Times Literary Supplement* by Martin Ceadel as an "absorbingly detailed study" which "will be welcomed both for its glimpse of Russell in an unfamiliar role and also for the light it sheds on the NCF."

Vellacott told *CA:* "I was always interested in writing. Studying history came about because of the influence of a remarkable teacher, Jean Rowntree. It only began to feel like 'my own thing' when I began to do original research. The arrival at McMaster University of the Bertrand Russell Archives was timed just right for me. By a further stroke of good fortune, research on Russell's peace activities during World War I led me to Catherine Marshall, and I was able to combine my two major interests: peace history and feminist history.

"I lived in South Africa from 1947 to 1952 but left because of apartheid. I became a Quaker in 1961, and that is a full-time occupation in itself."

BIOGRAPHICAL/CRITICAL SOURCES:

PERIODICALS

American Historical Review, April, 1982.
Times Literary Supplement, April 3, 1981.

*   *   *

VENDLER, Zeno 1921-

PERSONAL: Born December 22, 1921, in Devecser, Hungary; immigrated to United States, became naturalized citizen; son of Zeno Miklos and Vilma (Gubas) Vendler; married Semiramis Da Silva, May 28, 1964; children: David, Alexander. *Education:* Canisianum, Maastricht, Netherlands, S.T.L., 1952; Harvard University, Ph.D., 1959.

ADDRESSES: Office—Department of Philosophy, University of California, San Diego, Box 109, La Jolla, Calif. 92093.

CAREER: Boston College, Boston, Mass., instructor in philosophy, 1957-59; University of Pennsylvania, Philadelphia, research associate in linguistics, 1959-60; Cornell University, Ithaca, N.Y., assistant professor of philosophy, 1960-63; University of Pennsylvania, research associate in linguistics, 1963-64; Brooklyn College of the City University of New York, Brooklyn, N.Y., associate professor of philosophy, 1964-65; University of Calgary, Calgary, Alberta, associate professor, 1965-68, professor of philosophy, 1968-73; Rice University, Houston, Tex., Carolyn and Fred McManus Professor of Philosophy, 1973-75; University of California, San Diego, La Jolla, professor of philosophy, 1975—.

AWARDS, HONORS: Grant from Canada Council, 1968-69; fellow of National Endowment for the Humanities, 1977-79.

WRITINGS:

The Transformational Grammar of English Adjectives, Department of Linguistics, University of Pennsylvania, 1963.
Linguistics in Philosophy, Cornell University Press, 1967.
Adjectives and Nominalizations, Mouton, 1968.
Res Cogitans: An Essay in Rational Psychology, Cornell University Press, 1972.

The Matter of Minds, Clarendon, 1984.

Contributor to philosophy and linguistic journals.

BIOGRAPHICAL/CRITICAL SOURCES:

PERIODICALS

Times Literary Supplement, March 23, 1973, October 4, 1985.

* * *

VEVERS, (Henry) Gwynne 1916-1988

OBITUARY NOTICE—See index for *CA* sketch: Born November 13, 1916, in Girvan, Scotland; died July 24, 1988. Scientist, curator, administrator, translator, editor, and author. Vevers was known for his vast canon of works in which he discussed the sciences accessibly and simply. He spent most of his career at the Zoological Society of London, where he was aquarium curator from 1955 to 1981 and assistant director of science from 1966 to 1981. His many writings include *The British Seashore, The Underwater World, The Pocket Guide to Aquarium Fishes,* and, as editor, *Practical Encyclopaedia of Freshwater Tropical Aquarium Fishes.* Vevers also wrote many science books for children, and he translated more than fifty zoological volumes.

OBITUARIES AND OTHER SOURCES:

PERIODICALS

Times (London), July 27, 1988.

* * *

VINCENT, Gabrielle [a pseudonym]

PERSONAL: Born in Brussels, Belgium.

ADDRESSES: Home—Brussels, Belgium.

CAREER: Illustrator and author of books for children, 1980—.

WRITINGS:

SELF-ILLUSTRATED CHILDREN'S BOOKS IN ENGLISH TRANSLATION

Ernest et Celestine ont perdu Simeon, Duculot (Paris-Gembloux), 1981, published as *Ernest and Celestine,* Greenwillow, 1982.
Ernest et Celestine, musiciens des rues, Duculot, 1981, published as *Bravo, Ernest and Celestine!* Greenwillow, 1982.
Ernest et Celestine vont pique-niquer, Duculot, 1982, published as *Ernest and Celestine's Picnic,* Greenwillow, 1982.
Ernest et Celestine chez le photographe, Duculot, 1982, published as *Smile, Ernest and Celestine,* Greenwillow, 1982.
Le Patchwork, Duculot, 1982, published as *Ernest and Celestine's Patchwork Quilt,* Greenwillow, 1982.
La Tasse cassee, Duculot, 1982, published as *Breakfast Time, Ernest and Celestine,* Greenwillow, 1985.
Noel chez Ernest et Celestine, Duculot, 1983, published as *Merry Christmas, Ernest and Celestine,* Greenwillow, 1984.
Ernest et Celestine au musee, Duculot, 1985, published as *Where Are You, Ernest and Celestine?* Greenwillow, 1986.

SIDELIGHTS: Gabrielle Vincent is a painter and illustrator who decided as a child that she would be an artist, but she did not pursue her career as an author and illustrator until 1980. In 1981 her characters Ernest and Celestine were presented at the Bologna Bookfair, and the bear and mouse have been popular in Europe since then. Vincent's books are published in French by the Belgian publisher Duculot, but they have been translated and published in at least a dozen other countries as well.

BIOGRAPHICAL/CRITICAL SOURCES:

BOOKS

Children's Literature Review, Volume 13, Gale, 1987.

PERIODICALS

New York Times Book Review, March 30, 1986.

[Sketch verified by author's editor, Christiane Lapp]

* * *

VOGLER, Roger E. 1938-

PERSONAL: Born February 14, 1938, in Benton Harbor, Mich.; married, 1962; children: two. *Education:* University of California, Los Angeles, B.A., 1963; University of Arizona, M.A., 1966, Ph.D., 1967.

ADDRESSES: Home—1126 West Foothill Blvd., Suite 260, Upland, Calif. 91786. *Office*—Department of Psychology, Pomona College, Claremont, Calif. 91711.

CAREER: Pomona College, Claremont, Calif., began as assistant professor, 1967, became associate professor, professor of psychology, 1976—. Private practice of clinical psychology; clinical psychologist at Center for Behavior Change, Pomona; member of Foothills Psychological Associates, Upland, Calif. Research psychologist at Patton State Hospital, 1968—; research scholar at Max-Planck Institute of Psychiatry, Munich, West Germany, 1970-71; consultant to Veterans Administration.

MEMBER: European Association of Behavior Therapy, American Psychological Association.

AWARDS, HONORS: Grant from Department of Mental Hygiene, 1968; Humboldt fellow, 1970—.

WRITINGS:

The Better Way to Drink, Simon & Schuster, 1982.

Contributor to psychology journals.

SIDELIGHTS: Roger E. Vogler told *CA:* "Alcohol abuse is best conceptualized as a habit of varying degrees."

* * *

von TROTTA, Margarethe 1942-

PERSONAL: Born February 21, 1942, in Berlin, Germany; married second husband, Volker Schloendorff (a filmmaker); children: (first marriage) one son.

ADDRESSES: Office—c/o German Film and Television Academy, Pommernallee 1, 1 Berlin 19, West Germany.

CAREER: Screenwriter and director of motion pictures. Actress in stage productions during 1960s and, subsequently, in television productions and in motion pictures, including "Gods of the Plague," 1969, "A Free Woman," 1972, and "Coup de Grace," 1977.

AWARDS, HONORS: Golden Lion from Venice Film Festival, 1981, for "Marianne and Juliane."

WRITINGS:

SCREENPLAYS; AND DIRECTOR

(With husband, Volker Schloendorff; and director with Schloendorff) "Die verlorene Ehre der Katherina Blum" (adapted from the novel by Heinrich Boell), Bioskop-Film, 1975; released in the United States as "The Lost Honor of Katharina Blum," New World, 1975.

(With Luisa Francia) *Das zweite Erwachen der Christa Klages* (Bioskop-Film/WDR/First City Films/Blue Dolphin Films, 1977; released in the United States as "The Second Awakening of Christa Klages," New Line Cinema, 1979), Fischer Taschenbuch Verlag, 1980.

Schwestern; oder, Die Balance des Gluecks (Bioskop-Film, 1979; released in the United States as "Sisters; or, The Balance of Happiness," Cinema 5, 1982), Fischer Taschenbuch Verlag, 1979.

"Die bleierne Zeit" (title means "The Leaden Time"), Bioskop-Film, 1981; released in the United States as "Marianne and Juliane," New Yorker Films, 1982 (released in England as "The German Sisters").

Heller Wahn (Bioskop-Film/Les Films du Losange/West Deutscher Rundfunk, 1983; released in the United States as "Sheer Madness," R5/S8, 1985; [released in England as "Friends and Husbands"]), Fischer Taschenbuch Verlag, 1981.

Rosa Luxemburg (Bioskop-Film/Pro-Ject Film/Filmverlag der Autoren/Regina Ziegler Film/Baren Film/WDR, 1986; released in the United States by New Yorker Films, 1987), F. Greno, 1986.

OTHER SCREENPLAYS

(With husband, Volker Schloendorff) "Der ploetzliche Reichtum der armen Leute von Kombach," Hallelujah Films, 1970; released in the United States as "The Sudden Wealth of the Poor People of Kombach," New Yorker Films, 1974.

(With Schloendorff) "Strohfeuer," Hallelujah Films, 1972; released in the United States as "A Free Woman," New Yorker Films, 1974.

(With Genevieve Dormann and Jutta Bruckner) "Coup de Grace" (adapted from the novel by Marguerite Yourcenar), Argos Films, 1976; released in the United States by Cinema 5, 1978.

(With Schloendorff, Jean-Claude Carriere, and Kai Herrmann) "Die Faelschung" (title means "The Forgery"; adapted from the novel by Nicolas Born), Argos Films/Bioskop-Film/Artemis Film, 1981; released in the United States as "Circle of Deceit," United Artists Classics, 1982.

(With Dacia Maraini) "Paura e Amore" (title means "Love and Fear"), Erre-Produzione/Bioskop-Film/Cinemax, 1988.

SIDELIGHTS: Margarethe von Trotta is among the generation of German filmmakers that includes Werner Herzog, Wim Wenders, the late Rainer Werner Fassbinder, and von Trotta's husband, Volker Schloendorff. She began her film career as an actress, notably in films by Fassbinder and by Schloendorff, and she subsequently worked as a screenwriter in collaboration with her writer-director husband, but it is as writer and director of her own politico-feminist films that she is probably best known. In these works she has, to varying degrees, explored what Amy Taubin described in the *Village Voice* as "the emotional lives of intelligent, demanding, and desirous women." These films have earned von Trotta substantial recognition in Europe and the United States, with critics such as the *New Republic*'s Stanley Kauffmann calling her "one of the best living directors."

Von Trotta entered the film world in the late 1960s after acting on West German stages and appearing in television productions. Among her first works as an actress were Fassbinder's "Gods of the Plague" and "The American Soldier," where she was provided with merely rudimentary instructions and required to devise her own characterizations. Of Fassbinder and her other male directors she later recalled, "They just told me what to say and what to do and then left me alone."

In 1970 von Trotta obtained her first screenwriting credit by collaborating with Schloendorff on "The Sudden Wealth of the Poor People of Kombach," which Schloendorff also directed. The film, based on an actual event, concerns the capture, trial, and execution of seven peasants who had robbed a tax collector in the 1820s. The *New York Times*'s Vincent Canby found the film too solemn and detached.

More successful was von Trotta's work as both co-writer and lead actress in Schloendorff's 1972 film "A Free Woman." In this work she played a thirtyish divorcee struggling to start a career and obtain child custody in a decidedly male-dominated society. Howard Thompson, reviewing "A Free Woman" in the *New York Times*, wrote that von Trotta and Schloendorff "and the other performers and contributors have forged a fine, thoughtful and stimulating film that observantly mirrors a human condition, the traditional subordination of women, with truthful, biting irony." Thompson added, "It would be hard to find a more persuasive and appealing proponent of feminism than [von Trotta]."

In 1975 von Trotta made her directorial debut, collaborating with Schloendorff on "The Lost Honor of Katharina Blum." Adapted by von Trotta and Schloendorff from the novel by Heinrich Boell, this film concerns a housekeeper-waitress who becomes the subject of scandal after spending one night with a suspected terrorist. Although innocent of wrongdoing, Katharina Blum becomes the target of police harrassment and a newspaper slander. An investigation soon clears her of wrongdoing, but the intimidation and public humiliation continues, and her reputation is ruined by an opportunist reporter. Katharina eventually shoots him and joins a band of criminals.

Von Trotta's next major work was as co-screenwriter and lead actress in "Coup de Grace," Schloendorff's 1976 film set amid the post-World War I conflict between Allied forces and Bolsheviks in Latvia. The work's central figure is Sophie (played by von Trotta), an aristocrat whose family estate has become headquarters for a Bolshevik regiment. Despite political differences, Sophie falls in love with a Prussian officer—who, in turn, is attracted to her brother—and when her love proves unrequited, Sophie instigates a self-destructive political act. In his *New York Times* review, Vincent Canby described "Coup de Grace" as "vivid and haunting."

After "Coup de Grace" von Trotta devoted herself primarily to filmmaking, and with her ensuing works she became a leading artist in West Germany's then-thriving film community. In 1977 she completed "The Second Awakening of Christa Klages," her first work as solo director and her first writing credit independent of Schloendorff (collaborating, instead, with Luisa Francia). Christa Klages is a teacher who robs a bank to obtain funds necessary for sustaining a day nursery. Pursued by both the police and, for personal reasons, by one of the bank's female tellers, Christa flees with a former classmate to a Portuguese commune. Once there, however, they are rejected by the communers, and thus return to their homeland. Christa then hides in an abandoned apartment. Near suicide, she returns to the day nursery only to find that the employees and children are being evicted. Christa is soon captured, but the teller who had pursued her earlier refuses to identify her as a robber.

Writing in *Monthly Film Bulletin*, Thomas Elsaesser reported that "The Second Awakening of Christa Klages" "was immensely successful and intensely debated" upon release in 1977, a period of accelerated terrorism and public anxiety in West Germany. Elsaesser noted that the film was full of "anxiety, terror, guilt—this triad of negative emotions [that] is almost the trademark of the New German Cinema," and he added that with its controversial perspective it "formed part of the broad sweep that led the German cinema directly into political issues." *New York Times* critic Vincent Canby found the film compelling and provocative when he reviewed it in 1979. "It is never predictable," he wrote. "And while the plot is rather absurd, the film is emotionally and stylistically consistent." He added that novice director von Trotta was "a feminist of striking movie-making talent."

Von Trotta followed "The Second Awakening of Christa Klages" with "Sisters," a disturbing work about two sisters' undying bond. The film's principal figure is Maria, an industrious secretary supporting both herself and her sister, Anna, a meek biology student prone to melancholy. The sisters' relationship is complex, for Maria exerts nearly supervisorial control over Anna while simultaneously serving her. Although extremely close, the sisters experience increasing tension when Maria begins an affair with her boss's son. Anna becomes jealous, and her jealousy turns to rage. She berates Maria, then commits suicide. Despondent and guilt ridden, Maria immerses herself in work. At her job, however, she befriends Miriam, an affable typist. Maria soon exerts the same control over Miriam that she had with Anna, urging her to take school courses and taking her as a roommate. As Maria's authority increases, though, Miriam grows distrustful. She discovers Anna's diary and learns she is serving as the sister's replacement. Miriam then leaves, whereupon Maria vows to become Anna as well as be herself.

"Sisters" earned some impressive appraisals upon its American release in early 1982. The *New York Times*'s Janet Maslin described it as "a quietly accomplished film, and often a very good one, skillful in its examination of both the separateness and the similarity of [Maria and Anna]." Maslin admired von Trotta's direct pictorial style and her concentrated manner of narration, particularly as it related to characterization. "Indeed," wrote Maslin, "the film's strength lies in the meticulous, if somewhat dispassionate manner in which the sisters' natures are contrasted and interwoven." More enthusiastic was *New Republic*'s Stanley Kauffmann, who hailed the film as a major achievement. He called "Sisters" a "delicate, strange, lovely work" and praised von Trotta as a stunningly resourceful artist. "There is not one split second of waste or of haste in this film," he declared. "The making of it is perfect."

In 1981 von Trotta wrote and directed "Marianne and Juliane" which focuses on a feminist journalist and her terrorist sister. Their relationship, as is often the case in von Trotta's films, is both loving and troubling. Although equally dissatisfied with West German politics, they pursue change through radically different channels, and each woman resents the other woman's activities. Nonetheless, they are quite close, and when Marianne is captured and imprisoned, Juliane becomes increasingly involved with her sister's plight. She endures humiliating experiences visiting the prison and protests Marianne's dehumanizing living conditions, which include isolation and constant bright lights. Near exhaustion from the emotional and physical strain, Juliane agrees to a vacation with her lover, Wolfgang. While abroad, though, she learns of her sister's death—an apparent suicide. Juliane returns home and subsequently suffers a breakdown. Upon recovering, she pursues her own examination of Marianne's death and learns that her sister was probably murdered. Juliane consequently writes an article contradicting reports of Marianne's suicide, but unsympathetic editors at the feminist publication reject the article, claiming that Marianne's demise is no longer relevant. Juliane then returns home to raise Marianne's son.

"Marianne and Juliane" is probably von Trotta's most acclaimed film. In West Germany, where it bore particular relevance to a nation seemingly preoccupied with terrorism, the work launched her into the cinematic forefront, and in Italy it earned the Venice Film Festival's prestigious Golden Lion. American critics also received "Marianne and Juliane" as a major work. *New Republic*'s Stanley Kauffmann commended von Trotta's sensitivity and cited her extraordinary artistry. "Cinematically," he asserted, "the film is built with delicacy and strength." Sheila Benson expressed similar praise, writing in the *Los Angeles Times* that the film was "a miracle of imagery and observation" and that with it von Trotta "emerges as a director of international importance." Benson was especially impressed with von Trotta's abilities in rendering both the political and the personal. According to Benson, von Trotta had fashioned "a delicate and intelligent film, a flowing poem of memory and forgetting."

"Sheer Madness," von Trotta's next film, also proved a vivid account of two women's relationship. This film centers on the relationship of Olga, a feminist professor, and Ruth, a severely depressed artist. Their friendship begins when Olga consoles Ruth after her suicide attempt. Soon, to the chagrin of the demanding men in their lives, Olga and Ruth form a strong friendship. With Olga's help, Ruth prepares an exhibition of her unshown paintings. But Ruth's husband, resentful of the women's friendship, connives to prevent the exhibition, then tells Ruth that Olga's interest results from his own request that Olga help her. Crushed, Ruth again attempts sucide. She fails, however, and after recovering she accompanies Olga on a study trip. In returning they are confronted by Ruth's husband, who accuses Olga of stealing Ruth's affections. His anger results in violence. Soon afterwards, upon returning home from work, he is shot by Ruth. At her trial, she thanks Olga for her encouragement.

Critics shared less overall satisfaction with "Sheer Madness" than with von Trotta's two preceding films. Reviewers such as the *Chicago Tribune*'s Robert Blau found the film elliptical and unconvincing, while the *New York Times*'s Janet Maslin and *New Republic*'s Stanley Kauffmann complained that it was extremist and imprecise. Maslin and Kauffmann conceded, however, that von Trotta was nonetheless an accomplished filmmaker. Maslin wrote, "The extremist side of 'Sheer Madness' . . . is tempered at least to some degree by the skillfulness and humanity of Miss von Trotta's execution." And Kauffmann, who found the script for "Sheer Madness" "inferior" to that of either "Sisters" or "Marianne and Juliane," declared that "von Trotta's filmmaking . . . is wonderful." He cited her subdued visual technique and "evocative" editing as evidence that she was, despite the film's alleged flaws, "an extraordinary talent." Even more favorable was *Ms.* reviewer

Molly Haskell, who deemed "Sheer Madness" "an eerily honest film, as beautiful as it is appalling." Maslin called von Trotta "a director of astonishing depth and skill" and concluded that she was "one of the most important directors . . . of the 1980s."

In her next film, "Rosa Luxemburg," von Trotta fashioned a conventional, populist biography of the radical socialist. Beginning with Luxemburg's final imprisonment in 1916, then flashing back to the century's first years before establishing strict chronology, "Rosa Luxemburg" details Luxemburg's relatively bourgeois background and charts her rise within the socialist ranks. The film also addresses her conflicts within the socialist movement, in which she antagonized many with her frequently iconoclastic perspective, and elucidates—frequently with her own words—her advocacy of mass action and general strikes. The film ends in 1919 with a disturbing depiction of Luxemburg's capture and murder by German soldiers.

Like "Sheer Madness," "Rosa Luxemburg" drew a mixed response from American critics. Writing in the *Village Voice*, Amy Taubin found von Trotta's film a timely reflection of feminist concerns and affirmed that women participants from the "liberation movement of the late '60s and early '70s will find in the film . . . moving echoes of their struggles to gain recognition for the authority of their subjectivity and their daily experience." But another *Village Voice* writer, chief critic J. Hoberman, lamented the "gentility" of von Trotta's perspective and complained that von Trotta eliminated too many aspects of Luxemburg's life. The film, he declared, "is accommodating in ways that Luxemburg never was." Stanley Kauffmann, one of von Trotta's staunchest supporters, also acknowledged the complexity of Luxemburg's life, but he added that von Trotta had made "as good a film on this subject as is imaginable." He observed, "Her film cannot fully satisfy those who know Luxemburg or those who do not; still it is so beautifully made that it suggests the very powers it incompletely represents."

Since von Trotta's emergence as a major filmmaker, the German cinema has paradoxically diminished in international stature. Fassbinder's death in 1982, together with the departure of Wenders, Herzog, and Schloendorff to foreign projects, undermined West Germany's status as a leading producer of quality films. Von Trotta, however, has persevered. It is likely that she is now her nation's leading film artist, and as Stanley Kauffmann contended in 1987, she is "arguably the best filmmaker now at work."

BIOGRAPHICAL/CRITICAL SOURCES:

BOOKS

Phillips, Klaus, editor, *New German Filmmakers*, Ungar, 1985.

PERIODICALS

Monthly Film Bulletin, June, 1982, July, 1983, August, 1983.
Ms., December, 1983, May, 1987.
Nation, April 25, 1987.
New Republic, February 10, 1982, June 2, 1982, October 21, 1985, May 18, 1987.
New Statesman, May 14, 1982, July 1, 1983, January 20, 1984.
New York, May 24, 1982, June 1, 1987.
New York Times, June 19, 1974, September 26, 1974, October 3, 1975, February 6, 1978, May 17, 1979, January 31, 1982, February 11, 1982, April 22, 1982, October 20, 1985.
Village Voice, May 28, 1979, December 10, 1979, February 3, 1982, May 12, 1987.

—*Sketch by Les Stone*

W

WADE, Edwin L.   1940-

PERSONAL: Born July 1, 1947, in Inyokern, Calif.; son of Q. T. and Margret B. (Belneave) Wade; married. *Education:* California State University, Fullerton, B.A., 1969; University of Washington, Seattle, M.A., 1973, Ph.D., 1976.

ADDRESSES: Office—Philbrook Museum of Art, 2727 South Rockford Rd., Tulsa, Okla. 74114.

CAREER: Private curator of art in Seattle, Wash., 1972-73; School of American Research, Santa Fe, N.M., Weatherhead resident scholar, 1973-75; Harvard University, Cambridge, Mass., assistant director of Peabody Museum of Archaeology and Ethnology, and lecturer in anthropology, 1977-80; Philbrook Museum of Art, Tulsa, Okla., curator of art, 1981—.

AWARDS, HONORS: Western Heritage Wrangler Award from National Cowboy Hall of Fame, for *The Arts of the North American Indian,* and Governor's Arts Award, for exhibition "What Is Native American Art," both 1986.

WRITINGS:

America's Great Lost Expedition, Heard Museum, 1981.
Magic Images, University of Oklahoma Press, 1981.
Historic Hopi Ceramics, Harvard University Press, 1981.
As in a Vision: Masterworks of American Indian Art, University of Oklahoma Press, 1983.
Indianische Kunst im 20. Jahrhundert, Prestel-Vergel, 1984, revised English edition published as *One Hundred Years of Native American Art,* University of Oklahoma Press, in press.
The Arts of the North American Indian, Hudson Hills, 1986.

Contributor of articles to periodicals.

WORK IN PROGRESS: A variety of national and international projects concerned with the changing image of Native American and ethnic art as well as its art market and museum reception; a series of articles on America's obsession with spiritual issues.

SIDELIGHTS: Edwin L. Wade told *CA:* "I have been critically accused of a disdain for Western civilization which, upon mature reflection, is probably true. My unconventional career arose from running away as a teenager from the technological complexity of southern California to the then relative isolation of Hopi Indian country in Arizona. I rapidly realized there

were other ways to see reality and to ease one's frustrations. Though nice, not everyone needs a Malibu deck house and Porsche to find significance in life. More important, particularly to our beleaguered civilization, is the self-realization of some motivational directive that will allow our people a reason to sustain their lives and creative energies. Though perhaps cynical in its first hearing, I believe these are positive, constructive comments and, surprisingly to myself, they have revealed themselves as the core issue that has propelled my writings and investigations."

*   *   *

WAGGONER, Hyatt H(owe)   1913-1988

OBITUARY NOTICE—See index for *CA* sketch: Born November 19, 1913, in Pleasant Valley, N.Y.; died of emphysema, October 13, 1988, in Hanover, N.H. Educator, editor, and author. Waggoner was known for his expertise in the works of Nathaniel Hawthorne. He taught at the University of Kansas City for fourteen years and later at Brown University, from which he retired in 1980 after twenty-four years as professor of American literature. Among his writings are *Hawthorne: A Critical Study, American Poets From the Puritans to the Present, The Presence of Hawthorne,* and *American Visionary Poetry.* Waggoner also edited works by Hawthorne and contributed articles to many other volumes and periodicals.

OBITUARIES AND OTHER SOURCES:

PERIODICALS

New York Times, October 15, 1988.

*   *   *

WAILEY, Anthony Paul   1947-
(Tony Wailey)

PERSONAL: Born December 3, 1947, in Liverpool, England; son of John Llewellan (a factory worker) and Jane (a factory worker; maiden name, Smythe) Wailey. *Education:* Ruskin College, Oxford, diploma in history, 1975; University of Essex, B.A., 1977; University of Liverpool, Ph.D., 1980. *Religion:* Catholic.

ADDRESSES: Home—91 Alderney St., Pimlico, London SW1, England.

CAREER: Merchant seaman in Liverpool, England, 1963-68; building worker in Denmark and France, 1968-70; English teacher in Barcelona, Spain, 1970-72; building worker in Bristol, England, 1972-73; writer, 1975—. Part time adult education teacher at the City Literary Institute, London, England.

MEMBER: Liverpool Football Supporters Club.

AWARDS, HONORS: State mature scholarship, 1975.

WRITINGS:

(Contributor) Martyn Nightingale, editor, *Merseyside in Crisis*, Liverpool Research Group, 1980.
(With Paul Thompson and Trevor Lummis; under name Tony Wailey) *Living the Fishing*, Routledge & Kegan Paul, 1983.
The Balance of Strange Times, Picador, in press.

Contributor to periodicals, including *Footsteps, History Workshop,* and *Record.*

WORK IN PROGRESS: A novel, *The Difficult Match,* publication expected in 1990; *The Western Approaches,* a book about Liverpool and the Seaman's Union, publication expected in 1993.

SIDELIGHTS: Living the Fishing—by Paul Thompson, with Tony Wailey and Trevor Lummis—is a general survey of British fishing since the onset of industrialization. Based on 160 interviews with people involved in the industry, as well as documentary sources, the study looks at the moral and economic ramifications of fishing developments, focusing particularly on the coastal communities of Lancashire, East Anglia, Scotland, and Shetland; Thompson suggests that Britain must look to Shetland's adaptable, individualistic, egalitarian fishing society, in fact, for a model of future industry success. Describing *Living the Fishing* as "history from the inside," *Times Literary Supplement* reviewer Angus Calder determined, "The result is mostly convincing and always fascinating."

Wailey told *CA* that he speaks Spanish and French and likes football and travel. He names Ernest Hemingway's *A Farewell to Arms*—enjoyed on a ship in Spain in 1968—the most affecting book he has read.

He added: "My concerns are many, my career non-existent. The most difficult thing I find to do is to keep dancing when the heart gets broken and concrete fills the shoes. Writing is like waltzing in sand for the unpublished. The quick step would come easier if my work jived all over the newsstands, railway stations, and building concourses of the United States."

BIOGRAPHICAL/CRITICAL SOURCES:

PERIODICALS

Times Literary Supplement, March 2, 1984.

*   *   *

WAILEY, Tony
    See WAILEY, Anthony Paul

*   *   *

WAKEMAN, Carolyn   1943-

PERSONAL: Born October 11, 1943, in Connecticut; daughter of Willard C. and Edrie (Humphreys) Huntley; married second husband, Frederic Wakeman, Jr. (a professor), December 31,

1974; children: Matthew, Sarah. *Education:* Pembroke College (now Brown University), A.B. (cum laude), 1964; Washington University, A.M., 1968, Ph.D., 1980.

ADDRESSES: Home—New York, N.Y.

CAREER: Hope High School, Providence, R.I., English teacher, 1964-66; University of California, Berkeley, teaching associate in English composition, 1974-80; Beijing University of Foreign Studies, Beijing, China, assistant professor of English literature, 1980-82 and 1985-86; University of California, Berkeley, research associate at Center for Chinese Studies, 1986-87.

MEMBER: Association of Asian Studies, Columbia University Modern History Seminar.

AWARDS, HONORS: Award from Bay Area Book Reviewers Association, 1986, for *To the Storm.*

WRITINGS:

(Editor with husband, Frederic Wakeman, Jr.) *Conflict and Control in Late Imperial China,* University of California Press, 1975.
(With Yue Daiyun) *To the Storm: The Odyssey of a Revolutionary Chinese Woman* (autobiography), University of California Press, 1985.

Contributor of articles to *Journal of Asian Studies, Shakespeare Quarterly,* and *Foreign Literature* (China), and of book reviews to *New York Times, Los Angeles Times,* and *San Francisco Chronicle.*

WORK IN PROGRESS: A book, tentatively titled *Behind Chinese Walls,* "about the lives of teachers and students in one Chinese university over the past forty years"; an article, "Zhang Xinxin and the Writer's Choice," for *Critical Approaches to Chinese Women Writers.*

SIDELIGHTS: To the Storm: The Odyssey of a Revolutionary Chinese Woman is Yue Daiyun's personal account—retold by American teacher Carolyn Wakeman—of two decades of political purges in Maoist China. Yue was a third-generation university intellectual and dedicated Communist party member whose promising academic career and comfortable family life were shattered with false charges of "rightism" in 1958, reported Jerome B. Grieder in *Nation,* explaining that Yue spent the next twenty years "separated from the people"—denied teaching positions, socially ostracized, and removed from her family in reeducation episodes consisting of isolation, hard labor, and near starvation on collective farms. Under the new leadership of Deng Xiaoping, however, her political conviction was overturned in 1979, pronounced a casualty of the anti-intellectualism and political fanaticism that marked the Mao decades. Returned to her university post and to the Communist party as an honored veteran, Yue expresses scant bitterness over past sufferings, seeing the radical years as somehow necessary to the Chinese revolution and hoping that such sacrifices can be redeemed. "Even as I recalled the disappointments of my own life and the tragic loss of my friends," the *Nation* quoted her in *To the Storm,* "I realized that some flame still burned in my heart."

Commending Wakeman's sensitivity to both China and the English language, Jeffrey C. Kinkley wrote in the *Los Angeles Times Book Review* that he was intrigued by Yue's conclusion that "not a single step was taken in vain." He maintained, "The statement suggests a moral and perceptual gulf between traditional East and traditional West." Other critics expressed similar perplexity over the narrator's uncritical account, but they appreciated its candor and insider's view of modern China's most turbulent years. Reviewers also applauded Wakeman's thoughtful rendering of Yue's reminiscences, based on two years of notes and conversations and shaped into a first-person narrative. Writing that *To the Storm* "reads better than many novels," Kinkley related: "[Yue] has a novelist's memory, sufficient for Wakeman to have reconstructed an intimate diary of Yue's emotions and free associations." *Times Literary Supplement* critic Jonathan Mirsky similarly observed that "Wakeman has convincingly translated Yue's experiences and sentiments into her own words, synthesis and sequences." And discussing the autobiography in *Nation*, Grieder concluded that this account of personal tragedy and "a social and cultural disaster of awesome dimensions" "owe[s] much to the insight of [its] Western co-author."

Wakeman told *CA:* "In the fall of 1980, having recently completed a doctoral dissertation on Shakespeare's *Coriolanus*, I accompanied my husband to Beijing and began teaching English literature at the Beijing Foreign Studies University. Little did I know that this decision would change the shape of my future. After returning to the United States in 1982 I began writing and lecturing about China. The collaborative biography *To the Storm* gave me a chance to make available to others the compelling story of a Chinese woman, a university teacher whose life reflects the unfulfilled promise of China's revolution."

BIOGRAPHICAL/CRITICAL SOURCES:

PERIODICALS

Los Angeles Times Book Review, May 25, 1986.
Nation, July 5/12, 1986.
New York Review of Books, July 17, 1986.
New York Times Book Review, December 29, 1985.
Times Literary Supplement, August 22, 1986.
Washington Post Book World, June 21, 1987.

*   *   *

WALCOTT, John   1949-

PERSONAL: Born August 29, 1949, in Paterson, N.J.; son of Henry Richards, Jr. (an engineer) and Katharine (Fearing) Walcott; married Nancy Bittles, August 11, 1973; children: Jennifer, Allison. *Education:* Williams College, B.A., 1971.

ADDRESSES: Office—Wall Street Journal, 1025 Connecticut Ave. N.W., Washington, D.C. 20036. *Agent*—Theron Raines, Raines & Raines, 71 Park Ave., Suite 4A, New York, N.Y. 10016.

CAREER: Record, Hackensack, N.J., science writer, 1973-75, Washington correspondent, 1975-77; *Newsweek*, New York, N.Y., Washington correspondent, 1977-81, chief diplomatic correspondent in Washington, D.C., 1981-86; *Wall Street Journal*, New York City, national security correspondent in Washington, D.C., 1986—. U.S. media representative at UNESCO Conference on New World Information and Communication Order, Igls, Austria, 1983. Member of Georgetown University School of Foreign Service leadership seminar, 1985.

MEMBER: Overseas Writers Club (president, 1985-87), White House Correspondents Association.

AWARDS, HONORS: Edwin M. Hood Award for diplomatic correspondence from National Press Club, 1983; Sigma Delta Chi awards for coverage of nuclear weapons issues, the Mideast, and Central America, 1983, 1984, and 1985; Edward Weintal Prize for diplomatic reporting from Institute for the Study of Diplomacy, Georgetown University, 1988.

WRITINGS:

(With David C. Martin) *Best Laid Plans: The Inside Story of America's War Against Terrorism*, Harper, 1988.

BIOGRAPHICAL/CRITICAL SOURCES:

PERIODICALS

Washington Post Book World, July 17, 1988.

*   *   *

WALKER, Lou Ann   1952-

PERSONAL: Born December 9, 1952, in Hartford City, Ind.; daughter of Gale Freeman (a printer) and Doris Jean (a film librarian; maiden name, Wells) Walker; married Speed Vogel (a writer), September 8, 1986. *Education:* Attended Ball State University, 1971-73; Universite de Besancon, degree in French language and literature, 1975; Harvard University, B.A., 1976.

ADDRESSES: Home—New York, N.Y., and Sag Harbor, N.Y. *Agent*—Liz Darhansoff, 1220 Park Ave., New York, N.Y. 10128.

CAREER: Indianapolis News, Indianapolis, Ind., reporter, 1976; *New York* (magazine), New York, N.Y., assistant to executive editor, 1976-77; *Esquire*, New York City, associate editor, 1977-79; *Cosmopolitan*, New York City, assistant to executive editor, 1979-80; *Diversion* (magazine), New York City, associate editor, 1980-81; *Direct* (magazine), New York City, editor, 1981-82. Sign language interpreter for New York Society for the Deaf. Consultant on special project for handicapped people for Museum of Modern Art, 1980-85. Consultant to Broadway's Theater Development Fund and sign language advisor on many Broadway shows, 1984—.

MEMBER: Authors Guild.

AWARDS, HONORS: Rockefeller Foundation humanities fellowship, 1982-83; Christopher Award for *A Loss for Words*, 1987; National Endowment for the Arts creative writing grant, 1988.

WRITINGS:

Amy: The Story of a Deaf Child, photographs by Michael Abramson, Lodestar, 1985.
A Loss for Words: The Story of Deafness in a Family (autobiography; Book-of-the-Month Club editor's choice), Harper, 1986.

Contributor of articles to *American Health*, *Harvard Magazine*, *Ladies' Home Journal*, *New York Times*, *Parade*, *People*, and *Redbook*.

WORK IN PROGRESS: A novel, *Max Joly*.

SIDELIGHTS: The oldest hearing child of profoundly deaf parents, Lou Ann Walker became the family's intermediary with the hearing world at an early age, dealing directly with doctors, teachers, and merchants while her parents were frequently dismissed as unintelligent and incapable. Marked by public embarrassment and isolation, it was a life that "seemed extraordinarily fragile" on the outside, as Carol Eron quoted from Walker's autobiography in *Washington Post*. The family home, however, was warm and loving, with a devoted mother and jocular father who expressed their own brand of independence and joy in living. After college and career relocation, Walker was still troubled by the years of trying to shield her parents from the ignorance of outsiders, caught between their silent world and her world of hearing people. "There were unbreakable bonds between us," she wrote, according to Ursula Vils of the *Los Angeles Times*. "Yet there was also an unbroachable chasm."

In *A Loss for Words: The Story of Deafness in a Family*, Walker recounts her singular past in an attempt to understand it. Taking nearly four years to complete, the book served as a kind of emotional catharsis for an existence that at times left her feeling like "a robot of words and sounds for people." Like her parents before her, the author eventually learns that there are two ways to address the unalterable: to be bitter, or to proceed and enjoy life. Hoping that this story of "lovely people, spunky daughter" can "do some good" for others, Hugh Kenner wrote in the *New York Times Book Review:* "So profoundly other, then, is the unhearing culture that moving it into a language we learn by hearing took both gifts and a nearly savage determination." Pointing out the absence of self-pity "in this delicate, carefully drawn memoir," *Washington Post* critic Carol Eron reflected: "The effect of parental deafness on hearing children is a largely neglected subject."

Walker told *CA:* "Nothing is harder than writing a memoir. I can only hope that from here on, my work will be emotionally intense—but less wrenching for me.

"My husband, Speed, and I bike and run every day, and we spend the summers with friends in Europe. I'm fluent in French, and, although I have enough Italian to understand a greengrocer's recipes, I'm struggling with that language. I continue to discover the beauties of American Sign Language."

BIOGRAPHICAL/CRITICAL SOURCES:

BOOKS

Walker, Lou Ann, *A Loss for Words: The Story of Deafness in a Family*, Harper, 1986.

PERIODICALS

Los Angeles Times, March 30, 1987.
New York Times Book Review, October 5, 1986.
People, December 15, 1986.
Washington Post, November 7, 1986.

*   *   *

WALLICH, Henry C(hristopher)   1914-1988

OBITUARY NOTICE—See index for *CA* sketch: Born June 10, 1914, in Berlin, Germany; died of a brain tumor, September 15, 1988, in Washington, D.C. Economist, businessman, government official, educator, editor, and author. Wallich was an authority on international economics. He began his career with an Argentine export business in the 1930s, then ventured to New York City and worked as a security analyst for various companies. He taught at Yale University for twenty-three years, leaving in 1974 after five years as Seymour H. Knox Professor of Economics. His last career post was as a governor of the U.S. Federal Reserve, from which he retired in 1986 due to illness. Wallich's writings include *Monetary Problems of an Export Economy, The Financial System of Portugal, Mainsprings of the German Revival, The Cost of Freedom: A New Look at Capitalism*, and *The Modern Corporation and Social Responsibility*, which he wrote with Henry G. Manne. He also

edited and wrote the introduction to *Zwei Generationen im Deutschen Bankwesen*, which was written by Hermann Wallich and Paul Wallich.

OBITUARIES AND OTHER SOURCES:

BOOKS

Who's Who in American Politics, 10th edition, Bowker, 1985.

PERIODICALS

Chicago Tribune, September 18, 1988.
Los Angeles Times, September 17, 1988.
New York Times, September 16, 1988.
Washington Post, September 16, 1988.

*   *   *

WALLS, H(enry) J(ames)   1907-1988

OBITUARY NOTICE—See index for *CA* sketch: Born December 24, 1907, in Edinburgh, Scotland; died August 16, 1988. Scientist and author. Walls was a specialist in forensics. For eighteen years he worked for Britain's Home Office Forensic Science Laboratory. He left there in 1964 to become director of Scotland Yard's Metropolitan Police Laboratory, from which he retired in 1968. Walls wrote *Forensic Science* and, with A. R. Brownlie, *Drink, Drugs, and Driving*. In addition, he wrote an autobiography, titled *Expert Witness*, and books on photography, including *Photo Technique*.

OBITUARIES AND OTHER SOURCES:

BOOKS

Who's Who, 140th edition, St. Martin's, 1988.

PERIODICALS

Times (London), August 19, 1988.

*   *   *

WALMSLEY, Tom   1948-

PERSONAL: Born December 13, 1948, in Liverpool, Lancashire, England; immigrated to Canada, October 10, 1952, landed immigrant, November 30, 1953; son of Tom (an electrician) and Veda (a homemaker; maiden name, Orr) Walmsley; married Marie Smith, February, 1968 (divorced, January, 1969); married Brenda Hilimoniuk (an employee of Bell Canada), January 30, 1976 (divorced, December, 1976); married Diana Clifford (an editorial assistant), June 20, 1987.

ADDRESSES: Home—Toronto, Ontario, Canada. *Agent*—Joyce Ketay, 320 West 90th St., New York, N.Y. 10024.

CAREER: Worked odd jobs, including cleaning herring, selling newspapers, and doing carpet factory work; worked on assembly line at General Motors, 1968-69; heroin addict and thief, 1971-74; Pulp Press, Vancouver, British Columbia, editor, 1974-79; writer, 1975—.

MEMBER: Playwrights Union of Canada.

AWARDS, HONORS: Award from Pulp Press, 1978, for *Doctor Tin;* co-winner of the Floyd S. Chalmers Canadian Play Award from the Ontario Arts Council, 1983, for "White Boys."

WRITINGS:

Rabies (poems), Pulp Press, 1975.

The Workingman (one-act play; first produced in Vancouver, British Columbia, at the New Play Centre, May 20, 1975), Pulp Press, 1975.

Lexington Hero (poems), Pulp Press, 1976.

The Jones Boy (one-act play; first produced in Toronto, Ontario, at the Toronto Free Theatre, January 20, 1977), Pulp Press, 1977.

Doctor Tin (novel), Pulp Press, 1979.

Something Red (two-act play; first produced in Vancouver at the New Play Centre, September 2, 1978), Virgo Press, 1980.

(With Dolly Reisman) "Mr. Nice Guy" (two-act play), first produced in Toronto at Toronto Free Theatre, April 3, 1986.

Getting Wrecked (one-act juvenile play; first produced in Toronto at the Theatre Direct, April 12, 1985), published in *Your Voice and Mine 2*, Joan Green, editor, Holt, 1987.

White Boys (two-act play; first produced in Toronto at the Tarragon Theatre, March 13, 1982), Playwrights Canada, 1988 (also see below).

"White Boys" (film), Alternative Pictures, 1989 (also see above).

WORK IN PROGRESS: Screen adaptation of *The Workingman,* to be produced by Pepper-Prince Productions; another play.

SIDELIGHTS: Tom Walmsley, described in the Toronto *Globe and Mail* by critic Liam Lacey as the "unrepentant bad boy of Canadian letters," began his writing career while a heroin addict. He published his first volume of poems, *Rabies,* in 1975, but he is better known for his plays and his prize-winning novel, *Doctor Tin,* which has become a classic in the Canadian punk culture. Walmsley's art is primarily concerned with exploring the varied nature of sex and violence; its characters are usually mentally disturbed in one way or another. Though he stopped using drugs when he became serious about his literary ambitions, Walmsley's poetry and prose often draw on his experiences with the darker side of Canadian street life, which included stealing television sets, he admitted to Jack Kapica in another *Globe and Mail* article. Walmsley's work, however, is not in the strictest sense autobiographical. As interviewer John Saint-Louis explained in *Limelight* magazine, "While preparing myself to meet Tom Walmsley, I had horrid visions of encountering a deranged psychopath who might, for his own simple amusement, tie me up and then nonchalantly slice my jugular vein. To my relief, I met nothing of the sort. I spent a most enjoyable and interesting afternoon with a philanthropist who exuded an aura of gentleness and sensitivity. I listened to an expressive man speak with directness, sincerity and humour about his perceptions of himself, his work and the world around him."

"The Workingman," which analyzes the behavior of two men and a woman who are making a pornographic film when a hired killer takes over their apartment, was Walmsley's first produced play, debuting in Vancouver, British Columbia, in 1975. According to Kapica, "people walked out in droves." Walmsley's 1977 stage effort, "The Jones Boy," met with better success. Praised as "hard-hitting" by reviewer Ray Conlogue for the *Globe and Mail,* the play involves two heroin addicts, Lee and Wayne, who turn their girlfriends into prostitutes to pay for their expensive habits. In Conlogue's words, the women, Carol and Sally, "do it for love." He noted "the unmistakable imprint" that the work bears "of Walmsley's first-hand experience in the criminal subculture," and judged

that the author's "affection for the characters does not preclude an awareness that something is deeply wrong with them."

Proclaimed "ugly, violent and frightening," as well as "fascinating" by Matthew Fraser, critiquing in the *Globe and Mail,* Walmsley's 1978 "Something Red" concerns the relationships of four people—Bobby, Christine, Alex, and Elizabeth. Bobby is hiding from the police in his lover Christine's apartment; Alex, a former criminal accomplice of Bobby's, comes to visit with his girlfriend Elizabeth, described by Conlogue as "a jerk of a middle-class princess bored with college and adoring males." After the foursome share a few drinks, it becomes known that Bobby and Elizabeth also share a strange sexual partnership. "Bobby's psychosis," explained Conlogue, excites Elizabeth; she enjoys having Bobby caress her naked body with the edge of a switchblade knife, leading Fraser to announce that "'Something Red' probably best expresses [Walmsley's] attitude toward sado-masochism." Alex, in a jealous rage at discovering Elizabeth's preference for another man, challenges Bobby in a deadly game of Russian roulette.

Walmsley composed his popular novel, *Doctor Tin,* in response to a 1978 three-day novel-writing contest. Described by Jay Scott in a *Globe and Mail* article as "a psychedelic, sado-masochistic, bisexual re-write of [detective fiction author] Raymond Chandler," the book recounts the story of the destructive, anti-establishment A. J., alias Dr. Tin. As Walmsley declared in *Doctor Tin,* "A. J. was [bent on destroying] as much of their world as he could, at least a corner of it, to at least make a dent if he could not actually rend the fabric asunder. And he did go forth in the hopes of setting an example." Walmsley "fantasizes with the fevered directness of an action painter" in *Doctor Tin,* according to Scott, and the author confided in the interview with Saint-Louis that the novel pleased him greatly: "I know there are problems with it but I had the most fun writing it. I really felt like there was nothing coming between me and it. And it came right off the top of my head so it had a real purity about it for me."

"A Walmsley play without a corpse is a bit of an event," opined Carole Corbeil, discussing "White Boys" for the *Globe and Mail,* "not to mention a departure." "White Boys," hailed as "a radar-directed, heat-seeking comedy of manners" by Conlogue, concerns Wells and Wake, two unemployed roommates who are both enamored of Susan, a free spirit who has supposedly killed her husband—"for being boring," according to Conlogue. To Wells's and Wake's dismay, Susan ends up preferring the very straight-laced Robinson, who gives them part-time work doing paper collating. As Conlogue observed, "the outlines of Walmsley's customary concerns are here, but mellower than usual. There is the lurking violence, but nobody actually gets killed in the duration." He also noted that "White Boys" had an interesting subtheme—Wells and Wake may be latent homosexuals attracted to each other but hiding it by having affairs with women. "They are both so likeable, you kind of wish they would get it together," added Conlogue.

The 1986 "Mr. Nice Guy" took Walmsley and his co-author Dolly Reisman three years to write. The play centers on a couple trying to save their marriage with a cottage weekend. Roy, the husband, however, cannot keep himself from physically abusing his wife, Heather, and she decides to kill him. Both Walmsley and Reisman had discussed Ann Jones's book *Women Who Kill,* and in Lacey's words, "felt the theme of women's revenge against males had dramatic possibilities."

Walmsley told *CA:* "I am an alcoholic and a heroin addict, but I have not used either chemical for five years. All my life

I've been obsessed with the various manifestations of sex and violence, and I've been enraged over cinematic, literary, and other media depictions of either. My major influences have been novelists, such as Nelson Algren, William Burroughs, Chester Himes, and Philip K. Dick. I've also been influenced by the music of the Velvet Underground, Jimi Hendrix, Bob Dylan, and John Coltrane. I have no hobbies, but love to travel. So far, the two most inspirational cities for me have been Berlin and Istanbul.''

BIOGRAPHICAL/CRITICAL SOURCES:

BOOKS

Walmsley, Tom, *Doctor Tin*, Pulp Press, 1979.

PERIODICALS

Globe and Mail (Toronto), January 19, 1977, January 11, 1980, March 1, 1980, May 12, 1982, May 14, 1982, February 4, 1986, March 22, 1986, April 15, 1986.
Limelight, May, 1983.

—*Sketch by Elizabeth Thomas*

*　　　*　　　*

WARD, Jonas
　See COX, William R(obert)

*　　　*　　　*

WARREN, Lucian (Crissey)　1913-1988

OBITUARY NOTICE—See index for *CA* sketch: Born February 12, 1913, in Jamestown, N.Y.; died of cancer, October 12, 1988, in Issue, Md. Journalist. Warren spent most of his career in Washington, D.C., where he was bureau chief for the *Buffalo Courier-Express* from 1945 to 1968 and for the *Buffalo Evening News* from 1968 to 1978. He subsequently worked there as a free-lance writer and as a correspondent for the *Frederick News-Post*.

OBITUARIES AND OTHER SOURCES:

BOOKS

Who's Who in America, 45th edition, Marquis, 1988.

PERIODICALS

Washington Post, October 13, 1988.

*　　　*　　　*

WATERS, John (M.)　1946(?)-

BRIEF ENTRY: Born c. 1946 in Baltimore, Md. American filmmaker and author. Waters is most famous for writing and directing outrageous and satiric films, including ''Pink Flamingos'' (Saliva Films, 1972) and ''Polyester'' (New Line Cinema, 1981), both featuring the late transvestite actor Divine. Waters began his film career with creations like ''Mondo Trasho'' (Film-Makers, 1970) and gained notoriety with ''Pink Flamingos.'' This 1972 movie concerns two families vying for the title of the filthiest people alive and includes a scene in which one of the characters eats dog excrement. ''Polyester,'' though slightly more tame in its subject matter, nonetheless reflects Waters's alternative sense of humor as members of the movie audience are given scratch-and-sniff cards with scents like gasoline and smelly shoes to use at certain points during the film. In 1988 Waters released ''Hairspray'' (New Line

Cinema), a less odious piece with a parental guidance rating (PG) instead of the usual restricted (R) or ''X'' ratings of his previous efforts. The film spoofs two genres, the teen movie and the message movie, and has been generally well received. Waters has also written two books discussing his attraction to the trashier side of popular culture, *Shock Value* (Dell, 1981) and *Crackpot: The Obsessions of John Waters* (Macmillan, 1986).

BIOGRAPHICAL/CRITICAL SOURCES:

PERIODICALS

Biography News, May/June, 1975.
Chicago Tribune, February 14, 1988.
Publishers Weekly, July 17, 1981.

*　　　*　　　*

WATTEL, Harold Louis　1921-

PERSONAL: Born September 30, 1921, in Brooklyn, N.Y.; son of David Max and Carolyn (Abrams) Wattel; married Sara Gordon, September 1, 1946; children: Karen, Jill. *Education:* Queens College of the City (now of the City University) of New York, B.A., 1942; Columbia University, M.A., 1947; New School for Social Research, Ph.D. (magna cum laude), 1954. *Politics:* Democrat.

ADDRESSES: Home—181 Shepherd Lane, Roslyn Heights, N.Y. 11577. *Office*—Department of Economics, Hofstra University, 1000 Fulton Ave., Hempstead, N.Y. 11550.

CAREER: War Production Board, Washington, D.C., junior economist, 1942; U.S. Department of Agriculture, Washington, D.C., economist, 1946; Hofstra University, Hempstead, N.Y., began as instructor, 1946, became professor of economics, 1957, economist at Bureau of Business and Community Research, 1954 and 1957, and director of bureau, 1957-58, chairman of economics department, 1957-61, chairman of Division of Business, 1961—, dean of School of Business, 1965-73. Economic consultant with firm of Boni, Watkins & Mounteer (now National Economic Research Associates), 1952; economic consultant to consumer council of the governor of New York, 1955-58; consultant to New York State Moreland Commission on Alcoholic Beverage Control Law, the New York City office of the industrial commissioner, the legislative reference bureau of the University of Hawaii, Schenley Industries, Ralston Purina Co., American Can Co., U.S. Merchant Marine Academy, Bulova Watch Foundation, Waldbaum, United Technical Publications, and National Millinery Planning Board. Member of the Comprehensive Health Planning Council, 1970-75, and member of its board of directors in Nassau-Suffolk; vice-president and member of board of directors of New York state unit of American Lung Association, president of Nassau-Suffolk unit; member of State Citizen Council, Consumer-Farmer Foundation, Foundation for Economics, Cornell Cooperative Extension, and Nassau-Suffolk Regional Medical Program. *Military service:* U.S. Naval Reserve, 1942-46; became lieutenant.

MEMBER: American Economic Association, American Association of University Professors (president, 1953), Middle Atlantic Association of Colleges of Business Administration (president, 1970-71), New York State Environmental Health Association (vice-president), Cooperative Extension Association of Nassau County, Metropolitan Economic Association, Pi Gamma Mu, Omicron Chi Epsilon, Beta Gamma Sigma (honorary associate).

AWARDS, HONORS: Hazen Foundation fellow, 1951; Ford Foundation fellow, 1960; Distinguished Service Award from Hofstra University, 1986.

WRITINGS:

(Contributor) *The Suburban Community*, Putnam, 1958, reprinted in *Readings in General Sociology*, Houghton, 1964.

(Contributor with Alfred Oxenfeldt) Raymond McCarthy, editor, *Alcohol Education for Classroom and Community*, McGraw, 1964.

Proxy Fights as Managerial Revolutions, Hofstra University Yearbook of Business, 1966.

(With Patricia K. Putnam) *Intoxicating Liquor Laws in Hawaii and the Industry*, University of Hawaii, 1969.

(Editor) *Voluntarism and the Business Community*, Hofstra University Yearbook of Business, 1971.

(Editor) *Planning in Higher Education*, Hofstra University Yearbook of Business, 1975.

(Contributor) Richard Cyert, editor, *Management of Non-Profit Institutions*, Hofstra University Yearbook of Business, 1975.

(Editor) *Chief Executive Officer Compensation*, Hofstra University Yearbook of Business, 1978.

(Editor) *The Gross Personal Income Tax*, Hofstra University Yearbook of Business, 1981.

The Policy Consequences of John Maynard Keynes, M. E. Sharpe and Macmillan, 1986.

Author of annual *Millinery Industry*. Contributing editor of *Long Island Business*, 1954-59. Contributor to periodicals, including *Journal of Retailing* and *Collegiate News and Views*.

WORK IN PROGRESS: Research on government consumer protection agencies.

SIDELIGHTS: Harold Louis Wattel told *CA:* "I have always tried to live up to the motto of my alma mater: 'We learn in order to serve.' My interests have focused on matters of welfare and the ability of a society's economy to provide for its members.

"My book *The Policy Consequences of John Maynard Keynes* consists of a series of papers commemorating the hundredth anniversary of the birth of one of the world's greatest economists. In the United States Keynes' fame was tarnished by the business community's mistaken allegation that he was anti-business. Keynes was interested in saving capitalism from the consequences of some inherent weaknesses, including the failure of businesspeople to invest all that consumers wanted to save. That government could play a positive role was the Keynesian contention that set the teeth of the business community on edge. It is my contention that a government-business partnership to maintain full employment would have had a salutary effect on this nation. It is ironic that the present administration has inadvertently demonstrated that government deficits could play a positive role in the economy once the business community was willing to accommodate rather than discredit an administration attempting to maintain full employment."

*   *   *

WEARNE, Alan (Richard) 1948-

PERSONAL: Born July 23, 1948, in Melbourne, Australia. *Education:* Attended Monash University, 1967-68; LaTrobe University, B.A., 1973; Rusden College, Diploma in Education, 1977. *Politics:* Labour.

ADDRESSES: Home—83 Edgevale Rd., Kew, Melbourne, Victoria 3101, Australia.

CAREER: "My 'working' life has swung between the twin poles of the Australian Public Service and high school teaching in Melbourne schools, with occasional forays into life as a storeman. Next year, who knows?"

MEMBER: International P.E.N., Fellowship of Australian Authors.

AWARDS, HONORS: Several fellowships from Literature Board of Australia Council.

WRITINGS:

Public Relations (poems), Makar Press, 1972.
New Devil, New Parish (poems), University of Queensland Press, 1976.
The Nightmarkers (verse novel), Penguin Australia, 1986.
Out Here (verse novella), Blood Axe Books, 1987.

Poetry editor of *Meanjin*, 1984-87.

WORK IN PROGRESS: A volume of new and selected poems, tentatively titled *For the Public Sector;* a play in verse.

SIDELIGHTS: Alan Wearne told *CA:* "My career and its reputation seem to rest on my desire to be amongst those who are attempting to resurrect narrative verse. The highlight, so far, has been *The Nightmarkers*, a verse novel. One verse novel a lifetime being most reasonable an aim, I am slowly but inexorably moving into the world of verse drama. *The Nightmarkers* took eight years to write, and any play may take almost as long. So don't start queuing to see it."

*   *   *

WEAVER, Michael D. 1961-

PERSONAL: Born July 5, 1961, in Boston, Mass.; son of James A., Jr. (in U.S. Air Force) and Una Grace (Cooper) Weaver; married Angela Renee Marshall (an artist), December 18, 1987. *Education:* Community College of the Air Force, A.A.S., 1984. *Politics:* None. *Religion:* None.

ADDRESSES: Home and office—Danville, Va. *Agent*—Susan Protter, 110 West 40th St., New York, N.Y. 10018.

CAREER: Writer, 1981—; Dan River, Inc., Danville, Va., systems programmer, 1985-88. *Military service:* U.S. Air Force, computer programmer, 1981-85; became sergeant.

WRITINGS:

Wolf-Dreams (fantasy novel), Avon, 1987.
Mercedes Nights (science fiction), St. Martin's, 1987.
Nightreaver (fantasy novel), Avon, 1988.
My Father Immortal (science fiction), St. Martin's, 1989.
Bloodfang (fantasy novel), Avon, 1989.

SIDELIGHTS: Michael D. Weaver told *CA:* "I'm only just beginning. I also compose music and hope to produce my first album in the near future."

*   *   *

WEBB, Melody Rae 1946-

PERSONAL: Born April 1, 1946, in Gallup, N.Mex.; daughter of N. J. and Lorraine (a housewife; maiden name, Overson) Webb; married David S. Grauman, June 6, 1969 (divorced, October, 1980); married Robert M. Utley (a historian), November 12, 1980. *Education:* University of Arizona, B.A., 1968; California State College, San Francisco (now San Francisco State University), M.A., 1974; University of New Mexico, Ph.D., 1983.

ADDRESSES: Home—5 Vista Grande Court, Santa Fe, N.Mex. 87505. *Office*—National Park Service, P.O. Box 728, Santa Fe, N.Mex. 87504-0728.

CAREER: Junior high school history teacher in New Orleans, La., 1968-69; University of Alaska, Fairbanks, archaeologist, 1974; National Park Service, Fairbanks, research historian, 1975-79; National Park Service, Santa Fe, N.Mex., regional historian, 1980—. Research associate at University of Alaska, Fairbanks, 1975-80. El Dorado Volunteer Fire Department, lieutenant, 1982-85, assistant chief, 1985-86.

MEMBER: Organization of American Historians, Western History Association, New Mexico Historical Society, Alaska Historical Society, Washington State Historical Society.

AWARDS, HONORS: Seven Superior Service Awards from National Park Service.

WRITINGS:

Big Business in Alaska: The Kennecott Mines, 1898-1938, University of Alaska Cooperative Park Studies Unit, 1977.
Yukon Frontiers: A Historic Resource Study of the Proposed Yukon-Charley National Rivers, University of Alaska Cooperative Park Studies Unit, 1977.
Chronicles of a Cold, Cold War: The Paperwork Battle for Wrangel Island, University of Alaska Cooperative Park Studies Unit, 1981.
(Contributor) Michael Kennedy, editor, *Mining in Alaska's Past,* Alaska Historical Society, 1981.
The Last Frontier: A History of the Yukon Basin of Canada and Alaska, University of New Mexico Press, 1985.

Contributor to history journals.

WORK IN PROGRESS: A History of Indian Territory, completion expected in 1990.

SIDELIGHTS: Melody Rae Webb told *CA:* "In 1976 I knew nothing about writing a book and even less about surveying for historic sites in a roadless wilderness. My graduate training in history had equipped me for archival research, but only my love for the environment prepared me for an 'outdoor archives.' Fortunately for me, as I readied my backpack and freeze-dried food, a trapper from the Yukon River strolled into my office and declared that he wanted to know the history of 'his country.' When I realized that he knew the land and its resources better than I with my book learning, I asked him to be my guide. He agreed, but only if we did it his way.

"Thus I was launched into a three-month experience that gave me an intimate feeling for the past. I had to give up my freeze-dried food. Instead, we brought flour, baking powder, dried peas and beans, and rice. My trapper shot live meat each day—grouse, beaver, and, even once, a bear—and we cooked over a campfire for three meals a day. Mosquitoes harrassed us just as badly as they did the argonauts of the Klondike Gold Rush. Sun, wind, and rain added variation to our days as we trekked over swamplands, through mud and forests, and along creek banks, searching for old cabins, trails, or mining camps.

"As a result of my outdoor archives research, I was able to add personal dimension to the history of the Yukon Basin, captured in *The Last Frontier.* I had experienced first-hand the hardships and thrill of living history."

WEDEL, Waldo R(udolph)   1908-

PERSONAL: Born September 10, 1908, in Newton, Kan.; son of Peter John and Magdalena (Krehbeil) Wedel; married Mildred Ingram Mott, August 12, 1939; children: Waldo Mott, Frank Peter, Linda Margaret Wedel Greene. *Education:* Attended Bethel College of the Mennonite Church of North America (now Bethel College), North Newton, Kan., 1926-28; University of Arizona, B.A., 1930; University of Nebraska, M.A., 1931; University of California, Berkeley, Ph.D., 1936. *Religion:* Mennonite.

ADDRESSES: Home—5305 Ridgefield Rd., Bethesda, Md. 20816.

CAREER: Nebraska State Historical Society, Lincoln, archaeologist, 1936; National Museum of Natural History, Washington, D.C., assistant curator of archaeology, 1936-40, associate curator, 1941-49, curator, 1950-62, head curator of anthropology, 1962-64, senior archaeologist, 1965-76, emeritus archaeologist, 1976—. Field director of Smithsonian Institution's Missouri River Basin Surveys, Lincoln, 1946-50; conducted field research in the western United States and Mexico.

MEMBER: American Association for the Advancement of Science (fellow), Society for American Archaeology (president, 1948-49), National Academy of Sciences, Kansas Anthropological Association, Association of Iowa Anthropologists, Anthropological Society of Washington (president, 1951-52).

AWARDS, HONORS: Award in Biological Sciences from Washington Academy of Science, 1948, for studies of Great Plains Indian ecology; D.Sc. from University of Nebraska, 1972, and Kansas State University, 1985; Distinguished Service Award from Society for American Archaeology, 1986, for studies of Great Plains archaeology and ecology.

WRITINGS:

An Introduction to Pawnee Archeology, U.S. Government Printing Office, 1936.
Archeological Investigations at Buena Vista Lake, Kern County, California, U.S. Government Printing Office, 1941.
Archeological Investigations in Platte and Clay Counties, Missouri, U.S. Government Printing Office, 1943.
An Introduction to Kansas Archeology, U.S. Government Printing Office, 1959.
Prehistoric Man on the Great Plains, University of Oklahoma Press, 1961.
(Editor and author of introduction) *A Plains Archaeology Source Book: Selected Papers of the Nebraska State Historical Society,* Garland Publishing, 1985.
(Editor) John Dunbar and Samuel Allis, *The Dunbar-Allis Letters on the Pawnee,* Garland Publishing, 1985.
Central Plains Prehistory: Holocene Environments and Culture Change in the Republican River Basin, University of Nebraska Press, 1986.

Contributor to anthropology and archaeology journals.

WORK IN PROGRESS: Chapters on Great Plains Indian archaeology and ecology for new handbook on American Indians, for Smithsonian Institution.

BIOGRAPHICAL/CRITICAL SOURCES:

BOOKS

Ubelaker, Douglas H. and Herman J. Viola, editors, *Plains*

Indian Studies: A Collection of Essays in Honor of John C. Ewers and Waldo R. Wedel, Smithsonian Institution Press, 1982.

PERIODICALS

American Anthropologist, August, 1962.
American Historical Review, April, 1962.

*   *   *

WEININGER, Benjamin Isaac   1905-1988

OBITUARY NOTICE: Born March 15, 1905, in New York, N.Y.; died of cancer, heart trouble, and a bleeding ulcer, September 10, 1988, in Santa Barbara, Calif. Psychiatrist, educator, and author. Weininger will be remembered as the "Five-Cent Psychiatrist" who, inspired by a Charles Schulz "Peanuts" cartoon, set up a counseling booth on a street in Los Angeles, California. After earning a medical doctorate from the University of Illinois in 1931, Weininger began his career at Shepherd and Enoch Pratt Hospital in Towson, Maryland, before moving to Washington, D.C., where he helped found the Washington School of Psychiatry, taught, and maintained a private practice from 1937 to 1952. He then moved to California, practicing in Santa Barbara and founding the Southern California Counseling Center in Los Angeles, which provided low-cost therapy to walk-in patients. He was influential in applying religion and Eastern philosophies to psychoanalysis. Until shortly before his death, Weininger also counseled Vietnam war veterans. His books include *Simple Guide for the Perplexed: Psychological First Aid* and *Why Salt the Peanuts? Sayings of the Five Cent Psychiatrist.*

OBITUARIES AND OTHER SOURCES:

BOOKS

Biographical Directory of the Fellows and Members of the American Psychiatric Association, Bowker, 1977.

PERIODICALS

Los Angeles Times, September 11, 1988.
Washington Post, September 12, 1988.

*   *   *

WEINTRAUB, Wiktor   1908-1988

OBITUARY NOTICE—See index for *CA* sketch: Born April 10, 1908, in Zawiercie, Poland; died of cancer, July 14, 1988, in Cambridge, Mass. Educator and author. Weintraub was an authority on Slavic and Polish literature. He taught at Harvard University from 1950 to 1978, when he became professor emeritus after seven years as Alfred Jurzykowski Professor of Polish Language and Literature. Among his works in English translation are *The Poetry of Adam Mickiewicz* and *Literature as Prophecy.*

OBITUARIES AND OTHER SOURCES:

BOOKS

Directory of American Scholars, Volume III: *Foreign Languages, Linguistics, and Philology*, 8th edition, Bowker, 1982.

PERIODICALS

New York Times, July 16, 1988.

WEISSBERG, Michael P.   1942-

PERSONAL: Born July 14, 1942, in New York, N.Y. *Education:* Attended Colby College, 1960-61; New York University, B.A., 1964; Tufts University, M.D., 1968.

ADDRESSES: *Office*—Department of Psychiatry, School of Medicine, University of Colorado, 4200 East Ninth St., Denver, Colo. 80262. *Agent*—Gloria Loomis, 150 East 35th St., New York, N.Y. 10016.

CAREER: University of Colorado, Denver, assistant professor, 1971-78, associate professor of pyschiatry, 1978—.

MEMBER: American Psychiatric Association (fellow).

WRITINGS:

(With Steven Dubovsky) *Clinical Psychiatry in Primary Care*, Williams & Wilkins, 1978, 3rd edition, 1986.
Dangerous Secrets: Maladaptive Responses to Stress, Norton, 1983.

WORK IN PROGRESS: Two books titled *Freud's Amnesia and His Wish to Forget* and *The Shooting of Elaine Doe.*

BIOGRAPHICAL/CRITICAL SOURCES:

PERIODICALS

Times Literary Supplement, February 22, 1985.

*   *   *

WEISSMANN, Gerald   1930-

PERSONAL: Born August 7, 1930, in Vienna, Austria; immigrated to the United States, 1938, naturalized citizen, 1943; son of Adolf (a medical doctor) and Greta (Lustbader) Weissmann; married Ann Raphael, 1953; children: Andrew, Lisa Beth. *Education:* Columbia University, B.A., 1950; New York University, M.D., 1954.

ADDRESSES: *Office*—Department of Medicine, School of Medicine, New York University, 550 First Ave., New York, N.Y. 10016.

CAREER: Licensed to practice medicine in New York. Mt. Sinai Hospital, New York City, intern, 1954-55; Bellevue Hospital, New York City, resident and chief resident, 1955-58; Arthritis and Rheumatism Foundation, New York City, research fellow in biochemistry, 1958-59; New York University, New York City, instructor, 1959-61, assistant professor, 1961-65, associate professor, 1965-70, professor of medicine, 1970—, director of Division of Rheumatology, 1974—. Diplomate of American Board of Internal Medicine, 1963; U.S. Public Health Service special research fellow at Strangeways Research Laboratory, Cambridge University, 1960-61; senior investigator of Arthritis and Rheumatism Foundation, 1961-65; career investigator of Health Research Council of New York, 1966-70; investigator and instructor at Woods Hole Marine Biology Laboratory, 1970—; consultant to U.S. Food and Drug Administration and National Heart and Lung Institute; Rockefeller Foundation resident at the Villa Serbelloni, Bellagio, Italy, 1987; centennial lecturer at the Marine Biological Laboratory, 1988, and at Johns Hopkins Medical School, 1989.

MEMBER: American Society of Cell Biology, American Society of Biological Chemistry and Molecular Biology, American Society of Experimental Pathology, American Society for Clinical Investigation, American Rheumatism Association, Society for Experimental Biology and Medicine.

AWARDS, HONORS: Alessandro Robecchi Prize for Rheumatology from International League Against Rheumatism, 1972, for research on mechanisms of inflammation; Guggenheim fellow at Center of Immunology and Physiology, Paris, France, 1973-74; Marine Biology Laboratory Prize in cell biology, 1974 and 1979, for work in cell biology of inflammation.

WRITINGS:

The Woods Hole Cantata: Essays on Science and Society, Dodd, 1985.
They All Laughed at Christopher Columbus: Tales of Medicine and the Art of Discovery, Times Books, 1987.

WORK IN PROGRESS: The Treasure of Dougo: Essays on Art and Science.

SIDELIGHTS: Gerald Weissmann, a professor of medicine at New York University Medical Center, is the author of two volumes of essays on the art and science of medicine. The essays in his first collection, *The Woods Hole Cantata,* relate the science of medicine to its social context. One piece concerns a medical researcher who is a prisoner in a concentration camp. Another describes the fate of a severe schizophrenic whose physical illness is treated with new wonder drugs; the patient is then released to the community with little apparent regard for the psychological and social aspects of her illness. The author discusses a wide range of medical and social issues that reflect his own routine as a scientific researcher. Anna Fels, a reviewer for the *New York Times Book Review,* found Gerald Weissmann's insights ''original and provocative.'' She wrote: ''It is not only Dr. Weissmann's observations that enliven these essays, but also the palpable delight he derives from the occasions that gave rise to them.''

Weissmann's second volume of essays, *They All Laughed at Christopher Columbus,* was published in 1987. In an article for the *New York Times Book Review,* Martha Weinman Lear called the book a ''graceful, feisty collection'' that conveys ''the promise of adventure, of voyages of discovery, near-palpable each morning . . . when the laboratory doors are opened.'' Weissmann uses examples from his own practice to inform the general reader about the world of scientific discovery and to air his views on some of the medico-social issues of our time. An essay on one of his asthma patients allows the physician to discuss the fluctuations in the history of asthma treatment over the years and the debate between those who consider it a physical ailment and others who treat asthma as a psychosomatic disorder. A female AIDS victim prompts Weissmann to consider the fear of science that permeates our age. Lear recommended *They All Laughed at Christopher Columbus* as ''a book filled with graceful and generous themes, written in a spirit of caring that defines medicine in the fullest sense.''

Weissmann told *CA:* ''I have been writing all my life and am always pleased when someone actually reads my work, not in the course of duty, but in the pursuit of pleasure.''

BIOGRAPHICAL/CRITICAL SOURCES:

PERIODICALS

New York Times Book Review, September 29, 1985, April 5, 1987.

*   *   *

WERNER, Eric   1901-1988

OBITUARY NOTICE—See index for *CA* sketch: Born August

1, 1901, in Vienna, Austria; died of heart failure, July 28, 1988, in New York, N.Y. Musicologist, educator, and author. From 1939 to 1967 Werner was professor of liturgical music at the Jewish Institute of Religion, where he founded the School of Sacred Music of Hebrew Union College. He also taught at such institutions as the Eastman School of Music and the University of Jerusalem. His writings include *In the Choir Loft, The Sacred Bridge, Anthology of Hebrew Music,* and *Mendelssohn: A New Image of the Composer and His Age.*

OBITUARIES AND OTHER SOURCES:

BOOKS

Directory of American Scholars, Volume I: *History,* 8th edition, Bowker, 1982.

PERIODICALS

New York Times, July 31, 1988.

*   *   *

WHEELER, Monroe   1900-1988

OBITUARY NOTICE: Born February 13, 1900, in Evanston, Ill.; died August 14, 1988, in Manhattan, N.Y. Administrator, publisher, editor, and author. Wheeler was known for publishing quality books in Paris during the 1930s and later in New York City, for the Museum of Modern Art. He began his career in typographical design and book production while studying in England, France, and Germany in the early 1920s. In 1930, settling in Paris, Wheeler joined Barbara Harrison to establish Harrison of Paris, a company that would be recognized in Paris literary circles for producing books of intelligence and artistic sensibility at moderate prices. The firm published such works as Lord Byron's *Childe Harold's Pilgrimage* and Wheeler's own compilation, *A Typographical Commonplace-Book.* Wheeler joined the staff of the Museum of Modern Art in 1935 and, six years later, became head of the department of exhibitions and publications. In this capacity he oversaw the publication of more than 350 books on visual art. Although he retired in 1967, Wheeler remained active as a trustee and a member of the museum's International Council. He edited *Modern Painters and Sculptors as Illustrators, Britain at War,* and *Modern Drawings* and co-authored *Bonnard and His Environment.*

OBITUARIES AND OTHER SOURCES:

BOOKS

Dictionary of Literary Biography, Volume 4: *American Writers in Paris, 1920-1939,* Gale, 1980.
Who's Who in American Art, 1973, Bowker, 1976.

PERIODICALS

New York Times, August 17, 1988.

*   *   *

WHIDDEN, Mary Bess   1936-

PERSONAL: Born August 14, 1936, in San Angelo, Tex.; daughter of J. Edgar (a businessman) and Bess (Mullican) Whidden. *Education:* University of Texas at Austin, B.A. (summa cum laude), 1957, Ph.D., 1965; University of North Carolina at Chapel Hill, M.A., 1959. *Politics:* Democrat.

ADDRESSES: Home—421 Richmond S.E., Albuquerque, N.M. 87106. *Office*—Department of English, University of New Mexico, Albuquerque, N.M. 87131.

CAREER: Newspaper and television writer in San Angelo, Tex., 1955-57; dealer at Harrah's Casino, 1962; University of Texas at Austin, special instructor in English, 1962-63; University of New Mexico, Albuquerque, assistant professor, 1963-70, associate professor of English, 1970—.

MEMBER: Modern Language Association of America, Phi Beta Kappa, Phi Kappa Phi.

AWARDS, HONORS: Woodrow Wilson fellowship, 1958-59.

WRITINGS:

Provincial Matters (essays), University of New Mexico Press, 1986.

Author of regular column in *Century,* 1982-83. Contributor to magazines, including *Network, New Mexico,* and *Southwestern Discoveries.*

WORK IN PROGRESS: An anthology of humor by American women since 1920.

SIDELIGHTS: Mary Bess Whidden told *CA:* "I write to write well and play with words. My essays are satiric and funny. I am lazy and enjoy parties."

*   *   *

WHITBY, Thomas J.   1919-

PERSONAL: Born January 12, 1919, in Chicago, Ill.; son of Clement Marsh and Gertrude Margaret (Dean) Whitby; married Mary Elizabeth Darrow, November 20, 1948; children: Philip J., Irene G. Holland, Michael L., Daniel C., Helen M. Stamenkovic, Francis G. *Education:* University of Chicago, Ph.B., 1947, M.A., 1952.

ADDRESSES: Home—6983 South Washington St., Littleton, Colo. 80122.

CAREER: U.S. Library of Congress, Washington, D.C., supervisor of Cyrillic Union Subject Catalog, 1952-54, senior subject cataloger in subject cataloging division, 1954-59, Slavic science acquisitions specialist in science and technology division, 1959-61; Olin Mathieson Chemical Corp., New Haven, Conn., information scientist in metals division, 1961-63; Martin-Marietta Corp., Denver, Colo., chief librarian at Denver division, 1963-68; University of Denver, Denver, associate professor of librarianship, 1968-85, professor emeritus, 1985—.

MEMBER: American Society of Indexers, American Association for the Advancement of Science, American Association for the Advancement of Slavic Studies, Society for the Scientific Study of Sex.

WRITINGS:

(Wtih Tanja Lorkovic) *Introduction to Soviet National Bibliography,* Libraries Unlimited, 1979.
(With Suzanne G. Frayser) *Studies in Human Sexuality: A Selected Guide,* Libraries Unlimited, 1987.

Contributor to *Library Quarterly.*

WORK IN PROGRESS: Russian and Soviet Bibliography: 1073 to the Present, for Harrassowitz in West Germany.

SIDELIGHTS: Thomas J. Whitby told *CA:* "Although I concentrated in the past on library science, bibliography, and Soviet studies, my current interests are somewhat broader. Since my retirement in 1985 I have turned my attention to book

indexing and the study of human sexuality. In both of my books I have written about subjects on which there is a need for information and understanding. While Soviet national bibliography is a subject of limited interest to Americans, it nonetheless has attracted worldwide attention as nations attempt to cope with the information explosion. Human sexuality, on the other hand, is of interest to almost everyone; but surprisingly little has been done to produce useful bibliographic tools of a comprehensive nature. This is the reason why anthropologist Dr. Suzanne G. Frayser and I decided to join forces to compile *Studies in Human Sexuality,* a four-year reading and writing project that generated lengthy informative abstracts of the monographic literature in human sexuality. It is our intention to continue reading and abstracting the literature in this field with a view to producing further editions of our work and in the hope that *Studies* will become the standard reference work to the book literature in the field."

*   *   *

WHITE, Frank   1944-

PERSONAL: Born April 3, 1944, in Greenwood, Miss.; son of Frank C. (a civil engineer) and Mary Ann (a secretary/administrator; maiden name, Crow) White; married Cristin Lindstrom, July 17, 1976 (divorced, 1982); children: Ruth Richmond, Joshua Steele. *Education:* Harvard University, B.A. (magna cum laude), 1966; graduate study at Oxford University, 1966-69. *Politics:* Independent. *Religion:* "A personal approach that is all my own."

ADDRESSES: Home—Newton, Mass. *Office*—719 Washington St., Newton, Mass. 02160.

CAREER: WGBH-TV-FM, Boston, Mass., producer, writer, and commentator, 1969-70; Foundation 70, Inc., Wellesley, Mass., co-founder, 1970-72; Whitewood Stamps, Inc., Newton, Mass., executive vice-president, 1972-77; Strayton Corp., Wellesley, writer and account manager, 1978-79; Human Systems, Inc., founder and president, 1981—. Senior consultant to advanced technology practice of Hill & Knowlton, Inc.

MEMBER: National Space Society, Space Studies Institute, Phi Beta Kappa.

AWARDS, HONORS: National Merit Scholarship and Harvard National Scholarship, both 1962; named Rhodes Scholar, 1966.

WRITINGS:

The Overview Effect: Space Exploration and Human Evolution, Houghton, 1987.

Also author of *Citizens of the Universe,* 1988, and several articles on human activity in space.

WORK IN PROGRESS: SETI, a book about the search for extraterrestrial intelligence, completion expected in 1989.

SIDELIGHTS: Frank White told *CA:* "My primary interest is in how the exploration of outer space is affecting human awareness and human society. I believe that the 'exploration of outer space' is really 'evolution into the universe,' and that it is humanity's greatest adventure."

BIOGRAPHICAL/CRITICAL SOURCES:

PERIODICALS

Los Angeles Times, November 13, 1987.

WHITE, Susan J. 1949-

PERSONAL: Born September 15, 1949, in Brookline, Mass.; daughter of John William (a businessman) and Ruth (a teacher; maiden name, Jacobs; present surname, Farwell) Kendall; married James Floyd White (a professor), October 28, 1982; children: Todd Alan Hawkes. *Education:* Gordon College, B.A. (magna cum laude), 1975; Boston College, M.A., 1981; University of Notre Dame, M.A., 1984, Ph.D., 1987. *Religion:* Episcopalian.

ADDRESSES: Home and office—17840 Ponader Dr., South Bend, Ind. 46635.

CAREER: University of Notre Dame, Notre Dame, Ind., instructor in religion, 1985-86; Lincoln Theological College, Lincoln, England, lecturer in liturgics, 1987. Consultant to Section on Worship, Board of Discipleship of the United Methodist Church and Office of Worship of the Presbyterian Church of the United States of America.

MEMBER: North American Academy of Liturgy, Liturgical Conference, Associated Parishes, Societas Liturgica, Alcuin Club.

AWARDS, HONORS: Cushwa fellowship for the study of American Catholicism from University of Notre Dame, 1986.

WRITINGS:

Church Architecture, Abingdon, 1988.
Modern Liturgical Art in America, Pueblo Press, 1989.

Contributor to *Harper's Dictionary of Religious Education* and *Abingdon Dictionary of Pastoral Care.* Contributor to journals, including *Reformed Liturgy and Music* and *Faith and Form.*

WORK IN PROGRESS: Research on Protestant worship.

* * *

WILHOIT, Francis M(arion) 1920-

PERSONAL: Born April 24, 1920, in Carthage, N.C.; son of John Robert and Janie (McKenzie) Wilhoit. *Education:* Harvard University, A.B., 1949, M.P.A., 1952, Ph.D., 1958; attended University of Heidelberg, 1949-51, and University of Brussels, 1952-53.

ADDRESSES: Home—3103 University Ave., Apt. 6, Des Moines, Iowa 50311. *Office*—Department of Political Science, Drake University, 25th St. and University Ave., Des Moines, Iowa 50311.

CAREER: Bank of Pinehurst, Carthage, N.C., assistant cashier, 1937-42; language master at school in Jacksonville, Fla., 1953-55; Mercer University, Macon, Ga., assistant professor of history and government, 1955-57; University of Miami, Coral Gables, Fla., associate professor of government, 1957-61; Drake University, Des Moines, Iowa, professor of political science, 1961—. *Military service:* U.S. Army Air Forces, 1942-45; became staff sergeant.

MEMBER: American Political Science Association, Midwest Political Science Association, Metropolitan Opera Guild, Common Cause.

AWARDS, HONORS: Fulbright fellow in Belgium, 1952-53; Chastain Award from Southern Political Science Association, 1973.

WRITINGS:

The Politics of Massive Resistance, Braziller, 1973.
The Quest for Equality in Freedom, Transaction Books, 1979.

BIOGRAPHICAL/CRITICAL SOURCES:

PERIODICALS

American Historical Review, December, 1975.
Annals of the American Academy of Political and Social Science, November, 1974.*

* * *

WILKINSON, Norman Beaumont 1910-1983

OBITUARY NOTICE—See index for *CA* sketch: Born November 6, 1910, in Philadelphia, Pa.; died of a stroke, October 15, 1983. Historian, educator, researcher, editor, and author. Wilkinson was research director for the Eleutherian Mills-Hagley Foundation's Hagley Museum in Delaware from 1954 to 1975. He began his career as a history instructor at Muhlenberg College from 1942 to 1947 and worked as assistant state historian for the Pennsylvania History and Museum Commission from 1947 to 1954. He wrote such works as *Bibliography of Pennsylvania History; Explosives in History; The Brandywine Home Front During the Civil War; E. I. Du Pont, Botaniste: The Beginning of a Tradition;* and *Lammot du Pont and the American Explosives Industry, 1850-1884.* In addition, Wilkinson co-edited the volume *Writings in Pennsylvania.*

OBITUARIES AND OTHER SOURCES:

Date of death provided by Jacqueline Hinsley, research associate of Hagley Museum and Library.

* * *

WILLIAMS, Edward Bennett 1920-1988

OBITUARY NOTICE—See index for *CA* sketch: Born May 31, 1920, in Hartford, Conn.; died of cancer, August 13, 1988, in Washington, D.C. Lawyer, businessman, educator, and author. Williams was a prominent criminal attorney with considerable political expertise. During his many years of practice in Washington, D.C., where he eventually established the firm Williams & Connolly, Williams became known for his work with highly controversial defendants, including alleged mobster Frank Costello, racketeering union leader Jimmy Hoffa, controversial Senator Joseph McCarthy, and fugitive businessman Robert Vesco. In addition, he was a law professor at Georgetown University from 1946 to 1958. For his achievements and prominence Williams was often considered for presidential appointments—including the CIA directorship from presidents Gerald Ford and Ronald Reagan—which he rejected. Williams was also a longtime sports enthusiast. He owned the Washington Redskins football team for several years and was owner of the Baltimore Orioles baseball team at the time of his death. In 1962 he wrote *One Man's Freedom,* a book about individuals' rights in the United States.

OBITUARIES AND OTHER SOURCES:

BOOKS

Current Biography, H. W. Wilson, 1988.
Who's Who in America, 45th edition, Marquis, 1988.

PERIODICALS

Los Angeles Times, August 14, 1988.

New York Times, August 15, 1988.
Washington Post, August 14, 1988.

*   *   *

WILSON, Forbes (Kingsbury)   1910-

PERSONAL: Born February 16, 1910, in York, Maine; son of William and Adeline M. (Kingsbury) Wilson; married Ann J. Sewell, June 17, 1940; children: Barbara, Jacqueline, Sally, Nancy, Jean. *Education:* Yale University, B.S., 1931.

ADDRESSES: Home—167 Organug Rd., York, Maine 03909.

CAREER: Braden Copper Co., mining engineer, 1931-32; Crucero Mining Co., mining engineer, 1933-34; Timmins Ochali Mining Co., began as mine superintendent, became general superintendent and general manager, 1935-42; Nicaro Nickel Co., began as exploration engineer, became administrative manager, assistant general manager, and general manager, 1943-47; Rising & Nelson Slate Co., West Pawlet, Vt., president, 1948-50; Freeport Minerals, New York, N.Y., manager of mineral exploration, 1951-55, assistant vice-president, 1955-57, vice-president, 1957-71, senior vice-president, 1972-74; consulting mining engineer and writer, 1974—. Member of board of directors of Freeport Indonesia, Inc.

MEMBER: American Institute of Mining and Metallurgical Engineers, Mining and Metallurgical Society of America, Explorers Club, Mining Club, Yale Club, Darien Country Club.

AWARDS, HONORS: Daniel C. Jackling Award, 1977, for Wilson's "vision, determination, dedication and leadership in the conquest of the remote and rugged Ertsberg and the technical and human barriers to its development," Legion of Honor, 1980, both from American Institute of Mining and Metallurgical Engineers.

WRITINGS:

The Conquest of Copper Mountain, Atheneum, 1981.

Contributor to geology journals.

*   *   *

WILSON-KASTNER, Patricia   1944-

PERSONAL: Born September 18, 1944, in New York, N.Y.; daughter of Woodrow W. (an electrician) and May (a bookkeeper; maiden name, McDonough) Wilson; married G. Ronald Kastner (a fund-raising consultant), May 25, 1974. *Education:* University of Dallas, B.A., 1967, M.A., 1969; University of Iowa, Ph.D., 1973. *Politics:* Democrat. *Religion:* Episcopalian.

ADDRESSES: Home and office—General Theological Seminary, 175 Ninth Ave., New York, N.Y. 10011.

CAREER: United Theological Seminary of the Twin Cities, New Brighton, Minn., assistant professor, 1975-78, associate professor of theology, 1978-1982; General Theological Seminary, New York, N.Y., professor of preaching, 1982—. Priest associate at Christ and St. Stephen's Episcopal Church, 1984—.

MEMBER: American Academy of Religion, American Society of Church History, Conference of Angelican Theologians.

WRITINGS:

Coherence in a Fragmented World: Jonathan Edward's Theology of the Holy Spirit, University Press of America, 1978.

(Editor and contributor) *A Lost Tradition: Women Writers of the Early Church*, University Press of America, 1981.
Faith, Feminism, and the Christ, Fortress, 1983.

Contributor to religious journals, including *Christian Century* and *Witness*.

WORK IN PROGRESS: God's Grace Among Us: From the Return Into Eternity to the Transformation of Time; Theology in a Pastoral Context: From Academy to Community.

SIDELIGHTS: Patricia Wilson-Kastner's 1983 publication *Faith, Feminism, and the Christ* garnered praise from *Commonweal* contributor Mary Gerhart, who described its argument that "there is nothing exclusively male or female about clear thinking about personal experience" as one that is "complex but never pedantic" and who judged Wilson-Kastner's study "one of the finest books thus far on feminist theology."

Wilson-Kastner told *CA:* "I have found it an interesting and always challenging experience to be a woman in a male-dominated profession. Neither theology nor the Episcopal priesthood have been overly hospitable. On the other hand, it is exciting to participate in the transformation of a whole area of human culture. I am also cheered by the support from unexpected places in and outside the church. I investigate the history of women in the church in order to appreciate the breadth of what women have already done, and how little that has been appreciated. My interest in writing theology springs from my recognition that both the ways we think and what we think about are changing; I want to be a part of that process. My hope is that my work links past and present, pointing to the future."

BIOGRAPHICAL/CRITICAL SOURCES:

PERIODICALS

Commonweal, March 22, 1985.
Religious Studies Review, July, 1984.
Women's Review of Books, March, 1985.

*   *   *

WINDER, R(ichard) Bayly   1920-1988

OBITUARY NOTICE—See index for *CA* sketch: Born September 11, 1920, in Greensboro, N.C.; died of cancer, August 6, 1988, in Princeton, N.J. Educator, academic administrator, consultant, translator, editor, and author. Winder was an authority on Oriental and Arabic languages and literature. He taught at Princeton University from 1950 to 1966, when he became a professor in the departments of history and Near Eastern languages and literature at New York University. Among Winder's other posts at New York University were director of the graduate program in modern Near Eastern studies and dean of the faculty of arts and sciences. In addition, he was a consultant to organizations such as UNESCO and the American Field Service. His books include *An Introduction to Modern Arabic*, which he wrote with Farhat J. Ziadeh, and *Saudi Arabia in the Nineteenth Century*. Winder also edited such volumes as *Current Problems in North Africa* and *Near Eastern Round Table*.

OBITUARIES AND OTHER SOURCES:

BOOKS

The Writers Directory: 1984-1986, St. James Press, 1983.

PERIODICALS

Washington Post, August 12, 1988.

* * *

WIRTHS, Claudine (Turner) G(ibson) 1926-

PERSONAL: Born May 9, 1926, in Covington, Ga.; daughter of Count Dillon (a professor of geology) and Julia (Thompson) Gibson; married Theodore Wirths (a National Science Foundation executive), December 28, 1945; children: William, David. *Education:* University of Kentucky, A.B. (cum laude), 1946, M.A., 1948; American University, M.Ed., 1980; doctoral study at University of North Carolina at Chapel Hill. *Religion:* Episcopal.

ADDRESSES: Home—P.O. Box 335, Braddock Heights, Md. 21714.

CAREER: Yale University, New Haven, Conn., secretary and research assistant for departments of psychology and anthropology, 1946-47; North Carolina League for Crippled Children and Adults, Chapel Hill, program director, 1948-49; research psychologist with Savannah River Studies, Aiken, S.C., for University of North Carolina, 1950-52; City Police Department, Aiken, police psychologist, 1952-56; Kirk School, Aiken, head teacher in special education, 1956-58; homemaker, Aiken, 1958-62; social science consultant in Rockville, Md., 1962-77; Green Acres School, Rockville, elementary schoolteacher, 1977-78; special education intern at high school in Springfield, Va., 1978-79; Gaithersburg High School, Gaithersburg, Md., special education teacher, Md., 1979-81, coordinator of Learning Center, 1981-84; writer, 1984—; Frederick Community College, Frederick, Md., member of adjunct faculty, 1987—. Member of U.S. Department of Defense Advisory Committee on Women in the Services, 1960-63, Girl Guard Board of Salvation Army, 1961-62, board of directors of Montgomery County Mental Health Association, 1967-71, and advisory board of Maryland Department of Natural Resources, 1975-78.

MEMBER: Phi Beta Kappa.

AWARDS, HONORS: Conservation Award from Maryland Environment Trust, 1973; award from Maryland-Delaware Press Association, 1979, for feature story writing; American Library Association listed *I Hate School* as a "best book of 1986" and a "recommended book for reluctant young adults readers."

WRITINGS:

(With Richard H. Williams) *Lives Through the Years,* Atherton, 1965.
(With Mary Bowman-Kruhm) *I Hate School: How to Hang In and When to Drop Out* (juvenile), Harper, 1987.
(With Mary Bowman-Kruhm) *I Need a Job* (juvenile), J. Weston Walch, 1988.

Work represented in anthologies, including *Humpty Dumpty's Bedtime Stories,* Parents Magazine Press, 1971. Contributor to magazines and newspapers, including *Law and Order, Maryland, Christian Ministry, Journal of Learning Disabilities, Parks and Recreation,* and *Cat Fancy.*

WORK IN PROGRESS: A book, tentatively titled *Where's My Other Sock?: How to Get Organized and Drive Your Parents and Teachers Crazy,* for teenagers, with Mary Bowman-Kruhm, for Harper.

SIDELIGHTS: Claudine G. Wirths told *CA:* "I began writing almost as soon as I could read because of my good fortune at having the author of some of my favorite first books, Madge A. Bigham, living near me on St. Simons Island, Georgia. When I expressed my great fondness for her books, she urged me to write my own. My first work at age seven, 'The Tall Cat' (I'm six feet tall), was not published, but was highly satisfying to me, and I continued writing.

"First published with a brief article to the *Atlanta Journal* when I was fifteen, I had my first short story for children published in *Humpty Dumpty* some twenty years later. From my teens on there was the usual avalanche of rejection slips (which continues to this day), but I kept on writing. My first major children's book was put in my hands the day I turned sixty. Success takes a little longer for some of us!

"My interest in dropout students began in graduate school in 1948 when I learned about dyslexia. I was intrigued at the puzzle of how a bright child might fail to learn to read. I was soon to encounter many such children when I entered police work. Far too often, the child in trouble was learning disabled and a potential dropout. The frustration set up by the handicap of dyslexia turns school days into days of despair, and, unless the child receives special help (and sometimes even when they do), school becomes a permanent nightmare for the child and their parents.

"I was unable to give my full effort to this problem until I went back to graduate school a few years ago and took a degree in special education. Following this, I changed professions and have spent all my time since then writing, sudying, teaching, and lecturing on learning disabilities. Currently retired from public school teaching, I write full-time with a close friend and colleague, Dr. Mary Bowman-Kruhm, who is a reading specialist with over twenty-five years of work with special-need students. We share compassion for the student who has school problems and we hope to help them understand how they can best help themselves. Our books do not talk down to readers but they do use simple language and clear ideas.

"Writing as a twosome has solved many of the problems that kept me from writing success in the past. I now keep to writing schedules, have a built-in editor, and, best of all, have someone to talk to who is as passionately concerned about writing and about problems of the learning disabled as I am. We each have a Macintosh computer and have worked out a joint writing system that works for us. We split profits and problems right down the middle.

"*I Hate School* gives tips on surviving in school, since dropping out is basically a no-win solution. We advocate 'stepping out' with a career plan when school is no longer a viable option. Resources for problem solving are given. *I Need a Job* discusses successful job behavior in blue-collar and entry-level jobs. We found that few books for students deal with the rough realities of blue-collar jobs and how to survive them. This is not a book on how to fill out a resume.

"*Where's My Other Sock?* is a practical book on organization skills for teens. Like the other books we've written, it is in dialogue format. We offer help and hope to all kinds of young people—from the person who only needs some new storage ideas to the confirmed slob. With five children between us, my partner and I have seen all the variations! We hope to continue to write nonfiction, how-to books aimed at teens who don't really like books, but who can use a little loving and practical support—even if it is in a book."

AVOCATIONAL INTERESTS: Wild flowers, vegetable gardening, camping.

*　　*　　*

WISENTHAL, J. L.   1940-

PERSONAL: Born July 15, 1940, in Montreal, Quebec, Canada; son of Miles (a statistician) and Dorothy (Rosenbloom) Wisenthal; married Christine Gregory, May 21, 1964; children: Stephen, Rosalind. *Education:* Bishop's University, B.A., 1961; Oxford University, B.Litt., 1964; University of London, Ph.D., 1970. *Religion:* Jewish.

ADDRESSES: Home—3937 West 35th Ave., Vancouver, British Columbia, Canada V6N 2P1. *Office*—Department of English, University of British Columbia, 2075 Westbrook Pl., Vancouver, British Columbia, Canada V6T 1W5.

CAREER: University of British Columbia, Vancouver, instructor, 1964-66, assistant professor, 1966-73, associate professor, 1973-81, professor of English, 1981—, associate dean of faculty of arts, 1985—.

WRITINGS:

The Marriage of Contraries: Bernard Shaw's Middle Plays, Harvard University Press, 1974.
Shaw and Ibsen, University of Toronto Press, 1979.
Shaw's Sense of History, Clarendon Press, 1988.

WORK IN PROGRESS: Research on Carlyle, Macaulay, and nineteenth-century historiography.

*　　*　　*

WITT, Ronald Gene   1932-

PERSONAL: Born December 23, 1932, in Wayne, Mich.; son of Elmer M. (a lighting engineer) and Iris I. (a housewife; maiden name, Palmer) Witt; married Mary Ann Frese (a professor), June 13, 1965; children: Eric Frese, Martha Irleen, Daria Celeste. *Education:* University of Michigan, B.A., 1954; Harvard University, M.A., 1958, Ph.D., 1965. *Religion:* Presbyterian.

ADDRESSES: Home—173 West Margaret Lane, Hillsborough, N.C. 27278. *Office*—Department of History, Duke University, Durham, N.C. 27705.

CAREER: University of Strasbourg, Strasbourg, France, Fulbright lecturer in American civilization, 1955-56; Harvard University, Cambridge, Mass., instructor, 1965-68, assistant professor of history, 1968-71; Duke University, Durham, N.C., associate professor, 1971-80, professor of history, 1980—, director of Angier B. Duke Memorial Scholarship Program, 1981—.

MEMBER: Mediaeval Academy of America, Renaissance Society of America (member of council), American Historical Association, Society for Italian Historical Studies, Columbia University Seminar on the Renaissance.

AWARDS, HONORS: Fellow of Old Dominion Fund, 1968-69; grant from National Endowment for the Humanities, 1974; Guggenheim fellow, 1977-78; grants from American Council of Learned Societies, 1979 and 1983; fellow at National Humanities Center, 1983; Fulbright grant, 1985-86.

WRITINGS:

(Contributor) Julius Kirshner and Anthony Molho, editors, *Renaissance Studies in Honor of Hans Baron,* DeKalb, 1970.

Coluccio Salutati and His Public Letters, Droz, 1976.
(With Benjamin G. Kohl) *The Earthly Republic of the Italian Humanists,* University of Pennsylvania Press, 1978.
(Editor with wife, Mary Ann Witt, Frank Tirro, Ann Dunbar, and Charlotte Brown) *Cultural Roots and Continuities,* two volumes, Heath, 1980, 2nd edition, 1984.
Hercules at the Crossroads: The Life, Works, and Thought of Coluccio Salutati, Duke University Press, 1983.

Contributor to history journals.

WORK IN PROGRESS: The Origins of Italian Humanism.

SIDELIGHTS: Hercules at the Crossroads: The Life, Works, and Thought of Coluccio Salutati is a definitive study of Salutati, in which Witt traces the career of the fourteenth-century Florentine humanist from his humble beginnings to his position as a provincial notary and influential civil servant, until his death in 1406. Witt reconstructs Salutati's life and philosophy from letters and learned papers. Writing in review in *Renaissance Quarterly,* Nicolai Rubinstein complimented Witt on his "minute attention to detail" and "many penetrating insights."

Witt told *CA:* "I was drawn to the figure of Coluccio Salutati because he exemplified the lay humanist in the fourteenth century. Chancellor of Florence, father of a large family, he was both a committed scholar and a devout Christian. Before Salutati, humanism was a movement consisting of scattered geniuses without a center. Through his vast literary correspondence and his patronage of Greek studies, his own scholarly achievements and concern to train disciples in the city, Salutati was responsible for making Florence the capital of Italian humanism in the first half of the fifteenth century."

BIOGRAPHICAL/CRITICAL SOURCES:

PERIODICALS

American Historical Review, October, 1977.
Choice, November, 1983.
English Historical Review, October, 1979.
Journal of Modern History, June, 1984.
Renaissance Quarterly, Summer, 1985.
Speculum, October, 1979, April, 1985.

*　　*　　*

WOLFENDEN, George
See BEARDMORE, George

*　　*　　*

WONG, J(ohn) Y(ue-Wo)   1946-

PERSONAL: Born November 29, 1946, in Canton, China; son of Po and Mo-ching (Chan) Wong; married C. L. Tsang (a nursing sister), December 14, 1977; children: Kit-tsun, O-siang. *Education:* University of Hong Kong, B.A. (with honors), 1968; Oxford University, D.Phil., 1972.

ADDRESSES: Home—Hockingdon, 264 Johnston St., Annandale, Sydney, New South Wales 2038, Australia. *Office*—Department of History, University of Sydney, Sydney, New South Wales 2006, Australia.

CAREER: Oxford University, Oxford, England, research fellow at St. Antony's College, 1972-74; University of Sydney, Sydney, Australia, lecturer, 1974-78, senior lecturer in history, 1979—, and fellow of Research Institute for Asia and the Pacific. Honorary treasurer of Australia-China Chamber of Commerce and Industry, New South Wales branch.

MEMBER: Oriental Society of Australia (honorary secretary), Royal History Society (fellow).

WRITINGS:

Yeh Ming-ch'en: Viceroy of Liang Kuang, 1852-58, Cambridge University Press, 1976.
(Editor) *Anglo-Chinese Relations, 1839-1860: A Calendar of Chinese Documents in the British Foreign Office Records,* Oxford University Press, 1983.
The Origins of an Heroic Image: Sun Yatsen in London, Oxford University Press, 1986.
(Editor) *Sun Yatsen: His International Ideas and International Connections,* Wild Peony, 1987.
(Editor) *Australia-China Relations, 1986,* Australia-China Business Cooperation Committee, 1987.
(Editor) *Australia-China Relations, 1988,* Australia-China Business Cooperation Committee, 1988.

Honorary editor of the *New South Wales-Guangdong Economic Committee Bulletin.*

WORK IN PROGRESS: Research on the origins of the *Arrow* war.

SIDELIGHTS: J. Y. Wong told *CA:* "I like writing because I feel I am creating something when I write."

*   *   *

WOOD, David G.   1919-

PERSONAL: Born September 15, 1919, in Salt Lake City, Utah; son of Thomas George (a businessman) and Roxie Norma (a housewife; maiden name, Woodruff) Wood; married Maurine Redd, March 24, 1939; children: Roxie Carolyn, Denton Robert. *Education:* Attended University of Alberta. *Politics:* "Conservative-Populist." *Religion:* Agnostic.

ADDRESSES: Home—723 Madison Ave. S.W., Calgary, Alberta, Canada T2S 1K2.

CAREER: Picture Butte Progress (weekly newspaper), Alberta, publisher, 1939-42; J. J. Gibbons (advertising agency), Calgary, Alberta, junior account executive, 1941-43; CFRN (radio station), Edmonton, Alberta, continuity editor and special events broadcaster, 1943-45; Schofield & Wood Ltd. (advertising agency), Edmonton, partner; Mannix Group of companies, Calgary, public relations director, 1952-65; Western Co-operative Fertilizer Limited, Calgary, vice-president and secretary, 1965-83; communications consultant, 1983—, Calgary.

WRITINGS:

The Lougheed Legacy (biography), Key Porter Books, 1985.

WORK IN PROGRESS: A book on water as a North American resource, an issue which may cause conflict between Canada and the United States, publication expected in 1991.

SIDELIGHTS: David G. Wood told *CA:* "I chose to write about Peter Lougheed for three reasons: I had worked with the man both as politician and businessman for many years, and his story needed to be told; he was a pragmatist in politics and he did what he did primarily for the good of Alberta, believing it was then also good for Canada; he had a very great impact on the repatriated Canadian constitution and on the way the Canadian federation is now viewed."

BIOGRAPHICAL/CRITICAL SOURCES:

PERIODICALS

Globe and Mail (Toronto), March 8, 1986.

*   *   *

WOODHOUSE, Barbara (Blackburn)   1910-1988

OBITUARY NOTICE—See index for *CA* sketch: Born May 9, 1910, in Rathfarnham, County Dublin, Ireland; died following a stroke, July 8 (some sources say July 9), 1988, in Buckinghamshire, England. Animal trainer, filmmaker, and author. Woodhouse was an endearing, highly successful dog trainer. She insisted that her method, which relied on conviction, instinct, and sympathy, was infallible in training even the most incorrigible canine. In the 1980s she developed a substantial following in Britain through her television series "Training Dogs the Woodhouse Way." This popularity resulted in her selection as Britain's female television personality of 1980. Woodhouse produced and directed such films as "School for Problem Dogs" and "Love Me, Love My Dog." Among her published works are *Dog Training My Way, The Barbara Woodhouse Book of Dogs, The World of Dogs, Walkies: Dog Care the Woodhouse Way,* and *Talking to Animals,* an autobiography.

OBITUARIES AND OTHER SOURCES:

BOOKS

Current Biography, H. W. Wilson, 1985, August, 1988.

PERIODICALS

New York Times, July 11, 1988.
Times (London), July 11, 1988.

*   *   *

WOODRUFF, Marian
See GOUDGE, Eileen

*   *   *

WOODS, George A(llan)   1926-1988

OBITUARY NOTICE—See index for *CA* sketch: Born January 26, 1926, in Lake Placid, N.Y.; died of lung cancer, August 11, 1988, in Englewood, N.J. Journalist, editor, and author. Woods was children's book editor for the *New York Times* from 1963 to 1984, when he became editor of the *New York Times Large Type Weekly.* Prior to working at the *Times,* Woods held a variety of positions with the *New York Times Book Review.* His own writings include *Vibrations* and the mystery *Catch a Killer,* which won the 1974 Dorothy Canfield Fisher Award.

OBITUARIES AND OTHER SOURCES:

PERIODICALS

Chicago Tribune, August 14, 1988.
New York Times, August 13, 1988.
Publishers Weekly, August 26, 1988.
School Library Journal, September, 1988.

*   *   *

WOOLLS, (Esther) Blanche   1935-

PERSONAL: Born March 30, 1935; daughter of Arthur William and Esther Lennie Sutton; married; children: Paul. *Education:* Indiana University—Bloomington, A.B., 1958, M.A., 1962, Ph.D., 1973.

ADDRESSES: Home—270 Tennyson Ave., Pittsburgh, Pa. 15213. *Office*—Department of Library Science, University of Pittsburgh, Pittsburgh, Pa. 15260.

CAREER: Director of school libraries in Hammond, Ind., 1965-67, and Roswell, N.M., 1967-70; University of Pittsburgh, Pittsburgh, Pa., affiliated with university beginning in 1973, professor of library science and chairman of department, 1986—.

MEMBER: International Federation of Library Associations, International Association of School Librarians, American Library Association (member of council and committee on accreditation), American Association of School Librarians, Association for Library Service to Children, Association of Specialized and Cooperative Library Agencies, Library and Information Technology Association, Young Adult Services Division, Pennsylvania School Librarians Association, Pennsylvania Learning Resources Association (past president), Pennsylvania Library Association.

WRITINGS:

(Editor with Barbara Evans Markuson) *Networks for Networkers: Critical Issues in Cooperative Library Development,* Neal-Schuman, 1980.
(With David V. Loertscher, Ann Weeks, and Marvin Davis) *The Use of Technology in the Administrative Function of School Library Media Programs,* Hi Willow, 1983.
(Editor with Loertscher) *The Microcomputer Facility and the School Library Media Specialist,* American Library Association, 1986.
Grant Proposal Writing: A Handbook for School Library Media Specialists, Greenwood Press, 1986.
Managing School Library Media Programs, Libraries Unlimited, 1988.

Chairman of editorial advisory board of *Learning and Media.*

WORK IN PROGRESS: Supervising school library media programs.

SIDELIGHTS: Blanche Woolls told *CA* that she is "interested in the provision of excellent school library media center services for children. The services are provided to help the students learn and to help the teachers teach. Only as an afterthought are school library media specialists available to circulate materials. Furthermore, unless individuals responsible for the information needs of their clientele do everything they can to locate and supply the most up-to-date and relevant information from whatever source, they have no hope to claim success at their tasks. All students and teachers have a right to equal access to the information in this country, and only by sharing resources, knowledge, and skills will equal access occur."

*   *   *

WOOTTON, Barbara (Frances Adam)   1897-1988

OBITUARY NOTICE: Born in 1897; died July 11, 1988. Social scientist, public administrator, criminologist, and author. A noted sociologist and criminologist in England, Wootton was one of the first women appointed a British life peer. Becoming Baroness Wootton of Abinger upon her marriage to John Wesley Wootton (who was killed in World War I combat five weeks after their wedding), she studied economics at Cambridge University's Girton College, where she later was a fellow and director of studies in economics. In 1922 Wootton became a research officer for the Labour party and, four years later, became the first director of studies for classes in the extramural department of London University, where she specialized in adult education for seventeen years. She subsequently headed the department of economics, sociology, and social studies at Bedford College. In addition, Wootton served as a lay magistrate for nearly fifty years and as a chairman of juvenile courts in London for sixteen years. She was a member of four royal commissions as well as a governor of the British Broadcasting Corporation. Her many books include *Lament for Economics, End Social Inequality: A Programme for Ordinary People, Social Science and Social Pathology, Crime and the Criminal Law: Reflections of a Magistrate and Social Scientist, In a World I Never Made: Autobiographical Reflections,* and *Incomes Policy.*

OBITUARIES AND OTHER SOURCES:

PERIODICALS

Chicago Tribune, July 13, 1988, July 17, 1988.
Times (London), July 13, 1988.

*   *   *

WYNDHAM, Francis (Guy Percy)   1924-

BRIEF ENTRY: Born July 2, 1924, in London, England. British editor, journalist, and author. Wyndham, who is highly acclaimed for his volumes of short stories and his first novel, *The Other Garden* (J. Cape, 1987), gained popularity as a fiction writer after establishing himself as a journalist and editor. He worked as an editor for the London publishing house of Andre Deutsch from 1955 to 1958 before becoming the literary editor of *Queen* magazine in 1959. In 1964 Wyndham signed on as an assistant editor and staff writer for the London Sunday *Times,* where he remained until 1980. The stories in his well-received first collection, *Out of the War* (Duckworth), were written when Wyndham was a young man experiencing World War II, but the volume was not published until 1974. *The Other Garden* earned the Whitbread Literary Award for best first novel of 1987. Wyndham's other fiction includes the collection *Mrs. Henderson and Other Stories* (J. Cape, 1985). In addition, Wyndham co-edited a volume of writer Jean Rhys's correspondence, *The Letters of Jean Rhys* (Viking, 1984), and co-authored a biography of Soviet leader Leon Trotsky, titled *Trotsky: A Documentary* (Praeger, 1972).

BIOGRAPHICAL/CRITICAL SOURCES:

BOOKS

The Author's and Writer's Who's Who, 6th edition, reprinted, Burke's Peerage, 1971.

PERIODICALS

Observer, May 12, 1985.
Times Literary Supplement, January 31, 1975, October 2, 1987.

Y

YANIV, Avner 1942-

PERSONAL: Born December 20, 1942; son of Meir and Shulamit Yaniv; married Lo Michal; children: three. *Education:* Hebrew University of Jerusalem, B.A. (political science) and B.A. (English), both 1967; graduate study at London School of Economics and Political Science, London, 1968-69; Linacre College, Oxford, D.Phil., 1973.

ADDRESSES: Office—Department of Government, Georgetown University, Washington, D.C. 20057; Department of Political Science, University of Haifa, Haifa 31999, Israel.

CAREER: University of Haifa, Haifa, Israel, lecturer, 1973-79, senior lecturer, 1979-85, associate professor of political science, 1985—, chairman of Jewish-Arab Center, 1980-84, chairman of Professors Union, 1980-82, director of Institute of Middle Eastern Studies, 1980-84. Director of research project for Jerusalem van Leer Foundation, 1973-75; visiting fellow at Institute for Peace Research and Security Policy, University of Hamburg, 1978; visiting senior member of Linacre College, Oxford, 1979; visiting professor at Georgetown University, 1982-83, 1986-88, and University of Maryland at College Park, 1985; guest on television and radio programs. *Military service:* Israel Defense Forces, with reserve paratroopers battalion, 1961-75.

WRITINGS:

P.L.O.: A Profile, Inter-University Study Group on the Middle East (Jerusalem), 1974.
(Editor with Moshe Ma'oz, and contributor) *Syria Under Assad: Domestic Constraints and Regional Risks,* St. Martin's, 1986.
Deterrence Without the Bomb: The Politics of Israeli Strategy, Heath, 1987.
Dilemmas of Security: Politics, Strategy, and the Israeli Experience in Lebanon, Oxford University Press, 1987.

CONTRIBUTOR

Avigdor Levi, editor, *The Arab-Israeli Conflict: Risks and Opportunities,* Stratis, 1975.
Gabriel Ben-dor, editor, *The Palestinians and the Middle East Conflict,* Turtledove Publishing, 1978.
Asher Arian, editor, *The Elections in Israel, 1981,* Ramot Publishing, 1983.

Louis Rene Beres, editor, *Security or Armageddon,* Heath, 1985.
Aurel Braun, editor, *The Middle East in Global Strategy,* Westview, 1987.
Hirsh Goodman, editor, *Syria at the Crossroads,* Westview, 1988.
Yehuda Lukacs and Abdalla Battah, editors, *The Arab-Israeli Conflict: Twenty Years After the Six Day War,* Westview, 1988.
Gregory Mahler, editor, *Israel in the Post-Begin Era,* Westview, 1988.

Contributor of articles and reviews to periodicals, including *Washington Quarterly, International Security,* and *Journal of Politics.*

WORK IN PROGRESS: Israel Among the Nations: The Foreign Policy of the Jewish State, for Oxford University Press.

BIOGRAPHICAL/CRITICAL SOURCES:

PERIODICALS

New York Times Book Review, October 4, 1987.
Times Literary Supplement, March 11-17, 1988.

*   *   *

YEZIERSKA, Anzia 1885(?)-1970

PERSONAL: Surname is pronounced "Ye-*zyer*-ska"; born c. October 19, 1885 (some sources say 1880, 1881, or 1883), in Plinsk, Russian Poland; immigrated to United States, c. 1901, naturalized citizen, 1912; died of a stroke, November 21, 1970, in Ontario, Calif.; daughter of Bernard (a Talmudic scholar) and Pearl (a homemaker) Yezierska; married Jacob Gordon (an attorney), 1910 (marriage annulled, 1910); married Arnold Levitas (a teacher and textbook writer), 1911 (marriage ended, 1916); children: (second marriage) Louise. *Education:* Studied domestic science at Columbia University.

CAREER: Worked as a seamstress in a sweatshop, as a cook and domestic for a wealthy family, and in a factory, all on New York's Lower East Side, c. 1900-03; teacher of domestic science in an elementary school, c. 1908-10; translator for a project among Polish-speaking people in Philadelphia run by John Dewey through Columbia University, 1917-18; screenwriter in Hollywood, 1922; U.S. Government, Work Projects

Administration (WPA), Writers' Project, New York City, cataloger of trees in Central Park during the early 1930s; writer, 1915-69.

MEMBER: Authors' League of America.

AWARDS, HONORS: Prize for best short story of the year from Edward J. O'Brien, 1919, for "The Fat of the Land."

WRITINGS:

Hungry Hearts (short stories; contains "Wings," "Hunger," "The Lost Beautifulness," "The Free Vacation House," "The Miracle," "Where Lovers Dream," "Soap and Water," "The Fat of the Land," "My Own People," and "How I Found America"), Houghton, 1920, reprinted, Arno Press, 1975 (also see below).

Salome of the Tenements (novel), Boni & Liveright, c. 1923.

Children of Loneliness (short stories), Funk, 1923.

Bread Givers: A Struggle Between a Father of the Old World and a Daughter of the New (novel), introduction by Alice Kessler Harris, Doubleday, 1925, reprinted, Braziller, 1975.

Arrogant Beggar (novel), Doubleday, 1927.

All I Could Never Be (novel), Putnam, 1932.

Red Ribbon on a White Horse (autobiographical novel), introduction by W. H. Auden, Scribner, 1950, reprinted, Persea Books, 1981.

The Open Cage: An Anzia Yezierska Collection, edited with an introduction by Harris, afterword by Louise Levitas Henriksen, Persea Books, 1979.

Hungry Hearts and Other Stories (contains *Hungry Hearts* [also see above], and "This Is What $10,000 Did to Me," "Wild Winter Love," and "One Thousand Pages of Research"), preface by Henriksen, Persea Books, 1985.

Short story "The Fat of the Land" also included in *Best Short Stories of 1919,* edited by Edward J. O'Brien. Contributor of short stories to periodicals, including *Forum* and *Chicago Jewish Forum.*

SIDELIGHTS: Through her short stories and novels, Russian-born Jewish writer Anzia Yezierska reanimates her experience as a poor, young immigrant woman living on New York's Lower East Side at the turn of the twentieth century. Although largely drawn from episodes in her own life, Yezierska's prose plots are widely regarded as accurate depictions of the entire Jewish immigrant experience. Her female protagonists struggle against the restrictions of their traditional Judaic values and orthodox religion, striving for autonomy, prosperity, and acceptance in the new world.

Yezierska was born in the village of Plinsk near Warsaw in Russian Poland. Since the author never knew the date of her birth, she chose her own—October 19, 1883. Although the exact date remains unknown, historians and biographers, including Alice Kessler Harris who recently edited a collection of Yezierska's shorter works, now agree that 1885 was the probable year of the author's birth. According to most sources, Yezierska immigrated to the United States with her impoverished family in 1901. Her father, a Talmudic scholar, was not gainfully employed; he engaged in a tedious, full-time study of the sacred books and authoritative laws of the Jewish faith while his wife and children worked menial jobs and surrendered their meager wages to sustain the household.

Viewing America as a country of unlimited opportunities for determined, intelligent immigrants, Yezierska sought to free herself from the poverty and oppression of her highly conser-vative, patriarchal roots and begin a new life. Studying English at night and working in a sweatshop by day, she earned a scholarship to Columbia University three years after her arrival in the United States. Discontented in her subsequent role as a teacher of domestic science, she was married briefly in 1910. After an annulment that same year and another failed marriage that produced her only daughter, Yezierska relinquished her familial responsibilities to pursue a career in writing.

The author made her literary debut in 1915 with the publication of "Free Vacation House" in the December issue of *Forum.* The short story detailed the humiliating and insensitive treatment of the poor by charitable agencies, a subject Yezierska would again address in later writings. Four years after her first piece was published, American anthologist Edward J. O'Brien included her short story "The Fat of the Land" in his volume *Best Short Stories of 1919* and proclaimed it the best of the year. The award-winning tale centered on a newly affluent, elderly Jewish woman who finds herself yearning for the vibrance and kinship of her former East Side ghetto neighborhood.

In 1920, Yezierska published a collection of short works entitled *Hungry Hearts.* Hollywood producer Samuel Goldwyn based a 1922 silent film of the same name on the volume and turned the young writer into a celebrity. She moved to California to pursue a career in fiction and screenwriting but, removed from the milieu of the New York ghetto, was uninspired and virtually unable to write. Refusing a one hundred thousand dollar Hollywood writing contract, she returned to New York.

Back in her own neighborhood, Yezierska began her first novel, *Salome of the Tenements.* Its plot revolves around Sonya, a beautiful, headstrong, uneducated immigrant who falls in love with and marries Manning, a rational, upper-class American philanthropist. The marriage fails. In an excerpt of the book cited by Louise Maunsell Field in the *New York Times Book Review,* Yezierska attributed the faded romance to Manning's inherently "paler passions, paler needs, paler capacity—paler fire!" Field remarked, "Resentment . . . breathes through almost every page of the book," but conceded that Yezierska's powerful characterization made Sonya "a living human being" who is "real to [the reader], even when the incidents of her story are far from convincing; real in her ignorances and her crudities, her idealization of Manning and her ardent amorousness, her flaming desires and her complete egotism. . . . Sonya is drawn with strong, sure, vivid, strokes."

The author's subsequent works were, to the chagrin of many reviewers, built around the same themes that made her famous; she treated these themes, however, with a force and vigor that was consistently recognized by critics. The 1923 short story collection *Children of Loneliness* contained pieces similar in content and style to those in the *Hungry Hearts* anthology. A writer for the *New York Times Book Review,* referring to Yezierska's self-conscious and repeated use of familiar characters, noted that "it is almost always about herself that [the author] writes." The critic continued, "Her gift is not creative; she is a reporter and an autobiographist rather than a fiction writer." The title story, "Children of Loneliness," illuminates the gap that widens between immigrant parents of the old world and their Americanized children. An excerpt from the story published in the *New York Times Book Review* depicts young immigrant Rachel Ravinsky's harsh rejection of her unsophisticated parents, and indeed, of her entire culture: "To think I was born of these creatures! It's an insult to my soul." Yet, in keeping with Yezierska's established theme, the girl finds her relationship with an American-born man passionless and unfulfilling because he cannot understand her past. The *New York Times* critic allowed, "[*Children of Loneliness*] has color and a dramatic quality which, if it frequently slips into melodrama, nevertheless gives effectiveness to many of its scenes."

Similarly, Yezierska's 1927 novel *Arrogant Beggar* was censured as an "elaboration of the obvious" by a writer for the *Saturday Review*. The book portrays social service agencies as patronizing institutions run by incompetent members of the upper class. But beyond its "thin" characters and "trite" plot, the *Saturday Review* critic declared, "Surely never was a poor story better told. . . . Both scene and situation are . . . of the most familiar, but like an old room newly decorated they gleam beneath their author's furnishings."

Commenting on the aspirations of the foreign-born personalities that populate the author's works, Richard F. Shepard asserted in the *New York Times* that "Yezierska's people . . . did not want to find themselves. They wanted to lose themselves and find America, to shed Europe and to live the American dream." But a recurring motif of disappointment in success is evidenced by her characters' inability to find contentment as their desires are fulfilled and by the author's own anguished response to wealth and fame in Hollywood. "It was only when Yezierska had achieved . . . relative comforts," wrote Johanna Kaplan in the *New York Times Book Review*, "that she perceived herself as lost and disconnected, and ceased to thrive." For the writer and her characters, the satisfaction gained from becoming Americanized was tainted by an accompanying sense of alienation from the Jewish culture.

Conflict, tension, and a sense of bitter disillusionment inform Yezierska's work as her characters attempt to reconcile their old-world heritage with the promise of a new land. These emotions are vividly captured in *Bread Givers*, the writer's most successful novel. Considered an early piece of feminist literature, *Bread Givers* is Yezierska's first-person indictment of her father, fictionally represented by the character of Reb Smolinsky, for his patriarchal Jewish beliefs. Johan J. Smertenko, writing for the *Saturday Review of Literature*, credited her for the "fierce vitality" that distinguished the work, but went on to call that same vitality "unharnessed and little directed," the author's "undoing." The *New York Times Book Review*, however, unequivocally hailed the novel as a "colorful, almost barbaric tapestry" of "raw, uncontrollable poetry and a powerful, sweeping design."

In the 1932 novel *All I Could Never Be*, Yezierska expanded on the theme she introduced in *Salome of the Tenements*—that of the doomed romance between a poor, young immigrant woman and a wealthy, established American man. Critics agree that Yezierska imbued the work with the spirit of her own passion and restlessness. *All I Could Never Be* is a fictionalized account of the author's ill-fated romance with American educator and philosopher John Dewey. Yezierska met Dewey in 1917 when she attended a social and political philosophy seminar he was conducting at Columbia University. Dewey became her mentor and encouraged her literary pursuits; Yezierska's idea for a sober, intellectual American male to play against her fiery, uneducated immigrant heroine is said to have been based on her conception of Dewey. Echoing the sentiment of several reviewers, a writer for the *New York Times Book Review* faulted *All I Could Never Be* for its lack of original plot and character development, calling it a "story [Yezierska] has told before."

Over the next twenty years, Yezierska's literary reputation declined. She slipped into virtual obscurity as an author before her fictionalized autobiography, *Red Ribbon on a White Horse*, was published in 1950. The book takes its title from a ghetto proverb which holds that poverty enhances a wise man as does a red ribbon on a white horse. Chronicling the lean years of the Depression, her Hollywood and New England sojourns, emotional meetings with her father, and the idealized love affairs of her youth, *Red Ribbon on a White Horse* earned considerable acclaim as a work of great truth and passion. Nathan L. Rothman declared in *Saturday Review*, "Only a madman or a poet or a dreamer, only an artist would pause to ask the questions . . . Yezierska asked herself."

Literary critics generally recognize Yezierska's fiction as a distinctive and valid account of the Jewish immigrant experience from a woman's point of view. The author is remembered more for the honesty and intensity of her narratives than the skill with which she developed her plots and characters. Yezierska's later work of the 1950s and 1960s focused on the problems facing the wave of Puerto Rican immigrants to the mainland states and on the aged in America. "Take Up Your Bed and Walk," her last story to be published, was written from the perspective of an elderly Jewish woman and appeared in the *Chicago Jewish Forum* in 1969. This and several other short stories were compiled in a volume entitled *The Open Cage: An Anzia Yezierska Collection*, which was published in 1979, almost a decade after the author's death.

MEDIA ADAPTATIONS: Hungry Hearts was adapted by Julien Josephson for a silent film of the same title, released by Goldwyn, 1922. Sidney Olcott directed "Salome of the Tenements," a silent film based on the novel of the same name, in 1925.

BIOGRAPHICAL/CRITICAL SOURCES:

BOOKS

Contemporary Literary Criticism, Volume 46, Gale, 1988.
Dictionary of Literary Biography, Volume 28: *Twentieth-Century American Jewish Fiction Writers*, Gale, 1984.
Neidle, Cecyle S., *America's Immigrant Women*, Hippocrene, 1976.
Schoen, Carol B., *Anzia Yezierska*, Twayne, 1982.

PERIODICALS

New York Times, February 21, 1980.
New York Times Book Review, December 24, 1922, October 28, 1923, September 13, 1925, August 21, 1932, September 24, 1950, February 24, 1980.
Saturday Review, October 10, 1925, December 3, 1927, November 4, 1950.

OBITUARIES:

PERIODICALS

New York Times, November 23, 1970.*

—*Sketch by Barbara K. Carlisle*

* * *

YOFFE, Elkhonon (Hona) 1928-

PERSONAL: Born April 16, 1928, in Riga, Latvia (now U.S.S.R.); immigrated to United States, 1978, naturalized citizen, 1985; son of Zalman and Frida (Aizik) Yoffe; married Lydia Artushin (a university instructor in Russian), February

27, 1955; children: Mark. *Education:* Latvian State Conservatory, M.A. (percussion), 1952, M.A. (musicology), 1954.

ADDRESSES: Home—463 Coolidge, Birmingham, Mich. 48008. *Office*—Detroit Symphony Orchestra, Ford Auditorium, Detroit, Mich. 48226.

CAREER: Latvian State Symphony, Riga, U.S.S.R., timpanist, 1952-78; Juilliard School, New York, N.Y., orchestra librarian, 1979-82; Detroit Symphony Orchestra, Detroit, Mich., head librarian, 1982—. Teacher of music history for the Riga Ballet School, 1968-72; lecturer for Latvian State Philharmonic Society, 1972-78.

MEMBER: Major Symphony Orchestra Librarians Association.

WRITINGS:

Sitamie Instrumenti (title means "The Percussion Instruments"), Latvian State Publisher, 1962.
Marger Zarinsh: Suita-Nezimitis (title means "Marger Zarins: Ignoramus Suite"), Latvian State Publisher, 1965.
(With Allan Kenigsberg) *Dirizhor Edgar Tons* (title means "Conductor Edgar Tons"), Muzgiz [Moscow], 1974.
Tchaikovsky in America: The Composer's Visit in 1891 (main selection of Fine Arts Book Club), Oxford University Press, 1986.
(Translator from Latvian to Russian) Ruta U., *Bozhe, kan eshcho khotelos zhit* (title means "Dear God, I Wanted to Live"), Kontinent [Paris], 1987.

Contributor to Latvian and Russian journals.

WORK IN PROGRESS: Research for *Tchaikovsky's Music in America;* a screenplay based on *Tchaikovsky in America*.

SIDELIGHTS: Elkhonon Yoffe told *CA* that his immigration to the United States had a very positive effect on his life: "Here I found personal and creative freedom, a friendly and supportive atmosphere, and a new standard of living.

"I fell in love with my new profession as orchestra librarian. For the Detroit Symphony Orchestra I organize the distribution of all music materials for the concert season in cooperation with conductors, the concertmaster, section principals, and individual musicians to prepare the orchestra for rehearsals and performances. This is especially important in America where orchestras are limited in rehearsal time—much more than in Europe—for properly prepared materials can save the conductor a considerable amount of time.

"I was surprised by the outstanding popularity of Russian composer Petr Illich Tchaikovsky's music, such as his scores for the 'Nutcracker,' 'Swan Lake,' and 'Sleeping Beauty' ballets. This prompted me to study the subject in greater detail and resulted in my book *Tchaikovsky in America: The Composer's Visit in 1891*. Tchaikovsky himself wrote that he was surprised about his fame and welcome reception in 1891, during his only visit to America to participate in the opening festival of Carnegie Hall. The visit was an historically important event for America's musical life, and it was the culmination of the composer's popularity in this country."

*   *   *

YOGMAN, Michael W. 1947-

PERSONAL: Born March 1, 1947, in Bayonne, N.J.; son of Harvey (an educator) and Estelle (an educator; maiden name, Rapport) Yogman; married Elizabeth K. Ascher (a cardiologist), June 9, 1985; children: Madeline, Alexandra. *Education:* Williams College, B.A. (magna cum laude), 1968; attended University of Hull, 1968; Yale University, M.D., 1972; Harvard University, M.Sc., 1978. *Politics:* "Active." *Religion:* Jewish.

ADDRESSES: Home—14 Wyman Rd., Cambridge, Mass. 02138. *Office*—Infant Health and Development Program, Children's Hospital, 300 Longwood Ave., Boston, Mass. 02115.

CAREER: Yale-New Haven Hospital, New Haven, Conn., intern in pediatrics and internal medicine, 1972-73, resident in pediatrics, 1973-74; Children's Hospital, Boston, Mass., fellow in child development, 1974-76, assistant in medicine, 1976-79, associate, 1979-80, associate chief of Division of Child Development, 1980-84, director of Infant Health and Development Program, 1984—. Training in child psychotherapy at Judge Baker Guidance Clinic, 1976-77; associate pediatrician at Brigham and Women's Hospital, 1980—; member of pediatric staff of Beth Israel Hospital, Boston, 1980—, Mount Auburn Hospital, 1983—, and Cambridge Hospital, 1984—. Harvard University, clinical instructor, 1974-76, instructor, 1976-82, assistant professor of pediatrics, 1982—, member of Working Group on Early Life and Adolescent Health Policy, 1986—; lecturer at Yale University, Wright State University, University of Wisconsin—Madison, Johns Hopkins University, University of Calgary, Dalhousie University, Brown University, University of Massachusetts at Amherst, Northeastern University, Wheelock College, Boston University, State University of New York Downstate Medical Center, New School for Social Research, Radcliffe College, and Tufts University. Member of advisory panel of American Lung Association Project on Anticipatory Counseling, 1979; member of advisory board of Fatherhood Project; member of WNEV-TV AIDS Education Advisory Board and Cambridge Early Childhood Advisory Council.

MEMBER: World Association for Infant Psychiatry, International Conference on Infant Studies, Society for Pediatric Research, Ambulatory Pediatric Association, American Academy of Pediatrics (fellow), Society for Research in Child Development, Society for Developmental and Behavioral Pediatrics, National Center for Clinical Infant Programs, New England Pediatric Society, Massachusetts Public Health Association, Boston Institute for the Development of Infants and Parents, Phi Beta Kappa.

AWARDS, HONORS: Grants from National Foundation of the March of Dimes, 1981-83, 1984-86, Robert Wood Johnson Foundation, 1984-88, and Ross Laboratories, 1984.

WRITINGS:

(Editor with H. E. Fitzgerald and B. M. Lester; and contributor) *Theory and Research in Behavioral Pediatrics,* Plenum, Volume 1, 1982, Volume 2, 1984, Volume 3, 1986, Volume 4, 1988.
(Editor with T. Berry Brazelton) *In Support of Families,* Harvard University Press, 1986.
(Editor with Brazelton) *Affective Development in Infancy,* Ablex Publishing, 1986.
(Editor with H. William Taeusch) *Follow-Up Management of the High-Risk Infant,* Little, Brown, 1987.
(With K. V. Cook and Michelle Gersten) *Infant and Toddler Development: Active Organization of the Social World* (monograph), Current Problems in Pediatrics, 1988.

Member of editorial board of *Child Development,* 1980-84, 1987—, *Infant Mental Health Journal,* 1985—, and *Infants and Young Children,* 1988—.

CONTRIBUTOR

R. A. Hoekelman, P. A. Brunnel, S. B. Friedman, and other editors, *Principles of Pediatrics: Health Care of the Young*, McGraw, 1978, 2nd edition, 1986.

John G. Howells, editor, *Modern Perspectives in the Psychiatry of Infancy*, Brunner, 1979.

Michael Lewis and Leonard Rosenblum, editors, *The Child and Its Family*, Plenum, 1979.

H. B. Richardson, Jr., and M. J. Guralnick, editors, *Pediatric Education and the Needs of Young Exceptional Children*, University Park Press, 1979.

Vincent Smerglio, editor, *Newborns and Parents*, Lawrence Erlbaum Associates, 1981.

Kathleen Bloom, editor, *Prospective Issues in Infancy Research*, Lawrence Erlbaum Associates, 1981.

Harris Lieberman and R. J. Wurtman, editors, *Research Strategies for Assessing the Behavioral Effects of Foods and Nutrients*, MIT Press, 1982.

Stanley Cath, Alan Gurwitt, and J. M. Ross, editors, *Fatherhood*, Little, Brown, 1982.

Aidan Macfarlane, editor, *Progress in Child Health*, Churchill Livingstone, 1984.

Justin Call, Eleanor Galenson, and Robert Tyson, editors, *Frontiers in Infant Psychiatry*, Volume II, Basic Books, 1985.

Frank Pedersen and Phyllis Berman, editors, *Men's Transitions to Parenthood*, Lawrence Erlbaum Associates, 1987.

Phyllis Bronstein and C. P. Cowan, editors, *Fatherhood Today: Men's Changing Role in the Family*, Wiley, 1988.

S. Shelov, editor, *American Academy of Pediatrics Book of Baby and Child Care*, American Academy of Pediatrics, in press.

Also contributor to *Biological and Behavioral Determinants of Parental Behavior in Mammals*, edited by N. Krasnegor and R. Bridges, in press.

WORK IN PROGRESS: Research on the father-infant relationship.

SIDELIGHTS: Michael W. Yogman told *CA:* "As a pediatrician, I have been especially interested in the impact of public policy on children's health and development. In my writing I try to convey the need for a range of supports for families with young children, including home visits for families of high risk infants, high quality child care and enlightened parental leave policies, and a more involved role for fathers with infants and children. We depend on our children to shape our future toward a more compassionate and literate society, and we cannot afford to fail them."

* * *

YOSHIMASU Gozo 1939-

PERSONAL: Born February 22, 1939, in Tokyo, Japan; son of Kazuma (an engineer) and Etsu (an artist and teacher; maiden name, Aso) Yoshimasu; married Marilia (a singer), November 17, 1973. *Education:* Keio University, B.A., 1963.

ADDRESSES: Home—1-215-5 Kasumi-cho, Hachioji City 192, Japan. *Office*—Sawada Building Number 1, Apt. 305, 1-36-6 Komaba Meguro-Ku, Tokyo 153, Japan. *Agent*—c/o Katydid Books, 5746 Bridgeview, West Bloomfield, MI 48033.

CAREER: Sansai Finer Arts (magazine), Tokyo, Japan, chief editor, 1964-69; free-lance writer, 1970—. Fulbright visiting writer at University of Iowa, 1970-71; poet in residence at Oakland University, 1979-81; lecturer at institutions including Tama Art University, 1984—, and Asahi Cultural Center; has given poetry readings in the United States, Ireland, Netherlands, Brazil, India, Scotland, England, and Canada.

MEMBER: Japan Writers Association, Japan Pen Club.

AWARDS, HONORS: Takami Jun Prize from Takami Jun Poetry Committee, 1971, for *Shishu ogon Shihen*; Rekitei Prize from Rekitei Group, 1979, for *Neppu;* Hanatsubaki Modern Poetry Prize from Shiseido, 1984, for *Oshirisu ishi no kami.*

WRITINGS:

A Thousand Steps and More: Selected Poems and Prose 1964-1984, Katydid Books, 1987.

POETRY

Shuppatsu (title means "Departure"), Shingeijutsu-sha, 1964.
Shishu ogon shihen (title means "Collection of Golden Verses"), Shichosha, 1970.
Zuno no to (title means "Tower of the Brain), Seichi-sha, 1971.
Okoku (title means "Kingdom"), Kawadeshobo, 1973.
Waga akumabarai (title means "My Exorcism"), Seidosha, 1974.
Sosho de kakareta kawa (title means "River Written in Grass Ecriture"), Shichosha, 1977.
Gendai-shi bunko (title means "Selected Contemporary Poems"), Shichosha, Volume I, 1971, Volume II, 1978.
Yoshimasu Gozo shishu (title means "Complete Works of Yoshimasu Gozo"; includes *Shishu ogon shihen, Okoku, Shuppatsu*, and *Zuno no to*), five volumes, Kawadeshobo, 1978.
Neppu (title means "Devil's Wind"), Chuokoron-Sha, 1979.
Aozora (title means "Blue Sky"), Kawadeshobo, 1979.
Daibyoin waki ni sobietatsu kyojyu e no tegami (title means "A Letter to the Tall Tree Standing Next to the Great Hospital"), Chuokoron-Sha, 1983.
Oshirisu, ishi no kami, Shichosha, 1984; English edition published as "Osiris, God of Stone," translated and edited by Hiroaki Sato, St. Andrews Press, 1988.
Doido na manha (title means "Mad in the Morning"), translated by Jo Takahashi, edited by Masao Ohno, Numen (Rio de Janeiro), 1986.
Rasenka (title means "Song of Tornado") Kawadeshobo, 1989.

Also author of *Shinsen Yoshimasu Gozo shishu* (title means "New Selection of Poems by Gozo Yoshimasu"), 1978.

ESSAYS

Asa no tegami (title means "Morning Letter"), Ozawa Shoten, 1974.
Watashi wa moetatsu shinkiro (title means "I Am a Burning Mirage"), Ozawa Shoten, 1976.
Taiyo no kawa (title means "River of the Sun"), Ozawa Shoten, 1978.
Shizuka na basho (title means "Quiet Place"), Shoshi Yamada, 1981.
Rasenkei o sozoseyo (title means "Imagine, Spiral"), Ozawa Shoten, 1981.
Midori no toshi kagayaku gin (title means "Green City and Shining Silver"), Ozawa Shoten, 1985.
Uchifuruete iku jikan (title means "Time Trembles and Moves On "), Shichosha, 1987.

OTHER

Author of *Sora no koraju* (title means "Sky Collage"), 1978.

Work represented in anthologies, including *Post-War Japanese Poetry*, Penguin Books, 1972; *The Poetry of Postwar Japan*, edited by Kijima Hajime, University of Iowa Press, 1975; *The Iowa Review*, edited by Paul Engle, University of Iowa Press, 1976; *Writing From the World*, edited by Marilyn Chin and Walter Knupfer, University of Iowa Press, 1984. Contributor of articles, poems, and photographs to Japanese periodicals, including *Bungakkukai, Bungei, Eureka, Gendaishi Techo*, and *Umi*.

SIDELIGHTS: Yoshimasu Gozo told *CA:* ''I started to write poetry when I was in college, during the tumultuous times of the 1960s, but, even before, I felt attracted to poetry. When I was a boy I used to go for walks on the mountains near Tokyo looking for rocks. The mountain region on the outskirts of Tokyo was below sea level once and we can still find sea shells there. One day I smashed a sea-fashioned rock on my palm and a beautiful but horrible fossil of an echinoid appeared. In the fraction of time I broke the rock I saw something alive inside it. There was something organic which disappeared in one or two seconds, something which had existed for thousands of years but which died immediately—it disappeared in seconds. Thus my awareness of time began. The deep emotion I then experienced made me realize the propriety of such smashing action. In a way in my poetry I have tried to put the world on my palm and to break it with language. When I broke the fossil I felt as if I was groping the inner wall of some infinitely vast globular form; the end to which my poetry scampers is the center of that cloudiness where the power expressed through the poet has its infinitely powerful origin.

''Since the late 1960s I have been giving poetry readings to jazz or improvisational accompaniment. It started almost by accident. One day at a jazz spot in Tokyo the musicians asked me to read one of my poems. When the music started to play a strange power overcame me and an inner hidden oriental voice spoke with the power of jazz at a great speed. In some sense my text is influenced by my voice. When I write there is a 'vocal' text. There is a graphic form which I thought was impossible to read. Then I discovered that it was possible to read a comma. There are sound correspondences—and also the reading of the silent voice—it is the reading of silence. Gradually, through the breathing and the writing I approach different visions, of other worlds, through the blank, the comma. Typographical signs are very important: the hyphen, the comma, the apostrophe. I discovered this in Emily Dickinson; there is a silent voice in her. In Paul Celam, also. And Percy Bysshe Shelley. Poets sometimes feel an invisible language. It's not the cosmos, but something which comes, though invisibly, through the blank of the page.''

AVOCATIONAL INTERESTS: Photography, cinematography.

*   *   *

YOST, Elwy McMurran   1925-

PERSONAL: Born July 10, 1925, in Weston, Ontario, Canada; son of Elwy Honderich (a pickle manufacturer) and Annie Josephine (a housewife; maiden name, McMurran) Yost; married Lila Ragnhild Melby (a housewife), June 16, 1951; children: Christopher Monrad, Graham John Boz. *Education:* University of Toronto, B.A. (with honors), 1948. *Politics:* ''I vote for the candidate, not the party.'' *Religion:* Protestant, ''but

really a life-long searcher for some meaning to the universe and existence.''

ADDRESSES: Home—15 Sir Williams Lane, Islington, Ontario, Canada M9A 1T8.

CAREER: Toronto Star, Toronto, Ontario, in circulation department, 1948-52; Avro Aircraft, Malton, Ontario, human relations counselor, 1953-59; high school English teacher in Toronto, 1959-64; television panelist on ''Live a Borrowed Life,'' ''The Superior Sex,'' and ''Flashback,'' host of radio show ''It's Debatable'' and host of children's television show ''Passport to Adventure,'' for Canadian Broadcasting Corporation, 1959-68; Metropolitan Educational Television Association, Toronto, producer, 1964-66, executive director, 1967-70; TVOntario, Toronto, superintendent of regional liaison, 1970-73, executive producer and host of ''Saturday Night at the Movies,'' 1974—, ''Magic Shadows,'' 1974-88, and ''Rough Cuts,'' 1978-80; writer, 1988—. Professional actor in summer stock, with Midland Players and Niagara Born Players, 1946-53; chairman of Conestoga College Film Advisory Council, 1979-81. Patron of Youth Without Shelter, 1987-88. *Military service:* Canadian Army, 1944-45.

MEMBER: Alliance of Canadian Television and Radio Artists, Sons of the Desert.

WRITINGS:

(Contributor) Walt McDayter, editor, *The Media Mosaic*, Holt, c. 1970.
Magic Moments From the Movies, Doubleday, 1978.
Secret of the Lost Empire (juvenile), Scholastic TAB Publications, 1980.
Billy and the Bubbleship (juvenile), Scholastic TAB Publications, 1982, published as *The Mad Queen of Mordra*, Scholastic TAB Publications, 1987.

Author of radio scripts in the early 1960s, including ''The Lost City,'' ''A Long Time Till Harry Comes,'' and ''The Falls of Orellana,'' all for Canadian Broadcasting Corp. Contributor to periodicals, including *Bakka, Video Scene, Leisureways*, and *Counsellor and Higher Literacy;* contributor of film reviews to the *Toronto Star*.

WORK IN PROGRESS: An adult novel.

SIDELIGHTS: Elwy McMurran Yost told *CA:* ''I have always wanted to be a novelist like Robert Louis Stevenson or Jack London, or Theodore Dreiser, Sinclair Lewis, Max Braithwaite, or Pierre Berton of Canada. Now that I am semiretired, I am trying to do something about it.

''My first children's novel, *Secret of the Lost Empire*, took twenty-four years to write and to sell to a publisher; thus, I suppose I possess a certain 'stick-to-it-ivity.' My current adult novel is a huge, complicated, somewhat bizarre affair that may take five or seven years to complete—I hope I live long enough to see it through to completion.

''Movies were my first love. From the time I was five, my father always gave me a dime to attend the Saturday matinees, and always made me tell him the plots when I came home. A little later I started to draw and write my own comic strips (unpublished) and write poetry and movie reviews. My first adult book, *Magic Moments From the Movies*, was a chronicle of my favorite scenes from the whole history of movies and took five years to write. It was drawn from four volumes of film reviews that I had written over the years for my own enjoyment.

"*Secret of the Lost Empire* involved a boy's search for his father, lost seven years in the jungles and plateaus of Peru and the Amazon while looking for the highest waterfall on earth. *Billy and the Bubbleship*, now titled *The Mad Queen of Mordra*, concerns a boy of eleven or twelve who discovers a melting meteor one dark night in the forest behind his Ontario home. He takes some of the 'fluid' back to the chemistry lab in his house and produces a huge bubble—like a soap bubble, but very different in terms of its properties—that he can fly around in. He goes through a black hole into another universe where, on a strange 'flat' planet, he runs into conflict with a beautiful, mad queen, who presides over a city built on the bottom of a vast ocean.

"One thing I have learned about writing novels, juvenile and adult, is the amount of rewriting that is necessary. My juvenile books were each rewritten four or five times and were vastly improved with each draft. One has to fall in love with rewriting, unless one is some kind of genius, which I am not. Also, the role of one's editor is profound. Two editors from Scholastic TAB Publications worked closely with me for four years on my first juvenile, and even trained my wife, Lila, to be an editor so that she could edit each draft before it went to them. Writing books demands of an author an almost maniacal capacity for 'Fuss.' That should be the title of my autobiography someday."

*　　*　　*

YOUNG, Leontine R(uth)   1910-1988

OBITUARY NOTICE—See index for *CA* sketch: Born March 29, 1910, in Palmyra, N.Y.; died of lung cancer, July 28, 1988, in Princeton, N.J. Social worker, educator, administrator, and author. Young was a social worker in the state of New York during the 1940s and a member of the faculty at Columbia University from 1945 to 1952. She taught at Ohio State University throughout the remainder of the 1950s and worked as executive director of the Child Service Association in Newark, New Jersey, beginning in 1960. Among her writings are *The Treatment of Adolescent Girls in an Institution, Out of Wedlock, Life Among the Giants,* and *Wednesday's Children: A Study of Child Neglect and Abuse,* which influenced legislation on child abuse in New Jersey.

OBITUARIES AND OTHER SOURCES:

PERIODICALS

New York Times, July 30, 1988.

*　　*　　*

YOUNG, Mary Lou Daves   1918- (Mary Lawrence)

PERSONAL: Born May 17, 1918, in Newark, Ohio; married Delmer Daves (a writer and producer), 1938 (died August 15, 1977); married Samuel Doak Young (a banker), May 11, 1980 (died April 15, 1987); children: (first marriage) Michael Lawrence, Debby Daves Richards, Donna Daves Kent. *Education:* Attended Western College for Women, 1936-37, and University of California, Los Angeles, 1942-43.

ADDRESSES: Home—107 North Bentley Ave., Los Angeles, Calif. 90049; and 1730 Valdez Dr., La Jolla, Calif. 92037. *Agent*—Marshall Lee, 230 Fifth Ave., Suite 1808, New York, N.Y. 10001.

CAREER: Professional actress on stage, film, and television, 1937-73; interior decorator in Los Angeles, Calif., 1960-80. El Paso Museum of Art, member of board of trustees, 1981-86, president of board, 1986.

WRITINGS:

UNDER NAME MARY LAWRENCE

Mother and Child: One Hundred Works of Art With Commentaries by More Than One Hundred Distinguished People, Crowell, 1975.
Lovers: One Hundred Works of Art Celebrating Romantic Love, With Commentaries by the Distinguished and the Great (Literary Guild selection), A & W Publishers, 1982.
Children in Art, Balance House, in press.

SIDELIGHTS: Mary Lawrence told *CA:* "Each of my books contains one hundred color plates and encompasses art on a single theme from the year 500 B.C. through the work of Picasso."

BIOGRAPHICAL/CRITICAL SOURCES:

PERIODICALS

Los Angeles Times, January 3, 1982.

Z

ZECKHAUSER, Richard Jay 1940-

PERSONAL: Born November 1, 1940, in Philadelphia, Pa.; son of Julius Nathaniel and Estelle (Borgenicht) Zeckhauser; married Nancy Mackell Hoover, September 9, 1967; children: Bryn Gordon, Benjamin Rennell. *Education:* Harvard University, A.B. (summa cum laude), 1962, Ph.D., 1968.

ADDRESSES: Home—138 Irving St., Cambridge, Mass. 02138. *Office*—John F. Kennedy School of Government, Harvard University, 79 JFK St., Cambridge, Mass. 02138.

CAREER: Harvard University, Cambridge, Mass., assistant professor, 1968-70, associate professor, 1970-72, professor, 1972-88, Frank P. Ramsey Professor of Political Economy, 1988—, chairman of non-tenure appointments in economics, statistics, and analytic methods, 1972—, chairman of research committee, 1977—, and director of regulation project, 1977—, for John F. Kennedy School of Government, research associate for Business and Government Research Center and for Energy and Environmental Policy Center, associate of Eliot House. Founder, director, and principal of Niederhoffer, Cross, & Zeckhauser, Inc. (investment banking and commodity and currency trading firm), 1967-84; principal and director of Interactive Marketing Systems (computer-based marketing firm), 1984—; principal and director of Energy Recovery, Inc., 1985—; principal of Goldmark Capital Ltd. (investment bankers), 1986—; consultant to Rand Corporation, 1963—, and to private and government organizations. Member of board of trustees of Winsor School, Boston, Mass.

MEMBER: Association for Public Policy and Management (member of policy council).

WRITINGS:

(Editor and co-author of introduction) *Benefit Cost and Policy Analysis Annual, 1974,* Aldine, 1974.
(With Edith Stokey) *A Primer for Policy Analysis,* Norton, 1978.
(With Peter D. McClelland) *Demographic Dimensions of the New Republic,* Cambridge University Press, 1982.
(Editor with Derek Leebaert) *What Role for Government? Lessons From Policy Research,* Duke University Press, 1983.
(Editor with John Pratt) *Principals and Agents: The Structure of Business,* Harvard Business School Press, 1985.

(Editor with Winthrop Knowlton) *American Society, Public and Private Responsibilities,* Ballinger, 1986.
(Editor with Paul MacAvoy, William Stanbury, and George Yarrow) *Privatization and State-Owned Enterprise: Lessons From the United Kingdom, Canada, and the United States,* Kluwar Academic, 1988.

Contributor of more than one hundred articles to periodicals, including *American Economic Review, Econometrica, Journal of Chronic Diseases, Journal of Economic Theory, Journal of Human Resources, Journal of Political Economy, Journal of Public Economics, Management Science, Public Policy, Quarterly Journal of Economics, Western Economic Journal,* and *Yale Law Journal.*

Co-editor of *Energy Economics, Journal of Risk and Uncertainty,* and *Japan and the World Economy: International Journal of Economic Theory and Policy.*

WORK IN PROGRESS: Economic Paradigms and *Lives Versus Dollars,* as well as numerous articles; "research on commitment relationships in American society, and the role of shareholder voting in corporate governance."

*   *   *

ZERBE, Jerome (B.) 1904-1988

OBITUARY NOTICE—See index for *CA* sketch: Born July 24, 1904, in Euclid, Ohio; died after a long illness, August 19, 1988, in New York, N.Y. Photographer, editor, and author. Zerbe was best known for his photographs recording cafe society during the 1930s. He started his career as art editor of the Cleveland weekly *Parade* in the early 1930s, then moved to New York City and began frequenting the city's cafes and nightclubs for subject matter. In 1933 he commenced a longtime association with *Town and Country,* regularly contributing photographs and—from 1949 to 1974—working as society editor. Zerbe's pictures are collected in the volumes *People on Parade, El Morocco's Family Album, Les Pavillons,* and *Happy Times.* In addition, he wrote *The Art of Social Climbing.*

OBITUARIES AND OTHER SOURCES:

BOOKS

Who's Who in America, 40th edition, Marquis, 1978.

PERIODICALS

Chicago Tribune, August 25, 1988.
New York Times, August 23, 1988.

*   *   *

ZETTERLING, Mai (Elisabeth)   1925-

PERSONAL: Born May 24, 1925, in Vaesteras, Sweden; immigrated to England; daughter of Joel and Lina (Thoernblom) Zetterling; married Tutte Lemkow (an actor and dancer), 1944 (divorced, 1953); married David Hughes (a writer), 1958 (divorced, 1977); children: (first marriage) one son, one daughter. *Education:* Royal Theatre School of Drama (Stockholm), graduated in 1945.

ADDRESSES: Agent—c/o Douglas Rae Management Ltd., 28 Charing Cross Rd., London W.1, England.

CAREER: Actress, screenwriter, and director of motion pictures and stage and television productions; author. Actress in stage productions, including "The Wild Duck," 1948, "The Seagull," 1949, and "A Doll's House," 1953; actress in motion pictures, including "Hets," 1944, "The Girl in the Painting," 1948, and "The Truth About Women," 1958. Contributing director to documentary "Visions of Eight," 1973.

AWARDS, HONORS: Golden Lion from Venice Film Festival, 1963, for "The War Game."

WRITINGS:

BOOKS

(With husband, David Hughes) *The Cat's Tale* (for children), J. Cape, 1965.
Night Games (novel), Coward-McCann, 1966 (also see below).
In the Shadow of the Sun (short stories), J. Cape, 1975.
Bird of Passage (novel), St. Martin's, 1976.
All Those Tomorrows (autobiography), J. Cape, 1985, Grove, 1986.
The Crystal Castle (for children), Norsteots (Sweden), 1985.

Also author of children's book *The Rain's Hat* adapted from Zetterling's television production, 1979 (also see below).

SCREENPLAYS, AND DIRECTOR

(With husband, David Hughes) "Alskande par" (adapted from Agnes von Krustenstjierna's novel *The Misses von Pahlen*), 1964, released in the United States as "Loving Couples," Prominent Films, 1966.
(With Hughes) "Nattlek" (adapted from Zetterling's novel *Night Games;* also see above), 1966, released in the United States as "Night Games," Mondial Films, 1966.
(With Hughes) "Doktor Glas" (adapted from Hjalmar Soderberg's novel), 1967, released in the United States as "Doctor Glas," Twentieth Century-Fox, 1969.
(With Hughes) "Flickorna," 1968, released in the United States as "The Girls," Goran Lindgren, 1972.
(With Roy Minton and Jeremy Watt) "Scrubbers," Orion Classics, 1984.
"Amorosa," Swedish Film Institute, 1986.

Also writer, or co-writer, and director of television features and documentaries, including "The Polite Invasion," 1960, "Lords of Little Egypt," 1961, "The War Game," 1961, "The Prosperity Race," 1962, "The Do-It Yourself Democracy," 1963, "Vincent the Dutchman," 1971, "We har manga Namn" (title means "We Have Many Names"), 1976, "The Moon Is a Green Cheese," 1976, "The Native Squatter," 1977, "Stockholm," 1977, "The Rain's Hat," 1978, "Lady Policeman," 1979, and "Of Seals and Men," 1979.

SIDELIGHTS: Mai Zetterling is a writer and filmmaker who is probably best known, at least in the United States, for her sexually frank films from the 1960s. She entered the performing arts while still a teenager by performing in productions on the Swedish stage. In 1945, a year before she actually completed studies at the Royal Theatre School of Drama in Stockholm, she appeared in the Swedish film "Hets" (title means "Torment"), a gripping drama—written by Ingmar Bergman—about a naive student's doomed love for the mistress of a sadistic professor. Years later Zetterling still prized "Hets" as the work in which she delivered her finest performance.

During the next few years Zetterling distinguished herself on the Swedish stage and in Swedish films. In 1948, however, she left Sweden to work on the British stage, where she eventually appeared in works by Chekhov, Ibsen, and Shakespeare. Soon she was also acting in Hollywood film productions. But her experiences there left her increasingly dissatisfied with the acting profession, and after appearing in the Danny Kaye vehicle "Knock on Wood" she abandoned acting to work as a filmmaker.

In 1960 Zetterling obtained funding from British television to write—with her husband, David Hughes—and direct "The Polite Invasion," a short documentary about immigrant Swedes in Lapland. She next collaborated with Hughes on "Lords of Little Egypt," a brief film about gypsies that appeared on British television in 1961. Her first major work as director, however, was "The War Game," an independently produced short about children fighting for possession of a toy weapon. This film, which Zetterling wrote with Hughes, enjoyed great success at the 1964 Venice Film Festival, where it was accorded the prestigious Golden Lion.

On the strength of her success in Venice, Zetterling found funding for her first feature film, "Alskande par," released in the United States as "Loving Couples." This work, which Zetterling adapted with Hughes from a portion of Agnes von Krusenstjierna's long novel *The Misses von Pahlen*, recalls Bergman's "Brink of Life" by concerning itself with three pregnant women. But unlike Bergman's work, which focused on the more traumatic aspects of childbearing and birthgiving, Zetterling's "Loving Couples" details the romantic entanglements that resulted in three women's pregnancies. Two of the principal characters have conceived with men with whom they are not married, and the third woman, while bearing her own husband's child, loathes the spouse and longs for a more fulfilling relationship. Zetterling provides a largely sympathetic perspective on the women's predicaments, and with considerable frankness—even as regards the film's sexual aspects—she delineates the sexism and classism inherent in Victorian Sweden.

"Loving Couples" was described by *New York Times* reviewer A. H. Weiler as "an arresting, serious drama." In praising Zetterling's debut as writer and director of feature films, Weiler cited her candid handling of eroticism and commended her "genuine versatility." The reviewer complained only that the film seemed unnecessarily complicated, but added that this flaw was one of admirable ambition, noting that Zetterling's "initial effort behind the camera is bold . . . in presenting facets of amour, illicit and otherwise, at too great length." Despite this objection, Weiler concluded that Zetterling "proves she knows the directorial craft."

After completing "Loving Couples," Zetterling began writing books. In 1966 she published *Night Games,* a graphic, charged novel about a twisted mother-son relationship. The novel was followed that same year by Zetterling's film adaptation, "Natt-lek," released in the United States as "Night Games," which she directed from a script written with Hughes. Shown at the 1966 Venice Film Festival, "Night Games" outraged festival judges with its uncompromising portrait of crudity and per-version. Like the novel, the film centers on a young Swedish man's struggle to free himself from dominance by his disturbed mother, who had resorted to sexual manipulation in maintaining her authority. Haunted by memories of his mother's twisted cruelty, the son eventually destroys their home and thus, presumably, overcomes inhibitions caused by his traumatic, sordid experiences.

Reviewing "Night Games" in the *New York Times* review, Bosley Crowther commended Zetterling's directorial skill and her flair "in creating visual images." Crowther added, however, that the film's credibility was undermined by its unlikely preponderance of sordid sexual episodes. The reviewer expressed hope that such episodes were meant in jest, noting that he could "not otherwise comprehend what would be [Zetterling's] purpose in doing so many extravagantly bold and bizarre things that appear beyond any likely context of any level of Scandinavian life."

Zetterling followed "Night Games" with "Doktor Glas," released in the United States as "Doctor Glas," her adaptation—written with Hughes—of Hjalmar Soderberg's novel of love and murder. The protagonist is a lonely, emotionally withdrawn old man obsessed with his crime of passion. The circumstances of that crime are recounted in flashbacks that, in turn, serve as the film's main narrative. Earlier in his career, the doctor entertains sexual fantasies in which he couples with the vivacious young wife of an aging, physically unappealing pastor. Eventually, the young woman actually approaches the doctor and reveals her efforts to avoid sexual relations with her disgusting husband. The inhibited doctor responds by poisoning his secret love's spouse. The woman's affection is not forthcoming, however, and the doctor lives out his remaining years alone and haunted by memories.

With "Loving Couples" and "Night Games," Zetterling gained recognition as a filmmaker who frankly and unassumingly addressed the more shocking and troubling aspects of sexuality. She sustained that reputation with "Doctor Glas," but to such an extent that the *New York Times*'s Vincent Canby lamented Zetterling's seeming reluctance to sufficiently dramatize the narrative. Canby charged that the film was "totally devoid of passion" and added that Zetterling possessed "a talent for reducing everything—the magnificent, the banal and the bizarre—to the same set of commonplace statistics." He declared that "even scenes of sexual hallucination look like road-maps for a subconscious as flat as Iowa."

Zetterling's next film, "Flickorna," released in the United States as "The Girls," explored both private and professional lives of various women touring Sweden in a production of Aristophanes's "Lysistrata." Much of the film is about the dismal personal lives of two actresses: one, a mistress; the other, a harried mother. The actresses, and other women involved with the play, eventually perceive similarities between their own concerns and those of the anti-war women characters of "Lysistrata."

Roger Greenspun, who reviewed "The Girls" in the *New York Times* when the 1968 film received its belated American re-

lease in 1972, wrote that Zetterling rendered this realization only vaguely and, thus, unconvincingly. He wrote that "whatever its intentions, 'The Girls' never formulates a feminist manifesto, and its heroines seem only to divide their time between Greek comedy and soap opera." Noting the presence of leading Scandinavian actresses Harriet Andersson, Bibi Andersson, and Gunnel Lindblom, Greenspun declared that the movie's "goodness is wholly personal and largely incidental." He concluded, "That Mai Zetterling working with so much has arrived at so little is less an indication of new directions than of directorial failure."

In the years since completing "The Girls," Zetterling has pursued a variety of artistic ventures, producing children's books, a short story collection, an autobiography, and more novels. She has also worked more extensively in television, writing and directing numerous documentaries and features for Scandinavian and British networks. In addition, she has co-written and directed "Scrubbers," a feature film that *New York Times* critic Janet Maslin described as a graphic depiction of prison life. This work, released in 1984, may revive American interest in Zetterling. If so, she has many television productions still awaiting release or broadcast in the United States.

AVOCATIONAL INTERESTS: Gardening, cooking, philosophical ESP, alchemy.

BIOGRAPHICAL/CRITICAL SOURCES:

BOOKS

Smith, Sharon, *Women Who Make Movies,* Hopkinson & Blake, 1975.
Young, Vernon, *Cinema Borealis: Ingmar Bergman and the Swedish Ethos,* Avon, 1972.
Young, Vernon, *On Film: Unpopular Essays on a Popular Art,* Quadrangle, 1972.
Zetterling, Mai, *All Those Tomorrows,* J. Cape, 1985.

PERIODICALS

American Cinematographer, November, 1972.
Atlantic Monthly, January, 1967.
Cahiers du Cinema in English, December, 1966.
Films and Filming, April, 1974.
Listener, March 13, 1975.
London Review of Books, February 20, 1986.
New Statesman, October 7, 1966, January 30, 1976.
New York Times, September 20, 1966, December 20, 1966, April 7, 1969, April 30, 1972, June 7, 1972.
New York Times Book Review, December 18, 1966, December 26, 1976.
Observer, March 9, 1975, February 1, 1976.
Spectator, February 15, 1975.
Take One, November-December, 1970.
Time, November 18, 1966.
Times Literary Supplement, February 14, 1975.

—*Sketch by Les Stone*

*   *   *

ZIEGLER, Charles E. 1953-

PERSONAL: Born October 17, 1953, in Plymouth, Ind.; son of Charles A. and Justine D. (Harris) Ziegler. *Education:* Purdue University, B.A., 1975; University of Illinois at Urbana-Champaign, A.M., 1977, Ph.D., 1979.

ADDRESSES: Home—150 North Jane St., Louisville, Ky. 40206. *Office*—Department of Political Science, University of Louisville, Louisville, Ky. 40292.

CAREER: St. Leo College, St. Leo, Fla., assistant professor of political science, 1979-80; University of Louisville, Louisville, Ky., assistant professor, 1980-86, associate professor of political science, 1986—. National fellow at Hoover Institution on War, Revolution, and Peace, Stanford University, 1985-86; visiting associate professor of Soviet environmental policy, Oberlin College, 1987. International affairs fellow of Council on Foreign Relations, 1987-88. Member of Louisville Committee on Foreign Relations.

MEMBER: American Political Science Association, American Association for the Advancement of Slavic Studies, Southern Conference of Slavic Studies.

WRITINGS:

Policy Alternatives in Soviet Environmental Protection, Carl Beck Papers in Russian and East European Studies, University of Pittsburgh, 1982.

(Contributor) Paul B. Downing and Kenneth Hanf, editors, *International Comparisons in Implementing Pollution Laws,* Kluwer-Nijhoff, 1983.

(Contributor) Gavin Boyd and Gerald W. Hopple, editors, *Political Change and Foreign Policies,* Frances Pinter, 1987.

Environmental Policy in the U.S.S.R., University of Massachusetts Press, 1987.

Contributor to Soviet studies books and political science journals, including *British Journal of Political Science, Comparative Politics, Political Science Quarterly,* and *Technology Review.*

WORK IN PROGRESS: A study of the linkages between domestic politics and foreign policy in the Soviet Union, publication by International Institute for Strategic Studies, London, expected in 1989.

SIDELIGHTS: Charles E. Ziegler told *CA:* "I am particularly interested in diverse cultural experiences and their impact on political behavior. I am competent in Russian and have traveled to the Soviet Union, Eastern and Western Europe, Latin America, and the South Pacific. I was in Poland during the height of the Solidarity period, in the summer of 1981. I found that the heady optimism and talk about democracy was replaced by resignation and apathy after martial law.

"At the present time, Soviet environmental issues are being discussed and evaluated more openly than at any time in the past. There are many ecology clubs and nature preservation societies that have emerged under Mikhail Gorbachev's leadership. These groups operate outside the normal bureaucratic channels that have generally frustrated ecological progress. Furthermore, these groups mirror the broader liberalization taking place in the Soviet Union."

*　　　*　　　*

ZUMWALT, Elmo Russell III 1946(?)-1988

OBITUARY NOTICE: Born c. 1946 in Tulare, Calif.; died of cancer, August 13, 1988, in Fayetteville, N.C. Military officer, lawyer, and author. Son of the Vietnam admiral who authorized the use of Agent Orange—whose highly toxic and carcinogenic component dioxin cleared thick foliage hiding enemy guerillas—Zumwalt was heavily exposed to the chemical and suffered from lymphoma and Hodgkin's disease the last five years of his life. After graduating from the University of North Carolina in 1968, Zumwalt volunteered for the U.S. Navy and became a lieutenant junior grade, commanding a patrol boat in Vietnam from 1969 to 1970. During his service he swam through water containing Agent Orange, then believed harmless to humans. Later the defoliant was said to be the cause of the high rate of cancer in Vietnam veterans as well as birth defects in their offspring. Zumwalt's son, Russell, suffers from one such congenital disorder. After the war Zumwalt became a lawyer, and he never blamed his father for his affliction. They collaborated on *My Father, My Son,* in which they defended the decision to use Agent Orange as a means of reducing casualties in Vietnam. The work was also adapted for television.

OBITUARIES AND OTHER SOURCES:

PERIODICALS

Detroit Free Press, August 14, 1988.
Los Angeles Times, August 14, 1988.
New York Times, August 14, 1988.
Washington Post, August 14, 1988.

Contemporary Authors®

Cumulative Index
Volumes 1–126

This Index Includes References to All Entries in the Contemporary Authors Series

Contemporary Authors

Volume 126 brings the total coverage to more than 92,000 writers, both living and deceased, a large portion of whom are missing in similar works. Writers in fiction, general nonfiction, poetry, journalism, drama, motion pictures, television, and other fields are all included in CA. Each new volume contains sketches on authors not previously listed in the series. Cumulative index in even-numbered original volumes. All volumes in the series are in print.

Contemporary Authors New Revision Series

Provides completely updated information on authors listed in previous volumes of CA. Sketches from a number of volumes are assessed, and only entries requiring significant change are revised and published in the CA New Revision Series. Volumes 1-26 are in print.

(All volumes published under the former revision system, 1-4 through 41-44 First Revision, will remain in print.)

Contemporary Authors Permanent Series

Consists of updated listings for deceased and inactive authors removed from original volumes 9-36 when these volumes were revised. Two volumes only; both are in print.

Contemporary Authors Autobiography Series

Presents specially commissioned autobiographies by leading writers. Volumes 1-7 are in print.

Contemporary Authors Bibliographical Series

Contains primary and secondary bibliographies as well as analytical bibliographical essays. Volumes 1-2 are in print.

And to All Entries in These Gale Reference Works

Authors in the News

Reprints articles from American newspapers and magazines covering writers and other members of the communications media.

Black Writers

Combines in a single volume both newly written and completely updated CA sketches on more than four hundred twentieth-century black writers to provide in-depth information unavailable in any other single reference source.

Children's Literature Review

Includes excerpts from reviews, criticism, and commentary on works of children's authors and illustrators.

Concise Dictionary of American Literary Biography

Contains illustrated entries on major American authors selected and updated from the Dictionary of Literary Biography.

Contemporary Literary Criticism

Presents excerpts from current criticism of the works of today's novelists, poets, playwrights, short story writers, scriptwriters, and other creative writers.

Dictionary of Literary Biography

Encompasses three related series. Dictionary of Literary Biography furnishes overviews of authors and their work, placing them in the larger context of literary history. Dictionary of Literary Biography Documentary Series illuminates the careers of major figures through a selection of literary documents. Dictionary of Literary Biography Yearbook summarizes the past year's literary activity and includes updated and new author entries.

Short Story Criticism

Provides excerpts from criticism of the works of major short story writers of all eras and nationalities.

Something About the Author

Contains heavily illustrated sketches on juvenile and young adult authors and illustrators from all eras.

Something About the Author Autobiography Series

Presents specially commissioned autobiographies by prominent authors and illustrators of books for children.

Twentieth-Century Literary Criticism

Furnishes lengthy excerpts from criticism of the works of novelists, poets, playwrights, short story writers, and other creative writers who died between 1900 and 1960.

Yesterday's Authors of Books for Children

Consists of heavily illustrated sketches on children's authors who died before 1961.

Contemporary Authors

Cumulative Index • Volumes 1-126

Citations to entries in *Contemporary Authors* are identified as follows:

R after number	•	*Contemporary Authors* First Revision Volumes 1-44
Volume number only	•	*Contemporary Authors* Original Volumes 45-126
CANR	•	*Contemporary Authors* New Revision Series, Volumes 1-26
CAP	•	*Contemporary Authors* Permanent Series, Volumes 1-2
CAAS	•	*Contemporary Authors* Autobiography Series, Volumes 1-7
CABS	•	*Contemporary Authors* Bibliographical Series, Volumes 1-2

Citations to entries in other reference works are identified as follows:

AITN	•	*Authors in the News*, Volumes 1-2
BW	•	*Black Writers*
CDALB	•	*Concise Dictionary of American Literary Biography*, 1941-1968, 1640-1865, 1865-1917
CLC	•	*Contemporary Literary Criticism*, Volumes 1-50
CLR	•	*Children's Literature Review*, Volumes 1-16
DLB	•	*Dictionary of Literary Biography*, Volumes 1-76
DLBD	•	*Dictionary of Literary Biography Documentary Series*, Volumes 1-4
DLBY	•	*Dictionary of Literary Biography Yearbook*, 1980-1987
SAAS	•	*Something About the Author Autobiography Series*, Volumes 1-6
SATA	•	*Something About the Author*, Volumes 1-53
SSC	•	*Short Story Criticism*, Volumes 1-2
TCLC	•	*Twentieth-Century Literary Criticism*, Volumes 1-29
YABC	•	*Yesterday's Authors of Books for Children*, Volumes 1-2

INDEX

A. A.
See Willis, (George) Anthony Armstrong
A. E.
See Russell, George William
See also DLB 19
See also TCLC 3, 10
A. M.
See Megged, Aharon
Aach, Herb(ert) 1923-1985 Obituary 118
Aaker, David A(llen) 1938- 49-52
Aalben, Patrick
See Jones, Noel
Aallyn, Alysse
See Clark, Melissa
Aalto, (Hugo) Alvar (Henrik) 1898-1976
Obituary 65-68
Aardema, Verna
See Vugteveen, Verna Aardema
See also SATA 4
Aaron, Benjamin 1915- 23-24R
Aaron, Chester 1923- CANR-8
Earlier sketch in CA 21-22R
See also SATA 9
Aaron, Daniel 1912- CANR-7
Earlier sketch in CA 13-14R
Aaron, David (Laurence) 1938- 126
Aaron, Hank
See Aaron, Henry Louis
Aaron, Henry Louis 1934- Brief entry 104
Aaron, James Ethridge 1927- 23-24R
Aaron, R. I.
See Aaron, Richard Ithamar
Aaron, Richard Ithamar 1901-1987
Obituary 122
Aaron, Shirley L. 1941- 123
Aaron, Sidney
See Chayefsky, Sidney
Aaron, Stephen 1936- 124
Aaronovitch, Sam 1919- 13-14R
Aarons, Edward S(idney) 1916-1975 93-96
Obituary 57-60
Aarons, Slim 1916- Brief entry 106
Aaronson, Bernard S(eymour) 1924- 29-32R
Aarsleff, Hans 1925- 21-22R
Aaseng, Nate
See Aaseng, Nathan
Aaseng, Nathan 1953- 106
See also SATA 38, 51
Aasheim, Ashley 1942- 115
Abadinsky, Howard 1941- 110
Abagnale, Frank W., Jr. 1948- 112
Abajian, James De Tar 1914- 65-68
Abarbanel, Karin 1950- 65-68
Abarbanel, Sam X. 1914- Brief entry 106

Abasiyanik, Sait Faik 1906-1954
Brief entry 123
Abata, Russell M(ary) 1930- 113
Abate, Frank R(obert) 1951- 118
Abayakoon, Cyrus D. F. 1912- Brief entry .. 115
Abbaanano, Nicola 1901- 33-36R
Abbas, Khwaja Ahmad 1914- 57-60
Abbazia, Patrick 1937- 57-60
Abbe, Elfriede (Martha) 1919- 15-16R
Abbe, George (Bancroft) 1911- CANR-10
Earlier sketch in CA 25-28R
Abbensetts, Michael 1938- 104
Abberley, Aldwyn
See Cowie, Donald
Abbey, Edward 1927- CANR-2
Earlier sketch in CA 45-48
See also CLC 36
Abbey, Lloyd (Robert) 1943- 125
Brief entry 104
Abbey, Lynn
See Abbey, Marilyn Lorraine
Abbey, Margaret
See York, Margaret Elizabeth
Abbey, Marilyn Lorraine 1948- 119
Abbey, Merrill R. 1905- CANR-3
Earlier sketch in CA 1R
Abbington, John
See Gibson, Walter B(rown)
Abbot, Anthony
See Oursler, (Charles) Fulton
Abbot, Charles G(reeley) 1872-1973 77-80
Obituary 45-48
Abbot, Rick
See Sharkey, John Michael
Abbot, W(illiam) W(right) 1922-
Brief entry 110
Abbott, Willis J(ohn) 1863-1934
Brief entry 119
See also DLB 29
Abbott, Alice
See Borland, Kathryn Kilby
and Speicher, Helen Ross S(mith)
Abbott, Anthony S. 1935- 17-18R
Abbott, Berenice 1898- 106
Abbott, Carl (John) 1944- CANR-11
Earlier sketch in CA 65-68
Abbott, Claude Colleer 1889-1971 .... 7-8R
Obituary 89-92
Abbott, Eric Symes 1906-1983 Obituary ... 110
Abbott, Freeland K(night) 1919-1971 ..... CAP-2
Earlier sketch in CA 25-28
Abbott, George 1887- 93-96
Abbott, H(orace) Porter 1940- 45-48
Abbott, Jack Henry
See Abbott, Rufus Henry

Abbott, Jacob 1803-1879 .... SATA-22
See also DLB 1, 42
Abbott, James H(amilton) 1924- 77-80
Abbott, Jerry (Lynn) 1938- 45-48
Abbott, John J(amison) 1930- 17-18R
Abbott, John Janisen 17-18R
Abbott, Keith 1944- 121
Abbott, L(enwood) B(allard) 1908-1985
Obituary 117
Abbott, Lee K(ittredge) 1947- 124
See also CLC 48
Abbott, Manager Henry
See Stratemeyer, Edward L.
Abbott, Margaret Evans 1896-1976
Obituary 110
Abbott, Martin 1922-1977 .... 33-36R
Abbott, May L(aura) 1916- 9-10R
Abbott, Philip (R.) 1944- 126
Brief entry 106
Abbott, R(obert) Tucker 1919- CANR-4
Earlier sketch in CA 9-10R
Abbott, Raymond H(erbert) 1942- 57-60
Abbott, Richard H(enry) 1936- 33-36R
Abbott, Robert S. 1868-1940 .... DLB-29
Abbott, Rowland A(ubrey) S(amuel)
1909- 53-56
Abbott, Rufus Henry 1944- 107
Abbott, Sarah
See Zolotow, Charlotte S.
Abbott, Shirley 1934- 113
Abbott, Sidney 1937- 41-44R
Abbott, Walter M(atthew) 1923- 11-12R
Abbotts, John 1947- 73-76
Abboushi, W(asif) F(ahmi) 1931- 29-32R
Abbs, Peter 1942- 93-96
ABC
See Caddick, Arthur
Abcarian, Richard 1929- 33-36R
Abdallah, Omar
See Humbaraci, D(emir) Arslan
Abdel-Malek, Anouar 1924- 29-32R
Abdelsamad, Moustafa H(assan) 1941- ... 53-56
Abdul, Raoul 1929- 29-32R
See also SATA 12
Abdullah, Achmed 1881-1945 Brief entry .. 115
Abdullahi, Guda 1946- 93-96
Abdul-Rauf, Muhammad 1917- 101
Abe, Kobo 1924- CANR-24
Earlier sketch in CA 65-68
See also CLC 8, 22
Abeel, Erica (Hennefeld) 1937- 113
Brief entry 109
Abel, Alan (Irwin) 1928- CANR-12
Earlier sketch in CA 19-20R

Abel, Bob
See Abel, Robert
Abel, Elie 1920- CANR-8
Earlier sketch in CA 61-64
Abel, Ernest L(awrence) 1943- CANR-14
Earlier sketch in CA 41-44R
Abel, I(orwith) W(ilbur) 1908-1987
Obituary 123
Brief entry 105
Abel, Jeanne 1937- 19-20R
Abel, Lionel 1910- 61-64
Abel, Raymond 1911- SATA-12
Abel, Reuben 1911- 37-40R
Abel, Robert 1913(?)-1987 Obituary 122
Abel, Robert 1931-1981 .... CANR-11
Obituary 105
Earlier sketch in CA 65-68
Abel, Robert H(alsall) 1941- 102
Abel, Theodora M(ead) 1899- 57-60
Abel, Theodore 1896- 23-24R
Abel, Wilhelm 1904- Brief entry 119
Abeles, Elvin 1907- 104
Abell, Arunah S. 1806-1888 .... DLB-43
Abell, George O(gden) 1927-1983 .... CANR-3
Obituary 111
Earlier sketch in CA 9-10R
Abell, Kathleen 1938- 49-52
See also SATA 9
Abell, Kjeld 1901-1961 Obituary 111
See also CLC 15
Abell, Ron(ald F.) 1932- 119
Abella, Alex 1950- 93-96
Abella, Irving (Martin) 1940- 49-52
Abels, Harriette S(heffer) 1926- 121
See also SATA 50
Abels, Jules 1913- 61-64
Abel-Smith, Brian 1926- CANR-9
Earlier sketch in CA 21-22R
Abelson, Philip Hauge 1913- Brief entry .. 107
Abelson, Raziel A(lter) 1921- CANR-6
Earlier sketch in CA 11-12R
Abelson, Robert P(aul) 1928- 41-44R
Abend, Norman A(nchel) 1931- 33-36R
Aber, William M(cKee) 1929- 57-60
Aberbach, Joel D(avid) 1940- CANR-20
Earlier sketch in CA 45-48
Abercrombie, Barbara (Mattes) 1939- 81-84
See also SATA 16
Abercrombie, Lascelles 1881-1938
Brief entry 112
See also DLB 19
Abercrombie, M(innie) L(ouie) J(ohnson)
1909(?)-1984 Obituary 115

Abercrombie, M. L. Johnson
 See Abercrombie, M(innie) L(ouie) J(ohnson)
Abercrombie, Michael 1912-1979
 Obituary 115
Abercrombie, Nigel J(ames) 1908-1986 101
 Obituary 118
Abercrombie, Stanley 1935- 117
Aberg, Sherrill E. 1924- 21-22R
Aberle, David F(riend) 1918- 21-22R
Aberle, John Wayne 1919- 1R
Aberle, Kathleen Gough 1925- CANR-5
 Earlier sketch in CA 13-14R
Abernathy, David M(yles) 1933- 53-56
Abernathy, (M.) Elton 1913- 17-18R
Abernathy, M(abra) Glenn 1921- 13-14R
Abernathy, William J(ackson) 1933-1983 93-96
 Obituary 111
Abernethy, Francis Edward 1925- CANR-8
 Earlier sketch in CA 21-22R
Abernethy, George Lawrence 1910- 2R
Abernethy, Peter L(ink) 1935- 69-72
Abernethy, Robert G(ordon) 1927- 21-22R
 See also SATA 5
Abernethy, Thomas Perkins 1890-1975 CAP-1
 Obituary 111
 Earlier sketch in CA 19-20
Abernethy, Virginia 1934- 93-96
Abert, Donald B. 1907-1985 Obituary 116
Abisch, Roslyn Kroop 1927- CANR-10
 Earlier sketch in CA 21-22R
 See also SATA 9
Abisch, Roz
 See Abisch, Roslyn Kroop
Abish, Walter 1931- 101
 See also CLC 22
Able, James A(ugustus), Jr. 1928- 93-96
Ableman, Paul 1927- CANR-12
 Earlier sketch in CA 61-64
Abler, Ronald F. 1939- CANR-4
 Earlier sketch in CA 53-56
Abler, Thomas S(truthers) 1941- 101
Abley, Mark 1955- 120
Abodaher, David J. (Naiph) 1919- CANR-10
 Earlier sketch in CA 17-18R
 See also SATA 17
Abolafia, Yossi SATA-46
Abrahall, Clare Hoskyns
 See Hoskyns-Abrahall, Clare (Constance Drury)
Abraham, Claude K(urt) 1931- 23-24R
Abraham, George 1915- 110
Abraham, Gerald Ernest Heal 1904-1988 89-92
 Obituary 125
Abraham, Henry Julian 1921- CANR-18
 Earlier sketches in CA 5-6R, CANR-2
Abraham, Katherine 1922- 110
Abraham, Katy
 See Abraham, Katherine
Abraham, Louis Arnold 1893-1983
 Obituary 108
Abraham, M(annamplakkal) Francis 1939- 110
Abraham, Willard 1916- CANR-5
 Earlier sketch in CA 13-14R
Abraham, William E. 1934- 13-14R
Abraham, William I(srael) 1919- 25-28R
Abrahami, Izzy 1930- Brief entry 110
Abrahamian, Ervand 1940- 110
Abrahams, Doris Caroline 1901(?)-1982(?) Obituary 108
Abrahams, Edward 1949- 122
Abrahams, Gerald 1907-1980 102
 Obituary 97-100
Abrahams, Hilary (Ruth) 1938- SATA-29
Abrahams, Howard Phineas 1904- 57-60
Abrahams, Peter (Henry) 1919- CANR-26
 Earlier sketch in CA 57-60
 See also BW
 See also CLC 4
Abrahams, R(aphael) G(arvin) 1934- 25-28R
Abrahams, Robert David 1905- CAP-2
 Earlier sketch in CA 33-36
 See also SATA 4
Abrahams, Roger D(avid) 1933- CANR-24
 Earlier sketches in CA 11-12R, CANR-5
Abrahams, William Miller 1919- 61-64
Abrahamsen, Christine Elizabeth 1916- 101
Abrahamsen, David 1903- 65-68
Abrahamson, Mark J. 1939- 101
Abrahamsson, Bengt 1937- 97-100
Abrahms, Sally (Ellen) 1953- 113
Abram, H(arry) S(hore) 1931-1977 29-32R
Abram, Morris Berthold 1918- 108
Abramov, Emil
 See Draitser, Emil
Abramov, Fyodor Aleksandrovich 1920-1983 Obituary 109
Abramov, S(hene'ur) Zalman 1908-
 Brief entry 108
Abramovitz, Anita (Zeltner Brooks) 1914- 97-100
Abramowitz, Jack 1918- CANR-6
 Earlier sketch in CA 7-8R
Abramowitz, Shalom Jacob 1835(?)-1917
 Brief entry 118
Abrams, Alan E(dwin) 1941- 89-92
Abrams, Charles 1901-1970 CAP-2
 Earlier sketch in CA 23-24
Abrams, George J(oseph) 1918-1978 CANR-12
 Earlier sketch in CA 61-64
Abrams, Harry N(athan) 1904-1979
 Obituary 93-96
Abrams, Joy 1941- 77-80
 See also SATA 16
Abrams, Lawrence F. 124
 See also SATA 47
Abrams, Linsey 1951- CANR-18
 Earlier sketch in CA 102
Abrams, M(eyer) H(oward) 1912- CANR-13
 Earlier sketch in CA 57-60
 See also DLB 67
 See also CLC 24
Abrams, Mark 1906- 124
Abrams, Peter D(avid) 1936- 33-36R
Abrams, Philip 1933(?)-1981 Obituary 105
Abrams, Richard M. 1932- 13-14R
Abrams, Sam(uel) 1935- 21-22R
Abramsky, Chimen 1916- Brief entry 109
Abramson, Doris E. 1925- 25-28R
Abramson, Harold Alexander 1889-1980
 Obituary 102
Abramson, Harold J(ulian) 1934- 45-48
Abramson, Jesse P. 1904-1979 Obituary 89-92
Abramson, Joan 1932- 25-28R
Abramson, Martin 1921- 49-52
Abramson, Michael 1944- 69-72
Abramson, Paul R(obert) 1937- CANR-8
 Earlier sketch in CA 61-64
Abrash, Merritt 1930- 23-24R
Abrashkin, Raymond 1911-1960 115
 See also SATA 50
Abravanel, Elizabeth 1944- 112
Abravanel, Elliot D(on) 1942- 112
Abrecht, Mary Ellen (Benson) 1945- 69-72
Abreu, Maria Isabel 1919- 45-48
Abruzzo, Ben(jamine Lawrence) 1930-1985 Obituary 115
Absalom, Roger Neil Lewis 1929- 111
Abse, Dannie 1923- CANR-4
 Earlier sketch in CA 53-56
 See also CAAS 1
 See also DLB 27
 See also CLC 7, 29
Abse, David Wilfred 1915- 49-52
Abse, Joan 1926- 108
Abshire, David M. 1926- CANR-8
 Earlier sketch in CA 23-24R
Abt, Clark C(laus) 1929- CANR-21
 Earlier sketch in CA 69-72
Abt, Lawrence Edwin 1915- CANR-13
 Earlier sketch in CA 33-36R
Abt, Vicki 1942- 120
Abu Jaber, Kamel S(aleh) 1932- CANR-14
 Earlier sketch in CA 21-22R
Abu-Lughod, Ibrahim Ali 1929- CANR-10
 Earlier sketch in CA 5-6R
Abu-Lughod, Janet L(ouise) 1928- CANR-10
 Earlier sketch in CA 65-68
Abun-Nasr, Jamil Miri 1932- 69-72
Aby, Stephen H. 1949- 123
Abzug, Bella (Savitzky) 1920- Brief entry 104
Abzug, Martin 1916-1986 Obituary 119
Abzug, Robert H(enry) 1945- CANR-21
 Earlier sketch in CA 104
Academicas Mentor
 See Montagu, Ashley
Academic Investor
 See Reddaway, W(illiam) Brian
Accola, Louis W(ayne) 1937- CANR-12
 Earlier sketch in CA 29-32R
Ace, Goodman 1899-1982 61-64
 Obituary 106
Aceto, Vincent J(ohn) 1932- 106
Achard, George
 See Torres-Levin, Tereska (Szwarc)
Achard, Marcel
 See Ferreol, Marcel Auguste
Achebe, (Albert) Chinua(lumogu) 1930- CANR-26
 Earlier sketches in CA 4R, CANR-6
 See also BW
 See also SATA 38, 40
 See also CLC 1, 3, 5, 7, 11, 26
Achenbaum, W(ilbert) Andrew 1947- CANR-15
 Earlier sketch in CA 89-92
Acheson, Dean (Gooderham) 1893-1971 CAP-2
 Obituary 33-36R
 Earlier sketch in CA 25-28
Acheson, Patricia Castles 1924- 3R
Achilles
 See Lamb, Charles Bentall
Achinstein, Peter Jacob 1935- 111
Achtemeier, Elizabeth (Rice) 1926- CANR-8
 Earlier sketch in CA 17-18R
Achtemeier, Paul J(ohn) 1927- CANR-8
 Earlier sketch in CA 17-18R
Achyut
 See Birla, Lakshminiwas
Ackart, Robert 1921- 109
Acker, Alison 1928- 125
Acker, Duane Calvin 1931- 33-36R
Acker, Helen 73-76
Acker, Kathy 1948- 122
 Brief entry 117
 See also CLC 45
Acker, Robert Flint 1920- 89-92
Acker, William R. B. 1910(?)-1974
 Obituary 49-52
Ackerley, J(oe) R(andolph) 1896-1967 102
 Obituary 89-92
Ackerman, Bruce A. 1943- CANR-4
 Earlier sketch in CA 53-56
Ackerman, Carl W(illiam) 1890-1970 73-76
 Obituary 29-32R
Ackerman, Diane 1948- 57-60
Ackerman, Edward A. 1911-1973
 Obituary 41-44R
Ackerman, Eugene (Francis) 1888-1974 SATA-10
Ackerman, Forrest J(ames) 1916- 102
Ackerman, Gerald M(artin) 1928- CANR-1
 Earlier sketch in CA 45-48
Ackerman, J. Mark 1939- 53-56
Ackerman, James S(loss) 1919- 9-10R
Ackerman, Nathan W(ard) 1908-1971 CAP-2
 Earlier sketch in CA 29-32
Ackerman, Robert E(dwin) 1928- CANR-20
 Earlier sketch in CA 45-48
Ackerman, Robert K. 1933- 123
Ackerman, Robert W(illiam) 1910-1980 103
Ackerman, Susan Rose
 See Rose-Ackerman, Susan
Ackermann, Paul Kurt 1919- Brief entry 104
Ackermann, Robert John 1933-
 Brief entry 108
Ackerson, Duane (Wright, Jr.) 1942- 33-36R
Ackland, Rodney 1908- 57-60
Ackley, Charles Walton 1913-1975 41-44R
Ackley, Hugh Gardner 1915- 61-64
Ackley, Randall William 1931- CANR-6
 Earlier sketch in CA 53-56
Ackoff, Russell L(incoln) 1919- CANR-15
 Earlier sketch in CA 41-44R
Ackroyd, Joyce Irene 103
Ackroyd, Peter 1949- Brief entry 123
 See also CLC 34
Ackroyd, Peter R(unham) 1917- 25-28R
Ackworth, Robert Charles 1923- 5-6R
Acland, Alice
 See Wignall, Anne
Acland, James H. 1917-1976 41-44R
Acomb, Evelyn Martha
 See Acomb-Walker, Evelyn
Acomb, Frances (Dorothy) 1907-
 Brief entry 109
Acomb-Walker, Evelyn 1910- 85-88
Acorn, Milton 1923- 103
 See also DLB 53
 See also CLC 15
Acquaviva, Sabino Samele 1927- 101
Acquaye, Alfred Allotey 1939- 25-28R
Acre, Stephen
 See Gruber, Frank
Acred, Arthur 1926- 25-28R
Acs, Laszlo (Bela) 1931- SATA-32, 42
Acton, Edward J. 1949- CANR-2
 Earlier sketch in CA 45-48
Acton, Harold Mario Mitchell 1904- CANR-3
 Earlier sketch in CA 4R
Acton, Jay
 See Acton, Edward J.
Acton, Thomas (Alan) 1948- 57-60
Acuff, Frederick Gene 1931- Brief entry 110
Acuff, Selma Boyd 1924- 111
 See also SATA 45
Acuna, Rodolfo 1932- Brief entry 108
Acuna, Rudy
 See Acuna, Rudolfo
Aczel, Tamas 1921- 49-52
Ada, Alma Flor 1938- 123
 See also SATA 43
Adachi, Barbara (Curtis) 1924- 49-52
Adair, Cecil
 See Everett-Green, Evelyn
Adair, Dennis 1945- 107
Adair, Ian 1942- CANR-11
 Earlier sketch in CA 69-72
 See also SATA 53
Adair, Jack
 See Pavey, Don
Adair, James 1709(?)-1783(?) DLB-30
Adair, James R. 1923- 19-20R
Adair, John G(lenn) 1933- 49-52
Adair, Margaret Weeks ?-1971 CAP-1
 Earlier sketch in CA 13-14
 See also SATA 10
Adam, Ben
 See Drachman, Julian M(oses)
Adam, Cornel
 See Lengyel, Cornel Adam
Adam, Helen 1909- CANR-7
 Earlier sketch in CA 19-20R
Adam, Heribert 1936- 105
Adam, Jan 1920- 115
Adam, Michael 1919- 53-56
Adam, Ruth (Augusta) 1907- 23-24R
Adam, Thomas R(itchie) 1900- CAP-1
 Earlier sketch in CA 19-20
Adamczewski, Zygmunt 1921- 15-16R
Adamec, Ludwig W(arren) 1924- CANR-24
 Earlier sketches in CA 23-24R, CANR-9
Adamic, Alojzij 1899(?)-1951 Brief entry 109
Adamic, Louis
 See Adamic, Alojzij
 See also DLB 9
Adamov, Arthur 1908-1970 CAP-2
 Obituary 25-28R
 Earlier sketch in CA 17-18
 See also CLC 4, 25
Adams, A. Don
 See Cleveland, Philip Jerome
Adams, A. John 1931- 33-36R
Adams, Adrienne 1906- CANR-1
 Earlier sketch in CA 49-52
 See also SATA 8
Adams, Alexander B. 1917(?)-1984
 Obituary 112
Adams, Alice (Boyd) 1926- CANR-26
 Earlier sketch in CA 81-84
 See also DLBY 86
 See also CLC 6, 13, 46
Adams, Andy 1859-1935 YABC-1
Adams, Andy
 See Gibson, Walter B(rown)
Adams, Anne H(utchinson) 1935-1980 41-44R
Adams, Annette
 See Rowland, D(onald) S(ydney)
Adams, Ansel (Easton) 1902-1984 CANR-10
 Obituary 112
 Earlier sketch in CA 21-22R
 See also AITN 1
Adams, Arthur E(ugene) 1917- CANR-4
 Earlier sketch in CA 7-8R
Adams, Arthur Gray (Jr.) 1935- CANR-23
 Earlier sketch in CA 107
Adams, Arthur Merrihew 1908- 53-56
Adams, Arthur Stanton 1896-1980
 Obituary 102
Adams, Barbara
 See Gardner, Virginia (Marberry)
Adams, Bart
 See Bingley, David Ernest
Adams, Betsy
 See Pitcher, Gladys
Adams, Brooks 1848-1927 Brief entry 123
 See also DLB 47
Adams, Bruin
 See Ellis, Edward S(ylvester)
Adams, Captain Bruin
 See Ellis, Edward S(ylvester)
Adams, Captain J. F. C.
 See Ellis, Edward S(ylvester)
Adams, Cedric M. 1902-1961 Obituary 89-92
Adams, Charles Francis, Jr. 1835-1915
 Brief entry 113
 See also DLB 47
Adams, Charles J(oseph) 1924- CANR-24
 Earlier sketches in CA 17-18R, CANR-8
Adams, Charles Lynford 1929- 113
Adams, Charlotte 1899- Brief entry 107
Adams, Christopher
 See Hopkins, (Hector) Kenneth
Adams, Christopher
 See Hopkins, Kenneth
Adams, Chuck
 See Tubb, E(dwin) C(harles)
Adams, Cindy CANR-17
 Earlier sketch in CA 23-24R
Adams, Cleve F(ranklin) 1895-1949
 Brief entry 112
Adams, Clifton 1919- CANR-21
 Earlier sketch in CA 13-14R
Adams, Clinton 1918- 33-36R
Adams, Dale
 See Quinn, Elisabeth
Adams, Don(ald Kendrick) 1925- 33-36R
Adams, Donald K(napp) 1924-1987
 Obituary 123
 Brief entry 111
Adams, Donald R., Jr. 1940- Brief entry 113
Adams, Douglas Noel 1952- 106
 See also DLBY 83
 See also CLC 27
Adams, E(lie) M(aynard) 1919- 3R
Adams, Edith
 See Shine, Deborah
Adams, Elsie B(onita) 1932- 69-72
Adams, Eugenia
 See Owens, Virginia Stem
Adams, Evangeline (Smith) 1872(?)-1932
 Brief entry 121
Adams, F(rank) Ramsay 1883-1963 7-8R
Adams, Faith 1960- 121
Adams, Florence 1932- 49-52
Adams, Francis A(lexandre) 1874-1975
 Obituary 61-64
Adams, Frank C(lyde) 1916- 69-72
Adams, Franklin P(ierce) 1881-1960
 Obituary 93-96
 See also DLB 29
Adams, Frederick C(harles) 1941-
 Brief entry 105
Adams, George Matthew 1878-1962
 Obituary 93-96
Adams, George Worthington 1905- 41-44R
Adams, Georgia Sachs 1913- 37-40R
Adams, Glenda 1939- 104
Adams, Graham, Jr. 1928- 17-18R
Adams, Harlen M(artin) 1904- CAP-1
 Earlier sketch in CA 13-14
Adams, Harold 1923- 126
Adams, Harriet S(tratemeyer) 1892(?)-1982 19-20R
 Obituary 106
 See also SATA 1, 29
 See also AITN 2
Adams, Harrison CANR-26
 Earlier sketches in CA 19-20, CAP-2
Adams, Harry Baker 1924- Brief entry 106
Adams, Hazard 1926- 9-10R
 See also SATA 6
Adams, Henry (Brooks) 1838-1918
 Brief entry 104
 See also DLB 12, 47
 See also TCLC 4
Adams, Henry H(itch) 1917- CANR-13
 Earlier sketch in CA 21-22R
Adams, Henry Mason 1907- CAP-1
 Earlier sketch in CA 17-18
Adams, Henry T.
 See Ransom, Jay Ellis
Adams, Herbert Baxter 1850-1901 DLB-47
Adams, Herbert Mayow 1893-1985 CAP-2
 Obituary 115
 Earlier sketch in CA 25-28
Adams, Howard (Joseph) 1928- 89-92
Adams, J(ames) Donald 1891-1968 CANR-1
 Earlier sketch in CA 2R
Adams, J(ames) Mack 1933- 85-88
Adams, James E(dward) 1941- 73-76
Adams, James F(rederick) 1927- 19-20R
Adams, James Luther 1901- 41-44R
Adams, James R(owe) 1934- 41-44R

Adams, James Truslow 1878-1949
Brief entry 115
See also DLB 17
Adams, Jane (Ellen) 1940- 116
Adams, Jay Edward 1929- 126
Brief entry 108
Adams, Joey 1911- CANR-1
Earlier sketch in CA 49-52
Adams, John 1734-1826 .... DLB-31
Adams, John 1938- 111
Adams, John Clarke 1910- 3R
Adams, John Coldwell 1927- 121
Adams, John Cranford 1903-1986
Obituary 121
Adams, John D(avid) 1942- 115
Adams, John F(estus) 1930- 33-36R
Adams, John M(ilton) 1905-1981 107
Adams, John P. 1923(?)-1983 122
Obituary 111
Adams, John Paul
See Kinnaird, Clark
Adams, John Quincy 1767-1848 .... DLB-37
Adams, John R. 1900- 25-28R
Adams, Julian 1919- CANR-11
Earlier sketch in CA 25-28R
Adams, Justin
See Cameron, Lou
Adams, Kenneth Menzies 1922- 103
Adams, Kramer A. 1920- 11-12R
Adams, L(ouis) Jerold 1939- 49-52
Adams, Laura 1943- 53-56
Adams, Laurie 1941- 53-56
See also SATA 33
Adams, Lee (Richard) 1924- Brief entry 111
Adams, Leon D(avid) 1905- 45-48
Adams, Leonie (Fuller) 1899-1988 .... CAP-1
Obituary 125
Earlier sketch in CA 9-10
See also DLB 48
Adams, Les 1934- 97-100
Adams, Lowell
See Joseph, James (Herz)
Adams, Marion 1932- 41-44R
Adams, Mary (Grace Agnes) 1898-1984
Obituary 113
Adams, Maurice 1915(?)-1985 Obituary 116
Adams, Michael (Evelyn) 1920- 33-36R
Adams, Michael C(harles) C(orringham)
1945- 89-92
Adams, Mildred
See Kenyon, Mildred Adams
Adams, Nancy 1943(?)-1987 Obituary 123
Adams, Nathan Miller 1934- 45-48
Adams, Norman (Edward Albert) 1927- 114
Adams, Paul L(ieber) 1924- 61-64
Adams, Percy G(uy) 1914- CANR-4
Earlier sketch in CA 4R
Adams, Perseus 1933- 107
Adams, Philip R. 1908- 85-88
Adams, Phoebe-Lou 1918- 125
Brief entry 121
Adams, Rachel Leona White 1905(?)-1979
Obituary 93-96
Adams, Ramon Frederick 1889-1976
Obituary 65-68
Adams, Ramona Shepherd 1921- 106
Adams, Richard (George) 1920- CANR-3
Earlier sketch in CA 49-52
See also SATA 7
See also CLC 4, 5, 18
See also AITN 1, 2
Adams, Richard E(dward) W(ood) 1931- 106
Adams, Richard N(ewbold) 1924- CANR-12
Earlier sketch in CA 29-32R
Adams, Richard P(errill) 1917-1977 .... CAP-2
Obituary 69-72
Earlier sketch in CA 33-36
Adams, Robert (Franklin) 1932- 69-72
Adams, Robert H(ickman) 1937- CANR-22
Earlier sketch in CA 105
Adams, Robert Martin 1915- CANR-4
Earlier sketch in CA 5-6R
Adams, Robert McCormick 1926- CANR-12
Earlier sketch in CA 61-64
Adams, Robert P. 1910- 13-14R
Adams, Rolland Leroy 1905(?)-1979
Obituary 89-92
Adams, Russell B(aird), Jr. 1937- 69-72
Adams, Russell L. 1930- 53-56
Adams, Ruth Joyce SATA-14
Adams, Sally Pepper ?-197(?) 41-44R
Adams, Sam 1934- 57-60
Adams, Samuel 1722-1803 .... DLB-31, 43
Adams, Samuel A. 1933(?)-1988 Obituary 126
Adams, Sexton 1936- 25-28R
Adams, (Llewellyn) Sherman 1899-1986
Obituary 120
Adams, Stephen J(on) 1945- 111
Adams, T(homas) W(illiam) 1933- 25-28R
Adams, Terrence Dean 1935- 33-36R
Adams, Theodore Floyd 1898-1980 .... CAP-1
Obituary 97-100
Earlier sketch in CA 11-12
Adams, Thomas Boylston 1910- 114
Adams, Thomas F. 1927- 15-16R
Adams, Thomas Randolph 1921- 107
Adams, Tricia
See Kite, Pat
Adams, Val 1917(?)-1983 Obituary 109
Adams, Walter 1922- CANR-3
Earlier sketch in CA 2R
Adams, Willi Paul 1940- 105
Adams, William Howard Brief entry 105
Adams, William Taylor 1822-1897 .... SATA-28
See also DLB 42
Adams, William Yewdale 1927- Brief entry 104
Adamski, George 1891-1965 Obituary 112
Adam Smith, Janet (Buchanan) 1905- 113
Adam-Smith, Patricia Jean 1926- 105
Adam-Smith, Patsy
See Adam-Smith, Patricia Jean
Adamson, Alan (Herbert) 1919- 81-84
Adamson, David Grant 1927- 15-16R
Adamson, Donald 1939- 53-56
Adamson, Ed(ward Joseph) 1915(?)-1972
Obituary 37-40R
Adamson, Frank
See Adams, Robert (Franklin)
Adamson, Gareth 1925-1982(?) CANR-11
Obituary 106
Earlier sketch in CA 13-14R
See also SATA 30, 46
Adamson, George Worsley 1913- 107
See also SATA 30
Adamson, Graham
See Groom, Arthur William
Adamson, Hans Christian 1890-1968 .... 5-6R
Adamson, Joe
See Adamson, Joseph III
Adamson, Joseph III 1945- CANR-21
Earlier sketches in CA 45-48, CANR-1
Adamson, Joy(-Friederike Victoria)
1910-1980 .... CANR-22
Obituary 93-96
Earlier sketch in CA 69-72
See also SATA 11, 22
See also CLC 17
Adamson, Lesley
See Grant-Adamson, Lesley
Adamson, Walter L(uiz) 1946- 107
Adamson, Wendy Writson 1942- 53-56
See also SATA 22
Adamson, William Robert 1927- 23-24R
Adas, Michael 1943- 53-56
Adastra
See Mirepoix, Camille
Adburgham, Alison Haig 1912- CAP-1
Earlier sketch in CA 9-10
Adcock, Almey St. John 1894- 65-68
Adcock, Betty
See Adcock, Elizabeth S(harp)
Adcock, C(yril) John 1904- CAP-1
Earlier sketch in CA 19-20
Adcock, Elizabeth S(harp) 1938- 57-60
Adcock, Fleur 1934- CANR-11
Earlier sketch in CA 25-28R
See also DLB 40
See also CLC 41
Adcock, Frank Ezra 1886-1968 Obituary 106
Addams, Charles (Samuel) 1912-1988 .... CANR-12
Obituary 126
Earlier sketch in CA 61-64
See also CLC 30
Addanki, Sam 1932- 109
Adde, Leo 1927(?)-1975 Obituary 57-60
Addeo, Jovita A. 1939- 103
Addie, Bob 1911(?)-1982 Obituary 105
Addie, Pauline Betz 1919(?)- Brief entry 105
Addington, Arthur Charles 1939- 105
Addington, Larry H(olbrook) 1932- 33-36R
Addison, Gwen
See Harris, Al(fred)
Addison, Herbert 1889-1982 Obituary 108
Addison, Lloyd 1937- 45-48
Addison, William Wilkinson 1905- CANR-5
Earlier sketch in CA 13-14R
Addiss, Stephen 1935- 120
Addleshaw, George William Outram
1907(?)-1982 Obituary 107
Addona, Angelo F. 1925- 25-28R
See also SATA 14
Addy, George M(ilton) 1927- 21-22R
Addy, John 1915- 69-72
Addy, Ted
See Winterbotham, R(ussell) R(obert)
Ade, George 1866-1944 Brief entry 110
See also DLB 11, 25
Ade, Walter Frank Charles 1910- 53-56
Adelberg, Doris
See Orgel, Doris
Adelberg, Roy P. 1928- 17-18R
Adeler, Max
See Clark, Charles Heber
Adelman, Bob 1930- 69-72
Adelman, Clifford 1942- 41-44R
Adelman, Gary 1935- 33-36R
Adelman, Howard 1938- 25-28R
Adelman, Irma Glicman CANR-3
Earlier sketch in CA 5-6R
Adelman, Irving 1926- 21-22R
Adelman, Janet (Ann) 1941- 61-64
Adelman, M(orris) A(lbert) 1917- 126
Brief entry 104
Adelman, Saul J(oseph) 1944- 104
Adelmann, Frederick J(oseph) 1915- 49-52
Adelsberger, Lucie 1895-1971 Obituary 33-36R
Adelson, Daniel 1918- 69-72
Adelson, Joseph (Bernard) 1925- 19-20R
Adelson, Leone 1908- 61-64
See also SATA 11
Adelson, Sandra 1934- 105
Adelstein, Michael E. 1922- CANR-15
Earlier sketch in CA 33-36R
Aden, John M(ichael) 1918- 97-100
Adenauer, Konrad 1876-1967 Obituary 112
Adeney, David Howard 1911- 53-56
Ader, Paul (Fassett) 1919- 65-68
Aderman, Ralph M(erl) 1919- 5-6R
Ades, Dawn 1943- 103
Adiseshiah, Malcolm S(athianathan)
1910- 81-84
Adizes, Ichak 1937- 33-36R
Adkins, Arthur W(illiam) H(ope) 1929- 111
Brief entry 104
Adkins, Cecil (Dale) 1932- 115
Adkins, Dorothy C.
See Wood, Dorothy Adkins
Adkins, Jan 1944- 33-36R
See also SATA 8
See also CLR 7
Adkins, Nelson F(rederick) 1897-1976 73-76
Obituary 65-68
Adkins, Patrick H. 1948- 126
Adlard, John 1929- CANR-21
Earlier sketches in CA 57-60, CANR-6
Adlard, (P.) Mark 1932- 65-68
Adleman, Robert H. 1919- 25-28R
Adler, Alfred (F.) 1870-1937 Brief entry 119
Adler, B.
See Adler, William
Adler, Betty 1918-1973 .... CAP-1
Earlier sketch in CA 13-14
Adler, Bill
See Adler, William
Adler, C(arole) S(chwerdtfeger) 1932- CANR-19
Earlier sketch in CA 89-92
See also SATA 26
See also CLC 35
Adler, Carol 1938- 61-64
Adler, Christopher Edward 1954(?)-1984
Obituary 114
Adler, Cyrus 1863-1940 Brief entry 122
Adler, David A. 1947- CANR-23
Earlier sketches in CA 57-60, CANR-7
See also SATA 14
Adler, Denise Rinker 1908- 102
Adler, Elmer 1884-1962 Obituary 89-92
Adler, France-Michele 1942- 105
Adler, Freda 1934- CANR-11
Earlier sketch in CA 69-72
Adler, H. G. 1910- CANR-10
Earlier sketch in CA 25-28R
Adler, Hans A(rnold) 1921- 49-52
Adler, Helmut E(rnest) 1920- 33-36R
Adler, Irene
See Penzler, Otto
and Storr, Catherine (Cole)
Adler, Irving 1913- CANR-2
Earlier sketch in CA 7-8R
See also SATA 1, 29
Adler, Jack 73-76
Adler, Jacob 1873(?)-1974 Obituary 53-56
Adler, Jacob 1913- 17-18R
Adler, Jacob H(enry) 1919- 15-16R
Adler, John Hans 1912-1980 Obituary 97-100
Adler, Kathleen
See Jones, Kathleen Eve
Adler, Larry 1939- 105
See also SATA 36
Adler, Lucile 1922- 105
Adler, Lulla
See Rosenfeld, Lulla
Adler, Manfred 1936- 49-52
Adler, Margot 1946- 107
Adler, Max K(urt) 1905- CANR-3
Earlier sketch in CA 9-10R
Adler, Mortimer J(erome) 1902- CANR-7
Earlier sketch in CA 65-68
Adler, Norman Tenner 1941- CANR-20
Earlier sketch in CA 69-72
Adler, Peggy SATA-22
Adler, Renata 1938- CANR-22
Earlier sketches in CA 49-52, CANR-5
See also CLC 8, 31
Adler, Ruth 1915-1968 .... CANR-4
Obituary 25-28R
Earlier sketch in CA 7-8R
See also SATA 1
Adler, Selig 1909-1984 .... 7-8R
Obituary 114
Adler, Sol 1925- CANR-22
Earlier sketches in CA 19-20R, CANR-7
Adler, Warren 1927- CANR-11
Earlier sketch in CA 69-72
Adler, William 1929- CANR-7
Earlier sketch in CA 11-12R
Adler, William 1951- 124
Adlerblum, Nina H. 1882-1974 Obituary 49-52
Adoff, Arnold 1935- CANR-20
Earlier sketch in CA 41-44R
See also SATA 5
See also CLR 7
See also AITN 1
Adolph, E. F.
See Adolph, Edward F(rederick)
Adolph, Edward F(rederick) 1895-1986
Obituary 121
Adomeit, Ruth E(lizabeth) 1910- 111
Adon, Aaron Bar
See Bar-Adon, Aaron
Adony, Raoul
See Launay, Andre (Joseph)
Adorjan, Carol (Madden) 1934- CANR-14
Earlier sketch in CA 41-44R
See also SATA 10
Adorno, Theodor W(iesengrund)
1903-1969 89-92
Obituary 25-28R
Adrian, Arthur A(llen) 1906- CAP-2
Earlier sketch in CA 19-20
Adrian, Charles R. 1922- CANR-3
Earlier sketch in CA 2R
Adrian, Edgar Douglas 1889-1977
Obituary 73-76
Adrian, Mary
See Jorgensen, Mary Venn
Adrian, Rhys Brief entry 106
Adshead, Gladys L(ucy) 1896- 29-32R
See also SATA 3
Advani, Rukun 1955- 119
Ady, Endre 1877-1919 Brief entry 107
See also TCLC 11
Ady, Ronald W(illiam) 1934- 117
Adytum
See Curl, James Stevens
Adzigian, Denise Allard 1952- 97-100
Aebi, Ormond 1916- 89-92
Aeby, Jacquelyn CANR-24
Earlier sketch in CA 29-32R
Aero, Rita 112
Aers, David 1946- CANR-8
Earlier sketch in CA 61-64
Aeschliman, Michael D(avid) 1948- 113
Aesop 620(?)-564(?) B.C. CLR-14
Aesop, Abraham
See Newbery, John
Affabee, Eric
See Stine, R(obert) L(awrence)
Affron, Charles 1935- 21-22R
Afnan, Ruhi Muhsen 1899-1971 .... CAP-2
Earlier sketch in CA 29-32
Africa, Thomas Wilson 1927- 17-18R
Africano, Lillian 1935- CANR-11
Earlier sketch in CA 69-72
Aftel, Mandy 1948- 108
Afterman, Allen 1941- 103
Afton, Effie
See Harper, Frances Ellen Watkins
Agan, Patrick 1943- CANR-10
Earlier sketch in CA 65-68
Agan, Raymond J(ohn) 1919- 33-36R
Agan, (Anna) Tessie 1897- CAP-1
Earlier sketch in CA 17-18
Agapida, Fray Antonio
See Irving, Washington
Agar, Brian
See Ballard, (Willis) Todhunter
Agar, Herbert (Sebastian) 1897-1980 65-68
Obituary 102
Agar, Michael H(enry) 1945- CANR-2
Earlier sketch in CA 45-48
Agar, William (Macdonough) 1894-1972
Obituary 37-40R
Agard, H. E.
See Evans, Hilary
Agard, Nadema 1948- SATA-18
Agarossi, Elena 1940- CANR-20
Earlier sketch in CA 97-100
Agarwala, Amar N. 1917- CANR-13
Earlier sketch in CA 23-24R
Agassi, Joseph 1927- CANR-15
Earlier sketch in CA 41-44R
Agassiz, Jean Louis Rodolphe
1807-1873 .... DLB-1
Agay, Denes 1911- 69-72
Agbodeka, Francis 1931- CANR-4
Earlier sketch in CA 53-56
Agee, James (Rufus) 1909-1955
Brief entry 108
See also DLB 2, 26
See also CDALB 1941-1968
See also TCLC 1, 19
See also AITN 1
Agee, Joel 1940- Brief entry 105
Agee, Philip 1935- Brief entry 104
Agee, Warren Kendall 1916- 17-18R
Ager, Cecelia 1902-1981 Obituary 103
Ager, Derek Victor 1923- 107
Ageton, Arthur Ainsley 1900-1971 .... CANR-1
Obituary 29-32R
Earlier sketch in CA 3R
Aggeler, Geoffrey D(onovan) 1939- 97-100
Aggertt, Otis J. 1916-1973 .... 33-36R
Aghill, Gordon
See Silverberg, Robert
Aginsky, Bernard W(illard) 1905- 85-88
Aginsky, Burt W.
See Aginsky, Bernard W(illard)
Aginsky, Ethel G(oldberg) 1910- 41-44R
Agle, Nan Hayden 1905- CANR-3
Earlier sketch in CA 4R
See also SATA 3
Agnelli, Susanna 1922- 109
Agnew, Edith J(osephine) 1897- CAP-1
Earlier sketch in CA 17-18
See also SATA 11
Agnew, James Barron 1930- 89-92
Agnew, Patience McCormick-Goodhart
1913(?)-1976 Obituary 69-72
Agnew, Peter L(awrence) 1901-1969 .... CAP-2
Earlier sketch in CA 21-22
Agnew, Spiro T(heodore) 1918-
Brief entry 110
Agniel, Lucien D. 1919- 29-32R
Agnon, S(hmuel) Y(osef Halevi)
1888-1970 .... CAP-2
Obituary 25-28R
Earlier sketch in CA 17-18
See also CLC 4, 8, 14
Agonito, Rosemary (Giambattista) 1937- 122
Brief entry 112
Agor, Weston H(arris) 1939- 49-52
Agostinelli, Maria Enrica 1929- 33-36R
Agranoff, Robert 1936- CANR-14
Earlier sketch in CA 37-40R
Agree, Rose H. 1913- 21-22R
Agress, Hyman 1931- 89-92
Agress, Lynne 1941- 112
Agresto, John 1946- 115
Agronsky, Martin (Zama) 1915- 109
See also AITN 2
Aguero, Kathleen 1949- 73-76
Aguila, Pancho 1945- 105
Aguilar, Luis E. 1926- 23-24R
Aguilar, Rodolfo J(esus) 1936- 53-56
Aguilera, Donna Conant 37-40R

INDEX

Aguilera, Jaime Roldos
See Roldos Aguilera, Jaime
Aguilera Malta, Demetrio 1909- 124
Brief entry 111
Aguolu, Christian Chukwunedu 1940- CANR-19
Earlier sketch in CA 101
Agus, Irving A(braham) 1910-1984 CAP-2
Obituary 113
Earlier sketch in CA 33-36
Agus, Jacob Bernard 1911-1986 CANR-2
Obituary 120
Earlier sketch in CA 7-8R
Aguzzi-Barbagli, Danilo 1924- 49-52
Agwani, Mohammed Shafi 1928- CANR-7
Earlier sketch in CA 17-18R
Aharoni, Yohanan 1919-1976 CANR-15
Earlier sketch in CA 25-28R
Ahearn, Barry 1950- 110
Ahearn, Catherine 1949- 114
Ahern, Barnabas M. 1915- CANR-3
Earlier sketch in CA 7-8R
Ahern, James F(rancis) 1932-1986 41-44R
Obituary 118
Ahern, John F(rancis) 1936- 61-64
Ahern, Margaret McCrohan 1921- 15-16R
See also SATA 10
Ahern, Thomas Francis 1947- CANR-21
Earlier sketches in CA 45-48, CANR-1
Ahern, Tim(othy James) 1952- 115
Ahern, Tom
See Ahern, Thomas Francis
Aherne, Brian (de Lacy) 1902-1986
Obituary 118
Brief entry 117
Aherne, Owen
See Cassill, R(onald) V(erlin)
Ahern Emily M(artin)
See Martin, Emily
Ahituv, Niv 1943- 117
Ahl, Anna Maria 1926- SATA-32
Ahl, Frederick Michael 1941- 111
Ahlberg, Allan 1938- 114
Brief entry 111
See also SATA 35
Ahlberg, Janet 1944- 114
Brief entry 111
See also SATA 32
Ahlberg, William A. 1922(?)-1985
Obituary 116
Ahlborn, Richard Eighme 1933- 108
Ahlers, John C(larke) 1927-1983 Obituary 110
Ahlert, Richard 1921-1985 Obituary 117
Ahlstroem, G(oesta) W(erner) 1918- CANR-21
Earlier sketch in CA 45-48
Ahlstrom, G(osta) W(erner)
See Ahlstroem, G(oesta) W(erner)
Ahlstrom, Sydney E(ckman) 1919-1984 21-22R
Obituary 113
Ahmad, Ishtiaq 1937- 53-56
Ahmad, Nafis 1913- 17-18R
Ahmad, Suleiman M(uhammad) 1943- 110
Ahmann, Mathew H(all) 1931- 9-10R
Ahnebrink, Lars 1915- 5-6R
Ahnstrom, D(oris) N. 1915- 7-8R
Aho, James (Alfred) 1942- 107
Ahokas, Jaakko (Alfred) 1923- 65-68
Ahrari, Mohammed E. 1945- 120
Ahsen, Akhter 1931- CANR-25
Earlier sketches in CA 61-64, CANR-10
Ahuja, Savitri 1924- 112
Ai 1947- 85-88
See also CLC 4, 14
Aichinger, Helga 1937- CANR-19
Earlier sketch in CA 25-28R
See also SATA 4
Aichinger, Ilse 1921- 85-88
Aichinger, Peter 1933- CANR-11
Earlier sketch in CA 61-64
Aickman, Robert (Fordyce) 1914- CANR-3
Earlier sketch in CA 7-8R
Aidala, Thomas R(ichard) 1933-
Brief entry 112
Aidenoff, Abraham 1913-1976 37-40R
Obituary 61-64
Aidoo, (Christina) Ama Ata 1942- 101
See also BW
Aiguillette
See Hargreaves, Reginald (Charles)
Aiken, Clarissa Lorenz 1899- CAP-2
Earlier sketch in CA 21-22
See also SATA 12
Aiken, Conrad (Potter) 1889-1973 CANR-4
Obituary 45-48
Earlier sketch in CA 5-6R
See also SATA 3, 30
See also DLB 9, 45
See also CLC 1, 3, 5, 10
Aiken, George D(avid) 1892-1984
Obituary 114
Brief entry 111
Aiken, Henry David 1912-1982 CANR-1
Obituary 106
Earlier sketch in CA 4R
Aiken, Irene (Nixon) 93-96
Aiken, Joan (Delano) 1924- CANR-23
Earlier sketches in CA 9-10R, CANR-4
See also SATA 2, 30
See also SAAS 1
See also CLC 35
See also CLR 1
Aiken, John (Kempton) 1913- 101
Aiken, John R(obert) 1927- 33-36R
Aiken, Lewis R(oscoe), Jr. 1931- CANR-10
Earlier sketch in CA 25-28R
Aiken, Maurice C. 1909(?)-1983 Obituary 109
Aiken, Michael Thomas 1932- CANR-9
Earlier sketch in CA 21-22R
Aikin, Charles 1901- 7-8R
Aikman, Ann
See McQuade, Ann Aikman
Aikman, David (B. T.) 1944- 65-68
Aikman, Lonnelle (Davison) 1901(?)-1986
Obituary 121
Aimes, Angelica 1943- CANR-14
Earlier sketch in CA 81-84
Ainsbury, Ray
See Paine, Lauran (Bosworth)
and Verrill, A(lphues) Hyatt
Ainsbury, Roy
See Paine, Lauran (Bosworth)
Ainslie, Rosalynde 1932- 25-28R
Ainslie, Tom
See Carter, Richard
Ainsworth, Charles H(arold) 1935- 49-52
Ainsworth, Dorothy Sears 1894-1976
Obituary 69-72
Ainsworth, Ed(ward Maddin)
1902-1968 CANR-4
Earlier sketch in CA 5-6R
Ainsworth, G(eoffrey) C(lough) 1905- 73-76
Ainsworth, Harriet
See Cadell, (Violet) Elizabeth
Ainsworth, Katherine 1908- 29-32R
Ainsworth, Mary D(insmore) Salter
1913- CANR-8
Earlier sketch in CA 21-22R
Ainsworth, Norma CANR-5
Earlier sketch in CA 15-16R
See also SATA 9
Ainsworth, Patricia
See Bigg, Patricia Nina
Ainsworth, Ray
See Paine, Lauran (Bosworth)
Ainsworth, Roy
See Paine, Lauran (Bosworth)
Ainsworth, Ruth
See Gilbert, Ruth Gallard Ainsworth
See also SATA 7
Ainsworth, Thomas Hargraves, Jr. 1920- 123
Ainsworth, William Harrison
1805-1882 SATA-24
See also DLB 21
Ainsztein, Reuben 1917-1981 110
Obituary 108
Air Chief Marshal Lord Dowding
See Dowding, Hugh Caswell Tremenheere
Aird, Catherine
See McIntosh, Kinn Hamilton
Aird, Eileen M(argaret) 1945- 49-52
Airlie, Catherine
See MacLeod, Jean Sutherland
Airola, Paavo (Olavi) 1915- 81-84
Aislin
See Mosher, (Christopher) Terry
Aistis, Jonas 1908(?)-1973 Obituary 41-44R
Aistrop, Jack 1916- CANR-3
Earlier sketch in CA 4R
See also SATA 14
Aitchison, Janet 1962- 57-60
Aitken, A(dam) J(ack) 1921- CANR-7
Earlier sketch in CA 13-14R
Aitken, Amy 1952- 108
See also SATA 40
Aitken, Dorothy 1916- CANR-2
Earlier sketch in CA 49-52
See also SATA 10
Aitken, Douglas 1933- 115
Aitken, Hugh G(eorge) J(effrey) 1922- CANR-3
Earlier sketch in CA 2R
Aitken, Jonathan (William Patrick)
1942- 21-22R
Aitken, (John William) Max(well)
1910-1985 Obituary 116
Aitken, Thomas, Jr. 1910- 2R
Aitken, W(illiam) R(ussell) 1913- 41-44R
Aitken, William Maxwell
See Beaverbrook, William Maxwell Aitken
Aitkin, Don(ald Alexander) 1937- CANR-15
Earlier sketch in CA 93-96
Aitmatov, Chingiz 1928- 103
Ajami, Alfred M(ichel) 1948- Brief entry 110
Ajar, Emile
See Kacew, Romain
Ajay, Betty 1918- 69-72
Ajayi, J(acob) F(estus) Ade(niyi)
1929- CANR-18
Earlier sketch in CA 61-64
Ajegbo, Keith 1946- 122
Ajilvsgi, Geyata 1933- 124
Akaba, Suekichi 1910- SATA-46
Akaha, Tsuneo 1949- 120
Akanji, Sangodare
See Beier, Ulli
Akare, Thomas 1950- 109
Akashi, Yoji 1928- 33-36R
Ake, Claude 1939- CANR-10
Earlier sketch in CA 21-22R
Akehurst, M(ichael) B(arton) 1940- 25-28R
Akens, David S. 1921- CANR-12
Earlier sketch in CA 25-28R
Akenson, Donald Harman 1941- CANR-22
Earlier sketches in CA 57-60, CANR-7
Aker, George F(rederick) 1927- CANR-15
Earlier sketch in CA 41-44R
Akeret, Robert U(lrich) 1928- 45-48
Akers, Alan Burt
See Bulmer, (Henry) Kenneth
Akers, Charles W(esley) 1920- 15-16R
Akers, Floyd
See Baum, L(yman) Frank
Akers, Keith 1949- 112
Akers, Ronald L(ouis) 1939- CANR-1
Earlier sketch in CA 45-48
Akers, Susan Grey 1889-1984 Obituary 112
Akhmadulina, Bella Akhatovna 1937- 65-68
Akhmatova, Anna 1888-1966 CAP-1
Obituary 25-28R
Earlier sketch in CA 19-20
See also CLC 11, 25
Akhnaton, Askia
See Eckels, Jon
Akhurst, Bertram A. 1928- 45-48
Akin, Wallace E(lmus) 1923- 25-28R
Akin, William E(rnest) 1936- 116
Akinjogbin, I(saac) A(deagbo) 1930- CANR-12
Earlier sketch in CA 21-22R
Akins, Zoe 1886-1958 Brief entry 115
See also DLB 26
Akita, George 1926- 19-20R
Akmakjian, Hiag 1926- 57-60
Akpabot, Samuel Ekpe 1932- 101
Akrigg, G(eorge) P(hillip) V(ernon)
1913- 25-28R
Aksenov, Vassily
See Aksyonov, Vassily (Pavlovich)
See also CLC 22
Aksyonov, Vassily (Pavlovich) 1932- CANR-12
Earlier sketch in CA 53-56
See also CLC 37
Akutagawa Ryunosuke 1892-1927
Brief entry 117
See also TCLC 16
Aladjem, Henrietta H. 1917- 105
Alailima, Fay C. 1921- 33-36R
Alain
See Brustlein, Daniel
Alain-Fournier
See Fournier, Henri Alban
See also DLB 65
See also TCLC 6
Alajalov, Constantin 1900-1987 Obituary 123
See also SATA 53
Al-Amin, Jamil Abdullah 1943- 125
Brief entry 112
See also BW
Alan, Jack
See Green, Alan (Baer)
Alan, Sandy
See Ullman, Allan
Aland, Kurt 1915- CANR-12
Earlier sketch in CA 25-28R
Alas (y Urena), Leopoldo (Enrique Garcia)
1852-1901 Brief entry 113
See also TCLC 29
Alaya, Flavia (M.) 1935- 33-36R
al-Azm, Sadik J. 1934- CANR-9
Earlier sketch in CA 21-22R
Alazraki, Jaime 1934- CANR-21
Earlier sketch in CA 33-36R
Alba, Nanina 1915-1968 DLB-41
Alba, Richard D(enis) 1942- 109
Alba, Victor 1916- CANR-25
Earlier sketches in CA 23-24R, CANR-10
Alba de Gamez, Cielo Cayetana 1920- 93-96
Albanese, Catherine L(ouise) 1940- CANR-24
Earlier sketches in CA 65-68, CANR-9
Albaret, Celeste (Gineste) 1891-1984 73-76
Obituary 112
Albaugh, Edwin (Doll, Jr.) 1935- 89-92
Albaugh, Ralph M. 1909- CAP-1
Earlier sketch in CA 13-14
Albaum, Gerald (Sherwin) 1933- CANR-14
Earlier sketch in CA 37-40R
Albaum, Melvin 1936- 53-56
Albee, Edward (Franklin III) 1928- CANR-8
Earlier sketch in CA 7-8R
See also DLB 7
See also CDALB 1941-1968
See also CLC 1, 2, 3, 5, 9, 11, 13, 25
See also AITN 1
Albee, George Sumner 1905-1964 3R
Alber, Mike 1938- 25-28R
Albers, Anni 1899- CANR-2
Earlier sketch in CA 2R
Albers, Henry H. 1919- CANR-6
Earlier sketch in CA 2R
Albers, Josef 1888-1976 CANR-3
Obituary 65-68
Earlier sketch in CA 4R
Albert, A(braham) Adrian 1905-1972
Obituary 37-40R
Albert, Allan (Praigrod) 1945- Brief entry 116
Albert, Burton, Jr. 1936- CANR-23
Earlier sketches in CA 61-64, CANR-8
See also SATA 22
Albert, Ethel M(ary) 1918- 23-24R
Albert, Gail 1942- 108
Albert, Harold A. 29-32R
Albert, Linda 1939- 110
Albert, Louise 1928- 69-72
Albert, Marv 1943- 101
Albert, Marvin H. 73-76
Albert, Mimi (Abriel) 1940- 73-76
Albert, Peter J(oseph) 1946- 114
Albert, Walter E. 1930- 23-24R
Albertazzie, Ralph 1923- 101
Alberti, Rafael 1902- 85-88
See also CLC 7
Alberti, Robert E(dward) 1938- CANR-7
Earlier sketch in CA 61-64
Alberts, David Stephen 1942- 29-32R
Alberts, Frances Jacobs 1907- 5-6R
See also SATA 14
Alberts, Robert C(arman) 1907- 33-36R
Alberts, William W. 1925- 21-22R
Albertson, Chris 1931- 57-60
Albertson, Dean 1920- CANR-3
Earlier sketch in CA 2R
Albertyn, Dorothy
See Black, Dorothy
Albery, Nobuko 81-84
Albin, Peter S(teigman) 1934- 85-88
Albini, Joseph L(ouis) 1930- 61-64
Albinski, Henry Stephen 1931- CANR-23
Earlier sketches in CA 23-24R, CANR-8
Albinson, Jack
See Albinson, James P.
Albinson, James P. 1932- 57-60
Albion, Lee Smith SATA-29
Albion, Robert Greenhalgh 1896-1983 CANR-3
Obituary 110
Earlier sketch in CA 4R
Albornoz, Claudio Sanchez
See Sanchez Albornoz (y Mediuna),
Claudio
Albran, Kehlog
See Shacket, Sheldon R(ubin)
Albrand, Martha (a pseudonym)
1914-1981 CANR-11
Obituary 108
Earlier sketch in CA 13-14R
Albrecht, Lillie (Vanderveer) 1894- 7-8R
See also SATA 12
Albrecht, Milton C(harles) 1904- CANR-13
Earlier sketch in CA 33-36R
Albrecht, Robert C(harles) 1933- 23-24R
Albrecht, Ruth E. 1910- 17-18R
Albrecht, William P(rice) 1907- 73-76
Albrecht-Carrie, Rene 1904-1978 CANR-1
Earlier sketch in CA 3R
Albright, Bets Parker
See Albright, Elizabeth A.
Albright, Bliss (James F.) 1903- 33-36R
Albright, Daniel 1945- 125
Albright, Elizabeth A. 1920- 108
Albright, Horace M(arden) 1890-1987 124
Obituary 122
Albright, John Brannon 1930- 65-68
Albright, Joseph (Medill Patterson)
1937- 97-100
Albright, Peter 1926- 108
Albright, Raymond W(olf) 1901-1965 CAP-1
Earlier sketch in CA 9-10
Albright, Roger (Lynch) 1922- 106
Albright, Thomas 1935-1984 Obituary 112
Albright, William F(oxwell) 1891-1971
Obituary 33-36R
Albrow, Martin 1937- 33-36R
Albus, James Sacra 1935- 124
Alcala-Galiano, Juan Valera y
See Valera y Alcala-Galiano, Juan
Alcalde, E. L.
See Chaij, Fernando
Alcalde, Miguel
See Burgess, M(ichael) R(oy)
Alcantara, Ruben R(eyes) 1940- 105
Alcayaga, Lucila Godoy
See Godoy Alcayaga, Lucila
Alchemy, Jack
See Gershator, David
Alchian, Armen A(lbert) 1914- Brief entry 110
Alcibiade
See Praz, Mario
Alcock, Gudrun SATA-33
Alcock, John 1942- 125
Alcock, Vivien 1924- 110
See also SATA 38, 45
Alcorn, Alfred 1941- 122
Alcorn, John 1935- SATA-30, 31
Alcorn, Marvin D. 1902- 15-16R
Alcorn, Pat B(arker) 1948- 107
Alcorn, Robert Hayden 1909- 5-6R
Alcosser, Sandra (B.) 1944- Brief entry 124
Alcott, Amos Bronson 1799-1888 DLB-1
Alcott, Julia
See Cudlipp, Edythe
Alcott, Louisa May 1832-1888 YABC-1
See also DLB 1, 42
See also CDALB 1865-1917
See also CLR 1
Alcott, William Andrus 1789-1859 DLB-1
Alcyone
See Krishnamurti, Jiddu
Ald, Roy A(llison) CANR-24
Earlier sketch in CA 73-76
Alda, Alan 1936- 103
Alda, Arlene 1933- 114
See also SATA 36, 44
Aldan, Daisy 1923- CANR-25
Earlier sketches in CA 13-14R, CANR-8
Aldanov, M. A.
See Aldanov, Mark (Alexandrovich)
Aldanov, Mark (Alexandrovich)
1886(?)-1957 Brief entry 118
See also TCLC 23
Aldcroft, Derek H. 1936- CANR-12
Earlier sketch in CA 25-28R
Alden, Carella
See Remington, Ella-Carrie
Alden, Dauril 1926- 105
Alden, Douglas William 1912- 69-72
Alden, Isabella (Macdonald) 1841(?)-1930
Brief entry 120
See also YABC 2
See also DLB 42
Alden, Jack
See Barrows, (Ruth) Marjorie
Alden, John D. 1921- 17-18R
Alden, John R(ichard) 1908- CANR-11
Earlier sketch in CA 61-64
Alden, Michele
See Avallone, Michael (Angelo), Jr.
Alden, Robert L(eslie) 1937- 65-68
Alden, Sue
See Francis, Dorothy Brenner
Alder, Francis A(nthony) 1937- 61-64
Alder, Henry (Ludwig) 1922- 49-52
Alderfer, Clayton P. 1940- 37-40R

Alderfer, E. G.
See Alderfer, E. Gordon
Alderfer, E. Gordon 1915- 121
Alderfer, Harold F(reed) 1903- 11-12R
Alderman, Clifford Lindsey 1902- CANR-3
Earlier sketch in CA 3R
See also SATA 3
Alderman, Geoffrey 1944- 93-96
Alderman, (Barbara) Joy 1931- 61-64
Alderson, Jo(anne) Bartels 1930- 65-68
Alderson, Michael (Rowland) 1931-1988
Obituary 126
Alderson, (Arthur) Stanley 1927- 7-8R
Alderson, Sue Ann 1940- SATA-48
Alderson, William T(homas), Jr. 1926- 9-10R
Alding, Peter
See Jeffries, Roderic (Graeme)
Aldington, Richard 1892-1962 85-88
See also DLB 20, 36
See also CLC 49
Aldis, Dorothy (Keeley) 1896-1966 . . . . 3R
See also SATA 2
See also DLB 22
Aldiss, Brian W(ilson) 1925- CANR-5
Earlier sketch in CA 5-6R
See also CAAS 2
See also SATA 34
See also DLB 14
See also CLC 5, 14, 40
Aldon, Adair
See Meigs, Cornelia Lynde
Aldouby, Zwy H(erbert) 1931- 33-36R
Aldous, Allan (Charles) 1911- SATA-27
Aldous, Anthony Michael 1935- CANR-25
Earlier sketch in CA 69-72
Aldous, Tony
See Aldous, Anthony Michael
Aldred, Cyril 1914- CANR-6
Earlier sketch in CA 57-60
Aldrich, Ann
See Meaker, Marijane
Aldrich, C(larence) Knight 1914- 25-28R
Aldrich, Frederic DeLong 1899- CAP-1
Earlier sketch in CA 11-12
Aldrich, Jonathan 1936- Brief entry 112
Aldrich, Joseph C(offin) 1940- 114
Aldrich, Nelson Wilmarth, Jr. 1935-
Brief entry 110
Aldrich, Richard (Stoddard) 1902-1986
Obituary 119
Aldrich, Ruth I(sabelle) 105
Aldrich, Sandra Picklesimer 1945- 111
Aldrich, Thomas Bailey 1836-1907
Brief entry 111
See also SATA 17
See also DLB 42, 71, 74
Aldridge, A(lfred) Owen 1915- 17-18R
Aldridge, Adele 1934- 49-52
Aldridge, Alan 1943- 125
See also SATA 33
Aldridge, (Harold Edward) James
1918- CANR-13
Earlier sketch in CA 61-64
Aldridge, Jeffrey 1938- 25-28R
Aldridge, John W(atson) 1922- CANR-3
Earlier sketch in CA 2R
Aldridge, Josephine Haskell 73-76
See also SATA 14
Aldridge, Richard Boughton 1930- CANR-3
Earlier sketch in CA 9-10R
Aldrin, Edwin E(ugene), Jr. 1930- 89-92
Aldwinckle, Russell (Foster) 1911- 69-72
Aldyne, Nathan
See McDowell, Michael
Alegria, Fernando 1918- CANR-5
Earlier sketch in CA 11-12R
Alegria, Ricardo E. 1921- CANR-15
Earlier sketch in CA 25-28R
See also SATA 6
Aleichem, Sholom
See Rabinovitch, Sholem
See also TCLC 1
Aleixandre, Vicente 1898-1984 . . . . CANR-26
Obituary 114
Earlier sketch in CA 85-88
See also CLC 9, 36
Alejandro, Carlos Federico Diaz
See Diaz-Alejandro, Carlos Federico
Aleksin, Anatolii Georgievich 1924- 109
See also SATA 36
Aleman, Miguel 1903(?)-1983 Obituary 110
Alent, Rose Marie Bachem
See Bachem Alent, Rose M(arie Baake)
Alepoudelis, Odysseus
See Elytis, Odysseus
Aleshkovsky, Joseph 1929- Brief entry 121
Aleshkovsky, Yuz
See Aleshkovsky, Joseph
See also CLC 44
Alessandra, Anthony J(oseph) 1947- 103
Alessandrini, Federico 1906(?)-1983
Obituary 109
Alex, Ben (a pseudonym) 1946- 114
See also SATA 45
Alex, Marlee (a pseudonym) 1948- 114
See also SATA 45
Alexander, Albert 1914- 25-28R
Alexander, Alfred 1908-1983 Obituary 110
Alexander, Anna B(arbara Cooke) 1913- 57-60
See also SATA 1
Alexander, Anne
See Alexander, Anna B(arbara Cooke)
Alexander, Anthony Francis 1920- 2R
Alexander, Arthur (Wilson) 1927- 7-8R
Alexander, Bevin (Ray) 1928- 122
Alexander, Boyd 1913-1980 53-56
Obituary 97-100
Alexander, Charles
See Hadfield, (Ellis) Charles (Raymond)
Alexander, Charles C(omer) 1935- 15-16R
Alexander, Charles Stevenson 1916- CANR-2
Earlier sketch in CA 5-6R
Alexander, Christine 1893-1975 Obituary . . 61-64
Alexander, Christine (Anne) 1949- 117
Alexander, Colin James 1920- 15-16R
Alexander, Conel Hugh O'Donel
1909-1974 73-76
Alexander, David 1907-1973 . . . . 1R
Obituary 41-44R
Alexander, David M(ichael) 1945- 81-84
Alexander, Denis 1945- 45-48
Alexander, Edward 1936- 15-16R
Alexander, Edward P(orter) 1907- 33-36R
Alexander, Edwin P. 1905- 29-32R
Alexander, Eric 1910(?)-1982 Obituary 106
Alexander, Ernest R(obert) 1933- 103
Alexander, Faith
See Bentley, Margaret
Alexander, Floyce 1938- CANR-13
Earlier sketch in CA 33-36R
Alexander, Frances (Laura) 1888- 25-28R
See also SATA 4
Alexander, Frank 1943- 65-68
Alexander, Franklin Osborne 1897- CAP-2
Earlier sketch in CA 25-28
Alexander, Franz (Gabriel) 1891-1964 . . . . . .5-6R
Alexander, George Jonathan 1931- 73-76
Alexander, George M(oyer) 1914- 7-8R
Alexander, Gil
See Ralston, Gilbert A(lexander)
Alexander, Harold Lee 1934- 69-72
Alexander, Henry
See McAllister, Alister
Alexander, Herbert E(phraim) 1927- 41-44R
Alexander, Holmes (Moss) 1906-1985 61-64
Obituary 118
Alexander, Hubert G(riggs) 1909- 23-24R
Alexander, I. J. 1905(?)-1974 Obituary . . . 53-56
Alexander, Ian W(elsh) 1911- 13-14R
Alexander, J(onathan) J(ames) G(raham)
1935- CANR-13
Earlier sketch in CA 21-22R
Alexander, James 1691-1756 . . . . DLB-24
Alexander, James E(ckert) 1913- 73-76
Alexander, Jan
See Banis, Victor J(erome)
Alexander, Janet 1907- CANR-4
Earlier sketch in CA 9-10R
Alexander, Jean 1926- 49-52
Alexander, Joan
See Wetherell-Pepper, Joan Alexander
Alexander, Jocelyn Anne Arundel 1930- CANR-4
Earlier sketch in CA 4R
See also SATA 22
Alexander, John A(leck) 1912- 9-10R
Alexander, John Kurt 1941- 102
Alexander, John N. 1941- 69-72
Alexander, John T(horndike) 1940- 33-36R
Alexander, John W(esley) 1918- CANR-3
Earlier sketch in CA 5-6R
Alexander, Jon 1940- 33-36R
Alexander, Josephine 1909- 104
Alexander, (Charles) K(halil) 1923-1980
Obituary 103
Alexander, Kate
See Armstrong, Tilly
Alexander, Kathryn
See Caldwell, Kathryn (Smoot)
Alexander, Ken
See Alexander, Kenneth John Wilson
Alexander, Kenneth John Wilson 1922- 61-64
Alexander, L(ouis) G(eorge) 1932- CANR-19
Earlier sketch in CA 102
Alexander, Lawrence 1939- Brief entry 122
Alexander, Leo 1905-1985 Obituary 116
Alexander, Lewis M(cElwain) 1921- 21-22R
Alexander, Linda 1935- 23-24R
See also SATA 2
Alexander, Liza
See Campbell, Louisa D.
Alexander, Lloyd (Chudley) 1924- CANR-24
Earlier sketches in CA 1R, CANR-1
See also SATA 3, 49
See also DLB 52
See also CLC 35
See also CLR 1, 5
Alexander, Louis 1917- 121
Alexander, Marc 1929- CANR-14
Earlier sketch in CA 7-8R
Alexander, Marge
See Edwards, Roselyn
Alexander, Martha 1920- 85-88
See also SATA 11
Alexander, Marthann 1907- 53-56
Alexander, Martin 1930- 49-52
Alexander, Mary Jean McCutcheon 11-12R
Alexander, Meena 1951- 115
Alexander, Michael (Joseph) 1941- CANR-22
Earlier sketch in CA 45-48
Alexander, Michael Van Cleave 1937- 102
Alexander, Milton 1917- 17-18R
Alexander, Pamela 1948- 122
Alexander, Pat(ricia June) 1937- 113
Alexander, R(obert) McNeill 1934- 124
Alexander, R(obert) P(ercival)
1905(?)-1985 Obituary 117
Alexander, Rae Pace
See Alexander, Raymond Pace
Alexander, Ralph (Holland) 1936- 115
Alexander, Raymond Pace 1898-1974 97-100
See also SATA 22
Alexander, Ric
See Long, Richard A(lexander)
Alexander, Richard Dale 1929- 110
Alexander, Robert
See Gross, Michael (Robert)
Alexander, Robert
See Legat, Michael (Ronald)
Alexander, Robert J. 1918- CANR-18
Earlier sketches in CA 1R, CANR-3
Alexander, Robert Lester 1920- 108
Alexander, Robert William 1906(?)-1980
Obituary 97-100
Alexander, (Eben) Roy 1899(?)-1978 85-88
Obituary 81-84
Alexander, Roy 1928- 118
Alexander, Shana 1925- CANR-26
Earlier sketch in CA 61-64
Alexander, Sidney 1912- CANR-6
Earlier sketch in CA 11-12R
Alexander, Stanley Walter 1895-1980
Obituary 97-100
Alexander, Stella Tucker 1912- 105
Alexander, Sue 1933- CANR-19
Earlier sketches in CA 53-56, CANR-4
See also SATA 12
Alexander, Taylor Richard 1915- 107
Alexander, Theron 1913- CANR-3
Earlier sketch in CA 5-6R
Alexander, Thomas G(len) 1935- 65-68
Alexander, Thomas W(illiamson), Jr.
1930- 9-10R
Alexander, Vincent Arthur 1925-1980
Obituary 101
See also SATA 23
Alexander, W(illiam) M(ortimer) 1928- 69-72
Alexander, William M(arvin) 1912- 33-36R
Alexander, Yonah 1931- 61-64
Alexander, Zane
See Alexander, Harold Lee
Alexanderson, Gerald L(ee) 1933- 118
Alexandersson, Gunnar V(ilhelm) 1922- . .17-18R
Alexandre, Philippe 1932- 41-44R
Alexandrowicz, Charles Henry
1902-1975 . . . . CANR-1
Earlier sketch in CA 2R
Alexeev, Wassilij 1906- 89-92
Alexeieff, Alexandre A. 1901- SATA-14
Alexeyev, Constantin (Sergeivich)
See Stanislavsky, Constantin (Sergeivich)
Alexiou, Margaret 1939- 69-72
Alexis, Katina
See Strauch, Katina (Parthemos)
Aley, Albert 1919-1986 Obituary 118
Alfandary-Alexander, Mark 1923- 7-8R
al-Faruqi, Isma'il Raji 1921- CANR-13
Earlier sketch in CA 69-72
Alford, Bernard William Ernest 1937- 101
Alford, Norman (William) 1929- 37-40R
Alford, Robert R(oss) 1928- 41-44R
Alford, Terry (L.) 1945- Brief entry 110
Alfred, Richard
See Haverstock, Nathan Alfred
Alfred, William 1922- 15-16R
Alfven, Hannes O(lof) G(oesta) 1908- 29-32R
Algarin, Miguel 1941- CANR-20
Earlier sketch in CA 69-72
Algeo, John (Thomas) 1930- CANR-7
Earlier sketch in CA 19-20R
Alger, Horatio, Jr. 1832-1899 . . . . SATA-16
See also DLB 42
Alger, Leclaire (Gowans) 1898-1969 73-76
See also SATA 15
Alger, Philip Langdon 1894-1979 Obituary . . 109
Algery, Andre
See Coulet du Gard, Rene
Algren, Nelson 1909-1981 . . . . CANR-20
Obituary 103
Earlier sketch in CA 13-14R
See also DLB 9
See also DLBY 81, 82
See also CDALB 1941-1968
See also CLC 4, 10, 33
Alhaique, Claudio 1913- 29-32R
Ali, Ahmed 1910- CANR-15
Earlier sketch in CA 25-28R
Ali, Chaudhri Mohamad 1905-1980
Obituary 105
Ali, Muhammad 1942- Brief entry 116
Ali, Salim (A.) 1896-1987 Obituary 123
Ali, Schavi M(ali) 1948- CANR-26
Earlier sketches in CA 61-64, CANR-11
Ali, Tariq 1943- CANR-10
Earlier sketch in CA 25-28R
Aliano, Richard Anthony 1946- CANR-10
Earlier sketch in CA 65-68
Aliav, Ruth
See Kluger, Ruth
Aliber, Robert Z. 1930- CANR-25
Earlier sketches in CA 23-24R, CANR-8
Alibrandi, Tom 1941- CANR-12
Earlier sketch in CA 65-68
Alice (Mary Victoria Augusta Pauline),
Princess 1883-1981 Obituary 103
Aliesan, Jody 1943- CANR-7
Earlier sketch in CA 57-60
Alihan, Milla CAP-2
Earlier sketch in CA 29-32
Ali Khan, Shirley 1951- 118
Aliki
See Brandenberg, Aliki Liacouras
See also CLR 9
Alilunas, Leo John 1912- 17-18R
Alimayo, Chikuyo
See Franklin, Harold L(eroy)
Alinder, Martha Wheelock
See Wheelock, Martha E.
Alinsky, Saul (David) 1909-1972
Obituary 37-40R
Alioto, Robert F(ranklyn) 1933- 45-48
Alisky, Marvin (Howard) 1923- CANR-20
Earlier sketches in CA 13-14R, CANR-5
Alisov, Boris P. 1892-1972 Obituary 37-40R
Al-Issa, Ihsan 1931- 109
Alitto, Guy S(alvatore) 1942- 93-96
Alix, Ernest Kahlar 1939- Brief entry 112
Alkema, Chester Jay 1932- 53-56
See also SATA 12
Alker, Hayward R(ose), Jr. 1937- 17-18R
Alkire, Leland George, (Jr.) 1937- 101
Alkire, William Henry 1935- 107
Allaback, Steven Lee 1939- 97-100
Allaby, (John) Michael 1933- CANR-20
Earlier sketches in CA 45-48, CANR-1
Allaire, Joseph L(eo) 1929- 41-44R
Allamand, Pascale 1942- CANR-12
Earlier sketch in CA 69-72
See also SATA 12
Allan, Alfred K. 1930- 17-18R
Allan, D(avid) G(uy) C(harles) 1925- . . . CANR-15
Earlier sketch in CA 25-28R
Allan, Elkan 1922- 101
Allan, Harry T. 1928- 25-28R
Allan, J(ohn) David 1945- 41-44R
Allan, John B.
See Westlake, Donald E(dwin)
Allan, Lewis
See Meeropol, Abel
Allan, Mabel Esther 1915- CANR-18
Earlier sketches in CA 7-8R, CANR-2
See also SATA 5, 32
Allan, Mea 1909-1982 . . . . CANR-2
Obituary 107
Earlier sketch in CA 7-8R
Allan, Norman B. 1921- Brief entry 105
Allan, Robert Alexander 1914-1979
Obituary 106
Allan, Robin 1934- 107
Allan, Ted 1918- 77-80
See also DLB 68
Allana, Ghulam Ali 1906-1985 Obituary 115
Allana, Ghulamali
See Allana, Ghulam Ali
Allanbrook, Wye J(amison) 1943- 110
Alland, Alexander, Jr. 1931- 21-22R
Alland, Guy 1944- 69-72
Allard, Bessie Butler Newsom ?-1987
Obituary 122
Allard, Dean C(onrad) 1933- CANR-1
Earlier sketch in CA 45-48
Allard, Harry
See Allard, Harry G(rover), Jr.
Allard, Harry G(rover), Jr. 1928- 113
See also SATA 42
Allard, Michel (Adrien) 1924-1976
Obituary 65-68
Allard, Sven 1896-1975 . . . . CAP-2
Earlier sketch in CA 29-32
Allard, William Albert 1937- 115
Allardt, Erik 1925- CANR-13
Earlier sketch in CA 73-76
Allardt, Linda 1926- 126
Brief entry 104
Allardyce, Gilbert Daniel 1932- 33-36R
Allardyce, Paula
See Torday, Ursula
Allaun, Frank (Julian) 1913- 103
Allbeck, Willard Dow 1898- 21-22R
Allbeury, Ted
See Allbeury, Theodore Edward le
Bouthillier
Allbeury, Theodore Edward le Bouthillier
1917- CANR-5
Earlier sketch in CA 53-56
Allchin, A(rthur) M(acdonald) 1930- . . . CANR-17
Earlier sketch in CA 25-28R
Alldridge, James Charles 1910- 29-32R
Alldritt, Keith 1935- 25-28R
See also DLB 14
Allee, John Gage (Jr.) 1918-1987
Obituary 121
Allee, Marjorie Hill 1890-1945 . . . . SATA-17
Allegar, Daniel E(ugene) 1903- 33-36R
Allegro, John Marco 1923-1988 . . . . CANR-20
Obituary 124
Earlier sketches in CA 11-12R, CANR-4
Allen, A(rthur) B(ruce) 1903-1975 . . . . CAP-2
Earlier sketch in CA 23-24
Allen, A(rvon) Dale, Jr. 1935- 21-22R
Allen, Adam
See Epstein, Beryl (M. Williams)
and Epstein, Samuel
Allen, Adam
See Epstein, Beryl (Williams)
and Epstein, Samuel
Allen, Agnes Rogers 1893-1986 Obituary . . . 121
Allen, Alex B.
See Heide, Florence Parry
Allen, Allyn
See Eberle, Irmengarde
Allen, Anita
See Schenck, Anita A(llen)
Allen, Arthur A(ugustus) 1885-1964 . . . CANR-19
Earlier sketch in CA 2R
Allen, Barbara
See Stuart, (Violet) Vivian (Finlay)
Allen, Betsy
See Harrison, Elizabeth Cavanna
Allen, Betty (Jeanne) 1929- 113
Allen, Bob 1948- 118
Allen, Brian 1952- 126
Allen, Captain Quincy CANR-26
Earlier sketches in CA 19-20, CAP-2
Allen, Carl 1961- 69-72
Allen, Catherine Blanche 1883- 107
Allen, Cecil J(ohn) 1886-1973 . . . . CAP-2
Earlier sketch in CA 25-28

INDEX

Allen, Charles Livingstone 1913- 111
Allen, Charlotte Vale 1941- CANR-12
Earlier sketch in CA 69-72
Allen, Chester
See Holding, Vera Zumwalt
Allen, Chris 1929- 29-32R
Allen, Clabon Walter 1904-1987 Obituary ... 124
Allen, Clay
See Paine, Lauran (Bosworth)
Allen, Clifford Edward 1902- CAP-1
Earlier sketch in CA 9-10
Allen, Clifton Judson 1901- 108
Allen, Daniel 1947- 125
Allen, David 1925- 33-36R
Allen, David 1939- 115
Allen, David Elliston 1932- 25-28R
Allen, David F(ranklyn) 1943- 103
Allen, David Grayson 1943- 115
Allen, David W. 1922- Brief entry 113
Allen, Derek Fortrose 1910-1975 Obituary .. 114
Allen, Dick 1939- 33-36R
Allen, Diogenes 1932- CANR-25
Earlier sketches in CA 25-28R, CANR-10
Allen, Dizzy
See Allen, H(ubert) R(aymond)
Allen, Don Cameron 1903-1972 .... CANR-4
Earlier sketch in CA 5-6R
Allen, Donald Emerson 1917- 45-48
Allen, Donald M(erriam) 1912- CANR-10
Earlier sketch in CA 19-20R
Allen, Donald R. 1930- 45-48
Allen, Douglas (Malcolm) 1941- 113
Allen, Durward L(eon) 1910- 41-44R
Allen, Dwight W(illiam) 1931- 15-16R
Allen, E. C.
See Ward, Elizabeth Campbell
Allen, Edith Beavers 1920- 9-10R
Allen, Edith Marion CAP-1
Earlier sketch in CA 15-16
Allen, Edward D(avid) 1923- 49-52
Allen, Edward Heron
See Heron-Allen, Edward
Allen, Edward J(oseph) 1907- CAP-1
Earlier sketch in CA 17-18
Allen, Edward Switzer 1887-1985
Obituary 116
Allen, Elisabeth Offutt 1895- 57-60
Allen, (Evelyn) Elizabeth 1918- 121
Allen, Elizabeth 1955- 122
Allen, Elizabeth
See Thompson, Elizabeth Allen
Allen, Elizabeth Cooper
See Allen, Betty (Jeanne)
Allen, Eric 1916- Brief entry 111
Allen, Ethan 1738-1789 .... DLB-31
Allen, Everett S(locum) 1916- Brief entry ... 110
Allen, Francis A(lfred) 1919- 15-16R
Allen, Francis R(obbins) 1908- 77-80
Allen, Frank 1939- CANR-26
Earlier sketch in CA 109
Allen, Frederick G(arfield) 1936-1986 .. CANR-26
Obituary 121
Earlier sketch in CA 57-60
Allen, Frederick S(tetson) 1930-
Brief entry 112
Allen, G(eorge) C(yril) 1900-1982 .... CANR-3
Obituary 107
Earlier sketch in CA 4R
Allen, G(eorge) Francis 1907- CAP-1
Earlier sketch in CA 9-10
Allen, Garland E(dward) 1936- 53-56
Allen, Gary
See Allen, Frederick G(arfield)
Allen, Gay Wilson 1903- CANR-3
Earlier sketch in CA 7-8R
Allen, Geoffrey Francis 1902- CAP-1
Earlier sketch in CA 13-14
Allen, George 1808-1876 .... DLB-59
Allen, George (Herbert) 1922- 111
Allen, Gerald 1942- CANR-16
Earlier sketch in CA 93-96
Allen, Gertrude E(lizabeth) 1888- 61-64
See also SATA 9
Allen, Gilbert (Bruce) 1951- 111
Allen, Gina 1918- 4R
Allen, Grant 1848-1899 .... DLB-70
Allen, Gwenfread Elaine 1904- 61-64
Allen, H. Fredericka
See Allen, H(elena) G(ronlund)
Allen, H(elena) G(ronlund) 29-32R
Allen, H(ubert) R(aymond) 1919-1987
Obituary 122
Allen, Harold B(yron) 1902- CANR-10
Earlier sketch in CA 17-18R
Allen, Harold J(oseph) 1925- 45-48
Allen, Harry Cranbrook 1917- 7-8R
Allen, Hazel
See Hershberger, Hazel Kuhns
Allen, Henry
See Adams, Henry H(itch)
Allen, Henry Wilson 1912- 89-92
See also DLBY 85
Allen, Herman R. 1913(?)-1979 Obituary .. 89-92
Allen, (William) Hervey (Jr.) 1889-1949
Brief entry 108
See also DLB 9, 45
Allen, Howard W. 1931- 33-36R
Allen, Ida (Cogswell) Bailey 1885-1973
Obituary 110
Allen, Ira R. 1948- 65-68
Allen, Irene 1903- CAP-1
Earlier sketch in CA 15-16
Allen, Irving L(ewis), Jr. 1931- 110
Allen, Ivan, Jr. 1911- 109
Allen, Jack 1899- SATA-29
Allen, Jack 1914- CANR-4
Earlier sketch in CA 9-10R
Allen, James 1739-1808 .... DLB-31
Allen, James
See Ader, Paul (Fassett)
Allen, James B(rown) 1927- 105
Allen, James B(eekman) 1931- 105
Allen, James Egert 1896-1980 Obituary .. 97-100
Allen, James L(ovic), Jr. 1929- CANR-17
Earlier sketch in CA 33-36R
Allen, James Lane 1849-1925 .... DLB-71
Allen, James S. 1906(?)-1986 Obituary 120
Allen, James Smith 1949- 111
Allen, Jay Presson 1922- 73-76
See also DLB 26
Allen, Jeffrey (Yale) 1948- 112
See also SATA 42
Allen, Jeffrey G(rant) 1943- 116
Allen, Jerry 1911- 11-12R
Allen, Jim
See Allen, James L(ovic), Jr.
Allen, Johannes 1916-1973 .... CANR-14
Earlier sketch in CA 29-32R
Allen, John
See Perry, Ritchie (John Allen)
Allen, John Alexander 1922- 25-28R
Allen, John D(aniel) 1898-1972 .... CAP-2
Earlier sketch in CA 33-36
Allen, John Jay 1932- CANR-18
Earlier sketch in CA 33-36R
Allen, John Logan 1941- 85-88
Allen, John Stuart 1907-1982 Obituary 109
Allen, Jon L(ewis) 1931- 57-60
Allen, Jordan
See Dumke, Glenn S.
Allen, Judson B(oyce) 1932- CANR-17
Earlier sketch in CA 81-84
Allen, K. Eileen 1918- 113
Allen, Katharine Martin 1906(?)-1984
Obituary 113
Allen, Kenneth (William) 1941- 69-72
Allen, Kenneth S. 1913- 77-80
Allen, L(ouis) David 1940- Brief entry 117
Allen, Lafe Franklin 1914- Brief entry 111
Allen, Laura Jean Brief entry 110
See also SATA 53
Allen, Lawrence A. 1926- 45-48
Allen, Layman E(dward) 1927- 7-8R
Allen, Lee 1915-1969 .... CANR-1
Earlier sketch in CA 2R
Allen, Leonard 1915(?)-1981 Obituary 102
Allen, Leroy 1912- 65-68
See also SATA 11
Allen, Leslie Christopher 1935- CANR-13
Earlier sketch in CA 73-76
Allen, Leslie H. 1887(?)-1973 Obituary 49-52
Allen, Linda 1925- 102
See also SATA 33
Allen, Loring
See Allen, Robert Loring
Allen, Louis 1922- 41-44R
Allen, Louis A. 1917- 7-8R
Allen, M(arion) C. 1914- 9-10R
Allen, Marcus
See Donicht, Mark Allen
Allen, Marjorie 1931- 69-72
See also SATA 22
Allen, Marjory (Gill) 1897- CAP-1
Earlier sketch in CA 9-10
Allen, Mark
See Donicht, Mark Allen
Allen, Martha Mitten 1937- 125
Allen, Mary (Charlotte Chocqueel) 1909- 109
Allen, Mary
See Cleveland, Mary
Allen, Maury 1932- CANR-11
Earlier sketch in CA 17-18R
See also SATA 26
Allen, Merritt J(ames) 1918- 69-72
Allen, Merritt Parmelee 1892-1954 .... SATA-22
Allen, Michael (Derek) 1939- 77-80
Allen, Michael J(ohn) B(ridgman) 1941- 102
Allen, Minerva C(rantz) 1935- CANR-6
Earlier sketch in CA 57-60
Allen, Myron Sheppard 1901- CAP-1
Earlier sketch in CA 9-10
Allen, Nina (Stroemgren) 1935- SATA-22
Allen, Oliver E. 1922- 126
Allen, Pamela 1934- 126
See also SATA 50
Allen, Pat 1938- 118
Allen, Paul 1948- 81-84
Allen, Paula Gunn Brief entry 112
Allen, Peter Christopher 1905- 108
Allen, Phyllis (Greig) 65-68
Allen, Phyllis S(loan) 1908- 65-68
Allen, Polly Reynolds 1940- 110
Allen, R. Earl 1922- CANR-6
Earlier sketch in CA 9-10R
Allen, R(onald) R(oyce) 1930- 19-20R
Allen, Reginald E. 1931- CANR-13
Earlier sketch in CA 33-36R
Allen, Richard (Hugh Sedley) 1903- 25-28R
Allen, (Alexander) Richard 1929- CANR-11
Earlier sketch in CA 65-68
Allen, Richard C. 1926- CANR-17
Earlier sketch in CA 25-28R
Allen, Richard C.
See Taylor, John M(axwell)
Allen, Richard Sanders 1917- 21-22R
Allen, Richard V(incent) 1936- 21-22R
Allen, Roach Van 1917- 11-12R
Allen, Robert 1946- 97-100
Allen, Robert
See Garfinkel, Bernard Max
Allen, Robert C(lyde) 1950- 117
Allen, Robert Day 1927-1986 107
Obituary 125
Allen, Robert F(rances) 1928-1987 .... 33-36R
Obituary 123
Allen, Robert J. 1930- 15-16R
Allen, Robert L(ee) 1942- 101
See also BW
Allen, Robert Livingston 1916- 17-18R
Allen, Robert Loring 1921- CANR-6
Earlier sketch in CA 1R
Allen, Robert M. 1909-1979 .... CANR-2
Earlier sketch in CA 1R
Allen, Robert Porter 1905-1963 .... 5-6R
Allen, Robert S(haron) 1900-1981 .... CANR-6
Obituary 103
Earlier sketch in CA 57-60
Allen, Robert Thomas 1911- Brief entry 110
Allen, Rodney F. 1938- 61-64
See also SATA 27
Allen, Roger M(ichael) A(shley) 1942- 111
Allen, Ronald B(arclay) 1941- 114
Allen, Ronald Royce 1930- 113
Allen, Ross R(oundy) 1928- 33-36R
Allen, Roy (George Douglas) 1906-1983
Obituary 110
Allen, Rupert C(lyde) 1927- 65-68
Allen, Ruth
See Peterson, Esther (Allen)
Allen, Ruth Finney 1898-1979 93-96
Obituary 85-88
Allen, Sam
See Allen, M(arion) C.
Allen, Samuel W(ashington) 1917- CANR-26
Earlier sketch in CA 49-52
See also BW
See also SATA 9
See also DLB 41
Allen, Sarah (Pearson) Sawyer 1920- 89-92
Allen, Shirley Seifried 1921- 57-60
Allen, Shirley Walter 1883- CAP-2
Earlier sketch in CA 25-28
Allen, Stephen (Valentine Patrick William)
1921- CANR-18
Earlier sketch in CA 25-28R
Allen, Steve
See Allen, Stephen (Valentine Patrick William)
Allen, Sue P. 1913- 25-28R
Allen, Sydney (Earl), Jr. 1929- 29-32R
Allen, T. D.
See Allen, Terril Diener
Allen, Terril Diener 1908- CANR-2
Earlier sketch in CA 7-8R
See also SATA 35
Allen, Terry D.
See Allen, Terril Diener
Allen, Thomas B(enton) 1929- CANR-20
Earlier sketches in CA 15-16R, CANR-5
See also SATA 45
Allen, Tom
See Allen, Thomas B(enton)
Allen, Tony 1945- 77-80
Allen, Vernon L(esley) 1933- 29-32R
Allen, W(illiam) Sidney 1918- 49-52
Allen, Wallace (Wilbur) 1919- 118
Allen, Walter Ernest 1911- CANR-25
Earlier sketch in CA 61-64
See also CAAS 6
Allen, William 1940- 65-68
Allen, William A(ustin) 1916- CANR-13
Earlier sketch in CA 33-36R
Allen, William R(ichard) 1924- 17-18R
Allen, William Sheridan 1932- 15-16R
Allen, William Stannard 1913- 101
Allen, Woody 1935- 33-36R
See also DLB 44
See also CLC 16
Allende, Isabel 1942- Brief entry 125
See also CLC 39
Allendoerfer, Carl B(arnett) 1911-1974 . CANR-11
Earlier sketches in CA 17-18, CAP-2
Allen of Hurtwood, Lady
See Allen, Marjory (Gill)
Allentuch, Harriet Ray 1933- 13-14R
Allentuck, Andrew 1943- 111
Allentuck, Marcia Epstein 1928- 33-36R
Allerton, Mary
See Govan, Christine Noble
Alley, Brian 1933- 111
Alley, Henry Melton 1945- 112
Alley, Louis Edward 1914- 19-20R
Alley, Norman William 1895-1981
Obituary 115
Alley, Rewi 1897-1987 .... CANR-13
Obituary 124
Earlier sketch in CA 73-76
Alley, Robert S. 1932- 33-36R
Alley, Stephen L(ewis) 1915- Brief entry 110
Alleyn, Ellen
See Rossetti, Christina (Georgina)
Allgire, Mildred J. 1910- CAP-2
Earlier sketch in CA 25-28
Alliluyeva, Svetlana (Iosifovna Stalina)
1926- 57-60
Allin, Clinton Harrop
See Harrop-Allin, Clinton
Allin, Craig Willard 1946- CANR-25
Earlier sketch in CA 108
Allingham, Margery (Louise)
1904-1966 .... CANR-4
Obituary 25-28R
Earlier sketch in CA 5-6R
See also CLC 19
Allingham, Michael 1943- 97-100
Allingham, William 1824-1889 .... DLB-35
Allington, Richard L(loyd) 1947- 112
See also SATA 35, 39
Allinsmith, Wesley 1923- 85-88
Allinson, Beverley (Lynn Rouse) 1936- .. CANR-4
Earlier sketch in CA 49-52
Allinson, Gary D(ean) 1942- 77-80
Allis, Frederick Scouller, Jr. 1913- 115
Allis, Oswald T(hompson) 1880-1973
Obituary 37-40R
Allison, A(ntony) F(rancis) 1916- 106
Allison, Alexander Ward 1919- 7-8R
Allison, Anne Marie 1931- 114
Allison, Anthony C(lifford) 1928- CANR-25
Earlier sketch in CA 29-32R
Allison, Bob SATA-14
Allison, C(hristopher) FitzSimons 1927- CANR-4
Earlier sketch in CA 1R
Allison, Clay
See Keevill, Henry J(ohn)
Allison, E. M. A.
See Allison, Eric W(illiam)
and Allison, Mary Ann
Allison, Eric W(illiam) 1947- 122
Allison, Graham T(illett), Jr. 1940- CANR-2
Earlier sketch in CA 49-52
Allison, Harrison C(larke) 1917- 49-52
Allison, Henry E. 1937- Brief entry 110
Allison, John Murray 1889- 73-76
Allison, Joseph D(avid) 1950- 111
Allison, Linda 1948- 113
See also SATA 43
Allison, Marian
See Reid, Frances P(ugh)
Allison, Mary Ann 1949- 122
Allison, Michael Frederick Lister 1936- 57-60
Allison, Mike
See Allison, Michael Frederick Lister
Allison, Penny
See Katz, Carol
Allison, R(ichard) Bruce 1949- CANR-19
Earlier sketches in CA 49-52, CANR-3
Allison, Ralph B(rewster) 1931- 101
Allison, Rand
See McCormick, Wilfred
Allison, Rosemary 1953- 93-96
Allison, Roy (Anthony) 1957- 119
Allison, Sam
See Loomis, Noel M(iller)
Allman, James 1943- 112
Allman, John 1935- CANR-25
Earlier sketch in CA 85-88
Allman, T. D. 1944- CANR-17
Earlier sketch in CA 93-96
Allmendinger, David F(rederick), Jr.
1938- 61-64
See also SATA 35
Allon, Yigal 1918-1980 73-76
Obituary 97-100
Allott, Kenneth 1912-1973 Obituary 89-92
See also DLB 20
Allott, Miriam 1920- 112
Alloway, David N(elson) 1927- CANR-10
Earlier sketch in CA 23-24R
Alloway, Lawrence 1926- 41-44R
Allport, Gordon (Willard) 1897-1967 .... CANR-3
Obituary 25-28R
Earlier sketch in CA 1R
Allport, Susan 1950- 124
Allred, Donald M(ervin) 1923- 65-68
Allred, G. Hugh 1932- CANR-8
Earlier sketch in CA 61-64
Allred, Gordon T(hatcher) 1930- CANR-10
Earlier sketch in CA 17-18R
See also SATA 10
Allred, Ruel A(cord) 1929- 106
Allsen, Philip E(dmond) 1932- CANR-4
Earlier sketch in CA 53-56
Allsop, Kenneth 1920-1973 .... CANR-6
Earlier sketch in CA 3R
See also SATA 17
Allsopp, (Harold) Bruce 1912- CANR-18
Earlier sketches in CA 7-8R, CANR-2
Allston, Washington 1779-1843 .... DLB-1
Allswang, John M(yers) 1937- 41-44R
Allum, Nancy (Patricia Eaton) 1920- CAP-1
Earlier sketch in CA 9-10
Allvine, Fred C. 1936- 61-64
Allvine, Glendon 1893(?)-1977 Obituary ... 73-76
Allward, Maurice (Frank) 1923- CANR-19
Earlier sketches in CA 7-8R, CANR-3
Allwood, Martin (Samuel) 1916- 110
Allworth, Edward (Alfred) 1920- 101
Allyn, Jennifer
See Jones, Jeannette
Allyn, Paul
See Schosberg, Paul A.
Allyson, Kym
See Kimbro, John M.
Alman, David 1919- 9-10R
Al-Marayati, Abid A(min) 1931- 33-36R
Almaraz, Felix D(iaz), Jr. 1933- 33-36R
Almaz, Michael 1921- 81-84
Almedingen, E. M.
See Almedingen, Martha Edith von
See also SATA 3
See also CLC 12
Almedingen, Martha Edith von
1898-1971 .... CANR-1
Earlier sketch in CA 2R
Almon, Bert 1943- 110
Almon, Clopper, Jr. 1934- 21-22R
Almond, Gabriel Abraham 1911- CANR-18
Earlier sketch in CA 101
Almond, Linda Stevens 1881(?)-1987
Obituary 121
See also SATA 50
Almond, Paul 1931- 73-76
Almond, Richard 1938- 53-56
Almonte, Rosa
See Paine, Lauran (Bosworth)

Almquist, Don 1929- SATA-11
Almquist, Gregg (Andrew) 1948- 126
Almquist, L. Arden 1921- 29-32R
Almy, Millie 1915- 85-88
Aloian, David 1928- 25-28R
Aloma, Rene R(amon) 1947- 113
Alonso, Damaso 1898- Brief entry 110
See also CLC 14
Alonso, J(uan) M(anuel) 1936- 102
Alonso, Maria Teresa Manjon
See Manjon-Alonso, Maria Teresa
Alonso, William 1933- CANR-6
Earlier sketch in CA 9-10R
Alotta, Robert I(gnatius) 1937- CANR-14
Earlier sketch in CA 65-68
Aloysius, Sister Mary
See Schaldenbrand, Mary
Alpaugh, Craig 1945- 117
Alper, Benedict S(olomon) 1905- 49-52
Alper, M(ax) Victor 1944- 69-72
Alpern, Andrew 1938- CANR-11
Earlier sketch in CA 69-72
Alpern, David M(ark) 1942- 73-76
Alpern, Gerald D(avid) 1932- 53-56
Alperovitz, Gar 1936- 49-52
Alpers, Antony 1919- CANR-3
Earlier sketch in CA 3R
Alpers, Bernard J. 1900-1981 Obituary 105
Alpers, Edward Alter 1941- 109
Alpers, Paul (Joel) 1932- 85-88
Alpers, Svetlana (Leontief) 1936- 115
Alpert, Hollis 1916- CANR-23
Earlier sketches in CA 3R, CANR-6
Alpert, Mark (Lauren) 1947- 107
Alpert, Mark I(ra) 1942- 61-64
Alpert, Paul 1907- 41-44R
Alpert, Richard 1931- 89-92
Alphonso-Karkala, John B. 1923- CANR-14
Earlier sketch in CA 37-40R
Alphonso Karkala, John B.
See Alphonso-Karkala, John B.
Alplaus, N. Y.
See Rubin, Cynthia Elyce
Al-Qazzaz, Ayad (Sayyid Ali) 1941- 112
Alred, Gerald J(ames) 1943- 105
AlRoy, Gil Carl 1924-1985 CANR-17
Obituary 116
Earlier sketch in CA 41-44R
Alschuler, Rose Haas 1887-1979 CAP-2
Obituary 89-92
Earlier sketch in CA 25-28
Alsen, Eberhard 1939- 110
Alsop, George 1636-? DLB-24
Alsop, Gulielma Fell 1881-1978 Obituary 77-80
Alsop, Joseph (Wright) 1910- 122
Alsop, Mary O'Hara 1885-1980 CANR-4
Obituary 102
Earlier sketch in CA 9-10R
See also SATA 2, 24, 34
Alsop, Richard 1761-1815 DLB-37
Alsop, Stewart (Johonnot Oliver)
1914-1974 89-92
Obituary 49-52
Alsterlund, Betty
See Pilkington, Betty
Alstern, Fred
See Stern, Alfred
Alston, Mary Niven 1918- 33-36R
Alston, Patrick L(ionel) 1926- 25-28R
Alston, Walter Emmons 1911-1984
Obituary 113
Alston, William P(ayne) 1921- CANR-7
Earlier sketch in CA 7-8R
Alswang, Betty 1920(?)-1978 Obituary 77-80
Alt, David D. 1933- 49-52
Alt, Herschel 1897(?)-1981 Obituary 105
Alt, (Arthur) Tilo 1931- 41-44R
Alta 1942- 57-60
See also CLC 19
Altabe, Joan B. 1935- 53-56
Altbach, Edith Hoshino 1941- 57-60
Altbach, Philip G(eoffrey) 1941- CANR-10
Earlier sketch in CA 25-28R
Altenbernd, (August) Lynn 1918- CANR-1
Earlier sketch in CA 45-48
Alter, J(ohn) Cecil 1879-1964 5-6R
Alter, Jean V(ictor) 1925- 45-48
Alter, Joseph Dinsmore 1923- 111
Alter, Judith (MacBain) 1938- CANR-14
Earlier sketch in CA 81-84
See also SATA 52
Alter, Judy
See Alter, Judith (MacBain)
Alter, Robert B(ernard) 1935- CANR-1
Earlier sketch in CA 49-52
See also CLC 34
Alter, Robert Edmond 1925-1965 CANR-1
Earlier sketch in CA 3R
See also SATA 9
Alter, Stephen 1956- 109
Alterman, Nathan 1910-1970 Obituary 25-28R
Altfest, Karen Caplan 105
Alth, Max O(ctavious) 1927- CANR-17
Earlier sketch in CA 41-44R
Althauser, Robert P(ierce) 1939- 57-60
Althea
See Braithwaite, Althea
Alther, Lisa 1944- CANR-12
Earlier sketch in CA 65-68
See also CLC 7, 41
Althoff, Phillip 1941- 33-36R
Altholz, Josef L(ewis) 1933- 9-10R
Althouse, Larry
See Althouse, Lawrence Wilson
Althouse, LaVonne 1932- 19-20R
Althouse, Lawrence Wilson 1930- 101
Altick, Richard Daniel 1915- CANR-19
Earlier sketches in CA 3R, CANR-4
Altieri, Charles F(rancis) 1942- 106
Altizer, Thomas J(onathan) J(ackson)
1927- CANR-3
Earlier sketch in CA 1R
Altman, Dennis 1943- CANR-15
Earlier sketch in CA 33-36R
Altman, Edward I(ra) 1941- CANR-22
Earlier sketches in CA 57-60, CANR-7
Altman, Frances 1937- 65-68
Altman, Irwin 1928- 81-84
Altman, Irwin 1930- CANR-21
Earlier sketch in CA 69-72
Altman, Jack 1938- 21-22R
Altman, Larry
See Altman, Irwin
Altman, Nathaniel 1948- CANR-21
Earlier sketches in CA 57-60, CANR-6
Altman, Richard Charles 1932- 41-44R
Altman, Robert 1925- 73-76
See also CLC 16
Altman, Robert A. 1943- 29-32R
Altman, Thomas
See Black, Campbell
Altman, Wilfred 1927- CAP-1
Earlier sketch in CA 9-10
Altmann, Alexander 1906-1987 CANR-8
Obituary 122
Earlier sketch in CA 61-64
Altmann, Berthold 1902(?)-1977
Obituary 69-72
Altoma, Salih J(awad) 1929- 49-52
Altrocchi, Julia Cooley 1893-1972 CAP-1
Earlier sketch in CA 13-14
Altschul, Aaron Mayer 1914- 105
Altschul, b j 1948- 114
Altschul, Selig 1914- 108
Altschuler, Franz 1923- SATA-45
Altsheler, Joseph A(lexander)
1862-1919 YABC-1
Altshuler, Alan Anthony 1936- 108
Altshuler, Edward A. 1919- 19-20R
Aluko, Timothy Mofolorunso 1918- CANR-10
Earlier sketch in CA 65-68
See also BW
Alurista
See Urista, Alberto H.
Al-Van-Gar
See Radwanski, Pierre A(rthur)
Alvarez, A(lfred) 1929- CANR-3
Earlier sketch in CA 1R
See also DLB 14, 40
See also CLC 5, 13
Alvarez, Alejandro Rodriguez 1903-1965
Obituary 93-96
Alvarez, Eugene 1932- 57-60
Alvarez, John
See del Rey, Lester
Alvarez, Joseph A. 1930- CANR-17
Earlier sketch in CA 33-36R
See also SATA 18
Alvarez, Luis W(alter) 1911-1988 Obituary 126
Alvarez, Max Joseph 1960- 112
Alvarez, Walter C(lement) 1884-1978 CANR-10
Earlier sketch in CA 61-64
Alvarez-Altman, Grace (DeJesus) 1926- 33-36R
Alvarez del Vayo, Julio 1891-1975
Obituary 61-64
Alverson, Charles (E.) 1935- CANR-13
Earlier sketch in CA 25-28R
Alverson, Donna 1933- 65-68
Alverson, Marianne 1942- 126
Alves, Colin 1930- CANR-2
Earlier sketch in CA 7-8R
Alves, Marcio Moreira 1936- CANR-2
Earlier sketch in CA 45-48
Alves, Michael (Joseph) 1956- 118
Alvey, Edward, Jr. 1902- 53-56
Alvey, R(ichard) Gerald 1935- 121
Alvin, Juliette (Louise) ?-1982 77-80
Obituary 108
Alworth, E. P(aul) 1918- 25-28R
Alwyn, William 1905-1985 Obituary 117
Aly, Bower 1903- CANR-5
Earlier sketch in CA 5-6R
Aly, Lucile Folse 1913- 23-24R
Alyeshmerni, Mansoor 1943- 29-32R
Alyn, Marc (a pseudonym) 1937- 101
Alzado, Lyle (Martin) 1949- Brief entry 110
Alzaga, Florinda 1930- 73-76
Amabile, George 1936- 33-36R
Amacher, Richard Earl 1917- CANR-3
Earlier sketch in CA 3R
Amacher, Ryan C(uster) 1945- 105
Amadi, Elechi (Emmanuel) 1934- CANR-16
Earlier sketch in CA 29-32R
See also BW
Amado, Jorge 1912- 77-80
See also CLC 13, 40
Amadon, Dean 1912- 61-64
Amalrik, Andrei Alekseyevich 1938-1980
Obituary 102
Amamoo, Joseph Godson 1931- 13-14R
Aman, Mohammed M(ohammed)
1940- CANR-16
Earlier sketches in CA 49-52, CANR-1
Amanda
See Wynne-Tyson, Esme
Amann, Peter H. 1927- 61-64
Amann, Richard 1945- 106
Amann, Ronald 1943- 112
Amann, Victor F(rancis) 1927- 41-44R
Amanuddin, Syed 1934- CANR-17
Earlier sketches in CA 49-52, CANR-1
Amaral, Anthony 1930-1982 CANR-11
Earlier sketch in CA 21-22R
Amare, Rothayne
See Byrne, Stuart J(ames)
Amaron, Douglas 1914-1985 Obituary 117
Amary, Issam B(ahjat) 1942- CANR-8
Earlier sketch in CA 61-64
Amato, Joseph Anthony 1938- CANR-6
Earlier sketch in CA 57-60
Amatora, Sister Mary 9-10R
Amaya, Ismael E(liseo) 1928-1986
Obituary 120
Amaya, Mario (Anthony) 1933-1986 CANR-9
Obituary 119
Earlier sketch in CA 61-64
Amazing Randi, The
See Randi, James
Ambasz, Emilio 1943- 73-76
Amberg, George H. 1901-1971 Obituary 110
Amberg, (Martin) Hans 1913- 77-80
Amberg, Richard H(iller), Jr. 1942- 77-80
Amberg, Richard Hiller 1912-1967
Obituary 114
Ambhanwong, Suthilak 1924- CANR-18
Earlier sketch in CA 73-76
Ambirajan, Srinivasa 1936- CANR-7
Earlier sketch in CA 19-20R
Ambler, C(hristopher) Gifford 1886- SATA-29
Ambler, Effie 1936- 77-80
Ambler, Eric 1909- CANR-7
Earlier sketch in CA 9-10R
See also CLC 4, 6, 9
Ambler, John S(teward) 1932- 49-52
Ambrose, Alice
See Lazerowitz, Alice Ambrose
Ambrose, David (Edwin) 1943- Brief entry 116
Ambrose, Eric (Samuel) 1908- CAP-1
Earlier sketch in CA 11-12
Ambrose, John W(illiam), Jr. 1931- 57-60
Ambrose, Stephen Edward 1936- CANR-3
Earlier sketch in CA 1R
See also SATA 40
Ambrose, W. Haydn 1922- 25-28R
Ambrosi, Hans Georg 1925- 103
Ambrosini, Maria Luisa 33-36R
Ambroz, Oton 1905- 41-44R
Ambrus, Gyozo Laszlo 1935- CANR-11
Earlier sketch in CA 25-28R
See also SATA 41
Ambrus, Victor G.
See Ambrus, Gyozo Laszlo
See also SATA 1
See also SAAS 4
Amdur, Neil 1939- 106
Amdur, Nikki 1950- 111
Amelio, Ralph J. 1939- 37-40R
Amen, Carol 1934(?)-1987 Obituary 123
Amend, Victor E(arl) 1916- 33-36R
Ament, Pat 1946- 85-88
Amerine, Maynard A(ndrew) 1911- 41-44R
Ameringer, Charles D. 1926- 57-60
Amerman, Lockhart 1911-1969 CAP-2
Earlier sketch in CA 29-32
See also SATA 3
Amery, (Harold) Julian 1919- 61-64
Ames, Charles Edgar 1895-1972 CAP-2
Earlier sketch in CA 25-28
Ames, Delano L. 1906- 107
Ames, Elinor
See Ranzini, Addis Durning
Ames, Evelyn 1908- 57-60
See also SATA 13
Ames, Felicia
See Burden, Jean
Ames, Fisher 1758-1808 DLB-37
Ames, Francis H. 1900- 17-18R
Ames, Gerald 1906- 73-76
See also SATA 11
Ames, Jennifer
See Greig, Maysie
Ames, Jocelyn Green 7-8R
Ames, John 1944- 111
Ames, John Dawes 1904-1987 Obituary 122
Ames, Lee J(udah) 1921- CANR-18
Earlier sketches in CA 4R, CANR-3
See also SATA 3
Ames, Leslie
See Rigoni, Orlando (Joseph)
and Ross, W(illiam) E(dward) D(aniel)
Ames, Lois (Winslow Sisson) 1931- 101
Ames, Louise Bates 1908- CANR-18
Earlier sketches in CA 3R, CANR-3
Ames, Mary Clemmer 1831-1884 DLB-23
Ames, Mildred 1919- CANR-11
Earlier sketch in CA 69-72
See also SATA 22
Ames, Noel
See Barrows, (Ruth) Marjorie
Ames, Norma 1920- CANR-12
Earlier sketch in CA 29-32R
Ames, Rachel 1922- 97-100
Ames, Ruth M(argaret) 1918- 29-32R
Ames, (Polly) Scribner 1908- 69-72
Ames, Van Meter 1898-1985 CAP-1
Obituary 117
Earlier sketch in CA 15-16
Ames, Walter Lansing 1946- 106
Ames, Winslow 1907- CAP-2
Earlier sketch in CA 25-28
Ames-Lewis, Francis 1943- 108
Amey, Lloyd Ronald 1922- CANR-20
Earlier sketch in CA 45-48
Amfitheatrof, Erik 1931- 89-92
Amft, M(arian) J(anet) 1920-1985
Obituary 117
Ami, Ben
See Eliav, Arie L(ova)
Ami, Shlomo Ben
See Ben-Ami, Shlomo
Amichai, Yehuda 1924- 85-88
See also CLC 9, 22
Amick, Robert Gene 1933- 33-36R
Amidon, Bill (Vincent) 1935-1979 45-48
Obituary 103
Amiel, Barbara 1940- 101
Amiel, Joseph 1937- 101
Amin, Ali 1913(?)-1976 Obituary 65-68
Amin, Samir 1931- CANR-15
Earlier sketch in CA 89-92
Amini, Johari M.
See Kunjufu, Johari M. Amini
See also DLB 41
Amir, Menachem 1930- 45-48
Amis, Breton
See Best, Rayleigh Breton Amis
Amis, Kingsley (William) 1922- CANR-8
Earlier sketch in CA 11-12R
See also DLB 15, 27
See also CLC 1, 2, 3, 5, 8, 13, 40, 44
See also AITN 2
Amis, Martin (Louis) 1949- CANR-8
Earlier sketch in CA 65-68
See also DLB 14
See also CLC 4, 9, 38
Amishai-Maisels, Ziva
See Maisels, Maxine S.
Amling, Frederick 1926- Brief entry 112
Amlund, Curtis Arthur 1927- 21-22R
Ammar, Abbas 1907(?)-1974 Obituary 53-56
Amme, Carl H., Jr. 1913- 25-28R
Ammer, Christine (Parker) 1931- 106
Ammer, Dean S. 1926- CANR-7
Earlier sketch in CA 19-20R
Ammerman, David L(eon) 1938- 57-60
Ammerman, Gale Richard 1923- 107
Ammerman, Leila T(remaine) 1912- 33-36R
Ammerman, Robert R(ay) 1927- 15-16R
Ammon, Harry 1917- 73-76
Ammons, A(rchie) R(andolph) 1926- CANR-6
Earlier sketch in CA 9-10R
See also DLB 5
See also CLC 2, 3, 5, 8, 9, 25
See also AITN 1
Amo, Tauraatua i
See Adams, Henry (Brooks)
Amoaku, J. K. 1936- 45-48
Amon, Aline 1928- CANR-8
Earlier sketch in CA 61-64
See also SATA 9
Amor, Amos
See Harrell, Irene B(urk)
Amor, Anne Clark 1933- 112
Amore, Roy Clayton 1942- 105
Amory, Anne Reinberg 1931- 17-18R
Amory, Cleveland 1917- 69-72
See also AITN 1
Amory, Mark 1941- 114
Amos, William E. 1926- 17-18R
Amos, Winsom 1921- 49-52
Amosov, N.
See Amosov, N(ikolai) M(ikhailovich)
Amosov, N(ikolai) M(ikhailovich) 1913-
Brief entry 112
Amoss, Berthe 1925- CANR-14
Earlier sketch in CA 21-22R
See also SATA 5
Amplegirth, Antony
See Dent, Anthony Austen
Amprimoz, Alexandre 1948- CANR-15
Earlier sketch in CA 37-40R
Amram, David (Werner III) 1930- 29-32R
Amrine, Michael 1919(?)-1974 73-76
Obituary 49-52
Amsel, Abram 1922- 114
Amstead, B(illy) H(oward) 1921- 23-24R
Amster, Linda 1938- CANR-22
Earlier sketch in CA 45-48
Amsterdam, Morey 1914- Brief entry 111
Amstutz, Arnold E. 1936- 21-22R
Amstutz, Mark R(obert) 1944- 105
Amter, Joseph A. ?-1982 Obituary 109
Amundsen, Kirsten 1932- 37-40R
Amundsen, Roald Engelbregt Gravning
1872-1928 Brief entry 117
Amusin, Joseph 1910-1984 Obituary 113
Amuzegar, Jahangir 1920- CANR-15
Earlier sketch in CA 41-44R
Analyticus
See Wise, James Waterman
Anand, Mulk Raj 1905- 65-68
See also CLC 23
Anand, Valerie 1937- CANR-13
Earlier sketch in CA 73-76
Anania, Michael 1939- 25-28R
Anastaplo, George 1925- 37-40R
Anastas, Lila L. 1940- 122
Anastas, Peter 1937- CANR-1
Earlier sketch in CA 45-48
Anastasi, Anne 1908- CANR-17
Earlier sketches in CA 7-8R, CANR-2
Anastasio, Dina 1941- 107
See also SATA 30, 37
Anastasiou, Clifford (John) 1929- CANR-18
Earlier sketches in CA 49-52, CANR-3
Anastos, Andrea La Sonde (Melrose)
1951- 117
Anatol
See Schnitzler, Arthur
Anatol, A.
See Kuznetsov, Anatoli
Anaya, Rudolfo A(lfonso) 1937- CANR-1
Earlier sketch in CA 45-48
See also CAAS 4
See also CLC 23
Anber, Paul
See Baker, Pauline H(alpern)

Ancel, Marc 1902- CANR-12
Earlier sketch in CA 69-72
Anchell, Melvin 1919- 25-28R
Anchor, Robert 1937- 69-72
Anckarsvard, Karin Inez Maria 1915-1969 ..9-10R
Obituary 103
See also SATA 6
Ancona, George 1929- CANR-19
Earlier sketches in CA 53-56, CANR-4
See also SATA 12
Andelin, Helen B. 1920- 89-92
Andelman, Eddie 1936- 57-60
Andelman, Samuel L(ouis) 1916-
Brief entry 114
Andelson, Robert V(ernon) 1931- 33-36R
Andereich, Justus
See Steiner, Gerolf
Anders, Donna Carolyn 1938- 125
Anders, Edith (Mary) England 1899- CAP-1
Earlier sketch in CA 15-16
Anders, Evelyn 1916- 29-32R
Anders, Jeanne
See Anderson, Joan Wester
Anders, Leslie 1922- 15-16R
Anders, Sarah Frances 1927- 105
Andersch, Alfred 1914-1980 ....33-36R
Obituary 93-96
See also DLB 69
Andersch, Elizabeth Genevieve 1913- 7-8R
Andersdatter, Karla M(argaret) 1938- ... CANR-21
Earlier sketch in CA 104
See also SATA 34
Andersen, Arlow W. 1906- CAP-1
Earlier sketch in CA 11-12
Andersen, Benny (Allan) 1929- 101
Andersen, Christopher P(eter) 1949- ... CANR-14
Earlier sketch in CA 69-72
Andersen, D(ennis) R(ichard) 1947- 108
Andersen, Doris 1909- CANR-11
Earlier sketch in CA 23-24R
Andersen, Francis Ian 1925- 108
Andersen, Georg 1941- 112
Andersen, Hans Christian 1805-1875 .... YABC-1
See also CLR 6
Andersen, Jefferson 1955(?)-1979
Obituary 85-88
Andersen, Juel 1923- CANR-22
Earlier sketch in CA 105
Andersen, Kenneth E(ldon) 1933- 37-40R
Andersen, Kurt 1954- CANR-23
Earlier sketch in CA 106
Andersen, Marianne S(inger) 1934- 65-68
Andersen, Marion Lineaweaver
1912(?)-1971 Obituary 29-32R
Andersen, R(udolph) Clifton 1933- 33-36R
Andersen, Richard 1931- CANR-24
Earlier sketches in CA 57-60, CANR-8
Andersen, Richard 1946- 102
Andersen, Ted
See Boyd, Waldo T.
Andersen, Uell Stanley 1917- 3R
Andersen, Wayne V. 1928- 9-10R
Andersen, Wilhelm 1911- 29-32R
Andersen, Yvonne 1932- 29-32R
See also SATA 27
Anderson, A(rthur) J(ames) 1933- 106
Anderson, Alan H., Jr. 1943- 69-72
Anderson, Alan Ross 1925-1973 .... CAP-2
Obituary 45-48
Earlier sketch in CA 17-18
Anderson, Allan 1915- 97-100
Anderson, Alpha E. 1914-1970 .... CAP-2
Earlier sketch in CA 23-24
Anderson, Ann Kiemel 1945- 121
Anderson, Arthur J(ames) O(utram)
1907- CANR-15
Earlier sketch in CA 85-88
Anderson, B(asil) W(illiam) 1901-1984
Obituary 112
Anderson, Barbara 1948- 93-96
Anderson, Barbara Gallatin 1926-
Brief entry 111
Anderson, Barry (Franklin) 1935- 19-20R
Anderson, Bern 1900-1963 .... 1R
Anderson, Bernard Eric 1936- CANR-5
Earlier sketch in CA 53-56
Anderson, Bernhard Word 1916- CANR-8
Earlier sketch in CA 57-60
Anderson, Bernice G(oudy) 1894- 101
See also SATA 33
Anderson, Bertha Moore 1892- 7-8R
Anderson, Beverly
See Nemiro, Beverly Anderson
Anderson, Beverly M.
See Nemiro, Beverly Anderson
Anderson, Bob 1947- 69-72
Anderson, Brad(ley Jay) 1924- 106
See also SATA 31, 33
Anderson, C. Farley
See Mencken, H(enry) L(ouis)
and Nathan, George Jean
Anderson, C(arl) L(eonard) 1901- 25-28R
Anderson, Camilla M(ay) 1904- 33-36R
Anderson, Carl Dicmann 1912- 33-36R
Anderson, Carl L(ennart) 1919- 41-44R
Anderson, Carolyn 1941- 73-76
Anderson, Catherine Corley 1909- 4R
Anderson, Charles 1933- 49-52
Anderson, Charles Burroughs 1905-1985 ..65-68
Obituary 115
Anderson, Charles C. 1931- 29-32R
Anderson, Charles Roberts 1902- CANR-3
Earlier sketch in CA 1R
Anderson, Charles W(illiam) 1934- 11-12R
Anderson, Charlotte Maria 1923- 81-84
Anderson, Chester 1932- Brief entry 117
Anderson, Chester G(rant) 1923- 25-28R
Anderson, Chuck
See Anderson, Charles
Anderson, Clarence William 1891-1971 73-76
Obituary 29-32R
See also SATA 11
Anderson, Clifford
See Gardner, Richard (M.)
Anderson, Colena M(ichael) 1891- CANR-11
Earlier sketch in CA 21-22R
Anderson, Cortland 1935-1985 Obituary 118
Anderson, Courtney 1906- CAP-1
Earlier sketch in CA 19-20
Anderson, Dave
See Anderson, David Poole
See also AITN 2
Anderson, David D(aniel) 1924- CANR-5
Earlier sketch in CA 13-14R
Anderson, David L(eonard) 1919- 7-8R
Anderson, David Poole 1929- 89-92
Anderson, Dillon 1906-1974 .... 3R
Obituary 45-48
Anderson, Donald F(rancis) 1938- 53-56
Anderson, Donald K(ennedy), Jr. 1922- ..37-40R
Anderson, Doris (Hilda) 1925- 89-92
Anderson, Dwight G(ale) 1938- 107
Anderson, E. Ruth 1907- 93-96
Anderson, E.W. 1901-1981 Obituary 104
Anderson, Earl Robert 1943- 111
Anderson, Edgar 1920- CANR-13
Earlier sketch in CA 33-36R
Anderson, Einar 1909- 15-16R
Anderson, Elbridge Gerry 1907- 69-72
Anderson, Elliott 1944- 93-96
Anderson, Eloise Adell 1927- 53-56
See also SATA 9
Anderson, Emily 1891-1962 124
Anderson, Eric (Douglas) 1949- 106
Anderson, Erica 1914- 57-60
Anderson, Eugene N(ewton) 1900- 29-32R
Anderson, (William) Ferguson 1914- 107
Anderson, Frank J(ohn) 1919- CANR-4
Earlier sketch in CA 9-10R
Anderson, Fred 1949- 117
Anderson, Frederick Irving 1877-1947
Brief entry 112
Anderson, Freeman B(urket) 1922- 41-44R
Anderson, Gary Clayton 1948- 117
Anderson, Gary Lee 1939- Brief entry 115
Anderson, George
See Groom, Arthur William
Anderson, George
See Weissman, Jack
Anderson, George B. 1908(?)-1985
Obituary 114
Anderson, George Christian 1907-1976 ... CAP-2
Obituary 69-72
Earlier sketch in CA 29-32
Anderson, George K(umler) 1901- CAP-2
Earlier sketch in CA 23-24
Anderson, George L(aVerne)
1905-1971 ....CANR-9
Earlier sketch in CA 13-14R
Anderson, George Lee 1934- Brief entry 111
Anderson, Gerald Dwight 1944- 115
Anderson, Gerald H(arry) 1930- CANR-7
Earlier sketch in CA 19-20R
Anderson, Godfrey Tryggve 1909- 41-44R
Anderson, Grace Fox 1932- 121
See also SATA 43
Anderson, H(ugh) Allen (Jr.) 1950- 120
Anderson, H(obson) Dewey 1897-1975 65-68
Obituary 61-64
Anderson, Harold H(omer) 1897- CAP-2
Earlier sketch in CA 21-22
Anderson, Harry V(ernon) 1903-1983
Obituary 110
Anderson, Henry P. 1927- 33-36R
Anderson, Howard Jeremy 1915(?)-1983
Obituary 111
Anderson, Howard Peter 1932- 61-64
Anderson, Hugh 1920- 9-10R
Anderson, Ian Gibson 1933- 85-88
Anderson, Irvine H(enry) 1928- CANR-11
Earlier sketch in CA 69-72
Anderson, J(ohn) E(dward) 1903- 37-40R
Anderson, J(ohn) K(inloch) 1924- CANR-10
Earlier sketch in CA 19-20R
Anderson, J(ohn) Kerby 1951- 97-100
Anderson, J. N.
See Anderson, (James) Norman
(Dalrymple)
Anderson, J(ohn) R(ichard) L(ane)
1911-1981 ....CANR-18
Obituary 104
Earlier sketch in CA 25-28R
See also SATA 15, 27
Anderson, Jack(son Northman) 1922- ... CANR-6
Earlier sketch in CA 57-60
See also AITN 1
Anderson, Jack 1935- CANR-24
Earlier sketch in CA 33-36R
Anderson, James C(letus) 1943- 111
Anderson, James D(esmond) 1933- 49-52
Anderson, James E(lliott) 1933- CANR-21
Earlier sketches in CA 9-10R, CANR-6
Anderson, James F(rancis) 1910- 41-44R
Anderson, James G(eorge) 1936- 25-28R
Anderson, James LaVerne 1940-
Brief entry 111
Anderson, James M(axwell) 1933- 33-36R
Anderson, (Helen) Jean 1931- CANR-14
Earlier sketch in CA 41-44R
Anderson, Jeanne 1934(?)-1979 Obituary ..85-88
Anderson, Jennifer 1942- 57-60
Anderson, Jerry M(aynard) 1933- 41-44R
Anderson, Jessica (Margaret) Queale CANR-4
Earlier sketch in CA 11-12R
See also CLC 37
Anderson, Joan Wester 1938- CANR-24
Earlier sketches in CA 65-68, CANR-9
Anderson, John Bayard 1922- 33-36R
Anderson, John F(reeman) 1945- 53-56
Anderson, John K.
See Anderson, J(ohn) K(inloch)
Anderson, John L(onzo) 1905- 25-28R
Anderson, John M(ueller) 1914- 17-18R
Anderson, John Q. 1916-1975 .... CANR-3
Earlier sketch in CA 1R
Anderson, Jon (Victor) 1940- CANR-20
Earlier sketch in CA 25-28R
See also CLC 9
Anderson, Joy 1928- 25-28R
See also SATA 1
Anderson, Judith H(elena) 1940- 123
Anderson, Judith I(cke) 1939- 112
Anderson, Ken 1917- 25-28R
Anderson, Kenneth Norman 1921- CANR-18
Earlier sketch in CA 102
Anderson, Kristin
See Du Breuil, (Elizabeth) L(or)inda
Anderson, LaVere Francis Shoenfelt 1907- .. 101
See also SATA 27
Anderson, Lee 1896-1972 .... 1R
Obituary 37-40R
Anderson, Lee Stratton 1925- 101
Anderson, Leone Castell 1923- 126
See also SATA 49, 53
Anderson, Lester William 1918-1973 ....7-8R
Obituary 103
Anderson, Lindsay 1923- CLC-20
Anderson, Lindsay (Gordon) 1923-
Brief entry 125
See also CLC 20
Anderson, Lonzo
See Anderson, John L(onzo)
See also SATA 2
Anderson, Lucia (Lewis) 1922- 41-44R
See also SATA 10
Anderson, Luther A(dolph) 65-68
Anderson, M(ary) D(esiree) 1902- 11-12R
Anderson, Madeleine Paltenghi 1899- CAP-1
Earlier sketch in CA 19-20
Anderson, Madelyn Klein CANR-11
Earlier sketch in CA 69-72
See also SATA 28
Anderson, Maggie
See Anderson, Margaret
Anderson, Malcolm 1934- 33-36R
Anderson, Margaret (Vance) 1917- 21-22R
Anderson, Margaret 1948- 101
Anderson, Margaret Bartlett 1922- 9-10R
Anderson, Margaret C(aroline) 1886-1973 ... 108
Obituary 45-48
See also DLB 4
Anderson, Margaret J(ohnson) 1909- ... CANR-3
Earlier sketch in CA 3R
Anderson, Margaret J(ean) 1931- CANR-26
Earlier sketches in CA 69-72, CANR-11
See also SATA 27
Anderson, Martin 1936- CANR-9
Earlier sketch in CA 15-16R
Anderson, Marvin Walter 1933- 41-44R
Anderson, Mary 1939- CANR-16
Earlier sketches in CA 49-52, CANR-1
See also SATA 7
Anderson, Matthew Smith 1922- 13-14R
Anderson, Maxie (Leroy) 1934-1983
Obituary 115
Anderson, Maxwell 1888-1959 Brief entry .. 105
See also DLB 7
See also TCLC 2
Anderson, Mona 1910- CANR-6
Earlier sketch in CA 57-60
See also SATA 40
Anderson, Nancy Fix 1941- 126
Anderson, (James) Norman (Dalrymple)
1908- CANR-4
Earlier sketch in CA 11-12R
Anderson, Norman Dean 1928- CANR-15
Earlier sketch in CA 33-36R
See also SATA 22
Anderson, Norman G(ulden) 1913-
Brief entry 114
Anderson, O(rvil) Roger 1937- 33-36R
Anderson, Odin W(aldemar) 1914- 25-28R
Anderson, Olive M(ary) 1915- CANR-14
Earlier sketch in CA 81-84
Anderson, Olive Ruth 1926- 107
Anderson, P(aul) Howard 1947- 61-64
Anderson, Patrick (John MacAllister)
1915-1979 93-96
Obituary 85-88
See also DLB 68
Anderson, Patrick 1936- 33-36R
Anderson, Paul E. 1925- 33-36R
Anderson, Paul Seward 1913-1975 ..... CANR-6
Earlier sketch in CA 4R
Anderson, Paul Y. 1893-1938 .... DLB-29
Anderson, Peggy 1938- 93-96
Anderson, Poul (William) 1926- CANR-15
Earlier sketches in CA 2R, CANR-2
See also CAAS 2
See also SATA 39
See also DLB 8
See also CLC 15
Anderson, Quentin 1912- CANR-3
Earlier sketch in CA 1R
Anderson, R. C. 1883(?)-1976 Obituary ...69-72
Anderson, R(oy) C(laude) 1931- 124
Anderson, Rachel 1943- CANR-24
Earlier sketches in CA 21-22R, CANR-9
See also SATA 34
Anderson, Randall C. 1934- 41-44R
Anderson, Ray Sherman 1925- CANR-10
Earlier sketch in CA 65-68
Anderson, Raymond L(loyd) 1927- 106
Anderson, Richard
See Anderson, J(ohn) R(ichard) L(ane)
Anderson, Richard Chase 1934-
Brief entry 112
Anderson, Richard Lloyd 1926- 37-40R
Anderson, Robert (Woodruff) 1917- 21-22R
See also DLB 7
See also CLC 23
See also AITN 1
Anderson, Robert A(ndrew) 1944- 109
Anderson, Robert C(harles) 1930- 85-88
Anderson, Robert David 1942- 73-76
Anderson, Robert H(enry) 1918- 49-52
Anderson, Robert Mapes 1929- 108
Anderson, Robert N(orris) 1944- 126
Anderson, Robert Newton 1929- 49-52
Anderson, Robert T(homas) 1926- 9-10R
Anderson, Robert W(illiam) 1926- 19-20R
Anderson, Roberta 1942- 115
Brief entry 111
Anderson, Rodney Dean 1938- 108
Anderson, Ronald Kinloch 1911-1984
Obituary 111
Anderson, Roy 1936- 15-16R
Anderson, Roy
See Anderson, R(oy) C(laude)
Anderson, Roy Allan 1895- CANR-9
Earlier sketch in CA 15-16R
Anderson, Ruth I(rene) 1919- CANR-18
Earlier sketch in CA 4R
Anderson, Ruth Nathan 1934- 69-72
Anderson, Scarvia (Bateman) 1926- CANR-14
Earlier sketch in CA 41-44R
Anderson, Sherwood 1876-1941 121
Brief entry 104
See also DLB 4, 9
See also DLBD 1
See also TCLC 1, 10, 24
See also SSC 1
Anderson, Sparky
See Anderson, George Lee
Anderson, Stanford 1934- 25-28R
Anderson, Stanley Edwin 1900-1977 .... CANR-3
Earlier sketch in CA 1R
Anderson, Stanley V(ictor) 1928- 21-22R
Anderson, Sydney 1927- 106
Anderson, T(heodore) W(ilbur) 1918- 49-52
Anderson, Teresa 1944- 85-88
Anderson, Theodore R(obert) 1927- 41-44R
Anderson, Thomas 1929- 3R
Anderson, Thomas D. 1929- 111
Anderson, Tom 1910- 69-72
Anderson, Tommy (Nolan) 1918- 45-48
Anderson, Totton J(ames) 1909- 3R
Anderson, Verily (Bruce) 1915- CANR-3
Earlier sketch in CA 7-8R
Anderson, Vernon E(llsworth) 1908- CANR-5
Earlier sketch in CA 4R
Anderson, Virgil Antris 1899- CANR-16
Earlier sketch in CA 1R
Anderson, Virginia (R. Cronin) 1920- 21-22R
Anderson, Vivienne 1916- 19-20R
Anderson, W. B.
See Schultz, James Willard
Anderson, Wallace Ludwig 1917- 17-18R
Anderson, Walt
See Anderson, Walter Truett
Anderson, Walter 1944- 101
Anderson, Walter Truett 1933- 105
Anderson, Warren DeWitt 1920- 17-18R
Anderson, Wayne 1946- 107
Anderson, Wayne Jeremy 1908- 49-52
Anderson, Wendell B(ernhard) 1920- 105
Anderson, William A(verette) 1937-
Brief entry 114
Anderson, William Charles 1920- CANR-2
Earlier sketch in CA 7-8R
Anderson, William Davis 1938- 33-36R
Anderson, William Eugene 1926-
Brief entry 111
Anderson, William G(ary) 1945- 115
Anderson, William H(arry) 1905-1972 49-52
Anderson, William Robert 1921- 7-8R
Anderson, William Scovil 1927- 61-64
Anderson, Wilton T(homas) 1916- 17-18R
Anderson Imbert, Enrique 1910- CANR-26
Earlier sketches in CA 19-20R, CANR-10
Andersons, Edgars
See Anderson, Edgar
Anders-Richards, Donald 1928- 25-28R
Andersson, Ingvar 1899(?)-1974
Obituary 53-56
Andersson, Theodore 1903- 49-52
Andersson, Theodore M(urdock) 1934- ...25-28R
Anderton, David A(lbin) 1919- CANR-9
Earlier sketch in CA 65-68
Anderton, Joanne (Marie) Gast 1930- 61-64
Anderton, Johana Gast
See Anderton, Joanne (Marie) Gast
Andervont, Howard Bancroft 1898-1981
Obituary 103
Andonian, Jeanne (Beghian) 1891(?)-1976
Obituary 65-68
Andonov-Poljanski, Hristo 1927- CANR-9
Earlier sketch in CA 21-22R
Andouard
See Giraudoux, (Hippolyte) Jean
Andrade, Carlos Drummond de
See Drummond de Andrade, Carlos
See also CLC 18
Andrade, E(dward) N(eville) da C(osta)
1887-1971 .... CAP-1
Earlier sketch in CA 11-12

Andrade, Victor (Manuel) 1905- 69-72
Andrain, Charles F(ranklin) 1937- 69-72
Andre, Evelyn M(arie) 1924- CANR-11
Earlier sketch in CA 69-72
See also SATA 27
Andre, (Kenneth) Michael 1946- 114
Andre, Rae 1946- 116
Andreach, Robert J. 1930- 33-36R
Andreano, Ralph L(ouis) 1929- CANR-6
Earlier sketch in CA 7-8R
Andreas, Burton G(ould) 1921- 81-84
Andreas, Thomas
See Williams, Thomas (Andrew)
Andreasen, Alan R(obert) 1934- 65-68
Andreasen, Nancy C(oover) 1938- 108
Andreas-Salome, Lou 1861-1937 .... DLB-66
Andreassen, Karl
See Boyd, Waldo T.
Andree, Louise
See Coury, Louise Andree
Andree, R(ichard) V(ernon) 1919- CANR-8
Earlier sketch in CA 57-60
Andree, Robert G(erald) 1912-1987 .... 29-32R
Obituary 124
Andreissen, David
See Poyer, David
Andreopoulos, Spyros (George) 1929- 77-80
Andres, Glenn M(erle) 1941- 73-76
Andres, Stefan 1906-1970 Obituary 29-32R
See also DLB 69
Andresen, Jack
See Andresen, John H(enry), Jr.
Andresen, John H(enry), Jr. 1917- 57-60
Andresen, Julie
See Tetel, Julie
Andreski, Iris
See Gillespie, I(ris) S(ylvia)
Andreski, Stanislav Leonard 1919- 61-64
Andrew, David S. 1943- 123
Andrew, J(ames) Dudley 1945- CANR-9
Earlier sketch in CA 65-68
Andrew, John (Alfred III) 1943- 69-72
Andrew, Malcolm (Ross) 1945- 105
Andrew, Prudence (Hastings) 1924- CANR-1
Earlier sketch in CA 1R
Andrew, Warren 1910- 21-22R
Andrewes, Christopher Howard 1896- 17-18R
Andrewes, Patience
See Bradford, Patience Andrewes
Andrews, A. A.
See Paine, Lauran (Bosworth)
Andrews, Allen 1913- CANR-1
Earlier sketch in CA 49-52
Andrews, Arthur (Douglas, Jr.) 1923- 69-72
Andrews, Barry G(eoffrey) 1943- CANR-2
Earlier sketch in CA 49-52
Andrews, Bart 1945- CANR-24
Earlier sketches in CA 65-68, CANR-9
Andrews, Benny 1930- 106
See also SATA 31
Andrews, Bruce 1948- CANR-10
Earlier sketch in CA 49-52
Andrews, Burton (Allen) 1906- CAP-2
Earlier sketch in CA 33-36
Andrews, Charles M(cLean) 1863-1943
Brief entry 119
See also DLB 17
Andrews, Cicily Fairfield
See West, Rebecca
Andrews, Claire 1940- 33-36R
Andrews, Clarence A(delbert) 1912- CANR-20
Earlier sketch in CA 33-36R
Andrews, Donald H(atch) 1898-197(?) CAP-2
Earlier sketch in CA 23-24
Andrews, Dorothea Harris 1916-1976
Obituary 69-72
Andrews, E(ric) M(ontgomery) 1933- 93-96
Andrews, Eamonn 1922-1987 120
Obituary 124
Andrews, Edgar Harold 1932- 105
Andrews, Eleanor Lattimore
See Lattimore, Eleanor Frances
Andrews, Elton V.
See Pohl, Frederik
Andrews, Ernest E(ugene) 1932- 57-60
Andrews, F(rank) Emerson 1902-1978 .... CANR-1
Obituary 81-84
Earlier sketch in CA 4R
See also SATA 22
Andrews, (Earl) Frank 1937- 61-64
Andrews, Frank M(eredith) 1935- CANR-14
Earlier sketch in CA 41-44R
Andrews, George (Clinton) 1926- 21-22R
Andrews, George F(redrick) 1918- 65-68
Andrews, Henry N(athaniel), Jr. 1910- 93-96
Andrews, J. Cutler 1908-1972 Obituary 37-40R
Andrews, J(ames) S(ydney) 1934- 29-32R
See also SATA 4
Andrews, James David 1924- 53-56
Andrews, James Frederick 1936-1980
Obituary 107
Andrews, James J. C. 1943(?)-1985
Obituary 116
Andrews, James R(obertson) 1936-
Brief entry 117
Andrews, Jan 1942- 122
See also SATA 49
Andrews, John F(rank) 1942- 119
Andrews, John Henry 1939- 107
Andrews, John Malcolm 1936- 117
Andrews, John Williams 1898-1975
Obituary 57-60
Andrews, Julie 1935- 37-40R
See also SATA 7
Andrews, Keith 1930- 33-36R
Andrews, Kenneth R(ichmond) 1916- CANR-16
Earlier sketch in CA 1R
Andrews, Kevin 1924- 124
Andrews, Laura
See Coury, Louise Andree
Andrews, Lewis M. 1946- 65-68
Andrews, (William) Linton 1886-1972 .... 9-10R
Obituary 120
Andrews, Lucilla Mathew Brief entry 116
Andrews, Lyman 1938- 49-52
Andrews, Lynn V. Brief entry 125
Andrews, Margaret E(lizabeth) 33-36R
Andrews, Mark Edwin 1903- CAP-1
Earlier sketch in CA 19-20
Andrews, (Daniel) Marshall 1899(?)-1973
Obituary 45-48
Andrews, Mary Evans 5-6R
Andrews, Michael
See Andrews, Michael Alford
Andrews, Michael Alford 1939- 116
Andrews, Michael F(rank) 1916- 49-52
Andrews, Mike
See Andrews, Michael Alford
Andrews, Paul Revere 1906-1983
Obituary 110
Andrews, Peter 1931- CANR-11
Earlier sketch in CA 17-18R
Andrews, Ralph W(arren) 1897- 9-10R
Andrews, Raymond 1934- CANR-15
Earlier sketch in CA 81-84
See also BW
Andrews, Robert D.
See Andrews, (Charles) Robert Douglas (Hardy)
Andrews, (Charles) Robert Douglas (Hardy)
1908- CAP-1
Earlier sketch in CA 9-10
Andrews, Roy Chapman 1884-1960 .... SATA-19
Andrews, Stanley 1894- CANR-22
Earlier sketch in CA 45-48
Andrews, V(irginia) C(leo) ?-1986 .... CANR-21
Obituary 121
Earlier sketch in CA 97-100
See also SATA 50
Andrews, Wayne 1913-1987 .... CANR-3
Obituary 123
Earlier sketch in CA 9-10R
Andrews, William G(eorge) 1930- CANR-7
Earlier sketch in CA 7-8R
Andrews, William R(obert) 1937- 53-56
Andreyev, Leonid (Nikolaevich) 1871-1919
Brief entry 104
See also TCLC 3
Andreyev, Nikolay Efremych 1908-1982
Obituary 106
Andrezel, Pierre
See Blixen, Karen (Christentze Dinesen)
Andrian, Gustave W(illiam) 1918-
Brief entry 114
Andric, Ivo 1892-1975 81-84
Obituary 57-60
See also CLC 8
Andriekus, (Kazimieras) Leonardas
1914- 25-28R
Andrien, Kenneth James 1951- 120
Andriessen, Hendrik (Franciscus)
1892-1981 Obituary 108
Andriola, Alfred J. 1912-1983 Obituary 109
See also SATA 34
Andrist, Ralph K. 1914- CANR-20
Earlier sketches in CA 9-10R, CANR-5
See also SATA 45
Andropov, Yuri (Vladimirovich) 1914-1984
Obituary 111
Andros, Dee G(us) 1924- 69-72
Andros, Phil
See Steward, Samuel M(orris)
Andrus, (Vincent) Dyckman 1942- 102
Andrus, Hyrum L(eslie) 1924- 37-40R
Andrus, Paul 1931- 65-68
Andrus, Vera 1895- CAP-2
Earlier sketch in CA 21-22
Andrzejewski, Jerzy 1909-1983 .... 25-28R
Obituary 109
Andrzeyevski, George
See Andrzejewski, Jerzy
Anduze-Dufy, Raphael
See Coulet du Gard, Rene
Anees, Munawar Ahmad 1948- 123
An Elderly Spinster
See Wilson, Margaret (Wilhemina)
Anfousse, Ginette 1944- SATA-48
Angebert, Jean
See Bertrand, Michel
Angebert, Jean-Michel
See Bertrand, Michel
Angebert, Michel
See Bertrand, Michel
Angel, Daniel D. 1939- 33-36R
Angel, Heather 1941- CANR-25
Earlier sketch in CA 69-72
Angel, J(ohn) Lawrence 1915-1986 101
Obituary 120
Angel, Marc D(wight) 1945- 101
Angel, Marie 1923- CANR-15
Earlier sketch in CA 29-32R
See also SATA 47
Angelella, Michael 1953- 97-100
Angeles, Jose 1930- 33-36R
Angeles, Peter A. 1931- 33-36R
See also SATA 40
Angeles, Philip 1909- 7-8R
Angeli, Marguerite (Lofft) de
See de Angeli, Marguerite (Lofft)
Angelilli, Frank Joseph
See Angell, Frank Joseph
Angelin, Patricia 119
Angelino, Marie
See Garbutt, Janice (D.) Lovoos
Angelique, Pierre
See Bataille, Georges
Angell, Ernest 1889-1973 Obituary 37-40R
Angell, Frank Joseph 1919- 17-18R
Angell, George 1945- 101
Angell, James Burrill 1829-1916 .... DLB-64
Angell, James W(aterhouse) 1898-1986
Obituary 119
Angell, Judie 1937- 77-80
See also SATA 22
Angell, Madeline 1919- CANR-10
Earlier sketch in CA 65-68
See also SATA 18
Angell, (Ralph) Norman 1872(?)-1967 .... CAP-1
Earlier sketch in CA 13-14
Angell, Richard B(radshaw) 1918- 15-16R
Angell, Robert Cooley 1899- 101
Angell, Roger 1920- CANR-13
Earlier sketch in CA 57-60
See also CLC 26
Angell, Tony 1940- CANR-4
Earlier sketch in CA 53-56
Angelo, Bonnie Brief entry 113
Angelo, Frank 1914- CANR-4
Earlier sketch in CA 53-56
Angelo, Valenti 1897- 73-76
See also SATA 14
Angelocci, Angelo 1926- 23-24R
Angelou, Maya 1928- CANR-19
Earlier sketch in CA 65-68
See also BW
See also SATA 49
See also DLB 38
See also CLC 12, 35
Anger, Kenneth 1930- 106
Angermann, Gerhard O(tto) 1904- 65-68
Angier, Bradford CANR-7
Earlier sketch in CA 5-6R
See also SATA 12
Angier, Carole 1943- 120
Angier, Roswell P. 1940- 101
Angiolillo, Paul F(rancis) 1917- 105
Anglade, Jean 1915- CANR-20
Earlier sketch in CA 103
Angle, Paul M(cClelland) 1900-1975 .... CAP-2
Obituary 57-60
Earlier sketch in CA 21-22
See also SATA 20
Anglin, Douglas G(eorge) 1923- CANR-14
Earlier sketch in CA 37-40R
Anglo, Sydney 1934- 89-92
Anglund, Joan Walsh 1926- CANR-15
Earlier sketch in CA 7-8R
See also SATA 2
See also CLR 1
Ango, Fan D.
See Longyear, Barry Brookes
Angoff, Allan 1910- CANR-20
Earlier sketch in CA 45-48
Angoff, Charles 1902-1979 .... CANR-4
Obituary 85-88
Earlier sketch in CA 5-6R
Angremy, Jean-Pierre 1937- 106
Angress, R(uth) K(lueger) 1931- 37-40R
Angress, Werner T(homas) 1920- 13-14R
Angrist, Shirley S(arah) 1933- 25-28R
Angrist, Stanley W(olff) 1933- 25-28R
See also SATA 4
Anguizola, G. A.
See Anguizola, Gustave (A.)
Anguizola, Gustave (A.) 1927- Brief entry 116
Angus, Douglas Ross 1909- CANR-3
Earlier sketch in CA 1R
Angus, Fay 1929- CANR-15
Earlier sketch in CA 89-92
Angus, Ian
See Mackay, James (Alexander)
Angus, J(ohn) Colin 1907- 107
Angus, Margaret 1908- 21-22R
Angus, Sylvia 1921-1982 .... CANR-10
Earlier sketch in CA 61-64
Angus, Tom
See Powell, Geoffrey Stewart
Angus-Butterworth, Lionel Milner 1900- CANR-4
Earlier sketch in CA 53-56
Anhalt, Edward 85-88
See also DLB 26
Anicar, Tom
See Racina, Thom
Anikouchine, William A(lexander) 1929-
Brief entry 117
Anita
See Daniel, Anita
Ankenbrand, Frank, Jr. 1905- CAP-2
Earlier sketch in CA 19-20
Anker, Charlotte 1934- 93-96
Ankerson, Dudley (Charles) 1948- 126
Anmar, Frank
See Nolan, William F(rancis)
Anna, Timothy E. 1944- 101
Annan, Noel Gilroy 1916- 61-64
Annand, J(ames) K(ing) 1908- CANR-18
Earlier sketch in CA 101
Annandale, Barbara
See Bowden, Jean
Annas, George J. 1945- 77-80
Anne-Mariel
See Goud, Anne
Annensky, Innokenty Fyodorovich
1856-1909 Brief entry 110
See also TCLC 14
Anness, Milford E(dwin) 1918- 17-18R
Annett, Cora
See Scott, Cora Annett (Pipitone)
Annett, John 1930- 29-32R
Annis, Linda Ferrill 1943- 85-88
Annixter, Jane
See Sturtzel, Jane Levington
Annixter, Paul
See Sturtzel, Howard A(llison)
Anno, Mitsumasa 1926- CANR-4
Earlier sketch in CA 49-52
See also SATA 5, 38
See also CLR 2, 14
Anobile, Richard J(oseph) 1947- CANR-5
Earlier sketch in CA 53-56
Anobile, Ulla (Kakonen) 1945- 111
Anodos
See Coleridge, Mary E(lizabeth)
Anoff, I(sador) S(amuel) 1892- 45-48
Anon, Charles Robert
See Pessoa, Fernando (Antonio Nogueira)
Anouilh, Jean (Marie Lucien Pierre)
1910-1987 .... 17-18R
Obituary 123
See also CLC 1, 3, 8, 13, 40, 50
Anquillare, John 1942- 105
Ansbacher, Heinz L(udwig) 1904- CAP-1
Earlier sketch in CA 9-10
Ansbacher, Max G. 1935- 89-92
Ansberry, William F. 1926- 33-36R
Anschel, Eugene 1907- 53-56
Anschel, Kurt R. 1936- 41-44R
Anscombe, G(ertrude) E(lizabeth)
M(argaret) 1919- Brief entry 122
Anscombe, Isabelle (Mary) 1954- 108
Ansel, Walter (Charles) 1897-1977 45-48
Obituary 73-76
Ansell, Helen 1940- 25-28R
Ansell, Jack 1925-1976 .... 17-18R
Obituary 69-72
Anselm, Felix
See Pollak, Felix
Ansen, Alan 1922- CANR-4
Earlier sketch in CA 1R
Anshen, Melvin (Leon) 1912- 124
Ansley, Gladys Piatt 1906- 5-6R
Anslinger, Harry Jacob 1892-1975 .... CAP-1
Obituary 61-64
Earlier sketch in CA 11-12
Anson, Bill 1907-1983 Obituary 110
Anson, Cyril J(oseph) 1923- 49-52
Anson, Jay 1921-1980 81-84
Obituary 97-100
Anson, John
See Firth, (Frederick) Anson
Anson, Peter Frederick 1889- 9-10R
Anson, Robert Sam 1945- 125
Brief entry 115
Anspach, Donald F. 1942- 69-72
Anstey, Edgar 1917- CANR-3
Earlier sketch in CA 7-8R
Anstey, Edgar
See Slusser, George Edgar
Anstey, F.
See Guthrie, Thomas Anstey
Anstey, Roger T(homas) 1927- 13-14R
Anstey, Vera (Powell) 1889- CAP-1
Earlier sketch in CA 17-18
Anstruther, Godfrey 1903-1988 Obituary 126
Anstruther, James
See Maxtone Graham, James Anstruther
An Tai-sung 1931- Brief entry 113
Antell, Gerson 1926- 53-56
Antell, Will D. 1935- 104
See also SATA 31
Anthes, Richard A(llen) 1944- 107
Anthony
See Taber, Anthony Scott
Anthony, Barbara 1932- CANR-21
Earlier sketch in CA 103
See also SATA 29
Anthony, C. L.
See Smith, Dodie
Anthony, Catherine
See Adachi, Barbara (Curtis)
Anthony, David
See Smith, William Dale
Anthony, Diana 1951- 114
Anthony, Edward 1895-1971 73-76
Obituary 33-36R
See also SATA 21
Anthony, Evelyn
See Ward-Thomas, Evelyn Bridget Patricia Stephens
Anthony, Florence
See Ai
Anthony, Geraldine C(ecilia) 1919- CANR-11
Earlier sketch in CA 69-72
Anthony, Gordon
See Stannus, (James) Gordon (Dawson)
Anthony, Inid E. 1925- 104
Anthony, J(oseph) Garner 1899- 61-64
Anthony, James R(aymond) 1922- 49-52
Anthony, John
See Beckett, Ronald Brymer
Anthony, John
See Sabini, John Anthony
Anthony, Julie 1948- 106
Anthony, Katharine (Susan) 1877-1965
Obituary 25-28R
Anthony, Michael 1932- CANR-10
Earlier sketch in CA 19-20R
See also BW
Anthony, Peter
See Shaffer, Anthony (Joshua)
and Shaffer, Peter (Levin)
Anthony, Piers 1934- 23-24R
See also DLB 8
See also CLC 35
Anthony, Rebecca (Jespersen) 1950- 118
Anthony, Robert N(ewton) 1916- CANR-5
Earlier sketch in CA 15-16R

Anthony, Susan B(rownell) 1916- ... 89-92
Anthony, William G. 1934- ... 17-18R
Anthony, William P(hilip) 1943- ... CANR-13
Earlier sketch in CA 77-80
Anthrop, Donald F. 1935- Brief entry ... 111
Anticaglia, Elizabeth 1939- ... CANR-1
Earlier sketch in CA 45-48
See also SATA 12
Antico, John 1924- ... 29-32R
Antill, James Macquarie 1912- ... CANR-13
Earlier sketch in CA 33-36R
Antin, David 1932- ... 73-76
Antin, Mary 1881-1949 Brief entry ... 118
See also DLBY 84
Antoine, Marc
See Proust, (Valentin-Louis-George-Eugene-) Marcel
Antoine-Dariaux, Genevieve 1914- ... 57-60
Antolini, Margaret Fishback 1904-1985
Obituary ... 117
See also SATA 45
Anton, Frank Robert 1920- ... 41-44R
Anton, Hector R(oque) 1919- ... 73-76
Anton, John P(eter) 1920- ... CANR-9
Earlier sketch in CA 21-22R
Anton, Michael J(ames) 1940- ... 57-60
See also SATA 12
Anton, Rita (Kenter) 1920- ... 9-10R
Antonacci, Robert J(oseph) 1916- ... CANR-9
Earlier sketch in CA 7-8R
See also SATA 37, 45
Antoncich, Betty (Kennedy) 1913- ... 15-16R
Antone, Evan Haywood 1922- ... 126
Antoni
See Iranek-Osmecki, Kazimierz
Antoniak, Helen Elizabeth 1947- ... 105
Antonick, Robert J. 1939- ... 37-40R
Antoninus, Brother
See Everson, William (Oliver)
Antonio, Robert J(ohn) 1945- ... 120
Antonioni, Michelangelo 1912- ... 73-76
See also CLC 20
Antoniutti, Ildebrando 1898-1974
Obituary ... 53-56
Antonovsky, Aaron 1923- ... CANR-12
Earlier sketch in CA 29-32R
Antony, Jonquil 1916(?)-1980 ... 15-16R
Obituary ... 120
Antoun, Richard T(aft) 1932- ... 65-68
Antreasian, Garo Z(areh) 1922- ... 81-84
Antrim, Harry Thomas 1936- ... 33-36R
Antrim, William H. 1928- ... 69-72
Antrobus, John 1933- ... CANR-11
Earlier sketch in CA 57-60
Antschel, Paul 1920-1970 ... 85-88
See also CLC 10, 19
Anttila, Raimo (Aulis) 1935- ... 33-36R
Anvic, Frank
See Sherman, Jory (Tecumseh)
Anwar, Chairil 1922-1949 Brief entry ... 121
See also TCLC 22
Anweiler, Oskar 1925- ... CANR-9
Earlier sketch in CA 65-68
Anyon, G(eorge) Jay 1909- ... 7-8R
Anzovin, Steven 1954- ... 124
Aoki, Haruo 1930- ... 49-52
Aoki, Hisako 1942- ... 115
See also SATA 45
Aoki, Michiko Y(amaguchi) ... 107
Apel, Karl-Otto 1922- ... CANR-22
Earlier sketch in CA 105
Apel, Willi 1893- ... CANR-2
Earlier sketch in CA 2R
Apelian, Albert Solomon 1893-1986
Obituary ... 121
Apfel, Necia H(alpern) 1930- ... CANR-23
Earlier sketch in CA 107
See also SATA 41, 51
Apffel, Edmund R., Jr. 1948- ... 107
Apgar, Virginia 1909-1974 ... 73-76
Obituary ... 53-56
Aphrodite, J.
See Livingston, Carole
Apikuni
See Schultz, James Willard
Apilentz
See Apelian, Albert Solomon
Apitz, Bruno 1900-1979 Obituary ... 85-88
Aplon, Roger 1937- ... 119
Apolinar, Danny 1934- ... 61-64
Apollinaire, Guillaume
See Kostrowitzki, Wilhelm Apollinaris de
See also TCLC 3, 8
Aponte, Barbara (Ann) Bockus 1936-
Brief entry ... 111
Apostle, Chris(tos) N(icholas) 1935- ... 21-22R
Apostolon, Billy (Michael) 1930- ... 97-100
Apostolos-Cappadona, Diane 1948- ... 112
App, Austin Joseph 1902-1984 ... 101
Obituary ... 112
Appadorai, A(ngadipuram) 1902- ... 102
Appel, Alfred, Jr. 1934- Brief entry ... 113
Appel, Allan 1946- ... 77-80
Appel, Benjamin 1907-1977 ... CANR-6
Obituary ... 69-72
Earlier sketch in CA 13-14R
See also SATA 21, 39
Appel, Frederic C. 1935(?)-1984 Obituary ... 112
Appel, John J. 1921- ... 33-36R
Appel, Kenneth Ellmaker 1896-1979
Obituary ... 89-92
Appel, Libby E(ve Sundel) 1937- ... 117
Appel, Martin E(liot) 1948- ... CANR-15
Earlier sketch in CA 85-88
See also SATA 45
Appel, Marty
See Appel, Martin E(liot)
Appel, Willa 1946- ... 117
Appel, William 1939- ... 114
Appelbaum, Diana Karter 1953- ... 122
Appelbaum, Judith (Pilpel) 1939- ... CANR-14
Earlier sketch in CA 77-80
Appelbaum, Paul S(tuart) 1951- ... 108
Appelbaum, Stephen A(rthur) 1926- ... 101
Appelfeld, Aharon 1932- Brief entry ... 112
See also CLC 23, 47
Appelman, Hyman (Jedidiah) 1902- ... 5-6R
Appere, Guy 1923- ... 117
Appiah, Peggy 1921- ... 41-44R
See also SATA 15
Appignanesi, Lisa 1946- ... 49-52
Applbaum, Ronald L. 1943- ... CANR-7
Earlier sketch in CA 57-60
Apple, Margot ... SATA-42
Apple, Max (Isaac) 1941- ... CANR-19
Earlier sketch in CA 81-84
See also CLC 9, 33
Apple, Michael W(hitman) 1942- ... 109
Apple, R(aymond) W(alter), Jr. 1934- ... 89-92
Applebaum, Edmond L(ewis) 1924- ... 117
Applebaum, Samuel 1904- ... 65-68
Applebaum, Stan 1922- ... 85-88
See also SATA 45
Applebaum, William 1906-1979(?) ... CANR-6
Earlier sketch in CA 11-12R
Applebee, Arthur N(oble) 1946- ... CANR-14
Earlier sketch in CA 81-84
Appleby, Andrew Bell 1929-1980 ... 108
Appleby, David P. 1925- ... 110
Appleby, John T. 1909(?)-1974 Obituary ... 53-56
Appleby, Jon 1948- ... 33-36R
Appleby, Joyce Oldham 1929- ... CANR-11
Earlier sketch in CA 69-72
Applegarth, Margaret Tyson 1886-1976
Obituary ... 69-72
Applegate, James (Earl) 1923- ... 33-36R
Applegate, Richard 1913(?)-1979
Obituary ... 85-88
Applegath, John 1935- ... 115
Appleman, John Alan 1912-1982 ... CANR-2
Obituary ... 108
Earlier sketch in CA 7-8R
Appleman, M(arjorie) H. 1928- ... 118
Appleman, Margie
See Appleman, M(arjorie) H.
Appleman, Mark J(erome) 1917- ... 29-32R
Appleman, Philip (Dean) 1926- ... CANR-6
Earlier sketch in CA 15-16R
Appleman, Roy Edgar 1904- ... CAP-1
Earlier sketch in CA 9-10
Appleton, Arthur 1913- ... 93-96
Appleton, George 1902- ... 126
Appleton, James Henry 1919- ... CANR-2
Earlier sketch in CA 5-6R
Appleton, Jane (Frances) 1934- ... 102
Appleton, Jay
See Appleton, James Henry
Appleton, Lawrence
See Lovecraft, H(oward) P(hillips)
Appleton, Marion Brymner 1906- ... 105
Appleton, Sarah 1930- ... 37-40R
Appleton, Sheldon Lee 1933- ... 1R
Appleton, Victor ... CAP-2
Earlier sketch in CA 19-20
See also SATA 1
Appleton, Victor II ... 19-20R
See also SATA 1
Appleton, William S. 1934- ... 101
Appleton, William W(orthen) 1915-
Brief entry ... 113
Applewhite, Cynthia ... 89-92
Applewhite, E(dgar) J(arratt, Jr.) 1919- ... 89-92
Applewhite, Harriet Branson 1940- ... 106
Applewhite, James W(illiam) 1935- ... CANR-25
Earlier sketch in CA 85-88
Applewhite, Philip B(oatman) 1938- ... 112
Appley, Lawrence A. 1904- ... 121
Appley, M(ortimer) H(erbert) 1921- ... 15-16R
Appleyard, Donald 1928- ... CANR-4
Earlier sketch in CA 5-6R
Appleyard, Reginald Thomas 1927- ... 17-18R
Applezweig, M. H.
See Appley, M(ortimer) H(erbert)
Apps, Jerold W(illard) 1934- ... CANR-16
Earlier sketches in CA 49-52, CANR-1
Apps, Jerry
See Apps, Jerold W(illard)
apRoberts, Ruth ... 111
Apsler, Alfred 1907- ... CANR-3
Earlier sketch in CA 5-6R
See also SATA 10
Apt, (Jerome) Leon 1929- ... 53-56
Apte, Mahadev L(akshuman) 1931- ... 117
Apted, M(ichael) R. 1919- ... 25-28R
Aptekar, Jane 1935- ... 81-84
Apter, David Ernest 1924- ... CANR-3
Earlier sketch in CA 1R
Apter, Michael J(ohn) 1939- ... 29-32R
Apter, Samson 1910- ... 104
Aptheker, Bettina 1944- ... CANR-6
Earlier sketch in CA 29-32R
Aptheker, Herbert 1915- ... CANR-6
Earlier sketch in CA 5-6R
Aquarius, Qass
See Buskirk, Richard H(obart)
Aquilano, Nicholas Joseph 1930- ... 112
Aquin, Hubert 1929-1977 ... 105
See also DLB 53
See also CLC 15
Aquina, Sister Mary
See Weinrich, A(nna) K(atharina) H(ildegard)
Aquino, Benigno S(imeon), Jr. 1932-1983
Obituary ... 110
Aquino, Ninoy
See Aquino, Benigno S(imeon), Jr.
Arafat, Ibtihaj Said 1934- ... 85-88
Aragbabalu, Omidiji
See Beier, Ulli
Aragon, Louis 1897-1982 ... 69-72
Obituary ... 108
See also DLB 72
See also CLC 3, 22
Aragones, Sergio 1937- ... 122
See also SATA 39, 48
Araki, James T(omomasa) 1925- ... 15-16R
Arango, Jorge Sanin 1916- ... 61-64
Aranha, Ray 1939- Brief entry ... 112
Aranow, Edward Ross 1909- ... 41-44R
Araoz, Daniel Leon 1930- ... 108
Arapoff, Nancy 1930- ... 29-32R
Arasteh, A(bdol) Reza 1927- ... 105
Arata, Esther S(pring) 1918- ... 89-92
Arata, Luis O(scar) 1950- ... 115
Arbatov, G. A.
See Arbatov, Georgi (Arkadevich)
Arbatov, Georgi (Arkadevich) 1923- ... 116
Arbatov, Yuri Arkadevich
See Arbatov, Georgi (Arkadevich)
Arbeiter, Jean S(onkin) 1937- ... 106
Arberry, A(rthur) J(ohn) 1905-1969 ... CANR-4
Earlier sketch in CA 4R
Arbib, Robert
See Arbib, Robert S(imeon), Jr.
Arbib, Robert S(imeon), Jr. 1915-1987 ... 33-36R
Obituary ... 123
Arbingast, Stanley A(lan) 1910- ... CANR-10
Earlier sketch in CA 17-18R
Arbogast, William F. 1908-1979 Obituary ... 89-92
Arbuckle, Dorothy Fry 1910-1982
Obituary ... 108
See also SATA 33
Arbuckle, Dugald S(inclair) 1912- ... 13-14R
Arbuckle, Robert D(ean) 1940- ... 61-64
Arbuckle, W(endell) S(herwood) 1911-1987 Obituary ... 122
Arbuckle, Wanda Rector 1910- ... 41-44R
Arbuthnot, May Hill 1884-1969 ... 9-10R
See also SATA 2
Arbuthnott, Hugh (James) 1936- ... 125
Arbuzov, Alexei Nikolaevich 1908-1986 ... 69-72
Obituary ... 119
Arca, Julie Anne 1953- ... 111
Arcana, Judith 1943- ... 103
Arce, Hector 1935-1980 ... 97-100
Arceneaux, Thelma Hoffmann Tyler ... AITN-1
Arch, E. L.
See Payes, Rachel C(osgrove)
ar C'Halan, Reun
See Galand, Rene
Archambault, Paul 1937- ... 81-84
Archdeacon, Thomas J(ohn) 1942- ... 65-68
Archer, A. A.
See Joscelyn, Archie L.
Archer, Frank
See O'Connor, Richard
Archer, Fred 1915- ... CANR-7
Earlier sketch in CA 57-60
Archer, Fred C. 1916(?)-1974 Obituary ... 53-56
Archer, Gleason Leonard, Jr. 1916- ... 65-68
Archer, H(orace) Richard 1911-1978 ... CANR-6
Obituary ... 89-92
Earlier sketch in CA 15-16R
Archer, Herbert Winslow
See Mencken, H(enry) L(ouis)
Archer, Jane (a pseudonym) ... 113
Archer, Jeffrey (Howard) 1940- ... CANR-22
Earlier sketch in CA 77-80
See also CLC 28
Archer, John H(all) 1914- ... 101
Archer, Jules 1915- ... CANR-6
Earlier sketch in CA 9-10R
See also SATA 4
See also SAAS 5
See also CLC 12
Archer, Lee
See Ellison, Harlan
Archer, Marion Fuller 1917- ... 5-6R
See also SATA 11
Archer, Mildred 1911- ... 104
Archer, Myrtle (Lilly) 1926- ... 102
Archer, Nuala 1955- ... 121
Archer, Peter Kingsley 1926- ... CANR-2
Earlier sketch in CA 7-8R
Archer, Ron
See White, Theodore Edwin
Archer, S. E.
See Soderberg, Percy Measday
Archer, Sellers G. 1908- ... 17-18R
Archer, Stephen H(unt) 1928- ... 19-20R
Archer, Stephen M(urphy) 1934- ... 105
Archer, W(illiam) G(eorge) 1907-1979 ... 57-60
Obituary ... 125
Archer, William 1856-1924 Brief entry ... 108
See also DLB 10
Archerd, Armand ... 115
Brief entry ... 110
Archerd, Army
See Archerd, Armand
Archer Houblon, Doreen (Lindsay) 1899-1977 ... 106
Archibald, (Rupert) Douglas 1919- ... 101
Archibald, Douglas N(elson) 1933-
Brief entry ... 113
Archibald, James Montgomery 1920-1983
Obituary ... 110
Archibald, Joe
See Archibald, Joseph S(topford)
Archibald, John J. 1925- ... 5-6R
Archibald, Joseph S(topford) 1898-1986 ... CANR-5
Obituary ... 118
Earlier sketch in CA 9-10R
See also SATA 3, 47
Archibald, Sandra O(rr) 1945- ... 113
Archibald, William 1924-1970 Obituary ... 29-32R
Arciniegas, German 1900- ... CANR-10
Earlier sketch in CA 61-64
Arcone, Sonya 1925-1978 ... 21-22R
Obituary ... 77-80
Ard, Ben N(eal), Jr. 1922- ... CANR-12
Earlier sketch in CA 33-36R
Ard, William (Thomas) 1922-1962(?) ... 5-6R
Ardagh, John 1928- ... 25-28R
Ardalan, Nader 1939- ... 69-72
Arden, Barbi
See Stoutenburg, Adrien (Pearl)
Arden, Gothard Everett 1905- ... CAP-1
Earlier sketch in CA 11-12
Arden, J. E. M.
See Conquest, (George) Robert (Acworth)
Arden, Jane ... 61-64
Arden, John 1930- ... 15-16R
See also CAAS 4
See also DLB 13
See also CLC 6, 13, 15
Arden, Leon 1932- ... 107
Arden, Noele
See Dambrauskas, Joan Arden
Arden, William
See Lynds, Dennis
Ardener, Edwin (William) 1927-1987 ... 7-8R
Obituary ... 123
Ardies, Tom 1931- ... 33-36R
Ardizzone, Edward (Jeffrey Irving) 1900-1979 ... CANR-8
Obituary ... 89-92
Earlier sketch in CA 5-6R
See also SATA 1, 21, 28
See also CLR 3
Ardizzone, Tony 1949- ... 85-88
Ardley, Neil (Richard) 1937- ... 115
See also SATA 43
Ardmore, Jane Kesner 1915- ... 7-8R
Ardoin, John (Louis) 1935- ... 57-60
Ardrey, Robert 1908-1980 ... 33-36R
Obituary ... 93-96
Arecco, Vera Lustig
See Lustig-Arecco, Vera
Areeda, Phillip E. 1930- ... 23-24R
Arehart-Treichel, Joan 1942- ... CANR-6
Earlier sketch in CA 57-60
See also SATA 22
Arellanes, Audrey Spencer 1920- ... 33-36R
Arem, Joel E(dward) 1943- ... 89-92
Arena, Jay M(orris) 1909- ... 107
Arena, John I. 1929- ... CANR-20
Earlier sketch in CA 45-48
Arenas, Reinaldo 1943- Brief entry ... 124
See also CLC 41
Arendt, Hannah 1906-1975 ... CANR-26
Obituary ... 61-64
Earlier sketch in CA 19-20R
Arenella, Roy 1939- ... SATA-14
Arens, Richard 1921-1984 ... 73-76
Obituary ... 112
Arens, William 1940- ... 89-92
Arensberg, Ann 1937- ... 114
See also DLBY 82
Arensberg, Conrad Maynadier 1910- ... 61-64
Arenson, Gloria 1935- ... 118
Arent, Arthur 1904-1972 ... CAP-2
Obituary ... 33-36R
Earlier sketch in CA 23-24
Areskoug, Kaj 1933- ... 29-32R
Aresty, Esther B(radford) ... 9-10R
Areta, Mavis
See Winder, Mavis Areta
Arey, James A(rthur) 1936-1988 ... 41-44R
Obituary ... 125
Arey, Leslie Brainerd 1891-1988 Obituary ... 125
Argan, Giulio Carlo 1909- ... 65-68
Argenti, John 1926- ... 115
Argenti, Philip 1891(?)-1974 Obituary ... 49-52
Argenzio, Victor 1902- ... 53-56
Argersinger, Peter H(ayes) 1944-
Brief entry ... 112
Arghezi, Tudor
See Theodorescu, Ion N.
Argiro, Larry 1909- ... 5-6R
Argo, Ellen
See Johnson, Ellen Argo
Argow, Waldemar 1916- ... 23-24R
Arguedas, Jose Maria 1911-1969 ... 89-92
See also CLC 10, 18
Arguelles, Jose A(nthony) 1939- ... CANR-20
Earlier sketch in CA 45-48
Arguelles, Miriam Tarcov 1943- ... 45-48
Argueta, Manlio 1936- ... CLC-31
Argus
See Osusky, Stefan
Argus
See Phillips-Birt, Douglas Hextall Chedzey
Argyle, Aubrey William 1910- ... CAP-1
Earlier sketch in CA 17-18
Argyle, Michael 1925- ... CANR-25
Earlier sketches in CA 21-22R, CANR-9
Argyris, Chris 1923- ... CANR-20
Earlier sketches in CA 2R, CANR-5
Arian, Alan (Asher) 1938- ... CANR-1
Earlier sketch in CA 49-52
Arian, Edward 1921- ... 33-36R
Arias-Misson, Alain 1936- ... 77-80
Aridas, Chris 1947- ... 112

Ariel
See Moraes, Frank Robert
Aries, Philippe 1914-1984 89-92
Obituary 112
Arieti, James Alexander 1948- 108
Arieti, Silvano 1914-1981 .... CANR-10
Obituary 104
Earlier sketch in CA 21-22R
Arimond, Carroll 1909-1979 Obituary 89-92
Aring, Charles D(air) 1904- 49-52
Aris, Rutherford 1929- 117
Aristides
See Epstein, Joseph
Ariyoshi, Sawako 1931-1984 105
Obituary 113
Ariyoshi, Shoichiro 1939(?)-1979
Obituary 89-92
Arkell, Anthony John 1898-1980 102
Obituary 97-100
Arkhurst, Frederick S(iegfried) 1920- CANR-25
Earlier sketch in CA 29-32R
Arkhurst, Joyce Cooper 1921- 17-18R
Arkin, Alan (Wolf) 1934- 112
Brief entry 110
See also SATA 32
Arkin, David 1906- 21-22R
Arkin, Frieda 1917- CANR-11
Earlier sketch in CA 65-68
Arkin, Herbert 1906- 7-8R
Arkin, Joseph 1922- 7-8R
Arkin, Marcus 1926- 53-56
Arkley, Arthur J(ames) 1919- 112
Arksey, Laura L(ee) 1936- 119
Arkush, Arthur Spencer 1925-1979
Obituary 85-88
Arland, Marcel 1899-1986 .... DLB-72
Arlandson, Leone 1917- 29-32R
Arlen, Michael 1895-1956 Brief entry 120
See also DLB 36
Arlen, Michael J. 1930- CANR-13
Earlier sketch in CA 61-64
Arleo, Joseph 1933- 29-32R
Arley, Catherine 1935- CANR-2
Earlier sketch in CA 45-48
Arliss, Leslie 1901-1987 Obituary 124
Arlott, (Leslie Thomas) John 1914- 9-10R
Arlotto, Anthony (Thomas) 1939- 33-36R
Arlow, Jacob A. 1912- 53-56
Arlt, Roberto 1900-1942 Brief entry 123
See also TCLC 29
Armacost, Michael Hayden 1937- 101
Armah, Ayi Kwei 1939- CANR-21
Earlier sketch in CA 61-64
See also BW
See also CLC 5, 33
Armand, Louis 1905-1971 .... CAP-2
Obituary 33-36R
Earlier sketch in CA 29-32
Armatas, James P. 1931- 41-44R
Armatrading, Joan 1950- Brief entry 114
See also CLC 17
Armbrister, Trevor 1933- 89-92
Armbruster, Carl J. 1929- 33-36R
Armbruster, F(ranz) O(wen) 1929- 49-52
Armbruster, Francis E(dward) 1923- 29-32R
Armbruster, Frank
See Armbruster, Francis E(dward)
Armbruster, Maxim Ethan 1902- 1R
Armens, Sven 1921- 21-22R
Armentrout, Fred S(herman) 1946- 119
Armentrout, William W(infield) 1918- 33-36R
Armer, Alberta (Roller) 1904- 7-8R
See also SATA 9
Armer, J(ohn) Michael 1937- 106
Armer, Laura (Adams) 1874-1963 65-68
See also SATA 13
Armerding, Carl Edwin 1936- 104
Armerding, George D. 1899- 85-88
Armerding, Hudson Taylor 1918- CANR-11
Earlier sketch in CA 23-24R
Armes, Roy (Philip) 1937- CANR-13
Earlier sketch in CA 73-76
Armington, John Calvin 1923- 53-56
Armistead, Samuel (Gordon) 1927- 53-56
Armitage, A(rthur) L(lewellyn) 1916-1984
Obituary 112
Armitage, Angus 1902- CAP-1
Earlier sketch in CA 13-14
Armitage, David 1943- SATA-38
Armitage, E(dward) Liddall 1887- CAP-1
Earlier sketch in CA 9-10
Armitage, G(ary) E(dric) 1956- 121
Armitage, Merle 1893-1975 Obituary 61-64
Armitage, Michael John 1930- 117
Armitage, Ronda (Jacqueline) 1943- 121
See also SATA 38, 47
Armitage, Shelley S(ue) 1947- 121
Armory, Thomas 1691(?)-1788 .... DLB-39
Armour, John
See Paine, Lauran (Bosworth)
Armour, Leslie 1931- 110
Armour, Lloyd R. 1922- 29-32R
Armour, Richard 1906- CANR-4
Earlier sketch in CA 1R
See also SATA 14
Armour, Rollin Stely 1929- 33-36R
Arms, George (Warren) 1912- 5-6R
Arms, Johnson
See Halliwell, David (William)
Arms, Suzanne 1944- 57-60
Armstrong, (Walter) Alan 1936- 73-76
Armstrong, Ann Seidel 1917- 9-10R
Armstrong, Anne(tte) 1924- 13-14R
Armstrong, Anthony
See Willis, (George) Anthony Armstrong
Armstrong, Anthony C.
See Armstrong, Christopher J. R.
Armstrong, (Grace) April (Oursler) 1926- 89-92
Armstrong, Arthur Hilary 1909- 69-72
Armstrong, Benjamin Leighton 1923- 93-96
Armstrong, Brian G(ary) 1936- 69-72
Armstrong, Charles B. 1923-1985
Obituary 115
Armstrong, Charlotte 1905-1969 .... CANR-3
Obituary 25-28R
Earlier sketch in CA 1R
Armstrong, Christopher J(ohn) R(ichard)
1935- 69-72
Armstrong, Claude Blakely 1889-1982
Obituary 108
Armstrong, D(avid) M(alet) 1926- CANR-11
Earlier sketch in CA 25-28R
Armstrong, (James) David 1945- 107
Armstrong, David M(ichael) 1944- 57-60
Armstrong, Diana 1943- 107
Armstrong, Douglas Albert 1920- 9-10R
Armstrong, Edward Allworthy
1900-1978 .... CANR-4
Earlier sketch in CA 7-8R
Armstrong, (Annette) Elizabeth 1917- 25-28R
Armstrong, F. W.
See Wright, T. M.
Armstrong, Frederick H(enry) 1926- 33-36R
Armstrong, Garner Ted 1929(?)-
Brief entry 113
Armstrong, George D. 1927- SATA-10
Armstrong, Gerry (Breen) 1929- 15-16R
See also SATA 10
Armstrong, Gregory T(imon) 1933- 9-10R
Armstrong, Hamilton Fish 1893-1973 93-96
Obituary 41-44R
Armstrong, Henry
See Jackson, Henry
Armstrong, Henry H.
See Arvay, Harry
Armstrong, Herbert W. 1892-1986
Obituary 118
Brief entry 116
Armstrong, J(on) Scott 1937- CANR-1
Earlier sketch in CA 45-48
Armstrong, (A.) James 1924- 29-32R
Armstrong, John A(lexander, Jr.)
1922- CANR-3
Earlier sketch in CA 4R
Armstrong, John Borden 1926- 33-36R
Armstrong, John Byron 1917-1976 .... 5-6R
Obituary 65-68
Armstrong, Joseph Gravitt 1943- 101
Armstrong, Judith Mary 1935- 102
Armstrong, Keith F(rancis) W(hitfield)
1950- 29-32R
Armstrong, Leslie 1940- 124
Armstrong, (Daniel) Louis 1900-1971
Obituary 29-32R
Armstrong, Louise 117
Brief entry 111
See also SATA 33, 43
Armstrong, Marjorie Moore 1912- 89-92
Armstrong, Martin 1882-1974 Obituary 49-52
Armstrong, O(rland) K(ay) 1893-1987 93-96
Obituary 122
Armstrong, (Raymond) Paul 1912- 37-40R
Armstrong, Paul B(radford) 1949- 112
Armstrong, Richard 1903- 77-80
See also SATA 11
Armstrong, Richard G. 1932- 73-76
Armstrong, Robert H(oward) 1936- 108
Armstrong, Robert L(aurence) 1926- 29-32R
Armstrong, Robert Plant 1919-1984 .... 41-44R
Obituary 113
Armstrong, Roger D. 1939- 19-20R
Armstrong, Ruth Gallup 1891- CAP-1
Earlier sketch in CA 9-10
Armstrong, (Russell) Scott 1945- 108
Armstrong, Terence Ian Fytton
1912-1970 .... CAP-2
Obituary 29-32R
Earlier sketch in CA 17-18
Armstrong, Thomas 1899-1978 .... 7-8R
Obituary 103
Armstrong, Tilly 1927- CANR-23
Earlier sketch in CA 107
Armstrong, Wallace Edwin 1896-1980
Obituary 97-100
Armstrong, William A(lexander) 1912- 13-14R
Armstrong, William A(rthur) 1915- 17-18R
Armstrong, William H(oward) 1914- CANR-9
Earlier sketch in CA 19-20R
See also SATA 4
See also CLR 1
See also AITN 1
Armstrong, William M(artin) 1919- 49-52
Armstrong-Jones, Antony (Charles Robert)
1930- 118
Armstrong Jones, Tony
See Armstrong-Jones, Antony (Charles Robert)
Armytage, Walter Harry Green 1915- 9-10R
Arnade, Charles W(olfgang) 1927- 33-36R
Arnandez, Richard 1912- CANR-6
Earlier sketch in CA 15-16R
Arnason, David 1940- 114
Arnason, H(jorvardur) H(arvard)
1909-1986 .... CANR-13
Obituary 119
Earlier sketch in CA 61-64
Arnau, Frank
See Schmitt, Heinrich
Arnaud, Georges
See Girard, Henri Georges Charles Achille
Arnaz, Desi
See Arnaz y de Acha, Desiderio Alberto III
Arnaz y de Acha, Desiderio Alberto III
1917(?)-1986 Obituary 121
Brief entry 114
Arncliffe, Andrew
See Walker, Peter N.
Arndt, Elise 1943- 116
Arndt, Ernst H(einrich) D(aniel) 1899- CAP-2
Earlier sketch in CA 23-24
Arndt, H(einz) W(olfgang) 1915- CANR-10
Earlier sketch in CA 21-22R
Arndt, Karl John Richard 1903- CANR-23
Earlier sketches in CA 17-18R, CANR-7
Arndt, Ursula (Martha H.) SATA-39
Arndt, Walter W(erner) 1916- CANR-5
Earlier sketch in CA 13-14R
Arnebeck, Bob 1947- 108
Arneson, D(on) J(on) 1935- 106
See also SATA 37
Arnett, Caroline
See Cole, Lois Dwight
Arnett, Carroll 1927- CANR-11
Earlier sketch in CA 21-22R
Arnett, Harold E(dward) 1931- CANR-8
Earlier sketch in CA 21-22R
Arnett, Ross H(arold), Jr. 1919- CANR-17
Earlier sketches in CA 49-52, CANR-2
Arnette, Robert
See Silverberg, Robert
Arney, William Ray 1950- 110
Arnez, Nancy Levi 1928- 29-32R
Arnheim, Daniel D(avid) 1930- CANR-5
Earlier sketch in CA 11-12R
Arnheim, Rudolf 1904- CANR-3
Earlier sketch in CA 4R
Arno, Enrico 1913-1981 .... SATA-28, 43
Arno, Peter 1904-1968 73-76
Obituary 25-28R
Arnold, Adlai F(ranklin) 1914- 33-36R
Arnold, Alan 1922- 7-8R
Arnold, Alvin L(incoln) 1929- 93-96
Arnold, Anthony 1928- 111
Arnold, Armin H. 1931- CANR-18
Earlier sketches in CA 9-10R, CANR-3
Arnold, Arnold (Ferdinand) 1921- CANR-10
Earlier sketch in CA 19-20R
Arnold, Bob 1952- CANR-21
Earlier sketch in CA 105
Arnold, Bruce 1936- 93-96
Arnold, Carl
See Raknes, Ola
Arnold, Caroline 1944- CANR-24
Earlier sketch in CA 107
See also SATA 34, 36
Arnold, Carroll C(lyde) 1912- Brief entry 116
Arnold, Catharine 1959- 125
Arnold, Charles Harvey 1920- 65-68
Arnold, Charlotte E(lizabeth) Cramer 57-60
Arnold, Corliss Richard 1926- 49-52
Arnold, Denis Midgley 1926-1986 .... CANR-2
Obituary 119
Earlier sketch in CA 7-8R
Arnold, Edmund C(larence) 1913- CANR-3
Earlier sketch in CA 4R
Arnold, Edwin 1832-1904 .... DLB-35
Arnold, Edwin L(ester Linden)
1857(?)-1935 Brief entry 109
Arnold, Elliott 1912-1980 .... CANR-24
Obituary 97-100
Earlier sketch in CA 19-20R
See also SATA 5, 22
Arnold, Emily 1939- 109
See also SATA 50
Arnold, Emmy (von Hollander)
1884-1980 .... CANR-9
Earlier sketch in CA 23-24R
Arnold, Eve 1913- 112
Arnold, Francena H(arriet Long) 1888- CAP-1
Earlier sketch in CA 17-18
Arnold, G. L.
See Lichtheim, George
Arnold, Gary Howard 1942- Brief entry 117
Arnold, Guy 1932- CANR-11
Earlier sketch in CA 25-28R
Arnold, H(arry) J(ohn) P(hilip) 1932- CANR-2
Earlier sketch in CA 7-8R
Arnold, Heini
See Arnold, Johann Heinrich
Arnold, Herbert 1935- 37-40R
Arnold, Janet 1932- 93-96
Arnold, Johann Heinrich 1913-1982 122
Obituary 111
Arnold, John D(avid) 1933- 111
Arnold, Joseph H.
See Hayes, Joseph
Arnold, June (Davis) 1926- 21-22R
Arnold, L. J.
See Cameron, Lou
Arnold, Leslie
See Lazarus, A(rnold) L(eslie)
Arnold, Lloyd R. 1906-1970 .... CAP-2
Earlier sketch in CA 25-28
Arnold, Lois B(arber) 107
Arnold, Magda B(londiau) 1903- 5-6R
Arnold, Margot
See Cook, Petronelle Marguerite Mary
Arnold, Marilyn 1935- 122
Arnold, Mary Ann 1918- 65-68
Arnold, Matthew 1822-1888 .... DLB-32, 57
Arnold, Milo Lawrence 1903- 57-60
Arnold, Olga Moore 1900-1981 Obituary 102
Arnold, Oren 1900- CANR-2
Earlier sketch in CA 5-6R
See also SATA 4
Arnold, Pauline 1894-1974 .... CANR-2
Earlier sketch in CA 1R
Arnold, Peter 1931- 123
Arnold, Peter 1943- CANR-1
Earlier sketch in CA 49-52
Arnold, R. Douglas 1950- 101
Arnold, Ray Henry 1895- 5-6R
Arnold, Richard 1912- CANR-3
Earlier sketch in CA 9-10R
Arnold, Richard E(ugene) 1908- CAP-2
Earlier sketch in CA 33-36
Arnold, Richard K(lein) 1923- 69-72
Arnold, Robert E(vans) 1932- 49-52
Arnold, Rollo (Davis) 1926- 23-24R
Arnold, Ron 1937- CANR-25
Earlier sketch in CA 108
Arnold, Stephen H. 1942- 117
Arnold, Thomas 1795-1842 .... DLB-55
Arnold, Thurman Wesley 1891-1969 .... CAP-1
Earlier sketch in CA 15-16
Arnold, William Robert 1933- 29-32R
Arnold, William Van 1941- 110
Arnold-Baker, Charles 1918- 7-8R
Arnold-Forster, Mark 1920-1981 65-68
Obituary 105
Arnoldy, Julie
See Bischoff, Julia Bristol
Arnosky, Jim 1946- CANR-12
Earlier sketch in CA 69-72
See also SATA 22
See also CLR 15
Arnothy, Christine 1930- CANR-10
Earlier sketch in CA 65-68
Arnott, (Margaret) Anne 1916- CANR-13
Earlier sketch in CA 73-76
Arnott, J(ames) F(ullarton) 1914-1982
Obituary 108
Arnott, Kathleen 1914- 57-60
See also SATA 20
Arnott, Peter D(ouglas) 1931- CANR-3
Earlier sketch in CA 3R
Arnoux, Alexandre (Paul) 1884-1973
Obituary 37-40R
Arnov, Boris, Jr. 1926- CANR-3
Earlier sketch in CA 4R
See also SATA 12
Arnove, Robert Fred 1937- 111
Arnow, Harriette (Louisa) Simpson
1908-1986 .... CANR-14
Obituary 118
Earlier sketch in CA 9-10R
See also SATA 42, 47
See also DLB 6
See also CLC 2, 7, 18
Arnow, L(eslie) Earle 1909- 69-72
Arnstein, Flora Jacobi 1885- 7-8R
Arnstein, Helene S(olomon) 1915- 57-60
See also SATA 12
Arnstein, Walter L(eonard) 1930- CANR-23
Earlier sketches in CA 15-16R, CANR-5
Arntson, Herbert E(dward) 1911- 19-20R
See also SATA 12
Arny, Mary (Travis) 1909- 61-64
Arny, Thomas Travis 1940- 85-88
Aron, Jean-Paul 1925(?)-1988 Obituary 126
Aron, Raymond (Claude Ferdinand)
1905-1983 .... CANR-2
Obituary 111
Earlier sketch in CA 49-52
Aron, Robert 1898-1975 93-96
Obituary 57-60
Aronfreed, Justin 1930- 25-28R
Aronin, Ben 1904-1980 Obituary 102
See also SATA 25
Aronoff, Myron J(oel) 1940- CANR-24
Earlier sketch in CA 107
Aronson, Alex 1912- 45-48
Aronson, Alvin 1928- 25-28R
Aronson, David 1894-1988 Obituary 126
Aronson, Elliot 1932- CANR-12
Earlier sketch in CA 33-36R
Aronson, Harvey 1929- 85-88
Aronson, J(ay) Richard 1937- 81-84
Aronson, James (Allan) 1915-1988 .... 29-32R
Obituary 126
Aronson, Joseph 1898- CAP-1
Earlier sketch in CA 19-20
Aronson, Marvin L. 1925- 41-44R
Aronson, Shlomo 1936- 73-76
Aronson, Theo 1930- CANR-25
Earlier sketches in CA 11-12R, CANR-4
Aronson, Virginia 1954- CANR-25
Earlier sketch in CA 108
Arora, Shirley (Lease) 1930- 4R
See also SATA 2
Aros, Andrew A(lexandre) 1944- 97-100
Arout, Gabriel 1909-1982 Obituary 106
Arp, Bill
See Smith, Charles Henry
Arp, Hans
See Arp, Jean
Arp, Jean 1887-1966 81-84
Obituary 25-28R
See also CLC 5
Arpad, Joseph J(ohn) 1937- 49-52
Arpel, Adrien
See Newman, Adrien Ann
Arps, Louisa Ward 1901-1986 Obituary 118
Arquette, Cliff(ord) 1905-1974 Obituary 53-56
Arrabal
See Arrabal, Fernando
See also CLC 2, 9, 18
Arrabal, Fernando 1932- CANR-15
Earlier sketch in CA 11-12R
Arre, Helen
See Ross, Zola Helen
Arre, John
See Holt, John (Robert)
Arreola, Juan Jose 1918- Brief entry 113
Arrick, Fran CLC-30

Arrighi, Mel 1933-1986 ... CANR-18
Obituary ... 120
Earlier sketches in CA 49-52, CANR-1
Arrington, Leonard James 1917- ... CANR-9
Earlier sketch in CA 19-20R
Arrow, Kenneth J(oseph) 1921- ... CANR-13
Earlier sketch in CA 15-16R
Arroway, Francis M.
See Rosmond, Babette
Arrowood, (McKendrick Lee) Clinton 1939- ... SATA-19
Arrowsmith, Marvin Lawrence 1913-
Brief entry ... 116
Arrowsmith, Pat 1930- ... 101
Arrowsmith, William Ayres 1924- ... CANR-4
Earlier sketch in CA 9-10R
Arroyo, Antonio M. Stevens
See Stevens-Arroyo, Antonio M.
Arroyo, Stephen J(oseph) 1946- ... 61-64
Art, Robert (Jeffrey) 1942- ... 65-68
Artaud, Antonin 1896-1948 Brief entry ... 104
See also TCLC 3
Arteaga, Lucio 1924- ... 49-52
Arteaga, William De
See De Arteaga, William
Artes, Dorothy Beecher 1919- ... 57-60
Arther, Richard O. 1928- ... 17-18R
Arthos, John 1908- ... 9-10R
Arthur, Alan
See Edmonds, Arthur Denis
Arthur, Anthony 1937- ... 119
Arthur, Art(hur) 1911-1985 Obituary ... 116
Arthur, Burt
See Shappiro, Herbert (Arthur)
Arthur, Don(ald) R(amsay) 1917-1984 ... 29-32R
Obituary ... 114
Arthur, Elizabeth 1953- ... CANR-21
Earlier sketch in CA 105
Arthur, Eric (Ross) 1898-1982 Obituary ... 112
Arthur, Frank
See Ebert, Arthur Frank
Arthur, Gladys
See Osborne, Dorothy (Gladys) Yeo
Arthur, Herbert
See Shappiro, Herbert (Arthur)
Arthur, Hugh
See Christie-Murray, David (Hugh Arthur)
Arthur, Kay L(ee) 1932- ... 118
Arthur, Lee ... 122
Arthur, Martin (Forest) 1951- ... 116
Arthur, Max 1939- ... 121
Arthur, Percy E. 1910- ... CAP-1
Earlier sketch in CA 9-10
Arthur, Robert
See Feder, Robert Arthur
Arthur, Ruth M(abel) 1905-1979 ... CANR-4
Obituary ... 85-88
Earlier sketch in CA 11-12R
See also SATA 7, 26
See also CLC 12
Arthur, Thomas H. 1937- ... 122
Arthur, Tiffany
See Pelton, Robert W(ayne)
Arthur, Timothy Shay 1809-1885 ... DLB-3, 42
Arthur, Tom
See Arthur, Thomas H.
Arthur, William
See Neubauer, William Arthur
Arthurs, Peter 1933- ... 106
Artin, Thomas 1938- Brief entry ... 116
Artin, Tom
See Artin, Thomas
Artis, Vicki Kimmel 1945- ... 53-56
See also SATA 12
Artmann, H(ans) C(arl) 1921- ... 101
Artobolevsky, Ivan I. 1905-1977 Obituary ... 73-76
Artom, Guido 1906-1982 ... CANR-12
Earlier sketch in CA 29-32R
Arts, Herwig (W. J.) 1935- ... 113
Artz, Frederick B(inkerd) 1894-1983 ... CANR-18
Earlier sketch in CA 1R
Artzybasheff, Boris (Miklailovich) 1899-1965 ... SATA-14
Aruego, Ariane
See Dewey, Ariane
Aruego, Jose ... 37-40R
See also SATA 6
See also CLR 5
Arundale, G. S.
See Arundale, George S(ydney)
Arundale, George S(ydney) 1878-1945
Brief entry ... 119
Arundel, Honor (Morfydd) 1919-1973 ... CAP-2
Obituary ... 41-44R
Earlier sketch in CA 21-22
See also SATA 4, 24
See also CLC 17
Arundel, Jocelyn
See Alexander, Jocelyn Anne Arundel
Arundel, Russell M. 1903-1978 Obituary ... 77-80
Aruri, Naseer H. ... 113
Arvay, Harry 1925- ... CANR-8
Earlier sketch in CA 57-60
Arvay, Stephen 1937- ... 114
Arvill, Robert
See Boote, Robert Edward
Arvin, Kay K(rehbiel) 1922- ... 65-68
Arvin, (Frederic) Newton (Jr.) 1900-1963
Obituary ... 116
Arvio, Raymond Paavo 1930-1986 ... 77-80
Obituary ... 120
Ary, Donald E(ugene) 1930- ... 41-44R
Ary, Sheila M(ary Littleboy) 1929- ... 13-14R
Arya, Usharbudh 1934- ... 105
Arzhak, Nikolai
See Daniel, Yuli (Markovich)
Arzoomanian, Raffi
See Arzoomanian, Ralph Sarkis
Arzoomanian, Ralph Sarkis 1937- ... 118
Arzt, Max 1897-1975 Obituary ... 61-64
Asals, Frederick (John) 1935- ... 124
Asamani, Joseph Owusu 1934- ... 49-52
Asante, Molefi K(ete) 1942- ... CANR-21
Earlier sketch in CA 33-36R
Asare, Bediako
See Konadu, S(amuel) A(sare)
Asare, Meshack (Yaw) 1945- ... CANR-11
Earlier sketch in CA 61-64
Asbell, Bernard 1923- ... CANR-25
Earlier sketches in CA 45-48, CANR-1
Asbjoernsen, Peter Christen 1812-1885 ... SATA-15
Asbury, Herbert 1891-1963 Obituary ... 116
Ascani, Sparky (Wilson) 1922- ... 111
Asch, Frank 1946- ... 41-44R
See also SATA 5
Asch, Nathan 1902-1964 ... 109
See also DLB 4, 28
Asch, Peter 1937- Brief entry ... 114
Asch, Sholem 1880-1957 Brief entry ... 105
See also TCLC 3
Ascheim, Skip 1943- ... 53-56
Ascher, Abraham 1928- ... 81-84
Ascher, Carol 1941- ... 105
Ascher, Sheila ... CANR-23
Earlier sketch in CA 105
Ascher, William (Louis) 1947- ... 114
Ascherson, Neal 1932- ... 13-14R
Ascher/Straus
See Ascher, Sheila
and Straus, Dennis
Aschmann, Alberta 1921- ... CANR-7
Earlier sketch in CA 15-16R
Aschmann, Helen Tann ... 13-14R
Ascoli, Max 1898-1978 Obituary ... 77-80
Ash, Anthony Lee 1931- ... CANR-3
Earlier sketch in CA 49-52
Ash, Bernard 1910- ... CAP-1
Earlier sketch in CA 19-20
Ash, Brian 1936- Brief entry ... 114
Ash, Christopher (Edward) 1914- ... 4R
Ash, David W(ilfred) 1923- ... 11-12R
Ash, Douglas 1914- ... CANR-2
Earlier sketch in CA 7-8R
Ash, John 1948- Brief entry ... 123
See also DLB 40
Ash, Jutta 1942- ... SATA-38
Ash, Lee (Michael) 1917- ... 110
Ash, Mary Kay (Wagner) ... 112
Ash, Maurice Anthony 1917- ... 101
Ash, Rene Lee 1939- ... 57-60
Ash, Roberta
See Garner, Roberta
Ash, Sarah Leeds 1904- ... CAP-1
Earlier sketch in CA 9-10
Ash, Shalom
See Asch, Sholem
Ash, William Franklin 1917- ... CANR-18
Earlier sketches in CA 7-8R, CANR-2
Ashabranner, Brent (Kenneth) 1921- ... CANR-10
Earlier sketch in CA 7-8R
See also SATA 1
Ashbaugh, Nancy 1929- ... 73-76
Ashbee, Paul 1918- ... 93-96
Ashbery, John (Lawrence) 1927- ... CANR-9
Earlier sketch in CA 7-8R
See also DLB 5
See also DLBY 81
See also CLC 2, 3, 4, 6, 9, 13, 15, 25, 41
Ashbolt, Allan Campbell 1921- ... 104
Ashbrook, James B(arbour) 1925- ... CANR-14
Earlier sketch in CA 37-40R
Ashbrook, Joseph 1918-1980 ... 122
Obituary ... 117
Ashbrook, William (Sinclair) 1922- ... 29-32R
Ashburne, Jim G. 1912- ... 4R
Ashby, Cliff 1919- ... 25-28R
See also CAAS 6
Ashby, Eric 1904- ... 61-64
Ashby, Gwynneth 1922- ... 25-28R
See also SATA 44
Ashby, LaVerne 1922- ... 21-22R
Ashby, (Darrel) LeRoy 1938- ... 33-36R
Ashby, Lloyd W. 1905- ... 89-92
Ashby, Neal 1924- ... 89-92
Ashby, Philip Harrison 1916- ... 17-18R
Ashcraft, Allan Coleman 1928- ... 9-10R
Ashcraft, Laura 1945- ... 107
Ashcraft, Laurie
See Ashcraft, Laura
Ashcraft, Morris 1922- ... 45-48
Ashcroft, John (David) 1942- ... 112
Ashdown, Clifford
See Freeman, R(ichard) Austin
Ashdown, Dulcie M(argaret) 1946- ... 122
Brief entry ... 112
Ashdown, Paul G(eorge) 1944- ... 119
Ashe, Arthur (R., Jr.) 1943- ... CANR-18
Earlier sketch in CA 65-68
Ashe, Douglas
See Bardin, John Franklin
Ashe, Geoffrey (Thomas) 1923- ... CANR-12
Earlier sketch in CA 7-8R
See also SATA 17
Ashe, Gerald C. 1924(?)-1984 Obituary ... 112
Ashe, Gordon
See Creasey, John
Ashe, Mary Ann
See Lewis, Mary (Christianna)
Ashe, Penelope
See Greene, Robert W.
and Karman, Mal
and Young, Billie
Asheim, Lester E(ugene) 1914- ... 19-20R
Ashenfelter, David L. 1948- ... 108
Ashenfelter, Orley C(lark) 1942- ... CANR-8
Earlier sketch in CA 61-64
Asher, Don 1926- ... 73-76
Asher, Harry (Maurice Felix) 1909- ... CANR-2
Earlier sketch in CA 5-6R
Asher, John A(lexander) 1921- ... 23-24R
Asher, Maxine 1930- ... 105
Asher, Miriam
See Mundis, Hester
Asher, Robert 1944- ... 111
Asher, Robert Eller 1910- ... 61-64
Asher, Sandra Fenichel 1942- ... CANR-22
Earlier sketch in CA 105
Asher, Sandy
See Asher, Sandra Fenichel
See also SATA 34, 36
See also DLBY 83
Ashey, Bella
See Breinburg, Petronella
Ashford, Daisy
See Ashford, Margaret Mary
Ashford, Douglas E(lliott) 1928- ... CANR-16
Earlier sketch in CA 73-76
Ashford, Gerald 1907- ... 41-44R
Ashford, Janet Isaacs 1949- ... 113
Ashford, Jeffrey
See Jeffries, Roderic (Graeme)
Ashford, Margaret Mary 1881-1972
Obituary ... 33-36R
See also SATA 10
Ashford, (H.) Ray 1926- ... 65-68
Ashford, Theodore Askounes 1908-1987
Obituary ... 122
Ashley, A.
See Aasheim, Ashley
Ashley, Bernard 1935- ... CANR-25
Earlier sketch in CA 93-96
See also SATA 39, 47
See also CLR 4
Ashley, Elizabeth
See Salmon, Annie Elizabeth
Ashley, (Arthur) Ernest 1906- ... CAP-1
Earlier sketch in CA 15-16
Ashley, Franklin 1942- ... CANR-1
Earlier sketch in CA 45-48
Ashley, Graham
See Organ, John
Ashley, Jack 1922- ... 106
Ashley, Leonard R(aymond) N(elligan) 1928- ... CANR-24
Earlier sketches in CA 15-16R, CANR-9
Ashley, Maurice (Percy) 1907- ... 41-44R
Ashley, Michael (Raymond Donald) 1948- ... CANR-13
Earlier sketch in CA 69-72
Ashley, Nova Trimble 1911- ... 65-68
Ashley, Paul P(ritchard) 1896-1979 ... CANR-10
Obituary ... 85-88
Earlier sketch in CA 21-22R
Ashley, Perry J(onathan) 1928- ... 120
Ashley, Ray
See Abrashkin, Raymond
Ashley, Robert P(aul), Jr. 1915- ... 17-18R
Ashley, Rosalind Minor 1923- ... 69-72
Ashley, Sally 1935- ... 109
Ashley, Steven
See McCaig, Donald
Ashley-Montagu, Montague Francis
See Montagu, (Montague Francis) Ashley
Ashlin, John
See Cutforth, John Ashlin
Ashlock, Patrick (Robert) 1937- ... 61-64
Ashlock, Robert B. 1930- ... CANR-12
Earlier sketch in CA 29-32R
Ashman, Howard 1950- Brief entry ... 122
Ashmead, John, Jr. 1917- ... 1R
Ashmole, Bernard 1894-1988 ... 106
Obituary ... 124
Ashmore, Harry S(cott) 1916- ... 15-16R
Ashmore, Jerome 1901- ... CAP-2
Earlier sketch in CA 33-36
Ashmore, Lewis
See Raborg, Frederick A(shton), Jr.
Ashmore, Owen 1920- ... 106
Ashner, Sonie Shapiro 1938- ... 57-60
Ashryn, Veryl M. 1948- ... 119
Ashton, Ann
See Kimbro, John M.
Ashton, Dore 1928- ... CANR-2
Earlier sketch in CA 5-6R
Ashton, (Arthur) Leigh (Bolland) 1897-1983 Obituary ... 114
Ashton, Robert 1924- ... CANR-3
Earlier sketch in CA 1R
Ashton, (Margery) Violet 1908- ... 73-76
Ashton, Warren T.
See Adams, William Taylor
Ashton, Winifred 1888-1965 Obituary ... 93-96
Ashton-Warner, Sylvia (Constance) 1908-1984 ... 69-72
Obituary ... 112
See also CLC 19
Ashworth, Kenneth H(ayden) 1932- ... 41-44R
Ashworth, Mary Wells Knight 1903- ... 7-8R
Ashworth, Wilfred 1912- ... 15-16R
Ashworth, William 1920- ... 7-8R
Asimov, Isaac 1920- ... CANR-19
Earlier sketches in CA 2R, CANR-2
See also SATA 1, 26
See also DLB 8
See also CLC 1, 3, 9, 19, 26
See also CLR 12
Asimov, Janet
See Jeppson, Janet O(pal)
Asinof, Eliot 1919- ... CANR-7
Earlier sketch in CA 11-12R
See also SATA 6
Aska, Warabe
See Masuda, Takeshi
Askari, Hussaini Muhammad
See Pereira, Harold Bertram
Askenasy, Hans George 1930- ... 77-80
Askew, Jack
See Hivnor, Robert
Askew, William C(larence) 1910- ... 49-52
Askham, Francis
See Greenwood, Julia Eileen Courtney
Askin, A. Bradley 1943- ... 73-76
Askin, Alma 1911- ... 57-60
Askin, I(da) Jayne 1940- ... 109
Askwith, Betty Ellen 1909- ... CANR-13
Earlier sketch in CA 61-64
Askwith, Herbert 1889-1985 Obituary ... 117
Brief entry ... 113
Aslanapa, Oktay 1914- ... 37-40R
Aslet, Clive (William) 1955- ... 113
Aspaturian, Vernon V. 1922- ... 105
Aspel, Michael (Terence) 1933-
Brief entry ... 117
Aspell, Patrick J(oseph) 1930- ... 25-28R
Aspin, Les 1938- ... 108
Aspinall, (Honor) Ruth (Alastair) 1922- ... CANR-2
Earlier sketch in CA 7-8R
Aspinwall, Dorothy B(rown) 1910- ... 49-52
Aspiz, Harold 1921- ... 105
Aspler, Tony 1939- ... CANR-25
Earlier sketch in CA 105
Asprey, Robert B. 1923- ... CANR-6
Earlier sketch in CA 5-6R
Asprin, Robert Lynn 1946- ... 85-88
Aspy, David N(athanial) 1930- ... CANR-20
Earlier sketch in CA 45-48
Asquith, Cynthia Mary Evelyn (Charteris) 1887-1960 Obituary ... 110
Asquith, Glenn Hackney 1904- ... CANR-16
Earlier sketches in CA 1R, CANR-1
Asquith, Nan
See Pattinson, Nancy Evelyn
Asquith, Stewart 1948- ... 116
Assael, Henry 1935- ... 41-44R
Assagioli, Roberto 1893(?)-1974
Obituary ... 53-56
Asselbroke, Archibald Algernon 1923- ... 77-80
Asselin, E(dward) Donald 1903-1970 ... CAP-1
Earlier sketch in CA 11-12
Asselineau, Roger (Maurice) 1915- ... CANR-26
Earlier sketch in CA 97-100
Assensoh, A(kwasi) B(retuo) 1946(?)- ... 120
Assiac
See Fraenkel, Heinrich
Astaire, Fred 1899-1987 Obituary ... 122
Aster, Sidney 1942- ... CANR-10
Earlier sketch in CA 65-68
Astier, Pierre A(rthur) G(eorges) 1927- ... CANR-20
Earlier sketch in CA 45-48
Astill, Kenneth N. 1923- ... 53-56
Astin, Alexander W(illiam) 1932- ... CANR-7
Earlier sketch in CA 17-18R
Astin, Helen S(tavridou) 1932- ... 29-32R
Astiz, Carlos A. 1933- ... 25-28R
Astley, Joan Bright 1910- ... 33-36R
Astley, Juliet
See Lofts, Norah (Robinson)
Astley, Thea (Beatrice May) 1925- ... CANR-11
Earlier sketch in CA 65-68
See also CLC 41
Aston, Athina (Leka) 1934- ... 117
Aston, James
See White, T(erence) H(anbury)
Aston, Margaret 1932- ... 73-76
Aston, Michael (Anthony) 1946- ... 61-64
Aston, Trevor Henry 1925-1985 Obituary ... 118
Astor, (Francis) David (Langhorne) 1912-
Brief entry ... 113
Astor, Gavin 1918-1984 Obituary ... 113
Astor, Gerald (Morton) 1926- ... CANR-24
Earlier sketch in CA 107
Astor, Mary 1906-1987 ... CANR-3
Obituary ... 123
Earlier sketch in CA 5-6R
Astor, Michael Langhorne 1916-1980 ... 61-64
Obituary ... 97-100
Astor, Susan 1946- ... 105
Astrachan, Samuel 1934- ... 69-72
Astro, Richard 1941- ... 29-32R
Asturias, Miguel Angel 1899-1974 ... CAP-2
Obituary ... 49-52
Earlier sketch in CA 25-28
See also CLC 3, 8, 13
Aswad, Betsy (Becker) 1939- ... CANR-25
Earlier sketch in CA 104
Aswell, Mary Louise 1902-1984 Obituary ... 114
Aswin
See Nandakumar, Prema
Atamian, David 1892(?)-1978 Obituary ... 81-84
Atcheson, Richard 1934- ... 29-32R
Atchison, Sandra Dallas 1939- ... CANR-10
Earlier sketch in CA 17-18R
Atchity, Kenneth John 1944- ... CANR-16
Earlier sketches in CA 49-52, CANR-1
Atchley, Bob
See Atchley, Robert C.

Atchley, Dana W(inslow) 1941- 61-64
Atchley, Robert C. 1939- CANR-1
Earlier sketch in CA 45-48
Atene, Ann
See Atene, (Rita) Anna
Atene, (Rita) Anna 1922- SATA-12
Athanassiadis, Nikos 1904- CANR-17
Earlier sketch in CA 33-36R
Athans, George (Stanley), Jr. 1952- 104
Athas, Daphne 1923- CANR-3
Earlier sketch in CA 4R
Athay, R(obert) E. 1925- 33-36R
Athearn, Robert G(reenleaf) 1914- CANR-3
Earlier sketch in CA 4R
Atheling, William
See Pound, Ezra (Loomis)
Atheling, William, Jr.
See Blish, James (Benjamin)
Atherton, Alexine 1930- 37-40R
Atherton, Gertrude (Franklin Horn)
1857-1948 Brief entry 104
See also DLB 9
See also TCLC 2
Atherton, James C(hristian) 1915- 49-52
Atherton, James S(tephen) 1910- CAP-1
Earlier sketch in CA 15-16
Atherton, Lewis E. 1905- 1R
Atherton, Lucius
See Masters, Edgar Lee
Atherton, Maxine 5-6R
Atherton, Pauline
See Cochrane, Pauline A(therton)
Atherton, Sarah
See Bridgman, Sarah Atherton
Atherton, Wallace N(ewman) 1927- 49-52
Athey, Irene J(owett) 1919- 61-64
Athill, Diana 1917- CANR-2
Earlier sketch in CA 4R
Athlone, Countess of
See Alice (Mary Victoria Augusta
Pauline), Princess
Athos
See Walkerley, Rodney Lewis (de Burah)
Athos, Anthony G(eorge) 1934- CANR-19
Earlier sketch in CA 25-28R
Atil, Esin 1938- 113
Atiya, Aziz S. 1898- 7-8R
Atiyah, P(atrick) S(elim) 1931- 37-40R
Atiyeh, George N(icholas) 1923- 57-60
Atkeson, Ray A. 1907- CANR-11
Earlier sketch in CA 69-72
Atkey, Philip 1908-1985 Obituary 118
Brief entry 112
Atkin, Flora B(lumenthal) 1919- CANR-16
Earlier sketch in CA 93-96
Atkin, J. Myron 1927- 45-48
Atkin, Mary Gage 1929- 81-84
Atkin, William Wilson 1912(?)-1976
Obituary 65-68
Atkins, Burton M(ark) 1944- Brief entry 115
Atkins, Chester Burton 1924- Brief entry ... 113
Atkins, Chester G(reenough) 1948- 45-48
Atkins, Chet
See Atkins, Chester Burton
Atkins, G(eorge) Douglas 1943- 114
Atkins, G(eorge) Pope 1934- CANR-17
Earlier sketch in CA 33-36R
Atkins, Gary 1949- 126
Atkins, (Arthur) Harold 1910- 105
Atkins, Harry 1933- 25-28R
Atkins, Hedley (John Barnard) 1905-1983
Obituary 111
Atkins, Jack
See Harris, Mark
Atkins, James G. 1932- 17-18R
Atkins, Jim
See Atkins, James G.
Atkins, John (Alfred) 1916- CANR-19
Earlier sketches in CA 11-12R, CANR-3
Atkins, Josiah 1755(?)-1781 .... DLB-31
Atkins, Kenneth R(obert) 1920- 73-76
Atkins, Meg Elizabeth 102
Atkins, Oliver F. 1916-1977 73-76
Atkins, Ollie
See Atkins, Oliver F.
Atkins, P(eter) W(illiam) 1940- 117
Atkins, Paul Moody 1892-1977 Obituary ...69-72
Atkins, Russell 1926- CANR-25
Earlier sketches in CA 45-48, CANR-1
See also BW
See also DLB 41
Atkins, Stuart (Pratt) 1914- 25-28R
Atkins, Thomas R(adcliffe) 1939- CANR-8
Earlier sketch in CA 61-64
Atkinson, Allen SATA-46
Atkinson, Anthony Barnes 1944- CANR-11
Earlier sketch in CA 69-72
Atkinson, Basil F(erris) C(ampbell) 1895- ...7-8R
Atkinson, (Justin) Brooks 1894-1984 ..CANR-14
Obituary 111
Earlier sketch in CA 61-64
Atkinson, Carroll (Holloway) 1896- CAP-1
Earlier sketch in CA 15-16
Atkinson, David J(ohn) 1943- 107
Atkinson, Frank 1922- 108
Atkinson, Geoffrey 1955- 118
Atkinson, Hugh C(raig) 1933-1986 49-52
Obituary 120
Atkinson, James 1914- 25-28R
Atkinson, James B(lakely) 1934- 119
Atkinson, Jennifer (Elizabeth) McCabe
1937- Brief entry 116
Atkinson, John W(illiam) 1923- CANR-11
Earlier sketch in CA 23-24R
Atkinson, M. E.
See Frankau, Mary Evelyn Atkinson
Atkinson, Margaret Fleming 73-76
See also SATA 14
Atkinson, Mary
See Hardwick, Mollie
Atkinson, Phillip S. 1921- 25-28R
Atkinson, R(ichard) C(hatham) 1929- 17-18R
Atkinson, Ron 1932- 57-60
Atkinson, Ronald Field 1928- 17-18R
Atkinson, W. W.
See Atkinson, William Walker
Atkinson, Walter S(ydney) 1891-1978
Obituary 73-76
Atkinson, William Christopher 1902- 109
Atkinson, William Walker 1862-1932
Brief entry 120
Atkisson, Arthur A(lbert, Jr.) 1930- 61-64
Atkyns, Glenn C(hadwick) 1921- 49-52
Atlas, Helen Vincent 1931- 101
Atlas, Martin 1914- 5-6R
Atlas, Samuel 1899-1977 Obituary 73-76
Atmore, Anthony 1932- 25-28R
Attaway, Robert J(oseph) 1942- 49-52
Attaway, William 1911-1986 .... DLB-76
Attea, Mary
See Spahn, Mary Attea
Atteberry, William L(ouis) 1939- 53-56
Attenborough, Bernard George CANR-2
Earlier sketch in CA 49-52
Attenborough, David Frederick 1926- CANR-6
Earlier sketch in CA 4R
Attenborough, John 1908- 101
Atterton, Julian (Harold) 1956- 122
Atthill, Robin 1912- 69-72
Atticus
See Davies, Hunter
and Fleming, Ian (Lancaster)
and Pawle, Gerald
Attiyeh, Richard E. 1937- Brief entry 113
Attlee, C. R.
See Attlee, Clement R(ichard)
Attlee, Clement R(ichard) 1883-1967
Obituary 112
Attneave, Carolyn L(ewis) 1920- CANR-1
Earlier sketch in CA 45-48
Attridge, Derek 1945- 105
Attwell, Arthur A(lbert) 1917- 49-52
Attwood, William 1919- 21-22R
Atwater, C(onstance) Elizabeth (Sullivan)
1923- 15-16R
Atwater, Eastwood 1925- 110
Atwater, Florence (Hasseltine Carroll) SATA-16
Atwater, James David 1928- 101
Atwater, Lynn 1935- 111
Atwater, Montgomery Meigs 1904- 73-76
See also SATA 15
Atwater, Richard Tupper 1892-1948(?)
Brief entry 111
See also SATA 27
Atwood, Ann (Margaret) 1913- 41-44R
See also SATA 7
Atwood, Drucy
See Morrison, Eula Atwood
Atwood, Margaret (Eleanor) 1939- CANR-24
Earlier sketches in CA 49-52, CANR-3
See also SATA 50
See also DLB 53
See also CLC 2, 3, 4, 8, 13, 15, 25, 44
See also SSC 2
Atwood, Robert B. AITN-2
Atyeo, Don 1950- 93-96
Auberjonois, Fernand 1910- 77-80
Aubert, Alvin (Bernard) 1930- CANR-26
Earlier sketch in CA 81-84
See also BW
See also DLB 41
Aubert, Rosemary 1946- 113
Aubery, Pierre 1920- 37-40R
Aubey, Robert T(haddeus) 1930- 21-22R
Aubigny, Pierre d'
See Mencken, H(enry) L(ouis)
Aubin, Henry (Trocme) 1942- 77-80
Aubin, Penelope 1685-1731(?) DLB-39
Aubrey-Fletcher, Henry Lancelot
1887-1969 Obituary 111
Aubry, Claude B. 1914-1984 106
See also SATA 29, 40
Auburn, Mark Stuart 1945- 89-92
Auchincloss, Louis (Stanton) 1917- CANR-6
Earlier sketch in CA 1R
See also DLB 2
See also DLBY 80
See also CLC 4, 6, 9, 18, 45
Auchmuty, James Johnston 1909-1981 101
Obituary 109
Auchterlonie, Dorothy
See Green, Dorothy (Auchterlonie)
Audax
See Oaksey, John
Audemars, Pierre 1909- CANR-7
Earlier sketch in CA 19-20R
Auden, Renee
See West, Uta
Auden, W(ystan) H(ugh) 1907-1973 ....CANR-5
Obituary 45-48
Earlier sketch in CA 9-10R
See also DLB 10, 20
See also CLC 1, 2, 3, 4, 6, 9, 11, 14,
43
Audi, Robert (N.) 1941- 123
Audiard, Michel 1920-1985 Obituary 116
Audiberti, Jacques 1900-1965 Obituary ..25-28R
See also CLC 38
Auel, Jean M(arie) 1936- CANR-21
Earlier sketch in CA 103
See also CLC 31
Auer, J(ohn) Jeffery 1913- CANR-6
Earlier sketch in CA 11-12R
Auerbach, Aline B.
See Auerbach, Aline Sophie (Buchman)
Auerbach, Aline Sophie (Buchman)
1899(?)-1985 Obituary 116
Auerbach, Arnold M. 1912- 17-18R
Auerbach, Erich 1892-1957 Brief entry 118
Auerbach, Erna ?-1975 Obituary 61-64
Auerbach, George 1905(?)-1973 Obituary ..45-48
Auerbach, Jerold S(tephen) 1936- 21-22R
Auerbach, Jessica (Lynn) 1947- 114
Auerbach, Marjorie (Hoffberg) 9-10R
Auerbach, Nina 1943- CANR-15
Earlier sketch in CA 85-88
Auerbach, Stevanne 1938- CANR-24
Earlier sketches in CA 57-60, CANR-8
Auerbach, Stuart C(harles) 1935- 89-92
Auerbach, Sylvia CANR-4
Earlier sketch in CA 53-56
Aufricht, Hans 1902- 45-48
Augarde, Steve 1950- CANR-21
Earlier sketch in CA 104
See also SATA 25
Augarde, Tony 1936- 118
Augarten, Stan 1952- 115
Auge, Bud
See Auge, Henry J., Jr.
Auge, Henry J., Jr. 1930(?)-1983
Obituary 109
Augelli, John P(at) 1921- 17-18R
See also SATA 46
Aughtry, Charles Edward 1925- 7-8R
Augsburger, A(aron) Don(ald) 1925- 21-22R
Augsburger, David W. 1938- CANR-13
Earlier sketch in CA 33-36R
Augsburger, Myron S. 1929- CANR-6
Earlier sketch in CA 15-16R
Augspurger, Everett F. 1904(?)-1986
Obituary 118
Augstein, Rudolf (Karl) 1923- 110
Auguet, Roland (Jacques) 1935- 105
August, Eugene R(obert) 1935- 49-52
August, John
See De Voto, Bernard (Augustine)
Augustin, Ann Sutherland 1934- 57-60
Augustin, Pius 1934- 19-20R
Augustine, Erich
See Stoil, Michael Jon
Augustine, Norman R(alph) 1935- 121
Augustson, Ernest
See Ryden, Ernest Edwin
Augustus, Albert, Jr.
See Nuetzel, Charles (Alexander)
Aukerman, Dale 1930- 112
Aukerman, Robert C. 1910- 33-36R
Aukofer, Frank A(lexander) 1935- 65-68
Auld, Rhoda L(andsman) 105
Auleta, Michael S. 1909- CAP-2
Earlier sketch in CA 25-28
Auletta, Ken 1942- CANR-12
Earlier sketch in CA 69-72
Auletta, Richard P(aul) 1942- 53-56
Auletta, Robert 1940- 119
Brief entry 115
Aulicino, Armand 1920(?)-1983 Obituary ... 109
Aulick, June L. 1906- 25-28R
Ault, Donald D(uane) 1942- 81-84
Ault, Phil
See Ault, Phillip H(alliday)
Ault, Phillip H(alliday) 1914- CANR-18
Earlier sketch in CA 101
See also SATA 23
Ault, Rosalie Sain 1942- 107
See also SATA 38
Ault, Roz
See Ault, Rosalie Sain
Aultman, Donald S. 1930- 19-20R
Aultman, Richard E(ugene) 1933- CANR-9
Earlier sketch in CA 65-68
Aumann, Francis R(obert) 1901- 41-44R
Aumbry, Alan
See Bayley, Barrington J(ohn)
Aumont, Jean-Pierre 1913- 29-32R
Aune, Bruce (Arthur) 1933- 73-76
Aung, (Maung) Htin 1909- CANR-3
Earlier sketch in CA 7-8R
See also SATA 21
Aunger, Edmund A(lexander) 1949- 112
Auntie Deb
See Coury, Louise Andree
Auntie Louise
See Coury, Louise Andree
Aurand, Harold Wilson 1940- 41-44R
Aurand, L(eonard) W(illiam) 1920- 53-56
Aurandt, Paul Harvey 1918- 102
Aurelio, John R. 1937- 111
Aurelius
See Bourne, Randolph S(illiman)
Aurell, Tage 1895-1976 Obituary 113
Aurner, Robert R(ay) 1898- 7-8R
Aurthur, Robert Alan 1922-1978 81-84
Ausland, John C(ampbell) 1920- 93-96
Auslander, Audrey (May) Wurdemann
1911-1960 Obituary 116
Auslander, Joseph 1897-1965 Obituary 116
Ausmus, Harry Jack 1937- 115
Austen, Michael (Edward) 1951- 109
Austen, Ralph A. 1937- 25-28R
Auster, Nancy (Eileen) R(oss) 1926- 65-68
Auster, Paul 1947- CANR-23
Earlier sketch in CA 69-72
See also CLC 47
Austerlitz, Robert Paul 1923- 111
Austerman, Wayne R. 1948- 122
Austgen, Robert Joseph 1932- 23-24R
Austin, Alfred 1835-1913 .... DLB-35
Austin, Allan Edward 1929- 73-76
Austin, Allen 1922- 33-36R
Austin, Anthony 1919- 33-36R
Austin, (Mildred) Aurelia 53-56
Austin, Barbara Leslie
See Linton, Barbara Leslie
Austin, Brett
See Floren, Lee
Austin, Charles M(arshall) 1941- 69-72
Austin, David E(dwards) 1926- 29-32R
Austin, Elizabeth S. 1907- CAP-2
Earlier sketch in CA 25-28
See also SATA 5
Austin, Frank
See Faust, Frederick (Shiller)
Austin, Harry
See McInerny, Ralph
Austin, Henry Wilfred 1906- 101
Austin, James C(layton) 1923- 13-14R
Austin, James Henry 1925- 81-84
Austin, John 1922- 61-64
Austin, John Langshaw 1911-1960
Obituary 112
Austin, K(enneth) A(shurst) 1911- 102
Austin, Lettie J(ane) 1925- 65-68
Austin, Lewis 1936- 73-76
Austin, Lloyd James 1915- CAP-1
Earlier sketch in CA 13-14
Austin, M(ichel) M(ervyn) 1943- CANR-19
Earlier sketch in CA 85-88
Austin, Margot CAP-1
Earlier sketch in CA 9-10
See also SATA 11
Austin, Mary (Hunter) 1868-1934
Brief entry 109
See also DLB 9
See also TCLC 25
Austin, Mary C(arrington) 1915- 7-8R
Austin, Neal F(uller) 1926- 25-28R
Austin, (John) Norman 1937- 89-92
Austin, Oliver L(uther), Jr. 1903- 49-52
See also SATA 7
Austin, R. G.
See Gelman, Rita Golden
Austin, (Stewart) Reid 1931- 89-92
Austin, Richard B(uckner), Jr. 1930- 73-76
Austin, Stephen
See Stevens, Austin N(eil)
Austin, Timothy R(obert) 1952- 117
Austin, Tom
See Jacobs, Linda C.
Austin, William 1778-1841 .... DLB-74
Austin, William W(eaver) 1920- 23-24R
Austwick, John
See Lee, Austin
Ausubel, Herman 1920-1977 .... 1R
Obituary 69-72
Ausubel, Marynn H. 1913(?)-1980
Obituary 97-100
Auten, James H(udson) 1938- 41-44R
Auteur, Hillary
See Gottfried, Theodore Mark
Auth, Tony
See Auth, William Anthony, Jr.
Auth, William Anthony, Jr. 1942- 111
Brief entry 108
See also SATA 51
Autran Dourado, Waldomiro
See Dourado, Autran
Autrey, C. E. 1904- CANR-2
Earlier sketch in CA 4R
Autry, Ewart (Arthur) 1900- 15-16R
Autry, (Orvon) Gene 1907- Brief entry 112
Autry, James Arthur 1933- Brief entry 115
Autton, Norman William James 1920- 101
Auty, Phyllis 1910- CANR-2
Earlier sketch in CA 7-8R
Auty, Robert 1914-1978 Obituary 111
Auvert, Elizabeth CANR-14
Earlier sketch in CA 37-40R
Auvil, Kenneth W(illiam) 1925- 17-18R
Avakian, Arra S(teve) 1912- 85-88
Avakumovic, Ivan 1926- 41-44R
Avalle-Arce, Juan Bautista 1927- CANR-13
Earlier sketch in CA 33-36R
Avallone, Michael (Angelo), Jr. 1924- ...CANR-4
Earlier sketch in CA 7-8R
Avalon, Arthur
See Woodroffe, John George
Avanzini, John F. 1936- 122
Aveline, Claude 1901- CANR-6
Earlier sketch in CA 7-8R
Aveni, Anthony F(rancis) 1938- 81-84
Averbach, Albert 1902-1975 ....CAP-2
Earlier sketch in CA 21-22
Averill, E(dgar) W(aite) 1906-1980 53-56
Averill, Esther 1902- CANR-12
Earlier sketch in CA 29-32R
See also SATA 1, 28
Averill, John Hillier 1923-1984 Obituary 111
Averill, Lloyd J(ames) 1923- CANR-10
Earlier sketch in CA 23-24R
Averitt, Robert T(abor) 1931- 23-24R
Avery, Al
See Montgomery, Rutherford George
Avery, Burniece 1908- 73-76
Avery, Catherine B(arber) 1909- 57-60
Avery, Edwina Austin 1896-1983 Obituary .. 110
Avery, George C(ostas) 1926- 25-28R
Avery, Gillian (Elise) 1926- CANR-4
Earlier sketch in CA 9-10R
See also SATA 7
See also SAAS 6
Avery, Ira 1914- 81-84
Avery, James S. 1923- 126
Avery, Jeanne 1931- 111
Avery, June
See Rees, Joan

Avery, Kay 1908- 1R
See also SATA 5
Avery, Laurence G(reen) 1934- 33-36R
Avery, Lynn
See Cole, Lois Dwight
Avery, Martin 1955- 113
Avery, Mary Ellen 1927- 118
Avery, Peter 1923- 15-16R
Avery, Richard
See Cooper, Edmund
Avery, Robert J., Jr. 1911(?)-1983
Obituary 110
Avery, Robert Sterling 1917- 13-14R
Avery, Valerie 1940- 111
Avey, Albert E(dwin) 1886-1963 CAP-1
Earlier sketch in CA 17-18
Avey, Ruby 1927- CANR-16
Earlier sketch in CA 89-92
Avi
See Wortis, Avi
Aviad, Janet 1942- 115
Avice, Claude (Pierre Marie) 1925- CANR-24
Earlier sketches in CA 61-64, CANR-8
Avila, Lilian Estelle 45-48
Avineri, Shlomo 1933- 25-28R
Avirgan, Anthony Lance 1944- 112
Avirgan, Tony
See Avirgan, Anthony Lance
Avis, Paul (David Loup) 1947- 120
Avison, Margaret 1918- 17-18R
See also DLB 53
See also CLC 2, 4
Avison, N(eville) Howard 1934- 29-32R
Avi-Yonah, M(ichael) 1904-1974 CANR-6
Earlier sketch in CA 7-8R
Avnery, Uri 1923- CANR-25
Earlier sketch in CA 105
Avni, Abraham Albert 1921- 33-36R
Avramovic, Dragoslav 1919- CANR-17
Earlier sketch in CA 41-44R
Avrelin, M.
See Steinberg, Aaron Zacharovich
Avrett, Robert 1901- 1R
Avrett, Rosalind Case 1933- 110
Avrett, Roz
See Avrett, Rosalind Case
Avrich, Paul (Henry) 1931- CANR-5
Earlier sketch in CA 49-52
Avriel, Ehud 1917- 69-72
Avril, Pierre 1930- 29-32R
Avruch, Kevin Andrew 1950- 123
Avrutis, Raymond 1948- 69-72
Awa, Eme Onuoha 1921- 15-16R
Awad, Elias M. 1934- CANR-11
Earlier sketch in CA 17-18R
Awdry, Wilbert Vere 1911- 103
Awe, Chulho 1927- 33-36R
Awolowo, Obafemi Awo 1909-1987 CANR-14
Obituary 122
Earlier sketch in CA 65-68
Awoonor, Kofi 1935- CANR-15
Earlier sketch in CA 29-32R
See also BW
Axell, Herbert (Ernest) 1915- CANR-14
Earlier sketch in CA 81-84
Axelrad, Jacob 1899- 61-64
Axelrad, Sidney 1913-1976 122
Obituary 110
Axelrad, Sylvia Brody 1914- 104
Axelrod, Alan 1952- 110
Axelrod, D(avid) B(ruce) 1943- CANR-1
Earlier sketch in CA 45-48
Axelrod, George 1922- 65-68
Axelrod, Herbert Richard 1927- 85-88
Axelrod, Joseph 1918- 33-36R
Axelrod, Paul (Douglas) 1949- 110
Axelrod, Robert 1943- 33-36R
Axelrod, Steven Gould 1944- 81-84
Axelson, Eric (Victor) 1913- CANR-25
Earlier sketches in CA 21-22R, CANR-9
Axford, H. William 1925- 37-40R
Axford, Joseph Mack 1879-1970 CAP-2
Earlier sketch in CA 25-28
Axford, Lavonne B(rady) 1928- 33-36R
Axford, Roger W(illiam) 1920- 33-36R
Axinn, Donald E(verett) 1929- 125
Brief entry 115
Axinn, June 1923- 89-92
Axline, W. Andrew 1940- 25-28R
Axtell, James Lewis 1941- CANR-25
Earlier sketch in CA 108
Axthelm, Peter M(acrae) 1943- 107
Axton, David
See Koontz, Dean R(ay)
Axton, W(illiam) F(itch) 1926- 21-22R
Ayal, Igal 1942- 37-40R
Ayala, Francisco 1934- 85-88
Ayala, Mitzi 1941- 110
Ayandele, E(mmanuel) A(yankanmi)
1936- CANR-13
Earlier sketch in CA 21-22R
Ayars, Albert L(ee) 1917- 29-32R
Ayars, James S(terling) 1898- CANR-2
Earlier sketch in CA 5-6R
See also SATA 4
Ayatey, Siegfried B. Y. 1934- 25-28R
Ayatollah, The
See Khomeini, Ruhollah (Mussavi)
Ayckbourn, Alan 1939- 21-22R
See also DLB 13
See also CLC 5, 8, 18, 33
Aycock, Don M(ilton) 1951- 106
Aydelotte, William Osgood 1910- 57-60
Ayearst, Morley 1899-1983 CAP-2
Obituary 109
Earlier sketch in CA 29-32
Ayer, A(lfred) J(ules) 1910- CANR-5
Earlier sketch in CA 7-8R
Ayer, Frederick, Jr. 1917(?)-1974 73-76
Obituary 45-48
Ayer, Jacqueline 1930- 69-72
See also SATA 13
Ayer, Margaret ?-1981 CANR-13
Earlier sketch in CA 65-68
See also SATA 15
Ayers, Bradley Earl 1935- 69-72
Ayers, Donald Murray 1923- 17-18R
Ayers, Edward L(ynn) 1953- 115
Ayers, M(ichael) R(ichard) 1935- 25-28R
Ayers, Robert H(yman) 1918- 45-48
Ayers, Ronald 1948- 61-64
Ayers, Rose
See Greenwood, Lillian Bethel
Ayerst, David (George Ogilvy) 1904-
Brief entry 113
Aykroyd, Dan(iel Edward) 1952- 123
Aykroyd, Wallace Ruddell 1899-1979
Obituary 110
Aylen, Leo (William) 1935- CANR-19
Earlier sketch in CA 102
Aylesworth, Jim 1943- CANR-22
Earlier sketch in CA 106
See also SATA 38
Aylesworth, Thomas G(ibbons) 1927- CANR-26
Earlier sketches in CA 25-28R, CANR-10
See also SATA 4
See also CLR 6
Ayling, (Harold) Keith (Oliver) 1898-1976 73-76
Obituary 69-72
Ayling, Stanley (Edward) 1909- CANR-21
Earlier sketch in CA 45-48
Aylmer, Felix
See Jones, Felix Edward Aylmer
Aylmer, G(erald) E(dward) 1926- CANR-5
Earlier sketch in CA 13-14R
Aylward, Gladys 1902(?)-1970 Obituary 111
Aylward, Marcus
See Alexander, Marc
Aymar, Brandt 1911- CANR-16
Earlier sketch in CA 3R
See also SATA 22
Aymar, Gordon C(hristian) 1893- 7-8R
Ayme, Marcel (Andre) 1902-1967 89-92
See also DLB 72
See also CLC 11
Aymes, Sister Maria de la Cruz 23-24R
Aynes, Edith A(nnette) 1909- 45-48
Aynes, Pat Edith
See Aynes, Edith A(nnette)
Aynesworth, Hugh (G.) 1931- 120
Brief entry 115
Ayrault, Evelyn West 1922- 9-10R
Ayre, Robert (Hugh) 1900- 4R
Ayres, Alison
See Carter, Robert A(yres)
Ayres, Carole Briggs
See Briggs, Carole S(uzanne)
Ayres, James Eyvind 1939- 103
Ayres, Patricia Miller 1923-1985 Obituary 117
See also SATA 46
Ayres, Paul
See Aarons, Edward S(idney)
Ayres, Robert U(nderwood) 1932- CANR-16
Earlier sketch in CA 93-96
Ayres, Ruby M(ildred) 1883-1955
Brief entry 117
Ayrton, Elisabeth Walshe 1918- CANR-21
Earlier sketches in CA 7-8R, CANR-3
Ayrton, Michael 1921-1975 CANR-21
Obituary 61-64
Earlier sketches in CA 7-8R, CANR-9
See also CLC 7
Aytoun, William Edmonstoune
1813-1865 DLB-32
Ayub Khan, Mohammad 1907-1974 CAP-2
Earlier sketch in CA 23-24
Ayvazian, L. Fred 1919- 69-72
Azaid
See Zaidenberg, Arthur
Azar, Edward E. 1938- 49-52
Azarian, Mary 1940- 118
Azbel, Mark Ya. 1932- 105
Azcarate y Florez, Pablo de 1890-1971
Obituary 113
Azevedo, Ross E(ames) 105
Aziz, Sartaj 1929- 111
Aznavour, Charles
See Aznavourian, Varenagh
Aznavourian, Varenagh 1924- Brief entry 112
Azneer, J. Leonard 1921- 33-36R
Azorin
See Martinez Ruiz, Jose
See also CLC 11
Azoy, A(nastasio) C. M. 1891- CAP-1
Earlier sketch in CA 13-14
Azrael, Judith Anne 1938- CANR-10
Earlier sketch in CA 65-68
Azrin, Nathan H(arold) 1930- CANR-16
Earlier sketches in CA 45-48, CANR-1
Azuela, Mariano 1873-1952 Brief entry 104
See also TCLC 3
Azumi, Atsushi 1907- 102
Azumi, Koya 1930- 29-32R

B

B., Tania
See Blixen, Karen (Christentze Dinesen)
B. V.
See Thomson, James
Baack, Lawrence James 1943- 109
Baade, (Wilhelm Heinrich) W(alter)
1893-1960 Obituary 112
Baali, Fuad (G.) 1930- Brief entry 117
Baal-Teshuva, Jacob 1929- 7-8R
Baar, James A. 1929- 102
Baars, Conrad W(alterus) 1919-1981 CANR-8
Earlier sketch in CA 57-60
Baars, Donald Lee 1928- 121
Baarslag, Karl Herman William 1900-1984
Obituary 111
Baastad, Babbis Friis
See Friis-Baastad, Babbis Ellinor
Baatz, Charles A(lbert) 1916- 104
Baatz, Olga K. 1921- 104
Bab
See Gilbert, W(illiam) S(chwenck)
Baba, Meher 1894-1969 109
Obituary 106
Babb, Howard S(elden) 1924-1978 13-14R
Obituary 120
Babb, Hugh Webster 1887-197(?) CAP-1
Earlier sketch in CA 13-14
Babb, Janice Barbara
See Bentley, Janice Babb
Babb, Lawrence 1902- CAP-2
Earlier sketch in CA 33-36
Babb, Lawrence Alan 1941- Brief entry 105
Babb, Sanora 1907- 15-16R
Babbage, Stuart Barton 1916- CANR-8
Earlier sketch in CA 5-6R
Babbidge, Homer D(aniels), Jr.
1925-1984 CANR-13
Obituary 112
Earlier sketch in CA 61-64
Babbie, Earl (Robert) 1938- CANR-23
Earlier sketches in CA 61-64, CANR-8
Babbis, Eleanor
See Friis-Baastad, Babbis Ellinor
Babbitt, Bruce E(dward) 1938- 97-100
Babbitt, Irving 1865-1933 DLB-63
Babbitt, Natalie 1932- CANR-19
Earlier sketches in CA 49-52, CANR-2
See also SATA 6
See also SAAS 5
See also DLB 52
See also CLR 2
Babbitt, Robert
See Bangs, Robert B(abbitt)
Babcock, C(larence) Merton 1908- CANR-5
Earlier sketch in CA 5-6R
Babcock, Dennis Arthur 1948- 61-64
See also SATA 22
Babcock, Dorothy E(llen) 1931- 65-68
Babcock, Frederic 1896- 5-6R
Babcock, Frederick Morrison
1897(?)-1983 Obituary 110
Babcock, Havilah 1898-1964 122
Obituary 110
Babcock, Leland S. 1922- Brief entry 106
Babcock, Nicolas
See Lewis, Tom
Babcock, Robert J(oseph) 1928- 15-16R
Babe, Thomas 1941- 101
Babel, Isaac (Emanuilovich)
See Babel, Isaak (Emmanuilovich)
See also TCLC 13
Babel, Isaak (Emmanuilovich)
1894-1941(?) Brief entry 104
See also TCLC 2
Baber, Walter F(rank) 1953- 120
Babiiha, Thaddeo K(itasimbwa) 1945- 110
Babin, David E. 1925- 23-24R
Babin, Maria Teresa 1910- Brief entry 107
Babington, Anthony Patrick 1920- 61-64
Babits, Mihaly 1883-1941 Brief entry 114
See also TCLC 14
Babitz, Eve 1943- 81-84
Babitz, Sol 1911- 41-44R
Babladelis, Georgia 1931- CANR-8
Earlier sketch in CA 23-24R
Babris, Peter J. 1917- CANR-10
Earlier sketch in CA 21-22R
Babson, Marian 102
Babson, Roger W(ard) 1875-1967
Obituary 89-92
Babula, William 1943- CANR-21
Earlier sketch in CA 105
Bacall, Lauren 1924- 93-96
Bacchelli, Riccardo 1891-1985 29-32R
Obituary 117
See also CLC 19
Bacciocco, Edward J(oseph), Jr. 1935- 45-48
Bach, Alice (Hendricks) 1942- 101
See also SATA 27, 30
Bach, Bert C(oates) 1936- 23-24R
Bach, George Leland 1915- CANR-3
Earlier sketch in CA 4R
Bach, George Robert 1914- 104
Bach, Ira J(ohn) 1906-1985 115
Bach, Jean
See Greif, Martin
Bach, Kent 1943- 85-88
Bach, Marcus (Louis) 1906- Brief entry 115
Bach, Orville E(uing), Jr. 1946- 115
Bach, P.D.Q.
See Schickele, Peter
Bach, Richard (David) CANR-18
Earlier sketch in CA 11-12R
See also SATA 13
See also CLC 14
See also AITN 1
Bach, Wilfrid 1936- CANR-10
Earlier sketch in CA 61-64
Bacharach, Alfred L(ouis) 1891-1966 CAP-1
Earlier sketch in CA 11-12
Bacharach, Bert(ram Mark) 1898-1983
Obituary 110
Bache, Benjamin Franklin 1769-1798 DLB-43
Bache, William B. 1922- 25-28R
Bachelard, Gaston 1884-1962 97-100
Obituary 89-92
Bachem Alent, Rose M(arie Baake) 49-52
Bacher, June Masters 1918- 108
Bachman, David C(hristian) 1934- 124
Bachman, Fred 1949- 53-56
See also SATA 12
Bachman, Ingeborg 1926-1973 93-96
Obituary 45-48
Bachman, Jerald G(raybill) 1936- 41-44R
Bachman, John Walter 1916- 5-6R
Bachmann, Gideon 1927- 104
Bachmura, Frank T(homas) 1922- 45-48
Bachrach, Bernard S. 1939- 113
Bachrach, Judy 1948- 114
Bacik, James Joseph 1936- 105
Back, Joe (W.) 1899-1986 CAP-2
Obituary 120
Earlier sketch in CA 17-18
Back, Kurt W(olfgang) 1919- 13-14R
Backer, Dorothy 1925- 85-88
Backer, John H. 1902-1985 33-36R
Obituary 116
Backer, Morton 1918- 19-20R
Backgammon, Daisy
See Murray, John F(rancis)
Backhouse, Janet 1938- CANR-26
Earlier sketch in CA 109
Backhouse, Sally 1927- 23-24R
Backlund, Ralph T. 1918- 73-76
Backman, Carl W(ard) 1923- 19-20R
Backman, Jules 1910- CANR-3
Earlier sketch in CA 2R
Backman, Melvin (Abraham) 1919- 21-22R
Backman, Milton V., Jr. 1927- CANR-13
Earlier sketch in CA 33-36R
Backstrom, Charles H(erbert) 1926- 13-14R
Backus, Jean L(ouise) 1914-1986 33-36R
Obituary 119
Backus, Oswald P(rentiss) III 1921-1972 CAP-2
Obituary 37-40R
Earlier sketch in CA 33-36
Bacmeister, Rhoda W(arner) 1893- CAP-1
Earlier sketch in CA 15-16
See also SATA 11
Bacon, Daisy Sarah 1899(?)-1986
Obituary 118
Bacon, Delia 1811-1859 DLB-1
Bacon, Edmund N(orwood) 1910- 41-44R
Bacon, Edward 1906-1981 29-32R
Obituary 102
Bacon, Elizabeth 1914- 29-32R
See also SATA 3
Bacon, Elizabeth E(maline) 1904- CAP-1
Earlier sketch in CA 19-20
Bacon, Frances Atchinson 1903- 4R
Bacon, Joan Chase
See Bowden, Joan Chase
Bacon, John 1940- 53-56
Bacon, Josephine Dodge (Daskam)
1876-1961 97-100
See also SATA 48
Bacon, Lenice Ingram 1895- 45-48
Bacon, Margaret 106
Bacon, Margaret Frances
See Bacon, Peggy
See also SATA 50
Bacon, Margaret Hope 1921- 25-28R
See also SATA 6
Bacon, Marion 1901(?)-1975 Obituary 57-60
Bacon, Martha Sherman 1917-1981 85-88
Obituary 104
See also SATA 18, 27
See also CLR 3
Bacon, Nancy 1940- 93-96
Bacon, Peggy 1895-1987 CAP-2
Obituary 121
Earlier sketch in CA 23-24
See also SATA 2
Bacon, Phillip 1922- 41-44R
Bacon, R(onald) L(eonard) 1924- 104
See also SATA 26
Bacon, Thomas 1700(?)-1768 DLB-31
Bacon, Wallace A(lger) 1914- 19-20R
Bacote, Clarence A(lbert) 1906- CAP-2
Earlier sketch in CA 33-36
Bacovia, G.
See Vasiliu, Gheorghe
Bacovia, George
See Vasiliu, Gheorghe
See also TCLC 24
Bacque, James 1929- 101
Badash, Lawrence 1934- CANR-14
Earlier sketch in CA 37-40R
Badawi, M(ohamed) M(ustafa) 1925- CANR-1
Earlier sketch in CA 49-52
Badawi, Muhammed Mustafa
See Badawi, M(ohamed) M(ustafa)
Badcock, Christopher Robert 1946- 101
Baddeley, Alan D(avid) 1934- 69-72
Baddeley, Hermione 1906(?)-1986
Obituary 120
Baddeley, V.C. Clinton
See Clinton-Baddeley, V.C.
Bade, Jane (Ruth) 1932- 89-92
Bade, Patrick 1951- 89-92
Baden-Powell, Dorothy 1920- 103
Baden-Powell, Robert (Stephenson Smyth)
1857-1941 Brief entry 114
See also SATA 16
Bader, Douglas (Robert Steuart)
1910-1982 101
Obituary 107
Bader, Julia 1944- 69-72
Bader, Robert S(mith) 1925- 120

Badger, John d'Arcy 1917- 45-48
Badger, Ralph E(astman) 1890-1978 .... CAP-2
Obituary 73-76
Earlier sketch in CA 21-22
Badger, Reid 1942- 97-100
Badgley, John 1930- 37-40R
Badgley, Robin F(rancis) 1931- 101
Badham, Leslie (Stephen Ronald)
1908-1975 Obituary 114
Badia, Leonard F(rancis) 1934- 113
Badian, Ernst 1925- 37-40R
Badillo, Herman 1929- 85-88
Badinter, Elisabeth 1944- 118
Badough, Rose Marie 1938- 117
Badura-Skoda, Eva 1929- CANR-14
Earlier sketch in CA 37-40R
Baechler, Jean 1937- CANR-13
Earlier sketch in CA 73-76
Baeck, Leo 1873-1956 Brief entry 115
Baeder, John 1938- 111
Baehr, Consuelo 1938- 103
Baehr, Harry William 1907-1987 Obituary ... 123
Baehr, Patricia Goehner 1952- 103
Baen, James P. 1943- Brief entry 112
Baensch, Willy E(dward) 1893-1972
Obituary 37-40R
Baenziger, Hans 1917- 49-52
Baer, Adela S(wenson) 1931- 101
Baer, Curtis O. 1898- 49-52
Baer, Daniel J(oseph) 1929- 33-36R
Baer, Donald Merle 1931- 81-84
Baer, Earl E. 1928- 57-60
Baer, Edith R(uth) 1920- CANR-21
Earlier sketch in CA 104
Baer, Eleanora A(gnes) 1907- 9-10R
Baer, Gabriel 1919- CANR-2
Earlier sketch in CA 7-8R
Baer, George Webster 1935- 21-22R
Baer, Hans A. 1944- 119
Baer, Jean L. CANR-9
Earlier sketch in CA 15-16R
Baer, Jill
See Gilbert, (Agnes) Joan (Sewell)
Baer, John 1886-1970 Obituary 29-32R
Baer, Judith A(bbott) 1945- 81-84
Baer, Marianne 1932- 81-84
Baer, Max Frank 1912- 11-12R
Baer, Rosemary 1913- 41-44R
Baer, Walter S. III 1937- 65-68
Baer, Werner 1931- 11-12R
Baerg, Harry J(ohn) 1909- CANR-4
Earlier sketch in CA 11-12R
See also SATA 12
Baerwald, Hans H(erman) 1927- 33-36R
Baerwald, Sara 1948- 61-64
Baetjer, Anna M(edora) 1899-1984
Obituary 112
Baetzhold, Howard G(eorge) 1923- 29-32R
Baeuml, Franz H(einrich) 1926- 49-52
Baez, Joan (Chandos) 1941- CANR-26
Earlier sketch in CA 21-22R
Bagarag, Shibli
See Lawlor, Patrick Anthony
Bagby, George
See Stein, Aaron Marc
Bagby, Wesley M(arvin) 1922- CANR-16
Earlier sketch in CA 4R
Bagdikian, Ben Haig 1920- CANR-6
Earlier sketch in CA 11-12R
Bage, Robert 1728-1801 .... DLB-39
Bagehot, Walter 1826-1877 .... DLB-55
Bagg, Graham (William) 1917- 57-60
Bagg, Robert Ely 1935- CANR-15
Earlier sketch in CA 65-68
Baggaley, Andrew R(obert) 1923- 15-16R
Baggett, Nancy 1943- 117
Baggley, John (Samuel) 1940- 124
Bagin, Don(ald Richard) 1938- 77-80
Baginski, Frank 1938- 93-96
Bagley, Christopher 1937- 119
Bagley, Desmond 1923-1983 ....19-20R
Obituary 109
Bagley, Edward R(osecrans) 1926- CANR-5
Earlier sketch in CA 53-56
Bagley, J(ohn) J(oseph) 1908- CANR-2
Earlier sketch in CA 7-8R
Bagnel, Joan 1933- 49-52
Bagni, Gwen
See Dubov, Gwen Bagni
Bagnold, Enid 1889-1981 .... CANR-5
Obituary 103
Earlier sketch in CA 7-8R
See also SATA 1, 25
See also DLB 13
See also CLC 25
Bagramian, Ivan K(ristoforovich)
1897-1982 Obituary 107
Bagrjana, Elisaveta
See Belcheva, Elisaveta
Bagryana, Elisaveta
See Belcheva, Elisaveta
Bagster, Hubert
See Trumper, Hubert Bagster
Bagwell, Philip S(idney) 1914- CANR-13
Earlier sketch in CA 33-36R
Bagwell, William Francis, Jr. 1923- 33-36R
Bahadur, K(rishna) P(rakash) 1924- 57-60
Bahat, Dan 1938- 77-80
Bahl, Roy W. (Jr.) 1939- 23-24R
Bahlke, George W(ilbon) 1934- 29-32R
Bahlke, Valerie Worth 1933- CANR-15
Earlier sketch in CA 41-44R
Bahlman, Dudley Ward Rhodes 1923- 85-88
Bahm, Archie J(ohn) 1907- CANR-3
Earlier sketch in CA 11-12R
Bahmueller, Charles F(erdinand) 1942- 112
Bahn, Eugene 1906- 23-24R
Bahn, Margaret (Elizabeth) Linton
1907-1969 .... CAP-2
Earlier sketch in CA 25-28
Bahr, Edith-Jane 1926- 65-68
Bahr, Erhard 1932- 33-36R
Bahr, Hermann 1863-1934 Brief entry 121
Bahr, Howard M. 1938- CANR-12
Earlier sketch in CA 29-32R
Bahr, Jerome 1909- 33-36R
Bahr, Robert 1940- CANR-9
Earlier sketch in CA 65-68
See also SATA 38
Bahti, Tom SATA-31
Baier, Kurt Erich 1917- 65-68
Baigell, Matthew 1933- 107
Bailes, Kendall E(ugene) 1940- Brief entry .. 112
Bailey, Alfred Goldsworthy 1905- 25-28R
See also DLB 68
Bailey, Alfred M(arshall) 1894-1978 ....41-44R
Bailey, Alice A(nne La Trobe-Bateman)
1880(?)-1949 Brief entry 116
Bailey, Alice Cooper 1890- CAP-1
Earlier sketch in CA 15-16
See also SATA 12
Bailey, Anthony 1933- CANR-3
Earlier sketch in CA 3R
Bailey, Barry 1926- 107
Bailey, Bernadine (Freeman) 1901- CANR-7
Earlier sketch in CA 5-6R
See also SATA 14
Bailey, Beryl Loftman 1920(?)-1977
Obituary 69-72
Bailey, Carolyn Sherwin 1875-1961 73-76
See also SATA 14
Bailey, Charles W(aldo) II 1929- CANR-1
Earlier sketch in CA 1R
Bailey, Chris H(arvey) 1946- 65-68
Bailey, Conrad Charles Maitland 1922- 105
Bailey, D. F. 1950- 125
Bailey, D. R. Shackleton
See Shackleton Bailey, D(avid) R(oy)
Bailey, David (Royston) 1938- 120
Bailey, David C(harles) 1930- 45-48
Bailey, Derrick Sherwin 1910-1984 .... CANR-2
Obituary 112
Earlier sketch in CA 5-6R
Bailey, Don 1942- 93-96
Bailey, Dudley 1918- 19-20R
Bailey, Eric 1933- 33-36R
Bailey, F(rancis) Lee 1933- 89-92
Bailey, Frederick George 1924- CANR-9
Earlier sketch in CA 13-14R
Bailey, Frederick Marshman 1882-1967 ... CAP-1
Earlier sketch in CA 13-14
Bailey, George 1919- CANR-17
Earlier sketch in CA 25-28R
Bailey, Gerald Earl 1929- CANR-10
Earlier sketch in CA 25-28R
Bailey, Gordon Keith 1936- 112
Bailey, H(enry) C(hristopher) 1878-1961
Obituary 108
Bailey, Harold (Walter) 1899- 109
Bailey, Harry A(ugustine), Jr. 1932- 23-24R
Bailey, Helen Miller 1909- 15-16R
Bailey, Herbert S(mith), Jr. 1921-
Brief entry 112
Bailey, Hillary G(oodsell) 1894- 57-60
Bailey, Hugh C(oleman) 1929- 11-12R
Bailey, J(ames) Martin 1929- 49-52
Bailey, J(ames) O(sler) 1903-1979 ....17-18R
Obituary 126
Bailey, Jackson Holbrook 1925- CANR-21
Earlier sketch in CA 45-48
Bailey, James H(enry) 1919- 106
Bailey, James R(ichard) A(be) 1919- 53-56
Bailey, (Corinne) Jane 1943- 77-80
Bailey, Jane H(orton) 1916- CANR-4
Earlier sketch in CA 53-56
See also SATA 12
Bailey, Joan H(auser) 1922- 21-22R
Bailey, Joe A(llen) 1929- 37-40R
Bailey, John (Robert) 1940- 121
See also SATA 52
Bailey, John A(medee) 1929- 37-40R
Bailey, Kenneth K(yle) 1923- 23-24R
Bailey, Kenneth P. 1912- CANR-4
Earlier sketch in CA 53-56
Bailey, Lloyd Richard 1936- CANR-15
Earlier sketch in CA 85-88
Bailey, M(innie Elizabeth) Thomas 57-60
Bailey, Maralyn Collins (Harrison) 1941- 53-56
See also SATA 12
Bailey, Matilda
See Radford, Ruby L(orraine)
Bailey, Maurice Charles 1932- 53-56
See also SATA 12
Bailey, Norman A(lishan) 1931- CANR-13
Earlier sketch in CA 21-22R
Bailey, Patrick 1925- 57-60
Bailey, Paul 1937- CANR-16
Earlier sketch in CA 21-22R
See also DLB 14
See also CLC 45
Bailey, Paul Dayton 1906-1987 .... CANR-6
Obituary 124
Earlier sketch in CA 5-6R
Bailey, Pearl (Mae) 1918- CANR-14
Earlier sketch in CA 61-64
See also BW
Bailey, Philip James 1816-1902 .... DLB-32
Bailey, Ralph Edgar 1893- CAP-1
Earlier sketch in CA 17-18
See also SATA 11
Bailey, Raymond H(amby) 1938- CANR-8
Earlier sketch in CA 61-64
Bailey, Richard W(eld) 1939- CANR-10
Earlier sketch in CA 25-28R
Bailey, Robert, Jr. 1945- 49-52
Bailey, Robert W(ilson) 1943- CANR-21
Earlier sketch in CA 69-72
Bailey, Stephen Kemp 1916-1982 .... CANR-4
Obituary 106
Earlier sketch in CA 1R
Bailey, Sydney D(awson) 1916- CANR-12
Earlier sketch in CA 69-72
Bailey, Thomas A(ndrew) 1902-1983 ... CANR-18
Obituary 110
Earlier sketch in CA 19-20R
Bailey, Victor 1948- 125
Bailie, Victoria Worley 1894- CAP-1
Earlier sketch in CA 15-16
Bailkey, Nels M(artin) 1911- 33-36R
Baillen, Claude
See Delay-Tubiana, Claude
Baillie, Allan 1943- 118
Baillie, Hugh 1890-1966 Obituary 89-92
See also DLB 29
Baillie, Isobel 1895-1983 Obituary 110
Baillie, Kate 1957- 124
Baillie-Hamilton, George 1894-1986
Obituary 121
Baily, Charles M(ichael) 1944- 117
Baily, Leslie 1906-1976 .... CAP-2
Earlier sketch in CA 25-28
Baily, Nathan A(riel) 1920- CANR-6
Earlier sketch in CA 9-10R
Baily, Samuel L(ongstreth) 1936- 29-32R
Bailyn, Bernard 1922- CANR-8
Earlier sketch in CA 61-64
See also DLB 17
Bain, A(ndrew) D(avid) 1936- Brief entry ... 111
Bain, Carl E. 1930- 85-88
Bain, Chester A(rthur) 1912- 29-32R
Bain, Chester Ward 1919- 85-88
Bain, Joe S. 1912- 33-36R
Bain, Kenneth Bruce Findlater 1921-1985 ..93-96
Obituary 115
Bain, Kenneth Ray 1942- 104
Bain, Robert 1932- 77-80
Bain, Willard S., Jr. 1938- 25-28R
Bainbridge, Beryl 1933- CANR-24
Earlier sketch in CA 21-22R
See also DLB 14
See also CLC 4, 5, 8, 10, 14, 18, 22
Bainbridge, Geoffrey 1923- 7-8R
Bainbridge, John 1913- 13-14R
Bainbridge, William Sims 1940- 120
Baine, Rodney M(ontgomery) 1913- 69-72
Baines, Anthony C(uthbert) 1912- 7-8R
Baines, Frank 1915-1987 Obituary 124
Baines, Jocelyn 1925-1973 106
Obituary 104
Baines, John M. 1935- 41-44R
Baines, John Robert 1946- 123
Bains, Larry
See Sabin, Louis
Bainton, Roland H(erbert) 1894-1984 ... CANR-5
Obituary 113
Earlier sketch in CA 4R
Bair, Deirdre 1935- 81-84
Bair, Frank E. 1927- 102
Baird, A(lbert) Craig 1883- CAP-1
Earlier sketch in CA 13-14
Baird, Alexander (John) 1925- 11-12R
Baird, Bil
See Baird, William Britton
See also SATA 30, 52
Baird, Duncan H. 1917- 65-68
Baird, Forrest J. 1905- CAP-1
Earlier sketch in CA 19-20
Baird, Irene 1901-1981 .... DLB-68
Baird, J(oseph) Arthur 1922- CANR-3
Earlier sketch in CA 5-6R
Baird, J(oseph) L. 1933- 85-88
Baird, Jack
See Baird, John Charlton
Baird, Jay Warren 1936- 41-44R
Baird, Jesse Hays 1889- 15-16R
Baird, John Charlton 1938- 126
Baird, John D. 1941- 109
Baird, John Edward 1922- 17-18R
Baird, Joseph Armstrong (Jr.) 1922- ... CANR-12
Earlier sketch in CA 33-36R
Baird, Lorrayne Y. 1927- 112
Baird, Marie-Terese 1918- 57-60
Baird, Martha (Joanna) 1921-1981 .... CANR-9
Earlier sketch in CA 61-64
Baird, Nancy Disher 1935- CANR-15
Earlier sketch in CA 89-92
Baird, Patrick D(ouglas) 1912-1984
Obituary 112
Baird, Robert D(ahlen) 1933- 53-56
Baird, Ronald J(ames) 1929- 53-56
Baird, Russell N. 1922- 19-20R
Baird, Thomas (P.) 1923- CANR-21
Earlier sketches in CA 53-56, CANR-4
See also SATA 39, 45
Baird, W(illiam) David 1939- 41-44R
Baird, William (Robb) 1924- 15-16R
Baird, William Britton 1904-1987 106
Obituary 122
See also SATA 30
Baird-Smith, Robin 1946- 123
Bairstow, Jeffrey N(oel) 1939- CANR-8
Earlier sketch in CA 61-64
Baity, Elizabeth Chesley 1907- 29-32R
See also SATA 1
Bajema, Carl Jay 1937- CANR-12
Earlier sketch in CA 33-36R
Bakal, Carl 1918- 23-24R
Bakalar, James B. 1943- 97-100
Bakalis, Michael J. 1938- 85-88
Bakan, David 1921- 25-28R
Bakan, Paul 1928- 23-24R
Bakaric, Vladimir 1912-1983 Obituary 114
Bake, William A(lbert) 1938- 110
Bakeless, John (Edwin) 1894-1978 .... CANR-5
Obituary 118
Earlier sketch in CA 5-6R
See also SATA 9
Bakeless, Katherine Little 1895- 7-8R
See also SATA 9
Bakely, Don(ald Carlisle) 1928- 65-68
Baker, Adelaide N(ichols) 1894-1974 45-48
Baker, Adolph 1917- 53-56
Baker, Al AITN-1
Baker, Alan 1951- CANR-16
Earlier sketch in CA 97-100
See also SATA 22
Baker, (Allen) Albert 1910- 104
Baker, Alfred Thornton 1915(?)-1983
Obituary 110
Baker, Allison
See Crumbaker, Alice
Baker, Alton Wesley 1912- 33-36R
Baker, Asa
See Dresser, Davis
Baker, Augusta 1911- CANR-17
Earlier sketch in CA 1R
See also BW
See also SATA 3
Baker, Benjamin 1915- 3R
Baker, Betty D(oreen Flook) 1916- CANR-6
Earlier sketch in CA 9-10R
Baker, Betty Lou 1928- CANR-2
Earlier sketch in CA 4R
See also SATA 5
Baker, Bill 1936- 77-80
Baker, Bill
See Baker, C(harles) William
Baker, Bill Russell 1933- 57-60
Baker, Bobby
See Baker, Robert G.
and Baker, Alfred Thornton
Baker, C(harles) William 1919- 57-60
Baker, Carlos (Heard) 1909-1987 .... CANR-3
Obituary 122
Earlier sketch in CA 5-6R
Baker, Charlotte 1910- 19-20R
See also SATA 2
Baker, Christopher John 1948- Brief entry .. 117
Baker, D(onald) Philip 1937- 102
Baker, David (Anthony) 1954- 118
Baker, Dennis 1942- 107
Baker, Denys Val 1917-1984 .... CANR-6
Obituary 113
Earlier sketch in CA 9-10R
Baker, Donald G(ene) 1932- 33-36R
Baker, Donald N(oel) 1936- 23-24R
Baker, Donald W(hitelaw) 1923- CANR-12
Earlier sketch in CA 73-76
Baker, Dorothy 1907-1968 .... CANR-1
Obituary 25-28R
Earlier sketch in CA 4R
Baker, Eleanor Z(uckerman) 1932- CANR-8
Earlier sketch in CA 57-60
Baker, (Mary) Elizabeth (Gillette) 1923- .. CANR-3
Earlier sketch in CA 3R
See also SATA 7
Baker, Elizabeth Faulkner 1886(?)-1973 ... CAP-1
Obituary 41-44R
Earlier sketch in CA 15-16
Baker, Elliott 1922- CANR-2
Earlier sketch in CA 45-48
See also CLC 8
Baker, Elsie 1929- 65-68
Baker, Elsworth F. 1903- CAP-2
Earlier sketch in CA 25-28
Baker, Eric Wilfred 1899-1973 Obituary ...45-48
Baker, Eugene H. SATA-50
Baker, F(rederick) Sherman 1902-1976
Obituary 65-68
Baker, Frank 1910- 9-10R
Baker, Frank 1936- CANR-18
Earlier sketches in CA 49-52, CANR-2
Baker, Frank S. 1899(?)-1983 Obituary 109
Baker, Frank S(heaffer) 1910- 17-18R
Baker, Gary G. 1939- 23-24R
Baker, Gayle Cunningham 1950- 105
See also SATA 39
Baker, George 1915-1975 93-96
Obituary 57-60
Baker, George W(alter) 1915- 21-22R
Baker, Gilbert
See Baker, John Gilbert Hindley
Baker, Gladys L(ucille) 1910- 41-44R
Baker, Gordon Pratt 1910- 4R
Baker, Herbert G(eorge) 1920- 41-44R
Baker, Herschel Clay 1914- 61-64
Baker, Houston A., Jr. 1943- CANR-14
Earlier sketch in CA 41-44R
See also BW
See also DLB 67
Baker, Howard 1905- CAP-2
Earlier sketch in CA 19-20
Baker, Howard H(enry), Jr. 1925- 124
Brief entry 113
Baker, Hugh D. R. 1937- CANR-12
Earlier sketch in CA 25-28R
Baker, Ivon 1928- 73-76
Baker, J(ohn) A(lec) 1926- 25-28R
Baker, James C(alvin) 1935- 125
Brief entry 117
Baker, James Lawrence 1941- 53-56
Baker, James R(upert) 1925- 29-32R
Baker, James T. 1940- 85-88
Baker, James Volant 1903- 57-60
Baker, James W. 1924- 77-80
See also SATA 22
Baker, Jane Howard 1950- 110

INDEX

Baker, Janice E(dla) 1941- ... 57-60
See also SATA 22
Baker, Jean Hogarth H(arvey) 1933- ... 41-44R
Baker, Jeannie 1950- ... 97-100
See also SATA 23
Baker, Jeffrey J(ohn) W(heeler) 1931- ... CANR-1
Earlier sketch in CA 49-52
See also SATA 5
Baker, Jerry ... 105
See also AITN 2
Baker, Jim
See Baker, James W.
Baker, John 1901(?)-1971 Obituary ... 104
Baker, John C(hester) 1909- ... 106
Baker, John F(leetwood) 1901-1985
Obituary ... 117
Baker, John F. 1931- ... 85-88
Baker, John Gilbert Hindley 1910-1986
Obituary ... 119
Baker, John H(enry) 1936- ... 33-36R
Baker, John R(andal) 1900-1984 ... 49-52
Obituary ... 113
Baker, John W(esley) 1920- ... 61-64
Baker, Joseph E(llis) 1905- ... 33-36R
Baker, Josephine 1906-1975 Obituary ... 105
Baker, Keith Michael 1938- ... 57-60
Baker, Kenneth F(rank) 1908- ... 49-52
Baker, Laura Nelson 1911- ... CANR-5
Earlier sketch in CA 5-6R
See also SATA 3
Baker, Lawrence M(anning) 1907- ... CAP-1
Earlier sketch in CA 13-14
Baker, Leonard S(tanley) 1931-1984 ... 23-24R
Obituary ... 114
Baker, Letha Elizabeth (Mitts) 1913- ... 33-36R
Baker, Liva 1930- ... 29-32R
Baker, Lucinda 1916- ... 65-68
Baker, Lynn S. 1948- ... 109
Baker, M(ary) E(llen) Penny ... 45-48
Baker, Margaret 1890- ... CANR-6
Earlier sketch in CA 15-16R
See also SATA 4
Baker, Margaret J(oyce) 1918- ... CANR-22
Earlier sketches in CA 13-14R, CANR-7
See also SATA 12
Baker, Marilyn 1929- Brief entry ... 111
Baker, Mary Gladys Steel 1892-1974 ... CAP-1
Earlier sketch in CA 15-16
See also SATA 12
Baker, (Robert) Michael (Graham)
1938- ... 25-28R
See also SATA 4
Baker, Michael H(enry) C(hadwick)
1937- ... CANR-23
Earlier sketches in CA 57-60, CANR-8
Baker, Miriam Hawthorn
See Nye, Miriam (Maurine Hawthorn)
Baker
Baker, Nancy C(arolyn Moll) 1944- ... 81-84
Baker, Nelson B(laisdell) 1905- ... 17-18R
Baker, Nina (Brown) 1888-1957 ... SATA-15
Baker, Norma Jean 1926-1962 Obituary ... 113
Baker, Oleda 1934- ... 69-72
Baker, Paul R(aymond) 1927- ... CANR-19
Earlier sketches in CA 11-12R, CANR-4
Baker, Paul T(hornell) 1927- ... 33-36R
Baker, Pauline H(alpern) 1941- ... 105
Baker, Pearl Biddlecome 1907- ... 17-18R
Baker, Peter (Gorton) 1926- ... CANR-10
Earlier sketch in CA 23-24R
Baker, Philip John Noel
See Noel-Baker, Philip John
Baker, R(onald) J(ames) 1924- ... 33-36R
Baker, R. R.
See Baker, R(eginald) Robin
Baker, R(eginald) Robin 1944- ... 110
Baker, Rachel 1904-1978 ... 5-6R
Obituary ... 103
See also SATA 2, 26
Baker, Ray Stannard 1870-1946
Brief entry ... 118
Baker, Richard M., Jr. 1924- ... 15-16R
Baker, Richard St. Barbe 1889-1982 ... CAP-1
Obituary ... 110
Earlier sketch in CA 11-12
Baker, Richard Terrill 1913-1981 ... 3R
Obituary ... 104
Baker, Robert Allen, Jr. 1921- ... 108
Baker, Robert Andrew 1910- ... 109
Baker, Robert B(ernard) 1937- ... CANR-6
Earlier sketch in CA 53-56
Baker, Robert D(onald) 1927- ... 121
Baker, Robert G. 1928- ... 85-88
Baker, Robert J(unior) 1920- ... 116
Baker, Robert K(erry) 1948- ... 108
Baker, Robin
See Baker, R(eginald) Robin
Baker, Robin Campbell 1941- ... 17-18R
Baker, (John) Roger 1934- ... 25-28R
Baker, Rollin H(arold) 1916- ... 118
Baker, Ronald L(ee) 1937- ... 105
Baker, Ross K(enneth) 1938- ... 29-32R
Baker, Russell (Wayne) 1925- ... CANR-11
Earlier sketch in CA 57-60
See also CLC 31
Baker, Samm Sinclair 1909- ... CANR-21
Earlier sketches in CA 5-6R, CANR-3
See also SATA 12
Baker, Scott (MacMartin) 1947- ... 93-96
Baker, Sharon 1938- ... 117
Baker, Sheridan (Warner, Jr.) 1918- ... CANR-18
Earlier sketches in CA 7-8R, CANR-2
Baker, Stephen 1921- ... CANR-19
Earlier sketches in CA 1R, CANR-3
Baker, Susan (Catherine) 1942- ... 105
See also SATA 29
Baker, T(homas) F(rancis) Timothy
1935- ... 25-28R
Baker, T(homas) Lindsay 1947- ... 121
Baker, Thomas George Adames 1920- ... 108
Baker, Thomas Harrison 1933- ... 33-36R
Baker, Victor Richard 1945- ... 109
Baker, Wesley C. ... 23-24R
Baker, William Avery 1911- ... CANR-2
Earlier sketch in CA 7-8R
Baker, William D. 1924- ... 105
Baker, William E(dwin) 1935- ... 23-24R
Baker, William Howard
See McNeilly, Wilfred (Glassford)
Baker, William Joseph 1938- ... CANR-24
Earlier sketch in CA 97-100
Baker, William W(allace) 1921- ... 73-76
Baker-Carr, Janet 1934- ... 93-96
Baker White, John 1902- ... 101
Bakewell, K(enneth) G(raham) B(artlett)
1931- ... CANR-19
Earlier sketch in CA 102
Bakewell, Paul, Jr. 1889-1972 ... CAP-1
Earlier sketch in CA 11-12
Bakewell, Peter J(ohn) 1943- ... 119
Bakhtiar, Laleh Mehree 1938- ... 69-72
Bakhtin, Mikhail (Mikhailovich) 1895-1975
Obituary ... 113
Bakish, David (Joseph) 1937- ... 45-48
Bakjian, Andy 1915- ... 53-56
Bakke, E(dward) Wight 1903-1971
Obituary ... 110
Bakke, Mary S(terling) 1904-1987 ... 37-40R
Obituary ... 121
Bakken, Dick 1941- ... CANR-25
Earlier sketch in CA 106
Bakken, Henry Harrison 1896- ... CANR-11
Earlier sketch in CA 65-68
Bakker, Cornelius B(ernardus) 1929- ... 57-60
Bakker, Elna S(undquist) 1921- ... 69-72
Bakker-Rabdau, Marianne K(atherine)
1935- ... 73-76
Baklanoff, Eric N. 1925- ... CANR-13
Earlier sketch in CA 33-36R
Bakr el Toure, Askia Muhammad Abu
See Toure, Askia Muhammad Abu Bakr el
Bakshi, Ralph 1938(?)- Brief entry ... 112
See also CLC 26
Bakshian, Aram 1944- ... 102
Bakula, William J(ohn), Jr. 1936- ... 49-52
Bakwin, Harry 1894-1973 ... CAP-2
Obituary ... 45-48
Earlier sketch in CA 19-20
Bakwin, Ruth Morris 1898- ... 19-20R
Balaam
See Lamb, G(eoffrey) F(rederick)
Balaam, David N(orman) 1950- ... 112
Balaban, John B. 1943- ... CANR-12
Earlier sketch in CA 65-68
Balaban, Nancy 1928- ... 126
Balabkins, Nicholas (W.) 1926- ... 11-12R
Balachandran, M(adhavarao) 1938- ... 102
Balachandran, Sarojini 1934- ... CANR-18
Earlier sketch in CA 102
Balagura, Saul 1943- ... 81-84
Balakian, Nona 1919- ... 85-88
Balakian, Peter 1951- ... 102
Balanchine, George 1904-1983 ... 111
Obituary ... 109
Balancy, Pierre Guy Girald 1924-1979
Obituary ... 89-92
Balandier, Georges (Leon) 1920- ... CANR-8
Earlier sketch in CA 61-64
Balas, David L(aszlo) 1929- ... 33-36R
Balaskas, Arthur 1940- ... 103
Balaskas, Janet (Marion) 1946- ... 117
Balassa, Bela 1928- ... CANR-3
Earlier sketch in CA 1R
Balawyder, Aloysius 1924- ... CANR-15
Earlier sketch in CA 41-44R
Balbontin, Jose Antonio 1893- ... CAP-1
Earlier sketch in CA 11-12
Balbus
See Huxley, Julian (Sorell)
Balch, Glenn 1902- ... CANR-3
Earlier sketch in CA 3R
See also SATA 3
Balchen, Bernt 1899-1973 Obituary ... 45-48
Balchin, John Frederick 1937- ... 122
Balchin, Nigel (Marlin) 1908-1970 ... CANR-21
Obituary ... 29-32R
Earlier sketch in CA 97-100
Balchin, W(illiam) G(eorge) V(ictor)
1916- ... CANR-18
Earlier sketch in CA 101
Balcomb, Raymond E. 1923- ... 23-24R
Balcon, Michael 1896-1977 ... 77-80
Obituary ... 73-76
Bald, F(rederick) Clever 1897-1970 ... CAP-1
Earlier sketch in CA 13-14
Bald, R(obert) C(ecil) 1901-1965 ... CANR-6
Earlier sketch in CA 5-6R
Bald, Wambly 1902- ... DLB-4
Baldanza, Frank 1924- ... 3R
Baldelli, Giovanni 1914- ... 45-48
Balderson, Margaret ... 25-28R
Balderston, Frederick E(mery) 1923-
Brief entry ... 112
Balderston, John L.
See Balderston, John Lloyd
Balderston, John Lloyd 1889-1954
Brief entry ... 121
See also DLB 26
Balderston, Katharine Canby 1895-1979
Obituary ... 93-96
Baldick, Robert 1927-1972 Obituary ... 89-92
Baldinger, Stanley 1932- ... 29-32R
Baldinger, Wallace S(pencer) 1905- ... 3R
Baldree, J(asper) Martin, Jr. 1927- ... 53-56
Baldridge, Cyrus LeRoy 1889- ... SATA-29
Baldridge, Mary Humphrey 1937- ... 114
Baldrige, Letitia (Katherine) ... CANR-17
Earlier sketch in CA 25-28R
Baldry, Harold (Caparne) 1907- ... 19-20R
Balducci, Carolyn (Feleppa) 1946- ... 33-36R
See also SATA 5
Balducci, Ernesto 1922- ... CANR-12
Earlier sketch in CA 29-32R
Baldwin, Alex
See Butterworth, W(illiam) E(dmund III)
Baldwin, Anne Norris 1938- ... 29-32R
See also SATA 5
Baldwin, Arthur W. 1904(?)-1976
Obituary ... 69-72
Baldwin, Bates
See Jennings, John (Edward, Jr.)
Baldwin, Billy
See Baldwin, William, Jr.
Baldwin, Christina 1946- ... CANR-13
Earlier sketch in CA 77-80
Baldwin, Clara ... 61-64
See also SATA 11
Baldwin, David A. 1936- ... 19-20R
Baldwin, Dick
See Raborg, Frederick A(shton), Jr.
Baldwin, Ed(ward A.) 1935- ... 118
Baldwin, Edward R(obinson) 1935- ... CANR-21
Earlier sketch in CA 45-48
Baldwin, Faith 1893-1978 ... CANR-4
Obituary ... 77-80
Earlier sketch in CA 7-8R
See also AITN 1
Baldwin, Gordo
See Baldwin, Gordon C.
Baldwin, Gordon C. 1908- ... CANR-3
Earlier sketch in CA 4R
See also SATA 12
Baldwin, Hanson W(eightman) 1903- ... 61-64
Baldwin, James 1841-1925 Brief entry ... 111
See also SATA 24
Baldwin, James (Arthur) 1924-1987 ... CANR-24
Obituary ... 124
Earlier sketches in CA 3R, CANR-3
See also CABS 1
See also BW
See also SATA 9
See also DLB 2, 7, 33
See also DLBY 87
See also CDALB 1941-1968
See also CLC 1, 2, 3, 4, 5, 8, 13, 15,
17, 42, 50
Baldwin, John D. 1930- ... 101
Baldwin, John W(esley) 1929- ... 105
Baldwin, Joseph B(urkette) 1918- ... 111
Baldwin, Joseph Glover 1815-1864 ... DLB-3, 11
Baldwin, Joyce G(ertrude) 1921- ... CANR-8
Earlier sketch in CA 61-64
Baldwin, Leland D(ewitt) 1897-1981 ... 41-44R
Obituary ... 103
Baldwin, Margaret
See Weis, Margaret (Edith)
Baldwin, Marshall W(hithed) 1903-1975 ... 61-64
Obituary ... 57-60
Baldwin, Michael 1930- ... CANR-3
Earlier sketch in CA 9-10R
Baldwin, Monica 1896(?)-1975 Obituary ... 104
Baldwin, Ned
See Baldwin, Edward R(obinson)
Baldwin, Raymond Earl 1893-1986
Obituary ... 121
Baldwin, Rebecca
See Chappell, Helen
Baldwin, Richard S(heridan) 1910- ... 105
Baldwin, Robert E(dward) 1924- ... 41-44R
Baldwin, Roger (Nash) 1884-1981
Obituary ... 105
Baldwin, Roger E(dwin) 1929- ... 49-52
Baldwin, Stan(ley C.) 1929- ... CANR-17
Earlier sketches in CA 49-52, CANR-2
See also SATA 28
Baldwin, William, Jr. 1903-1983 Obituary ... 111
Baldwin, William Lee 1928- ... CANR-3
Earlier sketch in CA 1R
Bale, Robert Osborne 1912- ... 1R
Bales, Carol Ann 1940- ... 45-48
See also SATA 29
Bales, Jack
See Bales, James E(dward)
Bales, James D(avid) 1915- ... 5-6R
Bales, James E(dward) 1951- ... 107
Bales, Robert F(reed) 1916- ... 93-96
Bales, William Alan 1917- ... 7-8R
Balet, Jan (Bernard) 1913- ... 85-88
See also SATA 11
Baley, James A. 1918- ... CANR-5
Earlier sketch in CA 15-16R
Balfort, Neil
See Fanthorpe, R(obert) Lionel
Balfour, A. J.
See Balfour, Arthur James
Balfour, Arthur J.
See Balfour, Arthur James
Balfour, Arthur James 1848-1930
Brief entry ... 120
Balfour, Conrad George 1928- ... 53-56
Balfour, Henry H(allowell), Jr. 1940- ... 117
Balfour, James 1925- ... 25-28R
Balfour, John
See Moore, James
Balfour, Michael (Leonard) Graham
1908- ... CANR-6
Earlier sketch in CA 11-12R
Balfour, (John) Patrick Douglas
1904-1976 ... CANR-6
Earlier sketch in CA 9-10R
Balfour-Kinnear, George Purvis Russell
1888- ... 5-6R
Balian, Lorna 1929- ... CANR-19
Earlier sketches in CA 53-56, CANR-4
See also SATA 9
Baligh, Helmy H. 1931- ... 21-22R
Balikci, Asen 1929- ... 29-32R
Balinky, Alexander 1919- ... 21-22R
Balint, Michael 1896-1970 ... CAP-1
Earlier sketch in CA 9-10
Balis, Andrea F. 1948- ... 108
Balizet, Carol 1933- ... 114
Baljeu, Joost 1925- ... 97-100
Balk, Alfred (W.) 1930- ... 25-28R
Balk, H(oward) Wesley 1932- Brief entry ... 111
Balka, Marie
See Balkany, Marie (Romoka Zelinger) de
Balkany, Marie (Romoka Zelinger) de
1930- ... 104
Balke, Willem 1933- ... 107
Balkey, Rita
See Oleyar, Rita Balkey
Balkin, Richard 1938- ... 77-80
Ball, B. N.
See Ball, Brian N(eville)
Ball, Brian N(eville) 1932- ... 33-36R
Ball, (Frederick) Clive 1941- Brief entry ... 114
Ball, David 1937- ... 65-68
Ball, Desmond (John) 1947- ... CANR-24
Earlier sketch in CA 106
Ball, Donald W(inston) 1934-1976 ... 122
Obituary ... 110
Ball, Donna 1951- ... 108
Ball, Doris Bell (Collier) 1897-1987 ... CANR-18
Obituary ... 122
Earlier sketches in CA 4R, CANR-2
Ball, Edith L. 1905- ... 85-88
Ball, (Katherine) Eve(lyn) 1890-1984 ... 122
Obituary ... 114
Ball, F(rederick) Carlton 1911- ... 17-18R
Ball, George W(ildman) 1909- ... 73-76
Ball, Howard 1937- ... CANR-17
Earlier sketch in CA 33-36R
Ball, Jane Eklund 1921- ... 33-36R
Ball, John (Dudley, Jr.) 1911-1988 ... CANR-18
Obituary ... 126
Earlier sketches in CA 7-8R, CANR-3
Ball, John C. 1924- ... CANR-8
Earlier sketch in CA 7-8R
Ball, John M(iller) 1923- ... 33-36R
Ball, Joseph H. 1905- ... CAP-2
Earlier sketch in CA 23-24
Ball, Larry Durwood, Sr. 1940- ... 123
Ball, M(ary) Margaret 1909- ... 25-28R
Ball, Marion J(okl) 1940- ... CANR-15
Earlier sketch in CA 89-92
Ball, Nicole (Janice) 1948- ... 112
Ball, Robert Edward 1911- ... 108
Ball, Robert Hamilton 1902- ... 11-12R
Ball, Robert M(yers) 1914- ... 97-100
Ball, Sylvia Patricia 1936- ... 57-60
Ball, Zachary
See Janas, Frankie-Lee
and Masters, Kelly R.
Ballantine, Bill
See Ballantine, William (Oliver)
Ballantine, David 1926- ... 115
Ballantine, John (Winthrop) 1920- ... 53-56
Ballantine, John
See da Cruz, Daniel, Jr.
Ballantine, Joseph W. 1890(?)-1973
Obituary ... 41-44R
Ballantine, Lesley Frost
See Frost, Lesley
Ballantine, Richard 1940- ... CANR-1
Earlier sketch in CA 45-48
Ballantine, William (Oliver) 1911- ... 106
Ballantyne, David (Watt) 1924- ... CANR-10
Earlier sketch in CA 65-68
Ballantyne, Dorothy Joan (Smith) 1922- ... 7-8R
Ballantyne, R(obert) M(ichael)
1825-1894 ... SATA-24
Ballantyne, Sheila 1936- ... CANR-25
Earlier sketch in CA 101
Ballard, Allen B(utler, Jr.) 1930- ... 61-64
Ballard, Charles E. 1914(?)-1987 Obituary ... 123
Ballard, Dean
See Wilkes-Hunter, R(ichard)
Ballard, Edward Goodwin 1910- ... CANR-13
Earlier sketch in CA 33-36R
Ballard, I. Edward 1909(?)-1985 Obituary ... 117
Ballard, J(ames) G(raham) 1930- ... CANR-15
Earlier sketch in CA 7-8R
See also DLB 14
See also CLC 3, 6, 14, 36
See also SSC 1
Ballard, Joan Kadey 1928- ... 5-6R
Ballard, K. G.
See Roth, Holly
Ballard, Lowell C(lyne) 1904-1986 ... CAP-1
Obituary ... 120
Earlier sketch in CA 11-12
See also SATA 12, 49
Ballard, (Charles) Martin 1929- ... 25-28R
See also SATA 1
Ballard, Mignon Franklin 1934- ... 121
See also SATA 49
Ballard, P. D.
See Ballard, (Willis) Todhunter
Ballard, Robert D(uane) 1942- ... 112
Ballard, (Willis) Todhunter 1903- ... 15-16R
Ballard, W. T.
See Ballard, (Willis) Todhunter
Ballard, Willis T.
See Ballard, (Willis) Todhunter
Ballem, John 1925- ... 81-84
Ballen, Roger 1950- ... 103

Ballentine, Rudolph 1941- 114
Baller, Warren Robert 1900- 69-72
Ballet, Arthur H(arold) 1924- Brief entry 111
Balliett, Whitney 1926- CANR-13
Earlier sketch in CA 17-18R
Ballin, Caroline 19-20R
Ballingall, James (Gordon Mackie) 1958- 117
Ballinger, Bill S.
See Ballinger, William Sanborn
Ballinger, Harry (Russell) 1892- CAP-2
Earlier sketch in CA 23-24
Ballinger, James Lawrence 1919- 17-18R
Ballinger, Louise Bowen 1909- 15-16R
Ballinger, (Violet) Margaret (Livingstone) 1894-1980 CANR-13
Obituary 105
Earlier sketch in CA 61-64
Ballinger, Raymond A. 1907- 7-8R
Ballinger, William Sanborn 1912-1980 CANR-1
Obituary 97-100
Earlier sketch in CA 4R
Ballon, Robert J(ean) 1919- CANR-21
Earlier sketch in CA 45-48
Ballonoff, Paul A(lan) 1943- 57-60
Ballou, Arthur W. 1915- 25-28R
Ballou, Ellen B(artlett) 1905- CAP-2
Earlier sketch in CA 29-32
Ballowe, James 1933- CANR-12
Earlier sketch in CA 29-32R
Ballstadt, Carl A. 1931- 124
Balma, Michael J(ames) 1930- 19-20R
Balmain, Pierre (Alexandre) 1914-1982
Obituary 107
Balme, Maurice (George) 1925- 61-64
Balmer, Edwin 1883-1959 Brief entry 114
Balmont, Konstantin (Dmitriyevich) 1867-1943 Brief entry 109
See also TCLC 11
Balmuth, Miriam S. 124
Balogh, Penelope 1916-1975 CAP-2
Earlier sketch in CA 25-28
See also SATA 1, 34
Balogh, Thomas 1905-1985 57-60
Obituary 115
Balow, Tom 1931- 45-48
See also SATA 12
Baloyra, Enrique Antonio 1942- 111
Balsdon, (John Percy Vyvian) Dacre 1901-1977 CANR-13
Obituary 73-76
Earlier sketch in CA 7-8R
Balsdon, J.P.V.D.
See Balsdon, (John Percy Vyvian) Dacre
Balseiro, Jose Agustin 1900- 81-84
See also AITN 1
Balsiger, David (Wayne) 1945- CANR-11
Earlier sketch in CA 61-64
Balsley, Howard L(loyd) 1913- CANR-4
Earlier sketch in CA 3R
Balsley, Irol Whitmore 1912- 15-16R
Baltake, Joe 1945- 118
Baltazar, Eulalio R. 1925- 19-20R
Baltazzi, Evan Serge 1919- 65-68
Baltensperger, Peter 1938- 115
Balterman, Marcia Ridlon 1942- 25-28R
Baltes, Paul B. 1939- 89-92
Balthasar, Hans Urs von
See von Balthasar, Hans Urs
Balthazar, Earl E(dward) 1918- 53-56
Baltz, Howard B(url) 1930- 29-32R
Baltzell, E(dward) Digby 1915- 33-36R
Baltzer, Hans (Adolf) 1900- SATA-40
Balukas, Jean 1959- Brief entry 111
Balwers, Renato
See La Barre, Weston
Baly, (Alfred) Denis 1913- 19-20R
Baly, Monica Eileen 1914- 102
Balzano, Jeanne (Koppel) 1912- 5-6R
Balzer, Richard J(ay) 1944- 45-48
Balzer, Robert Lawrence 1912- 103
Bambara, Toni Cade 1939- CANR-24
Earlier sketch in CA 29-32R
See also BW
See also DLB 38
See also CLC 19
Bamber, Linda 1945- 109
Bamberger, Bernard J(acob) 1904-1980 CANR-6
Obituary 101
Earlier sketch in CA 13-14R
Bamberger, Carl 1902- CAP-2
Earlier sketch in CA 21-22
Bamberger, Fritz 1902-1984 Obituary 113
Bambrough, (John) Renford 1926- 61-64
Bamdad, A.
See Shamlu, Ahmad
Bamford, James 1946- 123
Bamford, Paul W(alden) 1921- 41-44R
Bamfylde, Walter
See Bevan, Tom
Bamm, Peter
See Emmrich, Curt
Bamman, Henry A. 1918- CANR-7
Earlier sketch in CA 5-6R
See also SATA 12
Ban, (Maria) Eva 1934- 73-76
Ban, Joseph D(aniel) 1926- CANR-23
Earlier sketches in CA 23-24R, CANR-8
Ban, Thomas A. 1929- CANR-10
Earlier sketch in CA 21-22R
Banani, Amin 1926- 33-36R
Banbury, Philip 1914- 102
Bance, Alan F. 1939- 111
Bancroft, Anne 1923- 57-60
Bancroft, Caroline 1900- CAP-2
Earlier sketch in CA 21-22
Bancroft, George 1800-1891 DLB-1, 30, 59
Bancroft, Griffing 1907- 29-32R
See also SATA 6
See also AITN 1
Bancroft, Hubert Howe 1832-1918 DLB-47
Bancroft, Iris (May Nelson) 1922- CANR-19
Earlier sketch in CA 102
Bancroft, Laura
See Baum, L(yman) Frank
Bancroft, Mary 1903- 118
Bancroft, Peter 1916- 41-44R
Bancroft, Robert
See Kirsch, Robert R.
Bandeira (Filho), Manuel (Carneiro de Sousa) 1886(?)-1968 Obituary 115
Bandel, Betty 1912- 106
See also SATA 47
Bander, Edward J. 1923- CANR-5
Earlier sketch in CA 15-16R
Bandera, V(ladimir) N(icholas) 1932- 33-36R
Bandi, Hans-Georg 1920- 85-88
Bandinelli, Ranuccio Bianchi 1901(?)-1975
Obituary 53-56
Bandman, Bertram 1930- 21-22R
Bandoff, Hope
See Guthrie, Thomas Anstey
Bandura, Albert 1925- 13-14R
Bandy, (Eugene) Franklin 1914-1987 CANR-24
Obituary 122
Earlier sketch in CA 33-36R
Bandy, Leland A. 1935- 77-80
Bandy, Melanie 1932- 114
Bandy, W(illiam) T(homas) 1903- 37-40R
Bandy, Way 1941(?)-1986 123
Obituary 120
Bane, Mary Jo 1942- 126
Brief entry 112
Bane, Michael 1950- 108
Banel, Joseph 1943- 45-48
Baner, Skulda Vanadis 1897-1964 CAP-1
Earlier sketch in CA 13-14
See also SATA 10
Banerjee, H(emendra) N(ath) 1929-
Brief entry 114
Banerji, Ranan B(ihari) 1928- CANR-11
Earlier sketch in CA 29-32R
Banerji, Sara 1932- 126
Banet, Doris Beatrice Robinson 1925- 5-6R
Banfield, A(lexander) W(illiam) F(rancis) 1918- 61-64
Banfield, Edward C(hristie) 1916- 57-60
See also AITN 1
Bang, Betsy 1912- 102
See also SATA 37, 48
Bang, Garrett
See Bang, Molly Garrett
Bang, Molly Garrett 1943- 102
See also SATA 24
See also CLR 8
Bangert, Ethel E(lizabeth) 1912- CANR-1
Earlier sketch in CA 45-48
Bangert, William V(alentine) 1911- 45-48
Bangerter, Lowell A(llen) 1941- CANR-26
Earlier sketches in CA 69-72, CANR-11
Bangham, Mary Dickerson 1896- CAP-2
Earlier sketch in CA 23-24
Banghart, Charles K(enneth) 1910(?)-1980
Obituary 97-100
Banghart, Kenneth
See Banghart, Charles K(enneth)
Bangley, Bernard 1935- 110
Bangs, Carl (Oliver) 1922- CANR-7
Earlier sketch in CA 19-20R
Bangs, Carol Jane 1949- 114
Bangs, John Kendrick 1862-1922
Brief entry 110
See also DLB 11
Bangs, Lester 1949(?)-1982 Obituary 106
Bangs, Richard 1950- 122
Bangs, Robert B(abbitt) 1914- 37-40R
Banham, (Peter) Reyner 1922-1988 29-32R
Obituary 125
Banis, Victor J(erome) 1937- 81-84
Banister, Gary L. 1948- 57-60
Banister, Manly (Miles) 1914- 41-44R
Banister, Margaret 1894(?)-1977
Obituary 73-76
Bank, Dena Citron 1912- 123
Bank, Mirra 1945- 102
Bank, Stephen Paul 1941- 110
Bank, Ted
See Bank, Theodore P(aul) II
Bank, Theodore P(aul) II 1923- 41-44R
Bank-Jensen, Thea
See Ottesen, Thea Tauber
Bankoff, George Alexis
See Milkomane, George Alexis Milkomanovich
Bankowsky, Richard James 1928- 1R
Banks, Ann 1943- 105
Banks, Arthur S. 1926- 33-36R
Banks, Carolyn 1941- CANR-23
Earlier sketch in CA 105
Banks, Hal N(orman) 1921- 102
Banks, Harlan Parker 1913- 89-92
Banks, Iain (Menzies) 1954- Brief entry 123
See also CLC 34
Banks, J(ohn) Houston 1911- 33-36R
Banks, James A(lbert) 1941- CANR-13
Earlier sketch in CA 33-36R
Banks, James Houston 1925- 89-92
Banks, Jane 1913- 65-68
Banks, Jimmy
See Banks, James Houston
Banks, Laura Stockton Voorhees 1908(?)-1980 Obituary 101
See also SATA 23
Banks, Lynne Reid
See Reid Banks, Lynne
See also CLC 23
Banks, Oliver 1941- 107
Banks, Richard L. 1920- 11-12R
Banks, Roger 1929- 107
Banks, Ronald F(illmore) 1934- 29-32R
Banks, Russell 1940- CANR-19
Earlier sketch in CA 65-68
See also CLC 37
Banks, Sara (Jeanne Gordon Harrell)
See Harrell, Sara (Jeanne) Gordon
See also SATA 26
Banks, Taylor
See Banks, Jane
Banks, William L(ove) 1928- 112
Bankson, Douglas (Henneck) 1920- 45-48
Bankwitz, Philip Charles Farwell 1924- 33-36R
Banner, Angela
See Maddison, Angela Mary
Banner, Charla Ann Leibenguth 1942- CANR-24
Earlier sketch in CA 106
Banner, Hubert Stewart 1891-1964 CAP-1
Earlier sketch in CA 11-12
Banner, James M(orrill), Jr. 1935- 49-52
Banner, Lois W(endland) 1939- CANR-1
Earlier sketch in CA 49-52
Banner, Melvin Edward 1914- 53-56
Banner, William Augustus 1915- 45-48
Bannerman, Helen (Brodie Cowan Watson) 1863(?)-1946 Brief entry 111
See also SATA 19
Bannerman, Mark
See Lewing, Anthony Charles
Bannerman, Roland
See Hartston, W(illiam) R(oland)
Bannerman, W. Mary 1894-1984 Obituary 114
Bannick, Nancy (Meredith) 1926- 41-44R
Banning, Evelyn I. 1903- 73-76
See also SATA 36
Banning, Lance (Gilbert) 1942- 89-92
Banning, Margaret Culkin 1891-1982 CANR-4
Obituary 105
Earlier sketch in CA 5-6R
Bannister, Don
See Bannister, Donald
Bannister, Donald 1928- CANR-9
Earlier sketch in CA 61-64
Bannister, Jo 1951- 119
Bannister, Pat
See Davis, Lou Ellen
Bannister, Patricia V. 1923- Brief entry 115
Bannister, Robert C(orwin), Jr. 1935- 23-24R
Bannister, Sally
See Pratt, James Norwood
Bannock, Graham 1932- 33-36R
Bannon, Barbara Anne 1928- 101
Bannon, John Francis 1905-1986 CANR-4
Obituary 119
Earlier sketch in CA 1R
Bannon, Laura ?-1963 3R
See also SATA 6
Bannon, Peter
See Durst, Paul
Banta, Martha 1928- 81-84
Banta, R(ichard) E(lwell) 1904- CAP-2
Earlier sketch in CA 33-36
Bantel, Linda 1943- 113
Banting, Peter M(yles) 1936- 112
Bantock, G(eoffrey) H(erman) 1914- CANR-11
Earlier sketch in CA 25-28R
Bantock, Gavin (Marcus August) 1939- 33-36R
Banton, Coy
See Norwood, Victor G(eorge) C(harles)
Banton, Michael (Parker) 1926- CANR-2
Earlier sketch in CA 7-8R
Banville, John 1945- Brief entry 117
See also DLB 14
See also CLC 46
Banville, Thomas G(eorge) 1924- 81-84
Bany, Mary A. 1913- 11-12R
Banz, George 1928- 29-32R
Banziger, Hans
See Baenziger, Hans
Bapu
See Khare, Narayan Bhaskar
Barabas, Steven 1904-1983 5-6R
Obituary 109
Barach, Alvan L(eroy) 1895-1977
Obituary 73-76
Barach, Arnold B(auer) 1913-1987 97-100
Obituary 122
Barack, Nathan A. 1913- 15-16R
Barackman, Floyd Hays, Jr. 1923- 115
Barackman, Paul F(reeman) 1894- 1R
Baracks, Barbara 1951- 106
Barada, Bill
See Barada, William Richard
Barada, William Richard 1913- 45-48
Bar-Adon, Aaron 1923- Brief entry 114
Baraheni, Reza 1935- 69-72
Barak, Gregg 1948- 114
Barak, Michael
See Bar-Zohar, Michael
Baraka, Imamu Amiri
See Jones, (Everett) LeRoi
See also BW
See also DLB 5, 7, 16, 38
See also CDALB 1941-1968
See also CLC 1, 2, 3, 5, 10, 14, 33
Baral, Robert 1910- CAP-1
Earlier sketch in CA 9-10
Baram, Phillip J(ason) 1938- 85-88
Baram, Robert 1919- Brief entry 112
Baran, Annette 1927- Brief entry 114
Baranet, Nancy Neiman 1933- 41-44R
Baranov, Alexander A. 1931(?)-1983
Obituary 109
Baranson, Jack 1924- 119
Barany, George 1922- 25-28R
Barasch, Frances K. 1928- 37-40R
Barasch, Marc Ian 1949- 113
Barasch, Moshe 1920- 97-100
Barash, Meyer 1916- 1R
Barash, Samuel T(heodore) 1921- 107
Barba, Harry 1922- CANR-1
Earlier sketch in CA 1R
Barbach, Lonnie (Villoldo) 1946- CANR-25
Earlier sketches in CA 61-64, CANR-9
Barbanell, Maurice 1902-1981 Obituary 113
Barbara, Dominick A. 1914- 37-40R
Barbare, Rholf
See Volkoff, Vladimir
Barbary, James
See Beeching, Jack
Barbash, Jack 1910- CANR-16
Earlier sketch in CA 4R
Barbe, Walter Burke 1926- 15-16R
See also SATA 45
Barbeau, Arthur E(dward) 1936- 49-52
Barbeau, Clayton C(harles) 1930- 73-76
Barbeau, Marius 1883-1969 Obituary 25-28R
Barbee, David E(dwin) 1936- 57-60
Barbee, Phillips
See Sheckley, Robert
Barbellion, W. N. P.
See Cummings, Bruce F(rederick)
See also TCLC 24
Barber, Antonia
See Anthony, Barbara
Barber, Benjamin R. 1939- CANR-12
Earlier sketch in CA 29-32R
Barber, Bernard 1918- CANR-14
Earlier sketch in CA 65-68
Barber, Charles (Laurence) 1915- CANR-22
Earlier sketches in CA 17-18R, CANR-7
Barber, Cyril J(ohn) 1934- CANR-9
Earlier sketch in CA 65-68
Barber, D(ulan) F(riar Whilberton) 1940- CANR-21
Earlier sketch in CA 61-64
Barber, James David 1930- CANR-6
Earlier sketch in CA 15-16R
Barber, James G(eoffrey) 1952- 110
Barber, Jesse 1893-1979 Obituary 85-88
Barber, John Warner 1798-1885 DLB-30
Barber, Joseph 1909-1982 Obituary 107
Barber, Lucie W(elles) 1922- 108
Barber, Lucy L(ombardi) 1882(?)-1974
Obituary 49-52
Barber, Lynda
See Graham-Barber, Lynda
Barber, Lynda Graham
See Graham-Barber, Lynda
Barber, Lynn 1944- 97-100
Barber, Noel (John Lysberg) 1909-1988
Obituary 126
Brief entry 115
Barber, Philip W. 1903-1981 Obituary 103
Barber, Red
See Barber, Walter Lanier
Barber, Richard (William) 1941- CANR-13
Earlier sketch in CA 33-36R
See also SATA 35
Barber, Richard J. 1932- 29-32R
Barber, Samuel 1910-1981 Obituary 103
Barber, Stephen Guy 1921-1980 69-72
Obituary 97-100
Barber, T(heodore) X(enophon) 1927- 41-44R
Barber, Walter Lanier 1908- Brief entry 113
Barber, Willard F(oster) 1909- CAP-2
Earlier sketch in CA 21-22
Barber, William Henry 1918- 7-8R
Barber, William Joseph 1925- CANR-8
Earlier sketch in CA 61-64
Barbera, Henry 1929- 105
Barbera, Jack 1945- 110
See also CLC 44
Barbera, Joe
See Barbera, Joseph Roland
Barbera, Joseph Roland 1911- SATA-51
Barberis
See Barberis, Franco
Barberis, Franco 1905- 25-28R
Barbero, Yves Regis Francois 1943- 57-60
Barbet, Pierre
See Avice, Claude (Pierre Marie)
Barbette, Jay
See Spicer, Bart
Barbotin, Edmond 1920- 57-60
Barbour, Alan G. 1933- Brief entry 117
Barbour, Arthur Joseph 1926- 57-60
Barbour, Brian M(ichael) 1943- 49-52
Barbour, Douglas (Fleming) 1940- CANR-11
Earlier sketch in CA 69-72
Barbour, Frances Martha 1895- 17-18R
Barbour, George 1890-1977 Obituary 73-76
Barbour, Hugh (Stewart) 1921- 23-24R
Barbour, Ian G(raeme) 1923- CANR-8
Earlier sketch in CA 21-22R
Barbour, J(ames) Murray 1897-1970 CAP-1
Earlier sketch in CA 11-12
Barbour, Kenneth Michael 1921- CANR-7
Earlier sketch in CA 7-8R
Barbour, Michael G(eorge) 1942- CANR-2
Earlier sketch in CA 49-52
Barbour, Nevill 1895-1972 7-8R
Obituary 103
Barbour, Philip L(emont) 1898- 11-12R
Barbour, Ralph Henry 1870-1944 SATA-16
See also DLB 22
Barbour, Roger W(illiam) 1919- 61-64

Barbour, Russell B. 1906- ... CAP-2
Earlier sketch in CA 23-24
Barbour, Ruth P(eeling) 1924- ... 89-92
Barbour, Thomas L.
See Lesure, Thomas B(arbour)
Barbrook, Alec
See Barbrook, Alexander Thomas
Barbrook, Alexander Thomas 1927- ... 45-48
Barbusse, Henri 1873-1935 Brief entry ... 105
See also DLB 65
See also TCLC 5
Barchek, James Robert 1935- ... 41-44R
Barchilon, Jacques 1923- ... CANR-5
Earlier sketch in CA 13-14R
Barchus, Agnes J(osephine) 1893- ... 97-100
Barcia, Jose Rubia
See Rubia Barcia, Jose
Barck, Oscar Theodore, Jr. 1902- ... 21-22R
Barclay, Andrew M(ichael) 1941- ... 113
Barclay, Ann
See Greig, Maysie
Barclay, Barbara 1938- ... 29-32R
Barclay, Bill
See Moorcock, Michael (John)
Barclay, Cyril Nelson 1896- ... 7-8R
Barclay, Glen St. J(ohn) 1930- ... 77-80
Barclay, Harold B. 1924- ... 11-12R
Barclay, Hartley Wade 1903-1978 ... 85-88
Obituary ... 81-84
Barclay, Isabel
See Dobell, I(sabel) M(arian) B(arclay)
Barclay, Oliver R(ainsford) 1919- ... CANR-8
Earlier sketch in CA 57-60
Barclay, Virginia
See McDonnell, Virginia B(leecker)
Barclay, William 1907-1978 ... 77-80
Obituary ... 73-76
Barclay, William Ewert
See Moorcock, Michael (John)
Barcus, James E(dgar) 1938- ... 23-24R
Barcus, Nancy B(idwell) 1937- ... 117
Barcynski, Leon Roger 1949- ... CANR-10
Earlier sketch in CA 93-96
Barcynski, Vivian G(odfrey) 1917- ... CANR-10
Earlier sketch in CA 61-64
Bard, Bernard 1927- ... 25-28R
Bard, Harry 1906-1976 ... 33-36R
Bard, James (Alan) 1925- ... 102
Bard, Morton 1924- ... 97-100
Bard, Patti 1935- ... 21-22R
Bard, Rachel 1921- ... 117
Bardach, John E(ugene) 1915- ... 41-44R
Bardarson, Hjalmar R(oegnvaldur) 1918- ... 57-60
Barden, Leonard (William) 1929- ... CANR-2
Earlier sketch in CA 3R
Bardens, Amey E. 1894(?)-1974
Obituary ... 53-56
Bardens, Dennis (Conrad) 1911- ... 7-8R
Bardi, Pietro Maria 1900- ... CANR-19
Earlier sketch in CA 85-88
Bardin, John Franklin 1916-1981 ... 81-84
Obituary ... 104
Bardis, Panos D(emetrios) 1924- ... CANR-10
Earlier sketch in CA 25-28R
Bard of Avondale
See Jacobs, Howard
Bardolph, Richard 1915- ... 61-64
Bardon, Edward J(ohn) 1933- ... 81-84
Bardon, Jack Irving 1925- ... 101
Bardos, Marie (Dupuis) 1935- ... 13-14R
Bardot, Louis 1896-1975 Obituary ... 61-64
Bardsley, Cuthbert K(illick) N(orman)
1907- ... CAP-2
Earlier sketch in CA 25-28
Bardwell, George E(ldred) 1924- ... 3R
Bardwick, Judith M(arcia) 1933- ... CANR-19
Earlier sketch in CA 103
Bare, Arnold Edwin 1920- ... SATA-16
Bare, Colleen Stanley ... 102
See also SATA 32
Barea, Arturo 1897-1957 Brief entry ... 111
See also TCLC 14
Bareham, Terence 1937- ... 109
Barell, John 1938- ... 111
Barendrecht, Cor W(illiam) 1934- ... 114
Baretski, Charles Allan 1918- ... 77-80
Barfield, (Arthur) Owen 1898- ... CANR-2
Earlier sketch in CA 7-8R
Barfoot, Audrey Ilma 1918-1964 ... 7-8R
Barfoot, Joan 1946- ... 105
See also CLC 18
Barford, Carol 1931- ... 89-92
Barford, Philip (Trevelyan) 1925- ... 93-96
Bargad, Warren 1940- ... 122
Bargar, B(radley) D(uffee) 1924- ... 19-20R
Bargate, Verity 1941(?)-1981 Obituary ... 103
Bargebuhr, Frederick P(erez) 1904- ... CAP-2
Earlier sketch in CA 33-36
Bargellini, Piero 1897-1980(?) Obituary ... 97-100
Barger, Harold 1907- ... CAP-2
Earlier sketch in CA 19-20
Barger, James (David) 1947- ... 57-60
Bar-Hillel, Yehoshua 1915-1975 Obituary ... 115
Baring, Arnulf Martin 1932- ... 41-44R
Baring, Maurice 1874-1945 Brief entry ... 105
See also DLB 34
See also TCLC 8
Baringer, William E(ldon) 1909- ... 1R
Baring-Gould, William Stuart 1913-1967
Obituary ... 25-28R
Barish, Jonas A. 1922- ... 23-24R
Barish, Matthew 1907- ... 57-60
See also SATA 12
Baritz, Loren 1928- ... 15-16R
Barjavel, Rene (Gustave Henri) 1911-
Brief entry ... 107
Bark, Dennis L(aistner) 1942- ... 117
Bark, William (Carroll) 1908- ... CAP-1
Earlier sketch in CA 13-14
Barkalow, Frederick Schenck, Jr. 1914- ... 61-64
Barkan, Elliott Robert 1940- ... 23-24R
Barkan, Leonard 1944- ... 122
Brief entry ... 116
Barkas, J. L. 1948- ... 57-60
Barkas, Janet
See Barkas, J. L.
Barkdoll, Robert S. 1913(?)-1984
Obituary ... 112
Barkee, Asouff
See Strung, Norman
Barker, A(rthur) J(ames) 1918-1981 ... CANR-7
Obituary ... 104
Earlier sketch in CA 15-16R
Barker, A(udrey) L(ilian) 1918- ... CANR-3
Earlier sketch in CA 11-12R
See also DLB 14
Barker, A(nthony) W(ilhelm) 1930- ... 113
Barker, Albert W. 1900- ... CANR-14
Earlier sketch in CA 73-76
See also SATA 8
Barker, Bill
See Barker, William J(ohn)
Barker, Carol (Minturn) 1938- ... 107
See also SATA 31
Barker, Carol M. 1942- ... 45-48
Barker, Charles Albro 1904- ... 93-96
Barker, Charles M., Jr. 1926- ... 15-16R
Barker, Cicely Mary 1895-1973 ... 121
Obituary ... 117
See also SATA 39, 49
Barker, Clive 1952- Brief entry ... 121
Barker, D(erek) R(oland) 1930- ... 7-8R
Barker, Dennis (Malcolm) 1929- ... CANR-14
Earlier sketch in CA 25-28R
Barker, Dudley 1910-1980(?) ... CANR-1
Obituary ... 102
Earlier sketch in CA 2R
Barker, E. M.
See Barker, Elsa (McCormick)
Barker, Elisabeth 1910-1986 Obituary ... 118
Barker, Elliott S(peer) 1886-1988 ... 89-92
Obituary ... 125
Barker, Elsa (McCormick) 1906- ... CAP-2
Earlier sketch in CA 17-18
Barker, Elver A. 1920- ... 25-28R
Barker, Eric 1905-1973 ... 1R
Obituary ... 41-44R
Barker, Ernest 1874-1960 ... 103
Obituary ... 93-96
Barker, Esther T(emperley) 1910- ... CANR-2
Earlier sketch in CA 49-52
Barker, Frank Granville 1923- ... CAP-1
Earlier sketch in CA 11-12
Barker, George Granville 1913- ... CANR-7
Earlier sketch in CA 9-10R
See also DLB 20
See also CLC 8, 48
Barker, Gerard A(rthur) 1930- ... 69-72
Barker, Graham H(arold) 1949- ... 106
Barker, Harley Granville
See Granville-Barker, Harley
See also DLB 10
Barker, Howard 1946- ... 102
See also DLB 13
See also CLC 37
Barker, Jack M. 1924(?)-1985 Obituary ... 117
Barker, James Nelson 1784-1858 ... DLB-37
Barker, Jane 1652-1727(?) ... DLB-39
Barker, Jane Valentine 1930- ... CANR-11
Earlier sketch in CA 65-68
Barker, John W(alton, Jr.) 1933- ... 19-20R
Barker, Joseph 1929- ... 103
Barker, Kenneth S(tacey) 1932- ... 110
Barker, Larry L(ee) 1941- ... CANR-17
Earlier sketch in CA 81-84
Barker, M(uhammad) A(bd-Al-)R(ahman)
1929- ... 116
Barker, Melvern 1907- ... CAP-1
Earlier sketch in CA 9-10
See also SATA 11
Barker, Myrtie Lillian 1910- ... 7-8R
Barker, Nancy Nichols 1925- Brief entry ... 114
Barker, Nicolas (John) 1932- ... 102
Barker, Pat 1943- ... 122
Brief entry ... 117
See also CLC 32
Barker, Philip 1929- ... 114
Barker, Ralph 1917- ... CANR-16
Earlier sketches in CA 2R, CANR-1
Barker, Robert L(ee) 1937- ... 25-28R
Barker, Rodney (Steven) 1942- ... 45-48
Barker, Roger Garlock 1903- ... CANR-11
Earlier sketches in CA 11-12, CAP-1
Barker, Ronald 1921(?)-1976 Obituary ... 65-68
Barker, S. Omar 1894- ... CAP-2
Earlier sketch in CA 17-18
See also SATA 10
Barker, Sally
See McMurry, Sarah L.
Barker, Sebastian 1945- ... 124
Barker, Shirley Frances 1911-1965 ... 5-6R
Barker, T(heodore Cardwell) 1923- ... CANR-5
Earlier sketch in CA 13-14R
Barker, T(erence) S(narr) 1941- ... CANR-21
Earlier sketch in CA 45-48
Barker, Thomas M. 1929- ... 23-24R
Barker, W(illiam) Alan 1923-1988(?) ... CANR-1
Obituary ... 125
Earlier sketch in CA 3R
Barker, Wendy B. 1942- ... 125
Barker, Will 1913-1983 ... 9-10R
Obituary ... 110
See also SATA 8
Barker, William J(ohn) ... 65-68
Barker, William P(ierson) 1927- ... 9-10R
Barker-Benfield, G(raham) J(ohn) 1941-
Brief entry ... 113
Barkhouse, Joyce 1913- ... 93-96
See also SATA 48
Barkin, Carol 1944- Brief entry ... 118
See also SATA 42, 52
Barkin, David Peter 1942- ... 37-40R
Barkin, Kenneth D(avid) 1939- ... 41-44R
Barkin, Solomon 1907- ... 9-10R
Barkins, Evelyn (Warner) 1919- ... 29-32R
Barkley, Deanne 1931- Brief entry ... 114
Barkley, James Edward 1941- ... SATA-6
Barkley, T(heodore) M(itchell) 1934- ... 120
Barkley, Vada Lee 1919- ... 57-60
Barkman, Alma 1939- ... 114
Barkman, Paul Friesen 1921- ... 17-18R
Barkow, Al 1932- ... CANR-4
Earlier sketch in CA 53-56
Barks, Carl 1901- ... 115
See also SATA 37
Barks, Coleman (Bryan) 1937- ... CANR-12
Earlier sketch in CA 25-28R
See also DLB 5
Barksdale, E(thelbert) C(ourtland) 1944- ... 57-60
Barksdale, Hiram C(ollier) 1921- ... 11-12R
Barksdale, Richard (Kenneth) 1915- ... 49-52
Barkton, S. Rush
See Brav, Stanley R(osenbaum)
Barkun, Michael 1938- Brief entry ... 114
Barkworth, Peter (Wynn) 1929- ... 107
Barlach, Ernst 1870-1938 ... DLB-56
Barlay, Bennett
See Crossen, Kendell Foster
Barlay, Stephen 1930- ... CANR-12
Earlier sketch in CA 25-28R
Barlett, Donald L(eon) 1936- ... 115
Barley, M. W.
See Barley, Maurice Willmore
Barley, Maurice Willmore 1909- ... 122
Barlin, Anne L(ief) 1916- ... 97-100
Barling, Charles
See Barling, Muriel Vere Mant
Barling, Muriel Vere Mant 1904- ... 7-8R
Barlough, J(effrey) Ernest 1953- ... 49-52
Barlow, Claude W(illis) 1907-1976 ... CAP-2
Earlier sketch in CA 33-36
Barlow, Frank 1911- ... CANR-3
Earlier sketch in CA 9-10R
Barlow, Genevieve 1910- ... 21-22R
Barlow, J(ames) Stanley (Jr.) 1924- ... 41-44R
Barlow, James 1921-1973 ... CAP-1
Obituary ... 41-44R
Earlier sketch in CA 13-14
Barlow, Jane 1857-1917 Brief entry ... 115
Barlow, Joel 1754-1812 ... DLB-37
Barlow, John A(lfred) 1924- ... 21-22R
Barlow, John D(enison) 1934- ... 120
Barlow, Judith E(llen) 1946- ... 107
Barlow, (Emma) Nora 1885- ... CAP-2
Earlier sketch in CA 25-28
Barlow, Robert O.
See Meyer, Heinrich
Barlow, Roger
See Leckie, Robert (Hugh)
Barlow, Samuel L(atham) M(itchell)
1892-1982 Obituary ... 107
Barlow, Sanna Morrison
See Rossi, Sanna Morrison Barlow
Barlow, T(homas) Edward 1931- ... CANR-3
Earlier sketch in CA 45-48
Barlow, Wilfred 1915- ... 101
Barlowe, Raleigh 1914- ... 19-20R
Barltrop, Robert 1922- ... CANR-19
Earlier sketch in CA 73-76
Barman, Alicerose 1919- ... 65-68
Barman, Charles R(oy) 1945- ... 106
Barmann, Lawrence Francis 1932- ... 9-10R
Barmash, Isadore 1921- ... CANR-17
Earlier sketches in CA 45-48, CANR-1
Barmine, Alexander (G.) 1899-1987
Obituary ... 125
Barna, George 1954- ... 114
Barna, Yon 1927- ... 53-56
Barnabas
See Blandford, Brian E(rnest)
Barnabas
See West, Charles Converse
Barnaby, (Charles) Frank 1927- ... CANR-13
Earlier sketch in CA 33-36R
Barnaby, Ralph S(tanton) 1893- ... 61-64
See also SATA 9
Barnard, (James) Alan 1928- ... 9-10R
Barnard, Charles N(elson III) 1924- ... CANR-1
Earlier sketch in CA 49-52
Barnard, Christiaan (Neethling) 1922- ... CANR-14
Earlier sketch in CA 61-64
Barnard, Ellsworth 1907- ... CANR-26
Earlier sketches in CA 21-22R, CANR-11
Barnard, F(rederick) M(echner) 1921- ... 25-28R
Barnard, Harry 1906-1982 ... CANR-3
Obituary ... 107
Earlier sketch in CA 7-8R
Barnard, Howard Clive 1884-1985 ... 85-88
Obituary ... 117
Barnard, J(ohn) Darrell 1906- ... 7-8R
Barnard, J(ohn) Lawrence 1912-1977 ... 77-80
Obituary ... 73-76
Barnard, John 1681-1770 ... DLB-24
Barnard, (Virail) John 1932- ... 33-36R
Barnard, Mary (Ethel) 1909- ... CAP-2
Earlier sketch in CA 21-22
See also CLC 48
Barnard, Robert 1936- ... CANR-20
Earlier sketch in CA 77-80
Barnard, William Dean 1942- ... 69-72
Bar-Natan, Moshe
See Louvish, Misha
Barne, Kitty
See Barne, Marion Catherine
Barne, Marion Catherine 1883-1957
Brief entry ... 112
Barner, Bob 1947- ... 93-96
See also SATA 29
Bar Ner, R.
See Brenner, Reeve R(obert)
Barnes, Adrienne Martine
See Martine-Barnes, Adrienne
Barnes, Barry 1943- ... 97-100
Barnes, Chesley Virginia
See Young, Chesley Virginia
Barnes, Clara Ernst 1895- ... 5-6R
Barnes, Clive (Alexander) 1927- ... CANR-26
Earlier sketch in CA 77-80
See also AITN 2
Barnes, Djuna 1892-1982 ... CANR-16
Obituary ... 107
Earlier sketch in CA 11-12R
See also DLB 4, 9, 45
See also CLC 3, 4, 8, 11, 29
Barnes, Douglas 1927- ... CANR-19
Earlier sketch in CA 103
Barnes, Elmer Tracey ... CANR-26
Earlier sketches in CA 19-20, CAP-2
Barnes, (Frank) Eric Wollencott
1907-1962 ... SATA-22
Barnes, Gregory Allen 1934- ... CANR-25
Earlier sketches in CA 25-28R, CANR-10
Barnes, Harry Elmer 1889-1968 ... 89-92
Obituary ... 25-28R
Barnes, Hazel E(stella) 1915- ... CANR-3
Earlier sketch in CA 5-6R
Barnes, Henry A. 1906-1968 ... CAP-1
Earlier sketch in CA 15-16
Barnes, Irston Roberts 1904-1988
Obituary ... 124
Barnes, J. 1944- ... 85-88
Barnes, J(ohn) A(rundel) 1918- ... 101
Barnes, Jack 1920- ... 89-92
Barnes, Jack 1940- ... CANR-9
Earlier sketch in CA 61-64
Barnes, James A(nderson) 1898- ... 11-12R
Barnes, James J(ohn) 1931- ... CANR-4
Earlier sketch in CA 11-12R
Barnes, James N(eil) 1944- ... 117
Barnes, Jane
See Casey, Jane Barnes
Barnes, Jim 1933- ... 108
Barnes, Joanna 1934- ... 57-60
Barnes, John 1908- ... CANR-2
Earlier sketch in CA 45-48
Barnes, (Ernest) John (Ward) 1917- ... 108
Barnes, John B(ertram) 1924- ... 33-36R
Barnes, Joseph Fels 1907-1970 Obituary ... 104
Barnes, Julian 1946- ... CANR-19
Earlier sketch in CA 102
See also CLC 42
Barnes, Kenneth Charles 1903- ... 106
Barnes, Leonard (John) 1895- ... CAP-2
Earlier sketch in CA 29-32
Barnes, Lilly I. 1935- ... 126
Barnes, Malcolm 1909(?)-1984 Obituary ... 114
See also SATA 41
Barnes, Margaret Ayer 1886-1967
Obituary ... 25-28R
See also DLB 9
Barnes, Mary 1923- ... 85-88
Barnes, Melvyn (Peter Keith) 1942- ... 122
Barnes, Patience P(lummer) 1932- ... 108
Barnes, Peter 1931- ... 65-68
See also DLB 13
See also CLC 5
Barnes, Phoebe 1908- ... CAP-2
Earlier sketch in CA 23-24
Barnes, R(ichard) G(ordon) 1932- ... 33-36R
Barnes, Ralph M(osser) 1900-1984 ... CAP-2
Obituary ... 114
Earlier sketch in CA 17-18
Barnes, Robert J(ay) 1925- ... 21-22R
Barnes, Robert M(orson) 1940- ... CANR-25
Earlier sketch in CA 45-48
Barnes, Sam(uel) G(ill) 1913- ... 15-16R
Barnes, Samuel H(enry) 1931- ... 23-24R
Barnes, Stephen Emory 1952- ... 105
Barnes, Steven
See Barnes, Stephen Emory
Barnes, Thomas Garden 1930- ... CANR-1
Earlier sketch in CA 1R
Barnes, Timothy David 1942- ... 114
Barnes, Valerie ... 115
Barnes, Viola Florence 1885- ... 3R
Barnes, Walter 1880-1969 Obituary ... 116
Barnes, William 1801-1886 ... DLB-32
Barness, Richard 1917- ... 65-68
Barnet, Richard J. ... 13-14R
Barnet, Sylvan 1926- ... CANR-4
Earlier sketch in CA 4R
Barnetson, William Denholm 1917-1981
Obituary ... 103
Barnett, A. Doak 1921- ... CANR-15
Earlier sketch in CA 5-6R
Barnett, Adam
See Fast, Julius
Barnett, Correlli (Douglas) 1927- ... CANR-15
Earlier sketch in CA 15-16R
Barnett, Franklin 1903- ... 69-72
Barnett, George L(eonard) 1915- ... 29-32R
Barnett, (Nicolas) Guy 1928- ... 19-20R
Barnett, H(omer) G(arner) 1906- ... 45-48
Barnett, Isobel (Morag) 1918-1980
Obituary ... 105
Barnett, James Monroe 1925- ... 114
Barnett, Joe R(ichard) 1933- ... 106

Barnett, L. David
See Laschever, Barnett D.
Barnett, Leo 1925- 29-32R
Barnett, Leonard (Palin) 1919- CANR-12
Earlier sketches in CA 13-14, CAP-1
Barnett, Lincoln (Kinnear) 1909-1979 102
Obituary 89-92
See also SATA 36
Barnett, Malcolm Joel 1941- 45-48
Barnett, Marva T(uttle) 1913- 57-60
Barnett, Maurice 1917-1980 Obituary 97-100
Barnett, Michael 1930- 57-60
Barnett, Moneta 1922-1976 .... SATA-33
Barnett, Naomi 1927- CANR-7
Earlier sketch in CA 5-6R
See also SATA 40
Barnett, Peter Herbert 1945- 124
Barnett, Richard B(aity) 1941- 105
Barnett, Richard C(hambers) 1932- 33-36R
Barnett, Robert W(arren) 1911- 126
Barnett, S(amuel) A(nthony) 1915- CANR-6
Earlier sketch in CA 13-14R
Barnett, Sanford 1909(?)-1988 Obituary 125
Barnett, Suzanne Wilson 1940- 120
Barnett, Ursula A(nnemarie) 1924- 123
Barnett, Vivian E(ndicott) 1944- 115
Barnette, Henlee H(ulix) 1911- 49-52
Barnette, W(arren) Leslie, Jr. 1910- CAP-1
Earlier sketch in CA 11-12
Barnewall, Gordon G(ouverneur) 1924- 121
Barney, Harry
See Lottman, Eileen
Barney, Kenneth D. 1921- 69-72
Barney, Laura D(reyfus) 1880(?)-1974
Obituary 53-56
Barney, LeRoy 1930- 33-36R
Barney, Maginel Wright 1881(?)-1966
Obituary 111
See also SATA 32, 39
Barney, Natalie (Clifford) 1878(?)-1972
Obituary 33-36R
See also DLB 4
Barney, Stephen A(llen) 1942- 102
Barney, William L(esko) 1943- 41-44R
Barnhart, Clarence L(ewis) 1900- 13-14R
See also SATA 48
Barnhart, Joe Edward 1931- 41-44R
Barnhill, Myrtle Fait 1896-1986 .... CAP-1
Obituary 119
Earlier sketch in CA 15-16
Barnhouse, Donald 103
Barnhouse, Donald Grey 1895-1960 123
Obituary 113
Barnhouse, Ruth Tiffany 1923- CANR-15
Earlier sketch in CA 85-88
Barnie, John 1941- 57-60
Barnitt, Nedda Lemmon 9-10R
Barnitz, Harry W. 1920-1973 .... CAP-2
Earlier sketch in CA 25-28
Barnoon, Shlomo 1940- 41-44R
Barnouw, Adriaan Jacob 1877-1968
Obituary 104
See also SATA 27
Barnouw, Erik 1908- CANR-12
Earlier sketch in CA 15-16R
Barnouw, Victor 1915- 85-88
See also SATA 28, 43
Barn Owl
See Howells, Roscoe
Barnright, Julia
See Bancroft, Iris (May Nelson)
Barns, John W(intour) B(aldwin)
1912-1974 Obituary 49-52
Barnsley, Alan Gabriel 1916-1986 ....13-14R
Obituary 121
Barnstone, Aliki 1956- 105
Barnstone, Howard 1923-1987 Obituary 122
Barnstone, Willis 1927- 17-18R
See also SATA 20
Barnum, Jay Hyde 1888(?)-1962 .... SATA-20
Barnum, Richard CANR-26
Earlier sketches in CA 19-20, CAP-2
See also SATA 1
Barnum, Vance CANR-26
Earlier sketches in CA 19-20, CAP-2
Barnum, W(illiam) Paul 1933- 29-32R
Barnwell, D. Robinson 1915- 19-20R
Barnwell, John (Gibbes, Jr.) 1947- 113
Barnwell, William Curtis 1943- 103
Baro, Gene 1924-1982 Obituary 112
Baroff, George Stanley 1924- 101
Baroja (y Nessi), Pio 1872-1956
Brief entry 104
See also TCLC 8
Barolini, Antonio 1910-1971 .... CANR-1
Earlier sketch in CA 2R
Barolini, Helen 1925- CANR-16
Earlier sketch in CA 73-76
Barolini, Teodolinda 1951- 124
Barolsky, Paul 1941- 81-84
Baron, (Joseph) Alexander 1917- CANR-14
Earlier sketch in CA 7-8R
Baron, David
See Pinter, Harold
Baron, Dennis E(mery) 1944- 110
Baron, Elizabeth Frank
See Frank-Baron, Elizabeth
Baron, Frank 1936- 119
Baron, Hans 1900- 19-20R
Baron, Herman 1941- 61-64
Baron, J. W.
See Krauzer, Steven M(ark)
Baron, Mary (Kelley) 1944- CANR-2
Earlier sketch in CA 49-52
Baron, Mikan
See Barba, Harry
Baron, Oscar 1908(?)-1976 Obituary 65-68
Baron, Othello
See Fanthorpe, R(obert) Lionel
Baron, Robert Alex 1920- 41-44R
Baron, Salo W(ittmayer) 1895- 69-72
Baron, Samuel H(askell) 1921- CANR-3
Earlier sketch in CA 11-12R
Baron, Virginia Olsen 1931- 25-28R
See also SATA 28, 46
Baron, (Ora) Wendy 1937- 41-44R
Baron Amulree
See Mackenzie, Basil William Sholto
Baron Corvo
See Rolfe, Frederick (William Serafino Austin Lewis Mary)
Barondess, Sue K(aufman) 1926-1977 .. CANR-1
Obituary 69-72
Earlier sketch in CA 3R
See also CLC 8
Baron de Teive
See Pessoa, Fernando (Antonio Nogueira)
Barone, Michael 1944- 93-96
Baron Lloyd of Hampstead
See Lloyd, Dennis
Baron of Remenham
See Thomas, (William) Miles (Webster)
Baroody, Jamil Murad 1905-1979
Obituary 85-88
Barooshian, (Dickran) Vahan 1932- 85-88
Barr, Alfred H(amilton), Jr. 1902-1981 49-52
Obituary 105
Barr, (Chester) Alwyn (Jr.) 1938- 33-36R
Barr, Anthony 1921- 109
Barr, Betty 1932- 97-100
Barr, Beverly 61-64
Barr, Densil Neve
See Buttrey, Douglas N(orton)
Barr, Donald 1921- 11-12R
See also SATA 20
Barr, Donald Roy 1938- 69-72
Barr, Doris W(ilson) 1923- 33-36R
Barr, George 1907- CANR-1
Earlier sketch in CA 3R
See also SATA 2
Barr, Gladys Hutchison 1904-1976 .... CANR-6
Earlier sketch in CA 1R
Barr, James 1924- CANR-20
Earlier sketches in CA 3R, CANR-4
Barr, Jeff 1941- 69-72
Barr, Jene
See Cohen, Jene Barr
See also SATA 16, 42
Barr, Jennifer 1945- 102
Barr, John J(ay) 1942- 61-64
Barr, Margaret Scolari 1901-1987
Obituary 124
Barr, Marleen Sandra 1953- 120
Barr, O(rlando) Sydney 1919- 15-16R
Barr, Pat(ricia Miriam) 1934- CANR-12
Earlier sketch in CA 23-24R
Barr, Robert 1850-1912 .... DLB-70
Barr, Robert R(ussell) 1931- 110
Barr, Stephen 1904- CAP-1
Earlier sketch in CA 15-16
Barr, Stringfellow 1897-1982 .... CANR-1
Obituary 106
Earlier sketch in CA 2R
Barr, Tony
See Barr, Anthony
Barr, William G. 1920(?)-1987 Obituary 121
Barraclough, Geoffrey 1908-1984 101
Obituary 114
Barraclough, Solon L(ovett) 1922- 41-44R
Barraga, Natalie Carter 1915- 41-44R
Barral, Mary-Rose 1925- 33-36R
Barranger, M(illy) S(later) 1937- CANR-12
Earlier sketch in CA 29-32R
Barratt, G. R. V.
See Barratt, Glynn (Richard V.)
Barratt, Glynn (Richard V.) 1944-
Brief entry 110
Barratt-Brown, Michael 1918- CANR-17
Earlier sketch in CA 97-100
Barrault, Jean-Louis 1910- 105
Barrax, Gerald William 1933- CANR-10
Earlier sketch in CA 65-68
See also BW
See also DLB 41
Barre, Michael Lee 1943- 118
Barrell, Geoffrey Richard 1917-1983
Obituary 111
Barrell, Sarah Webb 1946(?)-1979
Obituary 89-92
Barren, Charles (MacKinnon) 1913- CANR-4
Earlier sketch in CA 11-12R
Barreno, Maria Isabel
See Martins, Maria Isabel Barreno de Faria
See also AITN 1
Barrer, Gertrude
See Barrer-Russell, Gertrude
Barrera, Mario 1939- 97-100
Barrer-Russell, Gertrude 1921- SATA-27
Barres, Oliver 1921- 13-14R
Barreto, Afonso Henrique de Lima
See Lima Barreto, Afonso Henrique de
Barrett, Anne Mainwaring (Gillett) 1911- .. CAP-2
Earlier sketch in CA 29-32
Barrett, Bob 1925- 73-76
Barrett, C(harles) Kingsley 1917- CANR-25
Earlier sketches in CA 21-22R, CANR-10
Barrett, C(lifton) Waller 1901- 41-44R
Barrett, Clifford L(eslie) 1894-1971
Obituary 33-36R
Barrett, Dean 1942- 69-72
Barrett, Donald N(eil) 1920- 13-14R
Barrett, Edward L(ouis), Jr. 1917- 25-28R
Barrett, Ethel SATA-44
Barrett, Eugene F(rancis) 1921- 57-60
Barrett, George W(est) 1908- 17-18R
Barrett, George W. 1913(?)-1984
Obituary 114
Barrett, Gerald Van 1936- 37-40R
Barrett, Harold 1925- 81-84
Barrett, Harry B(emister) 1922- 85-88
Barrett, Henry Charles 1923- 53-56
Barrett, Ivan J. 1910- 49-52
Barrett, J(ohn) Edward 1932- 37-40R
Barrett, James H(enry) 1906- 33-36R
Barrett, James Lee 1929- 81-84
Barrett, John Gilchrist 1921- CANR-2
Earlier sketch in CA 5-6R
Barrett, John Henry 1913- 101
Barrett, Judi
See Barrett, Judith
Barrett, Judith 1941- 103
See also SATA 26
Barrett, Laurence I(rwin) 1935- 69-72
Barrett, Leonard E(manuel) 1920- 65-68
Barrett, Linton Lomas 1904- 7-8R
Barrett, Lois (Yvonne) 1947- 125
Barrett, Marvin 1920- CANR-11
Earlier sketch in CA 69-72
Barrett, Mary Ellin 1927- 19-20R
Barrett, Max 81-84
Barrett, Maye
See Barrett, Max
Barrett, Michael Dennis 1947- 85-88
Barrett, N. S.
See Barrett, Norman (S.)
Barrett, Nancy Smith 1942- 37-40R
Barrett, Nathan N(oble) 1933- 17-18R
Barrett, Norman (S.) 1935- CANR-24
Earlier sketch in CA 107
Barrett, Patricia 1914-1987 ....5-6R
Obituary 121
Barrett, Paul F(rancis) 1943- 117
Barrett, Raina
See Kelly, Pauline Agnes
Barrett, Ron 1937- SATA-14
Barrett, Rona 1936- 103
See also AITN 1
Barrett, Russel H(unter) 1919- 17-18R
Barrett, Susan (Mary) 1938- Brief entry 109
Barrett, (Roger) Syd 1946- CLC-35
Barrett, Sylvia 1914- 25-28R
Barrett, Ward J. 1927- 29-32R
Barrett, William (Christopher) 1913- ... CANR-11
Earlier sketch in CA 13-14R
See also CLC 27
Barrett, William E(dmund) 1900-1986 .. CANR-22
Obituary 120
Earlier sketch in CA 7-8R
See also SATA 49
Barrett, William R. 1922(?)-1977
Obituary 73-76
Barretto, Larry
See Barretto, Laurence Brevoort
Barretto, Laurence Brevoort 1890-1971
Obituary 33-36R
Barriault, Arthur 1915(?)-1976 Obituary 65-68
Barricelli, Jean-Pierre 1924- CANR-21
Earlier sketch in CA 105
Barrick, Mac E(ugene) 1933- 33-36R
Barrie, Alexander 1923- CANR-5
Earlier sketch in CA 4R
Barrie, Donald C(onway) 1905- 17-18R
Barrie, J(ames) M(atthew) 1860-1937
Brief entry 104
See also YABC 1
See also DLB 10
See also TCLC 2
See also CLR 16
Barrie, Jane
See Savage, Mildred (Spitz)
Barrie, Patricia 1946- 122
Barrier, (John) Michael 1940- 109
Barrier, Norman G(erald) 1940- CANR-4
Earlier sketch in CA 53-56
Barriger, John Walker 1899-1976
Obituary 69-72
Barrile, Jackie 1943- 117
Barrington, H. W.
See Brannon, William T.
Barrington, John
See Brownjohn, Alan
Barrington, Maurice
See Brogan, D(enis) W(illiam)
Barrington, Michael
See Moorcock, Michael (John)
Barrington, P. V.
See Barling, Muriel Vere Mant
Barrington, Pamela
See Barling, Muriel Vere Mant
Barrington, Thomas Joseph 1916- 104
Barrio, Raymond 1921- CANR-11
Earlier sketch in CA 25-28R
Barrio-Garay, Jose Luis 1932- 81-84
Barris, Alex 1922- 61-64
Barris, Chuck 1929- Brief entry 109
Barris, George 1925- SATA-47
Barritt, Denis P(hillips) 1914- 21-22R
Barro, Robert Joseph 1944- 97-100
Barrol, Grady
See Bograd, Larry
Barroll, John Leeds III 1928- 101
Barron, Ann Forman 69-72
Barron, Bruce 1960- 123
Barron, Charlie Nelms 1922-1977
Obituary 69-72
Barron, Ed
See Bernhardt, Clyde Edric Barron
Barron, Frank (Xavier) 1922- CANR-8
Earlier sketch in CA 5-6R
Barron, Fred 117
Barron, Gayle 1945- 109
Barron, Gloria Joan 1934- 81-84
Barron, Greg 1952- 110
Barron, Jerome A(ure) 1933- CANR-24
Earlier sketch in CA 45-48
Barron, Milton L. 1918- CANR-18
Earlier sketch in CA 1R
Barron, (Richard) Neil 1934- 102
Barrosse, Thomas 1926- 9-10R
Barrow, Andrew 1945- 97-100
Barrow, Geoffrey W(allis) S(teuart)
1924- CANR-7
Earlier sketch in CA 17-18R
Barrow, Harold M(arion) 1909- 106
Barrow, Henry 1906(?)-1985 Obituary 117
Barrow, John D(avid) 1952- 115
Barrow, Joseph Louis 1914-1981
Obituary 103
Barrow, Keith E. 1954-1983 Obituary 111
Barrow, Kenneth 1945- 119
Barrow, Leo (Lebron) 1925- Brief entry 110
Barrow, Pamela
See Howarth, Pamela
Barrow, R. H. 1894(?)-1984 Obituary 114
Barrow, Rhoda
See Lederer, Rhoda Catharine (Kitto)
Barrow, Robin 1944- CANR-10
Earlier sketch in CA 65-68
Barrow, Terence 1923- 41-44R
Barrow, Thomas C(hurchill) 1929- 23-24R
Barrow, William
See Fuller, Hoyt (William)
Barrows, Anita 1947- 49-52
Barrows, Chester L. 1892(?)-1975
Obituary 104
Barrows, (Ruth) Marjorie 1892(?)-1983 .. CAP-2
Obituary 109
Earlier sketch in CA 21-22
Barrows, R. M.
See Barrows, (Ruth) Marjorie
Barrows, Ruth
See Barrows, (Ruth) Marjorie
Barrows, Susanna Isabel 1944- 108
Barrows, Sydney (Biddle) 1952- 126
Barry, Anne 1940- 85-88
Barry, Colman J. 1921- 13-14R
Barry, Herbert III 1930- CANR-14
Earlier sketch in CA 37-40R
Barry, Iris 1895-1969 Obituary 104
Barry, Jack 1939- 69-72
Barry, Jackson G(ranville) 1926- 29-32R
Barry, James Donald 1926- 33-36R
Barry, James P(otvin) 1918- CANR-24
Earlier sketch in CA 37-40R
See also SATA 14
Barry, Jane (Powell) 1925- 7-8R
Barry, Jerome B(enedict) 1894-1975 .... 3R
Obituary 61-64
Barry, Jocelyn
See Bowden, Jean
Barry, John Vincent William 1903-1969 .... 3R
Obituary 103
Barry, Joseph (Amber) 1917- CANR-14
Earlier sketch in CA 57-60
Barry, June 1925- 15-16R
Barry, Katharina Watjen 1936- 9-10R
See also SATA 4
Barry, Kevin
See Laffan, Kevin (Barry)
Barry, Lucy (Brown) 1934- 19-20R
Barry, Margaret Stuart 1927- CANR-25
Earlier sketch in CA 106
Barry, Mary J(ane) 1928- 49-52
Barry, Mike
See Malzberg, Barry N(athaniel)
Barry, Philip 1896-1949 Brief entry 109
See also DLB 7
See also TCLC 11
Barry, Raymond Walker 1894- CAP-1
Earlier sketch in CA 17-18
Barry, Robert (Everett) 1931- CANR-2
Earlier sketch in CA 5-6R
See also SATA 6
Barry, Roger Graham 1935- 102
Barry, Scott 1952- 89-92
See also SATA 32
Barry, Sebastian 1955- 117
Barry, Spranger
See Kauffmann, Stanley
Barry, Stephen P. 1948(?)-1986 123
Obituary 120
Barry, William A(nthony) 1930- 115
Barry, William David 1946- 114
Barsacq, Andre 1909-1973 Obituary 41-44R
Barsacq, Leon 1906-1969 Obituary 113
Barsby, John A. 1935- 121
Barsh, Russel Lawrence 1950- 105
Barsis, Max 1894(?)-1973 Obituary 41-44R
Barsky, Arthur 1900(?)-1982(?) Obituary ... 106
Barson, John 1936- 85-88
Barsotti, C(harles) 1933- 65-68
Barstow, Anne Llewellyn 1929- 111
Barstow, Phyllida 1937- 121
Barstow, Stan(ley) 1928- CANR-1
Earlier sketch in CA 3R
See also DLB 14
Bart, Andre Schwarz
See Schwarz-Bart, Andre
Bart, Benjamin F(ranklin) 1917- 25-28R
Bart, Lionel 1930- 65-68
Bart, Pauline B(ernice) 1930- 53-56
Bart, Peter 1932- CANR-19
Earlier sketch in CA 93-96
Bartek, E(dward) J(ohn) 1921- 37-40R
Bartel, Pauline C(hristine) 1952- 81-84
Bartel, Roland 1919- 17-18R
Bartell, Ernest 1932- 33-36R

Bartell, Linda Lang 1948- 125
Bartels, Robert 1913- 15-16R
Bartels, Robert A. 1923- CANR-16
Earlier sketch in CA 1R
Bartels, Susan Ludvigson
See Ludvigson, Susan
Barten, Harvey H(arold) 1933- 33-36R
Bartenbach, Jean 1918- 115
See also SATA 40
Bartenieff, Irmgard 1900(?)-1981
Obituary 105
Barter, A(lice) K(nar) 1918- 57-60
Barth, Alan 1906-1979 .... CANR-5
Obituary 104
Earlier sketch in CA 2R
Barth, Charles P. 1895- CAP-2
Earlier sketch in CA 25-28
Barth, Christoph F. 1917- 29-32R
Barth, Edna 1914-1980 .... 41-44R
Obituary 102
See also SATA 7, 24
Barth, Fredrik 1928- CANR-11
Earlier sketch in CA 65-68
Barth, Gunther 1925- 103
Barth, J(ohn) Robert 1931- 29-32R
Barth, John (Simmons) 1930- CANR-23
Earlier sketches in CA 1R, CANR-5
See also CABS 1
See also DLB 2
See also CLC 1, 2, 3, 5, 7, 9, 10, 14, 27
See also AITN 1, 2
Barth, Karl 1886-1968 Obituary 25-28R
Barth, Lois
See Freihofer, Lois Diane
Barth, Markus Karl 1915- CANR-2
Earlier sketch in CA 7-8R
Barth, Peter S. 1937- CANR-25
Earlier sketch in CA 106
Barth, Richard 1943- 81-84
Barth, Roland S(awyer) 1937- CANR-1
Earlier sketch in CA 45-48
Barthel, Diane L(ee) 1949- 115
Barthel, Joan 1932- 114
Brief entry 111
Barthelme, Donald 1931- CANR-20
Earlier sketch in CA 21-22R
See also SATA 7
See also DLB 2
See also DLBY 80
See also CLC 1, 2, 3, 5, 6, 8, 13, 23, 46
See also SSC 2
Barthelme, Frederick 1943- 122
Brief entry 114
See also DLBY 85
See also CLC 36
Barthelmes, (Albert) Wes(ley, Jr.) 1922-1976 69-72
Obituary 65-68
Barthes, Roland 1915-1980 Obituary 97-100
See also CLC 24
Bartholomay, Julia A. 1923- 45-48
Bartholomew, Barbara 1941- Brief entry 118
See also SATA 42
Bartholomew, Bart
See Bartholomew, Frank H.
Bartholomew, Cecilia 1907- CAP-1
Earlier sketch in CA 13-14
Bartholomew, Ed(ward Ellsworth) 1914- .. 25-28R
Bartholomew, Frank H. 1898-1985
Obituary 115
Bartholomew, Jean
See Beatty, Patricia Robbins
Bartholomew, John Eric
See Morecambe, Eric
Bartholomew, Paul C(harles) 1907-1975 .... CANR-10
Earlier sketch in CA 17-18R
Bartier, Pierre 1945- 23-24R
Bartlett, Amy 1949- 124
Bartlett, Basil Hardington 1905-1985
Obituary 115
Bartlett, Bruce R(eeves) 1951- CANR-19
Earlier sketch in CA 89-92
Bartlett, C(hristopher) J(ohn) 1931- 17-18R
Bartlett, Charles (Leffingwell) 1921- 29-32R
Bartlett, David
See Mason, Madeline
Bartlett, Donald L. Brief entry 110
Bartlett, Elizabeth (Winters) CANR-9
Earlier sketch in CA 17-18R
Bartlett, Elsa Jaffe 1935- CANR-15
Earlier sketch in CA 33-36R
Bartlett, Eric George 1920- CANR-19
Earlier sketches in CA 7-8R, CANR-2
Bartlett, F. C.
See Bartlett, Frederic Charles
Bartlett, Frederic Charles 1886-1969
Obituary 115
Bartlett, Gerald (Robert) 1935- 21-22R
Bartlett, Harriett M(oulton) 1897-1987
Obituary 121
Bartlett, Hubert Moyse
See Moyse-Bartlett, Hubert
Bartlett, Irving H(enry) 1923- CANR-9
Earlier sketch in CA 23-24R
Bartlett, Jean Anne 1927- 97-100
Bartlett, John 1820-1905 .... DLB-1
Bartlett, Jonathan 1931- 93-96
Bartlett, Kathleen
See Paine, Lauran (Bosworth)
Bartlett, Kim 1941- 89-92
Bartlett, Lee Anthony 1950- 114
Bartlett, Margaret Farrington 1896- CANR-5
Earlier sketch in CA 5-6R
Bartlett, Marie (Swan) 1918- 21-22R
Bartlett, Merrill L(ewis) 1939- 117
Bartlett, Nancy W(hite) 1913-1972 .... CAP-2
Obituary 41-44R
Earlier sketch in CA 23-24
Bartlett, Paul 1909- CAP-2
Earlier sketch in CA 17-18
Bartlett, Philip A. CANR-26
Earlier sketches in CA 19-20, CAP-2
See also SATA 1
Bartlett, Phyllis 1908(?)-1973 Obituary 41-44R
Bartlett, Richard A(dams) 1920- CANR-2
Earlier sketch in CA 5-6R
Bartlett, Robert (John) 1950- 125
Bartlett, Robert Merrill 1899- CANR-2
Earlier sketch in CA 5-6R
See also SATA 12
Bartlett, Robert V(irgil) 1953- CANR-22
Earlier sketch in CA 104
Bartlett, Ruhl J. 1897- CAP-1
Earlier sketch in CA 11-12
Bartlett, Ruth 19-20R
Bartlett, Vernon 1894-1983 61-64
Obituary 108
Bartley, Diana E(sther) Pelaez-Rivera 1940- 69-72
Bartley, Leigh
See Riker, Leigh
Bartley, Numan V(ache) 1934- CANR-12
Earlier sketch in CA 69-72
Bartley, Robert L(eRoy) 1937- 97-100
Bartley, William Warren III 1934- CANR-15
Earlier sketch in CA 37-40R
Bartocci, Gianni 1925- 23-24R
Bartol, Cyrus Augustus 1813-1900 .... DLB-1
Bartole, Genevieve 1927- 101
Bartolome de Roxas, Juan
See Rubia Barcia, Jose
Barton, Allen H(oisington) 1924- CANR-10
Earlier sketch in CA 25-28R
Barton, Bruce Walter 1935- 89-92
Barton, Byron 1930- CANR-13
Earlier sketch in CA 57-60
See also SATA 9
Barton, Del 1925-1971 Obituary 103
Barton, Erle
See Fanthorpe, R(obert) Lionel
Barton, Eustace Robert 1854-1943
Brief entry 114
Barton, Fredrick (Preston) 1948- 119
Barton, H. Arnold 1929- 77-80
Barton, Harriett SATA-43
Barton, Humphrey (Douglas Elliott) 1900- CAP-2
Earlier sketch in CA 19-20
Barton, Jim Tom 123
Barton, John (Stuart) 1957- 114
Barton, John Bernard Adie 1928- 81-84
Barton, John H(ays) 1936- 111
Barton, John Mackintosh Tilney 1898- CAP-1
Earlier sketch in CA 17-18
Barton, Jon
See Harvey, John (Barton)
Barton, Lee
See Fanthorpe, R(obert) Lionel
Barton, Lew(is Randolph) 1918- 73-76
Barton, M. Xaveria 1910- Brief entry 105
Barton, Margaret D(over) 1902- CAP-1
Earlier sketch in CA 15-16
Barton, Mary Neill 1899- CAP-2
Earlier sketch in CA 19-20
Barton, May Hollis CANR-26
Earlier sketches in CA 19-20, CAP-2
See also SATA 1
Barton, Michael (Lee) 1943- 110
Barton, Richard F(leming) 1924- 61-64
Barton, Roger A(very) 1903-1976
Obituary 65-68
Barton, S. W.
See Whaley, Barton Stewart
Barton, Thomas Frank 1905- CANR-1
Earlier sketch in CA 45-48
Barton, V(ernon) Wayne 3R
Barton, Walter Elbert 1886-1983 Obituary .. 111
Barton, Wayne 1944- 124
Barton, Weldon V. 1938- 21-22R
Barton, William (Renald III) 1950- CANR-1
Earlier sketch in CA 45-48
Bartos, Otomar J(an) 1927- 105
Bartos-Hoeppner, Barbara 1923- CANR-10
Earlier sketch in CA 25-28R
See also SATA 5
Bartov, Hanoch 1926- Brief entry 117
Bartram, Graham 1946- 116
Bartram, John 1699-1777 .... DLB-31
Bartram, William 1739-1823 .... DLB-37
Bartran, Margaret 1913-1976 .... CAP-2
Earlier sketch in CA 29-32
Bartrum, Douglas A(lbert) 1907- CANR-6
Earlier sketch in CA 11-12R
Bartsch, Jochen 1906- SATA-39
Bartscht, Waltraud 1924- 41-44R
Bartusis, Mary Ann 1930- 101
Bartz, Albert E(dward) 1933- 23-24R
Bartz, Patricia McBride 1921- 102
Bartz, Wayne R(onald) 1938- 111
Baruch, Dorothy W(alter) 1899-1962 .... SATA-21
Baruch, Grace K. 1936(?)-1988 Obituary 126
Baruch, Ruth-Marion 1922- 29-32R
Baruk, Henri Marc 1897- 85-88
Barwick, Steven 1921- 15-16R
Barwood, Hal Brief entry 125
Baryshnikov, Mikhail (Nikolayevich) 1948-
Brief entry 113
Barzanti, Sergio 1925- 19-20R
Barzilay, Isaac Eisenstein 1915- 113
Barzini, Luigi (Giorgio, Jr.) 1908-1984 .... CANR-23
Obituary 112
Earlier sketch in CA 13-14R
Bar-Zohar, Michael 1938- CANR-12
Earlier sketch in CA 23-24R
Barzun, Jacques (Martin) 1907- CANR-22
Earlier sketch in CA 61-64
Bas, Joe 1932- 53-56
Bas, Rutger
See Rutgers van der Loeff-Basenau, An(na) Maria Margaretha
Basa, Eniko Molnar 1939- 77-80
Basart, Ann Phillips 1931- CANR-1
Earlier sketch in CA 3R
Basche, James 1926- 29-32R
Bascio, Patrick 1927- 119
Bascom, David 1912- 93-96
Bascom, Willard N. 1916- CANR-6
Earlier sketch in CA 2R
Bascom, William R(ussel) 1912-1981 .... 19-20R
Obituary 125
Basdekis, Demetrios 1930- 25-28R
Baseley, Godfrey 1904- 102
Basgoz, M(ehmet) Ilhan 1921- 113
Bash, Deborah M. Blumenthal 1940- 109
Bash, Frank N(ess) 1937- 107
Bash, Harry H(arvey) 1926- 89-92
Basham, Don W(ilson) 1926- 65-68
Basham, Richard Dalton 1945- 111
Basham, William Randolph 1933(?)-1986
Obituary 118
Bashevis, Isaac
See Singer, Isaac Bashevis
Bashevkin, Sylvia B. 1954- 121
Bashira, Damali 1951- 57-60
Bashshur, Rashid L. 1933- 89-92
Basichis, Gordon (Allen) 1947- 85-88
Basil, Douglas C. 1923- 41-44R
Basil, Otto 1901-1983 49-52
Obituary 113
Basile, Gloria Vitanza 1929- CANR-12
Earlier sketch in CA 69-72
Basile, Joseph 1912- CANR-11
Earlier sketch in CA 25-28R
Basile, Leon 1955- 113
Basile, Robert M(anlius) 1916- 53-56
Basilius, Harold A. 1905-1977 .... CANR-2
Earlier sketch in CA 1R
Basinger, Jeanine (Deyling) 1936- CANR-18
Earlier sketch in CA 97-100
Basiuk, Victor 1932- 93-96
Baskerville, Barnet 1916- 4R
Baskerville, Patricia 1951- 108
Baskett, John 1930- 97-100
Baskette, Floyd K(enneth) 1910- 33-36R
Baskin, Barbara H(olland) 1929- CANR-22
Earlier sketch in CA 103
Baskin, Esther Tane 1926(?)-1973
Obituary 37-40R
Baskin, Leonard 1922- 106
See also SATA 27, 30
Baskin, Robert E(dward) 1917-1983
Obituary 110
Baskin, Samuel 1921- 17-18R
Baskin, Wade 1924-1974 .... CAP-2
Earlier sketch in CA 23-24
Basler, Roy P(rentice) 1906- CANR-4
Earlier sketch in CA 5-6R
Basler, Thomas G(ordon) 1940- 103
Bason, Fred
See Bason, Frederick (Thomas)
Bason, Frederick (Thomas) 1907-1973 .... 7-8R
Obituary 89-92
Bason, Lillian 1913- 69-72
See also SATA 20
Bass, Altha Leah (Bierbower) 1892-1988 . CAP-2
Obituary 126
Earlier sketch in CA 23-24
Bass, Althea
See Bass, Altha Leah (Bierbower)
Bass, Bernard M(orris) 1925- CANR-19
Earlier sketches in CA 1R, CANR-4
Bass, Clarence B(eaty) 1922- 5-6R
Bass, Eben E(dward) 1924- 107
Bass, Ellen 1947- CANR-2
Earlier sketch in CA 49-52
Bass, George F(letcher) 1932- 122
Bass, Henry B(enjamin) 1897-1975
Obituary 57-60
Bass, Herbert Jacob 1929- CANR-1
Earlier sketch in CA 3R
Bass, Howard 1923- CANR-2
Earlier sketch in CA 7-8R
Bass, Howard L(arry) 1942- 69-72
Bass, Jack 1934- CANR-19
Earlier sketch in CA 29-32R
Bass, Jack A(lexander) 1946- 97-100
Bass, Kingsley B., Jr.
See Bullins, Ed
Bass, Lawrence W(ade) 1898- 49-52
Bass, Madeline Tiger 1934- 116
Bass, Milton R. 1923- 25-28R
Bass, Rick 1958- 126
Bass, Robert D(uncan) 1904- 61-64
Bass, T. J.
See Bassler, Thomas J(oseph)
See also DLBY 81
Bass, Thomas A. 1951- 124
Bass, Virginia W(auchope) 1905- 61-64
Bass, William M(arvin III) 1928- 41-44R
Bassan, Maurice 1929- 25-28R
Bassani, Giorgio 1916- 65-68
See also CLC 9
Basse, Eli 1904-1979 Obituary 93-96
Basseches, Michael 1950- 114
Bassermann, Lujo
See Schreiber, Hermann
Basset, Bernard 1909-1988 .... CANR-6
Obituary 125
Earlier sketch in CA 11-12R
Bassett, Edward Eryl 1940- 33-36R
Bassett, Flora Marjorie 1890(?)-1980
Obituary 97-100
Bassett, George William 1910- 102
Bassett, Glenn Arthur 1930- 19-20R
Bassett, (Mary) Grace 1927- 73-76
Bassett, Jack
See Rowland, D(onald) S(ydney)
Bassett, James E(lias) 1912-1978 61-64
Obituary 81-84
Bassett, Jeni 1960(?)- SATA-43
Bassett, John Earl, Jr. 1942- 123
Bassett, John Keith
See Keating, Lawrence A.
Bassett, John Spencer 1867-1928
Brief entry 122
See also DLB 17
Bassett, Lisa 1958- 126
Bassett, Marnie
See Bassett, Flora Marjorie
Bassett, Richard 1900- CAP-2
Earlier sketch in CA 25-28
Bassett, Ronald 1924- 81-84
Bassett, T(homas) D(ay) Seymour 1913- CANR-8
Earlier sketch in CA 23-24R
Bassett, William B. K. 1908- CAP-1
Earlier sketch in CA 9-10
Bassett, William Travis 1923- 11-12R
Bassett, William W. 1932- 25-28R
Bassiouni, M. Cherif 1937- 29-32R
Bassler, Thomas J(oseph) 1932- 115
Basso, Aldo P(eter) 1922- 65-68
Basso, (Joseph) Hamilton 1904-1964 89-92
Bassoff, Bruce 1941- 69-72
Basten, Fred E(rnest) CANR-22
Earlier sketches in CA 57-60, CANR-7
Bastias, Constantine 1901(?)-1972
Obituary 37-40R
Bastico, Ettore 1876-1972 Obituary 37-40R
Bastin, J(ohn) S(turgus) 1927- CANR-11
Earlier sketch in CA 23-24R
Bastlund, Knud 1925- 23-24R
Basu, Arindam 1948- 61-64
Basu, Asoke (Kumar) 1940- 106
Basu, Dipak R. 1951- 112
Basu, Kaushik 1952- 115
Basu, Romen 1923- CANR-13
Earlier sketch in CA 77-80
Bataille, Georges 1897-1962 101
Obituary 89-92
See also CLC 29
Bataille, Gretchen M. 1944- 102
Batbedat, Jean 1926- 37-40R
Batchelder, Alan Bruce 1931- 23-24R
Batchelder, Howard T(imothy) 1909- CAP-2
Earlier sketch in CA 19-20
Batcheller, John M. 1918- 45-48
Batchelor, C(larence) D(aniel) 1888-1977
Obituary 73-76
Batchelor, David 1943- CANR-18
Earlier sketch in CA 101
Batchelor, Edward, Jr. 1930- 110
Batchelor, John 1942- 93-96
Batchelor, John (Dennis) 1947- 109
Batchelor, John Calvin 1948- 105
Batchelor, Joy 1914- SATA-29
Batchelor, Julie F(rances) E(lizabeth) 1947- 109
Batchelor, Reg
See Paine, Lauran (Bosworth)
Batcher, Elaine Kotler 1944- 109
Bate, Lucy 1939- 69-72
See also SATA 18
Bate, Norman (Arthur) 1916- 4R
See also SATA 5
Bate, Sam 1907- 102
Bate, W(alter) Jackson 1918- 7-8R
See also DLB 67
Bateman, Barbara Dee 1933- 41-44R
Bateman, Robert (Moyes Carruthers) 1922-1973 .... CANR-7
Earlier sketch in CA 7-8R
Bateman, Walter L(ewis) 1916- 29-32R
Bates, Alan Lawrence 1923- 17-18R
Bates, Arthenia J. 1920- 57-60
Bates, Barbara S(nedeker) 1919- 17-18R
See also SATA 12
Bates, Betty
See Bates, Elizabeth
See also SATA 19
Bates, Carol Neuls
See Neuls-Bates, Carol
Bates, Caroline (Philbrick) 1932- 103
Bates, Charles C(arpenter) 1918- 121
Bates, Darrell 1913- CAP-1
Earlier sketch in CA 9-10
Bates, David Vincent 1922- 110
Bates, Elizabeth 1921- CANR-14
Earlier sketch in CA 77-80
Bates, H(erbert) E(rnest) 1905-1974 93-96
Obituary 45-48
See also CLC 46
Bates, Helen L. Z.
See Yakobson, Helen B(ates)
Bates, J(ames) Leonard 1919- 13-14R
Bates, Jefferson D(avis) 1920- CANR-15
Earlier sketch in CA 81-84
Bates, Jerome E. 1917- 17-18R
Bates, Katharine Lee 1859-1929 .... DLB-71
Bates, Kenneth Francis 1904- CAP-1
Earlier sketch in CA 13-14

Bates, Lucius Christopher 1901(?)-1980
Obituary 101
Bates, Margaret J(ane) 1918- 17-18R
Bates, Marston 1906-1974 CANR-7
Obituary 49-52
Earlier sketch in CA 7-8R
Bates, Paul A(llen) 1920- 37-40R
Bates, Peter Watson 1920- 102
Bates, Ralph Samuel 1906- 3R
Bates, Robert H(inrichs) 1942- CANR-11
Earlier sketch in CA 69-72
Bates, Robert L(atimer) 1912- 121
Brief entry 116
Bates, Ronald (Gordon Nudell) 1924- 25-28R
Bates, Scott 1923- 49-52
Bates, Stephen 1958- 122
Bates, Steven Latimer 1940- 114
Bates, Su
See Bates, Susannah (Vacella)
Bates, Susannah (Vacella) 1941- 112
Bates, Timothy M(ason) 1946- 53-56
Bateson, Charles (Henry) 1903- 69-72
Bateson, F(rederick) W(ilse) 1901-1978 CANR-6
Earlier sketch in CA 5-6R
Bateson, Gregory 1904-1980 41-44R
Obituary 101
Batey, Mavis 1921- 125
Batey, Richard (Alexander) 1933- 33-36R
Batey, Tom 1946- 107
See also SATA 41, 52
Bath, Philip Ernest 1898- CAP-1
Earlier sketch in CA 9-10
Batherman, Muriel
See Sheldon, Muriel
Bathke, Edwin A(lbert) 1936- 57-60
Bathke, Nancy E(dna) 1938- 57-60
Batho, Edith C(lara) 1895- CAP-1
Earlier sketch in CA 11-12
Bathurst, Sheila
See Sullivan, Sheila
Batista, Fulgencio
See Batista y Zaldivar, Fulgencio
Batista y Zaldivar, Fulgencio 1901-1973
Obituary 111
Batiuk, Thomas M(artin) 1947- 69-72
See also SATA 40
Batki, John 1942- 45-48
Batman, Richard (Dale) 1932- 124
Bator, Robert 1939- 115
Batra, Raveendra N(ath) 1943- 89-92
Batson, George (Donald) 1918-1977 33-36R
Obituary 73-76
Batson, Larry 1930- 57-60
See also SATA 35
Batson, Wade Thomas 1912- 125
Battaglia, Anthony 1939- 108
Battaglia, Aurelius 1910- SATA-33, 50
Battaglia, Elio Lee 1928- CANR-1
Earlier sketch in CA 4R
Battalia, O. William 1928- 45-48
Battan, Louis J(oseph) 1923- 15-16R
Battcock, Gregory 1938-1980 CANR-11
Obituary 105
Earlier sketch in CA 23-24R
Battelle, Phyllis (Marie) 1922- 77-80
Batten, Charles Linwood, Jr. 1942- 85-88
Batten, H(arry) Mortimer 1888-1958
Brief entry 112
See also SATA 25
Batten, Jack 1932- 49-52
Batten, James Knox 1936- 107
Batten, James William 1919- 33-36R
Batten, Jean (Gardner) 1909-1982 106
Obituary 123
Batten, Joyce Mortimer
See Mankowska, Joyce Kells Batten
Batten, Mary 1937- 41-44R
See also SATA 5
Batten, (Richard) Peter 1916- 97-100
Batten, Thomas Reginald 1904- 13-14R
Battenhouse, Roy W(esley) 1912- 13-14R
Batterberry, Ariane Ruskin 1935- CANR-13
Earlier sketch in CA 69-72
See also SATA 13
Batterberry, Michael Carver 1932- 77-80
See also SATA 32
Battersby, James L(yons) 1936- 41-44R
Battersby, Martin 1914(?)-1982 Obituary 106
Battersby, William J(ohn) 1904-1976 CANR-4
Earlier sketch in CA 7-8R
Battestin, Martin C(arey) 1930- 15-16R
Battin, B(rinton) W(arner) 1941- 112
Battin, Buck
See Battin, B(rinton) W(arner)
Battin, R(osabell) Ray 1925- CANR-6
Earlier sketch in CA 11-12R
Battin, Wendy 1953- 121
Battis, Emery John 1915- 4R
Battiscombe, E(sther) Georgina (Harwood)
1905- CANR-14
Earlier sketches in CA 9-10, CAP-1
Battista, Miriam 1912(?)-1980 Obituary 103
Battista, O(rlando) A(loysius) 1917- CANR-7
Earlier sketch in CA 15-16R
Battisti, Eugenio 1924- 37-40R
Battle, Allen Overton 1927- 41-44R
Battle, Gerald N(ichols) 1914- 57-60
Battle, Jean Allen 1914- 25-28R
Battle, Lois 1942- 106
Battle, Richard John Vulliamy 1907-1982
Obituary 107
Battle, Sol(omon Oden) 1934- 25-28R
Battles, (Roxy) Edith 1921- 41-44R
See also SATA 7
Battles, Ford Lewis 1915- 15-16R
Batto, Bernard Frank 1941- 57-60
Batts, Michael S. 1929- 41-44R
Batty, C(harles) D(avid) 1932- 19-20R
Batty, Joyce D(orothea) 1919- 17-18R
Batty, Linda Schmidt 1940- 61-64
Battye, Gladys Starkey 1915- Brief entry 111
Battye, Louis Neville 1923- 7-8R
Baty, Gordon B(ruce) 1938- 57-60
Baty, Roger M(endenhall) 1937- 77-80
Baty, Wayne 1925- CANR-5
Earlier sketch in CA 15-16R
Bauby, Cathrina 1927- 49-52
Bauchart
See Camus, Albert
Baudhuin, John S. 1948- 112
Baudouy, Michel-Aime 1909- CAP-2
Earlier sketch in CA 33-36
See also SATA 7
Bauduc, R.
See Segre, Dan V(ittorio)
Baudy, Nicolas 1904(?)-1971 Obituary 33-36R
Bauer, Caroline Feller 1935- 77-80
See also SATA 46, 52
Bauer, E. Charles 1916- 11-12R
Bauer, Erwin A. 1919- CANR-6
Earlier sketch in CA 11-12R
Bauer, Florence Marvyne CAP-2
Earlier sketch in CA 17-18
Bauer, Fred 1934- CANR-13
Earlier sketch in CA 29-32R
See also SATA 36
Bauer, George C. 1942- 73-76
Bauer, George Howard 1933- CANR-15
Earlier sketch in CA 29-32R
Bauer, (Jo) Hanna R(uth Goldsmith)
1918- 57-60
Bauer, Harry C(harles) 1902-1979 CAP-1
Obituary 85-88
Earlier sketch in CA 13-14
Bauer, Helen 1900- 5-6R
See also SATA 2
Bauer, Josef Martin 1901- CANR-5
Earlier sketch in CA 7-8R
Bauer, K(arl) Jack 1926-1987 CANR-10
Obituary 123
Earlier sketch in CA 25-28R
Bauer, Malcolm Clair 1914- 102
Bauer, Maria 1919- 117
Bauer, Marion Dane 1938- CANR-26
Earlier sketches in CA 69-72, CANR-11
See also SATA 20
Bauer, Nancy 1934- 113
Bauer, Peter Thomas 1915- 103
Bauer, Raymond A(ugustine)
1916-1977 CANR-11
Obituary 73-76
Earlier sketch in CA 61-64
Bauer, Robert A(lbert) 1910- 69-72
Bauer, Royal D(aniel) M(ichael) 1889- 33-36R
Bauer, Walter 1904- 101
Bauer, William Waldo 1892-1967 CANR-7
Earlier sketch in CA 5-6R
Bauer, Wolfgang L(eander) 1930- 15-16R
Bauer, Yehuda 1926- CANR-12
Earlier sketch in CA 29-32R
Bauerle, Ruth (Ellen) H(awkins) 1924- 112
Bauernfeind, Harry B. 1904- CAP-2
Earlier sketch in CA 19-20
Bauerschmidt, Marjorie 1926- SATA-15
Baugh, Albert C(roll) 1891-1981 107
Obituary 103
Baugh, Daniel A(lbert) 1931- 69-72
Baughan, Peter E(dward) 1934- 107
Baughman, Dorothy 1940- 65-68
Baughman, Ernest W(arren) 1916- 33-36R
Baughman, James L(ewis) 1952- 118
Baughman, James P(orter) 1936- 25-28R
Baughman, John Lee 1913- 97-100
Baughman, M(illard) Dale 1919- 41-44R
Baughman, Ray Edward 1925- CANR-22
Earlier sketches in CA 11-12R, CANR-4
Baughman, Ronald 1940- 122
Baughman, Urbanus E., Jr. 1905(?)-1978
Obituary 81-84
Baughn, William Hubert 1918- CANR-17
Earlier sketch in CA 3R
Baukhage, Hilmar Robert 1889-1976
Obituary 65-68
See also AITN 2
Bauland, Peter 1932- 25-28R
Baulch, Jerry T. 1913- 77-80
Baulch, Lawrence 1926- 25-28R
Baum, Allyn Z(elton) 1924- 17-18R
See also SATA 20
Baum, Bernard H(elmut) 1926- 37-40R
Baum, Dale 1943- 118
Baum, Daniel (Jay) 1934- CANR-6
Earlier sketch in CA 15-16R
Baum, David William 1940- 53-56
Baum, Gregory 1923- CANR-15
Earlier sketch in CA 25-28R
Baum, L(yman) Frank 1856-1919
Brief entry 108
See also SATA 18
See also DLB 22
See also TCLC 7
See also CLR 15
Baum, Louis 1948- 124
See also SATA 52
Baum, Louis F.
See Baum, L(yman) Frank
Baum, Paull F(ranklin) 1886-1964 7-8R
Obituary 103
Baum, Rainer C(arl) 1934- 107
Baum, Richard (Dennis) 1940- 57-60
Baum, Richard Fitzgerald 1913- 7-8R
Baum, Robert J(ames) 1941- CANR-17
Earlier sketch in CA 85-88
Baum, Thomas 1940- 65-68
Baum, Vicki 1888-1960 93-96
Baum, Willi 1931- 29-32R
See also SATA 4
Bauman, Clarence 1928- 45-48
Bauman, Edward Walter 1927- 106
Bauman, H(erman) Carl 1913- 9-10R
Baumann, Amy (Brown) Beeching
1922- 21-22R
See also SATA 10
Baumann, Carol Edler 1932- 33-36R
Baumann, Charles Henry 1926- 73-76
Baumann, Charly 1928- 89-92
Baumann, Edward (Weston) 1925- 109
Baumann, Elwood D. Brief entry 111
See also SATA 33
Baumann, Gerd 1953- 125
Baumann, Hans 1914- CANR-3
Earlier sketch in CA 7-8R
See also SATA 2
Baumann, Hans Felix S(iegismund)
1893-1985 Obituary 115
Baumann, Kurt 1935- CANR-13
Earlier sketch in CA 77-80
See also SATA 21
Baumann, Walter 1935- 29-32R
Baumbach, Jonathan 1933- CANR-12
Earlier sketch in CA 15-16R
See also CAAS 5
See also DLBY 80
See also CLC 6, 23
Baumback, Clifford M(ason) 1915- CANR-6
Earlier sketch in CA 57-60
Baume, Michael 1930- 25-28R
Baumel, Judith 1956- 125
Baumer, Franklin L(e Van) 1913-
Brief entry 110
Baumer, William H(enry) 1909- CANR-1
Earlier sketch in CA 2R
Baumgaertel, (Max) Walter 1902- 69-72
Baumgard, Herbert Mark 1920- 13-14R
Baumgardt, David 1890-1963 CANR-15
Obituary 103
Earlier sketch in CA 4R
Baumgartel, Walter
See Baumgaertel, (Max) Walter
Baumgarten, Sylvia 1933- 112
Baumgartner, Frederic J(oseph) 1945- 110
Baumgartner, John Stanley 1924- 9-10R
Bauml, Franz H.
See Baeuml, Franz H(einrich)
Baumol, William J(ack) 1922- CANR-24
Earlier sketches in CA 13-14R, CANR-7
Baumrin, Bernard H(erbert) 1934- 11-12R
Baumrin, Stefan
See Baumrin, Bernard H(erbert)
Baur, Francis G. 1930- 111
Baur, John E(dward) 1922- 11-12R
Baur, John I(reland) H(owe) 1909-1987
Obituary 122
Baus, Herbert M(ichael) 1914- CANR-11
Earlier sketch in CA 25-28R
Bausani, Alessandro 1921- 45-48
Bausch, Richard (Carl) 1945- 101
Bausch, Robert (Charles) 1945- 109
Bausch, William J. 1929- CANR-11
Earlier sketch in CA 29-32R
Bavarel, Michel (Joseph) 1940- 114
Bavier, Robert Newton (Jr.) 1918- 115
Bavin, Bill 1919- 73-76
Bavinck, J(ohan) H(erman) 1895-1965
Obituary 113
Bawden, Nina
See Kark, Nina Mary (Mabey)
See also DLB 14
See also CLR 2
Bawn, Mary
See Wright, Mary Pamela Godwin
Bax
See Baxter, Gordon F(rancis), Jr.
Bax, Clifford 1886-1962 Obituary 113
See also DLB 10
Bax, Martin C(harles) O(wen) 1933- 65-68
Bax, Roger
See Winterton, Paul
Baxandall, Rosalyn Fraad 1939- 81-84
Baxt, George 1923- 21-22R
Baxter, Angus 1912- 111
Baxter, Anne 1923-1985 114
Obituary 118
Brief entry 111
Baxter, Annette Kar 1926- CANR-4
Earlier sketch in CA 1R
Baxter, Batsell Barrett 1916- 33-36R
Baxter, Charles 1947- 57-60
See also CLC 45
Baxter, Craig 1929- CANR-26
Earlier sketches in CA 25-28R, CANR-11
Baxter, Douglas Clark 1942- 85-88
Baxter, Edna May 1890- CAP-1
Earlier sketch in CA 17-18
Baxter, Eric George 1918- 19-20R
Baxter, Eric P(eter) 1913- 9-10R
Baxter, George Owen
See Faust, Frederick (Shiller)
Baxter, Glen 1944- 109
Baxter, Gordon F(rancis), Jr. 1923- CANR-1
Earlier sketch in CA 45-48
Baxter, Hazel
See Rowland, D(onald) S(ydney)
Baxter, Ian F. G. CANR-11
Earlier sketch in CA 23-24R
Baxter, James Finney III 1893-1975 65-68
Baxter, James K(eir) 1926-1972 77-80
See also CLC 14
Baxter, James P(hinney) III 1893-1975
Obituary 57-60
Baxter, James Sidlow 1903- 73-76
Baxter, John 1939- CANR-25
Earlier sketch in CA 29-32R
Baxter, John
See Hunt, E(verette) Howard, Jr.
Baxter, Maurice Glen 1920- 15-16R
Baxter, Michael John 1944- 103
Baxter, Mike
See Baxter, Michael John
Baxter, Patricia E. W. 107
Baxter, Phyllis
See Wallmann, Jeffrey M(iner)
Baxter, Shane V.
See Norwood, Victor G(eorge) C(harles)
Baxter, Stephen B(artow) 1929- 19-20R
Baxter, Valerie
See Meynell, Laurence Walter
Baxter, William F(rancis) 1929- 89-92
Baxter, William T(hreipland) 1906- 107
Bay, Christian 1921- 33-36R
Bay, Howard 1912-1986 81-84
Obituary 121
Bayard, Jean 1923- 114
Baybars, Taner 1936- CANR-4
Earlier sketch in CA 53-56
Bayer, Eleanor
See Perry, Eleanor (Rosenfeld Bayer)
Bayer, Harold
See Gregg, Andrew K.
Bayer, Herbert 1900-1985 Obituary 117
Bayer, Jane E. ?-1985 Obituary 116
See also SATA 44
Bayer, Linda 1948- CANR-26
Earlier sketch in CA 107
Bayer, Oliver Weld
See Perry, Eleanor (Rosenfeld Bayer)
Bayer, Ronald 1943- 106
Bayer, Sylvia
See Glassco, John
Bayer, William 1939- 33-36R
Bayer-Berenbaum, Linda
See Bayer, Linda
Bayerle, Gustav 1931- 53-56
Bayes, Marjorie 1934- 115
Bayes, Ronald H(omer) 1932- CANR-10
Earlier sketch in CA 25-28R
Bayh, Birch E(vans), Jr. 1928- 41-44R
Bayh, Marvella (Hern) 1933-1979 93-96
Obituary 85-88
Bay Laurel, Alicia
See Laurel, Alicia Bay
Baylen, Joseph O(scar) 1920- CANR-10
Earlier sketch in CA 25-28R
Bayles, Ernest E(dward) 1897- 73-76
Bayles, Michael D(ale) 1941- CANR-18
Earlier sketches in CA 49-52, CANR-1
Bayless, John 1913(?)-1983 Obituary 109
Bayless, Kenneth 1913(?)-1972 Obituary 104
Bayless, Raymond 1920- 85-88
Bayley, Barrington J(ohn) 1937- CANR-14
Earlier sketch in CA 37-40R
Bayley, Charles C(alvert) 1907- 33-36R
Bayley, David H(ume) 1933- 15-16R
Bayley, Edwin Richard 1918- 108
Bayley, John (Oliver) 1925- 85-88
Bayley, Monica Worsley 1919- 111
Bayley, Nicola 1949- 118
See also SATA 41
Bayley, Peter Charles 1921- 101
Bayley, Stephen 1951- 106
Bayley, Viola (Powles) 1911- CANR-5
Earlier sketch in CA 7-8R
Baylis, John 1946- CANR-18
Earlier sketch in CA 101
Bayliss, John Clifford 1919- 13-14R
Bayliss, Timothy
See Baybars, Taner
Baylor, Byrd 1924- 81-84
See also SATA 16
See also CLR 3
Baylor, Robert 1925- 13-14R
Bayly, Joseph T(ate) 1920- 17-18R
Baym, Max I. 1895- 41-44R
Baym, Nina 1936- 112
Bayne, David C(owan) 1918- 41-44R
Bayne, Stephen F(ielding), Jr. 1908-1974
Obituary 45-48
Bayne-Jardine, C(olin) C(harles) 1932- 25-28R
Baynes, Cary F. 1873(?)-1977 Obituary 104
Baynes, Dorothy Colston
See Colston-Baynes, Dorothy
Baynes, John (Christopher Malcolm)
1928- 21-22R
Baynes, Ken 1934- Brief entry 110
Baynes, Pauline (Diana) 1922- 120
See also SATA 19
Baynham, Henry (W. F.) 1933- 29-32R
Bayrd, Edwin 1944- 97-100
Bays, Gwendolyn McKee 13-14R
Bazelon, David T. 1923- 17-18R
Bazelon, Irwin 1922- 102
Bazin, Andre 1918-1958 Brief entry 113
Bazin, Germain (Rene Michel) 1907- CANR-12
Earlier sketch in CA 7-8R
Bazin, Herve
See Herve-Bazin, Jean Pierre Marie
Bazin, Nancy Topping 1934- 41-44R
Bazley, Margaret C. 1938- 106
Bb
See Watkins-Pitchford, Denys James
Beach, Bert Beverly 1928- 57-60
Beach, Charles
See Reid, (Thomas) Mayne
Beach, Charles Amory CANR-26
Earlier sketches in CA 19-20, CAP-2
See also SATA 1
Beach, Dale S. 1923- 15-16R
Beach, David (Williams) 1938- 115

Beach, Earl F(rancis) 1912- ... 13-14R
Beach, Edward L(atimer) 1918- ... CANR-6
Earlier sketch in CA 5-6R
See also SATA 12
Beach, Frank Ambrose 1911-1988 ... 110
Obituary ... 125
Beach, Lynn
See Lance, Kathryn
Beach, Mark B. 1937- ... 69-72
Beach, Stewart T(aft) 1899-1979 ... 93-96
Obituary ... 85-88
See also SATA 23
Beach, Sylvia (Woodbridge) 1887-1962 ... 108
See also DLB 4
Beach, Vincent W(oodrow) 1917- ... 33-36R
Beach, (William) Waldo 1916- ... 61-64
Beachcomber
See Morton, John (Cameron Andrieu) Bingham (Michael)
Beachcroft, Nina 1931- ... CANR-19
Earlier sketch in CA 97-100
See also SATA 18
Beachcroft, T(homas) O(wen) 1902- ... CAP-1
Earlier sketch in CA 9-10
Beachey, Duane 1948- ... 112
Beachum, Larry M(ahon) 1948- ... 113
Beachy, Lucille 1935- ... 77-80
Beadell, Len 1923- ... 102
Beadle, Leigh P(atric) 1941- ... 65-68
Beadle, Muriel (McClure Barnett) 1915- ... 21-22R
Beadles, William T(homas) 1902- ... 19-20R
Beagle, Peter S(oyer) 1939- ... CANR-4
Earlier sketch in CA 11-12R
See also DLBY 80
See also CLC 7
Beaglehole, J(ohn) C(awte) 1901-1971 ... CAP-2
Obituary ... 33-36R
Earlier sketch in CA 21-22
Beakley, George Carroll, Jr. 1922- ... CANR-16
Earlier sketches in CA 45-48, CANR-1
Beal, Anthony (Ridley) 1925- ... 9-10R
Beal, George M(elvin) 1917- ... CANR-13
Earlier sketch in CA 23-24R
Beal, Graham W(illiam) J(ohn) 1947- ... 118
Beal, Gwyneth 1943- ... 69-72
Beal, John Robinson 1906(?)-1985
Obituary ... 116
Beal, M. F. 1937- ... 73-76
See also DLBY 81
Beal, Merrill D. 1898- ... CANR-5
Earlier sketch in CA 2R
Beal, Richard S(mith) 1945-1984 ... 122
Obituary ... 114
Beale, Betty ... 73-76
Beale, Calvin L(unsford) 1923- ... 3R
Beale, Christopher Griffin
See Griffin-Beale, Christopher
Beale, Howard 1898- ... 109
Beale, Howard K. 1899-1959 ... DLB-17
Beale, Walter H(enry) 1945- Brief entry ... 118
Bealer, Alex W(inkler III) 1921-1980 ... CANR-2
Obituary ... 97-100
Earlier sketch in CA 45-48
See also SATA 8, 22
Bealer, George Persson ... 113
Beales, Derek (Edward Dawson) 1931- ... CANR-16
Earlier sketch in CA 73-76
Beales, H(ugh) L(ancelot) 1889-1988
Obituary ... 125
Beales, Peter 1936- ... 122
Bealey, (Frank) William 1922- ... CANR-2
Earlier sketch in CA 7-8R
Beall, James Lee 1924- ... CANR-11
Earlier sketch in CA 65-68
Beall, Karen F(riedmann) 1938- ... 106
Beall, Otho T(hompson), Jr. 1908-1977
Obituary ... 113
Beals, Alan R(obin) 1928- ... 37-40R
Beals, Carleton 1893-1979 ... CANR-3
Earlier sketch in CA 4R
See also SATA 12
Beals, Frank Lee 1881-1972 ... 7-8R
Obituary ... 103
See also SATA 26
Beals, Ralph L(eon) 1901- ... 23-24R
Beam, Alvin Wesley 1912-1982 Obituary ... 107
Beam, C. Richard ... 45-48
Beam, George D(ahl) 1934- ... 69-72
Beam, Philip C(onway) 1910- ... 97-100
Beaman, Joyce Proctor 1931- ... 29-32R
Beame, Rona 1934- ... 45-48
See also SATA 12
Beamer, (George) Charles (Jr.) 1942- ... 121
See also SATA 43
Beamish, Annie O'Meara de Vic 1883- ... 15-16R
Beamish, Anthony Hamilton ?-1983
Obituary ... 109
Beamish, Huldine V. 1904- ... CAP-1
Earlier sketch in CA 13-14
Beamish, Noel de Vic
See Beamish, Annie O'Meara de Vic
Beamish, Tufton Victor Hamilton
See Chelwood, Tufton Victor Hamilton
Bean, Constance A(ustin) ... 41-44R
Bean, George E(wart) 1903- ... 25-28R
Bean, Henry (Schorr) 1945- ... 109
Bean, Keith F(enwick) 1911- ... CAP-1
Earlier sketch in CA 11-12
Bean, Lowell John 1931- ... 41-44R
Bean, Mabel Greene 1898(?)-1977
Obituary ... 73-76
Bean, Normal
See Burroughs, Edgar Rice
Bean, Orson 1928- ... 77-80
Bean, Walton (Elbert) 1914- ... 25-28R
Bean, William B(ennett) 1909- ... 111
Beaney, Jane
See Udall, Jan Beaney
Bear, Bullen
See Donnelly, Austin Stanislaus
Bear, David 1949- ... 106
Bear, Greg(ory Dale) 1951- ... 113
Bear, James A(dam), Jr. 1919- ... 21-22R
Bear, Joan 1918- ... 57-60
Bear, John (Boris) 1938- ... CANR-13
Earlier sketch in CA 73-76
Bear, Roberta Meyer 1942- ... 21-22R
Bearce, George D(onham) 1922- ... 11-12R
Bearchell, Charles 1925- ... 93-96
Beard, Belle Boone 1898-1984 Obituary ... 114
Beard, Charles A(ustin) 1874-1948
Brief entry ... 115
See also SATA 18
See also DLB 17
See also TCLC 15
Beard, Dan(iel Carter) 1859-1941 ... SATA-22
Beard, Estle S. 1908-1983 ... 111
Beard, Helen 1931- ... 113
Beard, James (Andrews) 1903-1985 ... CANR-15
Obituary ... 114
Earlier sketch in CA 81-84
Beard, James F(ranklin) 1919- ... 3R
Beard, Marna L(ouise) 1942- ... 112
Beard, Peter H. 1938- ... 13-14R
Beard, Robert Eric 1911-1983 Obituary ... 111
Bearden, James Hudson 1933- ... 23-24R
Bearden, Romare (Howard) 1914(?)-1988 ... 102
Obituary ... 125
See also SATA 22
Beardmore, Cedric
See Beardmore, George
Beardmore, George 1908-1979 ... 69-72
Obituary ... 126
See also SATA 20
Beardslee, John W(alter) III 1914- ... 37-40R
Beardsley, Charles Noel 1914- ... CANR-2
Earlier sketch in CA 4R
Beardsley, (John) Douglas 1941- ... 113
Beardsley, Elizabeth Lane ... 29-32R
Beardsley, John 1952- ... 109
Beardsley, (Betty) Lou 1925- ... 118
Beardsley, Monroe C(urtis) 1915-1985 ... 17-18R
Obituary ... 117
Beardsley, Richard K(ing) 1918-1978 ... CANR-11
Obituary ... 77-80
Earlier sketch in CA 17-18R
Beardsley, Theodore S(terling), Jr. 1930- ... 33-36R
Beardsworth, Millicent Monica 1915- ... 103
Beardwood, Roger 1932- ... 89-92
Beardwood, Valerie Fairfield ... 5-6R
Beare, Francis W(right) 1902- ... CANR-16
Earlier sketch in CA 4R
Beare, (M.A.) Nikki 1928- ... 37-40R
Bearman, Jane (Ruth) 1917- ... 105
See also SATA 29
Bearne, C(olin) G(erald) 1939- ... 97-100
Bearss, Edwin C(ole) 1923- ... CANR-10
Earlier sketch in CA 25-28R
Beaser, Herbert W. 1913(?)-1979
Obituary ... 85-88
Beasley, Jerry C(arr) 1940- ... CANR-14
Earlier sketch in CA 37-40R
Beasley, M. Robert 1918- ... 9-10R
Beasley, Maurine 1936- ... CANR-20
Earlier sketch in CA 104
Beasley, Rex 1925- ... 11-12R
Beasley, W(illiam) Conger, Jr. 1940- ... CANR-4
Earlier sketch in CA 53-56
Beasley, W(illiam) G(erald) 1919- ... 53-56
Beasley-Murray, George Raymond 1916- ... 65-68
Beason, Robert G(ayle) 1927- ... 114
Beath, Paul Robert 1905- ... 7-8R
Beaton, Alan A. 1947- ... 123
Beaton, Anne
See Washington, (Catherine) Marguerite Beauchamp
Beaton, Cecil (Walter Hardy) 1904-1980 ... 81-84
Obituary ... 93-96
Beaton, George
See Brenan, (Edward Fitz)Gerald
Beaton, (Donald) Leonard 1929-1971 ... CANR-4
Obituary ... 29-32R
Earlier sketch in CA 7-8R
Beaton, M. C.
See Chesney, Marion
Beaton-Jones, Cynon 1921- ... 7-8R
Beattie, Ann 1947- ... 81-84
See also DLBY 82
See also CLC 8, 13, 18, 40
Beattie, Carol 1918- ... 29-32R
Beattie, Edward J(ames), Jr. 1918- ... 106
Beattie, Jessie Louise 1896- ... CANR-17
Earlier sketches in CA 7-8R, CANR-2
Beattie, John (Hugh Marshall) 1915- ... 37-40R
Beattie, Sally 1941- ... 122
Beattie, Susan 1938- ... 123
Beatts, Anne Patricia 1947- ... 102
Beatty, Elizabeth
See Holloway, Teresa (Bragunier)
Beatty, Hetty Burlingame 1907-1971 ... 4R
Obituary ... 103
See also SATA 5
Beatty, Jerome, Jr. 1918- ... CANR-3
Earlier sketch in CA 9-10R
See also SATA 5
Beatty, John (Louis) 1922-1975 ... CANR-4
Obituary ... 57-60
Earlier sketch in CA 7-8R
See also SATA 6, 25
Beatty, Morgan 1902-1975 Obituary ... 61-64
Beatty, Patricia Robbins 1922- ... CANR-3
Earlier sketch in CA 4R
See also SATA 1, 30
See also SAAS 4
Beatty, Rita Gray 1930- ... 45-48
Beatty, Robert Owen 1924-1976 Obituary ... 69-72
Beatty, Warren
See Beaty, Warren
Beatty, William Alfred 1912-19(?) ... CAP-1
Earlier sketch in CA 13-14
Beatty, William K(ave) 1926- ... 41-44R
Beaty, Betty ... CANR-18
Earlier sketch in CA 73-76
Beaty, (Arthur) David 1919- ... CANR-18
Earlier sketches in CA 4R, CANR-2
Beaty, Janice J(anowski) 1930- ... 15-16R
Beaty, Jerome 1924- ... 85-88
Beaty, Shirley MacLean 1934- ... 103
Beaty, Warren 1937(?)- ... 126
Brief entry ... 109
Beaubien, Anne K(athleen) 1947- ... 123
Beauchamp, Edward R(obert) 1933- ... 61-64
Beauchamp, Gorman 1938- ... 121
Beauchamp, Kathleen Mansfield 1888-1923 Brief entry ... 104
Beauchamp, Kenneth L(loyd) 1939- ... 29-32R
Beauchamp, Pat
See Washington, (Catherine) Marguerite Beauchamp
Beauchamp, Tom L. 1939- ... CANR-13
Earlier sketch in CA 73-76
Beauchemin, Yves 1941- ... DLB-60
Beauclerk, Helen De Vere 1892-1969
Obituary ... 114
Beaudoin, Kenneth Lawrence 1913- ... 29-32R
Beaudouin, John T(yrell) 1920-
Brief entry ... 114
Beaufitz, William
See Critchley, Julian (Michael Gordon)
Beaufort, John (David) 1912- ... 104
Beaufre, Andre 1902-1975 ... 65-68
Obituary ... 57-60
Beaulac, Willard L(eon) 1899- ... 11-12R
Beaulieu, Victor-Levy 1945- ... DLB-53
Beauman, E(ric) Bentley ... 9-10R
Beauman, Katharine (Burgoyne) Bentley 1902- ... 102
Beaumont, Beverly
See von Block, Sylvia
Beaumont, Charles 1929-1967 ... 5-6R
Obituary ... 103
Beaumont, Charles Allen 1926- ... 3R
Beaumont, Cyril William 1891-1976 ... 13-14R
Obituary ... 65-68
Beaumont, Francis 1584(?)-1616 ... DLB-58
Beaumont, George Ernest 1888-1974
Obituary ... 49-52
Beaumont, Keith (Stanley) 1944- ... 118
Beaumont, Roger A(lban) 1935- ... 65-68
Beauregard, Erving E. 1920- ... 111
Beaurline, L(ester) A(lbert) 1927- ... 21-22R
Beausang, Michael F(rancis), Jr. 1936- ... 57-60
Beausay, Florence E(dith) 1911- ... 21-22R
Beausoleil, Beau 1941- ... CANR-14
Earlier sketch in CA 81-84
Beauvais, Robert 1911- ... 104
Beauvoir, Simone (Lucie Ernestine Marie Bertrand) de 1908-1986 ... 11-12R
Obituary ... 118
See also DLB 72
See also DLBY 86
See also CLC 1, 2, 4, 8, 14, 31, 44, 50
Beaver, Bruce (Victor) 1928- ... 97-100
Beaver, Frank E(ugene) 1938- ... 114
Beaver, Harold (Lothar) 1929- ... 21-22R
Beaver, (Jack) Patrick 1923- ... 33-36R
Beaver, Paul (Eli) 1953- ... 115
Beaver, R(obert) Pierce 1906- ... CANR-7
Earlier sketch in CA 5-6R
Beaver, Stanley H(enry) 1907-1984
Obituary ... 114
Beaverbrook, William Maxwell Aitken 1879-1964 ... 103
Obituary ... 89-92
Beazley, John Davidson 1885-1970
Obituary ... 115
Bebb, Russ(ell H.), Jr. 1930- ... 49-52
Bebell, Mildred Hoyt 1909- ... CAP-1
Earlier sketch in CA 15-16
Bebey, Francis 1929- ... CANR-25
Earlier sketch in CA 69-72
See also BW
Bebler, A(lex) Anton 1937- ... CANR-2
Earlier sketch in CA 49-52
Becerra, Rosina M. 1939- ... 122
Becher, Ulrich 1910- ... 101
See also DLB 69
Bechervaise, John Mayston 1910- ... CANR-5
Earlier sketch in CA 15-16R
Bechhoefer, Bernhard G. 1904- ... 2R
Bechko, Peggy Anne 1950- ... CANR-2
Earlier sketch in CA 49-52
Becht, J. Edwin 1918- ... 29-32R
Bechtel, Louise Seaman 1894-1985 ... CAP-2
Obituary ... 116
Earlier sketch in CA 29-32
See also SATA 4, 43
Bechtel, Paul M(oyer) 1909- ... 116
Bechtol, William M(ilton) 1931- ... 49-52
Beck, Aaron T(emkin) 1921- ... CANR-11
Earlier sketch in CA 23-24R
Beck, Alan M(arshall) 1942- ... CANR-21
Earlier sketch in CA 45-48
Beck, Barbara L. 1927- ... 17-18R
See also SATA 12
Beck, Calvin Thomas 1937- ... 97-100
Beck, Carl 1930- ... CANR-1
Earlier sketch in CA 1R
Beck, Clive 1939- ... 49-52
Beck, Doc
See Beck, Earl Clifton
Beck, Earl Clifton 1891-1977 Obituary ... 110
Beck, Earl R(ay) 1916- ... 33-36R
Beck, Emily M(orison) 1915- ... 114
Beck, Evelyn Torton 1933- ... CANR-13
Earlier sketch in CA 33-36R
Beck, Harry
See Paine, Lauran (Bosworth)
Beck, Helen L(ouise) 1908- ... 73-76
Beck, Henry G(abriel) J(ustin) 1914- ... 11-12R
Beck, Horace P(almer) 1920- ... 77-80
Beck, Hubert (F.) 1931- ... CANR-12
Earlier sketch in CA 29-32R
Beck, James (H.) 1930- ... 85-88
Beck, James Murray 1914- ... 101
Beck, Joan (Wagner) 1923- Brief entry ... 118
Beck, John Jacob, Jr. 1941- ... 53-56
Beck, Julian 1925-1985 ... 102
Obituary ... 117
Beck, Leslie 1907(?)-1978 Obituary ... 104
Beck, Lewis White 1913- ... CANR-2
Earlier sketch in CA 7-8R
Beck, M. Susan 1941- ... 113
Beck, Marilyn (Mohr) 1928- ... 65-68
Beck, Pamela 1954- ... 120
Beck, Paul 1933(?)-1985 Obituary ... 116
Beck, Phineas
See Chamberlain, Samuel
Beck, Robert Edward 1941- ... 104
Beck, Robert H(olmes) 1918- ... 29-32R
Beck, Robert Nelson 1924-1980 ... CANR-4
Earlier sketch in CA 3R
Beck, Thomas D(avis) 1943- ... 57-60
Beck, Toni 1925- ... 57-60
Beck, Victor Emanuel 1894-1963 ... 5-6R
Beck, Warren 1896-1986 ... CANR-3
Obituary ... 119
Earlier sketch in CA 1R
Beck, Warren Albert 1918- ... CANR-6
Earlier sketch in CA 5-6R
Beckel, Graham 1913- ... 3R
Beckelhymer, (Paul) Hunter 1919- ... CANR-3
Earlier sketch in CA 2R
Becker, A(dolph) C(arl), Jr. 1920- ... 65-68
Becker, Abraham S(amuel) 1927- ... 33-36R
Becker, Albert B. 1903-1972 ... CAP-2
Earlier sketch in CA 29-32
Becker, Arthur P(eter) 1918- ... 29-32R
Becker, B. Jay 1904-1987 ... 65-68
Obituary ... 123
Becker, Beril 1901- ... CAP-1
Earlier sketch in CA 9-10
See also SATA 11
Becker, Bill
See Becker, William
Becker, Bruce ... 57-60
Becker, Carl 1873-1945 ... DLB-17
Becker, Carol 1947- ... 124
Becker, Edith C. (Stepien) 1915- ... 15-16R
Becker, Ernest 1925-1974 ... 97-100
Becker, Florence
See Lennon, Florence Becker (Tanenbaum)
Becker, Gary S(tanley) 1930- ... CANR-11
Earlier sketch in CA 61-64
Becker, George J(oseph) 1908- ... CANR-7
Earlier sketch in CA 5-6R
Becker, Harold K(auffman) 1933- ... CANR-13
Earlier sketch in CA 29-32R
Becker, Howard Saul 1928- Brief entry ... 115
Becker, Irving 1945- ... 122
Becker, Jillian (Ruth) 1932- ... CANR-25
Earlier sketch in CA 77-80
Becker, John (Leonard) 1901- ... CAP-1
Earlier sketch in CA 11-12
See also SATA 12
Becker, John E(dward) 1930- ... 49-52
Becker, Joseph M(aria) 1908- ... CANR-7
Earlier sketch in CA 17-18R
Becker, Joyce 1936- ... SATA-39
Becker, Juergen 1932- ... DLB-75
Becker, Jurek 1937- ... 85-88
See also DLB 75
See also CLC 7, 19
Becker, Klaus
See Koch, Kurt E(mil)
Becker, Lawrence C(arlyle) 1939- ... 85-88
Becker, Lucille F(rackman) 1929- ... CANR-12
Earlier sketch in CA 29-32R
Becker, Manning H. 1922- ... 13-14R
Becker, Marion Rombauer 1903-1976 ... 37-40R
Obituary ... 69-72
Becker, Marvin Burton 1922- ... 107
Becker, May Lamberton 1873-1958
Brief entry ... 112
See also SATA 33
Becker, Murray 1909(?)-1986 Obituary ... 118
Becker, Olga
See Frank, Rudolf
Becker, Paula Lee 1941- ... 19-20R
Becker, Peter 1921- ... 53-56
Becker, Robert O(tto) 1923- ... 123
Becker, Robin 1951- ... 110
Becker, Ruby Wirt 1915- ... 33-36R
Becker, Russell J(ames) 1923- ... 37-40R
Becker, Samuel L(eo) 1923- ... CANR-7
Earlier sketch in CA 15-16R
Becker, Seymour 1934- ... 25-28R
Becker, Stephen (David) 1927- ... CANR-3
Earlier sketch in CA 7-8R
See also CAAS 1
Becker, Ted
See Becker, Theodore L(ewis)

Becker, Theodore L(ewis) 1932-
Brief entry 116
Becker, Thomas W(illiam) 1933- 7-8R
Becker, Walter 1950- CLC-26
Becker, Wesley C(lemence) 1928- 33-36R
Becker, William 1903(?)-1983 Obituary 110
Becker, William H(enry) 1943- 125
Beckerman, Bernard 1921-1985 .... CANR-19
Obituary 117
Earlier sketch in CA 4R
Beckerman, Wilfred 1925- CANR-7
Earlier sketch in CA 17-18R
Beckett, Ian F(rederick) W(illiam) 1950- 120
Beckett, J(ames) C(amlin) 1912-
Brief entry 114
Beckett, John A(ngus) 1916- 33-36R
Beckett, Kenneth A(lbert) 1929- CANR-10
Earlier sketch in CA 65-68
Beckett, Lucy 1942- 49-52
Beckett, Ralph L(awrence) 1923- 7-8R
Beckett, Ronald Brymer 1891- 7-8R
Beckett, Samuel (Barclay) 1906- 7-8R
See also DLB 13, 15
See also CLC 1, 2, 3, 4, 6, 9, 10, 11, 14, 18, 29
Beckett, Sheilah 1913- SATA-33
Beckey, Fred W(olfgang) 1923- 109
Beckford, George L(eslie Fitz-Gerald) 1934- 97-100
Beckford, William 1760-1844 .... DLB-39
Beckham, Barry (Earl) 1944- CANR-26
Earlier sketch in CA 29-32R
See also DLB 33
Beckham, Stephen Dow 1941- CANR-12
Earlier sketch in CA 61-64
Beckhart, Benjamin Haggott 1897-1975
Obituary 57-60
Beckingham, Charles Fraser 1914- 61-64
Beckinsale, Monica 1914- 69-72
Beckinsale, Robert Percy 1908- CANR-2
Earlier sketch in CA 7-8R
Becklake, Sue 1943- 120
Beckler, Marion Floyd 1889- CAP-1
Earlier sketch in CA 11-12
Beckles Willson, Robina (Elizabeth) 1930- CANR-20
Earlier sketches in CA 13-14R, CANR-5
Beckman, Aldo Bruce 1934- 73-76
Beckman, Delores 1914- 121
See also SATA 51
Beckman, Gail McKnight 1938- 53-56
Beckman, Gunnel 1910- CANR-15
Earlier sketch in CA 33-36R
See also SATA 6
See also CLC 26
Beckman, Kaj
See Beckman, Karin
Beckman, Karin 1913- SATA-45
Beckman, Patti
See Boeckman, Patti
Beckman, Per (Frithiof) 1913- SATA-45
Beckman, Robert C(harles) 1934- 120
Beckmann, David M(ilton) 1948- CANR-8
Earlier sketch in CA 61-64
Beckmann, George Michael 1926- 7-8R
Beckmann, Martin J(osef) 1924- 37-40R
Beckmann, Petr 1924- 69-72
Beckner, Weldon (Earnest) 1933- 33-36R
Beckovic, Matija 1939- 33-36R
Beckson, Karl 1926- CANR-2
Earlier sketch in CA 5-6R
Beckwith, B(rainerd) K(ellogg) 1902- 73-76
Beckwith, Burnham Putnam 1904- 33-36R
Beckwith, Charles E(milio) 1917- 37-40R
Beckwith, John Gordon 1918- 9-10R
Beckwith, Lillian
See Comber, Lillian
Beckwith, Paul 1905-1975 Obituary 113
Beckwith, Yvonne 106
Bedard, Michelle
See MacKenzie, Joan Finnigan
Bedard, Patrick Joseph 1941- 112
Bedau, Hugo Adam 1926- CANR-19
Earlier sketches in CA 11-12R, CANR-4
Bedall, Barbara G(ould) 1919- 33-36R
Beddall-Smith, Charles John 1916- 15-16R
Beddoe, Ellaruth
See Elkins, Ella Ruth
Beddoes, Richard H(erbert) 1926- 37-40R
Bede, Andrew
See Beha, Ernest
Bede, Jean-Albert 1903-1977 Obituary 69-72
Bedeian, Arthur G(eorge) 1946- 110
Bedell, George C(hester) 1928- 41-44R
Bedell, L. Frank 1888- CAP-1
Earlier sketch in CA 15-16
Bedell, Madelon (Jane Berns) 1922(?)-1986 Obituary 119
Bedells, Phyllis 1893-1985 Obituary 116
Bedford, A. N.
See Watson, Jane Werner
Bedford, Ann
See Rees, Joan
Bedford, Annie North
See Watson, Jane Werner
Bedford, Charles Harold 1929- 57-60
Bedford, Donald F.
See Fearing, Kenneth (Flexner)
Bedford, Emmett G(runer) 1922- 45-48
Bedford, Henry F(rederick) 1931- 11-12R
Bedford, Kenneth
See Paine, Lauran (Bosworth)
Bedford, Norton M(oore) 1916- 5-6R
Bedford, Sybille 1911- 11-12R
Bediako, Kwabena Asare
See Konadu, S(amuel) A(sare)
Bedikian, Antriganik A. 1886(?)-1980
Obituary 93-96
Bedinger, Margery 1891- 57-60
Bedinger, Singleton B(erry) 1907- 49-52
Bedini, Silvio A. 1917- CANR-13
Earlier sketch in CA 33-36R
Bednarik, Charles (Philip) 1925- 77-80
Bednarik, Chuck
See Bednarik, Charles (Philip)
Bedoukian, Kerop 1907-1981 93-96
See also SATA 53
Bedoyere, Michael De La
See De La Bedoyere, Michael
Bedrij, Orest (John) 1933- CANR-16
Earlier sketch in CA 85-88
Bedsole, Adolph 1914- 15-16R
Bee, Clair (Francis) 1900-1983 .... 4R
Obituary 109
Bee, (John) David (Ashford) 1931- 17-18R
Bee, Helen L. 1939- CANR-16
Earlier sketch in CA 89-92
Bee, Jay
See Brainerd, John W(hiting)
Bee, Robert L(awrence) 1938- 113
Beebe, (Ida) Ann 1919- 41-44R
Beebe, B(urdetta) F(aye)
See Johnson, B(urdetta) F(aye)
See also SATA 1
Beebe, Frank L(yman) 1914- 89-92
Beebe, Frederick S(essions) 1914-1973
Obituary 41-44R
Beebe, H. Keith 1921- 29-32R
Beebe, Lucius 1902-1966 Obituary 25-28R
Beebe, Maurice (Laverne) 1926- CANR-1
Earlier sketch in CA 4R
Beebe, Ralph K(enneth) 1932- 33-36R
Beebe, (Charles) William 1877-1962 73-76
See also SATA 19
Beeby, Betty 1923- SATA-25
Beeby, C(larence) E(dward) 1902- 109
Beech, George T(homas) 1931- 11-12R
Beech, Harold Reginald 1925- 25-28R
Beech, Keyes 1913- 33-36R
Beech, Robert (Paul) 1940- 33-36R
Beech, Webb
See Butterworth, W(illiam) E(dmund III)
Beecham, Justin
See Wintle, Justin (Beecham)
Beecham, Thomas 1879-1961 Obituary 112
Beechcroft, William
See Hallstead, William F(inn III)
Beecher, Catharine Esther 1800-1878 .... DLB-1
Beecher, Henry Ward 1813-1887 .... DLB-3, 43
Beecher, John 1904-1980 .... CANR-8
Obituary 105
Earlier sketch in CA 5-6R
See also CLC 6
See also AITN 1
Beecher, William (M.) 1933- 65-68
Beechert, Edward D. 1920- 124
Beechhold, Henry F(rank) 1928- 33-36R
Beechick, Ruth 1925- CANR-25
Earlier sketch in CA 108
Beeching, Jack 1922- CANR-13
Earlier sketch in CA 21-22R
See also SATA 14
Beechy, Winifred
See Beechy, Winifred Nelson
Beechy, Winifred Nelson 1915- 116
Beecroft, John William Richard 1902-1966 .... 5-6R
Beedell, Suzanne (Mollie) 1921- CANR-20
Earlier sketch in CA 69-72
Beeding, Francis
See Palmer, John (Leslie) and Saunders, Hilary Aidan St. George
Beegle, Charles William 1928- 106
Beegle, Dewey Maurice 1919- 5-6R
Beegle, J(oseph) Allan 1918- 119
Beek, Martin(us) A(drianus) 1909- 13-14R
Beekman, Allan 1913- 33-36R
Beekman, E(ric) M(ontague) 1939- CANR-14
Earlier sketch in CA 33-36R
Beekman, John 1918- 61-64
Beekman, Ross
See Dey, Frederic (Merrill) Van Rensselaer
Beeks, Graydon 1919- 65-68
Beeler, Nelson F(rederick) 1910- 69-72
See also SATA 13
Beeman, Richard R(oy) 1942- 77-80
Beer, Barrett L(ynn) 1936- 49-52
Beer, Edith Lynn 1930- CANR-11
Earlier sketch in CA 61-64
Beer, Eloise C. S. 1903- 13-14R
Beer, Ethel S(ophia) 1897-1975 .... CAP-2
Obituary 57-60
Earlier sketch in CA 25-28
Beer, Francis Anthony 1939- CANR-10
Earlier sketch in CA 25-28R
Beer, George L. 1872-1920 .... DLB-47
Beer, Jeanette (Mary Ayres) 124
Beer, John B(ernard) 1926- CANR-23
Earlier sketches in CA 5-6R, CANR-7
Beer, Kathleen Costello 1926- 25-28R
Beer, Lawrence W(ard) 1932- 37-40R
Beer, Lisl
See Beer, Eloise C. S.
Beer, Patricia 1924- CANR-13
Earlier sketch in CA 61-64
See also DLB 40
Beer, Ralph (Robert) 1947- 120
Beer, Samuel Hutchison 1911- 61-64
Beer, Vic
See Bird, Vivian
Beer, William Reed 1943- 112
Beerbohm, Henry Maximilian 1872-1956
Brief entry 104
See also DLB 34
See also TCLC 1, 24
Beers, Burton F(loyd) 1927- CANR-19
Earlier sketch in CA 4R
Beers, Dorothy Sands 1917- 49-52
See also SATA 9
Beers, Henry A. 1847-1926 .... DLB-71
Beers, Henry Putney 1907- 15-16R
Beers, Lorna 1897- 49-52
See also SATA 14
Beers, Paul Benjamin 1931- 102
Beers, V(ictor) Gilbert 1928- CANR-16
Earlier sketches in CA 49-52, CANR-1
See also SATA 9
Beery, Mary 1907- 5-6R
Beesly, Patrick 1913-1986 .... CANR-15
Obituary 120
Earlier sketch in CA 85-88
Beeson, Trevor Randall 1926- 93-96
Beeton, (Douglas) Ridley 1929- 93-96
Beevers, John (Leonard) 1911-1975 61-64
Beezley, P(aul) C. 1895- 7-8R
Beezley, William H(oward Taft) 1942- 49-52
Befu, Harumi 1930- 53-56
Beg, Toran
See McKillop, Norman
Begg, A(lexander) Charles 1912- 102
Begg, Howard Bolton 1896- 5-6R
Begg, Neil Colquhoun 1915- 102
Beggs, David W(hiteford) III 1931-1966 .... CAP-1
Earlier sketch in CA 15-16
Beggs, Donald L(ee) 1941- 33-36R
Beggs, Edward Larry 1933- 89-92
Begiebing, Robert J(ohn) 1946- 122
Begin, Menachem 1913- Brief entry 109
Begin, Menahem
See Begin, Menachem
Begleiter, Henri 1935- 119
Begley, James 1929- 25-28R
Begley, Kathleen A(nne) 1948- 77-80
See also SATA 21
Begnal, Michael H(enry) 1939- 73-76
Begner, Edith CANR-3
Earlier sketch in CA 3R
Beha, Ernest 1908- CAP-1
Earlier sketch in CA 13-14
Beha, Sister Helen Marie 1926- 21-22R
Behan, Brendan 1923-1964 73-76
See also DLB 13
See also CLC 1, 8, 11, 15
Behan, Leslie
See Gottfried, Theodore Mark
Behara, Devendra Nath 1940- 41-44R
Behee, John 1933- 112
Behle, William H(arroun) 1909- 7-8R
Behler, Ernst 1928- 41-44R
Behlmer, George K(inkel) 1948- 123
Behlmer, Rudy 1926- CANR-8
Earlier sketch in CA 57-60
Behm, Marc 1925- 101
Behm, William H(erman), Jr. 1922- 15-16R
Behme, Robert Lee 1924- 57-60
Behn, Aphra 1640(?)-1689 .... DLB-39
Behn, Harry 1898-1973 .... CANR-5
Obituary 53-56
Earlier sketch in CA 7-8R
See also SATA 2, 34
See also DLB 61
Behn, Noel 1928- Brief entry 116
Behney, John Bruce 1905- 101
Behnke, Charles A(lbert) 1891- CAP-2
Earlier sketch in CA 19-20
Behnke, Frances L. 33-36R
See also SATA 8
Behnke, John 1945- 69-72
Behnke, Leo 1933- 111
Behr, Edward 1926- CANR-3
Earlier sketch in CA 2R
Behr, Joyce 1929- SATA-15
Behr, Marion 1939- 105
Behrend, Jeanne 1911- 19-20R
Behrens, Earl (Charles) 1892-1985
Obituary 116
Behrens, Helen Kindler 1922- 61-64
Behrens, Herman D(aniel) 1901- 33-36R
Behrens, John C. 1933- CANR-14
Earlier sketch in CA 37-40R
Behrens, June York 1925- CANR-24
Earlier sketches in CA 17-18R, CANR-8
See also SATA 19
Behrens, Roy R(ichard) 1946- 110
Behrman, Carol H(elen) 1925- CANR-22
Earlier sketches in CA 61-64, CANR-7
See also SATA 14
Behrman, Cynthia F(ansler) 1931- 123
Behrman, Daniel 1923- 65-68
Behrman, Jack N(ewton) 1922- 29-32R
Behrman, Lucy Creevey
See Creevey, Lucy E.
Behrman, S(amuel) N(athaniel) 1893-1973 .... CAP-1
Obituary 45-48
Earlier sketch in CA 15-16
See also DLB 7, 44
See also CLC 40
Behrstock, Barry 1948- 106
Beichman, Arnold 1913- 49-52
Beichner, Paul E(dward) 1912- 33-36R
Beier, Ernst G(unter) 1916- 21-22R
Beier, Ulli 1922- CANR-4
Earlier sketch in CA 9-10R
Beigel, Allan 1940- 101
Beigel, Herbert 1944- 97-100
Beigel, Hugo George 1897- 37-40R
Beik, Paul H(arold) 1915- 15-16R
Beik, William (Humphrey) 1941- 123
Beilenson, Edna 1909-1981 85-88
Obituary 103
Beilenson, Laurence W. 1899-1988 .... 29-32R
Obituary 125
Beiler, Edna 1923- CANR-1
Earlier sketch in CA 4R
Beilharz, Edwin A(lanson) 1907-1986 .... 33-36R
Obituary 120
Beim, Norman 1923- 85-88
Beine, George Holmes 1893- 93-96
Beineix, Jean-Jacques 1946- 124
Beiner, Ronald 1953- 117
Beirne, Brother Killian 1896- 21-22R
Beirne, Gerald E(dward) 1936- 118
Beirne, Joseph Anthony 1911-1974 45-48
Obituary 53-56
Beiser, Arthur 1931- 93-96
See also SATA 22
Beiser, Germaine 1931- SATA-11
Beisner, Robert L(ee) 1936- 25-28R
Beissel, Henry Eric 1929- CANR-10
Earlier sketch in CA 65-68
Beisser, Arnold R(ay) 1925- 25-28R
Beistle, Shirley
See Climo, Shirley
Beit-Hallahmi, Benjamin 1943- 105
Beitler, Ethel Jane (Heinkel) 1906- CANR-2
Earlier sketch in CA 5-6R
Beitler, Stanley (Samuel) 1924- 5-6R
Beitz, Charles R(ichard) 1949- CANR-1
Earlier sketch in CA 49-52
Beitzell, Edwin Warfield 1905(?)-1984
Obituary 114
Beitzell, Robert (E.) 1930- Brief entry 115
Beitzinger, A(lfons) J(oseph) 1918- 45-48
Beizer, Boris 1934- 105
Beja, Morris 1935- 29-32R
Bejerot, Nils 1921- 29-32R
Bekessy, Jean
See Habe, Hans
Bekker, Hugo 1925- 41-44R
Bekker-Nielsen, Hans 1933- CANR-16
Earlier sketch in CA 25-28R
Belair, Felix, Jr. 1907-1978 Obituary 77-80
Belair, Richard L. 1934- 15-16R
See also SATA 45
Belaney, Archibald Stansfeld 1888-1938
Brief entry 114
See also SATA 24
Belanger, Jerome D(avid) 1938- 69-72
Belasco, David 1853-1931 Brief entry 104
See also DLB 7
See also TCLC 3
Belcastro, Joseph 1910- CAP-2
Earlier sketch in CA 19-20
Belch, Caroline Jean 1916- 45-48
Belchem, David
See Belchem, R(onald) F(rederick) K(ing)
Belchem, R(onald) F(rederick) K(ing) 1911-1981 122
Obituary 108
Belcher, Jerry 1930-1987 Obituary 124
Belcheva, Elisaveta 1893- CLC-10
Belden, Gail
See Belden, Louise Conway
Belden, Louise Conway 1910- 104
Belden, Wilanne Schneider 1925- CANR-23
Earlier sketch in CA 106
Belding, Robert E(dward) 1911- 33-36R
Beldone, Phil "Cheech"
See Ellison, Harlan
Belehradek, Jan 1896-1980 Obituary 97-100
Beleno
See Azuela, Mariano
Belew, M. Wendell 1922- 33-36R
Belfer, Nancy 1930- 85-88
Belfield, Eversley (Michael Gallimore) 1918- CANR-11
Earlier sketch in CA 25-28R
Belfiglio, Valentine J(ohn) 1934- CANR-11
Earlier sketch in CA 49-52
Belford, Lee A(rcher) 1913- 19-20R
Belfrage, Cedric 1904- CANR-3
Earlier sketch in CA 11-12R
Belfrage, Sally 1936- 105
Bel Geddes, Joan
See Geddes, Joan Bel
Belgion, (Harold) Montgomery 1892-1973 .... CAP-1
Earlier sketch in CA 13-14
Belgum, David 1922- CANR-6
Earlier sketch in CA 13-14R
Belin, David W. 1928- 85-88
Beling, Willard A(dolf) 1919- 53-56
Belinkov, Arkady Viktorovich 1922(?)-1970 Obituary 29-32R
Belisle, Louis-Alexandre 1902-1985
Obituary 117
Belitsky, A(braham) Harvey 1929- 33-36R
Belitt, Ben 1911- CANR-7
Earlier sketch in CA 13-14R
See also CAAS 4
See also DLB 5
See also CLC 22
Belk, Fred Richard 1937- 115
Belkin, Gary S(tuart) 1945- 114
Belkin, Samuel 1911-1976 .... CANR-6
Obituary 65-68
Earlier sketch in CA 2R
Belkind, Allen 1927- 29-32R
Belknap, B. H.
See Ellis, Edward S(ylvester)
Belknap, Boynton
See Ellis, Edward S(ylvester)
Belknap, Boynton, M.D.
See Ellis, Edward S(ylvester)

Belknap, Ivan (Carl) 1916- ... 5-6R
Belknap, Jeremy 1744-1798 ... DLB-30, 37
Belknap, Robert H(arlan) 1917- ... 45-48
Belknap, Robert L(amont) 1929- ... 33-36R
Belknap, S(ally) Yancey 1895- ... CAP-1
Earlier sketch in CA 11-12
Bell, A(rthur) Donald 1920- ... 25-28R
Bell, Adrian (Hanbury) 1901-1980 ... 97-100
Obituary ... 102
Bell, Alan P(aul) 1932- ... CANR-13
Earlier sketch in CA 33-36R
Bell, Anne Olivier 1916- ... 112
Bell, Arthur 1939-1984 ... 85-88
Obituary ... 112
Bell, Barbara Currier 1941- ... 115
Bell, Bernard W(illiam) 1936- Brief entry ... 117
Bell, Betty
See Bell, Lorna Beatrice
Bell, Carol
See Flavell, Carol Willsey Bell
Bell, Carolyn
See Rigoni, Orlando (Joseph)
Bell, Carolyn Shaw 1920- ... 29-32R
Bell, Charles G. 1929- ... 37-40R
Bell, Charles Greenleaf 1916- ... CANR-2
Earlier sketch in CA 4R
Bell, Chip R(ay) 1944- ... 121
Bell, (Arthur) Clive (Howard) 1881-1964 ... 97-100
Obituary ... 89-92
Bell, Colin (John) 1938- ... 29-32R
Bell, Corydon Whitten 1894- ... 7-8R
See also SATA 3
Bell, Daniel 1919- ... CANR-4
Earlier sketch in CA 2R
Bell, David R(obert) 1932- ... 93-96
Bell, David S(heffield) 1945- ... 61-64
Bell, David Victor John 1944- ... CANR-17
Earlier sketches in CA 45-48, CANR-1
Bell, Derrick Albert, Jr. 1930- ... 104
Bell, Earl Hoyt 1903-1963 ... 3R
Bell, Eileen 1907- ... 33-36R
Bell, Elizabeth Rose 1912- ... 106
Bell, Elliot V(allance) 1902-1983 Obituary ... 108
Bell, Emily Mary
See Cason, Mabel Earp
Bell, Gail Winther 1936- ... 41-44R
Bell, Geoffrey (Lakin) 1939- Brief entry ... 114
Bell, Geoffrey Foxall 1896-1984 Obituary ... 111
Bell, Gerald D(ean) 1937- ... 49-52
Bell, Gertrude (Wood) 1911- ... 15-16R
See also SATA 12
Bell, Gina
See Balzano, Jeanne (Koppel)
See also SATA 7
Bell, Gordon Bennett 1934- ... 104
Bell, H(arold) Idris 1879-1967 ... CAP-1
Earlier sketch in CA 13-14
Bell, Harry McAra 1899- ... CAP-1
Earlier sketch in CA 13-14
Bell, Herbert C(lifford Francis) 1881-1966
Obituary ... 113
Bell, Herbert W. 1922- ... 123
Bell, Irene Wood 1944- ... 89-92
Bell, J. Bowyer 1931- ... 19-20R
Bell, Jack L. 1904-1975 ... CANR-6
Obituary ... 61-64
Earlier sketch in CA 1R
Bell, James (Adrian) 1917- ... 73-76
Bell, James B. 1932- ... 101
Bell, James Edward 1941- ... 33-36R
Bell, James K(enton) 1937- ... 25-28R
Bell, James Madison 1826-1902 ... 124
Brief entry ... 122
See also BW
See also DLB 50
Bell, Janet
See Clymer, Eleanor
Bell, John (Donnelly) 1944- ... 97-100
Bell, John
See Johnson, Victor Hugo
Bell, John C. 1902(?)-1981 Obituary ... 103
Bell, John Elderkin 1913- ... 81-84
Bell, John Patrick 1935- ... 101
Bell, Joseph N. 1921- ... 7-8R
Bell, Josephine
See Ball, Doris Bell (Collier)
Bell, Joyce 1920- ... CANR-8
Earlier sketch in CA 57-60
Bell, Joyce Denebrink 1936- ... 19-20R
Bell, L. Nelson 1894-1973 ... CAP-1
Obituary ... 45-48
Earlier sketch in CA 19-20
Bell, Leland V(irgil) 1934- ... 49-52
Bell, Linda R. 1949- ... 117
Bell, Lorna Beatrice 1902- ... 117
Bell, Louise Price ... CAP-1
Earlier sketch in CA 9-10
Bell, Madison (Smartt) 1957- ... 111
See also CLC 41
Bell, Malcolm (H.) 1931- ... 122
Bell, Margaret E(lizabeth) 1898- ... CANR-1
Earlier sketch in CA 2R
See also SATA 2
Bell, Marvin 1937- ... 23-24R
See also DLB 5
See also CLC 8, 31
Bell, Mary Hayley
See Hayley Bell, Mary
Bell, Michael Davitt 1941- ... CANR-15
Earlier sketch in CA 81-84
Bell, Millicent (L.) ... 114
Bell, Neill 1946- ... 118
See also SATA 50
Bell, Norman (Edward) 1899- ... 61-64
See also SATA 11
Bell, Norman W. 1928- ... CANR-1
Earlier sketch in CA 4R
Bell, Oliver (Sydney) 1913- ... 53-56
Bell, Philip W(ilkes) 1924- ... CANR-26
Earlier sketch in CA 29-32R
Bell, Quentin (Claudian Stephen) 1910- ... 57-60
Bell, R(obert) C(harles) 1917- ... CANR-24
Earlier sketches in CA 19-20R, CANR-7
Bell, Raymond Martin 1907- ... 29-32R
See also SATA 13
Bell, Robert (Ivan) 1942- ... 101
Bell, Robert E(ugene) 1914- ... 37-40R
Bell, Robert Roy 1924- ... CANR-1
Earlier sketch in CA 4R
Bell, Robert S(tanley) W(arren) 1871-1921
Brief entry ... 115
See also SATA 27
Bell, Robert Vaughn 1924- ... 110
Bell, Roger 1947- ... 122
Bell, (Caroline) Rose (Buchanan) 1939- ... 29-32R
Bell, Roseann P. 1945- ... 120
Bell, Rudolph M(ark) 1942- ... 45-48
Bell, Sallie Lee ... CANR-1
Earlier sketch in CA 4R
Bell, Sarah Fore 1920- ... 53-56
Bell, Sidney 1929- ... 41-44R
Bell, Stephen (Scott) 1935- ... 65-68
Bell, Thelma Harrington 1896- ... 1R
See also SATA 3
Bell, Thornton
See Fanthorpe, R(obert) Lionel
Bell, Vicars W(alker) 1904- ... CAP-1
Earlier sketch in CA 15-16
Bell, W. L. D.
See Mencken, H(enry) L(ouis)
Bell, Wendell 1924- ... CANR-4
Earlier sketch in CA 3R
Bell, Whitfield Jenks, Jr. 1914- ... 105
Bell, William J. ... AITN-1
Bell, William Stewart 1921- ... 4R
Bell, Winifred 1914- ... CANR-9
Earlier sketch in CA 19-20R
Bellah, James Warner 1899-1976 ... 7-8R
Obituary ... 69-72
Bellah, Robert N(eelly) 1927- ... 21-22R
Bellairs, George
See Blundell, Harold
Bellairs, John 1938- ... CANR-24
Earlier sketches in CA 23-24R, CANR-8
See also SATA 2
Bellak, Leopold 1916- ... CANR-16
Earlier sketch in CA 85-88
Bellamy, Atwood C.
See Mencken, H(enry) L(ouis)
Bellamy, David (James) 1933- Brief entry ... 114
Bellamy, Edward 1850-1898 ... DLB-12
Bellamy, Francis Rufus 1886-1972
Obituary ... 33-36R
Bellamy, Guy 1935- ... CANR-9
Earlier sketch in CA 65-68
Bellamy, Harmon
See Bloom, Herman Irving
Bellamy, James A(ndrew) 1925- ... 49-52
Bellamy, Joe David 1941- ... CANR-15
Earlier sketch in CA 41-44R
Bellamy, Joseph 1719-1790 ... DLB-31
Bellamy, Peter 1914- Brief entry ... 117
Bellamy, Ralph 1904- ... 101
Bellan, Ruben C. 1918- ... 13-14R
Belle, Pamela 1952- ... 115
Beller, Anne Scott ... 77-80
Beller, Elmer Adolph 1894-1980
Obituary ... 97-100
Beller, Jacob 1896- ... CAP-2
Earlier sketch in CA 25-28
Beller, Joel 1926- ... 113
Beller, William Stern 1919- ... 7-8R
Bellerby, (Mary Eireen) Frances Parker
1899-1975 ... 101
Bellhouse, Alan Robert 1914-1980
Obituary ... 108
Belli, Angela 1935- ... 37-40R
Belli, Melvin M(ouron) 1907- ... 104
Bellin, Edward J.
See Kuttner, Henry
Bellingham, Brenda 1931- ... 123
See also SATA 51
Bellingham, Helen Mary Dorothea
See Beauclerk, Helen De Vere
Bellini delle Stelle, Pier Luigi
1920(?)-1984 Obituary ... 111
Bellis, David James 1944- ... 108
Bellman, Richard (Ernest) 1920-1984 ... CANR-12
Obituary ... 112
Earlier sketch in CA 69-72
Bellman, Samuel Irving 1926- ... CANR-7
Earlier sketch in CA 17-18R
Bellman, Willard F. 1920- ... 113
Bell-Metereau, Rebecca 1949- ... 122
Bello, Francis (Cesare) 1917-1987
Obituary ... 121
Belloc, (Joseph) Hilaire (Pierre)
1870-1953 Brief entry ... 106
See also YABC 1
See also DLB 19
See also TCLC 7, 18
Belloc, Joseph Peter Rene Hilaire
See Belloc, (Joseph) Hilaire (Pierre)
Belloc, Joseph Pierre Hilaire
See Belloc, (Joseph) Hilaire (Pierre)
Belloc, M. A.
See Lowndes, Marie Adelaide (Belloc)
Bellochio, Marco 1939- ... 110
Bellocq, Louise
See Boudat, Marie-Louise
Bellonci, Maria 1902-1986 Obituary ... 120
Bellone, Enrico 1938- ... 106
Bellony, Alice 1925- ... 118
Bellony-Rewald, Alice
See Bellony, Alice
Bellot, Leland J(oseph) 1936- Brief entry ... 115
Bellow, Saul 1915- ... 5-6R
See also CABS 1
See also DLB 2, 28
See also DLBY 82
See also DLBD 3
See also CDALB 1941-1968
See also CLC 1, 2, 3, 6, 8, 10, 13, 15,
25, 33, 34
See also AITN 2
Bellows, Fiona (Ann) 1941- ... 115
Bellows, James G(ilbert) 1922- ... 102
Bellows, Roger Marion 1905- ... 4R
Bellows, Thomas J(ohn) 1935- ... 45-48
Bellush, Bernard 1917- Brief entry ... 120
Bell-Villada, Gene Harold 1941- ... 105
Bellville, Cheryl Walsh 1944- ... 109
See also SATA 49
Bellville, Rod 1944- ... 117
Bell-Zano, Gina
See Balzano, Jeanne (Koppel)
See also SATA 7
Belmont, Eleanor Robson 1879-1979
Obituary ... 97-100
Belmont, Georges 1909- ... 29-32R
Belmont, Herman S. 1920- ... 41-44R
Belmonte, Thomas 1946- ... 93-96
Beloff, Max 1913- ... CANR-18
Earlier sketch in CA 7-8R
Beloff, Michael 1942- ... 21-22R
Beloff, Nora 1919- ... 106
Belok, Michael V(ictor) 1923- ... 33-36R
Beloof, Robert 1923- ... 21-22R
Belote, James H(ine) 1922- ... 33-36R
Belote, Julianne 1929- ... 61-64
Belote, William Milton 1922- ... 49-52
Belotserkovsky, Vladimir Naumovich Bill
See Bill-Belotserkovsky, Vladimir
Naumovich
Belous, Russell E. 1925- ... 25-28R
Belozersky, Andrei (Nicolaevich)
1905-1972 Obituary ... 37-40R
Belpre, Pura 1899-1982 ... 73-76
Obituary ... 109
See also SATA 16, 30
Belser, Lee 1925- ... 73-76
Belser, Reimond Karel Maria de 1929- ... CLC-14
Belshaw, Cyril S(hirley) 1921- ... 11-12R
Belshaw, Michael (Horace) 1928- ... 21-22R
Belsky, Dick 1945- ... 122
Belsley, David A(lan) 1939- ... 29-32R
Belth, Joseph M(orton) 1929- ... 112
Belting, Natalia Maree 1915- ... CANR-3
Earlier sketch in CA 1R
See also SATA 6
Belton, John Raynor 1931- ... 69-72
See also SATA 22
Beltran, Alberto 1923- ... SATA-43
Beltran, Miriam 1914- ... 33-36R
Beltran, Pedro (Gerardo) 1897-1979 ... 93-96
Obituary ... 85-88
Belushi, John 1949-1982 Obituary ... 106
Belveal, L(orenzo) Dee 1918- ... 23-24R
Belvedere, Lee
See Grayland, Valerie (Merle Spanner)
Bely, Andrey
See Bugayev, Boris Nikolayevich
See also TCLC 7
Bely, Jeanette L(obach) 1916- ... 33-36R
Belyi, Andrei
See Bugayev, Boris Nikolayevich
Belz, Carl 1937- ... CANR-26
Earlier sketches in CA 29-32R, CANR-11
Belz, Herman (Julius) 1937- ... 65-68
Bemelmans, Ludwig 1898-1962 ... 73-76
See also SATA 15
See also DLB 22
See also CLR 6
Bemis, Samuel Flagg 1891-1973 ... 11-12R
Obituary ... 45-48
See also DLB 17
Bemis, Stephen Edward 1937-1985
Obituary ... 115
Bemister, Henry
See Barrett, Harry B(emister)
Bemmy, Karen (Amy) 1955- ... 123
Bemporad, Jules (Richard) 1937- ... 122
Ben, Ilke
See Harper, Carol Ely
Benagh, Jim 1937- ... CANR-9
Earlier sketch in CA 57-60
Ben-Ami, Shlomo 1943- ... 116
Ben-Amos, Dan 1934- ... CANR-11
Earlier sketch in CA 69-72
Benamou, Michel J(ean) 1929-1978 ... CANR-3
Earlier sketch in CA 5-6R
Benante, Joseph P(hilip) 1936- ... 33-36R
Benarde, Melvin A(lbert) 1923- ... 25-28R
Benardete, Jane Johnson 1930- ... 45-48
Benario, Herbert W. 1929- ... 25-28R
Benarria, Allan
See Goldenthal, Allan Benarria
Benary, Margot
See Benary-Isbert, Margot
Benary-Isbert, Margot 1889-1979 ... CANR-4
Obituary ... 89-92
Earlier sketch in CA 7-8R
See also SATA 2, 21
See also CLC 12
See also CLR 12
Benasutti, Marion 1908- ... 21-22R
See also SATA 6
Benatar, Stephen (Royce) 1937- ... 110
Benavente (y Martinez), Jacinto
1866-1954 Brief entry ... 106
See also TCLC 3
Ben-Avraham, Chofetz Chaim
See Pickering, Stephen
Benbow, Charles (Clarence) 1929- ... 122
Bence, Evelyn ... 110
Bence-Jones, Mark 1930- ... CANR-5
Earlier sketch in CA 13-14R
Bench, Johnny (Lee) 1947- Brief entry ... 113
Benchley, Nathaniel (Goddard)
1915-1981 ... CANR-12
Obituary ... 105
Earlier sketches in CA 4R, CANR-2
See also SATA 3, 25, 28
Benchley, Peter (Bradford) 1940- ... CANR-12
Earlier sketch in CA 17-18R
See also SATA 3
See also CLC 4, 8
See also AITN 2
Benchley, Robert (Charles) 1889-1945
Brief entry ... 105
See also DLB 11
See also TCLC 1
Benda, Harry J(indrich) 1919- ... 11-12R
Benda, Julien 1867-1956 Brief entry ... 120
Bendavid, Avrom 1942- ... 41-44R
Ben-David, Joseph 1920-1986 Obituary ... 118
Bender, Coleman C. 1921- ... 33-36R
Bender, David L(eo) 1936- ... 123
Bender, David R(ay) 1942- ... 102
Bender, Frederic L(awrence) 1943- ... 69-72
Bender, Henry E(dwin), Jr. 1937- ... 33-36R
Bender, James F(rederick) 1905- ... 17-18R
Bender, Jay
See Deindorfer, Robert Greene
Bender, John B(ryant) 1940- ... 65-68
Bender, Louis W. 1927- ... CANR-14
Earlier sketch in CA 33-36R
Bender, Lucy Ellen 1942- ... 25-28R
See also SATA 22
Bender, Marylin 1925- ... CANR-12
Earlier sketch in CA 21-22R
Bender, Norman J(ohn) 1927- ... 118
Bender, Richard 1930- ... 45-48
Bender, Robert M. 1936- ... 33-36R
Bender, Ross Thomas 1929- ... 61-64
Bender, Stephen (Joseph) 1942- ... 61-64
Bender, Thomas 1944- ... CANR-12
Earlier sketch in CA 73-76
Bender, Todd K. 1936- ... CANR-24
Earlier sketches in CA 21-22R, CANR-9
Benderly, Beryl Lieff 1943- ... 108
Bendick, Jeanne 1919- ... CANR-2
Earlier sketch in CA 7-8R
See also SATA 2
See also SAAS 4
See also CLR 5
Bendick, Marc, Jr. 1946- ... 118
Bendick, Robert L(ouis) 1917- ... 61-64
See also SATA 11
Bendiner, Elmer 1916- ... CANR-7
Earlier sketch in CA 57-60
Bendiner, Kenneth Paul 1947- ... 119
Bendiner, Robert 1909- ... 11-12R
Bendit, Gladys Williams 1885- ... CAP-1
Earlier sketch in CA 13-14
Bendit, Laurence John 1898-1974 ... CAP-2
Earlier sketch in CA 25-28
Bendix, Reinhard 1916- ... CANR-4
Earlier sketch in CA 1R
Bendixson, Terence 1934- ... 93-96
Ben-Dov, Meir
See Bernet, Michael M.
Benecke, Gerhard ?-1985 Obituary ... 117
Benedek, Therese 1892-1977 ... 41-44R
Benedetti, Robert L(awrence) 1939- ... 29-32R
Benedetto, Arnold J(oseph) 1916-1966 ... 7-8R
Benedict, Bertram 1892(?)-1978 Obituary ... 77-80
Benedict, Burton 1923- ... 109
Benedict, Dianne 1941- ... 110
Benedict, Dorothy Potter 1889-1979 ... CAP-1
Obituary ... 93-96
Earlier sketch in CA 13-14
See also SATA 11, 23
Benedict, Elizabeth (a pseudonym) 1954-
Brief entry ... 126
Benedict, Joseph
See Dollen, Charles Joseph
Benedict, Lois Trimble 1902-1967 ... CAP-2
Earlier sketch in CA 19-20
See also SATA 12
Benedict, Marion 1923- ... 109
Benedict, Michael Les 1945- ... 45-48
Benedict, Rex 1920- ... 19-20R
See also SATA 8
Benedict, Robert P(hilip) 1924-1986 ... 41-44R
Obituary ... 119
Benedict, Stewart H(urd) 1924- ... 13-14R
See also SATA 26
Benedictus, David (Henry) 1938- ... CANR-24
Earlier sketch in CA 73-76
See also DLB 14
Benedikt, Michael 1935- ... CANR-7
Earlier sketch in CA 15-16R
See also DLB 5
See also CLC 4, 14
Benefield, June 1921- ... 45-48
Benell, Florence B(elle) 1912- ... 33-36R
Benell, Julie 1906(?)-1982 Obituary ... 105
Benello, C. George 1926- ... 33-36R
Ben-Ephraim, Gavriel 1946- ... 116
Benes, Jan 1936- ... 29-32R
Benet, Edouard
See Edwards, William B(ennett)
Benet, James 1914- ... CANR-8
Earlier sketch in CA 61-64

Benet, Juan 1927- CLC-28
Benet, Laura 1884-1979 CANR-6
Obituary 85-88
Earlier sketch in CA 9-10R
See also SATA 3, 23
Benet, Mary Kathleen 1943- 57-60
Benet, Stephen Vincent 1898-1943
Brief entry 104
See also YABC 1
See also DLB 4, 48
See also TCLC 7
Benet, Sula 1906-1982 89-92
Obituary 108
See also SATA 21, 33
Benet, William Rose 1886-1950
Brief entry 118
See also DLB 45
See also TCLC 28
Benetar, Judith 1941- 53-56
Benevolo, Leonardo 1923- 89-92
Ben-Ezer, Ehud 1936- CANR-24
Earlier sketches in CA 61-64, CANR-8
Benezra, Barbara (Beardsley) 1921- 15-16R
See also SATA 10
Benfield, Derek 1926- CANR-10
Earlier sketch in CA 23-24R
Benfield, G(raham) J(ohn) Barker
See Barker-Benfield, G(raham) J(ohn)
Benfield, Richard E. 1940- 77-80
Benford, Gregory (Albert) 1941- CANR-24
Earlier sketches in CA 69-72, CANR-12
See also DLBY 82
Benford, Harry (Bell) 1917- 89-92
Benford, Timothy B(artholomew)
1941- CANR-11
Earlier sketch in CA 69-72
Benge, Eugene J(ackson) 1896- CANR-9
Earlier sketch in CA 57-60
Bengelsdorf, Irving S. 1922- 57-60
Bengtson, Vern L. 1941- CANR-4
Earlier sketch in CA 49-52
Bengtsson, Arvid 1916- 33-36R
Ben-Gurion, David 1886-1973 101
Obituary 45-48
Benham, Leslie 1922- 9-10R
See also SATA 48
Benham, Lois (Dakin) 1924- 9-10R
See also SATA 48
Benham, Mary Lile 1914- 102
Ben-Horav, Naphthali
See Kravitz, Nathaniel
Ben-Horin, Meir 1918- CANR-14
Earlier sketch in CA 29-32R
Benichou, Paul 1908- 57-60
Beniger, James R. 1946- 111
Benington, John (Elson) 1921- 5-6R
Ben-Israel-Kidron, Hedva 33-36R
Benjamin, Alice
See Brooke, Avery (Rogers)
Benjamin, Anna Shaw 1925- 41-44R
Benjamin, Annette Francis 1928- 19-20R
Benjamin, Bry 1924- 19-20R
Benjamin, Burton Richard 1917-1988 101
Obituary 126
Benjamin, Claude (Max Edward Pohlman)
1911- 9-10R
Benjamin, Curtis G. 1901-1983 122
Obituary 111
Benjamin, Edward Bernard 1897- 69-72
Benjamin, Gerald 1945- 49-52
Benjamin, Harry 1885-1986 CAP-1
Obituary 120
Earlier sketch in CA 11-12
Benjamin, Herbert S(tanley) 1922- 5-6R
Benjamin, Joseph 1921- 57-60
Benjamin, Judy-Lynn
See del Rey, Judy-Lynn
Benjamin, Nora
See Kubie, Nora Gottheil Benjamin
Benjamin, Park 1809-1864 DLB-3, 59, 73
Benjamin, Philip (Robert) 1922-1966 7-8R
Obituary 25-28R
Benjamin, Robert (Irving) 1949- 109
Benjamin, Roger W. 1942- 37-40R
Benjamin, Ruth 1934- 125
Benjamin, William E(arl) 1942- 25-28R
Benjaminson, Peter 1945- CANR-12
Earlier sketch in CA 73-76
Benji, Thomas
See Robinson, Frank M(alcolm)
ben-Jochannan, Yosef 1918- CANR-12
Earlier sketch in CA 69-72
Benko, Stephen 1924- 11-12R
Benkovitz, Miriam J(eanette)
1911-1986 CANR-4
Obituary 119
Earlier sketch in CA 11-12R
Benn, Gottfried 1886-1956 Brief entry 106
See also DLB 56
See also TCLC 3
Benn, John Andrews 1904-1984 Obituary 115
Benn, Matthew
See Siegel, Benjamin
Bennani, B(en) M(ohammed) 1946- CANR-13
Earlier sketch in CA 61-64
Benne, Kenneth D(ean) 1908- 33-36R
Benner, Judith Ann 1942- 122
Benner, Ralph Eugene (Jr.) 1932- 33-36R
Bennet, Glin 1927- 123
Bennet, Ruth
See Straubing, Harold (Elk)
Bennett, A(bram) E(lting Hasbrouck)
1898- 65-68
Bennett, Addison C(urtis) 1918- CANR-7
Earlier sketch in CA 5-6R
Bennett, Adrian A(rthur) 1941- 53-56
Bennett, Alan 1934- 103
See also CLC 45
Bennett, Alice
See Ziner, Florence (Feenie)
Bennett, Anna Elizabeth 1914- 19-20R
Bennett, Archibald F. 1896- CAP-1
Earlier sketch in CA 15-16
Bennett, (Enoch) Arnold 1867-1931
Brief entry 106
See also DLB 10, 34
See also TCLC 5, 20
Bennett, Betty T. 115
Bennett, Boyce McLean, Jr. 1928- 115
Bennett, Bruce (William) 1952- 110
Bennett, Bruce L(anyon) 1917- 25-28R
Bennett, Charles 1899- DLB-44
Bennett, Charles 1901- CAP-1
Earlier sketch in CA 15-16
Bennett, Charles 1932- 25-28R
Bennett, Charles E(dward) 1910- 11-12R
Bennett, Christine
See Neubauer, William Arthur
Bennett, Daniel
See Gilmore, Joseph L(ee)
Bennett, Daphne Nicholson 41-44R
Bennett, David H. 1935- 25-28R
Bennett, Dennis J. 1917- CANR-20
Earlier sketch in CA 49-52
Bennett, Dorothea
See Young, Dorothea Bennett
Bennett, Dwight
See Newton, D(wight) B(ennett)
Bennett, E(thel) M. Granger 1891- CAP-1
Earlier sketch in CA 13-14
Bennett, E. N.
See Bennett, Ernest N(athaniel)
Bennett, Edward (Martin) 1924- 5-6R
Bennett, Edward M(oore) 1927- 33-36R
Bennett, Elizabeth
See Mitchell, Margaret (Munnerlyn)
Bennett, Ernest N(athaniel) 1868-1947
Brief entry 119
Bennett, Frances Grant 1899- CAP-2
Earlier sketch in CA 25-28
Bennett, Fredna W(illis) 1906- CAP-1
Earlier sketch in CA 9-10
Bennett, G. V.
See Bennett, Gareth Vaughan
Bennett, Gareth Vaughan 1929-1987
Obituary 124
Bennett, Geoffrey (Martin) 1909-1983 13-14R
Obituary 110
Bennett, George 1920- 5-6R
Bennett, George Harold 1930- 97-100
See also BW
Bennett, Gertrude Ryder 53-56
Bennett, Gordon A(nderson) 1940- 29-32R
Bennett, Gordon C. 1935- CANR-14
Earlier sketch in CA 33-36R
Bennett, Gwendolyn 1902-1981 DLB-51
Bennett, Gwendolyn B. 1902-1981 125
See also BW
Bennett, Hal
See Bennett, George Harold
See also DLB 33
See also CLC 5
Bennett, Hall
See Hall, Bennie Caroline (Humble)
Bennett, Harold (Zina) 1936- 41-44R
Bennett, Harve
See Fischman, Harve
Bennett, Howard Franklin 1911-1974 4R
Bennett, Isadora 1900-1980 Obituary 93-96
Bennett, J(ohn) G(odolphin) 1897-1974
Obituary 111
Bennett, Jack Arthur Walter 1911-1981 CANR-6
Obituary 103
Earlier sketch in CA 9-10R
Bennett, James D(avid) 1926- 61-64
Bennett, James Gordon 1795-1872 DLB-43
Bennett, James Gordon, Jr. 1841-1918 DLB-23
Bennett, James R(ichard) 1932- 33-36R
Bennett, James Thomas 1942- CANR-23
Earlier sketch in CA 106
Bennett, Jay 1912- CANR-11
Earlier sketch in CA 69-72
See also SATA 27, 41
See also SAAS 4
See also CLC 35
Bennett, Jean Francis
See Dorcy, Sister Mary Jean
Bennett, Jeremy
See Bennett, John Jerome Nelson
Bennett, Jill (Crawford) 1934- SATA-41
Bennett, Jill 1947- 106
Bennett, John 1865-1956 YABC-1
See also DLB 42
Bennett, John (Frederic) 1920- 29-32R
Bennett, John Jerome Nelson 1939- 21-22R
Bennett, John M(ichael) 1942- CANR-18
Earlier sketches in CA 49-52, CANR-2
Bennett, John W. 1918- 69-72
Bennett, John William 1915- CANR-4
Earlier sketch in CA 3R
Bennett, Jonathan (Francis) 1930- CANR-1
Earlier sketch in CA 45-48
Bennett, Joseph D. 1922-1972 3R
Obituary 33-36R
Bennett, Josephine Waters 1899-1975 3R
Obituary 103
Bennett, Judith ?-1979 Obituary 85-88
Bennett, Kay Curley 1922- 17-18R
Bennett, Lerone, Jr. 1928- CANR-25
Earlier sketches in CA 45-48, CANR-2
See also BW
Bennett, Linda L(eveque) 1946- 115
Bennett, Louise (Simone) 1919- CLC-28
Bennett, M. J.
See Bennett, Marcia J(oanne)
Bennett, Marcia J(oanne) 1945- 114
Bennett, Margaret E(laine) 1893- 7-8R
Bennett, Margot 1912-1980 Obituary 105
Bennett, Marion T(insley) 1914- 11-12R
Bennett, Melba Berry 1901-1968 CAP-2
Earlier sketch in CA 19-20
Bennett, Meridan 1927- 25-28R
Bennett, Michael 1943-1987 101
Obituary 122
Bennett, Mildred R. 1909- CAP-2
Earlier sketch in CA 25-28
Bennett, Neville 1937- CANR-19
Earlier sketch in CA 102
Bennett, Noel 1939- 45-48
Bennett, Norman Robert 1932- CANR-18
Earlier sketches in CA 9-10R, CANR-3
Bennett, Patrick (H.) 1931- 122
Bennett, Paul Lewis 1921- CANR-4
Earlier sketch in CA 1R
Bennett, Penelope Agnes 1938- 13-14R
Bennett, Rachel
See Hill, Margaret (Ohler)
Bennett, Rainey 1907- SATA-15
Bennett, Richard 1899- SATA-21
Bennett, Rita (Marie) 1934- CANR-20
Earlier sketch in CA 69-72
Bennett, Robert A(ndrew) 1927- CANR-5
Earlier sketch in CA 13-14R
Bennett, Robert D(onald) 1947- 118
Bennett, Robert L. 1931- 41-44R
Bennett, Robert Russell 1894-1981
Obituary 105
Bennett, Russell H(oradley) 1896- SATA-25
Bennett, Scott (Boyce) 1939- 33-36R
Bennett, Thomas L(eroy) 1942- 85-88
Bennett, Victor 1919- CANR-7
Earlier sketch in CA 7-8R
Bennett, W(illiam) R(obert) 1921- 13-14R
Bennett, William (Ira) 1941- 107
Bennett, William L. 1924- 19-20R
Bennett-Coverley, Louise 1919- 97-100
Bennett-England, Rodney Charles 1936- 61-64
Bennetts, Pamela 1922- 37-40R
Bennie, William A(ndrew) 1921- 69-72
Bennigsen, Alexandre (A.) 1913-1988(?)
Obituary 125
Benning, (Barbara) Lee Edwards 1934- 53-56
Bennion, Barbara Elisabeth 1930- 110
Bennis, Warren G. 1925- CANR-5
Earlier sketch in CA 53-56
Benoff, Mac 1915(?)-1972 Obituary 37-40R
Benoist-Mechin, Jacques 1901-1983 105
Obituary 109
Benoit, Emile 1910-1978 CANR-3
Obituary 77-80
Earlier sketch in CA 7-8R
Benoit, Jacques 1941- DLB-60
Benoit, Leroy James 1913- 33-36R
Benoit, Pierre 1886-1962 Obituary 93-96
Benoit, Pierre Maurice 1906-1987 41-44R
Obituary 122
Benoit, Richard 1899(?)-1969 Obituary 104
Benoliel, Jeanne Quint 1919- 49-52
Bense, Walter F(rederick) 1932- CANR-1
Earlier sketch in CA 45-48
Bensen, Alice R. 1911- 69-72
Bensen, Donald R. 1927- CANR-20
Earlier sketches in CA 9-10R, CANR-5
Bensko, John 1949- 105
Bensman, Joseph 1922- CANR-10
Earlier sketch in CA 23-24R
Bensol, Oscar
See Gilbert, Willie
Benson, A. George 1924- 69-72
Benson, B. A.
See Beyea, Basil
Benson, Ben(jamin) 1915-1959
Brief entry 112
Benson, C(arl) David 1942- 123
Benson, C. Randolph 1923- 29-32R
Benson, Carmen 1921- 57-60
Benson, Charles S(cott) 1922- CANR-8
Earlier sketch in CA 17-18R
Benson, Constantine Walter 1909-1982
Obituary 108
Benson, Daniel
See Cooper, Colin Symons
Benson, Dennis C(arroll) 1936- 37-40R
Benson, E(dward) F(rederic) 1867-1940
Brief entry 114
See also TCLC 27
Benson, Elizabeth P(olk) 1924- 93-96
Benson, Eugene 1928- 89-92
Benson, Frederick R. 1934- 33-36R
Benson, Frederick William 1948- CANR-19
Earlier sketch in CA 101
Benson, Gigi (Dian Daniels) 1941- 108
Benson, Ginny
See Benson, Virginia
Benson, Harry 1929- 108
Benson, Herbert 1935- 85-88
Benson, J(ack) L(eonard) 1920- 105
Benson, Jackson J. 1930- 25-28R
See also CLC 34
Benson, Jeffrey 1937- 120
Benson, Kathleen 1947- 85-88
Benson, Larry D(ean) 1929- 37-40R
Benson, Lyman (David) 1909- 49-52
Benson, Margaret H. Benson 1899- 7-8R
Benson, Mary 1919- CANR-17
Earlier sketches in CA 49-52, CANR-1
Benson, Maxine (Frances) 1939- 65-68
Benson, Rachel
See Jowitt, Deborah
Benson, Raymond 1955- 118
Benson, Richard
See Cooper, Saul
Benson, Robert G(reen) 1930- 29-32R
Benson, Robert S(later) 1942- 33-36R
Benson, Rolf Eric 1951- 102
Benson, Ruth Crego 1937- 41-44R
Benson, Sally 1900-1972 CAP-1
Obituary 37-40R
Earlier sketch in CA 19-20
See also SATA 1, 27, 35
See also CLC 17
Benson, Stella 1892-1933 Brief entry 117
See also DLB 36
See also TCLC 17
Benson, Stephana Vere 1909- 13-14R
Benson, Ted
See Benson, Frederick William
Benson, Thomas Godfrey 1899- CAP-1
Earlier sketch in CA 11-12
Benson, Thomas W(alter) 1937- CANR-19
Earlier sketch in CA 29-32R
Benson, Virginia 1923- 57-60
Benson, Warren S(ten) 1929- 114
Benson, William Howard 1902- 4R
Benstead, Steven 1951- 113
Bensted-Smith, Richard (Brian) 1929- 13-14R
Benstock, Bernard 1930- CANR-7
Earlier sketch in CA 17-18R
Benstock, Shari 1944- 97-100
Bent, Alan Edward 1939- CANR-4
Earlier sketch in CA 49-52
Bent, Charles N. 1935- 23-24R
Bent, Rudyard K(ipling) 1901- CANR-18
Earlier sketch in CA 3R
Benteen, John
See Haas, Ben(jamin) L(eopold)
Bentel, Pearl B(ucklen) 1901- CAP-2
Earlier sketch in CA 21-22
Benthall, Jonathan 1941- 41-44R
Bentham, Frederick 1911- 105
Bentham, Jay
See Bensman, Joseph
Benthic, Arch E.
See Stewart, Harris B(ates), Jr.
Benthul, Herman F(orrest) 1911- 33-36R
Bentley, Beth (Rita) 1928- 101
Bentley, Colin 1936- 118
Bentley, E(dmund) C(lerihew) 1875-1956
Brief entry 108
See also DLB 70
See also TCLC 12
Bentley, Eric (Russell) 1916- CANR-6
Earlier sketch in CA 7-8R
See also CLC 24
Bentley, G(erald) E(ades), Jr. 1930- CANR-4
Earlier sketch in CA 3R
Bentley, Gerald Eades 1901- 41-44R
Bentley, Howard Beebe 1925- 9-10R
Bentley, Janice Babb 1933- 15-16R
Bentley, Judith (McBride) 1945- CANR-23
Earlier sketch in CA 107
See also SATA 40
Bentley, Margaret 1926- CANR-25
Earlier sketch in CA 108
Bentley, Nicolas Clerihew 1907-1978 CANR-11
Obituary 81-84
Earlier sketch in CA 65-68
See also SATA 24
Bentley, Phyllis Eleanor 1894-1977 CANR-3
Earlier sketch in CA 4R
See also SATA 6, 25
Bentley, Richard
See Browning, Alice C(rolley)
Bentley, Roy 1947- SATA-46
Bentley, Sarah 1946- 29-32R
Bentley, Toni 1958- 123
Bentley, Ursula 1945- 125
Bentley, Virginia W(illiams) 1908- 57-60
Bentley-Taylor, David 1915- CANR-14
Earlier sketch in CA 77-80
Benton, Dorothy Gilchrist 1919- 57-60
Benton, F(red) Warren 1948- 119
Benton, Helen Hemingway 1902(?)-1974
Obituary 104
Benton, John Frederic 1931-1988 69-72
Obituary 124
Benton, John W. 1933- CANR-12
Earlier sketch in CA 29-32R
Benton, Joseph Nelson, Jr. 1924-1988
Obituary 124
Benton, Josephine Moffett 1905- 7-8R
Benton, Karla
See Rowland, D(onald) S(ydney)
Benton, Kenneth (Carter) 1909- CANR-1
Earlier sketch in CA 49-52
Benton, Lewis R(obert) 1920- 19-20R
Benton, (Joseph) Nelson (Jr.) 1924- 112
Brief entry 110
Benton, Patricia 1907- 5-6R
Benton, Peggie 1906- 49-52
Benton, Richard G(lasscock) 1938- 81-84
Benton, Robert (Douglass) 1932- CANR-2
Earlier sketch in CA 1R
See also DLB 44
Benton, Robert
See Buse, Renee
Benton, Thomas Hart 1889-1975 93-96
Obituary 53-56
Benton, Wilbourn Eugene 1917- 3R
Benton, Will
See Paine, Lauran (Bosworth)
Benton, William 1900-1973 CAP-1
Obituary 41-44R
Earlier sketch in CA 15-16
Bentov, Itzhak 1923(?)-1979 Obituary 85-88
Bentwich, Norman 1883-1971 Obituary 111
Bentz, Thomas 1943- 112

Bentz, William F(rederick) 1940- ... 53-56
ben Uzair, Salem
See Horne, Richard Henry
Benveniste, Asa 1925- ... 69-72
Benveniste, Emile 1902-1976 Obituary ... 115
Benveniste, Guy 1927- ... CANR-8
Earlier sketch in CA 61-64
Ben-Veniste, Richard 1943- Brief entry ... 114
Benvenisti, Meron (Shmuel) 1934- ... CANR-12
Earlier sketch in CA 65-68
Benward, Bruce (Charles) 1921- ... CANR-9
Earlier sketch in CA 9-10R
Beny, Roloff
See Beny, Wilfred Roy
Beny, Wilfred Roy 1924-1984 ... 23-24R
Obituary ... 112
Benyo, Richard (Stephen) 1946- ... CANR-13
Earlier sketch in CA 77-80
Ben-Yosef, Avraham C(haim)
See Matsuba, Moshe
Benz, Ernst (Wilhelm) 1907-1978 ... CANR-13
Earlier sketch in CA 15-16R
Benz, Frank L(eonard) 1930- ... 41-44R
Benzie, William 1930- ... 37-40R
Benziger, Barbara Field 1918- Brief entry ... 115
Benziger, James 1914- ... 13-14R
Ben-Zion
See Weinman, Benzion
Benzoni, Juliette (Andree Marguerite)
1920- ... CANR-18
Earlier sketch in CA 101
Beorse, Bryn 1896- ... 45-48
Bequaert, Lucia H(umes) ... 65-68
Beranek, Leo L(eroy) 1914- ... 7-8R
Beranek, William 1922- ... 5-6R
Berard, J(ules) Aram 1933- ... 17-18R
Berardo, Felix M(ario) 1934- ... CANR-24
Earlier sketches in CA 57-60, CANR-8
Berberova, Nina (Nikolaevna) 1901- ... CANR-14
Earlier sketch in CA 33-36R
Berbrich, Joan D. 1925- ... CANR-12
Earlier sketch in CA 29-32R
Berbusse, Edward J(oseph) 1912- ... 21-22R
Berch, William O.
See Coyne, Joseph E.
Berchen, Ursula 1919- ... 65-68
Berchen, William 1920- ... 65-68
Berck, Martin G(ans) 1928- ... 65-68
Berckman, Evelyn Domenica 1900- ... CANR-1
Earlier sketch in CA 3R
Bercovici, Rion 1903(?)-1976 Obituary ... 69-72
Bercovitch, Reuben 1923- ... 104
Bercovitch, Sacvan 1933- ... 41-44R
Berczeller, Richard 1902- ... 11-12R
Berdes, George R. 1931- ... 29-32R
Berdie, Douglas R(alph) 1946- ... 53-56
Berdie, Ralph F(reimuth) 1916-1974 ... CANR-11
Earlier sketch in CA 17-18R
Berding, Andrew H(enry) 1902- ... 7-8R
Berdyaev, Nicolas
See Berdyaev, Nikolai (Aleksandrovich)
Berdyaev, Nikolai (Aleksandrovich)
1874-1948 Brief entry ... 120
Bere, Rennie Montague 1907- ... 65-68
Bereday, George Z(ygmunt) F(ijalkowski)
1920-1983 ... CANR-4
Obituary ... 111
Earlier sketch in CA 4R
Bereiter, Carl 1930- Brief entry ... 113
Berelson, Bernard R(euben) 1912-1979 ... CANR-3
Obituary ... 89-92
Earlier sketch in CA 7-8R
Berelson, David 1943- ... 25-28R
Berelson, Howard 1940- ... SATA-5
Berenbaum, Linda Bayer
See Bayer-Berenbaum, Linda
Berends, Polly Berrien 1939- ... 108
See also SATA 38, 50
Berendsohn, Walter A(rthur) 1884- ... 33-36R
Berendt, Joachim Ernst 1922- ... CANR-12
Earlier sketch in CA 69-72
Berendzen, Richard (Earl) 1938- ... 85-88
Berenson, Conrad 1930- ... 11-12R
Berenstain, Jan(ice) ... CANR-14
Earlier sketch in CA 25-28R
See also SATA 12
Berenstain, Michael 1951- ... CANR-14
Earlier sketch in CA 97-100
See also SATA 45
Berenstain, Stan(ley) 1923- ... CANR-14
Earlier sketch in CA 25-28R
See also SATA 12
Bereny, Gail Rubin 1942- ... 85-88
Beresford, Anne 1929- ... 97-100
See also DLB 40
Beresford, Elisabeth ... 102
See also SATA 25
Beresford, J(ohn) D(avys) 1873-1947
Brief entry ... 112
Beresford, Maurice Warwick 1920- ... 13-14R
Beresford-Howe, Constance 1922- ... 53-56
See also AITN 2
Beresiner, Yasha 1940- ... CANR-12
Earlier sketch in CA 69-72
Beretta, Lia 1934- ... 17-18R
Berg, A(ndrew) Scott 1949(?)- ... 81-84
Berg, Adriane G(ilda) 1948- ... 119
Berg, Alan (David) 1932- ... CANR-22
Earlier sketch in CA 45-48
Berg, Barbara J. ... 124
Berg, Bjoern 1923- ... SATA-47
Berg, Darrel E. 1920- ... 17-18R
Berg, Dave
See Berg, David
Berg, David 1920- ... CANR-10
Earlier sketch in CA 21-22R
See also SATA 27
Berg, Fred Anderson 1948- ... 37-40R
Berg, Frederick S(ven) 1928- ... 53-56
Berg, Friedrich Kantor
See Kantor-Berg, Friedrich
Berg, Goesta 1903- ... 69-72
Berg, Irwin August 1913- ... 13-14R
Berg, Ivar E(lis), Jr. 1929- ... CANR-13
Earlier sketch in CA 23-24R
Berg, Jean Horton 1913- ... CANR-4
Earlier sketch in CA 53-56
See also SATA 6
Berg, Joan
See Victor, Joan Berg
Berg, Larry L(ee) 1939- ... 41-44R
Berg, Lasse 1943- ... CANR-12
Earlier sketch in CA 73-76
Berg, Leila Rita 1917- ... 101
Berg, Louis 1901-1972 Obituary ... 37-40R
Berg, Orley M. 1918- ... 19-20R
Berg, Paul Conrad 1921- ... 33-36R
Berg, Richard F(rederick) 1936- ... 115
Berg, Rick 1951- ... 93-96
Berg, Ron 1952- ... SATA-48
Berg, Stephen 1934- ... CANR-8
Earlier sketch in CA 15-16R
See also DLB 5
Berg, Thomas L(eRoy) 1930- ... 69-72
Berg, Viola Jacobson 1918- ... CANR-5
Earlier sketch in CA 53-56
Berg, William 1938- ... 97-100
Bergamini, David H(owland)
1928-1983 ... CANR-15
Obituary ... 110
Earlier sketch in CA 1R
Bergamini, John D. 1925(?)-1982
Obituary ... 108
Bergaust, Erik 1925-1978 ... 73-76
Obituary ... 77-80
See also SATA 20
Berge, Carol ... CANR-7
Earlier sketch in CA 15-16R
Bergel, Egon Ernst 1894-1969 ... CAP-2
Earlier sketch in CA 21-22
Bergen, Polly 1930- ... 57-60
Bergendoff, Conrad J(ohn) I(mmanuel)
1895- ... CANR-13
Earlier sketch in CA 33-36R
Bergengruen, Werner 1892-1964(?)
Obituary ... 114
See also DLB 56
Berger, Andrew J(ohn) 1915- ... CANR-14
Earlier sketch in CA 41-44R
Berger, Arthur Asa 1933- ... CANR-26
Earlier sketches in CA 25-28R, CANR-10
Berger, Bennett Maurice 1926- ... CANR-4
Earlier sketch in CA 1R
Berger, Bruce 1938- ... 112
Berger, Carl 1925- ... 11-12R
Berger, Colonel
See Malraux, (Georges-) Andre
Berger, David 1943- ... 115
Berger, Elmer 1908- ... 61-64
Berger, Evelyn Miller 1896- ... CANR-14
Earlier sketch in CA 37-40R
Berger, Gilda Brief entry ... 118
See also SATA 42
Berger, H. Jean 1924- ... 15-16R
Berger, Harry, Jr. 1924- ... 110
Berger, Hilbert J. 1920- ... 57-60
Berger, Ivan (Bennett) 1939- ... CANR-17
Earlier sketch in CA 97-100
Berger, John (Peter) 1926- ... 81-84
See also DLB 14
See also CLC 2, 19
Berger, John J(oseph) 1945- ... 69-72
Berger, Josef 1903-1971 ... 7-8R
Obituary ... 33-36R
See also SATA 36
Berger, Joseph 1924- ... 41-44R
Berger, Karen 1944- ... 122
Berger, Klaus 1901- ... CAP-1
Earlier sketch in CA 13-14
Berger, Marilyn 1935- ... 101
Berger, Marjorie Sue 1916- ... 15-16R
Berger, Mark L(ewis) 1942- Brief entry ... 109
Berger, Melvin H. 1927- ... CANR-4
Earlier sketch in CA 5-6R
See also SATA 5
See also SAAS 2
See also CLC 12
Berger, Meyer 1898-1959(?) Brief entry ... 120
See also DLB 29
Berger, Michael (Louis) 1943- ... CANR-14
Earlier sketch in CA 77-80
Berger, Morroe 1917-1981 ... CANR-4
Obituary ... 103
Earlier sketch in CA 1R
Berger, Nan 1914- ... 113
Berger, Peter Ludwig 1929- ... CANR-1
Earlier sketch in CA 1R
Berger, Phil 1942- ... CANR-12
Earlier sketch in CA 61-64
Berger, Rainer 1930- ... 37-40R
Berger, Raoul 1901- ... 93-96
Berger, Raymond M(ark) 1950- ... 109
Berger, Robert W(illiam) 1936- ... 49-52
Berger, Stuart 1953- ... 112
Berger, Suzanne E(lizabeth) 1944- ... 105
Berger, Terry 1933- ... 37-40R
See also SATA 8
Berger, Thomas (Louis) 1924- ... CANR-5
Earlier sketch in CA 2R
See also DLB 2
See also DLBY 80
See also CLC 3, 5, 8, 11, 18, 38
Berger, Yves 1934- ... 85-88
Bergeret, Ida Treat 1889(?)-1978
Obituary ... 77-80
Bergeron, David M(oore) 1938- ... CANR-2
Earlier sketch in CA 45-48
Bergeron, Paul H. 1938- ... 101
Bergeron, Victor (Jules, Jr.) 1902-1984 ... 89-92
Obituary ... 114
Berges, Marshall (William) 1921(?)-1988
Obituary ... 126
Bergeson, John B(rian) 1935- ... 69-72
Bergevin, Paul (Emile) 1906- ... CANR-2
Earlier sketch in CA 7-8R
Bergey, Alyce (Mae) 1934- ... CANR-7
Earlier sketch in CA 5-6R
See also SATA 45
Berggren, W(illiam) A(lfred) 1931- ... 123
Berghahn, Volker R(olf) 1938- ... CANR-20
Earlier sketch in CA 103
Bergier, Jacques 1912-1978 ... 85-88
Obituary ... 81-84
Bergin, Allen E. 1934- ... 45-48
Bergin, Kenneth Glenny 1911-1981
Obituary ... 103
Bergin, Thomas Goddard 1904-1987 ... CANR-3
Obituary ... 124
Earlier sketch in CA 11-12R
Bergman, Arlene Eisen 1942- ... 61-64
Bergman, Bernard A(aron) 1894-1980 ... 102
Obituary ... 97-100
Bergman, Bo 1869-1967 Obituary ... 25-28R
Bergman, David (L.) 1950- ... CANR-22
Earlier sketch in CA 106
Bergman, Floyd L(awrence) 1927- ... CANR-17
Earlier sketches in CA 49-52, CANR-2
Bergman, Hannah E(stermann) 1925- ... 69-72
Bergman, Hjalmar (Frederik Elgerus)
1883-1931 Brief entry ... 119
Bergman, (Shmuel) Hugo 1883-1975
Obituary ... 57-60
Bergman, (Ernst) Ingmar 1918- ... 81-84
See also CLC 16
Bergman, Ingrid 1915-1982 Obituary ... 107
Bergman, Jay Asa 1948- ... 110
Bergman, Jules (Verne) 1929-1987 ... 108
Obituary ... 121
Bergmann, Ernst W. 1896(?)-1977
Obituary ... 69-72
Bergmann, Fred L(ouis) 1916- ... 61-64
Bergmann, Frithjof H. 1930- ... 101
Bergmann, Peter G(abriel) 1915- ... 23-24R
Bergonzi, Bernard 1929- ... CANR-8
Earlier sketch in CA 17-18R
Bergonzo, Jean Louis 1939-19(?) ... CAP-2
Earlier sketch in CA 25-28
Bergquist, Laura (Cecelia) 1918-1982
Obituary ... 108
Bergreen, Laurence R. 1950- ... 104
Bergson, Abram 1914- ... 13-14R
Bergson, Leo
See Stebel, S(idney) L(eo)
Bergstein, Eleanor 1938- ... CANR-5
Earlier sketch in CA 53-56
See also CLC 4
Bergsten, C. Fred 1941- ... 111
Bergsten, Staffan 1932- ... CANR-6
Earlier sketch in CA 57-60
Bergstrom, Louise 1914- ... 29-32R
Beringause, Arthur F. 1919- ... 33-36R
Beringer, Richard E. 1933- ... 81-84
Berk, Fred 1911(?)-1980 Obituary ... 97-100
Berke, Joel S(ommers) 1936-1981 ... 110
Obituary ... 105
Berke, Joseph H(erman) 1939- ... 57-60
Berke, Roberta 1943- ... 106
Berkebile, Don(ald) H(erbert) 1926- ... CANR-8
Earlier sketch in CA 61-64
Berkebile, Fred D(onovan) 1900-1978 ... 5-6R
Obituary ... 103
See also SATA 26
Berkeley, Anthony
See Cox, A(nthony) B(erkeley)
Berkeley, David S(helley) 1917- ... 41-44R
Berkeley, Edmund 1912- Brief entry ... 112
Berkeley, Ellen Perry 1931- ... 110
Berkemeyer, William C. 1908- ... CAP-2
Earlier sketch in CA 25-28
Berkey, Barry Robert 1935- ... 69-72
See also SATA 24
Berkey, Helen 1898- ... CAP-2
Earlier sketch in CA 23-24
Berkhofer, Robert Frederick, Jr. 1931- ... 15-16R
Berkin, Carol Ruth 1942- ... CANR-11
Earlier sketch in CA 69-72
Berkley, George E(ugene) 1928-
Brief entry ... 113
Berkman, Edward O(scar) 1914- ... CANR-9
Earlier sketch in CA 61-64
Berkman, Harold W(illiam) 1926- ... CANR-21
Earlier sketches in CA 53-56, CANR-5
Berkman, Richard Lyle 1946- ... CANR-1
Earlier sketch in CA 45-48
Berkman, Sue 1936- ... 45-48
Berkman, Ted
See Berkman, Edward O(scar)
Berkoff, Steven 1937- ... 104
Berkove, Lawrence Ivan 1930- ... 106
Berkovits, Eliezer 1908- ... CANR-2
Earlier sketch in CA 4R
Berkovitz, Irving H(erbert) 1924- ... 57-60
Berkow, Ira 1940- ... 97-100
Berkowitz, Bernard 1909- ... AITN-1
Berkowitz, David Sandler 1913- ... 33-36R
Berkowitz, Freda Pastor 1910- ... CAP-1
Earlier sketch in CA 9-10
See also SATA 12
Berkowitz, Gerald M(artin) 1942- ... 110
Berkowitz, Leonard 1926- ... 125
Berkowitz, Luci 1938- ... 33-36R
Berkowitz, Marvin 1938- ... 29-32R
Berkowitz, Morris Ira 1931- ... 53-56
Berkowitz, Pearl H(enriette) 1921- ... 23-24R
Berkowitz, Sol 1922- ... CANR-1
Earlier sketch in CA 45-48
Berkowitz, William R(obby) 1939- ... 112
Berkson, Bill 1939- ... CANR-24
Earlier sketches in CA 21-22R, CANR-9
Berkson, William Koller 1944- ... 102
Berlak, Harold 1932- ... 33-36R
Berland, Alwyn 1920- ... 125
Berland, Theodore 1929- ... CANR-18
Earlier sketches in CA 7-8R, CANR-2
Berlanstein, Lenard R(ussell) 1947- ... 69-72
Berlant, Anthony 1941- Brief entry ... 112
Berlant, Tony
See Berlant, Anthony
Berle, Adolf A(ugustus), Jr. 1895-1971 ... CAP-2
Obituary ... 29-32R
Earlier sketch in CA 23-24
Berle, Beatrice Bishop 1902- ... 114
Berle, Milton 1908- ... 77-80
See also AITN 1
Berleant, Arnold 1932- ... 29-32R
Berlin, Ellin (Mackay) 1904(?)-1988 ... 65-68
Obituary ... 126
Berlin, Ira 1941- ... 101
Berlin, Irving 1888- ... 108
Berlin, Irving N. 1917- ... CANR-13
Earlier sketch in CA 23-24R
Berlin, Isaiah 1909- ... 85-88
Berlin, Michael J(oseph) 1938- ... 69-72
Berlin, Normand 1931- ... 57-60
Berlin, Richard Emmett 1894(?)-1986
Obituary ... 118
Berlin, Sven 1911- ... CANR-15
Earlier sketch in CA 85-88
Berlind, Bruce 1926- ... 33-36R
Berliner, Don 1930- ... CANR-21
Earlier sketch in CA 105
See also SATA 33
Berliner, Franz 1930- ... CANR-12
Earlier sketch in CA 29-32R
See also SATA 13
Berliner, Herman A(lbert) 1944- ... 77-80
Berliner, Joseph S(cholom) 1921- ... 69-72
Berlitz, Charles (L. Frambach) 1914- ... CANR-9
Earlier sketch in CA 7-8R
See also SATA 32
Berl-Lee, Maria
See Lee, Maria Berl
Berloni, William 1956- ... 77-80
Berlye, Milton K. 1915- ... 49-52
Berlyne, D(aniel) E(llis) 1924- ... 13-14R
Berman, Arthur I(rwin) 1925- ... 97-100
Berman, Bennett H(erbert) 1927- ... 105
Berman, Bruce D(avid) 1944- ... 41-44R
Berman, Claire 1936- ... CANR-10
Earlier sketch in CA 25-28R
Berman, Connie 1949- ... 93-96
Berman, Daniel M(arvin) 1928-1967 ... CANR-1
Earlier sketch in CA 1R
Berman, Ed 1941- ... 106
Berman, Edgar F(rank) 1915(?)-1987 ... 97-100
Obituary ... 124
Berman, Eleanor 1934- ... 85-88
Berman, Emile Zola 1902-1981 Obituary ... 104
Berman, Harold Joseph 1918- ... CANR-15
Earlier sketch in CA 89-92
Berman, Larry 1951- ... 93-96
Berman, Linda 1948- ... 113
See also SATA 38
Berman, Louise M(arguerite) 1928- ... 21-22R
Berman, Marshall 1940- ... 29-32R
Berman, Milton 1924- ... 1R
Berman, Morton 1924- ... CANR-2
Earlier sketch in CA 5-6R
Berman, Morton M(ayer) 1899-1986
Obituary ... 118
Berman, Paul (Lawrence) 1949- ... 110
Berman, Ronald 1930- ... 13-14R
Berman, Sanford 1933- ... 37-40R
Berman, Simeon M(oses) 1935- ... 49-52
Berman, Susan 1945- ... CANR-17
Earlier sketch in CA 65-68
Berman, William C(arl) 1932- ... 41-44R
Bermange, Barry 1933- ... 57-60
Bermant, Chaim 1929- ... CANR-6
Earlier sketch in CA 57-60
See also CLC 40
Bermant, Gordon 1936- ... 120
Bermel, Albert (Cyril) 1927- ... CANR-11
Earlier sketch in CA 69-72
Bermont, Hubert Ingram 1924- ... CANR-5
Earlier sketch in CA 9-10R
Bermosk, Loretta Sue 1918- ... CANR-3
Earlier sketch in CA 11-12R
Bern, Maria Rasputin Soloviev
1900(?)-1977 Obituary ... 73-76
Berna, Paul 1910- ... 73-76
See also SATA 15
Bernabei, Alfio 1941- ... CANR-14
Earlier sketch in CA 77-80
Bernadette
See Watts, (Anna) Bernadette
Bernal, Ignacio 1910- ... 97-100
Bernal, J(ohn) D(esmond) 1901-1971 ... 97-100
Obituary ... 33-36R
Bernal, Judith F. 1939- ... 57-60
Bernal, Martin Gardiner 1937- ... 104
Bernal y Garcia y Pimentel, Ignacio
1910- ... CANR-5
Earlier sketch in CA 9-10R

Bernanos, (Paul Louis) Georges
1888-1948 Brief entry ... 104
See also DLB 72
See also TCLC 3
Bernard, George 1939- ... 73-76
Bernard, George I. 1949- ... SATA-39
Bernard, Guy
See Barber, Stephen Guy
Bernard, H(arvey) Russell 1940- ... 41-44R
Bernard, Harold W. 1908- ... CANR-4
Earlier sketch in CA 3R
Bernard, Hugh Y(ancey), Jr. 1919- ... 23-24R
Bernard, Jack F. 1930- ... 21-22R
Bernard, Jacqueline (de Sieyes)
1921-1983 ... 23-24R
Obituary ... 117
See also SATA 8, 45
Bernard, Jay
See Sawkins, Raymond H(arold)
Bernard, Jean-Jacques 1888-1972
Obituary ... 37-40R
Bernard, John 1756-1828 ... DLB-37
Bernard, Kenneth 1930- ... 41-44R
Bernard, Kenneth A(nderson) 1906- ... 29-32R
Bernard, Laureat J(oseph) 1922- ... 25-28R
Bernard, Marley
See Graves, Susan B(ernard)
Bernard, Nelson T(ed), Jr. 1925- ... 123
Bernard, Oliver 1925- ... 15-16R
Bernard, Paul Peter 1929- ... 89-92
Bernard, Richard Marion 1948- ... 105
Bernard, Robert
See Martin, Robert Bernard
Bernard, Sidney 1918- ... 29-32R
Bernard, Stefan
See Baumrin, Bernard H(erbert)
Bernard, Thelma Rene 1940- ... 57-60
Bernard, Will 1915- ... 93-96
Bernard, William Spencer 1907-1986
Obituary ... 118
Bernardo, Aldo S(isto) 1920- ... CANR-4
Earlier sketch in CA 4R
Bernardo, James V. 1913- ... 17-18R
Bernardo, Stephanie 1947- ... 112
Bernarn, Terrave
See Burnett, David (Benjamin Foley)
Bernauer, George F. 1941- ... 29-32R
Bernays, Anne
See Kaplan, Anne Bernays
Bernays, Edward L. 1891- ... 17-18R
Bernazza, Ann Marie
See Haase, Ann Marie Bernazza
Bernbach, William 1911-1982 Obituary ... 108
Bernd, Joseph Laurence 1923- ... 19-20R
Berndt, Ronald Murray 1916- ... CANR-19
Earlier sketches in CA 5-6R, CANR-3
Berndt, Walter 1900(?)-1979 Obituary ... 89-92
Berndtson, Arthur 1913- ... 108
Berne, Eric (Lennard) 1910-1970 ... CANR-4
Obituary ... 25-28R
Earlier sketch in CA 7-8R
Berne, Leo
See Davies, L(eslie) P(urnell)
Berne, Patricia H(iggins) 1934- ... 110
Berne, Stanley 1923- ... CANR-1
Earlier sketch in CA 45-48
Berner, Carl Walter 1902- ... 49-52
Berner, Jeff 1940- ... 89-92
Berner, Robert B(arry) 1940- ... 41-44R
Bernert, Eleanor H.
See Sheldon, Eleanor Bernert
Bernet, Michael M. 1930- ... 25-28R
Bernhard, Thomas 1931- ... 85-88
See also CLC 3, 32
Bernhard, Virginia Purington 1937- ... 112
Bernhardsen, Bris
See Bernhardsen, (Einar) Christian
(Rosenvinge)
Bernhardsen, (Einar) Christian (Rosenvinge)
1923- ... 29-32R
Bernhardt, Clyde Edric Barron 1905-1986
Obituary ... 119
Bernhardt, Frances Simonsen 1932- ... 103
Bernhardt, Karl S. 1901-1967 ... CAP-1
Earlier sketch in CA 13-14
Bernheim, Evelyne 1935- ... 21-22R
Bernheim, Kayla F. 1946- ... 108
Bernheim, Marc 1924- ... 21-22R
Bernheimer, Martin 1936- ... 69-72
Bernier, Olivier 1941- ... 105
Berninghausen, David K(nipe) 1916- ... 111
Berns, Julie 1899(?)-1983 Obituary ... 111
Berns, Walter (Fred) 1919- ... CANR-24
Earlier sketch in CA 101
Bernstein, Alvin H(owell) 1939- ... 89-92
Bernstein, Anne C(arolyn) 1944- ... 105
Bernstein, Arnold 1920- ... 29-32R
Bernstein, Barton J(annen) 1936- ... 37-40R
Bernstein, Basil (Bernard) 1924-
Brief entry ... 119
Bernstein, Blanche 1912- ... 110
Bernstein, Burton 1932- ... CANR-21
Earlier sketches in CA 1R, CANR-4
Bernstein, Carl 1944- ... 81-84
See also AITN 1
Bernstein, David 1915(?)-1974 Obituary ... 53-56
Bernstein, Douglas A. 1942- ... 45-48
Bernstein, Gail Lee 1939- ... 115
Bernstein, Gerry 1927- ... 105
Bernstein, Harry 1909- ... CANR-1
Earlier sketch in CA 1R
Bernstein, Hillel 1892(?)-1977 Obituary ... 69-72
Bernstein, Irving 1916- Brief entry ... 114
Bernstein, J(erome) S(traus) 1936- ... 25-28R
Bernstein, Jacob 1946- ... 104
Bernstein, Jane 1949- ... 104
Bernstein, Jeremy 1929- ... 13-14R
Bernstein, Jerry Marx 1908-1969 ... CAP-2
Earlier sketch in CA 25-28
Bernstein, Joanne E(ckstein) 1943- ... CANR-13
Earlier sketch in CA 77-80
See also SATA 15
Bernstein, John Andrew 1944- ... 124
Bernstein, Joseph M(ilton) 1908(?)-1975
Obituary ... 57-60
Bernstein, Leonard 1918- ... CANR-21
Earlier sketches in CA 2R, CANR-2
Bernstein, Lewis 1915- ... 33-36R
Bernstein, Margery 1933- ... 57-60
Bernstein, Marilyn 1929- ... 21-22R
Bernstein, Marver H(illel) 1919- ... CANR-2
Earlier sketch in CA 1R
Bernstein, Marvin David 1923- ... 45-48
Bernstein, Merton C(lay) 1923- ... 19-20R
Bernstein, Michael Andre 1947- ... 124
Bernstein, Mordechai 1893-1983 Obituary ... 109
Bernstein, Morey 1919- ... 23-24R
Bernstein, Norman R. 1927- ... CANR-13
Earlier sketch in CA 33-36R
Bernstein, Paula 1944- ... 125
Bernstein, Philip S(idney) 1901- ... 49-52
Bernstein, Richard J(acob) 1932-
Brief entry ... 113
Bernstein, Richard K. 1934- ... 105
Bernstein, Seymour ... CANR-26
Earlier sketch in CA 109
Bernstein, Theodore M(enline)
1904-1979 ... CANR-3
Earlier sketch in CA 1R
See also SATA 12, 27
Bernstein, Thomas P(aul) 1937- ... 113
Bernstein, Walter 1919- ... 106
Bernzweig, Eli P. 1927- ... CANR-26
Earlier sketch in CA 29-32R
Berofsky, Bernard 1935- ... 89-92
Berque, Jacques Augustin 1910- ... 85-88
Berquist, Goodwin F(auntleroy) 1930- ... 23-24R
Berrellez, Robert 1920(?)-1985 Obituary ... 116
Berrett, LaMar C(ecil) 1926- ... 53-56
Berrian, Albert H. 1925- ... 37-40R
Berriault, Gina 1926- Brief entry ... 116
Berridge, Celia 1943- ... 110
Berridge, Elizabeth 1921- ... CANR-6
Earlier sketch in CA 57-60
Berridge, P(ercy) S(tuart) A(ttwood)
1901- ... 29-32R
Berrien, Edith Heal
See Heal, Edith
Berrien, F. Kenneth 1909-1971 ... CANR-1
Obituary ... 29-32R
Earlier sketch in CA 3R
Berrigan, Daniel 1921- ... CANR-11
Earlier sketch in CA 33-36R
See also CAAS 1
See also DLB 5
See also CLC 4
Berrigan, Edmund Joseph Michael, Jr.
1934-1983 ... CANR-14
Obituary ... 110
Earlier sketch in CA 61-64
Berrigan, Philip (Francis) 1923- ... CANR-11
Earlier sketch in CA 15-16R
Berrigan, Ted
See Berrigan, Edmund Joseph Michael,
Jr.
See also DLB 5
See also CLC 37
Berrill, Jacquelyn (Batsel) 1905- ... 19-20R
See also SATA 12
Berrill, N(orman) J(ohn) 1903- ... 19-20R
Berrington, Hugh B(ayard) 1928- ... 49-52
Berrington, John
See Brownjohn, Alan
Berrisford, Judith Mary
See Lewis, Judith Mary
Berry, Adrian M(ichael) 1937- ... CANR-25
Earlier sketches in CA 57-60, CANR-9
Berry, B. J.
See Berry, Barbara J.
Berry, Barbara J. 1937- ... 33-36R
See also SATA 7
Berry, Boyd M(cCulloch) 1939- ... 69-72
Berry, Brewton 1901- ... CANR-3
Earlier sketch in CA 4R
Berry, Brian J(oe) L(obley) 1934- ... CANR-5
Earlier sketch in CA 15-16R
Berry, Bryan 1930-1955 Brief entry ... 112
Berry, Burton Yost 1901- ... 85-88
Berry, Charles Edward Anderson 1931- ... 115
Berry, Charles H. 1930- ... 69-72
Berry, Chuck
See Berry, Charles Edward Anderson
See also CLC 17
Berry, Cicely 1926- ... 93-96
Berry, D. C. 1942- ... 45-48
Berry, David (Ronald) 1942- ... 29-32R
Berry, David (Adams) 1943- ... 108
Berry, Don (George) 1932- ... 106
Berry, Edmund G(rindlay) 1915- ... 3R
Berry, Edward I. 1940- ... 57-60
Berry, (Julia) Elizabeth 1920- ... 21-22R
Berry, Erick
See Best, (Evangel) Allena Champlin
Berry, Francis 1915- ... CANR-5
Earlier sketch in CA 5-6R
Berry, Frederic Aroyce, Jr. 1906-1978
Obituary ... 77-80
Berry, Geoffrey 1912-1988 Obituary ... 124
Berry, Helen
See Rowland, D(onald) S(ydney)
Berry, Henry 1926- ... 85-88
Berry, Herbert 1922- ... 111
Berry, I. William 1934- ... CANR-25
Earlier sketch in CA 105
Berry, Jack 1918- ... 37-40R
Berry, James 1932- ... 23-24R
Berry, James Gomer 1883-1968 Obituary ... 89-92
Berry, Jane Cobb 1915(?)-1979 Obituary ... 85-88
See also SATA 22
Berry, Jason 1949- ... 45-48
Berry, Jim 1946- ... 107
Berry, Jim
See Berry, James
Berry, Jo(ycelyn) 1933- ... CANR-18
Earlier sketch in CA 102
Berry, John Nichols (III) 1933- Brief entry ... 113
Berry, Jonas
See Ashbery, John (Lawrence)
Berry, Joy Wilt ... SATA-46
Berry, Katherine F(iske) 1877-19(?) ... CAP-2
Earlier sketch in CA 17-18
Berry, Lloyd E(ason) 1935- ... 15-16R
Berry, Lynn 1948- ... 61-64
Berry, Mary Frances 1938- ... CANR-14
Earlier sketch in CA 33-36R
See also BW
Berry, Nicholas O(rlando) 1936- ... 93-96
Berry, Paul 1919- ... 102
Berry, R(obert) J(ames) 1934- ... 121
Berry, Roland (Brian) 1951- ... 93-96
Berry, Ron(ald Anthony) 1920- ... 25-28R
Berry, Sister Mary Virginia 1908(?)-1987
Obituary ... 122
Berry, Stephen Ames 1947- ... 118
Berry, Thomas 1914- ... 23-24R
Berry, Thomas Edwin 1930- ... 102
Berry, Thomas Elliott 1917- ... 33-36R
Berry, Wallace Taft 1928- ... CANR-8
Earlier sketch in CA 19-20R
Berry, Wendell (Erdman) 1934- ... 73-76
See also DLB 5, 6
See also CLC 4, 6, 8, 27, 46
See also AITN 1
Berry, William D(avid) 1926- ... 73-76
See also SATA 14
Berry, William Turner 1888- ... CAP-2
Earlier sketch in CA 23-24
Berryman, Charles (Beecher) 1939- ... 112
Berryman, James Thomas 1902-1971
Obituary ... 93-96
Berryman, Jim
See Berryman, James Thomas
Berryman, John 1914-1972 ... CAP-1
Obituary ... 33-36R
Earlier sketch in CA 15-16
See also CABS 2
See also DLB 48
See also CDALB 1941-1968
See also CLC 1, 2, 3, 4, 6, 8, 10, 13,
25
Bersani, Leo 1931- ... CANR-5
Earlier sketch in CA 53-56
Berscheid, Ellen 1936- ... 25-28R
Bersianik, Louky 1930- ... DLB-60
Berson, Harold 1926- ... 33-36R
See also SATA 4
Berson, Lenora E. 1926- ... 93-96
Berssenbrugge, Mei-mei 1947- ... 104
Berst, Charles A(shton) 1932- ... 41-44R
Berst, Jesse ... 116
Bertcher, Harvey (Joseph) 1929- ... 85-88
Bertelson, David (Earl) 1934- ... 21-22R
Berthelot, Joseph A. 1927- ... 21-22R
Berthoff, Rowland (Tappan) 1921- ... 33-36R
Berthoff, Warner (Bement) 1925- ... CANR-2
Earlier sketch in CA 5-6R
Berthold, Dennis (Alfred) 1942- ... 117
Berthold, Margot 1922- ... 73-76
Berthold, Mary Paddock 1909- ... 53-56
Bertholf, Diana 1946- ... 115
Berthoud, Jacques (Alexandre) 1935- ... CANR-10
Earlier sketch in CA 19-20R
Berthrong, Donald J(ohn) 1922- ... 81-84
Berthrong, Evelyn Nagai
See Nagai Berthrong, Evelyn
Bertin, Charles-Francois
See Berlitz, Charles (L. Frambach)
Bertin, Jack
See Bertin, John
Bertin, John 1904-1963 Obituary ... 116
Bertin, Leonard M. 1918- ... 15-16R
Bertman, Stephen (Samuel) 1937- ... 45-48
Bertocci, Peter A(nthony) 1910- ... 17-18R
Bertolino, James 1942- ... CANR-17
Earlier sketches in CA 45-48, CANR-1
Bertolucci, Bernardo 1940- ... 106
See also CLC 16
Berton, Peter (Alexander Menquez) 1922- ... 77-80
Berton, Pierre 1920- ... CANR-2
Earlier sketch in CA 3R
See also DLB 68
Berton, Ralph 1910- ... 49-52
Bertonasco, Marc F(rancis) 1934- ... 89-92
Bertram, Anthony 1897-1978 Obituary ... 104
Bertram, (George) Colin (Lawder) 1911- ... 13-14R
Bertram, James Munro 1910- ... 65-68
Bertram, Jean De Sales ... CANR-12
Earlier sketch in CA 45-48
Bertram, Noel
See Fanthorpe, R(obert) Lionel
Bertram-Cox, Jean De Sales
See Bertram, Jean De Sales
Bertrand, Alvin L(ee) 1918- ... 45-48
Bertrand, Charles
See Carter, David C(harles)
Bertrand, Lewis 1897(?)-1974 Obituary ... 53-56
Bertrand, Michel 1944- ... CANR-13
Earlier sketch in CA 73-76
Berwanger, Eugene H. ... 21-22R
Berwick, Jean Shepherd 1929- ... 9-10R
Berwick, Keith (Bennet) 1928- ... 33-36R
Besag, Frank P. 1935- ... 119
Besanceney, Paul H. 1924- ... 45-48
Besant, Annie (Wood) 1847-1933
Brief entry ... 105
See also TCLC 9
Besas, Peter 1933- ... 77-80
Beschloss, Michael R(ichard) 1955- ... 101
Besdine, Matthew 1905(?)-1986 Obituary ... 120
Beshers, James M(onahan) 1931- ... 4R
Beshoar, Barron B(enedict) 1907- ... 69-72
Beskow, Bo 1906- ... CANR-11
Earlier sketch in CA 61-64
Beskow, Elsa (Maartman) 1874-1953 ... SATA-20
Besoyan, Rick 1924(?)-1970 Obituary ... 25-28R
Bessborough, Tenth Earl of
See Ponsonby, Frederick Edward Neuflize
Bessell, Peter (Joseph) 1921-1985
Obituary ... 117
Besser, Gretchen R(ous) 1928- ... CANR-14
Earlier sketch in CA 41-44R
Besser, Joe 1907-1988 Obituary ... 124
Besser, Milton 1911-1976 ... 69-72
Obituary ... 65-68
Bessette, Gerard 1920- ... CANR-14
Earlier sketch in CA 37-40R
See also DLB 53
Bessie, Alvah 1904-1985 ... CANR-2
Obituary ... 116
Earlier sketch in CA 5-6R
See also DLB 26
See also CLC 23
Bessie, Constance Ernst 1918(?)-1985
Obituary ... 115
Bessinger, Jess B(alsor), Jr. 1921- ... 15-16R
Bessom, Malcolm E(ugene) 1940-1988 ... 57-60
Obituary ... 126
Bessy, Maurice 1910- ... CANR-26
Earlier sketches in CA 65-68, CANR-10
Best, Adam
See Carmichael, William Edward
Best, Alan C.G. 1939- ... 111
Best, (Evangel) Allena Champlin
1892-1974 ... CAP-2
Earlier sketch in CA 25-28
See also SATA 2, 25
Best, Charles H(erbert) 1899-1978 ... 45-48
Obituary ... 103
Best, Ernest 1917- ... 114
Best, Ernest E. 1919- ... 112
Best, G. F. A.
See Best, Geoffrey (Francis Andrew)
Best, Gary A(llen) 1939- ... 33-36R
Best, Gary Dean 1936- ... 117
Best, Geoffrey (Francis Andrew) 1928-
Brief entry ... 114
Best, (Oswald) Herbert 1894- ... CAP-2
Earlier sketch in CA 25-28
See also SATA 2
Best, Hugh 1920- ... 115
Best, James J(oseph) 1938- ... 37-40R
Best, John Wesley 1909- ... 17-18R
Best, Judith A. 1938- ... 69-72
Best, Marc
See Lemieux, Marc
Best, Marshall A. 1901(?)-1982 Obituary ... 106
Best, Michael R. ... 37-40R
Best, Otto F(erdinand) 1929- ... CANR-25
Earlier sketch in CA 69-72
Best, Rayleigh Breton Amis 1905- ... CAP-1
Earlier sketch in CA 15-16
Best, Robin Hewitson ?-1984 Obituary ... 113
Best, Thomas W(aring) 1939- ... 29-32R
Bestall, A(lfred) E(dmeades) 1892-1986
Obituary ... 119
See also SATA 48
Beste, R(aymond) Vernon 1908- ... CANR-4
Earlier sketch in CA 4R
Bester, Alfred 1913-1987 ... CANR-12
Obituary ... 123
Earlier sketch in CA 15-16R
See also DLB 8
Besterman, Theodore (Deocatus Nathaniel)
1904-1976 Obituary ... 105
Bestic, Alan Kent 1922- ... 13-14R
Beston, Henry 1888-1968 Obituary ... 25-28R
Bestor, Arthur (Eugene, Jr.) 1908- ... CANR-6
Earlier sketch in CA 4R
Bestor, Dorothy K(och) ... 118
Bestul, Thomas H(oward) 1942- ... 53-56
Betancourt, Jeanne 1941- ... 49-52
See also SATA 43
Betancourt, Romulo 1908-1981 ... 104
Betenson, Lula Parker 1884- ... 61-64
Beth
See Winship, Elizabeth
Beth, Loren Peter 1920- ... CANR-3
Earlier sketch in CA 4R
Beth, Mary
See Miller, Mary Beth
Bethancourt, T. Ernesto
See Paisley, Tom
See also SATA 11
See also CLR 3
Bethe, H. A.
See Bethe, Hans Albrecht
Bethe, Hans A.
See Bethe, Hans Albrecht
Bethe, Hans Albrecht 1906- Brief entry ... 115
Bethel, Dell 1929- ... CANR-26
Earlier sketch in CA 29-32R
See also SATA 52
Bethel, Elizabeth Rauh 1942- ... 106
Bethel, Paul D(uane) 1919- ... 25-28R
Bethell, Jean (Frankenberry) 1922- ... CANR-3
Earlier sketch in CA 9-10R
See also SATA 8

Bethell, Nicholas William 1938- CANR-1
Earlier sketch in CA 45-48
Bethell, Tom 1940- 77-80
Bethers, Ray 1902- CAP-1
Earlier sketch in CA 11-12
See also SATA 6
Bethge, Eberhard 1909- 85-88
Bethlen, T. D.
See Silverberg, Robert
Bethmann, Erich Waldemar 1904- CAP-2
Earlier sketch in CA 23-24
Bethune, J. G.
See Ellis, Edward S(ylvester)
Bethune, J. H.
See Ellis, Edward S(ylvester)
Bethurum, F(rances) Dorothy 1897- CAP-2
Earlier sketch in CA 17-18
Beti, Mongo
See Biyidi, Alexandre
See also CLC 27
Betjeman, John 1906-1984 .... 11-12R
Obituary 112
See also DLB 20
See also DLBY 84
See also CLC 2, 6, 10, 34, 43
Betjeman, Penelope Chetwode
See Chetwode, Penelope
Betocchi, Carlo 1899- CANR-4
Earlier sketch in CA 9-10R
Bett, Walter R(eginald) 1903- CAP-1
Earlier sketch in CA 13-14
Bettelheim, Bruno 1903- CANR-23
Earlier sketch in CA 81-84
Bettelheim, Charles 1913- CANR-13
Earlier sketch in CA 73-76
Bettelheim, Frederick A(braham) 1923- 49-52
Betten, Neil B. 1939- 105
Bettenbender, John (I.) 1921-1988
Obituary 125
Bettenson, Henry (Scowcroft) 1908- 13-14R
Betteridge, Anne
See Potter, Margaret (Newman)
Betteridge, Don
See Newman, Bernard (Charles)
Betteridge, H(arold) T(homas) 1910- 5-6R
Bettersworth, John K(nox) 1909- CANR-2
Earlier sketch in CA 5-6R
Betti, Liliana 1939- 101
Betti, Ugo 1892-1953 Brief entry 104
See also TCLC 5
Bettina
See Ehrlich, Bettina Bauer
Bettis, Joseph Dabney 1936- 33-36R
Bettmann, Otto Ludwig 1903- 17-18R
See also SATA 46
Betts, Charles L(ancaster), Jr. 1908- 101
Betts, Donni 1948- CANR-5
Earlier sketch in CA 53-56
Betts, Doris (Waugh) 1932- CANR-9
Earlier sketch in CA 15-16R
See also DLBY 82
See also CLC 3, 6, 28
Betts, Emmett Albert 1903- 33-36R
Betts, George 1944- CANR-2
Earlier sketch in CA 45-48
Betts, Glynne Robinson 1934- 105
Betts, James
See Haynes, Betsy
Betts, John (Edward) 1939- 106
Betts, Raymond F. 1925- CANR-3
Earlier sketch in CA 3R
Betts, Richard K(evin) 1947- CANR-16
Earlier sketch in CA 85-88
Betts, William W(ilson), Jr. 1926- 33-36R
Betty, L(ewis) Stafford 1942- 118
Betz, Betty 1920- 4R
Betz, Eva Kelly 1897-1968 .... CAP-1
Earlier sketch in CA 11-12
See also SATA 10
Betz, Hans Dieter 1931- CANR-19
Earlier sketches in CA 53-56, CANR-4
Beuf, Ann H(ill) 1939- 85-88
Beum, Robert (Lawrence) 1929- 11-12R
Beurdeley, Michel 1911- 49-52
Beutel, William Charles 1930- 101
Beuttler, Edward Ivan Oakley 73-76
Bevan, Alistair
See Roberts, Keith (John Kingston)
Bevan, Aneurin 1897-1960 Obituary 106
Bevan, Bryan 1913- 13-14R
Bevan, E. Dean 1938- 33-36R
Bevan, Gloria Brief entry 117
Bevan, Jack 1920- 13-14R
Bevan, James (Stuart) 1930- 106
Bevan, Tom 1868-193(?) YABC-2
Bevenot, Maurice 1897-1980 Obituary 105
Beveridge, Albert J. 1862-1927 .... DLB-17
Beveridge, Andrew A(lan) 1945- 93-96
Beveridge, George David, Jr. 1922-1987 ... 102
Obituary 121
Beveridge, Meryle Secrest 1930- 81-84
Beveridge, Oscar Maltman 1913- 11-12R
Beveridge, William (Henry) 1879-1963
Obituary 112
Beveridge, William (Ian Beardmore) 1908- .. 106
Beverley, Mary Frances 1925- 120
Beverley, Robert 1673(?)-1722 ..... DLB-24, 30
BeVier, Michael J(udson) 97-100
Bevilacqua, Alberto 1934- CANR-26
Earlier sketch in CA 29-32R
Bevington, David M(artin) 1931- CANR-3
Earlier sketch in CA 3R
Bevington, Helen 1906- 15-16R
Bevis, Em Olivia 1932- CANR-1
Earlier sketch in CA 49-52
Bevis, H(erbert) U(rlin) 1902- CAP-2
Earlier sketch in CA 29-32
Bevis, James
See Cumberland, Marten
Bevlin, Marjorie Elliott 1917- 9-10R
Bewes, Richard 1934- CANR-20
Earlier sketch in CA 102
Bewick, Thomas 1753-1828 .... SATA-16
Bewkes, Eugene Garrett 1895- 7-8R
Bewley, Charles Henry 1888- 5-6R
Bewley, Marius 1918-1973 .... CANR-3
Obituary 41-44R
Earlier sketch in CA 5-6R
Bey, Isabelle
See Bosticco, (Isabel Lucy) Mary
Beye, Charles Rowan 1930- 93-96
Beyea, Basil 1910- 61-64
Beyer, (Richard) Andrew 1943- CANR-11
Earlier sketch in CA 69-72
Beyer, Audrey White 1916- 13-14R
See also SATA 9
Beyer, Edvard (Freydar) 1920- 121
Brief entry 116
Beyer, Evelyn M. 1907- CAP-2
Earlier sketch in CA 25-28
Beyer, Glenn H. 1913-1969 .... CANR-2
Earlier sketch in CA 3R
Beyer, Robert 1913(?)-1978 Obituary 77-80
Beyer, Steven L(arsen) 1943- 123
Beyer, Werner William 1911- 11-12R
Beyerchen, Alan 1945- 81-84
Beyerhaus, Peter (Paul Johannes)
1929- CANR-16
Earlier sketch in CA 93-96
Beyerlin, Walter W(ilhelm) 1929- 124
Beyers, Charlotte K(empner) 1931- 85-88
Beyfus, Drusilla 1927- 107
Beyle, Thad L. 1934- 37-40R
Beynon, Huw 1942- 107
Beynon, John
See Harris, John (Wyndham Parkes Lucas) Beynon
Beytagh, Gonville (Aubie) ffrench
See ffRench-Beytagh, Gonville (Aubie)
Bezencon, Jacqueline (Buxcel) 1924- ... SATA-48
Bezilla, Michael 1950- 111
Bezio, May Rowland ?-1977 Obituary 69-72
Bezruchka, Stephen (Anthony) 1943- 107
Bhagat, G(oberdhan) 1928- 29-32R
Bhagavatula, Murty S. 1921- 29-32R
Bhagwati, Jagdish N. 1934- 19-20R
Bhajan, Yogi
See Yogiji, Harbhajan Singh Khalsa
Bhaktivedanta Swami, A. C.
See Prabhupada, A. C. Bhaktivedanta
Bhana, Surendra 1939- 57-60
Bharati, Agehananda 1923- CANR-4
Earlier sketch in CA 4R
Bhardwaj, Surinder Mohan 1934- 45-48
Bharti, Ma Satya 1942- 102
Bhatia, Hans Raj 1904- 53-56
Bhatia, Jamunadevi 1919- 101
Bhatia, June
See Bhatia, Jamunadevi
Bhatia, Krishan 1926(?)-1974 Obituary 53-56
Bhatnagar, Joti 1935- 41-44R
Bhatt, Jagdish J(eyshanker) 1939- CANR-14
Earlier sketch in CA 77-80
Bhattacharji, Sukumari 1921- 33-36R
Bhattacharya, Bhabani 1906- CANR-9
Earlier sketch in CA 5-6R
Bhave, Vinoba 1895-1982 Obituary 108
Bhutto, Zulfikar Ali 1928-1979 .... CANR-11
Earlier sketch in CA 53-56
Biaggini, Adriana Ivancich 1930(?)-1983
Obituary 109
Biagi, Shirley 1944- CANR-15
Earlier sketch in CA 85-88
Bial, Morrison David 1917- 61-64
Bialik, Chaim Nachman 1873-1934 ..... TCLC-25
Bialk, Elisa
See Krautter, Elisa (Bialk)
Bialostocki, Jan 1921- 104
Bialostosky, Don H(oward) 1947- 120
Bianchi, Engene C(arl) 1930- 25-28R
Bianchi, Hombert 1912(?)-1980
Obituary 97-100
Bianchi, Robert S(teven) 1943- 109
Bianco, Lucien Andre 1930- CANR-15
Earlier sketch in CA 85-88
Bianco, Margery (Williams) 1881-1944
Brief entry 109
See also SATA 15
Bianco, Pamela 1906- 85-88
See also SATA 28
Biancolli, Louis Leopold 1907- 65-68
Biasin, Gian-Paolo 1933- 25-28R
Bibb, (David) Porter III 1937- 65-68
Bibby, Cyril 1914- CANR-7
Earlier sketch in CA 13-14R
Bibby, John F(ranklin) 1934- 45-48
Bibby, T(homas) Geoffrey 1917- CANR-4
Earlier sketch in CA 3R
Bibby, Violet 1908- 102
See also SATA 24
Bibee, John 1954- 112
Biberman, Edward 1904-1986 49-52
Obituary 118
Biberman, Herbert 1900-1971 .... CAP-1
Obituary 33-36R
Earlier sketch in CA 15-16
Bibesco, Marthe Lucie 1887-1973 93-96
Obituary 49-52
Bible, Charles 1937- 69-72
See also SATA 13
Bibo, Bobette
See Gugliotta, Bobette
Bicanic, Rudolf 1905-1968 85-88
Bice, Clare 1909-1976 .... SATA-22
Bichler, Joyce 1954- 107
Bichsel, Peter 1935- 81-84
See also DLB 75
Bick, Edgar Milton 1902-1978 Obituary ... 77-80
Bickel, Alexander M(ordecai)
1924-1974 .... CANR-1
Obituary 53-56
Earlier sketch in CA 4R
Bickelhaupt, David L(ynn) 1929- 69-72
Bickerman, Elias J(oseph) 1897-1981 .. CANR-20
Obituary 104
Earlier sketch in CA 25-28R
Bickers, Richard Leslie Townshend
1917- CANR-1
Earlier sketch in CA 45-48
Bickerstaff, Isaac
See Swift, Jonathan
Bickersteth, Geoffrey Langdale 1884-1974
Obituary 49-52
Bickerton, Derek 1926- 61-64
Bicket, Zenas J(ohan) 1932- 37-40R
Bickford, Elwood Dale 1927- 61-64
Bickham, Jack M(iles) 1930- CANR-23
Earlier sketches in CA 7-8R, CANR-8
Bickle, Judith Brundrett ?-19(?) CAP-1
Earlier sketch in CA 13-14
Bickley, R(obert) Bruce, Jr. 1942- CANR-9
Earlier sketch in CA 65-68
Bickman, Martin 1945- 104
Bida, Constantine 1916- CANR-13
Earlier sketch in CA 61-64
Bidart, Frank 19(?)- CLC-33
Bidault, Georges 1899-1983 Obituary 109
Biddiss, Michael Denis 1942- CANR-4
Earlier sketch in CA 53-56
Biddle, Arthur W(illiam) 1936- 45-48
Biddle, Bruce J(esse) 1928- CANR-7
Earlier sketch in CA 17-18R
Biddle, Francis (Beverley) 1886-1968 .... 5-6R
Obituary 103
Biddle, George 1885-1973 Obituary 45-48
Biddle, Katherine Garrison Chapin
1890-1977 .... CANR-5
Obituary 73-76
Earlier sketch in CA 5-6R
Biddle, Marcia McKenna 1931- 112
Biddle, Perry H(arvey), Jr. 1932- 57-60
Biddle, Phillips R. 1933- 37-40R
Biddle, Wayne 1948- 106
Biddle, William W(ishart) 1900-19(?) CAP-2
Earlier sketch in CA 17-18
Biderman, Albert D. 1923- CANR-23
Earlier sketches in CA 5-6R, CANR-8
Biderman, Sol 1936- 25-28R
Bidney, David 1908- 11-12R
Bidwell, Dafne (Mary) 1929- 97-100
Bidwell, Marjory Elizabeth Sarah 77-80
Bidwell, Percy W(ells) 1888-19(?) CAP-1
Earlier sketch in CA 9-10
Biebel, David B. 1949- 125
Bieber, Margarete 1879-1978 .... CANR-11
Obituary 77-80
Earlier sketch in CA 19-20R
Biebuyck, Daniel P. 1925- CANR-11
Earlier sketch in CA 25-28R
Biegel, John E(dward) 1925- 49-52
Biegel, Paul 1925- CANR-14
Earlier sketch in CA 77-80
See also SATA 16
Biehler, Robert F(rederick) 1927- 37-40R
Bielby, Cliff 1919-1984 Obituary 111
Bielenberg, Christabel 1909- 29-32R
Bieler, Ludwig 1906-1981 .... 7-8R
Obituary 103
Bielfield, Sidney 1904(?)-1984 Obituary 112
Bielski, Feliks
See Giergielewicz, Mieczyslaw F.
Bielyi, Sergei
See Hollo, Anselm
Biemiller, Carl L(udwig, Jr.) 1912-1979 121
Obituary 106
See also SATA 21, 40
Biemiller, Ruth Cobbett 1914- 37-40R
Bien, David Duckworth 1930- 5-6R
Bien, Joseph Julius 1936- CANR-5
Earlier sketch in CA 53-56
Bien, Peter (Adolph) 1930- 9-10R
Bienek, Horst 1930- 73-76
See also DLB 75
See also CLC 7, 11
Bienen, Henry Samuel 1939- 81-84
Bienenfeld, Florence L(ucille) 1929- CANR-23
Earlier sketch in CA 106
See also SATA 39
Bienstock, Mike
See Bienstock, Myron Joseph
Bienstock, Myron Joseph 1922- 9-10R
Bienvenu, Bernard J(efferson) 1925- 53-56
Bienvenu, Richard (Thomas) 1936- 61-64
Bier, Jesse 1925- CANR-3
Earlier sketch in CA 7-8R
Bier, William C(hristian) 1911-1980 ...... 33-36R
Obituary 97-100
Bierbaum, Margaret 1916- 33-36R
Bierbaum, Otto Julius 1865-1910 ...... DLB-66
Bierce, Ambrose (Gwinett) 1842-1914(?)
Brief entry 104
See also DLB 11, 12, 23, 71, 74
See also CDALB 1865-1917
See also TCLC 1, 7
Bierhorst, John (William) 1936- CANR-13
Earlier sketch in CA 33-36R
See also SATA 6
Bieri, Arthur Peter 1931- 61-64
Bierley, Paul E(dmund) 1926- CANR-13
Earlier sketch in CA 77-80
Bierman, Arthur K(almer) 1923- 85-88
Bierman, Harold, Jr. 1924- CANR-9
Earlier sketch in CA 19-20R
Bierman, Judah 1917- 114
Bierman, Mildred Thornton 1912- 5-6R
Bierman, Stanley M(elvin) 1935- 106
Biermann, Lillian
See Wehmeyer, Lillian (Mabel) Biermann
Biermann, Wolf 1936- 81-84
Biernatzki, William E(ugene) 1931- CANR-6
Earlier sketch in CA 57-60
Biers, William Richard 1938- CANR-23
Earlier sketch in CA 106
Bierstedt, Robert 1913- CANR-2
Earlier sketch in CA 1R
Biery, William (Richard) 1933- 57-60
Biesanz, Mavis Hiltunen 1919- 33-36R
Biesanz, Richard 1944- 112
Biesterveld, Betty Parsons 1923- CANR-1
Earlier sketch in CA 3R
Bietenholz, Peter G(erard) 1933- 101
Biezanek, Anne C(ampbell) 1927- 17-18R
Bigart, Robert James 1947- 33-36R
Bigelow, Donald N(evius) 1918- 41-44R
Bigelow, Gordon Ellsworth 1919- 110
Bigelow, Karl Worth 1898-1980
Obituary 97-100
Bigelow, Marybelle S(chmidt) 1923- 25-28R
Bigelow, Robert P(ratt) 1927- Brief entry ... 118
Bigelow, Robert Sydney 1918- 102
Bigg, Patricia Nina 1932- 102
Bigge, Morris L. 1908- 9-10R
Biggers, Earl Derr 1884-1933 Brief entry ... 108
Biggers, John Thomas 1924- CANR-2
Earlier sketch in CA 3R
Biggle, Lloyd, Jr. 1923- CANR-20
Earlier sketches in CA 13-14R, CANR-5
See also DLB 8
Biggs, Anselm G. 1914- 33-36R
Biggs, Bradley 1920- 124
Biggs, John B(urville) 1934- CANR-6
Earlier sketch in CA 57-60
Biggs, John, Jr. 1895-1979 Obituary 85-88
Biggs, Margaret Key 1933- 114
Biggs, (Marvin) Mouzon, Jr. 1941- 111
Biggs, Peter
See Rimel, Duane (Weldon)
Biggs-Davison, John (Alec) 1918- 13-14R
Bigiaretti, Libero 1906- CANR-12
Earlier sketch in CA 29-32R
Bigler, Vernon 1922- 21-22R
Bignell, Alan 1928- 103
Bigsby, C(hristopher) W(illiam) E(dgar)
1941- CANR-11
Earlier sketch in CA 25-28R
Bihalji-Merin, Oto 1904- CANR-15
Earlier sketch in CA 81-84
Bihler, Penny 1940- 77-80
Bijou, Sidney W(illiam) 1908- CANR-14
Earlier sketch in CA 37-40R
Bikel, Theodore 1924- CANR-1
Earlier sketch in CA 1R
Bikkie, James A(ndrew) 1929- 53-56
Biklen, Douglas Paul 1945- CANR-15
Earlier sketch in CA 85-88
Bilas, Richard A(llen) 1935- 53-56
Bilbo, Queenie ?-1972 Obituary 37-40R
Bilbow, Antony 1932- 25-28R
Bilderback, Dean Loy 1932- 97-100
Bilderback, Diane E(lizabeth) 1951- 110
Bileck, Marvin 1920- SATA-40
Bilek, Arthur J(ohn) 1929- 115
Bilich, Marion Yellin 1949- 114
Bilinsky, Yaroslav 1932- 13-14R
Bilkey, Warren J(oseph) 1920- 29-32R
Bill, Alfred Hoyt 1879-1964 107
See also SATA 44
Bill, J(ohn) Brent 1951- 117
Bill, James A(lban) 1939- Brief entry 114
Bill, Valentine T. 13-14R
Billam, Rosemary 1952- 123
Bill-Belotserkovsky, Vladimir Naumovich
1884-1970 Obituary 104
Biller, Henry B(urt) 1940- 114
Billetdoux, Francois (Paul) 1927- 21-22R
Billett, Roy O(ren) 1891- 13-14R
Billias, George Athan 1919- CANR-6
Earlier sketch in CA 11-12R
Billings, Charlene W(interer) 1941- CANR-24
Earlier sketch in CA 107
See also SATA 41
Billings, Charles E(dward) 1938- 121
Billings, Evelyn L(ivingston) 1918- 112
Billings, Ezra
See Halla, (Robert) Chris(tian)
Billings, Harold (Wayne) 1931- 25-28R
Billings, John Shaw 1898-1975 Obituary ... 104
Billings, Josh
See Shaw, Henry Wheeler
Billings, Peggy 1928- 25-28R
Billings, Richard N. 1930- 103
Billings, Robert 1949- 113
Billings, Warren M(artin) 1940- 61-64
Billings, William Dwight 1910- 113
Billingsley, Andrew 1926- 57-60
Billingsley, Edward Baxter 1910- CAP-2
Earlier sketch in CA 25-28
Billington, Dora May 1890-1968 .... CAP-1
Earlier sketch in CA 13-14
Billington, Elizabeth T(hain) 101
See also SATA 43, 50
Billington, James H(adley) 1929-
Brief entry 117
Billington, John
See Beaver, (Jack) Patrick
Billington, Joy 1931- 77-80
Billington, Michael 1939- 102
Billington, Monroe Lee 1928- 21-22R

Billington, Rachel 1942- 33-36R
See also CLC 43
See also AITN 2
Billington, Ray Allen 1903-1981 .... CANR-5
Obituary 103
Earlier sketch in CA 1R
Billington, Raymond John 1930- 110
Billmeyer, Fred Wallace, Jr. 1919- 85-88
Billout, Guy (Rene) 1941- CANR-26
Earlier sketch in CA 85-88
See also SATA 10
Bills, Robert E(dgar) 1916- 107
Bills, Scott L(aurence) 1948- 112
Billy, Andre 1882-1971 Obituary 29-32R
Bilow, Pat 1941- 106
Bilsland, Bilko
See Bilsland, E(rnest) C(harles)
Bilsland, E(rnest) C(harles) 1931- 69-72
Bimler, Richard William 1940- CANR-14
Earlier sketch in CA 41-44R
Binder, Aaron 1927- 57-60
Binder, David 1931- 65-68
Binder, Eando
See Binder, Otto O(scar)
Binder, Frederick M(elvin) 1931- 29-32R
Binder, Frederick Moore 1920- 41-44R
Binder, Leonard 1927- 61-64
Binder, Otto O(scar) 1911-1974 .... CANR-3
Obituary 53-56
Earlier sketch in CA 4R
Binder, Pearl
See Elwyn-Jones, Pearl Binder
Binding, Rudolf G. 1867-1938 .... DLB-66
Bindman, Arthur J(oseph) 1925- 45-48
Bindoff, Stanley Thomas 1908-1980 73-76
Obituary 102
Bindra, Dalbir 1922-1980 122
Obituary 117
Bing, Elisabeth D. 1914- CANR-11
Earlier sketch in CA 69-72
Bing, Rudolf 1902- 89-92
Bingaman, Ron 1936- 61-64
Binger, Carl A(lfred) L(anning) 1889-1976 73-76
Obituary 65-68
Binger, Norman H(enry) 1914- 33-36R
Binger, Walter 1888(?)-1979 Obituary 85-88
Bingham, (George) Barry 1906-1988
Obituary 126
Bingham, (George) Barry, Jr. 1933- 106
Bingham, Caleb 1757-1817 .... DLB-42
Bingham, Caroline 1938- CANR-10
Earlier sketch in CA 57-60
Bingham, Carson
See Cassiday, Bruce (Bingham)
Bingham, Charlotte (Mary Therese) 1942- CANR-11
Earlier sketch in CA 105
Bingham, David A(ndrew) 1926- 53-56
Bingham, Edwin R(alph) 1920- CANR-2
Earlier sketch in CA 5-6R
Bingham, Evangeline M(arguerite) L(adys) (Elliot) 1899- 65-68
Bingham, Jane Marie 1941- 104
Bingham, John (Michael Ward) 1908-1988 .... CANR-11
Obituary 126
Earlier sketch in CA 21-22R
Bingham, Jonathan Brewster 1914-1986 ....33-36R
Obituary 119
Bingham, June Rossbach 1919- 4R
Bingham, M(orley) P(aul) 1918- 49-52
Bingham, Madeleine (Mary Ebel) 1912-1988 .... CANR-11
Obituary 124
Earlier sketch in CA 13-14R
Bingham, Melinda 1950- 119
Bingham, Mindy
See Bingham, Melinda
Bingham, Richard D. 1937- 112
Bingham, Robert C(harles) 1927- 21-22R
Bingham, Robert E. 1925- 29-32R
Bingham, Robert Kamerer 1925(?)-1982
Obituary 107
Bingham, Sallie
See Ellsworth, Sallie Bingham
Bingham, Woodbridge 1901-1986
Obituary 119
Bingley, Clive (Hamilton) 1936- 19-20R
Bingley, D. E.
See Bingley, David Ernest
Bingley, David Ernest 1920- CANR-18
Earlier sketches in CA 45-48, CANR-2
Binham, Philip Frank 1924- 107
Binion, Rudolph 1927- CANR-4
Earlier sketch in CA 1R
bin Ishak, Yusof
See Ishak, Yusof bin
Binkley, Anne
See Rand, Ann (Binkley)
Binkley, Luther John 1925- 5-6R
Binkley, Olin T(rivette) 1908- 45-48
Binkley, William Campbell 1889-1970 107
Obituary 104
Binns, Archie (Fred) 1899- 73-76
Binns, J(ames) W(allace) 1940- 53-56
Binswanger, Ludwig 1881-1966 Obituary 107
Binyon, Claude 1905-1978 Obituary 77-80
Binyon, Helen 1904-1982(?) Obituary 114
Binyon, (Robert) Laurence 1869-1943
Brief entry 115
See also DLB 19
Binyon, T(imothy) J(ohn) 1936- 111
See also CLC 34
Binzen, Bill
See Binzen, William
See also SATA 24
Binzen, William 89-92
Biossat, Bruce 1910(?)-1974 Obituary 104
Biot, Francois 1923- 13-14R
Biow, Milton H. 1882(?)-1976 Obituary 65-68
Bioy Casares, Adolfo 1914- CANR-19
Earlier sketch in CA 29-32R
See also CLC 4, 8, 13
Biram, Brenda 1930(?)-1984 Obituary 112
Birch, Alison Wyrley 1922- 85-88
Birch, Anthony H(arold) 1924- CANR-5
Earlier sketch in CA 13-14R
Birch, Bruce C(harles) 1941- CANR-25
Earlier sketches in CA 65-68, CANR-10
Birch, Cyril 1925- 85-88
Birch, Daniel R(ichard) 1937- 101
Birch, David L. 1937- CANR-16
Earlier sketch in CA 25-28R
Birch, Herbert G. 1918-1973 Obituary 41-44R
Birch, L(ouis) C(harles) 1918- 120
Birch, Leo Bedrich 1902- 33-36R
Birch, Lionel ?-1982(?) Obituary 106
Birch, (Evelyn) Nigel (Chetwode) 1906-1981 Obituary 108
Birch, Reginald B(athurst) 1856-1943 .. SATA-19
Birch, William G(arry) 1909- 53-56
Birchall, Ian H(arry) 1939- 97-100
Bircham, Deric Neale 1934- 89-92
Bird, Al
See Mandel, Leon
Bird, Anthony (Cole) 1917- 13-14R
Bird, Brandon
See Evans, George Bird and Evans, Kay Harris
Bird, C.
See Ellison, Harlan
Bird, Caroline 1915- CANR-11
Earlier sketch in CA 19-20R
Bird, Cordwainer
See Ellison, Harlan
Bird, David 1926(?)-1987 Obituary 121
Bird, Dennis L(eslie) 1930- 116
Bird, Dorothy Maywood 1899- CAP-1
Earlier sketch in CA 17-18
Bird, Florence (Bayard) 1908- 97-100
Bird, George L(loyd) 1900- CANR-2
Earlier sketch in CA 5-6R
Bird, Harrison K. 1910- 85-88
Bird, Isabella L.
See Bishop, Isabella Lucy (Bird)
Bird, James Harold 1923- 102
Bird, Junius Bouton 1907-1982 Obituary 106
Bird, (Cyril) Kenneth 1887-1965 .... CAP-1
Earlier sketch in CA 13-14
Bird, Lewis P(enhall) 1933- CANR-17
Earlier sketch in CA 97-100
Bird, Patricia Amy 1941- CANR-22
Earlier sketches in CA 61-64, CANR-7
Bird, Richard (Miller) 1938- CANR-19
Earlier sketches in CA 11-12R, CANR-4
Bird, Sarah McCabe 1949- 111
Bird, Veronica 1932- 112
Bird, Vivian 1910- 102
Bird, W(illiam) Ernest 1890- CAP-1
Earlier sketch in CA 19-20
Bird, Wendell R(aleigh) 116
Bird, Will R. 1891- 13-14R
Bird, William 1889-1963 Obituary 112
See also DLB 4
Birdsall, Steve 1944- CANR-7
Earlier sketch in CA 53-56
Birdsell, Joseph B(enjamin) 1908- 119
Birdseye, Clarence (Frank) 1886-1956
Brief entry 122
Birdwell, Russell (Juarez) 1903-1977
Obituary 107
Birdwhistell, Ray L. 1918- 45-48
Birenbaum, Arnold 1939- 108
Birenbaum, Halina 1929- 45-48
Birenbaum, Harvey 1936- 109
Birenbaum, William M. 1923- 29-32R
Birimisa, George 1924- 89-92
Birkenhead, Lord
See Smith, Frederick Winston Furneaux
Birkenmayer, Sigmund Stanley 1923- 23-24R
Birket-Smith, Kaj 1893- CAP-1
Earlier sketch in CA 13-14
Birkin, Andrew (Timothy) 1945- 97-100
Birkin, Charles (Lloyd) 1907- 69-72
Birkley, Marilyn 1916- 41-44R
Birkner, Michael John 1950- 125
Birkos, Alexander S(ergei) 1936- 25-28R
Birks, Tony 1937- CANR-12
Earlier sketch in CA 69-72
Birksted-Breen, Dana 1946- 102
Birla, Ghanshyamdas 1894-1983 Obituary .. 110
Birla, Lakshminiwas N. 1909- CAP-1
Earlier sketch in CA 13-14
Birley, Julia (Davies) 1928- 13-14R
Birley, Robert 1903-1982 Obituary 110
Birmelin, Blair T. 1939- 117
Birmingham, David (Bevis) 1938- 19-20R
Birmingham, F(rederic) A(lexander) 1911-1982 .... CANR-11
Obituary 107
Earlier sketch in CA 17-18R
Birmingham, Frances A(therton) 1920- 17-18R
Birmingham, John 1951- 45-48
Birmingham, Lloyd 1924- SATA-12
Birmingham, Maisie 1914- 101
Birmingham, Stephen 1932- CANR-20
Earlier sketches in CA 49-52, CANR-2
See also AITN 1
Birmingham, Walter (Barr) 1913- 17-18R
Birn, Randi (Marie) 1935- 73-76
Birn, Raymond Francis 1935- 102
Birnbach, Martin 1929- 3R
Birnbaum, Eleazar 1929- 37-40R
Birnbaum, Louis 1909-1983 125
Birnbaum, Milton 1919- 33-36R
Birnbaum, Norman 1926- CANR-5
Earlier sketch in CA 53-56
Birnbaum, Philip 1904-1988 .... CANR-1
Obituary 125
Earlier sketch in CA 49-52
Birnbaum, Phyllis 1945- 102
Birnbaum, Stephen (Norman) 1937-
Brief entry 125
Birnbaum, Steve
See Birnbaum, Stephen (Norman)
Birnberg, Thomas B.
See Brooks, Thomas
Birne, Henry 1921- 17-18R
Birney, Alice L(otvin) 1938- 33-36R
Birney, (Alfred) Earle 1904- CANR-20
Earlier sketches in CA 3R, CANR-5
See also CLC 1, 4, 6, 11
Birnie, Whittlesey 1945- 97-100
Birnkrant, Arthur 1906(?)-1983 Obituary 108
Biro, B(alint) S(tephen) 1921- CANR-11
Earlier sketch in CA 25-28R
Biro, Charlotte Slovak 1904- 57-60
Biro, Val
See Biro, B(alint) S(tephen)
See also SATA 1
Biro, Yvette 111
Birren, Faber 1900- CANR-7
Earlier sketch in CA 13-14R
Birren, James E(mmett) 1918- 17-18R
Birse, A(rthur) H(erbert) 1889- CAP-2
Earlier sketch in CA 23-24
Birstein, Ann 17-18R
Birt, David 1936- CANR-13
Earlier sketch in CA 73-76
Bischof, Ledford Julius 1914- 11-12R
Bischoff, David F(redrick) 1951- 81-84
Bischoff, F(rederick) A(lexander) 1928- 89-92
Bischoff, Julia Bristol 1909-1970 .... CAP-2
Earlier sketch in CA 21-22
See also SATA 12
Bish, Robert L(ee) 1942- 53-56
Bishai, Wilson B. 1923- 33-36R
Bi Shang-guan
See Shen Congwen
Bisher, James F(urman) 1918- CANR-2
Earlier sketch in CA 5-6R
Bishin, William R(obert) 1939- 61-64
Bishir, John (William) 1933- 41-44R
Bishop, Bonnie 1943- 103
See also SATA 37
Bishop, Claire (Huchet) 73-76
See also SATA 14
Bishop, Crawford M. 1885- CAP-2
Earlier sketch in CA 17-18
Bishop, Curtis (Kent) 1912-1967 .... CAP-1
Earlier sketch in CA 11-12
See also SATA 6
Bishop, Donald
See Steward, Samuel M(orris)
Bishop, Donald G. 1907- CANR-3
Earlier sketch in CA 3R
Bishop, Donald H(arold) 1920- 105
Bishop, E. Morchard
See Stonor, Oliver
Bishop, Elizabeth 1911-1979 .... CANR-26
Obituary 89-92
Earlier sketch in CA 7-8R
See also CABS 2
See also SATA 24
See also DLB 5
See also CLC 1, 4, 9, 13, 15, 32
Bishop, Eugene C. 1909-1983 Obituary 109
Bishop, Ferman 1922- 23-24R
Bishop, Gavin 1946- 121
Bishop, George (Victor) 1924- CANR-2
Earlier sketch in CA 49-52
Bishop, George W(esley), Jr. 1910- 13-14R
Bishop, Gordon (Bruce) 1938- 118
Bishop, Ian Benjamin 1927- 106
Bishop, Isabella Bird
See Bishop, Isabella Lucy (Bird)
Bishop, Isabella L.
See Bishop, Isabella Lucy (Bird)
Bishop, Isabella Lucy (Bird) 1831-1904
Brief entry 123
Bishop, James 1929- 97-100
Bishop, James Alonzo 1907-1987 ....19-20R
Obituary 123
Bishop, Jim
See Bishop, James Alonzo
See also AITN 1, 2
Bishop, John 1908- 65-68
Bishop, John 1935- 105
See also CLC 10
Bishop, John L(yman) 1913-1974 .... CAP-2
Earlier sketch in CA 33-36
Bishop, John Melville 1946- CANR-13
Earlier sketch in CA 77-80
Bishop, John Peale 1892-1944 Brief entry .. 107
See also DLB 4, 9, 45
Bishop, Joseph W(arren), Jr. 1915-1985 ....33-36R
Obituary 116
Bishop, Leonard 1922- 15-16R
Bishop, Lloyd (Ormond) 1933- 114
Bishop, Louis Faugeres 1901(?)-1986 122
Obituary 119
Bishop, Maurice 1944-1983 123
Obituary 111
See also BW
Bishop, Maxine H. 1919- 25-28R
Bishop, Michael 1945- CANR-9
Earlier sketch in CA 61-64
See also AITN 2
Bishop, Morchard
See Stonor, Oliver
Bishop, Morris 1893-1973 .... CANR-6
Obituary 45-48
Earlier sketch in CA 4R
Bishop, Mrs. J. F.
See Bishop, Isabella Lucy (Bird)
Bishop, Pike
See Obstfeld, Raymond
Bishop, Robert 1938- CANR-15
Earlier sketch in CA 81-84
Bishop, Robert Lee 1931- 15-16R
Bishop, Ron 1922(?)-1988 Obituary 124
Bishop, Susan M. 1921(?)-1970 Obituary .. 104
Bishop, Tania Kroitor 1906- CAP-2
Earlier sketch in CA 29-32
Bishop, Thomas W(alter) 1929- CANR-18
Earlier sketches in CA 3R, CANR-1
Bishop, Tom
See Bishop, Thomas W(alter)
Bishop, W(illiam) Arthur 1923- 21-22R
Bishop, William W(arner), Jr. 1906- 17-18R
Bishop of Marsland
See Duncan, Ronald
Bishop of Truro
See Leonard, Graham Douglas
Bisignani, Joseph D(aniel) 1947- 112
Biskin, Miriam 1920- 21-22R
Bisque, Anatole
See Bosquet, Alain
Bissell, Claude T(homas) 1916- 101
Bissell, Elaine 81-84
Bissell, Richard (Pike) 1913-1977 .... CANR-6
Obituary 69-72
Earlier sketch in CA 4R
Bisset, Donald 1910- CANR-13
Earlier sketch in CA 33-36R
See also SATA 7
Bisset, Ronald 1950- 103
bissett, bill 1939- CANR-15
Earlier sketch in CA 69-72
See also DLB 53
See also CLC 18
Bissett, Donald J(ohn) 1930- 97-100
Bisson, Thomas N(oel) 1931- 119
Bissoondoyal, Basdeo 1906- CANR-11
Earlier sketch in CA 25-28R
Bisztray, George 1938- 106
Bita, Lili
See Zaller, Angelika Bita
Bite, Ben
See Schneck, Stephen
Bitker, Marjorie M. 1901- 77-80
Bitsios, Dimitri S. 1915-1984 Obituary 111
Bittel, Lester Robert 1918- CANR-21
Earlier sketches in CA 15-16R, CANR-6
Bitter, Francis 1902-1967 Obituary 113
Bitter, Gary G(len) 1940- CANR-14
Earlier sketch in CA 69-72
See also SATA 22
Bittermann, Henry J(ohn) 1904- 33-36R
Bittinger, Desmond W(right) 1905- 37-40R
Bittinger, Emmert F(oster) 1925- 37-40R
Bittker, Boris I(rving) 1916- Brief entry 109
Bittle, William E(lmer) 1926- 53-56
Bittlinger, Arnold 1928- 49-52
Bittner, Donald F(rancis) 1941- 122
Bittner, Vernon (John) 1932- 69-72
Bittner, William (Robert) 1921- 5-6R
Bitton, Davis 1930- CANR-14
Earlier sketch in CA 33-36R
Biven, W(illiam) Carl 1925- 21-22R
Bivins, John 1940- 85-88
Bixby, Jay Lewis
See Bixby, Jerome Lewis
Bixby, Jerome Lewis 1923- 17-18R
Bixby, Ray Z.
See Tralins, S(andor) Robert
Bixby, William (Courtney) 1920-1986 ... CANR-6
Obituary 118
Earlier sketch in CA 3R
See also SATA 6, 47
Bixler, Julius Seelye 1894-1985 Obituary 115
Bixler, Norma 1905- 49-52
Bixler, Paul (Howard) 1899- 69-72
Bixler, R(oy) Russell, Jr. 1927- 61-64
Biyidi, Alexandre 1932- 124
Brief entry 114
See also BW
Bizardel, Yvon 1891- 61-64
Bizzarro, Salvatore 1939- 53-56
Bjarme, Brynjolf
See Ibsen, Henrik (Johan)
Bjerke, Robert Alan 1939- 41-44R
Bjerke, Ward (Ollie) 1920- Brief entry 108
Bjerre, Jens 1921- 11-12R
Bjoerneboe, Jens 1920-1976 69-72
Obituary 65-68
Bjoernson, Bjoernstjerne (Martinius) 1832-1910 Brief entry 104
See also TCLC 7
Bjorklund, Lorence F. 1913-1978 ... SATA-32, 35
Bjorn, Thyra Ferre 1905-1975 .... CANR-3
Obituary 57-60
Earlier sketch in CA 5-6R
Bjornard, Reidar B(ernhard) 1917- 33-36R
Bjorneboe, Jens
See Bjoerneboe, Jens
Bjornson, Bjornstjerne (Martinius)
See Bjoernson, Bjoernstjerne (Martinius)
See also TCLC 7
Bjornson, Richard 1938- 77-80
Bjornson, (Kristjan) Val(dimar) 1906-1987
Obituary 121

Bjornstad, James 1940- ... 29-32R
Bjorset, Bryniolf
See Beorse, Bryn
Blachford, George 1913- ... 11-12R
Blachly, Frederick (Frank) 1881(?)-1975
Obituary ... 57-60
Blachly, Lou 1889- ... CAP-1
Earlier sketch in CA 13-14
Black, Albert George 1928- ... 45-48
Black, Algernon David 1900- ... CANR-2
Earlier sketch in CA 4R
See also SATA 12
Black, Angus 1943- ... 29-32R
Black, Antony 1936- ... 121
Black, Betty
See Schwartz, Betty
Black, Bonnie Lee 1945- ... 107
Black, Brady Forrest 1908- ... 102
Black, Campbell 1944- ... 89-92
Black, Charles
See Black, Charles L(und), Jr.
Black, Charles L(und), Jr. 1915- ... CANR-3
Earlier sketch in CA 1R
Black, Clinton Vane De Brosse 1918- ... 102
Black, Creed C(arter) 1925- ... 73-76
Black, Cyril Edwin 1915- ... CANR-3
Earlier sketch in CA 4R
Black, D. M.
See Black, David (Macleod)
Black, David (Macleod) 1941- ... 25-28R
See also DLB 40
Black, David
See Way, Robert E(dward)
Black, Dianne (a pseudonym) 1940- ... 97-100
Black, Dorothy 1899-1985 Obituary ... 115
Black, Dorothy 1914- ... 111
Black, Douglas M. 1896(?)-1977 Obituary ... 104
Black, Duncan 1908- ... CAP-2
Earlier sketch in CA 19-20
Black, E(dward) L(oring) 1915- ... 9-10R
Black, Earl 1942- ... 101
Black, Elizabeth 1908(?)-1987 Obituary ... 122
Black, Eugene C(harlton) 1927- ... 11-12R
Black, Eugene R(obert) 1898- ... CAP-2
Earlier sketch in CA 25-28
Black, Floyd H. 1888-1983 Obituary ... 111
Black, Gavin
See Wynd, Oswald Morris
Black, Hallie 1943- ... 108
Black, Harry George 1933- ... 61-64
Black, Hugh C(leon) 1920- ... 37-40R
Black, Hugo Lafayette 1886-1971
Obituary ... 33-36R
Black, Ian Stuart 1915- ... CANR-6
Earlier sketch in CA 9-10R
Black, Irma Simonton 1906-1972 ... CANR-6
Obituary ... 37-40R
Earlier sketch in CA 4R
See also SATA 2, 25
Black, Ishi
See Gibson, Walter B(rown)
Black, Ivan 1904(?)-1979 Obituary ... 85-88
Black, James A(llen) 1937- ... 121
Black, James Menzies 1913- ... CANR-5
Earlier sketch in CA 5-6R
Black, John N(icholson) 1922- ... CANR-13
Earlier sketch in CA 33-36R
Black, John Wilson 1906- ... CAP-1
Earlier sketch in CA 17-18
Black, Jonathan
See von Block, Bela W(illiam)
Black, Joseph E. 1921- ... 11-12R
Black, Kenneth, Jr. 1925- ... CANR-7
Earlier sketch in CA 15-16R
Black, Kitty
See Black, Dorothy
Black, Lionel
See Barker, Dudley
Black, Maggie
See Black, Margaret K(atherine)
Black, Malcolm Charles Lamont 1928- ... 85-88
Black, Mansell
See Trevor, Elleston
Black, Margaret K(atherine) 1921- ... CANR-14
Earlier sketch in CA 29-32R
Black, Martha E(llen) 1901- ... 33-36R
Black, Mary (Childs) 1922- ... CANR-13
Earlier sketch in CA 21-22R
Black, Matthew W(ilson) 1895- ... CAP-2
Earlier sketch in CA 25-28
Black, Max 1909- ... 61-64
Black, Michael L(awrence) 1940- ... 121
Black, Millard H. 1912- ... 25-28R
Black, Misha 1910- ... CAP-1
Earlier sketch in CA 11-12
Black, Nancy B(reMiller) 1941- Brief entry ... 107
Black, Percy 1922- ... 33-36R
Black, Robert 1946- ... 121
Black, Robert B(ruce) 1920- ... 109
Black, Robert C(lifford) III 1914- ... 41-44R
Black, Roe C(oddington) 1926- ... 89-92
Black, Stanley Warren III 1939- ... 45-48
Black, Susan Adams 1953- ... 105
See also SATA 40
Black, Theodore Michael 1919- ... 109
Black, Veronica
See Peters, Maureen
Black, William Joseph 1934(?)-1977
Obituary ... 73-76
Black, Winifred 1863-1936 ... DLB-25
Blackall, Eric Albert 1914- ... 65-68
Blackamore, Arthur 1679-? ... DLB-24, 39
Blackbeard, Bill 1926- ... 97-100
Blackburn, Alexander (Lambert) 1929- ... 97-100
See also DLBY 85
Blackburn, Barbara
See Leader, (Evelyn) Barbara (Blackburn)
Blackburn, Claire
See Jacobs, Linda C.
Blackburn, George M. III 1950- ... 123
Blackburn, Graham (John) 1940- ... CANR-22
Earlier sketch in CA 69-72
Blackburn, John (Fenwick) 1923- ... CANR-22
Earlier sketches in CA 3R, CANR-2
Blackburn, John(ny) Brewton 1952- ... SATA-15
Blackburn, Joyce Knight 1920- ... 17-18R
See also SATA 29
Blackburn, Laurence Henry 1897- ... 57-60
Blackburn, Michael 1954- ... 118
Blackburn, Norma Davis 1914- ... 69-72
Blackburn, Paul 1926-1971 ... 81-84
Obituary ... 33-36R
See also DLB 16
See also DLBY 81
See also CLC 9, 43
Blackburn, R(obert) M(artin) 1934- ... 119
Blackburn, Robert T. 1923- ... 121
Blackburn, Simon 1944- ... 49-52
Blackburn, Thomas (Eliel Fenwick)
1916-1977 ... 73-76
Obituary ... 113
See also DLB 27
Blackburn, Thomas C(arl) 1936- ... CANR-22
Earlier sketch in CA 69-72
Blackburne, Kenneth (William) 1907-1980
Obituary ... 105
Blackburne, Neville Alfred Edmund 1913- ... 53-56
Blacker, C(arlos) P(aton) 1895-1975
Obituary ... 57-60
Blacker, Carmen Elizabeth 1924- ... 11-12R
Blacker, Irwin R(obert) 1919-1985 ... CANR-3
Obituary ... 115
Earlier sketch in CA 3R
Blackett, Patrick (Maynard Stuart)
1897-1974 Obituary ... 49-52
Blackett, Veronica Heath 1927- ... 53-56
See also SATA 12
Blackey, Robert 1941- ... CANR-4
Earlier sketch in CA 53-56
Blackford, Charles Minor III 1898- ... 69-72
Blackford, Staige D(avis) 1931- ... 103
Blackhall, David Scott 1910- ... 7-8R
Blackham, Garth J. 1926- ... 33-36R
Blackham, H(arold) J(ohn) 1903- ... 23-24R
Black Hobart
See Sanders, (James) Ed(ward)
Blackie, Bruce L(othian) 1936- ... 57-60
Blackie, John (Ernest Haldane)
1904-1985 ... 73-76
Obituary ... 116
Blackie, Pamela 1917- ... 103
Blacking, John (Anthony Randoll)
1928- ... CANR-3
Earlier sketch in CA 11-12R
Blackledge, Ethel H(ale) ... CANR-11
Earlier sketch in CA 23-24R
Blackman, Audrey 1907- ... 109
Blackman, Sheldon 1935- ... 33-36R
Blackman, Victor 1922- ... 103
Blackmer, Donald L. M. 1929- ... 33-36R
Black-Michaud, Jacob 1938- ... 61-64
Blackmon, C(harles) Robert 1925- ... 33-36R
Blackmon, Rosemary Barnsdall
1921(?)-1983 Obituary ... 111
Blackmore, Charles (David) 1957- ... 124
Blackmore, Dorothy S. 1914- ... 41-44R
Blackmore, John T(homas) 1931- ... CANR-15
Earlier sketch in CA 41-44R
Blackmore, Peter 1909-1984 ... 9-10R
Obituary ... 114
Blackmore, R(ichard) D(oddridge)
1825-1900 Brief entry ... 120
See also DLB 18
See also TCLC 27
Blackmore, Robert Long 1919- ... 113
Blackmur, R(ichard) P(almer) 1904-1965 ... CAP-1
Obituary ... 25-28R
Earlier sketch in CA 11-12
See also DLB 63
See also CLC 2, 24
Blackoff, Edward M. 1934- ... 11-12R
Blackshear, Helen F(riedman) 1911- ... CANR-10
Earlier sketch in CA 25-28R
Blacksnake, George
See Richardson, Gladwell
Blackstock, Charity
See Torday, Ursula
Blackstock, Lee
See Torday, Ursula
Blackstock, Nelson 1944- ... 97-100
Blackstock, Paul W(illiam) 1913- ... 15-16R
Blackstock, Walter 1917- ... CANR-9
Earlier sketch in CA 5-6R
Blackstone, Bernard 1911-1983 ... 69-72
Obituary ... 111
Blackstone, Geoffrey Vaughan 1910- ... CAP-1
Earlier sketch in CA 9-10
Blackstone, Harry
See Blackstone, Harry (Bouton), Jr.
Blackstone, Harry (Bouton), Jr. 1934- ... 114
Blackstone, Tessa Ann Vosper 1942- ... CANR-19
Earlier sketch in CA 102
Blackstone, William T(homas) 1931- ... CANR-11
Earlier sketch in CA 17-18R
Black Tarantula, The
See Acker, Kathy
Blackton, Peter
See Wilson, Lionel
Blackwelder, Bernice Fowler 1902- ... 3R
Blackwelder, Boyce W. 1913- ... 19-20R
Blackwelder, Jerry 1950- ... 122
Blackwell, Basil (Henry) 1889-1984
Obituary ... 112
Blackwell, Betsy Talbot 1905(?)-1985
Obituary ... 115
Blackwell, (Samuel) Earl (Jr.) 1913- ... 81-84
Blackwell, James E(dward) 1926-
Brief entry ... 114
Blackwell, Leslie 1885- ... 9-10R
Blackwell, Lois S. 1943- ... 85-88
Blackwell, (Annie) Louise 1919-1977 ... 37-40R
Blackwell, Marilyn Johns 1948- ... 116
Blackwell, Muriel F(ontenot) 1929- ... 108
Blackwell, Richard Joseph 1929- ... 33-36R
Blackwell, Roger D(ale) 1940- ... 93-96
Blackwell, William L. 1929- ... 23-24R
Blackwood, Alan 1932- ... 110
Blackwood, Algernon (Henry) 1869-1951
Brief entry ... 105
See also TCLC 5
Blackwood, Andrew W(atterson)
1882-1966 ... 5-6R
Obituary ... 103
Blackwood, Andrew W(atterson), Jr.
1915- ... CANR-5
Earlier sketch in CA 1R
Blackwood, Caroline 1931- ... 85-88
See also DLB 14
See also CLC 6, 9
Blackwood, Cheryl Prewitt 1957- ... 108
Blackwood, Easley 1903- ... 115
Blackwood, George D(ouglas) 1919- ... 13-14R
Blackwood, James R. 1918- ... 23-24R
Blackwood, Paul Everett 1913- ... 102
Blade, Alexander
See Hamilton, Edmond
and Silverberg, Robert
Bladel, Roderick L(eRoy) ... 97-100
Bladen, Ashby 1929- ... 106
Bladen, V(incent) W(heeler) 1900- ... 61-64
Blades, Ann 1947- ... CANR-13
Earlier sketch in CA 77-80
See also SATA 16
See also CLR 15
Blades, Brian Brewer 1906-1977
Obituary ... 73-76
Blades, James 1901- ... 65-68
Bladow, Suzanne Wilson 1937- ... 61-64
See also SATA 14
Blaffer, Sarah C.
See Hrdy, Sarah Blaffer
Blagden, Cyprian 1906-1962 ... 4R
Blagden, David 1944- ... 53-56
Blagowidow, George 1923- ... 77-80
Blaher, Damian J(oseph) 1913- ... 21-22R
Blaich, Theodore Paul 1902- ... CAP-1
Earlier sketch in CA 13-14
Blaike, Avona
See MacIntosh, Joan
Blaikie, Robert J. 1923- ... 33-36R
Blaiklock, Edward Musgrave 1903- ... CANR-7
Earlier sketch in CA 19-20R
Blaine, James
See Avallone, Michael (Angelo), Jr.
Blaine, John
See Goodwin, Harold Leland
Blaine, Marge
See Blaine, Margery Kay
Blaine, Margery Kay 1937- ... 61-64
See also SATA 11
Blaine, Thomas R(obert) 1895- ... 106
Blaine, Tom R.
See Blaine, Thomas R(obert)
Blaine, William L(ee) 1931- ... 65-68
Blainey, Ann (Warriner) 1935- ... 25-28R
Blainey, Geoffrey (Norman) 1930- ... 25-28R
Blair
See Blair-Fish, Wallace Wilfrid
Blair, Anne Denton 1914- ... 110
See also SATA 46
Blair, Calvin Patton 1924- ... 15-16R
Blair, Carvel Hall 1924- ... 49-52
Blair, Charles E. 1920- ... 25-28R
Blair, Claude 1922- ... CANR-11
Earlier sketch in CA 7-8R
Blair, Clay Drewry, Jr. 1925- ... 77-80
See also AITN 2
Blair, Cynthia 1953- ... 118
Blair, (Robert) Dike 1919- ... 9-10R
Blair, Don 1933- ... 65-68
Blair, Dorothy L. 1890- ... 114
Blair, Dorothy S(ara Greene) 1913-
Brief entry ... 113
Blair, Edward H. 1938- ... CANR-7
Earlier sketch in CA 17-18R
Blair, Edward P(ayson) 1910- ... CANR-26
Earlier sketches in CA 13-14, CAP-1,
CANR-11
Blair, Eric Hugh 1903-1950 Brief entry ... 104
See also SATA 29
Blair, Everetta Love 1907- ... CAP-2
Earlier sketch in CA 25-28
Blair, Francis Preston 1791-1876 ... DLB-43
Blair, Frank 1915- ... 93-96
Blair, George S(imms) 1924- ... 17-18R
Blair, Glenn Myers 1908- ... 5-6R
Blair, Gwenda (Linda) 1943- ... 125
Blair, Harry Wallace 1938- ... 109
Blair, Helen 1910- ... SATA-29
Blair, J(oseph) Allen 1913- ... 89-92
Blair, James 1655(?)-1743 ... DLB-24
Blair, Jane N(emec) 1911- ... 57-60
Blair, Jay 1953- ... SATA-45
Blair, John Durburrow 1759-1823 ... DLB-37
Blair, John G(eorge) 1934- ... 15-16R
Blair, John M(alcolm) 1914-1976 ... 73-76
Obituary ... 69-72
Blair, Kay Reynolds 1942- ... 33-36R
Blair, Leon Borden 1917- ... 29-32R
Blair, Lorraine Louise 1899(?)-1984
Obituary ... 114
Blair, Lucile
See Yeakley, Marjory Hall
Blair, Paxton 1892-1974 Obituary ... 53-56
Blair, Peter Hunter
See Hunter Blair, Peter
Blair, Philip M(ark) 1928- ... 41-44R
Blair, Ruth Van Ness 1912- ... 21-22R
See also SATA 12
Blair, Sam 1932- ... 53-56
Blair, Shannon
See Kaye, Marilyn
Blair, Thomas (Lucien Vincent) 1926- ... 106
Blair, Walter 1900- ... CANR-18
Earlier sketches in CA 5-6R, CANR-3
See also SATA 12
Blair, Wilfrid
See Blair-Fish, Wallace Wilfrid
Blair-Fish, Wallace Wilfrid 1889-1968 ... CAP-2
Earlier sketch in CA 29-32
Blais, Madeleine 1947- ... 104
Blais, Marie-Claire 1939- ... 21-22R
See also CAAS 4
See also DLB 53
See also CLC 2, 4, 6, 13, 22
Blaisdell, Anne
See Linington, (Barbara) Elizabeth
Blaisdell, Anne
See Linington, Elizabeth
Blaisdell, Donald C(hristy) 1899-1988 ... 37-40R
Obituary ... 126
Blaisdell, Foster W(arren) 1927- ... 69-72
Blaisdell, Harold F. 1914- ... 65-68
Blaisdell, Paul H(enry) 1908- ... 61-64
Blaise, Clark 1940- ... CANR-5
Earlier sketch in CA 53-56
See also CAAS 3
See also DLB 53
See also CLC 29
See also AITN 2
Blake, Alfred
See Janifer, Laurence M(ark)
Blake, Andrew
See Janifer, Laurence M(ark)
Blake, Brian 1918- ... 109
Blake, Bud
See Blake, Julian Watson
Blake, Christina
See Chandler, Bryn
Blake, David H(aven) 1940- ... 41-44R
Blake, Eubie
See Blake, James Hubert
Blake, Eugene Carson 1906-1985
Obituary ... 116
Blake, Fay M(ontaug) 1920- ... 53-56
Blake, Gary 1944- ... CANR-15
Earlier sketch in CA 85-88
Blake, Gerald H(enry) 1936- ... 124
Blake, Harlan Morse 1923- ... 25-28R
Blake, I(srael) George 1902- ... 21-22R
Blake, J. W.
See Blake, John William
Blake, James 1922-1979 ... 93-96
Obituary ... 85-88
Blake, James Hubert 1883-1983 Obituary ... 109
Blake, Jennifer
See Maxwell, Patricia
Blake, John W.
See Blake, John William
Blake, John William 1911-1987 Obituary ... 122
Blake, Jonas
See Hardy, C. Colburn
Blake, Judith (Kincade) 1926- ... 3R
Blake, Julian Watson 1918- ... 65-68
Blake, Justin
See Bowen, John (Griffith)
Blake, Katherine
See Walter, Dorothy Blake
Blake, Kathleen 1944- ... 57-60
Blake, Kay
See Walter, Dorothy Blake
Blake, Ken
See Bulmer, (Henry) Kenneth
Blake, L(eslie) J(ames) 1913- ... CANR-11
Earlier sketch in CA 25-28R
Blake, Minden V(aughan) 1913- ... 69-72
Blake, Mindy
See Blake, Minden V.
Blake, Monica
See Muir, Marie
Blake, Nelson Manfred 1908- ... CANR-3
Earlier sketch in CA 1R
Blake, Nicholas
See Day Lewis, C(ecil)
Blake, Norman (Francis) 1934- ... 93-96
Blake, Olive
See Supraner, Robyn
Blake, Patricia 1933- ... 49-52
Blake, Patrick
See Egleton, Clive (Frederick)
Blake, Paul C. 1916- ... 25-28R
Blake, Peter (Jost) 1920- ... CANR-14
Earlier sketch in CA 65-68
Blake, Quentin 1932- ... CANR-11
Earlier sketch in CA 25-28R
See also SATA 9, 52
Blake, Reed H(arris) 1933- ... 57-60
Blake, Richard A(loysius) 1939- ... 93-96
Blake, Robert (Norman William) 1916- ... CANR-22
Earlier sketch in CA 9-10R
Blake, Robert 1949- ... SATA-42
Blake, Robert
See Davies, L(eslie) P(urnell)
Blake, Robert R(ogers) 1918- ... CANR-13
Earlier sketch in CA 23-24R
Blake, Robert W(illiam) 1930- ... 33-36R

Blake, Sally
See Saunders, Jean
Blake, Sally Mirliss 1925-1986 ....17-18R
Obituary 118
Blake, Stephanie
See Pearl, Jacques Bain
Blake, Vanessa
See Brown, May
Blake, Walker E.
See Butterworth, W(illiam) E(dmund III)
Blake, Wendon
See Holden, Donald
Blake, William 1757-1827 ..... SATA-30
Blake, William J(ames) 1894-1969 .....5-6R
Obituary 25-28R
Blakeborough, Jack Fairfax
See Fairfax-Blakeborough, John Freeman
Blakeborough, John Freeman Fairfax
See Fairfax-Blakeborough, John Freeman
Blakeley, Phyllis (Ruth) 1922- 61-64
Blakeley, Thomas J(ohn) 1931- CANR-3
Earlier sketch in CA 9-10R
Blakely, Allison 1940- 125
Blakely, R(obert) J(ohn) 1915- 37-40R
Blakemore, Colin (Brian) 1944- 85-88
Blakeney, Jay D.
See Chester, Deborah
Blaker, Alfred A(rthur) 1928- 65-68
Blakeslee, Alton (Lauren) 1913- 105
Blakeslee, Thomas R(obert) 1937- 101
Blakeston, Oswell 1907(?)-1985(?)
Obituary 116
Blakey, George T., Jr. 1939- 120
Blakey, Scott 1936- 85-88
Blakey, Walker Jameson 1940- 69-72
Blakiston, Georgiana 1903- 69-72
Blakiston, Noel 1905-1984 Obituary 115
Blakney, Raymond D. 1897(?)-1970
Obituary 104
Blalock, Hubert Morse, Jr. 1926- CANR-5
Earlier sketch in CA 13-14R
Blalock, Jane B. 1945- Brief entry 112
Blamires, David (Malcolm) 1936- CANR-14
Earlier sketch in CA 65-68
Blamires, Harry 1916- CANR-20
Earlier sketches in CA 9-10R, CANR-5
Blance, Ellen 1931- CANR-7
Earlier sketch in CA 57-60
Blanch, Lesley 1907- 102
Blanch, Robert J. 1938- 21-22R
Blanch, Stuart Yarworth 1918- 106
Blanchard, Allan E(dward) 1929- 69-72
Blanchard, B(irdsall) Everard 1909- 41-44R
Blanchard, Carroll Henry, Jr. 1928- 15-16R
Blanchard, Fessenden Seaver 1888-1963 .....5-6R
Blanchard, Howard L(awrence) 1909- 7-8R
Blanchard, J. Richard 1912- 89-92
Blanchard, Kendall A(llan) 1942- CANR-11
Earlier sketch in CA 69-72
Blanchard, Kenneth H(artley) 1939- 111
Blanchard, Nina 101
Blanchard, Paula (Barber) 1936- 81-84
Blanchard, Peter 1946- 117
Blanchard, Ralph Harrub 1890-1973 ..... CAP-1
Earlier sketch in CA 13-14
Blanchard, William H(enry) 1922- CANR-8
Earlier sketch in CA 23-24R
Blanche, Pierre 1927- 25-28R
Blanchet, Eileen 1924- 57-60
Blanchette, Oliva 1929- 53-56
Blanchot, Maurice 1907- Brief entry 117
See also DLB 72
Blanck, Gertrude 1914- 85-88
Blanck, Jacob Nathaniel 1906-1974 ..... CAP-1
Obituary 53-56
Earlier sketch in CA 11-12
Blanck, Rubin 1914- 25-28R
Blanco, Luis Anado 1903(?)-1975
Obituary 104
Blanco, Richard L(idio) 1926- 57-60
Blanco White, Amber 1887-1981 Obituary 105
Bland, Alexander
See Gosling, Nigel
Bland, E.
See Nesbit, E(dith)
Bland, Fabian
See Nesbit, E(dith)
Bland, Hester Beth 1906- 57-60
Bland, Jeffrey 1946- 106
Bland, Jennifer
See Bowden, Jean
Bland, Larry I(rvin) 1940- 109
Bland, Randall Walton 1942- CANR-5
Earlier sketch in CA 53-56
Blanda, George (Frederick) 1927-
Brief entry 114
Blandenship, Edward Gary 1943- 45-48
Blandford, Brian E(rnest) 1937- 118
Blandford, Percy William 1912- 9-10R
Blanding, Forrest H(arvey) 1917- 111
Blandino, Giovanni 1923- 23-24R
Blane, Gertrude
See Blumenthal, Gertrude
Blane, Howard T(homas) 1926- CANR-10
Earlier sketch in CA 25-28R
Blanford, James T. 1917- 33-36R
Blank, Blanche D(avis) 41-44R
Blank, George (W. III) 1945- 110
Blank, Joseph P. 1919- 93-96
Blank, Leonard 1927- CANR-12
Earlier sketch in CA 33-36R
Blank, Sheldon H(aas) 1896- 4R
Blankenship, A(lbert) B. 1914- CANR-7
Earlier sketch in CA 15-16R
Blankenship, Edward Gary 1943- 45-48
Blankenship, Lela (McDowell) 1886- 7-8R
Blankenship, William D(ouglas) 1934- 33-36R
Blankfort, (Seymour) Michael
1907-1982 ..... CANR-2
Obituary 107
Earlier sketch in CA 3R
Blanksten, George I(rving) 1917- CANR-1
Earlier sketch in CA 1R
Blanpied, Pamela Wharton 1937- 102
Blanshard, Brand 1892-1987 ..... CANR-16
Obituary 124
Earlier sketch in CA 4R
Blanshard, Paul 1892-1980 Obituary 93-96
Blanton, (Martha) Catherine 1907- 4R
Blantz, Thomas E(dward) 1934- 111
Blanzaco, Andre C. 1934- 29-32R
Blasco Ibanez, Vicente 1867-1928
Brief entry 110
See also TCLC 12
Blase, Melvin G(eorge) 1933- 33-36R
Blaser, Robin (Francis) 1925- CANR-8
Earlier sketch in CA 57-60
Blashford-Snell, John Nicholas 1936- CANR-19
Earlier sketch in CA 102
Blasier, (Stewart) Cole 1925- 23-24R
Blasing, Mutlu Konuk 1944- 89-92
Blasing, Randy 1943- 114
Blass, Birgit A(nnelise) 1940- 29-32R
Blass, Ron(ald J.) 1922-1984 Obituary 114
Blassingame, John W(esley) 1940- CANR-25
Earlier sketch in CA 49-52
See also BW
Blassingame, Wyatt Rainey 1909-1985 ..... CANR-3
Obituary 114
Earlier sketch in CA 4R
See also SATA 1, 34, 41
Blatchford, Christie 1951- 73-76
Blathwayt, Jean 1918- 106
Blatt, Burton 1927- CANR-14
Earlier sketch in CA 41-44R
Blatt, Sidney J(ules) 1928- 37-40R
Blatter, Dorothy (Gertrude) 1901- CAP-1
Earlier sketch in CA 11-12
Blatty, William Peter 1928- CANR-9
Earlier sketch in CA 7-8R
See also CLC 2
Blau, Abram 1907-1979 Obituary 85-88
Blau, Eric 1921- 85-88
Blau, Francine D(ee) 1946- CANR-25
Earlier sketch in CA 106
Blau, Herbert 1926- 111
Blau, Joseph L(eon) 1909-1986 .....9-10R
Obituary 121
Blau, Joshua 1919- CANR-7
Earlier sketch in CA 15-16R
Blau, Judith R. 1942- 122
Blau, Milton
See Blau, Eric
Blau, Peter M(ichael) 1918- CANR-1
Earlier sketch in CA 1R
Blau, Sheldon Paul 1935- 57-60
Blau, Tom 1913(?)-1984 Obituary 113
Blau, Yehoshua
See Blau, Joshua
Blau, Zena Smith 1922- CANR-1
Earlier sketch in CA 45-48
Blauer, Ettagale 1940- CANR-24
Earlier sketch in CA 103
See also SATA 49
Blaufarb, Douglas S(amuel) 1918- 85-88
Blaug, Mark 1927- CANR-16
Earlier sketches in CA 3R, CANR-1
Blaukopf, Kurt 1914- Brief entry 114
Blauner, Robert 1929- 17-18R
Blaushild, Babette 1927- 29-32R
Blaustein, Albert Paul 1921- CANR-19
Earlier sketches in CA 3R, CANR-1
Blaustein, Arthur I. 1933- CANR-10
Earlier sketch in CA 25-28R
Blaustein, Elliott H(arold) 1915- 41-44R
Blaustein, Esther 1935- 45-48
Blauw, Johannes 1912- 11-12R
Blaxland, John 1917- 7-8R
Blaxland, W(illiam) Gregory 1918- CANR-3
Earlier sketch in CA 9-10R
Blaylock, James P(aul) 1950- 110
Blayne, Sara
See Howl, Marcia (Yvonne Hurt)
Blayney, Margaret S(tatler) 1926- 53-56
Blayre, Christopher
See Heron-Allen, Edward
Blaze, Wayne 1951- 61-64
Blazek, Douglas 1941- 25-28R
Blazek, Ron(ald David) 1936- 111
Blazer, Dan G(erman) II 1944- 110
Blazer, J. S.
See Scott, Justin
Blazier, Kenneth D(ean) 1933- CANR-11
Earlier sketch in CA 69-72
Bleakley, David (Wylie) 1925- 102
Bleamer, Burton 1906(?)-1986 Obituary 118
Blechman, Barry M. 1943- 97-100
Blechman, Burt 1932- 21-22R
Bledlow, John
See Vale, (Henry) Edmund (Theodoric)
Bledsoe, Albert Taylor 1809-1877 ..... DLB-3
Bledsoe, Jerry 1941- 85-88
Bledsoe, Joseph C(ullie) 1918- 33-36R
Bledsoe, Thomas (Alexander) 1914- CANR-9
Earlier sketch in CA 13-14R
Bledsoe, William Ambrose 1906-1981
Obituary 104
Bleeck, Oliver
See Thomas, Ross (Elmore)
Bleeker, Mordecia
See Morgan, Fred Troy
Bleeker, Sonia
See Zim, Sonia Bleeker
See also SATA 2, 26
Blees, Robert A(rthur) 1922- 19-20R
Blegen, Carl (William) 1887-1971
Obituary 33-36R
Blegen, Theodore C. 1891-1969 ..... CANR-3
Earlier sketch in CA 5-6R
Blegvad, Erik 1923- 97-100
See also SATA 14
Blegvad, Lenore 1926- CANR-14
Earlier sketch in CA 69-72
See also SATA 14
Blehl, Vincent Ferrer 1921- 11-12R
Bleiberg, Robert Marvin 1924- 103
Bleich, Alan R. 1913- 15-16R
Bleich, Harold 1930(?)-1980 Obituary 93-96
Bleich, J(udah) David 1936- 116
Bleicher, Michael N(athaniel) 1935- 37-40R
Bleier, Robert Patrick 1946- 85-88
Bleier, Rocky
See Bleier, Robert Patrick
Blench, J(ohn) W(heatley) 1926- 15-16R
Blend, Charles D(aniels) 1918- 23-24R
Blenkinsopp, Joseph 1927- 37-40R
Bleser, Carol K. 1935- 107
Blesh, Rudi
See Blesh, Rudolph Pickett
Blesh, Rudolph Pickett 1899-1985 .....17-18R
Obituary 117
Blessing, Richard Allen 1939- 53-56
Bletter, Robert 1933(?)-1976 Obituary 61-64
Bletter, Rosemarie Haag 1939- 57-60
Blevins, James Lowell 1936- 106
Blevins, Leon W(ilford) 1937- 57-60
Blevins, William L. 1937- 33-36R
Blevins, Winfred (Ernest, Jr.) 1938- CANR-1
Earlier sketch in CA 45-48
Bleything, Dennis H(ugh) 1946- 61-64
Bleznick, Donald W(illiam) 1924- 21-22R
Blicker, Seymour 1940- 77-80
Blicq, Anthony 1926- 33-36R
Bligh, Norman
See Neubauer, William Arthur
Blight, John 1913- CANR-22
Earlier sketch in CA 69-72
Blinder, Alan S(tuart) 1945- 113
Blinder, Elliot 1949- 106
Blinderman, Abraham 1916- 61-64
Blinn, Johna
See Dorsey, Helen
Blinn, Walter Craig 1930- 61-64
Blish, James (Benjamin) 1921-1975 ..... CANR-3
Obituary 57-60
Earlier sketch in CA 3R
See also DLB 8
See also CLC 14
Blishen, Bernard Russell 1919- CANR-3
Earlier sketch in CA 4R
Blishen, Edward 1920- CANR-11
Earlier sketch in CA 19-20R
See also SATA 8
Bliss, A(lan) J(oseph) 1921-1985
Obituary 118
Bliss, Carey S(tillman) 1914- 41-44R
Bliss, Corinne Demas 1947- 104
See also SATA 37
Bliss, Dorothy E(lizabeth) 1916-1987 118
Obituary 124
Bliss, Edward, Jr. 1912- 41-44R
Bliss, George William 1918-1978 85-88
Obituary 81-84
Bliss, Lee 1943- 122
Bliss, (John) Michael 1941- 103
Bliss, Reginald
See Wells, H(erbert) G(eorge)
Bliss, Ronald G(ene) 1942- 53-56
See also SATA 12
Blissett, Marlan 1938- 41-44R
Blistein, Elmer M(ilton) 1920- 11-12R
Blitch, Fleming Lee
See Lee, Fleming
Blitchington, Evelyn G(rant) 1947- 114
Blits, Jan H. 1943- 110
Blitzstein, Marc 1905-1964 Obituary 110
Bliven, Bruce 1889-1977 .....37-40R
Obituary 69-72
Bliven, Bruce, Jr. 1916- CANR-7
Earlier sketch in CA 19-20R
See also SATA 2
Bliven, Naomi 1925- 33-36R
Blixen, Karen (Christentze Dinesen)
1885-1962 ..... CANR-22
Earlier sketches in CA 25-28, CAP-2
See also SATA 44
See also CLC 10
Blizzard, S(amuel) W(ilson, Jr.)
1914(?)-1976 Obituary 65-68
Bloch, Ariel A(lfred Karl) 1933- 41-44R
Bloch, Barbara 1925- CANR-24
Earlier sketch in CA 106
Bloch, Bertram 1892-1987 Obituary 122
Bloch, Blanche 1890-1980 Obituary 97-100
Bloch, Chana Florence 1940- 105
Bloch, Dorothy 1912- 93-96
Bloch, E. Maurice 25-28R
Bloch, Ernst 1885-1977 .....29-32R
Obituary 73-76
Bloch, Herbert A(aron David) 1904-1965 ..... 3R
Bloch, Herman D(avid) 1914- 29-32R
Bloch, Lucienne 1909- SATA-10
Bloch, Lucienne S(chupf) 1937- 93-96
Bloch, Marc 1886-1944 Brief entry 118
Bloch, Marie Halun 1910- CANR-19
Earlier sketches in CA 4R, CANR-4
See also SATA 6
Bloch, Robert (Albert) 1917- CANR-5
Earlier sketch in CA 5-6R
See also SATA 12
See also DLB 44
See also CLC 33
Blocher, Henri (Arthur) 1937- CANR-10
Earlier sketch in CA 65-68
Blochman, Lawrence G(oldtree)
1900-1975 ..... CAP-2
Obituary 53-56
Earlier sketch in CA 19-20
See also SATA 22
Block, Allan (Forrest) 1923- 49-52
Block, Andrew 1892-1985 Obituary 118
Block, Arthur John 1916(?)-1981
Obituary 105
Block, Eugene B. 1890- CANR-2
Earlier sketch in CA 7-8R
Block, Hal 1914(?)-1981 Obituary 104
Block, Herbert (Lawrence) 1909- 111
Block, Irvin 1917- 19-20R
See also SATA 12
Block, Irving (Leonard) 1930- 118
Block, Jack 1921- 33-36R
Block, Jack 1931- 53-56
Block, Jean Libman 5-6R
Block, Joel D(avid) 1943- CANR-15
Earlier sketch in CA 89-92
Block, Julian 1934- 106
Block, Lawrence 1938- CANR-6
Earlier sketch in CA 3R
Block, Libbie 1910(?)-1972 .....33-36R
Block, Marvin Avram 1903- 106
Block, Michael 1942- 101
Block, Ned Joel 1942- 117
Block, Paul, Jr. 1911-1987 Obituary 122
Block, Ralph 1889-1974 Obituary 45-48
Block, Rudolph
See Lessing, Bruno
Block, Seymour Stanton 1918- 89-92
Block, Stanley Byron 1939- 85-88
Block, Thomas H(arris) 1945- CANR-18
Earlier sketch in CA 101
Block, Walter (Edward) 1941- CANR-22
Earlier sketches in CA 57-60, CANR-6
Block, Zenas 1916- 107
Blocker, Clyde (Edward) 1918- 33-36R
Blocker, H(arry) Gene 1937- 116
Blockinger, Betty
See Blocklinger, Peggy O'More
Blocklinger, Peggy O'More 1895- 7-8R
Blocksma, Mary SATA-44
Blodgett, Beverley 1926- 57-60
Blodgett, E(dward) D(ickinson) 1935- 112
Blodgett, Geoffrey Thomas 1931- 17-18R
Blodgett, Harold William 1900- 15-16R
Blodgett, Harriet Eleanor 1919- 33-36R
Blodgett, Richard 1940- CANR-1
Earlier sketch in CA 49-52
Bloem, Diane Brummel 1935- CANR-16
Earlier sketch in CA 85-88
Bloesch, Donald G. 1928- 13-14R
Bloesser, Robert 1930- 37-40R
Blofeld, John (Eaton Calthorpe)
1913-1987 ..... CANR-19
Obituary 123
Earlier sketches in CA 53-56, CANR-4
Blok, Alexander (Alexandrovich)
1880-1921 Brief entry 104
See also TCLC 5
Blok, Anton 1935- 97-100
Blom, Gaston E(ugene) 1920- 25-28R
Blom, Karl Arne 1946- CANR-11
Earlier sketch in CA 69-72
Blom, Lynne Anne 1942- 120
Blom-Cooper, Louis Jacques 1926- 7-8R
Blond, Anthony 1928- 106
Blondel, Jean Fernand Pierre 1929- 101
Blondell, (Rose) Joan 1906(?)-1979 115
Obituary 93-96
Blood, Bob
See Blood, Robert O(scar), Jr.
Blood, Charles Lewis 1929- 73-76
See also SATA 28
Blood, Jerome W. 1926- 11-12R
Blood, Marje 41-44R
Blood, Matthew
See Dresser, Davis
Blood, Robert O(scar), Jr. 1921- CANR-3
Earlier sketch in CA 4R
Bloodstone, John
See Byrne, Stuart J(ames)
Bloom, Alan (Herbert Vawser) 1906- CANR-3
Earlier sketch in CA 9-10R
Bloom, Alexander 1947- 114
Bloom, Allan (David) 1930- Brief entry 125
Bloom, Claire 1931- 114
Bloom, Daniel Halevi 1949- 120
Bloom, Edward A(lan) 1914- CANR-2
Earlier sketch in CA 1R
Bloom, Erick Franklin 1944- 57-60
Bloom, Floyd E(lliott) 1936- 120
Bloom, Freddy 1914- 101
See also SATA 37
Bloom, Gordon F. 1918- 13-14R
Bloom, Harold 1930- 15-16R
See also DLB 67
See also CLC 24
Bloom, Harry 1913(?)-1981 Obituary 104
Bloom, Herman Irving 1908- 102
Bloom, John 1921- 7-8R
Bloom, John Porter 1924- 49-52
Bloom, Ken(neth) 1949- 115
Bloom, Lillian D. 1920- CANR-11
Earlier sketch in CA 17-18R
Bloom, Lloyd SATA-43

Bloom, Lynn (Marie) Z(immerman) 1934- ... CANR-21
Earlier sketches in CA 15-16R, CANR-6
Bloom, Melvyn H(arold) 1938- ... 45-48
Bloom, Murray Teigh 1916- ... 19-20R
Bloom, Pauline ... 41-44R
Bloom, Robert 1930- ... 17-18R
Bloom, Samuel William 1921- ... CANR-3
Earlier sketch in CA 11-12R
Bloom, Ursula 1893-1984 ... 25-28R
Obituary ... 114
Blooman, Percy A. 1906- ... CAP-1
Earlier sketch in CA 11-12
Bloomberg, Edward (Michael) 1937- ... 41-44R
Bloomberg, Marty
See Bloomberg, Max Arthur
Bloomberg, Max Arthur 1938- ... 101
Bloomberg, Morton 1936- ... 53-56
Bloome, Enid P. 1925- ... 85-88
Bloomer, Kent C(ress) 1935- ... 125
Bloomfield, Anthony John Westgate 1922- ... 4R
Bloomfield, Arthur (John) 1931- ... 65-68
Bloomfield, Arthur Irving 1914- ... 41-44R
Bloomfield, Aurelius
See Bourne, Randolph S(illiman)
Bloomfield, B(arry) C(ambray) 1931- ... CANR-5
Earlier sketch in CA 11-12R
Bloomfield, Harold H. 1944- ... CANR-9
Earlier sketch in CA 57-60
Bloomfield, Lincoln Palmer 1920- ... CANR-5
Earlier sketch in CA 1R
Bloomfield, Masse 1923- ... CANR-8
Earlier sketch in CA 61-64
Bloomfield, Maxwell H(erron III) 1931- ... 122
Brief entry ... 118
Bloomfield, Morton W(ilfred) 1913-1987 ... CANR-2
Obituary ... 122
Earlier sketch in CA 5-6R
Bloomingdale, Teresa 1930- ... CANR-21
Earlier sketch in CA 105
Bloomquist, Edward R. 1924- ... 29-32R
Bloomstein, Morris J. 1928- ... 25-28R
Blos, Joan W(insor) 1928- ... CANR-21
Earlier sketch in CA 101
See also SATA 27, 33
Blos, Peter 1904- ... 89-92
Bloss, F(red) Donald 1920- ... 53-56
Bloss, Meredith 1908-1982 Obituary ... 107
Blossom, Frederick A. 1878(?)-1974
Obituary ... 49-52
Blossom, Thomas 1912- ... 23-24R
Blotner, Joseph (Leo) 1923- ... CANR-13
Earlier sketch in CA 19-20R
See also AITN 1
Blotnick, Elihu 1939- ... 106
Blotnick, Srully (D.) 1941(?)- Brief entry ... 123
Blouet, Brian Walter 1936- ... CANR-15
Earlier sketch in CA 93-96
Blough, Glenn O(rlando) 1907- ... CAP-1
Earlier sketch in CA 11-12
See also SATA 1
Blough, Roger M(iles) 1904-1985
Obituary ... 117
Blount, Charles (Harold Clavell) 1913- ... 17-18R
Blount, Margaret 1924- ... 69-72
Blount, Roy (Alton), Jr. 1941- ... CANR-10
Earlier sketch in CA 53-56
See also CLC 38
Bloustein, Edward J. 1925- ... 41-44R
Blow, Suzanne (Katherine) 1932- ... 45-48
Bloy, Leon 1846-1917 Brief entry ... 121
See also TCLC 22
Blu, Karen I(sobell) 1941- ... 121
Blue, Betty (Anne) 1922- ... CANR-1
Earlier sketch in CA 45-48
Blue, Frederick Judd 1937- ... 53-56
Blue, Martha Ward 1942- ... 104
Blue, Rose 1931- ... CANR-14
Earlier sketch in CA 41-44R
See also SATA 5
Blue, Vida (Rochelle) 1949- Brief entry ... 112
Blue, Wallace
See Kraenzel, Margaret (Powell)
Blue, Zachary
See Stine, R(obert) L(awrence)
Bluebond-Langner, Myra 1948- ... 81-84
Blue Cloud, Peter (Aroniawenrate) 1933- ... 117
Bluefarb, Samuel 1919- ... 37-40R
Bluemle, Andrew (Waltz) 1929- ... 1R
Blues, Elwood
See Aykroyd, Dan(iel Edward)
Bluestein, Daniel Thomas 1943- ... 65-68
Bluestein, Gene 1928- ... 81-84
Bluestone, Barry A(lan) 1944- ... 115
Bluestone, George 1928- ... CANR-1
Earlier sketch in CA 4R
Bluestone, Max 1926- ... 15-16R
Bluh, Bonnie 1926- ... 97-100
Bluhm, Heinz 1907- ... CAP-1
Earlier sketch in CA 17-18
Bluhm, William T(heodore) 1923- ... 15-16R
Blum, Albert A(lexander) 1924- ... CANR-11
Earlier sketch in CA 7-8R
Blum, Carol (Kathlyn) O'Brien 1934- ... CANR-17
Earlier sketch in CA 101
Blum, D. Steven 1951- ... 118
Blum, David 1935- ... 107
Blum, Eleanor 1914- ... 3R
Blum, Fred 1932- ... 15-16R
Blum, Harold P. 1929- ... 103
Blum, Henrik L(eo) 1915- ... CANR-6
Earlier sketch in CA 11-12R
Blum, Jerome 1913- ... CANR-19
Earlier sketch in CA 1R
Blum, John Morton 1921- ... CANR-2
Earlier sketch in CA 7-8R
Blum, Lawrence A. 1943- ... 124
Blum, Leon 1872-1950 Brief entry ... 119
Blum, Lucille Hollander 1904- ... 101
Blum, Mark E. 1937- ... 121
Blum, Ralph ... AITN-1
Blum, Richard H(osmer Adams) 1927- ... 13-14R
Blum, Shirley Neilsen 1932- ... 33-36R
Blum, Stella 1916-1985 ... 97-100
Obituary ... 116
Blum, Virgil C(larence) 1913- ... 15-16R
Blum, William (Henry) 1933- ... 125
Blumberg, Arnold 1925- ... 33-36R
Blumberg, Dorothy Rose 1904- ... CAP-2
Earlier sketch in CA 25-28
Blumberg, Gary 1938- ... CANR-2
Earlier sketch in CA 45-48
Blumberg, Harry 1903- ... 73-76
Blumberg, Leonard U. 1920- ... 101
Blumberg, Morris B. 1917- ... 123
Blumberg, Myrna 1932- ... 23-24R
Blumberg, Nathan(iel) Bernard 1922- ... 41-44R
Blumberg, Paul (Marvin) 1935- Brief entry ... 113
Blumberg, Phillip I(rvin) 1919- ... 101
Blumberg, Rena J(oy) 1934- ... 109
Blumberg, Rhoda 1917- ... CANR-26
Earlier sketches in CA 65-68, CANR-9
See also SATA 35
Blumberg, Rhoda L(ois Goldstein) 1926- ... CANR-6
Earlier sketch in CA 57-60
Blumberg, Richard E(lliot) 1944- ... 113
Blumberg, Robert S(tephen) 1945- ... 57-60
Blume, Friedrich 1893-1975 ... 73-76
Blume, Judy (Sussman) 1938- ... CANR-13
Earlier sketch in CA 29-32R
See also SATA 2, 31
See also DLB 52
See also CLC 12, 30
See also CLR 2, 15
Blumenfeld, Gerry 1906- ... 23-24R
Blumenfeld, Hans 1892- ... CAP-2
Earlier sketch in CA 21-22
Blumenfeld, Harold 1905- ... 97-100
Blumenfeld, Meyer 1905-1980 Obituary ... 97-100
Blumenfeld, Samuel L(eon) 1926- ... 41-44R
Blumenfeld, (F.) Yorick 1932- ... 25-28R
Blumenson, Martin 1918- ... CANR-21
Earlier sketches in CA 4R, CANR-4
Blumenstock, David Irving 1913-1963
Obituary ... 116
Blumenthal, Arthur L. 1936- ... 29-32R
Blumenthal, David Reuben 1938- ... 112
Blumenthal, Eileen (Flinder) 1948- ... 120
Blumenthal, Fred(erick G.) 1919(?)-1986
Obituary ... 118
Blumenthal, Gerda Renee 1923- ... 1R
Blumenthal, Gertrude 1907-1971 Obituary ... 104
See also SATA 27
Blumenthal, Henry 1911-1987 ... 29-32R
Obituary ... 121
Blumenthal, L. Roy 1908-1975 Obituary ... 61-64
Blumenthal, Lassor Agoos 1926- ... 25-28R
Blumenthal, Michael C. 1949- ... 110
Blumenthal, Monica David 1930-1981 ... 73-76
Obituary ... 103
Blumenthal, Norm ... 97-100
Blumenthal, Shirley 1943- ... 108
See also SATA 46
Blumenthal, Sidney 1909- ... 106
Blumenthal, Susan
See Tribich, Susan
Blumenthal, Walter Hart 1883- ... CAP-1
Earlier sketch in CA 11-12
Blumin, Stuart M(ack) 1940- ... 65-68
Bluming, Mildred G. 1919- ... 106
Blumrich, Josef F(ranz) 1913- ... 93-96
Blumrosen, Alfred W(illiam) 1928- ... 53-56
Blunck, Hans Friedrich 1888-1961 ... DLB-66
Blundel, Anne
See Conley, Enid Mary
Blundell, Harold 1902- ... 101
Blunden, Edmund (Charles) 1896-1974 ... CAP-2
Obituary ... 45-48
Earlier sketch in CA 17-18
See also DLB 20
See also CLC 2
Blunden, Margaret (Anne) 1939- ... 23-24R
Blunk, Frank M. 1897(?)-1976 Obituary ... 69-72
Blunsden, John (Beresford) 1930- ... 57-60
Blunsdon, Norman (Victor Charles) 1915-1968 ... CAP-1
Earlier sketch in CA 13-14
Blunt, Anthony (Frederick) 1907-1983 ... 113
Obituary ... 109
Blunt, Don
See Booth, Edwin
Blunt, Wilfrid (Jasper Walter) 1901-1987 ... CANR-21
Obituary ... 121
Earlier sketches in CA 15-16R, CANR-5
Blunt, Wilfrid Scawen 1840-1922 ... DLB-19
Bluphocks, Lucien
See Seldes, Gilbert (Vivian)
Bluth, B(etty) J(ean) 1934- ... CANR-24
Earlier sketch in CA 106
Blutig, Eduard
See Gorey, Edward (St. John)
Bly, Amy Sprecher 1955- ... 126
Bly, Carol(yn) 1930- ... CANR-26
Earlier sketch in CA 108
Bly, Janet (Chester) 1945- ... 116
See also SATA 43
Bly, Nellie
See Cochrane, Elizabeth
Bly, Peter A(nthony) 1944- ... 116
Bly, Robert 1926- ... 5-6R
See also DLB 5
See also CLC 1, 2, 5, 10, 15, 38
Bly, Robert W(ayne) 1957- ... 117
See also SATA 48
Bly, Stephen A(rthur) 1944- ... 121
See also SATA 43
Bly, Thomas J. 1918(?)-1979 Obituary ... 85-88
Blyn, George 1919- ... CANR-14
Earlier sketch in CA 37-40R
Blyth, Alan 1929- ... CANR-1
Earlier sketch in CA 49-52
Blyth, Chay 1940- Brief entry ... 110
Blyth, Estelle 1882(?)-1983 Obituary ... 109
Blyth, Henry 1910-1983 ... 21-22R
Obituary ... 110
Blyth, Jeffrey 1926- ... 65-68
Blyth, John
See Hibbs, John
Blyth, Myrna 1939- ... CANR-10
Earlier sketch in CA 65-68
Blythe, (William) LeGette 1900- ... CANR-1
Earlier sketch in CA 3R
Blythe, Ronald (George) 1922- ... 7-8R
Blyton, Carey 1932- ... 49-52
See also SATA 9
Blyton, Enid (Mary) 1897-1968 ... 77-80
Obituary ... 25-28R
See also SATA 25
Boa, Kenneth 1945- ... CANR-8
Earlier sketch in CA 61-64
Boadella, David 1931- ... 53-56
Boadt, Lawrence 1942- ... 114
Boak, Arthur Edward Romilly 1888-1962 ... 5-6R
Boak, (Charles) Denis 1932- ... 13-14R
Boalch, Donald (Howard) 1914- ... 11-12R
Boalt, (Hans) Gunnar 1910- ... CANR-7
Earlier sketch in CA 57-60
Board, C(hester) Stephen 1942- ... 57-60
Board, Joseph B(reckinridge), Jr. 1931- ... 29-32R
Boardman, Arthur 1927- ... 61-64
Boardman, Charles C. 1932- ... 29-32R
Boardman, Eunice
See Meske, Eunice Boardman
Boardman, Fon Wyman, Jr. 1911- ... CANR-3
Earlier sketch in CA 4R
See also SATA 6
Boardman, Francis 1915-1976 Obituary ... 69-72
Boardman, Gwenn R.
See Petersen, Gwenn Boardman
See also SATA 12
Boardman, John 1927- ... 101
Boardman, Michael Moore 1945- ... 118
Boardman, Neil S(ervis) 1907- ... CAP-1
Earlier sketch in CA 13-14
Boardman, Peter (David) 1950-1982 ... 97-100
Obituary ... 108
Boardman, Thomas Leslie 1919-
Brief entry ... 111
Boardwell, Robert Lee 1926- ... 103
Boarino, Gerald L(ouis) 1931- ... 23-24R
Boarman, Patrick M(adigan) 1922- ... CANR-9
Earlier sketch in CA 15-16R
Boas, Claudio Villas
See Villas Boas, Claudio
Boas, Franz 1858-1942 Brief entry ... 115
Boas, Guy (Herman Sidney) 1896-1966 ... CAP-1
Earlier sketch in CA 11-12
Boas, Jacob 1943- ... 120
Boas, Louise Schutz 1885- ... 5-6R
Boas, Marie
See Hall, Marie Boas
Boas, Maurits Ignatius 1892- ... CANR-5
Earlier sketch in CA 3R
Boas, Orlando Villas
See Villas Boas, Orlando
Boase, Alan Martin 1902-1982 ... CANR-10
Obituary ... 108
Earlier sketch in CA 7-8R
Boase, Paul H(enshaw) 1915- ... 37-40R
Boase, Thomas Sherrer Ross 1898-1974 ... CAP-2
Earlier sketch in CA 23-24
Boase, Wendy 1944- ... 106
See also SATA 28
Boateng, E(rnest) A(mano) 1920- ... CANR-11
Earlier sketch in CA 23-24R
Boateng, Yaw Maurice
See Brunner, Maurice Yaw
Boatman, Don Earl 1913- ... 4R
Boatner, Mark Mayo III 1921- ... 21-22R
See also SATA 29
Boatright, Mody Coggin 1896-1970 ... CANR-3
Obituary ... 89-92
Earlier sketch in CA 7-8R
Boatwright, Howard (Leake, Jr.) 1918- ... 53-56
Boatwright, James III 1933-1988 ... 119
Obituary ... 126
Boaz, Martha (Tearosse) ... CANR-19
Earlier sketches in CA 9-10R, CANR-3
Boba, Imre 1919- ... 69-72
Bobb, Bernard E(arl) 1917- ... 5-6R
Bobbe, Dorothie de Bear 1905-1975 ... CAP-2
Obituary ... 57-60
Earlier sketch in CA 25-28
See also SATA 1, 25
Bobbitt, Philip 1948- ... 108
Bober, Harry 1915-1988 Obituary ... 125
Bober, Stanley 1932- ... CANR-11
Earlier sketch in CA 23-24R
Bobette
See Simenon, Georges (Jacques Christian)
Bobinski, George S(ylvan) 1929- ... 29-32R
Bobker, Lee R(obert) 1925- ... CANR-9
Earlier sketch in CA 53-56
Bobo, Lawrence (Douglas) 1958- ... 124
Bobri, Vladimir V. 1898- ... 105
Bobritsky, Vladimir
See Bobri, Vladimir V.
See also SATA 32, 47
Bobroff, Edith
See Marks, Edith Bobroff
Bobrow, Davis Bernard 1936- ... CANR-7
Earlier sketch in CA 57-60
Bobrow, Edwin E. 1928- ... CANR-24
Earlier sketches in CA 23-24R, CANR-8
Bobrowski, Johannes 1917-1965 ... 77-80
See also DLB 75
Bobst, Elmer H(olmes) 1884-1978 ... 122
Obituary ... 113
Bocca, Al
See Winter, Bevis (Peter)
Bocca, Geoffrey 1923-1983 Obituary ... 110
Bochco, Steven 1943- Brief entry ... 124
See also CLC 35
Bochenski, Innocentius M.
See Bochenski, Joseph M.
Bochenski, Joseph M. 1902- ... CANR-7
Earlier sketch in CA 5-6R
Bochner, Salomon 1899- ... 41-44R
Bochroch, Albert R(obert) 1909- ... 111
Bock, Alan W(illiam) 1943- ... 41-44R
Bock, Carl H(einz) 1930-19(?) ... CAP-2
Earlier sketch in CA 19-20
Bock, Fred 1939- ... CANR-10
Earlier sketch in CA 25-28R
Bock, Frederick 1916- ... 9-10R
Bock, Hal
See Bock, Harold I.
Bock, Harold I. 1939- ... 29-32R
See also SATA 10
Bock, Joanne 1940- ... 57-60
Bock, Paul J(ohn) 1922- ... 53-56
Bock, Philip K. 1934- ... CANR-11
Earlier sketch in CA 25-28R
Bock, William Sauts Netamux'we 1939- ... SATA-14
Bockelman, Wilfred 1920- ... 37-40R
Bockl, George 1909- ... 61-64
Bockle, Franz
See Boeckle, Franz
Bockmon, Guy Alan 1926- ... 7-8R
Bockstoce, John R(oberts) 1944- ... 121
Bockus, H(erman) William 1915- ... 53-56
Bocock, Robert (James) 1940- ... CANR-12
Earlier sketch in CA 69-72
Boczek, Boleslaw Adam 1922- ... CANR-4
Earlier sketch in CA 3R
Bod, Peter
See Vesenyi, Paul E.
Bodansky, Oscar 1901-1977 Obituary ... 73-76
Bodard, Lucien (Albert) 1914- Brief entry ... 116
Bodart, Joni
See Bodart-Talbot, Joni
Bodart-Talbot, Joni 1947- ... CANR-23
Earlier sketch in CA 106
Boddewyn, J(ean) J. 1929- ... CANR-17
Earlier sketch in CA 25-28R
Boddie, Charles Emerson 1911- ... 65-68
Boddington, Craig Thornton 1952- ... 111
Boddy, David 1940- ... 119
Boddy, Frederick A(rthur) 1914- ... 61-64
Boddy, William Charles 1913- ... 101
Bode, Carl 1911- ... CANR-20
Earlier sketches in CA 1R, CANR-3
Bode, Elroy 1931- ... CANR-10
Earlier sketch in CA 25-28R
Bode, Janet 1943- ... CANR-12
Earlier sketch in CA 69-72
Bode, Roy E. 1948- ... 77-80
Bodecker, N(iels) M(ogens) 1922-1988 ... CANR-4
Obituary ... 124
Earlier sketch in CA 49-52
See also SATA 8
Bodeen, DeWitt 1908-1988 ... CANR-10
Obituary ... 125
Earlier sketch in CA 25-28R
Bodell, Mary
See Pecsok, Mary Bodell
Boden, Hilda
See Bodenham, Hilda Morris
Boden, Margaret A. 1936- ... 93-96
Bodenham, Hilda Morris 1901- ... CANR-6
Earlier sketch in CA 11-12R
See also SATA 13
Bodenheim, Maxwell 1892-1954
Brief entry ... 110
See also DLB 9, 45
Bodenheimer, Edgar 1908- ... CANR-20
Earlier sketch in CA 33-36R
Bodet, Jaime Torres
See Torres Bodet, Jaime
Bodett, Thomas Edward 1955- ... 123
Bodett, Tom
See Bodett, Thomas Edward
Bodey, Hugh (Arthur) 1939- ... CANR-12
Earlier sketch in CA 61-64
Bodger, Joan
See Mercer, Joan Bodger
Bodian, Nat G. 1921- ... CANR-20
Earlier sketch in CA 103
Bodie, Idella F(allaw) 1925- ... 41-44R
See also SATA 12
Bodin, Paul 1909- ... 65-68
Bodine, Eunice
See Lapp, Eunice Willis Bodine
Bodington, Nancy H(ermione) 1912- ... 53-56
Bodington, Stephen 1909- ... 123
Bodker, Cecil 1927- ... CANR-13
Earlier sketch in CA 73-76
See also SATA 14
See also CLC 21
Bodkin, Cora 1944- ... 69-72

Bodkin, M(atthias) M'Donnell 1850-1933
Brief entry ... 114
See also DLB 70
Bodkin, Maud 1875- ... CAP-1
Earlier sketch in CA 11-12
Bodkin, Ronald G(eorge) 1936- ... 33-36R
Bodle, Yvonne Gallegos 1939- ... 33-36R
Bodley, Hal
See Bodley, Harley Ryan, Jr.
Bodley, Harley Ryan, Jr. 1936- ... 126
Bodmer, Walter Fred 1936- ... 102
Bodnar, John Edward 1944- ... 110
Bodo, Murray 1937- ... CANR-23
Earlier sketches in CA 57-60, CANR-7
Bodo, Peter T. 1949- ... 85-88
Bodoh, John J(ames) 1931- ... 45-48
Bodsworth, (Charles) Fred(erick) 1918- .. CANR-3
Earlier sketch in CA 1R
See also SATA 27
See also DLB 68
Bodwell, Richard
See Spring, Gerald M(ax)
Boeckle, Franz 1921- ... 101
Boeckman, Charles 1920- ... 15-16R
See also SATA 12
Boeckman, Patti ... 109
Boege, Ulrich Gustav 1940- ... 97-100
Boegehold, Betty (Doyle) 1913-1985 ... CANR-12
Obituary ... 115
Earlier sketch in CA 69-72
See also SATA 42
Boegner, Marc 1881-1970 Obituary ... 29-32R
Boehlke, Frederick J(ohn), Jr. 1926- ... 21-22R
Boehlke, Robert R(ichard) 1925- ... 5-6R
Boehlow, Robert H(enry) 1925- ... 53-56
Boehm, Christopher 1937- ... 121
Boehm, Eric H. 1918- ... 13-14R
Boehm, Herb
See Varley, John (Herbert)
Boehm, Karl 1894-1981 Obituary ... 105
Boehm, Sydney 1908- ... DLB-44
Boehm, William D(ryden) 1946- ... 61-64
Boehme, Lillian R.
See Rodberg, Lillian
Boehning, W. R.
See Bohning, W(olf) R(uediger)
Boehringer, Robert 1885(?)-1974
Obituary ... 53-56
Boelcke, Willi A(lfred) 1929- Brief entry ... 107
Boelen, Bernard J(acques) 1916- ... 41-44R
Boell, Heinrich (Theodor) 1917-1985 ... CANR-24
Obituary ... 116
Earlier sketch in CA 21-22R
See also DLB 69
See also DLBY 85
See also CLC 2, 3, 6, 9, 11, 15, 27, 39
Boeman, John (Sigler) 1923- ... 108
Boer, Charles 1939- ... 69-72
See also DLB 5
Boer, Harry R(einier) 1913- ... CANR-4
Earlier sketch in CA 3R
Boesch, Hans Heinrich 1911-1978
Obituary ... 116
Boesch, Mark J(oseph) 1917- ... 21-22R
See also SATA 12
Boesel, David 1938- ... 41-44R
Boesen, Victor 1908- ... 37-40R
See also SATA 16
Boesiger, Willi 1904- ... 102
Boeth, Richard 1933-1982 Obituary ... 107
Boetie, Dugmore 1920(?)-1966 Obituary ... 109
Boettcher, Henry J. 1893- ... CAP-1
Earlier sketch in CA 19-20
Boettcher, Robert B. 1941(?)-1984
Obituary ... 112
Boettinger, Henry M(aurice) 1924- ... 73-76
Boeve, Edgar G. 1929- ... 21-22R
Boewe, Charles (Ernst) 1924- ... 11-12R
Boff, Vic 1915- ... 103
Boffey, David Barnes 1945- ... 110
Bogaduck
See Lindsay, Harold Arthur
Bogan, James 1945- ... 103
Bogan, Louise 1897-1970 ... 73-76
Obituary ... 25-28R
See also DLB 45
See also CLC 4, 39, 46
Bogard, Travis (Miller) 1918- ... 69-72
Bogarde, Dirk
See Van Den Bogarde, Derek Jules
Gaspard Ulric Niven
See also DLB 14
See also CLC 19
Bogardus, Emory Stephen 1882-1973
Obituary ... 116
Bogart, Carlotta 1929- ... 61-64
Bogart, Leo 1921- ... CANR-14
Earlier sketch in CA 41-44R
Bogat, Shatan
See Kacew, Romain
Bogatyryov, Konstantin 1924(?)-1976
Obituary ... 65-68
Bogdanor, Vernon 1943- ... CANR-14
Earlier sketch in CA 81-84
Bogdanovich, Peter 1939- ... CANR-21
Earlier sketch in CA 7-8R
Bogen, James Benjamin 1935- ... 89-92
Bogen, Laurel Ann 1950- ... 112
Bogen, Nancy R(uth) 1932- ... 97-100
Boger, Louise Ade 1909- Brief entry ... 115
Bogert, L(otta) Jean 1888-1970 ... CAP-1
Earlier sketch in CA 11-12
Boggan, E(lton) Carrington 1943- ... 101
Boggess, Louise Bradford 1912- ... CANR-7
Earlier sketch in CA 15-16R
Boggs, Bill
See Boggs, William III
Boggs, James 1919- ... 77-80
Boggs, Jean Sutherland 1922- ... 108
Boggs, Marcus 1947- ... 108
Boggs, Ralph Steele 1901- ... CAP-1
Earlier sketch in CA 11-12
See also SATA 7
Boggs, W(ilmot) Arthur 1916- ... 19-20R
Boggs, Wade Hamilton, Jr. 1916- ... 13-14R
Boggs, William III 1942- ... 102
Bogin, George 1920- ... 104
Bogin, Ruth 1920- ... 122
Bogle, Donald ... AITN-1
Bogner, Norman 1935- ... CANR-15
Earlier sketch in CA 7-8R
See also AITN 2
Bogomolny, Robert L(ee) 1938- ... 121
Bogosian, Eric 1953- ... CLC-45
Bogoslovsky, Christina Stael
1888(?)-1974 Obituary ... 49-52
Bograd, Larry 1953- ... 93-96
See also SATA 33
See also CLC 35
Bogue, Allan G(eorge Britton) 1921- ... 107
Bogue, Jesse C. 1912(?)-1983 Obituary ... 111
Bogue, Lucile 1911- ... CANR-13
Earlier sketch in CA 37-40R
Boguslawski, Dorothy Beers 1911(?)-1978
Obituary ... 77-80
Bohan, Peter ... 33-36R
Bohana, Aileen Stein 1951- ... 103
Bohannan, Paul (James) 1920- ... 11-12R
Bohdal, Susi 1951- ... 97-100
See also SATA 22
Bohen, Halcyone H(arger) 1937- ... 108
Bohen, Sister Marian 1930- ... 7-8R
Bohi, Charles W(esley) 1940- ... 89-92
Bohi, M. Janette 1927- ... 25-28R
Bohlander, Jill 1936- ... 37-40R
Bohle, Bruce 1918- ... CANR-9
Earlier sketch in CA 21-22R
Bohle, Edgar (Henry) 1909- ... 3R
Bohlen, Charles Eustis 1904-1974
Obituary ... 111
Bohlen, Joe M(erl) 1919- ... 5-6R
Bohlke, L(andall) Brent 1942-1987 ... 124
Bohlman, (Mary) Edna McCaull 1897- ... CAP-1
Earlier sketch in CA 9-10
Bohlman, Herbert W(illiam) 1896- ... CAP-1
Earlier sketch in CA 19-20
Bohn, Frank 1878-1975 Obituary ... 57-60
Bohn, Joyce Illig 1940(?)-1976 Obituary ... 69-72
Bohn, Martin J(ohn), Jr. 1938- ... 116
Bohn, Ralph C. 1930- ... CANR-11
Earlier sketch in CA 19-20R
Bohner, Charles (Henry) 1927- ... 118
Bohnet, Michael 1937- ... 102
Bohning, W(olf) R(uediger) 1942- ... 111
Bohnstedt, John W(olfgang) 1927- ... 33-36R
Bohr, Niels (Henrik David) 1885-1962
Obituary ... 112
Bohr, R(ussell) L(eRoi) 1916- ... 25-28R
Bohr, Theophilus
See Thistle, Mel(ville William)
Bohrnstedt, George W(illiam) 1938- ... CANR-20
Earlier sketch in CA 33-36R
Bohrod, Aaron 1907- ... 23-24R
Boice, James Montgomery 1938- ... CANR-12
Earlier sketch in CA 29-32R
Boiko, Claire Taylor 1925- ... 93-96
Boiles, Charles Lafayette (Jr.) 1932- ... 65-68
Boime, Albert 1933- ... 125
Bois, J(oseph) Samuel 1892- ... 33-36R
Boisgilbert, Edmund
See Donnelly, Ignatius
Boissevain, Jeremy 1928- ... CANR-21
Earlier sketches in CA 57-60, CANR-6
Boissiere, Robert 1914- ... 119
Boissoneau, Robert 1937- ... 105
Boissonneau, Alice ... 101
Bok, Bart J(an) 1906-1983 ... 49-52
Obituary ... 110
Bok, Cary W(illiam) 1905-1970
Obituary ... 29-32R
Bok, Derek Curtis 1930- ... 106
Bok, Priscilla F(airfield) 1896- ... 49-52
Bok, Sissela Ann 1934- ... 112
Bokenkotter, Thomas 1924- ... CANR-17
Earlier sketch in CA 85-88
Bokser, Ben Zion 1907-1984 ... CANR-11
Obituary ... 111
Earlier sketch in CA 65-68
Bokum, Fanny Butcher 1888-1987 ... 37-40R
Obituary ... 122
Bokun, Branko 1920- ... 45-48
Boland, Bridget 1913-1988 ... 101
Obituary ... 124
Boland, Charles Michael 1917- ... 11-12R
Boland, Daniel 1891- ... CAP-1
Earlier sketch in CA 13-14
Boland, Eavan 1944- ... DLB-40
See also CLC 40
Boland, (Bertram) John 1913-1976 ... CANR-10
Earlier sketch in CA 9-10R
Boland, Lillian C(anon) 1919- ... 29-32R
Bolch, Ben W(ilsman) 1938- ... 57-60
Bolcom, William E(lden) 1938- ... 93-96
Bold, Alan 1943- ... 25-28R
Bolding, Amy 1910- ... 73-76
Boldt, Menno 1930- ... 120
Bolen, Jean Shinoda 1936- ... 110
Boles, Donald Edward 1926- ... CANR-18
Earlier sketch in CA 4R
Boles, Harold W(ilson) 1915- ... 17-18R
Boles, John B. 1943- ... CANR-14
Earlier sketch in CA 37-40R
Boles, Paul Darcy 1916-1984 ... CANR-4
Obituary ... 112
Earlier sketch in CA 9-10R
See also SATA 9, 38
Bolgan, Anne C(atherine) 1923- ... 41-44R
Bolgar, (Caius Coriolanus) R(obert) R(alph)
1913-1985 Obituary ... 117
Bolger, Philip C(unningham) 1927- ... CANR-6
Earlier sketch in CA 57-60
Bolian, Polly 1925- ... 33-36R
See also SATA 4
Bolin, Luis (A.) 1894-1969 ... CAP-2
Earlier sketch in CA 23-24
Boling, Katharine (Singleton) 1933- ... 57-60
Bolinger, Dwight (L.) 1907- ... CANR-7
Earlier sketch in CA 15-16R
Bolino, August C(onstantino) 1922- ... CANR-18
Earlier sketch in CA 4R
Bolitho, Archie A(rdella) 1886- ... CAP-1
Earlier sketch in CA 9-10
Bolitho, Harold 1939- ... 103
Bolitho, (Henry) Hector 1897-1974 ... CAP-1
Obituary ... 53-56
Earlier sketch in CA 9-10
Bolitho, Ray D.
See Blair, Dorothy S(ara Greene)
Bolkhovitinov, Nikolai Nikolaevich 1930- .. 97-100
Bolkosky, Sidney M(arvin) 1944- ... 65-68
Boll, Carl R. 1894- ... CAP-1
Earlier sketch in CA 17-18
Boll, David 1931- ... 21-22R
Boll, Ernest
See Boll, Theophilus E(rnest) M(artin)
Boll, Heinrich (Theodor) 1917-1985 ... CANR-24
Obituary ... 116
See also DLB 69
See also DLBY 85
See also CLC 2, 3, 6, 9, 11, 15, 27, 39
Boll, Heinrich (Theodor)
See Boell, Heinrich (Theodor)
See also DLB 69
See also DLBY 85
See also CLC 2, 3, 6, 9, 11, 15, 27, 39
Boll, Theo
See Boll, Theophilus E(rnest) M(artin)
Boll, Theophilus E(rnest) M(artin) 1902- .. 37-40R
Bolland, O(rlando) Nigel 1943- ... 110
Bolle, Kees W. 1927- ... CANR-17
Earlier sketch in CA 25-28R
Bollen, Roger 1942(?)- ... SATA-29
See also AITN 1
Bollens, John C(onstantinus)
1920-1983 ... CANR-3
Obituary ... 111
Earlier sketch in CA 3R
Boller, Paul Franklin, Jr. 1916- ... CANR-19
Earlier sketches in CA 4R, CANR-3
Bolles, (Edmund) Blair 1911- ... 9-10R
Bolles, Donald F. 1928-1976 ... 73-76
Obituary ... 65-68
Bolles, Richard Nelson 1927- ... CANR-1
Earlier sketch in CA 45-48
Bolles, Robert C(harles) 1928- ... 21-22R
Bollettieri, Nick J(ames) 1931- ... 110
Bolliger, Max 1929- ... 25-28R
See also SATA 7
Bolling, Hal
See Schwalberg, Carol(yn Ernestine
Stein)
Bolling, Richard (Walker) 1916- ... 19-20R
Bolling, Robert 1738-1775 ... DLB-31
Bolloten, Burnett 1909-1987 ... 93-96
Obituary ... 123
Bolman, Frederick deWolfe, Jr.
1912-1985 Obituary ... 117
Bolner, James (Jerome) 1936- ... 61-64
Bologna, Joseph ... 77-80
Bolognese, Don
See Bolognese, Donald Alan
Bolognese, Donald Alan 1934- ... 97-100
See also SATA 24
Bolognese, Elaine Raphael (Chionchio)
1933- ... 97-100
Bolotowsky, Ilya 1907-1981 Obituary ... 108
Bolshakoff, Serge 1901- ... 93-96
Bolster, John 1910-1984 ... 89-92
Obituary ... 111
Bolsterli, Margaret Jones 1931- ... 111
Bolt, Bruce A(lan) 1930- ... CANR-10
Earlier sketch in CA 65-68
Bolt, Carol 1941- ... 101
See also DLB 60
Bolt, David (Michael) Langstone 1927- .. CANR-6
Earlier sketch in CA 3R
Bolt, Ernest C(ollier), Jr. 1936- ... 77-80
Bolt, Lee
See Faust, Frederick (Shiller)
Bolt, Martin 1944- ... 118
Bolt, Robert (Oxton) 1924- ... 17-18R
See also DLB 13
See also CLC 14
Bolten, Steven E. 1941- ... 37-40R
Boltho, Andrea 1939- ... 69-72
Bolton, Carole 1926- ... CANR-1
Earlier sketch in CA 49-52
See also SATA 6
Bolton, Evelyn
See Bunting, Anne Evelyn
Bolton, Guy (Reginald) 1884-1979 ... 7-8R
Obituary ... 89-92
Bolton, Herbert, E. 1870-1953 ... DLB-17
Bolton, Isabel
See Miller, Mary Britton
Bolton, James 1917(?)-1981 Obituary ... 103
Bolton, John Robert 1948- ... 115
Bolton, Kenneth (Ewart) 1914- ... 9-10R
Bolton, Maisie Sharman 1915- ... 9-10R
Bolton, Muriel Roy 1909(?)-1983
Obituary ... 109
Bolton, Theodore 1889(?)-1973 Obituary .. 45-48
Bolton, W(hitney) F(rench) 1930- ... 17-18R
Bolton, Whitney 1900-1969 Obituary ... 25-28R
Bolus, James Michael 1943- ... 111
Bolus, Jim
See Bolus, James Michael
Boman, Thorleif Gustav 1894- ... 23-24R
Bomans, Godfried J(an) A(rnold)
1913-1971 ... CAP-2
Earlier sketch in CA 29-32
Bomar, Cora Paul 1913- ... 41-44R
Bombardieri, Merle 1949- ... 107
Bombeck, Erma 1927- ... CANR-12
Earlier sketch in CA 23-24R
See also AITN 1
Bombelles, Joseph T. 1930- ... 25-28R
Bomeli, Edwin C(larence) 1920- ... 21-22R
Bomkauf
See Kaufman, Bob (Garnell)
Bommarito, James W. 1922- ... 121
Bona, Mercy
See Ziegler, Alan
Bonachea, E(nrique) Rolando 1943- ... 41-44R
Bonacich, Edna 1940- ... 45-48
Bonanno, Margaret Wander 1950- ... 85-88
Bonansea, Bernardino M(aria) 1908- ... CANR-14
Earlier sketch in CA 41-44R
Bonaparte, Felicia 1937- ... CANR-11
Earlier sketch in CA 61-64
Bonatti, Walter 1930- ... CANR-23
Earlier sketch in CA 106
Bonavia, David Michael 1940-1988 ... 106
Obituary ... 126
Bonavia-Hunt, Noel Aubrey 1882-1965 ... CAP-1
Earlier sketch in CA 9-10
Bonbright, James C(ummings) 1891-1985 ... 3R
Obituary ... 117
Bond, B. J.
See Heneghan, James
Bond, Brian 1936- ... CANR-6
Earlier sketch in CA 57-60
Bond, Charles R(ankin), Jr. 1915- ... 124
Bond, Christopher Godfrey 1945- ... 101
Bond, Donald F(rederic) 1898-1987 ... 13-14R
Obituary ... 121
Bond, Douglas Danford 1911-1976
Obituary ... 69-72
Bond, E(dward) J(arvis) 1930- ... 114
Bond, Edward 1934- ... 25-28R
See also DLB 13
See also CLC 4, 6, 13, 23
Bond, Elaine 1924-1984 Obituary ... 112
Bond, Evelyn
See Hershman, Morris
Bond, Felicia 1954- ... SATA-49
Bond, Geoffrey 1924- ... 29-32R
Bond, Gladys Baker 1912- ... CANR-2
Earlier sketch in CA 5-6R
See also SATA 14
Bond, Harold 1939- ... CANR-11
Earlier sketch in CA 65-68
Bond, Horace Mann 1904-1972 ... CANR-1
Obituary ... 37-40R
Earlier sketch in CA 1R
Bond, J. Harvey
See Winterbotham, R(ussell) R(obert)
Bond, Jean Carey ... 106
Bond, Julian 1940- ... 49-52
See also BW
Bond, Marshall, Jr. 1908- ... CAP-2
Earlier sketch in CA 25-28
Bond, Mary Fanning Wickham 1898- ... 23-24R
Bond, Maurice Francis 1916-1983
Obituary ... 111
Bond, (Thomas) Michael 1926- ... CANR-24
Earlier sketches in CA 5-6R, CANR-4
See also SATA 6
See also SAAS 3
See also CLR 1
Bond, Mrs. James
See Bond, Mary Fanning Wickham
Bond, Nancy (Barbara) 1945- ... CANR-9
Earlier sketch in CA 65-68
See also SATA 22
See also CLR 11
Bond, Nelson S(lade) 1908- ... CAP-1
Earlier sketch in CA 19-20
Bond, Otto F(erdinand) 1885- ... 4R
Bond, Ray
See Smith, Richard Rein
Bond, Raymond T. 1893(?)-1981
Obituary ... 104
Bond, Richmond Pugh 1899- ... CAP-2
Earlier sketch in CA 33-36
Bond, Ruskin 1934- ... CANR-14
Earlier sketch in CA 29-32R
See also SATA 14
Bond, Simon 1947- ... 104
Bond, Ted
See Bond, E(dward) J(arvis)
Bond, William Henry 1915- ... 124
Bond, William J(oseph) 1941- ... CANR-26
Earlier sketch in CA 108
Bondanella, Peter Eugene 1943- ... CANR-10
Earlier sketch in CA 65-68
Bonderoff, Jason (Dennis) 1946- ... 97-100
Bondi, Joseph C. 1936- ... CANR-11
Earlier sketch in CA 29-32R
Bondurant, Joan V(alerie) 1918- ... 41-44R
Bone, Edith 1889(?)-1975 Obituary ... 57-60
Bone, Hugh A(lvin) 1909- ... CANR-3
Earlier sketch in CA 1R
Bone, Jesse F. 1916- ... 57-60
Bone, Quentin 1918- ... 85-88
Bone, Robert (Adamson) 1924- ... 69-72

Bone, Robert C(larke) 1917- 37-40R
Bonehill, Captain Ralph
See Stratemeyer,Edward L.
Bonelli, Robert Allen 1950- 112
Bonellie, Helen-Janet 1937- 41-44R
Bones, James C., Jr. 1943- 125
Bones, Jim, Jr.
See Bones, James C., Jr.
Boness, A. James 1928- 37-40R
Bonestell, Chesley 1888-1986 Obituary 119
See also SATA 48
Bonett, Emery
See Coulson, Felicity Carter
Bonett, John
See Coulson, John H(ubert) A(rthur)
Bonetti, Edward 1928- 93-96
Bonewits, Isaac
See Bonewits, P(hilip) E(mmons) I(saac)
Bonewits, P(hilip) E(mmons) I(saac)
1949- 93-96
Boney, Elaine E(mesette) 1921-
Brief entry 110
Boney, F(rancis) N(ash) 1929- CANR-15
Earlier sketch in CA 41-44R
Boney, Mary Lily
See Sheats, Mary Boney
Boney, William Jerry 1930- 23-24R
Bonfante, Larissa CANR-11
Earlier sketch in CA 69-72
Bongar, Emmet W(ald) 1919- 33-36R
Bongartz, Heinz
See Thorwald, Juergen
Bongartz, Roy 1924- 15-16R
Bongie, Laurence L(ouis) 1929- 61-64
Bonham, Barbara Thomas 1926- CANR-7
Earlier sketch in CA 19-20R
See also SATA 7
Bonham, Frank 1914- CANR-4
Earlier sketch in CA 11-12R
See also SATA 1, 49
See also SAAS 3
See also CLC 12
Bonham-Carter, Victor 1913- 9-10R
Bonham Carter, (Helen) Violet (Asquith)
1887-1969 .... CAP-2
Earlier sketch in CA 17-18
Bonheim, Helmut 1930- CANR-4
Earlier sketch in CA 3R
Bonhoeffer, Dietrich 1906-1945
Brief entry 122
Bonhomme, Denise 1926- 104
Boni, Albert 1892-1981 65-68
Obituary 104
Boni, Margaret Bradford 1893(?)-1974
Obituary 53-56
Bonime, Florence 1907- 49-52
Bonime, Walter 1909- CAP-2
Earlier sketch in CA 17-18
Bonine, Gladys Nichols 1907- CAP-1
Earlier sketch in CA 15-16
Bonington, Christian (John Storey)
1934- CANR-1
Earlier sketch in CA 45-48
Bonini, Charles P(ius) 1933- 13-14R
Bonino, Louise
See Williams, Louise Bonino
Bonjean, Charles M. 1935- 41-44R
Bonk, James 1932- 123
Bonk, Wallace J. 1923- 9-10R
Bonn, Pat
See Bonn, Patricia Carolyn
Bonn, Patricia Carolyn 1948- SATA-43
Bonn, Robert Lewis 1937- 125
Bonn, Thomas L. 1939- 109
Bonnamy, Francis
See Walz, Audrey Boyers
Bonnar, Alphonsus 1895-1968 .... CAP-1
Earlier sketch in CA 9-10
Bonnay, Charles (Louis) 1930-1986
Obituary 119
Bonnefoy, Yves 1923- 85-88
See also CLC 9, 15
Bonnell, Dorothy Haworth 1914- CANR-3
Earlier sketch in CA 4R
Bonnell, F(raser) C(larence) 1908-1983 118
Bonnell, F(lorence Rhodes) W(inn) 1915- ... 118
Bonnell, John Sutherland 1893- 7-8R
Bonner, Brian 1917- CANR-21
Earlier sketch in CA 104
Bonner, Gerald 1926- CANR-5
Earlier sketch in CA 11-12R
Bonner, James Calvin 1904- CANR-9
Earlier sketch in CA 11-12R
Bonner, Joey 1948- 122
Bonner, John Tyler 1920- 49-52
Bonner, Mary Graham 1890-1974 73-76
Obituary 49-52
See also SATA 19
Bonner, Michael
See Glasscock, Anne Bonner
Bonner, Parker
See Ballard, (Willis) Todhunter
Bonner, Paul Hyde 1893-1968 .... 4R
Obituary 103
Bonner, Raymond T(homas) 1942- 117
Bonner, Terry Nelsen
See Castoro, Laura A(nn)
and Krauzer, Steven M(ark)
and Raeschild, Sheila
and Yarbro, Chelsea Quinn
Bonner, Thomas, Jr. 1942- 110
Bonner, Thomas N(eville) 1923- 11-12R
Bonner, William H(omer) 1924- 53-56
Bonner, William Hallam 1899-1980
Obituary 115
Bonners, Susan SATA-48
Bonnette, Jeanne 1907- 41-44R
Bonnette, Victor
See Roy, Ewell Paul
Bonneville, Douglas A(lan) 1931- 21-22R
Bonney, Bill
See Keevill, Henry J(ohn)
Bonney, H(anning) Orrin 1903-1979 .....11-12R
Obituary 103
Bonney, Lorraine G(agnon) 1922- CANR-1
Earlier sketch in CA 45-48
Bonney, Merl E(dwin) 1902- CAP-2
Earlier sketch in CA 33-36
Bonney, (Mabel) Therese 1897-1978
Obituary 73-76
Bonnice, Joseph G(regory) 1930- 49-52
Bonnie, Richard J(effrey) 1945- CANR-4
Earlier sketch in CA 53-56
Bonnifield, Paul 1937- 104
Bonnor, William (Bowen) 1920- 11-12R
Bonny, Helen L(indquist) 1921- CANR-19
Earlier sketches in CA 49-52, CANR-2
Bono, Philip 1921- 101
Bonoma, T(homas) V(incent) 1946- CANR-15
Earlier sketch in CA 85-88
Bonomi, Patricia U(pdegraff) 1928- 85-88
Bonsal, Philip Wilson 1903- 85-88
Bonsall, Crosby Barbara (Newell) 1921- ...73-76
See also SATA 23
Bontecou, Eleanor 1890(?)-1976
Obituary 65-68
Bontempo, Charles J(oseph) 1931- 61-64
Bontemps, Arna Wendell 1902-1973 .... CANR-4
Obituary 41-44R
Earlier sketch in CA 1R
See also BW
See also SATA 2, 24, 44
See also DLB 48, 51
See also CLC 1, 18
See also CLR 6
Bontly, Thomas (John) 1939- 57-60
Bontrager, G(erald) Edwin 1939- 114
Bontrager, John K(enneth) 1923- 65-68
Bonvie, Thomas L. 1940- 114
Bony, Jean (Victor) 1908- 101
Bonzon, Paul-Jacques 1908-1978 93-96
See also SATA 22
Boodman, David M(orris) 1923- 23-24R
Boody, Shirley Bright 1919- 89-92
Boog Watson, Elspeth Janet 1900- CAP-1
Earlier sketch in CA 11-12
Booher, Dianna Daniels 1948- 103
See also SATA 33
Bookbinder, David J(oel) 1951- 101
Bookbinder, Robert 1950- 110
Bookchin, Murray 1921- CANR-1
Earlier sketch in CA 3R
Booker, Anton S.
See Randolph, Vance
Booker, Malcolm (Richard) 1915- 108
Booker, Simeon Saunders 1918- 11-12R
Bookman, Charlotte
See Zolotow, Charlotte S.
Book-Senninger, Claude 1928- 45-48
Bookspan, Martin 1926- 41-44R
Bookstein, Abraham 1940- 53-56
Boom, Alfred B. 1928- CANR-14
Earlier sketch in CA 25-28R
Boom, Corrie ten
See ten Boom, Corrie
Boon, Francis
See Bacon, Edward
Boon, Louis-Paul 1912-1979 .... CANR-13
Earlier sketch in CA 73-76
Boone, Bruce 1940- 112
Boone, Buford 1909(?)-1983 Obituary 109
Boone, Charles Eugene
See Boone, Pat
Boone, Daniel R. 1927- CANR-12
Earlier sketch in CA 33-36R
Boone, Debby
See Boone, Deborah Ann
Boone, Deborah Ann 1956- 110
Boone, Gene 1962- 113
Boone, Gray Davis 1938- 93-96
Boone, Louis E(ugene) 1941- CANR-15
Earlier sketch in CA 41-44R
Boone, Muriel 1893- 69-72
Boone, Pat 1934- CANR-2
Earlier sketch in CA 4R
See also SATA 7
Boontje
See Boon, Louis-Paul
Boore, W(alter) H(ugh) 1904- CANR-5
Earlier sketch in CA 7-8R
Boorer, Wendy 1931- CANR-6
Earlier sketch in CA 57-60
Boorman, Howard L(yon) 1920- 41-44R
Boorman, John 1933- 121
Brief entry 112
Boorman, Linda (Kay) 1940- 121
See also SATA 46
Boorman, Scott A(rcher) 1949- 29-32R
Boorstein, Edward 1915- 73-76
Boorstin, Daniel J(oseph) 1914- CANR-1
Earlier sketch in CA 3R
See also SATA 52
See also DLB 17
See also AITN 2
Boorstin, Paul (Terry) 1944- 103
Boos, Frank Holgate 1893-1968 .... CAP-2
Earlier sketch in CA 33-36
Boot, John C. G. 1936- 19-20R
Boote, Robert Edward 1920- 65-68
Booth, Alan R. 1934- Brief entry 107
Booth, Bradford A(llen) 1909-1968
Obituary 116
Booth, Catherine Bramwell
See Bramwell-Booth, Catherine
Booth, Charles Orrell 1918- 13-14R
Booth, Edwin CANR-7
Earlier sketch in CA 17-18R
Booth, Ernest Sheldon 1915-1984 53-56
See also SATA 43
Booth, Geoffrey
See Tann, Jennifer
Booth, George C(live) 1901- CAP-1
Earlier sketch in CA 11-12
Booth, Graham (Charles) 1935- SATA-37
Booth, Helen Sutton 1890(?)-1985
Obituary 117
Booth, Irwin
See Hoch, Edward D(entinger)
Booth, James 1945- 119
Booth, John A(llan) 1946- 111
Booth, John E(rlanger) 1919- 9-10R
Booth, Ken 1943- 102
Booth, Mark Haworth
See Haworth-Booth, Mark
Booth, Mark Warren 1943- 107
Booth, Martin 1944- 93-96
See also CAAS 2
See also CLC 13
Booth, Nyla 121
Booth, Pat(rick John) 1929- CAP-1
Earlier sketch in CA 9-10
Booth, Paul Henry Gore
See Gore-Booth, Paul Henry
Booth, Philip 1907-1981 106
Booth, Philip 1925- CANR-5
Earlier sketch in CA 5-6R
See also DLBY 82
See also CLC 23
Booth, Rosemary Frances 1928- 53-56
Booth, Stephen 1933- 69-72
Booth, Taylor L(ockwood) 1933- 53-56
Booth, Warren Scripps 1894-1987
Obituary 121
Booth, Wayne C(layson) 1921- CANR-3
Earlier sketch in CA 1R
See also CAAS 5
See also DLB 67
See also CLC 24
Boothby, Robert
See Boothby, Robert John Graham
Boothby, Robert John Graham 1900-1986 .. 117
Obituary 120
Boothroyd, (John) Basil 1910-1988 .... CANR-13
Obituary 124
Earlier sketch in CA 33-36R
Bootle, Stan Kelly
See Kelly-Bootle, Stan
Booton, (Catherine) Kage 1919- 61-64
Booty, John Everitt 1925- CANR-17
Earlier sketch in CA 85-88
Bopp, Karl Richard 1906-1979 Obituary 107
Bor, Josef 1906-1979 Obituary 115
Bor, Norman 1893(?)-1973 Obituary 104
Boraas, Roger S(tuart) 1926- 33-36R
Borah, Woodrow (Wilson) 1912- CANR-3
Earlier sketch in CA 7-8R
Borch, Ted
See Lund, A. Morten
Borchard, Ruth (Berendsohn) 1910- 15-16R
Borchardt, D(ietrich) H(ans) 1916- CANR-24
Earlier sketches in CA 23-24R, CANR-9
Borchardt, Frank L(ouis) 1938- 33-36R
Borchardt, Rudolf 1877-1945 .... DLB-66
Borchers, Gladys L. 1891- CAP-1
Earlier sketch in CA 17-18
Borchert, Gerald L(eo) 1932- CANR-14
Earlier sketch in CA 37-40R
Borchert, James 1941- 104
Borchert, Wolfgang 1921-1947 Brief entry .. 104
See also DLB 69
See also TCLC 5
Borden, Bob
See Rees, Clair (Francis)
Borden, Charles A. 1912-1968 ....7-8R
Borden, Henry 1901- 41-44R
Borden, Lee
See Deal, Borden
Borden, Leigh
See Deal, Borden
Borden, Linda 1951(?)- 125
Borden, Lizzie
See Borden, Linda
Borden, M.
See Saxon, Gladys Relyea
Borden, Mary 1886-1968 .... CAP-1
Obituary 25-28R
Earlier sketch in CA 15-16
Borden, Morton 1925- 11-12R
Borden, Neil Hopper 1895- CANR-6
Earlier sketch in CA 3R
Borden, Norman E(aston), Jr. 1907- 17-18R
Borden, Richard Carman 1900- CAP-1
Earlier sketch in CA 11-12
Borden, William (Vickers) 1938- CANR-25
Earlier sketches in CA 25-28R, CANR-10
Borderieux, Carita 1874-1953 Brief entry ... 113
Bordes, Francois 1919-1981 Obituary 103
Bordier, Georgette 1924- SATA-16
Bordin, Edward S. 1913- 57-60
Bordin, Ruth B(irgitta) 1917- CANR-11
Earlier sketch in CA 21-22R
Bordley, James III 1900- 69-72
Bordman, Gerald 1931- 107
Bordow, Joan (Wiener) 1944- 85-88
Borea, Phyllis Gilbert 1924- 29-32R
Boreham, Gordon F. 1928- 41-44R
Borek, Ernest 1911-1986 106
Obituary 118
Borel, Jacques 1925- CANR-13
Earlier sketch in CA 33-36R
Borel, Raymond C. 1927- 73-76
Borell, Helene
See Hegeler, Sten
Boreman, Jean 1909- CAP-2
Earlier sketch in CA 21-22
Boren, Henry C(harles) 1921- 17-18R
Boren, James H(arlan) 1925- 41-44R
Borenstein, Audrey F(arrell) 1930- CANR-13
Earlier sketch in CA 77-80
Borenstein, Emily 1923- 104
Borer, Mary (Irene) Cathcart 1906- CANR-4
Earlier sketch in CA 9-10R
Boretz, Allen 1900-1986 Obituary 119
Boretz, Alvin 1919- 124
Brief entry 118
Boretz, Benjamin (Aaron) 1934- 69-72
Borg, Bjoern (Rune) 1956- Brief entry 114
Borg, Bjorn
See Borg, Bjoern (Rune)
Borg, Dorothy 1902- 23-24R
Borg, Walter R(aymond) 1921- CANR-13
Earlier sketch in CA 33-36R
Borgen, Robert 1945- 124
Borges, Jorge Luis 1899-1986 .... CANR-19
Earlier sketch in CA 21-22R
See also DLBY 86
See also CLC 1, 2, 3, 4, 6, 8, 9, 10, 13,
19, 44, 48
Borgese, Elisabeth Mann 1918- CANR-24
Earlier sketch in CA 73-76
Borghese, Junio Valerio 1906(?)-1974
Obituary 53-56
Borglum, (James) Lincoln (De La Mothe)
1912-1986 122
Obituary 118
Borgmann, Albert 1937- 117
Borgmann, Dmitri A(lfred) 1927-1985 ....17-18R
Obituary 118
Borgo, Ludovico 1930- 65-68
Borgos, Seth 1952- 119
Borgstrom, Georg A(rne) 1912- 17-18R
Borgzinner, Jon A. 1938-1980 108
Obituary 97-100
Borhek, Mary V(irginia) 1922- 113
Borich, Michael 1949- 105
Boring, Edwin G(arrigues) 1886-1968 ... CANR-6
Earlier sketch in CA 3R
Boring, M(aynard) Eugene 1935- 107
Boring, Mel 1939- 106
See also SATA 35
Boring, Phyllis Zatlin
See Zatlin, Phyllis
Boris, Edna Z(wick) 1943- 113
Boris, Martin 1930- 89-92
Borja, Corinne 1929- 97-100
See also SATA 22
Borja, Robert 1923- 97-100
See also SATA 22
Bork, Alfred M. 1926- 17-18R
Bork, Robert H(eron) 1927- Brief entry 111
Borkin, Joseph 1911-1979 97-100
Obituary 89-92
Borklund, C(arl) W(ilbur) 1930- 21-22R
Borko, Harold 1922- 15-16R
Borkovec, Thomas D. 1944- 45-48
Borland, Barbara Dodge CAP-1
Earlier sketch in CA 9-10
Borland, Hal
See Borland, Harold Glen
See also SATA 5, 24
Borland, Harold Glen 1900-1978 .... CANR-6
Obituary 77-80
Earlier sketch in CA 4R
Borland, Kathryn Kilby 1916- CANR-4
Earlier sketch in CA 53-56
See also SATA 16
Borman, Kathryn M. 1941- 117
Borman, William Alan 1948- 126
Bormann, Ernest G(ordon) 1925- 17-18R
Born, Adolf 1930- SATA-49
Born, Ernest Alexander 1898- 102
Born, Max 1882-1970 ....7-8R
Obituary 25-28R
Borne, Dorothy
See Rice, Dorothy Mary
Borne, Lawrence Roger 1939- 121
Borneman, Ernest 1915- CANR-19
Earlier sketches in CA 9-10R, CANR-3
Borneman, H.
See Gottshall, Franklin Henry
Bornemann, Alfred H. 1908- 13-14R
Bornet, Vaughn Davis 1917- CANR-20
Earlier sketches in CA 3R, CANR-5
Bornheimer, Deane G(ordon) 1935- 89-92
Borning, Bernard C(arl) 1913- CANR-3
Earlier sketch in CA 3R
Bornkamm, Guenther 1905- Brief entry 116
Bornstein, Diane (Dorothy) 1942-1984 .. CANR-8
Obituary 112
Earlier sketch in CA 57-60
Bornstein, George (Jay) 1941- 29-32R
Bornstein, Morris 1927- CANR-2
Earlier sketch in CA 7-8R
Bornstein, Sam 1913- Brief entry 112
Bornstein-Lercher, Ruth 1927- CANR-8
Earlier sketch in CA 61-64
See also SATA 14
Borntrager, Karl A. 1892- 89-92
Borodacz, William ?-1986 Obituary 118
Borodin, George
See Milkomane, George Alexis
Milkomanovich
Boroff, David 1917-1965 .... CAP-1
Obituary 29-32R
Earlier sketch in CA 11-12
Boroson, Warren 1935- 23-24R
Borovski, Conrad 1930- 37-40R
Borovsky, Natasha 1924- 121

Borowitz, Albert (Ira) 1930- ... CANR-15
Earlier sketch in CA 85-88
Borowitz, Eugene B(ernard) 1924- ... CANR-1
Earlier sketch in CA 49-52
Borowski, Tadeusz 1922-1951 Brief entry ... 106
See also TCLC 9
Borras, Frank Marshall (?)-1980 Obituary ... 102
Borrello, Alfred 1931- ... 29-32R
Borrie, John 1915- ... 103
Borrie, Wilfred David 1913- ... 109
Borroff, Edith 1925- ... 65-68
Borroff, Marie 1923- ... CANR-2
Earlier sketch in CA 7-8R
Borror, Donald J(oyce) 1907- ... 4R
Borror, Gordon L(amar) 1936- ... 117
Borrow, George 1803-1881 ... DLB-21, 55
Borsch, Frederick Houk 1935- ... CANR-25
Earlier sketches in CA 25-28R, CANR-10
Borski, Lucia Merecka ... 73-76
See also SATA 18
Borsodi, Ralph 1888-1977 Obituary ... 73-76
Borson, Roo
See Borson, Ruth Elizabeth
Borson, Ruth Elizabeth 1952- ... 112
Borst, Raymond R(ichard) 1909- ... 107
Borsten, Orin 1912- ... 85-88
Borten, Helen Jacobson 1930- ... CANR-3
Earlier sketch in CA 5-6R
See also SATA 5
Borth, Christian C. 1895(?)-1976
Obituary ... 65-68
Bortin, George ... 114
Bortin, V. G.
See Bortin, George
and Bortin, Virginia
Bortin, Virginia 1936- ... 114
Bortner, Doyle M(cClean) 1915- ... 33-36R
Bortner, Morton 1925- ... 33-36R
Bortoli, Georges 1923- ... 65-68
Borton, Elizabeth
See Trevino, Elizabeth B(orton) de
Borton, John C., Jr. 1938- ... 29-32R
Borton, Terry
See Borton, John C., Jr.
Bortstein, Larry 1942- ... 33-36R
See also SATA 16
Bortz, Edward L(eRoy) 1896-1970 ... CAP-1
Earlier sketch in CA 11-12
Boruch, Robert F(rancis) 1942- ... 69-72
Borus, Michael E(liot) 1938-1987 ... 37-40R
Obituary ... 122
Borza, Eugene N(icholas) 1935- ... 25-28R
Bosanquet, Reggie
See Bosanquet, Reginald
Bosanquet, Reginald 1932-1984 Obituary ... 113
Bosch, David J(acobus) 1929- ... 118
Bosch, William Joseph 1928- ... 29-32R
Bosco, Antoinette (Oppedisano) 1928- ... 13-14R
Bosco, (Fernand Joseph Marius) Henri
1888-1976 ... 69-72
Obituary ... 65-68
See also DLB 72
Bosco, Jack
See Holliday, Joseph
Bosco, Monique 1927- ... DLB-53
Bose, Buddhadeva 1908- Brief entry ... 119
Bose, Irene Mott 1899(?)-1974 Obituary ... 53-56
Bose, N(irmal) K(umar) 1901-1972 ... CAP-2
Earlier sketch in CA 23-24
Bose, Tarun Chandra 1931- ... 45-48
Boserup, Ester 1910- ... 57-60
Boshell, Buris R(aye) 1923- ... 105
Boshell, Gordon 1908- ... 77-80
See also SATA 15
Boshinski, Blanche 1922- ... 21-22R
See also SATA 10
Boskin, Joseph 1929- ... 25-28R
Boskoff, Alvin 1924- ... 13-14R
Bosland, Chelcie Clayton 1901- ... 5-6R
Bosler, Raymond Thomas 1915- ... 112
Bosley, Harold A(ugustus) 1907-1975 ... 49-52
Obituary ... 53-56
Bosley, Keith 1937- ... CANR-6
Earlier sketch in CA 57-60
Boslooper, Thomas 1923- ... 81-84
Bosmajian, Haig Aram 1928- ... CANR-7
Earlier sketch in CA 17-18R
Bosmajian, Hamida 1936- ... 107
Bosquet, Alain 1919- ... 13-14R
Boss, Judy 1935- ... 57-60
Boss, Richard W(oodruff) 1937- ... 103
Bosschere, Jean de 1878(?)-1953
Brief entry ... 115
See also TCLC 19
Bosse, Malcolm J(oseph) 1933- ... 106
See also SATA 35
Bosserman, (Charles) Phillip 1931- ... 102
Bossert, Steven T(homas) 1948- ... 104
Bossom, Naomi 1933- ... 102
See also SATA 35
Bossone, Richard M. 1924- ... 33-36R
Bosticco, (Isabel Lucy) Mary ... 102
Bostick, William A(llison) 1913- ... 89-92
Boston, Charles K.
See Gruber, Frank
Boston, Lucy Maria (Wood) 1892- ... 73-76
See also SATA 19
See also CLR 3
Boston, Noel 1910-1966 ... CAP-1
Earlier sketch in CA 15-16
Boston, Robert 1940- ... 65-68
Bostwick, Burdette Edwards 1908- ... 106
Boswell
See Gordon, Giles (Alexander Esme)
Boswell, Barbara (S.) 1946- ... 122
Boswell, Charles (Meigs, Jr.) 1909- ... 5-6R
Boswell, Jackson Campbell 1934- ... 61-64
Boswell, Jeanetta 1922- ... CANR-22
Earlier sketch in CA 106
Boswell, John (Eastburn) 1947- ... 121
Boswell, Thomas 1947- ... 118
Bosworth, Allan R(ucker) 1901-1986 ... 4R
Obituary ... 120
Bosworth, Clifford Edmund 1928- ... CANR-7
Earlier sketch in CA 13-14R
Bosworth, David 1947- ... 113
Bosworth, Frank
See Paine, Lauran (Bosworth)
Bosworth, J. Allan 1925- ... SATA-19
Bosworth, Patricia 1933- ... 77-80
Bosworth, R(ichard) J(ames) B(oon)
1943- ... CANR-23
Earlier sketch in CA 106
Botein, Bernard 1900-1974 Obituary ... 45-48
Botel, Morton 1925- ... 105
Botham, Noel 1940- ... 104
Bothmer, Dietrich Felix von
See von Bothmer, Dietrich Felix
Bothwell, Jean ?-1977 ... CANR-3
Earlier sketch in CA 2R
See also SATA 2
Botjer, George (Francis) 1937- ... 97-100
Botkin, B(enjamin) A(lbert) 1901-1975 ... CAP-1
Obituary ... 57-60
Earlier sketch in CA 15-16
See also SATA 40
Botkin, James W. 1943- ... 112
Boto, Eza
See Biyidi, Alexandre
Botsch, Robert Emil 1947- ... 104
Botsford, Keith 1928- ... 9-10R
Botsford, Ward 1927- ... 110
Bott, George 1920- ... 104
Botta, Anne Charlotte (Lynch) 1815-1891 ... DLB-3
Bottel, Helen 1914- ... 25-28R
Botterill, Cal(vin Bruce) 1947- ... 57-60
Bottigheimer, Ruth B. 1939- ... 125
Bottiglia, William F(ilbert) 1912- ... 23-24R
Botting, Douglas (Scott) 1934- ... CANR-16
Earlier sketches in CA 45-48, CANR-1
See also SATA 43
Bottner, Barbara 1943- ... CANR-23
Earlier sketches in CA 61-64, CANR-8
See also SATA 14
Bottom, Raymond 1927- ... 33-36R
Bottome, Edgar M. 1937- ... 33-36R
Bottome, Phyllis
See Forbes-Dennis, Phyllis
Bottomley, Gordon 1874-1948 Brief entry ... 120
See also DLB 10
Bottomly, Heath 1919- ... 105
Bottomore, T(homas) B(urton) 1920- ... CANR-20
Earlier sketches in CA 9-10R, CANR-4
Bottoms, A(nthony) E(dward) 1939- ... 73-76
Bottoms, David 1949- ... CANR-22
Earlier sketch in CA 105
See also DLBY 83
Bottoms, Lawrence W(endell) 1908- ... 89-92
Bottrall, Margaret Florence Saumarez
1909- ... 104
Bottrall, (Francis James) Ronald 1906- ... 53-56
See also DLB 20
Botvinnik, Mikhail Moiseyevich 1911- ... 112
Botwinick, Jack 1923- ... 41-44R
Bouce, Paul-Gabriel 1936- ... 73-76
Bouchard, Lois Kalb 1938- ... 25-28R
Bouchard, Robert H. 1923- ... 19-20R
Boucher, Alan (Estcourt) 1918- ... CANR-24
Earlier sketches in CA 5-6R, CANR-9
Boucher, Anthony
See White, William A(nthony) P(arker)
See also DLB 8
Boucher, Frank 1901-1977 ... 122
Obituary ... 110
Boucher, John G(regory) 1930- ... 37-40R
Boucher, Jonathan 1738-1804 ... DLB-31
Boucher, Paul Edward 1893- ... CAP-1
Earlier sketch in CA 13-14
Boucher, Sandy 1936- ... 110
Boucher, Wayne I(rving) 1934- ... 53-56
Boucolon, Maryse 1937- ... 110
Boudat, Marie-Louise 1909- ... CAP-1
Earlier sketch in CA 11-12
Boudon, Raymond 1934- ... 49-52
Boudreau, Eugene H(oward) 1934- ... 45-48
Boudreaux, Patricia Duncan 1941- ... 33-36R
Bough, Lee
See Huser, (La)Verne (Carl)
Boughey, Arthur S(tanley) 1913-
Brief entry ... 113
Boughner, Daniel C(liness) 1909-1974 ... CAP-2
Obituary ... 49-52
Earlier sketch in CA 23-24
Boughton, James M(urray) 1940- ... 41-44R
Boughton, Willis A(rnold) 1885-1977
Obituary ... 73-76
Bouissac, Paul (Antoine Rene) 1934- ... 65-68
Boularan, Jacques 1890-1972 Obituary ... 37-40R
Boulby, Mark 1929- ... 37-40R
Boulding, Elise (Biorn-Hansen) 1920- ... CANR-26
Earlier sketches in CA 21-22R, CANR-8
Boulding, Kenneth E(wart) 1910- ... CANR-26
Earlier sketches in CA 5-6R, CANR-7
Boulet, Susan Seddon 1941- ... SATA-50
Boulger, James Denis 1931-1979 ... 109
Boulle, Pierre (Francois Marie-Louis)
1912- ... CANR-24
Earlier sketch in CA 11-12R
See also SATA 22
Boulogne, Jean 1942- ... 93-96
Boult, Adrian (Cedric) 1889-1983 ... 114
Obituary ... 109
Boult, S. Kye
See Cochrane, William E.
Boulting, John (Edward) 1913-1985
Obituary ... 116
Boulton, David 1935- ... CANR-15
Earlier sketch in CA 25-28R
Boulton, James T(hompson) 1924- ... 29-32R
Boulton, Jane 1921- ... 65-68
Boulton, Laura Theresa Craytor
1899(?)-1980 Obituary ... 110
Boulton, Marjorie 1924- ... CANR-9
Earlier sketch in CA 65-68
Boulton, Wayne G(ranberry) 1941- ... 115
Boultwood, Alban 1911- ... 118
Boulware, Marcus H(anna) 1907- ... CANR-1
Earlier sketch in CA 45-48
Bouma, Donald H(erbert) 1918- ... 41-44R
Bouma, Mary La Grand ... 93-96
Bouman, Pieter M(arinus) 1938- ... CANR-12
Earlier sketch in CA 29-32R
Bouman, Walter Richard 1929- ... 29-32R
Boumelha, Penelope Ann 1950- ... 110
Boumelha, Penny
See Boumelha, Penelope Ann
Boumphrey, Robert Stavely 1916(?)-1987
Obituary ... 123
Bouraoui, H(edi) A(ndre) 1932- ... CANR-25
Earlier sketches in CA 65-68, CANR-9
Bourbon, Ken
See Bauer, Erwin A.
Bourdeaux, Michael 1934- ... CANR-14
Earlier sketch in CA 33-36R
Bourdier, James A(aron) 1929-1987
Obituary ... 124
Bourdon, David 1934- ... CANR-13
Earlier sketch in CA 37-40R
See also SATA 46
Bourdon, Sylvia Diane Eve 1949- ... 85-88
Bouregy, Thomas 1909(?)-1978 Obituary ... 104
Bouret, Jean 1914- ... 85-88
Bourget, Paul (Charles Joseph)
1852-1935 Brief entry ... 107
See also TCLC 12
Bourgholtzer, Frank 1919- ... 25-28R
Bourguignon, Erika (Eichhorn) 1924- ... 85-88
Bourjaily, Monte Ferris 1894-1979 ... 97-100
Obituary ... 85-88
Bourjaily, Vance (Nye) 1922- ... CANR-2
Earlier sketch in CA 2R
See also CAAS 1
See also DLB 2
See also CLC 8
Bourke, Vernon J(oseph) 1907- ... CANR-3
Earlier sketch in CA 11-12R
Bourke-White, Margaret 1904-1971 ... CAP-1
Obituary ... 29-32R
Earlier sketch in CA 15-16
Bourliaguet, Leonce 1895-1965 ... 102
Bourliere, Francois (Marie Gabriel) 1913-
Brief entry ... 113
Bourne, Aleck William 1885(?)-1974
Obituary ... 53-56
Bourne, Charles P. 1931- ... 11-12R
Bourne, Dorothy D(ulles) 1893-19(?) ... CAP-2
Earlier sketch in CA 23-24
Bourne, Edward Gaylord 1860-1908 ... DLB-47
Bourne, Eulalia ... 97-100
Bourne, Frank Card 1914- ... 19-20R
Bourne, Geoffrey Howard 1909-1988 ... 33-36R
Obituary ... 126
Bourne, J(ohn) M. 1949- ... 124
Bourne, James R. 1897-19(?) ... CAP-2
Earlier sketch in CA 21-22
Bourne, Joanna Watkins 1949- ... 112
Bourne, John
See John, Owen
Bourne, Kenneth 1930- ... CANR-11
Earlier sketch in CA 25-28R
Bourne, L(arry) S(tuart) 1939- ... CANR-12
Earlier sketch in CA 33-36R
Bourne, Lesley
See Marshall, Evelyn
Bourne, Lyle E(ugene), Jr. 1932- ... 53-56
Bourne, Miriam Anne 1931- ... CANR-10
Earlier sketch in CA 21-22R
See also SATA 16
Bourne, Peter
See Jeffries, Graham Montague
Bourne, Peter Geoffrey 1939- ... CANR-7
Earlier sketch in CA 57-60
Bourne, Randolph S(illiman) 1886-1918
Brief entry ... 117
See also DLB 63
See also TCLC 16
Bourne, Ruth (May) 1897-1986 ... 33-36R
Obituary ... 120
Bourneuf, Alice E. 1912-1980 Obituary ... 102
Bourricaud, Francois 1922- ... CANR-26
Earlier sketch in CA 29-32R
Bouscaren, Anthony Trawick 1920- ... CANR-5
Earlier sketch in CA 3R
Bouscaren, T(imothy) Lincoln 1884- ... CAP-1
Earlier sketch in CA 11-12
Bousquet, Joe 1897-1950 ... DLB-72
Bousquet, Marie-Louis Valentin
1887(?)-1975 Obituary ... 104
Boussard, Jacques Marie 1910- ... 29-32R
Boustead, John Edmund Hugh 1895-1980
Obituary ... 97-100
Boutell, Clarence Burley 1908-1981
Obituary ... 104
Boutell, Clip
See Boutell, Clarence Burley
Boutet de Monvel, (Louis) M(aurice)
1850(?)-1913 ... SATA-30
Boutilier, Mary A(nn) 1943- ... 105
Bouton, James Alan 1939- ... 89-92
Bouton, Jim
See Bouton, James Alan
Bouvard, Marguerite Anne 1937- ... 37-40R
Bouvier, Emile 1906- ... 37-40R
Bouvier, Leon F(rancis) 1922- ... 105
Bova, Ben(jamin William) 1932- ... CANR-11
Earlier sketch in CA 7-8R
See also SATA 6
See also DLBY 81
See also CLC 45
See also CLR 3
Bovard, Oliver K. 1872-1945 ... DLB-25
Bovasso, Julie 1930- ... 25-28R
Bove, Emmanuel 1898-1945 ... DLB-72
Bove, Paul A(nthony) 1949- ... 125
Bovee, Courtland L(owell) 1944- ... 49-52
Bovee, Ruth
See Paine, Lauran (Bosworth)
Boven, William 1887(?)-1970 Obituary ... 104
Bovet, Eric D(avid) 1900- ... 118
Bovey, John (Alden, Jr.) 1913- ... 107
Bovis, H(enry) Eugene 1928- ... 29-32R
Bow, Russell 1925- ... 23-24R
Bowden, Betsy 1948- ... 107
Bowden, Edwin T(urner), Jr. 1924- ... CANR-8
Earlier sketch in CA 15-16R
Bowden, Elbert Victor 1924- ... CANR-15
Earlier sketch in CA 41-44R
Bowden, Gregory Houston 1948- ... 41-44R
Bowden, Henry Warner 1939- ... 49-52
Bowden, J(ocelyn) J(ean) 1927- ... 29-32R
Bowden, Jean 1925- ... CANR-7
Earlier sketch in CA 53-56
Bowden, Jim
See Spence, William John Duncan
Bowden, Joan Chase 1925- ... 89-92
See also SATA 38, 51
Bowden, Leonard (Walter) 1933- ... 17-18R
Bowden, Mary Weatherspoon 1941- ... 110
Bowden, Roland Heywood 1916- ... CANR-24
Earlier sketch in CA 106
Bowden, Susan White
See White-Bowden, Susan
Bowder, Diana (Ruth) 1942- ... 109
Bowditch, James L(owell) 1939- ... 89-92
Bowdle, Donald N(elson) 1935- ... 49-52
Bowdler, Roger 1934- ... 97-100
Bowe, Frank 1947- ... 104
Bowe, Gabriel P(aul) 1923- ... 23-24R
Bowe, Kate
See Taylor, Mary Ann
Bowe, (Paul Thomas) Patrick 1945- ... 106
Bowen, Barbara C(herry) 1937- ... 37-40R
Bowen, Betty Morgan
See West, Betty
Bowen, Catherine Drinker 1897-1973 ... CANR-15
Obituary ... 45-48
Earlier sketch in CA 5-6R
See also SATA 7
Bowen, Croswell 1905-1971 Obituary ... 33-36R
Bowen, David
See Bowen, Joshua David
Bowen, Desmond 1921- ... 33-36R
Bowen, Earl Kenneth 1918- ... 5-6R
Bowen, Edmund (John) 1898-1980
Obituary ... 105
Bowen, Elbert Russell 1918- ... 13-14R
Bowen, Elizabeth (Dorothea Cole)
1899-1973 ... CAP-2
Obituary ... 41-44R
Earlier sketch in CA 17-18
See also DLB 15
See also CLC 1, 3, 6, 11, 15, 22
Bowen, Emrys George 1900-1983
Obituary ... 111
Bowen, Ezra 1927- ... 85-88
Bowen, Francis 1811-1890 ... DLB-1, 59
Bowen, Haskell L. 1929- ... 41-44R
Bowen, Howard R(othmann) 1908- ... CANR-8
Earlier sketch in CA 23-24R
Bowen, (Ivor) Ian 1908-1984 ... 105
Obituary ... 115
Bowen, J(ean) Donald 1922- ... CANR-8
Earlier sketch in CA 19-20R
Bowen, James Keith 1932- ... 37-40R
Bowen, John 1916- ... 103
Bowen, John (Griffith) 1924- ... CANR-2
Earlier sketch in CA 4R
See also DLB 13
Bowen, Joshua David 1930- ... 105
See also SATA 22
Bowen, Marjorie
See Campbell, (Gabrielle) Margaret (Vere)
Bowen, Mary
See Hall, Mary Bowen
Bowen, Peter 1939- ... 57-60
Bowen, Ralph H(enry) 1919- ... 69-72
Bowen, Richard M. 1928- ... 23-24R
Bowen, Robert O. 1920- ... 11-12R
Bowen, Robert Sydney 1900-1977 ... 73-76
Obituary ... 69-72
See also SATA 21, 52
Bowen, Zack (Rhollie) 1934- ... 29-32R
Bowen-Judd, Sara (Hutton) 1922-1985 ... CANR-5
Obituary ... 117
Earlier sketch in CA 9-10R
Bower, Barbara
See Todd, Barbara Euphan
Bower, David A(llan) 1945- ... 37-40R
Bower, Donald E(dward) 1920- ... 77-80
Bower, Eli M(ichael) 1917- ... 89-92
Bower, Fay Louise 1929- ... 53-56
Bower, Gordon H(oward) 1932- ... 19-20R
Bower, Joseph L(yon) 1938- ... 112
Bower, Julia Wells 1903- ... 41-44R
Bower, Keith
See Beckett, Kenneth A(lbert)
Bower, Louise 1900- ... CAP-2
Earlier sketch in CA 21-22

Bower, Muriel 1921- ... 49-52
Bower, Robert T(urrell) 1919- ... 49-52
Bower, Sharon Anthony 1932- ... 65-68
Bower, William Clayton 1878- ... 7-8R
Bowering, George 1935- ... CANR-10
Earlier sketch in CA 21-22R
See also DLB 53
See also CLC 15, 47
Bowering, Marilyn R(uthe) 1949- ... 101
See also CLC 32
Bowers, C. A. 1935- ... 29-32R
Bowers, Claude, G. 1878-1958 ... DLB-17
Bowers, Edgar 1924- ... CANR-24
Earlier sketch in CA 7-8R
See also DLB 5
See also CLC 9
Bowers, Faubion 1917- ... 5-6R
Bowers, Fredson (Thayer) 1905- ... CANR-2
Earlier sketch in CA 5-6R
Bowers, George K. 1916- ... CANR-2
Earlier sketch in CA 3R
Bowers, John 1928- ... 33-36R
Bowers, John M. 1949- ... 126
Bowers, John Waite 1935- ... 41-44R
Bowers, Kenneth S. 1937- ... 97-100
Bowers, Margaretta K(eller) 1908- ... 5-6R
Bowers, Mary Beacom 1932- ... 105
Bowers, Neal 1948- ... 110
Bowers, Q(uentin) David 1938- ... CANR-16
Earlier sketch in CA 41-44R
Bowers, Ronald (Lee) 1941- ... 41-44R
Bowers, Warner Fremont 1906- ... 61-64
Bowers, William 1916-1987 ... 102
Obituary ... 122
Bowers, William J(oseph) 1935- ... 97-100
Bowers, William L(avalle) 1930-
Brief entry ... 114
Bowersock, G(len) W(arren) 1936- ... 81-84
Bowes, Anne LaBastille
See LaBastille, Anne
Bowett, Derek William 1927- ... CANR-6
Earlier sketch in CA 9-10R
Bowick, Dorothy Mueller
See Mueller, Dorothy
Bowie, David
See Jones, David Robert
See also CLC 17
Bowie, Janetta (Hamilton) 1907- ... 102
Bowie, Jim
See Norwood, Victor G(eorge) C(harles)
and Stratemeyer, Edward L.
Bowie, Norman E. 1942- ... CANR-13
Earlier sketch in CA 33-36R
Bowie, Robert R(ichardson) 1909- ... CAP-1
Earlier sketch in CA 11-12
Bowie, Sam
See Ballard, (Willis) Todhunter
Bowie, Walter Russell 1882-1969 ... CANR-3
Earlier sketch in CA 5-6R
Bowker, Francis E. 1917- ... 41-44R
Bowker, John (Westerdale) 1935- ... CANR-12
Earlier sketch in CA 25-28R
Bowker, Lee Harrington 1940- ... CANR-25
Earlier sketch in CA 108
Bowker, Margaret 1936- ... 25-28R
Bowker, R(obin) M(arsland) 1920- ... 65-68
Bowlby, John 1907- ... 49-52
Bowle, John (Edward) 1905-1985 ... CANR-1
Obituary ... 117
Earlier sketch in CA 4R
Bowler, Jan Brett
See Brett, Jan (Churchill)
Bowler, R(eginald) Arthur 1930- ... 57-60
Bowles, Chester (Bliss) 1901-1986 ... 69-72
Obituary ... 119
Bowles, D(elbert) Richard 1910- ... 33-36R
Bowles, Edmund A(ddison) 1925- ... 33-36R
Bowles, Ella Shannon 1886-1975
Obituary ... 57-60
Bowles, Frank H(amilton) 1907-1975 ... 15-16R
Obituary ... 57-60
Bowles, George A., Jr. 1924(?)-1986
Obituary ... 118
Bowles, Gordon Townsend 1904- ... CAP-1
Earlier sketch in CA 11-12
Bowles, Jane (Sydney) 1917-1973 ... CAP-2
Obituary ... 41-44R
Earlier sketch in CA 19-20
See also CLC 3
Bowles, John 1938- ... 106
Bowles, Kerwin
See Abeles, Elvin
Bowles, Norma L(ouise) ... 77-80
Bowles, Paul (Frederick) 1910- ... CANR-19
Earlier sketches in CA 4R, CANR-1
See also CAAS 1
See also DLB 5, 6
See also CLC 1, 2, 19
Bowles, Samuel III 1826-1878 ... DLB-43
Bowley, Rex Lyon 1925- ... 103
Bowling, Ann (Patricia) 1951- ... 113
Bowling, Jackson M(ichael) 1934- ... 7-8R
Bowman, Albert Hall 1921- ... 41-44R
Bowman, Alfred C(onner) 1904-1982 ... 117
Bowman, Bob
See Bowman, Robert T.
Bowman, Bruce 1938- ... 65-68
Bowman, Clell Edgar 1904- ... 105
Bowman, David J. 1919- ... 9-10R
Bowman, Derek 1931- ... 102
Bowman, Frank Paul 1927- ... 33-36R
Bowman, Henry A(delbert) 1903- ... CAP-1
Earlier sketch in CA 13-14
Bowman, Herbert E(ugene) 1917- ... 65-68
Bowman, James Cloyd 1880-1961 ... 97-100
See also SATA 23
Bowman, Jeanne
See Blocklinger, Peggy O'More
Bowman, John S(tewart) 1931- ... CANR-19
Earlier sketches in CA 9-10R, CANR-5
See also SATA 16
Bowman, John Wick 1894- ... CANR-6
Earlier sketch in CA 4R
Bowman, Karl M. 1888-1973 Obituary ... 41-44R
Bowman, Kathleen (Gill) 1942- ... 69-72
See also SATA 40, 52
Bowman, Larry G(ene) 1935- Brief entry ... 115
Bowman, LeRoy 1887-1971 Obituary ... 33-36R
Bowman, Locke E., Jr. 1927- ... CANR-2
Earlier sketch in CA 7-8R
Bowman, Louise Morey 1882-1944 ... DLB-68
Bowman, Marcelle 1914- ... 25-28R
Bowman, Mary D. 1924- ... 25-28R
Bowman, Mary Jean 1908- ... 33-36R
Bowman, Ned A(lan) 1932- ... 41-44R
Bowman, Paul Hoover 1914- ... 33-36R
Bowman, Peter 1917(?)-1985 Obituary ... 114
Bowman, Raymond Albert 1903-1979
Obituary ... 89-92
Bowman, Robert 1928- ... 25-28R
Bowman, Robert T. 1910- ... 73-76
Bowman, Sylvia E(dmonia) 1914- ... 1R
Bowman, Ward S(imon), Jr. 1911- ... 49-52
Bowmer, Angus L(ivingston) 1904-1979
Obituary ... 85-88
Bowne, Ford
See Brown, Forrest
Bowood, Richard
See Daniell, Albert Scott
Bowra, (Cecil) Maurice 1898-1971 ... CANR-2
Obituary ... 29-32R
Earlier sketch in CA 4R
Bowring, Richard (John) 1947- ... 114
Bowser, Eileen 1928- ... CANR-26
Earlier sketches in CA 69-72, CANR-11
Bowser, Frederick P(ark) 1937- ... 49-52
Bowser, Joan
See Bowser, Pearl
Bowser, Pearl 1931- ... CANR-13
Earlier sketch in CA 33-36R
Bowskill, Derek 1928- ... CANR-13
Earlier sketch in CA 77-80
Bowyer, (Raymond) Chaz 1926- ... CANR-15
Earlier sketch in CA 93-96
Bowyer, John W(alter) 1921- ... 37-40R
Bowyer, Mathew J(ustice) 1926- ... CANR-13
Earlier sketch in CA 37-40R
Box, Edgar
See Vidal, Gore
Box, Sydney 1907-1983 Obituary ... 109
Boxer, Charles Ralph 1904- ... 102
Boxer, (Charles) Mark (Edward)
1931-1988 Obituary ... 126
Boxerman, David Samuel 1945- ... 61-64
Boxill, Roger 1928- ... 126
Boxman
See Chambliss, William J(oseph)
Boy, Angelo V(ictor) 1929- ... 69-72
Boyajian, Cecile
See Starr, Cecile
Boyarsky, Bill 1936- ... 25-28R
Boyce, (Joseph) Chris(topher) 1943- ... 73-76
Boyce, David George 1942- ... 103
Boyce, George A(rthur) 1898- ... 53-56
See also SATA 19
Boyce, Gray Cowan 1899- ... 5-6R
Boyce, Joseph Nelson 1937- ... 102
Boyce, Richard Fyfe 1896-1985 ... 69-72
Obituary ... 116
Boyce, Ronald R(eed) 1931- ... CANR-18
Earlier sketches in CA 11-12R, CANR-3
Boycott, Desmond (Lionel) Morse
See Morse-Boycott, Desmond (Lionel)
Boyd, Alamo
See Bosworth, Allan R(ucker)
Boyd, Andrew (Kirk Henry) 1920- ... 1R
Boyd, Ann S.
See Schoonmaker, Ann
Boyd, Anne Morris 1884-1974 Obituary ... 113
Boyd, Beverly M(ary) 1925- ... 69-72
Boyd, Bob
See Boyd, Robert T(hompson)
Boyd, Carolyn Patricia 1944- ... 112
Boyd, Carse
See Stacton, David (Derek)
Boyd, Dean (Wallace) ... 5-6R
Boyd, E(lizabeth) 1904(?)-1974 Obituary ... 53-56
Boyd, Edward M. 1927- ... 120
Boyd, Frank
See Kane, Frank
Boyd, Harper W(hite), Jr. 1917- ... 15-16R
Boyd, Herb 1938- ... 110
Boyd, J(ohn) Francis 1910- ... 7-8R
Boyd, Jack 1932- ... 49-52
Boyd, James 1888-1944 ... DLB-9
Boyd, James M(oore) 1919- ... 33-36R
Boyd, James S(terling) 1917- ... 49-52
Boyd, John
See Upchurch, Boyd (Bradfield)
See also DLB 8
Boyd, John D. 1916- ... 25-28R
Boyd, Julian P(arks) 1903-1980 ... 65-68
Obituary ... 97-100
Boyd, Malcolm 1923- ... CANR-26
Earlier sketches in CA 5-6R, CANR-4
Boyd, (Charles) Malcolm 1932- ... 126
Boyd, Martin a Beckett 1893- ... CAP-1
Earlier sketch in CA 13-14
Boyd, Maurice 1921- ... 11-12R
Boyd, Mildred Worthy 1921- ... 17-18R
Boyd, Myron F(enton) 1909-1978 ... 41-44R
Boyd, Nancy
See Millay, Edna St. Vincent
Boyd, Neil
See DeRosa, Peter (Clement)
Boyd, Pauline
See Schock, Pauline
Boyd, R(obert) L(ewis) F(ullarton) 1922- ... 57-60
Boyd, Robert H. 1912- ... 53-56
Boyd, Robert S. 1928- ... 15-16R
Boyd, Robert T(hompson) 1914- ... 108
Boyd, Robin 1919- ... 17-18R
Boyd, Selma
See Acuff, Selma Boyd
Boyd, Shylah 1945- ... 61-64
Boyd, Sue Abbott 1921- ... CANR-14
Earlier sketch in CA 65-68
Boyd, Thomas (Alexander) 1898-1935
Brief entry ... 111
See also DLB 9
Boyd, Waldo T. 1918- ... CANR-12
Earlier sketch in CA 29-32R
See also SATA 18
Boyd, William 1885- ... 41-44R
Boyd, William 1952- ... 120
Brief entry ... 114
See also CLC 28
Boyd, William C(louser) 1903-1983
Obituary ... 109
Boyd, William Harland 1912- ... CANR-11
Earlier sketch in CA 69-72
Boyden, David D(odge) 1910-1986
Obituary ... 120
Boydston, Jo Ann 1924- ... 29-32R
Boyer, Brian D. 1939- ... 45-48
Boyer, Bruce Hatton 1946- ... 101
Boyer, Carl B(enjamin) 1906-1976
Obituary ... 65-68
Boyer, Dwight 1912- ... 65-68
Boyer, Elizabeth (Mary) 1913- ... 81-84
Boyer, Ernest LeRoy 1928- ... 110
Boyer, Harold W. 1908- ... 4R
Boyer, John (William) 1946- ... 103
Boyer, Mildred (Vinson) 1926- ... 112
Boyer, Paul Samuel 1935- ... CANR-18
Earlier sketches in CA 49-52, CANR-1
Boyer, Richard Edwin 1932- ... 23-24R
Boyer, Richard Lewis 1943- ... CANR-11
Earlier sketch in CA 69-72
Boyer, Richard O. 1903-1973 Obituary ... 45-48
Boyer, Robert
See Lake, Kenneth R(obert)
Boyer, Robert E(rnst) 1929- ... 41-44R
See also SATA 22
Boyer, Ruth Gasink 1913- ... 114
Boyer, Sophia Ames 1907(?)-1972
Obituary ... 37-40R
Boyer, William H(arrison) 1924- ... CANR-22
Earlier sketch in CA 106
Boyer, William W., (Jr.) 1923- ... 13-14R
Boyers, Margaret Anne ... 118
Boyers, Peggy
See Boyers, Margaret Anne
Boyers, Robert 1942- ... CANR-4
Earlier sketch in CA 53-56
Boyesen, Hjalmar Hjorth 1848-1895 . DLB-12, 71
Boyington, (Gregory) Pappy 1912-1988
Obituary ... 124
Boykin, James H(andy) 1914- ... CANR-2
Earlier sketch in CA 5-6R
Boylan, Boyd
See Whiton, James Nelson
Boylan, Brian Richard 1936- ... 81-84
Boylan, James (Richard) 1927- ... CANR-16
Earlier sketches in CA 4R, CANR-1
Boylan, Leona Davis 1910- ... 61-64
Boylan, Lucile 1906- ... CAP-1
Earlier sketch in CA 11-12
Boylan, Mary 1913(?)-1984 Obituary ... 112
Boyle, Andrew 1923- ... 5-6R
Boyle, Andrew Philip More 1919- ... 102
Boyle, Ann (Peters) 1916- ... CANR-26
Earlier sketch in CA 29-32R
See also SATA 10
Boyle, Charles 1951- ... 113
Boyle, Deirdre 1949- ... 110
Boyle, Edward Charles Gurney 1923-1981
Obituary ... 108
Boyle, Eleanor Vere (Gordon)
1825-1916 ... SATA-28
Boyle, Freddie M. 1915(?)-1984 Obituary ... 113
Boyle, Hal
See Boyle, Harold V(incent)
Boyle, Harold V(incent) 1911-1974 ... 101
Obituary ... 89-92
Boyle, Harry Joseph 1915- ... CANR-7
Earlier sketch in CA 13-14R
Boyle, J(ohn) A(ndrew) 1916-1979 ... CANR-9
Obituary ... 85-88
Earlier sketch in CA 61-64
Boyle, John Hunter 1930- ... 41-44R
Boyle, John P(hillips) 1931- Brief entry ... 114
Boyle, (Emily) Joyce 1901- ... CAP-1
Earlier sketch in CA 13-14
Boyle, Kay 1902- ... 15-16R
See also CAAS 1
See also DLB 4, 9, 48
See also CLC 1, 5, 19
Boyle, (C.) Kevin 1943- ... 123
Boyle, Mark
See Kienzle, William X(avier)
Boyle, Mary 1882(?)-1975 Obituary ... 53-56
Boyle, Patrick 1905-1982 ... CLC-19
Boyle, Robert (Richard) 1915- ... 15-16R
Boyle, Robert H. 1928- ... CANR-12
Earlier sketch in CA 19-20R
Boyle, Samuel J. III 1920-1985 Obituary ... 118
Boyle, Sarah Patton 1906- ... CAP-1
Earlier sketch in CA 15-16
Boyle, Stanley E(ugene) 1927- ... 41-44R
Boyle, T. Coraghessan 1948- ... 120
See also DLBY 86
See also CLC 36
Boyle, Ted Eugene 1933- ... 23-24R
Boyle, Thomas 1939- ... 118
Boyle, Timm
See Boyle, Timothy R(obert)
Boyle, Timothy R(obert) 1953- ... 118
Boylen, Margaret Currier 1921-1967 ... 3R
Obituary ... 103
Boyles, C(larence) S(cott), Jr. 1905- ... 3R
Boylston, Helen Dore 1895-1984 ... CANR-21
Obituary ... 113
Earlier sketch in CA 73-76
See also SATA 23, 39
Boyne, Walter J(ames) 1929- ... 107
Boynton, Lewis Delano 1909- ... CANR-6
Earlier sketch in CA 5-6R
Boynton, Peter S. 1920(?)-1971 Obituary ... 104
Boynton, Robert W(hitney) 1921-
Brief entry ... 117
Boynton, Sandra (Keith) 1953- ... SATA-38
Boynton, Sandra (Keith) 1953- ... 126
Boynton, Searles Roland 1926- ... 77-80
Boyum, Joy Gould 1934- ... 33-36R
Boyum, Keith O(rel) 1945- ... 102
Boz
See Dickens, Charles (John Huffam)
Bozarth-Campbell, Alla (Linda Renee)
1947- ... 105
Boze, Arthur Phillip 1945- ... 57-60
Bozeman, Adda B(ruemmer) 1908- ... CANR-3
Earlier sketch in CA 5-6R
Bozeman, Theodore Dwight 1942- ... 85-88
Braasch, William Frederick 1878- ... CAP-2
Earlier sketch in CA 29-32
Brabazon, James
See Seth-Smith, Leslie James
Brabb, George J(acob) 1925- ... 41-44R
Brabec, Barbara 1937- ... CANR-15
Earlier sketch in CA 93-96
Brabson, George Dana 1900- ... CAP-1
Earlier sketch in CA 19-20
Brace, Edward Roy 1936- ... CANR-19
Earlier sketch in CA 102
Brace, Geoffrey (Arthur) 1930- ... CANR-11
Earlier sketch in CA 69-72
Brace, Gerald Warner 1901-1978 ... 13-14R
Obituary ... 81-84
Brace, Richard Munthe 1915-1977 ... CANR-15
Obituary ... 69-72
Earlier sketch in CA 3R
Brace, Timothy
See Pratt, Theodore
Braceairdle, Cyril 1920- ... 45-48
Bracegirdle, Brian 1933- ... 101
Braceland, Francis J(ames) 1900-1985
Obituary ... 115
Bracewell, Ronald N(ewbold) 1921- ... 57-60
Bracewell-Milnes, (John) Barry 1931- ... CANR-13
Earlier sketch in CA 33-36R
Bracey, Howard E(dwin) 1905- ... 13-14R
Bracey, John H(enry, Jr.) 1941- ... 29-32R
Bracher, Frederick (George) 1905- ... 111
Bracher, Karl Dietrich 1922- ... CANR-17
Earlier sketches in CA 45-48, CANR-1
Bracher, Marjory (Louise) 1906- ... CAP-1
Earlier sketch in CA 15-16
Brack, Harold Arthur 1923- ... 17-18R
Brack, O M, Jr. 1938- ... 41-44R
Brack, Vektris
See Humphrys, Leslie George
Brackbill, Yvonne 1928- ... 23-24R
Bracken, Dorothy K(endall) ... 23-24R
Bracken, Joseph Andrew 1930- ... 37-40R
Bracken, Paul 1948- ... 115
Bracken, Peg 1920- ... CANR-6
Earlier sketch in CA 4R
Brackenbury, Alison 1953- ... DLB-40
Brackenridge, Hugh Henry
1748-1816 ... DLB-11, 37
Brackenridge, R(obert) Douglas 1932- ... 101
Bracker, Jon 1936- ... 17-18R
Brackett, Charles 1892-1969 Obituary ... 113
See also DLB 26
Brackett, Leigh (Douglass) 1915-1978 ... CANR-1
Obituary ... 77-80
Earlier sketch in CA 3R
See also DLB 8, 26
Brackman, Arnold C(harles) 1923-1983 ... CANR-2
Obituary ... 111
Earlier sketch in CA 5-6R
See also AITN 1
Brackney, William (Henry) 1948- ... 123
Bracy, William 1915- ... 61-64
Bradbrook, M(uriel) C(lara) 1909- ... CANR-23
Earlier sketches in CA 13-14R, CANR-7
Bradburn, Norman M. 1933- ... CANR-13
Earlier sketch in CA 37-40R
Bradburne, E(lizabeth) S. 1915- ... 25-28R
Bradbury, Bianca 1908- ... CANR-5
Earlier sketch in CA 13-14R
See also SATA 3
Bradbury, Dorothy E(dith) 1902-1984
Obituary ... 113
Bradbury, Edward P.
See Moorcock, Michael (John)
Bradbury, John M(ason) 1908-1969 ... CAP-1
Earlier sketch in CA 15-16
Bradbury, Katharine L(orraine) 1946- ... 111
Bradbury, Malcolm (Stanley) 1932- ... CANR-1
Earlier sketch in CA 2R
See also DLB 14
See also CLC 32
Bradbury, Parnell 1904- ... 13-14R
Bradbury, Peggy 1930- ... 65-68

Bradbury, Ray (Douglas) 1920- CANR-2
Earlier sketch in CA 4R
See also SATA 11
See also DLB 2, 8
See also CLC 1, 3, 10, 15, 42
See also AITN 1, 2
Braddock, Joseph (Edward) 1902-
Brief entry 117
Braddock, Richard R(eed) 1920-1974 1R
Obituary 103
Braddon, George
See Milkomane, George Alexis Milkomanovich
Braddon, Mary Elizabeth 1837(?)-1915
Brief entry 108
See also DLB 18, 70
Braddon, Russell (Reading) 1921- CANR-2
Earlier sketch in CA 4R
Braddy, Haldeen 1908-1980 17-18R
Obituary 101
Brade-Birks, S(tanley) Graham 1887- CAP-1
Earlier sketch in CA 15-16
Braden, Charles Samuel 1887- 5-6R
Braden, Irene A.
See Hoadley, Irene Braden
Braden, Spruille 1894-1978 Obituary 115
Braden, Thomas (Wardell) 1918-
Brief entry 113
Braden, Tom
See Braden, Thomas
Braden, Waldo W(arder) 1911- CANR-5
Earlier sketch in CA 7-8R
Braden, William 1930- 23-24R
Bradfield, James McComb 1917- 5-6R
Bradfield, Jolly Roger
See Bradfield, Roger
Bradfield, Nancy 1913- 29-32R
Bradfield, Richard 1896- CAP-2
Earlier sketch in CA 23-24
Bradfield, Roger 1924- 19-20R
Bradford, Adam, M.D.
See Wassersug, Joseph D.
Bradford, Alex 1927-1978 Obituary 112
Bradford, Andrew 1686-1742 DLB-43, 73
Bradford, Ann (Liddell) 1917- Brief entry 116
See also SATA 38
Bradford, Barbara Taylor 1933- 89-92
Bradford, Benjamin 1925- 85-88
Bradford, David F(rantz) 1939- 124
Bradford, Dennis E(arle) 1946- 118
Bradford, Ernle (Dusgate Selby) 1922-1986 101
Obituary 119
Bradford, Gamaliel 1863-1932 DLB-17
Bradford, James C(hapin) 1945- 111
Bradford, John 1749-1830 DLB-43
Bradford, Karleen 1936- 112
See also SATA 48
Bradford, Leland P(owers) 1905- CANR-9
Earlier sketch in CA 13-14R
Bradford, Leroy 1922- 105
Bradford, Lois J(ean) 1936- 104
See also SATA 36
Bradford, M(elvin) E(ustace) 1934- CANR-13
Earlier sketch in CA 77-80
Bradford, Patience Andrewes 1918- 33-36R
Bradford, Peter Amory 1942- 61-64
Bradford, Reed H(oward) 1912- 49-52
Bradford, Richard (Roark) 1932- CANR-2
Earlier sketch in CA 49-52
Bradford, Richard H(eadlee) 1938- 89-92
Bradford, Robert W(hitmore) 1918- 77-80
Bradford, Roy Hamilton 1920- 109
Bradford, Sax(ton) 1907-1966 4R
Bradford, Will
See Paine, Lauran (Bosworth)
Bradford, William 1590-1657 DLB-24, 30
Bradford, William C(astle) 1910- 9-10R
Bradford, William III 1719-1791 DLB-43, 73
Bradlaugh, Charles 1833-1891 DLB-57
Bradlee, Benjamin C(rowninshield) 1921- 61-64
See also AITN 2
Bradlee, Frederic 1920- 21-22R
Bradley, Alfred 1925- 105
Bradley, Bert E(dward) 1926- 41-44R
Bradley, Bill
See Bradley, William Warren
Bradley, Brigitte L(ooke) 1924- 37-40R
Bradley, C. Paul 1918- 106
Bradley, Concho
See Paine, Lauran (Bosworth)
Bradley, David (Henry, Jr.) 1950- CANR-26
Earlier sketch in CA 104
See also BW
See also DLB 33
See also CLC 23
Bradley, David G. 1916- 13-14R
Bradley, Duane
See Sanborn, Duane
Bradley, Ed 1911(?)-1983 Obituary 110
Bradley, Ed(ward R.) 1941- 113
Brief entry 108
See also BW
Bradley, Erwin S(tanley) 1906- CAP-2
Earlier sketch in CA 33-36
Bradley, Harold Whitman 1903- 33-36R
Bradley, Hassell 1930- 65-68
Bradley, Helen G(enevieve) 1932- 112
Bradley, Ian Campbell 1950- 103
Bradley, James V(andiver) 1924- 37-40R
Bradley, John (Francis Nejez) 1930- CANR-10
Earlier sketch in CA 25-28R
Bradley, John Lewis 1917- 29-32R
Bradley, Joseph F(rancis) 1917- 23-24R
Bradley, Kenneth (Granville) 1904- CAP-1
Earlier sketch in CA 13-14
Bradley, Marion Zimmer 1930- CANR-7
Earlier sketch in CA 57-60
See also DLB 8
See also CLC 30
Bradley, Marjorie D. 1931- 25-28R
Bradley, Matt 1947- 105
Bradley, Melanie (Rose) Choukas
See Choukas-Bradley, Melanie (Rose)
Bradley, Michael
See Blumberg, Gary
Bradley, Omar Nelson 1893-1981
Obituary 103
Bradley, Preston 1888-1983 Obituary 110
Bradley, R. C. 1929- CANR-14
Earlier sketch in CA 33-36R
Bradley, Ritamary 1916- 49-52
Bradley, Robert A(ustin) 1917- 21-22R
Bradley, Sam(uel McKee) 1917- 21-22R
Bradley, (Edward) Sculley 1897- 89-92
Bradley, Van Allen 1913-1984 37-40R
Obituary 114
Bradley, Virginia 1912- CANR-8
Earlier sketch in CA 61-64
See also SATA 23
Bradley, William 1934- 45-48
Bradley, William Aspenwall 1878-1939
Brief entry 107
See also DLB 4
Bradley, William L(ee) 1918- 23-24R
Bradley, William Warren 1943- 101
Bradlow, Edna Rom CAP-1
Earlier sketch in CA 9-10
Bradlow, Frank R(osslyn) 1913- CANR-13
Earlier sketches in CA 9-10, CAP-1
Bradner, Enos 1892-1984 57-60
Obituary 111
Bradshaw, Brendan 1937- 73-76
Bradshaw, George 1909(?)-1973
Obituary 45-48
Bradshaw, Gillian (Marucha) 1956- 103
Bradshaw, Jon (Wayne) 1937-1986
Obituary 121
Bradshaw, Terry (Paxton) 1948- 111
Bradshaw, Thornton F(rederick) 1917- 108
Bradstreet, Anne 1612(?)-1672 DLB-24
See also CDALB 1640-1865
Bradstreet, Vallerie
See Roby, Mary Linn
Bradt, A(cken) Gordon 1896-1983 57-60
Obituary 110
Bradway, John S(aeger) 1890- CAP-2
Earlier sketch in CA 33-36
Bradwell, James
See Kent, Arthur William Charles
Brady, Alexander 1896-1985 Obituary 117
Brady, Charles Andrew 1912- 5-6R
Brady, Darlene A(nn) 1951- 102
Brady, Dave 1913(?)-1988 Obituary 125
Brady, David W(illiam) 1940- Brief entry 114
Brady, Esther Wood 1905-1987 93-96
Obituary 123
See also SATA 31, 53
Brady, Frank 1924-1986 15-16R
Obituary 120
Brady, Frank 1934- CANR-9
Earlier sketch in CA 61-64
Brady, Gene P(aul) 1927- 107
Brady, George Stuart 1887-1977
Obituary 73-76
Brady, Gerald Peter 1929- 5-6R
Brady, Ignatius Charles 1911- 113
Brady, Irene 1943- CANR-20
Earlier sketch in CA 33-36R
See also SATA 4
Brady, James Winston 1928- CANR-21
Earlier sketch in CA 101
Brady, Jane 1934- Brief entry 113
Brady, John 1942- CANR-10
Earlier sketch in CA 65-68
Brady, John Paul 1928- CANR-5
Earlier sketch in CA 13-14R
Brady, Kristin 1949- 109
Brady, Leo 1917-1984 69-72
Obituary 114
Brady, Lillian 1902- 105
See also SATA 28
Brady, Mary Lou 1937- 106
Brady, Maureen 1943- 112
Brady, Maxine L. 1941- 69-72
Brady, Michael 1928- 93-96
Brady, Nicholas
See Levinson, Leonard
Brady, Peter
See Daniels, Norman
Brady, Sally Ryder 1939- 103
Brady, Terence 1939- 106
Brady, William S.
See Harvey, John (Barton)
Braenne, Berit 1918- 21-22R
Braestrup, Carl Bjorn 1897-1982 Obituary 107
Braestrup, Peter 1929- 97-100
Braff, Allan James 1930- 108
Braganti, Nancy (Sue) 1941- 117
Bragdon, Clifford R(ichardson) 1940- 57-60
Bragdon, Elspeth MacDuffie 1897- CANR-5
Earlier sketch in CA 5-6R
See also SATA 6
Bragdon, Henry Wilkinson 1906-1980 CANR-3
Obituary 97-100
Earlier sketch in CA 7-8R
Bragdon, Lillian Jacot 73-76
See also SATA 24
Bragg, Arthur N(orris) 1897- CAP-1
Earlier sketch in CA 17-18
Bragg, Bill
See Bragg, William Fredrick, Jr.
Bragg, Dobby
See Sykes, Roosevelt
Bragg, Mabel Caroline 1870-1945 SATA-24
Bragg, Melvyn 1939- CANR-10
Earlier sketch in CA 57-60
See also DLB 14
See also CLC 10
Bragg, Michael 1948- SATA-46
Bragg, Richard Geoffrey 1909- 121
Bragg, Sir W. H.
See Bragg, William Henry
Bragg, Sir William
See Bragg, William Henry
Bragg, Sir William Henry
See Bragg, William Henry
Bragg, William Fredrick, Jr. 1922- 109
Bragg, William Henry 1862-1942
Brief entry 123
Bragg, William Lawrence 1890-1971
Obituary 115
Braggin, Mary Vetterling
See Vetterling-Braggin, Mary (Katherine)
Braham, Allan (John Witney) 1937- 105
Braham, Randolph Lewis 1922- CANR-19
Earlier sketches in CA 3R, CANR-5
Brahms, Caryl
See Abrahams, Doris Caroline
Brahs, Stuart J(ohn) 1940- 57-60
Brahtz, John F(rederick) Peel 1918- 73-76
Braider, Donald 1923-1976 CAP-2
Obituary 65-68
Earlier sketch in CA 33-36
Braidwood, Robert John 1907- 108
Brailsford, Frances
See Wosmek, Frances
Braimah, Joseph Adam 1916- 61-64
Braiman, Susan 1943- 97-100
Brain, George B(ernard) 1920- 41-44R
Brain, J(oy) B(lundell) 1926- 118
Brain, James Lewton
See Lewton-Brain, James
Brain, Joseph J. 1920- 13-14R
Brain, Robert 1933- 73-76
Brainard, Harry Gray 1907- 1R
Brainard, Joe 1942- CANR-12
Earlier sketch in CA 65-68
Braine, John (Gerard) 1922-1986 CANR-1
Obituary 120
Earlier sketch in CA 2R
See also DLB 15
See also DLBY 86
See also CLC 1, 3, 41
Brainerd, Barron 1928- 33-36R
Brainerd, Charles Jon 1944- 103
Brainerd, John W(hiting) 1918- 57-60
Braithwaite, Althea 1940- CANR-18
Earlier sketch in CA 97-100
See also SATA 23
Braithwaite, (Eustace) E(dward) R(icardo) 1920- CANR-25
Earlier sketch in CA 106
See also BW
Braithwaite, Kenneth James
See Barrow, Kenneth
Braithwaite, Max 1911- 93-96
Braithwaite, William Stanley (Beaumont) 1878-1962 125
See also BW
See also DLB 50, 54
Brake, Mike 1936- 93-96
Brakel, Samuel J(ohannes) 1943- 33-36R
Brakhage, Stan 1933- CANR-15
Earlier sketch in CA 41-44R
Bralver, Eleanor 1913- 97-100
Braly, Malcolm 1925-1980 CANR-12
Obituary 97-100
Earlier sketch in CA 19-20R
Bram, Chris
See Bram, Christopher
Bram, Christopher 1952- 126
Bram, Elizabeth 1948- CANR-9
Earlier sketch in CA 65-68
See also SATA 30
Bram, Joseph 1904-1974 Obituary 110
Bramah, Ernest 1868-1942 DLB-70
Bramall, Eric 1927- 9-10R
Braman, Sandra 1951- 114
Bramann, Jorn K(arl) 1938- 119
Brambell, Wilfrid 1912- 113
Bramble, Forbes 1939- 89-92
Brameld, Theodore (Burghard Hurt) 1904-1987 17-18R
Obituary 123
Bramer, Jennie (Perkins) 1900- CAP-1
Earlier sketch in CA 13-14
Bramer, John C(onrad) Jr. 1924- 4R
Bramesco, Norton J. 1924- 106
Bramlett, John
See Pierce, John Leonard, Jr.
Brammell, P(aris) Roy 1900- 65-68
Brammer, Lawrence M(artin) 1922- 13-14R
Brammer, William 1930(?)-1978
Obituary 77-80
See also CLC 31
Brams, Stanley Howard 1910- 11-12R
Brams, Steven J(ohn) 1940- CANR-26
Earlier sketches in CA 61-64, CANR-10
Bramsch, Joan 1936- 122
Bramson, Leon 1930- CANR-4
Earlier sketch in CA 3R
Bramson, Robert M(ark) 1925- CANR-25
Earlier sketch in CA 108
Bramwell, Charlotte
See Kimbro, John M.
Bramwell, Dana G. 1948- 57-60
Bramwell, James Guy 1911- 9-10R
Bramwell-Booth, Catherine 1883-1987
Obituary 123
Branagan, Thomas 1774-1843 DLB-37
Brana-Shute, Gary 1945- 111
Branca, Albert A. 1916- 15-16R
Brancaforte, Benito 1934- 37-40R
Brancati, Vitaliano 1907-1954 Brief entry 109
See also TCLC 12
Brancato, Gilda 1949- 107
Brancato, Robin F(idler) 1936- CANR-11
Earlier sketch in CA 69-72
See also SATA 23
See also CLC 35
Branch, Alan E(dward) 1933- CANR-25
Earlier sketch in CA 105
Branch, Daniel Paulk 1931- 17-18R
Branch, Edgar Marquess 1913- 13-14R
Branch, Harold F(rancis) 1894-1966 7-8R
Branch, Kip 1947- 108
Branch, Mary 1910- CANR-10
Earlier sketch in CA 25-28R
Branch, Melville C(ampbell) 1913- CANR-14
Earlier sketch in CA 41-44R
Branch, William (Blackwell) 1927- CANR-16
Earlier sketch in CA 81-84
See also BW
See also DLB 76
Brand, C(larence) E(ugene) 1895- CAP-2
Earlier sketch in CA 23-24
Brand, Carl F(remont) 1892- 15-16R
Brand, Charles M(acy) 1932- 23-24R
Brand, Charles Peter 1923- 15-16R
Brand, Christianna
See Lewis, Mary (Christianna)
Brand, Clay
See Norwood, Victor G(eorge) C(harles)
Brand, Eugene L(ouis) 1931- CANR-8
Earlier sketch in CA 61-64
Brand, Garrison
See Brandner, Gary
Brand, Gerd 1921- Brief entry 113
Brand, Irene B. 1929- 124
Brand, Jeanne L(aurel) 1919- 15-16R
Brand, Max
See Faust, Frederick (Shiller)
Brand, Millen 1906-1980 21-22R
Obituary 97-100
See also CLC 7
Brand, Myles 1942- 37-40R
Brand, Oscar 1920- CANR-4
Earlier sketch in CA 4R
Brand, Peter
See Larsen, Erling
Brand, Sandra 1918- 85-88
Brand, Stewart 1938- 81-84
See also AITN 1
Brand, Susan
See Roper, Susan Bonthron
Brandabur, Edward 1930- 41-44R
Brande, Ralph T. 1921- 25-28R
Brandeis, Louis Dembitz 1856-1941
Brief entry 118
Brandel, Arthur Meyer 1913(?)-1980
Obituary 102
Brandel, Marc 1919- CANR-25
Earlier sketch in CA 108
Brandell, (Erik) Gunnar 1916- CANR-20
Earlier sketch in CA 103
Branden, Barbara CLC-44
Branden, Nathaniel 1930- 33-36R
Branden, Victoria (Fremlin) 101
Brandenberg, Aliki Liacouras 1929- CANR-12
Earlier sketches in CA 4R, CANR-4
See also SATA 2, 35
Brandenberg, Franz 1932- CANR-12
Earlier sketch in CA 29-32R
See also SATA 8, 35
Brandenburg, David J(ohn) 1920-1987
Obituary 123
Brandenburg, Frank R(alph) 1926- 13-14R
Brander, Michael (William) 1924- CANR-7
Earlier sketch in CA 53-56
Brandes, Georg (Morris Cohen) 1842-1927 Brief entry 105
See also TCLC 10
Brandes, Joseph 1928- 5-6R
Brandes, Norman Scott 1923- 57-60
Brandes, Paul D(ickerson) 1920- CANR-2
Earlier sketch in CA 45-48
Brandewyne, (Mary) Rebecca (Wadsworth) 1955- CANR-23
Earlier sketch in CA 107
Brandhorst, Carl T(heodore) 1898- CAP-2
Earlier sketch in CA 25-28
See also SATA 23
Brandi, John 1943- CANR-12
Earlier sketch in CA 73-76
Brandis, Marianne 1938- 117
Brandner, Gary 1933- CANR-17
Earlier sketches in CA 45-48, CANR-1
Brandon, Beatrice
See Krepps, Robert W(ilson)
Brandon, Brumsic, Jr. 1927- 61-64
See also SATA 9
Brandon, Curt
See Bishop, Curtis (Kent)
Brandon, Dick H. 1934-1981 CANR-10
Earlier sketch in CA 19-20R
Brandon, Donald (Wayne) 1926- 69-72
Brandon, Dorothy 1899(?)-1977 Obituary 69-72
Brandon, Frances Sweeney 1916- 9-10R
Brandon, Frank
See Bulmer, (Henry) Kenneth
Brandon, (Oscar) Henry 1916- 49-52
Brandon, James Rodger 1927- CANR-11
Earlier sketch in CA 69-72
Brandon, Jay (Robert) 1953- 119

Brandon, Joe
 See Davis, Robert P.
Brandon, John G(ordon) 1879(?)-1941
 Brief entry 112
Brandon, Johnny 105
Brandon, Joyce A(lmeta) 1938- 118
Brandon, Robert Joseph 1918- 105
Brandon, Robin
 See Brandon, Robert Joseph
Brandon, S(amuel) G(eorge) F(rederick)
 1907-1971 102
Brandon, Shelia
 See Rayner, Claire (Berenice)
Brandon, William 1914- 77-80
Brandon-Cox, Hugh 1917- 93-96
Brandreth, Gyles 1948- 65-68
 See also SATA 28
Brandreth, Henry R(enaud) T(urner)
 1914-1984 Obituary 114
Brandstatter, A(rthur) F. 1914- 107
Brandt, Alvin G. 1922- 13-14R
Brandt, Anthony 1936- 69-72
Brandt, Bill 1904(?)-1983 Obituary 111
Brandt, Carol 1904-1984 Obituary 114
Brandt, Catharine 1905- 106
 See also SATA 40
Brandt, Floyd S(tanley) 1930- 21-22R
Brandt, Harvey
 See Edwards, William B(ennett)
Brandt, Jane Lewis 1915- 97-100
Brandt, Keith
 See Sabin, Louis
Brandt, Leslie F. 1919- CANR-23
 Earlier sketches in CA 23-24R, CANR-8
Brandt, Lucile (Long Strayer) 1900- CANR-13
 Earlier sketch in CA 61-64
Brandt, Nat
 See Brandt, Nathan Henry, Jr.
Brandt, Nathan Henry, Jr. 1929- CANR-18
 Earlier sketch in CA 102
Brandt, Rex(ford Elson) 1914- CANR-5
 Earlier sketch in CA 13-14R
Brandt, Richard B(ooker) 1910-
 Brief entry 114
Brandt, Richard M(artin) 1922- 33-36R
Brandt, Roger
 See Crawford, William (Elbert)
Brandt, Sue R(eading) 1916- 25-28R
Brandt, Tom
 See Dewey, Thomas B.
Brandt, Vincent S. R. 1924- 37-40R
Brandt, William E(dward) 1920- 5-6R
Brandt, Willy 1913- 85-88
Brandt, Yanna Kroyt 1933- 104
Brandts, Robert (Percival) 1930- 69-72
Brandwein, Chaim N(aftali) 1920- 23-24R
Brandys, Marian 1912- 57-60
Branegan, James Augustus III 1950- 124
Branfield, John (Charles) 1931- CANR-14
 Earlier sketch in CA 41-44R
 See also SATA 11
Branfoot, Gwynneth
 See Holder, Gwynneth
Branick, Vincent P(atrick) 1941- 113
Branigan, Keith 1940- 124
Branin, M(anlif) Lelyn 1901- 85-88
Branley, Franklyn M(ansfield) 1915- CANR-14
 Earlier sketch in CA 33-36R
 See also SATA 4
 See also CLC 21
 See also CLR 13
Brann, Eva T(oni) H(elene) 1929- 93-96
Brannan, Robert Louis 1927- 21-22R
Brannen, Noah S(amuel) 1924- CANR-11
 Earlier sketch in CA 25-28R
Brannen, Ted R. 1924- 17-18R
Branner, Hans Christian 1903-1966 97-100
 Obituary 89-92
Branner, R(obert) 1927-1973 .... CANR-3
 Obituary 45-48
 Earlier sketch in CA 5-6R
Brannigan, Bill
 See Brannigan, William
Brannigan, William 1936- 65-68
Brannon, William T. 1906- CAP-1
 Earlier sketch in CA 15-16
Branscomb, (Bennett) Harvie 1894- 106
Branscum, Robbie 1937- CANR-8
 Earlier sketch in CA 61-64
 See also SATA 23
Bransford, Kent Jackson 1953- 97-100
Bransom, (John) Paul 1885-1979 .... SATA-43
Branson, David 1909- CANR-21
 Earlier sketch in CA 41-44R
Branson, Margaret Stimmann 1922- CANR-1
 Earlier sketch in CA 49-52
Branston, (Ronald Victor) Brian 1914- 53-56
Brant, Charles S(tanford) 1919- 25-28R
Brant, Irving (Newton) 1885-1976 .... 9-10R
 Obituary 69-72
Brant, Lewis
 See Rowland, D(onald) S(ydney)
Brantley, Cynthia Louise 1943- 109
Branyan, Robert L(ester) 1930- 104
Branzburg, Paul M(arshal) 1941- 73-76
Braque, Georges 1882-1963 Obituary 112
Brasch, Charles (Orwell) 1909-1973 114
 Obituary 104
Brasch, Ila Wales 1945- 57-60
Brasch, James D(aniel) 1929- 116
Brasch, Rudolph 1912- CANR-8
 Earlier sketch in CA 21-22R
Brasch, Walter Milton 1945- CANR-23
 Earlier sketches in CA 57-60, CANR-6
Brasher, Christopher William 1928- 7-8R
Brasher, N(orman) H(enry) 1922- 25-28R
Brasher, Nell 1912- CANR-7
 Earlier sketch in CA 61-64
Brasher, Thomas L(owber) 1912- 69-72
Brashers, H(oward) C(harles) 1930- CANR-8
 Earlier sketch in CA 7-8R
Brashler, William 1947- CANR-2
 Earlier sketch in CA 45-48
Brasier, Virginia 1910- 61-64
Brasier-Creagh, Patrick
 See Creagh, Patrick
Brasnett, Bertrand R(ippington)
 1893-1988 Obituary 124
Brason, Gill 1942- 112
Brass, Paul Richard 1936- 17-18R
Brassai
 See Halasz, Gyula
Brasselle, Keefe 1923(?)-1981 Obituary 104
Brassens, Georges 1921-1981 Obituary 105
Brasseur, Pierre
 See Espinasse, Albert
Braswell, George Wilbur, Jr. 1936- 112
Brater, Enoch 1944- 122
Brathwaite, Edward (Kamau) 1930- CANR-26
 Earlier sketches in CA 25-28R, CANR-11
 See also BW
 See also CLC 11
Brathwaite, Errol (Freeman) 1924- CANR-11
 Earlier sketches in CA 57-60, CANR-7
Brathwaite, Sheila R. 1914- 25-28R
Bratt, Elmer Clark 1901-1970 .... 3R
 Obituary 103
Bratt, John H(arold) 1909- CANR-9
 Earlier sketch in CA 19-20R
Bratter, Herbert Max 1900-1976 Obituary 65-68
Bratter, Thomas Edward 1939- 120
Brattgarg, Helge (Axel Kristian) 1920- 7-8R
Bratton, Fred Gladstone 1896-19(?) CAP-1
 Earlier sketch in CA 11-12
Bratton, Helen 1899- CAP-2
 Earlier sketch in CA 23-24
 See also SATA 4
Brattstrom, Bayard H(olmes) 1929- 57-60
Braude, Benjamin 1945- 111
Braude, Jacob M(orton) 1896-1970 .... CANR-5
 Earlier sketch in CA 5-6R
Braude, Michael 1909-1986 Obituary 121
Braude, Michael 1936- 17-18R
 See also SATA 23
Braude, William Gordon 1907- 33-36R
Braudel, Fernand (Paul) 1902-1985 .... CANR-14
 Obituary 117
 Earlier sketch in CA 93-96
Braudy, Leo 1941- 37-40R
Braudy, Susan (Orr) 1941- CANR-10
 Earlier sketch in CA 65-68
Brauer, Carl M(alcolm) 1946- 85-88
Brauer, George C(harles), Jr. 1925-
 Brief entry 113
Brauer, Jerald C(arl) 1921- CANR-13
 Earlier sketch in CA 33-36R
Brauer, Kinley J(ules) 1935- 21-22R
Brault, Gerard Joseph 1929- CANR-3
 Earlier sketch in CA 7-8R
Brault, Jacques 1933- DLB-53
Braun, Armin C(harles John) 1911-1986
 Obituary 120
Braun, Arthur E. 1876-1976 Obituary 69-72
Braun, Edward 1936- Brief entry 115
Braun, Eric 1921- 102
Braun, Henry 1930- 25-28R
Braun, Hugh 1902- 25-28R
Braun, J(oachim) Werner 1914-1972
 Obituary 37-40R
Braun, John R(ichard) 1928- 33-36R
Braun, Lev 1913- 41-44R
Braun, Richard Emil 1934- 9-10R
Braun, Sidney D(avid) 1912- CANR-10
 Earlier sketch in CA 65-68
Braun, Theodore E. D. 1933- CANR-7
 Earlier sketch in CA 15-16R
Braun, Thomas (Felix Rudry Gerhart)
 1935- 115
Braun, Volker 1939- DLB-75
Braunburg, Rudolf 1924- 109
Braund, Hal
 See Braund, Harold
Braund, Harold 1913-1988 61-64
 Obituary 124
Braunrot, Bruno 1936- 114
Braunstein, Daniel N(orman) 1938- 111
Braunstein, Mark M(athew) 1951- 113
Braunthal, Alfred 1898(?)-1980 Obituary 93-96
Braunthal, Gerard 1923- 15-16R
Braunthal, Julius 1891-1972 .... CAP-2
 Earlier sketch in CA 23-24
Brautigan, Richard (Gary) 1935-1984 53-56
 Obituary 113
 See also DLB 2, 5
 See also DLBY 80, 84
 See also CLC 1, 3, 5, 9, 12, 34, 42
Brav, Stanley R(osenbaum) 1908- 25-28R
Braverman, Harry 1920-1976 53-56
 Obituary 69-72
Braverman, Kate 1950- 89-92
Bravmann, Rene A. 1939- 85-88
Brawer, Florence B(lum) 1922- 37-40R
Brawley, Benjamin (Griffith) 1882-1939 125
 See also BW
Brawley, Ernest 1937- 53-56
Brawley, Paul Holm
 See Brawley, Paul L(eroy)
Brawley, Paul L(eroy) 1942-1988 73-76
 Obituary 126
Brawn, Dympna 1931- 25-28R
Brawne, Michael 1925- 73-76
Braxton, Joanne M. 1950- DLB-41
Bray, Alison
 See Rowland, D(onald) S(ydney)
Bray, Allen Farris III 1926- 9-10R
Bray, Douglas W. 1918- 15-16R
Bray, Howard 1929- 105
Bray, J(ohn) J(efferson) 1912- 102
Bray, Thomas 1656-1730 .... DLB-24
Bray, Virginia Elizabeth Nuckolls
 1895(?)-1979 Obituary 93-96
Bray, Warwick 1936- CANR-15
 Earlier sketch in CA 25-28R
Braybrooke, David 1924- CANR-18
 Earlier sketches in CA 11-12R, CANR-3
Braybrooke, Neville (Patrick Bellairs)
 1925- 7-8R
Brayce, William
 See Rowland, D(onald) S(ydney)
Brayman, Harold 1900-1988 73-76
 Obituary 124
Braymer, Marguerite
 See Dodd, Marguerite
Braymer, Marjorie Elizabeth 1911- 3R
 See also SATA 6
Braynard, Frank O. 1916- CANR-8
 Earlier sketch in CA 17-18R
Braza, Jacque
 See McKeag, Ernest L(ionel)
Brazeau, Peter (Alden) 1942-1986 111
 Obituary 119
Brazell, Karen 1938- 45-48
Brazelton, T(homas) Berry 1918- 97-100
Brazer, Harvey E(lliott) 1922- 111
Brazil, Angela 1869(?)-1947 Brief entry 112
Brazill, William J., Jr. 1935- 53-56
Brazos, Waco
 See Jennings, Michael Glenn
Breach, Robert Walter 1927- 15-16R
Breakwell, Glynis M(arie) 1952- 122
Brealey, Richard A. 1936- 53-56
Brean, Herbert (J.) 1907-1973 93-96
 Obituary 41-44R
Brearley, Denis 1940- 37-40R
Brears, Peter C(harles) D(avid) 1944- 102
Breasted, Charles 1898(?)-1980 Obituary 93-96
Breasted, James Henry 1865-1935 .... DLB-47
Breasted, James Henry, Jr. 1908-1983
 Obituary 109
Breathed, (Guy) Berke(ley) 1957- 110
Breathett, George 1925- 13-14R
Breatnac, Seamus
 See Walsh, James P(atrick)
Breault, William 1926- CANR-6
 Earlier sketch in CA 57-60
Brecher, Charles Martin 1945- CANR-4
 Earlier sketch in CA 53-56
Brecher, Edward M(oritz) 1911- CANR-7
 Earlier sketch in CA 13-14R
Brecher, Jeremy 1946- CANR-12
 Earlier sketch in CA 69-72
Brecher, Michael 1925- CANR-4
 Earlier sketch in CA 1R
Brecher, Ruth E(rnestine) 1911-1966 .... CAP-1
 Earlier sketch in CA 13-14
Brechner, Irv 1951- 110
Brecht, Arnold 1884-1977 77-80
 Obituary 73-76
Brecht, Bertolt 1898-1956 Brief entry 104
 See also DLB 56
 See also TCLC 1, 6, 13
Brecht, Edith 1895-1975 .... CAP-2
 Earlier sketch in CA 25-28
 See also SATA 6, 25
Brecht, Eugen Berthold Friedrich
 See Brecht, Bertolt
Brecht, George 1924- 106
Breck, Allen duPont 1914- CANR-9
 Earlier sketch in CA 13-14R
Breck, Vivian
 See Breckenfeld, Vivian Gurney
Breckenfeld, Vivian Gurney 1895- 5-6R
 See also SATA 1
Breckenridge, Adam Carlyle 1916- 29-32R
Breckinridge, Mary 1881-1965 Obituary 114
Breckler, Rosemary 1920- 101
Breda, Tjalmar
 See DeJong, David C(ornel)
Bredel, Willi 1901-1964 .... DLB-56
Bredemeier, Harry Charles 1920- CANR-8
 Earlier sketch in CA 7-8R
Bredemeier, Mary E(lizabeth) 1924- 81-84
Bredes, Don(ald) 1947- 110
Bredow, Miriam
 See Wolf, Miriam Bredow
Bredsdorff, Elias Lunn 1912- CAP-1
 Earlier sketch in CA 9-10
Bredsdorff, Jan 1942- CANR-13
 Earlier sketch in CA 21-22R
Bredvold, Louis I(gnatius) 1888-1977 .... 3R
 Obituary 103
Bree, Germaine 1907- CANR-4
 Earlier sketch in CA 1R
Breech, (Earl) James 1944- 114
Breed, Paul F. 1916- 33-36R
Breeden, Stanley 1938- 106
Breem, Wallace (Wilfred Swinburne)
 1926- Brief entry 113
Breen, Dana
 See Birksted-Breen, Dana
Breen, (Joseph) John 1942- 77-80
Breen, Jon L(inn) 1943- 119
Breen, Quirinus 1896-1975 .... CAP-2
 Earlier sketch in CA 33-36
Breen, Richard 1935- 110
Breen, Richard L. 1919-1967 Obituary 111
Breen, T(imothy) H(all) 1942- 101
Breen, William J(ames) 1937- 118
Breese, Dave
 See Breese, David W(illiam)
Breese, David W(illiam) 1926- 118
Breese, Gerald (William) 1912- 41-44R
Breeskin, Adelyn Dohme 1896-1986 .... 33-36R
 Obituary 119
Breetveld, Jim Patrick 1925- CANR-2
 Earlier sketch in CA 4R
Breeze, Katie 1929- 111
Breffort, Alexandre 1901-1971 Obituary 29-32R
Breger, Louis 1935- 69-72
Breggin, Peter R(oger) 1936- CANR-15
 Earlier sketch in CA 81-84
Bregman, Jacob I(srael Jack) 1923- 41-44R
Bregman, Jay 1940- 109
Brehm, Sharon S(tephens) 1945- 112
Brehm, Shirley A(lice) 1926- 69-72
Breig, Joseph A(nthony) 1905- 5-6R
Breihan, Carl W(illiam) 1916- CANR-1
 Earlier sketch in CA 4R
Breillat, Catherine 1950- 33-36R
Breimyer, Harold F(rederick) 1914- 19-20R
Breinburg, Petronella 1927- CANR-4
 Earlier sketch in CA 53-56
 See also SATA 11
Breines, Paul 1941- 61-64
Breines, Simon 1906- Brief entry 114
Breines, Winifred 1942- 113
Breisach, Ernst Adolf 1923- CANR-18
 Earlier sketch in CA 3R
Breisky, William J(ohn) 1928- 53-56
 See also SATA 22
Breit, Harvey 1909-1968 .... CANR-6
 Obituary 25-28R
 Earlier sketch in CA 5-6R
Breit, Marquita E(laine) 1942- 57-60
Breit, William (Leo) 1933- CANR-13
 Earlier sketch in CA 33-36R
Breitbart, Vicki 1942- 93-96
Breitenkamp, Edward C(arlton) 1913- CANR-25
 Earlier sketches in CA 25-28R, CANR-10
Breitman, George 1916-1986 .... CANR-7
 Obituary 119
 Earlier sketch in CA 61-64
Breitman, Richard D(avid) 1947- CANR-21
 Earlier sketch in CA 105
Breitner, I. Emery 1929- 57-60
Breland, Osmond P(hilip) 1910- 11-12R
Brelis, Dean 1924- 11-12R
Brelis, Matthew 1957- Brief entry 126
Brelis, Nancy (Burns) 1929- 21-22R
Brelsford, W(illiam) V(ernon) 1907- CAP-1
 Earlier sketch in CA 13-14
Breman, Paul 1931- 21-22R
Brembeck, Winston Lamont 1912-
 Brief entry 115
Bremer, Arthur H(erman) 1950-
 Brief entry 113
Bremer, Francis J(ohn) 1947- 93-96
Bremer, Lisa
 See Janas, Frankie-Lee
Bremner, Geoffrey 1930- 115
Bremner, John B(urton) 1920-1987
 Obituary 123
Bremner, Robert H(amlett) 1917- CANR-9
 Earlier sketch in CA 23-24R
Brems, Hans 1915- CANR-10
 Earlier sketch in CA 25-28R
Bremser, Bonnie 1939- DLB-16
Bremser, Ray 1934- 17-18R
 See also DLB 16
Bremyer, Jayne Dickey 1924- 61-64
Brenan, (Edward FitzGerald 1894-1987 .... CANR-3
 Obituary 121
 Earlier sketch in CA 4R
Brend, Ruth M(argaret) 1927- 105
Brendel, Otto Johannes 1901-1973 97-100
Brendon, Piers (George Rundle) 1940- 101
Brendtro, Larry K. 1940- 29-32R
Brener, Milton E. 1930- 29-32R
Brengelman, Fred(erick Henry) 1928-
 Brief entry 115
Brengelmann, Johannes Clemens 1920- 5-6R
Brenlove, Milovan S. 1948- 126
Brennan, Anne 1936- 109
Brennan, Bernard P(atrick) 1918- 5-6R
Brennan, Christopher
 See Kininmonth, Christopher
Brennan, Christopher John 1870-1932
 Brief entry 117
 See also TCLC 17
Brennan, Donald (George) 1926-1980
 Obituary 97-100
Brennan, Gale (Patrick) 1927- 125
 See also SATA 53
Brennan, John N(eedham) H(uggard)
 1914- CANR-20
 Earlier sketches in CA 4R, CANR-4
Brennan, Joseph Gerard 1910- CANR-3
 Earlier sketch in CA 3R
Brennan, Joseph K(illorin) 1952- 121
Brennan, Joseph Lomas 1903- CANR-2
 Earlier sketch in CA 5-6R
 See also SATA 6
Brennan, Joseph Payne 1918- CANR-19
 Earlier sketches in CA 4R, CANR-4
Brennan, Lawrence D(avid) 1915- 5-6R
Brennan, Louis A(rthur) 1911-1983 .... 19-20R
 Obituary 109
Brennan, Maeve 1917- 81-84
 See also CLC 5
Brennan, Matthew J. 1917- 106
Brennan, Maynard J. 1921- 13-14R
Brennan, Michael Joseph, Jr. 1928- 15-16R
Brennan, Neil F(rancis) 1923- 37-40R
Brennan, Niall 1918- 13-14R
Brennan, Nicholas (Stephen) 1948- 106

Brennan, Ray 1908(?)-1972 Obituary 37-40R
Brennan, Richard O(liver) 1916- 89-92
Brennan, Tim
See Conroy, John Wesley
Brennan, Will
See Paine, Lauran (Bosworth)
Brennand, Frank
See Lambert, Eric
Brennecke, John H(enry) 1934- 37-40R
Brenneman, Helen Good 1925- 23-24R
Brenner, Anita 1905-1974 49-52
Obituary 53-56
Brenner, Barbara (Johnes) 1925- CANR-12
Earlier sketch in CA 9-10R
See also SATA 4, 42
Brenner, Elizabeth 1954- 123
Brenner, Erma 1911- 69-72
Brenner, Fred 1920- SATA-34, 36
Brenner, Gerry 1937- 110
Brenner, Isabel
See Schuchman, Joan
Brenner, Lenni 1937- 117
Brenner, Marie 1949- 73-76
Brenner, Rebecca Summer 1945- CANR-10
Earlier sketch in CA 61-64
Brenner, Reeve R(obert) 1936- Brief entry .. 116
Brenner, Summer
See Brenner, Rebecca Summer
Brenner, Yehojachin Simon 1926- CANR-11
Earlier sketch in CA 21-22R
Brennert, Alan (Michael) 1954- 118
Brenni, Vito J(oseph) 1923- 49-52
Brent, Beryl
See Ince, Martin (Jeffrey)
Brent, Harold Patrick 1943- 33-36R
Brent, Harry
See Brent, Harold Patrick
Brent, Hope 1935(?)-1984 .... SATA-39
Brent, Iris
See Bancroft, Iris (May Nelson)
Brent, Jonathan 1949- 113
Brent, Peter (Ludwig) 1931-1984 ...... CANR-13
Obituary 114
Earlier sketch in CA 65-68
Brent, Stuart 73-76
See also SATA 14
Brentano, Bernard von 1901-1964 ...... DLB-56
Brentano, Robert 1926- 23-24R
Brent-Dyer, Elinor Mary 1895-1969 101
Brent of Bin Bin
See Franklin, (Stella Maraia Sarah) Miles
Brenton, Howard 1942- 69-72
See also DLB 13
See also CLC 31
Breo, Dennis L. 1942- 124
Brereton, Geoffrey 1906-1979 .... CANR-20
Earlier sketch in CA 25-28R
Bresee, Clyde W. 1916- 122
Bresky, Dushan 53-56
Breslau, Alan Jeffry 1926- 69-72
Breslauer, George W. 1946- CANR-12
Earlier sketch in CA 29-32R
Breslauer, Samuel Daniel 1942- 102
Breslin, Catherine 1936- 93-96
Breslin, Herbert H. 1924- 53-56
Breslin, James 1930- 73-76
Breslin, James E. 1935- 33-36R
Breslin, Jimmy
See Breslin, James
See also CLC 4, 43
See also AITN 1
Breslin, Mark 1952- 121
Breslin, Paul 1946- 111
Breslove, David 1891- 9-10R
Breslow, Lester 1915- 115
Breslow, Lou 1900(?)-1987 Obituary 124
Bressett, Kenneth E(dward) 1928- 93-96
Bressler, Leo A(lbert) 1911- 57-60
Bressler, Marion Ann 1921- 57-60
Bresson, Robert 1907- 110
See also CLC 16
Brestin, Dee 1944- 114
Bretall, Robert Walter 1913-1980 Obituary .. 110
Bretecher, Claire 1940- Brief entry 113
Bretnor, Reginald 1911- CANR-25
Earlier sketches in CA 65-68, CANR-10
Breton, Albert 1929- 61-64
Breton, Andre 1896-1966 .... CAP-2
Obituary 25-28R
Earlier sketch in CA 19-20
See also DLB 65
See also CLC 2, 9, 15
Bretscher, Paul G(erhardt) 1921- CANR-8
Earlier sketch in CA 17-18R
Brett, Bernard 1925- CANR-17
Earlier sketch in CA 97-100
See also SATA 22
Brett, Bill 1922- 122
Brett, David
See Campbell, Will D(avis)
Brett, Dorothy 1883-1977 Obituary 73-76
Brett, George P(latt), Jr. 1893-1984
Obituary 112
Brett, Grace N(eff) 1900-1975 ....11-12R
Obituary 120
See also SATA 23
Brett, Hawksley
See Bell, Robert S(tanley) W(arren)
Brett, Jan (Churchill) 1949- 116
See also SATA 42
Brett, John Michael
See Tripp, Miles (Barton)
Brett, Leo
See Fanthorpe, R(obert) Lionel
Brett, Mary Elizabeth 11-12R
Brett, Michael
See Tripp, Miles (Barton)
Brett, Molly
See Brett, Mary Elizabeth
Brett, Peter David 1943- 77-80
Brett, Raymond Laurence 1917- CANR-3
Earlier sketch in CA 1R
Brett, Simon (Anthony Lee) 1945- 69-72
Brettell, Richard (Robson) 1949- 124
Brett-James, (Eliot) Antony 1920-1984 .. CANR-7
Obituary 112
Earlier sketch in CA 7-8R
Bretton, Henry L. 1916- CANR-2
Earlier sketch in CA 5-6R
Brettschneider, Bertram D(onald)
1924-1986 ....33-36R
Obituary 121
Brett-Smith, Richard 1923- 21-22R
Brett-Young, Jessica (Hankinson)
1883-1970 .... CAP-1
Earlier sketch in CA 9-10
Bretuo, Akwasi
See Assensoh, A(kwasi) B(retuo)
Breuer, Bessie 1893-1975 .... CAP-2
Obituary 61-64
Earlier sketch in CA 17-18
Breuer, Ernest Henry 1902-1972 .... CAP-2
Earlier sketch in CA 19-20
Breuer, Georg 1919- 105
Breuer, Gustav J. 1915-1985 Obituary 114
Breuer, Gustl
See Breuer, Gustav J.
Breuer, Lee 1937- 110
Breuer, Marcel 1902-1981 .... CANR-5
Obituary 104
Earlier sketch in CA 7-8R
Breuer, Miles J(ohn) 1888-1947
Brief entry 112
Breuer, Reinhard 1946- 115
Breuer, William B(entley) 1924- 118
Breugelmans, Rene 1925- 103
Breunig, Jerome Edward 1917- 15-16R
Breunig, LeRoy C(linton) 1915- 61-64
Brew, Douglas James 1949(?)-1985
Obituary 117
Brew, J(ohn) O(tis) 1906- 61-64
Brewer, Annie M. 1925- 107
Brewer, D(erek) S(tanley) 1923- CANR-4
Earlier sketch in CA 1R
Brewer, Edward S(amuel) 1933- CANR-13
Earlier sketch in CA 33-36R
Brewer, (Lucie) Elisabeth 1923- 115
Brewer, Frances Joan 1913-1965 .... CAP-1
Earlier sketch in CA 11-12
Brewer, Fredric (Aldwyn) 1921- 17-18R
Brewer, Garry Dwight 1941- CANR-14
Earlier sketch in CA 33-36R
Brewer, J(ohn) Mason 1896-1975 .... CAP-2
Earlier sketch in CA 25-28
Brewer, Jack A. 1933- 23-24R
Brewer, James H. Fitzgerald 1916- 11-12R
Brewer, Jeutonne P. 1939- CANR-14
Earlier sketch in CA 77-80
Brewer, Kenneth W(ayne) 1941- 110
Brewer, Margaret L. 1929- 29-32R
Brewer, Priscilla J. 1956- 122
Brewer, Sally King 1947- SATA-33
Brewer, Sam Pope 1909(?)-1976
Obituary 65-68
Brewer, Thomas B. 1932- 21-22R
Brewer, William C. 1897(?)-1974
Obituary 53-56
Brewer, Wilmon 1895- 5-6R
Brewi, Janice 1933- 110
Brewington, Marion Vernon 1902-1974 .. CANR-3
Obituary 53-56
Earlier sketch in CA 5-6R
Brewster, Benjamin
See Folsom, Franklin (Brewster)
Brewster, Dorothy 1883-1979 .... CANR-3
Obituary 85-88
Earlier sketch in CA 1R
Brewster, Elizabeth (Winifred) 1922- ... CANR-25
Earlier sketches in CA 25-28R, CANR-10
See also DLB 60
Brewster, Patience 1952- 121
See also SATA 51
Brewster, Townsend 1924- 105
Brewton, John E(dmund) 1898- CANR-3
Earlier sketch in CA 5-6R
See also SATA 5
Brewton, Sara Westbrook ?-1976 122
Breyer, N(orman) L(ane) 1942- 49-52
Breyer, Stephen Gerald 1938- 107
Breytenbach, Breyten 1939(?)- Brief entry ... 113
See also CLC 23, 37
Breza, Tadeusz 1905(?)-1970 Obituary ...29-32R
Brezhnev, Leonid I(lyich) 1906-1982
Obituary 108
Brian
See Powell, Brian S(harples)
Brian, Alan B.
See Parulski, George R(ichard), Jr.
Brian, Denis 1923- 25-28R
Briand, Paul L., Jr. 1920- CANR-4
Earlier sketch in CA 2R
Briand, Rena 1935- 29-32R
Briarton, Grendel
See Bretnor, Reginald
Brice, Douglas 1916- 21-22R
Brice, Marshall Moore 1898- 19-20R
Brichant, Colette Dubois 1926- 15-16R
Brick, Howard 1953- 126
Brick, John 1922-1973 .... CAP-1
Obituary 45-48
Earlier sketch in CA 13-14
See also SATA 10
Brick, Michael 1922-1974 .... CANR-9
Earlier sketch in CA 15-16R
Bricker, Victoria Reifler 1940- 53-56
Brickhill, Paul Chester Jerome 1916- 11-12R
Bricklin, Mark Harris 1939- 111
Brickman, Marshall 1941- 81-84
Brickman, William Wolfgang
1913-1986 .... CANR-17
Obituary 119
Earlier sketches in CA 4R, CANR-1
Brickner, Richard P(ilpel) 1933- CANR-2
Earlier sketch in CA 5-6R
Bricktop
See Smith, Ada Beatrice Queen Victoria
Louisa Virginia
Bricuth, John
See Irwin, John T(homas)
Bridenbaugh, Carl 1903- CANR-4
Earlier sketch in CA 11-12R
Bridge, Ann
See O'Malley, Mary Dolling (Sanders)
Bridge, Don(ald) U(lysses) 1894-1984
Obituary 112
Bridge, Raymond 1943- 69-72
Bridgecross, Peter
See Cardinal, Roger (Thomas)
Bridgeman, Harriet 1942- 85-88
Bridgeman, Richard
See Davies, L(eslie) P(urnell)
Bridgeman, William Barton 1916- 9-10R
Bridger, Adam
See Bingley, David Ernest
Bridger, Gordon (Frederick) 1932- 65-68
Bridgers, Sue Ellen 1942- CANR-11
Earlier sketch in CA 65-68
See also SATA 22
See also SAAS 1
See also DLB 52
See also CLC 26
Bridges, Emily
See Bruggen, Carol (Holmes)
Bridges, Hal 1918- 1R
Bridges, Herb 1929- 110
Bridges, Howard
See Staples, Reginald Thomas
Bridges, James 1936- Brief entry 116
Bridges, Laurie
See Bruck, Lorraine
Bridges, Robert (Seymour) 1844-1930
Brief entry 104
See also DLB 19
See also TCLC 1
Bridges, William (Andrew) 1901- 33-36R
See also SATA 5
Bridges, William (Emery) 1933- CANR-13
Earlier sketch in CA 33-36R
Bridges-Adams, William 1889-1965 ...... CAP-1
Earlier sketch in CA 13-14
Bridgman, Elizabeth 1921- 73-76
Bridgman, Sarah Atherton 1889(?)-1975
Obituary 57-60
Bridgwater, (William) Patrick 1931- 7-8R
Bridie, James
See Mavor, Osborne Henry
See also DLB 10
See also TCLC 3
Bridson, Gavin (Douglas Ruthven) 1936- ... 105
Bridwell, Norman 1928- CANR-20
Earlier sketches in CA 13-14R, CANR-5
See also SATA 4
Briefs, Goetz Antony 1889-1974 .... CAP-2
Obituary 49-52
Earlier sketch in CA 21-22
Briegel, Ann C(arrick) 1915- 33-36R
Brien, Mimi 1929- 111
Brien, Raley
See McCulley, Johnston
Brier, Bob 1943- 102
Brier, Howard M(axwell) 1903-1969 ..... CAP-1
Earlier sketch in CA 13-14
See also SATA 8
Brier, Peter A. 1935- 105
Brier, Royce 1894-1975 Obituary 93-96
Brier, Warren Judson 1931- 25-28R
Brierley, David 1936- 107
Brierley, Susan S.
See Isaacs, Susan (Sutherland Fairhurst)
Briffault, Herma 1898-1981 Obituary 104
Briggs, Asa 1921- CANR-7
Earlier sketch in CA 5-6R
Briggs, Austin (Eugene), Jr. 1931- 29-32R
Briggs, B(arry B.) Bruce
See Bruce-Briggs, B(arry B.)
Briggs, Berta N. 1884(?)-1976 Obituary ...69-72
Briggs, Carl 1925- 114
Briggs, Carole S(uzanne) 1950- 110
See also SATA 47
Briggs, Charles Frederick 1804-1877 ..... DLB-3
Briggs, Charlie 1927- CANR-1
Earlier sketch in CA 49-52
Briggs, Desmond Lawther 1931- CANR-25
Earlier sketch in CA 108
Briggs, Dorothy Corkille 1924- 29-32R
Briggs, Ellis O(rmsbee) 1899-1976 73-76
Obituary 65-68
Briggs, F(red) Allen 1916- 33-36R
Briggs, Fred 1932- 73-76
Briggs, G. A. 1891(?)-1978 Obituary 104
Briggs, George M(cSpadden) 1919- 33-36R
Briggs, Jean 1925- 93-96
Briggs, Katharine Mary 1898-1980 .... CANR-12
Obituary 102
Earlier sketch in CA 9-10R
See also SATA 25
Briggs, Kenneth Arthur 1941- 101
Briggs, Kenneth R. 1934- 33-36R
Briggs, L(loyd) Cabot 1909-1975 .... CANR-3
Obituary 57-60
Earlier sketch in CA 5-6R
Briggs, Peter 1921-1975 .... CAP-2
Obituary 57-60
Earlier sketch in CA 25-28
See also SATA 31, 39
Briggs, R(obert) C(ook) 1915- 37-40R
Briggs, Raymond Redvers 1934- 73-76
See also SATA 23
See also CLR 10
Briggs, Shirley Ann 1918- 106
Briggs, Vernon M(ason), Jr. 1937- 73-76
Briggs, Walter Ladd 1919- 69-72
Brigham, Besmilr 1923- CANR-12
Earlier sketch in CA 29-32R
Brigham, John C(arl) 1942- 41-44R
Brighouse, Harold 1882-1958 Brief entry ... 110
See also DLB 10
Bright, Deborah (Sue Tomberg) 1949- ...97-100
Bright, Greg 1951- 93-96
Bright, John 1908- 5-6R
Bright, Pamela Mia 1914- 109
Bright, Richard (Eugene) 1931- 69-72
Bright, Robert 1902- 73-76
See also SATA 24
Bright, Sarah
See Shine, Deborah
Bright, William 1928- 33-36R
Brightbill, Charles K(estner) 1910-1966 ...... 2R
Obituary 103
Brightfield, Richard 1927- 118
See also SATA 53
Brightfield, Rick
See Brightfield, Richard
Brightman, Robert 1920- 105
Brighton, Howard 1925- 57-60
Brighton, Wesley, Jr.
See Lovin, Roger Robert
Brightwell, L(eonard) R(obert) 1889- ... SATA-29
Brignano, Russell C(arl) 1935- 57-60
Brignetti, Raffaello 1922(?)-1978 Obituary .. 104
Brigola, Alfredo L(uigi) 1923- 41-44R
Briles, Judith 1946- 106
Briley, John (Richard) 1925- 101
Brilhart, John K. 1929- 23-24R
Brill, Earl H(ubert) 1925- 19-20R
Brill, Leon 1915- 110
Brill, Steven 85-88
Brilliant, Ashleigh 1933- CANR-11
Earlier sketch in CA 65-68
Brilliant, Eleanor L(uria) 1930- 112
Brilliant, Richard 1929- 33-36R
Briloff, Abraham J(acob) 1917- 61-64
Brim, Orville G(ilbert), Jr. 1923- CANR-2
Earlier sketch in CA 5-6R
Brimberg, Stanlee 1947- 49-52
See also SATA 9
Brin, David 1950- CANR-24
Earlier sketch in CA 102
See also CLC 34
Brin, Herb(ert Henry) 1915- 49-52
Brin, Ruth Firestone 1921- CANR-8
Earlier sketch in CA 17-18R
See also SATA 22
Brinckerhoff, Sidney B(urr) 1933-
Brief entry 117
Brinckloe, Julie (Lorraine) 1950- 65-68
See also SATA 13
Brindel, June (Rachuy) 1919- 49-52
See also SATA 7
Brindle, Reginald Smith
See Smith Brindle, Reginald
Brindze, Ruth 1903- 73-76
See also SATA 23
Brinegar, David F(ranklin) 1910- 77-80
Brines, Russell (Dean) 1911- 69-72
Briney, Robert E(dward) 1933- CANR-19
Earlier sketches in CA 53-56, CANR-4
Bring, Mitchell 1951- 106
Bringhurst, Robert 1946- CANR-21
Earlier sketches in CA 57-60, CANR-6
Brinitzer, Carl 1907-1974 .... CANR-3
Obituary 53-56
Earlier sketch in CA 7-8R
Brink, Andre (Philippus) 1935- 104
See also CLC 18, 36
Brink, Carol Ryrie 1895-1981 .... CANR-3
Obituary 104
Earlier sketch in CA 2R
See also SATA 1, 27, 31
Brink, T(erry) L(ee) 1949- CANR-15
Earlier sketch in CA 89-92
Brink, Wellington 1895-1979 Obituary 85-88
Brinker, Paul A. 1919- 25-28R
Brinker, Robert Durie 1901-1983 Obituary .. 111
Brinkerhoff, Derricksen Morgan 1921- 85-88
Brinkley, Alan 1949- 107
Brinkley, Christie 1953- 122
Brinkley, David (McClure) 1920- 97-100
Brinkley, George A. (Jr.) 1931- 17-18R
Brinkley, Joel 1952- 102
Brinkley, Roberta Florence 1892(?)-1967
Obituary 112
Brinkley, William (Clark) 1917- CANR-11
Earlier sketch in CA 21-22R
Brinkman, George L(oris) 1942- 53-56
Brinkman, Grover 1903- 73-76
Brinks, Herbert J(ohn) 1935- CANR-12
Earlier sketch in CA 29-32R
Brinley, Bertrand R(ussell) 1917- 29-32R
Brinner, William M(ichael) 1924- 111
Brinnin, John Malcolm 1916- CANR-1
Earlier sketch in CA 1R
See also DLB 48
Brinsmead, H(esba) F(ay) 1922- CANR-10
Earlier sketch in CA 21-22R
See also SATA 18
See also SAAS 5
See also CLC 21

INDEX

Brinsmead, Hesba Fay
See Hungerford, Hesba (Fay) Brinsmead
Brint, Armand Ian 1952- ... 105
Brinton, (Clarence) Crane 1898-1968 ... 7-8R
Obituary ... 25-28R
Brinton, Henry 1901-1977 ... CANR-4
Earlier sketch in CA 2R
Brinton, Howard Haines 1884-1973 ... CANR-3
Earlier sketch in CA 7-8R
Brion, Guy
See Madsen, Axel
Brion, John M. 1922- ... 23-24R
Brion, Marcel 1895-1984 ... 124
Obituary ... 114
Briquebec, John
See Rowland-Entwistle, (Arthur) Theodore (Henry)
Brisbane, Albert 1809-1890 ... DLB-3
Brisbane, Arthur 1864-1936 ... DLB-25
Brisbane, Henry R.
See Ellis, Edward S(ylvester)
Brisbane, Holly E. 1927- ... 33-36R
Brisbane, Katharine 1932- ... CANR-23
Earlier sketch in CA 107
Brisbane, Robert Hughes 1913- ... 77-80
Brisco, P. A.
See Matthews, Patricia (Anne)
Brisco, Patty
See Matthews, Clayton (Hartley) and Matthews, Patricia (Anne)
Briscoe, D(avid) Stuart 1930- ... CANR-25
Earlier sketches in CA 17-18R, CANR-9
Briscoe, Jill (Pauline) 1935- ... CANR-8
Earlier sketch in CA 61-64
See also SATA 47
Briscoe, John 1938- ... 118
Briscoe, Mary Louise 1937- ... 109
Brisk, Melvin J. 1924-1981 Obituary ... 104
Briskin, Jacqueline 1927- ... CANR-13
Earlier sketch in CA 29-32R
Brisley, Joyce Lankester 1896- ... 97-100
See also SATA 22
Brisman, Leslie 1944- ... 61-64
Brissenden, Paul F(rederick) 1885-1974 ... CAP-2
Obituary ... 53-56
Earlier sketch in CA 17-18
Brissenden, R(obert) F(rancis) 1928- ... CANR-10
Earlier sketch in CA 23-24R
Brister, C(ommodore) W(ebster), Jr. 1926- ... CANR-7
Earlier sketch in CA 13-14R
Brister, Richard 1915- ... 13-14R
Bristol, Goldie M(ae) 1918- ... 121
Bristol, Julius
See Abel, Alan (Irwin)
Bristol, Lee Hastings, Jr. 1923-1979 ... CANR-4
Obituary ... 89-92
Earlier sketch in CA 7-8R
Bristow, Allen P. 1929- ... CANR-8
Earlier sketch in CA 21-22R
Bristow, Gwen 1903-1980 ... CANR-12
Obituary ... 102
Earlier sketch in CA 19-20R
Bristow, Robert O'Neil 1926- ... 25-28R
Bristowe, Anthony (Lynn) 1921-19(?) ... CAP-1
Earlier sketch in CA 11-12
Britain, Dan
See Pendleton, Don(ald Eugene)
Britchky, Seymour 1930- ... 102
Britindian
See Solomon, Samuel
Britsch, Ralph A(dam) 1912- ... 101
Britsch, Todd A(dam) 1937- ... 101
Britt, Albert 1874-1969 ... 5-6R
Obituary ... 103
See also SATA 28
Britt, Dell 1934- ... 25-28R
See also SATA 1
Britt, George (William Hughes) 1895-1988
Obituary ... 124
Britt, Steuart Henderson 1907-1979 ... CANR-2
Obituary ... 85-88
Earlier sketch in CA 1R
Brittain, Bill
See Brittain, William
Brittain, Frederick ?-1969 ... CANR-3
Earlier sketch in CA 7-8R
Brittain, Joan Tucker 1928- ... 37-40R
Brittain, John A(shleigh) 1923- ... 73-76
Brittain, Vera (Mary) 1893(?)-1970 ... CAP-1
Obituary ... 25-28R
Earlier sketch in CA 15-16
See also CLC 23
Brittain, William 1930- ... CANR-13
Earlier sketch in CA 77-80
See also SATA 36
Brittan, Gordon G(oodhue), Jr. 1939- ... 89-92
Brittan, Samuel 1933- ... 29-32R
Britten, Milton R(eese) 1924-1985 ... 125
Obituary ... 115
Britten Austin, Paul 1922- ... CANR-13
Earlier sketch in CA 23-24R
Britter, Eric V(alentine) B(lakeney) 1906-1977 Obituary ... 73-76
Brittin, Norman A(ylsworth) 1906- ... 19-20R
Brittin, Phil (Henry) 1953- ... 108
Britton, Bryce 1943- ... 110
Britton, Christopher (Q.) 1943- Brief entry ... 118
Britton, Dorothea S(prague) 1926- ... CANR-16
Earlier sketches in CA 45-48, CANR-1
Britton, Dorothy (Guyver) 1922- ... 107
Britton, John A(ndrew) 1943- ... 126
Britton, Karl (William) 1909-1983 ... 29-32R
Obituary ... 110
Britton, Kate
See Stegeman, Janet Allais
See also SATA 49
Britton, Louisa
See McGuire, Leslie Sarah
Britton, Mattie Lula Cooper 1914- ... 7-8R
Britton, Peter Ewart 1936- ... CANR-18
Earlier sketch in CA 97-100
Brivic, Sheldon Roy 1943- ... 122
Brkic, Jovan 1927- ... 41-44R
Bro, Bernard (Gerard Marie) 1925- ... CANR-17
Earlier sketch in CA 97-100
Bro, Harmon Hartzell 1919- ... 25-28R
Bro, Margueritte (Harmon) 1894-1977 ... 77-80
See also SATA 19, 27
Broad, C(harlie) D(unbar) 1887-1971 ... 101
Obituary ... 89-92
Broad, Charles Lewis 1900- ... 7-8R
Broad, Jay 1930- ... CANR-19
Earlier sketch in CA 97-100
Broadbent, Donald E(ric) 1926- ... 105
Broadbent, Edward 1936- ... 45-48
Broadbent, W. W. 1919- ... 69-72
Broaddus, J(ohn) Morgan, Jr. 1929- ... 21-22R
Broadfoot, Barry 1926- ... 89-92
Broadhead, Helen Cross 1913- ... 103
See also SATA 25
Broadhurst, Allan R. 1932- ... 5-6R
Broadhurst, Ronald Joseph Callender 1906- ... CAP-1
Earlier sketch in CA 11-12
Broadley, Margaret E(ricson) 1904-1985 ... 97-100
Obituary ... 117
Broadribb, Violet ... 41-44R
Broadus, Catherine 1929- ... 37-40R
Broadus, Loren, Jr. 1928- ... 37-40R
Broadus, Robert N(ewton) 1922- ... 73-76
Broadwell, Martin M. 1927- ... CANR-13
Earlier sketch in CA 73-76
Broat, I(sidore) G(erald) 1927- ... 97-100
Brobeck, Florence 1895-1979 Obituary ... 85-88
Broby-Johansen, R(udolf) 1900- ... CANR-12
Earlier sketch in CA 25-28R
Broce, Thomas Edward 1935- ... 69-72
Broch, Hermann 1886-1951 Brief entry ... 117
See also TCLC 20
Brochmann, Elizabeth 1938- ... 112
See also SATA 41
Brochu, Andre 1942- ... DLB-53
Brock, Alice May 1941- ... 41-44R
Brock, Arthur Guy Clutton
See Clutton-Brock, Arthur Guy
Brock, Ben
See Howells, Roscoe
Brock, Betty 1923- ... 29-32R
See also SATA 4
Brock, C(harles) E(dmund) 1870-1938 ... SATA-32, 42
Brock, D(ewey) Heyward 1941- ... 53-56
Brock, Delia
See Ephron, Delia
Brock, Dewey Clifton, Jr. 1930- ... 7-8R
Brock, Edwin 1927- Brief entry ... 119
See also DLB 40
Brock, Emma L(illian) 1886-1974 ... 5-6R
Obituary ... 103
See also SATA 8
Brock, Gavin
See Lindsay, (John) Maurice
Brock, Gerald Wayne 1948- ... 57-60
Brock, H(enry) M(atthew) 1875-1960 ... SATA-42
Brock, Horace 1908(?)-1981 Obituary ... 105
Brock, Horace Rhea 1927- ... 113
Brock, Lou(is Clark) 1939- Brief entry ... 113
Brock, Lynn
See McAllister, Alister
Brock, Mary Duncan Howe 1909(?)-1984
Obituary ... 112
Brock, Michael George 1920- ... 93-96
Brock, P. W.
See Brock, Patrick Willet
Brock, Patrick Willet 1902- ... 112
Brock, Peter (de Beauvoir) 1920- ... CANR-5
Earlier sketch in CA 11-12R
Brock, Rose
See Hansen, Joseph
Brock, Russell Claude 1903-1980
Obituary ... 105
Brock, Stanley E(dmunde) 1936- ... 57-60
Brock, Stuart
See Trimble, Louis P(reston)
Brock, Van(dall) K(line) 1932- ... CANR-11
Earlier sketch in CA 61-64
Brock, W(illiam) H(odson) 1936- ... 23-24R
Brock, William R(anulf) 1916- ... CANR-20
Earlier sketches in CA 4R, CANR-4
Brockbank, Reed 1923- ... 21-22R
Brockelman, Paul T(aylor) 1935- ... 110
Brockett, Eleanor Hall 1913-1967 ... CAP-1
Earlier sketch in CA 9-10
See also SATA 10
Brockett, Oscar Gross 1923- ... CANR-22
Earlier sketches in CA 15-16R, CANR-7
Brockley, Fenton
See Rowland, D(onald) S(ydney)
Brockman, C(hristian) Frank 1902- ... 5-6R
See also SATA 26
Brockman, David Drake
See Drake-Brockman, David
Brockman, Harold 1902-1980 Obituary ... 101
Brockman, James R(aymond) 1926- ... 110
Brockman, Norbert 1934- ... 73-76
Brockriede, Wayne Elmer 1922- ... CANR-4
Earlier sketch in CA 4R
Brockway, Allan R(eitz) 1932- ... 23-24R
Brockway, Edith E. 1914- ... 17-18R
Brockway, (Archibald) Fenner 1888-1988 ... CAP-1
Obituary ... 125
Earlier sketch in CA 11-12
Brockway, George P(ond) 1915- ... 123
Brockway, Thomas P(armelee) 1898- ... CAP-2
Earlier sketch in CA 17-18
Brockway, Wallace 1905-1972 Obituary ... 37-40R
Brod, Max 1884-1968 ... CANR-7
Obituary ... 25-28R
Earlier sketch in CA 7-8R
Brod, Ruth Hagy 1911-1980 Obituary ... 97-100
Brodatz, Philip 1915- ... 57-60
Brode, Douglas 1943- ... 57-60
Brode, Wallace R. 1900(?)-1974
Obituary ... 53-56
Broder, David S(alzer) 1929- ... 97-100
Broder, Patricia Janis 1935- ... CANR-6
Earlier sketch in CA 57-60
Broderick, Carlfred B(artholomew) 1932- ... CANR-10
Earlier sketch in CA 25-28R
Broderick, Damien Francis 1944- ... 111
Broderick, Dorothy M. 1929- ... 15-16R
See also SATA 5
Broderick, Francis L(yons) 1922- ... 101
Broderick, John C(aruthers) 1926- ... 4R
Broderick, John F. 1909- ... CAP-2
Earlier sketch in CA 33-36
Broderick, Richard L(awrence) 1927- ... CANR-1
Earlier sketch in CA 45-48
Broderick, Robert C(arlton) 1913- ... CANR-8
Earlier sketch in CA 23-24R
Brodeur, Paul (Adrian, Jr.) 1931- ... CANR-25
Earlier sketch in CA 7-8R
Brodeur, Ruth Wallace
See Wallace-Brodeur, Ruth
Brodhead, John R. 1814-1873 ... DLB-30
Brodhead, Michael John 1935- ... 105
Brodie, Bernard 1910-1978 ... CANR-10
Obituary ... 81-84
Earlier sketch in CA 17-18R
Brodie, Fawn M(cKay) 1915-1981 ... CANR-10
Obituary ... 102
Earlier sketch in CA 17-18R
Brodie, H(arlowe) Keith H(ammond) 1939- ... 103
Brodie, John (Riley) 1935- Brief entry ... 115
Brodie, Sally
See Cavin, Ruth (Brodie)
Brodin, Pierre Eugene 1909- ... 85-88
Brodine, Karen 1947- ... 123
Brodine, Virginia Warner 1915- ... 41-44R
Brodkey, Harold ... 111
Brodribb, (Arthur) Gerald (Norcott) 1915- ... 113
Brodsky, Archie 1945- ... CANR-7
Earlier sketch in CA 61-64
Brodsky, Beverly
See McDermott, Beverly Brodsky
Brodsky, Iosif Alexandrovich 1940- ... 41-44R
See also AITN 1
Brodsky, Joseph
See Brodsky, Iosif Alexandrovich
See also CLC 4, 6, 13, 36, 50
Brodsky, Louis Daniel 1941- ... 111
Brodsky, Michael Mark 1948- ... CANR-18
Earlier sketch in CA 102
See also CLC 19
Brodsky, Stanley L. 1939- ... 29-32R
Brodsky, Vera
See Lawrence, Vera Brodsky
Brodwin, Leonora Leet 1929- ... 53-56
Brody, Baruch A(lter) 1943- ... CANR-14
Earlier sketch in CA 33-36R
Brody, David 1930- ... 33-36R
Brody, Elaine 1923-1987 ... 37-40R
Obituary ... 123
Brody, J(acob) J(erome) 1929- ... 113
Brody, Jane E(llen) 1941- ... CANR-23
Earlier sketch in CA 102
Brody, Jules 1928- ... CANR-9
Earlier sketch in CA 13-14R
Brody, Marc
See Wilkes-Hunter, R(ichard)
Brody, Nathan 1935- ... 111
Brody, Polly 1919- ... 57-60
Brody, Saul Nathaniel 1938- ... 53-56
Brody, Sylvia
See Axelrad, Sylvia Brody
Broe, Mary Lynn 1946- ... 110
Broe, Ruth Hammond 1912(?)-1983
Obituary ... 110
Broeg, Bob
See Broeg, Robert M.
Broeg, Robert M. 1918- ... CANR-5
Earlier sketch in CA 13-14R
Broeger, Achim 1944- ... 107
See also SATA 31
Broehl, Wayne G(ottlieb), Jr. 1922- ... 11-12R
Broek, J(an) O(tto) M(arius) 1904-1974 ... CAP-2
Earlier sketch in CA 19-20
Broekel, Rainer Lothar 1923- ... CANR-19
Earlier sketches in CA 9-10R, CANR-3
See also SATA 38
Broekel, Ray
See Broekel, Rainer Lothar
Broeker, Galen 1920- ... 41-44R
Broekman, Marcel 1922- ... 57-60
Broer, Lawrence R(ichard) 1938- ... 69-72
Broer, Marion Ruth 1910- ... 13-14R
Broerman, Bruce M(artin) 1945- ... 126
Broesamle, John J(oseph) 1941- ... 57-60
Brof, Janet 1929- ... 37-40R
Brog, Molly (Jane) 1950- ... 113
Brogan, D(enis) W(illiam) 1900-1974 ... 97-100
Obituary ... 45-48
Brogan, Elise
See Urch, Elizabeth
Brogan, Frankie Fonde 1922- ... 109
Brogan, Gerald E(dward) 1924-1981 ... 29-32R
Obituary ... 104
Brogan, Jacqueline Vaught 1952- ... 125
Brogan, James E(dmund) 1941- ... 41-44R
Brogan, Phil(ip) F(rancis) 1896- ... 11-12R
Brogan, T(erry) V. F. 1951- ... 119
Broger, Achim
See Broeger, Achim
Broglie, Marguerite de 1897-1973
Obituary ... 37-40R
Broh, C(harles) Anthony 1945- ... 61-64
Broh-Kahn, Eleanor 1924- ... 45-48
Broido, Vera
See Cohn, Vera
Brokamp, Marilyn 1920- ... 49-52
See also SATA 10
Brokaw, Thomas John 1940- ... 108
Brokaw, Tom
See Brokaw, Thomas John
Brokensha, David W(arwick) 1923- ... 25-28R
Brokhin, Yuri 1934- ... 57-60
Brokhoff, John R(udolph) 1913- ... CANR-23
Earlier sketches in CA 61-64, CANR-8
Brolin, Brent C(ruse) 1940- ... 65-68
Bromage, Mary Cogan 1906- ... CAP-1
Earlier sketch in CA 15-16
Bromberg, Walter 1900- ... 65-68
Bromberger, Merry (Marie Louis) 1906-1979 Obituary ... 110
Bromberger, Serge Paul 1912- ... 29-32R
Brombert, Victor H. 1923- ... CANR-7
Earlier sketch in CA 13-14R
Brome, Richard 1590(?)-1652 ... DLB-58
Brome, (Herbert) Vincent ... CANR-14
Earlier sketch in CA 77-80
Bromell, Henry 1947- ... CANR-9
Earlier sketch in CA 53-56
See also CLC 5
Bromfield, Louis (Brucker) 1896-1956
Brief entry ... 107
See also DLB 4, 9
See also TCLC 11
Bromhall, Winifred ... SATA-26
Bromhead, Peter (Alexander) 1919- ... 61-64
Bromige, David (Mansfield) 1933- ... CANR-16
Earlier sketch in CA 25-28R
Bromiley, Geoffrey W(illiam) 1915- ... CANR-19
Earlier sketches in CA 5-6R, CANR-4
Bromke, Adam 1928- ... 15-16R
Bromley, David G(rover) 1941- ... 41-44R
Bromley, Dorothy Dunbar 1896-1986
Obituary ... 118
Bromley, Dudley 1948- ... 77-80
See also SATA 51
Bromley, Gordon 1910- ... 112
Bromley, John Carter 1937- ... 33-36R
Bromley, John Selwyn 1913-1985
Obituary ... 116
Brommer, Gerald F(rederick) 1927- ... CANR-21
Earlier sketch in CA 105
See also SATA 28
Bromwich, David (Lee) 1951- Brief entry ... 121
Bronaugh, Robert Brett 1947- ... 106
Brondfield, Jerome 1913- ... 73-76
See also SATA 22
Brondfield, Jerry
See Brondfield, Jerome
Broner, E(sther) M(asserman) 1930- ... CANR-25
Earlier sketches in CA 19-20R, CANR-8
See also DLB 28
See also CLC 19
Bronfeld, Stewart 1929- ... 109
Bronfenbrenner, Martin 1914- ... 13-14R
Bronfenbrenner, Urie 1917- ... CANR-16
Earlier sketch in CA 97-100
Bronin, Andrew 1947- ... 45-48
Bronk, William 1918- ... CANR-23
Earlier sketch in CA 89-92
See also CLC 10
Bronner, Edwin B(laine) 1920- ... CANR-22
Earlier sketches in CA 7-8R, CANR-7
Bronner, Simon J. 1954- ... 121
Bronner, Stephen Eric 1949- ... 113
Bronowski, Jacob 1908-1974 ... CANR-3
Obituary ... 53-56
Earlier sketch in CA 2R
Bronsen, David 1926- ... 37-40R
Bronson, Bertrand Harris 1902-1986 ... 61-64
Obituary ... 118
Bronson, Lita
See Bell, Louise Price
Bronson, Lynn
See Lampman, Evelyn Sibley
Bronson, Oliver
See Rowland, D(onald) S(ydney)
Bronson, Wilfrid Swancourt 1894-1985 ... 73-76
Obituary ... 116
See also SATA 43
Bronson, William (Knox) 1926-1976 ... 41-44R
Obituary ... 65-68
Bronson, Wolfe
See Raborg, Frederick A(shton), Jr.
Bronstein, Arthur J. 1914- ... 9-10R
Bronstein, Leo 1903(?)-1976 Obituary ... 65-68
Bronstein, Lev Davidovich
See Trotsky, Leon
Bronstein, Lynne 1950- ... 77-80
Bronstein, Yetta
See Abel, Jeanne
Bronte, Anne 1820-1849 ... DLB-21
Bronte, Charlotte 1816-1855 ... DLB-21
Bronte, D(iana) Lydia 1938- ... 125
Bronte, Emily 1818-1848 ... DLB-21, 32
Bronte, Louisa
See Roberts, Janet Louise
Bronwell, Arthur B. 1909- ... 33-36R
Brook, Barry S(helley) 1918- ... CANR-16
Earlier sketch in CA 25-28R
Brook, David 1932- ... 13-14R
Brook, G. L.
See Brook, George Leslie

Brook, George Leslie 1910-1987 .... CANR-5
Obituary 123
Earlier sketch in CA 9-10R
Brook, Judith (Penelope) 1926- 122
See also SATA 51
Brook, Judy
See Brook, Judith (Penelope)
Brook, Peter (Stephen Paul) 1925- 105
Brook, Victor John Knight 1887-1974 .... 4R
Obituary 103
Brooke, A. B.
See Jennings, Leslie Nelson
Brooke, Avery (Rogers) 1923- CANR-21
Earlier sketches in CA 57-60, CANR-6
Brooke, Brian 1911- 85-88
Brooke, Bryan (Nicholas) 1915- CANR-1
Earlier sketch in CA 45-48
Brooke, Carol
See Ramskill, Valerie Patricia Roskams
Brooke, Christopher N(ugent) L(awrence)
1927- CANR-18
Earlier sketches in CA 7-8R, CANR-2
Brooke, Dinah 1936- CANR-4
Earlier sketch in CA 49-52
Brooke, Eleanor (Golden) 1905(?)-1987
Obituary 122
Brooke, Frances 1724-1789 .... DLB-39
Brooke, George Mercer, Jr. 1914- 122
Brooke, Harold 1910- Brief entry 113
Brooke, Henry 1703(?)-1783 .... DLB-39
Brooke, (Bernard) Jocelyn 1908- 5-6R
Brooke, John 1920-1985 Obituary 118
Brooke, Joshua
See Miller, Victor (Brooke)
Brooke, L(eonard) Leslie 1862-1940 ... SATA-17
Brooke, Maxey 1913- 9-10R
Brooke, Nicholas Stanton 1924- 25-28R
Brooke, Rupert (Chawner) 1887-1915
Brief entry 104
See also DLB 19
See also TCLC 2, 7
Brooke, (Robert) Tal(iaferro) 1945- 93-96
Brooke-Haven, P.
See Wodehouse, P(elham) G(renville)
Brooke-Little, John 1927- CANR-10
Earlier sketch in CA 23-24R
Brooker, Clark
See Fowler, Kenneth A(brams)
Brooke-Rose, Christine 1926- 13-14R
See also DLB 14
See also CLC 40
Brookes, Edgar Harry 1897- CANR-3
Earlier sketch in CA 4R
Brookes, Kenneth John 1909-1984
Obituary 111
Brookes, Owen
See Barber, D(ulan) F(riar Whilberton)
Brookes, Pamela 1922- 25-28R
Brookes, Reuben Solomon 1914- CAP-1
Earlier sketch in CA 9-10
Brookhouse, (John) Christopher 1938- ...29-32R
Brookhouser, Frank 1912(?)-1975 .... 4R
Obituary 61-64
Brookins, Dana 1931- 69-72
See also SATA 28
Brookman, Denise Cass 1921- 4R
Brookman, Rosina Francesca 1932- 61-64
Brookner, Anita 1928- 120
Brief entry 114
See also DLBY 87
See also CLC 32, 34
Brookover, Wilbur B(one) 1911- 33-36R
Brooks, A(lfred) Russell 1906- CAP-2
Earlier sketch in CA 33-36
Brooks, Albert
See Einstein, Albert
Brooks, Anita
See Abramovitz, Anita (Zeltner Brooks)
See also SATA 5
Brooks, Anne Tedlock 1905- CANR-1
Earlier sketch in CA 4R
Brooks, B. David 1938- 113
Brooks, Bruce SATA-53
Brooks, C(larence) Carlyle 1888- CAP-1
Earlier sketch in CA 13-14
Brooks, Charles (Gordon) 1920- 115
Brooks, Charles B(enton) 1921- 3R
Brooks, Charles E(dward) 1921- 53-56
Brooks, Charles Timothy 1813-1883 ..... DLB-1
Brooks, Charles V. W. 1912- 77-80
Brooks, Charlotte K. 89-92
See also SATA 24
Brooks, Cleanth 1906- 17-18R
See also DLB 63
See also CLC 24
Brooks, D(avid) P. 1915- CANR-11
Earlier sketch in CA 25-28R
Brooks, David H(opkinson) 1929- 61-64
Brooks, Deems M(arkham) 1934- 69-72
Brooks, Douglas
See Brooks-Davies, Douglas
Brooks, Douglas L(ee) 1916- 114
Brooks, Elston (Harwood) 1930- 125
Brooks, Emerson M. 1905(?)-1982
Obituary 108
Brooks, Gary D(onald) 1942- 41-44R
Brooks, George E(dward), Jr. 1933- 33-36R
Brooks, Gladys Rice 1886(?)-1984
Obituary 111
Brooks, Glenn E(llis), Jr. 1931- 2R
Brooks, Gregory 1961- 102
Brooks, Gwendolyn 1917- CANR-1
Earlier sketch in CA 1R
See also BW
See also SATA 6
See also DLB 5, 76
See also CDALB 1941-1968
See also CLC 1, 2, 4, 5, 15, 49
See also AITN 1
Brooks, H(arold) Allen 1925- CANR-14
Earlier sketch in CA 81-84
Brooks, Harvey 1915- 25-28R
Brooks, Hindi Brief entry 115
Brooks, Hugh C. 1922- 29-32R
Brooks, Hunter O(tis) 1929- 77-80
Brooks, James L. 1940- 73-76
Brooks, Janice Young 1943- CANR-9
Earlier sketch in CA 65-68
Brooks, Jeremy 1926- CANR-7
Earlier sketch in CA 5-6R
See also DLB 14
Brooks, Jerome 1931- CANR-2
Earlier sketch in CA 49-52
See also SATA 23
Brooks, Jerome E(dmund) 1895(?)-1983
Obituary 109
Brooks, John (Nixon) 1920- CANR-6
Earlier sketch in CA 15-16R
Brooks, John
See Sugar, Bert Randolph
Brooks, Juanita 1898- Brief entry 114
Brooks, Karen 1949- 57-60
Brooks, Keith 1923- 17-18R
Brooks, (Frank) Leonard 1911- 13-14R
Brooks, LeRoy D(avis) II 1943-
Brief entry 113
Brooks, Lester 1924- CANR-13
Earlier sketch in CA 33-36R
See also SATA 7
Brooks, Louise 1906-1985 Obituary 117
Brooks, Lyman Beecher 1910-1984 122
Obituary 112
Brooks, Maria (Zagorska) 1933- 41-44R
Brooks, Maurice (Graham) 1900- SATA-45
Brooks, Mel
See Kaminsky, Melvin
See also DLB 26
See also CLC 12
Brooks, Nelson Herbert 1902-1978
Obituary 77-80
Brooks, Noah 1830-1903 .... DLB-42
Brooks, Pat 1931- CANR-7
Earlier sketch in CA 57-60
Brooks, Patricia 1926- CANR-11
Earlier sketch in CA 25-28R
Brooks, Paul 1909- CANR-7
Earlier sketch in CA 15-16R
Brooks, Peter 1938- CANR-1
Earlier sketch in CA 45-48
See also CLC 34
Brooks, Peter W(right) 1920- 9-10R
Brooks, Philip 1899(?)-1975 Obituary 104
Brooks, Polly Schoyer 1912- CANR-17
Earlier sketch in CA 4R
See also SATA 12
Brooks, Richard 1912- 73-76
See also DLB 44
Brooks, Richard Oliver 1934- 112
Brooks, Robert A(ngus) 1920-1976
Obituary 65-68
Brooks, Robert Emanuel 1941- 57-60
Brooks, Ron(ald George) 1948-
Brief entry 111
See also SATA 33
Brooks, Seth Rogers 1901-1987 Obituary ... 123
Brooks, Stewart M. 1923- CANR-9
Earlier sketch in CA 17-18R
Brooks, Terry 1944- CANR-14
Earlier sketch in CA 77-80
Brooks, Thomas 1941- 120
Brooks, Thomas R(eed) 1925- 73-76
Brooks, Tim(othy Haley) 1942- CANR-19
Earlier sketch in CA 102
Brooks, Van Wyck 1886-1963 .... CANR-6
Earlier sketch in CA 4R
See also DLB 45, 63
See also CLC 29
Brooks, W. Hal 1933- 57-60
Brooks, Walter R(ollin) 1886-1958
Brief entry 111
See also SATA 17
Brooks, William D(ean) 1929- 33-36R
Brooks-Davies, Douglas 1942- CANR-12
Earlier sketch in CA 73-76
Brook-Shepherd, (Frederick) Gordon
1918- CANR-3
Earlier sketch in CA 9-10R
Brookshier, Frank 93-96
Brookter, Marie 1934?- AITN-1
Broom, Leonard 1911- CANR-5
Earlier sketch in CA 15-16R
Broomall, Robert W(alter) 1946- 119
Broome, Charles L(arue) 1925- 41-44R
Broome, Harvey 1902-1968 122
Obituary 110
Broomell, Myron H(enry) 1906-1970 ..... CAP-1
Earlier sketch in CA 9-10
Broomfield, Gerald W(ebb) 1895-1976 .....7-8R
Obituary 103
Broomfield, J(ohn) H(indle) 1935- 25-28R
Broomsnodder, B(radley) MacKinley
1940- CANR-8
Earlier sketch in CA 15-16R
Brophy, Ann 1931- 106
Brophy, Brigid (Antonia) 1929- CANR-25
Earlier sketch in CA 7-8R
See also CAAS 4
See also DLB 14
See also CLC 6, 11, 29
Brophy, Donald F(rancis) 1934- CANR-10
Earlier sketch in CA 23-24R
Brophy, Elizabeth Bergen 1929- 61-64
Brophy, James David, Jr. 1926- CANR-3
Earlier sketch in CA 4R
Brophy, James J(oseph) 1912- 65-68
Brophy, Jere E(dward) 1940- CANR-2
Earlier sketch in CA 45-48
Brophy, Jim
See Brophy, James J(oseph)
Brophy, John 1899-1965 .... CAP-1
Earlier sketch in CA 11-12
Brophy, Liam 1910- 11-12R
Brophy, Robert J(oseph) 1928- CANR-5
Earlier sketch in CA 53-56
Brose, Olive J(ohnson) 1919- 41-44R
Brosman, Catharine Savage 1934- CANR-21
Earlier sketch in CA 61-64
See also CLC 9
Brosnahan, Leonard Francis 1922- 102
Brosnahan, Tom 1945- 119
Brosnan, James Patrick 1929- CANR-3
Earlier sketch in CA 4R
See also SATA 14
Brosnan, Jim
See Brosnan, James Patrick
Bross, Irwin D(udley) J(ackson) 1921- ...37-40R
Brossard, Chandler 1922- CANR-8
Earlier sketch in CA 61-64
See also CAAS 2
See also DLB 16
Brossard, Nicole 1943- 122
See also DLB 53
Brossier, Margaret 1918(?)-1984 Obituary .. 113
Brostowin, Patrick Ronald 1931- 15-16R
Brother Antoninus
See Everson, William (Oliver)
Brother Bob
See Buell, Robert Kingery
Brother Choleric
See van Zeller, Claud
Brothers, (M.) Jay 1931- 103
Brothers, Joyce (Diane Bauer) 1929- ... CANR-13
Earlier sketch in CA 23-24R
See also AITN 1
Brothers Hildebrandt, The
See Hildebrandt, Tim(othy)
Brotherston, James Gordon 1939- CANR-11
Earlier sketch in CA 25-28R
Brotherton, Manfred 1900(?)-1981
Obituary 102
Broude, Norma (Freedman) 1941- 113
Broudy, Harry S(amuel) 1905- CANR-3
Earlier sketch in CA 2R
Broue, Pierre 1926- CANR-12
Earlier sketch in CA 69-72
Brough, James 1918- 111
Brough, John 1917-1984 Obituary 111
Brough, R(obert) Clayton 1950- CANR-7
Earlier sketch in CA 57-60
Brougham, John 1810-1880 .... DLB-11
Broughton, Bradford B. 1926- 21-22R
Broughton, Diane 1943- 81-84
Broughton, Geoffrey 1927- 102
Broughton, Jack(sel Markham) 1925- 73-76
Broughton, James 1913- CANR-2
Earlier sketch in CA 49-52
See also DLB 5
Broughton, Panthea Reid 1940- CANR-7
Earlier sketch in CA 57-60
Broughton, Rhoda 1840-1920 .... DLB-18
Broughton, T(homas) Alan 1936- CANR-23
Earlier sketches in CA 45-48, CANR-2
See also CLC 19
Brouillette, Jeanne S. 4R
Broumas, Olga 1949- CANR-20
Earlier sketch in CA 85-88
See also CLC 10
Broun, Emily
See Sterne, Emma Gelders
Broun, Heywood 1888-1939 .... DLB-29
Broun, Heywood Hale 1918- CANR-12
Earlier sketch in CA 17-18R
Broun, Heywood Oren 1950(?)-1987
Obituary 124
Broun, Hob
See Broun, Heywood Oren
Broussard, Louis 1922- 25-28R
Broussard, Vivian L.
See Martinetz, V(ivian) L.
Brouwer, Luitzen Egbertus Jan 1881-1966
Obituary 116
Brovka, Petr (Pyatrus Ustinovich)
1905-1980 Obituary 105
Brow, Robert 1924- CANR-10
Earlier sketch in CA 23-24R
Broward, Donn
See Halleran, Eugene E(dward)
Broward, Robert C. 1926- 122
Browder, Earl Russell 1891(?)-1973
Obituary 45-48
Browder, Lesley H(ughes), Jr. 1935- 45-48
Browder, Olin L(orraine), Jr. 1913- 41-44R
Browder, Robert P(aul) 1921- 122
Browder, Sue 1946- 77-80
Browder, Walter Everett 1939- 53-56
Brower, Brock (Hendrickson) 1931- 25-28R
Brower, Charles Hendrickson 1901-1984 102
Obituary 113
Brower, Charlie
See Brower, Charles Hendrickson
Brower, Daniel R(oberts) 1936- 41-44R
Brower, David R(oss) 1912- CANR-9
Earlier sketch in CA 61-64
Brower, Kenneth (David) 1944- CANR-10
Earlier sketch in CA 25-28R
Brower, Linda A. 1945- 33-36R
Brower, Millicent CANR-15
Earlier sketch in CA 41-44R
See also SATA 8
Brower, Pauline 1929- 77-80
See also SATA 22
Brower, Reuben Arthur 1908-1975 ..... CANR-6
Obituary 57-60
Earlier sketch in CA 4R
Browin, Frances Williams 1898- CAP-1
Earlier sketch in CA 19-20
See also SATA 5
Brown, A(lfred) R(eginald) Radcliffe
See Radcliffe-Brown, A(lfred) R(eginald)
Brown, Alan A. 1929- CANR-16
Earlier sketch in CA 25-28R
Brown, Alan R. 1938- 105
Brown, Alberta L(ouise) 1894- CAP-1
Earlier sketch in CA 11-12
Brown, Alexander (Crosby) 1905- CANR-3
Earlier sketch in CA 2R
Brown, Alexis
See Baumann, Amy (Brown) Beeching
Brown, Alice Very
See Very, Alice (N.)
Brown, Allen 1926- 15-16R
Brown, Andreas Le 1933- 108
Brown, Anne Ensign 1937- 101
Brown, Anne S(eddon) K(insolving)
1906-1985 ....17-18R
Obituary 117
Brown, Annice Harris 1897- 45-48
Brown, Annora 1899-1987(?) Obituary 121
Brown, Anthony Eugene 1937- 89-92
Brown, Archibald Haworth 1938- CANR-20
Earlier sketch in CA 103
Brown, Arnold 1927- 117
Brown, Arthur A(llen) 1900- 73-76
Brown, Arthur Wayne 1917- CANR-8
Earlier sketch in CA 5-6R
Brown, Ashley 1923- CANR-20
Earlier sketches in CA 4R, CANR-3
Brown, B(artley) Frank 1917- CANR-4
Earlier sketch in CA 11-12R
Brown, B(essie) Katherine (Taylor)
1917- 15-16R
Brown, Barbara B(anker) 1917- 69-72
Brown, Barbara W(ood) 1928- 105
Brown, Beatrice C.
See Curtis Brown, Beatrice
Brown, Benjamin F. 1930- CANR-1
Earlier sketch in CA 45-48
Brown, Bernard E(dward) 1925- CANR-21
Earlier sketches in CA 4R, CANR-4
Brown, Bert R(obert) 1936- 41-44R
Brown, Beth CAP-2
Earlier sketch in CA 21-22
Brown, Betty
See Jones, Elizabeth B(rown)
Brown, Bill
See Brown, William L(ouis)
Brown, Billye Walker
See Cutchen, Billye Walker
Brown, Blanche R. (Levine) 1915- 13-14R
Brown, Bob
See Brown, Robert Carlton
and Brown, Robert Joseph
See also DLB 4, 45
Brown, Bob Burton 1925- 23-24R
Brown, Buck 1936- SATA-45
Brown, Calvin S(mith) 1909- 49-52
Brown, Camille 1917- 9-10R
Brown, Carl F(raser) 1910- 41-44R
Brown, Carol Williams 1941- 111
Brown, Carter
See Yates, A(lan) G(eoffrey)
Brown, Cassie 1919-1986 .... CANR-23
Earlier sketch in CA 45-48
Brown, Cecil 1907-1987 Obituary 123
Brown, Cecil H(ooper) 1944- 109
Brown, Cecil M(orris) 1943- 73-76
See also BW
See also DLB 33
Brown, Charles
See Cadet, John
Brown, Charles Brockden
1771-1810 .... DLB-37, 59, 73
See also CDALB 1640-1865
Brown, Charles H. 1910- 23-24R
Brown, Charles N(ikki) 1937- 93-96
Brown, Charles T(homas) 1912- 41-44R
Brown, Christopher P(aterson) 1939- .. CANR-10
Earlier sketch in CA 65-68
Brown, Christy 1932-1981 105
Obituary 104
See also DLB 14
Brown, Clarence (Fleetwood, Jr.) 1929-
Brief entry 112
Brown, Clark 1935- 25-28R
Brown, Claude 1937- 73-76
See also BW
See also CLC 30
Brown, Clifford Waters, Jr. 1942- 77-80
Brown, (John) Clive (Anthony) 1947- 121
Brown, Conrad 1922- SATA-31
Brown, Constantine 1889-1966 .... CAP-1
Earlier sketch in CA 11-12
Brown, Courtney C(onrades) 1904- 77-80
Brown, Croswell 1905(?)-1971 Obituary 104
Brown, Curtis F(ranklin) 1925- 61-64
Brown, Cynthia 1952- 121
Brown, Dale W. 1926- 37-40R
Brown, Daniel G(ilbert) 1924- 45-48

Brown, Daniel Russell
See Curzon, Daniel
Brown, Daphne Faunce
See Faunce-Brown, Daphne (Bridget)
Brown, David 1916- ... 15-16R
Brown, David (Alan) 1922-1982 Obituary ... 110
Brown, David (Clifford) 1929- ... 57-60
Brown, David
See Myller, Rolf
Brown, David E(arl) 1938- ... 113
Brown, David Grant 1936- ... 15-16R
Brown, David S(pringer) 1915- ... 29-32R
Brown, Deaver David 1943- ... 102
Brown, Dee (Alexander) 1908- ... CANR-11
Earlier sketch in CA 15-16R
See also CAAS 6
See also SATA 5
See also DLBY 80
See also CLC 18, 47
Brown, Delwin (Wray) 1935- Brief entry ... 117
Brown, Denise Scott 1931- ... 41-44R
Brown, Dennis A(lbert) 1926-1978 ... CANR-13
Earlier sketch in CA 61-64
Brown, Derek Ernest Denny
See Denny-Brown, Derek Ernest
Brown, Diana 1928- ... CANR-18
Earlier sketch in CA 101
Brown, Donald Eugene 1909- ... CAP-1
Earlier sketch in CA 15-16
Brown, Donald Fowler 1909- ... 41-44R
Brown, Donald Robert 1925- ... 41-44R
Brown, Doris E. 1910(?)-1975 Obituary ... 61-64
Brown, Dorothy
See Oxley, Dorothy (Anne)
Brown, Dorothy M. 1932- ... 125
Brown, Douglas (Frank Lambert) 1907- ... 25-28R
Brown, Douglas
See Gibson, Walter B(rown)
Brown, Drollene P. 1939- ... 122
See also SATA 53
Brown, Duane 1937- ... 33-36R
Brown, E(dward) K(illoran) 1905-1951
Brief entry ... 107
Brown, E(ugene) Richard 1942- ... CANR-18
Earlier sketch in CA 97-100
Brown, Edgar S., Jr. 1922- ... 9-10R
Brown, Edward J(ames) 1909- ... 25-28R
Brown, Eleanor Frances 1908- ... 29-32R
See also SATA 3
Brown, Eleanor Gertrude 1887-1968
Obituary ... 104
Brown, Elizabeth Louise 1924- ... 53-56
Brown, Elizabeth M(yers) 1915- ... 107
See also SATA 43
Brown, Emily Clara 1911- ... 53-56
Brown, Erik 1923- ... 114
Brown, Ernest Henry Phelps 1906- ... 108
Brown, Evelyn M. 1911- ... 21-22R
Brown, F(rancis) Andrew 1915- ... 41-44R
Brown, F. Keith 1913(?)-1976 Obituary ... 69-72
Brown, F(rancis Charles Claypon) Yeats
See Yeats-Brown, F(rancis Charles Claypon)
Brown, Fern G. 1918- ... CANR-17
Earlier sketch in CA 97-100
See also SATA 34
Brown, (Robert) Fletch 1923- ... 116
See also SATA 42
Brown, Forrest ... 49-52
Brown, (Ernest) Francis 1903- ... 73-76
Brown, Francis R(obert) 1914- ... 41-44R
Brown, Frank A(rthur), Jr. 1908- ... 69-72
Brown, Frank E(dward) 1908- ... 101
Brown, Frank London 1927-1962 ... DLB-76
Brown, Frederick 1934- ... 25-28R
Brown, Frederick G(ramm) 1932- ... CANR-12
Earlier sketch in CA 29-32R
Brown, Fredric (William) 1906-1972 ... 122
Obituary ... 33-36R
See also DLB 8
Brown, G(eorge) Neville 1932- ... 17-18R
Brown, Geoff 1932- ... 61-64
Brown, George
See Wertmuller, Lina
Brown, George Alfred George
See George-Brown, George Alfred
Brown, George Douglas 1869-1902 ... TCLC-28
Brown, George Earl 1883-1964 ... 5-6R
See also SATA 11
Brown, George Isaac 1923- ... 73-76
Brown, George Mackay 1921- ... CANR-12
Earlier sketch in CA 21-22R
See also CAAS 6
See also SATA 35
See also DLB 14, 27
See also CLC 5, 48
Brown, George Thompson 1921- ... 111
Brown, Gerald Saxon 1911- ... 11-12R
Brown, Gerald W(illiam) 1916- ... 33-36R
Brown, Giles T(yler) 1916- ... 19-20R
Brown, Ginny
See Brown, Virginia Sharpe
Brown, Gwilym Slater 1928-1974 ... 11-12R
Obituary ... 53-56
Brown, H. Rap
See Al-Amin, Jamil Abdullah
Brown, Harcourt 1900- ... CANR-20
Earlier sketch in CA 101
Brown, Harold O(gden) J(oseph)
1933- ... CANR-10
Earlier sketch in CA 25-28R
Brown, Harriett M. 1897- ... 7-8R
Brown, Harrison Scott 1917-1986 ... 69-72
Obituary ... 121
Brown, Harry (Peter McNab, Jr.)
1917-1986 ... 69-72
Obituary ... 120
See also DLB 26
Brown, Harry G(unnison) 1880-1975
Obituary ... 57-60
Brown, Harry M(atthew) 1921- ... CANR-10
Earlier sketch in CA 25-28R
Brown, Hazel E(lizabeth) 1893- ... 57-60
Brown, Helen Gurley 1922- ... CANR-5
Earlier sketch in CA 7-8R
Brown, Herbert Ross 1902- ... CAP-1
Earlier sketch in CA 15-16
Brown, Howard Mayer 1930- ... CANR-3
Earlier sketch in CA 4R
Brown, Hugh Auchincloss 1879-1975
Obituary ... 61-64
Brown, Huntington 1899- ... CAP-1
Earlier sketch in CA 19-20
Brown, Ida Mae 1908- ... CAP-2
Earlier sketch in CA 29-32
Brown, Ina Corinne ... 5-6R
Brown, Ina Ladd 1905- ... CAP-1
Earlier sketch in CA 13-14
Brown, Ira Vernon 1922- ... 5-6R
Brown, Irene Bennett 1932- ... CANR-12
Earlier sketch in CA 29-32R
See also SATA 3
Brown, Irving
See Adams, William Taylor
Brown, Irwin
See Murray, David Stark
Brown, Ivor (John Carnegie)
1891-1974 ... CANR-12
Obituary ... 49-52
Earlier sketch in CA 11-12R
See also SATA 5, 26
Brown, J(ames) Douglas 1898-1986
Obituary ... 118
Brown, J(oseph) P(aul) S(ummers)
1930- ... 61-64
Brown, James (Wiley) 1909- ... 77-80
Brown, James (Montgomery) 1921- ... 4R
Brown, James 1934- ... CANR-10
Earlier sketch in CA 65-68
Brown, James Alan Calvert 1922-1984
Obituary ... 114
Brown, James Bush
See Bush-Brown, James
Brown, James Cooke 1921- ... 29-32R
Brown, James I(saac) 1908- ... CANR-7
Earlier sketch in CA 17-18R
Brown, James Patrick 1948- ... 29-32R
Brown, James S(eay), Jr. 1944- ... 120
Brown, James Wilson 1913- ... 41-44R
Brown, Jamie 1945- ... CANR-20
Earlier sketch in CA 101
Brown, Janet 1947- ... 69-72
Brown, Jay A(llen) 1935- ... 110
Brown, Jeff
See Brown, Sevellon III
Brown, Jerry Earl 1940- ... 105
Brown, Jerry Wayne 1936- ... 25-28R
Brown, Jim (M.) 1940- ... 69-72
Brown, Jo Giese 1947- ... 108
Brown, Joan Sayers 1925(?)-1983
Obituary ... 110
Brown, Joe David 1915-1976 ... 13-14R
Obituary ... 65-68
See also SATA 44
Brown, John 1887- ... CAP-1
Earlier sketch in CA 13-14
Brown, John 1920- ... 7-8R
Brown, John (E.) 1934- ... 25-28R
Brown, John A. 1898- ... 112
Brown, John Arthur 1914- ... CANR-11
Earlier sketch in CA 17-18R
Brown, John Buchanan
See Buchanan-Brown, John
Brown, John Gracen 1936- ... 104
Brown, John J. 1916- ... 15-16R
Brown, John L(ackey) 1914- ... 49-52
Brown, John Mason 1900-1969 ... 9-10R
Obituary ... 25-28R
Brown, John Pairman 1923- ... 33-36R
Brown, John Russell 1923- ... CANR-11
Earlier sketch in CA 21-22R
Brown, Jonathan (M.) 1939- Brief entry ... 112
Brown, Joseph E(dward) 1929- ... CANR-6
Earlier sketch in CA 53-56
See also SATA 51
Brown, Judith Gwyn 1933- ... CANR-21
Earlier sketch in CA 93-96
See also SATA 20
Brown, Judith K. ... 124
Brown, Judith M(argaret) 1944- ... CANR-15
Earlier sketch in CA 41-44R
Brown, Julia (Prewitt) 1948- ... 93-96
Brown, Karl 1895(?)-1970 Obituary ... 104
Brown, Kenneth H. 1936- ... 13-14R
Brown, Kevin V. 1922- ... 89-92
Brown, Kitt
See Vandergriff, (Lola) Aola
Brown, L(aurence) B(inet) 1927- ... 65-68
Brown, L. Carl
See Brown, Leon Carl
Brown, L. J.
See Du Breuil, (Elizabeth) L(or)inda
Brown, Larry
See Brown, Lawrence, Jr.
Brown, Laurene Krasny 1945- ... 117
Brown, Lawrence, Jr. 1947- Brief entry ... 114
Brown, Lawrence R. 1904(?)-1986
Obituary ... 119
Brown, Lee Dolph 1890-1971 Obituary ... 29-32R
Brown, Leigh ... 65-68
Brown, Leland 1914- ... 1R
Brown, Lennox (John) 1934- ... 93-96
Brown, Leon Carl 1928- Brief entry ... 117
Brown, LeRoy Chester 1908- ... CANR-13
Earlier sketches in CA 11-12, CAP-1
Brown, Les(ter Louis) 1928- ... CANR-13
Earlier sketch in CA 33-36R
Brown, Leslie H(ilton) 1917-1980 ... CANR-7
Earlier sketch in CA 9-10R
Brown, Leslie Wilfrid 1912- ... 17-18R
Brown, Letitia Woods 1915-1976 ... 73-76
Obituary ... 69-72
Brown, Lloyd Arnold 1907-1966 ... CAP-1
Earlier sketch in CA 11-12
See also SATA 36
Brown, Louis M(orris) 1909- ... 49-52
Brown, Lyle C(larence) 1926- ... CANR-15
Earlier sketch in CA 41-44R
Brown, M(ary) L(oretta) T(herese) ... 15-16R
Brown, Mac Alister 1924- ... 89-92
Brown, Mahlon A.
See Ellis, Edward S(ylvester)
Brown, Mandy
See Brown, May
Brown, Marc Tolon 1946- ... 69-72
See also SATA 10, 53
Brown, Marcia 1918- ... 41-44R
See also SATA 7, 47
See also DLB 61
See also CLR 12
Brown, Marel 1899- ... 102
Brown, Margaret Wise 1910-1952
Brief entry ... 108
See also YABC 2
See also DLB 22
See also CLR 10
Brown, Margery (Wheeler) ... CANR-26
Earlier sketch in CA 25-28R
See also BW
See also SATA 5
Brown, Marian A. 1911- ... 73-76
Brown, Marilyn McMeen Miller 1938- ... CANR-6
Earlier sketch in CA 57-60
Brown, Marion Marsh 1908- ... CANR-3
Earlier sketch in CA 4R
See also SATA 6
Brown, Mark H(erbert) 1900- ... CAP-2
Earlier sketch in CA 21-22
Brown, Marshall 1945- ... 111
Brown, Marshall L. 1924- ... 23-24R
Brown, Marvin L., Jr. 1920- ... 53-56
Brown, Mary Ellen 1939- ... 117
Brown, Maurice F(red) 1928-1985 ... 41-44R
Obituary ... 116
Brown, May 1913- ... 118
Brown, Melissa Mather 1917- ... 121
Brown, Merle Elliott 1925-1978 ... 108
Brown, Michael 1931- ... 33-36R
Brown, Michael Barratt
See Barratt-Brown, Michael
Brown, Michael H(arold) 1952- ... 121
Brown, Michael John 1932- ... 29-32R
Brown, Milton Perry, Jr. 1928- ... 9-10R
Brown, Milton W(olf) 1911- Brief entry ... 113
Brown, Morna Doris 1907- ... CANR-5
Earlier sketch in CA 5-6R
Brown, Morris Cecil 1943- ... 37-40R
Brown, Moses
See Barrett, William (Christopher)
Brown, Muriel 1938- ... 107
Brown, Muriel W(hitbeck) 1892- ... CAP-2
Earlier sketch in CA 23-24
Brown, Murray 1929- ... 37-40R
Brown, Myra Berry 1918- ... CANR-3
Earlier sketch in CA 4R
See also SATA 6
Brown, Nathaniel Hapgood 1929- ... 101
Brown, Ned 1882(?)-1976 Obituary ... 65-68
Brown, Neville (George) 1932- ... 11-12R
Brown, Newell 1917- ... 97-100
Brown, Norman D(onald) 1935- ... 53-56
Brown, Norman O(liver) 1913- ... 21-22R
Brown, Oliver Madox 1855-1874 ... DLB-21
Brown, Palmer 1919- ... 107
See also SATA 36
Brown, Pamela Beatrice 1924- ... 13-14R
See also SATA 5
Brown, Parker B(oyd) 1928- ... 53-56
Brown, Paula 1925- ... 110
Brown, Peter 1926(?)-1984(?) Obituary ... 112
Brown, Peter (Robert Lamont) 1935- ... CANR-13
Earlier sketch in CA 23-24R
Brown, Peter Douglas 1925- ... CANR-16
Earlier sketch in CA 25-28R
Brown, Peter Lancaster
See Lancaster-Brown, Peter
Brown, R(eginald) Allen 1924- ... CANR-11
Earlier sketch in CA 7-8R
Brown, R(onald) G(ordon) S(clater)
1929- ... 29-32R
Brown, Rae
See Brown, Forrest
Brown, Ralph Adams 1908- ... 33-36R
Brown, Raymond Bryan 1923- ... 19-20R
Brown, Raymond E(dward) 1928- ... CANR-17
Earlier sketch in CA 97-100
Brown, Raymond George 1924- ... 109
Brown, Raymond Kay 1936- ... 102
Brown, Raymond Lamont
See Lamont-Brown, Raymond
Brown, Re Mona 1917- ... 41-44R
Brown, Rebecca 1956- ... 124
Brown, Rex V(andesteene) 1933- ... 53-56
Brown, Richard 1935- ... 114
Brown, Richard C(arl) 1917- ... CANR-17
Earlier sketches in CA 7-8R, CANR-2
Brown, Richard D(avid) 1939- ... 53-56
Brown, Richard E(ugene) 1937- ... 73-76
Brown, Richard H(olbrook) 1927- ... 11-12R
Brown, Richard H(arvey) 1940- ... 109
Brown, Richard Howard 1929- ... 57-60
Brown, Richard Maxwell 1927- ... CANR-11
Earlier sketch in CA 19-20R
Brown, Rita Mae 1944- ... CANR-11
Earlier sketches in CA 45-48, CANR-2
See also CLC 18, 43
Brown, Robert Carlton 1886-1959
Brief entry ... 107
Brown, Robert Craig 1935- ... 101
Brown, Robert D. 1924- ... CANR-20
Earlier sketch in CA 104
Brown, Robert E(ldon) 1907- ... 7-8R
Brown, Robert Edward 1945- ... CANR-15
Earlier sketch in CA 65-68
Brown, Robert Fath 1941- ... 111
Brown, Robert Goodell 1923- ... 33-36R
Brown, Robert Hanbury 1916- ... 112
Brown, Robert Joseph 1907- ... CANR-13
Earlier sketches in CA 9-10, CAP-1
See also SATA 14
Brown, Robert L. 1921- ... 23-24R
Brown, Robert McAfee 1920- ... CANR-7
Earlier sketch in CA 13-14R
Brown, Robert T(homas) 1943- ... 113
Brown, Robin 1937- ... 97-100
Brown, Roderick (Langmere) Haig-
See Haig-Brown, Roderick (Langmere)
Brown, Roger Glenn 1941- ... 77-80
Brown, Roger H(amilton) 1931- ... 11-12R
Brown, Roger William 1925- ... 15-16R
Brown, Ronald 1900- ... 81-84
Brown, Rosalie
See Moore, Rosalie (Gertrude)
See also SATA 9
Brown, Rosel George 1926-1967 Obituary ... 102
Brown, Rosellen 1939- ... CANR-14
Earlier sketch in CA 77-80
See also CLC 32
Brown, Rosemary (Eleanor) 1938-
Brief entry ... 115
Brown, Roswell
See Webb, Jean Francis
Brown, Roy (Frederick) 1921-1982 ... 65-68
Obituary ... 117
See also SATA 39, 51
Brown, Rustie 1930(?)-1988 Obituary ... 125
Brown, Sanborn C(onner) 1913-1981 ... CANR-11
Obituary ... 106
Earlier sketch in CA 17-18R
Brown, Sanford J(ay) 1946- ... 118
Brown, Sevellon III 1913-1983 Obituary ... 110
Brown, Seyom 1933- ... CANR-17
Earlier sketch in CA 65-68
Brown, Sheldon S. 1933- ... 122
Brown, Sheldon S. 1937- ... CANR-7
Earlier sketch in CA 53-56
Brown, Sidney DeVere 1925- ... 33-36R
Brown, Stanley (Branson) 1914- ... 49-52
Brown, Stanley C(oleman) 1928- ... 77-80
Brown, Stanley H(arold) 1927- ... 45-48
Brown, Stephen W. 1940- ... CANR-13
Earlier sketch in CA 33-36R
Brown, Sterling Allen 1901- ... CANR-26
Earlier sketch in CA 85-88
See also BW
See also DLB 48, 51, 63
See also CLC 1, 23
Brown, Steven R(andall) 1939- ... 49-52
Brown, Stuart C(ampbell) 1938- ... CANR-25
Earlier sketch in CA 29-32R
Brown, Stuart Gerry 1912- ... 23-24R
Brown, Susan Jenkins 1896- ... 85-88
Brown, T. E. 1830-1897 ... DLB-35
Brown, T(illman) Merritt 1913- ... 41-44R
Brown, Terence 1944- ... CANR-19
Earlier sketch in CA 102
Brown, Theo W(atts) 1934- ... CANR-8
Earlier sketch in CA 61-64
Brown, Theodore L(awrence) 1928- ... 33-36R
Brown, Theodore M(orey) 1925- ... 33-36R
Brown, Thomas H. 1930- ... 57-60
Brown, Tina 1953- ... 118
Brief entry ... 116
Brown, Tony
See Brown, W. Anthony
Brown, Tony
See Brown, William Anthony
Brown, Truesdell S(parhawk) 1906- ... 15-16R
Brown, Turner, Jr.
See Hample, Stuart
Brown, Velma Darbo 1921- ... 97-100
Brown, Vinson 1912- ... CANR-1
Earlier sketch in CA 4R
See also SATA 19
Brown, Virginia (Suggs) 1924- ... 69-72
Brown, Virginia Pounds 1916- ... 114
Brown, Virginia Sharpe 1916- ... 13-14R
Brown, W. Anthony 1933- Brief entry ... 110
Brown, W(illiam) Norman 1892-1975 ... 61-64
Obituary ... 57-60
Brown, Wallace 1933- ... 17-18R
Brown, Walter Lee 1924- ... 33-36R
Brown, Walter R(eed) 1929- ... CANR-2
Earlier sketch in CA 45-48
See also SATA 19
Brown, Warner
See Boroson, Warren
Brown, Warren (William) 1894-1978 ... 85-88
Obituary ... 81-84
Brown, Warren A. 1917(?)-1985 Obituary ... 117
Brown, Wayne 1944- ... 101
Brown, Weldon A(mzy) 1911- ... 65-68
Brown, Wenzell 1912- ... CANR-5
Earlier sketch in CA 1R

Brown, Wesley 1945- 125
See also BW
Brown, Wilfred (Banks Duncan) 1908-1985 ..... 9-10R
Obituary 116
Brown, Wilfred A(rthur) Gavin
See Gavin-Brown, Wilfred A(rthur)
Brown, Will
See Ainsworth, William Harrison
Brown, Will C.
See Boyles, C. S(cott), Jr.
Brown, William Anthony 1933- 125
See also BW
Brown, William Campbell 1928- 57-60
Brown, William E(nglish) 1907-1975 ..... CAP-2
Earlier sketch in CA 29-32
Brown, William Edward 1904- 126
Brown, William F(rank) 1920- 33-36R
Brown, William F(erdinand) 1928- 33-36R
Brown, William Hill 1765-1793 ..... DLB-37
Brown, William J. 97-100
Brown, William James 1889- 7-8R
Brown, William L(ouis) 1910-1964 ..... 4R
See also SATA 5
Brown, William Wells 1813-1884 ..... DLB-3, 50
Brown, Zenith Jones 1898-1983 ..... 11-12R
Obituary 110
Brown-Azarowicz, Marjory F. 1922- 33-36R
Brownback, Paul 1940- 113
Browne, Anthony (Edward Tudor) 1946- 97-100
See also SATA 44, 45
Browne, Barum
See Saunders, Hilary Aidan St. George
Browne, Charles Farrar 1834-1867 ..... DLB-11
Browne, Colette (Victoria) 1950- 121
Browne, Courtney 1915- 21-22R
Browne, Dik
See Browne, Richard
See also SATA 38
See also AITN 1
Browne, E(lliott) Martin 1900-1980 ..... CAP-2
Obituary 97-100
Earlier sketch in CA 25-28
Browne, G(erald) P(eter) 1930- 23-24R
Browne, Gary Lawson 1939- 101
Browne, George Stephenson 1890-1970 ..... CAP-2
Earlier sketch in CA 29-32
Browne, Hablot Knight 1815-1882 ..... SATA-21
Browne, Harry 1933- CANR-3
Earlier sketch in CA 49-52
Browne, Harry
See Browne, Henry
Browne, Henry 1918- 102
Browne, Howard 1908- 73-76
Browne, (Clyde) Jackson 1948(?)- 120
See also CLC 21
Browne, Joseph William 1914- 105
Browne, Joy 1944- 97-100
Browne, Malcolm W(ilde) 1931- 17-18R
Browne, Matthew
See Rands, William Brighty
Browne, Michael Dennis 1940- CANR-15
Earlier sketch in CA 29-32R
See also DLB 40
Browne, Ray B(roadus) 1922- CANR-11
Earlier sketch in CA 19-20R
Browne, Raymond 1897- 73-76
Browne, Richard 1917- SATA-38
Browne, Robert
See Karlins, Marvin
Browne, Robert S(pan) 1924- CANR-14
Earlier sketch in CA 37-40R
Browne, Roland A. 1910- 65-68
Browne, Sam
See Smith, Ronald Gregor
Browne, Theodore R. 1911(?)-1979
Obituary 81-84
Browne, Walter A(nderson) 1895- 37-40R
Browne, William P(aul) 1945- CANR-25
Earlier sketch in CA 109
Browne, Wynyard (Barry) 1911-1964
Obituary 113
See also DLB 13
Brownell, Blaine Allison 1942- 65-68
Brownell, John Arnold 1924- 21-22R
Brownell, W. C. 1851-1928 ..... DLB-71
Browning, Alice C(rolley) 1907-1985
Obituary 117
Browning, Christopher R(obert) 1944- 112
Browning, Columban
See Browning, William
Browning, David (George) 1938- 37-40R
Browning, Dixie Burrus 1930- 110
Browning, Don S(pencer) 1934- CANR-2
Earlier sketch in CA 49-52
Browning, (Grayson) Douglas 1929- 15-16R
Browning, Elizabeth 1924- 57-60
Browning, Elizabeth Barrett 1806-1861 ..... DLB-32
Browning, Frank 1946- 107
Browning, Gordon 1938- 37-40R
Browning, Iben 1918- Brief entry 113
Browning, J(ohn) D. 1942- 125
Browning, John S.
See Williams, Robert Moore
Browning, L. J.
See Du Breuil, (Elizabeth) L(or)inda
Browning, Mary 1887- CAP-1
Earlier sketch in CA 11-12
Browning, Norma Lee 1914- CANR-8
Earlier sketch in CA 61-64
Browning, Peter 1928- 104
Browning, Preston M(ercer), Jr. 1929- 57-60
Browning, Reed 1938- 57-60
Browning, Robert 1812-1889 ..... YABC-1
See also DLB 32
Browning, Robert 1914- CANR-13
Earlier sketch in CA 33-36R
Browning, Robert L(ynn) 1924- CANR-16
Earlier sketch in CA 85-88
Browning, Rufus P(utnam) 1934- 124
Browning, (Zerilda) Sinclair 1946- 112
Browning, Tod 1882-1962 Obituary 117
See also CLC 16
Browning, Wilfrid (Robert Francis) 1918- 7-8R
Browning, William 1921- 113
Brownjohn, Alan 1931- 25-28R
See also SATA 6
See also DLB 40
Brownlee, O(swald) H(arvey) 1917- 65-68
Brownlee, W(illiam H(ugh) 1917- 9-10R
Brownlee, W(ilson) Elliot, Jr. 1941- 69-72
Brownlee, Walter 1930- 57-60
Brownlie, Ian 1932- CANR-2
Earlier sketch in CA 5-6R
Brownlow, Cecil Alexander III 1926-1988
Obituary 124
Brownlow, Kevin 1938- CANR-12
Earlier sketch in CA 25-28R
Brownmiller, Susan 1935- 103
Brownrigg, Walter Grant 1940- 110
Brownson, Orestes Augustus 1803-1876 ..... DLB-1, 59, 73
Brownson, William C(larence), Jr. 1928- 69-72
Brownstein, Karen (Osney) 1944- 124
Brownstein, Michael 1943- 33-36R
Brownstein, Oscar Lee 1928- 113
Brownstein, Rachel M. 1937- 122
Brownstein, Ronald J. 1958- 106
Brownstein, Samuel C. 1909- 7-8R
Brownstone, David M. 1928- CANR-21
Earlier sketch in CA 104
Broxholme, John Franklin 1930- CANR-12
Earlier sketch in CA 65-68
Broxon, Mildred Downey 1944- 107
Broy, Anthony 1916- 102
Broyard, Anatole 1920- 105
Broyles, J(ohn) Allen 1934- 11-12R
Broyles, William Dodson, Jr. 1944- 73-76
Brozek, Josef (Maria) 1913- 45-48
Brozen, Yale 1917- 109
Bru, Hedin
See Jacobsen, Hans Jacob
Brubach, Holly 1953- 110
Brubacher, John Seiler 1898- CANR-1
Earlier sketch in CA 2R
Brubaker, Dale L(ee) 1937- CANR-4
Earlier sketch in CA 53-56
Brubaker, Earl R(oy) 1932- 107
Brubaker, Sterling 1924- 21-22R
Bruccoli, Matthew J(oseph) 1931- CANR-7
Earlier sketch in CA 11-12R
See also CLC 34
Bruce, Ben F., Jr. 1920- 13-14R
Bruce, Charles 1906-1971 ..... DLB-68
Bruce, Curt 1946- 97-100
Bruce, David (Kirkpatrick Este) 1898-1977
Obituary 105
Bruce, Debra 1951- 118
Bruce, Dickson D., Jr. 1946- 53-56
Bruce, Donald (James) 1930- 17-18R
Bruce, Dorita Fairlie 1885-1970 Obituary 107
See also SATA 27
Bruce, F(rederick) F(yvie) 1910- CANR-19
Earlier sketches in CA 2R, CANR-3
Bruce, George 1909- 65-68
Bruce, Harold (R., Jr.) 1934(?)-1987
Obituary 122
Bruce, Harry J. 1931- 23-24R
Bruce, Janet
See Campbell, Janet Bruce
Bruce, Jeannette M. 1922- 5-6R
Bruce, Lennart 1919- CANR-13
Earlier sketch in CA 33-36R
Bruce, Lenny
See Schneider, Leonard Alfred
See also CLC 21
Bruce, Leo
See Croft-Cooke, Rupert
Bruce, Mary 1927- 25-28R
See also SATA 1
Bruce, Maurice 1913(?)-1988 Obituary 125
Bruce, Monica
See Melaro, Constance L(oraine)
Bruce, Philip Alexander 1856-1933 ..... DLB-47
Bruce, R(aymon) R(ene) 1934- 89-92
Bruce, Richard
See Nugent, Richard Bruce
Bruce, Robert 1927- CAP-1
Earlier sketch in CA 9-10
Bruce, Robert V(ance) 1923- 53-56
Bruce, Shelley
See Merklinghaus, Michele
Bruce, Sylvia (Valerie) 1936- 33-36R
Bruce, Violet R(ose) 29-32R
Bruce-Briggs, B(arry B.) 112
Bruce Lockhart, Robin 1920- 25-28R
Bruce-Novoa
See Bruce-Novoa, John David
Bruce-Novoa, John David 1944-
Brief entry 117
Bruce-Novoa, Juan
See Bruce-Novoa, John David
Bruch, Hilde 53-56
See also AITN 1
Bruchac, Joseph III 1942- CANR-13
Earlier sketch in CA 33-36R
See also SATA 42
Bruchey, Stuart (Weems) 1917- 33-36R
Bruck, Lilly 1918- 109
Bruck, Lorraine 1921- SATA-46
Brucker, Clara (Hantel) 1892(?)-1980
Obituary 97-100
Brucker, Gene (Adam) 1924- Brief entry 114
Brucker, Herbert 1898-1977 ..... CANR-4
Obituary 69-72
Earlier sketch in CA 5-6R
Brucker, Roger W(arren) 1929- CANR-11
Earlier sketch in CA 65-68
Bruckman, Clyde 1894-1955 ..... DLB-26
Bruder, Judith 97-100
Bruegel, Johann Wolfgang 1905-1986 77-80
Obituary 121
Bruegel, John Wolfgang
See Bruegel, Johann Wolfgang
Brueggemann, Walter (A.) 1933-
Brief entry 117
Bruegmann, Robert 1948- 101
Bruehl, Anton 1900-1982 Obituary 110
Bruemmer, Fred 1929- 102
See also SATA 47
Bruening, William H(arry) 1943- 57-60
Bruess, Clint E. 1941- 33-36R
Bruff, Nancy
See Gardner, Nancy Bruff
Bruffee, Kenneth A. 1934- 37-40R
Bruford, Walter Horace 1894-1988
Obituary 126
Bruggen, Carol (Holmes) 1932- 117
Brugger, Bill
See Brugger, William
Brugger, Robert J. 1943- CANR-16
Earlier sketch in CA 85-88
Brugger, William 1941- CANR-12
Earlier sketch in CA 73-76
Bruggink, Donald J. 1929- CANR-7
Earlier sketch in CA 13-14R
Bruhn, Eric (Belton Evers) 1928-1986
Obituary 118
Bruhn, John Glyndon 1934- 89-92
Bruin, John
See Brutus, Dennis
Bruins, Elton J(ohn) 1927- 53-56
Bruland, Esther (Byle) 1956- 116
Bruller, Jean (Marcel) 1902- CANR-12
Earlier sketch in CA 65-68
Brulls, Christian
See Simenon, Georges (Jacques Christian)
Brumback, Carl V. 1917(?)-1987 Obituary 123
Brumbaugh, Robert Sherrick 1918- CANR-3
Earlier sketch in CA 5-6R
Brumbaugh, Thomas B(rendle) 1921- 49-52
Brumble, H(erbert) David III 1943- 107
Brumgardt, John R(aymond) 1946- 97-100
Brumm, Ursula 1919- 29-32R
Brummel, Mark Joseph 1933- 103
Brummet, R. Lee 1921- 23-24R
Brummitt, Wyatt B. 1897- 11-12R
Brun, Ellen 1933- 103
Brun, Henri 1939- 53-56
Bruna, Dick 1927- 112
See also SATA 30, 43
See also CLR 7
Brundage, Burr Cartwright 1912- 41-44R
Brundage, Dorothy J(une) 1930- 104
Brundage, James A(rthur) 1929- CANR-7
Earlier sketch in CA 5-6R
Brundage, John Herbert 1926- 101
Brundage, Percival F(lack) 1892-1979 101
Obituary 89-92
Brune, Lester H(ugo) 1926- CANR-13
Earlier sketch in CA 33-36R
Bruneau, Jean
See Sylvestre, (Joseph Jean) Guy
Bruneau, Thomas C. 1939- 53-56
Bruner, Edward M. 1924- 121
Bruner, Herbert B. 1894(?)-1974
Obituary 53-56
Bruner, Jerome S(eymour) 1915- CANR-1
Earlier sketch in CA 45-48
Bruner, Margaret E. (Baggerly) 1886-197(?) CAP-1
Earlier sketch in CA 17-18
Bruner, Richard W(allace) 1926- 49-52
Bruner, Wally 1931- 49-52
Brunet, Michel 1917-1985 ..... CANR-18
Obituary 117
Earlier sketch in CA 102
Brunette, Peter (Clark, Jr.) 1943- 126
Brunetti, Cledo 1910-1971 ..... CAP-2
Earlier sketch in CA 29-32
Brunetti, Mendor Thomas 1894-1979
Obituary 89-92
Brunhoff, Jean de 1899-1937 Brief entry 118
See also SATA 24
See also CLR 4
Brunhoff, Laurent de 1925- 73-76
See also SATA 24
See also CLR 4
Brunhouse, Robert Levere 1908- CANR-2
Earlier sketch in CA 49-52
Bruni, (Toni) Roxanna 1952- 114
Bruning, Nancy P(auline) 1948- CANR-23
Earlier sketch in CA 106
Brunn, Harry O(tis), Jr. 1919- 2R
Brunner, Edmund de S(chweinitz) 1889-1973 ..... CAP-1
Obituary 45-48
Earlier sketch in CA 15-16
Brunner, Elizabeth 1920-1983 Obituary 111
Brunner, James A(lbertus) 1923- 37-40R
Brunner, John (Kilian Houston) 1934- CANR-2
Earlier sketch in CA 1R
See also CLC 8, 10
Brunner, Maurice Yaw 1950- 103
Brunner, Theodore F(riederich) 1934- 33-36R
Brunnings, Florence E(mery) 1916- 112
Bruno, Frank
See St. Bruno, Albert Francis
Bruno, Frank J(oe) 1930- 107
Bruno, Harold R., Jr. 1928- 77-80
Bruno, James Edward 1940- 41-44R
Bruno, Michael 1921- 33-36R
Bruno, Vincent J. 1926- 65-68
Bruns, Frederick R., Jr. 1913(?)-1979
Obituary 85-88
Bruns, George 1914(?)-1983 Obituary 109
Bruns, J(ames) Edgar 1923- CANR-2
Earlier sketch in CA 5-6R
Bruns, William A(lan) 1942- 113
Bruns, William J(ohn), Jr. 1935- 37-40R
Brunskill, Ronald (William) 1929- 85-88
Brunstein, Karl (Avrum) 1933- 97-100
Brunt, P(eter) A(stbury) 1917- 101
Bruntjen, Scott 1943- 111
Brunton, David W(alter) 1929- 41-44R
Brunton, Paul 1898-1981 Obituary 115
Bruntz, George G. 1901- 7-8R
Brunvand, Jan Harold 1933- CANR-26
Earlier sketch in CA 108
Brus, Wlodzimierz 1921- 73-76
Brush, Craig B(alcombe) 1930- 21-22R
Brush, Douglas P(eirce) 1930- CANR-7
Earlier sketch in CA 57-60
Brush, John E(dwin) 1919- 33-36R
Brush, Judith M(arie) 1938- CANR-7
Earlier sketch in CA 57-60
Brush, Stephen G(eorge) 73-76
Brushwood, John S(tubbs) 1920- CANR-9
Earlier sketch in CA 21-22R
Brusiloff, Phyllis 1935- 57-60
Bruss, Elizabeth W(issman) 1944-1981 108
Brussel, Jacob 1900(?)-1979 Obituary 104
Brussel, James Arnold 1905- CANR-3
Earlier sketch in CA 4R
Brust, Harold
See Cheyney, (Reginald Evelyn) Peter (Southouse)
Brust, Steven K. (Zoltan) 1955- 115
Brustein, Robert S(anford) 1927- CANR-7
Earlier sketch in CA 11-12R
Bruster, Bill(y) G(lenn) 1940- 111
Brustlein, Daniel 1904- SATA-40
Brustlein, Janice Tworkov 9-10R
See also SATA 40
Bruteau, Beatrice 1930- 57-60
Bruton, Eric (Moore) 1915- CANR-23
Earlier sketches in CA 13-14R, CANR-5
Bruton, Henry J(ackson) 1921- 23-24R
Bruton, J(ack) G(ordon) 1914- 11-12R
Brutten, Gene J. 1928- 37-40R
Brutten, Milton 1922- 45-48
Brutus
See Spooner, John D.
Brutus, Dennis 1924- CANR-2
Earlier sketch in CA 49-52
See also BW
See also CLC 43
Bruun, Bertel 1937- 45-48
Bruun, (Arthur) Geoffrey 1898-1988 ..... 1R
Obituary 126
Bruun, Ruth Dowling 1937- 108
Bruyn, Kathleen 1903- CAP-2
Earlier sketch in CA 33-36
Bruzelius, Caroline 1949- 121
Bry, Adelaide 1920- 33-36R
Bry, Gerhard 1911- 41-44R
Bryan, Ashley F. 1923- CANR-26
Earlier sketch in CA 107
See also BW
See also SATA 31
Bryan, C(ourtlandt) D(ixon) B(arnes) 1936- CANR-13
Earlier sketch in CA 73-76
See also CLC 29
Bryan, Carter R(oyston) 1911- 33-36R
Bryan, Christopher 1935- CANR-20
Earlier sketch in CA 104
Bryan, Dorothy M. 1896(?)-1984 Obituary 114
See also SATA 39
Bryan, G(eorge) McLeod 1920- 4R
Bryan, George B(arton) 1939- 117
Bryan, J(oseph) III 1904- CANR-11
Earlier sketch in CA 61-64
Bryan, J(ack) Y(eaman) 1907- 73-76
Bryan, John E. 1931- CANR-4
Earlier sketch in CA 53-56
Bryan, Julien (Hequembourg) 1899-1974
Obituary 53-56
Bryan, M(erwyn) Leonard 1937- 103
Bryan, Marian K(nighton) 1900(?)-1974
Obituary 53-56
Bryan, Martin 1908- 2R
Bryan, Mavis
See O'Brien, Marian P(lowman)
Bryan, Michael
See Moore, Brian
Bryan, Mina R(uese) 1908-1985 Obituary 115
Bryan, Sharon 1943- 115
Bryan, (William) Wright 1905- 77-80
Bryans, Robert Harbinson 1928- CANR-11
Earlier sketch in CA 7-8R
Bryans, Robin
See Bryans, Robert Harbinson
Bryant, Anita
See Green, Anita Jane
Bryant, Arthur (Wynne Morgan) 1899-1985 105
Obituary 114
Bryant, Bear
See Bryant, Paul W(illiam)
Bryant, Bernice (Morgan) 1908- CAP-1
Earlier sketch in CA 9-10
See also SATA 11
Bryant, Beth Elaine 1936- 15-16R
Bryant, Cyril E(ric, Jr.) 1917- 61-64
Bryant, Donald C(ross) 1905- 13-14R

INDEX

Bryant, Dorothy 1930- ... CANR-19
Earlier sketches in CA 53-56, CANR-4
Bryant, Edward (Albert) 1928- ... CANR-11
Earlier sketch in CA 11-12R
Bryant, Edward (Winslow, Jr.) 1945- ... CANR-1
Earlier sketch in CA 45-48
Bryant, Gay 1945- ... CANR-13
Earlier sketch in CA 73-76
Bryant, Henry A(llen), Jr. 1943- ... CANR-4
Earlier sketch in CA 53-56
Bryant, J(oseph) A(llen), Jr. 1919- ... 5-6R
Bryant, James C(ecil), Jr. 1931- ... 49-52
Bryant, Jerry H(olt) 1928- ... 33-36R
Bryant, Katherine Cliffton 1912- ... 13-14R
Bryant, Keith L(ynn), Jr. 1937- ... 49-52
Bryant, Margaret M. 1900- ... CANR-4
Earlier sketch in CA 4R
Bryant, Paul W(illiam) 1913-1983 ... 111
Obituary ... 108
Bryant, Ralph C(lement) 1938- ... 117
Bryant, Robert H(arry) 1925- ... 23-24R
Bryant, Shasta M(onroe) 1924- ... 41-44R
Bryant, T(homas) Alton 1926- ... CANR-10
Earlier sketch in CA 25-28R
Bryant, Traphes L(emon) 1914- ... 77-80
Bryant, Verda E. 1910- ... CAP-2
Earlier sketch in CA 21-22
Bryant, William Cullen
1794-1878 ... DLB-3, 43, 59
See also CDALB 1640-1865
Bryant, Willis Rooks 1892-1965 ... 7-8R
Obituary ... 103
Bryce, Gladysann 1934- ... 116
Bryce, James 1934- ... 112
Bryce, Murray D(avidson) 1917- ... 13-14R
Brychta, Alex 1956- ... CANR-20
Earlier sketch in CA 103
See also SATA 21
Bryde, John F(rancis) 1920- ... 33-36R
Bryden, Bill
See Bryden, William Campbell Rough
Bryden, John Marshall 1941- ... CANR-1
Earlier sketch in CA 49-52
Bryden, John R(ennie) 1913- ... 33-36R
Bryden, William Campbell Rough 1942- ... 105
Bryer, Jackson R(obert) 1937- ... CANR-18
Earlier sketches in CA 9-10R, CANR-3
Bryer, (Alastair) Robin (Mornington)
1944- ... 111
Bryers, Paul 1945- ... 73-76
Bryfonski, Dedria (Anne) 1947- ... 101
Bryher
See Ellerman, Annie Winifred
Bryks, Rachmil 1912-1974 ... 97-100
Brymer, Jack 1915- ... 110
Brynildsen, Ken(neth) 1944- ... 110
Brynner, Yul
See Khan, Taidje
Bryson, Bernarda 1905- ... 49-52
See also SATA 9
Bryson, Conrey 1905- ... 93-96
Bryson, Phillip J(ames) 1939- ... 69-72
Bryson, Reid Allen 1920- ... 101
Bryson, W(illiam) Hamilton 1941- ... 114
Bryusov, Valery Yakovlevich 1873-1924
Brief entry ... 107
See also TCLC 10
Brzezinski, Zbigniew K(azimierz) 1928- ... CANR-5
Earlier sketch in CA 3R
Buba, Joy Flinsch 1904- ... SATA-44
Bubar, Margaret Weber 1920(?)-1978
Obituary ... 77-80
Bubb, Mel
See Whitcomb, Ian
Bube, Richard H. 1927- ... CANR-8
Earlier sketch in CA 23-24R
Bubeck, Mark I(rving) 1928- ... 61-64
Buber, Martin 1878-1965 ... 125
Obituary ... 25-28R
Bubner, Rudiger
See Bubner, Ruediger
Bubner, Ruediger 1941- ... 121
Buccellati, Giorgio 1937- ... 41-44R
Bucchieri, Theresa F. 1908- ... 73-76
Bucco, Martin 1929- ... CANR-14
Earlier sketch in CA 29-32R
Buchan, Alastair (Francis) 1918-1976 ... 73-76
Obituary ... 65-68
Buchan, Bryan 1945- ... 107
See also SATA 36
Buchan, David
See Womack, David A(lfred)
Buchan, James 1916- Brief entry ... 119
Buchan, John 1875-1940 Brief entry ... 108
See also YABC 2
See also DLB 34, 70
Buchan, Kate
See Erskine, Barbara
Buchan, Norman Findlay 1922- ... 109
Buchan, Perdita 1940- ... 21-22R
Buchan, Stuart 1942-1987 ... 57-60
Obituary ... 123
Buchan, Thomas Buchanan 1931- ... CANR-16
Earlier sketch in CA 25-28R
Buchan, Tom
See Buchan, Thomas Buchanan
Buchanan, A(lbert) Russell 1906- ... 13-14R
Buchanan, Annette 1933- ... 118
Buchanan, Betty (Joan) 1923- ... 101
Buchanan, Chuck
See Rowland, D(onald) S(ydney)
Buchanan, Colin O(gilvie) 1934- ... 25-28R
Buchanan, Cynthia 1942- ... CANR-1
Earlier sketch in CA 45-48
Buchanan, Cynthia D(ee) 1937- ... 7-8R
Buchanan, Daniel C(rump) 1892- ... 19-20R
Buchanan, (Eric) David 1933- ... 57-60
Buchanan, David A(lan) 1949- ... 118
Buchanan, Donald W(illiam) 1908-19(?) ... CAP-1
Earlier sketch in CA 11-12
Buchanan, Edna (Rydzik) 1946(?)-
Brief entry ... 125
Buchanan, George (Henry Perrott)
1904- ... CANR-3
Earlier sketch in CA 11-12R
Buchanan, George Wesley 1921- ... CANR-14
Earlier sketch in CA 37-40R
Buchanan, James J(unkin) 1925- ... 33-36R
Buchanan, James McGill 1919- ... CANR-22
Earlier sketches in CA 5-6R, CANR-3
Buchanan, Keith 1919- ... CANR-10
Earlier sketch in CA 23-24R
Buchanan, Laura
See King, Florence
Buchanan, Marie ... CANR-25
Earlier sketches in CA 65-68, CANR-10
Buchanan, Patrick
See Corley, Edwin (Raymond)
Buchanan, Pegasus 1920- ... 11-12R
Buchanan, R(obert) A(ngus) 1930- ... CANR-7
Earlier sketch in CA 17-18R
Buchanan, Robert 1841-1901 ... DLB-18, 35
Buchanan, Thomas G(ittings) 1919- ... 2R
Buchanan, Wiley T(homas), Jr.
1914-1986 Obituary ... 118
Buchanan, William
See Buck, William Ray
Buchanan, William J(esse) 1926- ... 73-76
Buchanan-Brown, John 1929- ... 102
Buchard, Robert 1931- ... 33-36R
Buchdahl, Gerd 1914- ... 57-60
Bucheister, Patt 1942- ... 122
Buchele, William Martin 1895- ... 57-60
Buchen, Irving H. 1930- ... 25-28R
Bucher, Bradley 1932- ... 37-40R
Bucher, Charles A(ugustus) 1912- ... CANR-3
Earlier sketch in CA 11-12R
Bucher, Francois 1927- ... CANR-3
Earlier sketch in CA 5-6R
Bucher, Glenn R(ichard) 1940- ... 57-60
Bucher, Magnus 1927- ... 41-44R
Buchheim, Lothar-Guenther 1918- ... 85-88
See also CLC 6
Buchheimer, Naomi Barnett
See Barnett, Naomi
Buchheit, Lee C(harles) 1950- ... 81-84
Buchler, Justus 1914- ... 5-6R
Buchman, Dian Dincin ... CANR-8
Earlier sketch in CA 61-64
Buchman, Frank N(athan) D(aniel)
1878-1961 Obituary ... 112
Buchman, Herman 1920- ... 41-44R
Buchman, Marion ... 121
Buchman, Randall L(oren) 1929- ... CANR-1
Earlier sketch in CA 45-48
Buchman, Sidney 1902-1975 ... 93-96
Obituary ... 61-64
See also DLB 26
Buchwald, Art(hur) 1925- ... CANR-21
Earlier sketch in CA 5-6R
See also SATA 10
See also CLC 33
See also AITN 1
Buchwald, Emilie 1935- ... CANR-2
Earlier sketch in CA 49-52
See also SATA 7
Buck, Ashley ?-1980 Obituary ... 97-100
Buck, Charles (Henry, Jr.) 1915- ... 33-36R
Buck, Doris P(itkin) 1898(?)-1980
Obituary ... 102
Buck, Edith V(irginia) 1919- ... 117
Buck, Frederick Silas ... 7-8R
Buck, George C(rawford) 1918- ... 69-72
Buck, Harry M(erwyn, Jr.) 1921- ... CANR-13
Earlier sketch in CA 33-36R
Buck, James H. 1924- ... 104
Buck, Joan Juliet 1948- ... CANR-25
Earlier sketch in CA 108
Buck, John Lossing 1890-1975 ... CANR-2
Obituary ... 61-64
Earlier sketch in CA 45-48
Buck, John N(elson) 1906- ... CAP-2
Earlier sketch in CA 29-32
Buck, Lewis 1925- ... 73-76
See also SATA 18
Buck, Margaret Waring 1910- ... 5-6R
See also SATA 3
Buck, Marion A(shby) 1909- ... CAP-1
Earlier sketch in CA 13-14
Buck, Paul H(erman) 1899-1978
Obituary ... 81-84
Buck, Pearl S(ydenstricker) 1892-1973 ... CANR-1
Obituary ... 41-44R
Earlier sketch in CA 2R
See also SATA 1, 25
See also DLB 9
See also CLC 7, 11, 18
See also AITN 1
Buck, Peggy S(ullivan) 1930- ... 65-68
Buck, Philip W(allenstein) 1900- ... 65-68
Buck, Robert N. 1914- ... 103
Buck, Stratton 1906- ... CAP-2
Earlier sketch in CA 17-18
Buck, Vernon E(llis) 1934- ... 37-40R
Buck, William Ray 1930- ... 4R
Buckeridge, Anthony (Malcolm) 1912- ... CANR-2
Earlier sketch in CA 49-52
See also SATA 6
Buckeye, Donald A(ndrew) 1930- ... 49-52
Buckholdt, David R. 1942- ... 101
Buckholtz, Eileen (Garber) 1949- ... 117
See also SATA 47
Buckhout, Robert 1935- ... 45-48
Buckingham, Burdette H. 1907(?)-1977
Obituary ... 73-76
Buckingham, Clyde E(dwin) 1907- ... CAP-1
Earlier sketch in CA 15-16
Buckingham, Edwin 1810-1833 ... DLB-73
Buckingham, James (William) 1932- ... 29-32R
Buckingham, Jamie
See Buckingham, James (William)
Buckingham, Joseph Tinker 1779-1861 ... DLB-73
Buckingham, Robert W(illiam) III ... 113
Buckingham, Walter S(amuel), Jr.
1924-1967 ... 1R
Obituary ... 103
Buckingham, Willis J(ohn) 1938- ... 29-32R
Buckland, Michael K(eeble) 1941- ... 97-100
Buckland, Raymond 1934- ... 73-76
Buckle, (Christopher) Richard (Sandford)
1916- ... 97-100
Buckler, Ernest 1908-1984 ... CAP-1
Obituary ... 114
Earlier sketch in CA 11-12
See also SATA 47
See also DLB 68
See also CLC 13
Buckler, John 1945- ... 121
Buckler, William Earl 1924- ... CANR-20
Earlier sketches in CA 1R, CANR-5
Buckley, Anthony D. 1945- ... 120
Buckley, Doris Heather
See Buckley Neville, Heather
Buckley, Fergus Reid 1930- ... 21-22R
Buckley, Fiona
See Anand, Valerie
Buckley, Francis J(oseph) 1928- ... CANR-13
Earlier sketch in CA 33-36R
Buckley, Helen E(lizabeth) 1918- ... CANR-3
Earlier sketch in CA 5-6R
See also SATA 2
Buckley, James Lane 1923- ... 61-64
Buckley, Jerome Hamilton 1917- ... CANR-3
Earlier sketch in CA 2R
Buckley, Julian Gerard 1905- ... 41-44R
Buckley, Mary L(orraine) ... 53-56
Buckley, Michael F. 1880(?)-1977
Obituary ... 69-72
Buckley, Michael J(oseph) 1931- ... 73-76
Buckley, Peter 1938- ... 112
Buckley, Priscilla 1921- ... 81-84
Buckley, Roger N(orman) 1937- ... 97-100
Buckley, Shawn 1943- ... 93-96
Buckley, Suzanne Shelton 1946- ... 108
Buckley, Thomas H(ugh) 1932- ... 29-32R
Buckley, Vincent (Thomas) 1925- ... 101
Buckley, Walter (Frederick) 1921- ... 121
Buckley, William F(rank), Jr. 1925- ... CANR-24
Earlier sketches in CA 4R, CANR-1
See also DLBY 80
See also CLC 7, 18, 37
See also AITN 1
Buckley Neville, Heather 1910- ... 103
Bucklin, Louis P(ierre) 1928- ... 97-100
Buckman, Peter 1941- ... CANR-11
Earlier sketch in CA 65-68
Buckmaster, Henrietta
See Stephens, Henrietta Henkle
See also SATA 6
Buckminster, Joseph Stevens
1784-1812 ... DLB-37
Bucknall, Barbara J(ane) 1933- ... CANR-14
Earlier sketch in CA 33-36R
Bucknell, Howard III 1924-1986 ... 125
Buckner, Robert (Henry) 1906- ... 3R
See also DLB 26
Buckner, Sally Beaver 1931- ... 61-64
Buckstead, Richard C(hris) 1929- ... 49-52
Buckvar, Felice (Spitz) 1938- ... 107
Buczkowski, Leopold 1905- ... 41-44R
Buday, George
See Buday, Gyorgy
Buday, Gyorgy 1907- ... 107
Budberg, Moura 1892(?)-1974 Obituary ... 53-56
Budbill, David 1940- ... 73-76
Budd, Edward C(arhart) 1920- ... 23-24R
Budd, Elaine 1925- ... 101
Budd, Kenneth George 1904-1972 ... CAP-1
Earlier sketch in CA 13-14
Budd, Lillian (Peterson) 1897- ... CANR-4
Earlier sketch in CA 2R
See also SATA 7
Budd, Louis J(ohn) 1921- ... CANR-3
Earlier sketch in CA 4R
Budd, Mavis ... CANR-19
Earlier sketch in CA 102
Budd, Richard W. 1934- ... 23-24R
Budd, Thomas ?-1698 ... DLB-24
Budd, William C(laude) 1923- ... 49-52
Buddee, Paul Edgar 1913- ... 103
Budden, Laura M(adeline) 1894- ... 7-8R
Bude, John
See Elmore, Ernest Carpenter
Budenz, Louis F(rancis) 1891-1972
Obituary ... 89-92
Budge, Ian 1936- ... CANR-12
Earlier sketch in CA 29-32R
Budgen, Frank Spencer Curtis 1882-1971
Obituary ... 29-32R
Budick, Sanford 1942- ... 33-36R
Budimir, (Simo) Velimir 1926- ... 65-68
Budinger, Peyton Bailey 1939- ... 114
Budoff, Penny Wise 1939- ... 110
Budrys, Algirdas Jonas 1931- ... CANR-20
Earlier sketches in CA 2R, CANR-4
See also DLB 8
Budrys, Algis
See Budrys, Algirdas Jonas
Budurowycz, Bohdan B(asil) 1921- ... CANR-3
Earlier sketch in CA 5-6R
Budzik, Janet K. Sims 1942- ... 37-40R
Budziszewski, J(ay Dalton) 1952- ... 125
Buechner, (Carl) Frederick 1926- ... CANR-11
Earlier sketch in CA 13-14R
See also DLBY 80
See also CLC 2, 4, 6, 9
Buechner, John C(harles) 1934- ... 23-24R
Buechner, Thomas S(charman) 1926- ... 49-52
Buehler, Curt F(erdinand) 1905-1985 ... 1R
Obituary ... 117
Buehlmann, Walbert 1916- ... 115
Buehnau, Ludwig
See Schreiber, Hermann
Buehner, Andrew J(ohn) 1905- ... 17-18R
Buehr, Walter Franklin 1897-1971 ... CANR-3
Obituary ... 33-36R
Earlier sketch in CA 5-6R
See also SATA 3
Buehrig, Edward H(enry) 1910- ... 37-40R
Buehrig, Gordon M. 1904- ... 101
Buel, Richard (Van Wyck), Jr. 1933- ... CANR-13
Earlier sketch in CA 73-76
Bueler, Lois E(aton) 1940- ... 57-60
Bueler, William Merwin 1934- ... 37-40R
Buell, Frederick H(enderson) 1942- ... 33-36R
Buell, John (Edward) 1927- ... 2R
See also DLB 53
See also CLC 10
Buell, Jon A. 1939- ... 102
Buell, Lawrence 1939- ... 49-52
Buell, Robert Kingery 1908-1971 ... CAP-2
Earlier sketch in CA 25-28
Buell, Victor P(aul) 1914- ... CANR-8
Earlier sketch in CA 21-22R
Buelow, George J. 1929- ... 21-22R
Buendia, Manuel
See Giron, Manuel Buendia Tellez
Buenker, John D(avid) 1937- ... CANR-16
Earlier sketches in CA 45-48, CANR-1
Bueno, Jose de la Torre 1905(?)-1980
Obituary ... 93-96
Bueno de Mesquita, Bruce James 1946- ... 108
Buergenthal, Thomas 1934- ... 37-40R
Buerkle, Jack Vincent 1923- ... 41-44R
Buero Vallejo, Antonio 1916- ... CANR-24
Earlier sketch in CA 106
See also CLC 15, 46
Bueschel, Richard M. 1926- ... CANR-26
Earlier sketches in CA 25-28R, CANR-11
Buetow, Harold A(ndrew) 1919- ... 53-56
Buettner-Janusch, John 1924- ... 49-52
Bufalari, Giuseppe 1927- ... CANR-16
Earlier sketch in CA 25-28R
Buferd, Norma Bradley 1937- ... 69-72
Buff, Conrad 1886-1975 ... SATA-19
Buff, Mary Marsh 1890-1970 Obituary ... 116
See also SATA 19
Buffa, Dudley W. 1940- ... 121
Buffalo Chuck
See Barth, Charles P.
Buffaloe, Neal D(ollison) 1924- ... 53-56
Buffington, Albert F(ranklin) 1905- ... 33-36R
Buffington, Robert (Ray) 1933- ... 21-22R
Bufkin, Ernest Claude, Jr. 1929- ... 101
Buford, Thomas O(liver) 1932- ... 29-32R
Bugayev, Boris Nikolayevich 1880-1934
Brief entry ... 104
Bugbee, Emma 1888(?)-1981 Obituary ... 105
See also SATA 29
Bugbee, Ruth Carson 1903- ... CANR-1
Earlier sketch in CA 1R
Bugental, James F(rederick) T(homas)
1915- ... CANR-25
Earlier sketches in CA 23-24R, CANR-10
Bugg, James L(uckin), Jr. 1920- ... 7-8R
Bugg, Ralph 1922- ... 73-76
Buggie, Frederick D(enman) 1929- ... 97-100
Buglass, Leslie J. 1917- ... 13-14R
Bugliarello, George 1927- ... 41-44R
Bugliosi, Vincent (T.) 1934- ... CANR-13
Earlier sketch in CA 73-76
Buhite, Russell D(evere) 1938- ... 101
Buhle, Mari Jo 1943- ... 108
Buhler, Charlotte B(ertha) 1893-197(?) ... CAP-2
Earlier sketch in CA 17-18
Buhler, Curt F(erdinand)
See Buehler, Curt F(erdinand)
Buhlmann, Walbert
See Buehlmann, Walbert
Buisseret, David 1934- ... 124
Buist, Charlotte
See Patterson, Charlotte (Buist)
Buist, Vincent 1919(?)-1979 Obituary ... 89-92
Buitenhuis, Peter (Martinus) 1925- ... 25-28R
Buitrago, Ann Mari 1929- ... 105
Bukalski, Peter J(ulian) 1941- ... CANR-15
Earlier sketch in CA 41-44R
Buker, George E(dward) 1923- ... 53-56
Bukharin, Nikolai (Ivanovich) 1888-1938
Brief entry ... 120
Bukowczyk, John J(oseph) 1950- ... 125
Bukowski, Charles 1920- ... 17-18R
See also DLB 5
See also CLC 2, 5, 9, 41
Buktenica, Norman A(ugust) 1930- ... 33-36R
Bulatkin, Eleanor Webster 1913- ... 33-36R
Bulatovic, Miodrag 1930- ... CANR-21
Earlier sketch in CA 5-6R
Buley, R(oscoe) Carlyle 1893-1968 ... CAP-2
Obituary ... 25-28R
Earlier sketch in CA 21-22
Bulfinch, Thomas 1796-1867 ... SATA-35
Bulgakov, Mikhail (Afanas'evich)
1891-1940 Brief entry ... 105
See also TCLC 2, 16
Bulger, William T(homas) 1927- ... 69-72

Bulgya, Alexander Alexandrovich
1901-1956 Brief entry 117
Bulka, Reuven P(inchas) 1944- 113
Bulkeley, Christy C. AITN-2
Bulkley, Dwight H(atfield) 1919- 105
Bull, Angela (Mary) 1936- CANR-24
Earlier sketches in CA 21-22R, CANR-9
See also SATA 45
Bull, Geoffrey Taylor 1921- CANR-3
Earlier sketch in CA 9-10R
Bull, George (Anthony) 1929- 115
Bull, Guyon B(oys) G(arrett) 1912- CANR-5
Earlier sketch in CA 7-8R
Bull, Hedley Norman 1932-1985 ....5-6R
Obituary 116
Bull, John 1914- 69-72
Bull, Norman John 1916- CANR-16
Earlier sketch in CA 93-96
See also SATA 41
Bull, Odd 1907- 81-84
Bull, Peter (Cecil) 1912-1984 .... CANR-11
Obituary 112
Earlier sketch in CA 25-28R
See also SATA 39
Bull, Robert J(ehu) 1920- 97-100
Bull, Storm 1913- 11-12R
Bull, William E(merson) 1909-1972 ...... CAP-1
Earlier sketch in CA 15-16
Bulla, Clyde Robert 1914- CANR-18
Earlier sketches in CA 7-8R, CANR-3
See also SATA 2, 41
See also SAAS 6
Bullard, E(dgar) John III 1942- 33-36R
Bullard, Fred Mason 1901- 25-28R
Bullard, Helen 1902- CANR-7
Earlier sketch in CA 17-18R
Bullard, Oral 1922- CANR-23
Earlier sketches in CA 61-64, CANR-8
Bullard, Pamela 1948- 106
Bullard, Roger A(ubrey) 1937- 33-36R
Bulle, Florence (Elizabeth) 1925- CANR-15
Earlier sketch in CA 93-96
Bulleid, H(enry) A(nthony) V(aughan)
1912- CANR-13
Earlier sketches in CA 9-10, CAP-1
Bullen, Dana R(ipley) 1931- 73-76
Bullen, Keith Edward 1906-1976 Obituary ... 106
Bullen, Robert 1926(?)-1976 Obituary 69-72
Buller, Herman 1923- 61-64
Bulliet, Richard W(illiams) 1940- CANR-7
Earlier sketch in CA 57-60
Bullingham, Rodney
See Sladen, Norman St. Barbe
Bullins, Ed 1935- CANR-24
Earlier sketch in CA 49-52
See also BW
See also DLB 7, 38
See also CLC 1, 5, 7
Bullis, Harry Amos 1890-1963 .... CAP-2
Earlier sketch in CA 17-18
Bullis, Jerald 1944- CANR-1
Earlier sketch in CA 49-52
Bullitt, John M(arshall) 1921-1985
Obituary 117
Bullitt, Orville H(orwitz) 1894-1979 ......33-36R
Obituary 89-92
Bullitt, Stimson 1919- 112
Bullitt, William C(hristian) 1891-1967
Obituary 89-92
Bullock, Alan Louis Charles 1914- 1R
Bullock, Alice 1904- 89-92
Bullock, Barbara
See Bullock-Wilson, Barbara
Bullock, C(larence) Hassell 1939- 89-92
Bullock, Charles S(pencer) III 1942- ... CANR-13
Earlier sketch in CA 33-36R
Bullock, Frederick W(illiam) B(agshawe)
1903-19(?) CANR-4
Earlier sketch in CA 7-8R
Bullock, Henry 1907(?)-1973 Obituary ...41-44R
Bullock, Michael 1918- CANR-7
Earlier sketch in CA 19-20R
Bullock, Paul 1924-1986 .... CANR-11
Obituary 118
Earlier sketch in CA 29-32R
Bullock-Wilson, Barbara 1945- 65-68
Bullough, Bonnie 1927- CANR-11
Earlier sketch in CA 69-72
Bullough, D(onald) A(uberon) 1928- 107
Bullough, Geoffrey 1901-1982 .... CANR-5
Obituary 106
Earlier sketch in CA 4R
Bullough, Vern (LeRoy) 1928- CANR-26
Earlier sketches in CA 9-10R, CANR-4,
11
Bullough, William A(lfred) 1933- 101
Bulman, Joan (Carroll Boone) 1904- 103
Bulman, Oliver (Meredith Boone)
1902-1974 Obituary 49-52
Bulmer, (Henry) Kenneth 1921- CANR-9
Earlier sketch in CA 15-16R
Bulmer, Martin 1943- 113
Bulmer, Ralph N(eville) H(ermon)
1928-1988 Obituary 126
Bulmer-Thomas, Ivor 1905- CAP-1
Earlier sketch in CA 11-12
Buloff, Joseph 1899(?)-1985 Obituary 115
Bulpin, T(homas) V(ictor) 1918- CANR-4
Earlier sketch in CA 11-12R
Bultmann, Rudolf Karl 1884-1976 ....7-8R
Obituary 65-68
Bulwer-Lytton, Edward 1803-1873 ...... DLB-21
Bumagin, Victoria E. 1923- 89-92
Bump, Jerome 1943- 109
Bumppo, Nathaniel John Balthazar
1940- 97-100
Bumppo, Natty
See Bumppo, Nathaniel John Balthazar
Bumpus, Jerry 1937- CANR-10
Earlier sketch in CA 65-68
See also DLBY 81
Bumstead, Kathleen Mary 1918-1987 121
See also SATA 53
Bumsted, J(ohn) M(ichael) 1938- 41-44R
Bunce, Alan 1939- 77-80
Bunce, Frank David 1907- CAP-1
Earlier sketch in CA 11-12
Bunce, Linda Susan (Staines) 1956- 107
Bunch, Charlotte (Anne) 1944- 126
Bunch, Clarence 53-56
Bunch, David R(oosevelt) 29-32R
Bunche, Ralph J(ohnson) 1904-1971 125
Obituary 33-36R
See also BW
Bunch-Weeks, Charlotte
See Bunch, Charlotte (Anne)
Bundy, Clarence E(verett) 1906- 85-88
Bundy, William P(utnam) 1917- 104
Bunge, Mario A(ugusto) 1919- 9-10R
Bunge, Nancy L(iddell) 1942- 124
Bunge, Robert Pierce 1930- 124
Bunge, Walter R(ichard) 1911- 25-28R
Bung Karno
See Sukarno, (Ahmed)
Buni, Andrew 1931- 21-22R
Bunim, Irving M. 1901(?)-1980 Obituary ... 103
Bunin, Catherine 1967- 93-96
See also SATA 30
Bunin, Ivan Alexeyevich 1870-1953
Brief entry 104
See also TCLC 6
Bunin, Sherry 1925- 93-96
See also SATA 30
Buning, Sietze
See Wiersma, Stanley M(arvin)
Bunke, H(arvey) Charles 1922- 11-12R
Bunker, Edward 1933- 41-44R
Bunker, Gerald Edward 1938- 37-40R
Bunker, Linda K. 1947- 111
Bunn, John T(homas) 1924- 37-40R
Bunn, John W. 1898- CAP-2
Earlier sketch in CA 23-24
Bunn, Ronald F(reeze) 1929- 21-22R
Bunn, Scott (Middelton) 1943- 111
Bunn, Thomas 1944- 69-72
Bunnell, Peter C(urtis) 1937- CANR-12
Earlier sketch in CA 33-36R
Bunnell, William S(tanley) 1925- CAP-1
Earlier sketch in CA 11-12
Bunt, Lucas N(icolaas) H(endrik) 1905- 69-72
Bunting, A. E.
See Bunting, Anne Evelyn
Bunting, Anne Evelyn 1928- CANR-19
Earlier sketches in CA 53-56, CANR-5
See also SATA 18
Bunting, Bainbridge 1913-1981 .... CANR-8
Earlier sketch in CA 61-64
Bunting, Basil 1900-1985 .... CANR-7
Obituary 115
Earlier sketch in CA 53-56
See also DLB 20
See also CLC 10, 39, 47
Bunting, Eve
See Bunting, Anne Evelyn
Bunting, Glenn (Davison) 1957- SATA-22
Bunting, Josiah 1939- 45-48
Bunuan, Josefina S(antiago) 1935- 33-36R
Bunuel, Luis 1900-1983 101
Obituary 110
See also CLC 16
Bunyan, John 1628-1688 .... DLB-39
Bunzel, John H(arvey) 1924- 17-18R
Buol, S(tanley) W(alter) 1934- 49-52
Burack, Abraham Saul 1908-1978 ...... CANR-4
Obituary 77-80
Earlier sketch in CA 11-12R
Burack, Elmer H(oward) 1927- CANR-16
Earlier sketch in CA 37-40R
Burack, Sylvia K. 1916- CANR-9
Earlier sketch in CA 21-22R
See also SATA 35
Burak, Linda (Gallina) 116
Buranelli, Vincent 1919- CANR-20
Earlier sketches in CA 11-12R, CANR-5
Burbank, Addison (Buswell)
1895-1961 .... SATA-37
Burbank, Garin 1940- 69-72
Burbank, Natt B(ryant) 1903- CAP-2
Earlier sketch in CA 25-28
Burbank, Nelson L(incoln) 1898- CAP-1
Earlier sketch in CA 11-12
Burbank, Rex James 1925- CANR-18
Earlier sketch in CA 1R
Burbidge, Peter George 1919-1985
Obituary 116
Burbridge, Branse 1921- 97-100
Burby, Raymond J(oseph) III 1942- ... CANR-11
Earlier sketch in CA 69-72
Burby, William E(dward) 1893- CAP-1
Earlier sketch in CA 11-12
Burch, Claire R. 1925- 101
Burch, Francis F(loyd) 1932- 29-32R
Burch, George Bosworth 1902-1973 122
Obituary 109
Burch, Jennings Michael 1941- 118
Burch, Mark H(etzel) 1953- 122
Burch, Mary Lou 1914- 104
Burch, Monte G. 1943- 103
Burch, Pat 1944- 57-60
Burch, Philip H. 1930- 106
Burch, Preston M. 1884-1978 Obituary ...77-80
Burch, Robert J(oseph) 1925- CANR-17
Earlier sketches in CA 5-6R, CANR-2
See also SATA 1
See also DLB 52
Burcham, Nancy A(nn) 1942- 89-92
Burchard, John Ely 1898-1975 .... CANR-6
Obituary 61-64
Earlier sketch in CA 3R
Burchard, Max N(orman) 1925- 23-24R
Burchard, Peter Duncan 1921- CANR-18
Earlier sketches in CA 5-6R, CANR-3
See also SATA 5
Burchard, Rachael C(aroline) 1921- 33-36R
Burchard, S. H.
See Burchard, Sue
Burchard, Sue 1937- CANR-19
Earlier sketches in CA 53-56, CANR-4
See also SATA 22
Burchardt, Bill
See Burchardt, William Robert
Burchardt, Nellie 1921- 21-22R
See also SATA 7
Burchardt, William Robert 1917- CANR-16
Earlier sketch in CA 89-92
Burchell, Mary
See Cook, Ida
Burchell, R(obert) A(rthur) 1941- 106
Burchett, Randall E. ?-1971 .... 3R
Obituary 103
Burchett, Wilfred (Graham) 1911-1983 .. CANR-2
Obituary 110
Earlier sketch in CA 49-52
Burchfield, Joe D(onald) 1937- 85-88
Burchfield, Robert William 1923- CANR-14
Earlier sketch in CA 41-44R
Burchwood, Katharine T(yler) 57-60
Burck, Jacob 1907-1982 Obituary 106
Burckel, Nicholas C(lare) 1943- CANR-19
Earlier sketch in CA 103
Burckhardt, C(arl) J(akob) 1891-1974 93-96
Obituary 49-52
Burd, Laurence Hull 1915-1983 Obituary ... 109
Burd, Van Akin 1914- 41-44R
Burda, R(obert) W(arren) 1932- 73-76
Burden, Jean 1914- CANR-3
Earlier sketch in CA 9-10R
Burden, William Douglas 1898-1978
Obituary 81-84
Burder, John 1940- 110
Burdett, Winston 1913- 29-32R
Burdette, Franklin L. 1911-1975 65-68
Obituary 61-64
Burdge, Rabel J(ames) 1937- 69-72
Burdick, Donald W(alter) 1917- 53-56
Burdick, Eric 1934- 29-32R
Burdick, Eugene (Leonard) 1918-1965 .....5-6R
Obituary 25-28R
See also SATA 22
Burdick, Loraine 1929- 57-60
Burdon, R(andal) M(athews) 1896- CAP-1
Earlier sketch in CA 13-14
Bureau, William H(obbs) 1913- 102
Buren, Martha Margareta Elisabet 1910- .. CAP-1
Earlier sketch in CA 13-14
Burfield, Eva
See Ebbett, (Frances) Eva
Burford, E(phraim) J(ohn) 1905- 124
Burford, Eleanor
See Hibbert, Eleanor Burford
Burford, Lolah 41-44R
Burford, Roger L(ewis) 1930- 41-44R
Burford, William (Skelly) 1927- CANR-7
Earlier sketch in CA 7-8R
Burg, Dale R(onda) 1942- CANR-23
Earlier sketch in CA 106
Burg, David
See Dolberg, Alexander
Burg, David F(rederick) 1936- 116
Burge, Doris 1909- 120
Burge, Ethel 1916- 65-68
Burgeon, G. A. L.
See Barfield, (Arthur) Owen
Burger, Albert E. 1941- 37-40R
Burger, Alfred 1905- 122
Burger, Angela Sutherland (Brown) 1936- ..81-84
Burger, Carl 1888-1967 .... CAP-2
Earlier sketch in CA 19-20
See also SATA 9
Burger, Chester 1921- 11-12R
Burger, Edward J(ames), Jr. 1933- 110
Burger, George V(anderkarr) 1927- 57-60
Burger, Henry G. 1923- CANR-15
Earlier sketch in CA 41-44R
Burger, Jack
See Burger, John R(obert)
Burger, John
See Marquard, Leo(pold)
Burger, John R(obert) 1942- 81-84
Burger, Nash K(err) 1908- CAP-2
Earlier sketch in CA 23-24
Burger, Robert E(ugene) 1931- 85-88
Burger, Robert S. 1913- 29-32R
Burger, Ronna Cheryl 1947- 117
Burger, Ruth (Pazen) 1917- 17-18R
Burger, Sarah Greene 1935- 69-72
Burgess, Ann Marie
See Gerson, Noel Bertram
Burgess, Anthony
See Wilson, John (Anthony) Burgess
See also DLB 14
See also CLC 1, 2, 4, 5, 8, 10, 13, 15,
22, 40
See also AITN 1
Burgess, C(hester) F(rancis) 1922- 21-22R
Burgess, Charles (Orville) 1932- 33-36R
Burgess, Christopher Victor 1921- 9-10R
Burgess, Em
See Burgess, Mary Wyche
Burgess, Eric (Alexander) 1912- 101
Burgess, Eric 1920- CANR-18
Earlier sketches in CA 5-6R, CANR-3
Burgess, (Frank) Gelett 1866-1951
Brief entry 113
See also SATA 30, 32
See also DLB 11
Burgess, Helen S(teers) 1906-1987
Obituary 123
Burgess, Jackson (Visscher) 1927- 11-12R
Burgess, Jane K. 1928- CANR-13
Earlier sketch in CA 73-76R
Burgess, John H(enry) 1923- 33-36R
Burgess, John Lawie 1912-1987 Obituary .. 121
Burgess, John W. 1844-1931 .... DLB-47
Burgess, Linda Cannon 1911- 73-76
Burgess, Lorraine Marshall 1913- 106
Burgess, M(argaret) Elaine 15-16R
Burgess, M(ichael) R(oy) 1948- CANR-6
Earlier sketch in CA 57-60
Burgess, Mary Wyche 1916- 61-64
See also SATA 18
Burgess, Michael
See Gerson, Noel Bertram
Burgess, Norman 1923- 25-28R
Burgess, Philip M(ark) 1939- CANR-16
Earlier sketch in CA 25-28R
Burgess, Robert F(orrest) 1927- CANR-11
Earlier sketch in CA 25-28R
See also SATA 4
Burgess, Robert H(errmann) 1913- CANR-5
Earlier sketch in CA 9-10R
Burgess, Robert L. 1938- 29-32R
Burgess, Thornton Waldo 1874-1965 73-76
See also SATA 17
See also DLB 22
Burgess, Trevor
See Trevor, Elleston
Burgess, W(arren) Randolph 1889-1978 .. CAP-2
Obituary 81-84
Earlier sketch in CA 29-32
Burgess-Kohn, Jane
See Burgess, Jane K.
Burgett, Donald R(obert) 1925- 21-22R
Burggraaff, Winfield J. 1940- Brief entry ... 114
Burghard, August 1901- CANR-7
Earlier sketch in CA 19-20R
See also AITN 2
Burghardt, Andrew Frank 1924- 5-6R
Burghardt, Walter J(ohn) 1914- CANR-19
Earlier sketches in CA 2R, CANR-4
Burgin, C(harles) David 1939- 73-76
Burgin, (Weston) Richard 1947- 25-28R
Burgos, Joseph A(gner), Jr. 1945- 106
Burgoyne, Elizabeth
See Pickles, M(abel) Elizabeth
Burgwyn, Diana 1937- 108
Burgwyn, Mebane Holoman 1914- 49-52
See also SATA 7
Burhoe, Ralph Wendell 1911- 17-18R
Buri, Fritz 1907- CANR-8
Earlier sketch in CA 19-20R
Burian, Jarka M(arsano) 1927- 33-36R
Burian, Richard M(artin) 1941- 121
Burich, Nancy J(ane) 1943- 29-32R
Burick, Si(mon) 1909-1986 85-88
Obituary 121
Burk, Bill E(ugene) 1932- 65-68
Burk, Bruce 1917- 61-64
Burk, John Daly 1772(?)-1808 .... DLB-37
Burke, Alan Dennis 1949- 106
Burke, Anna Mae Walsh 1938- 111
Burke, Avid J. 1906- 23-24R
Burke, C(letus) J(oseph) 1917-1973 45-48
Burke, Carl F(rancis) 1917- 25-28R
Burke, Carol 1950- CANR-14
Earlier sketch in CA 65-68
Burke, Colin Bradley 1936- 113
Burke, David 1927- CANR-23
Earlier sketch in CA 105
See also SATA 46
Burke, Desmond William Lardner
See Lardner-Burke, Desmond William
Burke, Edmund M. 1928- 11-12R
Burke, Fielding
See Dargan, Olive (Tilford)
Burke, Fred G(eorge) 1926- 13-14R
Burke, Gerald 1914- CANR-1
Earlier sketch in CA 45-48
Burke, J(ohn) Bruce 1933- 37-40R
Burke, J(ackson) F(rederick Augustine)
1915- CANR-12
Earlier sketch in CA 65-68
Burke, James 1936- 102
Burke, James Lee 1936- CANR-22
Earlier sketches in CA 15-16R, CANR-7
Burke, James Wakefield 1916- CANR-1
Earlier sketch in CA 45-48
Burke, John (Frederick) 1922- CANR-25
Earlier sketches in CA 7-8R, CANR-9
Burke, John
See O'Connor, Richard
Burke, John Emmett 1908- 37-40R
Burke, John Garrett 1917- 77-80
Burke, John J(oseph), Jr. 1942- 114
Burke, Jonathan
See Burke, John (Frederick)
Burke, Joseph (Terence Anthony) 1913- 103
Burke, Kenneth (Duva) 1897- 5-6R
See also DLB 45, 63
See also CLC 2, 24
Burke, Leda
See Garnett, David
Burke, Maggie
See Snyder, Marilyn

Burke, (Omar) Michael 1927- 73-76
Burke, Owen
See Burke, John (Frederick)
Burke, (Ulick) Peter 1937- CANR-16
Earlier sketch in CA 25-28R
Burke, Ralph
See Silverberg, Robert
Burke, Richard C(ullen) 1932- 53-56
Burke, Robert E(ugene) 1921- 21-22R
Burke, Russell 1946- 33-36R
Burke, S(amuel) M(artin) 1906- 49-52
Burke, Shifty
See Benton, Peggie
Burke, Stanley 1923- 101
Burke, T(homas) Patrick 1934- 121
Burke, Ted 1934(?)-1978 Obituary 77-80
Burke, Thomas 1886-1945 Brief entry 113
Burke, Tom 73-76
Burke, Vee
See Burke, Velma Whitgrove
Burke, Velma Whitgrove 1921- CANR-4
Earlier sketch in CA 53-56
Burke, Vincent John 1919-1973 122
Obituary 111
Burke, Virginia M. 1916- 45-48
Burke, W. Warner 1935- CANR-14
Earlier sketch in CA 37-40R
Burkert, Nancy Ekholm 1933- SATA-24
Burkert, Walter 1931- 103
Burket, Harriet 1908- 37-40R
Burkett, David (Young III) 1934- CANR-9
Earlier sketch in CA 65-68
Burkett, Eva M(ae) 1903- 33-36R
Burkett, Jack 1914- 101
Burkett, Molly 1932- CANR-9
Earlier sketch in CA 53-56
Burkey, Richard M(ichael) 1930- 93-96
Burkhalter, Barton R. 1938- CANR-11
Earlier sketch in CA 25-28R
Burkhardt, Richard Wellington 1918- 2R
Burkhart, Charles 1924- 15-16R
Burkhart, James A(ustin) 1914-1979 .... 9-10R
Burkhart, John E(rnest) 1927- 116
Burkhart, Kathryn Watterson 1942- 45-48
Burkhart, Kitsi
See Burkhart, Kathryn Watterson
Burkhart, Robert E(dward) 1937- 29-32R
Burkhead, Jesse 1916- CANR-3
Earlier sketch in CA 4R
Burkholder, J(ames) Peter 1954- 119
Burkholder, John Richard 1928- 115
Burkholz, Herbert 1932- CANR-11
Earlier sketch in CA 25-28R
Burkill, T(om) A(lec) 1912- 33-36R
Burkitt, Denis (Parsons) 1911- 112
Burkle, Howard R(ussell) 1925-
Brief entry 107
Burkman, Katherine H. 1934- 29-32R
Burkowsky, Mitchell R(oy) 1931- 29-32R
Burks, Ardath Walter 1915- 107
Burks, Arthur W(alter) 1915- 49-52
Burks, David D. 1924- 33-36R
Burks, Edward C. 1921(?)-1983 Obituary 111
Burks, Gordon E(ngledow) 1904- 4R
Burks, Ned
See Burks, Edward C.
Burl, (Harry) Aubrey (Woodruff) 1926- 97-100
Burland, Brian (Berkeley) 1931- CANR-23
Earlier sketches in CA 15-16R, CANR-7
See also SATA 34
Burland, C. A.
See Burland, Cottie (Arthur)
Burland, Cottie (Arthur) 1905- CANR-5
Earlier sketch in CA 5-6R
See also SATA 5
Burleigh, Anne Husted 1941- 29-32R
Burleigh, David Robert 1907- 4R
Burleigh, John H. S. 1894-1985 Obituary 116
Burley, George (Joseph) 1939- Brief entry 107
Burley, W(illiam) J(ohn) 1914- CANR-13
Earlier sketch in CA 33-36R
Burling, Robbins 1926- 17-18R
Burlingame, (William) Roger 1889-1967 .... 5-6R
See also SATA 2
Burlingame, Virginia (Struble) 1900- CAP-2
Earlier sketch in CA 23-24
Burlingham, Dorothy (Tiffany) 1891-1979 109
Obituary 93-96
Burma, John H(armon) 1913- CANR-5
Earlier sketch in CA 1R
Burman, Alice Caddy 1896(?)-1977 .... SATA-24
Burman, Ben Lucien 1896-1984 .... CANR-8
Obituary 114
Earlier sketch in CA 5-6R
See also SATA 6, 40
Burman, Jose Lionel 1917- 109
Burmeister, Edwin 1939- CANR-26
Earlier sketch in CA 29-32R
Burmeister, Eva (Elizabeth) 1899- CAP-1
Earlier sketch in CA 13-14
Burmeister, Jon 1933- 29-32R
Burmeister, Lou E(lla) 1928- CANR-26
Earlier sketch in CA 45-48
Burn, A(ndrew) R(obert) 1902- CANR-17
Earlier sketches in CA 4R, CANR-1
Burn, Barbara 1940- CANR-17
Earlier sketch in CA 85-88
Burn, Doris 1923- 29-32R
See also SATA 1
Burn, Duncan (Lyall) 1902-1988 Obituary 124
Burn, Gordon 1948- 123
Burn, J(oshua) Harold 1892-1982 .... CAP-1
Obituary 108
Earlier sketch in CA 11-12
Burn, Mary (Wynn) 1910- 122
Burnaby, John 1891-1978 .... CAP-1
Obituary 104
Earlier sketch in CA 13-14
Burnam, Tom 1913- 61-64
Burne, Glen
See Green, Alan (Baer)
Burne, Glenn S. 1921- 21-22R
Burne, Kevin G. 1925- 15-16R
Burner, David (B.) 1937- CANR-10
Earlier sketch in CA 25-28R
Burness, Tad
See Burness, Wallace B(inny)
Burness, Wallace B(inny) 1933- CANR-21
Earlier sketch in CA 69-72
Burnet, George Bain 1894- CAP-2
Earlier sketch in CA 23-24
Burnet, (Frank) Macfarlane 1899-1985 73-76
Obituary 117
Burnet, Mary E(dith) 1911- 53-56
Burnett, Alfred David 1937- CANR-19
Earlier sketch in CA 102
Burnett, Anne Pippin 1925- 113
Burnett, Avis 1937- 41-44R
Burnett, Ben G(eorge) 1924-1975 .... CANR-3
Earlier sketch in CA 4R
Burnett, Calvin 1921- 33-36R
Burnett, Collins W. 1914- CANR-3
Earlier sketch in CA 11-12R
Burnett, Constance Buel 1893-1975 .... 5-6R
See also SATA 36
Burnett, David (Benjamin Foley)
1931-1971 .... 11-12R
Obituary 33-36R
Burnett, David (Alan) 1946- 121
Burnett, Dorothy Kirk 1924- 7-8R
Burnett, Frances (Eliza) Hodgson
1849-1924 Brief entry 108
See also YABC 2
See also DLB 42
Burnett, Hallie Southgate (Zeisel) CANR-6
Earlier sketch in CA 13-14R
Burnett, Janet 1915- 49-52
Burnett, Joe Ray 1928- 17-18R
Burnett, John 1925- 57-60
Burnett, June 1936- 113
Burnett, Laurence 1907- 49-52
Burnett, Leo 1891-1971 Obituary 116
Burnett, Leon R. 1925(?)-1983 Obituary 109
Burnett, W(illiam) R(iley) 1899-1982 .... CANR-22
Obituary 106
Earlier sketch in CA 7-8R
See also DLB 9
Burnett, Whit(ney Ewing) 1899-1973 .... CAP-2
Obituary 41-44R
Earlier sketch in CA 13-14
Burnette, O(llen) Lawrence, Jr. 1927- 33-36R
Burney, Anton
See Hopkins, (Hector) Kenneth
Burney, Elizabeth (Mary) 1934- 23-24R
Burney, Eugenia 1913- 29-32R
Burney, Fanny 1752-1840 .... DLB-39
Burnford, Sheila (Philip Cochrane Every)
1918-1984 .... CANR-1
Obituary 112
Earlier sketch in CA 2R
See also SATA 3, 38
See also CLR 2
Burnham, Alan 1913-1984 .... 15-16R
Obituary 112
Burnham, David (Bright) 1933- 122
Burnham, Dorothy E(dith) 1921- 65-68
Burnham, (Linden) Forbes (Sampson)
1923-1985 Obituary 117
Burnham, J. W.
See Burnham, Jack (Wesley)
Burnham, Jack (Wesley) 1931- 115
Burnham, James 1905-1987 Obituary 123
Burnham, John
See Beckwith, Burnham Putnam
Burnham, John C(hynoweth) 1929- 33-36R
Burnham, Linda Frye 1940- 125
Burnham, Richard 1940- 118
Burnham, Robert Ward, Jr. 1913- 19-20R
Burnham, Sophy 1936- 41-44R
See also AITN 1
Burnham, Walter Dean 1930- 101
Burnim, Kalman A(aron) 1928- 2R
Burningham, John Mackintosh 1936- 73-76
See also SATA 16
See also CLR 9
Burnley, (John) David 1941- 117
Burnley, Judith CANR-16
Earlier sketch in CA 97-100
Burns, Aidan 1943- 121
Burns, Alan 1929- CANR-5
Earlier sketch in CA 11-12R
See also DLB 14
Burns, Alan Cuthbert 1887-1980 Obituary 102
Burns, Allan P. 1935- 125
Burns, Alma 1919- 81-84
Burns, Arthur F(rank) 1904-1987 .... 15-16R
Obituary 122
Burns, Betty 1909- CAP-2
Earlier sketch in CA 19-20
Burns, Bobby
See Burns, Vincent Godfrey
Burns, Carol 1934- 29-32R
Burns, Chester R(ay) 1937- 103
Burns, David D. 1942- 114
Burns, E(dward) Bradford 1932- 17-18R
Burns, Edward McNall 1897-1972 .... 1R
Obituary 103
Burns, Eedson Louis Millard
1897-1985 .... CANR-5
Obituary 117
Earlier sketch in CA 7-8R
Burns, Eveline M(abel Richardson)
1900-1985 Obituary 117
Burns, Geoff 1954- 115
Burns, George 1896- 112
Burns, Gerald P(hillip) 1918- 17-18R
Burns, Helen M(arie) 1922- 110
Burns, Hobert Warren 1925- 4R
Burns, James MacGregor 1918- CANR-19
Earlier sketch in CA 7-8R
Burns, James W(illiam) 1937- 33-36R
Burns, Jean (Ellen) 1934- 103
Burns, Jim 1936- 101
Burns, Joan Simpson 1927- 65-68
Burns, John Horne 1916-1953 Brief entry 115
See also DLBY 85
Burns, John McLauren 1932- Brief entry 109
Burns, John V. 1907- CAP-2
Earlier sketch in CA 33-36
Burns, Marilyn SATA-33
Burns, Michael 1947- 121
Burns, Norman T(homas) 1930- 69-72
Burns, Olive Ann 1924- 120
Burns, Paul C. CANR-4
Earlier sketch in CA 3R
See also SATA 5
Burns, Ralph J. 1901- CAP-2
Earlier sketch in CA 25-28
Burns, Ray
See Burns, Raymond (Howard)
Burns, Raymond (Howard) 1924- SATA-9
Burns, Rex (Sehler) 1935- CANR-13
Earlier sketch in CA 77-80
Burns, Richard Dean 1929- CANR-8
Earlier sketch in CA 19-20R
Burns, Richard W(ebster) 1920- 69-72
Burns, Robert Edward 1919- 111
Burns, Robert Grant 1938- CANR-16
Earlier sketch in CA 25-28R
Burns, Robert I(gnatius) 1921- CANR-26
Earlier sketches in CA 19-20R, CANR-7
Burns, Robert M(ilton) C(lark), Jr. 1940- 102
Burns, Ruby V(ermillion) 1901- 106
Burns, Scott
See Burns, Robert M(ilton) C(lark), Jr.
Burns, Sheila
See Bloom, Ursula
Burns, Tex
See L'Amour, Louis (Dearborn)
Burns, Thomas (Jr.) 1928- CANR-14
Earlier sketch in CA 41-44R
Burns, Thomas Stephen 1927- 49-52
Burns, Tom 1913- CANR-22
Earlier sketches in CA 5-6R, CANR-5
Burns, Vincent Godfrey 1893-1979 .... 41-44R
Obituary 85-88
See also AITN 2
Burns, Wayne 1918- CANR-1
Earlier sketch in CA 2R
Burns, William A. 1909- CANR-11
Earlier sketches in CA 13-14, CAP-1
See also SATA 5
Burns, Zed H(ouston) 1903- 33-36R
Burnshaw, Stanley 1906- 9-10R
See also DLB 48
See also CLC 3, 13, 44
Burnside, Wesley M(ason) 1918- 65-68
Buros, Oscar Krisen 1905-1978 Obituary 77-80
Burow, Daniel R(obert) 1931- CANR-11
Earlier sketch in CA 29-32R
Burr, Alfred Gray 1919- 25-28R
Burr, Anne 1937- 25-28R
See also CLC 6
Burr, Charles 1922(?)-1976 Obituary 69-72
Burr, Gray 1919- 69-72
Burr, John R(oy) 1933- 45-48
Burr, Keith 1946- 115
Burr, Lonnie 1943- 103
See also SATA 47
Burr, Samuel Engle, Jr. 1897-1987
Obituary 124
Burr, Wesley R(ay) 1936- 37-40R
Burrell, Berkeley G(raham) 1919-1979 .... 33-36R
Obituary 89-92
Burrell, David B(akewell) 1933- 33-36R
Burrell, Evelyn Patterson 1920- CANR-7
Earlier sketch in CA 53-56
Burrell, Roy E(ric) C(harles) 1923- 33-36R
Burridge, Kenelm (Oswald Lancelot)
1922- 93-96
Burrin, Frank K. 1920- 25-28R
Burrington, David E. 1931- 73-76
Burris, B. C(ullen) 1924- 21-22R
Burris-Meyer, Harold 1902- 41-44R
Burros, Marian (Fox) 89-92
Burroughs, Ben(jamin F.) 1918-1980 65-68
Obituary 122
Burroughs, Edgar Rice 1875-1950
Brief entry 104
See also SATA 41
See also DLB 8
See also TCLC 2
Burroughs, Jean Mitchell 1908- 65-68
See also SATA 28
Burroughs, John 1837-1921 Brief entry 109
See also DLB 64
Burroughs, Margaret G.
See Burroughs, Margaret Taylor (Goss)
Burroughs, Margaret Taylor (Goss)
1917- CANR-25
Earlier sketch in CA 23-24R
See also BW
See also DLB 41
Burroughs, Polly 1925- 25-28R
See also SATA 2
Burroughs, Raleigh (Simpson) 1901- 106
Burroughs, William (Seward), Jr.
1947-1981 73-76
Obituary 112
See also DLB 16
Burroughs, William S(eward) 1914- CANR-20
Earlier sketch in CA 9-10R
See also DLB 2, 8, 16
See also DLBY 81
See also CLC 1, 2, 5, 15, 22, 42
See also AITN 2
Burrow, James Gordon 1922- CANR-2
Earlier sketch in CA 5-6R
Burrow, John A(nthony) 1932- 97-100
Burrow, John W(yon) 1935- CANR-12
Earlier sketch in CA 21-22R
Burroway, Janet (Gay) 1936- CANR-12
Earlier sketch in CA 21-22R
See also CAAS 6
See also SATA 23
See also DLB 6
Burrowes, Michael Anthony Bernard 1937- 103
Burrowes, Mike
See Burrowes, Michael Anthony Bernard
Burrows, Abe
See Burrows, Abram Solman
Burrows, Abram Solman 1910-1985 110
Obituary 116
Burrows, David J(ames) 1936- 41-44R
Burrows, E(dwin) G(ladding) 1917- CANR-14
Earlier sketch in CA 77-80
Burrows, Fredrika Alexander 1908- CANR-6
Earlier sketch in CA 57-60
Burrows, James C. 1944- 29-32R
Burrows, John 1945- 101
Burrows, Miles 1936- 21-22R
Burrows, Millar 1889-1980 81-84
Obituary 97-100
Burrows, William E. 1937- 65-68
Burrows, William R(ichard) 1942- 117
Burrup, Percy E. 1910- 4R
Bursk, Christopher 1943- CANR-24
Earlier sketch in CA 85-88
Bursk, Edward C(ollins) 1907- CANR-5
Earlier sketch in CA 4R
Burstall, Aubrey F(rederic) 1902-1984
Obituary 113
Burstein, Alvin G(eorge) 1931- 85-88
Burstein, Chaya M(alamud) 1923- 126
Burstein, John 1949- CANR-21
Earlier sketch in CA 69-72
See also SATA 40
Burstein, Patricia (Ann) 1945- 108
Burstein, Paul 1946- 123
Burstiner, Irving 1919- 104
Burston, W. H. 1915-1981 Obituary 103
Burstyn, Harold L(ewis) 1930- CANR-5
Earlier sketch in CA 11-12R
Burt, Al(vin Victor, Jr.) 1927- 25-28R
Burt, Alfred LeRoy 1888- CAP-1
Earlier sketch in CA 9-10
Burt, Cyril (Lodowic) 1883-1971 .... CAP-1
Obituary 33-36R
Earlier sketch in CA 13-14
Burt, Donald X(avier) 1929- 116
Burt, Frances R(iemer) 1917- 69-72
Burt, Jesse Clifton 1921-1976 .... CANR-4
Earlier sketch in CA 9-10R
See also SATA 20, 46
Burt, John J. 1934- CANR-11
Earlier sketch in CA 29-32R
Burt, Larry W(ayne) 1950- 122
Burt, Leonard James 1892-1983 Obituary 114
Burt, Mala S(chuster) 1943- 112
Burt, Nathaniel 1913- 19-20R
Burt, Olive Woolley 1894- CANR-5
Earlier sketch in CA 7-8R
See also SATA 4
Burt, Robert Amsterdam 1939- 102
Burt, Roger B(ivens) 1939- 113
Burt, Samuel M(athew) 1915- 23-24R
Burt, Simon 1947- 123
Burt, William Henry 1903- 106
Burtchaell, James Tunstead 1934- CANR-11
Earlier sketch in CA 25-28R
Burtis, C(harles) Edward 1907- 41-44R
Burtle, James (L.) 1919- Brief entry 113
Burtness, Paul Sidney 1923- 19-20R
Burton, Anthony 1933- 61-64
Burton, Anthony 1934- 97-100
Burton, Arthur 1914-1982 .... CANR-10
Earlier sketch in CA 21-22R
Burton, Carl D. 1913- 4R
Burton, David H(enry) 1925- CANR-3
Earlier sketch in CA 49-52
Burton, Dolores Marie 1932- 25-28R
Burton, Dwight L(owell) 1922- 61-64
Burton, Edward J. 1917- 23-24R
Burton, (Alice) Elizabeth 1908- CANR-15
Earlier sketch in CA 65-68
Burton, Gabrielle 1939- 45-48
Burton, Genevieve 1912- 33-36R
Burton, H(arry) M(cGuire Philip)
1898(?)-1979 Obituary 93-96
Burton, Hal
See Burton, Harold Bernard
Burton, Harold Bernard 1908- 97-100
Burton, Hester (Wood-Hill) 1913- CANR-10
Earlier sketch in CA 9-10R
See also SATA 7
See also CLR 1
Burton, Ian 1935- 19-20R
Burton, Ivor Flower 1923- 109
Burton, Jane 105
Burton, Joe Wright 1907-1976 107
Burton, John A(ndrew) 1944- CANR-14
Earlier sketch in CA 65-68
Burton, John Wear 1915- 103

Burton, Katherine (Kurz) 1890-1969 ... 77-80
Burton, Leslie
See McGuire, Leslie Sarah
Burton, Lindy 1937- ... 25-28R
Burton, Lloyd E. 1922- ... 53-56
Burton, Marilee Robin 1950- ... 121
See also SATA 46
Burton, Martin A. 1911-1984 Obituary ... 114
Burton, Mary E(lizabeth) 1900- ... 106
Burton, Maurice 1898- ... CANR-9
Earlier sketch in CA 65-68
See also SATA 23
Burton, Nelson, Jr. 1942- ... 57-60
Burton, Orville Vernon 1947- ... 126
Burton, Philip 1904- ... 25-28R
Burton, Richard 1925-1984 Obituary ... 113
Burton, Richard F. 1821-1890 ... DLB-55
Burton, Robert (Wellesley) 1941- ... CANR-17
Earlier sketches in CA 45-48, CANR-1
See also SATA 22
Burton, Robert E(dward) 1927- ... CANR-13
Earlier sketch in CA 61-64
Burton, Robert H(enderson) 1934- ... 37-40R
Burton, Roger V(ernon) 1928- ... 45-48
Burton, S(amuel) H(olroyd) 1919- ... 102
Burton, Thomas
See Longstreet, Stephen
Burton, Thomas G(lenn) 1935- ... 105
Burton, Virginia Lee 1909-1968 ... CAP-1
Obituary ... 25-28R
Earlier sketch in CA 13-14
See also SATA 2
See also DLB 22
See also CLR 11
Burton, William Evans 1804-1860 ... DLB-73
Burton, William H(enry) 1890-1964 ... CANR-1
Earlier sketch in CA 3R
See also SATA 11
Burton, William L(ester) 1928- ... 21-22R
Burton-Bradley, Burton Gyrth 1914- ... 77-80
Burtschi, Mary 1911- ... CANR-19
Earlier sketches in CA 11-12R, CANR-5
Burtt, E(dwin) A. 1892- ... 7-8R
Burtt, Everett Johnson, Jr. 1914- ... 11-12R
Burtt, George 1914- ... CANR-11
Earlier sketch in CA 61-64
Burtt, Harold E(rnest) 1890- ... CAP-2
Earlier sketch in CA 17-18
Burwash, Peter 1945- ... 119
Bury, Frank
See Harris, Herbert
Bury, J(ohn) P(atrick) T(uer) 1908- ... 19-20R
Buryn, Ed(ward Casimir) 1934- ... 85-88
Busbee, Shirlee (Elaine) 1941- ... 77-80
Busby, Edith (A. Lake) ?-1964 Obituary ... 109
See also SATA 29
Busby, F. M. 1921- ... CANR-24
Earlier sketches in CA 65-68, CANR-9
Busby, John 1928- ... 116
Busby, Jonathan
See Allen, Eric
Busby, Mabel Janice
See Stanford, Sally
Busby, Roger (Charles) 1941- ... 105
Buscaglia, Felice Leonardo 1924- ... 112
Brief entry ... 110
Buscaglia, Leo F.
See Buscaglia, Felice Leonardo
Busch, Briton Cooper 1936- ... CANR-8
Earlier sketch in CA 23-24R
Busch, Francis X(avier) 1879-1975 ... CAP-1
Obituary ... 61-64
Earlier sketch in CA 13-14
Busch, Frederick 1941- ... 33-36R
See also CAAS 1
See also DLB 6
See also CLC 7, 10, 18, 47
Busch, Hans (Peter) 1914- ... 109
Busch, Julia 1940- ... 57-60
Busch, Niven 1903- ... CANR-7
Earlier sketch in CA 13-14R
See also DLB 44
Busch, Noel F(airchild) 1906-1985 ... 49-52
Obituary ... 117
Busch, Phyllis S. 1909- ... 107
See also SATA 30
Busch, Ronald 1928-1987 Obituary ... 123
Buschkuehl, Matthias 1953- ... 121
Buschkuhl, Matthias
See Buschkuehl, Matthias
Buse, R. F.
See Buse, Renee
Buse, Renee 1914(?)-1979 Obituary ... 85-88
Buse, Rueben C. 1932- ... 109
Busey, James L. 1916- ... 5-6R
Bush, Alan (Dudley) 1900- ... 110
Bush, Barbara Holstein 1935- ... CANR-12
Earlier sketch in CA 69-72
Bush, Barry (Michael) 1938- ... 110
Bush, Charlie Christmas 1888(?)-1973 ... 107
Obituary ... 104
Bush, Christopher
See Bush, Charlie Christmas
Bush, Clifford L(ewis) 1915- ... 33-36R
Bush, Donald J(ohn) ... 114
Bush, (John Nash) Douglas 1896-1983 ... 37-40R
Obituary ... 109
Bush, Eric Wheler 1899-1985 ... 65-68
Obituary ... 117
Bush, Frederic W(illiam) 1929- ... 125
Bush, George Edward, Jr. 1938- ... 109
Bush, George P(ollock) 1892- ... 19-20R
Bush, George S(idney) 1925- ... 110
Bush, Grace A(bhau) 1936- ... 104
Bush, Jim 1926- ... 57-60
Bush, John W(illiam) 1917-1976 ... CAP-2
Earlier sketch in CA 33-36
Bush, L(uther) Russ(ell III) 1944- ... 121
Bush, Larry
See Bush, Lawrence Dana
Bush, Lawrence Dana 1951- ... 109
Bush, Lewis William 1907- ... 81-84
Bush, Martin H(arry) 1930- ... CANR-12
Earlier sketch in CA 29-32R
Bush, Patricia (Jahns) 1932- ... CANR-24
Earlier sketch in CA 105
Bush, Richard C(larence) 1923-
Brief entry ... 114
Bush, Robert (Burton) 1917- ... 116
Bush, Robert (Ray) 1920-1972
Obituary ... 33-36R
Bush, Ronald ... CLC-34
Bush, Sargent, Jr. 1937- ... 65-68
Bush, Ted J. 1922- ... 19-20R
Bush, Vannevar 1890-1974 ... 97-100
Obituary ... 53-56
Bush, William (Shirley, Jr.) 1929- ... CANR-14
Earlier sketch in CA 37-40R
Busha, Charles Henry 1931- ... CANR-5
Earlier sketch in CA 53-56
Bush-Brown, James 1892-1985 ... 7-8R
Obituary ... 118
Bush-Brown, Louise 1896(?)-1973
Obituary ... 49-52
Bushell, Don(ald Gair), Jr. 1934-
Brief entry ... 113
Bushell, Raymond 1910- ... CANR-20
Earlier sketches in CA 15-16R, CANR-5
Bushey, Jerry 1941- ... CANR-25
Earlier sketch in CA 108
Bushinsky, Jay (Joseph Mason) 1932- ... 77-80
Bushman, Claudia L(auper) 1934- ... CANR-22
Earlier sketch in CA 106
Bushman, Richard L(yman) 1931- ... CANR-22
Earlier sketch in CA 21-22R
Bushmiller, Ernest Paul 1905-1982 ... 29-32R
Obituary ... 107
See also AITN 1
Bushmiller, Ernie
See Bushmiller, Ernest Paul
See also SATA 31
Bushnell, David S(herman) 1927- ... 41-44R
Bushrui, S(uheil) B(adi) 1929- ... 17-18R
Bushyager, Linda E(yster) 1947- ... 93-96
Busia, Kofi Abrefa 1913-1978 ... 69-72
Obituary ... 126
Buske, Morris Roger 1912- ... 13-14R
Buskin, Martin 1930-1976 Obituary ... 65-68
Buskirk, Richard H(obart) 1927- ... CANR-1
Earlier sketch in CA 1R
Busoni, Rafaello 1900-1962 Obituary ... 117
See also SATA 16
Buss, Arnold H. 1924- ... CANR-4
Earlier sketch in CA 1R
Buss, Claude Albert 1903- ... 109
Buss, Leo W. 1953- ... 121
Buss, Martin J(ohn) 1930- ... 33-36R
Bussard, Paul 1904-1983 Obituary ... 109
Bussche, Henri O(mer) A(ntoine) Van den
1920-1965 ... CANR-5
Earlier sketch in CA 7-8R
Busse, Thomas V(alentine) 1941-1986 ... 77-80
Obituary ... 119
Bussell, Harold L. 1941- ... 125
Bussey, Ellen M(arion) 1926- ... CANR-2
Earlier sketch in CA 49-52
Bussieres, Simone 1918- ... 53-56
Bustad, Leo Kenneth 1920- ... 106
Bustamante, A(gustin) Jorge 1938- ... 33-36R
Bustanoby, Andre S(teven) 1930- ... 101
Bustard, Robert 1938- ... 65-68
Busteed, Marilyn 1937- ... 61-64
Bustos, F(rancisco)
See Borges, Jorge Luis
Bustos Domecq, H(onorio)
See Bioy Casares, Adolfo
and Borges, Jorge Luis
Buswell, J(ames) Oliver, Jr. 1895- ... 5-6R
Butcher, Fanny
See Bokum, Fanny Butcher
Butcher, Geoffrey (Arthur John) 1936- ... 111
Butcher, Grace 1934- ... 25-28R
Butcher, H(arold) J(ohn) 1920- ... 23-24R
Butcher, Harry Cecil 1901-1985 Obituary ... 115
Butcher, James Neal 1933- ... CANR-14
Earlier sketch in CA 33-36R
Butcher, (Anne) Judith 1927- ... 57-60
Butcher, (Charles) Philip 1918- ... CANR-4
Earlier sketch in CA 4R
Butcher, Russell Devereux 1938- ... CANR-8
Earlier sketch in CA 61-64
Butcher, Thomas Kennedy 1914- ... CAP-1
Earlier sketch in CA 11-12
Butchvarov, Panayot K. 1933- ... 33-36R
Butck, Zulie
See Jones, Thomas W(arren)
Butel, Jane
See de Calles, Jane F. Butel
Butera, Mary C. 1925- ... 21-22R
Buteux, Paul E. 1939- ... 121
Buth, Lenore 1932- ... 89-92
Buthelezi, Gatsha 1928- ... 102
Butland, Gilbert J(ames) 1910- ... 21-22R
Butler, Albert 1923- ... CANR-5
Earlier sketch in CA 15-16R
Butler, Annie L(ouise) 1920- ... 33-36R
Butler, Arthur D. 1923- ... 4R
Butler, B. C.
See Butler, Basil Christopher
Butler, Basil Christopher 1902-1986 ... CANR-2
Obituary ... 120
Earlier sketch in CA 1R
Butler, Beverly Kathleen 1932- ... CANR-4
Earlier sketch in CA 2R
See also SATA 7
Butler, Bill
See Butler, Ernest Alton
and Butler, William Huxford
Butler, Bishop B. C.
See Butler, Basil Christopher
Butler, Charles Henry 1894-19(?) ... CAP-2
Earlier sketch in CA 23-24
Butler, Christina Violet 1884-1982
Obituary ... 106
Butler, Christopher
See Butler, Basil Christopher
Butler, Colin Gasking 1913- ... 109
Butler, David Edgeworth 1924- ... CANR-13
Earlier sketch in CA 7-8R
Butler, David Francis 1928- ... 41-44R
Butler, David Jonathon 1946- ... 69-72
Butler, E(dward) H(arry) 1913- ... 13-14R
Butler, Edgar W(ilbur) 1929- ... 77-80
Butler, Erica Bracher 1905- ... CAP-2
Earlier sketch in CA 17-18
Butler, Ernest Alton 1926- ... 33-36R
Butler, Francelia McWilliams 1913- ... CANR-3
Earlier sketch in CA 11-12R
Butler, G(eorge) Paul 1900- ... CAP-2
Earlier sketch in CA 17-18
Butler, George D. 1893- ... 19-20R
Butler, George Tyssen 1943- ... 103
Butler, Grace Kipp Pratt
See Pratt-Butler, Grace Kipp
Butler, (Frederick) Guy 1918- ... CANR-18
Earlier sketch in CA 101
Butler, Gwendoline Williams 1922- ... CANR-6
Earlier sketch in CA 11-12R
Butler, Hal 1913- ... 57-60
Butler, Iris 1905- ... 21-22R
Butler, Ivan
See Beuttler, Edward Ivan Oakley
Butler, J. Donald 1908- ... 1R
Butler, Jack 1944- ... 114
Butler, James 1904- ... CAP-1
Earlier sketch in CA 11-12
Butler, James H(armon) 1908- ... 41-44R
Butler, James R(amsay) M(ontagu)
1889-1975 ... CAP-1
Earlier sketch in CA 13-14
Butler, Jean Campbell (MacLaurin)
1918- ... 11-12R
Butler, Jean Rouverol 1916- ... 97-100
Butler, Jeffrey (Ernest) 1922- ... 65-68
Butler, Jerry P. 1944- ... 65-68
Butler, Joan
See Alexander, Robert William
Butler, John Alfred Valentine
1899-1977 ... CANR-5
Obituary ... 106
Earlier sketch in CA 5-6R
Butler, Joseph Thomas 1932- ... 15-16R
Butler, Joyce 1933- ... CANR-25
Earlier sketches in CA 65-68, CANR-9
Butler, Juan 1942-1981 ... DLB-53
Butler, Lionel Harry 1923-1981 ... 110
Obituary ... 105
Butler, Lucius (Albert, Jr.) 1928- ... 69-72
Butler, Margaret Gwendoline ... 104
Butler, Marilyn (Speers) 1937- ... 102
Butler, Mildred Allen 1897- ... CAP-2
Earlier sketch in CA 29-32
Butler, Natalie Sturges 1908- ... 53-56
Butler, Nathan
See Sohl, Jerry
Butler, Octavia E(stelle) 1947- ... CANR-24
Earlier sketches in CA 73-76, CANR-12
See also BW
See also DLB 33
See also CLC 38
Butler, Pat(rick) (Trevor) 1929- ... 7-8R
Butler, Rab
See Butler, Richard Austen
Butler, Richard 1925- ... CANR-8
Earlier sketch in CA 57-60
Butler, Richard
See Allbeury, Theodore Edward le
Bouthillier
Butler, Richard Austen 1902-1982
Obituary ... 106
Butler, Rick 1946- ... 97-100
Butler, Robert Albert 1934- ... CANR-11
Earlier sketch in CA 61-64
Butler, Robert Lee 1918- ... 57-60
Butler, Robert N(eil) 1927- ... 41-44R
Butler, Robert Olen (Jr.) 1945- ... 112
Butler, Rohan D'Olier 1917- ... 109
Butler, Ron(ald William) 1934- ... 69-72
Butler, Samuel 1835-1902 Brief entry ... 104
See also DLB 18, 57
See also TCLC 1
Butler, Sandra (Ada) 1938- ... 105
Butler, Stanley 1914- ... 57-60
Butler, Stefan Congrat
See Congrat-Butler, Stefan
Butler, Stuart Thomas 1926- ... 107
Butler, Suzanne
See Perreard, Suzanne Louise Butler
Butler, Ted
See Schweitzer, Darrell
Butler, Walter C.
See Faust, Frederick (Shiller)
Butler, Walter E(rnest) 1898- ... CANR-5
Earlier sketch in CA 7-8R
Butler, William 1929- ... 107
Butler, William E(lliott II) 1939- ... CANR-11
Earlier sketch in CA 25-28R
Butler, William F(rank) 1917-1972
Obituary ... 113
Butler, William Huxford 1934- ... 57-60
Butlin, Martin (Richard Fletcher)
1929- ... CANR-19
Earlier sketches in CA 7-8R, CANR-2
Butor, Michel (Marie Francois) 1926- ... 9-10R
See also CLC 1, 3, 8, 11, 15
Butow, Robert J. C. 1924- ... 13-14R
Butrym, Zofia Teresa 1927- ... 103
Butscher, Edward 1943- ... 97-100
Butt, (Howard) Edward, Jr. 1927- ... 57-60
Butt, (Dorcas) Susan 1938- ... 89-92
Buttaci, Sal(vatore) St. John 1941- ... CANR-9
Earlier sketch in CA 65-68
Buttel, Robert (William) 1923- ... 102
Buttenwieser, Paul (Arthur) 1938- ... 104
Butter, Peter (Herbert) 1921- ... 7-8R
Butterfield, Fox 1939- ... 119
Butterfield, Herbert 1900- ... 2R
Butterfield, Lyman H(enry) 1909-1982
Obituary ... 106
Butterfield, Roger (Place) 1907-1981 ... CAP-1
Obituary ... 103
Earlier sketch in CA 9-10
Butterfield, Stephen T(homas) 1942- ... 57-60
Butterick, George F. 1942-1988 ... CANR-11
Obituary ... 126
Earlier sketch in CA 69-72
Butters, Dorothy Gilman 1923- ... CANR-2
Earlier sketch in CA 4R
See also SATA 5
Butterworth, Douglas Stanley 1930- ... 108
Butterworth, Emma Macalik 1928- ... 105
See also SATA 43
Butterworth, F(rank) Edward (Jr.) 1917- ... 29-32R
Butterworth, Hezekiah 1839-1905 ... DLB-42
Butterworth, Lionel Milner Angus
See Angus-Butterworth, Lionel Milner
Butterworth, Michael 1924-1986 ... CANR-10
Obituary ... 121
Earlier sketch in CA 25-28R
Butterworth, Neil 1934- ... 125
Butterworth, Oliver 1915- ... 4R
See also SATA 1
Butterworth, W(illiam) E(dmund III)
1929- ... CANR-18
Earlier sketches in CA 2R, CANR-2
See also SATA 5
Butti, Ken(neth Michael) 1950- ... 104
Buttigieg, Anton 1912-1983 Obituary ... 109
Buttimer, Anne 1938- ... 37-40R
Buttinger, Joseph 1906- ... 21-22R
Buttinger, Muriel Gardiner 1901-1985 ... 77-80
Obituary ... 115
Buttitta, Anthony 1907- ... 81-84
Buttitta, Tony
See Buttitta, Anthony
Buttlar, Lois J(acqueline) 1934- ... 112
Buttle, Myra
See Purcell, Victor
Button, Daniel E(van) 1917- ... 89-92
Button, Dick 1929- ... 11-12R
Button, James W(ickham) 1942- ... 81-84
Button, Kenneth John 1948- ... CANR-20
Earlier sketch in CA 103
Button, (Henry) Warren 1922- ... 97-100
Buttress, Frederick Arthur 1908- ... 33-36R
Buttrey, Douglas N(orton) ... CANR-18
Earlier sketch in CA 101
Buttrick, George Arthur 1892-1980 ... 61-64
Obituary ... 93-96
Butts, David P. 1932- ... 11-12R
Butts, Jane Roberts 1929-1984 ... CANR-15
Earlier sketch in CA 41-44R
Butts, Porter (Freeman) 1903- ... 41-44R
Butts, R. Freeman 1910- ... 15-16R
Butwell, Richard 1929- ... CANR-1
Earlier sketch in CA 45-48
Butzer, Karl W(ilhelm) 1934- ... CANR-8
Earlier sketch in CA 23-24R
Buultjens, (Edward) Ralph 1936- ... CANR-4
Earlier sketch in CA 53-56
Buxbaum, Edith 1902- ... CAP-2
Earlier sketch in CA 25-28
Buxbaum, Martin 1912- ... 17-18R
Buxbaum, Melvin H. 1934- ... 53-56
Buxbaum, Robert C(ourtney) 1930- ... 97-100
Buxton, Anne (Arundel) Brief entry ... 115
Buxton, Anthony 1892(?)-1970 Obituary ... 104
Buxton, (Evelyn June) Bonnie 1940- ... 69-72
Buxton, Charles R(oberts) 1913- ... 65-68
Buxton, Claude E(lmo) 1912- Brief entry ... 114
Buxton, David Roden 1910- ... 104
Buxton, Edward F(ulton) 1917- ... 41-44R
Buxton, Harold J(ocelyn) 1880-1976
Obituary ... 104
Buxton, (Edward) John (Mawby) 1912- ... CANR-5
Earlier sketch in CA 9-10R
Buxton, Thomas H(amilton) 1940- ... 57-60
Buys, Donna 1944- ... 102
Buzan, Barry 1946- ... 119
Buzo, Alexander (John) 1944- ... CANR-17
Earlier sketch in CA 97-100
Buzzard, John Huxley 1912-1984 Obituary ... 112
Buzzati, Dino 1906-1972 Obituary ... 33-36R
See also CLC 36
Buzzell, Robert (Dow) 1933- ... 104
Buzzle, Buck
See Rubin, Charles J.
Buzzotta, V. R(alph) 1931- ... 37-40R
Byars, Betsy (Cromer) 1928- ... CANR-18
Earlier sketch in CA 33-36R
See also SATA 4, 46
See also SAAS 1
See also DLB 52
See also CLC 35
See also CLR 1, 16

Byatt, A(ntonia) S(usan Drabble)
  1936- CANR-13
  Earlier sketch in CA 13-14R
  See also DLB 14
  See also CLC 19
Bychowski, Gustav 1895-1972 Obituary ..33-36R
Byck, Robert 1933- 109
Bye, Beryl (Joyce Rayment) 1926- CANR-11
  Earlier sketch in CA 61-64
Bye, Ranulph (deBayeux) 1916- 53-56
Bye, Raymond T(aylor) 1892- 7-8R
Byerly, Henry Clement 1935- 53-56
Byerly, Kenneth R(hodes) 1908- 2R
Byers, David (Milner) 1941- 53-56
Byers, Edward A(dams) 1939- 119
Byers, Edward E. 1921- CANR-3
  Earlier sketch in CA 4R
Byers, (Amy) Irene 1906- CANR-3
  Earlier sketch in CA 11-12R
Byers, R(ichard) McCulloch 1913- 69-72
Byfield, Barbara Ninde 1930- CANR-4
  Earlier sketch in CA 4R
  See also SATA 8
Byham, William C(larence) 1936- CANR-17
  Earlier sketch in CA 25-28R
Bykau, Vasilii Uladzimiravich
  See Bykov, Vasily Vladimirovich
Bykov, Vasily Vladimirovich 1924- 102
Byles, Mather 1707-1788 ....DLB-24
Bylinsky, Gene ,Michael) 1930- 77-80
Bynagle, Hans E(dward) 1946- 120
Byng, Douglas 1893-1987 Obituary 123
Bynner, Witter 1881-1968 ....CANR-4
  Obituary 25-28R
  Earlier sketch in CA 3R
  See also DLB 54
Bynum, David E(liab) 1936- CANR-20
  Earlier sketch in CA 37-40R
Bynum, Terrell Ward 1941- CANR-18
  Earlier sketch in CA 101
Byock, Jesse L(ewis) 1945- 110
Byrd, Bobby
  See Byrd, Robert James
Byrd, C. L.
  See Rosenkrantz, Linda
Byrd, Cecil Kash 1913- 19-20R
Byrd, Eldon A(rthur) 1939- 45-48
Byrd, Elizabeth 1912- CANR-5
  Earlier sketch in CA 5-6R
  See also SATA 34
Byrd, Emmett
  See Hinden, Michael C(harles)
Byrd, John Crowe
  See Hinden, Michael C(harles)
Byrd, Martha 1930- 29-32R
Byrd, Richard E(dward) 1931- CANR-7
  Earlier sketch in CA 57-60
Byrd, Robert (John) 1942- SATA-33
Byrd, Robert James 1942- 65-68
Byrd, William II 1674-1744 ....DLB-24
Byrne, Charles Raymond 1916-1983
  Obituary 111
Byrne, David 1953(?)- CLC-26
Byrne, Donald E(dward), Jr. 1942- 73-76
Byrne, Donn (Erwin) 1931- CANR-20
  Earlier sketches in CA 11-12R, CANR-5
Byrne, Edmund F(rancis) 1933- 29-32R
Byrne, Edward M. 1935- 29-32R
Byrne, Frank L(oyola) 1928- 23-24R
Byrne, Gary C. 1942- 49-52
Byrne, Herbert Winston 1917- 4R
Byrne, James E. 1945- 81-84
Byrne, John 1940- 104
Byrne, John Keyes 1926- 102
  See also CLC 19
Byrne, Muriel St. Clare 1895-1983 ....CAP-1
  Obituary 111
  Earlier sketch in CA 17-18
Byrne, Peter 1925- 65-68
Byrne, Ralph
  See Burns, Ralph J.
Byrne, Richard Hill 1915- 21-22R
Byrne, Robert (Eugene) 1928- Brief entry ... 110
Byrne, Robert 1930- CANR-13
  Earlier sketch in CA 73-76
Byrne, Stuart J(ames) 1913- 102
Byrnes, Edward T(homas) 1929- 53-56
Byrnes, Eugene F. 1890(?)-1974
  Obituary 49-52
Byrnes, Garrett D(avis) 1904(?)-1985
  Obituary 118
Byrnes, James Francis 1879-1972
  Obituary 112
Byrnes, Joseph Francis 1939- 114
Byrnes, Robert F. 1917- CANR-10
  Earlier sketch in CA 25-28R
Byrnes, Thomas Edmund 1911- 15-16R
Byrom, James
  See Bramwell, James Guy
Byrom, (Robert) Michael 1925- 7-8R
Byron, Carl R(oscoe) 1948- 97-100
Byron, Christopher M. 1944- 77-80
Byron, Gilbert 1903- 17-18R
Byron, John
  See Armstrong, John Byron
Byron, William J(ames) 1927- 81-84
Bytwerk, Randall Lee 1950- 109
Bywater, William G(len), Jr. 1940- 61-64

C

C.3.3.
  See Wilde, Oscar (Fingal O'Flahertie
    Wills)

C. E. M.
  See Mastrangelo, Charles E.
Caballero, Ann Mallory 1928- 19-20R
Cabanis, Jose 1922- Brief entry 111
Cabaniss, J(ames) Allen 1911- 1R
  See also SATA 5
Cabarga, Leslie 1954- CANR-13
  Earlier sketch in CA 77-80
Cabassa, Victoria 1912- 49-52
Cabbell, Edward J. 1946- 121
Cabbell, Paul 1942- 53-56
Cabeen, David Clark 1886-19(?) CAP-1
  Earlier sketch in CA 13-14
Cabell, James Branch 1879-1958
  Brief entry 105
  See also DLB 9
  See also TCLC 6
Cabibi, John F(rank) J(oseph) 1912- 53-56
Cable, George Washington 1844-1925
  Brief entry 104
  See also DLB 12, 74
  See also TCLC 4
Cable, James (Eric) 1920- CANR-15
  Earlier sketch in CA 85-88
Cable, John L(aurence) 1934- CANR-21
  Earlier sketch in CA 69-72
Cable, Mary 1920- CANR-11
  Earlier sketch in CA 25-28R
  See also SATA 9
Cable, Thomas Monroe 1942- Brief entry ... 106
Cabot, Blake 1905(?)-1974 Obituary 53-56
Cabot, John Moors 1901-1981 Obituary 103
Cabot, Robert (Moors) 1924- 29-32R
Cabot, Thomas Dudley 1897- 93-96
Cabot, Tracy 1941- 81-84
Cabral, Alberto
  See White, Richard Alan
Cabral, Amilcar 1921-1973 Obituary 111
Cabral, O. M.
  See Cabral, Olga
Cabral, Olga 1909- CANR-10
  Earlier sketch in CA 25-28R
  See also SATA 46
Cabrera, James C. 1935- 109
Cabrera Infante, G(uillermo) 1929- 85-88
  See also CLC 5, 25, 45
Caccia-Dominioni, Paolo 1896- 21-22R
Cacciatore, Vera (Signorelli) 1911- CANR-5
  Earlier sketch in CA 7-8R
Cachia, Pierre J. E. 1921- CANR-11
  Earlier sketch in CA 25-28R
Cacoyannis, Michael 1922- 101
Cadbury, Henry J(oel) 1883-1974 ....CAP-1
  Obituary 53-56
  Earlier sketch in CA 15-16
Cadbury, Paul Strangman 1895-1984
  Obituary 114
Cadden, Joseph E. 1911(?)-1980
  Obituary 101
Caddick, Arthur 1911-1987 Obituary 122
Caddy, Alice
  See Burman, Alice Caddy
Cade, Alexander
  See Methold, Kenneth (Walter)
Cade, Toni
  See Bambara, Toni Cade
Cadell, (Violet) Elizabeth 1903- CANR-11
  Earlier sketch in CA 57-60
Cadenhead, Ivie E(dward), Jr. 1923- 41-44R
Cadet, John 1935- 77-80
Cadieux, Charles L. 1919- 57-60
Cadieux, (Joseph Arthur) Lorenzo
  1903-1976 49-52
  Obituary 103
Cadieux, (Joseph David Romeo) Marcel
  1915-1981 Obituary 108
Cadle, Dean 1920- 25-28R
Cadmus
  See Buchan, John
Cadogan, Alexander (George Montagu)
  1884-1968 Obituary 106
Cadogan, Mary (Rose) 1928- 106
Cadwallader, Clyde T(homas) 5-6R
Cadwallader, Sharon 1936- CANR-17
  Earlier sketches in CA 49-52, CANR-1
  See also SATA 7
Cady, Arthur 1920-1983 Obituary 109
Cady, Edwin Harrison 1917- CANR-4
  Earlier sketch in CA 2R
Cady, Ernest (Albert) 1899-1985 Obituary .. 117
Cady, (Walter) Harrison 1877(?)-1970
  Obituary 116
  See also SATA 19
Cady, Jack A(ndrew) 1932- CANR-9
  Earlier sketch in CA 65-68
Cady, John Frank 1901- CANR-4
  Earlier sketch in CA 1R
Cady, Steve (Noel) 1927- 45-48
Caedmon, Father
  See Wahl, Thomas (Peter)
Caefer, Raymond J(ohn) 1926- 17-18R
Caeiro, Alberto
  See Pessoa, Fernando (Antonio Nogueira)
Caemmerer, Richard R(udolph) 1904- CANR-5
  Earlier sketch in CA 1R
Caen, Herb (Eugene) 1916- CANR-1
  Earlier sketch in CA 1R
  See also AITN 1
Caesar, (Eu)Gene (Lee) 1927- CANR-1
  Earlier sketch in CA 3R
Cafferty, Bernard 1934- 41-44R
Cafferty, Pastora San Juan 1940- 114
Caffey, David L(uther) 1947- 45-48
Caffrey, John G(ordon) 1922- 17-18R
Caffrey, Kate CANR-1
  Earlier sketch in CA 49-52
Cagan, Phillip D(avid) 1927- 17-18R

Cage, John (Milton, Jr.) 1912- CANR-9
  Earlier sketch in CA 13-14R
  See also CLC 41
Caggiano, Philip 1949- 114
Cagle, Malcolm W(infield) 1918- 108
  See also SATA 32
Cagle, William R(ea) 1933- 65-68
Cagney, James (Francis, Jr.)
  1899(?)-1986 Obituary 118
  Brief entry 115
Cagney, Peter
  See Winter, Bevis (Peter)
Cahalan, (John) Don(ald) 1912- 102
Cahalane, Victor H(arrison) 1901- CAP-2
  Earlier sketch in CA 23-24
Cahan, Abraham 1860-1951 Brief entry 108
  See also DLB 9, 25, 28
Cahen, Alfred B. 1932- 17-18R
Cahill, Audrey Fawcett 1929- 23-24R
Cahill, Daniel J(oseph) 1929- 69-72
Cahill, Fred V(irgil), Jr. 1916-1984
  Obituary 112
Cahill, Gilbert A. 1912- Brief entry 107
Cahill, James F(rancis) 1926- CANR-6
  Earlier sketch in CA 1R
Cahill, Jane (Miller) 1901- CAP-2
  Earlier sketch in CA 23-24
Cahill, Kevin Michael 1936- CANR-18
  Earlier sketch in CA 102
Cahill, Rick 1950- 126
Cahill, Robert S. 1933- 15-16R
Cahill, Susan Neunzig 1940- 37-40R
Cahill, Thomas (Quinn) 1940- 49-52
Cahill, Tom
  See Cahill, Thomas (Quinn)
Cahn, Edgar S. 1935- 29-32R
Cahn, Rhoda 1922- 81-84
  See also SATA 37
Cahn, Robert 1917- 108
Cahn, Sammy 1913- 85-88
Cahn, Steven M. 1942- CANR-13
  Earlier sketch in CA 21-22R
Cahn, William 1912-1976 ....23-24R
  Obituary 69-72
  See also SATA 37
Cahn, Zvi 1896- CAP-2
  Earlier sketch in CA 23-24
Cahnman, Werner J(acob) 1902- 49-52
Caiden, Gerald E(lliot) 1936- CANR-14
  Earlier sketch in CA 29-32R
Caidin, Martin 1927- CANR-2
  Earlier sketch in CA 2R
  See also AITN 2
Caiger-Smith, Alan 1930- 13-14R
Caillois, Roger 1913-1978 ....CANR-13
  Obituary 85-88
  Earlier sketch in CA 25-28R
Caillou, Alan
  See Lyle-Smythe, Alan
Cain, Arthur H(omer) 1913- CANR-4
  Earlier sketch in CA 4R
  See also SATA 3
Cain, Bob
  See Cain, Robert Owen
Cain, Bruce E. 1948- 122
Cain, George 1943- DLB-33
Cain, Glen G. 1933- 21-22R
Cain, Guillermo
  See Cabrera Infante, G(uillermo)
Cain, Jackson
  See Gleason, Robert
Cain, James M(allahan) 1892-1977 ....CANR-8
  Obituary 73-76
  Earlier sketch in CA 17-18R
  See also CLC 3, 11, 28
  See also AITN 1
Cain, Mary (Dawson) 1904-1984 Obituary .. 112
Cain, Maureen 1938- 73-76
Cain, Michael Peter 1941- 93-96
Cain, Robert Owen 1934- 65-68
Cain, T. G. S. 1944- 124
Cain, Thomas H(enry) 1931- 93-96
Caine, (Thomas Henry) Hall 1853(?)-1931
  Brief entry 122
Caine, Jeffrey (Andrew) 1944- 85-88
Caine, Lynn 1924(?)-1987 Obituary 124
Caine, Mark
  See Raphael, Frederic (Michael)
Caine, Mitchell
  See Sparkia, Roy (Bernard)
Caine, Stanley P(aul) 1940- 41-44R
Caine, Sydney 1902- CAP-2
  Earlier sketch in CA 25-28
Caines, Jeannette (Franklin) SATA-43
Caird, George Bradford 1917-1984 61-64
  Obituary 112
Caird, Janet 1913- CANR-2
  Earlier sketch in CA 49-52
Cairncross, Alec
  See Cairncross, Alexander Kirkland
Cairncross, Alexander Kirkland 1911- ... CANR-8
  Earlier sketch in CA 61-64
Cairncross, Frances (Anne) 1944- 57-60
Cairney, John 1930- 105
Cairns, David 1904- CANR-11
  Earlier sketch in CA 61-64
Cairns, (Thomas) Dorian 1901-1972
  Obituary 37-40R
Cairns, Earle E(dwin) 1910- CANR-18
  Earlier sketch in CA 1R
Cairns, Grace Edith 1907- CANR-18
  Earlier sketch in CA 1R
Cairns, Huntington 1904-1985 ....CANR-5
  Obituary 114
  Earlier sketch in CA 53-56
Cairns, J(ames) F(ord) 1914- 105

Cairns, John C(ampbell) 1924- CANR-5
  Earlier sketch in CA 13-14R
Cairns, Thomas W(illiam) 1931- 23-24R
Cairns, Trevor 1922- 33-36R
  See also SATA 14
Cairns-Smith, A(lexander) G(raham) 1931- .. 123
Cairo, Jon
  See Romano, Deane Louis
Caitlin, Elise 1953- 111
Cake, Patrick
  See Welch, Timothy L.
Calabrese, Alphonse F. X. 1923- 69-72
Calabrese, Anthony 1938- 89-92
Calabresi, Guido 1932- CANR-20
  Earlier sketch in CA 41-44R
Calaferte, Louis 1928- CANR-17
  Earlier sketches in CA 45-48, CANR-1
Calais, Jean
  See Rodefer, Stephen
Calamandrei, Mauro 1925- 69-72
Calamari, John D(aniel) 1921- 37-40R
Calasibetta, Charlotte M(ankey) 1917- 103
Calde, Mark A(ugustine) 1945- 69-72
Caldecott, Moyra 1927- CANR-13
  Earlier sketch in CA 77-80
  See also SATA 22
Caldecott, Randolph (J.) 1846-1886 .... SATA-17
  See also CLR 14
Calder, Alexander 1898-1976 Obituary 111
Calder, Angus 1942- 29-32R
Calder, C(larence) R(oy), Jr. 1928- 81-84
Calder, Daniel Gillmore 1939- 103
Calder, Jason
  See Dunmore, John
Calder, Jenni 1941- CANR-1
  Earlier sketch in CA 45-48
Calder, Kent E(yring) 1948- 107
Calder, Lyn
  See Calmenson, Stephanie
Calder, Nigel (David Ritchie) 1931- CANR-11
  Earlier sketch in CA 21-22R
Calder, Ritchie
  See Ritchie-Calder, Peter Ritchie
Calder, Robert
  See Mundis, Jerrold
Calder, Robert Lorin 1941- 65-68
Calder-Marshall, Arthur 1908- 61-64
Calderon, Jose Vasconcelos
  See Vasconcelos (Calderon), Jose
Calderone, Mary S(teichen) 1904- 104
  See also AITN 1
Calderwood, Ivan E. 1899- 57-60
Calderwood, James D(ixon) 1917- CANR-3
  Earlier sketch in CA 5-6R
Calderwood, James L(ee) 1930- 21-22R
Caldicott, Helen (Mary) 1938- 124
  Brief entry 114
Caldwell, Ben(jamin) 1937- 124
  Brief entry 117
  See also BW
  See also DLB 38
Caldwell, Bettye (McDonald) 1924- 104
Caldwell, C(harles) Edson 1906-1974 .... CAP-2
  Earlier sketch in CA 29-32
Caldwell, Dan (Edward) 1948- 112
Caldwell, Edward S(abiston) 1928- 65-68
Caldwell, Erskine (Preston) 1903-1987 .. CANR-2
  Obituary 121
  Earlier sketch in CA 2R
  See also CAAS 1
  See also DLB 9
  See also CLC 1, 8, 14, 50
  See also AITN 1
Caldwell, Gaylon L(oray) 1920- 33-36R
Caldwell, Harry B(oynton) 1935- 37-40R
Caldwell, Helen F. 1904- 77-80
Caldwell, Inga Gilson 1897- 61-64
Caldwell, Irene Catherine (Smith)
  1908-1979 ....9-10R
  Obituary 103
Caldwell, James
  See Lowry, Robert (James Collas)
Caldwell, John 1928- CANR-12
  Earlier sketch in CA 73-76
Caldwell, John C(ope) 1913- CANR-13
  Earlier sketch in CA 23-24R
  See also SATA 7
Caldwell, Joseph H(erman) 1934- 23-24R
Caldwell, Kathryn (Smoot) 1942- 69-72
Caldwell, Louis O(liver) 1935- 69-72
Caldwell, Lynton (Keith) 1913- CANR-12
  Earlier sketch in CA 29-32R
Caldwell, (James Alexander) Malcolm
  1931-1978 ....CANR-17
  Earlier sketch in CA 25-28R
Caldwell, Marge 1914- 97-100
Caldwell, Nat(han Green) 1912-1985
  Obituary 115
Caldwell, Oliver Johnson 1904- 37-40R
Caldwell, Robert G(ranville) 1882-1976
  Obituary 65-68
Caldwell, Robert Graham 1904- 19-20R
Caldwell, (Janet Miriam) Taylor (Holland)
  1900-1985 ....CANR-5
  Obituary 116
  Earlier sketch in CA 5-6R
  See also CLC 2, 28, 39
Caldwell, William A(nthony) 1906-1986
  Obituary 119
Calef, Wesley (Carr) 1914- 13-14R
Caley, Rod
  See Rowland, Donald S(ydney)
Calhoon, Richard P(ercival) 1909- 57-60
Calhoon, Robert M(cCluer) 1935- CANR-4
  Earlier sketch in CA 53-56
Calhoun, Calfrey C. 1928- 37-40R

Calhoun, Chad
See Goulart, Ron(ald Joseph)
Calhoun, Charles W(illiam) 1948- 125
Calhoun, Conyus 1946- 111
Calhoun, Daniel F(airchild) 1929- 65-68
Calhoun, Don Gilmore 1914- 85-88
Calhoun, Donald W(allace) 1917- 104
Calhoun, Eric
See Turner, Robert H(arry)
Calhoun, James Frank 1941- 109
Calhoun, John Caldwell 1782-1850 ...... DLB-3
Calhoun, Mary
See Wilkins, Mary Huiskamp
See also SATA 2
Calhoun, Richard James 1926- 33-36R
Calhoun, Robert L(owery) 1896-1983
Obituary 110
Calhoun, Thomas 1940- 89-92
Calia, Vincent F(rank) 1926- 53-56
Calian, Carnegie Samuel 1933- 25-28R
Caliban
See Reid, J(ohn) C(owie)
Califano, Joseph A(nthony), Jr. 1931- ... CANR-2
Earlier sketch in CA 45-48
Calin, William (Compaine) 1936- CANR-11
Earlier sketch in CA 21-22R
Calisch, Edith Lindeman 1898-1984
Obituary 114
Calisher, Hortense 1911- CANR-22
Earlier sketches in CA 4R, CANR-1
See also DLB 2
See also CLC 2, 4, 8, 38
Calistro, Paddy
See Calistro McAuley, Patricia Ann
Calistro McAuley, Patricia Ann 1948- 118
Calitri, Charles J(oseph) 1916- 5-6R
Calitri, Princine 33-36R
Calkin, Homer Leonard 1912- 41-44R
Calkin, Ruth Harms 1918- 102
Calkins, Fay
See Alailima, Fay C.
Calkins, Franklin
See Stratemeyer, Edward L.
Calkins, Lucy McCormick 125
Calkins, Rodello 1920- Brief entry 105
Call, Alice E(lizabeth) LaPlant 1914- 13-14R
Call, Hughie Florence 1890- 7-8R
See also SATA 1
Calladine, Andrew G(arfield) 1941- 102
Calladine, Carole E(lizabeth) 1942- 102
Callaghan, Barry 1937- 101
Callaghan, Catherine A. 1931- 33-36R
Callaghan, Mary Rose 1944- 118
Callaghan, Morley Edward 1903- 9-10R
See also DLB 68
See also CLC 3, 14, 41
Callaghan, Thomas 1924- 114
Callahan, Charles C(lifford) 1910- CAP-2
Earlier sketch in CA 17-18
Callahan, Claire Wallis 1890- 7-8R
Callahan, Daniel 1930- 21-22R
Callahan, Dorothy M(onahan) 1934- 114
See also SATA 35, 39
Callahan, John
See Gallun, Raymond Z(inke)
Callahan, John F(rancis) 1912- 33-36R
Callahan, Nelson J. 1927- 33-36R
Callahan, North 1908- CANR-2
Earlier sketch in CA 1R
Callahan, Philip Serna 1923- 102
See also SATA 25
Callahan, Raymond (Aloysius) 1938- 69-72
Callahan, Sidney Cornelia 1933- 17-18R
Callahan, Sterling G. 1916- 21-22R
Callahan, Steven (Patrick) 1952- 120
Callan, Edward T. 1917- 17-18R
Callan, Jamie 1954- 109
Callan, John P(atrick) 1939- 111
Callan, Richard J(erome) 1932- 53-56
Callard, Maurice (Frederick Thomas)
1912- CANR-3
Earlier sketch in CA 1R
Callard, Thomas Henry 1912- 9-10R
Callas, Theo
See McCarthy, Shaun (Lloyd)
Callaway, Bernice (Anne) 1923- 121
See also SATA 48
Callaway, Joseph A(tlee) 1920- 65-68
Callaway, Kathy 1943- 107
See also SATA 36
Callcott, George H(ardy) 1929- 29-32R
Callcott, Margaret Law 1929- 61-64
Callcott, Wilfrid H(ardy) 1895-1969
Obituary 112
Calle, Francisco Rosillo
See Rosillo-Calle, Francisco
Callen, Larry
See Callen, Lawrence Willard, Jr.
Callen, Lawrence Willard, Jr. 1927- CANR-12
Earlier sketch in CA 73-76
See also SATA 19
Callen, William B. 1930- 23-24R
Callenbach, Ernest 1929- CANR-21
Earlier sketches in CA 57-60, CANR-6
Callender, Charles 1928- 41-44R
Callender, Julian
See Lee, Austin
Callender, Wesley P(ayne), Jr. 1923- 17-18R
Calleo, David P(atrick) 1934- CANR-10
Earlier sketch in CA 17-18R
Callihan, E(lmer) L(ee) 1903- CAP-2
Earlier sketch in CA 25-28
Callinan, Bernard James 1913- 110
Callis, Helmut G(unther) 1906- CANR-5
Earlier sketch in CA 53-56
Callis, Robert 1920- 37-40R
Callison, Brian 1934- 29-32R
Callister, Frank 1916- 13-14R
Callmann, Rudolf 1892-1976 69-72
Obituary 65-68
Callow, Alexander B., Jr. 1925- 21-22R
Callow, James T(homas) 1928- 41-44R
Callow, Philip Kenneth 1924- CANR-21
Earlier sketches in CA 13-14R, CANR-6
Calloway, Cab(ell III) 1907- Brief entry 113
Calloway, Doris Howes 1923- 21-22R
Callum, Myles 1934- 9-10R
Callwood, June 1924- CANR-24
Earlier sketch in CA 101
Calman, Alvin R(ose) 1895-1983 Obituary .. 110
Calman, Mel 1931- 126
Calmann, John 1935-1980 ....21-22R
Obituary 97-100
Calmann-Levy, Robert 1899-1982
Obituary 108
Calmenson, Stephanie 1952- CANR-24
Earlier sketch in CA 107
See also SATA 37, 51
Calmer, Edgar 1907-1986 .... CANR-20
Obituary 118
Earlier sketch in CA 69-72
See also DLB 4
Calmer, Ned
See Calmer, Edgar
Calmus, Lawrence 1943- 111
Calnan, T(homas) D(aniel) 1915- 29-32R
Calne, Roy Yorke 1930- 61-64
Calonne, David Stephen 1953- 114
Caltagirone, Carmen L(illian) 1950- 114
Calter, Paul (William) 1934- CANR-14
Earlier sketch in CA 41-44R
Calverley, C. S. 1831-1884 .... DLB-35
Calvert, Elinor H.
See Lasell, Elinor H.
Calvert, George Henry 1803-1889 .... DLB-1, 64
Calvert, John
See Leaf, (Wilbur) Munro
Calvert, Laura D. 1922- 37-40R
Calvert, Mary 1941- 93-96
Calvert, Monte A(lan) 1938- 21-22R
Calvert, Patricia 1931- CANR-21
Earlier sketch in CA 105
See also SATA 45
Calvert, Peter (Anthony Richard)
1936- CANR-11
Earlier sketch in CA 25-28R
Calvert, Robert, Jr. 1922- 25-28R
Calvez, Jean-Yves 1927- 57-60
Calvin, Henry
See Hanley, Clifford
Calvin, Ross 1890(?)-1970 Obituary 104
Calvin, William H(oward) 1939- 123
Calvino, Italo 1923-1985 .... CANR-23
Obituary 116
Earlier sketch in CA 85-88
See also CLC 5, 8, 11, 22, 33, 39
Calvocoressi, Peter (John Ambrose)
1912- 65-68
Cam, Helen Maud 1885-1968 .... CAP-1
Earlier sketch in CA 13-14
Camara, Helder Pessoa 1909- 61-64
Camber, Andrew
See Bingley, David Ernest
Cambon, Glauco (Gianlorenzo)
1921-1988 .... CANR-7
Obituary 125
Earlier sketch in CA 19-20R
Camden, Archie 1888-1979 114
Cameja, Pedro
See Camejo, Peter (Miguel)
Camejo, Pedro
See Camejo, Peter (Miguel)
Camejo, Pedro M.
See Camejo, Peter (Miguel)
Camejo, Peter (Miguel) 1939- 125
Brief entry 105
Camerini, Mario 1895-1981 Obituary 103
Cameron, A(rchibald) J(ames) 1920- 73-76
Cameron, Alan (Douglas Edward)
1938- CANR-8
Earlier sketch in CA 61-64
Cameron, Allan Gillies 1930- 102
Cameron, Allan W(illiams) 1938- 33-36R
Cameron, Angus de Mille 1913- 102
Cameron, Angus Fraser 1941-1983 122
Obituary 109
Cameron, Ann 1943- 101
See also SATA 27
Cameron, Betsy 1949- 101
Cameron, (Jack) Bruce 1913-1979 .... 2R
Cameron, Constance Carpenter 1937- 49-52
Cameron, D. A.
See Cameron, Donald (Allan)
Cameron, D. Y.
See Cook, Dorothy Mary
Cameron, David R(obertson) 1941- 73-76
Cameron, Deborah 1958- 126
Cameron, Donald (Allan) 1937- CANR-8
Earlier sketch in CA 23-24R
Cameron, Donald
See Bryans, Robert Harbinson
Cameron, Edna M. 1905- CAP-1
Earlier sketch in CA 9-10
See also SATA 3
Cameron, Eleanor (Frances) 1912- CANR-22
Earlier sketches in CA 4R, CANR-2
See also SATA 1, 25
See also DLB 52
See also CLR 1
Cameron, Eleanor Cranston 118
Cameron, Eleanor Elford 1910- 77-80
Cameron, Elizabeth
See Nowell, Elizabeth Cameron
Cameron, Elizabeth Jane 1910-1976 .... CANR-1
Obituary 69-72
Earlier sketch in CA 3R
See also SATA 30, 32
Cameron, Elspeth 1943- 113
Cameron, Frank T. 1909- CAP-1
Earlier sketch in CA 19-20
Cameron, George Glenn 1905-1979
Obituary 89-92
Cameron, Harold W. 1905- 81-84
Cameron, Hope
See Morritt, Hope
Cameron, Ian
See Payne, Donald Gordon
Cameron, J(ames) M(unro) 1910- CANR-2
Earlier sketch in CA 7-8R
Cameron, (Mark) James (Walter)
1911-1985 ....23-24R
Obituary 114
Cameron, James R(eese) 1929- 33-36R
Cameron, John 1914- 29-32R
Cameron, Julie
See Cameron, Lou
Cameron, Kate
See Du Breuil, (Elizabeth) L(or)inda
Cameron, Kenneth 1922- 103
Cameron, Kenneth Neill 1908- CANR-3
Earlier sketch in CA 11-12R
Cameron, Kenneth Walter 1908- CANR-24
Earlier sketches in CA 21-22R, CANR-8
Cameron, Kim S(terling) 1946- 109
Cameron, Lorna
See Fraser, Anthea
Cameron, Lou 1924- CANR-21
Earlier sketches in CA 3R, CANR-4
Cameron, M(alcolm) G(ordon) Graham
See Graham-Cameron, M(alcolm)
G(ordon)
Cameron, M. Graham
See Graham-Cameron, M(alcolm)
G(ordon)
Cameron, Mary Owen 1915- 15-16R
Cameron, Meribeth E(lliott) 1905- 1R
Cameron, Mike Graham
See Graham-Cameron, M(alcolm)
G(ordon)
Cameron, Neil 1920-1985 Obituary 115
Cameron, Peter 1959- 125
See also CLC 44
Cameron, Polly 1928- 17-18R
See also SATA 2
Cameron, Roderick (William) 1913-1985
Obituary 117
Brief entry 113
Cameron, Rondo (Emmett) 1925- CANR-5
Earlier sketch in CA 1R
Cameron, Sharon 1947- 123
Cameron, Silver Donald
See Cameron, Donald (Allan)
Cameron, William Bruce 1920- 37-40R
Cameron, William J(ames) 1926-
Brief entry 116
Cameron Watt, Donald 1928- CANR-14
Earlier sketch in CA 77-80
Camilleri, Joseph A. 1944- 117
Caminada, Jerome (Charles) 1911-1985
Obituary 117
Camm, John 1718-1778 .... DLB-31
Cammack, Floyd M(cKee) 1933- CANR-6
Earlier sketch in CA 11-12R
Cammann, Schuyler (van Rensselaer)
1912- 9-10R
Cammarata, Jerry F(rank) 1947- 81-84
Cammer, Leonard 1913- 65-68
Camner, James 1950- 108
Camoin, Francois Andre 1939- 61-64
Camp, Candace P(auline) 1949- 102
Camp, Charles L. 1893-1975 Obituary 61-64
See also SATA 31
Camp, Dalton Kingsley 1920- 61-64
Camp, Fred V(alterma) 1911- 49-52
Camp, James 1923- 33-36R
Camp, John (Michael Francis) 1915- 93-96
Camp, Roderic (Ai) 1945- CANR-18
Earlier sketch in CA 102
Camp, T(homas) Edward 1929- 13-14R
Camp, Walter (Chauncey) 1859-1925 ... YABC-1
Camp, Wesley D(ouglass) 1915- 19-20R
Camp, William (Newton Alexander) 1926- ..61-64
Campa, Arthur L(eon) 1905- 73-76
Campaigne, Jameson Gilbert 1914-1985 ..... 2R
Obituary 114
Campana, Dino 1885-1932 Brief entry 117
See also TCLC 20
Campanella, Francis B. 1936- 53-56
Campanile, Archille 1900(?)-1977
Obituary 69-72
Campanile, Pasquale Festa
See Festa Campanile, Pasquale
Campbell, A. C.
See Campbell, Andrew C.
Campbell, Alan K. 1923- CANR-3
Earlier sketch in CA 5-6R
Campbell, Alexander 1912-1977 61-64
Obituary 69-72
Campbell, Alistair 1907-1974 .... CAP-1
Earlier sketch in CA 17-18
Campbell, Alla (Linda Renee) Bozarth
See Bozarth-Campbell, Alla (Linda Renee)
Campbell, (Elizabeth) Andrea 1963- SATA-50
Campbell, Andrew C. 1923- Brief entry 114
Campbell, (Albert) Angus 1910-1980
Obituary 105
Campbell, Angus
See Chetwynd-Hayes, R(onald Henry
Glynn)
Campbell, Ann R. 1925- 21-22R
See also SATA 11
Campbell, Archibald Bruce 1881- CAP-1
Earlier sketch in CA 15-16
Campbell, Arnold Everitt 1906-1980
Obituary 108
Campbell, Arthur A(ndrews) 1924- 1R
Campbell, Ballard Crooker, Jr. 1940- 104
Campbell, Beatrice Murphy
See Murphy, Beatrice M.
Campbell, Bernard G(rant) 1930- 23-24R
Campbell, Blanche 1902- 5-6R
Campbell, Bruce
See Epstein, Samuel
Campbell, Camilla 1905- CAP-2
Earlier sketch in CA 25-28
See also SATA 26
Campbell, Carlos Cardozo 1937- 102
Campbell, Charles Arthur 1897-1974
Obituary 49-52
Campbell, Charles S(outter) 1911- 69-72
Campbell, Clive
See MacRae, Donald G.
Campbell, Colin Dearborn 1917- 33-36R
Campbell, Cy(ril Calvin) 1925- 97-100
Campbell, D(onald)
See Gilford, C(harles) B(ernard)
Campbell, D(onald) Ross 1939- 117
Campbell, Dan H(ampton) 1907-1974
Obituary 112
Campbell, David (Watt Ian) 1915-1979 ...97-100
Campbell, David A(itken) 1927- CANR-11
Earlier sketch in CA 25-28R
Campbell, David (John) Graham
See Graham-Campbell, David (John)
Campbell, David P. 1934- 23-24R
Campbell, Dennis M(arion) 1945- 73-76
Campbell, Don(ald Guy) 1922- 19-20R
Campbell, Donald 1940- 69-72
Campbell, Duane E(ugene) 1941- 116
Campbell, E(lwood) G(ordon) 1923- 107
Campbell, E. Simms 1906-1971 Obituary ..93-96
Campbell, Edward D(unscomb) C(hristian),
Jr. 1946- CANR-26
Earlier sketch in CA 106
Campbell, Edward F(ay), Jr. 1932- 15-16R
Campbell, Elizabeth McClure 1891- 37-40R
Campbell, Enid (Mona) 1932- 109
Campbell, Ernest Q(ueener) 1926- 37-40R
Campbell, Eugene Edward 1915- 23-24R
Campbell, Ewing 1940- CANR-13
Earlier sketch in CA 73-76
Campbell, F(enton) Gregory, Jr. 1939- 69-72
Campbell, Francis Stuart
See Kuehnelt-Leddihn, Erik (Maria) Ritter
von
Campbell, G(aylon) S(anford) 1940- 107
Campbell, George F(rederick) 1915- CANR-14
Earlier sketch in CA 65-68
Campbell, Graeme 1931- 77-80
Campbell, Hannah 11-12R
Campbell, Herbert James 1925- 97-100
Campbell, Hope 1925- CANR-10
Earlier sketch in CA 61-64
See also SATA 20
Campbell, Howard E(rnest) 1925- CANR-7
Earlier sketch in CA 57-60
Campbell, Ian 1899-1978 53-56
Obituary 103
Campbell, Ian 1942- CANR-25
Earlier sketches in CA 65-68, CANR-9
Campbell, J(ames) Arthur 1916- 53-56
Campbell, Jack K(enagy) 1927- 23-24R
Campbell, James 1920- 57-60
Campbell, James E(dward) 1945- 107
Campbell, James Edwin 1867-1896 ..... DLB-50
Campbell, James Howard 1928- 113
Campbell, James Marshall 1895-1977 73-76
Obituary 69-72
Campbell, Jane 1934- 41-44R
Campbell, Jane
See Edwards, Jane Campbell
Campbell, Janet Bruce 1955- 121
Campbell, (Mary) Jean 1943- 115
Campbell, Jeff(erson) H(olland) 1931- 41-44R
Campbell, Jeffrey
See Black, Campbell
Campbell, Jeremy 1931- 109
Campbell, Jim
See Campbell, James Howard
Campbell, Joan 1929- 109
Campbell, Joanna
See Bly, Carol(yn)
Campbell, John 1653-1728 .... DLB-43
Campbell, John 1947- 114
Campbell, John Coert 1911- CANR-3
Earlier sketch in CA 4R
Campbell, John Creighton 1941- 111
Campbell, John Franklin 1940(?)-1971
Obituary 33-36R
Campbell, John Lorne 1906- 29-32R
Campbell, John R(oy) 1933- 53-56
Campbell, John W(ood) 1910-1971 ...... CAP-2
Obituary 29-32R
Earlier sketch in CA 21-22
See also DLB 8
See also CLC 32
Campbell, Joseph 1904-1987 .... CANR-3
Obituary 124
Earlier sketch in CA 4R
Campbell, Judith
See Pares, Marion (Stapylton)
Campbell, Karen
See Beaty, Betty
Campbell, Karlyn Kohrs 1937- CANR-18
Earlier sketches in CA 53-56, CANR-4
Campbell, Keith 1938- 106

Campbell, Keith Oliver 1920- 110
Campbell, Ken 1941- 77-80
Campbell, Kenneth 1901(?)-1979
 Obituary 85-88
Campbell, Laurence R(andolph)
 1903-1987 126
Campbell, Lawrence James 1931- 106
Campbell, Litta Belle 1886-1980 .... CANR-5
 Earlier sketch in CA 5-6R
Campbell, Louisa D. 1958- 121
Campbell, Luke
 See Madison, Thomas A.
Campbell, Malcolm J(ames) 1930- CANR-21
 Earlier sketches in CA 57-60, CANR-6
Campbell, Margaret 69-72
Campbell, (Gabrielle) Margaret (Vere)
 1886-1952 Brief entry 116
Campbell, Margaret 1916- 106
Campbell, Maria 1940- 102
Campbell, Marjorie Wilkins 97-100
Campbell, Michael Mussen 1924-1984 102
 Obituary 113
Campbell, Oscar James, Jr. 1879-1970
 Obituary 29-32R
Campbell, Patricia J(ean) 1930- 103
 See also SATA 45
Campbell, Patricia Piatt 1901- 25-28R
Campbell, Patrick Gordon 1913-1980
 Obituary 102
Campbell, Patty
 See Campbell, Patricia J(ean)
Campbell, Paul N. 1923- 21-22R
Campbell, Penelope 1935- 33-36R
Campbell, Peter (Walter) 1926- CANR-11
 Earlier sketches in CA 13-14, CAP-1
Campbell, Peter Anthony 1935- 21-22R
Campbell, R. T.
 See Todd, Ruthven
Campbell, R. W.
 See Campbell, Rosemae Wells
Campbell, R(obert) Wright 1927- CANR-24
 Earlier sketches in CA 57-60, CANR-6,
 21
Campbell, (John) Ramsey 1946- CANR-7
 Earlier sketch in CA 57-60
 See also CLC 42
Campbell, Randolph B(luford) 1940- 41-44R
Campbell, Rex R. 1931- 41-44R
Campbell, Rita Ricardo
 See Ricardo-Campbell, Rita
Campbell, Robert 1922-1977 .... CANR-8
 Obituary 73-76
 Earlier sketch in CA 53-56
Campbell, Robert
 See Campbell, R(obert) Wright
Campbell, Robert B(lair) 1923- 69-72
Campbell, Robert C(harles) 1924- 49-52
Campbell, Robert Dale 1914- 11-12R
Campbell, Robert Wellington 1926- CANR-3
 Earlier sketch in CA 1R
Campbell, Rod 1945- SATA-44, 51
Campbell, Rosemae Wells 1909- 13-14R
 See also SATA 1
Campbell, (Ignatius) Roy (Dunnachie)
 1901-1957 Brief entry 104
 See also DLB 20
 See also TCLC 5
Campbell, Sheldon 1919- 41-44R
Campbell, Sid 1944- 118
Campbell, Stanley W(allace) 1926- 49-52
Campbell, Stephen K(ent) 1935- 49-52
Campbell, Thomas F. 1924- 21-22R
Campbell, Thomas M(oody) 1936- 49-52
Campbell, Tom D. 1938- 126
Campbell, Wilfred
 See Campbell, William
 See also TCLC 9
Campbell, Will D(avis) 1924- CANR-22
 Earlier sketches in CA 7-8R, CANR-7
Campbell, William 1858(?)-1918
 Brief entry 106
Campbell, William Edward March
 1893-1954 Brief entry 108
Campbell-Johnson, Alan 1913- 65-68
Campbell-Purdie, Wendy 1925- 21-22R
Campen, Richard N(ewman) 1912- 69-72
Camper, Shirley
 See Soman, Shirley
Campion, Joan 1940- 124
Campion, Nardi Reeder 1917- CANR-6
 Earlier sketch in CA 4R
 See also SATA 22
Campion, Rosamond
 See Rosmond, Babette
Campion, Sidney R(onald) 1891- CAP-1
 Earlier sketch in CA 9-10
Campion, Thomas 1567-1620 .... DLB-58
Camplin, Jamie (Robert) 1947- 97-100
Campling, Christopher R(ussell) 1925- 113
Campling, Elizabeth 1948- 123
 See also SATA 53
Campolo, Anthony, Jr. 1935- CANR-26
 Earlier sketches in CA 69-72, CANR-11
Campos, Alvaro de
 See Pessoa, Fernando (Antonio Nogueira)
Camps, Francis Edward 1905-1972 .... 37-40R
Campton, David 1924- CANR-20
 Earlier sketches in CA 7-8R, CANR-5
Camus, Albert 1913-1960 89-92
 See also DLB 72
 See also CLC 1, 2, 4, 9, 11, 14, 32
Camus, Raoul Francois 1930- 65-68
Camus, (Jean) Renaud (Gabriel) 1946- 108
Camuti, Louis J(oseph) 1893-1981 101
 Obituary 103
Canada, Lena 1942- 93-96
Canaday, John E(dwin) 1907-1985 .... CANR-7
 Obituary 116
 Earlier sketch in CA 13-14R
Canan, James William 1929- 61-64
Canary
 See Conn, Canary Denise
Canary, Robert H(ughes) 1939- CANR-11
 Earlier sketch in CA 29-32R
Canavan, Francis 1917- 118
Canaway, W(illiam) H(amilton) 1925- 93-96
Canby, Courtlandt 1914- 118
Canby, Henry Seidel 1878-1961 Obituary 89-92
Canby, Vincent 1924- 81-84
 See also CLC 13
Cancale
 See Desnos, Robert
Cancellare, Frank 1910-1985 Obituary 116
Cancian, Francesca M(icaela) 1937- 57-60
Cancian, Francis Alexander 1934- CANR-7
 Earlier sketch in CA 53-56
Cancian, Frank
 See Cancian, Francis Alexander
Candelaria, Frederick (Henry) 1929- 17-18R
Candelaria, Nash 1928- CANR-11
 Earlier sketch in CA 69-72
Candell, Victor 1903-1977 .... SATA-24
Candida
 See Hoffman, Lisa
Candilis, Wray O. 1927- CANR-10
 Earlier sketch in CA 25-28R
Candland, Douglas Keith 1934- CANR-2
 Earlier sketch in CA 5-6R
Candler, Julie 1919- 65-68
Candlin, Enid Saunders 1909- CANR-1
 Earlier sketch in CA 45-48
Candy, Edward
 See Neville, B(arbara) Alison (Boodson)
Cane, Melville (Henry) 1879-1980 .... CANR-8
 Obituary 97-100
 Earlier sketches in CA 4R, CANR-6
Canellopoulos, Panayiotis 1902-1986
 Obituary 120
Canemaker, John 1943- 81-84
Caner, Mary Paul 1893- CAP-2
 Earlier sketch in CA 21-22
Canetti, Elias 1905- CANR-23
 Earlier sketch in CA 21-22R
 See also CLC 3, 14, 25
Caney, Steven 1941- 104
Canfield, Cass 1897-1986 .... 41-44R
 Obituary 118
Canfield, (Fayette) Curtis 1903-1986
 Obituary 120
Canfield, D(elos) Lincoln 1903- 25-28R
Canfield, Dorothy
 See Fisher, Dorothy (Frances) Canfield
Canfield, Gae Whitney 1931- 113
Canfield, James D(avid) 1937- 117
Canfield, James K(eith) 1925- 25-28R
Canfield, James Lewis 1942- 121
Canfield, Jane White 1897-1984 109
 Obituary 112
 See also SATA 32, 38
Canfield, John A(lan) 1941- 37-40R
Canfield, Kenneth French 1909- CAP-1
 Earlier sketch in CA 15-16
Canfield, Leon Hardy 1886- 3R
Canfield, Muriel 1935- 115
Cang, Joel 1899-1974 .... CAP-2
 Earlier sketch in CA 29-32
Cangemi, Sister Marie Lucita 1920- 21-22R
Canham, Erwin D(ain) 1904-1982 .... CAP-1
 Obituary 105
 Earlier sketch in CA 13-14
Canham, Kingsley 1945- 57-60
Caniff, Milton (Arthur) 1907-1988 85-88
 Obituary 125
 See also AITN 1
Cann, Marjorie Mitchell 1924- 89-92
Cannam, Peggie 1925- 13-14R
Cannan, Denis 1919- CANR-7
 Earlier sketch in CA 57-60
Cannan, Gilbert E. 1884-1955 Brief entry 111
 See also DLB 10
Cannan, Joanna
 See Pullein-Thompson, Joanna Maxwell
Cannell, Kathleen Biggar (Eaton)
 1891-1974 106
 See also DLB 4
Cannell, Skipwith 1887-1957 .... DLB-45
Canning, Jeff(rey Michael) 1947- 73-76
Canning, John 1920- 89-92
Canning, Paul 1947- 126
Canning, Ray R(ussell) 1920- 41-44R
Canning, Victor 1911-1986 .... CANR-6
 Obituary 118
 Earlier sketch in CA 13-14R
Cannon, Alexander 1896-1963(?) Obituary 111
Cannon, Beth 1951- 69-72
Cannon, Bettie (Waddell) 1922- 126
Cannon, Bill
 See Cannon, William S.
Cannon, Cornelia (James) 1876-1969
 Obituary 109
 See also SATA 28
Cannon, Garland (Hampton) 1924- CANR-13
 Earlier sketch in CA 33-36R
Cannon, Grant Groesbeck 1911-1969
 Obituary 117
Cannon, Harold C(harles) 1930- 45-48
Cannon, Helen 1921- 101
Cannon, James Monroe III 1918- 2R
Cannon, James P. 1890(?)-1974
 Obituary 53-56
Cannon, Jimmy 1909-1973 Obituary 104
Cannon, John (Ashton) 1918- 49-52
Cannon, John
 See Newton, Michael
Cannon, Le Grand, Jr. 1899-1979
 Obituary 93-96
Cannon, Lou(is S.) 1933- 29-32R
Cannon, Mark W(ilcox) 1928- 15-16R
Cannon, Poppy
 See White, Poppy Cannon
Cannon, Ravenna
 See Mayhar, Ardath
Cannon, William Ragsdale 1916- CANR-18
 Earlier sketches in CA 1R, CANR-4
Cannon, William S. 1918- 29-32R
Canny, Nicholas P(atrick) 1944- 69-72
Cano-Ballesta, Juan 1932- CANR-1
 Earlier sketch in CA 49-52
Canon, Lance Kirkpatrick 1939- 45-48
Canovan, Margaret 1939- 81-84
Cansdale, George (Soper) 1909- 9-10R
Cant, Gilbert 1909-1982 Obituary 107
Cant, Reginald (Edward) 1914-1987
 Obituary 122
Cantacuzene, Julia 1876-1975 Obituary 61-64
Cantacuzino, Sherban 1928- 118
Cantalupo, Charles 1951- 126
Cantelon, John E(dward) 1924- 11-12R
Cantelon, Philip L(ouis) 1940- 124
Canterbery, E(stes) Ray 1935- 41-44R
Cantin, Eileen 1931- 53-56
Cantin, Eugene Thorpe 1944- 45-48
Cantinat, Jean 1902- 29-32R
Cantor, Arthur 1920- 29-32R
Cantor, Eli 1913- CANR-14
 Earlier sketch in CA 77-80
Cantor, Gilbert M. 1929(?)-1987 Obituary 122
Cantor, Leonard M(artin) 1927- 69-72
Cantor, Louis 1934- 29-32R
Cantor, Milton 1925- Brief entry 112
Cantor, Muriel G. 1923- CANR-12
 Earlier sketch in CA 33-36R
Cantor, Norman F(rank) 1929- 102
Cantor, Paul A(rthur) 1945- 89-92
Cantor, Paul David 1916-1979 Obituary 89-92
Cantori, Louis J. 1934- 29-32R
Cantrell, J(ohn) A(nthony) 1952- 123
Cantril, Albert H(adley) 1940- 111
Cantu, Robert Clark 1938- 108
Cantwell, Aston
 See Platt, Charles
Cantwell, Dennis P(atrick) 1940- 57-60
Cantwell, Lois 1951- 121
Cantwell, Robert Emmett 1908-1978 .... CANR-4
 Obituary 81-84
 Earlier sketch in CA 5-6R
 See also DLB 9
Cantzlaar, George La Fond 1906-1967 .... CAP-1
 Earlier sketch in CA 15-16
Canuck, Abe
 See Bingley, David Ernest
Canusi, Jose
 See Barker, S. Omar
Canutt, Enos Edward 1895(?)-1986
 Obituary 119
 Brief entry 114
Canutt, Yakima
 See Canutt, Enos Edward
Canzoneri, Robert (Wilburn) 1925- 19-20R
Capaldi, Nicholas 1939- 21-22R
Cape, Judith
 See Page, P(atricia) K(athleen)
Cape, Peter (Irwin) 1929- 108
Cape, William H(enry) 1920- 11-12R
Capeci, Dominic Joseph, Jr. 1940- 77-80
Capek, Karel 1890-1938 Brief entry 104
 See also TCLC 6
Capek, Milic 1909- CANR-4
 Earlier sketch in CA 4R
Capel, Roger
 See Sheppard, Lancelot C(apel)
Capelle, Russell B(eckett) 1917- 7-8R
Capen, Joseph 1658-1725 .... DLB-24
Capers, Gerald Mortimer, Jr. 1909- 5-6R
Capitan, William H(arry) 1933- 29-32R
Capitanchik, Maurice 1929(?)-1985
 Obituary 118
Capitman, William G(ardiner) 1921-1975 122
 Obituary 111
Capizzi, Michael 1941- 41-44R
Caplan, Arthur L(eonard) 1950- CANR-22
 Earlier sketch in CA 106
Caplan, David 1947- 105
Caplan, Edwin H(arvey) 1926- 41-44R
Caplan, Frank 1911(?)-1988 110
 Obituary 126
Caplan, Gerald 1917- CANR-18
 Earlier sketch in CA 25-28R
Caplan, Harry 1896- CAP-2
 Earlier sketch in CA 23-24
Caplan, Lionel 33-36R
Caplan, Ralph 1925- 15-16R
Caplan, Ronald Mervyn 1937- 107
Caplan, Theresa 110
Caplan, Thomas (Mark) 1946- 107
Caples, John 1900- 23-24R
Caplin, Alfred Gerald 1909-1979 57-60
 Obituary 89-92
 See also SATA 21
Caplovitz, David 1928- 41-44R
Caplow, Theodore 1920- CANR-20
 Earlier sketches in CA 4R, CANR-4
Capon, Edmund (George) 1940- 107
Capon, (Harry) Paul 1912-1969 .... 5-6R
 Obituary 103
Capon, Peter
 See Oakley, Eric Gilbert
Capon, Robert Farrar 1925- Brief entry 106
Caponigri, A(loysius) Robert 1915- 37-40R
Caporale, Rocco 1927- 37-40R
Capote, Truman 1924-1984 .... CANR-18
 Obituary 113
 Earlier sketch in CA 7-8R
 See also DLB 2
 See also DLBY 80, 84
 See also CDALB 1941-1968
 See also CLC 1, 3, 8, 13, 19, 34, 38
 See also SSC 2
Capouya, Emile 122
 Brief entry 118
Capp, Al
 See Caplin, Alfred Gerald
Capp, Glenn Richard 1910- CANR-3
 Earlier sketch in CA 1R
Capp, Richard 1935- 81-84
Cappadona, Diane Apostolos
 See Apostolos-Cappadona, Diane
Cappel, Constance 1936- CANR-10
 Earlier sketch in CA 21-22R
 See also SATA 22
Cappelluti, Frank Joseph 1935-1972 .... 37-40R
Capper, Douglas Parode 1898(?)-1979 .... 9-10R
 Obituary 103
Cappo, Joseph 1936- 77-80
Cappon, Daniel 1921- 19-20R
Cappon, Lester J(esse) 1900-1981 106
 Obituary 104
Capps, Benjamin (Franklin) 1922- CANR-7
 Earlier sketch in CA 7-8R
 See also SATA 9
Capps, Carroll M. 1917(?)-1971 Obituary 112
Capps, Clifford Lucille Sheats
 1902-1976 .... 37-40R
Capps, Donald E(ric) 1939- CANR-12
 Earlier sketch in CA 29-32R
Capps, Jack Lee 1926- 23-24R
Capps, Walter H(olden) 1934- CANR-12
 Earlier sketch in CA 29-32R
Cappy Dick
 See Cleveland, George
Capra, Frank 1897- 61-64
 See also CLC 16
Capra, Fritjof 1939- 107
Capretta, Patrick J(ohn) 1929- 21-22R
Caprio, Betsy
 See Caprio, Elizabeth Blair
Caprio, Elizabeth Blair 1933- 110
Caprio, Frank S(amuel) 1906- 101
Capron, Alexander Morgan 1944- 115
Capron, Jean F. 1924- 21-22R
Capron, Louis (Bishop) 1891- CAP-1
 Earlier sketch in CA 9-10
Capron, Walter Clark 1904-1979 .... CAP-1
 Obituary 89-92
 Earlier sketch in CA 17-18
Capron, William M(osher) 1920- 29-32R
Capstick, Peter Hathaway 1940- 102
Captain Kangaroo
 See Keeshan, Robert J.
Captain Wheeler
 See Ellis, Edward S(ylvester)
Captain X
 See Power-Waters, Brian
Caputi, Anthony (Francis) 1924- CANR-3
 Earlier sketch in CA 1R
Caputo, David A(rmand) 1943- 65-68
Caputo, Philip 1941- 73-76
 See also CLC 32
Caputo, Robert 1949- 101
Caradon, Lord
 See Foot, Hugh Mackintosh
Caraley, Demetrios 1932- 103
Caraman, Philip 1911- CANR-21
 Earlier sketches in CA 11-12R, CANR-6
Caramello, Charles 1948- 112
Carano, Paul 1919- 19-20R
Caras, Roger A(ndrew) 1928- CANR-5
 Earlier sketch in CA 4R
 See also SATA 12
Caras, Tracy 1953- 113
Carawan, Candie
 See Carawan, Carolanne M.
Carawan, Carolanne M. 1939- 19-20R
Carawan, Guy H., Jr. 1927- 19-20R
Caraway, Charless 1888-1977 125
Carballido, Emilio 1925- 33-36R
Carbaugh, Robert J(ohn) 1946- 65-68
Carbery, Thomas F. 29-32R
Carbine, Patricia (Theresa) 1931- 107
Carbonell, Reyes 1917- 9-10R
Carbonnier, Jeanne 1894-1974 .... CAP-2
 Earlier sketch in CA 33-36
 See also SATA 3, 34
Carbury, A.B.
 See Carr, Albert H. Z(olotkoff)
Carcopino, Jerome 1881(?)-1970
 Obituary 104
Card, Orson Scott 1951- 102
 See also CLC 44, 47, 50
Cardarelli, Joseph 1944- 77-80
Carden, Karen W(ilson) 1946- CANR-1
 Earlier sketch in CA 49-52
Carden, Maren Lockwood 53-56
Carden, Patricia J. 1935- 41-44R
Cardenal, Ernesto 1925- CANR-2
 Earlier sketch in CA 49-52
 See also CLC 31
Cardenas, Daniel N(egrete) 1917- CANR-26
 Earlier sketch in CA 45-48
Cardenas, Gilbert 1947- 97-100
Cardew, Cornelius 1936-1981 Obituary 108
Cardew, Michael (Ambrose) 1901-1983 49-52
 Obituary 109
Cardiff, Gray Emerson 1949- 89-92
Cardinal, Ora 1913- 111

Cardinal, Roger (Thomas) 1940- CANR-18
Earlier sketches in CA 45-48, CANR-1
Cardinal, Sister Mary Ora
See Cardinal, Ora
Cardona, George 1936- 119
Cardona-Hine, Alvaro 1926- CANR-5
Earlier sketch in CA 9-10R
Cardone, Samuel S(teve) 1938- 19-20R
Cardozo, Arlene Rossen 1938- CANR-19
Earlier sketch in CA 102
Cardozo, Benjamin N(athan) 1870-1938
Brief entry 117
Cardozo, Michael H. 1910- 33-36R
Cardozo, Nancy 103
Cardozo, Peter 1916- 61-64
Cardui, Van
See Wayman, Tony Russell
Cardui, Vanessa
See Wayman, Tony Russell
Cardus, Neville 1889-1975 .... CANR-11
Obituary 57-60
Earlier sketch in CA 61-64
Cardwell, D(onald) S(tephen) L(owell)
1919- 101
Cardwell, Guy A(dams) 1905- 15-16R
Care, Felicity
See Coury, Louise Andree
Care, Norman S. 1937- 25-28R
Careless, J(ames) M(aurice) S(tockford)
1919- 102
Carens, James Francis 1927- CANR-12
Earlier sketch in CA 61-64
Cares, Paul B. 1911- 11-12R
Caress, James M. 1947- 122
Caress, Jay
See Caress, James M.
Carette, Louis 1913- 85-88
Carew, Dorothy 1910(?)-1973 Obituary ..41-44R
Carew, Dudley Charles 1903-1981
Obituary 103
Carew, Jan (Rynveld) 1925- 77-80
See also SATA 40, 51
Carew, Jocelyn
See Aeby, Jacquelyn
Carew, John Mohun 1921-1980 .... CANR-7
Earlier sketch in CA 13-14R
Carew, Rod(ney Cline) 1945- 104
Carew, Tim
See Carew, John Mohun
Carewe, S. C.
See Du Breuil, (Elizabeth) L(or)inda
Carey, Anne
See Nevill, Barry St-John
Carey, Bonnie 1941- SATA-18
Carey, Diane 1954- 122
Carey, Eileen
See O'Casey, Eileen (Reynolds)
Carey, Ernestine Gilbreth 1908- 5-6R
See also SATA 2
See also CLC 17
Carey, Gary 1938- CANR-15
Earlier sketch in CA 57-60
Carey, James Charles 1915- 15-16R
Carey, Jane Perry (Clark) 1898-1981 73-76
Obituary 105
Carey, John 1934- CANR-6
Earlier sketch in CA 57-60
Carey, John A(ndrew) 1949- 109
Carey, Kenneth Moir 1908-1979 Obituary ... 108
Carey, M. V.
See Carey, Mary (Virginia)
Carey, Mary (Virginia) 1925- CANR-17
Earlier sketch in CA 81-84
See also SATA 39, 44
Carey, Mathew 1760-1839 .... DLB-37, 73
Carey, Michael (Sausmarez) 1913-1985
Obituary 118
Carey, Michael
See Burton, Edward J.
Carey, Michael L(awrence) 1948- 65-68
Carey, Mother Marme Aimee 1931- 15-16R
Carey, Omer L. 1929- CANR-23
Earlier sketches in CA 23-24R, CANR-8
Carey, Peter 1943- Brief entry 123
See also CLC 40
Carey, Richard John 1925- 53-56
Carey, Robert George 1926- Brief entry 108
Carey Evans, Olwen (Elizabeth) 1892- 126
Carey-Jones, N(orman) S(tewart) 1911- ..21-22R
Carfagne, Cyril
See Jennings, Leslie Nelson
Carfagno, Vincent R. 1935- 41-44R
Carfax, Catherine
See Fairburn, Eleanor
Cargas, Harry J(ames) 1932- CANR-21
Earlier sketches in CA 15-16R, CANR-6
Cargill, Jennifer S(ue) 1944- 109
Cargill, Oscar 1898-1972 .... CANR-15
Obituary 33-36R
Earlier sketch in CA 2R
Cargill, Robert L. 1929- 25-28R
Cargo, David N(iels) 1932- 57-60
Cargo, Robert T. 1933- 85-88
Cargoe, Richard
See Payne, (Pierre Stephen) Robert
Carhart, Arthur Hawthorne 1892- CAP-1
Earlier sketch in CA 9-10
Caridi, Ronald J. 1941- 25-28R
Carigiet, Alois 1902-1985 73-76
Obituary 119
See also SATA 24, 47
Carin, Arthur A. 1928- 29-32R
Carini, Edward 1923- 61-64
See also SATA 9
Carkeet, David 1946- 102
Carl, Beverly May 1932- CANR-4
Earlier sketch in CA 53-56
Carl, Lillian Stewart 1949- 118
Carle, Eric 1929- CANR-25
Earlier sketches in CA 25-28R, CANR-10
See also SATA 4
See also SAAS 6
See also CLR 10
Carlell, Lodowick 1602-1675 .... DLB-58
Carlen, Claudia 1906- 106
Carleton, Barbee Oliver 1917- 23-24R
Carleton, Captain L. C.
See Ellis, Edward S(ylvester)
Carleton, Captain Latham C.
See Ellis, Edward S(ylvester)
Carleton, Latham C.
See Ellis, Edward S(ylvester)
Carleton, Mark T. 1935- CANR-12
Earlier sketch in CA 33-36R
Carleton, R(eginal) Milton 1899-1986 69-72
Obituary 120
Carleton, Will(iam McKendree) 1845-1912
Brief entry 115
Carleton, William G(raves) 1903- CAP-2
Earlier sketch in CA 25-28
Carley, V(an Ness) Royal 1906-1976 ..... CAP-2
Earlier sketch in CA 29-32
See also SATA 20
Carli, Angelo 1937- 49-52
Carlile, Clark S(tites) 1912- 41-44R
Carlile, Henry 1934- 33-36R
Carlin, Gabriel S. 1921- 4R
Carlin, Thomas W(illard) 1918- 25-28R
Carline, Richard (Cotton) 1896-1980
Obituary 105
Carling, Francis 1945- 25-28R
Carlino, Lewis John 1932- 77-80
Carlinsky, Dan 1944- CANR-23
Earlier sketches in CA 21-22R, CANR-8
Carlisle, Carol Jones 1919- 29-32R
Carlisle, Clark
See Holding, James (Clark Carlisle, Jr.)
Carlisle, D. M.
See Cook, Dorothy Mary
Carlisle, Douglas H(ilton) 1921- 45-48
Carlisle, E(rvin) Fred 1935- 53-56
Carlisle, Fred 1915- 73-76
Carlisle, Henry (Coffin) 1926- CANR-15
Earlier sketch in CA 13-14R
See also CLC 33
Carlisle, Howard M(yron) 1928- 69-72
Carlisle, Lilian (Matarose) Baker 1912- 53-56
Carlisle, Olga Andreyev 1930- CANR-7
Earlier sketch in CA 13-14R
See also SATA 35
Carlisle, Regis 1955- CANR-17
Earlier sketch in CA 77-80
Carlisle, Rodney P. 1936- 45-48
Carlisle, Thomas (Fiske) 1944- 53-56
Carlisle, Thomas John 1913- CANR-18
Earlier sketch in CA 101
Carlock, John R(obert) 1921- 33-36R
Carlock, Lynn
See Cunningham, Marilyn
Carlon, Patricia Bernardette 13-14R
Carlquist, Sherwin 1930- 13-14R
Carls, (John) Norman 1907- CAP-2
Earlier sketch in CA 17-18
Carlsen, G(eorge) Robert 1917- CANR-24
Earlier sketches in CA 19-20R, CANR-8
See also SATA 30
Carlsen, James C(aldwell) 1927- 25-28R
Carlsen, Ruth C(hristoffer) 1918- CANR-24
Earlier sketches in CA 19-20R, CANR-8
See also SATA 2
Carlson, Andrew R(aymond) 1934- 29-32R
Carlson, Arthur E(ugene) 1923- 37-40R
Carlson, Avis D(ungan) 1896-1987 73-76
Obituary 121
Carlson, Bernice Wells 1910- CANR-2
Earlier sketch in CA 5-6R
See also SATA 8
Carlson, Betty 1919- CANR-2
Earlier sketch in CA 3R
Carlson, C. C.
See Carlson, Carole C.
Carlson, Carl Walter 1907- 49-52
Carlson, Carole C. 1925- 113
Carlson, Dale Bick 1935- CANR-3
Earlier sketch in CA 11-12R
See also SATA 1
Carlson, Daniel (Bick) 1960- 105
See also SATA 27
Carlson, Edgar M(agnus) 1908- 105
Carlson, Ellsworth C. 1917- Brief entry 105
Carlson, Elof Axel 1931- 45-48
Carlson, Eric W(alter) 1910- 25-28R
Carlson, Esther Elisabeth 1920- 5-6R
Carlson, Harry Gilbert 1930- 109
Carlson, John A(llyn) 1933- 29-32R
Carlson, Judith Lee 1952- 104
Carlson, Leland H(enry) 1908- 19-20R
Carlson, Lewis H(erbert) 1934- 41-44R
Carlson, Loraine 1923- CANR-14
Earlier sketch in CA 37-40R
Carlson, Marvin 1935- CANR-8
Earlier sketch in CA 23-24R
Carlson, Nancy L(ee) 1953- 110
See also SATA 45
Carlson, Natalie Savage 1906- CANR-3
Earlier sketch in CA 4R
See also SATA 2
See also SAAS 4
Carlson, P. M.
See Carlson, Patricia M(cElroy)
Carlson, Patricia M(cElroy) 1940- 114
Carlson, Paul Robins 1928- 101
Carlson, Raymond 1906-1983 Obituary 109
Carlson, Reynold Edgar 1901- CANR-4
Earlier sketch in CA 4R
Carlson, Richard 1912(?)-1977 Obituary ...73-76
Carlson, Richard Stocks 1942- 57-60
Carlson, Rick J. 1940- 65-68
Carlson, Robert E(ugene) 1922- 41-44R
Carlson, Ron(ald F.) 1947- 105
Carlson, Ronald L. 1934- CANR-13
Earlier sketch in CA 33-36R
Carlson, Roy L(incoln) 1930- 41-44R
Carlson, Ruth (Elizabeth) Kearney 1911- ..29-32R
Carlson, Theodore L(eonard) 1905- 45-48
Carlson, Vada F. 1897- CANR-10
Earlier sketch in CA 23-24R
See also SATA 16
Carlson, William H(ugh) 1898- CAP-2
Earlier sketch in CA 23-24
Carlson, William S(amuel) 1905- 4R
Carlston, Kenneth S. 1904- 5-6R
Carlstrom, Nancy White 1948- 121
See also SATA 48, 53
Carlton, Alva
See Delk, Robert Carlton
Carlton, Charles 1941- 53-56
Carlton, Charles Merritt 1928- 45-48
Carlton, David 1938- 103
Carlton, Henry F(isk) 1893(?)-1973
Obituary 41-44R
Carlton, Lessie 1903- 49-52
Carlton, Robert G(oodrich) 1927- 19-20R
Carlton, Roger
See Rowland, D(onald) S(ydney)
Carlton, Wendy 1949- 101
Carlut, Charles E. 1911- Brief entry 107
Carlyle, Jane Welsh 1801-1866 .... DLB-55
Carlyle, Thomas 1795-1881 .... DLB-55
Carm, Mac
See Armstrong, Keith F(rancis)
W(hitfield)
Carmack, Robert M. 1934- 45-48
Carman, Barry (Francis) 1922- 118
Carman, (William) Bliss 1861-1929
Brief entry 104
See also TCLC 7
Carman, Dulce
See Drummond, Edith Marie Dulce
Carman
Carman, J(ustice) Neale 1897-1972 ...... CAP-1
Earlier sketch in CA 9-10
Carman, Robert A(rchibald) 1931- CANR-7
Earlier sketch in CA 57-60
Carman, William Y(oung) 1909- 13-14R
Carmel, Catherine 1939- 69-72
Carmel, Hesi 1937- 103
Carmell, Aryeh 1917- 118
Carmen, Arlene 1936- 69-72
Carmen, Sister (M.) Joann 1941- 21-22R
Carmen Sylva
See Elisabeth (Ottilie Luise), Queen
(Pauline)
Carmer, Carl (Lamson) 1893-1976 ...... CANR-4
Obituary 69-72
Earlier sketch in CA 7-8R
See also SATA 30, 37
Carmer, Elizabeth Black 1904- SATA-24
Carmi, T.
See Charny, Carmi
Carmichael, Ann
See MacAlpine, Margaret H(esketh
Murray)
Carmichael, Ann G(ayton) 1947- 125
Carmichael, Calum M. 1938- 53-56
Carmichael, Carrie
See Carmichael, Harriet
See also SATA 40
Carmichael, D(ouglas) R(oy) 1941- 33-36R
Carmichael, Fred 1924- CANR-25
Earlier sketches in CA 19-20R, CANR-10
Carmichael, Harriet 115
Carmichael, Harry
See Ognall, Leopold Horace
Carmichael, Hoagland Howard 1899-1981
Obituary 108
Carmichael, Hoagy
See Carmichael, Hoagland Howard
Carmichael, Joel 1915- CANR-2
Earlier sketch in CA 1R
Carmichael, John P(eerless) 1902-1986
Obituary 119
Carmichael, Leonard 1898-1973 ....41-44R
Obituary 45-48
Carmichael, Oliver C(romwell) 1891-1966 . CAP-1
Earlier sketch in CA 9-10
Carmichael, Peter A(rchibald) 1897- CAP-2
Earlier sketch in CA 17-18
Carmichael, Stokely 1941- CANR-25
Earlier sketch in CA 57-60
See also BW
Carmichael, Thomas N(ichols)
1919-1972 .... CAP-2
Earlier sketch in CA 29-32
Carmichael, William Edward 1922- 37-40R
Carmilly, Moshe 1908- 41-44R
Carmines, Al(vin Allison, Jr.) 1936- 103
Carmody, Denise Lardner 1935- 93-96
Carmody, Jay 1900(?)-1973 Obituary 41-44R
Carmoy, Guy de 1907- 89-92
Carnac, Carol
See Rivett, Edith Caroline
Carnac, Levin
See Griffith-Jones, George Chetwynd
Carnahan, Walter H(ervey) 1891- CAP-1
Earlier sketch in CA 9-10
Carnall, Geoffrey 1927- 15-16R
Carnap, Rudolf P. 1891-1970 .... CAP-1
Obituary 29-32R
Earlier sketch in CA 9-10
Carnarvon, The Earl of
See Herbert, Henry George Alfred Marius
Victor Francis
Carnegie, Dorothy Vanderpool AITN-1
Carnegie, Raymond Alexander 1920- ... CANR-11
Earlier sketch in CA 23-24R
Carnegie, Sacha
See Carnegie, Raymond Alexander
Carnegy, Patrick 1940- 81-84
Carneiro, Maurina Pereira
See Pereira Carneiro, Maurina
Carnell, Corbin Scott 1929- CANR-10
Earlier sketch in CA 65-68
Carnell, E. J.
See Carnell, (Edward) John
Carnell, Edward John 1919-1967 .... CAP-1
Earlier sketch in CA 13-14
Carnell, (Edward) John 1912-1972 ......25-28R
Obituary 104
Carner, Mosco 1904-1985 .... CANR-12
Obituary 116
Earlier sketches in CA 11-12, CAP-1
Carnes, Conrad D(ew) 1936- 85-88
Carnes, Mark C(hristopher) 1950- 112
Carnes, Paul N(athaniel) 1921-1979
Obituary 85-88
Carnes, Ralph L(ee) 1931- 33-36R
Carnes, Valerie Folts-Bohanan 1945- 33-36R
Carnevali, Doris L(orrain) CANR-21
Earlier sketch in CA 69-72
Carney, Daniel 1944- 119
Carney, Dora Sanders 1903-1986
Obituary 120
Carney, James (Patrick) 1914- 21-22R
Carney, John J(oseph), Jr. 1932- 69-72
Carney, John Otis 1922- CANR-3
Earlier sketch in CA 1R
Carney, Matthew 1922- CANR-25
Earlier sketch in CA 108
Carney, Richard Edward 1929- 37-40R
Carney, T(homas) F(rancis) 1931- CANR-17
Earlier sketches in CA 49-52, CANR-1
Carney, W(illiam) Alderman 1922- 25-28R
Carnicelli, D(omenick) D. 1931- 61-64
Carnochan, W(alter) B(liss) 1930- 33-36R
Carnot, Joseph B(arry) 1941- 45-48
Carnoy, Martin 1938- CANR-10
Earlier sketch in CA 65-68
Caro, Francis G(eorge) 1936- CANR-11
Earlier sketch in CA 69-72
Caro, Robert A. 101
Caroe, Olaf Kirkpatrick 1892-1981 113
Carol, Bill J.
See Knott, William C(ecil, Jr.)
Carol, Jacqueline
See Cooper, Jacqueline
Caroli, Betty Boyd 1938- 118
Caroll, Nonie 1926- 103
Caron, Roger 1938- 89-92
Carona, Philip B(en) 1925- CANR-4
Earlier sketch in CA 4R
Caronia, Guiseppe 1884(?)-1977
Obituary 69-72
Caroselli, Remus F(rancis) 1916- 97-100
See also SATA 36
Carossa, Hans 1878-1956 .... DLB-66
Carosso, Vincent Phillip 1922- CANR-3
Earlier sketch in CA 9-10R
Carothers, J. Edward 1907- 41-44R
Carothers, Robert Lee 1942- 45-48
Carousso, Georges 1909- 89-92
Carozzi, Albert V(ictor) 1925- 53-56
Carp, Frances Merchant 1918- 23-24R
Carpelan, Bo (Gustaf Bertelsson) 1926- .. CANR-2
Earlier sketch in CA 49-52
See also SATA 8
Carpenter
See Arnold, June (Davis)
Carpenter, (John) Allan 1917- CANR-3
Earlier sketch in CA 9-10R
See also SATA 3
Carpenter, Andrew 1943- 93-96
Carpenter, Cal
See Carpenter, Clarence A(lfred)
Carpenter, Charles A. (Jr.) 1929- 33-36R
Carpenter, Charles H(ope), Jr. 1916- 111
Carpenter, Clarence A(lfred) 1921- 116
Carpenter, Clarence Ray 1905-1975
Obituary 57-60
Carpenter, David A(llen) 1949- 111
Carpenter, David C. 1941- 121
Carpenter, Delores Bird 1942- 126
Carpenter, Don(ald Richard) 1931- CANR-1
Earlier sketch in CA 45-48
See also CLC 41
Carpenter, Duffy
See Hurley, John J(erome)
Carpenter, Elizabeth Sutherland 1920- 41-44R
Carpenter, Frances 1890-1972 .... CANR-4
Obituary 37-40R
Earlier sketch in CA 5-6R
See also SATA 3, 27
Carpenter, Francis Ross 1925- 101
Carpenter, Fred
See Hand, (Andrus) Jackson
Carpenter, Frederic Ives (Jr.) 1903- 5-6R
Carpenter, Humphrey (William Bouverie)
1946- CANR-13
Earlier sketch in CA 89-92
Carpenter, J(ohn) D(avid) 1948- 115
Carpenter, James A. 1928- 37-40R
Carpenter, John A(lcott) 1921-1978 ......11-12R
Obituary 77-80
Carpenter, John Jo
See Reese, John (Henry)
Carpenter, John R. 1936- CANR-9
Earlier sketch in CA 65-68

Carpenter, Joyce Frances ... 33-36R
Carpenter, Kenneth J(ohn) 1923- ... 124
Carpenter, Liz
See Carpenter, Elizabeth Sutherland
Carpenter, Lucas 1947- ... 126
Carpenter, Margaret Haley ?-1985 ... 5-6R
Obituary ... 116
Carpenter, Marjorie 1896- ... 45-48
Carpenter, Michael (Anthony) 1940- ... 119
Carpenter, Mimi Gregoire 1947- ... 111
Carpenter, Nan Cooke 1912- ... 25-28R
Carpenter, Patricia (Healy Evans) 1920- ... 29-32R
See also SATA 11
Carpenter, Peter 1922- ... 15-16R
Carpenter, Rhys 1889-1980 ... 57-60
Obituary ... 93-96
Carpenter, Richard C(oles) 1916- ... 15-16R
Carpenter, Stephen Cullen ?-1820(?) ... DLB-73
Carpenter, William 1940- ... 106
Carpenter, Willow
See Browning, (Zerilda) Sinclair
Carpentier (y Valmont), Alejo
1904-1980 ... CANR-11
Obituary ... 97-100
Earlier sketch in CA 65-68
See also CLC 8, 11, 38
Carper, Jean Elinor 1932- ... CANR-7
Earlier sketch in CA 17-18R
Carper, L. Dean 1931- ... 49-52
Carpozi, George, Jr. 1920- ... CANR-11
Earlier sketch in CA 13-14R
Carr, A.H.Z.
See Carr, Albert H. Z(olotkoff)
Carr, Albert H. Z(olotkoff) 1902-1971 ... CANR-1
Obituary ... 33-36R
Earlier sketch in CA 4R
Carr, Annie Roe ... CANR-26
Earlier sketches in CA 19-20, CAP-2
Carr, Archie (Fairly, Jr.) 1909-1987 ... 15-16R
Obituary ... 122
Carr, Arthur C(harles) 1918- ... 37-40R
Carr, Arthur Japheth 1914- ... 57-60
Carr, Bruce (A.) 1938- ... 114
Carr, C(harles) T(elford) 1905-1976
Obituary ... 65-68
Carr, Catharine
See Wade, Rosalind Herschel
Carr, David William 1911- ... 37-40R
Carr, Donald Eaton 1903- ... 15-16R
Carr, Dorothy Stevenson Laird 1912- ... 9-10R
Carr, Edward Hallet 1892-1982 ... CANR-14
Obituary ... 108
Earlier sketch in CA 61-64
Carr, Edwin George 1937- ... 61-64
Carr, Emily 1871-1945 ... DLB-68
Carr, Gerald F(rancis) 1930- ... 118
Carr, Glyn
See Styles, (Frank) Showell
Carr, Gwen B. 1924- ... 41-44R
Carr, Harriett Helen 1899- ... CAP-1
Earlier sketch in CA 9-10
See also SATA 3
Carr, Herbert R(eginald) C(ulling)
1896-1986 Obituary ... 119
Carr, Ian (Henry Randell) 1933- ... 110
Carr, J(ames) L(loyd) 1912- ... 102
Carr, Janet Baker
See Baker-Carr, Janet
Carr, Jay Phillip 1936- ... 89-92
Carr, Jess(e Crowe, Jr.) 1930- ... CANR-12
Earlier sketch in CA 29-32R
Carr, (Bettye) Jo (Crisler) 1926- ... 21-22R
Carr, John C(harles) 1929- ... 53-56
Carr, John Dickson 1906-1977 ... CANR-3
Obituary ... 69-72
Earlier sketch in CA 49-52
See also CLC 3
Carr, John Laurence 1916- ... 49-52
Carr, Josephine 1952- ... 111
Carr, Lois Green 1922- ... 61-64
Carr, Margaret 1935- ... 105
Carr, Mary Jane 1899-1988 ... CAP-1
Obituary ... 124
Earlier sketch in CA 9-10
See also SATA 2
Carr, Michael Harold 1935- ... 109
Carr, Pat M(oore) 1932- ... CANR-14
Earlier sketch in CA 65-68
Carr, Philippa
See Hibbert, Eleanor Burford
Carr, Raymond 1919- ... CANR-8
Earlier sketch in CA 19-20R
Carr, Robert K(enneth) 1908-1979 ... 93-96
Obituary ... 85-88
Carr, Roberta
See Roberts, Irene
Carr, Robyn 1951- ... 115
Carr, Roland T. 1908(?)-1983 ... 122
Obituary ... 111
Carr, Stephen L(amoni) ... 57-60
Carr, Terry (Gene) 1937- ... 81-84
Carr, Virginia Mason
See Vaughan, Virginia M(ason)
Carr, Virginia Spencer 1929- ... 61-64
See also CLC 34
Carr, Warren Tyree 1917- ... 7-8R
Carr, William 1921- ... 73-76
Carr, William G(eorge) 1901- ... 53-56
Carr, William H(enry) A(lexander)
1924- ... CANR-7
Earlier sketch in CA 15-16R
Carraco, Carol Crowe
See Crowe-Carraco, Carol
Carranco, Lynwood 1921- ... CANR-21
Earlier sketches in CA 57-60, CANR-6
Carras, Mary C(alliope) ... 85-88
Carrasco, David ... 112
Carrel, Alexis 1873-1944 Brief entry ... 120
Carrel, Mark
See Paine, Lauran (Bosworth)
Carrell, Norman (Gerald) 1905- ... CAP-2
Earlier sketch in CA 25-28
Carrera Andrade, Jorge 1903-1978
Obituary ... 85-88
Carrick, A. B.
See Lindsay, Harold Arthur
Carrick, Carol 1935- ... CANR-17
Earlier sketches in CA 45-48, CANR-1
See also SATA 7
Carrick, Donald 1929- ... CANR-20
Earlier sketches in CA 53-56, CANR-5
See also SATA 7
Carrick, Edward
See Craig, Edward Anthony
Carrick, John
See Crosbie, (Hugh) Provan
Carrick, Malcolm 1945- ... CANR-14
Earlier sketch in CA 77-80
See also SATA 28
Carrier, Constance 1908- ... 33-36R
Carrier, Esther Jane 1925- ... 19-20R
Carrier, Jean-Guy 1945- ... 101
Carrier, Lark 1947- ... SATA-50
Carrier, Roch 1937- ... DLB-53
See also CLC 13
Carrier, Warren (Pendleton) 1918- ... CANR-18
Earlier sketches in CA 9-10R, CANR-3
Carrigan, Andrew G(ardner) 1935- ... CANR-1
Earlier sketch in CA 45-48
Carrigan, D(avid) Owen 1933- ... 25-28R
Carrigan, Richard A(lfred), Jr. 1932- ... 112
Carrighar, Sally ... 93-96
See also SATA 24
Carriker, Robert C(harles) 1940- ... 69-72
Carrillo, Lawrence W(ilbert) 1920- ... 15-16R
Carringer, Robert L. 1941- ... CANR-17
Earlier sketch in CA 97-100
Carrington, Charles Edmund 1897- ... 7-8R
Carrington, Frank G(amble, Jr.) 1936- ... 57-60
Carrington, George C(abell), Jr. 1928- ... 122
Brief entry ... 118
Carrington, Grant 1938- ... 104
Carrington, Leonora 1917- ... 124
Brief entry ... 114
Carrington, Molly
See Matthews, C(onstance) M(ary)
Carrington, Paul D(eWitt) 1931- ... 29-32R
Carrington, Richard (Temple Murray)
1921- ... 9-10R
Carrington, William Langley 1900-1970 ... CAP-1
Earlier sketch in CA 13-14
Carris, Joan Davenport 1938- ... 106
See also SATA 42, 44
Carrison, Daniel J. 1917- ... 37-40R
Carrithers, David W. 1943- ... 110
Carrithers, Gale H(emphill), Jr. 1932- ... 41-44R
Carrithers, Wallace M(axwell) 1911- ... 25-28R
Carrol, Shana
See Newcomb, Kerry
and Schaefer, Frank
Carroll, Anne Kristin
See Gales, Barbara J.
Carroll, Archie B(enjamin III) 1943- ... 109
Carroll, B(illy) D(an) 1940- ... 53-56
Carroll, Berenice A(nita) 1932- ... 41-44R
Carroll, C(armal) Edward 1923- ... 29-32R
Carroll, Carroll 1902- ... 101
Carroll, Charles Francis 1936- ... 53-56
Carroll, Curt
See Bishop, Curtis (Kent)
Carroll, Daniel B(ernard) 1928-1977 ... 41-44R
Carroll, Dennis 1940- ... 114
Carroll, Donald K(ingery) 1909- ... CAP-2
Earlier sketch in CA 17-18
Carroll, Elizabeth
See James, Elizabeth
Carroll, Faye 1937- ... 23-24R
Carroll, Gladys Hasty 1904- ... CANR-5
Earlier sketch in CA 3R
See also DLB 9
Carroll, Herbert A(llen) 1897- ... CAP-1
Earlier sketch in CA 11-12
Carroll, Jackson W(alker) 1932- ... CANR-16
Earlier sketch in CA 85-88
Carroll, James P. 1943(?)- ... 81-84
See also CLC 38
Carroll, Jeffrey 1950- ... 85-88
Carroll, Jim 1951- ... 45-48
See also CLC 35
Carroll, John 1735-1815 ... DLB-37
Carroll, John 1944- ... CANR-7
Earlier sketch in CA 57-60
Carroll, John B(issell) 1916- ... CANR-3
Earlier sketch in CA 1R
Carroll, John J(oseph) 1924- ... 15-16R
Carroll, John M(elvin) 1928- ... 37-40R
Carroll, John Millar 1925- ... CANR-23
Earlier sketches in CA 5-6R, CANR-8
Carroll, Jonathan 1949- ... CANR-21
Earlier sketch in CA 105
Carroll, Joseph T(homas) 1935- ... 102
Carroll, Joy 1924- ... 102
Carroll, Kenneth Lane 1924- ... 37-40R
Carroll, L(awrence) Patrick 1936- ... 111
Carroll, (Archer) Latrobe 1894- ... CANR-3
Earlier sketch in CA 4R
See also SATA 7
Carroll, Laura
See Parr, Lucy
Carroll, Lewis
See Dodgson, Charles Lutwidge
See also DLB 18
See also CLR 2
Carroll, Loren 1904-1978 ... 85-88
Obituary ... 81-84
Carroll, Martin
See Carr, Margaret
Carroll, Paul 1927- ... 25-28R
See also DLB 16
Carroll, Paul Vincent 1900-1968 ... 9-10R
Obituary ... 25-28R
See also DLB 10
See also CLC 10
Carroll, Peter N(eil) 1943- ... 102
Carroll, Phil 1895-1971 ... CAP-1
Earlier sketch in CA 13-14
Carroll, Raymond 1924- ... 126
See also SATA 47
Carroll, Robert
See Alpert, Hollis
Carroll, Robert P(eter) 1941- ... 105
Carroll, Rosalynn
See Katz, Carol
Carroll, Ruth (Robinson) 1899- ... CANR-1
Earlier sketch in CA 4R
Carroll, St. Thomas Marion
See Carroll, Tom M.
Carroll, Sheila Baker 1918(?)-1984
Obituary ... 113
Carroll, Sister Mary Gerald 1913- ... 23-24R
Carroll, Stephen J(ohn), Jr. 1930- ... 41-44R
Carroll, Ted
See Carroll, Thomas Theodore, Jr.
Carroll, Theodus 1928- ... 69-72
Carroll, Thomas J. 1909-1971 ... 2R
Obituary ... 103
Carroll, Thomas Theodore, Jr. 1925- ... 11-12R
Carroll, Tom M. 1950- ... 53-56
Carroll, Vern 1933- ... 57-60
Carroll, Vinnette (Justine) ... 123
Brief entry ... 114
See also BW
Carron, Malcolm 1917- Brief entry ... 105
Carrott, Richard G. 1924- ... 85-88
Carrouges, Michel
See Couturier, Louis (Joseph)
Carrow, Milton M(ichael) 1912- ... CANR-16
Earlier sketch in CA 25-28R
Carr-Saunders, Alexander (Morris)
1886-1966 ... CANR-20
Obituary ... 103
Earlier sketch in CA 3R
Carruth, Estelle 1910- ... 9-10R
Carruth, Gorton Veeder 1925- ... CANR-6
Earlier sketch in CA 57-60
Carruth, Hayden 1921- ... CANR-4
Earlier sketch in CA 9-10R
See also SATA 47
See also DLB 5
See also CLC 4, 7, 10, 18
Carruthers, Ben F(rederick) 1911- ... 114
Carruthers, Malcolm Euan 1938- ... 102
Carruthers, Peter 1952- ... 126
Carry, (Benjamin) Peter 1942- ... 105
Carryaway, Nick
See Murray, John F(rancis)
Carryl, Charles E. 1841-1920 ... DLB-42
Carsac, Francis
See Bordes, Francois
Carsberg, Bryan Victor 1939- ... CANR-12
Earlier sketch in CA 29-32R
Carse, James P(earce) 1932- ... 23-24R
Carse, Robert 1902-1971 ... CANR-1
Obituary ... 29-32R
Earlier sketch in CA 4R
See also SATA 5
Carskadon, Thomas R. 1901(?)-1983(?)
Obituary ... 108
Carson, Ada Lou 1932- ... 110
Carson, Alan 1951- ... 115
Carson, Captain James ... CANR-26
Earlier sketches in CA 19-20, CAP-2
Carson, Ciaran 1948- Brief entry ... 112
Carson, Clayborne 1944- ... 105
Carson, F(ranklin) John 1920- ... 11-12R
Carson, Gerald (Hewes) 1899- ... CANR-16
Earlier sketches in CA 4R, CANR-1
Carson, Hampton L(awrence) 1914- ... 5-6R
Carson, Herbert L(ee) 1929- ... 29-32R
Carson, J(ohn) Franklin 1920- ... 15-16R
See also SATA 1
Carson, Jane Dennison ?-1984 Obituary ... 114
Carson, Kit
See Carson, Xanthus
Carson, Mary 1934- ... 41-44R
Carson, Rachel Louise 1907-1964 ... 77-80
See also SATA 23
Carson, Ray F(ritziof) 1939- ... 61-64
Carson, Robert 1909-1983 ... 21-22R
Obituary ... 108
Carson, Robert B. 1934- ... CANR-6
Earlier sketch in CA 57-60
Carson, Robert C(harles) 1930- ... 29-32R
Carson, Ronald A(lan) 1940- ... 119
Carson, Rosalind
See Chittenden, Margaret
Carson, Ruth
See Bugbee, Ruth Carson
Carson, S. M.
See Gorsline, (Sally) Marie
Carson, William Glasgow Bruce 1891- ... 5-6R
Carson, Xanthus 1910- ... 57-60
Carstairs, George Morrison 1916- ... 69-72
Carstairs, Kathleen
See Pendower, Jacques
Carsten, Francis Ludwig 1911- ... 13-14R
Carstens, Grace Pearce ... 2R
Carstensen, Roger Norwood 1920- ... CANR-2
Earlier sketch in CA 5-6R
Carswell, Catherine 1879-1946 ... DLB-36
Carswell, Evelyn M(edicus) 1919- ... 57-60
Carswell, John (Patrick) 1918- ... CANR-21
Earlier sketch in CA 9-10R
Carswell, Leslie
See Stephens, Rosemary
Carte, Gene E(dward) 1938- ... 61-64
Carter, Alan 1936- ... 33-36R
Carter, Albert Howard 1913-1970 ... CAP-2
Earlier sketch in CA 25-28
Carter, Alfred Edward 1914- ... 33-36R
Carter, Amon Giles, Jr. 1919-1982
Obituary ... 111
Carter, Angela 1940- ... CANR-12
Earlier sketch in CA 53-56
See also DLB 14
See also CLC 5, 41
Carter, Ann
See Brooks, Anne Tedlock
Carter, Anne
See Brooks, Anne Tedlock
Carter, Anne Pitts 1925- Brief entry ... 106
Carter, Arthur M. 1911-1988 Obituary ... 125
Carter, Ashley
See Whittington, Harry (Benjamin)
Carter, Barbara (Ellen) 1925-1988 ... CANR-10
Obituary ... 126
Earlier sketch in CA 53-56
Carter, Boyd (George) 1908-1980 ... CANR-7
Earlier sketch in CA 13-14R
Carter, Bruce
See Hough, Richard (Alexander)
Carter, Burnham 1901(?)-1979 Obituary ... 89-92
Carter, Byron L. 1924- ... 23-24R
Carter, C(edric) O(swald) 1917-1984
Obituary ... 112
Carter, Carolle J(ean) 1934- ... 81-84
Carter, Charles Frederick 1919- ... CANR-20
Earlier sketches in CA 1R, CANR-4
Carter, Charles H(oward) 1927- ... 11-12R
Carter, Charles W(ebb) 1905- ... 21-22R
Carter, Dan T. 1940- ... 65-68
Carter, David C(harles) 1946- ... 45-48
Carter, Don E(arl) 1917- ... 73-76
Carter, Dorothy Sharp 1921- ... 49-52
See also SATA 8
Carter, E. Lawrence 1910- ... 25-28R
Carter, Edward Julian 1902-1982 ... 5-6R
Obituary ... 107
Carter, Elliott Cook 1908- ... 89-92
Carter, Ernestine Marie ?-1983 Obituary ... 110
Carter, Everett 1919- ... 13-14R
Carter, Forrest 1927(?)-1979 ... 107
See also SATA 32
Carter, Frances Monet 1923- ... 37-40R
Carter, Frances Tunnell ... 37-40R
Carter, George F(rancis) 1912- ... CANR-4
Earlier sketch in CA 7-8R
Carter, Gwendolen M(argaret) 1906- ... CANR-19
Earlier sketches in CA 1R, CANR-4
Carter, Harold 1925- ... 33-36R
Carter, Harry Graham 1901-1982 Obituary ... 106
Carter, Harvey L(ewis) 1904- ... 23-24R
Carter, Helene 1887-1960 ... SATA-15
Carter, Henry
See Leslie, Frank
Carter, Henry Hare 1905- ... 41-44R
Carter, (William) Hodding 1907-1972 ... CAP-1
Obituary ... 33-36R
Earlier sketch in CA 13-14
See also SATA 2, 27
Carter, Hugh 1895- ... 37-40R
Carter, Hurricane
See Carter, Rubin
Carter, J(ohn) Anthony 1943- ... 61-64
Carter, James E(dward) 1935- ... CANR-22
Earlier sketches in CA 57-60, CANR-7
Carter, James Earl, Jr. 1924- ... 69-72
Carter, James Puckette 1933- ... 33-36R
Carter, James Richard 1940- ... 33-36R
Carter, Jane (Borsch) Robbins
See Robbins-Carter, Jane (Borsch)
Carter, Janet 1938- ... 104
Carter, Jimmy
See Carter, James Earl, Jr.
Carter, John (Waynflete) 1905-1975 ... 7-8R
Obituary ... 57-60
Carter, John Franklin 1897-1967
Obituary ... 25-28R
Carter, John Mack 1928- ... 103
Carter, John Stewart 1912-1965 ... CAP-1
Earlier sketch in CA 11-12
Carter, John T(homas) 1921- ... 33-36R
Carter, Joseph 1912-1984 ... 49-52
Obituary ... 112
Carter, K(ay) Codell 1939- ... 110
Carter, Katharine J(ones) 1905- ... 5-6R
See also SATA 2
Carter, Landon 1710-1778 ... DLB-31
Carter, Lief Hastings 1940- ... CANR-6
Earlier sketch in CA 57-60
Carter, (Bessie) Lillian (Gordy) 1898-1983 ... 118
Obituary ... 111
Brief entry ... 105
Carter, Lin 1930- ... 41-44R
See also DLBY 81
Carter, Lonnie 1942- ... CANR-9
Earlier sketch in CA 65-68
Carter, Luther J(ordan) 1927- ... 57-60
Carter, M(argaret) L(ouise) 1948- ... 33-36R
Carter, Margaret (Mary) 1923- ... 107
Carter, Martin (Wylde) 1927- ... 102
Carter, Mary ... CANR-5
Earlier sketch in CA 9-10R
Carter, Mary Ellen 1923- ... 25-28R
Carter, Mary Kennedy ... 65-68
Carter, Neil 1913- ... 17-18R

Carter, Nevada
See Paine, Lauran (Bosworth)
Carter, Nicholas
See Dey, Frederic (Merrill) Van Rensselaer
Carter, Nick
See Avallone, Michael (Angelo), Jr.
and Ballard, (Willis) Todhunter
and Crider, (Allen) Bill(y)
and Dey, Frederic (Merrill) Van Rensselaer
and Hayes, Ralph E(ugene)
and Henderson, M(arilyn) R(uth)
and Lynds, Dennis
and Randisi, Robert J(oseph)
and Rasof, Henry
and Smith, Martin Cruz
and Stratemeyer, Edward L.
and Swain, Dwight V(reeland)
and Wallmann, Jeffrey M(iner)
Carter, Paul A(llen) 1926- ... CANR-13
Earlier sketch in CA 33-36R
Carter, Paul J(efferson), Jr. 1912-1975 ... CAP-2
Earlier sketch in CA 21-22
Carter, Peter 1929- ... 69-72
Carter, Phyllis Ann
See Eberle, Irmengarde
Carter, Ralph
See Neubauer, William Arthur
Carter, Randolph 1914- ... 101
Carter, Richard 1918- ... CANR-8
Earlier sketch in CA 61-64
Carter, Richard D(uane) 1929- ... 111
Carter, Robert A(yres) 1923- ... 33-36R
Carter, Robert M(ack) 1925- ... 33-36R
Carter, Roger 1939- ... 119
Carter, (Eleanor) Rosalynn (Smith) 1927- ... 113
Carter, Rubin 1937- Brief entry ... 113
Carter, Samuel III 1904- ... 57-60
See also SATA 37
Carter, Sebastian 1941- ... 126
Carter, Victor A(lbert) 1902- ... CAP-1
Earlier sketch in CA 9-10
Carter, William 1934- ... 33-36R
Carter, William Ambrose 1899- ... CAP-1
Earlier sketch in CA 17-18
Carter, William Beverly, Jr. 1921-1982
Obituary ... 110
Carter, William E. 1926-1983 ... 19-20R
Obituary ... 110
See also SATA 1, 35
Carter, William Lee 1925- ... 1R
Carter, Worrall Reed 1885(?)-1975
Obituary ... 57-60
Carterette, Edward C(alvin) 1921- ... 41-44R
Carter-Harrison, Paul
See Harrison, Paul Carter
Carter-Ruck, Peter F(rederick) 1914- ... 97-100
Cartey, Wilfred (George Onslow)
1931- ... CANR-25
Earlier sketch in CA 73-76
See also BW
Carthy, Mother Mary Peter 1911- ... 13-14R
Cartier, Xam Wilson 1949(?)- ... 125
See also BW
Cartland, Barbara (Hamilton) 1901- ... CANR-6
Earlier sketch in CA 11-12R
Cartledge, Paul 1947- ... 124
Cartledge, Samuel Antoine 1903- ... 3R
Cartlidge, Barbara 1922- ... 121
Cartlidge, Michelle 1950- ... 93-96
See also SATA 37, 49
Cartnal, Alan 1950- ... 105
Cartner, William Carruthers 1910- ... 73-76
See also SATA 11
Carto, Willis A(llison) 1926- ... 114
Cartter, Allan Murray 1922-1976 ... CANR-8
Earlier sketch in CA 5-6R
Cartwright, Desmond S(pencer) 1924- ... 89-92
Cartwright, Gary 1934- ... 89-92
Cartwright, James McGregor
See Jennings, Leslie Nelson
Cartwright, Joseph H. 1939- ... 73-76
Cartwright, N.
See Scofield, Norma Margaret Cartwright
Cartwright, Rosalind Dymond 1922- ... 81-84
Cartwright, Sally 1923- ... CANR-2
Earlier sketch in CA 49-52
See also SATA 9
Cartwright, Vanessa
See Preston, Harry
Cartwright, William H(olman) 1915- ... 9-10R
Carty, James William, Jr. 1925- ... 53-56
Caruba, Alan 1937- ... 65-68
Caruso, Enrico 1873-1921 Brief entry ... 115
Caruso, John Anthony 1907- ... 33-36R
Carus-Wilson, Eleanora M(ary) 1897- ... 7-8R
Caruth, Donald L(ewis) 1935- ... 29-32R
Caruthers, Osgood 1915-1985 Obituary ... 117
Caruthers, William Alexander 1802-1846 .. DLB-3
Carvajal, Ricardo
See Meneses, Enrique
Carvalho-Neto, Paulo de 1923- ... CANR-4
Earlier sketch in CA 53-56
Carvell, Fred J. 1934- ... 29-32R
Carver, Dave
See Bingley, David Ernest
Carver, Frank G(ould) 1928- ... 49-52
Carver, Fred D(onald) 1936- ... 29-32R
Carver, Jeffrey A(llan) 1949- ... CANR-18
Earlier sketch in CA 101
Carver, John
See Gardner, Richard (M.)
Carver, Jonathan 1710-1780 ... DLB-31
Carver, (Richard) Michael (Power)
1915- ... CANR-14
Earlier sketch in CA 69-72
Carver, Norman F., Jr. 1928- ... 41-44R
Carver, Raymond 1938-1988 ... CANR-17
Obituary ... 126
Earlier sketch in CA 33-36R
See also DLBY 84
See also CLC 22, 36
Carver, Saxon Rowe 1905- ... CAP-1
Earlier sketch in CA 13-14
Carvic, Heron ?-1980 ... 53-56
Obituary ... 103
Carwell, L'Ann
See McKissack, Patricia (L'Ann) C(arwell)
Cary
See Cary, Louis F(avreau)
Cary, Barbara Knapp 1912(?)-1975
Obituary ... 61-64
See also SATA 31
Cary, Bob 1921- ... 105
Cary, Diana Serra
See Cary, Peggy-Jean Montgomery
Cary, Harold Whiting 1903- ... CAP-1
Earlier sketch in CA 9-10
Cary, James Donald 1919- ... 5-6R
Cary, John H. 1926- ... 11-12R
Cary, (Arthur) Joyce (Lunel) 1888-1957
Brief entry ... 104
See also DLB 15
See also TCLC 1, 29
Cary, Jud
See Tubb, E(dwin) C(harles)
Cary, Lee J(ames) 1925- ... 29-32R
Cary, Louis F(avreau) 1915- ... SATA-9
Cary, Lucian 1886-1971 ... 33-36R
Cary, Otis 1921- ... 61-64
Cary, Peggy-Jean Montgomery 1918- ... 57-60
Cary, Richard 1909- ... 23-24R
Cary, William L(ucius) 1910-1983
Obituary ... 109
Cary, Zenja Saft 1932(?)-1983 Obituary ... 110
Caryl, Jean
See Kaplan, Jean Caryl Korn
Caryl, Warren 1920- ... 23-24R
Casada, James A(llen) 1942- ... 109
Casado, Pablo Gil 1931- ... 49-52
Casady, Cort (Boon) 1947- ... CANR-22
Earlier sketch in CA 105
Casady, Donald Rex 1926- ... 15-16R
Casalandra, Estelle
See Estelle, Sister Mary
Casale, Joan T(herese) 1935- ... 61-64
Casale, Ottavio M(ark) 1934- ... 104
Casals, Pablo
See Casals, Pau Carlos Salvador Defillo de
Casals, Pau Carlos Salvador Defillo de
1876-1973 ... 93-96
Obituary ... 45-48
Casas, Penelope 1943- ... 114
Casberg, Melvin Augustus 1909- ... 104
Cascio, Chuck 1946- ... 93-96
Casdorph, Herman Richard 1928- ... 101
Casdorph, Paul D(ouglas) 1932- ... 106
Case, Brian (David) 1937- ... 25-28R
Case, David 1937- ... 107
Case, Elinor Rutt 1914- ... 4R
Case, Fred E. 1918- ... CANR-4
Earlier sketch in CA 5-6R
Case, Geoffrey ... 77-80
Case, Jack Gaylord 1918(?)-1970
Obituary ... 104
Case, John 1944- ... 114
Case, Josephine Young 1907- ... CAP-2
Earlier sketch in CA 25-28
Case, Justin
See Gleadow, Rupert Seeley
Case, L. L.
See Lewin, Leonard C(ase)
Case, Leland D(avidson) 1900- ... 17-18R
Case, Lynn M(arshall) 1903- ... 15-16R
Case, Marshal T(aylor) 1941- ... 57-60
See also SATA 9
Case, Maurice 1910-1968 ... CAP-2
Earlier sketch in CA 19-20
Case, Michael
See Howard, Robert West
Case, Patricia J(une) 1952- ... 110
Case, Victoria 1897- ... 7-8R
Case, Walter 1909(?)-1983 Obituary ... 110
Casebier, Allan (Frank) 1934- ... 65-68
Casebier, Marjorie
See McCoy, Marjorie Casebier
Casebier, Virginia (Eleanor) 1918- ... 41-44R
Caseley, Judith 1951- ... 121
See also SATA 53
Caseleyr, Cam(ille Auguste Marie) 1909- .. CAP-1
Earlier sketch in CA 9-10
Casely-Hayford, J(oseph) E(phraim)
1866-1930 Brief entry ... 123
See also TCLC 24
Casement, Richard 1942-1982 Obituary ... 108
Casemore, Robert 1915- ... 73-76
Casewit, Curtis W(erner) 1922- ... CANR-21
Earlier sketches in CA 13-14R, CANR-6
See also SATA 4
Casey, Beatrice Vivian 1898(?)-1986
Obituary ... 120
Casey, Bill Harris 1930- ... 1R
Casey, Brigid 1950- ... 49-52
See also SATA 9
Casey, Daniel J(oseph) 1937- ... CANR-22
Earlier sketches in CA 57-60, CANR-6
Casey, Douglas R(obert) 1946- Brief entry .. 118
Casey, Edward Scott 1939- ... 102
Casey, Genevieve M(ary) 1916- ... 116
Casey, Gladys
See Grier, Barbara G(ene Damon)
Casey, Jack
See Casey, John
Casey, Jane Barnes 1942- ... 104
Casey, John (Dudley) 1939- ... CANR-23
Earlier sketch in CA 69-72
Casey, John 1950- ... 120
Casey, Juanita 1925- ... 49-52
See also DLB 14
Casey, Kevin 1940- ... 25-28R
Casey, Lawrence B. 1905-1977 ... 73-76
Obituary ... 69-72
Casey, Mart
See Casey, Michael T.
Casey, Michael 1947- ... 65-68
See also DLB 5
See also CLC 2
Casey, Michael T. 1922- ... 21-22R
Casey, Patrick
See Thurman, Wallace (Henry)
Casey, Richard Gardiner 1890-1976 ... 61-64
Obituary ... 65-68
Casey, Robert J(oseph) 1890-1962
Obituary ... 89-92
Casey, Rosemary 1904-1976 Obituary ... 65-68
Casey, Rosemary Alice (Christmann)
1922- ... 5-6R
Casey, Thomas Francis 1923- ... 15-16R
Casey, W. Wilson 1954- ... 107
Casey, Warren 1935- ... 101
See also CLC 12
Casey, William J(oseph) 1913-1987
Obituary ... 122
Casey, William Van Etten 1914- ... 57-60
Casgrain, Therese F. 1896(?)-1981 ... 110
Obituary ... 108
Cash, Anthony 1933- ... 102
Cash, Arthur H(ill) 1922- Brief entry ... 110
Cash, Grace (Savannah) 1915- ... 23-24R
Cash, Grady
See Cash, Grace (Savannah)
Cash, J(ames) Allan 1901- ... CANR-4
Earlier sketch in CA 7-8R
Cash, John R.
See Cash, Johnny
Cash, Johnny 1932- Brief entry ... 110
Cash, Joseph H(arper) 1927- ... 41-44R
Cash, Kevin (Richard) 1926-1985 ... 77-80
Obituary ... 115
Cash, Philip 1931- ... 106
Cash, Sebastian
See Smithells, Roger (William)
Cashen, Richard A(nthony) 1938- ... 112
Cashin, Edward J(oseph, Jr.) 1927- ... CANR-9
Earlier sketch in CA 21-22R
Cashin, Edward L(awrence)
See Cashin, Edward J(oseph, Jr.)
Cashin, James A. 1911-1982 ... CANR-10
Earlier sketch in CA 17-18R
Cashman, John
See Davis, Timothy Francis Tothill
Cashman, Paul Harrison 1924- ... 15-16R
Cashman, Sean Dennis 1943- ... 107
Cashmore, E. Ellis 1949- ... 116
Cashmore, Ernest
See Cashmore, E. Ellis
Caskey, John L. 1908- ... 15-16R
Casler, Lawrence (Ray) 1932- ... 49-52
Casmier, Adam A(nthony) 1934- ... 33-36R
Casmir, Fred L. 1928- ... 37-40R
Casner, A(ndrew) James 1907- ... CANR-4
Earlier sketch in CA 7-8R
Caso, Adolph 1934- ... CANR-7
Earlier sketch in CA 57-60
Casolaro, Daniel 1949- ... 114
Cason, Mabel Earp 1892-1965 ... CAP-1
Earlier sketch in CA 13-14
See also SATA 10
Casona, Alejandro
See Alvarez, Alejandro Rodriguez
See also CLC 49
Casotti, Fred 1923- ... 93-96
Caspari, Ernest W(olfgang) 1909- ... 41-44R
Caspary, Vera 1899-1987 ... CANR-9
Obituary ... 122
Earlier sketch in CA 13-14R
Casper, Barry M(ichael) 1939- ... 69-72
Casper, Bill, Jr.
See Casper, William Earl, Jr.
Casper, Billy
See Casper, William Earl, Jr.
Casper, Henry W. 1909- ... 37-40R
Casper, Jonathan D(avid) 1942- ... 53-56
Casper, Joseph Andrew 1941- ... 65-68
Casper, Leonard Ralph 1923- ... 2R
Casper, Linda Ty
See Ty-Casper, Linda
Casper, William Earl, Jr. 1931- ... 121
Casque, Sammy
See Davis, Sydney Charles Houghton
Casriel, H(arold) Daniel 1924-1983 ... 15-16R
Obituary ... 110
Cass, Carl Bartholomew 1901- ... CAP-1
Earlier sketch in CA 9-10
Cass, James (Michael) 1915- ... 101
Cass, Joan E(velyn) ... CANR-20
Earlier sketches in CA 4R, CANR-5
See also SATA 1
Cass, Ronald A(ndrew) 1949- ... 106
Cass, Zoe
See Low, Lois Dorothea
Cassady, Carolyn 1923- ... DLB-16
Cassady, Neal 1926-1968 ... DLB-16
Cassady, Ralph, Jr. 1900-1978 ... CANR-4
Obituary ... 77-80
Earlier sketch in CA 2R
Cassandra
See Connor, William (Neil)
Cassara, Ernest 1925- ... 41-44R
Cassata, Mary B. 1930- ... 121
Cassavant, Sharron Greer 1939- ... 125
Cassavetes, John 1929- ... 85-88
See also CLC 20
Cassedy, James H(iggins) 1919- ... 4R
Cassedy, Sylvia 1930- ... CANR-22
Earlier sketch in CA 105
See also SATA 27
Cassel, Don 1942- ... 110
Cassel, Lili
See Wronker, Lili Cassel
Cassel, Mana-Zucca 1891-1981 Obituary ... 103
Cassel, Russell N. 1911- ... 37-40R
Cassel, Virginia Cunningham ... 105
Cassell, Anthony K. 1941- ... 120
Cassell, Frank A(llan) 1941- ... 33-36R
Cassell, Frank Hyde 1916- ... 37-40R
Cassell, Richard A(llan) 1921- ... 23-24R
Cassell, Sylvia 1924- ... 5-6R
Cassells, Cyrus (Curtis III) 1957- ... 112
Cassells, John
See Duncan, W(illiam) Murdoch
Casselman, Karen Leigh 1942- ... 107
Cassels, Alan 1929- ... CANR-13
Earlier sketch in CA 33-36R
Cassels, Louis 1922-1974 ... CANR-4
Obituary ... 45-48
Earlier sketch in CA 9-10R
Casserley, H(enry) C(yril) 1903- ... CANR-9
Earlier sketch in CA 65-68
Casserley, Julian Victor Langmead 1909- .. 9-10R
Casserly, John J(oseph) 1927- ... 120
Cassiday, Bruce (Bingham) 1920- ... CANR-19
Earlier sketches in CA 1R, CANR-4
Cassidy, Claude
See Paine, Lauran (Bosworth)
Cassidy, Daniel J(ames) 1956- ... 119
Cassidy, Frederic Gomes 1907- ... 4R
Cassidy, George
See Vance, William E.
Cassidy, Harold G(omes) 1906- ... 25-28R
Cassidy, John 1928- ... 114
Cassidy, John A(lbert) 1908- ... 33-36R
Cassidy, John R(ufus) 1922- ... 89-92
Cassidy, Jude (Anne) 1955- ... 121
Cassidy, Michael 1936- ... 97-100
Cassidy, Richard J(oseph) 1942- ... 114
Cassidy, Vincent H. 1923- ... 21-22R
Cassidy, William L(awrence Robert) ... 103
Cassilis, Robert
See Edwardes, Michael (F. H.)
Cassill, Kay ... 89-92
Cassill, R(onald) V(erlin) 1919- ... CANR-7
Earlier sketch in CA 9-10R
See also CAAS 1
See also DLB 6
See also CLC 4, 23
Cassils, Peter
See Keele, Kenneth D(avid)
Cassin, Rene Samuel 1887-1976
Obituary ... 65-68
Cassinelli, C(harles) W(illiam, Jr.) 1925- ... 3R
Cassity, (Allen) Turner 1929- ... CANR-11
Earlier sketch in CA 17-18R
See also CLC 6, 42
Casso, Evans J(oseph) 1914- ... 57-60
Cassola, Albert M(aria) 1915- ... CAP-1
Earlier sketch in CA 9-10
Cassola, Carlo 1917-1987 ... 101
Obituary ... 121
Casson, Hugh Maxwell 1910- ... CANR-20
Earlier sketch in CA 103
Casson, Lionel 1914- ... CANR-3
Earlier sketch in CA 9-10R
Casstevens, Thomas W(illiam) 1937- ... 19-20R
Cast, David (Jesse Dale) 1942- ... 109
Castagna, Edwin 1909-1983 ... CAP-2
Obituary ... 111
Earlier sketch in CA 17-18
Castagnola, Lawrence A. 1933- ... CANR-12
Earlier sketch in CA 29-32R
Castaneda, Carlos 1931- ... 25-28R
See also CLC 12
Castaneda, Hector-Neri 1924- ... CANR-19
Earlier sketches in CA 7-8R, CANR-3
Castaneda, James A(gustin) 1933- ... 41-44R
Castel, Albert 1928- ... CANR-5
Earlier sketch in CA 1R
Castel, J(ean) G(abriel) 1928- ... CANR-25
Earlier sketches in CA 21-22R, CANR-9
Castellan, N(orman) John, Jr. 1939- ... 37-40R
Castellaneta, Carlo 1930- ... CANR-11
Earlier sketch in CA 13-14R
Castellano, Giuseppe 1893-1977 Obituary .. 73-76
Castellanos, Jane Mollie Robinson
1913- ... 11-12R
See also SATA 9
Castellanos, Rosario 1915-1974 Obituary .. 53-56
Castellon, Federico 1914-1971 ... SATA-48
Castells, Manuel 1942- ... 115
Castells, Matilde O(livella) 1929- ... 69-72
Castelnuovo-Tedesco, P(ietro) 1925- ... 21-22R
Castetter, William Benjamin 1914- ... CANR-4
Earlier sketch in CA 4R
Castillo, Edmund L. 1924- ... 29-32R
See also SATA 1
Castillo, Richard Griswold del
See Griswold del Castillo, Richard
Castillo Puche, Jose Luis 1919-
Brief entry ... 110
Castle, Anthony (Percy) 1938- ... 113
Castle, Charles 1939- ... 33-36R
Castle, Coralie 1924- ... 57-60
Castle, Damon
See Smith, Richard Rein

Castle, Edgar Bradshaw 1897-1973
Obituary ... 104
Castle, Emery N(eal) 1923- ... 4R
Castle, Frances
See Leader, (Evelyn) Barbara (Blackburn)
Castle, Kate ... 123
Castle, Keith 1927(?)-1985 Obituary ... 118
Castle, Lee
See Ogan, George F.
and Ogan, Margaret E. (Nettles)
Castle, Marian (Johnson) ... CAP-2
Earlier sketch in CA 17-18
Castle, Mort 1946- ... CANR-14
Earlier sketch in CA 81-84
Castle, Paul
See Howard, Vernon (Linwood)
Castle, Robert
See Hamilton, Edmond
Castle, Robert W., Jr. 1929- ... 25-28R
Castle, Sue G(aronzik) 1942- ... 105
Castle, Terry (Jacqueline) 1953- ... 112
Castle, Tony
See Castle, Anthony (Percy)
Castle, William 1914-1977 ... 77-80
Obituary ... 69-72
Castleman, Harry 1953- ... 109
Castleman, Michael 1950- ... 108
Castleman, (Esther) Riva 1930-
Brief entry ... 117
Castlemon, Harry
See Fosdick, Charles Austin
Castles, Francis G(eoffrey) 1943- ... CANR-17
Earlier sketch in CA 25-28R
Castles, Lance 1937- ... 25-28R
Castleton, Virginia 1925- ... 49-52
Castor, Grahame (Douglas) 1932- ... CANR-7
Earlier sketch in CA 15-16R
Castor, Henry 1909- ... 17-18R
Castoro, Laura A(nn) 1948- ... 124
Castro, Americo 1885-1972 ... 37-40R
Castro, Antonio 1946- ... 53-56
Castro, Fidel 1927- Brief entry ... 110
Castro, Jan Garden 1945- ... 120
Castro, Tony
See Castro, Antonio
Castro-Klaren, Sara 1942- ... 61-64
Castronovo, David 1945- ... 114
Castro Ruz, Fidel
See Castro, Fidel
Casty, Alan Howard 1929- ... CANR-4
Earlier sketch in CA 3R
Caswall, Edward 1814-1878 ... DLB-32
Caswell, Helen (Rayburn) 1923- ... 33-36R
See also SATA 12
Caswell, Margaret (Betsy) R(oss)
1903(?)-1982 Obituary ... 107
Catala, Rafael 1942- ... CANR-13
Earlier sketch in CA 73-76
Catalano, Donald B(ernard) 1920- ... 57-60
Catalano, Joseph S(tellario) 1928- ... 102
Cataldo, Michael F. 1947- ... 122
Catanese, Anthony James (Jr.) 1942- ... CANR-14
Earlier sketch in CA 29-32R
Catania, A(nthony) Charles 1936- ... 37-40R
Catanzariti, John 1942- ... 124
Cate, Benjamin W(ilson) 1931- ... 73-76
Cate, Curtis 1924- ... CANR-9
Earlier sketch in CA 53-56
Cate, Curtis Wolsey 1884-1976 Obituary ... 61-64
Cate, Dick
See Cate, Richard Edward Nelson
Cate, Richard Edward Nelson 1932- ... 73-76
See also SATA 28
Cate, Robert L(ouis) 1932- ... 111
Cate, William Burke 1924- ... 13-14R
Cateora, Philip Rene 1932- ... 7-8R
Cater, (Silas) Douglass 1923- ... CANR-1
Earlier sketch in CA 4R
Cates, Ray A., Jr. 1940- ... 29-32R
Cates, Tory
See Bird, Sarah McCabe
Cathcart, Helen ... CANR-2
Earlier sketch in CA 7-8R
Cathcart, Noble Aydelotte 1898-1988
Obituary ... 126
Cathcart, Robert S(tephen) 1923- ... 101
Cather, Willa (Sibert) 1873-1947
Brief entry ... 104
See also SATA 30
See also DLB 9, 54
See also DLBD 1
See also CDALB 1865-1917
See also TCLC 1, 11
See also SSC 2
Catherall, Arthur 1906- ... 7-8R
See also SATA 3
Cathers, David M. 1941- ... 111
Cathers, Ken 1951- ... 112
Catherwood, (Henry) Frederick (Ross)
1925- ... 106
Cathey, Cornelius Oliver 1908- ... 3R
Cathon, Laura E(lizabeth) 1908- ... 5-6R
See also SATA 27
Catledge, Turner 1901-1983 ... 57-60
Obituary ... 109
See also AITN 1
Catlin, George E(dward) G(ordon)
1896-1979 ... 13-14R
Obituary ... 85-88
Catlin, Warren Benjamin 1881-1968 ... 4R
Obituary ... 103
Catlin, Wynelle 1930- ... 65-68
See also SATA 13
Catling, Darrel (Charles) 1909- ... 7-8R
Catling, Patrick Skene 1925- Brief entry ... 115
Catlow, Joanna
See Lowry, Joan (Catlow)

Cato
See Howard, Peter D(unsmore)
Cato, Nancy (Fotheringham) 1917- ... CAP-1
Earlier sketch in CA 49-52
Catoir, John T. 1931- ... CANR-11
Earlier sketch in CA 25-28R
Caton, Charles E(dwin) 1928- ... 9-10R
Caton, Hiram P. 1936- ... CANR-4
Earlier sketch in CA 53-56
Caton-Thompson, Gertrude 1888-1985 ... 122
Obituary ... 116
Catron, Louis E. 1932- ... 45-48
Cattan, Henry 1906- ... 29-32R
Cattaui, Georges 1896-1974 ... CAP-2
Earlier sketch in CA 25-28
Cattell, Everett L(ewis) 1905- ... 4R
Cattell, Psyche 1893- ... 41-44R
Cattell, Raymond Bernard 1905- ... CANR-2
Earlier sketch in CA 7-8R
Catto, Max(well Jeffrey) 1909- ... 105
Catton, (Charles) Bruce 1899-1978 ... CANR-7
Obituary ... 81-84
Earlier sketch in CA 5-6R
See also SATA 2, 24
See also DLB 17
See also CLC 35
See also AITN 1
Catton, William Bruce 1926- ... CANR-1
Earlier sketch in CA 4R
Catton, William R(obert), Jr. 1926- ... 109
Catudal, Honore M(arc, Jr.) 1944- ... CANR-12
Earlier sketch in CA 69-72
Catz, Max
See Glaser, Milton
Caudell, Marian 1930- ... 121
See also SATA 52
Caudill, Harry M(onroe) 1922- ... CANR-14
Earlier sketch in CA 33-36R
Caudill, Rebecca 1899-1985 ... CANR-2
Obituary ... 117
Earlier sketch in CA 5-6R
See also SATA 1, 44
Caudill, William W(ayne) 1914-1983
Obituary ... 110
Caudwell, Christopher
See Sprigg, C(hristopher) St. John
Cauffield, Margaret E(ileen) 1932- ... 122
Caughey, John L(yon) 1941- ... 115
Caughey, John Walton 1902- Brief entry ... 106
Caulder, Colline 1945- ... 113
Cauldwell, Frank
See King, Francis H(enry)
Cauley, John R(owan) 1908-1976
Obituary ... 65-68
Cauley, Lorinda Bryan 1951- ... 101
See also SATA 43, 46
Cauley, Terry
See Cauley, Troy Jesse
Cauley, Troy Jesse 1902- ... CANR-1
Earlier sketch in CA 4R
Caulfield, Malachy Francis 1915- ... CANR-14
Earlier sketch in CA 77-80
Caulfield, Max
See Caulfield, Malachy Francis
Caulfield, Peggy F. 1926-1987 ... 7-8R
Obituary ... 123
See also SATA 53
Caulfield, Sean 1925- ... 108
Cauliflower, Sebastian
See Seldes, Gilbert (Vivian)
Cauman, Samuel 1910-1971 ... CAP-2
Earlier sketch in CA 23-24
See also SATA 48
Caunitz, William J. 1935- ... CLC-34
Caunitz, William J. 1935- Brief entry ... 125
Causley, Charles (Stanley) 1917- ... CANR-5
Earlier sketch in CA 9-10R
See also SATA 3
See also DLB 27
See also CLC 7
Caute, David 1936- ... CANR-1
Earlier sketch in CA 3R
See also CAAS 4
See also DLB 14
See also CLC 29
Cautela, Joseph R(ichard) 1927- ... 106
Cauthen, Baker James 1909-1985
Obituary ... 115
Cauthen, Irby Bruce, Jr. 1919- ... 111
Cauthen, W(ilfred) Kenneth 1930- ... CANR-7
Earlier sketch in CA 7-8R
Cauvin, Jean-Pierre (Bernard) 1936- ... 116
Cauwels, Janice M(arie) 1949- ... 110
Cava, Esther Laden 1916- ... 37-40R
Cavafy, C(onstantine) P(eter)
See Kavafis, Konstantinos Petrou
See also TCLC 2, 7
Cavaiani, Mabel 1919- ... CANR-21
Earlier sketches in CA 57-60, CANR-6
Cavalcanti, Alberto (de Almeida)
1897-1982 Obituary ... 107
Cavalier, Julian 1931- ... CANR-2
Earlier sketch in CA 49-52
Cavaliero, Glen 1927- ... CANR-13
Earlier sketch in CA 73-76
Cavallari, Alberto 1927- ... CANR-10
Earlier sketch in CA 23-24R
Cavallaro, Ann (Abelson) 1918- ... 5-6R
Cavallo, Diana 1931- ... CANR-2
Earlier sketch in CA 1R
See also SATA 7
Cavallo, Evelyn
See Spark, Muriel (Sarah)
Cavallo, Robert M. 1932- ... CANR-10
Earlier sketch in CA 65-68
Cavan, Romilly 1914(?)-1975 Obituary ... 61-64
Cavan, Sherri 1938- ... 19-20R

Cavanagh, Gerald F(rancis) 1931- ... 41-44R
Cavanagh, Helen (Carol) 1939- ... 104
See also SATA 37, 48
Cavanagh, John B. 1908-1983 Obituary ... 110
Cavanagh, John Richard 1904- ... CAP-2
Earlier sketch in CA 19-20
Cavanagh, Richard E(dward) 1946- ... 121
Cavanah, Frances 1899-1982 ... 15-16R
See also SATA 1, 31
Cavanaugh, Arthur 1926- ... 17-18R
Cavani, Liliana 1936- ... 110
Cavanna, Betty
See Harrison, Elizabeth Cavanna
See also SATA 1, 30
See also SAAS 4
See also CLC 12
Cavanna, Elizabeth Allen
See Harrison, Elizabeth Cavanna
Cave, Alfred A. 1935- ... 37-40R
Cave, Hugh Barnett 1910- ... CANR-2
Earlier sketch in CA 7-8R
Cave, Roderick (George James Munro)
1935- ... CANR-2
Earlier sketch in CA 7-8R
Cave, Thomas
See Steward, Samuel M(orris)
Cavell, Stanley (Louis) 1926- ... CANR-11
Earlier sketch in CA 61-64
Cavelti, Peter C(hristian) 1948- ... 116
Cavendish, J(ean) M(avis) 1932- ... 118
Cavendish, Richard 1930- ... CANR-20
Earlier sketches in CA 9-10R, CANR-5
Caveney, Philip (Richard) 1951- ... CANR-19
Earlier sketch in CA 102
Caverhill, Nicholas
See Kirk-Greene, Anthony (Hamilton
Millard)
Caverhill, William Melville 1910-1983
Obituary ... 111
Cavers, David F(arquhar) 1902-1988 ... 19-20R
Obituary ... 125
Cavert, Samuel McCrea 1888-1976 ... 37-40R
Cavert, Walter Dudley 1891- ... 1R
Caves, Richard E(arl) 1931- ... CANR-19
Earlier sketches in CA 4R, CANR-4
Cavett, Dick
See Cavett, Richard A.
Cavett, Richard A. 1936- ... 108
Cavin, Ruth (Brodie) 1918- ... CANR-8
Earlier sketch in CA 61-64
See also SATA 38
Cavitch, David 1933- ... 29-32R
Cavnes, Max P(arvin) 1922- ... 11-12R
Cavrell, Jean 1927- ... 107
Cawein, Madison 1865-1914 ... DLB-54
Cawelti, John G(eorge) 1929- ... 23-24R
Cawley, Linda 1949- ... 113
Cawley, Robert Ralston 1893-1973 ... CAP-2
Obituary ... 41-44R
Earlier sketch in CA 21-22
Cawley, Winifred 1915- ... 69-72
See also SATA 13
Cawood, John W. 1931- ... 33-36R
Caws, Ian 1945- ... 118
Caws, Mary Ann 1933- ... CANR-10
Earlier sketch in CA 25-28R
Caws, Peter (James) 1931- ... CANR-8
Earlier sketch in CA 17-18R
Cawthorne, Graham 1906(?)-1980
Obituary ... 97-100
Caxton, Pisistratus
See Lytton, Edward G(eorge) E(arle)
and L(ytton) Bulwer-Lytton, Baron
Cayce, Edgar E(vans) 1918- ... 23-24R
Cayce, Hugh Lynn 1907-1982 ... 25-28R
Obituary ... 107
Cayley, Michael (Forde) 1950- ... 53-56
Cayrol, Jean 1911- ... 89-92
See also CLC 11
Cayton, Andrew R(obert) L(ee) 1954- ... 126
Cayton, Horace R(oscoe) 1903-1970 ... CAP-1
Obituary ... 29-32R
Earlier sketch in CA 13-14
Cazalet-Keir, Thelma ... 25-28R
Cazamian, Louis Francois 1877-1965
Obituary ... 93-96
Cazden, Elizabeth 1950- ... 65-68
Cazden, Norman 1914- ... 37-40R
Cazden, Robert E. 1930- ... 33-36R
Cazeau, Charles J(ay) 1931- ... 104
Cazeaux, Isabelle 1926- ... 53-56
Cazel, Fred A(ugustus), Jr. 1921- ... 11-12R
Cazelles, Brigitte Jacqueline 1944- ... 102
Cazemajou, Jean 1924- ... 73-76
Cazet, Denys 1938- ... 108
See also SATA 41, 52
Cazzola, Gus 1934- ... 108
Cebula, Richard J(ohn) 1944- ... 111
Cebulash, Mel 1937- ... CANR-12
Earlier sketch in CA 29-32R
See also SATA 10
Cecchetti, Giovanni 1922- Brief entry ... 107
Cecelski, Elizabeth 1953- ... 119
Cech, John O(tto) 1944- ... 120
Cecil, (Edward Christian) David (Gascoyne)
1902-1986 ... CANR-13
Obituary ... 118
Earlier sketch in CA 61-64
Cecil, Henry
See Leon, Henry Cecil
Cecil, Hugh Mortimer
See Roberts, William
Cecil, Lamar (John Ryan, Jr.) 1932- ... 21-22R
Cecil, Lord David
See Cecil, (Edward Christian) David
(Gascoyne)

Cecil, R. H.
See Hewitt, Cecil Rolph
Cecil, Robert 1913- ... 53-56
Ceder, Georgiana Dorcas ... 2R
See also SATA 10
Cefkin, J. Leo 1916- ... 25-28R
Cegielka, Francis A(nthony) 1908- ... 37-40R
Ceitho, Dewi
See Jones, Evan David
Cela, Camilo Jose 1916- ... CANR-21
Earlier sketch in CA 21-22R
See also CLC 4, 13
Celaeno
See Harper, George W(illiam)
Celan, Paul
See Antschel, Paul
See also DLB 69
Celeste, Sister Marie ... 49-52
Celestino, Martha Laing 1951- ... 107
See also SATA 39
Celine, Louis-Ferdinand
See Destouches, Louis-Ferdinand
See also DLB 72
See also CLC 1, 3, 4, 7, 9, 15, 47
Cell, Edward (Charles) 1928- ... 21-22R
Cell, John W(hitson) 1935- ... 41-44R
Cellario, Alberto R. 1910(?)-1984
Obituary ... 112
Celler, Emanuel 1888-1981 Obituary ... 108
Celnik, Max 1933- ... 17-18R
Celoria, Francis (S. C.) 1926- ... 102
Cemach, Harry P(aul) 1917- ... 57-60
Cenci, Louis 1918- ... 17-18R
Cendrars, Blaise
See Sauser-Hall, Frederic
Censer, Jane T(urner) 1951- ... 123
Cente, H. F.
See Rocklin, Ross Louis
Center, Allen Harry 1912- ... CANR-4
Earlier sketch in CA 5-6R
Cento
See Cobbing, Bob
Centore, F. F. 1938- ... 25-28R
Ceram, C. W.
See Marek, Kurt W(illi)
Ceravolo, Joseph 1934-1988 ... 102
Obituary ... 126
Cerf, Bennett (Alfred) 1898-1971 ... CAP-2
Obituary ... 29-32R
Earlier sketch in CA 19-20
See also SATA 7
Cerf, Christopher (Bennett) 1941- ... 25-28R
See also SATA 2
Cerf, Jay H(enry) 1923-1974 ... CAP-2
Obituary ... 53-56
Earlier sketch in CA 19-20
Cerling, Charles (Edward), Jr. 1943- ... 111
Cermak, Laird S(cott) 1942- ... CANR-4
Earlier sketch in CA 53-56
Cermak, Martin
See Duchacek, Ivo D(uka)
Cerminara, Gina ... 17-18R
Cerney, James Vincent 1914- ... 23-24R
Cernuda (y Bidon), Luis 1902-1963
Obituary ... 89-92
Cerra, Frances 1946- ... 97-100
Cerri, Lawrence J. 1923- ... CANR-17
Earlier sketch in CA 89-92
Cerruti, James Smith 1918- ... 103
Certner, Simon 1909(?)-1979 Obituary ... 89-92
Cerutti, Maria Antonietta 1932- ... 25-28R
Cerutti, Toni
See Cerutti, Maria Antonietta
Cerutty, Percy Wells 1895-1975 ... CAP-2
Obituary ... 61-64
Earlier sketch in CA 25-28
Cervantes, Alfonso J(uan) 1920-1983
Obituary ... 110
Cervantes, Lucius F. 1914- ... 15-16R
Cerveri, Doris 1914- ... 101
Cervon, Jacqueline
See Moussard, Jacqueline
Cerwinske, Laura 1948- ... 111
Cerych, Ladislav 1925- ... CANR-7
Earlier sketch in CA 15-16R
Cesaire, Aime (Fernand) 1913- ... CANR-24
Earlier sketch in CA 65-68
See also BW
See also CLC 19, 32
Cesara, Manda
See Poewe, Karla
Cetin, Frank Stanley 1921- ... 4R
See also SATA 2
Cetron, Marvin Jerome 1930- ... 107
Cetta, Lewis T(homas) 1933- ... 53-56
Cevasco, George A(nthony) 1924- ... CANR-2
Earlier sketch in CA 5-6R
Chabe, Alexander M(ichael) 1923- ... 53-56
Chaber, M. E.
See Crossen, Kendell Foster
Chabod, Federico 1901-1960 Obituary ... 116
Chabrol, Claude 1930- ... 110
See also CLC 16
Chace, Isobel
See de Guise, Elizabeth (Mary Teresa)
Chace, James (Clarke) 1931- ... CANR-1
Earlier sketch in CA 3R
Chace, William M(urdough) 1938- ... 69-72
Chacholiades, Miltiades 1937- ... CANR-1
Earlier sketch in CA 45-48
Chacko, David 1942- ... 49-52
Chacko, George K(uttickal) 1930- ... CANR-13
Earlier sketch in CA 73-76
Chaconas, D(oris) J. 1938- ... 21-22R
Chadbourne, Richard M(cClain) 1922- ... 23-24R
Chadeayne, Lee 1933- ... 53-56
Chadourne, Marc 1896(?)-1975 Obituary ... 53-56

Chadwick, Bruce A(lbert) 1940- 97-100
Chadwick, Henry 1920- CANR-25
Earlier sketches in CA 21-22R, CANR-9
Chadwick, James 1891-1974 Obituary 49-52
Chadwick, Janet (Bachand) 1933- 97-100
Chadwick, (Gerald William St.) John 1915- 25-28R
Chadwick, John 1920- 4R
Chadwick, Lee 1909- 69-72
Chadwick, Lester CAP-2
Earlier sketch in CA 19-20
See also SATA 1
Chadwick, Margaret Lee (Gill) 1893-1984 Obituary 112
Chadwick, Nora Kershaw 1891-1972 ..... CAP-1
Earlier sketch in CA 15-16
Chadwick, (William) Owen 1916- CANR-19
Earlier sketches in CA 4R, CANR-1
Chadwick, Ronald P(aul) 1935- 116
Chadwin, Mark Lincoln 1939- CANR-17
Earlier sketch in CA 25-28R
Chaet, Bernard 1924- 69-72
Chafe, Wallace L. 1927- 29-32R
Chafe, William H(enry) 1942- CANR-12
Earlier sketch in CA 49-52
Chafetz, Henry 1916-1978 .... CANR-3
Obituary 73-76
Earlier sketch in CA 1R
Chafetz, Janet Saltzman 1942- 69-72
Chafetz, Morris E(dward) 1924- CANR-5
Earlier sketch in CA 13-14R
Chaffee, Allen CAP-1
Earlier sketch in CA 9-10
See also SATA 3
Chaffee, John 1946- 85-88
Chaffee, Steven Henry 1935- 106
Chaffin, Lillie D(orton) 1925- CANR-13
Earlier sketch in CA 33-36R
See also SATA 4
Chaffin, Yule M. 1914- 23-24R
Chafin, Andrew 1937- 53-56
Chagall, David 1930- CANR-3
Earlier sketch in CA 9-10R
Chagall, Marc 1887-1985 122
Obituary 114
Chagla, M(ohamedali) C(urrim) 1900-1981 Obituary 108
Chai, Chen kang 1916- 21-22R
Chai, Ch'u 1906- 9-10R
Chai, Hon-chan 1931- 23-24R
Chai, Winberg 1932- CANR-9
Earlier sketch in CA 5-6R
Chaij, Fernando 1909- CANR-8
Earlier sketch in CA 21-22R
Chaikin, Miriam 1928- CANR-14
Earlier sketch in CA 81-84
See also SATA 24
Chais, Pamela (Herbert) 1930- 73-76
Chaisson, Eric (Joseph) 1946- CANR-25
Earlier sketch in CA 108
Chajkowsky, William E(ugene) 1938- 116
Chakerian, Charles (Garabed) 1904- 45-48
Chakour, Charles M. 1929- 33-36R
Chakravarty, Amiya (Chandra) 1901- CANR-1
Earlier sketch in CA 1R
Chakravarty, Birendra Narayan 1904-1980(?) 102
Chalfant, Edward Allan 1921- 111
Chalfont, Alun
See Jones, (Alun) Arthur Gwynne
Chalhoub, Michael 1932- 89-92
Chalidze, Valery Nikolaevich 1938- 103
Chalk, John Allen 1937- 57-60
Chalk, Ocania 1927- CANR-1
Earlier sketch in CA 45-48
Chalker, Jack L(aurence) 1944- 73-76
Chall, Jeanne S(ternlicht) 1921- CANR-10
Earlier sketch in CA 25-28R
Challand, Helen J(ean) 1921- 121
Brief entry 118
Challans, Mary 1905-1983 81-84
Obituary 111
See also SATA 23, 36
Challice, Kenneth
See Hutchin, Kenneth Charles
Challinor, John 1894- 73-76
Challis, George
See Faust, Frederick (Shiller)
Challoner, H. K.
See Mills, J(anet) M(elanie) A(ilsa)
Challoner, Robert
See Butterworth, Michael
Chalmers, David Mark 1927- 25-28R
Chalmers, Eric Brownlie 1929- 102
Chalmers, Floyd S(herman) 1898- CAP-2
Earlier sketch in CA 25-28
Chalmers, George 1742-1825 .... DLB-30
Chalmers, Harvey II 1890-1971 Obituary 33-36R
Chalmers, John W. 1910- 93-96
Chalmers, Malcolm 1956- 120
Chalmers, Mary (Eileen) 1927- 5-6R
See also SATA 6
Chalon, Jean 1935- CANR-16
Earlier sketch in CA 97-100
Chalon, Jon
See Chaloner, John Seymour
Chaloner, John Seymour 1924- 93-96
Chaloner, W. H.
See Chaloner, William Henry
Chaloner, William Henry 1914-1987 Obituary 122
Chamberlain, Anne 1917- 77-80
Chamberlain, Betty 1908-1983 ....33-36R
Obituary 109
Chamberlain, Elinor 1901- CAP-1
Earlier sketch in CA 15-16
Chamberlain, Houston Stewart 1855-1927(?) Brief entry 120
Chamberlain, John (Rensselaer) 1903- 57-60
Chamberlain, Jonathan Mack 1928- 101
Chamberlain, Joseph Miles 1923- 107
Chamberlain, Margaret 1954- SATA-46
Chamberlain, Mary (Christina) 1947- 115
Chamberlain, Muriel Evelyn 1932- CANR-16
Earlier sketch in CA 93-96
Chamberlain, Narcisse 1924- 15-16R
Chamberlain, Neil Wolverton 1915- CANR-6
Earlier sketch in CA 13-14R
Chamberlain, (Arthur) Neville 1869-1940 Brief entry 113
Chamberlain, Robert Lyall 1923- 15-16R
Chamberlain, Samuel 1895-1975 .... CAP-2
Obituary 53-56
Earlier sketch in CA 23-24
Chamberlain, Samuel S. 1851-1916 .... DLB-25
Chamberlain, Wilson
See Crandall, Norma
Chamberlain, Wilt(on Norman) 1936- 103
Chamberland, Paul 1939- DLB-60
Chamberlin, E(ric) R(ussell) 1926- CANR-19
Earlier sketch in CA 97-100
Chamberlin, Enid C. S. 1900(?)-1982(?) Obituary 106
Chamberlin, J. E(ward) 1943- 85-88
Chamberlin, J(ohn) Gordon 1914- CANR-4
Earlier sketch in CA 3R
Chamberlin, Judi 1944- 81-84
Chamberlin, Leslie J(oseph) 1926- 53-56
Chamberlin, M. Hope 1920-1974 45-48
Obituary 49-52
Chamberlin, Mary 1914- 45-48
Chamberlin, Waldo 1905- 65-68
Chamberlin, William Henry 1897-1969 .....5-6R
See also DLB 29
Chambers, Aidan 1934- CANR-12
Earlier sketch in CA 25-28R
See also SATA 1
See also CLC 35
Chambers, Anne 1949- 126
Chambers, Anthony H(ood) 1943- 108
Chambers, Bradford 1922-1984 Obituary ... 113
See also SATA 39
Chambers, Charles Haddon 1860-1921 Brief entry 110
See also DLB 10
Chambers, Clarke A(lexander) 1921- 41-44R
Chambers, Dewey W. 1929- CANR-12
Earlier sketch in CA 29-32R
Chambers, Edward J(ames) 1925- 17-18R
Chambers, Frances 1940- 111
Chambers, Frank P(entland) 1900- CAP-1
Earlier sketch in CA 9-10
Chambers, Howard V.
See Lowenkopf, Shelly A(lan)
Chambers, Iain 1949- 126
Chambers, James 1948- Brief entry 124
Chambers, Jane 1937-1983 85-88
Obituary 109
Chambers, Jessie
See Lawrence, D(avid) H(erbert Richards)
Chambers, John W. 1933- 124
See also SATA 46
Chambers, Jonathan David 1898-1970 .. CANR-3
Earlier sketch in CA 4R
Chambers, Lenoir 1891-1970 111
Obituary 104
Chambers, Lucille Arcola 1909(?)-1988 Obituary 125
Chambers, M(erritt) M(adison) 1899- ... CANR-5
Earlier sketch in CA 9-10R
Chambers, Margaret Ada Eastwood 1911- 9-10R
See also SATA 2
Chambers, Mortimer Hardin, Jr. 1927- .. CANR-6
Earlier sketch in CA 11-12R
Chambers, Peggy
See Chambers, Margaret Ada Eastwood
Chambers, Peter
See Phillips, D(ennis) J(ohn Andrew)
Chambers, R(aymond) J(ohn) 1917- 17-18R
Chambers, Robin Bernard 1942- 103
Chambers, W(illiam) Walker 1913- 29-32R
Chambers, (David) Whittaker 1901-1961 Obituary 89-92
Chambers, William E. 1943- 73-76
Chambers, William Nisbet 1916- CANR-8
Earlier sketch in CA 7-8R
Chambers, William Trout 1896- CAP-1
Earlier sketch in CA 13-14
Chambers-Schiller, Lee Virginia 1948- 120
Chambertin, Ilya
See von Block, Bela W(illiam)
and von Block, Sylvia
Chambliss, Bill
See Chambliss, William J(oseph)
Chambliss, William C. 1908(?)-1975 Obituary 57-60
Chambliss, William J(ones) 1923- 15-16R
Chambliss, William J(oseph) 1933- CANR-14
Earlier sketch in CA 77-80
Chamelin, Neil Charles 1942- 69-72
Chametzky, Jules 1928- 33-36R
Chamlee, Ruth Miller 1893(?)-1983 Obituary 110
Champagne, Marian 1915- 7-8R
Champe, Flavia Waters 1902- 115
Champernowne, David (Gawen) 1912- 104
Champigny, Robert J(ean) 1922- 33-36R
Champion, Dick
See Champion, Richard Gordon
Champion, John C(arr) 1923- CANR-8
Earlier sketch in CA 17-18R
Champion, John E(lmer) 1922- 13-14R
Champion, Larry S(tephen) 1932- CANR-9
Earlier sketch in CA 23-24R
Champion, R(ichard) A(nnells) 1925- 29-32R
Champion, Richard Gordon 1931- 77-80
Champkin, Peter 1918- 7-8R
Champlin, Charles (Davenport) 1926- 69-72
Champlin, James R(aymond) 1928- 21-22R
Champlin, John Michael 1937- 110
Champlin, Joseph M(asson) 1930- CANR-20
Earlier sketches in CA 49-52, CANR-1
Champlin, Tim
See Champlin, John Michael
Champney, Freeman 1911- 25-28R
Chamson, Andre J(ules) L(ouis) 1900-1983 .... CANR-2
Obituary 111
Earlier sketch in CA 7-8R
Ch'An, Chu
See Blofeld, John (Eaton Calthorpe)
Ch'an, Chu
See Blofeld, John (Eaton Calthorpe)
Chan, Loren Briggs 1943- CANR-8
Earlier sketch in CA 57-60
Chanaidh, Fear
See Campbell, John Lorne
Chanakya
See Panikkar, K(avalam) Madhava
Chanan, Ben
See Yaffe, Richard
Chanan, Gabriel 1942- CANR-7
Earlier sketch in CA 57-60
Chanan, Michael 1946- 106
Chance, John Newton 1911-1983 102
Obituary 110
Chance, Jonathan
See Chance, John Newton
Chance, Michael R(obin) A(lexander) 1915- 85-88
Chance, Roger (James Ferguson) 1893-1987 Obituary 122
Chance, Stephen
See Turner, Philip
Chancellor, John 1900-1971 .... CAP-2
Earlier sketch in CA 23-24
Chancellor, John (William) 1927- 109
See also AITN 1
Chancellor, Paul 1900-1975 Obituary 57-60
Chand, Meira (Angela) 1942- 106
Chand, Munshi Prem
See Srivastava, Dhanpat Rai
Chand, Prem
See Srivastava, Dhanpat Rai
Chanda, Asok Kumar 1902- 19-20R
Chandler, A(rthur) Bertram 1912-1984 . CANR-13
Earlier sketch in CA 21-22R
Chandler, Alfred D(upont), Jr. 1918- CANR-4
Earlier sketch in CA 9-10R
Chandler, Alice 1931- 53-56
Chandler, Allison 1906- CAP-1
Earlier sketch in CA 9-10
Chandler, B. J. 1921- 2R
Chandler, Billy Jaynes 1932- 122
Chandler, Bryn 1945- 118
Chandler, Caroline A(ugusta) 1906-1979 ....17-18R
Obituary 93-96
See also SATA 22, 24
Chandler, David (Geoffrey) 1934- CANR-11
Earlier sketch in CA 25-28R
Chandler, David Leon CANR-16
Earlier sketches in CA 49-52, CANR-1
Chandler, David Porter 1933- 45-48
See also SATA 28
Chandler, E(dwin) Russell, Jr. 1932- 77-80
Chandler, Edna Walker 1908-1982 ...... CANR-4
Obituary 108
Earlier sketch in CA 4R
See also SATA 11, 31
Chandler, Frank
See Harknett, Terry
Chandler, George 1915- CANR-5
Earlier sketch in CA 9-10R
Chandler, Harry 1864-1944 .... DLB-29
Chandler, Howard 1915(?)-1981 Obituary ... 104
Chandler, Jennifer (Westwood) 1940- ... CANR-9
Earlier sketch in CA 65-68
Chandler, Lester Vernon 1905-1988 Obituary 126
Chandler, Linda S(mith) 1929- CANR-23
Earlier sketch in CA 106
See also SATA 39
Chandler, Margaret Kueffner 1922- 17-18R
Chandler, Norman 1899-1973 Obituary 89-92
Chandler, Otis 1927- 111
Chandler, Raymond 1888-1959 Brief entry 104
See also TCLC 1, 7
Chandler, Richard Eugene 1916- 5-6R
Chandler, Robert 1953- 112
See also SATA 40
Chandler, Robert Wilbur 1921- 102
Chandler, Ruth Forbes 1894-1978 .... 4R
Obituary 103
See also SATA 2, 26
Chandler, S(tanley) Bernard 1921- 21-22R
Chandler, T(ony) J(ohn) 1928- 107
Chandler, Tertius 1915- CANR-19
Earlier sketch in CA 102
Chandola, Anoop C. 1937- CANR-14
Earlier sketch in CA 37-40R
Chandonnet, Ann F. 1943- CANR-23
Earlier sketches in CA 61-64, CANR-8
Chandor, (Peter John) Anthony 1932- .. CANR-26
Earlier sketch in CA 29-32R
Chandos, Fay
See Swatridge, Irene Maude (Mossop)
Chandos, John
See McConnell, John Lithgow Chandos
Chandra, Pramod 1930- 77-80
Chandrasekhar, Sripati 1918- 89-92
Chaneles, Sol 1926- 41-44R
Chaney, Jill 1932- CANR-11
Earlier sketch in CA 25-28R
Chaney, Norman 1935- 110
Chaney, Otto Preston, Jr. 1931- 33-36R
Chaney, William A(lbert) 1922- 33-36R
Chang, Chen-chi 1920- Brief entry 115
Chang, Ch'eng-chi
See Chang, Chen-chi
Chang, Chung-yuan 1900- 117
Chang, Constance D(an) 1917- 61-64
Chang, Dae H(ong) 1928- CANR-6
Earlier sketch in CA 57-60
Chang, Garma C. C.
See Chang, Chen-chi
Chang, Hsin-hai 1898(?)-1972 ....7-8R
Chang, Isabelle C(hin) 1924- 21-22R
Chang, Jen-chi 1903- CAP-1
Earlier sketch in CA 11-12
Chang, Kia-Ngau 1889- 5-6R
Chang, Kwang-chih 1931- CANR-15
Earlier sketch in CA 41-44R
Chang, Lee
See Levinson, Leonard
Chang, Parris (Hsu-Cheng) 1936- CANR-6
Earlier sketch in CA 57-60
Chang, Raymond 1939- 121
Chang, Richard T(aiwon) 1933- 61-64
Chang-Rodriguez, Eugenio 1926- CANR-21
Earlier sketches in CA 9-10R, CANR-6
Chanin, Abraham (Solomon) 1921- 89-92
Chankin, Donald O(liver) 1934- 57-60
Channel, A. R.
See Catherall, Arthur
Channels, Vera G(race) 1915- 69-72
Channing, Edward (Perkins) 1856-1931 Brief entry 122
See also DLB 17
Channing, Edward Tyrrell 1790-1856 .. DLB-1, 59
Channing, Steven A. 1940- CANR-13
Earlier sketch in CA 33-36R
Channing, William Ellery 1780-1842 .. DLB-1, 59
Channing, William Ellery II 1817-1901 .... DLB-1
Channing, William Henry 1810-1884 .. DLB-1, 59
Channon, Henry 1897-1958 Brief entry 121
Chanover, E(dmond) Pierre 1932- 29-32R
Chanover, Hyman 1920- CANR-2
Earlier sketch in CA 49-52
Chansky, Norman M(orton) 1929- 21-22R
Chant, Barry (Mostyn) 1938- CANR-11
Earlier sketch in CA 65-68
Chant, Donald (Alfred) 1928- CANR-18
Earlier sketch in CA 101
Chant, Joy
See Rutter, Eileen Joyce
Chant, Ken(neth David) 1933- 89-92
Chantiles, Vilma Liacouras 1925- CANR-6
Earlier sketch in CA 57-60
Chantler, David T(homas) 1925- 93-96
Chao, Buwei Yang 1889-1981 61-64
Obituary 120
Chao, Evelina 1949- 120
Chao, Kang 1929- 33-36R
Chao, Paul 1919- 114
Chao, Yuen Ren 1892-1982 .... CAP-2
Obituary 106
Earlier sketch in CA 21-22
Chapel, Paul 1926- 25-28R
Chapelle, Howard I(rving) 1901-1975 .... CAP-2
Obituary 57-60
Earlier sketch in CA 25-28
Chapian, Marie 1938- CANR-22
Earlier sketch in CA 106
See also SATA 29
Chapin, Alene Olsen Dalton 1915(?)-1986 Obituary 119
See also SATA 47
Chapin, Dwight Allan 1938- 41-44R
Chapin, F(rancis) Stuart, Jr. 1916- CANR-2
Earlier sketch in CA 7-8R
Chapin, Harry (Forster) 1942-1981 105
Obituary 104
Chapin, Henry 1893-1983 93-96
Obituary 110
Chapin, June Roediger 1931- CANR-13
Earlier sketch in CA 37-40R
Chapin, Katherine Garrison
See Biddle, Katherine Garrison Chapin
Chapin, Kim 1942- CANR-9
Earlier sketch in CA 53-56
Chapin, Louis Le Bourgeois, Jr. 1918-1981 103
Chapin, Ned 1927- 15-16R
Chapin, Schuyler G(arrison) 1923- 77-80
Chapin, Victor 1919(?)-1983 Obituary 109
Chapin, William 1918- 37-40R
Chaplin, Bill
See Chaplin, W. W.
Chaplin, Charles Spencer 1889-1977 81-84
Obituary 73-76
See also CLC 16
Chaplin, Charlie
See Chaplin, Charles Spencer
See also DLB 44
Chaplin, George 1914- 69-72
See also AITN 2
Chaplin, James P(atrick) 1919- CANR-1
Earlier sketch in CA 1R
Chaplin, L(inda) Tarin 1941- 116
Chaplin, Sid(ney) 1916-1986 .... CANR-16
Obituary 118
Earlier sketches in CA 9-10, CAP-1
Chaplin, W. W. 1895(?)-1978 Obituary ...81-84

INDEX

Chapman, A(rthur) H(arry) 1924- CANR-19
Earlier sketch in CA 25-28R
Chapman, Abraham 1915- 45-48
Chapman, Allen CAP-2
Earlier sketch in CA 19-20
See also SATA 1
Chapman, Alvah H., Jr. AITN-2
Chapman, Brian 1923- 9-10R
Chapman, Carleton B(urke) 1915- 69-72
Chapman, Charles F(rederic) 1881-1976
Obituary 65-68
Chapman, Christine 1933- CANR-12
Earlier sketch in CA 73-76
Chapman, Clark Russell 1945- 110
Chapman, Colin 1937- CANR-26
Earlier sketch in CA 29-32R
Chapman, (William) Donald 1923- 109
Chapman, Dorothy Hilton 1934- 57-60
Chapman, Edmund H(aupt) 1906- CAP-1
Earlier sketch in CA 15-16
Chapman, (Constance) Elizabeth (Mann)
1919- CAP-1
Earlier sketch in CA 9-10
See also SATA 10
Chapman, Elwood N. 1916- 37-40R
Chapman, Frances
See Chapman, Frank M(onroe)
Chapman, Frank
See Chapman, Frank M(onroe)
Chapman, Frank M(onroe) 1930- 113
Chapman, G(eorge) W(arren) Vernon
1925- CANR-26
Earlier sketch in CA 29-32R
Chapman, Gaynor 1935- SATA-32
Chapman, George 1559(?)-1634 .... DLB-62
Chapman, Graham 1941- 116
See also CLC 21
Chapman, Guy (Patterson) 1889-1972 101
Obituary 89-92
Chapman, Hester W(olferstan)
1899-1976 .... CANR-9
Obituary 65-68
Earlier sketch in CA 9-10R
Chapman, J. Dudley 1928- CANR-8
Earlier sketch in CA 23-24R
Chapman, James (Keith) 1919- CANR-15
Earlier sketch in CA 41-44R
Chapman, Jean 97-100
See also SATA 34
Chapman, Jennifer 1950- 118
Chapman, John 1900-1972 Obituary 33-36R
Chapman, John Jay 1862-1933
Brief entry 104
See also TCLC 7
Chapman, John L(eslie) 1920- 2R
Chapman, John Roy 1927- CANR-15
Earlier sketch in CA 77-80
Chapman, John Stanton Higham
1891-1972 Obituary 107
See also SATA 27
Chapman, Joseph Irvine 1912- 61-64
Chapman, June R(amey) 1918- 7-8R
Chapman, Karen C. 1942- 65-68
Chapman, Kenneth F(rancis) 1910- CAP-1
Earlier sketch in CA 15-16
Chapman, Kenneth G. 1927- 15-16R
Chapman, Laura 1935- 105
Chapman, Loren J(ames) 1927- 53-56
Chapman, M(ary) Winslow 1903- 93-96
Chapman, Marie M(anire) 1917- CANR-11
Earlier sketch in CA 61-64
Chapman, Maristan
See Chapman, John Stanton Higham
Chapman, Nancy W(hisnant) Collins
See Collins-Chapman, Nancy W(hisnant)
Chapman, Phil 1944- 121
Chapman, Raymond 1924- CANR-2
Earlier sketch in CA 7-8R
Chapman, Richard Arnold 1937-
Brief entry 105
Chapman, Rick M. 1943- 49-52
Chapman, Robert (DeWitt) 1937- 107
Chapman, Robert L(undquist) 1920- 122
Chapman, Roger E(ddington) 1916- 23-24R
Chapman, Ronald (George) 1917- 7-8R
Chapman, Ruth 1912(?)-1979 Obituary 104
Chapman, Samuel Greeley 1929- CANR-9
Earlier sketch in CA 19-20R
Chapman, Stanley D(avid) 1935- CANR-9
Earlier sketch in CA 21-22R
Chapman, Stepan 41-44R
Chapman, Steven
See Chapman, Stepan
Chapman, Sydney 1888-1970 106
Chapman, Vera 1898- 81-84
See also SATA 33
Chapman, Victoria L(ynn) 1944- 57-60
Chapman, Walker
See Silverberg, Robert
Chapman-Mortimer, William Charles
1907- 13-14R
Chapnick, Howard 1922- 65-68
Chappel, Bernice M(arie) 1910- CANR-16
Earlier sketch in CA 89-92
Chappell, Clovis G(illham) 1882-1972 65-68
Chappell, Fred 1936- CANR-8
Earlier sketch in CA 7-8R
See also CAAS 4
See also DLB 6
See also CLC 40
Chappell, Gordon (Stelling) 1939- 57-60
Chappell, Helen 1947- 104
Chappell, Jeannette
See Kalt, Jeannette Chappell
Chappell, Mollie 102
Chappell, Vere Claiborne 1930- 7-8R
Chappell, Warren 1904- CANR-8
Earlier sketch in CA 19-20R
See also SATA 6
Chappell, William (Evelyn) 1908- 106
Chapple, Christopher 1954- 126
Chapple, Eliot D(ismore) 1909- 41-44R
Chapple, (Clement) Gerald 1937- 111
Chapple, J(ohn) A(lfred) V(ictor) 1928- ... 21-22R
Chapple, Richard L(ynn) 1944- 112
Chapple, Steve 1949- 77-80
Chaput, Donald (Charles) 1933- 122
Brief entry 117
Char, K. T. Narasimha
See Narasimha Char, K. T.
Char, Rene(-Emile) 1907-1988 .... 15-16R
Obituary 124
See also CLC 9, 11, 14
Char, Tin-Yuke 1905- 57-60
Char, Wai Jane Chun 1912- 118
Char, Yum
See Barrett, Dean
Charanis, Peter 1908-1985 .... 37-40R
Obituary 115
Charbonneau, Louis (Henry) 1924- 85-88
Charbonneau, Robert 1911-1967 .... DLB-68
Charby, Jay
See Ellison, Harlan
Charchat, Isaac 1904(?)-1985 Obituary 116
Chard, (Maire) Brigid 1934- 105
Chard, Judy 1916- CANR-14
Earlier sketch in CA 77-80
Chard, Leslie F. II 1934- 33-36R
Chardiet, Bernice (Kroll) 1927(?)- 103
See also SATA 27
Chardin, Pierre Teilhard de
See Teilhard de Chardin, (Marie Joseph)
Pierre
Chargaff, Erwin 1905- CANR-18
Earlier sketch in CA 101
Charhadi, Driss ben Hamed 13-14R
Chari, V. Krishna 1924- 19-20R
Charland, William (Alfred), Jr. 1937- 97-100
Charles, Amy M(arie) 1922- 116
Charles, C(arol) M(organ) 1931- CANR-1
Earlier sketch in CA 49-52
Charles, David
See Mondey, David (Charles)
Charles, Don C(laude) 1918- 11-12R
Charles, Donald
See Meighan, Donald Charles
Charles, Franklin
See Adams, Cleve F(ranklin)
Charles, Gerda CANR-1
Earlier sketch in CA 1R
See also DLB 14
Charles, Gordon H(ull) 1920- 104
Charles, Henry
See Harris, Marion Rose (Young)
Charles, Louis
See Stratemeyer, Edward L.
Charles, Mark
See Bickers, Richard Leslie Townshend
Charles, Nathanael
See Franklin, Benjamin V
Charles, Nicholas
See Kuskin, Karla (Seidman)
Charles, Ray
See Robinson, Ray Charles
Charles, Robert
See Smith, Robert Charles
Charles, Sascha 1896(?)-1972 Obituary .. 37-40R
Charles, Searle F(ranklin) 1923- 11-12R
Charles, Theresa
See Swatridge, Charles (John)
and Swatridge, Irene Maude (Mossop)
Charles, Will
See Willeford, Charles (Ray III)
Charles-Roux, Edmonde 1920- 85-88
Charles the Clown
See Kraus, Charles E.
Charleston, Robert E.
See Robinson, Charles M. III
Charleston, Robert Jesse 1916- 102
Charlesworth, Arthur Riggs 1911- 53-56
Charlesworth, Edward A(llison) 1949- 125
Charlesworth, James Clyde 1900-1974 .... 9-10R
Obituary 45-48
Charlesworth, John Kaye 1889- CAP-1
Earlier sketch in CA 9-10
Charlesworth, Maxwell John 1925- CANR-18
Earlier sketches in CA 4R, CANR-2
Charlier, Patricia (Mary) Simonet 1923- ... 37-40R
Charlier, Roger H(enri) 1921- CANR-13
Earlier sketch in CA 37-40R
Charlip, Remy 1929- 33-36R
See also SATA 4
See also CLR 8
Charlot, Jean 1898-1979 .... CANR-4
Earlier sketch in CA 7-8R
See also SATA 8, 31
Charlot, John (Pierre) 1941- 120
Charlot, Martin (Day) 1944- 114
Charlotte, Susan 1954- 109
Charlson, David
See Holmes, David Charles
Charlton, Donald Geoffrey 1925- CANR-17
Earlier sketches in CA 4R, CANR-1
Charlton, Evan 1912-1983 Obituary 110
Charlton, Jack
See Charlton, John
Charlton, James (Mervyn) 1939- 81-84
Charlton, John 1935- 109
Charlton, John
See Woodhouse, Martin (Charlton)
Charlton, Linda
See Murray, Linda Charlton
Charlton, Michael (Alan) 1923- SATA-34
Charlwood, D(onald) E(rnest) 1915- CANR-9
Earlier sketch in CA 23-24R
Charlwood, Don
See Charlwood, D(onald) E(rnest)
Charmatz, Bill 1925- 29-32R
See also SATA 7
Charnance, L. P.
See Hannaway, Patricia H(inman)
Charnas, Suzy McKee 1939- CANR-18
Earlier sketch in CA 93-96
Charney, Ann 102
Charney, David H. 1923- CANR-15
Earlier sketch in CA 81-84
Charney, George 1905(?)-1975 Obituary ... 61-64
Charney, Hanna K(urz) 1931- 49-52
Charney, Maurice (Myron) 1929- CANR-18
Earlier sketches in CA 9-10R, CANR-3
Charnin, Martin (Jay) 1934- 103
Charnley, John 1911-1982 Obituary 107
Charnley, Mitchell V(aughn) 1898- 69-72
Charnock, Joan 1903- CAP-2
Earlier sketch in CA 33-36
Charny, Carmi 1925- CANR-7
Earlier sketch in CA 15-16R
Charny, Israel W(olf) 1931- 57-60
Charosh, Mannis 1906- 29-32R
See also SATA 5
Charques, Dorothy (Taylor) 1899-1976 73-76
Obituary 65-68
Charriere, Henri 1906-1973 101
Charron, Shirley 1935- 69-72
Charry, Elias 1906- 69-72
Charter, S(teve) P. R. 1915(?)-1984
Obituary 114
Charteris, Hugo (Francis Guy) 1922-1970 ... 105
Obituary 89-92
Charteris, James Donald 1948- 117
Charteris, Leslie 1907- CANR-10
Earlier sketch in CA 7-8R
Charters, Alexander N(athaniel) 1916- 120
Charters, Ann (Danberg) 1936- CANR-9
Earlier sketch in CA 17-18R
Charters, Samuel (Barclay) 1929- CANR-9
Earlier sketch in CA 9-10R
Chartham, Robert
See Seth, Ronald (Sydney)
Chartier, Emilio
See Estenssoro, Hugo
Chartkoff, Joseph L(ouis) 1942- 119
Chartkoff, Kerry K(ona) 1943- 119
Charvat, Frank John 1918- 1R
Charvet, John 1938- CANR-15
Earlier sketch in CA 85-88
Chary, Frederick B(arry) 1939- 49-52
Charyn, Jerome 1937- CANR-7
Earlier sketch in CA 7-8R
See also CAAS 1
See also DLBY 83
See also CLC 5, 8, 18
Chasan, Daniel Jack 1943- 29-32R
Chase, A(lice) Elizabeth 1906- CAP-1
Earlier sketch in CA 11-12
Chase, Adam
See Fairman, Paul W.
and Marlowe, Stephen
and Thomson, James C(utting)
Chase, Alan (Louis) 1929- 2R
Chase, Alice
See McHargue, Georgess
Chase, Alston Hurd 1906- 5-6R
Chase, Borden
See Fowler, Frank
See also DLB 26
Chase, Chris AITN-1
Chase, Cleveland B(ruce) 1904(?)-1975
Obituary 53-56
Chase, Clinton I(rvin) 1927- 106
Chase, Cora G(ingrich) 1898- CANR-7
Earlier sketch in CA 61-64
Chase, Donald 1943- 53-56
Chase, Elaine R(aco) 1949- 114
Chase, Emily
See Sachs, Judith
and White, Carol
Chase, Gilbert 1906- 17-18R
Chase, Glen
See Levinson, Leonard
Chase, Harold W(illiam) 1922- CANR-4
Earlier sketch in CA 11-12R
Chase, Ilka 1905-1978 .... CANR-9
Obituary 77-80
Earlier sketch in CA 61-64
Chase, James Hadley
See Raymond, Rene (Brabazon)
Chase, James S(taton) 1932- 85-88
Chase, Judith Wragg 1907- 41-44R
Chase, Larry
See Chase, Lawrence
Chase, Lawrence 1943- 97-100
Chase, Loriene Eck 102
Chase, Loring D. 1916- 25-28R
Chase, Lyndon
See Chard, Judy
Chase, Mary (Coyle) 1907-1981 77-80
Obituary 105
See also SATA 17, 29
Chase, Mary Ellen 1887-1973 .... CAP-1
Obituary 41-44R
Earlier sketch in CA 15-16
See also SATA 10
See also CLC 2
Chase, Mildred Portney 1921- 106
Chase, Naomi Feigelson 1932- 104
Chase, Otta Louise 1909- 49-52
Chase, Philander D(ean) 1943- 124
Chase, Richard 1904-1988 61-64
Obituary 125
Chase, Samuel B(rown), Jr. 1932- 5-6R
Chase, Stuart 1888-1985 65-68
Obituary 117
Chase, Sylvia (Belle) 1938- 115
Brief entry 110
Chase, Virginia Lowell
See Perkins, Virginia Chase
Chase, W. Linwood 1897(?)-1983
Obituary 110
Chase-Riboud, Barbara (Dewayne Tosi)
1939- 113
See also BW
See also DLB 33
Chasin, Barbara 1940- 69-72
Chasins, Abram 1903-1987 .... CANR-14
Obituary 122
Earlier sketch in CA 37-40R
Chasman, Herbert 1938- 121
Chastain, Madye Lee 1908- 5-6R
See also SATA 4
Chasteen, Edgar R(ay) 1935- 33-36R
Chastenet de Castaing, Jacques
1893-1978 Obituary 77-80
Chaston, Gloria Duncan 1929- 69-72
Chatalbash, Ron 1959- 111
Chatelain, Nicolas 1913-1976 Obituary 65-68
Chatelet, Albert 1928- CANR-6
Earlier sketch in CA 13-14R
Chater, Elizabeth (Eileen) 1910- 111
Chatfield, (Earl) Charles (Jr.) 1934- 37-40R
Chatfield, Hale 1936- CANR-13
Earlier sketch in CA 33-36R
Chatfield, Michael 1934- CANR-10
Earlier sketch in CA 25-28R
Chatham, Doug(las) M. 1938- CANR-8
Earlier sketch in CA 61-64
Chatham, James R(ay) 1931- 33-36R
Chatham, Josiah G(eorge) 1914- 49-52
Chatham, Larry
See Bingley, David Ernest
Chatham, Russell 1939- 69-72
Chatman, Seymour B(enjamin) 1928- 37-40R
Chatov, Robert 1927- 105
Chatt, Orville K(eith) 1924- 53-56
Chatterje, Sarat Chandra 1876-1936(?)
Brief entry 109
Chatterjee, Margaret (Gantzer) 1925- ... CANR-20
Earlier sketches in CA 7-8R, CANR-3
Chatterji, Saratchandra
See Chatterje, Sarat Chandra
See also TCLC 13
Chatterji, Suniti Kumar 1890- 81-84
Chatterton, Wayne 1921- 37-40R
Chatwin, (Charles) Bruce 1940- 85-88
See also CLC 28
Chaudhuri, Haridas 1913- CANR-4
Earlier sketch in CA 7-8R
Chaudhuri, Sukanta 1950- 57-60
Chauffard, Rene-Jacques 1920(?)-1972
Obituary 37-40R
Chauncy, Charles 1705-1787 .... DLB-24
Chauncy, Nan(cen Beryl Masterman)
1900-1970 .... CANR-4
Earlier sketch in CA 3R
See also SATA 6
See also CLR 6
Chaundler, Christine 1887-1972 .... CAP-2
Earlier sketch in CA 29-32
See also SATA 1, 25
Chauvin, Remy 1913- 108
Chavasse, Michael Louis Maude
1923-1983 Obituary 110
Chavchavadze, Paul 1899-1971 .... CAP-2
Obituary 29-32R
Earlier sketch in CA 25-28
Chavel, Charles Ber 1906- CANR-4
Earlier sketch in CA 49-52
Chaves, Jonathan 1943- CANR-9
Earlier sketch in CA 65-68
Chavez, Angelico 1910- 93-96
Chavez, John R(ichard) 1949- 118
Chavez, Patricia 1934- 103
Chaviaras, Strates 1935- 105
Chayefsky, Paddy
See Chayefsky, Sidney
See also DLB 7, 44
See also DLBY 81
See also CLC 23
Chayefsky, Sidney 1923-1981 .... CANR-18
Obituary 104
Earlier sketch in CA 11-12R
Chayes, Abram 1922- CANR-14
Earlier sketch in CA 65-68
Chaytor, Lee
See Chater, Elizabeth (Eileen)
Chazanof, William 1915- 33-36R
Chaze, (Lewis) Elliott 1915- 113
Cheape, Charles Windsor 1945- 105
Cheatham, K(aryn) Follis 1943- 81-84
Cheavens, (Sam) Frank 1905- 33-36R
Cheavens, Martha Louise (Schuck)
1898-1975 Obituary 57-60
Check, Otto Premier
See Berman, Ed
Check, William A. 1943- 118
Checkland, S(ydney) G(eorge)
1916-1986 .... 17-18R
Obituary 118
Chedid, Andree 1920- CLC-47
Cheech
See Marin, Richard Anthony
Cheek, Frances Edith 1923- 41-44R
Cheeks, James E. 1930- 124
Cheesman, Paul R. 1921- CANR-1
Earlier sketch in CA 49-52
Cheetham, Erika 1939- 109

Cheetham, Hal
See Cheetham, J(ames) H(arold)
Cheetham, J(ames) H(arold) 1921- 108
Cheetham, Nicholas (John Alexander)
1910- CANR-15
Earlier sketch in CA 81-84
Cheever, Ezekiel 1615-1708 .... DLB-24
Cheever, George Barrell 1807-1890 ..... DLB-59
Cheever, John 1912-1982 .... CANR-5
Obituary 106
Earlier sketch in CA 7-8R
See also CABS 1
See also DLB 2
See also DLBY 80, 82
See also CDALB 1941-1968
See also CLC 3, 7, 8, 11, 15, 25
See also SSC 1
Cheever, Susan 1943- 103
See also DLBY 82
See also CLC 18, 48
Cheffins, Ronald I. 1930- 45-48
Cheifetz, Dan 1926- 69-72
Cheifetz, Philip M(orris) 1944- 53-56
Chein, Isidor 1912- Brief entry 105
Chejne, Anwar G(eorge) 1923-1983 .... CANR-18
Earlier sketch in CA 25-28R
Chekenian, Aram Haigaz 1900-1986
Obituary 119
Chekenian, Jane
See Gerard, Jane
Chekhonte, Antosha
See Chekhov, Anton (Pavlovich)
Chekhov, Anton (Pavlovich) 1860-1904 124
Brief entry 104
See also TCLC 3, 10
See also SSC 2
Chekhova, Olga 1897-1980 Obituary 97-100
Chekki, Dan(esh) A(yyappa) 1935- CANR-23
Earlier sketches in CA 61-64, CANR-7
Cheldelin, Larry V(ernon) 1945- 116
Chelf, Carl P. 1937- 37-40R
Chelius, James R(obert) 1943- 115
Chellis, Marcia 1940- 121
Chelminski, Rudolph 1934- 93-96
Chelton, John
See Durst, Paul
Chelwood, Tufton Victor Hamilton 1917- ...65-68
Chen, Anthony 1929- CANR-14
Earlier sketch in CA 37-40R
See also SATA 6
Chen, Ching-chih 1937- CANR-22
Earlier sketch in CA 106
Ch'En, Chi-yun 1933- 108
Chen, Chung-Hwan 1906- 45-48
Chen, Edwin (Hung-teh) 1934- Brief entry .. 116
Chen, Jack 1908- CANR-15
Earlier sketch in CA 41-44R
Chen, Janey 1922- 73-76
Ch'en, Jerome 1921- CANR-9
Earlier sketch in CA 15-16R
Chen, Joseph Tao 1925- 37-40R
Chen, Kan 1928- 49-52
Chen, Kenneth K(uan-) S(heng) 1907- 19-20R
Chen, King C(hing) 1926- CANR-4
Earlier sketch in CA 53-56
Chen, Kuan I. 1926- 41-44R
Chen, Lincoln C(hih-ho) 1942- 49-52
Chen, Nai-Ruenn 1927- CANR-9
Earlier sketch in CA 23-24R
Chen, Philip S(tanley) 1903-1978 ...... CANR-5
Earlier sketch in CA 9-10R
Chen, Samuel Shih-Tsai 1915- 41-44R
Chen, Theodore Hsi-En 1902- CANR-17
Earlier sketches in CA 2R, CANR-1
Chen, Tony
See Chen, Anthony
Chen, Vincent 1917- 37-40R
Chen, Yuan-tsung 1932- 106
Chenault, Lawrence R(oyce) 1897- CAP-2
Earlier sketch in CA 17-18
Chenault, Nell
See Smith, Linell Nash
Chenery, Hollis Burnley 1918- 111
Chenery, Janet (Dai) 1923- 103
See also SATA 25
Chenery, William Ludlow 1884-1974 97-100
Obituary 53-56
Chenevix Trench, Charles Pocklington
1914- 9-10R
Cheney, Anne 1944- 61-64
Cheney, Brainard (Bartwell) 1900- CAP-2
Earlier sketch in CA 25-28
Cheney, C. R.
See Cheney, Christopher Robert
Cheney, Christopher Robert 1906-1987
Obituary 123
Cheney, Cora 1916- CANR-4
Earlier sketch in CA 3R
See also SATA 3
Cheney, Ednah Dow (Littlehale)
1824-1904 .... DLB-1
Cheney, Frances Neel 1906- 33-36R
Cheney, Glenn Alan 1951- 109
Cheney, Jean E. 1921- 118
Cheney, Lois A. 1931- 29-32R
Cheney, Lynne 1941- 89-92
Cheney, Margaret 1921- 101
Cheney, Richard B(ruce) 1941- 113
Cheney, Robert S(impson) 1922- 118
Cheney, Roberta Carkeek 1912- 73-76
Cheney, Ruth G(ordon) 1908- 113
Cheney, Sheldon Warren 1886-1980
Obituary 102
Cheney, Ted
See Cheney, Theodore Albert
Cheney, Theodore A. Rees
See Cheney, Theodore Albert
Cheney, Theodore Albert 1928- CANR-23
Earlier sketches in CA 61-64, CANR-8
See also SATA 11
Cheney, Thomas E. 1901- 41-44R
Cheney-Coker, Syl 1945- 101
Cheng, Chu-yuan 1927- CANR-20
Earlier sketches in CA 15-16R, CANR-5
Cheng, F.T.
See Cheng, Tien-hsi
Cheng, Hang-Sheng 1927- 69-72
Cheng, Hou-Tien 1944- 69-72
Cheng, J(ames) Chester 1926- 9-10R
Cheng, James K(uo) C(hiang) 1936- 25-28R
Cheng, Judith 1955- SATA-36
Cheng, Ronald Ye-lin 1933- 41-44R
Cheng, Tien-hsi 1884-1970 Obituary 104
Cheng, Yi
See Cheng, James K(uo) C(hiang)
Cheng, Ying-wan 41-44R
Chen Hwei
See Stevenson, William
Chen Jia
See Shen Congwen
Chen Jo-hsi
See Tuann, Lucy H(siu-mei Chen)
Chennault, Anna (Chan) 1925- 61-64
Chennells, Roy D. 1912(?)-1981 Obituary .. 105
Chenneviere, Daniel
See Rudhyar, Dane
Chenoweth, Vida S. 1928- CANR-11
Earlier sketch in CA 25-28R
Cheraskin, Emanuel 1916- 53-56
Cherim, Stanley M(arshall) 1929- 53-56
Cherington, Paul Whiton 1918-1974 .... CANR-6
Obituary 53-56
Earlier sketch in CA 4R
Chermayeff, Ivan 1932- 97-100
See also SATA 47
Chermayeff, Serge 1900- 21-22R
Chernaik, Judith 1934- CANR-11
Earlier sketch in CA 61-64
Chernenko, Konstantin Ustinovich
1911-1985 Obituary 115
Cherner, Anne 1954- 109
Chernev, Irving 1900-1981 Obituary 105
Cherniavsky, Michael 1923(?)-1973
Obituary 41-44R
Chernik, Barbara E(ileen) 1938- 117
Chernin, Kim 1940- 107
Cherniss, Harold
See Cherniss, Harold Fredrik
Cherniss, Harold Fredrik 1904-1987 93-96
Obituary 123
Cherniss, Michael D(avid) 1940- 37-40R
Cherniss, Norman A(rnold) 1926-1984 122
Obituary 114
Chernoff, Dorothy A.
See Ernst, (Lyman) John
Chernoff, Goldie Taub 1909- 33-36R
See also SATA 10
Chernoff, John Miller 1947- 105
Chernofsky, Jacob L. 1928- 73-76
Chernow, Burt 1933- 110
Chernow, Carol 1934- 57-60
Chernow, Fred B. 1932- 57-60
Chernowitz, Maurice E. 1909-1977
Obituary 73-76
Cherns, Albert
See Cherns, Albert B(ernard)
Cherns, Albert B(ernard) 1921-1987
Obituary 122
Cherrington, Ernest H(urst), Jr. 1909- ...33-36R
Cherrington, John 1909- 116
Cherrington, Leon G. 1926- 33-36R
Cherry, C. Conrad 1937- CANR-11
Earlier sketch in CA 23-24R
Cherry, Caroline L(ockett) 1942- 57-60
Cherry, Carolyn Janice 1942- CANR-10
Earlier sketch in CA 65-68
Cherry, Charles L(ester) 1942- 57-60
Cherry, (Edward) Colin 1914-1979 ..... CANR-12
Obituary 93-96
Earlier sketch in CA 69-72
Cherry, George Loy 1905- 5-6R
Cherry, Gordon E(manuel) 1931- 125
Cherry, Kelly CANR-3
Earlier sketch in CA 49-52
See also DLBY 83
See also AITN 1
Cherry, Lynne 1952- SATA-34
Cherry, Sheldon H(arold) 1934- 49-52
Cherryh, C. J.
See Cherry, Carolyn Janice
See also DLBY 80
See also CLC 35
Cherryholmes, Anne
See Price, Olive
Chervin, Ronda 1937- CANR-21
Earlier sketches in CA 57-60, CANR-6
Cherwinski, Joseph 1915- CANR-5
Earlier sketch in CA 15-16R
Chesbro, George C(lark) 1940- 77-80
Chesebro, James William 1944- 108
Chesen, Eli S. 1944- 37-40R
Chesham, Henry
See Bingley, David Ernest
Chesham, Sallie CANR-26
Earlier sketch in CA 29-32R
Chesher, Kim 1955- CANR-19
Earlier sketch in CA 102
Chesher, Richard (Harvey) 1940- 106
Cheshire, David 1944- 97-100
Cheshire, Geoffrey Leonard 1917- CAP-1
Earlier sketch in CA 13-14
Cheshire, Herbert 1925(?)-1985 Obituary ... 118
Cheshire, Maxine 1930- 108
Cheskin, Louis 1909-1981 .... CANR-5
Obituary 105
Earlier sketch in CA 5-6R
Chesler, Bernice 1932- CANR-16
Earlier sketch in CA 25-28R
Chesler, Phyllis 1940- CANR-4
Earlier sketch in CA 49-52
Cheslock, Louis 1898- CAP-1
Earlier sketch in CA 11-12
Chesney, Inga L. 1928- 45-48
Chesney, Kellow (Robert) 1914- 29-32R
Chesney, Marion 1936- 115
Brief entry 111
Chesney, Weatherby
See Hyne, C(harles) J(ohn) Cutcliffe
(Wright)
Chesnoff, Richard Z(eltner) 1937- CANR-10
Earlier sketch in CA 25-28R
Chesnut, J(ames) Stanley 1926- 23-24R
Chesnutt, Charles W(addell) 1858-1932 125
Brief entry 106
See also BW
See also DLB 12, 50
See also TCLC 5
Chesnutt, David R(ogers) 1940- 122
Chess, Stella 1914- 85-88
Chess, Victoria 1939- 107
See also SATA 33
Chessare, Michele SATA-42
Chesser, Eustace 1902-1973 .... CANR-4
Obituary 45-48
Earlier sketch in CA 9-10R
Chessex, Jacques 1934- 65-68
Chessman, Caryl (Whittier) 1921-1960 73-76
Chessman, G(eorge) Wallace 1919- 15-16R
Chessman, Ruth (Green) 1910- CAP-2
Earlier sketch in CA 17-18
Chester, Alfred 1929(?)-1971 Obituary ...33-36R
See also CLC 49
Chester, Allan Griffith 1900-1976 Obituary .. 111
Chester, Deborah 1957- CANR-18
Earlier sketch in CA 102
Chester, Edward W(illiam) 1935- CANR-13
Earlier sketch in CA 23-24R
Chester, Laura 1949- CANR-9
Earlier sketch in CA 65-68
Chester, Michael (Arthur) 1928- CANR-1
Earlier sketch in CA 3R
Chester, (Daniel) Norman 1907-1986 109
Obituary 120
Chester, Peter
See Phillips, D(ennis) J(ohn Andrew)
Chesterman, Charles W(esley) 1913- 107
Chesterman, Clement (Clapton)
1894-1983 Obituary 110
Chesterson, Denise
See Robins, Denise (Naomi)
Chesterton, A(rthur) K(enneth) 1899- CAP-1
Earlier sketch in CA 11-12
Chesterton, G(ilbert) K(eith) 1874-1936
Brief entry 104
See also SATA 27
See also DLB 10, 19, 34, 70
See also TCLC 1, 6
See also SSC 1
Chestor, Rui
See Courtier, S(idney) H(obson)
Chetham-Strode, Warren 1896- CAP-1
Earlier sketch in CA 13-14
Chethimattam, John B(ritto) 1922- 25-28R
Chetin, Helen 1922- CANR-12
Earlier sketch in CA 29-32R
See also SATA 6
Chetwin, Grace 123
See also SATA 50
Chetwode, Penelope 1910-1986 102
Obituary 119
Chetwynd, Berry
See Rayner, Claire (Berenice)
Chetwynd, Tom 1938- 45-48
Chetwynd-Hayes, R(onald Henry Glynn)
1919- CANR-12
Earlier sketch in CA 61-64
Chetwynd-Talbot, Edward Hugh Frederick
1909- 116
Cheung, Steven N(g-) S(heong) 1935- ...25-28R
Cheuse, Alan 1940- 49-52
Chevalier, Christa 1937- CANR-24
Earlier sketch in CA 107
See also SATA 35
Chevalier, Elizabeth (Pickett) 1896-1984
Obituary 111
Chevalier, Haakon (Maurice) 1901-1985 ...61-64
Obituary 116
Chevalier, Louis 1911- 85-88
Chevalier, Maurice 1888-1972 Obituary ...33-36R
Chevalier, Paul Eugene George 1925- 106
Chevallier, Gabriel 1895-1969 Obituary 113
Chevallier, Raymond 1929- 103
Chevigny, Bell Gale 1936- 57-60
Chevigny, Paul G. 1935- 97-100
Cheville, Roy A(rthur) 1897- 97-100
Chew, Allen F. 1924- 33-36R
Chew, Peter 1924- 57-60
Chew, Ruth 1920- CANR-14
Earlier sketch in CA 41-44R
See also SATA 7
Cheyette, Irving 1904- CANR-22
Earlier sketch in CA 69-72
Cheyney, Arnold B. 1926- CANR-23
Earlier sketches in CA 23-24R, CANR-8
Cheyney, Edward P. 1861-1947 .... DLB-47
Cheyney, (Reginald Evelyn) Peter
(Southouse) 1896-1951 Brief entry 113
Chi, Madeleine 1930- CANR-11
Earlier sketch in CA 69-72
Chi, Richard Hu See-Yee 1918- 37-40R
Chi, Wen-shun 1910- 13-14R
Chiang Kai-shek 1886(?)-1975 Obituary 112
Chiang Pin-chin 1904-1986 Obituary 118
Chiang Yee 1903-1977 .... CANR-15
Obituary 73-76
Earlier sketch in CA 65-68
Chiara, Piero 1913-1986 .... CANR-8
Obituary 121
Earlier sketch in CA 53-56
Chiarenza, Carl 1935- 109
Chiari, Joseph 1911- CANR-4
Earlier sketch in CA 7-8R
Chiaromonte, Nicola ?-1972 Obituary 104
Chiba, Atsuko 1941(?)-1987 Obituary 123
Chibnall, Marjorie (McCallum) 1915- 29-32R
Chicago, Judy 1939- CANR-21
Earlier sketch in CA 85-88
Chichester, Francis (Charles) 1901-1972 .. CAP-1
Obituary 37-40R
Earlier sketch in CA 13-14
Chichester, Jane
See Longrigg, Jane Chichester
Chick, Edson M(arland) 1924- 23-24R
Chickering, Arthur W. 1927- 29-32R
Chickering, Roger (Philip) 1942- 73-76
Chickos, James Speros 1941- 49-52
Chicorel, Marietta 85-88
Chidsey, Donald Barr 1902-1981 .... CANR-2
Obituary 103
Earlier sketch in CA 5-6R
See also SATA 3, 27
Chidzero, Bernard Thomas Gibson 1927- 3R
Chief Standing Bear
See Standing Bear, Luther
Chieger, Bob 1945- 114
Chielens, Edward E(rnest) 1943- 53-56
Ch'ien, Ts'un-hsun
See Tsien, Tsuen-hsuin
Ch'ien Chung-shu 1910- CLC-22
Chiesa, Francesco 1871(?)-1973 Obituary .. 104
Chignon, Niles
See Lingeman, Richard R(oberts)
Chigounis, Evans 1931- 45-48
Chilcote, Ronald H. 1935- CANR-24
Earlier sketches in CA 21-22R, CANR-8
Chilcott, John H(enry) 1924- 41-44R
Child, Alan
See Langner, Lawrence
Child, Francis James 1825-1896 ..... DLB-1, 64
Child, Heather 1912- 11-12R
Child, Irvin L(ong) 1915- 41-44R
Child, John 1922- 93-96
Child, Julia 1912- CANR-19
Earlier sketch in CA 41-44R
Child, Kenneth 1916-1983 Obituary 111
Child, Lydia Maria 1802-1880 .... DLB-1, 74
Child, Philip 1898-1978 .... CAP-1
Earlier sketch in CA 13-14
See also SATA 47
See also DLB 68
See also CLC 19
Child, Roderick 1949- 25-28R
Childers, (Robert) Erskine 1870-1922
Brief entry 113
See also DLB 70
Childers, Thomas (Allen) 1940- 37-40R
Childress, Alice 1920- CANR-3
Earlier sketch in CA 45-48
See also BW
See also SATA 7, 48
See also DLB 7, 38
See also CLC 12, 15
See also CLR 14
Childress, James Franklin 1940- CANR-11
Earlier sketch in CA 65-68
Childress, William 1933- 41-44R
Childs, Barney 1926- 23-24R
Childs, Brevard S(prings) 1923-
Brief entry 117
Childs, C. Sand
See Childs, Maryanna
Childs, David (Haslam) 1933- CANR-14
Earlier sketch in CA 37-40R
Childs, George W. 1829-1894 .... DLB-23
Childs, H(alla) Fay (Cochrane)
1890-1971 .... CAP-1
Earlier sketch in CA 15-16
See also SATA 1, 25
Childs, Harwood Lawrence 1898-1972 ... CAP-2
Obituary 37-40R
Earlier sketch in CA 25-28
Childs, J(ames) Rives 1893-1987
Obituary 123
Childs, James Bennett 1896-1977
Obituary 73-76
Childs, Marilyn Grace Carlson 1923- 9-10R
Childs, Marquis W(illiam) 1903- CANR-12
Earlier sketch in CA 61-64
Childs, Maryanna 1910- 9-10R
Childs, Timothy 1941- 97-100
Childs, W(illiam) H(arold) J(oseph)
1905(?)-1983 Obituary 109
Chiles, Robert E(ugene) 1923- 17-18R
Chiles, Webb 1941- 108
Chill, Dan S(amuel) 1945- 69-72
Chilman, Catherine (Earles) S(treet) 1914- .. 121
Chilson, Richard William 1943- CANR-6
Earlier sketch in CA 57-60
Chilson, Robert 1945- 69-72
Chilton, Irma 1930- CANR-19
Earlier sketch in CA 103
Chilton, John (James) 1932- CANR-8
Earlier sketch in CA 61-64
Chilton, Lance 1944- 123
Chilton, Shirley R(ay) 1923- 77-80

Chilver, Guy (Edward Farquhar) 1910-1982 ... 109
Obituary ... 107
Chilver, Peter 1933- ... CANR-17
Earlier sketch in CA 25-28R
Chimaera
See Farjeon, Eleanor
Chin, Chuan
See Chi, Richard Hu See-Yee
Chin, Frank (Chew, Jr.) 1940- ... 33-36R
Chin, Richard (M.) 1946- ... 121
See also SATA 52
Chin, Robert 1918- ... 61-64
Chinard, Gilbert 1882(?)-1972 Obituary ... 104
Chinas, Beverly N(ewbold) 1924- ... 89-92
Chinery, Michael 1938- ... CANR-20
Earlier sketch in CA 103
See also SATA 26
Ching, James C(hristopher) 1926- ... 37-40R
Ching, Julia (Chia-yi) 1934- ... 101
Chinitz, Benjamin 1924- ... 9-10R
Chinmoy, Sri 1931- ... CANR-2
Earlier sketch in CA 49-52
Chinn, Laurene Chambers 1902-1978 ... 2R
Obituary ... 103
Chinn, Robert (Edward) 1928- ... 69-72
Chinn, William G. 1919- ... 33-36R
Chinoy, Ely 1921-1975 ... CANR-1
Obituary ... 57-60
Earlier sketch in CA 3R
Chinoy, Helen Krich 1922- ... 17-18R
Chinweizu 1943- ... 103
Chipasula, Frank (Mkalawile) 1949- ... 121
Chipman, Bruce L(ewis) 1946- ... 37-40R
Chipman, Donald E(ugene) 1928- ... 29-32R
Chipman, John S(omerset) 1926- ... 104
Chipp, D(onald) L(eslie) 1925- ... 108
Chipp, Herschel B(rowning) 1913- ... 25-28R
Chipperfield, Joseph Eugene 1912-1980(?) ... CANR-6
Earlier sketch in CA 9-10R
See also SATA 2
Chipperfield, Richard 1904-1988 Obituary ... 125
Chirenje, J. Mutero 1935- ... 65-68
Chirovsky, Nicholas L. 1919- ... CANR-4
Earlier sketch in CA 53-56
Chisholm, A(rthur) M(urray) 1872-1960 Obituary ... 114
Chisholm, A(lan) R(owland) 1888- ... 7-8R
Chisholm, Anne ... 109
Chisholm, Hugh J., Jr. 1913-1972 Obituary ... 37-40R
Chisholm, K. Lomneth 1919- ... 61-64
Chisholm, Mary K(athleen) 1924- ... 37-40R
Chisholm, Matt
See Watts, Peter Christopher
Chisholm, Michael (Donald Inglis) 1931- ... 37-40R
Chisholm, R(obert) F(erguson) 1904- ... CAP-2
Earlier sketch in CA 29-32
Chisholm, Roderick Milton 1916- ... 102
Chisholm, Roger K. 1937- ... 33-36R
Chisholm, Sam(uel) Whitten 1919- ... 5-6R
Chisholm, Shirley (Anita St. Hill) 1924- ... 29-32R
See also BW
Chisholm, William S(herman), Jr. 1931- ... 49-52
Chishti, Hakim M.
See Thomson, Robert
Chislett, (Margaret) Anne 1943- ... CLC-34
Chisolm, Lawrence W(ashington) 1929- ... 11-12R
Chissell, Joan Olive ... 61-64
Chitham, Edward (Harry Gordon) 1932- ... CANR-19
Earlier sketch in CA 103
Chitnis, Anand C. 1942- ... 123
Chitrabhanu, Gurudev Shree 1922- ... 89-92
Chittenden, Elizabeth F. 1903- ... 61-64
See also SATA 9
Chittenden, Hiram Martin 1858-1917 ... DLB-47
Chittenden, Margaret 1935- ... CANR-19
Earlier sketches in CA 53-56, CANR-4
See also SATA 28
Chittick, Donald Ernest 1932- ... 115
Chittick, William O(liver) 1937- ... 41-44R
Chittum, Ida 1918- ... CANR-14
Earlier sketch in CA 37-40R
See also SATA 7
Chitty, Arthur Benjamin 1914- ... CANR-20
Earlier sketches in CA 53-56, CANR-4
Chitty, Letitia 1897-1982 Obituary ... 108
Chitty, Susan Elspeth 1929- ... CAP-1
Earlier sketch in CA 9-10
Chitty, Thomas Willes 1926- ... 7-8R
See also CLC 11
Chitwood, B(illy) J(ames) 1931- ... 97-100
Chitwood, Marie Downs 1918- ... 9-10R
Chitwood, Oliver Perry 1874-1971 ... CAP-1
Earlier sketch in CA 13-14
Chiu, Hong-Yee 1932- ... 53-56
Chiu, Hungdah 1936- ... CANR-14
Earlier sketch in CA 37-40R
Chivers, Thomas Holley 1809-1858 ... DLB-3
Chi-wei
See Shu, Austin Chi-wei
Chlamyda, Jehudil
See Peshkov, Alexei Maximovich
Chloros, A(lexander) G(eorge) 1926-1982 Obituary ... 108
Chloros, Aleck George
See Chloros, A(lexander) G(eorge)
Chmaj, Betty E. 1930- ... 97-100
Chmielarz, Sharon 1940- ... 121
Chmielewski, Edward 1928- ... 13-14R
Ch'o, Chou
See Shu-Jen, Chou
Cho, Yong Hyo 1934- Brief entry ... 105
Cho, Yong Sam 1925- ... 5-6R
Choate, Ernest A(lfred) 1900- ... 49-52
Choate, Gwen Peterson 1922- ... 3R
Choate, J(ulian) E(rnest, Jr.) 1916- ... 33-36R
Choate, Judith (Newkirk) 1940- ... 105
See also SATA 30
Choate, R. G.
See Choate, Gwen Peterson
Chobanian, Aram V(an) 1929- ... 108
Chochlik
See Radwanski, Pierre A(rthur)
Chodes, John 1939- ... CANR-25
Earlier sketches in CA 61-64, CANR-9
Chodorov, Edward 1904-1988 ... 102
Obituary ... 126
Chodorov, Jerome 1911- ... CANR-15
Earlier sketch in CA 65-68
Chodorov, Stephan 1934- ... 17-18R
Chodorow, Nancy (Julia) 1944- ... 105
Chogyam Trungpa 1939-1987 ... CANR-12
Obituary ... 122
Earlier sketch in CA 25-28R
Choi Sunu 1916-1984 Obituary ... 115
Choldin, Marianna Tax 1942- ... CANR-26
Earlier sketch in CA 109
Choleric, Brother
See van Zeller, Claud
Chomette, Rene Lucien 1898-1981 Obituary ... 103
See also CLC 20
Chommie, John C(ampbell) 1914-1974 ... CAP-2
Earlier sketch in CA 29-32
Chomsky, A(vram) Noam 1928- ... 17-18R
Chomsky, William 1896-1977 ... 77-80
Obituary ... 73-76
Chong
See Chong, Thomas
Chong, Kyona-Jo
See Chung, Kyuna Cho
Chong, Peng-Khuan ... 25-28R
Chong, Thomas 1938- Brief entry ... 112
Chong, Tommy
See Chong, Thomas
Choper, Jesse H(erbert) 1935- ... CANR-5
Earlier sketch in CA 15-16R
Chopin, Kate
See Chopin, Katherine
See also DLB 12
See also CDALB 1865-1917
See also TCLC 5, 14
Chopin, Katherine 1851-1904 ... 122
Brief entry ... 104
Choquette, Adrienne 1915-1973 ... DLB-68
Choquette, Robert 1905- ... DLB-68
Chorafas, Dimitris N. 1926- ... CANR-20
Earlier sketches in CA 7-8R, CANR-4
Chorao, (Ann Mc)Kay (Sproat) 1936- ... CANR-19
Earlier sketches in CA 49-52, CANR-1
See also SATA 8
Chorell, Walentin 1912-1984(?) Obituary ... 111
Chorley, Katharine Campbell (Hopkinson) 1897-1986 Obituary ... 120
Chorley, R. J.
See Chorley, Richard John
Chorley, Richard J(ohn) 1927- ... 121
Chorley, Richard J.
See Chorley, Richard John
Chorley, Richard John 1927- Brief entry ... 116
Chorny, Merron 1922- ... 41-44R
Choron, Jacques 1904-1972 ... CAP-1
Obituary ... 33-36R
Earlier sketch in CA 9-10
Chorpenning, Charlotte (Lee Barrows) 1872-1955 Brief entry ... 114
See also SATA 37
Chothia, Jean 1944- ... 105
Chotzinoff, Samuel 1889-1964 Obituary ... 93-96
Chou, Ya-luu 1924- ... 41-44R
Choucri, Nazli 1943- ... CANR-14
Earlier sketch in CA 81-84
Choudhury, G(olam) W(ahed) 1926- ... CANR-17
Earlier sketch in CA 25-28R
Chou En-lai 1898-1976 Obituary ... 112
Choukas, Michael (Eugene) 1901- ... CAP-2
Earlier sketch in CA 17-18
Choukas-Bradley, Melanie (Rose) 1952- ... 124
Chouraqui, Andre (Nathanael) 1917- ... CANR-10
Earlier sketch in CA 65-68
Chow, Gregory C. 1929- ... 13-14R
Chow, Yung-Teh 1916- ... 37-40R
Chowder, Ken 1950- ... 102
Chowdhary, Savitri Devi (Dumra) 1907- ... CAP-1
Earlier sketch in CA 11-12
Chowning, Larry S(hepherd) 1949- ... 111
Choy, Bong-youn 1914- ... 69-72
Chrimes, Stanley Bertram 1907-1984 ... 7-8R
Obituary ... 113
Chrislock, Carl H(endrick) 1917- ... 45-48
Chrisman, Arthur Bowie 1889-1953 ... YABC-1
Chrisman, Harry E. 1906- ... 4R
Chrisman, Katherine (G.) 1940(?)-1987 Obituary ... 122
Christ, Carl F(inley) 1923- ... 21-22R
Christ, Carol T(ecla) 1944- ... 93-96
Christ, Henry I(rvine) 1915- ... CANR-2
Earlier sketch in CA 7-8R
Christ, John M(ichael) 1934- ... 106
Christ, Karl 1923- ... 120
Christ, Ronald 1936- ... CANR-10
Earlier sketch in CA 25-28R
Christaller, Walter 1893-1969 Obituary ... 115
Christelow, Eileen 1943- ... 111
See also SATA 35, 38
Christen, Robert J. 1928-1981 Obituary ... 108
Brief entry ... 107
Christensen, Ann 1946- ... 108
Christensen, Anna
See Mayer, Deborah Anne
Christensen, Clyde M. 1905- ... 53-56
Christensen, David E(mun) 1921- ... 15-16R
Christensen, Edward L. 1913- ... 25-28R
Christensen, Eleanor Ingalls 1913- ... 53-56
Christensen, Erwin O(ttomar) 1890- ... CAP-1
Earlier sketch in CA 13-14
Christensen, Francis 1902-19(?) ... CAP-2
Earlier sketch in CA 23-24
Christensen, Gardell Dano 1907- ... 9-10R
See also SATA 1
Christensen, Harold T(aylor) 1909- ... 45-48
Christensen, J(ack) A(rden) 1927- ... 53-56
Christensen, James L(ee) 1922- ... 97-100
Christensen, Jerome 1948- ... 110
Christensen, Jo Ippolito
See Christensen, Yolanda Maria Ippolito
Christensen, Otto H(enry) 1898- ... 33-36R
Christensen, Paul 1943- ... CANR-15
Earlier sketch in CA 77-80
Christensen, Sandra 1944- ... 110
Christensen, Yolanda Maria Ippolito 1943- ... CANR-7
Earlier sketch in CA 57-60
Christenson, Cornelia V(os) 1903- ... CAP-2
Earlier sketch in CA 33-36
Christenson, Evelyn (Carol) 1922- ... 117
Christenson, Larry 1928- ... CANR-8
Earlier sketch in CA 57-60
Christenson, Nordis 1929- ... 108
Christenson, Reo M. 1918- ... 37-40R
Christesen, Barbara 1940- ... 107
See also SATA 40
Christesen, Clement Byrne 1911- ... 102
Christgau, Alice Erickson 1902- ... CAP-2
Earlier sketch in CA 17-18
See also SATA 13
Christgau, John (Frederick) 1934- ... 103
Christgau, Robert (Thomas) 1942- ... 65-68
Christian, A. B.
See Yabes, Leopoldo Y(abes)
Christian, Barbara T. 1943- ... 110
See also BW
Christian, C(urtis) W(allace) 1927- ... 21-22R
Christian, Carol (Cathay) 1923- ... 53-56
Christian, Frederick
See Gehman, Richard (Boyd)
Christian, Garth Hood 1921-1967 ... CAP-1
Earlier sketch in CA 9-10
Christian, George (Eastland) 1927- ... 65-68
Christian, Glynn 1942- ... 115
Christian, Henry A(rthur) 1931- ... CANR-14
Earlier sketch in CA 33-36R
Christian, James L(ee) 1927- ... 57-60
Christian, Jill
See Dilcock, Noreen
Christian, John
See Dixon, Roger
Christian, Louise
See Grill, Nannette L.
Christian, Marcus Bruce 1900- ... 73-76
Christian, Mary Blount 1933- ... CANR-17
Earlier sketches in CA 45-48, CANR-1
See also SATA 9
Christian, Peter
See Steinbrunner, (Peter) Chris(tian)
Christian, Portia 1908- ... 103
Christian, Rebecca 1952- ... 107
Christian, Reginald Frank 1924- ... CANR-3
Earlier sketch in CA 5-6R
Christian, Roy Cloberry 1914- ... 93-96
Christian, Shirley (Ann) 1938- ... 125
Brief entry ... 119
Christian, William A(rmistead), Jr. 1944- ... 107
Christiani, Dounia Bunis 1913- ... 15-16R
Christians, Clifford Glenn 1939- ... 104
Christiansen, Arthur 1904-1963 ... 2R
Christiansen, Eugene Martin 1944- ... 121
Christiansen, Harley Duane 1930- ... CANR-4
Earlier sketch in CA 53-56
Christiansen, Keith 1947- ... 112
Christiansen, Michael Robin 1927-1984 Obituary ... 113
Christiansen, Richard (Dean) 1931- ... 121
Christianson, Elin B(allantyne) 1936- ... 111
Christianson, Gale E. 1942- ... 81-84
Christianson, John Robert 1934- ... 23-24R
Christie
See Ichikawa, Kon
Christie, Agatha (Mary Clarissa) 1890-1976 ... CANR-10
Obituary ... 61-64
Earlier sketch in CA 19-20R
See also SATA 36
See also DLB 13
See also CLC 1, 6, 8, 12, 39, 48
See also AITN 1, 2
Christie, George C(ustis) 1934- ... 37-40R
Christie, Hugh
See Christie-Murray, David (Hugh Arthur)
Christie, Ian R(alph) 1919- ... CANR-20
Earlier sketches in CA 7-8R, CANR-2
Christie, Jean 1912- ... 101
Christie, John Aldrich 1920- ... 65-68
Christie, Keith
See Haynes, Alfred H(enry)
Christie, Lindsay H. 1906(?)-1976 Obituary ... 61-64
Christie, Milton 1921- ... 17-18R
Christie, (Ann) Philippa ... CANR-4
Earlier sketch in CA 7-8R
Christie, Trevor L. 1905-1969 ... CAP-2
Earlier sketch in CA 21-22
Christie-Murray, David (Hugh Arthur) 1913- ... CANR-4
Earlier sketch in CA 53-56
Christine, Charles T(hornton) 1936- ... 33-36R
Christine, Dorothy Weaver 1934- ... 33-36R
Christ-Janer, Albert W. 1910-1973 ... CANR-4
Obituary ... 45-48
Earlier sketch in CA 1R
Christman, Don(ald) R. 1919- ... 17-18R
Christman, Elizabeth 1914- ... 89-92
Christman, Henry 1906-1980 Obituary ... 103
Christman, Henry Max 1932- ... 65-68
Christman, Luther (Parmalee) 1915- ... 124
Christman, R(aymond) J(ohn) 1919- ... 89-92
Christmas, Joyce 1939- ... 123
Christodoulou, Anastasios 1932- ... 120
Christoff, Peter K. 1911- ... 121
Christol, Carl Quimby 1914- ... CANR-4
Earlier sketch in CA 5-6R
Christoph, James B(ernard) 1928- ... CANR-4
Earlier sketch in CA 5-6R
Christopher, Beth
See Steinke, Ann (Elizabeth)
Christopher, Georgia B. 1932- ... 111
Christopher, Joe R(andell) 1935- ... CANR-4
Earlier sketch in CA 53-56
Christopher, John
See Youd, Samuel
See also CLR 2
Christopher, John B. 1914- ... 13-14R
Christopher, Kenneth
See Brophy, Donald F(rancis)
Christopher, Louise
See Hale, Arlene
Christopher, Matt(hew F.) 1917- ... CANR-5
Earlier sketch in CA 2R
See also SATA 2, 47
Christopher, Maurine (Brooks) ... 65-68
Christopher, Milbourne 1914(?)-1984 ... 105
Obituary ... 113
See also SATA 46
Christopher, Nicholas 1951- ... 108
Christopher, Robert Collins 1924- ... 102
Christophersen, Paul (Hans) 1911- ... 57-60
Christowe, Stoyan 1898- ... 65-68
Christy, Betty 1924- ... 57-60
Christy, George ... 11-12R
Christy, Howard Chandler 1873-1952 ... SATA-21
Christy, Joe
See Christy, Joseph M.
Christy, Joseph M. 1919- ... CANR-14
Earlier sketch in CA 29-32R
Christy, Marian 1932- ... 65-68
Christy, Teresa E(lizabeth) 1927- ... 73-76
Chroman, Eleanor 1937- ... 45-48
Chroman, Nathan 1929- ... 77-80
Chronic, Halka (Pattison) 1923- ... 118
Chroust, Anton-Hermann 1907- ... CAP-1
Earlier sketch in CA 9-10
Chruden, Herbert J(efferson) 1918- ... 5-6R
Chu, Arthur (T. S.) 1916- ... 81-84
Chu, Daniel 1933- ... 15-16R
See also SATA 11
Chu, Godwin C(hien) 1927- ... 114
Chu, Grace (Goodyear) 1916- ... 81-84
Chu, Grace Zia 1899- ... CANR-4
Earlier sketch in CA 5-6R
Chu, Kong 1926- ... 49-52
Chu, Louis H. 1915- ... 15-16R
Chu, Samuel C. 1929- ... 69-72
Ch'u, Tung-tsu 1910- ... CANR-2
Earlier sketch in CA 1R
Chu, Valentin (Yuan-ling) 1919- ... 9-10R
Chu, W. R.
See Chu, Arthur (T. S.)
Chubb, Elmer
See Masters, Edgar Lee
Chubb, Judith (Ann) 1947- ... 113
Chubb, Thomas Caldecot 1899-1972 ... CANR-6
Obituary ... 33-36R
Earlier sketch in CA 2R
Chubin, Barry 1943- ... 124
Chudacoff, Howard P(eter) 1943- ... 45-48
Chudley, Ron(ald Alexander) 1937- ... 110
Chuikov, Vasili Ivanovich 1900-1982 Obituary ... 106
Chukovskaya, Lydia (Korneeva) 1907- Brief entry ... 117
Chukovsky, Kornei (Ivanovich) 1882-1969 ... CANR-4
Obituary ... 25-28R
Earlier sketch in CA 7-8R
See also SATA 5, 34
Chulak, Armando ?-1975 Obituary ... 109
Chuman, Frank Fujio 1917- ... 69-72
Chun, Jinsie K(yung) S(hien) 1902- ... 49-52
Chun, Richard 1935- ... 65-68
Chung, Connie
See Chung, Constance Yu-Hwa
Chung, Constance Yu-Hwa 1946- Brief entry ... 119
Chung, Edward K(oo-Young) 1931- ... 107
Chung, Hyung C(han) 1931- ... 57-60
Chung, Joseph Sang-hoon 1929- ... 49-52
Chung, Kyung Cho 1921- ... 33-36R
Chung-yu, Chu
See Hsu, Benedict (Pei-Hsiung)
Chunn, Jay Carrington II 1938- ... 116
Chupack, Henry 1915- ... 49-52
Church, Albert M(arion) 1940- ... 111
Church, Benjamin 1734-1778 ... DLB-31
Church, Jeffrey
See Kirk, Richard (Edmund)
Church, Joseph 1918- ... 1R
Church, Margaret 1920- ... 15-16R
Church, Peter
See Nuttall, Jeff
Church, Ralph (Bruce) 1927- ... 37-40R
Church, Richard 1893-1972 ... CANR-3
Obituary ... 33-36R
Earlier sketch in CA 4R
See also SATA 3

Church, Robert L(eValley) 1938- 61-64
Church, Ronald James Harrison
See Harrison Church, Ronald James
Church, Roy A. 1935- 124
Church, Ruth Ellen (Lovrien) CANR-7
Earlier sketch in CA 5-6R
Church, Suzanne
See Bates, Susannah (Vacella)
Church, William Farr 1912- Brief entry 105
Churchill, Allen 1911-1988 97-100
Obituary 124
Churchill, Bill
See Churchill, Gail Winston
Churchill, Caryl 1938- CANR-22
Earlier sketch in CA 102
See also DLB 13
See also CLC 31
Churchill, Creighton 1912-1984 69-72
Obituary 114
Churchill, David 1935- 106
Churchill, E(lmer) Richard 1937- CANR-11
Earlier sketch in CA 17-18R
See also SATA 11
Churchill, Edward Delos 1895-1972
Obituary 37-40R
Churchill, Elizabeth
See Hough, Richard (Alexander)
Churchill, Gail Winston 1903(?)-1984
Obituary 112
Churchill, Guy E. 1926- 29-32R
Churchill, Joyce
See Harrison, M(ichael) John
Churchill, Linda R. 1938- CANR-11
Earlier sketch in CA 21-22R
Churchill, R(eginald) C(harles) 1916- 9-10R
Churchill, Randolph (Frederick Edward
Spencer) 1911-1968 Obituary 89-92
Churchill, Reba 1932(?)-1985 Obituary 116
Churchill, Rhona Adelaide 1913- 7-8R
Churchill, Samuel 1911- 17-18R
Churchill, Sarah (Millicent Hermione)
1914-1982 Obituary 107
Churchill, Winston (Leonard Spencer)
1874-1965 97-100
Churchland, Patricia Smith 1943- 123
Churchman, C(harles) West 1913- CANR-9
Earlier sketch in CA 23-24R
Churchman, Michael 1929- 37-40R
Chute, B(eatrice) J(oy) 1913-1987 .... 4R
Obituary 123
See also SATA 2, 53
Chute, Carolyn 1947- 123
See also CLC 39
Chute, Marchette (Gaylord) 1909- CANR-5
Earlier sketch in CA 4R
See also SATA 1
Chute, Robert M. 1926- 109
Chute, Rupert
See Cleveland, Philip Jerome
Chute, William J(oseph) 1914- 11-12R
Chwalek, Henryka C. 1918- 17-18R
Chwast, Jacqueline 1932- CANR-5
Earlier sketch in CA 49-52
See also SATA 6
Chwast, Seymour 1931- SATA-18
Chyet, Stanley F. 1931- 33-36R
Cialente, Fausta
See Terni-Cialente, Fausta
Cianciolo, Patricia Jean 1929- CANR-13
Earlier sketch in CA 37-40R
Ciaramitaro, Andrew James 1955- 110
Ciaramitaro, Barbara 1946- 107
Ciarcia, Steve 1947- 110
Ciardi, John (Anthony) 1916-1986 ...... CANR-5
Obituary 118
Earlier sketch in CA 7-8R
See also CAAS 2
See also SATA 1, 46
See also DLB 5
See also DLBY 86
See also CLC 10, 40, 44
Ciccorella, Aubra Dair 65-68
Cicellis, Kay 1926- CANR-3
Earlier sketch in CA 3R
Cicognani, Amleto Giovanni Cardinal
1883-1973 Obituary 45-48
Cicourel, Aaron V. 1928- 53-56
Cid Perez, Jose (Diego) 1906- CANR-4
Earlier sketch in CA 53-56
Ciechanowski, Jan 1888(?)-1973
Obituary 41-44R
Cienciala, Anna M(aria) 1929- 89-92
Cieplak, Tadeusz N(owak) 1918- CANR-11
Earlier sketch in CA 69-72
Cigler, Allan J(ames) 1943- 111
Cikovsky, Nicolai, Jr. 1933- 113
Cilffriw, Gwynfor
See Griffith, Thomas Gwynfor
Cimbollek, Robert (Carl) 1937- 57-60
Ciment, Michel 1938- 97-100
Cimino, Michael 1943- 105
See also CLC 16
Cinberg, Bernard L. 1905-1979 Obituary ..85-88
Cincinnatus
See Currey, Cecil B(arr)
Cinel, Dino 1941- 111
Cioffari, Vincenzo 1905- 17-18R
Cioffi, Lou(is James) 1926- 120
Brief entry 109
Cioran, E(mil) M. 1911- 25-28R
Cipes, Robert M. 1930- 23-24R
Ciplijauskaite, Birute 1929- CANR-14
Earlier sketch in CA 37-40R
Cipolla, Carlo M(anlio) 1922- CANR-18
Earlier sketches in CA 7-8R, CANR-2
Cipolla, Joan Bagnel
See Bagnel, Joan
Cipriano, Anthony (John) 1941- 102
Circus, Anthony
See Hoch, Edward D(entinger)
Circus, Jim
See Rosevear, John
Cire
See Hayden, Eric W(illiam)
Ciria, Alberto 1934- 73-76
Cirino, Linda D(avis) 1941- 65-68
Cirino, Robert 1937- 61-64
Cismaru, Alfred 1933- 61-64
Ciszek, Walter 1904- CAP-1
Earlier sketch in CA 13-14
Citati, Pietro 1930- CANR-4
Earlier sketch in CA 53-56
Citino, David 1947- 104
Citrine, Walter McLennan 1887-1983
Obituary 109
Cittafino, Ricardo
See Bickers, Richard Leslie Townshend
Ciuba, Edward J(oseph) 1935- 61-64
Civille, John R(aphael) 1940- CANR-11
Earlier sketch in CA 69-72
Cixous, Helene 1937- 126
Cizmar, Paula 1949- 122
Claassen, Harold 1905- CAP-2
Earlier sketch in CA 19-20
Clabaugh, Gary K(enneth) 1940- 69-72
Clabby, John 1911- 104
Clack, Robert Wood 1886-1964 122
Obituary 110
Claerbaut, David 1946- CANR-1
Earlier sketch in CA 45-48
Claffey, William J. 1925- 23-24R
Claflin, Edward 1949- 97-100
Clagett, John (Henry) 1916- CANR-6
Earlier sketch in CA 7-8R
Clagett, Marshall 1916- CANR-5
Earlier sketch in CA 1R
Claghorn, Charles Eugene 1911- 57-60
Clague, Ewan 1896-1987 ....29-32R
Obituary 122
Clague, Maryhelen 1930- 81-84
Claiborne, Craig 1920- CANR-5
Earlier sketch in CA 2R
Claiborne, Robert (Watson, Jr.) 1919- . CANR-12
Earlier sketch in CA 29-32R
Clain-Stefanelli, Vladimir 1914-1982 111
Obituary 108
Clair, Andree 29-32R
See also SATA 19
Clair, Bernard (Eddy) 1951- 102
Clair, Rene
See Chomette, Rene Lucien
See also CLC 20
Claire, Keith
See Andrews, Claire
Claire, Keith
See Andrews, Keith
Claire, William Francis 1935- CANR-7
Earlier sketch in CA 57-60
Clairmont, Elva 1937- 117
Clammer, David 1943- 69-72
Clampett, Bob 1914(?)-1984 Obituary 112
See also SATA 38
See also AITN 1
Clampett, Robert
See Clampett, Bob
See also SATA 44
Clampitt, Amy 110
See also CLC 32
Clance, Pauline Rose 1938- 126
Clancy, Francis Michael 1903-1986
Obituary 121
Clancy, John Gregory 1922- 13-14R
Clancy, Joseph P(atrick) 1928- CANR-18
Earlier sketch in CA 101
Clancy, King
See Clancy, Francis Michael
Clancy, Laurence James 1942- 108
Clancy, Laurie
See Clancy, Laurence James
Clancy, Thomas H(anley) 1923- CANR-7
Earlier sketch in CA 15-16R
Clancy, Thomas L., Jr. 1947- Brief entry ... 125
Clancy, Tom
See Clancy, Thomas L., Jr.
See also CLC 45
Clancy, William 1922-1982 Obituary 106
Clanton, (Orval) Gene 1934- 41-44R
Clanton, Gordon 1942- 57-60
Clapham, Arthur Roy 1904- 109
Clapham, John 1908- CANR-10
Earlier sketch in CA 25-28R
Clapp, James Gordon 1909-1970 .... CAP-1
Earlier sketch in CA 9-10
Clapp, Margaret (Antoinette) 1910-1974
Obituary 49-52
Clapp, Patricia 1912- CANR-10
Earlier sketch in CA 25-28R
See also SATA 4
See also SAAS 4
Clapp, Verner W(arren) 1901-1972
Obituary 37-40R
Clapper, Raymond 1892-1944 .... DLB-29
Clapperton, Richard 1934- 25-28R
Clar, C(harles) Raymond 1903- 37-40R
Clardy, Andrea Fleck 1943- CANR-17
Earlier sketch in CA 97-100
Clardy, J(esse) V. 1929- 33-36R
Clare, Elizabeth
See Cook, Dorothy Mary
Clare, Ellen
See Sinclair, Olga
Clare, Francis D.
See Aschmann, Alberta
Clare, George P. 1920- 111
Clare, Helen
See Hunter Blair, Pauline (Clarke)
Clare, John 1793-1864 .... DLB-55
Clare, Josephine 1933- 73-76
Clare, Margaret
See Maison, Margaret (Mary Bowles)
Clarens, Carlos (Figueredo y)
1936(?)-1987 ....21-22R
Obituary 121
Clareson, Thomas D(ean) 1926- CANR-18
Earlier sketches in CA 2R, CANR-2
Clarfield, Gerard Howard 1936- 103
Claridge, Gordon S. 1932- 21-22R
Clarie, Thomas C(ashin) 1943- 93-96
Clarin
See Alas (y Urena), Leopoldo (Enrique
Garcia)
Clarizio, Harvey F(rank) 1934- 33-36R
Clark, Admont Gulick 1919- 53-56
Clark, Al C.
See Goines, Donald
Clark, Alan 1928- 13-14R
Clark, Alfred Alexander Gordon 1900-1958
Brief entry 112
Clark, Alice S(andell) 1922- 41-44R
Clark, Andrew Hill 1911-1975 .... CAP-2
Earlier sketch in CA 25-28
Clark, Ann L(ivezey) 1913- CANR-7
Earlier sketch in CA 19-20R
Clark, Ann Nolan 1896- CANR-2
Earlier sketch in CA 5-6R
See also SATA 4
See also DLB 52
See also CLR 16
Clark, Anne 1909- 29-32R
Clark, Anne
See Amor, Anne Clark
Clark (of Herriotshall), Arthur Melville
1895- 9-10R
Clark, Badger
See Paine, Lauran (Bosworth)
Clark, Ben T. 1928- 53-56
Clark, Bill
See Clark, William A(rthur)
Clark, Billy C(urtis) 1928- CANR-22
Earlier sketch in CA 2R
Clark, (Robert) Brian 1932- 41-44R
See also CLC 29
Clark, Bruce B(udge) 1918- 69-72
Clark, Burton R(obert) 1921- 110
Clark, C. E. Frazer, Jr. 1925- 33-36R
Clark, C. H. Douglas 1890- CAP-2
Earlier sketch in CA 23-24
Clark, C(harles) M(anning) H(ope)
1915- 97-100
Clark, Carol (Lois) 1948- 57-60
Clark, Catherine Anthony (Smith)
1892-1977 .... CAP-1
Earlier sketch in CA 11-12
See also DLB 68
Clark, Champ 1923- 108
See also SATA 47
Clark, Charles E(dwin) 1929- 29-32R
Clark, Charles Heber 1841-1915
Brief entry 111
See also DLB 11
Clark, Charles Tallifero 1917- 15-16R
Clark, China (Debra) 1950- 45-48
Clark, Christopher (Anthony) Stuart
See Stuart-Clark, Christopher (Anthony)
Clark, Clifford E(dward), Jr. 1941- 81-84
Clark, Colin (Grant) 1905- CANR-8
Earlier sketch in CA 61-64
Clark, D.M.J.
See Clark, Douglas
Clark, David
See Hardcastle, Michael
Clark, David Allen
See Ernst, (Lyman) John
Clark, David Gillis 1933- 53-56
Clark, David Ridgley 1920- CANR-9
Earlier sketch in CA 17-18R
Clark, Dennis E. 1916- 29-32R
Clark, Dennis J. 1927- CANR-1
Earlier sketch in CA 1R
Clark, Diana Cooper
See Cooper-Clark, Diana
Clark, Dick
See Clark, Richard Wagstaff
Clark, Don(ald Rowlee) 1925- 57-60
Clark, Don(ald Henry) 1930- 29-32R
Clark, Donald E. 1933- CANR-8
Earlier sketch in CA 23-24R
Clark, Dora Mae 1893- 41-44R
Clark, Dorothy Park 1899- 5-6R
Clark, Douglas 1919- 114
Clark, E. Ritchie 1912- 122
Clark, Edward W(illiam) 1943- 123
Clark, Eleanor 1913- 11-12R
See also DLB 6
See also CLC 5, 19
Clark, Electa 1910- 69-72
Clark, Eliot (Candee) 1883-1980
Obituary 97-100
Clark, Ella E(lizabeth) 1896- 105
Clark, Ellery Harding, Jr. 1909- CANR-10
Earlier sketch in CA 65-68
Clark, Elmer Talmage 1886-1966 ....7-8R
Clark, Eric 1911- CANR-9
Earlier sketch in CA 13-14R
Clark, Eric 1937- 102
Clark, Eugenie 1922- 49-52
Clark, Evans 1888-1970 Obituary 104
Clark, Evert 1926(?)-1988 Obituary 126
Clark, F(rederick) Stephen 1908-1977 .. CANR-14
Earlier sketch in CA 21-22R
Clark, Francis 1919- 19-20R
Clark, Frank J(ames) 1922- CANR-17
Earlier sketch in CA 13-14R
See also SATA 18
Clark, Fred George 1890-1972 Obituary ..37-40R
Clark, Gail 1944- CANR-16
Earlier sketch in CA 97-100
Clark, Garel
See Garelick, May
Clark, Garth (Reginald) 1947- 115
Clark, George Norman 1890-1979 65-68
Obituary 85-88
Clark, George Sidney Roberts Kitson
See Kitson Clark, George Sidney Roberts
Clark, Gerald 1918- 13-14R
Clark, Gordon H(addon) 1902-1985 .... CANR-17
Earlier sketches in CA 3R, CANR-1
Clark, (John) Grahame (Douglas)
1907- CANR-10
Earlier sketch in CA 65-68
Clark, Gregory 1892-1977 Obituary 89-92
Clark, Harry 1917- 61-64
Clark, Harry Hayden 1901-1971 .... CAP-2
Earlier sketch in CA 29-32
Clark, Henry B(alsley) II 1930- CANR-8
Earlier sketch in CA 5-6R
Clark, Howard
See Haskin, Dorothy C(lark)
Clark, J(onathan) C(harles) D(ouglas)
1951- 121
Clark, J(ohn) H(oward) 1929- 106
Clark, J(eff) R(ay) 1947- CANR-22
Earlier sketch in CA 106
Clark, J. R.
See Clark, John R(ussell)
Clark, James Anthony 1907- 65-68
Clark, James C. 1947- 122
Clark, James M(ilford) 1930- 21-22R
Clark, James V(aughan) 1927- 13-14R
Clark, Jean C(ashman) 1920- 93-96
Clark, Jere Walton 1922- 23-24R
Clark, Jerome L. 1928- 37-40R
Clark, Jerry E(ugene) 1942- 73-76
Clark, Joan 1934- 93-96
Clark, John Desmond 1916- 61-64
Clark, John Drury 1907- 37-40R
Clark, John G(arretson) 1932- 19-20R
Clark, John Maurice 1884-1963 ....5-6R
Clark, John Pepper 1935- CANR-16
Earlier sketch in CA 65-68
See also BW
See also CLC 38
Clark, John R(ussell) 1927- 120
Clark, John R(ichard) 1930- 37-40R
Clark, John R(alph) K(ukeakalani) 1946- 101
Clark, John W(illiams) 1907- 13-14R
Clark, Joseph D(eadrick) 1893- CAP-2
Earlier sketch in CA 33-36
Clark, Joseph James 1893-1971 .... CAP-2
Obituary 29-32R
Earlier sketch in CA 19-20
Clark, Joseph L(ynn) 1881- CAP-2
Earlier sketch in CA 17-18
Clark, Katerina 1941- 110
Clark, Katharine (Jarman) 1911(?)-1986
Obituary 118
Clark, Keith 1939- 124
Clark, Kenneth (Mackenzie) 1903-1983 93-96
Obituary 109
Clark, Kenneth B(ancroft) 1914- 33-36R
See also BW
Clark, L. D. 1922- CANR-1
Earlier sketch in CA 2R
Clark, Laurence (Walter) 1914- 13-14R
Clark, LaVerne Harrell 1929- CANR-11
Earlier sketch in CA 15-16R
Clark, Leonard 1905-1981 .... CANR-7
Obituary 105
Earlier sketch in CA 13-14R
See also SATA 29, 30
Clark, Leonard H(ill) 1915- CANR-4
Earlier sketch in CA 53-56
Clark, Leroy D. CANR-11
Earlier sketch in CA 61-64
Clark, Lewis Gaylord 1808-1873 ..DLB-3, 64, 73
Clark, Lindley H(oag), Jr. 1920- 65-68
Clark, Lydia Benson
See Meaker, Eloise
Clark, Mabel Margaret (Cowie) 1903-1975 .. 101
Clark, Malcolm (Hamilton), Jr. 1917- 106
Clark, (Charles) Manning (Hope) 1915- 9-10R
Clark, Marden J. 1916- 61-64
Clark, Margaret Goff 1913- CANR-20
Earlier sketches in CA 3R, CANR-5
See also SATA 8
Clark, Marguerite Sheridan 1892(?)-1982
Obituary 107
Clark, Maria Louisa Guidish 1926- 5-6R
Clark, Marion L. 1943-1977 77-80
Obituary 73-76
Clark, Marjorie A. 1911- 33-36R
Clark, Mark (Wayne) 1896-1984 Obituary ... 112
Clark, (Bennett) Marsh 1928-1985 122
Obituary 117
Clark, Mary T. 37-40R
Clark, Mary Higgins 1931- CANR-16
Earlier sketch in CA 81-84
See also SATA 46
Clark, Mary Jane 1915- 57-60
Clark, Mary Lou
See Clark, Maria Louisa Guidish
Clark, Mary Margaret 1929- 113
Clark, Mary T(wibill) 102
Clark, Mavis Thorpe 1912- CANR-8
Earlier sketch in CA 57-60
See also SATA 8
See also SAAS 5
See also CLC 12

Clark, Melissa 1949- CANR-22
Earlier sketch in CA 104
Clark, Merle
See Gessner, Lynne
Clark, Michael D(orsey) 1937- 111
Clark, Miles (Morton) 1920- 23-24R
Clark, Naomi 1932- 77-80
Clark, Neal 1950- 113
Clark, Neil M(cCullough) 1890- 7-8R
Clark, Norman H(arold) 1925- 69-72
Clark, Parlin
See Trigg, Harry Davis
Clark, Patricia Finrow 1929- 17-18R
See also SATA 11
Clark, (William) Ramsey 1927- 29-32R
Clark, Randall 1957- 120
Clark, Richard Charles 1935- Brief entry 114
Clark, Richard Wagstaff 1929- Brief entry 113
Clark, Robert Alfred 1908- 101
Clark, Robert E(ugene) 1912- 41-44R
Clark, Robert E(dward) D(avid) 1906- CANR-21
Earlier sketch in CA 7-8R
Clark, Robert L(loyd), Jr. 1945- 103
Clark, Robert P(hillips) 1921- 126
Clark, Rolf 1937- 114
Clark, Romane Lewis 1925- 17-18R
Clark, Ronald Harry 1904- 110
Clark, Ronald William 1916-1987 25-28R
Obituary 122
See also SATA 2, 52
Clark, Ruth C(ampbell) 1920- 69-72
Clark, Samuel 1945- 89-92
Clark, Samuel Delbert 1910- CANR-11
Earlier sketches in CA 13-14, CAP-1
Clark, Septima Poinsette 1898-1987 7-8R
Obituary 124
Clark, Stephen R(ichard) L(yster) 1945- CANR-13
Earlier sketch in CA 77-80
Clark, Sue C(assidy) 1935- 41-44R
Clark, Sydney A(ylmer) 1890-1975 CANR-4
Obituary 57-60
Earlier sketch in CA 7-8R
Clark, Terry N(ichols) 1940- 25-28R
Clark, Thomas D(ionysious) 1903- CANR-4
Earlier sketch in CA 5-6R
Clark, Thomas Willard 1941- 81-84
Clark, Tom
See Clark, Thomas Willard
Clark, Truman R(oss) 1935- 61-64
Clark, Van D(eusen) 1909- CAP-1
Earlier sketch in CA 13-14
See also SATA 2
Clark, Virginia
See Gray, Patricia (Clark)
Clark, Walter Houston 1902- 37-40R
Clark, Walter Van Tilburg 1909-1971 9-10R
Obituary 33-36R
See also SATA 8
See also DLB 9
See also CLC 28
Clark, Wesley James 1950- 112
Clark, William (Donaldson) 1916-1985 29-32R
Obituary 116
Clark, William A(rthur) 1931- 33-36R
Clark, William Bedford 1947- 109
Clark, William Smith II 1900-1969 CAP-2
Earlier sketch in CA 25-28
Clarke, Anna 1919- CANR-18
Earlier sketch in CA 102
Clarke, Arthur C(harles) 1917- CANR-2
Earlier sketch in CA 4R
See also SATA 13
See also CLC 1, 4, 13, 18, 35
Clarke, Arthur G(ladstone) 1887- CAP-2
Earlier sketch in CA 17-18
Clarke, Austin 1896-1974 CAP-2
Obituary 49-52
Earlier sketch in CA 29-32
See also DLB 10, 20
See also CLC 6, 9
Clarke, Austin C(hesterfield) 1934- CANR-14
Earlier sketch in CA 25-28R
See also BW
See also DLB 53
See also CLC 8
Clarke, Basil F(ulford) L(owther) 1908-1978 CANR-4
Obituary 89-92
Earlier sketch in CA 7-8R
Clarke, Boden
See Burgess, M(ichael) R(oy)
Clarke, Brenda (Margaret Lilian) 1926- CANR-24
Earlier sketches in CA 65-68, CANR-9
Clarke, Captain Jafar
See Nesmith, Robert I.
Clarke, Charles (Richard Astley) 1944- 118
Clarke, Charles Galloway 1899-1983
Obituary 110
Clarke, Clorinda 1917- 25-28R
See also SATA 7
Clarke, D(erek) A(shdown) 1921- 125
Clarke, D(avid) Waldo 1907- 9-10R
Clarke, David E(gerton) 1920- 17-18R
Clarke, David Leonard 1937-1976
Obituary 111
Clarke, Derrick Harry 1919- 103
Clarke, Dorothy Clotelle
See Shadi, Dorothy Clotelle Clarke
Clarke, Dudley (Wrangel) 1899-1974 CAP-1
Earlier sketch in CA 15-16
Clarke, Duncan L(ynn) 1941- CANR-16
Earlier sketch in CA 97-100
Clarke, Dwight Lancelot 1885-1971 1R
Obituary 103
Clarke, Ernest George 1927- 102
Clarke, Garry E(vans) 1943- 77-80
Clarke, George Timothy CANR-1
Earlier sketch in CA 4R
Clarke, George Wallace
See Wallace-Clarke, George
Clarke, Gillian 1937- 106
See also DLB 40
Clarke, H. Harrison 1902- CANR-5
Earlier sketch in CA 3R
Clarke, Hans Thacher 1887-1972
Obituary 37-40R
Clarke, Harry Eugene, Jr. 1921- 5-6R
Clarke, Henry Charles 1899- 102
Clarke, Hockley
See Clarke, Henry Charles
Clarke, Howard William 1929- 37-40R
Clarke, Hugh Vincent 1919- CANR-19
Earlier sketch in CA 102
Clarke, I. F.
See Clarke, Ignatius (Ian) Frederick
Clarke, Ian
See Clarke, Ignatius (Ian) Frederick
Clarke, Ignatius (Ian) Frederick 1918- 116
Clarke, J(ohn) F(rederick) Gates 1905- CAP-1
Earlier sketch in CA 13-14
Clarke, Jack Alden 1924- 29-32R
Clarke, James F(ranklin) 1906- 69-72
Clarke, James Freeman 1810-1888 DLB-1, 59
Clarke, James Hall
See Rowland-Entwistle, (Arthur) Theodore (Henry)
Clarke, James W(eston) 1937- 110
Clarke, Joan (Lorraine) 1920- 104
Clarke, Joan B. 1921- SATA-27, 42
Clarke, Joan Dorn 1924- 11-12R
Clarke, John (Campbell) 1913-19(?) CAP-1
Earlier sketch in CA 15-16
Clarke, John
See Laklan, Carli
and Sontup, Dan(iel)
Clarke, John Henrik 1915- CANR-24
Earlier sketch in CA 53-56
See also BW
See also AITN 1
Clarke, John Joseph 1879- CANR-5
Earlier sketch in CA 7-8R
Clarke, Kenneth W(endell) 1917- 17-18R
Clarke, Lea
See Rowland-Entwistle, (Arthur) Theodore (Henry)
Clarke, Lige 1942- 41-44R
Clarke, Martin Lowther 1909- CANR-2
Earlier sketch in CA 7-8R
Clarke, Mary 1923- 104
Clarke, Mary Stetson 1911- CANR-8
Earlier sketch in CA 21-22R
See also SATA 5
Clarke, Mary Washington 1913- CANR-11
Earlier sketch in CA 25-28R
Clarke, Mary Whatley 1899- CANR-2
Earlier sketch in CA 7-8R
Clarke, Michael
See Newlon, (Frank) Clarke
Clarke, Nicholas Goodrick
See Goodrick-Clarke, Nicholas
Clarke, P(eter) F(rederick) 1942- 73-76
Clarke, Pauline
See Hunter Blair, Pauline (Clarke)
Clarke, Peter 1936- 104
Clarke, Rebecca Sophia 1833-1906
Brief entry 119
See also DLB 42
Clarke, Richard (William Barnes) 1910-1975 Obituary 115
Clarke, Richard
See Paine, Lauran (Bosworth)
Clarke, Robert
See Paine, Lauran (Bosworth)
and Platt, Charles
Clarke, Robin Harwood 1937- CANR-9
Earlier sketch in CA 15-16R
Clarke, Ron 1937- 107
Clarke, Ronald Francis 1933- 21-22R
Clarke, Shirley 1925- CLC-16
Clarke, Simon 1946- 122
Clarke, Stephan P(aul) 1945- 69-72
Clarke, Thomas E(mmet) 1918- 53-56
Clarke, Thomas Ernest Bennett 1907- CANR-19
Earlier sketch in CA 103
Clarke, Thurston 1946- CANR-13
Earlier sketch in CA 77-80
Clarke, Tom E(ugene) 1915- 5-6R
Clarke, William Dixon 1927- 5-6R
Clarke, William Kendall 1911(?)-1981
Obituary 104
Clarke, William M(alpas) 1922- CANR-15
Earlier sketch in CA 41-44R
Clarke, William Thomas 1932- 57-60
Clarke-Stewart, K(athleen) Alison 1932- 113
Clark-Kennedy, Archibald Edmund 1893-1985 Obituary 117
Clarkson, Adrienne 1939- 49-52
Clarkson, E(dith) Margaret 1915- CANR-20
Earlier sketches in CA 4R, CANR-5
See also SATA 37
Clarkson, Ewan 1929- CANR-17
Earlier sketch in CA 25-28R
See also SATA 9
Clarkson, Geoffrey P. E. 1934- CANR-2
Earlier sketch in CA 5-6R
Clarkson, Helen
See McCloy, Helen (Worrell Clarkson)
Clarkson, J. F.
See Tubb, E(dwin) C(harles)
Clarkson, Jan Nagel 1943- 93-96
Clarkson, Jesse Dunsmore 1897-1973 5-6R
Obituary 45-48
Clarkson, L(eslie) A(lbert) 1933- 73-76
Clarkson, Orman
See Richardson, Gladwell
Clarkson, Paul S(tephen) 1905- 29-32R
Clarkson, Stephen 1937- 41-44R
Clarkson, Tom 1913- 103
Clary, Jack 1932- 57-60
Clasen, Claus-Peter 1931- 41-44R
Clash, The
See Headon, (Nicky) Topper
and Jones, Mick
and Simonon, Paul
and Strummer, Joe
See also CLC 30
Clasper, Paul D(udley) 1923- 4R
Claspy, Everett M. 1907(?)-1973
Obituary 41-44R
Claster, Daniel S(tuart) 1932- 23-24R
Clatworthy, Nancy M(oore) K. 1924- 124
Claude, Richard (P.) 1934- 29-32R
Claudel, Alice Moser CANR-2
Earlier sketch in CA 49-52
Claudel, Paul (Louis Charles Marie) 1868-1955 Brief entry 104
See also TCLC 2, 10
Claudia, Sister Mary 1906- CAP-1
Earlier sketch in CA 9-10
Claudia, Susan
See Johnston, William
Claus, Hugo (Maurice Julius) 1929-
Brief entry 116
Claus, Marshall R. 1936-1970 CAP-2
Earlier sketch in CA 29-32
Clausen, Aage R. 1932- 49-52
Clausen, Andy 1943- Brief entry 117
See also DLB 16
Clausen, Connie 1923- 1R
Clausen, Dennis M(onroe) 1943- 106
Clausen, W. V.
See Clausen, Wendell (Vernon)
Clausen, Wendell (Vernon) 1923- 121
Clauser, Suzanne (P.) 1929- 37-40R
Clavel, Bernard (Charles Henri) 1923- CANR-2
Earlier sketch in CA 45-48
Clavel, Maurice 1920-1979 Obituary 85-88
Clavell, James (duMaresq) 1925- CANR-26
Earlier sketch in CA 25-28R
See also CLC 6, 25
Claverie, Jean 1946- SATA-38
Clawson, Marion 1905- CANR-10
Earlier sketch in CA 65-68
Clawson, Robert W(ayne) 1939- CANR-25
Earlier sketch in CA 108
Clay, Bertha M.
See Dey, Frederic (Merrill) Van Rensselaer
Clay, Cassius M.
See Clay, Cassius Marcellus
Clay, Cassius Marcellus 1810-1903
Brief entry 120
See also DLB 43
Clay, Cassius Marcellus
See Ali, Muhammad
Clay, Charles Travis 1885-1978 Obituary 77-80
Clay, Comer 1910- 45-48
Clay, Diskin 1938- 115
Clay, Duncan
See Diehl, W(illiam) W(ells)
Clay, Edith 1910- 125
Clay, Floyd M(artin) 1927- 45-48
Clay, Grady E. 1916- 93-96
Clay, James 1924- 17-18R
Clay, Jenny Strauss 125
Clay, Jim
See Clay, James
Clay, Lucius D(uBignon) 1897-1978 81-84
Obituary 77-80
Clay, Marie M(ildred) 1926- CANR-22
Earlier sketches in CA 61-64, CANR-8
Clay, Patrice 1947- 106
See also SATA 47
Clay, Roberta 1900- CAP-2
Earlier sketch in CA 29-32
Claybaugh, Amos L(incoln) 1917- 69-72
Claydon, Leslie Francis 1923- 53-56
Clayes, Stanley A(rnold) 1922- 29-32R
Claypool, Jane
See Miner, Jane Claypool
Clayre, Alasdair 1935-1984 102
Obituary 111
Clayton, Aileen Bowen 1918-1981 113
Clayton, Barbara
See Pluff, Barbara Littlefield
Clayton, Bruce 1939- 69-72
Clayton, C. Guy 1936- 122
Clayton, Charles C(urtis) 1902- 73-76
Clayton, Donald D(elbert) 1935- 65-68
Clayton, (Francis) Howard 1918- CANR-12
Earlier sketch in CA 29-32R
Clayton, Howard 1929- 65-68
Clayton, James E(dwin) 1929- 11-12R
Clayton, James L. 1931- CANR-12
Earlier sketch in CA 29-32R
Clayton, Jo 1939- 81-84
Clayton, John 1892-1979 33-36R
Obituary 89-92
Clayton, John
See Beevers, John (Leonard)
Clayton, John J(acob) 1935- CANR-11
Earlier sketch in CA 25-28R
Clayton, Keith (M.) 1928- CANR-11
Earlier sketch in CA 23-24R
Clayton, Paul C(lark) 1932- 61-64
Clayton, Richard Henry Michael 1907- CANR-4
Earlier sketch in CA 5-6R
Clayton, Susan
See Bailey, Alfred Goldsworthy
Clayton, Sylvia 103
Clayton, Thomas (Swoverland) 1932- 41-44R
Clayton, Thompson B(owker) 1904- 57-60
Claytor, Gertrude Boatwright 1890(?)-1973 Obituary 45-48
Cleage, Albert B., Jr. 1911- 65-68
Cleage, Pearl (Michelle) 1948- 41-44R
Cleall, Charles 1927- 7-8R
Clear, Todd R. 1949- 117
Cleare, John 1936- 65-68
Clearman, Brian (Patrick Joseph) 1941- 115
Cleary, Beverly (Atlee Bunn) 1916- CANR-19
Earlier sketches in CA 1R, CANR-2
See also SATA 2, 43
See also DLB 52
See also CLR 2, 8
Cleary, David Powers 1915- 106
Cleary, Florence Damon 1896- 81-84
Cleary, James W(illiam) 1927- 19-20R
Cleary, Johanna L. 1961- 122
Cleary, Jon 1917- CANR-26
Earlier sketches in CA 4R, CANR-3
Cleary, Robert E(dward) 1932- 41-44R
Cleator, P(hilip) E(llaby) 1908- 102
Cleaver, Anastasia N. CANR-18
Earlier sketch in CA 97-100
Cleaver, Bill 1920-1981 73-76
See also SATA 22, 27
See also DLB 52
See also CLR 6
Cleaver, Carole 1934- 49-52
See also SATA 6
Cleaver, Dale G. 1928- 17-18R
Cleaver, (Leroy) Eldridge 1935- CANR-16
Earlier sketch in CA 21-22R
See also BW
See also CLC 30
Cleaver, Elizabeth (Mrazik) 1939-1985 97-100
Obituary 117
See also SATA 23, 43
See also CLR 13
Cleaver, Hylton Reginald 1891-1961 73-76
See also SATA 49
Cleaver, Nancy
See Mathews, Evelyn Craw
Cleaver, Vera 1919- 73-76
See also SATA 22
See also DLB 52
See also CLR 6
Cleaver, William J(oseph) 1920-1981
Obituary 104
Cleaves, Emery N(udd) 1902- 33-36R
Cleaves, Freeman 1904- 4R
Cleaves, Peter S(hurtleff) 1943- 69-72
Clebsch, William Anthony 1923-1984 15-16R
Obituary 113
Clecak, Peter (E.) 1938- 41-44R
Cleckley, Hervey Milton 1903-1984 122
Obituary 111
Cleese, John (Marwood) 1939- 116
Brief entry 112
See also CLC 21
Cleeve, Brian (Talbot) 1921- CANR-16
Earlier sketches in CA 49-52, CANR-1
Clegg, Alec
See Clegg, Alexander Bradshaw
Clegg, Alexander Bradshaw 1909- 85-88
Clegg, Charles (Myron, Jr.) 1916- CANR-17
Earlier sketch in CA 25-28R
Clegg, Jerry S(tephen) 1933- 77-80
Clegg, John 1909- 118
Clegg, Reed K. 1907- CAP-1
Earlier sketch in CA 13-14
Clegg, Stewart (Roger) 1947- CANR-11
Earlier sketch in CA 69-72
Cleghorn, Reese 1930- 25-28R
Cleishbotham, Jebediah
See Scott, Sir Walter
Cleland, Charles C(arr) 1924- CANR-14
Earlier sketch in CA 41-44R
Cleland, Charles E(dward) 1936- 111
Cleland, David I. 1926- CANR-10
Earlier sketch in CA 25-28R
Cleland, Hugh
See Clarke, John (Campbell)
Cleland, John 1710-1789 DLB-39
Cleland, Mabel
See Widdemer, Mabel Cleland
Cleland, (Joseph) Max(well) 1942-
Brief entry 113
Cleland, Morton
See Rennie, James Alan
Cleland, W(illiam) Wendell 1888-1972
Obituary 37-40R
Clelland, Catherine
See Townsend, Doris McFerran
Clelland, Richard C(ook) 1921- 19-20R
Clem, Alan L(eland) 1929- CANR-3
Earlier sketch in CA 11-12R
Clemeau, Carol
See Esler, Carol Clemeau
Clemen, Wolfgang Hermann 1909- CANR-2
Earlier sketch in CA 2R
Clemence, Richard V(ernon) 1910- 1R
Clemenceau, Georges (Eugene Benjamin) 1841-1929 Brief entry 114
Clemenko, Harold B. 1905-1984 Obituary 113
Clemens, Alphonse H. 1905-1977
Obituary 73-76
Clemens, Bryan T. 1934- 97-100
Clemens, Cyril AITN-2
Clemens, Diane S(haver) 1936- 29-32R
Clemens, Rodgers
See Lovin, Roger Robert

Clemens, Samuel Langhorne 1835-1910
Brief entry 104
See also YABC 2
See also DLB 11, 12, 23, 64, 74
See also CDALB 1865-1917
Clemens, Virginia Phelps 1941- CANR-15
Earlier sketch in CA 85-88
See also SATA 35
Clemens, Walter C., Jr. 1933- CANR-7
Earlier sketch in CA 17-18R
Clement, A(lfred) J(ohn) 1915- 25-28R
Clement, Charles Baxter 1940- 105
Clement, Evelyn Geer 1926- 53-56
Clement, George H. 1909- 29-32R
Clement, Hal
See Stubbs, Harry C(lement)
See also DLB 8
Clement, Herbert F(lint) 1927- 81-84
Clement, Jane Tyson 1917- 25-28R
Clement, Roland C(harles) 1912- 49-52
Clement, Wallace 1949- 111
Clements, A(rthur) L(eo) 1932- 29-32R
Clements, Barbara Evans 1945- 89-92
Clements, Bruce 1931- CANR-5
Earlier sketch in CA 53-56
See also SATA 27
Clements, Colleen D(ianne) 1936- 110
Clements, E(llen) Catherine (Scott)
1920- 15-16R
Clements, E(ileen) H(elen) 1905- CAP-1
Earlier sketch in CA 9-10
Clements, Frank A. 1942- 93-96
Clements, Harold M., Sr. 1907- 69-72
Clements, John 1916- CANR-11
Earlier sketch in CA 69-72
Clements, Julia 1906- CAP-1
Earlier sketch in CA 13-14
Clements, Kendrick Alling 1939- 110
Clements, Marcelle 1948- 121
Clements, Robert John 1912- CANR-5
Earlier sketch in CA 4R
Clements, Robert W(illiam) 1939- 110
Clements, Ronald Ernest 1929- 15-16R
Clements, Tad S. 1922- 25-28R
Clements, Traverse 1900(?)-1977
Obituary 69-72
Clements, William 1933(?)-1983 Obituary .. 110
Clements, William M(orris) 1943- 106
Clemhout, Simone 1934- 73-76
Cleminshaw, Clarence Higbee 1902-1985
Obituary 116
Brief entry 106
Clemmons, Francois 1945- 41-44R
Clemmons, Robert S(tarr) 1910- CAP-2
Earlier sketch in CA 21-22
Clemmons, William (Preston) 1932- 57-60
Clemo, Jack
See Clemo, Reginald John
See also DLB 27
Clemo, Reginald John 1916- CANR-6
Earlier sketch in CA 13-14R
Clemo, Richard F(rederick) 1920-1976
Obituary 65-68
Clemoes, Peter Alan Martin 1920- 102
Clemons, Elizabeth
See Nowell, Elizabeth Cameron
Clemons, Harry 1879-19(?) CAP-1
Earlier sketch in CA 13-14
Clemons, Luiamae 1917- 73-76
Clemons, Walter, Jr. 1929- CANR-6
Earlier sketch in CA 4R
Clendenen, Clarence Clemens 1899- 3R
Clendenin, John C(ameron) 1903- 19-20R
Clendenin, William R(itchie) 1917-1979 ...13-14R
Obituary 120
Clendenning, John 1934- 123
Clendenning, Sheila T. 1939- 25-28R
Cleobury, Frank Harold 1892- CAP-1
Earlier sketch in CA 13-14
Clephane, Irene (Amy) 13-14R
Clepper, Henry (Edward) 1901-1987 .... CANR-1
Obituary 122
Earlier sketch in CA 45-48
Clepper, Irene E(lizabeth) 53-56
Clerc, Charles 1926- CANR-14
Earlier sketch in CA 37-40R
Clerici, Gianni 1930- 65-68
Clerihew, E.
See Bentley, E(dmund) C(lerihew)
Clerk, N. W.
See Lewis, C(live) S(taples)
Clery, (Reginald) Val(entine) 1924- CANR-3
Earlier sketch in CA 49-52
Cleugh, Mary F(rances) 1913- CANR-4
Earlier sketch in CA 3R
Cleve, Janita
See Rowland, D(onald) S(ydney)
Cleve, John
See Offutt, Andrew J(efferson V)
Cleveland, Bob
See Cleveland, George
Cleveland, Carles 1952- 85-88
Cleveland, Clifford S.
See Goldsmith, David H(irsh)
Cleveland, George 1903(?)-1985 Obituary .. 116
See also SATA 43
Cleveland, (James) Harlan 1918- CANR-4
Earlier sketch in CA 2R
Cleveland, Harold van B(uren) 1916- ... CANR-13
Earlier sketch in CA 23-24R
Cleveland, John
See McElfresh, (Elizabeth) Adeline
Cleveland, Leslie 1921- 102
Cleveland, Mary 1917- 104
Cleveland, Philip Jerome 1903- 11-12R
Cleveland, Ray L(eRoy) 1929- 21-22R
Cleveland, Sidney E(arl) 1919- 9-10R
Cleven, Cathrine
See Cleven, Kathryn Seward
Cleven, Kathryn Seward 4R
See also SATA 2
Clevenger, Ernest Allen, Jr. 1929- CANR-8
Earlier sketch in CA 57-60
Clevenger, Theodore, Jr. 1929- 41-44R
Clever, (Warren) Glenn 1918- 57-60
Cleverdon, (Thomas) Douglas (James)
1903-1987 ....29-32R
Obituary 123
Cleverley Ford, D(ouglas) W(illiam)
1914- CANR-11
Earlier sketch in CA 25-28R
Cleves, Bernard
See Moore, Bernard
Clevin, Joergen 1920- 29-32R
See also SATA 7
Clevin, Jorgen
See Clevin, Joergen
Clew, Jeffrey Robert 1928- CANR-21
Earlier sketches in CA 57-60, CANR-6
Clew, William J(oseph) 1904- 77-80
Clewes, Dorothy (Mary) 1907- CANR-3
Earlier sketch in CA 5-6R
See also SATA 1
Clewes, Howard (Charles Vivian)
1912(?)-1988 Obituary 125
Clews, Roy 1937- 65-68
Click, J(ohn) W(illiam) 1936- 57-60
Cliff, Jimmy
See Chambers, James
See also CLC 21
Cliff, Michelle 1946- 116
See also BW
Clifford, Craig Edward 1951- 125
Clifford, Derek Plint 1915- CANR-4
Earlier sketch in CA 7-8R
Clifford, Eth
See Rosenberg, Ethel (Clifford)
Clifford, Francis
See Thompson, A(rthur) L(eonard) B(ell)
Clifford, George 1934(?)-1985 Obituary 118
Clifford, Geraldine Joncich 1931- 25-28R
Clifford, H(enry) Dalton 1911- 9-10R
Clifford, Harold B(urton) 1893- CAP-1
Earlier sketch in CA 11-12
See also SATA 10
Clifford, James L(owry) 1901-1978 ..... CANR-6
Obituary 77-80
Earlier sketch in CA 3R
Clifford, John
See Bayliss, John Clifford
Clifford, John E(dward) 1935- 37-40R
Clifford, John Garry 1942- 53-56
Clifford, John McLean 1904-1979 85-88
Clifford, John W(illiam) 1918- 19-20R
Clifford, Laurie B(erry) 1948- 112
Clifford, Margaret Cort 1929- CANR-23
Earlier sketch in CA 25-28R
See also SATA 1
Clifford, Martin 1910- CANR-11
Earlier sketch in CA 25-28R
Clifford, Martin
See Hamilton, Charles Harold St. John
Clifford, Mary Louise Beneway 1926- ... CANR-3
Earlier sketch in CA 5-6R
See also SATA 23
Clifford, Nicholas R(owland) 1930- 21-22R
Clifford, Peggy
See Clifford, Margaret Cort
Clifford, Richard J(ohn) 1934- 112
Clifford, Sarah 1916-1976 .... CANR-11
Earlier sketch in CA 25-28R
Clifford, Theodore
See von Block, Sylvia
Cliffton, Katherine Potter
See Bryant, Katherine Cliffton
Clift, Virgil Alfred 1912- 9-10R
Clift, Wallace Bruce 1926- 110
Clifton, Bernice Marie 1901(?)-1985 ....7-8R
Obituary 116
Clifton, Bud
See Stacton, David (Derek)
Clifton, Fred J. 1935(?)-1984 Obituary 114
Clifton, Harry
See Hamilton, Charles Harold St. John
Clifton, Jack (Whitney) 1912- 106
Clifton, James A(lfonso) 1927- CANR-25
Earlier sketches in CA 25-28R, CANR-10
Clifton, James M(alcolm) 1930- 112
Clifton, Lewis
See Linedecker, Clifford L.
Clifton, (Thelma) Lucille 1936- CANR-24
Earlier sketches in CA 49-52, CANR-2
See also BW
See also SATA 20
See also DLB 5, 41
See also CLC 19
See also CLR 5
Clifton, Marguerite Ann 1925- 15-16R
Clifton, Mark (Irvin) 1906-1963 Obituary ... 117
Clifton-Taylor, Alec 1907-1985 125
Clignet, Remi Pierre 1931- 104
Climo, Shirley 1928- CANR-24
Earlier sketch in CA 107
See also SATA 35, 39
Clinard, Dorothy Long 1909- 5-6R
Clinard, Helen Hall 1931- 124
Clinard, Marshall B(arron) 1911- CANR-4
Earlier sketch in CA 7-8R
Clinard, Turner N(orman) 1917- 37-40R
Clinch, Nicholas (Bayard) 1930- 111
Clinchy, Everett R(oss) 1896-1986
Obituary 118
Cline, Bev
See Fink Cline, Beverly
Cline, Beverly
See Fink Cline, Beverly
Cline, Beverly Fink
See Fink Cline, Beverly
Cline, C(harles) Terry, Jr. 1935- CANR-25
Earlier sketches in CA 61-64, CANR-8
Cline, Catherine Ann 1927- 19-20R
Cline, Charles (William) 1937- CANR-7
Earlier sketch in CA 61-64
Cline, Denzel C(ecil) 1903- CAP-2
Earlier sketch in CA 21-22
Cline, Edward 1946- 101
Cline, Gloria Griffen 1929-1973 ....7-8R
Obituary 125
Cline, Joan
See Hamilton, Joan Lesley
Cline, Linda 1941- 65-68
Cline, Ray Steiner 1918- Brief entry 106
Cline, Rodney 1903- 61-64
Cline, Victor (Bailey) 1925- 65-68
Clinebell, Howard J., Jr. 1922- CANR-13
Earlier sketch in CA 33-36R
Clinton, (Lloyd) D(eWitt) 1946- 116
Clinton, Dirk
See Silverberg, Robert
Clinton, F. G.
See Campbell, R(obert) Wright
Clinton, Iris A. (Corbin) 1901- CAP-1
Earlier sketch in CA 11-12
Clinton, Jeff
See Bickham, Jack M(iles)
Clinton, Jon
See Prince, J(ack) H(arvey)
Clinton, Richard Lee 1938- CANR-23
Earlier sketches in CA 61-64, CANR-8
Clinton, Rupert
See Bulmer, (Henry) Kenneth
Clinton-Baddeley, V.C. 1911(?)-1970
Obituary 104
Clipman, William 1954- 106
Clipper, Lawrence Jon 1930- 49-52
Clish, (Lee) Marian 1946- SATA-43
Clissmann, Anne
See Clune, Anne
Clissold, (John) Stephen (Hallet)
1913-1982 110
Obituary 107
Clistier, Adeline
See Denny, Alma
Clithero, Myrtle E(ly) 1906- CAP-2
Earlier sketch in CA 25-28
Clithero, Sally
See Clithero, Myrtle E(ly)
Clive, Clifford
See Hamilton, Charles Harold St. John
Clive, Geoffrey 1927-1976 ....33-36R
Clive, John 1933- 103
Clive, John Leonard 1924- 85-88
Clive, Mary 1907- 21-22R
Clive, William
See Bassett, Ronald
Clodfelter, (William) Frank(lin) 1911- 103
Clodfelter, Micheal 1946- 69-72
Cloeren, Hermann J(osef) 1934- 41-44R
Cloete, Stuart 1897-1976 .... CANR-3
Obituary 65-68
Earlier sketch in CA 1R
Clogan, Paul M(aurice) 1934- 33-36R
Clogg, Clifford C(ollier) 1949- 112
Cloke, Richard 1916- CANR-11
Earlier sketch in CA 69-72
Clokey, Richard M(ontgomery) 1936-
Brief entry 107
Clones, N(icholas) J. 97-100
Clopton, Beverly Virginia B(eck) 106
Clor, Harry M(ortimer) 1929- 53-56
Clore, Gerald L(ewis, Jr.) 1939- 37-40R
Close, A. Kathryn 1908(?)-1973
Obituary 41-44R
Close, Frank (E.) 1945- 126
Close, Henry T(hompson) 1928- 4R
Close, Reginald Arthur 1909- 17-18R
Close, Upton
See Hall, Josef Washington
Closen, Michael L. 1949- 121
Closs, August 1898- CANR-2
Earlier sketch in CA 5-6R
Closs, Elizabeth
See Traugott, Elizabeth Closs
Clotfelter, Beryl E(dward) 1926- 53-56
Clotfelter, Cecil F. 1929- 53-56
Clotfelter, Mary (Eunice) L(ong) 103
Clothier, Peter (Dean) 1936- 65-68
Cloud, (Joseph) Fred (Jr.) 1925- 15-16R
Cloud, Patricia
See Strother, Pat Wallace
Cloud, Preston (Ercelle) 1912- 93-96
Cloud, Yvonne
See Kapp, Yvonne (Mayer)
Cloudsley-Thompson, J(ohn) L(eonard)
1921- CANR-23
Earlier sketches in CA 19-20R, CANR-8
See also SATA 19
Clough, Arthur Hugh 1819-1861 .... DLB-32
Clough, B(renda) W(ang) 1955- 116
Clough, Francis F(rederick) 1912- CAP-1
Earlier sketch in CA 9-10
Clough, Neil 1950- 112
Clough, Ralph Nelson 1916- Brief entry 105
Clough, Rosa Trillo 1906- 13-14R
Clough, Shepard B(ancroft) 1901- CANR-4
Earlier sketch in CA 1R
Clough, William 1911(?)-1976 Obituary ...69-72
Clough, William A. 1899- CAP-2
Earlier sketch in CA 21-22
Clough, Wilson O(ber) 1894- 17-18R
Clouse, Robert Gordon 1931- CANR-12
Earlier sketch in CA 29-32R
Clouser, John William 1932- 61-64
Clout, Hugh Donald 1944- CANR-15
Earlier sketch in CA 41-44R
Cloutier, Cecile
See Cloutier-Wojciechowska, Cecile
See also DLB 60
Cloutier, David 1951- CANR-7
Earlier sketch in CA 57-60
Cloutier-Wojciechowska, Cecile 1930- .. CANR-12
Earlier sketch in CA 65-68
Clover, Frank Metlar III 1940- 101
Clow, Martha de Mev 1932- 29-32R
Cloward, Richard Andrew 1926- 41-44R
Clower, Robert W(ayne) 1926- 89-92
Clowney, Edmund P(rosper) 1917- CANR-8
Earlier sketch in CA 5-6R
Clowse, Converse Dilworth 1929-
Brief entry 108
Clubb, Louise George 1930- 69-72
Clubb, O(liver) Edmund 1901- 37-40R
Clubb, Oliver E., Jr. 1929- 5-6R
Clubbe, John 1938- CANR-11
Earlier sketch in CA 25-28R
Cluff, Charles E. 1937- 65-68
Clugston, Richard 1938- 41-44R
Clum, John M(acKenzie) 1941- 69-72
Clun, Arthur
See Polsby, Nelson W(oolf)
Clune, Anne 1945- 103
Clune, Francis Patrick 1893-1971 .... CAP-2
Obituary 29-32R
Earlier sketch in CA 23-24
Clune, Frank
See Clune, Francis Patrick
Clune, Henry W. 1890- CANR-5
Earlier sketch in CA 2R
Clunies Ross, Anthony (Ian) 1932- 53-56
Clurman, Harold 1901-1980 .... CANR-2
Obituary 101
Earlier sketch in CA 4R
Cluster, Dick 1947- 97-100
Clute, Morrel J. 1912- 13-14R
Clute, Robert E(ugene) 1924- 41-44R
Clutha, Janet Paterson Frame 1924- CANR-2
Earlier sketch in CA 4R
Clutterbuck, David Ashley 1947- 113
Clutterbuck, Richard 1917- CANR-25
Earlier sketches in CA 23-24R, CANR-9
Clutton-Brock, Arthur Guy 1906- 110
Cluver, Eustace Henry 1894- CAP-1
Earlier sketch in CA 9-10
Cluysenaar, Anne (Alice Andree Jackson)
1936- 102
Clyde, Leslie
See Kipps, Harriet C(lyde)
Clyde, Norman Asa 1885-1972 ....41-44R
Clyde Cool
See Frazier, Walt(er)
Clymer, Eleanor 1906- CANR-9
Earlier sketch in CA 61-64
See also SATA 9
Clymer, (Joseph) Floyd 1895-1970
Obituary 104
Clymer, Kenton James 1943- Brief entry 109
Clymer, Reuben Swinburne 1878- CAP-1
Earlier sketch in CA 11-12
Clynder, Monica
See Muir, Marie
Clyne, James F. 1898(?)-1977 Obituary ...69-72
Clyne, Patricia (Edwards) 101
See also SATA 31
Clyne, Terence
See Blatty, William Peter
Clytus, John 1929- 29-32R
Cnudde, Charles F(rancis) 1938- CANR-26
Earlier sketch in CA 29-32R
Coad, F(rederick) Roy 1925- 103
Coad, Oral Sumner 1887- 45-48
Coade, Jessie 1911- 120
Coakley, Lakme 1912- 69-72
Coakley, Mary Lewis CAP-1
Earlier sketch in CA 15-16
Coakley, Michael 1947(?)-1988 Obituary ... 126
Coale, Samuel Chase 1943- CANR-11
Earlier sketch in CA 65-68
Coalson, Glo 1946- 103
See also SATA 26
Coan, Eugene V(ictor) 1943- 110
Coan, Otis W(elton) 1895- CAP-2
Earlier sketch in CA 33-36
Coan, Richard Welton 1928- CANR-12
Earlier sketch in CA 69-72
Coates, Austin 1922- 102
Coates, Belle 1896- 5-6R
See also SATA 2
Coates, Charles R(obert) 1915- 106
Coates, David 1946- 125
Coates, Donald R(obert) 1922- CANR-2
Earlier sketch in CA 49-52
Coates, Doreen (Frances) 1912- 107
Coates, Gary J(oseph) 1947- 110
Coates, Geoffrey Edward 1917- 37-40R
Coates, J(ohn) F(rancis) 1922- 123
Coates, Ken 1930- 123
Coates, Robert M(yron) 1897-1973 ....5-6R
Obituary 41-44R
See also DLB 4, 9
Coates, Ruth Allison 1915- 57-60
See also SATA 11
Coates, William Ames 1916-1973 ....37-40R
Coates, Willson H(avelock) 1899-1976 ...37-40R
Obituary 69-72
Coats, Alice M(argaret) 1905- 53-56
See also SATA 11
Coats, George W. 1936- 23-24R

INDEX

Coats, Peter 1910- CANR-1
Earlier sketch in CA 49-52
Coatsworth, Elizabeth (Jane)
1893-1986 CANR-4
Obituary 120
Earlier sketch in CA 7-8R
See also SATA 2, 49
See also DLB 22
See also CLR 2
Cobb, Alice 1909- 7-8R
Cobb, Carl W(esley) 1926- 21-22R
Cobb, Charles E., Jr. 1943- DLB-41
Cobb, David 1934- 112
Cobb, Faye Davis 1932- 9-10R
Cobb, Frank I. 1869-1923 DLB-25
Cobb, Geoffrey Belton 1892(?)-1971
Obituary 104
Cobb, Irvin S. 1876-1944 DLB-11, 25
Cobb, James Charles 1947- 112
Cobb, Jane
See Berry, Jane Cobb
Cobb, John B(oswell), Jr. 1925- CANR-2
Earlier sketch in CA 3R
Cobb, Jonathan 1946- 93-96
Cobb, Nathan 1943- 105
Cobb, R. C.
See Cobb, Richard (Charles)
Cobb, Richard (Charles) 1917- Brief entry 116
Cobb, Robert A. 1941- 69-72
Cobb, Roger W(illiam) 1941- 104
Cobb, Vicki 1938- CANR-14
Earlier sketch in CA 33-36R
See also SATA 8
See also SAAS 6
See also CLR 2
Cobban, Alfred 1901-1968 Obituary 111
Cobbett
See Ludovici, Anthony M(ario)
Cobbett, Richard
See Pluckrose, Henry (Arthur)
Cobbett, William 1762-1835 DLB-43
Cobbing, Bob 1920- 101
Cobbledick, James R. 1935- 97-100
Cobbs, John L(ewis) 1917- Brief entry 115
Cobbs, Price M(ashaw) 1928- 23-24R
Coben, Lawrence A(llan) 1926- 111
Coben, Stanley 1929- 122
Cober, Alan E(dwin) 1935- SATA-7
Cobham, Sir Alan
See Hamilton, Charles Harold St. John
Coble, John (Lawrence) 1924- 9-10R
Cobleigh, Ira U(nderwood) 1903- 81-84
Coblentz, Stanton A(rthur) 1896- CANR-21
Earlier sketch in CA 5-6R
Cobley, John 1914- 13-14R
Cobrin, Harry Aaron 1902- CAP-2
Earlier sketch in CA 29-32
Coburn, Andrew 1932- CANR-4
Earlier sketch in CA 53-56
Coburn, Broughton 1951- 111
Coburn, D(onald) L(ee) 1938- 89-92
See also CLC 10
Coburn, John Bowen 1914- CANR-2
Earlier sketch in CA 4R
Coburn, Karen Levin 1941- 65-68
Coburn, Kathleen 1905- 93-96
Coburn, L. J.
See Harvey, John (Barton)
Coburn, Louis 1915- 104
Coburn, Thomas B(owen) 1944- 110
Coburn, Walt 1889- CAP-1
Earlier sketch in CA 9-10
Cocagnac, Augustin Maurice(-Jean)
1924- CANR-17
Earlier sketch in CA 25-28R
See also SATA 7
Coccioli, Carlo 1920- CANR-9
Earlier sketch in CA 13-14R
Cochard, Thomas S(ylvester) 1893- 57-60
Cochet, Gabriel 1888-1973 Obituary 45-48
Cochran, Bert 1917-1984 45-48
Obituary 113
Cochran, Bobbye A. 1949- SATA-11
Cochran, Charles L(eo) 1940- 57-60
Cochran, Clarke E(dward) 1945- 107
Cochran, Elizabeth
See Cochrane, Elizabeth
Cochran, Hamilton 1898-1977 CANR-6
Obituary 73-76
Earlier sketch in CA 3R
Cochran, Jacqueline 1910(?)-1980
Obituary 101
Cochran, Jeff
See Durst, Paul
Cochran, John A(rthur) 1921- 122
Cochran, John R(obert) 1937- 41-44R
Cochran, Leslie H(ershel) 1939- CANR-2
Earlier sketch in CA 49-52
Cochran, Rice E.
See Monroe, Keith
Cochran, Thomas C(hilds) 1902- CANR-8
Earlier sketch in CA 61-64
See also DLB 17
Cochrane, A(rchibald) L(eman)
1909(?)-1988 Obituary 125
Cochrane, Arthur C(aspersz) 1909- CANR-4
Earlier sketch in CA 7-8R
Cochrane, Elizabeth 1867-1922 Brief entry 118
See also DLB 25
Cochrane, Eric W. 1928-1985 49-52
Obituary 118
Cochrane, Glynn 1940- 53-56
Cochrane, Hugh (Ferrier) 1923- 103
Cochrane, James D(avid) 1938- 29-32R
Cochrane, James L. 1941- CANR-13
Earlier sketch in CA 33-36R
Cochrane, Jennifer (Ann Frances) 1936- 102
Cochrane, Louise Morley 1918- 11-12R
Cochrane, Pauline A(therton) 1929- 110
Cochrane, Willard W(esley) 1914- CANR-11
Earlier sketch in CA 23-24R
Cochrane, William E. 1926- 97-100
Cochrane de Alencar, Gertrude E. L.
1906- 7-8R
Cochran-Smith, Marilyn 1951- 115
Coch-y-Bonddhu
See Arnold, Richard
Cockburn, Alexander 1941- Brief entry 123
Cockburn, (Francis) Claud 1904-1981 102
Obituary 105
Cockburn, Thomas Aiden 1912- 9-10R
Cockcroft, George Powers 1932- 116
Cockcroft, James D(onald) 1935- CANR-25
Earlier sketches in CA 25-28R, CANR-10
Cockcroft, John (Douglas) 1897-1967 CAP-2
Earlier sketch in CA 21-22
Cockerell, H(ugh) A(nthony) L(ewis)
1909- CAP-1
Earlier sketch in CA 13-14
Cockerell, Sydney M(orris) 1906-1987
Obituary 124
Cockerill, John A. 1845-1896 DLB-23
Cockett, Mary CANR-19
Earlier sketches in CA 9-10R, CANR-4
See also SATA 3
Cockfield, Jamie (Hartwell) 1945- 115
Cocking, Clive 1938- 105
Cocking, J(ohn) M(artin) 1914- 53-56
Cockrell, Amanda
See Crowe, Amanda Cockrell
Cockrell, Marian (Brown) 1909- CAP-2
Earlier sketch in CA 17-18
Cocks, Geoffrey (Campbell) 1948- 121
Cockshut, A(nthony) O(liver) J(ohn)
1927- CANR-10
Earlier sketch in CA 19-20R
Coco, James (Emil) 1930(?)-1987
Obituary 121
Cocozzella, Peter 1937- 37-40R
Cocozzoli, Gary R(ichard) 1951- 119
Cocteau, Jean (Maurice Eugene Clement)
1889-1963 CAP-2
Earlier sketch in CA 25-28
See also DLB 65
See also CLC 1, 8, 15, 16, 43
Codding, George A(rthur), Jr. 1923- CANR-13
Earlier sketch in CA 33-36R
Code, Grant Hyde 1896-1974 49-52
Codel, Martin 1903(?)-1973 Obituary 41-44R
Codel, Michael R(ichard) 1939- 73-76
Coder, S(amuel) Maxwell 1902- CANR-14
Earlier sketch in CA 37-40R
Codere, Helen (Frances) 1917- 69-72
Codevilla, (Maria) Angelo 1943- 61-64
Codrescu, Andrei 1946- CANR-13
Earlier sketch in CA 33-36R
See also CLC 46
Codrington, Kenneth de Burgh 1899-1986
Obituary 118
Cody, Al
See Joscelyn, Archie L.
Cody, C. S.
See Waller, Leslie
Cody, D(ouglas) Thane R(omney) 1932- 57-60
Cody, Fred 1916- 107
Cody, James P.
See Rohrbach, Peter Thomas
Cody, John 1925- 101
Cody, John J. 1930- 29-32R
Cody, Liza Brief entry 125
Cody, Martin L(eonard) 1941- 53-56
Cody, Morrill 1901- 125
Cody, Walt
See Norwood, Victor G(eorge) C(harles)
Coe, Charles Norton 1915- 4R
Coe, Christine Sadler
See Sadler, Christine
Coe, Douglas
See Epstein, Beryl (M. Williams)
and Epstein, Samuel
Coe, Fred(erick) 1914-1979 Obituary 85-88
Coe, Lloyd 1899(?)-1976 Obituary 69-72
See also SATA 30
Coe, Malcolm (James) 1930- 123
Coe, Max
See Bourne, Randolph S(illiman)
Coe, Michael Douglas 1929- CANR-19
Earlier sketches in CA 4R, CANR-4
Coe, Michelle E(ileen) 1917- 106
Coe, Peter 1929-1987 Obituary 122
Coe, Ralph T(racy) 1929- CANR-1
Earlier sketch in CA 2R
Coe, Richard L(ivingston) 1916- 65-68
Coe, Richard N(elson) 1923- CANR-12
Earlier sketch in CA 25-28R
Coe, Rodney Michael 1933- 41-44R
Coe, Tucker
See Westlake, Donald E(dwin)
Coe, William C(harles) 1930- 37-40R
Coel, Margaret 1937- 106
Coelho, George Victor 1918- CANR-1
Earlier sketch in CA 45-48
Coen, Ethan 1958- 126
Coen, Joel 1955- 126
Coen, Rena Neumann 1925- 15-16R
See also SATA 20
Coens, Sister Mary Xavier 1918- 21-22R
Coerr, Eleanor (Beatrice) 1922- CANR-11
Earlier sketch in CA 25-28R
See also SATA 1
Coetzee, J(ohn) M. 1940- 77-80
See also CLC 23, 33
Cofer, Charles N(orval) 1916- 37-40R
Cofer, Judith Ortiz 1952- 115
Coffee, Lenore J. 1897(?)-1984 Obituary 113
See also DLB 44
Coffey, Alan R. 1931- 33-36R
Coffey, Brian
See Koontz, Dean R(ay)
Coffey, (Helen) Dairine 1933- 21-22R
Coffey, J(oseph) I(rving) 1916- 41-44R
Coffey, John W(ill), Jr. 1925- 45-48
Coffey, Marilyn 1937- CANR-2
Earlier sketch in CA 45-48
Coffey, Robert E(dward) 1931- 65-68
Coffey, Thomas Patrick 1928- 120
Coffin, Arthur B. 1929- 29-32R
Coffin, Berton 1910- CANR-5
Earlier sketch in CA 11-12R
Coffin, David R(obbins) 1918- 5-6R
Coffin, Dean 1911- 33-36R
Coffin, Frank M(orey) 1919- 11-12R
Coffin, Geoffrey
See Mason, F(rancis) van Wyck
Coffin, George S(turgis) 1903- 7-8R
Coffin, Harold 1905(?)-1981 Obituary 104
Coffin, Harold Glen 1926- 115
Coffin, Joseph (John) 1899- 57-60
Coffin, Lewis A(ugustus) III 1932- 61-64
Coffin, Lyn 1943- 110
Coffin, Patricia 1912-1974 CAP-2
Obituary 49-52
Earlier sketch in CA 33-36
Coffin, Robert P(eter) Tristram 1892-1955
Brief entry 123
See also DLB 45
Coffin, Tristram 1912- 23-24R
Coffin, Tristram Potter 1922- CANR-2
Earlier sketch in CA 5-6R
Coffin, William Sloane, Jr. 1924- 103
Coffinet, Julien 1907- 61-64
Coffman, Barbara Frances 1907- CAP-1
Earlier sketch in CA 15-16
Coffman, Charles DeWitt 1909- 102
Coffman, Edward M. 1929- 33-36R
Coffman, Paul B(rown) 1900- CAP-2
Earlier sketch in CA 21-22
Coffman, Ramon Peyton 1896- CAP-2
Earlier sketch in CA 17-18
See also SATA 4
Coffman, Virginia (Edith) 1914- CANR-2
Earlier sketch in CA 49-52
Cofyn, Cornelius
See Saunders, Hilary Aidan St. George
Cogane, Gerald
See Fonarow, Jerry
Coger, Leslie Irene 1912- 21-22R
Coggan, (Frederick) Donald 1909- 17-18R
Coggin, Philip A(nnett) 1917- 117
Coggins, Jack (Banham) 1914- CANR-2
Earlier sketch in CA 7-8R
See also SATA 2
Coggins, Paul E. 1951- 126
Coggins, Ross 1927- 15-16R
Coghill, Nevill (Henry Kendall Aylmer)
1899-1980 CANR-11
Obituary 102
Earlier sketch in CA 13-14R
Coghlan, Brian (Laurence Dillon) 1926- 17-18R
Coghlan, Margaret M. 1920- 106
Cogley, John 1916-1976 CANR-2
Obituary 65-68
Earlier sketch in CA 45-48
Cogswell, Coralie (Norris) 1930- 15-16R
Cogswell, Fred(erick William) 1917- CANR-18
Earlier sketches in CA 7-8R, CANR-3
See also DLB 60
Cogswell, James A(rthur) 1922- 33-36R
Cogswell, Mason Fitch 1761-1830 DLB-37
Cogswell, Theodore R. 1918- CANR-4
Earlier sketch in CA 4R
Cohan, Avery B(erlow) 1914-1977 61-64
Obituary 69-72
Cohan, Tony 1939- 108
Cohane, John Philip 1911- 101
Cohane, Tim(othy) 1912- 9-10R
Cohart, Mary 1911- 57-60
Cohen, Aaron (Samuel) 1935- 110
Cohen, Aharon 1910- 69-72
Cohen, Albert 1895(?)-1981 Obituary 105
Cohen, Albert J. 1903(?)-1984 Obituary 114
Cohen, Albert Kircidel 1918- 13-14R
Cohen, Allan Y. 1939- 33-36R
Cohen, Amnon 1936- 85-88
Cohen, Anne Billings 1937- 57-60
Cohen, Anthea 1913- CANR-18
Earlier sketch in CA 97-100
Cohen, Arthur A(llen) 1928-1986 CANR-17
Obituary 120
Earlier sketches in CA 4R, CANR-1
See also DLB 28
See also CLC 7, 31
Cohen, Arthur M. 1927- 33-36R
Cohen, B(enjamin) Bernard 1922- 11-12R
Cohen, Barbara 1932- CANR-19
Earlier sketches in CA 53-56, CANR-4
See also SATA 10
Cohen, Benjamin J(erry) 1937- CANR-18
Earlier sketch in CA 101
Cohen, Benjamin Victor 1894-1983 CAP-1
Obituary 110
Earlier sketch in CA 11-12
Cohen, Bernard 1937- 103
Cohen, Bernard Lande 1902- 29-32R
Cohen, Bernard P. 1930- 45-48
Cohen, Bruce J. 1938- 89-92
Cohen, Carl 1931- CANR-5
Earlier sketch in CA 3R
Cohen, Charles 1943- 111
Cohen, Daniel (E.) 1936- CANR-20
Earlier sketches in CA 45-48, CANR-1
See also SATA 8
See also SAAS 4
Cohen, David 1952- 108
Cohen, David Steven 1943- 53-56
Cohen, Donna 1947- 122
Cohen, Dorothy H. 1915- Brief entry 105
Cohen, Edgar H. 1913- 29-32R
Cohen, Edmund D(avid) 1943- 57-60
Cohen, Edward H. 1941- Brief entry 115
Cohen, Edward M(artin) 1936- 23-24R
Cohen, Elaine (Marsha Perlman) 1938- 110
Cohen, Elie Aron 1909- 53-56
Cohen, Eliot A(sher) 1956- 113
Cohen, Florence Chanock 1927- 5-6R
Cohen, Gary B(ennett) 1948- 107
Cohen, Gary G. 1934- CANR-7
Earlier sketch in CA 57-60
Cohen, George Michael 1931- 81-84
Cohen, Harry 1936- 106
Cohen, (Henry) Hennig 1919- CANR-5
Earlier sketch in CA 3R
Cohen, Henry 1933- 33-36R
Cohen, Howard Martin 1926- Brief entry 107
Cohen, I. Bernard 1914- 69-72
Cohen, Ira Sheldon 1924- CANR-10
Earlier sketch in CA 5-6R
Cohen, Jacob 1918- 123
Cohen, Janet 1940- 126
Cohen, Jean Louise 1946- 111
Cohen, Jene Barr 1900-1985 CANR-3
Obituary 115
Earlier sketch in CA 5-6R
Cohen, Jerome Alan 1930- CANR-13
Earlier sketch in CA 49-52
Cohen, Jerome B(ernard) 1915-1986 9-10R
Obituary 121
Cohen, Joan Lebold 1932- CANR-13
Earlier sketch in CA 25-28R
See also SATA 4
Cohen, John 1911- CANR-6
Earlier sketch in CA 13-14R
Cohen, John Michael 1903- CANR-4
Earlier sketch in CA 7-8R
Cohen, Joseph 1926- CANR-10
Earlier sketch in CA 65-68
Cohen, Jozef 1921- 29-32R
Cohen, Judith Beth 1943- 118
Cohen, Kalman J(oseph) 1931- 15-16R
Cohen, Kathleen Rogers 1933- 53-56
Cohen, Keith 1945- 101
Cohen, Lawrence Jonathan 1923- 65-68
Cohen, Leonard (Norman) 1934- CANR-14
Earlier sketch in CA 21-22R
See also DLB 53
See also CLC 3, 38
Cohen, Margie K(anter) 1912- 109
Cohen, (Stephen) Marshall 1929- CANR-23
Earlier sketches in CA 45-48, CANR-2
Cohen, Martin A(aron) 1928- Brief entry 113
Cohen, Marvin 1931- CANR-17
Earlier sketch in CA 25-28R
Cohen, Matt 1942- 61-64
See also DLB 53
See also CLC 19
Cohen, Michael P. 1944- 121
Cohen, Mike
See Cohen, Morris
Cohen, Miriam 1926- 106
See also SATA 29
Cohen, Morris 1912- 17-18R
Cohen, Morris L(eo) 1927- 49-52
Cohen, Mortimer J. 1894-1972 Obituary 104
Cohen, Morton N(orton) 1921- CANR-5
Earlier sketch in CA 2R
Cohen, Myron 1903(?)-1986 Obituary 118
Cohen, Nancy Wainer 1947- 111
Cohen, Naomi W(iener) 1927- Brief entry 114
Cohen, Norm(an) 1936- 109
Cohen, Octavus Roy 1891-1959
Brief entry 112
Cohen, Paul Andrew 1934- 115
Cohen, Paul S. 1945- 123
Cohen, Peter Zachary 1931- CANR-12
Earlier sketch in CA 33-36R
See also SATA 4
Cohen, Richard Murry 1938- CANR-19
Earlier sketch in CA 103
Cohen, Robert 1938- CANR-12
Earlier sketch in CA 29-32R
Cohen, Robert Carl 1930- 57-60
See also SATA 8
Cohen, Roberta G. 1937- 49-52
Cohen, Ronald 1930- CANR-13
Earlier sketch in CA 33-36R
Cohen, Ronald Dennis 1940- 105
Cohen, Ronald Jay 1949- 97-100
Cohen, Rosalyn
See Higgins, Rosalyn (Cohen)
Cohen, S. Alan 1933- 29-32R
Cohen, S. Ralph 1917-1983 Obituary 110
Cohen, Sanford 1920- 1R
Cohen, Sara Kay Sherman 1943- 102
Cohen, Sarah Blacher 1936- 81-84
Cohen, Scott 1946- 116
Cohen, Selma Jeanne 1920- 25-28R
Cohen, Seymour Jay 1922- 25-28R
Cohen, Sharleen Cooper CANR-19
Earlier sketch in CA 97-100
Cohen, Sheldon S. 1931- 25-28R
Cohen, Sherry Suib 1934- 102
Cohen, Sidney 1910-1987 15-16R
Obituary 122
Cohen, Stanley 1928- CANR-15
Earlier sketch in CA 29-32R
Cohen, Stephen 1941- 118

Cohen, Stephen D(avid) 1942- ... 111
Cohen, Stephen F(rand) 1938- ... 49-52
Cohen, Stephen S. 1941- ... 33-36R
Cohen, Stephen Z(olman) 1931- ... 121
Cohen, Steve (Michael) 1951- ... 114
Cohen, Stewart 1940- ... 65-68
Cohen, Susan 1938- ... CANR-20
Earlier sketches in CA 53-56, CANR-5
Cohen, Warren I. 1934- ... CANR-9
Earlier sketch in CA 21-22R
Cohen, Wilbur J(oseph) 1913-1987 ... CANR-17
Obituary ... 122
Earlier sketch in CA 25-28R
Cohen, William A(lan) 1937- ... CANR-19
Earlier sketch in CA 103
Cohen, William B(enjamin) 1941- ... 37-40R
Cohen, William Howard 1927- ... 17-18R
Cohen, William S(ebastian) 1940- ... 108
Cohen, Yehudi A(ryeh) 1928- ... 113
Cohen-Solal, Annie 19(?)- ... CLC-50
Cohen-Stratyner, Barbara Naomi 1951- ... 113
Cohler, Bertram J(oseph) 1938- ... 109
Cohler, David Keith 1940- ... 104
Cohn, Adrian A. 1922- ... 25-28R
Cohn, Alan M(artin) 1926- ... 110
Cohn, Angelo 1914- ... CANR-4
Earlier sketch in CA 5-6R
See also SATA 19
Cohn, Arthur 1910- ... 110
Cohn, Dorrit 1924- ... 93-96
Cohn, Elchanan 1941- ... 73-76
Cohn, Haim H(erman) 1911- ... 45-48
Cohn, Helen Desfosses
See Desfosses, Helen
Cohn, Jan Kadetsky 1933- ... 102
Cohn, Jules 1930- ... 33-36R
Cohn, Keith E(van) 1935- ... 107
Cohn, Lester
See Cole, Lester
Cohn, Marguerite A. 1898(?)-1984
Obituary ... 113
Cohn, Marvin L(ester) 1924- ... 105
Cohn, Nik 1946- ... 102
Cohn, Norman 1915- ... 57-60
Cohn, Robert Greer 1921- ... 9-10R
Cohn, Roy M(arcus) 1927-1986 ... 108
Obituary ... 119
Cohn, Rubin (Goodman) 1911-1986 ... 57-60
Obituary ... 119
Cohn, Ruby 1922- ... 93-96
Cohn, Samuel Kline, Jr. 1949- ... 125
Cohn, Stanley H(arold) 1922- ... 29-32R
Cohn, Theodore 1923- ... 89-92
Cohn, Vera 1907- ... 97-100
Cohn, Victor (Edward) 1919- ... 65-68
Cohon, Barry
See Cohon, Baruch J(oseph)
Cohon, Baruch J(oseph) 1926- ... 29-32R
Cohon, Beryl David 1898- ... CANR-6
Earlier sketch in CA 1R
Coigney, Virginia 1917- ... 103
Coit, John Hamilton 1947(?)-1986
Obituary ... 118
Coit, Lew Garrison 1897(?)-1985 Obituary ... 116
Coit, Margaret Louise 1919- ... CANR-5
Earlier sketch in CA 1R
See also SATA 2
Cojeen, Robert H. 1920- ... 37-40R
Coke, Tom S(tephen) 1943- ... 115
Coke, Van Deren 1921- ... CANR-22
Earlier sketches in CA 15-16R, CANR-7
Coker, C(harles) F(rederick) W(illiams)
1932-1983 Obituary ... 110
Coker, Carolyn ... 125
Coker, Elizabeth Boatwright 1909- ... 45-48
Coker, Gylbert 1944- ... 93-96
Coker, Jerry 1932- ... CANR-6
Earlier sketch in CA 11-12R
Coker, Syl Cheney
See Cheney-Coker, Syl
Colacci, Mario 1910- ... 5-6R
Coladarci, Arthur Paul 1917- ... 5-6R
Colaiaco, James A(lfred) 1945- ... 115
Colander, Pat(ricia) 1952- ... 110
Colaneri, John Nunzio 1930- ... 103
Colaw, Emerson S. 1921- ... 13-14R
Colbach, Edward M(ichael) 1939- ... 69-72
Colbeck, Maurice 1925- ... CANR-5
Earlier sketch in CA 15-16R
Colberg, Marshall R(udolph) 1913- ... CANR-1
Earlier sketch in CA 1R
Colbert, Anthony 1934- ... 89-92
See also SATA 15
Colbert, Douglas A(lbert) 1933- ... 57-60
Colbert, Edwin Harris 1905- ... CANR-8
Earlier sketch in CA 61-64
Colbert, Evelyn S(peyer) 1918- ... 102
Colbert, James 1951- ... 122
Colbert, Roman 1921- ... 53-56
Colbourn, H(arold) Trevor 1927- ... 33-36R
Colburn, C(lyde) William 1939- ... 37-40R
Colburn, David Richard 1942- ... 110
Colburn, George A(bbott) 1938- ... 41-44R
Colby, Averil 1900-1983(?) Obituary ... 108
Colby, Benjamin N(ick) 1931- ... 61-64
Colby, C(arroll) B(urleigh) 1904-1977 ... CANR-6
Earlier sketch in CA 4R
See also SATA 3, 35
Colby, Douglas (Steven) 1954- ... 116
Colby, Elbridge 1891-1982 ... CAP-1
Obituary ... 108
Earlier sketch in CA 15-16
Colby, Jean Poindexter 1909- ... CANR-5
Earlier sketch in CA 4R
See also SATA 23
Colby, Joan 1939- ... CANR-13
Earlier sketch in CA 77-80
Colby, Robert A(lan) 1920- ... 53-56
Colby, Roy (Edward) 1910- ... 25-28R
Colby, Vineta (Blumoff) 1922- ... 11-12R
Colby, William Egan 1920- ... 81-84
Colchie, Elizabeth Schneider
See Schneider, Elizabeth (Susan)
Colden, Cadwallader 1688-1776 ... DLB-24, 30
Coldham, James D(esmond Bowden)
1924-1987 ... 113
Obituary ... 121
Coldrey, Jennifer (M.) 1940- ... 121
Coldsmith, Don(ald Charles) 1926- ... CANR-21
Earlier sketch in CA 105
Coldwell, David F(rederick) C(larke)
1923- ... 17-18R
Coldwell, Joan 1936- ... 106
Coldwell, M(ichael) J. 1888-1974
Obituary ... 53-56
Cole, Adrian 1949- ... 121
Cole, Allison
See Coker, Carolyn
Cole, Andrew Thomas, Jr. 1933- ... 102
Cole, Ann 1937- ... 65-68
Cole, Ann Kilborn
See Callahan, Claire Wallis
Cole, Annette
See Steiner, Barbara A(nnette)
Cole, Arthur C(harles) 1886-1976
Obituary ... 65-68
Cole, Barry 1936- ... CANR-16
Earlier sketch in CA 25-28R
See also DLB 14
Cole, Bill
See Cole, William Shadrack
Cole, Bruce 1938- ... CANR-15
Earlier sketch in CA 65-68
Cole, Burt 1930- ... 73-76
Cole, C. Donald 1923- ... 125
Cole, C(harles) Robert 1939- ... 65-68
Cole, Cannon
See Cook, Arlene Ethel
Cole, Charles C(hester), Jr. 1922- ... 118
Cole, Charles L(eland) 1927- ... 69-72
Cole, Charles Woolsey 1906-1978 ... CANR-22
Obituary ... 77-80
Earlier sketch in CA 69-72
Cole, Clifford A. 1915- ... 13-14R
Cole, Cozy
See Cole, William R.
Cole, Dandridge MacFarlan 1921- ... 13-14R
Cole, David C(hamberlin) 1928-
Brief entry ... 106
Cole, Davis
See Elting, Mary
Cole, Donald Barnard 1922- ... 5-6R
Cole, Doris 1938- ... 89-92
Cole, Douglas 1934- ... CANR-2
Earlier sketch in CA 5-6R
Cole, E(ugene) R(oger) 1930- ... CANR-19
Earlier sketches in CA 53-56, CANR-4
Cole, Eddie-Lou 1909- ... 65-68
Cole, Edward B(ender) 1923- ... 107
Cole, Edward C(yrus) 1904- ... 15-16R
Cole, Frank R(aymond) 1892- ... 69-72
Cole, G(eorge) D(ouglas) H(oward)
1889-1959 Brief entry ... 108
Cole, George F(raser) 1935- ... 65-68
Cole, Gordon
See Cole, Gordon H(enry)
Cole, Gordon H(enry) 1912-1988 Obituary ... 125
Cole, (Roger) Henri 1956- ... 121
Cole, Howard C(handler) 1934- ... 49-52
Cole, Hubert (Archibald Noel) 1908- ... CANR-5
Earlier sketch in CA 7-8R
Cole, J(ohn) A(lfred) 1905- ... CAP-1
Earlier sketch in CA 15-16
Cole, J. P.
See Cole, John P(eter)
Cole, Jack
See Stewart, John (William)
Cole, Jackson
See Germano, Peter B.
and Schisgall, Oscar
Cole, Janet
See Hunter, Kim
Cole, Jennifer
See Zach, Cheryl (Byrd)
Cole, Joan 1957- ... 113
Cole, Joanna 1944- ... 115
See also SATA 37, 49
See also CLR 5
Cole, John N(elson) 1923- ... 93-96
Cole, John P(eter) 1928- ... CANR-19
Earlier sketches in CA 5-6R, CANR-3
Cole, John Y(oung), Jr. 1940- ... CANR-19
Earlier sketch in CA 103
Cole, Jonathan R(ichard) 1942- ... 53-56
Cole, Juan R(icardo) I(rfan) 1952- ... 121
Cole, K. C. 1946- ... 105
Cole, (Edmund) Keith 1919- ... CANR-19
Earlier sketch in CA 102
Cole, Larry 1936- ... 45-48
Cole, Leonard A(aron) 1933- ... 81-84
Cole, Leonard Leslie 1909-1980 ... 103
Cole, Lester 1904(?)-1985 Obituary ... 117
Cole, Lewis 1946- ... 109
Cole, Lois Dwight 1903-1979 ... CANR-4
Obituary ... 104
Earlier sketch in CA 2R
See also SATA 10, 26
Cole, Luella (Winifred) 1893-19(?) ... CAP-1
Earlier sketch in CA 19-20
Cole, Margaret Alice ... CANR-6
Earlier sketch in CA 11-12R
Cole, Margaret Isabel 1893-1980 ... CANR-4
Obituary ... 97-100
Earlier sketch in CA 5-6R
Cole, Martha 1916(?)-1986 Obituary ... 118
Cole, Mary
See Hanna, Mary T.
Cole, Michael 1938- ... 97-100
Cole, Michelle 1940- ... 29-32R
Cole, Monica M(ary) 1922- ... 4R
Cole, Richard Cargill 1926- ... 124
Cole, Robert E(van) 1937- ... 69-72
Cole, Robert H. 1918- ... 33-36R
Cole, Roger L. 1933- ... 25-28R
Cole, Sandi Gelles
See Gelles-Cole, Sandi
Cole, Sheila R(otenberg) 1939- ... CANR-4
Earlier sketch in CA 53-56
See also SATA 24
Cole, Sonia (Mary) 1918-1982 ... 93-96
Obituary ... 106
Cole, Stephen 1941- ... 29-32R
Cole, Stephen
See Webbe, Gale D(udley)
Cole, Sylvan, Jr. 1918- ... 69-72
Cole, (Andrew) Thomas (Jr.) 1933- ... 33-36R
Cole, W(illiam) Owen 1931- ... 118
Cole, Wayne S. 1922- ... 23-24R
Cole, Wendell 1914- ... 23-24R
Cole, William (Rossa) 1919- ... CANR-7
Earlier sketch in CA 9-10R
See also SATA 9
Cole, William Earle 1904-1979 ... 17-18R
Obituary ... 126
Cole, William Graham 1917- ... 19-20R
Cole, William R. 1909-1981 Obituary ... 108
Cole, William Shadrack 1937- ... 101
Colean, Miles Lanier 1898- ... CAP-2
Earlier sketch in CA 21-22
Coleburt, J(ames) Russell 1920- ... 13-14R
Colecchia, Francesca Maria ... 89-92
Colegate, Isabel 1931- ... CANR-22
Earlier sketches in CA 17-18R, CANR-8
See also DLB 14
See also CLC 36
Colegrove, Kenneth 1886-1975 ... CANR-4
Obituary ... 53-56
Earlier sketch in CA 5-6R
Coleman, A(llan) D(ouglass) 1943- ... CANR-15
Earlier sketch in CA 73-76
Coleman, Almand R(ouse) 1905- ... CAP-2
Earlier sketch in CA 29-32
Coleman, Arthur 1924- ... 81-84
Coleman, Bernard D(avid) 1919- ... 25-28R
Coleman, Bill
See Coleman, William V(incent)
Coleman, Bob
See Coleman, Robert David
Coleman, Bruce P(umphrey) 1931- ... 37-40R
Coleman, Buck
See Richardson, Gladwell
Coleman, Clayton W(ebster) 1901- ... 29-32R
Coleman, D(onald) C(uthbert) 1920- ... 13-14R
Coleman, Dorothy Gabe 1935- ... 93-96
Coleman, Elliott 1906-1980 ... 19-20R
Obituary ... 97-100
Coleman, Emily Holmes 1899-1974 ... 105
See also DLB 4
Coleman, Emmett
See Reed, Ishmael
Coleman, Evelyn Scherabon
See Firchow, Evelyn Scherabon
Coleman, Felicia Slatkin 1916(?)-1981
Obituary ... 102
Coleman, Francis Xavier Jerome 1939- ... 108
Coleman, J(ohn) Winston, Jr. 1898-1983 ... 49-52
Coleman, James A(ndrew) 1921- ... 5-6R
Coleman, James C(ovington) 1914- ... CANR-1
Earlier sketch in CA 2R
Coleman, James S(amuel) 1926- ... 13-14R
Coleman, James Smoot 1919- ... 3R
Coleman, John R(oyston) 1921- ... CANR-1
Earlier sketch in CA 4R
See also AITN 1
Coleman, Kenneth 1916- ... CANR-8
Earlier sketch in CA 23-24R
Coleman, Lee
See Lapidus, Elaine
Coleman, Lonnie 1920-1982 ... 77-80
Obituary ... 107
Coleman, Lucile ... 73-76
Coleman, Marion (Reeves) Moore
1900- ... CANR-11
Earlier sketch in CA 17-18R
Coleman, Michael C(hristopher) 1946- ... 119
Coleman, Patricia R(egister) 1936- ... CANR-25
Earlier sketch in CA 109
Coleman, Patty R.
See Coleman, Patricia R(egister)
Coleman, Peter J(arrett) 1926- ... 7-8R
Coleman, Raymond James 1923- ... 49-52
Coleman, Richard J(ames) 1941- ... 41-44R
Coleman, Richard M(ark) 1951- ... 121
Coleman, Richard Patrick 1927- ... 33-36R
Coleman, Robert David 1951- ... 121
Coleman, Robert E(merson) 1928- ... CANR-7
Earlier sketch in CA 15-16R
Coleman, Robert William Alfred 1916- ... 11-12R
Coleman, Roy V. 1885-1971 Obituary ... 104
Coleman, Terry 1931- ... CANR-10
Earlier sketch in CA 15-16R
Coleman, Thomas R. 1942- ... 57-60
Coleman, Vernon 1946- ... 81-84
Coleman, Wanda 1946- ... 119
See also BW
Coleman, William L(eRoy) 1938- ... CANR-21
Earlier sketch in CA 69-72
See also SATA 34, 49
Coleman, William V(incent) 1932- ... CANR-25
Earlier sketches in CA 57-60, CANR-9
Coleman-Norton, P(aul) R(obinson)
1898-1971 Obituary ... 29-32R
Colen, B. D. 1946- ... CANR-23
Earlier sketch in CA 65-68
Colenbrander, Joanna 1908- ... 121
Coleridge, John
See Binder, Otto O(scar)
Coleridge, M. E.
See Coleridge, Mary E(lizabeth)
Coleridge, Mary E(lizabeth) 1861-1907
Brief entry ... 116
See also DLB 19
Coles, Alan 1927- ... 124
Coles, Cyril Henry 1899-1965 ... CAP-1
Earlier sketch in CA 9-10
Coles, Don 1928- ... 115
See also CLC 46
Coles, Flournoy (Arthur), Jr. 1915- ... 57-60
Coles, Harry L(ewis) 1920- ... 9-10R
Coles, John M(orton) 1930- ... CANR-12
Earlier sketch in CA 29-32R
Coles, Kaines Adlard 1901-1985 ... CAP-1
Obituary ... 117
Earlier sketch in CA 13-14
Coles, Manning
See Coles, Cyril Henry
Coles, Robert (Martin) 1929- ... CANR-3
Earlier sketch in CA 45-48
See also SATA 23
Coles, Robert R(eed) 1908(?)-1985
Obituary ... 116
Coles, S(ydney) F(rederick) Arthur 1896- ... 7-8R
Coles, Susan Vaughan Ebershoff
See Ebershoff-Coles, Susan Vaughan
Coles, William Allan 1930- ... 33-36R
Coles, William E., Jr. 1932- ... CANR-10
Earlier sketch in CA 61-64
Coletta, Paolo Enrico 1916- ... CANR-14
Earlier sketch in CA 41-44R
Colette, (Sidonie-Gabrielle) 1873-1954
Brief entry ... 104
See also DLB 65
See also TCLC 1, 5, 16
Colette, Jacques 1929- ... 89-92
Colford, Paul D(ennis) 1953- ... 110
Colford, William E(dward) 1908-1971 ... 7-8R
Obituary ... 33-36R
Colgin, Russell W(eymount) 1925- ... 121
Colgrave, Bertram 1888-1968 ... CAP-2
Earlier sketch in CA 25-28
Colie, Rosalie L(ittell) 1924-1972 Obituary ... 106
Colimore, Vincent J(erome) 1914- ... 37-40R
Colin, Ann
See Ure, Jean
Colin, Jean
See Bell, Joyce
Colina, Tessa Patterson 1915- ... CANR-7
Earlier sketch in CA 19-20R
Colinvaux, Paul (Alfred) 1930- ... CANR-14
Earlier sketch in CA 41-44R
Colish, Marcia L. 1937- ... CANR-10
Earlier sketch in CA 25-28R
Coll, Regina A(udrey) 1929- ... 112
Collard, Edgar Andrew 1911- ... 102
Collas, J. P. 1911-1984 Obituary ... 114
Colledge, Malcolm A(ndrew) R(ichard)
1939- ... CANR-10
Earlier sketch in CA 25-28R
Collen, Neil
See Lee, Lincoln
Coller, Richard Walter 1925- ... 119
Collett, Rosemary K(ing) 1931- ... 69-72
Colletta, Nat J(oseph) 1944- ... 104
Colley, Ann C(heetham) 1940- ... 112
Colley, Iain 1940- ... 97-100
Collias, Joe G. 1928- ... CANR-14
Earlier sketch in CA 41-44R
Collie, Michael (John) 1929- ... CANR-18
Earlier sketches in CA 49-52, CANR-3
Collier, (John) Basil 1908- ... CANR-2
Earlier sketch in CA 7-8R
Collier, Boyd D(ean) 1938- ... 57-60
Collier, Calhoun C(rofford) 1916- ... 25-28R
Collier, Christopher 1930- ... CANR-13
Earlier sketch in CA 33-36R
See also SATA 16
See also CLC 30
Collier, David 1942- ... 69-72
Collier, David S(wanson) 1923-1983 ... 21-22R
Obituary ... 111
Collier, Douglas
See Fellowes-Gordon, Ian (Douglas)
Collier, Ethel 1903- ... 65-68
See also SATA 22
Collier, Eugenia W(illiams) 1928- ... 49-52
Collier, Gaydell M(aier) 1935- ... 93-96
Collier, Gaylan Jane 1924- ... 37-40R
Collier, (Alan) Graham 1923- ... 19-20R
Collier, (James) Graham 1937- ... 105
Collier, Herbert L(eon) 1933- ... 103
Collier, James L(incoln) 1928- ... CANR-4
Earlier sketch in CA 9-10R
See also SATA 8
See also CLC 30
Collier, Jane
See Hampson, Zena
Collier, John 1901-1980 ... CANR-10
Obituary ... 97-100
Earlier sketch in CA 65-68
Collier, Johnnie Lucille
See Collier, Lucille Ann
Collier, Joy
See Millar, (Minna Henrietta) Joy
Collier, Kenneth Gerald 1910- ... CANR-18
Earlier sketch in CA 85-88
Collier, Leo(nard) D(awson) 1908- ... 7-8R
Collier, Louise Wilbourn 1925- ... 109

Collier, Lucille Ann 1919(?)- Brief entry 109
Collier, Lucy Ann
See Collier, Lucille Ann
Collier, Margaret
See Taylor, Margaret Stewart
Collier, Peter 1939- 65-68
Collier, Phyllis K(ay) 1939- 110
Collier, Richard 1924- CANR-25
Earlier sketches in CA 4R, CANR-5
Collier, Simon 1938- 23-24R
Collier, Zena
See Hampson, Zena
See also SATA 23
Colligan, Francis J(ames) 1908-19(?) CAP-2
Earlier sketch in CA 19-20
Collignon, Jean Henri 1918- 3R
Collignon, Joseph 1930- 89-92
Collin, Marion (Cripps) 1928- CANR-5
Earlier sketch in CA 9-10R
Collin, Richard H(arvey) 1932- 122
Collin, Richard Oliver 1940- 105
Collings, Ellsworth 1887- 73-76
Collings, I. J(illie) 115
Collings, Michael R(obert) 1947- 111
Collingwood, Charles (Cummings) 1917-1985 .... 29-32R
Obituary 117
Collingwood, R(obin) G(eorge) 1889(?)-1943 Brief entry 117
Collins, Alice H(esslein) 1907- 65-68
Collins, Arnold Quint 1935- 73-76
Collins, Barbara J(ane) 1929- CANR-6
Earlier sketch in CA 57-60
Collins, Barry 1941- 102
Collins, Barry E(merson) 1937- CANR-7
Earlier sketch in CA 13-14R
Collins, Beulah Stowe 1923-1983 122
Obituary 110
Collins, Carvel 1912- CANR-8
Earlier sketch in CA 17-18R
Collins, Charles C. 1919- 25-28R
Collins, Charles William 1880-1964
Obituary 89-92
Collins, Christopher 1936- 49-52
Collins, Cindy
See Smith, Richard Rein
Collins, Clark
See Reynolds, Dallas McCord
Collins, Colette
See Knaack, Twila
Collins, D.
See Bulleid, H(enry) A(nthony) V(aughan)
Collins, David A(lmon) 1931- 23-24R
Collins, David R(aymond) 1940- CANR-26
Earlier sketches in CA 29-32R, CANR-11
See also SATA 7
Collins, Desmond 1940- CANR-14
Earlier sketch in CA 73-76
Collins, Donald E(dward) 1934- 122
Collins, Douglas 1912-1972 Obituary 33-36R
Collins, F(rederick) Herbert 1890- CAP-1
Earlier sketch in CA 11-12
Collins, Fletcher, Jr. 1906- 53-56
Collins, Freda
See Collins, Frederica Joan Hale
Collins, Frederica Joan Hale 1904- CAP-1
Earlier sketch in CA 13-14
Collins, Gary (Ross) 1934- CANR-22
Earlier sketches in CA 57-60, CANR-7
Collins, George R(oseborough) 1917- CANR-1
Earlier sketch in CA 4R
Collins, Harold R(eeves) 1915- 25-28R
Collins, Henry 1917- 17-18R
Collins, Henry B(ascom), Jr. 1899-1987
Obituary 123
Collins, Herbert Ridgeway 1932- 118
Collins, Hunt
See Hunter, Evan
Collins, Jackie CANR-22
Earlier sketch in CA 102
Collins, James Daniel 1917- CANR-5
Earlier sketch in CA 2R
Collins, Jean E(lizabeth) 1948- 110
Collins, Joan 1933- 116
Collins, Jodie 1941- 121
Collins, John H. 1893- 4R
Collins, John J(oseph) 1946- 112
Collins, John Lawrence, Jr. 1929- CANR-19
Earlier sketch in CA 65-68
Collins, John M(artin) 1921- 49-52
Collins, Joseph B. 1898(?)-1975
Obituary 53-56
Collins, Joseph T. 1939- 120
Collins, Judith Graham 1942- 115
Collins, Judy (Marjorie) 1939- 103
Collins, June Irene 1935- 37-40R
Collins, Kathleen 1931-1988 119
Obituary 126
Collins, L(ewis) John 1905-1982 .... CAP-1
Obituary 108
Earlier sketch in CA 13-14
Collins, Larry
See Collins, John Lawrence, Jr.
Collins, Linda 1931- 125
See also CLC 44
Collins, Lorraine (Hill) 1931- 57-60
Collins, Mabel
See Cook, Mabel Collins
Collins, Margaret (Brandon James) 1909- .. 89-92
Collins, Marie (Margaret) 1935- 53-56
Collins, Marjorie A(nn) 1930- CANR-11
Earlier sketch in CA 65-68
Collins, Marva (Deloise Nettles) 1936- 111
Collins, Max Allan, (Jr.) 1948- 103
Collins, Meghan 1926- 101
Collins, Michael 1930- CANR-5
Earlier sketch in CA 53-56
Collins, Michael
See Lynds, Dennis
Collins, Mortimer 1827-1876 .... DLB-21, 35
Collins, Myron D(ean) 1901- CAP-1
Earlier sketch in CA 15-16
Collins, Myrtle T(elleen) 1915- 101
Collins, Nancy W.
See Collins-Chapman, Nancy W(hisnant)
Collins, Norman Richard 1907-1982 105
Obituary 107
Collins, Orvis F(loyd) 1918- 69-72
Collins, Pat(ricia) Lowery 1932- CANR-24
Earlier sketch in CA 107
See also SATA 31
Collins, Peter (Sheridan) 1942- 77-80
Collins, Philip (Arthur William) 1923- .. CANR-22
Earlier sketches in CA 7-8R, CANR-8
Collins, R(obert) G(eorge) 1926- 112
Collins, Raymond F(rancis) 1935- 112
Collins, Robert 1924- CANR-15
Earlier sketch in CA 89-92
Collins, Robert E(mmet) 1927- 69-72
Collins, Robert M. 1943- 110
Collins, Robert O(akley) 1933- CANR-22
Earlier sketches in CA 3R, CANR-4
Collins, Rowland Lee 1934-1985 .... 9-10R
Obituary 116
Collins, Ruth Philpott 1890-1975 .... CANR-4
Obituary 53-56
Earlier sketch in CA 2R
See also SATA 30
Collins, Thomas Hightower 1910- 102
Collins, Trish 1927- 106
Collins, Wilkie 1824-1889 .... DLB-18, 70
Collins, Will
See Corley, Edwin (Raymond)
Collins, William Alexander Roy 1900-1976
Obituary 69-72
Collins, William Bernard 1913- 7-8R
Collins-Chapman, Nancy W(hisnant) 1933- .. 112
Collinson, Laurence (Henry) 1925- 103
Collinson, Roger (Alfred) 1936- 110
Collis, John Stewart 1900-1984 61-64
Obituary 112
Collis, Kevin F(rancis) 1930- 107
Collis, Louise 1925- 21-22R
Collis, Maurice 1889-1973 .... CANR-4
Obituary 89-92
Earlier sketch in CA 5-6R
Collis, William Robert Fitzgerald 1900- CAP-1
Earlier sketch in CA 9-10
Collison, David (John) 1937- 105
Collison, Koder M(acklin) 1910- 53-56
Collison, Robert Lewis Wright 1914- CANR-2
Earlier sketch in CA 5-6R
Colliss, Gertrude Florence Mary (Jones) 1908- 7-8R
Collodi, Carlo
See Lorenzini, Carlo
See also CLR 5
Collom, Jack 1931- 77-80
Colloms, Brenda 1919- CANR-7
Earlier sketch in CA 61-64
See also SATA 40
Collyer, Mary 1716(?)-1763(?) DLB-39
Collyns, Robin 1940- 69-72
Colm, Gerhard 1897-1968 .... 5-6R
Obituary 103
Colman, Arthur D. 1937- 33-36R
Colman, Benjamin 1673-1747 .... DLB-24
Colman, E(rnest) A(drian) M(ackenzie) 1930- 57-60
Colman, George
See Glassco, John
Colman, Hila CANR-7
Earlier sketch in CA 15-16R
See also SATA 1, 53
Colman, John E. 1923- 23-24R
Colman, Juliet Benita 1944- 61-64
Colman, Libby Lee 1940- 33-36R
Colman, Morris 1899(?)-1981 .... SATA-25
Colmer, John (Anthony) 1921- CANR-15
Earlier sketch in CA 85-88
Colmer, Michael (J.) 1942- CANR-21
Earlier sketch in CA 69-72
Colodny, Robert G. 1915- CANR-14
Earlier sketch in CA 37-40R
Colombo, Dale
See Monroe, Keith
Colombo, Furio 1931- 111
Colombo, John Robert 1936- CANR-11
Earlier sketch in CA 25-28R
See also SATA 50
See also DLB 53
Colonel Sanders
See Sanders, Harland
Colonius, Lillian 1911- 23-24R
See also SATA 3
Colony, Horatio 1900-1977 .... 37-40R
Colorado, Antonio J.
See Colorado Capella, Antonio Julio
Colorado Capella, Antonio Julio 1903- 19-20R
See also SATA 23
Colp, Ralph, Jr. 1924- 126
Colquhoun, Archibald 1912-1964
Obituary 89-92
Colquhoun, Frank 1909- 106
Colquhoun, Ithell 1906-1988 .... 13-14R
Obituary 125
Colquhoun, Keith 1927- 102
Colquitt, Betsy Feagan 1926- 53-56
Colson, Charles W(endell) 1931- 102
Colson, Elizabeth 1917- 53-56
Colson, Frederick
See Geis, Richard E(rwin)
Colson, Greta (Scotchmur) 1913- CAP-1
Earlier sketch in CA 9-10
Colson, Howard P(aul) 1910- 29-32R
Colson, Laramie
See Richardson, Gladwell
Colston, Lowell G(wen) 1919-1985 53-56
Obituary 118
Colston-Baynes, Dorothy 1881(?)-1973
Obituary 104
Colt, Clem
See Nye, Nelson C(oral)
Colt, John W. 1900(?)-1983 Obituary 111
Colt, Martin
See Epstein, Beryl (M. Williams)
and Epstein, Samuel
Colt, Winchester Remington
See Hubbard, L(afayette) Ron(ald)
Colt, Zandra
See Stevenson, Florence
Coltart, James M(ilne) 1903-1986
Obituary 120
Colter, Cyrus 1910- CANR-10
Earlier sketch in CA 65-68
See also BW
See also DLB 33
Colter, Shayne
See Norwood, Victor G(eorge) C(harles)
Coltharp, Lurline H(ughes) 1913- 17-18R
Coltman, Ernest Vivian
See Dudley, Ernest
Coltman, Will
See Bingley, David Ernest
Colton, C(larence) E(ugene) 1914- CANR-2
Earlier sketch in CA 5-6R
Colton, Harold S(ellers) 1881-1970 .... CANR-3
Earlier sketch in CA 3R
Colton, Helen 1918- 57-60
Colton, James
See Hansen, Joseph
Colton, James B(yers) II 1908- 37-40R
Colton, Joel 1918- CANR-2
Earlier sketch in CA 4R
Colton, Timothy J. 1947- 124
Coltrane, James
See Wohl, James P(aul)
Colum, Padraic 1881-1972 73-76
Obituary 33-36R
See also SATA 15
See also CLC 28
Columbu, Franco 1941- 125
Columella
See Moore, Clement Clarke
Colver, A(nthony) Wayne 1923- 93-96
Colver, Alice Mary (Ross) 1892- 69-72
Colver, Anne 1908- CANR-2
Earlier sketch in CA 45-48
See also SATA 7
Colvert, James B(rumley) 1921- 116
Colvett, Latayne
See Scott, Latayne Colvett
Colville, Derek Kent 1923- Brief entry 105
Colville, John Rupert 1915-1987 .... CANR-10
Obituary 124
Earlier sketch in CA 61-64
Colvin, Brenda 1897-1981 Obituary 108
Colvin, Clare 1943- 123
Colvin, Elaine Wright 1942- 106
Colvin, Howard Montagu 1919- 61-64
Colvin, Ian G(oodhope) 1912-1975 .... CAP-2
Obituary 57-60
Earlier sketch in CA 19-20
Colvin, James
See Moorcock, Michael (John)
Colvin, Ralph W(hitmore) 1920-1981 107
Obituary 104
Colwell, C(harles) Carter 1932- 41-44R
Colwell, Eileen (Hilda) 1904- CANR-12
Earlier sketch in CA 29-32R
See also SATA 2
Colwell, Ernest Cadman 1901-1974 .... CANR-4
Obituary 53-56
Earlier sketch in CA 5-6R
Colwell, Richard J(ames) 1930- 69-72
Colwell, Robert 1931- 33-36R
Colwin, Laurie 1944- CANR-20
Earlier sketch in CA 89-92
See also DLBY 80
See also CLC 5, 13, 23
Colyer, Penrose 1940- CANR-20
Earlier sketches in CA 65-68, CANR-14
Coman, Dale Rex 1906- 81-84
Coman, Edwin Truman, Jr. 1903- 11-12R
Comaroff, John L(ionel) 1945- 125
Comaromi, John P(hillip) 1937- 111
Comay, Joan 103
Comber, Lillian 1916- CANR-3
Earlier sketch in CA 9-10R
Combs, A(rthur) W(right) 1912- CANR-10
Earlier sketch in CA 17-18R
Combs, Ann 1935- 117
Combs, David 1934- 108
Combs, Eugene 1934- 118
Combs, James E(verett) 1941- CANR-19
Earlier sketch in CA 101
Combs, Jerald A(rthur) 1937- 110
Combs, Richard Earl 1934- 33-36R
Combs, Robert
See Murray, John
Combs, (Elisha) Tram(mell, Jr.) 1924- 13-14R
Comden, Betty 1919- CANR-2
Earlier sketch in CA 49-52
See also DLB 44
Comeau, Arthur M. 1938- 61-64
Comer, James P(ierpont) 1934- 61-64
Comey, Dennis J. 1896-1987 Obituary 123
Comey, James Hugh 1947- 65-68
Comfort, Alex(ander) 1920- CANR-1
Earlier sketch in CA 4R
See also CLC 7
Comfort, Howard 1904- 37-40R
Comfort, Iris Tracy CANR-6
Earlier sketch in CA 13-14R
Comfort, Jane Levington
See Sturtzel, Jane Levington
Comfort, Mildred Houghton 1886- 9-10R
See also SATA 3
Comfort, Montgomery
See Campbell, (John) Ramsey
Comfort, Richard A(llen) 1933- 21-22R
Comidas, Chinas
See Genser, Cynthia
Comini, Alessandra 1934- 93-96
Comins, Ethel M(ae) CANR-8
Earlier sketch in CA 61-64
See also SATA 11
Comins, Jeremy 1933- CANR-14
Earlier sketch in CA 65-68
See also SATA 28
Comitas, Lambros 1927- Brief entry 113
Comito, Terry Allen 1935- 109
Commager, Henry Steele 1902- CANR-26
Earlier sketch in CA 21-22R
See also SATA 23
See also DLB 17
Commager, (Henry) Steele (Jr.) 1932-1984 Obituary 112
Commins, William Dollard, Sr. 1899-1983
Obituary 109
Commire, Anne CANR-21
Earlier sketch in CA 69-72
Committe, Thomas C. 1922- 65-68
Commoner, Barry 1917- 65-68
Como, (Michael) William 1925- 69-72
Comparetti, Alice 1907- 37-40R
Compere, Mickie
See Davidson, Margaret
Complo, Sister Jannita Marie 1935- 57-60
Comprone, Joseph J(ohn) 1943- CANR-5
Earlier sketch in CA 53-56
Compton, Ann
See Prebble, Marjorie Mary Curtis
Compton, Arthur Holly 1892-1962
Obituary 116
Compton, D(avid) G(uy) 1930- CANR-17
Earlier sketch in CA 25-28R
Compton, Guy
See Compton, D(avid) G(uy)
Compton, Henry (Pasfield) 1909- 9-10R
Compton, James V(incent) 1928- 29-32R
Compton, Piers 1903- 122
Compton-Burnett, I(vy) 1892-1969 .... CANR-4
Obituary 25-28R
Earlier sketch in CA 4R
See also DLB 36
See also CLC 1, 3, 10, 15, 34
Compton-Hall, (Patrick) Richard 1929- . CANR-24
Earlier sketch in CA 107
Comrey, Andrew Laurence 1923-
Brief entry 106
Comroe, Julius H(iram), Jr. 1911-1984 122
Obituary 113
Comstock, Anthony 1844-1915 Brief entry .. 110
See also TCLC 13
Comstock, Christine 1942- CANR-20
Earlier sketch in CA 104
Comstock, George Adolphe 1932- 124
Comstock, Helen 1893-1970 .... CANR-4
Obituary 89-92
Earlier sketch in CA 5-6R
Comstock, Henry B. 1908- CAP-2
Earlier sketch in CA 33-36
Comstock, Mary Bryce 1934- 105
Comstock, W(illiam) Richard 1928- 73-76
Comte, The Great
See Hawkesworth, Eric
Comus
See Ballantyne, R(obert) M(ichael)
Comyns, Barbara
See Comyns-Carr, Barbara Irene Veronica
Comyns-Carr, Barbara Irene Veronica 1912- 7-8R
Conacher, D(esmond) J(ohn) 1918- 25-28R
Conacher, J(ames) B(lennerhasset) 1916- 25-28R
Conan Doyle, Adrian Malcolm 1910-1970 ... 7-8R
Obituary 29-32R
Conan Doyle, Arthur
See Doyle, Arthur Conan
Conant, Eaton H. 1930- 53-56
Conant, Howard (Somers) 1921- CANR-8
Earlier sketch in CA 17-18R
Conant, James Bryant 1893-1978 .... 15-16R
Obituary 77-80
Conant, Kenneth John 1894- 2R
Conant, Ralph W(endell) 1926- CANR-14
Earlier sketch in CA 29-32R
Conant, Roger 1909- Brief entry 107
Conard, Alfred Fletcher 1911- 15-16R
Conard, Joseph W. 1911- 13-14R
Conard, Robert C. 1933- 126
Conarroe, Joel (Osborne) 1934- 29-32R
Conarroe, Richard R(iley) 1928- 69-72
Conaway, James (Alley) 1941- 33-36R
Conconi, Charles N. 1938- 77-80
Conde, Jesse C(lay) 1912- 57-60
Conde, Maryse
See Boucolon, Maryse
Condee, Ralph Waterbury 1916- 17-18R
Condit, Carl Wilbur 1914- CANR-4
Earlier sketch in CA 3R
Condit, Martha Olson 1913- 73-76
See also SATA 28
Condliffe, John B(ell) 1891-1981 .... CAP-1
Obituary 106
Earlier sketch in CA 15-16
Condon, David Rensing 1924- 114

Condon, E(dward) U(hler) 1902-1974
Obituary ... 112
Condon, Eddie 1905-1973 Obituary ... 45-48
Condon, George Edward 1916- ... CANR-1
Earlier sketch in CA 45-48
Condon, Jack
See Condon, John C(arl), Jr.
Condon, John C(arl), Jr. 1938- ... CANR-10
Earlier sketch in CA 23-24R
Condon, Richard (Thomas) 1915- ... CANR-23
Earlier sketches in CA 1R, CANR-2
See also CAAS 1
See also CLC 4, 6, 8, 10, 45
Condon, Robert 1921(?)-1972 Obituary ... 37-40R
Condor, Gladyn
See Davison, Gladys Patton
Condray, Bruno
See Humphrys, Leslie George
Condry, William Moreton 1918- ... 103
Cone, Carl B. 1916- ... 11-12R
Cone, Edward Toner 1917- ... 110
Cone, Fairfax Mastick 1903-1977 ... 73-76
Obituary ... 69-72
Cone, Ferne Geller 1921- ... 107
See also SATA 39
Cone, James H. 1938- ... 33-36R
Cone, John F(rederick) 1926- ... 17-18R
Cone, Molly Lamken 1918- ... CANR-16
Earlier sketches in CA 4R, CANR-1
See also SATA 1, 28
Cone, William F. 1919- ... 57-60
Conerly, Perian Collier 1926- ... 5-6R
Coney, Michael G(reatrex) 1932- ... 97-100
Confer, Vincent 1913- ... 21-22R
Conford, Ellen 1942- ... CANR-13
Earlier sketch in CA 33-36R
See also SATA 6
See also CLR 10
Confucius
See Lund, Philip R(eginald)
Congdon, Constance S. 1944- ... 123
Congdon, Herbert Wheaton 1876-1965 ... 5-6R
Congdon, Kirby 1924- ... CANR-7
Earlier sketch in CA 15-16R
Congdon, William Grosvenor 1912- ... CANR-24
Earlier sketches in CA 17-18R, CANR-7
Conger, (Seymour) Beach III 1912-1969
Obituary ... 115
Conger, John (Janeway) 1921- ... CANR-6
Earlier sketch in CA 13-14R
Conger, Lesley
See Suttles, Shirley (Smith)
Congrat-Butler, Stefan 1914(?)-1979 ... 103
Obituary ... 89-92
Congreve, Willard J(ohn) 1921- ... 57-60
Congreve, William 1670-1729 ... DLB-39
Conil, Jean 1917- ... CANR-13
Earlier sketch in CA 13-14R
Conine, (Odie) Ernest 1925- ... 69-72
Coniston, Ed
See Bingley, David Ernest
Conkin, Paul K(eith) 1929- ... 33-36R
Conkle, E(llsworth) P(routy) 1899- ... 65-68
Conklin, Barbara P. 1927- ... 109
Conklin, Gladys Plemon 1903- ... CANR-4
Earlier sketch in CA 2R
See also SATA 2
Conklin, Groff 1904-1968 ... CANR-3
Earlier sketch in CA 1R
Conklin, Harold C(olyer) 1926- ... 118
Conklin, John E(van) 1943- ... CANR-14
Earlier sketch in CA 37-40R
Conklin, Mike 1944- ... 120
Conklin, Paul ... 115
Brief entry ... 111
See also SATA 33, 43
Conkling, Hilda 1910- ... SATA-23
Conlay, Iris 1910- ... CAP-1
Earlier sketch in CA 11-12
Conley, Ellen Alexander 1938- ... CANR-20
Earlier sketch in CA 103
Conley, Enid Mary 1917- ... CANR-10
Earlier sketch in CA 65-68
Conley, John (Allan) 1912- ... 61-64
Conley, Phillip Mallory 1887- ... 69-72
Conley, Robert J(ackson) 1940- ... CANR-15
Earlier sketch in CA 41-44R
Conley, Verena Andermatt 1943- ... 117
Conlin, David A. 1897- ... 17-18R
Conlin, Joseph R. 1940- ... 49-52
Conlon, Denis J. 1932- ... 37-40R
Conlon, Kathleen (Annie) 1943-
Brief entry ... 114
Conly, Robert Leslie 1918(?)-1973 ... 73-76
Obituary ... 41-44R
See also SATA 23
Conn, Canary Denise 1949- ... 57-60
Conn, Charles Paul 1945- ... CANR-6
Earlier sketch in CA 57-60
Conn, Charles William 1920- ... CANR-10
Earlier sketch in CA 23-24R
Conn, Frances G. 1925- ... 33-36R
Conn, Jan E(velyn) 1952- ... 110
Conn, Martha Orr 1935- ... 93-96
Conn, Peter J. 1942- ... 33-36R
Conn, Stetson 1908- ... CAP-1
Earlier sketch in CA 9-10
Conn, Stewart 1936- Brief entry ... 117
Conn, Walter E(ugene) 1940- ... 110
Connable, Alfred 1931- ... 81-84
Connally, Eugenia (Maye) Horstman 1931- ... 103
Connell, Brian (Reginald) 1916- ... CANR-4
Earlier sketch in CA 4R
Connell, Evan S(helby), Jr. 1924- ... CANR-2
Earlier sketch in CA 4R
See also CAAS 2
See also DLB 2
See also DLBY 81
See also CLC 4, 6, 45
Connell, Francis J. 1888- ... CAP-1
Earlier sketch in CA 13-14
Connell, Jon 1952- ... 97-100
Connell, K(enneth) H(ugh) 1917-1973 ... CAP-2
Earlier sketch in CA 25-28
Connell, Kirk
See Chapman, John Stanton Higham
Connell, Maureen 1931- ... 104
Connell, William Fraser 1916- ... 104
Connellan, Leo 1928- ... 81-84
Connelly, Douglas 1949- ... 121
Connelly, Marc(us Cook) 1890-1980 ... 85-88
Obituary ... 102
See also SATA 25
See also DLB 7
See also DLBY 80
See also CLC 7
Connelly, Owen (Sergeson, Jr.) 1924- ... 19-20R
Connelly, Philip M(arshal) 1904(?)-1981
Obituary ... 104
Connelly, Thomas L(awrence) 1938- ... CANR-11
Earlier sketch in CA 19-20R
Connely, Willard 1888-1967 ... CAP-2
Earlier sketch in CA 17-18
Conner, Berenice Gillete 1908- ... 65-68
Conner, Floyd D(avis) 1951- ... 119
Conner, Patrick (Roy Mountifort) 1947- ... 106
Conner, Patrick Reardon 1907- ... 7-8R
Conner, Paul Willard 1937-1984 ... 17-18R
Obituary ... 114
Conner, Rearden
See Conner, Patrick Reardon
Conner, Valerie Jean 1945- ... 114
Conners, Bernard F. 1926- ... 41-44R
Conners, Kenneth Wray 1909- ... 29-32R
Connery, Donald S(tuart) 1926-
Brief entry ... 114
Connery, George Edward 1907(?)-1985
Obituary ... 116
Connery, John (R.) 1913-1987 Obituary ... 124
Connery, Robert H(owe) 1907- ... 41-44R
Connett, Eugene Virginius III 1891-1969 .. CAP-1
Earlier sketch in CA 13-14
Connette, Earle 1910- ... CAP-1
Earlier sketch in CA 15-16
Connick, C(harles) Milo 1917- ... 3R
Conniff, Frank 1914-1971 Obituary ... 93-96
Conniff, James C(lifford) G(regory) ... 23-24R
Conniff, Michael L(ee) 1942- ... 118
Conniff, Richard 1951- ... 124
Connolly, Cyril (Vernon) 1903-1974 ... CAP-2
Obituary ... 53-56
Earlier sketch in CA 21-22
Connolly, Francis X(avier) 1909-1965 ... CAP-1
Earlier sketch in CA 13-14
Connolly, Jerome P(atrick) 1931- ... SATA-8
Connolly, Paul
See Wicker, Thomas Grey
Connolly, Peter 1935- ... 103
See also SATA 47
Connolly, Ray 1940- ... 101
Connolly, Robert D(uggan, Jr.) 1917- ... 69-72
Connolly, Thomas Edmund 1918- ... CANR-4
Earlier sketch in CA 3R
Connolly, Vivian 1925- ... CANR-1
Earlier sketch in CA 49-52
Connor, J. Robert 1927- ... 123
Connor, Jim 1935- ... 107
Connor, John Anthony 1930- ... 15-16R
Connor, Joyce Mary 1929- ... CANR-10
Earlier sketch in CA 65-68
Connor, Kevin
See O'Rourke, Frank
Connor, Lawrence S(tanton) 1925- ... 89-92
Connor, Patricia 1943- ... 25-28R
Connor, Ralph
See Gordon, Charles William
Connor, Seymour V(aughan) 1923- ... 53-56
Connor, Susanna Pflaum
See Pflaum, Susanna Whitney
Connor, Tony
See Connor, John Anthony
See also DLB 40
Connor, W(alter) Robert 1934- ... 41-44R
Connor, Walter Downing 1942- ... 106
Connor, William (Neil) 1909(?)-1967
Obituary ... 25-28R
Connors, Bruton
See Rohen, Edward
Connors, Dorsey ... 45-48
Connors, John Stanley 1925-1984
Obituary ... 112
Connors, Joseph 1945- ... 106
Conolly, L(eonard) W(illiam) 1941- ... 106
Conolly, Violet 1901(?)-1988(?) Obituary ... 124
Conor, Glen
See Cooney, Michael
Conot, Robert E. 1929- ... CANR-2
Earlier sketch in CA 45-48
Conover, C(harles) Eugene 1903- ... 7-8R
Conover, Carole 1941- ... 89-92
Conover, Chris 1950- ... SATA-31
Conover, David (Beals) 1919-1983 ... 115
Conover, Hobart H. 1914- ... 15-16R
Conover, Jessica Arline Wilcox
See Jones, Candy
Conquest, Edwin Parker, Jr. 1931- ... 29-32R
Conquest, Ned
See Conquest, Edwin Parker, Jr.
Conquest, Owen
See Hamilton, Charles Harold St. John
Conquest, (George) Robert (Acworth)
1917- ... CANR-25
Earlier sketches in CA 15-16R, CANR-9
See also DLB 27
Conrad, Alfred Borys 1899(?)-1979
Obituary ... 104
Conrad, Andree 1945- ... 29-32R
Conrad, Barnaby (Jr.) 1922- ... CANR-6
Earlier sketch in CA 9-10R
Conrad, Brenda
See Brown, Zenith Jones
Conrad, David Eugene 1928- ... 17-18R
Conrad, Earl 1912-1986 ... CANR-10
Obituary ... 118
Earlier sketch in CA 1R
Conrad, Edna (G.) 1893- ... CAP-2
Earlier sketch in CA 33-36
Conrad, Hal
See Conrad, Harold
Conrad, Harold 1911- ... 112
Conrad, Jack (Randolph) 1923- ... 11-12R
Conrad, John W(ilfred) 1935- ... CANR-4
Earlier sketch in CA 53-56
Conrad, Jon(athan) J(ames) 1920- ... 114
Conrad, Joseph 1857-1924 Brief entry ... 104
See also SATA 27
See also DLB 10, 34
See also TCLC 1, 6, 13, 25
Conrad, Kenneth
See Lottich, Kenneth V(erne)
Conrad, L. K.
See Conrad, Andree
Conrad, Pam 1947- ... 121
See also SATA 49, 52
Conrad, Paul (Francis) 1924- ... 113
Conrad, Robert 1928- ... 41-44R
Conrad, Robert Arnold
See Hart, Moss
Conrad, Susan P(hinney) 1941-
Brief entry ... 113
Conrad, Sybil 1921- ... 23-24R
Conrad, Tod
See Wilkes-Hunter, R(ichard)
Conrad, Will C. 1882- ... CAP-1
Earlier sketch in CA 13-14
Conradis, Heinz 1907- ... CAP-1
Earlier sketch in CA 13-14
Conrads, Ulrich 1923- ... 9-10R
Conran, Anthony 1931- ... CANR-14
Earlier sketch in CA 65-68
Conran, Shirley (Ida) 1932- ... CANR-22
Earlier sketch in CA 103
Conran, Terence Orby 1931- ... 85-88
Conron, (Alfred) Brandon 1919- ... 17-18R
Conrow, Robert 1942- ... 57-60
Conroy, Barbara 1934- ... 111
Conroy, Charles W. 1922- ... 15-16R
Conroy, Frank 1936- ... 77-80
Conroy, (Francis) Hilary 1919- ... 115
Conroy, Jack
See Conroy, John Wesley
See also SATA 19
See also DLBY 81
Conroy, John Wesley 1899- ... CANR-3
Earlier sketch in CA 7-8R
Conroy, Mary 1941- ... 110
Conroy, Michael R(alph) 1945- ... CANR-9
Earlier sketch in CA 53-56
Conroy, Pat 1945- ... CANR-24
Earlier sketch in CA 85-88
See also DLB 6
See also CLC 30
See also AITN 1
Conroy, Patricia 1941- ... 93-96
Conroy, Peter V(incent), Jr. 1944- ... 53-56
Conroy, Robert
See Goldston, Robert (Conroy)
Considine, Bob
See Considine, Robert (Bernard)
See also AITN 2
Considine, Douglas M(axwell) 1915- ... CANR-11
Earlier sketch in CA 69-72
Considine, John J(oseph) 1897- ... 3R
Considine, Robert (Bernard) 1906-1975 ... 93-96
Obituary ... 61-64
Consilvio, Thomas 1947- ... 57-60
Consolo, Dominick P(eter) 1923- ... 33-36R
Constable, John W. 1922- ... 81-84
Constable, Trevor James 1925- ... 89-92
Constable, W(illiam) G(eorge) 1887-1976 ... 5-6R
Obituary ... 65-68
Constant, Alberta Wilson 1908-1981 ... CANR-4
Obituary ... 109
Earlier sketch in CA 4R
See also SATA 22, 28
Constantelos, Demetrios J. 1927- ... CANR-24
Earlier sketches in CA 21-22R, CANR-8
Constantin, James A. 1922- ... 13-14R
Constantin, Robert W(ilfrid) 1937- ... 25-28R
Constantine, David 1944- ... DLB-40
Constantine, Greg(ory John) 1938- ... 117
Constantine, K. C. (a pseudonym)
1935(?)- Brief entry ... 114
Constantine, Larry L(eRoy) 1943- ... CANR-14
Earlier sketch in CA 81-84
Constantine, Mildred 1914- ... 112
Brief entry ... 105
Constantine, Stephen 1947- ... 120
Constantino, Renato 1919- ... 118
Conton, William (Farquhar) 1925- ... 4R
Contoski, Victor 1936- ... CANR-17
Earlier sketch in CA 25-28R
Contosta, David R(ichard) 1945- ... 104
Contreras, Heles 1933- ... CANR-14
Earlier sketch in CA 37-40R
Converse, John Marquis 1909-1980
Obituary ... 102
Converse, Paul D(ulaney) 1889-1968 ... CAP-2
Earlier sketch in CA 17-18
Converse, Philip E. 1928- ... CANR-6
Earlier sketch in CA 13-14R
Convict Writer, The
See Torok, Lou
Conway, Alan (Arthur) 1920- ... CANR-2
Earlier sketch in CA 1R
Conway, Arlington B.
See Burns, Eedson Louis Millard
Conway, David 1939- ... 106
Conway, Denise
See Prebble, Marjorie Mary Curtis
Conway, Freda 1911- ... 25-28R
Conway, Gordon
See Hamilton, Charles Harold St. John
Conway, J(ohn) D(onald) 1905-1967 ... CANR-2
Earlier sketch in CA 2R
Conway, Jim 1932- ... 116
Conway, Joan Ditzel 1933- ... 97-100
Conway, John Seymour 1929- ... 25-28R
Conway, (Mary) Margaret 1935- ... 37-40R
Conway, Moncure Daniel 1832-1907 ... DLB-1
Conway, Peter
See Milkomane, George Alexis
Milkomanovich
Conway, Sally 1934- ... 116
Conway, Theresa (Ann) 1951- ... CANR-19
Earlier sketch in CA 103
Conway, Thomas D(aniel) 1934- ... 21-22R
Conway, Thomas Daniel 1933- ... 112
Conway, Tim
See Conway, Thomas Daniel
Conway, Tom
See Yates, A(lan) G(eoffrey)
Conway, Troy
See Avallone, Michael (Angelo), Jr.
Conway, Ward
See Westmoreland, Reg(inald Conway)
Conway, William J. 1904-1983 Obituary ... 110
Conybeare, Charles Augustus
See Eliot, T(homas) S(tearns)
Conyers, James E(rnest) 1932- ... 41-44R
Conyngham, William Joseph 1924- ... 53-56
Conyus
See Calhoun, Conyus
Conze, Edward J. D. 1904- ... 13-14R
Conzelman, James Gleason 1898-1970
Obituary ... 104
Conzelman, Jimmy
See Conzelman, James Gleason
Coogan, Daniel 1915- ... 21-22R
Coogan, John W(illiam) 1947- ... 107
Coogan, Joseph Patrick 1925- ... CANR-4
Earlier sketch in CA 3R
Coogan, Michael David 1942- Brief entry ... 112
Cook, Adrian 1940- ... 49-52
Cook, Alan Hugh 1922- ... 106
Cook, Albert Spaulding 1925- ... CANR-16
Earlier sketches in CA 1R, CANR-1
Cook, Alice H(anson) 1903- ... 115
Cook, Alice Rice 1899-1973 Obituary ... 41-44R
Cook, Ann Jennalie 1934- ... 105
Cook, Arlene Ethel 1936- ... 65-68
Cook, Bernadine 1924- ... SATA-11
Cook, Beverly Blair 1926- ... 37-40R
Cook, Blanche Wiesen 1941- ... CANR-4
Earlier sketch in CA 53-56
Cook, Bruce 1932- ... 33-36R
Cook, Chris(topher) 1945- ... CANR-23
Earlier sketches in CA 57-60, CANR-6
Cook, Daniel 1914- ... 33-36R
Cook, Daniel J(oseph) 1938- ... 53-56
Cook, David (John) 1929- ... 107
Cook, David 1940- ... CANR-22
Earlier sketch in CA 103
Cook, David A. 1945- ... 107
Cook, David C(harles) III 1912- ... 57-60
Cook, David T. 1946- ... 65-68
Cook, Don(ald Paul) 1920- ... CANR-14
Earlier sketch in CA 15-16R
Cook, Don Lewis 1928- ... 69-72
Cook, Dorothy Mary 1907- ... CANR-20
Earlier sketch in CA 103
Cook, Ebenezer 1667(?)-1732(?) ... DLB-24
Cook, Edward M(arks), Jr. 1944- ... 123
Brief entry ... 118
Cook, Elsa E(stelle) 1932- ... 125
Cook, Eugene 1917(?)-1986 Obituary ... 120
Cook, F(rederick) P. 1937- ... 93-96
Cook, Fred J(ames) 1911- ... CANR-23
Earlier sketches in CA 9-10R, CANR-3
See also SATA 2
Cook, Geoffrey 1946- ... 77-80
Cook, George Allan 1916- ... 23-24R
Cook, George S. 1920- ... 49-52
Cook, Gervis Frere
See Frere-Cook, Gervis
Cook, Gladys Emerson ... 5-6R
Cook, Gladys Moon 1907- ... 33-36R
Cook, Glen (Charles) 1944- ... 122
Cook, Glenn J. 1913- ... 25-28R
Cook, Gregory M(orton) 1942- ... 117
Cook, Harold Reed 1902- ... 15-16R
Cook, Hugh C(hristopher) B(ult) 1910- ... 57-60
Cook, Ida ?-1987(?) Obituary ... 121
Cook, (Harold) J. 1952- ... 120
Cook, J(ames) Gordon 1916- ... 11-12R
Cook, Jack
See Cook, John Augustine
Cook, (Harold) James 1926- ... 73-76
Cook, James Graham 1925-1966 ... 2R
Obituary ... 103
Cook, James W(yatt) 1932- ... 69-72
Cook, Jeffrey 1934- ... 97-100
Cook, Joan Marble 1920- ... 57-60
Cook, John Augustine 1940- ... 45-48

Cook, John Lennox 1923- ... 106
Cook, Joseph Jay 1924- ... CANR-2
Earlier sketch in CA 3R
See also SATA 8
Cook, Lennox
See Cook, John Lennox
Cook, Louise (Celia) 1942-1984 Obituary ... 112
Cook, Luther T(ownsend) 1901- ... 89-92
Cook, Lyn
See Waddell, Evelyn Margaret
Cook, Mabel Collins 1851-1927(?)
Brief entry ... 121
Cook, Margaret G(erry) 1903- ... 5-6R
Cook, Marjorie 1920- ... 81-84
Cook, Mark 1942- ... CANR-14
Earlier sketch in CA 37-40R
Cook, Mary Jane 1929- ... 93-96
Cook, Melva Janice 1919- ... CANR-9
Earlier sketch in CA 23-24R
Cook, Melvin A(lonzo) 1911- ... CANR-2
Earlier sketch in CA 49-52
Cook, (Will) Mercer 1903-1987 ... CANR-25
Obituary ... 124
Earlier sketch in CA 77-80
See also BW
Cook, Michael 1931- ... 123
Cook, Michael 1933- ... 93-96
See also DLB 53
Cook, Michael Lewis 1929- ... 112
Cook, Myra B. 1933- ... 23-24R
Cook, Nilla Cram 1908-1982 Obituary ... 108
Cook, Olive 1916- ... CANR-19
Earlier sketches in CA 7-8R, CANR-3
Cook, Olive Rambo 1892- ... 13-14R
Cook, P(auline) Lesley 1922- ... 15-16R
Cook, Paul H(arlin) 1950- ... 106
Cook, Peter D(onald) 1939- ... 112
Cook, Petronelle Marguerite Mary
1925- ... CANR-15
Earlier sketch in CA 81-84
Cook, Ramona Graham ... 5-6R
Cook, Ramsay 1931- ... CANR-25
Earlier sketch in CA 102
Cook, Raymond Allen 1919- ... 45-48
Cook, Reginald L. 1903- ... 65-68
Cook, Richard I(rving) 1927- ... 23-24R
Cook, Robert Andrew 1912- ... 117
Cook, Robert I. 1920- ... 33-36R
Cook, Robert William Arthur 1931- ... 25-28R
Cook, Robin 1940- ... 111
Brief entry ... 108
See also CLC 14
Cook, Robin
See Cook, Robert William Arthur
Cook, Roderick 1932- ... 9-10R
Cook, Roy
See Silverberg, Robert
Cook, Stanley 1922- ... 93-96
Cook, Stephani 1944- ... CANR-23
Earlier sketch in CA 106
Cook, Stephen 1949- ... 118
Cook, Stuart W(ellford) 1913- ... CANR-1
Earlier sketch in CA 4R
Cook, Sylvia (Carol) 1938- ... 49-52
Cook, Terry 1942- ... CANR-12
Earlier sketch in CA 73-76
Cook, Thomas H. 1947- ... 111
Cook, Thomas Ira 1907-1976 Obituary ... 111
Cook, W(illiam) Robert 1928- ... 115
Cook, Warren L. 1925- ... 37-40R
Cook, (George) Whitfield 1909- ... 107
Cook, William H(arleston) 1931- ... 104
Cook, William J(esse), Jr. 1938- ... 29-32R
Cook, William Wallace 1867-1933
Brief entry ... 116
Cooke, (Alfred) Alistair 1908- ... CANR-9
Earlier sketch in CA 57-60
See also AITN 1
Cooke, Ann
See Cole, Joanna
Cooke, Arthur
See Lowndes, Robert A(ugustine) W(ard)
Cooke, Barbara
See Alexander, Anna B(arbara Cooke)
Cooke, Barclay 1912-1981 ... 97-100
Obituary ... 105
Cooke, Bernard J. 1922- ... CANR-9
Earlier sketch in CA 15-16R
Cooke, Charles Harris 1904(?)-1977
Obituary ... 73-76
Cooke, David Coxe 1917- ... CANR-2
Earlier sketch in CA 2R
See also SATA 2
Cooke, Deryck (Victor) 1919-1976
Obituary ... 115
Cooke, Donald Ewin 1916-1985 ... CANR-4
Obituary ... 117
Earlier sketch in CA 4R
See also SATA 2, 45
Cooke, Edward F(rancis) 1923- ... 41-44R
Cooke, George Willis 1848-1923 ... DLB-71
Cooke, Gerald 1925- ... 13-14R
Cooke, Gilbert William 1899- ... CAP-1
Earlier sketch in CA 11-12
Cooke, Greville (Vaughan Turner) 1894- ... 13-14R
Cooke, Hereward Lester 1916-1973 ... CANR-1
Obituary ... 45-48
Earlier sketch in CA 3R
Cooke, Hope 1940- ... 108
Cooke, Jacob E(rnest) 1924- ... 2R
Cooke, James Francis 1875-1960
Obituary ... 115
Cooke, John Byrne 1940- ... 119
Cooke, John D(aniel) 1892-1972 Obituary ... 106
Cooke, John Esten 1830-1886 ... DLB-3
Cooke, John Estes
See Baum, L(yman) Frank
Cooke, John Fletcher
See Fletcher-Cooke, John
Cooke, Joseph R(obinson) 1926- ... 65-68
Cooke, M. E.
See Creasey, John
Cooke, Margaret
See Creasey, John
Cooke, Michael, F.R.C.S.
See Cook, Michael Lewis
Cooke, Michael G(eorge) 1934- ... 110
Cooke, Philip Pendleton 1816-1850 ... DLB-3, 59
Cooke, Robert (Gordon) 1930-1987 ... 101
Obituary ... 121
Cooke, Robert William 1935- ... 123
Cooke, Rose Terry 1827-1892 ... DLB-12, 74
Cooke, Terence James 1921-1983
Obituary ... 110
Cooke, Thomas D(arlington) 1933- ... 115
Cooke, William 1942- ... CANR-14
Earlier sketch in CA 33-36R
Cookridge, E. H.
See Spiro, Edward
Cookson, Catherine (McMullen) 1906- ... CANR-9
Earlier sketch in CA 15-16R
See also SATA 9
Cookson, Frank Barton 1912-1977
Obituary ... 69-72
Cookson, Peter W. 1913- ... 49-52
Cookson, Peter W., Jr. 1942- ... 121
Cookson, William 1939- ... 49-52
Cool, Joyce 1938- ... 111
Cool, Ola C. 1890(?)-1977 Obituary ... 69-72
Coolbrith, Ina 1841-1928 ... DLB-54
Coole, W. W.
See Kulski, Wladyslaw W(szebor)
Cooley, Denton A(rthur) 1920- ... 126
Cooley, John Kent 1927- ... 15-16R
Cooley, Lee Morrison 1919- ... CANR-3
Earlier sketch in CA 9-10R
Cooley, Leland Frederick 1909- ... CANR-4
Earlier sketch in CA 5-6R
Cooley, Margaret L. 1906(?)-1985
Obituary ... 117
Cooley, Peter (John) 1940- ... CANR-21
Earlier sketch in CA 69-72
Cooley, Richard A(llen) 1925- ... 21-22R
Coolidge, Archibald C(ary), Jr. 1928- ... 37-40R
Coolidge, Clark 1939- ... 33-36R
Coolidge, Harold Jefferson 1904-1985
Obituary ... 115
Coolidge, Olivia E(nsor) 1908- ... CANR-2
Earlier sketch in CA 5-6R
See also SATA 1, 26
Coolidge, Susan
See Woolsey, Sarah Chauncy
Cooling, Benjamin Franklin 1938- ... 53-56
Coolwater, John
See Conniff, James C(lifford) G(regory)
Coomaraswamy, A. K.
See Coomaraswamy, Ananda K(entish)
Coomaraswamy, Ananda K(entish)
1877-1947 Brief entry ... 115
Coombes, B. L. 1894(?)-1974 Obituary ... 53-56
Coombs, Charles Anthony 1918-1981 ... 109
Obituary ... 105
Coombs, Charles I(ra) 1914- ... CANR-19
Earlier sketches in CA 5-6R, CANR-4
See also SATA 3, 43
Coombs, Chick
See Coombs, Charles I(ra)
Coombs, Douglas (Stafford) 1924- ... 13-14R
Coombs, H. Samm 1928- ... 93-96
Coombs, Herbert Cole 1906- ... 93-96
Coombs, Murdo
See Davis, Frederick C(lyde)
Coombs, Orde M. 1939(?)-1984 ... CANR-25
Obituary ... 113
Earlier sketch in CA 73-76
See also BW
Coombs, Patricia 1926- ... CANR-1
Earlier sketch in CA 4R
See also SATA 3, 51
Coombs, (Robert) Peter 1913- ... 116
Coombs, Philip H(all) 1915- ... CANR-23
Earlier sketches in CA 17-18R, CANR-8
Coombs, Robert H(olman) 1934- ... 41-44R
Coomer, Joe 1958- ... 125
Coon, Carleton Stevens 1904-1981 ... CANR-2
Obituary ... 104
Earlier sketch in CA 5-6R
Coon, Gene L(ee) 1924-1973 ... CANR-15
Obituary ... 103
Earlier sketch in CA 2R
Coon, Martha Sutherland 1884- ... CAP-2
Earlier sketch in CA 25-28
Coon, Nelson 1895- ... 69-72
Coon, Stephen 1948- ... 57-60
Cooney, Barbara 1917- ... CANR-3
Earlier sketch in CA 5-6R
See also SATA 6
Cooney, Caroline B. 1947- ... 97-100
See also SATA 41, 48
Cooney, David M(artin) 1930- ... 17-18R
Cooney, Eugene J(erome) 1931- ... 45-48
Cooney, John 1942- ... 115
Cooney, Michael 1921- ... 25-28R
Cooney, Nancy Evans 1932- ... 105
See also SATA 42
Cooney, Seamus (Anthony) 1933- ... 53-56
Cooney, Timothy J. 1929- ... 107
Coons, Frederica Bertha (Safley) 1910- ... 17-18R
Coons, William R(ichard) 1934- ... 41-44R
Coontz, Otto 1946- ... 105
See also SATA 33
Coop, Howard 1928- ... 25-28R
Coope, Rosalys 1921- ... 45-48
Cooper, Alfred Morton 1890- ... CAP-1
Earlier sketch in CA 11-12
Cooper, Alice 1948- ... 106
Cooper, Allan 1954- ... 118
Cooper, Allan D. 1952- ... 121
Cooper, Arnold Cook 1933- ... 19-20R
Cooper, B(rian) Lee 1942- ... 117
Cooper, Barbara (Ann) 1929- ... 9-10R
Cooper, (Fraser) Barry 1943- ... 126
Cooper, Bernarr 1912- ... 41-44R
Cooper, Bev 1936- ... 119
Cooper, Brian (Newman) 1919- ... CANR-22
Earlier sketch in CA 4R
Cooper, Bruce M(ichael) 1925- ... CANR-9
Earlier sketch in CA 15-16R
Cooper, Bryan (Robert Wright) 1932- ... 25-28R
Cooper, C(hristopher) D(onald)
H(untington) 1942- ... 29-32R
Cooper, Carl
See Cooper, Kenneth C(arlton)
Cooper, Charles M(uhlenberg) 1909- ... 41-44R
Cooper, Charles W(illiam) 1904- ... CAP-2
Earlier sketch in CA 21-22
Cooper, Chester L. 1917- ... 29-32R
Cooper, Christopher (John) 1941- ... 107
Cooper, (Brenda) Clare 1935- ... 118
Cooper, Colin Symons 1926- ... 102
Cooper, Darien B(rown) 1934- ... 116
Cooper, Darien B(irla) 1937- ... CANR-16
Earlier sketches in CA 49-52, CANR-1
Cooper, David (Graham) 1931-1986 ... 97-100
Obituary ... 119
Cooper, David E. 1942- ... 49-52
Cooper, Derek Macdonald 1925- ... 102
Cooper, Diana (Olivia Winifred Maud
Manners) 1892(?)-1986 Obituary ... 119
Cooper, Dominic (Xavier) 1944- ... 65-68
Cooper, Douglas 1911-1984 Obituary ... 112
Cooper, Edmund 1926- ... 33-36R
Cooper, Elizabeth Ann 1927- ... 3R
Cooper, Elizabeth Keyser ... CANR-1
Earlier sketch in CA 4R
See also SATA 47
Cooper, Emmanuel 1938- ... CANR-3
Earlier sketch in CA 49-52
Cooper, Esther
See Kellner, Esther
Cooper, (C.) Everett
See Burgess, M(ichael) R(oy)
Cooper, Frank E(dward) 1910-1968 ... CAP-2
Earlier sketch in CA 21-22
Cooper, Giles (Stannus) 1918-1966
Obituary ... 113
See also DLB 13
Cooper, Gladys 1888-1971 Obituary ... 33-36R
Cooper, Gordon 1932- ... 61-64
See also SATA 23
Cooper, Grace Rogers 1924- ... 41-44R
Cooper, Hannah
See Spence, William John Duncan
Cooper, Harold E(ugene) 1928- ... 45-48
Cooper, Harold H. 1911(?)-1976
Obituary ... 69-72
Cooper, Harold R. 1911(?)-1978
Obituary ... 77-80
Cooper, Henry S(potswood) F(enimore), Jr.
1933- ... CANR-13
Earlier sketch in CA 69-72
Cooper, Henry St. John
See Creasey, John
Cooper, I(rving) S(pencer) 1922-1985 ... CANR-26
Obituary ... 117
Earlier sketch in CA 69-72
Cooper, J. California ... 125
See also BW
Cooper, Jacqueline 1924- ... 107
Cooper, James A. ... CANR-26
Earlier sketches in CA 19-20, CAP-2
Cooper, James Fenimore 1789-1851 ... SATA-19
See also DLB 3
See also CDALB 1640-1865
Cooper, James L(ouis) 1934- ... 53-56
Cooper, James M. 1939- ... 45-48
Cooper, Jamie Lee ... 9-10R
Cooper, Jane (Marvel) 1924- ... CANR-17
Earlier sketch in CA 25-28R
Cooper, Jeff 1920- ... 41-44R
Cooper, Jefferson
See Fox, G(ardner) F(rancis)
Cooper, Jeremy (Francis Peter) 1946- ... 93-96
Cooper, Jilly 1937- ... 105
Cooper, John 1934-1984 Obituary ... 113
Cooper, John C(harles) 1933- ... CANR-9
Earlier sketch in CA 23-24R
Cooper, John Cobb 1887- ... 5-6R
Cooper, John Dean
See Cooper, Jeff
Cooper, John E(llsworth) 1922- ... 25-28R
Cooper, John Irwin 1905- ... 41-44R
Cooper, John L. 1936- ... CANR-13
Earlier sketch in CA 21-22R
Cooper, John M(iller) 1912- ... 21-22R
Cooper, John Milton, Jr. 1940-
Brief entry ... 105
Cooper, John O(wen) 1938- ... 89-92
Cooper, John R. ... CAP-2
Earlier sketch in CA 19-20
See also SATA 1
Cooper, Joseph Bonar 1912- ... 19-20R
Cooper, Joseph D(avid) 1917-1975 ... CANR-4
Obituary ... 57-60
Earlier sketch in CA 5-6R
Cooper, Kay 1941- ... CANR-16
Earlier sketches in CA 45-48, CANR-1
See also SATA 11
Cooper, Kenneth C(arlton) 1948- ... 110
Cooper, Kenneth H(ardy) 1931-
Brief entry ... 126
Cooper, Kenneth Schaaf 1918- ... 9-10R
Cooper, Kent 1880-1965 Obituary ... 89-92
See also DLB 29
Cooper, Lee Pelham 1926- ... CANR-4
Earlier sketch in CA 5-6R
See also SATA 5
Cooper, Leslie M(uir) 1930- ... 41-44R
Cooper, Lester (Irving) 1919-1985 ... 108
Obituary ... 116
See also SATA 32, 43
Cooper, Lettice (Ulpha) 1897- ... CANR-5
Earlier sketch in CA 9-10R
See also SATA 35
Cooper, Louise 1952- ... 107
Cooper, Louise Field 1905- ... CANR-4
Earlier sketch in CA 4R
Cooper, Lynna
See Fox, G(ardner) F(rancis)
Cooper, Mae (Klein) ... 17-18R
Cooper, Mario 1905- ... 23-24R
Cooper, Martin Du Pre 1910-1986 ... 103
Obituary ... 118
Cooper, Matthew (Heald) 1952- ... 85-88
Cooper, Mattie Lula
See Britton, Mattie Lula Cooper
Cooper, Michael (John) 1930- ... 15-16R
Cooper, Michele F(reda) 1941- ... 85-88
Cooper, Morley
See Cooper, Alfred Morton
Cooper, Neil (Louis) 1930- ... 119
Cooper, Parley J(oseph) 1937- ... CANR-26
Earlier sketches in CA 65-68, CANR-10
Cooper, Patricia J(ean) 1936- ... 97-100
Cooper, Paul 1926- ... 49-52
Cooper, Paul F(enimore) 1900(?)-1970
Obituary ... 104
Cooper, Paulette 1944- ... 37-40R
Cooper, Peter Lee 1949- ... 111
Cooper, Philip (Jr.) 1926- ... 33-36R
Cooper, Phyllis 1939- ... 53-56
Cooper, Richard N(ewell) 1934- ... CANR-10
Earlier sketch in CA 25-28R
Cooper, Robert G(ravlin) 1943- ... 110
Cooper, Robert St. John 1905(?)-1984
Obituary ... 111
Cooper, Sandi E. 1936- ... 49-52
Cooper, Saul 1934- ... 3R
Cooper, Signe Skott 1921- ... CANR-4
Earlier sketch in CA 53-56
Cooper, Sister Mary Ursula 1925- ... 5-6R
Cooper, Sophie
See Amory, Mark
Cooper, Susan 1935- ... CANR-15
Earlier sketch in CA 29-32R
See also SATA 4
See also SAAS 6
See also CLR 4
Cooper, Sylvia 1903- ... CAP-2
Earlier sketch in CA 17-18
Cooper, Wayne 1938- ... 93-96
Cooper, Wendy (Lowe) 1919- ... CANR-6
Earlier sketch in CA 13-14R
Cooper, Wilhelmina (Behmenburg)
1939(?)-1980 Obituary ... 97-100
Cooper, Will 1929- ... 69-72
Cooper, William
See Hoff, Harry S(ummerfield)
Cooper, William F(razier) 1932- ... 69-72
Cooper, William Hurlbert 1924- ... 49-52
Cooper, William J(ames), Jr. 1940- ... 69-72
Cooper, William W(ager) 1914- ... 15-16R
Cooper, Wyatt (Emory) 1927-1978 ... 73-76
Obituary ... 77-80
See also AITN 2
Cooper-Clark, Diana 1945- ... 109
Cooper-Klein, Nina
See Cooper, Mae (Klein)
Cooperman, Hasye 1909- ... 37-40R
Cooperman, Stanley 1929-1976 ... CAP-2
Earlier sketch in CA 33-36
Coopersmith, Harry 1903- ... CAP-2
Earlier sketch in CA 21-22
Coopersmith, Jerome 1925- ... 73-76
Coopersmith, Stanley 1926- ... 21-22R
Cooter, Roger James 1948- ... 123
Cootner, Paul H(arold) 1930- ... 11-12R
Coover, James B(urrell) 1925- ... CANR-23
Earlier sketches in CA 57-60, CANR-6
Coover, Robert (Lowell) 1932- ... CANR-3
Earlier sketch in CA 45-48
See also DLB 2
See also DLBY 81
See also CLC 3, 7, 15, 32, 46
Coox, Alvin D(avid) 1924- ... 29-32R
Copani, Peter 1942- ... 89-92
Cope, David 1941- ... 33-36R
Cope, Edward A(llen) 1948- ... 121
Cope, Jack
See Cope, Robert Knox
Cope, Jackson I(rving) 1925- ... 103
Cope, Lewis 1934- ... 125
Cope, Myron 1929- ... 57-60
Cope, Oliver 1902- Brief entry ... 109
Cope, Robert Knox 1913- ... 9-10R
Cope, (Vincent) Zachary 1881-1974 ... CAP-1
Earlier sketch in CA 9-10
Copel, Sidney L(eroy) 1930- ... 23-24R
Copelan, Rachel 1934- ... 114
Copeland, Ann
See Furtwangler, Virginia W(alsh)
Copeland, Bill
See Copeland, Paul William
Copeland, Bonnie Chapman 1919- ... 101
Copeland, Carolyn Faunce 1930- ... 65-68

Copeland, E(dwin) Luther 1916- ... CANR-3
Earlier sketch in CA 11-12R
Copeland, Helen 1920- ... 25-28R
See also SATA 4
Copeland, James E(verett) 1937- ... 125
Copeland, James Isaac 1910- ... 106
Copeland, Lennie 1946- ... 120
Copeland, Melvin T. 1884-1975 ... CAP-2
Obituary ... 57-60
Earlier sketch in CA 21-22
Copeland, Miles 1916- ... 29-32R
Copeland, Morris A(lbert) 1895- ... CAP-1
Earlier sketch in CA 17-18
Copeland, Paul W. ... 105
See also SATA 23
Copeland, Paul William 1917- ... 25-28R
Copeland, Ray (M.) 1926-1984 Obituary ... 112
Copeland, Ross H. 1930- ... 25-28R
Copeland, Stewart (Armstrong) 1952- ... CLC-26
Copeland, Thomas Wellsted 1907-1979 ... 5-6R
Copeman, George H(enry) 1922- ... CANR-8
Earlier sketch in CA 7-8R
Copenhaver, Charles L(eonard) 1915-1982
Obituary ... 107
Coper, Rudolf 1904- ... CAP-1
Earlier sketch in CA 13-14
Copetas, A. Craig 1951- ... 121
Copi, Irving M(armer) 1917- ... CANR-5
Earlier sketch in CA 1R
Coplan, Kate M(ildred) 1901- ... 7-8R
Copland, Aaron 1900- ... 7-8R
Coplans, John (Rivers) 1920- Brief entry ... 112
Copleston, Frederick Charles (John Paul)
1907- ... CANR-7
Earlier sketch in CA 13-14R
Copley, Frederick S.
See Greif, Martin
Copley, Gerald L. C.
See Cole, Lester
Copley (Diana) Heather Pickering
1918- ... SATA-45
Coplin, William D(avid) 1939- ... CANR-12
Earlier sketch in CA 23-24R
Copman, Louis 1934- ... 57-60
Copp, Andrew James (III) 1916- ... 25-28R
Copp, E. Anthony 1945- ... 102
Copp, Jim
See Copp, Andrew James (III)
Coppa, Frank John 1937- ... CANR-13
Earlier sketch in CA 33-36R
Coppard, A(lfred) E(dgar) 1878-1957
Brief entry ... 114
See also YABC 1
See also TCLC 5
Coppard, Audrey 1931- ... 29-32R
Coppe, Abiezer
See Taylor, John (Alfred)
Coppee, Francois 1842-1908 ... TCLC-25
Coppel, Alec 1909(?)-1972 Obituary ... 33-36R
Coppel, Alfred 1921- ... CANR-10
Earlier sketch in CA 19-20R
See also DLBY 83
Copper, (Robert) Arnold (de Vignier)
1934- ... 97-100
Copper, John Franklin 1940- ... CANR-11
Earlier sketch in CA 69-72
Copper, Marcia S(nyder) 1934- ... 53-56
Copperman, Paul 1947- ... 101
Copperud, Roy H. 1915- ... 11-12R
Coppock, John (Oates) 1914- ... 13-14R
Coppock, John Terence 1921- ... 102
Coppock, Joseph D(avid) 1909- ... 49-52
Coppola, Francis Ford 1939- ... 77-80
See also DLB 44
See also CLC 16
Coppola, Raymond T(homas) 1947- ... 102
Coram, Christopher
See Walker, Peter N.
Corbalis, Judy 1941- ... 125
Corballis, Michael C(harles) 1936- ... 115
Corbally, John Edward, Jr. 1924- ... 5-6R
Corbett, Chan
See Schachner, Nat(han)
Corbett, Christopher 1951- ... 123
Corbett, Edward P(atrick) J(oseph)
1919- ... CANR-9
Earlier sketch in CA 17-18R
Corbett, Elizabeth (Frances) 1887-1981 ... CANR-2
Obituary ... 102
Earlier sketch in CA 5-6R
Corbett, Grahame ... 116
See also SATA 36, 43
Corbett, J(ack) Elliott 1920- ... 29-32R
Corbett, James A(rthur) 1908- ... 65-68
Corbett, Janice M. 1935- ... 37-40R
Corbett, (John) Patrick 1916- ... 17-18R
Corbett, Pearson H(arris) 1900- ... CAP-1
Earlier sketch in CA 9-10
Corbett, Richmond McLain 1902- ... CAP-1
Earlier sketch in CA 15-16
Corbett, Ruth 1912- ... 29-32R
Corbett, Scott 1913- ... CANR-23
Earlier sketches in CA 3R, CANR-1
See also SATA 2, 42
See also SAAS 2
See also CLR 1
Corbett, Thomas H(enry) 1938- ... 77-80
Corbett, W(illiam) J(esse) 1938- ... SATA-44, 50
Corbin, Arnold 1911- ... 9-10R
Corbin, Charles B. 1940- ... CANR-14
Earlier sketch in CA 29-32R
Corbin, Claire 1913- ... 41-44R
Corbin, Donald A(lvin) 1920- ... 33-36R
Corbin, H(ayman) Dan 1912- ... 41-44R
Corbin, Iris
See Clinton, Iris A. (Corbin)
Corbin, John B(oyd) 1935- ... CANR-22
Earlier sketch in CA 105
Corbin, Richard 1911-1988 ... CANR-3
Obituary ... 125
Earlier sketch in CA 7-8R
Corbin, Sabra Lee
See Malvern, Gladys
Corbin, William
See McGraw, William Corbin
Corbishley, Thomas 1903-1976 ... CANR-7
Obituary ... 65-68
Earlier sketch in CA 13-14R
Corbitt, Helen Lucy 1906-1978 ... CANR-4
Obituary ... 89-92
Earlier sketch in CA 7-8R
Corby, Dan
See Catherall, Arthur
Corcoran, Barbara 1911- ... CANR-11
Earlier sketch in CA 23-24R
See also CAAS 2
See also SATA 3
See also DLB 52
See also CLC 17
Corcoran, Gertrude B(eatty) 1922- ... 29-32R
Corcoran, Jean (Kennedy) 1926- ... 3R
Corcos, Lucille 1908-1973 ... 21-22R
See also SATA 10
Cord, Barry
See Germano, Peter B.
Cord, Robert L. 1935- ... 33-36R
Cord, Steven Benson 1928- ... 21-22R
Cord, William O. 1921- ... 37-40R
Cordasco, Francesco 1920- ... CANR-21
Earlier sketches in CA 13-14R, CANR-6
Cordelier, Maurice
See Giraudoux, (Hippolyte) Jean
Cordell, Alexander
See Graber, Alexander
Cordell, Richard Albert 1896- ... 1R
Corden, W(arner) M(ax) 1927- ... 33-36R
Corder, Brice W(ood) 1936- ... 53-56
Corder, Eric
See Mundis, Jerrold
Corder, George Edward 1904- ... 110
Corder, Jim(my Wayne) 1929- ... 17-18R
Cordier, Andrew W(ellington) 1901-1975
Obituary ... 106
Cordier, Gilbert
See Scherer, Jean-Marie Maurice
Cordier, Ralph Waldo 1902- ... 37-40R
Cordingley, Patrick 1944- ... 114
Cordingly, David 1938- ... 93-96
Cordis, Lonny
See Donson, Cyril
Cords, Nicholas J. 1929- ... 105
Cordtz, Dan 1927- ... 73-76
Cordwell, Miriam 1908-1986 ... 89-92
Obituary ... 120
Corea, Gena
See Corea, Genoveffa
Corea, Genoveffa 1946- ... 81-84
Corelli, Marie
See Mackay, Mary
See also DLB 34
Coren, Alan 1938- ... 69-72
See also SATA 32
Corey, Dorothy ... CANR-26
Earlier sketches in CA 69-72, CANR-11
See also SATA 23
Corey, Gerald F(rancis) 1937- ... 114
Corey, Paul (Frederick) 1903- ... CANR-2
Earlier sketch in CA 5-6R
Corey, Stephen 1948- ... 124
Corfe, Thomas Howell 1928- ... 103
See also SATA 27
Corfe, Tom
See Corfe, Thomas Howell
Corfield, Conrad Laurence 1893-1980
Obituary ... 105
Corfman, Eunice (Luccock) 1928-1980
Obituary ... 97-100
Corina, Maurice 1936- ... 57-60
Cork, Patrick
See Cockburn, (Francis) Claud
Cork, Richard (Graham) 1947- ... CANR-24
Earlier sketch in CA 107
Corke, Helen 1882- ... CAP-1
Earlier sketch in CA 9-10
Corke, Hilary 1921- ... 97-100
Corkey, R(obert) 1881-1966 ... CAP-1
Earlier sketch in CA 15-16
Corkran, David Hudson, Jr. 1902- ... 5-6R
Corkran, Herbert, Jr. 1924- ... 29-32R
Corle, Edwin 1906-1956 ... DLBY-85
Corless, Roger (Jonathan) 1938- ... 108
Corlett, William 1938- ... 103
See also SATA 39, 46
Corlew, Robert Ewing 1922- ... 110
Corley, (Thomas) Anthony (Buchanan)
1923- ... 2R
Corley, Edwin (Raymond) 1931-1981 ... CANR-12
Obituary ... 105
Earlier sketch in CA 25-28R
Corley, Ernest
See Bulmer, (Henry) Kenneth
Corley, Nora T(eresa) ... 118
Corley, Ray
See Corley, Edwin (Raymond)
Corley, Robert N(eil) 1930- ... CANR-19
Earlier sketches in CA 11-12R, CANR-3
Corliss, Charlotte N(uzum) 1932- ... 53-56
Corliss, William R(oger) 1926- ... CANR-16
Earlier sketches in CA 45-48, CANR-1
Cormack, Alexander James Ross 1942- ... 65-68
Cormack, James Maxwell Ross
1909-1975 ... CAP-1
Earlier sketch in CA 9-10
Cormack, M(argaret) Grant 1913- ... 3R
See also SATA 11
Cormack, Margaret Lawson 1912- ... 3R
Cormack, Maribelle B. 1902-1984 ... SATA-39
Cormack, Sandy
See Cormack, Alexander James Ross
Corman, Avery 1935- ... 85-88
Corman, Cid
See Corman, Sidney
See also CAAS 2
See also DLB 5
See also CLC 9
Corman, Sidney 1924- ... 85-88
Cormier, Bruno M. 1919- Brief entry ... 114
Cormier, Frank 1927- ... 23-24R
Cormier, Ramona 1923- ... 49-52
Cormier, Raymond J(oseph) 1938- ... CANR-19
Earlier sketches in CA 53-56, CANR-4
Cormier, Robert (Edmund) 1925- ... CANR-23
Earlier sketches in CA 3R, CANR-5
See also SATA 10, 45
See also DLB 52
See also CLC 12, 30
See also CLR 12
Cormillot, Albert E. J. 1938- ... 69-72
Corn, Alfred 1943- ... 104
See also DLBY 80
See also CLC 33
Corn, Ira George, Jr. 1921-1982 ... 85-88
Obituary ... 106
Cornea, Carol
See Koch, Kurt E(mil)
Cornebise, Alfred E(mile) 1929- ... 115
Cornehls, James V(ernon) 1936- ... 93-96
Cornelisen, Ann 1926- ... CANR-17
Earlier sketch in CA 25-28R
corneliszavandenheuvel
See van den Heuvel, Cornelisz A.
Cornelius, Carol 1942- ... 115
See also SATA 40
Cornelius, Temple H. 1891-1964 ... CAP-1
Earlier sketch in CA 11-12
Cornelius, Wanda Pyle 1936- ... 105
Cornell, Douglas B. 1906(?)-1982
Obituary ... 106
Cornell, Felix M. 1896(?)-1970 Obituary ... 104
Cornell, Francis Griffith 1906-1979
Obituary ... 89-92
Cornell, George W. 1920- ... 9-10R
Cornell, J.
See Cornell, Jeffrey
Cornell, James (Clayton, Jr.) 1938- ... CANR-11
Earlier sketch in CA 69-72
See also SATA 27
Cornell, Jean Gay 1920- ... CANR-1
Earlier sketch in CA 45-48
See also SATA 23
Cornell, Jeffrey 1945- ... SATA-11
Cornell, Katherine 1898(?)-1974 Obituary ... 49-52
Cornell, Tim 1946- ... 115
Corner, E. J. H.
See Corner, Edred John Henry
Corner, Edred John Henry 1906-
Brief entry ... 116
Corner, George W(ashington) 1889-1981 ... 102
Obituary ... 104
Corner, Philip 1933- ... 23-24R
Cornett, Joe D(elayne) 1935- ... 53-56
Corney, Estelle 1911- ... 115
Cornfeld, Gaalyah 1902- ... CANR-12
Earlier sketch in CA 73-76
Cornford, A(ndrew) J(ohn) 1942- ... 112
Cornforth, Maurice 1909-1980 ... CANR-4
Obituary ... 102
Earlier sketch in CA 5-6R
Corngold, Stanley Alan 1934- ... CANR-14
Earlier sketch in CA 37-40R
Cornillon, John Raymond Koppleman
1941- ... 17-18R
Cornish, Dudley T(aylor) 1915- ... 19-20R
Cornish, Edward (Seymour) 1927- ... CANR-25
Earlier sketch in CA 108
Cornish, Geoffrey (St. John) 1914- ... 125
Cornish, John (Buckley) 1914- ... 25-28R
Cornish, Sam(uel James) 1935- ... CANR-24
Earlier sketch in CA 41-44R
See also BW
See also SATA 23
See also DLB 41
Cornish, W(illiam) R(odolph) 1937- ... 29-32R
Cornman, James W(elton) 1929-1978 ... CANR-11
Earlier sketch in CA 69-72
Cornock, (John) Stroud 1938- ... 25-28R
Cornuelle, Richard C. 1927- ... 17-18R
Cornwall, E(spie) Judson 1924- ... CANR-6
Earlier sketch in CA 57-60
Cornwall, I(an) W(olfran) 1909- ... 11-12R
Cornwall, J. Spencer 1888(?)-1983
Obituary ... 109
Cornwall, James (Handyside) Marshall
See Marshall-Cornwall, James
(Handyside)
Cornwall, Jim
See Rikhoff, James C.
Cornwall, John 1928- ... 115
Cornwall, Martin
See Cavendish, Richard
Cornwall, Nellie
See Sloggett, Nellie
Cornwell, Bernard 1944- ... 104
Cornwell, David (John Moore) 1931- ... CANR-13
Earlier sketch in CA 7-8R
See also CLC 9, 15
Cornwell, Elmer E(ckert), Jr. 1924-
Brief entry ... 118
Cornwell, Smith
See Smith, David (Jeddie)
Coronel, Jorge Icaza
See Icaza Coronel, Jorge
Corporal Trim
See Bolger, Philip C(unningham)
Corradi, Gemma 1939- ... 23-24R
Corradi, Juan E. 1943- ... 113
Corrall, Alice Enid 1916- ... 7-8R
Corre, Alan D. 1931- ... 37-40R
Correa
See Galbraith, Jean
Correa, Gustavo 1914- ... 49-52
Correia-Afonso, John 1924- ... CANR-13
Earlier sketch in CA 33-36R
Corren, Grace
See Hoskins, Robert
Correu, Larry M. 1931- ... 114
Correy, Lee
See Stine, G(eorge) Harry
Corrie, Elva
See Clairmont, Elva
Corrigan, (Helen) Adeline 1909- ... 69-72
See also SATA 23
Corrigan, Barbara 1922- ... 57-60
See also SATA 8
Corrigan, Francis Joseph 1919- ... 7-8R
Corrigan, John D(avitt) 1900- ... 41-44R
Corrigan, John Thomas 1936- ... CANR-10
Earlier sketch in CA 65-68
Corrigan, Ralph L(awrence), Jr. 1937- ... 33-36R
Corrigan, Robert A(nthony) 1935- ... 9-10R
Corrigan, Robert W(illoughby) 1927- ... CANR-6
Earlier sketch in CA 7-8R
Corrin, Jay P(atrick) 1943- ... 125
Corrin, Sara 1918- ... 120
See also SATA 48
Corrin, Stephen ... 121
See also SATA 48
Corrington, John William 1932- ... CANR-8
Earlier sketch in CA 13-14R
See also DLB 6
Corriveau, Monique (Chouinard)
1927-1976 ... CANR-12
Obituary ... 122
Earlier sketch in CA 61-64
Corrothers, James D. 1869-1917 ... DLB-50
Corry, Emmett 1934- ... 111
Corry, J(ames) A(lexander) 1899-1985
Obituary ... 120
Corsa, Helen Storm 1915- ... 19-20R
Corsaro, Francesco Andrea 1924- ... 85-88
Corsaro, Frank
See Corsaro, Francesco Andrea
Corsaro, Maria C(ecelia) 1949- ... 107
Corsel, Ralph 1920- ... 25-28R
Corsi, Jerome R(obert) 1946- ... 89-92
Corsini, Raymond J. 1914- ... CANR-21
Earlier sketches in CA 4R, CANR-3
Corso, (Nunzio) Gregory 1930- ... 7-8R
See also DLB 5,16
See also CLC 1, 11
Corson, Fred Pierce 1896-1985 ... CAP-2
Obituary ... 115
Earlier sketch in CA 23-24
Corson, Hazel W. 1906- ... CANR-2
Earlier sketch in CA 2R
Corson, John J(ay) 1905- ... CANR-5
Earlier sketch in CA 1R
Corson, Richard ... 41-44R
Corson-Finnerty, Adam Daniel 1944- ... CANR-14
Earlier sketch in CA 81-84
Corstanje, Auspicius van
See van Corstanje, Charles
Corstanje, Charles van
See van Corstanje, Charles
Cort, David 1904-1983 ... 9-10R
Obituary ... 111
Cort, M. C.
See Clifford, Margaret Cort
Cort, Margaret
See Clifford, Margaret Cort
Cortada, James W(illiam) 1946-
Brief entry ... 114
Cortazar, Julio 1914-1984 ... CANR-12
Earlier sketch in CA 21-22R
See also CLC 2, 3, 5, 10, 13, 15, 33, 34
Cortazzi, (Henry Arthur) Hugh 1924- ... 115
Cortazzo, Carman 1936- ... 109
Corteen, Wes
See Norwood, Victor G(eorge) C(harles)
Cortes, Carlos E(liseo) 1934- ... CANR-8
Earlier sketch in CA 61-64
Cortes, Juan B(autista) 1925- ... 37-40R
Cortese, A(nthony) James 1917- ... 65-68
Cortesi, Lawrence
See Cerri, Lawrence J.
Cortez, Jayne 1936- ... CANR-13
Earlier sketch in CA 73-76
See also BW
See also DLB 41
Cortez-Villon, Juan
See Herzinger, Kim A(llen)
Cortinez, Carlos 1934- ... 123
Cortner, Richard C(arroll) 1935- ... 104
Cortright, Barbara 1927- ... 112
Cortright, David 1946- ... 57-60
Corty, Floyd L(ouis) 1916- ... 13-14R
Corwen, Leonard 1921- ... CANR-15
Earlier sketch in CA 93-96
Corwin, Adele Beatrice Lewis 1922- ... 123
Corwin, Cecil
See Kornbluth, C(yril) M.
Corwin, Edward S(amuel) 1878-1963 ... 122
Obituary ... 113
Corwin, Judith H(offman) 1946- ... 113
See also SATA 10

Corwin, Norman 1910- CANR-24
Earlier sketches in CA 4R, CANR-1
See also AITN 2
Corwin, Ronald G(ary) 1932- CANR-23
Earlier sketches in CA 19-20R, CANR-8
Cory, Caroline
See Freeman, Kathleen
Cory, Corrine
See Cory, Irene E.
Cory, Daniel 1904-1972 Obituary 37-40R
Cory, David 1872-1966 Obituary 25-28R
Cory, Desmond
See McCarthy, Shaun (Lloyd)
Cory, Howard L.
See Jardine, Jack
Cory, Irene E. 1910- 49-52
Cory, Jean-Jacques 1947- 57-60
Cory, Ray
See Marshall, Mel(vin D.)
Cory, William Johnson 1823-1892 .... DLB-35
Corya, I. E.
See Cory, Irene E.
Cosby, Bill
See Cosby, William Henry, Jr.
Cosby, William Henry, Jr. 1937- 81-84
See also BW
Cosby, Yvonne Shepard 1886(?)-1980
Obituary 97-100
Cose, Ellis Jonathan 1951- 119
Cosell, Howard 1920- 108
Cosentino, Andrew J(oseph) 1931- 120
Cosentino, Donald J(ohn) 1941- 108
Coser, Lewis A. 1913- CANR-4
Earlier sketch in CA 3R
Coser, Rose Laub 1916- 15-16R
Cosgrave, John O'Hara II 1908-1968 .... CANR-1
Earlier sketch in CA 4R
See also SATA 21
Cosgrave, Patrick 1941- 33-36R
Cosgrove, Carol Ann
See Twitchett, Carol Cosgrove
Cosgrove, Margaret (Leota) 1926- CANR-6
Earlier sketch in CA 9-10R
See also SATA 47
Cosgrove, Mark P. 1947- 85-88
Cosgrove, Maynard G(iles) 1895- 57-60
Cosgrove, Rachel
See Payes, Rachel C(osgrove)
Cosgrove, Richard A(lfred) 1941- 104
Cosgrove, Stephen E(dward) 1945- CANR-22
Earlier sketch in CA 69-72
See also SATA 40, 53
See also AITN 1
Cosh, (Ethel Eleanor) Mary 7-8R
Cosic, Dobrica 1921- Brief entry 122
See also CLC 14
Coskey, Evelyn 1932- 41-44R
See also SATA 7
Coslow, Sam 1905-1982 77-80
Obituary 106
Cosman, Carol 104
Cosman, Madeleine Pelner 1937-
Brief entry 105
Cosneck, Bernard Joseph 1912- 49-52
Cosner, Shaaron 1940- 116
See also SATA 43
Coss, Thurman L. 1926- 13-14R
Cossart, Theophilus
See Glass, Montague (Marsden)
Cosseboom, Kathy Groehn
See El-Messidi, Kathy Groehn
Cossi, Olga 1921- 81-84
Cosslett, Tess 1947- 115
Cossman, E(li) Joseph 1918- 19-20R
Cost, March
See Morrison, Margaret Mackie
Costa, Albert Bernard 1929- 13-14R
Costa, Gustavo 1930- 37-40R
Costa, Horacio (L.) de la 1916-1977
Obituary 112
Costa, Richard Hauer 1921- 21-22R
Costabel, Eva Deutsch 1924- 125
See also SATA 45
Costabel-Deutsch, Eva
See Costabel, Eva Deutsch
Costain, Thomas B(ertram) 1885-1965 .... 5-6R
Obituary 25-28R
See also DLB 9
See also CLC 30
Costantin, M(ary) M(cCaffrey) 1935- 45-48
Costantini, Humberto 1924(?)-1987
Obituary 122
See also CLC 49
Costas, Orlando E(nrique) 1942-1987 101
Obituary 124
Costas, Procope 1900(?)-1974 Obituary 53-56
Costello, Anne 1937- 102
Costello, Chris 1947- 107
Costello, David F(rancis) 1904- 33-36R
See also SATA 23
Costello, Donald P(aul) 1931- 19-20R
Costello, Elvis 1955- CLC-21
Costello, Grace Seymour 1883-1983
Obituary 110
Costello, John E(dward) 1943- 85-88
Costello, Joseph P(atrick) 1924- 115
Costello, Michael
See Detzer, Karl
Costello, Peter 1946- 93-96
Costello, William Aloysious 1904-1969 .... 4R
Obituary 103
Costelloe, M(artin) Joseph 1914- 41-44R
Coster, Robert
See Barltrop, Robert
Costigan, Daniel M. 1929- CANR-14
Earlier sketch in CA 33-36R
Costigan, Giovanni 1905- CAP-1
Earlier sketch in CA 15-16
Costigan, James 1928- 73-76
Costikyan, Edward N. 1924- 19-20R
Costinescu, Tristan
See Gross, Terence
Costis, Harry George 1928- 45-48
Costley, Bill
See Costley, William K(irkwood), Jr.
Costley, William K(irkwood), Jr. 1942- 81-84
Costonis, John J(oseph) 1937- CANR-4
Earlier sketch in CA 49-52
Cote, Richard G(eorge) 1934- 69-72
Cotes, Peter 1912- CANR-26
Earlier sketches in CA 7-8R, CANR-4
Cothem, Fayly H(ardcastle) 1926- 4R
Cothen, Joe H(erbert) 1926- 113
Cothran, J(oseph) Guy 1897- CAP-2
Earlier sketch in CA 29-32
Cothran, Jean 1910- 93-96
Cotich, Felicia 1926- 115
Cotler, Gordon 1923- 2R
Cotler, Sherwin B(arry) 1941- 65-68
Cotlow, Lewis N(athaniel) 1898-1987 65-68
Obituary 122
Cotner, Robert Crawford 1906- 37-40R
Cotner, Thomas E. 1916- 37-40R
Cott, Hugh B(amford) 1900-1987
Obituary 122
Cott, Jonathan 1942- 53-56
See also SATA 23
Cott, Nancy F. 1945- 81-84
Cottam, Clarence 1899-1974 97-100
See also SATA 25
Cottam, Keith M. 1941- 81-84
Cottam, Walter P(ace) 1894- CAP-1
Earlier sketch in CA 15-16
Cotten, Nell(ie) Wyllie 1908- 4R
Cotter, Charles H(enry) 1919- 13-14R
Cotter, Cornelius Philip 1924- CANR-1
Earlier sketch in CA 3R
Cotter, Edward F(rancis) 1917- CANR-6
Earlier sketch in CA 7-8R
Cotter, James Finn 1929- 33-36R
Cotter, Janet M(errill) 1914- 61-64
Cotter, Joseph S., Sr.
See Cotter, Joseph Seamon, Sr.
Cotter, Joseph Seamon, Jr. 1895-1919 .. DLB-50
Cotter, Joseph Seamon, Sr. 1861-1949 124
See also BW
See also DLB 50
See also TCLC 28
Cotter, Richard V(ern) 1930- CANR-14
Earlier sketch in CA 41-44R
Cotterell, Geoffrey 1919- 7-8R
Cotterell, (Francis) Peter 1930- CANR-1
Earlier sketch in CA 49-52
Cotterill, Rodney M(ichael) J(ohn) 1933- 118
Cottle, Charles
See Anderson, Robert C(harles)
Cottle, Thomas J. 1937- CANR-17
Earlier sketch in CA 33-36R
Cottle, William C(ullen) 1913- 41-44R
Cottler, Joseph 1899- CAP-2
Earlier sketch in CA 25-28
See also SATA 22
Cotton, (Thomas) Henry 1907-1987
Obituary 124
Cotton, John 1584-1652 .... DLB-24
Cotton, John 1925- CANR-11
Earlier sketch in CA 65-68
Cotton, John W(healdon) 1925- 33-36R
Cotton, Norris 1900- 103
Cottrell, Alan (Howard) 1919- CANR-10
Earlier sketch in CA 65-68
Cottrell, Alan P. 1935-1984 120
Cottrell, Alvin J. 1925(?)-1984 Obituary 112
Cottrell, (William) Fred(erick) 1903- 3R
Cottrell, Jack (Warren) 1938- CANR-23
Earlier sketch in CA 107
Cottrell, Leonard 1913-1974 .... CANR-4
Earlier sketch in CA 5-6R
See also SATA 24
Cottrell, Leonard S(later), Jr. 1899-1985 107
Obituary 115
Cottrell, Robert D(uane) 1930- 53-56
Couch, Arthur Thomas Quiller
See Quiller-Couch, Arthur Thomas
Couch, Helen F(ox) 1907- CAP-2
Earlier sketch in CA 17-18
Couch, Osma Palmer
See Tod, Osma Gallinger
Coudenhove-Kalergi, Richard N(icolas)
1894-1972 Obituary 37-40R
Coudert, Allison P(ierce) 1941- 110
Coudert, Jo 1923- 17-18R
Couffer, Jack 1924- CANR-1
Earlier sketch in CA 3R
Couger, J(ames) Daniel 1929- CANR-8
Earlier sketch in CA 53-56
Coughlan, John W. 1927- 21-22R
Coughlan, Margaret N(ourse) 1925- 107
Coughlan, (John) Robert 1914- 65-68
Coughlan, William C(arlisle), Jr. 1946- 115
Coughlin, Bernard J. 1922- 15-16R
Coughlin, Charles E(dward) 1891-1979
Obituary 97-100
Coughlin, George G(ordon) 1900- 107
Coughlin, Joseph Welter 1919- 4R
Coughlin, Violet L(ouise) 73-76
Coughran, Larry C. 1925- 21-22R
Coughtry, Jay 1945- 111
Couldery, Fred(erick) A(lan) J(ames)
1928- 11-12R
Coulet du Gard, Rene 1919- CANR-4
Earlier sketch in CA 53-56
Coulette, Henri Anthony 1927-1988 .... CANR-14
Obituary 125
Earlier sketch in CA 65-68
Coulling, Sidney Baxter 1924- 102
Couloumbis, Theodore A. 1935- CANR-7
Earlier sketch in CA 17-18R
Coulson, C(harles) A(lfred) 1910-1974 .. CANR-4
Earlier sketch in CA 7-8R
Coulson, Felicity Carter 1906- 11-12R
Coulson, John H(ubert) A(rthur) 1906- 11-12R
Coulson, Juanita (Ruth) 1933- CANR-26
Earlier sketches in CA 25-28R, CANR-9
Coulson, N. J.
See Coulson, Noel J(ames)
Coulson, Noel J(ames) 1928-1986 124
Obituary 120
Coulson, Robert 1924- 49-52
Coulson, Robert S(tratton) 1928- CANR-24
Earlier sketches in CA 23-24R, CANR-9
Coulson, William D(onald) E(dward)
1942- 89-92
Coulter, E(llis) Merton 1890-1981 .... CANR-3
Obituary 104
Earlier sketch in CA 11-12R
Coulter, Edwin M(artin) 1937- 104
Coulter, John (William) 1888-1980 .... CANR-3
Earlier sketch in CA 7-8R
See also DLB 68
Coulter, N(orman) Arthur, Jr. 1920- 65-68
Coulter, Stephen 1914- Brief entry 109
Coulton, James
See Hansen, Joseph
Council, Norman Briggs 1936- 102
Cound, John J(ames) 1928- 37-40R
Counsell, John William 1905-1987 57-60
Obituary 121
Counselman, Mary Elizabeth 1911- 106
Counsilman, James E(dward) 1920- 126
Count, Earl W(endel) 1899- 37-40R
Counter, Kenneth (Norman Samuel)
1930- 25-28R
Countess of Romanones
See Quintanilla, Maria Aline Griffith y
Dexter, Condesa de
Countryman, The
See Whitlock, Ralph
Countryman, Vern 1917- 15-16R
Counts, Charles Richard 1934- 49-52
Counts, George S(ylvester) 1889-1974 .... 5-6R
Obituary 53-56
Couper, Heather 1949- 124
Couper, J(ohn) M(ill) 1914- 45-48
Couperus, Louis (Marie Anne) 1863-1923
Brief entry 115
See also TCLC 15
Coupey, Philippe 1937- 104
Coupling, J. J.
See Pierce, John Robinson
Courage, James Francis 1903-1963 77-80
Courant, Richard 1888-1972 Obituary 33-36R
Couratin, Arthur Hubert 1902-1988
Obituary 126
Courlander, Harold 1908- CANR-18
Earlier sketches in CA 11-12R, CANR-3
See also SATA 6
Cournos, John 1881-1966 .... CAP-2
Earlier sketch in CA 13-14
See also DLB 54
Couroucli, Jennifer 1922- 29-32R
Course, Alfred George 1895- 9-10R
Course, Edwin 1922- 77-80
Coursen, Herbert R(andolph), Jr.
1932- CANR-19
Earlier sketches in CA 53-56, CANR-4
Court, Harold
See Swycaffer, Jefferson P(utnam)
Court, Margaret Smith 1942- Brief entry 106
Court, Sharon
See Rowland, D(onald) S(ydney)
Court, W(illiam) H(enry) B(assano)
1905(?)-1971 Obituary 104
Court, Wesli 1940- CANR-11
Earlier sketch in CA 69-72
Court, Wesli
See Turco, Lewis (Putnam)
Courtenay, Ashley (Reginald) 1888-1986
Obituary 121
Courtenay, William J(ames) 1935- 11-12R
Courter, Gay 1944- CANR-26
Earlier sketches in CA 57-60, CANR-7
Courthion, Pierre (Barthelemy) 1902- .. CANR-14
Earlier sketch in CA 81-84
Courtice, Katie 1942- 121
Courtier, S(idney) H(obson) 1904-197(?) . CAP-2
Earlier sketch in CA 25-28
Courtine, Robert 1910- CANR-14
Earlier sketch in CA 81-84
Courtis, Stuart Appleton 1874-1969
Obituary 105
See also SATA 29
Courtland, Roberta
See Dern, Erolie Pearl Gaddis
Courtneidge, Cicely 1893-1980 Obituary 105
Courtney, Dayle
See Goldsmith, Howard
Courtney, Gwendoline CAP-1
Earlier sketch in CA 9-10
Courtney, John
See Judd, Frederick Charles
Courtney, Nicholas (Piers) 1944- 113
Courtney, Ragan 1941- 97-100
Courtney, (John) Richard 1927- CANR-23
Earlier sketch in CA 105
Courtney, Robert
See Ellison, Harlan
and Robinson, Frank M(alcolm)
Courtney, William J(ohn) 1921- 102
Courtney, Winifred F(isk) 1918- 109
Courtwright, David T(odd) 1952- 110
Courville, Donovan A(mos) 1901- 45-48
Coury, Louise Andree 1895(?)-1983
Obituary 109
See also SATA 34
Couse, Harold C. 1925- 17-18R
Cousens, Frances Reissman 1913-1985
Obituary 115
Couser, G(riffith) Thomas 1946- 89-92
Cousins, Albert Newton 1919- 41-44R
Cousins, Geoffrey (Esmond) 1900- 25-28R
Cousins, Margaret 1905- CANR-1
Earlier sketch in CA 4R
See also SATA 2
Cousins, Norman 1915- CANR-13
Earlier sketch in CA 17-18R
Cousins, Peter Edward 1928- 104
Cousse, Raymond 1942- 101
Cousteau, Jacques-Yves 1910- CANR-15
Earlier sketch in CA 65-68
See also SATA 38
See also CLC 30
Cousteau, Philippe Pierre 1940-1979 .... 33-36R
Obituary 89-92
Coustillas, Pierre 1930- 73-76
Coutard, Wanda Lundy Hale 1902(?)-1982
Obituary 106
Coutinho, Joaquim 1886(?)-1978
Obituary 77-80
Couto, Richard A. 1941- CANR-15
Earlier sketch in CA 89-92
Coutts, Frederick Lee 1899- 109
Couture, Andrea 1943- 85-88
Couturier, Louis (Joseph) 1910- 101
Couzyn, Jeni 1942- 85-88
Covarrubias, Barbara Faith 1932- 113
Covatta, Anthony Gallo 1944- 53-56
Covell, Alan C(arter) 1952- 118
Covell, Jon Carter 1910- CANR-17
Earlier sketch in CA 97-100
Coven, Brenda 110
Coveney, James 1920- 41-44R
Coventry, Francis 1725-1754 .... DLB-39
Coventry, John 1915- 93-96
Cover, Arthur Byron 1950- 107
Cover, Robert M. 1943-1986 57-60
Obituary 119
Coverdale, John F(oy) 1940- 73-76
Coverley, Louise Bennett
See Bennett-Coverley, Louise
Covert, James Thayne 1932- 37-40R
Covert, Paul 1941- CANR-20
Earlier sketch in CA 103
Covey, Cyclone 1922- 21-22R
Covey, Stephen R. 1932- CANR-12
Earlier sketch in CA 33-36R
Covici, Pascal, Jr. 1930- 2R
Coville, Bruce 1950- CANR-22
Earlier sketch in CA 97-100
See also SATA 32
Coville, Walter J(oseph) 1914- CANR-5
Earlier sketch in CA 7-8R
Covin, Theron Michael 1947- 57-60
Covina, Gina 1952- 101
Covington, James W. 1917- 33-36R
Covington, Martin Vaden 1936- 37-40R
Covino, Frank 1931- 57-60
Covino, Joseph, Jr. 1954- 113
Covvey, H(arry) Dominic J(oseph) 1944- ... 110
Cowan, Alan
See Gilchrist, Alan W.
Cowan, Charles Donald 1923- 102
Cowan, Edward James 1944- 103
Cowan, G(ordon) 1933- 25-28R
Cowan, G(eorge) H(amilton) 1917- 17-18R
Cowan, Geoffrey 1942- 97-100
Cowan, George McKillop 1916- 102
Cowan, Gregory M(ac) 1935-1979 .... CANR-9
Earlier sketch in CA 65-68
Cowan, Henry J(acob) 1919- CANR-19
Earlier sketches in CA 53-56, CANR-4
Cowan, Ian Borthwick 1932- CANR-24
Earlier sketches in CA 61-64, CANR-8
Cowan, J(oseph) L(loyd) 1929- 25-28R
Cowan, James C(ostello) 1927- 29-32R
Cowan, Janice 1941- 97-100
Cowan, Louise (Shillingburg) 1916- 3R
Cowan, Lyn 1942- 116
Cowan, Michael H(eath) 1937- 23-24R
Cowan, Paul 1940-1988 Obituary 126
Cowan, Peter (Walkinshaw) 1914- CANR-25
Earlier sketches in CA 21-22R, CANR-9
Cowan, Richard O(lsen) 1934- 53-56
Cowan, Robert Granniss 1895- CAP-1
Earlier sketch in CA 11-12
Cowan, Ruth Schwartz 1941- 115
Cowan, Stuart DuBois 1917- 104
Cowan, Walter G(reaves) 1912- 120
Cowan, Wood (Messick) 1896-1977 69-72
Coward, Noel (Pierce) 1899-1973 .... CAP-2
Obituary 41-44R
Earlier sketch in CA 17-18
See also DLB 10
See also CLC 1, 9, 29
See also AITN 1
Cowart, David (Guyland) 1947- 104
Cowasjee, Saros 1931- CANR-20
Earlier sketches in CA 11-12R, CANR-5
Cowden, Dudley J(ohnstone) 1899- 41-44R
Cowden, Jeanne 1918- 85-88
Cowden, Joanna Dunlap 1933- 53-56
Cowdrey, A(lbert) E(dward) 1933- 17-18R
Cowdrey, (Michael) Colin 1932- 105
Cowell, (John) Adrian 1934- 103
Cowell, Cyril 1888- CAP-2
Earlier sketch in CA 21-22

Cowell, Frank Richard 1897- CANR-8
Earlier sketch in CA 53-56
Cowell, Henry Dixon 1897-1965 Obituary ... 116
Cowen, David L(aurence) 1909- 15-16R
Cowen, Emory L(eland) 1926- 69-72
Cowen, Eve
See Werner, Herma
Cowen, Frances
See Munthe, Frances
Cowen, Ida 1898- 45-48
Cowen, Robert Churchill 1927- 13-14R
Cowen, Ron(ald) 1944- 85-88
Cowen, Roy C(hadwell) 1930- CANR-12
Earlier sketch in CA 33-36R
Cowen, Zelman 1919- CANR-1
Earlier sketch in CA 1R
Cowgill, Donald O(len) 1911- 37-40R
Cowherd, Raymond Gibson 1909- 124
Cowie, Alexander 1896- 33-36R
Cowie, Donald 1911- 116
Cowie, Evelyn E(lizabeth) 1924- CANR-9
Earlier sketch in CA 13-14R
Cowie, Hamilton Russell 1931- 102
Cowie, Leonard W(allace) 1919- CANR-9
Earlier sketch in CA 13-14R
See also SATA 4
Cowie, Mervyn (Hugh) 1909- CAP-1
Earlier sketch in CA 9-10
Cowie, Peter 1939- CANR-18
Earlier sketches in CA 49-52, CANR-1
Cowle, Jerome Milton 1917- 93-96
Cowle, Jerry
See Cowle, Jerome Milton
Cowler, Rosemary (Elizabeth) 1925- 25-28R
Cowles, Fleur CANR-24
Earlier sketches in CA 11-12R, CANR-4
See also AITN 1
Cowles, Frank, Jr. 1918- 57-60
Cowles, Gardner 1861-1946 .... DLB-29
Cowles, Gardner A., Jr. 1903-1985
Obituary 116
Cowles, Ginny 1924- 57-60
Cowles, John, Sr. 1898-1983 Obituary 109
Cowles, Kathleen
See Krull, Kathleen
Cowles, Lois Thornburg 1909-1980
Obituary 101
Cowles, Mike
See Cowles, Gardner A., Jr.
Cowles, Raymond B(ridgeman) 1896-1975
Obituary 61-64
Cowles, S(amuel) Macon, Jr. 1916- 23-24R
Cowles, Virginia (Spencer) 1912-1983 ... CANR-12
Obituary 110
Earlier sketch in CA 65-68
Cowley, Joseph (Gilbert) 1923- 106
Cowley, (Cassia) Joy 1936- CANR-11
Earlier sketch in CA 25-28R
See also SATA 4
Cowley, Malcolm 1898- CANR-3
Earlier sketch in CA 5-6R
See also DLB 4, 48
See also DLBY 81
See also CLC 39
Cowlin, Dorothy
See Whalley, Dorothy
Cowling, Elizabeth 1910- Brief entry 110
Cowling, Ellis 1905- CAP-1
Earlier sketch in CA 15-16
Cowling, Maurice John 1926- CANR-3
Earlier sketch in CA 7-8R
Cowlishaw, Ranson 1894- 7-8R
Cowper, Richard
See Middleton-Murry, John (Jr.)
Cox, A(nthony) B(erkeley) 1893-1970 97-100
Cox, Albert W(esley) 1921- 53-56
Cox, Allan 1937- 93-96
Cox, Alva Irwin, Jr. 1925- 19-20R
Cox, Archibald 1912- 73-76
Cox, (Christopher) Barry 1931- 103
Cox, Bertha Mae (Hill) 1901- 19-20R
Cox, Bill 1910- 9-10R
Cox, C. Benjamin 1925- 97-100
Cox, Carol 1946- 117
Cox, Charles B(rian) 1928- 25-28R
Cox, Claire 1919- CANR-2
Earlier sketch in CA 5-6R
Cox, Constance 1915- CANR-24
Earlier sketches in CA 21-22R, CANR-9
Cox, David (Dundas) 1933- 119
Cox, Donald William 1921- CANR-4
Earlier sketch in CA 4R
See also SATA 23
Cox, Edith Muriel 102
Cox, Edward Finch 1946- 29-32R
Cox, Edward Franklin 1925- 33-36R
Cox, Edward Locksley 1943- 121
Cox, Edwin B(urk) 1930- 37-40R
Cox, Erle (Harold) 1873-1950 Brief entry ... 112
Cox, Eugene L. 1931- 21-22R
Cox, Frank D. 1933- 29-32R
Cox, Fred(erick) M(oreland) 1928- CANR-1
Earlier sketch in CA 45-48
Cox, G. William 1949(?)-1988 Obituary 125
Cox, Gary D(uane) 1947- 113
Cox, Geoffrey Sandford 1910- 103
Cox, George W(yatt) 1935- 115
Cox, Harvey (Gallagher, Jr.) 1929- 77-80
See also AITN 1
Cox, (William) Harvey 1939- 45-48
Cox, Hebe 1909- CAP-1
Earlier sketch in CA 13-14
Cox, Hugh Brandon
See Brandon-Cox, Hugh
Cox, Hugh S(towell) 1874-1969 .... CAP-2
Earlier sketch in CA 21-22
Cox, J(ohn) Gray 1952- 123
Cox, J. Halley 1910-1974 Obituary 112
Cox, Jack
See Cox, John Roberts
Cox, James Anthony 1926- 104
Cox, James M(elville) 1925- 13-14R
Cox, James Middleton, Jr. 1903-1974
Obituary 89-92
Cox, James W(illiam) 1923- 33-36R
Cox, Jeri
See Kimes, Beverly Rae
Cox, Joan (Irene) 1942- 101
Cox, John H(enry) 1907-1975 Obituary 115
Cox, John Roberts 1915-1981 .... CANR-14
Earlier sketch in CA 29-32R
See also SATA 9
Cox, John Stuart 1931- 117
Cox, Joseph A. 1896(?)-1980 Obituary ...97-100
Cox, Joseph Mason Andrew 1930- CANR-2
Earlier sketch in CA 49-52
See also BW
Cox, Joseph W(illiam) 1937- 81-84
Cox, Keith (Kohn) 1931- CANR-12
Earlier sketch in CA 69-72
Cox, Kevin R. 1939- 37-40R
Cox, LaWanda Fenlason 1909- 9-10R
Cox, Lee Sheridan 1916- 25-28R
Cox, Marie-Therese Henriette 1925- 105
Cox, Marion Monroe 1898-1983 Obituary ... 110
Cox, Martha Heasley 1919- 15-16R
Cox, Mary Elizabeth
See Headapohl, Betty R.
Cox, Maxwell E. 1922- 25-28R
Cox, Miriam Stewart 11-12R
Cox, Molly
See Cox, Marie-Therese Henriette
Cox, Oliver Cromwell 1901-1974 .... 3R
Obituary 103
Cox, P(atrick) Brian 45-48
Cox, Palmer 1840-1924 Brief entry 111
See also SATA 24
See also DLB 42
Cox, R(obert) David 1937- CANR-13
Earlier sketch in CA 29-32R
Cox, R(alph) Merritt 1939- 33-36R
Cox, Rachel Dunaway 1904- 33-36R
Cox, Reavis 1900- CAP-1
Earlier sketch in CA 15-16
Cox, Richard 1931- CANR-11
Earlier sketch in CA 21-22R
Cox, Richard Howard 1925- CANR-8
Earlier sketch in CA 13-14R
Cox, Thomas R(ichard) 1933- 53-56
Cox, Victoria
See Garretson, Victoria Diane
Cox, Wallace (Maynard) 1924-1973 97-100
Obituary 41-44R
Cox, Wally
See Cox, Wallace (Maynard)
See also SATA 25
Cox, Warren E(arle) 1895-1977 .... CAP-2
Obituary 69-72
Earlier sketch in CA 33-36
Cox, William E(dwin), Jr. 1930- 106
Cox, William R(obert) 1901-1988 ..... CANR-24
Obituary 126
Earlier sketches in CA 11-12R, CANR-6
See also SATA 31, 46
Cox, William Trevor 1928- CANR-4
Earlier sketch in CA 11-12R
See also CLC 9, 14
Coxe, Antony D(acres) Hippisley
See Hippisley Coxe, Antony D(acres)
Coxe, George Harmon 1901- 57-60
Coxe, Louis (Osborne) 1918- 13-14R
See also DLB 5
Coxe, Tench 1755-1824 .... DLB-37
Cox-George, Noah Arthur William
1915- CANR-6
Earlier sketch in CA 13-14R
Coxhead, Elizabeth 1909(?)-1979
Obituary 89-92
Cox-Johnson, Ann
See Saunders, Ann Loreille
Coy, Harold 1902- CANR-4
Earlier sketch in CA 7-8R
See also SATA 3
Coyle, David Cushman 1887-1969 ..... CANR-15
Obituary 103
Earlier sketch in CA 1R
Coyle, L(eslie) Patrick 1934- 110
Coyle, Lee
See Coyle, Leo (Perry)
Coyle, Leo (Perry) 1925- 41-44R
Coyle, William 1917- CANR-2
Earlier sketch in CA 4R
Coyne, John (P.) 1940- CANR-12
Earlier sketch in CA 93-96
Coyne, John R(ichard), Jr. 1935- 37-40R
Coyne, Joseph E. 1918- 13-14R
Coysh, A(rthur) W(ilfred) 1905- CANR-13
Earlier sketch in CA 73-76
Coysh, Victor 1906- CANR-8
Earlier sketch in CA 61-64
Coze, Paul 1903(?)-1974 Obituary 53-56
Cozzens, James Gould 1903-1978 ..... CANR-19
Obituary 81-84
Earlier sketch in CA 11-12R
See also DLB 9
See also DLBY 84
See also DLBD 2
See also CDALB 1941-1968
See also CLC 1, 4, 11
Crabb, Alfred Leland 1884- CAP-1
Earlier sketch in CA 13-14
Crabb, Cecil V., Jr. 1924- 13-14R
Crabb, E(dmund) W(illiam) 1912- CAP-1
Earlier sketch in CA 11-12
Crabb, Lawrence J(ames), Jr. 1944- ... CANR-14
Earlier sketch in CA 65-68
Crabb, Richard 1914- 23-24R
Crabbe, Buster
See Crabbe, Clarence Linden
Crabbe, Clarence Linden 1908-1983 ... CANR-11
Obituary 109
Earlier sketch in CA 69-72
Crabtree, Arthur B(amford) 1910- CAP-2
Earlier sketch in CA 17-18
Crabtree, Judith 1928- 118
Crabtree, T(homas) T(avron) 1924- 23-24R
Crackel, Theodore J(oseph) 1938- 33-36R
Crackers, Fritz
See Frank, Philip Norman
Cracknell, Basil Edward 1925- 103
Cracraft, James (Edward) 1939- 53-56
Cracroft, Richard Holton 1936- 53-56
Craddock, Charles Egbert
See Murfree, Mary Noailles
Craddock, Patricia (Bland) 1938- CANR-4
Earlier sketch in CA 53-56
Craddock, William J(ames) 1946- 85-88
Cradock, Thomas 1718-1770 .... DLB-31
Craft, Maurice 1932- CANR-11
Earlier sketch in CA 65-68
Craft, Michael 1928- 25-28R
Craft, Robert 1923- CANR-7
Earlier sketch in CA 11-12R
Craft, Ruth Brief entry 110
See also SATA 31
Crafts, Glenn Alty 1918- 11-12R
Crafts, Kathy 1952- 109
Crafts, Roger Conant 1911- 106
Cragg, D. J.
See Cragg, Dan
Cragg, Dan 1939- 115
Cragg, Gerald R(obertson) 1906- 61-64
Cragg, (Albert) Kenneth 1913- CANR-22
Earlier sketches in CA 17-18R, CANR-7
Craghan, John Francis 1936- 53-56
Crago, Hugh 1946- 116
Crago, Maureen 1939- 116
Crago, T(homas) Howard 1907- CAP-1
Earlier sketch in CA 15-16
Crahan, Margaret E(llen) 1939- 114
Craib, Ian 1945- 69-72
Craig, A. A.
See Anderson, Poul (William)
Craig, Albert M(orton) 1927- 37-40R
Craig, Alec
See Craig, Alexander George
Craig, Alexander George 1897- CAP-1
Earlier sketch in CA 9-10
Craig, Alisa
See MacLeod, Charlotte (Matilda Hughes)
Craig, Archibald Campbell 1888-1985
Obituary 117
Craig, Barbara M(ary St. George) 1914- ..37-40R
Craig, Bill 1930- 33-36R
Craig, Charlotte M(arie) 1929- 73-76
Craig, Christine (Angela) 1943- 120
Craig, Daniel H. 1811-1895 .... DLB-43
Craig, David 1932- CANR-14
Earlier sketch in CA 41-44R
Craig, David
See Tucker, James
Craig, Denys
See Stoll, Dennis G(ray)
Craig, Don(ald) Laurence 1946- 73-76
Craig, E(velyn) Quita 1917- 103
Craig, Edward Anthony 1905- 15-16R
Craig, Edward (Henry) Gordon 1872-1966
Obituary 25-28R
Craig, Eleanor 1929- 93-96
Craig, Elizabeth (Josephine)
1883-1980 .... CANR-11
Obituary 101
Earlier sketch in CA 11-12R
Craig, Georgia
See Dern, Erolie Pearl Gaddis
Craig, Gerald M(arquis) 1916- 9-10R
Craig, Gordon A(lexander) 1913- CANR-17
Earlier sketch in CA 25-28R
Craig, H(enry) A(rmitage) L(lewellyn)
1921-1978 85-88
Obituary 81-84
Craig, Hazel Thompson 1904- 2R
Craig, Helen 1934- 117
See also SATA 46, 49
Craig, James 1930- 73-76
Craig, Jasmine
See Cresswell, Jasmine (Rosemary)
Craig, Jean T. 1936- 7-8R
Craig, John David 1903- CAP-2
Earlier sketch in CA 17-18
Craig, John Eland
See Chipperfield, Joseph Eugene
Craig, John Ernest 1921- 101
See also SATA 23
Craig, John H(erbert) 1885- CAP-1
Earlier sketch in CA 9-10
Craig, Jonathan
See Smith, Frank E.
Craig, Larry
See Coughran, Larry C.
Craig, Lee
See Sands, Leo G(eorge)
Craig, M. F.
See Craig, Mary (Francis) S(hura)
Craig, M. Jean 73-76
See also SATA 17
Craig, M. S.
See Craig, Mary (Francis) S(hura)
Craig, Margaret (Maze) 1911-1964 .... 3R
See also SATA 9
Craig, Mary
See Craig, Mary (Francis) S(hura)
Craig, Mary (Francis) S(hura) 1923- ... CANR-26
Earlier sketches in CA 3R, CANR-4
See also SATA 6
Craig, Mary Shura
See Craig, Mary (Francis) S(hura)
Craig, (Elizabeth) May 1889(?)-1975 101
Obituary 89-92
Craig, Nancy
See Maslin, Alice
Craig, Pamela Tudor
See Tudor-Craig, Pamela
Craig, Peggy
See Kreig, Margaret B. (Baltzell)
Craig, Philip R. 1933- 25-28R
Craig, Raymond C. 1928- 124
Craig, Richard B(lythe) 1935- 53-56
Craig, Robert B(ruce) 1944- 49-52
Craig, Robert C(harles) 1921- 17-18R
Craig, Robert D(ean) 1934- CANR-14
Earlier sketch in CA 81-84
Craig, Vera
See Rowland, D(onald) S(ydney)
Craig, Webster
See Russell, Eric Frank
Craig, William Lane 1949- 116
Craige, Betty Jean 1946- 117
Craighead, Frank C(ooper), Jr. 1916- 97-100
Craighead, W(ade) Edward 1942-
Brief entry 118
Craigie, E(dward) Horne 1894- CAP-2
Earlier sketch in CA 25-28
Craik, Arthur
See Craig, Alexander George
Craik, Dinah Maria (Mulock)
1826-1887 .... SATA-34
See also DLB 35
Craik, Kenneth H(enry) 1936- CANR-1
Earlier sketch in CA 45-48
Craik, Thomas Wallace 1927- 106
Craik, W(endy) A(nn) 1934- 25-28R
Craille, Wesley
See Rowland, D(onald) S(ydney)
Crain, Jeff
See Meneses, Enrique
Crain, John 1926(?)-1979 Obituary 89-92
Crain, Robert L(ee) 1934- CANR-13
Earlier sketch in CA 21-22R
Crain, Sharie 1942- 77-80
Craine, Eugene R(ichard) 1917-1977 .....33-36R
Craker, Lyle E(ugene) 1941- 116
Cram, Mildred 1889- 49-52
Cramer, Clarence H(enley) 1905-1982 ... CANR-9
Earlier sketch in CA 13-14R
Cramer, George H. 1913- 23-24R
Cramer, Harold 1927- 29-32R
Cramer, J(an) S(olomon) 1928- 29-32R
Cramer, James 1915- 23-24R
Cramer, John Francis 1899-1967 .... CAP-1
Earlier sketch in CA 17-18
Cramer, Kathryn 1943- 25-28R
Cramer, Richard L(ouis) 1947- 102
Cramer, Richard S(eldon) 1928- 29-32R
Cramer, Stanley H. 1933- 29-32R
Cramp, Rosemary (Jean) 1929- 121
Crampton, C(harles) Gregory 1911- 21-22R
Crampton, Georgia Ronan 1925- 57-60
Crampton, Helen
See Chesney, Marion
Crampton, Roger C. 1929- 33-36R
Cranbrook, James L.
See Edwards, William B(ennett)
Cranch, Christopher Pearse
1813-1892 .... DLB-1, 42
Crandall, James E(dward) 1930- 41-44R
Crandall, Joy
See Martin, Joy
Crandall, Norma 1907- 69-72
Crandall, Robert Warren 1940- 124
Crandell, Anne (Elizabeth) Shaver
See Shaver-Crandell, Anne Elizabeth
Crandell, Richard F. 1901-1974 Obituary ..53-56
Crane, Alex
See Wilkes-Hunter, R(ichard)
Crane, Barbara (Joyce) 1934- 107
See also SATA 31
Crane, Bill
See Crane, William B.
Crane, Caroline 1930- CANR-19
Earlier sketches in CA 11-12R, CANR-3
See also SATA 11
Crane, Catherine C(owle) 1940- 101
Crane, Diana 1933- 89-92
Crane, Donald P(aul) 1933- 61-64
Crane, (Lauren) Edgar 1917- 17-18R
Crane, Edna Temple
See Eicher, (Ethel) Elizabeth
Crane, Elaine Forman 1939- 122
Crane, Frank H. 1912- 89-92
Crane, (Harold) Hart 1899-1932
Brief entry 104
See also DLB 4, 48
See also TCLC 2, 5
Crane, Hewitt D(avid) 1927- 116
Crane, Jacob L(eslie) 1892-1988 Obituary .. 125
Crane, James G(ordon) 1927- 15-16R
Crane, Jim
See Crane, James G(ordon)
Crane, Joan St. C(lair) 1927- 73-76
Crane, Julia G(orham) 1925- 41-44R
Crane, M. A.
See Wartski, Maureen (Ann Crane)
Crane, Milton 1917-1985 Obituary 117
Crane, Morley Benjamin 1890-1983
Obituary 110
Crane, Philip Miller 1930- 11-12R

Crane, R(onald) S(almon) 1886-1967 85-88
See also DLB 63
See also CLC 27
Crane, Richard (Arthur) 1944- 77-80
Crane, Robert
See Robertson, Frank C(hester)
and Sellers, Con(nie Leslie, Jr.)
Crane, Robert Dickson 1929- 81-84
Crane, Royston Campbell 1901-1977
Obituary 89-92
See also SATA 22
Crane, Stephen (Townley) 1871-1900
Brief entry 109
See also YABC 2
See also DLB 12, 54
See also CDALB 1865-1917
See also TCLC 11, 17
Crane, Sylvia E(ngel) 1918- 33-36R
Crane, Theodore Rawson 1929- 97-100
Crane, Verner W(inslow) 1889-1974
Obituary 113
Crane, Walter 1845-1915 ..... SATA-18
Crane, Wilder (Willard) 1928- 45-48
Crane, William B. 1904-1981 107
Crane, William D(wight) 1892- 5-6R
See also SATA 1
Crane, William Earl 1899- 103
Cranfield, Charles E(rnest) B(urland)
1915- CANR-18
Earlier sketches in CA 7-8R, CANR-2
Cranfield, Geoffrey Alan 1920- 7-8R
Cranford, Clarence William 1906- 2R
Cranford, Robert J(oshua) 1908- CAP-2
Earlier sketch in CA 17-18
Cranin, A(braham) Norman 1927- 73-76
Cranko, John 1927-1973 Obituary 45-48
Crankshaw, Edward 1909-1984 ..... CANR-23
Obituary 114
Earlier sketch in CA 25-28R
Cranny, Titus (Francis) 1921-1981 ..... 25-28R
Cranor, Phoebe 1923- 112
Cranston, Edward
See Fairchild, William
Cranston, Maurice (William) 1920- CANR-3
Earlier sketch in CA 5-6R
Cranston, Mechthild 53-56
Cranton, Elmer M(itchell) 1932- 118
Cranwell, John Philips 1904- 61-64
Crapanzano, Vincent 1939- CANR-5
Earlier sketch in CA 53-56
Crapol, Edward P(aul) 1936- 45-48
Crapps, Robert W. 1925- 53-56
Crapsey, Adelaide 1878-1914 ..... DLB-54
Crary, Catherine S. 1909- CAP-1
Earlier sketch in CA 15-16
Crary, Elizabeth (Ann) 1942- SATA-43
Crary, Margaret (Coleman) 1906- 7-8R
See also SATA 9
Crary, Ryland W(esley) 1913-1984
Obituary 113
Crase, Douglas 1944- 106
Crassweller, Robert D. 1915- 21-22R
Craster, John Montagu 1901-1975
Obituary 108
Crathern, Alice Tarbell 1894-1973
Obituary 110
Craton, Michael (John) 1931- 41-44R
Cratty, Bryant J. 1929- CANR-11
Earlier sketch in CA 25-28R
Craven, Avery (Odelle) 1885(?)-1980
Obituary 113
See also DLB 17
Craven, George M(ilton) 1929- 61-64
Craven, Margaret 1901-1980 103
See also CLC 17
Craven, Roy C., Jr. 1924- 69-72
Craven, Thomas 1889-1969 97-100
See also SATA 22
Craven, Wesley Frank (Jr.) 1905-1981 61-64
Obituary 103
Cravens, Gwyneth 85-88
Cravens, Hamilton 1938- 103
Craveri, Marcello 1914- 21-22R
Crawells, Carl
See Herm, Gerhard
Crawford, Alan 1953- 101
Crawford, Ann Fears 1932- CANR-9
Earlier sketch in CA 21-22R
Crawford, Bill
See Crawford, William Hulfish
Crawford, C(harles) Merle 1924- 45-48
Crawford, Char 1935- 57-60
Crawford, Charles 1752-1815(?) DLB-31
Crawford, Charles F. ?-1983 Obituary 109
Crawford, Charles O(len) 1934- 37-40R
Crawford, Charles P. 1945- CANR-24
Earlier sketch in CA 45-48
See also SATA 28
Crawford, Charles W(ann) 1931- CANR-8
Earlier sketch in CA 61-64
Crawford, Cheryl 1902-1986 Obituary 120
Brief entry 112
Crawford, Christina 1939- 85-88
Crawford, Clan, Jr. 1927- 57-60
Crawford, David L. 1890(?)-1974
Obituary 45-48
Crawford, Deborah 1922- 49-52
See also SATA 6
Crawford, Donald W(esley) 1938- 45-48
Crawford, F(rancis) Marion 1854-1909
Brief entry 107
See also DLB 71
See also TCLC 10
Crawford, Fred D. 1947- 117
Crawford, Fred Roberts 1924- CANR-2
Earlier sketch in CA 45-48
Crawford, Iain (Padruig) 1922- CANR-23
Earlier sketch in CA 3R
Crawford, James M. 1925- 89-92
Crawford, Jean 1907(?)-1976 Obituary 104
Crawford, Jerry L(eroy) 1934- 106
Crawford, Joan
See Le Sueur, Lucille
Crawford, Joanna 1941- 11-12R
Crawford, John E(dmund) 1904-1971 ..... CAP-2
Earlier sketch in CA 17-18
See also SATA 3
Crawford, John R. 1915(?)-1976
Obituary 65-68
Crawford, John Richard 1932- 106
Crawford, John S(herman) 1928- 106
Crawford, John W(illiam) 1914- 3R
Crawford, John W(illiam) 1936- CANR-4
Earlier sketch in CA 53-56
Crawford, Joyce 1931- 25-28R
Crawford, Kenneth G(ale) 1902-1983 81-84
Obituary 108
Crawford, Linda 1938- CANR-23
Earlier sketch in CA 65-68
Crawford, Marion (Kirk) 1910(?)-1988
Obituary 124
Crawford, Matsu W(offord) 1902- CAP-2
Earlier sketch in CA 17-18
Crawford, Max 1938- 77-80
Crawford, Mel 1925- SATA-33, 44
Crawford, Oliver 1917- 85-88
Crawford, Patricia 103
Crawford, Phyllis 1899- SATA-3
Crawford, Richard (Arthur) 1935- CANR-9
Earlier sketch in CA 57-60
Crawford, Robert
See Rae, Hugh C(rauford)
Crawford, Robert Platt 1893- CAP-2
Earlier sketch in CA 17-18
Crawford, Stanley (Gottlieb) 1937- 69-72
Crawford, T(erence Gordon) S(harman)
1945- 29-32R
Crawford, Tad 1946- Brief entry 114
Crawford, Thelmar Wyche 1905- 4R
Crawford, Theresa 1956- 110
Crawford, Vaughn Emerson 1917(?)-1981
Obituary 104
Crawford, Walter B(yron) 1919- 116
Crawford, William (Elbert) 1929- CANR-4
Earlier sketch in CA 3R
Crawford, William H. 1907(?)-1973
Obituary 104
Crawford, William Hulfish 1913-1982
Obituary 105
Crawford, William P(atrick) 1922- 106
Crawley, Aidan Merivale 1908- 61-64
Crawley, Alan 1887-1975 ..... DLB-68
Crawley, C(harles) W(illiam) 1899- 109
Crawley, Gerard M(arcus) 1938- 106
Crawley, Thomas Edward 1920- 111
Cray, Ed(ward) 1933- CANR-16
Earlier sketch in CA 81-84
Crayder, Dorothy 33-36R
See also SATA 7
Crayder, Teresa
See Colman, Hila
Crayon, Geoffrey
See Irving, Washington
Crayon, Porte
See Strother, David Hunter
Craz, Albert G. 1926- CANR-8
Earlier sketch in CA 17-18R
See also SATA 24
Creager, Alfred L(eon) 1910- 19-20R
Creagh, Patrick 1930- CANR-18
Earlier sketch in CA 25-28R
Creagh-Osborne, Richard 1928- CANR-7
Earlier sketch in CA 11-12R
Creamer, J. Shane 1929- Brief entry 116
Creamer, Robert W. 1922- 21-22R
Crean, John Edward, Jr. 1939- 41-44R
Crean, Patrick (G.) 1949- 123
Creasey, John 1908-1973 ..... CANR-8
Obituary 41-44R
Earlier sketch in CA 5-6R
See also CLC 11
Creasy, Robert K(enwood) 1934- 118
Creasy, Rosalind R. 110
Crechales, Anthony George 1926- 29-32R
Crechales, Tony
See Crechales, Anthony George
Crecine, John Patrick 1939- CANR-7
Earlier sketch in CA 57-60
Crecy, Jeanne
See Williams, Jeanne
Credland, Peter (Francis) 1946- 69-72
Credle, Ellis 1902- CANR-9
Earlier sketch in CA 15-16R
See also SATA 1
Credo
See Creasey, John
Creed, David
See Guthrie, James Shields
Creekmore, Betsey B(eeler) 1915- 69-72
Creekmore, Mildred C. 1905(?)-1987
Obituary 123
Creel, George 1876-1953 Brief entry 115
See also DLB 25
Creel, Herrlee G(lessner) 1905- 85-88
Creel, Stephen Melville 1938- 69-72
Creeley, Robert (White) 1926- CANR-23
Earlier sketch in CA 4R
See also DLB 5, 16
See also CLC 1, 2, 4, 8, 11, 15, 36
Creelman, James 1859-1915 ..... DLB-23
Creelman, Marjorie B(roer) 1908- CAP-2
Earlier sketch in CA 21-22
Creer, Thomas L(aselle) 1934- CANR-22
Earlier sketch in CA 69-72
Creese, Bethea CANR-5
Earlier sketch in CA 9-10R
Creese, Walter L(ittlefield) 1919- 125
Creeth, Edmund Homer 1928- 102
Creevey, Lucy E. 1940- 29-32R
Crefeld, Donna Carolyn Anders
See Anders, Donna Carolyn
Cregan, David (Appleton Quartus)
1931- CANR-1
Earlier sketch in CA 45-48
See also DLB 13
Creger, Ralph (Clinton) 1914- 15-16R
Cregier, Don M(esick) 1930- 69-72
Crehan, Stewart 1942- 118
Crehan, Thomas 1919- CANR-2
Earlier sketch in CA 7-8R
Creigh, Dorothy (Weyer) 1921- 105
Creighton, Don
See Drury, Maxine Cole
Creighton, Donald Grant 1902-1979 101
Obituary 93-96
Creighton, (Mary) Helen 1899- 41-44R
Creighton, Helen (Evelyn) 1914- 33-36R
Creighton, Joanne V(anish) 1942- 69-72
Creighton, Luella Bruce 1901- CAP-1
Earlier sketch in CA 17-18
Creighton, Thomas 1915(?)-1987
Obituary 123
Creighton, Thomas H(awk) 1904-1984 ..... CANR-6
Obituary 114
Earlier sketch in CA 7-8R
Crellin, John 1916- 69-72
Cremeans, Charles D(avis) 1915- 7-8R
Cremer, Jan 1940- 15-16R
Cremer, Robert Roger 1947- 61-64
Cremer, Robert Wyndham Ketton
See Ketton-Cremer, Robert Wyndham
Cremin, Lawrence A(rthur) 1925- 33-36R
Crena de Iongh, Mary (Dows Herter Norton)
1894(?)-1985 Obituary 116
Crena de Iongh, Daniel 1888-1970 ..... CAP-2
Obituary 29-32R
Earlier sketch in CA 25-28
Crennen, Robert Earl 1929-1984 Obituary 112
Crenner, James 1938- 13-14R
Crenshaw, James L. 1934- CANR-14
Earlier sketch in CA 37-40R
Crenshaw, Mary Ann CANR-8
Earlier sketch in CA 57-60
Crepeau, Richard C(harles) 1941- 105
Cressey, Donald R(ay) 1919-1987 ..... CANR-6
Obituary 123
Earlier sketch in CA 13-14R
Cressey, William W. 1939- 33-36R
Cresson, Bruce Collins 1930- 45-48
Cresswell, Helen 1934- CANR-8
Earlier sketch in CA 17-18R
See also SATA 1, 48
Cresswell, Jasmine (Rosemary) 1941- 110
Creston, Dormer
See Colston-Baynes, Dorothy
Creswell, K(eppel) A(rchibald) C(ameron)
1879- CAP-1
Earlier sketch in CA 9-10
Cretan, Gladys (Yessayan) 1921- 29-32R
See also SATA 2
Cretcher, Dorothy 1934- 112
Cretzmeyer, F(rancis) X(avier), Jr.
1913- 15-16R
Crevecoeur, Michel Guillaume Jean de
1735-1813 ..... DLB-37
Crew, Francis Albert Eley 1888-1973 ..... CAP-2
Earlier sketch in CA 17-18
Crew, Helen (Cecilia) Coale 1866-1941
Brief entry 121
See also YABC 2
Crew, Louie 1936- 81-84
Crewe, Jonathan V(ere) 1941- 116
Crews, Clyde F. 1944- 116
Crews, Donald 108
See also SATA 30, 32
See also CLR 7
Crews, Frederick C(ampbell) 1933- CANR-1
Earlier sketch in CA 3R
Crews, Harry (Eugene) 1935- CANR-20
Earlier sketch in CA 25-28R
See also DLB 6
See also CLC 6, 23, 49
See also AITN 1
Crews, Judson (Campbell) 1917- CANR-24
Earlier sketches in CA 15-16R, CANR-7
Crews, William J. 1931- 25-28R
Cribb, Larry 1934- 109
Cribbet, John E(dward) 1918- 19-20R
Cribbin, James J(oseph) 1915- 121
Crichton, James Dunlop 1907- CANR-5
Earlier sketch in CA 15-16R
Crichton, Jennifer 1957- 123
Crichton, John 1916- 19-20R
Crichton, Kyle Samuel 1896-1960
Obituary 89-92
Crichton, (John) Michael 1942- CANR-13
Earlier sketch in CA 25-28R
See also SATA 9
See also DLBY 81
See also CLC 2, 6
See also AITN 2
Crichton, Robert 1925- 17-18R
See also AITN 1
Crick, Bernard (Rowland) 1929- CANR-5
Earlier sketch in CA 1R
Crick, Donald Herbert 1916- 102
Crick, Francis (Harry Compton) 1916- 121
Brief entry 113
Crick, Michael (Lawrence) 1958- 118
Criddle, Joan D(ewey) 1935- 126
Criden, Joseph 1916- 77-80
Criden, Yosef
See Criden, Joseph
Crider, (Allen) Bill(y) 1941- 112
Cridland, Nancy C. 1932- 111
Crighton, John C(lark) 1903- 33-36R
Crighton, Richard E. 1921- 109
Crile, Barney
See Crile, George, Jr.
Crile, George, Jr. 1907- 89-92
Crim, Keith R(enn) 1924- 29-32R
Crim, Mort 1935- 41-44R
Crimmins, James Custis 1935- CANR-11
Earlier sketch in CA 5-6R
Crinkley, Richmond 1940- 29-32R
Cripe, Helen 1932- CANR-8
Earlier sketch in CA 61-64
Cripps, (Matthew) Anthony (Leonard)
1913- 13-14R
Cripps, L(ouise) L(ilian) 1914- 97-100
Cripps, Thomas (Robert) 1932- 97-100
Crisler, Fritz
See Crisler, Herbert Orin
Crisler, Herbert Orin 1899-1982 Obituary 107
Crisler, Lois (Brown) ?-1971 Obituary 104
Crisp, Anthony Thomas 1937- 101
Crisp, C(olin) G(odfrey) 1936- 37-40R
Crisp, Frank R(obson) 1915- 9-10R
Crisp, Norman James 1923- 93-96
Crisp, Quentin 1908- 116
Brief entry 109
Crisp, Robert (James) 1R
Crisp, Tony
See Crisp, Anthony Thomas
Crispin, A(nn) C(arol) 1950- 113
Crispin, Edmund
See Montgomery, (Robert) Bruce
See also CLC 22
Crispin, John 1936- 53-56
Crispin, Ruth Helen Katz 1940- 93-96
Crispo, John 1933- 37-40R
Crissey, Elwell 1899- CAP-2
Earlier sketch in CA 23-24
Crist, Judith (Klein) 1922- CANR-17
Earlier sketch in CA 81-84
See also AITN 1
Crist, Lyle M(artin) 1924- 53-56
Crist, Raymond E. 1904- 73-76
Crist, Steven G(ordon) 1956- 101
Cristabel
See Abrahamsen, Christine Elizabeth
Cristina, Frank
See Laughlin, Tom
Cristina, Teresa
See Laughlin, Tom
Cristofer, Michael 1945(?)- Brief entry 110
See also DLB 7
See also CLC 28
Cristol, Vivian 19-20R
Cristy, Ann
See Mittermeyer, Helen (Hayton
Monteith)
Cristy, R. J.
See De Cristoforo, R. J.
Criswell, Cloyd M. 1908- CAP-1
Earlier sketch in CA 17-18
Criswell, W(allie) A(mos) 1909- 19-20R
Critchfield, Howard J(ohn) 1920- 53-56
Critchfield, Richard (Patrick) 1931- CANR-16
Earlier sketch in CA 41-44R
Critchley, Edmund M(ichael) R(hys)
1931- 21-22R
Critchley, Julian (Michael Gordon) 1930- 85-88
Critchley, Lynne
See Radford, Richard F(rancis), Jr.
Critchley, T(homas) A(lan) 1919- 29-32R
Crites, Ronald W(ayne) 1945- CANR-18
Earlier sketch in CA 102
Crites, Stephen D(ecatur) 1931- 41-44R
Critic
See Martin, (Basil) Kingsley
Criticus
See Harcourt, Melville
and Roe, F(rederic) Gordon
Crittenden, Mabel (Buss) 1917- 103
Crnjanski, Milos 1893- CAP-1
Earlier sketch in CA 9-10
Crobaugh, Emma AITN-2
Croce, Arlene 1934- 104
Croce, Benedetto 1866-1952 Brief entry 120
Crocetti, Guido M. 1920-1979 85-88
Crocker, Helen Bartter 1929- 69-72
Crocker, Lester G(ilbert) 1912- CANR-5
Earlier sketch in CA 5-6R
Crocker, Lionel (George) 1897- CAP-2
Earlier sketch in CA 25-28
Crocker, Mary Wallace 1941- 93-96
Crocker, Thomas Dunstan 1936-
Brief entry 108
Crocker, Walter Russell 1902- 17-18R
Crockett, Albert Stevens 1873-1969
Obituary 89-92
Crockett, Christina
See Gray, Linda Crockett
Crockett, David 1786-1836 ..... DLB-3, 11
Crockett, G(eorge) Ronald 1906- CAP-1
Earlier sketch in CA 11-12
Crockett, H(arold) Dale 1933- 111
Crockett, James Underwood
1915-1979 ..... CANR-13
Obituary 89-92
Earlier sketch in CA 33-36R
Crockett, S(amuel) R(utherford)
1860-1914 Brief entry 116
Crocombe, Ronald G(ordon) 1929- 15-16R
Crofford, Emily (Ardell) 1927- 107

Crofford, Lena H(enrichson) 1908- CAP-1
Earlier sketch in CA 9-10
Croft, Julian (Charles Basset) 1941- 124
Croft, Michael (John) 1922-1986 Obituary .. 121
Croft, Peter John 1929-1984 122
Obituary 114
Croft, Sutton
See Lunn, Arnold
Croft-Cooke, Rupert 1903-1979 .... CANR-4
Obituary 89-92
Earlier sketch in CA 9-10R
Croft-Murray, Edward 1907-1980 Obituary .. 102
Crofton, Denis Hayes 1908- 109
Crofts, Freeman Wills 1879-1957
Brief entry 115
Crofts, John E(rnest) V(ictor) 1887-1972 . CAP-2
Earlier sketch in CA 25-28
Crofut, William E. III 1934- 25-28R
See also SATA 23
Crohn, Burrill B(ernard) 1884-1983
Obituary 110
Croise, Jacques
See Schakovskoy, Zinaida
Croizier, Ralph 1935- 61-64
Croll, Carolyn 1945- 123
See also SATA 52
Croly, Jane Cunningham 1829(?)-1901
Brief entry 118
See also DLB 23
Croman, Dorothy Young
See Rosenberg, Dorothy
Cromie, Alice Hamilton 1914- CANR-3
Earlier sketch in CA 11-12R
See also SATA 24
Cromie, Robert (Allen) 1909- CANR-16
Earlier sketches in CA 2R, CANR-1
Cromie, William J(oseph) 1930- 13-14R
See also SATA 4
Crommelynck, Fernand 1885-1970
Obituary 89-92
Crompton, Anne Eliot 1930- CANR-13
Earlier sketch in CA 33-36R
See also SATA 23
Crompton, John
See Lamburn, John Battersby Crompton
Crompton, Louis (William) 1925- 33-36R
Crompton, Margaret (Norah Mair) 1901- .. CAP-1
Earlier sketch in CA 13-14
Crompton, Richmal
See Lamburn, Richmal Crompton
Cromwell, Chester R. 1925- 89-92
Cromwell, Elsie
See Lee, Elsie
Cromwell, Harvey 1907- 17-18R
Cromwell, John 1887-1979 Obituary 89-92
Cromwell, John 1914(?)-1979 Obituary ...89-92
Cromwell, Link
See Kaye, Lenny
Cromwell, Richard Sidney 1925- 53-56
Cronbach, Abraham 1882-1965 .... 3R
See also SATA 11
Crone, Alla 1923- 113
Crone, G(erald) R(oe) 1899-1982 121
Crone, Moira 1952- 125
Crone, (Hans-) Rainer 1942- CANR-14
Earlier sketch in CA 33-36R
Crone, Ruth 1919- 9-10R
See also SATA 4
Croner, Helga 1914- 107
Croner, John A(lton) 1916- 121
Cronin, A(rchibald) J(oseph)
1896-1981 .... CANR-5
Obituary 102
Earlier sketch in CA 1R
See also SATA 25, 47
See also CLC 32
Cronin, Audrey Kurth 1958- 125
Cronin, George 1933- 101
Cronin, James E(mmet) 1908- CANR-24
Earlier sketch in CA 45-48
Cronin, John F(rancis) 1908- 37-40R
Cronin, Joseph M(arr) 1935- 49-52
Cronin, Sylvia 1929- 89-92
Cronin, Thomas E(dward) 1940- CANR-20
Earlier sketch in CA 85-88
Cronin, Vincent (Archibald Patrick)
1924- CANR-5
Earlier sketch in CA 9-10R
Cronkhite, Bernice Brown 1893-1983
Obituary 110
Cronkite, Walter (Leland, Jr.) 1916- 69-72
See also AITN 1, 2
Cronley, Jay 1943- 81-84
Cronne, H(enry) A(lfred) 1904- 65-68
Cronon, E(dmund) David 1924- CANR-1
Earlier sketch in CA 3R
Cronon, William (John) 1954- 111
Cronus, Diodorus
See Taylor, Richard
Cronyn, Hume 1911- 123
Crook, Bette (Jean) 1921- 73-76
Crook, Beverly Courtney 115
See also SATA 35, 38
Crook, Compton Newby 1908- 121
Crook, David 1910- 97-100
Crook, Howard (Hawthorne) 1937- 107
Crook, Isabel 1915- 97-100
Crook, J(ohn) A(nthony) 1921- 23-24R
Crook, J(oseph) Mordaunt 1937- 41-44R
Crook, Margaret Brackenbury 1886- CAP-1
Earlier sketch in CA 15-16
Crook, Roger H(awley) 1921- CANR-4
Earlier sketch in CA 2R
Crook, W. Melvin 1912(?)-1984 Obituary ... 112
Crook, William 1933- 102
Crookall, Robert 1890- 33-36R
Crookenden, Napier 1915- CANR-11
Earlier sketch in CA 69-72
Crooks, James B(enedict) 1933- 25-28R
Cropp, Ben(jamin) 1936- 33-36R
Cropper, Margaret 1886-1980 Obituary 102
Crosbie, John S(haver) 1920- CANR-12
Earlier sketch in CA 73-76
Crosbie, (Hugh) Provan 1912- 9-10R
Crosbie, Sylvia Kowitt 1938- 73-76
Crosby, Alexander L. 1906-1980 ....29-32R
Obituary 93-96
See also SATA 2, 23
Crosby, Alfred W., Jr. 1931- 19-20R
Crosby, Bing
See Crosby, Harry Lillis
Crosby, (Mary Jacob) Caresse 1892-1970
Obituary 25-28R
See also DLB 4, 48
Crosby, Donald A(llen) 1932- 53-56
Crosby, Donald F(rancis) 1933- 77-80
Crosby, Faye J. 1947- 114
Crosby, Harry 1898-1929 Brief entry 107
See also DLB 4, 48
Crosby, Harry H(erbert) 1919- CANR-5
Earlier sketch in CA 15-16R
Crosby, Harry Lillis 1904-1977 Obituary ...73-76
Crosby, Henry Grew
See Crosby, Harry
Crosby, Henry Sturgis
See Crosby, Harry
Crosby, James O'(Hea) 1924- 89-92
Crosby, Jeremiah
See Crosby, Michael (Hugh)
Crosby, John (Campbell) 1912- CANR-4
Earlier sketch in CA 1R
Crosby, John F. 1931- CANR-7
Earlier sketch in CA 17-18R
Crosby, Michael (Hugh) 1940- CANR-11
Earlier sketch in CA 19-20R
Crosby, Muriel (Estelle) 1908- 19-20R
Crosby, Philip B(ayard) 1926- 73-76
Crosby, Ruth 1897- 49-52
Crosby, Sumner McK(night) 1909-1982 ..13-14R
Obituary 108
Crosher, G. R. 69-72
See also SATA 14
Crosland, Andrew T(ate) 1944- 53-56
Crosland, (Charles) Anthony (Raven)
1918-1977 73-76
Obituary 69-72
Crosland, Margaret 1920- CANR-21
Earlier sketches in CA 49-52, CANR-1
Cross, Aleene (Ann) 1922- CANR-26
Earlier sketch in CA 29-32R
Cross, Amanda
See Heilbrun, Carolyn G(old)
Cross, Anthony (Glenn) 1936- CANR-17
Earlier sketch in CA 37-40R
Cross, (Alan) Beverley 1931- 102
Cross, Claire 1932- 23-24R
Cross, Colin (John) 1928-1985 .... CANR-7
Obituary 118
Earlier sketch in CA 9-10R
Cross, Donna Woolfolk 1947- 97-100
Cross, Frank Moore, Jr. 1921- 65-68
Cross, Gary Scott 1946- 115
Cross, George Lynn 1905- 125
Cross, Gilbert B. 1939- CANR-23
Earlier sketch in CA 105
See also SATA 51
Cross, Gillian (Clare) 1945- 111
See also SATA 38
Cross, Helen Reeder
See Broadhead, Helen Cross
Cross, Herbert James 1934- 45-48
Cross, Ira Brown 1880-1977 Obituary 106
Cross, James
See Parry, Hugh J(ones)
Cross, Jennifer 1932- 29-32R
Cross, John Keir 1914-1967 73-76
Cross, John R(ay) 1939- 120
Cross, K(enneth) G(ustav) W(alter)
1927-1967 .... CAP-1
Earlier sketch in CA 15-16
Cross, K(athryn) Patricia 1926- CANR-13
Earlier sketch in CA 33-36R
Cross, Leslie (Frank) 1909-1977 65-68
Obituary 89-92
Cross, M. Claire
See Cross, Claire
Cross, Milton (John) 1897-1975 Obituary ..53-56
Cross, Nigel 1942- 116
Cross, Ralph D(onald) 1931- CANR-17
Earlier sketch in CA 93-96
Cross, Richard 1950(?)-1983 Obituary 110
Cross, Richard K(eith) 1940- CANR-12
Earlier sketch in CA 33-36R
Cross, Robert Brandt 1914- 37-40R
Cross, Robert Dougherty 1924- 3R
Cross, Robert Singlehurst 1925- 7-8R
Cross, (Alfred) Rupert (Neal) 1912-1980
Obituary 102
Cross, (Alfred) Rupert (Neale) 1912-1980 ... 105
Cross, Samuel S(tephen) 1919- 45-48
Cross, Sister Mary Francilda
1902(?)-1984 Obituary 114
Cross, Stewart
See Drago, Harry Sinclair
Cross, T. T.
See da Cruz, Daniel, Jr.
Cross, Theodore L(amont) 1924- 45-48
Cross, Thomas B. 1949- 123
Cross, Victor
See Coffman, Virginia (Edith)
Cross, Wilbur Lucius III 1918- CANR-2
Earlier sketch in CA 4R
See also SATA 2
Crossan, Darryl
See Smith, Richard Rein
Crosscountry
See Campbell, Thomas F.
Crossen, Ken
See Crossen, Kendell Foster
Crossen, Kendell Foster 1910- CANR-4
Earlier sketch in CA 4R
Crosser, Paul K. 1902-1976 .... CANR-3
Earlier sketch in CA 3R
Crossette, George 1910-1984 Obituary 114
Crossley, Archibald M(addock) 1896-1985
Obituary 116
Crossley-Holland, Kevin 1941- 41-44R
See also SATA 5
See also DLB 40
Crossman, Richard (Howard Stafford)
1907-1974 61-64
Obituary 49-52
Croteau, John T(ougas) 1910- 9-10R
Crothers, George D. 1909- CAP-1
Earlier sketch in CA 15-16
Crothers, J(essie) Frances 1913- 33-36R
Crothers, Jessie F.
See Crothers, J(essie) Frances
Crothers, Rachel 1878(?)-1958 Brief entry .. 113
See also DLB 7
See also TCLC 19
Crotty, William J(oseph) 1936- CANR-13
Earlier sketch in CA 21-22R
Crouch, Bill, Jr.
See Crouch, William Maxwell, Jr.
Crouch, Harold (Arthur) 1940- CANR-15
Earlier sketch in CA 89-92
Crouch, Marcus 1913- CANR-23
Earlier sketches in CA 9-10R, CANR-5
See also SATA 4
Crouch, Steve 1915-1983 .... CANR-9
Obituary 109
Earlier sketch in CA 53-56
Crouch, Thomas W(illiam) 1932- 73-76
Crouch, Tom D. 1944- 106
Crouch, W(illiam) George (Alfred)
1903-1970 ....5-6R
Obituary 89-92
Crouch, William Maxwell, Jr. 1945- 126
Crouch, Winston Winford 1907-
Brief entry 106
Croudace, Glynn 1917- 29-32R
Crouse, Russell M. 1893-1966 77-80
Obituary 25-28R
Crouse, Timothy 1947- 77-80
Crouse, William H(arry) 1907- CANR-6
Earlier sketch in CA 7-8R
Crout, George C(lement) 1917- CANR-11
Earlier sketch in CA 29-32R
See also SATA 11
Crout, Robert Rhodes 1946- 116
Crouzet, Francois Marie-Joseph 1922- .. CANR-19
Earlier sketches in CA 9-10R, CANR-3
Croves, Hal
See Traven, B.
Crovitz, Herbert F(loyd) 1932- 29-32R
Crow, Alice (von Bauer) 1894-1966 ...... CAP-1
Earlier sketch in CA 15-16
Crow, C(harles) P(atrick) 1938- 102
Crow, Charles L(loyd) 1940- 112
Crow, Donna Fletcher 1941- CANR-25
Earlier sketch in CA 108
See also SATA 40
Crow, Duncan 1920- 85-88
Crow, Elizabeth Smith 1946- 103
Crow, Francis Luther
See Luther, Frank
Crow, Jeffrey J(ay) 1947- CANR-19
Earlier sketch in CA 85-88
Crow, John A(rmstrong) 1906- 13-14R
Crow, Lester D(onald) 1897-1983 .... CAP-1
Obituary 110
Earlier sketch in CA 15-16
Crow, Mark (Alan) 1948- 57-60
Crow, Martin M(ichael) 1901- CAP-2
Earlier sketch in CA 19-20
Crow, William Bernard 1895-1976 .... CAP-1
Obituary 65-68
Earlier sketch in CA 13-14
Crowbate, Ophelia Mae
See Smith, C. U.
Crowcroft, Andrew 1923- 23-24R
Crowcroft, Jane
See Crowcroft, Peter
Crowcroft, Peter 1923- 101
Crowder, Christopher M. D. 1922- 103
Crowder, Michael 1934-1988 .... CANR-1
Obituary 126
Earlier sketch in CA 2R
Crowder, Richard (Henry) 1909- CAP-1
Earlier sketch in CA 17-18
Crowe, Amanda Cockrell 1948- 101
Crowe, Bettina Lum 1911- 9-10R
See also SATA 6
Crowe, C. B.
See Gibson, Walter B(rown)
Crowe, Cecily (Teague) Brief entry 115
Crowe, Charles 1928- 17-18R
Crowe, Charles Monroe 1902-1978 .... 3R
Obituary 103
Crowe, E. Odell 1925(?)-1983 Obituary 110
Crowe, F. J.
See Johnston, Jill
Crowe, Frederick Ernest 1915- 111
Crowe, Gregory D(ennis) 1963- 116
Crowe, John
See Lynds, Dennis
Crowe, Kenneth C(harles) 1934- 103
Crowe, Philip Kingsland 1908-1976 65-68
Obituary 69-72
Crowe, Robert L(ee) 1937- 69-72
Crowe, Sylvia 1901- CAP-1
Earlier sketch in CA 9-10
Crowe-Carraco, Carol 1943- 93-96
Crowell, George H. 1931- 25-28R
Crowell, Grace Noll 1877-1969 107
See also SATA 34
Crowell, Joan 1921- 57-60
Crowell, Muriel Beyea 1916- 57-60
Crowell, Norton B. 1914- 11-12R
Crowell, Pers 1910- 29-32R
See also SATA 2
Crowell, Robert Leland 1909- 109
Crowfield, Christopher
See Stowe, Harriet (Elizabeth) Beecher
Crowl, Philip A(xtell) 1914- 110
Crowley, Aleister
See Crowley, Edward Alexander
See also TCLC 7
Crowley, Arthur McBlair 1945- 107
See also SATA 38
Crowley, Daniel J(ohn) 1921- CANR-9
Earlier sketch in CA 21-22R
Crowley, Edward Alexander 1875-1947
Brief entry 104
Crowley, Ellen T(eresa) 1943- CANR-17
Earlier sketch in CA 97-100
Crowley, Frances G(eyer) 1921- 105
Crowley, George (David) 1913-1987
Obituary 123
Crowley, J(oseph) Donald 1932- 122
Crowley, James B. 1929- 23-24R
Crowley, John 1942- 61-64
See also DLBY 82
Crowley, John Edward 1943- 53-56
Crowley, John W(illiam) 1945- 69-72
Crowley, Mart 1935- 73-76
See also DLB 7
Crowley, Mary C. 1915- 97-100
Crowley, Raymond 1895-1982 Obituary 106
Crown, David A. 1928- CANR-10
Earlier sketch in CA 25-28R
Crown, Paul 1928- 19-20R
Crownfield, Gertrude 1867-1945 .... YABC-1
Crowson, P(aul) S(piller) 1913- 53-56
Crowther, Betty 1939- 61-64
Crowther, (Francis) Bosley 1905-1981 65-68
Obituary 103
Crowther, Duane S(wofford) 1934- CANR-17
Earlier sketch in CA 25-28R
Crowther, Geoffrey 1907-1972 Obituary ..33-36R
Crowther, James Gerald 1899- 73-76
See also SATA 14
Crowther, Jean D(ecker) 1937- 120
Crowther, Wilma 1918- 7-8R
Crowther-Hunt, Norman Crowther
1920-1987 Obituary 121
Croxford, Leslie 1944- 81-84
Croxton, Anthony H(ugh) 1902- 61-64
Croxton, Frederick E(mory) 1899- CAP-2
Earlier sketch in CA 23-24
Croy, Homer 1883-1965 110
Obituary 89-92
See also DLB 4
Crozet, Charlotte 1926- 25-28R
Crozetti, R(uth G.) Warner
See Warner-Crozetti, R(uth G.)
Crozier, Brian (Rossiter) 1918- CANR-3
Earlier sketch in CA 11-12R
Crozier, Lorna 1948- 113
Crud
See Crumb, R(obert)
Cruden, Robert 1910- 33-36R
Cruger, Melvin J. 1925(?)-1983 Obituary ... 111
Cruickshank, Allan D(udley) 1907-1974
Obituary 53-56
Cruickshank, C. G.
See Cruickshank, Charles (Greig)
Cruickshank, Charles (Greig) 1914- CANR-25
Earlier sketches in CA 23-24R, CANR-9
Cruickshank, Helen Gere 1907- CAP-1
Earlier sketch in CA 13-14
Cruickshank, John 1924- CANR-20
Earlier sketches in CA 3R, CANR-4
Cruickshank, Marjorie 1920-1983 122
Obituary 111
Cruickshank, William M(ellon) 1915- 89-92
Cruikshank, George 1792-1878 .... SATA-22
Crumarums
See Crumb, R(obert)
Crumb, R(obert) 1943- 106
See also CLC 17
Crumbaker, Alice 1911- 81-84
Crumbaugh, James C(harles) 1912- 37-40R
Crumbley, D. Larry 1941- CANR-12
Earlier sketch in CA 29-32R
Crumbum
See Crumb, R(obert)
Crumley, James 1939- CANR-21
Earlier sketch in CA 69-72
See also DLBY 84
Crumm, Lloyd C(arlton), Jr. 1927- CANR-10
Earlier sketch in CA 65-68
Crummey, Robert O(wen) 1936- CANR-17
Earlier sketch in CA 25-28R
Crump, Barry (John) 1935- CANR-8
Earlier sketch in CA 13-14R
Crump, Fred H., Jr. 1931- CANR-19
Earlier sketches in CA 11-12R, CANR-3
See also SATA 11
Crump, Galbraith Miller 1929- 57-60
Crump, Geoffrey (Herbert) 1891- CAP-1
Earlier sketch in CA 13-14
Crump, J(ames) Irving 1887-1979 73-76
Obituary 89-92
See also SATA 21
Crump, Kenneth G(ordon), Jr. 1931- 23-24R

Crump, Spencer (M., Jr.) 1933- CANR-9
Earlier sketch in CA 23-24R
Crump, (Stephen) Thomas 1929- 49-52
Crumpacker, Laurie 1941- 118
Crumpet, Peter
See Buckley, Fergus Reid
Crumpler, Frank H(unter) 1935- 77-80
Crumpler, Gus H(unt) 1911- 69-72
Crumrine, N(orman) Ross II 1934- CANR-8
Earlier sketch in CA 15-16R
Crumski
See Crumb, R(obert)
Crum the Bum
See Crumb, R(obert)
Crunden, Reginald
See Cleaver, Hylton Reginald
Crunden, Robert M. 1940- CANR-15
Earlier sketch in CA 29-32R
Crunk
See Crumb, R(obert)
Cruse, Harold 77-80
Cruso, Thalassa 1909- 65-68
Crussi, F(rank) Gonzalez
See Gonzalez-Crussi, F(rank)
Crustt
See Crumb, R(obert)
Crutcher, Anne Neilson 1919-1983
Obituary 111
Crutcher, Chris(topher C.) 1946- 113
See also SATA 52
Cruz, Joan Carroll 1931- 73-76
Cruz, Ray(mond) 1933- SATA-6
Cruz, Victor Hernandez 1949- CANR-14
Earlier sketch in CA 65-68
See also BW
See also DLB 41
Cryer, Gretchen (Kiger) 1935- 123
Brief entry 114
See also CLC 21
Crying Wind
See Stafford, Linda (Crying Wind)
Crystal, David 1941- CANR-23
Earlier sketches in CA 17-18R, CANR-7
Crystal, John C(urry) 1920- 102
Csath, Geza 1887-1919 Brief entry 111
See also TCLC 13
Csicsery-Ronay, Istvan 1917- 21-22R
Csikos-Nagy, Bela 1915- 73-76
Csikszentmihalyi, Mihaly 1934- 125
Ctvrtek, Vaclav 1911-1976 Obituary 107
See also SATA 27
Cua, Antonio S. 1932- CANR-7
Earlier sketch in CA 17-18R
Cuban, Larry 1934- CANR-12
Earlier sketch in CA 29-32R
Cubas, Braz
See Dawes, Robyn M(ason)
Cuber, John F(rank) 1911- 9-10R
Cubeta, Paul Marsden 1925- 7-8R
Cuciti, Peggy L. 1949- 123
Cudahy, Brian J(ames) 1936- 41-44R
Cuddihy, John Murray 1922- 85-88
Cuddon, John Anthony 1928- CANR-19
Earlier sketches in CA 7-8R, CANR-3
Cuddy, Don 1925- 69-72
Cudjoe, Selwyn Reginald 1943- 118
Cudlip, David 1933- CLC-34
Cudlipp, Edythe 1929- CANR-12
Earlier sketch in CA 33-36R
Cudlipp, Hugh 1913- Brief entry 116
Cuelho, Art 1943- 61-64
Cuevas, Clara 1933- 57-60
Cuff, Barry
See Koste, Robert Francis
Cuff, Robert Dennis 1941- Brief entry 109
Cuffari, Richard 1925-1978 SATA-6, 25
Cuisenaire, Emile-Georges 1891(?)-1976
Obituary 61-64
Cuisenier, Jean 1927- CANR-20
Earlier sketch in CA 73-76
Culbert, David H(olbrook) 1943- 112
Culbert, Samuel Alan 1938- 69-72
Culbert, T(homas) Patrick 1930-
Brief entry 107
Culbertson, Don S(tuart) 1927- 11-12R
Culbertson, Hugh M. 77-80
Culbertson, J(ohn) M(athew) 1921- 11-12R
Culbertson, James T(homas) 1911- 118
Culbertson, Judi 1941- 85-88
Culbertson, Manie 1927- 49-52
Culbertson, Paul T(homas) 1905- 37-40R
Culex
See Stanier, Maida Euphemia Kerr
Culhane, Claire 1918- 118
Culhane, Shamus 1908- 121
Culican, William 1929(?)-1984 Obituary 113
Culkin, Ann Marie 1918- 9-10R
Cull, John G(uinn, Jr.) 1934- 41-44R
Cullen, Charles T(homas) 1940- 53-56
Cullen, Countee 1903-1946 124
Brief entry 108
See also BW
See also SATA 18
See also DLB 4, 48, 51
See also TCLC 4
Cullen, George Francis 1901-1980
Obituary 102
Cullen, Joseph P(atrick) 1920- 49-52
Cullen, Lee Stowell 1922- 103
Cullen, Maurice R(aymond), Jr. 1927- 73-76
Cullen, Patrick (Colborn) 1940- 29-32R
Cullen, Peta
See Pyle, Hilary
Culler, A(rthur) Dwight 1917- 17-18R
Culler, Annette Lorena
See Penney, Annette Culler
Culler, Jonathan 1944- 104
See also DLB 67
Culleton, Beatrice 1949- 120
Culley, Thomas R(obert) 1931- 33-36R
Culliford, Pierre 1928- 124
See also SATA 40
Culliford, Stanley George 1920- 65-68
Culligan, Joe
See Culligan, Matthew J(oseph)
Culligan, Matthew J(oseph) 1918- CANR-20
Earlier sketch in CA 81-84
Cullinan, Bernice Ellinger 1926- 104
Cullinan, Elizabeth 1933- CANR-11
Earlier sketch in CA 25-28R
Cullinan, Gerald 1916- 23-24R
Cullinane, Leo Patrick 1907(?)-1978
Obituary 77-80
Culliney, John L. 1942- 65-68
Cullingford, Cecil H(oward) D(unstan)
1904- CANR-7
Earlier sketch in CA 7-8R
Cullingford, Guy
See Taylor, Constance Lindsay
Cullingworth, J(ohn) Barry 1929- CANR-1
Earlier sketch in CA 4R
Cullman, Marguerite Wagner 1908- 1R
Cullman, W(illiam) Arthur 1914- 113
Cullman, W. Arthur 1914- Brief entry 111
Cullmann, Oscar 1902- 106
Cullop, Charles P. 1927- 25-28R
Cully, Iris V(irginia Arnold) 1914- CANR-17
Earlier sketches in CA 3R, CANR-1
Cully, Kendig Brubaker 1913- CANR-17
Earlier sketches in CA 2R, CANR-1
Culotta, Nino
See O'Grady, John (Patrick)
Culp, Delos Poe 1911- 17-18R
Culp, John H(ewett, Jr.) 1907- 29-32R
Culp, Louanna McNary 1901-1965 CAP-1
Earlier sketch in CA 15-16
See also SATA 2
Culp, Paula 1941- 57-60
Culpepper, R(ichard) Alan 1946- 115
Culpepper, Robert H(arrell) 1924- 77-80
Culross, Michael (Gerard) 1942- 33-36R
Culshaw, John (Royds) 1924-1980 CANR-11
Obituary 97-100
Earlier sketch in CA 23-24R
Culver, Dwight W(endell) 1921- 9-10R
Culver, Elsie Thomas 1898- CAP-2
Earlier sketch in CA 21-22
Culver, Kathryn
See Dresser, Davis
Culver, Kenneth Leon 1903- 103
Culver, Robert Duncan 1916- 120
Culver, Roger B(ruce) 1940- 104
Cum, R.
See Crumb, R(obert)
Cumberland, Charles C(urtis)
1914-1970 CANR-2
Earlier sketch in CA 4R
Cumberland, John H(ammett) 1924-
Brief entry 106
Cumberland, Kenneth Brailey 1913- 53-56
Cumberland, Marten 1892-1972 CAP-1
Earlier sketch in CA 11-12
Cumberland, William Henry 1929- 19-20R
Cumberlege, Marcus (Crossley) 1938- CANR-17
Earlier sketch in CA 97-100
Cumberlege, Vera 1908- 81-84
Cumbler, John T(aylor) 1946- 89-92
Cumes, J(ames) W(illiam) C(rawford)
1922- 73-76
Cuming, Geoffrey John 1917-1988 CANR-18
Obituary 125
Earlier sketches in CA 7-8R, CANR-3
Cuming, Pamela 1944- 107
Cumings, Bruce Glenn 1943- 107
Cumming, Patricia (Arens) 1932- CANR-11
Earlier sketch in CA 61-64
Cumming, Primrose Amy 1915- 33-36R
See also SATA 24
Cumming, Robert 1945- 106
Cumming, Robert Denoon 1916-
Brief entry 107
Cumming, William P(atterson) 1900- 33-36R
Cummings, Ann
See Rudolph, Lee (Norman)
Cummings, Arthur J. 1920(?)-1979
Obituary 89-92
Cummings, Betty Sue 1918- CANR-14
Earlier sketch in CA 73-76
See also SATA 15
Cummings, Bruce F(rederick) 1889-1919
Brief entry 123
Cummings, Charles 1940- 107
Cummings, D(onald) W(ayne) 1935- 101
Cummings, E(dward) E(stlin) 1894-1962 73-76
See also DLB 4, 48
See also CLC 1, 3, 8, 12, 15
Cummings, Florence
See Bonime, Florence
Cummings, Gary 1941(?)-1987 Obituary 125
Cummings, Jack
See Cummings, John W(illiam), Jr.
Cummings, Jean 1930- 33-36R
Cummings, John W(illiam), Jr. 1940- 117
Cummings, Larry L(ee) 1937- 53-56
Cummings, Milton C(urtis), Jr. 1933- 13-14R
Cummings, Monette 1914- 116
Cummings, Parke 1902-1987 CAP-1
Obituary 123
Earlier sketch in CA 13-14
See also SATA 2, 53
Cummings, Pat 1950- 122
See also SATA 42
Cummings, Paul 1933- CANR-8
Earlier sketch in CA 21-22R
Cummings, Ray(mond King) 1887-1957
Brief entry 113
See also DLB 8
Cummings, Richard (Marshall) 1938- 113
Cummings, Richard
See Gardner, Richard (M.)
Cummings, Richard LeRoy 1933- 45-48
Cummings, Scott 112
Cummings, Thomas G(erald) 1944- CANR-16
Earlier sketch in CA 97-100
Cummings, Violet M(ay) 1905- 57-60
Cummings, W(alter) T(hies) 1933- 3R
Cummins, D. Duane 1935- CANR-14
Earlier sketch in CA 37-40R
Cummins, Geraldine Dorothy 1890-1969 CAP-1
Earlier sketch in CA 9-10
Cummins, James 1948- 122
Cummins, Maria Susanna 1827-1866 YABC-1
See also DLB 42
Cummins, Paul F. 1937- 33-36R
Cummins, Walter (Merrill) 1936- CANR-15
Earlier sketch in CA 41-44R
Cundiff, Edward William 1919- CANR-4
Earlier sketch in CA 4R
Cundiff, Margaret Joan 1932- 112
Cundy, Henry Martyn 1913- 7-8R
Cuneo, Ernest (L.) 1905-1988 Obituary 125
Cuneo, Gilbert Anthony 1913-1978
Obituary 77-80
Cuneo, John R(obert) 1911- 53-56
Cuney, Waring
See Cuney, William Waring
Cuney, William Waring 1906-1976 125
See also BW
See also DLB 51
Cunha, Euclides (Rodrigues Pimenta) da
1866-1909 Brief entry 123
See also TCLC 24
Cunha, George Martin 1911- 25-28R
Cuninggim, Merrimon 1911- 41-44R
Cunliffe, Barrington Windsor 1939- CANR-24
Earlier sketches in CA 53-56, CANR-9
Cunliffe, Barry
See Cunliffe, Barrington Windsor
Cunliffe, Elaine 33-36R
Cunliffe, John Arthur 1933- CANR-11
Earlier sketch in CA 61-64
See also SATA 11
Cunliffe, Marcus (Falkner) 1922- CANR-10
Earlier sketch in CA 21-22R
See also SATA 37
Cunliffe, William Gordon 1929- 25-28R
Cunningham, Aline CANR-9
Earlier sketch in CA 57-60
Cunningham, Barry 1940- 73-76
Cunningham, Bob
See May, Julian
Cunningham, Captain Frank
See Glick, Carl (Cannon)
Cunningham, Cathy
See Cunningham, Chet
Cunningham, Chet 1928- CANR-19
Earlier sketches in CA 49-52, CANR-4
See also SATA 23
Cunningham, Dale S(peers) 1932- CANR-8
Earlier sketch in CA 15-16R
See also SATA 11
Cunningham, Donald H(ayward) 1935- CANR-20
Earlier sketch in CA 103
Cunningham, E. V.
See Fast, Howard (Melvin)
Cunningham, Floyd F(ranklin) 1899- CAP-1
Earlier sketch in CA 15-16
Cunningham, H(orace) H(erndon)
1913-1969 CAP-1
Earlier sketch in CA 11-12
Cunningham, Imogen 1883-1976
Obituary 65-68
Cunningham, J(ames) V(incent)
1911-1985 CANR-1
Obituary 115
Earlier sketch in CA 1R
See also DLB 5
See also CLC 3, 31
Cunningham, James F. 1901- CAP-2
Earlier sketch in CA 19-20
Cunningham, John D(onovan) 1933- 111
Cunningham, Joseph F. X. 1925- 69-72
Cunningham, Joseph Sandy 1928- 61-64
Cunningham, Julia (Woolfolk) 1916- CANR-19
Earlier sketches in CA 9-10R, CANR-4
See also SATA 1, 26
See also SAAS 2
See also CLC 12
Cunningham, Laura 1947- CANR-23
Earlier sketch in CA 85-88
Cunningham, Lawrence 1935- CANR-15
Earlier sketch in CA 85-88
Cunningham, Lyda Sue Martin 1938- 19-20R
Cunningham, Marilyn 1927- 125
Cunningham, Mary (Elizabeth) 1951- 114
Cunningham, Michael 1952- CLC-34
Cunningham, Michael A(lan) 1945- 41-44R
Cunningham, Noble E., Jr. 1926- 81-84
Cunningham, Paul James, Jr. 1917- 73-76
Cunningham, R(onnie) Walter 1932- 103
Cunningham, Richard 1939- 101
Cunningham, Robert Louis 1926- 41-44R
Cunningham, Robert M(aris), Jr. 1909- CANR-1
Earlier sketch in CA 49-52
Cunningham, Robert Stanley 1907- 53-56
Cunningham, Rosemary 1916- 9-10R
Cunningham, Virginia
See Holmgren, Virginia C(unningham)
Cunningham, W(infield) Scott
1899(?)-1986 Obituary 118
Cunninghame Graham, R(obert) B(ontine)
1852-1936 Brief entry 119
See also TCLC 19
Cunnington, Phillis 1887-1974 Obituary 53-56
Cunz, Dieter 1910-1969 CAP-2
Earlier sketch in CA 19-20
Cuomo, George (Michael) 1929- CANR-7
Earlier sketch in CA 7-8R
See also DLBY 80
Cuomo, Mario Matthew 1932- 103
Cupitt, Don 1934- CANR-14
Earlier sketch in CA 41-44R
Cuppleditch, David 1946- 116
Cuppy, Will(iam Jacob) 1884-1949
Brief entry 108
See also DLB 11
Cure, Karen 1949- CANR-9
Earlier sketch in CA 65-68
Curiae, Amicus
See Fuller, Edmund (Maybank)
Curie, Eve 1904- CAP-1
Earlier sketch in CA 9-10
See also SATA 1
Curie, Marie (Sklodowska) 1867-1934
Brief entry 118
Curl, David H. 1932- 93-96
Curl, Donald Walter 1935- 33-36R
Curl, James Stevens 1937- CANR-14
Earlier sketch in CA 37-40R
Curle, Adam
See Curle, Charles T. W.
Curle, Charles T. W. 1916- 33-36R
Curler, (Mary) Bernice 1915- 85-88
Curley, Arthur 1938- CANR-9
Earlier sketch in CA 21-22R
Curley, Charles 1949- 57-60
Curley, Daniel 1918- CANR-18
Earlier sketches in CA 11-12R, CANR-3
See also SATA 23
Curley, Dorothy Nyren
See Nyren, Dorothy Elizabeth
Curley, Michael J. 1900-1972 Obituary 37-40R
Curley, Walter J(oseph) P(atrick) 1922- 53-56
Curling, Audrey 61-64
Curling, Bill
See Curling, Bryan William Richard
Curling, Bryan William Richard 1911- 102
Curnow, (Thomas) Allen (Monro) 1911- 69-72
Curnow, Frank
See Atkinson, Frank
Curnow, Ray(mond) 1928- 117
Curran, Bob
See Curran, Robert
Curran, Charles A(rthur) 1913- 33-36R
Curran, Charles E. 1934- CANR-14
Earlier sketch in CA 23-24R
Curran, Charles John 1921-1980 Obituary 105
Curran, Dolores 1932- CANR-6
Earlier sketch in CA 57-60
Curran, Donald J. 1926- 45-48
Curran, Francis X. 1914- 17-18R
Curran, Jan Goldberg 1937- 101
Curran, Joseph M(aroney) 1932- 103
Curran, Mona (Elisa) 7-8R
Curran, Peter Malcolm 1922- 103
Curran, Phil(ip) R(ead) 1911- 73-76
Curran, Robert 1923- 89-92
Curran, Samuel (Crowe) 1912- 109
Curran, Stuart (Alan) 1940- 29-32R
Curran, Susan 1952- 113
Curran, Thomas J(oseph) 1929- 45-48
Curran, Ward S(chenk) 1935- 41-44R
Curran, William John 1925- 108
Curren, Polly 1917- CANR-4
Earlier sketch in CA 4R
Current, Richard N(elson) 1912- CANR-5
Earlier sketch in CA 2R
Current-Garcia, Eugene 1908- 19-20R
Currer-Briggs, Noel 1919- CANR-13
Earlier sketch in CA 73-76
Currey, Cecil B(arr) 1932- CANR-25
Earlier sketch in CA 25-28R
Currey, R(onald) F(airbridge) 1894-1983 CAP-1
Obituary 109
Earlier sketch in CA 9-10
Currey, R(alph) N(ixon) 1907- 93-96
Currey, Richard 1949- 117
Currie, Ann (Brooke Peterson)
1922(?)-1980 Obituary 102
Currie, Barton Wood 1878-1962 Obituary 116
Currie, David
See Allen, Sydney (Earl), Jr.
Currie, David P. 1936- Brief entry 106
Currie, Donald Glenne 1926-1984
Obituary 111
Currie, Ellen 19(?)- CLC-44
Currie, Lauchlin (Bernard) 1902- CANR-15
Earlier sketch in CA 73-76
Currie, Mary Montgomerie Lamb Singleton
See Fane, Violet
Currie, Robert 1937- 112
Currier, Alvin C. 1932- 23-24R
Currier, Frederick P(lumer) 1923- 85-88
Currier, Richard L(eon) 1940- 57-60
Curro, Evelyn Malone 1907- 7-8R
Curry, Andrew 1931- 57-60
Curry, Avon
See Bowden, Jean
Curry, David 1942- 69-72
Curry, Dean C(onrad) 1952- 118
Curry, Estell H. 1907- CAP-2
Earlier sketch in CA 23-24
Curry, F. Hayden 1940- 108
Curry, George E(dward) 1947- 69-72

Curry, Gladys J.
See Washington, Gladys J(oseph)
Curry, Jane L(ouise) 1932- ... CANR-24
Earlier sketches in CA 17-18R, CANR-7
See also SATA 1, 52
See also SAAS 6
Curry, Jennifer 1934- ... 77-80
Curry, Kenneth 1910- ... CANR-8
Earlier sketch in CA 17-18R
Curry, Leonard Preston 1929- ... 29-32R
Curry, Lerond (Loving) 1938- ... 33-36R
Curry, Martha Mulroy 1926- ... 61-64
Curry, Paul (J.) 1917-1986 ... 49-52
Obituary ... 118
Curry, Peggy Simson 1911-1987 ... CANR-12
Obituary ... 121
Earlier sketch in CA 33-36R
See also SATA 8, 50
Curry, Richard Orr 1931- ... 15-16R
Curry, Thomas A. 1901(?)-1976 Obituary ... 69-72
Curry, Windell
See Sujata, Anagarika
Curry-Lindahl, Kai 1917- ... CANR-19
Earlier sketches in CA 49-52, CANR-2
Curtayne, Alice 1898- ... 53-56
Curteis, Ian Bayley 1935- ... 103
Curti, Merle Eugene 1897- ... CANR-4
Earlier sketch in CA 5-6R
See also DLB 17
Curtin, James R(udd) 1922- ... 19-20R
Curtin, Mary Ellen 1922- ... 57-60
Curtin, Patricia (W.) Romero 1935- ... CANR-14
Earlier sketch in CA 37-40R
Curtin, Philip
See Lowndes, Marie Adelaide (Belloc)
Curtin, Phillip D. 1922- ... CANR-7
Earlier sketch in CA 13-14R
Curtin, William M(artin) 1927- ... 53-56
Curtis, Alan R(obert) 1936- ... 105
Curtis, Anthony 1926- ... CANR-18
Earlier sketch in CA 101
Curtis, (Hubert) Arnold 1917- ... CANR-12
Earlier sketch in CA 29-32R
Curtis, Bruce (Richard) 1944- ... SATA-30
Curtis, Carol Edwards 1943- ... 77-80
Curtis, Charles J(ohn) 1921- ... 21-22R
Curtis, Charles Ralph 1899- ... 7-8R
Curtis, Charlotte (Murray) 1928-1987 ... 9-10R
Obituary ... 122
See also AITN 2
Curtis, David Paul 1942- ... CANR-13
Earlier sketch in CA 23-24R
Curtis, Donald 1915- ... CANR-20
Earlier sketch in CA 103
Curtis, Edith Roelker 1893-1977 ... 1R
Obituary ... 103
Curtis, George William 1824-1892 ... DLB-1, 43
Curtis, Gerald 1904-1983 Obituary ... 109
Curtis, Howard J(ames) 1906-1972
Obituary ... 37-40R
Curtis, J(osiah) Montgomery 1905-1982
Obituary ... 108
Curtis, Jack 1922- ... 103
Curtis, Jackie
See Holder, John, Jr.
Curtis, James (Richard) 1953- ... 108
Curtis, James C. 1938- Brief entry ... 105
Curtis, James Malcolm 1940- ... 119
Curtis, Jared Ralph 1936- ... 101
Curtis, John
See Prebble, John Edward Curtis
Curtis, Lewis Perry 1900-1976 ... CAP-2
Obituary ... 65-68
Earlier sketch in CA 23-24
Curtis, Lindsay R(aine) 1916- ... 41-44R
Curtis, Lynn A(lan) 1943- ... 61-64
Curtis, Margaret James 1897- ... 3R
Curtis, Marjorie
See Prebble, Marjorie Mary Curtis
Curtis, Mark H(ubert) 1920- ... 5-6R
Curtis, Michael Raymond 1923- ... CANR-22
Earlier sketch in CA 103
Curtis, Norman 1914- ... 45-48
Curtis, Patricia 1924- ... CANR-18
Earlier sketch in CA 69-72
See also SATA 23
Curtis, Paul
See Czura, R(oman) P(eter)
Curtis, Peter
See Lofts, Norah (Robinson)
Curtis, Philip (Delacourt) 1920- ... 109
Curtis, Price
See Ellison, Harlan
Curtis, Richard (Alan) 1937- ... CANR-25
Earlier sketch in CA 106
See also SATA 29
Curtis, Richard Hale
See Levinson, Leonard
and Rothweiler, Paul Roger
Curtis, Richard Kenneth 1924- ... 4R
Curtis, Rosemary Ann (Stevens) 1935- ... 9-10R
Curtis, Sharon 1951- ... 126
Brief entry ... 116
Curtis, Thomas Bradford 1911- ... 61-64
Curtis, Thomas Dale 1952- ... 126
Brief entry ... 116
Curtis, Tom
See Curtis, Thomas Dale
Curtis, Tom
See Pendower, Jacques
Curtis, Tony 1925- ... 73-76
Curtis, Tony 1946- ... CANR-22
Earlier sketch in CA 106
Curtis, Wade
See Pournelle, Jerry (Eugene)
Curtis, Will
See Nunn, William Curtis
Curtis, William J(oseph) R. 1948- ... 110
Curtis Brown, Beatrice 1901-1974 ... CAP-2
Earlier sketch in CA 25-28
Curtiss, John S(helton) 1899- ... CAP-2
Earlier sketch in CA 19-20
Curtiss, Mina (Stein Kirstein) 1896-1985
Obituary ... 118
Curtiss, Ursula Reilly 1923-1984 ... CANR-5
Obituary ... 114
Earlier sketch in CA 4R
Curtler, Hugh Mercer 1937- ... CANR-15
Earlier sketch in CA 89-92
Curto, Josephine J. 1927- ... 19-20R
Curwin, Richard L(eonard) 1944- ... 77-80
Curzon, Clare
See Buchanan, Marie
Curzon, Daniel ... 73-76
Curzon, Lucia
See Stevenson, Florence
Curzon, Sam
See Krasney, Samuel A.
Curzon, Virginia
See Hawton, Hector
Cusac, Marian H(ollingsworth) 1932- ... 33-36R
Cusack, (Ellen) Dymphna 1902-198(?) ... CANR-11
Earlier sketch in CA 9-10R
Cusack, Lawrence X(avier) 1919- ... 5-6R
Cusack, Michael J(oseph) 1928- ... 69-72
Cush, Carol Gregor
See Gregor, Carol
Cushing, Barry E(dwin) 1945- ... CANR-4
Earlier sketch in CA 53-56
Cushing, Jane 1922- ... 29-32R
Cushing, Mary W(atkins) 189(?)-1974
Obituary ... 53-56
Cushing, Richard Cardinal
See Cushing, Richard James
Cushing, Richard James 1895-1970
Obituary ... 112
Cushion, John P(atrick) 1915- ... 93-96
Cushman, Clarissa Fairchild 1889-1980
Obituary ... 93-96
Cushman, Dan 1909- ... CANR-18
Earlier sketches in CA 5-6R, CANR-3
Cushman, Doug 1953- ... 117
Cushman, Jerome ... 2R
See also SATA 2
Cushman, Joseph David, Jr. 1925- ... 111
Cushman, Keith (Maxwell) 1942- ... 124
Cushman, Robert F(airchild) 1918- ... 77-80
Cushman, Stephen B. 1956- ... 123
Cusick, Philip A. 1937- ... 69-72
Cuskelly, Eugene James 1924- ... 7-8R
Cuskey, (Raymond) Walter 1934- ... 41-44R
Cuss, (Theodore Patrick) Camerer
1909(?)-1970 Obituary ... 104
Cussler, Clive (Eric) 1931- ... CANR-21
Earlier sketches in CA 45-48, CANR-1
Custer, Chester Eugene 1920- ... 41-44R
Custer, Clint
See Paine, Lauran (Bosworth)
Cusumano, Michael A. 1954- ... 125
Cutchen, Billye Walker 1930- ... CANR-13
Earlier sketch in CA 77-80
See also SATA 15
Cutcliffe, Stephen H(osmer) 1947- ... 116
Cutforth, John Ashlin 1911- ... 9-10R
Cutforth, Rene 1909(?)-1984 ... 123
Obituary ... 112
Cuthbert, Diana Daphne Holman-Hunt
1913- ... 4R
Cuthbert, Eleonora Isabel (McKenzie)
1902- ... CAP-1
Earlier sketch in CA 11-12
Cuthbert, Mary
See Hellwig, Monika Konrad
Cuthbertson, Gilbert Morris 1937- ... 57-60
Cuthbertson, Tom 1945- ... CANR-1
Earlier sketch in CA 45-48
Cutler, Bruce 1930- ... CANR-18
Earlier sketches in CA 4R, CANR-2
Cutler, Carl C(uster) 1878-1966 ... 4R
Obituary ... 103
Cutler, Carol 1926- ... CANR-19
Earlier sketch in CA 103
Cutler, Charles L(ocke, Jr.) 1930- ... 65-68
Cutler, Daniel S(olomon) 1951- ... 120
Cutler, Donald R. 1930- ... 23-24R
Cutler, (May) Ebbitt 1923- ... CANR-4
Earlier sketch in CA 49-52
See also SATA 9
Cutler, Irving H. 1923- ... CANR-9
Earlier sketch in CA 23-24R
Cutler, Ivor 1923- ... CANR-9
Earlier sketch in CA 7-8R
See also SATA 24
Cutler, Katherine Noble 1905- ... CANR-4
Earlier sketch in CA 5-6R
Cutler, Roland 1938- ... CANR-25
Earlier sketch in CA 102
Cutler, Samuel
See Folsom, Franklin (Brewster)
Cutler, William Worcester III 1941- ... 103
Cutler, Winnifred B(erg) 1944- ... 117
Cutlip, Scott M. 1915- ... 5-6R
Cutrate, Joe
See Spiegelman, Art
Cutrer, Thomas W(illiam) 1947- ... 123
Cutright, Paul Russell 1897- ... 65-68
Cutright, Phillips 1930- ... 5-6R
Cutshall, Alden 1911- ... CANR-3
Earlier sketch in CA 9-10R
Cutsumbis, Michael N(icholas) 1935- ... 45-48
Cutt, W(illiam) Towrie 1898-1981 ... 81-84
Obituary ... 115
See also SATA 16
Cutten, M. J.
See Cutten, Mervyn (James)
Cutten, Mervyn (James) 1916- ... 120
Cutter, Donald C(olgett) 1922- ... CANR-13
Earlier sketch in CA 33-36R
Cutter, Fred 1924- ... 57-60
Cutter, Robert Arthur 1930- ... CANR-8
Earlier sketch in CA 57-60
Cutter, Tom
See Randisi, Robert J(oseph)
Cutter, Tom
See Wallmann, Jeffrey M(iner)
Cutting, Edith E(lsie) 1918- ... 106
Cuttino, G(eorge) P(eddy) 1914- ... 23-24R
Cuttle, Evelyn Roeding ... 57-60
Cuttler, Charles D(avid) 1913- ... 29-32R
Cutts, John P. 1927-1986 ... 45-48
Obituary ... 121
Cutts, Richard 1923- ... 33-36R
Cutul, Ann-Marie 1945- ... 103
Cuyler, Louise E. 1908- ... 23-24R
Cuyler, Margery S(tuyvesant) 1948- ... 117
See also SATA 39
Cuyler, Stephen
See Bates, Barbara S(nedeker)
Cuyler, Susanna (Stevens) 1946- ... 61-64
Cykler, Edmund A(lbert) 1903- ... 11-12R
Cylwicki, Albert 1932- ... 116
Cynan
See Evans-Jones, Albert
Cynthia
See King, Florence
Cyr, Arthur 1945- ... 125
Cyr, Don(ald Joseph) 1935- ... 103
Cyr, John Edwin 1915- ... 103
Czaczkes, Shmuel Yosef
See Agnon, S(hmuel) Y(osef Halevi)
Czaja, Michael 1911- ... 57-60
Czaplinski, Suzanne 1943- ... 61-64
Czerniawski, Adam 1934- ... CANR-14
Earlier sketch in CA 37-40R
Czerny, Peter G(erd) 1941- ... 65-68
Czestochowski, Joseph S(tephen) 1950- ... 113
Czobor, Agnes 1920- ... 37-40R
Czura, R(oman) P(eter) 1913- ... 89-92

D

D. P.
See Wells, H(erbert) G(eorge)
Daane, Calvin J(ohn) 1925- ... 41-44R
Daane, James 1914- ... 23-24R
Dabberdt, Walter F. 1942- ... CANR-23
Earlier sketch in CA 107
Dabbs, Jack Autrey 1914- ... 17-18R
Dabbs, James McBride 1896-1970 ... CAP-1
Earlier sketch in CA 15-16
Dabcovich, Lydia ... 124
See also SATA 47
Dabit, Eugene 1898-1936 ... DLB-65
Dabkin, Edwin Franden 1898(?)-1976
Obituary ... 65-68
Dabney, Dick 1933-1981 ... 69-72
Obituary ... 105
Dabney, Joseph Earl 1929- ... 49-52
Dabney, Ross H. 1934- ... 23-24R
Dabney, Virginius 1901- ... CANR-1
Earlier sketch in CA 45-48
Dabney, William M(inor) 1919- ... 9-10R
Daborne, Robert 1580(?)-1628 ... DLB-58
D'Abreu, Gerald Joseph 1916-19(?) ... CAP-2
Earlier sketch in CA 19-20
Dabringhaus, Erhard 1917- ... 115
Dabrowska, Maria (Szumska) 1889-1965 ... 106
See also CLC 15
Dabydeen, Cyril 1945- Brief entry ... 122
Dabydeen, David 1955- ... 125
See also BW
See also CLC 34
DaCal, Ernesto Guerra 1911- ... CANR-19
Earlier sketches in CA 5-6R, CANR-4
Dace, Letitia (Skinner) 1941- ... 106
Dace, Tish
See Dace, Letitia (Skinner)
Dace, (Edwin) Wallace 1920- ... 61-64
Dacey, Norman F(ranklyn) 1908- ... CANR-2
Earlier sketch in CA 7-8R
Dacey, Philip 1939- ... CANR-14
Earlier sketch in CA 37-40R
Dachman, Ken 1958- ... 110
Dachs, David 1922-1980 ... CANR-11
Earlier sketch in CA 69-72
Dack, Gail Monroe 1901-1976 Obituary ... 111
da Cruz, Daniel, Jr. 1921- ... CANR-19
Earlier sketches in CA 7-8R, CANR-3
Dacy, Douglas Calvin 1927- Brief entry ... 104
Dadie, Bernard B(inlin) 1916- ... CANR-17
Earlier sketch in CA 25-28R
See also BW
Daedalus
See Bramesco, Norton J.
Daehlin, Reidar A. 1910- ... CAP-1
Earlier sketch in CA 17-18
Daem, Thelma (Mary) Bannerman 1914- ... 5-6R
Daemer, Will
See Miller, (H.) Bill(y)
and Wade, Robert (Allison)
Daemmrich, Horst S. 1930- ... CANR-1
Earlier sketch in CA 45-48
Daenzer, Bernard John 1916- ... 53-56
Dagan, Avigdor 1912- ... CANR-13
Earlier sketch in CA 33-36R
Dagenais, James J(oseph) 1928- ... 41-44R
Dager, Edward Z(icca) 1921- ... 61-64
Dagerman, Stig (Halvard) 1923-1954
Brief entry ... 117
See also TCLC 17
Dagg, Anne Innis 1933- ... CANR-11
Earlier sketch in CA 69-72
Daglish, Eric Fitch 1892-1966 ... 102
D'Agostino, Angelo 1926- ... 19-20R
D'Agostino, Dennis John 1957- ... 106
D'Agostino, Giovanna P. 1914- ... 57-60
D'Agostino, Joseph David 1929- ... 69-72
Dagover, Lil 1897-1980 Obituary ... 105
Daheim, Mary 1937- ... 110
Dahinden, Justus 1925- ... 81-84
Dahl, Arlene 1928- Brief entry ... 105
Dahl, Borghild (Margarethe) 1890-1984 ... CANR-2
Obituary ... 112
Earlier sketch in CA 3R
See also SATA 7, 37
Dahl, Curtis 1920- ... CANR-2
Earlier sketch in CA 4R
Dahl, Georg 1905- ... 85-88
Dahl, Gordon J. 1932- ... 49-52
Dahl, Linda 1949- ... 122
Dahl, Murdoch Edgcumbe 1914- ... CAP-1
Earlier sketch in CA 9-10
Dahl, Nils A(lstrup) 1911- ... 65-68
Dahl, Roald 1916- ... CANR-6
Earlier sketch in CA 1R
See also SATA 1, 26
See also CLC 1, 6, 18
See also CLR 1, 7
Dahl, Robert Alan 1915- ... 65-68
Dahlberg, Arthur O. ... 124
Dahlberg, Edward 1900-1977 ... 9-10R
Obituary ... 69-72
See also DLB 48
See also CLC 1, 7, 14
Dahlberg, Edwin T(heodore) 1892-1986 ... CAP-2
Obituary ... 120
Earlier sketch in CA 17-18
Dahlberg, Jane S. 1923- ... 23-24R
Dahlinger, John Cote 1923-1984 Obituary ... 114
Dahlstedt, Marden 1921- ... CANR-1
Earlier sketch in CA 45-48
See also SATA 8
Dahlstrand, Frederick Charles 1945- ... 111
Dahlstrom, Earl C(arl) 1914- ... 17-18R
Dahm, Charles W(illiam) 1937- ... 107
Dahms, Alan M(artin) 1937- ... 49-52
Dahmus, Joseph Henry 1909- ... 21-22R
Dahood, Mitchell (Joseph) 1922-1982 ... CANR-20
Obituary ... 106
Earlier sketch in CA 25-28R
Dahrendorf, Ralf 1929- ... CANR-3
Earlier sketch in CA 3R
Daiches, David 1912- ... CANR-7
Earlier sketch in CA 5-6R
Daigh, Ralph (Foster) 1907-1986 Obituary ... 121
Daigon, Arthur 1928- ... 33-36R
Daiken, Leslie Herbert 1912- ... 4R
Dailey, Charles A(lvin) 1923- ... 89-92
Dailey, Janet (Ann) 1944- ... CANR-17
Earlier sketch in CA 89-92
Daily, Jay E(lwood) 1923- ... 33-36R
Daims, Diva 1925- ... 113
Dain, Martin J. 1924- ... 15-16R
See also SATA 35
Dain, Norman 1925- ... 11-12R
Dain, Phyllis 1929- ... 69-72
Dainton, (William) Courtney 1920- ... 9-10R
Daiute, Robert James 1926- ... 13-14R
Dakers, Elaine Kidner 1905-1978 ... 85-88
Dakin, Arthur Hazard 1905- Brief entry ... 106
Dakin, D(avid) Martin 1908- ... 73-76
Dakin, Edwin Franden 1898-1976
Obituary ... 104
Dakin, (David) Julian 1939-1971 ... CAP-2
Earlier sketch in CA 25-28
Dalal, Nergis 1920- Brief entry ... 116
Daland, Robert T(heodore) 1919- ... 21-22R
Dalbor, John B(ronislaw) 1929- ... 17-18R
Dalcourt, Gerard J. 1927- ... 33-36R
Dale, (Mary) Alzina Stone 1931- ... 114
Dale, Antony 1912- ... 107
Dale, Arbie Myron, Jr. 1924- ... 122
Dale, Celia (Marjorie) ... CANR-3
Earlier sketch in CA 7-8R
Dale, Colin
See Lawrence, T(homas) E(dward)
See also TCLC 18
Dale, D(ion) M(urray) C(rosbie) 1930- ... 23-24R
Dale, Doris Cruger 1927- ... 116
Dale, Edgar 1900-1985 Obituary ... 117
Dale, Edward Everett 1879-1972 ... CANR-4
Earlier sketch in CA 5-6R
Dale, Edwin L., Jr. 1923- ... 69-72
Dale, Ernest 1917- ... 13-14R
Dale, George E.
See Asimov, Isaac
Dale, Jack
See Holliday, Joseph
Dale, James 1886-1985 ... CAP-2
Obituary ... 116
Earlier sketch in CA 33-36
Dale, John B. 1905- ... 13-14R
Dale, Kathleen 1895-1984 Obituary ... 112
Dale, Laura A(bbott) 1919-1983 Obituary ... 113
Dale, Magdalene L(arsen) 1904- ... 15-16R
Dale, Margaret J(essy) Miller 1911- ... CANR-19
Earlier sketches in CA 7-8R, CANR-3
See also SATA 39
Dale, Norman
See Denny, Norman (George)
Dale, Paul W(orthen) 1923- ... 25-28R
Dale, Peter (John) 1938- ... CANR-16
Earlier sketches in CA 45-48, CANR-1
See also DLB 40

Dale, Peter N(icholas) 1950- 126
Dale, Reginald R. 1907- 21-22R
Dale, Richard 1932- 33-36R
Dale, Richard
See Lansdale, Joe R(ichard)
Dale, Robert D(ennis) 1940- 113
Dale, Roman
See Czura, R(oman) P(eter)
d'Alelio, Ellen F. 1938- 17-18R
Dales, Douglas S. 1907(?)-1985 Obituary .. 114
Dales, Richard C(lark) 1926- CANR-24
Earlier sketch in CA 45-48
Daleski, H(illel) M(atthew) 1926- 33-36R
D'Alessandro, Robert (Philip) 1942- 61-64
Dalet, Roger (Charles) 1927- 107
Daley, Adeline 1922(?)-1984 Obituary 112
Daley, Arthur (John) 1904-1974 .... CAP-2
Obituary 45-48
Earlier sketch in CA 23-24
Daley, Bill
See Appleman, John Alan
Daley, Brian 1947- 126
Daley, Eliot A. 1936- 97-100
Daley, Janet 1944- 125
Daley, Joseph A(ndrew) 1927- 53-56
Daley, Robert 1930- CANR-24
Earlier sketches in CA 2R, CANR-2
Dalfiume, Richard Myron 1936- 25-28R
D'Alfonso, John 1918- 29-32R
Dalgleish, Oakley Hedley 1910-1963
Obituary 115
Dalgliesh, Alice 1893-1979 73-76
Obituary 89-92
See also SATA 17, 21
Dalglish, Edward R(ussell) 1913- 37-40R
Dali, Salvador (Domenech Felipe Jacinto)
1904- 104
Dall, Caroline Wells (Healey) 1822-1912 .. DLB-1
D'Allard, Hunter
See Ballard, (Willis) Todhunter
Dallas, Athena Gianakas
See Dallas-Damis, Athena G(ianakas)
Dallas, E. S. 1828-1879 .... DLB-55
Dallas, John
See Duncan, W(illiam) Murdoch
Dallas, Philip 1921- 61-64
Dallas, Ruth 1919- CANR-10
Earlier sketch in CA 65-68
Dallas, Sandra
See Atchison, Sandra Dallas
Dallas-Damis, Athena G(ianakas) 1925- 81-84
Dallek, Robert 1934- CANR-17
Earlier sketch in CA 25-28R
D'Allenger, Hugh
See Kershaw, John (Hugh D'Allenger)
Dallimore, Arnold A(rthur) 1911- 112
Dallin, Alexander 1924- CANR-19
Earlier sketches in CA 1R, CANR-5
Dallin, Leon 1918- CANR-1
Earlier sketch in CA 1R
Dallmann, Martha (Elsie) 1904- 4R
Dallmayr, Fred R(einhard) 1928- CANR-1
Earlier sketch in CA 49-52
Dally, Ann Mullins 1926- CANR-21
Earlier sketches in CA 7-8R, CANR-3
Dalmas, John
See Jones, John R(obert)
D'Alonzo, C(onstance) Anthony
1912-1972 Obituary 37-40R
Dalpadado, J(ames) Kingsley (Evold)
1922- 112
Dalphin, John R(obert) 1942- 118
Dal Poggetto, Newton Francis 1922- 61-64
d'Alpuget, Blanche 1944- 114
Dalrymple, Byron W(illiam) 1910- CANR-6
Earlier sketch in CA 57-60
Dalrymple, Douglas J(esse) 1934- 73-76
Dalrymple, Gertrude Bradley 1901(?)-1984
Obituary 113
Dalrymple, Ian (Murray) 1903- 115
Dalrymple, Jean 1910- CANR-5
Earlier sketch in CA 5-6R
Dalrymple, Willard 1921- 23-24R
Dalsass, Diana 1947- 106
Dalton, Alene
See Chapin, Alene Olsen Dalton
Dalton, Anne 1948- SATA-40
Dalton, Claire
See Burns, Alma
Dalton, Clive
See Clark, F(rederick) Stephen
Dalton, (John) David 1944- 97-100
Dalton, Dennis (Gilmore) 1938- 115
Dalton, Dorothy 1915- 21-22R
Dalton, Elizabeth 1936- 85-88
Dalton, Gene W(ray) 1928- 25-28R
Dalton, George 1926- Brief entry 106
D'Alton, Louis (Lynch) 1900-1951
Brief entry 110
See also DLB 10
Dalton, Priscilla
See Avallone, Michael (Angelo), Jr.
Dalton, Richard 1930- 57-60
Dalton, Stephen 1937- 85-88
Dalven, Rae 1904- 33-36R
Daly, Anne 1896- CAP-2
Earlier sketch in CA 29-32
Daly, Cahal Brendan 1917- 104
Daly, Carroll John 1889-1958 Brief entry ... 112
Daly, Christopher B. 1954- 126
Daly, Donald F(remont) 69-72
Daly, Edith Iglauer CANR-14
Earlier sketch in CA 77-80
Daly, Elizabeth 1878-1967 .... CAP-2
Obituary 25-28R
Earlier sketch in CA 23-24
Daly, Emily Joseph 1913- 9-10R
Daly, Faye Kennedy 1936- 97-100
Daly, Herman E. 1938- 89-92
Daly, Jim
See Stratemeyer, Edward L.
Daly, John Jay 1888(?)-1976 Obituary 69-72
Daly, Kathleen N(orah) Brief entry 115
See also SATA 37
Daly, (Arthur) Leo 1920- CANR-25
Earlier sketch in CA 105
Daly, Lowrie John 1914- 15-16R
Daly, Mary 1928- 25-28R
Daly, Mary Tinley 1904(?)-1979 85-88
Daly, Maureen
See McGivern, Maureen Daly
See also SATA 2
See also SAAS 1
See also CLC 17
Daly, Nicholas 1946- 111
See also SATA 37
Daly, Niki
See Daly, Nicholas
Daly, Robert 1943- 104
Daly, Robert Welter 1916-1975 .... 9-10R
Obituary 103
Daly, Saralyn R(uth) 1924- 57-60
Daly, Sister Mary Virginia 1925- 17-18R
Daly, T(homas) A(ugustine) 1871-1948
Brief entry 111
See also DLB 11
Dalzel, Peter
See Dalzel Job, P(atrick)
Dalzel Job, P(atrick) 1913- 13-14R
Dalzell, Robert (Fenton), Jr. 1937- 81-84
Dam, Hari N(arayan) 1921- 57-60
Dam, Kenneth W. 1932- CANR-12
Earlier sketch in CA 69-72
Damachi, (Godwin) Ukandi 1942- CANR-2
Earlier sketch in CA 45-48
Damas, Leon-Gontran 1912-1978 125
Obituary 73-76
See also BW
Damata, Ted 1909(?)-1988 Obituary 125
D'Amato, Alex 1919- CANR-18
Earlier sketch in CA 81-84
See also SATA 20
D'Amato, Anthony A. 1937- 29-32R
D'Amato, Barbara 1938- 69-72
D'Amato, Janet (Potter) 1925- CANR-18
Earlier sketches in CA 49-52, CANR-1
See also SATA 9
Damaz, Paul F. 1917- 7-8R
d'Amboise, Christopher 1960- 115
Dambrauskas, Joan Arden 1933- 104
D'Ambrosio, Charles A. 1932- 23-24R
D'Ambrosio, Richard A(nthony) 1927- 102
D'Ambrosio, Vinnie-Marie 1928- 45-48
Dame, Lawrence 1898- CAP-1
Earlier sketch in CA 11-12
D'Amelio, Dan 1927- 33-36R
Dameron, J(ohn) Lasley 1925- 53-56
Damerst, William A. 1923- 19-20R
Damiani, Bruno Mario 1942- 57-60
D'Amico, John Francis 1947(?)-1987
Obituary 124
Damis, John 1940- 118
Damm, John S. 1926- 37-40R
Damon, Gene
See Grier, Barbara G(ene Damon)
Damon, S(amuel) Foster 1893-1971 101
See also DLB 45
Damon, Virgil Green 1895-1972 .... CAP-1
Obituary 37-40R
Earlier sketch in CA 9-10
Damor, Hakji
See Lesser, R(oger) H(arold)
D'Amore, Arcangelo R. T. 1920-1986
Obituary 118
Damore, Leo 1929- 81-84
Damrosch, Helen
See Tee-Van, Helen Damrosch
Damrosch, Leopold, Jr. 1941- 45-48
Damsker, Matt(hew Harry) 1951- 108
Damtoft, Walter A(tkinson) 1922- 57-60
Dana, Amber
See Paine, Lauran (Bosworth)
Dana, Barbara 1940- CANR-8
Earlier sketch in CA 19-20R
See also SATA 22
Dana, Charles Anderson 1819-1897 ... DLB-3, 23
Dana, E. H.
See Hamel Dobkin, Kathleen
Dana, Richard
See Paine, Lauran (Bosworth)
Dana, Richard H(enry) 1927- CANR-15
Earlier sketch in CA 85-88
Dana, Richard Henry, Jr. 1815-1882 ... SATA-26
See also DLB 1
Dana, Robert (Patrick) 1929- 33-36R
Dana, Rose
See Ross, W(illiam) E(dward) D(aniel)
Danachair, Caoimhin O
See Danaher, Kevin
Danagher, Edward F. 1919- 11-12R
Danaher, Kevin 1913- 33-36R
See also SATA 22
Danan, Alexis 1889(?)-1979 Obituary 89-92
Danby, Hope (Smedley) 1899- CAP-1
Earlier sketch in CA 13-14
Danby, John B(lench) 1905-1983
Obituary 109
Danby, Mary
See Calvert, Mary
Danby, Miles William 1925- 13-14R
Dance, E(dward) H(erbert) 1894- 37-40R
Dance, F(rancis) E(sburn) X(avier)
1929- CANR-16
Earlier sketches in CA 4R, CANR-1
Dance, Frank E. X.
See Dance, F(rancis) E(sburn) X(avier)
Dance, Jim 1924(?)-1983 Obituary 110
Dance, S(tanley) Peter 1932- CANR-13
Earlier sketch in CA 69-72
Dance, Stanley (Frank) 1910- CANR-8
Earlier sketch in CA 17-18R
Dancer, J. B.
See Harvey, John (Barton)
Danco, Katharine L(eck) 1929- 112
Danco, Katy
See Danco, Katharine L(eck)
Danco, Leon A(ntoine) 1923- 112
Dancocks, Daniel G. 1950- 120
D'Ancona, Mirella Levi 1919- CANR-6
Earlier sketch in CA 53-56
Dancy, John Christopher 1920- 107
Dandrea, Don(ald E.) 1936- 120
D'Andrea, Kate
See Steiner, Barbara A(nnette)
D'Andrea, Paul 1939- 120
Dandridge, Ray G.
See Dandridge, Raymond Garfield
Dandridge, Raymond Garfield 1882-1930 ... 125
See also BW
See also DLB 51
Dandy, James Edgar 1903-1976 Obituary ... 104
Dane, Carl
See Adams, F(rank) Ramsay
Dane, Clemence
See Ashton, Winifred
See also DLB 10
Dane, Les(lie A.) 1925- 89-92
Dane, Mark
See Avallone, Michael (Angelo), Jr.
Dane, Mary
See Morland, Nigel
Dane, Nathan II 1916-1980 108
Obituary 97-100
Dane, Zel
See Timms, E(dward) V(ivian)
Daneff, Stephen Constantine 1931- 106
Daneke, Gregory A(llen) 1950- 112
Danelski, David J. 1930- 15-16R
Danenberg, Leigh 1893-1976 Obituary 69-72
Danford, Howard G(orby) 1904- CAP-1
Earlier sketch in CA 11-12
Danforth, Art(hur Louis) 1913(?)-1987
Obituary 122
Danforth, John 1660-1730 .... DLB-24
Danforth, Loring M(andell) 1949- 111
Danforth, Samuel I 1626-1674 .... DLB-24
Danforth, Samuel II 1666-1727 .... DLB-24
Dangaard, Colin (Edward) 1942- 85-88
D'angelo, Edward 1932- 37-40R
D'Angelo, Frank J(oseph) 1928- 120
D'Angelo, Lou
See D'Angelo, Luciano
D'Angelo, Luciano 1932- 33-36R
Dangerfield, Balfour
See McCloskey, (John) Robert
Dangerfield, Clint
See Norwood, Victor G(eorge) C(harles)
Dangerfield, George (Bubb) 1904-1986 .... 9-10R
Obituary 121
Dangerfield, Harlan
See Padgett, Ron
Dangerfield, Rodney 1922(?)- 102
Danhof, Clarence H(enry) 1911- 37-40R
Dani, Ahmad Hasan 1920- 13-14R
Daniel, Alan 1939- SATA-53
Daniel, Anita 1893(?)-1978 Obituary 77-80
See also SATA 23, 24
Daniel, Anne
See Steiner, Barbara A(nnette)
Daniel, Charles 1933- 114
Daniel, Cletus E(dward) 1943- 107
Daniel, (Elbert) Clifton, Jr. 1912-
Brief entry 113
Daniel, Colin
See Windsor, Patricia (Frances)
Daniel, Daniel 1890(?)-1981 Obituary 104
Daniel, Elna Worrell
See Stone, Elna
Daniel, Emmett Randolph 1935- 102
Daniel, Errol Valentine 111
Daniel, George Bernard, Jr. 1927- 15-16R
Daniel, Glenda 1943- 111
Daniel, Glyn (Edmund) 1914-1986 .... CANR-13
Obituary 121
Earlier sketch in CA 57-60
Daniel, Hawthorne 1890- 5-6R
See also SATA 8
Daniel, James 1916- 69-72
Daniel, Jerry C(layton) 1937- 33-36R
Daniel, John M. 1825-1865 .... DLB-43
Daniel, Julie Goldsmith 1949- CANR-14
Earlier sketch in CA 77-80
Daniel, Lee
See Reid, Daniel P. (Jr.)
Daniel, Lorne (MacLeod Lyons) 1953- 118
Daniel, Norman (Alexander) 1919- CANR-6
Earlier sketch in CA 57-60
Daniel, Pete 1938- CANR-14
Earlier sketch in CA 37-40R
Daniel, Price, Jr. 1941-1981 Obituary 103
Daniel, Ralph T(homas) 1921- 53-56
Daniel, Robert L(eslie) 1923- 33-36R
Daniel, Robert W(oodham) 1915- 25-28R
Daniel, Samuel 1562(?)-1619 .... DLB-62
Daniel, Stephen H(artley) 1950- 119
Daniel, Urcel 1908(?)-1984 Obituary 113
Daniel, Walter C(larence) 1922- 110
Daniel, Yuli (Markovich) 1925- 116
Daniele, Joseph William 1927- 89-92
Daniell, Albert Scott 1906-1965 .... CANR-3
Earlier sketch in CA 5-6R
Daniell, David Scott
See Daniell, Albert Scott
Daniell, Jere Rogers 1932- CANR-11
Earlier sketch in CA 29-32R
Daniell, Rosemary 1935- 118
Danielle, Maria 1945- 114
Danielli, James Frederic 1911-1984
Obituary 113
Daniells, Lorna M(cLean) 1918- CANR-18
Earlier sketch in CA 89-92
Daniells, Roy 1902-1979 57-60
See also DLB 68
Danielou, Alain 1907- CANR-14
Earlier sketch in CA 73-76
Danielou, Jean 1905-1974 .... CAP-2
Obituary 49-52
Earlier sketch in CA 23-24
Daniel-Rops, Henri
See Petiot, Henri Jules Charles
Daniels, Anna Kleegman 1893-1970
Obituary 29-32R
Daniels, Arlene Kaplan 1930- CANR-12
Earlier sketch in CA 29-32R
Daniels, Brett
See Adler, Renata
Daniels, Bruce C(olin) 1943- 122
Daniels, David 1933- 53-56
Daniels, Derick January 1926- Brief entry ... 112
Daniels, Dewey
See McKimmey, James
Daniels, Dorothy 1915- CANR-15
Earlier sketch in CA 89-92
Daniels, Douglas Henry 1943- 125
Daniels, Draper 1913-1983 53-56
Obituary 109
Daniels, Elizabeth Adams 1920- 37-40R
Daniels, Farrington 1889-1972 .... 5-6R
Obituary 37-40R
Daniels, Frank Arthur 1904-1986 Obituary .. 121
Daniels, Frank James 1900(?)-1983
Obituary 110
Daniels, George H. 1935- CANR-10
Earlier sketch in CA 25-28R
Daniels, George M(orris) 1927- 29-32R
Daniels, Guy 1919- 21-22R
See also SATA 7, 11
Daniels, Harold R(obert) 1919- 17-18R
Daniels, James R(aymond) 1956- 121
Daniels, Jim
See Daniels, James R(aymond)
Daniels, John Clifford 1915- 13-14R
Daniels, John S.
See Overholser, Wayne D.
Daniels, Jonathan 1902-1981 49-52
Obituary 105
Daniels, Josephus 1862-1948 Brief entry ... 122
See also DLB 29
Daniels, Kate 1953- 124
Daniels, Les(lie Noel III) 1943- CANR-24
Earlier sketches in CA 65-68, CANR-9
Daniels, Mary 1937- 93-96
Daniels, Max
See Gellis, Roberta L(eah Jacobs)
Daniels, Norman CANR-15
Earlier sketch in CA 89-92
Daniels, Norman 1942- CANR-22
Earlier sketch in CA 106
Daniels, Olga
See Sinclair, Olga
Daniels, Pamela 1937- 101
Daniels, R(obertson) Balfour 1900- 49-52
Daniels, Randy (Allan) 1949- 81-84
Daniels, Robert V(incent) 1926- CANR-2
Earlier sketch in CA 1R
Daniels, Roger 1927- CANR-23
Earlier sketches in CA 7-8R, CANR-8
Daniels, Sally 1931- 3R
Daniels, Shouri
See Ramanujan, Molly
Daniels, Steven Lloyd 1945-1973 .... 33-36R
Daniels, Velma Seawell 1931- 108
Danielson, Elena S(chafer) 1947- 116
Danielson, J. D.
See James, M. R.
Danielson, Michael N(ils) 1934- 33-36R
Danielson, Wayne Allen 1929- 77-80
Danielsson, Bengt (Emmerik) 1921- ... CANR-23
Earlier sketch in CA 107
Daniere, Andre L(ucien) 1926- 11-12R
Daniloff, Nicholas 1934- 85-88
Danilov, Victor J(oseph) 1924- CANR-21
Earlier sketches in CA 13-14R, CANR-6
Daninos, Pierre 1913- CANR-15
Earlier sketch in CA 77-80
Danish, Barbara 1948- 57-60
Dank, Gloria Rand 1955- 114
See also SATA 46
Dank, Leonard D(ewey) 1929- SATA-44
Dank, Milton 1920- CANR-11
Earlier sketch in CA 69-72
See also SATA 31
Danker, Frederick William 1920- CANR-5
Earlier sketch in CA 15-16R
Danker, W(illiam) John 1914- 15-16R
Dankleff, Richard E(lden) 1925- 114
Danky, James Philip 1947- CANR-12
Earlier sketch in CA 69-72
Danly, Robert Lyons 1947- 108
Dann, Colin (Michael) 1943- 108
Dann, Jack 1945- CANR-2
Earlier sketch in CA 49-52
Dann, John C(hristie) 1944- 126
Dann, Max 1955- 118
Dann, Uriel 1922- 25-28R

Dannay, Frederic 1905-1982 .... CANR-1
Obituary 107
Earlier sketch in CA 1R
See also CLC 11
Dannelley, Paul (Edward, Jr.) 1919- 122
Dannemiller, Lawrence 1925- 1R
Dannenfeldt, Karl H(enry) 1916- 25-28R
Danner, Margaret (Essie) 1915- 29-32R
See also BW
See also DLB 41
Dannett, Sylvia G. L. 1909- CANR-4
Earlier sketch in CA 2R
D'Annunzio, Gabriele 1863-1938
Brief entry 104
See also TCLC 6
Danoff, I. Michael 1940- 97-100
Danowski, T(haddeus) S(tanley) 1914-1987 .... 11-12R
Obituary 123
Danska, Herbert 1928- 29-32R
Danson, Lawrence Neil 1942- 85-88
d'Antibes, Germain
See Simenon, Georges (Jacques Christian)
Danto, Arthur C(oleman) 1924- 17-18R
Danto, Bruce L. 1927- CANR-7
Earlier sketch in CA 53-56
Danton, J(oseph) Periam 1908- 11-12R
Danton, Rebecca
See Roberts, Janet Louise
Dantzic, Cynthia Maris 1933- 101
Dantzig, George Bernard 1914- Brief entry .. 106
Danvers, Jack
See Caseleyr, Cam(ille Auguste Marie)
Danzig, Allan (Peter) 1931- 45-48
Danzig, Allison 1898-1987 .... 37-40R
Obituary 121
Danzig, Fred P(aul) 1925- 65-68
Danziger, Edmund J(efferson), Jr. 1938- ... 102
Danziger, Kurt 1926- 41-44R
Danziger, Marlies K(allmann) 1926- CANR-16
Earlier sketch in CA 25-28R
Danziger, Paula 1944- 115
Brief entry 112
See also SATA 30, 36
See also CLC 21
Danziger, Sheldon H. 1948- 119
Daoud, Hazim S. 1930-1976 122
Dapper, Gloria 1922- 19-20R
Dapping, William Osborne 1880-1969
Obituary 115
D'Aprix, Roger M. 1932- 33-36R
Darack, Arthur J. 1918- 115
Darbelnet, Jean (Louis) 1904- CANR-10
Earlier sketch in CA 25-28R
Darby, Catherine
See Peters, Maureen
Darby, Edwin Wheeler 1922- 125
Darby, Gene Kegley 1921- CANR-2
Earlier sketch in CA 5-6R
Darby, Henry Clifford 1909- 7-8R
Darby, J. N.
See Govan, Christine Noble
Darby, John 1940- 105
Darby, Michael 1944- 116
Darby, Patricia (Paulsen) 73-76
See also SATA 14
Darby, Ray(mond) 1912- 17-18R
See also SATA 7
d'Arch Smith, Timothy 1936- 15-16R
Darcy, Clare 102
D'Arcy, G(eorge) Minot 1930- 9-10R
D'Arcy, Jean (Marie) 1913-1983 Obituary ... 109
Darcy, Jean
See Lepley, Jean Elizabeth
D'Arcy, Margaretta 1934- 104
D'Arcy, Martin C(yril) 1888-1976 .... CANR-3
Obituary 69-72
Earlier sketch in CA 7-8R
D'Arcy, Pamela
See Roby, Mary Linn
D'Arcy, Paul F(rancis) 1921- 19-20R
d'Arcy, Willard
See Cox, William R(obert)
Darden, Lloyd (Nestor) 1931- Brief entry ... 113
Darden, Norma Jean 114
Darden, William R(aymond) 1936- 77-80
Dardess, John W(olfe) 1937- 45-48
Dardig, Jill C(arolyn) 1948- 69-72
Dardis, Tom 1926- CANR-9
Earlier sketch in CA 65-68
Dare, Evelyn
See Everett-Green, Evelyn
Dareff, Hal 1920- 65-68
Darga, Bert 1931- 110
Dargan, Olive (Tilford) 1869-1968
Obituary 111
Dargo, George 1935- 115
d'Argyre, Gilles
See Klein, Gerard
Dariaux, Genevieve Antoine
See Antoine-Dariaux, Genevieve
Darien, Peter
See Bassett, William B. K.
Daringer, Helen Fern 1892- CAP-2
Earlier sketch in CA 17-18
See also SATA 1
Dario, Ruben
See Sarmiento, Felix Ruben Garcia
See also TCLC 4
Darion, Joe
See Darion, Joseph
Darion, Joseph 1917- Brief entry 113
Dark, Alvin Ralph 1922- 105
Dark, Harris Edward 1922- 57-60
Dark, Johnny
See Norwood, Victor G(eorge) C(harles)
Dark, Philip J(ohn) C(rosskey) 1918- ... CANR-18
Earlier sketches in CA 49-52, CANR-2
Darke, Marjorie 1929- CANR-15
Earlier sketch in CA 81-84
See also SATA 16
Darley, F(elix) O(ctavius) C(arr) 1822-1888 .... SATA-35
Darley, John M(cConnon) 1938- 93-96
Darling, Arthur Burr 1892-1971 .... 5-6R
Obituary 33-36R
Darling, David J. SATA-44
Darling, Edward 1907-1974 .... CANR-3
Obituary 53-56
Earlier sketch in CA 49-52
Darling, Frank Clayton 1925- 19-20R
Darling, Frank Fraser
See Fraser Darling, Frank
Darling, Jay Norwood 1876-1962
Obituary 93-96
Darling, John R(othburn) 1937- 93-96
Darling, Kathy
See Darling, Mary Kathleen
Darling, Lois MacIntyre 1917- CANR-3
Earlier sketch in CA 5-6R
See also SATA 3
Darling, Louis, Jr. 1916-1970 .... CANR-3
Obituary 89-92
Earlier sketch in CA 7-8R
See also SATA 3, 23
Darling, Mary Kathleen 1943- CANR-4
Earlier sketch in CA 53-56
See also SATA 9
Darling, Richard L(ewis) 1925- 23-24R
Darlington, Alice B(enning) 1906-1973 ... CAP-2
Obituary 41-44R
Earlier sketch in CA 25-28
Darlington, C(yril) D(ean) 1903-1981 ... CANR-10
Obituary 108
Earlier sketch in CA 9-10R
Darlington, Charles F. 1904-1986 .... CAP-2
Obituary 119
Earlier sketch in CA 25-28
Darlington, Joy 1947- 89-92
Darlington, William Aubrey (Cecil) 1890- .. CAP-1
Earlier sketch in CA 15-16
Darlow, Michael (George) 1934- 104
Darlton, Clark
See Ernsting, Walter
Darmstadter, Joel 1928- 121
Darnay, Arsen (Julius) 1936- 111
Darnton, John (Townsend) 1941- 126
Brief entry 119
Darnton, Robert (Choate) 1939- 116
Brief entry 113
Darr, Ann 1920- CANR-7
Earlier sketch in CA 57-60
Darracott, Joseph C(orbould) 1934- 106
Darrah, William C(ulp) 1909- 57-60
Darrell, R(obert) D(onaldson) 1903-1988
Obituary 125
Darroch, Maurice A. 1903-19(?) CAP-2
Earlier sketch in CA 19-20
Darroch, Sandra Jobson 1942- 89-92
Darrow, Ralph C(arroll) 1918- 61-64
Darrow, Richard W(illiam) 1915-1976 .... 21-22R
Obituary 120
Darrow, Whitney (Jr.) 1909- CANR-14
Earlier sketch in CA 61-64
See also SATA 13
Dart, John 1936- 65-68
Dart, Raymond A(rthur) 1893- CAP-1
Earlier sketch in CA 13-14
Darton, G(erald) C(hristopher) 1913(?)-1987 Obituary 122
Darvas, Nicolas 1920- 61-64
Darveaux, Terry A(lan) 1943- 65-68
Darvill, Fred T(homas), Jr. 1927- CANR-6
Earlier sketch in CA 57-60
Darwall, Stephen L(eicester) 1946- 113
Darwin, Charles 1809-1882 .... DLB-57
Darwin, Len
See Darwin, Leonard
Darwin, Leonard 1916- SATA-24
Darwin, M. B.
See McDavid, Raven I(oor), Jr.
Dary, David A. 1934- CANR-13
Earlier sketch in CA 29-32R
Daryush, Elizabeth 1887-1977 .... CANR-3
Earlier sketch in CA 49-52
See also DLB 20
See also CLC 6, 19
Das, Deb Kumar 1935- 102
Das, Durga 1900-1974 .... CAP-2
Obituary 49-52
Earlier sketch in CA 29-32
Das, Gurcharan 1943- 33-36R
Das, Jagannath Prasad 1931- CANR-6
Earlier sketch in CA 57-60
Das, Kamala 1934- 101
Das, Manmath Nath 1926- CANR-8
Earlier sketch in CA 15-16R
Dasenbrock, Reed Way 1953- 125
Dasent, Sir George Webbe 1817-1896 .. SATA-29
Das Gupta, Jyotirindra 1933- 53-56
Dash, Irene G(olden) 125
Dash, Joan 1925- 49-52
Dash, Samuel 1925- Brief entry 105
Dash, Tony 1945- 33-36R
Dashiell, Alfred Sheppard 1901-1970
Obituary 89-92
Dashti, Ali 1894- 85-88
Dashwood, Edmee Elizabeth Monica de la Pasture 1890-1943 Brief entry 119
Dashwood, Robert Julian 1899- CAP-1
Earlier sketch in CA 13-14
da Silva, Howard 1909-1986 Obituary 118
DaSilva, Leon
See Wallmann, Jeffrey M(iner)
DaSilva, Zenia Sacks 1925- 121
Daskam, Josephine Dodge
See Bacon, Josephine Dodge (Daskam)
Dasmann, Raymond (Fredric) 1919- CANR-2
Earlier sketch in CA 7-8R
Dass, Ram
See Alpert, Richard
Dassault, Marcel (Bloch) 1892-1986
Obituary 119
Brief entry 115
Dassonville, Michel A(uguste) 1927- 73-76
Dater, Henry M. 1909(?)-1974 Obituary ... 49-52
Datesh, John Nicholas 1950- 97-100
Dathorne, O(scar) R(onald) 1934- CANR-26
Earlier sketch in CA 57-60
See also BW
Daube, David 1909- CANR-1
Earlier sketch in CA 4R
Daubeny, Peter (Lauderdale) 1921-1975 ... 61-64
Dauber, Kenneth Marc 1945- 114
Daudet, Leon 1867-1942 Brief entry 121
Dauenhauer, Richard L(eonard) 1942- .. CANR-11
Earlier sketch in CA 61-64
Dauer, Dorothea W. 1917- 37-40R
Dauer, Manning J(ulian) 1909- 89-92
Dauer, Rosamond 1934- CANR-10
Earlier sketch in CA 65-68
See also SATA 23
Dauer, Victor Paul 1909- 19-20R
Daugert, Stanley M(atthew) 1918- 19-20R
Daughdrill, James H(arold), Jr. 1934- 41-44R
Daughen, Joseph R(obert) 1935- 33-36R
Daugherty, Carroll R(oop) 1900-1988
Obituary 125
Daugherty, Charles Michael 1914- 73-76
See also SATA 16
Daugherty, James (Henry) 1889-1974 73-76
Obituary 49-52
See also SATA 13
Daugherty, Richard D(eo) 1922- 108
See also SATA 35
Daugherty, Sarah Bowyer 1949- 106
Daugherty, Sonia Medwedeff ?-1971
Obituary 104
See also SATA 27
Daughtrey, Anne Scott 1920- 19-20R
d'Aulaire, Edgar Parin 1898-1986 49-52
Obituary 119
See also SATA 5, 47
See also DLB 22
d'Aulaire, Ingri (Mortenson) 1904-1980 ... 49-52
Obituary 102
See also SATA 5, 24
See also DLB 22
Daumal, Rene 1908-1944 Brief entry 114
See also TCLC 14
Daunton, M(artin) J(ames) 1949- 125
Dauster, Frank (Nicholas) 1925- 53-56
Dauten, Carl Anton 1913-1976 .... CANR-3
Earlier sketch in CA 5-6R
Dauw, Dean C(harles) 1933- CANR-6
Earlier sketch in CA 53-56
D'Avanzo, Mario Louis 1931- 41-44R
Davar, Ashok 69-72
Dave, Shyam
See Gantzer, Hugh
Daveluy, Paule Cloutier 1919- 9-10R
See also SATA 11
Davenant, William 1606-1668 .... DLB-58
Davenport, Elaine 1946- 102
Davenport, Francine
See Tate, Velma
Davenport, Francis Garvin 1905-1975
Obituary 111
Davenport, Gene L(ooney) 1935- 33-36R
Davenport, Guy (Mattison, Jr.) 1927- .. CANR-23
Earlier sketch in CA 33-36R
See also CLC 6, 14, 38
Davenport, Gwen 1910- 11-12R
Davenport, John 1905-1987 Obituary 122
Davenport, Marcia 1903- 9-10R
Davenport, Robert DLB-58
Davenport, Spencer CANR-26
Earlier sketches in CA 19-20, CAP-2
Davenport, T(homas) R(odney) H(ope) 1926- 77-80
Davenport, Walter 1889-1971 Obituary 104
Davenport, William H. 1908- CANR-4
Earlier sketch in CA 4R
Daventry, Leonard John 1915- 19-20R
Daves, Delmer Lawrence 1904(?)-1977
Obituary 73-76
See also DLB 26
Daves, Francis Marion 1903- 45-48
Daves, Jessica 1898(?)-1974 Obituary 53-56
Daves, Michael 1938- 9-10R
See also SATA 40
Davey, Cyril J(ames) 1911- CANR-18
Earlier sketches in CA 7-8R, CANR-2
Davey, Frank 1907(?)-1983 Obituary 109
Davey, Frank
See Davey, Frankland Wilmot
See also DLB 53
Davey, Frankland Wilmot 1940- CANR-13
Earlier sketch in CA 65-68
Davey, Gilbert (Walter) 1913- CANR-12
Earlier sketches in CA 9-10, CAP-1
Davey, Harold W(illiam) 1915-1986 120
Davey, Jocelyn
See Raphael, Chaim
Davey, John
See Richey, David
Davey, Thomas A. 1954- 126
Daviau, Donald G(eorge) 1927- CANR-14
Earlier sketch in CA 81-84
David, A. R.
See David, A(nn) Rosalie
David, A(nn) Rosalie 1946- 114
David, Alfred 1929- 85-88
David, Anne 1924-1987 .... CANR-12
Obituary 122
Earlier sketch in CA 29-32R
David, Carl 1949- 108
David, Ed
See Wohlmuth, Ed
David, Emily
See Alman, David
David, Gerald 1941- 114
David, Heather M(acKinnon) 1937- 37-40R
David, Henry 1907-1984 Obituary 111
David, Henry P. 1923- CANR-6
Earlier sketch in CA 15-16R
David, Irene 1921- 110
David, Jack 1946- 110
David, Jay
See Adler, William
David, Jonathan
See Ames, Lee J(udah)
David, Joseph Ben
See Ben-David, Joseph
David, Lester 1914- CANR-14
Earlier sketch in CA 37-40R
David, Marjorie 1950- 112
David, Martin H(eidenhain) 1935- 37-40R
David, Michael Robert 1932- 53-56
David, Nicholas
See Morgan, Thomas Bruce
David, Paul A(llan) 1935- 97-100
David, Paul T(heodore) 1906- CANR-2
Earlier sketch in CA 5-6R
David, Rosalie
See David, A(nn) Rosalie
David, Saul 1921- 124
Brief entry 114
David, Stephen M(ark) 1934-1985 .... 33-36R
Obituary 115
David, William
See Sandman, Peter M(ark)
David-Neel, Alexandra 1868-1969
Obituary 25-28R
Davidow, Mike 1913- 57-60
Davidow-Goodman, Ann
See Goodman, Ann (Davidow)
Davids, Anthony 1923- 41-44R
Davids, Bob
See Davids, L(eonard) Robert
Davids, L(eonard) Robert 1926- 115
Davids, Lewis Edmund 1917- 37-40R
Davids, Richard Carlyle 1913- 97-100
Davidson, Abraham A. 1935- 53-56
Davidson, Alan Eaton 1924- 103
Davidson, Alastair 1939- 29-32R
Davidson, Alice Joyce 1932- 115
See also SATA 45
Davidson, Angus (Henry Gordon) 1898-1980 .... 25-28R
Obituary 97-100
Davidson, Arnold E(dward) 1936- 111
Davidson, Avram 1923- CANR-26
Earlier sketch in CA 101
See also DLB 8
Davidson, Basil 1914- CANR-17
Earlier sketches in CA 1R, CANR-1
See also SATA 13
Davidson, Bill
See Davidson, William
Davidson, Bill R.
See Davidson, William R.
Davidson, Caroline 1953- 122
Davidson, Cathy Notari 1949- CANR-23
Earlier sketch in CA 106
Davidson, Chalmers Gaston 1907- 29-32R
Davidson, Chandler 1936- 45-48
Davidson, Clarissa Start
See Lippert, Clarissa Start
Davidson, Clifford 1932- 45-48
Davidson, David 1908-1985 49-52
Obituary 117
Davidson, Diane 1924- 29-32R
Davidson, Donald (Grady) 1893-1968 ... CANR-4
Obituary 25-28R
Earlier sketch in CA 7-8R
See also DLB 45
See also CLC 2, 13, 19
Davidson, Donald 1917- CANR-2
Earlier sketch in CA 45-48
Davidson, E(phraim) E(dward) 1923- 33-36R
Davidson, Ellen Prescott 49-52
Davidson, Eugene (Arthur) 1902- CANR-3
Earlier sketch in CA 3R
Davidson, Eva Rucker 1894(?)-1974
Obituary 53-56
Davidson, F(rank) G(eoffrey) 1920- 29-32R
Davidson, Frank P(aul) 1918- 116
Davidson, Glen W(illiam) 1936- CANR-9
Earlier sketch in CA 61-64
Davidson, Gustav 1895-1971 Obituary ... 29-32R
Davidson, H(ilda) R(oderick) Ellis 1914- CANR-11
Earlier sketch in CA 17-18R
Davidson, Harold G(ordon) 1912- 65-68
Davidson, Henry A(lexander) 1905-1973
Obituary 45-48
Davidson, Herbert A(lan) 1932- 19-20R
Davidson, Hugh
See Hamilton, Edmond
Davidson, Hugh M(acCullough) 1918- 102
Davidson, Irwin Delmore 1906-1981
Obituary 105
Davidson, James Dale 1947- 107
Davidson, James West 1946- CANR-15
Earlier sketch in CA 85-88

INDEX

Davidson, Jeffrey P(hilip) 1951- ... 122
Davidson, Jessica 1915- ... CANR-14
Earlier sketch in CA 41-44R
See also SATA 5
Davidson, John 1857-1909 Brief entry ... 118
See also DLB 19
See also TCLC 24
Davidson, John
See Reid, Charles (Stuart)
Davidson, John Wells 1903-1986
Obituary ... 120
Davidson, Judith 1953- ... 116
See also SATA 40
Davidson, Julian M. 1931- ... 102
Davidson, Lionel 1922- ... CANR-1
Earlier sketch in CA 4R
See also DLB 14
Davidson, Margaret 1936- ... CANR-17
Earlier sketch in CA 25-28R
See also SATA 5
Davidson, Marion
See Garis, Howard R(oger)
Davidson, Marshall B(owman) 1907- ... 33-36R
Davidson, Mary R. 1885-1973 ... 5-6R
See also SATA 9
Davidson, Mary S. 1940- ... 107
Davidson, Max D. 1899(?)-1977
Obituary ... 73-76
Davidson, Michael 1944- ... 106
Davidson, Michael
See Rorvik, David M(ichael)
Davidson, Michael Childers 1897- ... 29-32R
Davidson, Mickie
See Davidson, Margaret
Davidson, Mildred 1935- ... 93-96
Davidson, Morris 1898-1979 ... 85-88
Davidson, Muriel 1924(?)-1983 Obituary ... 110
Davidson, Norman 1933- ... 119
Davidson, Paul 1930- ... CANR-6
Earlier sketch in CA 13-14R
Davidson, Philip (Grant) 1902- ... 73-76
Davidson, R.
See Davidson, Raymond
Davidson, Raymond 1926- ... SATA-32
Davidson, Robert F(ranklin) 1902- ... 49-52
Davidson, Roger H(arry) 1936- ... CANR-24
Earlier sketches in CA 21-22R, CANR-9
Davidson, Rosalie 1921- ... 69-72
See also SATA 23
Davidson, Sandra Calder 1935- ... 41-44R
Davidson, Sara 1943- ... 81-84
See also CLC 9
Davidson, Sol M. 1924- ... 17-18R
Davidson, William 1918- ... 93-96
Davidson, William R. 1929(?)-1987
Obituary ... 122
Davidson, William Robert 1919- ... 19-20R
Davidson-Houston, J(ames) Vivian
1901-1965 ... 7-8R
Davie, Donald (Alfred) 1922- ... CANR-1
Earlier sketch in CA 3R
See also CAAS 3
See also DLB 27
See also CLC 5, 8, 10, 31
Davie, Elspeth 1919- ... 126
Brief entry ... 120
Davie, Ian 1924- ... 102
Davie, Maurice R(ea) 1893-1964 ... 7-8R
Davie, Michael 1924- ... 57-60
Davie, Peter (Edward Sidney) 1936- ... 114
Davied, Camille
See Rose, Camille Davied
Davie-Martin, Hugh
See McCutcheon, Hugh Davie-Martin
Davies, A(lfred) Mervyn 1899-1976 ... 17-18R
Obituary ... 69-72
Davies, Ada Hilton 1893- ... CAP-2
Earlier sketch in CA 17-18
Davies, Alan T(rewartha) 1933- ... 33-36R
Davies, Alfred T(homas) 1930- ... 15-16R
Davies, Andrew (Wynford) 1936- ... 105
See also SATA 27
Davies, Bettilu D(onna) 1942- ... CANR-18
Earlier sketch in CA 101
See also SATA 33
Davies, Christie
See Davies, John Christopher Hughes
Davies, Colin
See Elliot, Ian
Davies, (George) Colliss (Boardman)
1912- ... CAP-1
Earlier sketch in CA 11-12
Davies, D(avid) Jacob 1916-1974 ... 7-8R
Obituary ... 103
Davies, Daniel R. 1911- ... 37-40R
Davies, David Margerison 1923- ... 7-8R
Davies, David Michael 1929- Brief entry ... 109
Davies, David W(illiam) 1908- ... CANR-3
Earlier sketch in CA 9-10R
Davies, Duncan (Sheppey) 1921-1987 ... 124
Obituary ... 122
Davies, Ebenezer Thomas 1903- ... CAP-1
Earlier sketch in CA 13-14
Davies, Eileen Winifred 1910- ... CAP-1
Earlier sketch in CA 13-14
Davies, Evelyn 1924- ... CANR-8
Earlier sketch in CA 61-64
Davies, Evelyn A(dele) 1915- ... 61-64
Davies, Harriet Vaughn 1879(?)-1978
Obituary ... 77-80
Davies, Horton (Marlais) 1916- ... CANR-7
Earlier sketch in CA 5-6R
Davies, Hugh Sykes 1909-1984(?)
Obituary ... 113
Davies, Hunter 1936- ... CANR-12
Earlier sketch in CA 57-60
See also SATA 45
Davies, (David) Ioan 1936- ... 21-22R
Davies, Ivor K(evin) 1930- ... 53-56
Davies, J. Clarence III 1937- ... 29-32R
Davies, J. Kenneth 1925- ... 57-60
Davies, James Chowning 1918- ... 45-48
Davies, Joan 1934- ... 124
See also SATA 47, 50
Davies, John Christopher Hughes 1941- ... 93-96
Davies, John Evan Weston 1914- ... 113
Brief entry ... 111
Davies, John Gordon 1919- ... 69-72
Davies, John K(enyon) 1937- ... 120
Davies, John Paton, Jr. 1908- ... 11-12R
Davies, L(eslie) P(urnell) 1914- ... CANR-9
Earlier sketch in CA 21-22R
Davies, Laurence 1926- ... 57-60
Davies, Mansel Morris 1913- ... 9-10R
Davies, Margaret C(onstance Brown)
1923- ... 9-10R
Davies, Margaret Lloyd 1935- ... 106
Davies, Marion
See Douras, Marion Cecilia
Davies, Martin Brett 1936- ... 102
Davies, Merton E(dward) 1917- ... 85-88
Davies, Morton Rees 1939- ... 37-40R
Davies, (Claude) Nigel (Byam) 1920- ... CANR-19
Earlier sketch in CA 102
Davies, Norman 1939- ... 41-44R
Davies, Oliver 1905- ... CAP-2
Earlier sketch in CA 25-28
Davies, P.C.W.
See Davies, Paul (Charles William)
Davies, Paul (Charles William) 1946- ... 106
Davies, (William Thomas) Pennar 1911- ... 13-14R
Davies, Peter 1937- ... 53-56
See also SATA 52
Davies, Piers (Anthony David) 1941- ... 103
Davies, R(onald) E. G. 1921- ... 17-18R
Davies, R(eginald) T(horne) 1923- ... 9-10R
Davies, R(obert) W(illiam) 1925- ... CANR-13
Earlier sketch in CA 33-36R
Davies, Ray(mond Douglas) 1944-
Brief entry ... 116
See also CLC 21
Davies, Rhys 1903-1978 ... CANR-4
Obituary ... 81-84
Earlier sketch in CA 9-10R
See also CLC 23
Davies, Richard Llewelyn
See Llewelyn-Davies, Richard
Davies, Richard O. 1937- ... 19-20R
Davies, (William) Robertson 1913- ... CANR-17
Earlier sketch in CA 33-36R
See also DLB 68
See also CLC 2, 7, 13, 25, 42
Davies, Rod 1941- ... 61-64
Davies, Rosemary Reeves 1925- ... 49-52
Davies, Rupert Eric 1909- ... CANR-18
Earlier sketches in CA 5-6R, CANR-3
Davies, Ruth A(nn) 1915- ... CANR-26
Earlier sketch in CA 29-32R
Davies, Samuel 1723-1761 ... DLB-31
Davies, Stan Gebler 1943- ... 65-68
Davies, Stanley Powell 1892-1985
Obituary ... 115
Davies, Stevan L(awrence) 1948- ... 107
Davies, Sumiko 1942- ... 126
See also SATA 46
Davies, T(refor) Rendall 1913- ... CAP-1
Earlier sketch in CA 9-10
Davies, Thomas 1941- ... 115
Davies, Thomas M(ockett), Jr. 1940- ... CANR-6
Earlier sketch in CA 57-60
Davies, Tom
See Davies, Thomas
Davies, W(illiam) H(enry) 1871-1940
Brief entry ... 104
See also DLB 19
See also TCLC 5
Davies, Walter C.
See Kornbluth, C(yril) M.
Davies, William David 1911- ... CANR-1
Earlier sketch in CA 1R
Davies, Wyndham (Roy) 1926- ... 25-28R
Davin, D(aniel) M(arcus) 1913- ... CANR-3
Earlier sketch in CA 9-10R
Davinson, Donald E(dward) 1932- ... CANR-3
Earlier sketch in CA 7-8R
Daviot, Gordon
See Mackintosh, Elizabeth
See also DLB 10
Davis, Adelle 1904-1974 ... 37-40R
Obituary ... 49-52
Davis, Allen F(reeman) 1931- ... CANR-25
Earlier sketches in CA 23-24R, CANR-10
Davis, Allen III 1929- ... 108
Davis, (William) Allison 1902-1983 ... 125
Obituary ... 111
Brief entry ... 106
See also BW
Davis, Andrew Jackson 1826-1910
Brief entry ... 120
Davis, Angela (Yvonne) 1944- ... CANR-10
Earlier sketch in CA 57-60
See also BW
Davis, Ann E(lizabeth) 1932- ... 69-72
Davis, Archie K. 1911- ... 124
Davis, Arthur G. 1915- ... 15-16R
Davis, Arthur Hoey 1868-1935 Brief entry ... 121
Davis, Arthur Kennard 1910- ... CAP-1
Earlier sketch in CA 13-14
Davis, Arthur Kyle, Jr. 1897-19(?) ... CAP-2
Earlier sketch in CA 17-18
Davis, Arthur P(aul) 1904- ... 61-64
See also BW
Davis, Audrey
See Paine, Lauran (Bosworth)
Davis, Barbara 1955- ... 108
Davis, Barbara Kerr 1946- ... 104
Davis, Ben Reeves 1927- ... 77-80
Davis, (Mary) Bernice
See Curler, (Mary) Bernice
Davis, Berrie 1922- ... 101
Davis, Bertram H(ylton) 1918- ... CANR-1
Earlier sketch in CA 4R
Davis, Bette
See Davis, Ruth Elizabeth
Davis, Bette J. 1923- ... 93-96
See also SATA 15
Davis, Bill C. 1951- ... 110
Davis, Brian 1925-1988 Obituary ... 126
Davis, Burke 1913- ... CANR-25
Earlier sketches in CA 1R, CANR-4
See also SATA 4
Davis, Calvin DeArmond 1927- ... 5-6R
Davis, Charles 1923- ... CANR-21
Earlier sketch in CA 5-6R
Davis, Charles A. 1795-1867 ... DLB-11
Davis, Charles T(witchell) 1918-1981 ... 125
See also BW
Davis, Charles T(ill) 1929- ... 37-40R
Davis, Christopher 1928- ... CANR-3
Earlier sketch in CA 9-10R
See also SATA 6
Davis, Cliff
See Smith, Richard Rein
Davis, Clive E(dward) 1914- ... 17-18R
Davis, Clyde Brion 1894-1962 ... 5-6R
See also DLB 9
Davis, Creath 1939- ... CANR-21
Earlier sketches in CA 57-60, CANR-6
Davis, Curtis Carroll 1916- ... CANR-6
Earlier sketch in CA 9-10R
Davis, Curtis Wheeler 1928-1986 Obituary ... 119
Davis, D(elbert) Dwight 1908-1965
Obituary ... 111
See also SATA 33
Davis, D(onald) Evan 1923-1979 ... 19-20R
Obituary ... 122
Davis, Daniel S(heldon) 1936- ... 45-48
See also SATA 12
Davis, Daphne ... 65-68
Davis, David Brion 1927- ... CANR-26
Earlier sketches in CA 19-20R, CANR-9
Davis, David C(harles) L. 1928- ... 33-36R
Davis, David Howard 1941- ... 53-56
Davis, Deane C(handler) 1900- ... 108
Davis, Dick 1945- ... DLB-40
Davis, Don
See Dresser, Davis
Davis, Donald Gordon, Jr. 1939- ... CANR-6
Earlier sketch in CA 53-56
Davis, Dorothy Salisbury 1916- ... CANR-14
Earlier sketch in CA 37-40R
Davis, Douglas (Matthew) 1933- ... 111
Davis, Douglas F(redell) 1935- ... 105
Davis, E. Adams
See Davis, Edwin Adams
Davis, Earl C(linton) 1938- ... 111
Davis, Earle (Rosco) 1905- ... 65-68
Davis, Edwin Adams 1904- ... CAP-2
Earlier sketch in CA 25-28
Davis, Eleanor Harmon 1909- ... 106
Davis, Elise Miller 1915- ... 69-72
Davis, Elizabeth
See Davis, Lou Ellen
Davis, Elizabeth G. 1910(?)-1974
Obituary ... 53-56
Davis, Elwood Craig 1896- ... CANR-3
Earlier sketch in CA 1R
Davis, F(loyd) James 1920- ... CANR-4
Earlier sketch in CA 3R
Davis, Fitzroy K. 1912-1980 ... 49-52
Obituary ... 102
Davis, Flora 1934- ... CANR-10
Earlier sketch in CA 65-68
Davis, Forest K(endall) 1918- ... 41-44R
Davis, Francis 1946- ... 123
Davis, Frank G(reene) 1915- ... 85-88
Davis, Frank Marshall 1905-1987 ... 125
Obituary ... 123
See also BW
See also DLB 51
Davis, Franklin M(ilton), Jr. 1918-1981 ... CANR-4
Earlier sketch in CA 3R
Davis, Fred 1925- ... 13-14R
Davis, Frederick Barton 1909-1975 ... CANR-17
Obituary ... 116
Earlier sketch in CA 3R
Davis, Frederick C(lyde) 1902-1977
Obituary ... 115
Davis, Garold N(eil) 1932- ... 41-44R
Davis, Gary A(lan) 1938- ... 106
Davis, Genevieve 1928- ... 65-68
Davis, Genny Wright 1948- ... 105
Davis, George 1939- ... CANR-9
Earlier sketch in CA 65-68
See also BW
Davis, George L(ittleton), Sr. 1921- ... 57-60
Davis, Gerry 1930- Brief entry ... 117
Davis, Gibbs 1953- ... 111
See also SATA 41, 46
Davis, Gil
See Gilmore, Don
Davis, Gilbert 1899-1983 Obituary ... 109
Davis, Gordon
See Hunt, E(verette) Howard, Jr.
and Levinson, Leonard
Davis, Gordon B(itter) 1930- ... CANR-4
Earlier sketch in CA 53-56
Davis, Grania 1943- ... CANR-16
Earlier sketch in CA 85-88
See also SATA 50
Davis, Grant Miller 1937- ... CANR-11
Earlier sketch in CA 29-32R
Davis, Gwen 1936- ... CANR-2
Earlier sketch in CA 3R
See also AITN 1
Davis, H(enry) Grady 1890- ... CAP-2
Earlier sketch in CA 21-22
Davis, Harley
See Green, Kay
Davis, Harold Eugene 1902-1988 ... CANR-1
Obituary ... 126
Earlier sketch in CA 3R
Davis, Harold Lenoir 1896-1960 Obituary ... 89-92
See also DLB 9
See also CLC 49
Davis, Harold S(eaton) 1919- ... 57-60
Davis, Harriet Eager 1892(?)-1974
Obituary ... 49-52
Davis, Harry Rex 1921- ... 3R
Davis, Henry P. 1894(?)-1970 Obituary ... 104
Davis, Herbert (John) 1893-1967 ... CANR-1
Earlier sketch in CA 3R
Davis, Hope Hale ... 25-28R
Davis, Hope Harding 1915(?)-1976
Obituary ... 69-72
Davis, Horace B(ancroft) 1898- ... 23-24R
Davis, Horance G(ibbs), Jr. 1924- ... 65-68
Davis, Howard V(aughn) 1915- ... 25-28R
Davis, Hubert J(ackson) 1904- ... 107
See also SATA 31
Davis, I(rene) M(ary) 1926- ... 61-64
Davis, J(ohn) Cary 1905- ... 41-44R
Davis, J. Morton 1929- ... 124
Davis, J(ames) William 1908- ... 102
Davis, Jack Leonard 1917- ... 106
Davis, James Allan 1929- ... CANR-1
Earlier sketch in CA 1R
Davis, James C(urran) 1895-1981
Obituary ... 108
Davis, James C(ushman) 1931-
Brief entry ... 117
Davis, James H. 1932- ... 89-92
Davis, James Kotsilibas
See Kotsilibas-Davis, James
Davis, James Richard 1936- ... 65-68
Davis, James Robert 1945- ... CANR-16
Earlier sketch in CA 85-88
See also SATA 32
Davis, James W(arren, Jr.) 1935- ... 29-32R
Davis, Jan Haddle 1950- ... 93-96
Davis, Jean Reynolds 1927- ... 61-64
Davis, Jean Walton 1909- ... 3R
Davis, Jed H(orace, Jr.) 1921- ... 17-18R
Davis, Jerome 1891-1979 ... CANR-3
Obituary ... 89-92
Earlier sketch in CA 5-6R
Davis, Jim
See Davis, James Robert
and Smith, Richard Rein
Davis, Jinnie Y(eh) 1945- ... 107
Davis, Joe 1901-1978 Obituary ... 112
Davis, Joe Lee 1906-1974 ... 5-6R
Obituary ... 103
Davis, Johanna 1937-1974 ... 41-44R
Obituary ... 53-56
Davis, John 1774-1854 ... DLB-37
Davis, John D(avid) 1937- ... 29-32R
Davis, John H(erbert) 1904- ... 29-32R
Davis, John H. 1929- ... CANR-18
Earlier sketch in CA 25-28R
Davis, John J(ames) 1936- ... 33-36R
Davis, John King 1884-1967 ... CAP-1
Earlier sketch in CA 9-10
Davis, Joseph C(ole) 1908- ... 97-100
Davis, Joseph S(tancliffe) 1885-1975 ... 101
Obituary ... 57-60
Davis, Judith 1925- ... 106
Davis, Julia 1900- ... CANR-1
Earlier sketch in CA 4R
See also SATA 6
Davis, Julian 1902(?)-1974 Obituary ... 53-56
Davis, K(eith) 1918- ... CANR-20
Earlier sketches in CA 4R, CANR-5
Davis, Karen Padgett 1942- ... 112
Davis, Keith F. 1952- ... 123
Davis, Ken(neth Pickett) 1906- ... 49-52
Davis, Kenneth Culp 1908- Brief entry ... 115
Davis, Kenneth R(exton) 1921- ... 19-20R
Davis, Kenneth S. 1912- ... 15-16R
Davis, Kingsley 1908- ... CANR-8
Earlier sketch in CA 15-16R
Davis, L(awrence) J(ames) 1940- ... CANR-11
Earlier sketch in CA 25-28R
Davis, Lance E(dwin) 1928- ... 53-56
Davis, Lanny J(esse) 1945- ... 57-60
Davis, Lawrence B(ennion) 1939- ... 45-48
Davis, Lennard J. 1949- ... 116
Davis, Lenwood G. 1939- ... 25-28R
Davis, Lew A(rter) 1930- ... 21-22R
Davis, Lloyd (Moore) 1931- ... 69-72
Davis, Lou Ellen 1936- ... 81-84
Davis, Louis E(lkin) 1918- ... 53-56
Davis, Louise Littleton 1921- ... 103
See also SATA 25
Davis, Loyal Edward 1896-1982 Obituary ... 107
Davis, Luther 1921- ... 105
Davis, M(orris) Edward 1899- ... 7-8R
Davis, Maggie (Hill) ... CANR-9
Earlier sketch in CA 15-16R
Davis, Maralee G.
See Gibson, Maralee G.
Davis, Marc 1934- ... 29-32R
Davis, Margaret Banfield 1903- ... CAP-1
Earlier sketch in CA 11-12
Davis, Margaret Thomson 1926- ... 102
See also DLB 14
Davis, Marguerite 1889- ... SATA-34

Davis, Marilyn K(ornreich) 1928- 5-6R
Davis, Martha 1942- CANR-4
Earlier sketch in CA 49-52
Davis, Mary L(ee) 1935- CANR-4
Earlier sketch in CA 49-52
See also SATA 9
Davis, Mary Octavia 1901- CAP-2
Earlier sketch in CA 25-28
See also SATA 6
Davis, Maxine
See McHugh, Maxine Davis
Davis, Melodie M(iller) 1951- 113
Davis, Melton S(amillow) 1910- 41-44R
Davis, (John) Michael 1940- 33-36R
Davis, Michael Justin 1925- 102
Davis, Mildred 77-80
Davis, Mildred Ann (Campbell) 1916- 5-6R
Davis, Millard C. 1930- 69-72
Davis, Monte 1949- 103
Davis, Morris 1933- CANR-11
Earlier sketch in CA 61-64
Davis, Morton D(avid) 1930- 65-68
Davis, Moshe 1916- CANR-20
Earlier sketches in CA 9-10R, CANR-4
Davis, Murray S(tuart) 1940- 53-56
Davis, Myrna (Mushkin) 1936- 69-72
Davis, Natalie Zemon 1928- 53-56
Davis, Neil 1934(?)-1985 Obituary 117
Davis, Neil
See Davis, T(homas) Neil
Davis, Nolan 1942- CANR-25
Earlier sketch in CA 49-52
See also BW
Davis, Norah Deakin 1941- 111
Davis, Norman 1913- Brief entry 106
Davis, Norman Maurice 1936- 69-72
Davis, Nuel Pharr 1915- 29-32R
Davis, Olivia 1922- 81-84
Davis, Ossie 1917- CANR-26
Earlier sketch in CA 112
See also BW
See also DLB 7, 38
Davis, Patrick (David Channer) 1925- 93-96
Davis, Paxton 1925- CANR-3
Earlier sketch in CA 9-10R
See also SATA 16
Davis, Peter (Frank) 1937- 107
Davis, Philip E(dward) 1927- 49-52
Davis, Philip J. 1923- 124
Davis, Polly Ann 1931- 102
Davis, R. G. 1933- 57-60
Davis, R(alph) H(enry) C(arless) 1918- .. CANR-6
Earlier sketch in CA 7-8R
Davis, Ralph C(urrier) 1894- 33-36R
Davis, Rebecca (Blaine) Harding
1831-1910 Brief entry 104
See also DLB 74
See also TCLC 6
Davis, Rex D. 1924- 11-12R
Davis, Richard CANR-26
Earlier sketches in CA 53-56, CANR-7
Davis, Richard Beale 1907- CANR-2
Earlier sketch in CA 5-6R
Davis, Richard Harding 1864-1916
Brief entry 114
See also DLB 12, 23
See also TCLC 24
Davis, Richard W. 1935- 33-36R
Davis, Robert 1881-1949 .... YABC-1
Davis, Robert Con 1948- CANR-23
Earlier sketch in CA 104
Davis, Robert Murray 1934- CANR-12
Earlier sketch in CA 33-36R
Davis, Robert P. 1929- CANR-3
Earlier sketch in CA 7-8R
Davis, Robert Ralph, Jr. 1941- 37-40R
Davis, Rocky 1927- 61-64
Davis, Ronald L(eroy) 1936- 37-40R
Davis, Rosemary 7-8R
Davis, Rosemary L.
See Davis, Rosemary
Davis, Roy Eugene 1931- CANR-6
Earlier sketch in CA 11-12R
Davis, Rupert (Charles) Hart
See Hart-Davis, Rupert (Charles)
Davis, Russell Gerard 1922- 7-8R
See also SATA 3
Davis, Ruth Elizabeth 1908- CANR-21
Earlier sketch in CA 61-64
Davis, Sammy, Jr. 1925- 108
Davis, Samuel 1930- 29-32R
Davis, Samuel Cole 1764-1809 .... DLB-37
Davis, Sandra T. W. 1937- 124
Davis, Sara deSaussure 1943- 125
Davis, Stanley Nelson 1924- 108
Davis, Steven Andrew 1947- 112
Davis, Stratford
See Bolton, Maisie Sharman
Davis, Suzanne
See Sugar, Bert Randolph
Davis, Sydney Charles Houghton 1887- 7-8R
Davis, Sylvan 1927(?)-1984 Obituary 112
Davis, T. N.
See Davis, T(homas) Neil
Davis, T(homas) Neil 1932- 123
Davis, Terence 1924- 21-22R
Davis, Thomas J(oseph) 1946- CANR-4
Earlier sketch in CA 53-56
Davis, Timothy Francis Tothill 1941- 81-84
Davis, Tom Edward 1929- 85-88
Davis, Verne Theodore 1889-1973 .... 4R
See also SATA 6
Davis, (Benton) Vincent (Jr.) 1930- CANR-23
Earlier sketches in CA 19-20R, CANR-7
Davis, W(illiam) Jackson 1942- 107
Davis, W(arren) Jefferson 1885-1973 .... CAP-2
Earlier sketch in CA 29-32
Davis, W(illiam) N(ewell), Jr. 1915- 81-84
Davis, Walter A(lbert III) 1942- 114
Davis, Walter Richardson 1928- 102
Davis, Wayne H(arry) 1930- 33-36R
Davis, Wiley H. 1913- 25-28R
Davis, William 1933- CANR-10
Earlier sketch in CA 65-68
Davis, William C(harles) 1946- CANR-23
Earlier sketches in CA 61-64, CANR-8
Davis, William H(atcher) 1939- 33-36R
Davis, William S(terling) 1943- 111
Davis, William Virgil 1940- CANR-23
Earlier sketch in CA 106
Davis, Winston (Bradley) 1939- 104
Davis-Friedmann, Deborah 1945- 118
Davis-Gardner, Angela 1942- 110
Davis-Goff, Annabel 1942- 85-88
Davison, Edward 1898-1970 Obituary 29-32R
Davison, Frank Dalby 1893-1970 Obituary .. 116
See also CLC 15
Davison, Geoffrey 1927- 110
Davison, Gladys Patton 1905- CAP-1
Earlier sketch in CA 15-16
Davison, Jane 1932(?)-1981 Obituary 104
Davison, Jean 1937- CANR-10
Earlier sketch in CA 65-68
Davison, Kenneth E(dwin) 1924- 11-12R
Davison, Lawrence H.
See Lawrence, D(avid) H(erbert Richards)
Davison, Ned J. 1926- 45-48
Davison, Peter 1928- CANR-3
Earlier sketch in CA 9-10R
See also CAAS 4
See also DLB 5
See also CLC 28
Davison, Roderic H(ollett) 1916- 37-40R
Davison, Verne E(lbert) 1904- 69-72
Davisson, Charles Nelson 1917- 25-28R
Davisson, William I. 1929- CANR-11
Earlier sketch in CA 19-20R
Davis-Weyer, Caecilia 1929- 41-44R
Davitt, Thomas E(dward) 1904-1980 .... 25-28R
Obituary 117
Davitz, Joel R(obert) 1926- Brief entry 114
Davy, Francis X(avier) 1916- 29-32R
Davy, George Mark Oswald 1898-1983
Obituary 110
Davy, John Charles 1927-1984 Obituary 114
Davys, Mary 1674-1732 .... DLB-39
Davys, Sarah
See Manning, Rosemary (Joy)
Dawdy, Doris Ostrander 53-56
Dawe, (Donald) Bruce 1930- CANR-11
Earlier sketch in CA 69-72
Dawe, Donald G. 1926- 33-36R
Dawe, Frederick
See Gettings, Fred
Dawe, (Chartres) Gerald 1952- 114
Dawe, Roger David 1934- CANR-3
Earlier sketch in CA 11-12R
Dawes, Dorothy
See Cooper, Parley J(oseph)
Dawes, Frank 1933- 69-72
Dawes, Nathaniel Thomas, Jr. 1937- 49-52
Dawes, Neville 1926- 13-14R
Dawes, Robyn M(ason) 1936- 37-40R
Dawidowicz, Lucy S. 1915- CANR-18
Earlier sketch in CA 25-28R
Dawis, Rene V(illanueva) 1928- 45-48
Dawisha, Adeed Isam 1944- CANR-18
Earlier sketch in CA 102
Dawisha, Karen (Lea) 1949- 120
Dawkins, Cecil 1927- 7-8R
Dawkins, Richard 1941- CANR-26
Earlier sketch in CA 69-72
Dawley, David 1941- 45-48
Dawley, Powel Mills 1907- 57-60
Dawlish, Peter
See Kerr, James Lennox
Dawn, C(larence) Ernest 1918- 61-64
Dawood, N(essim) J(oseph) 1927- 49-52
Dawson, Alan David 1942- 77-80
Dawson, Carl 1938- CANR-1
Earlier sketch in CA 45-48
Dawson, Christopher (Henry)
1889-1970 .... CANR-6
Obituary 29-32R
Earlier sketch in CA 3R
Dawson, Elizabeth
See Geach, Christine
Dawson, Elmer A. CAP-2
Earlier sketch in CA 19-20
See also SATA 1
Dawson, Fielding 1930- 85-88
See also CLC 6
Dawson, Frank G(ates, Jr.) 1925- 69-72
Dawson, George G(lenn) 1925- 37-40R
Dawson, Giles E(dwin) 1903- CAP-2
Earlier sketch in CA 19-20
Dawson, Grace S(trickler) 1891- 17-18R
Dawson, Howard A. 1895(?)-1979
Obituary 89-92
Dawson, Jan 1939(?)-1980 Obituary 101
Dawson, Jennifer CANR-10
Earlier sketch in CA 57-60
Dawson, Jerry F. 1933- 33-36R
Dawson, Joseph G(reen) III 1945- 110
Dawson, Mary 1919- 21-22R
See also SATA 11
Dawson, Mildred A(gnes) 1897- CANR-12
Earlier sketch in CA 17-18R
Dawson, Minnie E. 1906-1978 85-88
Dawson, Peter
See Faust, Frederick (Shiller)
Dawson, (John) Philip 1928- 21-22R
Dawson, Richard E(vans) 1939- 73-76
Dawson, Robert (Merril) 1941- 21-22R
Dawson, Robert L(ewis) 1943- 105
Dawson, William 1704-1752 .... DLB-31
Dawson-Scott, C(atharine) A(my)
1865-1934 Brief entry 113
Day, A(rthur) Grove 1904- CANR-23
Earlier sketches in CA 21-22R, CANR-8
Day, Alan Charles Lynn 1924- 1R
Day, Alan J(ohn) 1942- 105
Day, Albert Edward 1884-1973 .... CAP-2
Obituary 45-48
Earlier sketch in CA 23-24
Day, Albert M. 1897-1979 93-96
Obituary 85-88
Day, Alice Taylor 1928- 19-20R
Day, Benjamin Henry 1810-1889 .... DLB-43
Day, Beth (Feagles) 1924- CANR-18
Earlier sketches in CA 9-10R, CANR-3
See also SATA 33
Day, Bradford M(arshall) 1916- 104
Day, Clarence (Shepard, Jr.) 1874-1935
Brief entry 108
See also DLB 11
See also TCLC 25
Day, Clarence Burton 1889-1987 Obituary .. 121
Day, David 1944- 93-96
Day, Donald
See Harding, Donald Edward
Day, Dorothy 1897-1980 65-68
Obituary 102
See also DLB 29
Day, Douglas (Turner III) 1932- CANR-8
Earlier sketch in CA 9-10R
Day, Gardiner Mumford 1900-1981
Obituary 104
Day, George 1950- 117
Day, George Harold 1900- CAP-1
Earlier sketch in CA 13-14
Day, Gwynn McLendon 1908- CAP-1
Earlier sketch in CA 11-12
Day, Houston
See Day, Sam Houston
Day, J(ames) Edward 1914- 17-18R
Day, J(ohn) Laurence 1934- 65-68
Day, James F(rancis) 1917- 33-36R
Day, James Wentworth 1899-1983(?) .. CANR-10
Obituary 108
Earlier sketch in CA 13-14R
Day, John 1574(?)-1640(?) DLB-62
Day, John A(rthur) 1913- 17-18R
Day, John Patrick 1919- 7-8R
Day, John R(obert) 1917- CANR-9
Earlier sketch in CA 7-8R
Day, Kenneth 1912- 11-12R
Day, LeRoy Judson 1917- 23-24R
Day, Lincoln H(ubert) 1928- 19-20R
Day, Lucille 1947- 110
Day, M(ichael) H(erbert) 1927- 102
Day, Martin Steele 1917- CANR-7
Earlier sketch in CA 5-6R
Day, Maurice 1892- SATA-30
Day, Max
See Cassiday, Bruce (Bingham)
Day, Melvin Norman 1923- 109
Day, Michael
See Dempewolff, Richard F(rederic)
Day, Nancy Raines 1951- 111
Day, (Truman) Owen 1890- 69-72
Day, Paul Woodford 1916- 25-28R
Day, Peter (Morton) 1914- 1R
Day, Price 1907-1978 85-88
Obituary 81-84
Day, R(oss) H(enry) 1927- 29-32R
Day, Ralph L(ewis) 1926- CANR-7
Earlier sketch in CA 7-8R
Day, Richard B(ruce) 1942- 49-52
Day, Richard E. 1929- 33-36R
Day, Richard Hollis 1933- 114
Day, Robert Adams 1924- 53-56
Day, Sam Houston 1896-1984 Obituary 113
Day, Stacey B(iswas) 1927- 33-36R
Day, Thomas 1748-1789 .... YABC-1
See also DLB 39
Dayan, Moshe 1915-1981 .... CANR-22
Obituary 105
Earlier sketch in CA 23-24R
Dayan, Yael 1939- 89-92
See also AITN 1
Dayananda, James Yesupriya 1934- 81-84
Day Lewis, C(ecil) 1904-1972 .... CAP-1
Obituary 33-36R
Earlier sketch in CA 15-16
See also DLB 15, 20
See also CLC 1, 6, 10
Daynes, Byron W(ilford) 1937- 110
Daysh, G(eorge) H(enry) J(ohn)
1901-1987 Obituary 122
Dayton, Donald W(ilber) 1942- CANR-24
Earlier sketch in CA 69-72
Dayton, Edward R(isedorph) 1924- CANR-16
Earlier sketch in CA 85-88
Dayton, Eldorous L. 1906-1987 Obituary ... 122
Dayton, Irene 1922- CANR-6
Earlier sketch in CA 57-60
Dazai, Osamu
See Tsushima, Shuji
See also TCLC 11
d'Azevedo, Warren L. 1920- 93-96
Dazey, Agnes J(ohnston) CAP-2
Earlier sketch in CA 23-24
See also SATA 2
Dazey, Frank M. CAP-2
Earlier sketch in CA 23-24
See also SATA 2
Deacon, Eileen
See Geipel, Eileen
Deacon, George Edward Raven 1906-1984
Obituary 114
Deacon, Joseph John 1920- 69-72
Deacon, Richard 1922-1984 Obituary 113
Deacon, Richard
See McCormick, (George) Donald (King)
Deacon, Ruth E. 1923- 102
Deacon, William Arthur 1890-1977 .... DLB-68
Deadman, Ronald 1919-1988(?) Obituary ... 125
Deagon, Ann (Fleming) 1930- 57-60
Deak, Edward Joseph, Jr. 1943- 53-56
Deak, Francis 1899-1972 Obituary 33-36R
Deak, Istvan 1926- CANR-11
Earlier sketch in CA 25-28R
Deakin, Frederick William 1913- CANR-5
Earlier sketch in CA 7-8R
Deakin, James 1929- CANR-24
Earlier sketches in CA 21-22R, CANR-8
Deakin, Motley F. 1920- 120
Deakin, Rose 1937- 109
Deakins, Roger Lee 1933- 61-64
Deal, Babs H(odges) 1929- CANR-1
Earlier sketch in CA 1R
Deal, Borden 1922-1985 .... CANR-2
Obituary 114
Earlier sketch in CA 4R
See also DLB 6
Deal, William S(anford) 1910- CANR-3
Earlier sketch in CA 7-8R
Deale, Kenneth Edwin Lee 1907-19(?) ... CANR-4
Earlier sketch in CA 7-8R
Dealey, E(dward) M(usgrove) 1892-1969 . CAP-2
Earlier sketch in CA 23-24
Dealey, Ted
See Dealey, E(dward) M(usgrove)
deAlmeida, Hermione (Beatrice) 1950- 118
Dean, Abner 1910-1982 Obituary 107
Dean, Amber 1902-1985 .... CANR-2
Obituary 116
Earlier sketch in CA 5-6R
Dean, Anabel 1915- CANR-14
Earlier sketch in CA 37-40R
See also SATA 12
Dean, Barbara 1946- 113
Dean, Basil 1888- 69-72
Dean, Beryl 1911- 9-10R
Dean, Burton V(ictor) 1924- CANR-20
Earlier sketches in CA 45-48, CANR-1
Dean, Christopher G(eorge) 1940- 111
Dean, Dorothy 1932(?)-1987 Obituary 121
Dean, Dwight G(antz) 1918- 17-18R
Dean, E. Douglas 1916- 97-100
Dean, Edith M(ae) 1915- 111
Dean, Edwin R(obinson) 1933- 17-18R
Dean, Frances Mary 1905(?)-1983
Obituary 110
Dean, Herbert Morris 1938- 105
Dean, Howard E(dward) 1916- 41-44R
Dean, Ida
See Grae, Ida
Dean, Jeffrey S. 1939- 37-40R
Dean, (Alfreda) Joan 1925- 101
Dean, Joan FitzPatrick 1949- 118
Dean, Joel 1906- 33-36R
Dean, John
See Bumppo, Nathaniel John Balthazar
Dean, John A(urie) 1921- 53-56
Dean, John Wesley III 1938- 105
Dean, Karen Strickler 1923- CANR-26
Earlier sketch in CA 109
See also SATA 49
Dean, Leonard Fellows 1909- Brief entry ... 105
Dean, Luella Jo 1908(?)-1977 Obituary ... 69-72
Dean, Malcolm 1948- 105
Dean, Morton 1935- 69-72
Dean, Nancy 1930- 65-68
Dean, Nell Marr 1910- 21-22R
Dean, Roger 1944- Brief entry 114
Dean, Roy 1925- CANR-6
Earlier sketch in CA 57-60
Dean, Stanley (Rochelle) 1908- 73-76
Dean, Vera Micheles 1903-1972
Obituary 37-40R
Dean, Warren 1932- 29-32R
Dean, William D(enard) 1937- 37-40R
Dean, William F(rishe) 1899-1981
Obituary 105
Dean, Winton Basil 1916- CANR-10
Earlier sketch in CA 65-68
Dean, Yetive H(ornor) 1909- CAP-1
Earlier sketch in CA 9-10
de Andrade, Carlos Drummond
See Drummond de Andrade, Carlos
DeAndrea, William L(ouis) 1952- CANR-20
Earlier sketch in CA 81-84
Deane, Dee Shirley 1928- 81-84
Deane, Elisabeth
See Beilenson, Edna
Deane, Herbert Andrew 1921- 1R
Deane, James G(arner) 1923- 89-92
Deane, Lorna
See Wilkinson, Lorna Hilda Kathleen
Deane, Nancy H(ilts) 1939- 29-32R
Deane, Norman
See Creasey, John
Deane, Seamus (Francis) 1940- 118
Deane, Shirley Joan 1920- CANR-2
Earlier sketch in CA 3R
de Angeli, Marguerite (Lofft)
1889-1987 .... CANR-3
Obituary 122
Earlier sketch in CA 5-6R
See also SATA 1, 27, 51
See also DLB 22
See also CLR 1
See also AITN 2
DeAngelis, William 1943- 113
de Antonio, Emile 1922- 117
Brief entry 113

Dear, William (C.) 1937- 125
de Aragon, Ray John 1946- 115
Dearden, Harold 1882(?)-1962 Obituary 116
Dearden, James A(rthur) 1924-1976 .....33-36R
Dearden, James S(hackley) 1931- CANR-12
Earlier sketch in CA 25-28R
Dearden, John 1919- 33-36R
Deardorff, Robert 1912- 61-64
Deardorff, Tom 1940- 89-92
Dearing, James (William) 1959- 114
Dearing, Vinton Adams 1920- 110
Dearlove, John 1944- 97-100
DeArmand, Frances Ullmann
1904(?)-1984 ....7-8R
Obituary 112
See also SATA 10, 38
de Armas, Frederick A(lfred) 1945- 37-40R
de Armas, Jose R(afael) 1924- 113
DeArment, Robert K(endall) 1925- 93-96
Dearmer, Geoffrey 1893- CAP-2
Earlier sketch in CA 23-24
Dearmin, Jeannie Tarascou 1924- 7-8R
Dearstyne, Howard (Best) 1903-1979 121
Obituary 85-88
De Arteaga, William 1943- 111
Deary, Terry 1946- 110
See also SATA 41, 51
Deason, Hilary J(ohn) 1903- 73-76
d'Easum, Cedric (Godfrey) 1907- CANR-12
Earlier sketch in CA 73-76
d'Easum, Dick
See d'Easum, Cedric (Godfrey)
Deasy, C(ornelius) M(ichael) 1918- 93-96
Deasy, Mary (Margaret) 1914- 5-6R
Deaton, Charles W. 1942- 93-96
Deaton, John (Graydon) 1939- CANR-11
Earlier sketch in CA 61-64
Deats, Paul (Kindred), Jr. 1918- 13-14R
Deats, Randy 1954- 93-96
Deats, Richard L(ouis) 1932- 23-24R
Deaux, George 1931- 7-8R
Deaux, Kay 1941- 114
DeBakey, Michael E(llis) 1908- 73-76
de Banke, Cecile 1889-1965 .... CAP-1
Earlier sketch in CA 13-14
See also SATA 11
de Bary, Brett
See Nee, Brett de Bary
deBary, William Theodore 57-60
DeBeaubien, Philip Francis 1913-1979
Obituary 85-88
de Beausobre, Iulia
See Namier, Julia
de Beauvoir, Simone (Lucie Ernestine Marie Bertrand)
See Beauvoir, Simone (Lucie Ernestine Marie Bertrand) de
de Bedts, Ralph F(ortes) 1914- 11-12R
De Beer, E(smond) S(amuel) 1895- CAP-1
Earlier sketch in CA 13-14
de Beer, Gavin R(ylands) 1899-1972 ..... CAP-1
Earlier sketch in CA 15-16
DeBenedetti, Charles Louis 1943-1987 102
Obituary 121
DeBerard, Ella 1900- 73-76
Deberdt-Malaquais, Elisabeth 1937- 57-60
de Betancourt, Cressy
See Dobkin De Rios, Marlene
DeBetz, Barbara Holstein 123
de Beus, Jacobus Gysbertus 1909- 102
Debevec Henning, Sylvie Marie 1948- 109
Debicki, Andrew P(eter) 1934- 37-40R
Debicki, Roman 1896- 3R
de Blank, Joost 1908-1968 .... CAP-1
Earlier sketch in CA 13-14
De Blasis, Celeste (N.) 1946- CANR-4
Earlier sketch in CA 53-56
de Blij, Harm J(an) 1935- CANR-23
Earlier sketches in CA 15-16R, CANR-8
Debo, Angie 1890-1988 69-72
Obituary 124
DeBoer, John C(harles) 1923- CANR-26
Earlier sketch in CA 29-32R
DeBoer, John James 1903-1969 .... CANR-3
Earlier sketch in CA 3R
de Bois, Helma
See de Bois, Wilhelmina J. E.
de Bois, Wilhelmina J. E. 1923- 19-20R
de Boissiere, Ralph (Anthony) 1907- 106
DeBold, Richard C. 1927- 23-24R
DeBolt, Margaret Wayt 1930- 115
De Bona, Maurice, Jr. 1926- 65-68
de Bono, Edward 1933- CANR-10
Earlier sketch in CA 23-24R
De Bonville, Bob 1926- 69-72
De Borchgrave, Arnaud 1926- 73-76
De Borhegyi, Suzanne Sims 1926- 5-6R
de Born, Edith 25-28R
De Bow, James Dunwoody Brownson
1820-1867 .... DLB-3
DeBoy, James J(oseph), Jr. 1942- 113
Debray, (Jules) Regis 1942- 21-22R
Debreczeny, Paul 1932- CANR-12
Earlier sketch in CA 33-36R
De Breffny, Brian 1931- 77-80
Debrett, Hal
See Dresser, Davis
Debreu, Gerard 1921- CANR-23
Earlier sketch in CA 37-40R
de Brissac, Malcolm
See Dickinson, Peter
de Broca, Philippe (Claude Alex) 1933- 126
de Broglie, L.
See de Broglie, Louis (Victor Pierre Raymond)
de Broglie, Louis (Victor Pierre Raymond)
1892-1987 Obituary 122
de Brunhoff, Jean
See Brunhoff, Jean de
De Brunhoff, Laurent
See Brunhoff, Laurent de
de Bruyn, Guenter 1926- DLB-75
de Bruyn, Monica (Jean) G(rembowicz)
1952- 65-68
See also SATA 13
Debus, Allen G(eorge) 1926- CANR-14
Earlier sketch in CA 37-40R
Debussy, (Achille) Claude 1862-1918
Brief entry 118
de Calles, Jane F. Butel 1938- 126
Decalo, Samuel 1937- 121
de Camp, Catherine Crook 1907- CANR-20
Earlier sketches in CA 21-22R, CANR-9
See also SATA 12
DeCamp, Graydon 1934- 97-100
de Camp, L(yon) Sprague 1907- CANR-20
Earlier sketches in CA 2R, CANR-1, 9
See also SATA 9
See also DLB 8
de Campi, John Webb 1939- 69-72
De Campos, L.
See Dahl, Linda
De Canio, Stephen J(ohn) 1942- 57-60
De Capite, Raymond Anthony 1924- 2R
Decarie, Therese Gouin 1923- 41-44R
DeCarl, Lennard 1940- 81-84
de Castro, Fernando J(ose) 1937- 53-56
De Castro, Josue 1908-1973 ....33-36R
De Caux, Len
See De Caux, Leonard Howard
De Caux, Leonard Howard 1899- 29-32R
Decaux, Lucile
See Bibesco, Marthe Lucie
DeCecco, John Paul 1925- 19-20R
de Cervera, Alejo 1919- 23-24R
de Chair, Somerset (Struben) 1911- CANR-1
Earlier sketch in CA 45-48
DeChancie, John 1946- 118
Dechant, Emerald V(ictor) 1926- 11-12R
DeChant, John A(loysius) 1917-1974 .... CAP-2
Obituary 53-56
Earlier sketch in CA 23-24
de Chardin, Pierre Teilhard
See Teilhard de Chardin, (Marie Joseph) Pierre
deCharms, Richard Iv 1927- 41-44R
de Chasca, Edmund V(illela) 1903-
Brief entry 117
de Chatellerault, Victor
See Beaudoin, Kenneth Lawrence
Dechert, Charles R(ichard) 1927- CANR-10
Earlier sketch in CA 21-22R
de Chirico, Giorgio 1888-1978 89-92
Obituary 81-84
De Christoforo, Ron(ald) 1951- 81-84
Deci, Edward L(ewis) 1942- 53-56
Decker, Beatrice 1919- 61-64
Decker, Donald M(ilton) 1923- 37-40R
Decker, Duane 1910-1964 ....7-8R
See also SATA 5
Decker, Hannah S(hulman) 1937- 85-88
Decker, Leslie E(dward) 1930- 11-12R
Decker, Robert Owen 1927- 65-68
Decker, William 1926- Brief entry 115
Deckers, Jeanine 1933(?)-1985 Obituary ... 115
Deckert, Alice Mae 15-16R
DeClements, Barthe 1920- CANR-22
Earlier sketch in CA 105
See also SATA 35
De Cock, Liliane 1939- CANR-2
Earlier sketch in CA 45-48
Decolta, Ramon
See Whitfield, Raoul
DeConde, Alexander 1920- CANR-6
Earlier sketch in CA 5-6R
de Costa, (George) Rene 1939- 102
deCoste, Fredrik 1910- CAP-2
Earlier sketch in CA 21-22
DeCoster, Cyrus C(ole) 1914- 49-52
DeCourcy Hinds, Michael 1947- 114
DeCoursey, Virginia 1924- 114
deCoy, Robert H(arold), Jr. 1920- 25-28R
de Crespigny, (Richard) Rafe (Champion)
1936- 57-60
De Cristoforo, R(omeo) J(ohn) 1917- ... CANR-3
Earlier sketch in CA 11-12R
DeCrow, Karen 1937- 33-36R
Decter, Midge (Rosenthal) 1927- CANR-2
Earlier sketch in CA 45-48
Dedek, John F. 1929- 33-36R
Dederick, Robert 1919- Brief entry 116
de Dienes, Andre 1913- 41-44R
Dedijer, Vladimir 1914- CANR-4
Earlier sketch in CA 2R
Dedina, Michel 1933- 33-36R
Dedini, Eldon 1921- 65-68
Dedmon, Emmett 1918-1983 .... CANR-5
Obituary 110
Earlier sketch in CA 11-12R
Dee, Henry
See Torbett, Harvey Douglas Louis
Dee, Ruby
See Wallace, Ruby Ann
Deedy, John 1923- 33-36R
See also SATA 24
Deegan, Paul Joseph 1937- 102
See also SATA 38, 48
Deeken, Alfons 1932- 77-80
Deeley, Roger 1944- 53-56
Deelman, Christian Felling 1937-1964 .... CAP-1
Earlier sketch in CA 11-12
Deemer, Bill 1945- 17-18R
Deemer, Charles (Robert, Jr.) 1939- 73-76
Deen, Edith Alderman 1905- CANR-2
Earlier sketch in CA 7-8R
Deener, David R(ussell) 1920- 19-20R
Deeping, (George) Warwick 1877-1950
Brief entry 114
Deeps, Frederick
See Speed, F(rederick) Maurice
Deer, Irving 1924- 17-18R
Deer, Sandra 1940- CLC-45
Deese, Helen 1925- 126
Deese, James (Earle) 1921- CANR-5
Earlier sketch in CA 4R
Deeter, Allen C. 1931- 45-48
de Extramuros, Quixote
See Espino, Federico (Licsi, Jr.)
DeFalco, Joseph Michael 1931- 15-16R
DeFanti, Charles 1942- 89-92
DeFelice, Louise P(aula) 1945- 61-64
De Felitta, Frank (Paul) 1921- 61-64
Deferrari, Roy J(oseph) 1890-1969 ...... CAP-1
Earlier sketch in CA 13-14
DeFerrari, Sister Teresa Mary 1930- 9-10R
Deffner, Donald L(ouis) 1924- CANR-11
Earlier sketch in CA 17-18R
de Filippo, Eduardo 1900-1984 Obituary 114
de Fletin, P.
See Fielden, T(homas) P(erceval)
Defoe, Daniel 1660(?)-1731 .... SATA-22
See also DLB 39
de Fontaine, Felix Gregory 1834-1896 ... DLB-43
deFontaine, Wade Hampton 1893-1969 .....5-6R
Obituary 103
De Forbes
See Forbes, DeLoris (Florine) Stanton
Deford, Frank 1938- 33-36R
deFord, Miriam Allen 1888-1975 .... CANR-4
Earlier sketch in CA 3R
deFord, Sara (Whitcraft) 1916- 25-28R
DeForest, Charlotte B. 1879-1971 .... CAP-2
Earlier sketch in CA 25-28
De Forest, John William 1826-1906
Brief entry 119
See also DLB 12
De Forest, Lee 1873-1961 Obituary 112
de Forrest, Julie
See DeWitt, Edith Openshaw
de Fossard, R(onald) A(lfred) 1929- 41-44R
de Fox, Lucia Ungaro
See Lockert, Lucia (Alicia Ungaro Fox)
deFrance, Anthony
See DiFranco, Anthony (Mario)
DeFrancis, John 1911- Brief entry 106
DeFrees, Madeline 1919- CANR-4
Earlier sketch in CA 11-12R
deFreres, Sebastian J(ean) 1936- 121
de Funiak, William Q(uinby) 1901- 33-36R
de Gamez, Cielo Cayetana Alba
See Alba de Gamez, Cielo Cayetana
de Gamez, Tana
See Alba de Gamez, Cielo Cayetana
Degani, Meir H(ershtenkorn) 1909- 102
DeGarmo, Kenneth Scott 1943- 81-84
de Gaulle, Charles (Andre Joseph Marie)
1890-1970 Obituary 111
de Gaury, Gerald 1897-1984 ....15-16R
Obituary 112
Degen, Bruce 1945- 124
See also SATA 47
Degenhardt, Henry W(illiam) 1910- CANR-23
Earlier sketch in CA 106
De Gennaro, Angelo Anthony 1919- 15-16R
Degenshein, George A. 1918(?)-1979
Obituary 93-96
De George, Richard T(homas) 1933- ... CANR-17
Earlier sketches in CA 7-8R, CANR-2
DeGering, Etta Fowler 1898- CAP-1
Earlier sketch in CA 9-10
See also SATA 7
Degh, Linda 1920- 85-88
Deghy, Guy (Stephen) 1912- CAP-1
Earlier sketch in CA 9-10
DeGidio, Sandra 1943- 112
Degler, Carl N(eumann) 1921- CANR-3
Earlier sketch in CA 7-8R
Degler, Stanley E. 1929- 25-28R
Degnan, James Philip 1933- 41-44R
de Gourmont, Remy
See Gourmont, Remy de
De Graeff, Allen
See Blaustein, Albert Paul
de Graff, Robert F(air) 1895-1981
Obituary 105
See also DLBY 81
de Graffe, Richard
See St. Clair, Leonard
DeGraft, Joseph Coleman 1932- 73-76
de Graft-Johnson, John Coleman 1919- ..21-22R
de Gramont, Sanche
See Morgan, Ted
DeGrave, Philip
See DeAndrea, William L(ouis)
de Grazia, Alfred 1919- CANR-5
Earlier sketch in CA 15-16R
De Grazia, Ettore 1909-1982 .... CANR-13
Earlier sketch in CA 61-64
De Grazia, Sebastian 1917- 65-68
De Grazia, Ted
See De Grazia, Ettore
See also SATA 39
DeGre, Muriel (Harris) 1914-1971 .... CAP-1
Earlier sketch in CA 17-18
De Greene, Kenyon B(renton) CANR-14
Earlier sketch in CA 37-40R
De Gregori, Thomas R(oger) 1935- CANR-12
Earlier sketch in CA 29-32R
DeGregorio, William A(lfred) 1946- 117
DeGregory, Jerry L(ouis) 1945- 119
de Groat, Diane 1947- 107
See also SATA 31
DeGrood, David H. 1937- 33-36R
DeGroot, Alfred Thomas 1903- CANR-5
Earlier sketch in CA 5-6R
de Groot, Roy Andries 1910-1983
Obituary 110
deGros, J. H.
See Villiard, Paul
de Grummond, Lena Young CANR-1
Earlier sketch in CA 4R
See also SATA 6
de Grunwald, Constantine 9-10R
de Guadaloupe, Brother Jose
See Mojica, Jose
Deguine, Jean-Claude 1943- 81-84
de Guingand, Francis Wilfred 1900-1979
Obituary 89-92
de Guise, Elizabeth (Mary Teresa) 1934- 126
de Gunzburg, Nicholas
See Gunzburg, Nicholas de
deGuzman, Daniel 1911- 93-96
De Haan, Margaret
See Freed, Margaret De Haan
De Haan, Richard W. 1923- 23-24R
De Haas, Elsa 1901- 45-48
de Hamel, Christopher 1950- 120
de Hamel, Joan Littledale 1924- 103
de Hart, Allen 1926- 119
de Hartmann, Olga 1883(?)-1979
Obituary 89-92
de Hartog, Jan 1914- CANR-1
Earlier sketch in CA 2R
See also CLC 19
de Hevesy, Paul 1883-1988 Obituary 125
Dehn, Olive 1914- 117
Dehn, Paul (Edward) 1912-1976 89-92
Dehoney, W(illiam) Wayne 1918- 19-20R
de Hostos, E. M.
See Hostos (y Bonilla), Eugenio Maria de
de Hostos, Eugenio M.
See Hostos (y Bonilla), Eugenio Maria de
Dehqani-Tafti, H. B. 1920- 106
Dehr, Dorothy 1915- 29-32R
Dei-Anang, Michael 1909- 53-56
Deibler, William E. 1932- 89-92
Deighton, Lee C(ecil) 1906-1987 124
Obituary 122
Deighton, Len
See Deighton, Leonard Cyril
See also CLC 4, 7, 22, 46
Deighton, Leonard Cyril 1929- CANR-19
Earlier sketch in CA 11-12R
Deikman, Arthur J(oseph) 1929- 65-68
Deindorfer, Robert Greene 1922-1983 ... CANR-3
Obituary 109
Earlier sketch in CA 11-12R
Deindorfer, Scott 1967- 81-84
Deinzer, Harvey T. 1908- 17-18R
de longh, Mary (Dows Herter Norton) Crena
See Crena de longh, Mary (Dows Herter Norton)
Deiss, Joseph Jay 1915- CANR-14
Earlier sketch in CA 33-36R
See also SATA 12
Deitz, Susan 1934- 110
De Jaegher, Raymond-Joseph
1905-1980 .... CAP-2
Obituary 93-96
Earlier sketch in CA 21-22
De Jong, Arthur J(ay) 1934- 69-72
DeJong, David C(ornel) 1905-1967 ....5-6R
See also SATA 10
deJong, Dola 5-6R
See also SATA 7
De Jong, Gerald Francis 1921- 61-64
de Jong, Gerrit, Jr. 1892- 37-40R
De Jong, Gordon F(rederick) 1935- 25-28R
DeJong, Meindert 1906- 15-16R
See also SATA 2
See also DLB 52
See also CLR 1
De Jong, Peter 1945- 69-72
de Jonge, Alex 1938- CANR-5
Earlier sketch in CA 53-56
De Jonge, Marinus 1925- 123
de Jongh, James 1942- 85-88
de Journlet, Marie
See Little, Paul H(ugo)
de Jouvenel, Bertrand
See de Jouvenel des Ursins, Edouard Bertrand
de Jouvenel des Ursins, Edouard Bertrand
1903-1987 Obituary 121
De Jovine, F(elix) Anthony 1927-1976 .... CAP-2
Earlier sketch in CA 29-32
Deju, Raul A(ntonio) 1946- 53-56
DeKalb, Lorimer
See Knorr, Marian L(ockwood)
de Kay, James T(ertius) 1930- CANR-10
Earlier sketch in CA 25-28R
de Kay, Ormonde, Jr. 1923- 49-52
See also SATA 7
de Kerpely, Theresa 1898- 119
deKieffer, Donald (Eulette) 1945- 112
de Kiewiet, Cornelis W(illem) 1902-1986
Obituary 118
de Kiewiet, Cornelius W(illiam)
See De Kiewiet, Cornelis W(illem)
de Kiewit, Cornelis W(illem)
See de Kiewiet, Cornelis W(illem)
de Kiriline, Louise
See Lawrence, Louise de Kiriline
Dekker, Carl
See Laffin, John (Alfred Charles) and Lynds, Dennis
Dekker, George 1934- 104

Dekker, Thomas 1572(?)-1632 .... DLB-62
Dekle, Bernard 1905- 17-18R
Dekmejian, Richard Hrair 1933- 37-40R
Deknatel, F(rederick) B(rockway)
1905-1973 Obituary 45-48
Dekobra, Maurice
See Tessier, (Ernst) M(aurice)
De Koenigswerther, Edwin Raymond
1930- 49-52
DeKok, David (Paul) 1953- 124
DeKosky, Robert K. 1945- 93-96
DeKoster, Lester Ronald 1915- 13-14R
De Koven, Bernard 1941- 85-88
De Koven, Bernie
See De Koven, Bernard
Dekovic, Gene 1922- CANR-26
Earlier sketch in CA 108
deKruif, Paul (Henry) 1890-1971 ....9-10R
Obituary 29-32R
See also SATA 5, 50
de Kun, Nicolas 1923- 17-18R
De La Bedoyere, Michael 1900-1973
Obituary 104
Delacato, Carl H(enry) 1923- 41-44R
Delacorte, Peter 1943- 105
de la Costa, Horacio (L.)
See Costa, Horacio (L.) de la
Delacour, Jean
See Delacour, Jean Theodore
Delacour, Jean Theodore 1890-1985
Obituary 117
Delacre, Lulu 1957- SATA-36
DeLacy, Margaret (Eisenstein) 1951- 122
DeLaet, Sigfried J(an) 1914- CANR-18
Earlier sketches in CA 7-8R, CANR-3
Delafield, E. M.
See Dashwood, Edmee Elizabeth Monica
de la Pasture
See also DLB 34
de la Garza, Rodolfo O(ropea) 1942- 77-80
De Lage, Ida 1918- CANR-14
Earlier sketch in CA 41-44R
See also SATA 11
de La Glannege, Roger-Maxe
See Legman, G(ershon)
De La Grange, Henry Louis 1924- 69-72
de la Guardia, Ernesto, Jr. 1904-1983
Obituary 109
de Laguna, Frederica (Annis) 1906- 37-40R
de Laguna, Grace Mead A(ndrus)
1878-1978 .... CAP-1
Obituary 77-80
Earlier sketch in CA 11-12
Delahanty, Randolph
See Delehanty, Randolph
Delahay, E(ileen) A(vril) 1915-1982 ......25-28R
Obituary 117
De La Iglesia, Maria Elena 1936- 29-32R
de la Mare, Albinia Catherine 1932- 33-36R
de la Mare, Richard (Herbert Ingpen)
1901-1986 Obituary 118
de la Mare, Walter (John) 1873-1956
Brief entry 110
See also SATA 16
See also DLB 19
See also TCLC 4
DeLamarter, Jeanne
See Bonnette, Jeanne
DeLamotte, Roy Carroll 1917- CANR-15
Earlier sketch in CA 41-44R
DeLancey, Mark W(akeman) 1939- 93-96
Deland, Margaret(ta Wade Campbell)
1857-1945 Brief entry 122
Delaney, Bud
See Delaney, Francis, Jr.
Delaney, C(ornelius) F. 1938- CANR-16
Earlier sketch in CA 25-28R
Delaney, Daniel J(oseph) 1938- 41-44R
Delaney, Denis
See Green, Peter (Morris)
Delaney, Edmund T. 1914- 15-16R
Delaney, Francis, Jr. 1931- 57-60
Delaney, Franey
See O'Hara, John (Henry)
Delaney, Frank 1942- 126
Delaney, Harry 1932- 25-28R
See also SATA 3
Delaney, Jack J(ames) 1921- 21-22R
Delaney, John Joseph 1910-1985 ...... CANR-5
Obituary 115
Earlier sketch in CA 1R
DeLaney, Joseph Lawrence 1917- 102
Delaney, Lolo M(ae) 1937- 57-60
Delaney, Marshall
See Fulford, Robert
Delaney, Mary Murray 1913- 53-56
Delaney, Ned
See Delaney, Thomas Nicholas III
See also SATA 28
Delaney, Norman Conrad 1932- 37-40R
Delaney, Robert Finley 1925- CANR-6
Earlier sketch in CA 1R
Delaney, Shelagh 1939- 19-20R
See also DLB 13
See also CLC 29
Delaney, Steve 1938- 121
Brief entry 110
Delaney, Thomas Nicholas III 1951- ... CANR-10
Earlier sketch in CA 65-68
Delaney, William A(nthony) 1926- 106
de Lange, Nicholas (Robert Michael)
1944- CANR-15
Earlier sketch in CA 89-92
Delano, Anthony 1930- 102
Delano, Hugh 1933- 65-68
See also SATA 20
Delano, Isaac O. 1904- 25-28R
Delano, Kenneth J(oseph) 1934- 57-60
de Lantagne, Cecile
See Cloutier-Wojciechowska, Cecile
Delany, George (Battle) 1946- 114
Delany, Kevin F(rancis) X(avier) 1927- 73-76
Delany, Martin Robinson 1812-1885 .... DLB-50
Delany, Paul 1937- CANR-19
Earlier sketch in CA 29-32R
Delany, Samuel R(ay, Jr.) 1942- 81-84
See also BW
See also DLB 8, 33
See also CLC 8, 14, 38
Delany, Sheila 1940- 112
de la Pena, Augustin (Mateo) 1942- 115
Delaplane, Stanton Hill 1907-1988 ....25-28R
Obituary 125
Delaporte, Ernest P(ierre) 1924- 97-100
Delaporte, Theophile
See Green, Julien (Hartridge)
de la Portilla, Marta (Rosa) 1927- 61-64
De Lapp, Ardyce Lucile 1903- 97-100
DeLapp, George Leslie 1895- 102
De La Ramee, (Marie) Louise
1839-1908 .... SATA-20
de la Renta, Francoise de Langiade
1921(?)-1983 Obituary 110
De La Roche, Mazo 1879-1961 85-88
See also DLB 68
See also CLC 14
Delasanta, Rodney 1932- 33-36R
de las Cuevas, Raymon
See Harrington, Mark Raymond
de la Torre, Jose 1943- 112
De La Torre, Lillian
See McCue, Lillian Bueno
de la Torre, Victor Raul Haya
See Haya de la Torre, Victor Raul
DeLatte, Carolyn E(lizabeth) 1943- 112
Delattre, Pierre 1930- 105
Delatush, Edith G. 1921- 124
de Laubenfels, David J(ohn) 1925- 53-56
Delaunay, Charles 1911-1988 Obituary 125
de Launay, Jacques F(orment) 1924- ... CANR-3
Earlier sketch in CA 11-12R
Delaune, (Jewel) Lynn (de Grummond) .. CANR-21
Earlier sketch in CA 4R
See also SATA 7
DeLaura, David J(oseph) 1930- 23-24R
DeLaurentis, Louise Budde 1920- 7-8R
See also SATA 12
de la Warr, George Walter 1904-1969 .... CAP-1
Earlier sketch in CA 15-16
Delay, Claude
See Delay-Tubiana, Claude
Delay-Tubiana, Claude 1934- CANR-4
Earlier sketch in CA 53-56
Delbanco, Nicholas (Franklin) 1942- 19-20R
See also CAAS 2
See also DLB 6
See also CLC 6, 13
del Barco, Lucy Salamanca 19-20R
Del Boca, Angelo 1925- 25-28R
Delbridge, Rosemary 1949(?)-1981
Obituary 105
del Castillo, Michel 1933- 109
See also CLC 38
del Castillo, Richard Griswold
See Griswold del Castillo, Richard
Delcroix, Carlo 1896-1977 Obituary 73-76
Delderfield, Eric R(aymond) 1909- CANR-4
Earlier sketch in CA 53-56
See also SATA 14
Delderfield, Ronald Frederick 1912-1972 ...73-76
Obituary 37-40R
See also SATA 20
Delear, Frank J. 1914- CANR-9
Earlier sketch in CA 21-22R
Deledda, Grazia (Cosima) 1875(?)-1936
Brief entry 123
See also TCLC 23
DeLeeuw, Adele (Louise) 1899-1988 .... CANR-1
Obituary 125
Earlier sketch in CA 4R
See also SATA 1, 30
DeLeeuw, Cateau 1903-1975 .... CANR-3
Earlier sketch in CA 4R
de Leeuw, Hendrik 1891-1977 Obituary ...73-76
Delehanty, Randolph 1944- 123
de Leiris, Alain 1922- 73-76
DeLeon, David (Henry) 1947- Brief entry ... 114
de Lerma, Dominique-Rene 1928- CANR-1
Earlier sketch in CA 45-48
Delessert, Etienne 1941- CANR-13
Earlier sketch in CA 21-22R
See also SATA 27, 46
DeLey, Herbert (Clemone, Jr.) 1936- 21-22R
Delfano, M. M.
See Flammonde, Paris
Delfgaauw, Bernard(us Maria Ignatius)
1912- 23-24R
Delgado, Alan (George) 1909- CANR-5
Earlier sketch in CA 11-12R
Delgado, Jose Manuel R(odriguez)
1915- 29-32R
Delgado, Ramon (Louis) 1937- CANR-15
Earlier sketch in CA 85-88
D'Elia, Donald John 1933- 57-60
D'Elia, Maria
See Goudiss, Maria Agnes D'Elia
Delibes, Miguel
See Delibes Setien, Miguel
See also CLC 8, 18
Delibes Setien, Miguel 1920- CANR-1
Earlier sketch in CA 45-48
Deligiorgis, Stavros (George) 1933- 61-64
DeLillo, Don 1936- CANR-21
Earlier sketch in CA 81-84
See also DLB 6
See also CLC 8, 10, 13, 27, 39
de Lima, Agnes 1887(?)-1974 Obituary ...53-56
De Lima, Clara Rosa 1922- CANR-6
Earlier sketch in CA 57-60
de Lima, Sigrid 1921- 25-28R
Delinsky, Barbara (Ruth Greenberg) 1945- .. 111
de Lint, Charles (Henri Diederick Hoefsmit)
1951- 126
Delisle, Francoise 1886(?)-1974 Obituary ..53-56
De Lisser, Herbert George 1878-1944
Brief entry 109
See also TCLC 12
Delius, Anthony (Ronald St. Martin)
1916- CANR-12
Earlier sketch in CA 17-18R
Delk, Robert Carlton 1920- 45-48
Dell, Belinda
See Bowden, Jean
Dell, Christopher 1927- 65-68
Dell, E(dward) T(homas), Jr. 1923- 15-16R
Dell, Edmund 1921- 103
Dell, Floyd 1887-1969 Obituary 89-92
See also DLB 9
Dell, Jeffrey 1899-1985(?) Obituary 116
Dell, Roberta E(lizabeth) 1946- 81-84
Dell, Sidney 1918- CANR-17
Earlier sketches in CA 5-6R, CANR-2
Della Femina, Jerry 1936- Brief entry 111
Della-Piana, Gabriel M. 1926- 73-76
delle Stelle, Pier Luigi Bellini
See Bellini delle Stelle, Pier Luigi
Dellin, Lubomir A. D. 1920- 45-48
Dellinger, David (T.) 1915- 65-68
Delloff, Irving Arthur 1920- 15-16R
Delman, David 1924- Brief entry 115
Delmar, Ken 1941- 121
Del Mar, Marcia 1950- 105
Delmar, Roy
See Wexler, Jerome (LeRoy)
Delmar, Vina (Croter) 1905- 65-68
Delmer, Denis Sefton 1904- 5-6R
Delmonico, Andrea
See Morrison, Eula Atwood
De Loach, Allen (Wayne) 1939- CANR-16
Earlier sketch in CA 85-88
DeLoach, Charles F. 1927- 37-40R
DeLoach, Clarence, Jr. 1936- 57-60
Delon, Floyd G(urney) 1929- CANR-21
Earlier sketch in CA 69-72
de Lone, Richard H. 1940- 101
DeLone, Ruth
See Rankin, Ruth (DeLone) I(rvine)
DeLong, Lea Rosson 1947- 119
DeLong, Thomas A(nderton) 1935- CANR-25
Earlier sketch in CA 106
de Longchamps, Joanne (Cutten)
1923- CANR-3
Earlier sketch in CA 11-12R
De Lora, Joann S.
See Sandlin, Joann S(chepers) De Lora
DeLorean, John Z(achary) 1925- 122
DeLorenzo, Lorisa Mernette 1951- 117
DeLorenzo, Robert John 1947- 117
Deloria, Vine (Victor), Jr. 1933- CANR-20
Earlier sketches in CA 53-56, CANR-5
See also SATA 21
See also CLC 21
Delorme, Andre
See Julien, Charles-Andre
Delorme, Michele
See Cranston, Mechthild
Delort, Robert 1932- 102
de los Reyes, Gabriel 45-48
de los Rios, Francisco Giner
See Giner de los Rios, Francisco
Deloughery, Grace L. 1933- 33-36R
de Loune, Henry
See Popham, Peter (Nicholas Home)
Delp, Michael W(illiam) 1948- 77-80
Delpar, Helen 1936- 53-56
Delphos, Omar
See Ald, Roy A(llison)
del Rey, Judy-Lynn 1943-1986 124
Obituary 118
del Rey, Lester 1915- CANR-17
Earlier sketch in CA 65-68
See also SATA 22
See also DLB 8
Delta
See Dennett, Herbert Victor
Delton, Jina 1961- 106
Delton, Judy 1931- CANR-25
Earlier sketches in CA 57-60, CANR-8
See also SATA 14
Delton, Julie 1959- 108
DeLuca, A(ngelo) Michael 1912-1976 ....21-22R
Obituary 120
De Luca, Charles J. 1927- 73-76
De Lucca, John 1920- 41-44R
Delulio, John 1938- SATA-15
Delumeau, Jean 1923- 97-100
De Luna, Frederick Adolph 1928- 65-68
Delupis, Ingrid 1939- 103
Del Vecchio, John M(ichael) 1947- 110
See also CLC 29
Delving, Michael
See Williams, Jay
DeLynn, Jane 1946- 77-80
DeLyser, Femmy 1935- 110
Delzell, Charles F(loyd) 1920- CANR-2
Earlier sketch in CA 2R
Demac, Donna A. 1952- 121
de Madariaga, Isabel 1919- 107
Demaine, Don
See Drinkall, Gordon (Don)
de Man, Paul 1919(?)-1983 Obituary 111
See also DLB 67
de Mandiargues, Andre Pieyre
See Pieyre de Mandiargues, Andre
De Manio, Jack 1914- 61-64
Demant, Vigo Auguste 1893-1983
Obituary 109
de Mar, Esmeralda
See Mellen, Ida M(ay)
Demaray, Donald E(ugene) 1926- CANR-16
Earlier sketches in CA 3R, CANR-1
De Marco, Angelus A. 1916- 11-12R
De Marco, Arlene AITN-1
DeMarco, Donald 1937- CANR-24
Earlier sketches in CA 61-64, CANR-7
de Mare, Eric S. 1910- CANR-6
Earlier sketch in CA 9-10R
deMare, George 1912- 23-24R
Demarest, Bruce A(lvin) 1935- 118
Demarest, Chris(topher) L(ynn) 1951- 109
See also SATA 44, 45
Demarest, Doug
See Barker, Will
Demarest, Michael 1924(?)-1984 Obituary .. 112
Demarest, Phyllis Gordon 1911-1969
Obituary 104
Demarest, Rosemary Regina 1914- 116
Demarest, Victoria Booth(-Clibborn)
1890-1982 124
Obituary 112
Demaret, James Newton 1910-1983
Obituary 111
Demaret, Jimmy
See Demaret, James Newton
Demaret, Pierre 1943- CANR-12
Earlier sketch in CA 61-64
De Maria, Robert 1928- CANR-5
Earlier sketch in CA 1R
De Marinis, Rick 1934- CANR-25
Earlier sketches in CA 57-60, CANR-9
Demaris, Ovid
See Desmarais, Ovid E.
De Marly, Diana 1939- 125
DeMartini, Rodney J(ames) 1947- 113
De Martino, Manfred F(rank) 1924-
Brief entry 117
Demas, Vida 1927- 49-52
See also SATA 9
deMatteo, Donna 1941- 25-28R
de Mauny, Erik 1920- CANR-13
Earlier sketch in CA 33-36R
deMause, Lloyd 1931- 65-68
Dembo, L(awrence) S(anford) 1929- CANR-2
Earlier sketch in CA 1R
Dembry, R. Emmet
See Murfree, Mary Noailles
Demby, William 1922- 81-84
See also BW
See also DLB 33
de Medici, Marino 1933- 89-92
De Mejo, Oscar 1911- 111
See also SATA 40
Dement, William Charles 1928- Brief entry .. 105
De Mente, Boye 1928- CANR-8
Earlier sketch in CA 23-24R
de Menton, Francisco
See Chin, Frank (Chew, Jr.)
Demeny, Janos 1915- 118
Demers, James 1942- 97-100
de Mesne, Eugene (Frederick Peter
Cheshire) CANR-25
Earlier sketch in CA 41-44R
de Mesquita, Bruce James Bueno
See Bueno de Mesquita, Bruce James
de Messieres, Nicole 1930- 107
See also SATA 39
Demetillo, Ricaredo 1920- 102
Demetrakopoulos, Stephanie Anne 1937- ... 111
Demetrius, James Kleon 1924- CANR-13
Earlier sketch in CA 21-22R
Demetz, Peter 1922- CANR-14
Earlier sketch in CA 65-68
Demi
See Hitz, Demi
De Michael, Don(ald Anthony) 1928-1982
Obituary 106
Demijohn, Thom
See Disch, Thomas M(ichael)
and Sladek, John
de Milan, Sister Jean
See Jean, Gabrielle (Lucille)
D'Emilio, A. Edward 1919(?)-1987
Obituary 122
de Mille, Agnes
See Prude, Agnes George
DeMille, Alexandria
See Du Breuil, (Elizabeth) L(or)inda
De Mille, Cecil B(lount) 1881-1959
Brief entry 115
DeMille, Nelson 1943- CANR-25
Earlier sketches in CA 57-60, CANR-6
De Mille, Nelson
See Levinson, Leonard
de Mille, Richard 1922- CANR-13
Earlier sketch in CA 23-24R
Deming, Barbara 1917-1984 .... CANR-15
Earlier sketch in CA 85-88
Deming, Kirk
See Drago, Harry Sinclair
Deming, Louise Macpherson 1916-1976
Obituary 61-64
Deming, Philander 1829-1915 .... DLB-74
Deming, Richard 1915- CANR-3
Earlier sketch in CA 11-12R
See also SATA 24

Deming, Robert H. 1937- 21-22R
DeMirjian, Arto, Jr. 1931- 57-60
De Molen, Richard Lee 1938- 45-48
Demone, Harold W(ellington), Jr.
 1924- CANR-9
 Earlier sketch in CA 5-6R
De Monfried, Henri 1879(?)-1974
 Obituary 53-56
Demong, Phyllis 1920- 106
de Montalvo, Luis Galvez
 See Avalle-Arce, Juan Bautista
DeMonte, Claudia 1947- 114
de Montebello, Guy-Philippe Lannes
 1936- 45-48
de Montfort, Guy
 See Johnson, Donald McI(ntosh)
de Montherlant, Henry (Milon)
 See Montherlant, Henry (Milon) de
DeMontreville Polak, Doris 1904(?)-1974
 Obituary 49-52
De Mordaunt, Walter J(ulius) 1925- 33-36R
Demorest, Jean-Jacques 1920- 5-6R
Demorest, Stephen 1949- CANR-20
 Earlier sketch in CA 101
De Morny, Peter
 See Wynne-Tyson, Esme
Demos, Paul 1888-1983 Obituary 109
Demotes, Michael
 See Burgess, M(ichael) R(oy)
DeMott, Benjamin 1924- 5-6R
De Mott, Donald W(arren) 1928- 61-64
de Mourgues, Odette (Marie Helene Louise)
 1914-1988 ....7-8R
 Obituary 126
Dempewolff, Richard F(rederic) 1914- ... CANR-1
 Earlier sketch in CA 4R
Dempsey, David Knapp 1914- CANR-2
 Earlier sketch in CA 7-8R
Dempsey, Hugh Aylmer 1929- CANR-26
 Earlier sketches in CA 69-72, CANR-11
Dempsey, Jack
 See Dempsey, William Harrison
Dempsey, Lotta 101
Dempsey, Paul K(enneth) 1935- CANR-19
 Earlier sketch in CA 25-28R
Dempsey, Richard A(llen) 1932- 61-64
Dempsey, William Harrison 1895-1983 89-92
 Obituary 109
Dempster, Barry 1952- 113
Dempster, Chris 1943- 106
Dempster, Derek David 1924- 15-16R
Dempster, Stuart 1936- 104
Demske, James Michael 1922- 29-32R
Demura, Fumio 1940- CANR-12
 Earlier sketch in CA 61-64
Demuth, Norman (Frank) 1898-1968 .... CAP-1
 Earlier sketch in CA 13-14
Demuth, Patricia Brennan 1948- 118
 See also SATA 51
Den, Petr
 See Radimsky, Ladislaw
Denali, Peter
 See Holm, Don(ald Raymond)
de Natale, Francine
 See Malzberg, Barry N(athaniel)
Denbeaux, Fred J. 1914- 7-8R
Denbie, Roger
 See Green, Alan (Baer)
Denbigh, Kenneth George 1911- 106
Den Boer, James (Drew) 1937- CANR-10
 Earlier sketch in CA 23-24R
Denby, Edwin (Orr) 1903-1983 Obituary 110
 See also CLC 48
Dendel, Esther (Sietmann Warner) 1910- ... 102
Dender, Jay
 See Deindorfer, Robert Greene
Dendle, Brian J(ohn) 1936- 116
Dendy, Marshall C(oleman) 1902- CAP-2
 Earlier sketch in CA 17-18
DeNeef, Arthur Leigh 1942- 102
Deneen, James R. 1928- 45-48
Denenberg, Herbert S(idney) 1929- 37-40R
de Neufville, Richard 1939- 53-56
Denevan, William M(axfield) 1931- 41-44R
de Nevers, Noel (Howard) 1932- 37-40R
DeNevi, Donald P. 1937- 37-40R
Denfeld, Duane (Henry) 1939- 41-44R
Deng, William 1929- 13-14R
Dengler, Dieter 1938- 102
Dengler, Marianna (Herron) 1935- 102
Dengler, Sandy 1939- 112
 See also SATA 40
Denham, Alice 1933- 23-24R
Denham, Avery Strakosch ?-1970
 Obituary 104
Denham, Bertie 1927- 93-96
Denham, H(enry) M(angles) 1897- 61-64
Denham, John 1615-1669 .... DLB-58
Denham, Mary Orr 1918- CANR-2
 Earlier sketch in CA 4R
Denham, Reginald 1894-1983 .... CAP-1
 Obituary 109
 Earlier sketch in CA 15-16
Denham, Robert D(ayton) 1938- 53-56
Denham, Sully
 See Budd, Mavis
Denhardt, Robert Moorman 1912- 101
den Hollander, A(rie) Nicolaas Jan
 1906-1976 .... CAP-2
 Earlier sketch in CA 29-32
Denholm, Therese Mary Zita White 1933- ..9-10R
Denholtz, Elaine (Grudin) CANR-13
 Earlier sketch in CA 73-76
Dening, Greg 1931- 107
Denis, Armand 1896(?)-1971 Obituary 104
Denis, Charlotte
 See Plimmer, Charlotte
 and Plimmer, Denis
Denis, Julio
 See Cortazar, Julio
Denis, Manuel Maldonado
 See Maldonado-Denis, Manuel
Denis, Michaela Holdsworth 13-14R
Denis, Paul 1909- 21-22R
Denisoff, R. Serge 1939- 33-36R
Denison, Barbara 1926- 13-14R
Denison, Corrie
 See Partridge, Eric (Honeywood)
Denison, Edward F(ulton) 1915- 23-24R
Denison, (John) Michael (Terence
 Wellesley) 1915- 109
Denison, Norman 1925- 65-68
Denker, Henry 1912- 33-36R
 See also AITN 1
Denkler, Horst 1935- CANR-19
 Earlier sketches in CA 53-56, CANR-4
Denkstein, Vladimir 1906- 103
Denlinger, A(nna) Martha 1931- 113
Denman, D(onald) R(obert) 1911- CANR-8
 Earlier sketch in CA 61-64
Denmark, Florence L. 1932- 85-88
Denmark, Harrison
 See Zelazny, Roger (Joseph)
Dennehy, Raymond L(eo) 1934- 109
Dennes, William Ray 1898- 73-76
Dennett, Daniel C. 1942- 97-100
Dennett, Herbert Victor 1893- CANR-5
 Earlier sketch in CA 7-8R
Denney, Diana 1910- 104
 See also SATA 25
Denney, Myron Keith 1930- 102
Denney, Reuel (Nicholas) 1913- CANR-2
 Earlier sketch in CA 4R
Dennie, Joseph 1768-1812 .. DLB-37, 43, 59, 73
Denning, A. T.
 See Denning, Alfred Thompson
Denning, Alfred Thompson 1899-
 Brief entry 115
Denning, Basil W. 1928- 33-36R
Denning, Candace 1946- 125
Denning, Melita
 See Barcynski, Vivian G(odfrey)
Denning, Patricia
 See Willis, Corinne Denneny
Dennis, Arthur
 See Edmonds, Arthur Denis
Dennis, Benjamin G. 1929- 45-48
Dennis, Carl 1939- 77-80
Dennis, Charles 1946- CANR-17
 Earlier sketch in CA 65-68
Dennis, Deborah Ellis 1950- 116
Dennis, Everette E. 1942- 41-44R
Dennis, Henry C(harles) 1918- 41-44R
Dennis, Ian 1952- 125
Dennis, James M(unn) 1932- 102
Dennis, John V(alue) 1916- 107
Dennis, Landt 1937- 65-68
Dennis, Lane T(imothy) 1943- 93-96
Dennis, Lawrence 1893-1977 Obituary 73-76
Dennis, Morgan 1891?-1960 .... SATA-18
Dennis, Nigel (Forbes) 1912- 25-28R
 See also DLB 13, 15
 See also CLC 8
Dennis, Patrick
 See Tanner, Edward Everett III
Dennis, Peggy 1909- 77-80
Dennis, Peter (John) 1945- 41-44R
Dennis, Ralph AITN-1
Dennis, Richard (John) 1949- 118
Dennis, Robert C. 1920-1983 101
 Obituary 110
Dennis, Rutledge M(elvin) 1939- 115
Dennis, Suzanne Easton 1922- 25-28R
Dennis, Wayne 1905-1976 ....17-18R
 Obituary 69-72
Dennis, Wesley 1903-1966 .... SATA-18
Dennis-Jones, H(arold) 1915- CANR-8
 Earlier sketch in CA 57-60
Dennison, A(lfred) Dudley, Jr. 1914- CANR-9
 Earlier sketch in CA 57-60
Dennison, George (Harris) 1925-1987 101
 Obituary 123
 See also CAAS 6
Dennison, George M(arshel) 1935- 53-56
Dennison, Milo
 See Cantwell, Lois
Dennison, Peter (John) 1942- 124
Dennison, Sam 1926- 109
Dennison, Shane 1933- 73-76
Denniston, Denise 1946- 69-72
Denniston, Elinore 1900-1978 Obituary 81-84
 See also SATA 24
Denniston, Lyle (William) 1931- 65-68
Denny, Alma 1912- 89-92
Denny, Brian
 See Doughty, Bradford
Denny, Carol
 See Brandt, Carol
Denny, John Howard 1920- CAP-1
 Earlier sketch in CA 9-10
Denny, Ludwell 1894-1970 Obituary 29-32R
Denny, M(aurice) Ray 1918- CANR-14
 Earlier sketch in CA 41-44R
Denny, Norman (George) 1901-1982 107
 See also SATA 43
Denny-Brown, Derek Ernest 1901-1981
 Obituary 103
Dennys, Joyce (a pseudonym) 1895- 121
Dennys, Rodney Onslow 1911- 85-88
Denoeu, Francois 1898-1975 53-56
Denomme, Robert T. 1930- 25-28R
Denoon, Donald (John Noble) 1940- ... CANR-14
 Earlier sketch in CA 73-76
DeNovo, John A(ugust) 1916- 11-12R
Densen-Gerber, Judianne 1934- 37-40R
Denslow, W(illiam) W(allace)
 1856-1915 .... SATA-16
 See also CLR 15
Denson, John Lee 1903-1982 Obituary 108
Dent, Alan (Holmes) 1905-1978 .... CANR-5
 Earlier sketch in CA 9-10R
Dent, Anthony Austen 1915- CANR-15
 Earlier sketch in CA 25-28R
Dent, Colin 1921- 13-14R
Dent, Harold (Collett) 1894- CANR-5
 Earlier sketch in CA 7-8R
Dent, Harry (Shuler) 1930- 81-84
Dent, Lester 1904(?)-1959 Brief entry 112
Dent, Robert William 1917- 105
Dent, Thomas C(ovington) 1932- 125
 Brief entry 122
 See also BW
Dent, Tom
 See Dent, Thomas C(ovington)
 See also DLB 38
Dentan, Robert C(laude) 1907- CANR-2
 Earlier sketch in CA 1R
Dentinger, Jane 1951- 123
Dentinger, Stephen
 See Hoch, Edward D(entinger)
Dentler, Robert A(rnold) 1928- CANR-17
 Earlier sketches in CA 3R, CANR-1
Denton, Charles F(rederick) 1942- 37-40R
Denton, D. Keith 1948- 112
Denton, Daniel 1626(?)-1703 .... DLB-24
Denton, H(arry) M. 1882- CAP-1
 Earlier sketch in CA 11-12
Denton, J(effrey) H(oward) 1939- CANR-15
 Earlier sketch in CA 41-44R
Denton, Jeremiah A(ndrew), Jr. 1924- 69-72
Denton, Wallace 1928- 3R
d'Entreves, Alexander (Passerin)
 1902-1985 Obituary 118
Dentry, Robert
 See White, Osmar Egmont Dorkin
Denues, Celia 1915- 41-44R
Den Uyl, Douglas J(ohn) 1950- 117
Denver, Boone
 See Rennie, James Alan
Denver, Drake C.
 See Nye, Nelson C(oral)
Denver, Rod
 See Edson, J(ohn) T(homas)
Denver, Walt
 See Sherman, Jory (Tecumseh)
Denvir, Bernard 1917- 115
Denys, Teresa (a pseudonym) 1947- 105
Denzel, Justin F(rancis) 1917- CANR-4
 Earlier sketch in CA 53-56
 See also SATA 38, 46
Denzer, Ann Wiseman
 See Wiseman, Ann (Sayre)
Denzer, Peter W(orthington) 1921- 7-8R
Denzin, Norman K(ent) 1941- CANR-12
 Earlier sketch in CA 29-32R
de Obaldia, Rene
 See Obaldia, Rene de
de Oca, Marco Antonio Montes
 See Montes de Oca, Marco Antonio
de Oliveira, Paulo C(arlos) 1953- 114
Deon, Michel 1919- CANR-16
 Earlier sketch in CA 37-40R
De Palma, Brian (Russell) 1940- 109
 See also CLC 20
de Paola, Thomas Anthony 1934- CANR-2
 Earlier sketch in CA 49-52
 See also SATA 11
de Paola, Tomie
 See de Paola, Thomas Anthony
 See also DLB 61
 See also CLR 4
de Paor, Risteard
 See Power, Richard
Depas, Spencer 1925- 69-72
DePaul, Edith
 See Delatush, Edith G.
DePauw, Linda Grant 1940- CANR-9
 Earlier sketch in CA 21-22R
 See also SATA 24
Depel, Jim 1936- 73-76
de Pereda, Prudencio 1912- CANR-4
 Earlier sketch in CA 1R
Depestre, Rene 1926- Brief entry 113
Depew, Arthur M(c Kinley) 1896-1976 ...41-44R
Depew, Wally
 See Depew, Walter Westerfield
Depew, Walter Westerfield 1924- 5-6R
De Pietro, Albert 1913- 69-72
de Polman, Willem
 See Nichols, Dale (William)
De Polnay, Peter 1906-1984 73-76
 Obituary 114
DePorte, Anton W. 1928- 124
DePorte, Michael V(ital) 1939- 49-52
Depp, Roberta J. 1947- 101
de Pre, Jean-Anne
 See Avallone, Michael (Angelo), Jr.
DePree, Gladis (Lenore) 1933- 101
DePree, Gordon 1930- 101
Depta, Victor M(arshall) 1939- 49-52
De Puy, Norman R(obert) 1929- 97-100
Dequasie, Andrew 1929- 114
D'Erasmo, Martha 1939- 81-84
Derber, Milton 1915- Brief entry 106
Derby, George Horatio 1823-1861 .... DLB-11
Derby, Pat 1942- 69-72
de Regniers, Beatrice Schenk (Freedman)
 1914- CANR-26
 Earlier sketches in CA 13-14R, CANR-6
 See also SATA 2
 See also SAAS 6
Dereksen, David
 See Stacton, David (Derek)
Deren, Eleanora 1908(?)-1961 Obituary 111
Deren, Maya
 See Deren, Eleanora
 See also CLC 16
Derenberg, Walter J(ulius) 1903-1975
 Obituary 61-64
De Reneville, Mary Margaret Motley
 Sheridan 1912- 5-6R
de Reyna, Rudy 1914- CANR-10
 Earlier sketch in CA 57-60
Derfler, (Arnold) Leslie 1933- CANR-9
 Earlier sketch in CA 7-8R
deRham, Edith 1933- 15-16R
Derham, (Arthur) Morgan 1915- 13-14R
Der Hovanessian, Diana 124
Deric, Arthur J. 1926- 23-24R
Dering, Joan (Rosalind Cordelia) 1917- 9-10R
De Risi, William J(oseph) 1938- 53-56
de Rivera, Joseph H(osmer) 1932- 41-44R
Derleth, August (William) 1909-1971 .... CANR-4
 Obituary 29-32R
 Earlier sketch in CA 1R
 See also SATA 5
 See also DLB 9
 See also CLC 31
Derman, Lou 1914(?)-1976 Obituary 65-68
Derman, Sarah Audrey 1915- CANR-17
 Earlier sketch in CA 4R
 See also SATA 11
Dermid, Jack 1923- 49-52
Dermout, Maria
 See Dermout-Ingermann, Helena Antonia
 Maria Elisabeth
Dermout-Ingermann, Helena Antonia Maria
 Elisabeth 1888-1962 Obituary 114
Dern, Erolie Pearl Gaddis 1895-1966 .... CANR-6
 Obituary 25-28R
 Earlier sketch in CA 2R
Dern, Karl L(udwig) 1894- 57-60
Dern, Peggy
 See Dern, Erolie Pearl Gaddis
Dernburg, Thomas F(rederick) 1930- CANR-2
 Earlier sketch in CA 1R
Der Nersessian, Sirarpie 1896- 102
de Robeck, Nesta 1886- CAP-2
 Earlier sketch in CA 25-28
De Rochemont, Richard (Guertis)
 1903-1982 Obituary 108
de Rocher, Gregory (David) 1943- 114
DeRoin, Nancy 1934- 65-68
de Romaszkan, Gregor 1894- 15-16R
de Roo, Anne Louise 1931- 103
 See also SATA 25
de Roos, Robert (William) 1912- 11-12R
de Ropp, Robert S(ylvester) 1913- 19-20R
Deror, Yehezkel
 See Dror, Yehezkel
DeRosa, Peter (Clement) 1932- CANR-9
 Earlier sketch in CA 21-22R
DeRosier, Arthur H(enry), Jr. 1931- 29-32R
De Rosis, Helen A. 1918- 122
 Brief entry 107
De Rossi, Claude J(oseph) 1942- 53-56
Derossi, Flavia 1926- 112
de Rothschild, Pauline (Fairfax-Potter)
 1908(?)-1976 Obituary 65-68
de Rougemont, Denis 1906-1985
 Obituary 118
de Roussan, Jacques 1929- 123
 Brief entry 110
 See also SATA 31
Derr, Richard L(uther) 1930- 53-56
Derr, Thomas Sieger 1931- 53-56
Derrett, J(ohn) Duncan M(artin) 1922- . CANR-21
 Earlier sketches in CA 15-16R, CANR-6
Derrick, Graham
 See Raby, Derek Graham
Derrick, Lionel
 See Cunningham, Chet
Derrick, Paul 1916- CAP-1
 Earlier sketch in CA 9-10
Derricotte, Toi 1941- 113
Derrida, Jacques 1930- Brief entry 124
 See also CLC 24
Derriman, James Parkyns 1922- 106
Derry, John W(esley) 1933- CANR-3
 Earlier sketch in CA 5-6R
Derry, (Thomas) Ramsay 1939- 110
Derry, Thomas Kingston 1905- CANR-4
 Earlier sketch in CA 1R
Derry Down Derry
 See Lear, Edward
Dershowitz, Alan M. 1938- CANR-11
 Earlier sketch in CA 25-28R
Dersonnes, Jacques
 See Simenon, Georges (Jacques
 Christian)
Dertouzos, Michael L. 1936- 23-24R
Derum, James Patrick 1893- CAP-1
 Earlier sketch in CA 13-14
De Ruth, Jan 1922- 33-36R
Dervin, Brenda 1938- 29-32R
Dervin, Daniel A(rthur) 1935- 57-60
Derwent, Lavinia 69-72
 See also SATA 14
Derwin, Jordan 1931- 13-14R
Dery, Tibor 1894-1977 Obituary 73-76
Desai, Anita 1937- 81-84
 See also CLC 19, 37
Desai, Meghnad 1940- 126

Desai, P(rasannavadan) B(hagwanji) 1924- ... 29-32R
Desai, Ram 1926- ... 7-8R
Desai, Rashmi H(arilal) 1928- ... 15-16R
Desai, Rupin W(alter) 1934- ... 45-48
de Ste. Croix, G(eoffrey) E(rnest) M(aurice) 1910- ... 73-76
de Saint-Gall, Auguste Amedee
See Strich, Christian
de St. Jorre, John 1936- ... 102
de Saint-Luc, Jean
See Glassco, John
de Saint Phalle, Therese 1930- ... CANR-21
Earlier sketch in CA 29-32R
de Saint Phalle, Thibaut 1918- ... 108
DeSalvo, Joseph S(alvatore) 1938- ... 45-48
DeSalvo, Louise A(nita) 1942- ... CANR-23
Earlier sketch in CA 102
Desan, Wilfrid 1908- ... 61-64
Desani, G(ovindas) V(ishnoodas) 1909- ... 45-48
de Santillana, Giorgio Diaz 1902- ... CAP-1
Earlier sketch in CA 13-14
DeSantis, Mary Allen (Carpe) 1930- ... 9-10R
De Santis, Vincent P. 1918- ... CANR-4
Earlier sketch in CA 11-12R
De Santo, Charles P(asquale) 1923- ... 116
De Satge, John (Cosmo) 1928-1984 ... 124
Obituary ... 113
Desatnick, Robert L(awrence) 1931- ... 41-44R
de Sausmarez, (Lionel) Maurice 1915-1969 ... CAP-1
Earlier sketch in CA 11-12
de Saussure, Eric 1925- ... 105
Desbarats, Peter 1933- ... CANR-10
Earlier sketch in CA 17-18R
See also SATA 39
Desbiens, Jean-Paul 1927- ... DLB-53
Desborough, Vincent Robin d'Arba 1914-1978 Obituary ... 111
Descargues, Pierre 1925- ... CANR-14
Earlier sketch in CA 37-40R
Deschampsneufs, Henry Pierre Bernard 1911- ... CANR-6
Earlier sketch in CA 7-8R
de Schanschieff, Juliet Dymoke 1919- ... 106
Descharnes, Robert (Pierre) 1926- ... 69-72
Deschenaux, Jacques 1945- ... 61-64
Deschin, Celia Spalter 1903- ... 104
Deschin, Jacob 1900(?)-1983 Obituary ... 110
Deschler, Lewis 1905-1976 Obituary ... 65-68
Deschner, Donald (Anthony) 1933- ... 21-22R
Deschner, (Hans) Guenther 1941- ... 41-44R
Deschner, (Hans) Gunther
See Deschner, (Hans) Guenther
Deschner, John 1923- ... 81-84
de Schweinitz, Karl 1887-1975 ... 61-64
de Selincourt, Aubrey 1894-1962 ... 73-76
See also SATA 14
de Sena, Jorge 1919-1978 Obituary ... 77-80
De Seversky, Alexander P(rocofieff) 1894-1974 Obituary ... 53-56
DeSeyn, Donna E. 1933- ... 21-22R
Desfosses, Helen 1945- ... 41-44R
Des Gagniers, Jean 1929- ... CANR-9
Earlier sketch in CA 65-68
DeShazo, Edith K(ind) 1920- ... 61-64
DeShazo, Elmer Anthony 1924- ... 37-40R
Deshen, Shlomo 1935- ... 57-60
Deshler, G(eorge) Byron 1903- ... 53-56
DeSiano, Francis P(atrick) 1945- ... 112
De Sica, Vittorio 1901(?)-1974 Obituary ... 117
See also CLC 20
Desiderato, Otello 1926- ... 37-40R
De Simone, Daniel V. 1930- ... 25-28R
Desmarais, Barbara G.
See Taylor, Barbara G.
Des Marais, Louise M(ercier) 1923- ... 110
Desmarais, Ovid E. 1919- ... CANR-23
Earlier sketches in CA 4R, CANR-4
Desmond, Adrian J(ohn) 1947- ... CANR-8
Earlier sketch in CA 61-64
See also SATA 51
Desmond, Alice Curtis 1897- ... CANR-2
Earlier sketch in CA 4R
See also SATA 8
Desmond, (Clarice) J(oanne) Patrick (Scholes) 1910- ... 11-12R
Desmond, John 1909(?)-1977 Obituary ... 73-76
Desmond, John F(rancis) 1939- ... 112
Desmond, Ray 1925- ... 120
Desmond, Robert W(illiam) 1900- ... CANR-12
Earlier sketch in CA 73-76
Desmond, Shaw 1877-1960 Obituary ... 89-92
Desmonde, William H(erbert) 1921- ... 1R
Desnos, Robert 1900-1945 Brief entry ... 121
See also TCLC 22
De Sola, John
See Morland, Nigel
De Sola, Ralph 1908- ... 53-56
Desowitz, Robert S. 1926- ... 126
Despalatovic, Elinor Murray 1933- ... 105
Despert, J(uliette) Louise 1892- ... 69-72
Desplaines, Baroness Julie
See Jennings, Leslie Nelson
Despland, Michel 1936- ... 49-52
Despres, Leo A(rthur) 1932- ... 25-28R
Des Pres, Terrence 1939-1987 ... 73-76
Obituary ... 124
DesRochers, Alfred 1901-1978 ... DLB-68
Desrosiers, Leo-Paul 1896-1967 ... DLB-68
Dessau, Joanna 1921- ... CANR-24
Earlier sketch in CA 106
Dessauer, John H(ans) 1905- ... 104
Dessauer, John P(aul) 1924- ... 53-56
Dessel, Norman F(rank) 1932- ... 61-64
Dessen, Alan C(harles) 1935- ... 69-72
Dessent, Michael H(arold) 1942- ... 110
Dessi, Giuseppe 1909-1977 ... 65-68
Obituary ... 126
d'Estaing, Valery Giscard
See Giscard d'Estaing, Valery
De Steuch, Harriet Henry 1897(?)-1974 Obituary ... 49-52
Destler, Chester McArthur 1904-1984 ... CANR-16
Obituary ... 114
Earlier sketch in CA 5-6R
Destler, I. M. 1939- ... CANR-15
Earlier sketch in CA 89-92
Destouches, Louis-Ferdinand 1894-1961 ... 85-88
See also CLC 9, 15
Destry, Vince
See Norwood, Victor G(eorge) C(harles)
De Sua, William Joseph 1930- ... 15-16R
de Swaan, Abram 1942- ... CANR-13
Earlier sketch in CA 69-72
de Sylva, Donald Perrin 1928- ... 53-56
De Tabley, Lord 1835-1895 ... DLB-35
De Tarr, Francis 1926- ... 17-18R
Deter, Dean (Allen) 1945- ... 53-56
de Teran, Lisa St. Aubin
See St. Aubin de Teran, Lisa
Deterline, William A(lexander) 1927- ... CANR-8
Earlier sketch in CA 7-8R
de Terra, Helmut 1900-1981 Obituary ... 104
de Terra, Rhoda Hoff 1901- ... 2R
Detherage, May 1908- ... CAP-2
Earlier sketch in CA 23-24
Dethier, Vincent Gaston 1915- ... CANR-9
Earlier sketch in CA 65-68
Dethlefsen, Merle 1934- ... 119
Dethloff, Henry C(lay) 1934- ... 23-24R
De Thomasis, Louis 1940- ... 123
Detine, Padre
See Olsen, Ib Spang
de Tirtoff, Romain 1892- ... 69-72
Detjen, Ervin W(infred) 1909- ... CAP-2
Earlier sketch in CA 19-20
Detjen, Mary (Elizabeth) Ford 1904- ... CAP-1
Earlier sketch in CA 13-14
de Todany, James
See Beaudoin, Kenneth Lawrence
de Toledano, Ralph
See Toledano, Ralph de
de Tolignac, Gaston
See Griffith, D(avid Lewelyn) W(ark)
De Tolnay, Charles Erich 1899- ... 73-76
de Tonquedec, Jospeh
See Tonquedec, Joseph de
de Trevino, Elizabeth B.
See Trevino, Elizabeth B(orton) de
Detro, Gene 1935- ... CANR-12
Earlier sketch in CA 61-64
Detter, Ingrid
See Delupis, Ingrid
Detweiler, Robert 1932- ... 33-36R
Detwiler, Donald S(caife) 1933- ... 37-40R
Detz, Joan (Marie) 1951- ... 118
Detz, Phyllis 1911- ... CAP-2
Earlier sketch in CA 33-36
Detzer, David William 1937- ... 93-96
Detzer, Karl 1891- ... CAP-1
Earlier sketch in CA 9-10
Detzler, Jack J. 1922- ... 33-36R
Detzler, Wayne Alan 1936- ... 105
Deuchar, Margaret 1952- ... 113
Deuel, Thorne 1890-1984 Obituary ... 112
Deutrich, Mabel E. 1915- ... 5-6R
Deutsch, Alfred H(enry) 1914- ... 116
Deutsch, Arnold R. 1919- ... 101
Deutsch, Babette 1895-1982 ... CANR-4
Obituary ... 108
Earlier sketch in CA 4R
See also SATA 1, 33
See also DLB 45
See also CLC 18
Deutsch, Bernard Francis 1925- ... 15-16R
Deutsch, Eberhard Paul 1897-1980 Obituary ... 93-96
Deutsch, Eliot (Sandler) 1931- ... CANR-10
Earlier sketch in CA 65-68
Deutsch, Eva Costabel
See Costabel, Eva Deutsch
Deutsch, Harold C(harles) 1904- ... 21-22R
Deutsch, Helen 1906- ... 112
Brief entry ... 108
Deutsch, Helene (Rosenbach) 1884-1982 Obituary ... 106
Deutsch, Herbert A(rnold) 1932- ... 89-92
Deutsch, Hermann Bacher 1889-1970 Obituary ... 93-96
Deutsch, John James 1911-1976 Obituary ... 111
Deutsch, Karl W(olfgang) 1912- ... 41-44R
Deutsch, Marilyn Weisberg 1950- ... 102
Deutsch, Morton 1920- ... 1R
Deutsch, Ronald M(artin) 1928- ... CANR-4
Earlier sketch in CA 3R
Deutscher, Irwin 1923- ... 25-28R
Deutscher, Isaac 1907-1967 ... CANR-4
Obituary ... 25-28R
Earlier sketch in CA 5-6R
Deutscher, Max 1916(?)-1979 Obituary ... 93-96
Deutscher, Thomas (Brian) 1949- ... 124
Deutschkron, Inge 1922- ... 29-32R
Deutschman, Alan (Barry) 1965- ... 116
Devadutt, Vinjamuri E(verett) 1908- ... CAP-2
Earlier sketch in CA 23-24
De Vaere, Ulric Josef 1932- ... 3R
Devahuti, D. 1929- ... 45-48
Devajee, Ved
See Gool, Reshard
Deval, Gord 1930- ... 124
Deval, Jacques
See Boularan, Jacques
De Valera, Eamon 1882-1975 Obituary ... 89-92
De Valera, Sinead 1879(?)-1975 Obituary ... 53-56
See also SATA 30
de Valois, Ninette 1898- Brief entry ... 115
Devaney, John 1926- ... CANR-23
Earlier sketches in CA 19-20R, CANR-7
See also SATA 12
Devaraja, N(and) K(ishore) 1917- ... 104
Devas, Nicolette (Macnamara) 1911-1987(?) ... 13-14R
Obituary ... 122
DeVault, M(arion) Vere 1922- ... CANR-20
Earlier sketches in CA 1R, CANR-4
De Vaux, Roland 1903-1971 Obituary ... 33-36R
De Veaux, Alexis 1948- ... CANR-26
Earlier sketch in CA 65-68
See also BW
See also DLB 38
D'Evelyn, Katherine E(dith) 1899- ... 17-18R
Dever, Joseph 1919-1970 ... CAP-2
Obituary ... 29-32R
Earlier sketch in CA 19-20
Dever, William Gwinn 1933- Brief entry ... 109
Deveraux, Jude
See White, Jude Gilliam
de Vere, Aubrey 1814-1902 ... DLB-35
de Vere, Jane
See Watson, Julia
Deverell, William H(erbert) 1937- ... 115
Devereux, Frederick L(eonard), Jr. 1914- ... CANR-1
Earlier sketch in CA 49-52
See also SATA 9
Devereux, George 1908- ... 69-72
Devereux, Hilary 1919- ... 13-14R
Devereux, Robert (Essex) 1922- ... 5-6R
Deverson, Harry 1909(?)-1972 Obituary ... 104
De Vet, Charles V(incent) 1911- ... 102
Devi, Indra 1899- ... CAP-1
Earlier sketch in CA 13-14
Devi, Nila
See Woody, Regina Jones
Devi, Ragini 1894(?)-1982 Obituary ... 110
Deview, Lucille 1920- ... 73-76
De Vilbiss, Philip
See Mebane, John (Harrison)
Deville, Rene
See Kacew, Romain
de Villiers, Gerard 1929- ... 61-64
de Vilmorin, Louise Leveque
See Vilmorin, Louise Leveque de
de Vinck, Antoine 1924- ... 53-56
de Vinck, Catherine 1922- ... CANR-6
Earlier sketch in CA 57-60
de Vinck, (Baron) Jose M. G. A. 1912- ... 19-20R
Devine, D(avid) M(cDonald) 1920- ... CANR-1
Earlier sketch in CA 4R
Devine, Dominic
See Devine, D(avid) M(cDonald)
Devine, Donald J. 1937- ... 81-84
Devine, (Mary) Elizabeth 1938- ... 116
Devine, George 1941- ... CANR-1
Earlier sketch in CA 45-48
Devine, Janice 1909(?)-1973 Obituary ... 41-44R
Devine, (Joseph) Lawrence 1935- ... 73-76
Devine, Thomas G. 1928- ... 17-18R
DeVinney, Richard 1936- ... 45-48
Devins, Joseph H(erbert), Jr. 1930- ... 21-22R
DeVitis, Angelo A(nthony) 1925- ... 107
De Vito, Joseph Anthony 1938- ... 37-40R
Devkota, Laxmiprasad 1909-1959 Brief entry ... 123
See also TCLC 23
Devletoglou, Nicos E. 1936- ... 41-44R
Devlin, Bernadette (Josephine) 1947- ... 105
Devlin, Diana (Mary) 1941- ... 114
Devlin, Gerard M(ichael) 1933- ... 105
Devlin, Harry 1918- ... CANR-8
Earlier sketch in CA 65-68
See also SATA 11
Devlin, John C. 1911(?)-1984 Obituary ... 113
Devlin, John J(oseph), Jr. 1920- ... 37-40R
Devlin, L. Patrick 1939- ... 61-64
Devlin, Otis 1916- ... 117
Devlin, Patrick (Arthur) 1905- ... 69-72
Devlin, (Dorothy) Wende 1918- ... CANR-8
Earlier sketch in CA 61-64
See also SATA 11
DeVoe, Shirley Spaulding 1899- ... 77-80
Devol, Kenneth S(towe) 1929- ... 49-52
Devon, D. G.
See Demorest, Stephen
and Gross, Michael (Robert)
Devon, John Anthony
See Payne, (Pierre Stephen) Robert
Devor, John W(esley) 1901- ... CAP-1
Earlier sketch in CA 11-12
Devore, Irven 1934- ... 23-24R
DeVorkin, David H(yam) 1944- ... CANR-26
Earlier sketch in CA 108
De Vorsey, Louis, Jr. 1929- ... 21-22R
DeVos, George A(lphonse) 1922- ... CANR-11
Earlier sketch in CA 21-22R
De Vos, Karen Helder 1939- ... 102
de Vosjoli, Philippe L. Thyraud 1920- ... 29-32R
De Voto, Bernard (Augustine) 1897-1955 Brief entry ... 113
See also DLB 9
See also TCLC 29
de Vries, Anne 1904-1964 Obituary ... 116
De Vries, Carrow 1906- ... 53-56
deVries, Egbert 1901- ... 61-64
de Vries, Herbert A. 1917- ... CANR-13
Earlier sketch in CA 33-36R
de Vries, Jan 1943- ... CANR-26
Earlier sketch in CA 69-72
de Vries, Leonard
See Vries, Leonard de
de Vries, Manfred F. R. Kets
See Kets de Vries, Manfred F. R.
De Vries, Peter 1910- ... 17-18R
See also DLB 6
See also DLBY 82
See also CLC 1, 2, 3, 7, 10, 28, 46
de Vries, Rachel (Guido) 1947- ... 123
De Vries, Simon J(ohn) 1921- ... 57-60
De Vries, Walter (Dale) 1929- ... 69-72
Dew, Charles B(urgess) 1937- ... 21-22R
Dew, Donald 1928- ... 106
Dew, Edward MacMillan 1935- ... 81-84
Dew, Joan King 1932- ... 104
Dew, Robb (Reavill) Forman 1946- ... 104
de Waal, Frans 1948- ... 110
De Waal, Ronald Burt 1932- ... CANR-14
Earlier sketch in CA 37-40R
de Waal, Victor (Alexander) 1929- ... 29-32R
de Waal Malefijt, Annemarie 1914-1982 ... 61-64
Obituary ... 109
De Waard, E(lliott) John 1935- ... CANR-2
Earlier sketch in CA 49-52
See also SATA 7
Dewald, Paul A. 1920- ... 19-20R
Dewar, Deborah 1946(?)-1986 Obituary ... 118
Dewar, Diana Ill 1928(?)-1984 Obituary ... 112
Dewar, Margaret E(lizabeth) 1948- ... 114
Dewar, Mary (Williamson) 1921- ... 15-16R
Dewart, Leslie 1922- ... 9-10R
de Water, Frederic F(ranklyn) Van
See Van de Water, Frederic F(ranklyn)
Dewdney, Christopher 1951- ... 125
See also DLB 60
Dewdney, John Christopher 1928- ... 103
Dewdney, Selwyn (Hanington) 1909-1979 ... 69-72
See also DLB 68
DeWeerd, Harvey A. 1902- ... 73-76
DeWeese, Gene
See DeWeese, Thomas Eugene
DeWeese, Jean
See DeWeese, Thomas Eugene
DeWeese, Thomas Eugene 1934- ... CANR-24
Earlier sketches in CA 65-68, CANR-9
See also SATA 45, 46
De Welt, Don Finch 1919- ... CANR-1
Earlier sketch in CA 1R
de Wet, Hugh Oloff 1912(?)-1976(?) Obituary ... 104
Dewey, Ariane 1937- ... CANR-3
Earlier sketch in CA 49-52
See also SATA 7
Dewey, Bradley R. 1934- ... 29-32R
Dewey, Donald O(dell) 1930- ... 37-40R
Dewey, Edward R(ussell) 1895-1978 ... 41-44R
Dewey, Frank L. 1906- ... 122
Dewey, Godfrey 1887-1977 ... CAP-2
Obituary ... 73-76
Earlier sketch in CA 29-32
Dewey, Irene Sargent 1896- ... CAP-2
Earlier sketch in CA 17-18
Dewey, Jennifer (Owings) 1941- ... 126
See also SATA 48
Dewey, John 1859-1952 Brief entry ... 114
Dewey, Kenneth Francis 1940- ... 112
See also SATA 39
Dewey, Melvil 1851-1931 Brief entry ... 118
Dewey, Melville Louis Kossuth
See Dewey, Melvil
Dewey, Robert D(yckman) 1923- ... 9-10R
Dewey, Robert E(ugene) 1923- ... 13-14R
Dewey, Thomas B(lanchard) 1915- ... CANR-1
Earlier sketch in CA 3R
Dewhirst, Ian 1936- ... 102
Dewhurst, Eileen (Mary) 1929- ... 109
Dewhurst, J(ames) Frederic 1895-1967 ... CAP-2
Earlier sketch in CA 17-18
Dewhurst, Keith 1931- ... CANR-18
Earlier sketch in CA 61-64
Dewhurst, Kenneth 1919- ... CANR-2
Earlier sketch in CA 7-8R
deWit, Dorothy (May Knowles) 1916-1980 ... 113
Obituary ... 109
See also SATA 28, 39
DeWitt, Addison
See Newman, Kim (James)
DeWitt, Edith Openshaw 1920- ... 111
DeWitt, James
See Lewis, Mildred D.
DeWitt, John 1910(?)-1984 Obituary ... 113
Dewlen, Al 1921- ... CANR-2
Earlier sketch in CA 2R
de Wohl, Louis 1903-1961 Obituary ... 111
De Wolf, L. Harold 1905- ... CANR-2
Earlier sketch in CA 2R
DeWolf, Rose (Doris) 1934- ... CANR-11
Earlier sketch in CA 29-32R
de Wolfe, Ivor
See Hastings, Hubert de Cronin
de Wolfe, Ivy
See Hastings, Hubert de Cronin
Dewsbury, Donald A(llen) 1939- ... CANR-15
Earlier sketch in CA 89-92
Dexter, Al
See Poindexter, Clarence Albert
Dexter, Beverly L(iebherr) 1943- ... 114
Dexter, Byron (Vinson) 1900-1973 Obituary ... 113
Dexter, (Norman) Colin 1930- ... CANR-25
Earlier sketches in CA 65-68, CANR-10
Dexter, John
See Zachary, Hugh
Dexter, Lewis Anthony 1915- ... CANR-4
Earlier sketch in CA 11-12R
Dexter, Martin
See Faust, Frederick (Shiller)
Dexter, (Ellen) Pat(ricia) Egan ... 81-84
Dexter, Pete 1943- ... CLC-34

Dexter, Susan (Elizabeth) 1955- CANR-25
Earlier sketch in CA 108
Dey, Frederic (Merrill) Van Rensselaer
1865-1922 Brief entry 113
Dey, Joseph C(harles), Jr. 1907- CAP-1
Earlier sketch in CA 11-12
Dey, Marmaduke
See Dey, Frederic (Merrill) Van
Rensselaer
Deyermond, Alan D(avid) 1932- CANR-6
Earlier sketch in CA 13-14R
Deyneka, Anita 1943- CANR-26
Earlier sketches in CA 61-64, CANR-11
See also SATA 24
Deyneka, Peter (N., Sr.) 1898-1987
Obituary 123
de Young, M. H. 1849-1925 .... DLB-25
DeYoung, Mary 1949- 112
Deyrup, Astrith Johnson 1923- 65-68
See also SATA 24
Deza, Ernest C. 1923- 53-56
Dhalla, Nariman K. 1925- 25-28R
Dharmi, Santana 1914- CANR-20
Earlier sketch in CA 101
d'Harnoncourt, Anne (Julie) 1943- 120
Dhavamony, Mariasusai 1925- 33-36R
Dhiegh, Khigh (Alx) 93-96
Dhokalia, (Ramaa) Prasad 1925- 41-44R
Dhrymes, Phoebus J(ames) 1932- CANR-12
Earlier sketch in CA 29-32R
Diack, Hunter 1908-1974 .... CAP-2
Earlier sketch in CA 21-22
Dial, Joan 1937- CANR-24
Earlier sketch in CA 81-84
Diallo, Nafissatou (Niang) 1941-? 116
Diamano, Silmang
See Senghor, Leopold Sedar
Diamant, Lincoln 1923- 33-36R
Diamond, Ann
See McLean, Anne (Julia)
Diamond, Arthur Sigismund 1897- CAP-1
Earlier sketch in CA 9-10
Diamond, Cora A(nn) 1937- 121
Diamond, Donna 1950- 115
See also SATA 30, 35
Diamond, Edwin 1925- CANR-9
Earlier sketch in CA 15-16R
Diamond, Graham 1945- 85-88
Diamond, Harold J(ames) 1934- 110
Diamond, I(sidore) A. L. 1920-1988 81-84
Obituary 125
See also DLB 26
Diamond, Jacqueline
See Hyman, Jackie (Diamond)
Diamond, Jay 1934- CANR-14
Earlier sketch in CA 65-68
Diamond, John 1907- 109
Diamond, John 1934- 85-88
Diamond, Malcolm L(uria) 1924- 25-28R
Diamond, Marc 1944- 119
Diamond, Martin 1919-1977 77-80
Obituary 73-76
Diamond, Milton 1934- 89-92
Diamond, Neil 1941- 108
See also CLC 30
Diamond, Norma Joyce 1933- Brief entry ... 108
Diamond, Petra
See Sachs, Judith
Diamond, Rebecca
See Sachs, Judith
Diamond, Robert Mach 1930- CANR-7
Earlier sketch in CA 9-10R
Diamond, Sander A. 1942- 49-52
Diamond, Selma 1920-1985 Obituary 116
Diamond, Sigmund 1920- 3R
Diamond, Solomon 1906- 102
Diamond, Stanley 1922- 102
Diamond, Stephen A(rthur) 1946- 89-92
Diamond, William 1917- 65-68
Diamonstein, Barbaralee D. CANR-15
Earlier sketch in CA 85-88
Diara, Agadem Lumumba 1947- 65-68
Diara, Schavi M.
See Ali, Schavi M(ali)
Dias, Earl Joseph 1916- 23-24R
See also SATA 41
Diaz, Janet W(inecoff) 1935- 53-56
Diaz-Alejandro, Carlos Federico 1937-1985
Obituary 116
Diaz-Guerrero, Rogelio 1918- 101
Diaz Plaja, Guillermo 1909-1984 Obituary ... 113
di Bassetto, Corno
See Shaw, George Bernard
DiBattista, Maria 1947- 113
Dibb, Paul 1939- CANR-1
Earlier sketch in CA 45-48
Dibba, Ebou 1943- 124
Dibble, J(ames) Birney 1925- 17-18R
Dibble, Nancy Ann 1942- 103
Dibble, Vadna Davis 1902(?)-1983
Obituary 110
Dibdin, Michael 1947- 77-80
Dibelius, Otto (Friedrich Karl) 1880-1967
Obituary 114
Dibell, Ansen
See Dibble, Nancy Ann
Di Bella, Anna 1933- Brief entry 110
Dible, Donald M(eredith) 1936- 110
Dibner, Andrew Sherman 1926-
Brief entry 110
Dibner, Bern 1897- 107
Dibner, Martin 1911- CANR-4
Earlier sketch in CA 2R
DiBona, Joseph E. 1927- Brief entry 109
Di Cavalcanti, Emiliano 1898(?)-1976
Obituary 69-72
Dice, Lee R. 1889(?)-1976 Obituary 69-72
Di Certo, J(oseph) J(ohn) 1933- CANR-13
Earlier sketch in CA 23-24R
Di Cesare, Mario A(nthony) 1928- CANR-3
Earlier sketch in CA 5-6R
Dichter, Ernest 1907- 19-20R
Dichter, Harry 1900(?)-1978(?) Obituary ... 104
Di Cicco, Pier Giorgio 1949- CANR-17
Earlier sketch in CA 97-100
See also DLB 60
Dick, Bernard F(rancis) 1935- CANR-9
Earlier sketch in CA 21-22R
Dick, Daniel T. 1946- 61-64
Dick, Everett 1898- 25-28R
Dick, Ignace 1926- CANR-12
Earlier sketch in CA 25-28R
Dick, Kay 1915- CANR-15
Earlier sketch in CA 15-16R
Dick, Philip K(indred) 1928-1982 ...... CANR-16
Obituary 106
Earlier sketches in CA 49-52, CANR-2
See also DLB 8
See also CLC 10, 30
Dick, R. A.
See Leslie, Josephine Aimee Campbell
Dick, Robert C. 1938- 37-40R
Dick, Susan 1940- 120
Dick, Trella Lamson 1889-1974 .... 7-8R
See also SATA 9
Dick, Trevor J.O. 1934- Brief entry 106
Dick, William M(ilner) 1933- 41-44R
Dickason, David Howard 1907-1974 ..... CAP-2
Earlier sketch in CA 33-36
Dicke, Robert H(enry) 1916- 53-56
Dicken, E(ric) W(illiam) Trueman 1919- 9-10R
Dickens, A(rthus) G(eoffrey) 1910- 53-56
Dickens, Charles (John Huffam)
1812-1870 .... SATA-15
See also DLB 21, 55, 70
Dickens, Floyd, Jr. 1940- 111
Dickens, Frank
See Huline-Dickens, Frank William
Dickens, Jacqueline B(ass) 1941- 112
Dickens, Milton 1908- 2R
Dickens, Monica (Enid) 1915- CANR-2
Earlier sketch in CA 7-8R
See also SATA 4
Dickens, Norman
See Eisenberg, Lawrence B(enjamin)
Dickens, Peter (Gerald Charles)
1917-1987 124
Obituary 122
Dickens, Roy S(elman), Jr. 1938- CANR-9
Earlier sketch in CA 65-68
Dickenson, Fred 1909-1986 Obituary 119
Dickenson, James R. 1931- 65-68
Dicker, Eva Barash 1936- 107
Dicker, Ralph Leslie 1914- 65-68
Dickerman, Edmund H. 1935- Brief entry ... 110
Dickerson, F(rederick) Reed 1909- 17-18R
Dickerson, Grace Leslie 1911- 5-6R
Dickerson, John 1939- 57-60
Dickerson, Martha Ufford 1922- 81-84
Dickerson, Nancy H(anschman) 1930- 69-72
Dickerson, Oliver M(orton) 1875-1966
Obituary 106
Dickerson, Robert B(radford), Jr. 1955- 106
Dickerson, Roy Ernest 1886-1965 .... 7-8R
Obituary 103
See also SATA 26
Dickerson, William E(ugene) 1897-1971 .. CAP-2
Earlier sketch in CA 21-22
Dickey, Charley 1920- 69-72
Dickey, Franklin M(iller) 1921- 23-24R
Dickey, Glenn (Ernest, Jr.) 1936- CANR-4
Earlier sketch in CA 53-56
Dickey, James (Lafayette) 1923- CANR-10
Earlier sketch in CA 11-12R
See also CABS 2
See also DLB 5
See also DLBY 82
See also CLC 1, 2, 4, 7, 10, 15, 47
See also AITN 1, 2
Dickey, Lee
See Bremyer, Jayne Dickey
Dickey, R(obert) P(reston) 1936- CANR-25
Earlier sketch in CA 29-32R
Dickey, William 1928- CANR-24
Earlier sketch in CA 9-10R
See also DLB 5
See also CLC 3, 28
Dickie, Edgar P(rimrose) 1897- CAP-1
Earlier sketch in CA 11-12
Dickie, George (Thomas) 1926- 33-36R
Dickie, James 1934- 97-100
Dickie, John 1923- 13-14R
Dickie, Margaret (McKenzie) 1935- 123
Dickie-Clark, H(amish) F(indlay) 1922- ... 21-22R
Dickins, A. S. M.
See Dickins, Anthony (Stewart Mackay)
Dickins, Anthony (Stewart Mackay)
1914-1987 Obituary 124
Dickinson, A(lan) E(dgar) F(rederic)
1899- 73-76
Dickinson, A(rthur) T(aylor), Jr. 1925- 7-8R
Dickinson, Charles 1952- CLC-49
Dickinson, Donald C. 1927- 23-24R
Dickinson, Edward C(live) 1938- 61-64
Dickinson, Eleanor 1931- 65-68
Dickinson, Emily (Elizabeth)
1830-1886 .... SATA-29
See also DLB 1
See also CDALB 1865-1917
Dickinson, H(arry) T(homas) 1939- 33-36R
Dickinson, John 1732-1808 .... DLB-31
Dickinson, John K(ellogg) 1918- 25-28R
Dickinson, Jonathan 1688-1747 .... DLB-24
Dickinson, Leon T. 1912- 13-14R
Dickinson, Lois Stice 1898(?)-1970
Obituary 104
Dickinson, Margaret
See Muggeson, Margaret Elizabeth
Dickinson, Mary 1949- 110
See also SATA 41, 48
Dickinson, Patric Thomas 1914- CANR-3
Earlier sketch in CA 9-10R
See also DLB 27
Dickinson, Peter 1927- 41-44R
See also SATA 5
See also CLC 12, 35
Dickinson, Peter A(llen) 1926- 102
Dickinson, Richard D(onald) N(ye, Jr.)
1929- Brief entry 109
Dickinson, Robert Eric 1905- CANR-3
Earlier sketch in CA 5-6R
Dickinson, Ruth F(rankenstein) 1933- 37-40R
Dickinson, (William) Stirling 1909- CAP-2
Earlier sketch in CA 33-36
Dickinson, Susan 1931- 57-60
See also SATA 8
Dickinson, Thorold (Barron) 1903-1984 ... 45-48
Obituary 112
Dickinson, W(illiam) Croft 1897-1963 ... CANR-6
Earlier sketch in CA 3R
See also SATA 13
Dickinson, William Boyd 1908-1978 85-88
Obituary 81-84
Dick-Lauder, George (Andrew) 1917- 102
Dickler, Gerald 1912- 11-12R
Dickmeyer, Lowell A. 1939- 109
See also SATA 51
Dicks, Henry V(ictor) 1900- 102
Dicks, Russell Leslie 1906-1965 .... CAP-1
Earlier sketch in CA 15-16
Dickson, Carr
See Carr, John Dickson
Dickson, Carter
See Carr, John Dickson
Dickson, Charles W., Jr. 1926- 25-28R
Dickson, Donald R(ichard) 1951- 126
Dickson, Franklyn 1941- 53-56
Dickson, George E(dmond) 1918- 49-52
Dickson, Gordon R(upert) 1923- CANR-6
Earlier sketch in CA 9-10R
See also DLB 8
Dickson, Helen
See Reynolds, Helen Mary Greenwood
Campbell
Dickson, K. A.
See Dickson, Kwesi A(botsia)
Dickson, Kwesi A(botsia) 1929-
Brief entry 109
Dickson, (Horatio Henry) Lovat
1902-1987 .... 13-14R
Obituary 121
Dickson, Margaret (Smith) 1947- 114
Dickson, Mora (Hope-Robertson) 1918- . CANR-5
Earlier sketch in CA 15-16R
Dickson, Naida 1916- 37-40R
See also SATA 8
Dickson, Paul (Andrew) 1939- 33-36R
Dickson, Peter George Muir 1929- 13-14R
Dickson, Robert J(ames) 1919- 21-22R
Dickson, Stanley 1927- 53-56
Dickstein, Morris 1940- 85-88
Di Cyan, Erwin 1918- 37-40R
Didato, Salvatore V. 1926- 122
Brief entry 107
Didinger, Ray 1946- 93-96
Didion, Joan 1934- CANR-14
Earlier sketch in CA 5-6R
See also DLB 2
See also DLBY 81, 86
See also CLC 1, 3, 8, 14, 32
See also AITN 1
di Donato, Georgia 1932- 103
di Donato, Pietro 1911- 101
See also DLB 9
Didsbury, Howard F(rancis), Jr. 1924- 111
Didsbury, Peter 1946- 112
Diebold, Janet
See Sylvester, Janet Hart
Diebold, Janet Oline
See Sylvester, Janet Hart
Diebold, John (Theurer) 1926- 53-56
Diebold, William, Jr. 1918- CANR-6
Earlier sketch in CA 13-14R
Dieckmann, Ed(ward Adolph), Jr.
1920- CANR-21
Earlier sketch in CA 102
Dieckmann, Liselotte 1902- 97-100
Diederich, Bernard 1926- 77-80
Diefendorf, Barbara B(oonstoppel) 1946- ... 124
Diefendorf, Jeffry M(indlin) 1945- 104
Diefenthaler, Jon 1943- 124
Diego, Gerardo
See Diego Cendoya, Gerardo
Diego Cendoya, Gerardo 1896-1987
Obituary 123
Diehl, (Robert) Digby 1940- CANR-7
Earlier sketch in CA 53-56
Diehl, James M(ichael) 1938- 85-88
Diehl, Katharine Smith 1906- CAP-1
Earlier sketch in CA 11-12
Diehl, Kemper 1918- 118
Diehl, Lorraine B(uscaglia) 1940- 119
Diehl, W(illiam) W(ells) 1916- 19-20R
Diehl, William (Francis, Jr.) 1924- CANR-13
Earlier sketch in CA 101
Diehm, Floyd L(ee) 1925- Brief entry 110
Diekhoff, John S(iemon) 1905-1976 ..... CAP-2
Obituary 69-72
Earlier sketch in CA 29-32
Diekman, John R(aymond) 1946- 110
Diekmann, Godfrey 1908- CANR-2
Earlier sketch in CA 4R
Diel, Paul 1893- 103
Diener, Royce 1918- Brief entry 110
Dienes, C(harles) Thomas 1940- CANR-11
Earlier sketch in CA 69-72
Dienstag, Eleanor 1938- 65-68
Dienstein, William 1909- CAP-1
Earlier sketch in CA 17-18
Dierenfield, Richard B(ruce) 1922- 19-20R
Dierickx, C(harles) W(allace) 1921- 61-64
Dierks, Jack Cameron 1930- 29-32R
Diers, Carol Jean 1933- 33-36R
Diesing, Paul R. 1922- CANR-2
Earlier sketch in CA 1R
Dieska, L. Joseph 1913- 37-40R
Dieskau, Dietrich Fischer
See Fischer-Dieskau, Dietrich
Dieter, William 1929- 114
Dietl, (Kirsten) Ulla 1940- 33-36R
Dietrich, John E(rb) 1913- 17-18R
Dietrich, Noah 1889-1982 45-48
Obituary 106
Dietrich, R(ichard) F(arr) 1936- 23-24R
Dietrich, Richard V(incent) 1924- CANR-19
Earlier sketches in CA 53-56, CANR-4
Dietrich, Robert
See Hunt E(verette) Howard, Jr.
Dietrich, Wilson G. 1916- 25-28R
Dietz, Betty Warner
See Dietz, Elisabeth H.
Dietz, David H(enry) 1897-1984 .... CANR-2
Obituary 114
Earlier sketch in CA 1R
See also SATA 10, 41
Dietz, Elisabeth H. 1908- 29-32R
Dietz, Howard 1896-1983 53-56
Obituary 110
Dietz, Lew 1907- CANR-3
Earlier sketch in CA 5-6R
See also SATA 11
Dietz, Marjorie (Priscilla) J(ohnson)
1918- CANR-14
Earlier sketch in CA 65-68
Dietz, Norman D. 1930- CANR-10
Earlier sketch in CA 23-24R
Dietz, Peter O(wen) 1935- 33-36R
Dietze, Charles Edgar 1919- 69-72
Dietze, Gottfried 1922- 23-24R
Dietzel, Paul F(ranklin) 1924- 21-22R
Diez Del Corral, Luis 1911- 13-14R
Diez de Medina, Raul 1909(?)-1985
Obituary 117
DiFederico, Frank R. 1933(?)-1987
Obituary 125
DiFranco, Anthony (Mario) 1945- 118
See also SATA 42
Di Franco, Fiorenza 1932- CANR-17
Earlier sketches in CA 45-48, CANR-1
DiGaetani, John Louis 1943- 114
Digby, Joan (Hildreth) 1942- 126
Digby, John (Michael) 1938- 126
Digennaro, Joseph 1939- 53-56
Digges, Jeremiah
See Berger, Josef
Digges, Sister Mary Laurentia 1910- CAP-2
Earlier sketch in CA 21-22
Diggins, John P(atrick) 1935- 37-40R
Diggle, James 1944- CANR-13
Earlier sketch in CA 61-64
Diggory, James C(lark) 1920- CANR-9
Earlier sketch in CA 23-24R
Diggory, Terence (Elliott) 1951- 112
Diggs, Bernard James 1916- Brief entry 106
Diggs, Elizabeth 1939- 109
Diggs, Ellen Irene 114
Diggs, Irene
See Diggs, Ellen Irene
DiGiacomo, James J(oseph) 1924- 112
Di Girolamo, Vittorio 1928- 45-48
D'Ignazio, Fred(erick) 1949- 110
See also SATA 35, 39
Di Grazia, Thomas ?-1983 .... SATA-32
di Guisa, Giano
See Praz, Mario
Dihoff, Gretchen 1942- 41-44R
Dijkstra, Bram (Abraham Jan) 1938- 37-40R
Dike, Kenneth Onwuka 1917-1983
Obituary 111
Dikshit, R(amesh) D(utta) 1939- CANR-10
Earlier sketch in CA 65-68
Dikty, Julian May
See May, Julian
Dil, Zakhmi
See Hilton, Richard
DiLauro, Stephen 1950- 112
Dilcock, Noreen 1907- 103
Di Lella, Alexander A. 1929- 23-24R
DiLello, Richard 1945- 41-44R
Di Leo, Joseph H. 1902- 33-36R
Diles, Dave 1931- CANR-8
Earlier sketch in CA 57-60
Dilke, Annabel (Mary) 1942- CAP-1
Earlier sketch in CA 11-12
Dilke, Caroline (Sophia) 1940- 102
Dilke, Christopher Wentworth
1913(?)-1987 Obituary 125
Dilke, O(swald) A(shton) W(entworth)
1915- 69-72
Dilks, David (Neville) 1938- CANR-8
Earlier sketch in CA 61-64
Dill, Alonzo T(homas, Jr.) 1914- 37-40R
Dill, Clarence C(leveland) 1884-1978
Obituary 115
Dill, (George) Marshall, Jr. 1916- 4R

Dillard, Annie 1945- CANR-3
Earlier sketch in CA 49-52
See also SATA 10
See also DLBY 80
See also CLC 9
Dillard, Dudley 1913- 25-28R
Dillard, Emil L(ee) 1921- 57-60
Dillard, Heath (Portmann) 1933- 119
Dillard, J(oey) L(ee) 1924- CANR-14
Earlier sketch in CA 41-44R
Dillard, Polly Hargis 1916- CANR-5
Earlier sketch in CA 11-12R
See also SATA 24
Dillard, R(ichard) H(enry) W(ilde)
1937- CANR-10
Earlier sketch in CA 21-22R
See also CAAS 7
See also DLB 5
See also CLC 5
Dille, John M. 1921(?)-1971 Obituary 33-36R
Dille, Robert Crabtree 1924(?)-1983
Obituary 109
Dillehay, Ronald C(lifford) 1935- 23-24R
Dillenbeck, Marsden V. CAP-2
Earlier sketch in CA 25-28
Dillenberger, Jane 1916- CANR-23
Earlier sketches in CA 17-18R, CANR-7
Dillenberger, John 1918- CANR-17
Earlier sketches in CA 4R, CANR-2
Diller, Edward 1925- 85-88
Diller, Phyllis (Ada) 1917- CANR-22
Earlier sketch in CA 81-84
Dilles, James 1923- 1R
Dilley, Clyde H(obson) 1939- 113
Dilley, Frank B(rown) 1931- 15-16R
Dilliard, Irving (Lee) 1904- 21-22R
Dilligan, Robert J(ames) 1940- Brief entry 108
Dilling, Judith
See Rhoades, Judith G(rubman)
Dilling, Yvonne 1955- 118
Dillingham, Beth 1927- 53-56
Dillingham, William B(yron) 1930- 15-16R
Dillistone, Frederick W(illiam) 1903- CANR-5
Earlier sketch in CA 4R
Dillman, Audrey 1922(?)-1984 Obituary 113
Dillman, David D. 1900(?)-1983 Obituary 110
Dillon, Barbara 1927- 110
See also SATA 39, 44
Dillon, Bert 1937- 77-80
Dillon, Conley Hall 1906-1987 .... CANR-17
Obituary 123
Earlier sketch in CA 1R
Dillon, David 1941- 69-72
Dillon, Diane 1933- SATA-15, 51
Dillon, Eilis 1920- CANR-4
Earlier sketch in CA 9-10R
See also CAAS 3
See also SATA 2
See also CLC 17
Dillon, George 1906-1968 Obituary 89-92
Dillon, George Lewis 1944- 102
Dillon, J(ames) T(homas) 1940- 33-36R
Dillon, John M(yles) 1939- 77-80
Dillon, Lawrence S(amuel) 1910- CANR-25
Earlier sketch in CA 45-48
Dillon, Leo 1933- SATA-15, 51
Dillon, Martin 1949- 61-64
Dillon, Merton L. 1924- 13-14R
Dillon, Millicent (Gerson) 1925- CANR-12
Earlier sketch in CA 65-68
Dillon, Richard H(ugh) 1924- CANR-8
Earlier sketch in CA 19-20R
Dillon, Wallace Neil 1922- 3R
Dillon, Wilton S(terling) 1923- 37-40R
Dillow, Harry C. 1922- 123
Dilorenzo, Ronald Eugene 1931-
Brief entry 110
Dilson, Jesse 1914- 25-28R
See also SATA 24
Diltz, Bert Case 1894- CANR-9
Earlier sketch in CA 65-68
Dimancescu, Dan 1943- 113
di Marco, Gino
See Weiss, Irving J.
Di Marco, Luis Eugenio 1937- CANR-2
Earlier sketch in CA 45-48
Dimberg, Ronald G(ilbert) 1938- 61-64
Dimbleby, Jonathan 1944- 119
Brief entry 108
Di Meglio, Clara 1933- 97-100
DiMeglio, John E(dward) 1934- 77-80
DiMento, Joseph F(rank) 1947- 69-72
di Michele, Mary 1949- CANR-17
Earlier sketch in CA 97-100
Dimick, John M. 1898(?)-1983 Obituary 111
Dimick, Kenneth M. 1937- 29-32R
Dimmette, Celia (Puhr) 1896- CAP-2
Earlier sketch in CA 29-32
Dimmitt, Richard Bertrand 1925- 17-18R
Dimock, Edward Cameron, Jr. 1929- 102
Dimock, Gladys Ogden 1908- 7-8R
Dimock, Hedley G(ardiner) 1928- 5-6R
Dimock, Marshall E(dward) 1903- CANR-2
Earlier sketch in CA 1R
DiMona, Joseph 104
Dimond, E(dmunds) Grey 1918- 85-88
Dimond, Mary Clark 93-96
Dimond, Stanley E(llwood) 1905- 15-16R
Dimond, Stuart J. 1938-1981 .... 33-36R
Dimondstein, Geraldine 1926- 33-36R
Dimont, Madelon 1938- 41-44R
Dimont, Max I. 1912- 19-20R
Dimont, Penelope
See Mortimer, Penelope (Ruth)
Dimrecken, B. Grayer
See de Mille, Richard
Dimson, Wendy
See Baron, (Ora) Wendy
Din, Gilbert C. 1932- 118
Dinan, Carolyn 126
See also SATA 47
Dineley, David Lawrence 1927- 101
Diner, Hasia R(ena) 1946- CANR-9
Earlier sketch in CA 61-64
Diner, Steven J(ay) 1944- 110
Dinerman, Beatrice 1933- 13-14R
Dinerman, Helen Schneider 1921(?)-1974
Obituary 53-56
Dinerstein, Herbert S(amuel) 1919-
Brief entry 108
Dines, (Harry) Glen 1925- 9-10R
See also SATA 7
Dines, Michael 1916- 103
Dinesen, Isak
See Blixen, Karen (Christentze Dinesen)
See also CLC 10, 29
Ding, J. N.
See Darling, Jay Norwood
Dinges, John (Charles) 1941- 101
Dingle, Graeme 1945- 123
Dingle, Herbert 1890-1978 .... 13-14R
Obituary 122
Ding Ling
See Chiang Pin-chin
Dingman, Roger 1938- 93-96
Dings, John (Garetson) 1939- 41-44R
Dingwall, E(ric) J(ohn) 1890-1986 89-92
Obituary 120
Dingwall, W(illiam) Orr 1934- CANR-13
Earlier sketch in CA 21-22R
Dinhofer, A(lfred) 1929- 25-28R
Dinitz, Simon 1926- CANR-14
Earlier sketch in CA 37-40R
Dinkin, Robert J. 1940- Brief entry 107
Dinkmeyer, Don C. 1924- CANR-15
Earlier sketch in CA 41-44R
Dinman, Bertram David 1925- Brief entry 109
Dinnan, James A. 1929- 69-72
Dinneen, Betty 1929- CANR-8
Earlier sketch in CA 57-60
Dinnerstein, Harvey 1928- 112
See also SATA 42
Dinnerstein, Leonard 1934- CANR-24
Earlier sketches in CA 23-24R, CANR-9
Dino
See Dinhofer, A(lfred)
Dinsdale, Tim(othy Kay) 1924-1987 .... CANR-2
Obituary 124
Earlier sketch in CA 3R
See also SATA 11
Dinsky, Lazar 1891(?)-1976 Obituary 69-72
Dinsmore, Herman H. 1900(?)-1980
Obituary 97-100
Dintenfass, Mark 1941- CANR-11
Earlier sketch in CA 25-28R
See also DLBY 84
Dintiman, George B(lough) 1936- CANR-20
Earlier sketches in CA 53-56, CANR-5
Dinwiddie, Elza Teresa 110
Diole, Philippe V. 1908- 53-56
Diomede, John K.
See Effinger, George Alec
Dion, Gerard 1912- 41-44R
Dion, Sister Anita 1918- CANR-2
Earlier sketch in CA 7-8R
Dione, Robert L(ester) 1922- 57-60
Dionisopoulos, P(anagiotes) Allan
1921- 29-32R
Diop, Birago (Ismael) 1906- 125
See also BW
Diop, Cheikh Anta 1923-1986 125
Obituary 118
Brief entry 110
See also BW
Dior, Christian 1905-1957 Brief entry 115
DiOrio, Al(bert John) 1950- CANR-9
Earlier sketch in CA 57-60
Diotima
See Wynne-Tyson, Esme
DiPalma, Ray(mond) 1943- CANR-24
Earlier sketch in CA 29-32R
DiPasquale, Dominic 1932- 57-60
DiPego, Gerald F(rancis) 1941- 85-88
DiPerna, Paula 1949- 112
DiPersio, Michael S(alvatore) 1934- 110
Di Peso, Charles C(orradino) 1920- 57-60
Di Pietro, Robert Joseph 1932- CANR-7
Earlier sketch in CA 17-18R
Diplomaticus
See Guerra y Sanchez, Ramiro
Dipper, Alan 1922- 49-52
Dippie, Brian William 1943- CANR-25
Earlier sketch in CA 108
Dipple, Elizabeth 1937- 33-36R
di Prima, Diane 1934- CANR-13
Earlier sketch in CA 17-18R
See also DLB 5, 16
Dirac, P.A.M.
See Dirac, Paul A(drien) M(aurice)
Dirac, Paul A(drien) M(aurice) 1902-1984
Obituary 113
Dire, Eloise (Evangeline) Hodge 1907- 118
DiRenzo, Gordon J(ames) 1934- CANR-4
Earlier sketch in CA 53-56
Diringer, David 1900-1975 .... CANR-6
Obituary 57-60
Earlier sketch in CA 4R
Dirk
See Gringhuis, Richard H.
Dirk, R.
See Dietrich, Richard V(incent)
Dirks, Raymond L(ouis) 1934- 106
Dirks, Rudolph 1877-1968 Obituary 106
See also SATA 31
Dirksen, Alvin Joseph 1915- 110
Dirksen, Charles J(oseph) 1912- 5-6R
Dirksen, Louella Carver 1899-1979 103
Obituary 89-92
Dirlik, Arif 1940- 97-100
di Roccaferrera Ferrero, Giuseppe M.
1912- CANR-7
Earlier sketch in CA 15-16R
Dirrim, Allen Wendell 1929- 23-24R
Dirscherl, Denis 1934- 21-22R
Dirvin, Joseph I. 1917- CANR-2
Earlier sketch in CA 7-8R
Di Scala, Spencer M(ichael) 1941- 102
Disch, Thomas M(ichael) 1940- CANR-17
Earlier sketch in CA 23-24R
See also CAAS 4
See also DLB 8
See also CLC 7, 36
Dischell, Judy
See Lalli, Judy
Disher, Maurice Willson 1893-1969 .... CAP-1
Earlier sketch in CA 9-10
Dishman, Pat(ricia L.) 1939- 19-20R
d'Isly, Georges
See Simenon, Georges (Jacques
Christian)
Disney, Doris Miles 1907-1976 .... CANR-3
Obituary 65-68
Earlier sketch in CA 5-6R
Disney, Walt(er Elias) 1901-1966 Obituary 107
See also SATA 27, 28
See also DLB 22
Dison, Norma 1928- 53-56
Dispenza, Joseph Ernest 1942- 81-84
Disraeli, Benjamin 1804-1881 .... DLB-21, 55
Disraeli, Robert 1903- CAP-1
Earlier sketch in CA 11-12
Disston, Harry 1899- 41-44R
Distel, Peter
See Koch, Kurt E(mil)
Distler, Paul Francis 1911- 7-8R
Ditchburn, R(obert) W(illiam) 1903-1987 69-72
Obituary 122
Ditcum, Steve
See Crumb, R(obert)
Dito Und Idem
See Elisabeth (Ottilie Luise), Queen
(Pauline)
Ditsky, John (Michael) 1938- CANR-9
Earlier sketch in CA 65-68
Dittes, James E(dward) 1926- 61-64
Dittmer, Lowell 1941- 89-92
Ditton, James
See Clark, Douglas
Dittrich, John E(dward) 1931- 112
Ditzel, Paul C(alvin) 1926- 41-44R
Ditzen, Lowell Russell 1913-1987 .... 17-18R
Obituary 122
Ditzen, Rudolf 1893-1947 Brief entry 123
Ditzion, Sidney 1908-1975 .... 41-44R
Obituary 57-60
Divale, William T(ulio) 1942- 33-36R
Di Valentin, Maria Messuri 1911- CANR-5
Earlier sketch in CA 5-6R
See also SATA 7
Diverres, Armel Hugh 1914- 9-10R
Divine, Arthur Durham 1904-1987 103
Obituary 122
See also SATA 52
Divine, David
See Divine, Arthur Durham
Divine, Floy (Sherman) 1881-1986 113
Obituary 118
Divine, Robert A(lexander) 1929- CANR-20
Earlier sketches in CA 5-6R, CANR-3
Divine, Thomas F(rancis) 1900- 37-40R
DiVitto, Barbara A(nn) 1947- 118
Divoky, Diane 1939- 33-36R
Dix, Albert V. 1901(?)-1983 Obituary 109
Dix, Dorothea Lynde 1802-1887 .... DLB-1
Dix, Dorothy
See Gilmer, Elizabeth Meriwether
Dix, Robert H. 1930- 23-24R
Dix, William (Shepherd) 1910-1978
Obituary 77-80
Dixon, Bernard 1938- CANR-26
Earlier sketches in CA 65-68, CANR-10
Dixon, Christa Klingbeil 1935- 102
Dixon, Colin J. 1933- 105
Dixon, Dougal 1947- CANR-25
Earlier sketch in CA 107
See also SATA 45
Dixon, Franklin W. 19-20R
See also SATA 1
Dixon, George
See Willis, Ted
Dixon, Graham (Peter) 1956- 121
Dixon, H(arry) Vernor 1908- CAP-1
Earlier sketch in CA 9-10
Dixon, Janice T(horne) 1932- 107
Dixon, Jeane 1918- CANR-21
Earlier sketch in CA 65-68
Dixon, Jeanne 1936- 105
See also SATA 31
Dixon, John W(esley), Jr. 1919- CANR-3
Earlier sketch in CA 11-12R
Dixon, Joseph L(awrence) 1896- 61-64
Dixon, Kenneth L. 1915(?)-1986 Obituary 119
Dixon, Laurinda S. 1948- 126
Dixon, Marjorie (Mack) 1887- CAP-2
Earlier sketch in CA 23-24
Dixon, Paige
See Corcoran, Barbara
Dixon, Penelope A(nn) 1948- 113
Dixon, Peter L(ee) 1931- CANR-2
Earlier sketch in CA 45-48
See also SATA 6
Dixon, Pierson (John) 1904-1965 .... CAP-1
Earlier sketch in CA 15-16
Dixon, Richard Watson 1833-1900
Brief entry 122
See also DLB 19
Dixon, Robert G(alloway) 1920-1980
Obituary 97-100
Dixon, Roger 1930- 53-56
Dixon, Roger Edmund 1935-1983
Obituary 109
Dixon, Rosie
See Wood, Christopher (Hovelle)
Dixon, Ruth
See Barrows, (Ruth) Marjorie
Dixon, S(ydney) L(awrence) 1930- 69-72
Dixon, Stephen 1936- CANR-17
Earlier sketch in CA 89-92
Dixon, Wheeler Winston 1950- 121
Dizard, Wilson P(aul) 1922- 17-18R
Dizenzo, Charles (John) 1938- 25-28R
Dizney, Henry (Franklin) 1926- 33-36R
Djassi, Abel
See Cabral, Amilcar
Djeddah, Eli 1911- 37-40R
Djerassi, Carl 1923- Brief entry 111
Djonovich, Dusan J. 1920- 69-72
Dluhosch, Eric 1927- 25-28R
Dluznowsky, Moshe 1906-1977 Obituary 73-76
Dmytryshyn, Basil 1925- CANR-26
Earlier sketches in CA 21-22R, CANR-11
Doak, (Dearle) Donn(ell) 1930- 65-68
Doak, Wade Thomas 1940- CANR-6
Earlier sketch in CA 57-60
Doan, Daniel 1914- 103
Doan, Eleanor Lloyd CANR-1
Earlier sketch in CA 4R
Doane, Donald P(aul) 1911- 77-80
Doane, Gilbert H(arry) 1897- CAP-1
Earlier sketch in CA 11-12
Doane, Marion S.
See Woodward, Grace Steele
Doane, Pelagie 1906-1966 .... CANR-6
Earlier sketch in CA 4R
See also SATA 7
Dobb, Maurice (Herbert) 1900-1976 .... CANR-4
Obituary 69-72
Earlier sketch in CA 9-10R
Dobbie, Elliott Van Kirk 1907-1970
Obituary 111
Dobbin, John E. 1914-1979 .... 9-10R
Obituary 103
Dobbin, Muriel 1935- 118
Dobbins, Austin C(harles) 1919- 57-60
Dobbins, Charles G(ordon) 1908- CAP-1
Earlier sketch in CA 15-16
Dobbins, Dorothy Wyeth 1929- 69-72
Dobbins, Gaines Stanley 1886-1978 .... CANR-2
Earlier sketch in CA 3R
Dobbins, Marybelle King 1900- 41-44R
Dobbs, Betty Jo Teeter 1930- 69-72
Dobbs, Farrell 1907-1983 .... CANR-14
Obituary 111
Earlier sketch in CA 49-52
Dobbs, Greg 1946- 65-68
Dobbs, Kildare (Robert Eric) 1923- CANR-19
Earlier sketch in CA 102
Dobbyn, John F(rancis) 1937- 53-56
Dobelis, M(iervaldis) C(hristian) 1929- 116
Dobell, Byron (Maxwell) 1927- Brief entry 112
Dobell, I(sabel) M(arian) B(arclay) 1909- CAP-1
Earlier sketch in CA 17-18
See also SATA 11
Dobell, Sydney 1824-1874 .... DLB-32
Dober, Richard P. 11-12R
Dobie, Ann B(rewster) 1935- 106
Dobie, Bertha McKee 1890(?)-1974
Obituary 53-56
Dobie, Edith 1894-1975 .... CAP-2
Obituary 57-60
Earlier sketch in CA 23-24
Dobie, J(ames) Frank 1888-1964 .... CANR-6
Earlier sketch in CA 1R
See also SATA 43
Dobin, Abraham 1907- 53-56
Dobinson, Charles Henry 1903-1980
Obituary 102
Dobkin, Alexander 1908-1975 Obituary 57-60
See also SATA 30
Dobkin, Bruce H. 1947- 122
Dobkin, Kathleen Hamel
See Hamel Dobkin, Kathleen
Dobkin, Kathy
See Hamel Dobkin, Kathleen
Dobkin, Kaye
See Hamel Dobkin, Kathleen
Dobkin, Marjorie Housepian 1923- CANR-13
Earlier sketch in CA 33-36R
Dobkin De Rios, Marlene 1939- CANR-12
Earlier sketch in CA 61-64
Dobkins, J(ames) Dwight 1943- 49-52
Dobler, Bruce 1939- CANR-7
Earlier sketch in CA 53-56
Dobler, Lavinia G. 1910- CANR-2
Earlier sketch in CA 4R
See also SATA 6
Doblin, Alfred
See Doeblin, Alfred
See also TCLC 13
Dobner, Maeva Park 1918- 29-32R
Dobney, Frederick J(ohn) 1943- 53-56
Dobraczynski, Jan 1910- CAP-1
Earlier sketch in CA 11-12

Dobree, Bonamy 1891-1974 ... CANR-4
Obituary ... 53-56
Earlier sketch in CA 5-6R
Dobriansky, Lev E. 1918- ... CANR-2
Earlier sketch in CA 1R
Dobrin, Arnold 1928- ... CANR-11
Earlier sketch in CA 25-28R
See also SATA 4
Dobrin, Arthur 1943- ... CANR-8
Earlier sketch in CA 61-64
Dobrin, Ronald L. 1938- ... 120
Dobriner, William M(ann) 1922- ... 65-68
Dobrovolsky, Sergei P(avlovich) 1908- ... CAP-2
Earlier sketch in CA 33-36
Dobrow, Larry 1925- ... 123
Dobrowolski, Tomasz B. 1914(?)-1976
Obituary ... 65-68
Dobschiner, Johanna-Ruth 1925- ... 97-100
Dobson, Austin 1840-1921 ... DLB-35
Dobson, (Richard) Barrie 1931- ... 33-36R
Dobson, Christopher (Joseph Edward)
1927- ... 97-100
Dobson, Dennis 1919(?)-1979(?)
Obituary ... 104
Dobson, E. Philip 1910- ... CAP-1
Earlier sketch in CA 13-14
Dobson, Elinore (Lucille) 1934- ... 114
Dobson, Eric John 1913-1984 ... CANR-5
Obituary ... 112
Earlier sketch in CA 15-16R
Dobson, Eugene 1936- Brief entry ... 113
Dobson, James (Clayton, Jr.) 1936- ... 29-32R
Dobson, Jessie ?-1984 Obituary ... 113
Dobson, John M(cCullough) 1940- ... 37-40R
Dobson, Julia 1941- ... 106
See also SATA 48
Dobson, Julia M(argaret) 1937- ... 73-76
Dobson, Margaret J(une) 1931- ... 53-56
Dobson, Rosemary 1920- ... 77-80
Dobson, Terry 1937- ... 81-84
Dobson, Theodore E(lliott) 1946- ... 109
Dobson, William A(rthur) C(harles) H(arvey)
1913- ... 15-16R
Doby, John T(homas) 1920- Brief entry ... 114
Doby, Tibor 1914- ... 5-6R
Dobyns, Henry F(armer) 1925- ... CANR-15
Earlier sketch in CA 37-40R
Dobyns, Lloyd (Allen, Jr.) 1936- ... 119
Brief entry ... 110
Dobyns, Stephen 1941- ... CANR-18
Earlier sketches in CA 45-48, CANR-2
See also CLC 37
Dobzhansky, Theodosius 1900-1975 ... CAP-1
Obituary ... 61-64
Earlier sketch in CA 13-14
Doc Abraham
See Abraham, George
Docherty, James L.
See Raymond, Rene (Brabazon)
Docherty, Thomas 1955- ... 120
Dockeray, J(ames) C(arlton) 1907-1984 ... 45-48
Obituary ... 114
Dockery, Wallene T. 1941- ... CANR-22
Earlier sketch in CA 105
See also SATA 27
Dockrell, William Bryan 1929- ... CANR-14
Earlier sketch in CA 37-40R
Dockstader, Frederick J. 1919- ... 13-14R
Doc Lochard
See Lochard, Metz T(ullus) P(aul)
Doctorow, E(dgar) L(aurence) 1931- ... CANR-2
Earlier sketch in CA 45-48
See also DLB 2, 28
See also DLBY 80
See also CLC 6, 11, 15, 18, 37, 44
See also AITN 2
Doctors, Samuel I(saac) 1936- ... CANR-5
Earlier sketch in CA 53-56
Doctor X
See Nourse, Alan E(dward)
Doczi, George Frederic 1909- ... 113
Dodd, A(rthur) E(dward) 1913- ... 9-10R
Dodd, Anne W(escott) 1940- ... 93-96
Dodd, Arthur Herbert 1893(?)-1975
Obituary ... 57-60
Dodd, Bella V.
See Dodd, Maria Assunta Isabella Visono
Dodd, Charles (Harold) 1884-1973
Obituary ... 45-48
Dodd, David L(e Fevre) 1895-1988
Obituary ... 126
Dodd, Donald B(radford) 1940- ... CANR-6
Earlier sketch in CA 57-60
Dodd, Ed(ward) Benton 1902- ... 73-76
See also SATA 4
Dodd, Edward
See Dodd, Edward Howard, Jr.
Dodd, Edward Howard, Jr. 1905- ... 49-52
Dodd, James Harvey 1892-1969 ... 1R
Obituary ... 103
Dodd, Lynley (Stuart) 1941- ... CANR-25
Earlier sketch in CA 107
See also SATA 35
Dodd, Marguerite 1911- ... 7-8R
Dodd, Maria Assunta Isabella Visono
1904-1969 Obituary ... 111
Dodd, Philip W. 1904(?)-1983 Obituary ... 110
Dodd, Stuart C(arter) 1900-1975 ... 41-44R
Dodd, Susan M. 1946- ... 116
Dodd, Thomas J. 1907-1971 Obituary ... 29-32R
Dodd, Wayne (Donald) 1930- ... 33-36R
Dodd, William E. 1869-1940 ... DLB-17
Dodderidge, Esme 1916- ... 97-100
Dodds, E(ric) R(obertson) 1893-1979 ... 101
Dodds, Edward Charles 1899-1973
Obituary ... 115
Dodds, Gordon Barlow 1932- ... 5-6R
Dodds, John W(endell) 1902- ... 5-6R
Dodds, Robert Clyde 1918- ... 7-8R
Dodds, Robert H(ungerford) 1914-1976 ... CAP-2
Earlier sketch in CA 29-32
Dodds, Tracy 1952- ... 85-88
Dodek, Miriam (Joyce) Selker 1909-1986
Obituary ... 118
Doder, Dusko 1937- ... 102
Doderer, Heimito von
See von Doderer, Heimito
Dodge, Bayard 1888-1972 Obituary ... 111
Dodge, Bertha S(anford) 1902- ... CANR-2
Earlier sketch in CA 5-6R
See also SATA 8
Dodge, Calvert R(enaul) 1931- ... 61-64
Dodge, Daniel
See Du Breuil, (Elizabeth) L(or)inda
Dodge, David (Francis) 1910- ... 65-68
Dodge, David L(aurence) 1931-
Brief entry ... 112
Dodge, Dick 1918(?)-1974 Obituary ... 49-52
Dodge, Dorothy R(ae) 1927- ... 45-48
Dodge, Ernest Stanley 1913-1980 ... CANR-2
Obituary ... 97-100
Earlier sketch in CA 1R
Dodge, Fremont
See Grimes, Lee
Dodge, Gil
See Hano, Arnold
Dodge, H(arry) Robert 1929- ... 29-32R
Dodge, Langdon
See Wolfson, Victor
Dodge, Lowell 1940- ... 33-36R
Dodge, Marshall 1935- ... 89-92
Dodge, Mary (Elizabeth) Mapes
1831(?)-1905 Brief entry ... 109
See also SATA 21
See also DLB 42
Dodge, Nicholas A. 1933- ... 65-68
Dodge, Norton T(ownshend) 1927- ... CANR-16
Earlier sketch in CA 25-28R
Dodge, Peter 1926- ... 37-40R
Dodge, Richard Holmes 1926- ... CANR-8
Earlier sketch in CA 13-14R
Dodge, Steve
See Becker, Stephen (David)
Dodge, Wendell P(hillips) 1883-1976
Obituary ... 65-68
Dodgshon, Robert A(ndrew) 1941- ... 125
Dodgson, Charles Lutwidge 1832-1898 ... YABC-2
See also CLR 2
Dodson, Daniel B. 1918- ... CANR-3
Earlier sketch in CA 11-12R
Dodson, Fitzhugh (James) 1923- ... CANR-24
Earlier sketch in CA 29-32R
Dodson, James L. 1910- ... 53-56
Dodson, Kenneth MacKenzie 1907- ... 3R
See also SATA 11
Dodson, Leonidas 1900-1977 Obituary ... 111
Dodson, Oscar H(enry) 1905- ... 7-8R
Dodson, Owen (Vincent) 1914-1983 ... CANR-24
Obituary ... 110
Earlier sketch in CA 65-68
See also BW
See also DLB 76
Dodson, Richard S(licer), Jr. 1896- ... CAP-1
Earlier sketch in CA 11-12
Dodson, Susan 1941- ... 97-100
See also SATA 40, 50
Dodson, Tom 1914- ... 29-32R
Dodwell, Peter C(arpenter) 1930- ... 29-32R
Doebler, Charles H. 1925- ... 23-24R
Doebler, John (Willard) 1932- ... 89-92
Doeblin, Alfred 1878-1957 Brief entry ... 110
See also DLB 66
See also TCLC 13
Doehring, Donald G(ene) 1927- ... 29-32R
Doell, Charles E(dward) 1894- ... CAP-1
Earlier sketch in CA 15-16
Doely, Sarah Bentley
See Bentley, Sarah
Doenecke, Justus Drew 1938- ... CANR-20
Earlier sketch in CA 104
Doenim, Susan
See Effinger, George Alec
Doenitz, Karl 1891-1980 Obituary ... 103
Doerffler, Alfred 1884- ... 2R
Doering, Jeanne
See Zornes, Jeanne Doering
Doeringer, Peter B(rantley) 1941- ... CANR-12
Earlier sketch in CA 61-64
Doerksen, Nan 1934- ... 123
See also SATA 50
Doerkson, Margaret 1921- ... 105
Doermann, Humphrey 1930- ... 25-28R
Doernberg, Myrna 1939- ... 120
Doerr, Arthur H(arry) 1924- ... 41-44R
Doerr, Harriet 1910- ... 122
Brief entry ... 117
See also CLC 34
Doerschuk, Anna Beatrice 1880(?)-1974
Obituary ... 49-52
Doeser, Linda (Ann) 1950- ... 81-84
Doesticks, Q. K. Philander, P. B.
See Thomson, Mortimer
Doezema, Linda Pegman 1948- ... 102
Dogan, Mattei 1920- ... CANR-12
Earlier sketch in CA 25-28R
Dogg, Professor R. L.
See Berman, Ed
Doggett, Frank 1906- ... CANR-12
Earlier sketches in CA 21-22, CAP-2
Doggett, Rachel H. 1943- ... 124
Dogyear, Drew
See Gorey, Edward (St. John)
Dohan, Mary Helen 1914- ... 85-88
Dohen, Dorothy M. 1923-1984 Obituary ... 111
Doherty, Barbara 1931- ... 116
Doherty, Catherine de Hueck 1900- ... CANR-12
Earlier sketch in CA 65-68
Doherty, Charles Hugh 1913- ... 9-10R
See also SATA 6
Doherty, Dennis J. 1932- ... 102
Doherty, Eddie
See Doherty, Edward J(oseph)
Doherty, Edward J(oseph) 1890-1975 ... 65-68
Obituary ... 57-60
Doherty, Herbert J(oseph), Jr. 1926- ... 3R
Doherty, Ivy Duffy
See Doherty, Ivy R. Duffy
Doherty, Ivy R. Duffy 1922- ... CANR-5
Earlier sketch in CA 11-12R
Doherty, Robert W. 1935- ... 21-22R
Doherty, William 1911(?)-1984 Obituary ... 113
Doherty, William Thomas, Jr. 1923- ... 53-56
Dohme, Alvin R(obert) L(ouis) 1910- ... 110
Dohrenwend, Barbara Snell
1927-1982 ... CANR-11
Earlier sketch in CA 25-28R
Doig, Desmond 1921-1983 ... 69-72
Obituary ... 111
Doig, Ivan 1939- ... CANR-24
Earlier sketch in CA 81-84
Doig, Jameson W. 1933- ... CANR-15
Earlier sketch in CA 37-40R
Doimi di Delupis, Ingrid
See Delupis, Ingrid
Dolan, Anthony R(ossi) 1948- ... 73-76
Dolan, Edward F(rancis), Jr. 1924- ... 33-36R
See also SATA 31, 45
Dolan, Edwin G(eorge) 1943- ... 123
Dolan, Jay P(atrick) 1936- ... 81-84
Dolan, John Patrick 1923-1982(?) ... CANR-2
Obituary ... 106
Earlier sketch in CA 5-6R
Dolan, John Richard 1893- ... 9-10R
Dolan, Josephine A(loyse) 1913- ... 49-52
Dolan, Paul 1910- ... 9-10R
Dolan, Winthrop W(iggin) 1909- ... 57-60
Dolbeare, Kenneth M(arsh) 1930-
Brief entry ... 113
Dolberg, Alexander 1933- ... 33-36R
Dolbier, Maurice (Wyman) 1912- ... 65-68
Dolby, James L(ouis) 1926- ... 45-48
Dolce, Philip C(harles) 1941- ... 57-60
Dolch, Edward William 1889-1961 ... SATA-50
Dolch, Marguerite Pierce 1891-1978 ... SATA-50
Dolci, Danilo (Bruno Pietro) 1924-
Brief entry ... 116
Dolden, A(lfred) Stuart 1893- ... 105
Dole, Gertrude E(velyn) 1915- ... 41-44R
Dole, Jeremy H(askell) 1932- ... 17-18R
Dolezel, Lubomir 1922- ... 45-48
Dolgoff, Ralph L. 1932- ... 33-36R
Dolgoff, Sam 1902- ... 102
Dolgun, Alexander (Michael) 1926-1986 ... 104
Obituary ... 120
Doliber, Earl L(awrence) 1947- ... 49-52
Dolim, Mary N(uzum) 1925- ... 19-20R
Dolin, Anton
See Healey-Kay, (Sydney Francis) Patrick
(Chippendall)
Dolin, Edwin 1928- ... 45-48
Doliner, Roy 1932- ... CANR-16
Earlier sketches in CA 1R, CANR-1
Dolinger, Jane ... AITN-2
Dolinsky, Meyer 1923- ... 57-60
Dolinsky, Mike
See Dolinsky, Meyer
Dolit, Alan 1934- ... 61-64
Doll, (William) Richard (Shaboe) 1912- ... 108
Doll, Ronald C. 1913- ... CANR-8
Earlier sketch in CA 13-14R
Doll, Susan Marie 1954- ... 118
Dollar, Jimmy
See Shaginyan, Marietta Sergeyevna
Dollar, Truman E. 1937- ... 97-100
Dollard, John 1900(?)-1980 Obituary ... 102
Dollar Investor
See D'Ambrosio, Charles A.
Dollen, Charles Joseph 1926- ... CANR-21
Earlier sketches in CA 7-8R, CANR-6
Dolley, Michael 1925-1983 ... 123
Obituary ... 109
Dolliver, Barbara Babcock 1927- ... 7-8R
Dolloff, Eugene Dinsmore 1890-1972 ... 1R
Obituary ... 103
Dolmatch, Theodore B(ieley) 1924- ... 41-44R
Dolmetsch, Carl R(ichard, Jr.) 1924- ... 21-22R
Dolmetsch, Christopher L(ee) 1950- ... 111
Dolphin, Robert, Jr. 1935- ... 29-32R
Dols, Michael W(alters) 1942- ... 69-72
Dolson, Frank(lin Robert) 1933- ... 112
Dolson, Hildegarde
See Lockridge, Hildegarde (Dolson)
See also SATA 5
Doman, Glenn J(oseph) 1919- ... 61-64
Doman, June
See Beveridge, Meryle Secrest
Domanska, Janina ... CANR-11
Earlier sketch in CA 17-18R
See also SATA 6
See also AITN 1
Domaradzki, Theodore F(elix) 1910- ... CANR-1
Earlier sketch in CA 45-48
Domb, Cyril 1920- ... 109
Dombrowski, James A. 1897-1983
Obituary ... 109
Domecq, H(onorio) Bustos
See Bioy-Casares, Adolfo
and Borges, Jorge Luis
Domencich, Thomas A. ... 29-32R
Domergue, Maurice 1907- ... 25-28R
Dom Helder
See Camara, Helder Pessoa
Domhoff, G(eorge) William 1936- ... 45-48
Dominguez, Jorge Ignacio 1945- ... 102
Dominguez, Richard H(enry) 1941- ... 102
Domini, Jon
See LaRusso, Dominic A(nthony)
Domini, Rey
See Lorde, Audre (Geraldine)
Dominian, Jack 1929- ... 104
Dominic, R. B.
See Hennissart, Martha
and Latsis, Mary J(ane)
Dominic, Sister Mary
See Gallagher, Sister Mary Dominic
Dominick, Raymond Hunter III 1945- ... 110
Dominique
See Proust,
(Valentin-Louis-George-Eugene-)
Marcel
Domino, John
See Averill, Esther
Dominowski, Roger L. 1939- ... CANR-1
Earlier sketch in CA 45-48
Dominy, Eric (Norman) 1918- ... 11-12R
Domjan, Joseph (Spiri) 1907- ... CANR-24
Earlier sketches in CA 9-10R, CANR-3
See also SATA 25
Domke, Helmut Georg 1914-1974 ... CAP-1
Earlier sketch in CA 13-14
Domke, Martin 1892- ... CAP-1
Earlier sketch in CA 15-16
Dommen, Arthur J(ohn) 1934- ... 11-12R
Dommermuth, William P. 1925- ... 17-18R
Dommeyer, Frederick Charles 1909- ... 37-40R
Domville, Eric 1929- ... 41-44R
Don, A
See Stephen, Leslie
Donabedian, Avedis 1919- ... CANR-12
Earlier sketch in CA 73-76
Donagan, Alan (Harry) 1925- ... 5-6R
Donagan, Barbara (Galley) 1927- ... 17-18R
Donaghy, Henry J. 1930- ... 53-56
Donaghy, William A. 1910(?)-1975
Obituary ... 53-56
Donahoe, Bernard (Frances) 1932- ... 17-18R
Donahue, Don 1942- ... 69-72
Donahue, Francis J. 1917- ... 19-20R
Donahue, George T. 1911- ... 19-20R
Donahue, Jack 1917- ... CANR-17
Earlier sketch in CA 97-100
Donahue, June (Geserick) 1918(?)-1984
Obituary ... 111
Donahue, Kenneth 1915- ... 102
Donahue, Phil(lip John) 1935- ... 107
Donahue, Roy L(uther) 1908- ... CANR-15
Earlier sketch in CA 89-92
Donahue, Thomas John 1943- ... 112
Donald, Aida DiPace 1930- ... 21-22R
Donald, Anabel 1944- ... 122
Donald, Bruce H(arry) 1935- ... 111
Donald, David Herbert 1920- ... CANR-4
Earlier sketch in CA 11-12R
See also DLB 17
Donald, Larry W(atson) 1945- ... 93-96
Donald, Maxwell 1897-1978 Obituary ... 89-92
Donald, R. V.
See Floren, Lee
Donald, Vivian
See Mackinnon, Charles Roy
Donalds, Gordon
See Shirreffs, Gordon D(onald)
Donaldson, Betty 1923- ... 103
Donaldson, Bryna Stevens 1924- ... 116
Donaldson, E(thelbert) Talbot
1910-1987 ... CANR-2
Obituary ... 122
Earlier sketch in CA 49-52
Donaldson, Elvin F. 1903-1972 ... 1R
Obituary ... 103
Donaldson, Frances (Annesley) 1907- ... CANR-12
Earlier sketch in CA 61-64
Donaldson, Frances (Gertrude) F(laacke)
1892(?)-1987 Obituary ... 122
Donaldson, Gordon 1913- ... CANR-22
Earlier sketches in CA 13-14R, CANR-5
Donaldson, (Charles) Ian (Edward)
1935- ... CANR-12
Earlier sketch in CA 69-72
Donaldson, John W. 1893(?)-1979
Obituary ... 85-88
Donaldson, Kenneth 1908- ... 73-76
Donaldson, Malcolm 1884-1973 ... CAP-1
Earlier sketch in CA 9-10
Donaldson, Margaret 1926- ... CANR-20
Earlier sketch in CA 103
Donaldson, Norman 1922- ... 33-36R
Donaldson, Robert Herschel 1943- ... CANR-15
Earlier sketch in CA 85-88
Donaldson, Sam(uel Andrew) 1934- ... 111
Brief entry ... 109
Donaldson, Scott 1928- ... CANR-11
Earlier sketch in CA 25-28R
Donaldson, Stephen R. 1947- ... CANR-13
Earlier sketch in CA 89-92
See also CLC 46
Donaldson, (Charles) William 1935- ... 77-80
Donart, Arthur C(harles) 1936- ... 37-40R
Donat, Anton
See Donart, Arthur C(harles)
Donat, John (Annesley) 1933- ... 15-16R
Donato, Anthony 1909- ... CAP-1
Earlier sketch in CA 15-16
Donavan, John
See Morland, Nigel
Donawerth, Jane (Lynn) 1947- ... 118

Donceel, Joseph F. 1906- CANR-1
Earlier sketch in CA 4R
Donchess, Barbara (Briggs) 1922- 57-60
Dondis, Donis A(snin) 1924- 85-88
Donelson, Irene W(itmer) 1913- 19-20R
Donelson, Kenneth L(avern) 1927- 69-72
Donelson, Kenneth W(ilber) 1910- 19-20R
Donem, Sue
See Ross, Stanley Ralph
Doner, Mary Frances 1893- 15-16R
Doney, Willis (Frederick, Jr.) 1925- 21-22R
Donfried, Karl Paul 1940- 108
Donheiser, Alan D. 1936- 37-40R
Donicht, Mark Allen 1946- 93-96
Doniger, Lester (Laurence) 1909-1971
Obituary 104
Donin, Hayim Halevy 1928- 77-80
Donington, Robert 1907- 33-36R
Donis, Miles 1937-1979 .... 29-32R
Obituary 93-96
Donkin, Nance (Clare) 1915- CANR-20
Earlier sketch in CA 103
Donleavy, J(ames) P(atrick) 1926- CANR-24
Earlier sketch in CA 9-10R
See also DLB 6
See also CLC 1, 4, 6, 10, 45
See also AITN 2
Donley, Carol C(ram) 1937- 122
Donley, Marshall O(wen), Jr. 1932- CANR-14
Earlier sketch in CA 65-68
Donna, Natalie 1934-1979 .... CANR-6
Earlier sketch in CA 11-12R
See also SATA 9
Donnachie, Ian Lowe 1944- 105
Donnan, Marcia Jeanne 1932- 104
Donne, Maxim
See Duke, Madelaine (Elizabeth)
Donnell, David 1939(?)- CLC-34
Donnell, John C(orwin) 1919- 41-44R
Donnell, John D(ouglas) 1920- CANR-5
Earlier sketch in CA 53-56
Donnellan, Michael T(homas) 1931- 37-40R
Donnelley, Dixon 1915-1982 Obituary 105
Donnell-Kotrozo, Carol 1947- 113
Donnelly, Alton S(tewart) 1920- 23-24R
Donnelly, Austin Stanislaus 1923- 112
Donnelly, Desmond L(ouis) 1920- 15-16R
Donnelly, Doris (Krimper) 1940- 123
Donnelly, Dorothy (Boillotat) 1903- CANR-3
Earlier sketch in CA 5-6R
Donnelly, Esmond
See Oberdorf, Charles (Donnell)
Donnelly, Ignatius 1831-1901 Brief entry ... 110
See also DLB 12
Donnelly, James A. III 1929(?)-1984
Obituary 112
Donnelly, James H(oward), Jr. 1941- 29-32R
Donnelly, James S(tephen), Jr. 1943- 102
Donnelly, John 1941- 93-96
Donnelly, John Patrick 1934- 81-84
Donnelly, Joseph P(eter) 1905-1982 81-84
Obituary 108
Donnelly, Sister Gertrude Joseph 1920- .. 15-16R
Donner, Fred McGraw 1945- 106
Donner, Joern 1933- CANR-9
Earlier sketch in CA 13-14R
Donner, Stanley T(emple) 1910- 61-64
Donnison, David Vernon 1926- 106
Donnison, F(rank) S(iegfried) V(ernon)
1898- 3R
Donnison, Jean 1925- 77-80
Donnithorne, Audrey 1922- 17-18R
Donno, Elizabeth Story 1921- CANR-5
Earlier sketch in CA 1R
Donoghue, Denis 1928- CANR-16
Earlier sketch in CA 17-18R
Donoghue, Mildred R(ansdorf) CANR-10
Earlier sketch in CA 25-28R
Donoghue, Quentin 1937- 122
Donoghue, William E(lliott) 1941- 116
Donohoe, Thomas 1917- 53-56
Donohoe, Tom 1957- 123
Donohue, James F(itzgerald) 1934- 73-76
Donohue, John J. 1926- 122
Donohue, John K. 1909- CAP-1
Earlier sketch in CA 11-12
Donohue, John W(aldron) 1917- CANR-3
Earlier sketch in CA 5-6R
Donohue, Joseph (Walter, Jr.) 1935- 69-72
Donohue, Mark 1937-1975 57-60
Obituary 89-92
Donohue, Martin
See Gibson, Walter B(rown)
Donoso, Jose 1924- 81-84
See also CLC 4, 8, 11, 32
Donoughue, Bernard 1934- 17-18R
Donovan, Bonita R. 1947- 73-76
Donovan, Bonnie
See Donovan, Bonita R.
Donovan, Edward J(oseph) 1904- 5-6R
Donovan, Frank (Robert) 1906-1975 .... CANR-6
Obituary 61-64
Earlier sketch in CA 4R
See also SATA 30
Donovan, Hedley (Williams) 1914- 115
Brief entry 110
Donovan, James A., Jr. 1917- 23-24R
Donovan, James Britt 1916-1970 .... 9-10R
Obituary 89-92
Donovan, John 1919- CANR-2
Earlier sketch in CA 2R
Donovan, John 1928- 97-100
See also SATA 29
See also CLC 35
See also CLR 3
Donovan, John C(hauncey) 1920-1984 ... 37-40R
Obituary 114
Donovan, Josephine (Campbell) 1941- . CANR-24
Earlier sketch in CA 106
Donovan, Robert Alan 1921- 19-20R
Donovan, Robert J(ohn) 1912- CANR-18
Earlier sketches in CA 1R, CANR-2
Donovan, Timothy Paul 1927- 53-56
Donovan, William
See Berkebile, Fred D(onovan)
Donow, Herbert S(tanton) 1936- 112
Don Roberto
See Cunninghame Graham, R(obert)
B(ontine)
Donskoi, Mark Semyonovich 1901-1981
Obituary 103
Donson, Cyril 1919-1986 .... CANR-11
Earlier sketch in CA 23-24R
Don-Yehiya, Eliezer 1938- 111
Donze, Mary Terese 1911- CANR-25
Earlier sketch in CA 108
Doob, Anthony N(ewcomb) 1943- 33-36R
Doob, Leonard W(illiam) 1909- CANR-2
Earlier sketch in CA 5-6R
See also SATA 8
Doob, Penelope Billings Reed 1943- 53-56
Doody, Francis Stephen 1917- 15-16R
Doody, Margaret (Anne) 1939- CANR-11
Earlier sketch in CA 69-72
Doog, K. Caj
See Good, I(rving) John
Doohan, Leonard 1941- 118
Dooley, Arch R(ichard) 1925- 13-14R
Dooley, D(avid) J(oseph) 1921- CANR-16
Earlier sketch in CA 25-28R
Dooley, Ebon
See Ebon
Dooley, Howard J(ohn) 1944- 53-56
Dooley, John 1929(?)-1985 Obituary 119
Dooley, Patrick K(iaran) 1942- 53-56
Dooley, Peter C(hamberlain) 1937- 49-52
Dooley, Roger B(urke) 1920- CANR-22
Earlier sketch in CA 4R
Dooley, Thomas A(nthony) 1927-1961
Obituary 93-96
Dooley, William G(ermain) 1905(?)-1975
Obituary 57-60
Doolin, Dennis James 1933- 15-16R
Dooling, Dave
See Dooling, David, Jr.
Dooling, David, Jr. 1950- 125
Doolittle, Hilda 1886-1961 97-100
See also DLB 4, 45
See also CLC 14
Doolittle, Jerome (Hill) 1933- 53-56
Doone, Jice
See Marshall, James Vance
Dooren, Ingrid van
See van Dooren, Ingrid
Doorly, Ruth K. 1919- 25-28R
Doornkamp, John Charles 1938- CANR-7
Earlier sketch in CA 57-60
Dopuch, Nicholas 1929- 61-64
Dor, Ana
See Ceder, Georgiana Dorcas
Doran, Adelaide L(eMert) 1908- 116
Doran, Charles F(rancis) 1943- 73-76
Doran, Madeleine 1905- 121
Dorant, Gene
See Lent, D(ora) Geneva
Doray, Maya 1922- 45-48
Dorcy, Sister Mary Jean 1914- 9-10R
Dordick, Herbert S(halom) 1925- 116
Dore, Anita Wilkes 1914- 29-32R
Dore, Claire (Morin) 1934- 9-10R
Dore, (Louis Christophe Paul) Gustave
1832-1883 .... SATA-19
Dore, Ronald Philip 1925- CANR-15
Earlier sketch in CA 89-92
Doreian, Patrick 1942- 45-48
Doremus, Robert 1913- SATA-30
Doremus, Thomas Edmund 1922-1962 .... 2R
Doren, Marion (Walker) 1928- 125
Doreski, William 1946- CANR-17
Earlier sketches in CA 45-48, CANR-1
Dorey, T(homas) A(lan) 1921- 17-18R
Dorf, Richard C. 1933- 110
Dorff, Elliot N. 1943- 124
Dorfman, Ariel 1942- Brief entry 124
See also CLC 48
Dorfman, Dan 1932- 116
Brief entry 110
Dorfman, Eugene 1917- 29-32R
Dorfman, Gerald Allen 1939- 118
Dorfman, John 1947- CANR-12
Earlier sketch in CA 69-72
Dorfman, Joseph 1904- 45-48
Dorfman, Nancy S(chelling) 1922- 53-56
Dorfman, Nat N. 1895-1977 Obituary 73-76
Dorfman, Robert 1916- 17-18R
Dorge, Jeanne Emilie Marie
See Marie-Andre du Sacre-Coeur, Sister
Dorgeles, Roland 1886-1973 .... DLB-65
Doria, Charles 1938- 73-76
Dorian, Edith M(cEwen) 1900- CAP-1
Earlier sketch in CA 9-10
See also SATA 5
Dorian, Frederick 1902- CAP-1
Earlier sketch in CA 11-12
Dorian, Harry
See Hamilton, Charles Harold St. John
Dorian, Marguerite 19-20R
See also SATA 7
Dorian, Nancy C(urrier) 1936- 104
Dorin, Patrick C(arberry) 1939- CANR-15
Earlier sketch in CA 93-96
See also SATA 52
Doris, John Lawrence 1923- 102
Doris, Lillian 1899- 5-6R
Dorland, Henry
See Ash, Brian
Dorland, Michael 1948- 102
Dorliae, Peter Gondro 1935- 29-32R
Dorliae, Saint
See Dorliae, Peter Gondro
Dorman, Luke
See Bingley, David Ernest
Dorman, Michael 1932- CANR-5
Earlier sketch in CA 15-16R
See also SATA 7
Dorman, N. B. 1927- 106
See also SATA 39
Dorman, Sonya 1924- 73-76
Dormandy, Clara 1905- CAP-1
Earlier sketch in CA 9-10
d'Ormesson, Jean (Bruno Waldemar
Francois-de-Paule Lefevre) 1925-
Brief entry 111
Dormon, James H(unter), Jr. 1936- 23-24R
Dorn, Edward (Merton) 1929- 93-96
See also DLB 5
See also CLC 10, 18
Dorn, Frank 1901-1981 .... CANR-24
Obituary 104
Earlier sketch in CA 29-32R
Dorn, Jacob H(enry) 1939- 21-22R
Dorn, Phyllis Moore 1910(?)-1978
Obituary 77-80
Dorn, Sylvia O'Neill 1918- 69-72
Dorn, William S. 1928- 65-68
Dornan, James E., Jr. 1938(?)-1979
Obituary 85-88
Dornberg, John Robert 1931- CANR-1
Earlier sketch in CA 3R
Dornbusch, C(harles) E(mil) 1907- CAP-1
Earlier sketch in CA 9-10
Dorner, Peter Paul 1925- CANR-14
Earlier sketch in CA 37-40R
Doro, Edward 1910- 23-24R
Doro, Marion Elizabeth 1928- 89-92
Doroch, Efim Yakovlevitch 1908(?)-1972
Obituary 37-40R
Doronzo, Emmanuel 1903- 23-24R
Doroshkin, Milton 1914- 33-36R
Dorothy, R. D.
See Charques, Dorothy (Taylor)
Dorpalen, Andreas 1911-1982 .... 19-20R
Obituary 109
Dorr, Donal 1935- 118
Dorr, Rheta (Louise) Childe 1866-1948
Brief entry 116
See also DLB 25
Dorries, William (Lyle) 1923- 37-40R
Dorris, Michael Anthony 1945- CANR-19
Earlier sketch in CA 102
Dorris, R(obert) T. 1913- 29-32R
Dors, Diana
See Fluck, Diana
Dorsan, Luc
See Simenon, Georges (Jacques
Christian)
Dorsange, Jean
See Simenon, Georges (Jacques
Christian)
Dorsen, Norman 1930- 37-40R
Dorset, Gerald (Harris) 1920- 112
Dorset, Phyllis (Flanders) 1924- 25-28R
Dorset, Ruth
See Ross, W(illiam) E(dward) D(aniel)
Dorsett, Danielle
See Daniels, Dorothy
Dorsett, Lyle W(esley) 1938- CANR-9
Earlier sketch in CA 23-24R
Dorsey, David Frederick, Jr. 1934- 115
Dorsey, Hebe 1925-1987 Obituary 124
Dorsey, Helen 1928- 110
Dorsey, John M(orris) 1900- CANR-4
Earlier sketch in CA 5-6R
Dorsey, John R(ussell) 1938- 118
Dorsey, John Thornton, Jr. 1924- 111
Dorson, Richard M(ercer) 1916-1981 106
Obituary 105
See also SATA 30
Dorsonville, Max 1943- 65-68
Dorst, Jean (Pierre) 1924- CANR-19
Earlier sketches in CA 5-6R, CANR-3
Dorst, Tankred 1925- 41-44R
See also DLB 75
Dorwart, J(effrey) M(ichael) 1944- 97-100
Dorwart, Reinhold August 1911- 65-68
Dorworth, Alice Grey 1907- 5-6R
Dosa, Marta Leszlei 45-48
Doskocilova, Hana 1936- CANR-23
Earlier sketches in CA 61-64, CANR-8
Doskow, Minna 1937- 118
Dos Passos, John (Roderigo)
1896-1970 .... CANR-3
Obituary 29-32R
Earlier sketch in CA 2R
See also DLB 4, 9
See also DLBD 1
See also CLC 1, 4, 8, 11, 15, 25, 34
Doss, Helen (Grigsby) 1918- CANR-6
Earlier sketch in CA 9-10R
See also SATA 20
Doss, Margot Patterson CANR-12
Earlier sketch in CA 29-32R
See also SATA 6
Doss, Richard W(eller) 1933- Brief entry ... 112
Dossage, Jean
See Simenon, Georges (Jacques
Christian)
dos Santos, Joyce Audy Brief entry 118
See also SATA 42
Dossick, Philip 1941- 81-84
Doster, William C(lark) 1921- 13-14R
Dostoevski, Fedor Mikhailovich
1821-1881 .... SSC-2
Dothard, Robert Loos 1909(?)-1979
Obituary 85-88
Dotsenko, Paul 1894- 117
Dotson, Floyd 1917- 25-28R
Dotson, John L(ouis), Jr. 1937- 105
Dotson, Lillian O. 1921- 25-28R
Dotson, Robert Charles 1946- Brief entry ... 119
Dott, R(obert) H(enry), Jr. 1929- 53-56
Dottig
See Grider, Dorothy
Dotto, Lydia 1949- 125
Dotts, M. Franklin 1929- 57-60
Dotts, Maryann J. 1933- CANR-12
Earlier sketch in CA 33-36R
See also SATA 35
Doty, Brant Lee 1921- 19-20R
Doty, C(harles) Stewart 1928- 65-68
Doty, Carolyn 1941- CANR-23
Earlier sketch in CA 105
Doty, Gladys 1908- 53-56
Doty, Gresdna Ann 1931- 41-44R
Doty, James Edward 1922- 37-40R
Doty, Jean Slaughter 1929- CANR-2
Earlier sketch in CA 45-48
See also SATA 28
Doty, Richard (George) 1942- 109
Doty, Robert McIntyre 1933- 102
Doty, Roy 1922- CANR-8
Earlier sketch in CA 53-56
See also SATA 28
Doty, William G(uy) 1939- CANR-20
Earlier sketches in CA 53-56, CANR-5
Doty, William Lodewick 1919-1979 ..... CANR-1
Earlier sketch in CA 4R
Doubiago, Sharon 1946- 112
Doubleday, Neal Frank 1905-1976 .... 41-44R
Doubrovsky, Serge 1928- Brief entry 110
Doubtfire, Dianne (Abrams) 1918- CANR-17
Earlier sketches in CA 4R, CANR-1
See also SATA 29
Doucet, Clive 1946- 118
Doucette, Leonard E(ugene) 1936- 33-36R
Douds, Charles Tucker 1898-1982
Obituary 106
Dougall, Herbert E(dward) 1902- CAP-1
Earlier sketch in CA 19-20
Dougan, Michael B(ruce) 1944- 69-72
Dougherty, Betty 1922- 61-64
Dougherty, Charles 1922- SATA-18
Dougherty, Ching-yi (Hsu) 1915- 5-6R
Dougherty, David Mitchell 1903- 113
Dougherty, James (Patrick) 1937- 106
Dougherty, James E(dward) 1923-
Brief entry 111
Dougherty, Joanna Foster
See Foster, Joanna
Dougherty, John J(oseph) 1907-1986
Obituary 118
Dougherty, Jude P(atrick) 1930- 45-48
Dougherty, Philip H(ugh) 1923-1988
Obituary 126
Dougherty, Richard 1921-1986 .... CANR-2
Obituary 121
Earlier sketch in CA 1R
Dougherty, Richard M. 1935- 33-36R
Doughtie, Edward (Orth) 1935- 45-48
Doughty, Bradford 1921- 65-68
Doughty, Charles M(ontagu) 1843-1926
Brief entry 115
See also DLB 19, 57
See also TCLC 27
Doughty, Nina Beckett 1911- 53-56
Doughty, Oswald 1889- CAP-1
Earlier sketch in CA 9-10
Doughty, Paul L(arrabee) 1930- 85-88
Doughty, Robin W. 1941- 122
Douglas, Albert
See Armstrong, Douglas Albert
Douglas, Althea (Cleveland McCoy) 1926- ... 124
Douglas, Ann C.
See Welch, Ann Courtenay (Edmonds)
Douglas, Carole Nelson 1944- CANR-26
Earlier sketch in CA 107
Douglas, Charles H(erbert) 1926-
Brief entry 109
Douglas, Christopher
See Neill, Christopher Harry Douglas
Douglas, David C(harles) 1898-1982 73-76
Obituary 107
Douglas, Ellen
See Haxton, Josephine Ayres
Douglas, Ellen
See Williamson, Ellen Douglas
Douglas, Emily (Taft) 1899- 107
Douglas, George H(alsey) 1934- CANR-14
Earlier sketch in CA 81-84
Douglas, Glenn
See Duckett, Alfred
Douglas, Gregory A.
See Cantor, Eli
Douglas, Helen Bee
See Bee, Helen L.
Douglas, Helen Gahagan 1900-1980
Obituary 101
Douglas, J(ames) D(ixon) 1922- CANR-21
Earlier sketches in CA 13-14R, CANR-6
Douglas, James McM.
See Butterworth, W(illiam) E(dmund III)
Douglas, Jeff
See Offutt, Andrew J(efferson V)
Douglas, John (Frederick James) 1929- 116
Douglas, Kate
See Douglas, Kathleen
Douglas, Kathleen 1949- 117

Douglas, Kathryn
See Ewing, Kathryn
Douglas, Keith 1920-1944 .... DLB-27
Douglas, Leonard M(arvin) 1910-? CAP-2
Earlier sketch in CA 23-24
Douglas, Lloyd C.
See Douglas, Lloyd Cassel
Douglas, Lloyd Cassel 1877-1951
Brief entry 120
Douglas, Louis H(artwell) 1907- 21-22R
Douglas, Mack R. 1922- 21-22R
Douglas, Marjory Stoneman 1890- CANR-2
Earlier sketch in CA 1R
See also SATA 10
See also AITN 2
Douglas, Mary (Tew) 1921- 97-100
Douglas, Michael
See Crichton, (John) Michael
Douglas, Mike 1925- 89-92
Douglas, (George) Norman 1868-1952
Brief entry 119
See also DLB 34
Douglas, Paul Howard 1892-1976 69-72
Douglas, R. M.
See Mason, Douglas R(ankine)
Douglas, Robert
See Andrews, (Charles) Robert Douglas
(Hardy)
Douglas, Roy (Ian) 1924- CANR-13
Earlier sketch in CA 73-76
Douglas, Scott
See Smith, William Scott
Douglas, Shane
See Wilkes-Hunter, R(ichard)
Douglas, Thorne
See Haas, Ben(jamin) L(eopold)
Douglas, William A(llison) 1934- 45-48
Douglas, William O(rville) 1898-1980 .. CANR-21
Obituary 93-96
Earlier sketch in CA 9-10R
Douglas-Hamilton, James 1942- CANR-13
Earlier sketch in CA 33-36R
Douglas-Home, Alec
See Home, Alexander Frederick
Douglas-Home, Charles (Cospatrick)
1937-1985 Obituary 117
Douglas-Home, Henry 1907-1980 103
Obituary 101
Douglas-Home, Robin 1932-1968 .... CAP-2
Earlier sketch in CA 25-28
Douglas Home, William
See Home, William Douglas
Douglass, Amanda Hart
See Wallmann, Jeffrey M(iner)
Douglass, Barbara 1930- 114
See also SATA 40
Douglass, Billie
See Delinsky, Barbara (Ruth Greenberg)
Douglass, Donald McNutt 1899-1975 ....3R
Obituary 103
Douglass, Elisha Peairs 1915- 81-84
Douglass, Frederick 1817(?)-1895 ...... SATA-29
See also DLB 1, 43, 50
See also CDALB 1640-1865
Douglass, Harl R(oy) 1892- 5-6R
Douglass, Herbert Edgar 1927- CANR-13
Earlier sketch in CA 73-76
Douglass, James W. 1937- CANR-10
Earlier sketch in CA 25-28R
Douglass, Malcolm P(aul) 1923- CANR-13
Earlier sketch in CA 73-76
Douglass, Marcia Kent
See Doty, Gladys
Douglass, Paul F(ranklin) 1904- CANR-3
Earlier sketch in CA 5-6R
Douglass, Robert W. 1934- 57-60
Douglass, William 1691(?)-1752 ...... DLB-24
Douglass, William A(nthony) 1939- 69-72
Douglas-Scott-Montagu, Edward
See Montagu of Beaulieu, Edward John
Barrington
Doulis, Thomas 1931- CANR-11
Earlier sketch in CA 5-6R
Doulos, Jay
See Joyce, Jon L(oyd)
Doumato, Lamia 1947- 103
Dourado, Autran 1926- 25-28R
See also CLC 23
Douras, Marion Cecilia 1897-1961
Obituary 111
Douty, Esther M(orris) 1909-1978 ...... CANR-3
Obituary 85-88
Earlier sketch in CA 5-6R
See also SATA 8, 23
Douty, Norman F(ranklin) 1899- 49-52
Douvan, Elizabeth (Ann Malcolm) 1926- 106
Dove, Rita (Frances) 1952- 109
See also BW
See also CLC 50
Doveglion
See Villa, Jose Garcia
Dover, C(larence) J(oseph) 1919- 13-14R
Dover, K(enneth) J(ames) 1920- CANR-12
Earlier sketch in CA 25-28R
Dover Wilson, John 1881-1969
Obituary 25-28R
Dovey, Ken 1947- 120
Dovlatov, Sergei 1941- 115
Dow, Blanche H(innan) 1893-1973
Obituary 41-44R
Dow, Emily R. 1904- CAP-1
Earlier sketch in CA 11-12
See also SATA 10
Dow, George Francis 1868-1936
Brief entry 122
Dow, J(ose) Kamal 1936- 29-32R
Dow, Marguerite R(uth) 1926- 116

Dow, Neal 1906- 19-20R
Dow, Sterling 1903- CAP-2
Earlier sketch in CA 21-22
Dowd, Douglas F(itzgerald) 1919- 7-8R
Dowd, Laurence P(hillips) 1914- 17-18R
Dowd, Maxine
See Jensen, Maxine Dowd
Dowd, Merle E(dward) 1918- 85-88
Dowdell, Dorothy (Florence) Karns
1910- CANR-20
Earlier sketches in CA 11-12R, CANR-5
See also SATA 12
Dowden, Anne Ophelia 1907- CANR-18
Earlier sketches in CA 11-12R, CANR-3
See also SATA 7
Dowden, Edward 1843-1913 .... DLB-35
Dowden, George 1932- CANR-22
Earlier sketches in CA 53-56, CANR-4
Dowden, Wilfred S(ellers) 1917- 125
Dowdey, Clifford (Shirley, Jr.) 1904- 11-12R
Dowdey, Landon Gerald 1923- 89-92
See also SATA 11
Dowding, Hugh Caswell Tremenheere
1882-1970 Obituary 112
Dowdy, Andrew 1936- 49-52
Dowdy, Homer E(arl) 1922- 7-8R
Dowdy, Mrs. Regera
See Gorey, Edward (St. John)
Dowell, Coleman 1925-1985 ...... CANR-10
Obituary 117
Earlier sketch in CA 25-28R
Dowell, Jack (Larder) 1908- 57-60
Dowell, Richard W(alker) 1931- 116
Dower, Penn
See Pendower, Jacques
Dowie, James Iverne 1911- 41-44R
Dowie, Mark 1939- 85-88
Dowler, James Ross 1925- 29-32R
Dowley, D. M.
See Marrison, L(eslie) W(illiam)
Dowley, Timothy Edward 1946- CANR-18
Earlier sketch in CA 101
Dowling, Allan D. 1903-1983 Obituary 117
Dowling, Allen 1900- 29-32R
Dowling, Basil (Cairns) 1910- 97-100
Dowling, David (Hurst) 1950- 118
Dowling, Eddie 1894-1976 Obituary 65-68
Dowling, Harry Filmore 1904- 102
Dowling, Joseph A(lbert) 1926- 37-40R
Dowling, Maria 1955- 123
Dowling, Thomas, Jr. 1921- 85-88
Dowling, Tom
See Dowling, Thomas, Jr.
Down, Goldie (Malvern) 1918- CANR-26
Earlier sketches in CA 25-28R, CANR-11
Down, Michael (Graham) 1951- 118
Downard, William L. 1940- 49-52
Downer, Alan S(eymour) 1912-1970 .... CAP-1
Obituary 33-36R
Earlier sketch in CA 11-12
Downer, Marion 1892(?)-1971 Obituary ..33-36R
See also SATA 25
Downes, Bryan Trevor 1939- 33-36R
Downes, David A(nthony) 1927- 33-36R
Downes, Edward (Olin Davenport) 1911- 105
Downes, Kerry 1930- 119
Downes, Mollie Patricia Panter
See Panter-Downes, Mollie Patricia
Downes, Quentin
See Harrison, Michael
Downes, Randolph C(handler) 1901-1975 ..49-52
Obituary 61-64
Downey, Bill
See Downey, William L(eslie)
Downey, Fairfax D(avis) 1893- CANR-1
Earlier sketch in CA 2R
See also SATA 3
Downey, Glanville 1908- CANR-1
Earlier sketch in CA 1R
Downey, Harris 13-14R
Downey, James 1939- 101
Downey, Lawrence William (Lorne)
1921- 17-18R
Downey, Murray William 1910- CANR-1
Earlier sketch in CA 4R
Downey, William L(eslie) 1922- 110
Downie, Freda (Christina) 1929- 106
Downie, Jill 1938- CANR-25
Earlier sketch in CA 108
Downie, John 1931- CANR-26
Earlier sketch in CA 108
Downie, Leonard, Jr. 1942- CANR-1
Earlier sketch in CA 49-52
Downie, Mary Alice (Dawe) 1934- CANR-26
Earlier sketches in CA 25-28R, CANR-10
See also SATA 13
Downie, N(orville) M(organ) 1910- 17-18R
Downing, A(rthur) B(enjamin) 1915- 29-32R
Downing, Chris(tine) 1931- 57-60
Downing, Douglas 1957- 114
Downing, J., Major
See Davis, Charles A.
Downing, John (Allen) 1922- CANR-20
Earlier sketches in CA 53-56, CANR-5
Downing, Lester N. 1914- CANR-25
Earlier sketches in CA 25-28R, CANR-10
Downing, Major Jack
See Smith, Seba
Downing, Paul B(utler) 1938- 104
Downing, Warwick 1931- 53-56
Downs, Anthony 1930- 49-52
Downs, Brian W(esterdale) 1893-1984
Obituary 112
Downs, Cal W. 1936- 103
Downs, Donald (Alexander) 1948- 119
Downs, Hugh (Malcolm) 1921- CANR-2
Earlier sketch in CA 45-48

Downs, Hunton (Leache) 1918- 4R
Downs, Jacques M. 1926- 37-40R
Downs, James Francis 1926- 81-84
Downs, Lenthiel H(owell) 1915- 25-28R
Downs, Norton 1918-1985 ....1R
Obituary 114
Downs, Robert Bingham 1903- CANR-17
Earlier sketches in CA 1R, CANR-2
Downs, Robert C. S. 1937- CANR-1
Earlier sketch in CA 45-48
Downs, William Randall, Jr. 1914-1978 ... 81-84
Obituary 77-80
Dowse, Robert E. 1933- 21-22R
Dowse, (Dale) Sara 1938- 119
Dowsey-Magog, Paul 1950- 105
Dowson, Ernest Christopher 1867-1900
Brief entry 105
See also DLB 19
See also TCLC 4
Dowst, Somerby Rohrer 1926- 33-36R
Dowty, Alan K. 1940- 122
Doxey, Roy W(atkins) 1908- 41-44R
Doxey, William S(anford, Jr.) 1935- ... CANR-25
Earlier sketches in CA 65-68, CANR-9
Doxiadis, Constantinos Apostolos
1913-1975 ....41-44R
Obituary 57-60
Doyle, A. Conan
See Doyle, Arthur Conan
Doyle, Adrian M. C.
See Conan Doyle, Adrian Malcolm
Doyle, Arthur Conan 1859-1930 122
Brief entry 104
See also SATA 24
See also DLB 18, 70
See also TCLC 7
Doyle, Brian 1930- 53-56
Doyle, Charles (Desmond) 1928- CANR-26
Earlier sketches in CA 25-28R, CANR-11
Doyle, Charlotte Lackner 1937- 81-84
Doyle, Conan
See Doyle, Arthur Conan
Doyle, David
See Carter, David C(harles)
Doyle, Denis P. 1940- CANR-26
Earlier sketch in CA 109
Doyle, Don H(arrison) 1946- CANR-14
Earlier sketch in CA 81-84
Doyle, Donovan
See Boegehold, Betty (Doyle)
Doyle, Edward (Gerard) 1949- 118
Doyle, Edward Park 1907-1985 Obituary ... 115
Doyle, Esther M. 1910- 45-48
Doyle, Frank D. 1909(?)-1983 Obituary ... 109
Doyle, Gerald A. 1898(?)-1986 Obituary ... 119
Doyle, Harold Edmund
See Stearns, Harold Edmund
Doyle, James (Stephen) 1935- 73-76
Doyle, Jerry
See Doyle, Gerald A.
Doyle, John Robert, Jr. 1910- 25-28R
Doyle, Kirby 1932- DLB-16
Doyle, Mary Ellen 1932- 114
Doyle, Michael W. 1948- 120
Doyle, Mike
See Doyle, Charles (Desmond)
Doyle, Paul A. 1925- CANR-22
Earlier sketches in CA 15-16R, CANR-7
Doyle, Richard 1824-1883 .... SATA-21
Doyle, Richard 1948- 85-88
Doyle, Richard Edward 1929- 113
Doyle, Richard J(ames) 1923- 65-68
Doyle, Robert V(aughn) 1916- CANR-9
Earlier sketch in CA 65-68
Doyle, Sir A. Conan
See Doyle, Arthur Conan
Doyle, Sir Arthur Conan
See Doyle, Arthur Conan
Doyno, Victor A(nthony) 1937- 37-40R
Dozer, Donald Marquand 1905- CANR-1
Earlier sketch in CA 2R
Dozier, Craig Lanier 1920- 41-44R
Dozier, Edward P. 1916-1971 Obituary ..29-32R
Dozier, Robert R. 1932- 120
Dozier, Zoe
See Browning, Dixie Burrus
Dozois, Gardner R(aymond) 1947- 108
Dr. A
See Asimov, Isaac
and Silverstein, Alvin
Dr. Alphabet
See Morice, Dave
Dr. Hip
See Schoenfeld, Eugene
Dr. Hippocrates
See Schoenfeld, Eugene
Dr. NO
See Many, Seth E(dward)
Dr. Seuss
See Geisel, Theodor Seuss
See also CLR 9
Dr. Spektor
See Glut, Donald F(rank)
Drabble, Margaret 1939- CANR-18
Earlier sketch in CA 15-16R
See also SATA 48
See also DLB 14
See also CLC 2, 3, 5, 8, 10, 22
Drabble, Phil 1914- 102
Drabek, Jan 1935- 93-96
Drabek, Thomas E(dward) 1940- CANR-16
Earlier sketches in CA 45-48, CANR-1
Drache, Sharon 1943- 118
Drachkovitch, Milorad M. 1921- 19-20R
Drachler, Jacob 1909- 61-64
Drachler, Rose 1911- CANR-4
Earlier sketch in CA 53-56

Drachman, Edward Ralph 1940- 29-32R
Drachman, Julian M(oses) 1894- 61-64
Drachman, Theodore S(olomon) 1904- ...81-84
Drackett, Phil(ip Arthur) 1922- CANR-3
Earlier sketch in CA 9-10R
See also SATA 53
Draco, F.
See Davis, Julia
Drage, Charles H(ardinge) 1897- CANR-2
Earlier sketch in CA 7-8R
Drager, Marvin 1920- 81-84
Dragland, Stan L(ouis) 1942- 125
Dragnich, Alex N. 1912- CANR-15
Earlier sketch in CA 89-92
Drago, Edmund Leon 1942- 109
Drago, Harry Sinclair 1888-1979 113
Obituary 89-92
Drago, Sinclair
See Drago, Harry Sinclair
Dragon, Caroline
See Du Breuil, (Elizabeth) L(or)inda
Dragonette, Jessica (?)-1980 Obituary ...97-100
Dragonwagon, Crescent 1952- CANR-12
Earlier sketch in CA 65-68
See also SATA 11, 41
Drahos, Mary 1927- 116
Draitser, Emil 1937- CANR-18
Earlier sketch in CA 89-92
Drakakis, John 1944- 120
Drake, Albert (Dee) 1935- CANR-13
Earlier sketch in CA 33-36R
Drake, Alice Hutchins 1889(?)-1975
Obituary 61-64
Drake, Asa (a pseudonym) 113
Drake, Barbara (Ann) 1939- CANR-13
Earlier sketch in CA 33-36R
Drake, Bonnie
See Delinsky, Barbara (Ruth Greenberg)
Drake, Charles D(ominic) 1924- 116
Drake, David (Allen) 1945- CANR-17
Earlier sketch in CA 93-96
Drake, Donald C(harles) 1935- 85-88
Drake, Elizabeth 1948- 109
Drake, Francis Vivian 1894-1971 Obituary .. 104
Drake, Frank
See Hamilton, Charles Harold St. John
Drake, Frank D(onald) 1930- 19-20R
Drake, Frederick Charles 1937- 119
Drake, George Randolph 1938- CANR-11
Earlier sketch in CA 69-72
Drake, Harold Allen 1942- 97-100
Drake, Joan H(oward) CANR-24
Earlier sketch in CA 13-14R
Drake, Kimbal
See Gallagher, Rachel
Drake, Lisl
See Beer, Eloise C. S.
Drake, Michael 1935- CANR-16
Earlier sketch in CA 25-28R
Drake, Paul Winter 1944- 106
Drake, Richard Bryant 1925- 37-40R
Drake, Robert (Young, Jr.) 1930- 19-20R
Drake, (John Gibbs) St. Clair (Jr.) 1911- ..65-68
Drake, (Bryant) Stillman 1910- CANR-18
Earlier sketch in CA 41-44R
Drake, W. Anders
See Eshbach, Lloyd Arthur
Drake, W(inbourne) Magruder 1914- 41-44R
Drake, W(alter) Raymond 1913- CANR-5
Earlier sketch in CA 53-56
Drake, William D(onovan) 1922- 21-22R
Drake, William Daniel 1941- 69-72
Drake, William E(arle) 1903- CAP-1
Earlier sketch in CA 17-18
Drake-Brockman, David 1933- 114
Drakeford, John W. 1914- CANR-5
Earlier sketch in CA 4R
Dralle, Elizabeth (Mary) 1910- 4R
Drane, James F. 1930- CANR-7
Earlier sketch in CA 15-16R
Drane, John (William) 1946- CANR-15
Earlier sketch in CA 93-96
Drange, Theodore M. 1934- 37-40R
Dransfield, Michael (John Pender)
1948-1977 ....37-40R
Draper, Alfred 1924- CANR-13
Earlier sketch in CA 33-36R
Draper, Cena C(hristopher) 1907- CANR-10
Earlier sketch in CA 17-18R
Draper, Edgar 1926- 15-16R
Draper, (Ellinor) Elizabeth (Nancy)
1915- 17-18R
Draper, Hal 1914- CANR-24
Earlier sketches in CA 17-18R, CANR-7
Draper, Hastings
See Jeffries, Roderic (Graeme)
Draper, James T(homas), Jr. 1935- 89-92
Draper, Jo 1949- 119
Draper, John W. 1811-1882 .... DLB-30
Draper, John William 1893-1976 ...... CANR-16
Obituary 69-72
Earlier sketches in CA 9-10, CAP-1
Draper, Lyman C. 1815-1891 .... DLB-30
Draper, Norman R(ichard) 1931- 53-56
Draper, Ronald Philip 1928- 69-72
Draper, Theodore 1912- 13-14R
Draper, Thomas 1928- 108
Drapier, M. B.
See Swift, Jonathan
Drapkin, Herbert 1916- 33-36R
Drapkin, Israel 1906- 57-60
Draskovich, Slobodan M. 1910-1982 93-96
Obituary 108
Drath, Viola Herms 1926- CANR-14
Earlier sketch in CA 65-68
Drawbell, James Wedgwood 1899- 65-68

Drawson, Blair 1943- ... 85-88
See also SATA 17
Dray, William H(erbert) 1921- ... CANR-13
Earlier sketch in CA 33-36R
Drayer, Adam Matthew 1913- ... 9-10R
Drayham, James
See Mencken, H(enry) L(ouis)
Drayne, George
See McCulley, Johnston
Drazan, Joseph Gerald 1943- ... 110
Dreadstone, Carl
See Campbell, (John) Ramsey
Drebinger, John 1891(?)-1979 Obituary ... 89-92
Drefus, Jean-Paul Etienne 1909-1985
Obituary ... 117
Dreger, Georgia 1918- ... 115
Dreger, Ralph Mason 1913- ... 73-76
Dreher, Carl 1896-1976 ... 73-76
Dreher, Diane Elizabeth 1946- ... 119
Dreher, Melanie (Creagan) 1943- ... 114
Dreifort, John E. 1943- ... 45-48
Dreifus, Claudia 1944- ... CANR-1
Earlier sketch in CA 45-48
Dreifuss, Kurt 1897- ... CANR-16
Earlier sketches in CA 1R, CANR-1
Dreikurs, Rudolf 1897-1972 ... CANR-6
Obituary ... 33-36R
Earlier sketch in CA 3R
Dreiser, Theodore (Herman Albert)
1871-1945 Brief entry ... 106
See also DLB 9, 12
See also DLBD 1
See also CDALB 1865-1917
See also TCLC 10, 18
Dreiser, Vera ... 69-72
Dreiss, Joseph G. 1949- ... 125
Dreiss-Tarasovic, Marcia M(argaret)
1943- ... 65-68
Dreitzel, Hans Peter 1935- ... 41-44R
Drekmeier, Charles 1927- ... 4R
Drennen, D(onald) A(rthur) 1925- ... CANR-17
Earlier sketches in CA 4R, CANR-2
Dresang, Eliza (Carolyn Timberlake)
1941- ... 69-72
See also SATA 19
Dresbach, Glen Ward 1889-1968 ... 7-8R
Drescher, Joan E(lizabeth) 1939- ... 106
See also SATA 30
Drescher, John M(ummau) 1928- ... CANR-16
Earlier sketches in CA 49-52, CANR-1
Drescher, Sandra 1957- ... CANR-16
Earlier sketch in CA 85-88
Drescher, Seymour 1934- ... CANR-4
Earlier sketch in CA 11-12R
Drescher-Lehman, Sandra
See Drescher, Sandra
Dresner, Hal 1937- ... 15-16R
Dresner, Samuel H(ayim) 1923- ... CANR-9
Earlier sketch in CA 5-6R
Dressel, Paul L(eroy) 1910- ... CANR-3
Earlier sketch in CA 11-12R
Dresser, Davis 1904-1977 ... 77-80
Obituary ... 69-72
Dresser, Helen
See McCloy, Helen (Worrell Clarkson)
Dressman, Dennis L(ee) 1945- ... 106
Dressman, Denny
See Dressman, Dennis L(ee)
Dressman, John 1947- ... 122
Dretske, Frederick I(rwin) 1932- ... CANR-10
Earlier sketch in CA 25-28R
Dreux, William B(ehan) 1911- ... 89-92
Dreves, Veronica R. 1927-1986 Obituary ... 121
See also SATA 50
Drew, Bernard 1926(?)-1984 Obituary ... 111
Drew, Donald J. 1920- ... 57-60
Drew, Elizabeth 1887-1965 ... 5-6R
Drew, Elizabeth 1935- ... 104
Drew, Fraser Bragg Robert 1913- ... 13-14R
Drew, George A(lexander) 1894-1973
Obituary ... 113
Drew, Katherine Fischer 1923- ... 9-10R
Drew, Kenneth
See Cockburn, (Francis) Claud
Drew, Mary Anne
See Cassiday, Bruce (Bingham)
Drew, Morgan
See Price, Robert
Drew, Patricia (Mary) 1938- ... 77-80
See also SATA 15
Drew, Philip 1943- ... 107
Drew-Bear, Robert 1901- ... CAP-2
Earlier sketch in CA 33-36
Drewery, Mary 1918- ... 25-28R
See also SATA 6
Drewitz, Ingeborg 1923-1986 ... DLB-75
Drewry, Guy Carleton 1901- ... 5-6R
Drewry, Henry N. 1924- ... 97-100
Drewry, John E(ldridge) 1902-1983
Obituary ... 109
Drexel, Jay B.
See Bixby, Jerome Lewis
Drexler, Arthur 1925-1987 ... 97-100
Obituary ... 121
Drexler, J. F.
See Paine, Lauran (Bosworth)
Drexler, K(im) Eric 1955- ... 121
Drexler, Rosalyn 1926- ... 81-84
See also CLC 2, 6
Dreyer, Carl Theodor 1889-1968 Obituary ... 116
See also CLC 16
Dreyer, Edward C. 1937- ... 21-22R
Dreyer, Frederick 1932- ... 111
Dreyer, Peter (Richard) 1939- ... 81-84
Dreyfack, Raymond ... CANR-24
Earlier sketches in CA 65-68, CANR-9
Dreyfus, Edward A(lbert) 1937- ... 37-40R
Dreyfus, Fred
See Rosenblatt, Fred
Dreyfus, Hubert L(ederer) 1929- ... 33-36R
Dreyfus, Kay 1942- ... 124
Dreyfuss, Henry 1904-1972 ... 45-48
Obituary ... 37-40R
Dreyfuss, Joel 1945- ... 97-100
Dreyfuss, Larry 1928- ... 65-68
Dreyfuss, Randolph (Lowell) 1956- ... 97-100
Drial, J. E.
See Laird, Jean E(louise)
Dribben, Judith Strick 1923- ... 37-40R
Driberg, Thomas Edward Neil 1905-1976 ... 65-68
Obituary ... 104
Driberg, Tom
See Driberg, Thomas Edward Neil
Drieu la Rochelle, Pierre(-Eugene)
1893-1945 Brief entry ... 117
See also DLB 72
See also TCLC 21
Driftwood, Penelope
See De Lima, Clara Rosa
Drimmer, Frederick 1916- ... CANR-23
Earlier sketches in CA 61-64, CANR-7
Drinan, Adam
See Macleod, Joseph (Todd Gordon)
Drinan, Robert F(rederick) 1920- ... CANR-3
Earlier sketch in CA 11-12R
Dring, Nathaniel
See McBroom, R. Curtis
Drinkall, Gordon (Don) 1927- ... 9-10R
Drinkle, Ruth Wolfley 1903- ... 93-96
Drinkrow, John
See Hardwick, (John) Michael (Drinkrow)
Drinkwater, Francis Harold 1886- ... CANR-1
Earlier sketch in CA 3R
Drinkwater, John 1882-1937 Brief entry ... 109
See also DLB 10, 19
Drinkwater, Terry 1936- ... 69-72
Drinnon, Richard 1925- ... CANR-6
Earlier sketch in CA 13-14R
Driscoll, Gertrude 1898(?)-1975 Obituary ... 61-64
Driscoll, Peter (John) 1942- ... CANR-2
Earlier sketch in CA 49-52
Driscoll, R(obert) E(ugene) 1949- ... 85-88
Driskell, David Clyde 1931- ... 102
Driver, C(harles) J(onathan) 1939- ... 29-32R
Driver, Christopher (Prout) 1932- ... 57-60
Driver, Cynthia C.
See Lovin, Roger Robert
Driver, Donald 1922-1988 Obituary ... 125
Driver, Edwin D(ouglas) 1925- ... 114
Driver, Godfrey Rolles 1892-1975 ... CAP-2
Obituary ... 57-60
Earlier sketch in CA 21-22
Driver, Harold Edson 1907- ... CANR-6
Earlier sketch in CA 2R
Driver, Tom F(aw) 1925- ... CANR-1
Earlier sketch in CA 1R
Driving Hawk, Virginia
See Sneve, Virginia Driving Hawk
Droege, Thomas Arthur 1931- ... 113
Droescher, Vitus B(ernward) 1925- ... 33-36R
Drogheda, Earl of
See Moore, Charles Garrett Ponsonby
Droit, Michel (Arnould Arthur) 1923- ... CANR-11
Earlier sketch in CA 7-8R
Droppers, Carl Hyink 1918- ... 7-8R
Drop Shot
See Cable, George Washington
Dror, Yehezkel 1928- ... CANR-13
Earlier sketch in CA 21-22R
Drossaart Lulofs, H(endrik) J(oan)
1906- ... 15-16R
Drotar, David Lee 1952- ... 112
Drotning, Phillip T(homas) 1920- ... CANR-10
Earlier sketch in CA 25-28R
Drought, James (William) 1931-1983 ... CANR-20
Obituary ... 110
Earlier sketch in CA 7-8R
Drouin, Francis M. 1901- ... 37-40R
Drouin, Marie-Josee 1949- ... 116
Drowatzky, John N(elson) 1936- ... 89-92
Drower, E(thel) S(tefana May)
1879-1972 ... CAP-1
Earlier sketch in CA 11-12
Drown, Harold J(ames) 1904- ... 49-52
Drown, Merle 1943- ... 109
Drowne, Tatiana B(alkoff) 1913- ... 19-20R
Droz, Eugenie 1893(?)-1976 Obituary ... 104
Droze, Wilmon H(enry) 1924- ... CANR-10
Earlier sketch in CA 17-18R
Drubert, John H. 1925- ... 45-48
Druce, Christopher
See Pulling, Christopher Robert Druce
Drucker, H(enry) M(atthew) 1942- ... 106
Drucker, Malka 1945- ... CANR-14
Earlier sketch in CA 81-84
See also SATA 29, 39
Drucker, Mark L(ewis) 1947- ... 107
Drucker, Peter F(erdinand) 1909- ... 61-64
Drukker, J.
See Presser, (Gerrit) Jacob
Druks, Herbert 1937- ... CANR-9
Earlier sketch in CA 21-22R
Drum, Bob
See Drum, Robert F.
Drum, Robert F. 1918- ... 5-6R
Drumheller, Sidney J(ohn) 1923- ... 53-56
Drummond, Alison 1903- ... 112
Drummond, Donald F(rasier) 1914- ... CANR-4
Earlier sketch in CA 3R
Drummond, Dorothy W(eitz) 1928- ... 41-44R
Drummond, Edith Marie Dulce Carman
1883-1970 ... CAP-1
Earlier sketch in CA 9-10
Drummond, Ellen Lane 1897- ... 3R
Drummond, Harold D. 1916- ... CANR-12
Earlier sketch in CA 33-36R
Drummond, Ian (Macdonald) 1933- ... 37-40R
Drummond, J.
See Chance, John Newton
Drummond, Jack 1923(?)-1978 Obituary ... 81-84
Drummond, John 1900-1982 Obituary ... 106
Drummond, John Dodds 1944- ... 102
Drummond, June 1923- ... CANR-7
Earlier sketch in CA 13-14R
Drummond, Kenneth H(erbert) 1922- ... 19-20R
Drummond, Maldwin Andrew Cyril
1932- ... CANR-14
Earlier sketch in CA 73-76
Drummond, Richard H(enry) 1916- ... 41-44R
Drummond, (James) Roscoe 1902-1983 ... 104
Obituary ... 110
Drummond, V(iolet) H(ilda) 1911- ... 13-14R
See also SATA 6
Drummond, Walter
See Silverberg, Robert
Drummond, William Henry 1854-1907 ... TCLC-25
Drummond, William Joe 1944- ... 77-80
See also BW
Drummond de Andrade, Carlos 1902-1987
Obituary ... 123
See also CLC 18
Druon, Maurice (Samuel Roger Charles)
1918- ... CANR-12
Earlier sketch in CA 13-14R
Drury, Alan 1949- ... 106
Drury, Allen (Stuart) 1918- ... CANR-18
Earlier sketch in CA 57-60
See also CLC 37
Drury, Clare Marie
See Hoskyns-Abrahall, Clare (Constance Drury)
Drury, Clifford Merrill 1897- ... CANR-3
Earlier sketch in CA 9-10R
Drury, George H(erbert) 1940- ... 121
Drury, James Westbrook, 1919- ... 7-8R
Drury, John 1898-1972 ... 5-6R
Obituary ... 33-36R
Drury, Margaret Josephine 1937- ... 53-56
Drury, Maxine Cole 1914- ... 5-6R
Drury, Michael ... 49-52
Drury, Roger W(olcott) 1914- ... 65-68
See also SATA 15
Drury, S(hadia) B(asilious) 1950- ... 116
Drury, Treesa Way 1937- ... 53-56
Drury, William 1918- ... 125
Drutman, Irving 1910-1978 ... 85-88
Obituary ... 81-84
Druxman, Michael Barnett 1941- ... CANR-16
Earlier sketches in CA 49-52, CANR-1
Drvota, Mojmir 1923- ... 57-60
Dryansky, G. Y. ... 49-52
Dryden, Cecil P(earl) 1887- ... 25-28R
Dryden, Edgar A. 1937- ... 89-92
Dryden, John
See Rowland, D(onald) S(ydney)
Dryden, Ken(neth Wayne) 1947- ... 105
Dryden, Lennox
See Steen, Marguerite
Drysdale, Frank R(eiff) 1943- ... 89-92
Drysdale, George Russell 1912-1981
Obituary ... 108
Drysdale, Helena 1960- ... 125
Drysdale, Vera Louise 1923- ... 115
Drzazga, John 1907- ... CAP-1
Earlier sketch in CA 11-12
Drzemczewski, Andrew (Zbigniew) 1951- ... 116
D'Souza, Dinesh 1961- ... 118
Dua, R(am) P(arkash) 1930- ... 25-28R
Duan, Le
See Le Duan
Duane, Diane (Elizabeth) 1952- ... SATA-46
Duane, Jim
See Hurley, Vic
Duane, William 1760-1835 ... DLB-43
Duarte, Joseph S(imon) 1913- ... 57-60
Dubal, David 1944- ... 118
Duball, Michael
See Ald, Roy A(llison)
Duban, James 1951- ... 125
Dubanevich, Arlene 1950- ... 116
Dubay, Robert W. 1943- ... 65-68
DuBay, Sandra 1954- ... CANR-23
Earlier sketch in CA 107
Dubay, Thomas Edward 1921- ... CANR-6
Earlier sketch in CA 1R
DuBay, William H. 1934- ... 17-18R
Dube, Marcel 1930- Brief entry ... 117
See also DLB 53
Dube, Pierre Herbert 1943- ... CANR-10
Earlier sketch in CA 65-68
Dube, Rodolphe
See Hertel, Francois
Duberman, Lucile 1926- ... 69-72
Duberman, Martin 1930- ... CANR-2
Earlier sketch in CA 1R
See also CLC 8
Duberstein, Helen 1926- ... CANR-1
Earlier sketch in CA 45-48
Dubh, Cathal O
See Duff, Charles (St. Lawrence)
Dubie, Norman (Evans) 1945- ... CANR-12
Earlier sketch in CA 69-72
See also CLC 36
Dubin, Robert 1916- ... CANR-1
Earlier sketch in CA 45-48
Dubin, Samuel Sanford 1914- ... 37-40R
Dubinsky, David 1892-1982 Obituary ... 107
Dubitsky, Cora Marie 1933- ... 116
Dubkin, Lois Knudson 1911- ... 7-8R
du Blane, Daphne
See Groom, Arthur William
Dublin, Jack 1915- ... 23-24R
Dublin, Thomas Louis 1946- ... 101
Dubnick, Mel(vin Jay) 1946- ... 112
Dubnick, Randa Kay 1948- ... 112
Dubofsky, Melvyn 1934- ... CANR-16
Earlier sketches in CA 49-52, CANR-1
Dubois, Charles
See Counselman, Mary Elizabeth
Du Bois, David G(raham) 1925- ... 65-68
See also BW
Dubois, Elfrieda T(heresia Pichler) 1916- ... 9-10R
DuBois, Ellen Carol 1947- Brief entry ... 113
DuBois, Josiah Ellis, Jr. 1912-1983
Obituary ... 114
Dubois, M.
See Kent, Arthur William Charles
DuBois, Paul M(artin) 1945- ... 102
DuBois, Paul Z(inkhan) 1936- ... 111
DuBois, Rochelle (Lynn) Holt 1946- ... CANR-7
Earlier sketch in CA 57-60
DuBois, Rosemary
See Durrant, Rita D(elores)
Du Bois, Shirley Graham 1907(?)-1977 ... 77-80
Obituary ... 69-72
See also BW
See also SATA 24
Du Bois, W(illiam) E(dward) B(urghardt)
1868-1963 ... 85-88
See also BW
See also SATA 42
See also DLB 47, 50
See also CDALB 1865-1917
See also CLC 1, 2, 13
du Bois, William (Sherman) Pene
1916- ... CANR-17
Earlier sketch in CA 5-6R
See also SATA 4
See also DLB 61
See also CLR 1
Dubos, Jean (Porter) 1918(?)-1988
Obituary ... 126
Dubos, Rene (Jules) 1901-1982 ... 5-6R
Obituary ... 106
DuBose, Fred 1945- ... 118
DuBose, LaRocque (Russ) 1926- ... 23-24R
See also SATA 2
DuBose, Louise Jones 1901- ... CAP-1
Earlier sketch in CA 13-14
Dubout, C(harles) A(lbert) 1905-1976
Obituary ... 65-68
Dubov, Gwen Bagni ... 97-100
Dubov, Paul ?-1979 ... 97-100
Obituary ... 89-92
DuBow, Fredric L(ee) 1944- ... 25-28R
Du Breuil, (Elizabeth) L(or)inda 1924-1980 ... 104
DuBrin, Andrew J(ohn) 1935- ... CANR-15
Earlier sketch in CA 41-44R
Du Broff, Nedra 1931- ... 110
Du Broff, Sidney 1929- ... CANR-9
Earlier sketch in CA 21-22R
Dubrovin, Vivian 1931- ... CANR-9
Earlier sketch in CA 57-60
DuBruck, Alfred J(oseph) 1922- ... 37-40R
DuBruck, Edelgard (Conradt) 1925- ... 19-20R
Du Brul, Paul 1938(?)-1987 Obituary ... 125
Dubs, Homer H(asenpflug) 1892-1969 ... CAP-1
Earlier sketch in CA 15-16
Dubus, Andre 1936- ... CANR-17
Earlier sketch in CA 21-22R
See also CLC 13, 36
Dubus, Elizabeth Nell 1933- ... 110
Duby, Georges (Michel Claude) 1919- ... CANR-22
Earlier sketch in CA 104
Duca Minimo
See D'Annunzio, Gabriele
Du Cane, Peter 1901-1984 Obituary ... 114
du Cann, Charles Garfield Lott
1889(?)-1983 Obituary ... 109
Ducas, Dorothy 1905-1987 ... 5-6R
Ducasse, C(urt) J(ohn) 1881-1969 ... CANR-6
Earlier sketch in CA 4R
Duce, Robert 1908- ... 7-8R
Duchacek, Ivo D(uka) 1913-1988 ... CANR-1
Obituary ... 124
Earlier sketch in CA 3R
Du Chaillu, Paul (Belloni) 1835(?)-1903
Brief entry ... 112
See also SATA 26
Duchamp, (Henri-Robert) Marcel
1887-1968 ... 116
Obituary ... 110
Ducharme, Rejean 1941- ... DLB-60
Duche, Jean 1915- ... CANR-9
Earlier sketch in CA 9-10R
Duchene, Louis-Francois 1927- ... 105
Duchesne, Antoinette
See Paine, Lauran (Bosworth)
Duchesne, Jacques
See Saint-Denis, Michel Jacques
Duchesne, Janet 1930- Brief entry ... 111
See also SATA 32
Duchess of Windsor
See Windsor, (Bessie) Wallis Warfield (Spencer) Simpson
Duchin, Faye 1944- ... 125
Duckat, Walter Benjamin 1911- ... 29-32R
Ducker, Bruce 1938- ... 65-68
Duckert, Mary 1929- ... 53-56
Duckett, Alfred A. 1917(?)-1984 ... 45-48
Obituary ... 114
Duckett, Eleanor Shipley 1880(?)-1976
Obituary ... 69-72
Duckham, A(lec) N(arraway) 1903-1988 ... 73-76
Obituary ... 126
Duckham, Baron Frederick 1933- ... 103
Duckworth, Alistair M(cKay) 1936- ... 41-44R

Duckworth, F(rancis) R(obinson)
G(ladstone) 1881-1964 Obituary ... 113
Duckworth, George E(ckel) 1903-1972 .. CANR-1
Obituary ... 33-36R
Earlier sketch in CA 4R
Duckworth, Leslie Blakey 1904- ... 105
Ducornet, Erica 1943- ... CANR-14
Earlier sketch in CA 37-40R
See also SATA 7
Ducornet, Rikki
See Ducornet, Erica
Duda, Margaret B(arbalich) 1941- ... 65-68
Dudden, Arthur P(ower) 1921- ... CANR-3
Earlier sketch in CA 5-6R
Dudek, Louis 1918- ... CANR-1
Earlier sketch in CA 45-48
See also CLC 11, 19
Dudley, B(illy) J(oseph) 1931- ... 25-28R
Dudley, Barbara Hudson 1921- ... 65-68
Dudley, Carl Safford 1932- ... 116
Dudley, Donald Reynolds 1910-1972 ... CANR-4
Earlier sketch in CA 7-8R
Dudley, Edward 1926- ... 45-48
Dudley, Ernest 1908- ... 13-14R
Dudley, Geoffrey A(rthur) 1917- ... CANR-6
Earlier sketch in CA 15-16R
Dudley, Guilford A(llerton) 1921-1972 ... 41-44R
Dudley, Guilford, Jr. 1907- ... CAP-2
Earlier sketch in CA 19-20
Dudley, Helen
See Hope Simpson, Jacynth
Dudley, Jay
See Chapman, J. Dudley
Dudley, Lavinia P(ratt) 1891(?)-1984
Obituary ... 113
Dudley, Louise 1884- ... 73-76
Dudley, Martha Ward 1909(?)-1985
Obituary ... 117
See also SATA 45
Dudley, Nancy
See Cole, Lois Dwight
Dudley, Robert
See Baldwin, James
Dudley, Ruth H(ubbell) 1905- ... 61-64
See also SATA 11
Dudley Edwards, Ruth 1944- ... 107
Dudley-Smith, Timothy 1926- ... 103
Dudman, Richard (Beebe) 1918- ... 45-48
Due, Linnea A. 1948- ... 105
Dueker, Christopher W(ayne) 1939- ... 57-60
Dueker, Joyce S(utherlin) 1942- ... 57-60
Dueland, Joy V(ivian) ... 106
See also SATA 27
Duell, Charles Halliwell 1905-1970
Obituary ... 104
Duerr, Edwin 1904- ... 73-76
Duerrenmatt, Friedrich 1921- ... 17-18R
See also DLB 69
See also CLC 1, 4, 8, 11, 15, 43
Dufault, Peter Kane 1923- ... 33-36R
Duff, Annis (James) 1904(?)-1986
Obituary ... 120
See also SATA 49
Duff, Charles (St. Lawrence)
1894-1966 ... CANR-2
Earlier sketch in CA 4R
Duff, David (Skene) 1912- Brief entry ... 118
Duff, Ernest A(rthur) 1929- ... 25-28R
Duff, Gerald 1938- ... 45-48
Duff, John B. 1931- ... CANR-1
Earlier sketch in CA 45-48
Duff, Maggie
See Duff, Margaret K.
Duff, Margaret K. ... CANR-14
Earlier sketch in CA 37-40R
See also SATA 37
Duff, Raymond S(tanley) 1923- ... 23-24R
Duffee, David E(ugene) 1946- ... 104
Duffey, Bernard I. 1917- ... 114
Duffey, Margery 1926- ... 73-76
Duffield, Anne (Tate) 1893- ... CAP-1
Earlier sketch in CA 15-16
Duffin, Henry Charles 1884- ... CAP-1
Earlier sketch in CA 9-10
Duffus, R(obert) L(uther) 1888-1972 ... 101
Obituary ... 37-40R
Duffy, Ben
See Duffy, Bernard C.
Duffy, Bernard C. 1902-1972 Obituary ... 37-40R
Duffy, Bruce 19(?)- ... CLC-50
Duffy, Carol Ann 1955- ... 119
Duffy, Charles 1940- ... 104
Duffy, Clinton T(ruman) 1898-1982
Obituary ... 108
Duffy, Dennis 1938- ... 113
Duffy, Edmund 1899-1962 Obituary ... 93-96
Duffy, Elizabeth 1904-19(?) ... CAP-2
Earlier sketch in CA 19-20
Duffy, Francis R(amon) 1915- ... 49-52
Duffy, Helene (Krainovich) 1926- ... 19-20R
Duffy, John 1915- ... CANR-8
Earlier sketch in CA 19-20R
Duffy, John J(oseph) 1934- ... 57-60
Duffy, Maureen 1933- ... 25-28R
See also DLB 14
See also CLC 37
Duffy, Regis Anthony 1934- ... 110
Dufrechou, Carole
See Monroe, Carole
Dufty, William 1916- ... 65-68
Dugan, Alan 1923- ... 81-84
See also DLB 5
See also CLC 2, 6
Dugan, George 1909-1982 Obituary ... 107
Dugan, J(ohn) Raymond 1935- ... 121
Dugan, Jack
See Butterworth, W(illiam) E(dmund III)
Dugan, James (Thomas) 1912-1967 ... CANR-4
Earlier sketch in CA 5-6R
Dugan, Michael (Gray) 1947- ... CANR-14
Earlier sketch in CA 77-80
See also SATA 15
Dugard, C. J(ohn) R. 1936- ... 85-88
du Gard, Roger Martin
See Martin du Gard, Roger
Dugdale, Robert
See Hardy, Henry
Duggan, Alfred Leo 1903-1964 ... 73-76
See also SATA 25
Duggan, George Henry 1912- ... 17-18R
Duggan, Joseph J(ohn) 1938- ... 29-32R
Duggan, Mary M. 1921- ... 25-28R
Duggan, Maurice (Noel) 1922-1974 ... CANR-17
Obituary ... 53-56
Earlier sketch in CA 73-76
See also SATA 30, 40
Duggan, William 1952- ... 122
Duggan, William Redman 1915- ... 69-72
Duggans, Pat
See Connolly, Robert D(uggan, Jr.)
Dugger, Ronnie 1930- ... CANR-12
Earlier sketch in CA 21-22R
Duggins, James (Harry), Jr. 1933- ... 37-40R
Dughi, Nancy ... 3R
Dugmore, Clifford W(illiam) 1909- ... 13-14R
Duguid, Charles 1884- ... 109
Duguid, John Bright 1895-1980 Obituary ... 102
Duguid, Robert
See Pring-Mill, Robert D(uguid) F(orrest)
Duhamel, Georges 1884-1966 ... 81-84
Obituary ... 25-28R
See also DLB 65
See also CLC 8
Duhamel, Marcel 1900(?)-1977 Obituary ... 104
Duhamel, P(ierre) Albert 1920- ... 5-6R
du Hault, Jean
See Grindel, Eugene
Duhl, Leonard J. 1926- ... 13-14R
Duignan, Peter 1926- ... CANR-11
Earlier sketch in CA 13-14R
Duiker, William J(ohn) 1932- ... CANR-16
Earlier sketch in CA 85-88
Duis, Perry R. 1943- ... 124
Dujardin, Edouard (Emile Louis)
1861-1949 Brief entry ... 109
See also TCLC 13
du Jardin, Rosamond Neal 1902-1963 ... 3R
Obituary ... 103
See also SATA 2
Duka, Ivo
See Duchacek, Ivo D(uka)
Duke, Alvah (Carter) 1908- ... 45-48
Duke, Benjamin 1931- ... 49-52
Duke, Charles (Richard) 1940- ... CANR-11
Earlier sketch in CA 69-72
Duke, David C. 1940- ... 112
Duke, Donald Norman 1929- ... CANR-7
Earlier sketch in CA 19-20R
Duke, Forrest R(eagan) 1918- ... 77-80
Duke, James T(aylor) 1933- ... 65-68
Duke, John
See Chalmers, Floyd S(herman)
Duke, Judith S(ilverman) 1934- ... 118
Duke, Madelaine (Elizabeth) 1925- ... CANR-9
Earlier sketch in CA 57-60
Duke, Maurice 1934- ... 112
Duke, Michael Geoffrey Hare
See Hare Duke, Michael Geoffrey
Duke, Richard DeLaBarre 1930- ... 57-60
Duke, Robin (Antony Hare) 1916-1984
Obituary ... 115
Duke, Vernon 1903-1969 ... CAP-2
Earlier sketch in CA 29-32
Duke, Will
See Gault, William Campbell
Duke-Elder, Stewart 1898-1978 Obituary ... 77-80
Dukelsky, Vladimir
See Duke, Vernon
Duke Of Beaufort
See Somerset, Henry Hugh Arthur
FitzRoy
Duker, Abraham G(ordon) 1907- ... 53-56
Duker, Sam 1905-1978 ... 15-16R
Obituary ... 77-80
Dukert, Joseph M(ichael) 1929- ... CANR-3
Earlier sketch in CA 5-6R
Dukes, Ashley 1885-1959 Brief entry ... 110
See also DLB 10
Dukes, Paul 1889-1967 Obituary ... 112
Dukes, Paul 1934- ... CANR-9
Earlier sketch in CA 23-24R
Dukes, Philip
See Bickers, Richard Leslie Townshend
Dukes, Tyrone 1946(?)-1983 Obituary ... 110
Dukore, Bernard F. 1931- ... CANR-12
Earlier sketch in CA 25-28R
Dukore, Margaret Mitchell 1950- ... CANR-23
Earlier sketch in CA 106
Dulac, Edmund 1882-1953 ... SATA-19
Dulack, Thomas 1935- ... 25-28R
Dulany, Don E., Jr. 1928- ... 69-72
Dulany, Harris 1940- ... 33-36R
Dulieu, Jean
See van Oort, Jan
Dull, Jonathan R(omer) 1942- ... 69-72
Dulles, Allen W(elsh) 1893-1969 ... CAP-2
Earlier sketch in CA 23-24
Dulles, Avery (Robert) 1918- ... CANR-21
Earlier sketches in CA 9-10R, CANR-3
Dulles, Eleanor Lansing 1895- ... 9-10R
Dulles, Foster Rhea 1900-1970 ... CAP-1
Obituary ... 29-32R
Earlier sketch in CA 13-14
Dulles, John Foster 1888-1959 Brief entry .. 115
Dulles, John W(atson) F(oster) 1913- ... CANR-1
Earlier sketch in CA 4R
Duloup, Victor
See Volkoff, Vladimir
Dulsey, Bernard M. 1914- ... 11-12R
Dumarchais, Pierre 1882-1970 Obituary .. 29-32R
Dumarchey, Pierre
See Dumarchais, Pierre
Dumas, Alexandre 1802-1870 ... SATA-18
Dumas, Andre 1918- ... CANR-13
Earlier sketch in CA 73-76
Dumas, Claire
See Van Weddingen, Marthe
Dumas, Claudine
See Malzberg, Barry N(athaniel)
du Mas, Frank (Maurice) 1918- ... 106
Dumas, Frederic 1913- ... 69-72
Dumas, Gerald J. 1930- ... 25-28R
Dumas, Henry L. 1934-1968 ... 85-88
See also BW
See also DLB 41
See also CLC 6
Dumas, Jacqueline 1946- ... 123
Dumas, Philippe 1940- ... 107
See also SATA 52
du Maurier, Daphne 1907- ... CANR-6
Earlier sketch in CA 5-6R
See also SATA 27
See also CLC 6, 11
Dumbleton, William A(lbert) 1927- ... 37-40R
Dumenil, Lynn 1950- ... 125
Dumery, Henry 1920- ... 101
Dumezil, Georges (Edmond Raoul)
1898-1986 Obituary ... 120
Dumitriu, Petru 1924- Brief entry ... 116
Dumke, Edward J. 1946- ... 124
Dumke, Glenn S. 1917- ... 112
Dummett, Michael Anthony Eardley 1925- ... 102
Dumond, Dwight Lowell 1895-1976 ... 69-72
Obituary ... 65-68
Dumont, Jean-Paul 1940- ... CANR-12
Earlier sketch in CA 73-76
Dumoulin, Heinrich 1905- ... CANR-4
Earlier sketch in CA 5-6R
Dumpleton, John Le F(evre) 1924- ... 13-14R
Dumpty, Humpty S.
See Denenberg, Herbert S(idney)
Dun, Angus 1892-1971 Obituary ... 33-36R
Dun, Mao
See Yen-Ping, Shen
Dunas, Joseph C. 1900- ... 19-20R
Dunathan, Arni T(homas) 1936- ... 53-56
Dunaway, David King 1948- ... 107
Dunaway, John M(arson) 1945- ... 89-92
Dunayevskaya, Raya 1910-1987 Obituary ... 122
Dunbabin, J(ohn) P(aul) D(elacour)
1938- ... 69-72
Dunbabin, Jean 1939- ... 119
Dunbar, Alice
See Nelson, Alice Ruth Moore Dunbar
Dunbar, Alice Moore
See Nelson, Alice Ruth Moore Dunbar
Dunbar, Charles Stuart 1900- ... 107
Dunbar, David
See Baxter, Craig
Dunbar, Dorothy 1923- ... 11-12R
Dunbar, Edward
See Smith, David MacLeod
Dunbar, Ernest 1927- ... 25-28R
Dunbar, Janet 1901- ... CANR-6
Earlier sketch in CA 9-10R
Dunbar, John Greenwell 1930- ... 23-24R
Dunbar, Leslie W(allace) 1921- ... 125
Dunbar, Maxwell John 1914- ... 103
Dunbar, Paul Laurence 1872-1906 ... 124
Brief entry ... 104
See also BW
See also SATA 34
See also DLB 50, 54
See also CDALB 1865-1917
See also TCLC 2, 12
Dunbar, Robert E(verett) 1926- ... CANR-15
Earlier sketch in CA 85-88
See also SATA 32
Dunbar, Robert George 1907- ... 114
Dunbar, Tony 1949- ... 33-36R
Dunbar, Willis F(rederick) 1902-1970 ... CANR-4
Earlier sketch in CA 5-6R
Dunbar-Nelson, Alice
See Nelson, Alice Ruth Moore Dunbar
Dunbar-Nelson, Alice Moore
See Nelson, Alice Ruth Moore Dunbar
Dunbaugh, Frank Montgomery 1895- ... 45-48
Duncan, A(nthony) D(ouglas) 1930- ... 33-36R
Duncan, Alastair 1942- ... 117
Duncan, Alex
See Duke, Madelaine (Elizabeth)
Duncan, Alistair (Charteris) 1927- ... 61-64
Duncan, Archibald A(lexander) M(cBeth)
1926- ... 81-84
Duncan, Ardinelle Bean 1913- ... 4R
Duncan, (Reid) Bingham 1911- ... 85-88
Duncan, Bowie 1941- ... 33-36R
Duncan, C(yril) J(ohn) 1916- ... 25-28R
Duncan, Carl P(orter) 1921- Brief entry ... 115
Duncan, Charles T(homas) 1914- ... 19-20R
Duncan, Chester 1913- ... 93-96
Duncan, Clyde H. 1903- ... 19-20R
Duncan, David 1913- ... 7-8R
Duncan, David Douglas 1916- Brief entry ... 112
See also AITN 1
Duncan, Delbert J(ames) 1895- ... 41-44R
Duncan, Denis (Macdonald) 1920- ... CANR-23
Earlier sketch in CA 107
Duncan, Dora Angela
See Duncan, Isadora
Duncan, Dougal 1921- ... 102
Duncan, Elmer H(ubert) 1933- ... 69-72
Duncan, Florence Belle 1917(?)-1980
Obituary ... 97-100
Duncan, Frances (Mary) 1942- ... CANR-17
Earlier sketch in CA 97-100
See also SATA 48
Duncan, George
See Davison, Geoffrey
Duncan, Gregory
See McClintock, Marshall
Duncan, Helen (Harger Bodwell) 1902- ... 125
Duncan, Hugh Dalziel 1909-1970 ... CAP-2
Earlier sketch in CA 23-24
Duncan, Irma 1897-1977 ... 49-52
Obituary ... 73-76
Duncan, Isadora 1878(?)-1927 Brief entry .. 118
Duncan, Jane
See Cameron, Elizabeth Jane
Duncan, Joseph E(llis) 1921- ... 5-6R
Duncan, Julia Coley
See Sather, Julia Coley Duncan
Duncan, Julia K. ... CAP-2
Earlier sketch in CA 19-20
See also SATA 1
Duncan, Kenneth S(andilands) 1912- ... 9-10R
Duncan, Kunigunde 1886- ... 7-8R
Duncan, Lois 1934- ... CANR-23
Earlier sketches in CA 3R, CANR-2
See also SATA 1, 36
See also SAAS 2
See also CLC 26
Duncan, Marion Moncure 1913-1978
Obituary ... 77-80
Duncan, Norman 1871-1916 Brief entry ... 117
See also YABC 1
Duncan, Otis Dudley 1921- ... CANR-22
Earlier sketches in CA 13-14R, CANR-6
Duncan, Pam 1938- ... 37-40R
Duncan, Pope A(lexander) 1920- ... 15-16R
Duncan, Robert (Edward) 1919-1988 ... 11-12R
Obituary ... 124
See also DLB 5, 16
See also CLC 1, 2, 4, 7, 15, 41
Duncan, Robert F. 1890(?)-1974
Obituary ... 53-56
Duncan, Robert L(ipscomb) 1927- ... 106
See also CAAS 2
Duncan, Ronald 1914-1982 ... CANR-4
Obituary ... 107
Earlier sketch in CA 7-8R
See also DLB 13
Duncan, T. Bentley 1929- ... 77-80
Duncan, Thomas (William) 1905- ... CANR-1
Earlier sketch in CA 2R
Duncan, W(illiam) Murdoch 1909-1976 .. CANR-6
Earlier sketch in CA 15-16R
Duncan, W. R.
See Duncan, Robert L(ipscomb)
Duncan, W. Raymond 1936- ... 41-44R
Duncan, Wilbur H(oward) 1910- ... 116
Duncan, William (Robert) 1944- ... 115
Duncanson, Michael E(dward) 1948- ... 57-60
Duncombe, David C(ameron) 1928- ... 29-32R
Duncombe, Frances (Riker) 1900- ... 25-28R
See also SATA 25
Dundee, Robert
See Kirsch, Robert R.
Dundes, Alan 1934- ... CANR-26
Earlier sketches in CA 23-24R, CANR-9
Dundy, Elaine 1937- ... 97-100
Dunford, Judith 1933- ... 107
Dungan, David L(aird) 1936- ... 123
Dunham, Arthur 1893- ... 33-36R
Dunham, Barrows 1905- ... 7-8R
Dunham, Bob
See Dunham, Robert
Dunham, Donald Carl 1908- ... CANR-17
Earlier sketch in CA 4R
Dunham, H(enry) Warren 1906-1985 ... CANR-8
Obituary ... 118
Earlier sketch in CA 13-14R
Dunham, John L. 1939- ... 29-32R
Dunham, Katherine 1910- ... CANR-17
Earlier sketch in CA 65-68
See also BW
Dunham, Lowell 1910- ... 37-40R
Dunham, (Bertha) Mabel 1881-1957
Brief entry ... 114
Dunham, Montrew Goetz 1919- ... 19-20R
Dunham, Robert 1931- ... 69-72
Dunham, William Huse, Jr. 1901- ... 49-52
Dunhill, Alfred H(enry) 1896(?)-1971
Obituary ... 104
Dunhill, Mary 1907(?)-1988 Obituary ... 124
Dunkel, Harold Baker 1912- ... 5-6R
Dunkel, Richard H(adley) 1933- ... 73-76
Dunkell, Samuel (V.) 1919- Brief entry ... 115
Dunkelman, Ben(jamin) 1913- Brief entry ... 111
Dunkerley, Elsie Jeanette ?-1960 Obituary .. 116
Dunkerley, Roderic 1884- ... CAP-1
Earlier sketch in CA 13-14
Dunkin, Paul S(haner) 1905-1975 ... CAP-2
Earlier sketch in CA 33-36
Dunkle, William F(rederick), Jr. 1911- ... 53-56
Dunkley, Christopher 1944- ... 121
Dunkling, Leslie Alan 1935- ... CANR-14
Earlier sketch in CA 81-84
Dunkman, William E(dward) 1903- ... CAP-2
Earlier sketch in CA 25-28
Dunlap, Aurie N(ichols) 1907-1977 ... 37-40R
Dunlap, G(eorge) D(ale) 1923- ... 49-52
Dunlap, Jan ... 65-68
Dunlap, Jane
See Davis, Adelle
Dunlap, John 1747-1812 ... DLB-43
Dunlap, Joseph R(iggs) 1913- ... 85-88
Dunlap, Leslie W(hittaker) 1911- ... 37-40R

Dunlap, Lon
See McCormick, Wilfred
Dunlap, Orrin E(lmer), Jr. 1896-1970 .... CAP-1
Earlier sketch in CA 11-12
Dunlap, Thomas R(ichard) 1943- 126
Dunlap, William 1766-1839 .... DLB-30, 37, 59
Dunlay, Thomas W. 1944- 112
Dunleavy, Gareth W(inthrop) 1923- 33-36R
Dunleavy, Janet Egleson 1928- CANR-21
Earlier sketches in CA 57-60, CANR-6
Dunleavy, Patrick 1952- 123
Dunlop, Agnes M.R. ?-1982 .... CANR-9
Earlier sketch in CA 15-16R
Dunlop, Derrick Melville 1902-1980
Obituary 101
Dunlop, Douglas Morton 1909-1987
Obituary 123
Dunlop, Eileen (Rhona) 1938- CANR-14
Earlier sketch in CA 73-76
See also SATA 24
Dunlop, Ian G(eoffrey) D(avid) 1925- .. CANR-24
Earlier sketches in CA 9-10R, CANR-5
Dunlop, John B. 1942- 57-60
Dunlop, John Thomas 1914- CANR-5
Earlier sketch in CA 13-14R
Dunlop, Richard (B.) 1921- CANR-25
Earlier sketches in CA 17-18R, CANR-7
Dunlop, Robert 1953- 116
Dunmore, John 1923- CANR-23
Earlier sketch in CA 106
Dunmore, Spencer (Sambrook) 1928- .. CANR-13
Earlier sketch in CA 33-36R
Dunn, Alan (Cantwell) 1900-1974 .... CAP-2
Obituary 49-52
Earlier sketch in CA 33-36
Dunn, Carola 1946- 118
Dunn, Catherine M(ary) 1930- 37-40R
Dunn, Charles W(illiam) 1915- 49-52
Dunn, Delmer D(elano) 1941- 25-28R
Dunn, Donald H(arley) 1929- 33-36R
Dunn, Douglas (Eaglesham) 1942- CANR-2
Earlier sketch in CA 45-48
See also DLB 40
See also CLC 6, 40
Dunn, Edgar S(treeter), Jr. 1921- 9-10R
Dunn, Edward D. 1883(?)-1978 Obituary .. 77-80
Dunn, Esther Cloudman 1891-1977
Obituary 73-76
Dunn, Ethel (Deikman) 1932- 23-24R
Dunn, Frederick Sherwood 1893-1962
Obituary 113
Dunn, Halbert Louis 1896-1975 Obituary .. 61-64
Dunn, (Henry) Hampton 1916- 57-60
Dunn, Harold 1929- 9-10R
Dunn, Harris
See Doerffler, Alfred
Dunn, Harvey T(homas) 1884-1952 .... SATA-34
Dunn, Hugh Patrick 1916- 122
Dunn, James
See Wilkes-Hunter, R(ichard)
Dunn, James D(ouglas Grant) 1939- 73-76
Dunn, James Taylor 1912- CANR-20
Earlier sketches in CA 7-8R, CANR-4
Dunn, Jean 1921- 109
Dunn, Jerry G. 1916- CANR-11
Earlier sketch in CA 23-24R
Dunn, John (Montfort) 1940- CANR-11
Earlier sketch in CA 69-72
Dunn, Joseph (Willcox, Jr.) 1937- 122
Dunn, Judith F.
See Bernal, Judith F.
Dunn, Judy
See Spangenberg, Judith Dunn
Dunn, Katherine (Karen) 1945- 33-36R
Dunn, Kaye
See Dunham, Katherine
Dunn, Lloyd W. 1906- 57-60
Dunn, Marion Herndon 1920- 29-32R
Dunn, Mary Lois 1930- CANR-12
Earlier sketch in CA 61-64
See also SATA 6
Dunn, Mary Maples 1931- 114
Dunn, Nell
See Sandford, Nell Mary
Dunn, Patience (Louise Ralli) 1922- 7-8R
Dunn, Peter N(orman) 1926- 122
Dunn, Richard S(lator) 1928- Brief entry ... 112
Dunn, Ronald (Louis) 1936- Brief entry 120
Dunn, S. P.
See Dunn, Stephen P(orter)
Dunn, Samuel Watson 1918- CANR-5
Earlier sketch in CA 1R
Dunn, Si 1944- 77-80
Dunn, Stephen 1939- CANR-12
Earlier sketch in CA 33-36R
See also CLC 36
Dunn, Stephen P(orter) 1928- 124
Dunn, Stuart 1900- 57-60
Dunn, Thomas G(eorge) 1950- 119
Dunn, Thomas Tinsley 1901- 107
Dunn, Waldo H(ilary) 1882-1969 .... CAP-2
Earlier sketch in CA 21-22
Dunn, Walter Scott, Jr. 1928- 101
Dunn, William J. 1906- 33-36R
Dunn, William L(awrence, Jr.) 1924- 37-40R
Dunn, William Robert 1916- 113
Dunnahoo, Terry 1927- CANR-14
Earlier sketch in CA 41-44R
See also SATA 7
Dunnam, Maxie D(enton) 1934- 73-76
Dunnan, Nancy 1941- 112
Dunne, Colin 1937- 123
Dunne, Dominick 1925- 121
Dunne, Finley Peter 1867-1936 Brief entry .. 108
See also DLB 11, 23
See also TCLC 28
Dunne, George H(arold) 1905- CANR-5
Earlier sketch in CA 3R
Dunne, Gerald T. 1919- CANR-1
Earlier sketch in CA 45-48
Dunne, John Gregory 1932- CANR-14
Earlier sketch in CA 25-28R
See also DLBY 80
See also CLC 28
Dunne, John S(cribner) 1929- 15-16R
Dunne, (Christopher) Lee 1934- 120
Dunne, Mary Collins 1914- CANR-14
Earlier sketch in CA 41-44R
See also SATA 11
Dunne, Mary Jo
See Dunne, Mary Collins
Dunne, Philip 1908- CANR-11
Earlier sketches in CA 9-10, CAP-1
See also DLB 26
Dunne, Robert Williams 1895-1977
Obituary 69-72
Dunnell, Robert C(hester) 1942- 89-92
Dunner, Joseph 1908-1978 .... CANR-14
Earlier sketch in CA 21-22R
Dunnett, Alastair M(acTavish) 1908- 65-68
Dunnett, Dorothy 1923- CANR-3
Earlier sketch in CA 4R
Dunnett, Margaret (Rosalind) 1909-1977 ... 108
See also SATA 42
Dunnigan, Alice Allison 1906-1983 125
Obituary 109
See also BW
Dunning, Brad 1957- 102
Dunning, Bruce 1940- 77-80
Dunning, Chester S(idney) L(arson) 1949- .. 116
Dunning, Edward
See Gilbert, R(obert) A(ndrew)
Dunning, Eric (Geoffrey) 1936- 116
Dunning, John 1942- CANR-16
Earlier sketch in CA 93-96
Dunning, John H(arry) 1927- CANR-21
Earlier sketch in CA 104
Dunning, Lawrence 1931- 77-80
Dunning, Ralph Cheever 1878-1930
Brief entry 107
See also DLB 4
Dunning, Robert William 1938- CANR-20
Earlier sketches in CA 53-56, CANR-5
Dunning, (Arthur) Stephen (Jr.) 1924- . CANR-12
Earlier sketch in CA 25-28R
Dunning, William A. 1857-1922 .... DLB-17
Dunnington, Hazel Brain 1912- 21-22R
du Nouey, Pierre (-Andre-Leon) Lecomte
See Lecomte du Nouey, Pierre
(-Andre-Leon)
Dunoyer, Maurice
See Domergue, Maurice
Dunoyer De Segonzac, Andre 1884-1974
Obituary 53-56
Dunphy, Jack 1914- 25-28R
Dunrea, Olivier Jean-Paul Dominique
1953- 124
See also SATA 46
Dunsany, Edward John Moreton Drax
Plunkett 1878-1957 Brief entry 104
See also DLB 10
Dunsheath, Joyce (Houchen) 1902- 7-8R
Dunsheath, Percy 1886- 107
Dunsmore, Roger 1938- 110
Dunson, Josh 1941- 25-28R
Dunstan, Andrew
See Chandler, A(rthur) Bertram
Dunstan, Don(ald Allan) 1926- 110
Dunstan, Reginald (Ernest) 1914- 21-22R
Dunster, Mark 1927- 85-88
Dunsterville, G(alfrid) C. K. 1905- CAP-1
Earlier sketch in CA 9-10
Dunston, Arthur John 1922- 109
Dunton, (Arnold) Davidson 1912-1987
Obituary 121
Dunton, Samuel Cady 1910(?)-1975
Obituary 61-64
Dupee, F(rederick) W(ilcox) 1904-1979 ... CAP-1
Obituary 85-88
Earlier sketch in CA 13-14
du Perry, Jean
See Simenon, Georges (Jacques
Christian)
Dupin, August Dupont
See Taylor, John (Alfred)
Dupin, Jacques 1927- Brief entry 119
Duplessis, Yves
See Duplessis, Yvonne
Duplessis, Yvonne 1912- CANR-3
Earlier sketch in CA 9-10R
Dupont, Paul
See Frewin, Leslie Ronald
DuPont, Robert L(ouis), Jr. 1936- 125
Dupre, Catherine CANR-16
Earlier sketch in CA 25-28R
Dupre, J(osef) Stefan 1936- 102
Dupre, Louis CANR-18
Earlier sketches in CA 9-10R, CANR-3
Dupree, A(nderson) Hunter 1921- 11-12R
Dupree, Louis 1925- 41-44R
Dupree, Robert S(cott) 1940- 125
Dupres, Henri
See Fawcett, F(rank) Dubrez
Duprey, Richard A(llen) 1929- CANR-6
Earlier sketch in CA 7-8R
Dupuis, Adrian M(aurice) 1919- 11-12R
Dupuy, R(ichard) Ernest 1887-1975 .... CANR-6
Obituary 57-60
Earlier sketch in CA 4R
Dupuy, T(revor) N(evitt) 1916- CANR-18
Earlier sketches in CA 4R, CANR-2
See also SATA 4
Durac, Jack
See Rachman, Stanley Jack
Durack, Mary 1913- CANR-17
Earlier sketch in CA 97-100
Duram, James C(arl) 1939- CANR-4
Earlier sketch in CA 53-56
Duran, Gloria Diana Bradley 1924- 107
Duran, Manuel E. 1925- CANR-11
Earlier sketch in CA 25-28R
Duran, Richard (Paul) 1943- 114
Durand, G. Forbes
See Burgess, M(ichael) R(oy)
Durand, John Dana 1913-1981 .... CANR-9
Earlier sketch in CA 61-64
Durand, Loup 1933- 124
Durand, Loyal, Jr. 1902-1970 .... CAP-2
Earlier sketch in CA 21-22
Durand, Lucile
See Bersianik, Louky
Durand, Robert 1944- 57-60
Durandeaux, Jacques 1926- 25-28R
Durang, Christopher (Ferdinand) 1949- 105
See also CLC 27, 38
Durant, Ariel K(aufman) 1898-1981 .... CANR-4
Obituary 105
Earlier sketch in CA 11-12R
Durant, David N(orton) 1925- 77-80
Durant, Frederick C(lark) III 1916- 113
Durant, Henry 1902-1982 Obituary 107
Durant, John 1902- CANR-5
Earlier sketch in CA 9-10R
See also SATA 27
Durant, Stuart 1932- 104
Durant, Will(iam James) 1885-1981 .... CANR-4
Obituary 105
Earlier sketch in CA 11-12R
Durante, James Francis 1893-1980
Obituary 93-96
Durante, Jimmy
See Durante, James Francis
Duranty, Walter 1884-1957 .... DLB-29
Duras, Marguerite 1914- 25-28R
See also CLC 3, 6, 11, 20, 34, 40
Duratschek, (Mary) Claudia 1894- 37-40R
Duratschek, Sister Mary Claudia
See Duratschek, (Mary) Claudia
Durbahn, Walter E. 1895(?)-1981
Obituary 102
Durban, (Rosa) Pam 1947- 123
See also CLC 39
Durband, Alan 1927- CANR-20
Earlier sketches in CA 7-8R, CANR-2
Durbin, Brice 1899(?)-1983 Obituary 111
Durbin, Mary Lou 1927- 21-22R
Durbin, Richard Louis 1928- CANR-7
Earlier sketch in CA 53-56
Durbridge, Francis (Henry) 1912- CANR-24
Earlier sketches in CA 77-80, CANR-6
Durcan, Paul 1944- CLC-43
Durden, Robert Franklin 1925- 9-10R
Durey, Michael (John) 1947- 107
Durfee, David A(rthur) 1929- 29-32R
Durgnat, Raymond (Eric) 1932- 19-20R
Durham, Frank (Edington) 1935- 114
Durham, John 1925- 107
Durham, John
See Paine, Lauran (Bosworth)
Durham, John I. 1933- CANR-13
Earlier sketch in CA 29-32R
Durham, Mae
See Roger, Mae Durham
Durham, Marilyn 1930- 49-52
Durham, Philip 1912-1977 .... CANR-7
Earlier sketch in CA 11-12R
Durka, Gloria 1939- CANR-14
Earlier sketch in CA 65-68
Durkee, Mary C. 1921- 13-14R
Durkin, Barbara W(ernecke) 1944- 123
Durkin, Henry P(aul) 1940- 53-56
Durkin, Joseph Thomas 1903- CAP-1
Earlier sketch in CA 11-12
Durland, Frances Caldwell 1892- 113
Durland, William R(eginald) 1931- CANR-7
Earlier sketch in CA 57-60
Durnbaugh, Donald F. 1927- CANR-8
Earlier sketch in CA 21-22R
Durnin, Richard G(erry) 1920- 110
Durning, Addis
See Ranzini, Addis Durning
Duroche, Leonard L(eRoy) 1933- 37-40R
DuRocher, Richard J(ames) 1955- 118
Duroselle, Jean-Baptiste (Marie Lucien
Charles) 1917- CANR-18
Earlier sketches in CA 9-10R, CANR-3
Durr, Fred
See Durr, Frederick R(oland) E(ugene)
Durr, Frederick R(oland) E(ugene)
1921-1978 .... 37-40R
Durr, William Kirtley 1924- 15-16R
Durrani, Mahmood Khan 1914- CAP-1
Earlier sketch in CA 13-14
Durrant, Digby 1926- CANR-13
Earlier sketch in CA 21-22R
Durrant, Rita D(elores) 1923- 108
Durrant, Theo
See Offord, Lenore Glen
Durrell, Donald D(e Witt) 1903- CANR-8
Earlier sketch in CA 17-18R
Durrell, Gerald (Malcolm) 1925- CANR-25
Earlier sketches in CA 7-8R, CANR-4
See also SATA 8
Durrell, Jacqueline Sonia Rasen 1929- ... 23-24R
Durrell, Jacquie
See Durrell, Jacqueline Sonia Rasen
Durrell, Lawrence (George) 1912- 9-10R
See also DLB 15, 27
See also CLC 1, 4, 6, 8, 13, 27, 41
Durrell, Zoe C(ompton) 1910- 89-92
Durrenberger, Robert Warren 1918- ... CANR-10
Earlier sketch in CA 23-24R
Durrenmatt, Friedrich
See Duerrenmatt, Friedrich
See also DLB 69
See also CLC 1, 4, 8, 11, 15, 43
Durslag, Melvin 1921- 101
Durst, Paul 1921- 23-24R
d'Urstelle, Pierre
See Dorst, Jean (Pierre)
Durville, Hector 1849-1923 Brief entry 117
Dury, George H(arry) 1916- 113
Duryee, Mary Ballard 1896-1988 Obituary .. 125
Durzak, Manfred 1938- CANR-1
Earlier sketch in CA 49-52
du Sautoy, Peter (Francis De Courcy)
1921- 5-6R
Dusay, Katherine M(ulholland) 1943- 118
Duscha, Julius (Carl) 1924- 73-76
Dusenberry, William Howard 1908- CAP-1
Earlier sketch in CA 19-20
Dusenbury, Winifred L.
See Frazer, Winifred L(oesch)
Dushkin, Alexander M(ordecai) 1890-1976
Obituary 65-68
Dushnitzky-Shner, Sara 1913- 29-32R
Duska, Ronald 1937- 97-100
Duskin, Ruthie
See Feldman, Ruth Duskin
Dusky, Lorraine 1942- 85-88
Du Soe, Robert C. 1892-1958 .... YABC-2
Dussel, Enrique D. 1934- 89-92
Dussere, Carol
See Dussere, Carolyn T(homas)
Dussere, Carolyn T(homas) 1942- 103
Dussinger, John A(ndrew) 1935- 113
Duster, Alfreda Barnett 1904-1983
Obituary 109
Duster, Troy 1936- 29-32R
Dustin, Charles
See Giesy, J(ohn) U(lrich)
Duthie, Charles S. 1911- CAP-2
Earlier sketch in CA 29-32
Dutile, Fernand N(eville) 1940- 107
Dutourd, Jean Hubert 1920- 65-68
Dutt, R(ajani) Palme 1896-1974 .... CAP-1
Obituary 53-56
Earlier sketch in CA 11-12
Dutta, Reginald 1914- 61-64
Dutta, Rex
See Dutta, Reginald
Dutton, Bertha P(auline) 1903- 122
Brief entry 117
Dutton, Frederick G(ary) 1923- Brief entry .. 111
Dutton, Geoffrey (Piers Henry) 1922- .. CANR-17
Earlier sketches in CA 45-48, CANR-1
Dutton, H(arold) I. ?-1984 Obituary 116
Dutton, Joan Parry 1908- 11-12R
Dutton, John M(ason) 1926- 41-44R
Dutton, Mary 1922- 33-36R
Dutton, Paul 1943- 112
Dutton, Ralph (Stawell) 1898-1985 .... 13-14R
Obituary 116
Dutton, Richard Edward 1929- Brief entry .. 106
Dutz
See Davis, Mary Octavia
Duun, Olav 1876-1939 Brief entry 121
Duus, Masayo 1938- 89-92
Duus, Peter 1933- 25-28R
DuVal, F(rancis) Alan 1916- 33-36R
Duval, Jean-Jacques 1930- 69-72
DuVal, John 1940- 120
Duval, Katherine
See James, Elizabeth
Duval, Margaret
See Robinson, Patricia Colbert
Duvall, Evelyn Millis 1906- CANR-1
Earlier sketch in CA 4R
See also SATA 9
Duvall, Richard M. 1934- 45-48
Duvall, Robert (Selden) 1931- Brief entry ... 116
Duvall, W(illiam) Clyde (Jr.) 1917- 19-20R
DuVaul, Virginia C.
See Coffman, Virginia (Edith)
Duveen, Geoffrey 1883-1975 Obituary 61-64
Duveneck, Josephine Whitney 1891-1978 ... 114
Duverger, Maurice 1917- 65-68
Duvoisin, Roger Antoine 1904-1980 ... CANR-11
Obituary 101
Earlier sketch in CA 13-14R
See also SATA 2, 23, 30
See also DLB 61
DuWors, Richard E(dward) 1914- 45-48
Duy, Pham 1927- 61-64
Duyckinck, Evert Augustus
1816-1878 .... DLB-3, 64
Duyckinck, George Long 1823-1863 .... DLB-3
Dvoretzky, Edward 1930- CANR-14
Earlier sketch in CA 37-40R
Dvorkin, David 1943- 118
Dvornik, Francis 1893-1975 .... CANR-6
Obituary 61-64
Earlier sketch in CA 3R
Dwaraki, Leela 1942- 106
Dweck, Susan 1943- 33-36R
Dwiggins, Don 1913- CANR-23
Earlier sketches in CA 17-18R, CANR-8
See also SATA 4
Dwight, Allan
See Cole, Lois Dwight
Dwight, John Sullivan 1813-1893 .... DLB-1
Dwight, Olivia
See Hazzard, Mary
Dwight, Timothy 1752-1817 .... DLB-37

Dworkin, Andrea 1946- CANR-16
Earlier sketch in CA 77-80
See also CLC 43
Dworkin, Gerald 1937- 53-56
Dworkin, James B(arnet) 1948- 112
Dworkin, R. M.
See Dworkin, Ronald M(yles)
Dworkin, Rita 1928- 23-24R
Dworkin, Ronald
See Dworkin, Ronald M(yles)
Dworkin, Ronald M(yles) 1931-
Brief entry 123
Dwoskin, Charles 1922(?)-1980 Obituary 102
Dwoskin, Stephen 1939- 89-92
Dwyer, John 1930- 113
Dwyer, Judith A(nne) 1948- 117
Dwyer, K. R.
See Koontz, Dean R(ay)
Dwyer, T. Ryle 1944- 105
Dwyer, Thomas A. 1923- 115
Dwyer, Vincent Michael 1912-1987
Obituary 123
Dwyer-Joyce, Alice 1913- CANR-4
Earlier sketch in CA 53-56
Dyal, James A. 1928- CANR-10
Earlier sketch in CA 7-8R
Dyal, William M., Jr. 1928- 21-22R
Dyall, Valentine 1908-1985 Obituary 117
Dybek, Stuart 1942- 97-100
Dyck, Anni 1931- 25-28R
Dyck, Cornelius J(ohn) 1921- 89-92
Dyck, Harvey L(eonard) 1934- 69-72
Dyck, J. William 1918- 57-60
Dyck, Martin 1927- 41-44R
Dyckman, John William 1922-1987 .... CANR-2
Obituary 123
Earlier sketch in CA 3R
Dyckman, Thomas Richard 1932- CANR-13
Earlier sketch in CA 33-36R
Dye, Anne G.
See Phillips, Anne G(arvey)
Dye, Charles
See MacLean, Katherine
Dye, David L. 1925- 23-24R
Dye, Dwight L(atimer) 1931- 118
Dye, Frank Charles 1930- 103
Dye, H(ershel) Allan 1931- 93-96
Dye, Harold E(ldon) 1907- CANR-24
Earlier sketch in CA 29-32R
Dye, James W(ayne) 1934- 23-24R
Dye, Margaret 1932- 81-84
Dye, Thomas R(oy) 1935- CANR-12
Earlier sketch in CA 33-36R
Dyen, Isidore 1913- 53-56
Dyer, Beverly 1921- 61-64
Dyer, Braven 1900(?)-1983 Obituary 110
Dyer, Brian
See Petrocelli, Orlando R(alph)
and Rothery, Brian
Dyer, C. Raymond
See Dyer, Charles (Raymond)
Dyer, Charles (Raymond) 1928- 21-22R
See also DLB 13
Dyer, Elinor Mary Brent
See Brent-Dyer, Elinor Mary
Dyer, Esther R(uth) 1950- 102
Dyer, Frederick C. 1918- 19-20R
Dyer, Geoff 1958- 125
Dyer, George Bell 1903-1978 85-88
Obituary 81-84
Dyer, George E(dward) 1928-1974 .... 37-40R
Dyer, George J(ohn) 1927- 15-16R
Dyer, James (Frederick) 1934- 102
See also SATA 37
Dyer, John M. 1920- 13-14R
Dyer, John Percy 1902-1975 .... 3R
Obituary 103
Dyer, Judith Clements 1947- 112
Dyer, K(enneth) F(rank) 1939- 114
Dyer, Lucinda 1947- 105
Dyer, Raymond
See Dyer, Charles (Raymond)
Dyer, T(homas) A(llan) 1947- 101
Dyer, Thomas G(eorge) 1943- CANR-25
Earlier sketch in CA 107
Dyer, Wayne W(alter) 1940- CANR-25
Earlier sketch in CA 69-72
Dyer, William G(ibb) 1925- CANR-14
Earlier sketch in CA 41-44R
Dygard, Thomas J. 1931- CANR-15
Earlier sketch in CA 85-88
See also SATA 24
Dygat, Stanislaw 1914-1978 Obituary 111
Dygert, James H(erbert) 1934- CANR-10
Earlier sketch in CA 65-68
Dyk, Walter 1899-1972 Obituary 37-40R
Dyke, John 1935- CANR-12
Earlier sketch in CA 25-28R
See also SATA 35
Dykema, Karl W(ashburn) 1906-1970 .... CAP-2
Earlier sketch in CA 25-28
Dykeman, Richard M(ills) 1943- 93-96
Dykeman, Wilma CANR-1
Earlier sketch in CA 2R
Dykes, Archie R(eece) 1931- CANR-7
Earlier sketch in CA 17-18R
Dykes, Jack
See Owen, Jack
Dykes, Jeff(erson) C(henowth) 1900- CANR-17
Earlier sketches in CA 5-6R, CANR-2
Dykhuizen, George 1899- 49-52
Dykstra, Craig Richard 1947- 112
Dykstra, Gerald 1922- 45-48
Dykstra, Robert R. 1930- 25-28R
Dylan, Bob 1941- 41-44R
See also DLB 16
See also CLC 3, 4, 6, 12
Dymally, Mervyn M(alcolm) 1926- 41-44R
Dyment, Clifford (Henry) 1914-1971 .... CAP-1
Obituary 33-36R
Earlier sketch in CA 9-10
Dymoke, Juliet
See de Schanschieff, Juliet Dymoke
Dymond, Dorothy 1891-1985 Obituary 117
Dymond, Rosalind
See Cartwright, Rosalind Dymond
Dymsza, William A(lexander) 1920- CANR-2
Earlier sketch in CA 49-52
Dynes, Russell R(owe) 1923- CANR-23
Earlier sketches in CA 11-12R, CANR-6
Dyott, George (Miller) 1883-1972
Obituary 37-40R
Dyrness, William A(rthur) 1943- CANR-13
Earlier sketch in CA 33-36R
Dyroff, Jan Michael 1942- 61-64
Dyson, A(nthony) E(dward) 1928- 57-60
Dyson, Anne Jane 1912- 21-22R
Dyson, Freeman J(ohn) 1923- CANR-17
Earlier sketch in CA 89-92
Dyson, Geoffrey Harry George 1914-1981
Obituary 114
Dyson, George (Bernard) 1953- 126
Dyson, Lowell Keith 1929- 107
Dyson, R(obert) W(illiam) 1949- 123
Dywasuk, Colette Taube 1941- 45-48
Dziech, Billie Wright 1941- 113
Dziewanowski, M(arian) Kamil 1913- 29-32R
Dzwonkoski, Peter 1940- 123

E

E. V. B.
See Boyle, Eleanor Vere (Gordon)
Eade, Alfred Thompson 1891-1988
Obituary 125
Eadie, Donald 1919- 33-36R
Eadie, John W(illiam) 1935- 104
Eagan, Andrea Boroff 1943- 73-76
Eagan, Barbara Tiritilli 1935(?)-1986
Obituary 118
Eagar, Frances (Elisabeth Stuart)
1940-1978 61-64
Obituary 120
See also SATA 11
Eager, Edward McMaken 1911-1964 73-76
See also SATA 17
See also DLB 22
Eager, Mary Ann 1905(?)-1984 Obituary 111
Eager, Molly
See Eager, Mary Ann
Eagle, Chester (Arthur) 1933- 57-60
Eagle, Dorothy 1912- CANR-9
Earlier sketch in CA 23-24R
Eagle, Joanna 1934- 25-28R
Eagle, Mike 1942- SATA-11
Eagle, Robert H(arold) 1921-1969 .... CAP-2
Earlier sketch in CA 21-22
Eagles, Douglas Alan 1943- 110
Eaglesfield, Francis
See Guirdham, Arthur
Eagleson, John 1941- 53-56
Eagleton, Terence (Francis) 1943- CANR-23
Earlier sketches in CA 57-60, CANR-7
Eagleton, Terry
See Eagleton, Terence (Francis)
Eagleton, Thomas Francis 1929-
Brief entry 105
Eagly, Robert V(ictor) 1933- 49-52
Eaker, Ira
See Eaker, Ira C(larence)
Eaker, Ira C(larence) 1896-1987 Obituary 123
Eakin, Frank Edwin, Jr. 1936- 53-56
Eakin, Mary K(atherine) 1917- CANR-1
Earlier sketch in CA 4R
Eakin, Mary Mulford 1914-1980 126
Brief entry 106
Eakin, Paul John 1938- 120
Eakin, Richard M(arshall) 1910- 61-64
Eakin, Sue 1918- 69-72
Eakins, David W(alter) 1923- 49-52
Eakins, Pamela 1953- 117
Eales, John R(ay) 1910- 11-12R
Ealy, Lawrence O(rr) 1915- 33-36R
Eames, Alexandra 1942- 105
Eames, Andrew (John) 1958- 124
Eames, David 1934- 77-80
Eames, Edwin 1930- CANR-14
Earlier sketch in CA 41-44R
Eames, Elizabeth Ramsden 1921- 125
Eames, Hugh 1917- 45-48
Eames, John Douglas 1915- 69-72
Eames, S(amuel) Morris 1916- 57-60
Ear, The
See McLellan, Diana
Eardley, George C(harles) 1926- 57-60
Earhart, H(arry) Byron 1935- CANR-14
Earlier sketch in CA 37-40R
Earl, David M(agarey) 1911- 13-14R
Earl, Donald (Charles) 1931- 57-60
Earl, Johnrae 1919(?)-1978 Obituary 77-80
Earl, Lawrence 1915- 9-10R
Earl, Paul Hunter 1945- CANR-2
Earlier sketch in CA 49-52
Earle, (Mary) Alice Morse 1853(?)-1911
Brief entry 117
Earle, Jean
See Burge, Doris
Earle, Marilee
See Zdenek, Marilee
Earle, Olive L(ydia) 1888- 23-24R
See also SATA 7
Earle, Peter G. 1923- 17-18R
Earle, Ralph 1907- CANR-4
Earlier sketch in CA 1R
Earle, Timothy K. 1946- 125
Earle, William
See Johns, William Earle
Earle, William Alexander 1919- 85-88
Earley, Martha
See Westwater, Sister Agnes Martha
Earley, Tom 1911- CAP-2
Earlier sketch in CA 33-36
Earll, Tony
See Buckland, Raymond
Earl Mountbatten of Burma
See Mountbatten, Louis (Francis Albert
Victor Nicholas)
Earl of Arran
See Gore, Arthur Kattendyke S(trange)
D(avid) A(rchibald)
Earl of Carnarvon
See Herbert, Henry George Alfred Marius
Victor Francis
Earl of Longford
See Pakenham, Edward Arthur Henry
Earlson, Ian Malcolm
See Dorn, William S.
Early, James 1923- 45-48
Early, Richard E(lliott) 1908- 102
Early, Robert 1940- 49-52
Earnest, Ernest (Penney) 1901- 33-36R
Earney, Fillmore C(hristy) F(idelis) 1931- 57-60
Earnshaw, Anthony 1924- 53-56
Earnshaw, Brian 1929- CANR-11
Earlier sketch in CA 25-28R
See also SATA 17
Earp, Virgil
See Keevill, Henry J(ohn)
Eason, Ruth P. 1898(?)-1978 Obituary 81-84
Easson, James 1895-1979 .... 7-8R
Obituary 103
Easson, Roger R(alph) 1945- 112
Easson, William M(cAlpine) 1931- 65-68
East, Ben 1898- 33-36R
East, Bob 1920(?)-1985 Obituary 115
East, Charles 1924- 17-18R
East, John Marlborough 1936- 21-22R
East, John Porter 1931-1986 .... 17-18R
Obituary 119
East, Michael
See West, Morris L(anglo)
East, P. D. 1921-1971 .... 2R
Obituary 103
East, W(illiam) Gordon 1902- 69-72
Eastaugh, Kenneth 1929- 106
Eastaway, Edward
See Thomas, (Philip) Edward
Easterlin, Richard A(inley) 1926- 109
Easterman, Alexander Levvey 1890-1983
Obituary 110
Eastham, Thomas 1923- 77-80
Easthope, Gary 1945- 69-72
Eastin, Roy B(randon) 1917- 41-44R
Eastlake, William (Derry) 1917- CANR-5
Earlier sketch in CA 5-6R
See also CAAS 1
See also DLB 6
See also CLC 8
Eastland, Terry 1950- 97-100
Eastlick, John Taylor 1912- 106
Eastman, Addison J. 1918- 85-88
Eastman, Ann Heidbreder 1933- CANR-14
Earlier sketch in CA 37-40R
Eastman, Arthur M(orse) 1918- 23-24R
Eastman, Carol 116
See also DLB 44
Eastman, Charles 116
Eastman, Charles A(lexander)
1858-1939 .... YABC-1
Eastman, Edward Roe 1885- CAP-1
Earlier sketch in CA 13-14
Eastman, Frances Whittier 1915- 3R
Eastman, G. Don
See Oosterman, Gordon
Eastman, Harry Claude MacColl 1923-
Brief entry 105
Eastman, Joel Webb 1939- 15-16R
Eastman, John 1935- 117
Eastman, Lloyd E. 1929- 126
Brief entry 112
Eastman, Max (Forrester) 1883-1969 .... 11-12R
Obituary 25-28R
Eastman, May (Forrester) 1883- 11-12R
Eastman, P(hilip) D(ey) 1909-1986 107
Obituary 118
See also SATA 33, 46
Eastman, Richard M(orse) 1916- 17-18R
Eastman, Robert E. 1913- 93-96
Eastman, Roger (Herbert) 1931- 53-56
Easton, Allan 1916- CANR-20
Earlier sketches in CA 49-52, CANR-2
Easton, Carol 1933- 65-68
Easton, David 1917- 33-36R
Easton, Edward
See Malerich, Edward P.
Easton, Loyd D(avid) 1915- 21-22R
Easton, Robert (Olney) 1915- CANR-7
Earlier sketch in CA 15-16R
Easton, Stewart Copinger 1907- CANR-18
Earlier sketches in CA 1R, CANR-2
Easton, Thomas A(twood) 1944- 114
Eastwick, Ivy (Ethel) O(live) CANR-2
Earlier sketch in CA 5-6R
See also SATA 3
Eastwood, C(harles) Cyril 1916- 7-8R
Eastwood, Cyril
See Eastwood, C(harles) Cyril
Eatock, Marjorie 1927- 89-92
Eaton, Anne T(haxter) 1881-1971
Obituary 111
See also SATA 32
Eaton, Charles Edward 1916- CANR-20
Earlier sketches in CA 5-6R, CANR-2
Eaton, Clement 1898-1980 .... CANR-4
Obituary 118
Earlier sketch in CA 1R
Eaton, Evelyn (Sybil Mary) 1902- 53-56
Eaton, Faith (Sybil) 1927- 103
Eaton, George L.
See Verral, Charles Spain
Eaton, J(ohn) H(erbert) 1927- CANR-19
Earlier sketches in CA 3R, CANR-4
Eaton, Janet
See Givens, Janet E(aton)
Eaton, Jeanette 1886-1968 73-76
See also SATA 24
Eaton, John
See Bodington, Stephen
Eaton, John P. 126
Eaton, Joseph W. 1919- CANR-4
Earlier sketch in CA 4R
Eaton, Leonard K. 1922- 21-22R
Eaton, Marcia M(uelder) 1938- 113
Eaton, Theodore H(ildreth), Jr. 1907- 53-56
Eaton, Tom 1940- CANR-15
Earlier sketch in CA 41-44R
See also SATA 22
Eaton, Trevor 1934- 23-24R
Eaton, William Edward 1943- 69-72
Eauclaire, Sally 1950- 118
Eaves, James Clifton 1912- 13-14R
Eaves, Morris (Emery) 1944- 120
Eaves, T(homas) C(ary) Duncan 1918- 77-80
Eavey, Charles B(enton) 1889- 5-6R
Eavey, Louise Bone 1900- 5-6R
Eayrs, James George 1926- Brief entry 106
Eban, Abba (Solomon) 1915- CANR-26
Earlier sketch in CA 57-60
Eban, Aubrey
See Eban, Abba (Solomon)
Ebb, Fred 1935- CANR-24
Earlier sketch in CA 69-72
Ebbesen, Ebbe B(ruce) 1944- CANR-2
Earlier sketch in CA 49-52
Ebbett, (Frances) Eva 1925- 103
Ebbett, Eve
See Ebbett, (Frances) Eva
Ebejer, Francis 1925- CANR-16
Earlier sketch in CA 29-32R
Ebel, Alex 1927- SATA-11
Ebel, Henry 1938- 53-56
Ebel, Robert L(ouis) 1910- 89-92
Ebel, Suzanne
See Goodwin, Suzanne
Ebeling, Gerhard 1912- CANR-5
Earlier sketch in CA 9-10R
Ebeling, Walter 1907- 119
Ebenstein, Ronnie Sue 1946- 103
Ebenstein, William 1910-1976 .... CANR-6
Obituary 65-68
Earlier sketch in CA 2R
Eber, Dorothy (Margaret) Harley 1930- 41-44R
See also SATA 27
Eber, Irene 1929- 102
Eberhard, Wolfram 1909- CANR-2
Earlier sketch in CA 49-52
Eberhardt, Newman Charles 1912- 1R
Eberhardt, Peter
See Adams, Robert (Franklin)
Eberhart, Dikkon 1946- 93-96
Eberhart, George M(artin) 1950- 105
Eberhart, Mignon G(ood) 1899- 73-76
See also AITN 2
Eberhart, (Wilfred) Perry 1924- 19-20R
Eberhart, Richard 1904- CANR-2
Earlier sketch in CA 1R
See also DLB 48
See also CDALB 1941-1968
See also CLC 3, 11, 19
Eberle, Irmengarde 1898-1979 .... CANR-2
Obituary 85-88
Earlier sketch in CA 4R
See also SATA 2, 23
Eberle, Nancy (Oates) 1935(?)-1988
Obituary 125
Eberle, Paul 1928- 101
Eberman, (Gilbert) Willis 1917- 9-10R
Ebershoff-Coles, Susan Vaughan 1941- 102
Ebersohn, Wessel (Schalk) 1940- 97-100
Ebersole, A(lva) V(ernon), Jr. 1919- CANR-14
Earlier sketch in CA 37-40R
Eberstadt, Charles F. 1914(?)-1974
Obituary 53-56
Eberstadt, Fernanda 1960- CLC-39
Eberstadt, Isabel 1933- 126
Eberstadt, Lindley E. 1910(?)-1985
Obituary 115
Ebert, Alan 1935- CANR-16
Earlier sketch in CA 85-88
Ebert, Arthur Frank 1902-1984 .... 7-8R
Obituary 114
Ebert, John E(dward) 1922- 106
Ebert, Katherine 1921- 107
Ebert, Roger (Joseph) 1942- CANR-22
Earlier sketch in CA 69-72
Eberwein, Jane Donahue 1943- 111
Eberwein, Robert Thomas 1940- 111
Eblana, Sister 1907- CAP-1
Earlier sketch in CA 11-12
Eble, Kenneth Eugene 1923- CANR-19
Earlier sketches in CA 1R, CANR-4
Eblen, Jack Ericson 1936- 33-36R
Eblis, J. Philip
See Phillips, James W.
Ebon 1942- DLB-41

Ebon, Martin 1917- CANR-10
Earlier sketch in CA 23-24R
Ebsen, Buddy
See Ebsen, Christian
Ebsen, Christian 1908- 103
Ebsworth, (George Arthur) Raymond
1911- 4R
Eby, Cecil D(eGrotte) 1927- CANR-4
Earlier sketch in CA 1R
Eby, Richard E(ngle) 1912- 112
Eccles, David (McAdam) 1904- 53-56
Eccles, Frank 1923- 103
Eccles, Henry E. 1898- CAP-1
Earlier sketch in CA 15-16
Eccles, John Carew 1903- CANR-9
Earlier sketch in CA 65-68
Eccles, W(illiam) J(ohn) 1917- 9-10R
Eccles Williams, Ferelith 1920- CANR-21
Earlier sketch in CA 105
Eccli, Sandra Fulton 1936- 102
Echegaray (y Eizaguirre), Jose (Maria
Waldo) 1832-1916 Brief entry 104
See also TCLC 4
Echeruo, Michael J(oseph) C(hukwudalu)
1937- CANR-8
Earlier sketch in CA 57-60
Echevarria, Roberto Gonzalez
See Gonzalez-Echevarria, Roberto
Echeverria, Durand 1913- 9-10R
Echewa, T(homas) Obinkaram 1940- 73-76
Echlin, Edward P. 1930- 23-24R
Echo
See Proust,
(Valentin-Louis-George-Eugene-)
Marcel
Echols, Barbara E(llen) 1934- 106
Echols, John M(inor) 1913-1982 .... CANR-2
Obituary 107
Earlier sketch in CA 5-6R
Echols, Margit 1944- 97-100
Eck, Diana L. 1945- 107
Eckardt, A(rthur) Roy 1918- CANR-14
Earlier sketch in CA 37-40R
Eckardt, Alice L(yons) 1923- CANR-14
Earlier sketch in CA 37-40R
Eckaus, Richard S(amuel) 1926- 45-48
Eckblad, Edith Berven 1923- 17-18R
See also SATA 23
Eckbo, Garrett 1910- 25-28R
Ecke, Betty Tseng Yu-ho 1924- CANR-6
Earlier sketch in CA 7-8R
Ecke, Wolfgang 1927-1983 Obituary 111
See also SATA 37
Eckel, Malcolm W(illiam) 1912- 61-64
Eckel, Paul E(dward) 1908-1986 Obituary 119
Eckelberry, Grace Kathryn 1902- CAP-2
Earlier sketch in CA 33-36
Eckels, Jon CANR-3
Earlier sketch in CA 49-52
Ecker, Beverly A. 1938- 116
Ecker, H(erman) Paul 1922-1976 .... CAP-2
Earlier sketch in CA 29-32
Ecker-Racz, L. Laszlo 1906- 49-52
Eckerson, Olive Taylor 1901- 2R
Eckert, Allan W. 1931- CANR-14
Earlier sketch in CA 13-14R
See also SATA 27, 29
See also CLC 17
Eckert, Edward K(yle) 1943- 77-80
Eckert, Horst 1931- 37-40R
See also SATA 8
Eckert, Ruth E(lizabeth) 1905- 13-14R
Eckes, Alfred Edward, Jr. 1942- CANR-9
Earlier sketch in CA 61-64
Eckhardt, Bob
See Eckhardt, Robert Christian
Eckhardt, Robert Christian 1913- 85-88
Eckhardt, Tibor 1888-1972 Obituary 37-40R
Eckholm, Erik P(eter) 1949- CANR-6
Earlier sketch in CA 57-60
Eckley, Grace 1932- 45-48
Eckley, Mary M. 102
Eckley, Wilton Earl, Jr. 1929- 49-52
Eckman, Frederick (Willis) 1924- 33-36R
Eckman, Lester S(amuel) 1937- CANR-2
Earlier sketch in CA 49-52
Eckmar, F. R.
See De Hartog, Jan
Eckstein, Alexander 1915-1976 .... CANR-6
Obituary 69-72
Earlier sketch in CA 1R
Eckstein, Gustav 1890-1981 57-60
Obituary 104
Eckstein, Harry 1924- CANR-1
Earlier sketch in CA 3R
Eckstein, Jerome 1928- 114
Eckstein, Otto 1927-1984 .... CANR-14
Obituary 112
Earlier sketch in CA 15-16R
Eclov, Shirley
See Pfoutz, Shirley Eclov
Eco, Umberto 1932- CANR-12
Earlier sketch in CA 77-80
See also CLC 28
Economou, George 1934- 25-28R
Ecroyd, Donald H(owarth) 1923- CANR-4
Earlier sketch in CA 3R
Edari, Ronald S(amuel) 1943- 65-68
Edberg, Rolf 1912- CANR-26
Earlier sketches in CA 69-72, CANR-11
Eddings, David 1931- 110
Eddins, Dwight L. 1939- 33-36R
Eddison, E(ric) R(ucker) 1882-1945
Brief entry 109
See also TCLC 15
Eddison, John 1916- CANR-23
Earlier sketches in CA 61-64, CANR-8
Eddison, Roger (Tatham) 1916- CAP-1
Earlier sketch in CA 11-12
Eddleman, H(enry) Leo 1911- CANR-9
Earlier sketch in CA 13-14R
Eddy, C.M., Jr.
See Eddy, Clifford Martin, Jr.
Eddy, Clifford Martin, Jr. 1896-1967
Obituary 113
Eddy, Edward D(anforth, Jr.) 1921- 73-76
Eddy, Elizabeth M. 1926- 21-22R
Eddy, John J(ude) 1933- 73-76
Eddy, John P(aul) 1932- CANR-9
Earlier sketch in CA 61-64
Eddy, John Percy 1881-1975 Obituary 61-64
Eddy, Mary (Morse) Baker 1821-1910
Brief entry 113
Eddy, Paul 1944- CANR-15
Earlier sketch in CA 73-76
Eddy, Roger (Whittlesey) 1920- 17-18R
Eddy, Samuel K(ennedy) 1926- CANR-17
Earlier sketch in CA 3R
Ede, Janina 1937- SATA-33
Ede, Lisa S. 1947- 123
Edel, Abraham 1908- 3R
Edel, (Joseph) Leon 1907- CANR-22
Earlier sketches in CA 3R, CANR-1
See also CLC 29, 34
Edel, Matthew (David) 1941- 29-32R
Edelberg, Cynthia Dubin 1940- 89-92
Edelen, Georges 1924- 93-96
Edell, Celeste 3R
See also SATA 12
Edelman, Alice Fisher 1940- 112
Edelman, Bernard 1946- 126
Edelman, Elaine 113
See also SATA 50
Edelman, Gerald Maurice 1929- 112
Edelman, John W(alter) 1893-1971
Obituary 113
Edelman, Lily (Judith) 1915-1981 61-64
Obituary 102
See also SATA 22
Edelman, Marian Wright 1939- 124
See also BW
Edelman, Maurice 1911-1975 65-68
Obituary 61-64
Edelman, Murray 1919- 33-36R
Edelman, Nathan 1911-1971 Obituary 113
Edelman, Paul S. 1926- 9-10R
Edelsberg, Herman 1909-1986 Obituary 120
Edelson, Edward 1932- CANR-13
Earlier sketch in CA 19-20R
See also SATA 51
Edelson, Julie 1949- 122
Edelson, Marshall 1928- Brief entry 111
Edelstein, Arthur CANR-9
Earlier sketch in CA 65-68
Edelstein, David S(imeon) 1913- 61-64
Edelstein, J. M. 1924- 53-56
Edelstein, Morton A. 1925- 69-72
Edelstein, Scott 1954- 122
Edelstein, Stuart J. 1941- 122
Eden, Alvin N(oam) 1926- CANR-9
Earlier sketch in CA 61-64
Eden, (Robert) Anthony 1897-1977 77-80
Obituary 69-72
Eden, Dorothy (Enid) 1912-1982 81-84
Obituary 106
Eden, Laura
See Harrison, Claire E.
Eden, Robert 1942- 113
Edens, Cooper 1945- SATA-49
Edens, (Bishop) David 1926- 108
See also SATA 39
Eder, George Jackson 1900- 85-88
Eder, Richard (Gray) 1932- Brief entry 123
Edes, Benjamin 1732-1803 .... DLB-43
Edey, Maitland A(rmstrong) 1910- CANR-6
Earlier sketch in CA 57-60
See also SATA 25
Edgar, David 1948- CANR-12
Earlier sketch in CA 57-60
See also DLB 13
See also CLC 42
Edgar, Donald 1916- 121
Edgar, Frank Terrell Rhoades 1932- 69-72
Edgar, Josephine
See Mussi, Mary
Edgar, Ken(neth Frank) 1925- 49-52
Edgar, Neal Lowndes 1927-1983 69-72
Obituary 110
Edge, David O(wen) 1932- 73-76
Edge, Findley B(artow) 1916- 5-6R
Edgerton, Clyde (C.) 1944- Brief entry 118
See also CLC 39
Edgerton, Franklin 1885-1963 Obituary 110
Edgerton, Gary Richard 1952- 111
Edgerton, Harold Eugene 1903- CANR-5
Earlier sketch in CA 53-56
Edgerton, Joseph S. 1900(?)-1983
Obituary 109
Edgerton, Lucile Selk 1896-1987 Obituary 122
Edgerton, Robert B(reckenridge) 1931- 53-56
Edgerton, William B(enbow) 1914- 29-32R
Edgeworth, Maria 1767-1849 .... SATA-21
Edgington, Eugene S(inclair) 1924- 25-28R
Edgley, Charles K(enneth) 1943- 57-60
Edgley, Roy 1925- 29-32R
Edgren, Harry D(aniel) 1899- CAP-2
Earlier sketch in CA 33-36
Edgy, Wardore
See Gorey, Edward (St. John)
Edholm, O(tto) G(ustav) 1909-1985
Obituary 115
Edie, James M. 1927- 11-12R
Ediger, Peter J. 1926- 33-36R
Edinborough, Arnold 1922- 73-76
Edinger, Edward F(erdinand) 1922- 69-72
Edington, Andrew 1914- 73-76
Edison, Judith
See Paul, Judith Edison
Edison, Michael (G.) 1937- Brief entry 110
Edkins, Anthony 1927- 97-100
Edkins, Diana M(aria) 1947- 41-44R
Edler, Peter 1934- 107
Edlin, Herbert Leeson 1913-1976 .... CANR-9
Obituary 69-72
Earlier sketch in CA 61-64
Edlin, Rosabelle Alpern 1914- 11-12R
Edman, David 1930- 37-40R
Edman, Marion (Louise) 1901- CAP-1
Earlier sketch in CA 17-18
Edman, Victor Raymond 1900-1967 .... CANR-6
Earlier sketch in CA 3R
Edmands, Allan 1942- 117
Edmands, Dodie 1947- 116
Edmiston, (Helen) Jean (Mary) 1913- 13-14R
Edmiston, Susan 1940- 65-68
Edmond, Jay
See Jones, Jack
Edmond, Mary 1916- 121
Edmonds, Alan
See Edmonds, Arthur Denis
Edmonds, Ann C.
See Welch, Ann Courtenay (Edmonds)
Edmonds, Arthur Denis 1932- 73-76
Edmonds, C(ecil) J(ohn) 1889- CAP-1
Earlier sketch in CA 13-14
Edmonds, Charles
See Carrington, Charles Edmund
Edmonds, Helen G(rey) 1911- 65-68
Edmonds, I(vy) G(ordon) 1917- CANR-13
Earlier sketch in CA 33-36R
See also SATA 8
Edmonds, Jae
See Edmonds, James A.
Edmonds, James A. 1947- 118
Edmonds, Margaret Hammett 101
Edmonds, Margot
See Edmonds, Margaret Hammett
Edmonds, Paul
See Kuttner, Henry
Edmonds, R(obert) H(umphrey) G(ordon)
1920- 69-72
Edmonds, (Sheppard) Randolph
1900-1983 125
See also BW
See also DLB 51
Edmonds, Robert 1913- 112
Edmonds, Robin
See Edmonds, R(obert) H(umphrey)
G(ordon)
Edmonds, Ronald R. 1935-1983 Obituary 110
Edmonds, Vernon H. 1927- 37-40R
Edmonds, Walter D(umaux) 1903- CANR-2
Earlier sketch in CA 7-8R
See also SATA 1, 27
See also SAAS 4
See also DLB 9
See also CLC 35
Edmondson, Clifton Earl 1937- 102
Edmondson, G. C. 1922- CANR-26
Earlier sketches in CA 57-60, CANR-11
Edmondson, Garry C.
See Edmondson, G. C.
Edmondson, Wallace
See Ellison, Harlan
Edmonson, Harold A(rthur) 1937- 41-44R
Edmonson, Munro Sterling 1924- 33-36R
Edmund, Sean
See Pringle, Laurence P.
Edmunds, H(enry) Tudor 1897- 106
Edmunds, Malcolm 1938- 73-76
Edmunds, (Thomas) Murrell 1898- CANR-4
Earlier sketch in CA 4R
Edmunds, Simeon 1917- 17-18R
Edmunds, Stahrl W(illiam) 1917- 69-72
Edmundson, Bruce 1952- 126
Edom, Clifton C. 1907- 105
Edric, Robert
See Armitage, G(ary) E(dric)
Edrich, William J(ohn) 1916-1986
Obituary 120
Edsall, Florence S(mall) 1898(?)-1986
Obituary 119
Edsall, Marian (Stickney) 1920- 49-52
See also SATA 8
Edsall, Thomas Byrne 1941- 126
Edschmid, Kasimir
See Schmid, Eduard
See also DLB 56
Edson, Harold
See Hall, Asa Zadel
Edson, J(ohn) T(homas) 1928- CANR-12
Earlier sketch in CA 29-32R
Edson, Peter 1896-1977 Obituary 73-76
Edson, Russell 33-36R
See also CLC 13
Eduardi, Guillermo
See Edwards, William B(ennett)
Edwa
See Edwards, Bill
Edwardes, Allen
See Kinsley, D(aniel) A(llan)
Edwardes, Michael (F. H.) 1923- CANR-10
Earlier sketch in CA 57-60
Edwards, A. W. F. 1935- 73-76
Edwards, Al
See Nourse, Alan E(dward)
Edwards, Alexander
See Fleischer, Leonore
Edwards, Allen J(ack) 1926- 33-36R
Edwards, Allen L. 1914- CANR-10
Earlier sketch in CA 25-28R
Edwards, Anne 1927- CANR-13
Earlier sketch in CA 61-64
See also SATA 35
Edwards, Anne-Marie 1932- CANR-16
Earlier sketch in CA 85-88
Edwards, Anthony David 1936- 15-16R
Edwards, Audrey 1947- 81-84
See also SATA 31, 52
Edwards, Bertram
See Edwards, Herbert Charles
Edwards, Betty 1926- 105
Edwards, Bill 1929(?)-1987 Obituary 121
Edwards, Blake 1922- 81-84
Edwards, Bob
See Edwards, Robert Alan
Edwards, Bronwen Elizabeth
See Rose, Wendy
Edwards, Carl N(ormand) 1943- 57-60
Edwards, Cecile Pepin 1916- 5-6R
See also SATA 25
Edwards, Charles Edward 1930- 17-18R
Edwards, Charles Mundy, Jr. 1903-1985 45-48
Obituary 117
Edwards, Charlotte 29-32R
Edwards, Christine 1902- CAP-1
Earlier sketch in CA 19-20
Edwards, Clifford D(uane) 1934- 61-64
Edwards, Corwin D. 1901-1979 .... CANR-10
Obituary 85-88
Earlier sketch in CA 19-20R
Edwards, David C(harles) 1937- 41-44R
Edwards, David L(awrence) 1929- CANR-12
Earlier sketch in CA 7-8R
Edwards, David V(andeusen) 1941- 126
Brief entry 105
Edwards, Donald (Isaac) 1904- 65-68
Edwards, Donald Earl
See Harding, Donald Edward
Edwards, Dorothy 1903(?)-1934
Brief entry 122
Edwards, Dorothy 1914-1982 .... CANR-12
Obituary 107
Earlier sketch in CA 25-28R
See also SATA 4, 31
Edwards, Douglas 1917- 118
Brief entry 110
Edwards, Edgar O(wen) 1919- CANR-6
Earlier sketch in CA 2R
Edwards, Eli
See McKay, Festus Claudius
Edwards, Elizabeth
See Inderlied, Mary Elizabeth
Edwards, Elwyn Hartley 1927- CANR-8
Earlier sketch in CA 61-64
Edwards, F. E.
See Nolan, William F(rancis)
Edwards, Francis
See Brandon, Johnny
Edwards, Frank Allyn 1908-1967 .... CANR-1
Earlier sketch in CA 4R
Edwards, G(erald) B(asil) 1899-1976
Obituary 110
See also CLC 25
Edwards, Gawain
See Pendray, George Edward
Edwards, George 1914- 53-56
Edwards, George Charles III 1947- CANR-24
Earlier sketch in CA 107
Edwards, Gerald (Kenneth Savery) Hamilton
See Hamilton-Edwards, Gerald (Kenneth
Savery)
Edwards, Gillian (Mary) 1918- 25-28R
Edwards, Gunvor 107
See also SATA 32
Edwards, Gus 1939- 108
See also CLC 43
Edwards, Harry (Jr.) 1942- 111
Brief entry 109
Edwards, Harry
See Edwards, Henry James
Edwards, Harvey 1929- 25-28R
See also SATA 5
Edwards, Hazel (Eileen) 1945- 124
Edwards, Henry James 1893-1976 .... 13-14R
Obituary 122
Edwards, Herbert Charles 1912- 9-10R
See also SATA 12
Edwards, Hilton 1903- 65-68
Edwards, I(orwerth) E(iddon) S(tephen)
1909- CANR-7
Earlier sketch in CA 13-14R
Edwards, James Don(ald) 1926- CANR-4
Earlier sketch in CA 9-10R
Edwards, James Keith O'Neill 1920-1988
Obituary 126
Edwards, Jane Campbell 1932- 15-16R
See also SATA 10
Edwards, Jaroldeen 1932- 102
Edwards, Jerome E(arl) 1937- 37-40R
Edwards, Jimmy
See Edwards, James Keith O'Neill
Edwards, John 1943- 118
Edwards, John Milton
See Cook, William Wallace
Edwards, Jonathan 1703-1758 .... DLB-24
Edwards, Jonathan, Jr. 1745-1801 .... DLB-37
Edwards, Josephine Cunnington 1904- 15-16R
Edwards, Julia
See Stratemeyer, Edward L.
Edwards, Julia Spalding 1920- 37-40R
Edwards, Julie
See Andrews, Julie
Edwards, June
See Bhatia, Jamunadevi
Edwards, Junius 1929- DLB-33
Edwards, K(enneth) Morgan 1912- 5-6R
Edwards, Kate F(lournoy) 1877-1980 107

Edwards, Lee 1932- ... CANR-10
Earlier sketch in CA 25-28R
Edwards, Lee R. 1942- ... 124
Edwards, Linda Strauss 1948- ... 126
See also SATA 42, 49
Edwards, Lyford Paterson 1882-1984
Obituary ... 113
Edwards, Lynne 1943- ... 73-76
Edwards, Margaret (Alexander)
1902-1988 ... CAP-2
Obituary ... 125
Earlier sketch in CA 29-32
Edwards, Marie Babare ... 57-60
Edwards, Mark U(lin), Jr. 1946- ... CANR-10
Earlier sketch in CA 65-68
Edwards, Marvin L(ouis) 1915- ... 13-14R
Edwards, Max
See Benjamin, Claude (Max Edward Pohlman)
Edwards, Michael 1932- ... 85-88
Edwards, Michael 1938- ... CANR-22
Earlier sketch in CA 106
Edwards, Monica le Doux Newton 1912- ... 9-10R
See also SATA 12
Edwards, Nicky 1958- ... 122
Edwards, Norman
See White, Theodore Edwin and Carr, Terry (Gene)
Edwards, O(tis) C(arl), Jr. 1928- ... 53-56
Edwards, Oliver
See Haley, William (John)
Edwards, Olwen
See Gater, Dilys
Edwards, Owen Dudley 1938- ... CANR-7
Earlier sketch in CA 57-60
Edwards, P(rior) Max(imilian) H(emsley)
1914- ... 37-40R
Edwards, Page (Lawrence, Jr.) 1941- ... CANR-1
Earlier sketch in CA 45-48
Edwards, Paul 1923- ... 85-88
Edwards, Paul 1940- ... 123
Edwards, Paul Geoffrey 1926- ... 57-60
Edwards, Paul M(adison) 1933- ... 41-44R
Edwards, Peter (William) 1934- ... 109
Edwards, Philip 1923- ... CANR-12
Earlier sketch in CA 25-28R
Edwards, Phoebe
See Bloch, Barbara
Edwards, Phyllis Irene 1916-1984
Obituary ... 114
Edwards, R. M.
See Edwards, Roselyn
Edwards, (H. C.) Ralph 1894- ... CAP-1
Earlier sketch in CA 15-16
Edwards, Raoul D(urant) 1928-1987
Obituary ... 125
Edwards, Rem B(lanchard, Jr.) 1934- ... 37-40R
Edwards, Richard 1524-1566 ... DLB-62
Edwards, Richard Alan 1934- ... 69-72
Edwards, Richard C. 1944- ... CANR-2
Earlier sketch in CA 45-48
Edwards, Robert Alan 1947- ... 121
Edwards, Ron(ald George) 1930- ... 105
Edwards, Roselyn 1929- ... 25-28R
Edwards, Ruth Dudley
See Dudley Edwards, Ruth
Edwards, S. W.
See Sublette, Walter (Edwards)
Edwards, Sally (Cary) 1929- ... 25-28R
See also SATA 7
Edwards, Samuel
See Gerson, Noel Bertram
Edwards, Stephen
See Palestrant, Simon S.
Edwards, T(homas) Bentley 1906- ... CAP-2
Earlier sketch in CA 23-24
Edwards, Thomas R(obert) Jr. 1928- ... 5-6R
Edwards, Tilden Hampton, Jr. 1935- ... CANR-18
Earlier sketch in CA 102
Edwards, Verne E(rvie), Jr. 1924- ... 33-36R
Edwards, Ward 1927- ... 21-22R
Edwards, William 1896- ... CAP-1
Earlier sketch in CA 13-14
Edwards, William B(ennett) 1927- ... 5-6R
Edward VIII 1894-1972 Obituary ... 33-36R
Edwin, Brother B.
See Arnandez, Richard
Eekelaar, John M(ichael) 1942- ... 116
Eekman, Thomas 1923- ... 81-84
Eells, George 1922- ... CANR-14
Earlier sketch in CA 21-22R
Eells, Robert J(ames) 1944- ... 102
Efemey, Raymond (Frederick) 1928- ... 21-22R
Effinger, George Alec 1947- ... CANR-23
Earlier sketch in CA 37-40R
See also DLB 8
Efird, James M(ichael) 1932- ... CANR-14
Earlier sketch in CA 37-40R
Efron, Alexander 1897- ... CAP-2
Earlier sketch in CA 29-32
Efron, Arthur 1931- ... CANR-21
Earlier sketch in CA 69-72
Efron, Benjamin 1908- ... CANR-5
Earlier sketch in CA 5-6R
Efron, Edith Carol 1922- ... 102
Efron, Marina Ivanovna Tsvetaeva
See Tsvetaeva (Efron), Marina Ivanovna
Efron, Marshall 1938(?)- ... 126
Brief entry ... 112
Efros, Israel (Isaac) 1891-1981 ... 21-22R
Obituary ... 102
Efros, Susan Elyse 1947- ... 104
Efrot
See Efros, Israel (Isaac)
Egami, Tomi 1899- ... 61-64
Egan, Beresford Patrick 1905-1984
Obituary ... 111
Egan, David R(onald) 1943- ... 102
Egan, E(dward) W(elstead) 1922- ... CANR-9
Earlier sketch in CA 23-24R
See also SATA 35
Egan, Ferol 1923- ... 29-32R
Egan, Fred(erick Julian) 1905(?)-1986
Obituary ... 118
Egan, Gerard 1930- ... CANR-12
Earlier sketch in CA 29-32R
Egan, Harvey Daniel 1937- ... 113
Egan, John P. 1934- ... 110
Egan, Lesley
See Linington, (Barbara) Elizabeth
Egan, Lesley
See Linington, Elizabeth
Egan, Melinda A(nne) 1950- ... 102
Egan, Michael 1941- ... 45-48
Egan, Philip S(idney) 1920- ... 4R
Egan, Robert 1945- ... 77-80
Egbert, Donald Drew 1902-1973 ... CAP-2
Obituary ... 37-40R
Earlier sketch in CA 23-24
Egbert, Virginia Wylie
See Kilborne, Virginia Wylie
Egbuna, Obi B(enue Joseph) 1938- ... 102
Egejuru, Phanuel Akubueze ... 106
Egelhof, Joseph (Baird) 1919(?)-1980
Obituary ... 97-100
Eger, Jeffrey 1946- ... 125
Egermeier, Elsie E(milie) 1890- ... 5-6R
Egerton, Frank N(icholas) III 1936- ... 110
Egerton, George W(illiam) 1942- ... 85-88
Egerton, John (Walden) 1935- ... 85-88
Egerton, Lucy
See Malleson, Lucy Beatrice
Egg, Maria 1910- ... 29-32R
Egg-Benes, Maria
See Egg, Maria
Eggeling, Hans Friedrich 1878-1977 ... 4R
Obituary ... 73-76
Eggenberger, David 1918- ... 11-12R
See also SATA 6
Eggenschwiler, David 1936- ... 37-40R
Egger, M(aurice) David 1936- ... 57-60
Egger, Rowland (Andrews) 1908-1979 ... CANR-4
Earlier sketch in CA 5-6R
Eggers, J(ohn) Philip 1940- ... 33-36R
Eggers, William T. 1912- ... 29-32R
Eggert, Gerald G(ordon) 1926- ... 21-22R
Eggert, James Edward 1943- ... CANR-23
Earlier sketch in CA 107
Eggert, Jim
See Eggert, James Edward
Eggleston, Edward 1837-1902 Brief entry ... 111
See also SATA 27
See also DLB 12
Eggleston, Wilfrid 1901-1986 ... CANR-8
Obituary ... 119
Earlier sketch in CA 23-24R
Egielski, Richard 1952- ... SATA-11, 49
Egler, Frank E(dwin) 1911- ... 29-32R
Egleson, Janet F.
See Dunleavy, Janet Egleson
Egleton, Clive (Frederick) 1927- ... CANR-22
Earlier sketch in CA 103
Egoff, Sheila A. 1918- Brief entry ... 116
Egremont, Max 1948- ... 93-96
Eguchi, Shinichi 1914-1979 Obituary ... 85-88
Egypt, Ophelia Settle 1903-1984 ... 81-84
Obituary ... 112
See also SATA 16, 38
Ehle, John (Marsden, Jr.) 1925- ... 9-10R
See also CLC 27
Ehlers, Henry James 1907- ... 15-16R
Ehlert, Lois (Jane) 1934- ... SATA-35
Ehmann, James 1948- ... 109
Ehninger, Douglas W(agner)
1913-1979 ... CANR-4
Earlier sketch in CA 5-6R
Ehre, Edward 1905- ... 11-12R
Ehre, Milton 1933- ... 53-56
Ehrenberg, Miriam ... 124
Ehrenberg, Otto 1926- ... 124
Ehrenberg, Victor (Leopold) 1891-1976 ... CANR-4
Obituary ... 65-68
Earlier sketch in CA 7-8R
Ehrenbourg, Ilya (Grigoryevich)
See Ehrenburg, Ilya (Grigoryevich)
Ehrenburg, Ilya (Grigoryevich) 1891-1967 ... 102
Obituary ... 25-28R
See also CLC 18, 34
Ehrenburg, Ilyo (Grigoryevich)
See Ehrenburg, Ilya (Grigoryevich)
Ehrenfeld, David W(illiam) 1938- ... 81-84
Ehrenhalt, Alan 1947- ... 112
Ehrenpreis, Anne Henry 1927- ... 53-56
Ehrenpreis, Irvin 1920-1985 ... 121
Obituary ... 116
Brief entry ... 110
Ehrenreich, Barbara 1941- ... CANR-16
Earlier sketch in CA 73-76
Ehrenreich, Herman 1900(?)-1970
Obituary ... 104
Ehrenreich, John H. 1943- ... 125
Ehrensvaerd, Goesta (Carl Henrik)
1910- ... CANR-2
Earlier sketch in CA 49-52
Ehrenwald, Jan 1900-1988 ... CANR-2
Obituary ... 125
Earlier sketch in CA 49-52
Ehrenzweig, Albert A(rmin) 1906-1974 ... CAP-2
Earlier sketch in CA 29-32
Ehresmann, Donald L(ouis) 1937- ... 69-72
Ehresmann, Julia M. 1939- ... 33-36R
Ehret, Christopher 1941- ... 37-40R
Ehrhardt, Reinhold 1900- ... 29-32R
Ehrhart, W(illiam) D(aniel) 1948- ... CANR-7
Earlier sketch in CA 61-64
Ehricke, Krafft A(rnold) 1917-1984
Obituary ... 114
Ehrlich, Amy 1942- ... CANR-14
Earlier sketch in CA 37-40R
See also SATA 25
Ehrlich, Anne (Fitzhugh) Howland
1933- ... CANR-8
Earlier sketch in CA 61-64
Ehrlich, Arnold 1923- ... 33-36R
Ehrlich, Bettina Bauer 1903- ... CAP-1
Earlier sketch in CA 13-14
See also SATA 1
Ehrlich, Cyril 1925- ... 103
Ehrlich, Eugene H. 1922- ... CANR-5
Earlier sketch in CA 3R
Ehrlich, Everett M. 1950- ... 112
Ehrlich, Howard J. 1932- ... 19-20R
Ehrlich, Isaac 1938- ... 118
Ehrlich, Jack
See Ehrlich, John Gunther
Ehrlich, Jacob Wilburn 1900-1971
Obituary ... 33-36R
Ehrlich, Jake
See Ehrlich, Jacob Wilburn
Ehrlich, John Gunther 1930- ... CANR-4
Earlier sketch in CA 3R
Ehrlich, Leonard Harry 1924- ... 102
Ehrlich, Max 1909-1983 ... CANR-1
Obituary ... 115
Earlier sketch in CA 3R
Ehrlich, Nathaniel J(oseph) 1940- ... 53-56
Ehrlich, Otto Hild 1892-1979 Obituary ... 85-88
Ehrlich, Paul R(alph) 1932- ... CANR-8
Earlier sketch in CA 65-68
Ehrlich, Robert S. 1935- ... 23-24R
Ehrlich, Thomas 1934- ... 113
Ehrlich, Walter 1921- ... 53-56
Ehrlichman, John Daniel 1925- ... 65-68
Ehrman, John (Patrick William) 1920- ... CANR-26
Earlier sketches in CA 5-6R, CANR-4
Ehrman, Lee 1935- ... 69-72
Ehrmann, Herbert B(rutus) 1891-1970 ... CAP-2
Earlier sketch in CA 25-28
Ehrsam, Theodore George 1909- ... 45-48
Eibl-Eibesfeldt, Irenaeus 1928- ... CANR-3
Earlier sketch in CA 9-10R
Eibling, Harold Henry 1905-197(?) ... 37-40R
Eiby, George 1918- ... 53-56
Eich, Guenter 1907-1972 ... 111
Obituary ... 93-96
See also DLB 69
See also CLC 15
Eichelbaum, Stanley 1926- ... 73-76
Eichelberger, Clark M(ell) 1896-1980
Obituary ... 93-96
Eichelberger, Clayton L. 1925- ... 41-44R
Eichelberger, Rosa Kohler 1896- ... 102
Eichenbaum, Luise 1952- ... 126
Eichenberg, Fritz 1901- ... CANR-6
Earlier sketch in CA 57-60
See also SATA 9, 50
Eichenlaub, John Ellis 1922- ... CANR-4
Earlier sketch in CA 1R
Eicher, David J(ohn) 1961- ... 113
Eicher, (Ethel) Elizabeth ... 17-18R
Eicher, Joanne B(ubolz) 1930- ... 49-52
Eichhorn, David Max 1906- ... CAP-1
Earlier sketch in CA 11-12
Eichhorn, Werner 1899- ... 29-32R
Eichler, Margrit 1942- ... 107
See also SATA 35
Eichman, Mark 1949- ... 109
Eichner, Alfred S. 1937-1988 ... CANR-5
Obituary ... 124
Earlier sketch in CA 15-16R
Eichner, Hans 1921- ... CANR-19
Earlier sketches in CA 5-6R, CANR-4
Eichner, James A. 1927- ... 15-16R
See also SATA 4
Eichner, Maura 1915- ... CANR-14
Earlier sketch in CA 37-40R
Eichorn, Dorothy H(ansen) 1924- ... 49-52
Eickhoff, Andrew R(obert) 1924- ... 21-22R
Eicoff, Alvin Maurey 1921- ... 112
Eid, Leif 1908(?)-1976 Obituary ... 65-68
Eidelberg, Ludwig 1898-1970 ... CAP-1
Obituary ... 29-32R
Earlier sketch in CA 19-20
Eidelberg, Paul 1928- ... 23-24R
Eidenberg, Eugene 1939- ... 81-84
Eidesheim, Julie 1884-1972 Obituary ... 104
Eidsmoe, John 1945- ... 114
Eidsvik, Charles Vernon 1943- ... 101
Eidt, Robert C. 1923- ... 33-36R
Eiduson, Bernice T(abackman) 1921-1985 ... 1R
Eifert, Virginia (Louise) S(nider)
1911-1966 ... CANR-15
Earlier sketch in CA 1R
See also SATA 2
Eigen, Manfred 1927- ... 108
Eigen, Michael 1936- ... 115
Eigner, Edwin M(oss) 1931- ... 21-22R
Eigner, Larry
See Eigner, Laurence (Joel)
See also DLB 5
See also CLC 9
Eigner, Laurence (Joel) 1927- ... CANR-6
Earlier sketch in CA 9-10R
Eiland, Howard 1948- ... 111
Eiland, Murray L(ee) 1936- ... 85-88
Eilon, Samuel 1923- ... CANR-4
Earlier sketch in CA 7-8R
Eimer, D(ean) Robert 1927- ... 13-14R
Eimerl, Sarel (Henry) 1925- ... 21-22R
Einbond, Bernard Lionel 1937- ... 37-40R
Einhorn, Virginia Hilu
See Hilu, Virginia
Einsel, Mary E. 1929- ... 29-32R
Einsel, Naiad ... SATA-10
Einsel, Walter 1926- ... SATA-10
Einstein, Albert 1879-1955 Brief entry ... 121
Einstein, Albert 1947- ... 113
Brief entry ... 109
Einstein, Charles 1926- ... 65-68
Einstein, Elizabeth (Ann) 1939- ... 109
Einstein, Stanley 1934- ... CANR-4
Earlier sketch in CA 53-56
Einstoss, Ron 1930(?)-1977 Obituary ... 69-72
Einzig, Paul 1897-1973 ... CANR-5
Obituary ... 89-92
Earlier sketch in CA 11-12R
Einzig, Susan 1922- ... SATA-43
Eirelin, Glenn
See Evans, Glen
Eisdorfer, Carl 1930- ... 41-44R
Eisele, Albert A(lois) 1936- ... 41-44R
Eisele, Robert H. 1948- ... CANR-25
Earlier sketch in CA 108
Eiseley, Loren Corey 1907-1977 ... CANR-6
Obituary ... 73-76
Earlier sketch in CA 3R
See also CLC 7
Eiseman, Alberta 1925- ... 77-80
See also SATA 15
Eiseman, Alvord L. 1916- ... 112
Eisen, Carol G.
See Rinzler, Carol Eisen
Eisen, Jack 1925- ... 73-76
Eisenach, Eldon J(ohn) 1938- ... 106
Eisenberg, Azriel (Louis) 1903- ... CANR-10
Earlier sketch in CA 49-52
See also SATA 12
Eisenberg, Benjamin 1916-1984 Obituary ... 112
Eisenberg, Daniel Bruce 1946- ... CANR-6
Earlier sketch in CA 57-60
Eisenberg, Dennis (Harold) 1929- ... 25-28R
Eisenberg, Gerson G. 1909- ... 81-84
Eisenberg, Hershey H. 1927- ... 104
Eisenberg, Howard 1946- ... 101
Eisenberg, Larry 1919- ... 33-36R
Eisenberg, Lawrence B(enjamin) ... 77-80
Eisenberg, Lee 1946- ... CANR-9
Earlier sketch in CA 61-64
Eisenberg, Lisa 1949- ... 110
See also SATA 50
Eisenberg, Maurice 1902-1972 Obituary ... 37-40R
Eisenberg, Phyllis Rose 1924- ... 111
See also SATA 41
Eisenberg, Ralph 1930-1973 ... CANR-3
Obituary ... 45-48
Earlier sketch in CA 5-6R
Eisenberg, Ronald L(ee) 1945- ... CANR-13
Earlier sketch in CA 73-76
Eisenberger, Kenneth 1948- ... 81-84
Eisenbud, Jule 1908- ... 49-52
Eisendrath, Craig R. 1936- ... 49-52
Eisenhower, Dwight D(avid)
1890-1969 ... CANR-24
Earlier sketch in CA 65-68
Eisenhower, John S(heldon) D(oud)
1922- ... CANR-14
Earlier sketch in CA 33-36R
Eisenhower, Julie Nixon 1948- ... 114
Eisenhower, Milton S(tover) 1899-1985 ... 73-76
Obituary ... 116
Eisenman, Peter D(avid) 1932- ... 108
Eisenmenger, Robert Waltz 1926- ... 37-40R
Eisenschiml, Otto 1880-1963 ... 3R
Eisenson, Jon 1907- ... 19-20R
Eisenstadt, A(braham) S(eldin) 1920- ... CANR-4
Earlier sketch in CA 11-12R
Eisenstadt, Jill 1963- ... CLC-50
Eisenstadt, Shmuel N(oah) 1923- ... 25-28R
Eisenstaedt, Alfred 1898- ... 108
Eisenstat, Jane Sperry 1920- ... 4R
Eisenstein, Elizabeth L(ewisohn) 1923- ... 89-92
Eisenstein, Ira 1906- ... 21-22R
Eisenstein, James 1940- Brief entry ... 111
Eisenstein, Phyllis 1946- ... CANR-16
Earlier sketch in CA 85-88
Eisenstein, Sam(uel Abraham) 1932- ... CANR-16
Earlier sketch in CA 61-64
Eisenstein, Sergei (Mikhailovich)
1898-1948 Brief entry ... 114
Eiserer, Leonard Arnold 1948- ... 73-76
Eisinger, Chester E(manuel) 1915- ... 23-24R
Eisinger, Peter K(endall) 1942- ... 69-72
Eisler, Colin (Tobias) 1931- ... 85-88
Eisler, Frieda Goldman
See Goldman-Eisler, Frieda
Eisler, Georg 1928- Brief entry ... 106
Eisler, George B. 1892(?)-1983 Obituary ... 111
Eisler, Hanns 1898-1962 Obituary ... 116
Eisler, Lawrence 1920- ... 122
Eisler, Paul (Erich) 1922-1978 ... 61-64
Obituary ... 125
Eisler, Riane Tennenhaus 1931- ... 73-76
Eisman, Hy 1927- ... 65-68
Eisman, Mark 1948- ... 108
Eismann, Bernard N(orman) 1933- ... 4R
Eisner, Betty Grover 1915- ... 29-32R
Eisner, Elliot W(ayne) 1933- ... 123
Brief entry ... 118
Eisner, Gisela (Spanglet) 1925- ... CAP-1
Earlier sketch in CA 9-10
Eisner, Kurt 1867-1919 ... DLB-66
Eisner, Lotte (Henriette) 1896-1983 ... CANR-14
Obituary ... 111
Earlier sketch in CA 45-48
Eisner, Robert 1922- ... 107
Eisner, Sigmund 1920- ... 124

Eisner, Simon
See Kornbluth, C(yril) M.
Eisner, Victor 1921- ... 53-56
Eisner, Vivienne
See Margolis, Vivienne
Eisner, Will(iam Erwin) 1917- ... 108
See also SATA 31
Eiss, Harry Edwin 1950- ... 124
Eissenstat, Bernard W. 1927- ... 45-48
Eister, Allan W(ardell) 1915-1979 ... CANR-2
Earlier sketch in CA 45-48
Eiteman, David (Kurt) 1930- ... 45-48
Eiteman, Wilford J(ohn) 1902- ... CANR-4
Earlier sketch in CA 1R
Eitinger, Leo S(hua) 1912- ... CANR-16
Earlier sketch in CA 89-92
Eitington, Julius E. 1918- ... 120
Eitner, Lorenz E.A. 1919- ... CANR-5
Earlier sketch in CA 1R
Eitzen, Allan 1928- ... SATA-9
Eitzen, D(avid) Stanley 1934- ... CANR-19
Earlier sketches in CA 53-56, CANR-4
Eitzen, Ruth (Carper) 1924- ... 41-44R
See also SATA 9
Ekblaw, Sidney E(verette) 1903- ... 37-40R
Ekdahl, Janis (Kay) 1946- Brief entry ... 112
Ekeblad, Frederick A(lfred) 1917- ... 5-6R
Ekeh, Peter P(almer) 1937- ... 102
Ekeloef, (Bengt) Gunnar 1907-1968 ... 123
Obituary ... 25-28R
See also CLC 27
Ekelof, (Bengt) Gunnar
See Ekeloef, (Bengt) Gunnar
See also CLC 27
Ekins, Paul (Whitfield) 1950- ... 123
Ekirch, A(rthur) Roger 1950- ... 109
Ekirch, Arthur A., Jr. 1915- ... CANR-2
Earlier sketch in CA 7-8R
Ekker, Charles 1930- ... 37-40R
Eklund, Gordon (Stewart) 1945- ... CANR-24
Earlier sketch in CA 33-36R
See also DLBY 83
Eklund, Jane Mary
See Ball, Jane Eklund
Ekman, Paul 1934- ... CANR-14
Earlier sketch in CA 37-40R
Ekman, Rosalind 1933- ... 33-36R
Ekola, Giles C(hester) 1927- ... 17-18R
Ekstein, Rudolf 1912- ... CANR-4
Earlier sketch in CA 5-6R
Eksteins, Modris 1943- ... 77-80
Ekvall, Robert B(rainerd) 1898- ... CANR-5
Earlier sketch in CA 1R
Ekwall, Eldon E(dward) 1933- ... CANR-12
Earlier sketch in CA 29-32R
Ekwensi, C. O. D.
See Ekwensi, Cyprian (Odiatu Duaka)
Ekwensi, Cyprian (Odiatu Duaka) 1921- ... CANR-18
Earlier sketch in CA 29-32R
See also BW
See also CLC 4
Ela, Jonathan P(ell) 1945- ... 81-84
Elaine
See Leverson, Ada
See also TCLC 18
Elam, Richard M(ace, Jr.) 1920- ... 61-64
See also SATA 9
El-Aref, Aref ?-1973 Obituary ... 41-44R
Elashoff, Janet Dixon 1942- ... 61-64
Elath, Eliahu 1903- ... 13-14R
El-Ayouty, Yassin 1928- ... CANR-14
Earlier sketch in CA 29-32R
Elazar, Daniel J(udah) 1934- ... CANR-13
Earlier sketch in CA 21-22R
El-Baz, Farouk 1938- ... CANR-26
Earlier sketches in CA 25-28R, CANR-10
Elbert, Edmund J(oseph) 1923- ... 37-40R
Elbert, George A. 1911- ... 61-64
Elbert, Samuel H(oyt) 1907- ... CANR-5
Earlier sketch in CA 1R
Elbert, Virginie Fowler 1912- ... CANR-8
Earlier sketch in CA 61-64
Elbin, Paul Nowell 1905- ... 69-72
Elbing, Alvar O(liver), Jr. 1928- ... 21-22R
Elbing, Carol J(eppson) 1930- ... 21-22R
Elbogen, Paul 1894- ... 5-6R
Elborn, Geoffrey 1950- ... 109
Elbow, Peter (Henry) 1935- ... CANR-12
Earlier sketch in CA 65-68
Elbrecht, Paul G. 1921- ... 17-18R
El Bundukhari
See Dent, Anthony Austen
Elcock, Howard J(ames) 1942- ... CANR-12
Earlier sketch in CA 29-32R
El Crummo
See Crumb, R(obert)
Eldefonso, Edward 1933- ... CANR-14
Earlier sketch in CA 23-24R
Elder, Betty Doak 1938- ... 112
Elder, Ellen Rozanne 1940- ... 111
Elder, Gary 1939- ... 73-76
Elder, Glen(nard) H(oll), Jr. 1934- ... CANR-3
Earlier sketch in CA 49-52
Elder, John William 1933- ... 111
Elder, Karl 1948- ... 77-80
Elder, Leon
See Young, Noel
Elder, Lonne III 1931- ... CANR-25
Earlier sketch in CA 81-84
See also BW
See also DLB 7, 38, 44
Elder, Mark 1935- ... CANR-2
Earlier sketch in CA 49-52
Elder, Michael (Aiken) 1931- ... 33-36R
Elder, Rob(ert Laurie) 1938- ... 125
Elder, Robert E(llsworth) 1915- ... 1R
Elder, Shirley (A.) 1931- Brief entry ... 118
Eldersveld, Samuel James 1917- ... 111
Eldjarn, Kristjan (Thorarinsson) 1916-1982 Obituary ... 110
Eldred, Vince 1924- ... 69-72
Eldredge, H(anford) Wentworth 1909- ... 41-44R
Eldredge, Laurence H(oward) 1902- ... CAP-2
Earlier sketch in CA 25-28
Eldridge, Colin Clifford 1942- ... 107
Eldridge, Frank R. 1889(?)-1976
Obituary ... 69-72
Eldridge, J(ohn) E. T. 1936- ... CANR-11
Earlier sketch in CA 25-28R
Eldridge, Marian (Favel Clair) 1936- ... 118
Eldridge, Paul 1888- ... 9-10R
Eldridge, Retha Hazel (Giles) 1910- ... CAP-1
Earlier sketch in CA 13-14
Eleanor, Sister Joseph ... 25-28R
Elegant, Robert S(ampson) 1928- ... CANR-1
Earlier sketch in CA 4R
Elek, Paul 1906(?)-1976 Obituary ... 69-72
el-Erian, Abdullah Ali 1920-1981 Obituary ... 108
Elethea, Abba
See Thompson, James W.
Elevitch, M(orton) D. 1925- ... CANR-2
Earlier sketch in CA 49-52
Eley, Lynn W. 1925- ... CANR-16
Earlier sketch in CA 25-28R
Elfenbein, Julien 1897-1983 ... CANR-5
Obituary ... 109
Earlier sketch in CA 2R
Elfman, Blossom 1925- ... CANR-17
Earlier sketches in CA 45-48, CANR-2
See also SATA 8
Elford, Homer J. R. 1912- ... CANR-9
Earlier sketch in CA 23-24R
Elgar, Edward (William) 1857-1934
Brief entry ... 116
Elgar, Frank 1899- ... 102
Elgin, Kathleen 1923- ... 25-28R
See also SATA 39
Elgin, Mary
See Stewart, Dorothy Mary
Elgin, (Patricia Anne) Suzette Haden 1936- ... CANR-8
Earlier sketch in CA 61-64
Elgood, Robert (Francis Willard) 1948- ... 125
el Hajjam, Mohammed ben Chaib 1940- ... CANR-17
Earlier sketch in CA 97-100
Elia
See Lamb, Charles
Eliach, Yaffa 1935- ... 110
Eliade, Mircea 1907-1986 ... 65-68
Obituary ... 119
See also CLC 19
Elias, Albert J. 1920- ... 81-84
Elias, C(laude) E(dward), Jr. 1924- ... 13-14R
Elias, Christopher 1925- ... 33-36R
Elias, Eileen
See Davies, Eileen Winifred
Elias, Horace J(ay) 1910- ... CANR-16
Earlier sketch in CA 89-92
Elias, John L(awrence) 1933- ... CANR-25
Earlier sketch in CA 69-72
Elias, Robert H(enry) 1914- ... 61-64
Elias, Taslim Olawale 1914- ... CANR-21
Earlier sketches in CA 13-14R, CANR-6
Elias, Thomas S. 1942- ... 114
Eliason, Joyce 1934- ... 77-80
Eliav, Arie L(ova) 1921- ... CANR-11
Earlier sketch in CA 69-72
Elicker, Charles W. 1951-1978 Obituary ... 115
Elieff, Deanne D(esmond) 1926- ... 113
Elinson, Jack 1917- ... CANR-20
Earlier sketches in CA 45-48, CANR-2
Elioseff, Lee Andrew 1933- ... 17-18R
Eliot, Alexander 1919- ... CANR-1
Earlier sketch in CA 49-52
Eliot, Anne
See Cole, Lois Dwight
Eliot, Dan
See Silverberg, Robert
Eliot, George 1819-1880 ... DLB-21, 35, 55
Eliot, George Fielding 1894-1971
Obituary ... 29-32R
Eliot, John 1604-1690 ... DLB-24
Eliot, Sonny 1926- ... 81-84
Eliot, T(homas) S(tearns) 1888-1965 ... 7-8R
Obituary ... 25-28R
See also DLB 7, 10, 45, 63
See also CLC 1, 2, 3, 6, 9, 10, 13, 15, 24, 34, 41
Eliot, Thomas H(opkinson) 1907- ... 89-92
Eliot Hurst, M(ichael) E(liot) 1938- ... 57-60
Eliovson, Sima (Benveniste) 1919- ... CANR-20
Earlier sketches in CA 13-14R, CANR-5
Elis, Islwyn Ffowc 1924- ... 93-96
Elisabeth (Ottilie Luise), Queen (Pauline) 1843-1916 Brief entry ... 123
Eliscu, Frank 1912- ... 57-60
Elisofon, Eliot 1911-1973 Obituary ... 41-44R
See also SATA 21
Elison, George 1937- ... 53-56
Elizabeth Marie, Sister 1914- ... 11-12R
Elkholy, Abdo A. 1925- ... 23-24R
Elkin, Benjamin 1911- ... CANR-4
Earlier sketch in CA 4R
See also SATA 3
Elkin, Frederick 1918- ... 41-44R
Elkin, H. V.
See Hinkle, Vernon
Elkin, Judith Laikin 1928- ... CANR-19
Earlier sketches in CA 53-56, CANR-4
Elkin, Stanley L(awrence) 1930- ... CANR-8
Earlier sketch in CA 11-12R
See also DLB 2, 28
See also DLBY 80
See also CLC 4, 6, 9, 14, 27
Elkin, Stephen L(loyd) 1941- ... 93-96
Elkind, David 1931- ... CANR-1
Earlier sketch in CA 45-48
Elkins, Aaron J. 1935- ... 126
Elkins, Dov Peretz 1937- ... CANR-12
Earlier sketch in CA 29-32R
See also SATA 5
Elkins, Ella Ruth 1929- ... 25-28R
Elkins, Stanley Maurice 1925- ... 102
Elkins, T(homas) H(enry) 1926-
Brief entry ... 111
Elkins, William R. 1926- ... 33-36R
Elkon, Juliette
See Elkon-Hamelecourt, Juliette
Elkon-Hamelecourt, Juliette 1912- ... 57-60
Elkouri, Frank 1921- ... 69-72
Elkus, Jonathan Britton 1931- ... 111
Ellacott, S(amuel) E(rnest) 1911- ... CANR-3
Earlier sketch in CA 7-8R
See also SATA 19
Elledge, Jim 1950- ... CANR-19
Earlier sketch in CA 102
Elledge, Scott ... CLC-34
Elledge, W(aymon) Paul 1938- ... 25-28R
Ellen, Barbara 1938- ... 7-8R
Ellenberger, Henri F(rederic) 1905- ... CAP-2
Earlier sketch in CA 29-32
Ellenbogen, Eileen 1917- ... 104
Ellender, Raphael 1906-1972 Obituary ... 37-40R
Ellens, J(ay) Harold 1932- ... CANR-7
Earlier sketch in CA 57-60
Ellenson, Gene 1921- ... 57-60
Eller, John 1935- ... 105
Eller, Ronald D 1948- ... 110
Eller, Scott
See Holinger, William (Jaques)
Eller, Vernard (Marion) 1927- ... CANR-24
Earlier sketches in CA 23-24R, CANR-9
Eller, William 1921- ... 77-80
Ellerbeck, Rosemary (Anne L'Estrange) ... CANR-24
Earlier sketch in CA 106
Ellerbee, Linda 1944- ... 115
Brief entry ... 110
Ellerman, Annie Winifred 1894-1983 ... 104
Obituary ... 108
Ellery, John Blaise 1920- ... 9-10R
Ellet, Elizabeth F. 1818(?)-1877 ... DLB-30
Ellett, Marcella H. 1931- ... 23-24R
Ellfeldt, Lois 1910- ... 33-36R
Ellicott, V. L.
See Ellicott, Valcoulon MeMoyne
Ellicott, Valcoulon MeMoyne 1893-1983
Obituary ... 109
Ellin, E(lizabeth) M(uriel) 1905- ... CAP-2
Earlier sketch in CA 29-32
Ellin, Stanley (Bernard) 1916-1986 ... CANR-4
Obituary ... 119
Earlier sketch in CA 3R
Elling, Karl A(lwin) 1935- ... 25-28R
Elling, Ray H. 1929- ... 33-36R
Ellingsworth, Huber W. 1928- ... CANR-10
Earlier sketch in CA 21-22R
Ellington, Duke
See Ellington, Edward Kennedy
Ellington, Edward Kennedy 1899-1974 ... 97-100
Obituary ... 49-52
Ellington, James W(esley) 1927- ... 37-40R
Ellington, Mercer (Kennedy) 1919-
Brief entry ... 113
Ellington, Richard 1915(?)-1980 Obituary ... 102
Ellinwood, Leonard Webster 1905- ... 4R
Elliot, Asa
See Blinder, Elliot
Elliot, Daniel
See Feldman, Leonard
Elliot, Edith M(arie Farmer) 1912- ... 23-24R
Elliot, Elisabeth (Howard) 1926- ... CANR-6
Earlier sketch in CA 7-8R
Elliot, Geraldine
See Bingham, Evangeline M(arguerite) L(adys) (Elliot)
Elliot, Ian 1925- ... 69-72
Elliot, Jeffrey M. 1947- ... CANR-24
Earlier sketch in CA 106
Elliot, John 1898-1988 Obituary ... 126
Elliott, Alan C(urtis) 1952- ... CANR-18
Earlier sketch in CA 102
Elliott, Allan
See Elliott, K(enneth) A(llan) C(aldwell)
Elliott, Aubrey (George) 1917- ... 93-96
Elliott, Bob 1923- Brief entry ... 109
Elliott, Brian (Robinson) 1910- ... 25-28R
Elliott, Bruce (Walter Gardner Lively Stacy) 1915(?)-1973 Obituary ... 41-44R
Elliott, C(larence) Orville 1913- ... 33-36R
Elliott, Chip
See Elliott, E(scalus) E(mmert) III
Elliott, David W. 1939- ... 45-48
Elliott, Don
See Silverberg, Robert
Elliott, Donald 1928- ... 69-72
Elliott, Douglas B(yron) 1947- ... 113
Elliott, E(scalus) E(mmert) III 1945- ... 29-32R
Elliott, Emory 1942- ... CANR-23
Earlier sketch in CA 69-72
Elliott, Errol T(homas) 1894- ... 69-72
Elliott, George 1923- ... DLB-68
Elliott, George P(aul) 1918-1980 ... CANR-2
Obituary ... 97-100
Earlier sketch in CA 1R
See also CLC 2
Elliott, Harley 1940- ... CANR-4
Earlier sketch in CA 49-52
Elliott, Hugh (Francis Ivo) 1913-
Brief entry ... 112
Elliott, James Francis 1914-1981 Obituary ... 110
Elliott, Jan Walter 1939- ... 37-40R
Elliott, Janice 1931- ... CANR-8
Earlier sketch in CA 15-16R
See also DLB 14
See also CLC 47
Elliott, John 1938- ... 25-28R
Elliott, John E(d) 1931- ... CANR-5
Earlier sketch in CA 3R
Elliott, John H(uxtable) 1930- ... CANR-3
Earlier sketch in CA 7-8R
Elliott, John H(all) 1935- ... 126
Brief entry ... 113
Elliott, John R., Jr. 1937- ... 25-28R
Elliott, Jumbo
See Elliott, James Francis
Elliott, K(enneth) A(llan) C(aldwell) 1903-1986 ... 108
Obituary ... 119
Elliott, Kit 1936- ... 29-32R
Elliott, Lawrence 1924- ... CANR-21
Earlier sketches in CA 7-8R, CANR-3
Elliott, Leonard M. 1902- ... CAP-1
Earlier sketch in CA 13-14
Elliott, Lesley 1905- ... CANR-14
Earlier sketch in CA 77-80
Elliott, Malissa Childs 1929(?)-1979 ... 101
Obituary ... 85-88
Elliott, Mark Rowe 1947- ... CANR-24
Earlier sketch in CA 107
Elliott, Neil 1939- ... 25-28R
Elliott, Osborn 1924- ... CANR-12
Earlier sketch in CA 69-72
Elliott, P(hilip) R(oss) C(ourtney) 1943(?)-1983 Obituary ... 110
Elliott, Ralph H. 1925- ... CANR-2
Earlier sketch in CA 3R
Elliott, Raymond Pruitt 1904- ... 17-18R
Elliott, Richard V. 1934- ... 33-36R
Elliott, Robert
See Garfinkel, Bernard Max
Elliott, Robert B.
See Elliott, Bob
Elliott, Robert C(arl) 1914-1981 ... CANR-21
Earlier sketch in CA 1R
Elliott, Roberta ... 97-100
Elliott, Russell Richard 1912- ... 69-72
Elliott, Sarah M(cCarn) 1930- ... 41-44R
See also SATA 14
Elliott, Sheldon D(ouglass) 1906-1972
Obituary ... 33-36R
Elliott, Spencer H(ayward) 1883-1967 ... CAP-1
Earlier sketch in CA 11-12
Elliott, Sumner Locke 1917- ... CANR-21
Earlier sketches in CA 7-8R, CANR-2
See also CLC 38
Elliott, Susan (Anthony) 1947- ... 104
Elliott, Thomas Joseph 1941- ... 49-52
Elliott, Ward E(dward) Y(andell) 1937- ... 85-88
Elliott, William Douglas 1938- ... CANR-9
Earlier sketch in CA 65-68
Elliott, William III 1788-1863 ... DLB-3
Elliott, William M(arion), Jr. 1903- ... CAP-1
Earlier sketch in CA 9-10
Elliott, William Yandell 1896-1979
Obituary ... 85-88
Ellis, A. E. ... CLC-7
Ellis, Albert 1913- ... CANR-17
Earlier sketches in CA 2R, CANR-2
Ellis, Alec (Charles Owen) 1932- ... CANR-1
Earlier sketch in CA 45-48
Ellis, Alice Thomas
See Haycraft, Anna
See also CLC 40
Ellis, (Mary) Amabel (Nassau Strachey) Williams
See Williams-Ellis, (Mary) Amabel (Nassau Strachey)
Ellis, Amanda M. 1898-1969 ... CAP-2
Earlier sketch in CA 23-24
Ellis, Anyon
See Rowland-Entwistle, (Arthur) Theodore (Henry)
Ellis, Audrey ... CANR-10
Earlier sketch in CA 65-68
Ellis, B(yron) Robert 1940- ... 53-56
Ellis, Bret Easton 1964- ... 123
Brief entry ... 118
See also CLC 39
Ellis, Brooks (Fleming) 1897-1976
Obituary ... 65-68
Ellis, C(uthbert) Hamilton 1909- ... 13-14R
Ellis, Carl F., Jr. 1946- ... 121
Ellis, Carolyn Sue 1950- ... 122
Ellis, Charles D(aniel) 1937- Brief entry ... 115
Ellis, Charles Drummond 1895-1980
Obituary ... 105
Ellis, Charles Howard 1895- ... CAP-1
Earlier sketch in CA 13-14
Ellis, Clyde T(aylor) 1908- ... CAP-2
Earlier sketch in CA 23-24
Ellis, Dan C. 1949- ... 125
Ellis, David Maldwyn 1914- ... 9-10R
Ellis, Dock (Phillip, Jr.) 1945- Brief entry ... 111
Ellis, E. S.
See Ellis, Edward S(ylvester)
Ellis, Edward Robb 1911- ... 25-28R
Ellis, Edward S(ylvester) 1840-1916
Brief entry ... 122
See also YABC 1
See also DLB 42

INDEX

Ellis, Ella Thorp 1928- CANR-2
Earlier sketch in CA 49-52
See also SATA 7
Ellis, Elma I(srael) 1918- 33-36R
Ellis, Florence Hawley 1906- 61-64
Ellis, (J.) Frank(lyn) 1904(?)-1976
Obituary 65-68
Ellis, Frank Hale 1916- 73-76
Ellis, Frank K. 1933- 25-28R
Ellis, Harry Bearse 1921- CANR-2
Earlier sketch in CA 1R
See also SATA 9
Ellis, (Henry) Havelock 1859-1939
Brief entry 109
See also TCLC 14
Ellis, Helen E. (Oickle) 1926- 120
Ellis, Henry C(arlton) 1927- CANR-17
Earlier sketch in CA 97-100
Ellis, Herbert
See Wilson, Lionel
Ellis, Hilda Roderick
See Davidson, H(ilda) R(oderick) Ellis
Ellis, Howard S(ylvester) 1898- 49-52
Ellis, Howard W(oodrow) 1914- CANR-17
Earlier sketch in CA 4R
Ellis, Humphry F(rancis) 1907- 7-8R
Ellis, J(ames) H(ervey) S(tewart) 1893- CAP-2
Earlier sketch in CA 23-24
Ellis, J(ohn) R(ichard) 1938- 85-88
Ellis, Jack C(lare) 1922- 89-92
Ellis, Jack D. 1941- 121
Ellis, James 1935- 37-40R
Ellis, Jody 1925- 57-60
Ellis, John H. 1931- 125
Ellis, John M(artin) 1936- CANR-3
Earlier sketch in CA 49-52
Ellis, John Marion 1917- 49-52
Ellis, John O(liver) 1917- 85-88
Ellis, John Tracy 1905- CANR-5
Earlier sketch in CA 3R
Ellis, Joseph J(ohn) 1943- 53-56
Ellis, Joyce K. (Eileen) 1950- 116
Ellis, Julie 1933- Brief entry 111
Ellis, Kathy
See Bentley, Margaret
Ellis, Keith Stanley 1927- 102
Ellis, L(ewis) Ethan 1898-1977 CANR-4
Earlier sketch in CA 5-6R
Ellis, Landon
See Ellison, Harlan
Ellis, Leigh 1959- 105
Ellis, Leo R(oy) 1909- 11-12R
Ellis, M(adeleine) B(lanche) 1915- 69-72
Ellis, M(arion) LeRoy 1928- 37-40R
Ellis, Marc H. 1952- CANR-24
Earlier sketch in CA 107
Ellis, Mark Karl 1945- 103
Ellis, Mary Jackson 1916- CANR-17
Earlier sketch in CA 4R
Ellis, Mary Leith 1921- 23-24R
Ellis, Mel(vin Richard) 1912-1984 13-14R
Obituary 113
See also SATA 7, 39
Ellis, Norman R. 1924- 13-14R
Ellis, Olivia
See Wintle, Anne
Ellis, Peter Berresford 1943- CANR-21
Earlier sketch in CA 81-84
Ellis, Peter F(rancis) 1921- 115
Ellis, Ray C. 1898- CAP-2
Earlier sketch in CA 21-22
Ellis, Richard 1938- 104
Ellis, Richard E(manuel) 1937- 61-64
Ellis, Richard N(athaniel) 1939- 33-36R
Ellis, Richard White Bernard 1902- CAP-1
Earlier sketch in CA 15-16
Ellis, Roger (Melville) 1943- 126
Ellis, Ron(ald Walter) 1941- 77-80
Ellis, (Christopher) Royston (George)
1941- 7-8R
Ellis, Sarah 1952- 123
Ellis, Scott
See Schorr, Mark
Ellis, Ulrich Ruegg 1904-1981 Obituary 108
Ellis, Wesley
See Wallmann, Jeffrey M(iner)
Ellis, William 1918- 49-52
Ellis, William Donohue 1918- 49-52
Ellison, Alfred 1916- 1R
Ellison, Craig W(illiam) 1944- CANR-6
Earlier sketch in CA 57-60
Ellison, Fred P(ittman) 1922- Brief entry 113
Ellison, George R. 1907(?)-1983 Obituary 110
Ellison, Gerald Alexander 1910- CAP-1
Earlier sketch in CA 13-14
Ellison, Glenn 1911- 89-92
Ellison, Glenn "Tiger"
See Ellison, Glenn
Ellison, H(enry) L(eopold) 1903- CANR-6
Earlier sketch in CA 7-8R
Ellison, Harlan 1934- CANR-5
Earlier sketch in CA 5-6R
See also DLB 8
See also CLC 1, 13, 42
Ellison, Henry 1931-1965 7-8R
Ellison, Herbert J(ay) 1929- 15-16R
Ellison, James E. 1927- 15-16R
Ellison, James Whitfield 1929- CANR-1
Earlier sketch in CA 3R
Ellison, Jerome 1907-1981 29-32R
Obituary 104
Ellison, John Malcus 1889-1979 CANR-25
Earlier sketch in CA 4R
Ellison, Katherine (White) 1941- 101
Ellison, Lucile Watkins 1907(?)-1979 109
Obituary 93-96
See also SATA 22, 50
Ellison, Max 1914-1985 57-60
Obituary 116
See also AITN 1
Ellison, Ralph (Waldo) 1914- CANR-24
Earlier sketch in CA 11-12R
See also BW
See also DLB 2, 76
See also CDALB 1941-1968
See also CLC 1, 3, 11
Ellison, Randall Erskine 1904-1984
Obituary 113
Ellison, Reuben Young 1907- 15-16R
Ellison, Virginia H(owell) 1910- 33-36R
See also SATA 4
Ellison, William McLaren 1919(?)-1978
Obituary 81-84
Elliston, Frederick Allen 1944- 105
Elliston, Thomas R(alph) 1919-1977
Obituary 73-76
Elliston, Valerie Mae (Watkinson) 1929- 9-10R
Ellithorpe, Harold (Earle) 1925- 77-80
Ellman, Michael 1942- 45-48
Ellmann, Richard (David) 1918-1987 CANR-2
Obituary 122
Earlier sketch in CA 1R
See also DLBY 87
See also CLC 50
Ellsberg, Daniel 1931- 69-72
Ellsberg, Edward 1891- 7-8R
See also SATA 7
Ellsworth, L(ida) E(lizabeth) 1948- 118
Ellsworth, P(aul) T(heodore) 1897- 17-18R
Ellsworth, Ralph Eugene 1907- CANR-2
Earlier sketch in CA 3R
Ellsworth, S(amuel) George 1916- 45-48
Ellsworth, Sallie Bingham 1937- CANR-18
Earlier sketch in CA 1R
Ellsworth, Scott 1954- 109
Ellul, Jacques 1912- 81-84
Ellvinger, Barbara Anne Price
See Price, Barbara Anne Ellvinger
Ellwood, Edith E(lizabeth)
See Muesing-Ellwood, Edith E(lizabeth)
Ellwood, Gracia-Fay 1938- 29-32R
Ellwood, Robert S(cott), Jr. 1933- CANR-14
Earlier sketch in CA 41-44R
El Mallakh, Ragaei (William) 1925- 112
Elman, Richard 1934- 19-20R
See also CAAS 3
See also CLC 19
Elman, Robert 1930- CANR-3
Earlier sketch in CA 45-48
Elmandjra, Mahdi 1933- 89-92
Elmblad, Mary (B.) 1927- 108
El-Meligi, A(bdel) Moneim 1923- 19-20R
Elmen, Paul H. 1913- 89-92
Elmendorf, Mary Lindsay 1917- 57-60
Elmer, Carlos Hall 1920- 102
Elmer, Gary W. 1941- 122
Elmer, Irene (Elizabeth) 1937- 4R
El-Messidi, Kathy Groehn 1946- 57-60
Elmhirst, Leonard Knight 1893-1974
Obituary 115
Elmore, Ernest Carpenter 1901-1957
Brief entry 114
Elmore, (Carolyn) Patricia 1933- 114
See also SATA 35, 38
Elms, Alan C(linton) 1938- 69-72
Elmslie, Kenward 1929- CANR-25
Earlier sketches in CA 21-22R, CANR-9
Elmslie, William Alexander Leslie
1885-1965 CAP-1
Earlier sketch in CA 13-14
Elmstrom, George P. 1925- 5-6R
El Muhajir 1944- CANR-26
Earlier sketch in CA 49-52
See also BW
Elon, Amos 1926- Brief entry 121
Elovitz, Mark H(arvey) 1938- 69-72
Elphick, Richard Hall 1943- 112
Elphinstone, Francis
See Powell-Smith, Vincent (Walter Francis)
Elphinstone, Murgatroyd
See Kahler, Hugh (Torbert) MacNair
Elrick, George S(eefurth) 1921- 112
Elron
See Hubbard, L(afayette) Ron(ald)
el Ropo, Smokestack
See Perry, Charles
El Saadawi, Nawal 1931- 118
El Saffar, Ruth (Ann) 1941- 69-72
Elsasser, Albert B(ertrand) 1918- CANR-22
Earlier sketch in CA 69-72
Elsasser, Glen Robert 1935- 65-68
Elsberry, Terence 1943- 45-48
Elsbree, Langdon 1929- 33-36R
Else, Gerald Frank 1908-1982 61-64
Obituary 107
Elsea, Janet G(ayle) 1942- 119
Elsen, Albert E(dward) 1927- CANR-26
Earlier sketches in CA 7-8R, CANR-11
El-Shabazz, El Hajj Malik
See Little, Malcolm
El-Shabazz, El-Hajj Malik
See Little, Malcolm
Elshtain, Jean Bethke 1941- 106
Elsmere, Jane Shaffer 1932- 37-40R
Elsner, Gisela 1937- 9-10R
Elsner, Henry, Jr. 1930- 21-22R
Elsom, John Edward 1934- 65-68
Elson, Edward L(ee) R(oy) 1906- CANR-3
Earlier sketch in CA 5-6R
Elson, Lawrence M(cClellan) 1935- 53-56
Elson, R. N.
See Nelson, R(adell) Faraday
Elson, Robert T(ruscott) 1906-1987 77-80
Obituary 121
Elson, Ruth Miller 1917- 15-16R
Elspeth
See Bragdon, Elspeth MacDuffie
Elstar, Dow
See Gallun, Raymond Z(inke)
Elstob, Peter 1915- CANR-1
Earlier sketch in CA 3R
Elston, Allan Vaughan 1887-1976 CANR-3
Earlier sketch in CA 3R
Elston, Gene 1922- 33-36R
Elston, Robert 1934-1987 Obituary 124
Elston, Wilbur E(vans) 1913- Brief entry 112
Elstun, Esther N(ies) 1935- 117
Elsy, (Winifred) Mary 93-96
Elting, John R(obert) 1911- 112
Elting, Mary 1906- CANR-19
Earlier sketches in CA 9-10R, CANR-4
See also SATA 2
Elton, Edwin J(oel) 1939- 53-56
Elton, Geoffrey R(udolph) 1921- CANR-3
Earlier sketch in CA 11-12R
Elton, John
See Marsh, John
Elton, W(illiam) R. 1921- Brief entry 111
el-Toure, Askia Muhammad Abu Bakr
See Toure, Askia Muhammad Abu Bakr el
Eltringham, S(tewart) K(eith) 1929- 110
Eluard, Paul
See Grindel, Eugene
See also TCLC 7
El Uqsor
See Borgmann, Dmitri A(lfred)
Elvin, Drake
See Beha, Ernest
Elvin, Harold 1909-1985 CANR-4
Obituary 115
Earlier sketch in CA 7-8R
Elvin, (Herbert) Lionel 1905- CAP-1
Earlier sketch in CA 13-14
Elvin, Mark 1938- 73-76
Elward, James (Joseph) 1928- CANR-12
Earlier sketch in CA 29-32R
Elwart, Joan Potter 1927- 25-28R
See also SATA 2
Elwell, Fayette Herbert 1885- 7-8R
Elwell, Jerry MacElroy 1922- 57-60
Elwell, Stillman J. 1894-1977 Obituary 110
Elwell, Walter A(lexander) 1937- 119
Elwell-Sutton, L(aurence) P(aul)
1912-1984 5-6R
Obituary 114
Elwin, Malcolm 1903-1973 Obituary 89-92
Elwin, William
See Ebenstein, William
Elwood, Ann 1931- 125
See also SATA 52
Elwood, Catharyn 1903(?)-1975 Obituary 61-64
Elwood, Douglas J(ames) 1924- 116
Elwood, Muriel 1902- CAP-1
Earlier sketch in CA 9-10
Elwood, Roger 1943- CANR-10
Earlier sketch in CA 57-60
Elwyn-Jones, Pearl Binder 1904- 107
Ely, David 1927- 53-56
Ely, Donald P(aul) 1930- 29-32R
Ely, James W(allace), Jr. 1938- 73-76
Ely, John Hart 1938- 103
Ely, Paul (Henri) 1897-1975 Obituary 53-56
Ely, Virginia (Shackelford) 1899- CANR-24
Earlier sketch in CA 4R
Elytis, Odysseus 1911- 102
See also CLC 15, 49
Elzinga, Kenneth G(erald) 1941- CANR-13
Earlier sketches in CA 49-52, CANR-1
Emans, Robert 1934- 53-56
Emanuel, James A. 1921- CANR-12
Earlier sketch in CA 29-32R
See also BW
See also DLB 41
Ember, Carol R(uchlis) 1943- 77-80
Emberley, Barbara A(nne) 1932- CANR-5
Earlier sketch in CA 5-6R
See also SATA 8
See also CLR 5
Emberley, Ed(ward Randolph) 1931- CANR-5
Earlier sketch in CA 5-6R
See also SATA 8
See also CLR 5
Emberley, Michael 1960- 104
See also SATA 34
Embey, Philip
See Philipp, Elliot Elias
Emblen, D(onald) L(ewis) 1918- 33-36R
Embling, John 1952- 111
Emboden, William A., Jr. 1935- CANR-14
Earlier sketch in CA 41-44R
Embree, Ainslie Thomas 1921- CANR-2
Earlier sketch in CA 4R
Embry, Margaret Jacob 1919-1975 CANR-3
Earlier sketch in CA 1R
See also SATA 5
Emecheta, (Florence Onye) Buchi 1944- 81-84
See also BW
See also CLC 14, 48
Emeneau, Murray Barnson 1904- CANR-5
Earlier sketch in CA 1R
Emenegger, Bob
See Emenegger, Robert
Emenegger, Robert 1933- 102
Emenhiser, JeDon A(llen) 1933- 37-40R
Emerick, Kenneth F(red) 1925- 53-56
Emerson, Alice B. CAP-2
Earlier sketch in CA 19-20
See also SATA 1
Emerson, Caroline D. 1891-1973 CAP-1
Obituary 45-48
Earlier sketch in CA 17-18
Emerson, Caryl (Geppert) 1944- 123
Emerson, Connie 1930- 109
Emerson, (Alan) David 1900- CANR-2
Earlier sketch in CA 7-8R
Emerson, Donald (Conger) 1913- 21-22R
Emerson, Earl W. 1948- 123
Emerson, Everett Harvey 1925- CANR-22
Earlier sketches in CA 15-16R, CANR-5
Emerson, Frank C(reighton) 1936- 53-56
Emerson, H(enry) O(liver) 1893- CAP-2
Earlier sketch in CA 23-24
Emerson, James G(ordon), Jr. 1926- 19-20R
Emerson, Laura S(alome) 1907- CAP-1
Earlier sketch in CA 15-16
Emerson, Mary Lee
See Kennedy, Mary
Emerson, O. B. 1922- CANR-16
Earlier sketch in CA 25-28R
Emerson, Ralph Waldo
1803-1882 DLB-1, 59, 73
See also CDALB 1640-1865
Emerson, Ronald
See Scotland, James
Emerson, Ru 1944- 121
Emerson, Rupert 1899-1979 CANR-2
Obituary 85-88
Earlier sketch in CA 1R
Emerson, Thomas I(rwin) 1907- 21-22R
Emerson, William 1769-1811 DLB-37
Emerson, William K(eith) 1925- 41-44R
See also SATA 25
Emery, Alan E(glin) H(eathcote) 1928- 69-72
Emery, Allan C(omstock), Jr. 1919- 104
Emery, Anne (McGuigan) 1907- CANR-2
Earlier sketch in CA 3R
See also SATA 1, 33
Emery, David A(mos) 1920- 29-32R
Emery, Edwin 1914- CANR-11
Earlier sketch in CA 69-72
Emery, Fred 1933- 65-68
Emery, Gary 1942- 110
Emery, Kenneth Orris 1914- 107
Emery, Michael 1940- 73-76
Emery, Pierre-Yves 1929- 101
Emery, Robert F(irestone) 1927- 37-40R
Emery, Walter Byron 1907-1973 CANR-22
Earlier sketch in CA 1R
Emett, Rowland 1906- 102
Emig, Janet Ann 73-76
Emma, Ronald David 1920- 25-28R
Emmanuel, Philip D. 1909- CAP-1
Earlier sketch in CA 15-16
Emmanuel, Pierre
See Mathieu, Noel Jean
Emme, Eugene M(orlock) 1919-1985 CANR-8
Obituary 116
Earlier sketch in CA 15-16R
Emmel, Thomas C. 1941- Brief entry 111
Emmens, Carol Ann 1944- 106
See also SATA 39
Emmerich, Andre 1924- 9-10R
Emmerick, R(onald) E(ric) 1937- CANR-11
Earlier sketch in CA 25-28R
Emmerson, Donald K(enneth) 1940- CANR-14
Earlier sketch in CA 65-68
Emmerson, Henry Russell 1899- 7-8R
Emmerson, John K(enneth)
1908-1984 CANR-14
Obituary 112
Earlier sketch in CA 57-60
Emmerson, Richard Kenneth 1948- 106
Emmet, Dorothy Mary 1904- 9-10R
Emmet, E(ric) R(evell) 1909- 107
Emmett, Bruce 1949- 57-60
Emmitt, Robert (P.) 1925- 29-32R
Emmons, Charles F(rank) 1942- 110
Emmons, Della (Florence) Gould
1890-1983 Obituary 111
See also SATA 39
Emmons, Michael 1938- 107
Emmons, Nuel 1927- 125
Emmrich, Curt 1897-1975 CAP-2
Earlier sketch in CA 29-32
Emmrich, Kurt
See Emmrich, Curt
Emorey, N.
See Ellison, Jerome
Emory, Alan (Steuer) 1922- CANR-12
Earlier sketch in CA 69-72
Empey, Arthur Guy 1883-1963 Obituary 107
Empey, LaMar T. 1923- 29-32R
Employee X
See Fautsko, Timothy F(rank)
Empringham, Antoinette F(leur) 1939- 124
Empringham, Toni
See Empringham, Antoinette F(leur)
Empson, William 1906-1984 17-18R
Obituary 112
See also DLB 20
See also CLC 3, 8, 19, 33, 34
Emrich, Duncan (Black Macdonald)
1908-197(?) CANR-9
Earlier sketch in CA 61-64
See also SATA 11
Emshwiller, Carol 53-56
Emsley, Clare
See Plummer, Clare (Emsley)
Emsley, Michael Gordon 1930- 97-100
Emslie, M. L.
See Simpson, Myrtle L(illias)
Emswiler, Sharon Neufer 1944- 119
Emy, Hugh (Vincent) 1944- 77-80
Encausse, Gerard (Anaclet Vincent)
1865-1916 Brief entry 113

Encel, Sol
See Encel, Solomon
Encel, Solomon 1925- 115
Enchi, Fumiko (Ueda) 1905-1986 Obituary .. 121
See also CLC 31
Endacott, G(eorge) B(eer) 1901- 7-8R
Endacott, M(arie) Violet 1915- 11-12R
Ende, Jean 1947- 53-56
Ende, Michael 1930(?)- 124
Brief entry 118
See also SATA 42
See also DLB 75
See also CLC 31
See also CLR 14
Ende, Richard Chaffey von
See von Ende, Richard Chaffey
Endelman, Todd M(ichael) 1946- 125
Enderle, Judith (Ann) Ross 1941- CANR-22
Earlier sketch in CA 106
See also SATA 38
Enders, Richard
See Fenster, Robert
Endfield, Mercedes
See von Block, Bela W(illiam)
Endicott, Ruth Belmore CANR-26
Earlier sketches in CA 19-20, CAP-2
Endicott, Stephen Lyon 1928- 107
Endler, Norman S(olomon) 1931- CANR-9
Earlier sketch in CA 23-24R
Endo, Mitsuko 1942- 65-68
Endo, Shusaku 1923- CANR-21
Earlier sketch in CA 29-32R
See also CLC 7, 14, 19
Endore, (Samuel) Guy 1900-1970 ...... CANR-6
Obituary 25-28R
Earlier sketch in CA 2R
Endres, Clifford 1941- 108
Endy, Melvin B(ecker), Jr. 1938- 81-84
Enelow, Allen J(ay) 1922- CANR-7
Earlier sketch in CA 19-20R
Enfield, Carrie
See Smith, Susan Vernon
Engberg, Edward 1928- 21-22R
Engberg, Holger L(aessoe) 1930- 37-40R
Engberg, (Johanna) Susan 1940- 117
Engdahl, Sylvia Louise 1933- CANR-14
Earlier sketch in CA 29-32R
See also SATA 4
See also SAAS 5
See also CLR 2
Engebrecht, P(atricia) A(nn) 1935- 57-60
Engel, Alan S(tuart) 1932- 37-40R
Engel, Bernard F. 1921- 13-14R
Engel, Herbert M. 1918- 120
Engel, Howard 1931- 112
Engel, J. Ronald 1936- 124
Engel, James F. 1934- CANR-13
Earlier sketch in CA 23-24R
Engel, (Aaron) Lehman 1910-1982 ......41-44R
Obituary 107
Engel, Louis (Henry, Jr.) 1909-1982 .....21-22R
Obituary 108
Engel, Lyle Kenyon 1915-1986 85-88
Obituary 120
Engel, Madeline H(elena) 1941- 85-88
Engel, Marian 1933-1985 .... CANR-12
Earlier sketch in CA 25-28R
See also DLB 53
See also CLC 36
Engel, Mary June Montgomery
1920(?)-1985 Obituary 117
Engel, Monroe 1921- 7-8R
Engel, Pauline Newton 1918- 17-18R
Engel, Peter H. 1935- CANR-15
Earlier sketch in CA 81-84
Engel, S(rul) Morris (von) 1931- CANR-14
Earlier sketch in CA 37-40R
Engel, Salo 1908-1972 .... CAP-2
Earlier sketch in CA 33-36
Engel, Samuel G. 1904-1984 Obituary 112
Engelberg, Edward 1929- 37-40R
Engelhardt, Frederick
See Hubbard, L(afayette) Ron(ald)
Engelhart, Margaret S. 1924- 122
Engelking, L. L. 1903(?)-1980 Obituary 102
Engelman, Rose C. 1919(?)-1979
Obituary 89-92
Engelmann, Hugo O(tto) 1917- 41-44R
Engelmann, Larry 1941- 101
Engelmann, Ruth 1919- 106
Engelmann, Siegfried E. 1931- CANR-13
Earlier sketch in CA 23-24R
Engelmayer, Sheldon David 1945- 114
Engels, Donald (W.) 1946- 102
Engels, John David 1931- CANR-6
Earlier sketch in CA 15-16R
Engels, Norbert (Anthony) 1903- CAP-2
Earlier sketch in CA 17-18
Engeman, Thomas S(ledge) 1944- 109
Engen, Rodney K(ent) 1948- CANR-15
Earlier sketch in CA 65-68
Enger, Norman L. 1937- CANR-10
Earlier sketch in CA 25-28R
Engerman, Stanley L(ewis) 1936- 53-56
Enggass, Robert 1921- CANR-9
Earlier sketch in CA 13-14R
Engh, M(ary) J(ane) 1933- 69-72
Engh, Rohn 1938- 69-72
Engholm, Eva 1909- 93-96
Engl, Lieselotte 1918- 49-52
Engl, Theodor 1925- 49-52
England, Anthony Bertram 1939- 85-88
England, Barry 1932- 25-28R
England, E. M.
See Anders, Edith (Mary) England
England, E Squires
See Ball, Sylvia Patricia
England, George Allan 1877-1936
Brief entry 112
England, George W(illiam) 1927- 104
England, John C(arol) 1930- 116
England, Martha Winburn 1909- CAP-1
Earlier sketch in CA 11-12
England, Maurice Derrick 1908-1980 104
England, Rodney Charles Bennett
See Bennett-England, Rodney Charles
England, Wilbur Birch 1903- 4R
Engle, Eloise
See Paananen, Eloise (Katherine)
See also SATA 9
Engle, Jeff(rey) 1947- 103
Engle, John D(avid), Jr. 1922- CANR-25
Earlier sketches in CA 57-60, CANR-7
Engle, Louise Boardman Proctor
1897(?)-1987 Obituary 121
Engle, Parke F. 1900(?)-1984 Obituary 111
Engle, Paul (Hamilton) 1908- CANR-5
Earlier sketch in CA 1R
See also DLB 48
Engle, T(helburn) L(aRoy) 1901- 13-14R
Englebert, Victor 1933- 57-60
See also SATA 8
Englefield, Ronald 1891-1975 Obituary 105
Englekirk, John E(ugene) 1905-1983
Obituary 112
Engleman, Finis E(wing) 1895- 11-12R
Engler, Larry 1949- 53-56
Engler, Richard E(mil), Jr. 1925- 37-40R
Engler, Robert 1922- CANR-2
Earlier sketch in CA 3R
Englert, Clement Cyril 1910- CANR-5
Earlier sketch in CA 1R
English, Adrian J(oseph) 1939- 118
English, Arnold
See Hershman, Morris
English, Barbara (Anne) 1933- CANR-13
Earlier sketch in CA 33-36R
English, Charles
See Nuetzel, Charles (Alexander)
English, David 1931- 69-72
English, Deirdre (Elena) 1948- 85-88
English, E(ugene) Schuyler 1899-1981 107
Obituary 103
English, Earl (Franklin) 1905- 37-40R
English, Edward (H.) 19(?)-1973
Obituary 41-44R
English, Fenwick Walter 1939- CANR-1
Earlier sketch in CA 45-48
English, Isobel 1925- 53-56
English, James W(ilson) 1915- 21-22R
See also SATA 37
English, (Emma) Jean M(artin) 1937- 29-32R
English, John W(esley) 1940- 69-72
English, Maurice 1909-1983 .... CANR-12
Obituary 111
Earlier sketch in CA 9-10R
English, O(liver) Spurgeon 1901- CAP-2
Earlier sketch in CA 33-36
English, Ronald (Frederick) 1913- CAP-1
Earlier sketch in CA 9-10
English, Thomas H(opkins) 1895- CANR-2
Earlier sketch in CA 5-6R
English, Thomas Saunders 1928-
Brief entry 105
Englizian, H. Crosby 1923- 23-24R
Engquist, Richard 1933- 29-32R
Engren, Edith
See McCaig, Robert Jesse
Engs, Robert Francis 1943- 101
Engstrand, Iris (H.) Wilson 1935- 107
Engstrom, Ted W.
See Engstrom, Theodore W(ilhelm)
Engstrom, Theodore W(ilhelm) 1916- .. CANR-25
Earlier sketches in CA 65-68, CANR-9
Engstrom, W(infred) A(ndrew) 1925- 57-60
Enis, Ben M(elvin) 1942- CANR-22
Earlier sketches in CA 57-60, CANR-7
Enke, Stephen 1916-1974 65-68
Obituary 53-56
Enloe, Cynthia H(olden) 1938- CANR-17
Earlier sketch in CA 37-40R
Enlow, David R(oland) 1916- CANR-10
Earlier sketch in CA 7-8R
Ennes, James Marquis, Jr. 1933- 102
Ennis, Bruce J. 1940- Brief entry 110
Ennis, Robert H(ugh) 1927- CANR-10
Earlier sketch in CA 25-28R
Eno, Susan 101
Enoch, Kurt 1895-1982 Obituary 106
Enockson, Paul G(eorge) 1938- 110
Enomiya-Lassalle, Hugo M(akibi) 1898- ..23-24R
Enquist, Per Olov 1934- Brief entry 109
Enrick, Norbert Lloyd 1920- CANR-6
Earlier sketch in CA 15-16R
Enright, D(ennis) J(oseph) 1920- CANR-1
Earlier sketch in CA 4R
See also SATA 25
See also DLB 27
See also CLC 4, 8, 31
Enright, Elizabeth 1909-1968 61-64
Obituary 25-28R
See also SATA 9
See also DLB 22
See also CLR 4
Enright, Maureen Patricia Ford
1908(?)-1983 Obituary 111
Enroth, Clyde A(dolph) 1926- 37-40R
Enscoe, Gerald (Eugene) 1926- CANR-10
Earlier sketch in CA 5-6R
Ense, Wolfgang
See Frank, Rudolf
Ensign, Thomas 1940- 101
Ensign, Tod
See Ensign, Thomas
Ensley, Evangeline 1907- 122
Brief entry 114
Ensley, Francis Gerald 1907- CAP-1
Earlier sketch in CA 15-16
Enslin, Morton S(cott) 1897- 19-20R
Enslin, Theodore (Vernon) 1925- CANR-19
Earlier sketches in CA 53-56, CANR-4
See also CAAS 3
Ensminger, Marion Eugene 1908- CANR-16
Earlier sketches in CA 49-52, CANR-1
Ensor, Allison (Rash) 1935- 25-28R
Ensor, (Alick Charles) David(son)
1906-1987 Obituary 121
Enstrom, Robert (William) 1946- 104
Enteman, Willard F(inley) 1936- 33-36R
Entenza, John Dymock 1905-1984
Obituary 112
Enterline, James Robert 1932- 41-44R
Enthoven, Alain C(harles) 1930- 49-52
Entine, Alan D(avid) 1936- 23-24R
Entwisle, Doris R(oberts) 1924- 5-6R
Entwistle, Florence Vivienne 1889(?)-1982
Obituary 105
Entwistle, Harold 1923- 29-32R
Entwistle, Noel (James) 1936- CANR-16
Earlier sketch in CA 93-96
Entwistle, (Arthur) Theodore (Henry)
Rowland
See Rowland-Entwistle, (Arthur)
Theodore (Henry)
Enyeart, James L(yle) 1943- 113
Enys, Sarah L.
See Sloggett, Nellie
Enz, Jacob J(ohn) 1919- 41-44R
Enzensberger, Hans Magnus 1929- 119
Brief entry 116
See also CLC 43
Enzler, Clarence J. 1910(?)-1976
Obituary 69-72
Epafrodito
See Wagner, C(harles) Peter
Epand, Len 1950- 85-88
Epernay, Mark
See Galbraith, John Kenneth
Ephraim, Gavriel Ben
See Ben-Ephraim, Gavriel
Ephron, Delia 1944- CANR-12
Earlier sketch in CA 97-100
See also SATA 50
Ephron, Henry 1911- 73-76
Ephron, Nora 1941- CANR-12
Earlier sketch in CA 65-68
See also CLC 17, 31
See also AITN 2
Ephron, Phoebe (Wolkind) 1916-1971
Obituary 33-36R
Epler, Percy H. 1872-1975 Obituary 57-60
Epp, Eldon Jay 1930- CANR-7
Earlier sketch in CA 19-20R
Epp, Frank H(enry) 1929- 29-32R
Epp, Margaret A(gnes) 1913- CANR-3
Earlier sketch in CA 11-12R
See also SATA 20
Eppard, Philip B(lair) 1945- 112
Eppenbach, Sarah 1947- 114
Eppenstein, Louise (Kohn) 1892-1987
Obituary 123
Epperly, Elizabeth Rollins 1951- 106
Epperson, Gordon 1921- 25-28R
Eppie
See Naismith, Helen
Eppinga, Jacob D. 1917- 33-36R
Eppinger, Josh 1940- 89-92
Eppink, Norman R(oland) 1906- 53-56
Epple, Anne Orth 1927- 33-36R
See also SATA 20
Epps, Bernard 1936- DLB-53
Epps, Edgar G(ustavas) 1929- 49-52
Epps, Garrett 1950- 69-72
Epps, Preston H(erschel) 1888- 37-40R
Epps, Robert L(ee) 1932- 17-18R
Eppstein, John 1895-1988 Obituary 125
Epsilon
See Betjeman, John
Epstein, Ann Wharton
See Wharton, Annabel Jane
Epstein, Anne Merrick 1931- 69-72
See also SATA 20
Epstein, Barbara 1928- Brief entry 110
Epstein, Benjamin Robert 1912-1983 45-48
Obituary 109
Epstein, Beryl (M. Williams) 1910- CANR-18
Earlier sketches in CA 7-8R, CANR-2
See also SATA 1, 31
Epstein, Charlotte 1921- CANR-8
Earlier sketch in CA 61-64
Epstein, Cy(ril Robert) 1942- Brief entry 108
Epstein, Cynthia Fuchs 1933- CANR-14
Earlier sketch in CA 29-32R
Epstein, Daniel Mark 1948- CANR-2
Earlier sketch in CA 49-52
See also CLC 7
Epstein, David G(eorge) 1943- 69-72
Epstein, Dena J. 1916- 41-44R
Epstein, Edmund L(loyd) 1931- 118
Epstein, Edward Jay 1935- CANR-13
Earlier sketch in CA 19-20R
Epstein, Edwin M(ichael) 1937- 25-28R
Epstein, Ellen Robinson 1947- 115
Epstein, Erwin H(oward) 1939- 29-32R
Epstein, Eugene 1944- 69-72
Epstein, Fritz T(heodor) 1898-1979 .... CANR-22
Earlier sketch in CA 69-72
Epstein, Helen 1947- 89-92
Epstein, Howard M(ichael) 1927- 23-24R
Epstein, Jacob 1880-1959 Brief entry 120
Epstein, Jacob 1956- 114
See also CLC 19
Epstein, Jason 1928- 57-60
Epstein, Joseph 1937- 119
Brief entry 112
See also CLC 39
Epstein, Judith Sue 1947- 69-72
Epstein, Julius 1901-1975 Obituary 57-60
Epstein, Julius J. 1909- 124
Brief entry 113
See also DLB 26
Epstein, June CANR-13
Earlier sketch in CA 73-76
Epstein, Lee 1958- 119
Epstein, Leon D. 1919- 13-14R
Epstein, Leslie 1938- CANR-23
Earlier sketch in CA 73-76
See also CLC 27
Epstein, Melech (Michael) 1889(?)-1979
Obituary 89-92
Epstein, Morris 1921-1973 .... CAP-1
Obituary 45-48
Earlier sketch in CA 15-16
Epstein, Perle S(herry) 1938- CANR-9
Earlier sketch in CA 65-68
See also SATA 27
Epstein, Philip G. 1909-1952 Brief entry 117
See also DLB 26
Epstein, Samuel 1909- CANR-18
Earlier sketches in CA 9-10R, CANR-4
See also SATA 1, 31
Epstein, Samuel S(tanley) 1926- 115
Epstein, Seymour 1917- CANR-25
Earlier sketches in CA 3R, CANR-5
Epstein, William 1912- CANR-11
Earlier sketch in CA 69-72
Epstein, William H(enry) 1944- 61-64
Epton, Nina C(onsuelo) CANR-11
Earlier sketch in CA 5-6R
Equiano, Olaudah 1745(?)-1797 ..... DLB-37, 50
Eramus, M. Nott
See Stuber, Stanley I(rving)
Erasmus, Charles J(ohn) 1921- 1R
Erasmus, M. Nott
See Stuber, Stanley I(rving)
Erazmus, Edward T. 1920- Brief entry 106
Erb, Alta Mae 1891- CAP-1
Earlier sketch in CA 9-10
Erb, Paul 1894- 9-10R
Erb, Peter C. 1943- 113
Erbsen, Claude E. 1938- 89-92
Ercoli, Ercole
See Togliatti, Palmiro
Erdahl, Carol Syvertsen 1932- 108
Erdahl, Lowell O. 1931- 109
Erdman, David V(orse) 1911- CANR-17
Earlier sketches in CA 1R, CANR-1
Erdman, Howard Loyd 1935- 23-24R
Erdman, Loula Grace ?-1976 .... CANR-10
Earlier sketch in CA 7-8R
See also SATA 1
Erdman, Nikolai R. 1902(?)-1970
Obituary 29-32R
Erdman, Paul E(mil) 1932- CANR-13
Earlier sketch in CA 61-64
See also CLC 25
See also AITN 1
Erdoes, Richard 1912- 77-80
See also SATA 28, 33
Erdos, Paul L(ouis) 1914- 29-32R
Erdrich, Louise 1954- 114
See also CLC 39
Erdt, Terrence 1942- 106
Erenberg, Arthur 1909(?)-1980 Obituary 114
Erenberg, Lewis A. 1944- 125
Erenburg, Ilya (Grigoryevich)
See Ehrenburg, Ilya (Grigoryevich)
Erens, Patricia 1938- 93-96
Erhard, Ludwig 1897-1977 Obituary 112
Erhard, Thomas A. 1923- CANR-13
Earlier sketch in CA 33-36R
Erhard, Walter 1920- SATA-30
Eric, Kenneth
See Henley, Arthur
Erichsen, Heino R(ichard) 1924- 110
Erichsen-Nelson, Jean 1934- 109
Ericksen, Ephraim Gordon 1917- 7-8R
Ericksen, Gerald L(awrence) 1931- 29-32R
Ericksen, Kenneth J(errold) 1939- 37-40R
Ericksen, Stanford Clark 1911- Brief entry .. 108
Erickson, Arthur (Charles) 1924- 89-92
Erickson, Arvel Benjamin 1905-1974 ..... CAP-2
Earlier sketch in CA 21-22
Erickson, Bonnie H(eather) 1944- 112
Erickson, Carolly 1943- CANR-11
Earlier sketch in CA 69-72
Erickson, Don 1932- 110
Erickson, Donald A(rthur) 1925- 29-32R
Erickson, E(rnst) Walfred 1911- CANR-5
Earlier sketch in CA 7-8R
Erickson, Edsel L(ee) 1928- 53-56
Erickson, Erling Arthur 1934- 33-36R
Erickson, John 1929- 101
Erickson, Keith V. 1943- 29-32R
Erickson, M(elvin) E(ddy) 1918-19(?) 11-12R
Erickson, Marilyn T. 1936- 73-76
Erickson, Marion J. 1913- 17-18R
Erickson, Millard J. 1932- 93-96
Erickson, Milton H(yland) 1901-1980 106
Obituary 97-100
Erickson, Peter (Brown) 1945- 126
Erickson, Phoebe CANR-3
Earlier sketch in CA 1R
Erickson, Robert 1917- Brief entry 109
Erickson, Russell E(verett) 1932- 93-96
See also SATA 27

Erickson, Sabra Rollins 1912- ... CANR-5
Earlier sketch in CA 5-6R
See also SATA 35
Erickson, Stephen A(nthony) 1940- ... 85-88
Erickson, W(alter) Bruce 1938- ... 49-52
Ericson, Edward E(inar) 1939- ... 69-72
Ericson, Joe Ellis 1925- ... 41-44R
Ericson, Julia
See Leisy, James (Franklin)
Ericson, Walter
See Fast, Howard Melvin
Ericsson, Emily (Alice) 1904-1976
Obituary ... 65-68
Ericsson, Mary Kentra 1910- ... CANR-20
Earlier sketches in CA 4R, CANR-5
Ericsson, Ronald James 1935- ... 110
Erikson, Erik H(omburger) 1902- ... 25-28R
Erikson, Kai T(heodor) 1931- Brief entry ... 107
Erikson, Mel 1937- ... SATA-31
Erikson, Roy L. 1939(?)-1985 Obituary ... 116
Erikson, Stanley 1906- ... 37-40R
Eriksson, Buntel
See Bergman, (Ernst) Ingmar
Eriksson, Edward 1941- ... 77-80
Eriksson, Marguerite A. 1911- ... 13-14R
Eringer, Robert 1954- ... 114
Erisman, Fred (Raymond) 1937- ... 110
Erlander, Tage Fritiof 1901-1985 Obituary ... 116
Erlanger, Baba
See Trahey, Jane
Erlanger, Ellen (Louise) 1950- ... CANR-15
Earlier sketch in CA 85-88
See also SATA 52
Erlanger, Philippe 1903- ... CANR-20
Earlier sketches in CA 7-8R, CANR-5
Erlich, Alexander 1912-1985 Obituary ... 114
Erlich, Gloria C. ... 125
Erlich, Lillian (Feldman) 1910- ... CANR-5
Earlier sketch in CA 4R
See also SATA 10
Erlich, Victor 1914- ... CANR-3
Earlier sketch in CA 11-12R
Ermarth, Elizabeth 1939- ... 117
Ermine, Will
See Drago, Harry Sinclair
Ermolaev, Herman Sergei 1924- ... 107
Ernest, Victor (Hugo) 1911- ... CAP-2
Earlier sketch in CA 33-36
Ernest, William
See Berkebile, Fred D(onovan)
Ernharth, Ronald Louis 1936- ... 45-48
Erno, Richard B. 1923- ... 15-16R
Ernst, Barbara 1945- ... 65-68
Ernst, Carl Henry 1938- ... 45-48
Ernst, Clara
See Barnes, Clara Ernst
Ernst, Earle 1911- ... 5-6R
Ernst, Eldon G(ilbert) 1939- ... 85-88
Ernst, Jimmy 1920-1984 Obituary ... 112
Ernst, (Lyman) John 1940- ... 45-48
See also SATA 39
Ernst, Joseph Albert 1931- Brief entry ... 109
Ernst, Kathryn (Fitzgerald) 1942- ... CANR-12
Earlier sketch in CA 61-64
See also SATA 25
Ernst, Lisa Campbell 1957- ... 114
See also SATA 44
Ernst, Margaret Samuels 1894- ... CAP-1
Earlier sketch in CA 13-14
Ernst, Margot Klebe 1939- ... 23-24R
Ernst, Max 1891-1976 Obituary ... 65-68
Ernst, Morris L(eopold) 1888-1976 ... CANR-7
Obituary ... 65-68
Earlier sketch in CA 7-8R
Ernst, Paul 1866-1933 ... DLB-66
Ernst, Robert 1915- ... 23-24R
Ernst, Sheila 1941- ... 109
Ernsting, Walter 1920- ... 37-40R
Erny, Pierre Jean Paul 1933- ... CANR-13
Earlier sketch in CA 73-76
Eron, Carol (Lehman) 1945- ... 112
Eron, Leonard D(avid) 1920- Brief entry ... 110
Errington, Frederick (Karl) 1940- ... 104
Erskine, Barbara 1944- ... 123
Erskine, Chester 1904(?)-1986 Obituary ... 121
Erskine, Jim 1956- ... 107
Erskine, John 1879-1951 Brief entry ... 112
See also DLB 9
Erskine, Laurie York 1894(?)-1976
Obituary ... 69-72
Erskine, Margaret
See Williams, (Margaret) Wetherby
Erskine, Noel Leo ... 116
Erskine, Rosalind
See Longrigg, Roger (Erskine)
Erskine, Thomas L(eonard) 1939- ... 65-68
Erskine, Wilson Fiske 1911-1972(?) ... 4R
Erskine-Lindop, Audrey (Beatrice Noel)
1920-1986 ... 69-72
Obituary ... 121
Erte
See De Tirtoff, Romain
Ertel, (Richard) James 1922-1985 ... 9-10R
Obituary ... 117
Ertz, Susan 1894-1985 ... 5-6R
Obituary ... 116
Ervin, Janet Halliday 1923- ... 29-32R
See also SATA 4
Ervin, Sam(uel) J(ames), Jr. 1896-1985 ... 119
Obituary ... 115
Brief entry ... 113
Ervin, Susan
See Ervin-Tripp, Susan Moore
Ervin, Theodore Robert 1928- ... 15-16R
Ervine, St. John Greer 1883-1971
Obituary ... 29-32R
See also DLB 10
Ervin-Tripp, Susan Moore 1927- ... 53-56
Erwin, Annabel
See Barron, Ann Forman
Erwin, Edward (James) 1937- ... 29-32R
Erwin, John D(raper) 1883-1983 Obituary ... 109
Erwin, John Seymour 1911- ... 105
Erwin, Will
See Eisner, Will(iam Erwin)
Esau, Helmut 1941- ... 57-60
Esbensen, Barbara Juster ... SATA-53
Escandon, Ralph 1928- ... CANR-14
Earlier sketch in CA 37-40R
Escarpenter, Claudio 1922-1977 ... 17-18R
Obituary ... 120
Escarraz, Donald Ray 1932- ... 21-22R
Eschelbach, Claire John 1929- ... 1R
Escher, Franklin (Jr.) 1915- ... 11-12R
Escherich, Elsa Falk 1888- ... 5-6R
Eschholz, Paul A(nderson) 1942- ... CANR-14
Earlier sketch in CA 37-40R
Eschmeyer, R(einhart) E(rnst) 1898- ... 105
Eschmeyer, William N(eil) 1939- ... 112
Escott, Colin 1949- ... 107
Escott, Jonathan 1922- ... CANR-20
Earlier sketch in CA 65-68
Escott, Paul David 1947- ... 93-96
Escriva, Josemaria
See Escriva de Balaguer, Josemaria
Escriva de Balaguer, Josemaria
1902-1975 Obituary ... 57-60
Eseki, Bruno
See Mphahlele, Ezekiel
Esenin, Sergei (Alexandrovich) 1895-1925
Brief entry ... 104
See also TCLC 4
Esfandiary, F. M. ... CANR-8
Earlier sketch in CA 17-18R
Eshbach, Lloyd Arthur 1910- ... 118
Eshelman, Byron E(lias) 1915- ... 3R
Esherick, Joseph W(harton) 1942- ... 65-68
Eshleman, Clayton 1935- ... 33-36R
See also CAAS 6
See also DLB 5
See also CLC 7
Eshleman, Edwin D(uing) 1920-1985
Obituary ... 114
Eshleman, J. Ross 1936- ... 101
Eshmeyer, R. E.
See Eschmeyer, R(einhart) E(rnst)
See also SATA 29
Eskelin, Neil J(oyner) 1938- ... 33-36R
Eskelund, Karl 1918-1972 ... CAP-2
Earlier sketch in CA 23-24
Eskenazi, Gerald 1936- ... CANR-7
Earlier sketch in CA 61-64
Eskey, Kenneth 1930- ... 77-80
Eskin, Frada 1936- ... 37-40R
Eskow, John 1949- ... 105
Eskow, Seymour 1924- ... 11-12R
Esler, Anthony (James) 1934- ... CANR-26
Earlier sketches in CA 23-24R, CANR-8
Esler, Carol Clemeau 1935- ... 108
Esler, William K. 1930- ... CANR-5
Earlier sketch in CA 53-56
Esman, Aaron H(irsh) 1924- ... CANR-11
Earlier sketch in CA 61-64
Esman, Milton J. 1918- ... 81-84
Esmein, Jean 1923- ... 49-52
Esmond, Harriet
See Burke, John (Frederick)
Esohg, Lama
See Ghose, Amal
Eson, Morris E. 1921- ... 15-16R
Espeland, Pamela (Lee) 1951- ... 107
See also SATA 38, 52
Espenshade, Edward B(owman), Jr. 1910- ... 4R
Esper, Erwin A(llen) 1895-19(?) ... CAP-1
Earlier sketch in CA 15-16
Espey, John (Jenkins) 1913- ... CANR-25
Earlier sketches in CA 7-8R, CANR-4
Espinasse, Albert 1905-1972 Obituary ... 37-40R
'Espinasse, Margaret 1903(?)-1980
Obituary ... 114
Espino, Federico (Licsi, Jr.) 1939- ... 93-96
Espinosa, Jose E(dmundo) 1900-1967 ... CAP-2
Earlier sketch in CA 25-28
Espinosa, Rudy
See Espinoza, Rudolph Louis
Espinoza, Rudolph Louis 1933- ... 73-76
Esposito, John C(abrino) 1940- ... 33-36R
Esposito, John L(ouis) 1940- ... 116
Esposito, Joseph L(ouis) 1941- ... 114
Esposito, Phil(ip Anthony) 1942-
Brief entry ... 108
Espriu, Salvador 1913-1985 Obituary ... 115
See also CLC 9
Espy, Richard 1952- ... 105
Espy, Willard R(ichardson) 1910- ... CANR-2
Earlier sketch in CA 49-52
See also SATA 38
Esquenazi-Mayo, Roberto 1920- ... 45-48
Essame, Hubert 1896-1976 ... 49-52
Obituary ... 65-68
Esse, James
See Stephens, James
Esser, Robin 1933- ... 29-32R
Esses, Michael (Isaiah) 1923- Brief entry ... 110
Essex, Harry J. ... 33-36R
Essex, Mary
See Bloom, Ursula
Essex, Rosamund (Sibyl) 1900-1985 ... 107
Obituary ... 116
Essick, Robert N(ewman) 1942- ... CANR-19
Earlier sketches in CA 53-56, CANR-5
Esslin, Martin (Julius) 1918- ... 85-88
Esslinger, Dean R(obert) 1942- ... 61-64
Esslinger, Pat M.
See Carr, Pat M(oore)
Essoe, Gabe (Attila) 1944- ... 25-28R
Essop, Ahmed 1931- ... 123
Essrig, Harry 1912- ... 108
Estabrook, Robert Harley 1918- ... 69-72
Estabrooks, George H. 1896(?)-1973
Obituary ... 45-48
Estang, Luc 1911- ... 61-64
Estarellas, Juan 1918- ... CANR-2
Earlier sketch in CA 45-48
Estaver, Marguerite M. 1893- ... 97-100
Estelle, Sister Mary 1907- ... CAP-1
Earlier sketch in CA 11-12
Estenssoro, Hugo 1946- ... 69-72
Estep, Irene Compton ... 3R
See also SATA 5
Estep, W(illiam) R(oscoe), Jr. 1920- ... CANR-25
Earlier sketches in CA 13-14R, CANR-9
Esterbrook, Tom
See Hubbard, L(afayette) Ron(ald)
Estergreen, M. Morgan
See Estergreen, Marian Morgan
Estergreen, Marian Morgan 1910- ... 17-18R
Esterly, Glenn 1942- ... 33-36R
Estermann, Carlos ?-1976 Obituary ... 105
Esterow, Milton 1928- ... 19-20R
Estes, Bill 1941- ... 107
Estes, Eleanor 1906-1988 ... CANR-20
Obituary ... 126
Earlier sketches in CA 2R, CANR-5
See also SATA 7
See also DLB 22
See also CLR 2
Estes, J(oseph) Worth 1934- ... 104
Estes, John E(dward) 1939- ... 57-60
Estes, Rice 1907- ... CAP-1
Earlier sketch in CA 11-12
Estes, Richard J. 1942- ... 118
Estes, Steve(n Douglas) 1952- ... 97-100
Estes, Winston M(arvin) 1917-1982 ... 29-32R
Obituary ... 126
Estess, Ted L(ynn) 1942- ... 114
Estey, George F. 1924- ... 33-36R
Esthus, Raymond Arthur 1925- ... 15-16R
Estleman, Loren D. 1952- ... 85-88
See also CLC 48
Estner, Lois J(ane) 1947- ... 114
Estock, Anne (Martin) 1923- ... 4R
Estoril, Jean
See Allan, Mabel Esther
Estrada, Doris (Perkins) 1923- ... 19-20R
Estrada, Jacquelyn (Ann) 1946- ... 29-32R
Estrin, Herman A. 1915- ... CANR-7
Earlier sketch in CA 17-18R
Estroff, Sue E. 1950- ... 105
Esty, John Cushing, Jr. 1928- Brief entry ... 106
Eszterhas, Joe
See Eszterhas, Joseph A.
Eszterhas, Joseph A. Brief entry ... 124
Etchebaster, Pierre 1894-1980 ... 102
Obituary ... 97-100
Etchemendy, Nancy 1952- ... 106
See also SATA 38
Etcheson, Craig Carlyle 1955- ... 117
Etcheson, Warren W(ade) 1920- ... 41-44R
Etchison, Birdie L(ee) 1937- ... 106
See also SATA 38
Etchison, Dennis (William) 1943- ... 118
Brief entry ... 115
Eterovich, Adam S(lav) 1930- ... 49-52
Eterovich, Francis Hyacinth 1913- ... 37-40R
Ethell, Jeffrey L(ance) 1947- ... CANR-18
Earlier sketch in CA 101
Etheridge, Eugene Wesley 1925- ... 7-8R
Etherington, Charles Leslie 1903- ... 7-8R
Etherton, Michael (James) 1939- ... 121
Ethridge, James M(erritt) 1921- ... 114
Ethridge, Mark Foster 1896-1981 Obituary ... 103
Ethridge, Mark Foster, Jr. 1924-1985
Obituary ... 115
Ethridge, Willie Snow 1900-1983(?) ... 17-18R
Obituary ... 108
See also AITN 1
Etienne
See King-Hall, (William) Stephen
(Richard)
Etkin, Anne (Dunwody Little) 1923- ... 73-76
Etmekjian, James 1915- ... CANR-3
Earlier sketch in CA 5-6R
Eton, Robert
See Meynell, Laurence Walter
Etra, Jonathan 1952- ... 102
Ets, Marie Hall 1893- ... CANR-4
Earlier sketch in CA 3R
See also SATA 2
See also DLB 22
Ets-Hokin, Judith Diane 1938- ... 61-64
Etteldorf, Raymond P. 1911- ... 9-10R
Etter, Dave 1928- ... CANR-24
Earlier sketches in CA 19-20R, CANR-8
Etter, Les(ter Frederick) 1904- ... 25-28R
Etter, Patricia A. 1932- ... 120
Ettin, Andrew V(ogel) 1943- ... 124
Ettinger, Elzbieta 1925- ... 29-32R
Ettinger, Richard Prentice 1893-1971
Obituary ... 29-32R
Ettinger, Robert C(hester) W(ilson)
1918- ... 15-16R
Ettinghausen, Maurice Leon 1883-1974
Obituary ... 116
Ettinghausen, Richard 1906-1979 ... CANR-9
Obituary ... 85-88
Earlier sketch in CA 65-68
Ettleson, Abraham 1897- ... CAP-2
Earlier sketch in CA 23-24
Ettling, John 1944- ... 125
Ettlinger, Gerard H(erman) 1935- ... 61-64
Ettlinger, L(eopold) D(avid) 1913-
Brief entry ... 111
Etulain, Richard W(ayne) 1938- ... CANR-16
Earlier sketches in CA 45-48, CANR-1
Etzioni, Amitai (Werner) 1929- ... CANR-22
Earlier sketches in CA 2R, CANR-5
Etzioni, Minerva M(orales) 1938(?)-1985
Obituary ... 118
Etzkorn, K(laus) Peter 1932- ... 49-52
Etzkowitz, Henry 1940- ... 25-28R
Etzold, Thomas H(erman) 1945- ... CANR-14
Earlier sketch in CA 81-84
Eubank, (Weaver) Keith (Jr.) 1920- ... CANR-2
Earlier sketch in CA 7-8R
Eubank, Nancy 1934- ... 41-44R
Eubanks, Ralph T(ravis) 1920- ... 17-18R
Eucken, Rudolf (Christof) 1846-1926
Brief entry ... 119
Eulau, Heinz 1915- Brief entry ... 107
Eulenspiegel, Alexander
See Shea, Robert (Joseph)
Eulert, Don(ald Dean) 1935- ... CANR-18
Earlier sketches in CA 49-52, CANR-2
Euller, John E(lmer) 1926- ... 9-10R
Eulo, Ken 1939- ... 126
Brief entry ... 109
Eunson, (John) Dale 1904- ... 41-44R
See also SATA 5
Eunson, Robert C(harles) 1912-1975 ... 13-14R
Obituary ... 61-64
Euphan
See Todd, Barbara Euphan
Euphemides, Aristos
See von Koerber, Hans Nordewin
Eurich, Alvin C(hristian) 1902-1987 ... 17-18R
Obituary ... 123
Eurich, Nell 1919- ... CANR-12
Earlier sketch in CA 73-76
European
See Mosley, Oswald (Ernald)
Eusden, John (Dykstra) 1922- ... 45-48
Eustace, Cecil John 1903- ... 49-52
Eustace, May (Corcoran) 1904- ... 7-8R
Eustace, Robert
See Barton, Eustace Robert
Eustis, Alvin Allen, Jr. 1917- ... 102
Eustis, Laurette
See Murdock, Laurette P.
Eustis, O. B.
See Eustis, Orville B.
Eustis, Orville B. 1913-1986 ... 124
Euwe, Machgielis 1901-1981 Obituary ... 105
Euwe, Max
See Euwe, Machgielis
Evain, Elaine 1931- ... 57-60
Evan, Carol
See Goldsmith, Carol Evan
Evan, Evin
See Faust, Frederick (Shiller)
Evan, William (Martin) 1922- ... CANR-2
Earlier sketch in CA 3R
Evang, Karl 1902- ... 65-68
Evanier, David Brief entry ... 108
Evanoff, Vlad 1916- ... CANR-6
Earlier sketch in CA 5-6R
Evans, A(lfred) Alexander 1905- ... CAP-1
Earlier sketch in CA 9-10
Evans, Abbie Huston 1881- ... 57-60
Evans, Alan
See Stoker, Alan
Evans, Albert 1917- ... 85-88
Evans, Alice Frazer 1939- ... 112
Evans, Arthur Bruce 1948- ... 61-64
Evans, Barbara Lloyd
See Lloyd Evans, Barbara
Evans, Benjamin Ifor 1899-1982 Obituary ... 107
Evans, Bennett
See Berger, Ivan (Bennett)
Evans, Bergen (Baldwin) 1904-1978 ... CANR-4
Obituary ... 77-80
Earlier sketch in CA 5-6R
Evans, C(harles) Stephen 1948- ... CANR-13
Earlier sketch in CA 33-36R
Evans, (Jean) Cherry (Drummond) 1928- ... CAP-1
Earlier sketch in CA 9-10
Evans, Christopher (Riche) 1931-1979 ... 102
Evans, Clifford 1916(?)-1983 Obituary ... 110
Evans, Constance May 1890- ... 11-12R
Evans, D(avid) Ellis 1930- ... CANR-16
Earlier sketch in CA 25-28R
Evans, Dale
See Rogers, Dale Evans
Evans, David Allan 1940- ... 49-52
Evans, David Beecher 1928- Brief entry ... 105
Evans, David Huhn, Jr. 1944- ... 110
Evans, David R(ussell) 1937- ... CANR-17
Earlier sketch in CA 33-36R
Evans, David R(ichard) 1940- ... 116
Evans, David S(tanley) 1916- ... 41-44R
Evans, Debra 1953- ... 122
Evans, Don 1938- ... 111
Evans, Donald 1884-1921 Brief entry ... 123
See also DLB 54
Evans, Donald (Dwight) 1927- ... 41-44R
Evans, Donald P(aul) 1930- ... CANR-7
Earlier sketch in CA 57-60
Evans, Dorinda 1944- ... 121
Evans, E(myr) Estyn 1905- ... CANR-5
Earlier sketch in CA 5-6R
Evans, E(dward) Everett 1893-1958
Brief entry ... 113
Evans, Edward G(ordon), Jr. 1916- ... 45-48
Evans, Eli N. 1936- ... 45-48
See also AITN 1
Evans, Elizabeth 1932- ... 53-56

Evans, Ellen
See Du Breuil, (Elizabeth) L(or)inda
Evans, Emerald
See Du Breuil, (Elizabeth) L(or)inda
Evans, Eric J(ohn) 1945- ... 108
Evans, Eva (Knox) 1905- ... 73-76
See also SATA 27
Evans, Evan
See Faust, Frederick (Shiller)
Evans, F.M.G.
See Higham, Florence May Grier
Evans, (Francis) Fallon 1925- ... 1R
Evans, Fanny-Maude 1914- ... 117
Evans, Frances Monet Carter
See Carter, Frances Monet
Evans, Frank Bernard 1927- ... 114
Evans, G. B.
See Evans, Gwynne Blakemore
Evans, G. Blakemore
See Evans, Gwynne Blakemore
Evans, G(ayle) Edward 1937- ... 33-36R
Evans, G(eraint) N(antglyn) D(avies) 1935-1971 ... CAP-2
Earlier sketch in CA 33-36
Evans, G. R.
See Evans, Gillian (Rosemary)
Evans, Gareth Lloyd
See Lloyd Evans, Gareth
Evans, Geoffrey (Charles) 1901-1987 ... 19-20R
Obituary ... 121
Evans, George Bird 1906- ... CANR-2
Earlier sketch in CA 2R
Evans, George Ewart 1909-1988(?) ... 61-64
Obituary ... 124
Evans, George Henry 1805-1856 ... DLB-43
Evans, George W(illiam) II 1920- ... 21-22R
Evans, Gillian (Rosemary) 1944- ... 126
Evans, Glen 1921- ... 85-88
Evans, Gordon H(eyd) 1930- ... 15-16R
Evans, Gwynfor 1912- ... 61-64
Evans, Gwynne B.
See Evans, Gwynne Blakemore
Evans, Gwynne Blakemore 1912- ... 125
Evans, Harold 1911-1983 Obituary ... 109
Evans, Harold Matthew 1928- ... 41-44R
Evans, Harris
See Evans, George Bird
and Evans, Kay Harris
Evans, Harry 1896(?)-1988 Obituary ... 126
Evans, Herndon J. 1895-1976 ... 69-72
Evans, Hilary 1929- ... CANR-20
Earlier sketches in CA 3R, CANR-5
Evans, Howard Ensign 1919- ... CANR-6
Earlier sketch in CA 7-8R
Evans, Hubert Reginald 1892-1986 ... 103
Obituary ... 119
See also SATA 48
Evans, Humphrey (Marshall, Jr.) 1914- ... 29-32R
Evans, I(drisyn) O(liver) 1894-1977 ... CANR-15
Earlier sketch in CA 13-14R
Evans, Idella M(arie Crowe) 1924- ... 29-32R
Evans, Ilona 1918(?)-1980 Obituary ... 102
Evans, J(ames) A(llan) S(tewart) 1931- ... 37-40R
Evans, J. Martin 1935- ... 85-88
Evans, J(ack) N(aunton) 1920- ... 25-28R
Evans, J(ohn) Robert 1942- ... CANR-7
Earlier sketch in CA 57-60
Evans, Jacob A. 1920- ... 25-28R
Evans, James Allen 1926(?)-1983
Obituary ... 110
Evans, Jay 1925- ... 61-64
Evans, Jean 1939- ... 102
Evans, Jessica
See Lottman, Eileen
Evans, Joan 1893-1977 ... 15-16R
Obituary ... 73-76
Evans, John
See Browne, Howard
Evans, John Lewis 1930- ... 85-88
Evans, John W(alker) 1904- ... 33-36R
Evans, John X(avier) 1933- ... 37-40R
Evans, Jonathan
See Freemantle, Brian Harry
Evans, Joseph S., Jr. 1909(?)-1978 ... 85-88
Obituary ... 81-84
Evans, Joseph W(illiam) 1921- ... 23-24R
Evans, Julia (Rendel) 1913- ... 15-16R
Evans, K(athleen) M(arianne) 1911- ... 9-10R
Evans, Katherine (Floyd) 1901-1964 ... 5-6R
See also SATA 5
Evans, Kay Harris 1906- ... CANR-2
Earlier sketch in CA 2R
Evans, (Cyril) Kenneth 1917- ... 53-56
Evans, Kenneth R. 1938- Brief entry ... 110
Evans, Laurence 1923- ... 37-40R
Evans, Lawrence Watt 1954- ... 102
Evans, Lee
See Forrest, Richard (Stockton)
Evans, Lloyd (Lloyd Thomas) 1927- ... 69-72
Evans, Louis Hadley, Sr. 1897-1981 ... 116
Evans, Luther Harris 1902-1981 ... CANR-9
Obituary ... 106
Earlier sketch in CA 17-18R
Evans, M(edford) Stanton 1934- ... 65-68
Evans, Mari 1923- ... CANR-2
Earlier sketch in CA 49-52
See also BW
See also SATA 10
See also DLB 41
Evans, Mark ... 65-68
See also SATA 19
Evans, Marvin R(ussell) 1915- ... 49-52
Evans, Mary 1946- ... 122
Evans, Mary Ann
See Eliot, George
Evans, Max 1925- ... CANR-1
Earlier sketch in CA 4R
Evans, Medford (Bryon) 1907- ... 25-28R
Evans, Mel 1912(?)-1984 Obituary ... 112
Evans, Melbourne G(riffith) 1912- ... CAP-2
Earlier sketch in CA 33-36
Evans, Morgan
See Davies, L(eslie) P(urnell)
Evans, N(orman) Dean 1925- ... CANR-13
Earlier sketch in CA 21-22R
Evans, Nancy 1950- ... 77-80
Evans, Nathaniel 1742-1767 ... DLB-31
Evans, Oliver 1915- ... 19-20R
Evans, Olwen (Elizabeth) Carey
See Carey Evans, Olwen (Elizabeth)
Evans, Patricia Healy
See Carpenter, Patricia (Healy Evans)
Evans, Paul Richer 1925- Brief entry ... 106
Evans, Philip 1944- Brief entry ... 110
Evans, Rand B(oyd) 1942- Brief entry ... 107
Evans, Richard 1939- ... 106
Evans, Richard Evan 1898-1983 Obituary ... 109
Evans, Richard I(sadore) 1922-
Brief entry ... 108
Evans, Richard L(ouis) 1906-1971 ... 11-12R
Obituary ... 103
Evans, Robert Allen 1937- ... 112
Evans, Robert F(ranklin) 1930-1974 ... CAP-2
Earlier sketch in CA 23-24
Evans, Robert Henry 1937- ... 23-24R
Evans, Robert, Jr. 1932- ... 19-20R
Evans, Robert L(eonard) 1917- ... 49-52
Evans, Robert Owen 1919- ... 13-14R
Evans, Robert P. 1918- ... 13-14R
Evans, Rodney E(arl) 1939- ... 49-52
Evans, Rowland, Jr. 1921- ... CANR-15
Earlier sketch in CA 23-24R
Evans, Rupert N. 1921- ... 37-40R
Evans, Sara 1943- ... 93-96
Evans, Sebastian 1830-1909 ... DLB-35
Evans, Shirlee 1931- ... 61-64
Evans, Stanley G(eorge) 1912-1965 ... CAP-1
Earlier sketch in CA 9-10
Evans, Stuart 1934- ... 124
Brief entry ... 118
Evans, Susan H(ope) 1951- ... 115
Evans, Tabor
See Cameron, Lou
and Knott, William C(ecil, Jr.)
Evans, Thomas W(illiam) 1930- ... 45-48
Evans, Travers Moncure 1938- ... 57-60
Evans, Virginia Moran 1909- ... CANR-5
Earlier sketch in CA 7-8R
Evans, W(illiam) Glyn 1918- ... 89-92
Evans, W(illiam) McKee 1923- ... 23-24R
Evans, Walker 1903-1975 Obituary ... 89-92
Evans, (William Edis) Webster 1908- ... 41-44R
Evans, Wilbur 1913- ... 97-100
Evans, William 1895-1988 ... 81-84
Obituary ... 126
Evans, William David 1912-1985 Obituary ... 117
Evans, William Howard 1924- ... 23-24R
Evans, William R. 1938- ... 105
Evans Davies, Gloria 1932- ... 7-8R
Evansen, Virginia Besaw 1921- ... 13-14R
Evans-Jones, Albert 1895- ... 7-8R
Evans-Pritchard, Edward Evan 1902-1973 ... 65-68
Evarts, Esther
See Benson, Sally
Evarts, Hal G(eorge) 1887-1934
Brief entry ... 121
Evarts, Hal G. (Jr.) 1915- ... CANR-2
Earlier sketch in CA 49-52
See also SATA 6
Eve, Barbara
See Reiss, Barbara Eve
Eveland, Bill
See Eveland, Wilbur Crane
Eveland, Wilbur Crane 1918- ... 101
Eveling, (Harry) Stanley 1925- ... 61-64
Evely, Louis 1910- ... 85-88
Evelyn, Anthony
See Ward-Thomas, Evelyn Bridget Patricia Stephens
Evelyn, (John) Michael 1916- ... CANR-22
Earlier sketches in CA 5-6R, CANR-6
Evenhuis, Gertie 1932- ... 107
Evered, James F(letcher) 1928- ... 107
Everest, Allan S(eymour) 1913- ... CANR-26
Earlier sketches in CA 29-32R, CANR-11
Everett, Alexander Hill 1790-1847 ... DLB-59
Everett, Arthur (W., Jr.) 1914- ... 103
Everett, Donald E(dward) 1920- ... 9-10R
Everett, Edward 1794-1865 ... DLB-1, 59
Everett, Gail
See Hale, Arlene
Everett, Glenn D. 1921- ... 69-72
Everett, Peter 1931- ... 69-72
Everett, Peter W(illiam) 1924- ... 15-16R
Everett, T(homas) H(enry) 1903(?)-1986
Obituary ... 120
Everett, Walter 1936- ... 93-96
Everett-Green, Evelyn 1856-1932
Brief entry ... 114
Evergood, Philip 1901-1973 Obituary ... 41-44R
Everhart, James W(illiam), Jr. 1924- ... 89-92
Everhart, Jim
See Everhart, James W(illiam), Jr.
Everitt, Alan (Milner) 1926- ... CANR-11
Earlier sketch in CA 21-22R
Everitt, Arva Graham Johnson 1916(?)-1982 Obituary ... 107
Everitt, Bridget Mary 1924- ... 45-48
Everitt, C(harles) W(illiam) F(rancis) 1934- ... 65-68
Everitt, David Samuel 1952- ... 110
Everman, Welch D(uane) 1946- ... 57-60
Evernden, Margery 1916- ... 5-6R
See also SATA 5
Evers, (James) Charles 1923(?)-
Brief entry ... 111
Evers, Christopher 1940- ... 122
Eversley, D(avid) E(dward) C(harles) 1921- ... CANR-1
Earlier sketch in CA 4R
Eversole, Finley T. 1933- ... 9-10R
Everson, Dale Millar 1928- ... 17-18R
Everson, David H. 1941- ... 124
Everson, Ida Gertrude 1898- ... 37-40R
Everson, R(onald) G(ilmour) 1903- ... 19-20R
See also CLC 27
Everson, William (Oliver) 1912- ... CANR-20
Earlier sketch in CA 9-10R
See also DLB 5, 16
See also CLC 1, 5, 14
Everson, William Keith 1929- ... CANR-2
Earlier sketch in CA 4R
Everton, Macduff 1947- ... 104
Evertts, Eldonna L(ouise) 1917- ... 21-22R
Everwine, Peter Paul 1930- ... 73-76
Every, George 1909- ... CANR-6
Earlier sketch in CA 13-14R
Eves, Douglas 1922- ... 119
Evetts, Julia 1944- ... 69-72
Evins, Joseph Landon 1910- ... 61-64
Evitts, William J(oseph) 1942- ... 121
Brief entry ... 112
EVOE
See Knox, Edmund George Valpy
Evoy, John J(oseph) 1911- ... 5-6R
Evslin, Bernard 1922- ... CANR-9
Earlier sketch in CA 23-24R
See also SATA 28, 45
Evslin, Dorothy 1923- ... 57-60
Evtushenko, Evgenii Aleksandrovich
See Yevtushenko, Yevgeny (Alexandrovich)
Ewald, Wendy Taylor 1951- ... 120
Ewald, William Bragg, Jr. 1925- ... 107
Ewart, Andrew 1911- ... 17-18R
Ewart, Charles
See Lyte, Charles
Ewart, Gavin (Buchanan) 1916- ... CANR-17
Earlier sketch in CA 89-92
See also DLB 40
See also CLC 13, 46
Ewbank, Henry L(ee), Jr. 1924- ... 73-76
Ewbank, Walter F(rederick) 1918- ... CANR-17
Earlier sketch in CA 25-28R
Ewell, Barbara C(laire) 1947- ... 114
Ewell, Judith 1943- ... 107
Ewen, David 1907-1985 ... CANR-2
Obituary ... 118
Earlier sketch in CA 3R
See also SATA 4, 47
Ewen, Elizabeth 1943- ... 124
Ewen, Frederic 1899-1988 ... 73-76
Obituary ... 126
Ewen, Robert B. 1940- ... CANR-15
Earlier sketch in CA 37-40R
Ewen, Stuart 1945- ... CANR-12
Earlier sketch in CA 69-72
Ewens, James 1939- ... 116
Ewers, Hanns Heinz 1871-1943
Brief entry ... 109
See also TCLC 12
Ewers, John C(anfield) 1909- ... CANR-22
Earlier sketches in CA 19-20R, CANR-7
Ewert, David 1922- ... 105
Ewing, Alfred Cyril 1899-1973 ... CANR-4
Earlier sketch in CA 5-6R
Ewing, David Walkley 1923- ... CANR-5
Earlier sketch in CA 1R
Ewing, Donald M. 1895(?)-1978
Obituary ... 81-84
Ewing, Elizabeth 1904- ... 41-44R
Ewing, Frederick R.
See Sturgeon, Theodore Hamilton
Ewing, George W(ilmeth) 1923- ... 45-48
Ewing, John A(lexander) 1923- ... 125
Brief entry ... 105
Ewing, John Melvin 1925- ... 53-56
Ewing, John S(inclair) 1916- ... 13-14R
Ewing, Juliana (Horatia Gatty) 1841-1885 ... SATA-16
See also DLB 21
Ewing, Kathryn 1921- ... CANR-7
Earlier sketch in CA 61-64
See also SATA 20
Ewing, Sherman 1901-1975 Obituary ... 57-60
Ewton, Ralph W(aldo), Jr. 1938- ... 81-84
Ewy, Donna 1934- ... CANR-14
Earlier sketch in CA 33-36R
Ewy, Rodger 1931- ... CANR-14
Earlier sketch in CA 33-36R
Exall, Barry
See Nugent, John Peer
Excellent, Matilda
See Farson, Daniel (Negley)
Exell, Frank Kingsley 1902- ... 5-6R
Exley, Frederick (Earl) 1929- ... 81-84
See also DLBY 81
See also CLC 6, 11
See also AITN 2
Exley, Jo Ella Powell 1940- ... 122
Exman, Eugene 1900-1975 ... CAP-1
Obituary ... 61-64
Earlier sketch in CA 17-18
Ex - R. S. M.
See Lindsay, Harold Arthur
Exton, Clive (Jack Montague) 1930- ... 61-64
Exton, William, Jr. 1907- ... 45-48
Eyck, Frank 1921- ... CANR-11
Earlier sketch in CA 25-28R
Eye, Glen G(ordon) 1904- ... CANR-2
Earlier sketch in CA 49-52
Eyen, Jerome
See Eyen, Tom
Eyen, Tom 1941- ... CANR-22
Earlier sketch in CA 25-28R
Eyerly, Jeannette Hyde 1908- ... CANR-19
Earlier sketches in CA 4R, CANR-4
See also SATA 4
Eyestone, Robert 1942- ... 41-44R
Eykman, Christoph 1937- ... 41-44R
Eyles, Wilfred Charles 1891- ... CAP-2
Earlier sketch in CA 17-18
Eyre, Annette
See Worboys, Anne(tte Isobel) Eyre
Eyre, Dorothy
See McGuire, Leslie Sarah
Eyre, Katherine Wigmore 1901-1970
Obituary ... 104
See also SATA 26
Eyre, Richard M(elvin) 1944- ... CANR-13
Earlier sketch in CA 61-64
Eyre, Ronald 1929- ... 104
Eyre, S(amuel) R(obert) 1922- ... 23-24R
Eysenck, Hans J(urgen) 1916- ... CANR-25
Earlier sketches in CA 9-10R, CANR-4
Eysman, Harvey (Allen) 1939- ... 104
Eyster, C(harles) William 1917- ... 29-32R
Eyvindson, Peter (Knowles) 1946- ... 124
See also SATA 52
Ezekiel, Mordecai J(oseph) B(rill) 1899-1974 ... 65-68
Obituary ... 53-56
Ezekiel, Nissim 1924- ... 61-64
Ezekiel, Raphael S. 1931- ... 53-56
Ezekiel, Tish O'Dowd 1943- ... CLC-34
Ezell, Harry E(ugene) 1918-1974 ... 3R
Obituary ... 103
Ezell, John Samuel 1917- ... 1R
Ezell, Macel D. 1934- ... 77-80
Ezera, Kalu 1925- ... 15-16R
Ezergailis, Andrew 1930- ... 89-92
Ezorsky, Gertrude ... 89-92
Ezzell, Marilyn 1937- ... 109
See also SATA 38, 42

F

F.P.A.
See Adams, Franklin P(ierce)
Faas, Larry A(ndrew) 1936- ... 29-32R
Fabbri, Diego 1911-1980 Obituary ... 105
Fabbri, Nancy Rash 1940- ... 103
Fabe, Maxene 1943- ... 77-80
See also SATA 15
Faber, Adele 1928- ... 77-80
Faber, Charles F(ranklin) 1926- ... CANR-12
Earlier sketch in CA 29-32R
Faber, Doris (Greenberg) 1924- ... CANR-8
Earlier sketch in CA 17-18R
See also SATA 3
Faber, Frederick William 1814-1863 ... DLB-32
Faber, Harold 1919- ... CANR-8
Earlier sketch in CA 15-16R
See also SATA 5
Faber, John Henry 1918- ... 15-16R
Faber, Nancy W(eingarten) 1909-1976 ... 5-6R
Obituary ... 65-68
Faber, Richard Stanley 1924- ... 61-64
Faber-Kaiser, Andreas 1944- ... 73-76
Fabian, Donald L(eroy) 1919- ... 23-24R
Fabian, Josephine C(unningham) 1903-1984 ... CAP-1
Obituary ... 114
Earlier sketch in CA 9-10
Fabian, Robert (Honey) 1901-1978 ... 81-84
Obituary ... 77-80
Fabian, Ruth
See Quigley, Aileen
Fabinyi, Andrew 1908-1978 Obituary ... 108
Fabio, Sarah Webster 1928-1979 ... CANR-22
Earlier sketch in CA 69-72
See also BW
Fabisch, Judith Patricia 1938- ... CANR-19
Earlier sketch in CA 103
Fabos, Julius Gy(ula) 1932- ... 97-100
Fabre, Genevieve E. 1936- ... 109
Fabre, Jean Henri (Casimir) 1823-1915 ... SATA-22
Fabre, Michel J(acques) 1933- ... CANR-16
Earlier sketches in CA 45-48, CANR-1
Fabrega, Horacio, Jr. 1934- ... 73-76
Fabri, Ralph 1894-1975 ... CAP-2
Obituary ... 57-60
Earlier sketch in CA 19-20
Fabricand, Burton Paul 1923- ... 93-96
Fabricant, Carole 1944- ... 113
Fabricius, Johan (Johannes) 1899- ... CANR-5
Earlier sketch in CA 53-56
Fabrizio, Ray 1930- ... 33-36R
Fabrizius, Peter
See Fabry, Joseph B(enedikt)
and Knight, Max
Fabry, Joseph B(enedikt) 1909- ... 25-28R
Fabrycky, Wolter Joseph 1932- ... 21-22R
Fabun, Don 1920- ... 45-48
Fackenheim, Emil L(udwig) 1916- ... 23-24R
Facklam, Margery (Metz) 1927- ... CANR-21
Earlier sketches in CA 7-8R, CANR-6
See also SATA 20
Fackler, Eli
See Fackler, Elizabeth
Fackler, Elizabeth 1947- ... 118
Fackre, Gabriel Joseph 1926- ... CANR-7
Earlier sketch in CA 17-18R
Facos, James F(rancis) 1924- ... 41-44R
Factor, Regis A(nthony) 1937- ... 118

INDEX

Fader, Daniel 1930- 33-36R
Fader, Shirley Sloan 1931- CANR-14
Earlier sketch in CA 77-80
Faderman, Lillian 1940- CANR-16
Earlier sketch in CA 33-36R
Fadeyev, A.
See Bulgya, Alexander Alexandrovich
Fadeyev, Alexander
See Bulgya, Alexander Alexandrovich
Fadiman, Clifton (Paul) 1904- CANR-9
Earlier sketch in CA 61-64
See also SATA 11
Fadiman, Edwin, Jr. 1925- 29-32R
Fadiman, James 1939- 33-36R
Fadiman, Jeffrey A(ndrew) 1936- 116
Fadner, Frank (Leslie) 1910-1987 .... 11-12R
Obituary 123
Faegre, Torvald 1941- 89-92
Faelten, Sharon 1950- CANR-23
Earlier sketch in CA 106
Faessler, Shirley 1921(?)- 106
Fagan, Brian Murray 1936- CANR-14
Earlier sketch in CA 41-44R
Fagan, Edward R(ichard) 1924- CANR-20
Earlier sketches in CA 9-10R, CANR-5
Fage, John Donnelly 1921- CANR-7
Earlier sketch in CA 7-8R
Fagen, Donald 1948- CLC-26
Fagen, Richard R. 1933- CANR-22
Earlier sketches in CA 17-18R, CANR-7
Fagen, Stanley Alan 1936- 102
Fager, Charles E(ugene) 1942- 21-22R
Fagerstrom, Stan 1923- 57-60
Fagg, Elizabeth
See Olds, Elizabeth Fagg
Fagg, John (Edwin) 1916- 81-84
Fagg, William Buller 1914- 102
Fagles, Robert 1933- Brief entry 104
Fagley, Richard M(artin) 1910- 2R
Fagon, Alfred 1937-1986 Obituary 120
Fagothey, Austin 1901- CAP-1
Earlier sketch in CA 11-12
Fague, William Robert 1927- 109
Fagundo, Ana Maria 1938- 37-40R
Fagunwa, D(aniel) O(lorunfemi)
1910(?)-1963 Obituary 116
Fagyas, Maria 33-36R
Faherty, William B(arnaby) 1914- CANR-5
Earlier sketch in CA 7-8R
Fahey, Frank M(ichael) 1917- 101
Fahey, James C(harles) 1903-1974
Obituary 53-56
Fahlstrom, Oyvind (Axel Christian)
1928-1976 Obituary 69-72
Fahnestock, Beatrice Beck 1899(?)-1980
Obituary 97-100
Fahs, Ivan J. 1932- 45-48
Fahs, Sophia Blanche Lyon 1876-1978
Obituary 77-80
Fahy, Christopher 1937- CANR-11
Earlier sketch in CA 69-72
Fain, Haskell 1926- 33-36R
Fain, Tyrus Gerard 1933- 104
Fainlight, Ruth (Esther) 1931- CANR-26
Earlier sketches in CA 19-20R, CANR-8
Fainsod, Merle 1907-1972 .... CAP-1
Obituary 33-36R
Earlier sketch in CA 15-16
Fainstein, Norman Ira 1944- 102
Fainstein, Susan S. 1938- 93-96
Fainzilberg, Ilya Arnoldovich 1897-1937
Brief entry 120
Fair, A. A.
See Gardner, Erle Stanley
Fair, Charles M. 1916- CANR-10
Earlier sketch in CA 15-16R
Fair, Harold L(loyd) 1924- 89-92
Fair, James 1898(?)-1984 Obituary 112
Fair, James R(utherford), Jr. 1920- 29-32R
Fair, Marvin L(uke) 1897(?)-1983
Obituary 110
Fair, Ray C(larence) 1942- 29-32R
Fair, Ronald L. 1932- CANR-25
Earlier sketch in CA 69-72
See also BW
See also DLB 33
See also CLC 18
Fair, Sylvia 1933- 69-72
See also SATA 13
Fairbairn, Ann
See Tait, Dorothy
Fairbairn, Douglas 1926- 33-36R
Fairbairn, Garry L. 1947- 77-80
Fairbairn, Helen
See Southard, Helen Fairbairn
Fairbairn, Ian J(ohn) 1933- 53-56
Fairbairns, Zoe (Ann) 1948- CANR-21
Earlier sketch in CA 103
See also CLC 32
Fairbank, Alfred John 1895-1982 .... CANR-6
Obituary 106
Earlier sketch in CA 7-8R
Fairbank, John K(ing) 1907- CANR-3
Earlier sketch in CA 1R
Fairbanks, Carol 1935- 69-72
Fairbanks, Henry G(eorge) 1914-
Brief entry 112
Fairbrother, Nan 1913-1971 .... CANR-3
Obituary 33-36R
Earlier sketch in CA 7-8R
Fairburn, Eleanor 1928- CANR-8
Earlier sketch in CA 61-64
Fairchild, Hoxie Neale 1894-1973 .... 7-8R
Obituary 45-48
Fairchild, John B(urr) 1927- Brief entry 117
Fairchild, Louis W. 1901-1981 Obituary 105
Fairchild, William 73-76
Fairclough, Chris 1951- 112
Faire, Zabrina
See Stevenson, Florence
Fairfax, Ann
See Chesney, Marion
Fairfax, Beatrice
See Manning, Marie
and McCarroll, Marion C(lyde)
Fairfax, Felix
See Gibson, Walter B(rown)
Fairfax, John 1930- 97-100
Fairfax, John 1937- 49-52
Fairfax, Warwick (Oswald) 1901-1987
Obituary 121
Fairfax-Blakeborough, Jack
See Fairfax-Blakeborough, John Freeman
Fairfax-Blakeborough, John Freeman
1883-1978(?) 102
Fairfax-Lucy, Brian (Fulke
Cameron-Ramsay) 1898-1974 .... CAP-2
Earlier sketch in CA 29-32
See also SATA 6, 26
Fairfield, Darrell
See Larkin, Rochelle
Fairfield, James G(lencairn) T(homson)
1926- 126
Fairfield, John
See Livingstone, Harrison Edward
Fairfield, Leslie P(arke) 1941- Brief entry 107
Fairfield, Richard 1937- 41-44R
Fairfield, Roy P(hillip) 1918- 33-36R
Fairhall, David Keir 1934- 103
Fairholme, Elizabeth 1910- 97-100
Fairless, Caroline S. 1947- 105
Fairley, Barker 1887-1986 .... 1R
Obituary 121
Fairley, Irene R. 1940- 73-76
Fairley, James Stewart 1940- 102
Fairley, M(ichael) C(harles) 1937- CANR-14
Earlier sketch in CA 37-40R
Fairley, Peter 1930- CANR-24
Earlier sketch in CA 29-32R
Fairlie, Gerard 1899-1983 Obituary 109
See also SATA 34
Fairlie, Henry (Jones) 1924- 104
Fairman, Charles 1897- 45-48
Fairman, Herbert Walter 1907-1982 111
Obituary 108
Fairman, Honora C. 1927(?)-1978
Obituary 81-84
Fairman, Joan A(lexandra) 1935- 33-36R
See also SATA 10
Fairman, Paul W. 1916-1977 Obituary 114
Fairn, (Richard) Duncan 1906-1986
Obituary 119
Fairweather, Eileen 1954- 125
Fairweather, Eugene Rathbone 1920-
Brief entry 108
Fairweather, George W. 1921- 15-16R
Fairweather, Janet (Anne) 1945- 124
Fairweather, Sally (Hallberg) 1917- 112
Fairweather, Virginia 1922- 29-32R
Faison, S(amson) Lane, Jr. 1907- 89-92
Faissler, Margareta 1902- 7-8R
Fait, Hollis F. 1918- CANR-5
Earlier sketch in CA 1R
Faith, Barbara
See Covarrubias, Barbara Faith
Faith, (Richard) Mack 1944- 125
Faith, William Robert
See Fague, William Robert
Faithfull, Gail 1936- 57-60
See also SATA 8
Faiz, Faiz Ahmad 1912(?)-1984 Obituary 115
Fakhry, Majid 1923- 29-32R
Fakinos, Aris 1935- 81-84
Falassi, Alessandro 1945- 105
Falb, Lewis W(illiam) 1935- 102
Falck, (Adrian) Colin 1934- 65-68
Falco, Gian
See Papini, Giovanni
Falco, Maria J(osephine) 1932- CANR-12
Earlier sketch in CA 61-64
Falcoff, Mark 1941- 65-68
Falcon
See Nestle, John Francis
Falcon, Richard
See Shapiro, Samuel
Falcon, Walter P(hillip) 1936- 126
Brief entry 109
Falcon, William D(yche) 1932- 17-18R
Falcon-Barker, Ted 1923- 25-28R
Falconer, A. F.
See Falconer, Alexander Frederick
Falconer, Alexander Frederick 1908-1987
Obituary 122
Falconer, Alun ?-1973 Obituary 104
Falconer, James
See Kirkup, James
Falconer, Kenneth
See Kornbluth, C(yril) M.
Falconer, Lee N.
See May, Julian
Falero, Frank, Jr. 1937- 37-40R
Fales, Dean Abner, Jr. 1925- Brief entry 110
Fales, Edward (Daniel, Jr.) 1906- 97-100
Falk, Charles J(ohn) 1899-1971 .... CAP-2
Earlier sketch in CA 23-24
Falk, Doris Virginia 1919- Brief entry 111
Falk, Elsa
See Escherich, Elsa Falk
Falk, Eugene H(annes) 1913- 116
Falk, Gerhard 1931- 117
Falk, Harvey 1932- Brief entry 112
Falk, I(sidore) S(ydney) 1899-1984
Obituary 114
Falk, Irving A. 1921- 23-24R
Falk, Kathryn 1940- CANR-20
Earlier sketch in CA 97-100
Falk, Lee Harrison 1915- 97-100
Falk, Leslie A. 1915- 11-12R
Falk, Louis A. 1896(?)-1979 Obituary 85-88
Falk, Marvin W. 1943- 122
Falk, Minna Regina 1900-1983 Obituary 109
Falk, Pamela S. 1953- 122
Falk, Quentin 1948- 122
Falk, Richard A(nderson) 1930- CANR-12
Earlier sketch in CA 5-6R
Falk, Robert 1914- 89-92
Falk, Roger (Salis) 1910- 65-68
Falk, S(tephen) J(ohn) 1942- 124
Falk, Signi Lenea 1906- 7-8R
Falk, Stanley L(awrence) 1927- CANR-2
Earlier sketch in CA 3R
Falk, Susan Meyers 1942- 117
Falk, Toby
See Falk, S(tephen) J(ohn)
Falk, Ursula Adler 114
Falk, Ze'ev W(ilhelm) 1923- CANR-15
Earlier sketch in CA 21-22R
Falkender, Baroness Marcia
See Williams, Marcia
Falkirk, Richard
See Lambert, Derek
Falkland, Samuel
See Heijermans, Herman
Falkner, Leonard 1900- 23-24R
See also SATA 12
Falkner, Murry (Charles) 1899- CAP-2
Earlier sketch in CA 23-24
Falk-Roenne, Arne 1920- CANR-14
Earlier sketch in CA 23-24R
Falkus, Hugh Edward Lance 1917- 111
Fall, Bernard B. 1926-1967 .... CANR-6
Obituary 25-28R
Earlier sketch in CA 4R
Fall, Frieda Kay 1913- 41-44R
Fall, Thomas
See Snow, Donald Clifford
Fallaci, Oriana 1930- CANR-15
Earlier sketch in CA 77-80
See also CLC 11
Fallada, Hans
See Ditzen, Rudolf
See also DLB 56
Fallaw, Wesner 1907- 4R
Faller, Kevin 1920- CANR-4
Earlier sketch in CA 53-56
Fallere, Felicia
See Knist, F(rances) Emma
Fallers, Lloyd A(shton, Jr.) 1925-1974 .. CANR-4
Obituary 49-52
Earlier sketch in CA 9-10R
Falley, Margaret Dickson 1898-1983
Obituary 110
Fallon, Carlos 1909- 41-44R
Fallon, Eileen Brydon 1954- 118
Fallon, Frederic (Michael) 1944-1970 .... 41-44R
Fallon, George
See Bingley, David Ernest
Fallon, Jack
See Fallon, John W(illiam)
Fallon, John W(illiam) 1924- 77-80
Fallon, Martin
See Patterson, Henry
Fallon, Padraic 1905-1974 103
Obituary 89-92
Fallon, Peter 1951- Brief entry 106
Fallon, Robert T(homas) 1927- 121
Fallows, James M(ackenzie) 1949- CANR-2
Earlier sketch in CA 45-48
Falls, C(harles) B(uckles) 1874-1960
Obituary 116
See also SATA 27, 38
Falls, Cyril Bentham 1888- CAP-1
Earlier sketch in CA 13-14
Falls, Joe 1928- 77-80
Fallwell, Marshall Leigh, Jr. 1943- 69-72
Falorp, Nelson P.
See Jones, Stephen (Phillip)
Falstein, Louis 1909- 97-100
See also SATA 37
Faludy, George 1913- 21-22R
See also CLC 42
Faludy, Gyoergy
See Faludy, George
Falvey, Jack 1938- 122
Falwell, Jerry 1933- 102
Fama, Eugene F. 1939- Brief entry 113
Famiglietti, Eugene Paul 1931(?)-1980
Obituary 97-100
Famularo, Joseph John 1922- CANR-4
Earlier sketch in CA 1R
Fan, Kuang Huan 1932- 23-24R
Fanburg, Walter H. 1936- Brief entry 114
Fancher, Betsy 1928- DLBY-83
Fancher, Ewilda 1928- 61-64
Fancher, Raymond E(lwood), Jr. 1940- 69-72
Fanchon, Lisa
See Floren, Lee
Fancutt, Walter 1911- CANR-12
Earlier sketches in CA 9-10, CAP-1
Fandel, John 1925- CANR-23
Earlier sketch in CA 69-72
Fane, Bron
See Fanthorpe, R(obert) Lionel
Fane, Julian Charles 1927- CANR-6
Earlier sketch in CA 13-14R
Fane, Violet 1843-1905 .... DLB-35
Fang, Chaoying 1908(?)-1985 Obituary 116
Fang, Irving E. 1929- 49-52
Fang, Josephine (Maria) Riss 1922- 69-72
Fanger, Donald (Lee) 1929- 15-16R
Fann, K(uang) T(ih) 1937- 61-64
Fann, William E(dwin) 1930- CANR-2
Earlier sketch in CA 49-52
Fannin, Allen 1939- 69-72
Fanning, Buckner 1926- 69-72
Fanning, Charles (Frederick, Jr.) 1942- 81-84
Fanning, Leonard M(ulliken) 1888-1967 .... 7-8R
See also SATA 5
Fanning, Louis A(lbert) 1927- 69-72
Fanning, Michael 1942- 89-92
Fanning, Odom 1920- 53-56
Fanning, Robbie 1947- CANR-14
Earlier sketch in CA 77-80
Fanon, Frantz 1925-1961 116
Obituary 89-92
See also BW
Fanshawe, David 1942- 97-100
Fant, Joseph Lewis III 1928- 13-14R
Fant, Louis J(udson), Jr. 1931- 37-40R
Fanta, J. Julius 1907- 33-36R
Fante, John (Thomas) 1911-1983 .... CANR-23
Obituary 109
Earlier sketch in CA 69-72
See also DLBY 83
Fantel, Hans 1922- 49-52
Fanthorpe, Patricia Alice 1938- CANR-14
Earlier sketch in CA 89-92
Fanthorpe, R(obert) Lionel 1935- CANR-14
Earlier sketch in CA 73-76
Fantini, Mario D. 77-80
Farabee, Barbara 1944- 57-60
Faraday, Ann 1935- 77-80
Faragher, John Mack 1945- Brief entry 111
Farago, Ladislas 1906-1980 .... CANR-10
Obituary 102
Earlier sketch in CA 65-68
Farah, Caesar Elie 1929- 41-44R
Farah, Madelain 1934- 73-76
Farah, Nuruddin 1945- 106
Faralla, Dana 1909- 49-52
See also SATA 9
Faralla, Dorothy W.
See Faralla, Dana
Faramelli, Norman Joseph 1932-
Brief entry 109
Farau, Alfred 1904-1972 Obituary 37-40R
Farb, Peter 1929-1980 .... CANR-12
Obituary 97-100
Earlier sketch in CA 15-16R
See also SATA 12, 22
Farber, Bernard 1922- 23-24R
Farber, Donald C. CANR-13
Earlier sketch in CA 29-32R
Farber, Edward (Rolke) 1914-1982
Obituary 110
Farber, Joseph C. 1903- 33-36R
Farber, Leslie Hillel 1912-1981 110
Obituary 103
Farber, Marvin 1901- 49-52
Farber, Norma 1909-1984 102
Obituary 112
See also SATA 25, 38
See also DLB 61
Farber, Paul Lawrence 1944- 112
Farber, Seymour M(organ) 1912- 57-60
Farber, Stephen E. 1943- CANR-19
Earlier sketch in CA 103
Farber, Susan L. 1945- 106
Farber, Thomas (David) 1944- 103
Farberman, Harvey A(lan) 1939- 45-48
Farberow, Norman L(ouis) 1918- CANR-7
Earlier sketch in CA 19-20R
Farca, Marie C. 1935- 37-40R
Farel, Conrad
See Bardens, Dennis (Conrad)
Farely, Alison
See Poland, Dorothy (Elizabeth Hayward)
Farer, Tom J. 1935- CANR-8
Earlier sketch in CA 17-18R
Farewell, Nina
See Cooper, Mae (Klein)
Fargis, Paul (McKenna) 1939- CANR-13
Earlier sketch in CA 21-22R
Fargo, Doone
See Norwood, Victor G(eorge) C(harles)
Fargo, Joe
See Rikhoff, James C.
Fargue, Leon-Paul 1876(?)-1947
Brief entry 109
See also TCLC 11
Farhi, Moris 1935- CANR-13
Earlier sketch in CA 77-80
Faria, A(nthony) J(ohn) 1944- CANR-19
Earlier sketch in CA 102
Faricy, Robert L(eo) 1926- CANR-15
Earlier sketch in CA 37-40R
Faridi, S. N.
See Faridi, Shah Nasiruddin Mohammad
Faridi, Shah Nasiruddin Mohammad
1929- 29-32R
Faries, Clyde J. 1928- 37-40R
Faries, David A(llan) 1938- 112
Farigoule, Louis
See Romains, Jules
Farina, John 1950- 114
Farina, Richard 1936(?)-1966 81-84
Obituary 25-28R
See also CLC 9
Faris, (Earl) Barry 1889-1966 Obituary 114
Faris, Robert E. L(ee) 1907- 17-18R
Faris, Wendy B(ush) 1945- 115
Farish, Donald J(ames) 1942- 106
Farish, Margaret Kennedy 1918- 7-8R
Farjeon, (Eve) Annabel 1919- 53-56
See also SATA 11
Farjeon, Eleanor 1881-1965 .... CAP-1
Earlier sketch in CA 11-12
See also SATA 2

Farkas, Emil 1946- 69-72
Farkas, Philip 1914- 49-52
Farley, Carol 1936- CANR-25
Earlier sketches in CA 21-22R, CANR-10
See also SATA 4
Farley, (William) Edward 1929- 61-64
Farley, Eugene J. 1916- CANR-12
Earlier sketch in CA 33-36R
Farley, James A(loysius) 1888-1976
Obituary 65-68
Farley, Jean 1928- 23-24R
Farley, Miriam Southwell 1907(?)-1975
Obituary 57-60
Farley, Rawle 1922- 45-48
Farley, Walter (Lorimer) 1915- CANR-8
Earlier sketch in CA 19-20R
See also SATA 2, 43
See also DLB 22
See also CLC 17
Farley-Hills, David 1931- 73-76
Farlie, Barbara L(eitzow) 1936- 65-68
Farlow, John King
See King-Farlow, John
Farmacevten
See Holm, Sven (Aage)
Farmar, Hugh William 1908-1987
Obituary 123
Farmer, Albert J(ohn) 1894-1976 23-24R
Obituary 120
Farmer, Bernard James 1902- 7-8R
Farmer, Bertram Hughes 1916- 104
Farmer, Charles J(oseph) 1943- CANR-10
Earlier sketch in CA 57-60
Farmer, David Hugh 1923- 125
Farmer, Don 1938- 65-68
Farmer, Gary R(ay) 1923- 57-60
Farmer, Gene 1919-1972 Obituary 37-40R
Farmer, Herbert Henry 1892-1981(?)
Obituary 102
Farmer, Kathleen 1946- CANR-10
Earlier sketch in CA 65-68
Farmer, Laurence 1895(?)-1976 Obituary 65-68
Farmer, Martha L(ouise) 1912- 23-24R
Farmer, Norman K(ittrell, Jr.) 1934- 123
Farmer, Penelope (Jane) 1939- CANR-9
Earlier sketch in CA 15-16R
See also SATA 39, 40
See also CLR 8
Farmer, Peter 1950- SATA-38
Farmer, Philip Jose 1918- CANR-4
Earlier sketch in CA 3R
See also DLB 8
See also CLC 1, 19
Farmer, R. L.
See Lamont, Rosette C(lementine)
Farmer, Richard Neil 1928- CANR-8
Earlier sketch in CA 17-18R
Farmer, Robert Allen 1938- 23-24R
Farmer, William R(euben) 1921- 123
Brief entry 109
Farmer Jones
See Jones, Bryan L.
Farmiloe, Dorothy Alicia 1920- CANR-8
Earlier sketch in CA 61-64
Farnash, Hugh
See Luff, S(tanley) G(eorge) A(nthony)
Farndale, W(illiam) A(rthur) J(ames)
1916- CANR-11
Earlier sketch in CA 25-28R
Farner, Donald S(ankey) 1915- 53-56
Farnham, Burt
See Clifford, Harold B(urton)
Farnham, Emily 1912- 69-72
Farnham, Marynia F. 1900(?)-1979
Obituary 85-88
Farnham, Thomas J(avery) 1938- CANR-4
Earlier sketch in CA 53-56
Farnie, D(ouglas) A(ntony) 1926- CANR-12
Earlier sketch in CA 73-76
Farnsworth, Clyde A. 1908(?)-1984
Obituary 112
Farnsworth, Dana (Lyda) 1905-1986 61-64
Obituary 119
Farnsworth, E(dward) Allan 1928- 15-16R
Farnsworth, James
See Pohle, Robert W(arren), Jr.
Farnsworth, Jerry 1895- CAP-1
Earlier sketch in CA 15-16
Farnsworth, Lee W(infield) 1932- 33-36R
Farnsworth, Paul Randolph 1899- CAP-2
Earlier sketch in CA 29-32
Farnsworth, Robert M. 1929- 53-56
Farnum, K. T.
See Rips, Ervine M(ilton)
Farnworth, Warren 1935- 93-96
Farny, Michael H(olt) 1934- 65-68
Faron, Louis C. 1923- 11-12R
Farquhar, Aardvark Z. 1929- 113
Farquhar, Francis P(eloubet) 1887-1975 CAP-1
Obituary 57-60
Earlier sketch in CA 19-20
Farquhar, Margaret C(utting) 1905- 69-72
See also SATA 13
Farquharson, Alexander 1944- SATA-46
Farquharson, Charlie
See Harron, Don(ald)
Farquharson, Martha
See Finley, Martha
Farr, Bill
See Farr, William T.
Farr, David M. L. 1922- 37-40R
Farr, Diana (Pullein-Thompson) CANR-20
Earlier sketches in CA 15-16R, CANR-7
Farr, Dorothy M(ary) 1905- 77-80
Farr, Douglas
See Gilford, C(harles) B(ernard)
Farr, Finis (King) 1904-1982 CANR-1
Obituary 105
Earlier sketch in CA 3R
See also SATA 10
Farr, John
See Webb, Jack (Randolph)
Farr, Judith 1937- CANR-12
Earlier sketch in CA 29-32R
Farr, Kenneth R(aymond) 1942- 73-76
Farr, Michael 1924- 29-32R
Farr, Roger C. 33-36R
Farr, Sidney Saylor 1932- 114
Farr, Walter Greene, Jr. 1925- Brief entry 106
Farr, William T. 1934-1987 Obituary 121
Farra, Madame E.
See Fawcett, F(rank) Dubrez
Farrant, Leda 1927- 21-22R
Farrar, John C(hipman) 1896-1974 65-68
Obituary 53-56
Farrar, Lancelot Leighton, Jr. 1932- CANR-4
Earlier sketch in CA 53-56
Farrar, Larston Dawn 1915-1970 2R
Obituary 29-32R
Farrar, Margaret Petherbridge 1897-1984
Obituary 113
Farrar, Richard B(artlett), Jr. 1939- 65-68
Farrar, Ronald T(ruman) 1935- 33-36R
Farrar, Rowena Rutherford 1903- 108
Farrar, Susan Clement 1917- 101
See also SATA 33
Farrar-Hockley, Anthony Heritage 1924- 69-72
Farrell, Alan 1920- 15-16R
Farrell, Anne A. 1916- 25-28R
Farrell, Barry 1935(?)-1984 Obituary 114
Farrell, Ben
See Cebulash, Mel
Farrell, Bryan (Henry) 1923- CANR-2
Earlier sketch in CA 49-52
Farrell, C(larence) Frederick, Jr. 1934- 122
Farrell, Catharine
See O'Connor, Sister Mary Catharine
Farrell, Cliff 1899-1977 65-68
Obituary 125
Farrell, David
See Smith, Frederick E(screet)
Farrell, Desmond
See Organ, John
Farrell, Edith R(odgers) 1933- 122
Farrell, Edmund J(ames) 1927- 120
Farrell, Francis (Thomas) 1912-1983
Obituary 109
Farrell, Frank
See Farrell, Francis (Thomas)
Farrell, J(ames) G(ordon) 1935-1979 73-76
Obituary 89-92
See also DLB 14
See also CLC 6
Farrell, James T(homas) 1904-1979 CANR-9
Obituary 89-92
Earlier sketch in CA 5-6R
See also DLB 4, 9
See also DLBD 2
See also CLC 1, 4, 8, 11
Farrell, John J(oseph) 1934- Brief entry 110
Farrell, John Philip 1939- 102
Farrell, Kathleen (Amy) 1912- 7-8R
Farrell, Kirby 1942- 33-36R
Farrell, M. J.
See Keane, Mary Nesta (Skrine)
Farrell, Matthew Charles 1921- 49-52
Farrell, Melvin L(loyd) 1930- CANR-5
Earlier sketch in CA 13-14R
Farrell, Michael 1944- CANR-23
Earlier sketch in CA 69-72
Farrell, Patricia
See Zelver, Patricia (Farrell)
Farrell, Robert T(homas) 1938- 93-96
Farrell, Susan Caust 1944- 112
Farrell, William E. 1936(?)-1985 Obituary 115
Farrelly, M(ark) John 1927- 15-16R
Farren, David
See McFerran, Douglass David
Farren, Richard J.
See Betjeman, John
Farrer, Claire R(afferty) 1936- CANR-26
Earlier sketches in CA 65-68, CANR-10
Farrer, (Bryan) David 1906-1983 25-28R
Obituary 109
Farrer, Katharine Dorothy (Newton) 1911- 7-8R
Farrer, Keith Thomas Henry 1916- 110
Farrimond, John 1913- 102
Farrington, Benjamin 1891-1974 65-68
Obituary 53-56
See also SATA 20
Farrington, (Mary) Elizabeth Pruett
1898-1984 Obituary 113
Farrington, S(elwyn) Kip, Jr. 1904-1983 73-76
Obituary 109
See also SATA 20
Farris, John 101
Farris, Martin T(heodore) 1925- CANR-11
Earlier sketch in CA 21-22R
Farris, Paul L(eonard) 1919- 11-12R
Farrison, William Edward 1902- 29-32R
Farriss, N(ancy) M(arguerite) 1938- 25-28R
Farrow, J.
See Fonarow, Jerry
Farrow, James S.
See Tubb, E(dwin) C(harles)
Farson, Daniel (Negley) 1927- CANR-16
Earlier sketch in CA 93-96
Farson, (James Scott) Negley 1890-1960
Obituary 93-96
Farstad, Arthur L(eonard) 1935- 109
Farthing, Alison 1936- 117
See also SATA 36, 45
Farwell, Byron E. 1921- CANR-9
Earlier sketch in CA 15-16R
Farwell, George Michell 1911-1976 21-22R
Obituary 69-72
Farwell, Loring C(hapman) 1915-
Brief entry 111
Farzan, Massud 1936- 53-56
Fasana, Paul James 1933- CANR-14
Earlier sketch in CA 37-40R
Fasel, George W(illiam) 1938- 23-24R
Fasick, Adele M(ongan) 1930- 125
Fasold, Ralph W(illiam August) 1940- 29-32R
Fass, Paula S. 1947- Brief entry 112
Fassbinder, Rainer Werner 1946-1982 93-96
Obituary 106
See also CLC 20
Fassett, James 1904-1986 49-52
Obituary 121
Fassler, Joan (Grace) 1931- 61-64
See also SATA 11
Fast, Barbara 1924- 104
Fast, Howard (Melvin) 1914- CANR-1
Earlier sketch in CA 2R
See also SATA 7
See also DLB 9
See also CLC 23
Fast, Jonathan David 1948- 77-80
Fast, Julius 1919- CANR-11
Earlier sketch in CA 25-28R
Fastlife
See Grogan, Emmett
Fatchen, Max 1920- CANR-11
Earlier sketch in CA 25-28R
See also SATA 20
Fate, Terry 1949- 116
Fatemi, Nasrollah S(aifpour) 1910- 77-80
Father Xavier
See Hurwood, Bernhardt J.
Fatigati, (Frances) Evelyn 1948- 77-80
See also SATA 24
Fatio, Louise 1904- 37-40R
See also SATA 6
Fatjo, Thomas Joseph, Jr. 1940- 107
Fatouros, A(rghyrios) A. 1932- 15-16R
Fatout, Paul 1897- 23-24R
Fatt, Amelia 1943- 118
Faucher, Real 1940- 101
Faucher, W. Thomas 1945- 57-60
Faulhaber, Charles Bailey 1941- 53-56
Faulhaber, Martha 1926- 33-36R
See also SATA 7
Faulk, John Henry 1913- 102
Faulk, Odie B. 1933- CANR-14
Earlier sketch in CA 25-28R
Faulkner, Alex 1905(?)-1983 Obituary 109
Faulkner, Anne Irvin 1906- CANR-2
Earlier sketch in CA 4R
See also SATA 23
Faulkner, Charles H. 1937- 25-28R
Faulkner, Christopher G(raham) 1942- 125
Faulkner, Edwin J. 1900(?)-1987 Obituary 121
Faulkner, Elsie 1905- 65-68
Faulkner, Frank
See Ellis, Edward S(ylvester)
Faulkner, Harold Underwood 1890-1968 1R
Obituary 103
Faulkner, John 1901-1963 CANR-1
Earlier sketch in CA 2R
Faulkner, Joseph E. 1928- 45-48
Faulkner, Nancy
See Faulkner, Anne Irvin
Faulkner, Peter 1933- CANR-20
Earlier sketches in CA 7-8R, CANR-3
Faulkner, Ray (Nelson) 1906- 5-6R
Faulkner, Trader 1930- 102
Faulkner, Virginia (Louise) 1913-1980 CANR-11
Earlier sketch in CA 65-68
Faulkner, (Herbert Winthrop) Waldron
1898-1979 93-96
Obituary 85-88
Faulkner, William (Cuthbert) 1897-1962 81-84
See also DLB 9, 11, 44
See also DLBY 86
See also DLBD 2
See also CLC 1, 3, 6, 8, 9, 11, 14, 18, 28
See also SSC 1
Faulknor, Cliff(ord Vernon) 1913- CANR-8
Earlier sketch in CA 19-20R
Faulks, Neville 1908-1985 Obituary 118
Faunce, Roland Cleo 1905- 1R
Faunce, William A(lden) 1928- 25-28R
Faunce-Brown, Daphne (Bridget) 1938- 115
Faupel, John F(rancis) 1906- 7-8R
Faure, Lucie 1908-1977 Obituary 73-76
Faure, William C(aldwell), Jr. 1949- 109
Faurot, Albert 1914- 77-80
Faurot, Jean H(iatt) 1911- 29-32R
Faurot, Jeannette 1943- 106
Faurot, Ruth Marie 1916- 85-88
Fauset, Arthur Huff 25-28R
Fauset, Jessie Redmon 1884(?)-1961 109
See also BW
See also DLB 51
See also CLC 19
Fausold, Martin L. 1921- 23-24R
Fausset, Hugh I'Anson 1895-1965
Obituary 93-96
Faust, Clarence H(enry) 1901-1975
Obituary 57-60
Faust, Drew Gilpin 1947- 110
Faust, Frederick (Shiller) 1892-1944(?)
Brief entry 108
Faust, Irvin 1924- 33-36R
See also DLB 2, 28
See also DLBY 80
See also CLC 8
Faust, Naomi F(lowe) 61-64
Fausti, Remo P(hilip) 1917- 41-44R
Fauth, Robert T. 1916- 1R
Fautsko, Timothy F(rank) 1945- 85-88
Faux, Marian 1945- CANR-14
Earlier sketch in CA 81-84
Fava, Sylvia Fleis 1927- 115
Faverty, Frederic Everett 1902-1981 45-48
Obituary 104
Faville, David Ernest 1899-1970 1R
Obituary 103
Favret, Andrew G. 1925- 19-20R
Favretti, Rudy J(ohn) 1932- CANR-4
Earlier sketch in CA 53-56
Fawcett, Brian 1906- 102
Fawcett, Chris 1950- 107
Fawcett, Clara Hallard 1887- CAP-1
Earlier sketch in CA 15-16
Fawcett, Claude W(eldon) 1911- 49-52
Fawcett, F(rank) Dubrez 1891-1968 CAP-1
Earlier sketch in CA 9-10
Fawcett, J(ames) E(dmund) S(anford)
1913- 97-100
Fawcett, Ken(neth Richard) 1944- 104
Fawcett, Marion
See Sanderson, Sabina W(arren)
Fawcett, Robin P(owell) 1937- 119
Fawcett, Roger Knowlton 1909-1979
Obituary 89-92
Fawkes, Guy
See Benchley, Robert (Charles)
Fawkes, Richard (Brian) 1944- CANR-20
Earlier sketch in CA 103
Fax, Elton Clay 1909- CANR-15
Earlier sketch in CA 13-14R
See also SATA 25
Faxon, Alicia Craig 1931- 69-72
Faxon, Arba D. 1895(?)-1975 Obituary 61-64
Faxon, Lavinia
See Russ, Lavinia
Fay, Allen 1934- 123
Brief entry 118
Fay, Erica
See Stopes, Marie (Charlotte) Carmichael
Fay, Frederic L(eighton) 1890- CAP-2
Earlier sketch in CA 21-22
Fay, Gerard (Francis Arthur) 1913-1968 CAP-1
Earlier sketch in CA 15-16
Fay, Gordon S(haw) 1912- 53-56
Fay, John 1921- 57-60
Fay, Leo (Charles) 1920- 15-16R
Fay, Mary Helen
See Fagyas, Maria
Fay, Peter Ward 1924- 57-60
Fay, S(amuel) P(rescott), Jr. 1926- 89-92
Fay, Stanley
See Stanley, Fay Grissom (Shulman)
Fay, Stephen 1938- 25-28R
Fay, Thomas A(rthur) 1927- 102
Faye, Jean Pierre 1925- 102
Fayer, Mischa Harry 1902-1977 CANR-6
Earlier sketch in CA 1R
Fayerweather, John 1922- CANR-1
Earlier sketch in CA 3R
Fazakas, Ray 1932- 101
Fazakerley, George Raymond 1921- 13-14R
Fazal, M(uhammad) A(bul) 1939- 29-32R
Fazzano, Joseph E. 1929- 7-8R
Feagans, Lynne 1945- 117
Feagans, Raymond (John) 1953- 57-60
Feagin, Joe R(ichard) 1938- CANR-13
Earlier sketch in CA 37-40R
Feagles, Anita M(acRae) 1927- CANR-4
Earlier sketch in CA 4R
See also SATA 9
Feagles, Elizabeth
See Day, Beth (Feagles)
Feague, Mildred H. 1915- 29-32R
See also SATA 14
Feal-Deibe, Carlos 1935- 37-40R
Fear, David E. 1941- 53-56
Fear, Richard Arthur 1909- 125
Fear Chanaidh
See Campbell, John Lorne
Fearing, Kenneth (Flexner) 1902-1961 93-96
See also DLB 9
Fearon, George Edward 1901- CAP-1
Earlier sketch in CA 9-10
Fearon, John D(aniel) 1920- 37-40R
Fearon, Peter (Shaun) 1942- 29-32R
Fears, Gerald 81-84
Feather, John 1947- 122
Feather, Leonard G(eoffrey) 1914- 61-64
Feather, Norman 1904-1978 Obituary 111
Feather, Norman T(homas) 1930- 73-76
Featherstone, D.
See Warren, David
Featherstone, Helen 1944- 102
Featherstone, Joseph (Luke) 1940- 33-36R
Featherstonehaugh, Francis
See MacGregor, Alasdair Alpin (Douglas)
Feaver, George (Arthur) 1937- 29-32R
Feaver, J(ohn) Clayton 1911- CAP-2
Earlier sketch in CA 25-28
Feaver, William Andrew 1942- 103
Fecamps, Elise
See Creasey, John
Fecher, Charles A(dam) 1917- 81-84
Fecher, Constance
See Heaven, Constance
Fechter, Alyce Shinn 1909- CAP-1
Earlier sketch in CA 15-16
Feck, Luke 1935- 69-72
Fedde, Norman A(ndreas) 1914- 7-8R
Fedden, Henry (Romilly) 1908- 9-10R
Fedden, Robin
See Fedden, Henry (Romilly)

Fedder, Edwin H(ersh) 1929- 37-40R
Fedder, Norman J(oseph) 1934- CANR-25
Earlier sketches in CA 21-22R, CANR-9
Fedder, Ruth 1907- CANR-2
Earlier sketch in CA 5-6R
Feder, Bernard 1924- CANR-15
Earlier sketch in CA 33-36R
Feder, Ernest 1913- 37-40R
Feder, Jane 1940- 93-96
Feder, Jose 1917- 105
Feder, Karah (Tal) 1920- 17-18R
Feder, Lillian 41-44R
Feder, Paula (Kurzband) 1935- 105
See also SATA 26
Feder, Robert Arthur 1909-1969 Obituary 110
See also SATA 35
Federbusch, Simon
See Federbush, Simon
Federbush, Arnold 1935- 104
Federbush, Simon 1892(?)-1969 Obituary 115
Federico, Ronald Charles 1941- 89-92
Federman, Raymond 1928- CANR-10
Earlier sketch in CA 17-18R
See also DLBY 80
See also CLC 6, 47
Federoff, Alexander 1927(?)-1979
Obituary 89-92
Federspiel, J(uerg) F. 1931- CLC-42
Fedin, Konstantin A(lexandrovich)
1892-1977 81-84
Obituary 73-76
Fedler, Fred 1940- 97-100
Fedoroff, Alexander 1927-1979 CANR-5
Earlier sketch in CA 3R
Fedorov, Yevgeny Konstantinovich
1910-1981 Obituary 106
Feduccia, (John) Alan 1943- 124
Fedyshyn, Oleh S(ylvester) 1928- 49-52
Fee, Elizabeth 1946- 126
Fee, Gordon D(onald) 1934- 117
Feegel, John R(ichard) 1932- CANR-9
Earlier sketch in CA 57-60
Feeley, Kathleen 1929- 33-36R
Feeley, Malcolm McCollum 1942-
Brief entry 105
Feeley, Pat(ricia Falk) 1941- 81-84
Feelings, Muriel (Grey) 1938- 93-96
See also BW
See also SATA 16
See also CLR 5
Feelings, Thomas 1933- CANR-25
Earlier sketch in CA 49-52
See also BW
See also SATA 8
Feelings, Tom
See Feelings, Thomas
See also CLR 5
Feely, Terence John 1928- CANR-25
Earlier sketch in CA 106
Feenberg, Eugene 1906-1977 Obituary 73-76
Feeney, Leonard 1897-1978 81-84
Obituary 77-80
Feeney, Stephanie S(inger) 1939- 118
Feenstra, Henry John 1936- 37-40R
Feerick, John D(avid) 1936- 69-72
Fegan, Camilla 1939- 21-22R
Fegan, Patrick W. 1947- 111
Fegely, Thomas D(avid) 1941- 97-100
Fehl, Philipp P(inhas) 1920- 33-36R
Fehr, Howard Franklin 1901-1982
Obituary 106
Fehren, Henry 1920- CANR-9
Earlier sketch in CA 21-22R
Fehrenbach, T(heodore) R(eed, Jr.)
1925- CANR-1
Earlier sketch in CA 1R
See also SATA 33
Fehrenbacher, Don E. 1920- CANR-2
Earlier sketch in CA 1R
Fehrman, Carl (Abraham Daniel) 1915-
Brief entry 113
Feibes, Walter 1928- 53-56
Feibleman, James K(ern) 1904- CANR-22
Earlier sketches in CA 5-6R, CANR-7
See also AITN 2
Feibleman, Peter S(teinam) 1930- 110
Brief entry 108
Feider, Paul 1951- 114
Feied, Frederick (James) 1925- 13-14R
Feierman, Steven 1940- 53-56
Feifel, Herman 1915- 101
Feiffer, Jules 1929- 19-20R
See also SATA 8
See also DLB 7, 44
See also CLC 2, 8
Feig, Barbara Krane 1937- 104
See also SATA 34
Feig, Douglas 1946- 114
Feigelson, Naomi
See Chase, Naomi Feigelson
Feigenbaum, Lawrence H. 1918- 25-28R
Feigert, Frank B(rook) 1937- CANR-19
Earlier sketches in CA 53-56, CANR-4
Feigl, Herbert 1902- CAP-1
Earlier sketch in CA 13-14
Feigon, Lee (Nathan) 1945- 117
Fei-Kan, Li
See Li Fei-kan
Feikema, Feike
See Manfred, Frederick (Feikema)
Feil, Hila 1942- 37-40R
See also SATA 12
Feild, Reshad 1934- CANR-25
Earlier sketch in CA 69-72
Feilding, Charles (Rudolph) 1902- CAP-2
Earlier sketch in CA 25-28
Feilen, John
See May, Julian
Feiler, Seymour 1919- 41-44R
Fein, Albert 1930- 115
Fein, Helen 1934- 110
Fein, Irving A(shley) 1911- 69-72
Fein, John M(orton) 1922- 120
Fein, Judith 1941- 107
Fein, Leah Gold 49-52
Fein, Leonard J. 1934- 13-14R
Fein, Rashi 1926- 122
Fein, Richard J(acob) 1929- 45-48
Feinberg, Abraham L. 1899-1986 11-12R
Obituary 120
Feinberg, Barbara Jane 1938- CANR-22
Earlier sketch in CA 106
Feinberg, Barry (Vincent) 1938- 29-32R
Feinberg, Beatrice Cynthia Freeman
1915(?)-1988 CANR-25
Obituary 126
Earlier sketch in CA 81-84
Feinberg, Gerald 1933- CANR-12
Earlier sketch in CA 25-28R
Feinberg, Gloria (Granditer) 1923-
Brief entry 109
Feinberg, Hilda 49-52
Feinberg, Joel 1926- CANR-22
Earlier sketch in CA 17-18R
Feinberg, Lawrence B(ernard) 1940- 73-76
Feinberg, Leonard 1914- CANR-2
Earlier sketch in CA 5-6R
Feinberg, Mortimer R(obert) 1922- 102
Feinberg, Renee 1940- 112
Feinberg, Walter 1937- 57-60
Feinbloom, Deborah Heller 1940- 65-68
Feingold, Ben(jamin) F(ranklin)
1900-1982 97-100
Obituary 106
Feingold, Eugene (Neil) 1931- CANR-22
Earlier sketch in CA 17-18R
Feingold, Henry L(eo) 1931- 29-32R
Feingold, Jessica 1910- CAP-2
Earlier sketch in CA 25-28
Feingold, Michael 1945- 89-92
Feingold, S. Norman 1914- CANR-13
Earlier sketch in CA 13-14R
Feininger, Andreas (Bernhard Lyonel)
1906- CANR-20
Earlier sketch in CA 85-88
Feinman, Jeffrey 1943- CANR-10
Earlier sketch in CA 65-68
Feinsilver, Alexander 1910- 15-16R
Feinsilver, Lillian Mermin 1917- 29-32R
Feinsinger, Nathan Paul 1902-1983
Obituary 111
Feinstein, Alan (Shawn) 1931- 25-28R
Feinstein, Elaine 1930- 69-72
See also CAAS 1
See also DLB 14, 40
See also CLC 36
Feinstein, George W(illiamson) 1913- 73-76
Feinstein, Lloyd L(eonard) 1941- 113
Feinstein, Moshe 1895-1986 Obituary 118
Feinstein, Otto 1930- 104
Feinstein, Sherman C. 1923- CANR-7
Earlier sketch in CA 57-60
Feintuch, Burt H. 1949- 124
Feirstein, Bruce 1953- 108
Feirstein, Frederick 1940- CANR-1
Earlier sketch in CA 45-48
Feis, Herbert 1893-1972 CAP-1
Obituary 33-36R
Earlier sketch in CA 9-10
Feis, Ruth (Stanley-Brown) 1892- CAP-2
Earlier sketch in CA 19-20
Feise, Ernst 1884-1966 CAP-2
Earlier sketch in CA 17-18
Feist, Aubrey (Noel Lydston) 1903- 41-44R
Feit, E(wald) Edward 1924- CANR-10
Earlier sketch in CA 7-8R
Feitel, Donald G. 1925(?)-1976 Obituary 65-68
Feith, Herbert 1930- 4R
Feiwel, George R(ichard) 1929- CANR-23
Earlier sketches in CA 17-18R, CANR-8
Feiwel, Raphael Joseph 1907-1985
Obituary 117
Fejes, Claire 1920- CANR-13
Earlier sketch in CA 21-22R
Fejes, Endre 1923- 25-28R
Fejto, Francois (Philippe) 1909- 29-32R
Fekrat, M. Ali 1937- 45-48
Felber, Stanley B. 1932- 77-80
Feld, Bernard (David III) 1947- 125
Feld, Bernard T(aub) 1919- 104
Feld, Michael 1938- 33-36R
Feld, Rose Caroline 1895-1981 Obituary 105
Feld, Ross 1947- CANR-16
Earlier sketch in CA 33-36R
Feld, Werner (Joachim) 1910- CANR-24
Earlier sketches in CA 21-22R, CANR-8
Feldbaum, Eleanor G. 1935- 117
Feldberg, Michael 1943- 113
Feldenkrais, Moshe (Pinchas) 1904- 73-76
Felder, Paul
See Wellen, Edward (Paul)
Felder, Raoul Lionel 1934- 33-36R
Felderman, Eric 1944- 69-72
Feldkamp, Fred 1915(?)-1981 Obituary 105
Feldkamp, Phyllis 102
Feldman, Abraham J(ehiel) 1893-1977 81-84
Obituary 73-76
Feldman, Alan 1945- CANR-13
Earlier sketch in CA 73-76
Feldman, Anne (Rodgers) 1939- 73-76
See also SATA 19
Feldman, Annette Gerber 1913- 69-72
Feldman, Burton 1926- 33-36R
Feldman, Edmund Burke 1924- 33-36R
Feldman, Edwin B(arry) 1925- CANR-2
Earlier sketch in CA 7-8R
Feldman, Egal 1925- 125
Feldman, Ellen (Bette) 1941- CANR-18
Earlier sketch in CA 97-100
Feldman, George J(ay) 1904- CAP-1
Earlier sketch in CA 13-14
Feldman, Gerald D(onald) 1937- CANR-9
Earlier sketch in CA 21-22R
Feldman, Herbert (H. S.) 1910- 29-32R
Feldman, Irving (Mordecai) 1928- CANR-1
Earlier sketch in CA 1R
See also CLC 7
Feldman, Kenneth A. 1937- 29-32R
Feldman, Leon A(ryeh) 1921- CANR-16
Earlier sketch in CA 97-100
Feldman, Leonard 1927- 69-72
Feldman, Leslie AITN-1
Feldman, Louis H(arry) 1926- 53-56
Feldman, M(aurice) P(hilip) 1933- 41-44R
Feldman, Marty 1934(?)-1982 110
Obituary 108
Feldman, Robert A.
See Feldman, Robert Alan
Feldman, Robert Alan 1953- 123
Feldman, Ruth 1911- 106
Feldman, Ruth Duskin 1934- 119
Feldman, Samuel Nathan 1931- 25-28R
Feldman, Sandor S. 1891(?)-1973
Obituary 41-44R
Feldman, Saul D(aniel) 1943- 41-44R
Feldman, Sidney 1902(?)-1986 Obituary 121
Feldman, Silvia (Dash) 1928- 97-100
Feldman, Sol(omon) E. 1933- 25-28R
Feldman, Sophie 1930-1978 Obituary 108
Feldmann, Susan Judith 1928-1969
Obituary 104
Feldmeir, Daryle M(atthew) 1923-1987 73-76
Obituary 122
Feldon, Leah 1944- 97-100
Feldstein, Martin S(tuart) 1939- 73-76
Feldstein, Paul J(oseph) 1933- 89-92
Feldstein, Stuart A(lan) 1948- 113
Feldt, Allan Gunnar 1932- 41-44R
Feldzamen, A(lvin) N(orman) 1931- 25-28R
Felheim, Marvin 1914- 1R
Felice, Cynthia 1942- 107
Felix
See Vincent, Felix
Felix, David 1921- 45-48
Felix-Tchicaya, Gerald
See Tchicaya, Gerald Felix
Felkenes, George T(heodore) 1930- CANR-8
Earlier sketch in CA 57-60
Felker, Clay S(chuette) 1925- 73-76
Felker, Evelyn H. 1933- 57-60
Felker, Jere L. 1934- 23-24R
Felknor, Bruce L(ester) 1921- 21-22R
Fell, Barry
See Fell, H(oward) Barraclough
Fell, Derek (John) 1939- CANR-25
Earlier sketch in CA 108
Fell, H(oward) Barraclough 1917- 33-36R
Fell, James E(dward), Jr. 1944- 107
Fell, John L(ouis) 1927- 53-56
Fell, Joseph P(hineas) III 1931- CANR-6
Earlier sketch in CA 15-16R
Fellini, Federico 1920- 65-68
See also CLC 16
Fellman, Gordon 1934- 53-56
Fellman, Michael (Dinion) 1943- 45-48
Fellmeth, Robert C(harles) 1945- CANR-2
Earlier sketch in CA 49-52
Fellner, William John 1905-1983 CANR-2
Obituary 110
Earlier sketch in CA 1R
Fellowes, Anne
See Mantle, Winifred (Langford)
Fellowes-Gordon, Ian (Douglas) 1921- CANR-10
Earlier sketch in CA 7-8R
Fellows, Brian John 1936- 25-28R
Fellows, Donald Keith 1920- 41-44R
Fellows, Hugh P. 1915- 37-40R
Fellows, Jay 1940- CANR-11
Earlier sketch in CA 61-64
Fellows, Lawrence (Perry) 1924- 49-52
Fellows, Malcolm Stuart 1924- 11-12R
Fellows, Muriel H. 53-56
See also SATA 10
Fellows, Otis (Edward) 1908- CANR-1
Earlier sketch in CA 4R
Fellows, Richard A(stley) 1947- 121
Felmly, Lloyd McPherson 1894-1984
Obituary 112
Fels, Ludwig 1946- DLB-75
Fels, Rendigs 1917- 37-40R
Felsen, Henry Gregor 1916- CANR-1
Earlier sketch in CA 4R
See also SATA 1
See also SAAS 2
See also CLC 17
Felsenstein, Walter 1901-1975 Obituary 111
Felsenthal, Carol 1949- 108
Felsher, Howard D. 1927- 19-20R
Felstein, Ivor 1933- 41-44R
Felstiner, L. John, Jr. 1936- 45-48
Felt, Jeremy P(ollard) 1930- 23-24R
Felt, Margaret Elley 1917- 9-10R
Felter, Emma K. (Schroeder) 1896- CAP-1
Earlier sketch in CA 15-16
Felton, Bruce 1946- 65-68
Felton, Cornelius Conway 1807-1862 DLB-1
Felton, Harold William 1902- CANR-1
Earlier sketch in CA 3R
See also SATA 1
Felton, John Richard 1917- 89-92
Felton, Ronald Oliver 1909- CANR-3
Earlier sketch in CA 11-12R
See also SATA 3
Felton, Sandra 1935- 120
Felts, Shirley 1934- SATA-33
Feltskog, E(lmer) N. 1935- 37-40R
Felver, Charles S(tanley) 1916- 33-36R
Femiano, Samuel D. 1932- 21-22R
Femina, Jerry Della
See Della Femina, Jerry
Fen, Elisaveta
See Jackson, Lydia
Fenady, Andrew J. 1928- CANR-13
Earlier sketch in CA 77-80
Fenander, Elliot W(atkins) 1938- 21-22R
Fenberg, Matilda 1888(?)-1977 Obituary 73-76
Fenby, Eric (William) 1906- 25-28R
Fendell, Bob 1925- 57-60
Fendelman, Helaine Woll 1942- 69-72
Fenderson, Lewis H., Jr. 1907-1983 106
Obituary 111
See also SATA 37, 47
Fenelon, Fania 1918-1983 77-80
Obituary 111
Fenelon, Kevin G(erard) 1898-1983 73-76
Obituary 109
Feng, Chin
See Liu, Sydney (Chieh)
Fenger, Henning Johannes Hauch 1921- 73-76
Fenical, Marlin Edward 1907-1983
Obituary 110
Fenichel, Carol Hansen 1935- 119
Fenichell, Stephen 1956- 108
Fenick, Barbara 1951- 118
Fenik, Bernard Carl 1934- 122
Fenin, George N(icolaievich) 1916- 9-10R
Fenlon, Dick 1930- 89-92
Fenlon, Paul Edward 1921- 15-16R
Fenn, Charles (Henry) 1907- 9-10R
Fenn, Dan H(untington), Jr. 1923- CANR-1
Earlier sketch in CA 3R
Fenn, Elizabeth A. 1959- 115
Fenn, Henry Courtenay 1894-1978
Obituary 81-84
Fennario, David 1947- DLB-60
Fennell, Francis L(e Roy), Jr. 1942- 116
Fennell, John L(ister) I(llingworth)
1918- CANR-19
Earlier sketches in CA 3R, CANR-1
Fennell, William Oscar 1916- 101
Fennelly, Catherine 1918- 37-40R
Fennelly, John F(auntleroy) 1899-1974
Obituary 53-56
Fennelly, Parker W. 1891-1988 Obituary 125
Fennelly, Tony 1945- 119
Fennema, Owen Richard 1929- CANR-3
Earlier sketch in CA 49-52
Fenner, Carol Elizabeth 1929- CANR-3
Earlier sketch in CA 7-8R
See also SATA 7
Fenner, H(arry) Wolcott 1911-1972 CAP-2
Obituary 37-40R
Earlier sketch in CA 33-36
Fenner, James 1923- 37-40R
Fenner, James R.
See Tubb, E(dwin) C(harles)
Fenner, Kay Toy CAP-1
Earlier sketch in CA 9-10
Fenner, Mildred Sandison 1910- 33-36R
Fenner, Phyllis R(eid) 1899-1982 CANR-2
Obituary 106
Earlier sketch in CA 5-6R
See also SATA 1, 29
Fenner, Theodore (Lincoln) 1919- 37-40R
Fennimore, Keith John 1917- 57-60
Fenno, John 1751-1798 DLB-43
Fenno, R(ichard) Francis, Jr. 1926- 7-8R
Fensch, Edwin A. 1903- CAP-1
Earlier sketch in CA 15-16
Fensch, Thomas 1943- CANR-11
Earlier sketch in CA 25-28R
Fenster, Robert 1946- 113
Fenster, Valmai (Ruth) Kirkham
1939-1984 110
Obituary 114
Fensterheim, Herbert 1921- 112
Fenstermaker, J(oseph) Van 1933- 29-32R
Fenten, Barbara D(oris) 1935- CANR-5
Earlier sketch in CA 53-56
See also SATA 26
Fenten, D(onald) X. 1932- CANR-5
Earlier sketch in CA 33-36R
See also SATA 4
Fenton, Carroll Lane 1900-1969 CANR-6
Obituary 29-32R
Earlier sketch in CA 1R
See also SATA 5
Fenton, Clyde 1901-1982 Obituary 106
Fenton, Edward 1917- CANR-13
Earlier sketch in CA 9-10R
See also SATA 7
Fenton, Frank 1903-1971 Obituary 33-36R
Fenton, Freda
See Rowland, D(onald) S(ydney)
Fenton, James Martin 1949- 102
See also DLB 40
See also CLC 32
Fenton, John C(harles) 1921- CAP-1
Earlier sketch in CA 9-10
Fenton, John H(arold) 1921- 37-40R
Fenton, John Y(oung) 1933- 53-56
Fenton, Joseph Clifford 1906- 7-8R
Fenton, Mildred Adams 1899- 77-80
See also SATA 21
Fenton, Shane
See Stardust, Alvin
Fenton, Sophia Harvati 1914- 33-36R

Fenton, Thomas Patrick 1943- 89-92
Fenton, Thomas Trail 1930- 102
Fenton, William N(elson) 1908- 93-96
Fentress, John Simmons 1925(?)-1981
Obituary 104
Fenvessy, Stanley J(ohn) 1918- 106
Fenwick, Charles G(hequiere) 1880-1973
Obituary 41-44R
Fenwick, Kay
See Bean, Keith F(enwick)
Fenwick, (Ian Graham) Keith 1941- 102
Fenwick, Millicent Hammond 1910- 112
Fenwick, Patti
See Grider, Dorothy
Fenwick, Sheridan 1942- 69-72
Fenwick-Owen, Roderic (Franklin Rawnsley)
1921- Brief entry 111
Fenyvesi, Charles 1937- 102
Feola, Jose (Maria) 1926- 69-72
Feravolo, Rocco Vincent 1922- CANR-1
Earlier sketch in CA 1R
See also SATA 10
Ferazani, Larry 1938- 61-64
Ferber, Andrew 1935- 53-56
Ferber, Edna 1887-1968 ....7-8R
Obituary 25-28R
See also SATA 7
See also DLB 9, 28
See also CLC 18
See also AITN 1
Ferber, Ellen 1939- 102
Ferber, Robert 1922- 37-40R
Ferdinand, Theodore N(ichols) 1929- 23-24R
Ferdinand, Vallery III
See Salaam, Kalamu ya
Ferdon, Edwin N(elson), Jr. 1913- 21-22R
Ferejohn, John A(rthur) 1944- 53-56
Ferencz, Benjamin B(erell) 1920- CANR-19
Earlier sketch in CA 97-100
Fergus, Jan 1943- 125
Fergus, Patricia M(arguerita) 1918- 53-56
Ferguson, Alfred R(iggs) 1915-1974 .... CANR-6
Obituary 49-52
Earlier sketch in CA 1R
Ferguson, Annabelle Evelyn 1923- 102
Ferguson, Arthur B(owles) 1913- 5-6R
Ferguson, Bob
See Ferguson, Robert Bruce
Ferguson, C(harles) E(lmo) 1928- 19-20R
Ferguson, Cecil 1931- SATA-45
Ferguson, Charles Albert 1921- 69-72
Ferguson, Charles Austin 1937- 121
Ferguson, Charles W. 1901-1987 ....15-16R
Obituary 124
Ferguson, Chris(topher Wilson) 1944- 57-60
Ferguson, Clarence Clyde, Jr.
1924-1983 .... CANR-6
Obituary 111
Earlier sketch in CA 7-8R
Ferguson, David L. 1930- 73-76
Ferguson, Donald N(ivison) 1882-1985 .....5-6R
Obituary 116
Ferguson, E(lmer) James 1917- 61-64
Ferguson, Everett 1933- 33-36R
Ferguson, Franklin C(ole) 1934- 69-72
Ferguson, Harry 1903-1980 Obituary 97-100
Ferguson, Helen
See Kavan, Anna
Ferguson, Howard 1908- CAP-1
Earlier sketch in CA 11-12
Ferguson, J(ohn) Halcro 1920-1968 .... 1R
Obituary 103
Ferguson, James M(ilton) 1936- 23-24R
Ferguson, John 1921- CANR-25
Earlier sketches in CA 5-6R, CANR-8
Ferguson, John Henry 1907- 13-14R
Ferguson, M(ilton) Carr 1931- 49-52
Ferguson, Margaret W(illiams) 1948- 112
Ferguson, Marilyn 1938- 114
Brief entry 110
Ferguson, Mary Anne 1918- 77-80
Ferguson, Oliver W(atkins) 1924- 5-6R
Ferguson, Pamela 1943- 101
Ferguson, Peter R(oderick) I(nnes)
1933- CANR-3
Earlier sketch in CA 7-8R
Ferguson, Robert Bruce 1927- 69-72
See also SATA 13
Ferguson, Robert D(ouglas) 1921- 19-20R
Ferguson, Robert W(illiam) 1940- CANR-12
Earlier sketch in CA 61-64
Ferguson, Rowena 1904- 85-88
Ferguson, Samuel 1810-1886 .... DLB-32
Ferguson, Suzanne 1939- 57-60
Ferguson, Ted 1936- 65-68
Ferguson, Tom 1943- 107
Ferguson, Trevor 1947- 116
Ferguson, Walter (W.) 1930- 107
See also SATA 34
Ferguson, William (Rotch) 1943- 49-52
Ferguson, William M(cDonald) 1917- 117
Ferguson, William Scott 1875-1954 ..... DLB-47
Fergusson, Adam 1932- Brief entry 112
Fergusson, Bernard Edward 1911-1980 .. CANR-7
Obituary 102
Earlier sketch in CA 9-10R
Fergusson, Erna 1888-1964 .... CAP-1
Earlier sketch in CA 13-14
See also SATA 5
Fergusson, Francis (De Liesseline)
1904-1986 .... CANR-3
Obituary 121
Earlier sketch in CA 11-12R
Fergusson, Harvey 1890-1971 Obituary ..33-36R
Fergusson, James 1904-1973 Obituary 104
Fergusson, Rosalind (Joyce) 1953- 117
Fergusson Hannay, Doris 1902(?)-1982 . CANR-6
Obituary 107
Earlier sketch in CA 9-10R
Fericano, Paul F(rancis) 1951- CANR-12
Earlier sketch in CA 69-72
Ferkiss, Victor C(hristopher) 1925- 21-22R
Ferland, Carol 1936- 102
Ferlinghetti, Lawrence (Monsanto)
1919(?)- CANR-3
Earlier sketch in CA 7-8R
See also DLB 5, 16
See also CDALB 1941-1968
See also CLC 2, 6, 10, 27
Ferlita, Ernest (Charles) 1927- CANR-26
Earlier sketches in CA 29-32R, CANR-11
Ferm, Betty 1926- 23-24R
Ferm, Deane William 1927- CANR-13
Earlier sketch in CA 33-36R
Ferm, Max A(rnold) 1929- 116
Ferm, Robert Livingston 1931- 13-14R
Ferm, Vergilius (Ture Anselm)
1896-1974 ....9-10R
Obituary 49-52
Ferman, Edward L(ewis) 1937- 106
Ferman, Joseph W(olfe) 1906-1975
Obituary 104
Fermi, Enrico 1901-1954 Brief entry 115
Fermi, Laura 1907-1977 .... CANR-6
Earlier sketch in CA 2R
See also SATA 6, 28
Fermor, Patrick Leigh 1915- 81-84
Fern, Alan M(axwell) 1930- CANR-12
Earlier sketch in CA 33-36R
Fern, Eugene A. 1919-1987 .... CANR-16
Obituary 123
Earlier sketch in CA 4R
See also SATA 10
Fern, Fanny
See Parton, Sara Payson Willis
Fernald, John (Bailey) 1905-1985 .... CAP-2
Obituary 115
Earlier sketch in CA 23-24
Fernandez, Benedict J. (III) 1936- 85-88
Fernandez, Gladys Craven 1939- 106
Fernandez, Happy Craven
See Fernandez, Gladys Craven
Fernandez, James William 1930- CANR-23
Earlier sketch in CA 107
Fernandez, John P(eter) 1941- CANR-10
Earlier sketch in CA 65-68
Fernandez, Jose S(alvador) 1893-1967
Obituary 113
Fernandez, Joseph A. 1921- 37-40R
Fernandez, Julio A. 1936- 33-36R
Fernandez de la Reguera, Ricardo
1914- CANR-3
Earlier sketch in CA 7-8R
Fernandez-Marina, R(amon) 1909- 41-44R
Fernando, Ajith 1948- 122
Fernando, Lloyd 1926- 77-80
Fernea, Elizabeth Warnock 1927- CANR-12
Earlier sketch in CA 15-16R
Fernea, Robert Alan 1932- 33-36R
Fernett, Gene 1924- 49-52
Fernie, Eric (Campbell) 1939- 119
Ferns, H(enry) S(tanley) 1913- CANR-19
Earlier sketches in CA 5-6R, CANR-4
Fernsworth, Lawrence 1893(?)-1977(?)
Obituary 89-92
Ferracuti, Franco 1927- CANR-11
Earlier sketch in CA 25-28R
Ferrante, Don
See Gerbi, Antonello
Ferrante, Joan M(arguerite Aida) 1936- 85-88
Ferrar, Harold 1935- Brief entry 116
Ferrari, Enzo 1898-1988 Obituary 126
Ferrarini, Elizabeth M. 1948- 124
Ferraro, Gary P(aul) 1940- 89-92
Ferrars, E. X.
See Brown, Morna Doris
Ferrars, Elizabeth
See Brown, Morna Doris
Ferrater-Mora, Jose 1912- 3R
Ferre, Frederick 1933- 13-14R
Ferre, Gustave A. 1918- 4R
Ferre, Nels F(redrik) S(olomon)
1908-1971 .... CAP-2
Earlier sketch in CA 29-32
Ferreira de Castro, Jose Maria 1898-1974 ... 102
Obituary 49-52
Ferrell, Mallory Hope 1935- CANR-13
Earlier sketch in CA 33-36R
Ferrell, Robert H(ugh) 1921- CANR-22
Earlier sketches in CA 5-6R, CANR-6
Ferrell, Robert W(illingham) 1913- 15-16R
Ferreol, Marcel Auguste 1899-1974 97-100
Obituary 53-56
Ferrer, Aldo 1927- CANR-11
Earlier sketch in CA 25-28R
Ferrer, Gabriel (Francisco Victor) Miro
See Miro (Ferrer), Gabriel (Francisco
Victor)
Ferrer, Sister Vincent
See Doherty, Barbara
Ferreri, Marco 1928- 126
Ferres, John H(oward) 1932- 41-44R
Ferridge, Philippa 1933- CANR-18
Earlier sketch in CA 102
Ferrier, Janet Mackay 1919- 9-10R
Ferrier, Lucy
See Penzler, Otto
Ferril, Thomas Hornsby 1896- 65-68
Ferrini, Vincent 1913- DLB-48
Ferris, Helen Josephine 1890-1969 77-80
See also SATA 21
Ferris, James Cody CAP-2
Earlier sketch in CA 19-20
See also SATA 1
Ferris, Jean 1939- 116
See also SATA 50
Ferris, Norman (Bernard) 1931- 81-84
Ferris, Paul (Frederick) 1929- CANR-22
Earlier sketches in CA 7-8R, CANR-3
Ferris, Theodore P(arker) 1908-1972
Obituary 37-40R
Ferris, Timothy 1944- CANR-11
Earlier sketch in CA 69-72
Ferris, Tom
See Walker, Peter N.
Ferriss, Abbott Lamoyne 1915- 29-32R
Ferritor, Daniel Edward 1939- 49-52
Ferro, Marc 1924- 77-80
Ferro, Robert (Michael) 1941-1988 ....29-32R
Obituary 126
Ferron, Jacques 1921-1985 Brief entry 117
See also DLB 60
Ferron, Madeleine 1922- DLB-53
Ferruolo, Stephen C(arl) 1949- 120
Ferry, Anne Davidson 1930- 19-20R
Ferry, Charles 1927- CANR-16
Earlier sketch in CA 97-100
See also SATA 43
Ferry, David (Russell) 1924- 13-14R
Ferry, W(illiam) Hawkins 1914(?)-1988 61-64
Obituary 124
Fersh, Seymour H. 1926- CANR-14
Earlier sketch in CA 37-40R
Ferster, C(harles) B(ohris) 1922-1981 97-100
Obituary 102
Ferster, Dorothy C(oben) 1922- 111
Ferster, Marilyn B(ender)
See Gilbert, Marilyn B(ender)
Ferullo, Dan 1948- 106
Feshbach, Norma Deitch 1926- CANR-8
Earlier sketch in CA 61-64
Feshbach, Seymour 1925- CANR-8
Earlier sketch in CA 37-40R
Fesler, James W(illiam) 1911- 23-24R
Fesperman, John (Thomas, Jr.) 1925- .. CANR-2
Earlier sketch in CA 5-6R
Fess, Philip E. 1931- 33-36R
Fessel, Murray 1927- 21-22R
Fessenden, Katherine 1896(?)-1974
Obituary 53-56
Fessenden, Seth A(rthur) 1903-1976 ... CANR-10
Earlier sketch in CA 17-18R
Fessenko, Tatiana (Sviatenko) 1915- 13-14R
Fessier, Michael 1905(?)-1988 Obituary 126
Fessler, Loren W. 1923- 9-10R
Fest, Joachim C. 1926- 49-52
Fest, Thorrel B(rooks) 1910- CAP-1
Earlier sketch in CA 15-16
Festa Campanile, Pasquale 1927-1986
Obituary 118
Festa-McCormick, Diana 117
Festinger, Leon 1919- 3R
Fetherling, Dale 1941- 77-80
Fetler, Andrew 1925- 15-16R
Fetridge, William Harrison 1906- 73-76
Fetros, John G. 1932- 57-60
Fetscher, Iring 1922- CANR-12
Earlier sketch in CA 69-72
Fettamen, Ann
See Hoffman, Anita
Fetter, Elizabeth Head 1904-1973 ....7-8R
Obituary 41-44R
Fetter, Frank Whitson 1899- 106
Fetter, Richard (Leland) 1943- CANR-15
Earlier sketch in CA 89-92
Fetterley, Judith 1938- Brief entry 113
Fetterman, Elsie 1927- 97-100
Fetterman, John (Davis) 1920-1975 93-96
Obituary 61-64
Fettig, Art(hur John) 1929- CANR-13
Earlier sketch in CA 73-76
Fetz, Ingrid 1915- SATA-30
Fetzer, John F(rancis) 1931- 61-64
Feucht, Oscar E(mil) 1895- 103
Feuchtwanger, E(dgar) J(oseph)
1924- CANR-11
Earlier sketch in CA 69-72
Feuchtwanger, Lion 1884-1958 Brief entry .. 104
See also DLB 66
See also TCLC 3
Feuer, Avrohom Chaim 1946- 113
Feuer, Kathryn Beliveau 1926- 102
Feuer, Lewis S(amuel) 1912- CANR-3
Earlier sketch in CA 7-8R
Feuerlicht, Ignace CAP-2
Earlier sketch in CA 33-36
Feuerlicht, Roberta Strauss 1931- 19-20R
Feuerstein, Georg 1947- 123
Feuerstein, Phyllis A. 1930- 105
Feuerwerger, Marvin C(harles) 1950- 104
Feuerwerker, Albert 1927- CANR-8
Earlier sketch in CA 23-24R
Feulner, Edwin J(ohn), Jr. 1941- 115
Feulner, Patricia N(ancy) 1946- 105
Feur, D. C.
See Stahl, Fred Alan
Fewster, Kevin (John) 1953- 125
Fey, Harold E(dward) 1898- 19-20R
Feydeau, Georges (Leon Jules Marie)
1862-1921 Brief entry 113
See also TCLC 22
Feydy, Anne Lindbergh
See Sapieyevski, Anne Lindbergh
See also SATA 32
Feynman, R. P.
See Feynman, Richard Phillips
Feynman, Richard
See Feynman, Richard Phillips
Feynman, Richard P.
See Feynman, Richard Phillips
Feynman, Richard Phillips 1918-1988
Obituary 125
Brief entry 119
Fezler, William 1945- 122
ffolkes
See Davis, Brian
Ffolkes, Michael
See Davis, Brian
ffolliott, Rosemary 1934- 97-100
ffrench-Beytagh, Gonville (Aubie) 1912- 103
ffrench Blake, Neil (St. John) 1940- 69-72
ffrench Blake, Robert L(ifford) V(alentine)
1913- 61-64
Fiacc, Padraic
See O'Connor, Patrick Joseph
Fialkowski, Barbara 1946- 77-80
Fiammenghi, Gioia 1929- SATA-9
Fiandt, Mary K. 1914- 89-92
Fiarotta, Noel
See Ficarotta, Noel
See also SATA 15
Fiarotta, Phyllis
See Ficarotta, Phyllis
See also SATA 15
Fiber, Alan 102
Ficarotta, Noel 1944- CANR-11
Earlier sketch in CA 69-72
Ficarotta, Phyllis 1942- CANR-11
Earlier sketch in CA 69-72
Fichtelius, Karl-Erik 1924- 53-56
Fichter, Andrew J(ohn) 1945- 117
Fichter, George S. 1922- CANR-23
Earlier sketches in CA 17-18R, CANR-7
See also SATA 7
Fichter, Joseph 1908- CANR-19
Earlier sketches in CA 1R, CANR-4
Ficke, Arthur Davison 1883-1945 .... DLB-54
Ficken, Frederick A(rthur) 1910-1978
Obituary 81-84
Ficker, Victor B. 1937- CANR-13
Earlier sketch in CA 33-36R
Fickert, Kurt J(on) 1920- CANR-14
Earlier sketch in CA 37-40R
Fickett, Harold L., Jr. 1918- 15-16R
Fickett, Lewis P., Jr. 1926- 21-22R
Fickle, James Edward 1939- 106
Fickling, G. G.
See Fickling, Skip Forrest
Fickling, Skip Forrest 1925- 7-8R
Fidelio
See Hunt, Edgar H(ubert)
Fidler, James M. 1900-1988 Obituary 126
Fidler, Jimmie
See Fidler, James M.
Fidler, Kathleen (Annie) 1899-1980 .... CANR-20
Obituary 117
Earlier sketch in CA 25-28R
See also SATA 3, 45
Fidrych, Mark 1954- Brief entry 112
Fie, Jacquelyn Joyce 1937- 57-60
Fiedler, Fred E(dward) 1922- 23-24R
Fiedler, Jean(nette Feldman) CANR-11
Earlier sketch in CA 29-32R
See also SATA 4
Fiedler, Leslie A(aron) 1917- CANR-7
Earlier sketch in CA 11-12R
See also DLB 28, 67
See also CLC 4, 13, 24
Fiedler, Lois (Wagner) 1928- 17-18R
Fieg, Victor P. 1924- 106
Field, Adelaide (Anderson) 1916- 106
Field, Andrew 1938- CANR-25
Earlier sketch in CA 97-100
See also CLC 44
Field, Arthur J(ordan) 1927-1975 ....33-36R
Field, Barbara 1935- 110
Field, Carol 1940- 113
Field, Charles
See Rowland, D(onald) S(ydney)
Field, Daniel 1938- 65-68
Field, David D(udley) 1918- 73-76
Field, Dawn Stewart 1940- 57-60
Field, Dick 1912- 57-60
Field, Edward 1924- CANR-10
Earlier sketch in CA 13-14R
See also SATA 8
Field, Eleanor S. 1932- 122
Field, Elinor Whitney 1889-1980 Obituary ... 109
See also SATA 28
Field, Ernest R. 1925- 7-8R
Field, Eugene 1850-1895 .... SATA-16
See also DLB 23, 42
Field, Frances Fox 1913(?)-1977
Obituary 69-72
Field, Frank 1936- 21-22R
Field, Frank Chester
See Robertson, Frank C(hester)
Field, Frank McCoy 1887-1978 45-48
Obituary 103
Field, G(eorge) W(allis) 1914- 37-40R
Field, Gans T.
See Wellman, Manly Wade
Field, George B(rooks) 1929- 101
Field, Gordon Lawrence 1939- 17-18R
Field, Harry
See Field, Henry
Field, Hartry H(amlin) 1946- 124
Field, Hazel E(lizabeth) 1891-19(?) CAP-1
Earlier sketch in CA 19-20
Field, Henry 1902-1986 69-72
Obituary 118
Field, Irving M(edcraft) 1934- 25-28R
Field, James A(lfred), Jr. 1916- 25-28R
Field, Joanna
See Milner, Marion (Blackett)

Field, John (Leslie) 1910- 33-36R
Field, John P(aul) 1936- 37-40R
Field, Joyce W(olf) 1932- 29-32R
Field, Leslie A. 1926- 29-32R
Field, Mark G(eorge) 1923- 37-40R
Field, Michael 1915-1971 Obituary 29-32R
Field, Minna (Kagan) 25-28R
Field, Nathan 1587-1620(?) DLB-58
Field, Penelope
See Giberson, Dorothy (Dodds)
Field, Peter
See Hobson, Laura Z(ametkin)
Field, Phyllis Frances 1946- 107
Field, Rachel (Lyman) 1894-1942
Brief entry 109
See also SATA 15
See also DLB 9, 22
Field, Stanley 1911- CANR-9
Earlier sketch in CA 21-22R
Field, Thomas P(arry) 1914- 9-10R
Field, Walter S(herman) 1899- 49-52
Fielden, Charlotte 93-96
Fielden, T(homas) P(erceval) 1882- 7-8R
Fielder, Mildred (Craig) 1913- CANR-10
Earlier sketch in CA 15-16R
Fielding, A. W.
See Wallace, Alexander Fielding
Fielding, Daphne Winifred Louise 1904- ...9-10R
Fielding, G(ordon) J. 1934- 97-100
Fielding, Gabriel
See Barnsley, Alan Gabriel
Fielding, Henry 1707-1754 .... DLB-39
Fielding, Joy 1945- CANR-2
Earlier sketch in CA 49-52
Fielding, Nancy (Parker) 1913-1983
Obituary 111
Brief entry 108
Fielding, Raymond E. 1931- CANR-8
Earlier sketch in CA 17-18R
Fielding, Sarah 1710-1768 .... DLB-39
Fielding, Temple (Hornaday)
1913-1983 .... CANR-14
Obituary 109
Earlier sketch in CA 21-22R
Fielding, Waldo L. 1921- 45-48
Fielding, William J(ohn) 1886- 15-16R
Fielding, Xan
See Wallace, Alexander Fielding
Fields, Alan
See Duprey, Richard A(llen)
Fields, Arthur C. 1926(?)-1974 Obituary ...49-52
Fields, Beverly 1917- 49-52
Fields, Dorothy 1905-1974 93-96
Obituary 49-52
Fields, Gracie 1898-1979 Obituary 112
Fields, Howard K(enneth) 1938- 81-84
Fields, James Thomas 1817-1881 .... DLB-1
Fields, Jeff AITN-2
Fields, Joseph 1895-1966 Obituary 25-28R
Fields, Julia 1938- CANR-26
Earlier sketch in CA 73-76
See also BW
See also DLB 41
Fields, Kenneth (Wayne) 1939- Brief entry .. 110
Fields, Nora 49-52
Fields, Rick 1942- CANR-9
Earlier sketch in CA 65-68
Fields, Rona M(arcia) 1934- 69-72
Fields, Totie
See Feldman, Sophie
Fields, Victor A(lexander) 1901- 5-6R
Fields, W. C. 1880-1946 .... DLB-44
Fields, Wilbert J. 1917- 15-16R
Fields, Wilmer Clemont 1922- Brief entry ... 106
Fieler, Frank B(ernard) 1933- 41-44R
Fiene, Donald M(ark) 1930- 69-72
Fiene, Ernest 1894-1965 .... CAP-1
Earlier sketch in CA 13-14
Fiennes, Ranulph (Twisleton-Wykeham)
1944- CANR-20
Earlier sketches in CA 45-48, CANR-3
Fiennes, Richard
See Twisleton-Wykeham-Fiennes, Richard Nathaniel
Fiering, Norman Sanford 1935- 105
Fierro, Robert Daniel 1945- 109
Fierstein, Harvey (Forbes) 1954-
Brief entry 123
See also CLC 33
Fieser, Louis F(rederick) 1899-1977
Obituary 73-76
Fieser, Max E(ugene) 1930- 13-14R
Fiester, Mark (Lafayette) 1907- 65-68
Fieve, Ronald R(obert) 1930- Brief entry ... 107
Fife, Austin E(dwin) 1909- 53-56
Fife, Dale (Odile Hollerbach) 1901- CANR-19
Earlier sketch in CA 85-88
See also SATA 18
Fife, Robert Oldham 1918- 37-40R
Fifer, Ken 1947- 104
Fifield, William 1916-1987 .... CANR-9
Obituary 124
Earlier sketch in CA 15-16R
Fifo, Ray
See Glazar, Bob
Fifoot, Cecil Herbert Stuart 1899-1975
Obituary 107
Figes, Eva 1932- CANR-4
Earlier sketch in CA 53-56
See also DLB 14
See also CLC 31
Figgins, Ross 1936- CANR-11
Earlier sketch in CA 69-72
Figh, Margaret Gillis 1896- CAP-2
Earlier sketch in CA 29-32
Fighter Pilot, A
See Johnston, H(ugh) A(nthony) S(tephen)
Figler, Howard Elliot 1939- Brief entry 109
Figler, Stephen K(enneth) 1942- 117
Figueroa, John
See Figueroa, John J(oseph Maria)
Figueroa, John J(oseph Maria) 1920- 125
Brief entry 108
See also BW
Figueroa, John L(ewis) 1936- 65-68
Figueroa, Loida
See Figueroa-Mercado, Loida
Figueroa, Pablo 1938- 61-64
See also SATA 9
Figueroa-Chapel, Ramon 1935- 45-48
Figueroa-Mercado, Loida 1917- CANR-9
Earlier sketch in CA 57-60
Figurito, Joseph 1922- 29-32R
Fijan, Carol 1918- 53-56
See also SATA 12
Fikso, Eunice Cleland 1927- 7-8R
Filas, Francis L(ad) 1915-1985 .... CANR-2
Obituary 115
Earlier sketch in CA 5-6R
Filby, P(ercy) William 1911- CANR-3
Earlier sketch in CA 9-10R
Filene, Peter G. 1940- 21-22R
Filep, Robert Thomas 1931- CANR-19
Earlier sketches in CA 45-48, CANR-1
Filicchia, Ralph 1935- 103
Filip, Raymond 1950- 113
Filipovitch, Anthony J(oseph) 1947- 102
Filippo, Eduardo de
See de Filippo, Eduardo
Fill, Joseph Herbert 1924- Brief entry 112
Filler, Louis 1912- CANR-2
Earlier sketch in CA 1R
Fillmer, Henry Thompson 1932- 23-24R
Fillmore, Lowell 1882- CAP-1
Earlier sketch in CA 9-10
Fillmore, Parker H(oysted) 1878-1944 ... YABC-1
Fillmore, Roscoe Alfred 1887- 7-8R
Filmer, Henry
See Childs, J(ames) Rives
Filosa, Gary Fairmont Randolph de Marco II
1931- 65-68
Filreis, Alan 1956- 125
Filson, Floyd V(ivian) 1896- 61-64
Filson, John 1753(?)-1788 .... DLB-37
Filstrup, Chris
See Filstrup, E(dward) Christian
Filstrup, E(dward) Christian 1942- 113
See also SATA 43
Filstrup, Jane (Merrill) 1946- 110
Filstrup, Janie
See Filstrup, Jane (Merrill)
Filtzer, Donald 1948- 126
Finan, John J(oseph) 1925- 117
Finberg, H(erbert) P(atrick) R(eginald)
1900-1974 .... CAP-1
Obituary 53-56
Earlier sketch in CA 15-16
Finch, Christopher 1939- Brief entry 112
Finch, Donald George 1937- 53-56
Finch, Henry LeRoy 1918- 41-44R
Finch, Matthew
See Fink, Merton
Finch, Robert (Duer Claydon) 1900- ... CANR-24
Earlier sketches in CA 57-60, CANR-9
See also CLC 18
Finch(-Rayner), Sheila 1935- 121
Fincham, A(nthony) A(rthur) 1943- 117
Fincher, Cameron Lane 1926- 41-44R
Fincher, Ernest B(arksdale) 1910-1985 .. CANR-9
Obituary 115
Earlier sketch in CA 53-56
Finck, Furman J(oseph) 1900- CAP-2
Earlier sketch in CA 33-36
Fincke, Gary (William) 1945- 57-60
Finckenauer, James O(liver) 1939- 108
Finder, Joseph 1958- 113
Finder, Martin
See Salzmann, Siegmund
Findlater, Richard
See Bain, Kenneth Bruce Findlater
Findlay, Bruce Allyn 1895-1972 .... CAP-1
Earlier sketch in CA 13-14
Findlay, Campbell K(irkman) 1909- 7-8R
Findlay, David K. 1901- CAP-1
Earlier sketch in CA 13-14
Findlay, James Arthur 1883-1964
Obituary 111
Findlay, James F(ranklin), Jr. 1930- 49-52
Findlay, John N(iemeyer) 1903-1987 .... CANR-5
Obituary 123
Earlier sketch in CA 7-8R
Findlay, Robert R. 1932- 45-48
Findley, Carter Vaughn 1941- 102
Findley, Paul 1921- 29-32R
Findley, Timothy 1930- CANR-12
Earlier sketch in CA 25-28R
See also DLB 53
See also CLC 27
Findling, John Ellis 1941- 102
Fine, Anne 1947- 105
See also SATA 29
Fine, Benjamin 1905-1975 .... CANR-4
Obituary 57-60
Earlier sketch in CA 5-6R
Fine, Carla 1946- 112
Fine, Elsa Honig 1930- 49-52
Fine, Estelle
See Jelinek, Estelle C.
Fine, Gary Alan 1950- 111
Fine, I(sadore) V. 1918- 19-20R
Fine, John (Van Antwerp), Jr. 1939- 117
Fine, Judylaine 1948- 117
Fine, Nathan 1893(?)-1979 Obituary 89-92
Fine, Ralph Adam 1941- 29-32R
Fine, Reuben 1914- CANR-12
Earlier sketch in CA 17-18R
Fine, S(eymour) Morton 1930- 104
Fine, Seymour H(oward) 1925- 111
Fine, Sidney 1920- CANR-1
Earlier sketch in CA 1R
Fine, Warren 1943- 21-22R
Fine, William Michael 1924- 15-16R
Fineberg, Robert Gene 1940- 107
Finegan, Jack 1908- CANR-1
Earlier sketch in CA 1R
Finegan, T(homas) Aldrich 1929-
Brief entry 108
Fineman, Irving 1893- 5-6R
Finer, Leslie 1921- 15-16R
Finer, Samuel Edward 1915- 41-44R
Finestone, Harold 1920- Brief entry 110
Finestone, Harry 1920- 45-48
Fingarette, Herbert 1921- 77-80
Finger, Charles J(oseph) 1869(?)-1941
Brief entry 119
See also SATA 42
Finger, Seymour Maxwell 1915- 104
Finger, William R(atliff) 1947- 111
Fingerhut, Eugene R. 1932- 111
Fingesten, Peter 1916-1987 ....15-16R
Obituary 123
Finifter, Ada W(eintraub) 1938- CANR-21
Earlier sketch in CA 104
Fink, Arthur Emil 1903- 1R
Fink, Augusta 1916- CANR-13
Earlier sketch in CA 33-36R
Fink, Edith 1918- 61-64
Fink, Eli E. 1908(?)-1979 Obituary 85-88
Fink, Gary M. 1936- 53-56
Fink, Joanne 1954- 123
Fink, Joseph 1915- 57-60
Fink, Lawrence Alfred 1930- 97-100
Fink, Merton 1921- 9-10R
Fink, Paul Jay 1933- 53-56
Fink, Stevanne Auerbach
See Auerbach, Stevanne
Fink, William
See Mencken, H(enry) L(ouis)
Fink, William B(ertrand) 1916- 41-44R
See also SATA 22
Fink, Z(era) S(ilver) 1902- CAP-1
Earlier sketch in CA 9-10
Fink Cline, Beverly 1951- 113
Finke, Blythe Foote 1922- 65-68
See also SATA 26
Finke, Jack A. 1918(?)-1979 Obituary 89-92
Finkel, Donald 1929- CANR-9
Earlier sketch in CA 23-24R
Finkel, George (Irvine) 1909-1975 .... CAP-2
Earlier sketch in CA 17-18
See also SATA 8
Finkel, Lawrence S. 1925- 13-14R
Finkel, LeRoy 1939- 105
Finkelhor, David 1947- 118
Finkelhor, Dorothy Cimberg 1902- 110
Finkell, Max
See Catto, Max(well Jeffrey)
Finkelman, Paul 1949- CANR-22
Earlier sketch in CA 105
Finkelstein, Bonnie B(lumenthal) 1946- 85-88
Finkelstein, Jacob Joel 1922-1974
Obituary 53-56
Finkelstein, Leonid Vladimirovitch 1924- ..23-24R
Finkelstein, Louis 1895- 13-14R
Finkelstein, Marina S. 1921(?)-1972
Obituary 33-36R
Finkelstein, Milton 1920- 89-92
Finkelstein, Miriam 1928- 108
Finkelstein, Sidney 1910(?)-1974
Obituary 45-48
Finkle, Jason L(eonard) 1926- 23-24R
Finklehoffe, Fred F. 1910-1977 Obituary ...73-76
Finkler, Kaja 1935- 114
Finlator, John Haywood 1911- 102
Finlay, Campbell K(irkman) 1909- 7-8R
Finlay, David J(ames) 1934- CANR-16
Earlier sketch in CA 25-28R
Finlay, Fiona
See Stuart, (Violet) Vivian (Finlay)
Finlay, Ian Hamilton 1925- 81-84
See also DLB 40
Finlay, Matthew Henderson 1916- 13-14R
Finlay, William
See Mackay, James (Alexander)
Finlay, Winifred Lindsay Crawford
(McKissack) 1910- 9-10R
See also SATA 23
Finlayson, Ann 1925- 29-32R
See also SATA 8
Finlayson, Roderick (David) 1904- 81-84
Finler, Joel W(aldo) 1938- 77-80
Finletter, Thomas K(night) 1893-1980
Obituary 101
Finley, Gerald Eric 1931- 105
Finley, Glenna
See Witte, Glenna Finley
Finley, Harold M(arshall) 1916- 17-18R
Finley, James 1943- 97-100
Finley, Joseph E(dwin) 1919- 69-72
Finley, Lewis M(erren) 1929- 61-64
Finley, M(oses) I. 1912-1986 .... CANR-10
Obituary 119
Earlier sketch in CA 5-6R
Finley, Martha 1828-1909 Brief entry 118
See also SATA 43
See also DLB 42
Finman, Ted 1931- Brief entry 110
Finn, David 1921- 73-76
Finn, Doug(las Arthur) 1946- 118
Finn, Edward E(rnest) 1908- 115
Finn, Geraldine 1947- 118
Finn, James 1924- Brief entry 108
Finn, Jonathan 1884(?)-1971 Obituary ...29-32R
Finn, R. Welldon
See Finn, Reginald Patrick Arthur Welldon
Finn, Ralph L(eslie) 1912- CANR-9
Earlier sketch in CA 7-8R
Finn, Reginald Patrick Arthur Welldon
1900-1971 .... CANR-10
Earlier sketch in CA 13-14R
Finn, Rex Welldon
See Finn, Reginald Patrick Arthur Welldon
Finnegan, Robert
See Ryan, Paul William
Finnegan, Ruth H(ilary) 1933- CANR-12
Earlier sketch in CA 25-28R
Finneran, Richard J(ohn) 1943- CANR-12
Earlier sketch in CA 29-32R
Finnerty, Adam Daniel
See Corson-Finnerty, Adam Daniel
Finnerty, Daniel John
See Corson-Finnerty, Adam Daniel
Finney, Ben R(udolph) 1933- CANR-1
Earlier sketch in CA 45-48
Finney, Charles G(randison) 1905-1984 ... CAP-2
Obituary 112
Earlier sketch in CA 29-32
Finney, Gertrude Elva (Bridgeman) 1892- . CAP-1
Earlier sketch in CA 15-16
Finney, Gretchen Ludke 1901- 9-10R
Finney, Humphrey S. 1902- 97-100
Finney, Jack
See Finney, Walter Braden
See also DLB 8
Finney, Mark
See Muir, Kenneth (Arthur)
Finney, Nathaniel Solon 1903-1982
Obituary 108
Finney, Patricia 1958- 97-100
Finney, Paul B(urnham) 1929- 73-76
Finney, Shan 1944- 111
Finney, Theodore M(itchell) 1902- 61-64
Finney, Walter Braden 1911- Brief entry 110
Finnigan, Joan
See MacKenzie, Joan Finnigan
Finnin, (Olive) Mary 106
Finocchiaro, Mary (Bonomo) 1913- 29-32R
Fins, Alice 1944- 110
Finson, Jon W(illiam) 1950- 125
Fiore, Edith 1930- 85-88
Fiore, Michael V. 1934- 45-48
Fiore, Peter Amadeus 1927- 33-36R
Fiore, Robert Louis 1935- 73-76
Fiore, Silvestro 1921- 19-20R
Fiorenza, Elisabeth Schuessler 1938- 106
Fiorenza, Francis S(chuessler) 1941- 115
Fiori, Pamela A. 1944- 89-92
Fiorina, Morris Paul, Jr. 1946- 85-88
Fiorino, A(ngelo) John 1926- 29-32R
Fiorio, Franco Emilio 1912-1975 Obituary ..61-64
Firbank, Louis 1942- Brief entry 117
Firbank, (Arthur Annesley) Ronald
1886-1926 Brief entry 104
See also DLB 36
See also TCLC 1
Firchow, Evelyn Scherabon 1932- CANR-11
Earlier sketch in CA 23-24R
Firchow, Peter (Edgerly) 1937- 37-40R
Firebrace, Aylmer (Newton George) 1886- ...7-8R
Fires, Alicia
See Oglesby, Joseph
Fireside, Harvey 1929- 29-32R
Firestone, Harvey S(amuel), Jr.
1898-1973 Obituary 41-44R
Firestone, O(tto) J(ohn) 1913- 41-44R
Firestone, Tom
See Newcomb, Duane G(raham)
Firey, Walter Irving (Jr.) 1916- 1R
Firkins, Peter (Charles) 1926- 107
Firmage, George J(ames) 1928- 9-10R
Firmat, Gustavo (Francisco) Perez
See Perez-Firmat, Gustavo (Francisco)
Firmin, Charlotte 1954- CANR-23
Earlier sketch in CA 106
See also SATA 29
Firmin, Giles 1615-1697 .... DLB-24
Firmin, Peter 1928- CANR-17
Earlier sketch in CA 81-84
See also SATA 15
Firsoff, V(aldemar) Axel 1910- 93-96
First, Ruth 1925-1982 .... CANR-10
Obituary 107
Earlier sketch in CA 53-56
Firth, (Frederick) Anson 1902- 117
Firth, Grace (Ushler) 1922- 73-76
Firth, J. R.
See Firth, John Rupert
Firth, John Rupert 1890-1960 Obituary 116
Firth, Raymond (William) 1901- 65-68
Firth, Robert E. 1921- 77-80
Firth, Tony 1937(?)-1980 Obituary 97-100
Fisch, Edith L. 1923- 77-80
Fisch, Gerald G(rant) 1922- 15-16R
Fisch, Harold 1923- 37-40R
Fisch, Martin L. 1924- 109
Fisch, Max H(arold) 1900- 33-36R
Fisch, Richard 1926- Brief entry 106
Fischbach, Julius 1894- CANR-2
Earlier sketch in CA 7-8R
See also SATA 10
Fischel, Walter J(oseph) 1902-1973 .... CAP-2
Obituary 41-44R
Earlier sketch in CA 23-24

Fischer, Alfred (George) 1920- 73-76
Fischer, Ann 1919-1971 CAP-2
Earlier sketch in CA 25-28
Fischer, Arlene 1934- 111
Fischer, Bobby
See Fischer, Robert James
Fischer, Bruno 1908- 77-80
Fischer, Carl H(ahn) 1903- 17-18R
Fischer, Claude S(erge) 1948- 107
Fischer, David Hackett 1935- 17-18R
Fischer, Dietrich 1941- 117
Fischer, Donald E(dward) 1935- 41-44R
Fischer, Edward (Adam) 1914- CANR-16
Earlier sketches in CA 1R, CANR-1
Fischer, Ernst 1899-1972 Obituary 37-40R
Fischer, Fritz 1908- CANR-9
Earlier sketch in CA 65-68
Fischer, George 1923- CANR-9
Earlier sketch in CA 53-56
Fischer, George 1932- 25-28R
Fischer, Gerald C(harles) 1928- CANR-9
Earlier sketch in CA 23-24R
Fischer, J(ohn) L(yle) 1923- 19-20R
Fischer, Joel 1939- CANR-19
Earlier sketches in CA 53-56, CANR-4
Fischer, John 1910-1978 CANR-4
Obituary 81-84
Earlier sketch in CA 9-10R
Fischer, John Martin 1952- 124
Fischer, LeRoy H(enry) 1917- CANR-8
Earlier sketch in CA 17-18R
Fischer, Louis 1896-1970 CAP-1
Obituary 25-28R
Earlier sketch in CA 11-12
Fischer, Michael R(obert) 1949- 118
Fischer, Robert H. 1918- 37-40R
Fischer, Robert James 1943- 103
Fischer, Roger Adrian 1939- Brief entry 109
Fischer, Vera Kistiakowsky
See Kistiakowsky, Vera
Fischer, Victor 1924- Brief entry 110
Fischer, William F(rank) 1934- Brief entry 111
Fischer, Wolfgang Georg 1933- 33-36R
Fischer-Dieskau, Dietrich 1925- 97-100
Fischer-Galati, Stephen A(lexander) 1924-
Brief entry 117
Fischer-Nagel, Andreas 1951- 123
Fischer-Nagel, Heiderose 1956- 123
Fischetti, John 1916-1980 Obituary 102
Fischl, Viktor
See Dagan, Avigdor
Fischler, Stan(ley I.) Brief entry 116
See also SATA 36
Fischman, Harve 1930- Brief entry 113
Fischman, Leonard L(ipman) 1919- CANR-10
Earlier sketch in CA 15-16R
Fischtrom, Harvey 1933-1974 CAP-2
Obituary 53-56
Earlier sketch in CA 25-28
Fish, Byron 1908- 45-48
Fish, Julian
See Campbell, Blanche
Fish, Kenneth L(loyd) 1926- 29-32R
Fish, Margery (Townshend) 1892-1969 CANR-4
Earlier sketch in CA 7-8R
Fish, Peter Graham 1937- 69-72
Fish, Robert L. 1912-1981 CANR-13
Obituary 103
Earlier sketch in CA 13-14R
Fish, Roy J(ason) 1930- 123
Brief entry 118
Fish, Stanley Eugene 1938- Brief entry 112
See also DLB 67
Fishback, Margaret
See Antolini, Margaret Fishback
Fishbane, Michael A(lton) 1943- 113
Fishbein, Harold D(ennis) 1938- 126
Brief entry 105
Fishbein, Meyer H(arry) 1916- 41-44R
Fishbein, Morris 1889-1976 CANR-4
Obituary 69-72
Earlier sketch in CA 7-8R
Fishburn, Hummel 1901- CAP-1
Earlier sketch in CA 19-20
Fishburn, Janet Forsythe 1937- 108
Fishburn, Peter C(lingerman) 1936- 45-48
Fishel, Elizabeth 1950- 103
Fishel, Leslie H(enry), Jr. 1921- 23-24R
Fishel, Wesley R(obert) 1919-1977 73-76
Obituary 69-72
Fisher, A(rnold) Garth 1933- 104
Fisher, A(rthur) Stanley T(heodore) 1906- 93-96
Fisher, Aileen (Lucia) 1906- CANR-17
Earlier sketches in CA 5-6R, CANR-2
See also SATA 1, 25
Fisher, Alan 1929- 121
Fisher, Alan W(ashburn) 1939- 53-56
Fisher, Alden L(owell) 1928-1970 CAP-2
Earlier sketch in CA 25-28
Fisher, Allan C(arroll), Jr. 1919- 112
Fisher, Allan G(eorge) B(arnard)
1895-1976 33-36R
Fisher, Allen J. 1907(?)-1980 Obituary 102
Fisher, Ameel J(oseph) 1909- 104
Fisher, Arthur 1931- 110
Fisher, Barbara 1940- 104
See also SATA 34, 44
Fisher, Bart (Steven) 1943- 45-48
Fisher, Benjamin Franklin IV 1940- 112
Fisher, Bob
See Fisher, Robert Percival
Fisher, Bruce 1931- 118
Fisher, C(harles) William 1916- CANR-6
Earlier sketch in CA 7-8R
Fisher, Charles Alfred 1916-1982(?)
Obituary 105
Fisher, Clavin C(argill) 1912- 65-68
See also SATA 24
Fisher, Clay
See Allen, Henry Wilson
Fisher, David E(limelech) 1932- CANR-22
Earlier sketches in CA 53-56, CANR-4
Fisher, Dominic (Mayne Maitland) 1953- 124
Fisher, Don 1933(?)-1983 Obituary 111
Fisher, Dorothy (Frances) Canfield
1879-1958 Brief entry 114
See also YABC 1
See also DLB 9
Fisher, Douglas 1934- 102
Fisher, Douglas 1954- 118
Fisher, Douglas Mason 1919- 89-92
Fisher, Edward 1902- 2R
Fisher, Elizabeth 1941- 117
Fisher, Ernest Arthur 1887- 13-14R
Fisher, Esther Oshiver 1910- 85-88
Fisher, Eugene J(oseph) 1943- CANR-22
Earlier sketch in CA 105
Fisher, Florence (Anna) 1928- Brief entry 112
Fisher, Franklin M(arvin) 1934- 17-18R
Fisher, Fred L(ewis) 1911- CANR-5
Earlier sketch in CA 4R
Fisher, (Donald) Gary 1938- 103
Fisher, Gene H. 1922- 41-44R
Fisher, Gene L(ouis) 1947- 81-84
Fisher, George W. 1910(?)-1987 Obituary 124
Fisher, Glen H(arry) 1922- Brief entry 111
Fisher, Glenn W(illiam) 1924- 53-56
Fisher, Gordon N(eil) 1928-1985 Obituary 117
Fisher, Harold H. 1890-1975 Obituary 61-64
Fisher, Harvey Irvin 1916- 69-72
Fisher, Helen E(lizabeth) 1945- 108
Fisher, Humphrey J(ohn) 1933- 33-36R
Fisher, J(ohn) R(obert) 1943- CANR-1
Earlier sketch in CA 45-48
Fisher, J(oseph) Thomas 1936- 33-36R
Fisher, James (Maxwell McConnell)
1912-1970 126
Obituary 89-92
Fisher, James R(aymond), Jr. 1937- 81-84
Fisher, Joe 1947- 103
Fisher, Johanna 1922- 93-96
Fisher, John (Oswald Hamilton) 1909- 81-84
See also SATA 15
Fisher, John C(harles) 1927- 41-44R
Fisher, John H(urt) 1919- CANR-11
Earlier sketch in CA 21-22R
Fisher, Kenneth L(awrence) 1950- 118
Fisher, Kim N. 1948- 121
Fisher, Laine
See Howard, James A(rch)
Fisher, Laura Harrison 1934- 15-16R
See also SATA 5
Fisher, Lawrence V. 1923- 19-20R
Fisher, Lee 1908- 33-36R
Fisher, Leonard Everett 1924- CANR-2
Earlier sketch in CA 3R
See also SATA 4, 34
See also SAAS 1
See also DLB 61
Fisher, Lillian Estelle 1891- CAP-1
Earlier sketch in CA 15-16
Fisher, Lois H(amilton) 1936- 113
Fisher, Lois I. 1948- 113
See also SATA 35, 38
Fisher, Lois Jeannette 1909- 7-8R
Fisher, Louis 1934- 37-40R
Fisher, M(ary) F(rances) K(ennedy) 1908- 77-80
Fisher, Malcolm R(obertson) 1923-
Brief entry 110
Fisher, Margaret B(arrow) 1918- 17-18R
Fisher, Margery (Turner) 1913- 73-76
See also SATA 20
Fisher, Margot
See Paine, Lauran (Bosworth)
Fisher, Marvin 1927- 21-22R
Fisher, Mary L. 1928- 33-36R
Fisher, Michael John 1933- CANR-3
Earlier sketch in CA 2R
Fisher, Miles Mark 1899-1970 CAP-1
Earlier sketch in CA 15-16
Fisher, Miriam Louise (Scharfe) 1939- 15-16R
Fisher, Morris 1922- 21-22R
Fisher, Neal F(loyd) 1936- 106
Fisher, Nigel 1913- 102
Fisher, Norman George 1910-1972
Obituary 107
Fisher, Peter Jack 1930- 69-72
Fisher, Philip 1941- 113
Fisher, Philip A(rthur) 1907- 61-64
Fisher, R. A.
See Fisher, Ronald A(ylmer)
Fisher, Ralph Talcott, Jr. 1920- 41-44R
Fisher, Rhoda Lee 1924- 65-68
Fisher, Richard 1936- 19-20R
Fisher, Richard B(ernard) 1919- 77-80
Fisher, Robert (Tempest) 1943- CANR-26
Earlier sketch in CA 109
See also SATA 47
Fisher, Robert C(harles) 1930- 53-56
Fisher, Robert J(ay) 1924- 61-64
Fisher, Robert Percival 1935- 93-96
Fisher, Roger (Dummer) 1922- 37-40R
Fisher, Ronald A(ylmer) 1890-1962
Obituary 112
Fisher, Roy 1930- CANR-16
Earlier sketch in CA 81-84
See also DLB 40
See also CLC 25
Fisher, Rudolph 1897-1934 124
Brief entry 107
See also BW
See also DLB 51
See also TCLC 11
Fisher, Seymour 1922- CANR-12
Earlier sketch in CA 33-36R
Fisher, Shelton 1911-1985 Obituary 115
Fisher, Sidney Thomson 1908- 124
Fisher, Sterling Wesley 1899(?)-1978 85-88
Obituary 81-84
Fisher, Susan M(ichal) 1937- 119
Fisher, Sydney G.
See Fisher, Sydney George
Fisher, Sydney George 1856-1927
Brief entry 122
See also DLB 47
Fisher, Vardis (Alvero) 1895-1968 5-6R
Obituary 25-28R
See also DLB 9
See also CLC 7
Fisher, Wade
See Norwood, Victor G(eorge) C(harles)
Fisher, Wallace E. 1918- CANR-10
Earlier sketch in CA 23-24R
Fisher, Walter R. 1931- 15-16R
Fisher, Welthy Honsinger 1879-1980 CANR-2
Obituary 102
Earlier sketch in CA 4R
Fisher, Wesley Andrew 1944- 104
Fisher, William Bayne 1916-1984 65-68
Obituary 113
Fishler, Mary Shiverick 1920- 7-8R
Fishman, Betty G(oldstein) 1918- 7-8R
Fishman, Burton J(ohn) 1942- 45-48
Fishman, Charles 1942- CANR-7
Earlier sketch in CA 57-60
Fishman, George Samuel 1937- 25-28R
Fishman, Jack 1920- CANR-7
Earlier sketch in CA 9-10R
Fishman, Joshua A(aron) 1926- CANR-15
Earlier sketch in CA 41-44R
Fishman, Ken 1950- 105
Fishman, Leo 1914-1975 19-20R
Obituary 120
Fishman, Lew 1939- CANR-11
Earlier sketch in CA 61-64
Fishman, Robert (Lawrence) 1946- 112
Fishman, Sterling 1932- 45-48
Fishof, David 1956- 115
Fishwick, Marshall William 1923- CANR-6
Earlier sketch in CA 7-8R
Fisk, E(rnest) K(elvin) 1917- 19-20R
Fisk, McKee 1900- CAP-2
Earlier sketch in CA 21-22
Fisk, Nicholas 1923- CANR-11
Earlier sketch in CA 65-68
See also SATA 25
Fisk, Samuel 1907- 57-60
Fiske, Edward B. 1937- CANR-16
Earlier sketch in CA 85-88
Fiske, John 1608-1677 DLB-24
Fiske, John 1842-1901 DLB-47, 64
Fiske, Marjorie CANR-1
Earlier sketch in CA 45-48
Fiske, Roger E(lwyn) 1910- 13-14R
Fiske, Sharon
See Hill, Pamela
Fiske, Tarleton
See Bloch, Robert (Albert)
Fisketjon, Gary 1954- Brief entry 123
Fiskin, A(bram) M. I. 1916-1975 CAP-2
Earlier sketch in CA 23-24
Fison, Joseph Edward 1906-1972
Obituary 114
Fiss, Owen M(itchell) 1938- 112
Fiszel, Henryk 1910- 29-32R
Fiszman, Joseph R. 1921- 41-44R
Fitch, Alger Morton, Jr. 1919- 53-56
Fitch, Bob
See Fitch, Robert Beck
Fitch, Clarke
See Sinclair, Upton (Beall)
Fitch, (William) Clyde 1865-1909
Brief entry 110
See also DLB 7
Fitch, Donald S(heldon) 1949- 106
Fitch, Edwin M(edbery) 1902- CAP-2
Earlier sketch in CA 25-28
Fitch, George Ashmore 1883-1979
Obituary 85-88
Fitch, Geraldine T(ownsend) 1892(?)-1976
Obituary 69-72
Fitch, James Marston 1909- 89-92
Fitch, John IV
See Cormier, Robert (Edmund)
Fitch, Kenneth (Leonard) 1929- 49-52
Fitch, Lyle C(raig) 1913- 15-16R
Fitch, Raymond E(dward) 1930- 110
Fitch, Robert Beck 1938- 21-22R
Fitch, Stanley K. 1920- 29-32R
Fitch, Thomas 1700(?)-1774 DLB-31
Fitch, William Clyde 1865-1909 DLB-7
Fitch, Willis Stetson 1896(?)-1978
Obituary 81-84
Fite, Gilbert C(ourtland) 1918- 33-36R
Fite, James David 1933- 107
Fite, Mack
See Schneck, Stephen
Fitler, Mary Biddle 1878(?)-1966
Obituary 25-28R
Fitschen, Dale 1937- 77-80
See also SATA 20
Fitt, Mary
See Freeman, Kathleen
Fitter, Richard Sidney Richmond
1913- CANR-11
Earlier sketch in CA 65-68
Fitting, Greer A. 1943- 81-84
Fitting, James E. 1939- 45-48
Fitting, Melvin (Chris) 1942- CANR-11
Earlier sketch in CA 29-32R
Fitton, James 1899-1982 Obituary 106
Fitts, Dudley 1903-1968 93-96
Obituary 25-28R
Fitts, Henry (King) 1914- 113
Fitts, William Howard 1918- 21-22R
Fitz, Jean DeWitt 1912- 29-32R
Fitzalan, Roger
See Trevor, Elleston
Fitzell, John 1922- 13-14R
Fitzgerald, Arlene J. CANR-8
Earlier sketch in CA 23-24R
Fitzgerald, Barbara
See Value, Barbara Ann
Fitzgerald, Barry Charles 1939- 37-40R
FitzGerald, Brian Seymour Vesey
See Vesey-FitzGerald, Brian Seymour
FitzGerald, C(harles) P(atrick) 1902- CANR-11
Earlier sketch in CA 19-20R
Fitzgerald, Captain Hugh
See Baum, L(yman) Frank
Fitz-Gerald, Carolyn 1932- 41-44R
FitzGerald, Cathleen 1932-1987 33-36R
Obituary 121
See also SATA 50
Fitzgerald, E(dmund) V(alpy) K(nox)
1947- 73-76
FitzGerald, Edward 1809-1883 DLB-32
Fitzgerald, Edward 1898(?)-1982 Obituary 108
Fitzgerald, Edward Earl 1919- 73-76
See also SATA 20
Fitzgerald, Ellen
See Stevenson, Florence
Fitzgerald, Ernest A. 1925- CANR-12
Earlier sketch in CA 29-32R
Fitzgerald, F(rancis) A(nthony) 1940- SATA-15
Fitzgerald, F(rancis) Scott (Key)
1896-1940 123
Brief entry 110
See also DLB 4, 9
See also DLBY 81
See also DLBD 1
See also TCLC 1, 6, 14, 28
See also AITN 1
FitzGerald, Frances 1940- 41-44R
FitzGerald, Garret 1926- 109
Fitzgerald, George R. 1932- CANR-17
Earlier sketch in CA 97-100
Fitzgerald, Gerald (Pierce) 1930- 37-40R
Fitzgerald, Gerald E(dward) 1920- 25-28R
Fitz Gerald, Gregory 1923- CANR-1
Earlier sketch in CA 49-52
Fitzgerald, Hal
See Johnson, Joseph E(arl)
Fitzgerald, Harold Alvin 1896-1984
Obituary 114
Fitzgerald, Hiram E(arl) 1940- CANR-16
Earlier sketch in CA 77-80
Fitzgerald, Jack
See Shea, John Gerald
Fitzgerald, James A(ugustine) 1892- CANR-1
Earlier sketch in CA 1R
Fitzgerald, James V. 1889(?)-1976
Obituary 69-72
Fitzgerald, John
See Fazzano, Joseph E.
Fitzgerald, John D(ennis) 1907(?)-1988 93-96
Obituary 126
See also SATA 20
See also CLR 1
Fitzgerald, John Joseph 1928- 37-40R
Fitzgerald, Judith 1952- 113
Fitzgerald, Julia
See Watson, Julia
FitzGerald, Kathleen Whalen 1938- 109
Fitzgerald, Laurine Elisabeth 1930- 37-40R
Fitzgerald, Lawrence P(ennybaker)
1906-1976 CANR-2
Earlier sketch in CA 3R
Fitzgerald, Maury 1906(?)-1986 Obituary 121
Fitzgerald, Merni Ingrassia 1955- 124
See also SATA 53
Fitzgerald, Michael G(arrett) 1950- 77-80
Fitzgerald, Nancy 1951- 85-88
Fitzgerald, Patrick (John) 1928- 9-10R
Fitzgerald, Penelope 1916- 85-88
See also DLB 14
See also CLC 19
Fitzgerald, Randall 1950- 118
Fitzgerald, Richard (Ambrose) 1938- 45-48
Fitzgerald, Robert (Stuart) 1910-1985 CANR-1
Obituary 114
Earlier sketch in CA 2R
See also DLBY 80
See also CLC 39
FitzGerald, Robert D(avid) 1902- 19-20R
See also CLC 19
FitzGerald, Stephen (Arthur) 1938- 97-100
Fitzgerald, Tamsin 1950- 97-100
Fitzgerald, Thomas 1819-1891 DLB-23
Fitzgerald, Zelda (Sayre) 1900-1948 126
Brief entry 117
See also DLBY 84
FitzGibbon, (Robert Louis) Constantine
(Lee-Dillon) 1919-1983 CANR-2
Obituary 109
Earlier sketch in CA 4R
Fitzgibbon, Russell H(umke)
1902-1979 CANR-14
Earlier sketch in CA 65-68
FitzGibbon, Theodora (Joanne Eileen
Winifred) Rosling 1916- CANR-3
Earlier sketch in CA 7-8R
Fitzgibbons, James P. 1912(?)-1983
Obituary 110
Fitzhardinge, Joan Margaret 1912- CANR-23
Earlier sketches in CA 15-16R, CANR-6
See also SATA 2

INDEX

Fitzhenry, Robert Irvine 1918- 110
Fitzhugh, Louise 1928-1974 CAP-2
Obituary 53-56
Earlier sketch in CA 29-32
See also SATA 1, 24, 45
See also DLB 52
See also CLR 1
Fitzhugh, Robert Tyson 1906-1981
Obituary 104
Fitzhugh, William 1651(?)-1701 DLB-24
Fitzlyon, (Cecily) April (Mead) 1920- 7-8R
Fitzlyon, Kyril 1910- 93-96
Fitzmaurice, George 1877-1963 Obituary 93-96
Fitzmyer, Joseph A(ugustine) 1920- CANR-5
Earlier sketch in CA 9-10R
Fitzpatrick, Daniel Robert 1891-1969
Obituary 89-92
Fitzpatrick, James K(evin) 1942- 65-68
Fitzpatrick, Joseph P(atrick) 1913- 17-18R
Fitzpatrick, Kathryn 1934- 113
FitzPatrick, Paul Joseph 1894-1984
Obituary 111
Fitzpatrick, Tom 1927- Brief entry 111
FitzRalph, Matthew
See McInerny, Ralph
Fitz-Randolph, Jane (Currens) 1915- 103
See also SATA 51
Fitzroy, Rosamond
See Briggs, Desmond Lawther
Fitzsimmons, Cleo 1900- 1R
Fitzsimmons, Thomas 1926- CANR-15
Earlier sketch in CA 33-36R
Fitz-Simon, Christopher 1934- 113
Fitzsimons, Louise 1932- 61-64
Fitzsimons, M(athew) A(nthony) 1912- 13-14R
Fitzsimons, Neal 1928- 33-36R
FitzSimons, Raymund CANR-15
Earlier sketch in CA 33-36R
FitzSimons, Ruth M(arie Mangan) 53-56
Fitzwilliam, Michael
See Lyons, J. B.
Fivelson, Scott 1954- 117
Fix, Paul
See Morrison, Paul Fix
Fix, William R. 1941- CANR-15
Earlier sketch in CA 85-88
Fixler, Michael 1927- 15-16R
Fixx, James F(uller) 1932-1984 CANR-13
Earlier sketch in CA 73-76
Fixx, Jim
See Fixx, James F(uller)
Fizer, John 1925- 53-56
Fjelde, Rolf (Gerhard) 1926- 17-18R
Flach, Frederic F(rancis) 1927- 81-84
Flachmann, Michael 1942- 117
Flack, Audrey L. 1931- CANR-26
Earlier sketch in CA 106
Flack, Dora D(utson) 1919- CANR-21
Earlier sketches in CA 57-60, CANR-6
Flack, Elmer Ellsworth 1894- 17-18R
Flack, Marjorie 1897-1958 Brief entry 112
See also YABC 2
Flack, Naomi John White CANR-1
Earlier sketch in CA 1R
See also SATA 35, 40
Flacks, Niki 1943- 110
Flacks, Richard 1938- 49-52
Fladeland, Betty 1919- 45-48
Flader, Susan L. 1941- 81-84
Flagg, Fannie 1941- 111
Flagg, Kenneth
See Ayvazian, L. Fred
Flagstad, Kirsten 1895-1962 Obituary 112
Flaherty, Daniel Leo 1929- 89-92
Flaherty, David H(arris) 1940- 25-28R
Flaherty, Doug(las Ernest) 1939- 33-36R
Flaherty, Gloria 1938- 85-88
Flaherty, Joe 1936(?)-1983 Obituary 111
Flaherty, Robert J(oseph) 1884-1951
Brief entry 115
Flaherty, Robert Joseph 1933- 73-76
Flaherty, Vincent X. 1908(?)-1977
Obituary 73-76
Flaiano, Ennio 1910-1972 Obituary 37-40R
Flake, Chad J(ohn) 1929- 29-32R
Flamholtz, Eric 1943- 57-60
Flamm, Dudley 1931- 25-28R
Flamm, Gerald R(obert) 1916- 77-80
Flamm, Jerry
See Flamm, Gerald R(obert)
Flammarion, (Nicolas) Camille 1842-1925
Brief entry 120
Flammarion, Henri (Claude) 1910-1985
Obituary 117
Flammer, Philip M(eynard) 1928- 45-48
Flammonde, Paris 19-20R
Flanagan, Dorothy Belle
See Hughes, Dorothy B(elle)
Flanagan, John C(lemans) 1906- CANR-1
Earlier sketch in CA 4R
Flanagan, John T(heodore) 1906- 19-20R
Flanagan, Joseph David Stanislaus
1903- 13-14R
Flanagan, Mary 1943- 125
Flanagan, Neal M. 1920-1985 19-20R
Obituary 117
Flanagan, Owen J. 1949- 125
Flanagan, Robert (James) 1941- 33-36R
Flanagan, Thomas (James Bonner) 1923- 108
See also DLBY 80
See also CLC 25
Flanagan, William G(eorge) 1940- CANR-15
Earlier sketch in CA 93-96
Flanagan, William G(eorge) 1942- 119
Flanagan, William I. 1916(?)-1986
Obituary 118

Flanders, Helen Hartness 1890-1972 CAP-1
Obituary 33-36R
Earlier sketch in CA 15-16
Flanders, Henry Jackson, Jr. 1921- 33-36R
Flanders, James P(rescott) 1942- 69-72
Flanders, Jane (Hess) 1940- 110
Flanders, Michael (Henry) 1922-1975 CANR-4
Obituary 57-60
Earlier sketch in CA 7-8R
Flanders, Ned A. 1918- 37-40R
Flanders, Ralph Edward 1880-1970 CAP-1
Earlier sketch in CA 11-12
Flanders, Rebecca
See Ball, Donna
Flanders, Robert Bruce 1930- 19-20R
Flanery, E(dward) B(oyd) 1932- 61-64
Flanigan, Lloyd A(llen) 1933- 33-36R
Flanner, Hildegarde
See Monhoff, June Hildegarde Flanner
See also DLB 48
Flanner, Janet 1892-1978 CANR-13
Obituary 81-84
Earlier sketch in CA 65-68
See also DLB 4
Flannery, Edward H(ugh) 1912- 15-16R
Flannery, Harry W. 1900-1975 CAP-1
Obituary 57-60
Earlier sketch in CA 9-10
Flannery, James W(illiam) 1936-
Brief entry 110
Flannery, Peter 1951- 104
Flannery, Sean
See Hagberg, David J(ames)
Flasch, Joy 1932- 37-40R
Flaster, Donald J(ohn) 1932- 115
Flath, Arnold W(illiam), J. 1929- 65-68
Flato, Charles 1908(?)-1984 Obituary 111
Flattau, Edward 1937- 65-68
Flavell, Carol Willsey Bell 1939- 73-76
Flavell, John H(urley) 1928- CANR-11
Earlier sketch in CA 19-20R
Flavin, Martin 1883-1967 5-6R
Obituary 25-28R
See also DLB 9
Flavius, Brother
See Ellison, James E.
Flaxman, Traudl 1942- 25-28R
Flayderman, Phillip C(harles) 1930-1969 CAP-2
Earlier sketch in CA 23-24
Fleck, Betty
See Paine, Lauran (Bosworth)
Fleck, Henrietta 1903- 77-80
Fleck, Richard Francis 1937- CANR-18
Earlier sketch in CA 102
Flecker, (Herman) James Elroy 1884-1915
Brief entry 109
See also DLB 10, 19
Fleece, Jeffrey (Atkinson) 1920- 17-18R
Fleege, Urban H(erman) 1908- CANR-1
Earlier sketch in CA 45-48
Fleer, Jack D(avid) 1937- 25-28R
Fleeson, Doris 1901-1970 Obituary 93-96
See also DLB 29
Fleetwood, Frances 1902- CANR-17
Earlier sketches in CA 45-48, CANR-1
Fleetwood, Frank
See Fleetwood, Frances
Fleetwood, Hugh (Nigel) 1944- Brief entry 112
Fleetwood-Hesketh, (Charles) Peter
(Fleetwood) 1905-1985 Obituary 115
Flegg, (Henry) Graham 1924- 114
Fleischbein, Sister M. Catherine Frederic
1902- 5-6R
Fleischer, Jane
See Oppenheim, Joanne
Fleischer, Leonore Brief entry 109
See also SATA 47
Fleischer, Manfred P(aul) 1928- 29-32R
Fleischer, Max 1889-1972 Obituary 109
See also SATA 30
Fleischer, Nathaniel S. 1888(?)-1972
Obituary 37-40R
Fleischhauer-Hardt, Helga 1936- 102
See also SATA 30
Fleischman, Harry 1914- CANR-3
Earlier sketch in CA 5-6R
Fleischman, Paul 1952- 113
See also SATA 32, 39
Fleischman, (Albert) Sid(ney) 1920- CANR-5
Earlier sketch in CA 3R
See also SATA 8
See also CLR 1, 15
Fleischmann, Glen H(arvey) 1909- 33-36R
Fleischmann, Harriet 1904- CAP-2
Earlier sketch in CA 21-22
Fleischmann, Raoul H(erbert) 1885-1969
Obituary 115
Fleischmann, Wolfgang Bernard 1928- 116
Fleisher, Belton Mendel 1935- 69-72
Fleisher, Frederic 1933- 21-22R
Fleisher, Martin 1925- 45-48
Fleisher, Michael (Lawrence) 1942- 25-28R
Fleisher, Robbin 1951-1977 SATA-49, 52
Fleisher, Wilfried 1897(?)-1976 Obituary 65-68
Fleishman, Avrom (Hirsch) 1933- 21-22R
Fleishman, Edwin A(lan) 1927- CANR-11
Earlier sketch in CA 21-22R
Fleishman, Seymour 1918- Brief entry 111
See also SATA 32
Fleisser, Marieluise
See Haindl, Marieluise
See also DLB 56
Flemer, William III 1922- 61-64
Fleming, Alice Mulcahey 1928- CANR-2
Earlier sketch in CA 4R
See also SATA 9
Fleming, Amalia 1912-1986 Obituary 118

Fleming, Berry 1899- CANR-18
Earlier sketches in CA 1R, CANR-2
Fleming, C(harlotte) M(ary) 1894- 7-8R
Fleming, D(enna) F(rank) 1893- CANR-1
Earlier sketch in CA 1R
Fleming, David A(rnold) 1939- 93-96
Fleming, Donald M(ethuen) 1905-1986
Obituary 121
Fleming, Elizabeth P. 1888-1985 Obituary 119
See also SATA 48
Fleming, George J(oseph) 1917- 37-40R
Fleming, Gerald 1921- 53-56
Fleming, Guy
See Masur, Harold Q.
Fleming, H(orace) K(ingston) 1901- 33-36R
Fleming, Harold (Lee) 1927- 17-18R
Fleming, Harold M(anchester)
1900-19(?) CAP-2
Earlier sketch in CA 21-22
Fleming, Ian (Lancaster) 1908-1964 7-8R
See also SATA 9
See also CLC 3, 30
Fleming, Irene 1923(?)-1979 Obituary 89-92
Fleming, Jennifer Baker 1943- 77-80
Fleming, Joan Margaret 1908-1980 81-84
Obituary 102
Fleming, June 1935- 110
Fleming, Lady Amalia
See Fleming, Amalia
Fleming, Laurence (William Howie) 1929- 107
Fleming, Macklin 1911- 77-80
Fleming, Miles 1919- 29-32R
Fleming, Oliver
See MacDonald, Philip
Fleming, (Robert) Peter 1907-1971
Obituary 33-36R
Fleming, Ray(mond) 1945- 115
See also BW
Fleming, Robert H(enry) 1912-1984
Obituary 114
Fleming, Ronald Lee 1941- 108
Fleming, Sandford 1888- CAP-1
Earlier sketch in CA 9-10
Fleming, Susan 1932- CANR-14
Earlier sketch in CA 81-84
See also SATA 32
Fleming, Theodore B(owman), Jr. 1917- 45-48
Fleming, Thomas (James) 1927- CANR-10
Earlier sketch in CA 7-8R
See also SATA 8
See also CLC 37
Fleming, William (Coleman) 1909- 17-18R
Flemming, Nicholas Coit 1936- 97-100
Flemmons, Jerry 1936- 124
Flender, Harold 1924- 49-52
Flesch, Janos Laszlo 1933(?)-1983
Obituary 111
Flesch, Rudolf (Franz) 1911-1986 CANR-3
Obituary 120
Earlier sketch in CA 9-10R
Flesch, Y.
See Flesch, Yolande (Catarina)
Flesch, Yolande (Catarina) 1950- 122
Flescher, Irwin 1926- 37-40R
Flescher, Joachim 1906(?)-1976
Obituary 65-68
Fletcher, Adele (Whitely) 1898- CAP-1
Earlier sketch in CA 17-18
Fletcher, Alan Mark 1928- 73-76
Fletcher, Angus (John Stewart) 1930- 104
Fletcher, Anthony John 1941- 73-76
Fletcher, Arnold Charles 1917- 17-18R
Fletcher, Banister F.
See Fletcher, Banister Flight
Fletcher, Banister Flight 1866-1953
Brief entry 123
Fletcher, Barbara (Helen) 1935- 110
Fletcher, Basil Alais 1900-1983 65-68
Obituary 109
Fletcher, Bramwell 1904(?)-1988 Obituary 125
Fletcher, Charlie May Hogue 1897- 9-10R
See also SATA 3
Fletcher, Colin 1922- CANR-11
Earlier sketch in CA 13-14R
See also SATA 28
See also AITN 1
Fletcher, David
See Barber, D(ulan) F(riar Whilberton)
Fletcher, Dirk
See Cunningham, Chet
Fletcher, Geoffrey Scowcroft 1923- 103
Fletcher, George U.
See Pratt, (Murray) Fletcher
Fletcher, Grace Nies 1895- 7-8R
Fletcher, H(arry) L(utf) V(erne)
1902-197(?) CANR-4
Earlier sketch in CA 11-12R
Fletcher, Harold Roy 1907-1978 Obituary 111
Fletcher, Harris Francis 1892-1979 1R
Obituary 103
Fletcher, Harvey 1884-1981 Obituary 108
Fletcher, Helen Jill 1911- 9-10R
See also SATA 13
Fletcher, Henry Lancelot Aubrey
See Aubrey-Fletcher, Henry Lancelot
Fletcher, Ian 1920- Brief entry 124
Fletcher, (Minna) Inglis 7-8R
See also AITN 1
Fletcher, J(oseph) S(mith) 1863-1935
Brief entry 109
See also DLB 70
Fletcher, Jesse C. 1931- CANR-4
Earlier sketch in CA 11-12R
Fletcher, John 1579-1625 DLB-58
Fletcher, John (Walter James) 1937- CANR-15
Earlier sketch in CA 81-84
Fletcher, John C(aldwell) 1931- 124

Fletcher, John Gould 1886-1950
Brief entry 107
See also DLB 4, 45
Fletcher, Joseph (Francis III) 1905- CANR-11
Earlier sketch in CA 21-22R
Fletcher, Leon 1921- 49-52
Fletcher, Lucille
See Wallop, Lucille Fletcher
Fletcher, Marilyn P(endleton) 1940- 106
Fletcher, Marjorie 1941- Brief entry 113
Fletcher, Mary AITN-1
Fletcher, (William) Miles (III) 1946- 114
Fletcher, Richard E. 1917(?)-1983
Obituary 109
See also SATA 34
Fletcher, Rick
See Fletcher, Richard E.
Fletcher, Robert H. 1885(?)-1972
Obituary 37-40R
Fletcher, Roger A(nthony) 1942- 121
Fletcher, Ronald 1921- CANR-13
Earlier sketch in CA 33-36R
Fletcher, Sir Banister
See Fletcher, Banister Flight
Fletcher, William C(atherwood) 1932- 23-24R
Fletcher, William W(higham) 1918- CANR-15
Earlier sketch in CA 81-84
Fletcher, Winston 1937- 118
Fletcher-Cooke, John 1911- 102
Fleur, Anne 1901- SATA-31
Fleur, Paul
See Pohl, Frederik
Fleure, H. J.
See Fleure, Herbert John
Fleure, Herbert John 1877-1969 Obituary 115
Fleuridas, Ellie Rae
See Sherman, Eleanor Rae
Fleury, Delphine
See Amatora, Sister Mary
Flew, Antony G(arrard) N(ewton)
1923- CANR-18
Earlier sketches in CA 5-6R, CANR-3
Flexner, Eleanor 1908- 45-48
Flexner, James Thomas 1908- CANR-2
Earlier sketch in CA 4R
See also SATA 9
Flexner, Stuart Berg 1928- CANR-11
Earlier sketch in CA 15-16R
Flick, Carlos Thomas 1927- 89-92
Fliegel, Frederick C(hristian) 1925- 49-52
Flieger, Wilhelm 1931- 25-28R
Flier, Michael S(tephen) 1941- CANR-14
Earlier sketch in CA 37-40R
Fliess, Peter J(oachim) 1915- 21-22R
Flinders, Neil J. 1934- 21-22R
Flink, James J(ohn) 1932- Brief entry 112
Flink, Salomon J. 1906-1983 CANR-17
Earlier sketch in CA 2R
Flinn, M(ichael) W(alter) 1917-1983 CANR-13
Obituary 110
Earlier sketch in CA 19-20R
Flint, Betty M. 1920- 23-24R
Flint, Cort R(ay) 1915- 49-52
Flint, E. de P.
See Fielden, T(homas) P(erceval)
Flint, F(rank) S(tuart) 1885-1960 Obituary 113
See also DLB 19
Flint, Homer Eon 1892-1924 Brief entry 114
Flint, John E(dgar) 1930- 37-40R
Flint, Lucy 1954- 115
Flint, Timothy 1780-1840 DLB-73
Flippo, Chet 1943- 89-92
Flippo, Edwin B(ly) 1925- CANR-13
Earlier sketch in CA 33-36R
Flitner, David P(erkins), Jr. 1949- CANR-1
Earlier sketch in CA 45-48
See also SATA 7
Floan, Howard R(ussell) 1918- 19-20R
Floethe, Louise Lee 1913- CANR-2
Earlier sketch in CA 1R
See also SATA 4
Floethe, Richard 1901- 33-36R
See also SATA 4
Floherty, John Joseph 1882-1964 SATA-25
Flood, Charles Bracelen 1929- 41-44R
Flood, Curt(is Charles) 1938- Brief entry 115
Flood, E(dward) Thadeus 1932- 49-52
Flood, John M(ichael) 1947- 115
Flood, Kenneth Urban 1925- 11-12R
Flood, Robert G. 1935- CANR-22
Earlier sketch in CA 106
Flooglebuckle, Al
See Spiegelman, Art
Flook, Maria 1952- 110
Flora, Fletcher 1914-1969 CANR-3
Earlier sketch in CA 1R
Flora, James (Royer) 1914- CANR-3
Earlier sketch in CA 5-6R
See also SATA 1, 30
See also SAAS 6
Flora, Joseph M(artin) 1934- CANR-21
Earlier sketches in CA 15-16R, CANR-5
Flora, Paul 1922- Brief entry 113
Floren, Lee 1910- CANR-18
Earlier sketches in CA 5-6R, CANR-3
Florence, Philip Sargant 1890-1982
Obituary 106
Florence, Ronald 1942- CANR-15
Earlier sketch in CA 33-36R
Florentin, Eddy 1923- 49-52
Flores, Angel 1900- CANR-19
Earlier sketch in CA 103
Flores, Dan Louie 1948- 121
Flores, Ivan 1923- CANR-22
Earlier sketches in CA 19-20R, CANR-7
Flores, Janis 1946- CANR-26
Earlier sketches in CA 65-68, CANR-10

Flores, John 1943- 77-80
Florescu, Radu R. 1925- 41-44R
Florez, Pablo de Azcarate y
See Azcarate y Florez, Pablo de
Florian, Douglas 1950- 123
See also SATA 19
Florian, Tibor 1908- 73-76
Florin, Lambert F. 1905- CANR-7
Earlier sketch in CA 17-18R
Florinsky, Michael T(imothy)
1894-1981 .... CANR-15
Obituary 105
Earlier sketch in CA 1R
Floriot, Rene 1902-1975 Obituary 61-64
Florit, Eugenio 1903- 104
Florman, Samuel C(harles) 1925- 102
Florovsky, Georges (Vasilievich)
1893-1979 Obituary 111
Flory, Charles D(avid) 1902- 41-44R
Flory, Harry R. 1899-1976 Obituary 69-72
Flory, Jane Trescott 1917- CANR-3
Earlier sketch in CA 9-10R
See also SATA 22
Flory, Julia McCune 1882-1971 .... CAP-2
Obituary 29-32R
Earlier sketch in CA 21-22
Flory, Paul J(ohn) 1910-1985 Obituary 117
Floud, Roderick 1942- CANR-1
Earlier sketch in CA 45-48
Flournoy, Don Michael 1937- 126
Flower, Dean S. 1938- 21-22R
Flower, Desmond (John Newman) 1907- ..9-10R
Flower, Elizabeth Farquhar 1914- 103
Flower, Harry A(lfred) 1901- CAP-1
Earlier sketch in CA 11-12
Flower, (Harry) John 1936- 37-40R
Flower, Margaret Cameron Coss 61-64
Flower, (Walter) Newman 1879-1964
Obituary 109
Flower, Raymond (Charles) 1921- 108
Flowerdew, Phyllis 103
See also SATA 33
Flowers, Ann Moore 1923- 9-10R
Flowers, Betty S(ue) 1947- 65-68
Flowers, Charles 1942- 29-32R
Flowers, Charles E(ly, Jr.) 1920- 93-96
Flowers, John V(ictor) 1938- 106
Flowers, Paul Abbott 1905-1984 Obituary ... 112
Floyd, Barry Neil 1925- 33-36R
Floyd, Gareth 1940- SATA-31
Floyd, Harriet 1925- 69-72
Floyd, Lois Gray 1910(?)-1978 85-88
Obituary 81-84
Floyd, Samuel A(lexander), Jr. 1937- 115
Floyd, Troy S(mith) 1920- 37-40R
Floyd, W(illiam) E(dward) G(regory)
1939- 33-36R
Floyd, William Anderson 1928- 29-32R
Fluchere, Henri (Auguste) 1898-1987
Obituary 123
Fluchere, Henri 1914- 77-80
See also SATA 40
Fluck, Diana 1931-1984 Obituary 113
Fluck, Reginald Alan Paul 1928- 9-10R
Flume, Violet S(igoloff) 116
Flumiani, Carlo M(aria) 1911- CANR-9
Earlier sketch in CA 15-16R
Fluno, Robert Y(ounger) 1916- 33-36R
Flusser, Martin 1947- 73-76
Flute, Molly
See Lottman, Eileen
Fly, Claude L(ee) 1905- 97-100
Flyat, Sten G(unnar) 1911- 11-12R
Flying Officer X
See Bates, H(erbert) E(rnest)
Flynn, Barbara 1928- SATA-9
Flynn, Bernice (Lydia Carlson) 1922- 114
Flynn, Carol Houlihan 1945- 112
Flynn, Charles F(rederick) 1949- 57-60
Flynn, David H(oughton) 1953- 115
Flynn, Don
See Flynn, Donald R(obert)
Flynn, Donald R(obert) 1928- CANR-12
Earlier sketch in CA 29-32R
Flynn, Elizabeth Gurley 1890-1964
Obituary 111
Flynn, Fahey 1916-1983 Obituary 110
Flynn, George L. 1931- CANR-24
Earlier sketches in CA 65-68, CANR-9
Flynn, George Q(uitman) 1937- 25-28R
Flynn, Gerard (Cox) 1924- 41-44R
Flynn, Jackson
See Bensen, Donald R.
and Shirreffs, Gordon D(onald)
Flynn, James Joseph 1911- 23-24R
Flynn, James R. 1934- 21-22R
Flynn, John Joseph 1936- 19-20R
Flynn, John Thomas 1882-1964 Obituary ..89-92
Flynn, Leslie Bruce 1918- CANR-17
Earlier sketches in CA 1R, CANR-2
Flynn, Paul P(atrick) 1942- 37-40R
Flynn, Robert (Lopez) 1932- 29-32R
Flynt, Candace 1947- 102
Flynt, Larry AITN-2
Flynt, Wayne 1940- CANR-13
Earlier sketch in CA 37-40R
Flythe, Starkey S(harp), Jr. 1935- 69-72
Fo, Dario 1926- Brief entry 116
See also CLC 32
Foat Tugay, Emine 1897- CAP-1
Earlier sketch in CA 13-14
Foda, Aun
See Foxe, Arthur N(orman)
Fodaski-Black, Martha 1929- 73-76
Fodor, Eugene 1905- CANR-14
Earlier sketch in CA 21-22R
Fodor, M. W. 1890(?)-1977 Obituary 69-72
Fodor, Nandor 1895-1964 Obituary 112
Fodor, R(onald) V(ictor) 1944- CANR-15
Earlier sketch in CA 65-68
See also SATA 25
Foell, Earl W(illiam) 1929- 69-72
Foerster, Eberhard
See Weisenborn, Guenther
Foerster, Leona M(itchell) 1930- 89-92
Foerster, Lotte B(rand) 1910-1986 77-80
Obituary 119
Foerster, Norman 1887- 7-8R
Foff, Arthur R(aymond) 1925-1973 ...... CAP-2
Earlier sketch in CA 33-36
Fogarty, Jonathan Titulescu, Esq.
See Farrell, James T(homas)
Fogarty, Michael P(atrick) 1916- CANR-9
Earlier sketch in CA 21-22R
Fogarty, Robert S(tephen) 1938- CANR-9
Earlier sketch in CA 65-68
Fogel, Daniel
See Kahn-Fogel, Daniel (Mark)
Fogel, Daniel (Mark) Kahn
See Kahn-Fogel, Daniel (Mark)
Fogel, Ephim G(regory) 1920- 120
Fogel, Robert W(illiam) 1926- CANR-13
Earlier sketch in CA 77-80
Fogel, Ruby 19-20R
Fogelquist, Donald Frederick 1906- 69-72
Fogelson, Robert M(ichael) 1937- 81-84
Fogg, Sam R. 1917(?)-1987 Obituary 123
Fogle, Bruce 1944- 106
Fogle, French R(owe) 1912- 37-40R
Fogle, Richard Harter 1911- CANR-5
Earlier sketch in CA 7-8R
Foglio, Frank 1921- 57-60
Foiles, Keith Andrew 1926-1983 Obituary ... 109
Foin, Theodore C(hin) 1940- 93-96
Foisie, Jack 1919- 104
Fokkema, D(ouwe) W(essel) 1931- CANR-23
Earlier sketches in CA 19-20R, CANR-7
Fol, Alexander 1933- Brief entry 111
Foladare, Joseph 1909- 102
Folb, Edith A(rlene) 1938- 102
Folch-Ribas, Jacques 1928- 69-72
Foldessy, Edward P(atrick) 1941- 126
Folds, Thomas M. 93-96
Folejewski, Zbigniew 1910- CANR-7
Earlier sketch in CA 17-18R
Foley, Allen Richard 1898-1978 45-48
Obituary 77-80
Foley, (Anna) Bernice Williams 1902- .. CANR-12
Earlier sketch in CA 29-32R
See also SATA 28
Foley, Charles 1908- CAP-1
Earlier sketch in CA 15-16
Foley, Daniel J(oseph) 1913- CANR-5
Earlier sketch in CA 7-8R
Foley, Doug 1942- 57-60
Foley, Duncan K(arl) 1942- 93-96
Foley, Gerald (Patrick) 1936- CANR-11
Earlier sketch in CA 69-72
Foley, Helen
See Fowler, Helen Rosa Huxley
Foley, (Cedric) John 1917-1974 .... CANR-4
Obituary 53-56
Earlier sketch in CA 9-10R
Foley, John Miles 1947- 111
Foley, June 1944- 109
See also SATA 44
Foley, Leonard 1913- 89-92
Foley, (Mary) Louise Munro 1933- 37-40R
See also SATA 40
Foley, Martha 1897(?)-1977 117
Obituary 73-76
Foley, Mary Mix 1918- 102
Foley, Michael F(rancis) 1940-1984
Obituary 113
Foley, Paul 1914-1983 Obituary 111
Foley, Rae
See Denniston, Elinore
Foley, Richard 1947- 126
Foley, Richard N. 1910(?)-1980 Obituary ... 102
Foley, Scott
See Dareff, Hal
Foley, Vincent D. 1933- 57-60
Foley, William E. 1938- 33-36R
Foley, Winifred 1914- 102
Folk, Jerry 114
Folkard, Charles James 1878-1963
Obituary 109
See also SATA 28
Folke, Will
See Bloch, Robert (Albert)
Folkenflik, Robert 1939- Brief entry 111
Folkers, George Fulton 1929- 49-52
Folkerts, George W(illiam) 1938- 53-56
Folkman, Jerome (Daniel) 1907- CAP-2
Earlier sketch in CA 29-32
Folland, H(arold) F(reeze) 1906- 49-52
Follen, Eliza Lee (Cabot) 1787-1860 ..... DLB-1
Follett, Helen Thomas 1884(?)-1970
Obituary 107
See also SATA 27
Follett, James 1939- Brief entry 112
Follett, Ken(neth Martin) 1949- CANR-13
Earlier sketch in CA 81-84
See also DLBY 81
See also CLC 18
Follett, Robert J(ohn) R(ichard) 1928- .. CANR-23
Earlier sketches in CA 21-22R, CANR-8
Folley, Terence T. 1931- 21-22R
Folley, Vern L(eRoy) 1936- 49-52
Folliard, Edward T(homas) 1899-1976
Obituary 69-72
Follis, Anne Bowen 1947- 106
Follmann, J(oseph) F., Jr. 1908- CANR-7
Earlier sketch in CA 19-20R
Folmar, J. Kent
See Folmar, John Kent
Folmar, John Kent 1932- 116
Folmsbee, Stanley J(ohn) 1899-1974 .... CAP-2
Earlier sketch in CA 29-32
Folsom, Anne (Ferril) 1922- Brief entry 114
Folsom, Burton W(hitmore), Jr. 1947- 118
Folsom, Franklin (Brewster) 1907- CANR-2
Earlier sketch in CA 3R
See also SATA 5
Folsom, Jack
See Folsom, John B(entley)
Folsom, John B(entley) 1931- 45-48
Folsom, Kenneth E(verett) 1921- 21-22R
Folsom, Marion Bayard 1893- CAP-2
Earlier sketch in CA 17-18
Folsom, Marvin Hugh 1929- 57-60
Folsom, Michael (Brewster) 1938- 112
See also SATA 40
Folsom, Robert S(lade) 1915- 77-80
Folta, Jeannette R. 1934- 25-28R
Foltin, Lore Barbara 1913-19(?) CAP-2
Earlier sketch in CA 25-28
Foltz, William J(ay) 1936- 11-12R
Fomon, Samuel J(oseph) 1923- 53-56
Fonarow, Jerry 1935- CANR-4
Earlier sketch in CA 53-56
Fonda, Henry (Jaynes) 1905-1982
Obituary 107
Fonda, Peter 1939(?)- Brief entry 112
Fon Eisen, Anthony T. 1917- 15-16R
Foner, Eric 1943- CANR-12
Earlier sketch in CA 29-32R
Foner, Jack D(onald) 1910- 77-80
Foner, Nancy 1945- 53-56
Foner, Philip (Sheldon) 1910- CANR-3
Earlier sketch in CA 11-12R
Fong, Wen Chih 1930- 103
Fong-Torres, Ben 1945- 93-96
Fonseca, Aloysius Joseph 1915- CANR-9
Earlier sketch in CA 15-16R
Fonseca, John R. 1925- CANR-8
Earlier sketch in CA 19-20R
Fonstad, Karen Wynn 1945- 104
Fontaine, Andre 1910- 65-68
Fontaine, Andre (Lucien Georges)
1921- CANR-12
Earlier sketch in CA 25-28R
Fontaine, Joan 1917- 81-84
Fontana, Bernard L(ee) 1931- CANR-7
Earlier sketch in CA 19-20R
Fontana, Biancamaria 1952- 124
Fontana, Thomas M. 1951- Brief entry 113
Fontana, Vincent James 1923- 15-16R
Fontanet, Joseph 1921-1980 Obituary 105
Fontcreuse, Marquis de
See Jaeger, Cyril Karel Stuart
Fontenay, Charles L(ouis) 1917- 25-28R
Fontenelle, Don H(arris) 1946- 106
Fontenot, Chester J. 1950- 112
Fontenot, Mary Alice 1910- CANR-14
Earlier sketch in CA 37-40R
See also SATA 34
Fontenrose, Joseph 1903- 7-8R
Fonteyn, Margot
See Fonteyn de Arias, Margot
Fonteyn de Arias, Margot 1919- 117
Brief entry 110
Fonzi, Bruno 1913(?)-1976 Obituary 65-68
Foon, Dennis 1951- 111
Fooner, Michael 81-84
See also SATA 22
Foord, Archibald Smith 1914-1969 ...... CAP-1
Earlier sketch in CA 11-12
Foosaner, Samuel J. 1907(?)-1988
Obituary 125
Foot, Hugh Mackintosh 1907- 11-12R
Foot, M(ichael) R(ichard) D(aniell)
1919- CANR-3
Earlier sketch in CA 7-8R
Foot, Michael 1913- 108
Foot, Paul Mackintosh 1937- 17-18R
Foot, Philippa Ruth 1920- 101
Foote, A(von) Edward 1937- CANR-13
Earlier sketch in CA 73-76
Foote, Arthur 1911- 114
Foote, Darby Mozelle 1942- 61-64
Foote, Dorothy Norris (McBride) 1908- ... CAP-2
Earlier sketch in CA 21-22
Foote, Geoffrey 1950- 123
Foote, Horton 1916- 73-76
See also DLB 26
Foote, Shelby 1916- CANR-3
Earlier sketch in CA 5-6R
See also DLB 2, 17
Foote, Timothy (Gilson) 1926- 93-96
See also SATA 52
Foote, Victoria 1954- 118
Foote, Wilder 1905-1975 Obituary 57-60
Foote-Smith, Elizabeth 1913- 69-72
Footman, David (John) 1895-1983 97-100
Obituary 111
Footman, Robert 1916- 126
Footner, (William) Hulbert 1879-1944
Brief entry 114
Foran, Donald J. 1943- 33-36R
Forberg, Ati
See Forberg, Beate Gropius
See also SATA 22
Forberg, Beate Gropius 1925- 105
Forbes, Bryan 1926- 69-72
See also SATA 37
Forbes, Cabot L.
See Hoyt, Edwin P(almer), Jr.
Forbes, Calvin 1945- CANR-26
Earlier sketch in CA 49-52
See also BW
See also DLB 41
Forbes, Clarence A(llen) 1901- 77-80
Forbes, Colin
See Sawkins, Raymond H(arold)
Forbes, Daniel
See Kenyon, Michael
Forbes, DeLoris (Florine) Stanton
1923- CANR-5
Earlier sketch in CA 11-12R
Forbes, Donald (Galen) 1918-1987
Obituary 122
Forbes, Elliot 1917- 9-10R
Forbes, Eric Gray 1933-1984 .... CANR-10
Obituary 114
Earlier sketch in CA 65-68
Forbes, Esther 1891-1967 .... CAP-1
Obituary 25-28R
Earlier sketch in CA 13-14
See also SATA 2
See also DLB 22
See also CLC 12
Forbes, Graham B. CAP-2
Earlier sketch in CA 19-20
See also SATA 1
Forbes, Henry W(illiam) 1918- 4R
Forbes, J(ohn) V(an) G(elder) 1916- 9-10R
Forbes, Jack D. 1934- CANR-4
Earlier sketch in CA 1R
Forbes, Joanne R. (Triebel) 1930- 37-40R
Forbes, John Douglas 1910- 53-56
Forbes, Kathryn
See McLean, Kathryn (Anderson)
Forbes, Malcolm S(tevenson) 1919- 69-72
Forbes, Murray (M.) 1906-1987 Obituary ... 121
Forbes, (Christopher) Patrick 1925- 25-28R
Forbes, Rosita
See McGrath, Joan Rosita (Torr)
Forbes, Stanton
See Forbes, DeLoris (Florine) Stanton
Forbes, Thomas Rogers 1911- 41-44R
Forbes-Boyd, Eric 1897-1979 ....15-16R
Obituary 125
Forbes-Dennis, Phyllis 1884-1963
Obituary 93-96
Forbes-Robertson, Diana
See Sheean, Diana
Forbis, Judith 1934- 101
Forbis, William H. 1918- CANR-15
Earlier sketch in CA 37-40R
Forbus, Ina B(ell) 4R
Forcade, Robert J. 1935- 125
Force, Peter 1790-1868 .... DLB-30
Force, Roland W(ynfield) 1924- 41-44R
Force, William M. 1916- 21-22R
Forcey, Charles B(udd) 1925- CANR-1
Earlier sketch in CA 1R
Forche, Carolyn (Louise) 1950- 117
Brief entry 109
See also DLB 5
See also CLC 25
Forchheimer, Paul 1913- 53-56
Forcione, Alban Keith 1938- CANR-13
Earlier sketch in CA 33-36R
Ford, A(lec) G(eorge) 1926- 5-6R
Ford, Adam 1940- 111
Ford, Agnes Gibbs 1902- CAP-2
Earlier sketch in CA 21-22
Ford, Albert Lee
See Stratemeyer, Edward L.
Ford, Alice 1906- CAP-1
Earlier sketch in CA 19-20
Ford, Amasa B. 1922- 21-22R
Ford, Arthur A. 1897-1971 Obituary 112
Ford, Arthur L(ewis) 1937- 57-60
Ford, Barbara Brief entry 112
See also SATA 34
Ford, Betty
See Ford, Elizabeth Anne Bloomer
Ford, Boris 1917- 112
Ford, Brian J(ohn) 1939- CANR-15
Earlier sketch in CA 41-44R
See also SATA 49
Ford, Cathy Diane 1952- 105
Ford, Charles Henri 1913- CANR-13
Earlier sketch in CA 25-28R
See also DLB 4, 48
Ford, Colin John 1934- 85-88
Ford, Collier
See Ford, James L(awrence) C(ollier)
Ford, Corey 1902-1969 Obituary 25-28R
See also DLB 11
Ford, D(ouglas) W(illiam) Cleverley
1914- CANR-24
Earlier sketches in CA 61-64, CANR-9
Ford, Daniel (Francis) 1931- CANR-11
Earlier sketch in CA 17-18R
Ford, David
See Harknett, Terry
Ford, Donald (Frank William) 1924- 7-8R
Ford, Donald H(erbert) 1926- 41-44R
Ford, Edmund Brisco 1901-1988 85-88
Obituary 124
Ford, Edsel 1928-1970 .... CAP-1
Obituary 29-32R
Earlier sketch in CA 15-16
Ford, Edward (Charles) 1928- 89-92
Ford, Eileen (Otte) 1922- 120
Ford, Elaine 1938- CANR-19
Earlier sketch in CA 102
Ford, Elbur
See Hibbert, Eleanor Burford
Ford, Elizabeth
See Bidwell, Marjory Elizabeth Sarah

INDEX

Ford, Elizabeth Anne Bloomer 1918- ... CANR-23
Earlier sketch in CA 105
Ford, Florence
See Novelli, Florence
Ford, Ford Madox 1873-1939 Brief entry ... 104
See also DLB 34
See also TCLC 1, 15
Ford, Frank B(ernard) 1932- ... 85-88
Ford, Franklin L(ewis) 1920- ... 19-20R
Ford, Fred
See Doerffler, Alfred
Ford, George (Jr.) ... 107
See also SATA 31
Ford, George Barry 1885-1978 Obituary ... 81-84
Ford, George D. 1880(?)-1974 Obituary ... 53-56
Ford, George H(arry) 1914- ... CANR-2
Earlier sketch in CA 3R
Ford, George L(onnie) 1914- ... 7-8R
Ford, Gerald R(udolph, Jr.) 1913- ... 114
Brief entry ... 110
Ford, Gordon B(uell), Jr. 1937- ... CANR-13
Earlier sketch in CA 21-22R
Ford, Guy B(arrett) 1922- ... 5-6R
Ford, Harvey Seabury 1905(?)-1978
Obituary ... 73-76
Ford, Henry 1863-1947 Brief entry ... 115
Ford, Henry II 1917-1987 Obituary ... 123
Brief entry ... 111
Ford, Herbert Paul 1927- ... 19-20R
Ford, Hilary
See Youd, Samuel
Ford, Hildegarde
See Morrison, Velma Ford
Ford, Hugh D. 1925- Brief entry ... 114
Ford, J. Massingberd
See Ford, Josephine Massyngbaerde
Ford, James Allan 1920- ... CAP-1
Earlier sketch in CA 9-10
Ford, James L(awrence) C(ollier) 1907- ... 29-32R
Ford, Jesse Hill (Jr.) 1928- ... CANR-1
Earlier sketch in CA 2R
See also DLB 6
Ford, John 1586-? ... DLB-58
Ford, John 1895-1973 Obituary ... 45-48
See also CLC 16
Ford, Josephine Massyngbaerde ... 41-44R
Ford, Kathleen 1932- ... 25-28R
Ford, Kirk
See Spence, William John Duncan
Ford, Lee 1936- ... 25-28R
Ford, Leighton F. S. 1931- ... 19-20R
Ford, LeRoy 1922- ... 11-12R
Ford, Leslie
See Brown, Zenith Jones
Ford, Lewis
See Patten, Lewis B(yford)
Ford, Marcia
See Radford, Ruby L(orraine)
Ford, Marcus Peter 1950- ... 108
Ford, Margaret Patricia 1925- ... 9-10R
Ford, Mary Forker 1905- ... 11-12R
Ford, Murray J(ohn) S(tanley) 1923- ... 93-96
Ford, Nancy K(effer) 1906-1961 Obituary ... 109
See also SATA 29
Ford, Nick Aaron 1904-1982 ... CANR-11
Earlier sketch in CA 25-28R
See also BW
Ford, Norman D(ennis) 1921- ... CANR-10
Earlier sketch in CA 23-24R
Ford, Norrey
See Dilcock, Noreen
Ford, Patrick 1914- ... 23-24R
Ford, Paul F(rancis X.) 1947- ... CANR-22
Earlier sketch in CA 105
Ford, Percy 1894-1983 Obituary ... 110
Ford, Peter 1936- ... 126
Ford, Philip J(ohn) 1949- ... 115
Ford, Phyllis M(arjorie) 1928- ... CANR-13
Earlier sketch in CA 33-36R
Ford, R(obert) A(rthur) D(ouglass)
1915- ... CANR-19
Earlier sketch in CA 97-100
Ford, R(ichard) Clyde 1870-1951
Brief entry ... 121
Ford, Richard 1944- ... CANR-11
Earlier sketch in CA 69-72
See also CLC 46
Ford, Richard Brice 1935- ... 37-40R
Ford, Robert E. 1913-1975 ... CAP-2
Earlier sketch in CA 29-32
Ford, Robert N(icholas) 1909- ... 33-36R
Ford, Stephen 1949- ... 77-80
Ford, Thomas R(obert) 1923- ... 49-52
Ford, Thomas W(ellborn) 1924- ... 21-22R
Ford, W(illiam) Clay(ton, Jr.) 1946- ... 93-96
Ford, W(illiam) Herschel 1900- ... CANR-5
Earlier sketch in CA 9-10R
Ford, Webster
See Masters, Edgar Lee
Ford, Whitey
See Ford, Edward (Charles)
Ford, Worthington C. 1858-1941 ... DLB-47
Forde, Gerhard O(laf) 1927- ... 89-92
Forde-Johnston, James (Leo) 1927- ... CANR-3
Earlier sketch in CA 9-10R
Fordham, Frieda 1903-1988 Obituary ... 124
Fordham, Peta 1905- ... 106
Fordin, Hugh 1935- ... 57-60
Fordyce, Rachel (Poole) 1942- ... 121
Brief entry ... 118
Fore, William Frank 1928- ... 7-8R
Forell, George W(olfgang) 1919- ... CANR-16
Earlier sketches in CA 1R, CANR-1
Foreman, Carl 1914-1984 ... 41-44R
Obituary ... 113
See also DLB 26
Foreman, Clark H(owell) 1902-1977
Obituary ... 69-72
Foreman, Gene 1934- ... 77-80
Foreman, Harry 1915- ... 33-36R
Foreman, Kenneth Joseph 1891- ... CAP-2
Earlier sketch in CA 33-36
Foreman, L(eonard) L(ondon) 1901- ... CANR-5
Earlier sketch in CA 5-6R
Foreman, Lawton Durant 1913- ... 9-10R
Foreman, Michael 1938- ... CANR-10
Earlier sketch in CA 23-24R
See also SATA 2
Foreman, Richard 1937- ... 65-68
See also CLC 50
Foreman, Russell 1921- ... 77-80
Forer, Lois G(oldstein) 1914- ... 29-32R
Forer, Lucille K(remith) ... 37-40R
Forer, Mort 1922- ... 97-100
Fores, John 1914- ... 25-28R
Forest, Antonia ... 103
See also SATA 29
Forest, Ilse 1896- ... CAP-2
Earlier sketch in CA 19-20
Forest, Lee
See Woods, Clee
Forester, Bruce (Michael) 1939- ... CANR-25
Earlier sketch in CA 107
Forester, C(ecil) S(cott) 1899-1966 ... 73-76
Obituary ... 25-28R
See also SATA 13
See also CLC 35
Forester, Frank
See Herbert, Henry William
Foreyt, John P(aul) 1943- ... 118
Forez
See Mauriac, Francois (Charles)
Forgie, George B(arnard) 1941- ... 89-92
Forgus, Ronald (Henry) 1928- ... 41-44R
Forio, Robert
See Weiss, Irving J.
Forisha, Barbara L.
See Forisha-Kovach, Barbara L(usk)
Forisha-Kovach, Barbara L(usk) 1941- ... 107
Forkosch, Morris D(avid) 1908- ... 41-44R
Form, William H. 1917- ... 65-68
Forma, Warren 1923- ... 45-48
Forman, Brenda 1936- ... CANR-6
Earlier sketch in CA 9-10R
See also SATA 4
Forman, Celia Adler 1890(?)-1979
Obituary ... 85-88
Forman, Charles William 1916- ... 13-14R
Forman, Harrison 1904-1978 ... 5-6R
Obituary ... 77-80
Forman, Henry James 1879-1966 ... 7-8R
Forman, James Douglas 1932- ... CANR-19
Earlier sketches in CA 9-10R, CANR-4
See also SATA 8
Forman, Joan ... 102
Forman, Jonathan 1887-1974 ... CAP-2
Earlier sketch in CA 23-24
Forman, Leona S. 1940- ... 25-28R
Forman, Marc A(llan) 1935- ... 57-60
Forman, Max Leon 1909- ... 112
Forman, Milos 1932- ... 109
Forman, Robert E(dgar) 1924- ... 11-12R
Forman, Shepard (Lewis) 1938-
Brief entry ... 112
Forman, (James Adam) Sholto 1915- ... 25-28R
Formby, William A(rthur) 1943- ... 109
Formento, Dan 1954- ... 112
Formhals, Robert W(illard) Y(ates)
S(arguszko) 1919- ... 53-56
Formisano, Ronald P. 1939- Brief entry ... 115
Formwalt, Lee W(illiam) 1949- ... 119
Fornari, Franco 1921- ... CANR-12
Earlier sketch in CA 29-32R
Fornari, Harry D(avid) 1919- ... 69-72
Fornell, Earl Wesley 1915-1969 ... 1R
Obituary ... 103
Fornes, Maria Irene 1930- ... 25-28R
See also DLB 7
See also CLC 39
Forno, Lawrence J(oseph) 1943- ... 37-40R
Forrest, A(lfred) C(linton) 1916-1978 ... 49-52
Obituary ... 103
Forrest, Caleb
See Telfer, Dariel (Doris)
Forrest, David
See Forrest-Webb, Robert
Forrest, Derek W(illiam) 1926- ... 77-80
Forrest, Earle Robert 1883-1969 ... 3R
Obituary ... 103
Forrest, Felix C.
See Linebarger, Paul M(yron) A(nthony)
Forrest, Gary Gran 1943- ... 113
Forrest, James Taylor 1921- ... 115
Forrest, John Galbraith 1898-1982
Obituary ... 107
Forrest, Julian
See Wagenknecht, Edward (Charles)
Forrest, Julie de
See DeWitt, Edith Openshaw
Forrest, Leon 1937- ... CANR-25
Earlier sketch in CA 89-92
See also CAAS 7
See also BW
See also DLB 33
See also CLC 4
Forrest, Norman
See Morland, Nigel
Forrest, Richard (Stockton) 1932- ... CANR-25
Earlier sketches in CA 57-60, CANR-9
Forrest, Sybil
See Markun, Patricia Maloney
Forrest, W(illiam) G(eorge) 1925- ... 25-28R
Forrest, Wilbur S. 1887-1977 Obituary ... 69-72
Forrestal, Dan J(oseph), Jr. 1912- ... 77-80
Forrester, Frank H. 1919(?)-1986
Obituary ... 119
See also SATA 52
Forrester, Helen
See Bhatia, Jamunadevi
See also SATA 48
Forrester, Jay W(right) 1918- ... CANR-1
Earlier sketch in CA 45-48
Forrester, Larry 1924- ... 25-28R
Forrester, Leland S. 1905(?)-1978
Obituary ... 81-84
Forrester, Marian
See Schachtel, Roger (Bernard)
Forrester, Mary
See Humphries, Mary
Forrester, (William) Ray 1911- ... 23-24R
Forrester, Rex Desmond 1928- ... 103
Forrester, Victoria 1940- ... CANR-25
Earlier sketch in CA 108
See also SATA 35, 40
Forrest-Webb, Robert 1929- ... CANR-4
Earlier sketch in CA 49-52
Forsberg, (Charles) Gerald 1912- ... 102
Forsberg, Malcolm I. 1908- ... 21-22R
Forsberg, Roberta Jean 1914- Brief entry ... 105
Forsee, (Frances) Aylesa ... CANR-1
Earlier sketch in CA 4R
See also SATA 1
Forshay-Lunsford, Cin 1965- ... 119
Forssmann, Werner Theodor Otto
1904-1979 Obituary ... 111
Forster, Arnold 1912- ... 15-16R
Forster, E(dward) M(organ) 1879-1970 ... CAP-1
Obituary ... 25-28R
Earlier sketch in CA 13-14
See also DLB 34
See also CLC 1, 2, 3, 4, 9, 10, 13, 15,
22, 45
Forster, Kent 1916-1981 ... 23-24R
Obituary ... 125
Forster, Mark Arnold
See Arnold-Forster, Mark
Forster, Merlin H(enry) 1928- ... 41-44R
Forster, Peter 1926(?)-1982 Obituary ... 107
Forster, Robert 1926- ... 41-44R
Forstman, H(enry) Jackson 1929- ... 15-16R
Forsyth (Outram), Anne 1933- ... CANR-12
Earlier sketch in CA 29-32R
Forsyth, Bill 1948- ... 122
Forsyth, David J(ames) C(ameron)
1940- ... 41-44R
Forsyth, David P(ond) 1930- ... 9-10R
Forsyth, Frederick 1938- ... 85-88
See also CLC 2, 5, 36
Forsyth, George H(oward), Jr. 1901- ... 37-40R
Forsyth, Ilene (Haering) 1928- ... 37-40R
Forsyth, James (Law) 1913- ... 73-76
Forsyth, Richard S(andes) 1948- ... 116
Forsythe, Elizabeth 1927- ... 93-96
Forsythe, Irene
See Hanson, Irene (Forsythe)
Forsythe, Robert
See Crichton, Kyle Samuel
Forsythe, Sidney A. 1920- ... 41-44R
Fort, John 1942- ... 77-80
Fort, Paul 1872-1960 Obituary ... 114
Fort, Williams Edwards, Jr. 1905- ... 37-40R
Fortas, Abe 1910-1982 Obituary ... 106
Forte, Allen 1926- ... 41-44R
Forte, Dan 1935- ... 65-68
Forte, David F. 1941- ... 53-56
Fortebraccia, Donato
See Forte, Dan
Forten, Charlotte
See Grimke, Charlotte L(ottie) Forten
Forten, Charlotte L.
See Grimke, Charlotte L(ottie) Forten
See also DLB 50
See also TCLC 16
Fortes, Meyer 1906-1983 Obituary ... 109
Fortescue, William (Archer Irvine) 1945- ... 122
Fortman, Edmund J. 1901- ... CANR-11
Earlier sketch in CA 21-22R
Fortnum, Peggy
See Nuttall-Smith, Margaret Emily Noel
See also SATA 26
Fortune, T(imothy) Thomas 1856-1928
Brief entry ... 112
See also DLB 23
Forty, Adrian 1948- ... 123
Forty, George 1927- ... CANR-15
Earlier sketch in CA 89-92
Forward, Luke
See Patrick, Johnstone G(illespie)
Forward, Robert L(ull) 1932- ... CANR-20
Earlier sketch in CA 103
Forzano, Giovacchino 1884-1970 Obituary ... 104
Fosburgh, Hugh (Whitney) 1916-1976
Obituary ... 69-72
Fosburgh, Lacey 1942- ... CANR-22
Earlier sketch in CA 85-88
Fosburgh, Liza 1930- ... 112
Fosburgh, Pieter Whitney 1914(?)-1978
Obituary ... 77-80
Foscue, Edwin Jay 1899-1972 ... 4R
Obituary ... 103
Fosdick, Charles Austin 1842-1915
Brief entry ... 119
See also DLB 42
Fosdick, Harry Emerson 1878-1969
Obituary ... 25-28R
Fosdick, Raymond B(laine) 1883-1972
Obituary ... 37-40R
Foshay, Toby (Avard) 1950- ... 119
Foshee, John (Hugh) 1931- ... 69-72
Foskett, D(ouglas) J(ohn) 1918- ... CANR-5
Earlier sketch in CA 1R
Foskett, Daphne 1911- ... 102
Foskett, Reginald 1909-1973 ... CAP-2
Earlier sketch in CA 21-22
Foss, Christopher F(rank) 1946- ... 93-96
Foss, Dennis C(arleton) 1947- ... 104
Foss, Phillip Oliver ... 15-16R
Foss, William O(tto) 1918- ... 19-20R
Fosse, Alfred
See Jelly, George Oliver
Fosse, Bob
See Fosse, Robert Louis
See also CLC 20
Fosse, Robert Louis 1927-1987 Obituary ... 123
Brief entry ... 110
Fossedal, Gregory
See Fossedal, Gregory A.
Fossedal, Gregory A. 1959- ... 125
Fossey, Dian 1932-1985 ... 113
Obituary ... 118
Fossum, Robert H. 1923- ... 25-28R
Foster, Alan Dean 1946- ... CANR-22
Earlier sketches in CA 53-56, CANR-5
Foster, Brad W. 1955- ... SATA-34
Foster, Brian 1920- Brief entry ... 112
Foster, Carno A(ugustus) 1916- ... 41-44R
Foster, Catharine Osgood 1907- ... 65-68
Foster, Cedric 1900-1975 Obituary ... 89-92
Foster, Charles Howell 1913- ... 19-20R
Foster, Charles Irving 1898-197? ... 1R
Foster, Charles R(obert) 1927- ... 110
Foster, Charles William 1939- ... 57-60
Foster, Daniel W(illet) 1930- ... 108
Foster, David 1908- ... 97-100
Foster, David Manning 1944- ... CANR-18
Earlier sketch in CA 97-100
Foster, David William (Anthony) 1940- ... CANR-22
Earlier sketches in CA 21-22R, CANR-8
Foster, Don(ald) 1948- ... 33-36R
Foster, Donald (LeRoy) 1928- ... 53-56
Foster, Doris Van Liew 1899- ... 102
See also SATA 10
Foster, Dorothy 1936- ... 93-96
Foster, E(lizabeth) C(onnell) 1902- ... 53-56
See also SATA 9
Foster, Earl M(asters) 1940- ... 57-60
Foster, Edward Halsey 1942- ... CANR-18
Earlier sketches in CA 49-52, CANR-2
Foster, Elizabeth 1902- ... 85-88
See also SATA 12
Foster, Elizabeth 1905-1963 ... 4R
See also SATA 10
Foster, Elizabeth Read 1912- ... 106
Foster, F. Blanche 1919- ... 61-64
See also SATA 11
Foster, (Reginald) Francis 1896-1975 ... 109
Obituary ... 107
Foster, Frederick
See Godwin, John (Frederick)
Foster, G(eorge) Allen 1907-1969 ... 9-10R
See also SATA 26
Foster, Genevieve Stump 1893-1979 ... CANR-4
Obituary ... 89-92
Earlier sketch in CA 5-6R
See also SATA 2, 23
See also DLB 61
See also CLR 7
Foster, Genevieve W(akeman) 1902- ... 69-72
Foster, George
See Haswell, Chetwynd John Drake
Foster, George M(cClelland, Jr.) 1913-
Brief entry ... 113
Foster, H. Lincoln 1906- ... CAP-1
Earlier sketch in CA 19-20
Foster, Hal
See Foster, Harold (Rudolf)
See also AITN 2
Foster, Hannah Webster 1758-1840 ... DLB-37
Foster, Harold (Rudolf) 1892-1982
Obituary ... 107
See also SATA 31
Foster, Harold D(ouglas) 1943- ... 111
Foster, Henry H(ubbard), Jr.
1911-1988 ... CANR-2
Obituary ... 125
Earlier sketch in CA 1R
Foster, Herbert L(awrence) 1928- ... 57-60
Foster, Herbert W. 1920(?)-1979
Obituary ... 89-92
Foster, Idris Llywelyn 1911-1984 Obituary ... 113
Foster, Iris
See Posner, Richard
Foster, Jack Donald 1930- ... 29-32R
Foster, James C(aldwell) 1943- ... CANR-7
Earlier sketch in CA 57-60
Foster, Jeanne Robert (Ollivier)
1884-1970 Obituary ... 104
Foster, Joanna 1928- ... CANR-8
Earlier sketch in CA 5-6R
Foster, John 1648-1681 ... DLB-24
Foster, John 1915- ... 7-8R
Foster, John (Thomas) 1925- ... 33-36R
See also SATA 8
Foster, John (Andrew) 1941- ... 126
Foster, John Burt, Jr. 1945- ... 106
Foster, John L(awrence) 1930- ... 53-56
Foster, Joseph O'Kane 1898- ... 49-52
Foster, Julian F(rancis) S(herwood)
1926- ... 29-32R
Foster, K(enneth) Neill 1935- ... CANR-4
Earlier sketch in CA 53-56
Foster, Laura Louise (James) 1918- ... 17-18R
See also SATA 6
Foster, Lee 1923(?)-1977 Obituary ... 69-72
Foster, Lee Edwin 1943- ... 33-36R
Foster, Lynn 1952- ... 113

Foster, M(ichael) A(nthony) 1939- CANR-25
Earlier sketches in CA 57-60, CANR-9
Foster, Malcolm (Burton) 1931- 109
Foster, Margaret Lesser 1899(?)-1979
Obituary 89-92
See also SATA 21
Foster, Margery S(omers) 1914- 5-6R
Foster, Marguerite H. 1909- CAP-2
Earlier sketch in CA 21-22
Foster, Marian Curtis 1909-1978 73-76
Obituary 85-88
See also SATA 23
Foster, Marion
See Shea, Shirley
Foster, Mark Stewart 1939- 106
Foster, Martha S(tanding) 5-6R
Foster, Michael 1904-1956 Brief entry 110
See also DLB 9
Foster, Michael S(immler) 1942- 117
Foster, Nancy Haston 122
Foster, O'Kane
See Foster, Joseph O'Kane
Foster, Paul 1931- CANR-26
Earlier sketches in CA 21-22R, CANR-9
Foster, Peter 1947- CANR-25
Earlier sketch in CA 108
Foster, Philip (John) 1927- 69-72
Foster, Richard
See Crossen, Kendell Foster
Foster, Richard J(ames) 1942- CANR-15
Earlier sketch in CA 85-88
Foster, Robert A(lfred) 1949- 81-84
Foster, Ruel Elton 1916- 33-36R
Foster, Shirley 1943- 122
Foster, Timothy R(ichard) V(ernon) 1938- ... 112
Foster, Virginia Ramos 29-32R
Foster, Walter Roland 1925- Brief entry 116
Foster-Harris, William 1903(?)-1978
Obituary 104
Fothergill, (Arthur) Brian 1921- 19-20R
Fothergill, Philip G(ilbert) 1908- 7-8R
Fotheringham, Nick 1943- 121
Fottler, Myron David 1941- CANR-14
Earlier sketch in CA 37-40R
Foucault, Michel 1926-1984 105
Obituary 113
See also CLC 31, 34
Fougasse
See Bird, (Cyril) Kenneth
Fought, John G(uy) 1938- Brief entry 113
Fouhy, Ed(ward Michael) 1934- 69-72
Foulds, Elfrida Vipont 1902- CANR-4
Earlier sketch in CA 53-56
See also SATA 52
Foulke, Adrienne 1915- 65-68
Foulke, Robert (Dana) 1930- 45-48
Foulke, Roy Anderson 1896- CANR-1
Earlier sketch in CA 4R
Foulkes, A(lbert) Peter 1936- 37-40R
Foulkes, (William) David 1935- Brief entry .. 107
Foulkes, Fred K. 1941- CANR-12
Earlier sketch in CA 33-36R
Fountain, Charles (Francis) 1950- 118
Fountain, Leatrice 1924- 23-24R
Fouraker, Lawrence Edward 1923- 1R
Four Corners, George
See Viereck, George Sylvester
Fourest, Henri-Pierre 1911- Brief entry 109
Fourest, Michel
See Wynne-Tyson, (Timothy) Jon
(Lyden)
Fournet, Jean-Claude 1932- 124
Fournier, Frank
See Chapman, Frank M(onroe)
Fournier, Henri Alban 1886-1914
Brief entry 104
Fournier, Pierre 1916- CANR-16
Earlier sketch in CA 89-92
See also CLC 11
Fourth, Clifton
See Morse, H(enry) Clifton Iv
Fourth Brother, The
See Aung, (Maung) Htin
Foust, Paul J(ohn) 1920- 49-52
Fouste, E(thel) Bonita Rutledge 1926- 15-16R
Fout, John C(alvin) 1937- 57-60
Fowke, Edith (Margaret) 1913- 37-40R
See also SATA 14
Fowkes, Robert Allen 1913- Brief entry 106
Fowle, Eleanor Cranston
See Cameron, Eleanor Cranston
Fowler, Alastair (David Shaw) 1930- 15-16R
Fowler, Austin 1928- 23-24R
Fowler, Carolyn 117
Fowler, Charles B(runer) 1931- CANR-24
Earlier sketches in CA 57-60, CANR-8
Fowler, David Covington 1921- 1R
Fowler, David Henry 1924- Brief entry 112
Fowler, Don D. 1936- CANR-15
Earlier sketch in CA 33-36R
Fowler, Doreen (Angela) 1948- 119
Fowler, Douglas 1940- 57-60
Fowler, Elaine W(otten) 1914- 93-96
Fowler, Elizabeth Millspaugh 1921- 102
Fowler, Eugene Devlan 1890-1960 97-100
Obituary 89-92
Fowler, Frank 1900-1971 Obituary 113
Fowler, Gene 1931- CANR-20
Earlier sketches in CA 53-56, CANR-5
Fowler, Gene
See Fowler, Eugene Devlan
Fowler, George P(almer) 1909- 41-44R
Fowler, Guy 1893(?)-1966 Obituary 25-28R
Fowler, Harry (Jr.) 1934- CANR-1
Earlier sketch in CA 45-48
Fowler, Heather T.
See Remoff, Heather T(rexler)
Fowler, Helen Rosa Huxley 1917- CAP-1
Earlier sketch in CA 9-10
Fowler, James W(iley) III 1940- 104
Fowler, Jim
See Fowler, James W(iley) III
Fowler, John M(ajor) 1926- 103
Fowler, Kenneth A(brams) 1900-1987 ...... 7-8R
Obituary 122
Fowler, Marian (Elizabeth) 1929- 114
Fowler, Mark 1949- 65-68
Fowler, Mary Elizabeth 1911- CAP-2
Earlier sketch in CA 29-32
Fowler, Mary Jane
See Wheeler, Mary Jane
Fowler, (Edward) Michael (Coulson) 1929- .. 109
Fowler, Raymond Dalton, Jr. 1930-
Brief entry 110
Fowler, Raymond E(veleth) 1933- 85-88
Fowler, Richard A(lan) 1948- 113
Fowler, Robert H(oward) 1926- 73-76
Fowler, Roger 1938- 65-68
Fowler, Sandra (Lynn) 1937- 106
Fowler, Virginie
See Elbert, Virginie Fowler
Fowler, Wilfred 1907- CAP-1
Earlier sketch in CA 13-14
Fowler, Will 1922- 5-6R
Fowler, William Morgan, Jr. 1944- CANR-1
Earlier sketch in CA 45-48
Fowler, Wilton B(onham) 1936- 53-56
Fowles, Jib 1940- 69-72
Fowles, John 1926- CANR-25
Earlier sketch in CA 7-8R
See also SATA 22
See also DLB 14
See also CLC 1, 2, 3, 4, 6, 9, 10, 15,
33
Fowlie, Wallace 1908- CANR-5
Earlier sketch in CA 5-6R
Fox, Adam 1883-1977 .... CANR-10
Earlier sketches in CA 13-14, CAP-1
Fox, Aileen 1907- CANR-5
Earlier sketch in CA 7-8R
Fox, Alan John 15-16R
Fox, Alistair 1948- 116
Fox, Allan M(ark) 1948- 41-44R
Fox, Annette Baker 1912- Brief entry 109
Fox, Anthony
See Fullerton, Alexander (Fergus)
Fox, Bill
See Fox, William
Fox, Brian
See Ballard, (Willis) Todhunter
Fox, C(arol) Lynn 1948- 110
Fox, Charles Elliot 1878- CAP-1
Earlier sketch in CA 9-10
Fox, Charles Philip 1913- CANR-1
Earlier sketch in CA 1R
See also SATA 12
Fox, Col. Victor J.
See Winston, R(obert) A(lexander)
Fox, Connie
See Fox, Hugh (Bernard, Jr.)
Fox, Daniel Michael 1938- 112
Fox, David J(oseph) 1927- 15-16R
Fox, Dorothea Warren 1914- 61-64
Fox, Douglas A(llan) 1927- CANR-17
Earlier sketch in CA 41-44R
Fox, Douglas McMurray 1940- CANR-15
Earlier sketch in CA 33-36R
Fox, E(dward) Inman 1933- 17-18R
Fox, Edward J(ackson) 1913- 2R
Fox, Edward L. 1938- Brief entry 110
Fox, Edward Whiting 1911- Brief entry 106
Fox, Eleanor
See St. John, Wylly Folk
Fox, Fontaine Talbot, Jr. 1884-1964
Obituary 89-92
See also SATA 23
Fox, Frances Margaret
See Field, Frances Fox
Fox, Frank W(ayne) 1940- 109
Fox, Fred 1903(?)-1981 Obituary 104
See also SATA 27
Fox, Frederic Ewing 1917-1981 .... 4R
Obituary 103
Fox, Freeman
See Hamilton, Charles Harold St. John
Fox, G(ardner) F(rancis) 1911- CANR-5
Earlier sketch in CA 5-6R
Fox, G(eoffrey) P. 1938- CANR-11
Earlier sketch in CA 23-24R
Fox, Gail 1942- CANR-19
Earlier sketch in CA 103
Fox, George (Richard) 1934- 37-40R
Fox, Gilbert T(heodore) 1915- 69-72
Fox, Gill
See Fox, Gilbert T(heodore)
Fox, Grace (Estelle) 1899-1984 .... 37-40R
Obituary 111
Fox, Grace
See Anderson, Grace Fox
Fox, Grace Imogene 1907- 2R
Fox, H(enry) B(enjamin) 1910- 57-60
Fox, Harrison W(illiam), Jr. 1944- 126
Fox, Helen Morgenthau 1885(?)-1974
Obituary 45-48
Fox, Hugh (Bernard, Jr.) 1932- CANR-11
Earlier sketch in CA 25-28R
Fox, Jack C(urtis) 1925-1987 .... 21-22R
Obituary 122
Fox, Jack Vernon 1918-1982 Obituary 106
Fox, James (Lyttleton) 1945- 120
Fox, James M. 102
Fox, John 1906-1984 Obituary 114
Fox, John
See Todd, John (Murray)
Fox, John H(oward) 1925- CANR-8
Earlier sketch in CA 5-6R
Fox, John (William), Jr. 1862(?)-1919
Brief entry 108
See also DLB 9
Fox, John Roger 1896-1987 Obituary 125
Fox, Joseph M(ichael) 1934- 106
Fox, Karl A(ugust) 1917- CANR-7
Earlier sketch in CA 17-18R
Fox, Kenneth 1944- 125
Fox, Larry 106
See also SATA 30
Fox, Levi 1914- CANR-14
Earlier sketch in CA 77-80
Fox, Logan J(ordan) 1922- 53-56
Fox, Lorraine 1922-1976 .... SATA-11, 27
Fox, Lucia
See Lockert, Lucia (Alicia Ungaro Fox)
Fox, Marcia R(ose) 1942- 105
Fox, Mary Virginia 1919- CANR-12
Earlier sketch in CA 29-32R
See also SATA 39, 44
Fox, Matthew (Timothy) 1940- 126
Brief entry 109
Fox, Mem
See Fox, Merrion Frances
Fox, Merrion, Frances 1946- SATA-51
Fox, Michael A(llen) 1940- CANR-19
Earlier sketch in CA 103
Fox, Michael W(ilson) 1937- CANR-14
Earlier sketch in CA 73-76
See also SATA 15
Fox, Milton S. 1904-1971 Obituary 33-36R
Fox, Nancy L. 1917- 122
Fox, Norman A(rnold) 1911-1960
Obituary 114
Fox, Owen
See Farmer, Bernard James
Fox, Paula 1923- CANR-20
Earlier sketch in CA 73-76
See also SATA 17
See also DLB 52
See also CLC 2, 8
See also CLR 1
Fox, Ralph H(artzler) 1913-1973 Obituary .. 49-52
Fox, Ray Errol 1941- 85-88
Fox, Renee C(laire) 1928- 49-52
Fox, Richard G(abriel) 1939- 41-44R
Fox, Richard Wightman 1945- 93-96
Fox, Robert 1943- 77-80
Fox, Robert Barlow 1930- 15-16R
Fox, Robert J. 1927- CANR-17
Earlier sketches in CA 45-48, CANR-1
See also SATA 33
Fox, Ruth 1895- 73-76
Fox, Samuel 1905- CAP-2
Earlier sketch in CA 21-22
Fox, Samuel J. 1919- 53-56
Fox, Sharon E(lizabeth) 1938- 45-48
Fox, Siv Cedering 1939- 41-44R
Fox, Sonny 1925- 41-44R
Fox, Stephen
See Furthmann, Julius Grinnell
Fox, Stephen R. 1945- CANR-12
Earlier sketch in CA 29-32R
Fox, Ted
See Fox, Gilbert T(heodore)
Fox, Ted
See Fox, Theodore J.
Fox, Terry Curtis 1948- 117
Fox, Theodore J. 1954- 123
Fox, Uffa 1898-1972 Obituary 37-40R
Fox, V. Helen
See Couch, Helen F(ox)
Fox, Vernon (Brittain) 1916- 37-40R
Fox, Willard 1919- 21-22R
Fox, William 1919(?)-1985 Obituary 116
Fox, William Lloyd 1921- 17-18R
Fox, William McNair 1924- 5-6R
Fox, William Price (Jr.) 1926- CANR-11
Earlier sketch in CA 17-18R
See also DLB 2
See also DLBY 81
See also CLC 22
Fox, William Thornton Rickert 1912-
Brief entry 108
Fox, William W(ellington) 1909- 4R
Foxall, Raymond (Jehoiada Campbell)
1916- CANR-5
Earlier sketch in CA 9-10R
Foxe, Arthur N(orman) 1902-1982 ...... CANR-4
Obituary 108
Earlier sketch in CA 9-10R
Foxell, Nigel 1931- 97-100
Fox-Genovese, Elizabeth 1941- CANR-26
Earlier sketches in CA 65-68, CANR-10
Foxley, William M(cLachlan) 1926-1978 ... 77-80
Foxley-Norris, Christopher Neil 1917- 109
Fox-Lockert, Lucia
See Lockert, Lucia (Alicia Ungaro Fox)
Foxman, Sherri 1950- 112
Fox-Martin, Milton 1914(?)-1977
Obituary 69-72
Foxon, A(ndrew David) 1956- 121
Foxon, David Fairweather 1923- 102
Fox-Sheinwold, Patricia 102
Foxworth, Thomas G(ordon) 1937- 114
Foxx, Jack
See Pronzini, Bill
Foxx, Redd 1922- 89-92
Foxx, Richard M(ichael) 1944- CANR-17
Earlier sketches in CA 45-48, CANR-1
Foxx, Rosalind
See Haydon, June
and Simpson, Judith H(olroyd)
Foxx, Teralene S. 1939- 122
Foy, George 1952- 116
Foy, Kenneth R(ussell) 1922- 25-28R
Foy, Nancy 1934- CANR-2
Earlier sketch in CA 45-48
Fozdar, Jamshed K(hodadad) 1926- 49-52
Fracchia, Charles A(nthony) 1937- 89-92
Frackenpohl, Arthur R(oland) 1924- 19-20R
Frackman, Nathaline 1903(?)-1977
Obituary 69-72
Fraddle, Farragut
See Mearns, David Chambers
Fradin, Dennis Brindell 1945- 69-72
See also SATA 29
Fradkin, Elvira (Thekla) Kush
1890(?)-1972 Obituary 37-40R
Fradkin, Philip L(awrence) 1935- 107
Fraelich, Richard O(ddly) 1924- 7-8R
Fraenkel, Gerd 1919-1970 .... CAP-1
Earlier sketch in CA 11-12
Fraenkel, Gottfried S(amuel) 1901-1984
Obituary 114
Fraenkel, Heinrich 1897- 15-16R
Fraenkel, Jack R(unnels) 1932- 29-32R
Fraenkel, Michael 1896-1957 Brief entry 107
See also DLB 4
Fraenkel, Osmond K. 1888-1983 .... CAP-2
Obituary 109
Earlier sketch in CA 23-24
Frager, Robert 1940- 81-84
Frahm, Anne B. Schwerdt 1927- 9-10R
Fraiberg, Louis Benjamin 1913- 3R
Fraiberg, Selma 1918-1981 97-100
Obituary 105
Fraine, Harold G(eorge) 1900- 4R
Frair, Wayne Franklin 1926- 113
Fraistat, Neil (Richard) 1952- 122
Fraistat, Rose Ann C. 1952- 123
Frake, Warner
See Musciano, Walter A.
Frakes, George Edward 1932- 29-32R
Fraley, Oscar (B.) 1914- Brief entry 109
Fram, Eugene Harry 1929- 17-18R
Frame, Donald M(urdoch) 1911- 17-18R
Frame, Janet
See Clutha, Janet Paterson Frame
See also CLC 2, 3, 6, 22
Frame, Paul 1913- Brief entry 111
See also SATA 33
Framo, James L(awrence) 1922- CANR-15
Earlier sketch in CA 41-44R
Frampton, Hollis 1936-1984 Obituary 112
Frampton, Kenneth Brian 1930- 105
Frampton, Merle E(lbert) 1903- CAP-2
Earlier sketch in CA 25-28
Frampton, Peter (Kenneth) 1950-
Brief entry 117
Franc, Helen M. 1908- 103
Franca, Celia 1921- 89-92
Franca, Jose-Augusto 1922- CANR-19
Earlier sketch in CA 102
France, Anatole
See Thibault, Jacques Anatole Francois
See also TCLC 9
France, Anna Kay 1940- 103
France, Beulah Sanford 1891-1971
Obituary 33-36R
France, Claire
See Dore, Claire (Morin)
France, Evangeline
See France-Hayhurst, Evangeline
(Chaworth-Musters)
France, Harold L(eroy) 1930- 49-52
France, Malcolm 1928- 23-24R
France, Pierre Mendes
See Mendes-France, Pierre
France, Richard 1938- 93-96
See also DLB 7
France-Hayhurst, Evangeline
(Chaworth-Musters) 1904- CAP-1
Earlier sketch in CA 9-10
Francesca, Rosina
See Brookman, Rosina Francesca
Franchere, Ruth 73-76
See also SATA 18
Franchi, Eda
See Vickers, Antoinette L.
Francis, Anne
See Bird, Florence (Bayard)
and Wintle, Anne
Francis, Arlene 1912- 89-92
Francis, Arthur
See Gershwin, Ira
Francis, Basil (Hoskins) 1906- CAP-1
Earlier sketch in CA 13-14
Francis, C.D.E.
See Howarth, Patrick (John Fielding)
Francis, Cat
See Francis, Emile (Percy)
Francis, Charles
See Holme, Bryan
Francis, Clare 1946- CANR-15
Earlier sketch in CA 77-80
Francis, Claude 19(?)- CLC-50
Francis, Convers 1795-1863 .... DLB-1
Francis, Daniel 1947- 111
Francis, Daniel
See Cranny, Titus
Francis, (Alan) David 1900- 21-22R
Francis, David Noel 1904- 7-8R
Francis, Dee
See Haas, Dorothy F.
Francis, Dennis S. 1943(?)-1980 Obituary .. 102
Francis, Devon (Earl) 1901-1986 61-64
Obituary 118
Francis, Dick 1920- CANR-9
Earlier sketch in CA 7-8R
See also CLC 2, 22, 42

INDEX

Francis, Dorothy Brenner 1926- CANR-24
Earlier sketches in CA 21-22R, CANR-9
See also SATA 10
Francis, Emile (Percy) 1926- Brief entry 112
Francis, Frank Chalton 1901-1988 65-68
Obituary 126
Francis, Gloria A(ileen) 1930-1988
Obituary 125
Brief entry 113
Francis, H(erbert) E(dward, Jr.) 1924- . CANR-10
Earlier sketch in CA 25-28R
Francis, Helen Dannefer 1915- 15-16R
Francis, John M(ichael) 1939- 118
Francis, Marilyn 1920- CANR-3
Earlier sketch in CA 5-6R
Francis, Michael J(ackson) 1938- 89-92
Francis, Michel
See Cattaui, Georges
Francis, Mother Mary
See Aschmann, Alberta
Francis, Nelle (Trew) 1914- 37-40R
Francis, Pamela (Mary) 1926- 29-32R
See also SATA 11
Francis, Philip
See Lockyer, Roger
Francis, Philip S(heridan) 1918- 17-18R
Francis, R. Mabel 1880-19(?) CAP-2
Earlier sketch in CA 25-28
Francis, Richard (H.) 1945- CANR-24
Earlier sketch in CA 102
Francis, Robert (Churchill) 1901-1987 ... CANR-1
Obituary 123
Earlier sketch in CA 1R
See also CLC 15
Francis, Roy G. 1919- 1R
Francis, Wayne L(ouis) 1935- 41-44R
Francisco, Charles 1930- 109
Francisco, Clyde Taylor 1916- Brief entry ... 106
Francis-Williams, Lord
See Williams, Edward Francis
Franck, Frederick 1909- CANR-5
Earlier sketch in CA 3R
Franck, Harry Alverson 1881-1962
Obituary 110
Franck, Irene M(ary) 1941- CANR-21
Earlier sketch in CA 104
Franck, Phyllis 1928- 53-56
Franck, Sebastian
See Jacoby, Henry
Franck, Thomas M. 1931- 33-36R
Francke, Donald Eugene 1910-1978
Obituary 81-84
Francke, Kuno 1855-1930 .... DLB-71
Francke, Linda Bird 1939- CANR-15
Earlier sketch in CA 85-88
Franco, Jean 1914-1971 .... CAP-2
Earlier sketch in CA 25-28
Franco, Jean 1924- CANR-9
Earlier sketch in CA 23-24R
Franco, Johan (Henri Gustave) 1908- 97-100
Franco, Marjorie 114
See also SATA 38
Francoeur, Anna K(otlarchyk) 1940- 53-56
Francoeur, Robert T(homas) 1931- CANR-14
Earlier sketch in CA 37-40R
Francois, Andre 1915- 93-96
See also SATA 25
Francois, Pierre 1932- 19-20R
Francois, William E. 1924- CANR-5
Earlier sketch in CA 15-16R
Francoise
See Seignobosc, Francoise
Francois-Poncet, Andre 1887-1978
Obituary 73-76
Franda, Marcus F. 1937- CANR-9
Earlier sketch in CA 23-24R
Frandsen, Arden N. 1902- 3R
Frandsen, Julius 1907-1976 Obituary 69-72
Franey, Pierre 1921- CANR-15
Earlier sketch in CA 89-92
Frank, Adolph F(rederick) 1918- 106
Frank, Andre Gunder 1929- 21-22R
Frank, Anne 1929-1945(?) Brief entry 113
See also SATA 42
See also TCLC 17
Frank, Benis M. 1925- 37-40R
Frank, Benjamin 1902-1984 Obituary 113
Frank, Bernhard 1931- 105
Frank, Charles E(dward) 1911- 21-22R
Frank, Charles Paul 1935- Brief entry 112
Frank, Charles Raphael (Jr.) 1937- 37-40R
Frank, Daniel B. 1956- 117
Frank, Elizabeth 1945- 126
Brief entry 121
See also CLC 39
Frank, Florence Kiper 1885(?)-1976
Obituary 65-68
Frank, Gerold 1907- Brief entry 109
Frank, Goldalie 1908- CAP-1
Earlier sketch in CA 17-18
Frank, H(ans) Eric 1921- 49-52
Frank, Harry Thomas 1933-1980 53-56
Obituary 103
Frank, Helene
See Vautier, Ghislaine
Frank, Helmut J(ack) 1922- CANR-7
Earlier sketch in CA 19-20R
Frank, Irving 1910- CAP-2
Earlier sketch in CA 21-22
Frank, Isaiah 1917- CANR-1
Earlier sketch in CA 2R
Frank, Jacqueline ?-1982 Obituary 114
Frank, Janet
See Dunleavy, Janet Egleson
Frank, Jeffrey 1942- 21-22R
Frank, Jerome (New) 1889-1957
Brief entry 121
Frank, Jerome D(avid) 1909- CANR-3
Earlier sketch in CA 7-8R
Frank, John G. 1896(?)-1978 Obituary 81-84
Frank, Joseph 1916- CANR-1
Earlier sketch in CA 1R
Frank, Joseph (Nathaniel) 1918- 77-80
Frank, Josette 1893- CAP-1
Earlier sketch in CA 19-20
See also SATA 10
Frank, Katherine 124
Frank, Lawrence K(elso) 1890-1968 .... 3R
Obituary 103
Frank, Lee
See Griffin, Arthur J.
Frank, Leonhard 1882-1961 Obituary 116
See also DLB 56
Frank, Mary 1933- SATA-34
Frank, Melvin 1913- DLB-26
Frank, Melvin 1913(?)-1988 Obituary 126
Frank, Morton 1912- 102
Frank, Murray 1908-1977 ....37-40R
Obituary 73-76
Frank, Nathalie D. 1918- 11-12R
Frank, Pat (Harry Hart) 1907-1964 ....5-6R
Frank, Peter (Solomon) 1950- CANR-15
Earlier sketch in CA 81-84
Frank, Philip Norman 1943- 113
Frank, Philipp (G.) 1884-1966 Obituary ..25-28R
Frank, R., Jr.
See Ross, Frank (Xavier), Jr.
Frank, Reuven 1920- 81-84
Frank, Robert G(regg), Jr. 1943-
Brief entry 113
Frank, Robert J(oseph) 1939- 65-68
Frank, Robert Worth, Jr. 1914- 13-14R
Frank, Roberta 1941- 115
Frank, Ronald E(dward) 1933- CANR-18
Earlier sketches in CA 7-8R, CANR-3
Frank, Rudolf 1886-1979 121
Frank, Sheldon 1943- 77-80
Frank, Stanley B. 1908-1979 ....7-8R
Obituary 85-88
Frank, T. C.
See Laughlin, Tom
Frank, Thaisa 1943- 117
Frank, Waldo (David) 1889-1967 93-96
Obituary 25-28R
See also DLB 9, 63
Frank, William G.
See Frank, Rudolf
Frank, William L(uke) 1929- 106
Frankau, Mary Evelyn Atkinson 1899- CAP-1
Earlier sketch in CA 9-10
See also SATA 4
Frankau, Pamela 1908-1967 Obituary 25-28R
Frank-Baron, Elizabeth 1911(?)-1982
Obituary 108
Franke, C(arl) W(ilfred) 1928- 23-24R
Franke, Christopher 1941- 77-80
Franke, David 1938- 49-52
Franke, Herbert W. 1927- Brief entry 110
Franke, Holly L(ambro) 1943- 49-52
Frankel, A(rthur) Steven 1942- 53-56
Frankel, Bernice 61-64
See also SATA 9
Frankel, Charles 1917-1979 .... CANR-4
Obituary 89-92
Earlier sketch in CA 5-6R
Frankel, Edward 1910- 85-88
See also SATA 44
Frankel, Eliot 1922- 77-80
Frankel, Flo 1923- 105
Frankel, Hans H(ermann) 1916- 61-64
Frankel, Haskel 1926- 89-92
Frankel, Hermann F. 1899(?)-1977
Obituary 69-72
Frankel, J(oseph) 1913- CANR-3
Earlier sketch in CA 7-8R
Frankel, Julie 1947- 113
See also SATA 34, 40
Frankel, Max 1930- 65-68
Frankel, Otto (Herzberg) 1900- 108
Frankel, Sandor 1943- 33-36R
Frankel, Tobia (Brown) 1935(?)-1987
Obituary 122
Frankel, William 1917- 106
Frankel, Zygmunt 1929- 41-44R
Franken, Rose 1895(?)- DLBY-84
Franken, Rose (Dorothy) 1895(?)-1988
Obituary 125
Frankena, William K(laas) 1908- CANR-10
Earlier sketch in CA 19-20R
Frankenberg, Celestine Gilligan 9-10R
Frankenberg, Lloyd 1907-1975 .... CANR-6
Obituary 57-60
Earlier sketch in CA 2R
Frankenberg, Robert 1911- SATA-22
Frankenstein, Alfred Victor 1906-1981 ... CANR-2
Obituary 104
Earlier sketch in CA 3R
Frankenstein, Carl 1905- 9-10R
Frankenthal, Kate 1889-1976 Obituary 65-68
Frankfort, Ellen 1936-1987 ....29-32R
Obituary 122
Frankforter, A(lbertus) Daniel (III) 1939- ...81-84
Frankfurt, Harry Gordon 1929- 41-44R
Frankfurter, Felix 1882-1965 Brief entry 124
Frankl, Viktor E(mil) 1905- 65-68
Frankland, Mark 1934- 69-72
Frankland, (Anthony) Noble 1922- CANR-14
Earlier sketch in CA 65-68
Franklin, A.
See Arnold, Adlai F(ranklin)
Franklin, Ada C(rogman) ?-1983 Obituary ... 111
Franklin, Adele 1887(?)-1977 Obituary 69-72
Franklin, Alexander (John) 1921- 13-14R
Franklin, Alfred White 1905- CANR-7
Earlier sketch in CA 57-60
Franklin, Ben(jamin) A. 1927- 89-92
Franklin, Benjamin 1706-1790 ... DLB-24, 43, 73
See also CDALB 1640-1865
Franklin, Benjamin
See Hasek, Jaroslav (Matej Frantisek)
Franklin, Benjamin V 1939- 115
Franklin, Billy J(oe) 1940- 33-36R
Franklin, Bob 1949- 124
Franklin, Burt 1903-1972 .... CAP-1
Earlier sketch in CA 15-16
Franklin, Charles
See Usher, Frank (Hugh)
Franklin, Colin 1923- 77-80
Franklin, Denson Nauls 1914- 1R
Franklin, Edward Herbert 1930- 15-16R
Franklin, Elizabeth
See Campbell, Hannah
Franklin, Eugene
See Bandy, (Eugene) Franklin
Franklin, George E. 1890-1971 .... CAP-1
Earlier sketch in CA 19-20
Franklin, H. Bruce 1934- CANR-9
Earlier sketch in CA 5-6R
Franklin, Harold 1926- 29-32R
See also SATA 13
Franklin, Harold L(eroy) 1934- 57-60
Franklin, Harry 1906- CANR-12
Earlier sketches in CA 13-14, CAP-1
Franklin, J(ennie) E(lizabeth) 1937- 61-64
See also BW
Franklin, James 1697-1735 .... DLB-43
Franklin, Jay
See Carter, John Franklin
Franklin, Jerome L(ee) 1943- 102
Franklin, Jill (Leslie) 1928-1988 Obituary ... 125
Franklin, Jimmie Lewis 1939- 126
Brief entry 106
Franklin, Joe 1926- Brief entry 108
Franklin, John Hope 1915- CANR-26
Earlier sketches in CA 5-6R, CANR-3
See also BW
Franklin, Jon (Daniel) 1942- 104
Franklin, Kay 1933- 118
Franklin, Keith
See Foy, Kenneth R(ussell)
Franklin, Linda Campbell 1941- CANR-26
Earlier sketch in CA 105
Franklin, Marc A. 1932- 29-32R
Franklin, Marshall 1929- 53-56
Franklin, Max
See Deming, Richard
Franklin, (Stella Maraia Sarah) Miles
1879-1954 Brief entry 104
See also TCLC 7
Franklin, Nat
See Bauer, Erwin A.
Franklin, Olga 1912-1985 102
Obituary 115
Franklin, Penelope (Florence) 1948- 125
Franklin, R(alph) W(illiam) 1937- CANR-9
Earlier sketch in CA 23-24R
Franklin, Richard 1918- 21-22R
Franklin, S(amuel) Harvey 1928- CANR-26
Earlier sketch in CA 105
Franklin, Sidney 1903-1976 Obituary 65-68
Franklin, Steve
See Stevens, Franklin
Franklin, Ursula 1929- 112
Franklin, Wayne S(teven) 1945- 125
Franklyn, Charles Aubrey Hamilton
1896- 11-12R
Franklyn, Julian 1899-1970 Obituary 112
Franklyn, Robert Alan 1918- 89-92
Franko, Lawrence G. 1942- 37-40R
Frankowski, Leo 1943- 120
Franks, C(harles) E(dward) S(elwyn)
1936- 77-80
Franks, Claudia Stillman 1947- 117
Franks, Cyril Maurice 1923- 15-16R
Franks, Ed
See Brandon, Johnny
Franks, Felix 1926- 125
Franks, Kenny Arthur 1945- 123
Franks, Lucinda 1946- 53-56
Franks, Marlene Strong 1955- 125
Franks, Maurice R(udolph) 1942- 112
Franks, Robert S(leightholme) 1871-1963 ...7-8R
Fransella, Fay CANR-13
Earlier sketch in CA 25-28R
Frantz, Charles 1925- CANR-3
Earlier sketch in CA 5-6R
Frantz, Douglas 1949- 126
Frantz, Harry Warner 1891-1982 Obituary .. 106
Frantz, Joe B. 1917- CANR-1
Earlier sketch in CA 1R
Frantz, Ralph Jules 1902-1979 77-80
Obituary 89-92
See also DLB 4
Frantzen, Allen J. 1947- 121
Franz, Barbara E(van) 1946- 110
Franz, Carl 1944- 107
Franz, William S(trasser) 1945- 110
Franzblau, Abraham N(orman)
1901-1982 ....29-32R
Obituary 108
Franzblau, Rose N(adler) 1905-1979 .....29-32R
Obituary 89-92
Franzen, Gosta Knut 1906- 41-44R
Franzen, Lavern G(erhardt) 1926- CANR-7
Earlier sketch in CA 61-64
Franzen, Nils-Olof 1916- CANR-25
Earlier sketch in CA 29-32R
See also SATA 10
Franzero, Carlo Maria 1892-1986 .... CANR-5
Obituary 120
Earlier sketch in CA 2R
Franzero, Charles Marie
See Franzero, Carlo Maria
Franzius, Enno 1901- 25-28R
Franzmann, Martin H. 1907-1976 ...... CANR-3
Earlier sketch in CA 1R
Franzwa, Gregory M. 1926- CANR-9
Earlier sketch in CA 23-24R
Frary, Michael 1918- 77-80
Frasca, John (Anthony) 1916-1979 ..... CANR-3
Obituary 93-96
Earlier sketch in CA 49-52
Frascatoro, Gerald
See Hornback, Bert G(erald)
Frascino, Edward 1938- 114
Brief entry 111
See also SAAS 33, 48
Frascona, Joseph Lohengrin 1910- 17-18R
Frasconi, Antonio 1919- CANR-1
Earlier sketch in CA 1R
See also SATA 6, 53
Frase, Larry E. 1945- 41-44R
Frase, Robert W(illiam) 1912- 33-36R
Fraser, Alex
See Brinton, Henry
Fraser, Allan 1900- 57-60
Fraser, Amy Stewart 1892- CANR-9
Earlier sketch in CA 49-52
Fraser, Anthea CANR-25
Earlier sketches in CA 65-68, CANR-10
Fraser, Antonia (Pakenham) 1932- 85-88
See also SATA 32
See also CLC 32
Fraser, Arthur Ronald 1888-1974
Obituary 53-56
Fraser, Arvonne S. 1925- 33-36R
Fraser, B. Kay 1941- 69-72
Fraser, Betty
See Fraser, Elizabeth Marr
Fraser, Blair 1909-1968 .... CAP-2
Earlier sketch in CA 23-24
Fraser, Bruce (Donald) 1910- 109
Fraser, Colin 1935- 21-22R
Fraser, Conon 1930- CAP-1
Earlier sketch in CA 9-10
Fraser, D(onald) M(urray) 1946-1985 117
Fraser, (William) Dean 1916- 45-48
Fraser, Diane Lynch
See Lynch-Fraser, Diane
Fraser, Dorothy May 1903(?)-1980
Obituary 102
Fraser, Douglas 1910- 102
Fraser, Douglas Ferrar 1929- CANR-4
Earlier sketch in CA 4R
Fraser, Edith Emily Rose Oram 1903- CAP-1
Earlier sketch in CA 11-12
Fraser, Elise Parker 1903- 3R
Fraser, Elizabeth Marr 1928- SATA-31
Fraser, Eric (George) 1902-1983 ...... SATA-38
Fraser, Flora 1958- 124
Fraser, G(eorge) S(utherland) 1915-1980 ..85-88
Obituary 105
See also DLB 27
Fraser, George MacDonald 1925- CANR-2
Earlier sketch in CA 45-48
See also CLC 7
Fraser, Gordon Holmes 1898- CAP-1
Earlier sketch in CA 15-16
Fraser, Hamish 1913-1986 Obituary 120
Fraser, (William Jocelyn) Ian 1897-1974
Obituary 53-56
Fraser, J(ulius) T(homas) 1923- CANR-8
Earlier sketch in CA 61-64
Fraser, James
See White, Alan
Fraser, Jane
See Pilcher, Rosamunde
Fraser, Janet Hobhouse
See Hobhouse, Janet
Fraser, John 1931- 29-32R
Fraser, Kathleen 1937- 106
Fraser, Keath 1944- 125
Fraser, Maxwell
See Fraser, Dorothy May
Fraser, Morris 1941- 102
Fraser, Neil McCormick 1902- 7-8R
Fraser, Peter (Malcolm) 1928-1987 107
Obituary 121
Fraser, Peter (Shaw) 1932- 33-36R
Fraser, Raymond 1941- Brief entry 107
Fraser, Ronald
See Fraser, Arthur Ronald
Fraser, Ronald
See Tiltman, Ronald Frank
Fraser, Russell A(lfred) 1927- 37-40R
Fraser, Stewart Erskine 1929- CANR-10
Earlier sketch in CA 15-16R
Fraser, Stuart
See Wood, James (Alexander Fraser)
Fraser, Sylvia 1935- CANR-16
Earlier sketches in CA 45-48, CANR-1
Fraser, W(aller) B(rown) 1905- CAP-2
Earlier sketch in CA 25-28
Fraser, W(illiam) Hamish 1941- 103
Fraser, W(illiam) Lionel 18(?)-1965 ...... CAP-1
Earlier sketch in CA 9-10
Fraser Darling, Frank 1903-1979 61-64
Obituary 89-92
Fraser Harrison, Brian 1918- CAP-1
Earlier sketch in CA 9-10
Fraser Roberts, J(ohn) A(lexander)
See Roberts, J(ohn) A(lexander) Fraser
Frasier, James E(dwin) 1923- 17-18R
Frassanito, William A(llen) 1946- CANR-9
Earlier sketch in CA 57-60

Frasure, David W(illiam) 1942- ... 113
Fratcher, William F(ranklin) 1913- ... CANR-3
Earlier sketch in CA 5-6R
Frater Perdurabo
See Crowley, Edward Alexander
Fraticelli, Marco 1945- ... 118
Fratti, Mario 1927- ... 77-80
Frautschi, R(ichard) L(ane) 1926- ... 19-20R
Frawley, Ernest D(avid) 1920-1984
Obituary ... 114
Frawley, William John 1953- ... 114
Fraydas, Stan 1918- ... 57-60
Frayling, Christopher 1946- ... 110
Frayn, Michael 1933- ... 5-6R
See also DLB 13, 14
See also CLC 3, 7, 31, 47
Fraze, Candida (Merrill) 1945- ... 126
See also CLC 50
Frazee, Charles A(aron) 1929- ... 37-40R
Frazee, Steve 1909- ... CANR-5
Earlier sketch in CA 7-8R
Frazer, Andrew
See Marlowe, Stephen
Frazer, Fred
See Avallone, Michael (Angelo), Jr.
Frazer, J(ames) G(eorge) 1854-1941
Brief entry ... 118
Frazer, Mark Petrovich
See Maclean, Donald Duart
Frazer, Robert Caine
See Creasey, John
Frazer, Robert W(alter) 1911- ... 17-18R
Frazer, Sir James George
See Frazer, J(ames) G(eorge)
Frazer, William J(ohnson), Jr. 1924- ... 17-18R
Frazer, Winifred Dusenbury
See Frazer, Winifred L(oesch)
Frazer, Winifred L(oesch) ... 25-28R
Frazer-Hurst, Douglas 1883- ... CAP-1
Earlier sketch in CA 9-10
Frazetta, Frank 1928- ... 104
Frazier, Allie M. 1932- Brief entry ... 110
Frazier, Anitra 1937- ... 113
Frazier, Arthur
See Bulmer, (Henry) Kenneth
Frazier, Claude A(lbee) 1920- ... 29-32R
Frazier, Cliff(ord) 1934- Brief entry ... 109
Frazier, Edward Franklin 1894-1962
Obituary ... 108
Frazier, George 1911-1974 ... CAP-2
Obituary ... 49-52
Earlier sketch in CA 25-28
Frazier, Ian 1951- ... CLC-46
Frazier, Kendrick (Crosby) 1942- ... CANR-17
Earlier sketch in CA 101
Frazier, Neta Lohnes ... CANR-1
Earlier sketch in CA 2R
See also SATA 7
Frazier, Sarah
See Wirt, Winola Wells
Frazier, Shervert Hughes 1921- ... 85-88
Frazier, Thomas R(ichard) 1931- ... 33-36R
Frazier, Walt(er) 1945- ... 103
Frears, J(ohn) R(ussell) 1936- ... 107
Freas, Frank Kelly 1922- ... CANR-21
Earlier sketch in CA 102
Freburger, William J. 1940- ... 115
Frech, Frances 1923- ... 97-100
Freddi, Cris 1955- ... 106
Frede, Richard 1934- ... 69-72
Fredeman, William E(van) 1928- ... 33-36R
Fredenburgh, Franz A(lvah) 1906- ... 33-36R
Frederic, Harold 1856-1898 ... DLB-12, 23
Frederic, Mike
See Cox, William R(obert)
Frederic, Sister M. Catherine
See Fleischbein, M. Catherine Frederic
Frederick, Carl Louis 1942- ... 65-68
Frederick, Dick
See Dempewolff, Richard F(rederic)
Frederick, John
See Faust, Frederick (Shiller)
Frederick, John H(utchinson) 1896- ... 1R
Frederick, John Towner 1893-1975
Obituary ... 111
Frederick, Lee
See Nussbaum, Al(bert F.)
Frederick, Oswald
See Snelling, O(swald) F(rederick)
Frederick, Pauline 1908- ... 102
Frederick, Robert Allen 1928- ... CANR-3
Earlier sketch in CA 45-48
Fredericks, Carlton 1910-1987 ... CANR-7
Obituary ... 123
Earlier sketch in CA 53-56
See also AITN 1
Fredericks, Frank
See Franck, Frederick
Fredericks, Frohm
See Kerner, Fred
Fredericks, Pierce Griffin 1920-1985 ... 13-14R
Obituary ... 117
Fredericks, Vic
See Majeski, William
Frederika (Louise), Queen 1917-1981
Obituary ... 108
Frederiksen, Alan Ryle 1935- ... 113
Frederiksen, Martin W. 1930-1980
Obituary ... 101
Frederikson, Edna 1904- ... 49-52
Fredge, Frederique 1906- ... CAP-2
Earlier sketch in CA 21-22
Fredman, Alice G(reen) 1924- ... 102
Fredman, Henry John 1927- ... 29-32R
Fredman, John
See Fredman, Henry John
Fredman, Ruth Gruber 1934- ... 106
Fredricks, Edgar J(ohn) 1942- ... 25-28R
Fredrickson, George M(arsh) 1934- ... CANR-24
Earlier sketches in CA 19-20R, CANR-8
Fredrickson, Olive A(lta) 1901- ... 49-52
Fredriksson, Don 1926- ... 110
Fredriksson, Kristine 1940- ... 122
Free
See Hoffman, Abbie
Free, Ann Cottrell ... 9-10R
Free, James S(tillman) 1908- ... 77-80
Free, Lloyd A. 1908- ... 15-16R
Free, William Joseph 1933- ... 11-12R
Free, William Norris 1933- ... 25-28R
Freeborn, Brian (James) 1939- ... 65-68
Freeborn, Richard H. 1926- ... CANR-1
Earlier sketch in CA 3R
Freed, Alvyn M. 1913- ... CANR-8
Earlier sketch in CA 61-64
See also SATA 22
Freed, Arthur 1894-1973 Obituary ... 41-44R
Freed, Barry
See Hoffman, Abbie
Freed, Donald 1932- ... 85-88
Freed, Louis Franklin 1903- ... 7-8R
Freed, Lynn (R.) 1945- ... 108
Freed, Margaret De Haan 1917- ... 73-76
Freed, Ray 1939- ... 117
Freedberg, S(ydney) J(oseph) 1914- ... CANR-17
Earlier sketches in CA 1R, CANR-1
Freedeman, Charles E(ldon) 1926- ... 102
Freedgood, Lillian (Fischel) 1911- ... 15-16R
Freedgood, Morton 1912- Brief entry ... 108
See also AITN 1
Freedland, Michael 1934- ... CANR-11
Earlier sketch in CA 65-68
Freedland, Nat(haniel) 1936- ... 65-68
Freedley, George (Reynolds)
1904-1967 ... CANR-4
Earlier sketch in CA 5-6R
Freedman, Alfred M(ordecai) 1917- ... CANR-4
Earlier sketch in CA 49-52
Freedman, Arthur M(erton) 1916- ... 41-44R
Freedman, Benedict 1919- ... 69-72
See also SATA 27
Freedman, Dan 1952- ... 126
Freedman, Daniel X. 1921- ... 41-44R
Freedman, David M(ichael) 1949- ... 112
Freedman, David Noel 1922- ... CANR-1
Earlier sketch in CA 4R
Freedman, Hy 1914- ... 85-88
Freedman, Leonard 1924- ... CANR-1
Earlier sketch in CA 1R
Freedman, M(orris) David 1938- ... CANR-16
Earlier sketch in CA 41-44R
Freedman, Marcia K(ohl) 1922- ... CANR-10
Earlier sketch in CA 25-28R
Freedman, Maurice 1920-1975 ... CAP-2
Obituary ... 61-64
Earlier sketch in CA 25-28
Freedman, Mervin B. 1920- ... 29-32R
Freedman, Monroe H(enry) 1928-
Brief entry ... 107
Freedman, Morris 1920- ... CANR-3
Earlier sketch in CA 7-8R
Freedman, Nancy 1920- ... CANR-19
Earlier sketches in CA 45-48, CANR-1
See also SATA 27
Freedman, Paul H(arris) 1949- ... 122
Freedman, Ralph (William Bernard) 1920-
Brief entry ... 117
Freedman, Richard 1932- ... 77-80
Freedman, Robert Owen 1941- ... CANR-13
Earlier sketch in CA 33-36R
Freedman, Ronald 1917- ... CANR-6
Earlier sketch in CA 11-12R
Freedman, Russell (Bruce) 1929- ... CANR-23
Earlier sketches in CA 19-20R, CANR-7
See also SATA 16
Freedman, Samuel Sumner 1927- ... 112
Freedman, Warren 1921- ... 17-18R
Freehill, Maurice F(rancis) 1915- ... 7-8R
Freehling, Alison Goodyear 1941- ... 112
Freehof, Solomon B(ennett) 1892- ... 93-96
Freeland, Jay
See McLeod, John Freeland
Freeland, John Maxwell 1920- ... 13-14R
Freeland, Richard M. 1941- ... 81-84
Freeland, Stephen L. 1911(?)-1977
Obituary ... 69-72
Freeley, Austin J. 1922- ... 5-6R
Freeling, Nicolas 1927- ... CANR-17
Earlier sketches in CA 49-52, CANR-1
See also CLC 38
Freely, Maureen 1952- ... 97-100
Freeman, A. Myrick III 1936- ... 85-88
Freeman, Anne Frances 1936- ... 4R
Freeman, Arthur 1938- ... CANR-1
Earlier sketch in CA 2R
Freeman, Barbara C(onstance) 1906- ... 73-76
See also SATA 28
Freeman, Bill
See Freeman, William Bradford
Freeman, Bjorn
See Pratney, William Alfred
Freeman, C(lifford) Wade 1906- ... 7-8R
Freeman, Charles K. 1900-1980
Obituary ... 97-100
Freeman, Cynthia
See Feinberg, Beatrice Cynthia Freeman
Freeman, Darlene 1934- ... 29-32R
Freeman, Dave
See Freeman, David
Freeman, David 1922- ... 102
Freeman, David 1945- Brief entry ... 108
Freeman, David Hugh 1924- ... CANR-17
Earlier sketch in CA 1R
Freeman, Don 1908-1978 ... 77-80
See also SATA 17
Freeman, Donald Cary 1938- ... 53-56
Freeman, Donald McKinley 1931- ... CANR-15
Earlier sketch in CA 37-40R
Freeman, Douglas Southall 1886-1953
Brief entry ... 109
See also DLB 17
See also TCLC 11
Freeman, Eugene 1906- ... CANR-26
Earlier sketch in CA 41-44R
Freeman, G(raydon) L(a Verne) 1904- ... CANR-13
Earlier sketch in CA 13-14R
Freeman, Gary 1945- ... 93-96
Freeman, Gillian 1929- ... CANR-3
Earlier sketch in CA 7-8R
Freeman, Harrop A(rthur) 1907- ... 15-16R
Freeman, Harry 1906-1978 ... 77-80
Freeman, Howard E(dgar) 1929- ... CANR-23
Earlier sketches in CA 5-6R, CANR-6
Freeman, Ira Henry 1906- ... CAP-1
Earlier sketch in CA 15-16
Freeman, Ira Maximilian 1905- ... 73-76
See also SATA 21
Freeman, James Dillet 1912- ... 19-20R
Freeman, James Montague 1936- ... 102
Freeman, Jean Kenny 1929- ... 115
Freeman, Jean Todd 1929- ... 25-28R
Freeman, Jo 1945- ... CANR-8
Earlier sketch in CA 61-64
Freeman, John Crosby 1941- ... 15-16R
Freeman, Joseph 1897-1965 Obituary ... 89-92
Freeman, Kathleen 1897-1959 Brief entry ... 112
Freeman, Larry
See Freeman, G(raydon) L(a Verne)
Freeman, Lea David 1887(?)-1976
Obituary ... 69-72
Freeman, Legh Richmond 1842-1915 ... DLB-23
Freeman, Leslie J(ane) 1944- ... 106
Freeman, Linton C(larke) 1927- ... 69-72
Freeman, Lucy (Greenbaum) 1916- ... CANR-3
Earlier sketch in CA 5-6R
See also SATA 24
Freeman, Mae (Blacker) 1907- ... 73-76
See also SATA 25
Freeman, Margaret B. 1899-1980 ... 109
Obituary ... 97-100
Freeman, Margaret C(ooper) 1913- ... 57-60
Freeman, Margaret N(adgwick) 1915- ... 11-12R
Freeman, Mary Eleanor Wilkins 1852-1930
Brief entry ... 106
See also DLB 12
See also TCLC 9
See also SSC 1
Freeman, Max Herbert 1907- Brief entry ... 109
Freeman, Morton S(igmund) 1912- ... 118
Freeman, Paul 1929(?)-1980 Obituary ... 101
Freeman, Peter J.
See Calvert, Patricia
Freeman, R(ichard) Austin 1862-1943
Brief entry ... 113
See also DLB 70
See also TCLC 21
Freeman, R(ichard) B(roke) 1915-1986
Obituary ... 120
Freeman, Richard B(arry) 1944- ... CANR-15
Earlier sketch in CA 85-88
Freeman, Richard Borden 1908- ... CANR-17
Earlier sketch in CA 1R
Freeman, Roger A(dolf) 1904- ... 25-28R
Freeman, Roger A(nthony Wilson)
1928- ... CANR-26
Earlier sketches in CA 65-68, CANR-10
Freeman, Roger L(ouis) 1928- ... CANR-12
Earlier sketch in CA 69-72
Freeman, Ruth B(enson) 1906- ... 41-44R
Freeman, Ruth (Lazear) S(underlin)
1907- ... CANR-13
Earlier sketches in CA 15-16, CAP-1
Freeman, Susan Tax 1938- ... 85-88
Freeman, T(homas) W(alter) 1908-1988 ... 7-8R
Obituary ... 125
Freeman, Thomas 1919- ... 93-96
Freeman, Thomas Walter 1908- ... 7-8R
Freeman, Tony ... SATA-44
Freeman, Walter (Jackson, Jr.)
1895-1972 ... CAP-1
Obituary ... 33-36R
Earlier sketch in CA 17-18
Freeman, Warren S(amuel) 1911- ... 5-6R
Freeman, William Bradford 1938- ... SATA-48
Freeman-Grenville, Greville Stewart Parker
1918- ... CANR-3
Earlier sketch in CA 7-8R
Freeman-Ishill, Rose 1895- ... CAP-1
Earlier sketch in CA 9-10
Freemantle, Brian Harry 1936- ... CANR-16
Earlier sketch in CA 65-68
Freemon, Frank R(eed) 1938- ... 45-58
Freer, Coburn 1939- ... 125
Brief entry ... 105
Freer, Harold Wiley 1906- ... CAP-2
Earlier sketch in CA 21-22
Freese, Arthur S. 1917- ... 77-80
Freestrom, Hubert J. 1928- ... 37-40R
Freeth, Zahra 1925- ... 121
Fregault, Guy 1918-1977 ... 101
Frege, (Friedrich Ludwig) Gottlob
1848-1925 Brief entry ... 120
Fregly, Bert 1922- ... CANR-8
Earlier sketch in CA 57-60
Fregosi, Claudia (Anne Marie) 1946- ... 69-72
See also SATA 24
Frei, Eduardo
See Frei Montalva, Eduardo Frei
Frei, Hans W(ilhelm) 1922-1988 Obituary ... 126
Brief entry ... 111
Freiberg, Stanley K(enneth) 1923- ... 112
Freid, Jacob L. 1913- ... CANR-17
Earlier sketch in CA 3R
Freidel, Frank (Burt, Jr.) 1916- ... CANR-5
Earlier sketch in CA 3R
Freidenreich, Harriet Pass 1947- ... 114
Freides, Thelma K(atz) 1930- ... 49-52
Freidin, Seymour K(enneth) 1917- ... CANR-2
Earlier sketch in CA 4R
Freidson, Eliot 1923- ... CANR-8
Earlier sketch in CA 5-6R
Freihofer, Lois Diane 1933- ... 15-16R
Freilich, Joan S(herman) 1941- ... 57-60
Freilich, Morris 1928- ... 37-40R
Frei Montalva, Eduardo 1911-1982
Obituary ... 110
Freire, Paulo 1921- Brief entry ... 116
Freire-Maia, Newton 1918- ... 29-32R
Freitas, Margarete Elisabeth 1927- ... 45-48
Freivalds, John 1944- ... 69-72
Freixedo, Salvador 1923- ... 29-32R
Fremantle, Anne 1910- ... 15-16R
Fremgen, James Morgan 1933- ... 19-20R
Fremlin, Celia
See Goller, Celia (Fremlin)
Fremont, W. B.
See Bowers, Warner Fremont
Fremont-Smith, Eliot 1929- ... 105
Frenay, Henri 1905-1988 Obituary ... 126
French, Alfred 1916- ... 102
French, Alice 1850-1934 ... DLB-74
French, Allen 1870-1946 Brief entry ... 122
See also YABC 1
French, Ashley
See Robins, Denise (Naomi)
French, Bevan M(eredith) 1937- ... 97-100
French, Brandon 1944- ... 89-92
French, Calvin L(eonard) 1934- ... 53-56
French, Charles E(zra) 1923- ... CANR-1
Earlier sketch in CA 45-48
French, David 1939- ... 101
See also DLB 53
French, Doris
See Shackleton, Doris (Cavell)
French, Dorothy Kayser 1926- ... CANR-3
Earlier sketch in CA 9-10R
See also SATA 5
French, Edward L(ivingstone) 1916-1969 ... CAP-2
Earlier sketch in CA 21-22
French, Fiona 1944- ... 29-32R
See also SATA 6
French, Herbert E(liot) 1912- ... 45-48
French, Kathryn
See Mosesson, Gloria R(ubin)
French, Marilyn 1929- ... CANR-3
Earlier sketch in CA 69-72
See also CLC 10, 18
French, Michael 1944- ... 89-92
See also SATA 38, 49
French, Paul
See Asimov, Isaac
French, Peter 1918- ... 4R
French, Peter A(ndrew) 1942- ... CANR-17
Earlier sketches in CA 45-48, CANR-1
French, Philip (Neville) 1933- ... 103
French, R(obert) B(utler) D(igby)
1904-1981 ... CAP-2
Obituary ... 104
Earlier sketch in CA 25-28
French, R(oger) K(enneth) 1938- ... 118
French, Richard (De Land) 1947- ... CANR-11
Earlier sketch in CA 69-72
French, Ruth M. 1921(?)-1987 Obituary ... 122
French, Scott Robert 1948- ... 57-60
French, Simon 1957- ... CANR-22
Earlier sketch in CA 105
French, Warren G(raham) 1922- ... CANR-16
Earlier sketches in CA 1R, CANR-1
French, Wendell L(owell) 1923- ... 116
French, Will 1890(?)-1979 Obituary ... 89-92
French, William (Harold) 1926- ... 69-72
French, William Marshall 1907- ... CAP-1
Earlier sketch in CA 15-16
Frend, A.
See Cleveland, Philip Jerome
Frend, W(illiam) H(ugh) C(lifford)
1916- ... CANR-9
Earlier sketch in CA 21-22R
Freneau, Philip 1752-1832 ... DLB-37, 43
Frenkel, Jacob A(haron) 1943- ... 89-92
Frenkel, Richard E(ugene) 1924- ... 21-22R
Frentzen, Jeffrey 1956- ... 109
Frenz, Horst 1912- ... 29-32R
Frenzel, Louis (Earl), Jr. 1938- ... 112
Frere, A. S.
See Frere-Reeves, Alexander Stuart
Frere, Emile (George) 1917-1974 ... 41-44R
Frere, James Arnold 1920- ... 7-8R
Frere, Paul 1917- ... CANR-14
Earlier sketch in CA 7-8R
Frere, Sheppard (Sunderland) 1916- ... 21-22R
Frere-Cook, Gervis 1928- Brief entry ... 111
Frere-Reeves, Alexander Stuart 1892-1984
Obituary ... 114
Frerichs, A(lbert) C(hristian) 1910- ... CAP-2
Earlier sketch in CA 25-28
Freschet, Berniece (Louise Speck)
1927- ... CANR-11
Earlier sketch in CA 19-20R
Frese, Dolores Warwick 1936- ... CANR-9
Earlier sketch in CA 5-6R
Fretheim, Terence E(rling) 1936- ... CANR-11
Earlier sketch in CA 25-28R
Fretter, T. W.
See Andre, (Kenneth) Michael
Fretter, William Bache 1916- ... 113
Fretwell, Stephen DeWitt 1942- ... 53-56

Freuchen, (Lorence) Peter (Elfred)
1886-1957 Brief entry ... 114
Freud, Anna 1895-1982 ... 112
Obituary ... 108
Freud, Clement (Raphael) 1924- ... 102
Freud, Sigmund 1856-1939 Brief entry ... 115
Freudberg, Frank 1953- ... 118
Freudenberger, Herman 1922- ... 13-14R
Freudenheim, Leslie Ann Mandelson
1941- ... 69-72
Freudenheim, Yehoshua (Oskar)
1894-1975 ... CAP-2
Earlier sketch in CA 21-22
Freudenthal, Hans 1905- ... CANR-11
Earlier sketch in CA 25-28R
Freund, E(rnest) Hans 1905- ... 1R
Freund, Edith 1931- ... 118
Freund, Gerald 1930- ... CANR-1
Earlier sketch in CA 4R
Freund, Gisele 1912- ... 49-52
Freund, John E(rnst) 1921- ... 13-14R
Freund, Otto Kahn
See Kahn-Freund, Otto
Freund, Paul A(braham) 1908- ... 1R
Freund, Philip (Herbert) 1909- ... CANR-12
Earlier sketch in CA 13-14R
Freund, Rudolf 1915-1969 ... SATA-28
Freundlich, August L. 1924- ... 49-52
Frevert, Peter 1938- ... 81-84
Frew, David R(ichard) 1943- ... 77-80
Frewer, Glyn (M.) 1931- ... CANR-10
Earlier sketch in CA 15-16R
See also SATA 11
Frewin, Leslie Ronald 1917- ... CANR-11
Earlier sketch in CA 7-8R
Frey, Andrew 1905(?)-1983 Obituary ... 109
Frey, Erich A. 1931- ... 45-48
Frey, Frederick Ward 1929- ... 53-56
Frey, Henry A. 1923- ... 33-36R
Frey, John Andrew 1929- ... 89-92
Frey, Leonard H(amilton) 1927- ... 29-32R
Frey, Marlys
See Mayfield, Marlys
Frey, Richard L(incoln) 1905-1988 ... 89-92
Obituary ... 126
Freyer, Frederic
See Ballinger, William Sanborn
Freyre, Gilberto (de Mello) 1900-1987 ... 126
Brief entry ... 116
Freytag, Joseph
See Cooper, Parley J(oseph)
Freytag, Josephine
See Cooper, Parley J(oseph)
Friar, Kimon 1911- ... 85-88
Friar Tuck
See Tucker, Irwin St. John
Fribourg, Marjorie G. 1920- ... CANR-4
Earlier sketch in CA 3R
Frick, C. H.
See Irwin, Constance Frick
Frick, Constance
See Irwin, Constance Frick
Frick, Ford Christopher 1894-1978
Obituary ... 89-92
Frick, George F(rederick) 1925- ... 13-14R
Fricke, Cedric V. 1928- ... 15-16R
Fricker, E(dward) G(eorge) 1910- ... 125
Friday, Nancy 1937- ... 77-80
Friday, Peter
See Harris, Herbert
Frideres, James S(tephen) 1943- ... 113
Fridy, (William) Wallace 1910- ... CANR-17
Earlier sketch in CA 1R
Friebert, Stuart (Alyn) 1931- ... 65-68
Fried, Barbara 1924- ... 45-48
Fried, Charles 1935- ... CANR-12
Earlier sketch in CA 29-32R
Fried, Eleanor L.
See Furman, Eleanor L.
Fried, Emanuel 1913- ... 73-76
Fried, Erich 1921- ... 126
Brief entry ... 114
Fried, Eunice ... 124
Fried, Frederick 1908- ... 77-80
Fried, John J(ames) 1940- ... CANR-12
Earlier sketch in CA 33-36R
Fried, Jonathan L(ester) 1955- ... 113
Fried, Joseph P. 1939- ... 37-40R
Fried, Lawrence 1926-1983 Obituary ... 110
Fried, Marc (Allen) 1922- ... 77-80
Fried, Marc B(ernard) 1944- ... 77-80
Fried, Mary McKenzie Hill 1914- ... 93-96
Fried, Morton H(erbert) 1923-1986 ... 21-22R
Obituary ... 121
Fried, Peter A(lexander) 1943- ... 108
Fried, Richard M(ayer) 1941- ... 73-76
Fried, William 1945- ... 57-60
Friedan, Betty (Naomi) 1921- ... CANR-18
Earlier sketch in CA 65-68
Friedberg, Ardy 1935- ... 108
Friedberg, Gertrude (Tonkonogy) ... 21-22R
Friedberg, Joan Brest 1927- ... 124
Friedberg, Maurice 1929- ... CANR-5
Earlier sketch in CA 1R
Friede, Eleanor Kask 1920- ... 101
Friedelbaum, Stanley H(erman) 1927- ... 37-40R
Friedell, Aaron 1890(?)-1985 Obituary ... 116
Frieden, Bernard J. 1930- ... CANR-10
Earlier sketch in CA 15-16R
Frieden, Ken(neth) 1955- ... 118
Friedenberg, Edgar Zodiag 1921- ... 65-68
Friedenberg, Walter Drew 1928- ... 89-92
Friedenreich, Harriet Pass
See Freidenreich, Harriet Pass
Friedenthal, Richard 1896-1979 ... 103
Obituary ... 89-92
Frieder, Emma 1891- ... CAP-2
Earlier sketch in CA 33-36
Friederich, Werner P(aul) 1905- ... 15-16R
Friederichsen, Kathleen (Hockman)
1910- ... 19-20R
Friedgut, Theodore H. 1931- ... 89-92
Friedheim, Robert L(yle) 1934- ... CANR-12
Earlier sketch in CA 21-22R
Friedkin, William 1939- ... 107
Friedl, Ernestine 1920- ... 37-40R
Friedl, John 1945- ... CANR-4
Earlier sketch in CA 53-56
Friedlaender, Saul 1932- Brief entry ... 117
Friedlaender, Walter (Ferdinand)
1873-1966 Obituary ... 115
Friedland, Ronald Lloyd 1937-1975 ... CAP-2
Obituary ... 57-60
Earlier sketch in CA 33-36
Friedland, Ronnie 1945- ... 106
Friedland, Seymour 1928- ... CANR-17
Earlier sketch in CA 25-28R
Friedland, William H. 1923- ... 13-14R
Friedlander, Albert H(oschander)
1927- ... CANR-25
Earlier sketches in CA 23-24R, CANR-9
Friedlander, Howard 1941- ... 105
Friedlander, Joanne K(ohn) 1930- ... 61-64
See also SATA 9
Friedlander, Saul
See Friedlaender, Saul
Friedlander, Stanley Lawrence 1938- ... 17-18R
Friedlander, Walter A(ndreas) 1891- ... 37-40R
Friedman, Alan
See Horowitz, Shel Alan
Friedman, Alan J(acob) 1942- ... 125
Friedman, Alan Warren 1939- ... 25-28R
Friedman, Albert B(arron) 1920- ... CANR-17
Earlier sketch in CA 1R
Friedman, Alice R. 1900- ... 41-44R
Friedman, Arnold D'Arcy 1900-1981
Obituary ... 109
Friedman, Arnold P(hineas) 1909- ... CANR-1
Earlier sketch in CA 45-48
Friedman, Avner 1932- ... 53-56
Friedman, B(ernard) H(arper) 1926- ... CANR-3
Earlier sketch in CA 2R
See also CLC 7
Friedman, Bernard 1896-1983 Obituary ... 110
Friedman, Bruce Jay 1930- ... CANR-25
Earlier sketch in CA 11-12R
See also DLB 2, 28
See also CLC 3, 5
Friedman, Charles 1902-1984 Obituary ... 113
Friedman, David 1945- ... 89-92
Friedman, Edward Ludwig 1903- ... 3R
Friedman, Elizabeth 1893(?)-1980
Obituary ... 102
Friedman, Estelle (Ehrenwald) 1920- ... 5-6R
See also SATA 7
Friedman, Frieda 1905- ... SATA-43
Friedman, Hal
See Friedman, Harold
Friedman, Harold 1942- ... 89-92
Friedman, Herbert 1916- Brief entry ... 112
Friedman, Ina R(osen) 1926- ... 53-56
See also SATA 41, 49
Friedman, Irving S(igmund) 1915- ... CANR-3
Earlier sketch in CA 45-48
Friedman, Isaiah 1921- ... 53-56
Friedman, Jerrold David
See Gerrold, David
Friedman, John Block 1934- ... 125
Friedman, John S(aul) 1942- ... 118
Friedman, Josephine Troth 1928- ... 77-80
Friedman, Josh(ua M.) 1941- Brief entry ... 126
Friedman, Josh Alan 1956- ... 122
Friedman, Joy Troth
See Friedman, Josephine Troth
Friedman, Judi 1935- ... 65-68
See also AITN 2
Friedman, Julian R. 1920(?)-1983
Obituary ... 111
Friedman, Kathi V(allone) 1943- ... 114
Friedman, Ken(neth Scott) ... 65-68
Friedman, Kenneth 1939- ... 25-28R
Friedman, Lawrence J. 1940- ... 53-56
Friedman, Lawrence Meir 1930- ... CANR-5
Earlier sketch in CA 15-16R
Friedman, Lenemaja 1924- ... 61-64
Friedman, Leon 1933- ... 81-84
Friedman, Lester David 1945- ... 108
Friedman, Marcia 1925- ... 57-60
Friedman, Marvin 1930- ... SATA-33, 42
Friedman, Maurice S(tanley) 1921- ... 15-16R
Friedman, Max Motel 1899(?)-1988
Obituary ... 125
Friedman, Melvin J(ack) 1928- ... 21-22R
Friedman, Meyer 1910- Brief entry ... 113
Friedman, Michael H(enry) 1945- ... 101
Friedman, Michael J(an) 1955- ... 119
Friedman, Michaele Thompson 1944- ... 111
Friedman, Mickey
See Friedman, Michaele Thompson
Friedman, Milton 1912- ... CANR-22
Earlier sketches in CA 1R, CANR-1
Friedman, Murray 1926- ... 57-60
Friedman, Myles I(van) 1924- ... CANR-6
Earlier sketch in CA 57-60
Friedman, Nancy 1950- ... 107
Friedman, Norman 1925- ... CANR-1
Earlier sketch in CA 1R
Friedman, Paul 1899-1972 Obituary ... 37-40R
Friedman, Paul 1937- ... 122
Friedman, Paul Belais 1953- ... 110
Friedman, Ralph 1916- ... 69-72
Friedman, Rochelle (Rame) 1942- ... 112
Friedman, Rose D(irector) ... CANR-22
Earlier sketch in CA 101
Friedman, (Eve) Rosemary (Tibber)
1929- ... CANR-21
Earlier sketches in CA 7-8R, CANR-3
Friedman, Roslyn Berger 1924- ... 19-20R
Friedman, Roy 1934- ... 25-28R
Friedman, Sanford 1928- ... 73-76
Friedman, Sara Ann 1935- ... 77-80
Friedman, Saul S. 1937- ... 57-60
Friedman, Stuart 1913- ... 2R
Friedman, Susan Stanford 1943- ... 109
Friedman, Thomas L(oren) 1953- ... 109
Friedman, Warner G(eorge) 1934- ... 97-100
Friedman, Winifred 1923(?)-1975
Obituary ... 61-64
Friedmann, Arnold 1925- ... 41-44R
Friedmann, Deborah Davis
See Davis-Friedmann, Deborah
Friedmann, Georges 1902(?)-1977
Obituary ... 104
Friedmann, Herbert 1900-1987 ... 106
Obituary ... 122
Friedmann, John 1926- ... CANR-15
Earlier sketch in CA 85-88
Friedmann, Thomas 1947- ... 118
Friedmann, Wolfgang (Gaston)
1907-1972 ... CANR-6
Earlier sketch in CA 3R
Friedmann, Yohanan 1936- ... 33-36R
Friedrich, Anton
See Strich, Christian
Friedrich, Carl Joachim 1901-1984 ... 69-72
Obituary ... 113
Friedrich, Dick
See Friedrich, Richard
Friedrich, Gustav W(illiam) 1941-
Brief entry ... 111
Friedrich, Otto (Alva) 1929- ... CANR-3
Earlier sketch in CA 5-6R
See also SATA 33
Friedrich, Paul 1927- ... CANR-12
Earlier sketch in CA 29-32R
Friedrich, Priscilla 1927- ... 113
See also SATA 39
Friedrich, Richard 1936- ... 103
Friedrichs, Christopher R(ichard) 1947- ... 89-92
Friedrichs, Robert W(inslow) 1923- ... 49-52
Friedson, Anthony M(artin) 1924- ... 108
Friel, Brian 1929- ... 21-22R
See also DLB 13
See also CLC 5, 42
Frielink, A(braham) Barend 1917- ... 21-22R
Friend, Joseph H(arold) 1909-1972 ... CAP-2
Earlier sketch in CA 25-28
Friend, Krebs 1895(?)-1967(?) ... DLB-4
Friend, Robert 1913- ... CANR-7
Earlier sketch in CA 13-14R
Friendlich, Dick
See Friendlich, Richard J.
Friendlich, Richard J. 1909- ... CAP-1
Earlier sketch in CA 15-16
See also SATA 11
Friendly, Alfred 1911-1983 ... 101
Obituary ... 111
Friendly, Fred W. 1915- ... CANR-14
Earlier sketch in CA 23-24R
Friendly, Henry Jacob 1903-1986 ... 103
Obituary ... 118
Frier, Bruce W(oodward) 1943- ... 125
Friermood, Elisabeth Hamilton 1903- ... CANR-1
Earlier sketch in CA 1R
See also SATA 5
Fries, Albert Charles 1908- ... CANR-4
Earlier sketch in CA 1R
Fries, Fritz Rudolf 1935- ... CANR-11
Earlier sketch in CA 25-28R
See also DLB 75
Fries, James Franklin 1938- ... 89-92
Fries, Robert Francis 1911- ... 106
Friesen, Garry 1947- ... 114
Friesen, Gerald 1943- ... 120
Friesen, Patrick 1945- ... 113
Friesner, Esther M.
See Friesner-Stutzman, Esther M.
Friesner-Stutzman, Esther M. 1951- ... 125
Friess, Horace L(eland) 1900-1975 ... 65-68
Obituary ... 61-64
Friggens, Arthur (Henry) 1920- ... 103
Friis, Babbis
See Friis-Baastad, Babbis Ellinor
Frils, Erik J(ohan) 1913- ... 69-72
Friis, Harald T(rap) 1893-1976 Obituary ... 65-68
Friis-Baastad, Babbis Ellinor 1921-1970 ... 19-20R
See also SATA 7
See also CLC 12
Frijling-Schreuder, E(lisabeth) C. M.
1908- ... 61-64
Frillmann, Paul W. 1911-1972 ... CAP-2
Obituary ... 37-40R
Earlier sketch in CA 25-28
Frimbo, E. M.
See Whitaker, Rogers E(rnest) M(alcolm)
Friml, Rudolf 1879-1972 Obituary ... 37-40R
Frimmer, Steven 1928- ... 33-36R
See also SATA 31
Frimoth, Lenore B(eck) 1927- ... 5-6R
Frings, Ketti 1915-1981 ... 101
Obituary ... 103
Frings, Manfred S. 1925- ... CANR-26
Earlier sketches in CA 17-18R, CANR-8
Frink, Maurice 1895-1972 ... CAP-2
Earlier sketch in CA 25-28
Frinta, Mojmir S(vatopluk) 1922- ... 25-28R
Fripp, Patricia 1945- ... 93-96
Frisbie, Louise K(elley) 1913- ... 61-64
Frisbie, Margery (Rowbottom) 1923- ... 5-6R
Frisbie, Richard P(atrick) 1926- ... CANR-17
Earlier sketches in CA 5-6R, CANR-2
Frisby, Terence (Peter Michael) 1932- ... 65-68
Frisch, Karl (Ritter) von 1886-1982 ... 85-88
Obituary ... 115
Frisch, Max (Rudolf) 1911- ... 85-88
See also DLB 69
See also CLC 3, 9, 14, 18, 32, 44
Frisch, Michael H(erbert) 1942- ... 126
Frisch, Morton J. 1923- ... 33-36R
Frisch, O(tto) R(obert) 1904- ... 11-12R
Frisch, Paul Z. 1926(?)-1977 Obituary ... 73-76
Frisch, Ragnar Anton Kittil 1895-1973
Obituary ... 115
Frischauer, Willi 1906- ... CANR-7
Earlier sketch in CA 7-8R
Frischer, Bernard D(avid) 1949- ... 113
Frischwasser-Ra'Anan, H. F.
See Ra'Anan, Uri
Friskey, Margaret (Richards) 1901- ... CANR-2
Earlier sketch in CA 5-6R
See also SATA 5
Frison, George C(arr) 1924- ... 93-96
Fritchman, Stephen Hole 1902-
Brief entry ... 105
Frith, H(arold) J(ames) 1921- ... 102
Frith, Nigel (Andrew Silver) 1941- ... 69-72
Fritsch, Albert Joseph 1933- ... 102
Fritsch, Bruno 1926- ... CANR-11
Earlier sketch in CA 69-72
Fritsch, Charles Theodore 1912- ... 112
Fritschler, A. Lee 1937- ... 33-36R
Fritz
See Whitehall, Harold
Fritz, Henry E(ugene) 1927- ... 19-20R
Fritz, Jean (Guttery) 1915- ... CANR-16
Earlier sketches in CA 4R, CANR-5
See also SATA 1, 29
See also SAAS 2
See also DLB 52
See also CLR 2, 14
Fritz, Leah 1931- ... 93-96
Fritze, Julius Arnold 1918- ... 103
Fritzsch, Harald 1943- ... 113
Frobish, Nestle J(ohn) 1930- ... 101
Froboess, Harry (August) 1899- ... CAP-2
Earlier sketch in CA 17-18
Froehlich, Gustav 1902-1987 Obituary ... 124
Froehlich, Margaret W(alden) 1930- ... 115
Froelich, Robert E. 1929- ... CANR-3
Earlier sketch in CA 45-48
Frohlich, Gustav
See Froehlich, Gustav
Frohlich, Norman 1941- ... 77-80
Frohman, Charles E(ugene) 1901-1976 ... CAP-2
Earlier sketch in CA 29-32
Frohock, W(ilbur) M(errill) 1908-1984 ... 73-76
Obituary ... 113
Froissard, Lily Powell ... CANR-25
Earlier sketch in CA 45-48
Froissart, Jean 1338(?)-1410(?) ... SATA-28
Froman, Elizabeth Hull 1920-1975 ... CAP-1
Obituary ... 53-56
Earlier sketch in CA 15-16
See also SATA 10
Froman, Lewis A(crelius), Jr. 1935- ... 5-6R
Froman, Robert (Winslow) 1917- ... CANR-1
Earlier sketch in CA 4R
See also SATA 8
Frome, David
See Brown, Zenith Jones
Frome, Michael 1920- ... CANR-16
Earlier sketches in CA 4R, CANR-1
Fromer, Margot J(oan) 1939- ... 110
Fromkin, David 1932- ... 109
Fromkin, Howard L(arry) 1939- ... 121
Brief entry ... 118
Fromkin, Victoria A(lexandria) 1923- ... 89-92
Fromm, Erich 1900-1980 ... 73-76
Obituary ... 97-100
Fromm, Erika 1910- ... 9-10R
Fromm, Gary 1933- ... CANR-7
Earlier sketch in CA 17-18R
Fromm, Gloria G(likin) 1931- Brief entry ... 112
Fromm, Harold 1933- ... 23-24R
Fromm, Herbert 1905- ... CANR-1
Earlier sketch in CA 49-52
Fromm, Lilo 1928- ... 81-84
See also SATA 29
Fromme, Babbette Brandt 1925- ... 106
Frommer, Harvey 1937- ... CANR-26
Earlier sketch in CA 103
See also SATA 41
Frommer, Myrna 1941- ... 111
Froncek, Thomas (Walter) 1942- ... 81-84
Frondizi, Risieri 1910- ... 41-44R
Frontier, Tex
See Miller, J(ames) P.
Frooks, Dorothy 1899- ... 57-60
Froomkin, Joseph 1927- ... CANR-13
Earlier sketch in CA 23-24R
Frosch, Thomas Richard 1943- ... 69-72
Froscher, Wingate 1918- ... 1R
Frost, A(rthur) B(urdett) 1851-1928 ... SATA-19
Frost, Carol 1948- ... CANR-11
Earlier sketch in CA 69-72
Frost, David (Paradine) 1939- ... 69-72
Frost, Erica
See Supraner, Robyn
Frost, Ernest 1918- ... 9-10R
Frost, Everett L(loyd) 1942- ... 65-68
Frost, Frank (Jasper) 1929- ... 89-92
Frost, Frederick
See Faust, Frederick (Shiller)
Frost, Gavin 1930- ... CANR-1
Earlier sketch in CA 45-48

Frost, Gerhard Emanuel 1909- CAP-1
Earlier sketch in CA 9-10
Frost, Gregory 1951- 118
Frost, Helen 1898- CAP-1
Earlier sketch in CA 13-14
Frost, James A(rthur) 1918- 37-40R
Frost, Jason
See Obstfeld, Raymond
Frost, Joe L. 1933- 25-28R
Frost, Joni
See Paine, Lauran (Bosworth)
Frost, Lawrence A(ugust) 1907- CANR-26
Earlier sketches in CA 69-72, CANR-11
Frost, Lesley 1899-1983 .... 21-22R
Obituary 110
See also SATA 14, 34
Frost, Leslie Miscampbell 1895-1973
Obituary 41-44R
Frost, M(ax) Gilbert 1908- CAP-1
Earlier sketch in CA 13-14
Frost, Marjorie 1914- 25-28R
Frost, Paul
See Castle, Anthony (Percy)
Frost, Peter Kip 1936- 33-36R
Frost, Richard 1929- 33-36R
Frost, Richard H(indman) 1930- 25-28R
Frost, Richard T. 1926-1972 .... CAP-1
Obituary 37-40R
Earlier sketch in CA 15-16
Frost, Robert (Lee) 1874-1963 89-92
See also SATA 14
See also DLB 54
See also CLC 1, 3, 4, 9, 10, 13, 15, 26, 34, 44
Frost, Robert Carlton 1926- 53-56
Frost, Roon 1943- 126
Frost, S. E., Jr. 1899- CAP-2
Earlier sketch in CA 19-20
Frost, Stanley Brice 1913- 61-64
Frost, William 1917- 41-44R
Frostic, Gwen 1906- 19-20R
Frostick, Michael 1917- 9-10R
Frothingham, Octavius Brooks 1822-1895 .... DLB-1
Froude, James Anthony 1818-1894 .. DLB-18, 57
Frow, John 1948- 120
Froy, Herald
See Deghy, Guy (Stephen)
and Waterhouse, Keith Spencer
Frucht, Phyllis 1936- 57-60
Fruchtenbaum, Arnold G(enekovich) 1943- CANR-11
Earlier sketch in CA 61-64
Fruchter, Benjamin 1914- 1R
Fruchter, Norman D. 81-84
Frude, Neil 1946- 114
Fruehling, Rosemary T(herese) 1933- .. CANR-13
Earlier sketch in CA 33-36R
Frugoni, Cesare 1881-1978 Obituary 73-76
Fruhan, William E(dward), Jr. 1943- 41-44R
Frum, Barbara 1937- 101
Fruman, Norman 1923- 37-40R
Frumkes, Lewis Burke 1939- 114
Frumkin, Gene 1928- CANR-4
Earlier sketch in CA 9-10R
Frumkin, Robert M. 1928- CANR-9
Earlier sketch in CA 23-24R
Fruton, Joseph S(tewart) 1912- 49-52
Fruzzetti, Lina M(aria) 1942- 113
Fry, Alan 1931- CANR-1
Earlier sketch in CA 45-48
Fry, Barbara 1932- 25-28R
Fry, C(harles) George 1936- CANR-14
Earlier sketch in CA 37-40R
Fry, Christine 1943- 107
Fry, Christopher 1907- CANR-9
Earlier sketch in CA 17-18R
See also DLB 13
See also CLC 2, 10, 14
Fry, David
See Roper, William L(eon)
Fry, Dennis Butler 1907-1983 109
Obituary 110
Fry, Donald K(lein, Jr.) 1937- 25-28R
Fry, E(dwin) Maxwell 1899-1987 65-68
Obituary 123
Fry, Earl H(oward) 1947- 102
Fry, Edward Bernard 1925- CANR-5
Earlier sketch in CA 9-10R
See also SATA 35
Fry, Hilary G. 1922- 19-20R
Fry, Howard T(yrrell) 1919- 37-40R
Fry, John 1930- 93-96
Fry, Maggie Culver 1900- AITN-1
Fry, Maxwell
See Fry, E(dwin) Maxwell
Fry, Michael G(raham) 1934- CANR-23
Earlier sketch in CA 69-72
Fry, P(atricia) Eileen 1947- 104
Fry, Plantagenet Somerset
See Somerset Fry, (Peter George Robin) Plantagenet
Fry, Roger (Eliot) 1866-1934 Brief entry 115
Fry, Ronald W(illiam) 1949- 57-60
Fry, Rosalie Kingsmill 1911- 9-10R
See also SATA 3
Fry, Thomas Frederick 1919- 118
Fry, Tom
See Fry, Thomas Frederick
Fry, William F(inley, Jr.) 1924- 5-6R
Fryatt, Norma R. 57-60
Fryburger, Vernon R(ay), Jr. 1918- 4R
Fryd, Norbert 1913-1976 Obituary 65-68
Frydman, Szajko 1911- 25-28R
Frye, (Charles) Alton 1936- 21-22R
Frye, Ellen 1940- 49-52
Frye, John 1910- 49-52
Frye, Keith 1935- 53-56
Frye, (Herman) Northrop 1912- CANR-8
Earlier sketch in CA 5-6R
See also DLB 67, 68
See also CLC 24
Frye, Richard N(elson) 1920- CANR-3
Earlier sketch in CA 5-6R
Frye, Roland Mushat 1921- 9-10R
Frye, William R(uggles) 1918- 73-76
Fryer, Donald S.
See Sidney-Fryer, Donald
Fryer, Holly C(laire) 1908- CAP-1
Earlier sketch in CA 19-20
Fryer, Jonathan 1950- 85-88
Fryer, Judith 1939- 69-72
Fryer, Mary Beacock 1929- 97-100
Fryer, William T. 1900(?)-1980 Obituary .. 93-96
Frykenberg, Robert Eric 1930- 25-28R
Fryklund, Verne C(harles) 1896-1980 .... 13-14R
Obituary 126
Frykman, John H(arvey) 1932- 33-36R
Frym, Gloria 1947- 105
Frymier, Jack R(immel) 1925- 19-20R
Fryscak, Milan 1932- 53-56
Fuchida, Mitsuo 1902(?)-1976 Obituary ... 65-68
Fuchs, Daniel 1909- 81-84
See also CAAS 5
See also DLB 9, 26, 28
See also CLC 8, 22
Fuchs, Daniel 1934- CANR-14
Earlier sketch in CA 37-40R
See also CLC 34
Fuchs, Elinor 1933- 105
Fuchs, Erich 1916- 29-32R
See also SATA 6
Fuchs, Estelle 57-60
Fuchs, Guenter Bruno 1928-1977
Obituary 114
Fuchs, Jacob 1939- 23-24R
Fuchs, Jerome H(erbert) 1922- 69-72
Fuchs, Josef 1912- 21-22R
Fuchs, Lawrence H. 1927- CANR-5
Earlier sketch in CA 3R
Fuchs, Lucy 1935- CANR-12
Earlier sketch in CA 73-76
See also SATA 52
Fuchs, Roland J(ohn) 1933- CANR-14
Earlier sketch in CA 81-84
Fuchs, Victor R(obert) 1924- CANR-18
Earlier sketches in CA 1R, CANR-2
Fuchs, Vivian (Ernest) 1908- CANR-21
Earlier sketch in CA 104
Fuchshuber, Annegert 1940- 112
See also SATA 43
Fucilla, Joseph G(uerin) 1897- 89-92
Fucini, Joseph J(ames) 1951- 120
Fucini, Suzy 1951- 120
Fudge, William Kingston 1904-1985
Obituary 116
Fuegi, John 1936- 37-40R
Fueloep-Miller, Rene 1891-1963 Obituary ... 110
Fuentes, Carlos 1928- CANR-10
Earlier sketch in CA 69-72
See also CLC 3, 8, 10, 13, 22, 41
See also AITN 2
Fuentes, Martha Ayers 1923- 73-76
Fuentes, Roberto 1934- 57-60
Fuentes Mohr, Alberto 1928(?)-1979
Obituary 85-88
Fuerer-Haimendorf, Christoph von 1909- CANR-13
Earlier sketch in CA 15-16R
Fuermann, George Melvin 1918- 103
Fufuka, Karama
See Morgan, Sharon A(ntonia)
Fugard, Athol 1932- 85-88
See also CLC 5, 9, 14, 25, 40
Fugard, Sheila 1932- 125
See also CLC 48
Fugate, Bryan I(rven) 1943- 120
Fugate, Francis L(yle) 1915- 25-28R
Fugate, Joe K. 1931- 23-24R
Fugate, Roberta B(auslin) 1917- 111
Fugate, Terence (McCuddy) 1930- 5-6R
Fugitt, Eva D(raper) 1929- 110
Fuhrman, Ellsworth R(aymond) 1946- 112
Fuhrman, Lee 1903(?)-1977 Obituary 73-76
Fuhrmann, Joseph T(heodore) 1940- 73-76
Fuhro, Wilbur J. 1914- 11-12R
Fujikawa, Gyo 1908- 113
See also SATA 30, 39
Fujita, Tamao 1905- 37-40R
See also SATA 7
Fujiwara, Michiko 1946- 77-80
See also SATA 15
Fujiwara, Yoichi 1909- CANR-22
Earlier sketch in CA 105
Fuka, Vladimir 1926-1977 Obituary 104
See also SATA 27
Fukei, Gladys Arlene (Harper) 1920- 15-16R
Fuks, Ladislav 1923- 118
Fukuda, Haruko 1946- 109
Fukuda, Tsutomu 1905- 103
Fukui, Haruhiro 1935- 29-32R
Fukutake, Tadashi 1917- CANR-5
Earlier sketch in CA 13-14R
Fukuyama, Yoshio 1921- 41-44R
Fulbright, J(ames) William 1905- 9-10R
Fulbrook, Mary (Jean Alexandra) 1951- 121
Fulco, William J(ames) 1936- 49-52
Fuld, James J. 1916- 23-24R
Fuld, Leonard M. 1953- 120
Fulda, Carl H. 1909-1975 .... CAP-2
Earlier sketch in CA 33-36
Fuldauer, Ivan 1927- 69-72
Fuldheim, Dorothy (Snell) 1893- 49-52
Fulford, Robert 1932- 89-92
Fulford, Roger (Thomas Baldwin) 1902-1983 65-68
Obituary 109
Fulks, Bryan 1897- 97-100
Full, Harold 1919- 17-18R
Fuller, Alfred C(arl) 1885-1973 Obituary ... 45-48
Fuller, Beverley 1927- 69-72
Fuller, Blair 1927- 9-10R
Fuller, Catherine Leuthold 1916- 29-32R
See also SATA 9
Fuller, Charles (H., Jr.) 1939- 112
Brief entry 108
See also BW
See also DLB 38
See also CLC 25
Fuller, Curtis G. 1912- Brief entry 120
Fuller, Daniel P(ayton) 1925- Brief entry 112
Fuller, David O(tis) 1903- 53-56
Fuller, Dorothy Mason 1898- 101
Fuller, Edgar 1904-1973 Obituary 45-48
Fuller, Edmund (Maybank) 1914- 77-80
See also SATA 21
Fuller, Edward C. 1907- 53-56
Fuller, Elizabeth 1946- 113
Fuller, Harold 1940- 65-68
Fuller, Helen 1914(?)-1972 Obituary 37-40R
Fuller, Henry Blake 1857-1929 Brief entry ... 108
See also DLB 12
Fuller, Hoyt (William) 1927-1981 53-56
Obituary 103
See also BW
Fuller, Iola
See McCoy, Iola Fuller
Fuller, Jack (William) 1946- Brief entry 125
Fuller, Jean (Violet) Overton 1915- CANR-19
Earlier sketches in CA 7-8R, CANR-4
Fuller, John (Harold) CAP-1
Earlier sketch in CA 9-10
Fuller, John (Leopold) 1937- CANR-9
Earlier sketch in CA 21-22R
See also DLB 40
Fuller, John Frederick Charles 1878-1966 . CAP-1
Earlier sketch in CA 15-16
Fuller, John G(rant, Jr.) 1913- CANR-2
Earlier sketch in CA 1R
Fuller, Ken 1946- 125
Fuller, Lois Hamilton 1915- 4R
See also SATA 11
Fuller, Lon (Luvois) 1902-1978 .... CAP-2
Obituary 77-80
Earlier sketch in CA 33-36
Fuller, Margaret
See Ossoli, Sarah Margaret (Fuller marchesa d')
Fuller, Miriam Morris 1933- 37-40R
Fuller, Paul E(ugene) 1932- 73-76
Fuller, Peter (Michael) 1947- 97-100
Fuller, R(ichard) Buckminster (Jr.) 1895-1983 .... CANR-12
Obituary 109
Earlier sketch in CA 11-12R
Fuller, Reginald H(orace) 1915- CANR-18
Earlier sketches in CA 5-6R, CANR-3
Fuller, Robert C(harles) 1952- 116
Fuller, Roger
See Tracy, Don(ald Fiske)
Fuller, Roy (Broadbent) 1912- 7-8R
See also DLB 15, 20
See also CLC 4, 28
Fuller, Sam
See Fuller, Samuel (Michael)
Fuller, Samuel (Michael) 1911(?)-
Brief entry 112
Fuller, Samuel 1912- DLB-26
Fuller, Sarah Margaret 1810-1850 .... DLB-1, 59, 73
See also CDALB 1640-1865
Fuller, Thomas C(harles) 1918- 126
Fuller, Wayne E(dison) 1919- 15-16R
Fuller, William A(lbert) 1924- 41-44R
Fullerton, Alexander (Fergus) 1924- CANR-23
Earlier sketches in CA 19-20R, CANR-7
Fullerton, Gail Jackson 1927- 37-40R
Fullerton, Gail Putney
See Fullerton, Gail Jackson
Fullinwider, Robert King 1942- 108
Fullinwider, S. P(endleton) 1933-
Brief entry 109
Fullmer, Daniel W(arren) 1922- CANR-13
Earlier sketch in CA 33-36R
Fullmer, June Z(immerman) 1920- 25-28R
Fulmer, Robert M(arion) 1939- CANR-10
Earlier sketch in CA 57-60
Fulop-Miller, Rene
See Fueloep-Miller, Rene
Fulton, A(lbert) R(ondthaler) 1902- 1R
Fulton, Alice 1952- 116
Fulton, Gere (Burke) 1939- 53-56
Fulton, Len 1934- 57-60
See also DLBY 86
Fulton, Norman 1927- 37-40R
Fulton, Paul C(edric) 1901-1985 .... CAP-1
Obituary 118
Earlier sketch in CA 15-16
Fulton, Robert Lester 1926- Brief entry 105
Fulton, Robin 1937- CANR-16
Earlier sketch in CA 33-36R
See also DLB 40
Fults, John Lee 1932- 53-56
See also SATA 33
Fultz, Walter J. 1924(?)-1971 Obituary 104
Fulweiler, Howard Wells 1932- 77-80
Fumento, Rocco 1923- 2R
Funabashi, Seiichi 1904(?)-1976
Obituary 65-68
Funai, Mamoru (Rolland) 1932- SATA-46
Fundaburk, Emma Lila 1922- 41-44R
Funderburk, Guy B(ernard) 1902- 45-48
Funderburk, Thomas R(ay) 1928- 19-20R
Fung, Gong
See Goon, Fook Mun
Fung, Raymond (Wai Man) 1940- 123
Funigiello, Philip J. 1939- 65-68
Funk, Arthur Layton 1914- 23-24R
Funk, Charles Earle, Jr. 1913- 122
Funk, Peter V(an) K(euren) 1921- CANR-13
Earlier sketch in CA 21-22R
Funk, Rainer 1943- 109
Funk, Robert W(alter) 1926- 33-36R
Funk, Thompson 1911- CANR-2
Earlier sketch in CA 49-52
See also SATA 7
Funk, Tom
See Funk, Thompson
Funk, Wilfred (John) 1883-1965 Obituary .. 89-92
Funke, Lewis 1912- 49-52
See also SATA 11
Funston, Richard Y(ork) 1943- 123
Brief entry 118
Funt, Julian 1907(?)-1980 Obituary 97-100
Funt, Marilyn 1937- 102
Fuoss, Robert Martin 1912-1980
Obituary 93-96
Furbank, P(hilip) N(icholas) 1920- CANR-18
Earlier sketch in CA 21-22R
Furbee, Leonard J. 1896(?)-1975
Obituary 61-64
Furchgott, Terry 1948- 105
See also SATA 29
Furcolo, Foster 1917- 117
Furer, Howard B(ernard) 1934- 33-36R
Furer-Haimendorf, Christoph von
See Fuerer-Haimendorf, Christoph von
Furey, Michael
See Ward, Arthur Henry Sarsfield
Furfey, Paul Hanly 1896- CAP-2
Earlier sketch in CA 23-24
Furgurson, Ernest B(aker, Jr.) 1929- 73-76
Furgurson, Pat
See Furgurson, Ernest B(aker, Jr.)
Furley, David John 1922- 108
Furlong, Monica (Mavis) 1930- Brief entry .. 117
Furlonge, Geoffrey (Warren) 1903-1984
Obituary 114
Furman, Bess 1894-1969 Obituary 115
Furman, Eleanor L. 1913- CANR-12
Earlier sketch in CA 29-32R
Furman, Laura 1945- 104
See also DLBY 86
Furman, Roger 1924(?)-1983 Obituary 111
Furnas, J(oseph) C(hamberlain) 1905- 77-80
Furneaux, Robin
See Smith, Frederick William Robin
Furneaux, Rupert 1908- CANR-1
Earlier sketch in CA 4R
Furness, Edna L(ue) 1906- 37-40R
Furness, Horace Howard 1833-1912 .... DLB-64
Furness, William Henry 1802-1896 .... DLB-1
Furnier, Vincent Damon
See Cooper, Alice
Furnish, Dorothy Jean 1921- 106
Furnish, Victor Paul 1931- CANR-25
Earlier sketches in CA 23-24R, CANR-10
Furniss, Edgar S(tephenson) 1890-1972
Obituary 37-40R
Furniss, Norman Francis 1922- 1R
Furniss, Tim 1948- 109
See also SATA 49
Furniss, W(arren) Todd 1921- 57-60
Furphy, Joseph 1843-1912 .... TCLC-25
Furrer, Juerg 1939- 69-72
Furry, Elda 1890-1966 113
Obituary 89-92
Furse, John 1932- 109
Furst, Alan 1941- CANR-12
Earlier sketch in CA 69-72
Furst, Lilian Renee 1931- CANR-18
Earlier sketch in CA 102
Furtado, Celso 1920- CANR-25
Earlier sketches in CA 17-18R, CANR-9
Furth, Alex
See Sasuly, Richard
Furth, George 1932- 73-76
Furth, Hans G. 1920- 45-48
Furthman, Jules
See Furthmann, Julius Grinnell
See also DLB 26
Furthmann, Julius Grinnell 1888-1966
Obituary 113
Furtwangler, Albert (J.) 1942- 118
Furtwangler, Virginia W(alsh) 1932- 118
Furukawa, Toshi 1924- CANR-2
Earlier sketch in CA 45-48
See also SATA 24
Fusco, Margie 1949- 85-88
Fusero, Clemente 1913-1975 81-84
Fusfeld, Daniel R(oland) 1922- 45-48
Fuson, Benjamin Willis 1911- 37-40R
Fuson, Robert H(enderson) 1927- 89-92
Fuss, Peter 1932- CANR-9
Earlier sketch in CA 23-24R
Fussell, Betty
See Fussell, Betty Harper
Fussell, Betty Harper 1927- 121
Fussell, Edwin 1922- 53-56
Fussell, G(eorge) E(dwin) 1889- CANR-3
Earlier sketch in CA 7-8R
Fussell, Paul 1924- CANR-21
Earlier sketches in CA 19-20R, CANR-8
Fussner, F(rank) Smith 1920- CANR-5
Earlier sketch in CA 1R
Futrell, Allan W. 1952- 123
Futrell, Gene Allen 1928- 107

Futrelle, Jacques 1875-1912 Brief entry ... 113
See also TCLC 19
Futuyma, Douglas Joel 1942- ... 108
Fye, W(allace) Bruce (III) 1946- ... 126
Fyffe, Don(ald Lewis) 1925- ... 25-28R
Fyleman, Rose (Amy) 1877-1957
Brief entry ... 111
See also SATA 21
Fyler, John (Morgan) 1943- ... 89-92
Fyodorov, Yevgeny Konstantinovich
See Fedorov, Yevgeny Konstantinovich
Fysh, Wilmot Hudson 1895- ... 17-18R
Fyson, J(enny) G(race) 1904- ... CAP-2
Earlier sketch in CA 21-22
See also SATA 42
Fyvel, T. R.
See Feiwel, Raphael Joseph
Fyvel, Tosco Raphael
See Feiwel, Raphael Joseph

G

G. B.
See Boas, Guy (Herman Sidney)
Gaa, Charles J(ohn) 1911- ... 19-20R
Gaan, Margaret 1914- ... 81-84
Gaard, David 1945- ... 25-28R
Gaathon, A(ryeh) L(udwig) 1898- ... 49-52
Gabbard, Glen O(wens) 1949- ... 126
Gabbard, Krin 1948- ... 126
Gabbard, Lucina P(aquet) 1922- ... 110
Gabbett, Harry 1910(?)-1985 Obituary ... 116
Gabel, (W.) Creighton 1931- Brief entry ... 106
Gabel, Joseph 1912- ... 101
Gabel, Margaret 1938- ... 33-36R
Gabel, Medard 1946- ... CANR-11
Earlier sketch in CA 65-68
Gabin, Sanford B(yron) 1936- ... 114
Gable, Tom 1944- ... 93-96
Gablehouse, Charles 1928- ... 21-22R
Gablik, Suzi 1934- ... 33-36R
Gabo, Naum 1890-1977 ... CAP-2
Obituary ... 73-76
Earlier sketch in CA 33-36
Gabor, Dennis 1900-1979 ... 17-18R
Obituary ... 120
Gabor, Georgia M. 1930- ... 108
Gabor, Mark 1939- ... 81-84
Gaboury, Antonio 1919- ... CANR-2
Earlier sketch in CA 45-48
Gabre-Medhin, Tsegaye (Kawessa) 1936- ... 101
Gabre-Tsadick, Marta 1932- ... 115
Gabriel, A(strik) L. 1907- ... CANR-6
Earlier sketch in CA 7-8R
Gabriel, H(enry) 1922- ... 77-80
Gabriel, Joyce 1949- ... 97-100
Gabriel, Jueri (Evald) 1940- ... 93-96
Gabriel, Mabel McAfee 1884(?)-1976
Obituary ... 65-68
Gabriel, Philip L(ouis) 1918- ... 93-96
Gabriel, Ralph Henry 1890-1987 ... 13-14R
Obituary ... 122
Gabriel, Richard Alan 1942- Brief entry ... 104
Gabriel, Roman 1940- Brief entry ... 107
Gabriel-Robinet, Louis 1909-1975
Obituary ... 61-64
Gabrielson, Frank 1911(?)-1980 Obituary ... 93-96
Gabrielson, Ira N(oel) 1889-1977 ... CAP-1
Obituary ... 73-76
Earlier sketch in CA 9-10
Gabrielson, James B. 1917- ... 29-32R
Gabrys, Ingrid Schubert
See Schubert-Gabrys, Ingrid
Gach, Gary 1947- ... 77-80
Gach, Michael Reed 1952- ... 110
Gackenbach, Dick 1927- ... 115
See also SATA 30, 48
Gadamer, Hans-Georg 1900- ... 85-88
Gadd, David 1912- ... 57-60
Gadd, Maxine 1940- ... 116
Gadda, Carlo Emilio 1893-1973 ... 89-92
See also CLC 11
Gaddes, Peter
See Sheldon, Peter
Gaddis, J. Wilson 1910(?)-1975 Obituary ... 57-60
Gaddis, John Lewis 1941- ... 45-48
Gaddis, Peggy
See Dern, Erolie Pearl Gaddis
Gaddis, Thomas E(ugene) 1908-1984 ... CANR-16
Obituary ... 114
Earlier sketch in CA 29-32R
Gaddis, Vincent H. 1913- ... 15-16R
See also SATA 35
Gaddis, William 1922- ... CANR-21
Earlier sketch in CA 19-20R
See also DLB 2
See also CLC 1, 3, 6, 8, 10, 19, 43
Gaddy, C(urtis) Welton 1941- ... 61-64
Gadler, Steve J. 1905- ... 97-100
See also SATA 36
Gadney, Reg 1941- ... CANR-18
Earlier sketches in CA 49-52, CANR-3
Gado, Frank 1936- ... 49-52
Gadpaille, Warren J(oseph) 1924- ... 61-64
Gaebelein, Frank Ely 1899- ... CANR-2
Earlier sketch in CA 13-14R
Gaeddert, Lou Ann (Bigge) 1931- ... CANR-13
Earlier sketch in CA 73-76
See also SATA 20
Gaedeke, Ralph M(ortimer) 1941- ... CANR-24
Earlier sketches in CA 65-68, CANR-9
Gaeng, Paul A. 1924- ... 37-40R
Gaer, Joseph 1897-1969 ... 9-10R
Obituary ... 122
Gaer, Yossef
See Gaer, Joseph
Gaess, Roger 1943- ... 104
Gaff, Jerry G(ene) 1936- ... 85-88
Gaffney, Edward McGlynn, Jr. 1941- ... 114
Gaffney, James 1931- ... CANR-6
Earlier sketch in CA 57-60
Gaffney, (Merrill) Mason 1923- ... CANR-3
Earlier sketch in CA 49-52
Gag, Flavia 1907-1979 ... 7-8R
Obituary ... 104
See also SATA 24
Gag, Wanda (Hazel) 1893-1946
Brief entry ... 113
See also YABC 1
See also DLB 22
See also CLR 4
Gagan, Bernard 1915-1984 Obituary ... 112
Gagarin, Michael 1942- ... 89-92
Gagarin, Yuri (Alekseevich) 1934-1968
Obituary ... 112
Gage, Diane 1954- ... 116
Gage, Edwin 1943- ... 85-88
Gage, Joy P. 1930- ... 114
Gage, Nathaniel Lees 1917- ... 69-72
Gage, Nicholas
See Ngagoyeanes, Nicholas
Gage, William 1915-1973 ... CAP-2
Earlier sketch in CA 25-28
Gage, William W(hitney) 1925- ... 15-16R
Gage, Wilson
See Steele, Mary Q(uintard Govan)
Gager, John Goodrich, Jr. 1937-
Brief entry ... 104
Gager, Nancy Land 1932(?)-1980
Obituary ... 93-96
Gagliano, Frank 1931- ... CANR-1
Earlier sketch in CA 45-48
Gagliardo, John G(arver) 1933- ... 23-24R
Gagliardo, Ruth Garver 1895(?)-1980
Obituary ... 104
See also SATA 22
Gagne, Cole 1954- ... 112
Gagne, Robert M(ills) 1916- ... 121
Brief entry ... 116
Gagnier, Ed 1936- ... 65-68
Gagnier, Regenia (A.) 1953- ... 126
Gagnon, Jean-Louis 1913- ... 23-24R
Gagnon, John H(enry) 1931- ... 33-36R
Gagnon, Madeleine 1938- ... DLB-60
Gagnon, Paul Adelard 1925- Brief entry ... 104
Gahagan, Helen
See Douglas, Helen Gahagan
Gahagan, Jayne D. 1929(?)-1983
Obituary ... 110
Gaherty, Sherry 1951- ... 57-60
Gail, Marzieh ... CANR-11
Earlier sketch in CA 69-72
Gailey, Harry A(lfred) 1926- ... CANR-16
Earlier sketches in CA 45-48, CANR-1
Gailey, James H(erbert), Jr. 1916- ... 7-8R
Gailmor, William S. 1910(?)-1970
Obituary ... 104
Gaine, Hugh 1726-1807 ... DLB-43
Gainer, Bernard 1944- Brief entry ... 109
Gaines, Bill
See Gaines, William Maxwell
Gaines, Charles (Latham, Jr.) 1942- ... 119
Gaines, Diana 1912- ... 1R
Gaines, Ernest J(ames) 1933- ... CANR-24
Earlier sketches in CA 11-12R, CANR-6
See also BW
See also DLB 2, 33
See also DLBY 80
See also CLC 3, 11, 18
See also AITN 1
Gaines, Jack
See Gaines, Jacob
Gaines, Jacob 1918- ... 101
Gaines, Pierce Welch 1905- ... 15-16R
Gaines, Richard L. 1925- ... 49-52
Gaines, William Maxwell 1922- Brief entry ... 108
Gainham, Sarah
See Ames, Rachel
Gains, Larry 1900-1983 Obituary ... 110
Gainsbrugh, Glen M. 1949- ... 25-28R
Gainsbrugh, Martin R(euben) 1907-1977
Obituary ... 69-72
Gainsburg, Joseph (Charles) 1894- ... 7-8R
Gainza Paz, Alberto 1899-1977 ... 77-80
Obituary ... 73-76
Gaiser, Gerd 1908-1976 ... DLB-69
Gaite, Francis
See Coles, Cyril Henry
Gaither, Gant 1917- ... 11-12R
Gaither, Norman 1937- ... 112
Gaitskell, Charles D(udley) 1908- ... 29-32R
Gaitskell, H.T.N.
See Gaitskell, Hugh (Todd Naylor)
Gaitskell, Hugh (Todd Naylor) 1906-1963
Obituary ... 112
Gajdusek, Robert Elemer 1925- ... 102
Gajdusek, Robin
See Gajdusek, Robert Elemer
Gal, Allon 1934- ... CANR-1
Earlier sketch in CA 45-48
Gal, Hans 1890- ... 5-6R
Gal, Istvan 1912-1982 Obituary ... 107
Gal, Laszlo 1933- ... SATA-32, 52
Galai, Shmuel 1933- ... 107
Galambos, Louis (Paul) 1931- ... 81-84
Galamian, Ivan (Alexandrovitch)
1903-1981 Obituary ... 108
Galand, Rene 1923- ... CANR-24
Earlier sketch in CA 45-48
Galanoy, Terry 1927- ... CANR-4
Earlier sketch in CA 45-48
Galanskov, Yuri 1939(?)-1972 Obituary ... 37-40R
Galantay, Ervin Yvan 1930- ... 101
Galante, Pierre 1909- ... 15-16R
Galanter, Eugene 1924- ... 1R
Galanter, Marc 1931- ... 122
Galarza, Ernesto 1905-1984 Obituary ... 113
Galassi, Jonathan (White) 1949- ... 101
Galati, Stephen A(lexander) Fischer
See Fischer-Galati, Stephen A(lexander)
Galatopoulos, Stelios 1932- Brief entry ... 110
Galay, Ted 1941- ... 122
Galbraith, Clare K(earney) 1919- ... 33-36R
Galbraith, Georgie Starbuck 1909-1980 ... CAP-1
Obituary ... 97-100
Earlier sketch in CA 9-10
Galbraith, Jean 1906- ... 37-40R
Galbraith, John Kenneth 1908- ... 21-22R
Galbraith, John S. 1916- ... CANR-6
Earlier sketch in CA 5-6R
Galbraith, Madelyn 1897-1976 ... CAP-2
Earlier sketch in CA 33-36
Galbraith, Vivian Hunter 1889-1976 ... 73-76
Obituary ... 69-72
Galbreath, Robert (Carroll) 1938- ... 41-44R
Galdone, Paul 1907(?)-1986 ... CANR-13
Obituary ... 121
Earlier sketch in CA 73-76
See also SATA 17, 49
See also CLR 16
Galdos, Benito Perez
See Perez Galdos, Benito
Gale, Barry 1935- ... 110
Gale, Bill
See Gale, William
Gale, Elliot N(yman) 1938- Brief entry ... 110
Gale, Herbert M(orrison) 1907- ... CAP-1
Earlier sketch in CA 15-16
Gale, John
See Gaze, Richard
Gale, Linda A(nn) 1939- ... 112
Gale, Patrick (Evelyn Hugh Sadler) 1962- ... 124
Gale, Raymond F(loyd) 1918- ... 25-28R
Gale, Richard M. 1932- ... 25-28R
Gale, Richard Nelson 1896-1982 Obituary ... 107
Gale, Robert L(ee) 1919- ... CANR-18
Earlier sketches in CA 11-12R, CANR-3
Gale, Vi ... 33-36R
Gale, William 1925- ... 97-100
Gale, William C.
See Giles, Carl H(oward)
Gale, William Daniel 1906- ... 107
Gale, Zona 1874-1938 Brief entry ... 105
See also DLB 9
See also TCLC 7
Galeano, Eduardo (Hughes) 1940- ... CANR-13
Earlier sketch in CA 29-32R
Galella, Ron 1931- ... CANR-14
Earlier sketch in CA 53-56
See also AITN 1
Galenson, Walter 1914- ... CANR-11
Earlier sketch in CA 25-28R
Gales, Barbara J. 1940- ... CANR-14
Earlier sketch in CA 81-84
Galewitz, Herb 1928- ... CANR-14
Earlier sketch in CA 41-44R
Galfo, Armand J. 1924- ... 17-18R
Galiano, Juan Valera y Alcala
See Valera y Alcala-Galiano, Juan
Galich, Alexander 1918(?)-1977 Obituary ... 73-76
Galilea, Segundo 1928- ... 105
Galinsky, Ellen 1942- ... CANR-9
Earlier sketch in CA 65-68
See also SATA 23
Galinsky, G(otthard) Karl 1942- ... 33-36R
Gall, Auguste Amedee de Saint
See Strich, Christian
Gall, Elizabeth Cornelia 1898- ... 37-40R
Gall, Meredith D(amien) 1942- ... CANR-21
Earlier sketches in CA 53-56, CANR-6
Gall, Morris 1907- ... 45-48
Gall, Sally M(oore) 1941- ... 110
Gallager, Gale
See Oursler, Will(iam Charles)
Gallagher, Buell Gordon 1904- ... 65-68
Gallagher, Charles A(ugustus) 1927- ... CANR-9
Earlier sketch in CA 61-64
Gallagher, David P. 1944- ... 45-48
Gallagher, Dorothy 1935- ... 65-68
Gallagher, Edward J. 1892(?)-1978
Obituary ... 81-84
Gallagher, Idella J(ane Smith) 1917-
Brief entry ... 108
Gallagher, J(ames) Roswell 1903- ... 57-60
Gallagher, James J(ohn) 1926- ... 114
Gallagher, John F(redrick) 1936- ... 19-20R
Gallagher, (John) Joseph 1929- ... 122
Gallagher, Kent G(rey) 1933- ... 33-36R
Gallagher, Louis J(oseph) 1885-1972
Obituary ... 37-40R
Gallagher, (Joseph) Mark 1953- ... 123
Gallagher, Marsha V. 1943- ... 117
Gallagher, Mary 1947- ... 97-100
Gallagher, Matthew P(hilip) 1919- ... 5-6R
Gallagher, Maureen 1938- ... 118
Gallagher, Neil 1941- ... 114
Gallagher, Patricia ... CANR-11
Earlier sketch in CA 65-68
Gallagher, Patrick (Francis) 1930- ... 45-48
Gallagher, Rachel ... 89-92
Gallagher, Richard (Farrington) 1926- ... CANR-6
Earlier sketch in CA 3R
Gallagher, Richard
See Levinson, Leonard
Gallagher, Robert E(mmett) 1922- ... 13-14R
Gallagher, Sister Mary Dominic 1917- ... 19-20R
Gallagher, Tess 1943- ... 106
See also CLC 18
Gallagher, Thomas (Michael) ... CANR-5
Earlier sketch in CA 1R
Gallagher, Vera 1917- ... 115
Gallagher, William Davis 1808-1894 ... DLB-73
Gallagher, William M. 1923-1975
Obituary ... 89-92
Gallaher, Art, Jr. 1925- ... CANR-3
Earlier sketch in CA 2R
Gallaher, John G(erard) 1928- ... 126
Brief entry ... 112
Gallahue, David L(ee) 1943- ... CANR-13
Earlier sketch in CA 77-80
Gallahue, John (Jeremiah) 1930-
Brief entry ... 110
Gallant, Christine C. 1940- Brief entry ... 106
Gallant, Mavis 1922- ... 69-72
See also DLB 53
See also CLC 7, 18, 38
Gallant, Roy A(rthur) 1924- ... CANR-4
Earlier sketch in CA 7-8R
See also SATA 4
See also CLC 17
Gallant, T(homas) Grady 1920- ... 5-6R
Gallati, Mary Ernestine ... 7-8R
Gallati, Robert R. J. 1913- ... CANR-1
Earlier sketch in CA 3R
Galle, F(rederick) C(harles) 1919- ... 61-64
Galle, William 1938- ... 93-96
Gallegly, J(oseph) S(tephen) 1898- ... 5-6R
Gallen, John (J.) 1932- Brief entry ... 113
Galler, David 1929- ... 25-28R
Galler, Meyer 1914- ... 89-92
Gallerite, The
See Bason, Frederick (Thomas)
Gallery, Dan
See Gallery, Daniel V.
Gallery, Daniel V. 1901-1977 ... 15-16R
Obituary ... 69-72
Gallico, Paul (William) 1897-1976 ... CANR-23
Obituary ... 69-72
Earlier sketch in CA 7-8R
See also SATA 13
See also DLB 9
See also CLC 2
See also AITN 1
Gallie, Duncan (Ian Dunbar) 1946- ... 123
Gallie, Menna (Patricia Humphreys)
1920- ... CANR-1
Earlier sketch in CA 2R
Gallie, W(alter) B(ryce) 1912- ... 85-88
Galligan, Edward L(awrence) 1926- ... 126
Gallimard, Gaston 1881-1975 Obituary ... 61-64
Gallimore, Ronald 1938- ... 65-68
Gallin, Sister Mary Alice 1921- ... 13-14R
Gallinger, Osma Couch
See Tod, Osma Gallinger
Gallison, Kate
See Gallison, Kathleen
Gallison, Kathleen 1939- ... 120
Gallistel, C(harles) R(ansom) 1941- ... 119
Gallix, Francois 1939- ... CANR-26
Earlier sketch in CA 109
Gallman, Waldemar J(ohn) 1899-1980 ... CAP-1
Obituary ... 101
Earlier sketch in CA 11-12
Gallner, Sheldon M(ark) 1949- ... 53-56
Gallo, Max 1932- ... 85-88
Gallo, Rose Adrienne 1938- Brief entry ... 107
Gallois, Claire 1938- ... CANR-18
Earlier sketch in CA 85-88
Gallon, Arthur J(ames) 1915- ... 57-60
Gallop, David 1928- ... 65-68
Gallop, Jane 1952- ... 107
Galloping Gourmet
See Kerr, Graham
Galloway, A(llan) D(ouglas) 1920- ... 25-28R
Galloway, David D(arryl) 1937- ... CANR-16
Earlier sketch in CA 21-22R
Galloway, George Barnes 1898-1967 ... 1R
Obituary ... 103
Galloway, John C. 1915-1970 ... CAP-2
Earlier sketch in CA 25-28
Galloway, Jonathan F(uller) 1939- ... 77-80
Galloway, Joseph L(ee) 1941- ... CANR-12
Earlier sketch in CA 73-76
Galloway, Margaret C(ecilia) 1915- ... 13-14R
Galloway, Patricia Kay 1945- ... 112
Galloway, Priscilla 1930- ... 112
Gallu, Samuel ... 85-88
See also AITN 2
Gallucci, Robert L(ovis) 1946- ... 61-64
Gallun, Raymond Z(inke) 1911- ... CANR-9
Earlier sketch in CA 65-68
Gallup, Dick 1941- ... 33-36R
Gallup, Donald (Clifford) 1913- ... CANR-11
Earlier sketch in CA 25-28R
Gallup, George (Horace) 1901-1984 ... CANR-13
Earlier sketch in CA 15-16R
Gallwey, W. Timothy 1938- ... CANR-4
Earlier sketch in CA 53-56
Gallwitz, Klaus 1930- Brief entry ... 109
Galouye, Daniel Francis 1920- ... 9-10R
Galper, Harvey 1937- ... 119
Galster, George C(harles) 1948- ... 126
Galston, Arthur William 1920- ... 102
Galsworthy, John 1867-1933 Brief entry ... 104
See also DLB 10, 34
See also TCLC 1
Galt, Alfreda Sill ... 114
Galt, Serena
See Donald, Anabel
Galt, Thomas Franklin, Jr. 1908- ... 7-8R
See also SATA 5
Galt, Tom
See Galt, Thomas Franklin, Jr.
Galton, Francis 1822-1911 Brief entry ... 121

Galton, Lawrence 1913- CANR-6
Earlier sketch in CA 57-60
Galub, Jack 1915- 85-88
Galus, Henry S(tanley) 1923- 7-8R
Galvez de Montalvo, Luis
See Avalle-Arce, Juan Bautista
Galvin, Brendan 1938- CANR-24
Earlier sketches in CA 45-48, CANR-1
See also DLB 5
Galvin, James 1951- CANR-26
Earlier sketch in CA 108
See also CLC 38
Galvin, John R(ogers) 1929- CANR-13
Earlier sketch in CA 23-24R
Galvin, Patrick Joseph 1927- CANR-18
Earlier sketch in CA 102
Galvin, Thomas J(ohn) 1932- CANR-10
Earlier sketch in CA 15-16R
Galway, James 1939- Brief entry 105
Gam, Rita (Elenore) 1927- 45-48
Gambaccini, Peter 1950- 105
Gambill, Edward Lee 1936- 112
Gambino, Thomas D(ominic) 1942- 101
Gamble, Andrew (Michael) 1947- CANR-12
Earlier sketch in CA 69-72
Gamble, Frederick (John) 1904- CAP-1
Earlier sketch in CA 9-10
Gamble, Mary
See Murry, Mary Middleton
Gamble, Michael (Wesley) 1943- 110
Gamble, Sidney David 1890-1968 CAP-1
Earlier sketch in CA 11-12
Gamble, Teri (Susan) Kwal 1947- 110
Gambrell, Herbert (Pickens) 1898- 1R
Gambrill, Eileen 1934- CANR-15
Earlier sketch in CA 89-92
Gambs, John S(ake) 1899- 15-16R
Gamer, Robert E(manuel) 1938- 65-68
Gamerman, Martha 1941- 77-80
See also SATA 15
Gamm, David B(ernard) 1948- 69-72
Gammage, Allen Z. 1917- CANR-11
Earlier sketch in CA 5-6R
Gammage, Bill
See Gammage, William Leonard
Gammage, William Leonard 1942- CANR-10
Earlier sketch in CA 57-60
Gammell, Stephen 1943- SATA-53
Gammell, Susanna Valentine Mitchell
1897(?)-1979 Obituary 85-88
Gammie, John G(lenn) 1929- 121
Gammon, Roland I. 1920-1981 49-52
Obituary 103
Gammon, Samuel Rhea (III) 1924-
Brief entry 112
Gammond, Peter 1925- CANR-14
Earlier sketch in CA 81-84
Gamoran, Mamie (Goldsmith) 1900- CANR-3
Earlier sketch in CA 5-6R
Gamow, George 1904-1968 102
Obituary 93-96
Gamson, William A. 1934- CANR-13
Earlier sketch in CA 33-36R
Gamst, Frederick C(harles) 1936- CANR-11
Earlier sketch in CA 29-32R
Gance, Abel 1889-1981 Obituary 108
Ganci, Dave 1937- 115
Gandalac, Lennard
See Berne, Eric (Lennard)
Gandee, Lee R(auss) 1917- 33-36R
Gandevia, Bryan Harle 1925- CANR-22
Earlier sketch in CA 106
Gandhi, Indira (Priyadarshini Nehru)
1917-1984 Obituary 113
Gandhi, M. K.
See Gandhi, Mohandas Karamchand
Gandhi, Mahatma
See Gandhi, Mohandas Karamchand
Gandhi, Mohandas Karamchand
1869-1948 Brief entry 121
Gandley, Kenneth Royce 1920- CANR-12
Earlier sketch in CA 69-72
Gandolfo, Joe M. 1936- 105
Gandossy, Robert P. 1951- 120
Gangel, Kenneth O(tto) 1935- CANR-17
Earlier sketch in CA 25-28R
Gangemi, Kenneth 1937- 29-32R
Gangewere, Robert J(ay) 1936- 89-92
Ganley, Albert Charles 1918- 13-14R
Ganley, Gladys Dickens 1929- 113
Ganley, Oswald Harold 1929- 112
Ganly, Helen (Mary) 1940- 125
Gann, Ernest Kellogg 1910- CANR-1
Earlier sketch in CA 4R
See also CLC 23
See also AITN 1
Gann, L(ewis) H(enry) 1924- CANR-3
Earlier sketch in CA 7-8R
Gannett, Frank E(rnest) 1876-1957
Brief entry 117
See also DLB 29
Gannett, Lewis Stiles 1891-1966
Obituary 89-92
Gannett, Ruth Chrisman (Arens)
1896-1979 SATA-33
Gannett, Ruth Stiles 1923- 21-22R
See also SATA 3
Gannon, Frank 1952- 126
Gannon, Robert Haines 1931- CANR-4
Earlier sketch in CA 11-12R
See also SATA 8
Gannon, Robert I(gnatius) 1893-1978 CAP-1
Obituary 77-80
Earlier sketch in CA 15-16
Gannon, Thomas M(ichael) 1936- CANR-26
Earlier sketch in CA 109
Gans, Bruce Michael 1951- 81-84
Gans, Eric L. 1941- 33-36R
Gans, Herbert J. 1927- CANR-6
Earlier sketch in CA 1R
Gans, Roma 1894- 77-80
See also SATA 45
Gansberg, Judith M. 1947- 85-88
Ganshof, Francois-Louis 1895- CAP-2
Earlier sketch in CA 19-20
Gans-Ruedin, E(rwin) 1915- 65-68
Ganss, George Edward 1905- 49-52
Gant, Chuck
See Galub, Jack
Gant, Jonathan
See Adams, Clifton
Gant, Matthew
See Hano, Arnold
Gant, Phyllis 1922- 57-60
Gant, Richard
See Freemantle, Brian Harry
Gantner, Neilma 1922- 104
Gantos, Jack
See Gantos, John (Bryan), Jr.
Gantos, John (Bryan), Jr. 1951- CANR-15
Earlier sketch in CA 65-68
See also SATA 20
Gantry, Susan Nadler 1947- 61-64
Gantt, Fred, Jr. 1922-197(?) CANR-3
Earlier sketch in CA 11-12R
Gantt, William Andrew Horsley 1893-1980 102
Obituary 97-100
Gantz, Charlotte Orr 1909- 49-52
Gantzer, Hugh 1931- 61-64
Ganz, Arthur (Frederick) 1928- 49-52
Ganz, David L(awrence) 1951- 105
Ganz, Margaret 1927- 45-48
Ganz, Yaffa 1938- 115
See also SATA 52
Ganzalass, Martin Richard 1941- 33-36R
Ganzel, Dewey Alvin, Jr. 1927- 25-28R
Gapanov, Boris 1934(?)-1972 Obituary 37-40R
Gar, The
See Garfinkel, Charles H.
Gara, Larry 1922- 53-56
Garab, Arra M. 1930- 81-84
Garagiola, Joe
See Garagiola, Joseph Henry
Garagiola, Joseph Henry 1926- 126
Garard, Ira D(ufresne) 1888- 73-76
Garavaglia, Louis A(ubrey) 1940- 119
Garb, Solomon 1920- CANR-9
Earlier sketch in CA 15-16R
Garbarino, Joseph W. 1919- 53-56
Garbarino, Merwyn S(tephens) 77-80
Garber, Emil 1901(?)-1985 Obituary 115
Garber, Eugene K. 1932- CANR-6
Earlier sketch in CA 57-60
Garber, Frederick 1929- 53-56
Garber, Lawrence (Arnold) 1937- 122
Garber, Lee O(rville) 1900- 37-40R
Garbett, Colin (Campbell) 1881- CAP-1
Earlier sketch in CA 9-10
Garbini, Giovanni 1931- CANR-25
Earlier sketches in CA 21-22R, CANR-9
Garbo, Norman 1919- CANR-9
Earlier sketch in CA 17-18R
Garbutt, Bernard 1900- Brief entry 110
See also SATA 31
Garbutt, Janice (D.) Lovoos 124
Garceau, Oliver 1911- CAP-2
Earlier sketch in CA 29-32
Garchik, Morton (Lloyd) 1929- 119
Garcia, Ann O'Neal 1939- 108
Garcia, C(elso-) R(amon) 1921- 118
Garcia, F(laviano) Chris 1940- CANR-4
Earlier sketch in CA 53-56
Garcia, George Haddad
See Haddad-Garcia, George
Garcia, Mario R(amon) 1947- 77-80
Garcia Castaneda, Salvador 1932- 61-64
Garcia Lorca, Federico 1898-1936
Brief entry 104
See also TCLC 1, 7
Garcia Marquez, Gabriel (Jose) 1928- CANR-10
Earlier sketch in CA 33-36R
See also CLC 2, 3, 8, 10, 15, 27, 47
Gard, Janice
See Latham, Jean Lee
Gard, Joyce
See Reeves, Joyce
Gard, Richard A(bbott) 1914- CANR-1
Earlier sketch in CA 1R
Gard, Robert Edward 1910- 85-88
See also SATA 18
Gard, Roger Martin du
See Martin du Gard, Roger
Gard, (Sanford) Wayne 1899-1986 2R
Obituary 120
See also SATA 49
Gardam, Jane 1928- CANR-18
Earlier sketches in CA 49-52, CANR-2
See also SATA 28, 39
See also DLB 14
See also CLC 43
See also CLR 12
Garden, Alexander 1685(?)-1756 DLB-31
Garden, Bruce
See Mackay, James (Alexander)
Garden, Edward J(ames) C(larke) 1930- 25-28R
Garden, Graeme 1943- 107
Garden, John
See Fletcher, H(arry) L(utf) V(erne)
Garden, Nancy 1938- CANR-13
Earlier sketch in CA 33-36R
See also SATA 12
Garden, Robert Hal 1937- 69-72
Gardiner, C(linton) Harvey 1913- CANR-16
Earlier sketches in CA 1R, CANR-1
Gardiner, Charles Wrey 1901-1981
Obituary 103
Gardiner, Dorothy 1894-1979 Obituary 93-96
Gardiner, Glenn Lion 1896-1962 3R
Gardiner, Judy 1922- CANR-9
Earlier sketch in CA 21-22R
Gardiner, Mary Summerfield 1896-1982
Obituary 106
Gardiner, Muriel
See Buttinger, Muriel Gardiner
Gardiner, Patrick (Lancaster) 1922- CANR-5
Earlier sketch in CA 1R
Gardiner, Robert K. A. 1914- 21-22R
Gardiner, Robert W(orthington) 1932- 53-56
Gardiner, Stephen 1925- 97-100
Gardinier, David E(lmer) 1932- 112
Gardiol, Rita M(azzetti) 81-84
Gardner, Alan (Harold) 1925- 21-22R
Gardner, Angela Davis
See Davis-Gardner, Angela
Gardner, Anne
See Shultz, Gladys Denny
Gardner, Beau SATA-50
Gardner, (Robert) Brian 1931- 13-14R
Gardner, Carl 1931- 107
Gardner, D(avid) Bruce 1924- 49-52
Gardner, David P(ierpont) 1933- 21-22R
Gardner, Dic
See Gardner, Richard (M.)
Gardner, Dorothy E. M. 1900-1972 CAP-2
Earlier sketch in CA 23-24
Gardner, E(dward) Clinton 1920- 15-16R
Gardner, Eldon J(ohn) 1909- 41-44R
Gardner, Erle Stanley 1889-1970 CANR-13
Obituary 25-28R
Earlier sketch in CA 7-8R
Gardner, Frank Matthias 1908-1980
Obituary 109
Gardner, G(erald) B(rosseau) 1884-1964
Obituary 112
Gardner, Gerald 1929- CANR-5
Earlier sketch in CA 2R
Gardner, Helen (Louise) 1908- 97-100
Gardner, Herb CLC-44
Gardner, Howard 1943- CANR-9
Earlier sketch in CA 65-68
Gardner, Hugh 1910-1986 Obituary 120
See also SATA 49
Gardner, Hy 1908- 101
Gardner, Isabella (Stewart) 1915-1981 97-100
Obituary 104
Gardner, Jack Irving 1934- 102
Gardner, Jani 1943- 25-28R
Gardner, Jeanne LeMonnier 1925- 19-20R
See also SATA 5
Gardner, Jeffrey
See Fox, G(ardner) F(rancis)
Gardner, John Champlin, Jr. 1933-1982 65-68
Obituary 107
See also SATA 31, 40
See also DLB 2
See also DLBY 82
See also CLC 2, 3, 5, 7, 8, 10, 18, 28, 34
See also AITN 1
Gardner, John E(dward) 1917- 17-18R
Gardner, John Edmund 1926- CANR-15
Earlier sketch in CA 103
See also CLC 30
Gardner, John W(illiam) 1912- CANR-4
Earlier sketch in CA 1R
Gardner, Joseph L. 1933- 29-32R
Gardner, Lawrence
See Brannon, William T.
Gardner, Leonard 1934- Brief entry 111
Gardner, Lewis 1943- 65-68
Gardner, Lloyd C(alvin) 1934- CANR-3
Earlier sketch in CA 11-12R
Gardner, (Alice) Lucille 1913- 69-72
Gardner, Marilyn 101
Gardner, Martin 1914- 73-76
See also SATA 16
Gardner, Mary 1936- 124
Gardner, Mary A(delaide) 1920- 21-22R
Gardner, Nancy Bruff 1915- 15-16R
Gardner, Noel
See Kuttner, Henry
Gardner, Paul 69-72
Gardner, R(ufus) H(allette III) 1918- 33-36R
Gardner, Ralph D(avid) 1923- CANR-6
Earlier sketch in CA 15-16R
Gardner, Richard (M.) 1931- CANR-10
Earlier sketch in CA 21-22R
See also SATA 24
Gardner, Richard A. 1931- 33-36R
See also SATA 13
Gardner, Richard Kent 1928- 69-72
Gardner, Richard N(ewton) 1927- 89-92
Gardner, Riley W(etherell) 1921- 13-14R
Gardner, Robert 1911- 61-64
Gardner, Robert 1929- SATA-43
Gardner, Sheldon 1934- 104
See also SATA 33
Gardner, Virginia (Marberry) 1904- 112
Gardner, Wanda Kirby 1914- 73-76
Gardner, Wayland Downing 1928- 73-76
Gardner, William Earl 1928- CANR-18
Earlier sketches in CA 7-8R, CANR-3
Gardner, William Henry 1902-1969 CAP-1
Earlier sketch in CA 15-16
Gardner, Wynelle B. 1918- 65-68
Gardner-Smith, Percival 1888-1985 CAP-2
Obituary 116
Earlier sketch in CA 17-18
Gardons, S. S.
See Snodgrass, W(illiam) D(e Witt)
Garduk, Harry David 1910(?)-1985
Obituary 116
Gare, Fran
See Mandell, Fran Gare
Gareau, Etienne 1915- 45-48
Gareau, Frederick H(enry) 1923- 5-6R
Gareffa, Peter M(ichael) 1952- 118
Garelick, May 1910- 73-76
See also SATA 19
Garetz, Mark 1953- 112
Garfield, Brian (Wynne) 1939- CANR-6
Earlier sketch in CA 2R
Garfield, Eugene 1925- 114
Garfield, Evelyn Picon 1940- CANR-25
Earlier sketches in CA 57-60, CANR-9
Garfield, James B. 1881-1984 Obituary 112
See also SATA 6, 38
Garfield, Leon 1921- 17-18R
See also SATA 1, 32
See also CLC 12
Garfield, Patricia L(ee) 1934- 85-88
Garfield, Sol L(ouis) 1918- CANR-12
Earlier sketch in CA 29-32R
Garfield, Sydney 1916(?)-1988 Obituary 124
Garfinkel, Alan 1941- CANR-21
Earlier sketch in CA 105
Garfinkel, Bernard Max 1929- CANR-17
Earlier sketch in CA 25-28R
Garfinkel, Charles H. 1939- 112
Garfinkel, Charlie
See Garfinkel, Charles H.
Garfinkel, Herbert 1920- 1R
Garfinkel, Perry 1948- 121
Garfinkle, Adam M. 1951- 112
Garfinkle, Louis (Alan) 1928- Brief entry 112
Garfitt, Roger 1944- CANR-13
Earlier sketch in CA 33-36R
Garforth, Francis William 1917- 9-10R
Garfunkel, Louis X. 1897(?)-1972
Obituary 37-40R
Gargan, Edward T(homas) 1922-
Brief entry 111
Gargan, William (Michael) 1950- 111
Gargan, William Dennis 1905-1979
Obituary 106
Garibaldi, Gerald 1951- 108
Gariepy, Henry 1930- CANR-2
Earlier sketch in CA 49-52
Garioch, Robert Sutherland 1909-1981 103
Garis, Howard R(oger) 1873-1962 73-76
See also SATA 13
See also DLB 22
Garis, Robert (Erwin) 1925- 19-20R
Garitano, Rita 1939- 118
Garlan, Patricia Wallace 1926- 120
Garland, Bennett
See Garfield, Brian (Wynne)
Garland, Charles T(albot) 1910(?)-1976
Obituary 69-72
Garland, George
See Roark, Garland
Garland, (Hannibal) Hamlin 1860-1940
Brief entry 104
See also DLB 12, 71
See also TCLC 3
Garland, Hazel (Barbara) 1913-1988
Obituary 125
Garland, Madge 1900- 25-28R
Garland, Mary 1922- 89-92
Garland, Phyl(lis T.) 1935- 69-72
Garland, Robert (Sandford John) 1947- 120
Garlick, Peter C(yril) 1923- 41-44R
Garlick, Raymond 1926- CANR-4
Earlier sketch in CA 53-56
Garlington, Phil 1943- 81-84
Garlington, Warren K(ing) 1923- 11-12R
Garlinski, Jozef 1914- 108
Garment, Grace R. 1927(?)-1976
Obituary 104
Garmey, Jane 1942- 114
Garmon, William S. 1926- 21-22R
Garms, Walter I(rving, Jr.) 1925- 120
Garn, Edwin Jacob 1932- 107
Garn, Jake
See Garn, Edwin Jacob
Garneau, Michel 1939- DLB-53
Garneau, (Hector de) Saint-Denys
1912-1943 Brief entry 111
See also TCLC 13
Garner, Alan 1934- CANR-15
Earlier sketch in CA 73-76
See also SATA 18
See also CLC 17
Garner, Claud Wilton 1891- 11-12R
Garner, Dwight L. 1913- 25-28R
Garner, Graham
See Rowland, D(onald) S(ydney)
Garner, H(essle) F(ilmore) 1926- 73-76
Garner, Harry Hyman 1910- 17-18R
Garner, Helen 1942- Brief entry 124
Garner, Hugh 1913-1979 69-72
See also DLB 68
See also CLC 13
Garner, Joseph John Saville 1908-1983
Obituary 111
Garner, (Samuel) Paul 1910- 37-40R
Garner, Roberta 1943- 85-88
Garner, Rolf
See Berry, Bryan
Garner, (Lafayette) Ross 1914- 33-36R
Garner, Wendell R(ichard) 1921- CANR-11
Earlier sketch in CA 5-6R
Garner, William 1920- CANR-12
Earlier sketch in CA 29-32R
Garner, William R(obin) 1936- 21-22R
Garnet, Eldon 1946- CANR-9
Earlier sketch in CA 61-64

Garnett, A(rthur) Campbell 1894-1970 ... CANR-2
Earlier sketch in CA 1R
Garnett, Bill
See Garnett, William John
Garnett, Christopher Browne 1906-1975
Obituary ... 61-64
Garnett, David 1892-1981 ... CANR-17
Obituary ... 103
Earlier sketch in CA 5-6R
See also DLB 34
See also CLC 3
Garnett, Eve C. R. ... CANR-2
Earlier sketch in CA 4R
See also SATA 3
Garnett, Henrietta (Catherine Vanessa)
1945- ... 125
Garnett, Richard (Duncan Carey) 1923- ... 7-8R
Garnett, Roger
See Morland, Nigel
Garnett, Tay 1894(?)-1977 Obituary ... 73-76
Garnett, William John 1941- ... 102
Garnham, Nicholas 1937- ... 33-36R
Garofalo, Reebee
See Garofalo, Robert L.
Garofalo, Robert L. 1944- ... 77-80
Garoogian, Andrew 1928- Brief entry ... 113
Garoogian, Rhoda 1933- ... CANR-19
Earlier sketch in CA 102
Garos, Stephanie
See Katz, Steve
Garoyan, Leon 1925- ... CANR-5
Earlier sketch in CA 4R
Garrad, Larch S(ylvia) 1936- ... 61-64
Garrard, Gene
See Garrard, Jeanne Sue
Garrard, J(ohn) G(ordon) 1934-
Brief entry ... 114
Garrard, Jeanne Sue ... 81-84
Garrard, L(ancelot) A(ustin) 1904- ... CAP-1
Earlier sketch in CA 9-10
Garrard, Mary D(ubose) 1937- ... 125
Garraty, John A. 1920- ... CANR-2
Earlier sketch in CA 1R
See also SATA 23
See also DLB 17
Garreau, Joel 1948- ... 101
Garret, Maxwell R. 1917- ... 106
See also SATA 39
Garretson, Lucy Reed 1936- ... 97-100
Garretson, Robert L. 1920- ... 19-20R
Garretson, Victoria Diane 1945- ... 108
See also SATA 44
Garrett, Albert Charles 1915-1983
Obituary ... 109
Garrett, Alfred B. 1906- ... 5-6R
Garrett, Charles 1925-1977 Obituary ... 73-76
Garrett, Clarke 1935- ... 73-76
Garrett, Eileen J(eanette) 1893-1970 ... CAP-2
Earlier sketch in CA 25-28
Garrett, Franklin M(iller) 1906- ... 57-60
Garrett, Garet 1878-1954 Brief entry ... 122
Garrett, George (Palmer) 1929- ... CANR-1
Earlier sketch in CA 2R
See also CAAS 5
See also DLB 2, 5
See also DLBY 83
See also CLC 3, 11
Garrett, Gerald R. 1940- ... CANR-12
Earlier sketch in CA 73-76
Garrett, Gerard 1928- ... 73-76
Garrett, Helen 1895- ... SATA-21
Garrett, Howard 1931- ... 61-64
Garrett, James Leo, Jr. 1925- ... CANR-13
Earlier sketch in CA 33-36R
Garrett, (Ruth) Jane 1914- ... 105
Garrett, Jennifer 1960- ... 122
Garrett, John (Allen) 1920- ... CANR-16
Earlier sketch in CA 33-36R
Garrett, Leonard J(oseph) 1926- ... 17-18R
Garrett, Leslie 1931- ... 19-20R
Garrett, Lillian ... 29-32R
Garrett, Peter K. 1940- ... 25-28R
Garrett, Richard 1920- ... CANR-16
Earlier sketch in CA 81-84
Garrett, Romeo Benjamin 1910- ... 37-40R
Garrett, Stephen A(rmour) 1939- ... 111
Garrett, Thomas M(ichael) 1924- ... CANR-5
Earlier sketch in CA 4R
Garrett, Thomas S(amuel) 1913-1980 ... CANR-3
Earlier sketch in CA 3R
Garrett, Tom
See Garrett, Thomas S(amuel)
Garrett, Truman
See Judd, Margaret Haddican
Garrett, Wendell D(ouglas) 1929- ... 9-10R
Garrett, William 1890-1967 ... CAP-1
Earlier sketch in CA 11-12
Garrigan, Owen (Walter) 1928- ... 23-24R
Garrigue, Jean 1914-1972 ... CANR-20
Obituary ... 37-40R
Earlier sketch in CA 7-8R
See also CLC 2, 8
Garrigue, Sheila 1931- ... 69-72
See also SATA 21
Garrison, Barbara 1931- ... SATA-19
Garrison, Christian (Bascom) 1942- ... 65-68
Garrison, Dee 1934- ... 125
Garrison, Frederick
See Sinclair, Upton (Beall)
Garrison, James (Dale) 1943- ... 61-64
Garrison, Jim (C.) 1921- Brief entry ... 111
Garrison, Joan
See Neubauer, William Arthur
Garrison, Karl C(laudius) 1900- ... 37-40R
Garrison, Omar V. 1913- ... 33-36R
Garrison, Paul 1918- ... 122
Garrison, Phil
See Brandner, Gary
Garrison, R. Benjamin 1926- ... CANR-5
Earlier sketch in CA 13-14R
Garrison, Webb B(lack) 1919- ... CANR-18
Earlier sketches in CA 1R, CANR-2
See also SATA 25
Garrison, William Lloyd 1805-1879 ... DLB-1, 43
See also CDALB 1640-1865
Garrison, Winfred Ernest 1874-1969 ... CANR-6
Earlier sketch in CA 1R
Garrity
See Gerrity, David James
Garrity, Dave
See Gerrity, David James
Garrity, Devin Adair 1905-1981 ... 107
Obituary ... 103
Garrity, Joan Terry 1940- ... 69-72
See also AITN 1
Garrity, Richard (George) 1903- ... 77-80
Garrity, Terry
See Garrity, Joan Terry
Garrod, Rene J(eannette) 1954- ... 120
Garrow, David J(effries) 1953- ... 93-96
Garroway, Dave
See Garroway, David Cunningham
Garroway, David Cunningham 1913-1982
Obituary ... 107
Garry, Charles R. 1909- ... 73-76
Garside, Charles, Jr. 1927-1987 Obituary ... 122
Garside, Roger R(amsay) 1938- ... 107
Garskof, Michele Hoffnung
See Hoffnung, Michele
Garson, Barbara ... 33-36R
Garson, Clee
See Fairman, Paul W.
Garson, G(eorge) David 1943- ... CANR-4
Earlier sketch in CA 53-56
Garson, Helen Sylvia 1925- ... 107
Garson, Noel George 1931- ... 29-32R
Garson, Paul 1946- ... 49-52
Garst, Doris Shannon 1894- ... 4R
See also SATA 1
Garst, John Fredric 1932- ... 45-48
Garst, Robert E(dward) 1900-1980 ... 108
Obituary ... 97-100
Garst, Shannon
See Garst, Doris Shannon
Garstang, Jack
See Garstang, James Gordon
Garstang, James Gordon 1927- ... 13-14R
Garstein, Oskar Bernhard 1924- ... 13-14R
Gart, Murray Joseph 1924- ... 103
Garten, Hugh F(rederick) 1904-1975 ... CANR-3
Earlier sketch in CA 7-8R
Gartenberg, Egon 1911- ... 57-60
Gartenberg, Leo 1906- ... 11-12R
Garth, Will
See Hamilton, Edmond
and Kuttner, Henry
Garthoff, Raymond L(eonard) 1929- ... 7-8R
Garthwaite, Malaby
See Dent, Anthony Austen
Garthwaite, Marion H(ook) 1893- ... 5-6R
See also SATA 7
Gartland, Robert Aldrich 1927- ... 19-20R
Gartman, Louise 1920- ... 17-18R
Gartner, Alan 1935- ... CANR-15
Earlier sketch in CA 33-36R
Gartner, Carol B(licker) 1935- ... 114
Gartner, Chloe (Maria) 1916- ... CANR-20
Earlier sketches in CA 2R, CANR-5
Gartner, Lloyd P. 1927- ... CANR-2
Earlier sketch in CA 1R
Gartner, Michael G(ay) 1938- ... 77-80
Garton, Charles 1926- ... CANR-21
Earlier sketch in CA 45-48
Garton, Janet 1944- ... 114
Garton, Jean Staker 1929- ... 114
Garton, Malinda D(ean) (?)-1976 ... 1R
Obituary ... 103
See also SATA 26
Garton, Nancy Wells 1908- ... 7-8R
Garton, Nina R. 1905- ... CAP-2
Earlier sketch in CA 21-22
Garve, Andrew
See Winterton, Paul
Garver, Richard B(ennett) 1934- ... 33-36R
Garvey, Amy Jacques 1896(?)-1973
Obituary ... 45-48
Garvey, Edward B. 1914- ... 41-44R
Garvey, Gerald (Thomas) 1935-
Brief entry ... 112
Garvey, John 1944- ... CANR-14
Earlier sketch in CA 65-68
Garvey, Marcus (Moziah, Jr.) 1887-1940 ... 124
Brief entry ... 120
See also BW
Garvey, Mona 1934- ... 29-32R
Garvey, Robert 1908-1983 ... 107
Obituary ... 109
Garvey, Terence Willcocks 1915- ... 103
Garvie, A(lexander) F(emister) 1934- ... 73-76
Garvin, Charles D. 1929- ... CANR-6
Earlier sketch in CA 57-60
Garvin, (Hilda) Katharine 1904- ... 7-8R
Garvin, Lawrence 1945- ... 53-56
Garvin, Paul L(ucian) 1919- ... CANR-5
Earlier sketch in CA 15-16R
Garvin, Philip 1947- ... 73-76
Garvin, Richard M. 1934- ... 49-52
Garvin, Thomas Christopher 1943- ... 113
Garvin, Tom
See Garvin, Thomas Christopher
Garvin, William 1922- ... 25-28R
Garwood, Darrell (Nelson) 1909- ... 29-32R
Gary, Romain
See Kacew, Romain
See also CLC 25
Garza, Roberto J(esus) 1934- ... 104
Garzilli, Enrico 1937- ... 41-44R
Gascar, Pierre
See Fournier, Pierre
See also CLC 11
Gascoigne, Bamber 1935- ... CANR-10
Earlier sketch in CA 25-28R
Gascoigne, Marguerite
See Lazarus, Marguerite
Gascon, The
See Miller, F(rederick) W(alter)
G(ascoyne)
Gascoyne, David (Emery) 1916- ... CANR-10
Earlier sketch in CA 65-68
See also DLB 20
See also CLC 45
Gash, Jonathan
See Grant, John
Gash, Norman 1912- ... CANR-1
Earlier sketch in CA 3R
Gaskell, Elizabeth Cleghorn 1810-1865 ... DLB-21
Gaskell, Jane 1941- ... CANR-11
Earlier sketch in CA 7-8R
Gaskell, (John) Philip (Wellesley) 1926- ... CANR-3
Earlier sketch in CA 7-8R
Gaskell, Thomas F. 1916- ... 17-18R
Gaskill, Harold V. 1905-1975 Obituary ... 57-60
Gaskin, Catherine 1929- ... CANR-10
Earlier sketch in CA 65-68
Gaskin, David Edward 1939- ... 69-72
Gasnick, Roy M(ichael) 1933- ... 117
Gasparini, Graziano 1926- ... 41-44R
Gasparotti, Elizabeth Seifert 1897-1983 ... CANR-2
Obituary ... 110
Earlier sketch in CA 3R
Gasper, Louis 1911- ... 13-14R
Gasperini, Jim 1952- ... 122
See also SATA 49
Gasque, W(oodrow) Ward 1939- ... CANR-15
Earlier sketch in CA 65-68
Gass, William H(oward) 1924- ... 19-20R
See also DLB 2
See also CLC 1, 2, 8, 11, 15, 39
Gassan, Arnold 1930- ... 73-76
Gassert, Robert G(eorge) 1921- ... 17-18R
Gasset, Jose Ortega y
See Ortega y Gasset, Jose
Gassier, Pierre 1915- ... 49-52
Gassner, John Waldhorn 1903-1967 ... CANR-3
Obituary ... 25-28R
Earlier sketch in CA 2R
Gassner, Julius S(tephen) 1915- ... 37-40R
Gast, Kelly P.
See Edmondson, G. C.
Gaster, T(heodor) Herzl 1906- ... 73-76
Gastil, Raymond D(uncan) 1931- ... 29-32R
Gastmann, Albert (Lodewijk) 1921- ... 97-100
Gaston, Edwin W(illmer), Jr. 1925- ... CANR-2
Earlier sketch in CA 1R
Gaston, Georg M(eri-) A(kri) 1938- ... 109
Gaston, Jerry (Collins) 1940- ... CANR-1
Earlier sketch in CA 45-48
Gaston, Wilber
See Gibson, Walter B(rown)
Gat, Dimitri V(sevolod) 1936- ... 29-32R
Gatch, Milton McC(ormick, Jr.) 1932- ... 29-32R
Gatell, Frank Otto 1931- ... 9-10R
Gatenby, Greg 1950- ... 97-100
Gatenby, Rosemary 1918- ... CANR-9
Earlier sketch in CA 21-22R
Gater, Dilys 1944- ... 112
See also SATA 41
Gates, Hubert 1913(?)-1980 Obituary ... 101
Gates, Arthur Irving 1890-1972
Obituary ... 37-40R
Gates, David Murray 1921- ... 81-84
Gates, Doris 1901-1987 ... CANR-1
Obituary ... 124
Earlier sketch in CA 4R
See also SATA 1, 34
See also SAAS 1
See also DLB 22
Gates, Frieda 1933- ... 93-96
See also SATA 26
Gates, Henry Louis, Jr. 1950- ... CANR-25
Earlier sketch in CA 109
See also BW
See also DLB 67
Gates, J(eannette) M(cPherson) 1924- ... CANR-7
Earlier sketch in CA 57-60
Gates, Jean Key 1911- ... 33-36R
Gates, John A(lexander) 1898- ... 5-6R
Gates, John D. 1939- ... 89-92
Gates, John Floyd 1915- ... 1R
Gates, Lewis E. 1860-1924 ... DLB-71
Gates, Lillian Francis 1901- ... CAP-2
Earlier sketch in CA 25-28
Gates, Natalie ... 23-24R
Gates, Norman T(immins) 1914- ... 77-80
Gates, Paul W(allace) 1901- ... CANR-2
Earlier sketch in CA 1R
Gates, Robbins L(adew) 1922- ... 15-16R
Gates, William Byram 1917-1975
Obituary ... 61-64
Gatewood, Willard B., Jr. 1931- ... 17-18R
Gathercole, Adrienne Lois
See Kaeppler, Adrienne Lois
Gatheridge, R. Edward
See Wilson, Robert (Edward)
Gathorne-Hardy, Jonathan G. 1933- ... 104
See also SATA 26
Gatley, Jimmy 1931(?)-1985 Obituary ... 115
Gatley, Richard Harry 1936- ... 101
Gatlin, Douglas S. 1928- ... 21-22R
Gatlin, Lila L(ee) 1928- ... 101
Gatner, Elliott S(herman) M(ozian)
1914- ... CANR-3
Earlier sketch in CA 11-12R
Gato, J. A.
See Keller, John E(sten)
Gattegno, Caleb 1911-1988 Obituary ... 126
Gattey, Charles Neilson 1921- ... CANR-20
Earlier sketches in CA 13-14R, CANR-5
Gatti, Arthur Gerard 1942- ... 65-68
Gatti, Daniel Jon 1946- ... 45-48
Gatti, Enzo
See Gatti, Vincenzo
Gatti, Richard DeY 1947- ... 45-48
Gatti, Vincenzo 1942- ... CANR-8
Earlier sketch in CA 61-64
Gattmann, Eric 1925- ... 49-52
Gatty, Juliana Horatia
See Ewing, Juliana (Horatia Gatty)
Gatty, Margaret Scott 1809-1873 ... SATA-27
Gatty, Ronald 1929- ... 85-88
Gatzke, Hans W(ilhelm) 1915-1987 ... CANR-5
Obituary ... 123
Earlier sketch in CA 1R
Gauch, Patricia Lee 1934- ... CANR-9
Earlier sketch in CA 57-60
See also SATA 26
Gauchat, Dorothy 1921- ... 97-100
Gaudet, Frederick J(oseph) 1902-1977 ... 7-8R
Obituary ... 73-76
Gaudiose, Dorothy M(arie) 1920- ... 89-92
Gauer, Harold 1914- ... 15-16R
Gaugh, Harry F. ... 116
Gauld, Charles A(nderson) 1911- ... 15-16R
Gaulden, Ray 1914- ... CANR-8
Earlier sketch in CA 17-18R
Gauldie, Enid 1928- ... CANR-14
Earlier sketch in CA 77-80
Gauldie, (William) Sinclair 1918- ... 33-36R
Gaulle, Charles (Andre Joseph Marie) de
See de Gaulle, Charles (Andre Joseph
Marie)
Gault, Clare 1925- ... 97-100
See also SATA 36
Gault, Frank 1926-1982 ... CANR-11
Earlier sketch in CA 69-72
See also SATA 30, 36
Gault, Mark
See Cournos, John
Gault, William Campbell 1910- ... CANR-16
Earlier sketches in CA 49-52, CANR-1
See also SATA 8
Gaumnitz, Jack E(rwin) 1935- ... 120
Gaumnitz, Walter Herbert 1891-1979
Obituary ... 89-92
Gaunt, Leonard 1921- ... CANR-3
Earlier sketch in CA 7-8R
Gaunt, Michael
See Robertshaw, (James) Denis
Gaunt, Peter
See Eshbach, Lloyd Arthur
Gaunt, William 1900-1980 ... CANR-6
Obituary ... 97-100
Earlier sketch in CA 9-10R
Gauquelin, Michel (Roland) 1928- ... 57-60
Gaur, Albertine 1932- ... 121
Gaus, Gerald F. 1952- ... 112
Gaustad, Edwin Scott 1923- ... CANR-1
Earlier sketch in CA 4R
Gaver, Becky
See Gaver, Rebecca
Gaver, Jack 1906-1974 ... 97-100
Obituary ... 53-56
Gaver, Jessyca (Russell) 1915- ... CANR-9
Earlier sketch in CA 53-56
Gaver, Mary Virginia 1906- ... 1R
Gaver, Rebecca 1952- ... SATA-20
Gavett, J(oseph) William 1921- ... 25-28R
Gavett, Thomas W(illiam) 1932- ... 15-16R
Gavin
See Frost, Gavin
Gavin, Amanda
See Gibson-Jarvie, Clodagh
Gavin, Bill
See Gavin, William S.
Gavin, Catherine ... CANR-1
Earlier sketch in CA 4R
Gavin, Eileen A. 1931- ... 45-48
Gavin, James M(aurice) 1907- ... CAP-1
Earlier sketch in CA 15-16
Gavin, Jamila 1941- ... 110
Gavin, Thomas 1941- ... 85-88
Gavin, Thomas F. 1910- ... 108
Gavin, William
See Houston, Douglas (Norman)
Gavin, William S. 1907(?)-1985 Obituary ... 114
Gavin-Brown, Wilfred A(rthur) 1904- ... CAP-1
Earlier sketch in CA 9-10
Gavron, Daniel 1935- ... CANR-12
Earlier sketch in CA 29-32R
Gavronsky, Serge 1932- ... CANR-9
Earlier sketch in CA 65-68
Gavshon, Arthur L(eslie) 1916- ... 7-8R
Gaw, Walter A. 1904- ... 1R
Gawain, Shakti 1948- ... 93-96
Gawaine, John
See Hamilton-Hill, Donald
Gawron, Jean Mark 1953- ... 103
Gawsworth, John
See Armstrong, Terence Ian Fytton
and Bates, H(erbert) E(rnest)
Gawthrop, Louis C. 1930- ... 81-84
Gaxotte, Pierre 1895-1982 ... 111
Obituary ... 108
Gay, A. Nolder
See Koelsch, William Alvin

Gay, Amelia
See Hogarth, Grace (Weston Allen)
Gay, Carlo T(eofilo) E(berhard) 1913- ... 49-52
Gay, Ebenezer 1696-1787 ... DLB-24
Gay, Francis
See Gee, H(erbert) L(eslie)
Gay, John E(dward) 1942- ... 81-84
Gay, Kathlyn 1930- ... CANR-25
Earlier sketches in CA 21-22R, CANR-8
See also SATA 9
Gay, Peter (Jack) 1923- ... CANR-18
Earlier sketch in CA 13-14R
Gay, Volney P(atrick) 1948- ... 117
Gay, Zhenya 1906-1978 ... 73-76
See also SATA 19
Gaya-Nuno, Juan Antonio 1913-1975 ... 81-84
Gayarre, Charles E. A. 1805-1895 ... DLB-30
Gay-Crosier, Raymond 1937- ... CANR-15
Earlier sketch in CA 41-44R
Gaydos, Michael J. 1940- ... 53-56
Gaye, Carol
See Shann, Renee
Gaye, Marvin (Penze) 1939-1984 Obituary ... 112
See also CLC 26
Gay-Kelly, Doreen 1952- ... 61-64
Gayle, Addison, Jr. 1932- ... CANR-13
Earlier sketch in CA 25-28R
See also BW
Gayle, Emma
See Fairburn, Eleanor
Gayle, Marilyn
See Hoff, Marilyn
Gayle, Stephen H. 1948(?)-1982 Obituary ... 107
Gayles, Anne Richardson 1923- ... 53-56
Gaylin, Willard (M.) 1925- ... CANR-13
Earlier sketch in CA 23-24R
Gaylord, Billy
See Gaylord, William (Gilbert)
Gaylord, Edward King 1873-1974
Obituary ... 89-92
Gaylord, Sherwood Boyd 1914-
Brief entry ... 105
Gaylord, William (Gilbert) 1945-1985 ... 69-72
Obituary ... 118
Gayn, Mark J. 1909-1981 Obituary ... 105
Gayre, G(eorge) R(obert) 1907- ... CANR-4
Earlier sketch in CA 7-8R
Gayre of Gayre, R.
See Gayre, G(eorge) R(obert)
Gayre of Gayre and Nigg, Robert
See Gayre, G(eorge) R(obert)
Gazaway, Rena 1910- ... CAP-2
Earlier sketch in CA 29-32
Gazda, George M(ichael) 1931- ... CANR-13
Earlier sketch in CA 61-64
Gazdanov, Gaito 1903-1971 Obituary ... 104
Gazdanov, Georgii
See Gazdanov, Gaito
Gaze, Richard 1917- ... 4R
Gazell, James A(lbert) 1942- ... 49-52
Gazi, Stephen 1914-1978 ... 45-48
Obituary ... 103
Gazis, Denos C(onstantinos) 1930- ... 57-60
Gazley, John G(erow) 1895- ... 61-64
Gazzaniga, Michael S(aunders) 1939- ... 121
Gdanski, Marek
See Thee, Marek
Geach, Christine 1930- ... CANR-10
Earlier sketch in CA 25-28R
Geach, Patricia Sullivan 1916- ... 29-32R
Geach, Peter Thomas 1916- ... 103
Gealt, Adelheid (Medicus) 1946- ... 114
Geanakoplos, Deno John 1916- ... CANR-2
Earlier sketch in CA 1R
Geaney, Dennis J(oseph) 1914- ... CANR-20
Earlier sketches in CA 7-8R, CANR-5
Gear, C. William 1935- ... 53-56
Gear, Sheila 1942- ... 114
Geare, Michael 1919- ... 117
Geare, Mildred Mahler 1888(?)-1977
Obituary ... 73-76
Gearey, John 1926- ... CANR-23
Earlier sketch in CA 45-48
Gearhart, Sally Miller 1931- ... 57-60
Gearheart, B(ill) R. 1928- ... CANR-9
Earlier sketch in CA 23-24R
Gearing, Catherine 1916- ... 103
Gearing, Fred(erick) O(smond) 1922- ... 29-32R
Gearing-Thomas, G.
See Norwood, Victor G(eorge) C(harles)
Geary, Douglas 1931- ... 13-14R
Geary, Frederick Charles 1886(?)-1975(?)
Obituary ... 104
Geary, Herbert Valentine (Rupert)
1894-1965 ... CAP-1
Earlier sketch in CA 9-10
Geary, Patrick J(oseph) 1948- ... 104
Geary, Roger 1950- ... 123
Geasland, Jack
See Geasland, John Buchanan, Jr.
Geasland, John Buchanan, Jr. 1944- ... 81-84
Gebhard, Anna Laura Munro 1914- ... 7-8R
Gebhard, Bruno (Frederic) 1901- ... 73-76
Gebhard, Paul H(enry) 1917- ... 5-6R
Gebhart, Benjamin 1923- ... 53-56
Gebler, Carlo (Ernest) 1954- Brief entry ... 119
See also CLC 39
Gebler, Ernest 1915- ... CANR-3
Earlier sketch in CA 7-8R
Geck, Francis J(oseph) 1900- ... 73-76
Geckle, George L. 1939- ... 77-80
Gecys, Casimir C. 1904- ... CAP-2
Earlier sketch in CA 19-20
Gedda, George 1941- ... 77-80
Geddes, Charles L(ynn) 1928- ... CANR-2
Earlier sketch in CA 49-52
Geddes, Gary 1940- ... DLB-60
Geddes, Joan Bel 1916- ... 57-60
Geddes, Virgil 1897- ... DLB-4
Geddie, John 1937- ... 69-72
Gedo, John E. 1927- ... 121
Gedo, Mary M(athews) 1925- ... 104
Geduld, Harry M(aurice) 1931- ... CANR-20
Earlier sketches in CA 11-12R, CANR-5
Gedye, George Eric Rowe 1890-1970
Obituary ... 93-96
Gee, H(erbert) L(eslie) 1901-1977 ... 11-12R
Obituary ... 103
See also SATA 26
Gee, Maurice (Gough) 1931- ... 97-100
See also SATA 46
See also CLC 29
Geemis, Joseph (Stephen) 1935- ... 69-72
Geen, Russell Glenn 1932- ... CANR-22
Earlier sketch in CA 104
Geer, Charles 1922- ... 108
See also SATA 32, 42
Geer, Stephen (DuBois) 1930- ... 69-72
Geer, William D. 1906(?)-1976 Obituary ... 104
Geertz, Clifford 1926- ... 33-36R
Geertz, Hildred 1927- ... 77-80
Geeslin, Campbell 1925- ... 102
Geffen, Maxwell Myles 1896-1980
Obituary ... 102
Geffen, Roger 1919- ... 17-18R
Gefvert, Constance J(oanna) 1941- ... 53-56
Gega, Peter C(hristopher) 1924- ... 73-76
Geggus, David Patrick 1949- ... 114
Geherin, David J(ohn) 1943- ... CANR-17
Earlier sketch in CA 101
Gehlbach, Frederick Renner 1935- ... 106
Gehlen, Reinhard 1902-1979 Obituary ... 89-92
Gehman, Betsy Holland 1932- ... 19-20R
Gehman, Christian 1948- ... 119
Gehman, Henry Snyder 1888- ... 13-14R
Gehman, Richard (Boyd) 1921-1972 ... CANR-16
Obituary ... 33-36R
Earlier sketch in CA 3R
Gehr, Mary ... SATA-32
Gehrels, Franz 1922- ... 101
Gehri, Alfred 1896(?)-1972 Obituary ... 33-36R
Gehris, Paul 1934- ... 45-48
Geier, Arnold 1926- ... 4R
Geier, Woodrow A. 1914- ... 21-22R
Geigel Polanco, Vicente 1904-1979
Obituary ... 85-88
Geiger, Don(ald) Jesse 1923- ... 7-8R
Geiger, H(omer) Kent 1922- ... CANR-5
Earlier sketch in CA 1R
Geiger, Louis G. 1913- ... 13-14R
Geiger, Ray(mond Aloysius) 1910- ... 118
See also AITN 1
Geiger, Theodore 1915- Brief entry ... 114
Geipel, Eileen 1932- ... 107
See also SATA 30
Geipel, John 1937- ... CANR-13
Earlier sketch in CA 73-76
Geiringer, Irene (Steckel) 1899-1983
Obituary ... 111
Geiringer, Karl 1899- ... 13-14R
Geis, Darlene Stern ... CANR-5
Earlier sketch in CA 1R
See also SATA 7
Geis, Florence L(indauer) 1933- ... CANR-8
Earlier sketch in CA 57-60
Geis, Gilbert 1925- ... CANR-6
Earlier sketch in CA 11-12R
Geis, Richard E(rwin) 1927- ... 101
Geisel, Helen 1898-1967 Obituary ... 107
See also SATA 26
Geisel, Theodor Seuss 1904- ... CANR-13
Earlier sketch in CA 15-16R
See also SATA 1, 28
See also DLB 61
See also CLR 1
Geiser, Robert L(ee) 1931- ... 97-100
Geisert, Arthur 1941- ... 120
See also SATA 52
Geisinger, David L. 1938- ... 110
Geisler, Norman L(eo) 1932- ... CANR-10
Earlier sketch in CA 25-28R
Geismar, L(udwig) L(eo) 1921- ... CANR-11
Earlier sketch in CA 25-28R
Geismar, Maxwell (David) 1909-1979 ... 4R
Obituary ... 104
Geissman, Erwin William 1920-1980
Obituary ... 101
Geist, Harold 1916- ... CANR-22
Earlier sketches in CA 17-18R, CANR-7
Geist, Kenneth L(ee) 1936- ... 81-84
Geist, Robert John 1912- ... 41-44R
Geist, Roland C. 1896- ... 89-92
Geist, Sidney 1914- Brief entry ... 112
Geist, Valerius 1938- ... CANR-8
Earlier sketch in CA 61-64
Geitgey, Doris A. 1920- ... 53-56
Geiwitz, P(eter) James 1938- ... CANR-11
Earlier sketch in CA 29-32R
Gelatt, Roland 1920-1986 ... 13-14R
Obituary ... 121
Gelb, Alan
See Gelb, Alan Lloyd
Gelb, Alan Lloyd 1950- ... 126
Gelb, Arthur 1924- ... CANR-21
Earlier sketch in CA 3R
Gelb, Barbara (Stone) 1926- ... CANR-21
Earlier sketch in CA 3R
Gelb, Ignace J(ay) 1907-1985 ... 11-12R
Obituary ... 118
Gelb, Joyce 1940- ... 61-64
Gelb, Leslie H(oward) 1937- ... CANR-19
Earlier sketch in CA 103
Gelb, Norman 1929- ... 108
Gelbart, Larry (Simon) 1923- ... 73-76
See also CLC 21
Gelber, Harry G. 1926- ... 25-28R
Gelber, Jack 1932- ... CANR-2
Earlier sketch in CA 4R
See also DLB 7
See also CLC 1, 6, 14
Gelber, Lionel (Morris) 1907- ... 15-16R
Gelber, Steven M(ichael) 1943- ... 53-56
Geld, Ellen Bromfield 1932- ... 37-40R
Geldard, Frank A(rthur) 1904-1984 ... 41-44R
Obituary ... 114
Geldart, William 1936- ... SATA-15
Gelderman, Carol Wettlaufer 1935- ... 105
Gelernt, Jules 1928- ... 23-24R
Gelfand, Elissa D(eborah) 1949- ... 114
Gelfand, Lawrence Emerson 1926- ... CANR-3
Earlier sketch in CA 7-8R
Gelfand, Morris Arthur 1908- ... 49-52
Gelfman, Dick 1947- ... 122
Gelfman, Judith S(chlein) 1937- ... 65-68
Gelfond, Rhoda 1946- ... CANR-12
Earlier sketch in CA 49-52
Gelinas, Paul J. 1911- ... 41-44R
See also SATA 10
Gell, Frank
See Kowet, Don
Gell, Paul (Frederick William) 1928- ... 116
Gellatly, Peter 1923- Brief entry ... 111
Geller, Allen 1941- ... 25-28R
Geller, Bruce 1930-1978 Obituary ... 77-80
Geller, Evelyn
See Gottesfeld, Evelyn
Geller, Uri 1946- ... 69-72
Gellerman, Saul W(illiam) 1929- ... CANR-8
Earlier sketch in CA 5-6R
Gellert, Judith 1925- ... 33-36R
Gellert, Lew
See Wellen, Edward (Paul)
Gelles, Richard J. 1946- ... CANR-22
Earlier sketches in CA 61-64, CANR-8
Gelles, Sandi
See Gelles-Cole, Sandi
Gelles-Cole, Sandi 1949- ... 121
Gelley, Alexander 1933- Brief entry ... 108
Gellhorn, Ernst 1893-1973 ... CAP-2
Earlier sketch in CA 21-22
Gellhorn, Martha Ellis 1908- ... 77-80
See also DLBY 82
See also CLC 14
Gellhorn, Walter 1906- ... 13-14R
Gellinek, Christian 1930- ... CANR-9
Earlier sketch in CA 23-24R
Gellinek, Janis Little
See Solomon, Janis Little
Gellis, Roberta L(eah Jacobs) 1927- ... CANR-22
Earlier sketches in CA 7-8R, CANR-3
Gellman, Estelle Sheila 1941- ... 53-56
Gellman, Irwin F(rederick) 1942- ... CANR-1
Earlier sketch in CA 45-48
Gellner, Ernest (Andre) 1925- ... CANR-22
Earlier sketches in CA 7-8R, CANR-4
Gellner, John 1907- ... 29-32R
Gellrich, Jesse M. 1942- ... 118
Gelman, David Graham 1926- ... 103
Gelman, Mitch(ell Barry) 1962- ... 124
Gelman, Rita Golden 1937- ... CANR-16
Earlier sketch in CA 81-84
See also SATA 51
Gelman, Steve 1934- ... CANR-16
Earlier sketch in CA 25-28R
See also SATA 3
Gelman, Woodrow 1915(?)-1978 Obituary ... 104
Gelman, Woody
See Gelman, Woodrow
Gelmis, Joseph S(tephan) 1935- ... 45-48
Gelperin, L.
See Halpern, Leivick
Gelpi, Albert 1931- ... 33-36R
Gelpi, Barbara Charlesworth 1933- ... 112
Gelpi, Donald L. 1934- ... CANR-7
Earlier sketch in CA 17-18R
Geltman, Max 1906(?)-1984 Obituary ... 112
Gelula, Abner Joseph 1906-1985 Obituary ... 116
Gelven, (Charles) Michael 1937- ... 29-32R
Gelzer, Matthias 1886-1974 ... CAP-2
Earlier sketch in CA 25-28
Gemme, Francis Robert 1934- ... 23-24R
Gemme, Leila Boyle 1942- ... 81-84
Gemmell, Alan Robertson 1913- ... 114
Gemmett, Robert J(ames) 1936- ... 33-36R
Gemmill, Jane Brown 1898- ... 1R
Gemmill, Paul F. 1890(?)-1976 Obituary ... 69-72
Gemming, Elizabeth 1932- ... CANR-9
Earlier sketch in CA 65-68
See also SATA 11
Gems, (Iris) Pam(ela) 1925- ... 107
See also DLB 13
Genauer, Emily 1911- ... 106
Gendel, Evelyn W. 1916(?)-1977 Obituary ... 104
See also SATA 27
Gendell, Murray 1924- ... CANR-5
Earlier sketch in CA 9-10R
Gendlin, Eugene T. 1926- ... 3R
Gendron, George M. 1949- ... 93-96
Gendzier, Irene Lefel 1936- ... 23-24R
Gendzier, Stephen J(ules) 1930- ... 33-36R
General, Lloyd 1924(?)-1986 Obituary ... 119
Genet
See Flanner, Janet
Genet, Jean 1910-1986 ... CANR-18
Earlier sketch in CA 13-14R
See also DLB 72
See also DLBY 86
See also CLC 1, 2, 5, 10, 14, 44, 46
Genevoix, Maurice Charles Louis
1890-1980 Obituary ... 102
See also DLB 65
Geng, Veronica 1941- ... 124
Brief entry ... 119
Genn, Calder
See Gillie, Christopher
Gennaro, Joseph F(rancis), Jr. 1924- ... 101
See also SATA 53
Genne, Elizabeth Steel 1911- Brief entry ... 108
Genne, William H. 1910- ... 17-18R
Genovese, Eugene D(ominick) 1930- ... CANR-10
Earlier sketch in CA 69-72
See also DLB 17
Genoves Tarazaga, Santiago 1923-
Brief entry ... 107
Gensemer, Robert Eugene 1936-
Brief entry ... 110
Genser, Cynthia 1950- ... 69-72
Gensler, Kinereth 1922- ... 116
Genszler, G(eorge) William II 1915- ... CANR-9
Earlier sketch in CA 65-68
Gent, Peter 1942- ... 89-92
See also DLBY 82
See also CLC 29
See also AITN 1
Genthe, Charles V(incent) 1937- ... 29-32R
Gentil, Richard 1917- ... 102
Gentile, Gennaro L. 1946- ... 115
Gentile, Giovanni 1875-1944 Brief entry ... 119
Gentle, Mary 1956- ... 106
See also SATA 48
Gentleman, David (William) 1930- ... CANR-15
Earlier sketch in CA 25-28R
See also SATA 7
Gentles, Frederick (Ray) 1912- ... 29-32R
Gentry, Byron B. 1913- ... 15-16R
Gentry, Curt 1931- ... CANR-5
Earlier sketch in CA 11-12R
Gentry, Dwight L. 1919- ... 1R
Gentry, Marshall Bruce 1953- ... 121
Gentry, Peter
See Newcomb, Kerry
and Schaefer, Frank
Gentz, William Howard 1918- ... 107
Gentzler, J(ennings) Mason 1930- ... 93-96
Geoff
See Dyson, Geoffrey Harry George
Geoffrey, Theodate
See Wayman, Dorothy G.
Geoghegan, Sister Barbara 1902- ... CAP-1
Earlier sketch in CA 11-12
Geoghegan, Thomas Dolan 1917(?)-1987
Obituary ... 121
Georgakas, Dan 1938- ... CANR-22
Earlier sketches in CA 45-48, CANR-1
George, Alexander Lawrence 1920- ... 15-16R
George, Alfred Raymond 1912- ... 108
George, Charles H(illes) 1922- ... 11-12R
George, Chief Dan 1899-1981 ... 110
Obituary ... 108
George, Claude Swanson, Jr. 1920- ... 15-16R
George, Collins Crusor 1909- ... 77-80
George, Dan
See George, Chief Dan
George, David
See Vogenitz, David George
George, E(dgar) Madison 1907-1975 ... 4R
Obituary ... 103
George, Emery E(dward) 1933- ... CANR-16
Earlier sketch in CA 41-44R
George, Eugene
See Chevalier, Paul Eugene George
George, Henry 1839-1897 ... DLB-23
George, Hermon, Jr. 1945- ... 126
George, Jay
See Strachan, J(ohn) George
George, Jean Craighead 1919- ... CANR-25
Earlier sketch in CA 7-8R
See also SATA 2
See also DLB 52
See also CLC 35
See also CLR 1
George, John E(dwin) 1936- ... 53-56
George, John L(othar) 1916- ... 7-8R
See also SATA 2
George, Jonathan
See Burke, John (Frederick)
and Theiner, George (Fredric)
George, M(ary) Dorothy ... CAP-1
Earlier sketch in CA 15-16
George, Malcom F(arris) 1930- ... 57-60
George, Marion
See Benjamin, Claude (Max Edward
Pohlman)
George, Mary Carolyn Hollers Jutson
1930- ... CANR-12
Earlier sketch in CA 73-76
George, Mary Yanaga 1940- ... 29-32R
George, N(orvil) L(ester) 1902- ... CAP-2
Earlier sketch in CA 29-32
George, Nelson 1957- ... 119
George, Peter 1924-1966 Obituary ... 25-28R
George, Richard R(obert) 1943- ... 104
George, Robert Esmonde Gordon
1890-1969 ... CAP-1
Earlier sketch in CA 11-12
George, Rolf 1930- ... 110
George, Roy E(dwin) 1923- ... CANR-14
Earlier sketch in CA 37-40R
George, S(idney) C(harles) 1898- ... 53-56
See also SATA 11
George, Sally 1945- ... 105
George, Sara 1947- ... 65-68
George, Stefan (Anton) 1868-1933
Brief entry ... 104
See also TCLC 2, 14

George, Susan Akers 1934- 77-80
George, W(illiam) Lloyd 1900(?)-1975
Obituary 53-56
See also SATA 30
George, W(illiam) R(ichard) P(hilip)
1912- 69-72
George, Wilfred R(aymond) 1928- 111
George, Wilma
See Crowther, Wilma
George-Brown, George Alfred 1914-1985
Obituary 116
Brief entry 110
Georges, Georges Martin
See Simenon, Georges (Jacques Christian)
Georges, Robert A(ugustus) 1933- 111
Georgescu-Roegen, Nicholas 1906- CANR-9
Earlier sketch in CA 23-24R
Georges-Michel, Michel 1883-1985
Obituary 116
Georgi, Charlotte CANR-17
Earlier sketches in CA 2R, CANR-2
Georgiana, Sister
See Terstegge, Mabel Alice
Georgiou, Constantine 1927- 15-16R
See also SATA 7
Georgiou, Steven Demetre 1948- 101
Georgopoulos, Basil S(pyros) 1926- 73-76
Gephart, William J(ay) 1928- 69-72
Geraci, Philip C. 1929- 77-80
Gerald, J(ames) Edward 1906- 5-6R
Gerald, John Bart 1940- CANR-22
Earlier sketches in CA 7-8R, CANR-7
Gerald, Ziggy
See Zeigerman, Gerald
Gerard, Albert S(tanislas) 1920- CANR-13
Earlier sketch in CA 29-32R
Gerard, Andrew
See Gatti, Arthur Gerard
Gerard, Charles (Franklin) 1914- 29-32R
Gerard, Dave 1909- 53-56
Gerard, David 1923- 77-80
Gerard, Elaine
See Ryder, Eileen
Gerard, Gaston
See Ostergaard, G(eoffrey) N(ielsen)
Gerard, H(arold) B(enjamin) 1923-
Brief entry 110
Gerard, Jane 1930- 2R
Gerard, Jean Ignace Isidore
1803-1847 .... SATA-45
Gerard, Jules B(ernard) 1929- 110
Gerard, Karen (Nina) 1932- 120
Gerard, Louise 1878(?)-1970 Obituary 104
Gerard, Ralph W(aldo) 1900-1974
Obituary 49-52
Gerard-Libois, Jules C. 1923- 33-36R
Geras, Adele (Daphne) 1944- CANR-19
Earlier sketch in CA 97-100
See also SATA 23
Geras, Norman (Myron) 1943- CANR-19
Earlier sketch in CA 102
Gerasimov, Gennadi (Ivanovitch) 1930- 69-72
Gerasimov, Innokentii Petrovich
1905-1985 Obituary 115
Gerasimov, Mikhail Mikhaylovich
1907-1970 Obituary 107
Gerassi, John 1931- CANR-8
Earlier sketch in CA 7-8R
Geraud, (Charles Joseph) Andre
1882-1974 69-72
Obituary 53-56
Gerber, Albert B(enjamin) 1913- 17-18R
Gerber, Barbara (Lin) 1942- 117
Gerber, Bobbie
See Gerber, Barbara (Lin)
Gerber, Dan 1940- 33-36R
Gerber, David A(llison) 1944- 77-80
Gerber, Douglas E(arl) 1933- CANR-15
Earlier sketch in CA 29-32R
Gerber, Ellen W. 1936- Brief entry 107
Gerber, Helmut E. 1920-1981 .... CANR-10
Earlier sketch in CA 23-24R
Gerber, Israel J(oshua) 1918- 77-80
Gerber, John 1907(?)-1981 Obituary 103
Gerber, John C(hristian) 1908- 102
Gerber, Merrill Joan 1938- CANR-26
Earlier sketches in CA 15-16R, CANR-10
Gerber, Philip Leslie 1923- Brief entry 108
Gerber, Rudolph Joseph 1938- 105
Gerber, Sanford E(dwin) 1933- CANR-1
Earlier sketch in CA 49-52
Gerber, William 1908- 37-40R
Gerbers, Teresa 1933- 53-56
Gerbi, Antonello 1904-1976 77-80
Gerbner, George 1919- CANR-1
Earlier sketch in CA 45-48
Gerboth, Walter W(illiam) 1925-1984 ....15-16R
Obituary 112
Gerden, Friedrich Carl
See Greve, Felix Paul (Berthold Friedrich)
Gerdes, Florence Marie 1919- 25-28R
Gerdts, William H. 1929- CANR-10
Earlier sketch in CA 15-16R
Gergely, Tibor 1900-1978 107
Obituary 106
See also SATA 20
Gergen, Kenneth J(ay) 1934- 33-36R
Gerhard, Happy 1920- 57-60
Gerhardi, William Alexander
See Gerhardie, William Alexander
Gerhardie, William Alexander
1895-1977 .... CANR-18
Obituary 73-76
Earlier sketch in CA 25-28R
See also DLB 36
See also CLC 5
Gerhardt, Lydia A(nn) 1934- CANR-10
Earlier sketch in CA 61-64
Gerhart, Gail M. 1943- 85-88
Gerhart, Genevra 1930- 57-60
Gerig, Reginald R(oth) 1919- 57-60
Gerin, Winifred 1901(?)-1981 .... CANR-20
Obituary 104
Earlier sketch in CA 25-28R
Geringer, Laura 1948- 107
See also SATA 29
Gerlach, Barbara A(nn) 1946- 114
Gerlach, Don R(alph) 1932- 9-10R
Gerlach, John 1941- 101
Gerlach, Larry R(euben) 1941- Brief entry .. 109
Gerlach, Luther P(aul) 1930- 41-44R
Gerlach, Russel L(ee) 1939- 89-92
Gerlach, Vernon S(amuel) 1922- 61-64
Gerler, William R(obert) 1917- 65-68
See also SATA 47
Germain, Edward B. 1937- 89-92
Germain, Walter 1889-1962 Obituary 112
German, Donald R(obert) 1931-1986 ... CANR-22
Obituary 119
Earlier sketches in CA 57-60, CANR-7
German, Gene Arlin 1933- 45-48
German, Joan W(olfe) 1933- CANR-22
Earlier sketches in CA 57-60, CANR-7
German, Tony 1924- 97-100
Germane, Gayton E. 1920- CANR-18
Earlier sketches in CA 1R, CANR-2
Germani, Gino 1911-1979 .... CANR-7
Earlier sketch in CA 53-56
Germanicus
See Dunner, Joseph
Germann, A(lbert) C(arl) 1921- 1R
Germann, Richard Wolf 1930- 104
Germano, Peter B. 1913- Brief entry 116
Germany, (Vera) Jo(sephine) CANR-9
Earlier sketch in CA 65-68
Germar, Herb
See Germar, William H(erbert)
Germar, William H(erbert) 1911- 23-24R
Germeshausen, Anna Louise 1906-1968
Obituary 108
Germino, Dante (Lee) 1931- 53-56
Germond, Jack W. 1928- 112
Brief entry 108
Gernert, Eleanor Towles 1928- 37-40R
Gernes, Sonia 1942- 107
Gernsback, Hugo 1884-1967 Obituary 93-96
See also DLB 8
Gernsheim, Helmut 1913- CANR-22
Earlier sketches in CA 7-8R, CANR-5
Gernstein, Mordicai Brief entry 117
See also SATA 36
Geroely, Kalman
See Gabel, Joseph
Gerold, Karl 1906-1973 Obituary 41-44R
Gerold, William 1932- 17-18R
Geroly, Kalman
See Gabel, Joseph
Gerosa, Guido 1933- 73-76
Gerould, Daniel C. 1928- 29-32R
Gerow, Edwin 1931- 53-56
Gerow, Josh(ua R.) 1941- 103
Gerrard, Jean 1933- 115
See also SATA 51
Gerrard, Roy 1935- 110
See also SATA 45, 47
Gerrietts, John 1912- 77-80
Gerring, Ray H. 1926- 13-14R
Gerrish, B(rian) A(lbert) 1931- CANR-4
Earlier sketch in CA 5-6R
Gerrity, David James 1923- CANR-4
Earlier sketch in CA 2R
Gerrold, David 1944- 93-96
See also DLB 8
Gerschenkron, Alexander (Pavlovich)
1904-1978 .... CANR-1
Earlier sketch in CA 45-48
Gersh, Harry 1912- CANR-1
Earlier sketch in CA 4R
Gershator, David 1937- 115
Gershator, Phillis 1942- 102
Gershen, Martin 1924-1985 ....33-36R
Obituary 114
Gershenson, Daniel E(noch) 1935- 5-6R
Gershman, Herbert S. 1926-1971 .... CAP-2
Obituary 33-36R
Earlier sketch in CA 25-28
Gershon, Karen
See Tripp, Karen
Gershoy, Leo 1897-1975 .... CAP-1
Obituary 57-60
Earlier sketch in CA 13-14
Gershwin, Ira 1896-1983 Obituary 110
Brief entry 108
Gerson, Corinne 1927- CANR-25
Earlier sketch in CA 93-96
See also SATA 37
Gerson, Louis Leib 1921- 19-20R
Gerson, Noel Bertram 1914- 81-84
See also SATA 22
Gerson, Walter (Max) 1935- 41-44R
Gerson, Wolfgang 1916- 33-36R
Gersoni, Diane 1947- 53-56
Gersoni-Stavn, Diane
See Gersoni, Diane
Gerstad, John (Leif) 1924-1981 103
Obituary 105
Gerstein, Arnold A. 1940- 124
Gerstein, Linda (Groves) 1938- Brief entry .. 110
Gerstein, Mordicai 1935- SATA-47
Gerstenberger, Donna Lorine 1929- CANR-4
Earlier sketch in CA 7-8R
Gerster, Georg (Anton) 1928- 37-40R
Gerster, Patrick G(eorge) 1942- 57-60
Gerstine, Jack
See Gerstine, John
Gerstine, John 1915- 7-8R
Gerstl, Joel E. 1932- 21-22R
Gerstle, Kurt H(erman) 1923- 53-56
Gerstner, Edna Suckau 1914- 2R
Gerstner, John H(enry) 1914- CANR-2
Earlier sketch in CA 1R
Gert, Bernard 1934- 29-32R
Gerteiny, Alfred G(eorges) 1930- 21-22R
Gerteis, Louis S(axton) 1942- 45-48
Gerth, Donald Rogers 1928- 45-48
Gerth, Hans Heinrich 1908-1978
Obituary 81-84
Gertler, Menard M. 1919- 11-12R
Gertler, T. 121
Brief entry 116
See also CLC 34
Gertman, Samuel 1915- 1R
Gertz, Elmer 1906- CANR-11
Earlier sketch in CA 15-16R
Gertz, Theodore G(erson) 1936- 115
Gertzog, Irwin N(orman) 1933- 29-32R
Gerulaitis, Leonardas Vytautas 1928- 77-80
Gervais, C(harles) H(enry) 1946- 97-100
Gervais, Marty
See Gervais, C(harles) H(enry)
Gervasi, Frank H(enry) 1908- CAP-1
Earlier sketch in CA 15-16
Gerwig, Anna Mary (Gerwig) 1907- CAP-2
Earlier sketch in CA 17-18
Gerwin, Donald 1937- 25-28R
Gerzon, Mark 81-84
Gesch, Dorothy K(atherine) 1923- 29-32R
Gesch, Roy G(eorge) 1920- 23-24R
Geschickter, Charles F(reeborn)
1901-1987 Obituary 123
Geschwender, James A(rthur) 1933- 41-44R
Gesell, Arnold Lucius 1880-1961 Obituary .. 116
Geserick, June
See Donahue, June (Geserick)
Gesner, Carol 1922- 29-32R
Gesner, Clark 1938- 109
See also SATA 40
Gesner, Elsie Miller 1919- 17-18R
Gessert, Kate Rogers 1948- 113
Gessner, Lynne 1919- CANR-10
Earlier sketch in CA 25-28R
See also SATA 16
Geston, Mark S(ymington) 1946- 102
See also DLB 8
Gethers, Peter 1953- 103
Gething, Thomas W(ilson) 1939- 41-44R
Getlein, Dorothy Woolen 1921- 9-10R
Getlein, Frank 1921- CANR-6
Earlier sketch in CA 9-10R
Gettel, Ronald 1931- 112
Gettens, Rutherford John 1900(?)-1974
Obituary 49-52
Gettings, Eunice J. 1901(?)-1978
Obituary 81-84
Gettings, Fred 1937- 123
Gettleman, Marvin E. 1933- 37-40R
Gettleman, Susan
See Braiman, Susan
Getty, Gerald W(inkler) 1913- 57-60
Getty, Hilda F. 1938- 61-64
Getty, J(ean) Paul 1892-1976 69-72
Obituary 65-68
Getty, Mary Ann 1943- 114
Getz, Gene A(rnold) 1932- CANR-12
Earlier sketch in CA 29-32R
Getz, Malcolm 1945- CANR-18
Earlier sketch in CA 101
Getz, Oscar 1897-1983 Obituary 110
Getzels, Jacob Warren 1912- 45-48
Getzoff, Carole 1943- 61-64
Geubtner, Virginia Reidel
See Reidel-Geubtner, Virginia
Gevirtz, Don L(ee) 1928- 121
Gevirtz, Eliezer 1950- 121
See also SATA 49
Gevirtz, Stanley 1929-1988 Obituary 126
Brief entry 109
Gewe, Raddory
See Gorey, Edward (St. John)
Gewecke, Clifford George, Jr. 1932- 23-24R
Gewehr, Wolf M(ax) 1939- CANR-1
Earlier sketch in CA 45-48
Gewirth, Alan 1912- Brief entry 107
Gewirtz, Jacob L(eon) 1924- 45-48
Gewirtz, Leonard Benjamin 1918- 1R
Geyer, Alan (Francis) 1931- 9-10R
Geyer, Georgie Anne 1935- CANR-17
Earlier sketch in CA 29-32R
Geyl, Pieter (Catharinus Arie) 1887-1966 ... 103
Obituary 89-92
Geyman, John P. 1931- CANR-14
Earlier sketch in CA 37-40R
Gezi, Kal
See Gezi, Kalil I(smail)
Gezi, Kalil I(smail) 1930- CANR-17
Earlier sketch in CA 25-28R
Ghadimi, Hossein 1922- 61-64
Ghai, Dharam P. 1936- CANR-15
Earlier sketch in CA 21-22R
Gheddo, Piero 1929- CANR-15
Earlier sketch in CA 73-76
Ghelardi, Robert (Anthony) 1939- 69-72
Ghelderode, Michel de 1898-1962 85-88
See also CLC 6, 11
Gheorghiu, (Constantin) Virgil 1916- 33-36R
Gherity, James Arthur 1929- 17-18R
Ghigna, Charles 1946- 77-80
Ghine, Wunnakyawhtin U Ohn
See Maurice, David (John Kerr)
Ghiotto, Renato 1923- 49-52
Ghiradella, Robert 1934- 114
Ghiselin, Brewster 1903- CANR-13
Earlier sketch in CA 13-14R
See also CLC 23
Ghiselin, Michael T(enant) 1939- 49-52
Ghiselli, Edwin E(rnest) 1907- 37-40R
Ghnassia, Maurice (Jean-Henri) 1920- 49-52
Ghose, Amal 1929- 106
Ghose, Sri Chinmoy Kumar
See Chinmoy, Sri
Ghose, Sudhin(dra) N(ath) 1899- 7-8R
Ghose, Zulfikar 1935- 65-68
See also CLC 42
Ghosh, Amitav 1956- CLC-44
Ghosh, Arun Kumar 1930- CANR-26
Earlier sketches in CA 23-24R, CANR-10
Ghosh, Dipali 1945- 124
Ghosh, Jyotis Chandra 1904(?)-1975
Obituary 57-60
Ghosh, Tapan 1928- 53-56
Ghougassian, Joseph P(eter) 1944- 49-52
Ghurye, G(ovind) S(adashiv) 1893- CANR-3
Earlier sketch in CA 5-6R
Giacosa, Giuseppe 1847-1906 Brief entry ... 104
See also TCLC 7
Giacumakis, George, Jr. 1937- 41-44R
Giallombardo, Rose (Mary) 1925- 61-64
Giamatti, A(ngelo) Bartlett 1938- 97-100
Giamatti, Valentine 1911-1982 Obituary 106
Gianakaris, C(onstantine) J(ohn) 1934- ...25-28R
Giannaris, George (B.) 1936- CANR-22
Earlier sketches in CA 45-48, CANR-2
Giannestras, Nicholas James 1909-1978
Obituary 105
Giannetti, Louis D. 1937- 33-36R
Giannone, Richard 1934- 21-22R
Giannoni, Carlo Borromeo 1939- 41-44R
Giap Vo Nguyen
See Vo Nguyen Giap
Giardina, Anthony 1950- 118
Giardina, Denise 1951- 119
Giauque, William Francis 1895-1982
Obituary 106
Gibaldi, Joseph 1942- CANR-15
Earlier sketch in CA 89-92
Gibans, Nina Freedlander 1932- 116
Gibb, Hamilton (Alexander Rosskeen)
1895-1971 .... CANR-6
Obituary 33-36R
Earlier sketch in CA 4R
Gibb, Jack (Rex) 1914- 17-18R
Gibb, Lee
See Deghy, Guy (Stephen)
and Waterhouse, Keith (Spencer)
Gibbard, Graham S(tewart) 1942- 53-56
Gibbens, T(revor) C(harles) N(oel)
1912-1983 Obituary 111
Gibberd, Frederick 1908-1984 Obituary 111
Gibbon, Lewis Grassic
See Mitchell, James Leslie
See also TCLC 4
Gibbon, (William) Monk 1896-1987 69-72
Obituary 124
Gibbon, Vivian 1917- 103
Gibbons, Barbara (Halloran) 1934- CANR-10
Earlier sketch in CA 61-64
Gibbons, Bob
See Gibbons, Robert
Gibbons, Brian 1938- CANR-11
Earlier sketch in CA 25-28R
Gibbons, Don C(ary) 1926- Brief entry 110
Gibbons, Euell (Theophilus) 1911-1975 ... CAP-2
Obituary 61-64
Earlier sketch in CA 23-24
See also AITN 1
Gibbons, Faye 1938- 109
Gibbons, Felton L(ewis) 1929- 124
Gibbons, (Raphael) Floyd (Phillips)
1887-1939 Brief entry 113
See also DLB 25
Gibbons, Gail 1944- CANR-12
Earlier sketch in CA 69-72
See also SATA 23
See also CLR 8
Gibbons, Helen Bay 1921- 17-18R
Gibbons, J. Whitfield 1939- 114
Gibbons, John William 1907-1983
Obituary 109
Gibbons, Kaye 1960- CLC-50
Gibbons, Maurice 1931- 89-92
Gibbons, Reginald 1947- CANR-18
Earlier sketch in CA 97-100
Gibbons, Robert 1949- 116
Gibbons, Stella 1902- 13-14R
Gibbons, Whit
See Gibbons, J. Whitfield
Gibbons, William DLB-73
Gibbs, A(twood) James 1922- 19-20R
Gibbs, A(nthony) M(atthews) 1933- 33-36R
Gibbs, Alonzo (Lawrence) 1915- CANR-5
Earlier sketch in CA 5-6R
See also SATA 5
Gibbs, Anthony 1902-1975 .... CAP-2
Earlier sketch in CA 29-32
Gibbs, Barbara 1912- 25-28R
Gibbs, C. Earl 1935- 69-72
Gibbs, Esther 1904- 57-60
Gibbs, George 1870-1942 Brief entry 120
Gibbs, Henry
See Rumbold-Gibbs, Henry St. John Clair
Gibbs, Jack P(orter) 1927- 122
Brief entry 118
Gibbs, James A.
See Gibbs, James Atwood
Gibbs, James Atwood 1922- CANR-11
Earlier sketch in CA 69-72

Gibbs, Jim
See Gibbs, James Atwood
Gibbs, Joanifer 1947- 57-60
Gibbs, John G(amble) 1930- 41-44R
Gibbs, Mark 1920- 7-8R
Gibbs, Mary Ann
See Bidwell, Marjory Elizabeth Sarah
Gibbs, (Cecilia) May 1877-1969 Obituary ... 104
See also SATA 27
Gibbs, Paul T(homas) 1897- 11-12R
Gibbs, Peter Bawtree 1903- 2R
Gibbs, Philip (Hamilton) 1877-1962
Obituary 89-92
Gibbs, Rafe
See Gibbs, Raphael Sanford
Gibbs, Raphael Sanford 1912- 7-8R
Gibbs, Tony
See Gibbs, Wolcott, Jr.
Gibbs, William E. 1936-19(?) CAP-2
Earlier sketch in CA 21-22
Gibbs, Wolcott, Jr. 1935- 85-88
See also SATA 40
Gibbs-Smith, Charles Harvard
1909-1981 ..... CANR-4
Obituary 108
Earlier sketch in CA 11-12R
Gibbs-Wilson, Kathryn (Beatrice)
1930- CANR-10
Earlier sketch in CA 65-68
Gibby, Robert Gwyn 1916- 13-14R
Giberson, Dorothy (Dodds) CANR-2
Earlier sketch in CA 3R
Gibian, George 1924- CANR-19
Earlier sketches in CA 1R, CANR-5
Giblin, Charles Homer 1928- 41-44R
Giblin, James Cross 1933- CANR-24
Earlier sketch in CA 106
See also SATA 33
Gibney, Frank (Bray) 1924- CANR-11
Earlier sketch in CA 69-72
Gibney, Harriet
See Harvey, Harriet
Gibney, Sheridan 1904(?)-1988 Obituary ... 125
Giboire, Clive (John) 1945- 118
Gibran, Jean 1933- 69-72
Gibran, Kahlil 1883-1931 Brief entry 104
See also TCLC 1, 9
Gibson, Alexander Dunnett 1901-1978
Obituary 77-80
Gibson, Anne (E.) 1954- 125
Gibson, Arrell Morgan 1921- 41-44R
Gibson, Charles (Edmund) 1916- 7-8R
Gibson, Charles 1920- 21-22R
Gibson, Charline 1937- 69-72
Gibson, D. Parke 1930-1979 93-96
Obituary 85-88
Gibson, Derlyne 1936- 23-24R
Gibson, Donald B. 1933- 25-28R
See also BW
Gibson, E(rnest) Dana 1906- 29-32R
Gibson, E(dward) Lawrence 1935- 93-96
Gibson, Elizabeth 1949- 118
Gibson, Elsie (Edith) 1907- 61-64
Gibson, Eva 1939- 114
Gibson, Evan K(eith) 1909- 105
Gibson, Frank K. 1924- 37-40R
Gibson, George H(orner) 1932-
Brief entry 114
Gibson, Gerald Don 1938- 104
Gibson, Gertrude Hevener 1906- 5-6R
Gibson, Gifford Guy 1943- 77-80
Gibson, Graeme 1934- DLB-53
Gibson, H(amilton) B(ertie) 1914- 102
Gibson, Harry Clark
See Hubler, Richard Gibson
Gibson, James (Charles) 1919- 117
Gibson, James C.
See Gibson, James (Charles)
Gibson, James J(erome) 1904- 85-88
Gibson, James L(awrence) 1935- CANR-8
Earlier sketch in CA 5-6R
Gibson, James W(illiam) 1932- 41-44R
Gibson, Janice T(horne) 1934- 41-44R
Gibson, John 1907- 33-36R
Gibson, John M(endinghall) 1899-19(?) 2R
Gibson, Josephine
See Hine, Al(fred Blakelee)
and Hine, Sesyle Joslin
Gibson, Karon Rose (White) 1946- 105
Gibson, Maralee G. 1924- 17-18R
Gibson, Margaret 1944- 77-80
Gibson, Margaret 1948- 103
Gibson, Miles 1947- CANR-18
Earlier sketch in CA 102
Gibson, Morgan 1929- CANR-14
Earlier sketch in CA 25-28R
Gibson, (William) Morris(on) 1916- 117
Gibson, Nevin H(erman) 1915- 49-52
Gibson, Raymond E(ugene) 1924- 23-24R
Gibson, Reginald Walter 1901- CAP-1
Earlier sketch in CA 13-14
Gibson, Richard (Thomas) 1931- 41-44R
Gibson, Robert (Donald Davidson) 1927- ..65-68
Gibson, Robert L(eone) 1927- 121
Gibson, Robert William, Jr. 1923- 107
Gibson, Ronald George 1909- 109
Gibson, Rosemary
See Newell, Rosemary
Gibson, Shirley 1927- 103
Gibson, (William) Walker 1919- CANR-1
Earlier sketch in CA 1R
Gibson, Walter B(rown) 1897-1985 110
Obituary 118
Brief entry 108
Gibson, Walter Samuel 1932- 102
Gibson, Wilfrid Wilson 1878-1962
Obituary 113
See also DLB 19
Gibson, William 1914- CANR-9
Earlier sketch in CA 9-10R
See also DLB 7
See also CLC 23
Gibson, William (Ford) 1948- Brief entry ... 126
See also CLC 39
Gibson, William Carleton 1913- 19-20R
Gibson, William E(dward) 1944- 33-36R
Gibson, William M(erriam) 1912- 121
Gibson-Jarvie, Clodagh 1923- 105
Gichon, Mordechai 1922- 89-92
Gicovate, Bernard 1922- 37-40R
Gidal, Nachum
See Gidal, Tim N(achum)
Gidal, Peter 1946- 103
Gidal, Sonia (Epstein) 1922- CANR-14
Earlier sketch in CA 7-8R
See also SATA 2
Gidal, Tim N(achum) 1909- CANR-20
Earlier sketches in CA 5-6R, CANR-14
See also SATA 2
Gidalewitsch, Nachum
See Gidal, Tim N(achum)
Giddings, James Louis 1909-1964 ..... CAP-1
Earlier sketch in CA 11-12
Giddings, John Calvin 1930- 109
Giddings, Paula 1948- 125
See also BW
Giddings, Robert (Lindsay) 1935- CANR-9
Earlier sketch in CA 23-24R
Giddins, Gary 1948- CANR-13
Earlier sketch in CA 77-80
Giddy, Ian H. 1948- 114
Gide, Andre (Paul Guillaume) 1869-1951 ... 124
Brief entry 104
See also DLB 65
See also TCLC 5, 12
Gideonse, Harry David 1901-1985
Obituary 115
Gidley, Charles
See Wheeler, (Charles) Gidley
Gidley, (Gustavus) M(ick) 1941- 102
Gidlow, Elsa 1898-1986 77-80
Obituary 119
Gidney, James B. 1914- 45-48
Giedion, Sigfried 1888(?)-1968 Obituary 116
Giegling, John A(llan) 1935- 29-32R
See also SATA 17
Giele, Janet Z(ollinger) 1934- 114
Gielgud, Gwen Bagni
See Dubov, Gwen Bagni
Gielgud, (Arthur) John 1904- Brief entry ... 111
Gielgud, Val (Henry) 1900- CANR-5
Earlier sketch in CA 9-10R
Giere, Ronald N(elson) 1938- CANR-4
Earlier sketch in CA 49-52
Giergielewicz, Mieczyslaw F. 1901-1983 .. CAP-2
Obituary 113
Earlier sketch in CA 25-28
Gierow, Karl Ragnar (Knut) 1904-1982
Obituary 108
Giersch, Julius
See Arnade, Charles W(olfgang)
Giertz, Bo H(arald) 1905- CANR-9
Earlier sketch in CA 23-24R
Gies, Frances 1915- CANR-9
Earlier sketch in CA 25-28R
Gies, Joseph (Cornelius) 1916- CANR-9
Earlier sketch in CA 7-8R
Gies, Thomas G(eorge) 1921- 33-36R
Giesbrecht, Martin Gerhard 1933- CANR-4
Earlier sketch in CA 53-56
Giesey, Ralph E(dwin) 1923- 25-28R
Giessler, Phillip Bruce 1938- CANR-8
Earlier sketch in CA 61-64
Giesy, J(ohn) U(lrich) 1877-1947
Brief entry 112
Giff, Patricia Reilly 1935- CANR-18
Earlier sketch in CA 101
See also SATA 33
Giffen, Daniel H. 1938- 107
Giffin, Frederick Charles 1938- 41-44R
Giffin, James Manning 1935- 105
Giffin, Sidney F. 1907-1977 Obituary 73-76
Gifford, Barry (Colby) 1946- CANR-9
Earlier sketch in CA 65-68
See also CLC 34
Gifford, Denis 1927- CANR-18
Earlier sketch in CA 101
Gifford, Don (Creighton) 1919- 53-56
Gifford, Edward S(tewart), Jr. 1907- CAP-2
Earlier sketch in CA 19-20
Gifford, Francis Newton
See Gifford, Frank
Gifford, Frank 1930- Brief entry 109
Gifford, Griselda 1931- CANR-24
Earlier sketch in CA 107
See also SATA 42
Gifford, (Charles) Henry 1913- 17-18R
Gifford, James Fergus, Jr. 1940- 57-60
Gifford, Prosser 1929- CANR-18
Earlier sketch in CA 101
Gifford, Terry 1946- CANR-24
Earlier sketch in CA 106
Gifford, Thomas (Eugene) 1937- 77-80
Gifford-Jones, W.
See Walker, Kenneth Francis
Giggal, Kenneth 1927- CANR-20
Earlier sketch in CA 104
Giglio, Ernest D(avid) 1931- 33-36R
Giguere, Diane 1937- 25-28R
See also DLB 53
Giguere, Roland 1929- DLB-60
Gih, Andrew 1901- 23-24R
Gil, David G(eorg) 1924- CANR-12
Earlier sketch in CA 29-32R
Gil, Federico Guillermo 1915- CANR-2
Earlier sketch in CA 1R
Gilb, Corinne Lathrop 1925- 17-18R
Gilbar, Steven 1941- 106
Gilbert, Alan Graham 1944- 112
Gilbert, Allan H. 1888- 9-10R
Gilbert, Amy M(argaret) 1895- 49-52
Gilbert, Ann
See Taylor, Ann
Gilbert, Anna
See Lazarus, Marguerite
Gilbert, Anne 1927- CANR-7
Earlier sketch in CA 57-60
Gilbert, Anthony
See Malleson, Lucy Beatrice
Gilbert, Arlene E(lsie) 1934- 49-52
Gilbert, Arthur 1926-1976 ..... CANR-9
Earlier sketch in CA 19-20R
Gilbert, Ben W(illiam) 1918- 45-48
Gilbert, Benjamin Franklin 1918- CANR-22
Earlier sketches in CA 17-18R, CANR-7
Gilbert, Bentley B(rinkerhoff) 1924- 25-28R
Gilbert, Bill 1931- 105
Gilbert, Celia 1932- 115
Gilbert, Charles 1913- 41-44R
Gilbert, Christine B(ell) 1909- 103
Gilbert, Christopher 1949- 120
See also BW
Gilbert, Creighton (Eddy) 1924- CANR-15
Earlier sketch in CA 33-36R
Gilbert, David T(hompson) 1953- 106
Gilbert, Doris Wilcox 17-18R
Gilbert, Doug 1938-1979 Obituary 104
Gilbert, Douglas 1942- 53-56
Gilbert, Douglas L. 1925- 15-16R
Gilbert, Edmund W(illiam) 1900-1973 65-68
Gilbert, Edwin 1907-1976 77-80
Obituary 69-72
Gilbert, Felix 1905- Brief entry 106
Gilbert, George 1922- 69-72
Gilbert, Glenn Gordon 1936- CANR-13
Earlier sketch in CA 33-36R
Gilbert, Gordon Allan 1942- 103
Gilbert, Gorman 1943- 114
Gilbert, Gustave M. 1911-1977 Obituary ...69-72
Gilbert, Harriett 1948- CANR-9
Earlier sketch in CA 57-60
See also SATA 30
Gilbert, Harry 1946- 106
Gilbert, Herman Cromwell 1923- CANR-12
Earlier sketch in CA 29-32R
Gilbert, Jack 1925- 123
Brief entry 116
Gilbert, Jack G(lenn) 1934- 25-28R
Gilbert, James 1935- 29-32R
Gilbert, Jarvey 1917- 33-36R
Gilbert, (Agnes) Joan (Sewell) 1931- 21-22R
See also SATA 10
Gilbert, John (Raphael) 1926- 107
See also SATA 36
Gilbert, Julie Goldsmith
See Daniel, Julie Goldsmith
Gilbert, Manu
See West, Joyce (Tarlton)
Gilbert, Marilyn B(ender) 1926- CANR-1
Earlier sketch in CA 4R
Gilbert, Martin 1936- 11-12R
Gilbert, Michael (Francis) 1912- CANR-1
Earlier sketch in CA 1R
Gilbert, Milton 1909(?)-1979 Obituary 93-96
Gilbert, Miriam
See Presberg, Miriam Goldstein
Gilbert, Nan
See Gilbertson, Mildred Geiger
Gilbert, Neil 1940- 77-80
Gilbert, R(obert) A(ndrew) 1942- 124
Gilbert, Robert E(mile) 1939- 53-56
Gilbert, Rod(rigue Gabriel) 1941-
Brief entry 109
Gilbert, Russell Wieder 1905-1985 45-48
Obituary 115
Gilbert, Ruth Gallard Ainsworth 1908- ... CANR-4
Earlier sketch in CA 9-10R
Gilbert, S(tuart) R(eid) 1948- 101
Gilbert, Sandra M(ortola) 1936- CANR-14
Earlier sketch in CA 41-44R
Gilbert, Sara (Dulaney) 1943- CANR-6
Earlier sketch in CA 57-60
See also SATA 11
Gilbert, Stephen 1912- 25-28R
Gilbert, W(illiam) S(chwenck) 1836-1911
Brief entry 104
See also SATA 36
See also TCLC 3
Gilbert, Willie 1916- 45-48
Gilbert, (Lerman) Zack 1925- 65-68
Gilberts, Helen 1909- 29-32R
Gilbertson, Merrill Thomas 1911- 11-12R
Gilbertson, Mildred Geiger 1908- CANR-2
Earlier sketch in CA 5-6R
See also SATA 2
Gilbo, Patrick F(rancis) 1937- 107
Gilboa, Amir 1917-1984 Obituary 114
Gilboa, Yehoshua A. 1918- 29-32R
Gilborn, Alice 1936- 69-72
Gilbreath, Alice 1921- CANR-25
Earlier sketches in CA 25-28R, CANR-10
See also SATA 12
Gilbreath, (Larry) Kent 1945- 45-48
Gilbreth, Frank B., Jr. 1911- 9-10R
See also SATA 2
See also CLC 17
Gilbreth, Lillian Moller 1878-1972
Obituary 33-36R
Gilcher, Edwin L. 1909- 29-32R
Gilchrist, Agnes A(ddison) 1907-1976
Obituary 65-68
Gilchrist, Alan W. 1913- 21-22R
Gilchrist, Andrew (Graham) 1910- CANR-26
Earlier sketch in CA 109
Gilchrist, Ellen 1935- 116
Brief entry 113
See also CLC 34, 48
Gilchrist, J(ohn Thomas) 1927- 25-28R
Gilday, Robert M. 1925(?)-1980 Obituary ... 101
Gilden, Bert 1915(?)-1971 ..... CAP-1
Obituary 29-32R
Earlier sketch in CA 11-12
Gilden, K.B.
See Gilden, Bert
and Gilden, Katya
Gilden, Katya 11-12R
Gilder, Eric 1911- CANR-15
Earlier sketch in CA 89-92
Gilder, George F. 1939- CANR-26
Earlier sketches in CA 17-18R, CANR-9
See also AITN 1
Gilder, Richard Watson 1844-1909 ..... DLB-64
Gilder, Rosamond de Kay 1891-1986 ..... 1R
Obituary 120
Gildersleeve, Basil 1831-1924 ..... DLB-71
Gildersleeve, Thomas R(obert) 1927- 29-32R
Gildner, Gary 1938- CANR-12
Earlier sketch in CA 33-36R
Gildner, Judith 1943- 89-92
Gildrie, Richard P(eter) 1945- 73-76
Gildzen, Alex 1943- 41-44R
Gilead, Zerubavel 1912- 123
Giles, C(harles) W(ilfred) Scott
See Scott-Giles, C(harles) W(ilfred)
Giles, Carl H(oward) 1935- 29-32R
Giles, Elizabeth
See Holt, John (Robert)
Giles, Frederick John 1928- 93-96
Giles, Geoffrey J(ohn) 1947- 122
Giles, Gordon A.
See Binder, Otto O(scar)
Giles, Henry 1809-1882 ..... DLB-64
Giles, James R(ichard) 1937- 73-76
Giles, Janice Holt 1909-1979 ..... CANR-3
Earlier sketch in CA 1R
Giles, John 1921- 104
Giles, Kris
See Nielsen, Helen Berniece
Giles, Mary E(lizabeth) 1934- 108
Giles, Molly 1942- 126
See also CLC 39
Giles, Raymond
See Holt, John (Robert)
Giles, Robert H(artmann) 1933-
Brief entry 122
Gilfillan, Edward S(mith), Jr. 1906- 57-60
Gilfond, Henry CANR-24
Earlier sketches in CA 23-24R, CANR-9
See also SATA 2
Gilford, C(harles) B(ernard) 1920- 17-18R
Gilford, Madeline Lee 1923- 85-88
Gilge, Jeanette 1924- 61-64
See also SATA 22
Gilgen, Albert R(udolph) 1930- 37-40R
Gilgoff, Alice 1946- 85-88
Gilgun, John F(rancis) 1935- 117
Gilhooley, Jack
See Gilhooley, John
Gilhooley, John 1940- 85-88
Gilhooley, Leonard 1921- 37-40R
Gilien, Sasha 1925(?)-1971 Obituary 33-36R
Giliomee, Hermann (Buhr) 1938- 102
Gilison, Jerome Martin 1935- 103
Gilkes, A(ntony) N(ewcombe) 1900- 5-6R
Gilkey, Langdon (Brown) 1919- CANR-7
Earlier sketch in CA 19-20R
Gilkyson, Bernice Kenyon 1898(?)-1982
Obituary 106
Gill, Alan
See Gillepsie, Alfred
Gill, Bartholomew
See McGarrity, Mark
Gill, Bob 1931- 4R
Gill, Brendan 1914- 73-76
Gill, (Ronald) Crispin 1916- CANR-12
Earlier sketch in CA 21-22R
Gill, David (Lawrence William) 1934- ... CANR-12
Earlier sketch in CA 29-32R
Gill, Derek (Lewis Theodore) 1919- CANR-19
Earlier sketches in CA 49-52, CANR-4
See also SATA 9
Gill, Dominic 1941- 106
Gill, (Arthur) Eric (Rowton Peter Joseph)
1882-1940 Brief entry 120
Gill, Evan Robertson 1892- 11-12R
Gill, Frederick (Cyril) 1898- 7-8R
Gill, I(nayat) K(hera) 1924- 61-64
Gill, Jerry H. 1933- CANR-12
Earlier sketch in CA 33-36R
Gill, John Edward 1938- 106
Gill, Joseph 1901- CANR-3
Earlier sketch in CA 9-10R
Gill, Kay 1944- 111
Gill, Margery Jean 1925- SATA-22
Gill, Merton M(ax) 1914- 122
Gill, Patrick
See Creasey, John
Gill, Peter 1939- CANR-22
Earlier sketch in CA 103
Gill, Richard 1922- 41-44R
Gill, Richard T(homas) 1927- CANR-13
Earlier sketch in CA 23-24R
Gill, Traviss 1891- CAP-1
Earlier sketch in CA 13-14
Gillan, Garth J. 1939- 102
Gillan, Patricia Wagstaff 1936- 102

INDEX

Gillchrest, Muriel Noyes 1905- 25-28R
Gillelan, G(eorge) Howard 1917- CANR-6
Earlier sketch in CA 2R
Gillen, Lucy
See Stratton, Rebecca
Gillen, Mollie 1908- 41-44R
Gillen, Robert L(eonard) 1946- 114
Gillenson, Lewis William 1918- 7-8R
Giller, Robert M(aynard) 1942- 124
Gilles, Albert S(imeon), Sr. 1888- 57-60
Gilles, Anthony E(ugene) 1945- 114
Gilles, Daniel 1917- 103
Gillese, John Patrick 1920- 13-14R
Gillespie, A(braham) Lincoln, Jr.
1895-1950 Brief entry 115
See also DLB 4
Gillespie, Alfred 1924- 77-80
Gillespie, Dizzy
See Gillespie, John Birks
Gillespie, Gerald 1933- CANR-10
Earlier sketch in CA 25-28R
Gillespie, I(ris) S(ylvia) 1923- 65-68
Gillespie, James E(rnest), Jr. 1940- 53-56
Gillespie, Janet Wicks 1913- 7-8R
Gillespie, John Birks 1917- 104
Gillespie, John E. 1921- 17-18R
Gillespie, John T(homas) 1928- CANR-13
Earlier sketch in CA 73-76
Gillespie, Kingsley 1895-1984 Obituary 112
Gillespie, Link
See Gillespie, A(braham) Lincoln, Jr.
Gillespie, Marcia Ann AITN-2
Gillespie, Neal C(ephas) 1933- 33-36R
Gillespie, Robert B(ryne) 1917- 110
Gillespie, Robert W. 1922(?)-1983
Obituary 110
Gillespie, Susan
See Turton-Jones, Edith Constance
(Bradshaw)
Gillet, Lev 1892(?)-1980 Obituary 97-100
Gillett, Charlie 1942- 33-36R
Gillett, Eric (Walkey) 1893-1978 CANR-3
Earlier sketch in CA 7-8R
Gillett, J(ohn) D(avid) 1913- 49-52
Gillett, Margaret 1930- CANR-17
Earlier sketches in CA 1R, CANR-2
Gillett, Mary (Bledsoe) CAP-2
Earlier sketch in CA 25-28
See also SATA 7
Gillette, Arnold S(impson) 1904- CANR-2
Earlier sketch in CA 1R
Gillette, Henry Sampson 1915- 7-8R
See also SATA 14
Gillette, J(ay) Michael 1939- 113
Gillette, Michael
See Gillette, J(ay) Michael
Gillette, Paul 1938- 53-56
Gillette, Virginia M(ary) 1920- 57-60
Gillette, William 1933- 108
Gillham, Bill
See Gillham, W(illiam) E(dwin) C(harles)
Gillham, D. G. 1921- 21-22R
Gillham, W(illiam) E(dwin) C(harles) 1936- 113
See also SATA 42
Gilliam, Dorothy B(utler) 1936- 97-100
Gilliam, Florence DLB-4
Gilliam, Stan 1946- SATA-35, 39
Gilliam, Terry (Vance) 1940- 113
Brief entry 108
See also CLC 21
Gillian, Jerry
See Gilliam, Terry (Vance)
Gillian, Kay
See Smith, Kay Nolte
Gilliatt, Penelope (Ann Douglass) 1932- 15-16R
See also DLB 14
See also CLC 2, 10, 13
See also AITN 2
Gillie, Christopher 1914- 102
Gillie, Oliver (John) 1937- CANR-12
Earlier sketch in CA 65-68
Gillies, John 1925- CANR-12
Earlier sketch in CA 73-76
Gillies, Mary Davis 1900- CAP-2
Earlier sketch in CA 25-28
Gilligan, Edmund 1898-1973 Obituary 45-48
Gilligan, Sonja Carl 1936- 57-60
Gilliland, Alexis A(rnaldus) 1931- CANR-25
Earlier sketch in CA 108
Gilliland, Charles
See Muller, Charles G(eorge Geoffrey)
Gilliland, Charles Edward, Jr. 1916-1975
Obituary 110
Gilliland, (Cleburne) Hap 1918- CANR-5
Earlier sketch in CA 53-56
Gillin, Caroline J(ulia) 1932- 45-48
Gillin, Donald George 1930- 33-36R
Gillin, John P(hilip) 1907-1973 41-44R
Obituary 45-48
Gillingham, John (Bennett) 1940- CANR-18
Earlier sketch in CA 97-100
Gillings, Richard John 1902- 77-80
Gillion, Kenneth Lowell (Oliver) 1929- 93-96
Gillis, Daniel 1935- 106
Gillis, Everett A(lden) 1914- CANR-15
Earlier sketch in CA 41-44R
Gillis, John R. 1939- 33-36R
Gillis, Patricia Ingle 1932- Brief entry 108
Gillis, Phyllis 1945- 116
Gillispie, Charles C(oulston) 1918- 13-14R
Gillman, Olga Marjorie 1894- 7-8R
Gillman, Richard 1929- 17-18R
Gillmer, Thomas C(harles) 1911- CANR-6
Earlier sketch in CA 57-60
Gillmer, Tom
See Gillmer, Thomas C(harles)
Gillmor, C(harles) Stewart 1938- 45-48
Gillmor, Daniel S. 1917(?)-1975 Obituary 61-64
Gillmor, Donald M(iles) 1926- 41-44R
Gillmor, Frances 1903- CAP-2
Earlier sketch in CA 17-18
Gillmore, David 1934- 23-24R
Gillmore, Margalo 1897-1986 Obituary 119
Gillon, Adam 1921- CANR-8
Earlier sketch in CA 7-8R
Gillon, Diana (Pleasance Case) 1915- 15-16R
Gillon, Meir Selig 1907- 15-16R
Gillon, Werner 1905- 126
Gillott, Jacky 1939-1980 102
See also DLB 14
Gillquist, Peter E. 1938- CANR-12
Earlier sketch in CA 29-32R
Gilluly, James 1896-1980 Obituary 102
Gillum, Helen L(ouise) 1909- 69-72
Gilman, C(harles) Malcolm B(rookfield)
1898-1981 107
Gilman, Caroline (Howard)
1794-1888 DLB-3, 73
Gilman, Charlotte (Anna) Perkins (Stetson)
1860-1935 Brief entry 106
See also TCLC 9
Gilman, Dorothy
See Butters, Dorothy Gilman
Gilman, Esther 1925- SATA-15
Gilman, George G.
See Harknett, Terry
Gilman, J. D.
See Fishman, Jack
and Orgill, Douglas
Gilman, James
See Gilmore, Joseph L(ee)
Gilman, Richard 1925- CANR-5
Earlier sketch in CA 53-56
Gilman, Robert Cham
See Coppel, Alfred
Gilman, Sander L(awrence) 1944- CANR-5
Earlier sketch in CA 53-56
Gilman, Stephen 1917- 107
Gilman, William 1909-1978 3R
Gilman, William H(enry) 1911-1976 17-18R
Obituary 65-68
Gilmer, Ann
See Ross, W(illiam) E(dward) D(aniel)
Gilmer, B(everley) von Haller 1909- CANR-5
Earlier sketch in CA 5-6R
Gilmer, Elizabeth Meriwether
1861(?)-1951 Brief entry 114
See also DLB 29
Gilmer, Francis Walker 1790-1826 DLB-37
Gilmer, (Frank) Walker 1935- 33-36R
Gilmer, Wesley, Jr. 1928- 115
Gilmore, Alec 1928- 93-96
Gilmore, Al-Tony 1946- CANR-7
Earlier sketch in CA 57-60
Gilmore, Cecile
See MacMillan, Cecile
Gilmore, Charles L(ee) 33-36R
Gilmore, Christopher Cook 1940- CANR-17
Earlier sketch in CA 101
Gilmore, Daniel F(rancis) 1922-1988 65-68
Obituary 126
Gilmore, Don 1930- 29-32R
Gilmore, Eddy (Lanier King) 1907- 7-8R
Gilmore, Edith Spacil 1920- 4R
Gilmore, Gene 1920- 33-36R
Gilmore, Grant 1910-1982 Obituary 111
Gilmore, Harold L(awrence) 1931- 53-56
Gilmore, Haydn 1928- 85-88
Gilmore, Iris 1900- 97-100
See also SATA 22
Gilmore, J. Herbert, Jr. 1925- 33-36R
Gilmore, Jene Carlton 1933- 33-36R
Gilmore, John 1935- 25-28R
Gilmore, Joseph L(ee) 1929- 81-84
Gilmore, Maeve ?-1983 102
Obituary 110
Gilmore, Mary (Jean Cameron) 1865-1962 114
See also SATA 49
Gilmore, Richard 1943- 107
Gilmore, Thomas B(arry, Jr.) 1932- 73-76
Gilmore, William J(ames) 1945- 120
Gilmour, David 1944- CLC-35
Gilmour, Garth (Hamilton) 1925- CAP-1
Earlier sketch in CA 9-10
Gilmour, H. B. 1939- 81-84
Gilmour, Robert S(cott) 1940- 69-72
Gilmour, Robin 1943- 124
Gilner, Elias 1888(?)-1976 Obituary 65-68
Gilot, Francoise 1921- 108
Gilpatrick, Eleanor G(ottesfocht) 1930- CANR-9
Earlier sketch in CA 23-24R
Gilpin, Alan 1924- CANR-11
Earlier sketch in CA 25-28R
Gilpin, Alec Richard 1920- 45-48
Gilpin, John 1930-1983 Obituary 114
Gilpin, Laura 1891-1979 Obituary 111
Gilpin, Robert G., Jr. 1930- 5-6R
Gilray, J. D.
See Mencken, H(enry) L(ouis)
Gilroy, Frank D(aniel) 1925- 81-84
See also DLB 7
See also CLC 2
Gilroy, Harry 1908(?)-1981 Obituary 104
Gilroy, Thomas Laurence 1951- 103
Gilroy, Tom
See Gilroy, Thomas Laurence
Gilson, Barbara
See Gilson, Charles James Louis
Gilson, Charles James Louis 1878-1943 YABC-2
Gilson, Etienne Henry 1884-1978 102
Obituary 81-84
Gilson, Goodwin Woodrow 1918- 17-18R
Gilson, Jamie 1933- 111
See also SATA 34, 37
Gilson, Thomas Q(uinleven) 1916- 7-8R
Gilstrap, Robert L(awrence) 1933- 9-10R
Gilzean, Elizabeth Houghton Blanchet
1913- 9-10R
Gimbel, John 1922- CANR-2
Earlier sketch in CA 2R
Gimbutas, Marija (Alseika) 1921- 13-14R
Gimmestad, Victor E(dward) 1912-1982 57-60
Obituary 109
Gimpel, Herbert J. 1915- 17-18R
Gimpel, Jean 1918- 69-72
Gimson, Alfred Charles 1917-1985 7-8R
Obituary 116
Ginandes, Shepard 1928- 41-44R
Ginder, Richard 1914- 65-68
Gindin, James 1926- CANR-2
Earlier sketch in CA 5-6R
Giner de los Rios, Francisco 1839-1915
Brief entry 105
Gingell, Benjamin Broughton 1924- 104
Ginger, Ann Fagan 1925- CANR-19
Earlier sketches in CA 53-56, CANR-4
Ginger, Helen 1916- 19-20R
Ginger, John 1933- 25-28R
Gingerich, Martin E(llsworth) 1933- 118
Gingerich, Melvin 1902-1975 CAP-2
Earlier sketch in CA 25-28
Gingerich, Owen (Jay) 1930- CANR-22
Earlier sketches in CA 53-56, CANR-5
Ginglend, David R. 1913- 17-18R
Gingold, Hermione (Ferdinanda)
1897-1987 7-8R
Obituary 122
Gingrich, Arnold 1903-1976 13-14R
Obituary 69-72
Gingrich, F(elix) Wilbur 1901- CAP-2
Earlier sketch in CA 17-18
Giniger, Carol Virginia Wilkins
1929(?)-1985 Obituary 117
Giniger, Kenneth Seeman 1919- CANR-3
Earlier sketch in CA 7-8R
Ginn, Robert Jay, Jr. 1946- 107
Ginnings, Harriett W.
See Harriett
Ginns, Patsy (Lee) M(oore) 1937- 69-72
Ginns, Ronald 1896- CAP-1
Earlier sketch in CA 11-12
Ginori Lisci, Leonardo 1908-1987
Obituary 122
Ginott, Haim G. 1922-1973 Obituary 45-48
Ginsberg, Allen 1926- CANR-2
Earlier sketch in CA 2R
See also DLB 5, 16
See also CDALB 1941-1968
See also CLC 1, 2, 3, 4, 6, 13, 36
See also AITN 1
Ginsberg, Benjamin 1947- 121
Ginsberg, Joanne
See Summerfield, Joanne
Ginsberg, Leon H(erman) 1936- 105
Ginsberg, Louis 1895-1976 15-16R
Obituary 65-68
Ginsberg, Morris 1889-1970 Obituary 116
Ginsberg, Robert 1937- 25-28R
Ginsburg, Herbert (Paul) 1939- CANR-12
Earlier sketch in CA 73-76
Ginsburg, Mirra CANR-11
Earlier sketch in CA 19-20R
See also SATA 6
Ginsburg, Ruth Bader 1933- 53-56
Ginsburg, Seymour 1927- CANR-13
Earlier sketch in CA 21-22R
Ginsburgh, Robert N(eville) 1923- 15-16R
Ginsburgs, George 1932- CANR-4
Earlier sketch in CA 53-56
Ginsbury, Norman 1902- 7-8R
Ginter, Maria 1922- 105
Ginther, John R(obert) 1922- Brief entry 107
Gintis, Herbert 1940- 57-60
Ginzberg, Eli 1911- CANR-8
Earlier sketch in CA 5-6R
Ginzberg, Yevgeniya 1906(?)-1977
Obituary 69-72
Ginzburg, Natalia 1916- 85-88
See also CLC 5, 11
Ginzburg, Ralph 1929- 21-22R
Giono, Jean 1895-1970 CANR-2
Obituary 29-32R
Earlier sketch in CA 45-48
See also DLB 72
See also CLC 4, 11
Giordan, Alma Roberts 1917- 57-60
Giordan, Marion ?-1983 Obituary 110
Giordanetti, Elmo 1925-1984 Obituary 113
Giorno, John 1936- 33-36R
Gioseffi, Daniela 1941- CANR-3
Earlier sketch in CA 45-48
Giovacchini, Peter L(ouis) 1922- 101
Giovannetti, Alberto 1913- 9-10R
Giovanni, Nikki 1943- CANR-18
Earlier sketch in CA 29-32R
See also CAAS 6
See also BW
See also SATA 24
See also DLB 5, 41
See also CLC 2, 4, 19
See also CLR 6
See also AITN 1
Giovannitti, Len 1920- 15-16R
Giovanopoulos, Paul (Arthur) 1939- SATA-7
Giovene, Andrea 1904- 85-88
See also CLC 7
Gipe, George 1933-1986 77-80
Obituary 120
Gippius, Zinaida (Nikolayevna) 1869-1945
Brief entry 106
Gipson, Fred(erick Benjamin)
1908-1973 CANR-3
Obituary 45-48
Earlier sketch in CA 3R
See also SATA 2, 24
Gipson, John (Durwood) 1932- 61-64
Gipson, Lawrence Henry 1880-1971 CANR-3
Obituary 33-36R
Earlier sketch in CA 7-8R
See also DLB 17
Giragosian, Newman H. 1922- 93-96
Girard, Hazel Batten 1901- 112
Girard, Henri Georges Charles Achille
1917-1987 Obituary 121
Girard, James P(reston) 1944- 69-72
Girard, Joe 1928- CANR-9
Earlier sketch in CA 77-80
Girard, Linda (Walvoord) 1942- 114
See also SATA 41
Girard, Marvin Eugene 1924- 112
Girard, Mustang Marve
See Girard, Marvin Eugene
Girard, Rene N(oel) 1923- CANR-4
Earlier sketch in CA 9-10R
Girard, Robert C(olby) 1932- 101
Girardi, Joe
See Girard, Joe
Girardot, Norman J(ohn) 1943- 110
Giraud, Marcel 1900- 77-80
Giraudoux, (Hippolyte) Jean 1882-1944
Brief entry 104
See also DLB 65
See also TCLC 2, 7
Girdlestone, Cuthbert Morton
1895-1975 CANR-3
Obituary 65-68
Earlier sketch in CA 7-8R
Girion, Barbara 1937- CANR-15
Earlier sketch in CA 85-88
See also SATA 26
Girling, John L(awrence) S(cott) 1926- 106
Girling, Richard 1945- 108
Girod, Gerald R(alph) 1939- 53-56
Girod, Gordon H. 1920- 1R
Girodias, Maurice 1919- Brief entry 112
Girodo, Michel 1945- 81-84
Giron, Manuel Buendia Tellez
1926(?)-1984 Obituary 112
Gironella, Jose Maria 1917- 101
See also CLC 11
Giroud, Francoise 1916- CANR-17
Earlier sketch in CA 81-84
See also AITN 1
Giroux, E. X.
See Shannon, Doris
Giroux, Henry A(rmand) 1943- 112
Giroux, Joan 1922- 93-96
Giroux, Robert 1914- 107
Girson, Rochelle 23-24R
Girtin, Thomas 1913- 9-10R
Girtin, Tom
See Girtin, Thomas
Girvan, Helen (Masterman) 1891- 73-76
Girvetz, Harry K(enneth) 1910-1974
Obituary 111
Girzaitis, Loretta 1920- CANR-2
Earlier sketch in CA 49-52
Giscard, Valery
See Giscard d'Estaing, Valery
Giscard d'Estaing, Valery 1926-
Brief entry 111
Gish, Arthur G. 1939- 29-32R
Gishford, Anthony (Joseph) 1908-1975
Obituary 53-56
Gisolfi, Anthony M. 1909- CAP-2
Earlier sketch in CA 17-18
Gisselquist, David 1947- 112
Gissen, Max 1909(?)-1984 Obituary 114
Gissing, George (Robert) 1857-1903
Brief entry 105
See also DLB 18
See also TCLC 3, 24
Gist, Noel P(itts) 1899- CANR-1
Earlier sketch in CA 2R
Gist, Ronald R. 1932- 23-24R
Gitchoff, G(eorge) Thomas 1938- 53-56
Gitchoff, Tom
See Gitchoff, G(eorge) Thomas
Gitelman, Zvi Y(echiel) 1940- Brief entry 112
Gitin, David (Daniel) 1941- CANR-2
Earlier sketch in CA 49-52
Gitin, Maria (Brians) 1946- CANR-8
Earlier sketch in CA 61-64
Gitisetan, Dariush 118
Gitisetan, Darrin Dariush
See Gitisetan, Dariush
Gitlin, Murray 1903- 4R
Gitlin, Todd 1943- CANR-25
Earlier sketch in CA 29-32R
Gitlow, A(braham) Leo 1918- 1R
Gitlow, Benjamin 1891-1965 Obituary 89-92
Gittell, Marilyn 1931- CANR-9
Earlier sketch in CA 21-22R
Gittelsohn, Roland B(ertram) 1910- CANR-2
Earlier sketch in CA 5-6R
Gittelson, Celia 105
Gitter, A. George 1926- 102
Gittinger, J(ames) Price 41-44R
Gittings, Jo (Grenville) Manton 1919- CANR-3
Earlier sketch in CA 5-6R
See also SATA 3
Gittings, John 1938- CANR-9
Earlier sketch in CA 21-22R
Gittings, Robert (William Victor) 1911- 25-28R
See also SATA 6
Gittins, Diana 1946- 113
Gittleman, Edwin 1929- 21-22R

Gittleman, Sol 1934- 65-68
Gittler, Joseph B(ertram) 1912- 37-40R
Giudici, Ann Couper 1929- 73-76
Giuliani, George A. 1938- 120
Giunti, Renato 1905-1983 Obituary 109
Giurlani, Aldo
See Palazzeschi, Aldo
Giuseppi, John (Anthony) 1900- CAP-2
Earlier sketch in CA 23-24
Giuttari, Theodore Richard 1931- 29-32R
Givens, David B(radley) 1944- 119
Givens, Janet E(aton) 1932- 111
Givens, John 1943- 77-80
Givner, Abraham 1944- 89-92
Givner, Joan Mary 1936- CANR-25
Earlier sketch in CA 108
Gizycka, Eleanor M.
See Patterson, Eleanor Medill
Gizzi, Michael 1949- 117
Gjertsen, Derek 1933- 125
Glaab, Charles N(elson) 1927- CANR-8
Earlier sketch in CA 5-6R
Glad, Betty 1929- 21-22R
Glad, Donald 1915- 15-16R
Glad, Paul W(ilbur) 1926- 73-76
Gladden, E(dgar) Norman 1897- 21-22R
Gladden, Vivianne Cervantes 1927- 102
Glade, William P(atton), Jr. 1929- 41-44R
Gladilin, Anatoly (Tikhonovich) 1935- .. CANR-18
Earlier sketch in CA 101
Gladish, David F(rancis) 1928- 41-44R
Gladkov, Fyodor (Vasilyevich)
1883-1958 ....TCLC-27
Gladney Glasserow, Marion 1925- 118
Gladstone, Arthur M. 1921- 97-100
Gladstone, Eve
See Werner, Herma
Gladstone, Gary 1935- 29-32R
See also SATA 12
Gladstone, Josephine 1938- 21-22R
Gladstone, M(yron) J. 1923- 53-56
See also SATA 37
Gladstone, Maggie
See Gladstone, Arthur M.
Gladstone, Meredith 1939- 69-72
Gladstone, William Ewart 1809-1898 .... DLB-57
Gladwin, William Zachary
See Zollinger, Gulielma
Gladych, B. Michael 1910- 5-6R
Glaeser, Ernst 1902-1963 .... DLB-69
Glaettli, Walter E(ric) 1920- 21-22R
Glahe, Fred R(ufus) 1934- CANR-14
Earlier sketch in CA 37-40R
Glaister, John 1892-1971 Obituary 104
Glamis, Walter
See Schachner, Nat(han)
Glanville, Brian (Lester) 1931- CANR-3
Earlier sketch in CA 7-8R
See also SATA 42
See also DLB 15
See also CLC 6
Glanville, Maxwell 1918- 85-88
Glanville, Ranulph 1946- 114
Glanz, Edward C(oleman) 1924- 1R
Glanz, Rudolf 1892-1978 .... CANR-3
Earlier sketch in CA 49-52
Glanzman, Louis S. 1922- SATA-36
Glapthorne, Henry 1610-1643(?) DLB-58
Glaser, Daniel 1918- 61-64
Glaser, Dianne E(lizabeth) 1937- 77-80
See also SATA 31, 50
Glaser, E(ric) M(ichael) 1913- 23-24R
Glaser, Edward 1918-1972 Obituary 37-40R
Glaser, Eleanor Dorothy
See Zonik, Eleanor Dorothy
Glaser, Elton 1945- 111
Glaser, Eva Schocken 1918-1982 Obituary .. 105
Glaser, Isabel Joshlin 1929- 77-80
Glaser, Kurt 1914- CANR-5
Earlier sketch in CA 1R
Glaser, Lynn 1943- 21-22R
Glaser, Milton 1929- CANR-11
Earlier sketch in CA 17-18R
See also SATA 11
Glaser, Robert 1921- CANR-7
Earlier sketch in CA 17-18R
Glaser, Rollin Oliver 1932- CANR-10
Earlier sketch in CA 25-28R
Glaser, William A(rnold) 1925- CANR-21
Earlier sketches in CA 1R, CANR-6
Glasgow, Douglas G. 108
Glasgow, Ellen (Anderson Gholson)
1873(?)-1945 Brief entry 104
See also DLB 9, 12
See also TCLC 2, 7
Glasgow, Eric 1924- 69-72
Glasgow, Gordon H(enry) H(arper)
1926- 29-32R
Glasgow, Jack
See Larson, Doran
Glasgow, Mary Cecilia 1905-1983
Obituary 111
Glasheen, Adaline 1920- 101
Glasheen, Patrick 1897- CAP-1
Earlier sketch in CA 13-14
Glaskin, G(erald) M(arcus) 1923- CANR-5
Earlier sketch in CA 53-56
Glaskowsky, Nicholas A(lexander), Jr.
1928- CANR-3
Earlier sketch in CA 5-6R
Glaspell, Susan (Keating) 1882(?)-1948
Brief entry 110
See also YABC 2
See also DLB 7, 9
Glasrud, Bruce (Alden) 1940- 41-44R
Glass, Albert J(ulius) 1908-1983 Obituary .. 109
Glass, Andrew SATA-46
Glass, Andrew J(ames) 1935- 65-68
Glass, Bill 1935- CANR-13
Earlier sketch in CA 73-76
Glass, David Victor 1911-1978 85-88
Obituary 81-84
Glass, Ian Cameron 1926- 77-80
Glass, Joanna (McClelland) 1936- 81-84
Glass, John F(ranklin) 1936- 53-56
Glass, Justine C.
See Corrall, Alice Enid
Glass, Malcolm (Sanford) 1936- CANR-20
Earlier sketch in CA 104
Glass, Montague (Marsden) 1877-1934
Brief entry 117
See also DLB 11
Glass, Sandra
See Shea, Robert (Joseph)
Glass, Stanley T(homas) 1932- 21-22R
Glassberg, B(ertrand) Y(ounker)
1902-19(?) CAP-1
Earlier sketch in CA 15-16
Glassburner, Bruce 1920- 33-36R
Glassco, John 1909-1981 .... CANR-15
Obituary 102
Earlier sketch in CA 15-16R
See also DLB 68
See also CLC 9
Glasscock, Amnesia
See Steinbeck, John (Ernst)
Glasscock, Anne Bonner 1924- 3R
Glasse, Robert Marshall 1929- 29-32R
Glasser, Allen 1918- 9-10R
Glasser, Paul H(arold) 1929- CANR-15
Earlier sketch in CA 29-32R
Glasser, Ronald J. 1940(?)- CLC-37
Glasser, Selma 110
Glasser, Stephen A(ndrew) 1943- 53-56
Glasser, William 1925- 73-76
Glasserow, Mario N.
See Gladney Glasserow, Marion
Glasserow, Marion Gladney
See Gladney Glasserow, Marion
Glassford, Wilfred
See McNeilly, Wilfred (Glassford)
Glassgold, Peter 1939- 103
Glassie, Henry H(aywood) 1914-1987
Obituary 124
Glassman, Bernard Tetsugen 1939- 112
Glassman, Jon David 1944- 69-72
Glassman, Joyce
See Johnson, Joyce
Glassman, Michael 1899- 15-16R
Glassman, Peter Joel 1945- 113
Glassman, Ronald M. 1937- Brief entry 111
Glassner, Lester 1939- 107
Glassner, Martin Ira 1932- CANR-15
Earlier sketch in CA 41-44R
Glasson, Thomas Francis 1906- CAP-1
Earlier sketch in CA 9-10
Glassop, (Jack) Lawson 1913-1966 .... CAP-1
Earlier sketch in CA 9-10
Glasstone, Victor 1924- CANR-10
Earlier sketch in CA 65-68
Glatstein, Jacob 1896-1971 Obituary 33-36R
Glatthorn, Allan A. 1924- 15-16R
Glatzer, Hal 1946- 57-60
Glatzer, Nahum Norbert 1903- CANR-7
Earlier sketch in CA 13-14R
Glauber, Uta (Heil) 1936- 29-32R
See also SATA 17
Glaus, Marlene 1933- 23-24R
Glauser, Friedrich 1896-1938 .... DLB-56
Glavin, John P(atrick) 1933- 57-60
Glazar, Bob 1954- 115
Glaze, Andrew (Louis III) 1920- CANR-24
Earlier sketches in CA 17-18R, CANR-8
Glaze, Eleanor 1930- 49-52
Glaze, Thomas E(dward) 1914- 2R
Glazebrook, G(eorge) P(arkin) de
T(wenebrokes) 1899- 102
Glazebrook, Philip 1937- 29-32R
Glazener, Mary U(nderwood) 1921- 19-20R
Glazer, Daphne (Fae) 1938- 119
Glazer, Nathan 1923- 5-6R
Glazer, Nona Y.
See Glazer-Malbin, Nona
Glazer, Sidney 1905-1983 .... 1R
Obituary 111
Glazer, Tom 1914- CANR-8
Earlier sketch in CA 61-64
See also SATA 9
Glazer-Malbin, Nona 1932- 33-36R
Glazier, Kenneth MacLean 1912- 11-12R
Glazier, Lyle (Edward) 1911- 37-40R
Glazier, Stephen 1947- 108
Glazner, Joseph Mark 1945- 104
Gleadow, Rupert Seeley 1909-1974 ....9-10R
Obituary 103
Gleasner, Diana (Cottle) 1936- CANR-15
Earlier sketch in CA 65-68
See also SATA 29
Gleason, Abbott 1938- CANR-21
Earlier sketch in CA 104
Gleason, Eugene Franklin 1914- 4R
Gleason, Gene
See Gleason, Eugene Franklin
Gleason, Harold 1892- CAP-1
Earlier sketch in CA 9-10
Gleason, John (Marquis) 1942- 107
Gleason, John J(ames), Jr. 1934- 120
Gleason, Judith 1929- CANR-9
Earlier sketch in CA 61-64
See also SATA 24
Gleason, Ralph J(oseph) 1917-1975 65-68
Obituary 61-64
Gleason, Robert 1945- 118
Gleason, Robert J(ames) 1906- 73-76
Gleason, Robert Walter 1917- CANR-4
Earlier sketch in CA 1R
Gleason, S(arel) Everett 1905-1974
Obituary 53-56
Gleaves, Robert M(ilnor) 1938- 53-56
Gleaves, Suzanne 1904- 11-12R
Gleckner, Robert Francis 1925- CANR-17
Earlier sketches in CA 3R, CANR-2
Gledhill, Alan 1895-1983 .... CAP-1
Obituary 110
Earlier sketch in CA 9-10
Gleeson, Ruth (Ryall) 1925- 9-10R
Gleiman, Lubomir 1923- 41-44R
Gleisser, Marcus D(avid) 1923- 19-20R
Gleitman, Lila R. 1929- 114
Glen, Duncan (Munro) 1933- CANR-12
Earlier sketch in CA 21-22R
Glen, Eugene
See Fawcett, F(rank) Dubrez
Glen, Frank Grenfell 1933- 106
Glen, J(ohn) Stanley 1907-1986 .... CAP-1
Obituary 118
Earlier sketch in CA 9-10
Glen, Robert S. 1925- 29-32R
Glenday, Alice 1920- 57-60
Glendenning, Donn
See Paine, Lauran (Bosworth)
Glendenning, Raymond Carl 1907-1974
Obituary 114
Glendinning, Richard 1917- 21-22R
See also SATA 24
Glendinning, Sally
See Glendinning, Sara W(ilson)
Glendinning, Sara W(ilson) 1913- CANR-2
Earlier sketch in CA 49-52
See also SATA 24
Glendinning, Victoria 1937- Brief entry 120
See also CLC 50
Glendon, Mary Ann 1938- 41-44R
Glenn, Armon 1912- 107
Glenn, Christine Genevieve 1947- 115
Glenn, Edmund S(tanislas) 1915- 113
Glenn, Frank 1901-1982 Obituary 106
Glenn, Harold T(heodore) 1910- CANR-5
Earlier sketch in CA 7-8R
Glenn, Jacob B. 1905-1974 .... CANR-4
Obituary 49-52
Earlier sketch in CA 9-10R
Glenn, James
See Paine, Lauran (Bosworth)
Glenn, Jerry (Hesmer, Jr.) 1938- 45-48
Glenn, Lois (Ruth) 1941- 61-64
Glenn, Mel 1943- 123
See also SATA 45, 51
Glenn, Morton B(ernard) 1922- 61-64
Glenn, Norval Dwight 1933- 17-18R
Glennon, James 1900- 25-28R
Glennon, Maurade 1926- 25-28R
Glenny, Lyman A. 1918- CANR-7
Earlier sketch in CA 19-20R
Glenny, Michael Valentine 1927- 102
Gles, Margaret Breitmaier 1940- 57-60
See also SATA 22
Gleser, Goldine C(ohnberg) 1915- 17-18R
Gless, Darryl James 1945- 102
Glessing, Robert J(ohn) 1930- 29-32R
Gliauda, Jurgis 1906- CANR-3
Earlier sketch in CA 5-6R
Glick, Carl (Cannon) 1890-1971 ....7-8R
Obituary 103
See also SATA 14
Glick, Edward Bernard 1929- CANR-8
Earlier sketch in CA 23-24R
Glick, G(arland) Wayne 1921- 25-28R
Glick, Paul C(harles) 1910- 5-6R
Glick, Paula Brown
See Brown, Paula
Glick, Ruth (Burtnick) 1942- CANR-16
Earlier sketch in CA 89-92
Glick, Thomas F(rederick) 1939- CANR-15
Earlier sketch in CA 29-32R
Glick, Virginia Kirkus 1893-1980 .... CAP-2
Obituary 101
Earlier sketch in CA 21-22
See also SATA 23
Glick, Wendell 1916- 111
Glickman, Albert S(eymour) 1923- 53-56
Glickman, Arthur P. 1940- 61-64
Glickman, Beatrice Marden 1919- 102
Glickman, S(teven) Craig 1947- 116
Glickman, Susan 1953- 116
Glicksberg, Charles Irving 1900- CANR-2
Earlier sketch in CA 1R
Glicksman, Abraham M(orton) 1911- 5-6R
Glidden, Frederick D(illey) 1908-1975 .... CAP-2
Obituary 61-64
Earlier sketch in CA 21-22
Glidden, Horace Knight 1901- CAP-1
Earlier sketch in CA 15-16
Glidewell, John Calvin 1919- CANR-23
Earlier sketches in CA 15-16R, CANR-7
Glieberman, Herbert A(llen) 1930- 112
Gliewe, Unada (Grace) 1927- CANR-12
Earlier sketch in CA 29-32R
See also SATA 3
Glikes, Erwin 1937- 15-16R
Glimcher, Arnold B. 1938- 81-84
Glines, Carroll V(ane), Jr. 1920- CANR-2
Earlier sketch in CA 2R
See also SATA 19
Gliozzo, Charles 1932- 45-48
Glissant, Edouard 1928- CLC-10
Glisson, Jerry (Lee) 1923- 113
Gloag, John (Edwards) 1896-1981 .... CANR-10
Obituary 104
Earlier sketch in CA 65-68
Gloag, Julian 1930- CANR-10
Earlier sketch in CA 65-68
See also CLC 40
See also AITN 1
Glob, Peter Vilhelm 1911-1985 97-100
Obituary 117
Globe, Leah Ain 1900- 107
See also SATA 41
Glock, Charles Y(oung) 1919- CANR-5
Earlier sketch in CA 53-56
Glock, Marvin D(avid) 1912- 23-24R
Gloer, (William) Hulitt 1950- 126
Glogau, Art(hur H.) 1922- 53-56
Glogau, Lillian Flatow Fleischer 1925- 85-88
Glogowski, Maryruth F(rancine) P(helps)
1950- 120
Glorfeld, Louis E(arl) 1916- 53-56
Glos, Raymond E(ugene) 1903- 23-24R
Glovach, Linda 1947- CANR-14
Earlier sketch in CA 37-40R
See also SATA 7
Glover, Albert Gould 1942- 89-92
Glover, Bob
See Glover, Robert H.
Glover, Denis (James Matthews)
1912-1980 77-80
Obituary 101
See also SATA 7
Glover, Donald E(llsworth) 1933- 116
Glover, Harry 1912- 77-80
Glover, Janice 1919- 17-18R
Glover, John D(esmond) 1915- CANR-2
Earlier sketch in CA 5-6R
Glover, Judith 1943- CANR-22
Earlier sketch in CA 106
Glover, Leland E(llis) 1917- 9-10R
Glover, Michael 1922- CANR-23
Earlier sketches in CA 19-20R, CANR-8
Glover, Robert H. 1946- 116
Glover, (David) Tony "Harp Dog"
1939- 15-16R
Glowacki, Janusz 1938- 116
Glubb, John Bagot 1897-1986 .... CANR-5
Obituary 118
Earlier sketch in CA 9-10R
Glubb Pasha
See Glubb, John Bagot
Glubok, Shirley (Astor) 1933- CANR-4
Earlier sketch in CA 5-6R
See also SATA 6
See also CLR 1
Gluck, Carol 1941- 126
Gluck, Felix 1923-1981 Obituary 103
See also SATA 25
Gluck, Herb 1925- CANR-2
Earlier sketch in CA 45-48
Gluck, Jay 1927- CANR-12
Earlier sketch in CA 21-22R
Gluck, Louise 1943- 33-36R
See also DLB 5
See also CLC 7, 22, 44
Gluck, Robert 1947- 113
Gluckin, Doreen Sandra 1949- 108
Gluckman, Max 1911-1975 ....9-10R
Obituary 57-60
Glucksberg, Harold 1939- 105
Glueck, Eleanor T(ouroff) 1898-1972 .... CANR-9
Obituary 37-40R
Earlier sketches in CA 17-18, CAP-2
Glueck, Louise
See Gluck, Louise
See also DLB 5
See also CLC 7, 22
Glueck, Nelson 1900-1971 .... CAP-2
Earlier sketch in CA 17-18
Glueck, Sheldon 1896-1980 .... CANR-9
Obituary 97-100
Earlier sketch in CA 5-6R
Glueck, William F(rank) 1934-1980 ....33-36R
Glueckauf, Eugen 1906-1981 Obituary 108
Gluss, Brian 1930- 104
Glustrom, Simon W. 1924- 21-22R
Glut, Donald F(rank) 1944- CANR-13
Earlier sketch in CA 33-36R
Gluyas, Constance 1920- Brief entry 115
Gluzman, Brian
See Gluss, Brian
Glyn, Anthony 1922- 53-56
Glyn, Caroline 1947- CANR-5
Earlier sketch in CA 11-12R
Glyn, Richard Hamilton 1907-1980 105
Obituary 102
Glynn, James A. 1941- 57-60
Glynn, Jeanne Davis 1932- 29-32R
Glynn, Prudence (Loveday) 1935-1986
Obituary 120
Glynn, Thomas P(eter) 1935- 93-96
Glynne-Jones, M(arjorie) L(ilian) 1936-
Brief entry 111
Glynne-Jones, William 1907- 7-8R
See also SATA 11
Gmelch, George 1944- 103
Gmelch, Sharon Bohn 1947- 103
Gmelch, Walter H(oward) 1947- 112
Gnaegy, Charles 1938- 89-92
Gnagey, Thomas D(avid) 1938- 49-52
Gnagy, Jon
See Gnagy, Michael Jacques
Gnagy, Michael Jacques 1907(?)-1981
Obituary 103
Gnarowski, Michael 1934- 41-44R
Gniffke, Rudolf
See Hartmann, Rudolf A.
Gnosticus
See Weschcke, Carl L(ouis)
Gnuse, Robert K(arl) 1947- 121

Go, Puan Seng 1904- ... CAP-2
Earlier sketch in CA 29-32
Goacher, Denis 1925- ... 104
Goaman, Muriel
See Cox, Edith Muriel
Gobar, Ash 1930- ... 41-44R
Gobbato, Imero 1923- ... SATA-39
Gobbi, Tito 1915-1984 Obituary ... 112
Brief entry ... 105
Goble, Dorothy ... 93-96
See also SATA 26
Goble, Frank G. 1917- ... 112
Goble, (Lloyd) Neil 1933- ... 29-32R
Goble, Paul 1933- ... CANR-16
Earlier sketch in CA 93-96
See also SATA 25
Goble, Warwick (?)-1943 ... SATA-46
Gocek, Matilda A(rkenbout) 1923- ... CANR-1
Earlier sketch in CA 49-52
Gockel, Herman W. 1906- ... CANR-1
Earlier sketch in CA 1R
Godard, Jean-Luc 1930- ... 93-96
See also CLC 20
Godbold, E(dward) Stanly, Jr. 1942- ... 37-40R
Godbout, Jacques 1933- Brief entry ... 125
See also DLB 53
Goddard, Alfred
See Harper, Carol Ely
Goddard, Burton L(eslie) 1910- ... 23-24R
Goddard, Donald 1934- ... CANR-11
Earlier sketch in CA 17-18R
Goddard, Gladys Benjamin 1881(?)-1976
Obituary ... 61-64
Goddard, J(ack) R. 1930- ... 29-32R
Goddard, Kenneth (William) 1946- ... 110
Goddard, Morrill 1865-1937 ... DLB-25
Goddard, Robert Hutchings 1882-1945
Brief entry ... 118
Goddard, William 1740-1817 ... DLB-43
Godden, Geoffrey 1929- ... 102
Godden, Jon 1906-1984 ... 77-80
Obituary ... 112
Godden, (Margaret) Rumer 1907- ... CANR-4
Earlier sketch in CA 7-8R
See also SATA 3, 36
Gode, Alexander
See Gode von Aesch, Alexander
(Gottfried Friedrich)
Godechot, Jacques Leon 1907- ... CANR-25
Earlier sketches in CA 65-68, CANR-9
Godefroy, Vincent 1912- ... 69-72
Godel, Kurt
See Goedel, Kurt
Gode von Aesch, Alexander (Gottfried
Friedrich) 1906-1970 ... CAP-1
Earlier sketch in CA 9-10
See also SATA 14
Godey, John
See Freedgood, Morton
Godey, Louis A. 1804-1878 ... DLB-73
Godfrey, Cuthbert John ... 7-8R
Godfrey, (William) Dave 1938- ... CANR-11
Earlier sketch in CA 69-72
See also DLB 60
Godfrey, Eleanor S(mith) 1914- ... 69-72
Godfrey, Ellen 1942- ... 113
Godfrey, Frederick M. 1901-1974 ... CAP-1
Earlier sketch in CA 13-14
Godfrey, Henry F. 1906-1975 ... CAP-2
Earlier sketch in CA 25-28
Godfrey, Jane
See Bowden, Joan Chase
Godfrey, Laurie R(ohde) 1945- ... 113
Godfrey, Lionel (Robert Holcombe) 1932- ... 81-84
Godfrey, Martyn N. 1949- ... 126
Godfrey, Michael A. 1940- ... CANR-14
Earlier sketch in CA 81-84
Godfrey, Peter 1917- ... 124
Godfrey, Thomas 1736-1763 ... DLB-31
Godfrey, Vincent H. 1895(?)-1975
Obituary ... 57-60
Godfrey, William
See Youd, Samuel
Godin, Gabriel 1929- ... 73-76
Godine, David R(ichard) 1944- ... 101
Godley, John
See Kilbracken, John (Raymond Godley)
Godly, J. P.
See Plawin, Paul
Godman, Arthur 1916- ... CANR-24
Earlier sketch in CA 106
Godolphin, Francis R(ichard) B(orroum)
1903-1974 ... 65-68
Obituary ... 53-56
Godown, Marian Bailey ... 103
Godoy Alcayaga, Lucila 1889-1957
Brief entry ... 104
Godsey, John Drew 1922- ... 13-14R
Godshalk, William Leigh 1937- ... 41-44R
Godson, John 1937- ... 77-80
Godson, Joseph 1913-1986 Obituary ... 120
Godson, Roy (S.) 1942- Brief entry ... 111
Godwin, Anthony Richard James Wylie
1920(?)-1976 Obituary ... 104
Godwin, Gail 1937- ... CANR-15
Earlier sketch in CA 29-32R
See also DLB 6
See also CLC 5, 8, 22, 31
Godwin, Gaylord 1906(?)-1979 Obituary ... 85-88
Godwin, George (Stanley) 1889- ... 5-6R
Godwin, Harry 1901-1985 ... 109
Obituary ... 117
Godwin, John (Frederick) 1922- ... CANR-19
Earlier sketch in CA 102
Godwin, John 1929- ... CANR-16
Earlier sketches in CA 4R, CANR-1
Godwin, Joscelyn 1945- ... CANR-12
Earlier sketch in CA 69-72
Godwin, Parke 1816-1904 Brief entry ... 119
See also DLB 3, 64
Godwin, Tony
See Godwin, Anthony Richard James
Wylie
Godwin, William 1756-1836 ... DLB-39
Goebbels, Josef
See Goebbels, (Paul) Joseph
Goebbels, (Paul) Joseph 1897-1945
Brief entry ... 115
Goebbels, Joseph Paul
See Goebbels, (Paul) Joseph
Goebel, Dorothy (Burne) 1898-1976 ... 69-72
Obituary ... 65-68
Goebel, Julius, Jr. 1893(?)-1973
Obituary ... 45-48
Goedecke, W(alter) Robert 1928- ... 29-32R
Goedel, Kurt 1906-1978 Obituary ... 108
Goedertier, Joseph M. 1907- ... CAP-2
Earlier sketch in CA 25-28
Goedicke, Hans 1926- ... CANR-19
Earlier sketches in CA 45-48, CANR-1
Goedicke, Patricia (McKenna) 1931- ... CANR-11
Earlier sketch in CA 25-28R
Goedicke, Victor (Alfred) 1912- ... 17-18R
Goel, M(adan) Lal 1936- ... 53-56
Goeller, Carl 1930- ... 23-24R
Goelz, Paul Cornelius 1914- ... 109
Goen, Clarence C(urtis), Jr. 1924- ... 2R
Goen, Rayburne Wyndham, Jr. 1942- ... 107
Goen, Tex, Jr.
See Goen, Rayburne Wyndham, Jr.
Goeney, William M(orton) 1914- ... 5-6R
Goerdt, Arthur L(inus) 1912- ... 41-44R
Goergen, Donald 1943- ... 61-64
Goering, Helga
See Wallmann, Jeffrey M(iner)
Goerling, Lars 1931-1966 ... CAP-2
Obituary ... 25-28R
Earlier sketch in CA 21-22
Goerner, E(dward) A(lfred) 1929- ... 49-52
Goertz, Donald C(harles) 1939- ... 53-56
Goertzel, Ted George 1942- ... 69-72
Goes, Albrecht 1908- ... DLB-69
Goetchius, Eugene Van Ness 1921- ... 118
Goethals, George W. 1920- ... 13-14R
Goetsch-Trevelyan, Katherine
See Trevelyan, Katherine
Goettel, Elinor 1930- ... 29-32R
See also SATA 12
Goetz, Billy E. 1904- ... CAP-1
Earlier sketch in CA 13-14
Goetz, Delia 1898- ... 73-76
See also SATA 22
Goetz, Ignacio L. 1933- ... 37-40R
Goetz, Joseph (William) 1933- ... 118
Goetz, Lee Garrett 1932- ... 25-28R
Goetze, Albrecht E. R. 1897-1971
Obituary ... 33-36R
Goetzmann, William H. 1930- ... 23-24R
Goetz-Stankiewicz, Marketa ... 122
Goff, Charles Ray 1889-1984 Obituary ... 114
Goff, Frederick Richmond 1916-1982 ... CANR-7
Obituary ... 108
Earlier sketch in CA 17-18R
Goff, James R., Jr. 1957- ... 126
Goff, Martyn 1923- ... CANR-2
Earlier sketch in CA 7-8R
Goffart, Walter (Andre) 1934- ... CANR-16
Earlier sketch in CA 37-40R
Goffe, Thomas 1592(?)-1629 ... DLB-58
Goffen, Rona 1944- ... 121
Goffin, Raymond C. 1890(?)-1976
Obituary ... 65-68
Goffman, Erving 1922-1982 ... CANR-9
Obituary ... 108
Earlier sketch in CA 23-24R
Goffstein, M(arilyn) B(rooke) 1940- ... CANR-9
Earlier sketch in CA 21-22R
See also SATA 8
See also DLB 61
See also CLR 3
Gofman, John W(illiam) 1918- ... 65-68
Goforth, Ellen
See Francis, Dorothy Brenner
Gogarty, Oliver St. John 1878-1957
Brief entry ... 109
See also DLB 15, 19
See also TCLC 15
Goggin, Dan 1943- ... 126
Goggin, Terrence P(atrick) 1941- ... 103
Gogisgi
See Arnett, Carroll
Goh, Cheng-Teik 1943- ... 41-44R
Gohdes, Clarence Louis Frank 1901- ... 13-14R
Gohman, Fred Joseph 1918- ... 7-8R
Goines, Donald 1937-1974 Obituary ... 114
See also DLB 33
See also AITN 1
Goines, Donald 1937(?)-1974 ... 124
See also BW
Goins, Ellen H(aynes) 1927-1979 ... CANR-26
Earlier sketch in CA 33-36R
Goist, Park Dixon 1936- ... 37-40R
Goitein, S(helomo) D(ov) 1900-1985 ... CANR-8
Obituary ... 115
Earlier sketch in CA 61-64
Goitein, Solomon Dob Fritz
See Goitein, S(helomo) D(ov)
Gokak, Vinayak Krishna 1909- ... 69-72
Gokhale, Balkrishna Govind 1919- ... CANR-4
Earlier sketch in CA 1R
Gokhale, Namita 1956- ... 123
Golan, Aviezer 1922- ... 104
Golan, Matti 1936- ... 101
Golann, Cecil Paige 1921- ... 33-36R
See also SATA 11
Golann, Stuart E(ugene) 1936- ... 57-60
Golant, William 1937- ... 65-68
Golay, Frank H(indman) 1915- ... CANR-1
Earlier sketch in CA 2R
Golbin, Andree 1923- ... SATA-15
Golburgh, Stephen J. 1935- ... 21-22R
Gold, Aaron 1937-1983 ... 101
Obituary ... 109
Gold, Alan R(obert) 1948- ... 45-48
Gold, Artie 1947- ... 114
Gold, Barbara K(irk) 1945- ... 110
Gold, Don 1931- ... CANR-9
Earlier sketch in CA 61-64
Gold, Doris B. 1919- ... CANR-9
Earlier sketch in CA 23-24R
Gold, Douglas 1894- ... CAP-1
Earlier sketch in CA 11-12
Gold, Herbert 1924- ... CANR-17
Earlier sketch in CA 11-12R
See also DLB 2
See also DLBY 81
See also CLC 4, 7, 14, 42
Gold, Ivan 1932- ... CANR-3
Earlier sketch in CA 5-6R
Gold, Joseph 1933- ... 21-22R
Gold, Lee 1919(?)-1985 Obituary ... 116
Gold, Martin 1931- ... 29-32R
Gold, Michael
See Granich, Irving
See also DLB 9, 28
Gold, Milton J. 1917- ... 17-18R
Gold, Phyllis
See Goldberg, Phyllis
See also SATA 21
Gold, Robert S(tanley) 1924- ... 53-56
Gold, Seymour M(urray) 1933- ... CANR-21
Earlier sketch in CA 41-44R
Gold, Sharlya ... CANR-8
Earlier sketch in CA 61-64
See also SATA 9
Gold, Victor Roland 1924- ... 53-56
Gold, William E(mil) 1912- ... 69-72
Goldbarth, Albert 1948- ... CANR-6
Earlier sketch in CA 53-56
See also CLC 5, 38
Goldbeck, David M. 1942- ... 49-52
Goldbeck, Frederick E(rnest) 1902- ... 102
Goldbeck, Nikki 1947- ... 49-52
Goldbeck, Willis 1899(?)-1979 Obituary ... 89-92
Goldberg, Alvin Arnold 1931- ... 41-44R
Goldberg, Anatol 1910-1982 Obituary ... 117
See also CLC 34
Goldberg, Arnold I(rving) 1929- ... CANR-19
Earlier sketch in CA 103
Goldberg, Arthur J(oseph) 1908- ... 65-68
Goldberg, Barney 1918- ... 23-24R
Goldberg, Benjamin 1915- ... 120
Goldberg, Carl 1938- ... CANR-18
Earlier sketches in CA 49-52, CANR-3
Goldberg, Dick 1947- ... 97-100
See also DLB 7
Goldberg, Dorothy K(urgans)
1909(?)-1988 ... 103
Obituary ... 124
Goldberg, E(lliott) Marshall 1930- ... CANR-26
Earlier sketches in CA 69-72, CANR-11
Goldberg, Edward M(orris) 1931- ... 53-56
Goldberg, Fats
See Goldberg, Larry
Goldberg, George 1935- ... 69-72
Goldberg, Gerald Jay 1929- ... 49-52
Goldberg, Harvey E(llis) 1939- ... CANR-25
Earlier sketch in CA 45-48
Goldberg, Herb 1937- ... CANR-9
Earlier sketch in CA 61-64
Goldberg, Herbert S. 1926- ... 5-6R
See also SATA 25
Goldberg, Herman Raphael 1915- ... CANR-5
Earlier sketch in CA 11-12R
Goldberg, Hillel 1946- ... 116
Goldberg, Hyman 1908(?)-1970 Obituary ... 104
Goldberg, Jacob 1948- ... 120
Goldberg, Jan
See Curran, Jan Goldberg
Goldberg, Joan Rachel 1955- ... 110
Goldberg, Jonathan 1943- ... 122
Goldberg, Joseph P(hilip) 1918- ... 37-40R
Goldberg, Kenneth P(hilip) 1945- ... 116
Goldberg, Larry 1934- ... 113
Goldberg, Leah 1911-1970 Obituary ... 25-28R
Goldberg, Lester 1924- ... 126
Goldberg, Louis 1908- ... 13-14R
Goldberg, Louis
See Grant, Louis T(heodore)
Goldberg, Lucianne Cummings 1935- ... 85-88
Goldberg, M(ilton) A(llan) 1919-1970 ... CAP-2
Earlier sketch in CA 25-28
Goldberg, M(elvyn) Hirsh 1942- ... 73-76
Goldberg, Marie Waife
See Waife-Goldberg, Marie
Goldberg, Maxwell Henry 1907- ... CANR-24
Earlier sketch in CA 103
Goldberg, Miriam Levin 1914- ... 41-44R
Goldberg, Moses H(aym) 1940- ... CANR-15
Earlier sketch in CA 93-96
Goldberg, Nathan 1903(?)-1979 Obituary ... 85-88
Goldberg, Norman L(ewis) 1906- ... 81-84
Goldberg, P(ercy) Selvin 1917- ... 7-8R
Goldberg, Philip 1944- ... CANR-15
Earlier sketch in CA 85-88
Goldberg, Phyllis 1941- ... 57-60
Goldberg, Ray A(llan) 1926- ... 49-52
Goldberg, Reuben L(ucius) 1883-1970 ... CANR-9
Earlier sketch in CA 5-6R
Goldberg, Robert Alan 1949- ... 105
Goldberg, RoseLee 1947- ... 120
Goldberg, Rube
See Goldberg, Reuben L(ucius)
Goldberg, Samuel Louis 1926- ... 112
Goldberg, Sidney 1931- ... 77-80
Goldberg, Stan J. 1939- ... 49-52
See also SATA 26
Goldberg, Steven 1941- ... 53-56
Goldberger, Arthur Stanley 1930- ... 9-10R
Goldberger, Judith M. 1948- ... 112
Goldberger, Nancy Rule 1937- ... 124
Goldberger, Paul (Jesse) 1950-
Brief entry ... 122
Golde, Peggy 1930- ... 37-40R
Golde, Roger A(llan) 1934- ... 69-72
Goldemberg, Isaac 1945- ... CANR-11
Earlier sketch in CA 69-72
Goldemberg, Rose Leiman ... CANR-2
Earlier sketch in CA 49-52
Golden, Arthur 1924- ... 33-36R
Golden, Harry (Lewis) 1902-1981 ... CANR-2
Obituary ... 104
Earlier sketch in CA 2R
Golden, Harry, Jr. 1928(?)-1988 Obituary ... 125
Golden, James L. 1919- Brief entry ... 109
Golden, Jeffrey S. 1950- ... 33-36R
Golden, L(ouis) L(awrence) L(ionel)
1909(?)-1983 ... 23-24R
Obituary ... 111
Golden, Leon 1930- ... 19-20R
Golden, Marita 1950- ... 111
See also BW
Golden, Morris 1926- ... 3R
Golden, Robert Edward 1945- ... 65-68
Golden, Ruth I(sbell) 1910- ... CAP-2
Earlier sketch in CA 17-18
Golden, Samuel A(dler) 1909- Brief entry ... 110
Golden, Sean V(alentine) 1948- ... 107
Golden, Sherry (Lazar) 1945- ... 123
Goldenbaum, Sally 1941- ... 124
Goldenberg, Edie N. 1945- ... 69-72
Goldenberg, Herbert 1926- ... 41-44R
Goldenberg, I(sidore) Ira 1936- ... 110
Goldenberg, Robert 1942- ... 109
Golden Silver
See Storm, Hyemeyohsts
Goldensohn, Barry 1937- ... 77-80
Goldenson, Daniel R. 1944- ... 25-28R
Goldenson, Robert M(yar) 1908- ... 29-32R
Goldenthal, Allan Benarria 1920- ... 19-20R
Goldfader, Edward H. 1930- ... 29-32R
Goldfarb, Clare R(osett) 1934- ... 113
Goldfarb, Nathan 1913- ... 15-16R
Goldfarb, Ronald L. 1933- ... CANR-9
Earlier sketch in CA 23-24R
Goldfarb, Russell M. 1934- ... 37-40R
Goldfarb, Sally F(ay) 1957- ... 104
Goldfeder, Cheryl
See Pahz, (Anne) Cheryl Suzanne
Goldfeder, James
See Pahz, James Alon
Goldfeder, Jim
See Pahz, James Alon
Goldfein, Donna 1933- ... 116
Goldfrank, David M. ... 118
Goldfrank, Esther S(chiff) 1896- ... 61-64
Goldfrank, Helen Colodny 1912- ... CANR-3
Earlier sketch in CA 2R
See also SATA 6
Goldfried, Marvin R(obert) 1936- ... 37-40R
Goldgar, Bertrand A(lvin) 1927- ... 65-68
Goldhaber, Gerald Martin 1944- ... CANR-9
Earlier sketch in CA 57-60
Goldhamer, Herbert 1907-1977 ... CANR-2
Earlier sketch in CA 45-48
Goldhurst, Richard 1927- ... 57-60
Goldhurst, William 1929- ... 5-6R
Goldie, Frederick 1914-1980 Obituary ... 105
Goldie, Terrence William 1950- ... 113
Goldie, Terry
See Goldie, Terrence William
Goldin, Augusta 1906- ... CANR-7
Earlier sketch in CA 19-20R
See also SATA 13
Goldin, Grace 1916- ... 115
Goldin, Judah 1914- ... 33-36R
Goldin, Kathleen Mckinney 1943-
Brief entry ... 118
Goldin, Milton 1927- ... 61-64
Goldin, Stephen 1947- ... 77-80
Golding, Lawrence A(rthur) 1926- ... 61-64
Golding, Louis 1907- ... CAP-1
Earlier sketch in CA 9-10
Golding, Martin Philip 1930- ... 101
Golding, Morton J(ay) 1925- ... 21-22R
Golding, Peter 1947- ... 103
Golding, William (Gerald) 1911- ... CANR-13
Earlier sketch in CA 7-8R
See also DLB 15
See also CLC 1, 2, 3, 8, 10, 17, 27
Goldknopf, David 1918- ... 53-56
Goldman, A(ndrew) E. O. 1947- ... 57-60
Goldman, Alan H(arris) 1945- ... 93-96
Goldman, Albert 1927- ... CANR-9
Earlier sketch in CA 19-20R
Goldman, Alex J. 1917- ... 49-52
Goldman, Alvin I(ra) 1938- ... 77-80
Goldman, Alvin L. 1938- ... CANR-1
Earlier sketch in CA 45-48
Goldman, Arnold (Melvyn) 1936- ... 17-18R
Goldman, Bernard 1922- ... 53-56
Goldman, Bo 1932- ... 112
Brief entry ... 109
Goldman, Bruce (Eliot) 1942- ... 61-64
Goldman, Carl A(lexander) 1942- ... 101
Goldman, Charles R(emington) 1930- ... 53-56
Goldman, Dave 1927- ... 107

Goldman, Emma 1869-1940 Brief entry 110
See also TCLC 13
Goldman, Eric (Frederick) 1915- 7-8R
Goldman, Frederick 1921- 81-84
Goldman, George D(avid) 1923- 107
Goldman, Howard H(irsch) 1949- 112
Goldman, Irving 1911- 29-32R
Goldman, Jacquelin (Roberta) 1934- 69-72
Goldman, James A. 1927- CANR-1
Earlier sketch in CA 45-48
Goldman, Lee A. 1946- 25-28R
Goldman, Leo 1920- 85-88
Goldman, Lorraine 1940- 111
Goldman, Louis 1925- 125
Goldman, Marcus Selden 1894- 41-44R
Goldman, Marshall I(rwin) 1930- 9-10R
Goldman, Martin (Raymond Rubin)
1920- 69-72
Goldman, Martin 1950(?)-1984 Obituary ... 113
Goldman, Merle 1931- 33-36R
Goldman, Michael (Paul) 1936- CANR-8
Earlier sketch in CA 17-18R
Goldman, Norma Wynick 1922- 110
Goldman, Peter (Louis) 1933- CANR-24
Earlier sketches in CA 21-22R, CANR-8
Goldman, Phyllis W. 1927- 29-32R
Goldman, Ralph M(orris) 1920- 89-92
Goldman, Richard Franko 1910-1980 ... CANR-5
Obituary 93-96
Earlier sketch in CA 11-12R
Goldman, Ronald 23-24R
Goldman, Sheldon 1939- 23-24R
Goldman, Sherli E(vens) 1930- 25-28R
Goldman, Shifra M(eyerowitz) 1926- ... CANR-25
Earlier sketch in CA 106
Goldman, Susan 1939- 65-68
Goldman, William W. 1931- 9-10R
See also DLB 44
See also CLC 1, 48
Goldman-Eisler, Frieda 1909(?)-1982
Obituary 105
Goldmann, Lucien 1913-1970 .... CAP-2
Earlier sketch in CA 25-28
See also CLC 24
Goldmann, Nahum 1895-1982 Obituary 107
Goldmark, Peter C(arl) 1906-1977 77-80
Obituary 73-76
Goldner, Bernard (Burton) 1919- 5-6R
Goldner, Jack 1900- CAP-2
Earlier sketch in CA 25-28
Goldner, Nancy 1943- 57-60
Goldner, Orville (Charles) 1906- 53-56
Goldovsky, Boris 1908- CANR-16
Earlier sketch in CA 81-84
Goldring, Douglas 1887-1960 Obituary 93-96
Goldring, Patrick (Thomas Zachary)
1921- 29-32R
Goldsberry, Steven 1949- CLC-34
Goldsborough, June 1923- SATA-19
Goldscheider, Calvin 1941- 122
Brief entry 108
Goldscheider, Ludwig 1896- 7-8R
Goldschmidt, Clara Malraux
See Malraux, Clara (Goldschmidt)
Goldschmidt, Walter Rochs 1913- 9-10R
Goldschmidt, Yaagov 1927- 29-32R
Goldsen, Rose Kohn 1918- 1R
Goldsmith
See Miller, Lynne (Ellen)
Goldsmith, Arnold L(ouis) 1928- 41-44R
Goldsmith, Arthur (A., Jr.) 1926- CANR-5
Earlier sketch in CA 15-16R
Goldsmith, Barbara 1931- CANR-5
Earlier sketch in CA 53-56
Goldsmith, Carol Evan 1930- 29-32R
Goldsmith, David H(irsh) 1933- 117
Goldsmith, Donald 1943- 77-80
Goldsmith, Edward 104
Goldsmith, Emanuel S(idney) 1935-
Brief entry 109
Goldsmith, Howard 1943- CANR-21
Earlier sketch in CA 101
See also SATA 24
Goldsmith, Ilse Sondra (Weinberg)
1933- 37-40R
Goldsmith, Jack 1931- 57-60
Goldsmith, Joel S. 1892(?)-1964 Obituary .. 109
Goldsmith, John 1947- 125
Goldsmith, John Herman Thorburn
1903-1987 Obituary 122
See also SATA 52
Goldsmith, Oliver 1728-1774 .... SATA-26
See also DLB 39
Goldsmith, Peter
See Priestley, J(ohn) B(oynton)
Goldsmith, Raymond W(illiam) 1904-1988 .. 115
Obituary 126
Goldsmith, Robert Hillis 1911- 49-52
Goldsmith, Sharon S(weeney) 1948- 57-60
Goldsmith, Walter (Kenneth) 1938- 120
Goldson, Rae L(illian) Segalowitz 1893- 7-8R
Goldstein, Abraham 1903(?)-1982
Obituary 106
Goldstein, Abraham S(amuel) 1925- 33-36R
Goldstein, Alvin H., Sr. 1902-1972
Obituary 33-36R
Goldstein, Arthur D(avid) 1937- 73-76
Goldstein, Bernard R. 1938- 57-60
Goldstein, David 1933- CANR-11
Earlier sketch in CA 19-20R
Goldstein, Donald M(aurice) 1932- CANR-26
Earlier sketch in CA 108
Goldstein, E. Ernest 1918- 11-12R
Goldstein, Edward 1923- 11-12R
Goldstein, Ernest A. 1933- 110
See also SATA 52
Goldstein, Gersham 1938- Brief entry 108
Goldstein, Howard 1922- 93-96
Goldstein, Irwin L. 1937- 41-44R
Goldstein, Israel 1896-1986 53-56
Obituary 119
Goldstein, Jack 1930- 73-76
Goldstein, Jeffrey H(askell) 1942- CANR-14
Earlier sketch in CA 81-84
Goldstein, Jerome 1931- 101
Goldstein, Joan 1932- 114
Goldstein, Jonathan A(mos) 1929- 25-28R
Goldstein, Joseph 1923- 19-20R
Goldstein, Kenneth M(ichael) 1940- 33-36R
Goldstein, Kenneth S. 1927- Brief entry 107
Goldstein, Laurence 1937(?)-1972
Obituary 33-36R
Goldstein, Laurence 1943- 93-96
Goldstein, Leo S. 1924- 15-16R
Goldstein, Leon J. 1927- 69-72
Goldstein, Lisa 1953- CANR-25
Earlier sketch in CA 108
Goldstein, Malcolm 1925- 49-52
Goldstein, Marc 1948- 109
Goldstein, Martin E(ugene) 1939- 41-44R
Goldstein, Melvyn C. 1938- 121
Goldstein, Michael J(oseph) 1930- 103
Goldstein, Milton 1915- CANR-24
Earlier sketch in CA 45-48
Goldstein, Nathan 1927- CANR-16
Earlier sketches in CA 45-48, CANR-1
See also SATA 47
Goldstein, Philip 1910- 53-56
See also SATA 23
Goldstein, Rhoda L.
See Blumberg, Rhoda L(ois Goldstein)
Goldstein, Richard 1944- 25-28R
Goldstein, Roberta Butterfield 1917- 11-12R
Goldstein, Ruth M(artha) 1913- 113
Goldstein, Ruth Tessler 1924- 69-72
Goldstein, Sidney 1927- CANR-25
Earlier sketches in CA 23-24R, CANR-9
Goldstein, Stanley 1922- 103
Goldstein, Stephen R(obert) 1938- CANR-13
Earlier sketch in CA 61-64
Goldstein, Stewart 1941- 65-68
Goldstein, Thomas Eugene 1913-
Brief entry 108
Goldstein, William Isaac 1932- 15-16R
Goldstein-Jackson, Kevin 1946- 106
Goldstine, Herman Heine 1913- 110
Goldston, Robert (Conroy) 1927- CANR-13
Earlier sketch in CA 17-18R
See also SATA 6
Goldstone, Aline L(ewis) 1878(?)-1976
Obituary 65-68
Goldstone, Harmon H(endricks) 1911- 77-80
Goldstone, Herbert 1921- 77-80
Goldstone, Lawrence A.
See Treat, Lawrence
Goldstone, Richard H. 1921- 33-36R
Goldsworthy, David 1938- 33-36R
Goldsworthy, Graeme 1934- 114
Goldsworthy, Peter 1951- 118
Goldthorpe, J(ohn) E(rnest) 1921- 49-52
Goldthorpe, Rhiannon 1934- 126
Goldthwaite, Eaton K. 1907- 25-28R
Goldthwaite, Richard A. 1933- Brief entry .. 108
Goldwater, Barry (Morris) 1909- 41-44R
Goldwater, Eleanor Lowenstein
1909(?)-1980 Obituary 102
Goldwater, John AITN-1
Goldwater, Robert 1907-1973 Obituary ...41-44R
Goldwater, Walter Delmar 1907-1985
Obituary 116
Goldwin, Robert Allen 1922- 102
Goldwyn, Robert M(alcolm) 1930- 122
Gole, Victor Leslie 1903- CANR-23
Earlier sketch in CA 107
Goleman, Daniel 1946- 111
Golembiewski, Robert T(homas)
1932- CANR-21
Earlier sketches in CA 5-6R, CANR-6
Golenbock, Peter 1946- CANR-8
Earlier sketch in CA 57-60
Golenpaul, Ann 1907(?)-1986 Obituary 119
Golf, Loyal E.
See Golv, Loyal E(ugene)
Golffing, Francis (Charles) 1910- CANR-5
Earlier sketch in CA 5-6R
Goliard, Roy
See Shipley, Joseph T(wadell)
Golightly, Bonnie H(elen) 1919- 2R
Goll, Reinhold W(eimar) 1897- 7-8R
See also SATA 26
Gollan, Robin 1917- 13-14R
Gollancz, Victor 1893-1967 Obituary 116
Golledge, Reginald G(eorge) 1937- 41-44R
Goller, Celia (Fremlin) 1914- CANR-5
Earlier sketch in CA 13-14R
Golley, Frank Benjamin 1930- Brief entry ... 106
Gollin, Gillian Lindt
See Lindt, Gillian
Gollings, Franklin O. A. 1919- 23-24R
Gollmar, Robert H. 1903(?)-1987
Obituary 123
Gollwitzer, Heinz 1917- 25-28R
Gologor, Ethan 1940- 101
Golomb, Claire 1928- 103
Golomb, Louis 1943- CANR-16
Earlier sketch in CA 85-88
Golombek, Harry 1911- 103
Golon, Serge(anne) 1903-1972
Obituary 37-40R
Golovine, Michael N(icholas) 1903-1965 ....5-6R
Golson, G. Barry 1944- 69-72
Golv, Loyal E(ugene) 1926- CANR-1
Earlier sketch in CA 4R
Golz, R(einhardt) Lud 1936- CANR-5
Earlier sketch in CA 13-14R
Gom, Leona 1946- 116
Gombault, Charles Henri 1907-1983
Obituary 110
Gomberg, Adeline Wishengrad 1915- 19-20R
Gomberg, William 1911-1985 ....17-18R
Obituary 118
Gombossy, Zoltan
See Gabel, Joseph
Gombrich, E(rnst) H(ans Josef) 1909- ... CANR-5
Earlier sketch in CA 53-56
Gombrowicz, Witold 1904-1969 .... CAP-2
Obituary 25-28R
Earlier sketch in CA 19-20
See also CLC 4, 7, 11, 49
Gomery, Douglas 1945- 110
Gomez, David F(ederico) 1940- 49-52
Gomez, Joseph A(nthony) 1942- 104
Gomez, Rudolph 1930- 53-56
Gomez de la Serna, Ramon 1888-1963
Obituary 116
See also CLC 9
Gomez-Gil, Alfredo 1936- 41-44R
See also AITN 1
Gomori, George 1934- CANR-9
Earlier sketch in CA 23-24R
Gompertz, Rolf 1927- CANR-11
Earlier sketch in CA 69-72
Gongora, Maria Eugenia 1948- 104
Gonick, Jean 1950- 121
Gontarski, S(tanley) E. 1942- 114
Gontier, Fernande 19(?)- CLC-50
Gonzales, John
See Terrall, Robert
Gonzales, Manuel G(arcia) 1943- 111
Gonzales, Pancho
See Gonzales, Richard Alonzo
Gonzales, Richard Alonzo 1928-
Brief entry 105
Gonzales, Sylvia Alicia 1943- 77-80
Gonzalez, Alfonso 1927- 41-44R
Gonzalez, Angel 1925- CANR-15
Earlier sketch in CA 85-88
Gonzalez, Arturo 1928- 77-80
Gonzalez, Catherine Gunsalus
See Gunsalus Gonzalez, Catherine
Gonzalez, Edward 1933- Brief entry 109
Gonzalez, Gloria 1940- CANR-24
Earlier sketch in CA 65-68
See also SATA 23
Gonzalez, Jaime Jose 1925- 103
Gonzalez, Justo L(uis) 1937- CANR-16
Earlier sketch in CA 29-32R
Gonzalez, N(estor) V(icente) M(adali)
1915- CANR-2
Earlier sketch in CA 4R
Gonzalez, Nancie L(oudon) 1929- 103
Gonzalez, Richard F(lorentz) 1927- 114
Gonzalez, Sergio A(ntonio) Torres
See Torres Gonzalez, Sergio A(ntonio)
Gonzalez-Aller, Faustino 1922- 81-84
Gonzalez-Crussi, F(rank) 1936- 126
Brief entry 121
Gonzalez-Echevarria, Roberto 1943- 106
Gonzalez-Gerth, Miguel 1926- 69-72
Gonzalez Lopez, Emilio 1903- CANR-2
Earlier sketch in CA 49-52
Gonzalez-Mena, Janet 1937- 111
Gonzalez-Paz, Elsie E. 1913- 45-48
Gonzalez-Wippler, Migene 1936- 109
Gooby, Peter Taylor
See Taylor-Gooby, Peter
Gooch, Bob
See Gooch, Robert M(iletus)
Gooch, Brison D(owling) 1925- 13-14R
Gooch, Bryan Niel Shirley 1937- 93-96
Gooch, George Peabody 1873-1968 ....7-8R
Gooch, John 1945- 126
Gooch, Robert M(iletus) 1919- CANR-13
Earlier sketch in CA 77-80
Gooch, Stan(ley Alfred) 1932- CANR-14
Earlier sketch in CA 77-80
Gooch, Steve 1945- CANR-20
Earlier sketch in CA 101
Good, Carter V(ictor) 1897- 7-8R
Good, David F(ranklin) 1943- 125
Good, Edwin M(arshall) 1928- CANR-11
Earlier sketch in CA 17-18R
Good, H(arry) G(ehman) 1880-1971 .... 2R
Obituary 103
Good, I(rving) John 1916- CANR-3
Earlier sketch in CA 5-6R
Good, Lawrence R. 1924- 15-16R
Good, Paul 1929- 85-88
Good, Robert Crocker 1924- 73-76
Good, Thomas L(indall) 1943- CANR-22
Earlier sketches in CA 57-60, CANR-8
Goodacre, Elizabeth Jane 1929- 102
Goodall, Daphne Machin
See Machin Goodall, Daphne (Edith)
Goodall, Jane 1934- CANR-2
Earlier sketch in CA 45-48
Goodall, John Strickland 1908- 33-36R
See also SATA 4
Goodall, Leonard E. 1937- 85-88
Goodall, Marcus C(ampbell) 1914- 33-36R
Goodall, Melanie
See Drachman, Julian M(oses)
Goodall, Norman 1896-1985 Obituary 115
Goodall, Vanne Morris
See Morris-Goodall, Vanne
Goodavage, Joseph F. 1925- 25-28R
Goodbody, Slim
See Burstein, John
Goodchild, Peter 1939- 106
Goode, Barry 1938- 118
Goode, Diane 1949- SATA-15
Goode, Erich 1938- CANR-16
Earlier sketches in CA 49-52, CANR-1
Goode, Gerald 1899(?)-1983 Obituary 111
Goode, James 1924- 123
Goode, James M. 1939- 93-96
Goode, John 1927- 103
Goode, Kenneth G. 1932- 49-52
Goode, Richard (Benjamin) 1916- 17-18R
Goode, Ruth 1905- 77-80
Goode, Stephen H(ogue) 1924- CANR-2
Earlier sketch in CA 45-48
Goode, Stephen Ray 1943- CANR-18
Earlier sketch in CA 57-60
See also SATA 40
Goode, William Josiah 1917- 102
Goodell, Charles E(llsworth) 1926-1987 ...81-84
Obituary 121
Goodell, Donald (James) 1938- 45-48
Goodell, John S. 1939- 73-76
Goodell, Rae 1944- 77-80
Goodenough, Erwin R(amsdell)
1893-1965 ....7-8R
Goodenough, Evelyn
See Pitcher, Evelyn G(oodenough)
Goodenough, Ward Hunt 1919- CANR-2
Earlier sketch in CA 4R
Goodenow, Earle 1913- SATA-40
Gooders, John 1937- CANR-6
Earlier sketch in CA 57-60
Goodfellow, Peter 1935- 115
Goodfield, (Gwyneth) June 1927- 9-10R
Goodfriend, Arthur 1907- 5-6R
Goodgold, Edwin 1944- CANR-23
Earlier sketch in CA 21-22R
Goodhart, Arthur Lehman 1891-1978 85-88
Obituary 81-84
Goodhart, Robert S(tanley) 1909- 89-92
Goodheart, Barbara 1934- 33-36R
Goodheart, Eugene 1931- CANR-18
Earlier sketches in CA 5-6R, CANR-3
Goodin, Gayle 1938- 33-36R
Goodin, Robert Edward 1950- CANR-22
Earlier sketch in CA 105
Gooding, Cynthia 1924- 33-36R
Gooding, John (Ervine) 1940- 21-22R
Gooding, Judson 1926- 73-76
Gooding, Kathleen (Tinney) 116
Goodis, David 1917-1967 .... 1R
Goodkin, Sanford R(onald) 1929- 104
Goodkind, Henry M. 1904(?)-1970
Obituary 104
Goodlad, John I. 1920- CANR-19
Earlier sketches in CA 7-8R, CANR-3
Goodman, A(lvin) Harold 1924- 103
Goodman, A(dolph) W(inkler) 1915- 57-60
Goodman, Ann (Davidow) 1932- 107
Goodman, Arnold Abraham 1913- 109
Goodman, Benjamin David 1909(?)-1986
Obituary 119
Goodman, Benny
See Goodman, Benjamin David
Goodman, Celia (Mary) 1916- 123
Goodman, Charles S(chaffner) 1916- 33-36R
Goodman, David (Allen) 1941- 119
Goodman, David Michael 1936- 19-20R
Goodman, David S. 1917- 29-32R
Goodman, Deborah Lerme 1956- 121
See also SATA 49, 50
Goodman, Edward J(ulius) 1916- 111
Goodman, Elaine 1930- 37-40R
See also SATA 9
Goodman, Elizabeth B. 1912- 25-28R
Goodman, Ellen (Holtz) 1941- 104
Goodman, Elliot R(aymond) 1923- 1R
Goodman, Emily Jane 1940- 65-68
Goodman, Eugene B(enedict) 1922- 113
Goodman, Felicitas D(aniels) 1914- CANR-23
Earlier sketches in CA 53-56, CANR-4
Goodman, George J(erome) W(aldo)
1930- 21-22R
Goodman, Grant K(ohn) 1924- CANR-15
Earlier sketch in CA 41-44R
Goodman, Harriet Wilinsky 111
Goodman, Herman 1894-1971 Obituary 105
Goodman, James M(arion) 1929- 117
Goodman, Jay S. 1940- 37-40R
Goodman, Joan Elizabeth 1950- 126
See also SATA 50
Goodman, Jonathan 1931- CANR-13
Earlier sketch in CA 33-36R
Goodman, Joseph Irving 1908- 102
Goodman, Kenneth S. 1927- 25-28R
Goodman, Lenn Evan 1944- 53-56
Goodman, Leonard H(enry) 1941- 103
Goodman, Linda 1925- 89-92
Goodman, Louis Wolf 1942- 25-28R
Goodman, Mark 1939- 126
Goodman, Michael B(arry) 1949- 107
Goodman, Mitchell 1923- CANR-4
Earlier sketch in CA 4R
Goodman, (Henry) Nelson 1906- 45-48
Goodman, Norman 1934- CANR-17
Earlier sketches in CA 49-52, CANR-1
Goodman, Paul 1911-1972 .... CAP-2
Obituary 37-40R
Earlier sketch in CA 19-20
See also CLC 1, 2, 4, 7
Goodman, Percival 1904- 2R
Goodman, Philip 1911- 33-36R
Goodman, Randolph 1908- CANR-2
Earlier sketch in CA 7-8R
Goodman, Rebecca Gruver 1931- 77-80
Goodman, Richard Merle 1932- CANR-18
Earlier sketch in CA 102
Goodman, Roger B. 1919- CANR-9
Earlier sketch in CA 23-24R

Goodman, Ronald A. 1938- 73-76
Goodman, Rubin Robert 1913-1978
Obituary 81-84
Goodman, Saul 1919- 103
Goodman, Seymour S. 1931- CANR-22
Earlier sketch in CA 45-48
Goodman, Sonya
See Arcone, Sonya
Goodman, Stanley J(oshua) 1910- 110
Goodman, Steve 1948-1984 Obituary 113
Goodman, Steven M(ichael) 1957- 126
Goodman, Walter 1927- CANR-7
Earlier sketch in CA 9-10R
See also SATA 9
Goodnough, David L. 1930- 93-96
Goodnow, Henry F(rank) 1917- 15-16R
Goodnow, Jacqueline (Jarrett) 1924- CANR-5
Earlier sketch in CA 15-16R
Goodovitch, I(srael) M(eir) 1934- 25-28R
Goodpaster, Andrew J(ackson) 1915- 109
Goodpaster, Kenneth E(dwin) 1944- CANR-17
Earlier sketch in CA 97-100
Goodreau, William Joseph, Jr. 1931- 4R
Goodrich, David L(loyd) 1930- 85-88
Goodrich, Donna Clark 1938- 117
Goodrich, Foster E(dward) 1908-1972
Obituary 37-40R
Goodrich, Frances 1890(?)-1984 Obituary 111
See also DLB 26
Goodrich, Frances C. 1933- 23-24R
Goodrich, L(uther) Carrington
1894-1986 CANR-2
Obituary 120
Earlier sketch in CA 7-8R
Goodrich, Leland Matthew 1899- 81-84
Goodrich, Lloyd 1897-1987 69-72
Obituary 122
Goodrich, Norma Lorre 1917- 53-56
Goodrich, Robert E(dward), Jr. 1909- 33-36R
Goodrich, Samuel Griswold 1793-1860 SATA-23
See also DLB 1, 42, 73
Goodrich, William Lloyd 1910(?)-1975
Obituary 61-64
Goodrick, Edward W(illiam) 1913- 111
Goodrick-Clarke, Nicholas 1953- 123
Goodrum, Charles A(lvin) 1923- CANR-12
Earlier sketch in CA 25-28R
Goodsall, Robert Harold 1891-19(?) CANR-4
Earlier sketch in CA 7-8R
Goodsell, Charles T(rue) 1932- CANR-8
Earlier sketch in CA 61-64
Goodsell, Fred Field 1880-1976 3R
Obituary 69-72
Goodsell, Jane Neuberger 1921(?)-1988
Obituary 126
Goodson, Felix E(mmett) 1922- 49-52
Goodspeed, Donald J(ames) 1919- 5-6R
Goodspeed, Edgar Johnson 1871-1962
Obituary 93-96
Goodspeed, Peter 1944- 110
Goodstein, David B. 1932(?)-1985
Obituary 116
Goodstein, Leonard D(avid) 1927- CANR-13
Earlier sketch in CA 33-36R
Goodstein, Marvin (Elias) 1927- 125
Goodstein, R(euben) L(ouis) 1912-1985 53-56
Obituary 116
Goodwin, Albert 1906- 5-6R
Goodwin, Bennie Eugene II 1933- 112
Goodwin, Craufurd D(avid) W(ycliffe)
1934- CANR-14
Earlier sketch in CA 37-40R
Goodwin, Dave 1926- 113
Goodwin, Derek 1920- 93-96
Goodwin, Donald W(illiam) 1931- 65-68
Goodwin, Doris (Helen) Kearns 1943- CANR-23
Earlier sketch in CA 103
Goodwin, Eugene D.
See Kaye, Marvin (Nathan)
Goodwin, Geoffrey (Lawrence) 1916- 106
Goodwin, H(arry) Eugene 1922- 126
Goodwin, Hal
See Goodwin, Harold Leland
Goodwin, Harold 1919- 57-60
Goodwin, Harold Leland 1914- CANR-2
Earlier sketch in CA 4R
See also SATA 13, 51
Goodwin, John Lonnen 1921- 108
Goodwin, John R(obert) 1929- 77-80
Goodwin, Leonard 1929- 41-44R
Goodwin, Mark
See Matthews, Stanley G(oodwin)
Goodwin, (Trevor) Noel 1927- 124
Goodwin, R(ichard) M(urphey) 1913- CANR-12
Earlier sketch in CA 29-32R
Goodwin, Richard N(aradhof) 1931-
Brief entry 111
Goodwin, Robert L. 1928(?)-1983
Obituary 109
Goodwin, Stephen 1943- CANR-8
Earlier sketch in CA 57-60
See also DLBY 82
Goodwin, Suzanne CANR-14
Earlier sketch in CA 77-80
Goodwyn, Floyd L(owell) 1940- 113
Goodwyn, Lawrence 1928- 23-24R
Goody, Joan Edelman 1935- 17-18R
Goodyear, Frank H., Jr. 1944- 122
Goodyear, John H(enry) III 1941- 111
Gookin, Daniel 1612-1687 DLB-24
Gool, Reshard 1931- 97-100
Goolagong, Evonne 1951- 89-92
Goold-Adams, Richard 1916- 13-14R
Goon, Fook Mun 1917(?)-1984 Obituary 113
Gooneratne, (Malini) Yasmine 1935- CANR-18
Earlier sketch in CA 29-32R
Goor, Nancy (Ruth Miller) 1944- 113
See also SATA 34, 39
Goor, Ron(ald Stephen) 1940- 113
See also SATA 34, 39
Goossen, Agnes
See Epp, Margaret A(gnes)
Goossen, Irvy W. 37-40R
Goot, Mary Vander
See Vander Goot, Mary
Gopal, Sarvepalli 1923- 104
Gopalakrishnan, Chennat 1936- 112
Gopen, George D(avid) 1945- 113
Gorak, Jan 1952- 126
Goralski, Robert 1928-1988 105
Obituary 125
Goran, Lester 1928- 45-48
Goran, Morris 1918- CANR-2
Earlier sketch in CA 3R
Gorbanevskaya, Natalya 1936- 111
Gorbatov, Alexander V. 1891(?)-1973
Obituary 45-48
Gorden, Raymond L(owell) 1919- 53-56
Gordenker, Leon 1923- 23-24R
Gordett, Marea (Beth) 1949- 117
Gordh, George (Rudolph) 1912- 13-14R
Gordimer, Nadine 1923- CANR-3
Earlier sketch in CA 5-6R
See also CLC 3, 5, 7, 10, 18, 33
Gordin, Richard Davis 1928- 53-56
Gordis, Robert 1908- CANR-9
Earlier sketch in CA 13-14R
Gordon, Ad
See Hano, Arnold
Gordon, Alan F. 1947- 102
Gordon, Albert I(saac) 1903-1968 CAP-1
Earlier sketch in CA 11-12
Gordon, Alex
See Cotler, Gordon
Gordon, Alison (Ruth) 1943- 121
Gordon, Alvin J. 1912- 33-36R
Gordon, Ambrose, Jr. 1920-1987 33-36R
Obituary 122
Gordon, Andrew (Mark) 1945- 115
Gordon, Angela
See Paine, Lauran (Bosworth)
Gordon, Anne Wolrige
See Wolrige Gordon, Anne
Gordon, Antoinette K. 1892(?)-1975
Obituary 57-60
Gordon, Archibald Victor Dudley
1913-1984 Obituary 114
Gordon, Archie
See Gordon, Archibald Victor Dudley
Gordon, Arthur 1912- 5-6R
Gordon, Barbara 1935- CANR-17
Earlier sketch in CA 89-92
Gordon, Barry (Lewis John) 1934- 102
Gordon, Bernard K. 1932- 85-88
Gordon, Bernard Ludwig 1931- 29-32R
See also SATA 27
Gordon, Bertram M(artin) 1943- 101
Gordon, Beverly 1948- 93-96
Gordon, Burton L(e Roy) 1920- 114
Gordon, Caroline 1895-1981 CAP-1
Obituary 103
Earlier sketch in CA 11-12
See also DLB 4, 9
See also DLBY 81
See also CLC 6, 13, 29
Gordon, Charles William 1860-1937
Brief entry 109
Gordon, Colonel H. R.
See Ellis, Edward S(ylvester)
Gordon, Cyrus H(erzl) 1908- CANR-5
Earlier sketch in CA 4R
Gordon, Dane R. 1925- 33-36R
Gordon, David Cole 1922- 25-28R
Gordon, David J. 1929- Brief entry 105
Gordon, Diana
See Andrews, Lucilla Mathew
Gordon, Diana R(ussell) 1938- 49-52
Gordon, Donald
See Payne, Donald Gordon
Gordon, Donald Craigie 1911- 19-20R
Gordon, Donald E(dward) 1931-1984
Obituary 112
Gordon, Donald Ramsay 1929- CANR-14
Earlier sketch in CA 37-40R
Gordon, Doreen
See Chard, Judy
Gordon, Dorothy 1893-1970 73-76
See also SATA 20
Gordon, Edmund Wyatt 1921- 37-40R
Gordon, Edwin 1927- CANR-10
Earlier sketch in CA 17-18R
Gordon, Ernest 1916- CANR-2
Earlier sketch in CA 1R
Gordon, (Alexander) Esme 1910- 108
Gordon, Esther S(aranga) 1935- CANR-7
Earlier sketch in CA 53-56
See also SATA 10
Gordon, Ethel Edison 1915- 53-56
Gordon, Felice 1939- 97-100
Gordon, Frederick CANR-26
Earlier sketches in CA 19-20, CAP-2
See also SATA 1
Gordon, Fritz
See Jarvis, Fred(erick) G(ordon, Jr.)
Gordon, Gary
See Edmonds, I(vy) G(ordon)
Gordon, George
See Hasford, (Jerry) Gustav
Gordon, George Byron 1911- 33-36R
Gordon, George J(acob) 1943- 111
Gordon, George N(ewton) 1926- CANR-5
Earlier sketch in CA 1R
Gordon, Gerald 1909- CAP-1
Earlier sketch in CA 13-14
Gordon, Giles (Alexander Esme) 1940- 41-44R
See also DLB 14
Gordon, Gordon 1912- CANR-7
Earlier sketch in CA 5-6R
Gordon, Guanetta Stewart 37-40R
Gordon, Hal
See Goodwin, Harold Leland
Gordon, Harold J(ackson), Jr. 1919- 33-36R
Gordon, Harry
See Gordon, Henry Alfred
Gordon, (Charles) Harry (Clinton) Pirie
See Pirie-Gordon, (Charles) Harry
(Clinton)
Gordon, Henry Alfred 1925- CANR-5
Earlier sketch in CA 53-56
Gordon, I(an) R(obert) F(raser) 1939- 69-72
Gordon, Ian
See Fellowes-Gordon, Ian (Douglas)
Gordon, Ian A(listair) 1908- CANR-11
Earlier sketch in CA 25-28R
Gordon, Ida L. 1907- CAP-2
Earlier sketch in CA 33-36
Gordon, Ira J(ay) 1923-1978 CANR-26
Earlier sketch in CA 69-72
Gordon, (Gilbert) James 1918- 61-64
Gordon, Jane
See Lee, Elsie
Gordon, Jeffie Ross
See Enderle, Judith (Ann) Ross
and Tessler, Stephanie Gordon
Gordon, Joanne J(oy) 1956- 108
Gordon, John (Rutherford) 1890-1974
Obituary 104
Gordon, John (William) 1925- CANR-11
Earlier sketch in CA 103
Gordon, John
See Gesner, Clark
Gordon, John Fraser 1916- CANR-22
Earlier sketch in CA 105
Gordon, John Steele 1944- 57-60
Gordon, Kermit 1916-1976 Obituary 65-68
Gordon, Kurtz
See Kurtz, C(larence) Gordon
Gordon, Leland J(ames) 1897- 41-44R
Gordon, Leonard 1935- 53-56
Gordon, Leonard A. 1938- 37-40R
Gordon, Leonard H. D. 1928- 29-32R
Gordon, Lesley
See Elliott, Lesley
Gordon, Lew
See Baldwin, Gordon C.
Gordon, Lillian L. 1925-1977 29-32R
Gordon, Lincoln 1913- 117
Gordon, (Irene) Linda 1940- CANR-25
Earlier sketches in CA 65-68, CANR-10
Gordon, Lois G. 1938- CANR-13
Earlier sketch in CA 33-36R
Gordon, Lou 1917(?)-1977 Obituary 69-72
Gordon, Margaret (Anna) 1939- SATA-9
Gordon, Margaret T(aber) 1939- 81-84
Gordon, Mark 1942- 118
Gordon, Mary (Catherine) 1949- 102
See also DLB 6
See also DLBY 81
See also CLC 13, 22
Gordon, Mary Ebbitt
See Winters, Catherine (Mary)
Gordon, Michael 1940- 41-44R
Gordon, Michael (David) 1952- 123
Gordon, Mildred 1912-1979 CANR-7
Obituary 85-88
Earlier sketch in CA 5-6R
See also SATA 24
Gordon, Mitchell 1925- 7-8R
Gordon, Myron J(ules) 1920- CANR-6
Earlier sketch in CA 5-6R
Gordon, Nancy
See Heinl, Nancy G(ordon)
Gordon, Noah 1926- 17-18R
Gordon, Oliver
See Emerson, H(enry) O(liver)
Gordon, Patricia 1909- 21-22R
Gordon, Percival Hector 1884-1975 41-44R
Gordon, Peter
See Wilkes-Hunter, R(ichard)
Gordon, R(ichard) L(aurence) 1920-
Brief entry 114
Gordon, Ray
See Wainwright, Gordon Ray
Gordon, Rex
See Hough, S(tanley) B(ennett)
Gordon, Richard
See Ostlere, Gordon (Stanley)
Gordon, Richard L(ewis) 1934- 29-32R
Gordon, Robert A(aron) 1908-1978 CANR-4
Obituary 77-80
Earlier sketch in CA 5-6R
Gordon, Robert C(oningsby) 1921- 5-6R
Gordon, Robert J. 1947- 121
Gordon, Ruth 1896-1985 81-84
Obituary 117
Gordon, Samuel 1907(?)-1984 Obituary 114
Gordon, Sanford D(aniel) 1924- 33-36R
Gordon, Selma
See Lanes, Selma Gordon
Gordon, Shirley 1921- 97-100
See also SATA 41, 48
Gordon, Sol 1923- CANR-4
Earlier sketch in CA 53-56
See also SATA 11
See also CLC 26
Gordon, Steve 1938(?)-1982 Obituary 108
Gordon, Stewart
See Shirreffs, Gordon D(onald)
Gordon, Strathearn 1902-1983 Obituary 109
Gordon, Suzanne 1945- CANR-4
Earlier sketch in CA 49-52
Gordon, Sydney 1914- 29-32R
Gordon, Theodore J. 1930- 17-18R
Gordon, Thomas 1918- 29-32R
Gordon, Tom
See Thomas, Gordon
Gordon, Walter Kelly 1930- 33-36R
Gordon, Walter L(ockhart) 1906-1987 97-100
Obituary 122
Gordon, Wendell (Chaffee) 1916- 19-20R
Gordone, Charles 1925- 93-96
See also BW
See also DLB 7
See also CLC 1, 4
Gordons, The
See Gordon, Gordon
and Gordon, Mildred
Gordon Walker, Patrick (Chrestien)
1907- 29-32R
Gordon-Watson, Mary 1948- 112
Gordy, Berry, Sr. 1888-1978 102
Gore, Albert (Arnold) 1907- Brief entry 112
Gore, Arthur Kattendyke S(trange) D(avid)
A(rchibald) 1910-1983 Obituary 109
Gore, Christopher 1946(?)-1988 Obituary 125
Gore, John Francis 1885-1983 Obituary 110
Gore, Robert Hayes 1886-1972 Obituary 89-92
Gore, William Jay 1924- 11-12R
Goreau, Angeline 1951- 102
Gore-Booth, Paul Henry 1909-1984
Obituary 113
Gorecki, Jan 1926- 57-60
Gorelick, Bryna Siegel
See Siegel-Gorelick, Bryna
Gorelick, Molly C. 1920- 23-24R
See also SATA 9
Gorelik, Mordecai 1899- CAP-2
Earlier sketch in CA 23-24
Goren, Arthur A(ryeh) 1926- Brief entry 111
Goren, Charles H(enry) 1901- 69-72
Goren, Judith 1933- 61-64
Gorenko, Anna Andreevna
See Akhmatova, Anna
Gorenstein, Paul 1934- 114
Gorenstein, Shirley 1928- 73-76
Gorer, Geoffrey (Edgar) 1905-1985 69-72
Obituary 116
Gores, Joe
See Gores, Joseph N(icholas)
Gores, Joseph N(icholas) 1931- CANR-10
Earlier sketch in CA 25-28R
Gorey, Edward (St. John) 1925- CANR-9
Earlier sketch in CA 7-8R
See also SATA 27, 29
See also DLB 61
Gorey, Hays 57-60
Gorham, Charles Orson 1911-1975 CANR-6
Obituary 61-64
Earlier sketch in CA 1R
See also SATA 36
Gorham, J(eanne) U(rich) 1920- 53-56
Gorham, Maurice Anthony Coneys 1902- 9-10R
Gorham, Michael
See Folsom, Franklin (Brewster)
Gorkin, Jess 1913-1985 Obituary 115
Gorky, Maxim
See Peshkov, Alexei Maximovich
See also TCLC 8
Gorling, Lars
See Goerling, Lars
Gorman, Beth
See Paine, Lauran (Bosworth)
Gorman, Burton W(illiam) 1907- 29-32R
Gorman, George H. 1916-1982 Obituary 106
Gorman, Ginny
See Zachary, Hugh
Gorman, John Andrew 1938- 41-44R
Gorman, Katherine ?-1972 CAP-2
Earlier sketch in CA 29-32
Gorman, Ralph 1897-1972 Obituary 37-40R
Gorman, T. Walter 1916(?)-1972
Obituary 37-40R
Gorman, Thomas David 1919-1986 123
Obituary 120
Gorman, Tom
See Gorman, Thomas David
Gormley, Beatrice 1942- 113
See also SATA 35, 39
Gormley, Gerard (Joseph) 1931- CANR-14
Earlier sketch in CA 81-84
Gormley, Mike 1945- 69-72
Gorn, Janice L(eonora) 1915- 53-56
Gorn, Mordechai Martin 1890-1986
Obituary 119
Gorney, Roderic 1924- 73-76
Gorney, Sondra 1918- 45-48
Gornick, Vivian 1935- 101
Goro, Fritz 1901-1986 Obituary 121
Gorodetsky, Gabriel 1945- 69-72
Gorog, Judith (Allen) 1938- 114
See also SATA 39
Gorrell, Robert Mark 1914- CANR-5
Earlier sketch in CA 3R
Gorsline, Douglas (Warner) 1913-1985 CANR-9
Obituary 116
Earlier sketch in CA 61-64
See also SATA 11, 43
Gorsline, (Sally) Marie 1928- 106
See also SATA 28
Gorsline, S. M.
See Gorsline, (Sally) Marie
Gorst, Elliot Marcet 1885-1973 Obituary 104
Gortner, Ross A(iken), Jr. 1912- 5-6R
Gortner, Willis Alway 1913- 108
Gorton, Richard A. 1932- CANR-7
Earlier sketch in CA 57-60

Goryan, Sirak
See Saroyan, William
Goscilo, Helena 1945- 118
Goscinny, Rene 1926-1977 117
Obituary 113
See also SATA 39, 47
Gosden, Freeman F(isher) 1899-1982
Obituary 108
Gosden, Peter Henry John Heather 1927- .. 93-96
Gosdin, Rex 1938(?)-1983 Obituary 109
Gose, Elliott B(ickley), Jr. 1926- 33-36R
Goshay, Robert C. 1931- 15-16R
Goshen, Charles E(rnest) 1916- CANR-13
Earlier sketch in CA 21-22R
Goshgarian, Gary 1942- 112
Goshorn, Elizabeth 1953- 61-64
Goslin, David A. 1936- 9-10R
Gosling, J(ustin) C(yril) B(ertrand) 1930- .. 77-80
Gosling, John Neville 1905- 7-8R
Gosling, Nigel 1909-1982 Obituary 106
Gosling, Paula 1939- 111
Gosling, William Flower 1901- 7-8R
Goslovich, Marianne
See Brown, Morris Cecil
Gosnell, Betty
See Gosnell, Elizabeth Duke Tucker
Gosnell, Elizabeth Duke Tucker 1921- 29-32R
Gosnell, Harold F(oote) 1896- 41-44R
Goss, Clay 1946- 57-60
Gosse, Edmund (William) 1849-1928
Brief entry 117
See also DLB 57
See also TCLC 28
Gosselin, Chris(topher C.) 1929- 110
Gosset, W(illiam) P(atrick) 1946- 126
Gossett, Philip 1941- CANR-15
Earlier sketch in CA 89-92
Gossett, Thomas F. 1916- 13-14R
Gossman, Lionel 1929- CANR-7
Earlier sketch in CA 17-18R
Gostelow, Mary 1943- CANR-8
Earlier sketch in CA 61-64
Goswami, Maggie 1937- 117
Gotesky, Rubin 1906- 45-48
Gotfurt, Frederick 1902(?)-1973 Obituary 104
Gotlieb, Phyllis Fay (Bloom) 1926- CANR-7
Earlier sketch in CA 15-16R
See also CLC 18
Gotlieb, Sondra 1936- Brief entry 111
Gotoff, Harold C(harles) 1936- Brief entry .. 112
Gots, Ronald E(ric) 1943- 65-68
Gotshalk, D(ilman) W(alter) 1901-1973 .. CANR-6
Earlier sketch in CA 1R
Gott, K(enneth) D(avidson) 1923- 81-84
Gott, Richard (Willoughby) 1938- 81-84
Gottehrer, Barry H. 1935- 13-14R
Gotterer, Malcolm H(arold) 1924- 37-40R
Gottesfeld, Evelyn 1948- 104
Gottesfeld, Mary L. 1926(?)-1984
Obituary 113
Gottesman, Irving I(sadore) 1930- 37-40R
Gottesman, Ronald 1933- CANR-13
Earlier sketch in CA 33-36R
Gottesman, S. D.
See Kornbluth, C(yril) M.
and Lowndes, Robert A(ugustine) W(ard)
and Pohl, Frederik
Gottfried, Alex 1919- 1R
Gottfried, Manfred 1900-1985 Obituary 117
Gottfried, Martin 1933- CANR-14
Earlier sketch in CA 23-24R
Gottfried, Robert Steven 1949- 111
Gottfried, Theodore Mark 1928- CANR-18
Earlier sketch in CA 33-36R
Gottlieb, Adolph 1903-1974 Obituary 49-52
Gottlieb, Alan M(erril) 1947- 125
Gottlieb, Alex 1906-1988 Obituary 126
Gottlieb, Beatrice M. 1889(?)-1979
Obituary 89-92
Gottlieb, Bernhardt Stanley 1898- 2R
Gottlieb, Carla 1912- 119
Gottlieb, Darcy 1922- 77-80
Gottlieb, Elaine 61-64
Gottlieb, Gerald 1923- 5-6R
See also SATA 7
Gottlieb, Lois Davidson 1926- 17-28R
Gottlieb, Moshe R(aphael) 1931- 113
Gottlieb, Naomi R(uth) 1925- 57-60
Gottlieb, Paul 1936- 93-96
Gottlieb, Robert A(dams) 1931-
Brief entry 125
Gottlieb, Robin (Grossman) 1928- CANR-2
Earlier sketch in CA 4R
Gottlieb, (Anne Ruth) Vera 1945- 117
Gottlieb, William P(aul) 1917- 101
See also SATA 24
Gottman, John M(ordechai) 1942- CANR-12
Earlier sketch in CA 69-72
Gottschalk, Elin Toona
See Toona, Elin(-Kai)
Gottschalk, Louis (Reichenthal)
1899-1975 .... CANR-9
Obituary 57-60
Earlier sketch in CA 15-16R
Gottschalk, Louis A(ugust) 1916- CANR-19
Earlier sketches in CA 53-56, CANR-5
Gottschalk, Paul A. 1939- 61-64
Gottschalk, Shimon S. 1929- 89-92
Gottschalk, Stephen 1940- 77-80
Gottsegen, Abby J. 1956- 105
Gottsegen, Gloria Behar 1930- 77-80
Gottshall, Franklin Henry 1902- CANR-2
Earlier sketch in CA 7-8R
Gottwald, Norman Karol 1926- 108
Gotwals, Vernon (Detwiler, Jr.) 1924- 5-6R
Gotz, Ignacio L.
See Goetz, Ignacio L.
Gotzsche, Anne-Lise 1939- 97-100
Goud, Anne 1917- 61-64
Goudeket, Maurice 1889-1977 Obituary 69-72
Goudey, Alice E. 1898- 73-76
See also SATA 20
Goudge, Eileen 1950- 126
Goudge, Elizabeth (de Beauchamp)
1900-1984 .... CANR-5
Obituary 112
Earlier sketch in CA 7-8R
See also SATA 2, 38
Goudie, Andrew Shaw 1945- CANR-17
Earlier sketches in CA 49-52, CANR-1
Goudinoff, Peter Alexis 1941- 112
Goudiss, Maria Agnes D'Elia 1941- 114
Goudsmit, Samuel A(braham) 1902-1978
Obituary 81-84
Gouge, Orson
See Larner, Jeremy
Gough, Barry Morton 1938- CANR-11
Earlier sketch in CA 61-64
Gough, Catherine
See Mulgan, Catherine
See also SATA 24
Gough, John W(iedhofft) 1900- 15-16R
Gough, Kathleen
See Aberle, Kathleen Gough
Gough, Philip 1908- SATA-45
Gough, Vera 25-28R
Gougov, Nikola Delchev 1914- 45-48
Goulart, Frances Sheridan 1938- CANR-25
Earlier sketches in CA 57-60, CANR-7
Goulart, Ron(ald Joseph) 1933- CANR-7
Earlier sketch in CA 25-28R
See also SATA 6
Gould, Alan
See Canning, Victor
Gould, Alfred Ernest 1909- 7-8R
Gould, Beatrice Blackmar 1898- CAP-2
Earlier sketch in CA 25-28
Gould, Bruce Grant 1942- CANR-22
Earlier sketch in CA 45-48
Gould, Carol C. 1946- 103
Gould, Cecil (Hilton Monk) 1918- CANR-9
Earlier sketch in CA 21-22R
Gould, Chester 1900-1985 77-80
Obituary 116
See also SATA 43, 49
Gould, Douglas Parsons 1919- 2R
Gould, Ed(win Orrin) 1936- CANR-16
Earlier sketch in CA 93-96
Gould, Felix CAP-1
Earlier sketch in CA 11-12
Gould, James A(dams) 1922- 33-36R
Gould, James Warren 1924- CANR-2
Earlier sketch in CA 5-6R
Gould, Jay R(eid) 1906- CANR-24
Earlier sketch in CA 45-48
Gould, Jean R(osalind) 1919- CANR-21
Earlier sketches in CA 5-6R, CANR-3
See also SATA 11
Gould, Joan 1927- 107
Gould, John (Thomas) 1908- 65-68
Gould, John A(llen) 1944- 57-60
Gould, Joseph E(dmund) 1912- 11-12R
Gould, Josiah B(ancroft) 1928- 45-48
Gould, Joy
See Boyum, Joy Gould
Gould, Leroy C. 1937- 93-96
Gould, Leslie 1902-1977 Obituary 73-76
Gould, Lettie
See Paxson, Ethel
Gould, Lewis L(udlow) 1939- 41-44R
Gould, Lilian CANR-2
Earlier sketch in CA 49-52
See also SATA 6
Gould, Lois 77-80
See also CLC 4, 10
Gould, Marilyn 1928- SATA-15
Gould, Mary Earle 1885- 7-8R
Gould, Maurice M. 1909- CANR-5
Earlier sketch in CA 7-8R
Gould, Milton Samuel 1909- 93-96
Gould, Peter R(obin) 1932- 3R
Gould, Philip 1925- 124
Gould, Randall 1898(?)-1979 Obituary 89-92
Gould, Richard A(llan) 1939- CANR-7
Earlier sketch in CA 53-56
Gould, Roger L(ouis) 1935- Brief entry 110
Gould, Ronald 1904- 102
Gould, Shirley (Goldman) 81-84
Gould, Stephen Jay 1941- CANR-10
Earlier sketch in CA 77-80
Gould, Wallace 1882-1940 .... DLB-54
Gould, Warwick 1947- 110
Gould, Wesley Larson 1917- CANR-2
Earlier sketch in CA 2R
Gould, William B(enjamin) 1936-
Brief entry 118
Goulden, Joseph C. (Jr.) 1934- CANR-8
Earlier sketch in CA 17-18R
Goulden, Mark 1896(?)-1980 Obituary 101
Goulder, Grace
See Izant, Grace Goulder
Goulding, Brian 1933- 103
Goulding, Dorothy Jane 1923- 65-68
Goulding, Peter Geoffrey 1920- 106
Goulding, Ray(mond Walter) 1922- 85-88
Gouldner, Alvin W(ard) 1920-1980 .... CANR-17
Obituary 102
Earlier sketch in CA 13-14R
Goulet, Vivian G(loria) 1911- 41-44R
Goulet, Denis A. 1931- CANR-15
Earlier sketch in CA 41-44R
Goulet, John 1942- 85-88
Goulet, Robert (Joseph) 1924- 3R
Goulet, Rosalina Morales 1930- 119
Goulett, Harlan M(ador) 1927-1969 .... CAP-2
Earlier sketch in CA 21-22
Goulianos, Joan Rodman 1939- 49-52
Gouliashki, (Stoianov) Andrei 1914- CANR-19
Earlier sketch in CA 101
Goullart, Peter 1902- CAP-1
Earlier sketch in CA 13-14
Goulson, Carlyn Floyd 1922- 113
Goulson, Cary F.
See Goulson, Carlyn Floyd
Gourdie, Thomas 1913- CANR-1
Earlier sketch in CA 4R
Gourevitch, Doris-Jeanne 19-20R
Gourevitch, Peter A(lexis) 1943- 112
Gourhan, Andre (Georges Leandre) Leroi
See Leroi-Gourhan, Andre (Georges
Leandre)
Gouri, Haim 1923- 103
Gourlay, Elizabeth 1917- 112
Gourley, G(erald) Douglas 1911- 2R
Gourley, Jay 1947- 73-76
Gourlie, Norah Dundas CAP-1
Earlier sketch in CA 9-10
Gourmont, Remy de 1858-1915
Brief entry 109
See also TCLC 17
Gourse, Leslie 1939- 4R
Gourvish, T(erry) R. 1943- 125
Gouzenko, Igor 1919-1982 Obituary 107
Govan, Christine Noble 1898- CANR-2
Earlier sketch in CA 4R
See also SATA 9
Govan, Thomas P(ayne) 1907-1979 .... CANR-2
Earlier sketch in CA 45-48
Gove, Philip Babcock 1902-1972 .... CAP-1
Obituary 37-40R
Earlier sketch in CA 13-14
Gove, Samuel K(imball) 1923- 33-36R
Gove, Walter R(oberts) 1938- 118
Goveia, Elsa V(esta) 1925- 21-22R
Govenar, Alan B(ruce) 1952- 109
Gover, (John) Robert 1929- 11-12R
Govern, Elaine 1939- 53-56
See also SATA 26
Govier, Katherine 1948- CANR-18
Earlier sketch in CA 101
Govinda, Anagarika Brahmacari 1898- .. CANR-14
Earlier sketch in CA 23-24R
Govinda, Lama Anagarika Brahmacari
See Govinda, Anagarika Brahmacari
Govoni, Albert P(eter) 1914-1982 53-56
Obituary 108
Govoni, Laura E. 1914- 33-36R
Govorchin, Gerald Gilbert 1912- 13-14R
Gow, Donald 1920- 41-44R
Gow, Ronald 1897- CANR-13
Earlier sketches in CA 25-28, CAP-2
Gowan, Donald E(lmer) 1929- 69-72
Gowan, John Curtis 1912-1986 .... CANR-5
Obituary 121
Earlier sketch in CA 13-14R
Gowans, Alan 1923- CANR-18
Earlier sketches in CA 1R, CANR-2
Gowar, Antonia
See Dunford, Judith
and Margolis, Susanna
Gowen, (Samuel) Emmett 1902- CAP-1
Earlier sketch in CA 11-12
Gowen, James A(nthony) 1928- 17-18R
Gower, Herschel 1919- 5-6R
Gowers, Ernest (Arthur) 1880-1966
Obituary 89-92
Gowin, D(ixie) Bob 1925- CANR-26
Earlier sketch in CA 108
Gowing, Lawrence (Burnett) 1918- 11-12R
Gowing, Margaret (Margaret Mary) 1921- .. 81-84
Gowing, Peter Gordon 1930- 53-56
Gowland, Mariano E(zequiel) 1933- 7-8R
Goy, Richard J(ohn) 1947- 118
Goyder, George Armin 1908- 105
Goyen, (Charles) William 1915-1983 .... CANR-6
Obituary 110
Earlier sketch in CA 7-8R
See also DLB 2
See also DLBY 83
See also CLC 5, 8, 14, 40
See also AITN 2
Goyeneche, Gabriel
See Avalle-Arce, Juan Bautista
Goyer, Robert S(tanton) 1923- CANR-16
Earlier sketch in CA 41-44R
Goytisolo, Juan 1931- 85-88
See also CLC 5, 10, 23
Gozzi, Raymond D(ante) 1920- 116
Graaf, Peter
See Youd, Samuel
Grabar, Andre 1896- 111
Grabar, Oleg 1929- 124
Grabbe, Paul 1902- 93-96
Graber, Alexander 1914- CANR-1
Earlier sketch in CA 2R
See also SATA 7
Graber, Doris A. 1923- CANR-13
Earlier sketch in CA 33-36R
Graber, Gerry S(amuel) 1928- 81-84
Graber, Richard (Fredrick) 1927- 85-88
See also SATA 26
Grabianski, Janusz 1928-1976 .... CANR-2
Earlier sketch in CA 45-48
See also SATA 30, 39
Grabill, Joseph L. 1931- 29-32R
Grabner-Haider, Anton 1940- 73-76
Grabo, Norman Stanley 1930- 1R
Graboff, Abner 1919- 107
See also SATA 35
Grabois, Aryeh 1930- 105
Grabosky, Peter Nils 1945- 85-88
Grabow, Stephen (Harris) 1943- 121
Grabowski, Z(bigniew) Anthony 1903- 7-8R
Graburn, Nelson H(ayes) H(enry) 1936- . CANR-1
Earlier sketch in CA 45-48
Gracchus, Sidney J(oseph) 1930- 97-100
Grace, F(rances Jane) 111
See also SATA 45
Grace, Gerald R(upert) 1936- CANR-22
Earlier sketch in CA 45-48
Grace, Helen K(ennedy) 1935- 53-56
Grace, J. Peter 1913- 126
Grace, Joan C(arroll) 1921- 61-64
Grace, John Patrick 1942- 112
Grace, Joseph
See Hornby, John (Wilkinson)
Grace, Sherrill E(lizabeth) 1944- 110
Grace, William J(oseph), Jr. 1948- 111
Grace, William Joseph 1910- CAP-1
Earlier sketch in CA 13-14
Gracey, Harry L(ewis) 1933- 41-44R
Gracia, Jorge J(esus) E(miliano) 1942- 109
Gracie, Archibald 1859-1912 Brief entry 122
Gracq, Julien
See Poirier, Louis
See also CLC 11, 48
Gracy, David B(ergen) II 1941- CANR-16
Earlier sketch in CA 25-28R
Gracza, Margaret Young 1928- 15-16R
Grad, Bonnie L(ee) 1949- 117
Grad, Eli 1928- 115
Grad, Frank P. 1924- 33-36R
Grade, Arnold (Edward) 1928- 29-32R
Grade, Chaim 1910-1982 93-96
Obituary 107
See also CLC 10
Gradidge, Roderick 1929- 117
Gradon, Pamela O(live) E(lizabeth)
1915- 97-100
Gradwohl, David M(ayer) 1934- 125
Grady, Don(ald Wyndham) 1929- 115
Grady, Henry W. 1850-1889 .... DLB-23
Grady, James (Thomas) 1949- CANR-22
Earlier sketch in CA 104
Grady, Ronan Calistus, Jr. 1921- 49-52
Grady, Tex
See Webb, Jack (Randolph)
Grae, Ida 1918- 97-100
Graeber, Charlotte Towner SATA-44
Graebner, Alan 1938- 61-64
Graebner, Norman A. 1915- CANR-24
Earlier sketches in CA 15-16R, CANR-7
Graebner, Walter 1909- CAP-1
Earlier sketch in CA 15-16
Graebner, William Sievers 1943- 104
Graedon, Joe (David) 1945- 77-80
Graef, Hilda C(harlotte) 1907- 7-8R
Graeff, Grace M. 1918- 23-24R
Graeme, Bruce
See Jeffries, Graham Montague
Graeme, David
See Jeffries, Graham Montague
Graeme, Roderic
See Jeffries, Roderic (Graeme)
Graeme, Sheila 1944- 25-28R
Graf, Le Roy Philip 1915- 41-44R
Graf, Oskar Maria 1894-1967 Obituary 115
See also DLB 56
Graf, Rudolf F. 1926- 11-12R
Grafe, Felix
See Greve, Felix Paul (Berthold Friedrich)
Graff, George 1886-1973 Obituary 41-44R
Graff, Gerald (Edward) 1937- 29-32R
Graff, Henry F(ranklin) 1921- CANR-17
Earlier sketches in CA 1R, CANR-1
Graff, Polly Anne Colver
See Colver, Anne
Graff, S. Stewart 1908- 49-52
See also SATA 9
Grafton, Ann
See Owens, Thelma
Grafton, Carl 1942- 53-56
Grafton, David 1930- 126
Grafton, Sue 1940- 108
Graglia, Lino A(nthony) 1930- 69-72
Graham, A(lexander) John 1930- CANR-8
Earlier sketch in CA 15-16R
Graham, A(lexander) S(teel) 1917- 104
Graham, Ada 1931- CANR-4
Earlier sketch in CA 29-32R
See also SATA 11
Graham, Aelred 1907-1984 .... CANR-5
Obituary 114
Earlier sketch in CA 7-8R
Graham, Alice Walworth 1905- CANR-5
Earlier sketch in CA 2R
Graham, Alistair (Dundas) 1938- 49-52
Graham, Andrew Guillemard 1913-1981
Obituary 103
Graham, Angus (Charles) 1919- 17-18R
Graham, Billy
See Graham, William Franklin
Graham, Brenda Knight 1942- 103
See also SATA 32
Graham, Carlotta
See Wallmann, Jeffrey M(iner)
Graham, Caroline 1931- 119
Graham, Charles S.
See Tubb, E(dwin) C(harles)
Graham, Charlotte
See Bowden, Joan Chase
Graham, Clarence H. 1906-1971
Obituary 33-36R
Graham, David (Duane) 1927- 69-72
Graham, Desmond 1940- 73-76
Graham, Don B. 1940- CANR-18
Earlier sketch in CA 102

INDEX

Graham, Donald W(ilkinson) 1903- CAP-2
  Earlier sketch in CA 29-32
Graham, Eleanor 1896-1984 73-76
  Obituary 112
  See also SATA 18, 38
Graham, Elizabeth
  See Edmonds, Arthur Denis
Graham, Frank, Jr. 1925- CANR-4
  Earlier sketch in CA 11-12R
  See also SATA 11
Graham, Fred P(atterson) 1931- 37-40R
Graham, Gene S(wann) 1924- 41-44R
Graham, George J(ackson), Jr. 1938- ... 45-48
Graham, George Rex 1813-1894 .... DLB-73
Graham, Gerald (Sandford) 1903-1988 .. 102
  Obituary 126
Graham, Grace 1910- CAP-1
  Earlier sketch in CA 13-14
Graham, Harry Edward 1940- 29-32R
Graham, Henry 1930- 103
Graham, Howard Jay 1905- CAP-2
  Earlier sketch in CA 33-36
Graham, Hugh
  See Barrows, (Ruth) Marjorie
Graham, Hugh Davis 1936- CANR-13
  Earlier sketch in CA 23-24R
Graham, Ian (James Alastair) 1923- ... CANR-2
  Earlier sketch in CA 45-48
Graham, Ilse 1914- CANR-8
  Earlier sketch in CA 57-60
Graham, J. W. 1925- 93-96
Graham, J(ames) Walter 1906- 4R
Graham, James
  See Patterson, Henry
Graham, John 1926- 33-36R
  See also SATA 11
Graham, John
  See Phillips, David Graham
Graham, John Alexander 1941- 25-28R
Graham, John Remington 1940- 33-36R
Graham, John Thomas 1928- ., ...53-56
Graham, Jorie 1951- 111
  See also CLC 48
Graham, Jory 1925-1983 .... CANR-13
  Obituary 109
  Earlier sketch in CA 29-32R
Graham, Joseph M. 1911(?)-1971
  Obituary 104
Graham, Katharine (Meyer) 1917- 105
  See also AITN 1
Graham, (George) Kenneth 1936- 77-80
Graham, Kennon
  See Harrison, David L(ee)
Graham, Larry
  See Graham, Lawrence (Otis)
Graham, Lawrence (Otis) 1962- 116
Graham, Lawrence S(herman) 1936- ... 45-48
Graham, Lee E. 1913(?)-1977 Obituary ...73-76
Graham, Lloyd M. 1889- 97-100
Graham, Loren R. 1933- CANR-13
  Earlier sketch in CA 21-22R
Graham, Lorenz (Bell) 1902- CANR-25
  Earlier sketch in CA 9-10R
  See also BW
  See also SATA 2
  See also SAAS 5
  See also DLB 76
  See also CLR 10
Graham, Malcolm 1923- 53-56
Graham, Margaret Althea 1924- 11-12R
Graham, Margaret Bloy 1920- 77-80
  See also SATA 11
Graham, Matthew
  See Arnold, Peter
Graham, Michael 1898-1972 Obituary 104
Graham, Michael Angelo 1921-1985
  Obituary 117
Graham, Milton D(uke) 1916- 45-48
Graham, Neile 1958- 113
Graham, (Roger) Neill 1941- CANR-26
  Earlier sketch in CA 109
Graham, Neill
  See Duncan, W(illiam) Murdoch
Graham, Otis L., Jr. 1935- CANR-11
  Earlier sketch in CA 21-22R
Graham, Patricia Albjerg 1935- 25-28R
Graham, Peter W(illiam) 1951- 121
Graham, Philip Leslie 1915-1963
  Obituary 89-92
Graham, R(obert) B(ontine) Cunninghame
  See Cunninghame Graham, R(obert)
  B(ontine)
Graham, Rachel (Metcalf) 1895- CAP-1
  Earlier sketch in CA 15-16
Graham, Ramona
  See Cook, Ramona Graham
Graham, Richard 1934- CANR-15
  Earlier sketch in CA 29-32R
Graham, Robert
  See Haldeman, Joe (William)
Graham, Robert G. 1925- CANR-12
  Earlier sketch in CA 25-28R
Graham, Robin Lee 1949- 49-52
  See also SATA 7
Graham, Ruth
  See Evans, Jean
Graham, Sean 1920- 21-22R
Graham, Sheilah 1908(?)- 108
  See also AITN 1
Graham, Shirley
  See Du Bois, Shirley Graham
  See also DLB 76
Graham, Sonia
  See Sinclair, Sonia
Graham, Stephen 1884-1975 Obituary ...93-96
Graham, (Maude Fitzgerald) Susan
  1912- 19-20R

Graham, Thomas F(rancis) 1923- 23-24R
Graham, Tom
  See Lewis, (Harry) Sinclair
Graham, Vanessa
  See Fraser, Anthea
Graham, Victor E(rnest) 1920- 93-96
Graham, Virginia
  See Guttenberg, Virginia
Graham, W(illiam) Fred 1930- 33-36R
Graham, W(illiam) S(ydney) 1918-1986 ...73-76
  Obituary 118
  See also DLB 20
  See also CLC 29
Graham, William Franklin 1918- CANR-20
  Earlier sketch in CA 9-10R
Graham, Winston (Mawdsley) 1910- ... CANR-22
  Earlier sketches in CA 49-52, CANR-2
  See also CLC 23
Graham-Barber, Lynda 1944- 113
  See also SATA 42
Graham-Cameron, M.
  See Graham-Cameron, M(alcolm)
  G(ordon)
Graham-Cameron, M(alcolm) G(ordon)
  1931- 123
  See also SATA 45, 53
Graham-Cameron, Mike
  See Graham-Cameron, M(alcolm)
  G(ordon)
Graham-Campbell, David (John) 1912- 113
Grahame, Kenneth 1859-1932 Brief entry ... 108
  See also YABC 1
  See also DLB 34
  See also CLR 5
Graham Scott, Peter 1923- 108
Graham-White, Anthony 1940- 61-64
Graham-Yooll, Andrew M(ichael) 1944- ... 108
Grahn, Judith L. 1940- 122
  Brief entry 116
Grahn, Judy
  See Grahn, Judith L.
Grainger, A(nthony) J(ohn) 1929- 33-36R
Grainger, J(ohn) H(erbert) 1917- 77-80
Grainger, Margaret 1936- 116
Gralapp, Leland Wilson 1921- 15-16R
Gram, Harold A(lbert) 1927- 25-28R
Gram, Moltke (Stefanus) 1938- CANR-13
  Earlier sketch in CA 69-72
Gramatky, Hardie 1907-1979 .... CANR-3
  Obituary 85-88
  Earlier sketch in CA 2R
  See also SATA 1, 23, 30
  See also DLB 22
  See also AITN 1
Grambs, Jean D(resden) 1919- CANR-7
  Earlier sketch in CA 17-18R
Gramet, Charles 3R
Gramick, Jeannine 1942- 113
Grammaticus
  See Blaiklock, Edward Musgrave
Grampp, William D(yer) 1914- 33-36R
Grams, Armin 1924- 45-48
Granados, Paul
  See Kent, Arthur William Charles
Granat, Robert 1925- CANR-2
  Earlier sketch in CA 2R
Granatstein, J(ack) L(awrence) 1939- .. CANR-10
  Earlier sketch in CA 25-28R
Granbeck, Marilyn
  See Henderson, M(arilyn) R(uth)
Granberg, W(ilbur) J(ohn) 1906- 5-6R
Granberry, Edwin 1897- CAP-2
  Earlier sketch in CA 21-22
Granby, Milton
  See Wallmann, Jeffrey M(iner)
Grand, Samuel 1912- 107
  See also SATA 42
Granda, Chabuca
  See Larco, Isabel Granda
Grande, Luke M. 1922- CANR-2
  Earlier sketch in CA 7-8R
Grande Vitesse
  See Walkerley, Rodney Lewis (de Burah)
Grandfield, Raymond J(oseph) 1931- 53-56
Grandower, Elissa
  See Waugh, Hillary Baldwin
Grandville, J. J.
  See Gerard, Jean Ignace Isidore
Grandville, Jean Ignace Isidore Gerard
  See Gerard, Jean Ignace Isidore
Grandy, Richard (Edward) 1942- 77-80
Grange, Chris
  See Gnaegy, Charles
Grange, Cyril 1900- CAP-1
  Earlier sketch in CA 15-16
Grange, Peter
  See Nicole, Christopher Robin
Granger, Bruce Ingham 1920- 1R
Granger, Byrd Howell 1912- 107
Granger, Clive W(illiam) J(ohn) 1934- .. CANR-8
  Earlier sketch in CA 11-12R
Granger, Darius John
  See Marlowe, Stephen
Granger, Margaret Jane 1925(?)-1977
  Obituary 104
  See also SATA 27
Granger, Peggy
  See Granger, Margaret Jane
Granich, Irving 1894-1967 97-100
  Obituary 45-48
Granick, David 1926- 2R
Granick, Harry 1898- 85-88
Granik, (S.) Theodore 1906-1970
  Obituary 89-92
Granit, Arthur 1917- 120
Granite, Harvey R. 1927- CANR-15
  Earlier sketch in CA 33-36R

Granite, Tony
  See Politella, Dario
Grannis, Chandler B(rinkerhoff) 1912-
  Brief entry 111
Granovetter, Mark S. 1943- 85-88
Granovsky, Anatoli 1922-1974 Obituary ..53-56
Granowsky, Alvin 1936- 21-22R
Gransden, Antonia 1928- 77-80
Granstaff, Bill 1925- SATA-10
Grant, Alan
  See Kennington, (Gilbert) Alan
Grant, Alexander T(homas) K(ingdom)
  1906- 53-56
Grant, Ambrose
  See Raymond, Rene (Brabazon)
Grant, Anthony
  See Pares, Marion (Stapylton)
Grant, Barbara M(oll) 1932- 53-56
Grant, Ben
  See Henderson, M(arilyn) R(uth)
Grant, Brian W. 1939- CANR-7
  Earlier sketch in CA 57-60
Grant, Bruce 1893-1977 .... CANR-6
  Obituary 69-72
  Earlier sketch in CA 1R
  See also SATA 5, 25
Grant, Bruce Alexander 1925- 107
Grant, C.B.S.
  See Haga, Enoch J.
Grant, Charles L. 1942- 85-88
Grant, Cynthia D. 1950- CANR-20
  Earlier sketch in CA 104
  See also SATA 33
Grant, David
  See Thomas, Craig (David)
Grant, Don
  See Glut, Donald F(rank)
Grant, Donald J. 1939-1984 Obituary 113
Grant, Dorothy 1927- 114
Grant, Dorothy Fremont 1900- CAP-2
  Earlier sketch in CA 23-24
Grant, Elliott Mansfield 1895-1969 ..... CANR-5
  Earlier sketch in CA 7-8R
Grant, Ellsworth Strong 1917- 57-60
Grant, Eva 1907- 49-52
  See also SATA 7
Grant, Evva H. 1913-1977 Obituary 104
  See also SATA 27
Grant, Frederick C(lifton) 1891-1974 .... 1R
  Obituary 49-52
Grant, George (Parkin) 1918-1988
  Obituary 126
Grant, Gerald 1938- 81-84
Grant, Gordon 1875-1962 102
  See also SATA 25
Grant, Gwen(doline Ellen) 1940- CANR-22
  Earlier sketch in CA 106
  See also SATA 47
Grant, H. Roger 1943- 89-92
Grant, Harry J(ohnston) 1881-1963
  Obituary 114
  See also DLB 29
Grant, Hilda Kay 1910- 4R
Grant, Isabel F(rances) 1887-1983
  Obituary 110
Grant, J(ohn) B(arnard) 1940- CANR-6
  Earlier sketch in CA 57-60
Grant, Jack
  See Grant, J(ohn) B(arnard)
Grant, James Edward 1905-1966 Obituary .. 113
  See also DLB 26
Grant, James G. 1926(?)-1979 Obituary ...89-92
Grant, James Russell 1924- CANR-17
  Earlier sketch in CA 101
Grant, Jane (Cole) 1895-1972 .... CAP-2
  Obituary 33-36R
  Earlier sketch in CA 25-28
Grant, Jane
  See Leader, (Evelyn) Barbara (Blackburn)
Grant, Joan
  See Kelsey, Joan Marshall
Grant, Joanne B(enzel) 1940- 106
Grant, John 1933- 77-80
Grant, John E(rnest) 1925- 41-44R
Grant, John J. 1932- 53-56
Grant, John Webster 1919- CANR-6
  Earlier sketch in CA 7-8R
Grant, Judith 1929- 21-22R
Grant, Kay 23-24R
Grant, Kerry S. 1945- 121
Grant, Landon
  See Gribble, Leonard (Reginald)
Grant, (Alice) Leigh 1947- SATA-10
Grant, Louis T(heodore) 1943- 53-56
Grant, Madeleine Parker 1895- 73-76
Grant, Margaret
  See Franken, Rose (Dorothy)
Grant, Mary A(melia) 1890- CAP-2
  Earlier sketch in CA 25-28
Grant, Mary Kathryn 1941- 81-84
Grant, Matthew G.
  See May, Julian
Grant, Maxwell
  See Gibson, Walter B(rown)
  and Lynds, Dennis
Grant, Michael 1914- CANR-25
  Earlier sketches in CA 4R, CANR-4
Grant, Myrna (Lois) 1934- CANR-4
  Earlier sketch in CA 53-56
  See also SATA 21
Grant, Neil 1938- CANR-15
  Earlier sketch in CA 33-36R
  See also SATA 14
Grant, Nigel (Duncan Cameron) 1932- ... CANR-7
  Earlier sketch in CA 17-18R
Grant, Ozro F. 1908- CAP-2
  Earlier sketch in CA 21-22

Grant, Richard B(abson) 1925- CANR-4
  Earlier sketch in CA 3R
Grant, Robert B(ruce) 1933- 45-48
Grant, Robert M(cQueen) 1917- 65-68
Grant, Roderick 1941- Brief entry 112
Grant, Skeeter
  See Spiegelman, Art
Grant, Ulysses S. III 1881-1968 Obituary ... 111
Grant, Verne E(dwin) 1917- 53-56
Grant, Vernon W(esley) 1904- 17-18R
Grant, W(illiam) Leonard 1914- 19-20R
Grant, Wilson Wayne 1941- 97-100
Grant, Wyn(ford) 1947- 114
Grant, Zalin (Belton) 1941- 73-76
Grant-Adamson, Lesley 1942- 121
Grantham, Alexander (William George
  Herder) 1899- CAP-2
  Earlier sketch in CA 19-20
Grantham, Dewey Wesley 1921- CANR-1
  Earlier sketch in CA 1R
Grantland, Keith
  See Beaumont, Charles
Granton, Ester Fannie 1914(?)-1980
  Obituary 101
Grant Wallace, Lewis
  See Wallace, Lewis Grant
Granville, Joseph E(nsign) 1923- 65-68
Granville, W. Wilfred 1905- CAP-1
  Earlier sketch in CA 9-10
Granville-Barker, Harley 1877-1946
  Brief entry 104
  See also TCLC 2
Grape, Oliver
  See Wood, Christopher (Hovelle)
Grapho
  See Oakley, Eric Gilbert
Grass, Guenter (Wilhelm) 1927- CANR-20
  Earlier sketch in CA 13-14R
  See also DLB 75
  See also CLC 1, 2, 4, 6, 11, 15, 22, 32,
  49
Grassi, Joseph A(ugustus) 1922- CANR-19
  Earlier sketch in CA 103
Grasso, Domenico 1917- 73-76
Grasty, Charles H. 1863-1924 .... DLB-25
Grathwohl, Larry D(avid) 1947- 65-68
Grattan, C(linton) Hartley 1902-1980 . CANR-1
  Obituary 101
  Earlier sketch in CA 4R
Grattan, Virginia L(ee) 1932- 115
Grattan-Guinness, I. 1941- 73-76
Gratton, Thomas
  See Hulme, T(homas) E(rnest)
Gratus, Jack 1935- 93-96
Grau, Joseph A(ugust) 1921- 65-68
Grau, Shirley Ann 1929- CANR-22
  Earlier sketch in CA 89-92
  See also DLB 2
  See also CLC 4, 9
Graubard, Mark A. 1904- CANR-5
  Earlier sketch in CA 1R
Graubard, Paul S. 1932- 103
Graubard, Stephen R(ichards) 1924-
  Brief entry 113
Graubart, David 1907(?)-1984 Obituary ... 112
Grauer, Ben(jamin Franklin) 1908-1977
  Obituary 69-72
Grauer, Neil A(lbert) 1947- 122
Grauman, Lawrence, Jr. 1935- 33-36R
Graupe, Daniel 1934- 41-44R
Graupera, Carlos M(anuel) 1915- 49-52
Grava, Sigurd 1934- 77-80
Gravagnuolo, Benedetto 1949- 112
Grave, S(elwyn) A(lfred) 1916- 5-6R
Gravel, Fern
  See Hall, James Norman
Gravel, Mike 1930- 41-44R
Gravely, William B(ernard) 1939- 49-52
Graver, Jane (Ann) 1931- 117
Graver, Lawrence 1931- 25-28R
Graver, Suzanne 1936- 117
Graversen, Pat 1935- 109
Graves, Allen W(illis) 1915- 17-18R
Graves, Barbara Farris 1938- 41-44R
Graves, Charles Parlin 1911-1972 ... CANR-4
  Obituary 37-40R
  Earlier sketch in CA 5-6R
  See also SATA 4
Graves, Edgar B(aldwin) 1898-1983
  Obituary 109
Graves, Eleanor MacKenzie 1926- 102
Graves, John (Alexander III) 1920- ... CANR-9
  Earlier sketch in CA 13-14R
  See also DLBY 83
Graves, Leon B(erneil) 1946- 29-32R
Graves, Nora Calhoun 1914- 73-76
Graves, Phillip E(arl) 1945- 115
Graves, Richard 1715-1804 .... DLB-39
Graves, Richard L(atshaw) 1928- 57-60
Graves, Richard L(ayton) 1931- 53-56
Graves, Richard Perceval 1945- CANR-26
  Earlier sketches in CA 65-68, CANR-9
  See also CLC 44
Graves, Robert (von Ranke) 1895-1985 . CANR-5
  Obituary 117
  Earlier sketch in CA 5-6R
  See also SATA 45
  See also DLB 20
  See also DLBY 85
  See also CLC 1, 2, 6, 11, 39, 44, 45
Graves, Susan B(ernard) 1933- 41-44R
Graves, Tricia
  See Graversen, Pat
Graves, W(illiam) Brooke 1899- CAP-1
  Earlier sketch in CA 9-10
Graves, Wallace 1922- 33-36R
Graveson, R(onald) H(arry) 1911- 122

Grawbarger, Josephine (Clara) 1908- 121
Grawoig, Sheila
See Raeschild, Sheila
Gray, Alasdair 1934- 126
See also CLC 41
Gray, Alexander 1882-1968 7-8R
Gray, Alfred O(rren) 1914- CANR-7
Earlier sketch in CA 19-20R
Gray, Amlin 1946- CLC-29
Gray, Angela
See Daniels, Dorothy
Gray, Anne 1931- CANR-9
Earlier sketch in CA 65-68
Gray, Asa 1810-1888 DLB-1
Gray, Barry 1916- 61-64
Gray, Basil 1904- CAP-1
Earlier sketch in CA 9-10
Gray, Betsy
See Poole, Gray Johnson
Gray, Bettyanne 1934- 81-84
Gray, Bradford H(itch) 1942- 57-60
Gray, Captain Bill
See Gray, William Bittle
Gray, Charles A(ugustus) 1938- 19-20R
Gray, Clifford F. 1930- 25-28R
Gray, Darrell 1945- 65-68
Gray, David 1838-1861 DLB-32
Gray, David 1927-1983 Obituary 110
Gray, Dorothea Helen Forbes ?-1983
Obituary 110
Gray, Dorothy (Kamer) 1936- 69-72
Gray, Dorothy Kate 1918- 102
Gray, Douglas 1930- 117
Gray, Dulcie CANR-24
Earlier sketches in CA 7-8R, CANR-3
Gray, Dwight E(lder) 1903- CAP-2
Earlier sketch in CA 23-24
Gray, Eden 1907- 93-96
Gray, Edna Redmond 1905(?)-1983
Obituary 110
Gray, Edwyn 1927- 41-44R
Gray, Elizabeth Janet
See Vining, Elizabeth Gray
Gray, Ellington
See Jacob, Naomi Ellington
Gray, Ernest
See Gray, Ernest Alfred
Gray, Ernest A.
See Gray, Ernest Alfred
Gray, Ernest Alfred 1908- 118
Gray, Farnum 1940- 49-52
Gray, Floyd (Francis) 1926- CANR-10
Earlier sketch in CA 25-28R
Gray, Francine du Plessix 1930- CANR-11
Earlier sketch in CA 61-64
See also CAAS 2
See also CLC 22
Gray, Genevieve S(tuck) 1920- 33-36R
See also SATA 4
Gray, George Hugh 1922- CANR-7
Earlier sketch in CA 17-18R
Gray, Gibson 1922- 33-36R
Gray, Giles Wilkeson 1889- 7-8R
Gray, Gordon 1909-1982 Obituary 109
Gray, H(enry) Peter 1924- Brief entry 111
Gray, Harold (Lincoln) 1894-1968 107
See also SATA 32, 33
Gray, Harold James 1907- 107
Gray, Harriet
See Robins, Denise (Naomi)
Gray, J(esse) Glenn 1913-1977 37-40R
Obituary 73-76
Gray, J(ames) M(artin) 1930- 53-56
Gray, J(ohn) Richard 1929- CANR-5
Earlier sketch in CA 3R
Gray, J(ohn) Stanley 1894- CAP-2
Earlier sketch in CA 17-18
Gray, Jack 1927- 103
Gray, James 1899- 13-14R
Gray, James H(enry) 1906- 97-100
Gray, James R(obert) 1921- 33-36R
Gray, Jane
See Evans, Constance May
Gray, Jeffrey A(lan) 1934- 104
Gray, Jenny
See Gray, Genevieve S(tuck)
Gray, John (Henry) 1866-1934 Brief entry 119
See also TCLC 19
Gray, John 1913- 11-12R
Gray, John E(dmund) 1922- 65-68
Gray, John Milner 1889-1970 Obituary 29-32R
Gray, John Morgan 1907- 103
Gray, John Rodger 1913-1984 Obituary 113
Gray, John S(tephens) 1910- 73-76
Gray, John W(ylie) 1935- 19-20R
Gray, Juanita R(uth) 1918- 61-64
Gray, Lee Learner 1924- 73-76
Gray, Linda Crockett 1943- 109
Gray, Margaret K. 1949- 123
Gray, Marian
See Pierce, Edith Gray
Gray, Marianne 1947- 110
Gray, Martin 1926- CANR-14
Earlier sketch in CA 77-80
See also AITN 1
Gray, Mayo Loiseau 1938- 104
Gray, Michael H(aslam) 1946- 103
Gray, Nicholas Stuart 1922-1981 CANR-11
Obituary 103
Earlier sketch in CA 21-22R
See also SATA 4, 27
Gray, Nicolete (Mary) 1911- 103
Gray, Nigel 1941- 85-88
See also SATA 33
Gray, (Lucy) Noel (Clervaux) 1898-1983 65-68
See also SATA 47
Gray, Oscar S(halom) 1926- 29-32R
Gray, Parke H. 1936(?)-1987 Obituary 121
Gray, Patricia (Clark) 29-32R
See also SATA 7
Gray, Patsey
See Gray, Patricia (Clark)
Gray, Peter 1908- 41-44R
Gray, Philip
See Perlman, Jess
Gray, Ralph D(ale) 1933- CANR-24
Earlier sketches in CA 21-22R, CANR-8
Gray, Richard
See Gray, J(ohn) Richard
Gray, Richard B(utler) 1922- CANR-2
Earlier sketch in CA 1R
Gray, Richard G(eorge) 1932-1984
Obituary 114
Gray, Robert F(red) 1912- 19-20R
Gray, Robert Keith 1923- 4R
Gray, Robert Mack 1922- 13-14R
Gray, Ronald (Douglas) 1919- CANR-22
Earlier sketches in CA 17-18R, CANR-7
Gray, Ronald Francis 1918- 7-8R
Gray, Russell
See Fischer, Bruno
Gray, Simon 1936- 23-24R
See also CAAS 3
See also DLB 13
See also CLC 9, 14, 36
See also AITN 1
Gray, Spalding 1941- CLC-49
Gray, Stephen E. 1925- 73-76
Gray, Tony
See Gray, George Hugh
Gray, Vanessa
See Aeby, Jacquelyn
Gray, Wellington Burbank 1919-1977 1R
Obituary 103
Gray, William Bittle 1891-1974 CANR-11
Earlier sketch in CA 13-14R
Gray, William R(alph) 1946- 97-100
Gray, Wood 1905(?)-1977 Obituary 69-72
Graybar, Lloyd J(oseph) 1938- 57-60
Graybeal, David M(cConnell) 1921- 17-18R
Graybill, Florence Curtis 1898- 97-100
Graybill, Ron(ald D.) 1944- 33-36R
Grayeff, Felix 1906- 77-80
Grayland, Eugene C(harles)
1916-1976 CANR-11
Earlier sketches in CA 9-10, CAP-1
Grayland, V. Merle
See Grayland, Valerie (Merle Spanner)
Grayland, Valerie (Merle Spanner) CANR-11
Earlier sketch in CA 9-10R
See also SATA 7
Graymont, Barbara 81-84
Graysmith, Robert 1942- 117
Grayson, A(lbert) K(irk) 1935- 41-44R
Grayson, Alice Barr
See Grossman, Jean Schick
Grayson, Benson Lee 1932- 93-96
Grayson, C(harles) Jackson, Jr. 1923- 106
Grayson, Cary Travers, Jr. 1919- CANR-10
Earlier sketch in CA 17-18R
Grayson, Cecil 1920- 13-14R
Grayson, Charles 1905-1973 Obituary 41-44R
Grayson, David
See Baker, Ray Stannard
Grayson, Henry (Wesley) 1910- 41-44R
Grayson, Janet 1934- 53-56
Grayson, L(inda) M(ary) 1947- 89-92
Grayson, Marion F. 1906-1976 CANR-4
Obituary 69-72
Earlier sketch in CA 5-6R
Grayson, Melvin J(ay) 1924- 45-48
Grayson, Richard (A.) 1951- CANR-14
Earlier sketch in CA 85-88
See also CLC 38
Grayson, Robert A. 1927- 33-36R
Grayson, Ruth (King) 1926- 73-76
Grayson, William John 1788-1863 DLB-3, 64
Graystone, Lynn
See Brennan, Joseph Lomas
Grayzel, Solomon 1896-1980 CANR-4
Earlier sketch in CA 4R
Grazhdanin, Misha
See Burgess, M(ichael) R(oy)
Graziano, Anthony M(ichael) 1932- 93-96
Grealey, Thomas Louis 1916- 81-84
Grealis, Walt(er) 1929- 77-80
Grealy, Desmond 1923(?)-1979 Obituary 85-88
Grean, Stanley 1920- 29-32R
Greanias, George C. 1948- 126
Great Merlini, The
See Rawson, Clayton
Greatorex, Wilfred 1921- 103
Greaves, H(arold) R(ichard) G(oring)
1907- 5-6R
Greaves, (Brian) John 1898- 103
Greaves, Margaret 1914- CANR-18
Earlier sketch in CA 25-28R
See also SATA 7
Greaves, Percy L(aurie), Jr. 1906- 49-52
Greaves, Richard L(ee) 1938- CANR-16
Earlier sketch in CA 33-36R
Greaves, William 1926- 125
See also BW
Grebanier, Bernard (David N.)
1903-1977 CANR-10
Earlier sketch in CA 23-24R
Grebe, Maria Ester 1928- 25-28R
Greben, Stanley E(dward) 1927- 120
Greber, Judith 1939- 116
Grebstein, Lawrence C(harles) 1937- 29-32R
Grebstein, Sheldon Norman 1928- CANR-5
Earlier sketch in CA 1R
Greco, Jose 1918- 85-88
Greco, Margaret
See Fry, Barbara
Gree, Alain 1936- 89-92
See also SATA 28
Greeley, Andrew M(oran) 1928- CANR-7
Earlier sketch in CA 7-8R
See also CAAS 7
See also CLC 28
Greeley, Dana McLean 1908-1986
Obituary 119
Greeley, Horace 1811-1872 DLB-3, 43
Greeley, Valerie 1953- 118
Green, A(dwin) Wigfall 1900-1971(?) CAP-1
Earlier sketch in CA 9-10
Green, Abel 1900-1973 Obituary 41-44R
Green, Adam
See Weisgard, Leonard Joseph
Green, Adolph 1915- Brief entry 110
See also DLB 44
Green, Alan (Baer) 1906-1975 53-56
Obituary 57-60
Green, Alan Singer 1907- 85-88
Green, Andrew (Malcolm) 1927- CANR-12
Earlier sketch in CA 73-76
Green, Anita Jane 1940- 85-88
Green, Anna Katharine 1846-1935
Brief entry 112
Green, Anne (Mitchell) 1947- 120
Green, Anne M. 1922- 1R
Green, Arnold W(ilfred) 1914- 5-6R
Green, Arthur S(amuel) 1927- 5-6R
Green, Ben K. 1911(?)-1974 Obituary 115
See also AITN 1
Green, Benny
See Green, Bernard
Green, Bernard 1927- 25-28R
Green, Betty Radley 1926-1978 Obituary 111
Green, Bryan S(tuart) W(estmacott)
1901- CAP-1
Earlier sketch in CA 13-14
Green, Celia (Elizabeth) 1935- 65-68
Green, Constance McLaughlin 1897-1975 9-10R
Obituary 61-64
Green, D.
See Casewit, Curtis W(erner)
Green, Daniel W(illiam) E(dward) 1958- 121
Green, David 1942- 77-80
Green, David Bronte 1910- 13-14R
Green, David M(arvin) 1932- 41-44R
Green, Deborah 1948- 104
Green, Dennis Howard 1922- 110
Green, Donald E(dward) 1936- CANR-1
Earlier sketch in CA 45-48
Green, Donald Ross 1924- 37-40R
Green, Dorothy (Auchterlonie) 1915- 112
Green, Duff 1791-1875 DLB-43
Green, Edith Pinero 1929- CANR-15
Earlier sketch in CA 77-80
Green, Edward 1920- 15-16R
Green, Edwin 1948- 116
Green, Elizabeth A(dine) H(erkimer)
1906- 23-24R
Green, Elmer Ellsworth 1917- 103
Green, Ernestene L(everne) 1939- 57-60
Green, Evelyn Everett
See Everett-Green, Evelyn
Green, F(rederick) C(harles) 1891-1964
Obituary 89-92
Green, Fitzhugh 1917- 77-80
Green, Fletcher Melvin 1895-1978 CANR-6
Earlier sketch in CA 1R
Green, Frederick Pratt 1903- 102
Green, Galen 1949- 57-60
Green, George D(avid) 1938- Brief entry 114
Green, George MacEwan 1931- 81-84
Green, George S(herman) 1930- 97-100
Green, Georgia M. 1944- 93-96
Green, Gerald 1922- CANR-8
Earlier sketch in CA 15-16R
See also DLB 28
Green, Gil(bert) 1906- 73-76
Green, H(enry) Gordon 1912- 110
Green, Hannah 73-76
See also CLC 3
Green, Hannah
See Greenberg, Joanne (Goldenberg)
Green, Harold P(aul) 1922- 13-14R
Green, Harvey 1946- 115
Green, Henry
See Yorke, Henry Vincent
See also DLB 15
See also CLC 2, 13
Green, Hollis Lynn 1933- 103
Green, J(ames) C. R. 1949- 104
Green, James L(eroy) 1919- 17-18R
Green, Jane 1937- 61-64
See also SATA 9
Green, Jane Nugent 1918- 61-64
Green, Janet 1939- 112
Green, Jeffrey P(hillip) 1944- 111
Green, Jerome Frederic 1928- 125
Green, Jerry
See Green, Jerome Frederic
Green, Jim 1941- 114
Green, Joann 1938- 115
Green, John Alden 1925- CANR-3
Earlier sketch in CA 7-8R
Green, John F. 1943- 126
Green, John L(afayette), Jr. 1929- CANR-22
Earlier sketch in CA 45-48
Green, Jonas 1712-1767 DLB-31
Green, Jonathan (William) 1939- CANR-9
Earlier sketch in CA 61-64
Green, Joseph 1706-1780 DLB-31
Green, Joseph 1931- 29-32R
Green, Joseph F(ranklin), Jr. 1924- 15-16R
Green, Judith
See Galbraith, Jean
and Rodriguez, Judith Green
Green, Julien (Hartridge) 1900- 21-22R
See also DLB 4, 72
See also CLC 3, 11
Green, Kay 1927- 117
Green, Landis K(night) 1940- 57-60
Green, Lawrence W(inter) 1940- CANR-12
Earlier sketch in CA 69-72
Green, Leslie Claude 1920- 13-14R
Green, Lewis 1946- 125
Green, Lewis W(allace) 1932- 119
Green, Louis 1929- 45-48
Green, Marc Edward 1943- 117
Green, Margaret (Murphy) 1926- CANR-1
Earlier sketch in CA 2R
Green, Mark J(oseph) 1945- 41-44R
Green, Martin (Burgess) 1927- CANR-9
Earlier sketch in CA 17-18R
Green, Martyn 1899-1975 Obituary 57-60
Green, Mary McBurney 1896- CAP-2
Earlier sketch in CA 29-32
Green, Mary Moore 1906- CAP-1
Earlier sketch in CA 13-14
See also SATA 11
Green, Maureen Patricia 1933- 101
Green, (James) Maurice (Spurgeon)
1906-1987 Obituary 123
Green, Maurice B(erkeley) 1920- 77-80
Green, Maurice R(ichard) 1922- 15-16R
Green, Maury 1916- 29-32R
Green, Michael Frederick 1927- CANR-19
Earlier sketch in CA 102
Green, Milton D(ouglas) 1903- 41-44R
Green, Morton 1937- 57-60
See also SATA 8
Green, Norma B(erger) 1925- 41-44R
See also SATA 11
Green, O. O.
See Durgnat, Raymond (Eric)
Green, Otis H(oward) 1898- 9-10R
Green, Paul (Eliot) 1894-1981 CANR-3
Obituary 103
Earlier sketch in CA 5-6R
See also DLB 7, 9
See also DLBY 81
See also CLC 25
See also AITN 1
Green, Paul E(dgar) 1927- CANR-11
Earlier sketch in CA 69-72
Green, Peter (Morris) 1924- CANR-4
Earlier sketch in CA 5-6R
Green, Peter
See Bulmer, (Henry) Kenneth
Green, Phyllis 1932- CANR-17
Earlier sketches in CA 45-48, CANR-1
See also SATA 20
Green, Rayna (Diane) 1942- 114
Green, Reginald Herbold 1935- CANR-17
Earlier sketch in CA 25-28R
Green, Richard AITN-1
Green, Richard 1936- Brief entry 111
Green, Robert
See Smith, Richard Rein
Green, Robert D(avid) 1942- 77-80
Green, Robert L(ee) 1933- CANR-15
Earlier sketch in CA 65-68
Green, Roger C(urtis) 1932- CANR-24
Earlier sketch in CA 45-48
Green, Roger James 1944- 123
See also SATA 52
Green, Roger (Gilbert) Lancelyn
1918-1987 CANR-2
Obituary 123
Earlier sketch in CA 4R
See also SATA 2, 53
Green, Roland (James) 1944- 77-80
Green, Ronald Michael 1942- 85-88
Green, Rosalie B(eth) 1917- 4R
Green, Rose Basile 1914- CANR-15
Earlier sketch in CA 41-44R
Green, Samuel 1921(?)-1983 Obituary 111
Green, Samuel 1948- 77-80
Green, Sharon 1942- 120
Green, Sheila Ellen 1934- CANR-17
Earlier sketches in CA 4R, CANR-2
See also SATA 8
Green, Smith Wendell 1917(?)-1987
Obituary 124
Green, Stanley 1923- CANR-17
Earlier sketches in CA 4R, CANR-1
Green, Susan 1941- 81-84
Green, Thomas Andrew 1940- 125
Green, Thomas F. 1927- 57-60
Green, Thomas J(ohn) 1946- 113
Green, Timothy (Seton) 1936- CANR-22
Earlier sketches in CA 49-52, CANR-5
Green, Vivian Hubert Howard 1915- 9-10R
Green, William 1926- 53-56
Green, William A., Jr. 1935- 85-88
Green, William Baillie 1927- 118
Green, William M(ark) 1929- 45-48
Greenacre, Phyllis 1894- 5-6R
Greenall, Jack 1905-1983 Obituary 110
Greenawalt, R(obert) Kent 1936- 33-36R
Greenaway, Catherine 1846-1901
Brief entry 113
Greenaway, George W(illiam) 1903- 118
Greenaway, Gladys 1901- 93-96
Greenaway, Kate
See Greenaway, Catherine
See also YABC 2
See also CLR 6
Greenbank, Anthony Hunt 1933- CANR-19
Earlier sketches in CA 49-52, CANR-4
See also SATA 39

INDEX

Greenbaum, Fred 1930- 37-40R
Greenbaum, Leonard 1930- 21-22R
Greenbaum, Sidney 1929- CANR-15
Earlier sketch in CA 33-36R
Greenberg, Alvin (David) 1932- 33-36R
Greenberg, Arthur
See Granit, Arthur
Greenberg, Barbara L(evenson) 1932- 53-56
Greenberg, Bernard 1922- 69-72
Greenberg, Bernard L(ouis) 1917- 41-44R
Greenberg, Bradley S(ander) 1934- 104
Greenberg, Carl 1908-1984 Obituary 114
Greenberg, Clement 1909- CANR-2
Earlier sketch in CA 1R
Greenberg, Daniel A. 1934- 5-6R
Greenberg, Daniel S. 1931- 29-32R
Greenberg, Dolores 1934- 112
Greenberg, Douglas 1947- 117
Greenberg, Edward (Seymour) 1942- 53-56
Greenberg, Eliezer 1897(?)-1977
Obituary 69-72
Greenberg, Eric Rolfe 1945- 114
Greenberg, Harvey R. 1935- 33-36R
See also SATA 5
Greenberg, Herbert 1935- 25-28R
Greenberg, Ira A(rthur) 1924- CANR-2
Earlier sketch in CA 49-52
Greenberg, Ivan 1908-1973 85-88
Greenberg, Jae W. 1894(?)-1974
Obituary 104
Greenberg, James B(rian) 1945- 105
Greenberg, Jan W(eingarten) 1943- 118
Greenberg, Joanne (Goldenberg)
1932- CANR-14
Earlier sketch in CA 7-8R
See also SATA 25
See also CLC 7, 30
Greenberg, Joseph Harold 1915- 102
Greenberg, Judith Anne
See Azrael, Judith Anne
Greenberg, Kenneth R(ay) 1930- 57-60
Greenberg, Kenneth S. 1947- 124
Greenberg, Louis M. 1933- Brief entry 112
Greenberg, Martin Harry 1941- 49-52
Greenberg, Milton 1927- 25-28R
Greenberg, Morrie
See Greenberg, Morris S.
Greenberg, Morris S. 1924- 33-36R
Greenberg, Moshe 1928- 15-16R
Greenberg, Paul 1937- 69-72
Greenberg, Pearl 1927- 93-96
Greenberg, Polly 1932- 85-88
See also SATA 43, 52
Greenberg, Robert Arthur 1930- CANR-4
Earlier sketch in CA 1R
Greenberg, Selig 1904- 49-52
Greenberg, Selma 1930- 29-32R
Greenberg, Sidney 1917- CANR-3
Earlier sketch in CA 9-10R
Greenberg, Simon 1901- CANR-14
Earlier sketch in CA 77-80
Greenberg, Stan 1931- 119
Greenberg, Stanley Bernard 1945- 53-56
Greenberg, Uri Zvi 1898-1981 Obituary 103
Greenberger, Allen J(ay) 1937- 41-44R
Greenberger, Howard 1924- 45-48
Greenberger, Martin 1931- CANR-8
Earlier sketch in CA 61-64
Greenbie, Barrie B(arstow) 1920- 107
Greenbie, Marjorie Barstow 1889(?)-1976
Obituary 61-64
Greenblat, Cathy S(tein) 1940- Brief entry .. 118
Greenblatt, Augusta 1912- CANR-6
Earlier sketch in CA 57-60
Greenblatt, Edwin 1920- 49-52
Greenblatt, M(anuel) H(arry) 1922-1972 .. CAP-2
Earlier sketch in CA 17-18
Greenblatt, Robert Benjamin 1906-1987 .. CAP-1
Obituary 123
Earlier sketch in CA 11-12
Greenblatt, Stephen J(ay) 1943- 49-52
Greenblum, Joseph 1925- 23-24R
Greenburg, Dan 1936- CANR-25
Earlier sketches in CA 13-14R, CANR-9
Greenburger, Francis 1949- 85-88
Greenburger, Ingrid Elisabeth 1913- 104
Greene, A(lvin) C(arl) 1923- CANR-14
Earlier sketch in CA 37-40R
Greene, Adam
See Scott, Peter Dale
Greene, Anthony Hamilton Millard Kirk
See Kirk-Greene, Anthony (Hamilton Millard)
Greene, Asa 1789-1838 ....DLB-11
Greene, Bert 1923-1988 ....CANR-6
Obituary 125
Earlier sketch in CA 57-60
Greene, Bette 1934- CANR-4
Earlier sketch in CA 53-56
See also SATA 8
See also CLC 30
See also CLR 2
Greene, Bob
See Greene, Robert Bernard, Jr.
Greene, Carla 1916- CANR-1
Earlier sketch in CA 4R
See also SATA 1
Greene, Carol SATA-44
Greene, Charles Jerome 1910-1983
Obituary 110
Greene, Constance C(larke) 1924- CANR-8
Earlier sketch in CA 61-64
See also SATA 11
Greene, David B(eckwith) 1939- 117
Greene, David H. 1913- 23-24R
Greene, David L(ouis) 1944- Brief entry 114
Greene, David M(ason) 1920- 118
Greene, Donald J(ohnson) 1916- CANR-2
Earlier sketch in CA 1R
Greene, Ellin 1927- 77-80
See also SATA 23
Greene, Felix 1909-1985 ....CANR-6
Obituary 116
Earlier sketch in CA 3R
Greene, Fred
See Cadet, John
Greene, Gael CANR-10
Earlier sketch in CA 13-14R
See also CLC 8
Greene, Graham 1904- 15-16R
See also SATA 20
See also DLB 13, 15
See also DLBY 85
See also CLC 1, 3, 6, 9, 14, 18, 27, 37
See also AITN 2
Greene, Harris 1921- 15-16R
Greene, Harry A. 1889- CAP-2
Earlier sketch in CA 17-18
Greene, Harry J(oseph) 1906- 57-60
Greene, Herbert 1898- CAP-1
Earlier sketch in CA 9-10
Greene, Howard R. 1937- 61-64
Greene, Hugh (Carleton) 1910-1987 102
Obituary 121
Greene, Jack P(hillip) 1931- CANR-18
Earlier sketches in CA 11-12R, CANR-3
Greene, James H. 1915- 17-18R
Greene, Janet (Churchill) 1917- 5-6R
Greene, Janice Presser
See Presser, Janice
Greene, Jay E(lihu) 1914- CANR-5
Earlier sketch in CA 5-6R
Greene, Jerry
See Greene, Charles Jerome
Greene, John C(olton) 1917- 89-92
Greene, John William, Jr. 1946- 89-92
Greene, Johnny
See Greene, John William, Jr.
Greene, Jonathan Edward 1943- CANR-12
Earlier sketch in CA 33-36R
Greene, Laura 1935- CANR-23
Earlier sketch in CA 107
See also SATA 38
Greene, Lawrence J. 1943- 113
Greene, Lee S(eifert) 1905- CANR-5
Earlier sketch in CA 13-14R
Greene, Leonard M(ichael) 1918- 109
Greene, Lorenzo Johnston 1899-1988
Obituary 124
Greene, Mabel
See Bean, Mabel Greene
Greene, Mark R. 1923- CANR-5
Earlier sketch in CA 2R
Greene, Maxine 1917- CANR-13
Earlier sketch in CA 23-24R
Greene, Mott T(uthill) 1945- 110
Greene, Naomi 1942- 45-48
Greene, Nathanael 1935- 25-28R
Greene, Owen (John) 1954- 124
Greene, Pamela
See Forman, Joan
Greene, Philip L(eon) 1924- Brief entry 113
Greene, Reynolds W(illiam), Jr. 1924- .. CANR-2
Earlier sketch in CA 5-6R
Greene, Richard C. 1941- 111
Greene, Richard Leighton 1904-1983 ... CANR-2
Obituary 111
Earlier sketch in CA 5-6R
Greene, Robert 1558-1592 ....DLB-62
Greene, Robert
See Deindorfer, Robert Greene
Greene, Robert Bernard, Jr. 1947- 107
Greene, Robert W. 1929- 104
Greene, Robert W(illiam) 1933-
Brief entry 111
Greene, Ruth Altman 1896- 73-76
Greene, Sara
See Strong, June
Greene, Shirley E(dward) 1911- 3R
Greene, Stephanie 1953- 61-64
Greene, Stephen 1914-1979 Obituary 89-92
Greene, Thomas M(cLernon) 1926- 9-10R
Greene, Victor R(obert) 1933- 25-28R
Greene, Vivian AITN-2
Greene, Wade 1933- SATA-11
Greene, Walter E. 1929- 25-28R
Greene, Wilda 1911- CANR-9
Earlier sketch in CA 23-24R
Greene, William C. 1933- 15-16R
Greene, Yvonne
See Flesch, Yolande (Catarina)
Greenebaum, Louise G(uggenheim)
1919- 69-72
Greener, Leslie 1900-1974 ....CAP-2
Earlier sketch in CA 21-22
Greener, Michael (John) 1931- 25-28R
Greenewalt, Crawford Hallock 1902- CANR-2
Earlier sketch in CA 2R
Greenfeder, Paul 1925(?)-1983 Obituary 109
Greenfeld, Howard CANR-19
Earlier sketch in CA 81-84
See also SATA 19
Greenfeld, Josh 1927(?)- Brief entry 116
Greenfield, Darby
See Ward, Philip
Greenfield, Edward 1928- Brief entry 110
Greenfield, Eloise 1929- CANR-19
Earlier sketches in CA 49-52, CANR-1
See also BW
See also SATA 19
See also CLR 4
Greenfield, Gerald Michael 1943- 114
Greenfield, Harry I. 1922- Brief entry 109
Greenfield, Howard 1937(?)-1986
Obituary 118
Greenfield, Irving A. 1928- 33-36R
Greenfield, James Lloyd 1924- 73-76
Greenfield, Jeff 1943- CANR-24
Earlier sketch in CA 37-40R
Greenfield, Jerome 1923- 7-8R
Greenfield, Jerry
See Greenfield, Jerome
Greenfield, Jonas Carl 1926- Brief entry 110
Greenfield, Meg 1930- Brief entry 123
Greenfield, Norman S(amuel) 1923- 41-44R
Greenfield, Patricia Marks 1940- CANR-24
Earlier sketches in CA 21-22R, CANR-9
Greenfield, Sidney M(artin) 1932- 21-22R
Greenfield, Stanley B(rian) 1922- 11-12R
Greenfield, Thelma N. 1922- 25-28R
Greengold, Jane
See Stevens, Jane Greengold
Greengrass, Mark 1949- 118
Greengroin, Artie
See Brown, Harry (Peter McNab, Jr.)
Greenhalgh, P(eter) A(ndrew) L(ivsey)
1945- CANR-1
Earlier sketch in CA 49-52
Greenhaus, Thelma Nurenberg
1903-1984 69-72
Obituary 113
See also SATA 45
Greenhaw, H(arold) Wayne 1940- CANR-24
Earlier sketches in CA 23-24R, CANR-9
Greenhill, Basil (Jack) 1920- CANR-17
Earlier sketches in CA 7-8R, CANR-2
Greenhood, (Clarence) David 1895-1983 .... 2R
Obituary 109
Greenhouse, Linda 1947- 77-80
Greenhow, Robert 1800-1854 ....DLB-30
Greenhut, Melvin L. 1921- 15-16R
Greening, Hamilton
See Hamilton, Charles Harold St. John
Greenland, Colin 1954- 117
Greenlaw, Jean-Pierre 1910- 69-72
Greenlaw, Paul S(tephen) 1930- CANR-5
Earlier sketch in CA 2R
Greenleaf, Barbara Kaye 1942- 29-32R
See also SATA 6
Greenleaf, Peter 1910- 85-88
See also SATA 33
Greenleaf, Richard Edward 1930- 25-28R
Greenleaf, Robert Kiefner 1904- 125
Greenleaf, Stephen (Howell) 1942- 102
Greenleaf, William 1917- 9-10R
Greenlee, Douglas 1935-1979 45-48
Obituary 103
Greenlee, J(acob) Harold 1918- 19-20R
Greenlee, James W(allace) 1933- CANR-11
Earlier sketch in CA 69-72
Greenlee, Sam 1930- 69-72
See also BW
Greenlick, Merwyn R(onald) 1935- 41-44R
Greenman, Robert 1939- 115
Greenman, Russell Lester 1904-1983
Obituary 111
Greenough, Horatio 1805-1852 ....DLB-1
Greenough, Sarah 1951- 126
Greenough, William Croan 1914- 15-16R
Greenslade, S(tanley) L(awrence)
1905-1977 Obituary 111
Greenson, Ralph R(omeo) 1911-
Brief entry 114
Greenspan, Bud 1927- 103
Greenspan, Cappy Petrash
See Greenspan, Constance Anne Petrash
Greenspan, Charlotte L. 1921- 33-36R
Greenspan, Constance Anne Petrash
1932(?)-1983 Obituary 110
Greenspan, Elaine 1929- 110
Greenspan, Emily 1953- 124
Greenspan, Sophie 1906- 97-100
Greenspoon, Leonard J(ay) 1945- 111
Greenspun, H(erman) M(ilton) 1909- CAP-2
Earlier sketch in CA 21-22
See also AITN 2
Greenspun, Hank
See Greenspun, H(erman) M(ilton)
Greenspun, Roger (Austin) 1929- 102
Greenstein, Fred I(rwin) 1930- CANR-4
Earlier sketch in CA 49-52
Greenstock, David Lionel 1912- 9-10R
Greenstone, J. David 1937- 25-28R
Greenup, Ruth (Robinson) 1912(?)-1984
Obituary 113
Greenwald, Harold 1910- CANR-4
Earlier sketch in CA 1R
Greenwald, Jerry 1923- 57-60
Greenwald, Sheila
See Green, Sheila Ellen
Green-Wanstall, Kenneth 1918- 15-16R
Greenway, Hugh D(avids) S(cott) 1935- 73-76
Greenway, John 1919- 11-12R
Greenway, Roger S(elles) 1934- CANR-4
Earlier sketch in CA 53-56
Greenwell, Dora 1821-1882 ....DLB-35
Greenwood, David Charles 1927-1984 61-64
Obituary 112
Greenwood, Duncan 1919- 21-22R
Greenwood, Edward Alister 1930- CANR-12
Earlier sketch in CA 29-32R
Greenwood, Frank 1924- CANR-10
Earlier sketch in CA 25-28R
Greenwood, Gordon 1913- CANR-9
Earlier sketch in CA 21-22R
Greenwood, Gordon E(dward) 1935- 37-40R
Greenwood, Grace
See Lippincott, Sara Jane Clarke
Greenwood, Julia Eileen Courtney 1910- .. CAP-1
Earlier sketch in CA 13-14
Greenwood, Kathryn Moore 1922- 93-96
Greenwood, Lillian Bethel 1932- 104
Greenwood, Marianne (Hederstrom)
1926- CANR-6
Earlier sketch in CA 11-12R
Greenwood, Ned H. 1932- Brief entry 110
Greenwood, Ted
See Greenwood, Edward Alister
Greenwood, Theresa 1936- 29-32R
Greenwood, Val D(avid) 1937- 73-76
Greenwood, Walter 1903-1974 93-96
Obituary 53-56
See also DLB 10
Greer, Ann Lennarson 1944- 53-56
Greer, Art(hur Ellis, Jr.) 1929- 81-84
Greer, Ben 1948- 102
See also DLB 6
Greer, Carlotta C(herryholmes)
1879-1965 ....CAP-1
Earlier sketch in CA 15-16
Greer, Francesca
See Janas, Frankie-Lee
Greer, Georgeanna H(errmann) 1922- ... CANR-6
Earlier sketch in CA 57-60
Greer, Germaine 1939- 81-84
See also AITN 1
Greer, Herb 1929- CANR-8
Earlier sketch in CA 7-8R
Greer, Louise 1899- CAP-1
Earlier sketch in CA 15-16
Greer, Philip 1930-1985 Obituary 116
Greer, Rebecca Ellen 1935- 103
Greer, Richard
See Silverberg, Robert
Greer, Rita 1942- 97-100
Greer, Scott (Allen) 1922- 45-48
Greer, Thomas H(oag) 1914- 23-24R
Greeson, Janet 1952- 121
Greet, Brian Aubrey 1922- 105
Greet, Kenneth (Gerald) 1918- CANR-25
Earlier sketches in CA 7-8R, CANR-6
Greet, T(homas) Y(oung) 1923- 15-16R
Greet, William Cabell 1901-1972
Obituary 37-40R
Greever, William S(t. Clair) 1916- 5-6R
Greeves, Frederic 1903-1985 Obituary 115
Greevy, David U(pton) 1953- 112
Greg, W. R. 1809-1881 ....DLB-55
Greger, Debora 1949- 112
Gregersen, Edgar (Alstrup) 1937- 120
Gregg, Andrew K. 1929- CANR-15
Earlier sketch in CA 29-32R
Gregg, Charles T(hornton) 1927- CANR-14
Earlier sketch in CA 81-84
Gregg, Davis W(einert) 1918- 17-18R
Gregg, Hubert 1916- 102
Gregg, James E(rwin) 1927- 23-24R
Gregg, James R. 1914- 23-24R
Gregg, Jess 1926- 61-64
Gregg, John E(dwin) 1925- 45-48
Gregg, Larry
See Leighton, Lauren G(ray)
Gregg, Linda (Alouise) 1942- 113
Gregg, Martin
See McNeilly, Wilfred (Glassford)
Gregg, Pauline 7-8R
Gregg, Richard A(lexander) 1927- 15-16R
Gregg, Robert J(ohn) 1912- Brief entry 110
Gregg, Walter H(arold) 1919- 73-76
See also SATA 20
Gregg, William H. 1904(?)-1983 Obituary .. 109
Gregor, A(nthony) James 1929- 57-60
Gregor, Arthur 1923- CANR-11
Earlier sketch in CA 25-28R
See also SATA 36
See also CLC 9
Gregor, Carol 1943- 117
Gregor, Howard F(rank) 1920- CANR-2
Earlier sketch in CA 7-8R
Gregor, Lee
See Pohl, Frederik
Gregor, Rex H. 1922- 15-16R
Gregori, Leon 1919- SATA-15
Gregorian, Joyce Ballou 1946- CANR-24
Earlier sketch in CA 107
See also SATA 30
Gregorian, Vartan 1935- 29-32R
Gregorich, Barbara 1943- 117
Gregorios, Paulos Mar 1922- CANR-11
Earlier sketch in CA 25-28R
Gregorowski, Christopher 1940- CANR-15
Earlier sketch in CA 89-92
See also SATA 30
Gregory, Bettina 1946- 69-72
Gregory, Chuck
See Gnaegy, Charles
Gregory, Diana (Jean) 1933- 97-100
See also SATA 42, 49
Gregory, Dick 1932- CANR-7
Earlier sketch in CA 45-48
See also BW
Gregory, Elizabeth
See Gilford, C(harles) B(ernard)
Gregory, Freida 1938- 69-72
Gregory, H(ollingsworth) F(ranklin) 1906- ..69-72
Gregory, Harry
See Gottfried, Theodore Mark
Gregory, Hilton
See Ferguson, Charles W.
Gregory, Horace (Victor) 1898-1982 ... CANR-22
Obituary 106
Earlier sketches in CA 7-8R, CANR-3
See also DLB 48
Gregory, Isabella Augusta (Persse)
1852-1932 Brief entry 104
See also DLB 10
See also TCLC 1

Gregory, J. Dennis
See Williams, John A(lfred)
Gregory, James 1912- 77-80
Gregory, Jean
See Ure, Jean
Gregory, K(enneth) J(ohn) 1938- 107
Gregory, Kenneth (Malcolm) 1921- 73-76
Gregory, Lisa
See Camp, Candace P(auline)
Gregory, Lydia
See Carey, Diane
Gregory, Mark
See Burch, Monte G.
Gregory, Paul Roderick 1941- 53-56
Gregory, Peter 1924- 41-44R
Gregory, R(ichard) L(angton) 1923- 57-60
Gregory, Richard Claxton
See Gregory, Dick
Gregory, Robert G(ranville) 1924- 41-44R
Gregory, Robert Lloyd 1892- 29-32R
Gregory, Ross 1933- 29-32R
Gregory, Roy 1935- 37-40R
Gregory, Ruth W(ilhelmine) 1910- 77-80
Gregory, Sean
See Hossent, Harry
Gregory, Sinda 1947- 115
Gregory, Stephan
See Pendleton, Don(ald Eugene)
Gregory, Stephen
See Penzler, Otto
Gregory, Susan 1945- 108
Gregory, Thomas B(ernard) 1940- 45-48
Gregory, Timothy E(dmund) 1943- 111
Gregory, Vahan 1927- 69-72
Gregory, Violet L(efler) 1907- CANR-8
Earlier sketch in CA 57-60
Gregory, William King 1876-1970
Obituary 29-32R
Gregory, Yvonne 1919(?)-1979 Obituary ..89-92
Gregson, Paul
See Oakley, Eric Gilbert
Gregston, Gene 1925- 81-84
Greider, William (F.) 117
Greif, E(dwin) Charles 1915- 1R
Greif, Martin 1938- CANR-25
Earlier sketches in CA 65-68, CANR-10
Greiff, Barrie S(anford) 1935- Brief entry ... 114
Greig, Cicely ?-1983 Obituary 116
Greig, Maysie 1902-1971 102
Obituary 104
Greiner, Donald J(ames) 1940- CANR-16
Earlier sketches in CA 45-48, CANR-1
Greinke, (Lawrence) Eric 1948- 41-44R
Greisman, Joan Ruth 1937- 103
See also SATA 31
Grele, Ronald J(ohn) 1934- 73-76
Gremillion, Joseph 1919- 102
Gremmels, Marion Louise Chapman 1924- .. 111
Grenander, M(ary) E(lizabeth) 1918- CANR-4
Earlier sketch in CA 53-56
Grendahl, J(ay) Spencer 1943- 29-32R
Grendler, Paul F(rederick) 1936- 41-44R
Grendon, Edward
See LeShan, Lawrence L(ee)
Grendon, Stephen
See Derleth, August (William)
Grene, Marjorie (Glicksman) 1910- CANR-25
Earlier sketches in CA 13-14R, CANR-8
Grenelle, Lisa
See Munroe, Elizabeth L(ee)
Grenfell, Joyce (Irene) 1910-1979 ..... CANR-20
Obituary 89-92
Earlier sketch in CA 81-84
Grenier, Judson A(chille) 1930- 89-92
Grenier, Mildred 1917- CANR-12
Earlier sketch in CA 29-32R
Grennan, Margaret R(ose) 41-44R
Grenville, Bryan P(eter) 1955- 117
Grenville, J(ohn) A(shley) S(oames)
1928- CANR-5
Earlier sketch in CA 11-12R
Grenville, Kate 1950- 118
Grenville, Pelham
See Wodehouse, P(elham) G(renville)
Grenyer, Norman 1913-1983 Obituary 110
Gresham, Anthony
See Russell, Roy
Gresham, Claude Hamilton, Jr. 1922- ... CANR-8
Earlier sketch in CA 7-8R
Gresham, Elizabeth (Fenner) 1904- 81-84
Gresham, Grits
See Gresham, Claude Hamilton, Jr.
Gresham, Perry E(pler) 1907- 45-48
Gresser, Seymour 1926- 29-32R
Gresser, Sy
See Gresser, Seymour
Gressley, Gene M(aurice) 1931- CANR-10
Earlier sketch in CA 17-18R
Greteman, James 1933- 112
Greteman, Jim
See Greteman, James
Gretz, Susanna 1937- 29-32R
See also SATA 7
Gretzer, John SATA-18
Gretzky, Walter 1938- 120
Greulach, Victor A(ugust) 1906- 49-52
Greve, Elsa
See Greve, Felix Paul (Berthold Friedrich)
Greve, Felix Paul (Berthold Friedrich)
1879-1948 Brief entry 104
Greville, Fulke 1554-1628 .... DLB-62
Grew, James Hooper 1906- 103
Grew, Raymond 1930- 13-14R
Grewdead, Roy
See Gorey, Edward (St. John)
Grewer, Eira M(ary) 1931- 21-22R
Grex, Leo
See Gribble, Leonard (Reginald)
Grey, Abby (Bartlett) Weed 1903(?)-1983
Obituary 110
Grey, Anthony 1938- 29-32R
Grey, Beryl (Elizabeth) 1927- 109
Grey, Brenda
See Mackinlay, Leila Antoinette Sterling
Grey, Carenna Jane
See Kalpakian, Laura Anne
Grey, Carol
See Lowndes, Robert A(ugustine) W(ard)
Grey, Charles
See Tubb, E(dwin) C(harles)
Grey, David Lennox 1935- 93-96
Grey, Dorothy 1913- 120
Grey, Elizabeth
See Hogg, Elizabeth (Tootill)
Grey, Georgina
See Roby, Mary Linn
Grey, Ian 1918- CANR-2
Earlier sketch in CA 7-8R
Grey, Jerry 1926- CANR-20
Earlier sketches in CA 53-56, CANR-5
See also SATA 11
Grey, Lindsey
See Peel, Colin D(udley)
Grey, Marian Powys 1883(?)-1972
Obituary 104
Grey, Robert Waters 1943- 49-52
Grey, Robin
See Gresham, Elizabeth (Fenner)
Grey, Vivian (Hoffman) 17-18R
Grey, Zane 1872(?)-1939 Brief entry 104
See also DLB 9
See also TCLC 6
Grey Owl
See Belaney, Archibald Stansfeld
Greyser, Stephen A. 1935- 33-36R
Gri
See Denney, Diana
Gribbin, John 1946- 113
Gribbin, Lenore S. 1922- 33-36R
Gribbin, William James 1943- CANR-17
Earlier sketches in CA 45-48, CANR-1
Gribble, Charles E(dward) 1936- 41-44R
Gribble, Harry Wagstaff (Graham)
1891(?)-1981 Obituary 102
Gribble, James 1938- 29-32R
Gribble, Jennifer 1937- 116
Gribble, Leonard (Reginald) 1908- CANR-7
Earlier sketch in CA 53-56
Gribbons, Warren D(avid) 1921- 29-32R
Grice, Frederick 1910- CANR-3
Earlier sketch in CA 11-12R
See also SATA 6
Grice, Grimes
See Kamp, Irene Kittle
Grice, Julia (Haughey) 1940- CANR-16
Earlier sketch in CA 77-80
Gridban, Volsted
See Tubb, E(dwin) C(harles)
Grider, Dorothy 1915- SATA-31
Gridley, Marion E(leanor) 1906-1974 45-48
Obituary 103
See also SATA 26, 35
Gridley, Roy E. 1935- Brief entry 109
Gridzewski, Mieczylawski 1895(?)-1970
Obituary 104
Grieb, Kenneth J. 1939- CANR-12
Earlier sketch in CA 29-32R
Grieb, Lyndal 1940- 61-64
Grieder, Josephine 1939- 53-56
Grieder, Terence 1931- 114
Grieder, Theodore 1926- 45-48
Grieder, Walter 1924- 41-44R
See also SATA 9
Grieg, Michael 1922- 19-20R
Grieg, (Johan) Nordahl (Brun) 1902-1943
Brief entry 107
See also TCLC 10
Grier, B. R. 1913- 25-28R
Grier, Barbara G(ene Damon) 1933- 107
Grier, Edward F(rancis) 1917- 121
Grier, Eldon 1917- 113
Grier, Frances Belle Powner
1886(?)-1980(?) Obituary 104
Grier, Roosevelt 1932- 113
Grier, Rosey
See Grier, Roosevelt
Grierson, Edward 1914- CANR-4
Earlier sketch in CA 3R
Grierson, Francis Durham 1888-1972
Obituary 104
Grierson, Herbert John Clifford 1886-1960
Obituary 93-96
Grierson, John 1898-1972 Obituary 116
Grierson, John 1909-1977 .... CAP-2
Obituary 69-72
Earlier sketch in CA 19-20
Grierson, (Monica) Linden 1914- CAP-1
Earlier sketch in CA 9-10
Gries, Tom 1923(?)-1977 Obituary 69-72
Griese, Arnold A(lfred) 1921- CANR-1
Earlier sketch in CA 49-52
See also SATA 9
Grieson, Ronald Edward 1943- CANR-1
Earlier sketch in CA 49-52
Griesse, Carolyn 1941- 107
Griessman, Benjamin Eugene 1934- 41-44R
Griest, Guinevere L(indley) 1924- 65-68
Grieve, Andrew W. 1925- 11-12R
Grieve, C(hristopher) M(urray) 1892-1978 ..7-8R
Obituary 85-88
See also CLC 11, 19
Grieves, Forest L(eslie) 1938- 53-56
Grifalconi, Ann 1929- CANR-9
Earlier sketch in CA 7-8R
See also SATA 2
Griff
See Fawcett, F(rank) Dubrez
and McKeag, Ernest L(ionel)
Griffen, Edmund
See Du Breuil, (Elizabeth) L(or)inda
Griffen, (James) Jeff(erds) 1923- 15-16R
Griffin, A(rthur) H(arold) 1911- CANR-9
Earlier sketch in CA 21-22R
Griffin, Al 1919- 33-36R
Griffin, Anne J.
See Griffin, Arthur J.
Griffin, Arthur J. 1921- CANR-1
Earlier sketch in CA 49-52
Griffin, Barbara C(ook) 1945- 53-56
Griffin, Bryan F(rederick) 120
Brief entry 113
Griffin, C. F.
See Fikso, Eunice Cleland
Griffin, C. S.
See Griffin, Clifford S(tephen)
Griffin, C(harles) W(illiam) 1925- 53-56
Griffin, Charles C(arroll) 1902-1976
Obituary 65-68
Griffin, Charles Henry 1922- 19-20R
Griffin, Clifford S(tephen) 1929-
Brief entry 111
Griffin, (George) Dan(iel) 1937-1984
Obituary 112
Griffin, David Ray 1939- 77-80
Griffin, Donald (Redfield) 1915- CANR-15
Earlier sketch in CA 37-40R
Griffin, Dustin H(adley) 1943- 120
Griffin, Edward M(ichael) 1937- 89-92
Griffin, Emilie Russell Dietrich 1936- ... CANR-21
Earlier sketch in CA 103
Griffin, Ernest G(eorge) 1916- 25-28R
Griffin, Gerald G(ehrig) 1933- CANR-9
Earlier sketch in CA 57-60
Griffin, Gillett Good 1928- SATA-26
Griffin, Glen C. 1934- CANR-17
Earlier sketch in CA 29-32R
Griffin, (Arthur) Gwyn 1922(?)-1967
Obituary 89-92
Griffin, Jacqueline P. 1927- 33-36R
Griffin, James A. 1934- 29-32R
Griffin, John Howard 1920-1980 .... CANR-2
Obituary 101
Earlier sketch in CA 2R
See also AITN 1
Griffin, John Q(uealy) 1948- 77-80
Griffin, Judith Berry 108
See also SATA 34
Griffin, Keith B(roadwell) 1938- CANR-7
Earlier sketch in CA 57-60
Griffin, (Samuel) Marvin 1907-1982
Obituary 108
Griffin, Mary 1916- 61-64
Griffin, Mary Claire 1924- 19-20R
Griffin, Peter CLC-39
Griffin, Robert 1936- 53-56
Griffin, Russell M(organ) 1943- 114
Griffin, Stuart 1917- 7-8R
Griffin, Susan 1943- CANR-3
Earlier sketch in CA 49-52
Griffin, W. E. B.
See Butterworth, W(illiam) E(dmund III)
Griffin, Walter 1937- 73-76
Griffin, (Henry) William 1935- 93-96
Griffin, William D(enis) 1936- 122
Griffin, William Lloyd 1938- 21-22R
Griffin-Beale, Christopher 1947- 118
Griffiss, James E(dward) 1928-
Brief entry 118
Griffith, A. Kinney 1897- CANR-17
Earlier sketch in CA 2R
Griffith, A(rthur) Leonard 1920- CANR-5
Earlier sketch in CA 9-10R
Griffith, Albert J(oseph, Jr.) 1932- 37-40R
Griffith, Benjamin Woodward, Jr.
1922- CANR-20
Earlier sketches in CA 1R, CANR-5
Griffith, Corinne 1898(?)-1979 Obituary ...89-92
Griffith, D(avid Lewelyn) W(ark)
1875-1948 Brief entry 119
Griffith, Elizabeth 1727(?)-1793 .... DLB-39
Griffith, Ernest S(tacey) 1896- 13-14R
Griffith, Francis 1906- 106
Griffith, G(uy) T(hompson) 1908-1985
Obituary 117
Griffith, George
See Griffith-Jones, George Chetwynd
Griffith, Helen V(irginia) 1934- CANR-22
Earlier sketch in CA 105
See also SATA 39
Griffith, Jeannette
See Eyerly, Jeannette Hyde
Griffith, Jerry 1932- 53-56
Griffith, Kathryn 1923- 73-76
Griffith, Kenneth 1921- CANR-21
Earlier sketch in CA 69-72
Griffith, Lawrence
See Griffith, D(avid Lewelyn) W(ark)
Griffith, Leon Odell 1921- CANR-2
Earlier sketch in CA 3R
Griffith, Lucille B(lanche) 1905- 17-18R
Griffith, Patricia Browning 1935- CANR-13
Earlier sketch in CA 77-80
Griffith, Paul 1921-1983 ....23-24R
Obituary 109
Griffith, Richard (Edward) 1912-1969 ... CANR-6
Earlier sketch in CA 1R
Griffith, Robert 1940- 45-48
Griffith, Samuel Blair II 1906-1983
Obituary 109
Griffith, Thomas 1915- 23-24R
Griffith, Thomas Gwynfor 1926- 103
Griffith, William E(dgar) 1920- 61-64
Griffith, Winthrop 1931- 11-12R
Griffith-Jones, George Chetwynd
1857-1906 Brief entry 112
Griffith-Jones, Stephany 1947- 126
Griffiths, A(lan) Bede 1906- CANR-7
Earlier sketch in CA 13-14R
Griffiths, Brian 1941- 120
Griffiths, Bryn(lyn) David 1933- 101
Griffiths, Daniel E(dward) 1917- 25-28R
Griffiths, G(ordon) D(ouglas) 1910-1973 .. CAP-2
Earlier sketch in CA 21-22
See also SATA 20
Griffiths, G. D.
See Griffiths, (Edith) Grace (Chalmers)
Griffiths, (Edith) Grace (Chalmers)
1921- CANR-22
Earlier sketch in CA 106
Griffiths, Helen 1939- CANR-25
Earlier sketches in CA 19-20R, CANR-7
See also SATA 5
See also SAAS 5
Griffiths, John C(harles) 1934- 108
Griffiths, John Gwyn 1911- 106
Griffiths, Kitty Anna 105
Griffiths, Louise (Benckenstein) 1907- 3R
Griffiths, (Thomas) Mel(vin) 1910- 85-88
Griffiths, Michael C(ompton) 1928- CANR-14
Earlier sketch in CA 37-40R
Griffiths, Naomi 1934- 101
Griffiths, Paul (Anthony) 1947- 107
Griffiths, Percival Joseph 1899- 103
Griffiths, Ralph A(lan) 1937- CANR-22
Earlier sketch in CA 105
Griffiths, Richard M(athias) 1935- CANR-8
Earlier sketch in CA 17-18R
Griffiths, Robert David 1952- 118
Griffiths, Robert L. III
See Pauker, John
Griffiths, Sally 1934- 25-28R
Griffiths, Trevor 1935- 97-100
See also DLB 13
See also CLC 13
Griffiths, Vincent Llewellyn 1902(?)-1984
Obituary 113
Grigg, Charles M(eade) 1918- 13-14R
Grigg, John (Edward Poynder) 1924- 104
Griggs, Charles Irwin 1902- 1R
Griggs, Earl Leslie 1899- 73-76
Griggs, Gary B(ruce) 1943- 118
Griggs, Lee 1928- 69-72
Griggs, Sutton Elbert 1872-1930(?)
Brief entry 123
See also DLB 50
Griggs, Tamar 1941- 77-80
Grignon, Claude-Henri 1894-1976 ...... DLB-68
Grigoli, Valorie 1955- 122
Grigorovich, Yuri Nikolayevich 1927- 126
Grigsby, Gordon 1927- CANR-19
Earlier sketch in CA 97-100
Grigson, Geoffrey (Edward Harvey)
1905-1985 .... CANR-20
Obituary 118
Earlier sketch in CA 25-28R
See also DLB 27
See also CLC 7, 39
Grigson, Jane 1928- CANR-20
Earlier sketches in CA 49-52, CANR-1
Grill, Johnpeter Horst 1943- 112
Grill, Nannette L. 1935- 65-68
Grilli, Peter M. 1942- 120
Grilliot, Harold J(ohn) 1937- 107
Grillo, John 1942- Brief entry 117
Grillo, Ralph David 1940- 49-52
Grillo, Virgil 1938- 53-56
Grim, John A(llen) 1946- 117
Grim, Patrick 1950- 115
Grim, Ronald E(ugene) 1946- 118
Grimal, Pierre Antoine 1912- CANR-7
Earlier sketch in CA 13-14R
Grimaldi, J(ohn) V. 1916- CANR-19
Earlier sketches in CA 5-6R, CANR-3
Grimault, Berthe 1940- 13-14R
Grimble, Ian 1921- CANR-18
Earlier sketches in CA 7-8R, CANR-2
Grimble, Reverend Charles James
See Eliot, T(homas) S(tearns)
Grime, Harol (Riley) 1896-1984 Obituary ... 114
Grimes, Alan P. 1919- CANR-1
Earlier sketch in CA 1R
Grimes, (Lewis) Howard 1915- 25-28R
Grimes, Johnnie Marie 103
Grimes, Joseph E(vans) 1928- 37-40R
Grimes, Lee 1920- 61-64
Grimes, Martha 117
Brief entry 113
Grimes, Nikki 1950- 77-80
Grimes, Orville F(rank), Jr. 1943- 106
Grimes, Paul 1924- 77-80
Grimes, Ronald L. 1943- CANR-17
Earlier sketches in CA 45-48, CANR-1
Grimes, W(illiam) H(enry) 1892-1972
Obituary 33-36R
Grimke, Angelina (Emily) Weld 1880-1958 .. 124
See also BW
See also DLB 50, 54
Grimke, Charlotte L(ottie) Forten
1837(?)-1914 124
Brief entry 117
See also BW
Grimley, Mildred H(ess) 1919- 5-6R
Grimm, Charles John 1898(?)-1983
Obituary 111
Grimm, Charlie
See Grimm, Charles John

Grimm, Cherry Barbara 1930- ... 101
See also SATA 43
Grimm, Hans 1875-1959 ... DLB-66
Grimm, Harold J(ohn) 1901- ... 13-14R
Grimm, Jacob Ludwig Karl 1785-1863 . SATA-22
Grimm, Reinhold 1931- ... CANR-23
Earlier sketches in CA 61-64, CANR-8
Grimm, Wilhelm Karl 1786-1859 ... SATA-22
Grimm, William C(arey) 1907- ... 49-52
See also SATA 14
Grimond, Joseph 1913- ... 108
Grimsditch, Herbert Borthwick 1898-1971
Obituary ... 104
Grimshaw, Allen Day 1929- ... CANR-9
Earlier sketch in CA 65-68
Grimshaw, James A(lbert), Jr. 1940- ... 109
Grimshaw, Mark
See McKeag, Ernest L(ionel)
Grimshaw, Nigel (Gilroy) 1925- ... CANR-17
Earlier sketch in CA 101
See also SATA 23
Grimsley, Gordon
See Groom, Arthur William
Grimsley, Linda 1940- ... 81-84
Grimsley, Ronald 1915- ... CANR-3
Earlier sketch in CA 7-8R
Grimsley, Will (Henry) 1914- ... 33-36R
Grimstead, Hettie 1903- Brief entry ... 115
Grimsted, David Allen 1935- ... 25-28R
Grimsted, Patricia Kennedy 1935- ... 77-80
Grindal, Bruce T. 1940- ... 41-44R
Grindal, Gracia (Marie) 1943- ... 116
Grindea, Miron 1909- ... CANR-5
Earlier sketch in CA 7-8R
Grindel, Carl W(illiam) 1905- ... 85-88
Grindel, Eugene 1895-1952 Brief entry ... 104
Grindel, John Anthony 1937- ... 65-68
Grindell, Robert M(aclean) 1933- ... 15-16R
Grinder, Michael 1942- ... 61-64
Grindle, Carleton
See Page, Gerald W(ilburn)
Grindley, John (Thomas Ellam) 1926- ... 25-28R
Grindley, (Jane) Sally 1953- ... 121
Grindrod, Muriel (Kathleen) 1902- ... 7-8R
Gringhuis, Dirk
See Gringhuis, Richard H.
Gringhuis, Richard H. 1918-1974 ... CANR-5
Earlier sketch in CA 2R
See also SATA 6, 25
Grinnell, David
See Wollheim, Donald A(llen)
Grinnell, George Bird 1849-1938 ... SATA-16
Grinnell, Isabel Hoopes 1899(?)-1988
Obituary ... 124
Grinsell, Leslie Valentine 1907- ... CANR-3
Earlier sketch in CA 9-10R
Grinspoon, Lester 1928- ... 81-84
Grinstead, David 1939- ... 105
Grinstein, Alexander 1918- ... CANR-5
Earlier sketch in CA 15-16R
Gripari, Pierre 1925- ... 29-32R
Gripe, Maria (Kristina) 1923- ... CANR-17
Earlier sketch in CA 29-32R
See also SATA 2
See also CLR 5
Grise, Jeannette
See Thomas, Jeannette Grise
Grisewood, Harman (Joseph Gerard)
1906- ... CAP-2
Earlier sketch in CA 29-32
Grisez, Germain G. 1929- ... CANR-21
Earlier sketches in CA 15-16R, CANR-6
Grisham, Noel 1916- ... CANR-10
Earlier sketch in CA 25-28R
Grispino, Joseph Aloysius 1922- ... 17-18R
Grissim, John 1941- ... 113
Griswold, Charles L., Jr. 1951- ... 123
Griswold, Erwin N(athaniel) 1904- ... CAP-1
Earlier sketch in CA 15-16
Griswold, Lawrence T. 1904(?)-1984
Obituary ... 113
Griswold, Rufus Wilmot 1815-1857 ... DLB-3, 59
Griswold, Wesley S(outhmayd) 1909- ... 3R
Griswold del Castillo, Richard 1942- ... 101
Gritsch, Eric W. 1931- ... CANR-10
Earlier sketch in CA 23-24R
Grivas, Theodore 1922- ... 9-10R
Grizzard, Lewis 1946- Brief entry ... 123
Grob, Alan 1932- Brief entry ... 113
Grob, Gerald N. 1931- ... CANR-20
Earlier sketches in CA 1R, CANR-5
Grobman, Alex 1946- ... 116
Groch, Judith (Goldstein) 1929- ... 9-10R
See also SATA 25
Grode, Redway
See Gorey, Edward (St. John)
Grodnick, Susan 1951- ... 122
Groemping, Franz A(lbert) 1909(?)-1987
Obituary ... 123
Groenbjerg, Kirsten A(ndersen) 1946- .. CANR-15
Earlier sketch in CA 85-88
Groene, Bertram Hawthorne 1923- ... 45-48
Groene, Janet 1936- ... 37-40R
Groenhoff, Edwin L. 1924- ... 57-60
Groennings, Sven O. 1934- ... 45-48
Groenoset, Dagfinn 1920- ... 93-96
Groeschel, Benedict J(oseph) 1933- ... 115
Grof, Stanislav 1931- ... 73-76
Groff, Patrick J(ohn) 1924- ... 41-44R
Groff, Warren F(rederick) 1924- ... 53-56
Grogan, Emmett 1942-1978 ... 41-44R
Groh, Ed(win Charles) 1910- ... 49-52
Groh, George W. 1922-1984 ... 85-88
Obituary ... 114
Grohman, Joann Sills 1928- ... 107
Grohskopf, Bernice ... CANR-3
Earlier sketch in CA 5-6R
See also SATA 7
Groia, Phil(ip) 1941- ... 53-56
Grol, Lini R(icharda) 1913- ... CANR-25
Earlier sketches in CA 61-64, CANR-8
See also SATA 9
Grollman, Earl A. 1925- ... 23-24R
See also SATA 22
Grollman, Sharon Hya 1954- ... CANR-15
Earlier sketch in CA 81-84
Grollmes, Eugene E. 1931- ... 29-32R
Gromacki, Robert Glenn 1933- ... CANR-19
Earlier sketches in CA 53-56, CANR-4
Gromada, Thaddeus V(ladimir) 1929- ... 45-48
Groman, George L. 1928- ... 23-24R
Grombach, John V(alentin) 1901- ... 103
Gronbeck, Bruce E(lliott) 1941-
Brief entry ... 118
Gronbjerg, Kirsten A(ndersen)
See Groenbjerg, Kirsten A(ndersen)
Grondona, L(eo) St. Clare 1890-1982 ... 103
Obituary ... 108
Groneman, Chris Harold 1906- ... CANR-1
Earlier sketch in CA 4R
Gronert, Bernard G(eorge) 1920-1985
Obituary ... 116
Gronewold, Sue Ellen
See Gronewold, Susan Ellen
Gronewold, Susan Ellen 1947- ... 115
Groninger, William C. 1928(?)-1983
Obituary ... 111
Gronowicz, Antoni 1913-1985 ... 25-28R
Obituary ... 117
Groocock, J(ohn) M(ichael) 1929- ... 57-60
Groom, Arthur William 1898-1964 ... CANR-1
Earlier sketch in CA 4R
See also SATA 10
Groom, Bernard 1892- ... CAP-2
Earlier sketch in CA 21-22
Groom, Nigel 1924- ... 117
Groom, Winston 1943- ... 85-88
Groome, Thomas H(enry) 1945- ... 110
Gropius, Walter 1883-1969 Obituary ... 25-28R
Gropman, Donald S(heldon) 1936- ... 101
Gropp, Louis (Oliver) 1935- ... 120
Gropper, William 1897-1977 ... 102
Obituary ... 89-92
Grosbard, Ulu 1929- ... 25-28R
Grose, B(url) Donald 1943- ... CANR-22
Earlier sketch in CA 45-48
Grose, Christopher (Waldo) 1939-
Brief entry ... 114
Grose, Peter (Bolton) 1934- Brief entry ... 119
Groseclose, Elgin E. 1899-1983 ... CAP-2
Obituary ... 109
Earlier sketch in CA 21-22
Groseclose, Kel(vin) 1940- ... 113
Grosman, Brian A(llen) 1935- ... 73-76
Grosman, Ladislav 1921- ... 102
Grosman, Tatyana 1904-1982 Obituary ... 107
Grosofsky, Leslie
See Gross, Leslie
Gross, Alan 1947- ... CANR-24
Earlier sketch in CA 89-92
See also SATA 43
Gross, Albert C. 1947- ... 125
Gross, Anthony 1905-1984 Obituary ... 114
Gross, Beatrice 1935- ... 77-80
Gross, Ben Samuel 1891-1979 ... 97-100
Obituary ... 89-92
Gross, Bertram M(yron) 1912- ... CANR-9
Earlier sketch in CA 15-16R
Gross, Beverly 1938- ... 29-32R
Gross, Carl H. 1911- ... 15-16R
Gross, Daniel R(ussell) 1942- ... 53-56
Gross, David C(harles) 1923- ... 102
Gross, Ernest A(rnold) 1906- ... 7-8R
Gross, Feliks 1906- ... CANR-12
Earlier sketch in CA 29-32R
Gross, Franz B(runo) 1919- ... 29-32R
Gross, Gerald 1932- ... 11-12R
Gross, Hanns 1928- ... 41-44R
Gross, Harvey S(eymour) 1922- ... CANR-8
Earlier sketch in CA 15-16R
Gross, Helen Shimota 1931- ... 11-12R
Gross, Irma H(annah) 1892- ... CAP-1
Earlier sketch in CA 15-16
Gross, James A. 1933- ... 57-60
Gross, Joel 1951- ... CANR-14
Earlier sketch in CA 29-32R
Gross, Johannes Heinrich 1916- ... 29-32R
Gross, John 1935- ... 29-32R
Gross, John J. 1912-1970 ... CAP-2
Earlier sketch in CA 25-28
Gross, John Owen 1894-1971 ... CAP-2
Earlier sketch in CA 17-18
Gross, Kenneth 1954- ... 118
Gross, Kenneth G. 1939- ... 25-28R
Gross, Leonard 1928- ... 118
Brief entry ... 112
Gross, Leslie 1927- ... 7-8R
Gross, Llewellyn (Zwicker) 1914- ... 25-28R
Gross, Martin (Arnold) 1934- ... CANR-11
Earlier sketch in CA 15-16R
Gross, Martin L(ouis) 1925- ... CANR-7
Earlier sketch in CA 9-10R
Gross, Mary Anne 1943- ... 49-52
Gross, Michael 1891(?)-1979 Obituary ... 97-100
Gross, Michael (Robert) 1952- ... CANR-20
Earlier sketch in CA 93-96
Gross, Milt 1895-1953 ... DLB-11
Gross, Milton ... AITN-1
Gross, Milton 1912(?)-1973 Obituary ... 41-44R
Gross, Neal 1920-1981 Obituary ... 108
Gross, Phyllis P(ennebaker) 1915- ... 93-96
Gross, Richard Edmund 1920- ... CANR-1
Earlier sketch in CA 2R
Gross, Ronald 1935- ... CANR-5
Earlier sketch in CA 7-8R
Gross, Ruth Belov 1929- ... SATA-33
Gross, S(amuel Harry) 1933- ... 45-48
Gross, Sarah Chokla 1906-1976 ... 61-64
Obituary ... 65-68
See also SATA 9, 26
Gross, Seymour L. 1926- ... CANR-3
Earlier sketch in CA 1R
Gross, Sheldon H(arvey) 1921- ... 81-84
Gross, Shelley 1938- ... 21-22R
Gross, Shelly
See Gross, Sheldon H(arvey)
Gross, Stuart D. 1914- ... 57-60
Gross, Suzanne 1933- ... 19-20R
Gross, Terence 1947- ... 101
Gross, Theodore L(awrence) 1930- ... CANR-14
Earlier sketch in CA 41-44R
Gross, Walter 1923- ... 21-22R
Gross, William Joseph 1894- ... CAP-1
Earlier sketch in CA 11-12
Grossack, Irvin Millman 1927- ... 97-100
Grossack, Martin Myer 1928- ... CANR-6
Earlier sketch in CA 11-12R
Grossbach, Robert 1941- ... CANR-13
Earlier sketch in CA 33-36R
Grossbart, Ted A. 1946- ... 126
Grossberger, Lewis 1940(?)- Brief entry ... 121
Grossen, Neal E. 1943- ... 93-96
Grosser, Alfred 1925- ... CANR-20
Earlier sketches in CA 45-48, CANR-2
Grosser, Arthur E(dward) 1934- ... 116
Grosser, Morton 1931- ... CANR-17
Earlier sketch in CA 97-100
Grosshans, Henry 1921- ... 29-32R
Grossholtz, Jean 1929- ... 15-16R
Grossinger, Richard (Selig) 1944- ... CANR-19
Earlier sketch in CA 103
Grossinger, Tania 1937- ... CANR-4
Earlier sketch in CA 53-56
Grosskurth, Phyllis 1924- ... CANR-9
Earlier sketch in CA 15-16R
Grossman, Alfred 1927- ... 7-8R
Grossman, Allen (R.) 1932- ... CANR-16
Earlier sketches in CA 4R, CANR-1
Grossman, Edith Marian 1936- ... 108
Grossman, Ellie ... 110
Grossman, Frances Kaplan 1939- ... 57-60
Grossman, Gary H(oward) 1948- ... 69-72
Grossman, Herbert 1934- ... 17-18R
Grossman, Jean Schick 1894-1972
Obituary ... 37-40R
Grossman, Joan (Adess) 1940- ... 120
Grossman, Joan Delaney 1928- ... 111
Grossman, Julian 1931- ... 53-56
Grossman, Kurt R. 1897-1972 Obituary ... 33-36R
Grossman, Lawrence 1945- ... 65-68
Grossman, Lee 1931- ... 69-72
Grossman, Louis Irwin 1901-1988
Obituary ... 125
Grossman, Manuel Lester 1939-
Brief entry ... 106
Grossman, Martin (Allen) 1943- ... CANR-13
Earlier sketch in CA 77-80
Grossman, Martin A. 1951- ... 102
Grossman, Mary Louise 1930- ... 77-80
Grossman, Morton Charles 1919- ... CANR-2
Earlier sketch in CA 4R
Grossman, Nancy 1940- ... SATA-29
Grossman, Richard L(ee) 1921- ... 97-100
Grossman, Robert 1940- ... SATA-11
Grossman, Ronald P(hilip) 1934- ... 21-22R
Grossman, Samuel 1897- ... 53-56
Grossman, Sebastian P. 1934- ... 23-24R
Grossman, Shelly 1928(?)-1975 Obituary .. 57-60
Grossman, Vasily (Semenovich)
1905-1964 Brief entry ... 124
See also CLC 41
Grossman, William L(eonard) 1906-1980 . CAP-2
Obituary ... 97-100
Earlier sketch in CA 23-24
Grossmann, Reinhardt S. 1931- ... CANR-20
Earlier sketch in CA 33-36R
Grossu, Sergiu 1920- ... CANR-8
Earlier sketch in CA 57-60
Grossvogel, David I. 1925- ... CANR-4
Earlier sketch in CA 1R
Grosswirth, Marvin 1931-1984 ... 33-36R
Obituary ... 112
Grosvenor, Donna K(erkam) 1938- ... 109
Grosvenor, Gilbert (Hovey) 1875-1966
Obituary ... 93-96
Grosvenor, Kali Diana 1960- ... 69-72
Grosvenor, Melville Bell 1901-1982 ... 69-72
Obituary ... 106
Grosvenor, Verta Mae 1938- ... 69-72
See also BW
Groten, Dallas 1951- ... 115
Groth, Alexander J(acob) 1932- ... CANR-14
Earlier sketch in CA 41-44R
Groth, Jeanette L(ue) 1947- ... 111
Groth, John 1908- ... 101
See also SATA 21
Groth, John (August) 1908-1988 ... 101
Obituary ... 125
See also SATA 21
Grotjahn, Martin 1904- ... CANR-15
Earlier sketch in CA 41-44R
Grotowski, Jerzy 1933- Brief entry ... 105
Groulx, Lionel 1878-1967 ... DLB-68
Grounds, Roger (Ransford Paterson)
1938- ... 97-100
Grounds, Vernon C(arl) 1914- ... 122
Groundwater, William 1906(?)-1982
Obituary ... 106
Groupe, Darryl R.
See Bunch, David R(oosevelt)
Groussard, Serge 1921- ... 108
Grout, Donald Jay 1902-1987 ... 102
Obituary ... 121
Grout, Jack 1910- ... 69-72
Grout, Ruth E(llen) 1901- ... CAP-2
Earlier sketch in CA 17-18
Grove, Fred(erick) 1913- ... CANR-17
Earlier sketches in CA 3R, CANR-2
Grove, Frederick Philip
See Greve, Felix Paul (Berthold Friedrich)
See also TCLC 4
Grove, Jack William 1920- ... 7-8R
Grove, Lee E(dmonds) ?-1971 Obituary ... 104
Grove, Pearce S(eymour) 1930- ... 73-76
Grove, Will O.
See Brister, Richard
Grovelands, Sarah
See Schneider, Myra
Grover, David H(ubert) 1925- ... 15-16R
Grover, David S(teele) 1939- ... 89-92
Grover, John W(agner) 1927- ... 77-80
Grover, Linda 1934- ... 29-32R
Grover, Philip 1929- ... 104
Groves, Colin Peter 1942- ... 61-64
Groves, Don(ald) George ... 106
Groves, Francis Richard 1889- ... CAP-1
Earlier sketch in CA 13-14
Groves, Georgina
See Symons, (Dorothy) Geraldine
Groves, H(arry) E(dward) 1921- ... 5-6R
Groves, Harold M(artin) 1897- ... 5-6R
Groves, Naomi Jackson 1910- ... 117
Groves, Paul 1930- ... CANR-17
Earlier sketch in CA 93-96
Groves, Reg(inald) 1908- ... 13-14R
Groves, Ruth Clouse 1902- ... CAP-2
Earlier sketch in CA 17-18
Grow, Lawrence 1939- ... CANR-25
Earlier sketches in CA 73-76, CANR-10
Grozny, I. L.
See Berger, Ivan (Bennett)
Grub, Phillip D. 1932- ... CANR-14
Earlier sketch in CA 25-28R
Grubar, Francis S(tanley) 1924- ... 33-36R
Grubb
See Crumb, R(obert)
Grubb, Davis Alexander 1919-1980 ... CANR-4
Obituary ... 101
Earlier sketch in CA 2R
See also DLB 6
Grubb, Frederick (Crichton-Stuart) 1930- ... 101
Grubb, Kenneth George 1900-1980 ... CAP-1
Obituary ... 97-100
Earlier sketch in CA 9-10
Grubb, Norman (Percy) 1895- ... CANR-13
Earlier sketches in CA 15-16, CAP-1
Grubb, W. Norton 1948- ... 110
Grubbs, David H(arold) 1929- ... 117
Grubbs, Donald H. 1936- ... 81-84
Grubbs, Frank Leslie, Jr. 1931- ... 29-32R
Grubbs, Robert L(owell) 1919- ... CANR-2
Earlier sketch in CA 2R
Grube, Georges M(aximilien) A(ntoine)
1899- ... CAP-1
Earlier sketch in CA 13-14
Grubel, Herbert G(unter) 1934- ... CANR-5
Earlier sketch in CA 9-10R
Gruber, Frank 1904-1969 ... CAP-1
Obituary ... 25-28R
Earlier sketch in CA 13-14
Gruber, Frederick C(harles) 1903- ... 49-52
Gruber, Gary R. 1940- ... CANR-24
Earlier sketches in CA 53-56, CANR-9
Gruber, Helmut 1928- ... 103
Gruber, Howard E(rnest) 1922- ... 119
Brief entry ... 113
Gruber, Ira D(empsey) 1934- Brief entry ... 110
Gruber, Jacob W(illiam) 1921- ... 1R
Gruber, Joseph John, Jr. 1930- ... CANR-6
Earlier sketch in CA 7-8R
Gruber, Katherine 1952- ... 123
Gruber, Martin Jay 1937- ... CANR-8
Earlier sketch in CA 53-56
Gruber, Ruth ... CANR-12
Earlier sketch in CA 25-28R
Gruber, Terry (deRoy) 1953- ... 97-100
Gruberg, Martin 1935- ... 33-36R
Grubian, Motel 1909(?)-1972 Obituary ... 104
Grudin, Louis 1898- ... 1R
Gruelle, John (Barton) 1880-1938
Brief entry ... 115
See also SATA 32, 35
Gruelle, Johnny
See Gruelle, John (Barton)
See also DLB 22
Gruelle, Worth ... AITN-2
Gruen, Erich S(tephen) 1935- Brief entry ... 111
Gruen, John 1926- ... CANR-8
Earlier sketch in CA 17-18R
Gruen, Victor (David) 1903-1980 ... CANR-10
Obituary ... 97-100
Earlier sketch in CA 15-16R
Gruen, Yetta Fisher ... 125
Gruenbaum, Adolf 1923- ... CANR-20
Earlier sketches in CA 9-10R, CANR-5
Gruenbaum, Ludwig
See Gaathon, A(ryeh) L(udwig)
Gruenberg, Benj(amin) C(harles)
1875-1965 ... CAP-1
Earlier sketch in CA 13-14
Gruenberg, Sidonie Matsner 1881-1974 .. CAP-1
Obituary ... 49-52
Earlier sketch in CA 15-16
See also SATA 2, 27
Gruenberger, Fred J(oseph) 1918- ... 118

Grueneberg, Hans 1907-1982 Obituary 108
Gruenhagen, Robert W. 1932- 29-32R
Gruening, Ernest (Henry) 1887-1974 49-52
Gruenstein, Peter 1947- 77-80
Gruenther, Alfred M(aximilian) 1899-1983
Obituary 109
Gruffydd, Peter 1935- 104
Gruhn, Carrie Myers 1907- CAP-1
Earlier sketch in CA 11-12
Gruits, Patricia Beall 1923- 105
Gruliow, Leo 1913- 5-6R
Grumbach, Doris (Isaac) 1918- CANR-9
Earlier sketch in CA 5-6R
See also CAAS 2
See also CLC 13, 22
Grumbling Gourmet, The
See Chapman, Frank M(onroe)
Grumelli, Antonio 1928- 37-40R
Grumet, Robert Steven 1949- 102
Grumich, Charles A. 1905(?)-1981
Obituary 104
Grumley, Michael 1941-1988 ..... 29-32R
Obituary 125
Grumme, Marguerite (Evelyn) 5-6R
Grummer, Arnold E(dward) 1923- 106
See also SATA 49
Grun, Bernard 1901-1972 Obituary 37-40R
Grunbaum, Adolf
See Gruenbaum, Adolf
Grund, Josef Carl 1920- 73-76
Grundberg, Andy
See Grundberg, John Andrew
Grundberg, John Andrew 1947- 103
Grundlehner, Philip 1945- 115
Grundstein, Nathan D(avid) 1913- CANR-15
Earlier sketch in CA 37-40R
Grundt, Leonard 1936- 57-60
Grundy, J(ohn) B(rownsdon) C(lowes)
1902-1987 Obituary 123
Grundy, J(ohn) Owen 1911-1985 Obituary 114
Grundy, Joan 1920- 109
Grundy, Kenneth W(illiam) 1936- CANR-12
Earlier sketch in CA 73-76
Grundy, Lester H. 1914(?)-1985 Obituary 116
Gruneau, Richard S(teven) 1948- 110
Gruneberg, Hans
See Grueneberg, Hans
Grunfeld, Frederic V(olker) 1929-1987 ..... CANR-18
Obituary 124
Earlier sketch in CA 73-76
Grunge
See Crumb, R(obert)
Grunlan, Stephen Arthur 1942- CANR-18
Earlier sketch in CA 101
Grunwald, Constantine de
See de Grunwald, Constantine
Grunwald, Henry Anatole 1922- 107
Grunwald, Joseph 1920- 115
Grunwald, Lisa 1959- 120
See also CLC 44
Grunwald, Stefan 1933- 29-32R
Grupp, Stanley E(ugene) 1927- 53-56
Grusa, Jiri 1938- 117
Grusd, Edward Elihu 1904- CAP-2
Earlier sketch in CA 19-20
Gruskin, Alan D(aniel) 1904-1970 ..... CAP-1
Obituary 29-32R
Earlier sketch in CA 11-12
Gruson, Edward S. 1929- 45-48
Gruss, Edmond C(harles) 1933- 53-56
Grutz, Mariellen Procopio 1946- 93-96
Grutzmacher, Harold M(artin), Jr.
1930- 29-32R
Gruver, Rebecca
See Goodman, Rebecca Gruver
Gruver, William R. II 1929- 45-48
Grylls, David (Stanway) 1947- 85-88
Grylls, Rosalie Glynn 65-68
Grynberg, Henryk 1936- 29-32R
Gryst, Edward (George) 1911- 2R
Grzimek, Bernhard (Klemens Maria H. P.)
1909-1987 Obituary 121
Guadaloupe, Brother Jose de
See Mojica, Jose
Guado, Sergio
See Gerosa, Guido
Guandagnolo, Joseph F(rancis) 1912- 5-6R
Guandolo, John 1919- 21-22R
Guaragna, Salvatore 1893-1981 Obituary 105
Guard, Dave
See Guard, David
Guard, David 1934- 77-80
Guardia, Ernesto de la, Jr.
See de la Guardia, Ernesto, Jr.
Guardo, Carol Joan 1939- 103
Guare, John 1938- CANR-21
Earlier sketch in CA 73-76
See also DLB 7
See also CLC 8, 14, 29
Guarendi, Raymond N(icholas) 1952- 120
Guareschi, Giovanni 1908-1968 105
Obituary 25-28R
Guarino, M(artin) Vincent 1939- 41-44R
Guback, Thomas H(enry) 1937- 25-28R
Gubar, Susan (David) 1944- 108
Gubern, Santiago (Garriga-Nogues)
1933- CANR-2
Earlier sketch in CA 45-48
Gubert, Betty Kaplan 1934- 112
Gubrium, Jaber F(andy) 1943- CANR-4
Earlier sketch in CA 53-56
Gubser, Nicholas J. 1938- 19-20R
Guccione, Robert, Jr. AITN-2
Guches, Richard (Clement) 1938- 115
Guck, Dorothy 1913- 49-52
See also SATA 27
Gudde, Erwin G(ustav) 1889-1969 ..... CANR-4
Earlier sketch in CA 5-6R
Gudenian, Haig (Krikor) 1918-1985(?)
Obituary 115
Guder, Eileen (Likens) 1919- 17-18R
Gudiol, Jose
See Gudiol i Ricart, Josep
Gudiol i Ricart, Josep 1904- 81-84
Gudiol Ricart, Jose M.
See Gudiol i Ricart, Josep
Gudiol Ricart, Josep
See Gudiol i Ricart, Josep
Gudjonsson, Halldor Kiljan 1902- 103
Gudschinsky, Sarah C(aroline)
1919-1975 ..... CAP-2
Earlier sketch in CA 33-36
Guede, Norina (Maria Esterina) Lami
1913- 9-10R
Guehenne, Jean
See Guehenno, Jean Marcel Jules Marie
Guehenno, Jean Marcel Jules Marie
1890-1978 Obituary 104
Guelich, Robert A(llison) 1939- CANR-17
Earlier sketches in CA 45-48, CANR-2
Guemple, Lee 1930- 41-44R
Guenette, Robert (Homer) 1935- 25-28R
Guenter, Erich
See Eich, Guenter
Guenther, Charles (John) 1920- 29-32R
Guenther, Herbert V. 1917- 73-76
Guenther, John (Lewis) CANR-9
Earlier sketch in CA 5-6R
Guenther, (Robert) Wallace 1929- 65-68
Guerard, Albert Joseph 1914- CANR-2
Earlier sketch in CA 3R
See also CAAS 2
Guerin, Wilfred L(ouis) 1929- 17-18R
Guerlac, Henry (Edward) 1910-1985
Obituary 116
Guerlac, Rita 1916- 116
Guerney, Bernard G(uilbert), Jr. 1930- 93-96
Guerney, Bernard Guilbert 1894-1979
Obituary 85-88
Guernsey, Bruce H(ubbard) 1944- 108
Guernsey, James Lee 1923- 37-40R
Guernsey, Otis L(ove), Jr. 1918- 89-92
Guerny, Gene
See Gurney, Gene
Guerra, Emilio Louis 1909-1980
Obituary 97-100
Guerrant, Edward Owings 1911- 23-24R
Guerra y Sanchez, Ramiro 1880-1970
Obituary 104
Guerrero, Rogelio Diaz
See Diaz-Guerrero, Rogelio
Guerrette, Richard H(ector) 1930- 49-52
Guerrier, Dennis 1923- 29-32R
Guers-Villate, Yvonne 1924- 41-44R
Guess, Edward Preston 1925- 73-76
Guest, A(nthony) G(ordon) 1930- CANR-1
Earlier sketch in CA 2R
Guest, Barbara 1920- CANR-11
Earlier sketch in CA 25-28R
See also DLB 5
See also CLC 34
Guest, Edgar A(lbert) 1881-1959
Brief entry 112
Guest, Harry
See Guest, Henry Bayly
Guest, Henry Bayly 1932- CANR-9
Earlier sketch in CA 65-68
Guest, Ivor (Forbes) 1920- CANR-20
Earlier sketches in CA 7-8R, CANR-2
Guest, Judith (Ann) 1936- CANR-15
Earlier sketch in CA 77-80
See also CLC 8, 30
Guett, Dieter 1924- 65-68
Gueulette, David G(eorge) 1941- 111
Guevara, Che
See Guevara (Serna), Ernesto
Guevara (Serna), Ernesto 1928-1967
Obituary 111
Guevremont, Germaine 1893-1968 ..... DLB-68
Guffey, George R(obert) 1932- Brief entry 118
Guffin, Gilbert L. 1906- 17-18R
Gugas, Chris 1921- 97-100
Gugelyk, M(yron) Ted 1938- 120
Guggenheim, Edward Armand 1901-1970
Obituary 104
Guggenheim, Hans Georg 1927- 125
Guggenheim, Harry Frank 1890-1971
Obituary 89-92
Guggenheim, Marguerite 1898-1979
Obituary 105
Guggenheim, Peggy
See Guggenheim, Marguerite
Guggenheimer, Richard 1906-1977 ..... 41-44R
Obituary 69-72
Guggenmos, Josef 1922- 81-84
Guggisberg, C(harles) A(lbert) W(alter)
1913- 81-84
Gugliotta, Bobette 1918- CANR-14
Earlier sketch in CA 41-44R
See also SATA 7
Guhin, Michael A(lan) 1940- 41-44R
Guice, John D(avid) W(ynne) 1931- 41-44R
Guicharnaud, June 1922- 93-96
Guido, (Cecily) Margaret 1912- 65-68
Guild, Lurelle Van Arsdale 1898- CAP-2
Earlier sketch in CA 29-32
Guild, Nicholas M. 1944- 93-96
See also CLC 33
Guild, Thelma S(croggs) 1911- 118
Guild, Vera Palmer 1906- Brief entry 106
Guilds, John C(aldwell, Jr.) 1924- 77-80
Guiles, Fred Lawrence 1920- CANR-12
Earlier sketch in CA 25-28R
Guilford, J(oy) Paul 1897- CANR-4
Earlier sketch in CA 1R
Guilford, Joan S. 1928- 29-32R
Guillaume, Alfred 1888-19(?) CAP-1
Earlier sketch in CA 15-16
Guillaume, Jeanette G. Flierl 1899- 2R
See also SATA 8
Guille, Frances V(ernor) 1908-1975 45-48
Obituary 61-64
Guillemin, Henri 1903- 81-84
Guillemin, Jacques
See Sartre, Jean-Paul
Guillen, Jorge 1893-1984 89-92
Obituary 112
See also CLC 11
Guillen (y Batista), Nicolas (Cristobal)
1902- 125
Brief entry 116
See also BW
See also CLC 48
Guillet, Edwin C(larence) 1898-1975 107
Guillet, Jacques 1910- 102
Guillevic, (Eugene) 1907- 93-96
See also CLC 33
Guillois
See Desnos, Robert
Guillot, Rene 1900-1969 49-52
See also SATA 7
Guilloux, Louis 1899-1980 Obituary 104
See also DLB 72
Guilmartin, John Francis, Jr. 1940- 53-56
Guimary, Donald L(ee) 1932- 73-76
Guimond, James K. 1936- 25-28R
Guin, Wyman (Woods) 1915- 102
Guinagh, Kevin (Joseph) 1897- 17-18R
Guinan, Michael D(amon) 1939- 117
Guinee, Kathleen K. 1902(?)-1982
Obituary 109
Guiney, Louise Imogen 1861-1920 ..... DLB-54
Guiney, Mortimer 1930- 53-56
Guinn, Paul (Spencer, Jr.) 1928- 15-16R
Guinness, Bryan (Walter) 1905- 102
Guinness, (Ian) Os(wald) 1941- 65-68
Guinther, John 1927- CANR-11
Earlier sketch in CA 69-72
Guion, Robert M(organ) 1924- CANR-7
Earlier sketch in CA 17-18R
Guirdham, Arthur 1905- 103
Guisewite, Cathy (Lee) 1950- 113
Brief entry 111
Guisinger, Stephen Edward 1941- 103
Guitar, Mary Anne 1922- Brief entry 113
Guiterman, Arthur 1871-1943 Brief entry 120
See also DLB 11
Guither, Harold D. 1927- 29-32R
Gula, Richard M(ichael) 1947- 109
Gula, Robert J(ohn) 1941- 97-100
Gulick, Bill
See Gulick, Grover C.
Gulick, Edward Vose 1915- 113
Gulick, Grover C. 1916- CANR-17
Earlier sketch in CA 33-36R
Gulick, Robert Lee, Jr. 1912-1987
Obituary 122
Gulik, Robert H(ans) van
See van Gulik, Robert H(ans)
Gulker, Virgil G. 1947- 65-68
Gullace, Gino 1925- CANR-17
Earlier sketch in CA 69-72
Gullans, Charles (Bennett) 1929- CANR-18
Earlier sketches in CA 4R, CANR-4
Gullason, Thomas A(rthur) 1924- CANR-8
Earlier sketch in CA 23-24R
Gulley, Halbert E(dison) 1919- CANR-6
Earlier sketch in CA 5-6R
Gulley, Norman 1920- 33-36R
Gullick, Charles Francis William Rowley
1907- 7-8R
Gullick, Etta 1916- 89-92
Gullick, John M(ichael) 1916- 15-16R
Gulliford, Andrew 1953- 120
Gulliford, Ronald 1920- 13-14R
Gulliver, Harold S. 1935- 97-100
Gulliver, Lemuel
See Hastings, Macdonald
Gulston, Charles 1913-1981 122
Gummere, Richard M(ott), Jr. 1912- 45-48
Gump, Richard (Benjamin) 1906- CAP-1
Earlier sketch in CA 9-10
Gump, Sally
See Stanford, Sally
Gumpertz, Robert 1925- 69-72
Gunders, Henry 1924- 29-32R
Gundersheimer, Karen SATA-44
Gundersheimer, Werner L. 1937- 53-56
Gunderson, Doris V. 29-32R
Gunderson, Frank L(ester) 1902-1983
Obituary 110
Gunderson, Keith (Robert) 1935- 33-36R
Gunderson, Robert Gray 1915- 1R
Gundrey, Elizabeth 1924- CANR-6
Earlier sketch in CA 13-14R
See also SATA 23
Gundry, Robert H(orton) 1932- 29-32R
Gundry, Stanley Norman 1937- 114
Gundy, Elizabeth 112
Gundy, H(enry) Pearson) 1905- 45-48
Guney, Yilmaz 1937(?)-1984 Obituary 113
Gunji, Masakatsu 1913- 29-32R
Gunlicks, Arthur B. 1936- 126
Gunn, Bill
See Gunn, William Harrison
See also DLB 38
See also CLC 5
Gunn, Christopher Eaton 1944- 117
Gunn, Diana Maureen 1926- CANR-18
Earlier sketch in CA 97-100
Gunn, Drewey Wayne 1939- 57-60
Gunn, Elizabeth
See Gunn, Diana Maureen
Gunn, Giles B(uckingham) 1938- 57-60
Gunn, Helen Montgomery 1900(?)-1987
Obituary 122
Gunn, J(ohn) A(lexander) W(ilson)
1937- CANR-20
Earlier sketch in CA 25-28R
Gunn, James E(dwin) 1923- CANR-22
Earlier sketches in CA 11-12R, CANR-5
See also CAAS 2
See also SATA 35
See also DLB 8
Gunn, John (Charles) 1937- 49-52
Gunn, Mrs. Aneas 1870-1961 Obituary 115
Gunn, Neil M(iller) 1891-1973 Obituary 37-40R
See also DLB 15
Gunn, Peter (Nicholson) 1914- CANR-18
Earlier sketches in CA 25-28R, CANR-10
Gunn, Sister Agnes Marie 1928- 17-18R
Gunn, Thom(son William) 1929- CANR-9
Earlier sketch in CA 17-18R
See also DLB 27
See also CLC 3, 6, 18, 32
Gunn, William Harrison 1934- CANR-25
Earlier sketches in CA 13-14R, CANR-12
See also BW
See also AITN 1
Gunnars, Kristjana 1948- 113
See also DLB 60
Gunnarsson, Gunnar 1889-1975 Obituary 61-64
Gunnell, Bryn 1933- 103
Gunnell, John G. 1933- 25-28R
Gunneweg, Antonius H. J. 1922- CANR-16
Earlier sketch in CA 89-92
Gunning, Monica Olwen 1930- 65-68
Gunning, Robert 1908-1980 ..... CAP-2
Obituary 97-100
Earlier sketch in CA 25-28
Gunsalus Gonzalez, Catherine 1934-
Brief entry 107
Gunston, Bill
See Gunston, William Tudor
Gunston, William Tudor 1927- CANR-19
Earlier sketches in CA 49-52, CANR-3
See also SATA 9
Gunstone, A(ntony) J. H. 1937(?)-1984
Obituary 112
Gunter, (J.) Bradley (Hunt) 1940- 29-32R
Gunter, Pete A(ddison) Y(ancey)
1936- CANR-15
Earlier sketch in CA 33-36R
Gunterman, Bertha Lisette 1886(?)-1975
Obituary 104
See also SATA 27
Gunther, A(lbert) E(verard) 1903- 29-32R
Gunther, Bernard 1929- CANR-2
Earlier sketch in CA 45-48
Gunther, Gerald 1927- CANR-13
Earlier sketch in CA 33-36R
Gunther, John 1901-1970 ..... 11-12R
Obituary 25-28R
See also SATA 2
Gunther, Max 1927- 15-16R
Gunther, Peter F. 1920- 11-12R
Gunther, Richard (Paul) 1946- 103
Gunton, Sharon R(ose) 1952- 102
Guntrip, Harry
See Guntrip, Henry James Samuel
Guntrip, Henry James Samuel
1901-1975 ..... CANR-5
Earlier sketch in CA 7-8R
Gunzburg, Nicholas de 1904-1981
Obituary 103
Guppy, Nicholas (Gareth Lechmere)
1925- CANR-6
Earlier sketch in CA 7-8R
Gupta, Brijen K(ishore) 1929- CANR-16
Earlier sketches in CA 45-48, CANR-1
Gupta, Marie (Jacqueline) 1946- 57-60
Gupta, Pranati Sen
See Sen Gupta, Pranati
Gupta, Ram Chandra 1927- CANR-13
Earlier sketch in CA 23-24R
Gupta, S(ushil) (Kumar) 1927- 57-60
Gupta, Shiv K(umar) 1930- 57-60
Gupta, Sulekh Chandra 1928- 15-16R
Guptara, Prabhu S(iddhartha) 1949- 81-84
Guptill, Nathanael M(ann) 1917- 45-48
Gura, Philip F(rancis) 1950- 111
Gurdus, Luba Krugman 1914- 120
Gurik, Robert 1932- DLB-60
Gurin, Joel 1953- 108
Gurko, Leo 1914- CANR-5
Earlier sketch in CA 5-6R
See also SATA 9
Gurko, Miriam 1910(?)-1988 ..... 4R
Obituary 126
See also SATA 9
Gurman, Alan S(tephen) 1945- CANR-5
Earlier sketch in CA 53-56
Gurnee, Jeanne 1926- 93-96
Gurnee, Russell H(ampton) 1922- 107
Gurney, A(lbert) R(amsdell), Jr. 1930- 77-80
See also CLC 32, 50
Gurney, Gene 1924- CANR-9
Earlier sketch in CA 7-8R
Gurney, George 1939- 119
Gurney, J. Eric CANR-2
Earlier sketch in CA 4R
Gurney, Nancy Jack 1915(?)-1973
Obituary 45-48
Gurney, Peter
See Gurney, A(lbert) R(amsdell), Jr.
Gurr, Andrew (John) 1936- 33-36R
Gurr, David 1936- Brief entry 125

Gurr, Ted Robert 1936- CANR-16
Earlier sketch in CA 41-44R
Gurrey, Percival 1890-1980 Obituary 97-100
Gurtov, Melvin 1941- Brief entry 112
Gurwitsch, Aron 1901-1973 CAP-1
Obituary 41-44R
Earlier sketch in CA 15-16
Gusfield, Joseph R. 1923- 53-56
Gusikoff, Lynne
See Hawes, Lynne Gusikoff Salop
Guss, Donald L(eroy) 1929- 17-18R
Guss, Leonard M. 1926- 21-22R
Gussman, Boris (William) 1914- 5-6R
Gussow, Alan 1931- Brief entry 111
Gussow, Joan Dye 1928- 29-32R
Gussow, Mel 1933- 107
Gustaf, King of Sweden 1882-1973
Obituary 45-48
Gustafson, Alrik 1903-1970 4R
Obituary 103
Gustafson, Anita 1942- 112
See also SATA 45
Gustafson, Donald F. 1934- 11-12R
Gustafson, James 1949- 125
Gustafson, James M(oody) 1925- 25-28R
Gustafson, Jim
See Gustafson, James
Gustafson, Paula Catherine 1941- 106
Gustafson, Ralph (Barker) 1909- CANR-8
Earlier sketch in CA 23-24R
See also CLC 36
Gustafson, Richard C(larence) 1933-1977
Obituary 111
Gustafson, Richard F(olke) 1934- 19-20R
Gustafson, Sarah R.
See Riedman, Sarah R(egal)
Gustafson, Scott 1956- SATA-34
Gustafson, W(illiam) Eric 1933- 57-60
Gustafsson, Lars 1936- 85-88
Gustaitis, Rasa 1934- 25-28R
Gustavson, Carl G(ustav) 1915- 19-20R
Gustin, Lawrence Robert 1937- 57-60
Gustkey, Earl 1940- 57-60
Gut, Gom
See Simenon, Georges (Jacques Christian)
Gutch, John 1905-1988 Obituary 124
Gutcheon, Beth R(ichardson) 1945- CANR-2
Earlier sketch in CA 49-52
Gutek, Gerald L(ee) 1935- CANR-17
Earlier sketch in CA 81-84
Gutenberg, Arthur W(illiam) 1920- 37-40R
Guterman, Norbert 1900-1984 Obituary 113
Guterman, Simeon L(eonard) 1907- 41-44R
Guterman, Stanley S(anford) 1934- 29-32R
Gutheim, Frederick 1908- CANR-9
Earlier sketch in CA 23-24R
Guthke, Karl S(iegfried) 1933- CANR-15
Earlier sketch in CA 41-44R
Guthman, Edwin 1919- 33-36R
Guthman, William H(arold) 1924- 57-60
Guthmann, Harry G. 1896- 3R
Guthrie, A(lfred) B(ertram), Jr. 1901- CANR-24
Earlier sketch in CA 57-60
See also DLB 6
See also CLC 23
Guthrie, Anne 1890-1979 5-6R
See also SATA 28
Guthrie, Arlo (Davy) 1947- 113
Guthrie, David
See Allen, H(ubert) R(aymond)
Guthrie, Donald 1916- CANR-23
Earlier sketches in CA 13-14R, CANR-7
Guthrie, Harvey Henry, Jr. 1924- 13-14R
Guthrie, Hugh
See Freeman, John Crosby
Guthrie, Hunter 1901-1974 65-68
Obituary 53-56
Guthrie, Isobel
See Grieve, C(hristopher) M(urray)
Guthrie, James Shields 1931- CANR-15
Earlier sketch in CA 33-36R
Guthrie, James W. 1936- 41-44R
Guthrie, John 1908- 106
Guthrie, John A(lexander) 1907- 1R
Guthrie, Judith Bretherton 1905(?)-1972
Obituary 37-40R
Guthrie, Marjorie (Greenblatt Mazia)
1917-1983 Obituary 117
Guthrie, Ramon 1896-1973 5-6R
Obituary 45-48
See also DLB 4
Guthrie, Robert V(al) 1930- 53-56
Guthrie, Russell Dale 1936- Brief entry 106
Guthrie, T.
See Guthrie, (William) Tyrone
Guthrie, Thomas Anstey 1856-1934
Brief entry 113
Guthrie, (William) Tyrone 1900-1971 123
Obituary 29-32R
Guthrie, William Keith Chambers
1906-1981 CANR-11
Obituary 103
Earlier sketch in CA 65-68
Guthrie, Woodrow Wilson 1912-1967 113
Obituary 93-96
Guthrie, Woody
See Guthrie, Woodrow Wilson
See also CLC 35
Gutierrez, Donald 1932- 109
Gutierrez-Vega, Zenaida 1924- CANR-19
Earlier sketch in CA 41-44R
Gutin, Bernard 1934- 112
Gutkin, Harry 1915- 101
Gutkind, Erwin A(nton) 1886-1968 CANR-8
Earlier sketch in CA 7-8R
Gutkind, Lee 1943- CANR-20
Earlier sketches in CA 53-56, CANR-5
Gutkind, Peter C(laus) W(olfgang) 1925- 116
Gutman, Bill SATA-43
Gutman, Herbert G(eorge) 1928-1985 65-68
Obituary 116
Gutman, Judith Mara 1928- 21-22R
Gutman, Kellie O. 1952- 124
Gutman, Naham 1899(?)-1981 Obituary 102
See also SATA 25
Gutman, Richard J(ay) S(tephen) 1949- 101
Gutman, Robert 1926- 45-48
Gutman, Robert W. 1925- 25-28R
Gutman, Walter
See Gutman, Walter Knowlton
Gutman, Walter Knowlton 1903-1986
Obituary 119
Gutmann, James 1897- CAP-2
Earlier sketch in CA 21-22
Gutmann, Joseph 1923- CANR-17
Earlier sketches in CA 49-52, CANR-1
Gutmann, Myron P. 1949- Brief entry 105
Gutnik, Martin J(erome) 1942- CANR-3
Earlier sketch in CA 49-52
Gutsche, Thelma 1915- 23-24R
Gutstein, Morris A(aron) 1905-1987
Obituary 122
Gutt, Dieter
See Guett, Dieter
Guttenberg, Barnett 89-92
Guttenberg, Virginia 1914- 81-84
Guttentag, Marcia 1932-1977 CANR-8
Earlier sketch in CA 57-60
Gutteridge, Anne C(hristine) 1943- 108
Gutteridge, Bernard 1916-1985 Obituary 117
Gutteridge, Don(ald George) 1937- CANR-9
Earlier sketch in CA 65-68
Gutteridge, Lindsay 1923- 49-52
Gutteridge, Richard (Joseph Cooke) 1911- 122
Gutteridge, William F(rank) 1919- 15-16R
Gutterson, Herbert (Lindsley, Jr.) 1915- 9-10R
Gutting, Gary (Michael) 1942- 103
Guttmacher, Alan F(rank) 1898-1974 CANR-6
Obituary 49-52
Earlier sketch in CA 4R
Guttmacher, Manfred S(chanfarber)
1898-1966 CAP-1
Earlier sketch in CA 11-12
Guttmann, Alexander 29-32R
Guttmann, Allen 1932- CANR-16
Earlier sketches in CA 4R, CANR-1
Guttridge, Leonard F(rancis) 1918- 85-88
Guttsman, Wilhelm Leo 1920- 11-12R
Gutwirth, Samuel William 1903-1983
Obituary 111
Gutzke, Manford G(eorge) 1896- 17-18R
Guy, Anne W(elsh) 5-6R
Guy, David 1948- 105
Guy, Harold A. 1904- 17-18R
Guy, Ray 1939- DLB-60
Guy, Rosa (Cuthbert) 1928- CANR-14
Earlier sketch in CA 17-18R
See also BW
See also SATA 14
See also DLB 33
See also CLC 26
See also CLR 13
Guyer, Paul 1948- CANR-24
Earlier sketch in CA 105
Guymer, (Wilhelmina) Mary 1909- SATA-50
Guyot, James F(ranklin) 1932- 53-56
Guyton, Arthur C(lifton) 1919- CANR-7
Earlier sketch in CA 19-20R
Guzie, Tad W(alter) 1934- CANR-5
Earlier sketch in CA 15-16R
Guzman, Ralph C. 1924-1985 Obituary 117
Guzzo, Sandra E(lizabeth) 1941- 120
Guzzwell, John 1930- 13-14R
Gwaltney, Francis Irby 1921- CANR-2
Earlier sketch in CA 4R
Gwaltney, John Langston 1928- 77-80
Gwendolyn
See Bennett, (Enoch) Arnold
Gwilliam, Kenneth M(ason) 1937- 17-18R
Gwin, Lucy 1943- 109
Gwinup, Thomas 1932- 73-76
Gwirtzman, Milton S. 1933- 29-32R
Gwyn, Julian 1937- 57-60
Gwyn, Richard J. 1934- CANR-17
Earlier sketch in CA 25-28R
Gwyn, W(illiam) B(rent) 1927- CANR-5
Earlier sketch in CA 15-16R
Gwynn, Denis (Rolleston) 1893- CAP-1
Earlier sketch in CA 13-14
Gwynn, Mary 1952- 111
Gwynn, Robin D(avid) 1942- 121
Gwynne, Erskine 1898-1948 Brief entry 107
See also DLB 4
Gwynne, Fred(erick Hubbard) 1926- 113
See also SATA 27, 41
Gwynne, Oscar A.
See Ellis, Edward S(ylvester)
Gwynne, Oswald A.
See Ellis, Edward S(ylvester)
Gwynne, Peter 1941- 89-92
Gwynne-Jones, Allan 1892-1982 Obituary 107
Gwynne-Thomas, E(ric) H(ubert) 1917- 120
Gyftopoulos, Elias Panayiotis 1927- 104
Gyldenvand, Lily M. 1917- CANR-6
Earlier sketch in CA 15-16R
Gyllenhammar, Pehr G(ustaf) 1935- CANR-13
Earlier sketch in CA 73-76
Gyoergyi, Albert (von Nagyrapolt) Szent
See Szent-Gyoergyi, Albert (von Nagyrapolt)
Gyorgy, Andrew 1917- 122
Gyorgyey, Clara 1936- 77-80
Gyorgyi, Albert (von Nagyrapolt) Szent
See Szent-Gyoergyi, Albert (von Nagyrapolt)
Gysbers, Norman C(harles) 1932- 61-64
Gysin, Brion 1916-1986 117
Obituary 120
Brief entry 113
See also DLB 16
Gzowski, Peter 1934- 106

H

H. D.
See Doolittle, Hilda
See also CLC 3, 8, 14, 31, 34
H. F. E.
See Everett-Green, Evelyn
H. M. S.
See Kirk-Greene, Anthony (Hamilton Millard)
H. M. W.
See Wang, Hui-Ming
Haaby, Lawrence O. 1915- 33-36R
Haac, Oscar A(lfred) 1918- 33-36R
Haack, Susan 1945- 61-64
Haaf, Beverly T(erhune) 1936- 97-100
Haaften, Julia Van
See Van Haaften, Julia
Haag, Jessie Helen 1917- CANR-5
Earlier sketch in CA 15-16R
Haaker, Ann M. 25-28R
Haakonssen, Knud 1947- 124
Haan, Aubrey Edwin 1908- 1R
Haar, Charles M(onroe) 1920- 33-36R
Haar, Francis 1908- 53-56
Haar, Franklin B. 1906- CAP-1
Earlier sketch in CA 11-12
Haar, Jaap ter
See ter Haar, Jaap
See also CLR 15
Haar, James 1929- 21-22R
Haarer, Alec Ernest 1894-1970 CANR-4
Earlier sketch in CA 7-8R
Haarhoff, Theodore Johannes 1892-1971 CAP-1
Earlier sketch in CA 13-14
Haas, Albert E. 1917- 23-24R
Haas, Ben(jamin) L(eopold) 1926-1977 CANR-8
Obituary 73-76
Earlier sketch in CA 9-10R
Haas, Carolyn Buhai 1926- CANR-9
Earlier sketch in CA 65-68
See also SATA 43
Haas, Charles A. 1947- 125
Haas, Charlie 1952- 73-76
Haas, Dorothy F. CANR-20
Earlier sketches in CA 7-8R, CANR-3
See also SATA 43, 46
See also SAAS 43
Haas, Ernst 1921-1986 Obituary 120
Haas, Ernst B(ernard) 1924- 81-84
Haas, Gerda (Schild) 1922- 110
Haas, Harold I(rwin) 1925- 29-32R
Haas, Irene 1929- 97-100
See also SATA 17
Haas, Irvin 1916- 41-44R
Haas, J(ohn) Eugene 1926- 41-44R
Haas, James E(dward) 1943- CANR-7
Earlier sketch in CA 61-64
See also SATA 40
Haas, Jessie 1959- 114
Haas, Kenneth B(rooks), Sr. 1898- CANR-6
Earlier sketch in CA 57-60
Haas, Kurt 53-56
Haas, LaVerne 1942- 49-52
Haas, Lynne 1939- 65-68
Haas, Marilyn L(oomis) 1931- 117
Haas, Mary Odin 1910- CAP-1
Earlier sketch in CA 13-14
Haas, Mary R(osamond) 1910- 11-12R
Haas, Merle S. 1896(?)-1985 Obituary 114
See also SATA 41
Haas, Michael 1938- 53-56
Haas, Raymond Michael 1935- 37-40R
Haas, Robert Bartlett 1916- Brief entry 108
Haas, Robert Lewis 1936- 101
Haase, Ann Marie Bernazza 1942- 33-36R
Haase, John 1923- CANR-14
Earlier sketch in CA 7-8R
Haavikko, Paavo Juhani 1931- 106
See also CLC 18, 34
Habbema, Koos
See Heijermans, Herman
Habe, Hans 1911-1977 CANR-2
Obituary 73-76
Earlier sketch in CA 45-48
Habel, Norman C. 1932- 17-18R
Habenstreit, Barbara 1937- 29-32R
See also SATA 5
Haber, Audrey 1940- CANR-13
Earlier sketch in CA 33-36R
Haber, Carole R. 1951- 124
Haber, Eitan 1940- 104
Haber, Heinz 1913- 73-76
Haber, Jack 1939-1984 69-72
Obituary 114
Haber, Joyce 1932- 65-68
Haber, Louis 1910- 29-32R
See also SATA 12
Haber, Ralph Norman 1932- 33-36R
Haber, Samuel 1928- 9-10R
Haber, Tom Burns 1900- CAP-2
Earlier sketch in CA 17-18
Haber, William 1899- CAP-2
Earlier sketch in CA 21-22
Haberer, Joseph 1929- 65-68
Haberler, Gottfried 1900- 103
Haberly, David T(ristram) 1942- 106
Haberly, Loyd 1896-1981 105
Obituary 103
Haberman, Daniel 1933- 110
Haberman, David A. 1928- 126
Haberman, Donald (Charles) 1933- 21-22R
Haberman, Martin 1932- 57-60
Haberman, Shelby J(oel) 1947- 103
Habermann, Helen M(argaret) 1927- 53-56
Habermas, Juergen 1929- 109
Habermas, Jurgen
See Habermas, Juergen
Haberstroh, Chadwick John 1927- 41-44R
Habgood, John Stapylton 1927- CANR-22
Earlier sketches in CA 15-16R, CANR-5
Habig, Marion A(lphonse) 1901-1984 CANR-20
Obituary 114
Earlier sketches in CA 7-8R, CANR-5
Hablutzel, Philip 1935- 37-40R
Habsburg-Lothringen, Geza Louis Eusebius Gebhard Ralphael Albert Maria von
See von Habsburg-Lothringen, Geza Louis Eusebius Gebhard Ralphael Albert Maria
Hach, Clarence Woodrow 1917- 13-14R
Hachey, Thomas E(ugene) 1938- 37-40R
Hachten, Harva 108
Hachten, William Andrews 1924- 107
Hacikyan, A(gop) J. 1931- 33-36R
Hack, Walter G. 1925- 29-32R
Hackady, Hal Brief entry 105
Hacker, Andrew 1929- CANR-1
Earlier sketch in CA 1R
Hacker, Carlotta 1931- 118
Hacker, Frederick J. 1914- Brief entry 104
Hacker, Jeffrey H. 1954- 125
Hacker, Leonard
See Hackett, Buddy
Hacker, Louis M(orton) 1899-1987 17-18R
Obituary 122
Hacker, Marilyn 1942- 77-80
See also CLC 5, 9, 23
Hacker, Mary Louise 1908- CAP-2
Earlier sketch in CA 17-18
Hacker, Rose (Goldbloom) 1906- 13-14R
Hacker, Shyrle 1910- 101
Hackes, Peter Sidney 1924- 102
Hackett, Albert 1900- DLB-26
Hackett, Blanche Ann 1924- 73-76
Hackett, Buddy 1924- Brief entry 108
Hackett, Cecil Arthur 1908- 13-14R
Hackett, Charles J(oseph) 1915- 73-76
Hackett, Donald F. 1918- 29-32R
Hackett, Francis 1883-1962 108
Obituary 89-92
Hackett, Herbert L(ewis) 1917-1964 2R
Hackett, Jan Michele 1952- 105
Hackett, John W. 1924- 17-18R
Hackett, John Winthrop 1910- 89-92
Hackett, Laura Lyman 1916- 17-18R
Hackett, Lee
See Arkley, Arthur J(ames)
Hackett, Marie G. 1923- 37-40R
Hackett, Pat 105
Hackett, Paul 1920- 29-32R
Hackett, Peter 1940- Brief entry 108
Hackett, Philip 1941- 77-80
Hackett, Roger F(leming) 1922- 77-80
Hackett, William H. Y., Jr. 1921(?)-1986
Obituary 118
Hackford, Robert 1921(?)-1983 Obituary 111
Hackforth-Jones, (Frank) Gilbert 1900- 15-16R
Hacking, Ian 1936- 69-72
Hackleman, Michael A(lan) 1946- 106
Hackler, James C(ourtland) 1930- 112
Hackman, J(ohn) Richard 1940- CANR-1
Earlier sketch in CA 49-52
Hackman, Martha L. 1912- 29-32R
Hackney, Alan 1924- 7-8R
Hackney, Sheldon 1933- 41-44R
Hackney, Vivian 1914- 23-24R
Hackwell, W. John 1942- 126
Hadas, Moses 1900-1966 CANR-6
Obituary 25-28R
Earlier sketch in CA 1R
Hadas, Pamela White 1946- CANR-16
Earlier sketch in CA 93-96
Hadas, Rachel 1948- 111
Hadawi, Sami 1904- CANR-13
Earlier sketch in CA 23-24R
Haddad, George M. 1910- 17-18R
Haddad, Robert M(itchell) 1930- 69-72
Haddad, William Frederick 1928-
Brief entry 108
Haddad, Yvonne Y(azbeck) 1935- CANR-25
Earlier sketch in CA 108
Haddad-Garcia, George 1954- 107
Haddan, Eugene E. 1918- Brief entry 108
Hadden, Jeffrey K(eith) 1936- 106
Hadden, Maude Miner 1880-1967 CAP-2
Earlier sketch in CA 17-18
Haddix, Cecille
See Haddix-Kontos, Cecille P.
Haddix-Kontos, Cecille P. 1937- 69-72
Haddo, Oliver
See Puechner, Ray
Haddock, Sally 1954- 121
Haddon, Christopher
See Palmer, John (Leslie)
Haddox, John H(erbert) 1929- 45-48
Hader, Berta (Hoerner) 1890(?)-1976 73-76
Obituary 65-68
See also SATA 16
Hader, Elmer Stanley 1889-1973 73-76
See also SATA 16

Hadfield, Alice M(ary) 1908- CANR-26
Earlier sketch in CA 108
Hadfield, (Ellis) Charles (Raymond)
1909- CANR-26
Earlier sketches in CA 13-14R, CANR-7
Hadfield, E. C. R.
See Hadfield, (Ellis) Charles (Raymond)
Hadfield, Miles H(eywood) 1903-1982 CAP-1
Obituary 106
Earlier sketch in CA 15-16
Hadfield, Vic(tor Edward) 1940-
Brief entry 106
Hadham, John
See Parkes, James William
Hadik, Laszlo 1932(?)-1973 Obituary 45-48
Hadingham, Evan 1951- 102
Hadley, Arthur T. 1924- 89-92
Hadley, Charles D(avid), Jr. 1942- 110
Hadley, Eleanor M(artha) 1916- 29-32R
Hadley, Franklin
See Winterbotham, R(ussell) R(obert)
Hadley, Hamilton 1896- CAP-1
Earlier sketch in CA 9-10
Hadley, Jay 1947- 114
Hadley, Lee 1934- CANR-19
Earlier sketch in CA 101
See also SATA 38, 47
Hadley, Leila 1925- CANR-14
Earlier sketch in CA 41-44R
Hadley, Michael L(lewellyn) 1936- 118
Hadley, Morris 1894-1979 Obituary 85-88
Hadley Chase, James
See Raymond, Rene (Brabazon)
Hadlich, Roger L(ee) 1930- Brief entry 108
Hadlow, Leonard Harold 1908- CAP-1
Earlier sketch in CA 13-14
Hadrill, Andrew (Frederic) Wallace
See Wallace-Hadrill, Andrew (Frederic)
Hadrill, John Michael Wallace
See Wallace-Hadrill, John Michael
Hadwiger, Don F. 1930- 21-22R
Haeberle, Erwin J(akob) 1936- 29-32R
Haebich, Kathryn A. 1899- 7-8R
Haedrich, Marcel (pseudonym) 1913- 85-88
Haefele, John W(illiam) 1913- 3R
Haefner, Richard 1929- 108
Haegerstrand, (Stig) Torsten (Erik) 1916-
Brief entry 116
Haegg, Tomas 1938- 111
Haegglund, Bengt 1920- CANR-10
Earlier sketch in CA 25-28R
Haekkerup, Per 1915-1979 Obituary 85-88
Haenicke, Diether H. 1935- 33-36R
Haentzschel, Adolph T(heodore)
1881-1971 2R
Obituary 103
Haering, Bernhard 1912- CANR-9
Earlier sketch in CA 7-8R
Haertling, Peter 1933- CANR-22
Earlier sketch in CA 101
See also DLB 75
Haessler, Herbert A(lfred) 1926- 125
Haessly, Jacqueline 1937- 120
Hafemeister, David W(alter) 1934- 124
Hafen, Ann Woodbury 1893-1970
Obituary 111
Hafen, Brent Q(ue) 1940- 112
Hafen, LeRoy R(euben) 1893- 65-68
Hafer, W(illiam) Keith 108
Haffenden, Philip Spencer 1926- 61-64
Haffner, J. Lilliwhite
See Speed, F(rederick) Maurice
Hafley, James 1928- 17-18R
Hafner, Lawrence E. 1924- CANR-10
Earlier sketch in CA 25-28R
Hafner, Marylin 1925- SATA-7
Haga, Enoch J. 1931- 25-28R
Hagan, Arthur Peter 1912- 107
Hagan, Charles B(anner) 1905- 37-40R
Hagan, Chet 1922- CANR-25
Earlier sketch in CA 107
Hagan, John T(homas) 1926- 25-28R
Hagan, Kenneth J(ames) 1936- 41-44R
Hagan, Patricia
See Howell, Patricia Hagan
Hagan, William T(homas) 1918- CANR-8
Earlier sketch in CA 5-6R
Hagar, George
See Maria Del Rey, Sister
Hagarty, Britt 1949- 110
Hagberg, David J(ames) 1942- 106
Hagbrink, Bodil 1936- 104
Hage, Jerald 1932- 37-40R
Hagedorn, Hermann 1882-1964 Obituary 116
Hagedorn, Robert (Bruce) 1925- 49-52
Hagee, John C(harles) 1940- CANR-3
Earlier sketch in CA 45-48
Hagelman, Charles W(illiam), Jr. 1920- 21-22R
Hagelstange, Rudolf 1912-1984 81-84
See also DLB 69
Hageman, Howard G(arberich) 1921- CANR-5
Earlier sketch in CA 3R
Hagen, Clifford (Warren, Jr.) 1943- 29-32R
Hagen, Elizabeth Pauline 1915- 13-14R
Hagen, Everett E(inar) 1906- CANR-1
Earlier sketch in CA 2R
Hagen, John Milton 1902- 57-60
Hagen, John William 1940- 61-64
Hagen, Lorinda
See Du Breuil, (Elizabeth) L(or)inda
Hagen, Richard L(ionel) 1935- 93-96
Hagen, Uta 1919- 77-80
Hager, Alice Rogers 1894-1969 5-6R
Obituary 103
See also SATA 26
Hager, Henry B. 1926- 19-20R
Hager, Jean 1932- 101
Hager, Robert M. 1938- 65-68
Hager, Thomas Arthur 1953- 126
Hagerman, Paul Stirling 1949- 106
Hagerstrand, (Stig) Torsten (Erik)
See Haegerstrand, (Stig) Torsten (Erik)
Hagerty, James C(ampbell) 1909-1981
Obituary 103
Hagerty, Nancy K. 1935- 33-36R
Hagerty, Sheward 1930-1983 Obituary 109
Hagg, G. Eric 1908(?)-1979 Obituary 85-88
Hagg, Tomas
See Haegg, Tomas
Haggai, Thomas Stephens 1931- 93-96
Haggard, H(enry) Rider 1856-1925
Brief entry 108
See also SATA 16
See also DLB 70
See also TCLC 11
Haggard, Howard W. 1902- 121
Haggard, Merle 1937- Brief entry 112
Haggard, Paul
See Longstreet, Stephen
Haggard, Raymond (Gordon Rider) 1921-
Brief entry 109
Haggard, Virginia 1915- 122
Haggard, William
See Clayton, Richard Henry Michael
Haggerson, Nelson L. 1927- 41-44R
Haggerty, Brian A(rthur) 1943- 113
Haggerty, James J(oseph) 1920- 41-44R
See also SATA 5
Haggerty, P(atrick) E(ugene) 1914-1980
Obituary 105
Haggett, Peter 1933- 73-76
Haggie, Paul 1949- 124
Haggin, B(ernard) H. 1900-1987 CANR-18
Obituary 122
Earlier sketch in CA 102
Hagiwara, Michio Peter 1932- CANR-13
Earlier sketch in CA 73-76
Hagler, Erwin Harrison 1947- 120
Hagler, Skeeter
See Hagler, Erwin Harrison
Haglund, Elaine J(ean) 1937- 109
Hagman, Bette 1922- 53-56
Hagman, Donald Gerald 1932-1982
Obituary 114
Hagner, Donald Alfred 1936- 110
Hagon, Priscilla
See Allan, Mabel Esther
Hagopian, John V. 1923- 41-44R
Hagopian, Mark N. 1940- 49-52
Hagstrom, Jerry 1947- 111
Hagstrom, Julie 1950- 111
Hagstrom, Warren Olaf 1930- 21-22R
Hagstrum, Jean (Howard) 1913- 17-18R
Hague, Douglas Chalmers 1926- CANR-20
Earlier sketch in CA 69-72
Hague, Harlan 1932- 116
Hague, (Susan) Kathleen 1949- 125
See also SATA 45, 49
Hague, Michael R. 1948- 123
Brief entry 111
See also SATA 32, 48
Hague, Richard 1947- 126
Hague, William Edward, Jr. 1919- 85-88
Hagy, Ruth Geri
See Brod, Ruth Hagy
Hahn, Emily 1905- CANR-1
Earlier sketch in CA 3R
See also SATA 3
Hahn, Fred 1906- 45-48
Hahn, Gloria 1926-1987 Obituary 123
Hahn, H. George 1942- 107
Hahn, Hannelore CANR-3
Earlier sketch in CA 7-8R
See also SATA 8
Hahn, Harlan 1939- 33-36R
Hahn, James (Sage) 1947- CANR-17
Earlier sketches in CA 49-52, CANR-2
See also SATA 9
Hahn, (Mona) Lynn 1949- CANR-17
Earlier sketches in CA 49-52, CANR-2
See also SATA 9
Hahn, Mary Downing 1937- 122
See also SATA 44, 50
Hahn, Otto 1879-1968 Obituary 112
Hahn, Paul H. 1932- 117
Hahn, Robert H. 1920- 123
Hahn, Robert O(scar) 1916- 69-72
Hahn, Roger 1932- 33-36R
Hahn, Steven 1951- 123
Hahner, June E(dith) 1940- CANR-11
Earlier sketch in CA 25-28R
Hahon, James
See Swift, Patrick
Haiblum, Isidore 1935- CANR-19
Earlier sketches in CA 53-56, CANR-4
Haidu, Peter 1931- 37-40R
Haig, Alexander M(eigs), Jr. 1924-
Brief entry 124
Haig, (Irvine Reid) Stirling 1936- 33-36R
Haigaz, Aram
See Chekenian, Aram Haigaz
Haig-Brown, Roderick (Langmere)
1908-1976 CANR-4
Obituary 69-72
Earlier sketch in CA 7-8R
See also SATA 12
See also CLC 21
Haigerty, Leo James 1924- 1R
Haigh, Christopher 1944- 126
Haight, Amanda 1939- 77-80
Haight, Anne Lyon 1895-1977 CAP-2
Obituary 73-76
Earlier sketch in CA 33-36
See also SATA 30
Haight, Gordon S(herman) 1901-1985 CAP-2
Obituary 118
Earlier sketch in CA 25-28
Haight, John McVickar, Jr. 1917- 29-32R
Haight, M. R. 1938- 124
Haight, Mabel V. Jackson
See Jackson-Haight, Mabel V.
Hail, Marshall 1905- 7-8R
Haile, H(arry) G(erald) 1931- 65-68
Hailey, Arthur 1920- CANR-2
Earlier sketch in CA 3R
See also DLBY 82
See also CLC 5
See also AITN 2
Hailey, Elizabeth Forsythe 1938- CANR-15
Earlier sketch in CA 93-96
See also CAAS 1
See also CLC 40
Hailey, Johanna
See Howl, Marcia (Yvonne Hurt)
Hailey, Johanna
See Jarvis, Sharon
Hailey, Oliver 1932- CANR-15
Earlier sketch in CA 41-44R
Hailey, Sheila 1927- 85-88
Hailperin, Herman 1899-1973 7-8R
Obituary 103
Hailstones, Thomas J(ohn) 1919- 41-44R
Hailwood, Mike
See Hailwood, Stanley Michael Bailey
Hailwood, Stanley Michael Bailey
1940-1981 Obituary 108
Haiman, Franklyn S(aul) 1921- 37-40R
Haimann, Theo 1911- CANR-2
Earlier sketch in CA 5-6R
Haime, Agnes Irvine Constance (Adams)
1884- CAP-1
Earlier sketch in CA 9-10
Haimes, Norma 53-56
Haimowitz, Morris (Loeb) 1918- 37-40R
Haimowitz, Natalie Reader 1923- 53-56
Haimson, Leopold Henri 1917- 126
Brief entry 109
Hainaux, Rene 1918- 73-76
Haindl, Marieluise 1901-1974 Obituary 49-52
Haine, Edgar A. 1908- 97-100
Haines, Charles 1928- 41-44R
Haines, Charles G(rove) 1906-1976
Obituary 65-68
Haines, Edward Burdette 1910-1984
Obituary 112
Haines, Francis 1899- 5-6R
Haines, Francis D., Jr. 1923- 53-56
Haines, Gail Kay 1943- CANR-14
Earlier sketch in CA 37-40R
See also SATA 11
Haines, George H(enry), Jr. 1937- 33-36R
Haines, Harry B. 1949(?)-1984 Obituary 112
Haines, John (Meade) 1924- CANR-13
Earlier sketch in CA 19-20R
See also DLB 5
Haines, John
See Richardson, Gladwell
Haines, Max 1931- CANR-15
Earlier sketch in CA 85-88
Haines, Pamela Mary 1929- CANR-24
Earlier sketch in CA 106
Haines, Perry Franklin 1889- 5-6R
Haines, Walter W(ells) 1918- 1R
Haines, William Wister 1908- CAP-1
Earlier sketch in CA 9-10
Haining, Peter 1940- CANR-1
Earlier sketch in CA 45-48
See also SATA 14
Hainworth, Henry Charles 1914- 109
Hair, Donald S(herman) 1937- 69-72
Hair, P(aul) E(dward) H(edley) 1926- 25-28R
Hair, William Ivy 1930- 29-32R
Haire, Wilson John 1932- 101
Haislip, Harvey (Shadle) 1889-1978 2R
Obituary 103
Haislip, John 1925- 33-36R
Haislip, Martha Pratt 1889(?)-1984
Obituary 112
Haithcox, John Patrick 1933- 29-32R
Haj, Fareed 1935- 29-32R
Hake, Thomas Gordon 1809-1895 DLB-32
Hakeda, Yoshito S. 1924(?)-1983
Obituary 110
Hakes, Joseph Edward 1916- 11-12R
Hakim, Seymour 1933- 65-68
Hakutani, Yoshinobu 1935- 101
Halaby, Najeeb E(lias) 1915- Brief entry 107
Halacy, D(aniel) S(tephen), Jr. 1919- CANR-9
Earlier sketch in CA 7-8R
See also SATA 36
Halal, William E. 1933- 123
Halam, Ann
See Jones, Gwyneth A.
Halas, Celia (Mary) 1922- 103
Halas, George Stanley 1895-1983
Obituary 111
Halas, John 1912- 108
Halasz, Gyula 1899-1984 126
Obituary 113
Halasz, Nicholas 1895-1985 19-20R
Obituary 116
Halbach, Edward C(hristian), Jr. 1931- 93-96
Halberg, Arvo Kusta
See Hall, Gus
Halberstadt, John 1941- 49-52
Halberstadt, William Harold 1930- 4R
Halberstam, David 1934- CANR-10
Earlier sketch in CA 69-72
Halberstam, Michael J(oseph)
1932-1980 CANR-10
Obituary 102
Earlier sketch in CA 65-68
Halbert, Frederic (Leslie) 1945- 122
Brief entry 118
Halbert, Sandra (Edith) 1943- 123
Halbrook, Stephen P. 121
Halcomb, Ruth 1936- 97-100
Halcrow, Harold Graham 1911- 19-20R
Haldane, A(rchibald) R(ichard) B(urdon)
1900-1982 120
Obituary 108
Haldane, J(ohn) B(urdon) S(anderson)
1892-1964 101
Haldane, R(obert) A(ylmer) 1907- 69-72
Haldane, Roger John 1945- SATA-13
Haldane-Stevenson, James Patrick
1910- CANR-14
Earlier sketch in CA 45-48
Haldeman, Charles (Heuss) 1931- 7-8R
Haldeman, H(arry) R(obbins) 1926- 81-84
Haldeman, Jack C(arroll II) 1941-
Brief entry 119
Haldeman, Joe (William) 1943- CANR-6
Earlier sketch in CA 53-56
See also DLB 8
Haldeman, Linda (Wilson) 1935- 85-88
Hale, Agnes Burke 1890-1981 Obituary 103
Hale, Allean Lemmon 1914- 33-36R
Hale, Arlene 1924-1982 CANR-1
Earlier sketch in CA 1R
See also SATA 49
Hale, Charles A(dams) 1930- 25-28R
Hale, Clarence B(enjamin) 1905- 69-72
Hale, David G(eorge) 1938- 45-48
Hale, Dennis 1944- 25-28R
Hale, Edward Everett 1822-1909
Brief entry 119
See also SATA 16
See also DLB 1, 42, 74
Hale, Francesca
See Halpern, Frances J(oy)
Hale, Francis Joseph 1922- 53-56
Hale, Frank (Wilbur), Jr. 1927- 65-68
Hale, Helen
See Mulcahy, Lucille Burnett
Hale, Irina 1932- 105
See also SATA 26
Hale, J. Russell 1918- 101
Hale, Jade
See Hyatt, Betty H(ale)
Hale, Janet Campbell 1947- 49-52
Hale, John (Barry) 1926- 102
Hale, John Rigby 1923- CANR-19
Earlier sketch in CA 102
Hale, Judson (Drake) 1933- 69-72
Hale, Julian A(nthony) S(tuart) 1940- 41-44R
Hale, Kathleen 1898- 73-76
See also SATA 17
Hale, Keith 1955- 126
Hale, Leo Thomas
See Ebon
Hale, Leon 1921- CANR-10
Earlier sketch in CA 19-20R
Hale, (Charles) Leslie 1902-1985 CAP-1
Obituary 116
Earlier sketch in CA 15-16
Hale, Linda (Howe) 1929- 5-6R
See also SATA 6
Hale, Lionel Ramsay 1909-1977 Obituary 107
Hale, Lucretia P.
See Hale, Lucretia Peabody
Hale, Lucretia Peabody 1820-1900
Brief entry 122
See also SATA 26
See also DLB 42
Hale, Margaret
See Higonnet, Margaret Randolph
Hale, Michael
See Bullock, Michael
Hale, Nancy 1908-1988 5-6R
Obituary 126
See also SATA 31
See also DLBY 80
Hale, Nathan Cabot 1925- 53-56
Hale, Oron James 1902- 13-14R
Hale, Patricia Whitaker 1922- 53-56
Hale, Philip
See Eastwood, C(harles) Cyril
Hale, Richard W(alden) 1909-1976
Obituary 65-68
Hale, Robert Beverly 1901-1985 Obituary 117
Hale, Robert William 1937- 114
Hale, Sarah Josepha (Buell)
1788-1879 DLB-1, 42, 73
Hale, Wanda
See Coutard, Wanda Lundy Hale
Hale, William 1940- 125
Hale, William Harlan 1910-1974 93-96
Obituary 49-52
Hales, Ann
See Hales-Tooke, Ann (Mary Margaret)
Hales, E(dward) E(lton) Y(oung) 1908- 85-88
Hales, Edward John 1927- 106
Hales, Loyde (Wesley) 1933- 89-92
Hales, Norman
See Young, Vernon
Hales-Tooke, Ann (Mary Margaret) 1926- 123
Brief entry 116
Halevi, Z'ev ben Shimon
See Kenton, Warren
Haley, Alex (Palmer) 1921- 77-80
See also BW
See also DLB 38
See also CLC 8, 12

Haley, Andrew G(allagher) 1904- ... CAP-1
Earlier sketch in CA 15-16
Haley, Bruce Everts 1933- Brief entry ... 108
Haley, Earl. J. 1898(?)-1987 Obituary ... 122
Haley, Gail E(inhart) 1939- ... CANR-14
Earlier sketch in CA 21-22R
See also SATA 28, 43
Haley, James L(ewis) 1951- ... 77-80
Haley, Jay 1923- ... CANR-9
Earlier sketch in CA 23-24R
Haley, Joseph E. 1915- ... 15-16R
Haley, K(enneth) H(arold) D(obson)
1920- ... 25-28R
Haley, Margaret Angela 1861-1939
Brief entry ... 112
Haley, Michael 1952- ... 109
Haley, Neale ... 41-44R
See also SATA 52
Haley, (Harry) Russell 1934- ... 118
Haley, William (John) 1901-1987 Obituary .. 123
Half, Robert 1918- ... 107
Haliburton, Thomas Chandler
1796-1865 ... DLB-11
Halifax, Joan (Squire) 1942- ... 85-88
Halio, Jay L(eon) 1928- ... CANR-10
Earlier sketch in CA 25-28R
Halivni, David
See Weiss, David
Halivni, David Weiss
See Weiss, David
Halkett, John G(eorge) 1933- ... 57-60
Halkin, Shimon 1899- ... 53-56
Halkin, Simon
See Halkin, Shimon
Hall, Adam
See Trevor, Elleston
Hall, Adele 1910- ... 4R
See also SATA 7
Hall, Adrian 1927- ... CANR-22
Earlier sketch in CA 106
Hall, Al(fred) Rupert 1920- ... 9-10R
Hall, Alice Clay 1900- ... 73-76
Hall, Andrew 1935- ... 21-22R
Hall, Angus 1932- ... CANR-13
Earlier sketch in CA 21-22R
Hall, Ann
See Duckert, Mary
Hall, Anna Gertrude 1882-1967 ... CAP-1
Earlier sketch in CA 11-12
See also SATA 8
Hall, Anthony Stewart 1945- ... 102
Hall, Ariel Perry 1906- ... 69-72
Hall, Arlene Stevens 1923- ... 19-20R
Hall, Asa Zadel 1875-1965 ... CANR-4
Earlier sketch in CA 3R
Hall, Austin 1882(?)-1933 Brief entry ... 114
Hall, Aylmer
See Hall, Norah E. L.
Hall, B(axter) C(larence) 1936- ... CANR-9
Earlier sketch in CA 57-60
Hall, B. K. 1932- ... 106
Hall, Bennie Caroline (Humble) ... 4R
Hall, Borden
See Yates, Raymond F(rancis)
Hall, Brian P(atrick) 1935- ... CANR-9
Earlier sketch in CA 61-64
See also SATA 31
Hall, C(onstance) Margaret 1937- ... CANR-12
Earlier sketch in CA 73-76
Hall, Calvin (Springer) 1909- ... 13-14R
Hall, Cameron
See del Rey, Lester
Hall, Cameron P(arker) 1898- ... 49-52
Hall, Carolyn Vosburg 1927- ... 61-64
Hall, Caryl
See Hansen, Caryl (Hall)
Hall, Challis A(lva), Jr. 1917-1968 ... 1R
Obituary ... 103
Hall, Charles A(rthur) M(ann) 1924-
Brief entry ... 107
Hall, Clarence W(ilbur) 1902-1985
Obituary ... 114
Hall, Claudia
See Floren, Lee
Hall, Clifton L. 1898- ... CAP-1
Earlier sketch in CA 11-12
Hall, D(onald) J(ohn) 1903- ... 13-14R
Hall, Daniel George Edward 1891-1979 ... 103
Hall, David D(risko) 1936- ... 125
Brief entry ... 108
Hall, Don 1929- ... 110
Hall, Don Alan 1938- ... 108
Hall, Donald (Andrew, Jr.) 1928- ... CANR-2
Earlier sketch in CA 7-8R
See also CAAS 7
See also SATA 23
See also DLB 5
See also CLC 1, 13, 37
Hall, Donald Ray 1933- ... 33-36R
Hall, Dorothy Judd ... 122
Hall, Douglas 1931- ... SATA-43
Hall, Douglas John 1928- ... CANR-14
Earlier sketch in CA 69-72
Hall, Douglas Kent 1938- ... 33-36R
Hall, Edward Twitchell (Jr.) 1914- ... 65-68
Hall, Elizabeth 1929- ... CANR-14
Earlier sketch in CA 65-68
Hall, Elizabeth Cornelia 1898- ... 37-40R
Hall, Elvajean 1910- ... CANR-8
Earlier sketch in CA 15-16R
See also SATA 6
Hall, Eric J(ohn) 1933- ... 97-100
Hall, Evan
See Halleran, Eugene E(dward)
Hall, F. H. 1926- ... 77-80
Hall, Fernau ... 102
Hall, Frederic Sauser
See Sauser-Hall, Frederic
Hall, Gene E(rwin) 1941- ... 93-96
Hall, Geoffrey Fowler 1888-1970 ... CAP-1
Earlier sketch in CA 13-14
Hall, George 1941- ... CANR-15
Earlier sketch in CA 85-88
Hall, George F(ridolph) 1908- ... CANR-22
Earlier sketch in CA 45-48
Hall, George R. 1930- ... 123
Hall, Georgette Brockman 1915- ... 57-60
Hall, Geraldine M(arion) 1935- ... 33-36R
Hall, Gimone 1940- ... CANR-15
Earlier sketch in CA 29-32R
Hall, Gladys 1891(?)-1977 Obituary ... 73-76
Hall, Gordon Langley
See Simmons, Dawn Langley
Hall, Gus 1910- Brief entry ... 108
Hall, Gwendolyn Midlo 1929- ... 41-44R
Hall, H(essel) Duncan 1891-1976 ... CAP-2
Obituary ... 65-68
Earlier sketch in CA 29-32
Hall, Halbert Weldon 1941- ... 53-56
Hall, Haywood 1898- ... 77-80
Hall, Helen 1892- ... 104
Hall, Henry M(arion) 1877- ... 5-6R
Hall, J(ohn) C(live) 1920- ... 101
Hall, J(ames) Curtis 1926- ... 53-56
Hall, J. De P.
See McKelway, St. Clair
Hall, J. Tillman 1916- ... CANR-6
Earlier sketch in CA 4R
Hall, Jacquelyn (Dowd) 1943- ... 97-100
Hall, James 1793-1868 ... DLB-73, 74
Hall, James 1918- ... 102
Hall, James (Herrick, Jr.) 1933- ... 53-56
Hall, James
See Kuttner, Henry
Hall, James Andrew 1935- ... 118
Hall, James B(yron) 1918- ... CANR-1
Earlier sketch in CA 3R
Hall, James Baker 1935- ... 116
Hall, James Norman 1887-1951
Brief entry ... 123
See also SATA 21
See also TCLC 23
Hall, James W(illiam) 1937- ... CANR-22
Earlier sketch in CA 45-48
Hall, Jay C.
See Hall, John C.
Hall, Jean R(ogers) 1941- ... 105
Hall, Jerome 1901- ... CAP-1
Earlier sketch in CA 11-12
Hall, Jesse
See Boesen, Victor
Hall, John 1937- ... 93-96
Hall, John C. 1915- ... 57-60
Hall, John F. 1919- ... CANR-17
Earlier sketch in CA 1R
Hall, John O. P. 1911- ... 11-12R
Hall, John Whitney 1916- ... 25-28R
Hall, Josef Washington 1894-1960
Obituary ... 89-92
Hall, Joseph (Sargent) 1906- ... 41-44R
Hall, Julie (Ann) 1943- Brief entry ... 110
Hall, Kathleen M(ary) 1924- ... CANR-3
Earlier sketch in CA 7-8R
Hall, Katy
See McMullan, Kate Hall
Hall, Kendall
See Heath, Harry E(ugene), Jr.
Hall, Kenneth F(ranklin) 1926- ... 19-20R
Hall, Kermit L(ance) 1944- ... 101
Hall, Laurence James 1940- ... 97-100
Hall, Lawrence Sargent 1915- ... 4R
Hall, (Frederick) Leonard 1899- ... 65-68
Hall, Leslie 1948- ... 126
Hall, Linda B(iesele) 1939- ... CANR-23
Earlier sketch in CA 106
Hall, Livingston 1903- ... CAP-2
Earlier sketch in CA 21-22
Hall, Louis Brewer 1920- ... 110
Hall, Luella J(emima) 1890-1973 ... 45-48
Obituary ... 103
Hall, Lynn 1937- ... CANR-25
Earlier sketches in CA 23-24R, CANR-9
See also SATA 2, 47
See also SAAS 4
Hall, Malcolm 1945- ... CANR-4
Earlier sketch in CA 49-52
See also SATA 7
Hall, Manly Palmer 1901- ... 93-96
Hall, Marie Boas 1919- ... 11-12R
Hall, Marjory
See Yeakley, Marjory Hall
Hall, Mark W. 1943- ... 33-36R
Hall, Martin Hardwick 1925- ... 33-36R
Hall, Mary Ann 1942- ... 116
Hall, Mary Bowen 1932- ... 23-24R
Hall, MaryAnne 1934- ... CANR-25
Earlier sketch in CA 29-32R
Hall, Michael Garibaldi 1926- ... 15-16R
Hall, Monty 1924- Brief entry ... 108
Hall, N(orman) John 1933- ... CANR-12
Earlier sketch in CA 61-64
Hall, Nancy Lee 1923- ... 57-60
Hall, Natalie Watson 1923- ... 7-8R
Hall, Noel (Frederick) 1902-1983 Obituary .. 109
Hall, Norah E. L. 1914- ... 97-100
Hall, O. M.
See Hall, Oakley (Maxwell)
Hall, Oakley (Maxwell) 1920- ... CANR-3
Earlier sketch in CA 9-10R
Hall, Patrick 1932- ... 21-22R
Hall, Penelope C(oker) 1933- ... 19-20R
Hall, Peter (Geoffrey) 1932- ... CANR-24
Earlier sketches in CA 17-18R, CANR-8
Hall, Phil 1953- ... 102
Hall, R(obert) Cargill 1937- ... CANR-1
Earlier sketch in CA 49-52
Hall, (Marguerite) Radclyffe 1886(?)-1943
Brief entry ... 110
See also TCLC 12
Hall, Richard (Seymour) 1925- ... CANR-9
Earlier sketch in CA 17-18R
Hall, (Patrick) Richard Compton
See Compton-Hall, (Patrick) Richard
Hall, Richard H(ammond) 1934- ... CANR-13
Earlier sketch in CA 77-80
Hall, Robert A(nderson), Jr. 1911- ... CANR-5
Earlier sketch in CA 13-14R
Hall, Robert Benjamin 1918- ... 57-60
Hall, Robert Burnett, Jr. 1923- Brief entry .. 109
Hall, Robert E(lliott) 1924- ... CANR-13
Earlier sketch in CA 19-20R
Hall, Robert E(rnest) 1943- ... 114
Hall, Robert Lee 1941- ... 73-76
Hall, Robert T(om) 1938- Brief entry ... 110
Hall, Rodney 1935- ... 109
Hall, Roger (Wolcott) 1919- ... 29-32R
Hall, Roger 1945- ... 112
Hall, Rosalys Haskell 1914- ... 11-12R
See also SATA 7
Hall, Ross H(ume) 1926- ... 61-64
Hall, Rubylea (Ray) 1910- ... CAP-2
Earlier sketch in CA 17-18
Hall, Ruth 1933(?)-1981 Obituary ... 104
Hall, Steven (Leonard) 1960- ... 93-96
Hall, Susan 1940- ... 57-60
Hall, T(homas) William 1921- ... 118
Hall, Ted Byron 1902- ... CAP-2
Earlier sketch in CA 33-36
Hall, Thor 1927- ... 37-40R
Hall, Tom T. 1936- ... 102
Hall, Tony
See Hall, Anthony Stewart
Hall, Tord (Erik Martin) 1910- ... 29-32R
Hall, Trevor H(enry) 1910- ... CANR-16
Earlier sketch in CA 29-32R
Hall, Van Beck 1934- ... 45-48
Hall, Vernon, Jr. 1913- ... CANR-3
Earlier sketch in CA 7-8R
Hall, Wade H. 1934- ... CANR-6
Earlier sketch in CA 7-8R
Hall, Walter (Earl, Jr.) 1940- ... CANR-13
Earlier sketch in CA 21-22R
Hall, Wayne E(dward) 1947- ... 105
Hall, William N(orman) 1915-1974
Obituary ... 53-56
Hall, Willis 1929- ... 101
Hall, Wilson (Dudley) 1922- ... 69-72
Halla, (Robert) Chris(tian) 1949- ... CANR-18
Earlier sketch in CA 77-80
Hallahan, William H(enry) Brief entry ... 109
Hallahmi, Benjamin Beit
See Beit-Hallahmi, Benjamin
Hallam, Arthur Henry 1811-1833 ... DLB-32
Hallam, (Samuel Benoni) Atlantis 1915- ... 5-6R
Hallam, Elizabeth M. 1950- ... 123
Hallam, H(erbert) E(noch) 1923- ... 23-24R
Hallam, J(ohn) Harvey 1917- ... 13-14R
Hallas, Richard
See Knight, Eric (Mowbray)
Hallberg, Charles William 1899- ... CAP-1
Earlier sketch in CA 17-18
Hallberg, Edmond C. 1931- Brief entry ... 111
Hallberg, Peter 1916- ... CANR-4
Earlier sketch in CA 53-56
Hall-Clarke, James
See Rowland-Entwistle, (Arthur)
Theodore (Henry)
Halle, Jean-Claude 1939- ... CANR-17
Earlier sketch in CA 93-96
Halle, Katherine Murphy ... 41-44R
Halle, Kay
See Halle, Katherine Murphy
Halle, Louis J(oseph) 1910- ... CANR-2
Earlier sketch in CA 4R
Halleck, Fitz-Greene 1790-1867 ... DLB-3
Halleck, Seymour L(eon) 1929- ... CANR-13
Earlier sketch in CA 21-22R
Haller, Archibald O(rben), Jr. 1926- ... 45-48
Haller, Bill
See Bechko, Peggy Anne
Haller, Dorcas Woodbury 1946- ... 117
See also SATA 46
Haller, Ellis M(etcalf) 1915-1981 Obituary .. 103
Haller, John Samuel, Jr. 1940- ... 61-64
Haller, Mark H(ughlin) 1928- ... CANR-5
Earlier sketch in CA 11-12R
Haller, Mike 1945- ... 110
Haller, Robert S(pencer) 1933- ... CANR-2
Earlier sketch in CA 2R
Haller, Robin Meredith 1944- ... 65-68
Haller, William 1885-1974 Obituary ... 49-52
Halleran, Eugene E(dward) 1905- ... 4R
Hallet, Jean-Pierre 1927- ... 19-20R
Hallett, Ellen Kathleen 1899- ... CAP-1
Earlier sketch in CA 15-16
Hallett, Garth L(ie) 1927- ... CANR-13
Earlier sketch in CA 69-72
Hallett, George H(ervey), Jr. 1895-1985
Obituary ... 116
Hallett, Graham 1929- ... CANR-16
Earlier sketch in CA 25-28R
Hallett, Judith Peller 1944- ... 124
Hallett, Kathryn J(osephine) 1937- ... 57-60
Hallett, Robin 1926- ... 103
Halley, Anne 1928- ... 121
Halley, Laurence
See O'Keeffe, Laurence
Hallgarten, George W(olfgang) F(elix)
1901-1975 ... 65-68
Obituary ... 57-60
Hallgarten, Peter A(lexander) 1931- ... 97-100
Hallgarten, Siegfried Fritz 1902- ... CANR-18
Earlier sketches in CA 7-8R, CANR-3
Hallgren, Chris 1947- ... 115
Halliburton, David (Garland) 1933-
Brief entry ... 116
Halliburton, Richard 1900-1939
Brief entry ... 114
Halliburton, Rudia, Jr. 1929- ... 81-84
Halliburton, Warren J. 1924- ... CANR-24
Earlier sketch in CA 33-36R
See also BW
See also SATA 19
Halliday, Brett
See Dresser, Davis
and Terrall, Robert
Halliday, David 1948- ... 113
Halliday, Dorothy
See Dunnett, Dorothy
Halliday, E(rnest) M(ilton) 1913- ... 3R
Halliday, Ena
See Baumgarten, Sylvia
Halliday, F(rank) E(rnest) 1903-1982 ... CANR-2
Obituary ... 106
Earlier sketch in CA 2R
Halliday, Fred 1937- ... 53-56
Halliday, James
See Symington, David
Halliday, Jerry 1949- ... 69-72
Halliday, Jon 1939- ... 97-100
Halliday, M(ichael) A(lexander) K(irkwood)
1925- ... 126
Brief entry ... 112
Halliday, Michael
See Creasey, John
Halliday, Richard 1905-1973 Obituary ... 41-44R
Halliday, Tim (Richard) 1945- ... 112
Halliday, William R(oss) 1926- ... 49-52
See also SATA 52
Hallie, Philip P. 1922- ... CANR-9
Earlier sketch in CA 15-16R
Hallier, Amedee 1913- ... 73-76
Halligan, Nicholas 1917- ... CANR-5
Earlier sketch in CA 13-14R
Hallin, Emily Watson ... CANR-26
Earlier sketches in CA 25-28R, CANR-10
See also SATA 6
Hallinan, Hazel Hunkins 1891(?)-1982
Obituary ... 106
Hallinan, Nancy 1921- ... CANR-3
Earlier sketch in CA 9-10R
Hallinan, P(atrick) K(enneth) 1944- ... CANR-11
Earlier sketch in CA 69-72
See also SATA 37, 39
Hallinan, Vincent 1896- ... 4R
Hallion, Richard P(aul, Jr.) 1948- ... 41-44R
Halliwell, David (William) 1936- ... CANR-11
Earlier sketch in CA 65-68
Halliwell, Leslie 1929- ... CANR-16
Earlier sketches in CA 49-52, CANR-1
Hall-Jones, Frederick George 1891-1982
Obituary ... 108
Hallman, Frank Curtis 1943(?)-1975
Obituary ... 104
Hallman, G(eorge) Victor III 1930- ... 101
Hallman, Howard W(esley) 1928- ... 116
Hallman, Ralph J(efferson) 1911- ... 13-14R
Hallman, Ruth 1929- ... CANR-15
Earlier sketch in CA 85-88
See also SATA 28, 43
Hallo, William W. 1928- ... CANR-15
Earlier sketch in CA 37-40R
Hallock, G. B. F.
See Hallock, Gerard B(enjamin) F(leet)
Hallock, Gerard B(enjamin) F(leet)
1856-1953 Brief entry ... 122
Hallock, Robert Lay 1898(?)-1986
Obituary ... 120
Halloran, Richard (Colby) 1930- ... 29-32R
Halloway, Vance 1916- ... 53-56
Hallowell, A(lfred) Irving 1892-1974 ... 7-8R
Obituary ... 53-56
Hallowell, Christopher L. 1945- ... 93-96
Hallowell, John H(amilton) 1913- ... CANR-5
Earlier sketch in CA 15-16R
Hallpike, C. R. 1938- ... 41-44R
Hall-Quest, (Edna) Olga W(ilbourne)
1899-1986 ... 7-8R
Obituary ... 118
See also SATA 11, 47
Halls, Geraldine (Mary) 1919- ... 103
Halls, W(ilfred) D(ouglas) 1918- ... CANR-5
Earlier sketch in CA 3R
Hallstead, William F(inn III) 1924- ... CANR-21
Earlier sketches in CA 5-6R, CANR-6
See also SATA 11
Hallstein, Walter 1901-1982 Obituary ... 106
Hallstroem, Per (August Leonard)
1866-1960 Obituary ... 116
Hallstrom, Per (August Leonard)
See Hallstroem, Per (August Leonard)
Hallus, Tak
See Robinett, Stephen (Allen)
Hallward, Michael 1889- ... 49-52
See also SATA 12
Halm, George N(ikolaus) 1901- ... 23-24R
Halman, Talat Sait 1931- ... CANR-4
Earlier sketch in CA 53-56
Halmos, Paul 1911-1977 ... CANR-8
Earlier sketch in CA 17-18R
Halper
See Halpern, Leivick
Halper, Albert 1904-1984 ... CANR-3
Obituary ... 111
Earlier sketch in CA 7-8R
See also DLB 9
Halper, Nathan 1908(?)-1983 Obituary ... 110

Halper, Thomas 1942- ... 41-44R
Halperin, David M(artin) 1952- ... 117
Halperin, Don A(kiba) 1925- ... 57-60
Halperin, Edwin G. 1935(?)-1987
Obituary ... 123
Halperin, Irving 1922- ... 29-32R
Halperin, John 1941- ... CANR-6
Earlier sketch in CA 53-56
Halperin, Mark (Warren) 1940- ... CANR-9
Earlier sketch in CA 65-68
Halperin, Maurice 1906- ... 73-76
Halperin, Morton H. 1938- ... CANR-3
Earlier sketch in CA 11-12R
Halperin, S(amuel) William 1905-1979 ... 97-100
Obituary ... 85-88
Halperin, Samuel 1930- ... CANR-1
Earlier sketch in CA 1R
Halpern, A(braham) M(eyer) 1914- ... 19-20R
Halpern, Barbara Kerewsky
See Kerewsky-Halpern, Barbara
Halpern, Barbara Strachey 1912- ... 106
Halpern, Ben(jamin) 1912- Brief entry ... 115
Halpern, Daniel 1945- ... 33-36R
See also CLC 14
Halpern, Frances J(oy) ... 114
Halpern, Howard Marvin 1929- ... 93-96
Halpern, Joel M. 1929- ... CANR-3
Earlier sketch in CA 7-8R
Halpern, L.
See Halpern, Leivick
Halpern, Leivick 1888-1962 Obituary ... 114
Halpern, Manfred 1924- ... 11-12R
Halpern, Martin 1929- ... CANR-7
Earlier sketch in CA 5-6R
Halpern, Oscar Saul 1912- ... 97-100
Halpern, Paul G. 1937- ... 45-48
Halpern, Paul J(oseph) 1942- ... CANR-7
Earlier sketch in CA 57-60
Halpern, Stephen Mark 1940- ... 57-60
Halpert, Inge D. 1926- ... 23-24R
Halpert, Stephen 1941- ... 37-40R
Halpin, Andrew W(illiams) 1911- ... 19-20R
Halprin, Anna Schuman 1920- ... 85-88
Halprin, Lawrence 1916- ... 41-44R
Hals, Ronald M. 1926- ... 33-36R
Halsall, Elizabeth 1916- ... 33-36R
Halsall, Eric 1920- ... 107
Halsband, Robert 1914- ... CANR-8
Earlier sketch in CA 19-20R
Halsell, Grace (Eleanor) 1923- ... CANR-13
Earlier sketch in CA 23-24R
See also SATA 13
See also AITN 1
Halsey, A(lbert) H(enry) 1923- ... CANR-7
Earlier sketch in CA 17-18R
Halsey, Elizabeth 1890- ... CAP-2
Earlier sketch in CA 17-18
Halsey, Elizabeth Tower 1903(?)-1976
Obituary ... 65-68
Halsey, George Dawson 1889-1970 ... 4R
Obituary ... 103
Halsey, Margaret (Frances) 1910- ... 81-84
Halsey, Martha T. 1932- ... CANR-14
Earlier sketch in CA 37-40R
Halsey, William D(arrach) 1918-
Brief entry ... 117
Halsman, Philippe 1906-1979 ... CANR-10
Obituary ... 89-92
Earlier sketch in CA 23-24R
Halstead, Murat 1829-1908 ... DLB-23
Halstead, William Perdue 1906-1982
Obituary ... 109
Halsted, Anna Roosevelt 1906-1975
Obituary ... 61-64
See also SATA 30
Halstock, Max
See Caulfield, Malachy Francis
Halter, Carl 1915- ... 17-18R
Halter, Jon C(harles) 1941- ... CANR-13
Earlier sketch in CA 61-64
See also SATA 22
Halton, David 1940- ... 73-76
Halton, Eugene Rochberg
See Rochberg-Halton, Eugene
Haltrecht, Montague 1932- ... 29-32R
Halverson, Alton C. O. 1922- ... 61-64
Halverson, Richard C. 1916- ... CANR-3
Earlier sketch in CA 1R
Halverson, Richard P(aul) 1941- ... 109
Halverson, William H(agen) 1930- ... 37-40R
Halvorson, Arndt L(eroy) 1915- ... CANR-3
Earlier sketch in CA 7-8R
Halward, Leslie G. 1904(?)-1976
Obituary ... 65-68
Ham, Wayne 1938- ... CANR-11
Earlier sketch in CA 21-22R
Hamachek, Don E. 1933- ... 17-18R
Hamada, Hirosuke 1893- ... 45-48
Hamady, Walter ... AITN-1
Hamalainen, Pekka Kalevi 1938- ... 97-100
Hamalian, Leo 1920- ... CANR-2
Earlier sketch in CA 5-6R
See also SATA 41
Hamberg, Daniel 1924- ... 1R
Hamberger, Conrad P. 1900- ... 15-16R
Hamberger, John 1934- ... 69-72
See also SATA 14
Hambletonian
See Fairfax-Blakeborough, John Freeman
Hamblett, Theora 1895(?)-1977 Obituary ... 69-72
Hamblin, C(harles) L(eonard) 1922- ... 25-28R
Hamblin, Dora Jane 1920- ... 37-40R
See also SATA 36
Hamblin, Douglas H. 1923- ... 115
Hamblin, Robert L(ee) 1927- ... 97-100
Hamblin, W. K. 1928- ... 53-56
Hambrick-Stowe, Charles E(dwin) 1948- ... 125
Hamburg, Carl H(einz) 1915- ... 37-40R
Hamburg, David A(llen) 1925- Brief entry ... 109
Hamburg, Morris 1922- Brief entry ... 114
Hamburger, Ernest 1891(?)-1980
Obituary ... 97-100
Hamburger, Estelle 1898(?)-1983
Obituary ... 110
Hamburger, Kaete 1896- ... CANR-14
Earlier sketch in CA 29-32R
Hamburger, Max 1897-1970 ... CAP-2
Earlier sketch in CA 17-18
Hamburger, Michael (Peter Leopold)
1924- ... CANR-2
Earlier sketch in CA 7-8R
See also CAAS 4
See also DLB 27
See also CLC 5, 14
Hamburger, Michael J(ay) 1938- ... CANR-3
Earlier sketch in CA 45-48
Hamburger, Philip 1914- ... 5-6R
Hamburger, Robert (A., Jr.) 1943- ... CANR-8
Earlier sketch in CA 61-64
Hamburgh, Max 1922- ... 61-64
Hamby, Alonzo L. 1940- ... CANR-15
Earlier sketch in CA 37-40R
Hamel, Peter Michael 1947- ... 97-100
Hamel Dobkin, Kathleen 1945- ... 110
Hamelin, Louis-Edmond 1923- ... 110
Hamell, Patrick Joseph 1910- ... CAP-1
Earlier sketch in CA 15-16
Hamelman, Paul W(illiam) 1930-1976 ... 41-44R
Hamer, David Allan 1938- ... 45-48
Hamer, Frank 1929- ... 105
Hamer, Mick 1946- ... 109
Hamer, Philip (May) 1891-1971 Obituary ... 104
Hamermesh, Daniel S(elim) 1943-
Brief entry ... 110
Hamermesh, Morton 1915- ... 5-6R
Hamerow, Theodore S(tephen) 1920- ... 49-52
Hamerstrom, Frances 1907- ... 69-72
See also SATA 24
Hames, (Alice) Inez 1892- ... 29-32R
Hamey, J(ohn) A(nthony) 1956- ... 109
Hamey, L(eonard) A(rnold) 1918- ... 109
Hamil, Sharon Hide 1939- ... 122
Hamil, Thomas Arthur 1928- ... 73-76
See also SATA 14
Hamill, Denis 1951- ... 110
Hamill, Ethel
See Webb, Jean Francis
Hamill, Pete 1935- ... CANR-18
Earlier sketch in CA 25-28R
See also CLC 10
Hamill, Robert H(offman) 1912-1975 ... CAP-2
Earlier sketch in CA 33-36
Hamilton, Adam
See Henderson, M(arilyn) R(uth)
Hamilton, (John) Alan 1943- ... 115
Hamilton, Alex John 1939- ... 103
Hamilton, Alexander 1712-1756 ... DLB-31
Hamilton, Alexander 1755(?)-1804 ... DLB-37
Hamilton, Alfred Starr 1914- ... 53-56
Hamilton, Alice
See Cromie, Alice Hamilton
Hamilton, B(ertram) L(awson) St. John
1914- ... 15-16R
Hamilton, Beth Alleman 1927- ... 110
Hamilton, (Arthur Douglas) Bruce
1900-1974 Obituary ... 109
Hamilton, Buzz
See Hemming, Roy
Hamilton, Carl 1914- ... 53-56
Hamilton, Carlos D. 1908- ... 69-72
Hamilton, Charles 1913- ... CANR-20
Earlier sketches in CA 7-8R, CANR-3
Hamilton, Charles D(aniel) 1940-
Brief entry ... 112
Hamilton, Charles F(ranklin) 1915- ... 89-92
Hamilton, Charles Granville
1905-1984 ... CANR-15
Earlier sketch in CA 41-44R
Hamilton, Charles Harold St. John
1875-1961 ... 73-76
See also SATA 13
Hamilton, Charles Vernon 1929- ... 77-80
Hamilton, Charles W(alter) 1890- ... 7-8R
Hamilton, Cicely (Mary) 1872-1952
Brief entry ... 113
See also DLB 10
Hamilton, Clare
See Lawless, Bettyclare Hamilton
Hamilton, Clive
See Lewis, C(live) S(taples)
Hamilton, Dave
See Troyer, Byron L(eRoy)
Hamilton, David (Boyce, Jr.) 1918- ... 29-32R
Hamilton, David (Peter) 1935- ... 119
Hamilton, David 1939- ... 126
Hamilton, (Charles) Denis 1918-1988 ... 109
Obituary ... 125
Hamilton, Donald (Bengtsson) 1916- ... CANR-18
Earlier sketches in CA 4R, CANR-2
Hamilton, Dorothy (Drumm) 1906-1983 ... 33-36R
Obituary ... 110
See also SATA 12, 35
Hamilton, Earl J(efferson) 1899- ... CAP-1
Earlier sketch in CA 9-10
Hamilton, Edith 1867-1963 ... 77-80
See also SATA 20
Hamilton, Edmond 1904-1977 ... CANR-3
Earlier sketch in CA 2R
See also DLB 8
See also CLC 1
Hamilton, Edward G. 1897- ... CAP-1
Earlier sketch in CA 11-12
Hamilton, Eleanor Poorman 1909- ... CANR-2
Earlier sketch in CA 1R
Hamilton, (Muriel) Elizabeth (Mollie)
1906- ... CAP-1
Earlier sketch in CA 9-10
See also SATA 23
Hamilton, Elizabeth 1928- ... 97-100
Hamilton, Ernest
See Merril, Judith
Hamilton, Eugene (Jacob) Lee
See Lee-Hamilton, Eugene (Jacob)
Hamilton, Floyd (Garland) 1908(?)-1984
Obituary ... 113
Hamilton, Franklin
See Silverberg, Robert
Hamilton, Franklin Willard 1923- ... 33-36R
Hamilton, Gail
See Corcoran, Barbara
Hamilton, Gene 1943- ... 120
Hamilton, George Baillie
See Baillie-Hamilton, George
Hamilton, George Rostrevor 1888-1967
Obituary ... 93-96
Hamilton, Hamish 1900-1988 Obituary ... 125
Hamilton, Henry W. 1898- ... 33-36R
Hamilton, Hervey
See Robins, Denise (Naomi)
Hamilton, Holman 1910-1980 ... CANR-10
Obituary ... 97-100
Earlier sketch in CA 13-14R
Hamilton, Horace E(rnst) 1911- ... 21-22R
Hamilton, Howard Devon 1920- ... 13-14R
Hamilton, (Robert) Ian 1938- ... 106
See also DLB 40
Hamilton, J(ames) A(lan) B(ousfield)
1899-1971 Obituary ... 116
Hamilton, J(ames) Wallace 1900-1968 ... CAP-1
Earlier sketch in CA 13-14
Hamilton, Jack
See Brannon, William T.
Hamilton, James Robertson 1921- ... 103
Hamilton, Janet 1951- ... 114
Hamilton, Jean Tyree 1909- ... 33-36R
Hamilton, Joan Lesley 1942- ... 102
Hamilton, John
See Hayden, Sterling
Hamilton, John Maxwell 1947- ... 121
Hamilton, Julia
See Watson, Julia
Hamilton, Katie 1945- ... 118
Hamilton, Kay
See DeLeeuw, Cateau
Hamilton, Kenneth (Morrison) 1917- ... 17-18R
Hamilton, Marshall Lee 1937- ... 37-40R
Hamilton, Mary (E.) 1927- ... 123
Hamilton, Michael (Pollock) 1927- ... 29-32R
Hamilton, Milton W(heaton) 1901- ... CAP-1
Earlier sketch in CA 15-16
Hamilton, Mollie
See Kaye, M(ary) M(argaret)
Hamilton, Morse 1943- ... 108
See also SATA 35
Hamilton, Nancy 1908-1985 Obituary ... 115
Hamilton, Neill Q. 1925- ... 61-64
Hamilton, (Charles) Nigel 1944- ... 101
Hamilton, (Anthony Walter) Patrick
1904-1962 Obituary ... 113
See also DLB 10
Hamilton, Patrick Macfarlan 1892-1977
Obituary ... 108
Hamilton, Paul
See Dennis-Jones, H(arold)
Hamilton, Peter (Edward) 1947- ... 73-76
Hamilton, Raphael N(oteware) 1892- ... CAP-2
Earlier sketch in CA 29-32
Hamilton, Richard 1922- Brief entry ... 116
Hamilton, Richard F(rederick) 1930- ... CANR-26
Earlier sketch in CA 108
Hamilton, Robert W. ... CANR-26
Earlier sketches in CA 19-20, CAP-2
Hamilton, Ronald 1909- ... 15-16R
Hamilton, Russell G(eorge) 1934- ... 61-64
Hamilton, Seena M. 1926- ... 17-18R
Hamilton, Virginia 1936- ... CANR-20
Earlier sketch in CA 25-28R
See also BW
See also SATA 4
See also DLB 33, 52
See also CLC 26
See also CLR 1, 11
Hamilton, W(illiam) B(askerville)
1908-1972 ... CAP-1
Obituary ... 37-40R
Earlier sketch in CA 17-18
Hamilton, W(illis) D(avid) 1936- ... 105
Hamilton, Wade
See Floren, Lee
Hamilton, Wallace 1919-1983 ... CANR-15
Obituary ... 110
Earlier sketch in CA 85-88
Hamilton, Walter 1908-1988 ... 109
Obituary ... 124
Hamilton, William 1939- ... CANR-15
Earlier sketch in CA 69-72
Hamilton, William B(aillie) 1930- ... 102
Hamilton, William, Jr. 1924- ... 53-56
Hamilton-Edwards, Gerald (Kenneth Savery)
1906- ... CANR-14
Earlier sketch in CA 21-22R
Hamilton-Hill, Donald 1915-1985 Obituary ... 117
Hamizrachi, Yoram 1942- ... 107
Hamlet, Ova
See Lupoff, Richard A(llen)
Hamley, Dennis 1935- ... CANR-26
Earlier sketches in CA 57-60, CANR-11
See also SATA 39
Hamlin, Charles Hughes 1907- ... 69-72
Hamlin, Gladys E(va) ... 37-40R
Hamlin, Griffith Askew 1919- ... 37-40R
Hamlin, Marjorie (Day) 1921- ... 105
Hamlin, Wilfrid G(ardiner) 1918- ... 93-96
Hamm, Charles Edward 1925- ... 103
Hamm, Cleve 1927(?)-1984 Obituary ... 112
Hamm, Edward Frederick, Jr. 1908-1985
Obituary ... 115
Hamm, Glenn B(ruce) 1936-1980 ... 53-56
Obituary ... 125
Hamm, Jack 1916- ... CANR-9
Earlier sketch in CA 7-8R
Hamm, Marie Roberson 1917- ... 65-68
Hamm, Michael Franklin 1943- ... 89-92
Hamm, Robert M(acGowan) 1950- ... 116
Hamm, Russell Leroy 1926- ... CANR-2
Earlier sketch in CA 7-8R
Hammack, David C(onrad) 1941- ... 115
Hammack, James W., Jr. 1937- ... 81-84
Hamman, Henry (Longley) 1946- ... 119
Hamman, Ray T(racy) 1945- ... 69-72
Hammar, Russell A(lfred) 1920- ... 104
Hammarskjoeld, Dag (Hjalmar Agne Carl)
1905-1961 ... 77-80
Hammarskjold, Dag
See Hammarskjoeld, Dag (Hjalmar Ange
Carl)
Hammel, Eric M(axwell) 1946- ... 107
Hammel, Faye 1929- ... CANR-5
Earlier sketch in CA 3R
Hammen, Carl Schlee 1923- ... 53-56
Hammen, Oscar J(ohn) 1907- ... CAP-2
Earlier sketch in CA 25-28
Hammer, Carl, Jr. 1910- ... 53-56
Hammer, David Harry 1893(?)-1978
Obituary ... 81-84
Hammer, Emanuel F(rederick) 1926- ... 29-32R
Hammer, Jacob
See Oppenheimer, Joel (Lester)
Hammer, Jeanne-Ruth 1912- ... 9-10R
Hammer, Jefferson J(oseph) 1933- ... 41-44R
Hammer, Kenneth M. 1918- ... 85-88
Hammer, Richard 1928- ... CANR-11
Earlier sketch in CA 25-28R
See also SATA 6
Hammer, Signe ... 102
Hammerman, Donald R. 1925- ... 15-16R
Hammerman, Gay M(orenus) 1926- ... 33-36R
See also SATA 9
Hammerstein, Oscar (Greeley Glendenning)
II 1895-1960 ... 101
Hammes, John A(nthony) 1924- ... 13-14R
Hammes, Tobi Gillian Sanders
1948(?)-1987 Obituary ... 122
Hammett, (Samuel) Dashiell 1894-1961 ... 81-84
See also CLC 3, 5, 10, 19, 47
See also AITN 1
Hammick, Georgina 1939- ... 126
Hammil, Joel 1909- ... 114
Hamming, Richard W. 1915- ... 57-60
Hammon, Jupiter 1711-? ... DLB-31, 50
Hammond, Albert L(anphier) 1892-1970 ... 4R
Obituary ... 103
Hammond, Antony Derek 1938- ... 114
Hammond, Brean S(imon) 1951- ... 119
Hammond, Charles Montgomery, Jr.
1922- ... 106
Hammond, Dorothy 1924- ... 69-72
Hammond, Edwin Hughes 1919- ... 13-14R
Hammond, Gerald (Arthur Douglas) 1926- ... 107
Hammond, Guyton B(owers) 1930- ... 17-18R
Hammond, J(ames) D(illard) 1933- ... CANR-22
Earlier sketch in CA 45-48
Hammond, Jane
See Poland, Dorothy (Elizabeth Hayward)
Hammond, John (Henry, Jr.) 1910-1987 ... 106
Obituary ... 123
Hammond, John ?-1663 ... DLB-24
Hammond, Keith
See Kuttner, Henry
Hammond, Laurence ... 104
Hammond, Lawrence 1925- ... 81-84
Hammond, Mac (Sawyer) 1926- ... 19-20R
Hammond, Mason 1903- ... 65-68
Hammond, N(icholas) G(eoffrey)
L(empriere) 1907- ... CANR-21
Earlier sketches in CA 13-14R, CANR-5
Hammond, Norman 1944- ... CANR-19
Earlier sketches in CA 49-52, CANR-3
Hammond, Paul 1947- ... 57-60
Hammond, Paul Y(oung) 1929- ... CANR-2
Earlier sketch in CA 4R
Hammond, Peter B(oyd) 1928- ... 69-72
Hammond, Philip C. 1924- ... 5-6R
Hammond, Phillip E(verett) 1931- ... CANR-7
Earlier sketch in CA 19-20R
Hammond, Ralph
See Hammond Innes, Ralph
Hammond, Richard J(ames) 1911-1982 ... 61-64
Obituary ... 122
Hammond, Ross W(illiam) 1918- ... 33-36R
Hammond, Thomas T(aylor) 1920- ... 9-10R
Hammond, W(illiam) Rogers 1920- ... 45-48
Hammond, Winifred G(raham) 1899- ... 107
See also SATA 29
Hammond Innes, Ralph 1913- ... CANR-26
Earlier sketches in CA 5-6R, CANR-4
Hammonds, Michael (Galen) 1942- ... 45-48
Hammontree, Marie (Gertrude) 1913- ... 5-6R
See also SATA 13
Hamner, Earl (Henry), Jr. 1923- ... 73-76
See also DLB 6
See also CLC 12
See also AITN 2
Hamner, Robert Daniel 1941- ... 106
Hamod, (Hamode) Sam(uel) 1936- ... CANR-22
Earlier sketch in CA 45-48
Hamori, Laszlo Dezso 1911- ... 9-10R
Hamovitch, Mitzi Berger 1924- ... 112

INDEX

Hamp, Eric P(ratt) 1920- 17-18R
Hampden, John 1898- 109
Hampden-Turner, Charles M. 1934- 33-36R
Hampl, Patricia 1946- CANR-21
Earlier sketch in CA 104
Hample, Stuart 1926- 108
Hampsch, George H(arold) 1927- 15-16R
Hampshire, Joyce Gregorian
See Gregorian, Joyce Ballou
Hampshire, Stuart (Newton) 1914-
Brief entry 116
Hampshire, Susan 1942- Brief entry 112
Hampson, Anne 117
Brief entry 111
Hampson, (Richard) Denman 1929- SATA-15
Hampson, Frank 1918(?)-1985 Obituary 117
See also SATA 46
Hampson, Norman 1922- 25-28R
Hampson, Zena 1926- CANR-19
Earlier sketches in CA 4R, CANR-3
Hampton, Christopher 1929- CANR-4
Earlier sketch in CA 53-56
Hampton, Christopher (James) 1946- 25-28R
See also DLB 13
See also CLC 4
Hampton, David
See Fairclough, Chris
Hampton, David R(ichard) 1933- 81-84
Hampton, H(arold) Duane 1932- 33-36R
Hampton, Kathleen 1923- 4R
Hampton, Mark
See Norwood, Victor G(eorge) C(harles)
Hampton, Robert E. 1924- 33-36R
Hampton, William (Albert) 1929- CANR-13
Earlier sketch in CA 33-36R
Hamre, Leif 1914- CANR-4
Earlier sketch in CA 5-6R
See also SATA 5
Hamrick, Samuel J., Jr. 1929- 120
Brief entry 115
Hams, Thomas M., Jr. 1928- 11-12R
Hamsa, Bobbie 1944- 106
See also SATA 38, 52
Hamscher, Albert N(elson) 1946- 73-76
Hamsher, J. Herbert 1938- 57-60
Hamshere, Cyril (Eric) 1912- 41-44R
Hamson, C. J.
See Hamson, Charles John
Hamson, Charles John 1905-1987
Obituary 124
Hamsun, Knut
See Pedersen, Knut
See also TCLC 2, 14
Hamsund, Knut Pedersen
See Pedersen, Knut
Han, Henry H. 1932- 125
Han, Seung Soo 1936- CANR-2
Earlier sketch in CA 45-48
Han, Sungjoo 1940- 53-56
Han, Suyin 1917- 19-20R
Hanagan, Eva (Helen) 1923- 101
Hanagan, Michael Patrick 1947- 109
Hanaghan, Jonathan 1887-1967 65-68
Hanami, Tadashi (Akamatsu) 1930- 89-92
Hanan, Patrick Dewes 1927- 106
Hanau, Laia 1916- 89-92
Hanawalt, Barbara A(nn) 1941- 101
Hanbury, Victor
See Losey, Joseph (Walton)
Hanbury-Tenison, Marika 1938-1982 104
Obituary 108
Hanbury-Tenison, (Airling) Robin 1936- 57-60
Hance, Kenneth G(ordon) 1903- 85-88
Hance, William A(dams) 1916- 11-12R
Hanchett, William 1922- 33-36R
Hancock, Alice Van Fossen 1890- 2R
Hancock, Carla 89-92
Hancock, Carol Helen Brooks
See Hancock, Morgan
Hancock, Edward L(eslie) 1930- CANR-1
Earlier sketch in CA 45-48
Hancock, Geoffrey 1946- CANR-19
Earlier sketch in CA 101
Hancock, Harold B(ell) 1913- 53-56
Hancock, Joy Bright 1898-1986 Obituary 120
Hancock, Keith
See Hancock, W(illiam) K(eith)
Hancock, Leslie 1941- 23-24R
Hancock, Lyn 1938- 77-80
Hancock, M. Donald 1939- 33-36R
Hancock, Malcolm 1936- 25-28R
Hancock, Mary A. 1923- 37-40R
See also SATA 31
Hancock, Maxine 1942- CANR-8
Earlier sketch in CA 61-64
Hancock, Morgan 1941- 103
Hancock, Niel Anderson 1941- CANR-21
Earlier sketch in CA 97-100
Hancock, Ralph Lowell 1903- CAP-1
Earlier sketch in CA 9-10
Hancock, Roger Nelson 1929- 97-100
Hancock, Sheila 1942- 49-52
Hancock, Sibyl 1940- CANR-16
Earlier sketches in CA 49-52, CANR-1
See also SATA 9
Hancock, Taylor 1920- 97-100
Hancock, W(illiam) K(eith) 1898-1988 .... CANR-5
Obituary 126
Earlier sketch in CA 7-8R
Hand, G(eoffrey) J(oseph Philip Macaulay)
1931- 25-28R
Hand, J(oan) C(arole) 1943- 57-60
Hand, (Andrus) Jackson 1913- CANR-10
Earlier sketch in CA 61-64
Hand, John
See Pierson, John H(erman) G(roesbeck)
Hand, Thomas A(lypius) 1915- 13-14R
Hand, Wayland D(ebs) 1907-1986 .... 41-44R
Obituary 120
Handel, Gerald 1924- CANR-11
Earlier sketch in CA 23-24R
Handelman, Howard 1943- 57-60
Handelman, John R(obert) 1948- 77-80
Handelsman, Judith Florence 1948- 61-64
Handforth, Thomas (Schofield) 1897-1948
Brief entry 120
See also SATA 42
Handke, Peter 1942- 77-80
See also CLC 5, 8, 10, 15, 38
Handl, Irene 1902(?)-1987 103
Obituary 124
Handler, Jerome S(idney) 1933- 53-56
Handler, Joel F. 1932- Brief entry 113
Handler, Julian Harris 1922- 21-22R
Handler, Meyer Srednick 1905-1978
Obituary 77-80
Handler, Milton 1903- 61-64
Handler, Philip 1917-1981 .... 33-36R
Obituary 105
Handley, Graham Roderick 1926- CANR-24
Earlier sketch in CA 105
Handley-Taylor, Geoffrey 1920- CANR-7
Earlier sketch in CA 7-8R
Handlin, Mary (Flug) 1913-1976 .... CAP-2
Obituary 65-68
Earlier sketch in CA 33-36
Handlin, Oscar 1915- CANR-23
Earlier sketches in CA 3R, CANR-5
See also DLB 17
Handman, Herbert Ira 1932- 89-92
Handover, P(hyllis) M(argaret)
1923(?)-1974 .... 9-10R
Obituary 53-56
Handscombe, Richard 1935- 37-40R
Handville, Robert (Tompkins) 1924- SATA-45
Handy, Edward Smith Craighill
1893(?)-1980 Obituary 102
Handy, Robert T(heodore) 1918- CANR-2
Earlier sketch in CA 7-8R
Handy, Rollo 1927- 11-12R
Handy, Toni 1930- 97-100
Handy, W(illiam) C(hristopher) 1873-1958
Brief entry 121
Handy, William J. 1918- 45-48
Hane, Mikiso 1922- CANR-15
Earlier sketch in CA 81-84
Hane, Roger 1940-1974 .... SATA-20
Hanenkrat, Frank (Thomas) 1939- 93-96
Haner, F(rederick) T(heodore) 1929- 53-56
Hanes, Bailey C(ass) 1915- 77-80
Hanes, Elizabeth Sill 2R
Hanes, Frank Borden 1920- 1R
Hanes, Mary (a pseudonym) 1940(?)-
Brief entry 117
Haney, David P. 1938- CANR-21
Earlier sketches in CA 57-60, CANR-6
Haney, Eleanor H(umes) 1931- Brief entry 114
Haney, John B. 1931- 29-32R
Haney, Lynn 1941- CANR-1
Earlier sketch in CA 49-52
See also SATA 23
Haney, Thomas K. 1936- 15-16R
Haney, Thomas R. 45-48
Haney, William V. 1925- 17-18R
Hanff, Helene CANR-3
Earlier sketch in CA 7-8R
See also SATA 11
Hanfmann, George M(axim) A(nossov)
1911-1986 Obituary 118
Brief entry 117
Hanford, Lloyd D(avid) 1901-1979 .... CANR-11
Earlier sketch in CA 15-16R
Hanford, S. A. 1898-1978 Obituary 81-84
Hang, T(ing-)Y(ung) 1908(?)-1987
Obituary 122
Hangen, (Putnam) Welles 1930- 9-10R
Hanifi, M(ohammed) Jamil 1935- 61-64
Hanigan, James Patrick 1938- 125
Haning, Bob
See Haning, James R(obert)
Haning, James R(obert) 1928- CANR-2
Earlier sketch in CA 45-48
Hanke, Howard August 1911- 1R
Hanke, Lewis (Ulysses) 1905- 65-68
Hankey, Cyril Patrick 1886-1973 .... 4R
Obituary 103
Hankey, Rosalie A.
See Wax, Rosalie (Amelia) H.
Hankey, Roy 1932- 108
Hankin, (Edward Charles) St. John (Emile
Clavering) 1869-1909 Brief entry 110
See also DLB 10
Hankins, Clabe
See McDonald, Erwin L(awrence)
Hankins, Frank Hamilton 1877-1970
Obituary 104
Hankins, John Erskine 1905- 49-52
Hankins, Norman E(lijah) 1935- CANR-11
Earlier sketch in CA 61-64
Hankins, Thomas Leroy 1933- 108
Hankinson, Cyril (Francis James) 1895- CAP-1
Earlier sketch in CA 9-10
Hankla, Cathryn 1958- 116
Hanks, Lucien M(ason) 1910- 37-40R
Hanks, Stedman Shumway 1889-1979
Obituary 85-88
Hanle, Dorothea Zack 1917- 13-14R
Hanley, Boniface Francis 1924- 9-10R
Hanley, Clifford 1922- CANR-23
Earlier sketches in CA 9-10R, CANR-3
See also DLB 14
Hanley, Elizabeth
See Du Breuil, (Elizabeth) L(or)inda
Hanley, Evelyn A(lice) 1916-1980 .... 41-44R
Obituary 97-100
Hanley, Gerald (Anthony) 1916- CANR-6
Earlier sketch in CA 3R
Hanley, Hope Anthony 1926- CANR-5
Earlier sketch in CA 11-12R
Hanley, James 1901-1985 73-76
Obituary 117
See also CLC 3, 5, 8, 13
Hanley, Katharine Rose 1932- 37-40R
Hanley, Michael F. IV 1941- 65-68
Hanley, Mike
See Hanley, Michael F. IV
Hanley, Theodore Dean 1917- 7-8R
Hanley, Thomas O'Brien 1918- CANR-1
Earlier sketch in CA 1R
Hanley, William 1931- 41-44R
Hanlon, Emily 1945- 77-80
See also SATA 15
Hanlon, John J(oseph) 1912- 57-60
Hanmer, Davina
See Courtney, Nicholas (Piers)
Hann, C. M. 1953- 121
Hann, Jacquie 1951- CANR-13
Earlier sketch in CA 73-76
See also SATA 19
Hanna, Alfred Jackson 1893-1978 .... CANR-2
Earlier sketch in CA 45-48
Hanna, Bill
See Hanna, William
Hanna, David 1917- CANR-6
Earlier sketch in CA 57-60
Hanna, Frank A(llan) 1907-1978 Obituary 111
Hanna, J. Marshall 1907- CANR-24
Earlier sketch in CA 1R
Hanna, John Paul 1932- CANR-1
Earlier sketch in CA 45-48
Hanna, Lavone Agnes 1896- 13-14R
Hanna, Mary Carr 1905- 45-48
Hanna, Mary T. 1935- 97-100
Hanna, Paul R(obert) 1902- 45-48
See also SATA 9
Hanna, S(uhail) S(alim) 1943- 126
Hanna, Thomas 1928- CANR-1
Earlier sketch in CA 1R
Hanna, William 1910- SATA-51
Hanna, William John 1931- CANR-8
Earlier sketch in CA 61-64
Hannaford, John 1918- 45-48
Hannah, (Juliel) Barbara 1891- 97-100
Hannah, Barry 1942- 110
Brief entry 108
See also DLB 6
See also CLC 23, 38
Hannak, Johann Jacques 1892- CAP-1
Earlier sketch in CA 9-10
Hannam, Charles 1925- CANR-11
Earlier sketch in CA 61-64
See also SATA 50
Hannan, Joseph F(rancis) 1923- CANR-3
Earlier sketch in CA 9-10R
Hannas, Linda 1913- 113
Hannau, Hans W(alter) 1904- CANR-10
Earlier sketch in CA 23-24R
Hannavy, John Michael 1946- CANR-11
Earlier sketch in CA 69-72
Hannaway, Patricia H(inman) 1929- 61-64
Hannaway, Patti
See Hannaway, Patricia H(inman)
Hannay, Allen 1946- 109
Hannay, Doris Fergusson
See Fergusson Hannay, Doris
Hannay, James 1827-1873 .... DLB-21
Hannay, Margaret Patterson 1944- CANR-21
Earlier sketch in CA 104
Hanneman, Audre (Louise) 1926- 23-24R
Hanney, Peter 1930-1976 Obituary 105
Hannibal
See Alexander, Stanley Walter
Hannibal, Edward 1936- 29-32R
Hannifin, Jerry (Bernard) 1917- 77-80
Hanning, Hugh 1925- 25-28R
Hanning, Robert William 1938- 93-96
Hannula, Reino 1918- 105
Hannum, Alberta Pierson 1906-1985 65-68
Obituary 115
Hano, Arnold 1922- CANR-5
Earlier sketch in CA 9-10R
See also SATA 12
Hanrahan, Barbara 1939- Brief entry 121
Hanrahan, John D(avid) 1938- CANR-15
Earlier sketch in CA 77-80
Hanrieder, Wolfram F. 1931- CANR-23
Earlier sketches in CA 23-24R, CANR-8
Hans, Valerie P(atricia) 1951- 126
Hansberry, Lorraine (Vivian) 1930-1965 109
Obituary 25-28R
See also BW
See also DLB 7, 38
See also CDALB 1941-1968
See also CLC 17
Hansel, C(harles) E(dward) M(ark) 1917-
Brief entry 115
Hansel, Robert R(aymond) 1936-
Brief entry 110
Hansell, Antonina
See Looker, Antonina (Hansell)
Hansen, Al(fred Earl) 1927- 19-20R
Hansen, Alvin H(arvey) 1887-1975 .... CAP-1
Obituary 57-60
Earlier sketch in CA 15-16
Hansen, Bertrand Lyle 1922- 9-10R
Hansen, Carl (Francis) 1906-1983 .... CANR-2
Obituary 110
Earlier sketch in CA 5-6R
Hansen, Carol
See Fenichel, Carol Hansen
Hansen, Caryl (Hall) 1929- 108
See also SATA 39
Hansen, Cecil
See Huffaker, Clair
Hansen, Cecil Dan
See Huffaker, Clair
Hansen, Chadwick (Clarke) 1926- 29-32R
Hansen, Donald A(ndrew) 1933- 73-76
Hansen, Donald Charles 1935- 33-36R
Hansen, Emmanuel 1937- 104
Hansen, Flemming 1938- 93-96
Hansen, Forest Warnyr 1931- 45-48
Hansen, Gary B(arker) 1935- CANR-21
Earlier sketches in CA 11-12R, CANR-3
Hansen, Harry 1884-1977 73-76
Obituary 69-72
Hansen, Joseph 1923- CANR-16
Earlier sketch in CA 29-32R
See also CLC 38
Hansen, Joyce 1942- 105
See also SATA 39, 46
Hansen, Kenneth H(arvey) 1917- 13-14R
Hansen, Klaus J(uergen) 1931- 21-22R
Hansen, Mary Lewis (Patterson) 1933- 17-18R
Hansen, Niles M(aurice) 1937- CANR-13
Earlier sketch in CA 25-28R
Hansen, Norman J. 1918- 29-32R
Hansen, Richard H(erbert) 1929- 4R
Hansen, Rodney Thor 1940- 53-56
Hansen, Roger D(ennis) 1935- 105
Hansen, Ron 1947- CANR-17
Earlier sketch in CA 89-92
Hansen, Rosanna 1947- 105
Hansen, Terrence Leslie 1920-1974 .... 37-40R
Hansen, W(illiam) Lee 1928- 29-32R
Hansen, William F(reeman) 1941- 49-52
Hanser, Richard (Frederick) 1909-1981 .... CANR-8
Earlier sketch in CA 5-6R
See also SATA 13
Hanshew, Thomas W. 1857-1914
Brief entry 113
Hansi
See Hirschmann, Maria Anne
Hanson, A(lbert) H(enry) 1913-1971 .... CANR-4
Obituary 89-92
Earlier sketch in CA 7-8R
Hanson, Agnes O(lin) 1905- 107
Hanson, Anne Coffin 1921- 23-24R
Hanson, Anthony Tyrrell 1916- CANR-24
Earlier sketches in CA 23-24R, CANR-9
Hanson, Dirk 1950- 111
Hanson, E(ugene) Kenneth 1930- 13-14R
Hanson, Earl D(orchester) 1927- CANR-12
Earlier sketch in CA 73-76
Hanson, Earl Parker 1899-1978 .... 41-44R
Hanson, Eric O. 1942- 125
Hanson, F(ridolf) Allan 1939- 41-44R
Hanson, Harvey 1941- 65-68
Hanson, Howard (Harold) 1896-1981
Obituary 103
Hanson, Howard Gordon 1931- 23-24R
Hanson, Irene (Forsythe) 1898- 49-52
Hanson, Isabel 1929- 106
Hanson, James Arthur 1940- 49-52
Hanson, Jim 1953- 97-100
Hanson, Joan 1938- CANR-15
Earlier sketch in CA 33-36R
See also SATA 8
Hanson, Joseph E. 1894(?)-1971
Obituary 104
See also SATA 27
Hanson, June Andrea 1941- 97-100
Hanson, Kenneth O(stlin) 1922- CANR-7
Earlier sketch in CA 53-56
See also CLC 13
Hanson, Kristine 1958- 123
Hanson, Michael James 1942- 61-64
Hanson, Norwood Russell 1924-1967 .... CANR-8
Earlier sketch in CA 7-8R
Hanson, Paul D(avid) 1939- 61-64
Hanson, Pauline 45-48
Hanson, Peggy 1934- CANR-12
Earlier sketch in CA 29-32R
Hanson, Philip 1936- 103
Hanson, R(ichard) P(atrick) C(rosland)
1916- CANR-9
Earlier sketch in CA 23-24R
Hanson, Richard S(imon) 1931- 37-40R
Hanson, Robert Carl 1926- 37-40R
Hanson, Robert P(aul) 1918- 11-12R
Hanson, Ruth Katie 1900- 7-8R
Hanson, Simon
See Hanson, Richard S(imon)
Hanson, William S(tewart) 1950- 123
Hansten, Philip D. 1943- 33-36R
Hanushek, Eric Alan 1943- 41-44R
Hanzlicek, C(harles) G(eorge) 1942- CANR-12
Earlier sketch in CA 73-76
Hao, Qian
See Qian Hao
Hao, Yen-ping 1934- 53-56
Hapgood, Charles Hutchins 1904- 19-20R
Hapgood, David 1926- 15-16R
Hapgood, Fred 1942- 93-96
Hapgood, Ruth K(nott) 1920- 49-52
Happe, Peter 1932- 45-48
Happel, Robert A. 1916- 2R
Happel, Stephen 1944- 114
Happold, F(rederick) C(rossfield) 1893- 101
Haq, Mahbub ul 1934- 15-16R
Harald, Eric
See Boesen, Victor
Haraldsson, Erlendur 1931- 101
Harap, Henry 1893-1981 Obituary 104
Harap, Louis 1904- 57-60
Harari, Ehud 1935- 65-68
Harary, Keith 1953- 120

Harary, Stuart Blue
See Harary, Keith
Harasymiw, Bohdan 1936- 124
Haraway, Donna Jeanne 1944- 73-76
Harbach, Otto (Abels) 1873-1963
Obituary 112
Harbage, Alfred (Bennett) 1901-1976 CANR-5
Obituary 65-68
Earlier sketch in CA 5-6R
Harbaugh, John W(arvelle) 1926- 49-52
Harbaugh, William Henry 1920- 1R
Harberger, Arnold C. 1924- CANR-6
Earlier sketch in CA 15-16R
Harbert, Earl N(orman) 1934- CANR-13
Earlier sketch in CA 33-36R
Harbert, Mary Ann 1945- 61-64
Harbeson, Georgiana Brown 1894(?)-1980
Obituary 101
Harbeson, Gladys Evans 21-22R
Harbeson, John Willis 1938- 57-60
Harbin, Calvin E(dward) 1916- 23-24R
Harbin, Robert
See Williams, Ned
Harbinson, Robert
See Bryans, Robert Harbinson
Harbinson, W(illiam) A(llen) 1941- CANR-25
Earlier sketches in CA 61-64, CANR-9
Harbison, Frederick Harris 1912-1976
Obituary 65-68
Harbison, Peter 1939- 65-68
Harbison, Robert 1940- 102
Harbottle, Michael (Neale) 1917- 29-32R
Harbron, John D(avison) 1924- 11-12R
Harburg, E(dgar) Y(ipsel) 1896-1981 85-88
Obituary 103
Harburg, Yip
See Harburg, E(dgar) Y(ipsel)
Harbury, Colin (Desmond) 1922- 102
Harcave, Sidney S(amuel) 1916- 19-20R
Harcleroad, Fred F(arley) 1918- CANR-23
Earlier sketches in CA 19-20R, CANR-8
Harcourt, Ellen Knowles 1890(?)-1984
Obituary 111
See also SATA 36
Harcourt, G(eoffrey) C(olin) 1931- CANR-16
Earlier sketch in CA 25-28R
Harcourt, Melville 1909- 7-8R
Harcourt, Palma CANR-14
Earlier sketch in CA 77-80
Harcourt, Peter 1931- 81-84
Hard, Edward W(ilhelm), Jr. 1939- 85-88
Hard, Frederick 1897- CAP-2
Earlier sketch in CA 25-28
Hard, Margaret (Steel) 1888(?)-1974
Obituary 49-52
Hard, T. W.
See Hard, Edward W(ilhelm), Jr.
Hard, Walter (Rice) 1882-1966 Obituary 116
Hardach, Gerd 1941- 105
Hardaway, Francine 1941- 81-84
Hardcastle, Michael 1933- CANR-12
Earlier sketch in CA 25-28R
See also SATA 38, 47
Harden, Donald B(enjamin) 1901- 5-6R
Harden, Edgar F(rederick) 1932- 123
Harden, Ian (John) 1954- 126
Harden, Oleta Elizabeth (McWhorter)
1935- 37-40R
Harden, (John) William 1903- 93-96
Harder, Eleanor (Loraine) 1925- 37-40R
Harder, Geraldine Gross 1926- 53-56
Harder, Raymond Wymbs, Jr. 1920- 85-88
Hardesty, Nancy A(nn) 1941- CANR-23
Earlier sketches in CA 57-60, CANR-8
Hardesty, Sarah 1951- 126
Hardesty, Von 1939- 112
Hardgrave, Robert L(ewis), Jr. 1939- CANR-11
Earlier sketch in CA 25-28R
Hardie, Frank 1911- 33-36R
Hardiman, James W. 1919- 33-36R
Hardin, Charles M(eyer) 1908- 49-52
Hardin, Clement
See Newton, D(wight) B(ennett)
Hardin, Garrett James 1915- CANR-9
Earlier sketch in CA 17-18R
Hardin, J. D.
See Riefe, Alan
and Sheldon, Walter J.
Hardin, James N(eal) 1939- 114
Hardin, Paul III 1931- 25-28R
Hardin, Peter
See Vaczek, Louis
Hardin, Richard F(rancis) 1937- 45-48
Hardin, Robert 1934- 77-80
Hardin, Tim 1941(?)-1981 Obituary 102
Hardin, Tom
See Bauer, Erwin A.
Hardin, Wes
See Keevill, Henry J(ohn)
Harding, A(nthony) F(ilmer) 1946- 77-80
Harding, Barbara 1926- 41-44R
Harding, Bertita (Leonarz de) 1902- 5-6R
Harding, Carl B.
See Barker, Elver A.
Harding, D(ouglas) E(dison) 1909-
Brief entry 116
Harding, D(enys Clement) W(yatt)
1906- CANR-16
Earlier sketches in CA 15-16, CAP-1
Harding, D(ennis) W(illiam) 1940- 41-44R
Harding, Davis P. 1915(?)-1970 Obituary 104
Harding, Donald Edward 1916- CANR-4
Earlier sketch in CA 53-56
Harding, Harold F(riend) 1903- 37-40R
Harding, Harry (Jr.) 1946- 109
Harding, Jack 1914- 29-32R
Harding, James 1929- CANR-14
Earlier sketch in CA 33-36R
Harding, John 1948- 97-100
Harding, Kenneth
See Little, Paul H(ugo)
Harding, Lee 1937- 106
See also SATA 31, 32
Harding, Maria
See Goudiss, Maria Agnes D'Elia
Harding, Matt
See Floren, Lee
Harding, Matthew Whitman
See Floren, Lee
Harding, Neil 1942- 125
Harding, Peter
See Burgess, M(ichael) R(oy)
Harding, Sandra G. 1935- 120
Harding, Susan Friend 1946- 126
Harding, T(imothy) D. 1948- 85-88
Harding, Thomas G(rayson) 1937- 21-22R
Harding, Virginia Hamlet 1909- 45-48
Harding, Walter Roy 1917- CANR-17
Earlier sketches in CA 1R, CANR-1
Harding, Wes
See Keevill, Henry J(ohn)
Harding, William Harry 1945- 93-96
Hardinge, Helen (Mary Cecil) 1901- CAP-2
Earlier sketch in CA 29-32
Hardingham, John (Frederick Watson)
1916- CAP-1
Earlier sketch in CA 11-12
Hardison, O(sborne) B(ennett, Jr.)
1928- CANR-6
Earlier sketch in CA 5-6R
Hardman, John (David) 1944- 45-48
Hardman, Keith (Jordan) 1931- 116
Hardman, Richards Lynden 1924- 15-16R
Hardon, John A(nthony) 1914- CANR-2
Earlier sketch in CA 2R
Hardoy, Jorge Enrique 1926- 33-36R
Hardt, Helga Fleischhauer
See Fleischhauer-Hardt, Helga
Hardt, J(ohn) Pearce 1922- CANR-3
Earlier sketch in CA 5-6R
Hardwick, Adam
See Connor, John Anthony
Hardwick, Clyde T(homas) 1915- 5-6R
Hardwick, Elizabeth 1916- CANR-3
Earlier sketch in CA 7-8R
See also DLB 6
See also CLC 13
Hardwick, Homer
See Rogers, Paul (Patrick)
Hardwick, (John) Michael (Drinkrow)
1924- CANR-2
Earlier sketch in CA 49-52
Hardwick, Mollie CANR-2
Earlier sketch in CA 49-52
Hardwick, Richard Holmes, Jr. 1923- CANR-9
Earlier sketch in CA 7-8R
See also SATA 12
Hardwick, Sylvia
See Doherty, Ivy R. Duffy
Hardy, Adam
See Bulmer, (Henry) Kenneth
Hardy, Alan 1932- 73-76
Hardy, Alexander G(eorge) 1920-1973
Obituary 45-48
Hardy, Alice Dale CANR-26
Earlier sketches in CA 19-20, CAP-2
See also SATA 1
Hardy, Alister C(lavering) 1896-1985 85-88
Obituary 116
Hardy, Barbara (Gladys) 85-88
Hardy, C. Colburn 1910- CANR-21
Earlier sketches in CA 53-56, CANR-6
Hardy, David A(ndrews) 1936- CANR-8
Earlier sketch in CA 61-64
See also SATA 9
Hardy, Dennis 1941- 124
Hardy, Douglas
See Andrews, (Charles) Robert Douglas
(Hardy)
Hardy, Edward R(ochie) 1908- CAP-1
Earlier sketch in CA 15-16
Hardy, Eric 61-64
Hardy, Evelyn 1902- 23-24R
Hardy, Henry 1949- 113
Hardy, J(ohn) P(hillips) 1933- 25-28R
Hardy, Jason
See Oxley, William
Hardy, John Edward 1922- 13-14R
Hardy, Jon 1958- 123
See also SATA 53
Hardy, Jonathan G. Gathorne
See Gathorne-Hardy, Jonathan G.
Hardy, Laura
See Holland, Sheila
Hardy, Leroy C(lyde) 1927- 29-32R
Hardy, Melissa Arnold 1952- 102
Hardy, Michael (James Langley) 1933- 25-28R
Hardy, Peter 1931- 65-68
Hardy, Richard E(arl) 1938- 37-40R
Hardy, Richard P(eter) 1940- 117
Hardy, Ronald Harold 1919- 7-8R
Hardy, Stuart
See Schisgall, Oscar
Hardy, Thomas 1840-1928 123
Brief entry 104
See also DLB 18, 19
See also TCLC 4, 10, 18
See also SSC 2
Hardy, Tom 1943- 116
Hardy, W(illiam) G(eorge) 1895-1979 CANR-5
Earlier sketch in CA 7-8R
Hardy, Willene S(chaefer) 1937- 112
Hardy, William M(arion) 1922- CANR-2
Earlier sketch in CA 2R
Hardyck, Curtis D(ale) 1929- 29-32R
Hare, A(lexander) Paul 1923- CANR-2
Earlier sketch in CA 2R
Hare, Bill
See Hare, William Moorman
Hare, Cyril
See Clark, Alfred Alexander Gordon
Hare, David 1947- 97-100
See also DLB 13
See also CLC 29
Hare, Douglas Robert Adams 1929- 45-48
Hare, Eric B. 1894- CAP-1
Earlier sketch in CA 15-16
Hare, F(rederick) Kenneth 1919- CANR-14
Earlier sketch in CA 37-40R
Hare, John 1935- 21-22R
Hare, Nathan 1934- CANR-24
Earlier sketch in CA 41-44R
See also BW
Hare, Norma Q(uarles) 1924- 101
See also SATA 41, 46
Hare, Peter H. 1935- 33-36R
Hare, R(ichard) M(ervyn) 1919- CANR-2
Earlier sketch in CA 7-8R
Hare, Richard (Gilbert) 1907-1966 CAP-1
Earlier sketch in CA 13-14
Hare, Ronald 1899- 77-80
Hare, Thomas Blenman
See Hare, Thomas William
Hare, Thomas William 1952- 122
Hare, Van Court, Jr. 1929- 25-28R
Hare, William 1944- 111
Hare, William Moorman 1934- 101
Hare Duke, Michael Geoffrey 1925- 111
Harel, Isser 1912- CANR-10
Earlier sketch in CA 65-68
Hareven, Shulamith 1931- Brief entry 117
Hareven, Tamara K. 1937- CANR-13
Earlier sketch in CA 25-28R
Harewood, George Henry Hubert Lascelles
1923- 125
Harford, David K(ennedy) 1947- 49-52
Harford, Henry
See Hudson, W(illiam) H(enry)
Harger, Rolla N(eil) 1890-1983 Obituary 114
Harger, William Henderson 1936- 57-60
Hargrave, John Gordon 1894-1982
Obituary 110
Hargrave, Leonie
See Disch, Thomas M(ichael)
Hargrave, O. T. 1936- 33-36R
Hargrave, Rowena 1906- 33-36R
Hargraves, Thomas
See Ainsworth, Thomas Hargraves, Jr.
Hargreaves, Harry 1922- 7-8R
Hargreaves, John D(esmond) 1924- 9-10R
Hargreaves, Mary W(ilma) M(assey)
1914- CANR-14
Earlier sketch in CA 37-40R
Hargreaves, Reginald (Charles) 1888- CAP-1
Earlier sketch in CA 9-10
Hargreaves, (Charles) Roger 1935-1988
Obituary 126
Hargreaves-Mawdsley, W(illiam) Norman
1921-1980 CANR-7
Earlier sketch in CA 9-10R
Hargroder, Charles M(erlin) 1926- 73-76
Hargrove, Barbara Watts 1924- 33-36R
Hargrove, Erwin C. 1930- Brief entry 111
Hargrove, James 1947- 120
See also SATA 50
Hargrove, Jim
See Hargrove, James
Hargrove, Katharine T. 33-36R
Hargrove, Marion 1919- DLB-11
Hargrove, Merwin Matthew 1910- 11-12R
Hargrove, Nancy Duvall 1941- 97-100
Hargrove, Richard J(ohn), Jr. 1941- 116
Harik, Iliya F. 1934- CANR-16
Earlier sketch in CA 25-28R
Haring, Bernard
See Haering, Bernhard
Haring, Firth 1937- 25-28R
Haring, Jo 1934- 116
Haring, Joseph E(merick) 1931- 33-36R
Haring, Norris G. 1923- CANR-2
Earlier sketch in CA 2R
Haring, Philip S(myth) 1915- 37-40R
Harington, Donald 1935- CANR-7
Earlier sketch in CA 15-16R
Harjo, Joy 1951- 114
Hark, Mildred
See McQueen, Mildred Hark
Harkabi, Yehoshafat 1921- 73-76
Harkavy, Robert E(dward) 1936- 111
Harkaway, Hal
See Stratemeyer, Edward L.
Harker, Kenneth 1927- 97-100
Harker, Ronald 1909- 77-80
Harkey, Ira B(rown), Jr. 1918- 57-60
Harkey, William G. 1914- 25-28R
Harkins, Arthur M(artin) 1936- 97-100
Harkins, Paul W(illiam) 1911- 116
Harkins, Philip 1912- 29-32R
See also SATA 6
Harkins, William E(dward) 1921- 33-36R
Harkness, Bruce 1923- 13-14R
Harkness, D(avid) W(illiam) 1937- CANR-15
Earlier sketch in CA 29-32R
Harkness, David J(ames) 1913- CANR-3
Earlier sketch in CA 9-10R
Harkness, Edward 1947- 77-80
Harkness, Georgia (Elma) 1891-1974 CANR-6
Obituary 53-56
Earlier sketch in CA 1R
Harkness, Gladys Estelle Suiter
1908(?)-1973 Obituary 41-44R
Harkness, Jack
See Harkness, John Leigh
Harkness, John Leigh 1918- 120
Harkness, Marjory Gane 1880-19(?) CAP-2
Earlier sketch in CA 23-24
Harknett, Terry 1936- CANR-21
Earlier sketches in CA 57-60, CANR-6
Harlan
See Shaw, William Harlan
Harlan, Elizabeth 1945- 111
See also SATA 35, 41
Harlan, Glen
See Cebulash, Mel
Harlan, John Marshall 1899-1971
Obituary 33-36R
Harlan, Louis R(udolph) 1922- CANR-25
Earlier sketch in CA 23-24R
See also CLC 34
Harlan, William K(eith) 1938- 45-48
Harle, Elizabeth
See Roberts, Irene
Harlequin
See Reed, A(lexander) W(yclif)
Harley, John
See Marsh, John
Harling, Thomas
See Eastham, Thomas
Harlow, Enid 1939- 102
Harlow, Francis H(arvey) 1928- 57-60
Harlow, Harry F(rederick) 1905- 97-100
Harlow, Joan Hiatt 1932- 89-92
Harlow, LeRoy F(rancis) 1913- 85-88
Harlow, Lewis A(ugustus) 1901- CAP-1
Earlier sketch in CA 13-14
Harlow, Neal 1908- 109
Harlow, Robert 1923- DLB-60
Harlow, Samuel Ralph 1885-1972 2R
Obituary 37-40R
Harlow, W(illiam) M(orehouse)
1900-1986 13-14R
Obituary 119
Harman, Alec
See Harman, Richard Alexander
Harman, Barbara Leah 1946- 126
Harman, Claire
See Schmidt, Claire Harman
Harman, David 1944- 105
Harman, Fred 1902(?)-1982 Obituary 106
See also SATA 30
Harman, Gilbert H(elms) 1938- 73-76
Harman, Harry E. III 1917- 116
Harman, Hugh 1903-1982 Obituary 108
See also SATA 33
Harman, Jane
See Harknett, Terry
Harman, Jeanne Perkins 1919- CANR-11
Earlier sketch in CA 69-72
Harman, Mark 1951- 118
Harman, Nicholas 1933- 101
Harman, P(eter) M(ichael) 1943- 110
Harman, R. Alec
See Harman, Richard Alexander
Harman, Richard Alexander 1917- CANR-5
Earlier sketch in CA 11-12R
Harman, Willis W(alter) 1918- 7-8R
Harmel, Robert 1950- 110
Harmelink, Barbara (Mary) 61-64
See also SATA 9
Harmer, Mabel 1894- 11-12R
See also SATA 45
Harmer, Ruth Mulvey 1919- 9-10R
Harmin, Merrill 1928- 89-92
Harmon, A(llen) J(ackson) 1926- 21-22R
Harmon, Frederick G(ardner) 1932- 119
Harmon, Gary L. 1935- 37-40R
Harmon, Glynn 1933- 45-48
Harmon, H. H.
See Williams, Robert Moore
Harmon, James Judson 1933- 23-24R
Harmon, Jim
See Harmon, James Judson
Harmon, Lily 1912- 105
Harmon, Lyn S. 1930- 21-22R
Harmon, Margaret 1906- 69-72
See also SATA 20
Harmon, Maurice 1930- CANR-9
Earlier sketch in CA 23-24R
Harmon, Nolan B(ailey) 1892- 89-92
Harmon, (Norman) Paul 1942- 122
Harmon, Robert Bartlett 1932- CANR-23
Earlier sketches in CA 17-18R, CANR-8
Harmon, Susanna M(arie) 1940- 57-60
Harmon, William (Ruth) 1938- CANR-14
Earlier sketch in CA 33-36R
See also CLC 38
Harms, Ernest 1895-1974 CAP-1
Obituary 49-52
Earlier sketch in CA 13-14
Harms, John 1900- 17-18R
Harms, Leroy Stanley 1928- CANR-8
Earlier sketch in CA 53-56
Harms, Robert T(homas) 1932- 37-40R
Harms, Valerie 1940- CANR-2
Earlier sketch in CA 49-52
Harmsel, Henrietta Ten
See Ten Harmsel, Henrietta
Harmsen, Dorothy B. Bahneman 103
Harmsen, Frieda 1931- 107
Harmston, Olivia
See Weber, Nancy
Harmsworth, Esmond Cecil 1898-1978
Obituary 89-92
Harnack, Curtis (Arthur) 1927- CANR-22
Earlier sketches in CA 4R, CANR-2
Harnack, R(obert) Victor 1927- 15-16R

Harnack, William J. 1953- 125
Harnan, Terry 1920- 45-48
See also SATA 12
Harnden, Ruth Peabody 73-76
Harned, David Baily 1932- Brief entry 112
Harner, James L(owell) 1946- 110
Harner, Michael J(ames) 1929- Brief entry .. 114
Harness, Charles L(eonard) 1915-
Brief entry 113
See also DLB 8
Harnett, Bertram 1923- 119
Harnett, Cynthia (Mary) 1893-1981 .... CAP-1
Obituary 111
Earlier sketch in CA 9-10
See also SATA 5, 32
Harnetty, Peter 1927- 37-40R
Harnik, Bernard 1910- 93-96
Harnsberger, Caroline Thomas 1902- 61-64
Harnwell, Gaylord Probasco 1903-1982
Obituary 106
Haro, Robert P(eter) 1936- 33-36R
Harodoy, Jorge Enrique 1926- 33-36R
Harold, Fred(erick) G(ordon) 1937- 118
Haroldson, William
See King, Harold
Haroutunian, Joseph 1904-1968 Obituary 111
Harper, Anita 1943- 114
See also SATA 41
Harper, Bill
See Harper, William A(rthur)
Harper, Carol Ely 61-64
Harper, Daniel
See Brossard, Chandler
Harper, David
See Corley, Edwin (Raymond)
Harper, Douglas A(lbert) 1948- 117
Harper, Elaine
See Hallin, Emily Watson
Harper, F. E. W.
See Harper, Frances Ellen Watkins
Harper, Floyd H(enry) 1899-1978
Obituary 77-80
Harper, Frances E. W.
See Harper, Frances Ellen Watkins
Harper, Frances E. Watkins
See Harper, Frances Ellen Watkins
Harper, Frances Ellen
See Harper, Frances Ellen Watkins
Harper, Frances Ellen Watkins 1825-1911 125
Brief entry 111
See also BW
See also DLB 50
See also TCLC 14
Harper, George Mills 1914- Brief entry 114
Harper, George W(illiam) 1927- 113
Harper, Harold W. 89-92
Harper, Harry H(alsted), Jr. 1910-1983
Obituary 110
Harper, Howard 1904- 19-20R
Harper, Howard M(orrall), Jr. 1930- CANR-22
Earlier sketch in CA 21-22R
Harper, J(ohn) Russell 1914-1983 .... CANR-13
Earlier sketch in CA 33-36R
Harper, James E(dwin) 1927- 41-44R
Harper, Joan (Marie) 1932- 101
Harper, John C(arsten) 1924- 103
Harper, John Dickson 1910- 103
Harper, Karen 1945- 114
Harper, Kate
See Harper, Katherine E(rna)
Harper, Katherine E(rna) 1946- 103
Harper, M(ichael) J(ohn) K(ennedy) 1935- .. 116
Harper, Marvin Henry 1901- 49-52
Harper, Mary Wood
See Dixon, Jeanne
Harper, Michael 1931- CANR-15
Earlier sketch in CA 65-68
Harper, Michael S(teven) 1938- CANR-24
Earlier sketch in CA 33-36R
See also BW
See also DLB 41
See also CLC 7, 22
Harper, Mrs. F. E. W.
See Harper, Frances Ellen Watkins
Harper, Paula (Hays) 1938- 105
Harper, Robert A(lexander) 1924- 17-18R
Harper, Robert J(ohnston) C(raig)
1927- 13-14R
Harper, Stephen (Dennis) 1924- 97-100
Harper, Tom 1923(?)-1983 Obituary 110
Harper, Wilhelmina 1884-1973 .... CAP-1
Earlier sketch in CA 17-18
See also SATA 4, 26
Harper, William A(rthur) 1944- 77-80
Harpham, Geoffrey Galt 1946- 111
Harpole, Charles H(enry) 1943- 111
Harpole, Patricia Chayne 1933- 37-40R
Harpur, Patrick 1950- 114
Harr, Wilber C. 1908-1971 .... 1R
Obituary 103
Harragan, Betty Lehan 1921- CANR-17
Earlier sketch in CA 77-80
Harrah, Barbara K. 1938- 107
Harrah, David 1926- 7-8R
Harrah, David Fletcher 1949- 65-68
Harrah, Michael 1940- 115
See also SATA 41
Harral, Stewart 1906-1964 .... 5-6R
Harrar, E(llwood) S(cott) 1905- CAP-1
Earlier sketch in CA 11-12
Harrar, J(acob) George 1906-1982
Obituary 110
Harre, John 1931- 23-24R
Harre, (Horace) Rom(ano) 1927- CANR-21
Earlier sketches in CA 5-6R, CANR-2
Harrell, Allen W(aylan) 1922- 29-32R
Harrell, Costen J(ordan) 1885- 7-8R
Harrell, David Edwin, Jr. 1930- CANR-15
Earlier sketch in CA 37-40R
Harrell, Irene B(urk) 1927- CANR-25
Earlier sketches in CA 23-24R, CANR-9
Harrell, John G(rinnell) 1922- CANR-18
Earlier sketches in CA 11-12R, CANR-3
Harrell, Sara (Jeanne) Gordon 1940- 105
Harrell, (Clyde) Stevan 1947- 106
Harrell, Thomas Willard 1911- 1R
Harrelson, Walter (Joseph) 1919- 11-12R
Harrer, Heinrich 1912- CANR-7
Earlier sketch in CA 17-18R
Harrier, Richard C(harles) 1923- 122
Brief entry 117
Harries, Joan 1922- 107
See also SATA 39
Harries, Karsten 1937- 25-28R
Harries, Richard (Douglas) 1936- 116
Harriett 1905- 77-80
Harriford, Daphne
See Harris, Marion Rose (Young)
Harrigan, Anthony (Hart) 1925- 21-22R
Harrigan, Kathryn Rudie 1951- CANR-26
Earlier sketch in CA 109
Harrigan, Stephen 1948- 122
Harriman, Ann 1932- 111
Harriman, Averell
See Harriman, W(illiam) Averell
Harriman, Edward 1922- 114
Harriman, Margaret 1928- 21-22R
Harriman, Richard L(evet) 1944- 33-36R
Harriman, Sarah 1942- 57-60
Harriman, W(illiam) Averell 1891-1986
Obituary 119
Brief entry 111
Harrington, Alan 1919- 73-76
Harrington, Charles (Christopher)
1942- CANR-9
Earlier sketch in CA 65-68
Harrington, Curtis 1928- 103
Harrington, Denis J(ames) 1932- 69-72
Harrington, Donald Szantho 1914- 21-22R
Harrington, Elbert W(ellington) 1901- 37-40R
Harrington, Evelyn Davis 1911- CANR-4
Earlier sketch in CA 7-8R
Harrington, Geri CANR-21
Earlier sketches in CA 57-60, CANR-6
Harrington, Harold David 1903-1981 .... CANR-11
Earlier sketch in CA 25-28R
Harrington, Jack 1918- 57-60
Harrington, Jeremy 1932- 41-44R
Harrington, Joseph Daniel 1923- 89-92
Harrington, K.
See Bean, Keith F(enwick)
Harrington, Lyn
See Harrington, Evelyn Davis
See also SATA 5
Harrington, Mark Raymond 1882-1971 .... CAP-2
Earlier sketch in CA 17-18
Harrington, Michael 1928- CANR-19
Earlier sketch in CA 19-20R
Harrington, Norman W. 1922(?)-1987
Obituary 123
Harrington, (Peter) Ty(rus) 1951- 102
Harrington, William 1931- CANR-19
Earlier sketches in CA 11-12R, CANR-4
Harriott, Edwin Thomas 1933- 117
Harriott, Ted
See Harriott, Edwin Thomas
Harris, Alan 1928- 7-8R
Harris, Albert J(osiah) 1908- CANR-5
Earlier sketch in CA 2R
Harris, Alex(ander Eisemann) 1949- 124
Harris, Alf(red) 1928- 53-56
Harris, Alice Kessler 1941- CANR-14
Earlier sketch in CA 37-40R
Harris, Andrea
See Connolly, Vivian
and Walker, Irma Ruth (Roden)
Harris, Andrew
See Poole, Frederick King
Harris, Ann Sutherland 1937- 126
Harris, Aurand 1915- CANR-16
Earlier sketch in CA 93-96
See also SATA 37
Harris, Barbara J. 1942- 115
Harris, Barbara S(eger) 1927- 49-52
Harris, Ben(jamin) Charles 1907-1978 57-60
Obituary 89-92
Harris, Ben(jamin) M(axwell) 1923- CANR-2
Earlier sketch in CA 5-6R
Harris, Benjamin (?)-1720(?) DLB-42, 43
Harris, Bernice K(elly) 1892-1973 .... 5-6R
Obituary 45-48
Harris, Bertha 1937- 29-32R
Harris, Beulah ?-1970 Obituary 104
Harris, Bill 1933- 109
Harris, Brian
See King, Harold
Harris, Brownie 1949- 107
Harris, Carl V(ernon) 1937- 97-100
Harris, Charlaine 1951- 105
Harris, Charles 1923- 102
Harris, Charles B(urt) 1940- 53-56
Harris, Charles H(ouston) III 1937- 15-16R
Harris, Chauncy D(ennison) 1914- 29-32R
Harris, Chester W(illiam) 1910- CAP-1
Earlier sketch in CA 11-12
Harris, Christie (Lucy) Irwin 1907- CANR-6
Earlier sketch in CA 7-8R
See also SATA 6
See also CLC 12
Harris, Clyde E., Jr. 23-24R
Harris, Colver
See Colver, Anne
Harris, Curtis C(lark), Jr. 1930- 53-56
Harris, Cyril 1891- CAP-1
Earlier sketch in CA 11-12
Harris, Dale B(enner) 1914- 15-16R
Harris, Daniel A(rthur) 1942- 89-92
Harris, David (Victor) 1946- 69-72
Harris, David W. 1948- Brief entry 107
Harris, Del(mer William) 1937- CANR-8
Earlier sketch in CA 61-64
Harris, Donald 1931- 126
Harris, Dorothy Joan 1931- CANR-1
Earlier sketch in CA 45-48
See also SATA 13
Harris, Douglas H(ershel, Jr.) 1930- 25-28R
Harris, Edward Arnold 1910-1976
Obituary 65-68
Harris, Elliot 1932- 25-28R
Harris, Ernest E(dward) 1914- 33-36R
Harris, Errol E(ustace) 1908- CANR-18
Earlier sketches in CA 49-52, CANR-2
Harris, F(rank) Brayton 1932- 21-22R
Harris, Frank 1856(?)-1931 Brief entry 109
See also TCLC 24
Harris, Fred (Roy) 1930- CANR-26
Earlier sketch in CA 77-80
Harris, Frederick John 1943- 57-60
Harris, Gene Gray 1929- 17-18R
Harris, George Washington
1814-1869 .... DLB-3, 11
Harris, Geraldine (Rachel) 1951- 116
Harris, Gertrude (Margaret) 1916- 57-60
Harris, H(arold) A(rthur) 1902- 49-52
Harris, Helen(a Barbara Mary) 1927- 61-64
Harris, Herbert 1911- 102
Harris, Herbert 1914(?)-1974 Obituary 49-52
Harris, Hyde
See Harris, Timothy Hyde
Harris, Ian (Anthony) 1937- 107
Harris, Irving David 1914- 13-14R
Harris, Jacqueline L. 1929- 126
Harris, James E(dward) 1928- 126
Brief entry 110
Harris, Jana 1947- 105
Harris, Jane Allen 1918- 4R
Harris, Jane Gary 111
Harris, Janet 1932-1979 .... 33-36R
Obituary 93-96
See also SATA 4, 23
Harris, Janice Hubbard 1943- 118
Harris, Jay S(tephen) 1938- 85-88
Harris, Jed
See Horowitz, Jacob
Harris, Jessica L.
See Milstead, Jessica L(ee)
Harris, Joel Chandler 1848-1908
Brief entry 104
See also YABC 1
See also DLB 11, 23, 42
See also TCLC 2
Harris, John (Roy) 1915- CANR-2
Earlier sketch in CA 5-6R
Harris, John 1916- 93-96
Harris, John (Wyndham Parkes Lucas)
Beynon 1903-1969 102
Obituary 89-92
See also CLC 19
Harris, John S(harp) 1917- 29-32R
Harris, John S(terling) 1929- 65-68
Harris, Jonathan 1921- 121
See also SATA 52
Harris, Joseph E(arl) 1929- 122
Brief entry 117
Harris, Joseph Pratt 1896-1985 .... 3R
Obituary 115
Harris, Julian (Earle) 1896- 2R
Harris, Julie 1925- 103
Harris, Karen H(arriman) 1934- CANR-22
Earlier sketch in CA 103
Harris, Kathleen
See Humphries, Adelaide M.
Harris, Kathryn Gibbs
See Gibbs-Wilson, Kathryn (Beatrice)
Harris, Kenn 1947- 116
Harris, Kenneth 1904-1983 Obituary 109
Harris, Larry M.
See Janifer, Laurence M(ark)
Harris, Lavinia
See Johnston, Norma
Harris, Leon A., Jr. 1926- CANR-3
Earlier sketch in CA 9-10R
See also SATA 4
Harris, Leonard 1929- CANR-9
Earlier sketch in CA 65-68
Harris, Lloyd J(ohn) 1947- 61-64
Harris, Lorle K(empe) 1912- 97-100
See also SATA 22
Harris, Louis 1921- 13-14R
Harris, Louise 1903- CANR-7
Earlier sketch in CA 19-20R
Harris, M(iddleton) A. 1908-1977
Obituary 111
Harris, MacDonald
See Heiney, Donald (William)
Harris, Madalene 1925- 105
Harris, Marcia Lee 1951- 109
Harris, Marie 1943- CANR-20
Earlier sketch in CA 104
Harris, Marilyn
See Springer, Marilyn Harris
Harris, Marion Rose (Young) 1925- CANR-12
Earlier sketches in CA 9-10, CAP-1
Harris, Marjorie Silliman 1890- CAP-1
Earlier sketch in CA 13-14
Harris, Mark 1922- CANR-2
Earlier sketch in CA 7-8R
See also CAAS 3
See also DLB 2
See also DLBY 80
See also CLC 19
Harris, Mark C(harles) 1955- 113
Harris, Mark Jonathan 1941- CANR-21
Earlier sketch in CA 104
See also SATA 32
Harris, Marshall (Dees) 1903- CANR-1
Earlier sketch in CA 4R
Harris, Marvin 1927- 124
Brief entry 110
Harris, Mary B(ierman) 1943- 53-56
Harris, Mary Imogene 49-52
Harris, Mary K. 1905-1966 .... CAP-1
Earlier sketch in CA 15-16
Harris, Mary Law 1892(?)-1980 Obituary 102
Harris, Maynard L(awrence) 1902-1974
Obituary 116
Harris, Michael (Terry) 1948- 125
Harris, Michael H(ope) 1941- 57-60
Harris, Michael R(ichard) 1936- 29-32R
Harris, Miles F(itzgerald) 1913- CANR-6
Earlier sketch in CA 7-8R
Harris, P(eter) B(ernard) 1929- 104
Harris, Patricia 57-60
Harris, Philip R(obert) 1926- CANR-25
Earlier sketches in CA 17-18R, CANR-8
Harris, R(ansom) Baine 1927- 73-76
Harris, R(obert) J(ohn) C(ecil)
1922-1980 .... CANR-15
Earlier sketch in CA 65-68
Harris, R(obert) Laird 1911- CANR-1
Earlier sketch in CA 4R
Harris, Radie 65-68
Harris, Rex 1904-1985 Obituary 118
Harris, Richard (S.) 1928(?)-1987
Obituary 123
Harris, Richard 1934- 107
Harris, Richard 1955- 126
Harris, Richard Colebrook 1936- 97-100
Harris, Richard H. 1942- 103
Harris, Richard J(ohn) 1948- 115
Harris, Richard N(elson) 1942- 77-80
Harris, Ricky 1922- 103
Harris, Robert (Jennings) 1907- 5-6R
Harris, Robert Dalton 1921- 93-96
Harris, Robert Harry 1941- 108
Harris, Robert Samuel 1904-1983
Obituary 111
Harris, Robert T(aylor) 1912- 7-8R
Harris, Robie H. SATA-53
Harris, Robin
See Shine, Deborah
Harris, Robin S(utton) 1919- 21-22R
Harris, Roger
See Wilson, R(oger) H(arris) L(ebus)
Harris, Ronald W(alter) 1916- 7-8R
Harris, Rosemary (Jeanne) CANR-13
Earlier sketch in CA 33-36R
See also SATA 4
Harris, Roy J. 1903(?)-1980 Obituary 93-96
Harris, S(eymour) E(dwin) 1897-1974 65-68
Obituary 53-56
Harris, Sara Lee
See Stadelman, S(ara) L(ee)
Harris, Sheldon H(oward) 1928- 37-40R
Harris, Sherwood 1932- 97-100
See also SATA 25
Harris, Stephen E. 1943- Brief entry 111
Harris, Stephen L(eRoy) 1937- 29-32R
Harris, Steven Michael 1957- 121
Harris, (William) Stewart 1922- 104
Harris, Styron 1936- 112
Harris, Sydney J(ustin) 1917-1986 .... CANR-11
Obituary 120
Earlier sketch in CA 61-64
Harris, T George 1924- 69-72
Harris, Thistle Y.
See Stead, Thistle Yolette
Harris, Thomas 1940(?)- 113
Harris, Thomas A(nthony) 1913(?)- 93-96
Harris, Thomas Cunningham 1908-1985
Obituary 114
Harris, Thomas Harold 1933- 125
Harris, Thomas J. 1892(?)-1983 Obituary .. 109
Harris, Thomas O(rville) 1935- 73-76
Harris, Timothy Hyde 1946- 101
Harris, (Jonathan) Toby 1953- 118
Harris, Tom
See Harris, Thomas Cunningham
Harris, Trudier 1948- 115
Harris, Walter A. 1929- 29-32R
Harris, Warren G(ene) 1936- CANR-26
Earlier sketch in CA 77-80
Harris, Wendell V. 1932- 111
Harris, William Bliss 1901(?)-1981
Obituary 104
Harris, William C. 1933- 23-24R
Harris, William Foster
See Foster-Harris, William
Harris, William Hamilton 1944- 111
Harris, William J(oseph) 1942- CANR-19
Earlier sketches in CA 53-56, CANR-5
Harris, William McKinley, Sr. 1941- 126
Harris, (Theodore) Wilson 1921- CANR-11
Earlier sketch in CA 65-68
See also BW
See also CLC 25
Harrison, Allan E(ugene) 1925- CANR-6
Earlier sketch in CA 57-60
Harrison, Barbara 1941- CANR-12
Earlier sketch in CA 29-32R
Harrison, Barbara Grizzuti 1934- CANR-15
Earlier sketch in CA 77-80

Harrison, Bennett 1942- 53-56
Harrison, Bernard 1933- 93-96
Harrison, Beverly Wildung 1932- 111
Harrison, Bill
See Harrison, William C.
Harrison, Billy R. 1937- 121
Harrison, Brian Fraser
See Fraser Harrison, Brian
Harrison, C. William 1913- 107
See also SATA 35
Harrison, Carey 1944- 61-64
Harrison, Charles Yale 1898-1954 ...... DLB-68
Harrison, Chip 1952- 29-32R
Harrison, Claire E. 1946- 111
Harrison, Cynthia Ellen 1946- 57-60
Harrison, David L(akin) 1926- 117
Harrison, David L(ee) 1937- 93-96
See also SATA 26
Harrison, Deloris 1938- 61-64
See also SATA 9
Harrison, Don(ald Dean) 1941- 112
Harrison, Edward Hardy 1926- 116
Harrison, Elizabeth Cavanna 1909- CANR-6
Earlier sketch in CA 9-10R
Harrison, Eric George William Warde
1893-1987 Obituary 124
Harrison, Everett F(alconer) 1902- CAP-1
Earlier sketch in CA 11-12
Harrison, Francis Llewelyn 1905-1987
Obituary 124
Harrison, Frank Llewelyn
See Harrison, Francis Llewelyn
Harrison, Frank R(ussell) III 1935- 53-56
Harrison, Fred 1917- 29-32R
Harrison, Frederic 1831-1923 .... DLB-57
Harrison, G(eorge) B(agshawe) 1894- ... CANR-3
Earlier sketch in CA 1R
Harrison, George Russell 1898-1979 ..... CAP-2
Earlier sketch in CA 19-20
Harrison, Hank 1940- 41-44R
Harrison, Harry (Max) 1925- CANR-21
Earlier sketches in CA 4R, CANR-5
See also SATA 4
See also DLB 8
See also CLC 42
Harrison, Helen Amy 1943- 114
Harrison, Helen P(atricia) 1935- 102
Harrison, Howard 1930- 7-8R
Harrison, J(ohn) F(letcher) C(lews)
1921- CANR-10
Earlier sketch in CA 25-28R
Harrison, J(ames) P. 77-80
Harrison, James (Thomas) 1937- CANR-8
Earlier sketch in CA 15-16R
Harrison, Jay S(molens) 1927-1974
Obituary 53-56
Harrison, Jim
See Harrison, James (Thomas)
See also DLBY 82
See also CLC 6, 14, 33
Harrison, Joan (Mary) 1909- 104
Harrison, John A(rmstrong) 1915-
Brief entry 111
Harrison, John Baugham 1907- 1R
Harrison, John M(arshall) 1914- 25-28R
Harrison, John R(aymond) 1933- 101
See also AITN 2
Harrison, K(enneth) C(ecil) 1915- CANR-3
Earlier sketch in CA 9-10R
Harrison, Keith Edward 1932- 73-76
Harrison, Louise C(ollbran) 1908- CAP-1
Earlier sketch in CA 11-12
Harrison, Lowell H(ayes) 1922- 37-40R
Harrison, M(ichael) John 1945- 53-56
Harrison, Marcus 1924- 102
Harrison, Martin 1930- 49-52
Harrison, Mary
See Fabbri, Nancy Rash
Harrison, Max 69-72
Harrison, Michael 1907- 97-100
Harrison, Michael A. 1936- 126
Harrison, Michelle Jessica 1942- 109
Harrison, Molly 1909- 108
See also SATA 41
Harrison, Nicolas 1937(?)-1984 Obituary ... 114
Harrison, Paul Carter 1936- 125
Brief entry 117
See also BW
See also DLB 38
Harrison, Paul M. 1923- 53-56
Harrison, Randall P(aul) 1929- CANR-11
Earlier sketch in CA 69-72
Harrison, Ray(mond Vincent) 1928- 126
Harrison, Raymond H. 1911- 17-18R
Harrison, Richard A(rnold) 1945- 107
Harrison, Richard John 1920- 109
Harrison, Robert (Ligon) 1932- 25-28R
Harrison, Roland Kenneth 1920- 49-52
Harrison, Rosina 1899- 102
Harrison, (Thomas) Ross 1943- CANR-9
Earlier sketch in CA 61-64
Harrison, Royden John 1927- 17-18R
Harrison, S(ydney) Gerald 1924- 13-14R
Harrison, Sarah 1946- 102
Harrison, Saul I. 1925- CANR-10
Earlier sketch in CA 21-22R
Harrison, Selig S(eidenman) 1927- 85-88
Harrison, Stanley R. 1927- 41-44R
Harrison, Ted
See Harrison, Edward Hardy
Harrison, Tony 1937- 65-68
See also DLB 40
See also CLC 43
Harrison, Wallace (Kirkman) 1895-1981
Obituary 108
Harrison, Whit
See Whittington, Harry (Benjamin)
Harrison, Wilfrid 1909- CAP-1
Earlier sketch in CA 11-12
Harrison, William 1933- CANR-9
Earlier sketch in CA 19-20R
Harrison, William C. 1919- 25-28R
Harrison Church, Ronald James 1915- ...15-16R
Harriss, C(lement) Lowell 1912- CANR-2
Earlier sketch in CA 1R
Harriss, Joseph 1936- 57-60
Harriss, R(obert) P(reston) 1902- 73-76
Harriss, Will(ard Irvin) 1922- 111
See also CLC 34
Harrisse, Henry 1829-1910 .... DLB-47
Harrity, Richard 1907-1973 Obituary 41-44R
Harrod, Leonard Montague 1905- 15-16R
Harrod, Roy Forbes 1900-1978 ....9-10R
Obituary 103
Harrold, William E(ugene) 1936- 41-44R
Harron, Don(ald) 1924- 104
Harrop-Allin, Clinton 1936- 107
Harroun, Catherine 1907- 109
Harrow, Benjamin 1888-1970 Obituary 104
Harrowe, Fiona
See Hurd, Florence
Harrower, Elizabeth 1928- 101
Harrower, Molly 1906- 5-6R
Harry, M.
See Lewis, Sasha Gregory
Harsany, Peter 1913- 111
Harsch, Ernest 1951- 69-72
Harsch, Hilya
See Jelly, George Oliver
Harsch, Joseph C(lose) 1905- 102
Harsent, David 1942- 93-96
See also DLB 40
Harsh, George 1908(?)-1980 Obituary 93-96
Harsh, Wayne C. 1924- CANR-15
Earlier sketch in CA 29-32R
Harshaw, Ruth H(etzel) 1890-1968
Obituary 107
See also SATA 27
Harshbarger, David Dwight 1938- 53-56
Harson, Sley
See Ellison, Harlan
Harss, Luis 1936- 17-18R
Harstad, Peter Tjernagel 1935- 37-40R
Harston, Ruth 1944- 41-44R
Hart, A(rthur) Tindal 1908- 9-10R
Hart, Albert Bushnell 1854-1943
Brief entry 116
See also DLB 17
Hart, Albert Gailord 1909- CAP-2
Earlier sketch in CA 23-24
Hart, Alexandra 1939- CANR-6
Earlier sketch in CA 57-60
Hart, Allan H(untley) 1935- 106
Hart, Archibald D(aniel) 1932- CANR-15
Earlier sketch in CA 93-96
Hart, Barry
See Bloom, Herman Irving
Hart, Basil Henry Liddell
See Liddell Hart, Basil Henry
Hart, Benjamin 1958- 126
Brief entry 118
Hart, Bruce 1938- 107
See also SATA 39
Hart, Carol 1944- 65-68
Hart, Carole 1943- 107
See also SATA 39
Hart, Carolyn G(impel) 1936- CANR-25
Earlier sketch in CA 15-16R
Hart, David K(irkwood) 1933- 123
Brief entry 117
Hart, Donald J(ohn) 1917- 11-12R
Hart, Douglas C. 1950- 101
Hart, Edward J(ack) 1941- 53-56
Hart, Edward L. 1916- CANR-14
Earlier sketch in CA 37-40R
Hart, Ellis
See Ellison, Harlan
Hart, Ernest H(untley) 1910- 102
Hart, Frances (Newbold) Noyes
1890-1943 Brief entry 112
Hart, Francis
See Paine, Lauran (Bosworth)
Hart, Francis Dudley 1909- CANR-25
Earlier sketch in CA 108
Hart, Gary (Warren) 1936(?)- 124
Brief entry 114
Hart, Gavin 1939- 106
Hart, George L. III 1942- 93-96
Hart, H(erbert) L(ionel) A(dolphus)
1907- CANR-2
Earlier sketch in CA 4R
Hart, Henry C(owles) 1916- 1R
Hart, Henry Hersch 1886-1968 .... CAP-1
Earlier sketch in CA 9-10
Hart, Herbert Michael 1928- 11-12R
Hart, Hornell (Norris) 1888-1967 Obituary ... 111
Hart, James D(avid) 1911- CANR-1
Earlier sketch in CA 1R
Hart, Jane (Meyers) 1922- 107
Hart, Jeffrey Allen 1947- 109
Hart, Jim Allee 1914- 13-14R
Hart, John 1942- 109
Hart, John 1948- CANR-11
Earlier sketch in CA 65-68
Hart, John E(dward) 1917- 33-36R
Hart, John Fraser 1924- 37-40R
Hart, John Lewis 1931- CANR-4
Earlier sketch in CA 49-52
Hart, Johnny
See Hart, John Lewis
See also AITN 1
Hart, Jon
See Harvey, John (Barton)
Hart, Joseph 1945- 85-88
Hart, Judith 1924- 109
Hart, Kate
See Kramer, Roberta
Hart, Kitty 1926- 117
Hart, Larry 1920- 33-36R
Hart, Lois B(orland) 1941- 117
Hart, Marie 1932- 41-44R
Hart, Marilyn M(cGuire) 1926- 45-48
Hart, Matthew 1945- 125
Hart, Milton R. 1896(?)-1983 Obituary 109
Hart, Moss 1904-1961 109
Obituary 89-92
See also DLB 7
Hart, Oliver 1723-1795 .... DLB-31
Hart, Patricia Susan 1950- 118
Hart, Patrick 1925- 53-56
Hart, Ray L(ee) 1929- 29-32R
Hart, Richard (Harry) 1908- CAP-1
Earlier sketch in CA 9-10
Hart, Robert A(llan) 1929- Brief entry 117
Hart, Roderick P(atrick) 1945- 106
Hart, Sandra Lynn Housby 1948- CANR-25
Earlier sketch in CA 108
Hart, Stan 1929- 118
Hart, Stephanie 1949- 97-100
Hart, Sue
See Hart, Susanne
Hart, Susanne 1927- CANR-20
Earlier sketch in CA 102
Hart, V(orhis) Donn 1918- 15-16R
Hart, Walter 1906(?)-1973 Obituary 45-48
Hart, Winston Scott 1903(?)-1979
Obituary 89-92
Hartcup, Adeline 1918- 116
Hartcup, Guy 1919- 29-32R
Hart-Davis, Duff 1936- 29-32R
Hart-Davis, Phyllida
See Barstow, Phyllida
Hart-Davis, Rupert (Charles) 1907-
Brief entry 115
Harte, (Francis) Bret(t) 1836(?)-1902
Brief entry 104
See also SATA 26
See also DLB 12, 64, 74
See also CDALB 1865-1917
See also TCLC 1, 25
Harte, Marjorie
See McEvoy, Marjorie Harte
Harte, Samantha
See Hart, Sandra Lynn Housby
Harte, Thomas Joseph 1914-1974
Obituary 53-56
Hartel, Klaus Dieter
See Vandenberg, Philipp
Hartendorp, A(bram) V(an) H(eyningen)
1893- CAP-1
Earlier sketch in CA 15-16
Harter, Eugene C(laudius) 1926- 119
Harter, Helen (O'Connor) 1905- 7-8R
Harter, Hugh A(nthony) 1922- 110
Harter, Kenneth W. 1912(?)-1984
Obituary 112
Harter, Lafayette George, Jr. 1918- 9-10R
Hartford, Claire 1913- 29-32R
Hartford, Ellis F(ord) 1905- CAP-1
Earlier sketch in CA 13-14
Hartford, (George) Huntington II 1911- ...17-18R
Hartford, Margaret E(lizabeth) 1917- 41-44R
Hartford, Via
See Donson, Cyril
Harth, Erica 116
Harth, Erich 1919- 107
Harth, (John) Phillip 1926- Brief entry 116
Harth, Robert 1940- 33-36R
Harthan, John Plant 1916- 102
Harthoorn, A(ntonie) M(arinus) 1923- 53-56
Hartich, Alice 1888- CAP-2
Earlier sketch in CA 17-18
Harting, Emilie Clothier 1942- 73-76
Hartje, Robert G(eorge) 1922- 25-28R
Hartjen, Clayton A(lfred) 1943- 69-72
Hartke, Vance 1919- 25-28R
Hartland, Michael 1941- 110
Hartlaub, Felix 1913(?)-1945 .... DLB-56
Hartlaub, G(ustav) F(riedrich) 1884-1963
Obituary 112
Hartley, Dorothy 1893-1985 105
Obituary 118
Hartley, Ellen (Raphael) 1915-1980 ..... CANR-4
Earlier sketch in CA 7-8R
See also SATA 23
Hartley, Fred Allan III 1953- 106
See also SATA 41
Hartley, John I(rvin) 1921- 7-8R
Hartley, Keith 1940- 115
Hartley, L(eslie) P(oles) 1895-1972 45-48
Obituary 37-40R
See also DLB 15
See also CLC 2, 22
Hartley, Livingston 1900- 61-64
Hartley, Lodwick (Charles) 1906-1979 ... CANR-1
Earlier sketch in CA 1R
Hartley, Margaret L(ohlker) 1909-1983 ...97-100
Obituary 110
Hartley, Marie 1905- 11-12R
Hartley, Marsden 1877-1943 Brief entry 123
See also DLB 54
Hartley, Peter (Roy) 1933- 103
Hartley, Rachel M. 1895- 7-8R
Hartley, Robert F(rank) 1927- CANR-11
Earlier sketch in CA 69-72
Hartley, Shirley Foster 1928- CANR-13
Earlier sketch in CA 73-76
Hartley, William B(rown) 1913-1980 .... CANR-4
Earlier sketch in CA 7-8R
See also SATA 23
Hartling, Peter
See Haertling, Peter
See also DLB 75
Hartman, Berl
See Hartman, Berl Mendelson
Hartman, Berl Mendelson 1938- 122
Hartman, (Howard) Carl 1917- 122
Hartman, Carl 1928- 104
Hartman, Charles O(ssian) 1949- 108
Hartman, Chester W(arren) 1936- 57-60
Hartman, David N. 1921- 15-16R
Hartman, Evert 1937- 113
See also SATA 35, 38
Hartman, Geoffrey H. 1929- 125
Brief entry 117
See also DLB 67
See also CLC 27
Hartman, George E(dward) 1926- 41-44R
Hartman, Hermene D(emaris) 1948- 122
Hartman, Jan 1938- 65-68
Hartman, Jane E(vangeline) 1928- CANR-22
Earlier sketch in CA 105
See also SATA 47
Hartman, John J(acob) 1942- 49-52
Hartman, Louis F(rancis) 1901-1970 ..... CAP-2
Earlier sketch in CA 23-24
See also SATA 22
Hartman, Mary S(usan) 1941- 81-84
Hartman, Nancy Carol 1942- 53-56
Hartman, Olov 1906-1982 .... CANR-14
Earlier sketch in CA 29-32R
Hartman, Patience
See Zawadsky, Patience
Hartman, Rachel (Frieda) 1920-1972 ....7-8R
Obituary 33-36R
Hartman, Rhondda Evans 1934- 61-64
Hartman, Robert K(intz) 1940- 41-44R
Hartman, Robert S. 1910-1973 .... CAP-2
Obituary 45-48
Earlier sketch in CA 17-18
Hartman, Roger
See Mehta, Rustam Jehangir
Hartman, Shirley 1929- 57-60
Hartman, William E(llis) 1919- 69-72
Hartman, William T(aylor) 1942- 117
Hartmann, Betsy
See Hartmann, Elizabeth
Hartmann, Edward George 1912- 41-44R
Hartmann, Elizabeth 1951- 126
Hartmann, Ernest 1934- 21-22R
Hartmann, Franz 1838-1912 Brief entry 115
Hartmann, Frederick Howard 1922- CANR-16
Earlier sketches in CA 2R, CANR-1
Hartmann, Heinz 1894-1970 Obituary 104
Hartmann, Helmut Henry 1931- 105
Hartmann, Klaus 1925- 21-22R
Hartmann, Michael 1944- 97-100
Hartmann, Rudolf A. 1937- Brief entry 111
Hartmann, Sadakichi 1867-1944 .... DLB-54
Hartmann, Susan M(arie) 1940- 41-44R
Hartmann, William K(enneth) 1939- 69-72
Hartnack, Justus 1912- 41-44R
Hartnett, D(avid) W(illiam) 1952- 122
Hartnett, Ken(neth Owen) 1934- 118
Hartnoll, Phyllis 1906- 81-84
Hartocollis, Peter 1922- CANR-1
Earlier sketch in CA 45-48
Hartog, Diana 1942- 123
Hartog, Joseph 1933- 102
Hartshorn, Ruth M. 1928- SATA-11
Hartshorne, Charles 1897- CANR-4
Earlier sketch in CA 9-10R
Hartshorne, Richard 1899- 7-8R
Hartshorne, Thomas L(lewellyn) 1935- ...37-40R
Hart-Smith, William 1911- CANR-11
Earlier sketch in CA 23-24R
Hartsoe, Colleen Ivey 1925- 109
Hartston, W(illiam) R(oland) 1947- 116
Hartsuch, Paul Jackson 1902- 57-60
Hartt, Julian 1916(?)-1984 Obituary 113
Hartung, Albert Edward 1923- 103
Hartup, Willard W(ert) 1927- 25-28R
Hartwell, Dickson Jay 1906-1981 .... CAP-1
Obituary 103
Earlier sketch in CA 11-12
Hartwell, Nancy
See Callahan, Claire Wallis
Hartwell, Ronald Max 1921- 25-28R
Hartwick, Sylvia
See Doherty, Ivy R. Duffy
Hartwig, Marie (Dorothy) 1906- 1R
Hartwig, Richard E(ric) 1942- 118
Harty, (Fredric) Russell 1934-1988
Obituary 125
Hartz, Fred R. 1933- 122
Hartz, Jim AITN-2
Hartz, Louis 1919-1986 Obituary 118
Hartzler, Daniel David 1941- 61-64
Haruf, Kent 19(?)- CLC-34
Harvard, Andrew Carson 1949- 69-72
Harvard, Charles
See Gibbs-Smith, Charles Harvard
Harvard, Stephen 1948- 57-60
Harvester, Simon
See Rumbold-Gibbs, Henry St. John Clair
Harvey, Andrew 1952- Brief entry 126
Harvey, Anne 1933- 121
Harvey, Anthony Peter 1940- 106
Harvey, Barbara (Fitzgerald) 1928- 116
Harvey, Brett 1936- 126
Harvey, C(harles) J(ohn) D(errick)
1922- 11-12R
Harvey, David 1935- 123
Harvey, David (W.) 1935- Brief entry 117
Harvey, David Dow 1931- 65-68
Harvey, Donald J(oseph) 1922- 41-44R
Harvey, Earle Sherburn 1906- 109

Harvey, Edith 1908(?)-1972 Obituary ... 104
See also SATA 27
Harvey, Edward Burns 1939- ... 41-44R
Harvey, Frank 1912-1981 Obituary ... 105
Harvey, Frank (Laird) 1913- ... 7-8R
Harvey, Geoffrey 1943- ... 126
Harvey, Gina P(aula) 1922- ... 45-48
Harvey, Harriet 1924- ... 109
Harvey, Ian Douglas 1914-1987 ... CAP-1
Obituary ... 121
Earlier sketch in CA 9-10
Harvey, James C(ardwell) 1925- ... 45-48
Harvey, James O. 1926- ... 17-18R
Harvey, Joan M(argaret) 1918- ... 102
Harvey, John (Barton) 1938- ... 125
Harvey, John B.
See Harvey, John (Barton)
Harvey, John F(rederick) 1921- ... CANR-23
Earlier sketches in CA 15-16R, CANR-8
Harvey, John Hooper 1911- ... CANR-21
Earlier sketches in CA 7-8R, CANR-6
Harvey, John Robert 1942- ... 93-96
Harvey, Jonathan 1939- ... 61-64
Harvey, Karen (E.) G(iddens) 1944- ... 117
Harvey, Kenneth 1919(?)-1979 Obituary ... 89-92
Harvey, Lashley Grey 1900- ... 37-40R
Harvey, Maria Luisa Alvarez 1938- ... 53-56
Harvey, Marian 1927- ... 89-92
Harvey, Michael G. 1944- ... 110
Harvey, Mose Lofley 1910-1985 Obituary ... 115
Harvey, Nancy Lenz 1935- ... 65-68
Harvey, Nigel 1916- ... CANR-13
Earlier sketch in CA 73-76
Harvey, O. J. 1927- ... 37-40R
Harvey, P(aul) D(ean) A(dshead) 1930- ... 112
Harvey, Paul
See Aurandt, Paul Harvey
Harvey, Rachel
See Bloom, Ursula
Harvey, Richard B(lake) 1930- ... 49-52
Harvey, Robert 1884- ... 7-8R
Harvey, Ruth C(harlotte) 1918-1980 ... 1R
Obituary ... 102
Harvey, Van A(ustin) 1926- ... 33-36R
Harvey, Virginia I(sham) 1917- ... 57-60
Harvey, William Burnett 1922- ... 41-44R
Harvey Wood, (Elizabeth) Harriet 1934- ... 123
Harvie-Watt, George Steven 1903- ... 109
Harward, Donald W. 1939- ... 93-96
Harward, Timothy Blake 1932- ... 25-28R
Harwell, Ann (Manning) J. 1936- ... 57-60
Harwell, Ernie
See Harwell, William Earnest
Harwell, Richard Barksdale 1915- ... CANR-17
Earlier sketches in CA 4R, CANR-2
Harwell, William Earnest 1918- Brief entry ... 116
Harwick, B. L.
See Keller, Beverly (Lou)
Harwin, Brian
See Henderson, LeGrand
Harwit, Martin Otto 1931- ... 105
Harwood, Alan 1935- ... 113
Harwood, Alice (Mary) ... 7-8R
Harwood, (Henry) David 1938- ... 104
Harwood, Edwin 1939- ... 29-32R
Harwood, Gina
See Battiscombe, E(sther) Georgina (Harwood)
Harwood, Gwen(doline Nessie) 1920- ... 97-100
Harwood, Jonathan 1943- ... 103
Harwood, Lee 1939- ... CANR-9
Earlier sketch in CA 21-22R
See also DLB 40
Harwood, Pearl Augusta (Bragdon) 1903- ... 13-14R
See also SATA 9
Harwood, Raymond C(harles) 1906-1987
Obituary ... 122
Harwood, Ronald 1934- ... CANR-4
Earlier sketch in CA 4R
See also DLB 13
See also CLC 32
Harzfeld, Lois 1932- ... 107
Hasan, Saiyid Zafar 1930- ... 73-76
Hasbrouck, Kenneth E. 1916- ... 49-52
Hasegawa, Nyozekan 1875-1969 Obituary ... 111
Hasegawa, Tsuyoshi 1941- ... 109
Hasek, Jaroslav (Matej Frantisek) 1883-1923 Brief entry ... 104
See also TCLC 4
Hasel, Gerhard F(ranz) 1935- ... CANR-15
Earlier sketch in CA 41-44R
Haselden, Kyle (Emerson) 1913-1968 ... 5-6R
Haseler, Stephen Michael Alan 1942- ... 85-88
Haseley, Dennis ... SATA-44
Hasenclever, Herbert Frederick 1924-1978
Obituary ... 81-84
Hasford, (Jerry) Gustav 1947- ... 85-88
Hashmi, Aurangzeb Alamgir 1951- ... CANR-16
Earlier sketch in CA 77-80
Haskell, Arnold L(ionel) 1903-1981(?) ... CANR-7
Obituary ... 102
Earlier sketch in CA 5-6R
See also SATA 6
Haskell, Douglas 1899-1979 Obituary ... 89-92
Haskell, Edward Froehlich 1906-
Brief entry ... 105
Haskell, Francis (James Herbert) 1928- ... CANR-6
Earlier sketch in CA 11-12R
Haskell, John Duncan, Jr. 1941- ... CANR-25
Earlier sketch in CA 107
Haskell, Martin R(oy) 1912- ... 41-44R
Haskett, Edythe Rance 1915- ... 23-24R
Haskin, Dorothy C(lark) 1905- ... 5-6R
Haskin, Gretchen 1936- ... 103
Haskins, Barbara
See Stone, Barbara Haskins
Haskins, Charles Homer 1870-1937 ... DLB-47
Haskins, George Lee 1915- ... CANR-1
Earlier sketch in CA 1R
Haskins, Ilma 1919- ... 45-48
Haskins, James S. 1941- ... CANR-25
Earlier sketch in CA 33-36R
See also BW
See also SATA 9
See also CLR 3
Haskins, Jim
See Haskins, James S.
See also SAAS 4
Haskins, Sam(uel Joseph) 1926- ... 103
Haslam, Gerald W. 1937- ... CANR-11
Earlier sketch in CA 29-32R
Hasler, Eveline 1937- ... 106
Hasler, Joan 1931- ... 29-32R
See also SATA 28
Haslerud, George M(artin) 1906- ... 45-48
Hasley, Louis (Leonard) 1906- ... 37-40R
Hasley, Lucile (Charlotte Hardman) 1909- ... CAP-1
Earlier sketch in CA 11-12
Hasling, John 1928- ... 33-36R
Haslip, Joan 1912- ... 107
Hasluck, Paul (Meernaa Caedwalla) 1905- ... 109
Haspel, Eleanor C. 1944- ... 69-72
Hass, C(harles) Glen 1915- ... 17-18R
Hass, Eric 1905(?)-1980 Obituary ... 102
Hass, Hans 1919- ... 108
Hass, Michael 1938- ... 37-40R
Hass, Robert 1941- ... 111
See also CLC 18, 39
Hassall, Anthony J. 1939- ... 126
Hassall, Christopher (Vernon) 1912-1963
Obituary ... 89-92
Hassall, Joan 1906- ... SATA-43
Hassall, Mark (William Cory) 1940- ... CANR-13
Earlier sketch in CA 73-76
Hassall, William Owen 1912- ... 15-16R
Hassan, Ihab Habib 1925- ... CANR-19
Earlier sketches in CA 7-8R, CANR-3
Hassan, William Ephraim, Jr. 1923- ... 33-36R
Hasse, John Edward 1948- ... 119
Hassel, David John 1923- ... 113
Hassel, Odd 1897-1981 Obituary ... 108
Hassel, Sven 1917- ... 93-96
Hassenger, Robert (Leo) 1937- ... 21-22R
Hassing, Per 1916- ... 37-40R
Hassinger, Edward W(esley) 1925- ... 125
Hassler, Donald M. (II) 1937- ... CANR-14
Earlier sketch in CA 41-44R
Hassler, Jon (Francis) 1933- ... CANR-21
Earlier sketch in CA 73-76
See also SATA 19
Hassler, Warren W., Jr. 1926- ... 9-10R
Hassler, William T(homas) 1954- ... 104
Hassrick, Peter H(eyl) 1941- ... CANR-16
Earlier sketches in CA 49-52, CANR-1
Hast, Adele 1931- ... 119
Hastings, Adrian 1929- ... CANR-23
Earlier sketches in CA 19-20R, CANR-7
Hastings, Alan
See Williamson, Geoffrey
Hastings, Arthur Claude 1935- ... 37-40R
Hastings, Beverly
See Barkin, Carol
and James, Elizabeth
Hastings, Cecily Mary Eleanor 1924- ... 7-8R
Hastings, Graham
See Jeffries, Roderic (Graeme)
Hastings, Harrington
See Marsh, John
Hastings, Hubert de Cronin 1902-1986 ... 109
Obituary ... 121
Hastings, Hudson
See Kuttner, Henry
Hastings, Ian 1912- ... 45-48
Hastings, Macdonald 1909- ... CANR-9
Earlier sketch in CA 53-56
Hastings, March
See Levinson, Leonard
Hastings, Margaret 1910- ... 41-44R
Hastings, (Macdonald) Max 1945- ... 81-84
Hastings, Michael (Gerald) 1938- ... 97-100
Hastings, Paul G(uiler) 1914- ... CANR-24
Earlier sketch in CA 2R
Hastings, Philip Kay 1922- ... 102
Hastings, Phyllis (Dora Hodge) ... CANR-8
Earlier sketch in CA 9-10R
Hastings, Robert J. 1924- ... 122
Hastings, Robert Paul 1933- ... 73-76
Hastings, Roderic
See Jeffries, Graham Montague
Hastings, Selina ... CLC-44
Hastings, William T(homson) 1881- ... 7-8R
Haston, Dougal 1940-1977 Obituary ... 105
Hastorf, Albert H(erman) 1920- ... 97-100
Hasty, Ronald W. 1941- ... CANR-4
Earlier sketch in CA 53-56
Haswell, Chetwynd John Drake 1919- ... 41-44R
Haswell, Harold Alanson, Jr. 1912- ... 45-48
Haswell, Jock
See Haswell, Chetwynd John Drake
Haszard, Patricia Moyes 1923- ... CANR-13
Earlier sketch in CA 19-20R
Hatch, Alden 1898-1975 ... 65-68
Obituary ... 57-60
Hatch, (Alden) Denison 1935- ... 33-36R
Hatch, Elvin (James) 1937- ... 45-48
Hatch, Eric S(towe) 1902(?)-1973
Obituary ... 41-44R
Hatch, James V(ernon) 1928- ... 41-44R
Hatch, John (Charles) 1917- ... 11-12R
Hatch, Mary Cottam 1912-1970 Obituary ... 109
See also SATA 28
Hatch, Nathan O(rr) 1946- Brief entry ... 109
Hatch, Preble D(elloss) K(ellogg) 1898- ... CAP-2
Earlier sketch in CA 23-24
Hatch, Raymond N(orris) 1911- ... 21-22R
Hatch, Richard A(llen) 1940- ... CANR-9
Earlier sketch in CA 21-22R
Hatch, Robert McConnell 1910- ... 93-96
Hatch, William H(enry) P(aine) 1875-1972
Obituary ... 37-40R
Hatcher, George W. 1906(?)-1983
Obituary ... 110
Hatcher, Harlan (Henthorne) 1898- ... CAP-2
Earlier sketch in CA 19-20
Hatcher, John 1942- ... 33-36R
Hatcher, John S(outhall) 1940- ... 97-100
Hatcher, Nat(han) B(razzell) 1897- ... 4R
Hatcher, Robert Anthony 1937- ... 93-96
Hatcher, William S(pottswood) 1935- ... 123
Hatem, Mohamed Abdel-Kader
See Hatim, Muhammad 'Abd al-Qadir
Hatfield, Antoinette Kuzmanich 1929- ... 85-88
Hatfield, Dorothy B(lackmon) 1921- ... 53-56
Hatfield, Elaine (Catherine) 1937- ... CANR-17
Earlier sketches in CA 25-28R, CANR-10
Hatfield, Henry Caraway 1912- ... 65-68
Hatfield, Julie (Stockwell) 1940- ... 126
Hatfield, Mark O(dom) 1922- ... 77-80
Hatfield, Michael (Vernon) 1935- ... 119
Hathaway, Baxter L. 1909- ... CANR-5
Earlier sketch in CA 3R
Hathaway, Bo 1942- ... 106
Hathaway, Dale E(rnest) 1925- ... 9-10R
Hathaway, Jan
See Neubauer, William Arthur
Hathaway, Lulu (Bailey) 1903- ... 13-14R
Hathaway, Mavis
See Avery, Ira
Hathaway, Nancy 1946- ... 108
Hathaway, Richard Dean 1927- ... 125
Hathaway, Sibyl Collings 1884-1974 ... 4R
Obituary ... 103
Hathaway, Starke R(osecrans) 1903-1984 ... 5-6R
Obituary ... 113
Hathaway, William 1944- ... 73-76
Hathcock, Louise ... 4R
Hathorn, Richmond Y(ancey) 1917- ... CANR-1
Earlier sketch in CA 2R
Hatim, Muhammad 'Abd al-Qadir 1918- ... 89-92
Hatlen, Burton (Norval) 1936- ... 109
Hatley, George B(erton) 1924- ... 106
Hatlo, Jimmy 1898-1963 Obituary ... 93-96
See also SATA 23
Hatmon, Paul W. 1921- ... 106
Hatt, Harold E(rnest) 1932- ... 21-22R
Hatta, Mohammed 1902-1980 Obituary ... 97-100
Hattaway, Herman (Morell) 1938- ... 65-68
Hattaway, Michael 1941- ... 116
Hatteras, Amelia
See Mencken, H(enry) L(ouis)
Hatteras, Owen
See Mencken, H(enry) L(ouis)
and Nathan, George Jean
Hatteras, Owen
See Nathan, George Jean
See also TCLC 18
Hatteras, Owen III
See McDavid, Raven I(oor), Jr.
Hatterer, Lawrence J(ohn) 1925-
Brief entry ... 118
Hattersley, Ralph (Marshall, Jr.) 1921- ... 103
Hattersley, Roy (Sydney George) 1932- ... 103
Hattersley-Smith, Geoffrey (Francis) 1923- ... 118
Hattery, Lowell H(arold) 1916- ... 19-20R
Hatton, Ragnhild Marie 1913- ... CANR-12
Earlier sketch in CA 25-28R
Hatton, Robert Wayland 1934- ... 37-40R
Hatton, Thomas J(enison) 1935- ... 114
Hattwick, Richard E(arl) 1938- ... 73-76
Hatvary, George Egon ... 53-56
Hatzenbuehler, Ronald L(ee) 1945- ... 117
Hatzfeld, Helmut A(nthony) 1892-1979 ... 97-100
Obituary ... 85-88
Hauberg, Clifford A(lvin) 1906- ... 37-40R
Hauck, Allan 1925- ... 3R
Hauck, Paul A(nthony) 1924- ... CANR-14
Earlier sketch in CA 41-44R
Hauck, Richard Boyd 1936- ... 53-56
Hauerwas, Stanley Martin 1940- ... 57-60
Haug, C(harles) James 1946- ... 116
Haugaard, Erik Christian 1923- ... CANR-3
Earlier sketch in CA 7-8R
See also SATA 4
See also CLR 11
Haugaard, William Paul 1929- ... 25-28R
Hauge, Sharon K(aye) 1943- ... 116
Haugen, Edmund Bennett 1913- ... 19-20R
Haugen, Einar (Ingvald) 1906- ... CANR-25
Earlier sketches in CA 21-22R, CANR-9
Haugh, Richard (Stanley) 1942- ... CANR-9
Earlier sketch in CA 57-60
Haugh, Robert F(ulton) 1910- ... 61-64
Haughey, John C. 1930- ... 77-80
Haughey, Thomas Brace 1943- ... 113
Haught, James A(lbert, Jr.) 1932-
Brief entry ... 122
Haught, John F(rancis) 1942- ... 85-88
Haughton, Claire Shaver 1901- ... 85-88
Haughton, Rosemary (Luling) 1927- ... 7-8R
Haughton, Sidney Henry 1888-1982
Obituary ... 107
Haughton-James, Jean Rosemary
1924-1981 Obituary ... 105
Haugland, Vern(on Arnold) 1908-1984 ... 93-96
Obituary ... 113
Hauk, Maung
See Hobbs, Cecil (Carlton)
Haule, James M(ark) 1945- ... 109
Hauman, Doris 1898- ... SATA-32
Hauman, George 1890-1961 ... SATA-32
Haun, Paul 1906-1969 ... CAP-2
Earlier sketch in CA 17-18
Hau'Ofa, Epeli 1939- ... 124
Haupt, Christopher (Charles Herbert) Lehmann
See Lehmann-Haupt, Christopher (Charles Herbert)
Haupt, Zygmunt 1907(?)-1975 Obituary ... 61-64
Hauptly, Denis J(ames) 1945- ... 118
Hauptman, Terry 1947- ... 111
Hauptmann, Carl 1858-1921 ... DLB-66
Hauptmann, Gerhart (Johann Robert) 1862-1946 Brief entry ... 104
See also DLB 66
See also TCLC 4
Haury, Emil W(alter) 1904- ... 65-68
Hausdorff, Don 1927- ... 45-48
Hauser, Bengamin Gayelord 1895-1984
Obituary ... 114
Brief entry ... 111
Hauser, Carl Maria 1895-1985 Obituary ... 117
Hauser, Charles McCorkle 1929- ... 69-72
Hauser, Gayelord
See Hauser, Bengamin Gayelord
Hauser, Hillary 1944- ... CANR-11
Earlier sketch in CA 69-72
Hauser, Margaret L(ouise) 1909- ... CAP-1
Earlier sketch in CA 11-12
See also SATA 10
Hauser, Marianne 1910- ... CANR-13
Earlier sketches in CA 11-12, CAP-1
See also DLBY 83
Hauser, Phillip M(orris) 1909- ... 17-18R
Hauser, Robert Mason 1942- ... 109
Hauser, Thomas 1946- ... 85-88
Hauser, William B(arry) 1939- ... 69-72
Hausknecht, Murray 1925- ... 37-40R
Hausknecht, Richard 1929- ... 121
Hausman, Gerald 1945- ... CANR-17
Earlier sketches in CA 45-48, CANR-2
See also SATA 13
Hausman, Gerry
See Hausman, Gerald
Hausman, Patricia 1953- ... CANR-26
Earlier sketch in CA 107
Hausman, Warren H. 1939- ... 17-18R
Hausmann, Bernard A(ndrew) 1899- ... CAP-2
Earlier sketch in CA 23-24
Hausmann, Manfred 1898-1986 Obituary ... 120
Hausmann, Winifred 1922- ... CANR-26
Earlier sketches in CA 21-22R, CANR-11
Hausrath, Alfred Hartmann 1901- ... 41-44R
Haussig, Hans Wilhelm 1916- ... 29-32R
Hauther, Brenda 1951- ... 113
Hautzig, Deborah 1956- ... 89-92
See also SATA 31
Hautzig, Esther Rudomin 1930- ... CANR-20
Earlier sketches in CA 2R, CANR-5
See also SATA 4
Havard, William C(lyde), Jr. 1923- ... CANR-5
Earlier sketch in CA 2R
Havel, J(ean) E(ugene Martial) 1928- ... 41-44R
Havel, Vaclav 1936- ... 104
See also CLC 25
Havelock, Christine Mitchell 1924- ... 85-88
Havelock, Eric A(lfred) 1903-1988 ... CAP-1
Obituary ... 125
Earlier sketch in CA 15-16
Havelock, Eric A. 1903- ... CAP-1
Earlier sketch in CA 15-16
Havelock, Ronald G(eoffrey) 1935- ... 85-88
Haveman, Robert H. 1936- ... 19-20R
Havemann, Ernest (Carl) 1912- ... 4R
Havemann, Joel 1943- ... 85-88
Havemann, Robert (Hans Gunther) 1910-1982 Obituary ... 110
Havemeyer, Loomis 1886-1971
Obituary ... 33-36R
Haven, Richard 1924- ... 25-28R
Havens, Daniel F(rederick) 1931- ... 69-72
Havens, George R(emington) 1890-1977 ... CANR-4
Obituary ... 73-76
Earlier sketch in CA 7-8R
Havens, Gordon 1903-1983 Obituary ... 111
Havens, Leston Laycock 1924- ... 119
Havens, Murray Clark 1932- ... 41-44R
Havens, Shirley E(lise) 1925- ... 89-92
Havens, Thomas R. H. 1939- ... CANR-15
Earlier sketch in CA 41-44R
Haver, Ronald D. 1939- ... 109
Haverkamp-Begemann, Egbert 1923- ... CANR-11
Earlier sketch in CA 19-20R
Haverstick, John (Mitchell) 1919- ... 25-28R
Haverstock, Mary Sayre 1932- ... 81-84
Haverstock, Nathan Alfred 1931- ... 53-56
Haviaras, Stratis
See Chaviaras, Strates
See also CLC 33
Havighurst, Alfred F(reeman) 1904- ... 33-36R
Havighurst, Marion Boyd (?)-1974 ... CAP-1
Obituary ... 49-52
Earlier sketch in CA 13-14
Havighurst, Robert J(ames) 1900- ... 23-24R
Havighurst, Walter (Edwin) 1901- ... CANR-1
Earlier sketch in CA 3R
See also SATA 1
Haviland, Virginia 1911-1988 ... CANR-12
Obituary ... 124
Earlier sketch in CA 17-18R
See also SATA 6
Havill, Steven 1945- ... CANR-25
Earlier sketch in CA 108
Havis, Allan 1951- ... 108
Havlice, Patricia Pate 1943- ... CANR-12
Earlier sketch in CA 29-32R

Havlik, John F(ranklin) 1917-1984 ..... CANR-24
Earlier sketch in CA 45-48
Havoc, June 1916- 107
Havran, Martin J. 1929- CANR-1
Earlier sketch in CA 2R
Havrevold, Finn 1905- 109
Havrilesky, Thomas M(ichael) 1939- ... CANR-19
Earlier sketches in CA 53-56, CANR-4
Haw, Richard Claude 1913- CAP-1
Earlier sketch in CA 9-10
Hawes, Evelyn (Johnson) 15-16R
See also AITN 1
Hawes, Frances Cooper (Richmond) 1897- CAP-1
Earlier sketch in CA 9-10
Hawes, Gene R(obert) 1922- CANR-18
Earlier sketches in CA 7-8R, CANR-3
Hawes, Grace M. 1926- 69-72
Hawes, Hampton 1929(?)-1977 Obituary .. 69-72
Hawes, John T. 1906(?)-1983 Obituary 109
Hawes, Joseph M(ilton) 1938- 53-56
Hawes, Judy 1913- 33-36R
See also SATA 4
Hawes, Louis 1931- 114
Hawes, Lynne Gusikoff Salop 1931- ... CANR-22
Earlier sketch in CA 106
Hawes, William (Kenneth) 1931- 77-80
Hawgood, John Arkas 1905-1971
Obituary 104
Hawk, Alex
See Garfield, Brian (Wynne)
Hawk, Grace E. 1905-1983 Obituary 110
Hawk, Philip B(ovier) 1874-1966 Obituary .. 116
Hawke, David Freeman 1923- CANR-18
Earlier sketch in CA 102
Hawke, Gary Richard 1942- 102
Hawke, Nancy
See Nugent, Nancy
Hawke, Simon
See Yermakov, Nicholas
Hawken, William R. 1917- CANR-5
Earlier sketch in CA 9-10R
Hawker, Robert Stephen 1803-1875 .... DLB-32
Hawkes, (Charles Francis) Christopher 1905- Brief entry 105
Hawkes, Glenn R(ogers) 1919- 17-18R
Hawkes, (Jessie) Jacquetta (Hopkins) 1910- CANR-15
Earlier sketch in CA 69-72
Hawkes, John (Clendennin Burne, Jr.) 1925- CANR-2
Earlier sketch in CA 4R
See also DLB 2, 7
See also DLBY 80
See also CLC 1, 2, 3, 4, 7, 9, 14, 15, 27, 49
Hawkes, Robert E(rnest) 1930- 113
Hawkes, Terence 1932- 17-18R
Hawkesworth, (Elizabeth) Celia 1942- 121
Hawkesworth, Eric 1921- 29-32R
See also SATA 13
Hawking, S. W.
See Hawking, Stephen W(illiam)
Hawking, Stephen W(illiam) 1942- Brief entry 126
Hawkins, A. Desmond
See Hawkins, (Alec) Desmond
Hawkins, Angus 1953- 126
Hawkins, Arthur 1903- CANR-8
Earlier sketch in CA 21-22R
See also SATA 19
Hawkins, Brett W(illiam) 1937- CANR-11
Earlier sketch in CA 21-22R
Hawkins, (Alec) Desmond 1908- CANR-9
Earlier sketch in CA 65-68
Hawkins, Edward H. 1934- 85-88
Hawkins, Frances P(ockman) 1913- 105
Hawkins, Gary J(ames) 1937- 115
Hawkins, Gerald S(tanley) 1928- 19-20R
Hawkins, Gordon 1919- 41-44R
Hawkins, Harriett B(loker) 1934- Brief entry 112
Hawkins, Hugh (Dodge) 1929- 1R
Hawkins, Jack
See Hawkins, John Edward
Hawkins, Jim 1944- 73-76
Hawkins, John C(harles) 1948- 106
Hawkins, John Edward 1910-1973 120
Obituary 111
Hawkins, John Noel 1944- CANR-8
Earlier sketch in CA 61-64
Hawkins, John P. 1946- 120
Hawkins, Odie 1937- 57-60
Hawkins, Peter S(tephen) 1945- 110
Hawkins, (Helena Ann) Quail 1905- 17-18R
See also SATA 6
Hawkins, Robert 1923- CANR-14
Earlier sketch in CA 21-22R
Hawkins, Robert O(usley), Jr. 1938- 117
Hawkins, Walter Everette 1883 ?- DLB-50
Hawkins, William (Waller) 1912- 4R
Hawkinson, John (Samuel) 1912- 23-24R
See also SATA 4
Hawkinson, Lucy (Ozone) 1924-1971 103
See also SATA 21
Hawks, Howard (Winchester) 1896-1977
Obituary 73-76
Hawksworth, Henry D. 1933- 73-76
Hawley, Amos H(enry) 1910- 37-40R
Hawley, Beatrice
See Jagel, Beatrice Hawley
Hawley, Cameron 1905-1969 ..... 1R
Obituary 25-28R
Hawley, Donald Frederick 1921- 108
Hawley, Donald Thomas 1923- CANR-11
Earlier sketch in CA 65-68
Hawley, Ellis W. 1929- CANR-7
Earlier sketch in CA 19-20R
Hawley, Florence M.
See Ellis, Florence Hawley
Hawley, Gessner G. 1906(?)-1983
Obituary 110
Hawley, Henrietta Ripperger 1890(?)-1974
Obituary 49-52
Hawley, Isabel (Allen) L(ockwood) 1935- CANR-7
Earlier sketch in CA 57-60
Hawley, Jane Stouder 1936- 23-24R
Hawley, John Stratton 1941- 110
Hawley, Mabel C. CANR-26
Earlier sketches in CA 19-20, CAP-2
See also SATA 1
Hawley, Richard A. 1945- 123
Hawley, Robert C(oit) 1933- CANR-22
Earlier sketches in CA 57-60, CANR-7
Hawley, Willis D(avid) 1938- 114
Haworth, Lawrence 1926- 5-6R
Haworth, Mary
See Young, Mary Elizabeth Reardon
Haworth-Booth, Mark 1944- 124
Haworth-Booth, Michael 1896- 7-8R
Haws, Duncan 1921- 97-100
Hawthorn, Jeremy 1942- 97-100
Hawthorne, Captain R. M.
See Ellis, Edward S(ylvester)
Hawthorne, (Ivy Ellen) Jennie Crawley 1916- CAP-1
Earlier sketch in CA 9-10
Hawthorne, Julian 1846-1934 ..... TCLC-25
Hawthorne, Nathaniel 1804-1864 ..... YABC-2
See also DLB 1, 74
See also CDALB 1640-1865
Hawton, Hector 1901- 15-16R
Haxton, Josephine Ayres 1921- 115
Hay, David M(cKechnie) 1935- 53-56
Hay, Dennis 1952- 105
Hay, Denys 1915- 13-14R
Hay, Eloise K(napp) 1926- 11-12R
Hay, Jacob 1920- 25-28R
Hay, James G(ordon) 1936- CANR-4
Earlier sketch in CA 53-56
Hay, John (Milton) 1838-1905 Brief entry .. 108
See also DLB 12, 47
Hay, John 1915- CANR-9
Earlier sketch in CA 65-68
See also SATA 13
Hay, Leon Edwards 25-28R
Hay, Peter 1935- 21-22R
Hay, Robert D(ean) 1921- CANR-8
Earlier sketch in CA 61-64
Hay, Sara Henderson 1906-1987 ..... CAP-1
Obituary 123
Earlier sketch in CA 15-16
Hay, Stephen N(orthup) 1925- 7-8R
Hay, Thomas Robson 1888-1974
Obituary 49-52
Hay, Timothy
See Brown, Margaret Wise
Haya de la Torre, Victor Raul 1895-1979
Obituary 89-92
Hayakawa, S(amuel) I(chiye) 1906- CANR-20
Earlier sketch in CA 15-16R
Hayami, Yujiro 1932- 77-80
Hayano, David M(amoru) 1942- 115
Hayaseca y Eizaguirre, Jorge
See Echegaray (y Eizaguirre), Jose (Maria Waldo)
Hayashi, Tetsumaro 1929- CANR-14
Earlier sketch in CA 37-40R
Hayashi Fumiko 1904-1951 ..... TCLC-27
Haycock, Ken(neth) Roy 1948- 104
Haycock, Ronald G. 1942- 123
Haycraft, Anna 122
Haycraft, Howard 1905- 23-24R
See also SATA 6
Haycraft, Molly Costain 1911- 15-16R
See also SATA 6
Hayden, Albert A(rthur) 1923- 33-36R
Hayden, C. Gervin
See Wicker, Randolfe Hayden
Hayden, Carl T(rumbull) 1877-1972
Obituary 33-36R
Hayden, Dolores 1945- CANR-9
Earlier sketch in CA 65-68
Hayden, Donald E(ugene) 1915- CANR-10
Earlier sketch in CA 25-28R
Hayden, Eric W(illiam) 1919- CANR-2
Earlier sketch in CA 5-6R
Hayden, Gwendolen Lampshire 1904- .. SATA-35
Hayden, Howard K. 1930- 19-20R
Hayden, Jay
See Paine, Lauran (Bosworth)
Hayden, Jay G. 1884-1971 Obituary 89-92
Hayden, John O(lin) 1932- CANR-10
Earlier sketch in CA 25-28R
Hayden, Julia Elizabeth 1939(?)-1981
Obituary 104
Hayden, Julie
See Hayden, Julia Elizabeth
Hayden, Martin S(choll) 1912- 69-72
Hayden, (Holden) Mike 1920-1984 120
Hayden, Naura 1942- CANR-12
Earlier sketch in CA 73-76
Hayden, Robert C(arter), Jr. 1937- CANR-24
Earlier sketch in CA 69-72
See also BW
See also SATA 28, 47
Hayden, Robert E(arl) 1913-1980 ..... CANR-24
Obituary 97-100
Earlier sketch in CA 69-72
See also CABS 2
See also BW
See also SATA 19, 26
See also DLB 5, 76
See also CDALB 1941-1968
See also CLC 5, 9, 14, 37
Hayden, Sterling 1916-1986 111
Obituary 119
Hayden, Stirling
See Hayden, Sterling
Hayden, Thomas E(mmet) 1939- 107
Hayden, Tom
See Hayden, Thomas E(mmet)
Hayden, Torey L(ynn) 1951- 103
Haydn, Hiram 1907-1973 ..... CAP-1
Obituary 45-48
Earlier sketch in CA 9-10
Haydn, Richard 1905-1985 Obituary 115
Haydon, A(lbert) Eustace 1880-1975
Obituary 61-64
Haydon, Glen 1896-1966 ..... CAP-1
Earlier sketch in CA 9-10
Haydon, June 1932- 109
Haydon, Roger (Malcolm) 1950- 118
Hayek, F(riedrich) A(ugust von) 1899- .. CANR-20
Earlier sketch in CA 93-96
Hayes, Alden C(ary) 1916- 57-60
Hayes, Alfred 1911-1985 106
Obituary 117
Hayes, Ann L(ouise) 1924- 25-28R
Hayes, Anna Hansen 1886- 3R
Hayes, Bartlett (Harding, Jr.) 1904-1988 .. 77-80
Obituary 124
Hayes, Billy 97-100
Hayes, Carlton J(oseph) H(untley) 1882-1964 ..... CANR-3
Earlier sketch in CA 1R
See also SATA 11
Hayes, Dorsha 77-80
Hayes, Douglas A(nderson) 1918- CANR-18
Earlier sketch in CA 2R
Hayes, E(ugene) Nelson 1920- 29-32R
Hayes, Edward C. 1937- 45-48
Hayes, Edward L(ee) 1931- 29-32R
Hayes, Elvin 1945- Brief entry 111
Hayes, Francis Clement 1904- CAP-2
Earlier sketch in CA 21-22
Hayes, Geoffrey 1947- CANR-25
Earlier sketches in CA 65-68, CANR-9
See also SATA 26
Hayes, Grace Person 1919- 33-36R
Hayes, Harold T(homas) P(ace) 1926- .. CANR-22
Earlier sketch in CA 69-72
Hayes, James T(homas) 1923- 29-32R
Hayes, John F. 1904- CAP-1
Earlier sketch in CA 13-14
See also SATA 11
Hayes, John H(aralson) 1934- CANR-21
Earlier sketch in CA 69-72
Hayes, John Michael 1919- 108
See also DLB 26
Hayes, John P(hillip) 1949- CANR-15
Earlier sketch in CA 93-96
Hayes, John R(ichard) 1929- 108
Hayes, John S. 1910-1981 Obituary 108
Hayes, Joseph 1918- CANR-7
Earlier sketch in CA 17-18R
Hayes, Louis D. 1940- 29-32R
Hayes, Margaret 1925- 21-22R
Hayes, Mary Anne 1956- 105
Hayes, Mary-Rose 1939- 102
Hayes, Nelson (Taylor) 1903-1971 ..... 4R
Obituary 33-36R
Hayes, Paul J(ames) 1922- 57-60
Hayes, Paul Martin 1942- 77-80
Hayes, Penny (a pseudonym) 1940- 121
Hayes, Ralph E(ugene) 1927- CANR-15
Earlier sketch in CA 21-22R
Hayes, Robert M(ayo) 1926- 11-12R
Hayes, Samuel P(erkins) 1910- CANR-3
Earlier sketch in CA 5-6R
Hayes, Sheila 1937- CANR-22
Earlier sketch in CA 106
See also SATA 50, 51
Hayes, Steven C(harles) 1948- 112
Hayes, W. Woodrow
See Hayes, Wayne Woodrow
Hayes, Wayland J(ackson) 1893-1972 .... CAP-1
Earlier sketch in CA 13-14
Hayes, Wayne Woodrow 1913-1987
Obituary 121
Hayes, Will 5-6R
See also SATA 7
Hayes, William D(imitt) 1913- 7-8R
See also SATA 8
Hayes, Wilson
See Gibbs-Wilson, Kathryn (Beatrice)
Hayes, Woody
See Hayes, Wayne Woodrow
Hayes, Zachary (Jerome) 1932- 115
Hayford, Fred Kwesi 1937- 45-48
Hayford, Harrison (Mosher) 1916- 118
Hayford, J(oseph) E(phraim) Casely
See Casely-Hayford, J(oseph) E(phraim)
Hayford, Taria
See Haydon, June
Hayley Bell, Mary 25-28R
Hayman
See Peel, H(azel) M(ary)
Hayman, Carol Bessent 1927- 53-56
Hayman, David 1927- CANR-7
Earlier sketch in CA 17-18R
Hayman, John L(uther), Jr. 1929- 25-28R
Hayman, LeRoy 1916- 85-88
Hayman, Max 1908- 19-20R
Hayman, Ronald 1932- CANR-18
Earlier sketch in CA 25-28R
See also CLC 44
Haymes, Robert C. 1931- 33-36R
Hayn, Annette 1922- 65-68
Haynal, Andre (Emeric) 1930- 120
Hayne, Paul Hamilton 1830-1886 ..... DLB-3, 64
Haynes, Alfred H(enry) 1910- 7-8R
Haynes, Anne
See Madlee, Dorothy (Haynes)
Haynes, Betsy 1937- CANR-8
Earlier sketch in CA 57-60
See also SATA 37, 48
Haynes, Brian 1939- 111
Haynes, Glynn W(alker) 1936- 65-68
Haynes, James 1932- 110
Haynes, Lincoln 1924- 116
Haynes, Linda
See Swinford, Betty (June Wells)
Haynes, Maria S(chnee) 1912- 25-28R
Haynes, Mary 1938- 111
Haynes, Pat
See McKeag, Ernest L(ionel)
Haynes, Renee (Oriana) 1906- 49-52
Haynes, Richard F(rederick) 1935- 49-52
Haynes, Robert Talmadge, Jr. 1926- 4R
Haynes, Robert Vaughn 1929- 41-44R
Haynes, Sybille 1926- 57-60
Haynes, William Warren 1921- CANR-8
Earlier sketch in CA 5-6R
Haynie, Hugh 1927- 121
Haynie, Sandra (B.) 1943- Brief entry 121
Hays, (Lawrence) Brooks 1898-1981 ..... CAP-1
Obituary 105
Earlier sketch in CA 11-12
Hays, David G(lenn) 1928- CANR-14
Earlier sketch in CA 21-22R
Hays, Elinor Rice 1R
Hays, H(offman) R(eynolds) 1904-1980 ... 81-84
Obituary 105
See also SATA 26
Hays, Helen Ireland 1903- 61-64
Hays, Paul R. 1903-1980 ..... CAP-2
Obituary 93-96
Earlier sketch in CA 19-20
Hays, Peter L. 1938- 33-36R
Hays, R. Vernon 1902- 89-92
Hays, Richard D. 1942- 37-40R
Hays, Robert Glenn 1935- 53-56
Hays, Samuel Pfrimmer 1921- 103
Hays, Terence E(ugene) 1942- 69-72
Hays, Wilma Pitchford 1909- CANR-5
Earlier sketch in CA 1R
See also SATA 1, 28
See also SAAS 3
Haystead, Wes
See Haystead, Wesley
Haystead, Wesley 1942- CANR-22
Earlier sketches in CA 57-60, CANR-6
Hayter, Alethea 1911- 29-32R
Hayter, Earl W(iley) 1901- 41-44R
Hayter, Stanley William 1901-1988
Obituary 125
Hayter, William Goodenough 1906- CANR-9
Earlier sketch in CA 21-22R
Haythornthwaite, Philip John 1951- CANR-19
Earlier sketch in CA 103
Hayton, Richard Neil 1916- 57-60
Hayward, Brooke 1937- 81-84
Hayward, Charles H(arold) 1898- CANR-7
Earlier sketch in CA 9-10R
Hayward, Jack 1931- CANR-21
Earlier sketches in CA 57-60, CANR-6
Hayward, John F(orrest) 1916-1983 ..... 11-12R
Obituary 109
Hayward, John F(rank) 1918- 5-6R
Hayward, Linda 1943- 112
See also SATA 39
Hayward, Max 1925(?)-1979 93-96
Obituary 85-88
Hayward, Richard 1893- CAP-1
Earlier sketch in CA 9-10
Hayward, Richard
See Kendrick, Baynard H(ardwick)
Haywood, Carolyn 1898- CANR-20
Earlier sketches in CA 7-8R, CANR-5
See also SATA 1, 29
Haywood, Charles 1904- CANR-22
Earlier sketch in CA 3R
Haywood, Dixie 1933- 105
Haywood, Eliza 1693(?)-1756 ..... DLB-39
Haywood, H(erbert) Carl(ton) 1931- CANR-3
Earlier sketch in CA 49-52
Haywood, Harry
See Hall, Haywood
Haywood, John Alfred 1913- 19-20R
Haywood, Richard Mansfield 1905-1977 .. CAP-2
Obituary 69-72
Earlier sketch in CA 33-36
Haywood, Richard Mowbray 1933- 25-28R
Hazam, Louis J. 1911-1983 Obituary 110
Hazan, Marcella (Maddalena) 1924-
Brief entry 116
Hazan, Victor 1928- 114
Hazard, David 1955- 116
Hazard, Harry W(illiams) 1918- 122
Hazard, Jack
See Booth, Edwin
Hazard, John N(ewbold) 1909- 1R
Hazard, Leland 1893- 17-18R
Hazard, Patrick D. 1927- 13-14R
Hazel, Paul 1944- 114
Hazelrigg, Meredith K(ent) 1942- 33-36R
Hazelton, Alexander
See Armstrong, William A(lexander)

Hazelton, Roger 1909- CANR-16
Earlier sketches in CA 4R, CANR-1
Hazen, Allen T(racy) 1904- CAP-1
Earlier sketch in CA 13-14
Hazen, Barbara Shook 1930- CANR-22
Earlier sketch in CA 105
See also SATA 27
Hazen, Helen 1943- 116
Hazen, Margaret Hindle 1948- 126
Hazen, Robert M(iller) 1948- 112
Hazlehurst, Cameron 1941- 103
Hazleton, Lesley 1945- Brief entry 126
Hazlett, Bill
See Hazlett, William Scott
Hazlett, William Scott 1931-1983 Obituary .. 110
Hazlitt, Henry 1894- CANR-3
Earlier sketch in CA 5-6R
Hazlitt, Joseph
See Strage, Mark
Hazo, Robert G. 1931- 23-24R
Hazo, Samuel (John) 1928- CANR-8
Earlier sketch in CA 7-8R
Hazzard, Lowell B(restel) 1898-1978
Obituary 77-80
Hazzard, Mary 1928- 105
Hazzard, Shirley 1931- CANR-4
Earlier sketch in CA 9-10R
See also DLBY 82
See also CLC 18
Heacox, Cecil E. 1903- 101
Head, Alice Maud 1886-1981 Obituary 116
Head, Ann
See Morse, Anne Christensen
Head, Bessie 1937-1986 .... CANR-25
Obituary 119
Earlier sketch in CA 29-32R
See also BW
See also CLC 25
Head, Constance 1939- 37-40R
Head, Edith 1898(?)-1981 Obituary 105
Head, Gay
See Hauser, Margaret L(ouise)
Head, Gwen 1940- 89-92
Head, K(enneth) Maynard 1938- 110
Head, (Joanne) Lee 1931-1983 65-68
Obituary 110
Head, Matthew
See Canaday, John E(dwin)
Head, Richard G(lenn) 1938- 53-56
Head, Robert V. 1929- CANR-15
Earlier sketch in CA 41-44R
Head, Sydney W(arren) 1913- CANR-9
Earlier sketch in CA 65-68
Head, Timothy E. 1934- 15-16R
Headapohl, B. R.
See Headapohl, Betty R.
Headapohl, Betty R. 1940- 122
Headings, Mildred J. 1908- 37-40R
Headington, Bonnie Jay 1940- 114
Headington, Christopher John Magenis
1930- Brief entry 106
Headley, Elizabeth
See Harrison, Elizabeth Cavanna
Headley, Gwyn 1946- 125
Headley, Joel T. 1813-1897 .... DLB-30
Headon, (Nicky) Topper 1956(?)- CLC-30
Headstrom, (Birger) Richard 1902- CANR-13
Earlier sketches in CA 4R, CANR-2
See also SATA 8
Heady, Earl O(rel) 1916- CANR-8
Earlier sketch in CA 19-20R
Heady, Eleanor B(utler) 1917- 41-44R
See also SATA 8
Heady, Harold F(ranklin) 1916- 53-56
Heagney, Anne 1901- 7-8R
Heal, Edith 1903- CANR-2
Earlier sketch in CA 4R
See also SATA 7
Heal, Jeanne (Bennett) 1917- CAP-1
Earlier sketch in CA 9-10
Heald, Charles Brehmer 1882-1974
Obituary 49-52
Heald, Edward Thornton 1885- 17-18R
Heald, Morrell 1922- Brief entry 111
Heald, Timothy (Villiers) 1944- CANR-2
Earlier sketch in CA 49-52
Healey, B. J.
See Healey, Ben (James)
Healey, Ben (James) 1908- CANR-17
Earlier sketch in CA 77-80
Healey, Brooks
See Albert, Burton, Jr.
Healey, Denis Winston 1917- 110
Healey, F(rancis) G(eorge) 1903- CAP-2
Earlier sketch in CA 21-22
Healey, James 1936- 53-56
Healey, James Stewart 1931- 57-60
Healey, Joseph G(raham) 1938- 116
Healey, Larry 1927- 101
See also SATA 42, 44
Healey, Robert (Mathieu) 1921- 61-64
Healey-Kay, (Sydney Francis) Patrick
(Chippendall) 1904-1983 Obituary 111
Healy, David F(rank) 1926- 19-20R
Healy, Dermot 1947- 114
Healy, Fleming 1911- 7-8R
Healy, George Robert 1923- 19-20R
Healy, George W(illiam), Jr. 1905-1980 ...69-72
Obituary 125
Healy, John D(elaware) 1921- 93-96
Healy, Kent T(enney) 1902-1985 Obituary .. 114
Healy, Patrick III 1910- Brief entry 110
Healy, Paul F(rancis) 1915-1984 ....17-18R
Obituary 114
Healy, Richard J. 1916- 25-28R
Healy, Sean D(esmond) 1927- CANR-11
Earlier sketch in CA 25-28R
Healy, Sister Kathleen 61-64
Healy, Timothy S. 1923- 41-44R
Heaney, John J. 1925- CANR-5
Earlier sketch in CA 9-10R
Heaney, Seamus (Justin) 1939- CANR-25
Earlier sketch in CA 85-88
See also DLB 40
See also CLC 5, 7, 14, 25, 37
Heap, Desmond 1907- CANR-15
Earlier sketches in CA 9-10, CAP-1
Heaps, Willard A(llison) 1908- 85-88
See also SATA 26
Heard, (George) Alexander 1917- 17-18R
Heard, (Henry Fitz) Gerald 1889-1971 .... CAP-2
Obituary 29-32R
Earlier sketch in CA 21-22
Heard, H. F.
See Heard, (Henry Fitz) Gerald
Heard, J(oseph) Norman 1922- 11-12R
Heard, Nathan C(liff) 1936- CANR-25
Earlier sketch in CA 53-56
See also BW
See also DLB 33
Hearder, Harry 1924- 5-6R
Hearn, Charles R(alph) 1937- 77-80
Hearn, Emily
See Valleau, Emily
Hearn, Janice W. 1938- 65-68
Hearn, John 1920- 97-100
Hearn, (Patricio) Lafcadio (Tessima Carlos)
1850-1904 Brief entry 105
See also DLB 12
See also TCLC 9
Hearn, M(illard) F(illmore, Jr.) 1938- 115
Hearn, Sneed
See Gregg, Andrew K.
Hearnden, Arthur (George) 1931- 65-68
Hearne, Betsy Gould 1942- 114
See also SATA 38
Hearne, John (Edgar Caulwell) 1926- 125
Brief entry 116
See also BW
Hearnshaw, Leslie Spencer 1907- 89-92
Hearon, Shelby 1931- CANR-18
Earlier sketch in CA 25-28R
See also AITN 2
Hearsey, John E(dward) N(icholl)
1928- CANR-8
Earlier sketch in CA 7-8R
Hearst, David Whitmire 1915-1986
Obituary 119
Hearst, George Randolph 1904-1972
Obituary 89-92
Hearst, James 1900-1983 .... CANR-15
Earlier sketch in CA 85-88
Hearst, William Randolph 1863-1951
Brief entry 118
See also DLB 25
Heartman, Harold
See Mebane, John (Harrison)
Heasman, Kathleen Joan 1913- CAP-1
Earlier sketch in CA 9-10
Heater, Derek (Benjamin) 1931- CANR-6
Earlier sketch in CA 57-60
Heath, Catherine 1924- 93-96
See also DLB 14
Heath, Charles C(hastain) 1921- 69-72
Heath, Charles D(ickinson) 1941- 121
See also SATA 46
Heath, Douglas H(amilton) 1925- 17-18R
Heath, Dwight B(raley) 1930- CANR-7
Earlier sketch in CA 17-18R
Heath, Edward Richard George 1916- 33-36R
Heath, G. Louis 1944- 37-40R
Heath, Harry E(ugene), Jr. 1919- 85-88
Heath, (Ernest) James 1920- 17-18R
Heath, Jim F(rank) 1931- 29-32R
Heath, Mary Ellen 1928- 115
Heath, Monica
See Fitzgerald, Arlene J.
Heath, (Charles) Monro 1899-1966 ...... CAP-1
Earlier sketch in CA 9-10
Heath, Peter (Lauchlan) 1922- 41-44R
Heath, Robert L. 1941- 126
Heath, Robert W. 1931- 13-14R
Heath, Roy 1917- 11-12R
Heath, Roy A(ubrey) K(elvin) 1926- 106
Heath, Royton E(dward) 1907- 9-10R
Heath, Sandra
See Wilson, Sandra
Heath, Terrence (George) 1936- 97-100
Heath, Veronica
See Blackett, Veronica Heath
Heath, William (Webster) 1929- 2R
Heathcott, Mary
See Keegan, Mary Heathcott
Heath-Stubbs, John (Francis Alexander)
1918- 13-14R
See also DLB 27
Heat-Moon, William Least
See Trogdon, William (Lewis)
See also CLC 29
Heaton, Charles Huddleston 1928- CANR-20
Earlier sketch in CA 2R
Heaton, Eric William 1920- 61-64
Heaton, Herbert 1890-1973 ....7-8R
Obituary 41-44R
Heaton, Peter 1919- 104
Heaton, Rose Henniker 1884-1975
Obituary 61-64
Heaton-Ward, William Alan 1919- 102
Heatter, Gabriel 1890-1972 Obituary 89-92
Heaven, Constance 1911- CANR-18
Earlier sketches in CA 49-52, CANR-2
See also SATA 7
Hebard, Edna L(aura Henriksen) 1913- 9-10R
Hebb, D(onald) O(lding) 1904-1985 ..... CANR-2
Obituary 118
Earlier sketch in CA 2R
Hebblethwaite, Brian Leslie 1939- 109
Hebblethwaite, Peter 1930- 69-72
Hebden, Mark
See Harris, John
Hebert, Anne 1916- 85-88
See also DLB 68
See also CLC 4, 13, 29
Hebert, Ernest 1941- 102
Hebert, F(elix) Edward 1901-1979 110
Obituary 106
Hebert, (Arthur) Gabriel 1886-1963 .... 3R
Hebert, Jacques 1923- CANR-11
Earlier sketch in CA 25-28R
See also DLB 53
Hebert, Tom 1938- 69-72
Hebson, Ann (Hellebusch) 1925- 19-20R
Hechinger, Fred M(ichael) 1920- 77-80
Hechler, Ken 1914- 109
Hecht, Anthony (Evan) 1923- CANR-6
Earlier sketch in CA 11-12R
See also DLB 5
See also CLC 8, 13, 19
Hecht, Ben 1894-1964 85-88
See also DLB 7, 9, 25, 26, 28
See also CLC 8
Hecht, George J(oseph) 1895-1980
Obituary 97-100
See also SATA 22
Hecht, Henri Joseph 1922- 29-32R
See also SATA 9
Hecht, James L(ee) 1926- 33-36R
Hecht, Joseph C. 1924- 29-32R
Hecht, Marie B(ergenfeld) 1918- 21-22R
Hecht, Robert A(nthony) 1929- 114
Hecht, Roger 1926- 17-18R
Hecht, Warren Jay 1946- 103
Hechter, Michael 1943- 69-72
Hechtkopf, Henryk 1910- SATA-17
Hechtlinger, Adelaide 1914- 29-32R
Heck, Bessie Holland 1911- 7-8R
See also SATA 26
Heck, Frank H(opkins) 1904-1983 69-72
Obituary 126
Heck, Harold J(oseph) 1906- 41-44R
Heck, Peter M. 1937- 53-56
Heck, Suzanne Wright 1939- 53-56
Heckart, Barbara Hooper 1937- 118
Heckart, Beverly Anne 1938- 103
Heckel, Robert V. 1925- 11-12R
Heckelmann, Charles N(ewman) 1913- 49-52
Hecker, Isaac Thomas 1819-1888 .... DLB-1
Heckert, J(osiah) Brooks 1893- 7-8R
Heckler, Jonellen (Beth) 1943- 109
Heckman, Hazel 1904- 21-22R
Heckman, William O(scar) 1921- 21-22R
Heckmann, Wolf 1929- 114
Heckscher, August 1913- 3R
Hedayat, Sadeq 1903-1951 Brief entry 120
See also TCLC 21
Hedberg, Nancy 1944- 122
Hedde, Wilhelmina G(enevava) 1895- 7-8R
Hedden, Walter Page 1898(?)-1976
Obituary 65-68
Hedden, Worth Tuttle 1896-1985 .... CAP-2
Obituary 117
Earlier sketch in CA 21-22
Hedderwick, Mairi 1939- SATA-30
Hederman, Thomas M(artin), Jr.
1911-1985 Obituary 114
Hedge, Frederic Henry 1805-1890 .... DLB-1, 59
Hedge, Leslie (Joseph) 1922- 11-12R
Hedgeman, Anna Arnold 1899- CAP-1
Earlier sketch in CA 15-16
Hedges, Bob A(tkinson) 1919- 45-48
Hedges, David (Paget) 1930- 45-48
Hedges, Elaine R(yan) 1927- CANR-7
Earlier sketch in CA 57-60
Hedges, Inez (Kathleen) 1947- 116
Hedges, Joseph
See Harknett, Terry
Hedges, Sid(ney) G(eorge) 1897-1974 .. CANR-4
Earlier sketch in CA 11-12R
See also SATA 28
Hedges, Trimble R(aymond) 1906- CAP-2
Earlier sketch in CA 21-22
Hedges, Ursula M. 1940- 29-32R
Hedges, William L(eonard) 1923- 37-40R
Hedin, Mary 103
Hedley, George (Percy) 1899- CAP-2
Earlier sketch in CA 19-20
Hedley, (Gladys) Olwen 1912- CANR-9
Earlier sketch in CA 61-64
Hedlund, Ronald D(avid) 1941- 33-36R
Hedren, Paul L(eslie) 1949- 114
Hedrick, Addie M. 1903- CAP-2
Earlier sketch in CA 25-28
Hedrick, Basil C(alvin) 1932- CANR-21
Earlier sketch in CA 33-36R
Hedrick, Floyd D(udley) 1927- 33-36R
Hedrick, Joan Doran 1944- 107
Hedrick, Travis K. 1904(?)-1977
Obituary 69-72
Heeney, Brian 1933- 89-92
Heer, David MacAlpine 1930- 15-16R
Heer, John E(dward), Jr. 1921-19(?)
Obituary 113
Heer, Nancy Whittier 33-36R
Heeresma, Heere 1932- 25-28R
Heeresma Inc.
See Heeresma, Heere
Heermance, J. Noel 1939- 25-28R
Heerwagen, Paul K. 1895- 29-32R
Heezen, Bruce C(harles) 1924-1977 49-52
Obituary 69-72
Heffer, Eric S(amuel) 1922- 123
Heffern, Richard 1950- 61-64
Heffernan, James A(nthony) W(alsh)
1939- 25-28R
Heffernan, Michael 1942- CANR-18
Earlier sketch in CA 77-80
Heffernan, Patrick
See O'Heffernan, Patrick
Heffernan, Paul 1905(?)-1983 Obituary 110
Heffernan, Thomas (Patrick Carroll)
1939- 81-84
Heffernan, Thomas Farel 1933- 107
Heffernan, Thomas J(ohn Andrew) 1944- ... 125
Heffernan, William A. 1937- 25-28R
Heffley, Wayne 1927- 11-12R
Heffner, Richard D(ouglas) 1925- 69-72
Heffron, Dorris 1944- 49-52
Hefley, James C(arl) 1930- CANR-7
Earlier sketch in CA 13-14R
Heflin, Donald
See Wallmann, Jeffrey M(iner)
Hefner, Hugh (Marston) 1926- Brief entry .. 110
See also AITN 1
Hefner, Paul
See Tabori, Paul
Hefner, Robert W(illiam) 1952- 119
Hefter, Richard 1942- CANR-23
Earlier sketch in CA 107
See also SATA 31
Hegarty, Edward J. 1891- CANR-5
Earlier sketch in CA 2R
Hegarty, Ellen 1918- 37-40R
Hegarty, Reginald Beaton 1906-1973 ..... CAP-1
Obituary 41-44R
Earlier sketch in CA 15-16
See also SATA 10
Hegarty, Sister M(ary) Loyola
See Hegarty, Ellen
Hegarty, Walter 1922- 65-68
Hegel, Richard 1927- CANR-6
Earlier sketch in CA 57-60
Hegel, Robert Earl 1943- 108
Hegeler, Sten 1923- 107
Hegeman, Elizabeth Blair 1942- 61-64
Hegener, Mark Paul 1919-1988 Obituary ... 125
Heger, Theodore Ernest 1907- 33-36R
Hegesippus
See Schonfield, Hugh J(oseph)
Heggoy, Alf Andrew 1938- CANR-14
Earlier sketch in CA 37-40R
Hegi, Ursula 1946- 104
Heginbotham, Stanley J. 1938-
Brief entry 106
Heglar, Mary Schnall 1934- 49-52
Hegner, William 1928- 93-96
Hegre, Theodore A. 1908-1984 Obituary ... 115
Hegstad, Roland R(ex) 1926- 57-60
Heiber, Helmut 1924- 49-52
Heiby, Walter A(lbert) 1918- 21-22R
Heichberger, Robert Lee 1930- 53-56
Heichelheim, Fritz M(oritz) 1901-1968
Obituary 116
Heicher, Merlo K. W. 1882-1967 .... CAP-1
Earlier sketch in CA 13-14
Heidbreder, Margaret Ann
See Eastman, Ann Heidbreder
Heide, Florence Parry 1919- CANR-19
Earlier sketch in CA 93-96
See also SATA 32
See also SAAS 6
Heide, Robert 1939- CANR-20
Earlier sketch in CA 103
Heidegger, Martin 1889-1976 81-84
Obituary 65-68
See also CLC 24
Heideman, Eugene P. 1929- 69-72
Heiden, Carol A. 1939- 57-60
Heiden, Konrad 1901-1966 Obituary 116
Heidenreich, Charles A(lbert) 1917- 25-28R
Heidenstam, (Carl Gustaf) Verner von
1859-1940 Brief entry 104
See also TCLC 5
Heiderstadt, Dorothy 1907- CANR-1
Earlier sketch in CA 4R
See also SATA 6
Heidi, Gloria 69-72
Heidingsfield, Myron S. 1914-1969 .... 4R
Obituary 103
Heidish, Marcy Moran 1947- 101
See also DLBY 82
Heiferman, Ronald Ian 1941- 61-64
Heifetz, Harold 1919- CANR-10
Earlier sketch in CA 25-28R
Heifetz, Milton D. 1921- 57-60
Heifner, Jack 1946- 105
See also CLC 11
Heiges, P. Myers 1887-1968 .... CAP-1
Earlier sketch in CA 15-16
Heijermans, Herman 1864-1924
Brief entry 123
See also TCLC 24
Heijke, John 1927- 21-22R
Heikal, Muhammed Hassanein 1923-
Brief entry 112
Heil, John 112
Heil, Ruth 1947- 112
Heilbron, J(ohn) L(ewis) 1934- CANR-19
Earlier sketches in CA 53-56, CANR-4
Heilbroner, Joan Knapp 1922- 2R
Heilbroner, Robert L(ouis) 1919- CANR-21
Earlier sketches in CA 1R, CANR-4
Heilbronner, Walter L(eo) 1924- 25-28R
Heilbrun, Carolyn G(old) 1926- CANR-1
Earlier sketch in CA 45-48
See also CLC 25
Heilbrun, Lois Hussey 1922(?)-1987
Obituary 123

Heilbrunn, Otto 1906-1969 ... CAP-1
Earlier sketch in CA 15-16
Heilig, Matthias R. 1881-? ... CAP-2
Earlier sketch in CA 23-24
Heiliger, Edward Martin 1909- ... 13-14R
Heilman, Arthur (William) 1914- ... CANR-5
Earlier sketch in CA 5-6R
Heilman, Grant 1919- ... 53-56
Heilman, Joan Rattner ... CANR-21
Earlier sketches in CA 57-60, CANR-6
See also SATA 50
Heilman, Robert Bechtold 1906- ... CANR-9
Earlier sketch in CA 15-16R
Heilman, Samuel C(hiel) 1946- ... 69-72
Heilner, Van Campen 1899-1970
Obituary ... 29-32R
Heim, Alice (Winifred) 1913- ... CANR-14
Earlier sketch in CA 33-36R
Heim, Bruno Bernard 1911- ... 89-92
Heim, Kathleen M(cEntee) 1948- ... 111
Heim, Ralph Daniel 1895- ... 73-76
Heiman, Ernest J(ean) 1930- ... CANR-4
Earlier sketch in CA 53-56
Heiman, Grover G(eorge, Jr.) 1920- ... CANR-6
Earlier sketch in CA 5-6R
Heiman, Judith 1935- ... 3R
Heiman, Marcel 1909-1976 Obituary ... 65-68
Heimann, Susan 1940- ... 33-36R
Heimarck, Theodore 1906- ... 7-8R
Heimbeck, Raeburne S(eeley) 1930- ... 29-32R
Heimberg, Marilyn Markham
See Ross, Marilyn (Ann) Heimberg
Heimdahl, Ralph 1909- ... 69-72
Heimer, Mel(vin Lytton) 1915-1971 ... CANR-4
Obituary ... 29-32R
Earlier sketch in CA 2R
Heimert, Alan (Edward) 1928- ... 7-8R
Heimler, Eugene 1922- ... CANR-8
Earlier sketch in CA 13-14R
Heimlich, Henry Jay 1920- ... 102
Heimsath, Charles H. 1928- ... 19-20R
Hein, Eleanor C(harlotte) 1933- ... 61-64
Hein, John 1921- ... CANR-16
Earlier sketches in CA 45-48, CANR-1
Hein, Leonard William 1916- ... 53-56
Hein, Lucille Eleanor 1915- ... CANR-2
Earlier sketch in CA 7-8R
See also SATA 20
Hein, Marvin Lester 1925- ... 125
Hein, Norvin 1914- ... 61-64
Hein, Piet 1905- ... CANR-4
Earlier sketch in CA 49-52
Hein, Rolland Neal 1932- ... 112
Heinberg, Paul (Julius) 1924- ... CANR-23
Earlier sketch in CA 45-48
Heindel, Richard Heathcote 1912-1979
Obituary ... 89-92
Heine, Carl 1936- ... 57-60
Heine, Lala Koehn
See Koehn-Heine, Lala
Heine, Ralph W(illiam) 1914- ... 41-44R
Heine, William C(olbourne) 1919- ... 97-100
Heineman, Benjamin Walter, Jr. 1944- ... 105
Heineman, Helen 1936- ... 125
Heinemann, George Alfred 1918- ... SATA-31
Heinemann, Katherine 1918- ... 77-80
Heinemann, Larry C(urtiss) 1944- ... 110
See also CLC 50
Heinemann, Ronald L(ynton) 1939- ... 112
Heinen, Hubert (Plummer) 1937- ... 41-44R
Heiney, Donald (William) 1921- ... CANR-3
Earlier sketch in CA 3R
See also CLC 9
Heinke, Clarence H. 1912- ... 53-56
Heinl, Nancy G(ordon) 1916- ... 81-84
Heinl, Robert Debs, Jr. 1916-1979 ... CANR-4
Obituary ... 85-88
Earlier sketch in CA 7-8R
Heinlein, Robert A(nson) 1907-1988 ... CANR-20
Obituary ... 125
Earlier sketches in CA 2R, CANR-1
See also SATA 9
See also DLB 8
See also CLC 1, 3, 8, 14, 26
Heinrich, Bernd 1940- ... 109
Heinrich, Willi 1920- ... CANR-15
Earlier sketch in CA 93-96
See also DLB 75
Heinrichs, Waldo H(untley), Jr. 1925- ... 122
Heins, A(rthur) James 1931- ... 7-8R
Heins, Ethel L(eah) 1918- ... 102
Heins, Marjorie 1946- ... 69-72
Heins, Paul 1909- ... 69-72
See also SATA 13
Heinsohn, A(ugereau) G(ray), Jr. 1896- ... CAP-1
Earlier sketch in CA 11-12
Heinsohn, Thomas William 1934-
Brief entry ... 118
Heinsohn, Tommy
See Heinsohn, Thomas William
Heintz, Ann Christine 1930- ... CANR-8
Earlier sketch in CA 61-64
Heintz, Bonnie L(ee) 1924- ... 69-72
Heintz, John 1936- ... 45-48
Heintze, Carl 1922- ... 57-60
See also SATA 26
Heintzelman, Donald S(haffer) 1938- ... CANR-16
Earlier sketch in CA 93-96
Heinz, G.
See Gerard-Libois, Jules C.
Heinz, W(ilfred) C(harles) 1915- ... CANR-4
Earlier sketch in CA 5-6R
See also SATA 26
Heinz, William Frederick 1899-1976 ... CANR-12
Earlier sketch in CA 61-64
Heinze, Robert H(arold) 1920-1984
Obituary ... 113
Heinzelman, Kurt 1947- ... 101
Heinzen, Mildred
See Masters, Mildred
Heinzerling, Larry E(dward) 1945- ... 73-76
Heinzerling, Lynn Louis 1906-1983
Obituary ... 111
Heinzman(n), George (Melville) 1916- ... 2R
Heirich, Max 1931- ... 29-32R
Heise, David R(euben) 1937- ... 89-92
Heise, Edward Tyler 1912- ... 1R
Heise, Kenan 1933- ... 57-60
Heisenberg, Werner 1901-1976 Obituary ... 65-68
Heiser, Charles B(ixler), Jr. 1920- ... 45-48
Heiser, Victor George 1893-1972
Obituary ... 33-36R
Heiserman, Arthur Ray 1929-1975 ... CANR-15
Obituary ... 103
Earlier sketch in CA 1R
Heiserman, David L(ee) 1940- ... CANR-8
Earlier sketch in CA 61-64
Heisey, Alan Milliken 1928- ... 57-60
Heiskell, John Netherland 1872-1972
Obituary ... 89-92
Heisler, Martin O. 1938- ... CANR-23
Earlier sketch in CA 45-48
Heiss, Jerold (Sheldon) 1930- ... 126
Brief entry ... 111
Heissenbuettel, Helmut 1921- ... 81-84
See also DLB 75
Heissenbuttel, Helmut
See Heissenbuettel, Helmut
See also DLB 75
Heisserer, Andrew Jackson 1935- ... 111
Heitler, Walter (Heinrich) 1904-1981 ... CANR-8
Earlier sketch in CA 13-14R
Heitman, Sidney 1924- ... 11-12R
Heitner, Robert R. 1920- ... 5-6R
Heitzmann, William Ray 1948- ... CANR-17
Earlier sketch in CA 97-100
Heizer, Robert Fleming 1915-1979 ... 102
Hekker, Terry 1932- ... 97-100
Hekman, Susan J(ean) 1949- ... 114
Helbig, Alethea K. 1928- ... CANR-17
Earlier sketch in CA 97-100
Helbing, Terry 1951- ... 89-92
Helbling, Robert E(ugene) 1923- ... 49-52
Helck, C. Peter 1893- ... CANR-1
Earlier sketch in CA 3R
Held, David 1951- ... 110
Held, Jack Preston 1926- ... 33-36R
Held, Jacqueline 1936- ... CANR-14
Earlier sketch in CA 73-76
Held, Joseph 1930- ... 45-48
Held, Julius Samuel 1905- ... 103
Held, Peter
See Vance, John Holbrook
Held, R(over) Burnell 1921- ... 33-36R
Held, Ray E(ldred) 1918- ... 45-48
Held, Richard 1922- ... 41-44R
Held, Virginia (Potter) 1929- ... CANR-16
Earlier sketches in CA 1R, CANR-1
Helder, Dom
See Camara, Helder Pessoa
Heldman, Dan C(hristopher) 1943- ... 110
Heldman, Gladys M(edalie) 1922-
Brief entry ... 111
Heleniak, Kathryn Moore ... 110
Helfen, Otto J. Maenchen
See Maenchen, Otto John
Helfert, Erich A(nton) 1931- ... 9-10R
Helfgott, Daniel (Andrew) 1952- ... CANR-22
Earlier sketch in CA 106
Helfgott, Roy B. 1925- ... 81-84
Helfman, Elizabeth S(eaver) 1911- ... CANR-5
Earlier sketch in CA 5-6R
See also SATA 3
Helfman, Harry 1910- ... 25-28R
See also SATA 3
Helforth, John
See Doolittle, Hilda
Helfritz, Hans 1902- ... 41-44R
Helgerson, Richard 1940- ... 116
Helgesen, Sally 1948- ... 115
Helion, Jean 1904-1987 Obituary ... 124
Helitzer, Florence (Saperstein) 1928- ... 19-20R
Hellberg, Hans-Eric 1927- ... CANR-18
Earlier sketch in CA 101
See also SATA 38
Hellegers, Andre E. 1926-1979 Obituary ... 85-88
Heller, J(ohn) A(nthony) 1935- ... 61-64
Hellenhofferu, Vojtech Kapristian z
See Hasek, Jaroslav (Matej Frantisek)
Heller
See Iranek-Osmecki, Kazimierz
Heller, Abraham M. 1898-1975 Obituary ... 57-60
Heller, Bernard 1896-1976 Obituary ... 65-68
Heller, Celia S(topnicka) ... 37-40R
Heller, David (A.) 1922-1968 ... CAP-1
Earlier sketch in CA 9-10
Heller, David 1957- ... 124
Heller, Dawn Hansen 1932- ... 125
Heller, Deane Fons 1924- ... 9-10R
Heller, Erich 1911- ... CANR-8
Earlier sketch in CA 13-14R
Heller, Francis H(oward) 1917- ... 1R
Heller, H(einz) Robert 1940- ... CANR-22
Earlier sketch in CA 69-72
Heller, Herbert L. 1908- ... 21-22R
Heller, Jean 1942- ... 73-76
Heller, John 1896(?)-1987 Obituary ... 124
Heller, John H(erbert) 1921- ... 114
Heller, Joseph 1923- ... CANR-8
Earlier sketch in CA 7-8R
See also CABS 1
See also DLB 2, 28
See also DLBY 80
See also CLC 1, 3, 5, 8, 11, 36
See also AITN 1
Heller, Keith 1949- ... 119
Heller, Linda 1944- ... 108
See also SATA 40, 46
Heller, Mark (Francis) 1914- ... CANR-10
Earlier sketch in CA 61-64
Heller, Michael (David) 1937- ... CANR-26
Earlier sketch in CA 45-48
Heller, Mike
See Hano, Arnold
Heller, Peter 1920- ... CANR-14
Earlier sketch in CA 41-44R
Heller, Rachelle S(ara) 1943- ... 111
Heller, Reinhold (August Friedrich) 1940- ... 77-80
Heller, Robert 1899(?)-1973 Obituary ... 41-44R
Heller, Robert W(illiam) 1933- ... 25-28R
Heller, Shelly
See Heller, Rachelle S(ara)
Heller, Sipa 1897(?)-1980 Obituary ... 97-100
Heller, Trudy (Marie) 1944- ... 115
Heller, Walter W(olfgang) 1915-1987 ... 21-22R
Obituary ... 122
Heller, Wilson Battin 1893-1983 Obituary ... 110
Hellerman, Herbert 1927- ... 53-56
Hellerstein, David (Joel) 1953- ... 120
Hellerstein, Jerome R. 1907- ... CAP-1
Earlier sketch in CA 13-14
Hellerstein, Kathryn (Ann) 1952- ... 114
Hellie, Ann 1925- ... CANR-15
Earlier sketch in CA 77-80
Hellie, Richard 1937- ... CANR-14
Earlier sketch in CA 33-36R
Hellinga, Wytze (Gs) 1908-1985 Obituary ... 116
Hellinger, Douglas A(lan) 1948- ... CANR-21
Earlier sketch in CA 69-72
Hellinger, Stephen H(enry) 1948- ... CANR-21
Earlier sketch in CA 69-72
Hellison, Donald R(aymond) 1938- ... 53-56
Hellman, Anna 1902(?)-1972 Obituary ... 33-36R
Hellman, Arthur D(avid) 1942- ... 69-72
Hellman, C(larisse) Doris 1910-1973
Obituary ... 41-44R
Hellman, Geoffrey T(heodore) 1907-1977 ... 69-72
Obituary ... 73-76
Hellman, Hal
See Hellman, Harold
Hellman, Harold 1927- ... CANR-10
Earlier sketch in CA 25-28R
See also SATA 4
Hellman, Hugo E. 1908- ... CAP-2
Earlier sketch in CA 19-20
Hellman, Judith Adler 1945- ... 113
Hellman, Lillian (Florence) 1905-1984 ... 13-14R
Obituary ... 112
See also DLB 7
See also DLBY 84
See also CLC 2, 4, 8, 14, 18, 34, 44
See also AITN 1, 2
Hellman, Peter 1943- ... 107
Hellman, Robert 1919-1984 ... 17-18R
Obituary ... 113
Hellmann, Donald C(harles) 1933- ... 45-48
Hellmann, Ellen 1908- ... 106
Hellmann, John 1948- ... CANR-24
Earlier sketch in CA 105
Hellmuth, Jerome 1911- ... 15-16R
Hellmuth, William Frederick, Jr. 1920- ... CANR-4
Earlier sketch in CA 2R
Hellstrom, Ward 1930- ... 33-36R
Hellwig, Monika Konrad 1929- ... 37-40R
Helly, Dorothy O. 1931- ... 122
Hellyer, A(rthur) G(eorge) L(ee) 1902- ... CANR-19
Earlier sketches in CA 9-10R, CANR-4
Hellyer, Arthur
See Hellyer, A(rthur) G(eorge) L(ee)
Hellyer, Clement David 1914- ... 118
Hellyer, David Tirrell 1913- ... 17-18R
Hellyer, Jill 1925- ... 118
Hellyer, Paul (Theodore) 1923- ... CANR-14
Earlier sketch in CA 69-72
Helm, Bertrand P. 1929- ... 37-40R
Helm, Ernest Eugene 1928- ... CANR-2
Earlier sketch in CA 1R
Helm, Everett 1913- ... 49-52
Helm, P(eter) J(ames) 1916- ... CANR-3
Earlier sketch in CA 9-10R
Helm, Robert Meredith 1917- ... 17-18R
Helm, Thomas (William) 1919- ... 7-8R
Helmer, John 1946- ... 41-44R
Helmer, William F. 1926- ... 33-36R
Helmer, William J(oseph) 1936- ... 73-76
Helmericks, Bud
See Helmericks, Harmon R.
Helmericks, Constance (Chittenden)
1918-1987 ... 9-10R
Obituary ... 122
Helmericks, Harmon R. 1917- ... 29-32R
Helmering, Doris Wild 1942- ... 65-68
Helmers, George Dow 1906- ... 61-64
Helmholz, R(ichard) H(enry) 1940- ... 61-64
Helmi, Jack
See Sands, Leo G(eorge)
Helming, Ann 1924-19(?) ... CANR-2
Earlier sketch in CA 4R
Helminiak, Daniel A. 1942- ... 126
Helmker, Judith Anne 1940- ... 33-36R
Helmlinger, (Benita) Trudy 1943- ... 69-72
Helmore, G(eoffrey) A(nthony) 1922- ... 29-32R
Helm-Pirgo, Marian 1897- ... 77-80
Helmreich, Ernst Christian 1902- ... 1R
Helmreich, Jonathan Ernst 1936-
Brief entry ... 105
Helmreich, Paul C(hristian) 1933- ... 53-56
Helmreich, Robert Louis 1937- ... 65-68
Helmreich, William B. 1945- ... 105
Helms, Jesse (Alexander, Jr.) 1921-
Brief entry ... 124
Helms, Randel 1942- ... 49-52
Helms, Roland Thomas, Jr. 1940- ... 102
Helms, Tom
See Helms, Roland Thomas, Jr.
Helmstadter, Gerald C. 1925- ... 15-16R
Heloise
See Reese, Heloise (Bowles)
Helper, Rose ... 77-80
Helpern, Milton 1902-1977 ... 73-76
Obituary ... 69-72
Helprin, Mark 1947- ... 81-84
See also DLBY 85
See also CLC 7, 10, 22, 32
Helps, Racey 1913-1971 ... CAP-2
Obituary ... 29-32R
Earlier sketch in CA 23-24
See also SATA 2, 25
Helson, Harry 1898- ... CAP-1
Earlier sketch in CA 11-12
Helterman, Jeffrey A. 1942- ... 103
Helton, David (Kirby) 1940- ... 25-28R
Helton, Tinsley 1915- ... 1R
Helvick, James
See Cockburn, (Francis) Claud
Helweg, Hans H. 1917- ... 126
See also SATA 33, 50
Helwig, David (Gordon) 1938- ... 33-36R
See also DLB 60
Helyar, Jane Penelope Josephine
1933- ... CANR-26
Earlier sketches in CA 21-22R, CANR-10
Hembree, Charles R. 1938- ... 33-36R
Hemdahl, Reuel Gustaf 1903-1977 ... 37-40R
Hemenway, Robert 1921- ... 33-36R
Hemenway, Ruby 1884(?)-1987 Obituary ... 123
Hemery, Eric 1914- ... 111
Hemesath, Caroline 1899- ... 61-64
Hemingway, Ernest 1899-1961 ... 77-80
See also DLB 4, 9
See also DLBY 81, 87
See also DLBD 1
See also CLC 1, 3, 6, 8, 10, 13, 19, 30, 34, 39, 41, 44, 50
See also SSC 1
Hemingway, Gregory H. 1931(?)-
Brief entry ... 112
Hemingway, Leicester C. 1915-1982
Obituary ... 107
Hemingway, Maggie 1946- ... 125
Hemingway, Mary Welsh 1908-1986 ... 73-76
Obituary ... 121
Hemingway, Patricia Drake 1926-1978 ... 69-72
Obituary ... 73-76
Hemingway, Taylor
See Rywell, Martin
Heminway, John (H., Jr.) 1944- ... 25-28R
Hemleben, Sylvester John 1902- ... CAP-2
Earlier sketch in CA 25-28
Hemley, Cecil Herbert 1914-1966 ... CANR-1
Obituary ... 25-28R
Earlier sketch in CA 3R
Hemley, Elaine Gottlieb
See Gottlieb, Elaine
Hemlow, Joyce 1906- ... 7-8R
Hemming, John (Henry) 1935- ... CANR-12
Earlier sketch in CA 29-32R
Hemming, Roy 1928- ... 61-64
See also SATA 11
Hemmings, F(rederic) W(illiam) J(ohn)
1920- ... 97-100
Hemmings, Susan 1941- ... 118
Hempel, Amy 1951- Brief entry ... 118
See also CLC 39
Hempel, Carl G.
See Hempel, Carl Gustav
Hempel, Carl Gustav 1905- Brief entry ... 116
Hemphill, A. Marcus 1930(?)-1986
Obituary ... 120
Hemphill, Betty
See Hemphill, Elizabeth Anne
Hemphill, Charles F., Jr. 1917- ... 101
Hemphill, Christopher (Glenn) 1950-1987
Obituary ... 122
Hemphill, Elizabeth Anne 1920- ... 115
Hemphill, George 1922- ... 15-16R
Hemphill, Herbert Waide, Jr. 1929- ... 116
Hemphill, John K(nox) 1919- ... 53-56
Hemphill, Martha Locke 1904-1973 ... 37-40R
See also SATA 37
Hemphill, Paul 1936- ... CANR-12
Earlier sketch in CA 49-52
See also DLBY 87
See also AITN 2
Hemphill, W(illiam) Edwin 1912- ... 21-22R
Hempstone, Smith 1929- ... CANR-1
Earlier sketch in CA 3R
Hempton, David 1952- ... 125
Hemschemeyer, Judith 1935- ... 49-52
Henaghan, Jim 1919- ... 102
Henahan, Donal 1921- Brief entry ... 111
Henault, Marie (Josephine) 1921- ... 33-36R
Henbest, Nigel 1951- ... 124
See also SATA 52
Henchman, Daniel 1689-1761 ... DLB-24
Hencken, Hugh O'Neill 1902-1981
Obituary ... 104
Hendee, John C(lare) 1938- ... 93-96
Hendel, Charles William 1890-1982 ... CANR-13
Obituary ... 108
Earlier sketches in CA 15-16, CAP-1

Hendel, Samuel 1909-1984 ... CANR-1
Obituary ... 113
Earlier sketch in CA 4R
Hendelson, William H. 1904-1975
Obituary ... 104
Henderley, Brooks ... CANR-26
Earlier sketches in CA 19-20, CAP-2
See also SATA 1
Henderlite, Rachel 1905- ... 2R
Hendershot, Ralph 1896(?)-1979
Obituary ... 89-92
Henderson, Alexander (John) 1910- ... CAP-1
Earlier sketch in CA 15-16
Henderson, Algo D(onmyer) 1897-1988 . CANR-1
Obituary ... 126
Earlier sketch in CA 1R
Henderson, Alice Corbin 1881-1949 ... DLB-54
Henderson, Archibald 1877-1963
Obituary ... 93-96
Henderson, Archibald 1916- ... 53-56
Henderson, Bert C. 1904- ... CAP-1
Earlier sketch in CA 9-10
Henderson, Bill 1941- ... 33-36R
Henderson, Brian 1941- ... 112
Henderson, C(rispin) A(listair) P(oland)
1955- ... 119
Henderson, C(harles) William 1925- ... 65-68
Henderson, Charles, Jr. 1923- ... 45-48
Henderson, Charles P(ackard), Jr.
1941- ... 41-44R
Henderson, Dan Fenno 1921- ... 19-20R
Henderson, David 1942- ... CANR-10
Earlier sketch in CA 25-28R
See also BW
See also DLB 41
Henderson, Dion (Winslow) 1921-1984 .. CANR-5
Obituary ... 114
Earlier sketch in CA 9-10R
Henderson, Donald
See Laughlin, Tom
Henderson, Dwight F. 1937- ... 41-44R
Henderson, Edwin Bancroft 1883-1977
Obituary ... 116
Henderson, Eva Pendleton 1890- ... 115
Henderson, F. C.
See Mencken, H(enry) L(ouis)
Henderson, G(eorge) P(atrick) 1915- ... 29-32R
Henderson, G(eorge) P(oland) 1920- ... 37-40R
Henderson, George (David Smith)
1931- ... 25-28R
Henderson, George L(eslie) 1925- ... 69-72
Henderson, George Wylie 1904- ... 125
See also BW
See also DLB 51
Henderson, Gordon 1950- ... SATA-53
Henderson, Harold G(ould) 1889-1974
Obituary ... 53-56
Henderson, Harold H(ale) 1928- ... 114
Henderson, Harry B(rinton), Jr. 1914-
Brief entry ... 109
Henderson, Ian 1910-1969 ... CAP-2
Earlier sketch in CA 17-18
Henderson, Isabel 1933- ... 25-28R
Henderson, James 1934- ... CANR-13
Earlier sketch in CA 33-36R
Henderson, James Youngblood 1944- ... 110
Henderson, Jean Carolyn Glidden 1916- ... 102
Henderson, Jennifer 1929- ... 107
Henderson, John 1906(?)-1982 Obituary ... 108
Henderson, John 1915- ... 7-8R
Henderson, John S(teele) 1919- ... 5-6R
Henderson, John W(illiam) 1910- ... 25-28R
Henderson, K(enneth) D(avid) D(ruitt)
1903- ... CAP-1
Earlier sketch in CA 15-16
Henderson, Katherine Usher 1937- ... 126
Henderson, Kathy 1949- ... 123
See also SATA 53
Henderson, (Alan) Keith 1883-1982 ... 107
Obituary ... 106
Henderson, Keith M. 1934- ... 23-24R
Henderson, Laurance G. 1924(?)-1977
Obituary ... 73-76
Henderson, Laurence 1928- ... 53-56
Henderson, Lawrence W. 1921- ... 103
Henderson, LeGrand 1901-1965 ... 5-6R
See also SATA 9
Henderson, Linda Dalrymple 1948- ... 124
Henderson, Lois T(hompson) 1918- ... 81-84
Henderson, M(arilyn) R(uth) 1927- ... 77-80R
Henderson, Mary
See Mavor, Osborne Henry
Henderson, Mary C. 1928- ... 77-80
Henderson, Michael (Douglas) 1932- ... 110
Henderson, Nancy 1943- ... 41-44R
Henderson, Nancy Wallace 1916- ... 97-100
See also SATA 22
Henderson, Paul (III) 1939- Brief entry ... 122
Henderson, Peter 1904-1983 ... 108
Obituary ... 111
Henderson, Philip (Prichard)
1906-1977 ... CANR-14
Obituary ... 104
Earlier sketches in CA 9-10, CAP-1
Henderson, Randall 1888- ... CAP-1
Earlier sketch in CA 13-14
Henderson, Richard 1924- ... CANR-20
Earlier sketches in CA 13-14R, CANR-5
Henderson, Richard B(eveir) 1921- ... 77-80
Henderson, Richard I(van) 1926- ... CANR-11
Earlier sketch in CA 69-72
Henderson, Robert 1906- ... 106
Henderson, Robert M. 1926- ... 33-36R
Henderson, Robert W(augh) 1920- ... 4R
Henderson, Robert William 1888-1985
Obituary ... 117
Henderson, S(hirley) P(rudence) A(nn)
1929- ... 37-40R
Henderson, Stephen E. 1925- ... 29-32R
See also BW
Henderson, Sylvia
See Ashton-Warner, Sylvia (Constance)
Henderson, Thomas W(alter) 1949- ... 73-76
Henderson, Vivian (Wilson) 1923-1976 ... 65-68
Obituary ... 61-64
Henderson, W(illiam) O(tto) 1904- ... CANR-4
Earlier sketch in CA 2R
Henderson, William III 1922- ... 17-18R
Henderson, William L(eroy) 1927- ... 33-36R
Henderson, Zenna (Chlarson) 1917- ... CANR-1
Earlier sketch in CA 2R
See also SATA 5
See also DLB 8
Henderson-Howat, Gerald
See Howat, Gerald Malcolm David
Hendin, David (Bruce) 1945- ... 41-44R
Hendin, Herbert (Martin) 1926-
Brief entry ... 117
Hendin, Josephine 1946- ... 102
Hendley, Coit (Taylor), Jr. 1920-1985
Obituary ... 116
Hendon, William S(cott) 1933- ... 45-48
Hendra, Tony ... 102
Hendren, Ron 1945- ... 77-80
Hendrich, Paula Griffith 1928- ... CANR-1
Earlier sketch in CA 4R
Hendrick, George 1929- ... CANR-23
Earlier sketches in CA 13-14R, CANR-8
Hendrick, Irving G(uilford) 1936- ... 81-84
Hendrick, Ives 1898-1972 ... CAP-1
Obituary ... 33-36R
Earlier sketch in CA 11-12
Hendrick, T(homas) W(illiam) 1909- ... 108
Hendricks, Faye N(eidhold) 1913- ... 69-72
Hendricks, Frances Wade Kellam 1900- ... 37-40R
Hendricks, Gay 1945- ... 73-76
Hendricks, George D. 1913- ... 5-6R
Hendricks, J(ames) Edwin 1935- ... CANR-15
Earlier sketch in CA 41-44R
Hendricks, Robert J(oseph) 1944- ... 45-48
Hendricks, Walter 1892-1979 Obituary ... 103
Hendricks, William Lawrence 1929- ... CANR-17
Earlier sketches in CA 49-52, CANR-2
Hendrickson, David C. 1953- ... 126
Hendrickson, Donald E(ugene) 1941- ... 93-96
Hendrickson, James E. 1932- ... 21-22R
Hendrickson, Paul 1944- ... 108
Hendrickson, Robert 1933- ... CANR-1
Earlier sketch in CA 49-52
Hendrickson, Robert A(ugustus)
1923- ... CANR-12
Earlier sketch in CA 29-32R
Hendrickson, Walter Brookfield, Jr.
1936- ... CANR-1
Earlier sketch in CA 3R
See also SATA 9
Hendrie, Don(ald Franz), Jr. 1942- ... CANR-18
Earlier sketches in CA 49-52, CANR-3
Hendriks, A(rthur) L(emiere) 1922- ... 97-100
Hendriksen, Eldon Sende 1917- ... 15-16R
Hendry, Allan 1950- ... 106
Hendry, J(ames) F(indlay) 1912- ... 29-32R
Hendry, Thomas 1929- ... 69-72
Hendry, Tom
See Hendry, Thomas
Hendy, Philip (Anstiss) 1900-1980
Obituary ... 102
Henegan, Lucius Herbert, Jr.
1902(?)-1979 Obituary ... 85-88
Heneghan, James 1930- ... SATA-53
Heneman, Herbert Gerhard, Jr. 1916- ... CANR-1
Earlier sketch in CA 1R
Henfil
See Souza Filho, Henrique de
Henfrey, Colin (Vere Fleetwood) 1941- ... 15-16R
Henfrey, Norman 1929- ... 25-28R
Henig, Gerald S(heldon) 1942- ... 57-60
Henig, Martin (Edward) 1942- ... 114
Henig, Robin Marantz 1953- ... 108
Henig, Ruth B(eatrice) 1943- ... 49-52
Henig, Suzanne 1936- ... CANR-2
Earlier sketch in CA 45-48
Henige, David 1938- ... 103
Heninger, S(imeon) K(ahn), Jr. 1922- ... CANR-1
Earlier sketch in CA 1R
Henisch, Heinz K. 1922- ... 73-76
Henissart, Paul 1923- ... 29-32R
Henke, Dan (Ferdinand) 1924- ... 53-56
Henke, Emerson O(verbeck) 1916- ... CANR-12
Earlier sketch in CA 17-18R
Henkel, Barbara Osborn 1921- ... 11-12R
Henkel, Stephen C. 1933- ... 37-40R
Henkels, Robert M(acAllister), Jr. 1936- ... 57-60
Henkes, Kevin 1960- ... 114
See also SATA 43
Henkes, Robert 1922- ... CANR-13
Earlier sketch in CA 33-36R
Henkin, Harmon 1940(?)-1980 Obituary ... 101
Henkin, Louis 1917- ... CANR-13
Earlier sketch in CA 33-36R
Henle, Faye ?-1972 Obituary ... 37-40R
Henle, Fritz 1909- ... 73-76
Henle, James 1891(?)-1973 Obituary ... 37-40R
Henle, Jane 1913- ... 77-80
Henle, Mary 1913- ... 33-36R
Henle, Robert John 1909- ... 110
Henle, Theda O. 1918- ... 33-36R
Henley, Arthur 1921- ... 21-22R
Henley, Beth
See Henley, Elizabeth Becker
See also DLBY 86
See also CLC 23
Henley, Elizabeth Becker 1952- ... 107
Henley, Gail 1952- ... CANR-21
Earlier sketch in CA 89-92
Henley, Karyn 1952- ... 102
Henley, Nancy Eloise Main 1934-
Brief entry ... 106
Henley, Norman 1915- ... 17-18R
Henley, Virginia 1935- ... 109
Henley, W(illiam) Ballentine 1905- ... 61-64
Henley, Wallace (Boynton) 1941- ... CANR-14
Earlier sketch in CA 65-68
Henley, William Ernest 1849-1903
Brief entry ... 105
See also DLB 19
See also TCLC 8
Henn, Harry George 1919- ... 45-48
Henn, Thomas Rice 1901-1974 ... CANR-4
Earlier sketch in CA 7-8R
Hennacy, Ammon 1893-1970 Obituary ... 104
Henne, Frances E. 1906-1985 Obituary ... 118
Hennedy, Hugh L(ouis) 1929- ... 41-44R
Henneman, John Bell, Jr. 1935- ... 45-48
Hennesey, James J. 1926- ... 33-36R
Hennessey, Caroline
See von Block, Bela W(illiam)
and von Block, Sylvia
Hennessey, R(oger) A(nthony) S(ean)
1937- ... 29-32R
Hennessy, Bernard C. 1924- ... 15-16R
Hennessy, David James George 1932- . CANR-22
Earlier sketch in CA 106
Hennessy, James Pope
See Pope-Hennessy, James
Hennessy, Jossleyn (Michael Stephen
Philip) 1903- ... 9-10R
Hennessy, Mary L. 1927- ... 23-24R
Hennessy, Max
See Harris, John
Hennessy, Peter 1947- ... 123
Hennessy, Thomas C(hristopher) 1916- ... 115
Hennig, Margaret (Marie) 1940- ... 81-84
Henning, Charles N(athaniel) 1915- ... 1R
Henning, Daniel H(oward) 1931- ... CANR-2
Earlier sketch in CA 45-48
Henning, Edward B. 1922- ... 19-20R
Henning, Standish 1932- Brief entry ... 107
Henning, Sylvie Marie Debevec
See Debevec Henning, Sylvie Marie
Henninger, G. Ross 1898-1984 Obituary ... 112
Hennings, Dorothy Grant 1935- ... CANR-4
Earlier sketch in CA 53-56
Hennings, Josephine Silva 1899(?)-1985
Obituary ... 117
Hennissart, Martha ... 85-88
Henrey, Madeleine 1906- ... CANR-6
Earlier sketch in CA 13-14R
Henrey, Mrs. Robert
See Henrey, Madeleine
Henrey, Robert
See Henrey, Madeleine
Henri, Adrian (Maurice) 1932- ... CANR-15
Earlier sketch in CA 25-28R
Henri, Florette 1908-1985 ... 73-76
Obituary ... 117
Henri, G.
See Clement, George H.
Henrichsen, Walt(er Arlie), Jr. 1934- ... 89-92
Henricks, Kaw
See Wolfe, Charles Keith
Henries, A. Doris Banks 1913(?)-1981 ... 125
Obituary ... 103
See also BW
Henries, Doris
See Henries, A. Doris Banks
Henriksen, Thomas H(ollinger) 1939- ... 112
Henriod, Lorraine 1925- ... 45-48
See also SATA 26
Henriques, Veronica 1931- ... 102
Henry, Avril (Kay) 1935- ... 123
Henry, Bessie Walker 1921- ... 9-10R
Henry, Bill
See Henry, William Mellors
Henry, Buck 1930- ... 77-80
See also DLB 26
Henry, Carl F(erdinand) H(oward)
1913- ... CANR-21
Earlier sketches in CA 13-14R, CANR-6
Henry, (William) Claud 1914- ... 45-48
Henry, Daniel
See Kahnweiler, Daniel-Henry
Henry, David Dodds 1905- ... 106
Henry, David Lee
See Hill, R. Lance
Henry, Eric P(utnam) 1943- ... 108
Henry, Fran Worden 1948- ... 111
Henry, Frances 1931- ... 77-80
Henry, Francoise 1902-1982 Obituary ... 106
Henry, Harold Wilkinson 1926- ... 37-40R
Henry, Harriet
See De Steuch, Harriet Henry
Henry, James P(aget) 1914- ... 104
Henry, James S(helburne) 1950- ... 49-52
Henry, Janet Cope 1925(?)-1986 Obituary ... 118
Henry, Jeanne Heffernan 1940- ... 105
Henry, Joanne Landers 1927- ... 17-18R
See also SATA 6
Henry, Joseph B. 1901- ... CAP-2
Earlier sketch in CA 17-18
Henry, Jules 1904-1969 Obituary ... 109
Henry, Kenneth 1920- ... 57-60
Henry, Laurin L(uther) 1921- ... 2R
Henry, Marguerite ... CANR-9
Earlier sketch in CA 19-20R
See also SATA 11
See also DLB 22
See also CLR 4
Henry, Marion
See del Rey, Lester
Henry, O.
See Porter, William Sydney
See also TCLC 1, 19
Henry, Oliver
See Porter, William Sydney
Henry, Peter 1926- ... 109
Henry, Robert Selph 1889-1970 ... CANR-17
Obituary ... 103
Earlier sketch in CA 1R
See also DLB 17
Henry, Shirley 1925(?)-1972 Obituary ... 33-36R
Henry, Sondra 1930- ... 119
Henry, T. E.
See Rowland-Entwistle, (Arthur)
Theodore (Henry)
Henry, Vera 1909(?)-1987 ... CAP-2
Obituary ... 123
Earlier sketch in CA 21-22
Henry, W. P. 1929- ... 19-20R
Henry, Will
See Allen, Henry Wilson
Henry, William A(lfred) III 1950-
Brief entry ... 116
Henry, William Earl 1917- Brief entry ... 108
Henry, William Mellors 1890-1970
Obituary ... 89-92
Henschel, Elizabeth Georgie ... 107
Henschke, Alfred
See Klabund
Hensey, Frederick G(erald) 1931- ... 89-92
Hensey, Fritz
See Hensey, Frederick G(erald)
Henshall, A(udrey) S(hore) 1927- ... 11-12R
Henshaw, James Ene 1924- ... 101
Henshaw, Richard 1945- ... 101
Henshaw, Tom 1924- ... 103
Henshel, Richard L(ee) 1939- ... 57-60
Hensley, Charles S(tanley) 1919- ... 41-44R
Hensley, Jeff (Lane) 1947- ... 117
Hensley, Joe L. 1926- ... CANR-14
Earlier sketch in CA 33-36R
Hensley, (Malcolm) Stewart 1914(?)-1976
Obituary ... 65-68
Henslin, James M(arvin) 1937- ... CANR-15
Earlier sketch in CA 41-44R
Henson, Clyde E(ugene) 1914- ... 5-6R
Henson, James Maury 1936- ... 124
Brief entry ... 106
See also SATA 43
Henson, Jim
See Henson, James Maury
Henson, Margaret Swett 1924- ... 122
Henstra, Friso 1928- ... SATA-8
Henthorn, William E(llsworth) 1928- ... 41-44R
Hentoff, Nat(han Irving) 1925- ... CANR-25
Earlier sketches in CA 2R, CANR-5
See also CAAS 6
See also SATA 27, 42
See also CLC 26
See also CLR 1
Henty, G(eorge) A(lfred) 1832-1902
Brief entry ... 112
See also DLB 18
Hentz, Caroline Lee (Whiting) 1800-1856 . DLB-3
Henwood, James N. J. 1932- ... 29-32R
Henze, Donald F(rank) 1928- ... 23-24R
Hepburn, Andrew H. 1899(?)-1975
Obituary ... 57-60
Hepburn, James Gordon 1922- ... 85-88
Hepburn, Ronald W(illiam) 1927- ... 13-14R
Hepner, Harry W(alker) 1893-1984 ... 29-32R
Obituary ... 114
Hepner, James O(rville) 1933- ... 57-60
Heppenheimer, T(homas) A(dolph)
1947- ... CANR-16
Earlier sketch in CA 93-96
Heppenstall, Margit Strom 1913- ... 23-24R
Heppenstall, (John) Rayner 1911-1981 ... 4R
Obituary ... 103
See also CLC 10
Hepple, Alex 1904(?)-1983 Obituary ... 111
Hepple, Bob (Alexander) 1934- ... CANR-12
Earlier sketch in CA 29-32R
Hepple, Peter 1927- ... 81-84
Heppner, Sam(uel) 1913-1983 ... 25-28R
Obituary ... 109
Hepworth, James B. 1910- ... 1R
Hepworth, James Michael 1938- ... CANR-13
Earlier sketch in CA 73-76
Hepworth, Mike
See Hepworth, James Michael
Hepworth, (Charles) Philip 1912- ... 17-18R
Her
See Deal, Borden
Herail, Rene James 1939- ... 118
Herald, Earl Stannard 1914-1973 Obituary .. 112
Herald, George William 1911- ... 73-76
Herald, Kathleen
See Peyton, Kathleen Wendy
Heraud, Brian J(eremy) 1934- ... 73-76
Heravi, Mehdi 1940- ... 29-32R
Herber, Bernard P. 1929- ... 21-22R
Herber, Harold L. 1929- ... 108
Herber, Lewis
See Bookchin, Murray
Herberg, Will 1909-1977 ... 73-76
Obituary ... 69-72
Herberger, Charles F. 1920- ... 41-44R
Herbers, John N. 1923- ... 33-36R
Herbert, A(lan) P(atrick) 1890-1971 ... 97-100
Obituary ... 33-36R
See also DLB 10
Herbert, Anthony B(ernard) 1930- ... 77-80
Herbert, Arthur
See Shappiro, Herbert (Arthur)
Herbert, Cecil
See Hamilton, Charles Harold St. John

Herbert, Cynthia Ridgeway 1943- 118
Herbert, David T(homas) 1935- CANR-18
Earlier sketches in CA 49-52, CANR-2
Herbert, Don 1917- 29-32R
See also SATA 2
Herbert, Eugenia W(arren) 1929- 93-96
Herbert, Frank (Patrick) 1920-1986 ..... CANR-5
Obituary 118
Earlier sketch in CA 53-56
See also SATA 9, 37, 47
See also DLB 8
See also CLC 12, 23, 35, 44
Herbert, Gilbert 1924- CANR-23
Earlier sketch in CA 107
Herbert, Henry George Alfred Marius Victor Francis 1898-1987 Obituary 123
Herbert, Henry William 1807-1858 .... DLB-3, 73
Herbert, Ian 1939- 111
Herbert, (Edward) Ivor (Montgomery) 1925- CANR-19
Earlier sketches in CA 53-56, CANR-4
Herbert, James 1943- 81-84
Herbert, Jean (Daniel Fernand) 1897-1980 .... CANR-9
Earlier sketch in CA 17-18R
Herbert, John (David) 1924- CANR-13
Earlier sketch in CA 23-24R
Herbert, John
See Brundage, John Herbert
See also DLB 53
Herbert, Kevin (Barry John) 1921- 17-18R
Herbert, Marie 1941- 69-72
Herbert, Martin 1933- 103
Herbert, Miranda C(arleton) 1950- 97-100
Herbert, Robert L(ouis) 1929- CANR-5
Earlier sketch in CA 11-12R
Herbert, Theodore T(erence) 1942- CANR-15
Earlier sketch in CA 65-68
Herbert, Thomas Walter, Jr. 1938- 104
Herbert, Victor 1927- 112
Herbert, Wally
See Herbert, Walter William
Herbert, Walter William 1934- CANR-15
Earlier sketch in CA 69-72
See also SATA 23
Herbert, (Alfred Francis) Xavier 1901-1984 69-72
Obituary 114
Herbert, Zbigniew 1924- 89-92
See also CLC 9, 43
Herbertson, Gary J. 1938- 25-28R
Herblock
See Block, Herbert (Lawrence)
Herbrand, Jan(ice M.) 1931- 49-52
Herbruck, Christine Comstock
See Comstock, Christine
Herbst, Anthony F(rancis) 1941- 114
Herbst, Josephine (Frey) 1897-1969 .... 7-8R
Obituary 25-28R
See also DLB 9
See also CLC 34
Herbst, Jurgen (F. H.) 1928- 37-40R
Herbst, Robert L(eroy) 1935- 61-64
Herburger, Guenter 1932- DLB-75
Hercules, Frank (E. M.) CANR-2
Earlier sketch in CA 2R
See also BW
See also DLB 33
Herd, Dale 1940- 61-64
Herdan, Gustav 1897- 2R
Herdeck, Donald E. 1924- 53-56
Herdt, Gilbert H(enry) 1949- 105
Herdt, Sheryll (Enette) Patterson 1941- 57-60
Hereford, John
See Fletcher, H(arry) L(utf) V(erne)
Heren, Louis (P.) 1919- CANR-12
Earlier sketch in CA 25-28R
Herfindahl, Orris C(lemens) 1918-1972 ... 41-44R
Obituary 37-40R
Herge
See Remi, Georges
See also CLR 6
Hergenhahn, B(aldwin) R(oss) 1934- 123
Brief entry 118
Hergesheimer, Joseph 1880-1954
Brief entry 109
See also DLB 9
See also TCLC 11
Herget, Paul 1908(?)-1981 Obituary 105
Herian, V.
See Gregorian, Vartan
Heriat, Philippe
See Payelle, Raymond-Gerard
Herington, C. J(ohn) 1924- CANR-15
Earlier sketch in CA 29-32R
Heriot, Angus 1927- 7-8R
Heriteau, Jacqueline 1925- CANR-16
Earlier sketches in CA 45-48, CANR-1
Herity, Michael 1929- 49-52
Herken, Gregg (Franklin) 1947- CANR-20
Earlier sketch in CA 104
Herkimer, L(awrence) R(ussell) 1925(?)- 110
See also SATA 42
Herlihy, David 1930- 41-44R
Herlihy, James Leo 1927- CANR-2
Earlier sketch in CA 1R
See also CLC 6
Herlin, Hans 1925- 77-80
Herling, John 1907- Brief entry 112
Herm, Gerhard 1931- CANR-22
Earlier sketch in CA 104
Hermalyn, Gary 1952- 123
Herman, A(rthur) L(udwig) 1930- 65-68
Herman, Ben 1927- 104
Herman, Charlotte 1937- CANR-15
Earlier sketch in CA 41-44R
See also SATA 20
Herman, Donald L. 1928- CANR-4
Earlier sketch in CA 53-56
Herman, Esther 1935- 102
Herman, George E(dward) 1920- 69-72
Herman, George R(ichard) 1925- 5-6R
Herman, Jan (Jacob) 1942- 45-48
Herman, John R(ufus) 1928- 119
Herman, Judith 1943- 49-52
Herman, Justin B. 1907(?)-1983 Obituary .. 111
Herman, Kenneth Neil 1954- 77-80
Herman, Louis Jay 1925- 53-56
Herman, Marguerite Shalett 1914-1977 ... 41-44R
Herman, Masako 103
Herman, Melvin (Jerome) 1922-
Brief entry 111
Herman, Melvin 1922(?)-1983 Obituary 109
Herman, Simon N(athan) 1912- 29-32R
Herman, Sondra R(enee) 1932- 25-28R
Herman, Stanley M. 1928- 25-28R
Herman, Vic(tor J.) 1919- 107
Herman, Victor 1916(?)-1985 Obituary 115
Herman, Walter
See Wager, Walter H(erman)
Herman, William 1926- 126
Hermand, Jost 1930- CANR-14
Earlier sketch in CA 41-44R
Hermann, Donald H(arold) J(ames) 1943- CANR-17
Earlier sketches in CA 45-48, CANR-2
Hermann, Edward J(ulius) 1919- 17-18R
Hermann, John 1917- 49-52
Hermann, Philip J. 1916- 117
Hermann, (Theodore) Placid 1909-19(?) .. CAP-1
Earlier sketch in CA 15-16
Hermanns, Peter
See Brannon, William T.
Hermanns, William 1895- CANR-15
Earlier sketch in CA 37-40R
Hermans, Willem Frederik 1921- CAP-1
Earlier sketch in CA 9-10
Hermansen, Gustav 1909- 117
Hermansen, John 1918- 45-48
Hermanson, Dennis (Everett) 1947- SATA-10
Hermeren, Goeran A. 1938- CANR-15
Earlier sketch in CA 89-92
Hermes
See Flammarion, (Nicolas) Camille
Hermes, Patricia 1936- CANR-22
Earlier sketch in CA 104
See also SATA 31
Hermlin, Stephan 1915- DLB-69
Hern, (George) Anthony 1916- 23-24R
Hern, Nicholas 1944- 115
Hernadi, Paul 1936- CANR-15
Earlier sketch in CA 41-44R
Hernandez, Al 1909- CAP-2
Earlier sketch in CA 21-22
Hernandez, Amado V. 1903-1970
Obituary 112
Hernandez, Frances 1926- 37-40R
Hernandez, Juana Amelia 45-48
Hernandez, Luis F. 1923- 61-64
Hernandez, Pedro F(elix) 1925- 45-48
Herndl, George C. 1927- 33-36R
Herndon, Booton 1915- CANR-4
Earlier sketch in CA 9-10R
Herndon, James 1926- 89-92
Herndon, Venable 1927- 109
Herner, Charles H. 1930- 29-32R
Hernes, Helga Maria 1938- CANR-20
Earlier sketch in CA 103
Hernon, Peter 1944- CANR-8
Earlier sketch in CA 61-64
Hernton, Calvin C(oolidge) 1934- CANR-26
Earlier sketches in CA 11-12R, CANR-3
See also BW
See also DLB 38
Hero, Alfred O(livier), Jr. 1924- 21-22R
Herold, Brenda 1948- 33-36R
Herold, J(ean) Christopher 1919-1964 .... CAP-1
Earlier sketch in CA 9-10
Heron, Alasdair I(ain) C(ampbell) 1942- 115
Heron, David Winston 1920- 112
Heron, Laurence Tunstall 1902- 49-52
Heron, Patrick 1920- 109
Heron-Allen, Edward 1861-1943
Brief entry 113
Herpel, George L(loyd) 1921- CANR-15
Earlier sketch in CA 41-44R
Herr, Dan(iel J.) 1917- 2R
Herr, Edwin L. 1933- 37-40R
Herr, Ethel 1936- 112
Herr, Michael 1940(?)- 89-92
Herr, Pamela (Staley) 1939- 126
Herr, Richard 1922- 4R
Herrero, Stephen M(atthew) 1939- 118
Herreshoff, David 1921- 21-22R
Herreshoff, L. Francis 1890-1972 .... CAP-1
Obituary 37-40R
Earlier sketch in CA 13-14
Herrick, Bruce Hale 1936- CANR-7
Earlier sketch in CA 19-20R
Herrick, Joy Field 1930- 101
Herrick, Marvin Theodore 1899-1966 ... CANR-1
Earlier sketch in CA 1R
Herrick, Neal Q(uentin) 1927- 49-52
Herrick, Robert (Welch) 1868-1938
Brief entry 119
See also DLB 9,12
Herrick, Robert L(ee) 1930- 61-64
Herrick, Tracy Grant 1933- 112
Herrick, Walter R(ussell), Jr. 1918- 23-24R
Herrick, William 1915- CANR-9
Earlier sketch in CA 23-24R
See also DLBY 83
Herridge, Robert 1914(?)-1981 Obituary 104
Herring, George C., Jr. 1936- CANR-14
Earlier sketch in CA 41-44R
Herring, Hubert Clinton 1889-1967
Obituary 105
Herring, Jack W(illiam) 1925- 115
Herring, Ralph A(lderman) 1901-19(?) ... CAP-2
Earlier sketch in CA 21-22
Herring, Reuben 1922- CANR-7
Earlier sketch in CA 19-20R
Herring, Robert H(erschel) 1938- CANR-21
Earlier sketch in CA 105
Herrington, James L(awrence) 1928- 73-76
Herrington, Pat
See Herrington, Patricia (Murphy)
Herrington, Patricia (Murphy) 1927- 114
Herrington, Stuart A. 1941- 109
Herriot, James
See Wight, James Alfred
See also CLC 12
Herriot, Peter 1939- CANR-25
Earlier sketch in CA 29-32R
Herriott, Robert E. 1929- CANR-7
Earlier sketch in CA 17-18R
Herrmann, Dorothy 1941- 107
See also CLC 44
Herrmann, Frank 1927- CANR-10
Earlier sketch in CA 21-22R
Herrmann, John 1900-1959 Brief entry 107
See also DLB 4
Herrmann, Klaus J(acob) 1929- 37-40R
Herrmann, Luke John 1932- 103
Herrmann, Nina 1943- 77-80
Herrmann, R(obert) L(awrence) 1928- 109
Herrmann, Richard K. 1952- 124
Herrmann, Robert O(mer) 1932- 41-44R
Herrmann, Taffy
See Herrmann, Dorothy
Herrmanns, Ralph 1933- CANR-18
Earlier sketches in CA 9-10R, CANR-3
See also SATA 11
Herrnstadt, Richard L. 1926- 33-36R
Herrnstein, Barbara
See Smith, Barbara Herrnstein
Herrnstein, Richard J(ulius) 1930-
Brief entry 107
Herron, Don 1952- 111
Herron, Edward A(lbert) 1912- 5-6R
See also SATA 4
Herron, Ima Honaker 1899- CAP-2
Earlier sketch in CA 25-28
Herron, Lowell William 1916- 2R
Herron, Orley R., Jr. 1933- CANR-12
Earlier sketch in CA 25-28R
Herron, Shaun 1912- 29-32R
Herron, William George 1933- 37-40R
Herschberger, Ruth (Margaret) 1917- 33-36R
Herschensohn, Bruce 1932- 69-72
Herscher, Uri David 1941- 107
Hersey, George Leonard 1927- 41-44R
Hersey, Jean 1902- CANR-3
Earlier sketch in CA 11-12R
Hersey, John (Richard) 1914- 17-18R
See also SATA 25
See also DLB 6
See also CLC 1, 2, 7, 9, 40
Hersey, William Dearborn 1910- CAP-1
Earlier sketch in CA 11-12
Hersh, Burton 1933- 73-76
Hersh, Jacques 1935- 103
Hersh, Reuben 1927- 125
Hersh, Seymour M. 1937- CANR-15
Earlier sketch in CA 73-76
See also AITN 1
Hershan, Stella K. 1915- 33-36R
Hershatter, Richard Lawrence 1923- 81-84
Hershberg, David 1935- 45-48
Hershberger, Hazel Kuhns 5-6R
Hershenson, David Bert 1933- 41-44R
Hershenson, Maurice (Eugene) 1933- 41-44R
Hersher, Leonard 1925- 41-44R
Hershey, Burnet 1896-1971 .... CAP-2
Obituary 33-36R
Earlier sketch in CA 25-28
Hershey, Daniel 1931- CANR-16
Earlier sketch in CA 89-92
Hershey, Ed
See Hershey, Edward (Norman)
Hershey, Edward (Norman) 1944-
Brief entry 118
Hershey, Gerald L. 1931- 53-56
Hershey, Lenore 104
Hershey, Nathan 1930- 117
Hershey, Robert Delp 1909- 69-72
Hershfield, Harry 1885-1974 Obituary 53-56
Hershhorn, Bernard S(eymour) 1928- 119
Hershkowitz, Leo 1924- 25-28R
Hershman, Morris 1926- CANR-5
Earlier sketch in CA 53-56
Hershon, Robert 1936- CANR-13
Earlier sketch in CA 33-36R
Herskovits, Frances Shapiro 1897-1972
Obituary 33-36R
Herskowitz, Herbert Bennett 1925- 17-18R
Herskowitz, Mickey 81-84
Herst, Herman, Jr. 1909- CANR-2
Earlier sketch in CA 4R
Herstein, I(srael) N(athan) 1923-1988
Obituary 125
Herstein, Sheila R. 1942- 119
Hertel, Francois 1905-1985 .... DLB-68
Herter, Christian A(rchibald) 1895-1966
Obituary 116
Hertling, G(unter) H. 1930- 41-44R
Hertling, James E. 1935- 93-96
Hertsens, Marcel 1918- 9-10R
Hertweck, Alma Louise 1937- 122
Hertz, Aleksander 1895-1983 Obituary 109
Hertz, David Michael 1954- 125
Hertz, Grete Janus 1915- 101
See also SATA 23
Hertz, Jackoline G. 1920- 69-72
Hertz, Jacky
See Hertz, Jackoline G.
Hertz, Karl H(erbert) 1917- 73-76
Hertz, Leah 1937-1988 Obituary 126
Hertz, Peter Donald 1933- 37-40R
Hertz, Richard C(ornell) 1916- 21-22R
Hertz, Solange (Strong) 1920- 7-8R
Hertzberg, Arthur 1921- 19-20R
Hertzberg, Hazel W(hitman) 1918-1988 73-76
Obituary 126
Hertzberg, Hendrik 1943- 126
Hertzberg, Sidney 1910-1984 Obituary 114
Hertzler, Daniel 1925- 115
Hertzler, Joyce O(ramel) 1895-1975 .... 1R
Obituary 103
Hertzler, Lois Shank 1927- 57-60
Hertzman, Lewis 1927- 11-12R
Herum, John (Maurice) 1931- 61-64
Herve, Jean-Luc
See Humbaraci, D(emir) Arslan
Herve-Bazin, Jean Pierre Marie 1911- 81-84
Hervent, Maurice
See Grindel, Eugene
Hervey, Evelyn
See Keating, H(enry) R(eymond) F(itzwalter)
Hervey, Jane
See McGaw, Naomi Blanche Thoburn
Hervey, Michael 1920- 11-12R
Herwig, Holger H(einrich) 1941- CANR-7
Earlier sketch in CA 61-64
Herz, Irene 1948- 93-96
Herz, Jerome Spencer 45-48
Herz, Jerry
See Herz, Jerome Spencer
Herz, John H(ermann) 1908- 41-44R
Herz, Martin F(lorian) 1917-1983 .... CANR-9
Obituary 111
Earlier sketch in CA 23-24R
Herz, Peggy 1936- 37-40R
Herz, Stephanie M(argarette) 1900- 101
Herzberg, Donald Gabriel 1925-1980
Obituary 101
Herzberg, Joseph Gabriel 1907-1976
Obituary 65-68
Herzberger, Maximillian Jacob 1899-1982
Obituary 106
Herzel, Catherine (Williams) 1908- 5-6R
Herzfeld, Thomas J. 1945- 107
Herzinger, Kim A(llen) 1946- 114
Herzka, Heinz (Stefan) 1935- 37-40R
Herzog, Arthur (III) 1927- CANR-9
Earlier sketch in CA 19-20R
Herzog, Chaim 1918- 103
Herzog, E.
See Maurois, Andre
Herzog, Frederick 1925- 116
Herzog, Gerard 1920- 104
Herzog, John P(hillip) 1931- 29-32R
Herzog, Kristin (K. H.) 1929- 114
Herzog, Peter Emilius 1925- 125
Herzog, Stephen J(oel) 1938- 33-36R
Herzog, Werner 1942- 89-92
See also CLC 16
Herzstein, Robert Edwin 1940- CANR-7
Earlier sketch in CA 57-60
Hesburgh, Theodore M(artin) 1917- 13-14R
Heschel, Abraham Joshua 1907-1972 ... CANR-4
Obituary 37-40R
Earlier sketch in CA 7-8R
Heseltine, George Coulehan 1895-1980
Obituary 97-100
Heseltine, Nigel 1916- 9-10R
Heskes, Irene 1928- 93-96
Hesketh, (Charles) Peter (Fleetwood) Fleetwood
See Fleetwood-Hesketh, (Charles) Peter (Fleetwood)
Hesketh, Phoebe Rayner 1909- CANR-14
Earlier sketches in CA 9-10, CAP-1
Heskett, J(ames) L(ee) 1933- CANR-8
Earlier sketch in CA 13-14R
Hesky, Olga ?-1974 .... CAP-2
Obituary 53-56
Earlier sketch in CA 25-28
Hesla, David H(eimarck) 1929- 33-36R
Heslep, Robert D(urham) 1930- 37-40R
Heslin, Jo-Ann 1946- CANR-16
Earlier sketch in CA 93-96
Heslin, Richard 1936- 37-40R
Heslop, J. Malan 1923- 37-40R
Hespro, Herbert
See Robinson, Herbert Spencer
Hess, Albert G(unter) 1909- CAP-1
Earlier sketch in CA 19-20
Hess, Alexander 1898(?)-1981 Obituary 105
Hess, Bartlett L(eonard) 1910- CANR-21
Earlier sketch in CA 61-64
Hess, Beth B(owman) CANR-24
Earlier sketches in CA 65-68, CANR-9
Hess, Earl J(ohn) 1955- 118
Hess, Eckhard H(einrich) 1916-1986 57-60
Obituary 118
Hess, Gary R(ay) 1937- 21-22R
Hess, Hannah S(pier) 1934- 45-48
Hess, Hans 1908-1975 Obituary 53-56
Hess, J(ohn) Daniel 1937- 116
Hess, John L(oft) 1917- 102
Hess, John M(ilton) 1929- 23-24R
Hess, Karen 1918- 105
Hess, Karl 1923- 81-84

Hess, Lilo 1916- CANR-12
Earlier sketch in CA 33-36R
See also SATA 4
Hess, Margaret Johnston 1915- CANR-21
Earlier sketches in CA 57-60, CANR-6
Hess, Robert D(aniel) 1920- CANR-13
Earlier sketch in CA 23-24R
Hess, Robert L. 1932- 29-32R
Hess, (Walther Richard) Rudolf
1894-1987 Obituary 123
Hess, Stephen 1933- CANR-10
Earlier sketch in CA 19-20R
Hess, Thomas B(aer) 1920-1978 81-84
Obituary 77-80
Hess, William N. 1925- 29-32R
Hesse, Hermann 1877-1962 CAP-2
Earlier sketch in CA 17-18
See also SATA 50
See also DLB 66
See also CLC 1, 2, 3, 6, 11, 17, 25
Hesse, Mary (Brenda) 1924- CANR-12
Earlier sketch in CA 19-20R
Hesselgesser, Debra 1939- 69-72
Hesselgrave, David J(ohn) 1924- 81-84
Hesseltine, William Best 1902-1963 4R
Hessert, Paul 1925- 33-36R
Hessing, Dennis
See Dennis-Jones, H(arold)
Hession, Charles H(enry) 1911- 33-36R
Hession, Roy 1908- 81-84
Hessler, Gene 1928- 73-76
Hesslink, George K. 1940-1980 21-22R
Obituary 120
Hest, Amy 1950- 115
Hester, Hubert Inman 1895- CANR-5
Earlier sketch in CA 5-6R
Hester, Hugh Bryan 1895-1983 Obituary 111
Hester, James J. 1931- 37-40R
Hester, Kathleen B. 1905- CAP-2
Earlier sketch in CA 19-20
Hester, Marcus B. 1937- 33-36R
Hester, Randolph Thompson, Jr. 1944- 113
Hester, Thomas R(oy) 1946- 113
Hesterman, Vicki 1951- 112
Heston, Alan (Wiley) 1934- 97-100
Heston, Charlton 1924- 110
Brief entry 108
Heston, Edward 1908(?)-1973 Obituary 45-48
Heston, Leonard L(ancaster) 1930- 101
Heth, Meir 1932- 23-24R
Hetherington, (Hector) Alastair 1919- 109
Hetherington, Eileen Mavis (Plenderleith)
1926- 115
Hetherington, Hugh W(illiam) 1903- 5-6R
Hetherington, John (Aikman) 1907-1974 93-96
Obituary 53-56
Hetherington, Norriss Swigart 1942- 126
Hethmon, Robert H(enry) 1925- 15-16R
Hettinger, Herman Strecker 1902-1972
Obituary 37-40R
Hettlinger, Richard F(rederick) 1920- CANR-7
Earlier sketch in CA 19-20R
Hetzell, Margaret Carol 1917-1978 85-88
Obituary 81-84
Hetzler, Florence M(ary) 1926- CANR-25
Earlier sketch in CA 107
Hetzler, Stanley Arthur 1919- 37-40R
Hetzron, Robert 1937- 33-36R
Heuer, John (Michael) 1941- CANR-14
Earlier sketch in CA 69-72
Heuer, Kenneth John 1927- 110
See also SATA 44
Heuman, William 1912-1971 CANR-7
Earlier sketch in CA 7-8R
See also SATA 21
Heumann, Milton 1947- 110
Heuscher, Julius E(rnst) 1918- 11-12R
Heuss, John 1908-1966 CAP-1
Earlier sketch in CA 9-10
Heussler, Robert 1924- CANR-8
Earlier sketch in CA 5-6R
Heussner, Ralph C(lyde), Jr. 1949- 119
Heuterman, Thomas H(enry) 1934- 101
Heuvelmans, Bernard (Joseph Pierre)
1916- 97-100
Heuvelmans, Martin 1903- 49-52
Heuyer, Georges 1884-1977 Obituary 73-76
Hevener, John W(atts) 1933- 103
Heward, Edmund (Rawlings) 1912- 93-96
Heward, William L(ee) 1949- CANR-4
Earlier sketch in CA 53-56
Hewat, Alexander 1743(?)-1824 DLB-30
Hewens, Frank Edgar 1912- 45-48
Hewer, Humphrey Robert 1903-1974
Obituary 105
Hewes, Agnes Danforth 1874-1963
Obituary 113
See also SATA 35
Hewes, Cady
See De Voto, Bernard (Augustine)
Hewes, Dorothy W. 1922- 37-40R
Hewes, Hayden 1943- 85-88
Hewes, Henry 1917- 13-14R
Hewes, Jeremy Joan 1944- 77-80
Hewes, Laurence (Ilsley) 1902- 105
Hewes, Leslie 1906- 41-44R
Hewett, Anita 1918- 21-22R
See also SATA 13
Hewett, Dorothy Coade 1923- 97-100
Hewett, John H(arris) 1952- 115
Hewett, William S. 1924- 21-22R
Hewins, Geoffrey Shaw 1889- CAP-1
Earlier sketch in CA 9-10
Hewins, Ralph Anthony 1909-1984(?) CAP-1
Obituary 112
Earlier sketch in CA 9-10
Hewison, Robert 1943- 81-84
Hewitson, John Nelson 1917- 29-32R
Hewitt, Arthur Wentworth 1883- 69-72
Hewitt, Bernard (Wolcott) 1906- 13-14R
Hewitt, Cecil Rolph 1901- CANR-18
Earlier sketch in CA 102
Hewitt, David (Sword) 1942- 118
Hewitt, Don (S.) 1922- Brief entry 119
Hewitt, Emily Clark 1944- CANR-2
Earlier sketch in CA 45-48
Hewitt, Foster (William) 1903(?)-1985
Obituary 115
Hewitt, Garnet (William) 1939- 110
Hewitt, Geof (George F.) 1943- 33-36R
Hewitt, H(erbert) J(ames) 1890- 13-14R
Hewitt, James 1928- CANR-21
Earlier sketches in CA 57-60, CANR-6
Hewitt, Jean D(aphne) 1925- 77-80
Hewitt, John (Harold) 1907-1987 CANR-16
Obituary 123
Earlier sketch in CA 97-100
See also DLB 27
Hewitt, John P(aul) 1941- 53-56
Hewitt, Philip Nigel 1945- 81-84
Hewitt, Robert L. 1917(?)-1983 Obituary 111
Hewitt, Sue Whitsett 1919(?)-1984
Obituary 111
Hewitt, William Henry 1936- 17-18R
Hewlett, Dorothy (?)-1979 Obituary 85-88
Hewlett, Frank West 1909(?)-1983
Obituary 110
Hewlett, Maurice (Henry) 1861-1923
Brief entry 121
See also DLB 34
Hewlett, Richard Greening 1923- 9-10R
Hewlett, Roger S. 1911(?)-1977 Obituary 73-76
Hewlett, Sylvia Ann 1946- 123
Brief entry 118
Hewlett, Virginia B. 1912(?)-1979
Obituary 85-88
Hewson, John 1930- 37-40R
Hewton, Eric 1934- 126
Hexham, Irving 1943- 125
Hexner, Ervin Paul 1893-1968 7-8R
Obituary 103
Hext, Harrington
See Phillpotts, Eden
Hextall, David
See Phillips-Birt, Douglas Hextall Chedzey
Hexter, J(ack) H. 1910- 13-14R
Hey, John D(enis) 1944- 106
Hey, Nigel S(tewart) 1936- 33-36R
See also SATA 20
Heyd, David 1945- 118
Heydenburg, Harry E. 1891(?)-1979
Obituary 89-92
Heydenreich, Ludwig Heinrich 1903-
Brief entry 105
Heydon, Peter Richard 1913-1971 CAP-1
Earlier sketch in CA 19-20
Heyduck-Huth, Hilde 1929- 57-60
See also SATA 8
Heyel, Carl 1908- CANR-22
Earlier sketches in CA 19-20R, CANR-7
Heyen, William 1940- 33-36R
See also DLB 5
See also CLC 13, 18
Heyer, Georgette 1902-1974 93-96
Obituary 49-52
Heyer, Marilee 1942- 125
Heyerdahl, Thor 1914- CANR-22
Earlier sketches in CA 7-8R, CANR-5
See also SATA 2, 52
See also CLC 26
Heyler, David B., Sr. 1905(?)-1983
Obituary 110
Heyliger, William 1884-1955 YABC-1
Heym, Georg (Theodor Franz Arthur)
1887-1912 Brief entry 106
See also TCLC 9
Heym, Stefan 1913- CANR-4
Earlier sketch in CA 9-10R
See also DLB 69
See also CLC 41
Heyman, Abigail 1942- 57-60
Heyman, Ken(neth Louis) 1930- 112
See also SATA 34
Heyman, Neil Michael 1937- 113
Heymann, Frederick Gotthold 1900-1983
Obituary 111
Heymanns, Betty 1932- 85-88
Heymanson, Randal 1903-1984 Obituary 113
Heyn, Ernest V(ictor) 1904- Brief entry 111
Heyne, Paul 1931- 89-92
Heynen, Jim 1940- 77-80
Heyns, Barbara 1943- 85-88
Heyrman, Christine Leigh 1950- 115
Heyse, Paul (Johann Ludwig von)
1830-1914 Brief entry 104
See also TCLC 8
Heyst, Axel
See Grabowski, Z(bigniew) Anthony
Heyward, Carter 1945- 65-68
Heyward, Dorothy (Hartzell Kuhns)
1890-1961 Obituary 112
See also DLB 7
Heyward, (Edwin) DuBose 1885-1940
Brief entry 108
See also SATA 21
See also DLB 7, 9, 45
Heywood, Christopher 1928- 41-44R
Heywood, Hugh Christopher Lempriere
1896-1987 Obituary 122
Heywood, Karen 1946- SATA-48
Heywood, Lorimer D. 1899(?)-1977
Obituary 73-76
Heywood, Philip 1938- 69-72
Heywood, Rosalind 1895- 89-92
Heywood, Terence CAP-1
Earlier sketch in CA 9-10
Heywood, Thomas 1573(?)-1641 DLB-62
Heyworth, Peter (Lawrence Frederick)
1921- 65-68
Heyworth-Dunne, James ?-1974 Obituary 53-56
Hezel, Francis X(avier) 1939- 118
Hiaasen, Carl 1953- CANR-22
Earlier sketch in CA 105
Hian
See Higginson, William J(ohn)
Hiat, Elchik
See Katz, Menke
Hibbard, George Richard 1915- 85-88
Hibbard, Howard 1928-1984 CANR-9
Obituary 114
Earlier sketch in CA 53-56
Hibben, Frank Cummings 1910- CANR-2
Earlier sketch in CA 1R
Hibberd, Andrew Stuart 1893-1983(?)
Obituary 111
Hibberd, Jack 1940- 103
Hibbert, Christopher 1924- CANR-2
Earlier sketch in CA 4R
See also SATA 4
Hibbert, Eleanor Burford 1906- CANR-9
Earlier sketch in CA 17-18R
See also SATA 2
See also CLC 7
Hibbett, Howard (Scott) 1920- 106
Hibbs, Ben 1901-1975 65-68
Obituary 104
Hibbs, Douglas A(lbert), Jr. 1944- CANR-3
Earlier sketch in CA 49-52
Hibbs, John 1925- CANR-19
Earlier sketch in CA 103
Hibbs, Paul 1906- CAP-1
Earlier sketch in CA 15-16
Hibdon, James E(dward) 1924- 25-28R
Hick, John (Harwood) 1922- CANR-22
Earlier sketches in CA 9-10R, CANR-6
Hickel, Walter J(oseph) 1919- 41-44R
Hicken, Victor 1921- 21-22R
Hickerson, J(ohn) Mel(ancthon) 1897- 25-28R
Hickey, Edward Shelby 1928(?)-1978 85-88
Obituary 81-84
Hickey, Joseph J(ames) 1907- 41-44R
Hickey, Michael 1929- 102
Hickey, Neil 1931- 1R
Hickey, Raymond 1936- 114
Hickey, William
See Driberg, Thomas Edward Neil
Hickford, Jessie 1911- 53-56
Hickin, Norman E(rnest) 1910- CANR-15
Earlier sketch in CA 85-88
Hickinbotham, Tom 1903-1983 Obituary 111
Hickler, Holly 1923- 117
Hickling, C(harles) F(rederick) 1902-1977
Obituary 117
Hickman, Bert G(eorge), Jr. 1924- 108
Hickman, C(harles) Addison 1916- 103
Hickman, Charles 1905-1983 Obituary 109
Hickman, (Gertrud) Hannah 1928- 123
Hickman, Hoyt L(eon) 1927- 121
Hickman, Janet 1940- CANR-10
Earlier sketch in CA 65-68
See also SATA 12
Hickman, Martha Whitmore 1925- CANR-26
Earlier sketches in CA 25-28R, CANR-10
See also SATA 26
Hickman, Martin B(erkeley) 1925- 65-68
Hickman, Peggy 1906- 73-76
Hickman, Tracy Raye 1955- 126
Hickok, Dorothy Jane 1912- 73-76
Hickok, Lorena A. 1892(?)-1968 73-76
See also SATA 20
Hickok, Robert (Blair) 1927- 61-64
Hickok, Will
See Harrison, C. William
Hicks, Charles B(alch) 1916- 7-8R
Hicks, Clifford B. 1920- CANR-24
Earlier sketches in CA 5-6R, CANR-9
See also SATA 50
Hicks, Darryl E(dwin) 1948- 120
Hicks, David E. 1931- CANR-7
Earlier sketch in CA 11-12R
Hicks, Donald A(lbert) 1947- 111
Hicks, Eleanor B.
See Coerr, Eleanor (Beatrice)
Hicks, George L(eon) 1935- 65-68
Hicks, Granville 1901-1982 CANR-13
Obituary 107
Earlier sketch in CA 9-10R
Hicks, Harvey
See Stratemeyer, Edward L.
Hicks, J. L.
See Hicks, Jim(my Lyn)
Hicks, Jack 1942- 97-100
Hicks, James L. 1915(?)-1986 Obituary 118
Hicks, Jim(my Lyn) 1937- 107
Hicks, John (Richard) 1904- CANR-13
Earlier sketch in CA 65-68
Hicks, John (Kenneth) 1918- 25-28R
Hicks, John D(onald) 1890-1972 CANR-2
Earlier sketch in CA 4R
Hicks, John Edward 1890(?)-1971
Obituary 104
Hicks, John H(arland) 1919- 45-48
Hicks, John V(ictor) 1907- 110
Hicks, Raymond L. 1926- 61-64
Hicks, Robert E(lden) 1920- Brief entry 109
Hicks, Roger W(illiam) 1950- 124
Hicks, Ronald G(raydon) 1934- 73-76
Hicks, Tyler Gregory 1921- 103
Hicks, Ursula Kathleen (Webb) 1896-1985 103
Obituary 117
Hicks, Warren B(raukman) 1921- 33-36R
Hicks, Wilson 1897-1970 Obituary 29-32R
Hicky, Daniel Whitehead 1902- AITN-1
Hidden, (Frederick) Norman 1913- 77-80
Hidore, John J. 1932- CANR-21
Earlier sketches in CA 57-60, CANR-6
Hidy, Muriel E(mmie) 1906- 97-100
Hidy, Ralph W(illard) 1905- 7-8R
Hieatt, A(llen) Kent 1921- 21-22R
Hieatt, Constance B(artlett) 1928- CANR-23
Earlier sketches in CA 5-6R, CANR-8
See also SATA 4
Hiebel, Friedrich 1903- CANR-11
Earlier sketch in CA 65-68
Hiebert, Clarence 1927- 61-64
Hiebert, D(avid) Edmond 1910- 19-20R
Hiebert, Paul (Gerhardt) 1892-1987 CANR-17
Earlier sketches in CA 23-24, CAP-2
See also DLB 68
Hiebert, Ray Eldon 1932- CANR-7
Earlier sketch in CA 17-18R
See also SATA 13
Hiernaux, Jean 1921- 57-60
Hieronymus, Clara (Booth) 1913- 73-76
Hiers, John Turner 1945- 102
Hiers, Richard H(yde) 1932- 53-56
Hiesberger, Jean Marie 1941- 41-44R
Hiesinger, Kathryn B(loom) 1943- 119
Hiestand, Dale L(eroy) 1925- 41-44R
Hifler, Joyce (Sequichie) 1925- 21-22R
Higashiuchi, Yoshio 1915(?)-1987
Obituary 122
Higbe, (Walter) Kirby 1915-1985 Obituary 116
Higbee, Edward (Counselman) 1910- 15-16R
Higbee, Kenneth Leo 1941- 101
Higby, Mary Jane 25-28R
Higdon, David Leon 1939- 77-80
Higdon, Hal 1931- CANR-3
Earlier sketch in CA 11-12R
See also SATA 4
Higenbottam, Frank 1910-1982 Obituary 117
Higenbottom, Frank 1910- 25-28R
Higgie, Lincoln William 1938- 7-8R
Higginbotham, A(loysius) Leon, Jr. 1928- 110
Higginbotham, (Prieur) Jay 1937- CANR-17
Earlier sketch in CA 93-96
Higginbotham, John E. 1933- 29-32R
Higginbotham, R(obert) Don 1931- 17-18R
Higginbotham, Sanford Wilson 1913-
Brief entry 105
Higginbotham, Virginia 1935- 115
Brief entry 110
Higginbottom, J(effrey) Winslow
1945- SATA-29
Higgins, A(lbert) C(orbin) 1930- 37-40R
Higgins, A(ngus) J(ohn) B(rockhurst)
1911- 13-14R
Higgins, Aidan 1927- 11-12R
See also DLB 14
Higgins, Alice 1924(?)-1974 Obituary 53-56
Higgins, Chester (Archer, Jr.) 1946- 73-76
Higgins, Colin 1941-1988 33-36R
Obituary 126
See also DLB 26
Higgins, Dick
See Higgins, Richard C(arter)
Higgins, Don 1928- CANR-14
Earlier sketch in CA 25-28R
Higgins, George V(incent) 1939- CANR-17
Earlier sketch in CA 77-80
See also CAAS 5
See also DLB 2
See also DLBY 81
See also CLC 4, 7, 10, 18
Higgins, Ink
See Weiss, Morris S(amuel)
Higgins, Jack
See Patterson, Henry
Higgins, James E(dward) 1926- 73-76
Higgins, Jean C. 1932- 29-32R
Higgins, Joan 1948- 125
Higgins, John A(loysius) 1931- CANR-13
Earlier sketch in CA 77-80
Higgins, John J(oseph) 1935- 45-48
Higgins, Judith Holden 1930- 102
Higgins, Lionel G(eorge) 1891-1985 123
Higgins, Marguerite 1920-1966 5-6R
Obituary 25-28R
Higgins, Paul C. 1950- 106
Higgins, Paul Lambourne 1916- CANR-17
Earlier sketches in CA 3R, CANR-2
Higgins, Reynold Alleyne 1916- 25-28R
Higgins, Richard C(arter) 1938- CANR-8
Earlier sketch in CA 13-14R
Higgins, Ronald 1929- 81-84
Higgins, Rosalyn (Cohen) 1937- CANR-3
Earlier sketch in CA 11-12R
Higgins, Thomas J(oseph) 1899- CANR-5
Earlier sketch in CA 1R
Higgins, Trumbull 1919- 19-20R
Higgins, W(illiam) Robert 1938- 37-40R
Higginson, Fred H(all) 1921- 1R
Higginson, Margaret V(aliant) 1923- 105
Higginson, Thomas Wentworth
1823-1911 DLB-1, 64
Higginson, William J(ohn) 1938- 123
Higgs, David (Clive) 1939- 61-64
Higgs, E(ric) S(idney) 1908-1976 11-12R
Obituary 69-72
Higgs, Gerald B. 1921- 106
Higgs, Gertrude Monro
See Monro-Higgs, Gertrude
Higgs, Robert J(ackson) 1932- 115
High, Dallas M. 1931- 21-22R
High, Monique Raphel 1949- CANR-21
Earlier sketch in CA 102
High, Philip E(mpson) 1914- 97-100

High, Stanley (Hoflund) 1895-1961
Obituary ... 89-92
Higham, Charles 1931- ... CANR-17
Earlier sketch in CA 33-36R
Higham, David 1895-1978 ... CANR-2
Earlier sketch in CA 4R
Higham, David (Michael) 1949- ... 126
See also SATA 50
Higham, Florence May Grier 1896-1980
Obituary ... 97-100
Higham, John 1920- ... CANR-6
Earlier sketch in CA 1R
Higham, Robin (David Stewart) 1925- ... CANR-1
Earlier sketch in CA 2R
Higham, Roger 1935- ... 33-36R
Higham, T. F.
See Higham, Thomas Farrant
Higham, Thomas Farrant 1890-1975
Obituary ... 116
Highberger, Ruth 1917- ... 65-68
Highet, Gilbert (Arthur) 1906-1978 ... CANR-6
Obituary ... 73-76
Earlier sketch in CA 1R
Highet, Helen
See MacInnes, Helen (Clark)
Highland, Dora
See Avallone, Michael (Angelo), Jr.
Highland, Monica
See Espey, John (Jenkins)
and Kendall, Lisa See
and See, Carolyn (Penelope)
Highsmith, (Mary) Patricia 1921- ... CANR-20
Earlier sketches in CA 3R, CANR-1
See also CLC 2, 4, 14, 42
Highsmith, Richard M(organ), Jr. 1920- ... 37-40R
Hightower, Florence Cole 1916-1981 ... 4R
Obituary ... 103
See also SATA 4, 27
Hightower, John M(urmann) 1909-1987
Obituary ... 121
Hightower, Paul
See Collins, Thomas Hightower
Highwater, Jamake (Mamake) 1942- ... CANR-10
Earlier sketch in CA 65-68
See also CAAS 7
See also SATA 30, 32
See also DLB 52
See also DLBY 85
See also CLC 12
Higley, John (Clark) 1938- Brief entry ... 116
Higman, B(arry) W(illiam) 1943- ... 81-84
Higman, Francis M(ontgomery) 1935- ... CANR-12
Earlier sketch in CA 25-28R
Hignett, Sean 1934- ... 49-52
Higonnet, Margaret Randolph 1941- ... 61-64
Higonnet, Patrice Louis-Rene 1938- ... 65-68
Higson, James D(oran) 1925- ... 49-52
Hijirida, Kyoko 1937- ... 126
Hijuelos, Oscar 1951- ... 123
Hikmet, Nazim 1902-1963 Obituary ... 93-96
See also CLC 40
Hilary, Christopher 1927(?)-1979
Obituary ... 89-92
Hilberg, Raul 1926- ... 33-36R
Hilberry, Conrad (Arthur) 1928- ... CANR-10
Earlier sketch in CA 25-28R
Hilborn, Ann 1942- ... 109
Hilborn, Harry (Warren) 1900- ... CAP-2
Earlier sketch in CA 33-36
Hildebidle, John 1946- ... 114
Hildebrand, George H(erbert) 1913- ... CANR-8
Earlier sketch in CA 17-18R
Hildebrand, Grant 1934- ... 57-60
Hildebrand, Joel H(enry) 1881-1983 ... CAP-1
Obituary ... 109
Earlier sketch in CA 11-12
Hildebrand, Verna 1924- ... CANR-13
Earlier sketch in CA 33-36R
Hildebrandt, Franz 1909-1985 ... 118
Hildebrandt, Greg 1939- ... 104
See also SATA 33
Hildebrandt, Tim(othy) 1939- ... 122
Brief entry ... 111
See also SATA 33
Hildebrandts, The
See Hildebrandt, Tim(othy)
Hilder, Rowland 1905- ... SATA-36
Hilderbrand, Robert Clinton 1947- ... 105
Hildesheimer, Wolfgang 1916- ... 101
See also DLB 69
See also CLC 49
Hildick, E. W.
See Hildick, (Edmund) Wallace
See also SAAS 6
Hildick, (Edmund) Wallace 1925- ... 25-28R
See also SATA 2
Hildreth, Gertrude Howell 1898-1984
Obituary ... 112
Hildreth, Margaret Holbrook 1927- ... 89-92
Hildreth, Richard 1807-1865 ... DLB-1, 30, 59
Hildum, Donald C(layton) 1930- ... 23-24R
Hildyard, Nicholas 1955- ... 122
Hilfer, Anthony Channell 1936- ... 73-76
Hilfiker, David 1945- ... 123
Hilgard, Ernest R(opiequet) 1904- ... 113
Hilgartner, Stephen 1956- ... 111
Hilger, Sister Mary Inez 1891-1977 ... 73-76
Hilken, Glen A. 1936- ... 61-64
Hill, Ab
See Hill, Abram (Barrington)
Hill, Abram (Barrington) 1910(?)-1986
Obituary ... 120
Hill, Adrian Keith Graham 1895-1977 ... 77-80
Hill, Alexis
See Craig, Mary (Francis) S(hura)
Hill, Alexis
See Glick, Ruth (Burtnick)
Hill, Alfred T(uxbury) 1908- ... 21-22R
Hill, Archibald A(nderson) 1902- ... 49-52
Hill, Arthur Norman 1920(?)-1988
Obituary ... 125
Hill, Barrington Julian Warren 1915- ... 7-8R
Hill, Bennett D(avid) 1934- ... 111
Hill, Bob
See Hill, Robert C(ecil)
Hill, Brian (Merrikin) 1896- ... CAP-1
Earlier sketch in CA 9-10
Hill, Carol (Dechellis) 1942- ... 77-80
Hill, Charles William, Jr. 1940- ... 125
Hill, (John Edward) Christopher 1912- ... CANR-22
Earlier sketches in CA 9-10R, CANR-4
Hill, Claude 1911- ... 23-24R
Hill, Clifford S. 1927- ... CANR-7
Earlier sketch in CA 13-14R
Hill, Daniel G., Jr. 1896(?)-1979
Obituary ... 89-92
Hill, Dave
See Hill, David Charles
Hill, David Charles 1936- ... CANR-11
Earlier sketch in CA 19-20R
Hill, Deborah 1936- ... 108
Hill, Dee
See Zucker, Dolores Mae Bolton
Hill, Denise 1919- ... CANR-23
Earlier sketch in CA 106
Hill, (Richard) Desmond 1920-1984 ... 7-8R
Obituary ... 114
Hill, Devra Z.
See Zucker, Dolores Mae Bolton
Hill, Dilys M(ary) 1935- ... 61-64
Hill, Donald (Routledge) 1922- ... 122
Hill, Donald Hamilton
See Hamilton-Hill, Donald
Hill, Donna (Marie) ... CANR-25
Earlier sketches in CA 15-16R, CANR-7
See also SATA 24
Hill, Douglas (Arthur) 1935- ... CANR-4
Earlier sketch in CA 53-56
See also SATA 39
Hill, Draper
See Hill, L(eroy) Draper, Jr.
Hill, Earle 1941- ... 33-36R
Hill, Eileen
See Stack, Nicolete Meredith
Hill, Elizabeth Starr 1925- ... 17-18R
See also SATA 24
Hill, Ellen Wise 1942- ... 77-80
Hill, Eric 1927- ... SATA-53
See also CLR 13
Hill, Ernest 1915- ... 53-56
Hill, Errol Gaston 1921- ... CANR-26
Earlier sketch in CA 45-48
See also BW
Hill, Evan 1919- ... CANR-5
Earlier sketch in CA 11-12R
Hill, Fiona
See Pall, Ellen Jane
Hill, (Charles) Fowler 1901(?)-1973
Obituary ... 37-40R
Hill, (James William) Francis 1899-1980
Obituary ... 108
Hill, Frank Ernest 1888-1969 ... 73-76
Hill, Gene 1928- ... 97-100
Hill, Geoffrey (William) 1932- ... CANR-21
Earlier sketch in CA 81-84
See also DLB 40
See also CLC 5, 8, 18, 45
Hill, George E(dward) 1907- ... CAP-1
Earlier sketch in CA 17-18
Hill, George Roy 1921- ... 122
Brief entry ... 110
See also CLC 26
Hill, Gladwin 1914- ... 25-28R
Hill, Grace Brooks ... CANR-26
Earlier sketches in CA 19-20, CAP-2
See also SATA 1
Hill, Grace Livingston 1865-1947 ... YABC-2
Hill, (Norman) Graham 1929-1975
Obituary ... 108
Hill, H. D. N.
See Disston, Harry
Hill, Hamlin (Lewis) 1931- ... CANR-18
Earlier sketches in CA 11-12R, CANR-3
Hill, Harold E(verett) 1905- ... CANR-11
Earlier sketch in CA 69-72
Hill, Helen
See Miller, Helen Hill
Hill, Helen M(orey) 1915- ... 57-60
See also SATA 27
Hill, Henry Bertram 1907- ... 1R
Hill, Herbert 1924- ... 65-68
Hill, Hyacinthe
See Anderson, Virginia (R. Cronin)
Hill, I(saac) William 1908- ... 65-68
Hill, J(ohn) C(ampbell) 1888- ... 37-40R
Hill, James
See Jameson, (Margaret) Storm
Hill, James N(ewlin) 1934- ... 33-36R
Hill, Jane Bowers 1950- ... 126
Hill, Jim Dan 1897- ... CAP-1
Earlier sketch in CA 11-12
Hill, John Hugh 1905- ... CANR-5
Earlier sketch in CA 2R
Hill, John L. 1960- ... 124
Hill, John P(aul) 1936- ... 29-32R
Hill, John S(tanley) 1929- ... 37-40R
Hill, John Wiley 1890-1977 Obituary ... 69-72
Hill, Kathleen Louise 1917- ... CANR-3
Earlier sketch in CA 9-10R
See also SATA 4
Hill, Kay
See Hill, Kathleen Louise
Hill, Ken(neth) 1937- ... 108
Hill, King
See Robertson, Frank C(hester)
Hill, Knox C(alvin) 1910- ... CAP-1
Earlier sketch in CA 19-20
Hill, L(eslie) A(lexander) 1918- ... 23-24R
Hill, L(eroy) Draper, Jr. 1935- ... CANR-12
Earlier sketch in CA 17-18R
Hill, Larry D(ean) 1935- ... 73-76
Hill, Lawrence 1912-1988 Obituary ... 125
Hill, Lawson (Traphagen) 1927- ... 118
Hill, Lee H(alsey) 1899-1974 ... 37-40R
Obituary ... 45-48
Hill, Leslie Pinckney 1880-1960 ... 125
See also BW
See also DLB 51
Hill, Lew
See Skene-Melvin, (Lewis) David (St. Columb)
Hill, Lorna 1902- ... CANR-14
Earlier sketches in CA 9-10, CAP-1
See also SATA 12
Hill, Lowell Dean 1930- ... 114
Hill, M(elba) Anne 1953- ... 123
Hill, Margaret (Ohler) 1915- ... CANR-16
Earlier sketches in CA 4R, CANR-1
See also SATA 36
Hill, Marnesba D. 1913- ... 101
Hill, Marvin S(idney) 1928- ... 61-64
Hill, Mary A. 1939- ... 102
Hill, Mary Raymond 1923- ... CANR-6
Earlier sketch in CA 57-60
Hill, Mary V. 1941- ... 102
Hill, Meg
See Hill, Margaret (Ohler)
Hill, Meredith
See Craig, Mary (Francis) S(hura)
Hill, Mike 1944- ... 122
Hill, Monica
See Watson, Jane Werner
Hill, Nancy Klenk 1936- ... 108
Hill, Napoleon 1883(?)-1970 Obituary ... 104
Hill, Nellie
See Hill, Ellen Wise
Hill, Norman Llewellyn 1895- ... 7-8R
Hill, Pamela 1920- ... CANR-16
Earlier sketches in CA 49-52, CANR-1
Hill, Pati ... 69-72
Hill, Peter Proal 1926- ... 33-36R
Hill, Philip G(eorge) 1934- ... 33-36R
Hill, Polly
See Humphreys, Mary Eglantyne Hill
Hill, R(ufus) Carter 1945- ... 110
Hill, R. Lance 1943- ... CANR-11
Earlier sketch in CA 65-68
Hill, Ralph Nading 1917-1987 ... CANR-1
Obituary ... 124
Earlier sketch in CA 4R
Hill, Rebecca 1944- ... 111
Hill, Reginald (Charles) 1936- ... 73-76
Hill, Reuben (Lorenzo, Jr.) 1912-1985
Obituary ... 117
Hill, Richard 1901- ... CANR-1
Earlier sketch in CA 1R
Hill, Richard (Fontaine) 1941- ... 33-36R
Hill, Richard E. 1920- ... 33-36R
Hill, Richard Johnson 1925- ... CANR-4
Earlier sketch in CA 9-10R
Hill, Robert C(ecil) 1929- ... 118
Hill, Robert W(hite) 1919-1982 ... 9-10R
Obituary ... 107
See also SATA 12, 31
Hill, Rosalind M(ary) T(heodosia) 1908- ... CAP-1
Earlier sketch in CA 11-12
Hill, Roscoe E(arl) 1936- ... 37-40R
Hill, Rowland
See Wallace-Clarke, George
Hill, Roy Gerald 1926- ... 111
Hill, Ruth A.
See Viguers, Ruth Hill
Hill, Ruth Beebe 1913- ... 89-92
Hill, Ruth Livingston
See Munce, Ruth Hill
Hill, Samuel E(rvin) 1913- ... 17-18R
Hill, Samuel S(mythe), Jr. 1927- ... CANR-5
Earlier sketch in CA 11-12R
Hill, Selima 1945- ... 117
Hill, "Sir" John 1714(?)-1775 ... DLB-39
Hill, Stephen 1946- ... 111
Hill, Susan 1942- ... 33-36R
See also DLB 14
See also CLC 4
Hill, Thomas English 1909- ... 13-14R
Hill, W. M.
See Dodd, Edward Howard, Jr.
Hill, W(illiam) Speed 1935- ... 41-44R
Hill, Walter 1942- Brief entry ... 109
See also DLB 44
Hill, Weldon
See Scott, William R(alph)
Hill, West T(hompson), Jr. 1915- ... 37-40R
Hill, Wilhelmina 1902- ... 57-60
Hill, William Joseph 1924- ... 37-40R
Hill, Winfred F(arrington) 1929- ... 29-32R
Hillaby, John (D.) 1917- Brief entry ... 109
Hillam, Ray C. 1928- Brief entry ... 107
Hillard, James M(ilton) 1920- ... 73-76
Hillary, Edmund (Percival) 1919- ... 112
Hillary, Peter 1954- ... 123
Hillas, Julian
See Dashwood, Robert Julian
Hillbruner, Anthony 1914- ... 41-44R
Hillcourt, William 1900- ... 93-96
See also SATA 27
Hillegas, Mark R(obert) 1926- ... 33-36R
Hillel, Yehoshua Bar
See Bar-Hillel, Yehoshua
Hillenbrand, Barry R. 1941- ... 73-76
Hillenbrand, Martin Joseph 1915- ... 108
Hiller, Catherine 1946- ... 106
Hiller, Doris
See Nussbaum, Al(bert) F.
Hiller, Flora
See Hurd, Florence
Hiller, Herbert L. 1931- ... 125
Hiller, Ilo (Ann) 1938- ... 121
Hiller, Lejaren A(rthur), Jr. 1924- ... 1R
Hillerbrand, Hans J(oachim) 1931-
Brief entry ... 111
Hillerich, Robert L(ee) 1927- ... 112
Hillerman, Anne 1949- ... 118
Hillerman, Tony 1925- ... CANR-21
Earlier sketch in CA 29-32R
See also SATA 6
Hillers, Delbert R(oy) 1932- ... 77-80
Hillers, H(erman) W(illiam) 1925- ... 73-76
Hillert, Margaret 1920- ... CANR-17
Earlier sketches in CA 49-52, CANR-1
See also SATA 8
See also AITN 1
Hillery, George A(nthony), Jr. 1927- ... 25-28R
Hilles, Frederick W(hiley) 1900-1975 ... 5-6R
Obituary ... 61-64
Hillgarth, J(ocelyn) N(igel) 1929- ... 37-40R
Hillgruber, Andreas 1925- ... 106
Hilliard, Jan
See Grant, Kay
Hilliard, Noel (Harvey) 1929- ... CANR-7
Earlier sketch in CA 11-12R
See also CLC 15
Hilliard, Robert L. 1925- ... 107
Hilliard, Sam B(owers) 1930- ... 61-64
Hillier, Bevis 1940- ... 29-32R
Hillier, Jack R(onald) 1912- ... CANR-3
Earlier sketch in CA 7-8R
Hillier, James Martin 1941- ... 113
Hillier, Jim
See Hillier, James Martin
Hillier, Tristram (Paul) 1905-1983
Obituary ... 114
Hilliker, Grant 1921- ... 33-36R
Hilling, David 1935- ... CANR-12
Earlier sketch in CA 29-32R
Hillinger, Brad 1952- ... 73-76
Hillis, Charles Richard 1913- ... 13-14R
Hillis, Dave 1945- ... 57-60
Hillis, Dick
See Hillis, Charles Richard
Hillix, W(illiam) A(llen) 1927- ... 89-92
Hillman, Arthur 1909-1985 Obituary ... 115
Hillman, Barry L(eslie) 1942- ... 102
Hillman, Howard 1934- ... CANR-20
Earlier sketch in CA 41-44R
Hillman, James 1926- ... 89-92
Hillman, Martin
See Hill, Douglas (Arthur)
Hillman, Priscilla 1940- ... 108
See also SATA 39, 48
Hillman, Ruth Estelyn 1925- ... 53-56
Hillocks, George, Jr. 1934- ... 53-56
Hill-Reid, William Scott 1890- ... 7-8R
Hills, C(harles) A(lbert) R(eis) 1955- ... CANR-23
Earlier sketch in CA 106
See also SATA 39
Hills, Christopher B. 1926- ... 114
Hills, Denis (Cecil) 1913- ... CANR-10
Earlier sketch in CA 65-68
Hills, George 1918- ... 25-28R
Hills, L(awrence) Rust 1924- ... 25-28R
Hills, Lee 1906- ... 101
See also AITN 2
Hills, P. J.
See Hills, Philip J(ames)
Hills, Patricia Gorton Schulze 1936- ... 103
Hills, Philip J(ames) 1933- Brief entry ... 117
Hills, Stuart Lee 1932- ... 33-36R
Hills, Theo(dore) L(ewis) 1925- ... 7-8R
Hills, Tina ... AITN-2
Hillson, Maurie 1925- ... 17-18R
Hillstrom, Tom 1943- ... 102
Hillus, Wilhelm
See Hillers, H(erman) W(illiam)
Hillway, Tyrus 1912- ... CANR-4
Earlier sketch in CA 2R
Hillyard, Brian P. 1949- ... 111
Hillyer, Robert (Silliman) 1895-1961
Obituary ... 89-92
See also DLB 54
Hilscher, Herb(ert H.) 1902-1987
Obituary ... 122
Hilsdale, (Eric) Paul 1922- ... 11-12R
Hilsenrath, Edgar 1926- ... 49-52
Hilsman, Roger 1919- ... 5-6R
Hilt, Douglas Richard 1932- ... 65-68
Hiltebeital, Alf 1942- ... 103
Hiltner, Seward 1909-1984 ... CANR-1
Obituary ... 114
Earlier sketch in CA 3R
Hilton, Alec
See Chesser, Eustace
and Fullerton, Alexander
Hilton, Alice Mary 1924- ... 29-32R
Hilton, Bruce 1930- ... CANR-8
Earlier sketch in CA 7-8R
Hilton, Conrad N(icholson) 1887-1979
Obituary ... 81-84
Hilton, Della (Marion) 1934- ... 69-72
Hilton, Earl (Raymond) 1914- ... 23-24R
Hilton, George W(oodman) 1925- ... CANR-4
Earlier sketch in CA 1R
Hilton, Howard H(oyt, Jr.) 1926- ... 105
Hilton, Irene Pothus ... 3R
See also SATA 7

Hilton, James 1900-1954 Brief entry ... 108
See also SATA 34
See also DLB 34
See also TCLC 21
Hilton, John Buxton 1921- ... CANR-5
Earlier sketch in CA 53-56
Hilton, Lewis B. 1920- ... CANR-8
Earlier sketch in CA 57-60
Hilton, (Howard) Nelson 1950- ... 110
Hilton, Peter 1913- ... 69-72
Hilton, R(odney) H(oward) Brief entry ... 112
Hilton, Ralph 1907- ... 29-32R
See also SATA 8
Hilton, Richard 1894- ... CAP-1
Earlier sketch in CA 9-10
Hilton, Rodney
See Hilton, R(odney) H(oward)
Hilton, Ronald 1911- ... 29-32R
Hilton, Suzanne 1922- ... CANR-12
Earlier sketch in CA 29-32R
See also SATA 4
Hilton, Thomas Leonard 1924- ... 13-14R
Hilton Smith, Robert D(ennis) ?-1974
Obituary ... 53-56
Hilts, Philip J(ames) 1947- ... 110
Hilu, Virginia 1929(?)-1976 Obituary ... 104
Hilvert, John (Peter Paul) 1945- ... 124
Him
See Deal, Borden
Him, George 1900-1982 Obituary ... 106
See also SATA 30
Himber, Jacob 1907- ... 105
Himelick, (James) Raymond 1910- ... 33-36R
Himelstein, Morgan Y(ale) 1926- ... 5-6R
Himes, Chester (Bomar) 1909-1984 ... CANR-22
Obituary ... 114
Earlier sketch in CA 25-28R
See also BW
See also DLB 2, 76
See also CLC 2, 4, 7, 18
Himes, Joseph S(andy) 1908- ... 25-28R
Himler, Ann 1946- ... 53-56
See also SATA 8
Himler, Ronald (Norbert) 1937- ... CANR-5
Earlier sketch in CA 53-56
See also SATA 6
Himmelfarb, Gertrude 1922- ... 49-52
Himmelfarb, Milton 1918- ... 101
Himmelheber, Diana Martin 1938- ... 19-20R
Himmelman, John (Carl) 1959- ... 114
See also SATA 47
Himmelstein, Jerome L(ionel) 1948- ... 113
Himstreet, William Charles 1923- ... CANR-16
Earlier sketches in CA 1R, CANR-1
Hinchliff, Peter Bingham 1929- ... 102
Hinchliffe, Arnold P. 1930- ... CANR-14
Earlier sketch in CA 77-80
Hinckle, Warren James III 1938- ... 89-92
Hinckley, Barbara 1937- ... 57-60
Hinckley, Helen
See Jones, Helen Hinckley
Hinckley, Ted C(harles) 1925- ... 57-60
Hind, Dolores (Ellen) 1931- ... SATA-49, 53
Hind, Robert James 1931- ... 45-48
Hinde, Richard Standish Elphinstone
1912- ... CAP-1
Earlier sketch in CA 9-10
Hinde, Robert Aubrey 1923- ... 109
Hinde, Thomas
See Chitty, Thomas Willes
See also CLC 6, 11
Hinde, Wendy 1919- ... 103
Hindemith, Paul 1895-1963 Obituary ... 112
Hinden, Michael C(harles) 1941- ... 109
Hinderer, Walter (Hermann) 1934- ... CANR-1
Earlier sketch in CA 45-48
Hindin, Nathan
See Bloch, Robert (Albert)
Hinding, Andrea 1942- ... 126
Hindle, Brooke 1918- ... CANR-23
Earlier sketches in CA 15-16R, CANR-7
Hindle, Lee J(ohn) 1965- ... 117
Hindle, W(ilfred) H(ope) 1903-1967 ... CAP-2
Earlier sketch in CA 23-24
Hindley, Geoffrey 1935- ... 109
Hindman, Jane F(erguson) 1905- ... CANR-10
Earlier sketch in CA 25-28R
Hindman, Jo(sephine Long) 1910- ... 97-100
Hinds, Dudley S. 1926- ... 115
Hinds, E. M.
See Hinds, (Evelyn) Margery
Hinds, (Evelyn) Margery ... 9-10R
Hinds, Michael deCourcy
See deCourcy Hinds, Michael
Hindus, Maurice (Gerschon) 1891-1969
Obituary ... 25-28R
Hindus, Michael S(tephen) 1946- ... 105
Hindus, Milton Henry 1916- ... CANR-7
Earlier sketch in CA 19-20R
Hine, Al(fred Blakelee) 1915- ... CANR-2
Earlier sketch in CA 1R
Hine, (William) Daryl 1936- ... CANR-20
Earlier sketches in CA 2R, CANR-1
See also DLB 60
See also CLC 15
Hine, Frederick R. 1925- ... 37-40R
Hine, James R. 1909- ... CANR-17
Earlier sketches in CA 45-48, CANR-2
Hine, Robert Van Norden, Jr. 1921- ... CANR-1
Earlier sketch in CA 1R
Hine, Sesyle Joslin 1929- ... 15-16R
Hine, Thomas 1947- ... 123
Hine, Virginia H(aglin) 1920- ... 97-100
Hiner, Louis C(hase) 1919- ... 73-76
Hines, Anna G(rossnickle) 1946- ... 114
See also SATA 45, 51
Hines, Barry (Melvin) 1939- ... 102
Hines, Bede F(rancis) 1918- ... 45-48
Hines, Earl Kenneth 1905-1983 Obituary ... 109
Hines, Fatha
See Hines, Earl Kenneth
Hines, Neal O(ldfield) 1908- ... CANR-2
Earlier sketch in CA 7-8R
Hines, Paul (David) 1934- ... 29-32R
Hines, Robert Stephan 1926- ... CANR-3
Earlier sketch in CA 9-10R
Hines, Thomas S(pight) 1936- ... CANR-5
Earlier sketch in CA 53-56
Hines, William H. 1909(?)-1976 Obituary ... 65-68
Hinger, Charlotte 1940- ... 123
Hingley, Ronald F(rancis) 1920- ... 7-8R
Hingorani, R(up) C. 1925- ... CANR-26
Earlier sketch in CA 29-32R
Hinkel, John V.
See Hinkel, John Vincent
Hinkel, John Vincent 1906-1986 Obituary ... 121
Hinkemeyer, Michael T(homas) 1940- ... CANR-11
Earlier sketch in CA 69-72
Hinkle, Douglas P(addock) 1923- ... 69-72
Hinkle, Gerald H(ahn) 1931- ... 89-92
Hinkle, Olin Ethmer 1902- ... 3R
Hinkle, Vernon 1935- ... 109
Hinkson, James 1943- ... 69-72
Hinkson, Katharine Tynan
See Tynan, Katharine
Hinkson, Pamela 1900(?)-1982 Obituary ... 107
Hinman, Charlton (Joseph Kadio)
1911-1977 ... CANR-3
Obituary ... 89-92
Earlier sketch in CA 5-6R
Hinman, George W., Jr. 1891-1977
Obituary ... 73-76
Hinman, Robert B(enedict) 1920- ... 5-6R
Hinnebusch, Paul (Gerard) 1917- ... 114
Hinnebusch, William A(quinas) 1908- ... 37-40R
Hinnells, John R(ussell) 1941- ... 49-52
Hinrichsen, Max (Henry) 1901-1965 ... CAP-1
Earlier sketch in CA 13-14
Hinshaw, Cecil E(ugene) 1911- ... 15-16R
Hinshaw, H(orton) Corwin 1902- ... 104
Hinshaw, Randall (Weston) 1915- ... CANR-15
Earlier sketch in CA 41-44R
Hinshaw, Robert E(ugene) 1933- ... 57-60
Hinshaw, Seth B(ennett) 1908- ... 112
Hinshelwood, Cyril (Norman) 1897-1967
Obituary ... 116
Hinsley, F(rancis) H(arry) 1918- ... 17-18R
Hinson, E(dward) Glenn 1931- ... CANR-8
Earlier sketch in CA 21-22R
Hinson, (Grady) Maurice 1930- ... CANR-17
Earlier sketches in CA 45-48, CANR-2
Hinterhoff, Eugene 1895- ... CAP-1
Earlier sketch in CA 9-10
Hintikka, (Kaarlo) Jaakko (Juhani)
1929- ... CANR-2
Earlier sketch in CA 2R
Hinton, Ann Pearlman 1941- ... 108
Hinton, Bernard L. 1937- ... 33-36R
Hinton, Harold C(lendenin) 1924- ... 19-20R
Hinton, John 1926- ... 49-52
Hinton, Nigel 1941- ... 85-88
Hinton, Richard W.
See Angoff, Charles
Hinton, S(usan) E(loise) 1950- ... 81-84
See also SATA 19
See also CLC 30
See also CLR 3
Hinton, Sam 1917- ... 73-76
See also SATA 43
Hinton, Ted C. 1904(?)-1977 Obituary ... 73-76
Hinton, William H. 1919- ... CANR-18
Earlier sketch in CA 25-28R
Hintz, (Loren) Martin 1945- ... CANR-12
Earlier sketch in CA 65-68
See also SATA 39, 47
Hintze, Guenther 1906- ... CAP-2
Earlier sketch in CA 21-22
Hintze, Naomi A. 1909- ... CANR-1
Earlier sketch in CA 45-48
Hinxman, Margaret 1924- ... 124
Hinz, Evelyn J. 1938- ... CANR-10
Earlier sketch in CA 65-68
Hipp, George
See Abrams, George J(oseph)
Hippisley Coxe, Antony D(acres)
1912-1988 ... 103
Obituary ... 124
Hippius, Zinaida
See Gippius, Zinaida (Nikolayevna)
See also TCLC 9
Hipple, Theodore W(allace) 1935- ... CANR-10
Earlier sketch in CA 65-68
Hipple, Walter J(ohn), Jr. 1921- ... 41-44R
Hippler, Arthur E(dwin) 1935- ... 57-60
Hipps, Juanita Redmond 1913(?)-1979
Obituary ... 85-88
Hipskind, Judith 1945- ... 97-100
Hipskind, Verne K(enneth) 1925-1975 ... CAP-2
Earlier sketch in CA 21-22
Hirano, Marsha
See Hirano-Nakanishi, Marsha J(oyce)
Hirano-Nakanishi, Marsha J(oyce) 1949- ... 119
Hiraoka, Kimitake 1925-1970 ... 97-100
Obituary ... 29-32R
Hiro, Dilip ... CANR-14
Earlier sketch in CA 77-80
Hirsch, Abby 1946- ... 45-48
Hirsch, Barbara B. 1938- ... 73-76
Hirsch, Charles S. 1942- ... 105
Hirsch, David H. 1930- ... 97-100
Hirsch, E(ric) D(onald), Jr. 1928- ... 25-28R
See also DLB 67
Hirsch, Edward 1950- ... CANR-20
Earlier sketch in CA 104
See also CLC 31, 50
Hirsch, Ernest A(lbert) 1924-1977 ... CANR-11
Earlier sketch in CA 25-28R
Hirsch, Foster (Lance) 1943- ... CANR-17
Earlier sketches in CA 45-48, CANR-2
Hirsch, Fred 1931-1978 ... 25-28R
Obituary ... 77-80
Hirsch, Herbert 1941- ... CANR-15
Earlier sketch in CA 41-44R
Hirsch, Karen 1941- ... 105
Hirsch, Lester M. 1925- ... 17-18R
Hirsch, Linda 1949- ... 105
Hirsch, Marianne 1949- ... 113
Hirsch, Mark David 1910- ... 89-92
Hirsch, Miriam F. 1927- ... 106
Hirsch, Monroe J(erome) 1917- ... 41-44R
Hirsch, Morris Isaac 1915- ... 103
Hirsch, Phil 1926- ... 102
See also SATA 35
Hirsch, S. Carl 1913- ... CANR-2
Earlier sketch in CA 7-8R
See also SATA 2
Hirsch, Seev 1931- ... 33-36R
Hirsch, Steven R(ichard) 1937- ... 113
Hirsch, Thomas L. 1931- ... 49-52
Hirsch, Walter 1919- ... 15-16R
Hirsch, Werner Z. 1920- ... CANR-7
Earlier sketch in CA 19-20R
Hirsch, William Randolph
See Kitman, Marvin
and Lingeman, Richard R(oberts)
Hirschberg, Cornelius 1901- ... CAP-2
Earlier sketch in CA 17-18
Hirschfeld, Albert 1903- ... CANR-2
Earlier sketch in CA 1R
Hirschfeld, Burt 1923- Brief entry ... 111
Hirschfeld, Charles 1913- Brief entry ... 105
Hirschfeld, Herman 1905- ... CAP-1
Earlier sketch in CA 15-16
Hirschfield, Robert S(idney) 1928- ... 45-48
Hirschhorn, Clive 1940- ... CANR-9
Earlier sketch in CA 57-60
Hirschhorn, Howard H(arvey) 1931- ... CANR-16
Earlier sketch in CA 93-96
Hirschhorn, Richard Clark 1933- ... 69-72
Hirschi, Ron 1948- ... 120
Hirschi, Travis 1935- ... CANR-13
Earlier sketch in CA 77-80
Hirschman, Albert O. 1915- ... CANR-16
Earlier sketches in CA 1R, CANR-1
Hirschman, Jack 1933- ... CANR-22
Earlier sketch in CA 105
Hirschmann, Linda (Ann) 1941- ... 106
See also SATA 40
Hirschmann, Maria Anne ... 85-88
Hirschmeier, Johannes 1921- ... CANR-5
Earlier sketch in CA 13-14R
Hirsh, James E(ric) 1946- ... 109
Hirsh, M(ary) E(lizabeth) 1947- ... 125
Hirsh, Marilyn 1944-1988 ... CANR-16
Obituary ... 126
Earlier sketches in CA 49-52, CANR-1
See also SATA 7
Hirshberg, Al(bert Simon) 1909-1973 ... CANR-4
Obituary ... 41-44R
Earlier sketch in CA 4R
See also SATA 38
Hirshfield, Daniel S. 1942- ... 29-32R
Hirshson, Stanley Philip 1928- ... 2R
Hirst, David W(ayne) 1920- ... 37-40R
Hirst, Paul H(eywood) 1927- ... 65-68
Hirst, Paul Quentin 1946- ... 104
Hirst, Rodney Julian 1920- ... 11-12R
Hirst, Stephen M(ichael) 1939- ... 53-56
Hirst, Wilma E(llis) 1914- ... 15-16R
Hirt, Michael L(eonard) 1934- ... 9-10R
Hisamatsu, (Hoseki) Shin'ichi 1889- ... 81-84
Hiscock, Bruce 1940- ... 122
Hiscock, Eric 1899- ... 109
Hiscock, Eric C(harles) 1908-1986 ... 107
Obituary ... 120
Hiscocks, C(harles) Richard 1907- ... 53-56
Hiser, Iona Seibert ... CANR-2
Earlier sketch in CA 3R
See also SATA 4
Hiskett, Mervyn 1920- ... 61-64
Hislop, Codman 1906- ... CAP-2
Earlier sketch in CA 33-36
Hisrich, Robert D(ale) 1944- ... 112
Hiss, Alger 1904- ... 33-36R
Hiss, Tony 1941- ... 77-80
Hissey, Jane (Elizabeth) 1952- ... 124
Hitchcock, Alfred (Joseph) 1899-1980
Obituary ... 97-100
See also SATA 24, 27
See also CLC 16
Hitchcock, Alma Reville 1899-1982
Obituary ... 107
Hitchcock, George 1914- ... CANR-13
Earlier sketch in CA 33-36R
Hitchcock, H(ugh) Wiley 1923- ... CANR-17
Earlier sketches in CA 45-48, CANR-1
Hitchcock, Henry-Russell 1903-1987 ... 125
Obituary ... 122
Hitchcock, James 1938- ... 33-36R
Hitchcock, Raymond (John) 1922- ... 85-88
Hitchcock, Susan Tyler 1950- ... CANR-18
Earlier sketch in CA 102
Hitchens, Dolores 1908(?)-1973 Obituary ... 45-48
Hitchin, Martin Mewburn 1917- ... 13-14R
Hitching, (John) Francis 1933- ... 103
Hitchman, James H. 1932- ... 37-40R
Hitchman, Janet 1916-1980 ... 23-24R
Obituary ... 97-100
Hite, James (Cleveland) 1941- ... 53-56
Hite, Molly 1947- ... 124
Hite, Shere D. 1942- ... 81-84
Hitiris, Theodore 1938- ... 41-44R
Hitler, Adolf 1889-1945 Brief entry ... 117
Hitrec, Joseph George 1912-1972 ... CAP-2
Earlier sketch in CA 17-18
Hitsman, J(ohn) Mackay 1917-1970 ... CAP-1
Earlier sketch in CA 17-18
Hitt, Russell T(rovillo) 1905- ... 4R
Hitt, William D(ee) 1929- ... 49-52
Hitte, Kathryn 1919- ... 21-22R
See also SATA 16
Hitti, Philip K(huri) 1886-1978 ... CANR-6
Obituary ... 81-84
Earlier sketch in CA 2R
Hitz, Demi 1942- ... CANR-8
Earlier sketch in CA 61-64
See also SATA 11
Hitz-Holman, Betsy
See Holman, Betsy Hitz
Hively, Pete (Chester) 1934- ... 69-72
Hivnor, Robert 1916- ... 65-68
Hix, Charles (Arthur) 1942- ... CANR-21
Earlier sketch in CA 102
Hixon, Don L(ee) 1942- ... 73-76
Hixson, Joseph R(andolph) 1927- ... 65-68
Hixson, Richard F. 1932- ... 23-24R
Hixson, William B(utler), Jr. 1940- ... 37-40R
Hjelte, George 1893-1979 ... CANR-23
Earlier sketch in CA 29-32R
Hjortsberg, William (Reinhold) 1941- ... 33-36R
Hlasko, Marek 1933(?)-1969 Obituary ... 25-28R
Hlybinny, Vladimir
See Seduro, Vladimir
Hnizdovsky, Jacques 1915- ... SATA-32
Ho, Alfred K(uo-liang) 1919- ... 25-28R
Ho, Minfong 1951- ... 77-80
See also SATA 15
Ho, Ping-ti 1917- ... CANR-11
Earlier sketch in CA 5-6R
Hoa, Nguyen-Dinh
See Nguyen-dinh-Hoa
Hoadley, Irene Braden 1938- ... 29-32R
Hoadley, Walter E(vans) 1916- ... 102
Hoag, Edwin 1926- ... 15-16R
Hoagland, Edward 1932- ... CANR-2
Earlier sketch in CA 3R
See also SATA 51
See also DLB 6
See also CLC 28
Hoagland, Everett (III) 1942- ... CANR-25
Earlier sketch in CA 33-36R
See also BW
See also DLB 41
Hoagland, Jimmie Lee 1940- ... 101
Hoagland, John 1947(?)-1984 Obituary ... 112
Hoagland, Kathleen M(ary) Dooher
1909(?)-1984 ... 7-8R
Obituary ... 112
Hoagland, Mahlon B(ush) 1921- ... 85-88
Hoang Van Chi 1915- ... CANR-7
Earlier sketch in CA 13-14R
Hoare, Merval Hannah 1914- ... 103
Hoare, Robert J(ohn) 1921-1975 ... CANR-6
Earlier sketch in CA 11-12R
See also SATA 38
Hoare, Wilber W., Jr. 1921-1976
Obituary ... 65-68
Hoban, Lillian 1925- ... CANR-23
Earlier sketch in CA 69-72
See also SATA 22
Hoban, Russell (Conwell) 1925- ... CANR-23
Earlier sketch in CA 7-8R
See also SATA 1, 40
See also DLB 52
See also CLC 7, 25
See also CLR 3
Hoban, Tana ... CANR-23
Earlier sketch in CA 93-96
See also SATA 22
See also CLR 13
Hobart, Alice Nourse 1882-1967 ... 7-8R
Obituary ... 25-28R
Hobart, Alice Tisdale
See Hobart, Alice Nourse
Hobart, Billie 1935- ... 49-52
Hobart, Lois (Elaine) ... 5-6R
See also SATA 7
Hobbing, Enno 1920- ... 89-92
Hobbs, Albert Hoyt 1940- ... 125
Hobbs, Anne
See Purdy, Anne S.
Hobbs, Cecil (Carlton) 1907- ... 23-24R
Hobbs, Charles R(ene) 1931- ... 15-16R
Hobbs, (Carl) Fredric 1931- ... 81-84
Hobbs, Herschel Harold 1907- ... CANR-2
Earlier sketch in CA 7-8R
Hobbs, J. Kline 1928- ... 108
Hobbs, John Leslie 1916-1964 ... 7-8R
Hobbs, Michael 1934- ... 111
Hobbs, Perry
See Blackmur, R(ichard) P(almer)
Hobbs, Peter V(ictor) 1936- ... 53-56
Hobbs, Richard (Wright) 1931- ... 123
Brief entry ... 118
Hobbs, Robert C(arleton) 1946- ... CANR-24
Earlier sketch in CA 106
Hobbs, William (Beresford) 1939- ... 21-22R
Hobbs, Williston C. 1925(?)-1978
Obituary ... 81-84
Hobby, Bertram Maurice 1905-1983
Obituary ... 110
Hobby, Gladys L(ounsbury) 1910- ... 119
Hobby, Oveta Culp 1905- ... 81-84
Hobby, William P. 1932- ... 85-88
Hobday, Victor C(arr) 1914- ... 97-100

Hobel, Phil
See Fanthorpe, R(obert) Lionel
Hoben, John B. 1908- ... 37-40R
Hoberecht, Earnest 1918- ... 23-24R
Hoberman, Gerald 1943- ... 111
Hoberman, Mary Ann 1930- ... 41-44R
See also SATA 5
Hobfoll, Stevan E(arl) 1951- ... 123
Hobgood, Burnet M. 1922- ... 101
Hobhouse, Christina 1941- ... 25-28R
Hobhouse, Hermione 1934- ... CANR-15
Earlier sketch in CA 41-44R
Hobhouse, Janet 1948- ... 57-60
Hobhouse, Penelope
See Malins, Penelope
Hobkirk, Michael D(algliesh) 1924- ... 119
Hobley, Leonard Frank 1903- ... CANR-5
Earlier sketch in CA 13-14R
Hobsbaum, Philip (Dennis) 1932- ... CANR-3
Earlier sketch in CA 9-10R
See also DLB 40
Hobsbawm, Eric J(ohn Ernest) 1917- ... CANR-3
Earlier sketch in CA 5-6R
Hobson, Anthony (Robert Alwyn) 1921- ... 33-36R
Hobson, Burton (Harold) 1933- ... CANR-2
Earlier sketch in CA 7-8R
See also SATA 28
Hobson, Edmund (Schofield) 1931- ... 45-48
Hobson, Fred Colby, Jr. 1943- ... CANR-5
Earlier sketch in CA 53-56
Hobson, Geary 1941- ... 122
Hobson, Hank
See Hobson, Harry
Hobson, Harold 1904- ... 81-84
Hobson, Harry 1908- ... CAP-1
Earlier sketch in CA 9-10
Hobson, Julius W(ilson) 1922(?)-1977 ... 102
See also BW
Hobson, Laura Z(ametkin) 1900-1986 ... 19-20R
Obituary ... 118
See also SATA 52
See also DLB 28
See also CLC 7, 25
Hobson, Mary 1926- ... 106
Hobson, Polly
See Evans, Julia (Rendel)
Hobson, William 1911- ... 103
Hobzek, Mildred J(ane) 1919- ... 101
Hoch, Edward D(entinger) 1930- ... CANR-11
Earlier sketch in CA 29-32R
Hoch, Paul L(awrence) 1942- ... 65-68
Hochbaum, H(ans) Albert 1911- ... 103
Hochfield, George 1926- ... 2R
Hochhuth, Rolf 1931- ... 7-8R
See also CLC 4, 11, 18
Ho Chi Minh 1890(?)-1969 Obituary ... 112
Hochman, Harold M(arvin) 1936- ... 108
Hochman, Sandra 1936- ... 7-8R
See also DLB 5
See also CLC 3, 8
Hochman, Shel 1944- ... 69-72
Hochman, Shirley D(ean) 1917- ... 61-64
Hochman, Stanley Richard 1928- ... 103
Hochschild, Adam 1942- ... 125
Brief entry ... 121
Hochschild, Arlie Russell 1940- ... 57-60
See also SATA 11
Hochschild, Harold K. 1892-1981
Obituary ... 103
Hochstein, Rolaine ... CANR-23
Earlier sketch in CA 45-48
Hochstetter, Leo D. 1911(?)-1987
Obituary ... 122
Hochwaelder, Fritz 1911-1986 ... 29-32R
Obituary ... 120
See also CLC 36
Hochwald, Werner 1910- ... 19-20R
Hochwalder, Fritz
See Hochwaelder, Fritz
See also CLC 36
Hockaby, Stephen
See Mitchell, Gladys (Maude Winifred)
Hockenberry, Hope
See Newell, Hope Hockenberry
Hocker, Karla
See Hoecker, Karla
Hockett, Charles F(rancis) 1916- ... 19-20R
Hocking, Anthony 1938- ... 102
Hocking, Brian 1914-1974 ... CAP-2
Earlier sketch in CA 17-18
Hocking, Mary (Eunice) 1921- ... CANR-18
Earlier sketch in CA 101
See also CLC 13
Hocking, William Ernest 1873-1966 ... CAP-1
Earlier sketch in CA 13-14
Hockley, G(raham) C(harles) 1931- ... 29-32R
Hockney, David 1937- Brief entry ... 116
Hocks, Richard A(llen) 1936- ... 81-84
Hodder-Williams, Christopher 1926- ... CANR-1
Earlier sketch in CA 2R
Hode, W(illiam) Stanley 1903- ... 17-18R
Hodeir, Andre 1921- ... CANR-15
Earlier sketch in CA 85-88
Hodes, Aubrey 1927- ... 33-36R
Hodes, Scott 1937- ... 49-52
Hodgart, Matthew (John Caldwell)
1916- ... CANR-9
Earlier sketch in CA 7-8R
Hodge, Alan 1915-1979 Obituary ... 89-92
Hodge, David W(ayne) 1935- ... 61-64
Hodge, Francis (Richard) 1915- ... CANR-12
Earlier sketch in CA 33-36R
Hodge, Gene (Meany) 1898- ... 45-48
Hodge, James L(ee) 1935- ... 41-44R
Hodge, Jane Aiken 1917- ... CANR-3
Earlier sketch in CA 7-8R
Hodge, Marshall Bryant 1925-19(?) ... CAP-2
Earlier sketch in CA 23-24
Hodge, P(aul) W(illiam) 1934- ... CANR-14
Earlier sketch in CA 33-36R
See also SATA 12
Hodge, William H(oward) 1932- ... CANR-15
Earlier sketch in CA 65-68
Hodgell, P(atricia) C(hristine) 1951- ... 109
See also SATA 42
Hodges, C(yril) Walter 1909- ... CANR-5
Earlier sketch in CA 15-16R
See also SATA 2
Hodges, Carl G. 1902-1964 ... 7-8R
See also SATA 10
Hodges, Devon Leigh 1950- ... 125
Hodges, Donald Clark 1923- ... CANR-24
Earlier sketches in CA 53-56, CANR-6
Hodges, Doris M(arjorie) 1915- ... CANR-11
Earlier sketch in CA 25-28R
Hodges, Elizabeth Jamison ... 11-12R
See also SATA 1
Hodges, Gil(bert Ray) 1924-1972
Obituary ... 109
Hodges, Graham R(ushing) 1915- ... 5-6R
Hodges, Harold Mellor 1922- ... 19-20R
Hodges, Henry (Woolmington MacKenzie)
1920- ... 37-40R
Hodges, Henry G. 1888- ... 7-8R
Hodges, Herbert Arthur 1905-1976 ... 73-76
Obituary ... 69-72
Hodges, John C(unyus) 1892-1967 ... 5-6R
Obituary ... 103
Hodges, Louis W. 1933- ... 81-84
Hodges, Luther (Hartwell) 1898-1974
Obituary ... 53-56
Hodges, Margaret Moore 1911- ... CANR-2
Earlier sketch in CA 1R
See also SATA 1, 33
Hodges, Richard E(dwin) 1928- ... CANR-15
Earlier sketch in CA 41-44R
Hodges, Turner
See Morehead, Albert H(odges)
Hodges, Zane Clark 1932- ... CANR-15
Earlier sketch in CA 41-44R
Hodgetts, A(lfred) Birnie 1911- ... 101
Hodgetts, Blake Christopher 1967- ... 114
See also SATA 43
Hodgetts, J(ohn) E(dwin) 1917- ... 13-14R
Hodgetts, Richard M(ichael) 1942- ... CANR-23
Earlier sketches in CA 57-60, CANR-8
Hodgins, Bruce W(illard) 1931- ... 37-40R
Hodgins, Eric 1899-1971 ... 104
Obituary ... 29-32R
Hodgins, Jack 1938- ... 93-96
See also DLB 60
See also CLC 23
Hodgkin, Robert Allason 1916- ... 102
Hodgkin, Robin A.
See Hodgkin, Robert Allason
Hodgkin, Thomas Lionel 1910-1982
Obituary ... 115
Hodgkinson, Anthony 1916-1983 ... 126
Hodgkinson, Christopher 1928- ... 115
Hodgkinson, Edith 1959- ... 117
Hodgkinson, Liz 1943- ... 124
Hodgkinson, Marie Elisabeth
1921(?)-1983 Obituary ... 110
Hodgkiss, A(lan) G(eoffrey) 1921- ... 124
Hodgman, Helen 1945- Brief entry ... 117
See also DLB 14
Hodgson, D(avid) H(argraves) 1939- ... 25-28R
Hodgson, David
See Lewis, David
Hodgson, Derek 1929- ... 118
Hodgson, Godfrey (Michael Talbot)
1934- ... 25-28R
Hodgson, John A(lfred) 1945- ... 125
Hodgson, Leonard 1889-1969 ... CAP-1
Earlier sketch in CA 9-10
Hodgson, Margaret
See Ballinger, (Violet) Margaret (Livingstone)
Hodgson, Marshall G. S. 1922-1968 ... CAP-2
Earlier sketch in CA 21-22
Hodgson, Martha (Keeling) 1906- ... 57-60
Hodgson, Norma
See Russell, Norma Hull Lewis
Hodgson, Pat 1928- ... CANR-7
Earlier sketch in CA 57-60
Hodgson, Peter Crafts 1934- ... CANR-15
Earlier sketch in CA 29-32R
Hodgson, Peter E(dward) 1928- ... 11-12R
Hodgson, Phyllis 1909- ... CAP-1
Earlier sketch in CA 13-14
Hodgson, Ralph 1871-1962 ... 102
See also DLB 19
Hodgson, Richard Sargeant 1924- ... CANR-7
Earlier sketch in CA 15-16R
Hodgson, Robert D(avid) 1923- ... 7-8R
Hodgson, William Hope 1877(?)-1918
Brief entry ... 111
See also DLB 70
See also TCLC 13
Hodin, J(osef) P(aul) 1905- ... 41-44R
Hodnett, Edward 1901-1984 ... CANR-5
Obituary ... 114
Earlier sketch in CA 13-14R
Hodsdon, Nicholas E(dward) 1941- ... 49-52
Hodsdon, Nick
See Hodsdon, Nicholas E(dward)
Hodson, Henry V(incent) 1906- ... CANR-3
Earlier sketch in CA 7-8R
Hoebel, Edward Adamson 1906- ... CANR-1
Earlier sketch in CA 4R
Hoecker, Karla 1901- ... CANR-2
Earlier sketch in CA 49-52
Hoehling, A(dolph) A. 1915- ... CANR-1
Earlier sketch in CA 1R
Hoehling, Mary 1914- ... 93-96
Hoehn, Richard A(lbert) 1936- ... 116
Hoehner, Harold W. 1935- ... 37-40R
Hoekema, Anthony A(ndrew) 1913- ... 11-12R
Hoeksema, Gertrude 1921- ... 106
Hoel, Robert F(loyd) 1942- ... 53-56
Hoelterhoff, Manuela (Vali) 1949- ... 120
Brief entry ... 114
Hoelzel, Alfred 1934- ... 41-44R
Hoenig, J(ulius) 1916- ... 29-32R
Hoenig, Sidney B(enjamin) 1907-1979 ... CANR-2
Earlier sketch in CA 45-48
Hoeniger, F(rederick) David 1921- ... 41-44R
Hoenigswald, Henry M(ax) 1915- ... 13-14R
Hoequist, Charles Ernest, Jr. 1954- ... 108
Hoest, Bill
See Hoest, William P.
Hoest, William P. 1926- ... CANR-23
Earlier sketch in CA 69-72
Hoetink, H(armannus) 1931- ... 23-24R
Hoeveler, Diane Long 1949- ... 102
Hoexter, Corinne K. 1927- ... 49-52
See also SATA 6
Hoey, Joanne Nobes 1936- ... 106
Hofer, Philip 1898-1984 Obituary ... 114
Hoff, Carol 1900- ... CAP-2
Earlier sketch in CA 21-22
See also SATA 11
Hoff, Ebbe Curtis 1906- ... 57-60
Hoff, Harry S(ummerfield) 1910- ... CANR-20
Earlier sketches in CA 4R, CANR-2
Hoff, Marilyn 1942- ... CANR-7
Earlier sketch in CA 17-18R
Hoff, Syd(ney) 1912- ... CANR-4
Earlier sketch in CA 5-6R
See also SATA 9
See also SAAS 4
Hoffa, James R(iddle) 1913-1975(?)
Obituary ... 109
Hoffecker, Carol E(leanor) 1938- ... 85-88
Hoffecker, (John) Savin 1908- ... 5-6R
Hoffeld, Donald R(aymond) 1933- ... 29-32R
Hoffeld, Laura 1946(?)-1982 Obituary ... 106
Hoffenberg, Jack 1906-1977 ... 81-84
Hoffenberg, Mason 1922(?)-1986
Obituary ... 119
Hoffenstein, Samuel Goodman 1890-1947
Brief entry ... 111
See also DLB 11
Hoffer, Charles R(ussell) 1929- ... CANR-22
Earlier sketches in CA 15-16R, CANR-7
Hoffer, Eric 1902-1983 ... CANR-18
Obituary ... 109
Earlier sketch in CA 15-16R
Hoffer, Thomas William 1938- ... 118
Hoffer, William 1943- ... 65-68
Hofferbert, Richard I(ra) 1937- ... 29-32R
Hoffine, Lyla 1897- ... 2R
Hoffman, Abbie 1936- ... CANR-8
Earlier sketch in CA 21-22R
Hoffman, Abraham 1938- ... 106
Hoffman, Adeline M(ildred)
1908-1979 ... CANR-23
Earlier sketch in CA 29-32R
Hoffman, Alice 1952- ... 77-80
Hoffman, Anita 1942- ... 69-72
Hoffman, Arthur S. 1926- ... CANR-10
Earlier sketch in CA 25-28R
Hoffman, Arthur W(olf) 1921- ... 5-6R
Hoffman, Bengt R(uno) 1913- ... 69-72
Hoffman, Bernard G(ilbert) 1925- ... 41-44R
Hoffman, Betty Hannah 1918- ... 9-10R
Hoffman, Calvin 1908(?)-1986 Obituary ... 118
Hoffman, Charles Fenno 1806-1884 ... DLB-3
Hoffman, Daniel (Gerard) 1923- ... CANR-4
Earlier sketch in CA 3R
See also DLB 5
See also CLC 6, 13, 23
Hoffman, David Herbert 1932(?)-1985
Obituary ... 115
Hoffman, Dominic M. 1913- ... 116
Hoffman, Donald S(tone) 1936- ... 57-60
Hoffman, Edward ... 106
Hoffman, Edwin D. ... 101
See also SATA 49
Hoffman, Elizabeth P(arkinson) 1921- ... 77-80
Hoffman, Frederick J(ohn) 1909-1967 ... CANR-6
Earlier sketch in CA 4R
Hoffman, Gail 1896- ... 5-6R
Hoffman, George W(alter) 1914- ... 13-14R
Hoffman, Harry G. 1911(?)-1977
Obituary ... 69-72
Hoffman, Helmut 1912- ... CANR-17
Earlier sketch in CA 3R
Hoffman, Herbert H(einz) 1928- ... 117
Hoffman, Hester R(osalyn) 1895- ... CAP-1
Earlier sketch in CA 9-10
Hoffman, Jo Ann S. 1942- ... 81-84
Hoffman, Joseph G(ilbert) 1909-1974 ... 65-68
Obituary ... 53-56
Hoffman, Joy 1954- ... 108
Hoffman, Julius Jennings 1895-1983
Obituary ... 110
Hoffman, L. Richard 1930- ... 13-14R
Hoffman, Lee 1932- ... CANR-18
Earlier sketch in CA 25-28R
Hoffman, Lisa 1919- ... 29-32R
Hoffman, Lois Wladis 1929- ... 13-14R
Hoffman, Mark S. 1952- ... 125
Hoffman, Marshall 1942- ... 106
Hoffman, Michael Allen 1944- ... 106
Hoffman, Michael J(erome) 1939- ... 29-32R
Hoffman, Nancy Jo 1942- ... 107
Hoffman, Paul 1934-1984 ... CANR-1
Obituary ... 112
Earlier sketch in CA 45-48
Hoffman, Philip T(homas) 1947- ... 119
Hoffman, Phyllis M(iriam) 1944- ... CANR-12
Earlier sketch in CA 29-32R
See also SATA 4
Hoffman, Richard L(ester) 1937-1981 ... CANR-23
Earlier sketch in CA 29-32R
Hoffman, Robert C. 1899(?)-1985
Obituary ... 116
Hoffman, Robert L. 1937- ... 37-40R
Hoffman, Ronald 1941- Brief entry ... 112
Hoffman, Rosekrans 1926- ... CANR-15
Earlier sketch in CA 89-92
See also SATA 15
Hoffman, Ross John Swartz 1902- ... 65-68
Hoffman, Stanley 1944- ... 77-80
See also CLC 5
Hoffman, Willa M(athews) 1914- ... 61-64
Hoffman, William 1925- ... CANR-9
Earlier sketch in CA 21-22R
Hoffman, William M(oses) 1939- ... CANR-11
Earlier sketch in CA 57-60
See also CLC 40
Hoffmann, Ann (Marie) 1930- ... 37-40R
Hoffmann, Banesh 1906-1986 ... CANR-3
Obituary ... 119
Earlier sketch in CA 7-8R
Hoffmann, Charles 1921- ... 106
Hoffmann, Charles G. 1921- ... 15-16R
Hoffmann, Donald 1933- ... 25-28R
Hoffmann, E(rnst) T(heodor) A(madeus)
1776-1822 ... SATA-27
Hoffmann, Eleanor 1895- ... CAP-1
Earlier sketch in CA 15-16
Hoffmann, Erik P(eter) 1939- ... CANR-13
Earlier sketch in CA 33-36R
Hoffmann, Felix 1911-1975 ... CAP-2
Obituary ... 57-60
Earlier sketch in CA 29-32
See also SATA 9
Hoffmann, Frank W(illiam) 1949- ... 106
Hoffmann, Hilde 1927- ... 25-28R
Hoffmann, Leon-Francois 1932- ... 49-52
Hoffmann, Malcolm A(rthur) 1912- ... 65-68
Hoffmann, Margaret Jones 1910- ... CANR-2
Earlier sketch in CA 5-6R
See also SATA 48
Hoffmann, Peggy
See Hoffmann, Margaret Jones
Hoffmann, Peter (Conrad Werner)
1930- ... CANR-14
Earlier sketch in CA 81-84
Hoffmann, Peter R. 1935- ... 108
Hoffmann, Stanley 1928- ... CANR-5
Earlier sketch in CA 15-16R
Hoffmann, Stanley (H.) 1928- ... CANR-14
Earlier sketch in CA 81-84
Hoffmann, Yoel 1937- ... 97-100
Hoffmeister, Adolf 1903-1973 Obituary ... 41-44R
Hoffmeister, Donald F(rederick) 1916- ... 53-56
Hoffnung, Michele 1944- ... 81-84
Hofheinz, Roy Mark, Jr. 1935- ... 110
Hofinger, Johannes 1905- ... CAP-1
Earlier sketch in CA 19-20
Hofling, Charles K(reimer) 1920- ... 41-44R
Hofman, Anton
See Hollo, Anselm
Hofmann, Adele Dellenbaugh 1926- ... 97-100
Hofmann, Hans 1923- ... CANR-4
Earlier sketch in CA 3R
Hofmann, Melita C(ecelia) ?-1976 ... 5-6R
Obituary ... 69-72
Hofmann, Michael 1957- ... DLB-40
Hofmann, Paul Leopold 1912- ... 107
Hofmann, William J(ohn) 1931- ... 114
Hofmannsthal, Hugo von 1874-1929
Brief entry ... 106
See also TCLC 11
Hofsinde, Robert 1902-1973 ... 73-76
Obituary ... 45-48
See also SATA 21
Hofsommer, Don(ovan) L(owell)
1938- ... CANR-24
Earlier sketches in CA 65-68, CANR-9
Hofstadter, Albert 1910- ... 33-36R
Hofstadter, Douglas R(ichard) 1945- ... 105
Hofstadter, Richard 1916-1970 ... CANR-4
Obituary ... 29-32R
Earlier sketch in CA 4R
See also DLB 17
Hofstede, Geert H.
See Hofstede, Gerard H(endrik)
Hofstede, Gerard H(endrik) 1928- ... CANR-15
Earlier sketch in CA 41-44R
Hofstetter, Richard R(yan) 1956- ... 117
Hofvendahl, Russ(ell Lloyd) 1921- ... 116
Hogan, Bernice Harris 1929- ... CANR-7
Earlier sketch in CA 15-16R
See also SATA 12
Hogan, Dennis P. 1950- ... 110
Hogan, Desmond 1950- ... 102
See also DLB 14
Hogan, Inez 1895- ... CANR-1
Earlier sketch in CA 4R
See also SATA 2
Hogan, James P(atrick) 1941- ... CANR-15
Earlier sketch in CA 81-84
Hogan, John Charles 1919- ... 17-18R
Hogan, John D. 1927- ... 45-48
Hogan, Judy 1937- ... CANR-16
Earlier sketch in CA 77-80
Hogan, Lawrence D(aniel) 1944- ... 124
Hogan, Linda 1947- ... 120
Hogan, Michael 1943- ... CANR-14
Earlier sketch in CA 77-80

INDEX

Hogan, Paul 1927- 61-64
Hogan, (Robert) Ray 1908- CANR-4
Earlier sketch in CA 9-10R
Hogan, Robert (Goode) 1930- CANR-19
Earlier sketches in CA 4R, CANR-1
Hogan, Robert F(rancis) 1927- 41-44R
Hogan, Thom(as Eugene, Jr.) 1952- 103
Hogan, Ursula 1899- 5-6R
Hogan, Willard N(ewton) 1909- CAP-2
Earlier sketch in CA 21-22
Hogan, William Francis 1930- 25-28R
Hogan, William T. 1919- 97-100
Hogarth, Burne 1911- 93-96
Hogarth, Charles
See Bowen, (Ivor) Ian
and Creasey, John
Hogarth, Douglas
See Phillips-Birt, Douglas Hextall Chedzey
Hogarth, Emmett
See Polonsky, Abraham (Lincoln)
Hogarth, Grace (Weston Allen) 1905- 89-92
Hogarth, John
See Finnin, (Olive) Mary
Hogarth, Jr.
See Kent, Rockwell
Hogarth, (Arthur) Paul 1917- 49-52
See also SATA 41
Hogben, Lancelot T. 1895-1975 73-76
Obituary 61-64
Hogbin, H(erbert) Ian 1904- 9-10R
Hogbotel, Sebastian
See Gott, K(enneth) D(avidson)
Hoge, Cecil C(unningham), Sr. 1913- 116
Hoge, Dean R(ichard) 1937- 53-56
Hoge, James O(tey) 1944- 89-92
Hoge, Phyllis
See Thompson, Phyllis Hoge
Hoge, Warren McClamroch 1941- 102
Hogendorn, Jan S(tafford) 1937- CANR-14
Earlier sketch in CA 37-40R
Hogg, Beth
See Hogg, Elizabeth (Tootill)
Hogg, Clayton L(eRoy) 1924- 104
Hogg, Elizabeth (Tootill) 1917- CANR-10
Earlier sketch in CA 7-8R
Hogg, Garry 1902-1976 .... CANR-10
Earlier sketch in CA 23-24R
See also SATA 2
Hogg, Helen (Battles) Sawyer 1905- 69-72
Hogg, Ian V(ernon) 1926- CANR-12
Earlier sketch in CA 29-32R
Hogg, Oliver Frederick Gillilan 1887-1979 ..93-96
Obituary 85-88
Hogg, Quintin McGarel 1907- CANR-14
Earlier sketches in CA 11-12, CAP-1
Hogg, Robert (Lawrence) 1942- 53-56
Hogg, W(illiam) Richey 1921- 2R
Hoggart, Richard 1918- 9-10R
Hogins, James Burl 1936- 53-56
Hogner, Dorothy Childs 33-36R
See also SATA 4
Hogner, Nils 1893-1970 77-80
See also SATA 25
Hogrefe, Pearl CAP-1
Earlier sketch in CA 15-16
Hogrogian, Nonny 1932- CANR-2
Earlier sketch in CA 45-48
See also SATA 7
See also SAAS 1
See also CLR 2
Hogue, Arthur R(eed) 1906-1986 ....37-40R
Obituary 118
Hogue, C(harles) B(illy) 1928- 69-72
Hogue, Charles Leonard 1935- 105
Hogue, Richard 1946- 49-52
Hogue, W. Lawrence 1951- 126
Hoguet, Susan Ramsay 1945- 119
Hogwood, Christopher (Jarvis Haley)
1941- Brief entry 120
Hoh, Diane 1937- 120
See also SATA 48, 52
Hohenberg, Dorothy Lannuier
1905(?)-1977 Obituary 73-76
Hohenberg, John 1906- CANR-6
Earlier sketch in CA 13-14R
Hohenberg, Paul M(arcel) 1933- 25-28R
Hohendahl, Peter Uwe 1936- CANR-17
Earlier sketches in CA 45-48, CANR-2
Hohenstein, C(harles) Louis 1930- 116
Hohenstein, Henry J(ohn) 1931- 53-56
Hohenzollern, Friedrich Wilhelm (Victor
Albert) 1859-1941 Brief entry 120
Hohimer, Frank 1928- 57-60
Hohl, Ludwig 1904-1980 .... DLB-56
Hohler, Robert T(illman) 1951- 123
Hohlfelder, Robert Lane 1938- 45-48
Hohlwein, Kathryn Joyce 1930- 125
Hohn, Hazel (Stamper) 7-8R
Hohnen, David 1925- 21-22R
Hohoff, Tay
See Torrey, Therese von Hohoff
Hoig, Stan(ley Warlick) 1924- CANR-1
Earlier sketch in CA 1R
Hoijer, Harry 1904-1976 73-76
Obituary 65-68
Hoisington, Harland 1896(?)-1973
Obituary 45-48
Hoke, Helen L. 1903- 73-76
See also SATA 15
Hoke, John (Lindsay) 1925- 41-44R
See also SATA 7
Holabird, Katharine 1948- 121
Holaday, Allan Gibson 1916- 37-40R
Holan, Vladimir 1905-1980 Obituary 114
Holbeach, Henry
See Rands, William Brighty
Holbeche, Philippa Jack 1919- CAP-1
Earlier sketch in CA 9-10
Holberg, Ruth L(angland) 1889- 5-6R
See also SATA 1
Holbik, Karel 1920- 37-40R
Holbo, Paul Sothe 1929- 25-28R
Holborn, Hajo 1902-1969 .... CAP-2
Earlier sketch in CA 25-28
Holborn, Louise W. 1898-19(?) CAP-2
Earlier sketch in CA 25-28
Holborn, Mark 1949- 104
Holbrook, Bill 1921- 61-64
Holbrook, David (Kenneth) 1923- CANR-3
Earlier sketch in CA 7-8R
See also DLB 14, 40
Holbrook, Jennifer Kearns 1931- 102
Holbrook, Peter
See Glick, Carl (Cannon)
Holbrook, Sabra
See Erickson, Sabra Rollins
Holbrook, Stewart Hall 1893-1964 .... CAP-1
Earlier sketch in CA 9-10
See also SATA 2
Holburn, James 1900-1988 Obituary 124
Holck, Manfred, Jr. 1930- 19-20R
Holcomb, Adele M(ansfield) 1930- 113
Holcomb, Donald F(rank) 1925- 97-100
Holcomb, George L. 1911- 45-48
Holcomb, Jerry (Leona) 1927- 25-28R
Holcombe, Arthur N(orman) 1884-1977 .. CAP-2
Obituary 73-76
Earlier sketch in CA 29-32
Holcombe, Randall G(regory) 1950- 111
Holcroft, Thomas 1745-1809 .... DLB-39
Holden, Anthony (Ivan) 1947- 101
Holden, Anton 1934- 108
Holden, Curry
See Holden, William Curry
Holden, David (Shipley) 1924-1977 ......41-44R
Holden, Donald 1931- CANR-18
Earlier sketches in CA 45-48, CANR-2
Holden, Edith 1871-1920 Brief entry 113
Holden, Elizabeth Rhoda 1943- CANR-16
Earlier sketch in CA 97-100
Holden, Genevieve
See Pou, Genevieve Long
Holden, George S(cott) 1926- 106
Holden, Inez 1906-1974 Obituary 53-56
Holden, Jonathan 1941- CANR-16
Earlier sketches in CA 45-48, CANR-1
Holden, Matthew
See Parkinson, Roger
Holden, Matthew, Jr. 1931- 57-60
Holden, Molly 1927-1981 ....25-28R
See also DLB 40
Holden, Paul E. 1894(?)-1976 Obituary ...65-68
Holden, Raymond (Peckham)
1894-1972 .... CANR-4
Obituary 37-40R
Earlier sketch in CA 7-8R
Holden, Ursula 1921- CANR-22
Earlier sketch in CA 101
See also CLC 18
Holden, Vincent F. 1911-1972 Obituary ..37-40R
Holden, W. C.
See Holden, William Curry
Holden, W(illis) Sprague 1909-1973 .... 1R
Obituary 45-48
Holden, William Curry 1898(?)-
Brief entry 117
Holder, Bob N.
See Mullarky, Taylor
Holder, Glenn 1906- 41-44R
Holder, Gwynneth 1943- 119
Holder, John, Jr. 1947-1985 103
Obituary 116
Holder, Ray 1913- 102
Holder, William G. 1937- CANR-10
Earlier sketch in CA 25-28R
Holdgate, Martin Wyatt 1931- 109
Holdheim, William Wolfgang 1926- CANR-2
Earlier sketch in CA 1R
Holding, Charles H. 1897- CAP-1
Earlier sketch in CA 11-12
Holding, Elizabeth Sanxay 1889-1955
Brief entry 111
Holding, James (Clark Carlisle, Jr.)
1907- 25-28R
See also SATA 3
Holding, Vera Zumwalt 1894-1984
Obituary 114
Holditch, W(illiam) Kenneth 1933- 119
Holdren, Bob R. 1922- 37-40R
Holdren, John P(aul) 1944- 33-36R
Holdstock, Robert (P.) CLC-39
Holdsworth, Christopher (John) 1931- 124
Holdsworth, Irene CAP-1
Earlier sketch in CA 9-10
Holdsworth, Mary (Zvegintzov) 1908- CAP-1
Earlier sketch in CA 15-16
Hole, Christina 1896-1985 Obituary 118
Hole, Tahu Ronald Charles Pearce
1908-1985 Obituary 118
Holenstein, Elmar 1937- CANR-11
Earlier sketch in CA 65-68
Holford, Ingrid 1920- 102
Holford, William Graham 1907-1975
Obituary 108
Holiday, F(rederick) W(illiam) 1921- 25-28R
Holiday, Homer
See DeBeaubien, Philip Francis
Holinger, William (Jacques) 1944- 123
Holisher, Desider 1901-1972 .... CAP-2
Obituary 37-40R
Earlier sketch in CA 19-20
See also SATA 6
Holl, Adelaide Hinkle 1910- CANR-2
Earlier sketch in CA 4R
See also SATA 8
Holl, Adolf 1930- 101
Holl, Jack M. 1937- 57-60
Holl, Kristi D(iane) 1951- 114
See also SATA 51
Holladay, Sylvia A(gnes) 1936- 57-60
Holladay, William L(ee) 1926- 53-56
Holland, Ada Morehead 1911- 122
Holland, Alma Boice 29-32R
Holland, Barbara A(dams) 1925- 57-60
Holland, Brud
See Holland, Jerome H(eartwell)
Holland, Cecelia (Anastasia) 1943- CANR-9
Earlier sketch in CA 17-18R
Holland, Cecil Fletcher 1907-1978
Obituary 77-80
Holland, Deborah K(atherine) 1947- 57-60
Holland, DeWitte T(almage) 1923- 45-48
Holland, Elizabeth (Anne) 1928- 124
Holland, Francis Ross, Jr. 1927- 33-36R
Holland, Gail Bernice 1940- 126
Holland, Glen A. 1920- 37-40R
Holland, Harrison M(elsher) 1921- 117
Holland, Hilda 1901(?)-1975 Obituary 57-60
Holland, Isabelle 1920- CANR-25
Earlier sketches in CA 21-22R, CANR-10
See also SATA 8
See also CLC 21
Holland, Jack 1947- 105
Holland, Jack H. 1922- 81-84
Holland, James C(larence) 1935- 112
Holland, James Gordon 1927- 1R
Holland, James R. 1944- 37-40R
Holland, Janice 1913-1962 73-76
See also SATA 18
Holland, Jerome H(eartwell) 1916-1985
Obituary 114
Holland, John L(ewis) 1919- CANR-17
Earlier sketch in CA 25-28R
See also SATA 20
Holland, Joyce (Flint) 1921- 5-6R
Holland, Joyce
See Morice, Dave
Holland, Katrin
See Albrand, Martha
Holland, Kel
See Whittington, Harry (Benjamin)
Holland, Kenneth 1948- 118
Holland, Kenneth J(ohn) 1918- 33-36R
Holland, Laurence B(edwell) 1920-1980 ..19-20R
Obituary 102
Holland, Louise Adams 1893- 89-92
Holland, Lynwood M. 1905- 41-44R
Holland, Lys
See Gater, Dilys
Holland, Marcus
See Caldwell, (Janet Miriam) Taylor
(Holland)
Holland, Marion 1908- 61-64
See also SATA 6
Holland, Norman N(orwood) 1927- 17-18R
See also DLB 67
Holland, Patricia G. 1940- 115
Holland, Philip Welsby 1917- 109
Holland, Robert 1940- 33-36R
Holland, Sheila 1937- CANR-15
Earlier sketch in CA 85-88
Holland, Thomas E(dward) 1934- 53-56
Holland, Tim 1931- 57-60
Holland, Tom 1947- 126
Holland, Vyvyan (Beresford) 1886-1967 ..97-100
Obituary 25-28R
Holland, William E. 1940- 124
Hollander, A(rie) Nicolaas Jan den
See den Hollander, A(rie) Nicolaas Jan
Hollander, Hans 1899-1986 103
Obituary 120
Hollander, Herbert S. 1904(?)-1976
Obituary 69-72
Hollander, John 1929- CANR-1
Earlier sketch in CA 4R
See also SATA 13
See also DLB 5
See also CLC 2, 5, 8, 14
Hollander, Lee M(ilton) 1880- 1R
Hollander, Paul 1932- CANR-13
Earlier sketch in CA 37-40R
Hollander, Paul
See Silverberg, Robert
Hollander, Phyllis 1928- CANR-18
Earlier sketch in CA 97-100
See also SATA 39
Hollander, Richard Isaac 1912-1985
Obituary 117
Hollander, Robert 1933- CANR-5
Earlier sketch in CA 13-14R
Hollander, Sophie Smith 1911- 15-16R
Hollander, Stanley C(harles) 1919- 37-40R
Hollander, Zander 1923- CANR-18
Earlier sketch in CA 65-68
Hollands, Roy (Derrick) 1924- 114
Hollaway, Otto 1903- 69-72
Hollberg, John
See Hall, Gus
Holldobler, Turid 1939- SATA-26
Holleb, Arthur Irving 1921- 103
Hollender, Edward A. 1899- 105
Hollenweger, Walter J(acob) 1927- CANR-19
Earlier sketches in CA 53-56, CANR-4
Holler, Frederick L. 1921- 97-100
Holler, Ronald F. 1938- 53-56
Holleran, Andrew 1943(?)- CLC-38
Holles, Everett R. 1904(?)-1978 Obituary ..77-80
Holles, Robert Owen 1926- CANR-18
Earlier sketches in CA 7-8R, CANR-3
Holley, Bobbie Lee 1927- 33-36R
Holley, Edward Gailon 1927- CANR-6
Earlier sketch in CA 7-8R
Holley, Frederick S. 1924- 109
Holley, I(rving) B(rinton), Jr. 1919- CANR-14
Earlier sketch in CA 37-40R
Holley, Marietta 1836(?)-1926 Brief entry ... 118
See also DLB 11
Holli, Melvin G(eorge) 1933- CANR-26
Earlier sketches in CA 25-28R, CANR-11
Hollick, Ann L(orraine) 1941- 57-60
Holliday, Barbara Gregg 1917- 73-76
Holliday, James
See Gray, Simon
Holliday, Joe
See Holliday, Joseph
Holliday, Joseph 1910- CAP-2
Earlier sketch in CA 29-32
See also SATA 11
Hollindale, Peter 1936- 103
Holling, Holling C(lancy) 1900-1973
Obituary 106
See also SATA 15, 26
Hollingdale, R(eginald) J(ohn) 1930- 102
Hollinghurst, Alan 1954- 114
Hollings, Michael 1921- 81-84
Hollingshead, August deBelmont
1907-1980 ....13-14R
Obituary 120
Hollingshead, (Ronald) Kyle 1941- CANR-11
Earlier sketch in CA 23-24R
Hollingsworth, Alvin C(arl) 1930- SATA-39
Hollingsworth, Dorothy Frances 1916- 85-88
Hollingsworth, Harold M(arvin) 1932- 53-56
Hollingsworth, J(oseph) Rogers 1932- . CANR-22
Earlier sketches in CA 13-14R, CANR-7
Hollingsworth, Kent 1929- 81-84
Hollingsworth, Lyman B(urgess) 1919- 45-48
Hollingsworth, Margaret 1942- 123
See also DLB 60
Hollingsworth, Mary H(ead) 1910- 69-72
Hollingsworth, Paul M. 1932- 29-32R
Hollingworth, Clare 1911- 121
Hollinrake, Roger (Barker) 1929- 115
Hollis, C(harles) Carroll 1911- 125
Hollis, (Maurice) Christopher 1902-1977 ...73-76
Obituary 69-72
Hollis, Daniel W(alker) 1922- 5-6R
Hollis, Daniel W(ebster) III 1942- 118
Hollis, Florence 1907-1987 Obituary 123
Hollis, Harry Newcombe, Jr. 1938- 57-60
Hollis, Helen Rice 1908- 61-64
Hollis, James R(ussell) 1940- 41-44R
Hollis, Jim
See Summers, Hollis (Spurgeon, Jr.)
Hollis, Joseph W(illiam) 1922- 25-28R
Hollis, Lucile U(ssery) 1921- 25-28R
Hollis, Marcia 1937- 114
Hollister, Bernard C(laiborne) 1938- CANR-3
Earlier sketch in CA 49-52
Hollister, C(harles) Warren 1930- CANR-25
Earlier sketches in CA 4R, CANR-1
Hollister, Charles A(mmon) 1918- 17-18R
Hollister, George E(rwin) 1905- CAP-2
Earlier sketch in CA 17-18
Hollister, Herbert A(llen) 1933- 104
Hollister, Leo E. 1920- CANR-14
Earlier sketch in CA 23-24R
Hollister, William G(ray) 1915- 122
Hollmann, Clide John 1896-1966 ....7-8R
Hollo, Anselm 1934- CANR-9
Earlier sketch in CA 21-22R
See also DLB 40
Hollom, Philip Arthur Dominic 1912- 15-16R
Hollon, W. Eugene 1913- CANR-2
Earlier sketch in CA 1R
See also AITN 1
Hollow, John Walter 1939- 111
Holloway, Brenda W(ilmar) 1908- CAP-1
Earlier sketch in CA 9-10
Holloway, David 1924- 107
Holloway, (Rufus) Emory 1885-1977 49-52
Obituary 73-76
Holloway, (Percival) Geoffrey 1918- 49-52
Holloway, George (Edward Talbot)
1921- 25-28R
Holloway, Harry (Albert) 1925- 11-12R
Holloway, James Y(oung) 1927- 53-56
Holloway, John 1920- CANR-3
Earlier sketch in CA 7-8R
See also DLB 27
Holloway, Joseph E(dward) 1948- 111
Holloway, Marcella M(arie) 1913- 89-92
Holloway, Mark 1917- 21-22R
Holloway, Maurice 1920- 11-12R
Holloway, Robert J. 1921- 15-16R
Holloway, Stanley 1890-1982 Obituary 106
Holloway, Teresa (Bragunier) 1906- 19-20R
See also SATA 26
Holloway, Thomas H(alsey) 1944- 106
Holloway, W(illiam) V(ernon) 1903- CANR-2
Earlier sketch in CA 1R
Hollowell, John 1945- 102
Hollowood, Albert Bernard 1910-1981 .....9-10R
Obituary 103
Holly, J(ohn) Fred 1915- CANR-6
Earlier sketch in CA 5-6R
Holly, Joan C(arol) 1932- CANR-1
Earlier sketch in CA 4R
Holly, Joan Hunter
See Holly, Joan C(arol)
Holly, Michael Ann 1944- 121
Hollyday, Frederic B(lackmar) M(umford)
1928- 45-48
Holm, (Else) Anne (Lise) 1922- 19-20R
See also SATA 1

Holm, Bill
See Holm, Oscar William
Holm, Don(ald Raymond) 1918- 33-36R
Holm, John Cecil 1904-1981 Obituary 116
Holm, Marilyn D. (Franzen) 1944- 19-20R
Holm, Oscar William 1925- Brief entry 117
Holm, Sven (Aage) 1902- CAP-1
Earlier sketch in CA 11-12
Holman, Betsy Hitz 1951- 119
Holman, Bob
See Holman, Robert
Holman, C(larence) Hugh 1914-1981 ... CANR-21
Earlier sketch in CA 5-6R
Holman, Dennis (Idris) 1915- 9-10R
Holman, Felice 1919- CANR-18
Earlier sketches in CA 7-8R, CANR-3
See also SATA 7
Holman, Harriet R. 1912- 37-40R
Holman, L(loyd) Bruce 1939- 61-64
Holman, Mary A(lida) 1933- 93-96
Holman, Portia Grenfell 1903-1983
Obituary 109
Holman, Robert 1936- 116
Holman, William R(oger) 1926- 49-52
Holmans, Alan Edward 1934- 3R
Holme, Bryan 1913- 103
See also SATA 26
Holme, (Edith) Constance 1880(?)-1955
Brief entry 118
See also DLB 34
Holme, K. E.
See Hill, (John Edward) Christopher
Holme, Thea 1903- 41-44R
Holmelund, Paul 1890- 7-8R
Holmer, Paul L(eroy) 1916- 37-40R
Holmes, Ann 1936(?)-1985 Obituary 114
Holmes, Arthur 1890-1965 Obituary 116
Holmes, Arthur F. 1924- 33-36R
Holmes, Barbara Ware 1945- 120
Holmes, Burnham 1942- 97-100
Holmes, C. Raymond 1929- 57-60
Holmes, Charles M(ason) 1923- 29-32R
Holmes, Charles S(hiveley) 1916-1976 ...41-44R
Obituary 61-64
Holmes, Charles Warfield 1931-1984
Obituary 112
Holmes, Colin 1938- CANR-11
Earlier sketch in CA 25-28R
Holmes, David Charles 1919- 9-10R
Holmes, David M(orton) 1929- 33-36R
Holmes, Douglas 1933- 41-44R
Holmes, Edward M(orris) 1910- CANR-14
Earlier sketch in CA 37-40R
Holmes, Efner Tudor 1949- 65-68
Holmes, Eric M(ills) 1943- 121
Holmes, Frank Wakefield 1924- 109
Holmes, Frederic L(awrence) 1932- 93-96
Holmes, Geoffrey (Shorter) 1928- 25-28R
Holmes, Grant
See Fox, James M.
Holmes, H. H.
See White, William A(nthony) P(arker)
Holmes, Jack D(avid) L(azarus) 1930- .. CANR-24
Earlier sketch in CA 41-44R
Holmes, Jay
See Holmes, Joseph Everett
Holmes, Jeffrey 1934- 120
Holmes, John (Albert) 1904-1962
Obituary 115
Holmes, John 1913- 104
Holmes, John
See Souster, (Holmes) Raymond
Holmes, John Clellon 1926-1988 .... CANR-4
Obituary 125
Earlier sketch in CA 9-10R
See also DLB 16
Holmes, John Haynes 1879-1964
Obituary 89-92
Holmes, John L. 1925- 115
Holmes, John W(endell) 1910- Brief entry .. 109
Holmes, Jon 1948- 114
Holmes, Joseph Everett 1922- CANR-1
Earlier sketch in CA 3R
Holmes, Joseph R. 1928(?)-1983
Obituary 109
Holmes, Kenneth L(loyd) 1915- 37-40R
Holmes, Kim R(ene) 1952- 111
Holmes, Lowell D(on) 1925- 33-36R
Holmes, Marjorie (Rose) 1910- CANR-23
Earlier sketches in CA 3R, CANR-5
See also SATA 43
See also AITN 1
Holmes, Martin (Rivington) 1905- CANR-1
Earlier sketch in CA 49-52
Holmes, (John) Michael (Aleister) 1931- ..25-28R
Holmes, Michael Stephan 1942- 77-80
Holmes, Nancy 1921- 69-72
Holmes, Olive 1911- 115
Holmes, Oliver Wendell 1809-1894 .... SATA-34
See also DLB 1
See also CDALB 1640-1865
Holmes, Oliver Wendell, Jr. 1841-1935
Brief entry 114
Holmes, Parker Manfred 1895- CAP-1
Earlier sketch in CA 13-14
Holmes, Paul Allen 1901-1985 .... CAP-2
Obituary 114
Earlier sketch in CA 19-20
Holmes, Paul Carter 1926- CANR-11
Earlier sketch in CA 23-24R
Holmes, Peggy 1898- 121
Holmes, Raymond
See Souster, (Holmes) Raymond
Holmes, Richard 1945- Brief entry 126
Holmes, (Edward) Richard 1946- CANR-25
Earlier sketch in CA 106
Holmes, Rick
See Hardwick, Richard Holmes, Jr.
Holmes, Robert A(lexander) 1943- 57-60
Holmes, Robert L(awrence) 1935- 41-44R
Holmes, Robert Merrill 1925- 89-92
Holmes, Thomas K. CANR-26
Earlier sketches in CA 19-20, CAP-2
Holmes, Tiffany 1944- 97-100
Holmes, Tommy 1903-1975 Obituary 57-60
Holmes, Urban T(igner) 1900-1972 ...... CAP-2
Earlier sketch in CA 21-22
Holmes, W(ilfred) J(ay) 1900- 29-32R
Holmes, William Kersley 1882- CAP-1
Earlier sketch in CA 9-10
Holmgren, Helen Jean 1930- 97-100
See also SATA 45
Holmgren, Norah 1939- 102
Holmgren, Sister George Ellen
See Holmgren, Helen Jean
Holmgren, Virginia C(unningham) 1909- 107
See also SATA 26
Holmquist, Anders 1933- 29-32R
Holmquist, Eve 1921- 53-56
See also SATA 11
Holmstrand, Marie Juline (Gunderson)
1908- 5-6R
Holmstrom, (John) Edwin 1898- CAP-1
Earlier sketch in CA 11-12
Holmstrom, Lynda Lytle 1939- 33-36R
Holmvik, Oyvind 1914- 19-20R
Holod, Renata O. 1942- 119
Holoien, Martin O. 1928- 112
Holquist, (James) Michael 1935- CANR-17
Earlier sketches in CA 45-48, CANR-2
Holroyd, Michael (de Courcy Fraser)
1935- CANR-18
Earlier sketches in CA 53-56, CANR-4
Holroyd, Sam
See Burton, S(amuel) H(olroyd)
Holroyd, Stuart 1933- 93-96
Holsaert, Eunice ?-1974 Obituary 53-56
Holsinger, Jane Lumley 17-18R
Holske, Katherine ?-1973 Obituary 104
Holsopple, Barbara 1943- 73-76
Holst, Hermann E. von 1841-1904 ..... DLB-47
Holst, Imogen (Clare) 1907-1984 Obituary .. 112
Holst, Johan J(oergen) 1937- CANR-11
Earlier sketch in CA 25-28R
Holst, Lawrence E(berhardt) 1929- 61-64
Holsti, Kalevi J(acque) 1935- 23-24R
Holsti, Ole R(udolf) 1933- CANR-11
Earlier sketch in CA 25-28R
Holt, Andrew
See Anhalt, Edward
Holt, Edgar Crawshaw 1900-1975 ...... CANR-6
Obituary 61-64
Earlier sketch in CA 3R
Holt, Elizabeth B(asye) G(ilmore)
1906(?)-1987 124
Holt, Gavin
See Rodda, Charles
Holt, Helen
See Paine, Lauran (Bosworth)
Holt, (Laurence) James 1939- 25-28R
Holt, John 1721-1784 .... DLB-43
Holt, John (Caldwell) 1923-1985 69-72
Obituary 117
Holt, John (Robert) 1926- CANR-11
Earlier sketch in CA 25-28R
Holt, John Agee 1920- 1R
Holt, Kaare 1917- Brief entry 111
Holt, Kare
See Holt, Kaare
Holt, L. Emmett, Jr. 1895-1974 Obituary ..53-56
Holt, Lee E(lbert) 1912- 13-14R
Holt, Margaret 1937- 17-18R
See also SATA 4
Holt, Margaret Van Vechten (Saunders)
1899-1963 Obituary 111
See also SATA 32
Holt, Michael (Paul) 1929- CANR-5
Earlier sketch in CA 53-56
See also SATA 13
Holt, Michael F(itzgibbon) 1940- 81-84
Holt, Pat Mayo 1920- 111
Holt, Rackham
See Holt, Margaret Van Vechten
(Saunders)
Holt, Robert R(utherford) 1917- CANR-15
Earlier sketch in CA 41-44R
Holt, Robert T. 1928- 37-40R
Holt, Rochelle L.
See DuBois, Rochelle (Lynn) Holt
See also SATA 41
Holt, Stephen
See Thompson, Harlan (Howard)
Holt, Tex
See Joscelyn, Archie L.
Holt, Thelma Jewett 1913- 29-32R
Holt, Thomas J(ung) 1928- 102
Holt, Victoria
See Hibbert, Eleanor Burford
Holt, Will 1929- 105
Holt, William 1897-1977 .... CAP-1
Obituary 69-72
Earlier sketch in CA 17-18
Holtan, Orley I. 1933- 33-36R
Holtby, Robert Tinsley 1921- 108
Holter, Don W. 1905- 37-40R
Holthusen, Hans Egon 1913- 45-48
See also DLB 69
Holtje, Herbert F(ranklin) 1931- CANR-8
Earlier sketch in CA 61-64
Holton, Felicia Antonelli 1921- 69-72
Holton, Gerald (James) 1922- 15-16R
Holton, Leonard
See Wibberley, Leonard (Patrick
O'Connor)
Holton, (William) Milne 1931- 41-44R
Holton, Richard H(enry) 1926- Brief entry .. 107
Holtrop, William Frans 1908- 57-60
Holtz, Avraham 1934- 29-32R
Holtz, Barry W(illiam) 1947- 109
Holtz, Herman R(alph) 1919- 105
Holtze, Sally Holmes 1952- 123
Holtzman, Abraham 1921- CANR-2
Earlier sketch in CA 3R
Holtzman, Harry 1912-1987 Obituary 123
Holtzman, Jerome 1926- CANR-4
Earlier sketch in CA 53-56
Holtzman, Paul D(ouglas) 1918- 33-36R
Holtzman, Wayne H(arold) 1923- CANR-15
Earlier sketch in CA 37-40R
Holtzman, Will 1951- 102
Holub, Miroslav 1923- CANR-10
Earlier sketch in CA 21-22R
See also CLC 4
Holub, Robert C(harles) 1949- 114
Holum, Dianne 1951- 123
Holway, John 1929- 57-60
Holyer, Erna Maria 1925- CANR-12
Earlier sketch in CA 29-32R
See also SATA 22
Holyer, Ernie
See Holyer, Erna Maria
Holz, Loretta (Marie) 1943- CANR-10
Earlier sketch in CA 65-68
See also SATA 17
Holz, Robert K(enneth) 1930- 53-56
Holzapfel, Rudolf Patrick 1938- CAP-1
Earlier sketch in CA 11-12
Holzberger, William George 1932- 53-56
Holzel, Thomas Martin 1940- 126
Holzel, Tom
See Holzel, Thomas Martin
Holzer, Hans 1920- CANR-22
Earlier sketches in CA 13-14R, CANR-7
Holzer, Harold 1949- 116
Holzman, Franklyn Dunn 1918- 61-64
Holzman, Philip Seidman 1922- 37-40R
Holzman, Red
See Holzman, William
Holzman, Robert S(tuart) 1907- CANR-2
Earlier sketch in CA 1R
Holzman, William 1920- 101
Holzner, Burkart 1931- 93-96
Hom, Ken 1949- CANR-26
Earlier sketch in CA 109
Homan, Robert Anthony 1929- 7-8R
Homans, Abigail Adams 1879-1974
Obituary 104
Homans, George Caspar 1910- 107
Homans, Peter 1930- CANR-11
Earlier sketch in CA 23-24R
Homberger, Eric (Ross) 1942- CANR-23
Earlier sketch in CA 106
Homburger, Erik
See Erikson, Erik H(omburger)
Home, Alexander Frederick 1903- 102
Home, Charles (Cospatrick) Douglas
See Douglas-Home, Charles (Cospatrick)
Home, Henry Douglas
See Douglas-Home, Henry
Home, Michael
See Bush, Charlie Christmas
Home, William Douglas 1912- 102
See also DLB 13
Homel, Michael W. 1944- 126
Homer, Frederic D(onald) 1939- 65-68
Homer, Sidney 1902-1983 Obituary 110
Homer, Williams Innes 1929- 15-16R
Homes, Geoffrey
See Mainwaring, Daniel
Homewood, Charles H. 1914(?)-1984
Obituary 112
Homewood, Harry
See Homewood, Charles H.
Homola, Priscilla 1947- 116
Homola, Samuel 1929- 97-100
Homosap
See Nuttall, Jeff
Homrighausen, Elmer George 1900- 45-48
Homsher, Lola Mae 1913- 2R
Homze, Alma C. 1932- 29-32R
See also SATA 17
Homze, Edward L. 1930- 33-36R
Honan, Park 1928- CANR-14
Earlier sketch in CA 77-80
Honan, William H(olmes) 1930- 123
Honce, Charles E. 1895-1975 Obituary 61-64
Honderich, Ted 1933- CANR-14
Earlier sketch in CA 33-36R
Hone, Joseph 1937- CANR-14
Earlier sketch in CA 65-68
Hone, Ralph E(merson) 1913- CANR-9
Earlier sketch in CA 23-24R
Honey, Martha S(pencer) 1945- 112
Honey, P(atrick) J(ames) 1922- 13-14R
Honey, William (Houghton) 1910- 33-36R
Honeycombe, Gordon 1936- CANR-15
Earlier sketch in CA 77-80
Honeycutt, Benjamin L(awrence) 1938- 57-60
Honeycutt, Roy L(ee), Jr. 1926- 41-44R
Honeyman, Brenda
See Clarke, Brenda (Margaret Lilian)
Hong, Edna H. 1913- CANR-9
Earlier sketch in CA 21-22R
Hong, Howard V(incent) 1912- CANR-9
Earlier sketch in CA 21-22R
Hong, Jane Fay 1954- 93-96
Hong, Yong Ki 1929(?)-1979 Obituary 85-88
Honhart, Frederick L(ewis III) 1943- 112
Honig, Donald 1931- CANR-24
Earlier sketches in CA 19-20R, CANR-9
See also SATA 18
Honig, Edwin 1919- CANR-4
Earlier sketch in CA 7-8R
See also DLB 5
See also CLC 33
Honig, Louis 1911-1977 77-80
Obituary 73-76
Honigfeld, Gilbert
See Howard, Gilbert
Honigmann, E(rnst) A(nselm) J(oachim)
1927- CANR-9
Earlier sketch in CA 21-22R
Honigmann, John J(oseph) 1914-1977 .. CANR-2
Earlier sketch in CA 1R
Honnalgere, Gopal 1944- 73-76
Honness, Elizabeth H. 1904- 25-28R
See also SATA 2
Honnold, John Otis, Jr. 1915- CANR-8
Earlier sketch in CA 15-16R
Honore, Antony Maurice 1921- CANR-1
Earlier sketch in CA 3R
Honour, Hugh 1927- 103
Honourable Member for X
See de Chair, Somerset (Struben)
Honri, Peter 1929- 103
Hoobler, Dorothy CANR-11
Earlier sketch in CA 69-72
See also SATA 28
Hoobler, Thomas CANR-11
Earlier sketch in CA 69-72
See also SATA 28
Hood, Buck 1907(?)-1983 Obituary 110
Hood, David Crockett 1937- 37-40R
Hood, Donald W(ilbur) 1918- 37-40R
Hood, Dora (Ridout) 1885- CAP-2
Earlier sketch in CA 17-18
Hood, F(rancis) C(ampbell) 1895-1971 ... CAP-1
Earlier sketch in CA 13-14
Hood, Flora M(ae) 1898- 5-6R
Hood, Graham 1936- 77-80
Hood, Hugh (John Blagdon) 1928- CANR-1
Earlier sketch in CA 49-52
See also DLB 53
See also CLC 15, 28
Hood, Joseph F. 1925- 33-36R
See also SATA 4
Hood, Margaret Page 1892- 3R
Hood, Robert E. 1926- 23-24R
See also SATA 21
Hood, Sarah
See Killough, (Karen) Lee
Hood, (Martin) Sinclair (Frankland)
1917- CANR-9
Earlier sketch in CA 21-22R
Hood, William (Joseph) 1920- CANR-26
Earlier sketch in CA 109
Hoofnagle, Keith Lundy 1941- 15-16R
Hoogasian-Villa, Susie 1921-1978 ....17-18R
Obituary 114
Hoogenboom, Ari (Arthur) 1927- CANR-25
Earlier sketch in CA 45-48
Hoogenboom, Olive 1927- 23-24R
Hoogestraat, Wayne E. 7-8R
Hook, Andrew 1932- 53-56
Hook, Diana ffarington 1918- 61-64
Hook, Donald D(wight) 1928- CANR-4
Earlier sketch in CA 53-56
Hook, Frances 1912- 105
See also SATA 27
Hook, Frank S(cott) 1922- 23-24R
Hook, J(ulius) N(icholas) 1913- CANR-17
Earlier sketches in CA 5-6R, CANR-2
Hook, Judith 1941(?)-1984 Obituary 113
Hook, Martha 1936- 105
See also SATA 27
Hook, Sidney 1902- CANR-7
Earlier sketch in CA 11-12R
Hooke, Nina Warner 1907- 73-76
Hooker, C(lifford) A(lan) 1942- CANR-19
Earlier sketches in CA 49-52, CANR-4
Hooker, Craig Michael 1951- 57-60
Hooker, Frances
See Horovitz, Frances Margaret
Hooker, James Ralph 1929- 21-22R
Hooker, (Peter) Jeremy 1941- CANR-22
Earlier sketch in CA 77-80
See also DLB 40
See also CLC 43
Hooker, Richard
See Hornberger, H. Richard
Hooker, Richard J(ames) 1912- 122
Hooker, Ruth 1920- 69-72
See also SATA 21
Hooker, Stanley (George) 1907-1984
Obituary 112
Hooker, Thomas 1586-1647 .... DLB-24
Hookham, Hilda Henriette (Kuttner)
1915- 9-10R
Hooks, G(aylor) Eugene 1927- 4R
Hooks, Gene
See Hooks, G(aylor) Eugene
Hooks, William H(arris) 1921- CANR-19
Earlier sketch in CA 81-84
See also SATA 16
Hoole, Daryl Van Dam 1934- 23-24R
Hoole, W(illiam) Stanley 1903- CANR-7
Earlier sketch in CA 17-18R
Hooper, Byrd
See St. Clair, Byrd Hooper
Hooper, David (Vincent) 1915- 85-88
Hooper, Douglas 1927- CANR-18
Earlier sketch in CA 25-28R
Hooper, Finley (Allison) 1922- 123
Hooper, Hedley Colwill 1919- 124
Hooper, John W(illiam) 1926- 29-32R

Hooper, Johnson Jones 1815-1862 ... DLB-3,11
Hooper, Kay 1957- ... 122
Hooper, Meredith (Jean) 1939- ... CANR-22
Earlier sketch in CA 106
See also SATA 28
Hooper, Paul F(ranklin) 1938- ... CANR-18
Earlier sketch in CA 101
Hooper, Peter
See Hooper, Hedley Colwill
Hooper, Walter (McGehee) 1931- ... CANR-22
Earlier sketches in CA 17-18R, CANR-7
Hooper, William Loyd 1931- ... CANR-19
Earlier sketches in CA 5-6R, CANR-3
Hoopes, Clement R. 1906-1979 ... 73-76
Obituary ... 89-92
Hoopes, David S. 1928- ... 118
Hoopes, Donelson F(arquhar) 1932- ... 33-36R
Hoopes, James 1944- ... CANR-10
Earlier sketch in CA 65-68
Hoopes, Lyn Littlefield 1953- ... 120
See also SATA 44, 49
Hoopes, Ned E(dward) 1932- ... 17-18R
See also SATA 21
Hoopes, Robert (Griffith) 1920- ... CANR-1
Earlier sketch in CA 2R
Hoopes, Roy 1922- ... CANR-15
Earlier sketch in CA 21-22R
See also SATA 11
Hoopes, Townsend Walter 1922- ... 97-100
Hoople, Cheryl G. Brief entry ... 111
See also SATA 32
Hoops, Richard A(llen) 1933- ... 41-44R
Hoor, Elvie (Marie Mortensen) Ten
See Ten Hoor, Elvie (Marie Mortensen)
Hoornik, Ed(uard Jozef Antonie Marie)
1910-1970 Obituary ... 104
Hoos, Ida Russakoff 1912- ... 19-20R
Hooson, David J. M. 1926- ... 19-20R
Hooten, William J(arvis) 1900- ... 61-64
Hooton, Charles
See Rowe, Vivian C(laud)
Hoover, Calvin Bryce 1897-1974 ... CAP-1
Obituary ... 49-52
Earlier sketch in CA 13-14
Hoover, Dorothy Estheryne 1918- ... 49-52
Hoover, Dwight W(esley) 1926- ... 33-36R
Hoover, Edgar M. 1907- ... 13-14R
Hoover, F(rancis) Louis 1913- ... 41-44R
Hoover, H(elen) M(ary) 1935- ... CANR-22
Earlier sketch in CA 105
See also SATA 33, 44
Hoover, Hardy 1902- ... 29-32R
Hoover, Helen (Drusilla Blackburn)
1910-1984 ... 21-22R
Obituary ... 113
See also SATA 12, 39
Hoover, Herbert (Clark) 1874-1964 ... 108
Obituary ... 89-92
Hoover, Herbert Theodore 1930- ... 106
Hoover, J(ohn) Edgar 1895-1972 ... CANR-2
Obituary ... 33-36R
Earlier sketch in CA 3R
Hoover, John P. 1910- ... 53-56
Hoover, Kenneth H(arding) 1920- ... CANR-7
Earlier sketch in CA 57-60
Hoover, Marjorie L(awson) 1910- ... 41-44R
Hoover, Mary B(idgood) 1917- ... 93-96
Hoover, Thomas 1941- ... 102
Hopcraft, Arthur 1932- ... CANR-14
Earlier sketch in CA 25-28R
Hope, A(lec) D(erwent) 1907- ... 21-22R
See also CLC 3
Hope, A(shley) Guy 1914- ... 25-28R
Hope, Amanda
See Lewis, Judith Mary
Hope, Andrew
See Hern, (George) Anthony
Hope, Bob 1903- ... 101
Hope, Brian
See Creasey, John
Hope, C(harles) E(velyn) G(raham)
1900-1971 ... CAP-1
Earlier sketch in CA 15-16
Hope, Christopher (David Tully) 1944- ... 106
Hope, David
See Fraser, Douglas
Hope, Felix
See Williamson, Claude C(harles) H.
Hope, Jack 1940- ... 81-84
Hope, Jane 1938- ... 110
Hope, Karol ... 93-96
Hope, Laura Lee ... 19-20R
See also SATA 1
Hope, Margaret
See Knight, Alanna
Hope, Marjorie (Cecelia) 1923- ... 29-32R
Hope, Norman Victor 1908-1983 Obituary ... 110
Hope, Quentin M(anning) 1923- ... 13-14R
Hope, Ronald (Sidney) 1921- ... CANR-3
Earlier sketch in CA 9-10R
Hope, Welborn 1903- ... 29-32R
Hope-Jones, Arthur 1911-1984 Obituary ... 112
Hopes, David Brendan 1953- ... CANR-26
Earlier sketch in CA 109
Hope Simpson, Jacynth 1930- ... CANR-7
Earlier sketch in CA 13-14R
See also SATA 12
Hope-Wallace, Philip (Adrian) 1911-1979
Obituary ... 93-96
Hopewell, S(ydney) 1924- ... 25-28R
Hopf, Alice
See Hopf, Alice (Martha) L(ightner)
Hopf, Alice (Martha) L(ightner)
1904-1988 ... CANR-9
Obituary ... 124
Earlier sketch in CA 19-20R
See also SATA 5
Hopke, William E. 1918- ... 21-22R
Hopkin, Alannah 1949- ... 109
Hopkins, A. T.
See Turngren, Annette
Hopkins, Antony 1921- ... CANR-17
Earlier sketch in CA 101
Hopkins, Bill 1928- ... 11-12R
Hopkins, C(harles) Howard 1905- ... 123
Hopkins, Clark 1895-1976 Obituary ... 109
See also SATA 34
Hopkins, David 1948- ... 122
Hopkins, Donald R(oswell) 1941- ... 123
Hopkins, Fred W(right), Jr. 1935- ... 69-72
Hopkins, George E(mil) 1937- ... 33-36R
Hopkins, Gerard Manley 1844-1889 ... DLB-35, 57
Hopkins, Harry 1913- ... 29-32R
Hopkins, J(ohn) F(eely) 1922- ... 102
Hopkins, J. L. 1938- ... 77-80
Hopkins, Jack W(alker) 1930- ... 25-28R
Hopkins, James Franklin 1909- ... 1R
Hopkins, Jasper (Stephen, Jr.) 1936- ... CANR-14
Earlier sketch in CA 37-40R
Hopkins, Jerry 1935- ... CANR-18
Earlier sketch in CA 25-28R
Hopkins, John (Richard) 1931- ... 85-88
See also CLC 4
Hopkins, Joseph G(erard) E(dward)
1909- ... CANR-5
Earlier sketch in CA 1R
See also SATA 11
Hopkins, Joseph Martin 1919- ... 49-52
Hopkins, (Hector) Kenneth 1914-1988 ... CANR-1
Obituary ... 125
Earlier sketch in CA 3R,
Hopkins, Kenneth 1914- ... CANR-17
Earlier sketches in CA 3R, CANR-1
Hopkins, Lee (Wallace) ... 57-60
Hopkins, Lee Bennett 1938- ... 25-28R
See also SATA 3
See also SAAS 4
Hopkins, Lemuel 1750-1801 ... DLB-37
Hopkins, Lightnin'
See Hopkins, Sam
Hopkins, Lyman
See Folsom, Franklin (Brewster)
Hopkins, Marjorie 1911- ... 21-22R
See also SATA 9
Hopkins, Mark W(yatt) 1931- ... 29-32R
Hopkins, Milton 1906-1983 Obituary ... 109
Hopkins, Nicholas S(nowden) 1939- ... 77-80
Hopkins, Pauline Elizabeth 1859-1930 ... DLB-50
See also TCLC 28
Hopkins, Prynce (C.) 1885-1970 ... CAP-2
Earlier sketch in CA 21-22
Hopkins, Pryns
See Hopkins, Prynce (C.)
Hopkins, Raymond F(rederick) 1939- ... 49-52
Hopkins, Robert A. 1923- ... 89-92
Hopkins, Robert S(ydney) ... 115
Hopkins, Sam 1912-1982 Obituary ... 106
Hopkins, Samuel 1721-1803 ... DLB-31
Hopkins, Terence K(ilbourne) 1928- ... 11-12R
Hopkins, Thomas (McCaffrey Moore)...
Hopkins, Thomas H(ollis) 1945- ... 116
Hopkins, Thomas J(ohns) 1930- ... 37-40R
Hopkins, Viola
See Winner, Viola Hopkins
Hopkins, Vivian C. 1909- ... CAP-2
Earlier sketch in CA 33-36
Hopkinson, Diana 1912- ... 29-32R
Hopkinson, Francis 1737-1791 ... DLB-31
Hopkinson, Henry Thomas 1905- ... 19-20R
Hopkirk, Peter 1930- ... 107
Hopley, George
See Hopley-Woolrich, Cornell George
Hopley-Woolrich, Cornell George
1903-1968 ... CAP-1
Earlier sketch in CA 13-14
Hoppe, Art(hur Watterson) 1925- ... CANR-3
Earlier sketch in CA 7-8R
Hoppe, Eleanor Sellers 1933- ... 73-76
Hoppe, Emil Otho 1878- ... 11-12R
Hoppe, Joanne 1932- ... 81-84
See also SATA 42
Hoppe, Ronald A. 1931- ... 45-48
Hoppen, K(arl) Theodore 1941- ... 119
Hoppenstedt, Elbert M. 1917- ... 3R
Hopper, Columbus B(urwell) 1931- ... 33-36R
Hopper, David H. 1927- ... 23-24R
Hopper, Dennis 1936- ... 114
Hopper, Hedda
See Furry, Elda
Hopper, John 1934- ... 17-18R
Hopper, Nancy J. 1937- ... 115
See also SATA 35, 38
Hopper, R(obert) J(ohn) 1910-1987 ... 123
Hopper, Robert 1945- ... CANR-9
Earlier sketch in CA 65-68
Hopper, Vincent Foster 1906-1976 ... CANR-6
Obituary ... 61-64
Earlier sketch in CA 1R
Hoppin, Richard H(allowell) 1913- ... 41-44R
Hoppock, Robert 1901- ... 1R
Hopson, Dan, Jr. 1930- ... 23-24R
Hopson, Janet L(ouise) 1950- ... 89-92
Hopwood, Robert R. 1910- ... CAP-1
Earlier sketch in CA 13-14
Hora, F. Bayard 1909(?)-1984 Obituary ... 112
Horak, M. Stephan 1920- ... 11-12R
Horan, Francis Harding 1900-1978
Obituary ... 81-84
Horan, James David 1914-1981 ... CANR-9
Obituary ... 105
Earlier sketch in CA 13-14R
Horan, (Harold) Joseph Taaffe
1898(?)-1985 Obituary ... 117
Horan, William D. 1933- ... 25-28R
Horatio
See Proust,
(Valentin-Louis-George-Eugene-)
Marcel
Horatio, Algernon ... 89-92
Horatio, Jane
See Cudlipp, Edythe
Horbach, Michael 1924-1986 ... CANR-25
Obituary ... 120
Earlier sketch in CA 29-32R
Horchler, Richard (Thomas) 1925- ... 5-6R
Horchow, (Samuel) Roger 1928- ... 106
Horder, Mervyn 1910- ... 104
Hordern, William (Edward) 1920- ... 13-14R
Hordon, Harris E(ugene) 1942- ... 53-56
Horecky, Paul Louis 1913- ... CANR-2
Earlier sketch in CA 7-8R
Horelick, Arnold L(awrence) 1928- ... CANR-8
Earlier sketch in CA 17-18R
Horgan, Denis E. 1941- ... 101
Horgan, Edward R. 1934- ... 109
Horgan, John J(oseph) 1910- ... 61-64
Horgan, John Joseph 1881-1967 Obituary ... 116
Horgan, Paul 1903- ... CANR-9
Earlier sketch in CA 13-14R
See also SATA 13
See also DLBY 85
See also CLC 9
Hori, Ichiro 1910-1974 ... CAP-2
Earlier sketch in CA 25-28
Horie, Shigeo 1903- ... CAP-1
Earlier sketch in CA 13-14
Horikoshi, Jiro 1904(?)-1982 Obituary ... 110
Horka-Follick, Lorayne Ann 1940- ... 29-32R
Horkheimer, Max 1895-1973 Obituary ... 41-44R
Horman, Richard E. 1945- ... 29-32R
Horn, D(avid) B(ayne) 1901-1969 ... CANR-6
Earlier sketch in CA 4R
Horn, Daniel 1934- ... 21-22R
Horn, Edward Newman 1903(?)-1976
Obituary ... 65-68
Horn, Francis H(enry) 1908- ... 53-56
Horn, George F(rancis) 1917- ... CANR-8
Earlier sketch in CA 7-8R
Horn, Henry Eyster 1913- ... 23-24R
Horn, Jeanne P. 1925- ... 5-6R
Horn, John L(eonard) 1928- ... CANR-14
Earlier sketch in CA 37-40R
Horn, Linda L(ouise) 1947- ... 101
Horn, Maurice 1931- ... CANR-22
Earlier sketch in CA 89-92
Horn, Pamela (Lucy Ray) 1936- ... 69-72
Horn, Peter (Rudolf Gisela) 1934- ... 103
Horn, Peter
See Kuttner, Henry
Horn, Pierre L(aurence) 1942- ... 119
Horn, Richard 1954- ... 105
Horn, Robert M. 1933- ... 29-32R
Horn, Siegfried H(erbert) 1908- ... 37-40R
Horn, Stefan F. 1900- ... CAP-1
Earlier sketch in CA 15-16
Horn, (John) Stephen 1931- ... 15-16R
Horn, Stephen (McCaffrey Moore) 1931- ... 45-48
Horn, Thomas D. 1918- ... 13-14R
Horn, Vivi 1878(?)-1971 Obituary ... 104
Horn, Walter (William) 1908- ... 23-24R
Hornback, Bert G(erald) 1935- ... CANR-22
Earlier sketch in CA 29-32R
Hornbaker, Alice 1927- ... 77-80
Hornbein, Thomas Frederic 1930- ... 53-56
Hornberger, H. Richard ... 105
Hornberger, Theodore 1906-1975 ... CANR-3
Earlier sketch in CA 5-6R
Hornblow, Arthur, Jr. 1893-1976 ... 89-92
Obituary ... 65-68
See also SATA 15
Hornblow, Leonora (Schinasi) 1920- ... 73-76
See also SATA 18
Hornblower, Harry C.
See Shriver, Harry C(lair)
Hornbruch, Frederick William, Jr. 1913- ... 109
Hornby, John (Wilkinson) 1913- ... 9-10R
Hornby, Leslie 1949- ... 103
Hornby, Richard 1938- ... 89-92
Hornby, William H(arry) 1923- ... 106
Horne, A(lexander) D(ouglas) 1932- ... 109
Horne, Alistair (Allan) 1925- ... CANR-9
Earlier sketch in CA 5-6R
Horne, Bernard Shea 1905-1970 Obituary ... 104
Horne, Chevis Ferber 1914- ... CANR-16
Earlier sketch in CA 97-100
Horne, Cynthia Miriam 1939- ... 7-8R
Horne, Donald (Richmond) 1921- ... CANR-20
Earlier sketch in CA 103
Horne, Frank (Smith) 1899-1974 ... 125
Obituary ... 53-56
See also BW
See also DLB 51
Horne, Geoffrey 1916- ... 9-10R
Horne, Howard
See Payne, (Pierre Stephen) Robert
Horne, Hugh Robert 1915- ... 7-8R
Horne, Kenneth 1900-1975 Obituary ... 115
Horne, Lewis 1932- ... 110
Horne, Peter 1947- ... 69-72
Horne, R(alph) A(lbert) 1929- ... 106
Horne, Richard Henry 1803-1884 ... SATA-29
See also DLB 32
Horne, Roman L(emuel) 1901-1987
Obituary ... 121
Horne, Shirley (Faith) 1919- ... 49-52
Horner, Althea (Jane) 1926- ... 81-84
See also SATA 36
Horner, Dave 1934- ... 17-18R
See also SATA 12
Horner, David Stuart 1900(?)-1983(?)
Obituary ... 111
Horner, George F(rederick) 1899-1974 ... CAP-2
Earlier sketch in CA 33-36
Horner, J. C.
See Horner, John Curwen
Horner, John Curwen 1922- ... 103
Horner, Joyce Mary 1903-1980 Obituary ... 112
Horner, Kenric Lancaster 1902-1973
Obituary ... 111
Horner, Lance
See Horner, Kenric Lancaster
Horner, Thomas Marland 1927- ... 37-40R
Horner, Tom (Julian) 1913- ... 121
Horner, Winifred Bryan 1922- ... 118
Horney, Karen (Clementine Theodore
Danielsen) 1885-1952 Brief entry ... 114
Horngren, Charles T(homas) 1926- ... 57-60
Hornig, Doug 1943- ... 117
Hornik, Edith Lynn
See Beer, Edith Lynn
Hornman, Wim 1920- Brief entry ... 106
Hornos, Axel 1907- ... CAP-2
Earlier sketch in CA 29-32
See also SATA 20
Hornsby, Albert Sidney 1898(?)-1978
Obituary ... 104
Hornsby, Alton, Jr. 1940- ... 37-40R
Hornsby, Ken 1934- ... 105
Hornsby, Roger A. 1926- ... 21-22R
Hornsby-Smith, Michael P(eter) 1932- ... 126
Hornstein, Harvey A. 1938- ... 53-56
Hornstein, Lillian Herlands 1909- ... 45-48
Hornstein, Reuben Aaron 1912- ... 106
Hornung, Clarence Pearson 1899- ... CANR-9
Earlier sketch in CA 17-18R
Hornung, E(rnest) W(illiam) 1866-1921
Brief entry ... 108
See also DLB 70
Hornung, Erik 1933- ... 117
Hornung, Maximilian 1942- ... 107
Horobin, Ian M. 1899-1976 Obituary ... 69-72
Horovitz, Frances Margaret 1938-1983
Obituary ... 111
Horovitz, Israel 1939- ... 33-36R
See also DLB 7
Horovitz, Michael 1935- ... 81-84
Horowitz, Al
See Horowitz, I(srael) A.
Horowitz, David 1903- ... 69-72
Horowitz, David (Joel) 1939- ... 15-16R
Horowitz, David A. 1941- ... 89-92
Horowitz, David Charles 1937- ... 89-92
Horowitz, Donald L(eonard) 1939- ... 126
Horowitz, Edward 1904- ... CANR-4
Earlier sketch in CA 3R
Horowitz, Esther 1920- ... 49-52
Horowitz, Gene 1930- ... 77-80
Horowitz, Helen Lefkowitz 1942- ... 125
Horowitz, I(srael) A. 1907-1973
Obituary ... 41-44R
Horowitz, Ira 1934- ... 41-44R
Horowitz, Irving Louis 1929- ... 41-44R
Horowitz, Jacob 1900-1979 Obituary ... 89-92
Horowitz, Joseph 1948- ... 109
Horowitz, Laura (Godofsky) 1943-1983
Obituary ... 110
Horowitz, Leonard M(artin) 1937- ... 37-40R
Horowitz, Lois 1940- ... 119
Horowitz, Mardi J(on) 1934- ... 33-36R
Horowitz, Michael M. 1933- ... CANR-15
Earlier sketch in CA 41-44R
Horowitz, Morris A(aron) 1919- ... CANR-9
Earlier sketch in CA 65-68
Horowitz, Robert S. 1924- ... 9-10R
Horowitz, Shel Alan 1956- ... 120
Horrell, C. William 1918- ... CANR-13
Earlier sketch in CA 61-64
Horrock, Berta Crone 1896(?)-1983
Obituary ... 110
Horrock, Nicholas (Morton) 1936- ... 49-52
Horrocks, Brian (Gwynne) 1895-1985
Obituary ... 114
Horrocks, Edna M. 1908- ... CAP-2
Earlier sketch in CA 17-18
Horrocks, John E(dwin) 1913- ... 7-8R
Horsbrugh, Ian 1941- ... 111
Horsburgh, David Michael 1923-1984
Obituary ... 114
Horsburgh, H(oward) J(ohn) N(eate)
1918- ... 25-28R
Horsefield, J(ohn) Keith 1901- ... 7-8R
Horsely, Ramsbottom
See Berne, Eric (Lennard)
Horseman, Elaine Hall 1925- ... 15-16R
Horsley, David
See Bingley, David Ernest
Horsley, James (Allen) 1938- ... 45-48
Horsman, Reginald 1931- ... CANR-17
Earlier sketches in CA 4R, CANR-2
Horst, Irvin B(uckwalter) 1915- ... 41-44R
Horst, Samuel (Levi) 1919- ... 21-22R
Horstman, Allen (Henry) 1943- ... 122
Horton, Arthur MacNeill, Jr. 1947- ... 114
Horton, Felix Lee
See Floren, Lee
Horton, Frank E. 1939- ... 29-32R
Horton, George Moses 1797(?)-1883(?) ... DLB-50
Horton, James O(liver) 1943- ... 114
Horton, John (William) 1905- ... CANR-18
Earlier sketches in CA 9-10R, CANR-3
Horton, Louise 1916- ... CANR-2
Earlier sketch in CA 49-52
Horton, Lowell 1936- ... 53-56
Horton, Patricia Campbell 1943- ... 89-92
Horton, Paul Burleigh 1916- ... CANR-20
Earlier sketch in CA 1R
Horton, Paul Chester 1942- ... 106
Horton, Rod W(illiam) 1910- ... 49-52

Horton, Russell M. 1946- ... 97-100
Horton, Stanley M(onroe) 1916- ... CANR-6
Earlier sketch in CA 57-60
Horton, Susan R. 1941- ... 109
Horvat, Branko 1928- ... 53-56
Horvath, Betty 1927- ... 19-20R
See also SATA 4
Horvath, Janos 1921- ... 41-44R
Horvath, Joan 1944- ... 81-84
Horvath, Odon von
See Horvath, Oedoen von
Horvath, Oedoen von 1901-1938
Brief entry ... 118
Horvath, Violet M. 1924- ... 29-32R
Horwich, Frances R(appaport) 1908- ... CAP-1
Earlier sketch in CA 15-16
See also SATA 11
Horwitz, Elinor Lander ... CANR-13
Earlier sketch in CA 77-80
See also SATA 33, 45
Horwitz, Julius 1920-1986 ... CANR-12
Obituary ... 119
Earlier sketch in CA 9-10R
See also CLC 14
Horwitz, Richard P(aul) 1949- ... 122
Horwitz, Simi L(ouise) 1949- ... 103
Horwitz, Sylvia L(aibman) 1911- ... 61-64
Horwood, Harold (Andrew) 1923- ... CANR-25
Earlier sketches in CA 21-22R, CANR-9
See also DLB 60
Hoselitz, Bert(hold) F(rank) 1913- ... CANR-1
Earlier sketch in CA 1R
Hosford, Bowen I. 1916- ... CANR-24
Earlier sketch in CA 107
Hosford, Dorothy (Grant) 1900-1952 ... SATA-22
Hosford, Jessie 1892- ... 41-44R
See also SATA 5
Hosford, Philip L(ewis) 1926- ... 57-60
Hosford, Ray E. 1933- ... 85-88
Hosie, Stanley W(illiam) 1922- ... 25-28R
Hosier, Helen Kooiman 1928- ... CANR-8
Earlier sketch in CA 61-64
Hosier, Peter
See Clark, Douglas
Hosken, Fran(ziska) P(orges) 1919- ... CANR-6
Earlier sketch in CA 57-60
Hoskin, Cyril Henry 1911(?)-1981
Obituary ... 102
Hosking, Eric (John) 1909- ... CANR-17
Earlier sketch in CA 101
Hosking, Geoffrey A(lan) 1942- ... CANR-19
Earlier sketch in CA 85-88
Hoskins, Katharine Bail 1924- ... 65-68
Hoskins, Katherine (de Montalant) 1909- . CAP-2
Earlier sketch in CA 25-28
Hoskins, Robert 1933- ... 29-32R
Hoskins, William George 1908- ... 13-14R
Hoskyns-Abrahall, Clare (Constance
Drury) ... 29-32R
See also SATA 13
Hosley, Richard 1921- ... CANR-8
Earlier sketch in CA 7-8R
Hosmer, Charles B(ridgham), Jr. 1932- ... 15-16R
Hosmon, Robert Stahr 1943- ... 45-48
Hosokawa, Bill
See Hosokawa, William K.
Hosokawa, William K. 1915- ... CANR-11
Earlier sketch in CA 29-32R
Hospers, John, Jr. 1918- ... CANR-2
Earlier sketch in CA 1R
Hospital, Janette Turner 1942- ... 108
See also CLC 42
Hoss, Marvin Allen 1929- ... 29-32R
Hoss, Norman 1923(?)-1983 Obituary ... 111
Hossent, Harry 1916- ... CAP-1
Earlier sketch in CA 9-10
Hostetler, Beulah Stauffer 1926- ... 126
Hostetler, Marian 1932- ... CANR-24
Earlier sketches in CA 65-68, CANR-9
Hostetter, B(enjamin) Charles 1916- ... CANR-1
Earlier sketch in CA 4R
Hostler, Charles W(arren) 1919- ... 23-24R
Hostos, E. M. de
See Hostos (y Bonilla), Eugenio Maria de
Hostos, Eugenio M. de
See Hostos (y Bonilla), Eugenio Maria de
Hostos, Eugenio Maria
See Hostos (y Bonilla), Eugenio Maria de
Hostos (y Bonilla), Eugenio Maria de
1839-1903 Brief entry ... 123
See also TCLC 24
Hostovsky, Egon 1908-1973 Obituary ... 89-92
Hostrop, Richard Winfred 1925- ... 25-28R
Hotaling, Edward 1937- ... 77-80
Hotchkiss, Bill 1936- ... 104
Hotchkiss, Jeanette 1901- ... 23-24R
Hotchkiss, Ralf D. 1947- ... 33-36R
Hotchner, A(aron) E(dward) 1920- ... 69-72
Hotchner, Tracy 1950- ... 102
Hothem, Lar(ry Lee) 1938- ... 106
Hothersall, David 1940- ... 111
Hotson, John H(argrove) 1930- ... 25-28R
Hotspur
See Curling, Bryan William Richard
Hottois, James W. 1943- ... 77-80
Hotz, Robert B(ergmann) 1914- ... 101
Hou, Chi-ming 1924- ... 23-24R
Hou, Fu-Wu
See Houn, Franklin W.
Houblon, Doreen (Lindsay) Archer
See Archer Houblon, Doreen (Lindsay)
Houchin, Thomas D(ouglas) 1925- ... 77-80
Houck, Carter 1924- ... CANR-14
Earlier sketch in CA 77-80
See also SATA 22
Houck, John W(illiam) 1931- ... CANR-11
Earlier sketch in CA 29-32R
Houdini
See Lovecraft, H(oward) P(hillips)
Houdini, Merlin X.
See Borgmann, Dmitri A(lfred)
Houedard, Pierre-Sylvester 1924- ... 103
Houfe, Simon (Richard) 1942- ... CANR-19
Earlier sketch in CA 103
Hougan, Carolyn 19(?)- ... CLC-34
Hougan, James Richard 1942- ... 77-80
Hougan, Jim
See Hougan, James Richard
Hough, (Helen) Charlotte 1924- ... CANR-5
Earlier sketch in CA 9-10R
See also SATA 9
Hough, Denny C. 1925(?)-1983 Obituary ... 111
Hough, Emerson 1857-1923 Brief entry ... 120
See also DLB 9
Hough, George A(nthony) III 1920- ... 121
Brief entry ... 117
Hough, Graham (Goulder) 1908- ... CANR-25
Earlier sketch in CA 69-72
Hough, Henry Beetle 1896-1985 ... CANR-2
Obituary ... 116
Earlier sketch in CA 1R
Hough, Henry W(ade) 1906-197(?) ... 25-28R
Obituary ... 122
Hough, Hugh 1924-1986 ... 73-76
Obituary ... 119
Hough, Jerry F(incher) 1935- Brief entry ... 114
Hough, John T., Jr. 1946- ... 33-36R
Hough, Joseph C(arl), Jr. 1933- ... 23-24R
Hough, Judy Taylor 1932- ... 124
See also SATA 51
Hough, Lindy Downer 1944- ... CANR-8
Earlier sketch in CA 61-64
Hough, Louis 1914- ... 37-40R
Hough, Richard (Alexander) 1922- ... CANR-18
Earlier sketches in CA 5-6R, CANR-3
See also SATA 17
Hough, S(tanley) B(ennett) 1917- ... CANR-3
Earlier sketch in CA 7-8R
Houghteling, James L(awrence), Jr. 1920- ... 5-6R
Houghton, Bernard 1935- ... 77-80
Houghton, Diane 1940- ... 123
Houghton, Elizabeth
See Gilzean, Elizabeth Houghton Blanchet
Houghton, Eric 1930- ... CANR-2
Earlier sketch in CA 4R
See also SATA 7
Houghton, George William 1905- ... 13-14R
Houghton, Neal D(oyle) 1895- ... CAP-2
Earlier sketch in CA 25-28
Houghton, (Charles) Norris 1909- ... 23-24R
Houghton, Peter 1938- ... 119
Houghton, Samuel G(ilbert) 1902-1975 ... 65-68
Houghton, (William) Stanley 1881-1913
Brief entry ... 110
See also DLB 10
Houghton, Walter Edwards 1904-1983 ... CAP-1
Obituary ... 109
Earlier sketch in CA 9-10
Houlden, J(ames) L(eslie) 1929- ... 77-80
Houle, Cyril O(rvin) 1913- ... CANR-3
Earlier sketch in CA 5-6R
Houlehen, Robert J. 1918- ... 49-52
See also SATA 18
Houlgate, Deke 1930- ... 61-64
Hoult, Norah 1898-1984 Obituary ... 112
Hoult, Thomas Ford 1920- Brief entry ... 116
Houn, Franklin W. 1920- ... 23-24R
Hounsome, Terry 1944- ... 109
Houpt, Katherine Albro 1939- ... 105
Hourani, George F(adlo) 1913-1984 ... CANR-23
Earlier sketch in CA 45-48
Hours, Madeleine 1915- ... 49-52
Hours-Miedan, Madeleine
See Hours, Madeleine
Hours-Miedan, Magdeleine
See Hours, Madeleine
House, Anne W.
See McCauley, Elfrieda B(abnick)
House, Charles (Albert) 1916- ... 25-28R
House, Ernest R(obert) 1937- ... CANR-23
Earlier sketch in CA 45-48
House, Gloria 1941- ... 117
House, H(ershel) Wayne 1948- ... 119
House, John William 1919-1984 ... 106
Obituary ... 112
House, Karen Elliott 1947- Brief entry ... 125
House, Kurt D(uane) 1947- ... 104
House, Robert Burton 1892- ... CAP-1
Earlier sketch in CA 11-12
House, Robert J. 1932- ... 101
House, Robert W(illiam) 1920- ... 53-56
House, Ruth Sizemore 1946- ... 116
House, Victor 1893-1983 Obituary ... 109
Household, Geoffrey (Edward West)
1900-1988 ... 77-80
Obituary ... 126
See also SATA 14
See also CLC 11
Houselander, (Frances) Caryll 1901-1954
Brief entry ... 110
See also SATA 31
Houseman, Barton L(eroy) 1933- ... 61-64
Houseman, Gerald L. 1935- ... 108
Houseman, John 1902- Brief entry ... 110
Housepian, Marjorie
See Dobkin, Marjorie Housepian
Houser, Caroline ... 115
Housley, Norman (James) 1952- ... 108
Housman, A(lfred) E(dward) 1859-1936 ... 125
Brief entry ... 104
See also DLB 19
See also TCLC 1, 10
Housman, Laurence 1865-1959
Brief entry ... 106
See also SATA 25
See also DLB 10
See also TCLC 7
Houston, Beverle (Ann) 1936-1988 ... 89-92
Obituary ... 124
Houston, C(larence) Stuart 1927- ... 119
Houston, David 1938- ... 118
Houston, Douglas (Norman) 1947- ... 123
Houston, James A(rchibald) 1921- ... 65-68
See also SATA 13
See also CLR 3
Houston, James D. 1933- ... 25-28R
Houston, James M(ackintosh) 1922- ... 13-14R
Houston, Jean Brief entry ... 115
Houston, Jeanne (Toyo) Wakatsuki 1934- ... 103
Houston, Joan 1928- ... 19-20R
Houston, John Porter 1933-1987 ... CANR-3
Obituary ... 123
Earlier sketch in CA 11-12R
Houston, Neal B. 1928- ... 41-44R
Houston, Peyton (H.) 1910- ... CANR-1
Earlier sketch in CA 49-52
Houston, R. B.
See Rae, Hugh C(rauford)
Houston, Robert 1935- ... 37-40R
Houston, W(illiam) Robert, Jr. 1928- ... CANR-18
Earlier sketches in CA 5-6R, CANR-3
Houston, Will
See Paine, Lauran (Bosworth)
Houston, William Neil 1948- ... 123
Houtart, Francois 1925- ... 13-14R
Houthakker, Hendrik S(amuel) 1924- ... 17-18R
Houton, Kathleen
See Kilgore, Kathleen
Houts, Marshall (Wilson) 1919- ... CANR-13
Earlier sketch in CA 23-24R
Houts, Peter S. 1933- ... 49-52
Hovannisian, Richard G. 1932- ... 23-24R
Hovda, Robert W(alker) 1920- ... CANR-3
Earlier sketch in CA 11-12R
Hovde, A(nnis) J(orgen) 1917- ... 112
Hovde, Christian A(rneson) 1922- ... 7-8R
Hovde, Howard 1928- ... 25-28R
Hovell, Lucille A. (Peterson) 1916- ... 7-8R
Hovell, Lucy A.
See Hovell, Lucille A. (Peterson)
Hoverland, H. Arthur 1928- ... 45-48
Hoversten, Chester E. 1922- ... 7-8R
Hovey, E(lwyn) Paul 1908- ... CANR-1
Earlier sketch in CA 3R
Hovey, Richard 1864-1900 ... DLB-54
Hovey, Richard B(ennett) 1917- ... 25-28R
Hovey, Sonya 1898-1960 Obituary ... 113
Hoveyda, Fereydoun 1924- ... 101
Hovick, Rose Louise 1914(?)-1970
Obituary ... 113
Hoving, Thomas 1931- ... 101
Howald, Reed Anderson 1930- ... 57-60
Howar, Barbara 1934- ... 89-92
See also AITN 1, 2
Howard, A(rthur) E(llsworth) Dick 1933- ... 15-16R
Howard, Alan 1922- ... SATA-45
Howard, Alan 1934- ... CANR-20
Earlier sketch in CA 37-40R
Howard, Alvin Wendell 1922-1975 ... 33-36R
Howard, Alyssa
See Buckholtz, Eileen (Garber)
Howard, Alyssa
See Glick, Ruth (Burtnick)
Howard, Alyssa
See Titchener, Louise
Howard, Anthony (Michell) 1934- ... 109
Howard, Barbara 1930- ... 53-56
Howard, Ben(jamin Willis) 1944- ... 73-76
Howard, Bion B. 1912- ... 15-16R
Howard, Blanche 1923- ... 101
Howard, C(hester) Jeriel 1939- ... CANR-14
Earlier sketch in CA 29-32R
Howard, Carleton
See Howe, Charles H(orace)
Howard, Cecil
See Smith, Cecil (Howard III)
Howard, Charles Frederick 1904- ... 17-18R
Howard, Christopher 1913- ... 23-24R
Howard, Clark ... 122
Howard, Clive ?-1974 Obituary ... 53-56
Howard, Constance (Mildred) 1910- ... CANR-11
Earlier sketch in CA 69-72
Howard, Coralie
See Cogswell, Coralie (Norris)
Howard, D(erek) L(ionel) 1930- ... CANR-8
Earlier sketch in CA 7-8R
Howard, Daniel F(rancis) 1928- ... 41-44R
Howard, David M(orris) 1928- ... CANR-10
Earlier sketch in CA 25-28R
Howard, Deborah (Janet) 1946- ... 124
Howard, Dick 1943- ... 77-80
Howard, Don (Marcel) 1940- ... CANR-22
Earlier sketch in CA 106
Howard, Donald R(oy) 1927-1987 ... CANR-1
Obituary ... 121
Earlier sketch in CA 3R
Howard, Dorothy (Arlynne) 1912- ... 65-68
Howard, Dorothy Gray 1902- ... 93-96
Howard, Edmund (Bernard Carlo) 1909- ... 85-88
Howard, Edward G(arfield) 1918(?)-1972
Obituary ... 104
Howard, Edwin 1924- ... 65-68
Howard, Edwin J(ohnston) 1901- ... CAP-1
Earlier sketch in CA 11-12
Howard, Elizabeth Jane 1923- ... CANR-8
Earlier sketch in CA 5-6R
See also CLC 7, 29
Howard, Frances Minturn Brief entry ... 111
Howard, Fred D(avid) 1919- ... CANR-19
Earlier sketches in CA 3R, CANR-4
Howard, Frederick James 1904- ... 109
Howard, Gerald J(ohn) 1950- ... 108
Howard, Gilbert 1934- ... 49-52
Howard, Harold P. 1905- ... CAP-2
Earlier sketch in CA 33-36
Howard, Harry Nicholas 1902-1987 ... 49-52
Obituary ... 123
Howard, Hartley
See Ognall, Leopold Horace
Howard, Helen Addison 1904- ... CANR-3
Earlier sketch in CA 5-6R
Howard, Ian P. 1927- ... 23-24R
Howard, J. Grant 1929- ... 125
Howard, J. Woodford, Jr. 1931- ... 33-36R
Howard, James A(rch) 1922- ... CANR-8
Earlier sketch in CA 15-16R
Howard, James H(enri) 1925- ... 41-44R
Howard, James K(enton) 1943- ... 85-88
Howard, James T(homas) 1934- ... 101
Howard, Jane (Temple) 1935- ... CANR-13
Earlier sketch in CA 29-32R
Howard, Jean
See MacGibbon, Jean
Howard, Jessica
See Schere, Monroe
Howard, John (Arnold) 1916- ... 41-44R
Howard, John
See Hewitt, John (Harold)
Howard, John R(obert) 1933- ... 53-56
Howard, John Tasker 1890-1964
Obituary ... 89-92
Howard, Joseph Leon 1917- ... CANR-1
Earlier sketch in CA 1R
Howard, Joyce 1922- ... 7-8R
Howard, Kenneth I(rwin) 1932- ... 115
Howard, Kenneth Samuel 1882-1972 ... 9-10R
Obituary ... 103
Howard, Kez
See Houston, David
Howard, Lee M(ilton) 1922- ... 108
Howard, Leigh
See Lee Howard, Leon Alexander
Howard, Leon 1903-1982 ... 109
Howard, Leon Alexander Lee
See Lee Howard, Leon Alexander
Howard, Leslie G(raham) 1947- ... 114
Howard, Lowell B(ennett) 1925- ... 15-16R
Howard, Mark
See Rigsby, Howard
Howard, Mary
See Mussi, Mary
Howard, Maureen 1930- ... 53-56
See also DLBY 83
See also CLC 5, 14, 46
Howard, Michael (Eliot) 1922- ... CANR-2
Earlier sketch in CA 1R
Howard, Michael S. 1922-1974 Obituary ... 53-56
Howard, Moses L(eon) 1928- ... 109
Howard, Munroe 1913-1974 ... CAP-2
Earlier sketch in CA 23-24
Howard, Nona
See Luxton, Leonora Kathrine
Howard, Oliver Otis 1830-1909 Brief entry ... 109
Howard, Patricia (Lowe) 1937- ... CANR-7
Earlier sketch in CA 17-18R
Howard, Paul Jack 1908-1984 Obituary ... 113
Howard, Peter D(unsmore) 1908-1965 ... CAP-1
Earlier sketch in CA 11-12
Howard, Philip 1933- ... 65-68
Howard, Prosper
See Hamilton, Charles Harold St. John
Howard, Richard 1929- ... CANR-25
Earlier sketch in CA 85-88
See also DLB 5
See also CLC 7, 10, 47
See also AITN 1
Howard, Richard C. 1929- ... 53-56
Howard, Robert 1926- ... 41-44R
Howard, Robert Ervin 1906-1936
Brief entry ... 105
See also TCLC 8
Howard, Robert West 1908- ... CANR-1
Earlier sketch in CA 4R
See also SATA 5
Howard, Roger 1938- ... CANR-17
Earlier sketch in CA 93-96
Howard, Ronnalie Roper
See Roper, Ronnalie J.
Howard, Ross 1946- ... 120
Howard, Roy Joseph 1925- ... 112
Howard, Roy Wilson 1883-1964 Obituary ... 89-92
See also DLB 29
Howard, Sidney 1891-1939 ... DLB-7, 26
Howard, Stanley E. 1888(?)-1980
Obituary ... 102
Howard, Ted
See Howard, Theodore Korner
Howard, Theodore Korner 1915- ... 103
Howard, Thomas 1930- ... 37-40R
Howard, Thomas T(rumbull) 1935- ... 111
Howard, Troy
See Paine, Lauran (Bosworth)
Howard, Vechel
See Rigsby, Howard
Howard, Vernon (Linwood) 1918- ... 108
See also SATA 40
Howard, Warren F.
See Pohl, Frederik
Howard, Warren Starkie 1930- ... 7-8R
Howard-Hill, Trevor Howard 1933- ... 85-88
Howard-Williams, Jeremy (Napier)
1922- ... CANR-22
Earlier sketch in CA 106

Howarth, David (Armine) 1912- ... CANR-25
Earlier sketches in CA 13-14R, CANR-9
See also SATA 6
Howarth, Donald 1931- ... 25-28R
Howarth, Pamela 1954- ... 102
Howarth, Patrick (John Fielding) 1916- ... 77-80
Howarth, Stephen (William Russell) 1953- ... CANR-25
Earlier sketch in CA 107
Howarth, T(homas) E(dward) B(rodie) 1914-1988(?) Obituary ... 125
Howarth, W(illiam) D(river) 1922- ... 45-48
Howarth, William Louis 1940- ... CANR-20
Earlier sketch in CA 37-40R
Howat, Gerald Malcolm David 1928- ... CANR-16
Earlier sketch in CA 93-96
Howat, John K(eith) 1937- ... 49-52
Howatch, Joseph 1935- ... 65-68
Howatch, Susan 1940- ... CANR-24
Earlier sketch in CA 45-48
See also AITN 1
Howe, Charles H(orace) 1912- ... 53-56
Howe, Charles L. 1932- ... 19-20R
Howe, Christopher (Barry) 1937- ... 121
Howe, Daniel Walker 1937- ... 29-32R
Howe, Deborah 1946-1978 ... 105
See also SATA 29
Howe, Doris Kathleen ... CANR-3
Earlier sketch in CA 49-52
Howe, E. W. 1853-1937 ... DLB-12, 25
Howe, Ellic 1910- ... 25-28R
Howe, Fanny 1940- ... 117
See also SATA 52
See also CLC 47
Howe, Florence 1929- ... 124
Brief entry ... 109
Howe, G(eorge) Melvyn 1920- ... 101
Howe, George Frederick 1901-1988
Obituary ... 124
Howe, George Locke 1898(?)-1977
Obituary ... 69-72
Howe, Helen 1905-1975 ... CAP-2
Obituary ... 57-60
Earlier sketch in CA 23-24
Howe, Henry 1816-1893 ... DLB-30
Howe, Hubert S(hattuck), Jr. 1942- ... 57-60
Howe, Irving 1920- ... CANR-21
Earlier sketch in CA 9-10R
See also DLB 67
Howe, James 1946- ... CANR-22
Earlier sketch in CA 105
See also SATA 29
See also CLR 9
Howe, James Robinson 1935- ... 69-72
Howe, Jonathan Trumbull 1935- ... 29-32R
Howe, Josephine (Mary) O'Connor
See O'Connor Howe, Josephine (Mary)
Howe, Julia Ward 1819-1910 Brief entry ... 117
See also DLB 1
See also TCLC 21
Howe, Leland W(right) 1940- ... 123
Brief entry ... 118
Howe, Louise Kapp 1934-1984 Obituary ... 111
Howe, Mark Anthony DeWolfe 1864-1960
Obituary ... 89-92
Howe, Nelson 1935- ... 33-36R
Howe, Quincy 1900-1977 ... 49-52
Obituary ... 69-72
Howe, Reuel L(anphier) 1905- ... 23-24R
Howe, Richard J. 1937- ... 77-80
Howe, Russell Warren 1925- ... 49-52
Howe, Tina 1937- ... 109
See also CLC 48
Howe, W(arren) Asquith 1910- ... 29-32R
Howe, William Hugh 1928- ... 65-68
Howell, Barbara 1937- ... 49-52
Howell, Benjamin Franklin 1890-1976
Obituary ... 65-68
Howell, Clark, Sr. 1863-1936 ... DLB-25
Howell, Clinton T. 1913- ... 29-32R
Howell, David Arthur Russell 1936- ... 109
Howell, Elsworth Seaman 1915-1987
Obituary ... 122
Howell, Evan P(ark) 1839-1905
Brief entry ... 119
See also DLB 23
Howell, Helen (Jane) 1934- ... 57-60
Howell, James Edwin 1928- ... CANR-20
Earlier sketch in CA 2R
Howell, John
See Hall, Gus
Howell, John C(hristian) 1924- ... CANR-9
Earlier sketch in CA 21-22R
Howell, John M(ichael) 1933- ... 33-36R
Howell, Joseph T(oy III) 1942- ... CANR-24
Earlier sketch in CA 45-48
Howell, Leon 1936- ... 25-28R
Howell, Michael J. 1932(?)-1986 Obituary ... 118
Howell, Pat 1947- ... SATA-15
Howell, Patricia Hagan 1939- ... 81-84
Howell, Reet 1945- ... 110
Howell, Richard W(esley) 1926- ... 57-60
Howell, Robert Lee 1928- ... 25-28R
Howell, Roger (Jr.) 1936- ... CANR-11
Earlier sketch in CA 21-22R
Howell, S.
See Styles, (Frank) Showell
Howell, Thomas 1944- ... 73-76
Howell, Virginia
See Ellison, Virginia H(owell)
Howell, Wilbur Samuel 1904- ... 33-36R
Howell, William C(arl) 1932- ... 93-96
Howells, J(ames) Harvey 1912- ... 97-100
Howells, John G(wilym) 1918- ... CANR-24
Earlier sketches in CA 23-24R, CANR-9
Howells, Roscoe 1919- ... 104
Howells, William Dean 1837-1920
Brief entry ... 104
See also DLB 12, 64, 74
See also CDALB 1865-1917
See also TCLC 7, 17
Howells, William White 1908- ... CANR-19
Earlier sketches in CA 1R, CANR-2
Hower, Edward 1941- ... 106
Hower, Ralph M(erle) 1903-1973 ... 3R
Obituary ... 45-48
Howes, Alan B(arber) 1920- Brief entry ... 112
Howes, Barbara 1914- ... 9-10R
See also CAAS 3
See also SATA 5
See also CLC 15
Howes, Connie B. 1933- ... 89-92
Howes, Frank Stewart 1891-1974
Obituary ... 115
Howes, Michael 1904- ... 61-64
Howes, Paul Griswold 1892-1984 ... 29-32R
Obituary ... 113
Howes, Raymond F(loyd) 1903- ... CAP-1
Earlier sketch in CA 17-18
Howes, Robert Gerard 1919- ... CANR-4
Earlier sketch in CA 1R
Howes, Royce (Bucknam) 1901-1973 ... CAP-2
Obituary ... 41-44R
Earlier sketch in CA 19-20
Howes, Wright 1882-1978 Obituary ... 104
Howick, William Henry 1924- ... 33-36R
Howie, Carl G(ordon) 1920- ... 15-16R
Howith, Harry 1934- ... 25-28R
Howitzer, Bronson
See Hardman, Richards Lynden
Howker, Janni 1957- ... SATA-46
See also CLR 14
Howkins, John 1945- ... CANR-14
Earlier sketch in CA 65-68
Howl, Marcia (Yvonne Hurt) 1947- ... 121
Howland, Bette 1937- ... 85-88
Howland, Harold Edward 1913-1980
Obituary ... 102
Howlett, Duncan 1906- ... 107
Howlett, John (Reginald) 1940- ... CANR-12
Earlier sketch in CA 69-72
Howorth, Beckett 1902- ... 114
Howorth, M. K.
See Black, Margaret K(atherine)
Howorth, Muriel ... CAP-1
Earlier sketch in CA 9-10
Howse, Ernest Marshall 1902- ... 49-52
Howson, Susan 1945- ... 113
Howton, F(rank) William 1925- ... 29-32R
Hoxie, Frederick E(ugene) 1947- ... 117
Hoxie, R(alph) Gordon 1919- ... 103
Hoy, Cyrus H. 1926- ... 21-22R
Hoy, David 1930- ... 17-18R
Hoy, James F(ranklin) 1939- ... 57-60
Hoy, John C. 1933- ... CANR-9
Earlier sketch in CA 21-22R
Hoy, Nina
See Roth, Arthur J(oseph)
Hoye, Anna Scott 1915- ... 15-16R
Hoyem, Andrew 1935- ... 9-10R
See also DLB 5
Hoyer, George W. 1919- ... CANR-4
Earlier sketch in CA 3R
Hoyer, H(arvey) Conrad 1907- ... 33-36R
Hoyer, Mildred N(aeher) ... 57-60
Hoyland, Michael 1925- ... 23-24R
Hoyle, Fred 1915- ... CANR-3
Earlier sketch in CA 7-8R
Hoyle, Geoffrey 1942- ... CANR-6
Earlier sketch in CA 53-56
See also SATA 18
Hoyle, Martha Byrd
See Byrd, Martha
Hoyle, Peter 1939- ... 124
Hoyles, J(ames) Arthur 1908- ... 7-8R
Hoyt, Charles Alva 1931- ... 33-36R
Hoyt, Charles K(ing) 1938- ... 110
Hoyt, Clark 1942- ... 69-72
Hoyt, Edwin P(almer), Jr. 1923- ... CANR-1
Earlier sketch in CA 3R
See also SATA 28
Hoyt, Elizabeth E(llis) 1893- ... 37-40R
Hoyt, Erich 1950- ... 106
Hoyt, Herman A(rthur) 1909- ... 29-32R
Hoyt, Homer 1896-1984 ... CANR-1
Obituary ... 114
Earlier sketch in CA 1R
Hoyt, Jo Wasson 1927- ... 21-22R
Hoyt, Joseph B(ixby) 1913- ... 5-6R
Hoyt, Kenneth B(oyd) 1924- ... CANR-1
Earlier sketch in CA 45-48
Hoyt, Mary Finch 1924(?)- ... 107
Hoyt, Murray 1904- ... 9-10R
Hoyt, Olga (Gruhzit) 1922- ... 25-28R
See also SATA 16
Hoyt, (Edwin) Palmer 1897-1979
Obituary ... 89-92
Hoyt, Robert S(tuart) 1918-1971 Obituary ... 111
Hoyt, Waite (Charles) 1899-1984 Obituary ... 113
Hozeny, Tony 1946- ... 61-64
Hozjusz
See Dobraczynski, Jan
Hrabal, Bohumil 1914- ... 106
See also CLC 13
Hrdy, Sarah Blaffer 1946- ... 107
Hromadka, Josef L(ukl) 1889-1971 ... CAP-1
Earlier sketch in CA 9-10
Hruska-Cortes, Elias 1943- ... 45-48
Hruza, Zdenek 1926- ... 61-64
Hsia, Adrian (Rue Chun) 1938- ... 77-80
Hsia, C(hih)-T(sing) 1921- ... CANR-17
Earlier sketches in CA 2R, CANR-2
Hsia, David Yi-Yung 1925-1972
Obituary ... 33-36R
Hsia, Hsiao
See Liu, Wu-chi
Hsia, Tsi-an 1916-1965 ... CAP-2
Earlier sketch in CA 25-28
Hsiang, Yeh
See Liu, Sydney (Chieh)
Hsiao, Katharine H(uei-Ying Huang) 1923- ... 77-80
Hsiao, Kung-Chuan 1897- ... 3R
Hsiao, Tso-liang 1910- ... 3R
Hsiung, James Chieh 1935- ... 37-40R
Hsu, Benedict (Pei-Hsiung) 1933- ... 69-72
Hsu, Cho-yun 1930- ... CANR-9
Earlier sketch in CA 17-18R
Hsu, Francis L(ang) K(wang) 1909- ... CANR-16
Earlier sketches in CA 3R, CANR-1
Hsu, Immanuel C. Y. 1923- ... 1R
Hsu, Kai-yu 1922-1982 ... CANR-14
Earlier sketch in CA 21-22R
Hsueh, Chun-tu 1922- ... CANR-15
Earlier sketch in CA 41-44R
Hsun, Lu
See Shu-Jen, Chou
See also TCLC 3
Hsu Ying 1935- ... 124
Htin Aung, U.
See Aung, (Maung) Htin
Hu, Shi Ming
See Hu, Shu Ming
Hu, Shu Ming 1927- ... 85-88
Hu, Sze-Tsen 1914- ... 41-44R
Huaco, George A. 1927- ... 17-18R
Huang, David S(hih-Li) 1930- ... 9-10R
Huang, Parker (Po-fei) 1914- ... CANR-2
Earlier sketch in CA 45-48
Huang, Philip Chung-Chih 1940-
Brief entry ... 105
Huang, Po-fei
See Huang, Parker (Po-fei)
Huang, Ray (Jen-yu) 1918- ... CANR-8
Earlier sketch in CA 61-64
Huang, Stanley S(hang) C(hien) 1923- ... 77-80
Huan Yue
See Shen Congwen
Hubach, Robert R(ogers) 1916- ... 1R
Hubartt, Paul L(eroy) 1919- ... 7-8R
Hubbard, Barbara Marx 1929- ... 103
Hubbard, D(onald) L(ee) 1929- ... 21-22R
Hubbard, David Allan 1928- ... CANR-16
Earlier sketch in CA 33-36R
Hubbard, David G(raham) 1920- ... 33-36R
Hubbard, Don 1926- ... 109
Hubbard, Edward (Horton) 1937- ... 124
Hubbard, Frank T. 1921(?)-1976
Obituary ... 65-68
Hubbard, Freeman (Henry) 1894- ... 5-6R
Hubbard, George (Barron) 1884-1958
Brief entry ... 122
Hubbard, J(ake) T(imothy) W(illiam) 1935- ... 124
Hubbard, (Frank Mc)Kin(ney) 1868-1930
Brief entry ... 113
See also DLB 11
Hubbard, L(afayette) Ron(ald) 1911-1986 ... CANR-22
Obituary ... 118
Earlier sketch in CA 77-80
See also CLC 43
Hubbard, Lucien 1889(?)-1971
Obituary ... 33-36R
Hubbard, Margaret Ann
See Priley, Margaret Hubbard
Hubbard, P(hilip) M(aitland) 1910-1980 ... 85-88
Obituary ... 97-100
Hubbard, Paul H. 1900(?)-1983 Obituary ... 109
Hubbard, Preston John 1918- ... 7-8R
Hubbard, (Andrew) Ray 1924- ... 103
Hubbard, Robert Hamilton 1916- ... CANR-21
Earlier sketch in CA 1R
Hubbard, Ruth 1924- ... 116
Hubbard, Thomas Leslie Wallan 1905- ... CAP-1
Earlier sketch in CA 13-14
Hubbard, William 1621(?)-1704 ... DLB-24
Hubbell, Harriet Weed 1909- ... 7-8R
Hubbell, Harry M. 1881-1971 Obituary ... 29-32R
Hubbell, Jay B(roadus) 1885-1979 ... CANR-17
Obituary ... 116
Earlier sketch in CA 1R
Hubbell, John G(erard) 1927- ... 65-68
Hubbell, Lindley Williams 1901- ... CAP-1
Earlier sketch in CA 15-16
Hubbell, Patricia 1928- ... 17-18R
See also SATA 8
Hubbell, Richard Whittaker 1914- ... 13-14R
Hubbell, Sue 1935- ... 120
Hubbs, Carl Leavitt 1894-1979 Obituary ... 89-92
Hubbs, G(uy) Ward 1952- ... 114
Hubenka, Lloyd J(ohn) 1931- ... 49-52
Huber, Jack T(ravis) 1918- ... 23-24R
Huber, Joan 1925- ... CANR-13
Earlier sketch in CA 77-80
Huber, Leonard Victor 1903- ... CANR-6
Earlier sketch in CA 57-60
Huber, Morton Wesley 1923- ... 17-18R
Huber, Richard M(iller) 1922- ... 33-36R
Huber, Thomas 1937- ... 29-32R
Huber, Thomas Michael 1944- ... 112
Huberman, Edward 1910- ... 15-16R
Huberman, Elizabeth Duncan Lyle 1915- ... 15-16R
Huberman, Leo 1903-1968 ... CANR-4
Earlier sketch in CA 1R
Hubert, James Lee 1947- ... 73-76
Hubert, Jim
See Hubert, James Lee
Hubert, Renee Riese 1916- ... 61-64
Hubin, Allen J. 1936- ... 33-36R
Hubka, Betty (Josephine Morgan) 1924- ... 13-14R
Hubka, Thomas C. 1946- ... 126
Hubler, David 1941- ... 110
Hubler, Edward L(orenzo) 1902-1965 ... CAP-1
Earlier sketch in CA 13-14
Hubler, Herbert Clark 1910- ... 85-88
Hubler, Richard Gibson 1912- ... CANR-2
Earlier sketch in CA 3R
Hubley, Faith Elliot 1924- ... 81-84
See also SATA 48
Hubley, John 1914-1977 ... SATA-24, 48
Huby, Pamela M(argaret Clark) 1922- ... 21-22R
Huch, Friedrich 1873-1913 ... DLB-66
Huch, Ricarda (Octavia) 1864-1947
Brief entry ... 111
See also DLB 66
See also TCLC 13
Huchel, Peter 1903- ... 81-84
Huck, Gabe (Donald Joseph) 1941- ... 112
Huckaby, Elizabeth (Paisley) 1905- ... 106
Huckaby, Gerald 1933- ... 33-36R
Hucker, Charles O(scar) 1919- ... 69-72
Huckins, Wesley C. 1918- ... 23-24R
Huckleberry, E(vermont) R(obbins) 1894- ... CANR-11
Earlier sketch in CA 61-64
Huckshorn, Robert J(ack) 1928- ... 97-100
Hudd, Roy 1936- ... 105
Huddle, David 1942- ... 57-60
See also CLC 49
Huddle, Frank, Jr. 1943- ... 37-40R
Huddleston, Eugene L(ee) 1931- ... CANR-19
Earlier sketch in CA 102
Huddleston, Lee Eldridge 1935- ... 21-22R
Huddleston, Rodney D(esmond) 1937- ... 33-36R
Huddy, Delia 1934- ... CANR-19
Earlier sketch in CA 25-28R
Hudgens, A(lice) Gayle 1941- ... 37-40R
Hudgins, H(erbert) C(ornelius), Jr. 1932- ... 33-36R
Hudnut, Robert K(ilborne) 1934- ... CANR-17
Earlier sketch in CA 25-28R
Hudoba, Michael 1913-1984 Obituary ... 113
Hudon, Edward Gerard 1915- ... 7-8R
Hudson, Alec
See Holmes, W(ilfred) J(ay)
Hudson, Arthur Palmer 1894(?)-1978
Obituary ... 111
Hudson, Charles M(elvin, Jr.) 1932- ... 33-36R
Hudson, Danny L. 1940- ... 122
Hudson, Darril 1931- ... 45-48
Hudson, Derek (Rommel) 1911- ... 9-10R
Hudson, Geoffrey Francis 1903-1974
Obituary ... 49-52
Hudson, Gladys W(atts) 1926- ... 33-36R
Hudson, Gossie Harold 1930- ... 93-96
Hudson, Helen
See Lane, Helen
Hudson, Henry Norman 1814-1886 ... DLB-64
Hudson, Henry T(homas) 1932- ... 118
Hudson, Herman 1923- ... 97-100
Hudson, James A(lbert) 1924- ... 33-36R
Hudson, James J(ackson) 1919- ... 25-28R
Hudson, James R. 1933- ... 124
Hudson, Jean B(arlow) 1915- ... 93-96
Hudson, Jeffery
See Crichton, (John) Michael
Hudson, John A(llen) 1927- ... 25-28R
Hudson, Kenneth 1916- Brief entry ... 117
Hudson, (Margaret) Kirsty 1947- ... 107
See also SATA 32
Hudson, Liam 1933- ... CANR-12
Earlier sketch in CA 29-32R
Hudson, Lois Phillips 1927- ... 3R
Hudson, Marc 1947- ... 116
Hudson, Meg
See Koehler, Margaret Hudson
Hudson, Michael C(raig) 1938- ... 37-40R
Hudson, Michael Huckleberry 1939- ... CANR-13
Earlier sketch in CA 33-36R
Hudson, (Arthur) Palmer 1892- ... CAP-2
Earlier sketch in CA 19-20
Hudson, Peggy
See Herz, Peggy
Hudson, R(obert) Lofton 1910- ... 15-16R
Hudson, Randolph H(oyt) 1927- ... 19-20R
Hudson, Richard (McLain, Jr.) 1925- ... 65-68
Hudson, Robert
See Oleksy, Walter
Hudson, Robert P(aul) 1926- ... 116
Hudson, Robert Vernon 1932- ... 109
Hudson, Theodore R. ... 45-48
Hudson, W(illiam) H(enry) 1841-1922
Brief entry ... 115
See also SATA 35
See also TCLC 29
Hudson, Wilma J(ones) 1916- ... 33-36R
Hudson, Wilson Mathis 1907- ... 102
Hudson, Winthrop Still 1911- ... CANR-2
Earlier sketch in CA 3R
Hudspeth, Robert N. 1936- ... 103
Huebel, Harry Russell 1943- ... 77-80
Huebener, Theodore 1895-1983 Obituary ... 111
Huebner, Anna (Ismelda Mathews) 1877(?)-1974 Obituary ... 53-56
Huebner, Klaus H(ermann) 1916- ... 126
Huegli, A(lbert) G(eorge) 1913- ... 15-16R
Huelsman, Richard J(oseph) 1921- ... 111
Huelsmann, Eva 1928- ... SATA-16
Huerlimann, Bettina 1909-1983 ... 109
Obituary ... 110
See also SATA 34, 39
Huerlimann, Ruth 1939- ... 107
See also SATA 31, 32
Huessy, Hans R. 1921- ... 21-22R
Hueter, John E(dwin) 1918- ... 114

Huether, Anne Frances
See Freeman, Anne Frances
Huey, F. B., Jr. 1925- ... CANR-23
Earlier sketch in CA 106
Huey, Lynda 1947- ... 65-68
Hufana, A(lejandrino) G. 1926- ... 77-80
Hufbauer, Karl (George) 1937- ... 109
Huff, Afton (A.) W(alker) 1928- ... 65-68
Huff, Betty Tracy ... 25-28R
Huff, Darrell 1913- ... CANR-5
Earlier sketch in CA 3R
Huff, Robert 1924- ... CANR-6
Earlier sketch in CA 13-14R
Huff, T(om) E. 1938(?)- ... 93-96
See also AITN 2
Huff, Vaughn E(dward) 1935- ... 29-32R
Huffaker, Clair 1927- ... 113
Huffaker, Sandy 1943- ... SATA-10
Huffard, Grace Thompson 1892- ... CAP-1
Earlier sketch in CA 11-12
Huffert, Anton M. 1912- ... 13-14R
Huffman, Carolyn 1928- ... 69-72
Huffman, Claire (De Cesare Licari) ... 116
Huffman, Franklin E(ugene) 1934- ... CANR-12
Earlier sketch in CA 29-32R
Huffman, James Lamar 1941- ... 102
Huffman, Laurie 1916- ... 45-48
Huffman, Tom ... SATA-24
Hufford, Susan 1940- ... CANR-9
Earlier sketch in CA 57-60
Hufschmidt, Maynard Michael 1912- ... CANR-15
Earlier sketch in CA 41-44R
Hufton, Olwen H. 1938- ... 21-22R
Hug, Bernal D(ean) 1896- ... 57-60
Huggan, Isabel 1943- ... 119
Huggett, Frank E(dward) 1924- ... CANR-19
Earlier sketches in CA 9-10R, CANR-3
Huggett, Joyce 1937- ... 126
Huggett, Richard 1929- ... 53-56
Huggett, William Turner ... 53-56
Huggins, Alice Margaret 1891-1971 ... CAP-1
Earlier sketch in CA 17-18
Huggins, Charles B(renton) 1901-
Brief entry ... 115
Huggins, Nathan Irvin 1927- ... CANR-25
Earlier sketch in CA 29-32R
See also BW
Hughart, Barry ... CLC-39
Hughes, Alan 1935- ... 97-100
Hughes, Alice 1899(?)-1977 Obituary ... 104
Hughes, Andrew 1937- ... 61-64
Hughes, Anthony John 1933- ... 11-12R
Hughes, Arthur Joseph 1928- ... 17-18R
Hughes, Arthur Montague D'Urban
1873-1974 Obituary ... 49-52
Hughes, B(asil) P(erronet) 1903- ... 61-64
Hughes, C(hristopher) J(ohn) 1918- ... 17-18R
Hughes, C. J. Pennethorne
See Hughes, (Charles James)
Pennethorne
Hughes, Catharine R(achel) 1935-1987 ... 41-44R
Obituary ... 123
Hughes, Charles C(ampbell) 1929- ... 41-44R
Hughes, Charles L(loyd) 1933- ... CANR-11
Earlier sketch in CA 19-20R
Hughes, (John) Cledwyn 1920-1978 ... 15-16R
Obituary ... 126
Hughes, Colin
See Creasey, John
Hughes, Colin A(nfield) 1930- ... CANR-25
Earlier sketches in CA 23-24R, CANR-9
Hughes, Daniel 1929- ... 33-36R
Hughes, Daniel T(homas) 1930- ... 89-92
Hughes, David (John) 1930- Brief entry ... 116
See also DLB 14
See also CLC 48
Hughes, Dean 1943- ... CANR-22
Earlier sketch in CA 106
See also SATA 33
Hughes, Dean Aubrey 1908(?)-1987
Obituary ... 122
Hughes, Dorothy (Berry) 1910- ... CAP-2
Earlier sketch in CA 33-36
Hughes, Dorothy B(elle) 1904- ... 104
Hughes, Douglas A(llan) 1938- ... 29-32R
Hughes, Eden
See Butterworth, W(illiam) E(dmund III)
Hughes, Elizabeth
See Zachary, Hugh
Hughes, Emmet John 1920-1982 ... 69-72
Obituary ... 107
Hughes, Erica 1931- ... 109
Hughes, Everett Cherrington 1897-1983 ... 103
Obituary ... 108
Hughes, Felicity 1938- ... 33-36R
Hughes, G(eorge) E(dward) 1918- ... 23-24R
Hughes, Gerald (Thomas) 1930- ... 117
Hughes, Gervase 1905- ... 9-10R
Hughes, Glyn 1935- ... CANR-13
Earlier sketch in CA 33-36R
Hughes, Graham 1928- ... 57-60
Hughes, Gwilym Fielden 1899- ... 97-100
Hughes, H(enry) Stuart 1916- ... CANR-2
Earlier sketch in CA 3R
Hughes, Harold K(enneth) 1911- ... 11-12R
Hughes, Helen (Gintz) 1928- ... 15-16R
Hughes, Howard (Robard) 1905-1976
Obituary ... 112
Hughes, Irene Finger ... 103
Hughes, J(ohnson) Donald 1932- ... CANR-10
Earlier sketch in CA 65-68
Hughes, James Monroe 1890-1971 ... 1R
Obituary ... 103
Hughes, James Pennethorne
See Hughes, (Charles James)
Pennethorne
Hughes, James Quentin 1920- ... CANR-6
Earlier sketch in CA 13-14R
Hughes, James W(ilfred) 1934- ... 77-80
Hughes, (Robert) John 1930- ... CANR-4
Earlier sketch in CA 1R
Hughes, John 1950(?)- Brief entry ... 124
Hughes, John A(nthony) 1941- ... 41-44R
Hughes, John Jay 1928- ... 57-60
Hughes, John L(ewis) 1938- ... 77-80
Hughes, John Paul 1920-1974 ... 1R
Obituary ... 53-56
Hughes, Jonathan R(oberts) T(yson)
1928- ... 81-84
Hughes, Judith M(arkham) 1941- ... 33-36R
Hughes, Judy 1943- ... 69-72
Hughes, Kathleen W. 1927(?)-1977
Obituary ... 69-72
Hughes, Ken(neth) 1922- ... CANR-16
Earlier sketch in CA 7-8R
Hughes, (James) Langston 1902-1967 ... CANR-1
Obituary ... 25-28R
Earlier sketch in CA 1R
See also BW
See also SATA 4, 33
See also DLB 4, 7, 48, 51
See also CLC 1, 5, 10, 15, 35, 44
Hughes, Leo 1908- ... 41-44R
Hughes, Margaret Kelly 1894(?)-1980
Obituary ... 101
Hughes, Marija Matich ... 97-100
Hughes, Mary 1951- ... 122
Hughes, Mary Gray 1930- ... 61-64
Hughes, Mary Louise 1910- ... 29-32R
Hughes, Matilda
See MacLeod, Charlotte (Matilda Hughes)
Hughes, Merrit Y(erkes) 1893-1970 ... CAP-1
Earlier sketch in CA 17-18
Hughes, Monica (Ince) 1925- ... CANR-23
Earlier sketch in CA 77-80
See also SATA 15
See also CLR 9
Hughes, Nathaniel Cheairs, Jr. 1930- ... 17-18R
Hughes, Owain (Gardner Collingwood)
1943- ... 21-22R
Hughes, Patrick 1939- ... 61-64
Hughes, Paul L(ester) 1915- ... 9-10R
Hughes, (Charles James) Pennethorne
1907-1967 ... CAP-2
Earlier sketch in CA 21-22
Hughes, Philip 1895-1967 ... CAP-2
Earlier sketch in CA 17-18
Hughes, Philip Edgcumbe 1915- ... CANR-18
Earlier sketches in CA 9-10R, CANR-3
Hughes, (James) Quentin 1920- ... 29-32R
Hughes, R(ichard) E(dward) 1927- ... CANR-6
Earlier sketch in CA 5-6R
Hughes, Richard (Arthur Warren)
1900-1976 ... CANR-4
Obituary ... 65-68
Earlier sketch in CA 7-8R
See also SATA 8, 25
See also DLB 15
See also CLC 1, 11
Hughes, Richard 1906-1984 Obituary ... 111
Hughes, Richard 1941- ... 107
Hughes, Riley 1914-1981 ... 107
Obituary ... 103
Hughes, Robert 1929(?)-1972 Obituary ... 37-40R
Hughes, Robert (Studley Forrest) 1938(?)- ... 112
Brief entry ... 110
Hughes, Russell C. 1893(?)-1982
Obituary ... 108
Hughes, Russell Meriwether 1898(?)-1988
Obituary ... 124
Hughes, Sam
See Wilks, Brian
Hughes, Shirley 1927- ... CANR-24
Earlier sketch in CA 85-88
See also SATA 16
See also CLR 15
Hughes, Stephen Ormsby 1924- ... 61-64
Hughes, Ted 1930- ... CANR-1
Earlier sketch in CA 2R
See also SATA 27, 49
See also DLB 40
See also CLC 2, 4, 9, 14, 37
See also CLR 3
Hughes, Terry A. 1933- ... 65-68
Hughes, Theodore E(rmond) 1942- ... 116
Hughes, Thomas 1822-1896 ... SATA-31
See also DLB 18
Hughes, Thomas M(ears) 1927- ... 65-68
Hughes, Thomas Parke 1923- ... 29-32R
Hughes, Virginia
See Campbell, Hope
Hughes, Walter (Llewellyn) 1910- ... CANR-1
Earlier sketch in CA 4R
See also SATA 26
Hughes, William J., Jr. 1897(?)-1974
Obituary ... 45-48
Hughes, William W(auters) 1918- ... 126
Hughes, Zach
See Zachary, Hugh
Hughes, Zachary
See Zachary, Hugh
Hughey, Ruth Willard 1899- ... 1R
Hugill, Stan(ley) James 1906- ... CAP-2
Earlier sketch in CA 23-24
Hugo, Grant
See Cable, James (Eric)
Hugo, Herbert W. 1930(?)-1979
Obituary ... 89-92
Hugo, Richard F(ranklin) 1923-1982 ... CANR-3
Obituary ... 108
Earlier sketch in CA 49-52
See also DLB 5
See also CLC 6, 18, 32
Hugo, Victor (Marie) 1802-1885 ... SATA-47
Huhta, James K(enneth) 1937- ... 37-40R
Huie, William Bradford 1910-1986 ... CANR-7
Obituary ... 121
Earlier sketch in CA 11-12R
See also AITN 1
Huie, William O(rr) 1911- ... 23-24R
Huisken, Ronald H(erman) 1946- ... 93-96
Hula, Harold L. 1930- ... 25-28R
Hulbert, Jack 1892-1978 Obituary ... 115
Hulet, Claude Lyle 1920- ... CANR-9
Earlier sketch in CA 53-56
Hulicka, Irene M(ackintosh) 1927- ... 37-40R
Hulicka, Karel 1913- ... 41-44R
Huline-Dickens, Frank William 1931- ... 107
See also SATA 34
Hulke, Malcolm 1924- ... 81-84
Hull, Cary Schuler 1946- ... 106
Hull, Charles
See Charles, Gordon H(ull)
Hull, David L(ee) 1935- ... 77-80
Hull, David Stewart 1938- ... 25-28R
Hull, Denison Bingham 1897- ... 37-40R
Hull, Eleanor (Means) 1913- ... CANR-19
Earlier sketches in CA 11-12R, CANR-4
See also SATA 21
Hull, Eric Traviss
See Harnan, Terry
Hull, Eugene L(eslie) 1928- ... 37-40R
Hull, George F. 1909(?)-1974 Obituary ... 53-56
Hull, Gloria T(heresa Thompson)
1944- ... CANR-25
Earlier sketch in CA 108
See also BW
Hull, H. Braxton
See Jacobs, Helen Hull
Hull, Helen (Rose) 1888(?)-1971 ... CAP-1
Obituary ... 29-32R
Earlier sketch in CA 9-10
Hull, J(ohn) H(owarth) E(ric) 1923- ... 25-28R
Hull, Jesse Redding
See Hull, Jessie Redding
Hull, Jessie Redding 1932- ... 109
See also SATA 51
Hull, Katharine 1921-1977 ... 29-32R
See also SATA 23
Hull, Lynda 1954- ... 126
Hull, Marion A(da) 1911- ... 105
Hull, Opal
See Lehnus, Opal (Hull)
Hull, Oswald 1919- ... 25-28R
Hull, R(ichard) F(rancis) C(arrington)
1913(?)-1974 Obituary ... 53-56
Hull, Raymona E. 1907- ... 116
Hull, Raymond 1919-1985 ... CANR-11
Obituary ... 116
Earlier sketch in CA 25-28R
Hull, Richard W. 1940- ... CANR-25
Earlier sketch in CA 45-48
Hull, Roger H. 1942- ... 25-28R
Hull, Suzanne W(hite) 1921- ... 125
Hull, William (Doyle) 1918- ... CANR-5
Earlier sketch in CA 13-14R
Hull, William E(dward) 1930- ... CANR-24
Earlier sketches in CA 17-18R, CANR-7
Hulland, J(ennifer) R(osemary) 1936- ... 122
Hulley, Clarence C(harles) 1905- ... 41-44R
Hulme, Hilda Mary 1914- ... 77-80
Hulme, Kathryn 1900-1981 ... CAP-1
Obituary ... 104
Earlier sketch in CA 9-10
Hulme, Keri 1947- ... 125
See also CLC 39
Hulme, T(homas) E(rnest) 1883-1917
Brief entry ... 117
See also DLB 19
See also TCLC 21
Hulme, William E(dward) 1920- ... CANR-5
Earlier sketch in CA 13-14R
Hulse, Clark 1947- ... 106
Hulse, Erroll 1931- ... CANR-21
Earlier sketch in CA 104
Hulse, James Warren 1930- ... 11-12R
Hulse, (Herman) LaWayne 1922- ... 29-32R
Hulse, Michael (William) 1955- ... 118
Hulse, Stewart H(arding), Jr. 1931- ... CANR-14
Earlier sketch in CA 33-36R
Hult, Ruby El 1912- ... 57-60
Hulteng, John L. 1921- ... CANR-13
Earlier sketch in CA 33-36R
Hultgren, Thor 1902- ... CAP-1
Earlier sketch in CA 17-18
Hultman, Charles W(illiam) 1930- ... CANR-1
Earlier sketch in CA 1R
Hults, Dorothy Niebrugge 1898- ... CAP-1
Earlier sketch in CA 9-10
See also SATA 6
Humbaraci, D(emir) Arslan 1923- ... 49-52
Humbard, (Alpha) Rex (Emmanuel) 1919-
Brief entry ... 111
Humber, William 1949- ... 124
Humble, Richard 1945- ... CANR-17
Earlier sketches in CA 45-48, CANR-2
Humble, William F(rank) 1948- ... 21-22R
Hume, Arthur W. J. G. Ord
See Ord-Hume, Arthur W. J. G.
Hume, Basil
See Hume, George Haliburton
Hume, (Alexander) Brit(ton) 1943- ... 126
Brief entry ... 119
Hume, Fergus(on Wright) 1859-1932
Brief entry ... 109
See also DLB 70
Hume, George Haliburton 1923- ... 126
Hume, John E. N., Jr. 1915-1986
Obituary ... 118
Hume, John Robert 1939- ... 106
Hume, Kathryn 1945- ... 57-60
Hume, Lotta Carswell ... CAP-1
Earlier sketch in CA 9-10
See also SATA 7
Hume, Martha 1947- ... 112
Hume, Paul Chandler 1915- ... 102
Hume, Robert D. 1944- ... CANR-12
Earlier sketch in CA 29-32R
Hume, Ruth Fox 1922-1980 Obituary ... 97-100
See also SATA 22, 26
Hume, Stephen 1947- ... 125
Humes, D(ollena) Joy 1921- ... 1R
Humes, H(arold) L. 1926- ... 7-8R
Humes, James C. 1934- ... CANR-1
Earlier sketch in CA 45-48
Humes, John Portner 1921-1985 Obituary ... 117
Humes, Samuel 1930- ... 7-8R
Humez, Jean McMahon 1944- ... 124
Humfrey, C.
See Osborne, C(harles) H(umfrey)
C(aulfeild)
Hummel, Berta 1909-1946 ... SATA-43
Hummel, Charles E. 1923- ... 19-20R
Hummel, Madeline
See Moore, Madeline (Roberta)
Hummel, Ray O(rvin), Jr. 1909- ... 33-36R
Hummel, Ruth Stevenson 1929- ... 7-8R
Hummel, Sister Maria Innocentia
See Hummel, Berta
Humphreville, Frances Tibbetts 1909- ... 9-10R
Humphrey, David C(hurchill) 1937- ... 85-88
Humphrey, Henry (III) 1930- ... 77-80
See also SATA 16
Humphrey, Hubert Horatio 1911-1978 ... 69-72
Obituary ... 73-76
Humphrey, J(ames) Edward 1918- ... 93-96
Humphrey, James (Earl) 1939- ... 45-48
Humphrey, James H(arry) 1911- ... CANR-23
Earlier sketches in CA 61-64, CANR-8
Humphrey, Michael (Edward) 1926- ... 29-32R
Humphrey, Paul 1915- ... 110
Humphrey, Robert L. 1923- ... 57-60
Humphrey, William 1924- ... 77-80
See also DLB 6
See also CLC 45
Humphreys, A(rthur) R(aleigh) 1911-1988
Obituary ... 126
Humphreys, Alexander J(eremiah)
1913- ... 33-36R
Humphreys, Alice Lee 1893- ... 7-8R
Humphreys, (Travers) Christmas
1901-1983 ... 77-80
Obituary ... 109
Humphreys, David 1752-1818 ... DLB-37
Humphreys, Emyr Owen 1919- ... CANR-24
Earlier sketches in CA 7-8R, CANR-3
See also DLB 15
See also CLC 47
Humphreys, Graham 1945- ... SATA-32
Humphreys, J(ohn) R(ichard) Adams
1918- ... CANR-22
Earlier sketch in CA 3R
Humphreys, Josephine 1945- Brief entry ... 121
See also CLC 34
Humphreys, (Robert Allan) Laud
1930-1988 ... 29-32R
Obituary ... 126
Humphreys, Mary Eglantyne Hill 1914- ... CANR-6
Earlier sketch in CA 7-8R
Humphreys, Susan L.
See Lowell, Susan
Humphreyville, Theresa R. 1918- ... 13-14R
Humphries, Adelaide M. 1898- ... CAP-1
Earlier sketch in CA 15-16
Humphries, Helen Speirs Dickie 1915- ... CAP-1
Earlier sketch in CA 9-10
Humphries, (John) Jefferson 1955- ... 114
Humphries, Mary 1905- ... 53-56
Humphries, (George) Rolfe 1894-1969 ... CANR-3
Obituary ... 25-28R
Earlier sketch in CA 5-6R
Humphries, Sydney Vernon 1907- ... 103
Humphry, Derek 1930- ... 41-44R
Humphrys, Geoffrey
See Humphrys, Leslie George
Humphrys, Leslie George 1921- ... 107
Humpstone, Charles Cheney 1931- ... 49-52
Huncke, Herbert 1915- ... DLB-16
Hundley, Joan Martin 1921- ... 45-48
Hundley, Norris (Cecil), Jr. 1935- ... CANR-8
Earlier sketch in CA 17-18R
Huneker, James Gibbons 1857-1921 ... DLB-71
Huneryager, S(herwood) G(eorge) 1933- ... 1R
Hungerford, Cy(rus Cotton) 1889(?)-1983
Obituary ... 109
Hungerford, Edward Buell 1900- ... 37-40R
Hungerford, Harold R(alph) 1928- ... 33-36R
Hungerford, Hesba (Fay) Brinsmead 1922- ... 124
Hungerford, Mary Jane 1913- ... 77-80
Hungerford, Pixie
See Brinsmead, H(esba) F(ay)
Hungry Wolf, Adolf 1944- ... 115
Hungry Wolf, Beverly 1950- ... 117
Hunker, Henry L. 1924- ... 15-16R
Hunkin, Timothy Mark Trelawney 1950- ... 102
See also SATA 53
Hunkins, Francis P(eter) 1938- ... 57-60
Hunkins, Lee(cynth) 1930- ... 108
Hunnex, Milton D(eVerne) 1917- ... 29-32R
Hunnings, Neville March 1929- ... CANR-12
Earlier sketch in CA 25-28R
Hunnisett, Basil 1923- ... 119
Hunsaker, David M(alcolm) 1944- ... 33-36R
Hunsberger, Edith Mae 1927- ... 109
Hunsberger, Warren S(eabury) 1911- ... 41-44R
Hunsehe, Raymond W. 1891(?)-1983
Obituary ... 111

Hunsinger, George 1945- 65-68
Hunsinger, Paul 1919- 33-36R
Hunsinger, Walter (William) 1923- 122
Hunt, Abby Campbell 1933(?)-1985
Obituary 116
Hunt, Barbara
See Watters, Barbara H(unt)
Hunt, Bernice (Kohn) 1920- CANR-21
Earlier sketch in CA 9-10R
Hunt, Charles Butler 1906- 110
Hunt, Charlotte
See Hodges, Doris M(arjorie)
Hunt, Chester L. 1912- CANR-5
Earlier sketch in CA 13-14R
Hunt, Clarence
See Holman, C(larence) Hugh
Hunt, Dave
See Hunt, David C(harles Hadden)
Hunt, David (Wathen Stather) 1913- 102
Hunt, David 1942- 33-36R
Hunt, David C(harles Hadden) 1926- CANR-9
Earlier sketch in CA 57-60
Hunt, David C(urtis) 1935- CANR-16
Earlier sketch in CA 89-92
Hunt, Douglas 1918- 13-14R
Hunt, E(verette) Howard, Jr. 1918- CANR-2
Earlier sketch in CA 45-48
See also CLC 3
See also AITN 1
Hunt, E. K. 1937- 77-80
Hunt, Earl B. 1933- 93-96
Hunt, Earl W(ilbur) 1926- 85-88
Hunt, Edgar H(ubert) 1909- CAP-1
Earlier sketch in CA 9-10
Hunt, Elgin F(raser) 1895-1978 4R
Hunt, Everett Lee 1890(?)-1984 Obituary 112
Hunt, Florine E(lizabeth) 1928- 15-16R
Hunt, Francis CANR-26
Earlier sketches in CA 19-20, CAP-2
Hunt, Frazier 1885-1967 Obituary 93-96
Hunt, Garry Edward 1942- 115
Hunt, Geoffrey 1915(?)-1974 Obituary 104
Hunt, George Laird 1918- 49-52
Hunt, George W(illiam) 1937- 120
Hunt, Gill
See Tubb, E(dwin) C(harles)
Hunt, Gladys M. 1926- CANR-13
Earlier sketch in CA 29-32R
Hunt, (Leslie) Gordon 1906-1970 CAP-2
Earlier sketch in CA 29-32
Hunt, H(arry) Draper 1935- 37-40R
Hunt, Harrison
See Ballard, (Willis) Todhunter
Hunt, Herbert James 1899-1973 Obituary 89-92
Hunt, Hugh 1911- CANR-3
Earlier sketch in CA 5-6R
Hunt, Ignatius 1920- 17-18R
Hunt, Inez Whitaker 1899- CAP-1
Earlier sketch in CA 17-18
Hunt, Irene 1907- CANR-8
Earlier sketch in CA 19-20R
See also SATA 2
See also DLB 52
See also CLR 1
Hunt, J(oseph) McVicker 1906- 37-40R
Hunt, J. William, Jr. 1930- 53-56
Hunt, James Gerald 1932- CANR-14
Earlier sketch in CA 65-68
Hunt, (Henry Cecil) John 1910- 109
Hunt, John
See Paine, Lauran (Bosworth)
Hunt, John Dixon 1936- CANR-17
Earlier sketch in CA 85-88
Hunt, John J. 1929- 33-36R
Hunt, John P(aul) 1915-1988 33-36R
Obituary 124
Hunt, John W(esley) 1927- 21-22R
Hunt, Joyce 1927- CANR-22
Earlier sketch in CA 106
See also SATA 31
Hunt, June 1944- 103
Hunt, Kari (Eleanor B.) 1920- 41-44R
Hunt, Kellogg W(esley) 1912- 7-8R
Hunt, Kenneth E(dward) 1917(?)-1978
Obituary 104
Hunt, Kyle
See Creasey, John
Hunt, Lawrence J. 1920- 7-8R
Hunt, Leon (Gibson) 1931- 65-68
Hunt, Linda 1940- 106
See also SATA 39
Hunt, Mabel Leigh 1892-1971 CAP-1
Obituary 106
Earlier sketch in CA 9-10
See also SATA 1, 26
Hunt, Maurice P. 1915- 25-28R
Hunt, Morton M(agill) 1920- CANR-21
Earlier sketch in CA 7-8R
See also SATA 22
Hunt, Nan
See Ray, N(ancy) L(ouise)
Hunt, Nancy (Ridgely) 1927- 103
Hunt, Nigel
See Greenbank, Anthony Hunt
Hunt, Noel Aubrey Bonavia
See Bonavia-Hunt, Noel Aubrey
Hunt, Noreen 1931- 103
Hunt, Norman C.
See Crowther-Hunt, Norman Crowther
Hunt, Norman Crowther Crowther
See Crowther-Hunt, Norman Crowther
Hunt, Patricia 1922(?)-1983 Obituary 120
Hunt, Patricia Joan CANR-21
Earlier sketch in CA 103
Hunt, Penelope
See Napier, Priscilla
Hunt, Peter 1922- 5-6R
Hunt, Peter (Leonard) 1945- 113
Hunt, Ray(mond) C(hamp), Jr. 1919- 122
Hunt, Raymond G(eorge) 1928- CANR-3
Earlier sketch in CA 11-12R
Hunt, Richard (Paul) 1921- 73-76
Hunt, Richard N(orman) 1931- 11-12R
Hunt, Robert C(ushman) 1934- CANR-9
Earlier sketch in CA 21-22R
Hunt, Sam 1946- 110
Hunt, Tim(othy A.) 1949- 121
Hunt, Todd T. 1938- 15-16R
Hunt, V. Daniel 1939- 111
Hunt, Virginia Lloyd 1888(?)-1977
Obituary 73-76
Hunt, William 1934- CANR-3
Earlier sketch in CA 49-52
Hunt, William A(lvin) 1903-1986 Obituary 118
Hunt, William Dudley, Jr. 1922-1987 CANR-14
Obituary 122
Earlier sketch in CA 33-36R
Hunt, William Gibbes 1791-1833 DLB-73
Hunt, William R(aymond) 1929- 93-96
Hunter, A(rchibald) M(acbride) 1906- CANR-6
Earlier sketch in CA 9-10R
Hunter, Alan (James Herbert) 1922- CANR-18
Earlier sketches in CA 9-10R, CANR-3
Hunter, Allan A(rmstrong) 1893- 7-8R
Hunter, Anson
See Orrmont, Arthur
Hunter, Beatrice Trum 1918- CANR-22
Earlier sketches in CA 19-20R, CANR-7
Hunter, Bernice Thurman 1922- 119
See also SATA 45
Hunter, Bruce (William) 1952- 123
Hunter, C. Bruce 1917- 61-64
Hunter, Captain Marcy
See Ellis, Edward S(ylvester)
Hunter, Christine
See Hunter, Maud L(ily)
Hunter, Clark 124
Hunter, Clingham, M.D.
See Adams, William Taylor
Hunter, Dard 1883-1966 CAP-1
Obituary 25-28R
Earlier sketch in CA 15-16
Hunter, Doris A. 1929- 37-40R
Hunter, Edith Fisher 1919- 107
See also SATA 31
Hunter, Edward 1902-1978 7-8R
Obituary 77-80
Hunter, Elizabeth
See de Guise, Elizabeth (Mary Teresa)
Hunter, Evan 1926- CANR-5
Earlier sketch in CA 7-8R
See also SATA 25
See also DLBY 82
See also CLC 11, 31
Hunter, Frederick J(ames) 1916- 33-36R
Hunter, Geoffrey (Basil Bailey) 1925- 33-36R
Hunter, George E.
See Ellis, Edward S(ylvester)
Hunter, Gordon C. 1924- 106
Hunter, Hall
See Marshall, Edison
Hunter, Henry MacGregor 1929-
Brief entry 109
Hunter, Hilda 1921- 49-52
See also SATA 7
Hunter, Howard Eugene 1929- 41-44R
Hunter, J(ames) A(lston) H(ope)
1902- CANR-14
Earlier sketches in CA 9-10, CAP-1
Hunter, J(ohn) F(letcher) M(acGregor)
1924- 37-40R
Hunter, J(ames) Paul 1934- CANR-24
Earlier sketches in CA 21-22R, CANR-9
Hunter, Jack D(ayton) 1921- CANR-6
Earlier sketch in CA 7-8R
Hunter, James H(ogg) 1890- 85-88
Hunter, Jane (Harlow) 1949- 125
Hunter, Jim 1939- CANR-7
Earlier sketch in CA 11-12R
See also DLB 14
Hunter, Joan
See Yarde, Jeanne Betty Frances
Hunter, Joe
See McNeilly, Wilfred (Glassford)
Hunter, John
See Ballard, (Willis) Todhunter
and Hunter, Maud L(ily)
Hunter, John M(erlin) 1921- 13-14R
Hunter, Kim 1922- 61-64
Hunter, Kristin (Eggleston) 1931- CANR-13
Earlier sketch in CA 13-14R
See also BW
See also SATA 12
See also DLB 33
See also CLC 35
See also CLR 3
See also AITN 1
Hunter, Leigh
See Etchison, Birdie L(ee)
Hunter, Leona Wesley
See Greif, Martin
Hunter, Leslie S(tannard) 1890-1983 CAP-1
Obituary 110
Earlier sketch in CA 19-20
Hunter, Lieutenant Ned
See Ellis, Edward S(ylvester)
Hunter, Louis C. 1898(?)-1984 Obituary 112
Hunter, Louise H(arris) 41-44R
Hunter, Mac
See Hunter, Henry MacGregor
Hunter, Marjorie 1922- 69-72
Hunter, Marvin H(erbert) 1930-
Brief entry 111
Hunter, Mary Vann 1937- 107
Hunter, Maud L(ily) 1910- CANR-4
Earlier sketch in CA 9-10R
Hunter, Mel 1927- 93-96
See also SATA 39
Hunter, Michael (Cyril William) 1949- 104
Hunter, Milton R(eed) 1902-1975
Obituary 104
Hunter, Mollie
See McIlwraith, Maureen Mollie Hunter
See also CLC 21
Hunter, Ned
See Ellis, Edward S(ylvester)
Hunter, Norman (George Lorimer)
1899- CANR-15
Earlier sketch in CA 93-96
See also SATA 26
Hunter, Norman Charles 1908-1971
Obituary 29-32R
See also DLB 10
Hunter, Richard 1923-1981 Obituary 105
Hunter, Robert E(dwards) 1940- CANR-15
Earlier sketch in CA 41-44R
Hunter, Robert Grams 1927- 93-96
Hunter, Rodello
See Calkins, Rodello
Hunter, Sam 1923- CANR-8
Earlier sketch in CA 13-14R
Hunter, Stephen 1946- CANR-19
Earlier sketch in CA 102
Hunter, Thomas 1932- 108
Hunter, Tim 1947- 85-88
Hunter, Valancy
See Meaker, Eloise
Hunter, Vickie
See Hunter, Victoria Alberta
Hunter, Victoria Alberta 1929- 7-8R
Hunter, William A(lbert) 1908- 13-14R
Hunter, William B(ridges), Jr. 1915- 77-80
Hunter Blair, Pauline (Clarke) 1921- 29-32R
See also SATA 3
Hunter Blair, Peter 1912-1982 Obituary 108
Brief entry 107
Hunting, Constance 1925- CANR-23
Earlier sketch in CA 45-48
Huntington, Anna Hyatt 1876-1973
Obituary 45-48
Huntington, (E.) Gale 1902- 11-12R
Huntington, Harriet E(lizabeth) 1909- CANR-5
Earlier sketch in CA 7-8R
See also SATA 1
Huntington, Henry S., Jr. 1892-1981
Obituary 103
Huntington, John (Willard) 1940- 112
Huntington, Madge 1937- 126
Huntington, Samuel P(hillips) 1927- CANR-1
Earlier sketch in CA 1R
Huntington, Thomas W(aterman)
1893-1973 Obituary 45-48
Huntington, Virginia 1889- 21-22R
Huntley, Chester Robert 1911-1974 97-100
Obituary 49-52
See also AITN 1
Huntley, Chet
See Huntley, Chester Robert
Huntley, Frank Livingstone 1902- 33-36R
Huntley, H(erbert) E(dwin) 1892- CAP-1
Earlier sketch in CA 13-14
Huntley, James L(ewis) 1914- 101
Huntley, James Robert 1923- CANR-12
Earlier sketch in CA 29-32R
Huntley, Timothy Wade 1939- 102
Hunton, Mary
See Gilzean, Elizabeth Houghton-Blanchet
Hunton, Richard E(dwin) 1924- 21-22R
Huntress, Keith G(ibson) 1913- 7-8R
Huntsberger, John (Paul) 1931- 5-6R
Huntsberry, William E(mery) 1916- CANR-2
Earlier sketch in CA 3R
See also SATA 5
Hunzicker, Beatrice Plumb 1886- 7-8R
Hupka, Robert 1919- 61-64
Huppe, Bernard F. 1911- CANR-3
Earlier sketch in CA 5-6R
Huppert, George 1934- 29-32R
Hurd, Charles (Wesley Bolick)
1903-1968 CAP-1
Earlier sketch in CA 11-12
Hurd, Clement (G.) 1908-1988 CANR-24
Obituary 124
Earlier sketches in CA 29-32R, CANR-9
See also SATA 2
Hurd, Douglas (Richard) 1930- CANR-10
Earlier sketch in CA 25-28R
Hurd, Edith (Thacher) 1910- CANR-24
Earlier sketches in CA 13-14R, CANR-9
See also SATA 2
Hurd, Florence 1918- CANR-19
Earlier sketch in CA 103
Hurd, John C(oolidge), Jr. 1928- 17-18R
Hurd, Michael John 1928- CANR-12
Earlier sketch in CA 65-68
Hurd, (John) Thacher 1949- CANR-24
Earlier sketch in CA 106
See also SATA 45, 46
Hure, Anne 1918- 11-12R
Hureau, Jean (Emile Pierre) 1915-
Brief entry 110
Hurewitz, J(acob) C(oleman) 1914- CANR-2
Earlier sketch in CA 1R
hurkey, rooan
See Holzapfel, Rudolf Patrick
Hurkos, Peter 1911-1988 Obituary 125
Hurlbut, Allen F. 1910-1983 Obituary 110
Hurlbut, Cornelius S(earle), Jr. 1906- CANR-11
Earlier sketch in CA 25-28R
Hurlbutt, Robert H(arris), III 1924- 15-16R
Hurley, Alfred F(rancis) 1928- 97-100
Hurley, Doran 1900-1964 5-6R
Hurley, F(orrest) Jack 1940- CANR-25
Earlier sketch in CA 45-48
Hurley, Jane (Hezel) 1928- 15-16R
Hurley, John 1928- CANR-13
Earlier sketch in CA 33-36R
Hurley, John J(erome) 1930- 104
Hurley, Kathy 1947- 109
Hurley, Leslie J(ohn) 1911- 49-52
Hurley, Mark J(oseph, Jr.) 1919- 53-56
Hurley, Neil 1925- 29-32R
Hurley, Vic 1898-1978 3R
Obituary 103
Hurley, W(illiam) Maurice 1916- 37-40R
Hurley, Wilfred G(eoffrey) 1895-1973 CAP-2
Obituary 45-48
Earlier sketch in CA 17-18
Hurley, William James, Jr. 1924- 9-10R
Hurlimann, Bettina
See Huerlimann, Bettina
See also SATA 34, 39
Hurlimann, Ruth
See Huerlimann, Ruth
See also SATA 31, 32
Hurlock, Elizabeth B. 1898- 41-44R
Hurlow, (Wilma) Janet 1939- 118
Hurm, Ken 1934- 106
Hurne, Ralph 1932- 21-22R
Hurok, Sol(omon) 1888-1974 Obituary 49-52
Hursch, Carolyn J(udge) 41-44R
Hurst, A(lexander) A(nthony) 1917- 5-6R
Hurst, Charles G., Jr. 1928- 37-40R
Hurst, Fannie 1889-1968 CAP-1
Obituary 25-28R
Earlier sketch in CA 15-16
Hurst, G(eorge) Cameron III 1941- 85-88
Hurst, James M(arshall) 1924- 29-32R
Hurst, M(ichael) E(liot) Eliot
See Eliot Hurst, M(ichael) E(liot)
Hurst, Michael (Charles) 1931- 23-24R
Hurst, Norman 1944- 53-56
Hurst, Richard Maurice 1938- 101
Hurst, Virginia Radcliffe 1914(?)-1976
Obituary 69-72
Hurstfield, Joel 1911-1980 CANR-6
Obituary 102
Earlier sketch in CA 53-56
Hurston, Zora Neale 1903-1960 85-88
See also BW
See also DLB 51
See also CLC 7, 30
Hurt, Freda M(ary) E(lizabeth) 1911- 103
Hurt, Henry 1942- 106
Hurt, James (Riggins) 1934- CANR-23
Earlier sketch in CA 45-48
Hurt, Ray Douglas 1946- 125
Hurtgen, Andre O(scar) 1932- 81-84
Hurvitz, Leon Nahum 1923- 106
Hurwitz, Abraham B. 1905- 29-32R
Hurwitz, Edith F(arber) 1941- 108
Hurwitz, Howard L(awrence) 1916- 37-40R
Hurwitz, Johanna 1937- CANR-25
Earlier sketches in CA 65-68, CANR-10
See also SATA 20
Hurwitz, Ken 1948- 33-36R
Hurwitz, Samuel J(ustin) 1912-1972 CAP-2
Earlier sketch in CA 25-28
Hurwitz, Stephan 1901-1981 Obituary 103
Hurwood, Bernhardt J. 1926-1987 25-28R
Obituary 121
See also SATA 12, 50
Husar, John 1937- 81-84
Husband, William Hollow 1899(?)-1978
Obituary 81-84
Huse, Dennis P(aul) 1944- 115
Huseman, Richard C. 1939- Brief entry 109
Husen, Torsten 1916- CANR-9
Earlier sketch in CA 23-24R
Huser, (La)Verne (Carl) 1931- CANR-22
Earlier sketch in CA 106
Huson, Paul (Anthony) 1942- CANR-12
Earlier sketch in CA 29-32R
Huss, Roy 1927- 25-28R
Hussein, Taha 1889-1973 Obituary 45-48
Husserl, Edmund (Gustav Albrecht)
1859-1938 Brief entry 116
Hussey, David Edward 1934- CANR-9
Earlier sketch in CA 57-60
Hussey, John A(dam) 1913- 61-64
Hussey, Maurice Percival 1925- 9-10R
Hussman, Lawrence Eugene, Jr. 1932- 115
Huste, Annemarie 1943- 57-60
Husted, Darrell 1931- 81-84
Huston, Anne Marshall 116
Huston, Fran
See Miller, R. S.
Huston, James Alvin 1918- CANR-15
Earlier sketch in CA 41-44R
Huston, John (Marcellus) 1906-1987 73-76
Obituary 123
See also DLB 26
See also CLC 20
Huston, Luther A. 1888- CAP-2
Earlier sketch in CA 21-22
Huston, Mervyn James 1912- CANR-8
Earlier sketch in CA 61-64
Hustvedt, Lloyd (Merlyn) 1922- 21-22R
Huszar, George B(ernard) de 1919-19(?) CAP-2
Earlier sketch in CA 19-20
Hutchcroft, Vera 1923- 102
Hutchens, Eleanor Newman 1919- 15-16R
Hutchens, John Kennedy 1905- 65-68
Hutchens, Paul 1902-1977 61-64
See also SATA 31
Hutcheson, Richard G(ordon), Jr. 1921- 107
Hutchin, Kenneth Charles 1908- 110
Hutchings, Alan Eric 1910- 4R

Hutchings, Arthur (James Bramwell)
1906- CANR-6
Earlier sketch in CA 7-8R
Hutchings, Bill
See Hutchings, William Bruce
Hutchings, Edward, Jr. 1912- 126
Hutchings, Margaret (Joscelyne) 1918- .. CANR-3
Earlier sketch in CA 9-10R
Hutchings, Monica Mary 1917- 11-12R
Hutchings, Patrick A(elfred) 1929- CANR-4
Earlier sketch in CA 53-56
Hutchings, Raymond 1924- CANR-12
Earlier sketch in CA 33-36R
Hutchings, William Bruce 1948- 111
Hutchins, Carleen Maley 1911- 17-18R
See also SATA 9
Hutchins, Charles R. 1928- 123
Hutchins, Francis Gilman 1939- 21-22R
Hutchins, Hazel J. 1952- 123
See also SATA 51
Hutchins, Maude (Phelps McVeigh) 61-64
Hutchins, Myldred Flanigan 1910- 112
Hutchins, Pat 1942- CANR-15
Earlier sketch in CA 81-84
See also SATA 15
Hutchins, Robert Maynard 1899-1977 69-72
Hutchins, Ross Elliott 1906- CANR-5
Earlier sketch in CA 9-10R
See also SATA 4
Hutchinson, Arthur Stuart Menteth
1879-1971 Obituary 29-32R
Hutchinson, C(ecil) Alan 1914- 29-32R
Hutchinson, David (Christopher) 1960- 119
Hutchinson, Eliot Dole 1900- 61-64
Hutchinson, G(eorge) Evelyn 1903- CANR-14
Earlier sketches in CA 13-14, CAP-1
Hutchinson, George 1920-1980
Obituary 97-100
Hutchinson, H(ugh) Lester 1904- 17-18R
Hutchinson, John 1921- 45-48
Hutchinson, Joseph (Burtt) 1902-1988 109
Obituary 124
Hutchinson, Margaret Massey 1904- CAP-1
Earlier sketch in CA 15-16
Hutchinson, Mary Jane 1924- 106
Hutchinson, Michael E. 1925- 17-18R
Hutchinson, (William Patrick Henry) Pearse
1927- 103
Hutchinson, Peter 1943- CANR-8
Earlier sketch in CA 61-64
Hutchinson, Ray Coryton 1907-1975 .... CANR-3
Obituary 61-64
Earlier sketch in CA 4R
Hutchinson, Richard Wyatt 1894-1970 .....7-8R
Obituary 89-92
Hutchinson, Robert 1924- 15-16R
Hutchinson, Thomas 1711-1780 .... DLB-30, 31
Hutchinson, Vernal 1922- 49-52
Hutchinson, Veronica S(omerville)
1895-1961 Obituary 111
Hutchinson, Warner Alton, Jr. 1929- 110
Hutchinson, William K(enneth) 1945- 102
Hutchinson, William M(iller) 1916- 112
Hutchison, (William) Bruce 1901- 103
Hutchison, Chester Smith 1902- CAP-2
Earlier sketch in CA 17-18
Hutchison, (Dorothy) Dwight
1890(?)-1975 Obituary 57-60
Hutchison, E(arl) R. 1926- CANR-10
Earlier sketch in CA 25-28R
Hutchison, Emery 1919(?)-1985 Obituary ... 116
Hutchison, Harold Frederick 1900- CANR-4
Earlier sketch in CA 2R
Hutchison, Jane Campbell 1932- 37-40R
Hutchison, John Alexander 1912- 69-72
Hutchison, Sidney C(harles) 1912- 25-28R
Hutchison, William Robert 1930- 21-22R
Huth, Angela 1938- CANR-20
Earlier sketch in CA 85-88
Huth, Marta 1898- Brief entry 106
Huth, Mary Jo(sephine) 1929- 103
Huth, Tom 1941- 97-100
Huthmacher, J. Joseph 1929- 21-22R
See also SATA 5
Hutmacher (MacLean), Barbara Anne
1926- 112
Hutman, Norma Louise 1935- 25-28R
Hutschnecker, Arnold A. 1898- 81-84
Hutson, Anthony Brian Austen 1934- 93-96
Hutson, James H(oward) 1937- 85-88
Hutson, Jan 1932- 106
Hutson, Joan 1929- 89-92
Hutt, Maurice George 1928- 15-16R
Hutt, Max L. 1908- 57-60
Hutt, W(illiam) H(arold) 1899-1988 57-60
Obituary 125
Huttenback, Robert A. 1928- 25-28R
Huttig, Jack W(ilfred) 1919- 53-56
Huttner, Matthew 1915-1975 Obituary 104
Hutto, Nelson (Allen) 1904- CAP-1
Earlier sketch in CA 9-10
See also SATA 20
Hutton, Ann 1929- 108
Hutton, Clarke 1898- 107
Hutton, Geoffrey 1928- 41-44R
Hutton, Ginger
See Hutton, Virginia Carol
Hutton, Harold 1912- 102
Hutton, J(oseph) Bernard 1911-? CANR-14
Earlier sketch in CA 21-22R
Hutton, J(ohn) H(enry) 1885-1968 ...... CAP-1
Earlier sketch in CA 13-14
Hutton, James 1902-1980 77-80
Hutton, John (Harwood) 1928- 107
Hutton, Malcolm 1921- CANR-24
Earlier sketch in CA 107
Hutton, Richard 1949- 109
Hutton, Richard Holt 1826-1897 .... DLB-57
Hutton, Virginia Carol 1940- 77-80
Hutton, Warwick 1939- CANR-9
Earlier sketch in CA 61-64
See also SATA 20
Huus, Helen 1913- CANR-1
Earlier sketch in CA 3R
Huvos, Kornel 1913- 49-52
Huws, Daniel 1932- 81-84
Huxhold, Harry N(orman) 1922- 61-64
Huxley, Aldous Leonard 1894-1963 85-88
See also DLB 36
See also CLC 1, 3, 4, 5, 8, 11, 18, 35
Huxley, Anthony J(ulian) 1920- CANR-22
Earlier sketches in CA 9-10R, CANR-7
Huxley, Elspeth (Josceline Grant) 1907- ...77-80
Huxley, George 1932- 23-24R
Huxley, Herbert H(enry) 1916- 7-8R
Huxley, Judith 1927(?)-1983 Obituary 111
Huxley, Julian (Sorell) 1887-1975 ...... CANR-7
Obituary 57-60
Earlier sketch in CA 11-12R
Huxley, Laura Archera 15-16R
Huxley, T. H. 1825-1895 .... DLB-57
Huxley-Blythe, Peter J(ames) 1925- 17-18R
Huxtable, Ada Louise (Landman) 1921- 120
Huxtable, (William) John (Fairchild)
1912- 13-14R
Huy, Nguyen Ngoc
See Nguyen Ngoc Huy
Huyck, Dorothy Boyle 1925(?)-1979
Obituary 89-92
Huyck, Margaret Hellie 1939- 49-52
Huyck, Peter H(azelwood) 1940- 107
Huyck, Willard 1945(?)- Brief entry 111
Huygen, Wil(librord Joseph) 1922- CANR-15
Earlier sketch in CA 81-84
Huyghe, Rene (Louis) 1906- CANR-20
Earlier sketch in CA 81-84
Huyler, Jean Wiley 1935- CANR-13
Earlier sketch in CA 69-72
Huynh, Quang Nhuong 1946- 107
Huysmans, Charles Marie Georges
1848-1907 Brief entry 104
Huysmans, Joris-Karl
See Huysmans, Charles Marie Georges
See also TCLC 7
Huzar, Eleanor G(oltz) 1922- 85-88
Hy, Ronald John 1942- 115
Hyam, Ronald 1936- 97-100
Hyams, Barry 1911- 15-16R
Hyams, Edward (Solomon) 1910-1975 .. CANR-8
Obituary 61-64
Earlier sketch in CA 5-6R
Hyams, Joe
See Hyams, Joseph
Hyams, Joseph 1923- CANR-22
Earlier sketches in CA 17-18R, CANR-7
Hyatt, Betty H(ale) 1927- 125
Hyatt, Carole S. 1935- 93-96
Hyatt, Daniel
See James, Daniel (Lewis)
Hyatt, I. Ralph 1927- 115
Hyatt, J(ames) Philip 1909- 9-10R
Hyatt, Richard Herschel 1944- 101
Hybels, Bill 1951- 126
Hybels, Saundra 1938- 57-60
Hyde, Anthony 1946(?)- CLC-42
Hyde, Charles K(eith) 1945- 116
Hyde, Dayton O(gden) 25-28R
See also SATA 9
Hyde, Douglas (Arnold) 1911- Brief entry ... 109
Hyde, Elisabeth 1953- 122
Hyde, Fillmore 1896(?)-1970 Obituary 104
Hyde, George E. 1882- 7-8R
Hyde, Harford M(ontgomery) 1907- 5-6R
Hyde, Hawk
See Hyde, Dayton O(gden)
Hyde, Janet Shibley 1948- CANR-10
Earlier sketch in CA 65-68
Hyde, L(ouis) K(epler, Jr.) 1901- CAP-1
Earlier sketch in CA 13-14
Hyde, Laurence 1914- 17-18R
Hyde, Margaret Oldroyd 1917- CANR-1
Earlier sketch in CA 1R
See also SATA 1, 42
See also CLC 21
Hyde, Mary (Morley Crapo) 1912- 49-52
Hyde, Shelley
See Reed, Kit
Hyde, Simeon, Jr. 1919- 21-22R
Hyde, Stuart W(allace) 1923- 61-64
Hyde, Tracy Elliot
See Venning, Corey
Hyde, W. Lewis 1945- 104
Hyde, Wayne Frederick 1922- 4R
See also SATA 7
Hyden, (Sten Gustav Vilhelm) Goeran
1938- CANR-20
Earlier sketch in CA 103
Hyder, Clyde Kenneth 1902- 33-36R
Hyder, O(liver) Quentin 1930- Brief entry ... 105
Hyer, James Edgar 1923- 77-80
Hyer, Paul Van 1926- 104
Hyers, M. Conrad 1933- 33-36R
Hyett, Barbara Helfgott 1945- 120
Hygen, Johan B(ernitz) 1911- 23-24R
Hyink, Bernard L(ynn) 1913- 45-48
Hyland, Douglas K(irk) S(amuel) 1949- 124
Hyland, Drew A(lan) 1939- CANR-15
Earlier sketch in CA 89-92
Hyland, Jean Scammon 1926- 49-52
Hyland, Paul 1947- 121
Hyland, (Henry) Stanley 1914- 9-10R
Hylander, Clarence J(ohn) 1897-1964 ......7-8R
See also SATA 7
Hylton, Delmer P(aul) 1920- 17-18R
Hyma, Albert 1893- 19-20R
Hyman, Alan 1910- 102
Hyman, Ann 1936- 53-56
Hyman, B(arbara) D(avis) 1947- 125
Hyman, David N(eil) 1943- CANR-22
Earlier sketches in CA 57-60, CANR-7
Hyman, Dick 1904- CANR-7
Earlier sketch in CA 19-20R
Hyman, Frieda Clark 1913- 5-6R
Hyman, Harold M(elvin) 1924- 5-6R
Hyman, Helen Kandel 1920- 105
Hyman, Herbert H(iram) 1918-1985 .....23-24R
Obituary 118
Hyman, Irwin A(braham Meltzer) 1935- 93-96
Hyman, Jackie (Diamond) 1949- 108
Hyman, Jeremy (A.) 125
Hyman, Lawrence W. 1919- 41-44R
Hyman, Paula 1946- 89-92
Hyman, Richard J(oseph) 1921- CANR-1
Earlier sketch in CA 45-48
Hyman, Robin P(hilip) 1931- CANR-15
Earlier sketch in CA 41-44R
See also SATA 12
Hyman, Ronald T. 1933- CANR-25
Earlier sketches in CA 23-24R, CANR-9
Hyman, Sidney 1917- 102
Hyman, Stanley Edgar 1919-1970 85-88
Obituary 25-28R
Hyman, Trina Schart 1939- CANR-2
Earlier sketch in CA 49-52
See also SATA 7, 46
See also DLB 61
Hymans, Jacques Louis 1937- 57-60
Hymes, Dell H(athaway) 1927- 15-16R
Hymes, Lucia M(anley) 1907- 5-6R
See also SATA 7
Hymoff, Edward 1924- 17-18R
Hynd, Alan 1904(?)-1974 Obituary 45-48
Hyndman, Donald W(illiam) 1936- 57-60
Hyndman, Jane Andrews Lee
1912-1978 .... CANR-5
Obituary 89-92
Earlier sketch in CA 7-8R
See also SATA 1, 23, 46
Hyndman, Robert Utley 1906-1973 97-100
See also SATA 18
Hynds, Frances Jane 1929- 77-80
Hyne, C(harles) J(ohn) Cutcliffe (Wright)
1865-1944 Brief entry 111
Hynek, J(osef) Allen 1910-1986 81-84
Obituary 119
Hyneman, Charles S(hang) 1900-1985 ... CAP-1
Obituary 114
Earlier sketch in CA 13-14
Hynes, Samuel (Lynn) 1924- 105
Hyslop, Beatrice F. 1900(?)-1973
Obituary 45-48
Hyslop, James H(ervey) 1854-1920
Brief entry 123
Hyslop, Lois Boe 1908- 41-44R
Hysom, John L(eland, Jr.) 1934- 115
Hytier, Jean (Pierre) 1899-1983 Obituary ... 109

I

I. W.
See Watts, Isaac
Iacocca, Lee
See Iacocca, Lido Anthony
Iacocca, Lido Anthony 1924- 125
Iacone, Salvatore J(oseph) 1945- CANR-15
Earlier sketch in CA 85-88
Iacuzzi, Alfred 1896-1977 Obituary 73-76
Ian, Janis 1951- Brief entry 105
See also CLC 21
Iannelli, Richard 1949- 118
Ianni, Francis A(nthony) J(ames) 1926- ...45-48
Ianniello, Lynne Young 1925- 19-20R
Iannone, Jeanne
See Balzano, Jeanne (Koppel)
See also SATA 7
Iannone, Ron(ald Vincent) 1940- 53-56
Iannuzzi, John Nicholas 1935- 93-96
Iatrides, John O(restes) 1932- CANR-10
Earlier sketch in CA 25-28R
Ibanez, Carlos G. Velez
See Velez-Ibanez, Carlos G(uillermo)
Ibanez, Vicente Blasco
See Blasco Ibanez, Vicente
Ibarguengoitia, Jorge 1928-1983 124
Obituary 113
See also CLC 37
Ibarra, Crisostomo
See Yabes, Leopoldo Y(abes)
Ibbotson, Eva 1925- CANR-15
Earlier sketch in CA 81-84
See also SATA 13
Ibbotson, M. C(hristine) 1930- 25-28R
See also SATA 5
Ibele, Oscar Herman 1917- Brief entry 106
Ibingira, G(race) S(tuart) K(atebarirwe)
1932- 103
Ibrahim, Abdel-Sattar 1939- 69-72
Ibrahim, Ibrahim Abdelkader 1923- 15-16R
Ibsen, Henrik (Johan) 1828-1906
Brief entry 104
See also TCLC 2, 8, 16
Ibuka, Masaru 1908- 102
Ibuse, Masuji 1898- CLC-22
Icaza Coronel, Jorge 1906-1978 89-92
Obituary 85-88
Ice, Jackson Lee 1925- 25-28R
Icenhower, Joseph Bryan 1913- CANR-5
Earlier sketch in CA 7-8R
Ichikawa, Kon 1915- 121
See also CLC 20
Ichikawa, Satomi 1949- 126
Brief entry 116
See also SATA 36, 47
Icks, Robert J(oseph) 1900- 41-44R
Icolari, Daniel Leonardo 1942- 17-18R
Iddon, Don 1913(?)-1979 Obituary 89-92
Ide, Richard S(myth) 1943- 120
Idelsohn, Abraham Zevi 1882-1938
Brief entry 109
Iden, William
See Green, William M(ark)
Idle, Eric 1943- 116
See also CLC 21
Idone, Christopher 1937- 122
Idriess, Ion L. 1891(?)-1979 Obituary 89-92
Iduarte (Foucher), Andres 1907- 33-36R
Idyll, C(larence) P(urvis) 1916- CANR-8
Earlier sketch in CA 11-12R
Ierardi, Francis B. 1886-1970 Obituary 104
Ifft, James B(rown) 1935- 53-56
Ifkovic, Edward 1943- CANR-8
Earlier sketch in CA 61-64
Iggers, Georg G(erson) 1926- 25-28R
Iggers, Wilma Abeles 1921- 25-28R
Iggulden, John Manners 1917- 11-12R
Iglauer, Edith
See Daly, Edith Iglauer
Iglehart, Alfreda P(aulette) 1950- 109
Iglehart, Louis Tillman 1915-1981
Obituary 104
Iglesias, Mario 1924- CANR-25
Earlier sketch in CA 45-48
Iglitzin, Lynne 1931- 41-44R
Ignatieff, George 1913- 119
Ignatow, David 1914- 9-10R
See also CAAS 3
See also DLB 5
See also CLC 4, 7, 14, 40
Ignotus, Paul 1901-1978 .... CANR-8
Obituary 77-80
Earlier sketch in CA 7-8R
Igo, John N., Jr. 1927- 15-16R
Igoe, James (Thomas) 1935- 108
Igoe, (Lesly) Lynn Moody 1937- 108
Ihde, Don 1934- CANR-13
Earlier sketch in CA 33-36R
Ihimaera, Witi 1944- 77-80
See also CLC 46
Ihnat, Steve 1935(?)-1972 Obituary 33-36R
Iiams, Thomas M. Jr. 1928- 11-12R
Iino, (David) Norimoto 1918- 61-64
Ike, Nobutaka 1916- 21-22R
Ikeda, Daisaku 1928- 85-88
Ikeda, Kiyoshi 1928- Brief entry 104
Ikejiani, Okechukwu 1917- 17-18R
Ikenberry, Oliver Samuel 1908- 53-56
Ikerman, Ruth C. (Percival) 1910- 15-16R
Ikle, Fred Charles 1924- 45-48
Iko, Momoko 1940- CANR-14
Earlier sketch in CA 77-80
Ilardi, Vincent 1925- 29-32R
Ilardo, Joseph A(nthony) 1944- 89-92
Ilchman, Warren Frederick 1934- CANR-1
Earlier sketch in CA 2R
Iles, Bert
See Ross, Zola Helen
Iles, Francis
See Cox, A(nthony) B(erkeley)
Ilf, Ilya
See Fainzilberg, Ilya Arnoldovich
See also TCLC 21
Ilg, Frances L(illian) 1902-1981 107
Obituary 104
Ilgen, Thomas
See Ilgen, Thomas L.
Ilgen, Thomas L. 1946- 120
Ilich, John 1933- 106
Ilie, Paul 1932- CANR-10
Earlier sketch in CA 25-28R
Illan, Jose M(anuel) 1924- 45-48
Illes, Robert E(noch) 1914- 103
Illiano, Antonio 1934- 41-44R
Illich, Ivan D. 1926- CANR-10
Earlier sketch in CA 53-56
See also AITN 2
Illick, Joseph E. 1934- 17-18R
Illingworth, Frank (M. B.) 1908- CANR-5
Earlier sketch in CA 7-8R
Illingworth, John 1904(?)-1980
Obituary 97-100
Illingworth, Neil 1934- 15-16R
Illingworth, Ronald Stanley 1909- CANR-3
Earlier sketch in CA 9-10R
Illwitzer, Elinor G. 1934- 29-32R
Illyes, Gyula 1902-1983 114
Obituary 109
Ilowite, Sheldon A. 1931- 106
See also SATA 27
Ilsey, Dent
See Chapman, John Stanton Higham
Ilsley, Dent
See Chapman, John Stanton Higham
Ilsley, Velma (Elizabeth) 1918- CANR-3
Earlier sketch in CA 11-12R
See also SATA 12
Ilson, Robert (Frederick) 1937- 124
Iltinger, Paula 1944- 124
Ilyin, Mikhail Andreyevich 1878-1942
Brief entry 119
Imamura, Anne E(lizabeth Sommers)
1946- 126
Imamura, Shigeo 1922- 77-80
Imber, Gerald 1941- 89-92
Imbrie, John 1925- Brief entry 107
Imbrie, Katherine P(almer) 1952- 104

Imbs, Bravig (Wilbur Eugene) 1904-1946
Brief entry ... 107
See also DLB 4
Imerti, Arthur D. 1915- ... 37-40R
Imfeld, Al 1935- ... CANR-13
Earlier sketch in CA 69-72
Imhoof, Maurice Lee 1930- Brief entry ... 108
Immaculata, Sister
See Maxwell, Sister Mary
Immel, Mary Blair 1930- ... CANR-6
Earlier sketch in CA 15-16R
See also SATA 28
Immerman, Leon Andrew 1952- ... 103
Immerwahr, Sara Anderson 1914-
Brief entry ... 108
Immoos, Thomas 1918- ... CANR-15
Earlier sketch in CA 85-88
Immroth, John Phillip 1936-1976 ... CAP-2
Earlier sketch in CA 33-36
Imperato, Pascal James 1937- Brief entry ... 106
Impey, Oliver (Richard) 1936- ... 108
Imrie, Richard
See Pressburger, Emeric
Inada, Lawson Fusao 1938- ... 33-36R
Inalcik, Halil 1916- ... 49-52
Inayat-Khan, Pir Vilayat 1916- ... 93-96
Inbau, Fred E. 1909- ... CANR-1
Earlier sketch in CA 2R
Inber, Vera Mikhailovna 1893-1972
Obituary ... 37-40R
Ince, Basil A(ndre) 1933- ... 57-60
Ince, Martin (Jeffrey) 1952- ... 110
Ince, W(alter) N(ewcombe) 1927(?)-1988
Obituary ... 126
Inch, Morris Alton 1925- ... CANR-11
Earlier sketch in CA 29-32R
Inchbald, Elizabeth 1753-1821 ... DLB-39
Inciardi, James A(nthony) 1939- ... CANR-8
Earlier sketch in CA 61-64
Inclan, Ramon (Maria) del Valle
See Valle-Inclan, Ramon (Maria) del
Incogniteau, Jean-Louis
See Kerouac, Jean-Louis Lebrid de
Ind, Allison 1903-1974 ... CAP-1
Earlier sketch in CA 15-16
Indelman, Elchanan Chonon 1908(?)-1983
Obituary ... 109
Indelman-Yinnon, Moshe 1895(?)-1977
Obituary ... 73-76
Inderlied, Mary Elizabeth 1945- ... 49-52
Indik, Bernard P(aul) 1932- ... 33-36R
Inez, Colette 1931- ... 37-40R
Infield, Glenn (Berton) 1920-1981 ... CANR-5
Obituary ... 103
Earlier sketch in CA 7-8R
Ing, Dean 1931- ... CANR-23
Earlier sketch in CA 106
Ingalls, Daniel H(enry) H(olmes) 1916- ... 17-18R
Ingalls, David Sinton 1899-1985 Obituary ... 116
Ingalls, Jeremy 1911- ... 4R
Ingalls, Rachel (Holmes) 1940- Brief entry ... 123
See also CLC 42
Ingalls, Robert Paul 1941- ... 110
Brief entry ... 107
Ingard, K(arl) Uno 1921- ... 33-36R
Ingarden, Roman Witold 1893-1970
Obituary ... 113
Ingate, Mary 1912- ... 73-76
Ingbar, Mary Lee 1926- ... 41-44R
Inge, M(ilton) Thomas 1936- ... CANR-25
Earlier sketches in CA 17-18R, CANR-9
Inge, W. R.
See Inge, William Ralph
Inge, William Motter 1913-1973 ... 9-10R
See also DLB 7
See also CDALB 1941-1968
See also CLC 1, 8, 19
Inge, William Ralph 1860-1954
Brief entry ... 116
Ingelfinger, Franz Joseph 1910-1980
Obituary ... 97-100
Ingelow, Jean 1820-1897 ... SATA-33
See also DLB 35
Ingermann, Helena Antonia Maria Elisabeth Dermout
See Dermout-Ingermann, Helena Antonia Maria Elisabeth
Ingersol, Jared
See Paine, Lauran (Bosworth)
Ingersoll, David E(dward) 1939- ... 41-44R
Ingersoll, John H. 1925- ... 73-76
Ingersoll, Ralph (McAllister) 1900-1985 ... CAP-1
Obituary ... 115
Earlier sketch in CA 13-14
Ingersoll, Robert Franklin 1933- ... 104
Ingham, Colonel Frederic
See Hale, Edward Everett
Ingham, Daniel
See Lambot, Isobel
Ingham, Jennie 1944- ... 108
Ingham, Kenneth 1921- ... 110
Brief entry ... 108
Ingham, (Ann) Mary 1947- ... 120
Ingham, Richard Arnison 1935- ... 104
Ingham, Robert E(dward) 1934- ... 108
Ingilby, Joan Alicia 1911- ... 9-10R
Ingle, Clifford 1915- ... 29-32R
Ingle, Dwight Joyce 1907- ... CAP-1
Earlier sketch in CA 9-10
Ingleby, Terry 1901- ... 106
Ingles, G(lenn) Lloyd 1901- ... CAP-1
Earlier sketch in CA 19-20
Inglis, Brian (St. John) 1916- ... CANR-23
Earlier sketches in CA 19-20R, CANR-7
Inglis, David Rittenhouse 1905- ... CANR-5
Earlier sketch in CA 7-8R
Inglis, James 1927- ... 21-22R
Inglis, John K(enneth) 1933- ... 106
Inglis, R(obert) M(orton) G(all) 1910-1975 ... CANR-8
Earlier sketch in CA 13-14R
Inglis, Ruth Langdon 1927- ... CANR-1
Earlier sketch in CA 49-52
Inglis, Stuart J(ohn) 1923- ... 41-44R
Ingman, Nicholas 1948- ... SATA-52
Ingold, Gerard (Antoine Hubert) 1922- ... CANR-23
Earlier sketch in CA 106
Ingold, Klara (Schmid) 1913- ... 61-64
Ingraham, Barton L(ee) 1930- ... 119
Ingraham, Joseph Holt 1809-1860 ... DLB-3
Ingraham, Leonard W(illiam) 1913- ... 25-28R
See also SATA 4
Ingraham, Mark H(oyt) 1896-1982 ... 61-64
Obituary ... 109
Ingraham, Vernon L. 1924- ... 33-36R
Ingram, Anne (Whitten) Bower 1937- ... 102
Ingram, (Mildred Rebecca) Bowen (Prewett) ... 37-40R
Ingram, Collingwood 1880-1981 ... 61-64
Obituary ... 103
Ingram, Derek (Thynne) 1925- ... 9-10R
Ingram, Forrest L(eo) 1938- ... 53-56
Ingram, Gregory Keith 1944- ... 77-80
Ingram, Helen Moyer 1937- ... CANR-22
Earlier sketch in CA 105
Ingram, James C(arlton) 1922- ... 5-6R
Ingram, (Archibald) Kenneth 1882-1965 ... CAP-1
Earlier sketch in CA 13-14
Ingram, Thomas Henry 1924- ... CANR-2
Earlier sketch in CA 49-52
Ingram, Tom
See Ingram, Thomas Henry
Ingram, William 1930- ... 41-44R
Ingram, Willis J.
See Harris, Mark
Ingrams, Doreen 1906- ... CANR-12
Earlier sketch in CA 33-36R
See also SATA 20
Ingrams, Richard (Reid) 1937- ... 103
Ingrao, Charles W(illiam) 1948- ... 101
Ingstad, Helge Marcus 1899- ... 65-68
Ingwersen, Faith 1934- ... CANR-15
Earlier sketch in CA 69-72
Ingwersen, Niels 1935- ... CANR-15
Earlier sketch in CA 69-72
Inkeles, Alex 1920- ... CANR-1
Earlier sketch in CA 3R
Inkiow, (Janakiev) Dimiter 1932- ... 101
Inkster, Ian 1949- ... 113
Inlow, Gail M(aurice) 1910- ... CANR-4
Earlier sketch in CA 5-6R
Inman, Arthur Crew 1895-1963 ... 122
Inman, Billie (Jo) Andrew 1929- ... CANR-12
Earlier sketch in CA 29-32R
Inman, Jack (Ingles) 1919- ... 25-28R
Inman, John 1805-1850 ... DLB-73
Inman, Robert (Anthony) 1931- ... 17-18R
Inman, Will 1923- ... CANR-12
Earlier sketch in CA 25-28R
Inmerito
See Javitch, Daniel Gilbert
Inmon, W(illiam) H(arvey) 1945- ... 110
Innaurato, Albert (F.) 1948(?)- ... 122
Brief entry ... 115
See also CLC 21
Innerhofer, Franz 1944- ... 101
Innes, Brian 1928- ... CANR-14
Earlier sketch in CA 23-24R
Innes, C(atherine) L(ynette) 1940- ... 123
Innes, Christopher David 1941- ... 107
Innes, Frank C. 1934- ... 45-48
Innes, Hammond
See Hammond Innes, Ralph
Innes, Jean
See Saunders, Jean
Innes, Michael
See Stewart, J(ohn) I(nnes) M(ackintosh)
Innes, Ralph Hammond
See Hammond Innes, Ralph
Innes, Rosemary E(lizabeth Jackson) ... 25-28R
Innes, Stephen 1946- ... 116
Innis, Donald Quayle 1924- ... 41-44R
Innis, Pauline B. (Coleman) 1918- ... CANR-4
Earlier sketch in CA 4R
Inoue, Yukitoshi 1945- ... 25-28R
Inouye, Daniel K(en) 1924- ... 25-28R
Insall, Donald W(illiam) 1926- ... 61-64
Insana, Tino 1948- ... 123
Insel, Deborah (June) 1949- ... 110
Insight, James
See Coleman, Robert William Alfred
Insingel, Mark 1935- Brief entry ... 110
Insolia, Anthony Edward 1926- ... 120
Intriligator, Michael D(avid) 1938- ... 53-56
Inwood, M(ichael) J(ames) 1944- ... 117
Inyart, Gene
See Namovicz, Gene Inyart
See also SATA 6
Ionesco, Eugene 1912- ... 9-10R
See also SATA 7
See also CLC 1, 4, 6, 9, 11, 15, 41
Ionescu, Ghita G. 1913- ... 103
Iongh, Mary (Dows Herter Norton) Crena de
See Crena de Iongh, Mary (Dows Herter Norton)
Iorio, James 1921- ... 61-64
Iorio, John 1925- ... 49-52
Iorizzo, Luciano J(ohn) 1930- ... 73-76
Ipcar, Dahlov (Zorach) 1917- ... CANR-9
Earlier sketch in CA 19-20R
See also SATA 1, 49
Ippolito, Donna 1945- ... 104
Ipsen, D(avid) C(arl) 1921- ... 33-36R
Iqbal, Afzal 1919- ... CANR-26
Earlier sketches in CA 61-64, CANR-10
Iqbal, Muhammad 1873-1938 ... TCLC-28
Iqbal, Sabiha 1950- ... 111
Iranek-Osmecki, Kazimierz 1897-1984 ... 49-52
Obituary ... 113
Irby, Kenneth (Lee) 1936- ... CANR-22
Earlier sketch in CA 69-72
Ireland, David 1927- ... 25-28R
Ireland, Earl (Crowell) 1928- ... 7-8R
Ireland, Joe C. 1936- ... 73-76
Ireland, Kevin (Mark) 1933- ... 73-76
Ireland, Norma Olin 1907- ... CANR-3
Earlier sketch in CA 9-10R
Ireland, Patrick
See O'Doherty, Brian
Ireland, Robert M(ichael) 1937- ... CANR-25
Earlier sketch in CA 45-48
Iremonger, Lucille (d'Oyen) ... CANR-6
Earlier sketch in CA 9-10R
Iremonger, Valentin 1918- ... 101
Ireson, Barbara (Francis) 1927- ... CANR-21
Earlier sketch in CA 5-6R
Ireton, Rollo
See Shirley, Ralph
Irfani, Suroosh 1947- ... 118
Irgang, Jacob 1930- ... 85-88
Iribarne, Louis 1940- ... 123
Irion, Mary Jean 1922- ... 23-24R
Irion, Paul E(rnst) 1922- ... 23-24R
Irion, Ruth (Hershey) 1921- ... 65-68
Irish, Donald P(aul) 1919- ... 49-52
Irish, Jerry ... 125
Irish, Marian D(oris) 1909- ... 9-10R
Irish, Richard K. 1932- ... 65-68
Irish, William
See Hopley-Woolrich, Cornell George
Iriye, Akira 1934- ... CANR-11
Earlier sketch in CA 25-28R
Irland, David
See Green, Julien (Hartridge)
Iron, Ralph
See Schreiner, Olive (Emilie Albertina)
Ironmaster, Maximus
See Wilkinson, John (Donald)
Ironside, Henry Allan 1876-1951
Brief entry ... 115
Ironside, Virginia 1944- ... 120
Irsfeld, John H(enry) 1937- ... 65-68
Irvin, Bob
See Irvin, Robert W.
Irvin, Fred 1914- ... SATA-15
Irvin, Rea 1881-1972 Obituary ... 93-96
Irvin, Robert W. 1933-1980 Obituary ... 103
Irvine, Betty Jo 1943- ... 77-80
Irvine, Demar (Buel) 1908- ... 33-36R
Irvine, John Henry 1951- ... 119
Irvine, Keith 1924- ... 29-32R
Irvine, Lucy 1956- ... 118
Irvine, R(obert) R(alstone) 1936- ... CANR-15
Earlier sketch in CA 81-84
Irvine, Sidney H(erbert) 1931- Brief entry ... 106
Irvine, William 1906-1964 Obituary ... 106
Irving, Alexander
See Hume, Ruth Fox
Irving, Blanche M(cDaniel) 1904- ... 114
Irving, Brian William 1932- ... 53-56
Irving, Clifford Michael 1930- ... CANR-2
Earlier sketch in CA 2R
See also AITN 1
Irving, Clive 1933- ... CANR-22
Earlier sketch in CA 85-88
Irving, David (John Cawdell) 1938- ... CANR-25
Earlier sketch in CA 13-14R
Irving, Edward B(urroughs), Jr. 1923-
Brief entry ... 112
Irving, Gordon 1918- ... 25-28R
Irving, Henry
See Kanter, Hal
Irving, John (Winslow) 1942- ... 25-28R
See also DLB 6
See also DLBY 82
See also CLC 13, 23, 38
Irving, R(obert) L(ock) Graham 1877-1969 ... CAP-1
Earlier sketch in CA 15-16
Irving, Robert
See Adler, Irving
Irving, T(homas) B(allantine) 1914- ... 37-40R
Irving, Washington 1783-1859 ... YABC-2
See also DLB 3, 11, 30, 59, 73, 74
See also CDALB 1640-1865
See also SSC 2
Irwin, Ann(abelle Bowen) 1915- ... CANR-19
Earlier sketch in CA 101
See also SATA 38, 44
Irwin, Constance Frick 1913- ... CANR-5
Earlier sketch in CA 4R
See also SATA 6
Irwin, Cynthia C.
See Irwin-Williams, Cynthia (Cora)
Irwin, David 1933- ... 53-56
Irwin, Francis William 1905- Brief entry ... 105
Irwin, G. H.
See Palmer, Raymond A.
Irwin, George 1910-1971 ... 41-44R
Irwin, Grace (Lilian) 1907- ... 17-18R
See also DLB 68
Irwin, Graham W(ilkie) 1920- ... 121
Brief entry ... 118
Irwin, Hadley
See Hadley, Lee
and Irwin, Ann(abelle Bowen)
Irwin, Inez Haynes 1873-1970 ... 102
Irwin, James W. 1891(?)-1977 Obituary ... 73-76
Irwin, John T(homas) 1940- ... 53-56
Irwin, John V(aleur) 1915- ... CANR-1
Earlier sketch in CA 45-48
Irwin, Keith Gordon 1885-1964 ... 7-8R
See also SATA 11
Irwin, Margaret 1889-1967 Obituary ... 93-96
Irwin, P. K.
See Page, P(atricia) K(athleen)
Irwin, (Joseph) Paul 1940- ... 107
Irwin, Raymond 1902- ... CAP-1
Earlier sketch in CA 9-10
Irwin, Robert (Graham) 1946- ... 121
Irwin, Ruth Beckey 1906- ... 29-32R
Irwin, Theodore 1907- ... 65-68
Irwin, Vera Rushforth 1913- ... 33-36R
Irwin, W(illiam) R(obert) 1915- ... 65-68
Irwin, Will(iam Henry) 1873-1948
Brief entry ... 117
See also DLB 25
Irwin-Williams, Cynthia (Cora) 1936- ... CANR-1
Earlier sketch in CA 45-48
Isaac, Erich 1928- ... 45-48
Isaac, Glynn Llewelyn 1937-1985
Obituary ... 117
Isaac, Joanne 1934- ... 25-28R
See also SATA 21
Isaac, Joseph Ezra 1922- ... 115
Isaac, Paul E(dward) 1926- ... 19-20R
Isaac, Rael Jean (Isaacs) 1933- ... 17-18R
Isaac, Rhys L(lywelyn) 1937- ... 113
Isaac, Stephen 1925- ... 33-36R
Isaacs, Alan 1925- ... CANR-3
Earlier sketch in CA 11-12R
Isaacs, Bernard 1924- ... 107
Isaacs, E. Elizabeth 1917- ... 7-8R
Isaacs, Edith Somborn 1884-1978
Obituary ... 77-80
Isaacs, Harold Robert 1910-1986 ... CANR-2
Obituary ... 119
Earlier sketch in CA 3R
Isaacs, Jacob
See Kranzler, George G(ershon)
Isaacs, Neil D. 1931- ... CANR-9
Earlier sketch in CA 7-8R
Isaacs, Norman Ellis 1908- ... 81-84
Isaacs, Stan 1929- ... 15-16R
Isaacs, Stephen D(avid) 1937- ... 81-84
Isaacs, Susan (Sutherland Fairhurst) 1885-1948 Brief entry ... 120
Isaacs, Susan 1943- ... CANR-20
Earlier sketch in CA 89-92
See also CLC 32
Isaacson, Joel 1930- Brief entry ... 114
Isaacson, Robert L. 1928- ... CANR-7
Earlier sketch in CA 17-18R
Isaacson, Walter (Seff) 1952- ... 112
Isaak, Robert A(llen) 1945- ... CANR-13
Earlier sketch in CA 61-64
Isadora, Rachel Brief entry ... 111
See also SATA 32
See also CLR 7
Isais, Juan M. 1926- ... 29-32R
Isakovsky, Mikhail Vasilyevich 1900-1973
Obituary ... 41-44R
Isaksson, Ulla (Margareta Lundberg) 1916- Brief entry ... 109
Isard, Walter 1919- ... 114
Brief entry ... 112
Isban, Samuel 1905- ... CANR-2
Earlier sketch in CA 49-52
Isbister, Clair
See Isbister, Jean Sinclair
Isbister, Jean Sinclair 1915- ... CANR-18
Earlier sketches in CA 3R, CANR-1
Ise, John 1885-196(?) ... CAP-1
Earlier sketch in CA 13-14
Isely, Flora Kunigunde Duncan
See Duncan, Kunigunde
Isely, Helen Sue (Pearson) 1917-1978 ... 7-8R
Obituary ... 120
Iseminger, Gary 1937- ... 37-40R
Isenberg, Irwin M. 1931-1979 ... CANR-11
Earlier sketch in CA 19-20R
Isenberg, Seymour 1930- ... 33-36R
Isenhour, Thomas Lee 1939- ... 57-60
Iser, Wolfgang 1926- ... 57-60
Ishak, Fayek (Matta) 1922- ... 41-44R
Ishak, Yusof bin 1910(?)-1970 Obituary ... 104
Isham, Charlotte H(ickock) 1912- ... 73-76
See also SATA 21
Isham, Linda (Rose) 1938- Brief entry ... 107
Ishee, John A. 1934- ... CANR-18
Earlier sketch in CA 25-28R
Isherwood, Christopher (William Bradshaw) 1904-1986 ... 13-14R
Obituary ... 117
See also DLB 15
See also DLBY 86
See also CLC 1, 9, 11, 14, 44
Isherwood, Robert M. 1935- ... 126
Ishida, Takeshi 1923- ... CANR-16
Earlier sketch in CA 97-100
Ishigo, Estelle 1899- ... 61-64
Ishiguro, Kazuo 1954- ... 120
See also CLC 27
Ishikawa Takuboku 1886(?)-1912
Brief entry ... 113
See also TCLC 15
Ishino, Iwao 1921- ... 19-20R
Ish-Kishor, Judith 1892-1972 ... 3R
Obituary ... 103
See also SATA 11
Ish-Kishor, Sulamith 1896-1977 ... 73-76
Obituary ... 69-72
See also SATA 17
Ishlon, Deborah 1925- ... 4R
Ishmael, Woodi 1914- ... SATA-31
Ishmole, Jack 1924- ... 49-52

Ishwaran, K(arigoudar) 1922- 49-52
Isichei, Elizabeth 1939- CANR-5
Earlier sketch in CA 53-56
Isis
See Torbett, Harvey Douglas Louis
Iskander, Fazil 1929- 102
See also CLC 47
Islam, A(bul) K(hair) M(uhammed) Aminul
1933- 41-44R
Islam, Kazi Nazrul 1899(?)-1976
Obituary 69-72
Isle, Walter (Whitfield) 1933- 25-28R
Isler, Betty
See Isler, Elizabeth
Isler, Elizabeth 1915- 114
Ismach, Arnold H(arvey) 1930- 85-88
Ismael, Tareq Y. 125
Ismail, A. H. 1923- 25-28R
Isogai, Hiroshi 1940- 102
Ispahani, Mirza Abol Hassan 1902-1981
Obituary 108
Israel, Abby 1942- 107
Israel, Charles E(dward) 1920- 3R
Israel, Elaine 1945- CANR-9
Earlier sketch in CA 53-56
See also SATA 12
Israel, Fred L. 1934- CANR-12
Earlier sketch in CA 19-20R
Israel, Gerard 1928- 81-84
Israel, Jerry (Michael) 1941- 29-32R
Israel, John (Warren) 1935- 21-22R
Israel, Jonathan I. 1946- 109
Israel, Marion Louise 1882-1973 .... 3R
Obituary 103
See also SATA 26
Israel, Martin 1927- 109
Israel, Saul 1910- CAP-1
Earlier sketch in CA 15-16
Israeloff, Roberta 1952- 118
Israelowitz, Oscar 1949- 113
Issachar
See Stanford, J(ohn) K(eith)
Issawi, Charles Philip 1916- CANR-20
Earlier sketches in CA 7-8R, CANR-4
Isser, Natalie 1927- 53-56
Issler, Anne Roller 1892- 49-52
Iswolsky, Helene 1896-1975 .... 7-8R
Obituary 61-64
Italiaander, Rolf (Bruno Maximilian)
1913- CANR-23
Earlier sketches in CA 7-8R, CANR-6
Iterson, S(iny) R(ose) Van
See Van Iterson, S(iny) R(ose)
Itse, Elizabeth M(yers) 1930- CANR-1
Earlier sketch in CA 49-52
Itule, Bruce D. 1947- 125
Itzin, Catherine 1944- CANR-14
Earlier sketch in CA 77-80
Itzkoff, Seymour W(illiam) 1928- 33-36R
Ivan, Martha Miller Pfaff 1909- CAP-2
Earlier sketch in CA 19-20
Ivancevich, John M(ichael) 1939- CANR-25
Earlier sketch in CA 29-32R
Ivanov, Miroslav 1929- 81-84
Ivanov, Vsevolod Vyacheslavovich
1895-1963 Obituary 93-96
Ivanov, Vyacheslav Ivanovich 1866-1949
Brief entry 122
Ivask, George 1910-1986 Obituary 118
Ivask, Ivar Vidrik 1927- CANR-24
Earlier sketch in CA 37-40R
See also CLC 14
Ivens, Michael 1924- 7-8R
Ivens, Virginia R(uth) 1922- 105
Ivers, Larry E(dward) 1936- 77-80
Iversen, Gudmund R(agnvaldsson)
1934- CANR-4
Earlier sketch in CA 53-56
Iversen, Nick 1951- 73-76
Iverson, Genie 1942- CANR-9
Earlier sketch in CA 65-68
See also SATA 52
Iverson, Jeffrey (James) 1934- 105
Iverson, Lucille K(arin) 1925- 61-64
Iverson, Peter James 1944- 106
Ives, Burl (Icle Ivanhoe) 1909- 103
Ives, Charles Edward 1874-1954
Brief entry 113
Ives, Colta Feller 1943- 118
Ives, Edward D(awson) 1925- 25-28R
Ives, Lawrence
See Woods, Frederick
Ives, Morgan
See Bradley, Marion Zimmer
Ives, Sandy
See Ives, Edward D(awson)
Ives, Sumner 1911- 11-12R
Ivey, Allen E(ugene) 1933- CANR-2
Earlier sketch in CA 49-52
Ivey, Donald 1918- 89-92
Ivey, James Burnett 1925- 119
Ivey, Jim
See Ivey, James Burnett
Ivie, Robert L(ynn) 1945- 115
Ivie, Robert M. 1930- 9-10R
Ivnev, Riurik
See Kovalev, Mikhail A(leksandrovich)
Ivory, James (Francis) 1928- Brief entry 109
Ivry, Alfred Lyon 1935- CANR-1
Earlier sketch in CA 45-48
Ivy, Ralph 1938- 120
Iwamatsu, Jun Atsushi 1908- 73-76
See also SATA 14
Iwaszkiewicz, Jaroslaw 1894-1980
Obituary 97-100
Iwata, Masakazu 1917- 17-18R
Iyengar, B(ellur) K(rishnamachar)
S(undararaja) 1918- 97-100
Iyengar, K(odaganallur) R(amaswami)
Srinivasa 1908- CANR-8
Earlier sketch in CA 7-8R
Iyengar, S. Kesava 1894- 19-20R
Iyer, Raghavan (Narasimhan) 1930- CANR-22
Earlier sketches in CA 57-60, CANR-6
Izant, Grace Goulder 1893- CAP-1
Earlier sketch in CA 9-10
Izard, Barbara 1926- 29-32R
Izard, Carroll E(llis) 1923- CANR-4
Earlier sketch in CA 49-52
Izban, Samuel
See Isban, Samuel
Izenberg, Gerald N(athan) 1939- 105
Izenour, George Charles 1912- 93-96
Izzo, Herbert J(ohn) 1928- 41-44R

J

"J"
See Garrity, Joan Terry
J. L.-M.
See Lees-Milne, James
Jaanus, Maire 1940- 120
Jabay, Earl 1925- 21-22R
Jabber, Fuad (Amin)
See Jabber, Paul
Jabber, Paul 1943- 113
Jabez
See Nicol, Eric (Patrick)
Jablon, Howard 1939- 116
Jablonski, Edward 1922- CANR-18
Earlier sketches in CA 2R, CANR-2
Jablonski, Ronald E. 1929- Brief entry 104
Jablow, Martha M(oraghan) 1944- 112
Jabs, Carolyn 1950- 110
Jac, Lee
See Morton, Lee Jack, Jr.
Jaccottet, Philippe 1925- Brief entry 116
Jack, Daniel Thomson 1901-1984
Obituary 115
Jack, Donald Lamont 1924- CANR-3
Earlier sketch in CA 2R
Jack, Homer A(lexander) 1916- CANR-14
Earlier sketch in CA 41-44R
Jack, Ian 1923- 57-60
Jack, R. D. S.
See Jack, Ronald D(yce) S(adler)
Jack, R(obert) Ian 1935- CANR-3
Earlier sketch in CA 49-52
Jack, Ronald D(yce) S(adler) 1941- 120
Jackendoff, Ray S. 1945- CANR-6
Earlier sketch in CA 53-56
Jacker, Corinne L(itvin) 1933- 19-20R
Jackins, Harvey 1916- CANR-17
Earlier sketches in CA 49-52, CANR-1
Jacklin, Anthony 1944- 85-88
Jacklin, Tony
See Jacklin, Anthony
Jackman, E(dwin) R(ussell) 1894-19(?) .. CAP-1
Earlier sketch in CA 15-16
Jackman, Jarrell C(lark) 1943- 120
Jackman, Leslie (Arthur James) 1919- 29-32R
Jackman, Michael R. 1952- 120
Jackman, Robert W(illiam) 1946- 124
Jackman, Stuart 1922- CANR-18
Earlier sketch in CA 101
Jackman, Sydney W(ayne) 1925- CANR-19
Earlier sketches in CA 3R, CANR-1
Jackowska, Nicki 1942- 119
Jacks, L(awrence) P(earsall) 1860-1955
Brief entry 113
Jacks, Oliver
See Gandley, Kenneth Royce
Jackson, A(lexander) B(rooks) 1925- 104
Jackson, Alan 1938- 101
Jackson, Albert 1943- 93-96
Jackson, Albina
See Geis, Richard E(rwin)
Jackson, Allan 1905(?)-1976 Obituary 65-68
Jackson, Angela 1951- DLB-41
Jackson, Anna J. 1926- 103
Jackson, Anne 1896(?)-1984 .... SATA-37
Jackson, Anne
See Jackson, Anna J.
Jackson, Anthony 1926- CANR-11
Earlier sketch in CA 69-72
Jackson, Archibald Stewart 1922- 61-64
Jackson, Arlene M(arjorie) 1938- 118
Jackson, Arthur 1921- Brief entry 104
Jackson, B(erkley) R. 1937- 25-28R
Jackson, Barbara (Ward) 1914-1981 .... CANR-6
Obituary 103
Earlier sketch in CA 45-48
Jackson, Barbara Garvey Seagrave
1929- 21-22R
Jackson, Basil 1920- CANR-8
Earlier sketch in CA 57-60
Jackson, Blyden 1910- 57-60
Jackson, Brian 1933(?)-1983 Obituary 110
Jackson, Brooks 1941- 97-100
Jackson, Bruce 1936- 89-92
Jackson, C(hester) O(scar) 1901- CAP-1
Earlier sketch in CA 15-16
Jackson, C(aary) Paul 1902- CANR-6
Earlier sketch in CA 7-8R
See also SATA 6
Jackson, Caary
See Jackson, C(aary) Paul
Jackson, Carlton (Luther) 1933- 21-22R
Jackson, Carole 104
Jackson, Charles (Reginald) 1903-1968 101
Obituary 25-28R
Jackson, Charles O. 1935- 126
Brief entry 112
Jackson, Christine E(lisabeth) 1936- 121
Jackson, Clarence J.-L.
See Bulliet, Richard W(illiams)
Jackson, Dave
See Jackson, J. David
Jackson, David Cooper 1931- 109
Jackson, Derrick 1939- 77-80
Jackson, Diane 1938- 115
Jackson, Don(ald) D(e Avila) 1920-1968 .. CAP-1
Earlier sketch in CA 11-12
Jackson, Donald (Dean) 1919-1987 .... 19-20R
Obituary 124
Jackson, Donald Dale 1935- CANR-19
Earlier sketches in CA 49-52, CANR-1
Jackson, Dorothy Virginia Steinhauer
1924- 13-14R
Jackson, Douglas N. 1929- 37-40R
Jackson, E. F.
See Tubb, E(dwin) C(harles)
Jackson, Edgar (Newman) 1910- CANR-13
Earlier sketch in CA 77-80
Jackson, Ellen B. 1943- 110
Jackson, Elmore 1910- 112
Jackson, Esther Merle 1922- 15-16R
Jackson, Everatt
See Muggeson, Margaret Elizabeth
Jackson, Frank 1951- 120
Jackson, Franklin Jefferson
See Watkins, Mel
Jackson, Gabriel 1921- 21-22R
Jackson, Gabriele Bernhard 1934- 29-32R
Jackson, Geoffrey (Holt Seymour)
1915-1987 61-64
Obituary 123
See also SATA 53
Jackson, George (Lester) 1941-1971 120
Obituary 111
See also BW
Jackson, George D. 1929- 81-84
Jackson, George S(tuyvesant) 1906-1976 . CAP-1
Obituary 61-64
Earlier sketch in CA 17-18
Jackson, Gordon 1934- 104
Jackson, Graham 1949- 112
Jackson, Guida M. 1930- CANR-16
Earlier sketch in CA 93-96
Jackson, Harvey H(ardaway III) 1943- 119
Jackson, Helen Hunt 1830-1885 .... DLB-42, 47
Jackson, Henry 1912-1988 Obituary 126
Jackson, Henry Martin 1912-1983
Obituary 110
Jackson, Herbert C(ross) 1917- 9-10R
Jackson, Herbert G., Jr. 1928- 37-40R
Jackson, J. David 1944- CANR-18
Earlier sketch in CA 81-84
Jackson, J. P.
See Atkins, (Arthur) Harold
Jackson, Jacqueline 1928- 45-48
Jackson, Jacquelyne Johnson 1932- 37-40R
Jackson, James Charles 1936-1979
Obituary 117
Jackson, James P(ierre) 1925- CANR-14
Earlier sketch in CA 77-80
Jackson, Jesse 1908-1983 .... 25-28R
Obituary 109
See also BW
See also SATA 2, 29, 48
See also CLC 12
Jackson, John Archer 1929- 13-14R
Jackson, John E(dgar) 1942- 101
Jackson, John Howard 1932- 41-44R
Jackson, John N(icholas) 1925- CANR-14
Earlier sketch in CA 37-40R
Jackson, Jon A(nthony) 1938- 81-84
Jackson, Jonathan (Charles) 1966- 116
Jackson, Joseph 1924-1987 .... CANR-11
Obituary 122
Earlier sketches in CA 9-10, CAP-1
Jackson, Joseph Hollister 1912- 120
Jackson, Joy J(uanita) 1928- 29-32R
Jackson, Julia A(ndreasen) 1939- 119
Jackson, Karl (Dion) 1942- 102
Jackson, Katherine Gauss 1904-1975
Obituary 57-60
Jackson, (William) Keith 1928- CANR-8
Earlier sketch in CA 61-64
Jackson, Kenneth T. 1939- 21-22R
Jackson, Kevin Goldstein
See Goldstein-Jackson, Kevin
Jackson, Laura (Riding) 1901- 65-68
See also DLB 48
See also CLC 7
Jackson, Louise A(llen) 1937- 93-96
Jackson, Lowell G(eorge) 1934- 118
Jackson, Lucille
See Strauss, (Mary) Lucille Jackson
Jackson, Lydia 1900(?)-1983 Obituary 110
Jackson, MacDonald P. 1938- 125
Jackson, Mae 1946- 81-84
Jackson, Mahalia 1901-1972 Obituary 33-36R
Jackson, Margaret Weymouth 1895-1974
Obituary 115
See also AITN 1
Jackson, Mark
See Kurz, Ron
Jackson, Martin A(lan) 1941- 89-92
Jackson, Mary 1924- 61-64
Jackson, Melvin H. 1914(?)-1983
Obituary 111
Jackson, Michael P. 1947- 125
Jackson, Miles M(errill) 1929- 41-44R
Jackson, Neta J. 1944- CANR-18
Earlier sketch in CA 89-92
Jackson, Neville
See Glaskin, G(erald) M(arcus)
Jackson, Nora
See Tennant, Nora Jackson
Jackson, Norman 1932- CANR-17
Earlier sketch in CA 25-28R
Jackson, O. B.
See Jackson, C(aary) Paul
Jackson, Paul R. 1905- CAP-1
Earlier sketch in CA 15-16
Jackson, Percival Ephrates 1891-1970 .. CANR-3
Earlier sketch in CA 2R
Jackson, Philip W(esley) 1928- 23-24R
Jackson, R. E.
See Innes, Rosemary E(lizabeth Jackson)
Jackson, R(ichard) Eugene 1941- 109
Jackson, R(ichard) W(illiam) 1939- 119
Jackson, Reggie
See Jackson, Reginald Martinez
Jackson, Reginald Martinez 1946-
Brief entry 112
Jackson, Richard 1946- 110
Jackson, Richard A(rlen) 1937- 125
Jackson, Robert 1911- 9-10R
Jackson, Robert B(lake) 1926- CANR-6
Earlier sketch in CA 7-8R
See also SATA 8
Jackson, Robert J. 1936- 25-28R
Jackson, Robert L(owell) 1935- 73-76
Jackson, Robert Louis 1923- 109
Jackson, Robert S(umner) 1926- 29-32R
Jackson, Ruth A. 45-48
Jackson, Sally
See Kellogg, Jean (Defrees)
Jackson, Sam
See Trumbo, Dalton
Jackson, Sara
See Thomas, Sara (Sally)
Jackson, Scoop
See Jackson, Henry Martin
Jackson, Shirley 1919-1965 .... CANR-4
Obituary 25-28R
Earlier sketch in CA 1R
See also SATA 2
See also DLB 6
See also CDALB 1941-1968
See also CLC 11
Jackson, Stanley W(ebber) 1920- 124
Jackson, Stephanie
See Werner, Vivian
Jackson, Teague 1938- 93-96
Jackson, W(illiam) A(rthur) Douglas
1923- 45-48
Jackson, W(illiam) G(odfrey) F(othergill)
1917- 25-28R
Jackson, W(illiam) T(homas) H(obdell)
1915-1983 .... CANR-1
Obituary 117
Earlier sketch in CA 3R
Jackson, W(illiam) Turrentine 1915- 13-14R
Jackson, Wallace 1930- 114
Jackson, Wes 1936- CANR-22
Earlier sketches in CA 49-52, CANR-3
Jackson, William Vernon 1926- CANR-13
Earlier sketch in CA 23-24R
Jackson, Wilma 1929- CANR-12
Earlier sketch in CA 73-76
Jackson-Haight, Mabel V. 1912- 25-28R
Jaco, E(gbert) Gartly 1923- CANR-1
Earlier sketch in CA 1R
Jacob, Alaric 1909- 7-8R
Jacob, Charles E. 1931- CANR-5
Earlier sketch in CA 15-16R
Jacob, Ernest Fraser 1894-1971 .... CANR-3
Earlier sketch in CA 4R
Jacob, Francois 1920- 102
Jacob, Fred E. 1899- 105
Jacob, Gordon (Percival Septimus)
1895-1984 Obituary 113
Jacob, Helen Pierce 1927- 69-72
See also SATA 21
Jacob, Herbert 1933- 77-80
Jacob, John 1950- 126
Jacob, Margaret C(andee) 1943- CANR-16
Earlier sketch in CA 65-68
Jacob, (Cyprien-)Max 1876-1944
Brief entry 104
See also TCLC 6
Jacob, Nancy L. 1943- 29-32R
Jacob, Naomi Ellington 1884(?)-1964
Obituary 115
Jacob, Paul 1940- 103
Jacob, Philip E(rnest) 1914- CANR-4
Earlier sketch in CA 53-56
Jacobi, Carl (Richard) 1908- CAP-1
Earlier sketch in CA 13-14
Jacobi, Jolande (Szekacs) 1890- 9-10R
Jacobi, Kathy SATA-42
Jacobowitz, Ellen 1948- 121
Jacobs, Al(bert T.) 1903-1985 Obituary 115
Jacobs, Arthur (David) 1922- CANR-21
Earlier sketches in CA 7-8R, CANR-4
Jacobs, Barry (Douglas) 1932- 101
Jacobs, Bradford (McElderry) 1920- 121
Jacobs, Clyde E(dward) 1925- 37-40R
Jacobs, Dan(iel) N(orman) 1924- CANR-4
Earlier sketch in CA 7-8R
Jacobs, David Michael 1942- 57-60
Jacobs, Diane 1948- 73-76
Jacobs, Donald M(artin) 1937- 110
Jacobs, Flora Gill 1918- CANR-21
Earlier sketch in CA 1R
See also SATA 5
Jacobs, Francine 1935- CANR-18
Earlier sketches in CA 49-52, CANR-1
See also SATA 42, 43
Jacobs, Frank 1929- CANR-6
Earlier sketch in CA 13-14R
See also SATA 30

Jacobs, G(enevieve) Walker 1948- ... 49-52
Jacobs, Garry (Lawrence) 1946- ... 120
Jacobs, Glenn 1940- ... 29-32R
Jacobs, Harold 1941- ... 45-48
Jacobs, Harvey (Collins) 1915- ... 21-22R
Jacobs, Harvey 1930- ... 29-32R
Jacobs, Hayes B(enjamin) 1919- ... 11-12R
Jacobs, Helen Hull 1908- ... 9-10R
See also SATA 12
Jacobs, Herbert (Austin) 1903-1987 ... 15-16R
Obituary ... 122
Jacobs, Howard 1908- ... 65-68
Jacobs, James B. 1947- ... CANR-18
Earlier sketch in CA 101
Jacobs, Jane 1916- ... CANR-15
Earlier sketch in CA 21-22R
Jacobs, Jerome L. 1931- ... 89-92
Jacobs, Jerry 1932- ... CANR-11
Earlier sketch in CA 29-32R
Jacobs, Jill
See Bharti, Ma Satya
Jacobs, Jim 1942- ... 97-100
See also CLC 12
Jacobs, John (Kedzie) 1918- ... 23-24R
Jacobs, Joseph 1854-1916 Brief entry ... 111
See also SATA 25
Jacobs, Laurence Wile 1939- ... 53-56
Jacobs, Leah
See Gellis, Roberta L(eah Jacobs)
Jacobs, Leland Blair 1907- ... 73-76
See also SATA 20
Jacobs, Lewis 1906- ... 77-80
Jacobs, Linda C. 1943- ... 29-32R
See also SATA 21
Jacobs, Lou(is), Jr. 1921- ... CANR-9
Earlier sketch in CA 23-24R
See also SATA 2
Jacobs, Louis 1920- ... CANR-17
Earlier sketches in CA 3R, CANR-1
Jacobs, Melville 1902-1971 ... 4R
Obituary ... 103
Jacobs, Michael (Stephen) 1955- ... 123
Jacobs, Milton 1920- ... 37-40R
Jacobs, Nehama 1951- ... 126
Jacobs, Norman (Gabriel) 1924- ... 77-80
Jacobs, Paul 1918-1978 ... 13-14R
Obituary ... 73-76
Jacobs, Pepita Jimenez 1932- ... 19-20R
Jacobs, Philip E. 1914(?)-1985 Obituary ... 116
Jacobs, Renee 1962- ... 125
Jacobs, Robert D(urene) 1918- ... 41-44R
Jacobs, Roderick A(rnold) 1934- ... 23-24R
Jacobs, Ruth Harriet 1924- ... CANR-15
Earlier sketch in CA 89-92
Jacobs, Sheldon 1931- ... 106
Jacobs, Sophia Yarnall 1902- ... 106
Jacobs, Sue-Ellen 1936- ... 111
Jacobs, Susan
See Quinn, Susan
See also SATA 30
Jacobs, T. C. H.
See Pendower, Jacques
Jacobs, Travis Beal 1936- Brief entry ... 113
Jacobs, Vernon K(enneth) 1936- ... 117
Jacobs, Vivian 1916(?)-1981 Obituary ... 103
Jacobs, W(illiam) W(ymark) 1863-1943
Brief entry ... 121
See also TCLC 22
Jacobs, Walter Darnell 1922- ... 19-20R
Jacobs, Wilbur R(ipley) 1918- ... 15-16R
Jacobs, William Jay 1933- ... CANR-7
Earlier sketch in CA 57-60
See also SATA 28
Jacobsen, Hans Jacob 1901-1987
Obituary ... 122
Jacobsen, Josephine 1908- ... CANR-23
Earlier sketch in CA 33-36R
See also CLC 48
Jacobsen, Lydik S. 1897(?)-1976
Obituary ... 69-72
Jacobsen, Lyle E. 1929- ... 15-16R
Jacobsen, Marion Leach 1908- ... 61-64
Jacobsen, O(le) Irving 1896- ... CAP-2
Earlier sketch in CA 25-28
Jacobsen, Phebe R(obinson) 1922- ... 73-76
Jacobsen, Thorkild 1904- Brief entry ... 105
Jacobsohn, Gary J. 1946- ... 89-92
Jacobson, Bernard Isaac 1936- ... 109
Jacobson, Beverly 1927- ... 113
Jacobson, Boyd 1942- ... 118
Jacobson, Cliff 1940- ... 85-88
Jacobson, Dan 1929- ... CANR-25
Earlier sketches in CA 2R, CANR-2
See also DLB 14
See also CLC 4, 14
Jacobson, Daniel 1923- ... 53-56
See also SATA 12
Jacobson, David B(ernard) 1928- ... 53-56
Jacobson, Edith 1897(?)-1978 Obituary ... 85-88
Jacobson, Edmund 1888- ... 11-12R
Jacobson, Ethel ... 37-40R
Jacobson, Frederick L(awrence) 1938- ... 49-52
Jacobson, Gary Charles 1944- ... 109
Jacobson, Gerald F. 1922-1987 Obituary ... 123
Jacobson, Harold Karan 1929- ... CANR-19
Earlier sketches in CA 11-12R, CANR-3
Jacobson, Helen S(altz) 1921- ... CANR-6
Earlier sketch in CA 57-60
Jacobson, Howard Boone 1925- ... 2R
Jacobson, Jon 1938- ... 61-64
Jacobson, Julius 1922- ... 45-48
Jacobson, Marcia 1941- ... 115
Jacobson, Michael F. 1943- ... CANR-13
Earlier sketch in CA 77-80
Jacobson, Morris K(arl) 1906- ... CANR-3
Earlier sketch in CA 45-48
See also SATA 21
Jacobson, Nils Olof 1937- Brief entry ... 110
Jacobson, Nolan Pliny 1909- ... CANR-23
Earlier sketches in CA 21-22R, CANR-8
Jacobson, Robert (Marshall) 1940-1987 ... 89-92
Obituary ... 122
Jacobson, Rodolfo 1915- ... 41-44R
Jacobson, Sheldon A(lbert) 1903- ... 37-40R
Jacobson, Sibyl C(hafer) 1942- ... 65-68
Jacobson, Stephen A. 1934- ... 97-100
Jacobson, Steve
See Jacobson, Stephen A.
Jacobstein, J(oseph) Myron 1920- ... 53-56
Jacobus, Donald L(ines) 1887-1970 ... CANR-4
Earlier sketch in CA 5-6R
Jacobus, Elaine Wegener 1908- ... 33-36R
Jacobus, Lee A. 1935- ... CANR-13
Earlier sketch in CA 33-36R
Jacobus, Mary 1944- ... 105
Jacoby, Henry 1905- ... 77-80
Jacoby, Joseph E. 1944- ... 97-100
Jacoby, Neil H(erman) 1909-1979 ... CANR-10
Obituary ... 89-92
Earlier sketch in CA 23-24R
Jacoby, Oswald 1902-1984 ... 107
Obituary ... 113
Jacoby, Russell 1945- ... CANR-15
Earlier sketch in CA 77-80
Jacoby, Stephen M(ichael) 1940- ... 57-60
Jacoby, Susan ... 108
Jacopetti, Alexandra
See Hart, Alexandra
See also SATA 14
Jacot, B. L.
See Jacot de Boinod, Bernard Louis
Jacot, Michael 1924- ... 104
Jacot de Boinod, Bernard Louis
1898-1977 ... 11-12R
Obituary ... 77-80
Jacoway, Elizabeth 1944- ... 110
Jacqueline
See Carpentier (y Valmont), Alejo
Jacqueney, Mona G(raubart) ... 41-44R
Jacqueney, Theodore 1943(?)-1979
Obituary ... 89-92
Jacques, David (Lawson) 1948- ... 123
Jacques, Robin 1920- ... SATA-30, 32
See also SAAS 5
Jacquet, Constant Herbert, Jr. 1925- ... 106
Jaded Observer
See Zolf, Larry
Jados, Stanley S. 1912-1977 ... 33-36R
Jaediker, Kermit 1912(?)-1986 Obituary ... 118
Jaeger, Cyril Karel Stuart 1912- ... 3R
Jaeger, Edmund C(arroll) 1887-1983 ... CAP-2
Obituary ... 110
Earlier sketch in CA 23-24
Jaeger, Harry J., Jr. 1919(?)-1979
Obituary ... 85-88
Jaeger, Lorenz Cardinal 1892-1975
Obituary ... 57-60
Jaeger, Walter H(enry) E(dward)
1902(?)-1982 Obituary ... 108
Jaen, Didier Tisdel 1933- ... 29-32R
Jaenen, Cornelius John 1927- ... CANR-15
Earlier sketch in CA 85-88
Jaffa, George
See Wallace-Clarke, George
Jaffa, Harry V(ictor) 1918- ... 33-36R
Jaffe, A(bram) J. 1912- ... 5-6R
Jaffe, Aniela 1903- ... 125
Jaffe, Bernard 1896-1986 ... 5-6R
Obituary ... 121
Jaffe, Dan 1933- ... CANR-17
Earlier sketch in CA 25-28R
Jaffe, Dennis T(heodore) 1946- ... CANR-15
Earlier sketch in CA 89-92
Jaffe, Elsa
See Bartlett, Elsa Jaffe
Jaffe, Eugene D. 1937- ... 37-40R
Jaffe, Frederick S. 1925-1978 ... CANR-5
Earlier sketch in CA 9-10R
Jaffe, Gabriel Vivian 1923- ... 15-16R
Jaffe, Harold 1938- ... 29-32R
Jaffe, Hilde 1927- ... 105
Jaffe, Irma B(lumenthal) ... CANR-1
Earlier sketch in CA 45-48
Jaffe, Joseph 1924- Brief entry ... 113
Jaffe, Louis Leventhal 1905- ... 21-22R
Jaffe, (Andrew) Michael 1923- ... 23-24R
Jaffe, Nora Crow 1944- ... 106
Jaffe, Rona 1932- ... CANR-24
Earlier sketch in CA 73-76
See also AITN 1
Jaffe, Sam(uel Adason) 1929(?)-1985
Obituary ... 115
Jaffe, Sandra Sohn 1943- ... 101
Jaffe, Sherril 1945- ... CANR-19
Earlier sketch in CA 103
Jaffe, William 1898-1980 ... 57-60
Obituary ... 122
Jaffee, Al(lan) 1921- Brief entry ... 116
See also SATA 37
Jaffee, Dwight M. 1943- ... 57-60
Jaffin, David 1937- ... CANR-15
Earlier sketch in CA 65-68
Jagel, Beatrice Hawley 1944(?)-1985
Obituary ... 116
Jagendorf, Moritz (Adolf) 1888-1981 ... 5-6R
Obituary ... 102
See also SATA 2, 24
Jager, Okke 1928- ... CANR-23
Earlier sketches in CA 61-64, CANR-8
Jager, Ronald (Albert) 1932- ... 41-44R
Jaggard, Geoffrey (William) 1902-1970 ... CAP-2
Earlier sketch in CA 21-22
Jagger, John Hubert 1880- ... CAP-1
Earlier sketch in CA 9-10
Jagger, Mick 1944- ... CLC-17
Jagger, Peter (John) 1938- ... CANR-21
Earlier sketch in CA 103
Jagoda, Robert 1923- ... 73-76
Jahan, Rounaq 1944- ... 49-52
Jaher, Frederic Cople 1934- ... 9-10R
Jahn, Ernst A(dalbert) 1929- ... 69-72
Jahn, Janheinz 1918-1973 Obituary ... 111
Jahn, Joseph C. 1914(?)-1984 Obituary ... 113
Jahn, Joseph Michael 1943- ... CANR-5
Earlier sketch in CA 49-52
See also SATA 28
Jahn, Melvin E(dward) 1938- ... 9-10R
Jahn, Michael
See Jahn, Joseph Michael
Jahn, Mike
See Jahn, Joseph Michael
Jahnn, Hans Henny 1894-1959 ... DLB-56
Jahoda, Gloria (Adelaide Love)
1926-1980 ... CANR-4
Obituary ... 104
Earlier sketch in CA 1R
See also AITN 1
Jahoda, Gustav 1920- Brief entry ... 114
Jahsmann, Allan Hart 1916- ... 106
See also SATA 28
Jain, Girilal 1922- ... 11-12R
Jain, Ravindra Kumar 1937- ... 29-32R
Jain, Sagar C. 1930- ... CANR-10
Earlier sketch in CA 25-28R
Jain, Sharad Chandra 1933- ... CANR-21
Earlier sketch in CA 25-28R
Jaini, Padmanabh S. 1923- ... 103
Jakes, John (William) 1932- ... CANR-10
Earlier sketch in CA 57-60
See also DLBY 83
See also CLC 29
Jakle, John Allais 1939- ... 107
Jakobovits, Immanuel 1921- ... 108
Jakobovits, Leon Alex 1938- ... 25-28R
Jakobson, Roman 1896-1982 ... 77-80
Obituary ... 107
Jaksch, Wenzel 1896-1966 ... CAP-1
Earlier sketch in CA 13-14
Jakubauskas, Edward B(enedict) 1930- ... 57-60
Jakubowski, Patricia (Ann) 1941- ... 65-68
James, Alan Geoffrey 1943- ... 104
James, Allen
See Allen, James L(ovic), Jr.
James, Amalia
See Neggers, Carla A(malia)
James, Andrew
See Kirkup, James
James, Anne Eleanor Scott
See Scott-James, Anne Eleanor
James, Anthony
See Hanna, David
James, (Eliot) Antony Brett
See Brett-James, (Eliot) Antony
James, Bernard (Joseph) 1922-
Brief entry ... 110
James, Bessie (Williams) Rowland
1895-1974 ... 107
James, Bill
See James, George W(illiam)
James, Brian
See Thomas, Gordon
and Tierney, John Lawrence
James, Bruno S(cott) 1906- ... 5-6R
James, (David) Burnett (Stephen)
1919-1987 ... 7-8R
Obituary ... 122
James, C. B.
See Coover, James B(urrell)
James, C(yril) L(ionel) R(obert) 1901- ... 125
Brief entry ... 117
See also BW
See also CLC 33
James, C. W.
See Cumes, J(ames) W(illiam) C(rawford)
James, Cary A(mory) 1935- ... 29-32R
James, Charles J(oseph) 1944- ... CANR-5
Earlier sketch in CA 53-56
James, Charles L(yman) 1934- ... 29-32R
James, Clive 1939- Brief entry ... 105
James, Coy Hilton 1915- ... 103
James, Cy
See Watts, Peter Christopher
James, Cynthia
See Cresswell, Jasmine (Rosemary)
James, D(orris) Clayton 1931- ... 29-32R
James, D(avid) G(wilym) 1905-1968 ... CANR-4
Earlier sketch in CA 4R
James, Daniel (Lewis) 1911-1988
Obituary ... 125
James, David 1955- ... 119
James, David
See Hagberg, David J(ames)
James, Denise ... 29-32R
James, Diana
See Gunn, Diana Maureen
James, Don(ald H.) 1905- ... CANR-2
Earlier sketch in CA 4R
James, Dorothy Buckton 1937-
Brief entry ... 109
James, Dynely
See Mayne, William (James Carter)
James, Edgar C. 1933- ... CANR-5
Earlier sketch in CA 15-16R
James, Edward (Frank Willis) 1907-1984
Obituary ... 115
James, Edward
See Masur, Harold Q.
James, Edward T(opping) 1917- ... 33-36R
James, Edwin
See Gunn, James E(dwin)
James, Edwin Oliver 1889-1972 ... CAP-1
Earlier sketch in CA 15-16
James, Eleanor 1912- ... 41-44R
James, Elizabeth 1942- ... 121
See also SATA 39, 45, 52
James, Eric Arthur 1925- ... CAP-1
Earlier sketch in CA 9-10
James, Estelle 1935- ... 37-40R
James, F(rank) Cyril 1903-1973 Obituary ... 114
James, Fleming, Jr. 1904- ... CAP-1
Earlier sketch in CA 17-18
James, Gene Gray 1934- ... 114
James, George W(illiam) 1949- ... 109
James, H(enry) Thomas 1915- ... 25-28R
James, Harry Clebourne 1896-1978 ... CANR-4
Earlier sketch in CA 7-8R
See also SATA 11
James, Heather 1914- ... 45-48
James, Henry 1843-1916 Brief entry ... 104
See also DLB 12, 71, 74
See also CDALB 1865-1917
See also TCLC 2, 11, 24
James, Howard (Anthony, Jr.) 1935-
Brief entry ... 111
James, Hunter 1932- ... 114
James, Jean Rosemary Haughton
See Haughton-James, Jean Rosemary
James, (David) John ... 45-48
James, John 1633(?)-1729 ... DLB-24
James, Josef C. 1916(?)-1973 Obituary ... 45-48
James, Joseph B. 1912- ... 19-20R
James, Josephine
See Sterne, Emma Gelders
James, Judith
See Jennings, Leslie Nelson
James, Kristin
See Camp, Candace P(auline)
James, Leigh Franklin
See Little, Paul H(ugo)
James, Leonard F(rank) 1904- ... 49-52
James, Lloyd E.
See Laughlin, Tom
James, (William) Louis (Gabriel) ... CANR-6
Earlier sketch in CA 13-14R
James, M. R. 1940- ... 57-60
James, Marlise Ann 1945- ... 57-60
James, Matthew
See Lucey, James D(ennis)
James, Michael 1922(?)-1981 Obituary ... 104
James, Monica
See Nonhebel, Clare
James, Montague (Rhodes) 1862-1936
Brief entry ... 104
See also TCLC 6
James, Muriel ... 85-88
James, Naomi 1949- ... 102
James, Noel David Glaves 1911- ... 107
James, Norah C(ordner) ... 29-32R
James, P. D.
See White, Phyllis Dorothy James
See also CLC 18, 46
James, Paul 1921- ... 125
James, Paul
See Warburg, James Paul
James, Peter N. 1940- ... 57-60
James, Philip
See del Rey, Lester
and Moorcock, Michael (John)
James, Philip S(eaforth) 1914- ... CAP-1
Earlier sketch in CA 9-10
James, Preston E(verett) 1899- ... 45-48
James, Rebecca
See Elward, James (Joseph)
James, Robert A. 1946-1983 Obituary ... 109
James, Robert C(larke) 1918- ... 5-6R
James, Robert (Vidal) Rhodes
See Rhodes James, Robert (Vidal)
James, Robin (Irene) 1953- ... 126
See also SATA 50
James, Ronald
See Preston, James
James, Simon
See Kunen, James Simon
James, Stanton
See Flemming, Nicholas Coit
James, Susan
See Griffin, Arthur J.
James, Sydney V(incent, Jr.) 1929- ... CANR-21
Earlier sketch in CA 4R
James, Thelma Gray 1899-1988 ... 7-8R
Obituary ... 124
James, Theodore E(arle) 1913- ... 57-60
James, Theodore, Jr. 1934- ... 33-36R
James, Thomas N.
See Neal, James T(homas)
James, Trevor
See Constable, Trevor James
James, (Arthur) Walter 1912- ... 7-8R
James, Walter S.
See Sheldon, Walter J.
James, Warren E(dward) 1922- ... 45-48
James, Weldon (Bernard) 1912- ... 1R
James, Will(iam Roderick) 1892-1942 ... SATA-19
James, William 1842-1910 Brief entry ... 109
See also TCLC 15
James, William
See Craddock, William J(ames)
James, William C(losson) 1943- ... 126
James, William M.
See Harknett, Terry
James, William M.
See Harvey, John (Barton)
James, William Milbourne 1881- ... CAP-1
Earlier sketch in CA 11-12
James, Wilma Roberts 1905- ... 105
Jameson, Eric
See Trimmer, Eric J.

Jameson, Fredric 1934- DLB-67
Jameson, J. Franklin 1859-1937 DLB-17
Jameson, Judith
See Neyland, James (Elwyn)
Jameson, Kenneth (Ambrose) 1913- 77-80
Jameson, Kenneth P(eter) 1942- 112
Jameson, Samuel H(aig) 1896- 45-48
Jameson, (Margaret) Storm 1891-1986 81-84
Obituary 120
See also DLB 36
Jameson, Vic(tor Loyd) 1924- 19-20R
Jamieson, Bob
See Jamieson, Robert John
Jamieson, Paul F(letcher) 1903- CAP-1
Earlier sketch in CA 9-10
Jamieson, Robert John 1943- 116
Brief entry 110
Jamison, A(lbert) Leland 1911- 89-92
Jamison, Andrew 1948- 29-32R
Jamme, Albert (Joseph) 1916- 7-8R
Jampolsky, Gerald G(ershan) 1925- 111
Jan
See Noble, John (Appelbe)
Jan, Emerson
See Bixby, Jerome Lewis
Jan, George P(okung) 1925- 21-22R
Janas, Frankie-Lee 1908- CANR-24
Earlier sketch in CA 106
Jancar, Barbara Wolfe 1935- Brief entry 111
Jance, J. A.
See Jance, Judith A(nn)
Jance, Judith A(nn) 1944- 118
See also SATA 50
Janda, Kenneth (Frank) 1935- 15-16R
Jandl, Ernst 1925- CLC-34
Jandl, H(enry) Ward 1946- 121
Jandt, Fred E(dmund) 1944- 53-56
Jandy, Edward Clarence 1899-1980
Obituary 97-100
Jane, Mary Childs 1909- CANR-4
Earlier sketch in CA 1R
See also SATA 6
Jane, Nancy 1946- 89-92
Janeczko, Paul B(ryan) 1945- CANR-22
Earlier sketch in CA 104
See also SATA 53
Janes, Edward C. 1908- 93-96
See also SATA 25
Janes, J(oseph) Robert 1935- 123
See also SATA 50
Janes, Percy 1922- 113
Janes, Regina (Mary) 1946- 120
Janeshutz, Patricia M(arie) 1947- 121
Janeshutz, Trish
See Janeshutz, Patricia M(arie)
Janeway, Eliot 1913- Brief entry 112
Janeway, Elizabeth (Hall) 1913- CANR-2
Earlier sketch in CA 45-48
See also SATA 19
See also AITN 1
Janger, Allen R(obert) 1932- CANR-12
Earlier sketch in CA 29-32R
Janger, Kathleen N. 1940- 125
Janice
See Brustlein, Janice Tworkov
Janifer, Laurence M(ark) 1933- CANR-5
Earlier sketch in CA 9-10R
Janik, Allan (Stanley Peter) 1941- 53-56
Janik, Carolyn 1940- CANR-15
Earlier sketch in CA 89-92
Janik, Del Ivan 1945- 117
Janik, Phyllis 1944- 111
Janis, Irving L(ester) 1918- CANR-23
Earlier sketches in CA 19-20R, CANR-8
Janis, J(ack) Harold 1910- 15-16R
Jankelevitch, Vladimir 1903-1985
Obituary 117
Janko, Richard 1955- 111
Jankowsky, Kurt Robert 1928- 37-40R
Janner, Greville Ewan 1928- CANR-8
Earlier sketch in CA 13-14R
Janos, Andrew C(saba) 1934- 106
Janosch
See Eckert, Horst
Janov, Arthur 1924- 116
Janovy, John, Jr. 1937- CANR-19
Earlier sketch in CA 97-100
Janowitz, Morris 1919- 13-14R
Janowitz, Phyllis 93-96
Janowitz, Tama 1957- 106
See also CLC 43
Janowski, Tadeus M(arian) 1923- 53-56
Janowsky, Oscar Isaiah 1900- CANR-5
Earlier sketch in CA 7-8R
Janrup, (Ruth) Birgit 1931- 97-100
Jans, Zephyr
See Zekowski, Arlene
Jansen, Clifford J. 1935- 33-36R
Jansen, G(odfrey) H(enry) 1919- 114
Jansen, Godfrey
See Jansen, G(odfrey) H(enry)
Jansen, Jared
See Cebulash, Mel
Jansen, John Frederick 1918- 23-24R
Jansen, Robert B(ruce) 1922- 81-84
Janson, Anthony F(rederick) 1943- 121
Janson, Donald 1921- 5-6R
Janson, Dora Jane (Heineberg) 1916- 106
See also SATA 31
Janson, H(orst) W(oldemar) 1913-1982 CANR-4
Obituary 107
Earlier sketch in CA 1R
See also SATA 9
Janson, Hank
See Hobson, Harry
and Norwood, Victor G(eorge) C(harles)
Janson-Smith, Celina 1909-1985 Obituary 118
Janssen, Al(fred Guthrie) 1949- 121
Janssen, Lawrence H(arm) 1921- 15-16R
Janssens, Paul Mary 53-56
Jansson, Tove Marika 1914- 17-18R
See also SATA 3, 41
See also CLR 2
Janta, Alexander 1908-1974 101
Obituary 53-56
Jantsch, Erich 1929-1980 CANR-10
Earlier sketch in CA 65-68
Jantscher, Gerald R. 1939(?)-1987
Obituary 123
Jantzen, Hans 1881-1967 Obituary 111
Jantzen, Steven L(loyd) 1941- 77-80
Janus
See Clery, (Reginald) Val(entine)
Janus, Grete
See Hertz, Grete Janus
Janus, Sam Shep 1930- Brief entry 111
Januz, Lauren Robert 1939- 108
Janzen, John M(arvin) 1937- 81-84
Jaques, Elliott 1917- CANR-6
Earlier sketch in CA 13-14R
Jaques, Faith 1923- CANR-20
Earlier sketch in CA 103
See also SATA 21
Jaques, Florence Page 1890-1972 103
Obituary 104
Jaques, Francis Lee 1887-1969 SATA-28
Jaquette, Jane Stallmann 1942-
Brief entry 105
Jaquin, Noel 1894(?)-1974 Obituary 112
Jaquith, Priscilla 1908- 121
See also SATA 51
Jaramillo, Samuel 1925- 41-44R
Jarchow, Merrill E(arl) 1910- CANR-14
Earlier sketch in CA 41-44R
Jardim, Anne 1936- 107
Jardim, Vasco S. 1900(?)-1983 Obituary 111
Jardine, Alice (Ann) 1951- 117
Jardine, Jack 1931- 23-24R
Jareed
See Faridi, Shah Nasiruddin Mohammad
Jares, Joe 1937- CANR-12
Earlier sketch in CA 33-36R
Jarmain, W. Edwin 1938- 13-14R
Jarman, Cosette C(otterell) 1909- CAP-2
Earlier sketch in CA 21-22
Jarman, Mark Anthony 1955- 118
Jarman, Rosemary Hawley 1935- CANR-2
Earlier sketch in CA 49-52
See also SATA 7
Jarman, Thomas Leckie 1907- CANR-4
Earlier sketch in CA 7-8R
Jarman, Walton Maxey 1904-1980
Obituary 108
Jarmuth, Sylvia L. 1912- 25-28R
Jarnow, Jeannette 1909- 53-56
Jaroch, F(rancis) A(nthony) Randy 1947- 89-92
Jaroch, Randy
See Jaroch, F(rancis) A(nthony) Randy
Jarolimek, John 1921- Brief entry 114
Jaron, Lou
See Spender, Lynne
Jarreau, Al(wyn Lopez) 1940- 117
Brief entry 116
Jarrell, John W. 1908(?)-1978 Obituary 81-84
Jarrell, Mary Von Schrader 1914- 77-80
See also SATA 35
Jarrell, Randall 1914-1965 CANR-6
Obituary 25-28R
Earlier sketch in CA 7-8R
See also CABS 2
See also SATA 7
See also DLB 48, 52
See also CDALB 1941-1968
See also CLC 1, 2, 6, 9, 13, 49
See also CLR 6
Jarrett, (John) Derek 1928- 57-60
Jarrett, H(arold) Reginald 1916- CANR-3
Earlier sketch in CA 9-10R
Jarrett, James Louis 1917- 53-56
Jarrett, Marjorie 1923- 105
Jarrett, Roxanne
See Werner, Herma
Jarriel, Thomas Edwin 1934- 120
Brief entry 109
Jarriel, Tom
See Jarriel, Thomas Edwin
Jarrott, Mattie L. 1881(?)-1973
Obituary 41-44R
Jarry, Alfred 1873-1907 Brief entry 104
See also TCLC 2, 14
Jarvie, Clodagh Gibson
See Gibson-Jarvie, Clodagh
Jarvie, I(an) C(harles) 1937- 53-56
Jarvis, Ana C(ortesi) 1936- CANR-14
Earlier sketch in CA 65-68
Jarvis, Charles E(fthemios) 1921- 111
Jarvis, E. K.
See Bloch, Robert (Albert)
and Ellison, Harlan
and Fairman, Paul W.
and Silverberg, Robert
Jarvis, F(rank) Washington 1939- 37-40R
Jarvis, Fred(erick) G(ordon, Jr.) 1930- 33-36R
Jarvis, Howard (Arnold) 1902(?)-1986 122
Obituary 120
Brief entry 111
Jarvis, Jennifer M(ary) 1935- 13-14R
Jarvis, Martin 1941- CANR-25
Earlier sketch in CA 105
Jarvis, Rupert Charles 1899- 103
Jarvis, Sharon 1943- 119
Jarvis, William Don(ald) 1913- CAP-1
Earlier sketch in CA 15-16
Jasen, David A(lan) 1937- 29-32R
Jasenas, Michael 1912- Brief entry 113
Jashemski, Wilhelmina Feemster 1910- CAP-1
Earlier sketch in CA 15-16
Jasmin, Claude 1930- 123
See also DLB 60
Jasner, W. K.
See Watson, Jane Werner
Jasny, Naum 1883- CAP-1
Earlier sketch in CA 9-10
Jason
See Munro, (Macfarlane) Hugh
and Stannus, (James) Gordon (Dawson)
Jason, Johnny
See Glut, Donald F(rank)
Jason, Kathrine 1953- 126
Jason, Philip K(enneth) 1941- 114
Jason, Stuart
See Avallone, Michael (Angelo), Jr.
and Floren, Lee
Jason, Stuart
See Floren, Lee
Jaspan, Norman 103
Jaspers, Karl (Theodor) 1883-1969 122
Obituary 25-28R
Jaspersohn, William 1947- 102
Jassal, Harjinder (Singh) 1938- 111
Jassem, Kate
See Oppenheim, Joanne
Jassy, Marie-France Perrin
See Perrin Jassy, Marie-France
Jastak, Joseph Florian 1901-1979 CANR-4
Obituary 85-88
Earlier sketch in CA 7-8R
Jastrow, Robert 1925- CANR-18
Earlier sketch in CA 23-24R
Jauch, Lawrence R. 1943- 112
Jauncey, James H(enry) 1916- CANR-20
Earlier sketches in CA 1R, CANR-5
Jauss, Anne Marie 1907- CANR-4
Earlier sketch in CA 1R
See also SATA 10
Jauss, David 1951- 121
Jaussi, Laureen Richardson 1934- 73-76
Javitch, Daniel Gilbert 1941- 103
Javits, Benjamin A(braham) 1894-1973
Obituary 41-44R
Javits, Eric Moses 1931- 1R
Javits, Jacob K(oppel) 1904-1986 CANR-17
Obituary 118
Earlier sketches in CA 1R, CANR-1
Jawien, Andrzej
See John Paul II, Pope
Jaworska, Wladyslawa Jadwiga 1910- 53-56
Jaworski, Leon 1905-1982 CAP-1
Obituary 108
Earlier sketch in CA 15-16
Jaworskyj, Michael 1921- 61-64
Jaxon, Milt
See Kimbro, John M.
Jay, Antony (Rupert) 1930- 25-28R
Jay, Bill 1940- Brief entry 117
Jay, Charlotte
See Halls, Geraldine (Mary)
Jay, Donald
See Meyer, Charles R(obert)
Jay, Douglas (Patrick Thomas) 1907- CANR-12
Earlier sketch in CA 65-68
Jay, Elisabeth 1947- 124
Jay, Eric George 1907- 7-8R
Jay, G. S.
See Halls, Geraldine (Mary)
Jay, Hilda L(ease) 1921- 117
Jay, James M(onroe) 1927- 53-56
Jay, John 1745-1829 DLB-31
Jay, Karla 1947- 85-88
Jay, M(argaret) Ellen 1946- 118
Jay, Marion
See Spalding, Ruth
Jay, Martin (Evan) 1944- 53-56
Jay, Mel
See Fanthorpe, R(obert) Lionel
Jay, Peter 1937- 109
Jay, Peter (Anthony Charles) 1945- 97-100
Jay, Peter A. 1940- 101
Jay, Robert Ravenelle 1925- Brief entry 106
Jay, Ruth I(ngrid) 1920- 93-96
Jay, Ruth Johnson
See Jay, Ruth I(ngrid)
Jay, Simon
See Alexander, Colin James
Jayawardena, Visakha Kumari 1931- 45-48
Jayme, William North 1925- 9-10R
Jayne, Lieutenant R. H.
See Ellis, Edward S(ylvester)
Jayne, Sears 1920- 13-14R
Jaynes, Clare
See Mayer, Jane Rothschild
Jaynes, Julian 1923- 41-44R
Jaynes, Richard A(ndrus) 1935- 65-68
Jaynes, Roger W. 1946- 85-88
Jaynes, Ruth 1899- CAP-2
Earlier sketch in CA 25-28
Jazayery, M(ohammad) Ali 1924- CANR-9
Earlier sketch in CA 21-22R
Jeake, Samuel, Jr.
See Aiken, Conrad (Potter)
Jeal, Tim 1945- CANR-9
Earlier sketch in CA 21-22R
Jean, Gabrielle (Lucille) 1924- CANR-14
Earlier sketch in CA 37-40R
Jean, Marcel 1900- 25-28R
Jean-Louis
See Kerouac, Jean-Louis Lebrid de
Jeannerat, Pierre Gabriel 1902- 7-8R
Jeanniere, Abel 1921- 49-52
Jeans, Marylu Terral 1914- 89-92
Jeansonne, Glen 1946- 122
Jebb, (Hubert Miles) Gladwyn 1900- 21-22R
Jedamus, Paul 1923- 37-40R
Jedlitzka, Maria
See Jeritza, Maria
Jedrey, Christopher M(ichael) 1949- 101
Jedrzejewicz, Waclaw 1893- 25-28R
Jeef, Kalle
See Tshiamala, Kabasele
Jeeves, Malcolm A(lexander) 1926- CANR-12
Earlier sketch in CA 29-32R
Jeffares, A(lexander) Norman 1920- CANR-16
Earlier sketch in CA 85-88
Jeffer, Marsha 1940- 41-44R
Jefferds, Vincent H(arris) 1916- SATA-49
Jefferies, (John) Richard 1848-1887 SATA-16
Jefferies, Susan Herring 1903- CAP-1
Earlier sketch in CA 13-14
Jefferis, Barbara (Tarlton) 1917- 81-84
Jeffers, H(arry) Paul 1934- 93-96
Jeffers, Jo
See Johnson, Joan Helen
Jeffers, Lance 1919-1985 CANR-25
Earlier sketch in CA 65-68
See also BW
See also DLB 41
Jeffers, (John) Robinson 1887-1962 85-88
See also DLB 45
See also CLC 2, 3, 11, 15
Jeffers, Susan 97-100
See also SATA 17
Jefferson, Alan 1921- CANR-13
Earlier sketch in CA 33-36R
Jefferson, Blanche (Waugaman) 1909- 5-6R
Jefferson, Carter (Alfred) 1927- 17-18R
Jefferson, Ian
See Davies, L(eslie) P(urnell)
Jefferson, Janet
See Mencken, H(enry) L(ouis)
Jefferson, Omar Xavier
See Jefferson, Xavier T(homas)
Jefferson, Roland S. 1939- 111
See also BW
Jefferson, Sarah
See Farjeon, (Eve) Annabel
Jefferson, Thomas 1743-1826 DLB-31
See also CDALB 1640-1865
Jefferson, Xavier T(homas) 1952- CANR-13
Earlier sketch in CA 73-76
Jeffery, Grant 1924- 1R
Jeffery, Ransom 1943- 23-24R
Jefferys, Allan 93-96
Jefford, Bat
See Bingley, David Ernest
Jeffress, Philip W. 1941- Brief entry 111
Jeffrey, Adi-Kent Thomas 1916- 37-40R
Jeffrey, Christopher
See Leach, Michael
Jeffrey, David Lyle 1941- CANR-24
Earlier sketches in CA 57-60, CANR-7
Jeffrey, Julie Roy 1941- 93-96
Jeffrey, L(illian) H(amilton) 1915- 4R
Jeffrey, Lloyd Nicholas 1918- 37-40R
Jeffrey, Mildred (Mesurac) 7-8R
Jeffrey, Richard Carl 1926- 103
Jeffrey, Ruth
See Bell, Louise Price
Jeffrey, William
See Pronzini, Bill
and Wallmann, Jeffrey M(iner)
Jeffrey, William P., Jr. 1919- 57-60
Jeffreys, Harold 1891- 109
Jeffreys, J. G.
See Healey, Ben (James)
Jeffreys, Montagu Vaughan Castelman
1900-1985 CANR-4
Obituary 117
Earlier sketch in CA 7-8R
Jeffreys-Jones, Rhodri 1942- CANR-13
Earlier sketch in CA 77-80
Jeffries, Charles Joseph 1896-1972 CANR-4
Earlier sketch in CA 7-8R
Jeffries, Derwin J(ames) 1915- 57-60
Jeffries, Graham Montague
1900-1982 CANR-25
Earlier sketch in CA 77-80
Jeffries, John Worthington 1942- 103
Jeffries, Lewis I(ngles) 1942- 103
Jeffries, Ona (Griffin) 1893(?)-1973
Obituary 41-44R
Jeffries, Roderic (Graeme) 1926- CANR-25
Earlier sketches in CA 19-20R, CANR-9
See also SATA 4
Jeffries, Virginia M(urrill) 1911- 5-6R
Jeffs, Julian 1931- 37-40R
Jeffs, Rae 1921- 25-28R
Jefkins, Frank William 1920- CANR-9
Earlier sketch in CA 13-14R
Jehlen, Myra 1940- 101
Jelagin, Juri 1910-1987 Obituary 123
Jelakowitch, Ivan
See Heijermans, Herman
Jelavich, Barbara 1923- 53-56
Jelenski, Constantin 1922- 101
Jelinek, Estelle C. 1935- 102
Jelinek, Hena Maes
See Maes-Jelinek, Hena
Jellema, Roderick 1927- 41-44R
Jellicoe, (Patricia) Ann 1927- 85-88
See also DLB 13
See also CLC 27
Jellicoe, Geoffrey Alan 1900- 13-14R
Jellicoe, Sidney 1906-1973 CAP-2
Earlier sketch in CA 33-36
Jellinek, George 1919- 89-92
Jellinek, J(oseph) Stephan 1930- 81-84
Jellinek, Paul 1897- 13-14R
Jellison, Charles Albert, Jr. 1924- 3R

Jelly, George Oliver 1909- ... 103
Jemie, Onwuchekwa 1940- ... 89-92
Jemyma
See Holley, Marietta
Jena, Ruth Michaelis
See Ratcliff, Ruth
Jencks, Charles 1939- ... CANR-2
Earlier sketch in CA 49-52
Jencks, Christopher 1936- ... CANR-2
Earlier sketch in CA 49-52
Jencks, Harlan W(ardell) 1941- ... 111
Jenison, Don P. 1897- ... CANR-7
Earlier sketch in CA 19-20R
Jenkin, A(lfred) K(enneth) Hamilton
1900-1980 Obituary ... 102
Jenkins, Alan 1914- ... CANR-6
Earlier sketch in CA 57-60
Jenkins, Cecil 1927- ... 107
Jenkins, Clive 1926- ... CANR-5
Earlier sketch in CA 13-14R
Jenkins, Dan (Thomas B.) 1929- ... 126
Brief entry ... 111
Jenkins, David 1928- ... 97-100
Jenkins, David E(dward) 1925- Brief entry .. 114
Jenkins, Dorothy Helen 1907-1972
Obituary ... 37-40R
Jenkins, (Margaret) Elizabeth (Heald)
1905- ... CANR-13
Earlier sketch in CA 73-76
Jenkins, Emyl 1941- ... 114
Jenkins, Ferrell 1936- ... CANR-6
Earlier sketch in CA 57-60
Jenkins, Frances Briggs 1905- ... CAP-2
Earlier sketch in CA 25-28
Jenkins, Geoffrey 1920- ... CANR-16
Earlier sketch in CA 7-8R
Jenkins, (Thomas) Gilmour 1894-1981
Obituary ... 108
Jenkins, Gladys Gardner 1901- ... CANR-4
Earlier sketch in CA 3R
Jenkins, Gordon (Hill) 1910-1984
Obituary ... 112
Jenkins, Gwyn 1919- ... 2R
Jenkins, Hal
See Jenkins, Harold L.
Jenkins, Harold 1909- ... 9-10R
Jenkins, Harold L. 1909(?)-1987 Obituary .. 124
Jenkins, Holt M. 1920- ... 19-20R
Jenkins, Hugh (Gater) 1908- ... 104
Jenkins, Iredell 1909- ... 106
Jenkins, James J(erome) 1923- ... 15-16R
Jenkins, Jerry B(ruce) 1949- ... CANR-20
Earlier sketches in CA 49-52, CANR-5
Jenkins, John (Robert Graham) 1928- ... 45-48
Jenkins, John Geraint 1929- ... 21-22R
Jenkins, John H(olmes III) 1940- ... CANR-10
Earlier sketch in CA 65-68
Jenkins, Kenneth V(incent) 1930- ... 53-56
Jenkins, Linda Walsh 1944- ... 111
Jenkins, Louis 1942- ... CANR-4
Earlier sketch in CA 53-56
Jenkins, Marie M(agdalen) 1909- ... 41-44R
See also SATA 7
Jenkins, Michael (Romilly Heald) 1936- ... 25-28R
Jenkins, Nancy (Harmon) 1937- ... 109
Jenkins, Patricia 1927-1982 ... 106
Jenkins, Peter 1951- ... 89-92
Jenkins, Phyllis
See Schwalberg, Carol(yn Ernestine
Stein)
Jenkins, Ray(mond Leonard) 1935- ... 103
Jenkins, Reese V(almer) 1938- ... 65-68
Jenkins, (John) Robin 1912- ... CANR-1
Earlier sketch in CA 4R
See also DLB 14
Jenkins, Romilly James Heald
1907-1969 ... CANR-5
Earlier sketch in CA 7-8R
Jenkins, Roy Harris 1920- ... CANR-13
Earlier sketch in CA 9-10R
Jenkins, Simon 1943- ... 81-84
Jenkins, Will(iam) F(itzgerald)
1896-1975 ... CANR-4
Obituary ... 57-60
Earlier sketch in CA 9-10R
Jenkins, William A(twell) 1922- ... 61-64
See also SATA 9
Jenkins, William Marshall, Jr. 1918-
Brief entry ... 105
Jenkinson, Edward B(ernard) 1930- ... 23-24R
Jenkinson, Michael 1938- ... 25-28R
Jenks, Almet 1892-1966 ... CAP-1
Earlier sketch in CA 13-14
Jenks, C(larence) Wilfred 1909-1973 ... CANR-4
Earlier sketch in CA 11-12R
Jenks, George C(harles) 1850-1929
Brief entry ... 119
Jenks, James M. 1922- ... 122
Jenks, Randolph 1912- ... 11-12R
Jenkyns, Chris 1924- ... SATA-51
Jenkyns, Richard (Henry Austen) 1949- ... 108
Jenner, Bruce 1949- ... 110
Jenner, Chrystie 1950- ... 77-80
Jenner, Delia 1944- ... 23-24R
Jenner, Heather
See James, Heather
Jenner, Philip Norman 1921- ... 89-92
Jenner, W(illiam) J(ohn) F(rancis)
1940- ... CANR-12
Earlier sketch in CA 29-32R
Jenness, Aylette 1934- ... 25-28R
Jennifer, Susan
See Hoskins, Robert
Jennings, Coleman A(lonzo) 1933- ... 124
Jennings, Dana Close 1923- ... 53-56
Jennings, Dean Southern 1905-1969
Obituary ... 89-92
Jennings, Edward M(orton III) 1936- ... 29-32R
Jennings, Elizabeth (Joan) 1926- ... CANR-8
Earlier sketch in CA 61-64
See also CAAS 5
See also DLB 27
See also CLC 5, 14
Jennings, Gary (Gayne) 1928- ... CANR-9
Earlier sketch in CA 7-8R
See also SATA 9
Jennings, (William) Ivor 1903-1965 ... 5-6R
Jennings, James M(urray) 1924- ... 37-40R
Jennings, Jerry (Edward) 1935- ... CANR-7
Earlier sketch in CA 53-56
Jennings, Jesse David 1909- ... CANR-13
Earlier sketch in CA 33-36R
Jennings, John (Edward, Jr.) 1906-1973 . CAP-1
Obituary ... 45-48
Earlier sketch in CA 13-14
Jennings, Lane (Eaton) 1944- ... CANR-19
Earlier sketch in CA 102
Jennings, Leslie Nelson 1890-1972 ... CAP-1
Earlier sketch in CA 9-10
Jennings, Marianne Moody 1953- ... 118
Jennings, Michael Glenn 1931- ... CANR-24
Earlier sketch in CA 69-72
Jennings, Patrick
See Mayer, S(ydney) L(ouis)
Jennings, Paul (Francis) 1918- ... CANR-19
Earlier sketches in CA 9-10R, CANR-4
Jennings, Peter (Charles) 1938-
Brief entry ... 114
Jennings, Phillip C. 1946- ... 126
Jennings, Raymond P(olson) 1924- ... 110
Jennings, Richard (Wormington) 1907- ... 19-20R
Jennings, Robert
See Hamilton, Charles Harold St. John
Jennings, Robert E(dward) 1931- ... CANR-11
Earlier sketch in CA 61-64
Jennings, S. M.
See Meyer, Jerome Sydney
Jennings, Talbot 1895(?)-1985 Obituary ... 116
Jennings, Ted C(harles) 1949- ... 81-84
Jennings, Vivien ... 61-64
Jennings, Waylon 1937- ... CLC-21
Jennings, William Dale 1917- ... 25-28R
Jennison, C. S.
See Starbird, Kaye
Jennison, Christopher 1938- ... 53-56
Jennison, Keith Warren 1911- ... 73-76
See also SATA 14
Jennison, Peter S(axe) 1922- ... CANR-4
Earlier sketch in CA 9-10R
Jenny, Hans H(einrich) 1922- ... 103
Jenoff, Marvyne 1942- ... 117
Jens, Walter 1923- ... CANR-15
Earlier sketch in CA 89-92
See also DLB 69
Jensen, Ad(olph) E. 1899-1965 ... CAP-2
Earlier sketch in CA 19-20
Jensen, Alan F(rederick) 1938- ... 53-56
Jensen, Albert C(hristian) 1924- ... 85-88
Jensen, Andrew F(rederick), Jr. 1929- ... 57-60
Jensen, Ann ... 23-24R
Jensen, Arthur R(obert) 1923- ... CANR-2
Earlier sketch in CA 4R
Jensen, Clayne R. 1930- ... CANR-8
Earlier sketch in CA 17-18R
Jensen, De Lamar 1925- ... CANR-7
Earlier sketch in CA 11-12R
Jensen, Dwight 1934- ... 85-88
Jensen, Frede 1926- ... 57-60
Jensen, Gordon Duff 1926- Brief entry ... 106
Jensen, Gwendolyn Evans 1936- ... 57-60
Jensen, H. James 1933- ... 25-28R
Jensen, Irene K(hin Khin Myint) 1925- ... 69-72
Jensen, Irving L. 1920- ... CANR-7
Earlier sketch in CA 19-20R
Jensen, J(ohn) Vernon 1922- ... 49-52
Jensen, Jo
See Pelton, Beverly Jo
Jensen, John H(jalmar) 1929- ... 23-24R
Jensen, John Martin 1893- ... CAP-1
Earlier sketch in CA 15-16
Jensen, Julie
See McDonald, Julie
Jensen, Larry Cyril 1938- ... 106
Jensen, Laura (Linnea) 1948- ... 103
See also CLC 37
Jensen, Lawrence N(eil) 1924- ... 17-18R
Jensen, Lloyd 1936- ... 61-64
Jensen, Margaret Ann 1948- ... 123
Jensen, Marlene 1947- ... 81-84
Jensen, Mary Ten Eyck Bard 1904-1970 ... 5-6R
Obituary ... 29-32R
Jensen, Maxine Dowd 1919- ... 65-68
Jensen, Merrill (Monroe) 1905-1980 ... 77-80
Obituary ... 112
See also DLB 17
Jensen, Michael C(ole) 1939- ... 49-52
Jensen, Niels 1927- ... 49-52
See also SATA 25
Jensen, Ole Klindt
See Klindt-Jensen, Ole
Jensen, Oliver (Ormerod) 1914- ... CANR-10
Earlier sketch in CA 25-28R
Jensen, Paul K. 1916- ... 19-20R
Jensen, Paul M(orris) 1944- ... 53-56
Jensen, Pauline Marie (Long) 1900- ... CAP-2
Earlier sketch in CA 17-18
Jensen, Peter
See Wallmann, Jeffrey M(iner)
Jensen, Richard C(arl) 1936- ... 49-52
Jensen, Richard J. 1941- ... 33-36R
Jensen, Robert (Earl) 1938- ... 111
Jensen, Rolf (Arthur) 1912- ... 21-22R
Jensen, Rosalie (Seymour) 1938- ... 57-60
Jensen, Vernon H(ortin) 1907- ... 106
Jensen, Virginia Allen 1927- ... CANR-1
Earlier sketch in CA 45-48
See also SATA 8
Jensi, Muganwa Nsiku
See Shorter, Aylward
Jenson, Robert W(illiam) 1930- ... CANR-9
Earlier sketch in CA 7-8R
Jenson, William R(obert) 1946- ... 101
Jentleson, Bruce W. 1951- ... 124
Jentz, Gaylord A. 1931- ... CANR-14
Earlier sketch in CA 25-28R
Jenyns, R(oger) Soame 1904-1976 ... 73-76
Obituary ... 69-72
Jenyns, Soame
See Jenyns, R(oger) Soame
Jephcott, E(dmund) F(rancis) N(eville)
1938- Brief entry ... 115
Jeppson, J. O.
See Jeppson, Janet O(pal)
Jeppson, Janet O(pal) 1926- ... CANR-19
Earlier sketch in CA 49-52
See also SATA 46
Jepsen, Stanley M(arius) 1912- ... 77-80
Jerdee, Thomas H(arlan) 1927- ... 118
Jeremias, Joachim 1900- ... CANR-11
Earlier sketch in CA 7-8R
Jeremy, Sister Mary ... 7-8R
Jerina, Carol 1947- ... 126
Jeritza, Maria 1887-1982 Obituary ... 107
Jermain, Clive 1966(?)-1988 Obituary ... 124
Jerman, James (Auguste) 1920- ... 123
Jerman, Sylvia Paul
See Cooper, Sylvia
Jernick, Ruth 1948- ... 107
Jerome, Jerome K(lapka) 1859-1927
Brief entry ... 119
See also DLB 10, 34
See also TCLC 23
Jerome, John 1932- ... CANR-2
Earlier sketch in CA 45-48
Jerome, Joseph
See Sewell, Brocard
Jerome, Judson (Blair) 1927- ... CANR-20
Earlier sketches in CA 9-10R, CANR-4
Jerome, Lawrence E(dmund) 1944- ... 77-80
Jerome, Mark
See Appleman, Mark J(erome)
Jerome, Stuart 1918(?)-1983 Obituary ... 111
Jerrybilt
See Shields, Gerald R.
Jersild, Arthur T(homas) 1902- ... CANR-21
Earlier sketch in CA 4R
Jersild, Paul T(homas) 1931- ... 37-40R
Jervell, Jacob 1925- ... CANR-23
Earlier sketches in CA 61-64, CANR-8
Jeschke, Marlin 1929- ... 45-48
Jeschke, Susan 1942- ... 77-80
See also SATA 27, 42
Jeske, Richard Lee 1936- ... 111
Jesmer, Elaine 1939- ... 49-52
See also AITN 1
Jespersen, James 1934- ... 103
Jesse, F(ryniwyd) Tennyson 1889-1958
Brief entry ... 112
Jesse, Michael
See Baldwin, Michael
Jessel, Camilla (Ruth) 1937- ... CANR-23
Earlier sketch in CA 104
See also SATA 29
Jessel, George (Albert) 1898-1981 ... 89-92
Obituary ... 103
Jessel, John
See Weinbaum, Stanley Grauman
Jessen, Carl A. 1887(?)-1978 Obituary ... 77-80
Jessey, Cornelia
See Sussman, Cornelia Silver
Jessner, Lucie Ney 1896-1979 Obituary ... 93-96
Jessop, Thomas Edmund 1896- ... 9-10R
Jessor, Richard 1924- ... 41-44R
Jessup, Frances
See Van Briggle, Margaret F(rances)
Jessup
Jessup, John K(nox) 1907-1979 ... 101
Obituary ... 89-92
Jessup, Michael H(yle) 1937- Brief entry ... 109
Jessup, Paul F(rederick) 1939- ... 111
Jessup, Philip C(aryl) 1897-1986 ... 77-80
Obituary ... 118
Jessup, Richard 1925(?)-1982 Obituary ... 108
Jesty, P(eter) H(ugh) 1948- ... 121
Jeter, Jacky
See Jeter, Jacquelyn I.
Jeter, Jacquelyn I. 1935- ... 25-28R
Jett, Stephen C(linton) 1938- ... CANR-10
Earlier sketch in CA 25-28R
Jette, Fernand 1921- ... 5-6R
Jeune, Paul 1950- ... 101
Jevons, Frederic, Raphael 1929- ... 61-64
Jevons, Marshall
See Breit, William (Leo)
and Elzinga, Kenneth G(erald)
Jewell, Derek 1927-1985 ... CANR-20
Earlier sketches in CA 33-36R, CANR-13
Jewell, Edmund F. 1896(?)-1978
Obituary ... 81-84
Jewell, Malcolm E(dwin) 1928- ... CANR-5
Earlier sketch in CA 4R
Jewell, Nancy 1940- ... CANR-7
Earlier sketch in CA 61-64
See also SATA 41
Jewett, Alyce Lowrie (Williams) 1908- ... CAP-1
Earlier sketch in CA 13-14
Jewett, Ann E(lizabeth) 1921- ... 93-96
Jewett, Claudia L(owe) 1939- ... 112
Jewett, Eleanore Myers 1890-1967 ... 7-8R
See also SATA 5
Jewett, Paul King 1919- ... 53-56
Jewett, Robert 1933- ... CANR-2
Earlier sketch in CA 45-48
Jewett, (Theodora) Sarah Orne 1849-1909
Brief entry ... 108
See also SATA 15
See also DLB 12, 74
See also TCLC 1, 22
Jewison, Norman (Frederick) 1926-
Brief entry ... 113
Jewsbury, Geraldine 1812-1880 ... DLB-21
Jezard, Alison 1919- ... 29-32R
See also SATA 34
Jezer, Marty 1940- ... 109
Jezewski, Bohdan O(lgierd) 1900-1980 ... 7-8R
Obituary ... 103
Jha, Akhileshwar 1932- ... 107
Jha, Lakshmi Kant 1913-1988 Obituary ... 125
Jhabvala, Ruth Prawer 1927- ... CANR-2
Earlier sketch in CA 4R
See also CLC 4, 8, 29
Jianou, Ionel 1905- ... CANR-9
Earlier sketch in CA 23-24R
Jidejian, Nina 1921- ... 29-32R
Jiler, John 1946- ... 114
See also SATA 35, 42
Jiles, Paulette 1943- ... 101
See also CLC 13
Jillson, Joyce 1950- ... 111
Jimenez, Janey (Renee) 1953- ... 77-80
Jimenez (Mantecon), Juan Ramon
1881-1958 Brief entry ... 104
See also TCLC 4
Jinks, William Howard, Jr. 1938- ... 41-44R
Jipson, Wayne R(ay) 1931- ... 45-48
Jiskogo
See Harrington, Mark Raymond
Jo, Yung-Hwan 1932- ... 45-48
Joachim, Leo H. 1898-1985 Obituary ... 117
Joan, Polly 1933- ... 101
Joans, Ted 1928- ... CANR-25
Earlier sketches in CA 45-48, CANR-2
See also BW
See also DLB 16, 41
Jobb, Jamie 1945- ... 85-88
See also SATA 29
Jobe, Brock (William) 1948- ... 118
Jobes, Gertrude Blumenthal 1907- ... CAP-1
Earlier sketch in CA 11-12
Jobson, Gary Alan 1950- ... 93-96
Jobson, Hamilton 1914- ... 73-76
Jobson, Sandra
See Darroch, Sandra Jobson
Jocelyn, Richard
See Clutterbuck, Richard
Jochnowitz, George 1937- ... 49-52
Joedicke, Juergen 1925- ... 19-20R
Joel, Asher Alexander 1912- ... 108
Joel, Billy
See Joel, William Martin
See also CLC 26
Joel, William Martin 1949- ... 108
Joels, Merrill E. 1915- ... 25-28R
Joelson, Annette 1903-1971 Obituary ... 29-32R
Joerns, Consuelo ... 114
Brief entry ... 111
See also SATA 33, 44
Joers, Lawrence E(ugene) C(laire)
1900- ... 41-44R
Joesting, Edward Henry 1925- ... 103
Jofen, Jean 1922- ... 37-40R
Joffe, Josef 1944- ... 126
Joffe, Joyce 1940- ... 77-80
Johannes, John R. 1943- ... 111
Johannes, R.
See Moss, Rose
Johannesen, Richard L(ee) 1937- ... 17-18R
Johannesson, Olof
See Alfven, Hannes O(lof) G(oesta)
Johanningmeier, E(rwin) V(irgil) 1937- ... 104
Johannis, Theodore B(enjamin), Jr.
1914- ... 33-36R
Johannsen, Hano D. 1933- ... 29-32R
Johannsen, Robert Walter 1925- ... 1R
Johansen, Bruce Elliott 1950- ... 110
Johansen, Dorothy O. 1904- ... CAP-1
Earlier sketch in CA 13-14
Johanson, Donald C(arl) 1943- ... 107
Johanson, Stanley Morris 1933- ... 45-48
Johansson, Thomas (Hugo) B(ernard)
1943- ... CANR-19
Earlier sketch in CA 102
John, Angela V. 1948- ... 125
John, B.
See John, Elizabeth Beaman
John, Betty
See John, Elizabeth Beaman
John, Colin
See Hagan, Chet
John, Dane
See Major, Alan P(ercival)
John, DeWitt 1915-1985 Obituary ... 117
John, Elizabeth Beaman 1907- ... CANR-8
Earlier sketch in CA 5-6R
John, Errol 1924-1988 Obituary ... 126
John, Helen James 1930- ... 61-64
John, Owen 1918- Brief entry ... 117
John, Robert ... 29-32R
John, Sandra D(eanne Thompson) 1951- ... 114
John, Vera P.
See John-Steiner, Vera P(olgar)
Johnn, David
See Engle, John D(avid), Jr.
John Paul I, Pope 1912-1978 ... 81-84
John Paul II, Pope 1920- Brief entry ... 106
Johnpoll, Bernard K(eith) 1918- ... CANR-24
Earlier sketches in CA 21-22R, CANR-9

Johns, Albert Cameron 1914- CANR-6
Earlier sketch in CA 49-52
Johns, Avery
See Cousins, Margaret
Johns, Claude J., Jr. 1930- 77-80
Johns, Edward Alistair 1936- 45-48
Johns, Elizabeth 1937- 121
Johns, Eric 1907-1975 Obituary 116
Johns, Foster
See Seldes, Gilbert (Vivian)
Johns, Geoffrey
See Warner, (George) Geoffrey John
Johns, Glover S., Jr. 1911(?)-1976
Obituary 65-68
Johns, Janetta
See Quin-Harkin, Janet
Johns, John E(dwin) 1921- 9-10R
Johns, June 1925- 57-60
Johns, Kenneth
See Bulmer, (Henry) Kenneth
Johns, Marston
See Fanthorpe, R(obert) Lionel
Johns, Ray E(arl) 1900- 41-44R
Johns, Richard A(lton) 1929- 19-20R
Johns, Warren L. 1929- 23-24R
Johns, Whitey
See White, John I(rwin)
Johns, William Earle 1893-1968 73-76
Johnsen, Trevor Bernard Meldal
See Meldal-Johnsen, Trevor Bernard
Johnsgard, Karin L(uisa) 1964- 118
Johnsgard, Paul A(ustin) 1931- CANR-17
Earlier sketches in CA 49-52, CANR-1
Johnson, A.
See Johnson, Annabell Jones
Johnson, A. E.
See Johnson, Annabell Jones
and Johnson, Edgar Raymond
Johnson, Alan P(ackard) 1929- 19-20R
Johnson, Albert (Franklin) 1904- CANR-6
Earlier sketch in CA 9-10R
Johnson, Alden Porter 1914-1972
Obituary 104
Johnson, Allen 85-88
Johnson, Allison H(eartz) 1910- 41-44R
Johnson, Alvin 1874-1971 Obituary 29-32R
Johnson, Amandus 1877-1974 Obituary ... 49-52
Johnson, Andrew N(isseu) 1887-1982 61-64
Obituary 120
Johnson, Ann Cox
See Saunders, Ann Loreille
Johnson, Annabell Jones 1921- 9-10R
See also SATA 2
Johnson, Arno Hollock 1901-1985
Obituary 116
Johnson, Arnold W(aldemar) 1900- CAP-1
Earlier sketch in CA 13-14
Johnson, Arthur Menzies 1921- 21-22R
Johnson, Arthur W(illiam) 1920- 117
Johnson, Aubrey Rodway 1901-1985
Obituary 117
Johnson, Audrey P(ike) 1915- CANR-15
Earlier sketch in CA 93-96
Johnson, B(owen) C(harleston) 1945- 107
Johnson, B(urdetta) F(aye) 1920- CANR-3
Earlier sketch in CA 4R
Johnson, B(asil) L(eonard) C(lyde) 1919- ... 120
Johnson, B(ryan) S(tanley William)
1933-1973 .... CANR-9
Obituary 53-56
Earlier sketch in CA 9-10R
See also DLB 14, 40
See also CLC 6, 9
Johnson, Barbara F(erry) 1923- 73-76
Johnson, Barclay G(iddings) 1909-1985
Obituary 116
Johnson, Barry L(ynn) 1934- 33-36R
Johnson, Barry L(ee) 1943- 61-64
Johnson, Bea ?-1976 Obituary 65-68
Johnson, Ben E(ugene) 1940- CANR-8
Earlier sketch in CA 61-64
Johnson, Benj. F., of Boone
See Riley, James Whitcomb
Johnson, Benjamin A. 1937- CANR-9
Earlier sketch in CA 23-24R
Johnson, Benjamin F., of Boone
See Riley, James Whitcomb
Johnson, Benton 1928- 81-84
Johnson, Bernard 1933- 33-36R
Johnson, Bertha French 1906- 41-44R
Johnson, Beth 1953- 118
Johnson, Bradford 1937- 57-60
Johnson, Brian (Martin) 1925- CANR-23
Earlier sketch in CA 106
Johnson, Bruce 1933- 33-36R
Johnson, Burges 1877-1963 Obituary 89-92
Johnson, Byron Lindberg 1917- 21-22R
Johnson, C. Edward
See Johnson, Carl E(dward)
Johnson, C. F.
See Goulart, Frances Sheridan
Johnson, Carl E(dward) 1937- 25-28R
Johnson, Carl G(raves) 1915- 101
Johnson, Carol Virginia 1928- CANR-6
Earlier sketch in CA 9-10R
Johnson, Carroll B(ernard) 1938- 73-76
Johnson, Cecil Edward 1927- 33-36R
Johnson, Chalmers A(shby) 1931- CANR-6
Earlier sketch in CA 5-6R
Johnson, Charlene
See Crawford, Char
Johnson, Charles (Richard) 1948- 116
See also BW
See also DLB 33
See also CLC 7
Johnson, Charles Benjamin 1928-1980 .. CANR-4
Earlier sketch in CA 7-8R
Johnson, Charles Ellicott 1920-1969 .... 1R
Obituary 103
Johnson, Charles R. 1925- 65-68
See also SATA 11
Johnson, Charles S(purgeon) 1893-1956 ... 125
See also BW
See also DLB 51
Johnson, Charles S.
See Edwards, William B(ennett)
Johnson, Charles W(illiam) 1934- 107
Johnson, Charlotte Buel
See von Wodtke, Charlotte Buel Johnson
See also SATA 46
Johnson, Christine 1943- 123
Johnson, Christopher 1931- CANR-8
Earlier sketch in CA 13-14R
Johnson, Christopher Howard 1937-
Brief entry 106
Johnson, Chuck
See Johnson, Charles R.
Johnson, Clair 1915(?)-1980 Obituary ... 97-100
Johnson, Claudia Alta (Taylor) 1912- 89-92
Johnson, Claudia D(urst) 1938- 114
Johnson, Clive (White, Jr.) 1930- 29-32R
Johnson, Crockett
See Leisk, David Johnson
Johnson, Curt(is Lee) 1928- 33-36R
Johnson, Curtiss Sherman 1899- 45-48
Johnson, D(onald) Barton 1933- 33-36R
Johnson, D(avid) Bruce 1942- 61-64
Johnson, D(avid) Gale 1916- 19-20R
Johnson, D(ana) William 1945- 97-100
See also SATA 23
Johnson, Dale A(rthur) 1936- 37-40R
Johnson, Dave W(illiam) 1931- 93-96
Johnson, David 1927- CANR-8
Earlier sketch in CA 15-16R
Johnson, David G(eorge) 1906- 9-10R
Johnson, David Lawrence 1943- 114
Johnson, David Ralph 1942- 117
Johnson, Deidre A(nn) 1953- 116
Johnson, Denis 1949- 121
Brief entry 117
Johnson, Diane 1934- CANR-17
Earlier sketch in CA 41-44R
See also DLBY 80
See also CLC 5, 13, 48
Johnson, Don 1934- 116
Johnson, Donald Bruce 1921-1981 .... CANR-25
Earlier sketch in CA 1R
Johnson, Donald M(cEwen) 1909- 4R
Johnson, Donald McI(ntosh) 1903- CANR-8
Earlier sketch in CA 7-8R
Johnson, Donna Kay 1935- 106
Johnson, Donovan A(lbert) 1910- CANR-5
Earlier sketch in CA 7-8R
Johnson, Doris McNeely 1941- 111
Johnson, Dorothy Biddle 1887(?)-1974
Obituary 53-56
Johnson, Dorothy E(thel) 1920- 53-56
Johnson, Dorothy M(arie) 1905-1984 ... CANR-6
Obituary 114
Earlier sketch in CA 5-6R
See also SATA 6, 40
Johnson, Dorris 1914- 109
Johnson, Douglas W(ayne) 1934- CANR-21
Earlier sketches in CA 57-60, CANR-6
Johnson, E(dgar) A(gustus) J(erome)
1900-1972 .... CAP-1
Obituary 37-40R
Earlier sketch in CA 17-18
Johnson, E(arly) Ashby 1917- 33-36R
Johnson, E(ugene) Harper SATA-44
Johnson, E. Ned
See Johnson, Enid
Johnson, E(mil) Richard 1937- 104
Johnson, E(dward) W(arren) 1941- 29-32R
Johnson, Earl, Jr. 1933- CANR-10
Earlier sketch in CA 61-64
Johnson, Earl S.
See Johnson, Earl Shepard
Johnson, Earl Shepard 1894-1986
Obituary 119
Johnson, Edgar 1901-1972 .... 9-10R
Obituary 125
Johnson, Edgar Raymond 1912- 9-10R
See also SATA 2
Johnson, Edward 1598-1672 .... DLB-24
Johnson, Edward A(ndrew) 1915- 37-40R
Johnson, Edwin Clark (Toby) 1945- CANR-25
Earlier sketch in CA 107
Johnson, Eleanor
See Seymour, Dorothy Jane Z(ander)
Johnson, Eleanor Murdock 1892-1987
Obituary 123
Johnson, Electa Search 1909- 4R
Johnson, Elizabeth 1911-1984 .... CANR-4
Obituary 117
Earlier sketch in CA 1R
See also SATA 7, 39
Johnson, Ellen Argo 1933-1983 .... CANR-13
Obituary 110
Earlier sketch in CA 73-76
Johnson, Ellen Argo
See Argo, Ellen
Johnson, Ellen H. 1910- CANR-15
Earlier sketch in CA 37-40R
Johnson, Elmer Douglas 1915- CANR-3
Earlier sketch in CA 9-10R
Johnson, Elmer Hubert 1917- 15-16R
Johnson, Enid 1892- 73-76
Johnson, Eola 1909- 49-52
Johnson, Eric W(arner) 1918- CANR-4
Earlier sketch in CA 5-6R
See also SATA 8
Johnson, Evelyne 1922- CANR-21
Earlier sketch in CA 69-72
See also SATA 20
Johnson, Eyvind (Olof Verner)
1900-1976 73-76
Obituary 69-72
See also CLC 14
Johnson, Falk S(immons) 1913- 19-20R
Johnson, Fenton 1888-1958 124
Brief entry 118
See also BW
See also DLB 45, 50
Johnson, Ferd 1905- 69-72
Johnson, Forrest B(ryant) 1935- 106
Johnson, Franklyn A(rthur) 1921- CANR-4
Earlier sketch in CA 1R
Johnson, Frederick 1932- 73-76
Johnson, Fridolf (Lester) 1905-1988 103
Obituary 126
Johnson, Frosty
See Johnson, Forrest B(ryant)
Johnson, G(eorge) Orville 1915- CANR-4
Earlier sketch in CA 1R
Johnson, Gaylord 1884- CAP-1
Earlier sketch in CA 9-10
See also SATA 7
Johnson, Geoffrey 1893-1966 .... CAP-1
Earlier sketch in CA 13-14
Johnson, George 1917- 7-8R
Johnson, George (Laclede) 1952- 123
Johnson, Georgia Douglas (Camp)
1886-1966 125
See also BW
See also DLB 51
Johnson, Gerald White 1890-1980 85-88
Obituary 97-100
See also SATA 19, 28
See also DLB 29
Johnson, Gertrude F(alk) 1929- 57-60
Johnson, Greer 1920(?)-1974 Obituary 53-56
Johnson, H(arold) B(enjamin), Jr.
1931- 29-32R
Johnson, H(erbert) Webster 1906- CANR-4
Earlier sketch in CA 5-6R
Johnson, Halvard 1936- 33-36R
Johnson, Harold L. 1924- 13-14R
Johnson, Harold Scholl 1929- 37-40R
Johnson, Harold V. 1897- CANR-5
Earlier sketch in CA 4R
Johnson, Harper
See Johnson, E(ugene) Harper
Johnson, Harriett 1908-1987 Obituary 123
See also SATA 53
Johnson, Harry Alleyn 1921- 45-48
Johnson, Harry G(ordon) 1923-1977 .... 5-6R
Obituary 69-72
Johnson, Harry L. 1929- 29-32R
Johnson, Harry Morton 1917- 9-10R
Johnson, Harvey L(eroy) 1904- 37-40R
Johnson, Haynes Bonner 1931- CANR-12
Earlier sketch in CA 7-8R
Johnson, Helen (Louise) Kendrick
1844(?)-1917 Brief entry 123
Johnson, Helene 1907- DLB-51
Johnson, Henry
See Hammond, John (Henry, Jr.)
Johnson, Herbert A(lan) 1934- CANR-4
Earlier sketch in CA 5-6R
Johnson, Herbert J. 1933- 29-32R
Johnson, Hildegard Binder 1908- CANR-3
Earlier sketch in CA 9-10R
Johnson, Howard Albert 1915-1974 .... 1R
Obituary 49-52
Johnson, Hugh 1939- CANR-16
Earlier sketch in CA 93-96
Johnson, Humphrey Wynne 1925-1976
Obituary 61-64
Johnson, Irma Bolan 1903- CANR-1
Earlier sketch in CA 3R
Johnson, Irving McClure 1905- 4R
Johnson, J. R.
See James, C(yril) L(ionel) R(obert)
Johnson, Jack
See Johnson, John Arthur
Johnson, Jalmar Edwin 1905- 7-8R
Johnson, James A(llen) 1932- Brief entry ... 110
Johnson, James Craig 1944- 53-56
Johnson, James E(dgar) 1927- 77-80
Johnson, James H(enry) 1930- CANR-11
Earlier sketch in CA 25-28R
Johnson, James J(ay) 1939- 33-36R
Johnson, James L. 1927- CANR-9
Earlier sketch in CA 21-22R
Johnson, James P(earce) 1937- 81-84
Johnson, James Ralph 1922- CANR-2
Earlier sketch in CA 4R
See also SATA 1
Johnson, James Rosser 1916- 9-10R
Johnson, James Turner 1938- 61-64
Johnson, James Weldon 1871-1938 125
Brief entry 104
See also BW
See also SATA 31
See also DLB 51
See also TCLC 3, 19
Johnson, James William 1927- 53-56
Johnson, Jane 1951- 110
See also SATA 48
Johnson, Jane M(axine) 1914- 49-52
Johnson, Jann
See Johnson, Paula Janice
Johnson, (Hettie) Jean 1937- 126
Johnson, Jean Dye 1920- 23-24R
Johnson, Jerry Mack 1927- CANR-4
Earlier sketch in CA 53-56
Johnson, Jim
See Johnson, James A(llen)
Johnson, Jinna
See Johnson, Virginia
Johnson, Joan D. 1929- Brief entry 106
Johnson, Joan Helen 1931- 61-64
Johnson, Joan J. 1942- 122
Johnson, Joe Donald 1943- 57-60
Johnson, John Arthur 1878-1946
Brief entry 115
Johnson, John Bockover, Jr. 1912-1972
Obituary 106
Johnson, John E(mil) 1929- 110
See also SATA 34
Johnson, John J. 1912- 9-10R
Johnson, John M(yrton) 1941- 93-96
Johnson, Johnni 1922- 13-14R
Johnson, Joseph A., Jr. 1914(?)-1979
Obituary 89-92
Johnson, Joseph E(arl) 1946- 37-40R
Johnson, Joseph M. 1883(?)-1973
Obituary 45-48
Johnson, Josephine W(inslow) 1910- 25-28R
Johnson, Joy Duvall 1932- 110
Johnson, Joyce 1935- Brief entry 125
Johnson, Karen 1939- 69-72
Johnson, Kathryn 1929- 33-36R
Johnson, Keith B(arnard) 1933- 29-32R
Johnson, Kendall 1928- 69-72
Johnson, Kenneth G(ardner) 1922- 41-44R
Johnson, Kenneth M(itchell) 1903- 5-6R
Johnson, Kristi Planck 1944- 57-60
Johnson, L. D. 1916- 33-36R
Johnson, La Verne B(ravo) 1925- 65-68
See also SATA 13
Johnson, Lady Bird
See Johnson, Claudia Alta (Taylor)
Johnson, Lemuel A. 1941- 53-56
Johnson, LeRoy C. 1937- 126
Johnson, Lewis Kerr 1904- 1R
Johnson, Lincoln F., Jr. 1920- 81-84
Johnson, Lionel (Pigot) 1867-1902
Brief entry 117
See also DLB 19
See also TCLC 19
Johnson, Loch K. 1942- 121
Johnson, Lois Smith 1894- CAP-1
Earlier sketch in CA 9-10
See also SATA 6
Johnson, Lois Walfrid 1936- CANR-6
Earlier sketch in CA 57-60
See also SATA 22
Johnson, Louis 1924- CANR-18
Earlier sketch in CA 101
Johnson, Luke Timothy 1943- Brief entry ... 107
Johnson, Lyndon Baines 1908-1973 ... CANR-23
Obituary 41-44R
Earlier sketch in CA 53-56
Johnson, Lynn Eric 1932- Brief entry 108
Johnson, M. Glen 1936- 41-44R
Johnson, M. L.
See Abercrombie, M(innie) L(ouie) J(ohnson)
Johnson, Malcolm (Malone) 1904-1976 ... 69-72
Obituary 65-68
Johnson, Malcolm L. 1937- 69-72
Johnson, Manly 1920- 89-92
Johnson, Margaret 1926- 37-40R
Johnson, Margaret S(weet) 1893-1964
Obituary 113
See also SATA 35
Johnson, Marilue Carolyn 1931- CANR-1
Earlier sketch in CA 45-48
Johnson, Marion Georgina Wikeley
1912-1980 .... 11-12R
Obituary 97-100
Johnson, Mark 1949- 115
Johnson, Marshall D. 1935- 33-36R
Johnson, Mary Anne 1943- 53-56
Johnson, Mary Ellen 1949- 120
Johnson, Mary Frances K. 1929(?)-1979
Obituary 104
See also SATA 27
Johnson, Mary Louise
See King, Mary Louise
Johnson, Mary Ritz 1904- CAP-1
Earlier sketch in CA 9-10
Johnson, Maryanna 1925- 33-36R
Johnson, Maud Battle 1918(?)-1985
Obituary 117
See also SATA 46
Johnson, Maurice (O.) 1913-1978 ..... CANR-20
Earlier sketch in CA 1R
Johnson, Mauritz (Jr.) 1922- 41-44R
Johnson, Mel
See Malzberg, Barry N(athaniel)
Johnson, Mendal W(illiam) 1928-1976 101
Johnson, Merle Allison 1934- 37-40R
Johnson, Michael L(illard) 1943- CANR-19
Earlier sketches in CA 53-56, CANR-4
Johnson, Mike
See Sharkey, John Michael
Johnson, Milton 1932- SATA-31
Johnson, Nancy E(dith) 1941- 125
Johnson, Neil (James) 1955- 123
Johnson, Nicholas 1934- 29-32R
Johnson, Niel M(elvin) 1931- 41-44R
Johnson, Nora 1933- 106
Johnson, Nunnally 1897-1977 81-84
Obituary 69-72
See also DLB 26
Johnson, Olga Weydemeyer 1901- CAP-2
Earlier sketch in CA 29-32
Johnson, Oliver A(dolph) 1923- CANR-12
Earlier sketch in CA 29-32R
Johnson, Owen 1878-1952 .... DLBY-87

INDEX

Johnson, Pamela Hansford 1912-1981 .. CANR-2
Obituary ... 104
Earlier sketch in CA 2R
See also DLB 15
See also CLC 1, 7, 27
Johnson, Patrick Spencer 1938- ... 9-10R
Johnson, Paul (Bede) 1928- ... 17-18R
Johnson, Paul C(ornelius) 1904- ... 81-84
Johnson, Paul E(manuel) 1898- ... 15-16R
Johnson, Paul Victor 1920- ... 3R
Johnson, Paula Janice 1946- ... 106
Johnson, Pauline B. ... 1R
Johnson, Penelope D(elafield) 1938- ... 124
Johnson, Peter 1930- ... 65-68
Johnson, Philip A(rthur) 1915- ... 15-16R
Johnson, Philip Cortelyou 1906-
Brief entry ... 106
Johnson, Phyllis (Anne) 1937-1985 ... 126
Brief entry ... 108
Johnson, Pierce 1921- ... 41-44R
Johnson, Quentin G. 1930- ... 11-12R
Johnson, R(obbin) S(inclair) 1946- ... 29-32R
Johnson, Rachel H(arris) 1887-1983
Obituary ... 110
Johnson, Ralph W(hitney) 1923- ... 77-80
Johnson, Ray(mond Edward) 1927- ... 17-18R
Johnson, Ray DeForest 1926- ... 65-68
Johnson, Raynor C(arey) 1901-
Brief entry ... 115
Johnson, Richard
See Richey, David
Johnson, Richard A(ugust) 1937- ... 37-40R
Johnson, Richard B(righam) 1914-1977 .. 41-44R
Johnson, Richard C. 1919- ... 33-36R
Johnson, Richard D(avid) 1927- ... 109
Johnson, Richard N(ewhall) 1900-1971
Obituary ... 104
Johnson, Richard R(igby) 1942- ... 116
Johnson, Richard Tanner
See Pascale, Richard Tanner
Johnson, Robert A. 1921- ... 61-64
Johnson, Robert C(lyde) 1919- ... 5-6R
Johnson, Robert Erwin 1923- ... 37-40R
Johnson, Robert I(var) 1933- ... 53-56
Johnson, Robert J. 1933- ... 23-24R
Johnson, Robert L. 1919- ... 33-36R
Johnson, Robert L(eon, Jr.) 1930- ... 33-36R
Johnson, Robert Owen 1926- ... 33-36R
Johnson, Robert Sherlaw 1932- ... 61-64
Johnson, Robert W(illard) 1921- ... 19-20R
Johnson, Roger N(ylund) 1939- ... 53-56
Johnson, Ronald 1935- ... CANR-20
Earlier sketches in CA 9-10R, CANR-4
Johnson, Ronald C. 1927- ... 81-84
Johnson, Ronald M(aberry) 1936- ... 126
Brief entry ... 108
Johnson, Rossall J(ames) 1917- ... 21-22R
Johnson, Ruby Kelley 1928- ... 33-36R
Johnson, Ruth I.
See Jay, Ruth I(ngrid)
Johnson, (Walter) Ryerson 1901- ... CANR-2
Earlier sketch in CA 7-8R
See also SATA 10
Johnson, S(amuel) Lawrence
1909-1978 ... CANR-12
Earlier sketch in CA 29-32R
Johnson, Sabina Thorne
See Thorne, Sabina
Johnson, Sam Houston 1914(?)-1978 ... 89-92
Obituary ... 81-84
Johnson, Samuel 1696-1772 ... DLB-24
Johnson, Samuel 1709-1784 ... DLB-39
Johnson, Samuel 1822-1882 ... DLB-1
Johnson, Samuel A(ugustus) 1895- ... 17-18R
Johnson, Sherman E(lbridge) 1908- ... 53-56
Johnson, Sherman Ellsworth 1896-1978
Obituary ... 77-80
Johnson, Shirley K(ing) 1927- ... 11-12R
See also SATA 10
Johnson, Siddie Joe 1905-1977 Obituary ... 106
See also SATA 20
Johnson, Sonia 1936- ... 118
Johnson, Spencer 1938- ... 110
See also SATA 38
Johnson, Stanley (Patrick) 1940- ... CANR-13
Earlier sketch in CA 23-24R
Johnson, Stanley J. F. 1920(?)-1978
Obituary ... 77-80
Johnson, Stanley L(ewis) 1920- ... 17-18R
Johnson, (John) Stephen 1947- ... 107
Johnson, (Edward) Stowers ... 7-8R
Johnson, Sylvia A. ... SATA-52
Johnson, Thomas Frank 1920- ... 9-10R
Johnson, Thomas Herbert 1902-1985 ... 124
Johnson, Thomas William 1946-
Brief entry ... 110
Johnson, Una E. Brief entry ... 109
Johnson, Uwe 1934-1984 ... CANR-1
Obituary ... 112
Earlier sketch in CA 3R
See also DLB 75
See also CLC 5, 10, 15, 40
Johnson, Van L(oran) 1908- ... 37-40R
Johnson, Vernon E(dwin) 1920- ... 93-96
Johnson, Victor Hugo 1912- Brief entry ... 110
Johnson, Virginia 1914-1975 ... CAP-2
Earlier sketch in CA 33-36
Johnson, Virginia E. 1925- ... 21-22R
Johnson, Virginia W(eisel) 1910- ... 19-20R
Johnson, W. Bolingbroke
See Bishop, Morris
Johnson, W(illiam) Branch 1893- ... CANR-5
Earlier sketch in CA 7-8R
Johnson, W(illiam) E(rnest) 1858-1931
Brief entry ... 122
Johnson, W(alter) R(alph) 1933- ... CANR-9
Earlier sketch in CA 65-68
Johnson, W(endell) Stacy 1927- ... CANR-17
Earlier sketches in CA 1R, CANR-2
Johnson, Walter 1915-1985 ... 89-92
Obituary ... 116
Johnson, Walter Frank, Jr. 1914- ... 7-8R
Johnson, Warren Arthur 1937- ... 33-36R
Johnson, Wayne G(ustave) 1930- ... 113
Johnson, Wendell (Andrew Leroy)
1906-1965 ... CANR-1
Earlier sketch in CA 2R
Johnson, Willard R(aymond) 1935- ... 105
Johnson, William Alexander 1932- ... 7-8R
Johnson, William C(lark, Jr.) 1945- ... CANR-8
Earlier sketch in CA 61-64
Johnson, William R. ... CANR-25
Earlier sketches in CA 17-18R, CANR-7
See also SATA 38
Johnson, William Weber 1909- ... 17-18R
See also SATA 7
Johnson, Winifred (MacNally) 1905- ... 7-8R
Johnson Abercrombie, M. L.
See Abercrombie, M(innie) L(ouie)
J(ohnson)
Johnson-Marshall, Percy E. A. 1915- ... 23-24R
John-Steiner, Vera P(olgar) ... 121
Johnston, A(aron) Montgomery 1915- .. CANR-11
Earlier sketch in CA 29-32R
Johnston, Agnes Christine
See Dazey, Agnes J(ohnston)
Johnston, Alan (William) 1942- ... 103
Johnston, Albert H. 1914- ... 69-72
Johnston, Angus James II 1916- ... 11-12R
Johnston, Annie Fellows 1863-1931
Brief entry ... 116
See also SATA 37
See also DLB 42
Johnston, (William) Arnold 1942- ... 77-80
Johnston, Arthur 1924- ... 23-24R
Johnston, Arvin Harry 1906- ... 2R
Johnston, Basil H. 1929- ... CANR-11
Earlier sketch in CA 69-72
See also DLB 60
Johnston, Bernard 1934- ... 19-20R
Johnston, Bernice Houle 1914-1971 ... CAP-2
Earlier sketch in CA 33-36
Johnston, Brenda A(rlivia) 1944- ... 57-60
Johnston, Brian 1932- ... 65-68
Johnston, Bruce F(oster) 1919- ... CANR-14
Earlier sketch in CA 41-44R
Johnston, Charles (Hepburn)
1912-1986 ... CANR-5
Obituary ... 119
Earlier sketch in CA 15-16R
Johnston, Colin 1946- ... 108
Johnston, Dan 1912- ... 123
Johnston, (William) Denis 1901-1984 ... CAP-2
Obituary ... 113
Earlier sketch in CA 21-22
See also DLB 10
Johnston, Dorothy Grunbock 1915- ... CANR-5
Earlier sketch in CA 7-8R
Johnston, Ellen Turlington 1929- ... 65-68
Johnston, Fran(ces Jonsson) 1925- ... 15-16R
Johnston, Francis E. 1931- ... CANR-4
Earlier sketch in CA 53-56
Johnston, George 1913- ... CANR-15
Earlier sketch in CA 89-92
Johnston, George (Benson) 1913- ... CANR-20
Earlier sketches in CA 2R, CANR-5
Johnston, George Burke 1907- ... CAP-1
Earlier sketch in CA 17-18
Johnston, Gordon (Frederick) 1920-1983 ... 122
Johnston, H(ugh) A(nthony) S(tephen)
1913-1967 ... CAP-2
Earlier sketch in CA 21-22
See also SATA 14
Johnston, H(ugh) J(ames) M(orton)
1939- ... 41-44R
Johnston, Hank
See Johnston, Henry
Johnston, Henry 1922- ... 25-28R
Johnston, Herbert (Leo) 1912- ... 7-8R
Johnston, Hugh Buckner 1913- ... 69-72
Johnston, Jennifer 1930- ... 85-88
See also DLB 14
See also CLC 7
Johnston, Jill 1929- ... 53-56
Johnston, Johanna 1914(?)-1982 ... CANR-7
Obituary ... 108
Earlier sketch in CA 57-60
See also SATA 12, 33
Johnston, John H(ubert) 1921- ... 11-12R
Johnston, John M. 1898(?)-1979
Obituary ... 89-92
Johnston, Kenneth R(ichard) 1938- ... 121
Johnston, Leonard 1920- ... CANR-11
Earlier sketch in CA 15-16R
Johnston, Lynn (Beverley) 1947- ... 110
Johnston, Mary 1870-1936 Brief entry ... 109
See also DLB 9
Johnston, Minton C(oyne) 1900- ... 7-8R
Johnston, Mireille 1940- ... 49-52
Johnston, Norma ... 105
See also SATA 29
Johnston, Norman (Bruce) 1921- ... CANR-18
Earlier sketch in CA 93-96
Johnston, Norman J. 1918- ... 120
Johnston, Portia
See Takakjian, Portia
Johnston, R(onald) J(ohn) 1941- ... CANR-18
Earlier sketch in CA 101
Johnston, Randolph W(ardell) 1904- ... CANR-15
Earlier sketch in CA 85-88
Johnston, Richard Malcolm 1822-1898 .. DLB-74
Johnston, Richard W(yckoff) 1915-1981
Obituary ... 104
Johnston, Robert Kent 1945- ... 104
Johnston, Ronald 1926- ... 15-16R
Johnston, Russell G. 1933- ... 118
Johnston, S(amuel) Paul 1899-1985
Obituary ... 117
Johnston, Susan Taylor 1942- ... CANR-15
Earlier sketch in CA 41-44R
Johnston, Terry C(onrad) 1947- ... 113
Johnston, Thomas 1945- ... 104
Johnston, Thomas E. 1931- ... 15-16R
Johnston, Tony
See Johnston, Susan Taylor
See also SATA 8
Johnston, Velma B. 1912(?)-1977
Obituary ... 69-72
Johnston, Wayne 1958- ... 125
Johnston, William 1924- ... 85-88
Johnston, William 1925- ... 33-36R
Johnston, William M(urray) 1936- ... 37-40R
Johnstone, Charles 1719(?)-1800(?) ... DLB-39
Johnstone, D(onald) Bruce 1909- ... 104
Johnstone, Henry W(ebb), Jr. 1920- ... 1R
Johnstone, Iain 1943- ... 108
Johnstone, Kathleen Yerger 1906- ... 9-10R
Johnstone, Lammy Olcott 1949- ... CANR-14
Earlier sketch in CA 81-84
Johnstone, Parker Lochiel 1903- ... 69-72
Johnstone, Rex
See Chapman, Frank M(onroe)
Johnstone, Robert 1951- ... 118
Johnstone, Robert Morton, Jr. 1939- ... 81-84
Johnstone, T(homas) M(uir) 1924-1983
Obituary ... 114
Johnstone, Ted
See McDaniel, David (Edward)
Johnstone, William D(avid) G(ordon)
1935- ... 77-80
Johnston-Saint, Peter 1889-1974
Obituary ... 53-56
John XXIII, Pope 1881-1963 Obituary ... 113
Joiner, Charles A(drian) 1932- ... 77-80
Joiner, Charles W(ycliffe) 1916- ... CANR-1
Earlier sketch in CA 4R
Joiner, Edward Earl 1924- ... 49-52
Joiner, Verna J(ones) 1896- ... 4R
Joki, Virginia (Carville) 1909(?)-1986
Obituary ... 120
Jolas, Eugene 1894-1952 Brief entry ... 107
See also DLB 4, 45
Joliat, Eugene 1910- ... 49-52
Joliffe, John E(dward) A(ustin) 1891-1964 .. 7-8R
Jolin, Stephen Towne 1941- ... 45-48
Jolivet, R(egis) 1891-1966 ... CAP-1
Earlier sketch in CA 9-10
Joll, (Dowrish) Evelyn (Louis) 1925- ... 101
Joll, James (Bysse) 1918- ... CANR-7
Earlier sketch in CA 7-8R
Jolley, (Monica) Elizabeth 1923- ... CLC-46
Jolley, (Stephen) Nicholas 1948- ... 120
Jolliffe, H(arold) R(ichard) 1904-1978 ... 4R
Obituary ... 103
Jolly, Alison 1937- ... CANR-15
Earlier sketch in CA 41-44R
Jolly, Clifford J. 1939- Brief entry ... 108
Jolly, Cyril Arthur 1910- ... CAP-1
Earlier sketch in CA 9-10
Jolly, Hugh R. 1918-1986 ... 85-88
Obituary ... 118
Jolly, W(illiam) P(ercy) 1922- ... CANR-4
Earlier sketch in CA 53-56
Jolly Cholly
See Grimm, Charles John
Jolson, Marvin A(rnold) 1922- ... CANR-1
Earlier sketch in CA 49-52
Joly, Cyril Bencraft 1918- ... CAP-1
Earlier sketch in CA 9-10
Jonas, A(dolphe) David 1913- ... 107
Jonas, Ann 1919- ... 105
Jonas, Ann 1932- Brief entry ... 118
See also SATA 42, 50
See also CLR 12
Jonas, Arthur 1930- ... 13-14R
Jonas, Carl 1913-1976 ... 9-10R
Obituary ... 69-72
Jonas, Doris F(rances) 1916- ... CANR-8
Earlier sketch in CA 61-64
Jonas, George 1935- ... 29-32R
Jonas, Gerald 1935- ... 65-68
Jonas, Hans 1903- ... CANR-23
Earlier sketches in CA 61-64, CANR-7
Jonas, Ilsedore B. 1920- ... 33-36R
Jonas, Klaus W(erner) 1920- ... CANR-2
Earlier sketch in CA 1R
Jonas, Manfred 1927- ... CANR-8
Earlier sketch in CA 21-22R
Jonas, Norman N. 1931-1988 Obituary ... 125
Jonas, Paul 1922- ... CANR-13
Earlier sketch in CA 73-76
Jonas, Steven 1936- ... 89-92
Jonassen, Christen T(onnes) 1912- ... 41-44R
Joncich, Geraldine
See Clifford, Geraldine Joncich
Jones, A(rnold) H(ugh) M(artin)
1904-1970 Obituary ... 89-92
Jones, A(rthur) Morris 1899- ... CAP-1
Earlier sketch in CA 13-14
Jones, Adam Mars
See Mars-Jones, Adam
Jones, Adrienne 1915- ... 33-36R
See also SATA 7
Jones, Alan Griffith 1943- ... CANR-19
Earlier sketch in CA 103
Jones, Alan Moore, Jr. 1942- ... 53-56
Jones, Alan William 1940- ... 117
Jones, Alexander 1906-1970 ... CANR-2
Obituary ... 103
Earlier sketch in CA 2R
Jones, Allan Gwynne
See Gwynne-Jones, Allan
Jones, Andrew 1921- ... 93-96
Jones, Andrew (Eric) 1950- ... 111
Jones, Annabel
See Lewis, Mary (Christianna Milne)
Jones, Annabel
See Lewis, Mary (Christianna)
Jones, Antony Armstrong
See Armstrong-Jones, Antony (Charles
Robert)
Jones, Archer 1926- ... CANR-18
Earlier sketches in CA 1R, CANR-4
Jones, Archie N(eff) 1900- ... CAP-1
Earlier sketch in CA 15-16
Jones, Arthur F(rederick) 1945- ... 81-84
Jones, Arthur Glyn Prys
See Prys-Jones, Arthur Glyn
Jones, (Alun) Arthur Gwynne 1919-
Brief entry ... 120
Jones, Arthur Hope
See Hope-Jones, Arthur
Jones, Arthur (Mervyn) Keppel
See Keppel-Jones, Arthur (Mervyn)
Jones, Arthur Llewellyn 1863-1947
Brief entry ... 104
Jones, Aubrey 1911- ... 103
Jones, Barbara (Mildred) 1917(?)-1978 .. CANR-4
Obituary ... 81-84
Earlier sketch in CA 1R
Jones, Bessie 1902-1984 Obituary ... 114
Jones, Betty Millsaps 1940- ... 109
Jones, Bill
See Jones, William David Anthony
Jones, Billy M(ac) 1925- ... CANR-25
Earlier sketches in CA 21-22R, CANR-10
Jones, Bob
See Jones, Robert Reynolds, Jr.
Jones, Bobby
See Jones, Robert Tyre, Jr.
Jones, Brian 1938- Brief entry ... 119
Jones, Bryan L. 1945- ... 110
Jones, C(lifton) Clyde 1922- ... 109
Jones, C. M.
See Jones, Clarence Medlycott
Jones, Calico
See Richardson, Gladwell
Jones, Candy 1925- ... 107
Jones, Capt. Wilbur
See Edwards, William B(ennett)
Jones, Carolyn (Sue) 1933-1983 ... 29-32R
Obituary ... 110
Jones, Charles 1910- ... CAP-1
Earlier sketch in CA 9-10
Jones, Charles Alfred 1921-1982 Obituary .. 107
Jones, Charles C., Jr. 1831-1893 ... DLB-30
Jones, Charles Edwin 1932- ... CANR-23
Earlier sketch in CA 49-52
Jones, Charles M(artin) 1912- ... SATA-53
Jones, Charles O(scar) 1931- ... CANR-7
Earlier sketch in CA 19-20R
Jones, Charles W(illiams) 1905- ... 15-16R
Jones, Cheslyn Peter Montague
1918-1987(?) Obituary ... 125
Jones, Christina Hendry 1896- ... 73-76
Jones, (Audrey) Christine 1937- ... 61-64
Jones, Christopher 1937- ... 23-24R
Jones, Chuck
See Jones, Charles M(artin)
Jones, Clarence Medlycott 1913(?)-1986
Obituary ... 118
Jones, Clifford M(erton) 1902- ... 17-18R
Jones, Craig 1945- ... 81-84
Jones, Cranston E(dward) 1918- ... CANR-26
Earlier sketch in CA 2R
Jones, Cyril Meredith 1904- ... CAP-2
Earlier sketch in CA 23-24
Jones, D(ennis) F(eltham) Brief entry ... 111
Jones, D(ouglas) G(ordon) 1929- ... CANR-13
Earlier sketch in CA 29-32R
See also DLB 53
See also CLC 10
Jones, D(avid) Gareth 1940- ... 106
Jones, D(onald) L(ewis) 1925- ... 25-28R
Jones, D(avid) Mervyn 1922- ... 21-22R
Jones, Daisy (Marvel) 1906- ... 17-18R
Jones, Dan Burne 1908- ... 65-68
Jones, Daniel 1881-1967 ... CANR-6
Earlier sketch in CA 5-6R
Jones, David (Michael) 1895-1974 ... 9-10R
Obituary ... 53-56
See also DLB 20
See also CLC 2, 4, 7, 13, 42
Jones, David Arthur 1946- ... CANR-13
Earlier sketch in CA 73-76
Jones, David Pryce
See Pryce-Jones, David
Jones, David Rhodes 1932- ... 101
Jones, David Richard 1942- ... 125
Jones, David Robert 1947- ... 103
Jones, Diana Wynne 1934- ... CANR-26
Earlier sketches in CA 49-52, CANR-4
See also SATA 9
See also CLC 26
Jones, Dolores Blythe 1947- ... 120
Jones, Don 1924- ... 125
Jones, (Gene) Donald 1931- ... CANR-15
Earlier sketch in CA 85-88
Jones, Donald (Lawrence) 1938- ... 19-20R
Jones, Dorothy Holder ... 9-10R
Jones, Douglas C(lyde) 1924- ... CANR-12
Earlier sketch in CA 21-22R
See also SATA 52
Jones, Duane
See Jones, Dorothy Holder
Jones, DuPre Anderson 1937- ... 21-22R

Jones, E(li) Stanley 1884-1973 ... 93-96
  Obituary ... 41-44R
Jones, E(ndsley) Terrence 1941- ... 33-36R
Jones, E(lbert) Winston 1911- ... 13-14R
Jones, Ebenezer 1820-1860 ... DLB-32
Jones, (Hilary) Edgar 1953- ... 118
Jones, Edgar A(llen), Jr. 1921- ... 89-92
Jones, Edward A(llen) 1903- ... 25-28R
Jones, Edward E(llsworth) 1926- ... 17-18R
Jones, Edward H(arral), Jr. 1922- ... 15-16R
Jones, Eldred D(urosimi) 1925- ... 45-48
Jones, Elizabeth B(rown) 1907- ... 61-64
Jones, Elizabeth Orton 1910- ... 77-80
  See also SATA 18
Jones, Elwyn 1923-1982 ... CANR-21
  Obituary ... 106
  Earlier sketch in CA 69-72
Jones, Emlyn (David) 1912-1975 ... CAP-2
  Earlier sketch in CA 23-24
Jones, Emrys 1920- ... 17-18R
Jones, Enid (Mary) Huws 1911- ... 49-52
Jones, Eric Lionel 1936- ... 104
Jones, Ernest 1819-1868 ... DLB-32
Jones, (Alfred) Ernest 1879-1958
  Brief entry ... 121
Jones, Evan 1915- ... CANR-6
  Earlier sketch in CA 9-10R
  See also SATA 3
Jones, Evan David 1903-1987 Obituary ... 122
Jones, Eve (Spiro-John) 1924- ... 2R
Jones, Everett L(ee) 1915- ... 15-16R
Jones, Ezra Earl 1939- ... 57-60
Jones, F(rank) Lancaster 1937- ... 29-32R
Jones, Faustine Childress
  See Jones-Wilson, Faustine C(hildress)
Jones, Felix Edward Aylmer 1889- ... CAP-1
  Earlier sketch in CA 9-10
Jones, Francis P(rice) 1890- ... 9-10R
Jones, Frank 1937- ... 119
Jones, Frank E(dward) 1917- ... 15-16R
Jones, Frank Pierce 1905-1975 Obituary ... 110
Jones, Franklin Ross 1921- ... 53-56
Jones, Frederick George Hall
  See Hall-Jones, Frederick George
Jones, G(eorge) Curtis 1911- ... CANR-3
  Earlier sketch in CA 5-6R
Jones, G(wyn) O(wain) 1917- ... 25-28R
Jones, G(eorge) William 1931- ... CANR-11
  Earlier sketch in CA 21-22R
Jones, Gareth (Elwyn) 1939- ... CANR-19
  Earlier sketch in CA 102
Jones, Garth N(elson) 1925- ... 81-84
Jones, Gary M(artin) 1925- ... 19-20R
Jones, Gayl 1949- ... 77-80
  See also BW
  See also DLB 33
  See also CLC 6, 9
Jones, Gene 1928- ... 21-22R
Jones, Geoffrey (Gareth) 1952- ... 122
Jones, George Chetwynd Griffith
  See Griffith-Jones, George Chetwynd
Jones, George Fenwick 1916- ... CANR-7
  Earlier sketch in CA 13-14R
Jones, George Hilton 1924- ... 33-36R
Jones, George Thaddeus 1917- ... 53-56
Jones, Geraldine 1951- ... SATA-43
Jones, Geraldine
  See McCaughrean, Geraldine
Jones, Gillingham
  See Hamilton, Charles Harold St. John
Jones, (Morgan) Glyn 1905- ... CANR-3
  Earlier sketch in CA 9-10R
  See also DLB 15
Jones, Gordon W(illis) 1915- ... 45-48
Jones, Goronwy J(ohn) 1915- ... 11-12R
Jones, Guy Salisbury
  See Salisbury-Jones, Guy
Jones, Gwen 1951(?)-1988 Obituary ... 124
Jones, Gwendolyn ... 33-36R
Jones, Gwilym Peredur 1892-1975
  Obituary ... 57-60
Jones, Gwyn 1907- ... 124
  Brief entry ... 117
  See also DLB 15
Jones, Gwyneth A. 1952- ... 107
Jones, H(ouston) G(wynne) 1924- ... CANR-13
  Earlier sketch in CA 33-36R
Jones, H(enry) John F(ranklin) 1924- ... 9-10R
Jones, Hardin Blair 1914-1978 Obituary ... 77-80
Jones, Harold 1904- ... CANR-15
  Earlier sketch in CA 85-88
  See also SATA 14
Jones, Harold
  See Page, Gerald W(ilburn)
Jones, Harriet
  See Marble, Harriet Clement
Jones, Harry Lee 1921(?)-1983 Obituary ... 110
Jones, Helen 1917- ... 105
Jones, Helen Hinckley 1903- ... CANR-5
  Earlier sketch in CA 7-8R
  See also SATA 26
Jones, Helen L(ouise) 1903-1973
  Obituary ... 104
  See also SATA 22
Jones, (Max Him) Henri 1921- ... 41-44R
Jones, Henry Albert 1889-1981 Obituary ... 103
Jones, Henry Arthur 1851-1929
  Brief entry ... 110
  See also DLB 10
Jones, Hettie 1934- ... 81-84
  See also SATA 27, 42
Jones, Hortense P. 1918- ... 61-64
  See also SATA 9
Jones, Howard 1940- ... 85-88
Jones, Howard Mumford 1892-1980 ... 85-88
  Obituary ... 97-100
Jones, Howard P(alfry) 1899-1973
  Obituary ... 111
Jones, Hugh 1692(?)-1760 ... DLB-24
Jones, Iris Sanderson 1932- ... 73-76
Jones, J. Farragut
  See Levinson, Leonard
  and Streib, Dan(iel Thomas)
Jones, J(ohn) Ithel 1911- ... CAP-2
  Earlier sketch in CA 25-28
Jones, Jack 1884-1970 Obituary ... 115
Jones, Jack 1913-1984 Obituary ... 113
  Brief entry ... 109
Jones, Jack 1924- ... 85-88
Jones, Jack
  See Jones, James Larkin
Jones, Jacqueline 1948- ... 122
  See also BW
Jones, James 1921-1977 ... CANR-6
  Obituary ... 69-72
  Earlier sketch in CA 2R
  See also DLB 2
  See also CLC 1, 3, 10, 39
  See also AITN 1, 2
Jones, James C(linton) 1922- ... 69-72
Jones, James Henry 1907(?)-1977
  Obituary ... 73-76
Jones, James Larkin 1913- ... 109
Jones, James T. 1948- ... 124
Jones, Jeanie Schmit Kayser
  See Kayser-Jones, Jeanie Schmit
Jones, Jeanne 1937- ... CANR-12
  Earlier sketch in CA 61-64
Jones, Jeannette 1944- ... 110
Jones, Jenkin Lloyd 1911- ... 9-10R
Jones, Jessie Mae Orton 1887(?)-1983
  Obituary ... 111
  See also SATA 37
Jones, Jimmy
  See Jones, Clarence Medlycott
Jones, Jo ... 33-36R
Jones, Joanna
  See Burke, John (Frederick)
Jones, Johanna 1909- ... 118
Jones, John Bush 1940- ... 33-36R
Jones, John Griffin 1955- ... 113
Jones, John J.
  See Lovecraft, H(oward) P(hillips)
Jones, John Paul, Jr. 1912- ... CANR-11
  Earlier sketch in CA 69-72
Jones, John R(obert) 1926- ... 116
Jones, Joseph Jay 1908- ... CANR-16
  Earlier sketches in CA 1R, CANR-1
Jones, Joseph L. 1897-1980 Obituary ... 102
Jones, Judith Paterson 1938- ... 106
Jones, K. Westcott
  See Westcott-Jones, K(enneth)
Jones, Karen Midkiff 1948- ... 104
Jones, Katharine M(acbeth) 1900- ... 7-8R
Jones, Kathleen 1922- ... 81-84
Jones, Kathleen Eve 1944- ... 102
Jones, Kaylie (Ann) 1960- ... 123
Jones, Ken D(uane) 1930- ... 49-52
Jones, Kenley 1935- ... 69-72
Jones, Kenneth E(ffner) 1920- ... 57-60
Jones, Kenneth Glyn 1915- ... 115
Jones, Kenneth LaMar 1931- ... 53-56
Jones, Kenneth S. 1919- ... 21-22R
Jones, Kenneth W. 1934- Brief entry ... 113
Jones, Landon Y(oung) 1943- ... 105
Jones, Leon 1936- ... 101
Jones, Leonidas M(onroe), Sr. 1923- ... 45-48
Jones, (Everett) LeRoi 1934- ... 21-22R
  See also CLC 1, 2, 3, 5, 10, 14
Jones, Leroy P. 1941- ... 118
Jones, Lewis 1897-1939 ... DLB-15
Jones, Lewis Pinckney 1916- ... 61-64
Jones, Linda Phillips
  See Phillips-Jones, Linda
Jones, Lloyd S(cott) 1931- ... CANR-4
  Earlier sketch in CA 4R
Jones, Louis C(lark) 1908- ... 5-6R
Jones, Lyndon Hamer 1927- ... CANR-22
  Earlier sketch in CA 103
Jones, M(arjorie) L(ilian) Glynne
  See Glynne-Jones, M(arjorie) L(ilian)
Jones, Madeline Adams 1913- ... 23-24R
Jones, Madison (Percy, Jr.) 1925- ... CANR-7
  Earlier sketch in CA 13-14R
  See also CLC 4
Jones, Major J. 1919- ... 33-36R
Jones, Major Joseph
  See Thompson, William Tappan
Jones, Malcolm V(ince) 1940- ... 103
Jones, Maldwyn Allen 1922- ... CANR-4
  Earlier sketch in CA 1R
Jones, Marc Edmund 1888- ... 33-36R
Jones, Margaret Boone ... 25-28R
Jones, Margaret E. W. 1938- ... 37-40R
Jones, Marvin 1886-1976 Obituary ... 65-68
Jones, Mary (Elizabeth) 1942- ... 120
Jones, Mary Alice 1898(?)-1980 ... 19-20R
  Obituary ... 118
  See also SATA 6
Jones, Mary Brush 1925- ... 25-28R
Jones, Mary Voell 1933- ... 21-22R
Jones, Maxwell (Shaw) 1907- ... 25-28R
Jones, Maynard Benedict 1904-1972
  Obituary ... 93-96
Jones, McClure ... 112
  See also SATA 34
Jones, Mervyn 1922- ... CANR-1
  Earlier sketch in CA 45-48
  See also CAAS 5
  See also CLC 10
Jones, Michael (Christopher Emlyn)
  1940- ... CANR-20
  Earlier sketch in CA 104
Jones, Michael Owen 1942- ... 101
Jones, Mick 1956(?)- ... CLC-30
Jones, Miriam
  See Schuchman, Joan
Jones, Morris Val 1914- ... 7-8R
Jones, Nard
  See Jones, Maynard Benedict
Jones, Nettie 19(?)- ... CLC-34
Jones, Noel 1939- ... 81-84
Jones, O(wen) R(ogers) 1922- ... 2R
Jones, Oakah L., Jr. 1930- ... CANR-8
  Earlier sketch in CA 17-18R
Jones, Orlando
  See Looker, Antonina (Hansell)
Jones, P(eter) M(ichael) 1949- ... 122
Jones, Pat
  See Jones, Virgil Carrington
Jones, Paul Davis 1940- ... 49-52
Jones, Paul J. 1897(?)-1974 Obituary ... 53-56
Jones, Pearl Binder Elwyn
  See Elwyn-Jones, Pearl Binder
Jones, Peggy 1947- ... 109
Jones, Penelope 1938- ... CANR-14
  Earlier sketch in CA 81-84
  See also SATA 31
Jones, Peter 1920- ... 103
Jones, Peter 1921- ... 7-8R
Jones, Peter (Austin) 1929- ... CANR-4
  Earlier sketch in CA 53-56
Jones, Peter d'Alroy 1931- ... CANR-20
  Earlier sketches in CA 7-8R, CANR-3
Jones, Peter Gaylord 1929- ... 73-76
Jones, Philip Howard 1937- ... 102
Jones, Phillip L. 1928(?)-1979 Obituary ... 89-92
Jones, Pirkle 1914- ... 29-32R
Jones, Preston 1936-1979 ... 73-76
  Obituary ... 89-92
  See also DLB 7
  See also CLC 10
Jones, R(ichard) Ben(jamin) 1933- ... CANR-12
  Earlier sketch in CA 25-28R
Jones, Ray O. 1930- ... 89-92
Jones, Raymond F. 1915- Brief entry ... 106
Jones, Rebecca C(astaldi) 1947- ... CANR-22
  Earlier sketch in CA 106
  See also SATA 33
Jones, Reginald L(anier) 1931- ... 45-48
Jones, Reginald Victor 1911- ... 103
Jones, Richard 1926- ... CANR-2
  Earlier sketch in CA 49-52
Jones, Richard 1953- ... 121
Jones, Richard Allan 1943- ... 103
Jones, Richard Granville 1926- ... 112
Jones, Richard H(utton) 1914- ... 49-52
Jones, Richard M(atthew) 1925- ... 93-96
Jones, Robert B(rinkley) 1942- ... 114
Jones, Robert Emmet 1928- ... CANR-2
  Earlier sketch in CA 1R
Jones, Robert Epes 1908- ... CAP-1
  Earlier sketch in CA 13-14
Jones, Robert F(rancis) 1934- ... CANR-2
  Earlier sketch in CA 49-52
  See also CLC 7
Jones, Robert H(uhn) 1927- ... CANR-2
  Earlier sketch in CA 5-6R
Jones, Robert O(wen) 1928- ... 29-32R
Jones, Robert R(ussell) 1927- ... 69-72
Jones, Robert Reynolds, Jr. 1911- ... CANR-11
  Earlier sketch in CA 25-28R
Jones, Robert Tyre, Jr. 1902-1971
  Obituary ... 113
Jones, Robin Lloyd
  See Lloyd-Jones, Robin
Jones, Rod 1953- ... CLC-50
Jones, Rodney W(illiam) 1943- ... 113
Jones, Roger (Winston) 1939- ... 101
Jones, Roger Stanley 1934- ... 113
Jones, Royston Oscar 1925-1974 ... 85-88
Jones, Ruby Aileen Hiday 1908- ... CAP-1
  Earlier sketch in CA 11-12
Jones, Russell 1918-1979 ... 106
  Obituary ... 89-92
Jones, Russell Bradley 1894- ... 3R
Jones, Ruth Ann 1928- ... 107
Jones, Ruth Dorval ... 93-96
Jones, Sally Roberts 1935- ... 102
Jones, Sandy 1943- ... CANR-15
  Earlier sketch in CA 85-88
Jones, Sanford W.
  See Thorn, John
Jones, Scott N. 1929- ... 29-32R
Jones, Seaborn (Gustavus), Jr. 1942- ... 104
Jones, Stacy V(anderhoof) 1894- ... 3R
Jones, Stanley L(lewellyn) 1918- ... 9-10R
Jones, Stephen (Phillip) 1935- ... CANR-2
  Earlier sketch in CA 49-52
Jones, Stephen D(wight) 1948- ... 112
Jones, T(homas) Anthony 1940- ... 110
Jones, Tad
  See Jones, Thaddeus B.
Jones, Terry 1942- ... 116
  Brief entry ... 112
  See also SATA 51
  See also CLC 21
Jones, Thaddeus B. 1952- ... 125
Jones, Thomas B. 1929- ... 25-28R
Jones, Thomas M(artin) 1916- ... 29-32R
Jones, Thomas W(arren) 1947- ... 53-56
Jones, Tim(othy) Wynne
  See Wynne-Jones, Tim(othy)
Jones, Tom 1928- ... CANR-6
  Earlier sketch in CA 53-56
Jones, Tony Armstrong
  See Armstrong-Jones, Antony (Charles
  Robert)
Jones, Trevor Arthur 1936- ... 105
Jones, Trevor David 1908-1984 Obituary ... 114
Jones, Tristan 1924- ... 73-76
Jones, Turkel
  See McKimmey, James
Jones, Vane A. 1917- ... 21-22R
Jones, Vernon 1897- ... 53-56
Jones, (Charles) Victor 1919- ... 7-8R
Jones, Virgil Carrington 1906- ... CANR-2
  Earlier sketch in CA 2R
Jones, Volcano
  See Mitchell, Adrian
Jones, W(alton) Glyn 1928- ... 49-52
Jones, W(alter) Paul 1891- ... CAP-1
  Earlier sketch in CA 11-12
Jones, W(illiam) T(homas) 1910- ... 37-40R
Jones, Walter Benton 1893- ... 2R
Jones, Webb
  See Henley, Arthur
Jones, Weyman (B.) 1928- ... 19-20R
  See also SATA 4
Jones, Wilbur Devereux 1916- ... CANR-2
  Earlier sketch in CA 1R
Jones, William Alfred 1817-1900 ... DLB-59
Jones, William David Anthony 1946- ... 113
Jones, William Glynne
  See Glynne-Jones, William
Jones, William H(ugh) 1939-1982 ... 112
  Obituary ... 108
Jones, William M(cKendrey) 1927- ... CANR-7
  Earlier sketch in CA 61-64
Jones, William Monarch
  See Guthrie, Thomas Anstey
Jones, William P(owell) 1901- ... 4R
Jones, William R(onald) 1933- ... 104
Jones, Willis Knapp 1895- ... 13-14R
Jones, Zelda
  See Schuchman, Joan
Jones-Evans, Eric 1898- ... 21-22R
Jones-Jackson, Pat
  See Jones-Jackson, Patricia
Jones-Jackson, Patricia 1946-1986
  Obituary ... 124
Jones-Ryan, Maureen 1943- ... 93-96
Jones-Wilson, Faustine C(hildress) 1927- ... 77-80
Jong, Erica 1942- ... CANR-26
  Earlier sketch in CA 73-76
  See also DLB 2, 5, 28
  See also CLC 4, 6, 8, 18
  See also AITN 1
Jongeward, Dorothy 1925- ... CANR-3
  Earlier sketch in CA 49-52
Jonk, Clarence 1906- ... 5-6R
  See also SATA 10
Jonnes, Jill 1952- ... 121
Jonsen, Albert R(upert) 1931- ... CANR-11
  Earlier sketch in CA 25-28R
Jonson, Ben 1572(?)-1637 ... DLB-62
Jonsson, Snaebjorn 1888(?)-1978
  Obituary ... 81-84
Joos, Martin (George) 1907- ... CAP-1
  Earlier sketch in CA 15-16
Joosse, Barbara M(onnot) 1949- ... 109
  See also SATA 52
Joost, Nicholas (Teynac) 1916-1980 ... 15-16R
  Obituary ... 97-100
Joplin, Scott 1868-1917 Brief entry ... 123
Jopp, Hal
  See Jopp, Harold Dowling, Jr.
Jopp, Harold Dowling, Jr. 1946- ... 57-60
Joralemon, Ira B(eaman) 1884-1975
  Obituary ... 61-64
Joravsky, David 1925- ... CANR-2
  Earlier sketch in CA 1R
Jordan, Alexis Hill
  See Glick, Ruth (Burtnick)
Jordan, Alexis Hill
  See Titchener, Louise
Jordan, Alma Theodora 1929- ... 33-36R
Jordan, Amos A(zariah) 1922- ... 33-36R
Jordan, Barbara (Charline) 1936- ... 123
  Brief entry ... 113
  See also BW
Jordan, Bill
  See Jordan, William
Jordan, Borimir 1933- ... 89-92
Jordan, Carrie
  See Cudlipp, Edythe
Jordan, Clarence L(eonard) 1912-1969 ... CAP-2
  Earlier sketch in CA 23-24
Jordan, Dale R(oderick) 1931- ... 45-48
Jordan, David K. 1942- ... 61-64
Jordan, David M(alcolm) 1935- ... 33-36R
Jordan, David P(aul) 1939- ... 57-60
Jordan, David William 1940- ... 93-96
Jordan, Don
  See Howard, Vernon (Linwood)
Jordan, Donald A. 1936- ... 65-68
Jordan, E(mil) L(eopold) 1900- ... SATA-31
Jordan, Franklin Everard 1904(?)-1983
  Obituary ... 110
Jordan, Gail
  See Dern, Erolie Pearl Gaddis
Jordan, Gerald Ray 1896-1964 ... CAP-1
  Earlier sketch in CA 13-14
Jordan, Gilbert John 1902- ... 49-52
Jordan, Gill
  See Gilbert, George
Jordan, Grace Edgington ... CANR-2
  Earlier sketch in CA 4R
Jordan, Hope Dahle 1905- ... CANR-13
  Earlier sketch in CA 77-80
  See also SATA 15
Jordan, Jael (Michal) 1949- ... SATA-30
Jordan, John 1930- ... 103
Jordan, John E(mory) 1919- ... CANR-20
  Earlier sketch in CA 1R

Jordan, June 1936- ... CANR-25
Earlier sketch in CA 33-36R
See also BW
See also SATA 4
See also DLB 38
See also CLC 5, 11, 23
See also CLR 10
Jordan, Leonard
See Levinson, Leonard
Jordan, Lewis 1912-1983 Obituary ... 111
Jordan, Lois B(reedlove) 1912- ... 57-60
Jordan, Mildred 1901- ... CAP-2
Earlier sketch in CA 25-28
See also SATA 5
Jordan, Mildred Arlene 1918- ... 110
Jordan, Monica
See Caruba, Alan
Jordan, Neil 1950(?)- Brief entry ... 124
Jordan, Norman 1938- ... 33-36R
Jordan, Pascual 1902-1982(?) Obituary ... 112
Jordan, Pat(rick M.) 1941- ... 33-36R
See also CLC 37
Jordan, Philip D(ean) 1940- ... 110
Jordan, Philip Dillon 1903- ... 11-12R
Jordan, Robert Paul 1921- ... 29-32R
Jordan, Robert S(mith) 1929- ... CANR-1
Earlier sketch in CA 45-48
Jordan, Robin 1947- ... 65-68
Jordan, Ruth 1926- ... CANR-7
Earlier sketch in CA 57-60
Jordan, Stello 1914- ... 29-32R
Jordan, Terry G(ilbert) 1938- ... CANR-9
Earlier sketch in CA 21-22R
Jordan, Thomas E(dward) 1929- ... 120
Jordan, Thurston C., Jr. 1940- ... 25-28R
Jordan, Wayne 1903(?)-1979 Obituary ... 85-88
Jordan, Weymouth T(yree) 1912-1968 ... CAP-2
Earlier sketch in CA 17-18
Jordan, Wilbur K(itchener) 1902-1980 ... CANR-5
Obituary ... 97-100
Earlier sketch in CA 5-6R
Jordan, William 1941- Brief entry ... 118
Jordan, William A. 1928- ... 33-36R
Jordan, William H., Jr. 1944- ... 114
Jordan, William J(ohnston) 1924- ... 114
Jordan, William S(tone), Jr. 1917- ... 15-16R
Jordan, Winthrop D(onaldson) 1931- ... 25-28R
Jordan, Z(bigniew) A(ntoni) 1911-1977 ... 25-28R
Obituary ... 89-92
Jordan-Smith, Paul 1885(?)-1971
Obituary ... 104
Jorden, Eleanor Harz ... CANR-8
Earlier sketch in CA 7-8R
Jordy, William H(enry) 1917- ... CANR-25
Earlier sketch in CA 3R
Jorgens, Jack J(ohnstone) 1943- ... 65-68
Jorgensen, Ivar
See Ellison, Harlan
and Fairman, Paul W.
Jorgensen, James (Aleck) 1931- ... CANR-19
Earlier sketch in CA 103
Jorgensen, James D(ale) 1932- ... 41-44R
Jorgensen, Joseph G(ilbert) 1934- ... CANR-7
Earlier sketch in CA 61-64
Jorgensen, Mary Venn ... CANR-1
Earlier sketch in CA 2R
See also SATA 36
Jorgensen, Neil 1934- ... 53-56
Jorgenson, Ivar
See Silverberg, Robert
Jorgenson, Lloyd P. 1912- ... 125
Jorn, Asger 1914-1973 Obituary ... 41-44R
Jorstad, Erling (Theodore) 1930- ... CANR-12
Earlier sketch in CA 29-32R
Joscelyn, Archie L. 1899- ... CANR-5
Earlier sketch in CA 3R
Jose, F(rancisco) Sionil
See Sionil Jose, F(rancisco)
Jose, James R(obert) 1939- ... 29-32R
Josefowitz, Natasha 1926- ... 114
Josefsberg, Milt 1911-1987 ... 81-84
Obituary ... 124
Joselovitz, Ernest A. 1942- ... 108
Joselow, Beth Baruch 1948- ... 114
Joseph, Alexander 1907-1976 ... 13-14R
Obituary ... 120
Joseph, Bertram L(eon) 1915-1981 ... CANR-6
Obituary ... 104
Earlier sketch in CA 7-8R
Joseph, David I(glauer) 1941- ... 9-10R
Joseph, Dov 1899-1980 Obituary ... 93-96
Joseph, Franz
See Schnaubelt, Franz Joseph
Joseph, James (Herz) 1924- ... CANR-2
Earlier sketch in CA 4R
See also SATA 53
Joseph, Jenny 1932- ... CANR-25
Earlier sketch in CA 107
See also DLB 40
Joseph, Joan 1939- ... CANR-17
Earlier sketch in CA 25-28R
See also SATA 34
Joseph, John 1923- ... 1R
Joseph, Jonathan
See Fineman, Irving
Joseph, Joseph M(aron) 1903-1979 ... 5-6R
See also SATA 22
Joseph, M(ichael) K(ennedy)
1914-1981 ... CANR-6
Earlier sketch in CA 9-10R
Joseph, Marie ... 109
Joseph, Marjory L(ockwood) 1917- ... 77-80
Joseph, Mark (Chester) 1946- ... 120
Joseph, Richard 1910-1976 ... CANR-6
Obituary ... 69-72
Earlier sketch in CA 3R
Joseph, Stephen 1921-1967 ... 11-12R
Obituary ... 103
Joseph, Stephen M. 1938- ... 25-28R
Joseph, William A(llen) 1947- ... 118
Josephs, Ray 1912- ... 9-10R
Josephs, Stephen
See Dolmatch, Theodore B(ieley)
Josephson, Clifford A. 1922- ... 19-20R
Josephson, Elmer A. 1909- ... 121
Josephson, Halsey D. 1906(?)-1977
Obituary ... 69-72
Josephson, Hannah 1900-1976 ... CAP-2
Obituary ... 69-72
Earlier sketch in CA 29-32
Josephson, Harold 1942- ... 61-64
Josephson, Matthew 1899-1978 ... 81-84
Obituary ... 77-80
See also DLB 4
Josephy, Alvin M., Jr. 1915- ... CANR-8
Earlier sketch in CA 19-20R
Josey, E(lonnie) J(unius) 1924- ... 29-32R
Joshee, O(m) K(umar) 1934- ... 117
Joshi, Irene M(arian) 1934- ... 110
Joshi, Shivkumar 1916- ... 77-80
Joshua, Wynfred 1930- ... 29-32R
Josiah Allen's Wife
See Holley, Marietta
Josipovici, Gabriel 1940- ... 37-40R
See also DLB 14
See also CLC 6, 43
Joskow, Paul L. 1947- ... 124
Joslin, Sesyle
See Hine, Sesyle Joslin
See also SATA 2
Jospe, Alfred 1909- ... 106
Joss, John 1934- ... 101
Josselyn, John ?-1675 ... DLB-24
Josten, Josef 1913-1985 Obituary ... 118
Joubert, Andre J. 1924- ... 49-52
Joubert, Ingrid 1942- ... 110
Joudry, Patricia 1921- ... 65-68
Jouhandeau, Marcel Henri 1888-1979
Obituary ... 85-88
Jourard, Sidney M(arshall) 1926-1974 ... CANR-6
Obituary ... 53-56
Earlier sketch in CA 7-8R
Jourdain, Alice M. 1923- ... 53-56
Jourdain, Rose (Leonora) 1932- ... 89-92
Journet, Charles 1891-1975 ... 65-68
Obituary ... 57-60
Journlet, Marie de
See Little, Paul H(ugo)
Jouve, Pierre Jean 1887-1976 Obituary ... 65-68
See also CLC 47
Jouvenel, Bertrand de
See de Jouvenel des Ursins, Edouard Bertrand
Jouvet, Jean
See Strich, Christian
Jovanovich, William (Iliya) 1920- ... 107
Jowett, Garth Samuel 1940- ... CANR-10
Earlier sketch in CA 65-68
Jowett, Paul (Melville) 1959- ... 120
Jowitt, Deborah 1934- ... 103
Joy, Barbara Ellen 1898- ... 7-8R
Joy, David Anthony Welton 1942- ... CANR-20
Earlier sketch in CA 103
Joy, Donald Marvin 1928- ... 15-16R
Joy, Edward T(homas) 1909- ... 9-10R
Joy, Kenneth Ernest 1908- ... CAP-2
Earlier sketch in CA 23-24
Joy, Thomas Alfred 1904- ... 102
Joyce, Adrien
See Eastman, Carol
Joyce, Bill
See Joyce, William
Joyce, Brian T(homas) 1938- ... 106
Joyce, Bruce R(ogers) 1930- Brief entry ... 114
Joyce, Ernest 1899-1975 ... CAP-2
Earlier sketch in CA 33-36
Joyce, J(ames) Avery 1902-1987 ... CANR-10
Obituary ... 121
Earlier sketch in CA 65-68
See also SATA 11, 50
Joyce, James (Augustine Aloysius)
1882-1941 ... 126
Joyce, James (Augustus Aloysius)
1882-1941 Brief entry ... 104
See also DLB 10, 19, 36
See also TCLC 3, 8, 16
Joyce, James Daniel 1921- ... 9-10R
Joyce, Jon L(oyd) 1937- ... CANR-10
Earlier sketch in CA 65-68
Joyce, Julia
See Tetel, Julie
Joyce, Mary Rosera 1930- ... 29-32R
Joyce, R(oger) B(ilbrough) 1924- ... CANR-1
Earlier sketch in CA 45-48
Joyce, Robert E(dward) 1934- ... 29-32R
Joyce, William 1959(?)- ... 124
See also SATA 46
Joyce, William L(eonard) 1942- ... 111
Joyce, William W(alter) 1934- ... CANR-15
Earlier sketch in CA 85-88
Joyner, Charles W. 1935- ... 37-40R
Joyner, Jerry 1938- ... 107
See also SATA 34
Joyner, William T. 1934- ... 23-24R
Joynson, R(obert) B(illington) 1922- ... 57-60
Joynt, Carey Bonthron 1924- ... 124
Joynt, Robert R(ichard) 1915- ... 106
Jozsef, Attila 1905-1937 Brief entry ... 116
See also TCLC 22
Jucker, Sita 1921- ... CANR-12
Earlier sketch in CA 29-32R
See also SATA 5
Jucovy, Milton Edward 1918- ... 109
Juda, L(yon) 1923- ... 11-12R
Judah, Aaron 1923- ... 103
Judah, J(ay) Stillson 1911- ... 21-22R
Judd, Cyril
See Kornbluth, C(yril) M.
and Merril, Judith
and Pohl, Frederik
Judd, Deane B(rewster) 1900-1972 ... CAP-1
Earlier sketch in CA 13-14
Judd, Denis (O'Nan) 1938- ... CANR-13
Earlier sketch in CA 25-28R
See also SATA 33
Judd, Dennis R. 1943- ... CANR-16
Earlier sketch in CA 93-96
Judd, Frances K. ... CAP-2
Earlier sketch in CA 19-20
See also SATA 1
Judd, Frederick Charles 1914- ... CANR-6
Earlier sketch in CA 7-8R
Judd, Gerrit P(armele) 1915-1971 ... 5-6R
Obituary ... 29-32R
Judd, H(oward) Stanley 1936- ... CANR-21
Earlier sketch in CA 69-72
Judd, Harrison
See Daniels, Norman
Judd, Larry R. 1937- ... 45-48
Judd, Margaret Haddican 1906- ... 5-6R
Judd, Robert 1939- ... 85-88
Judd, Sara (Hutton) Bowen
See Bowen-Judd, Sara (Hutton)
Judd, Sylvester 1813-1853 ... DLB-1
Judelle, Beatrice 1908- ... 33-36R
Judge, Harry George 1928- ... 124
Judson, Clara Ingram 1879-1960 ... SATA-27, 38
Judson, David (Malcolm) 1941- ... 93-96
Judson, Horace Freeland 1931- ... 89-92
Judson, John 1930- ... CANR-12
Earlier sketch in CA 13-14R
Judson, Lewis Van Hagen 1893-1973
Obituary ... 41-44R
Judson, Margaret Atwood 1899- ... 102
Judson, Sylvia Shaw 1897- ... 41-44R
Judson, William
See Corley, Edwin (Raymond)
Judy, Marvin T(hornton) 1911- ... 33-36R
Judy, Stephen
See Tchudi, Stephen N.
Judy, Stephen N.
See Tchudi, Stephen N.
Judy, Susan J(ane) 1944- ... 107
Judy, Will(iam Lewis) 1891- ... 7-8R
Juel, Donald H. 1942- ... 114
Juel-Nielsen, Niels 1920- ... 106
Juengel, Eberhard 1934- Brief entry ... 118
Juenger, Ernst 1895- ... CANR-21
Earlier sketch in CA 101
See also DLB 56
Juergens, George Ivar 1932- ... 109
Juergensen, Hans 1919- ... CANR-8
Earlier sketch in CA 21-22R
Juergensmeyer, Jane Stuart
See Stuart, Jane
Juergensmeyer, John Eli 1934- ... 41-44R
Jugenheimer, Donald W(ayne) 1943- ... 125
Juhasz, Anne McCreary 1922- ... 53-56
Juhasz, Leslie A.
See Shepard, Leslie Albert
Juhasz, Suzanne 1942- ... 85-88
Jukes, (James Thomas) Geoffrey 1928- ... 29-32R
Jukes, Mavis 1947- Brief entry ... 121
See also SATA 43
Jukic, Ilija 1901-1977 ... 49-52
Obituary ... 103
Julesberg, Elizabeth Rider Montgomery
1902-1985 ... CANR-3
Obituary ... 115
Earlier sketch in CA 2R
See also SATA 3, 34
Jules-Rosette, Bennetta (Washington)
1948- ... 112
Juliard, Pierre 1939- ... 41-44R
Julie
See Robbins, June
Julien, Charles-Andre 1891- ... 103
Julie of Colorado Springs
See Robbins, June
Julier, Virginia Cheatham 1918- ... 5-6R
Julin, Joseph R. 1926- ... 37-40R
Juline, Ruth Bishop
See Ritchie, Ruth
Julitte, Pierre (Gaston Louis) 1910- ... 37-40R
Julius
See Curling, Bryan William Richard
Jullian, Philippe 1919-1977 ... 73-76
Julty, Sam 1927- ... 61-64
July, Robert W(illiam) 1918- ... 41-44R
Jumper, Andrew Albert 1927- ... 17-18R
Jumpp, Hugo
See MacPeek, Walter G.
Jun, Jong S(up) 1936- ... 53-56
June, Jennie
See Croly, Jane Cunningham
Jung, C(arl) G(ustav) 1875-1961 ... 117
Jung, Hwa Yol 1932- ... 37-40R
Jung, John A. 1937- ... 17-18R
Jung, Leo 1892-1987 Obituary ... 124
Junge, Mark G(ene) 1943- ... 122
Jungel, Eberhard
See Juengel, Eberhard
Junger, Ernst
See Juenger, Ernst
See also DLB 56
Jungk, Robert 1913- ... 85-88
Jungle Doctor
See White, Paul Hamilton Hume
Jungreis, Esther 1936- ... 110
Juniper, D(ean) F(rancis) 1929- ... CANR-18
Earlier sketch in CA 97-100
Junius
See Luxemburg, Rosa
Junker, Karin Stensland 1916- ... CANR-3
Earlier sketch in CA 11-12R
Junkins, Donald 1931- ... 33-36R
Junor, John 1919- ... 108
Jupo, Frank J. 1904- ... CANR-2
Earlier sketch in CA 7-8R
See also SATA 7
Jupp, James 1932- ... CANR-11
Earlier sketch in CA 23-24R
Jupp, Kenneth 1939- ... 65-68
Juptner, Joseph Paul 1913- ... 7-8R
Jur, Jerzy
See Lerski, George Jan
Jurek, Martin 1942- ... 77-80
Jurgela, Constantine R. 1904-1988
Obituary ... 124
Jurgens, Curt 1912-1982 Obituary ... 107
Jurgens, W(illiam) A(nthony) 1928- ... 41-44R
Jurgensen, Barbara (Bitting) 1928- ... 19-20R
Juris, Hervey A(sher) 1938- ... CANR-5
Earlier sketch in CA 53-56
Jurjevich, Ratibor-Ray (Momchila)
1915- ... 37-40R
Jurji, Edward J. 1907- ... 15-16R
Jurnak, Sheila
See Raeschild, Sheila
Jussim, Estelle 1927- ... 81-84
Just, Ward S(wift) 1935- ... 25-28R
See also CLC 4, 27
Juster, F. Thomas 1926- ... CANR-2
Earlier sketch in CA 45-48
Juster, Norton 1929- ... CANR-13
Earlier sketch in CA 13-14R
See also SATA 3
Justice, Blair 1927- ... CANR-1
Earlier sketch in CA 45-48
Justice, Donald (Rodney) 1925- ... CANR-26
Earlier sketch in CA 7-8R
See also DLBY 83
See also CLC 6, 19
Justice, William G(ross), Jr. 1930- ... CANR-20
Earlier sketches in CA 53-56, CANR-5
Justiciar
See Powell-Smith, Vincent (Walter Francis)
Justus, May 1898- ... 9-10R
See also SATA 1
Juta, Jan 1895- ... 49-52
Juta, Rene
See Juta, Jan
Jutikkala, Eino Kaarlo Ilmari 1907- ... CAP-1
Earlier sketch in CA 9-10
Jutson, Mary Carolyn Hollers
See George, Mary Carolyn Hollers Jutson
Juvenilia
See Taylor, Ann
Juvenis
See Bourne, Randolph S(illiman)
Juviler, Peter H(enry) 1926- ... 77-80
Jwaideh, Nizar 1933(?)-1988 Obituary ... 124

K

Kaapu, Myrtle King 1898-1985 Obituary ... 119
Kaba, Lansine 1941- ... 61-64
Kabadi, Sunder 1898(?)-1983 Obituary ... 111
Kabaphe, Konstantinos Petrou
See Kavafis, Konstantinos Petrou
Kabaphes, Konstantinos Petrou
See Kavafis, Konstantinos Petrou
Kabasele, Joseph
See Tshiamala, Kabasele
Kabbani, Rana 1958- ... 125
Kabdebo, Tamas
See Kabdebo, Thomas
Kabdebo, Thomas 1934- ... CANR-23
Earlier sketches in CA 53-56, CANR-7
See also SATA 10
Kabibble, Osh
See Jobb, Jamie
Kabotie, Fred 1900- ... 118
Kabraji, Fredoon 1897- ... CAP-1
Earlier sketch in CA 13-14
Kac, Arthur W(ayne) 1904- ... 117
Kac, Mark 1914-1984 Obituary ... 114
Kacew, Romain 1914-1980 ... 108
Obituary ... 102
Kacew, Roman
See Kacew, Romain
Kachru, Braj B(ehari) 1932- ... CANR-23
Earlier sketches in CA 61-64, CANR-8
Kaczer, Illes 1887- ... CAP-1
Earlier sketch in CA 9-10
Kadai, Heino Olavi 1931- ... 21-22R
Kadans, Joseph M(ichael) 1912- ... 118
Kadesch, Robert R(udstone) 1922- ... 57-60
See also SATA 31
Kadic, Ante 1910- Brief entry ... 107
Kadish, Ferne 1940- ... 61-64
Kadish, Mortimer Raymond 1916-
Brief entry ... 106
Kadler, Eric H(enry) 1922- ... 29-32R
Kadushin, Alfred 1916- ... 25-28R
Kadushin, Charles 1932- ... 25-28R
Kaegi, Walter Emil, Jr. 1937- ... CANR-10
Earlier sketch in CA 25-28R
Kael, Pauline 1919- ... CANR-6
Earlier sketch in CA 45-48
Kaelbling, Rudolf 1928- ... 19-20R
Kaelin, Eugene F(rancis) 1926- ... 45-48

INDEX

Kaellberg, Sture 1928- ... CANR-25
Earlier sketch in CA 107
Kaempfert, Wade
See del Rey, Lester
Kaempffert, Waldemar (Bernhard) 1877-1956 Brief entry ... 113
Kaeppler, Adrienne Lois 1935- Brief entry ... 107
Kaese, Harold 1909(?)-1975 Obituary ... 57-60
Kaestle, Carl F(rederick) 1940- ... 85-88
Kaestner, Dorothy 1920- ... 61-64
Kaestner, Erich 1899-1974 ... 73-76
Obituary ... 49-52
See also SATA 14
See also DLB 56
See also CLR 4
Kaeuper, Richard W(illiam) 1941- Brief entry ... 115
Kafe, Joseph Kofi Thompson 1933- ... 49-52
Kafka, Franz 1883-1924 ... 126
Brief entry ... 105
See also TCLC 2, 6, 13, 29
Kafka, Sherry 1937- ... 21-22R
Kafka, Vincent W(infield) 1924- ... 61-64
Kafker, Frank A. 1931- ... 37-40R
Kafu
See Nagai Sokichi
Kagan, Abram S. 1889(?)-1983 Obituary ... 111
Kagan, Andrew 1947- ... 123
Kagan, Benjamin 1914- ... 21-22R
Kagan, Donald 1932- ... CANR-9
Earlier sketch in CA 23-24R
Kagan, Jerome 1929- ... CANR-24
Earlier sketches in CA 7-8R, CANR-2
Kagan, Richard (Lauren) 1943- ... 57-60
Kagan, Richard C(lark) 1938- ... 53-56
Kagan, Robert A. 1938- ... 126
Kagan-Kans, Eva 1928- ... 49-52
Kaganoff, Nathan M. 1926- ... 126
Brief entry ... 108
Kagy, Frederick D(avid) 1917- ... 15-16R
Kahan, Gerald 1923- ... 33-36R
Kahan, Stanley 1931- ... 7-8R
Kahan, Stuart 1936- ... 93-96
Kahane, Claire 1935- ... 126
Kahane, Howard 1928- ... CANR-1
Earlier sketch in CA 49-52
Kahane, Meir (David) 1932- Brief entry ... 112
Kahin, Audrey R. 1934- ... 121
Kahl, Ann Hammel 1929- ... 17-18R
Kahl, Joseph A(lan) 1923- Brief entry ... 109
Kahl, M(arvin) P(hilip) 1934- ... 107
See also SATA 37
Kahl, Virginia 1919- ... CANR-2
Earlier sketch in CA 49-52
See also SATA 38, 48
Kahle, Roger (Raymond) 1943- ... 33-36R
Kahlenberg, Mary Hunt 1940- ... CANR-2
Earlier sketch in CA 45-48
Kahler, Erich Gabriel 1885-1970 ... CANR-7
Obituary ... 29-32R
Earlier sketch in CA 5-6R
Kahler, Hugh (Torbert) MacNair 1883-1969 ... 102
Kahler, Woodland 1895- ... 3R
Kahm, H(arold) S. ... 101
Kahn, Albert E(ugene) 1912-1979 ... 118
Obituary ... 89-92
Kahn, Alfred E(dward) 1917- ... 41-44R
Kahn, Alfred J. 1919- ... CANR-15
Earlier sketch in CA 5-6R
Kahn, Alice 1943- ... 119
Kahn, Arnold Dexter 1939- ... 101
Kahn, Balthazar
See Carlisle, Thomas (Fiske)
Kahn, David 1930- ... CANR-12
Earlier sketch in CA 25-28R
Kahn, E(ly) J(acques), Jr. 1916- ... 65-68
Kahn, Ely Jacques 1884-1972 Obituary ... 37-40R
Kahn, Frank J(ules) 1938- ... 33-36R
Kahn, Gilbert 1912-1971 ... CANR-6
Earlier sketch in CA 4R
Kahn, Grace Leboy 1891-1983 Obituary ... 109
Kahn, Hannah 1911- ... CANR-14
Earlier sketch in CA 77-80
See also AITN 2
Kahn, Herman 1922-1983 ... 65-68
Obituary ... 110
Kahn, Herta Hess 1919- ... 25-28R
Kahn, James 1947- ... 109
Kahn, James M. 1903(?)-1978 Obituary ... 77-80
Kahn, Joan 1914- ... 77-80
See also SATA 48
Kahn, Judd 1940- ... 101
Kahn, Kathy 1945- ... 41-44R
Kahn, Lawrence E(dwin) 1937- ... 103
Kahn, Lothar 1922- ... 25-28R
Kahn, Louis I. 1901-1974 Obituary ... 49-52
Kahn, Ludwig W(erner) 1910- ... 41-44R
Kahn, Margaret 1949- ... 101
Kahn, Michael D. 1936- ... 109
Kahn, Peggy
See Katz, Bobbi
Kahn, Richard (Ferdinand Karn) 1905- ... 97-100
Kahn, Robert I(rving) 1910- ... 7-8R
Kahn, Robert L(ouis) 1918- ... CANR-10
Earlier sketch in CA 17-18R
Kahn, Roger 1927- ... 25-28R
See also SATA 37
See also CLC 30
Kahn, Samuel 1897-1981 Obituary ... 106
Kahn, Sanders A(rthur) 1919-1987 ... 89-92
Obituary ... 121
Kahn, Sandra S(utker) 1942- ... 106
Kahn, Sholom J(acob) 1918- ... 102
Kahn, Si(mon) 1944- ... 33-36R
Kahn, Stephen 1940- ... 7-8R
Kahn, Steve
See Kahn, Stephen
Kahn, Sy M. 1924- ... CANR-10
Earlier sketch in CA 25-28R
Kahn, Theodore C(harles) 1912- ... 33-36R
Kahn-Fogel, Daniel (Mark) 1948- ... 97-100
Kahn-Freund, Otto 1900-1979 Obituary ... 108
Kahnweiler, Daniel-Henry 1884-1979 ... 29-32R
Obituary ... 85-88
Kahrl, George M(orrow) 1904- ... 105
Kahrl, Stanley J. 1931- ... 11-12R
Kahrl, William L. 1946- ... 109
Kaid, Lynda Lee 1948- ... CANR-16
Earlier sketch in CA 89-92
Kaikini, P(rabhakar) R(amrao) 1912- ... 61-64
Kaiko, Takeshi 1930- ... 104
Kaim-Caudle, Peter Robert 1916- ... 23-24R
Kain, John F(orrest) 1935- ... 29-32R
Kain, Malcolm
See Oglesby, Joseph
Kain, Richard M(organ) 1908- ... CANR-2
Earlier sketch in CA 7-8R
Kain, Richard Y(erkes) 1936- ... 37-40R
Kain, Saul
See Sassoon, Siegfried (Lorraine)
Kains, Josephine
See Goulart, Ron(ald Joseph)
Kainz, Howard Paul 1933- ... 114
Kairys, Anatolijus 1914- ... 102
Kaisari, Uri 1899(?)-1979 Obituary ... 85-88
Kaiser, Artur 1943- ... 97-100
Kaiser, Bill
See Sumner, David (W. K.)
Kaiser, Christopher B(arina) 1941- ... 114
Kaiser, Daniel H. 1945- ... 126
Kaiser, Edward J(ohn) 1935- ... 93-96
Kaiser, Edwin George 1893-1984 ... 45-48
Obituary ... 114
Kaiser, Ernest 1915- ... CANR-16
Earlier sketches in CA 49-52, CANR-1
Kaiser, Frances E(lkan) 1922- ... 57-60
Kaiser, Georg 1878-1945 Brief entry ... 106
See also TCLC 9
Kaiser, Harvey H. 1936- ... CANR-14
Earlier sketch in CA 81-84
Kaiser, Leo M(ax) 1918- ... 116
Kaiser, Otto 1924- ... 85-88
Kaiser, Robert Blair 1930- ... 9-10R
Kaiser, Robert G(reeley) 1943- ... 65-68
Kaiser, Walter (Jacob) 1931- ... CANR-15
Earlier sketch in CA 37-40R
Kaiser, Walter Christian, Jr. 1933- ... 114
Kaiser, Ward L(ouis) 1923- ... 53-56
Kaiser Wilhelm II
See Hohenzollern, Friedrich Wilhelm (Victor Albert)
Kaitz, Edward M. 1928- ... CANR-13
Earlier sketch in CA 29-32R
Kajencki, Francis C(asimir) 1918- ... 115
Kakapo, Leilani 1939- ... CANR-9
Earlier sketch in CA 19-20R
Kakar, Sudhir 1938- ... 33-36R
Kaki
See Heinemann, Katherine
Kakimoto, Kozo 1915- ... SATA-11
Kakonen, Ulla
See Anobile, Ulla (Kakonen)
Kakonis, Thomas E. 1930- ... 57-60
Kakonis, Tom E.
See Kakonis, Thomas E.
Kakugawa, Frances H(ideko) 1936- ... 77-80
Kaland, William J. 1915(?)-1983 Obituary ... 111
Kalashnikoff, Nicholas 1888-1961 ... 73-76
See also SATA 16
Kalb, Bernard 1932- Brief entry ... 109
Kalb, Jonah 1926- ... CANR-4
Earlier sketch in CA 53-56
See also SATA 23
Kalb, Marvin L. 1930- ... 5-6R
Kalb, S(am) William 1897- ... 33-36R
Kalberer, Augustine 1917- ... 61-64
Kalcheim, Lee 1938- ... 85-88
Kaldor, Mary 1946- ... 93-96
Kale, Arvind and Shanta
See Gantzer, Hugh
Kalechofsky, Roberta 1931- ... CANR-2
Earlier sketch in CA 49-52
See also DLB 28
Kaledin, Eugenia 1929- ... 109
Kalem, T(heodore) E(ustace) 1919-1985 Obituary ... 116
Kalemkerian, Zarouhi 1874(?)-1971 Obituary ... 104
Kalenik, Sandra 1945- ... 73-76
Kaler, James Otis 1848-1912 Brief entry ... 120
See also SATA 15
See also DLB 42
Kales, Emily Fox 1944- ... 23-24R
Kaletski, Alexander 1946- Brief entry ... 118
See also CLC 39
Kalia, Narendra Nath 1942- ... 112
Kalich, Jacob 1891-1975 Obituary ... 89-92
Kalich, Robert 1947- ... 106
Kalicki, Jan H(enryk) 1948- ... 65-68
Kalijarvi, Thorsten V(alentine) 1897-1980 . CAP-1
Obituary ... 97-100
Earlier sketch in CA 19-20
Kalin, Martin (Gregory) 1943- ... 53-56
Kalin, Robert 1921- ... CANR-8
Earlier sketch in CA 61-64
Kalin, Rudolf 1938- ... 45-48
Kalina, Sigmund 1911-1977 ... CANR-3
Earlier sketch in CA 49-52
Kalins, Dorothy (G.) 1942- ... CANR-17
Earlier sketch in CA 25-28R
Kalinsky, George 1936- ... CANR-2
Earlier sketch in CA 49-52
Kalish, Betty McKelvey 1913- ... 45-48
Kalish, Donald 1919- ... 11-12R
Kalish, Richard A(llan) 1930- ... CANR-25
Earlier sketches in CA 7-8R, CANR-10
Kalisher, Simpson 1926- ... 17-18R
Kallas, James (Gus) 1928- ... CANR-10
Earlier sketch in CA 17-18R
Kallaus, Norman F. 1924- ... 33-36R
Kallberg, Sture
See Kaellberg, Sture
Kallen, (Marc) Christian 1950- ... 120
Kallen, Horace M(eyer) 1882-1974 ... 93-96
Obituary ... 49-52
Kallen, Laurence 1944- ... 41-44R
Kallen, Lucille ... 97-100
Kallenbach, Joseph E(rnest) 1903- ... 77-80
Kallenbach, W(illiam) Warren 1926- ... 11-12R
Kallesser, Michael 1886(?)-1975 Obituary ... 61-64
Kallet, Arthur 1902-1972 Obituary ... 33-36R
Kallet, Marilyn 1946- ... 104
Kallich, Martin 1918- ... CANR-2
Earlier sketch in CA 5-6R
Kallifatides, Theodor 1938- ... CANR-15
Earlier sketch in CA 85-88
Kallir, Jane K(atherine) 1954- ... CANR-25
Earlier sketch in CA 109
Kallir, Otto 1894-1978 ... 49-52
Obituary ... 81-84
Kallman, Chester (Simon) 1921-1975 ... CANR-3
Obituary ... 53-56
Earlier sketch in CA 45-48
See also CLC 2
Kallmann, Helmut Max 1922- ... 108
Kallsen, T(heodore) J(ohn) 1915- ... 7-8R
Kalman, Harold David 1943- ... 103
Kalme, Egils 1909- ... 81-84
Kalmijn, Jo 1905- ... CAP-2
Earlier sketch in CA 21-22
Kalmus, Ain
See Mand, Ewald
Kalnay, Francis 1899- ... 49-52
See also SATA 7
Kalnoky, Ingeborg L(ouise) 1909- ... 61-64
Kalow, Gert 1921- ... 29-32R
Kalow, Gisela 1946- ... 107
See also SATA 32
Kalpakian, Laura Anne 1945- ... CANR-15
Earlier sketch in CA 81-84
Kals, W(illiam) S(teven) 1910- ... CANR-24
Earlier sketch in CA 45-48
Kalstone, David (Michael) 1932-1986 Obituary ... 119
Kalstone, Shirlee A(nn) 1932- ... CANR-8
Earlier sketch in CA 61-64
Kalt, Bryson R. 1934- ... 33-36R
Kalt, Jeannette Chappell 1898(?)-1976 Obituary ... 69-72
Kaltenborn, Hans Von 1878-1965 Obituary ... 93-96
Kalter, Joanmarie 1951- ... 102
Kalu, Ogbu Uke 1944- ... 93-96
Kaluger, George 1921- ... 29-32R
Kaluger, Meriem Fair 1921- ... 81-84
Kalven, Harry, Jr. 1914-1974 Obituary ... 53-56
Kalyanaraman, Aiyaswamy 1903- ... CAP-2
Earlier sketch in CA 33-36
Kamarck, Andrew M(artin) 1914- ... CANR-10
Earlier sketch in CA 21-22R
Kamarck, Lawrence 1927- ... 73-76
Kamath, M(adhav) V(ithal) 1921- ... CANR-21
Earlier sketch in CA 69-72
Kambu, Joseph
See Amamoo, Joseph Godson
Kamen, Betty 1925- ... 114
Kamen, Gloria 1923- ... 114
See also SATA 9
Kamen, Henry Arthur 1936- ... CANR-7
Earlier sketch in CA 7-8R
Kamen, Isai
See Stein, Jess
Kamen, Martin D(avid) 1913- ... 118
Kamen, Si 1920- ... 114
Kamenetsky, Ihor 1927- ... CANR-4
Earlier sketch in CA 2R
Kamenetz, Rodger 1950- ... 112
Kamenka, Eugene 1928- ... CANR-2
Earlier sketch in CA 5-6R
Kamerman, Jack B. 1940- ... 115
Kamerman, Sheila B(rody) 1928- ... CANR-10
Earlier sketch in CA 65-68
Kamerman, Sylvia E.
See Burack, Sylvia K.
Kamerschen, David R(oy) 1937- ... 53-56
Kamien, Marcia 1940- ... CANR-22
Earlier sketch in CA 105
Kamil, Alan C(urtis) 1941- Brief entry ... 109
Kamil, Jill 1930- ... CANR-7
Earlier sketch in CA 57-60
Kamin, Leon J. 1927- ... 103
Kamin, Nick
See Antonick, Robert J.
Kamins, Jeanette ... 5-6R
Kamins, Robert Martin 1918- Brief entry ... 105
Kaminska, Ida 1899-1980 Obituary ... 97-100
Kaminskaya, Dina 1920- ... 115
Kaminski, Margaret (Joan) 1944- ... CANR-8
Earlier sketch in CA 61-64
Kaminsky, Alice R. ... 33-36R
Kaminsky, Howard 1940- ... 105
Kaminsky, Jack 1922- ... 23-24R
Kaminsky, Marc 1943- ... CANR-24
Earlier sketches in CA 53-56, CANR-5
Kaminsky, Melvin 1926- ... CANR-16
Earlier sketch in CA 65-68
Kaminsky, Peretz 1916- ... 33-36R
Kaminsky, Stuart M(elvin) 1934- ... 73-76
Kaminsky, Susan Stanwood 1937- ... 115
Brief entry ... 110
Kamisar, Yale 1929- ... CANR-13
Earlier sketch in CA 69-72
Kamitses, Zoe 1941- ... 111
Kamm, Antony 1931- ... 117
Kamm, (Jan) Dorinda 1952- ... CANR-14
Earlier sketch in CA 37-40R
Kamm, Herbert 1917- ... 69-72
Kamm, Jacob Oswald 1918- ... 7-8R
Kamm, Josephine (Hart) 1905- ... CANR-5
Earlier sketch in CA 11-12R
See also SATA 24
Kamm, Phyllis S. 1918- ... 112
Kamman, Madeleine M(arguerite Pin) 1930- ... 85-88
Kamman, William 1930- ... 25-28R
Kammen, Michael G(edaliah) 1936- ... CANR-22
Earlier sketch in CA 25-28R
Kammerer, Gladys M. 1909-1970 ... CANR-16
Obituary ... 103
Earlier sketch in CA 3R
Kammeyer, Kenneth C(arl) W(illiam) 1931- ... 29-32R
Kamp, Irene Kittle 1910-1985 Obituary ... 116
Kampelman, Max M. 1920- ... 41-44R
Kampen, Irene Trepel 1922- ... CANR-1
Earlier sketch in CA 3R
Kampen, Michael Edwin 1939- Brief entry .. 110
Kampf, Abraham 1920- ... 23-24R
Kampf, Avram
See Kampf, Abraham
Kampf, Louis 1929- ... 33-36R
Kampov, Boris Nikolayevich 1908-1981 ... 108
Obituary ... 104
Kamrany, Nake M. 1934- ... CANR-14
Earlier sketch in CA 37-40R
Kamstra, Leslie D. 1920- ... 69-72
Kanahele, George Sanford 1930- ... 102
Kanazawa, Masakata 1934- ... 25-28R
Kanazawa, Roger
See Kanazawa, Masakata
Kandaouroff, Berice 1912- ... 33-36R
Kandel, Denise Bystryn 1933- ... 13-14R
Kandel, I(saac) L(eon) 1881-1965 ... CANR-3
Earlier sketch in CA 4R
Kandel, Lenore 1932- ... DLB-16
Kandel, Thelma E. 1932- ... 111
Kandell, Alice S. 1938- ... CANR-13
Earlier sketch in CA 33-36R
See also SATA 35
Kandinsky, Nina 1896(?)-1980 ... 101
Kandinsky, Wassily 1866-1944 Brief entry .. 118
Kando, Thomas M. 1941- ... CANR-2
Earlier sketch in CA 49-52
Kane, Aarno
See Kagan, Andrew
Kane, Basil G(odfrey) 1931- ... CANR-24
Earlier sketch in CA 69-72
Kane, Dennis Cornelius 1918- ... 41-44R
Kane, E. B. 1944- ... 57-60
Kane, Edward J(ames) 1935- ... 41-44R
Kane, Frank 1912-1968 ... 7-8R
Obituary ... 25-28R
Kane, Frank R. 1925- ... 77-80
Kane, George 1916- ... 103
Kane, H. Victor 1906- ... 29-32R
Kane, Harnett T(homas) 1910-1984 Obituary ... 113
Kane, Henry Bugbee 1902-1971 ... 73-76
See also SATA 14
Kane, J. Herbert 1910- ... 97-100
Kane, Jack
See Baker, (Allen) Albert
Kane, James
See Germano, Peter B.
Kane, Jim
See Germano, Peter B.
Kane, John Joseph 1909- ... CAP-2
Earlier sketch in CA 13-14
Kane, Julia
See Robins, Denise (Naomi)
Kane, L. A.
See Mannetti, Lisa
Kane, Pablo
See Zachary, Hugh
Kane, Paul
See Simon, Paul
Kane, Peter E(vans) 1932- ... 112
Kane, Robert S. 1925- ... CANR-23
Earlier sketches in CA 9-10R, CANR-7
Kane, Robert W. 1910- ... SATA-18
Kane, Thomas S. 1925- ... 114
Kane, William Everett 1943- ... 49-52
Kane, Wilson
See Bloch, Robert (Albert)
Kanet, Roger E(dward) 1936- ... CANR-14
Earlier sketch in CA 33-36R
Kanetzke, Howard W(illiam) 1932- ... 112
See also SATA 38
Kanfer, Allen 1905(?)-1983 Obituary ... 110
Kanfer, Frederick H. 1925- ... CANR-15
Earlier sketch in CA 41-44R
Kanfer, Stefan 1933- ... 103
Kang, Shin T. 1935- ... 33-36R
Kang, Younghill 1903-1972 Obituary ... 37-40R
Kanin, Garson 1912- ... CANR-7
Earlier sketch in CA 7-8R
See also DLB 7
See also CLC 22
See also AITN 1
Kanin, Michael 1910- ... 61-64
Kanin, Ruth 1920- ... 107
Kanitz, Walter 1910- ... 97-100
Kaniuk, Yoram 1930?- ... CLC-19
Kaniut, Larry (LeRoy) 1942- ... 114
Kann, Robert A. 1906-1981 Obituary ... 105

Kannappan, Subbiah 1927- ... 93-96
Kanner, Catherine 1954- ... 123
Kanner, Leo 1894-1981 ... 17-18R
Obituary ... 103
Kanof, Abram 1903- ... 29-32R
Kanovsky, Eliyahu 1922- ... 33-36R
Kansil, Joli 1943- ... 81-84
Kant, Hermann 1926- ... DLB-75
Kantar, Edwin B(ruce) 1932- ... 41-44R
Kanter, Arnold 1945- ... 89-92
Kanter, Hal 1918- ... 81-84
Kanter, Rosabeth Moss 1943- ... CANR-14
Earlier sketch in CA 77-80
Kanto, Peter
See Zachary, Hugh
Kantonen, T(aito) A(lmar) 1900- ... 33-36R
Kantor, Hal 1924- ... 77-80
Kantor, Harry 1911- ... CANR-2
Earlier sketch in CA 1R
Kantor, Herman I. 1909- ... 57-60
Kantor, James 1927-1974 ... CAP-2
Earlier sketch in CA 21-22
Kantor, Leonard 1924(?)-1984 Obituary ... 112
Kantor, MacKinlay 1904-1977 ... 61-64
Obituary ... 73-76
See also DLB 9
See also CLC 7
Kantor, Marvin 1934- ... CANR-2
Earlier sketch in CA 49-52
Kantor, Seth 1926- ... 81-84
Kantor-Berg, Friedrich 1908-1979
Obituary ... 89-92
Kantorovich, L(eonid) V(italevich)
1912-1986 Obituary ... 119
Kantowicz, Edward Robert 1943- ... 114
Kantrowitz, Arnie 1940- ... 77-80
Kantrowitz, Joanne Spencer 1931- ... 81-84
Kantzer, Kenneth S(ealer) 1917- ... 106
Kanwar, Mahfooz A. 1939- ... 37-40R
Kany, Charles E(mil) 1895-1968 ... CANR-3
Earlier sketch in CA 1R
Kanya-Forstner, A(lexander) S(ydney)
1940- ... CANR-17
Earlier sketch in CA 25-28R
Kanza, Thomas R. (Nsenga) 1933- ... CANR-5
Earlier sketch in CA 53-56
Kanzawa, Toshiko
See Furukawa, Toshi
Kanzer, Mark 1908- ... 37-40R
Kao, Charles C. L. 1932- ... 85-88
Kapel, Andrew
See Burgess, M(ichael) R(oy)
Kapel, David E(dward) 1932- ... 125
Kapelner, Alan ... 7-8R
Kapelrud, Arvid Schou 1912- ... 102
Kapfer, Miriam B(ierbaum) 1935- ... 33-36R
Kapfer, Philip G(ordon) 1936- ... 33-36R
Kapitsa, Pyotr L(eonidovich) 1894-1984
Obituary ... 112
Kaplan, Abraham 1918- ... 13-14R
Kaplan, Allan 1932- ... 33-36R
Kaplan, Andrew (Gary) 1941- ... 125
Kaplan, Anne Bernays 1930- ... CANR-5
Earlier sketch in CA 3R
See also SATA 32
Kaplan, Arthur 1925- ... 7-8R
Kaplan, Benjamin 1911- ... 1R
Kaplan, Bernard 1944- ... CANR-2
Earlier sketch in CA 49-52
Kaplan, Berton H(arris) 1930- ... 61-64
Kaplan, Bess 1927- ... 85-88
See also SATA 22
Kaplan, Boche 1926- ... CANR-10
Earlier sketch in CA 23-24R
See also SATA 24
Kaplan, Charles 1919- ... 9-10R
Kaplan, David Gordon 1908- ... 61-64
Kaplan, David Michael 1946- ... CLC-50
Kaplan, Edward 1946- ... CANR-11
Earlier sketch in CA 69-72
Kaplan, Eugene H(erbert) 1932- ... 81-84
Kaplan, Flora S(tewart) ... 109
Kaplan, Fred 1937- ... CANR-14
Earlier sketch in CA 41-44R
Kaplan, Fred Michael 1954- Brief entry ... 121
Kaplan, Frederick I(srael) 1920- ... 23-24R
Kaplan, H. Roy 1944- ... 89-92
Kaplan, Harold 1916- ... 19-20R
Kaplan, Helen Singer 1929- ... 102
See also AITN 1
Kaplan, Howard 1950- ... 69-72
Kaplan, Howard B(ernard) 1932- ... CANR-22
Earlier sketches in CA 61-64, CANR-8
Kaplan, Hymen R. 1910- ... 102
Kaplan, Irma 1900- ... 29-32R
See also SATA 10
Kaplan, Jack A(rnold) 1947- ... 57-60
Kaplan, Jacob J. 1920- ... CANR-10
Earlier sketch in CA 23-24R
Kaplan, Janice Ellen 1955- ... 117
Kaplan, Jean Caryl Korn 1926- ... 7-8R
See also SATA 10
Kaplan, Jim 1944- ... 126
Kaplan, Johanna 1942- ... 77-80
See also DLB 28
Kaplan, Joseph 1916(?)-1980 Obituary ... 97-100
Kaplan, Justin 1925- ... CANR-8
Earlier sketch in CA 19-20R
Kaplan, Lawrence Jay 1915- ... 21-22R
Kaplan, Lawrence S(amuel) 1924- ... 33-36R
Kaplan, Leonard 1918(?)-1977 Obituary ... 69-72
Kaplan, Martin (Harold) 1950- ... 65-68
Kaplan, Martin F(rancis) 1940- ... 93-96
Kaplan, Max 1911- ... CANR-20
Earlier sketches in CA 4R, CANR-5
Kaplan, Milton 1910- ... 65-68
Kaplan, Mordecai M(enahem) 1881-1983
Obituary ... 111
Kaplan, Morton A. 1921- ... CANR-7
Earlier sketch in CA 7-8R
Kaplan, Norman Mayer 1931- ... 110
Kaplan, Philip 1916- ... 13-14R
Kaplan, Richard 1929- ... 73-76
Kaplan, Robert B. 1928- ... CANR-22
Earlier sketches in CA 13-14R, CANR-7
Kaplan, S(aul) Howard 1938- ... 25-28R
Kaplan, Samuel 1935- ... 21-22R
Kaplan, Sidney 1913- ... 85-88
Kaplan, Stuart R(onald) 1932- ... CANR-21
Earlier sketches in CA 49-52, CANR-2
Kaplan, Sydney Janet 1939- ... 110
Kaplan, William 1957- ... 126
Kapler, Aleksei (Yaklovlevich)
1904(?)-1979 Obituary ... 89-92
Kaplon, Morton F(ischel) 1921- ... 23-24R
Kaplow, Herb(ert Elias) 1927- ... 119
Brief entry ... 110
Kaplow, Jeffry 1937- ... 17-18R
Kapoor, Ashok 1940- ... 85-88
Kapoor, Sukhbir Singh 1935- ... 109
Kapp, K(arl) William 1910-1976 ... CANR-8
Obituary ... 65-68
Earlier sketch in CA 5-6R
Kapp, Reginald Otto 1885-1966 ... 7-8R
Kapp, Yvonne (Mayer) 1903- ... 103
Kappauf, William Emil (Jr.) 1913- ... 106
Kappel, Philip 1901- ... CAP-1
Earlier sketch in CA 15-16
Kappelman, Murray M(artin) 1931- ... 73-76
Kappel-Smith, Diana 1951- ... 121
Kappen, Charles Vaughan 1910- ... 11-12R
Kaprow, Allan 1927- ... 105
Kapsner, Oliver L(eonard) 1902- ... 116
Kapstein, I(srael) J(ames) 1904-1983
Obituary ... 110
Kaptchuk, Ted J(ack) 1947- ... 110
Kapur, Harish 1929- ... CANR-15
Earlier sketch in CA 85-88
Kapuscinski, Ryszard 1932- ... 114
Kapusta, Paul
See Bickers, Richard Leslie Townshend
Karageorge, Michael
See Anderson, Poul (William)
Karageorghis, Vassos 1929- ... CANR-15
Earlier sketch in CA 81-84
Karamanski, Theodore J. 1953- ... 126
Karan, Pradyumna P(rasad) 1930- ... 114
Karanikas, Alexander 1916- ... 33-36R
Karapanou, Margarita 1946- ... 101
See also CLC 13
Karas, Jim 1949-1981 ... 126
Obituary ... 108
Karas, Joza 1926- ... 124
Karas, Phyllis 1944- ... 105
Karasu, Toksoz B(yram) 1935- ... 105
Karasz, Ilonka 1896-1981 ... SATA-29
Karbo, Joe 1925(?)-1980 Obituary ... 115
Kardiner, Abram 1891-1981 ... 107
Obituary ... 104
Kardish, Laurence 1945- ... 49-52
Kardouche, G(eorge) Khalil 1935- ... 19-20R
Karel, Leonard 1912- ... 49-52
Karen
See Aldrich, Sandra Picklesimer
Karen, Robert L(e Roy) 1925- ... 73-76
Karen, Ruth 1922-1987 ... CANR-11
Obituary ... 123
Earlier sketch in CA 19-20R
See also SATA 9
Karg, Elissa Jane 1951- ... 23-24R
Karger, Delmar William 1913- ... CANR-8
Earlier sketch in CA 17-18R
Kargon, Robert Hugh 1938- ... 45-48
Kariel, Henry S. 1924- ... 13-14R
Karin, Sidney 1943- ... 126
Karina
See Goud, Anne
Kariuki, Josiah Mwangi 1929- ... 107
Kark, Nina Mary (Mabey) 1925- ... CANR-8
Earlier sketch in CA 17-18R
See also SATA 4
Karkala, John A.
See Alphonso-Karkala, John B.
Karkala, John B.A.
See Alphonso-Karkala, John B.
Karkhanis, Sharad 1935- ... 110
Karkoschka, Erhard 1923- ... 45-48
Karl, Barry D(ean) 1927- ... 102
Karl, Frederick R(obert) 1927- ... CANR-3
Earlier sketch in CA 5-6R
See also CLC 34
Karl, Jean E(dna) 1927- ... CANR-12
Earlier sketch in CA 29-32R
See also SATA 34
Karl, Roger
See Trouve, Roger
Karlan, Richard 1919- ... 17-18R
Karlen, Arno 1937- ... CANR-5
Earlier sketch in CA 1R
Karlen, Delmar 1912- ... CANR-2
Earlier sketch in CA 7-8R
Karlgren, (Klas) Bernhard (Johannes)
1889- ... CAP-1
Earlier sketch in CA 9-10
Karlin, Eugene 1918- ... SATA-10
Karlin, Jules 1899- ... CAP-2
Earlier sketch in CA 25-28
Karlin, Muriel S.
See Trachman, Muriel Karlin
Karlin, Robert 1918- ... 9-10R
Karlins, Marvin 1941- ... CANR-17
Earlier sketch in CA 25-28R
Karlowich, Robert A. 1927- ... 125
Karlsson, Elis (Viktor) 1905- ... CAP-1
Earlier sketch in CA 15-16
Karlsson, T. Edward 1915(?)-1984
Obituary ... 113
Karman, James W. 1947- ... 126
Karman, Mal 1944- ... 103
Karmel, Alex 1931- ... 23-24R
Karmel, Roberta S(arah) 1937- ... 108
Karmel-Wolfe, Henia 1923- ... 49-52
Karmen, Roman Lazarevich 1906-1978
Obituary ... 77-80
Karmi, Abdul Karim 1907(?)-1980
Obituary ... 102
Karmi, Hasan Said 1908- ... 45-48
Karmin, Monroe William 1929- ... 101
Karnad, Girish 1938- ... 65-68
Karnes, Merle B(riggs) 1916- ... 85-88
Karnes, Thomas L(indas) 1914- ... 23-24R
Karney, Beulah Mullen ... 13-14R
Karniewski, Janusz
See Wittlin, Thaddeus (Andrew)
Karno, Bung
See Sukarno, (Ahmed)
Karnow, Stanley 1925- ... 57-60
Karol, Alexander
See Kent, Arthur William Charles
Karol, K. S.
See Kewes, Karol
Karolevitz, Bob
See Karolevitz, Robert F.
Karolevitz, Robert F. 1922- ... CANR-22
Earlier sketches in CA 17-18R, CANR-7
Karolides, Nicholas J(ames) 1928- ... 21-22R
Karolyi, Catherine (Andrassy) 1898-1985
Obituary ... 116
Karon, Bertram Paul 1930- ... CANR-7
Earlier sketch in CA 61-64
Karp, Abraham J. 1921- ... CANR-18
Earlier sketches in CA 5-6R, CANR-3
Karp, Alan 1947- ... 107
Karp, David 1922- ... CANR-1
Earlier sketch in CA 1R
Karp, Ivan C. 1926- ... 17-18R
Karp, Laurence E(dward) 1939- ... 77-80
Karp, Lila 1933- ... 25-28R
Karp, Mark 1922- ... 1R
Karp, Naomi J. 1926- ... 81-84
See also SATA 16
Karp, Stephen A(rnold) 1928- ... CANR-6
Earlier sketch in CA 1R
Karpat, Kemal H(asim) 1925- ... CANR-11
Earlier sketch in CA 69-72
Karpatkin, Marvin M. 1926-1975
Obituary ... 53-56
Karpau, Uladzimir
See Karpov, Vladimir
Karpel, Bernard 1911-1986 ... 106
Obituary ... 118
Karpel, Craig S. 1944- ... 65-68
Karpeles, Maud 1885- ... 25-28R
Karpf, Holly W. 1946- ... 37-40R
Karpin, Fred L(eon) 1913-1986 ... CANR-9
Obituary ... 119
Earlier sketch in CA 15-16R
Karplus, Walter J. 1927- ... 21-22R
Karpman, Harold L(ew) 1927- ... 77-80
Karpov, Vladimir 1912(?)-1977 Obituary ... 73-76
Karr, E(arl) R(alph) 1918- ... 3R
Karr, Phyllis Ann 1944- ... CANR-18
Earlier sketch in CA 101
Karras, Alex(ander G.) 1935- ... 107
Karrass, Chester L. 1923- ... 101
Karren, Keith J(ohn) 1943- ... 116
Karrer, Paul 1889-1971 Obituary ... 113
Karris, Robert J(oseph) 1938- ... CANR-5
Earlier sketch in CA 53-56
Karsavina, Jean (Faterson) 1908- ... 101
Karsavina, Tamara 1885-1978 Obituary ... 77-80
Karsch, Robert F(rederick) 1909- ... 77-80
Karsen, Sonja (Petra) 1919- ... 41-44R
Karsh, Bernard 1921- ... 103
Karsh, Yousuf 1908- ... 33-36R
Karshner, Roger 1928- ... 33-36R
Karsten, Peter 1938- ... CANR-13
Earlier sketch in CA 37-40R
Karta, Nat
See Norwood, Victor G(eorge) C(harles)
Kartiganer, Donald M. 1937- ... 97-100
Karu, Baruch 1899-1972 Obituary ... 104
Karve, Dinakar Dhondo 1899-1980 ... 7-8R
Obituary ... 103
Karve, Irawati (Karmarkar) 1905-1970 ... CAP-1
Earlier sketch in CA 19-20
Kary, Elizabeth N. (a pseudonym) 1947- ... 122
Kasack, Hermann 1896-1966 ... DLB-69
Kasarda, John Dale 1945- ... 103
Kaschnitz, Marie Luise
See von Kaschnitz-Weinberg, Marie Luise
See also DLB 69
Kasdan, Lawrence 1949- ... 109
Kasdan, Sara (Moskovitz) 1911- ... 2R
Kasdorf, Hans 1928- ... 116
Kase, Francis J(oseph) 1910- ... 23-24R
Kaselow, Joseph 1912-1986 Obituary ... 119
Kaser, David 1924- ... 17-18R
Kaser, Michael (Charles) 1926- ... CANR-10
Earlier sketch in CA 17-18R
Kaser, Paul 1944- ... 104
Kash, Don E(ldon) 1934- ... CANR-9
Earlier sketch in CA 23-24R
Kashdan, Isaac 1905-1985 Obituary ... 115
Kashima, Tetsuden 1940- ... 81-84
Kashiwagi, Isami 1925- ... SATA-10
Kashner, Rita 1942- ... 105
Kaslow, Florence W(hiteman) 1930- ... CANR-18
Earlier sketches in CA 45-48, CANR-1
Kasper, Sydney H. 1911- ... 4R
Kasperson, Roger E. 1938- ... 29-32R
Kasrils, Ronald 1938- ... 29-32R
Kass, Jerome 1923(?)-1973 Obituary ... 104
Kass, Jerome 1937- ... 57-60
Kass, Norman 1934- ... 29-32R
Kass, Ray 1944- ... 118
Kassalow, Everett M(alcolm) 1918- ... CANR-25
Earlier sketch in CA 45-48
Kassebaum, Gene G(irard) 1929- ... 19-20R
Kassem, Lou ... SATA-51
Kassewitz, Jack 1914(?)-1984 Obituary ... 112
Kassis, Hanna (Emmanuel) 1932- ... 125
Kassof, Allen 1930- ... 23-24R
Kasson, John F(ranklin) 1944- ... 81-84
Kassorla, Irene Chamie 1931- ... 110
Kast, Fremont E. 1926- ... 23-24R
Kastan, David Scott 1946- ... 109
Kastein, Shulamith 1903-1983 ... 105
Obituary ... 110
Kastel, Warren
See Silverberg, Robert
Kastenbaum, Robert (Jay) 1932- ... CANR-9
Earlier sketch in CA 15-16R
Kaster, Joseph 1912-19(?) ... CAP-1
Earlier sketch in CA 19-20
Kastl, Albert J(oseph) 1939- ... 57-60
Kastl, Lena 1942- ... 61-64
Kastle, Herbert D(avid) 1924-1987 ... CANR-1
Obituary ... 123
Earlier sketch in CA 1R
Kastner, Erich
See Kaestner, Erich
See also SATA 14
See also DLB 56
See also CLR 4
Kastner, Jonathan 1937- ... 25-28R
Kastner, Joseph 1907- ... 85-88
Kastner, Marianna 1940- ... 25-28R
Kastner, Patricia Wilson
See Wilson-Kastner, Patricia
Kasulis, T(homas) P(atrick) 1948- ... 124
Kasuya, Masahiro 1937- ... 110
See also SATA 51
Kaszner, Kurt
See Serwicher, Kurt
Kaszubski, Marek 1951- ... 105
Kataev, Evgeny Petrovich 1903-1942
Brief entry ... 120
Katahn, Martin 1928- ... 114
Katan, Norma-Jean 1936- ... 113
Katayev, Valentin (Petrovich) 1897-1986
Obituary ... 119
Brief entry ... 117
Katcha, Vahe
See Katchadourian, Vahe
Katchadourian, Herant A(ram) 1933- ... CANR-20
Earlier sketch in CA 103
Katchadourian, Vahe 1928- ... CANR-25
Earlier sketch in CA 29-32R
Katchen, Carole 1944- ... 61-64
See also SATA 9
Katchmer, George Andrew 1916- ... 3R
Kateb, George (Anthony) 1931- ... 123
Brief entry ... 118
Katen, Thomas Ellis 1931- ... 53-56
Kater, Michael H(ans) 1937- ... 114
Kates, Brian 1946- ... 119
Kates, Carol A. 1943- ... 115
Kates, Gary (Richard) 1952- ... 125
Kates, Robert W. 1929- ... CANR-24
Earlier sketches in CA 17-18R, CANR-8
Kathman, Michael D(ennis) 1943- ... 109
Kathryn
See Searle, Kathryn Adrienne
Kati
See Rekai, Kati
Katicic, Radoslav 1930- ... 37-40R
Katkov, George 1903-1985 Obituary ... 115
Katkov, Norman 1918- ... 15-16R
Kato, Hidetoshi 1930- ... 115
Kato, Shuichi 1919- ... 37-40R
Kato, Tsuyoski 1943- ... 126
Katona, Edita 1913- ... 69-72
Katona, George 1901-1981 Obituary ... 104
Katona, Robert 1949- ... SATA-21
Katope, Christopher G. 1918- ... 21-22R
Katoppo, (Henriette) Marianne 1943- ... 123
Katrovas, Richard 1953- ... 126
Katsarakis, Joan Harries
See Harries, Joan
Katsaros, Thomas 1926- ... 57-60
Katsh, Abraham I(saac) 1908- ... CANR-8
Earlier sketch in CA 7-8R
Katsh, Salem M(ichael) 1948- ... 110
Kattan, Naim 1928- ... CANR-11
Earlier sketch in CA 69-72
See also DLB 53
Katterjohn, Arthur D. 1930(?)-1980
Obituary ... 93-96
Katz, Abraham 1926- ... 49-52
Katz, Albert M(ichael) 1938- ... 93-96
Katz, Alfred 1938- ... 77-80
Katz, Alfred
See Allan, Alfred K.
Katz, Arthur M. 1942- ... 124
Katz, Basho
See Gatti, Arthur Gerard
Katz, Benjamin 1904-1985 Obituary ... 115
Katz, Bobbi 1933- ... CANR-16
Earlier sketch in CA 37-40R
See also SATA 12
Katz, Carol 1939- ... 115
Katz, Daniel 1903- ... 41-44R
Katz, Elias 1912- ... 29-32R
Katz, Ellis 1938- ... 29-32R
Katz, Eve 1938- ... CANR-1
Earlier sketch in CA 45-48

Katz, Fred(eric Phillip) 1938- 49-52
See also SATA 6
Katz, Fred E(mil) 1927- 77-80
Katz, Friedrich 1927- Brief entry 113
Katz, Gloria 1945(?)- 107
Katz, Herbert Melvin 1930- 103
Katz, Irving I. 1907- 4R
Katz, Jack 1944- 111
Katz, Jacob 1904- CANR-4
Earlier sketch in CA 1R
Katz, Jane B(resler) 1934- 85-88
See also SATA 33
Katz, Jay 1922- 118
Katz, John Stuart 1938- CANR-14
Earlier sketch in CA 37-40R
Katz, Jonathan 1938- 85-88
Katz, Josef 1918- 53-56
Katz, Joseph 1910- CANR-2
Earlier sketch in CA 1R
Katz, Judith Milstein 1943- 106
Katz, Leon 1919- CANR-20
Earlier sketches in CA 49-52, CANR-4
Katz, Leonard 1926- 21-22R
Katz, Lewis R(obert) 1938- 116
Katz, Lilian G(onshaw) 1932- 111
Katz, Marjorie P.
See Weiser, Marjorie P(hillis) K(atz)
Katz, Martin 1929- 23-24R
Katz, Marvin C(harles) 1930- 25-28R
Katz, Menke 1906- CANR-11
Earlier sketch in CA 15-16R
Katz, Michael B(arry) 1939- CANR-13
Earlier sketch in CA 33-36R
Katz, Michael M. 1956(?)-1988 Obituary 126
Katz, Michael Ray 1944- CANR-18
Earlier sketch in CA 102
Katz, Mickey
See Katz, Myron Meyer
Katz, Milton 1907- CAP-1
Earlier sketch in CA 11-12
Katz, Mort 1925- CANR-11
Earlier sketch in CA 61-64
Katz, Myron Meyer 1909-1985 81-84
Obituary 116
Katz, Robert 1933- CANR-11
Earlier sketch in CA 25-28R
Katz, Robert L. 1917- 9-10R
Katz, Samuel 1914- CANR-12
Earlier sketch in CA 25-28R
Katz, Sanford N. 1933- CANR-13
Earlier sketch in CA 33-36R
Katz, Shmuel
See Katz, Samuel
Katz, Stan
See Chapman, Frank M(onroe)
Katz, Stanley Nider 1934- 11-12R
Katz, Steve 1935- CANR-12
Earlier sketch in CA 25-28R
See also DLBY 83
See also CLC 47
Katz, Susan 1944(?)-1982 Obituary 107
Katz, William 1940- 85-88
Katz, William A(rmstrong) 1924- CANR-10
Earlier sketch in CA 25-28R
Katz, William Loren 1927- CANR-9
Earlier sketch in CA 21-22R
See also SATA 13
Katzander, Howard L. 1911(?)-1983
Obituary 110
Katzenbach, John 1950- 119
Katzenbach, Maria 1953- 77-80
Katzenbach, William E. 1904-1975
Obituary 61-64
Katzenstein, Mary Fainsod 1945- 93-96
Katzenstein, Peter J(oachim) 1945- CANR-17
Earlier sketch in CA 93-96
Ka-Tzetnik 135633 29-32R
Katzman, Allen 1937- 29-32R
Katzman, Anita 1920- 57-60
Katzman, David Manners 1941- CANR-5
Earlier sketch in CA 53-56
Katzman, Martin T(heodore) 1941- 111
Katznelson-Shazar, Rachel 1888-1975
Obituary 61-64
Katzner, Kenneth 1930- 7-8R
Kau, Michael Y. M.
See Kau, Ying-mao
Kau, Ying-mao 1934- Brief entry 114
Kauder, Emil 1901- 17-18R
Kaufelt, David Allan 1939- CANR-16
Earlier sketches in CA 45-48, CANR-1
Kauffeld, Carl F. 1911-1974 Obituary 49-52
Kauffman, Christmas Carol 1902- 1R
Kauffman, Christopher J. 1936- 107
Kauffman, Donald T(homas) 1920- CANR-11
Earlier sketch in CA 25-28R
Kauffman, Dorotha S(trayer) 1925- 17-18R
Kauffman, Draper L. 1946- 108
Kauffman, George B(ernard) 1930- 19-20R
Kauffman, Henry J. 1908- 13-14R
Kauffman, James M(ilton) 1940- CANR-7
Earlier sketch in CA 57-60
Kauffman, Janet 1945- 117
See also DLBY 86
See also CLC 42
Kauffman, Joseph F(rank) 1921- CANR-1
Earlier sketch in CA 45-48
Kauffman, Milo (Franklin) 1898- 89-92
Kauffmann, C. Michael 1931- 125
Kauffmann, Georg (Friedrich) 1925- 49-52
Kauffmann, Lane 1921- 19-20R
Kauffmann, (Franklin) Lane 1922(?)-1988
Obituary 125
Kauffmann, Samuel Hay 1898-1971
Obituary 89-92
Kauffmann, Stanley 1916- CANR-6
Earlier sketch in CA 7-8R
Kaufman, Arnold S. 1927- 25-28R
Kaufman, Arthur 1934- CANR-25
Earlier sketch in CA 107
Kaufman, Barry Neil 1942- CANR-17
Earlier sketch in CA 97-100
Kaufman, Bel CANR-13
Earlier sketch in CA 15-16R
Kaufman, Bob (Garnell) 1925-1986 CANR-22
Obituary 118
Earlier sketch in CA 41-44R
See also BW
See also DLB 16, 41
See also CLC 49
Kaufman, Burton I. 1940- 33-36R
Kaufman, Daniel 1949- 85-88
Kaufman, Debra Renee 1941- 109
Kaufman, Donald D(avid) 1933- 29-32R
Kaufman, Edmund George 1891- 73-76
Kaufman, George S. 1889-1961 108
Obituary 93-96
See also DLB 7
See also CLC 38
Kaufman, Gerald (Bernard) 1930- 23-24R
Kaufman, Gershen 1943- 117
Kaufman, Gloria (Shapiro) 1929- 122
Kaufman, Gordon Dester 1925- CANR-7
Earlier sketch in CA 13-14R
Kaufman, H(arold) G(erson) 1939- 69-72
Kaufman, Herbert 1922- Brief entry 115
Kaufman, I(sadore) 1892-1978 Obituary 77-80
Kaufman, Irving 1920- 21-22R
Kaufman, Jacob J(oseph) 1914- 41-44R
Kaufman, Joe 1911- 107
See also SATA 33
Kaufman, Lloyd 1927- 93-96
Kaufman, Martin 1940- 109
Kaufman, Mervyn D. 1932- 7-8R
See also SATA 4
Kaufman, Paul 1886-1979 Obituary 89-92
Kaufman, Paula T. 1946- 126
Kaufman, Philip 1936- 121
Brief entry 112
Kaufman, Polly W(elts) 1929- 114
Kaufman, Robert 1931- CANR-25
Earlier sketch in CA 17-18R
Kaufman, Roger (Alexander) 1932- CANR-9
Earlier sketch in CA 53-56
Kaufman, Rosamond (Arleen) V(an)
P(oznak) 1923- CANR-7
Earlier sketch in CA 11-12R
Kaufman, Sherwin A. 1920- CANR-10
Earlier sketch in CA 25-28R
Kaufman, Shirley 1923- 49-52
Kaufman, Sidney 1910-1983 Obituary 110
Kaufman, Stuart Bruce 1942- 123
Kaufman, Sue
See Barondess, Sue K(aufman)
See also CLC 3, 8
Kaufman, Wallace 1939- CANR-10
Earlier sketch in CA 25-28R
Kaufman, William I(rving) 1922- CANR-24
Earlier sketches in CA 13-14R, CANR-7
Kaufman, Wolfe 1905(?)-1970 Obituary 29-32R
Kaufmann, Angelika 1935- SATA-15
Kaufmann, Harry 1927- 45-48
Kaufmann, Helen L(oeb) 1887- CANR-7
Earlier sketch in CA 5-6R
Kaufmann, Henry William 1913- 41-44R
Kaufmann, John 1931- 81-84
See also SATA 18
Kaufmann, Myron S. 1921- 25-28R
Kaufmann, R(alph) James 1924- 13-14R
Kaufmann, U(rlin) Milo 1934- 41-44R
Kaufmann, Ulrich George 1920- 23-24R
Kaufmann, Walter 1921-1980 CANR-1
Obituary 101
Earlier sketch in CA 1R
Kaufmann, Walter 1933- 61-64
Kaufmann, William J(ohn) III 1942- 93-96
Kaufmann, William W. 1918- 13-14R
Kaul, Donald 1934- 65-68
Kaula, Edna Mason 1906- 7-8R
See also SATA 13
Kaumeyer, Dorothy 1914- Brief entry 105
Kauper, Paul Gerhardt 1907-1974 CANR-6
Obituary 49-52
Earlier sketch in CA 4R
Kaur, Sardarni Premka 1943- 77-80
Kausler, Donald H(arvey) 1927- 19-20R
Kauth, Benjamin 1914- 7-8R
Kautsky, Karl (Johann) 1854-1938
Brief entry 123
Kauvar, Gerald B(luestone) 1938- 45-48
Kavafis, Konstantinos Petrou 1863-1933
Brief entry 104
Kavaler, Lucy 1930- CANR-22
Earlier sketches in CA 57-60, CANR-7
See also SATA 23
Kavaler, Rebecca 1932- CANR-16
Earlier sketch in CA 89-92
Kavan, Anna 1901-1968 CANR-6
Earlier sketch in CA 7-8R
See also CLC 5, 13
Kavanagh, Aidan 1929- 112
Kavanagh, Dan(iel) 1946- 125
Kavanagh, Dan
See Barnes, Julian
Kavanagh, James H. 1948- 126
Kavanagh, Jennifer 1947- 119
Kavanagh, Michael 1945- 118
Kavanagh, P(atrick) J(oseph Gregory)
1931- 81-84
See also DLB 40
Kavanagh, Patrick (Joseph) 1904-1967 123
Obituary 25-28R
See also DLB 15, 20
See also CLC 22
Kavanaugh, Cynthia
See Daniels, Dorothy
Kavanaugh, Ian
See Webb, Jean Francis
Kavanaugh, James J(oseph) 1934- CANR-17
Earlier sketch in CA 13-14R
Kavanaugh, John F(rancis) 1941- 115
Kavanaugh, Kieran 1928- 25-28R
Kavanaugh, Robert E. 1926- 29-32R
Kavasch, E(lizabeth) Barrie 1942- 110
Kavenagh, W(illiam) Keith 1926- 37-40R
Kavesh, Robert A(llyn) 1927- 19-20R
Kavet, Robert 1924- 37-40R
Kavifis, Konstantinos Petrou
See Kavafis, Konstantinos Petrou
Kavli, Guthorm 1917- CAP-1
Earlier sketch in CA 9-10
Kavner, Richard S. 1936- 93-96
Kavolis, Vytautas 1930- 25-28R
Kawabata, Yasunari 1899-1972 93-96
Obituary 33-36R
See also CLC 2, 5, 9, 18
Kawahito, Kiyoshi 1939- 37-40R
Kawai, Kazuo 1904-1963 1R
Kawakami, Tovo S(uvemoto) 1916- 33-36R
Kawin, Bruce F. 1945- CANR-13
Earlier sketch in CA 37-40R
Kawin, Ethel ?-1969 CAP-1
Earlier sketch in CA 11-12
Kay, Barbara Ann 1929- 13-14R
Kay, Brian Ross 1924- 1R
Kay, David A(llen) 1940- Brief entry 114
Kay, Donald 1939- 57-60
Kay, E(lizabeth) Alison 1928- 65-68
Kay, Ellen
See DeMille, Nelson
Kay, Ernest 1915- CANR-24
Earlier sketches in CA 13-14R, CANR-6
Kay, George 1936- 21-22R
Kay, George
See Lambert, Eric
Kay, Harry 1919- 25-28R
Kay, Helen
See Goldfrank, Helen Colodny
Kay, J(ohn) A(nderson) 1948- 119
Kay, Jane Holtz 1938- CANR-22
Earlier sketch in CA 106
Kay, Kenneth (Edmond) 1915- CANR-6
Earlier sketch in CA 9-10R
Kay, Mara CANR-2
Earlier sketch in CA 7-8R
See also SATA 13
Kay, Mary
See Ash, Mary Kay (Wagner)
Kay, Norman (Forber) 1929- 45-48
Kay, (Sydney Francis) Patrick (Chippendall)
Healey
See Healey-Kay, (Sydney Francis) Patrick
(Chippendall)
Kay, Paul 1934- 41-44R
Kay, Reed 1925- 77-80
Kay, Ronald
See Knox-Mawer, Ronald
Kay, Terence 1918- 19-20R
Kay, Teresa
See de Kerpely, Theresa
Kay, Terry (Winter) 1938- 110
Kay, Terry
See Kay, Terence
Kay, Thomas O(bed) 1932- 3R
Kay, (Albert) William 1930-1976 CAP-2
Earlier sketch in CA 29-32
Kay, Zell
See Kemp, Roy Z(ell)
Kayal, Joseph M(itchell) 1942- 57-60
Kayal, Philip M(itchell) 1943- 57-60
Kaye, Alan
See Horowitz, Shel Alan
Kaye, Barbara
See Muir, Marie
Kaye, Bruce (Norman) 1939- 93-96
Kaye, Buddy 1918- 81-84
Kaye, Danny 1913-1987 Obituary 121
See also SATA 50
Kaye, Evelyn 1937- 57-60
Kaye, Geraldine (Hughesdon) 1925- CANR-22
Earlier sketches in CA 15-16R, CANR-7
See also SATA 10
Kaye, H. R.
See Knox, Hugh (Randolph)
Kaye, Harvey E(arle) 1927- 101
Kaye, Harvey J(ordan) 1949- 121
Kaye, Hilary 1950- 116
Kaye, Howard L. 1951- 126
Kaye, Joanne
See Payes, Rachel C(osgrove)
Kaye, Julian B(ertram) 1925- 1R
Kaye, Kenneth Peter 1946- 111
Kaye, Lenny 1946- Brief entry 121
Kaye, M(ary) M(argaret) 1909- CANR-24
Earlier sketch in CA 89-92
See also CLC 28
Kaye, Marilyn 1949- CANR-24
Earlier sketch in CA 107
Kaye, Marvin (Nathan) 1938- CANR-19
Earlier sketches in CA 53-56, CANR-5
Kaye, Mollie
See Kaye, M(ary) M(argaret)
Kaye, Myrna 1930- 57-60
Kaye, Peggy 1948- 116
Kaye, Philip A. 1920- 37-40R
Kaye, Phyllis Johnson 102
Kaye-Smith, Sheila 1887-1956 Brief entry 118
See also DLB 36
See also TCLC 20
Kayira, Legson Didimu 1940- 17-18R
See also BW
Kaymor, Patrice Maguilene
See Senghor, Leopold Sedar
Kaysen, Carl 1920- CANR-11
Earlier sketch in CA 19-20R
Kayser, Elmer Louis 1896-1985 37-40R
Obituary 116
Kayser, Hugh F. 1926- 107
Kayser-Jones, Jeanie Schmit 1935- 105
Kaysing, Bill
See Kaysing, William C.
Kaysing, William C. 1922- 33-36R
Kayyali, Abdul-Wahhab (Said) 1939-1981
Obituary 108
Kazakov, Yuri Pavlovich 1927- 7-8R
Kazamias, Andreas M. 1927- 19-20R
Kazan, Elia 1909- 21-22R
See also CLC 6, 16
Kazan, Frances 1946- 125
Kazantzakis, Nikos 1883-1957 Brief entry 105
See also TCLC 2, 5
Kazarian, Edward A(rshak) 1931- 53-56
Kazdin, Alan E(dward) 1945- 104
Kazee, Buell H(ilton) 1900-1976 Obituary 111
Kazemzadeh Firuz 1924- 23-24R
Kazickas, Jurate C(atherine) 1943- 102
Kazimiroff, Theodore L. 1941- 109
Kazin, Alfred 1915- CANR-1
Earlier sketch in CA 4R
See also CABS 1
See also DLB 67
See also CLC 34, 38
Kazis, Richard 1952- 112
Kazmer, Daniel (Raphael) 1947- 102
Kazmier, Leonard J(ohn) 1930- 107
Kazziha, Walid W. 1941- 65-68
Keach, Richard L(eroy) 1919- 89-92
Kealey, Edward J(oseph) 1936- CANR-14
Earlier sketch in CA 37-40R
Kealy, Sean P(atrick) 1937- 114
Kean, Benjamin Harrison 1912- 103
Kean, Charles Duell 1910-1963 5-6R
Kean, Edmund (Stanley) 1915- 102
Keane, Betty Winkler 1914- 93-96
Keane, Bil 1922- CANR-13
Earlier sketch in CA 33-36R
See also SATA 4
Keane, John B. 1928- 29-32R
See also DLB 13
Keane, Mary Nesta (Skrine) 1904- 114
Brief entry 108
Keane, Molly
See Keane, Mary Nesta (Skrine)
See also CLC 31
Keane, Patrick J(oseph) 1939- CANR-1
Earlier sketch in CA 45-48
Keaney, Marian 1944- 103
Kearey, Charles 1916- 45-48
Kearley, F(loyd) Furman 1932- 57-60
Kearney, Hugh Francis 1924- 7-8R
Kearney, James R(obert III) 1929- 25-28R
Kearney, Jean Nylander 1923- 65-68
Kearney, Robert N(orman) 1930- 81-84
Kearney, Ruth Elizabeth
See Carlson, Ruth (Elizabeth) Kearney
Kearns, Doris Helen
See Goodwin, Doris (Helen) Kearns
Kearns, Francis E(dward) 1931- 29-32R
Kearns, Frank 1917(?)-1986 Obituary 119
Kearns, Frank T. 1903-1984 Obituary 111
Kearns, James A(loysius) III 1949- 29-32R
Kearns, Lionel 1937- CANR-11
Earlier sketch in CA 19-20R
Kearns, Martha 1945- 57-60
Kearns, Michael S. 1947- 126
Kearny, Edward N. III 1936- 29-32R
Kearny, Jillian
See Goulart, Ron(ald Joseph)
Keasey, Carol Tomlinson
See Tomlinson-Keasey, Carol
Keast, James D. 1930- 25-28R
Keast, William R(ea) 1914- 15-16R
Keates, Jonathan 19(?)- CLC-34
Keating, Bern
See Keating, Leo Bernard
Keating, Charlotte Matthews 1927- 33-36R
Keating, Diane 1940- CANR-18
Earlier sketch in CA 101
Keating, Edward M. 1925- 15-16R
Keating, H(enry) R(eymond) F(itzwalter)
1926- CANR-18
Earlier sketch in CA 33-36R
Keating, John J. 1918(?)-1975 Obituary 61-64
Keating, L(ouis) Clark 1907- 21-22R
Keating, Lawrence A. 1903-1966 7-8R
See also SATA 23
Keating, Leo Bernard 1915- 29-32R
See also SATA 10
Keating, Michael (F.) 1932- 49-52
Keating, Tom 1917-1984 Obituary 112
Keaton, Buster 1895-1966 CLC-20
Keats, Charles B. 1905- CAP-1
Earlier sketch in CA 15-16
Keats, Ezra Jack 1916-1983 77-80
Obituary 109
See also SATA 14, 34
See also DLB 61
See also CLR 1
See also AITN 1
Keats, John (C.) 1920- 73-76
Keats, Mark 1905- 77-80
Keaveney, Arthur 1951- 124
Keaveney, Sydney Starr 1939- 53-56
Keay, Frederick 1915- 33-36R
Keay, John (Stanley Melville) 1941- 65-68
Kebbe, Charles Maynard 1913- 114
Kebin, Jodi
See Lawrence, Jodi

Keble, John 1792-1866 ... DLB-32, 55
Kebschull, Harvey G(ustav) 1932- ... 41-44R
Keck, Leander Earl 1928- ... 104
Keddell, Georgina (Murray) 1913- ... 25-28R
Keddie, Nikki R(agozin) 1930- ... CANR-13
Earlier sketch in CA 25-28R
Kedgley, Susan (Jane) 1948- ... 61-64
Kedourie, Elie 1926- ... CANR-10
Earlier sketch in CA 21-22R
Kedzie, Daniel Peter 1930- ... 17-18R
Kee, (Alexander) Alistair 1937- ... 89-92
Kee, Howard Clark 1920- ... CANR-10
Earlier sketch in CA 23-24R
Kee, Robert 1919- Brief entry ... 113
Keeble, John 1944- ... CANR-14
Earlier sketch in CA 29-32R
See also DLBY 83
Keech, William J(ohn) 1904- ... CAP-1
Earlier sketch in CA 9-10
Keech, William R(obertson) 1939- ... 25-28R
Keedy, Mervin L(averne) 1920- ... CANR-5
Earlier sketch in CA 53-56
Keefe, Carolyn 1928- ... 57-60
Keefe, Donald Joseph 1924- ... 37-40R
Keefe, John Edwin 1942- ... 107
Keefe, Michael 1946- ... 93-96
Keefe, Robert 1938- ... 89-92
Keefe, Susan E. 1947- ... 126
Keefe, Terry 1940- ... 125
Keefer, Catherine
See Ogan, George F.
and Ogan, Margaret E. (Nettles)
Keefer, T(ruman) Frederick 1930- ... 23-24R
Keeffe, Barrie (Colin) 1945- Brief entry ... 116
See also DLB 13
Keegan, Frank L. 1925- ... 45-48
Keegan, Marcia 1943- ... 49-52
See also SATA 9
Keegan, Mary Heathcott 1914- ... CANR-3
Earlier sketch in CA 7-8R
Keegan, Terence J(ames) 1939- ... 117
Keegan, Warren J(oseph) 1936- ... 57-60
Keel, Frank
See Keeler, Ronald F(ranklin)
Keel, John A.
See Kiehle, John Alva
Keele, Kenneth D(avid) 1909- ... 7-8R
Keele, Reba Lou 1941- Brief entry ... 106
Keeler, Mary Frear 1904- ... 77-80
Keeler, Ronald F(ranklin) 1913-1983 ... 107
See also SATA 47
Keeley, Edmund (Leroy) 1928- ... CANR-22
Earlier sketches in CA 1R, CANR-1
Keeley, James 1867-1934 ... DLB-25
Keeley, Joseph C(harles) 1907- ... 25-28R
Keeley, Steve 1949- ... 93-96
Keeling, Clinton Harry 1932- ... CANR-7
Earlier sketch in CA 11-12R
Keeling, E. B.
See Curl, James Stevens
Keeling, Jill Annette (Shaw) 1923- ... CANR-12
Earlier sketches in CA 9-10, CAP-1
Keely, Charles C(larke), Jr. 1934-1985
Obituary ... 116
Keely, Harry Harris 1904- ... 65-68
Keely, Jane 1922- ... 107
Keen, Benjamin 1913- Brief entry ... 114
Keen, (John) Ernest 1937- ... 33-36R
Keen, Geraldine
See Norman, Geraldine (Lucia)
Keen, M. H.
See Keen, Maurice Hugh
Keen, Martin L. 1913- ... 33-36R
See also SATA 4
Keen, Maurice
See Keen, Maurice Hugh
Keen, Maurice Hugh 1933- ... 122
Keen, Tommy 1923- ... 108
Keenan, Angela Elizabeth 1890-1983 ... 61-64
Obituary ... 111
Keenan, Boyd R(aymond) 1928- ... 17-18R
Keenan, Deborah (Anne) 1950- ... CANR-11
Earlier sketch in CA 69-72
Keenan, Desmond (Joseph) 1933- ... 125
Keenan, Joseph H(enry) 1900-1977
Obituary ... 73-76
Keenan, Martha 1927- ... 77-80
Keene, Burt
See Bickers, Richard Leslie Townshend
Keene, Carolyn ... 19-20R
Keene, Donald 1922- ... CANR-5
Earlier sketch in CA 1R
See also CLC 34
Keene, J(ames) Calvin 1908- ... CAP-1
Earlier sketch in CA 17-18
Keene, James A(llen) 1932- ... 109
Keene, R. D.
See Keene, Raymond D(ennis)
Keene, Ray
See Keene, Raymond D(ennis)
Keene, Raymond D(ennis) 1948-
Brief entry ... 112
Keener, Frederick M(ichael) 1937- ... CANR-15
Earlier sketch in CA 53-56
Keeney, Charles James 1912- ... 7-8R
Keeney, Chuck
See Keeney, Charles James
Keeney, Ralph L(yons) 1944- ... CANR-16
Earlier sketch in CA 97-100
Keeney, William (Echard) 1922- ... CANR-15
Earlier sketch in CA 41-44R
Keenleyside, Hugh Llewellyn 1898- ... CAP-1
Earlier sketch in CA 17-18
Keenleyside, T(erence) A(shley) 1940- ... 77-80
Keeny, S. M.
See Keeny, Spurgeon Milton
Keeny, Spurgeon Milton 1893-1988
Obituary ... 126
Keep, Carolyn 1940- ... 65-68
Keep, David (John) 1936- ... 61-64
Keep, John (Leslie Howard) 1926- ... 11-12R
Keeping, Charles 1924- ... CANR-11
Earlier sketch in CA 21-22R
See also SATA 9
Keeping, Charles (William James)
1924-1988 ... CANR-11
Obituary ... 125
Earlier sketch in CA 21-22R
See also SATA 9
Keery, Sam 1929- ... 124
Kees, Beverly (Ann) 1941- ... 81-84
Keese, Parton 1926- ... 109
Keesecker, William Francis 1918- ... 33-36R
Keeshan, Robert J. 1927- ... CANR-5
Earlier sketch in CA 7-8R
See also SATA 32
Keesing, Nancy (Florence) 1923- ... CANR-6
Earlier sketch in CA 11-12R
Keeslar, Oreon 1907- ... CAP-1
Earlier sketch in CA 13-14
Keeton, Elizabeth B(aker) 1919- ... 29-32R
Keeton, George Williams 1902- ... 13-14R
Keeton, Kathy ... AITN-2
Keeton, Kathy 1939- ... 125
Keeton, Morris Teuton 1917- ... CANR-4
Earlier sketch in CA 2R
Keeton, Robert E(rnest) 1919- ... CANR-2
Earlier sketch in CA 5-6R
Keeton, William T(insley) 1933-1980 ... 124
Obituary ... 105
Keever, Jack 1938- ... 53-56
Keevill, Henry J(ohn) 1914- ... CAP-1
Earlier sketch in CA 9-10
Keezer, Dexter Merriam 1895- ... 1R
Kefferstan, Jean
See Pedrick, Jean
Kegan, Adrienne Koch 1912-1971
Obituary ... 33-36R
Kegel, Charles H. 1924- ... 1R
Kegley, Charles W(illiam), Jr. 1944- ... 114
Kegley, Charles William 1912- ... CANR-2
Earlier sketch in CA 5-6R
Kehayan, V. Alex 1944- ... 110
Kehl, D(elmar) G(eorge) 1936- ... 33-36R
Kehl, James Arthur 1922- ... 112
Kehle, Roberta L(unsford) 1936- ... 116
Kehm, Freda (Irma) S(amuels) ... CAP-2
Earlier sketch in CA 29-32
Kehoe, Constance (DeMuzio) 1933- ... 15-16R
Kehoe, Monika 1909- ... 21-22R
Kehoe, Patrick E(mmett) 1941- ... 57-60
Kehoe, William F. 1933- ... 15-16R
Kehrer, Daniel M(ark) 1953- ... 120
Kehrer, James P(aul) 1951- ... 117
Keidel, Eudene 1921- ... 109
Keidel, Levi (Jr.) 1927- ... 115
Keifetz, Norman 1932- ... 89-92
Keiger, John F(rederick) V(ictor) 1952- ... 125
Keightley, David N(oel) 1932- ... 97-100
Keil, (Harold) Bill 1926- ... 81-84
Keil, Sally Van Wagenen 1946- ... 89-92
Keillor, Garrison
See Keillor, Gary (Edward)
See also DLBY 87
See also CLC 40
Keillor, Gary (Edward) 1942- ... 117
Brief entry ... 111
Keim, Charles J. 1921- ... CANR-13
Earlier sketch in CA 33-36R
Keimberg, Allyn
See Kimbro, John M.
Keinzley, Frances 1922- ... 85-88
Keir, Christine
See Popescu, Christine
Keir, David E(dwin) 1906-1969 ... CAP-1
Earlier sketch in CA 9-10
Keir, David Lindsay 1895-1973 ... CAP-2
Earlier sketch in CA 21-22
Keirstead, Burton Seely 1907- ... 7-8R
Keiser, Bea(trice) 1931- ... 97-100
Keiser, Norman F(red) 1930- ... 15-16R
Keislar, Evan R(ollo) 1913- ... 23-24R
Keisling, Bill
See Keisling, William
Keisling, William 1958- ... 113
Keisman, Michael E(dward) 1932- ... 25-28R
Keister, Elinore
See Dobson, Elinore (Lucille)
Keitges, Julie 1940- ... 110
Keith, Agnes Newton 1901- ... 19-20R
Keith, Carlton
See Robertson, Keith (Carlton)
Keith, David
See Steegmuller, Francis
Keith, Donald
See Monroe, Keith
Keith, Elmer (Merrifield) 1899- ... 101
Keith, Eros 1942- ... 114
See also SATA 52
Keith, Hal 1934- ... SATA-36
Keith, Hamish
See Chapman, James (Keith)
Keith, Harold Verne 1903- ... CANR-2
Earlier sketch in CA 7-8R
See also SATA 2
Keith, Herbert F. 1895- ... 37-40R
Keith, J. Kilmeny
See Malleson, Lucy Beatrice
Keith, Jean E. 1921-1979 Obituary ... 85-88
Keith, Jennie 1942- ... 116
Keith, Judith 1923- ... 49-52
Keith, K. Wymand 1924- ... 33-36R
Keith, Larry Ficquette 1947- ... 97-100
Keith, Lee
See Sunners, William
Keith, Michael
See Hubbard, L(afayette) Ron(ald)
Keith, Noel L. 1903- ... 57-60
Keith, Robert
See Applebaum, Stan
Keith, Ronald (A.) 1914(?)-1985 Obituary ... 117
Keith, Sam 1921- ... 65-68
Keith, Stuart 1931- ... 126
Keith, W(illiam) J(ohn) 1934- ... CANR-11
Earlier sketch in CA 17-18R
Keithley, Erwin M. 1905- ... 73-76
Keithley, George 1935- ... 37-40R
Keith-Lucas, Alan 1910- ... CANR-20
Earlier sketches in CA 7-8R, CANR-2
Keith-Lucas, Bryan 1912- ... 107
Keith-Spiegel, Patricia 1939- ... 41-44R
Keith X
See Armstrong, Keith F(rancis)
W(hitfield)
Kekes, John 1936- ... 65-68
Kekkonen, Sylvi 1900(?)-1974 Obituary ... 53-56
Kelber, Magda 1908- ... 7-8R
Kelch, Ray Alden 1923- ... 85-88
Kelder, Diane 1934- ... CANR-18
Earlier sketch in CA 25-28R
Keldysh, Mstislav V(sevolodovich)
1911-1978 Obituary ... 77-80
Kele, Max H(erschel) 1936- Brief entry ... 114
Keleher, Will(iam Aloysius) 1886-1972
Obituary ... 37-40R
Keleman, Stanley 1931- ... CANR-14
Earlier sketch in CA 81-84
Kelemen, Pal 1894- ... 104
Kelen, Emery 1896-1978 ... 9-10R
Obituary ... 103
See also SATA 13, 26
Kelen, Stephen 1912- ... 107
Kelf-Cohen, Reuben 1895- ... 49-52
Kelikian, Hampar 1899(?)-1983 Obituary ... 110
Kell, Joseph
See Wilson, John (Anthony) Burgess
Kell, Richard (Alexander) 1927- ... CANR-8
Earlier sketch in CA 7-8R
Kellam, Sheppard (Gordon) 1931- ... 73-76
Kelland, Clarence Budington 1881-1964
Obituary ... 89-92
Kellar, Kenneth C(hambers) 1906- ... 45-48
Kellaway, Frank (Gerald) 1922- ... 9-10R
Kellaway, George P(ercival) 1909- ... CAP-2
Earlier sketch in CA 23-24
Kelleam, Joseph E(veridge) 1913-1975 ... 107
See also SATA 31
Kelleher, Catherine McArdle 1939- ... 125
Brief entry ... 115
Kelleher, Patrick J(oseph) 1917-1985
Obituary ... 116
Kelleher, Stephen J(oseph) 1915- ... 69-72
Kelleher, Victor (Michael Kitchener) 1939- ... 126
See also SATA 52
Keller, Allan 1904- ... 29-32R
Keller, Betty 1930- ... 121
Keller, Beverly (Lou) ... CANR-17
Earlier sketches in CA 49-52, CANR-1
See also SATA 13
Keller, Charles 1942- ... CANR-2
Earlier sketch in CA 49-52
See also SATA 8
Keller, Clair W(ayne) 1932- ... 53-56
Keller, Dean H(oward) 1933- ... 53-56
Keller, Dick 1923- ... SATA-36
Keller, Dolores Elaine 1926- ... 104
Keller, Edward A(nthony) 1942- ... 73-76
Keller, Evelyn Fox 1936- ... 125
Keller, Frances Richardson 1914- ... 81-84
Keller, Franklin J. 1887(?)-1976 Obituary ... 65-68
Keller, Fred S(immons) 1899- ... CANR-11
Earlier sketch in CA 69-72
Keller, Gail Faithfull
See Faithfull, Gail
Keller, George 1928- ... 123
Keller, Helen (Adams) 1880-1968 ... 101
Obituary ... 89-92
Keller, Holly Brief entry ... 118
See also SATA 42
Keller, Howard H(ughes) 1941- ... 45-48
Keller, Irene (Barron) 1927- ... 116
See also SATA 36
Keller, James Gregory 1900-1977
Obituary ... 69-72
Keller, John E(sten) 1917- ... 45-48
Keller, Karl 1933- ... CANR-12
Earlier sketch in CA 57-60
Keller, Marti 1948- ... 97-100
Keller, Mitzie Stuart ... 111
Keller, Mollie ... SATA-50
Keller, Morton 1929- ... 5-6R
Keller, Suzanne 1930- ... 65-68
Keller, Thomas F(ranklin) 1931- ... CANR-3
Earlier sketch in CA 11-12R
Keller, W(alter) D(avid) 1900- ... 41-44R
Keller, Werner (Rudolf August Wolfgang)
1909-19(?) ... CANR-13
Earlier sketch in CA 23-24R
Kellerman, Barbara 1939- ... 110
Kellerman, Faye 1952- ... 120
Kellerman, Jonathan 1949- ... 106
See also CLC 44
Kellett, Arnold 1926- ... CANR-19
Earlier sketch in CA 103
Kelley, Alden D(rew) 1903- ... 1R
Kelley, Alice van Buren 1944- ... 81-84
Kelley, Allen C(harles) 1937- ... 104
Kelley, Arleon L(eigh) 1935- ... 115
Kelley, (Albert) Ben 1936- ... 45-48
Kelley, Brooks Mather 1929- ... 111
Kelley, Cecil B., Sr. 1911(?)-1987
Obituary ... 123
Kelley, Dean M(aurice) 1926- ... 81-84
Kelley, Donald R(eed) 1931- ... CANR-12
Earlier sketch in CA 29-32R
Kelley, Earl Clarence 1895- ... 5-6R
Kelley, Edith Summers 1884-1956
Brief entry ... 109
See also DLB 9
Kelley, Eugene J(ohn) 1922- ... 13-14R
Kelley, H. N. 1911- ... 45-48
Kelley, Hubert (Williams), Jr. 1926- ... 5-6R
Kelley, J(ohn) Charles 1913- ... 97-100
Kelley, Jane Holden 1928- ... 45-48
Kelley, Joanna (Elizabeth) 1910- ... CAP-2
Earlier sketch in CA 23-24
Kelley, Jonathan ... 107
Kelley, Joseph J(ohn), Jr. 1914- ... CANR-8
Earlier sketch in CA 61-64
Kelley, Kevin J. 1948- ... 120
Kelley, Kitty 1942- ... 81-84
Kelley, Leo P(atrick) 1928- ... CANR-24
Earlier sketch in CA 107
See also SATA 31, 32
Kelley, Mary 1943- ... 124
Kelley, Maurice (Willyle) 1903- ... 119
Kelley, Page H(utto) 1924- ... 25-28R
Kelley, Ray
See Paine, Lauran (Bosworth)
Kelley, Robert 1925- ... 25-28R
Kelley, Robert E(mmett) 1938- ... 53-56
Kelley, Ruby M.
See Johnson, Ruby Kelley
Kelley, Stanley, Jr. 1926- ... 13-14R
Kelley, True (Adelaide) 1946- ... CANR-23
Earlier sketch in CA 105
See also SATA 39, 41
Kelley, William 1929- ... CANR-6
Earlier sketch in CA 7-8R
See also BW
Kelley, William Melvin 1937- ... 77-80
See also DLB 33
See also CLC 22
Kelley, William T(homas) 1917- ... 37-40R
Kelley, Win 1923- ... 89-92
Kellin, Sally Moffet 1932- ... 61-64
See also SATA 9
Kelling, Furn L. 1914- ... 19-20R
See also SATA 37
Kelling, George W(alton) 1944- ... CANR-9
Earlier sketch in CA 57-60
Kelling, Hans-Wilhelm 1932- ... 37-40R
Kellison, Stephen G. 1942- ... 53-56
Kellman, Steven G. 1947- ... 112
Kellner, Bruce 1930- ... CANR-11
Earlier sketch in CA 29-32R
Kellner, Douglas Mackay 1943- ... 116
Kellner, Esther ... 13-14R
Kellner, L. 1904- ... 5-6R
Kellock, Archibald P.
See Mavor, Osborne Henry
Kellogg, Alfred Latimer 1915- ... 41-44R
Kellogg, Ansel Nash 1832-1886 ... DLB-23
Kellogg, Charles Edwin 1902-1980
Obituary ... 97-100
Kellogg, Charles Flint 1909- ... CAP-2
Earlier sketch in CA 23-24
Kellogg, Gene
See Kellogg, Jean (Defrees)
Kellogg, James C. III 1915-1980 Obituary ... 103
Kellogg, Jean (Defrees) 1916-1978 ... CANR-7
Earlier sketch in CA 9-10R
See also SATA 10
Kellogg, Marion S(chuyler) 1920- ... 120
Kellogg, Marjorie 1922- ... 81-84
See also CLC 2
Kellogg, Mary Alice 1948- ... 81-84
Kellogg, Steven 1941- ... CANR-1
Earlier sketch in CA 49-52
See also SATA 8
See also DLB 61
See also CLR 6
Kellogg, Virginia 1907-1981 Obituary ... 108
Kellogg, Winthrop N(iles) 1898-1971 ... 1R
Kellough, Richard Dean 1935- ... 53-56
Kellow, Kathleen
See Hibbert, Eleanor Burford
Kellow, Norman B. 1914- ... 21-22R
Kellum, D(avid) F(ranklin) 1936- ... 61-64
Kelly, Alfred H. 1907-1976 ... 5-6R
Obituary ... 65-68
Kelly, Alison 1913- ... 105
Kelly, Balmer H(ancock) 1914- ... 19-20R
Kelly, C(harles) Brian 1935- ... 89-92
Kelly, C.M.O.
See Gibbs, (Cecilia) May
Kelly, Carla 1947- ... 118
Kelly, Charles E. 1920(?)-1985 Obituary ... 114
Kelly, Charles Patrick Bernard
1891(?)-1971 Obituary ... 29-32R
Kelly, Clarence 1941- ... 61-64
Kelly, Commando
See Kelly, Charles E.
Kelly, Dave
See Kelly, David M(ichael)
Kelly, David M(ichael) 1938- ... CANR-12
Earlier sketch in CA 29-32R
Kelly, Edward H(anford) 1930- ... 37-40R
Kelly, Emmett (Leo) 1898-1979 Obituary ... 85-88
Kelly, Eric Philbrook 1884-1960 Obituary ... 93-96
See also YABC 1
Kelly, Faye L(ucius) 1914- ... 23-24R
Kelly, Frank K. 1914- ... CANR-16
Earlier sketches in CA 1R, CANR-1
Kelly, Frederic Joseph 1922- ... 53-56
Kelly, Gail P(aradise) 1940- ... 81-84
Kelly, Gary F(rank) 1943- ... 89-92

Kelly, George A. 1916- ... CANR-11
Earlier sketch in CA 17-18R
Kelly, George Armstrong 1932-1987
Obituary ... 125
Kelly, George E. 1887-1974 Obituary ... 49-52
See also DLB 7
See also AITN 1
Kelly, George V(incent) 1919- ... 93-96
Kelly, George W. 1894- ... CANR-9
Earlier sketch in CA 65-68
Kelly, Gerald R(ay) 1930- ... 29-32R
Kelly, Grace (Patricia) 1929-1982 Obituary ... 107
Kelly, Guy
See Moore, Nicholas
Kelly, Henry Ansgar 1934- ... 25-28R
Kelly, Ian
See Kelly, John Spence
Kelly, James B(urton) 1905- ... 49-52
Kelly, James Plunkett 1920- ... 53-56
Kelly, Jeffrey A(llen) 1948- ... 114
Kelly, Joan 1928(?)-1982 Obituary ... 107
Kelly, Joan Berlin 1939- ... 107
Kelly, John 1921- ... 73-76
Kelly, John M., Jr. 1919- ... 13-14R
Kelly, John Maurice 1931- ... 109
Kelly, John N(orman) D(avidson) 1909- ... CANR-5
Earlier sketch in CA 7-8R
Kelly, John Rivard 1939- ... 103
Kelly, John Spence 1934- ... 125
Kelly, Joyce 1933- ... 106
Kelly, Karen 1935- ... 101
Kelly, Kathleen Sheridan White 1945- ... 49-52
Kelly, L(ouis) G(erard) 1935- ... 107
Kelly, Laurence 1933- ... CANR-15
Earlier sketch in CA 81-84
Kelly, Lawrence C(harles) 1932- ... CANR-8
Earlier sketch in CA 23-24R
Kelly, Leo J. 1925- ... 41-44R
Kelly, (Alison) Linda 1936- ... 103
Kelly, M(ilton) T(erry) 1947- ... CANR-19
Earlier sketch in CA 97-100
Kelly, Mahlon (George) 1939- ... 53-56
Kelly, Marguerite (Lelong) 1932- ... 65-68
Kelly, Martha Rose 1914-1983 ... 69-72
See also SATA 37
Kelly, Marty
See Kelly, Martha Rose
Kelly, Mary Coolican 1927- ... CANR-2
Earlier sketch in CA 4R
Kelly, Mary J(osephine) 1944- ... 117
Kelly, Maurice Anthony 1931- ... 53-56
Kelly, Maurice N. 1919- ... 23-24R
Kelly, Nora (Hickson) 1910- ... 101
Kelly, Patrick
See Allbeury, Theodore Edward le Bouthillier
Kelly, Paula 1949- ... 114
Kelly, Pauline Agnes 1936- ... 45-48
Kelly, Philip John 1896-1972 ... 7-8R
Obituary ... 37-40R
Kelly, Ralph
See Geis, Darlene Stern
Kelly, Ray
See Paine, Lauran (Bosworth)
Kelly, Regina Z(immerman) 1898- ... CANR-2
Earlier sketch in CA 4R
See also SATA 5
Kelly, Richard 1937- ... 107
Kelly, Richard J(ohn) 1938- ... 41-44R
Kelly, Rita Mae 1939- ... 81-84
Kelly, Robert 1935- ... 17-18R
See also DLB 5
Kelly, Robert Glynn 1920- ... 1R
Kelly, Rosalie (Ruth) ... CANR-11
Earlier sketch in CA 61-64
See also SATA 43
Kelly, Russell 1949- ... 123
Kelly, Stan
See Kelly-Bootle, Stan
Kelly, Stephen E(ugene) 1919-1978 ... 110
Obituary ... 104
Kelly, Thomas 1909- ... CAP-1
Earlier sketch in CA 9-10
Kelly, Thomas 1929- ... 109
Kelly, Tim 1935- ... 15-16R
Kelly, Walt(er Crawford) 1913-1973 ... 73-76
Obituary ... 45-48
See also SATA 18
Kelly, William Leo 1924- ... 15-16R
Kelly, William W(atkins) 1928- ... 11-12R
Kelly-Bootle, Stan 1929- ... 110
Kelly-Gadol, Joan ... 61-64
Kelm, Karlton 1908(?)-1987 Obituary ... 121
Kelman, Charles D. 1930- ... 110
Kelman, Herbert C(hanoch) 1927- ... 15-16R
Kelman, Mark 1951- ... 93-96
Kelman, Steven 1948- ... CANR-12
Earlier sketch in CA 29-32R
Kelsay, Isabel Thompson 1905- ... 121
Kelsen, Hans 1881-1973 Obituary ... 115
Kelsey, Alice Geer 1896- ... 5-6R
See also SATA 1
Kelsey, Joan Marshall 1907- ... 7-8R
Kelsey, Morton T(rippe) 1917- ... CANR-26
Earlier sketches in CA 23-24R, CANR-10
Kelsey, Robert J(ohn) 1927- ... 103
Kelso, Louis O. 1913- ... 25-28R
Kelso, Ruth 1885-1986 Obituary ... 119
Kelson, Allen H(oward) 1940- ... CANR-13
Earlier sketch in CA 77-80
Keltner, John W(illiam) 1918- ... 29-32R
Kelton, Elmer 1926- ... CANR-12
Earlier sketch in CA 21-22R
See also AITN 1
Kelvin, Norman 1924- Brief entry ... 118
Kemal, Salim 1948- ... 125
Kemal, Yashar 1923- ... 89-92
See also CLC 14, 29
Kemble, Fanny 1809-1893 ... DLB-32
Kemble, James ... CAP-2
Earlier sketch in CA 29-32
Kemelman, Harry 1908- ... CANR-6
Earlier sketch in CA 11-12R
See also DLB 28
See also CLC 2
See also AITN 1
Kemeny, Jean A(lexander) 1930- ... 117
Kemeny, John G(eorge) 1926- ... 33-36R
Kemeny, Peter 1938-1975 ... 53-56
Obituary ... 89-92
Kemerer, Frank R(obert) 1940- ... CANR-26
Earlier sketches in CA 65-68, CANR-10
Kemmerer, Donald L(orenzo) 1905- ... 4R
Kemp, Anthony 1939- ... CANR-25
Earlier sketch in CA 105
Kemp, Arnold 1938- Brief entry ... 110
Kemp, Bernard Peter 1942- ... 107
Kemp, Betty 1916- ... 11-12R
Kemp, Charles F. 1912- ... CANR-5
Earlier sketch in CA 9-10R
Kemp, Diana Moyle 1919- ... CAP-1
Earlier sketch in CA 9-10
Kemp, Edward C. 1929- ... 81-84
Kemp, Gene 1926- ... CANR-12
Earlier sketch in CA 69-72
See also SATA 25
Kemp, Jack (French) 1935- ... 109
Kemp, Jerrold E(dwin) 1921- ... 77-80
Kemp, John C(rocker) 1942- ... 93-96
Kemp, Lysander (Schaffer, Jr.) 1920- ... CANR-1
Earlier sketch in CA 45-48
Kemp, Martin (John) 1942- ... 108
Kemp, Patrick S(amuel) 1932- ... 53-56
Kemp, Peter (Mant Macintyre) 1915- ... 25-28R
Kemp, Robert 1908-1967 ... CAP-1
Earlier sketch in CA 15-16
Kemp, Roy Z(ell) 1910- ... 9-10R
Kemp, Tom 1921- ... 25-28R
Kempe, C(harles) Henry 1922-1984 ... 122
Kemper, Donald J. 1929- ... 21-22R
Kemper, Inez 1906- ... CAP-1
Earlier sketch in CA 13-14
Kemper, Rachel H. 1931- ... 102
Kemper, Robert V(an) 1945- ... 104
Kemperman, Steve (Richard) 1955- ... 108
Kempfer, Lester Leroy 1932- ... 49-52
Kempher, Ruth Moon 1934- ... CANR-17
Earlier sketch in CA 25-28R
Kempner, Mary Jean 1913-1969 ... CAP-2
Earlier sketch in CA 29-32
See also SATA 10
Kempner, S. Marshall 1898- ... 85-88
Kempowski, Walter 1929- Brief entry ... 122
See also DLB 75
Kempster, Mary Yates 1911- ... CAP-1
Earlier sketch in CA 9-10
Kempster, Norman 1936- ... 77-80
Kempton, James Murray, Jr.
1945(?)-1971 Obituary ... 33-36R
Kempton, Jean Goldschmidt 1946(?)-1971
Obituary ... 33-36R
Kempton, Jean Welch 1914- ... 49-52
See also SATA 10
Kempton, (James) Murray 1918- ... 97-100
Kempton, Richard 1935- ... 106
Kemsley, Viscount
See Berry, James Gomer
Kemsley, William George, Jr. 1928- ... 85-88
Kendal, Geoffrey
See Bragg, Richard Geoffrey
Kendal, Wallis 1937- ... 107
Kendall, Aubyn 1919- ... 107
Kendall, Carol (Seeger) 1917- ... CANR-25
Earlier sketches in CA 5-6R, CANR-7
See also SATA 11
Kendall, David Evan 1944- ... 29-32R
Kendall, Dorothy Steinbomer 1912- ... 57-60
Kendall, E(dith) Lorna 1921- ... 5-6R
Kendall, Edward C(alvin) 1886-1972
Obituary ... 111
Kendall, Elaine (Becker) 1929- ... 17-18R
Kendall, Elizabeth B(emis) 1947- ... 81-84
Kendall, Gordon
See Lewitt, Shariann (N.)
Kendall, Henry Madison 1901-1966 ... 7-8R
Kendall, Kenneth E(verett) 1913- ... 45-48
Kendall, Lace
See Stoutenburg, Adrien (Pearl)
Kendall, Laurel 1947- ... 121
Kendall, Lisa See 1955- ... CANR-25
Earlier sketch in CA 111
Kendall, Lyle H(arris), Jr. 1919- ... 17-18R
Kendall, Marjorie 1930- ... 121
Kendall, Maurice (George) 1907-1983
Obituary ... 109
Kendall, Paul Murray 1911-1973 ... CAP-1
Earlier sketch in CA 15-16
Kendall, R(obert) T(illman) 1935- ... 93-96
Kendall, Robert 1934- ... CANR-6
Earlier sketch in CA 15-16R
Kendall, T(homas) Robert 1935- ... 69-72
Kendall, Willmoore 1909-1967 ... CANR-6
Earlier sketch in CA 5-6R
Kendle, John Edward 1937- ... 61-64
Kendler, Howard H(arvard) 1919- ... 17-18R
Kendrake, Carleton
See Gardner, Erle Stanley
Kendrick, Baynard H(ardwick)
1894-1977 ... CANR-4
Obituary ... 69-72
Earlier sketch in CA 4R
Kendrick, David Andrew 1937- ... CANR-9
Earlier sketch in CA 23-24R
Kendrick, Frank J(enness) 1928- ... 41-44R
Kendrick, John (Stafford) 1917- ... 121
Kendrick, John W(hitefield) 1917-
Brief entry ... 110
Kendrick, Thomas Downing 1895- ... 81-84
Kendrick, Walter 1947- ... 112
Kendricks, James
See Fox, G(ardner) F(rancis)
Kendris, Christopher 1923- ... CANR-24
Earlier sketches in CA 5-6R, CANR-7
Keneally, Thomas (Michael) 1935- ... CANR-10
Earlier sketch in CA 85-88
See also CLC 5, 8, 10, 14, 19, 27, 43
Kenealy, James P. 1927- ... 93-96
See also SATA 29, 52
Kenealy, Jim
See Kenealy, James P.
Keneas, Alexander 1938(?)-1984 Obituary ... 113
Kenelly, John W(illis Jr.) 1935- ... 25-28R
Kenen, Isaiah Leo 1905- ... 107
Kenen, Peter B(ain) 1932- ... CANR-22
Earlier sketches in CA 5-6R, CANR-7
Kenesson, Frank G. 1913(?)-1985
Obituary ... 119
Kenez, Peter 1937- ... 29-32R
Kenian, Paul Roger
See Clifford, Martin
Kenin, Richard (Metz) 1947-1983
Obituary ... 111
Keniston, Kenneth 1930- ... 25-28R
Kenkel, William F(rancis) 1925- ... 61-64
Kenna, Peter 1930- ... 61-64
Kennamer, Lorrin, Jr. 1924- ... CANR-6
Earlier sketch in CA 5-6R
Kennan, George Frost 1904- ... CANR-2
Earlier sketch in CA 3R
Kennan, Kent (Wheeler) 1913- ... 3R
Kennard-Davis, Arthur (Shelley) 1910- ... CAP-1
Earlier sketch in CA 9-10
Kennaway, James (Pebles Ewing)
1928-1968 ... 103
Obituary ... 89-92
Kennealy (Morrison), Patricia 1946- ... 120
Kennebeck, Edwin 1924- ... 41-44R
Kennebeck, Paul 1943- ... 53-56
Kennecott, G. J.
See Viksnins, George J(uris)
Kennedy, Adam ... CANR-24
Earlier sketch in CA 107
See also AITN 1
Kennedy, Adrienne (Lita) 1931- ... CANR-26
Earlier sketch in CA 103
See also BW
See also DLB 38
Kennedy, Andrew (Karpati) 1931- ... 61-64
Kennedy, Archibald Edmund Clark
See Clark-Kennedy, Archibald Edmund
Kennedy, Betty 1926- ... 121
Kennedy, Brendan 1970- ... 123
Kennedy, Bruce M. 1929- ... 57-60
Kennedy, Carol ... CANR-21
Earlier sketch in CA 105
Kennedy, Caroline 1944- ... 125
Kennedy, Charles J(oseph) 1935-1984
Obituary ... 114
Kennedy, Chuck
See Kennedy, Charles J(oseph)
Kennedy, D. James 1930- ... 61-64
Kennedy, Dane K(eith) 1951- ... 126
Kennedy, David M. 1941- ... CANR-13
Earlier sketch in CA 29-32R
Kennedy, Dennis (Edward) 1940- ... 120
Kennedy, Don H(enry) 1911- ... 61-64
Kennedy, Dorothy M(intzlaff) 1931- ... 116
See also SATA 53
Kennedy, Eddie C. 1910- ... 89-92
Kennedy, Edward Moore 1932- ... 110
Kennedy, Edward R(idgway) 1923(?)-1975
Obituary ... 104
Kennedy, Elliot
See Godfrey, Lionel (Robert Holcombe)
Kennedy, Eugene C(ullen) 1928- ... 25-28R
Kennedy, Gail 1900-1972 Obituary ... 33-36R
Kennedy, Gavin 1940- ... CANR-9
Earlier sketch in CA 61-64
Kennedy, George 1899(?)-1977 Obituary ... 73-76
Kennedy, George (Alexander) 1928- ... CANR-2
Earlier sketch in CA 5-6R
Kennedy, Gerald (Hamilton) 1907- ... CANR-6
Earlier sketch in CA 7-8R
Kennedy, Harold J. 1915(?)-1988
Obituary ... 124
Kennedy, Hubert (Collings) 1931- ... 93-96
Kennedy, J(ames) Hardee 1915- ... 15-16R
Kennedy, James
See Monahan, James (Henry Francis)
Kennedy, James G(ettier) 1932- ... 81-84
Kennedy, James William 1905- ... CANR-1
Earlier sketch in CA 4R
Kennedy, James Y(oung) 1916- ... 77-80
Kennedy, Jimmy 1903(?)-1984 Obituary ... 112
Kennedy, John Fitzgerald 1917-1963 ... CANR-1
Earlier sketch in CA 1R
See also SATA 11
Kennedy, John J(oseph) 1914- ... 57-60
Kennedy, John Pendleton 1795-1870 ... DLB-3
Kennedy, Joseph Charles 1929- ... CANR-4
Earlier sketch in CA 2R
See also SATA 14
See also CLC 8
Kennedy, Judith M(ary) 1935- ... 41-44R
Kennedy, Kathleen 1947(?)-1975
Obituary ... 57-60
Kennedy, Kenneth A(drian) R(aine)
1930- ... CANR-1
Earlier sketch in CA 45-48
Kennedy, Kieran A. 1935- ... 37-40R
Kennedy, L. D. 1924- ... 45-48
Kennedy, Leigh 1951- ... 122
Kennedy, Lena
See Smith, Lena (Kennedy)
Kennedy, Leonard Anthony 1922- ... 37-40R
Kennedy, Leonard M(ilton) 1925- ... 73-76
Kennedy, Ludovic Henry Coverley 1919- ... 65-68
Kennedy, Malcolm D(uncan) 1895- ... 11-12R
Kennedy, Margaret 1896-1967 Obituary ... 25-28R
See also DLB 36
Kennedy, Marilyn Moats 1943- ... 109
Kennedy, Mary ... 102
Kennedy, Michael 1926- ... CANR-23
Earlier sketches in CA 15-16R, CANR-5
Kennedy, Moorhead 1930- ... 123
Kennedy, P(eter) J(ohn) 1925- ... 123
Kennedy, Paul E(dward) 1929- ... SATA-33
Kennedy, Paul Michael 1945- ... CANR-9
Earlier sketch in CA 65-68
Kennedy, Ralph Dale 1897-1965 ... 4R
Kennedy, Raymond A. 1934- ... 5-6R
Kennedy, Richard 1910- ... 102
Kennedy, (Jerome) Richard 1932- ... CANR-26
Earlier sketches in CA 57-60, CANR-7
See also SATA 22
Kennedy, Richard S(ylvester) 1920- ... CANR-3
Earlier sketch in CA 5-6R
Kennedy, Robert E(mmet), Jr. 1937- ... 37-40R
Kennedy, Robert F(rancis) 1925-1968 ... CANR-1
Earlier sketch in CA 1R
Kennedy, Robert F(rancis), Jr. 1954- ... 110
Kennedy, Robert L(ee) 1930- ... 57-60
Kennedy, Robert Woods 1911- ... 49-52
Kennedy, Roger G(eorge) 1926- ... 115
Kennedy, Rose (Fitzgerald) 1890- ... 53-56
Kennedy, Sighle Aileen 1919- ... 53-56
Kennedy, Stetson 1916- ... 7-8R
Kennedy, Susan Estabrook 1942- ... 45-48
Kennedy, T(eresa) A. 1953- ... 114
See also SATA 35, 42
Kennedy, T(homas) F(illans) 1921- ... 53-56
Kennedy, Ted
See Kennedy, Edward Moore
Kennedy, Teresa
See Kennedy, T(eresa) A.
Kennedy, Theodore Reginald 1936- ... 105
Kennedy, Thomas 1920- ... 116
Kennedy, Thomas C. 1937- ... 125
Kennedy, William 1928- ... CANR-14
Earlier sketch in CA 85-88
See also DLBY 85
See also CLC 6, 28, 34
Kennedy, William B(ean) 1926- ... 116
Kennedy, William J(ohn) 1942- ... 117
Kennedy, X. J.
See Kennedy, Joseph Charles
See also DLB 5
See also CLC 42
Kennedy-Martin, Ian 1936- ... 101
Kenneggy, Richard
See Nettell, Richard (Geoffrey)
Kennel, LeRoy E(ldon) 1930- ... 77-80
Kennell, Ruth Epperson 1893-1977 ... CAP-2
Earlier sketch in CA 29-32
See also SATA 6, 25
Kennelly, Brendan 1936- ... CANR-5
Earlier sketch in CA 9-10R
See also DLB 40
Kenner, Charles Leroy 1933- ... 25-28R
Kenner, (William) Hugh 1923- ... 23-24R
See also DLB 67
Kennerly, David Hume 1947- ... 101
See also AITN 2
Kennerly, Karen 1940- ... 33-36R
Kennett, (Houn) Jiyu 1924- ... 93-96
Kennett, Lee 1931- ... 23-24R
Kennett, Peggy Teresa Nancy
See Kennett, (Houn) Jiyu
Kenney, Alice P(atricia) 1937-1985 ... CANR-10
Obituary ... 115
Earlier sketch in CA 25-28R
Kenney, Douglas C. 1947(?)-1980 ... 107
Obituary ... 101
Kenney, Edwin James, Jr. 1942- ... 53-56
Kenney, George Churchill 1889- ... CAP-1
Earlier sketch in CA 11-12
Kenney, John Paul 1920- ... 17-18R
Kenney, Lona B(ronberg) 1921- ... 115
Kenney, Susan (McIlvaine) 1941- ... 115
Kenney, Sylvia W. 1922-19(?) ... CAP-1
Earlier sketch in CA 19-20
Kennick, W(illiam) E(lmer) 1923- ... 15-16R
Kennington, (Gilbert) Alan 1906-1986
Obituary ... 121
Kennington, Alice Eve 1935- ... 119
Kennon, Donald R. 1948- ... 122
Kenny, Anthony
See Kenny, Anthony John Patrick
Kenny, Anthony John Patrick 1931- ... CANR-23
Earlier sketch in CA 101
Kenny, Charles J.
See Gardner, Erle Stanley
Kenny, Ellsworth Newcomb 1909-1971 ... 5-6R
Obituary ... 103
See also SATA 26
Kenny, Herbert Andrew 1912- ... 41-44R
See also SATA 13
Kenny, James Andrew 1933- ... CANR-26
Earlier sketch in CA 107
Kenny, Jean
See Freeman, Jean Kenny
Kenny, John P. 1909- ... 17-18R
Kenny, John Peter 1916- ... CANR-1
Earlier sketch in CA 45-48

Kenny, Kathryn
See Bowden, Joan Chase
and Krull, Kathleen
and Sanderlin, Owenita (Harrah)
and Stack, Nicolete Meredith
Kenny, Kevin
See Krull, Kathleen
Kenny, Mary 1936- 108
Kenny, Michael 1923- CANR-5
Earlier sketch in CA 4R
Kenny, Nicholas Napoleon 1895-1975
Obituary 89-92
Kenny, Nick
See Kenny, Nicholas Napoleon
Kenny, Shirley (Elise) Strum 1934- 45-48
Kenny, Vincent 1919- 45-48
Kenny, W. Henry 1918- 37-40R
Kenofer, C(harles) Louis 1923- 69-72
Kenoyer, Natlee Peoples 1907- CANR-5
Earlier sketch in CA 5-6R
Kenrick, Donald Simon 1929- 81-84
Kenrick, Tony 1935- 104
Kenshalo, Daniel R(alph) 1922- 41-44R
Kensinger, George
See Fichter, George S.
Kent, Alexander
See Reeman, Douglas Edward
Kent, Allegra 1938(?)- 126
Brief entry 105
Kent, Allen 1921- CANR-18
Earlier sketches in CA 11-12R, CANR-3
Kent, Arden
See Marion, Frieda
Kent, Arthur William Charles 1925- 102
Kent, Bill
See Kent, Carleton Volney, Jr.
Kent, Carleton Volney, Jr. 1909-1985
Obituary 114
Kent, Cromwell
See Sparshott, Francis (Edward)
Kent, David
See Lambert, David (Compton)
Kent, Deborah Ann 1948- 103
See also SATA 41, 47
Kent, Donald P(eterson) 1916-1972 .... 19-20R
Obituary 120
Kent, Edward Allen 1933- 45-48
Kent, Ernest W(illiam) 1940- 104
Kent, Fortune
See Toombs, John
Kent, Frank (Richardson, Jr.)
1907(?)-1978 Obituary 81-84
Kent, Frank R(ichardson) 1877-1958
Brief entry 121
See also DLB 29
Kent, George O(tto) 1919- 37-40R
Kent, George W. 1928- 25-28R
Kent, Harold W(infield) 1900- 65-68
Kent, Homer A(ustin), Jr. 1926- CANR-3
Earlier sketch in CA 9-10R
Kent, Jack
See Kent, John Wellington
Kent, John Henry Somerset 1923- 9-10R
Kent, John Wellington 1920-1985 .... CANR-16
Obituary 117
Earlier sketch in CA 85-88
See also SATA 24, 45
Kent, Katherine
See Dial, Joan
Kent, Kelvin
See Kuttner, Henry
Kent, Leonard J. 1927- 77-80
Kent, Louise Andrews 1886-1969 .... CANR-4
Obituary 25-28R
Earlier sketch in CA 4R
Kent, Malcolm 1932- 45-48
Kent, Mallory
See Lowndes, Robert A(ugustine) W(ard)
Kent, Margaret 1894- CAP-2
Earlier sketch in CA 25-28
See also SATA 2
Kent, Noel J(ay) 1944- 111
Kent, Nora 1899- CAP-1
Earlier sketch in CA 9-10
Kent, Pete
See Richardson, Gladwell
Kent, Philip
See Bulmer, (Henry) Kenneth
Kent, Rockwell 1882-1971 .... CANR-4
Obituary 29-32R
Earlier sketch in CA 5-6R
See also SATA 6
Kent, Sherman 1903-1986 53-56
Obituary 118
See also SATA 20, 47
Kent, Simon
See Catto, Max(well Jeffrey)
Kent, Stella
See Phillips, Stella
Kent, Tony
See Crechales, Anthony George
Kent, Valerie 1947- 114
Kentfield, Calvin 1924- 7-8R
Kenton, Leslie 1941- 113
Kenton, Maxwell
See Hoffenberg, Mason
and Southern, Terry
Kenton, Warren 1933- 29-32R
Kenward, James (Macara) 1908- 7-8R
Kenward, Jean 1920- 108
See also SATA 42
Kenward, Michael 1945- 103
Kenworthy, Brian J(ohn) 1920- 103
Kenworthy, Leonard S. 1912- CANR-1
Earlier sketch in CA 1R
See also SATA 6
Kenyatta, Jomo 1891(?)-1978 124
Obituary 113
See also BW
Kenyon, Bernice
See Gilkyson, Bernice Kenyon
Kenyon, Ernest M(onroe) 1920- 85-88
Kenyon, F(rank) W(ilson) 1912- CANR-1
Earlier sketch in CA 3R
Kenyon, J(ohn) P(hilipps) 1927- CANR-3
Earlier sketch in CA 9-10R
Kenyon, James William 1910- CAP-1
Earlier sketch in CA 9-10
Kenyon, Jane 1947- 118
Kenyon, Karen 1938- 106
Kenyon, Kate
See Ransom, Candice F.
Kenyon, Kathleen Mary 1906-1978 .... CANR-13
Earlier sketch in CA 21-22R
Kenyon, Ley 1913- 13-14R
See also SATA 6
Kenyon, Michael 1931- CANR-12
Earlier sketch in CA 15-16R
Kenyon, Mildred Adams 1894-1980 108
Obituary 105
Kenyon, Paul
See Freedland, Nat(haniel)
Kenyon, Robert O.
See Kuttner, Henry
Kenyon, W. A.
See Kenyon, Walter Andrew
Kenyon, Walter
See Kenyon, Walter Andrew
Kenyon, Walter A.
See Kenyon, Walter Andrew
Kenyon, Walter Andrew 1917-1986
Obituary 121
Kenzer, Robert C. 1955- 126
Keogh, Dermot (Francis) 1945- 126
Keogh, James 1916- 45-48
Keogh, Lilian Gilmore 1927- 11-12R
Keohane, Nannerl O(verholser) 1940- 106
Keohane, Robert O. 1941- 45-48
Kepes, Gyorgy 1906- 101
Kepes, Juliet A(ppleby) 1919- 69-72
See also SATA 13
Kephart, Horace 1862-1931 Brief entry 119
Kephart, Newell C. 1911-1973 .... CAP-2
Earlier sketch in CA 17-18
Kephart, William M. 1921- 41-44R
Kepler, Thomas Samuel 1897-1963 .... 4R
Keppel, Sonia 1900-1986 107
Obituary 120
Keppel-Jones, Arthur (Mervyn) 1909- 118
Kepple, Ella Huff 1902- CAP-2
Earlier sketch in CA 17-18
Keppler, Ann B(lystad) 1946- 117
Keppler, C(arl) F(rancis) 1909- 19-20R
Keppler, Herbert 1925- 85-88
Keppler, Victor 1904-1987 Obituary 124
Ker, Neil Ripley 1908-1982 Obituary 107
Ker, William Paton 1855-1923 Brief entry 121
Kerber, August Frank 1917- 23-24R
Kerber, Linda K(aufman) 1940- Brief entry .. 115
Kerby, Bill 1937- 104
Kerby, Joe Kent 1933- 53-56
Kerby, Philip Pearce 1911- Brief entry 116
Kerby, Robert L(ee) 1934- 41-44R
Kerby, Susan Alice
See Burton, (Alice) Elizabeth
Kercheval, Jesse Lee 1956- 126
Kerckhoff, Alan C(hester) 1924- 113
Kerek, Andrew 1936- 102
Kerekes, Tibor 1893-1969 .... CAP-2
Earlier sketch in CA 17-18
Kerensky, Alexandr Fedorovich 1881-1970
Obituary 113
Kerensky, Oleg 1930- CANR-12
Earlier sketch in CA 29-32R
Kerensky, V(asil) M(ichael) 1930- 53-56
Keres, Paul (Petrovich) 1916-1975
Obituary 57-60
Kerestesi, Michael 1929- 109
Kereszty, Roch A(ndrew) 1933- 29-32R
Kerewsky-Halpern, Barbara 1931- 102
Kerigan, Florence 1896- 29-32R
See also SATA 12
Kerin, Roger A(nthony) 1947- CANR-26
Earlier sketch in CA 109
Kerkvliet, Benedict J(ohn) 1943- 93-96
Kerlan, Irvin 1912-1963 .... 7-8R
Kerlinger, Fred N(ichols) 1910- CANR-2
Earlier sketch in CA 49-52
Kerman, Cynthia Earl 1923- 57-60
Kerman, Gertrude Lerner 1909- 7-8R
See also SATA 21
Kerman, Joseph Wilfred 1924- CANR-15
Earlier sketch in CA 65-68
Kerman, Judith (Berna) 1945- 77-80
Kerman, Sheppard 1928- CANR-26
Earlier sketch in CA 85-88
Kermani, Taghi Thomas 1929- 25-28R
Kermode, (John) Frank 1919- CANR-1
Earlier sketch in CA 2R
Kern, Alfred 1924- 33-36R
Kern, Canyon
See Raborg, Frederick A(shton), Jr.
Kern, E. R.
See Kerner, Fred
Kern, Edith 1912- 113
Kern, Gary 1938- 65-68
Kern, Gregory
See Tubb, E(dwin) C(harles)
Kern, Janet (Rosalie) 1924- 7-8R
Kern, Jean B(ordner) 1913- 85-88
Kern, Mary Margaret 1906- 101
Kern, Robert W(illiam) 1934- CANR-7
Earlier sketch in CA 61-64
Kern, Seymour 1913- 93-96
Kern, Stephen 1943- 69-72
Kern, Walter O(tto) 1930- 117
Kernaghan, Eileen 1939- 111
Kernan, Alvin B(ernard) 1923- 49-52
Kernan, Jerome B(ernard) 1932- 25-28R
Kernan, Julia K. 1901(?)-1988 Obituary 125
Kernan, Michael 1927- 81-84
Kerner, Fred 1921- CANR-22
Earlier sketches in CA 9-10R, CANR-6
Kernochan, Sarah 1947- 73-76
Kernodle, George R(iley) 1907- 65-68
Kerns, Frances Casey 1937- 81-84
Kerns, J(ames) Alexander 1894-1975
Obituary 104
Kerns, Robert Louis 1929- 77-80
Kerouac, Jack
See Kerouac, Jean-Louis Lebrid de
See also DLB 2, 16
See also DLBD 3
See also CDALB 1941-1968
See also CLC 1, 2, 3, 5, 14, 29
Kerouac, Jan
See Hackett, Jan Michele
See also DLB 16
Kerouac, Jean-Louis Lebrid de
1922-1969 .... CANR-26
Obituary 25-28R
Earlier sketch in CA 5-6R
See also AITN 1
Kerouac, John
See Kerouac, Jean-Louis Lebrid de
Kerpelman, Larry C(yril) 1939- 37-40R
Kerr, Alex(ander McBride) 1921- 61-64
Kerr, Alex A. 1922- 125
Kerr, Andy
See Kerr, Alex A.
Kerr, Barbara 1913- 89-92
Kerr, Ben
See Ard, William (Thomas)
Kerr, Carole
See Carr, Margaret
Kerr, Catherine 1945- 102
Kerr, Clark 1911- CANR-22
Earlier sketches in CA 45-48, CANR-1
Kerr, D(onald) G(ordon) G(rady)
1913-1976 .... CANR-6
Earlier sketch in CA 1R
Kerr, Donna H(anneman) 1944- 112
Kerr, Elizabeth M. 1905- 37-40R
Kerr, Frederick
See Kerner, Fred
Kerr, Graham 1934- 108
Kerr, Harry P(rice) 1928- 7-8R
Kerr, Homer L(ee) 1921- 120
Kerr, Howard Hastings 1931- 103
Kerr, Hugh Thomson 1909- 103
Kerr, James Lennox 1899-1963 102
Kerr, James Stolee 1928- 19-20R
Kerr, Jean 1923- CANR-7
Earlier sketch in CA 7-8R
See also CLC 22
Kerr, Jessica 1901- CAP-2
Earlier sketch in CA 29-32
See also SATA 13
Kerr, Joan P. 1921- 81-84
Kerr, (Anne-) Judith 1923- 93-96
See also SATA 24
Kerr, K(athel) Austin 1938- 25-28R
Kerr, Lois
See Cardozo, Lois S(teinmetz)
Kerr, M. E.
See Meaker, Marijane
See also SAAS 1
See also CLC 12, 35
Kerr, Malcolm (Hooper) 1931-1984 97-100
Obituary 111
Kerr, Norman D.
See Sieber, Sam Dixon
Kerr, Orpheus C.
See Newell, Robert Henry
Kerr, Phyllis Forbes 1942- 120
Kerr, Robert (a pseudonym) 1899- 69-72
Kerr, Rose Netzorg 1892-1974 .... CAP-2
Earlier sketch in CA 23-24
Kerr, Stanley E. 1894(?)-1976 Obituary 69-72
Kerr, Walter (Francis) 1913- CANR-7
Earlier sketch in CA 7-8R
Kerrigan, (Thomas) Anthony 1918- CANR-4
Earlier sketch in CA 49-52
See also CLC 4, 6
Kerrigan, Catherine 1939- 117
Kerrigan, Kate Lowe
See Rickett, Frances
Kerrigan, William J(oseph) CANR-2
Earlier sketch in CA 49-52
Kerry, Frances
See Kerigan, Florence
Kerry, Lois
See Duncan, Lois
Kersell, John E(dgar) 1930- 45-48
Kersey, Katharine C(lark) 1935- 116
Kersh, Cyril 1925- 104
Kersh, Gerald 1911-1968 Obituary 25-28R
Kershaw, Alister (Nasmyth) 1921- CANR-19
Earlier sketches in CA 7-8R, CANR-3
Kershaw, Gordon Ernest 1928- 85-88
Kershaw, John (Hugh D'Allenger) 73-76
Kershner, Howard E(ldred) 1891- 73-76
Kershner, Richard B(randon) 1913-1982
Obituary 110
Kerslake, Susan 1943- CANR-17
Earlier sketch in CA 93-96
Kersnowski, Frank L. 1934- 41-44R
Kertesz, Andre 1894-1985 85-88
Obituary 117
Kertesz, Louise 1939- 102
Kertesz, Stephen D(enis) 1904- CAP-2
Earlier sketch in CA 21-22
Kertzer, David I(srael) 1948- 106
Kertzer, Morris Norman 1910-1983 .... CANR-1
Obituary 111
Earlier sketch in CA 4R
Ker Wilson, Barbara 1929- CANR-7
Earlier sketch in CA 7-8R
See also SATA 20
Kerwood, John R. 1942- 53-56
Kesey, Ken (Elton) 1935- CANR-22
Earlier sketch in CA 4R
See also DLB 2, 16
See also CLC 1, 3, 6, 11, 46
Keshet, Harry F(inkelstein) 1940- 109
Keshishian, John M. 1923- 25-28R
Kesich, Veselin 1921- Brief entry 111
Kesler, (William) Jackson (II) 1938- 102
Kesler, Jay 1935- CANR-26
Earlier sketches in CA 61-64, CANR-8
Kess, Joseph Francis 1942- 65-68
Kessel, Dmitri 1902- 120
Kessel, John (Joseph Vincent) 1950- 120
Kessel, John H(oward) 1928- CANR-21
Earlier sketch in CA 23-24R
Kessel, Joseph (Elie) 1898-1979 105
Obituary 89-92
See also DLB 72
Kessel, Joyce Karen 1937- 105
See also SATA 41
Kessel, Lipmann 1914- 13-14R
Kessel, Martin 1901- DLB-56
Kessell, John L(ottridge) 1936- 93-96
Kesselman, Judi R.
See K-Turkel, Judi
Kesselman, Louis Coleridge 1919-1974
Obituary 110
Kesselman, Mark J. CANR-14
Earlier sketch in CA 37-40R
Kesselman-Turkel, Judi
See K-Turkel, Judi
Kesselring, Joseph (Otto) 1902-1967 .... CLC-45
Kessen, William 1925- CANR-1
Earlier sketch in CA 1R
Kessler, Diane Cooksey 1947- 57-60
Kessler, Edward 1927- 61-64
Kessler, Ethel 1922- 121
Brief entry 115
See also SATA 37, 44
Kessler, Francis P(aschal) 1944- 109
Kessler, Frank
See Kessler, Francis P(aschal)
Kessler, Gail 1937- 65-68
Kessler, Henry H(oward) 1896-1978
Obituary 73-76
Kessler, Herbert L(eon) 1941- 125
Kessler, Jascha (Frederick) 1929- CANR-8
Earlier sketch in CA 19-20R
See also CLC 4
Kessler, Kaye (Warren) 1923- 112
Kessler, Leonard P. 1921- 77-80
See also SATA 14
Kessler, Milton 1930- CANR-2
Earlier sketch in CA 4R
Kessler, Rod 1949- 117
Kessler, Ronald (Borek) 1943- CANR-13
Earlier sketch in CA 69-72
Kessler, Sheila 57-60
Kessler, Walter R. 1913-1978 Obituary 81-84
Kessner, Lawrence 1957- 109
Kessner, Thomas 1946- CANR-11
Earlier sketch in CA 69-72
Kesteloot, Lilyan 1931- CANR-19
Earlier sketch in CA 73-76
Kesten, Hermann 1900- DLB-56
Kester, Dana R(ay) 1943- 116
Kesterson, David B(ert) 1938- 41-44R
Kesterton, Wilfred (Harold) 1914- 41-44R
Kesteven, G. R.
See Crosher, G. R.
Kestner, Joseph A(loysius) 1943- 89-92
Ketch, Jack
See Tibbetts, John C(arter)
Ketcham, Carl H(untington) 1923- 29-32R
Ketcham, Charles B(rown) 1926- 29-32R
Ketcham, Hank
See Ketcham, Henry King
Ketcham, Henry King 1920- 105
See also SATA 27, 28
Ketcham, Howard 1902-1982 Obituary 106
Ketcham, Katherine 1949- 118
Ketcham, Orman W(eston) 1918- CANR-9
Earlier sketch in CA 23-24R
Ketcham, Ralph (Louis) 1927- CANR-4
Earlier sketch in CA 11-12R
Ketcham, Rodney K(enneth) 1909- CANR-4
Earlier sketch in CA 2R
Ketchum, Carlton Griswold 1892- 85-88
Ketchum, Creston Donald 1922- 11-12R
Ketchum, J.
See Frentzen, Jeffrey
Ketchum, Jack
See Paine, Lauran (Bosworth)
Ketchum, Marshall D(ana) 1905- CAP-1
Earlier sketch in CA 17-18
Ketchum, Richard M(alcolm) 1922- 25-28R
Ketchum, Robert Glenn 1947- CANR-23
Earlier sketch in CA 107
Ketchum, William C(larence), Jr.
1931- CANR-12
Earlier sketch in CA 33-36R
Keteyian, Armen 1953- 122
Kets de Vries, Manfred F. R. 1942- 111
Kett, Joseph F. 1938- 25-28R

Kettelkamp, Larry (Dale) 1933- ... CANR-16
Earlier sketch in CA 29-32R
See also SATA 2
See also SAAS 3
See also CLC 12
Ketterer, David (Anthony Theodor) 1942- ... CANR-21
Earlier sketches in CA 53-56, CANR-4
Ketterman, Grace H(orst) 1926- ... CANR-22
Earlier sketch in CA 106
Kettl, Donald F. 1952- ... 111
Kettle, Arnold (Charles) 1916-1986 ... CANR-6
Obituary ... 121
Earlier sketch in CA 11-12R
Kettle, Jocelyn Pamela 1934- ... 25-28R
Kettle, Pamela
See Kettle, Jocelyn Pamela
Kettle, Peter
See Glover, Denis (James Matthews)
Kettner, Elmer Arthur 1906-1964 ... 3R
Kettner, James H(arold) 1944- ... 89-92
Ketton-Cremer, Robert Wyndham 1906-1969 Obituary ... 106
Keucher, William F. 1918- ... 49-52
Keuls, Eva C(lara) 1928- ... 123
Keuls, Hans 1910-1985 Obituary ... 117
Keun, Irmgard 1905-1982 ... DLB-69
Kevan, Martin 1949- ... 110
Keve, Paul W(illard) 1913- ... CANR-6
Earlier sketch in CA 11-12R
Kevern, Barbara
See Shepherd, Donald (Lee)
Keveson, Peter 1919-1986 Obituary ... 118
Kevin, Jodi
See Lawrence, Jodi
Kevles, Bettyann 1938- ... CANR-11
Earlier sketch in CA 69-72
See also SATA 23
Kevles, Daniel J(erome) 1939- ... 85-88
Kew, Stephen 1947- ... 103
Kewes, Karol 1924- ... 9-10R
Key, Alexander (Hill) 1904-1979 ... CANR-6
Obituary ... 89-92
Earlier sketch in CA 5-6R
See also SATA 8, 23
Key, Jack D(ayton) 1934- ... 112
Key, Mary Ritchie 1924- ... CANR-16
Earlier sketches in CA 45-48, CANR-1
Key, Ted
See Key, Theodore
Key, Theodore 1912- ... 13-14R
Key, V(aldimer) O(rlando), Jr. 1908-1963 ... 4R
Key, William H(enry) 1919- ... 45-48
Key, Wilson Bryan 1925- ... CANR-2
Earlier sketch in CA 49-52
Keyes, Claire J. 1938- ... 126
Keyes, Daniel 1927- ... CANR-26
Earlier sketches in CA 19-20R, CANR-10
See also SATA 37
Keyes, Edward 1927- ... 103
Keyes, Evelyn 1919(?)- ... 85-88
Keyes, Fenton 1915- ... 107
See also SATA 34
Keyes, Frances Parkinson 1885-1970 ... CANR-7
Obituary ... 25-28R
Earlier sketch in CA 5-6R
Keyes, Kenneth S(cofield), Jr. 1921- ... CANR-24
Earlier sketches in CA 19-20R, CANR-8
Keyes, Langley Carleton, Jr. 1938- ... 25-28R
Keyes, Margaret Frings 1929- ... 57-60
Keyes, Noel
See Keightley, David N(oel)
Keyes, Ralph 1945- ... CANR-3
Earlier sketch in CA 49-52
Keyfitz, Nathan 1913- ... CANR-10
Earlier sketch in CA 25-28R
Keyishian, Harry 1932- ... 61-64
Keylock, Leslie R(obert) 1933- ... 117
Keylor, Arthur (W.) 1920(?)-1981
Obituary ... 104
Keylor, William R(obert) 1944- ... 89-92
Keynes, Edward 1940- ... 120
Keynes, Geoffrey Langdon 1887-1982 ... 103
Obituary ... 107
Keynes, John Maynard 1883-1946
Brief entry ... 114
Keynes, Richard Darwin 1919- ... 114
Keys, Ancel 1904- ... 61-64
Keys, Donald (Fraser) 1924- ... 115
Keys, Ivor Christopher Banfield 1919- ... 103
Keys, John D. 1938- ... 9-10R
Keys, Thomas Edward 1908- ... CAP-1
Earlier sketch in CA 11-12
Keyser, Daniel J. 1935- ... 121
Keyser, (George) Gustave 1910- ... 77-80
Keyser, Lester Joseph 1943- ... 105
Keyser, Marcia 1933- ... 116
See also SATA 42
Keyser, Samuel Jay 1935- ... 106
Keyser, Sarah
See McGuire, Leslie Sarah
Keyser, William R(ussell) 1916- ... 69-72
Keyserling, Eduard von 1855-1918 ... DLB-66
Keyserling, Leon H. 1908-1987 ... 61-64
Obituary ... 123
Keyssar, Alexander 1947- ... 121
Keyt, David (Alan) 1930- ... 1R
Kezdi, Paul 1914- ... 77-80
Kezys, Algimantas 1928- ... CANR-14
Earlier sketch in CA 81-84
Kgositsile, Keorapetse (William) 1938- ... CANR-25
Earlier sketch in CA 77-80
See also BW
Khadduri, Majid 1909- ... CANR-2
Earlier sketch in CA 1R
Khaketla, B. M.
See Khaketla, B(ennett) Makalo
Khaketla, B(ennett) Makalo 1913-
Brief entry ... 113
Khalatbari, Adel-Sultan 1901(?)-1977
Obituary ... 69-72
Khan, Hassina
See Ali Khan, Shirley
Khan, Lurey 1927- ... 97-100
Khan, (Chaudhri) Muhammad Zafrulla 1893-1985 Obituary ... 117
Khan, Pir Vilayat Inayat
See Inayat-Khan, Pir Vilayat
Khan, Shirley Ali
See Ali Khan, Shirley
Khan, Taidje 1920(?)-1985 Obituary ... 117
Khan, Zillur Rahman 1938- ... CANR-14
Earlier sketch in CA 41-44R
Khanna, J(aswant) L(al) 1925- ... 23-24R
Khanshendel, Chiron
See Rose, Wendy
Kharasch, Robert Nelson 1926- ... 103
Khare, Narayan Bhaskar 1882- ... CAP-1
Earlier sketch in CA 11-12
Kharitonov, Yevgeny 1941(?)-1981
Obituary ... 104
Khatchadourian, Haig 1925- ... 53-56
Khatena, Joe
See Khatena, Joseph
Khatena, Joseph 1925- ... 116
Khazzoom, J. Daniel 1932- ... 17-18R
Khedouri, Franklin 1944- ... 101
Kher, Inder Nath 1933- ... 93-96
Khera, S(ucha) S(ingh) 1903- ... 13-14R
Kherdian, David 1931- ... 21-22R
See also CAAS 2
See also SATA 16
See also CLC 6, 9
Khlebnikov, Velimir
See Khlebnikov, Viktor Vladimirovich
See also TCLC 20
Khlebnikov, Viktor Vladimirovich 1885-1922 Brief entry ... 117
Khodasevich, Vladislav (Felitsianovich) 1886-1939 Brief entry ... 115
See also TCLC 15
Khomaini, Ayatollah Sayyed Ruholla Mousavi
See Khomeini, Ruhollah (Mussavi)
Khomeini, Ayatollah
See Khomeini, Ruhollah (Mussavi)
Khomeini, Ayatollah Ruhollah
See Khomeini, Ruhollah (Mussavi)
Khomeini, Imam
See Khomeini, Ruhollah (Mussavi)
Khomeini, Ruhollah (Mussavi) 1900(?)- ... 117
Khornak, Lucille 1953- ... 110
Khosla, G(opal) D(as) 1901- ... 113
Khouri, Fred J(ohn) 1916- ... 25-28R
Khouri, Mounah A(bdallah) 1918- ... 114
Khrushchev, Nikita Sergeyevich 1894-1971 ... 112
Khumeini, Ruhollah
See Khomeini, Ruhollah (Mussavi)
Kiang, Ying-cheng ... 19-20R
Kianto, Ilmari 1874-1970 Obituary ... 29-32R
Kibbe, Pat (Hosley) ... 125
Kibbee, Roland 1914-1984 Obituary ... 113
Kibler, James Everett, Jr. 1944- ... CANR-22
Earlier sketch in CA 105
Kibler, Robert J(oseph) 1934- ... 29-32R
Kibler, William W. 1942- ... 37-40R
Kibre, Pearl 1902(?)-1985 Obituary ... 116
Kicknosway, Faye 1936- ... CANR-7
Earlier sketch in CA 57-60
Kicza, John E(dward) 1947- ... 120
Kidd, Aline H(alstead) 1922- ... 19-20R
Kidd, David Lundy 1926- ... CANR-1
Earlier sketch in CA 1R
Kidd, Elisabeth
See Triegel, Linda (Jeanette)
Kidd, Harry 1917- ... 29-32R
Kidd, J(ames) R(obbins) 1915- ... CANR-3
Earlier sketch in CA 7-8R
Kidd, J. Roby
See Kidd, J(ames) R(obbins)
Kidd, Ronald 1948- ... 116
See also SATA 42
Kidd, Russ
See Donson, Cyril
Kidd, Virginia 1921- ... CANR-10
Earlier sketch in CA 65-68
Kidd, Walter E. 1917- ... 23-24R
Kiddell, John 1922- ... 29-32R
See also SATA 3
Kiddell-Monroe, Joan 1908- ... CAP-1
Earlier sketch in CA 13-14
Kidder, Barbara (Ann) 1933- ... 41-44R
Kidder, J(onathan) Edward (Jr.) 1922- ... 107
Kidder, Rushworth M(oulton) 1944- ... 77-80
Kidder, Tracy 1945- ... 109
Kiddle, Lawrence B(ayard) 1907- ... 33-36R
Kidner, (Frank) Derek 1913- ... 41-44R
Kidney, Dorothy Boone 1919- ... CANR-3
Earlier sketch in CA 11-12R
Kidney, Walter C(urtis) 1932- ... CANR-19
Earlier sketches in CA 53-56, CANR-4
Kido, Koichi 1890(?)-1977 Obituary ... 69-72
Kidwell, Carl 1910- ... SATA-43
Kidwell, Catherine (Arthelia) 1921- ... 109
Kieckhefer, Richard 1946- ... 93-96
Kiefer, Bill
See Kiefer, Tillman W.
Kiefer, Christie Weber 1937- ... 103
Kiefer, Frederick (Paul) 1945- ... 114
Kiefer, Irene 1926- ... CANR-11
Earlier sketch in CA 69-72
See also SATA 21
Kiefer, Tillman W. 1898- ... CAP-2
Earlier sketch in CA 29-32
Kiefer, Warren 1929- ... 77-80
Kiefer, William Joseph 1925- ... 1R
Kiehle, John Alva 1930- Brief entry ... 115
Kiell, Norman 1916- ... CANR-5
Earlier sketch in CA 13-14R
Kiell, Paul J(acob) 1930- ... 124
Brief entry ... 118
Kielland, Alexander Lange 1849-1906
Brief entry ... 104
See also TCLC 5
Kiely, Benedict 1919- ... CANR-2
Earlier sketch in CA 3R
See also DLB 15
See also CLC 23, 43
Kiemel, Ann
See Anderson, Ann Kiemel
Kieniewicz, Stefan 1907- ... 29-32R
Kienzle, William X(avier) 1928- ... CANR-9
Earlier sketch in CA 93-96
See also CAAS 1
See also CLC 25
Kiepper, Shirley Morgan 1933- ... 37-40R
Kieran, John Francis 1892-1981 ... 101
Obituary ... 105
Kieran, Sheila 1930- ... 97-100
Kierland, Joseph Scott 1937- ... 61-64
Kierman, Frank Algerton, Jr. 1914- ... 125
Kiernan, Brian 1937- ... 107
Kiernan, Robert F(rancis) 1940- ... 115
Kiernan, Thomas ... 113
Kiernan, (E.) V(ictor) G(ordon) 1913- ... CANR-11
Earlier sketch in CA 25-28R
Kiernan, Walter 1902-1978 Obituary ... 73-76
Kies, Cosette (Nell) 1936- ... 124
Kiesel, Stanley 1925- ... 104
See also SATA 35
Kieser, Rolf 1936- ... 77-80
Kiesler, Charles A(dolphus) 1934- ... CANR-10
Earlier sketch in CA 25-28R
Kiesler, Sara B(eth) 1940- ... CANR-16
Earlier sketch in CA 25-28R
Kiesling, Christopher (Gerald) 1925-1986 ... CANR-12
Obituary ... 120
Earlier sketch in CA 29-32R
Kiesling, Herbert J. 1934- ... 45-48
Kiester, Edwin, Jr. 1927- ... 110
Kieszak, Kenneth 1939- ... 89-92
Kiev, Ari 1933- ... CANR-3
Earlier sketch in CA 11-12R
Kiev, I. Edward 1905-1975 Obituary ... 104
Kiger, Joseph Charles 1920- ... 125
Kihl, Armand
See Ald, Roy A(llison)
Kihss, Peter (Frederick) 1912(?)-1984
Obituary ... 114
Kijima Hajime
See Kojima Shozo
Kikel, Rudy (John) 1942- ... 117
Kiker, B(ill) F(razier) 1937- ... 61-64
Kiker, Douglas 1930- ... 65-68
Kikukawa, Cecily H(arder) 1919- ... 113
See also SATA 35, 44
Kilander, H(olger) Frederick 1900-1969 ... CAP-2
Earlier sketch in CA 17-18
Kilborne, Virginia Wylie 1912- ... 21-22R
Kilbourn, Jonathan 1916(?)-1976
Obituary ... 65-68
Kilbourn, William (Morley) 1926- ... CANR-11
Earlier sketch in CA 21-22R
Kilbracken, John (Raymond Godley) 1920- ... 7-8R
Kilburn, Henry
See Rigg, H(enry Hemmingway) K(ilburn)
Kilburn, Robert E(dward) 1931- ... 17-18R
Kilby, Clyde Samuel 1902-1986 ... CANR-9
Obituary ... 120
Earlier sketch in CA 13-14R
Kilby, Peter 1935- ... CANR-17
Earlier sketch in CA 25-28R
Kildahl, John P. 1927- ... 89-92
Kildahl, Phillip A. 1912- ... 23-24R
Kildare, Maurice
See Richardson, Gladwell
Kilduff, (Mary) Dorrell 1901- ... 7-8R
Kiley, Dan (Edward) 1942- Brief entry ... 125
Kiley, Frederick 1932- ... CANR-15
Earlier sketch in CA 37-40R
Kiley, Jed
See Kiley, John Gerald
See also DLB 4
Kiley, John Gerald 1889-1962 Obituary ... 112
Kiley, Margaret A(nn) ... 53-56
Kilgallen, Dorothy (Mae) 1913-1965
Obituary ... 89-92
Kilgallen, James L. 1888(?)-1982
Obituary ... 108
Kilgore, James C(olumbus) 1928- ... 33-36R
Kilgore, John
See Paine, Lauran (Bosworth)
Kilgore, Kathleen 1946- ... 109
See also SATA 42
Kilgore, William J(ackson) 1917- ... 45-48
Kilgour, John Graham 1937- ... 105
Kilgour, Raymond L(incoln) 1903- ... CAP-1
Earlier sketch in CA 15-16
Kilian, Crawford 1941- ... CANR-22
Earlier sketch in CA 105
See also SATA 35
Kilina, Patricia
See Warren, Patricia Nell
Killam, (Gordon) Douglas 1930- ... CANR-3
Earlier sketch in CA 49-52
Killanin, Lord
See Morris, Michael
Kille, Mary F. 1948- ... 33-36R
Killeen, Jacqueline 1931- ... 61-64
Killen, Linda 1945- ... 118
Killenberg, George A(ndrew) 1917- ... 77-80
Killens, John Oliver 1916-1987 ... CANR-26
Obituary ... 123
Earlier sketch in CA 77-80
See also CAAS 2
See also BW
See also DLB 33
See also CLC 10
Killian, Ida F(aith) 1910- ... 65-68
Killian, James R(hyne), Jr. 1904-1988 ... 97-100
Obituary ... 124
Killian, Larry
See Wellen, Edward (Paul)
Killian, Lewis M(artin) 1919- ... 9-10R
Killian, Ray A. 1922- ... 21-22R
Killigrew, Thomas 1612-1683 ... DLB-58
Killilea, Marie (Lyons) 1913- ... 7-8R
See also SATA 2
Killinger, George G(lenn) 1908- ... 102
Killinger, John 1933- ... 81-84
Killingley, Carl A(rthur) 1918- ... 118
Killingsworth, Frank R. 1873(?)-1976
Obituary ... 65-68
Killion, Katheryn L. 1936- ... 17-18R
Killion, Ronald G(ene) 1931- ... 61-64
Killorin, Joseph I(gnatius) 1926- ... 111
Killough, (Karen) Lee 1942- ... CANR-15
Earlier sketch in CA 89-92
Killy, Jean-Claude 1943- Brief entry ... 115
Kilmann, Peter R(ichard) 1945- ... 118
Kilmar, (Alfred) Joyce 1886-1918 ... DLB-45
Kilmartin, Edward J(ohn) 1923- ... 17-18R
Kilmer, (Alfred) Joyce 1886-1918
Brief entry ... 120
Kilmer, Kenton 1909- ... 1R
Kilmister, C(live) W(illiam) 1924- ... 119
Kilodney, Crad (a pseudonym) 1948- ... 115
Kilpatrick, Carroll 1913- ... 69-72
Kilpatrick, F(ranklin) P(eirce) 1920- ... 21-22R
Kilpatrick, James Jackson 1920- ... CANR-1
Earlier sketch in CA 1R
See also AITN 1, 2
Kilpatrick, Sarah
See Underwood, Mavis Eileen
Kilpatrick, Terrence 1920- ... 81-84
Kilreon, Beth
See Walker, Barbara (Jeanne) K(erlin)
Kilroy, Thomas 1934- ... 53-56
Kilson, Marion 1936- ... 37-40R
Kilson, Martin Luther, Jr. 1931- ... 103
Kilvert, B. Cory, Jr. 1930- ... 45-48
Kim
See Simenon, Georges (Jacques Christian)
Kim, C(hong-) I(k) Eugene 1930- ... 37-40R
Kim, Chin W. 1936- ... 37-40R
Kim, Chong Lim 1937- ... 114
Kim, Choong Soon 1938- ... 116
Kim, David U(ngchon) 1932- ... 109
Kim, Hee-Jin 1927- ... 106
Kim, Helen 1899-1970 ... CAP-1
Earlier sketch in CA 15-16
Kim, Hyung-chan 1938- ... 57-60
Kim, Ilpyong J(ohn) 1931- ... 53-56
Kim, Jung-Gun 1933- ... 53-56
Kim, K(wan) H(o) 1936- ... 29-32R
Kim, Kwan-Bong 1936- ... 37-40R
Kim, Kyung-Won 1936- ... 29-32R
Kim, Richard C(hong) C(hin) 1923- ... 29-32R
Kim, Richard E. 1932- ... 7-8R
Kim, Samuel S(oonki) 1935- ... 104
Kim, Se-Jin 1933- ... 53-56
Kim, Seung Hee 1936- ... 29-32R
Kim, Sung Bok 1932- Brief entry ... 113
Kim, Yong Choon 1935- ... 57-60
Kim, Yong-ik 1920- ... 19-20R
Kim, Yoon Hough 1934-1976 ... 33-36R
Kim, Young Hum 1920- ... 23-24R
Kimball, Arthur G(ustaf) 1927- ... 41-44R
Kimball, Dean 1912- ... 69-72
Kimball, Gayle 1943- ... 107
Kimball, George 1943- ... 53-56
Kimball, John P. 1941- ... CANR-2
Earlier sketch in CA 45-48
Kimball, John W(ard) 1931- ... CANR-15
Earlier sketch in CA 93-96
Kimball, Michael 1949- ... 120
Kimball, Nancy
See Upson, Norma
Kimball, Penn T(ownsend) 1915- ... CANR-18
Earlier sketch in CA 102
Kimball, Philip 1941- ... 117
Kimball, Richard Laurance 1939- ... CANR-7
Earlier sketch in CA 53-56
Kimball, Robert Eric 1939- Brief entry ... 106
Kimball, Solon T(oothaker) 1909- ... 21-22R
Kimball, Spencer L(evan) 1918- ... CANR-1
Earlier sketch in CA 1R
Kimball, Spencer W(oolley) 1895-1985 ... 45-48
Obituary ... 117
Kimball, Stanley B(uchholz) 1926- ... CANR-26
Earlier sketches in CA 17-18R, CANR-10
Kimball, Warren F. 1935- ... 25-28R
Kimball, Yeffe 1914-1978 ... SATA-37
Kimberley, Hugh
See Morland, Nigel
Kimberly, Gail ... 81-84
Kimble, Daniel Porter 1934- ... 41-44R
Kimble, David 1921- ... 13-14R
Kimble, George H(erbert) T(inley) 1908- ... 108
Kimble, Gregory A(dams) 1917- ... 21-22R
Kimbrell, Grady 1933- ... 33-36R
Kimbro, Harriet 1937- ... 112
Kimbro, Jean
See Kimbro, John M.

Kimbro, John M. 1929- CANR-2
Earlier sketch in CA 45-48
Kimbrough, Emily 1899- 19-20R
See also SATA 2
Kimbrough, Katheryn
See Kimbro, John M.
Kimbrough, Ralph B(radley) 1922- 73-76
Kimbrough, Richard B(enito) 1931- 41-44R
Kimbrough, Robert (Alexander III)
1929- CANR-6
Earlier sketch in CA 11-12R
Kimbrough, Sara Dodge 1901- 93-96
Kimche, David 103
Kimenye, Barbara 1940(?)- 101
Kimes, Beverly Rae 1939- 122
Brief entry 107
Kimmel, Arthur S(andor) 1930- 41-44R
Kimmel, Douglas C(harles) 1943- 53-56
Kimmel, Eric A. 1946- CANR-3
Earlier sketch in CA 49-52
See also SATA 13
Kimmel, Jo 1931- CANR-4
Earlier sketch in CA 53-56
Kimmel, Margaret Mary 1938- 124
See also SATA 43
Kimmel, Melvin 1930- 25-28R
Kimmel, Stanley (Preston) 1894(?)-1982
Obituary 109
Kimmel, William (Breyfogel) 1908-1982
Obituary 109
Kimmelman, Elaine 1925- 111
Kimmens, Andrew C(harles) 1942- 124
Kimmey, John Lansing 1922- Brief entry 108
Kimmich, Christoph M(artin) 1939- 69-72
Kimmich, Flora (Graham Horne) 1939- 106
Kimpel, Ben D(rew) 1915- 57-60
Kimpel, Ben F(ranklin) 1905- 1R
Kimrey, Grace (Evelyn) Saunders
1910- CANR-24
Earlier sketch in CA 45-48
Kim Ronyoung
See Hahn, Gloria
Kimura, Jiro 1949- 85-88
Kincaid, Alan
See Rikhoff, James C.
Kincaid, Jamaica 1949- 125
See also BW
See also CLC 43
Kincaid, James R(ussell) 1937- CANR-15
Earlier sketch in CA 65-68
Kincaid, Suzanne (Moss) 1936- 9-10R
Kinch, Sam E., Jr. 1940- 45-48
Kincheloe, Raymond McFarland 1909- 61-64
Kincl, (Gladys) Kay Owens 1955- 106
Kindall, Alva Frederick 1906- 1R
Kindem, Gorham A(nders) 1948- 125
Kinder, Faye 1902- 7-8R
Kinder, Gary 1946- 109
Kinder, James S. 1895- 15-16R
Kinder, Kathleen
See Potter, Kathleen Jill
Kinder, Marsha 1940- CANR-15
Earlier sketch in CA 41-44R
Kinderlehrer, Jane 1913- 106
Kindleberger, Charles P(oor), II 1910- .. CANR-12
Earlier sketch in CA 73-76
Kindley, Jeffrey 1945- Brief entry 125
Kindred, Alton R(ichard) 1922- 109
Kindred, Leslie W(ithrow) 1905- 41-44R
Kindred, Wendy (Good) 1937- 37-40R
See also SATA 7
Kindregan, Charles P(eter) 1935- CANR-10
Earlier sketch in CA 23-24R
Kineji, Maborushi
See Gibson, Walter B(rown)
Kinert, Reed (Charles) 1911(?)- 107
Kines, Pat Decker 1937- 65-68
See also SATA 12
Kines, Thomas Alvin 1922- 15-16R
Kines, Tom
See Kines, Thomas Alvin
King, Adam
See Hoare, Robert J(ohn)
King, Adele Cockshoot 1932- CANR-8
Earlier sketch in CA 13-14R
King, Alan 1927- 89-92
King, Alec Hyatt
See King, Alexander Hyatt
King, Alexander 1909- 110
King, Alexander Hyatt 1911- 124
King, Alfred M. 1933- 25-28R
King, Algin B(raddy) 1927- CANR-15
Earlier sketch in CA 41-44R
King, Alison
See Martini, Teri
King, Alvy L(eon) 1932- 33-36R
King, Annette 1941- 33-36R
King, Anthony (Stephen) 1934- 17-18R
King, Archdale Arthur 1890-1972 .... CAP-1
Earlier sketch in CA 17-18
King, Ben F(rank) 1937- 57-60
King, Bert T(homas) 1927- 45-48
King, Betty (Alice) 1919- 103
King, Betty Patterson 1925- 11-12R
King, Billi
See Caulder, Colline
King, Billie Jean 1943- CANR-10
Earlier sketch in CA 53-56
See also SATA 12
King, Bruce ?-1976 Obituary 61-64
King, Bruce A. 1933- CANR-19
Earlier sketches in CA 53-56, CANR-4
King, C(lyde) Richard 1924- CANR-11
Earlier sketch in CA 69-72
King, Captain Charles
See King, Charles
King, Cecil
See King, Cecil H(armsworth)
King, Cecil H(armsworth) 1901-1987 110
Obituary 122
King, Charles 1844-1933 Brief entry 122
King, Charles (Lester) 1922- 57-60
King, Clarence (Rivers) 1842-1901
Brief entry 110
See also DLB 12
King, Clarence 1884(?)-1974 Obituary 53-56
King, (David) Clive 1924- 104
See also SATA 28
King, Clyde S(tuart) 1919- 17-18R
King, Coretta Scott 1927- 29-32R
See also BW
King, Cynthia 1925- 29-32R
See also SATA 7
King, Daniel P(atrick) 1942- CANR-4
Earlier sketch in CA 53-56
King, Deborah 1950- 112
King, Donald B. 1913- 15-16R
King, Edith W(eiss) 1930- CANR-14
Earlier sketch in CA 33-36R
King, Edmund J(ames) 1914- CANR-2
Earlier sketch in CA 7-8R
King, Edmund L(udwig) 1914- CANR-13
Earlier sketch in CA 33-36R
King, Edward L. 1928- 81-84
King, Elizabeth A.
See Abravanel, Elizabeth
King, Florence 1936- CANR-7
Earlier sketch in CA 57-60
See also DLBY 85
See also AITN 1
King, Francis Edward 1931- 61-64
King, Francis H(enry) 1923- CANR-1
Earlier sketch in CA 2R
See also DLB 15
See also CLC 8
King, Francis P(aul) 1922- 15-16R
King, Frank A.
See King, Franklin Alexander
King, Frank H(enry) H(aviland) 1926- 119
King, Frank O. 1883-1969 Obituary 89-92
See also SATA 22
King, Franklin Alexander 1923- 45-48
King, Frederick Murl 1916- CANR-2
Earlier sketch in CA 5-6R
King, General Charles
See King, Charles
King, Glen D. 1925- 11-12R
King, Grace (Elizabeth) 1852(?)-1932
Brief entry 116
See also DLB 12
King, Harold 1945- CANR-7
Earlier sketch in CA 57-60
King, Helen H(ayes) 1937- 33-36R
King, Homer W. 1907- CAP-1
Earlier sketch in CA 15-16
King, Horace Maybray
See Maybray-King, Horace
King, Irving H(enry) 1935- 89-92
King, Ivan R(obert) 1927- 89-92
King, Jack
See Dowling, Allen
King, James 1942- 121
King, James Cecil 1924- CANR-14
Earlier sketch in CA 41-44R
King, James G. 1898(?)-1979 Obituary 89-92
King, James T(errell) 1933- 37-40R
King, James W. 1920- 9-10R
King, Janet Kauffman 1935- Brief entry 110
King, Jere Clemens 1910- 5-6R
King, Jerome Babcock 1927- 103
King, (Frederick) Jerry 1941- 97-100
King, Joan (M.) 1930- 123
King, Joe 1909(?)-1979 Obituary 85-88
King, John
See McKeag, Ernest L(ionel)
King, John Edward 1947- 102
King, John L(afayette) 1917- 41-44R
King, John N. 1945- 113
King, John O(zias) 1923- Brief entry 108
King, John Q. Taylor 1921- 25-28R
King, Josie
See Germany, (Vera) Jo(sephine)
King, K. DeWayne (Dewey) 1925- 13-14R
King, Kathleen (Marie) 1948- 114
King, Kimball 1934- 110
King, Larry 1933- Brief entry 111
King, Larry L. 1929- CANR-24
Earlier sketch in CA 15-16R
King, Leila Pier 1882-1981 Obituary 105
King, Leslie John 1934- Brief entry 106
King, Lester S(now) 1908- 33-36R
King, Louise W(ooster) CANR-7
Earlier sketch in CA 13-14R
King, Marcet (Alice Hines) 1922- 25-28R
King, Margaret L(eah) 1947- 123
King, Marian 1900(?)-1986 .... CANR-2
Obituary 118
Earlier sketch in CA 5-6R
See also SATA 23, 47
King, Marjorie Cameron 1909- 33-36R
King, Mark 1945- 61-64
King, Martha L. 1918- Brief entry 109
King, Martin
See Marks, Stan(ley)
King, Martin Luther, Jr. 1929-1968 .... CAP-2
Earlier sketch in CA 25-28
See also BW
See also SATA 14
King, Martin Luther, Sr. 1899-1984 125
Obituary 117
See also BW
King, Mary Louise 1911- 23-24R
King, Michael
See Buse, Renee
and Kahane, Meir (David)
King, Michael J(ulius) 1941- 119
King, Morton Brandon 1913- 102
King, Noel Q(uixote) 1922- CANR-19
Earlier sketches in CA 3R, CANR-4
King, Norman A.
See Tralins, S(andor) Robert
King, O. H. P. 1902- 2R
King, Patricia 1930- 7-8R
King, Paul
See Drackett, Phil(ip Arthur)
King, Pauline 1917- 119
King, Peggy Cameron
See King, Marjorie Cameron
King, Peter 1925- 125
King, Philip 1904- 103
King, Philip B(urke) 1903-1987 125
Obituary 122
King, Preston (Theodore) 1936- CANR-26
Earlier sketches in CA 23-24R, CANR-10
King, Ray A(iken) 1933- 21-22R
King, Richard A(ustin) 1929- 23-24R
King, Richard G. 1922- 37-40R
King, Richard H. 1942- 77-80
King, Richard L(ouis) 1937- CANR-1
Earlier sketch in CA 45-48
King, Robert B. 1949- 125
King, Robert Charles 1928- 19-20R
King, Robert G. 1929- 23-24R
King, Robert H(arlen) 1935- 45-48
King, Robert L. 1950- 77-80
King, Robert R(ay) 1942- CANR-8
Earlier sketch in CA 61-64
King, Robin 1919- 5-6R
King, Roma Alvah, Jr. 1914- CANR-1
Earlier sketch in CA 1R
King, Ronald (Wilfred) 1914- 107
King, Rufus 1917- 25-28R
King, Ruth Rodney
See Manley, Ruth Rodney King
King, Spencer B(idwell), Jr. 1904- CAP-1
Earlier sketch in CA 17-18
King, Stanley H(all) 1921- Brief entry 110
King, Stella 69-72
King, Stephen (Edwin) 1947- CANR-1
Earlier sketch in CA 61-64
See also SATA 9
See also DLBY 80
See also CLC 12, 26, 37
King, Stephen W(illiam) 1947- 61-64
King, T(homas) J(ames) 1925- 37-40R
King, Tabitha 1949- 105
King, Teri 1940- 89-92
King, Terry Johnson 1929-1978 .... 17-18R
Obituary 77-80
King, Thomas M(ulvihill) 1929- 57-60
King, Tony 1947- 109
See also SATA 39
King, Veronica
See King, Florence
King, Vincent
See Vinson, Rex Thomas
King, Willard L. 1893-1981 .... 3R
Obituary 103
King, William Donald Aelian 1910- 89-92
King, William R(ichard) 1938- CANR-8
Earlier sketch in CA 23-24R
King, Winston L(ee) 1907- 41-44R
King, Woodie, Jr. 1937- CANR-25
Earlier sketch in CA 103
See also BW
See also DLB 38
Kingdon, Frank 1894-1972 Obituary 33-36R
Kingdon, John W(ells) 1940- 25-28R
Kingdon, Robert M(cCune) 1927- 21-22R
Kingdon, Roger 1891-1984 Obituary 113
Kingery, Robert E(rnest) 1913-1978 .... 11-12R
Obituary 103
King-Farlow, John 1932- 111
King-Hall, Magdalen 1904-1971 .... CAP-1
Obituary 29-32R
Earlier sketch in CA 9-10
King-Hall, (William) Stephen (Richard)
1893-1966 .... 7-8R
King-Hele, Desmond (George) 1927- CANR-14
Earlier sketch in CA 29-32R
Kinghorn, A(lexander) M(anson) 1926- 93-96
Kinghorn, Kenneth Cain 1930- CANR-14
Earlier sketch in CA 41-44R
Kinglake, Alexander William 1809-1891 .. DLB-55
Kingman, Dong (Moy Shu) 1911- 112
See also SATA 44
Kingman, Lee
See Natti, (Mary) Lee
See also SATA 1
See also SAAS 3
See also CLC 17
Kingman, Russ 1917- CANR-17
Earlier sketch in CA 101
Kingry, Philip L. 1942- 53-56
Kingsbury, Arthur 1939- 29-32R
Kingsbury, Donald (MacDonald) 1929- 124
Kingsbury, Jack Dean 1934- 37-40R
Kingsbury, John M(erriam) 1928- CANR-6
Earlier sketch in CA 15-16R
Kingsbury, Robert C(arrick) 1924- CANR-2
Earlier sketch in CA 4R
Kingsland, Leslie William 1912- 69-72
See also SATA 13
Kingsland, Sharon E. 1951- 124
Kingsley, Charles 1819-1875 .... YABC-2
See also DLB 21, 32
Kingsley, Charlotte Mary
See Hanshew, Thomas W.
Kingsley, Daniel T(hain) 1932- 117
Kingsley, Emily Perl 1940- 107
See also SATA 33
Kingsley, Henry 1830-1876 .... DLB-21
Kingsley, Michael J. 1918(?)-1972
Obituary 37-40R
Kingsley, Sidney 1906- 85-88
See also DLB 7
See also CLC 44
Kingsley-Smith, Terence 1940- 57-60
King-Smith, Dick 1922- CANR-22
Earlier sketch in CA 105
See also SATA 38, 47
Kingsnorth, George W(illiam) 1924- 7-8R
Kingston, Albert J(ames) 1917- 23-24R
Kingston, Jeremy Henry Spencer 1931- 103
Kingston, Maxine (Ting Ting) Hong
1940- CANR-13
Earlier sketch in CA 69-72
See also SATA 53
See also DLBY 80
See also CLC 12, 19
Kingston, Syd
See Bingley, David Ernest
Kingston, (Frederick) Temple 1925- CANR-12
Earlier sketch in CA 33-36R
Kingston-Mann, Esther 112
King-Stoops, Joyce 1923- 81-84
Kininmonth, Christopher 1917- 53-56
Kinkade, Richard P(aisley) 1939- CANR-14
Earlier sketch in CA 37-40R
Kinkaid, Matt
See Adams, Clifton
Kinkaid, Wyatt E.
See Jennings, Michael Glenn
Kinkead, Eugene (Francis) 1906- CANR-1
Earlier sketch in CA 1R
Kinkead-Weekes, Mark 1931- 124
Kinkley, Jeffrey C(arroll) 1948- 125
Kinley, Phyllis (Elaine Gillespie) 1930- 3R
Kinloch, A. Murray 1923- 103
Kinmonth, Earl H. 1946- 107
Kinnaird, Clark 1901-1983 .... CANR-1
Obituary 111
Earlier sketch in CA 45-48
Kinnaird, John (William) 1924-1980 124
Obituary 97-100
Kinnaird, William M(cKee) 1928- 101
Kinnamon, Keneth 1932- 37-40R
Kinnane, John F. 1921-1987 Obituary 123
Kinnard, Douglas 1921- CANR-14
Earlier sketch in CA 77-80
Kinnear, Elizabeth K. 1902- CAP-2
Earlier sketch in CA 33-36
Kinnear, Michael 1937- 37-40R
Kinneavy, James Louis 1920- 69-72
Kinneir, (Richard) Jock 1917- 121
Kinnell, Galway 1927- CANR-10
Earlier sketch in CA 11-12R
See also DLB 5
See also DLBY 87
See also CLC 1, 2, 3, 5, 13, 29
Kinney, Arthur F(rederick) 1933- CANR-14
Earlier sketch in CA 37-40R
Kinney, C. Cle(land) 1915- 11-12R
See also SATA 6
Kinney, Francis S(herwood) 1915- 106
Kinney, Harrison 1921- 1R
See also SATA 13
Kinney, James (Joseph) 1942- 120
Kinney, James R(oser) 1902(?)-1978
Obituary 81-84
Kinney, Jean Stout 1912- 11-12R
See also SATA 12
Kinney, Lucien Blair 1895-1971 .... CAP-2
Earlier sketch in CA 23-24
Kinney, Peter 1943- 73-76
Kinney, Richard 1924(?)-1979 Obituary 85-88
Kinnicutt, Susan Sibley 1926- 77-80
Kinnison, William A(ndrew) 1932- 23-24R
Kinor, Jehuda
See Rothmuller, Aron Marko
Kinoshita Junji 1914- 124
Kinross, Lord
See Balfour, (John) Patrick Douglas
Kinsbruner, Jay 1939- 25-28R
Kinsel, Paschal 1895(?)-1976 Obituary 69-72
Kinsella, Paul L. 1923- 21-22R
Kinsella, Thomas 1928- CANR-15
Earlier sketch in CA 17-18R
See also DLB 27
See also CLC 4, 19
Kinsella, W(illiam) P(atrick) 1935- CANR-21
Earlier sketch in CA 97-100
See also CAAS 7
See also CLC 27, 43
Kinsey, Alfred C(harles) 1894-1956
Brief entry 115
Kinsey, Barry Allan 1931- 19-20R
Kinsey, Elizabeth
See Clymer, Eleanor
Kinsey-Jones, Brian
See Ball, Brian N(eville)
Kinsley, D(aniel) A(llan) 1939- 45-48
Kinsley, James 1922-1984 .... CANR-2
Obituary 114
Earlier sketch in CA 1R
Kinsolving, Charles McIlvaine 1893-1984
Obituary 114
Kinstler, Everett Raymond 1926- 33-36R
Kinter, Judith 1928- 109
Kintgen, Eugene R(obert), Jr. 1942- 116
Kintner, Earl W(ilson) 1912- CANR-1
Earlier sketch in CA 45-48
Kintner, Robert Edmonds 1909-1980
Obituary 103
Kintner, William R(oscoe) 1915- CANR-6
Earlier sketch in CA 7-8R

Kinton, Jack F(ranklin) 1939- ... CANR-7
Earlier sketch in CA 57-60
Kintsch, Walter 1932- ... 29-32R
Kinzer, Betty 1922- ... 21-22R
Kinzer, Donald Louis 1914- ... 53-56
Kinzer, H(arless) M(ahlon) 1923(?)-1975
Obituary ... 57-60
Kinzer, Nora Scott 1936- ... 126
Brief entry ... 106
Kiparsky, Valentin (Julius Alexander)
1904- ... 17-18R
Kiple, Kenneth F(ranklin) 1939- ... 120
Kipling, (Joseph) Rudyard 1865-1936 ... 120
Brief entry ... 105
See also YABC 2
See also DLB 19, 34
See also TCLC 8, 17
Kiplinger, Austin H(untington) 1918- ... 57-60
Kiplinger, Willard Monroe 1891-1967
Obituary ... 89-92
Kipnis, Claude 1938-1981 ... 107
Obituary ... 103
Kippax, Janet 1926- ... 97-100
Kipphardt, Heinar 1922-1982 ... 89-92
Obituary ... 108
Kippley, John F(rancis) 1930- ... 29-32R
Kippley, Sheila K. 1939- ... 61-64
Kipps, Harriet C(lyde) 1926- ... 124
Kiraly, Bela (Kalman) 1912- ... CANR-8
Earlier sketch in CA 61-64
Kirby, (George) Blaik 1928- ... 77-80
Kirby, D(avid) P(eter) 1936- ... 25-28R
Kirby, David G. 1942- ... 101
Kirby, David K(irk) 1944- ... 53-56
Kirby, Douglas J. 1929- ... 25-28R
Kirby, E(dward) Stuart 1909- ... CANR-22
Earlier sketches in CA 15-16R, CANR-7
Kirby, Emily B(aruch) 1929- ... 117
Kirby, F(rank) E(ugene) 1928- ... 65-68
Kirby, Gilbert W(alter) 1914- ... 103
Kirby, Jack Temple 1938- ... 25-28R
Kirby, Jean
See McDonnell, Virginia B(leecker)
Kirby, Jean
See Robinson, Chaille Howard (Payne)
Kirby, John B(yron) 1938- ... 105
Kirby, M(ary) Sheelah Flanagan 1916- ... 7-8R
Kirby, Mark
See Floren, Lee
Kirby, Rollin 1875-1952 Brief entry ... 118
Kirby, Thomas Austin 1904- ... 5-6R
Kirchhofer, Alfred H. 1892(?)-1985
Obituary ... 117
Kirchhoff, Frederick (Thomas) 1942- ... 111
Kirchner, Audrey Burie 1937- ... CANR-12
Earlier sketch in CA 73-76
Kirchner, Glenn 1930- ... 29-32R
Kirchner, Walther 1905- ... CANR-1
Earlier sketch in CA 1R
Kirchwey, Freda 1893-1976 ... 93-96
Obituary ... 61-64
Kirdar, Uner 1933- ... 23-24R
Kirgis, Frederic L(ee), Jr. 1934- ... 125
Kirk, Alexandra
See Woods, Sherryl
Kirk, Clara M(arburg) 1898-1976 ... CAP-1
Obituary ... 69-72
Earlier sketch in CA 17-18
Kirk, Cooper 1920- ... 116
Kirk, David 1935- ... 29-32R
Kirk, Donald 1938- ... 37-40R
Kirk, Donald R. 1935- ... 57-60
Kirk, Elizabeth D(oan) 1937- ... 53-56
Kirk, G(eoffrey) S(tephen) 1921- ... CANR-2
Earlier sketch in CA 5-6R
Kirk, George (Eden) 1911- ... 1R
Kirk, H(enry) David 1918- ... CANR-11
Earlier sketch in CA 17-18R
Kirk, Irene 1926- ... CANR-6
Earlier sketch in CA 7-8R
Kirk, Irina
See Kirk, Irene
Kirk, James A(lbert) 1929- ... 37-40R
Kirk, Jeremy
See Powell, Richard (Pitts)
Kirk, Jerome (Richard) 1937- ... 49-52
Kirk, John Esben 1905-1975 Obituary ... 57-60
Kirk, John T(homas) 1933- ... 49-52
Kirk, Lydia (Chapin) 1896-1984 Obituary ... 114
Kirk, Mary Wallace 1889- ... 57-60
Kirk, Michael
See Knox, William
Kirk, Philip
See Levinson, Leonard
Kirk, R.
See Dietrich, Richard V(incent)
Kirk, Richard (Edmund) 1931- ... 13-14R
Kirk, Robert Warner ?-1980 ... 9-10R
Obituary ... 103
Kirk, Roger E(dward) 1930- ... 41-44R
Kirk, Russell (Amos) 1918- ... CANR-20
Earlier sketches in CA 1R, CANR-1
See also AITN 1
Kirk, Ruth (Kratz) 1925- ... CANR-9
Earlier sketch in CA 15-16R
See also SATA 5
Kirk, Samuel A(lexander) 1904- ... CANR-1
Earlier sketch in CA 45-48
Kirk, T(homas) H(obson) 1899- ... CAP-2
Earlier sketch in CA 23-24
Kirk, Ted
See Bank, Theodore P(aul) II
Kirk, Wayne
See Kock, Winston E(dward)
Kirkbride, Norma Jean 1924(?)-1983
Obituary ... 111
Kirkbride, Ronald (de Levington) 1912- ... CANR-2
Earlier sketch in CA 3R
Kirkconnell, Watson 1895-1977 ... 125
Obituary ... 108
See also DLB 68
Kirkendall, Don(ald M.) 1923- ... 49-52
Kirkendall, Lester A(llen) 1903- ... CANR-5
Earlier sketch in CA 4R
Kirkendall, Richard Stewart 1928- ... 77-80
Kirk-Greene, Anthony (Hamilton Millard)
1925- ... CANR-11
Earlier sketch in CA 61-64
Kirk-Greene, Anthony H. M.
See Kirk-Greene, Anthony (Hamilton Millard)
Kirk-Greene, Christopher Walter Edward
1926- ... 13-14R
Kirkham, E. Bruce 1938- ... 37-40R
Kirkham, George L. 1941- ... 77-80
Kirkham, Michael 1934- ... 25-28R
Kirkland, Bryant M(ays) 1914- ... 21-22R
Kirkland, Caroline M. 1801-1864 ... DLB-3, 73, 74
Kirkland, Edward Chase 1894-1975 ... CANR-6
Obituary ... 104
Earlier sketch in CA 2R
Kirkland, Joseph 1830-1893 ... DLB-12
Kirkland, Wallace W. 1891(?)-1979
Obituary ... 89-92
Kirkland, Will
See Hale, Arlene
Kirkman, James S(pedding) 1906- ... 93-96
Kirkpatrick, Diane 1933- ... 53-56
Kirkpatrick, Donald L(ee) 1924- ... 41-44R
Kirkpatrick, Doris (Upton) 1902- ... 93-96
Kirkpatrick, Dow (Napier) 1917- ... 23-24R
Kirkpatrick, Evron M(aurice) 1911- ... 57-60
Kirkpatrick, Frank 1924- ... 108
Kirkpatrick, Ivone Augustine 1897-1964 ... CAP-1
Earlier sketch in CA 9-10
Kirkpatrick, Jean 1923- ... 81-84
Kirkpatrick, Jeane D(uane) J(ordan)
1926- ... CANR-7
Earlier sketch in CA 53-56
Kirkpatrick, John 1905- ... 45-48
Kirkpatrick, Lyman B(ickford), Jr. 1916- ... 33-36R
Kirkpatrick, Oliver (Austin) 1911- ... 49-52
Kirkpatrick, Ralph 1911-1984 ... 49-52
Obituary ... 112
Kirkpatrick, Samuel A(lexander) III
1943- ... 41-44R
Kirkpatrick, Smith 1922- ... 49-52
Kirkup, James 1918- ... CANR-2
Earlier sketch in CA 3R
See also CAAS 4
See also SATA 12
See also DLB 27
See also CLC 1
Kirkus, Virginia
See Glick, Virginia Kirkus
Kirkwood, Ellen Swan 1904- ... 25-28R
Kirkwood, G(ordon) M(acdonald) 1916- ... 93-96
Kirkwood, James 1930- ... CANR-6
Earlier sketch in CA 4R
See also CLC 9
See also AITN 2
Kirkwood, Jim
See Kirkwood, James
Kirkwood, Kenneth P. 1899-1968 ... 37-40R
Kirn, Ann Minette 1910- ... 93-96
Kirp, David L(eslie) 1944- ... 109
Kirsch, Anthony Thomas 1930- ... 103
Kirsch, Arthur C(lifford) 1932- ... 15-16R
Kirsch, Charlotte 1942- ... 109
Kirsch, Herbert 1924(?)-1978 Obituary ... 104
Kirsch, Leonard Joel 1934-1977 ... 37-40R
Kirsch, Paul John 1914- ... 108
Kirsch, Robert R. 1922-1980 ... CANR-13
Obituary ... 102
Earlier sketch in CA 33-36R
Kirsch, Sarah 1935- ... DLB-75
Kirschen, Leonard 1908-1983 Obituary ... 109
Kirschenbaum, Aaron 1926- ... 33-36R
Kirschenbaum, Howard 1944- ... 89-92
Kirschner, Allen 1930- ... 29-32R
Kirschner, Fritz
See Bickers, Richard Leslie Townshend
Kirschner, Joseph 1930- ... 121
Kirschner, Linda Rae 1939- ... 33-36R
Kirschten, Ernest 1902-1974 ... CAP-1
Obituary ... 49-52
Earlier sketch in CA 11-12
Kirshenbaum, Jerry 1938- ... 107
Kirshenblatt-Gimblett, Barbara 1942- ... CANR-15
Earlier sketch in CA 81-84
Kirshner, Gloria Ifland ... 41-44R
Kirsner, Douglas 1947- ... 77-80
Kirsner, Robert 1921- ... 23-24R
Kirst, Hans Hellmut 1914- ... 104
See also DLB 69
Kirst, Michael W(eile) 1939- ... CANR-24
Earlier sketch in CA 45-48
Kirstein, George G(arland) 1909-1986
Obituary ... 118
Kirstein, Lincoln (Edward) 1907-
Brief entry ... 117
Kirsten, Grace 1900- ... 104
Kirtland, G. B.
See Hine, Al(fred Blakelee)
and Hine, Sesyle Joslin
Kirtland, Helen Johns 1890(?)-1979
Obituary ... 89-92
Kirtland, Kathleen 1945- ... 65-68
Kirvan, John J. 1932- ... CANR-10
Earlier sketch in CA 23-24R
Kirwan, Albert D(ennis) 1904-1971 ... CANR-4
Earlier sketch in CA 4R
Kirwan, Laurence Patrick 1907- ... 3R
Kirwan, Molly (Morrow) 1906- ... CAP-1
Earlier sketch in CA 13-14
Kirwin, Harry Wynne 1911-1963 ... 4R
Kirzner, Israel M(ayer) 1930- ... CANR-3
Earlier sketch in CA 1R
Kis, Danilo 1935- ... 118
Brief entry ... 109
Kisamore, Norman D(ale) 1928- ... 5-6R
Kiser, Clyde V(ernon) 1904- ... 25-28R
Kiser, Lisa J. 1949- ... 114
Kish, G. Hobab
See Kennedy, Gerald (Hamilton)
Kish, George 1914- ... CANR-1
Earlier sketch in CA 1R
Kish, Kathleen Vera 1942- ... CANR-12
Earlier sketch in CA 69-72
Kish, Leslie 1910- ... CAP-1
Earlier sketch in CA 19-20
Kishel, Patricia G(unter) 1948- ... 117
Kishida, Eriko 1929- ... CANR-7
Earlier sketch in CA 53-56
See also SATA 12
Kishon, Ephraim 1924- ... CANR-2
Earlier sketch in CA 49-52
Kishtainy, Khalid 1929- ... 115
Kisiel, Marie 1929- ... 112
Kisinger, Grace Gelvin (Maze) 1913-1965 ... CAP-1
Earlier sketch in CA 13-14
See also SATA 10
Kisker, George W. 1912- ... 21-22R
Kismaric, Carole 1942- ... CANR-23
Earlier sketches in CA 33-36R, CANR-8
Kisner, James (Martin, Jr.) 1947- ... 113
Kisor, Henry (Du Bois) 1940- ... 73-76
Kissam, Edward 1943- ... 61-64
Kissane, John M(ichael) 1928- ... 53-56
Kissane, Leedice McAnelly 1905- ... CAP-2
Earlier sketch in CA 25-28
Kissen, Fan(ny) 1904- ... CAP-1
Earlier sketch in CA 15-16
Kissick, Gary 1946- ... 118
Kissin, Eva H. 1923- ... 29-32R
See also SATA 10
Kissinger, Henry A(lfred) 1923- ... CANR-2
Earlier sketch in CA 2R
Kissinger, Warren S(tauffer) 1922- ... 116
Kissling, Dorothy (Hight) 1904-1969
Obituary ... 105
Kissling, Fred R., Jr. 1930- ... 23-24R
Kiste, Robert Carl 1936- ... 61-64
Kister, Kenneth F. 1935- ... 25-28R
Kistiakowsky, George B(ogdan)
1900-1982 Obituary ... 108
Kistiakowsky, Vera 1928- ... 23-24R
Kistler, Mark O(liver) 1918- ... 77-80
Kistner, Robert William 1917- ... CANR-13
Earlier sketch in CA 61-64
Kitagawa, Daisuke 1910- ... CAP-2
Earlier sketch in CA 17-18
Kitagawa, Joseph M. 1915- ... CANR-2
Earlier sketch in CA 1R
Kitano, Harry H. L. 1926- ... 29-32R
Kitao, T(imothy) Kaori 1933- ... 106
Kitchel, Denison 1908- ... 105
Kitchen, Helen (Angell) ... CANR-23
Earlier sketches in CA 11-12R, CANR-8
Kitchen, Herminie B(roedel) 1901-1973 ... CAP-1
Earlier sketch in CA 17-18
Kitchen, Martin 1936- ... CANR-26
Earlier sketches in CA 61-64, CANR-10
Kitchen, Paddy 1934- ... CANR-21
Earlier sketch in CA 25-28R
Kitchener, Richard Frank 1941- ... 124
Kitcher, Philip 1947- ... 113
Kitchin, Laurence 1913- ... 104
Kite, Larry
See Schneck, Stephen
Kite, Pat 1940- ... 119
Kitman, Marvin 1929- ... 101
Kitson, Jack William 1940- ... 25-28R
Kitson Clark, George Sydney Roberts
1900-1975 ... CANR-14
Earlier sketch in CA 23-24R
Kitt, Eartha (Mae) 1928- ... 77-80
Kitt, Tamara
See de Regniers, Beatrice Schenk
(Freedman)
Kittelson, David James 1931- ... 119
Kittler, Glenn D. 1920(?)-1986 Obituary ... 119
Kitto, Crispin 1951- ... 119
Kitto, H(umphrey) D(avy) F(indley)
1897-1982 ... CAP-1
Obituary ... 105
Earlier sketch in CA 11-12
Kittredge, William 1932- ... 111
Kittrie, Nicholas N(orbert Nehemiah)
1928- ... 81-84
Kituomba
See Odaga, Asenath (Bole)
Kitzinger, Ernst 1912- ... 108
Kitzinger, Sheila 1929- ... 37-40R
Kitzinger, U(we) W(ebster) 1928- ... CANR-1
Earlier sketch in CA 2R
Kivenson, Gilbert 1920- ... 112
Kivy, Peter Nathan 1934- ... 103
Kiyota, Minoru 1923- ... 113
Kizer, Carolyn (Ashley) 1925- ... CANR-24
Earlier sketch in CA 65-68
See also CAAS 5
See also DLB 5
See also CLC 15, 39
Kjelgaard, James Arthur 1910-1959
Brief entry ... 109
See also SATA 17
Kjelgaard, Jim
See Kjelgaard, James Arthur
Kjome, June C(reola) 1920- ... 7-8R
Klaas, Joe 1920- ... CANR-12
Earlier sketch in CA 29-32R
Klaassen, Leo(nardus) H(endrik)
1920- ... CANR-26
Earlier sketches in CA 23-24R, CANR-11
Klaassen, Walter 1926- ... 115
Klabund 1890-1928 ... DLB-66
Kladstrup, Don(ald) 1943- ... 77-80
Klafs, Carl E. 1911- ... 13-14R
Klagsbrun, Francine (Lifton) ... 21-22R
See also SATA 36
Klaiber, Jeffrey L. 1943- ... 85-88
Klaich, Dolores 1936- ... 49-52
Klaidman, Stephen 1938- ... 125
Klainikite, Anne
See Gehman, Betsy Holland
Klaits, Barrie 1944- ... 73-76
See also SATA 52
Klaits, Joseph (Aaron) 1942- ... 126
Klamer, Arjo 1953- ... 116
Klamkin, Charles 1923- ... 61-64
Klamkin, Lynn 1950- ... 45-48
Klamkin, Marian 1926- ... CANR-1
Earlier sketch in CA 49-52
Klann, Margaret L. 1911- ... 77-80
Klaperman, Gilbert 1921- ... 49-52
See also SATA 33
Klaperman, Libby Mindlin 1921-1982 ... 9-10R
Obituary ... 107
See also SATA 31, 33
Klapp, Orrin E. 1915- ... 9-10R
Klapper, Charles F(rederick) 1905- ... CAP-1
Earlier sketch in CA 9-10
Klapper, Joseph T(homas) 1917-1984
Obituary ... 112
Klapper, M(olly) Roxana 1937- ... 53-56
Klapper, Marvin 1922- ... 19-20R
Klappert, Peter 1942- ... 33-36R
See also DLB 5
Klappholz, Kurt 1913-1975 Obituary ... 61-64
Klapthor, Margaret B(rown) 1922- ... 119
Klare, George R(oger) 1922- ... 5-6R
Klare, Hugh J(ohn) 1916- ... 103
Klaren, Peter F(lindell) 1938- ... 57-60
Klarsfeld, Beate 1939- ... 65-68
Klarsfeld, Serge 1935- ... 115
Klass, Allan Arnold 1907- ... 65-68
Klass, Morton 1927- ... CANR-5
Earlier sketch in CA 1R
See also SATA 11
Klass, Perri 1958- ... 126
Klass, Philip J. 1919- ... 25-28R
Klass, Shelia Solomon 1927- ... CANR-13
Earlier sketch in CA 37-40R
See also SATA 45
Klass, Sholom 1916- ... 23-24R
Klassen, Frank Roy 1910- ... 113
Klassen, Peter J(ames) 1930- ... CANR-1
Earlier sketch in CA 45-48
Klassen, Randolph Jacob 1933- ... 61-64
Klassen, Walter
See Klaassen, Walter
Klassen, William 1930- ... CANR-10
Earlier sketch in CA 25-28R
Klauber, John 1917-1981 Obituary ... 104
Klauber, Laurence M(onroe) 1883-1968
Obituary ... 105
Klauck, Daniel L. 1947- ... 69-72
Klauder, Francis John 1918- ... 53-56
Klaue, Lola Shelton 1903- ... 5-6R
Klause, John L(ouis) 1943- ... 118
Klausler, Alfred P(aul) 1910- ... 23-24R
Klausmeier, Herbert J. 1915- ... CANR-20
Earlier sketches in CA 3R, CANR-5
Klausner, Abraham J. 1915- ... 108
Klausner, Lawrence D(avid) 1939- ... 110
Klausner, Margot 1905-1976(?) Obituary ... 61-64
Klausner, Samuel Z(undel) 1923- ... 17-18R
Klavans, J(odie) K(ay) 1956- ... 118
Klaw, Spencer 1920- ... 25-28R
Klawans, Harold L(eo) 1937- ... 106
Klayman, Maxwell Irving 1917- ... 29-32R
Klebe, Charles Eugene 1907- ... CAP-2
Earlier sketch in CA 23-24
Klebe, Gene
See Klebe, Charles Eugene
Kleberger, Ilse 1921- ... CANR-15
Earlier sketch in CA 41-44R
See also SATA 5
Klee, James B(utt) 1916- ... 109
Kleeberg, Irene (Flitner) Cumming
1932- ... CANR-12
Earlier sketch in CA 61-64
Kleene, Stephen Cole 1909- ... 41-44R
Klees, Fredric (Spang) 1901- ... CAP-2
Earlier sketch in CA 19-20
Klehr, Harvey 1945- ... 111
Kleiler, Frank Munro 1914- ... 89-92
Kleiman, Robert 1918- ... 15-16R
Klein, A(braham) M(oses) 1909-1972 ... 101
Obituary ... 37-40R
See also DLB 68
See also CLC 19
Klein, Aaron E. 1930- ... CANR-19
Earlier sketch in CA 25-28R
See also SATA 28, 45
Klein, Alan F(redric) 1911- ... 57-60
Klein, Alexander 1918- ... CANR-14
Earlier sketch in CA 5-6R
Klein, Arnold William 1945- ... 37-40R
Klein, Bernard 1921- ... 17-18R
Klein, Carole (Doreen) 1934- Brief entry ... 118
Klein, Charlotte 1925- ... 101
Klein, Daniel Martin 1939- ... CANR-11
Earlier sketch in CA 61-64
Klein, Dave 1940- ... 89-92

Klein, David 1919- CANR-18
Earlier sketches in CA 4R, CANR-1
Klein, David Ballin 1897- 41-44R
Klein, Donald C(harles) 1923- 25-28R
Klein, Donald W(alker) 1929- Brief entry 114
Klein, Doris F.
See Jonas, Doris F(rances)
Klein, Edward 1936- 69-72
Klein, Elizabeth 1939- 110
Klein, Ernest 1899- CAP-2
Earlier sketch in CA 21-22
Klein, Fannie J. 1903-1984 Obituary 113
Klein, Fred 1932- Brief entry 115
Klein, Frederic Shriver 1904- 15-16R
Klein, Gene 1921- 126
Klein, Gerard 1937- 49-52
Klein, Gerda Weissmann 1924- 116
See also SATA 44
Klein, H(erbert) Arthur 15-16R
See also SATA 8
Klein, Herbert Sanford 1936- CANR-17
Earlier sketch in CA 93-96
Klein, Heywood 1954(?)-1984 Obituary 111
Klein, Holger Michael 1938- 65-68
Klein, Isaac 1905- 57-60
Klein, Jeffrey B. 1948- 77-80
Klein, Joe
See Klein, Joseph
Klein, John J(acob) 1929- 17-18R
Klein, Joseph 1946- 85-88
Klein, Josephine (F. H.) 1926- 2R
Klein, Julius 1901-1984 Obituary 112
Klein, K. K.
See Turner, Robert H(arry)
Klein, Karl
See Sala, Charles
Klein, Lawrence R(obert) 1920-
Brief entry 116
Klein, Leonore (Glotzer) 1916- CANR-1
Earlier sketch in CA 4R
See also SATA 6
Klein, Marcus 1928- 11-12R
Klein, Martin A. 1934- 23-24R
Klein, Marymae E. 1917- 97-100
Klein, Maury 1939- 33-36R
Klein, Maxine 1934- CANR-10
Earlier sketch in CA 61-64
Klein, Melanie 1882-1960 Obituary 111
Klein, Milton M(artin) 1917- 93-96
Klein, Mina C(ooper) 37-40R
See also SATA 8
Klein, Muriel Walzer 1920- 29-32R
Klein, Norma 1938- CANR-15
Earlier sketch in CA 41-44R
See also SATA 7
See also SAAS 1
See also CLC 30
See also CLR 2
Klein, Philip A(lexander) 1927- 17-18R
Klein, Philip Shriver 1909- CANR-1
Earlier sketch in CA 3R
Klein, Randolph Shipley 1942- 73-76
Klein, Richard C. 1916(?)-1983 Obituary 111
Klein, Richard G. 1941- 120
Klein, Richard M. 1923- CANR-25
Earlier sketch in CA 108
Klein, Robin 1936- 116
See also SATA 45
Klein, Rose (Shweitzer) 1918- 21-22R
Klein, Stanley 1930- 57-60
Klein, Stanley D. 1936- 77-80
Klein, Stuart M(arc) 1932- Brief entry 111
Klein, Suzanne Marie 1940- 57-60
Klein, T(heodore) E(ibon) D(onald) 1947- 119
See also CLC 34
Klein, Ted U. 1926- 25-28R
Klein, Thomas D(icker) 1941- 61-64
Klein, Walter J(ulian) 1923- 69-72
Klein, Woody 1929- 15-16R
Kleinbauer, W(alter) Eugene 1937- 37-40R
Kleinbaum, Abby Wettan 1943- 113
Kleinberg, Seymour 1933- 105
Kleine, Glen 1936- 73-76
Kleine-Ahlbrandt, W(illiam) Laird 1932- 29-32R
Kleiner, Art 1954- 124
Kleinfeld, Gerald R. 1936- 103
Kleinfeld, Judith S. 1944- CANR-15
Earlier sketch in CA 77-80
Kleinfeld, Vincent A. 1907- CANR-10
Earlier sketch in CA 19-20R
Kleinfield, N(athan) R(ichard) 1950- CANR-18
Earlier sketch in CA 97-100
Kleinfield, Sonny
See Kleinfield, N(athan) R(ichard)
Kleinhans, Theodore John 1924- 7-8R
Kleinke, Chris (Lynn) 1944- CANR-15
Earlier sketch in CA 89-92
Kleinman, Arthur (Michael) 1941- CANR-22
Earlier sketch in CA 105
Kleinman, Ruth 1929- 125
Kleinmann, Jack H(enry) 1932- 21-22R
Kleinmuntz, Benjamin 1930- 33-36R
Kleinzahler, August 1949- 125
Klejment, Anne M. 1950- CANR-17
Earlier sketch in CA 101
Klem, Kaye Wilson 1941- 89-92
Klement, Frank L(udwig) 1908- 9-10R
Klemer, Richard Hudson 1918-1972 .... CANR-4
Obituary 37-40R
Earlier sketch in CA 7-8R
Klemesrud, Judy 1939(?)-1985 89-92
Obituary 117
Klemin, Diana 49-52
Klemke, E(lmer) D. 1926- CANR-10
Earlier sketch in CA 25-28R
Klemm, Edward G., Jr. 1910- 57-60
See also SATA 30
Klemm, Roberta K(ohnhorst) 1884- 61-64
See also SATA 30
Klemm, W(illiam) R(obert) 1934- 93-96
Klemperer, Otto 1885-1973 Obituary 116
Klempner, Irving M(ax) 1924- 53-56
Klempner, John 1898(?)-1972 Obituary 37-40R
Klenbort, Charlotte
See Sempell, Charlotte
Klenicki, Leon 1930- 106
Klenk, Robert W(illiam) 1934- 29-32R
Klenz, William 1915- 7-8R
Klerer, Melvin 1926- 21-22R
Klerman, Lorraine V(ogel) 1929- CANR-15
Earlier sketch in CA 81-84
Klett, Guy S(oulliard) 1897- CAP-1
Earlier sketch in CA 13-14
Kleuser, Louise C(aroline) 1889(?)-1976
Obituary 65-68
Klevin, Jill Ross 1935- 111
See also SATA 38, 39
Klewin, W(illiam) Thomas 1921- 29-32R
Kleyman, Paul (Fred) 1945- 57-60
Kliban, B(ernard) 1935- 106
See also SATA 35
Klibansky, Raymond 1905- Brief entry 117
Kliever, Lonnie D(ean) 1931- 29-32R
Kliewer, Evelyn 1933- 101
Kliewer, Warren 1931- CANR-2
Earlier sketch in CA 45-48
Kligerman, Jack 1938- 85-88
Kligman, Ruth 1930- 101
Klima, Ivan 1931- CANR-17
Earlier sketch in CA 25-28R
Kliman, Gilbert W(allace) 1929- 117
Klimas, Antanas 1924- 41-44R
Klimas, John E(dward) 1927-1975
Obituary 111
Klimek, David E(rnest) 1941- 89-92
Klimenko, Michael 1924- 73-76
Klimentov, Andrei Platonovich 1899-1951
Brief entry 108
Klimisch, Sister Mary Jane 1920- 17-18R
Klimo, Jake
See Klimo, Vernon
Klimo, Vernon 1914- 101
Klimowicz, Barbara 1927- 21-22R
See also SATA 10
Klin, George 1931- 53-56
Klinck, Carl Frederick 1908- 17-18R
Klinck, George Alfred 1903-1973 .... 9-10R
Obituary 103
Klindt-Jensen, Ole 1918-1980 .... CANR-10
Obituary 101
Earlier sketch in CA 21-22R
Kline, George L(ouis) 1921- CANR-9
Earlier sketch in CA 17-18R
Kline, Linda 1940- 126
Kline, Lloyd W. 1931- 33-36R
Kline, Morris 1908- CANR-2
Earlier sketch in CA 5-6R
Kline, Nancy Meadors 1946- 57-60
Kline, Nathan S(chellenberg) 1916-1983 81-84
Obituary 109
Kline, Peter 1936- 25-28R
Kline, Suzy 1943- 120
See also SATA 48
Kline, Thomas J(efferson) 1942- 85-88
Klineberg, Stephen L(ouis) 1940- 77-80
Klinefelter, Walter 1899- CANR-3
Earlier sketch in CA 9-10R
Klineman, George A(lfred) 1947- 107
Kling, Robert E(dward), Jr. 1920- 29-32R
Kling, Simcha 1922- 15-16R
Kling, Woody 1926(?)-1988 Obituary 125
Klingelhofer, E(dwin) L(ewis) 1920- 124
Klinger, Eric 1933- CANR-13
Earlier sketch in CA 33-36R
Klinger, Kurt 1914- 19-20R
Klinghoffer, Arthur Jay 1941- 65-68
Klingman, Lawrence (Lewis) 1918-1986
Obituary 120
Klingstedt, Joe Lars 1938- 53-56
Klink, Johanna L. 1918- CANR-8
Earlier sketch in CA 61-64
Klinkowitz, Jerome 1943- CANR-1
Earlier sketch in CA 45-48
Klipper, Miriam Z(eldner) 108
Klise, Eugene Storm 1908- 7-8R
Klise, Thomas S. 1928- 57-60
Klobuchar, James John 1928- 73-76
Klobuchar, Jim
See Klobuchar, James John
Kloepfer, Marguerite (Fonnesbeck)
1916- 97-100
Kloesel, Christian Johannes Wilhelm
1942- 113
Kloetzli, Walter, (Jr.) 1921- 3R
Klonglan, Gerald E(dward) 1936- 41-44R
Klonis, N. I.
See Clones, N(icholas) J.
Klonsky, Milton 1921(?)-1981 Obituary 105
Kloos, Peter 1936- 93-96
Klooster, Fred H. 1922- 3R
Klopf, Donald W(illiam) 1923- CANR-15
Earlier sketch in CA 89-92
Klopfer, Donald S(imon) 1902-1986
Obituary 119
Klopfer, Peter H(ubert) 1930- 85-88
Klopfer, Walter G(eorge) 1923- 89-92
Kloppenburg, Boaventura 1919- CANR-15
Earlier sketch in CA 65-68
Klos, Frank W(illiam), Jr. 1924- 15-16R
Klose, Kevin 1940- 53-56
Klose, Norma Cline 1936- 19-20R
Klosinski, Emil 1922- 65-68
Kloss, Phillips 1902- CAP-1
Earlier sketch in CA 15-16
Kloss, Robert J(ames) 1935- 45-48
Kloss, Robert Marsh 1938- 65-68
Klosty, James (Michael) 1943- Brief entry 112
Klotman, Phyllis Rauch 93-96
Klotman, Robert Howard 1918- 53-56
Klots, Alexander Barrett 1903- 107
Klotter, James C(hristopher) 1947- 77-80
Klotter, John C(harles) 1918- 93-96
Klotz, Lynn C(harles) 1940- 116
Klubertanz, George Peter 1912- 7-8R
Kluckhohn, Frank L. 1907-1970 .... 7-8R
Obituary 29-32R
Klueger, Ruth
See Kluger, Ruth
Klug, Eugene F(rederick Adolf) 1917- CANR-1
Earlier sketch in CA 45-48
Klug, Ron(ald) 1939- CANR-24
Earlier sketch in CA 107
See also SATA 31
Kluge, Alexander 1932- 81-84
See also DLB 75
Kluge, Eike-Henner W. 1942- 61-64
Kluge, P(aul) F(rederick) 1942- CANR-16
Earlier sketch in CA 73-76
Kluger, James R. 1939- 29-32R
Kluger, Richard 1934- CANR-6
Earlier sketch in CA 9-10R
Kluger, Ruth 1914-1980 116
Obituary 108
Klugh, Henry E(licker, III) 1927- 53-56
Kluwe, Mary Jean 1905-1975 .... CAP-2
Earlier sketch in CA 23-24
Kmoch, Hans 1897(?)-1973 Obituary 41-44R
Knaack, Twila 1944- 119
Knachel, Philip A(therton) 1926- 23-24R
Knack, Martha C(arol) 1948- 118
Knaplund, Paul (Alexander) 1885-1964 .... CAP-1
Earlier sketch in CA 11-12
Knapp, Bettina (Liebowitz) CANR-21
Earlier sketches in CA 13-14R, CANR-6
Knapp, David A(llan) 1938- 41-44R
Knapp, Herbert W. 1931- 105
Knapp, J(ohn) Merrill 1914- 53-56
Knapp, James F(ranklin) 1940- 107
Knapp, John (Allen) II 1940- 116
Knapp, Joseph G(rant) 1900-1983 .... 37-40R
Obituary 110
Knapp, Joseph G(eorge) 1924- 41-44R
Knapp, Lewis M(ansfield) 1894- 23-24R
Knapp, Mark L(ane) 1938- 81-84
Knapp, Mary L. 1931- 105
Knapp, Peggy A(nn) 1937- 119
Knapp, Robert Hampden 1915-1974 .... CAP-2
Obituary 53-56
Earlier sketch in CA 15-16
Knapp, Ron 1952- 103
See also SATA 34
Knapp, Ronald Gary 1940- 112
Knapp, Ronald J(ames) 1935- 119
Knapp, Samuel Lorenzo 1783-1838 .... DLB-59
Knapper, Christopher (Kay) 1940- CANR-12
Earlier sketch in CA 29-32R
Knapton, Ernest John 1902- CANR-1
Earlier sketch in CA 4R
Knaub, Richard K. 1928- 41-44R
Knaus, William A. 1946- 105
Knauth, Percy 1914- 57-60
Knauth, Victor W. 1895(?)-1977
Obituary 73-76
Kneale, Matthew (Nicholas Kerr) 1960- 125
Knebel, Fletcher 1911- CANR-1
Earlier sketch in CA 1R
See also CAAS 3
See also SATA 36
See also CLC 14
See also AITN 1
Knecht, R(obert) J(ean) 1926- CANR-13
Earlier sketch in CA 33-36R
Knechtges, David R(ichard) 1942- 65-68
Kneebone, Geoffrey Thomas 1918- 5-6R
Kneese, Allen V(ictor) 1930- CANR-8
Earlier sketch in CA 15-16R
Knef, Hildegard 1925- CANR-4
Earlier sketch in CA 45-48
Kneller, John W(illiam) 1916- 17-18R
Knelman, Fred H. 1919- 102
Knelman, Martin 1943- 73-76
Knepler, Henry (William) 1922- 23-24R
Knezevich, Stephen J(oseph) 1920- CANR-10
Earlier sketch in CA 7-8R
Knickerbocker, Charles H(errick) 1922- 13-14R
Knickerbocker, Diedrich
See Irving, Washington
Knickerbocker, Kenneth L(eslie) 1905- 5-6R
Knickmeyer, Steve 1944- 85-88
Knies, Elizabeth 1941- 109
Knifesmith
See Cutler, Ivor
Kniffen, Fred B(owerman) 1900- 2R
Knigge, Robert (R.) 1921(?)-1987
Obituary 121
See also SATA 50
Knight, Adam
See Lariar, Lawrence
Knight, Alan 1946- 125
Knight, Alanna CANR-15
Earlier sketch in CA 81-84
Knight, Alice Valle 1922- 81-84
Knight, Anne (Katherine) 1946- SATA-34
Knight, Arthur 1916- 41-44R
Knight, Arthur Winfield 1937- CANR-19
Earlier sketches in CA 53-56, CANR-4
Knight, B(etty) Carolyn 1944- 118
Knight, Bernard 1931- CANR-2
Earlier sketch in CA 49-52
Knight, Bertram 1904- 103
Knight, Charles 1910- 109
Knight, Charles Landon AITN-2
Knight, Charles W. 1891- CAP-1
Earlier sketch in CA 9-10
Knight, Clayton 1891-1969 .... CAP-1
Earlier sketch in CA 9-10
Knight, Damon (Francis) 1922- CANR-17
Earlier sketches in CA 49-52, CANR-3
See also SATA 9
See also DLB 8
Knight, David
See Prather, Richard S(cott)
Knight, David C(arpenter) 1925- 73-76
See also SATA 14
Knight, David Marcus 1936- CANR-7
Earlier sketch in CA 57-60
Knight, Doug(las E.) 1925- 85-88
Knight, Douglas M(aitland) 1921- CANR-2
Earlier sketch in CA 49-52
Knight, Eric (Mowbray) 1897-1943 .... SATA-18
Knight, Etheridge 1931- CANR-23
Earlier sketch in CA 23-24R
See also BW
See also DLB 41
See also CLC 40
Knight, Everett 1919- 33-36R
Knight, Francis Edgar 1905- 73-76
See also SATA 14
Knight, Frank
See Knight, Francis Edgar
Knight, Frank H(yneman) 1885-1972
Obituary 33-36R
Knight, Franklin Willis 1942- 101
Knight, Frida 1910- CANR-2
Earlier sketch in CA 49-52
Knight, G(ilfred) Norman 1891-1978 .... CANR-17
Earlier sketch in CA 25-28R
Knight, G(eorge) Wilson 1897-1985 .... CANR-10
Obituary 115
Earlier sketch in CA 15-16R
Knight, Gareth
See Wilby, Basil Leslie
Knight, Geoffrey Egerton 1921- 122
Knight, George Angus Fulton 1909- 4R
Knight, Glee 1947-1975 57-60
Obituary 120
Knight, H(erbert) Ralph 1895- CAP-2
Earlier sketch in CA 25-28
Knight, Harold V(incent) 1907- 23-24R
Knight, Hattie M. 1908-1976 .... CAP-2
Earlier sketch in CA 29-32
Knight, Hilary 1926- 73-76
See also SATA 15
Knight, Hugh McCown 1905- 5-6R
Knight, Ione Kemp 1922- 37-40R
Knight, Isabel F(rances) 1930- 25-28R
Knight, James
See Schneck, Stephen
Knight, James A(llen) 1918- CANR-6
Earlier sketch in CA 15-16R
Knight, Janet M(argaret) 1940- 93-96
Knight, John S. III AITN-2
Knight, John Shively 1894-1981 93-96
Obituary 103
See also DLB 29
See also AITN 2
Knight, K(enneth) G(raham) 1921- 25-28R
Knight, Karl F. 1930- 17-18R
Knight, Mallory T.
See Hurwood, Bernhardt J.
Knight, Margaret K(ennedy) Horsey
1903- CAP-1
Earlier sketch in CA 9-10
Knight, Max 1909- 93-96
Knight, Maxwell 1900- CAP-1
Earlier sketch in CA 13-14
Knight, Michael E(mery) 1935- 105
Knight, Norman L(ouis) 1895- CAP-2
Earlier sketch in CA 23-24
Knight, Oliver (Holmes) 1919- 21-22R
Knight, Paul Emerson 1925- 13-14R
Knight, R(oy) C(lement) 1907- 15-16R
Knight, Richard S. 1936- 115
Knight, Robin 1943- 73-76
Knight, Roderic C(opley) 1942- 61-64
Knight, Ruth Adams 1898-1974 .... 5-6R
Obituary 49-52
See also SATA 20
Knight, Sarah Kemble 1666-1727 .... DLB-24
Knight, Stephen 1951-1985 69-72
Obituary 117
Knight, Thomas J(oseph) 1937- 102
Knight, Thomas S(tanley, Jr.) 1921- 17-18R
Knight, Vick R(alph), Jr. 1928- CANR-16
Earlier sketches in CA 45-48, CANR-1
Knight, Vick (Ralph), Sr. 1908-1984
Obituary 112
Knight, W(illiam) Nicholas 1939- 37-40R
Knight, Walker L(eigh) 1924- CANR-13
Earlier sketch in CA 37-40R
Knight, Wallace E(dward) 1926- CANR-11
Earlier sketch in CA 65-68
Knightley, Phillip 1929- 25-28R
Knight-Patterson, W. M.
See Kulski, Wladyslaw Wszebor
Knights, John Keell 1930(?)-1981
Obituary 102
Knights, L(ionel) C(harles) 1906- CANR-3
Earlier sketch in CA 7-8R
Knights, Peter R(oger) 1938- 37-40R
Knights, Ward A(rthur), Jr. 1927- 97-100
Knigin, Michael Jay 1942- 85-88
Kniker, Charles Robert 1936- 77-80
Knipe, Humphry 1941- 37-40R
Knipe, Wayne Bishop III 1946- 53-56
Knipschield, Don(ald Harold) 1940- 5-6R
Kniskern, David Paul 1948- 112

Knist, F(rances) Emma 1948- CANR-5
Earlier sketch in CA 53-56
Knister, Raymond 1899-1932 .... DLB-68
Knittel, John (Herman Emanuel)
1891-1970 Obituary 104
Knobel, Lance 1956- 121
Knoblauch, C(yril) H. 1945- 124
Knobler, Nathan 1926- 33-36R
Knobler, Peter (Stephen) 1946- 97-100
Knoblock, Edward 1874-1945 Brief entry 108
See also DLB 10
Knock, Warren 1932- 65-68
Knoebl, Kuno 1936- 25-28R
Knoepfle, John 1923- CANR-12
Earlier sketch in CA 13-14R
Knoepflmacher, U(lrich) C(amillus)
1931- CANR-10
Earlier sketch in CA 15-16R
Knoerle, Jeanne 1928- 45-48
Knoke, David (Harmon) 1947- CANR-26
Earlier sketches in CA 65-68, CANR-10
Knoles, (Michael Clive) David 1896- 7-8R
Knoles, George Harmon 1907- 7-8R
Knoll, Erwin 1931- 89-92
Knoll, Gerald M. 1942- 29-32R
Knoll, Paul W(endell) 1937- 107
Knoll, Robert Edwin 1922- CANR-5
Earlier sketch in CA 2R
Knollenberg, Bernhard 1892-1973 .... CAP-2
Obituary 41-44R
Earlier sketch in CA 21-22
Knoop, Faith Yingling 1896- 97-100
Knop, Werner 1912(?)-1970 Obituary 29-32R
Knopf, Alfred A. 1892-1984 106
Obituary 113
See also DLBY 84
Knopf, Edwin H. 1899-1982(?) Obituary 105
Knopf, Irwin J(ay) 1924- 119
Knopf, Kenyon A(lfred) 1921- 77-80
Knopf, Terry Ann 1940- CANR-17
Earlier sketch in CA 25-28R
Knopp, Josephine Zadovsky 1941- 103
Knorr, Albert Scofield 1929- 25-28R
Knorr, Dandi 1949- 112
Knorr, Klaus (Eugene) 1911- Brief entry 113
Knorr, Marian L(ockwood) 1910- 102
Knott, Bill
See Knott, William C(ecil, Jr.)
Knott, John R(ay), Jr. 1937- 57-60
Knott, Kim 1955- 124
Knott, Leonard L(ewis) 1905- 107
Knott, Will C.
See Knott, William C(ecil, Jr.)
Knott, William C(ecil, Jr.) 1927- CANR-22
Earlier sketches in CA 5-6R, CANR-7
See also SATA 3
Knotts, Howard (Clayton, Jr.) 1922- CANR-11
Earlier sketch in CA 69-72
See also SATA 25
Knowland, A(nthony) S(tephen) 1919- 116
Knowland, William Fife 1908-1974
Obituary 89-92
Knowler, John 1933(?)-1979 Obituary 85-88
Knowles, A(lbert) Sidney, Jr. 1926- 101
Knowles, Alison 1933- CANR-8
Earlier sketch in CA 19-20R
Knowles, Anne 1933- 102
See also SATA 37
Knowles, Asa S(mallidae) 1909- 29-32R
Knowles, Clayton 1908-1978 81-84
Obituary 73-76
Knowles, (Michael Clive) David
1896-1974 .... CANR-4
Obituary 53-56
Earlier sketch in CA 7-8R
Knowles, Dorothy 1906- 25-28R
Knowles, Henry P(aine) 1912- 61-64
Knowles, John 1926- 17-18R
See also SATA 8
See also DLB 6
See also CLC 1, 4, 10, 26
Knowles, John H(ilton) 1926-1979 101
Obituary 85-88
Knowles, Joseph W(illiam) 1922- 23-24R
Knowles, Louis L(eonard) 1947- 29-32R
Knowles, Mabel Winifred 1875-1949
Brief entry 122
Knowles, Malcolm Shepherd 1913- CANR-5
Earlier sketch in CA 7-8R
Knowles, Yereth K(ahn) 1920- 93-96
Knowlton, Derrick 1921- CANR-6
Earlier sketch in CA 57-60
Knowlton, Edgar C(olby), Jr. 1921- 41-44R
Knowlton, James 1943- 120
Knowlton, Robert A(lmy) 1914-1968 .... 3R
Obituary 103
Knowlton, William H. 1927- 19-20R
Knox, Alexander 1907- 81-84
Knox, Bernard M(acGregor) W(alker)
1914- Brief entry 117
Knox, Bill
See Knox, William
Knox, Calvin M.
See Silverberg, Robert
Knox, Caroline 1938- 120
Knox, Cleone
See King-Hall, Magdalen
Knox, Collie T. 1897-1977 77-80
Obituary 73-76
Knox, David H., Jr. 1943- 41-44R
Knox, Donald E(dward) 1936-1986 45-48
Obituary 119
Knox, Edmund George Valpy 1881-1971 112
Obituary 29-32R
Knox, (Mary) Eleanor Jessie 1909- SATA-30
Knox, Frank 1874-1944 .... DLB-29
Knox, George A(lbert) 1918- 121
Knox, Henry M(acdonald) 1916- 13-14R
Knox, Hugh (Randolph) 1942- 103
Knox, Israel 1906-1986 Obituary 119
Knox, James
See Brittain, William
Knox, John 1900- 13-14R
Knox, John Armory 1850-1906 .... DLB-23
Knox, John Ballenger 1909- CAP-1
Earlier sketch in CA 9-10
Knox, Katharine McCook 1890(?)-1983
Obituary 110
Knox, (Thomas) Malcolm 1900-1980 103
Obituary 97-100
Knox, Robert Buick 1918- 25-28R
Knox, Ronald A(rbuthnott) 1888-1957
Brief entry 111
Knox, Sanka (Lutins) 1906-1984 Obituary 112
Knox, Vera Huntingdon 11-12R
Knox, Warren Barr 1925- 49-52
Knox, William 1928- CANR-1
Earlier sketch in CA 2R
Knox-Johnston, Robin 1939- CANR-15
Earlier sketch in CA 29-32R
Knox-Mawer, Ronald 1925- 123
Knox-Mawer, Ronnie
See Knox-Mawer, Ronald
Knudsen, Hans August Heinrich
1886-1971 Obituary 29-32R
Knudsen, James 1950- 111
See also SATA 42
Knudson, Danny (Alan) 1940- CANR-11
Earlier sketch in CA 61-64
Knudson, R. R.
See Knudson, Rozanne
Knudson, Richard L(ewis) 1930- CANR-20
Earlier sketch in CA 104
See also SATA 34
Knudson, Rozanne 1932- CANR-15
Earlier sketch in CA 33-36R
See also SATA 7
Knuemann, Carl H(einz) 1922- 77-80
Knusel, Jack L(eonard) 1923- 25-28R
Knuth, Helen 1912- 53-56
Knutson, Harold Christian 1928- 112
Knutson, Jeanne N(ickell) 1934- 41-44R
Knutson, Kent S(iguart) 1924-1973 .... CAP-2
Obituary 41-44R
Earlier sketch in CA 33-36
Knutson, Roger M. 1933- 126
Knye, Cassandra
See Disch, Thomas M(ichael)
Ko, Kanzein
See Isogai, Hiroshi
Ko, Won 1925- 61-64
Kobal, John 1943- CANR-11
Earlier sketch in CA 61-64
Kobayashi, Masako Matsuno 1935- CANR-13
Earlier sketch in CA 5-6R
Kobayashi, Noritake 1932- 53-56
Kobayashi, Tetsuya 1926- 69-72
Kober, Arthur 1900-1975 .... CAP-1
Obituary 57-60
Earlier sketch in CA 13-14
See also DLB 11
Kobler, Arthur L(eon) 1920- 15-16R
Kobler, (Albert) John (Jr.) 1910- 65-68
Kobler, (Mary) Turner S. 1930- 37-40R
Kobrak, Peter 1936- 104
Kobre, Sidney 1907- 65-68
Kobrin, David 1941- 41-44R
Kobrin, Janet 1942- 57-60
Kobryn, A(llen) P(aul) 1949- 93-96
Koch, C(hristopher) J(ohn) 1932- CLC-42
Koch, Charlotte 85-88
Koch, Claude (F.) 1918- 11-12R
Koch, Dorothy Clarke 1924- 7-8R
See also SATA 6
Koch, Edward I(rving) 1924- 113
Koch, Eric 1919- 69-72
Koch, H(annsjoachim) W(olfgang)
1933- CANR-15
Earlier sketch in CA 93-96
Koch, Hans-Gerhard 1913- 17-18R
Koch, Helen L(ois) 1895- CAP-2
Earlier sketch in CA 21-22
Koch, Howard 1902- 73-76
See also DLB 26
Koch, James Harold 1926- 106
Koch, Joanne 1940- CANR-15
Earlier sketch in CA 69-72
Koch, Kenneth 1925- CANR-6
Earlier sketch in CA 4R
See also DLB 5
See also CLC 5, 8, 44
Koch, Kurt E(mil) 1913-1987 107
Obituary 122
Koch, Lew(is) Z. 1935- 69-72
Koch, Michael 1916(?)-1981 Obituary 103
Koch, Raymond 85-88
Koch, Richard 1921- 29-32R
Koch, Robert 1918- 9-10R
Koch, Stephen 1941- 77-80
Koch, Thilo 1920- CANR-11
Earlier sketch in CA 25-28R
Koch, Thomas J(ohn) 1947- 61-64
Koch, Thomas Walter 1933- 17-18R
Koch, William H., Jr. 1923- 19-20R
Kochan, Lionel 1922- 105
Kochan, Miriam (Louise) 1929- 103
Kochan, Paul C(ranston) 1906- 45-48
Kochan, Thomas A(nton) 1947- 123
Kochanek, Stanley A(nthony) 1934- 116
Kochen, Manfred 1928- 21-22R
Kochenburger, Ralph J. 1919- 53-56
Kocher, Eric 1912- 57-60
Kocher, Paul H(arold) 1907- 65-68
Kochetov, Vsevolod A(nisimovich)
1912-1973 Obituary 45-48
Kochiss, John (Matthew) 1926- 97-100
Kochka, Mary Murray 1894(?)-1984
Obituary 112
Kochman, Thomas 1936- 37-40R
Kock, Winston E(dward) 1909-1982 110
Kockelmans, Joseph J(ohn) 1923- 117
Brief entry 113
Kocsis, J. C.
See Paul, James
Kocsis, Robert
See Kossez, Robes
Kodaly, Zoltan 1882-1967 Obituary 112
Kodama, Sanehide 1932- 120
Kodanda Rao, Pandurangi 1889- 13-14R
Koda Rohan
See Koda Shigeyuki
Koda Shigeyuki 1867-1947 Brief entry 121
Kodera, Takashi James 1945- 111
Koehler, Alan (Robert) 1928- 13-14R
Koehler, G(eorge) Stanley 1915- 37-40R
Koehler, George E. 1930- 25-28R
Koehler, Ludmila 1917- 53-56
Koehler, Lyle P(eter) 1944- 109
Koehler, Margaret (Hudson) 85-88
Koehler, Nikki 1951- 25-28R
Koehler, W(illiam) R. 1914- 9-10R
Koehler, Wolfgang 1887-1967 Obituary 111
Koehn, Ilse
See Van Zwienen, Ilse Charlotte Koehn
Koehn, Lala
See Koehn-Heine, Lala
Koehn-Heine, Lala 1936- 112
Koelsch, William Alvin 1933- 104
Koen, Ross Y. 1918- 3R
Koenig, Allen Edward 1939- 23-24R
Koenig, C(lyde) Eldo 1919- 21-22R
Koenig, Duane (Walter) 1918- 37-40R
Koenig, Franz 1905- 101
Koenig, Fritz H(ans) 1940- 53-56
Koenig, John (Thomas) 1938- 102
Koenig, Laird 29-32R
Koenig, Linda Lee 1948- 113
Koenig, Louis William 1916- 1R
Koenig, Rene 1906- CANR-15
Earlier sketch in CA 81-84
Koenig, Samuel 1899-1972 .... CAP-2
Obituary 37-40R
Earlier sketch in CA 17-18
Koenig, Walter 1936- 104
Koenigsberg, Moses 1879-1945 .... DLB-25
Koenigsberger, H(elmut) G(eorg) 1918- 33-36R
Koenigswald, (Gustav Heinrich) Ralph von
See von Koenigswald, (Gustav Heinrich)
Ralph
Koenker, Diane 1947- 112
Koenker, Ernest Benjamin 1920-
Brief entry 106
Koenner, Alfred 1921- CANR-18
Earlier sketch in CA 101
Koepf, Michael 1940- 81-84
Koepke, Paul 1918- 114
Koepke, Wulf 1928- CANR-16
Earlier sketch in CA 93-96
Koeppel, Gary 1938- 49-52
Koeppen, Wolfgang 1906- DLB-69
Koerner, James D. 1923- 9-10R
Koerner, Stephan 1913- 1R
Koerner, W(illiam) H(enry) D(avid)
1878-1938 .... SATA-21
Koerte, Mary Norbert 1934- 103
Koertge, Noretta 1935- CANR-22
Earlier sketch in CA 106
Koertge, Ronald 1940- CANR-25
Earlier sketches in CA 65-68, CANR-9
See also SATA 53
Koestenbaum, Peter 1928- CANR-13
Earlier sketch in CA 29-32R
Koestenbaum, Phyllis 1930- CANR-25
Earlier sketch in CA 107
Koester, Helmut 1926- 110
Koestler, Arthur 1905-1983 .... CANR-1
Obituary 109
Earlier sketch in CA 1R
See also DLBY 83
See also CLC 1, 3, 6, 8, 15, 33
Koestler, Cynthia 1928(?)-1983 Obituary 114
Koethe, John (Louis) 1945- 49-52
Koff, Richard Myram 1926- CANR-15
Earlier sketch in CA 89-92
Kofoed, Jack
See Kofoed, John C.
Kofoed, John C. 1894-1979 .... 5-6R
Obituary 93-96
Kofsky, Frank (Joseph) 1935- 57-60
Kogan, Bernard Robert 1920- 11-12R
Kogan, Deborah
See Kogan Ray, Deborah
See also SATA 50
Kogan, Herman 1914- CANR-20
Earlier sketches in CA 9-10R, CANR-5
Kogan, Judith 1956- 126
Kogan, Leonard S(aul) 1919-1976
Obituary 65-68
Kogan, Maurice 1930- 107
Kogan, Norman 1919- 4R
Kogan Ray, Deborah 1940- CANR-22
Earlier sketches in CA 57-60, CANR-7
Kogawa, Joy Nozomi 1935- CANR-19
Earlier sketch in CA 101
Kogiku, K(iichiro) C(hris) 1927- 33-36R
Koginos, Manny T. 1933- 21-22R
Kogos, Frederick 1907-1974 .... CAP-2
Obituary 53-56
Earlier sketch in CA 29-32
Koh, Byung Chul 1936- 17-18R
Koh, Sung Jae 1917- 19-20R
Kohak, Erazim V. 1933- CANR-14
Earlier sketch in CA 37-40R
Kohake, Rosanne 1951- 114
Kohan, Rhea 89-92
Kohanski, Alexander S(iskind) 1902-1987 108
Obituary 123
Kohavi, Y.
See Stern, Jay B(enjamin)
Kohen-Raz, Reuven 1921- 37-40R
Kohfeldt, Mary Lou 1939- 119
Kohl, Benjamin G. 1938- 126
Kohl, Herbert 1937- CANR-14
Earlier sketch in CA 65-68
See also SATA 47
Kohl, Irene C(aistor) 1927- 119
Kohl, James (Virgil) 1942- 57-60
Kohl, Marvin 1932- 85-88
Kohlberg, Lawrence 1927-1987 125
Obituary 122
Kohlenberg, Robert J(oseph) 1937- 111
Kohler, Foy D(avid) 1908- 29-32R
Kohler, Heinz 1934- 23-24R
Kohler, Julilly H(ouse) 1908-1976 77-80
Obituary 69-72
See also SATA 20
Kohler, Mary C.
See Kohler, Mary Conway
Kohler, Mary Conway 1903-1986 Obituary 119
Kohler, Saul 1928- 69-72
Kohler, Sister Mary Hortense 1892- 7-8R
Kohler, Wolfgang
See Koehler, Wolfgang
Kohlmeier, Louis M(artin), Jr. 1926- 49-52
Kohls, R. L.
See Kohls, Richard L(ouis)
Kohls, Richard L(ouis) 1921- 126
Brief entry 106
Kohlstedt, Sally Gregory 1943- 69-72
Kohmescher, Matthew Franklin 1921- 113
Kohn, Alexander 1919- 123
Kohn, Alfie 1957- 122
Kohn, Bernice
See Hunt, Bernice (Kohn)
See also SATA 4
Kohn, Clyde F(rederick) 1911- Brief entry 109
Kohn, Eugene 1887-1977 Obituary 69-72
Kohn, George C(hilds) 1940- CANR-19
Earlier sketch in CA 103
Kohn, Hans 1891-1971 .... CANR-4
Obituary 29-32R
Earlier sketch in CA 1R
Kohn, Howard 1947- 124
Kohn, Jacob 1881-1968 .... 5-6R
Obituary 103
Kohn, John S. (Van E.) 1906-1976
Obituary 104
Kohn, Melvin L(ester) 1928- 41-44R
Kohn, Richard H(enry) 1940- 115
Kohn, Walter S(amuel) G(erst) 1923- 107
Kohner, Frederick 1905-1986 .... CANR-1
Obituary 119
Earlier sketch in CA 1R
See also SATA 10, 48
Kohout, Pavel 1928- CANR-3
Earlier sketch in CA 45-48
See also CLC 13
Kohr, Louise Hannah 1903- 41-44R
Kohs, Samuel C(almin) 1890-1984
Obituary 111
Koht, Halvdan 1873-1965 85-88
Kohut, Heinz 1913-1981 .... CANR-1
Obituary 105
Earlier sketch in CA 45-48
Kohut, Les
See Kohut, Nester C(larence)
Kohut, Nester C(larence) 1925- 45-48
Koidahl, Ilona 1924- 97-100
Koide, Tan 1938-1986 .... SATA-50
Koi Hai
See Palmer, (Nathaniel) Humphrey
Koilpillai, (Jesudas) Charles 41-44R
Koilpillai, Das
See Koilpillai, (Jesudas) Charles
Koinange, Mbiyu (Peter) 1907-1981
Obituary 108
Koiner, Richard B. 1929- 19-20R
Koizumi, Yakumo
See Hearn, (Patricio) Lafcadio (Tessima
Carlos)
Kojecky, Roger 1943- 85-88
Kojima, Naomi 1950- 109
Kojima, Takashi 1902- CAP-1
Earlier sketch in CA 9-10
Kojima Shozo 1928- 69-72
Kokoschka, Oskar 1886-1980 109
Obituary 93-96
Kokyshev, Lazor 1933(?)-1975 Obituary 104
Kolaja, Jiri Thomas 1919- 9-10R
Kolakowski, Leszek 1927- 49-52
Kolars, Frank 1899-1973 .... 7-8R
Obituary 37-40R
Kolasky, John 1915- 25-28R
Kolatch, Alfred Jacob 1916- 107
Kolatch, Jonathan 1943- 41-44R
Kolb, Annette 1870-1967 .... DLB-66
Kolb, Carolyn 1942- 89-92
Kolb, David A(llen) 1939- CANR-15
Earlier sketch in CA 65-68
Kolb, Erwin J(ohn) 1924- 37-40R
Kolb, Gwin Jackson 1919- 2R
Kolb, Harold H(utchinson), Jr. 1933- CANR-12
Earlier sketch in CA 29-32R
Kolb, (Gwin) Jack (II) 1946- 125
Kolb, John F. 1916(?)-1974 Obituary 53-56
Kolb, Ken(neth) 1926- 21-22R
Kolb, Lawrence 1911-1972 Obituary 37-40R

Kolb, Philip 1907- CANR-4
Earlier sketch in CA 53-56
Kolba, St. Tamara 97-100
See also SATA 22
Kolbas, Grace Holden 1914- 93-96
Kolbe, Henry E(ugene) 1907- 5-6R
Kolbenheyer, Erwin Guido 1878-1962 .... DLB-66
Kolbenschlag, Madonna (Claire) 1935-
Brief entry 115
Kolbrek, Loyal 1914- 29-32R
Kolchin, Peter 1943- 41-44R
Kolde, Endel Jakob 1917- CANR-1
Earlier sketch in CA 45-48
Kolenda, Konstantin 1923- 15-16R
Kolers, Paul A. 1926- 97-100
Kolesar, Paul 1927- 105
Kolesnik, Walter B(ernard) 1923- CANR-2
Earlier sketch in CA 7-8R
Kolevzon, Edward R. 1913(?)-1976
Obituary 69-72
Kolin, Philip C(harles) 1945- 119
Kolins, William 1926(?)-1973 Obituary 104
Kolinski, Charles J(ames) 1916- 19-20R
Kolinsky, Martin 1936- CANR-8
Earlier sketch in CA 61-64
Koljevic, Svetozar 1930- CANR-7
Earlier sketch in CA 19-20R
Kolker, Robert Phillip 1940- 112
Kolko, Gabriel 1932- CANR-4
Earlier sketch in CA 5-6R
Kolkowicz, Roman 1929- Brief entry 116
Kollat, David T(ruman) 1938- 41-44R
Kollek, Teddy
See Kollek, Theodore
Kollek, Theodore 1911- CAP-2
Earlier sketch in CA 29-32
Koller, Charles W. 1896(?)-1983 61-64
Obituary 109
Koller, James 1936- CANR-18
Earlier sketches in CA 49-52, CANR-2
See also CAAS 5
Koller, John M. 1938- 33-36R
Koller, Larry
See Koller, Lawrence Robert
Koller, Lawrence Robert 1912-1967 .... CANR-6
Earlier sketch in CA 4R
Koller, Marvin Robert 1919- 15-16R
Kollmar, Dick
See Kollmar, Richard Tompkins
Kollmar, Richard Tompkins 1910-1971
Obituary 89-92
Kollock, Will(iam Raymond) 1940- 33-36R
Kollontai, Alexandra (Mikhailovna)
1872-1952 Brief entry 112
Kollstedt, Paula Lubke 1946- 113
Kolmogorov, Andrei Nikolayevich
1903-1987 Obituary 123
Kolnai, Aurel (Thomas) 1900-1973 103
Kolodin, Irving 1908-1988 93-96
Obituary 125
Kolodny, Annette 1941- CANR-8
Earlier sketch in CA 61-64
See also DLB 67
Kolodny, Ralph (Leonard) 1923- 116
Kolodziej, Edward Albert 1935- 97-100
Kolon, Nita
See Onadipe, (Nathaniel) Kola(wole)
Kolosimo, Peter 1922- CANR-7
Earlier sketch in CA 53-56
Kolson, Clifford J(ohn) 1920- 11-12R
Kolstoe, Oliver P(aul) 1920- 17-18R
Koltun, Frances Lang 69-72
Kolumban, Nicholas 1937- 111
Kolve, Carolee Nance 1946- 122
Kolyer, John (McNaughton) 1933- CANR-11
Earlier sketch in CA 69-72
Komai, Akira 1908(?)-1983 Obituary 111
Komaiko, Jean R. 1922(?)-1984 Obituary 114
Komarnicki, Tytus 1896- CAP-1
Earlier sketch in CA 9-10
Komarovsky, Mirra CAP-1
Earlier sketch in CA 17-18
Komatsu Sakyo 1931- Brief entry 113
Kome, Penney 1948- 116
Komer, Robert W(illiam) 1922- 108
Komisar, Lucy 1942- 33-36R
See also SATA 9
Kommers, Donald P. 1932- 116
Komoda, Beverly 1939- 85-88
See also SATA 25
Komoda, Kiyo 1937- SATA-9
Komroff, Manuel 1890-1974 .... CANR-4
Obituary 53-56
Earlier sketch in CA 4R
See also SATA 2, 20
See also DLB 4
Konadu, Asare
See Konadu, S(amuel) A(sare)
Konadu, S(amuel) A(sare) 1932- CANR-26
Earlier sketch in CA 23-24R
See also BW
Konczacki, Zbigniew Andrzej 1917- CANR-10
Earlier sketch in CA 21-22R
Kondoleon, Harry 1955- 112
Kondracke, Morton 1939- Brief entry 119
Kondrashin, Kiril (Petrovich) 1914-1981
Obituary 108
Kondrashov, Stanislav (Nikolaevich)
1928- 69-72
Konecky, Edith 1922- 69-72
Konefsky, Samuel J. 1915-1970
Obituary 29-32R
Konek, Carol (Wolfe) 1934- Brief entry 114
Koner, Marvin 1921(?)-1983 Obituary 109
Kong, Shiu Loon 1934- 108
Konick, Marcus 1914- 37-40R
Konig, David Thomas 1947- 97-100
Konig, Franz
See Koenig, Franz
Konig, Fritz H(ans)
See Koenig, Fritz H(ans)
Konig, Rene
See Koenig, Rene
Konigsberg, Conrad Isidore 1916- 23-24R
Konigsburg, E(laine) L(obl) 1930- CANR-17
Earlier sketch in CA 21-22R
See also SATA 4, 48
See also DLB 52
See also CLR 1
Koning, Hans
See Koningsberger, Hans
Koningsberger, Hans 1921- CANR-2
Earlier sketch in CA 4R
See also SATA 5
Konkel, Wilbur Stanton 1912- 111
Konkle, Janet Everest 1917- 4R
See also SATA 12
Konner, Alfred
See Koenner, Alfred
Konner, Linda 1951- 102
Konner, Melvin Joel 1946- Brief entry 116
Konnyu, Leslie 1914- CANR-7
Earlier sketch in CA 15-16R
Konopka, Gisela 1910- 9-10R
Konovalov, Sergey 1899-1982 Obituary 106
Konrad, Evelyn 1930- 33-36R
Konrad, George
See Konrad, Gyoergy
Konrad, Gyoergy 1933- 85-88
See also CLC 4, 10
Konrad, James
See Maclean, Charles
Konstan, David 1940- 113
Kontos, Cecille
See Haddix-Kontos, Cecille P.
Kontos, Peter G(eorge) 1935-1977 .... CANR-17
Obituary 115
Earlier sketch in CA 25-28R
Konvitz, Jeffrey 1944- CANR-7
Earlier sketch in CA 53-56
Konvitz, Milton Ridvas 1908- CANR-4
Earlier sketch in CA 2R
Konwicki, Tadeusz 1926- 101
See also CLC 8, 28
Koo, Anthony Y(ing) C(hang) 1918- 57-60
Koo, Samuel 1941- 77-80
Koo, V(i) K(yuin) Wellington 1888-1985 81-84
Obituary 117
Koob, C(harles) Albert 1920- 41-44R
Koob, Derry D(elos) 1933- 37-40R
Koob, Joseph E. II 1948- 121
Koob, Theodora (J. Foth) 1918- 5-6R
See also SATA 23
Kooiker, Leonie
See Kooyker-Romijn, Johanna Maria
Kooiman, Gladys 1927- 89-92
Kooiman, Helen W.
See Hosier, Helen Kooiman
Koon, George William 1942- 116
Koon, Helene Wickham 1924- 120
Koonce, Ray F. 1913- 11-12R
Koonts, Jones Calvin 1924- 49-52
Koontz, Dean R(ay) 1945- CANR-19
Earlier sketch in CA 108
Koontz, Harold 1908-1984 .... 41-44R
Obituary 112
Koonz, Claudia Brief entry 126
Koop, Katherine C. 1923- 19-20R
Koop, Theodore Frederick 1907(?)-1988
Obituary 126
Koopman, LeRoy George 1935- 101
Koopmans, Tjalling (Charles) 1910-1985
Obituary 115
Koopowitz, Harold 1940- 114
Kooser, Ted
See Kooser, Theodore
Kooser, Theodore 1939- CANR-15
Earlier sketch in CA 33-36R
Kootz, Samuel Melvin 1898-1982
Obituary 107
Kooyker-Romijn, Johanna Maria 1927- 107
See also SATA 48
Kooyker-Romyn, Johanna Maria
See Kooyker-Romijn, Johanna Maria
Kopal, Zdenek 1914- 93-96
Kopelev, Lev (Zinovievich) 1912- 123
Kopelev, Raissa (Davydovna) Orlova
See Orlova-Kopelev, Raissa (Davydovna)
Kopelman, Arie 1937- 113
Koperwas, Sam 1948- CANR-22
Earlier sketch in CA 105
Kopf, David 1930- 89-92
Kopff, E(dward) Christian 1946- 117
Kopit, Arthur (Lee) 1937- 81-84
See also DLB 7
See also CLC 1, 18, 33
See also AITN 1
Kopkind, Andrew D(avid) 1935- 29-32R
Koplin, H(arry) T(homas) 1923- 33-36R
Koplinka, Charlotte
See Lukas, Charlotte Koplinka
Koplitz, Eugene D(e Vere) 1928- 37-40R
Kopman, H(enri Marshall) 1918- 89-92
Kopp, Anatole 1915- CANR-12
Earlier sketch in CA 29-32R
Kopp, Harriet Green 41-44R
Kopp, O(swald) W. 1918- 33-36R
Kopp, Richard L. 1934- CANR-13
Earlier sketch in CA 33-36R
Kopp, Sheldon B(ernard) 1929- 37-40R
Kopp, William LaMarr 1930- 65-68
Koppel, Lillian 1926- 108
Koppel, Shelley R(uth) 1951- 108
Koppel, Ted 1940(?)- 103
Kopper, Edward A(nthony), Jr. 1937- CANR-15
Earlier sketch in CA 69-72
Kopper, Lisa (Esther) 1950- SATA-51
Kopper, Philip (Dana) 1937- 97-100
Kopperman, Paul Edward 1945- 69-72
Koppett, Leonard 1923- CANR-11
Earlier sketch in CA 25-28R
Koppitz, Elizabeth M(unsterberg)
1919-1983 .... CANR-14
Obituary 111
Earlier sketch in CA 13-14R
Koppman, Lionel 1920- CANR-6
Earlier sketch in CA 11-12R
Kops, Bernard 1926- 5-6R
See also DLB 13
See also CLC 4
Kopulos, Stella 1906- 49-52
Kopycinski, Joseph V(alentine) 1923- 33-36R
Korach, Mimi 1922- SATA-9
Koran, Dennis 1947- 120
Korb, Lawrence J(oseph) 1939- 77-80
Korbel, John 1918- 11-12R
Korbel, Josef 1909-1977 .... 37-40R
Obituary 73-76
Korbonski, Andrzej 1927- 9-10R
Korbonski, Stefan 1903- CANR-5
Earlier sketch in CA 5-6R
Korda, Michael Vincent 1933- 107
Kordel, Lelord 1904- 106
Koren, Edward 1935- CANR-11
Earlier sketch in CA 25-28R
See also SATA 5
Koren, Henry J(oseph) 1912- 9-10R
Korenbaum, Myrtle 1915- 57-60
Korenblit, Joan B(ravo) 1952- 113
Korey, William 1922- Brief entry 112
Korfker, Dena 1908- CANR-17
Earlier sketch in CA 3R
Korg, Jacob 1922- CANR-2
Earlier sketch in CA 5-6R
Korges, James 1930-1975 .... CAP-2
Earlier sketch in CA 25-28
Korinets, Iurii Iosifovich
See Korinetz, Yuri (Iosifovich)
Korinetz, Yuri (Iosifovich) 1923- CANR-11
Earlier sketch in CA 61-64
See also SATA 9
See also CLR 4
Korman, A. Gerd 1928- 53-56
Korman, Gordon 1963- 112
See also SATA 41, 49
Korman, Keith 1956- 102
Kormendi, Ferenc 1900-1972 Obituary 37-40R
Kormondy, Edward J(ohn) 1926- CANR-13
Earlier sketch in CA 33-36R
Korn, Alfons L(udwig) 1906-1986 93-96
Obituary 119
Korn, Bertram Wallace 1918-1979 .... CANR-1
Earlier sketch in CA 2R
Korn, Frank J(ames) 1935- 115
Korn, Henry James 1945- 69-72
Korn, Noel 1923- 73-76
Korn, Peggy
See Liss, Peggy K.
Korn, Walter 1908- 73-76
Kornai, J(anos) 1928- 13-14R
Kornblatt, Joyce Reiser 1944- 106
Kornbluh, Marvin 1927-1987 Obituary 124
Kornblum, Allan 1949- 69-72
Kornblum, Cinda 1950- 69-72
Kornblum, Sylvan 1927- 41-44R
Kornbluth, C(yril) M. 1923-1958
Brief entry 105
See also DLB 8
See also TCLC 8
Kornbluth, Jesse 1946- CANR-17
Earlier sketch in CA 25-28R
Korneichuk, Aleksandr Y. 1905-1972
Obituary 33-36R
Korner, Stephan
See Koerner, Stephan
Kornfeld, Anita Clay 1928- 97-100
Kornfeld, Robert J(onathan) 1919- 104
Kornhauser, David H(enry) 1918- CANR-14
Earlier sketch in CA 41-44R
Kornhauser, William 1925- 2R
Kornrich, Milton 1933- 19-20R
Korol, Alexander G. 1900- 7-8R
Korolenko, V. G.
See Korolenko, Vladimir Galaktionovich
Korolenko, Vladimir
See Korolenko, Vladimir Galaktionovich
Korolenko, Vladimir G.
See Korolenko, Vladimir Galaktionovich
Korolenko, Vladimir Galaktionovich
1853-1921 Brief entry 121
See also TCLC 22
Korotkin, Judith 1931- 53-56
Korr, Charles Paul 1939- 112
Kors, Alan Charles 1943- 77-80
Kort, Carol 1945- 106
Kort, Wesley A(lbert) 1935- 37-40R
Korte, Mary Norbert
See Koerte, Mary Norbert
Korten, David C(raig) 1937- CANR-15
Earlier sketch in CA 41-44R
Kortepeter, C(arl) Max 1928- CANR-26
Earlier sketch in CA 41-44R
Korth, Francis N(icholas) 1912- 25-28R
Kortner, Peter 1924- 33-36R
Korty, Carol 1937- 77-80
See also SATA 15
Korty, John Van Cleave 1936- 106
Kory, Robert B(ruce) 1950- 65-68
Korzenny, Felipe 1947- 116
Korzybski, Alfred (Habdank Skarbek)
1879-1950 Brief entry 123
Kos, Erih 1913- Brief entry 106
Kosa, John 1914-1972 .... 5-6R
Kosch, Erich
See Kos, Erih
Koschade, Alfred 1928- 21-22R
Kosel, Janice E. 1948- 116
Koshetz, Herbert 1907(?)-1977 Obituary 73-76
Koshi, George M. 1911- CAP-2
Earlier sketch in CA 29-32
Koshland, Ellen 1947- CANR-13
Earlier sketch in CA 33-36R
Kosinski, Jerzy (Nikodem) 1933- CANR-9
Earlier sketch in CA 17-18R
See also DLB 2
See also DLBY 82
See also CLC 1, 2, 3, 6, 10, 15
Kosinski, Leonard V. 1923- 25-28R
Koskoff, David E(lihu) 1939- 49-52
Koslow, Jules 1916- CANR-6
Earlier sketch in CA 3R
Kosmala, Hans 1904(?)-1981 Obituary 104
Kosof, Anna 1945- 85-88
Koss, Stephen E(dward) 1940-1984 .... 25-28R
Obituary 114
Kossez, Robes 1935- CANR-12
Earlier sketch in CA 29-32R
Kossin, Sandy (Sanford) 1926- SATA-10
Kosslyn, Stephen Michael 1948- 117
Kossmann, Rudolf R(ichard) 1934- 37-40R
Kossoff, David 1919- 61-64
Kost, Mary Lu 1924- 45-48
Kost, Robert John 1913- 3R
Kostash, Myrna 1944- 65-68
Koste, Robert Francis 1933- 81-84
Kostelanetz, Andre 1901-1980 Obituary 107
Kostelanetz, Richard C(ory) 1940- 15-16R
See also CLC 28
Kosten, Andrew 1921- 2R
Koster, Donald N(elson) 1910- 53-56
Koster, John (Peter, Jr.) 1945- CANR-5
Earlier sketch in CA 53-56
Koster, R(ichard) M(orton) 1934- 37-40R
Kostich, Dragos D. 1921- CANR-10
Earlier sketch in CA 5-6R
Kostis, Nicholas 103
Kostiuk, Hryhory 1902- 77-80
Kostka, Edmund Karl 1915- 17-18R
Kostrowitzki, Wilhelm Apollinaris de
1880-1918 Brief entry 104
Kostrubala, Thaddeus 1930- 101
Kostyu, Frank A(lexander) 1919- CANR-1
Earlier sketch in CA 49-52
Kosygin, Alexei Nikolayevich 1904-1980
Obituary 102
Kot, Stanislaw 1886(?)-1976 Obituary 65-68
Kotarba, Joseph A(nthony) 1947- 111
Kotarbinski, Tadeusz (Marian) 1886-1981
Obituary 105
Kotcheff, Ted
See Kotcheff, William Theodore
Kotcheff, William Theodore 1931- 115
Kothari, Rajni 1928- 33-36R
Kotin, Armine Avakian
See Mortimer, Armine Kotin
Kotker, Norman 1931- CANR-10
Earlier sketch in CA 25-28R
Kotker, Zane 1934- CANR-3
Earlier sketch in CA 49-52
Kotler, Milton 1935- CANR-25
Earlier sketch in CA 29-32R
Kotler, Philip 1931- CANR-13
Earlier sketch in CA 33-36R
Kotlowitz, Robert 1924- 33-36R
See also CLC 4
Kotowska, Monika 1942- 93-96
Kotowski, Joanne 1930- 57-60
Kotre, John N(icholas) 1940- 81-84
Kotrozo, Carol Donnell
See Donnell-Kotrozo, Carol
Kotschevar, Lendal H(enry) 1908- CANR-10
Earlier sketch in CA 19-20R
Kotschnig, Walter M(aria) 1901-1985
Obituary 117
Kotsilibas-Davis, James 1940- 106
Kotsuji, Abraham S(etsuzau) 1899-1973 .... CAP-1
Obituary 45-48
Earlier sketch in CA 15-16
Kott, Jan 1914- 13-14R
Kottler, Dorothy 1918- 97-100
Kottman, Richard N(orman) 1932- 25-28R
Kotz, David M(ichael) 1943- 81-84
Kotz, Mary Lynn 1936- 104
Kotz, Nick 1932- 29-32R
Kotz, Samuel 1930- CANR-7
Earlier sketch in CA 15-16R
Kotzin, Michael C(harles) 1941- 37-40R
Kotzwinkle, William 1938- CANR-3
Earlier sketch in CA 45-48
See also SATA 24
See also CLC 5, 14, 35
See also CLR 6
Koubourlis, Demetrius J(ohn) 1938- 57-60
Koufax, Sandy
See Koufax, Sanford
Koufax, Sanford 1935- 89-92
Kouhi, Elizabeth 1917- 126
See also SATA 49
Koulack, David 1938- 102
Koumoulides, John (Thomas Anastassios)
1938- 41-44R
Koupernik, Cyrille 1917- 57-60
Kourdakov, Sergei 1951-1973 Obituary 115
Kousoulas, D(imitrios) George 1923- 19-20R
Kousser, J(oseph) Morgan 1943- 57-60
Koutoukas, H. M. 1947- 69-72
Koutoukas, H.M.
See Rivoli, Mario

Kouts, Anne 1945- 29-32R
See also SATA 8
Kouts, Hertha Pretorius 1922-1973 2R
Obituary 103
Kouwenhoven, John A(tlee) 1909- 1R
Kouyoumdjian, Dikran
See Arlen, Michael
Kovach, Barbara L(usk) Forisha
See Forisha-Kovach, Barbara L(usk)
Kovach, Bill 1932- CANR-11
Earlier sketch in CA 69-72
Kovach, Francis J(oseph) 1918- 61-64
Kovacs, Alexander 1930(?)-1977
Obituary 73-76
Kovacs, Imre 1913-1980 23-24R
Obituary 102
Kovaleff, Theodore Philip 1943- 116
Kovalev, Mikhail A(leksandrovich)
1893-1981 Obituary 108
Kovalik, Nada 1926- 25-28R
Kovalik, Vladimir 1928- 25-28R
Kovarik, Bill
See Kovarik, William
Kovarik, William 1951- 113
Kovarsky, Irving 1918- 29-32R
Kovel, Joel S. 1936- CANR-14
Earlier sketch in CA 29-32R
Kovel, Ralph CANR-23
Earlier sketches in CA 17-18R, CANR-8
Kovel, Terry 1928- CANR-23
Earlier sketches in CA 17-18R, CANR-8
Kovner, Aba 1918-1987 Obituary 123
Kovner, B.
See Adler, Jacob
Kovrig, Bennett 1940- CANR-12
Earlier sketch in CA 29-32R
Kowalewski, David 1943- 112
Kowalski, Frank 1907- 37-40R
Kowet, Don 1937- CANR-10
Earlier sketch in CA 57-60
Kowit, Steve 1938- 118
Kowitt, Sylvia
See Crosbie, Sylvia Kowitt
Kowitz, Gerald T(homas) 1928- 33-36R
Kownslar, Allan O(wen) 1935- 61-64
Koyama, Kosuke 1929- CANR-7
Earlier sketch in CA 57-60
Koykka, Arthur S(idney) 1937- 116
Koyre, Alexandre 1892-1964 Obituary 111
Kozak, Jan B(lahoslav) 1889(?)-1974
Obituary 45-48
Kozak, Roman 1948(?)-1988 Obituary 126
Kozar, Andrew Joseph 1930- 103
Kozelka, Paul 1909- CAP-2
Earlier sketch in CA 25-28
Kozer, Jose 1940- CANR-2
Earlier sketch in CA 49-52
Kozicki, Henry 1924- 103
Kozicki, Richard J(oseph) 1929- 125
Brief entry 118
Koziebrodzki, Leopold B(olesta) 1906- 41-44R
Kozintsev, Grigori (Mikhailovich)
1905-1973 53-56
Kozlenko, William 1917- 57-60
Kozloff, Max 1933- Brief entry 114
Kozlow, Mark J.
See Newton, Michael
Kozlowski, Theodore T(homas) 1917- CANR-19
Earlier sketches in CA 9-10R, CANR-4
Kozol, Jonathan 1936- CANR-16
Earlier sketch in CA 61-64
See also CLC 17
Kozoll, Michael 1940?- CLC-35
Kozulin, Alex 1949- 122
Kpomassie, Tete-Michel 1941- 123
Kraay, Colin M(ackennal) 1918-1982
Obituary 116
Kracmar, John Z. 1916- 37-40R
Krader, Lawrence 1919- 21-22R
Kraditor, Aileen S. 1928- 15-16R
Kraehe, Enno E(dward) 1921- 9-10R
Kraemer, Kenneth L(eo) 1936- 111
Kraemer, Richard H(oward) 1920- CANR-4
Earlier sketch in CA 53-56
Kraenzel, Carl F(rederick) 1906- 73-76
Kraenzel, Margaret (Powell) 1899- 4R
Kraf, Elaine 1946- CANR-11
Earlier sketch in CA 65-68
See also DLBY 81
Krafft, C(onrad) James 1923- 119
Krafft, Jim
See Krafft, C(onrad) James
Krafft, Maurice 1946- CANR-10
Earlier sketch in CA 65-68
Krafsur, Richard Paul 1940- 103
Kraft, Barbara 1939- 97-100
Kraft, Betsy Harvey 1937- 89-92
Kraft, Charles H(oward) 1932- CANR-16
Earlier sketches in CA 45-48, CANR-1
Kraft, Charlotte 1922- 103
Kraft, Dean 1950- 114
Kraft, Eric (Lance) 1944- 118
Kraft, Hy(man Solomon) 1899-1975 41-44R
Obituary 57-60
Kraft, Joseph 1924-1986 9-10R
Obituary 118
Kraft, Ken(neth) 1907- CANR-1
Earlier sketch in CA 4R
Kraft, Kenneth H., Sr. 1896-1983
Obituary 111
Kraft, Leo 1922- 41-44R
Kraft, Leonard E(dward) 1923- 29-32R
Kraft, Robert Alan 1934- 37-40R
Kraft, Stephanie (Barlett) 1944- 105
Kraft, Virginia 1932- 21-22R
Kraft, Walter Andreas
See Friedlander, Walter A(ndreas)
Kraft, William F. 1938- 33-36R
Kragen, Jinx
See Morgan, Judith A(dams)
Krahn, Fernando 1935- CANR-11
Earlier sketch in CA 65-68
See also SATA 31, 49
See also CLR 3
Kraig, Bruce 1939- CANR-18
Earlier sketch in CA 102
Krailsheimer, Alban John 1921- CANR-2
Earlier sketch in CA 5-6R
Kraines, Oscar 1916- 97-100
Kraines, Samuel H(enry) 1906- 77-80
Krajenke, Robert William 1939- 29-32R
Krajewski, Frank R. 1938- CANR-10
Earlier sketch in CA 65-68
Krajewski, Robert J(oseph) 1940- 97-100
Krakel, Dean Fenton 1923- 45-48
Krakowski, Lili 1930- 85-88
Kramarz, Joachim 1931- 25-28R
Kramer, A(lfred) T(heodore) 1892- CAP-1
Earlier sketch in CA 11-12
Kramer, Aaron 1921- CANR-12
Earlier sketch in CA 23-24R
Kramer, Anthony SATA-42
Kramer, Bernard M(ordecai) 1923- 77-80
Kramer, Charles 1915-1988 Obituary 125
Kramer, Dale 1936- CANR-5
Earlier sketch in CA 53-56
Kramer, Daniel C(aleb) 1934- 53-56
Kramer, Edith 1916- 33-36R
Kramer, Edna E.
See Kramer-Lassar, Edna Ernestine
Kramer, Eugene F(rancis) 1921- 37-40R
Kramer, Frank Raymond 1908- CAP-1
Earlier sketch in CA 11-12
Kramer, Gene 1927- 69-72
Kramer, George
See Heuman, William
Kramer, Hilton 1928- 113
Brief entry 109
Kramer, Jack 1923- 41-44R
Kramer, Jane 1938- 102
Kramer, Joel (Herbert) 1937- 97-100
Kramer, John Eichholtz, Jr. 1935- 108
Kramer, Jonathan M. 1946- 121
Kramer, Judith Rita 1933-1970 3R
Obituary 103
Kramer, Kathryn 19(?)- CLC-34
Kramer, Larry 1935- 126
Brief entry 124
See also CLC 42
Kramer, Lawrence (Eliot) 1946- 120
Kramer, Leonie Judith 1924- CANR-17
Earlier sketch in CA 81-84
Kramer, Mark (William) 1944- CANR-17
Earlier sketch in CA 97-100
Kramer, Milton D. 1915-1973 Obituary 37-40R
Kramer, Nancy 1942- 101
Kramer, Nora 1896(?)-1984 107
Obituary 113
See also SATA 26, 39
Kramer, (Simon) Paul 1914- 21-22R
Kramer, Paul J(ackson) 1904- CANR-1
Earlier sketch in CA 45-48
Kramer, Rita 1929- 69-72
Kramer, Roberta 1935- 103
Kramer, Roland Laird 1898- 7-8R
Kramer, Samuel Noah 1897- 11-12R
Kramer, Ted
See Steward, Samuel M(orris)
Kramer, Victor A. 1939- CANR-16
Earlier sketch in CA 85-88
Kramer-Lassar, Edna Ernestine 1902-1984 107
Obituary 113
Kramish, Arnold 1923- CANR-7
Earlier sketch in CA 7-8R
Krammer, Arnold Paul 1941- CANR-11
Earlier sketch in CA 61-64
Kramon, Florence 1920- 25-28R
Kramrisch, Stella 1898- CAP-2
Earlier sketch in CA 21-22
Kranidas, Kathleen
See Collins, Kathleen
Krantz, Hazel Newman 1920- CANR-16
Earlier sketches in CA 3R, CANR-1
See also SATA 12
Krantz, Judith 1927- CANR-11
Earlier sketch in CA 81-84
Krantz, Les(lie Jay) 1945- 120
Kranz, E(dwin) Kirker 1949- 33-36R
Kranz, Stewart D(uane) 1924- 101
Kranzberg, Melvin 1917- CANR-11
Earlier sketch in CA 21-22R
Kranzler, David 1930- 93-96
Kranzler, George G(ershon) 1916- CANR-12
Earlier sketch in CA 57-60
See also SATA 28
Kranzler, Gershon
See Kranzler, George G(ershon)
Krapf, Norbert 1943- 117
Krapp, R. M.
See Adams, Robert Martin
Krar, Stephen Frank 1924- CANR-20
Earlier sketches in CA 53-56, CANR-4
Kraselchik, R.
See Dyer, Charles (Raymond)
Krasilovsky, M(arvin) William 1926- 61-64
Krasilovsky, Phyllis 1926- CANR-11
Earlier sketch in CA 29-32R
See also SATA 1, 38
See also SAAS 5
Kraske, Robert Brief entry 116
See also SATA 36
Kraslow, David 1926- 29-32R
Krasna, Norman 1909-1984 Obituary 114
See also DLB 26
Krasne, Betty
See Levine, Betty K(rasne)
Krasner, Jack Daniel 1921-1978 CANR-3
Earlier sketch in CA 49-52
Krasner, Leonard 1924- 33-36R
Krasner, Stephen D(avid) 1942- CANR-15
Earlier sketch in CA 85-88
Krasner, William 1917- CANR-15
Earlier sketch in CA 37-40R
Krasney, Samuel A. 1922- 2R
Krasnow, Erwin G(ilbert) 1936- 103
Krasovskaya, Vera 1915- Brief entry 106
Krass, Alfred C(harles) 1936- 116
Krasser, Wilhelm 1925(?)-1979 Obituary 89-92
Krassner, Paul 1932- CANR-11
Earlier sketch in CA 21-22R
Krasso, Miklos 1929(?)-1986 Obituary 118
Kratcoski, Peter C(harles) 1936- 111
Kratochvil, Paul 1932- 25-28R
Kratos
See Power, Norman S(andiford)
Kratovil, Robert 1910- CANR-5
Earlier sketch in CA 5-6R
Kratzenstein, Jossef J. 1904- CAP-2
Earlier sketch in CA 17-18
Krauch, Velma 1916- 37-40R
Kraues, Judith E. 101
Kraus, Albert L(awson) 1920- 41-44R
Kraus, Barbara 1929-1977 102
Kraus, Bruce R. 1954- 97-100
Kraus, C(lyde) Norman 1924- CANR-15
Earlier sketch in CA 41-44R
Kraus, Charles E. 1946- 111
Kraus, George 1930- 25-28R
Kraus, Hans P(eter) 1907- CAP-2
Earlier sketch in CA 29-32
Kraus, Joanna Halpert 1937- CANR-21
Earlier sketch in CA 104
Kraus, Joe 1939- CANR-15
Earlier sketch in CA 89-92
Kraus, Joseph 1925- CANR-4
Earlier sketch in CA 53-56
Kraus, Karl 1874-1936 Brief entry 104
See also TCLC 5
Kraus, Michael 1901- 5-6R
Kraus, Richard G(ordon) 1923- CANR-11
Earlier sketch in CA 13-14R
Kraus, Robert 1925- 33-36R
See also SATA 4
Kraus, Sidney 1927- CANR-10
Earlier sketch in CA 7-8R
Kraus, W. Keith 1934- 21-22R
Krause, Frank H(arold) 1942- 104
Krause, Harry D(ieter) 1932- 33-36R
Krause, Herbert 1905-1976 49-52
Obituary 103
Krause, Lawrence Berle 1929- 113
Krause, Pat 1930- 114
Krause, Sydney J(oseph) 1925- 21-22R
Krause, Walter 1917- CANR-1
Earlier sketch in CA 2R
Kraushaar, John L. 1917- 45-48
Kraushaar, Otto F(rederick) 1901- 37-40R
Krauskopf, Konrad B(ates) 1910- 77-80
Krauss, Bob
See Krauss, Robert G.
Krauss, Bruno
See Bulmer, (Henry) Kenneth
Krauss, Ellis S(aunders) 1944- CANR-8
Earlier sketch in CA 61-64
Krauss, Herbert Harris 1940- 85-88
Krauss, Paul Gerhardt 1905- 3R
Krauss, Robert G. 1924- CANR-2
Earlier sketch in CA 1R
Krauss, Robert M. 1931- 17-18R
Krauss, Rosalind E(pstein) 1940- 81-84
Krauss, Ruth (Ida) 1911- CANR-13
Earlier sketches in CA 3R, CANR-1
See also SATA 1, 30
See also DLB 52
Krausz, Ernest 1931- 104
Krausz, Michael 1942- CANR-4
Earlier sketch in CA 53-56
Krausz, Norman G(eorge) P(hilip) 1920- 41-44R
Kraut, Benny 1947- 113
Krauthammer, Charles 1950- Brief entry 121
Krautheimer, Richard 1897- 103
Krautter, Elisa (Bialk) CANR-1
Earlier sketch in CA 1R
See also SATA 1
Krauze, Andrzej 1947- SATA-46
Krauzer, Steven M(ark) 1948- CANR-25
Earlier sketch in CA 109
Kravetz, Nathan 1921- 11-12R
Kravis, Irving B(ernard) 1916- CANR-7
Earlier sketch in CA 17-18R
Kravitz, Nathan
See Kravitz, Nathaniel
Kravitz, Nathaniel 1905- 49-52
Krawiec, Richard 1952- 122
Krawiec, T(heophile) S(tanley) 1913- CANR-10
Earlier sketch in CA 25-28R
Krawitz, Henry 1947- 45-48
Krawitz, Herman E(verett) 1925- 61-64
Krawitz, Ruth (Lifshitz) 1929- 9-10R
Kraybill, Donald B(rubaker) 1945- 69-72
Krebs, Alfred H. 1920- 23-24R
Krebs, Hans (Adolf) 1900-1981 Obituary 108
Krech, David 1909-1977 Obituary 73-76
Krech, Shepard III 1944- 119
Kredel, Fritz 1900-1973 Obituary 41-44R
See also SATA 17
Kredenser, Gail 1936- 21-22R
Kreeft, Peter 1937- CANR-14
Earlier sketch in CA 81-84
Krefetz, Gerald 1932- CANR-15
Earlier sketch in CA 33-36R
Krefetz, Ruth 1931-1972 CAP-2
Obituary 37-40R
Earlier sketch in CA 33-36
Kregel, J(an) A(llen) 1944- 41-44R
Kreh, Bernard 1925- 57-60
Kreider, Barbara 1942- 41-44R
Kreider, Carl 1914- 37-40R
Kreider, Jan F(rederick) 1942- 111
Kreidl, John Francis 1939- 81-84
Kreig, Margaret B. (Baltzell) 1922- 13-14R
Krein, David F(rederick) 1942- 85-88
Kreindler, Lee (Stanley) 1924- 17-18R
Kreingold, Shana 1889(?)-1972
Obituary 37-40R
Kreinin, Mordechai 1930- 9-10R
Kreisel, Henry 1922- 61-64
Kreiser, B(ernard) Robert 1943- 116
Kreisler, Fritz 1875-1962 Obituary 115
Kreisman, Leonard T(heodore) 1925- 15-16R
Kreisman, Marvin 1933(?)-1979(?)
Obituary 102
Kreitler, Hans 1916- 45-48
Kreitler, Shulamith 1938- 45-48
Krejci, Jaroslav 1916- CANR-14
Earlier sketch in CA 41-44R
Kremen, Bennett 1936- 57-60
Kremenliev, Boris A(ngeloff) 1911-1988 45-48
Obituary 125
Krementz, Jill 1940- CANR-23
Earlier sketch in CA 41-44R
See also SATA 17
See also CLR 5
See also AITN 1, 2
Kremer, Laura Evelyn 1921- 103
Kremer, William F. 1919- 69-72
Kreml, Anne Lee 1930- 21-22R
Krempel, Daniel S(partakus) 1926- 33-36R
Kren, George M. 1926- 102
Krenek, Ernst 1900- 57-60
Krenkel, John H(enry) 1906- CAP-2
Earlier sketch in CA 33-36
Krensky, Stephen (Alan) 1953- CANR-13
Earlier sketch in CA 73-76
See also SATA 41, 47
Krentel, Mildred White 1921- 5-6R
Krents, Harold Eliot 1944-1987 37-40R
Obituary 121
Krentz, Edgar (Martin) 1928- 23-24R
Krepps, Robert W(ilson) 1919-1980 CANR-1
Earlier sketch in CA 1R
Kresge, George Joseph, Jr.
See Kreskin
Kresh, Paul 1919- CANR-13
Earlier sketch in CA 15-16R
Kreskin 1935- 101
Kress, Nancy 1948- 126
Kress, Paul F(rederick) 1935- 29-32R
Kress, Robert (Lee) 1932- CANR-8
Earlier sketch in CA 61-64
Kress, Roy A(lfred) 1916- 107
Kress, Stephen W. 1945- 122
Kressel, Kenneth 1942- 119
Kressy, Michael 1936- CANR-8
Earlier sketch in CA 61-64
Kretsch, Robert W. 1913(?)-1979
Obituary 89-92
Kretzmann, Adalbert Raphael 1903- CAP-1
Earlier sketch in CA 15-16
Kretzmann, Norman 1928- 49-52
Kretzmer, Herbert 1925- 105
Kreuder, Ernst 1903-1972 DLB-69
Kreuger, Miles 1934- 81-84
Kreusler, Abraham A(rthur) 1897- 65-68
Kreuter, Kent 1932- 29-32R
Kreuzer, James R. 1913-1971 CAP-1
Earlier sketch in CA 11-12
Kreve (Mickevicius), Vincas 1882-1954 TCLC-27
Krevitsky, Nathan I. 1914- 9-10R
Krevitsky, Nik
See Krevitsky, Nathan I.
Krevolin, Nathan 1927- CANR-14
Earlier sketch in CA 41-44R
Krewer, Semyon E(fimovich) 1915- 105
Kreyche, Gerald F. 1927- 37-40R
Kreyche, Robert J. 1920- 13-14R
Kreymborg, Alfred 1883-1966 Obituary 25-28R
See also DLB 4, 54
Krich, A. M.
See Krich, Aron
Krich, Aron 1916- 120
Krich, Aron M.
See Krich, Aron
Krich, John 1951- 108
Krieg, Saul 1917- 81-84
Kriegel, Gail 1942- 108
Kriegel, Harriet 104
Kriegel, Leonard 1933- CANR-12
Earlier sketch in CA 33-36R
Krieger, Leonard 1918- CANR-7
Earlier sketch in CA 17-18R
Krieger, Murray 1923- CANR-2
Earlier sketch in CA 3R
See also DLB 67
Krieghbaum, Hillier (Hiram) 1902- CANR-2
Earlier sketch in CA 5-6R
Kriegman, Oscar M(arvin) 1930- 9-10R
Kriensky, Morris (Edward) 1917- 57-60
Krier, James E(dward) 1939- 81-84
Kriesberg, Louis 1926- CANR-12
Earlier sketch in CA 29-32R
Krikorian, Yervant H(ovhannes)
1892-1977 CANR-2
Obituary 73-76
Earlier sketch in CA 45-48
Krim, Seymour 1922- CANR-4
Earlier sketch in CA 7-8R
See also DLB 16

Krimerman, Leonard Isaiah 1934- ... 17-18R
Krims, Milton Robert 1904(?)-1988
Obituary ... 126
Krimsky, Joseph (Hayylm) 1883(?)-1971
Obituary ... 104
Krimsky, Sheldon 1941- ... 113
Kring, Hilda Adam 1921- ... 77-80
Kring, Walter Donald 1916- ... 116
Krinsky, Carol Herselle 1937- ... 37-40R
Kripalani, J(iwatram) B(hagwandas)
1888-1982 Obituary ... 110
Kripke, Dorothy Karp ... 19-20R
See also SATA 30
Krippendorff, Klaus 1932- ... 77-80
Krippner, Stanley (Curtis) 1932- ... CANR-15
Earlier sketch in CA 81-84
Krisch, Henry 1931- Brief entry ... 111
Krise, Raymond (Owens, Jr.) 1949- ... 109
Krisher, Bernard 1931- ... CANR-18
Earlier sketch in CA 77-80
Krishna, Gopi
See Shivpuri, Gopi Krishna
Krishnamurti, Jiddu 1895-1986 ... CANR-11
Obituary ... 118
Earlier sketch in CA 61-64
Krislov, Alexander
See Lee Howard, Leon Alexander
Krislov, Joseph 1927- ... 41-44R
Krislov, Samuel 1929- ... CANR-18
Earlier sketches in CA 9-10R, CANR-3
Krispyn, Egbert 1930- ... 15-16R
Kriss, Ronald P(aul) 1934- ... 69-72
Kristein, Marvin M(ichael) 1926- ... 29-32R
Kristeller, Paul Oskar 1905- ... CANR-6
Earlier sketch in CA 9-10R
Kristian, Hans
See Neerskov, Hans Kristian
Kristof, Jane 1932- ... 29-32R
See also SATA 8
Kristof, Ladis K(ris) D(onabed) 1918- ... 61-64
Kristof, Nicholas D(onabet) 1959- ... 126
Kristofferson, Kris 1936- ... 104
See also CLC 26
Kristol, Irving 1920- ... 25-28R
Kritsick, Stephen M(ark) 1951- ... 112
Kritzeck, James 1930- ... 5-6R
Krizay, John 1926- ... 61-64
Krleza, Miroslav 1893-1981 ... 97-100
Obituary ... 105
See also CLC 8
Krmpotic, Vesna 1932- ... CANR-20
Earlier sketch in CA 102
Kroc, Ray(mond Albert) 1902-1984 ... 118
Obituary ... 111
Kroch, Adolph A. 1882-1978 Obituary ... 81-84
Krochmal, Arnold 1919- ... CANR-14
Earlier sketch in CA 69-72
Krochmal, Connie 1949- ... 41-44R
Krock, Arthur 1887-1974 ... CAP-2
Obituary ... 49-52
Earlier sketch in CA 33-36
See also DLB 29
See also AITN 1
Krodel, Gerhard 1926- ... 61-64
Kroeber, A(lfred) L(ouis) 1876-1960
Obituary ... 110
Kroeber, Clifton B(rown) 1921- ... 110
Kroeber, Donald W(alter) 1934- ... 115
Kroeber, Karl 1926- ... 57-60
Kroeber, Theodora (Kracaw) 1897-1979 ... CANR-5
Obituary ... 89-92
Earlier sketch in CA 5-6R
See also SATA 1
Kroeber-Quinn, Theodora
See Kroeber, Theodora (Kracaw)
Kroeger, Arthur 1908- ... 15-16R
Kroeger, Frederick P(aul) 1921- ... 33-36R
Kroepcke, Karol
See Krolow, Karl (Gustav Heinrich)
Kroetsch, Robert 1927- ... CANR-8
Earlier sketch in CA 19-20R
See also DLB 53
See also CLC 5, 23
Kroetz, Franz Xaver 1946- ... CLC-41
Kroger, William S. 1906- ... CAP-1
Earlier sketch in CA 13-14
Krohn, Ernst C(hristopher) 1888-1975 ... 37-40R
See also AITN 1
Krohn, Norman Odya 1920- ... 116
Krohn, Robert 1937- ... 45-48
Kroll, Burt
See Rowland, D(onald) S(ydney)
Kroll, Ernest 1914- ... 97-100
Kroll, Francis Lynde 1904-1973 ... CAP-1
Earlier sketch in CA 15-16
See also SATA 10
Kroll, John (Leon) 1925-1986 Obituary ... 119
Kroll, Judith 1943- ... 65-68
Kroll, Morton 1923- ... 49-52
Kroll, Steven 1941- ... CANR-25
Earlier sketches in CA 65-68, CANR-9
See also SATA 19
Krolow, Karl (Gustav Heinrich) 1915- ... 81-84
Kromer, Helen ... 93-96
Kromminga, John H(enry) 1918- ... 77-80
Kronegger, Maria Elisabeth 1932- ... 25-28R
Kronenberg, Henry Harold 1902- ... 1R
Kronenberg, Maria Elizabeth 1881(?)-1970
Obituary ... 104
Kronenberger, Louis 1904-1980 ... CANR-2
Obituary ... 97-100
Earlier sketch in CA 4R
Kroner, Richard 1884- ... 9-10R
Kronhausen, Eberhard W(ilhelm) 1915- ... CANR-6
Earlier sketch in CA 11-12R
Kronhausen, Phyllis C(armen) 1929- ... CANR-6
Earlier sketch in CA 11-12R
Kronick, David A(braham) 1917- ... 11-12R
Kronick, Joseph G. 1953- ... 122
Kroninger, Robert H(enry) 1923- ... 15-16R
Kronk, Gary (Wayne) 1956- ... 115
Kronman, Anthony T(ownsend) 1945- ... 113
Kronstadt, Henry L(ippin) 1915- ... 73-76
Kronus, Sidney J., Jr. 1937- Brief entry ... 107
Krook, Dorothea 1920- ... 123
Krooss, Herman E. 1912-1975 ... CAP-2
Obituary ... 57-60
Earlier sketch in CA 17-18
Kropf, Linda S(toddart) 1947- ... 49-52
Kropf, Richard W(illiam Bartlett)
1932- ... CANR-10
Earlier sketch in CA 65-68
Kropotkin, Peter (Aleksieevich) 1842-1921
Brief entry ... 119
Kropp, Lloyd ... 25-28R
Kropp, Paul (Stephan) 1948- ... 112
See also SATA 34, 38
Krosby, H(ans) Peter 1929- ... 89-92
Krosney, Mary Stewart 1939- ... 19-20R
Krotki, Karol J(ozef) 1922- ... 41-44R
Krotkov, Yuri 1917- ... 102
See also CLC 19
Krout, John Allen 1896-1979 ... 97-100
Obituary ... 85-88
Kruchkow, Diane 1947- ... 69-72
Kruck, William E(vert) 1942- ... 114
Krueger, Anne O. 1934- ... CANR-15
Earlier sketch in CA 37-40R
Krueger, Christoph 1937- ... 33-36R
Krueger, Hardy 1928- ... 77-80
Krueger, John R(ichard) 1927- ... CANR-10
Earlier sketch in CA 21-22R
Krueger, Ralph R. 1927- ... CANR-2
Earlier sketch in CA 49-52
Krueger, Robert B(lair) 1928- ... 57-60
Krueger, Thomas A. 1936- ... 21-22R
Kruess, James 1926- ... CANR-5
Earlier sketch in CA 53-56
See also SATA 8
See also CLR 9
Krug, Edward August 1911-1980 ... CANR-4
Earlier sketch in CA 5-6R
Krug, Mark M. 1915- Brief entry ... 109
Krug, Samuel E(dward) 1943- ... 121
Kruger, Arthur N(ewman) 1916- ... CANR-1
Earlier sketch in CA 2R
Kruger, Daniel H(erschel) 1922- ... 25-28R
Kruger, Hardy
See Krueger, Hardy
Kruger, Mollee (Coppel) 1929- ... CANR-21
Earlier sketch in CA 69-72
Kruger, Paul
See Sebenthal, R(oberta) E(lizabeth)
Kruger, (Charles) Rayne ... 7-8R
Kruglak, Haym 1909- ... 53-56
Kruise, Carol Sue 1939- ... 125
Krukowski, Lucian 1929- ... 125
Krulewitch, Melvin Levin 1895-1978 ... 103
Krulik, Stephen 1933- ... CANR-8
Earlier sketch in CA 17-18R
Krull, Felix
See White, Stanley
Krull, Kathleen 1952- ... 106
See also SATA 39, 52
Krumb
See Crumb, R(obert)
Krumboltz, John D(wight) 1928-
Brief entry ... 110
Krumgold, Joseph (Quincy) 1908-1980 ... CANR-7
Obituary ... 101
Earlier sketch in CA 11-12R
See also SATA 1, 23, 48
See also CLC 12
Krumm, John McGill 1913- ... 109
Krummel, Donald William 1929- ... 106
Krumpelmann, John T(heodore) 1892- ... 41-44R
Krumwitz
See Crumb, R(obert)
Krupat, Arnold 1941- ... 126
Krupat, Edward 1945- ... 77-80
Krupnik, Baruch
See Karu, Baruch
Krupp, E(dwin) C(harles) 1944- ... CANR-21
Earlier sketch in CA 105
See also SATA 53
Krupp, Nate 1935- ... CANR-10
Earlier sketch in CA 21-22R
Krupp, Robin Rector 1946- ... SATA-53
Krupp, Sherman Roy 1926-1988 ... 3R
Obituary ... 125
Krusch, Werner E. 1927- ... 7-8R
Kruschke, Earl R(oger) 1934- ... 41-44R
Kruse, Alexander Z. 1888(?)-1972
Obituary ... 33-36R
Kruse, Harry D(ayton) 1900-1977
Obituary ... 73-76
Kruse, John 1919- ... 114
Krush, Beth 1918- ... SATA-18
Krush, Joe 1918- ... SATA-18
Krusich, Walter S(teve) 1922- ... 49-52
Kruskal, William H(enry) 1919- ... 33-36R
Kruss, James
See Kruess, James
See also CLR 9
Kruszewski, Z. Anthony 1928- Brief entry ... 113
Krutch, Joseph Wood 1893-1970 ... CANR-4
Obituary ... 25-28R
Earlier sketch in CA 2R
See also DLB 63
See also CLC 24
Krutilla, John Vasil 1922- ... CANR-9
Earlier sketch in CA 23-24R
Krutzch, Gus
See Eliot, T(homas) S(tearns)
Kruuk, Hans 1937- ... 61-64
Kruzas, Anthony T(homas) 1914- ... CANR-17
Earlier sketches in CA 1R, CANR-2
Krymow, Virginia P(auline) 1930- ... 69-72
Krypton
See Graham, Lloyd M.
Krysl, Marilyn 1943- ... 105
Krythe, Maymie Richardson ... 19-20R
Krzywan, Jozef
See Krotki, Karol J(ozef)
Krzyzaniak, Marian 1911- ... 11-12R
Krzyzanowski, Jerzy R(oman) 1922- ... 37-40R
Krzyzanowski, Ludwik 1907(?)-1986
Obituary ... 118
Kselman, Thomas A. 1948- ... 110
K-Turkel, Judi 1934- ... CANR-8
Earlier sketch in CA 61-64
Kubal, David L(awrence) 1936- ... 45-48
Kubat, Daniel 1928- Brief entry ... 114
Kubeck, James (Ernest) 1920- ... 17-18R
Kubek, Anthony 1920- ... 104
Kubelka, Susanna 1942- ... 113
Kube-McDowell, Michael P(aul) 1954- ... 119
Kubiak, T(imothy) J(ames) 1942- ... 61-64
Kubiak, William J. 1929- ... 33-36R
Kubicek, Robert V(incent) 1935- ... 29-32R
Kubie, Eleanor Gottheil 1899-1988 ... 7-8R
Obituary ... 126
See also SATA 39
Kubie, Lawrence S. 1896(?)-1973
Obituary ... 45-48
Kubie, Nora Benjamin
See Kubie, Eleanor Gottheil
Kubin, Alfred 1877-1959 Brief entry ... 112
See also TCLC 23
Kubinyi, Laszlo 1937- ... 85-88
See also SATA 17
Kubis, Pat 1928- ... 25-28R
Kubler, George (Alexander) 1912- ... 11-12R
Kubler-Ross, Elisabeth
See Kuebler-Ross, Elisabeth
Kublin, Hyman 1919- ... 9-10R
Kubly, Herbert (Oswald Nicholas)
1915- ... CANR-4
Earlier sketch in CA 7-8R
Kubo, Sakae 1926- ... CANR-7
Earlier sketch in CA 57-60
Kubose, Gyomay M(asao) 1905- ... 49-52
Kubota, Akira 1932- ... 37-40R
Kubrick, Stanley 1928- ... 81-84
See also DLB 26
See also CLC 16
Kucera, Henry 1925- ... 21-22R
Kucharek, Casimir (Anthony) 1928- ... 57-60
Kucharski, Kasimir
See Koch, Kurt E(mil)
Kucharsky, David (Eugene) 1931- ... 65-68
Kucherov, Alexander 1927-1985 Obituary ... 117
Kucich, John (Richard) 1952- ... 112
Kuczkir, Mary 1933- ... 115
Brief entry ... 111
Kuczynski, Pedro-Pablo 1938- ... 77-80
Kudian, Mischa ... 107
Kudrle, Robert Thomas 1942- ... 112
Kuebler-Ross, Elisabeth 1926- ... 25-28R
Kuehl, John 1928- ... 21-22R
Kuehl, Linda 1939(?)-1978 Obituary ... 104
Kuehl, Warren F(rederick) 1924- ... CANR-7
Earlier sketch in CA 17-18R
Kuehn, Dorothy Dalton
See Dalton, Dorothy
Kuehn, Thomas James 1950- ... 116
Kuehnelt-Leddihn, Erik (Maria) Ritter von
1909- ... CANR-20
Earlier sketches in CA 9-10R, CANR-3
Kuemmerly, Walter 1903- ... 49-52
Kuen, Alfred (F.) 1921- ... CANR-25
Earlier sketch in CA 107
Kuenan, Philip Henry 1902-1976 Obituary ... 116
Kueng, Hans 1928- ... 53-56
Kuenne, Robert E(ugene) 1924- ... 5-6R
Kuenstler, Morton 1927- ... SATA-10
Kuenzli, Alfred E(ugene) 1923- ... 17-18R
Kuesel, Harry N. 1892(?)-1977 Obituary ... 73-76
Kuester, David 1938- ... 53-56
Kuether, Edith Lyman 1915- ... 49-52
Kufeldt, George 1923- ... 37-40R
Kuffler, Stephen 1913-1980 Obituary ... 105
Kufner, Herbert L(eopold) 1927- ... 7-8R
Kugel, James 1945- ... 29-32R
Kugelman, Richard 1908- ... 41-44R
Kugelmass, J. Alvin 1910-1972 ... CANR-4
Obituary ... 33-36R
Earlier sketch in CA 7-8R
Kuh, Charlotte 1892(?)-1985 Obituary ... 115
See also SATA 43
Kuh, Edwin 1925-1986 ... 23-24R
Obituary ... 119
Kuh, Frederick Robert 1895-1978
Obituary ... 89-92
Kuh, Katharine W. 1904- ... 13-14R
Kuh, Richard H. 1921- ... 23-24R
Kuhatschek, Jack 1949- ... 122
Kuhl, Ernest Peter 1881- ... 41-44R
Kuhlken, Ken(neth Wayne) 1945- ... 102
Kuhlman, James A(llen) 1941- ... 85-88
Kuhlman, John M(elville) 1923- ... 17-18R
Kuhlman, Kathryn 1910(?)-1976 ... CANR-12
Obituary ... 65-68
Earlier sketch in CA 57-60
Kuhlmann, Susan 1942- ... 85-88
Kuhn, Alfred 1914- ... CANR-3
Earlier sketch in CA 11-12R
Kuhn, Annette 1945- ... 111
Kuhn, Bowie (Kent) 1926- ... 126
Kuhn, Edward, Jr. 1924(?)-1979 ... 102
Obituary ... 93-96
Kuhn, Ferdinand 1905-1978 ... 5-6R
Obituary ... 81-84
Kuhn, Harold B(arnes) 1911- ... 49-52
Kuhn, Irene Corbally ... CAP-1
Earlier sketch in CA 9-10
Kuhn, Karl F(rancis) 1939- ... 65-68
Kuhn, Maggie
See Kuhn, Margaret E.
Kuhn, Margaret E. 1905- Brief entry ... 109
Kuhn, Martin A(rno) 1924- ... 9-10R
Kuhn, Reinhard 1930- ... 45-48
Kuhn, Thomas S(amuel) 1922- ... CANR-11
Earlier sketch in CA 21-22R
Kuhn, Tillo E. 1919- ... 5-6R
Kuhn, William Ernst 1922- ... 37-40R
Kuhn, Wolfgang Erasmus 1914- ... 5-6R
Kuhne, Cecil 1952- ... 93-96
Kuhne, Marie (Ahnighito Peary)
1893-1978 Obituary ... 77-80
Kuhner, Herbert 1935- ... 25-28R
Kuhns, Dennis R(ay) 1947- ... 113
Kuhns, Dorothy
See Heyward, Dorothy (Hartzell Kuhns)
Kuhns, Grant (Wilson) 1929- ... 9-10R
Kuhns, Richard (Francis, Jr.) 1924- ... 37-40R
Kuhns, William 1943- ... 23-24R
Kuhse, Helga 1940- ... 122
Kuic, Vukan 1923- ... 37-40R
Kuiper, Gerard Peter 1905-1973 ... CAP-2
Obituary ... 45-48
Earlier sketch in CA 17-18
Kuisel, Richard F(rancis) 1935- ... 23-24R
Kuist, J(ames) M(arquis) 1935- ... 124
Kuitert, H(arminus) Martinus 1924- ... 25-28R
Kujawa, Duane 1938- ... 33-36R
Kujoth, Jean Spealman 1935-1975 ... CAP-2
Earlier sketch in CA 25-28
See also SATA 30
Kukla, Robert J(ohn) 1932- ... 49-52
Kuklick, Bruce 1941- ... 41-44R
Kuleshov, Arkady A. 1914-1978 Obituary ... 77-80
Kulick, John
See Pinchot, Ann (Kramer)
Kulkarni, Hemant B(alvantrao) 1916- ... CANR-1
Earlier sketch in CA 45-48
Kulkarni, R(amchandra) G(anesh) 1931- ... 29-32R
Kulkarni, Venkatesh S(rinivas) 1945- ... 113
Kulkin, Mary-Ellen
See Siegel, Mary-Ellen Kulkin
Kullman, Harry 1919-1982 ... 93-96
See also SATA 35
Kulshrestha, Chirantan 1946- ... 107
Kulski, Julian (Eugeniusz) 1929- ... CANR-14
Earlier sketch in CA 21-22R
Kulski, Wladyslaw W(szebor) 1903- ... 5-6R
Kulstein, David J. 1916-1974 ... CAP-2
Earlier sketch in CA 25-28
Kultermann, Udo 1927- ... 85-88
Kulukundis, Elias 1937- ... 21-22R
Kumar, Krishna 1942- ... 109
Kumar, Satish 1933- ... 112
Kumar, Shiv K(umar) 1921- ... CANR-7
Earlier sketch in CA 9-10R
Kumbel,
See Hein, Piet
Kumin, Maxine (Winokur) 1925- ... CANR-21
Earlier sketches in CA 2R, CANR-1
See also SATA 12
See also DLB 5
See also CLC 5, 13, 28
See also AITN 2
Kummel, Bernhard 1919- ... 33-36R
Kummerly, Walter
See Kuemmerly, Walter
Kunce, Joseph T(yree) 1928- ... 41-44R
Kuncewicz, Maria (Szczepanska) 1899- ... CAP-1
Earlier sketch in CA 9-10
Kuncewiczowa, Maria
See Kuncewicz, Maria (Szczepanska)
Kundera, Milan 1929- ... CANR-19
Earlier sketch in CA 85-88
See also CLC 4, 9, 19, 32
Kundsin, Ruth Blumfeld 1916- ... 106
Kunen, James Simon, 1948- ... 25-28R
Kunene, Mazisi (Raymond) 1930- ... 125
See also BW
Kuner, M(ildred) C(hristophe) 1922- ... 41-44R
Kunert, Guenter 1929- ... DLB-75
Kung, Hans
See Kueng, Hans
Kung, Shien Woo 1905- ... 2R
Kunhappa, Murkot 1905- ... 69-72
Kunhardt, Dorothy (Meserve) 1901-1979 ... 107
Obituary ... 93-96
See also SATA 22, 53
Kunhardt, Philip B(radish) Jr. 1928- ... 85-88
Kunhi Krishnan, T(aramal) V(anmeri)
1919- ... 61-64
Kuniczak, W(ieslaw) S(tanislaw) 1930- ... 85-88
Kuniholm, Bruce Robellet 1942- ... 93-96
Kuniholm, Whitney 1954- ... 112
Kunin, Madeleine May 1933- ... 93-96
Kunin, Richard A(llen) 1932- ... 107
Kunitz, Joshua 1896(?)-1980 Obituary ... 97-100
Kunitz, Stanley (Jasspon) 1905- ... CANR-26
Earlier sketch in CA 41-44R
See also DLB 48
See also CLC 6, 11, 14
Kunjufu, Johari M. Amini 1935- ... 41-44R
See also BW
Kunkel, Francis L(eo) 1921- ... 45-48
Kunnes, Richard 1941- ... 33-36R
Kuno, Susumu 1933- ... 41-44R
Kunreuther, Howard Charles 1938- ... 25-28R
Kunst, David W(illiam) 1939- ... 85-88
Kunstler, James Howard 1948- ... CANR-18
Earlier sketch in CA 101

Kunstler, Morton
See Kuenstler, Morton
Kunstler, William M(oses) 1919- CANR-5
Earlier sketch in CA 9-10R
Kuntz, J(ohn) Kenneth 1934- CANR-9
Earlier sketch in CA 23-24R
Kuntz, Kenneth A. 1916- 3R
Kuntz, Paul G. 1915- 5-6R
Kuntzleman, Charles T(homas) 1940- .. CANR-22
Earlier sketches in CA 57-60, CANR-7
Kunz, Marji 1939(?)-1979 Obituary 89-92
Kunz, Phillip Ray 1936- CANR-19
Earlier sketch in CA 37-40R
Kunz, Roxane (Brown) 1932- 121
See also SATA 53
Kunz, Virginia B(rainard) 1921- 21-22R
Kunze, Reiner 1933- 93-96
See also DLB 75
See also CLC 10
Kunzle, David Mark 1936- CANR-5
Earlier sketch in CA 53-56
Kunzur, Sheela
See Geis, Richard E(rwin)
Kuo, Ping-chia 1908- 7-8R
Kuo, Shirley W. Y. 1930- 115
Kuo, Ting-yee 1904(?)-1975 Obituary 61-64
Kuo Mo-Jo 1892-1978 Obituary 77-80
Kup, Alexander Peter 1924- CANR-9
Earlier sketch in CA 15-16R
Kup, Karl 1903-1981 Obituary 104
Kuper, Adam (Jonathan) 1941- CANR-20
Earlier sketch in CA 103
Kuper, Hilda Beemer 1911- CANR-2
Earlier sketch in CA 3R
Kuper, Jack 1932- 23-24R
Kuper, Leo 1908- CANR-11
Earlier sketch in CA 21-22R
Kuper, Yuri
See Kuperman, Yuri
Kuperman, Yuri 1940- 102
Kupfer, Fern 1946- 106
Kupferberg, Herbert 1918- 29-32R
See also SATA 19
Kupferberg, Naphtali 1923- CANR-13
Earlier sketch in CA 21-22R
Kupferberg, Tuli
See Kupferberg, Naphtali
See also DLB 16
Kupperman, Joel J. 1936- 33-36R
Kupperman, Karen O(rdahl) 1939- 111
Kuprin, Aleksandr Ivanovich 1870-1938
Brief entry 104
See also TCLC 5
Kuralt, Charles Bishop 1934- 89-92
Kurath, Gertrude Prokosch 1903- 15-16R
Kurath, Hans 1891- 9-10R
Kuratomi, Chizuko 1939- CANR-10
Earlier sketch in CA 21-22R
See also SATA 12
Kurdsen, Stephen
See Noon, Brian
Kurelek, William 1927-1977 .... CANR-3
Earlier sketch in CA 49-52
See also SATA 8, 27
See also CLR 2
Kurian, George 1928- 107
Kurien, C(hristopher) T(homas) 1931- .. CANR-13
Earlier sketch in CA 33-36R
Kurihara, Kenneth Kenkichi 1910-1972 .. CANR-6
Obituary 37-40R
Earlier sketch in CA 3R
Kurkjian, Stephen A. 1944(?)- Brief entry ... 116
Kurkul, Edward 1916- 25-28R
Kurland, Gerald 1942- CANR-14
Earlier sketch in CA 41-44R
See also SATA 13
Kurland, Michael (Joseph) 1938- CANR-11
Earlier sketch in CA 61-64
See also SATA 48
Kurland, Philip B. 1921- CANR-7
Earlier sketch in CA 9-10R
Kurman, George 1942- 53-56
Kurnitz, Harry 1909-1968 Obituary 25-28R
Kuroda, Yasumasa 1931- 45-48
Kuropas, Myron B(ohdon) 1932- 45-48
Kurosawa, Akira 1910- 101
See also CLC 16
Kurowski, Eugeniusz
See Dobraczynski, Jan
Kurrik, Maire Jaanus 1940- 101
Kursh, Charlotte Olmsted 1912- 9-10R
Kursh, Harry 1919- 9-10R
Kurten, Bjorn (Olof) 1924- CANR-20
Earlier sketch in CA 25-28R
Kurth-Voigt, Lieselotte E. 1923-
Brief entry 110
Kurtis, Arlene Harris 1927- 25-28R
Kurtis, Bill
See Kurtis, William Horton
Kurtis, William Horton 1940- Brief entry 124
Kurtz, C(larence) Gordon 1902- 65-68
Kurtz, David L(ee) 1941- 41-44R
Kurtz, Donna Carol 1943- 93-96
Kurtz, Ernest 1935- 112
Kurtz, Harold 1913- 17-18R
Kurtz, Irma 1935- 118
Kurtz, Katherine (Irene) 1944- CANR-25
Earlier sketch in CA 29-32R
Kurtz, Kenneth H(assett) 1928- 33-36R
Kurtz, Lester R. 1949- 126
Kurtz, Michael L(ouis) 1941- 107
Kurtz, Paul 1925- CANR-25
Earlier sketches in CA 13-14R, CANR-5
Kurtz, Stephen G(uild) 1926- 11-12R
Kurtzman, Jeffrey G(ordon) 1940- 110
Kurtzman, Joel 1947- 29-32R
Kurtz-Phelan, James L(anham) 1946- 49-52
Kurys, Diane 1949- 125
Kurz, Artur R.
See Scortia, Thomas N(icholas)
Kurz, Isolde 1853-1944 .... DLB-66
Kurz, Mordecai 1934- CANR-12
Earlier sketch in CA 29-32R
Kurz, Otto 1908-1975 107
Obituary 104
Kurz, Paul Konrad 1927- 29-32R
Kurz, Ron 1940- CANR-14
Earlier sketch in CA 81-84
Kurzer, Siegmund F. 1907(?)-1973
Obituary 104
Kurzman, Dan 1927- CANR-14
Earlier sketch in CA 69-72
Kurzman, Paul A(lfred) 1938- CANR-13
Earlier sketch in CA 33-36R
Kurzweg, Bernhard F. 1926- 17-18R
Kurzweil, Arthur 1951- 97-100
Kurzweil, Edith 110
Kurzweil, Zvi Erich 1911- CAP-1
Earlier sketch in CA 11-12
Kusan, Ivan 1933- CANR-6
Earlier sketch in CA 9-10R
Kusche, Larry
See Kusche, Lawrence David
Kusche, Lawrence David 1940- CANR-5
Earlier sketch in CA 53-56
Kusenberg, Kurt 1904-1983 .... DLB-69
Kushel, Gerald 1930- CANR-11
Earlier sketch in CA 25-28R
Kushner, David Z(arkeri) 1935- 53-56
Kushner, Donn 1927- 113
See also SATA 52
Kushner, Harold S(amuel) 1935- 107
Kushner, Harvey W(olf) 1941- 110
Kushner, Howard Irvin 1943- 81-84
Kushner, Irving 1929- 119
Kushner, Rose 1929- 61-64
Kushner, Sam 1915(?)-1987 Obituary 123
Kusin, Vladimir V(ictor) 1929- CANR-13
Earlier sketch in CA 33-36R
Kuske, Martin 1940- 97-100
Kuskin, Karla (Seidman) 1932- CANR-22
Earlier sketches in CA 3R, CANR-4
See also SATA 2
See also SAAS 3
See also CLR 4
Kuslan, Louis I(saac) 1922- CANR-1
Earlier sketch in CA 45-48
Kusmer, Kenneth Leslie 1945- 102
Kusnick, Barry A. 1910- 53-56
Kusniewicz, Andrzej 1904- 107
Kuspit, Donald B(urton) 1935- 97-100
Kussmaul, Ann (Sturm) 1945- 110
Kustermeir, Rudolf 1893(?)-1977
Obituary 73-76
Kustow, Michael (David) 1939- Brief entry .. 106
Kutash, Samuel Benjamin 1912-1979 ... CANR-2
Earlier sketch in CA 4R
Kuten, Jay 1935- Brief entry 108
Kuter, Laurence S(herman) 1905-1979
Obituary 113
Kutler, Stanley I. 1934- 23-24R
Kutner, Luis 1908- 109
Kutner, Nanette 1906?-1962 .... 4R
Kutsche, Paul 1927- 114
Kutscher, Charles L(awrence) 1936- 77-80
Kutsky, Roman Joseph 1922- Brief entry ... 110
Kuttna, Mari 1934-1983 Obituary 109
Kuttner, Henry 1915-1958 Brief entry 107
See also DLB 8
See also TCLC 10
Kuttner, Paul 1931- CANR-13
Earlier sketch in CA 77-80
See also SATA 18
Kutz, LeRoy M. 1922- 15-16R
Kutza, Elizabeth Ann 111
Kuwayama, George 1925- 116
Kuykendall, Eleanor 1938- Brief entry 109
Kuykendall, Jack L(awrence) 1940- 57-60
Kuykendall, Ralph S(impson) 1885-1963 ...... 3R
Kuzma, Greg 1944- 33-36R
See also CLC 7
Kuzma, Kay 1941- CANR-23
Earlier sketch in CA 106
See also SATA 39
Kuznets, Simon (Smith) 1901-1985
Obituary 116
Brief entry 108
Kuznetsov, (Edward) 1939- 57-60
Kuznetsov, Anatoli 1929-1979 Obituary ... 89-92
Kuzniewski, Anthony J(oseph) 1945- 107
Kvale, Velma R(uth) 1898- CAP-2
Earlier sketch in CA 25-28
See also SATA 8
Kvam, Wayne (Eugene) 1938- 45-48
Kvasnicka, Robert M(ichael) 1935- 97-100
Kwabena Nketia, J. H.
See Nketia, J(oseph) H(anson) Kwabena
Kwan, Kian M(oon) 1929- 17-18R
Kwant, R. C.
See Kwant, Remigius C(ornelis)
Kwant, Remigius C(ornelis) 1918- CANR-18
Earlier sketches in CA 9-10R, CANR-3
Kwant, Remy C.
See Kwant, Remigius C(ornelis)
Kwanten, Luc 1944- 93-96
Kwavnick, David 1940- 45-48
Kweder, Adele 1910- 5-6R
Kweder, David James 1905- 5-6R
Kweit, Robert W(illiam) 1946- 112
Kwiatkowska, Hanna Yaxa 1907(?)-1980
Obituary 97-100
Kwitny, Jonathan 1941- CANR-23
Earlier sketches in CA 49-52, CANR-1
Kwolek, Constance
See Porcari, Constance Kwolek
Kyburg, Henry (Guy) E(ly), Jr. 1928- ... CANR-8
Earlier sketch in CA 5-6R
Kyd, Thomas 1558-1594 .... DLB-62
Kyd, Thomas
See Harbage, Alfred (Bennett)
Kydd, Sam(uel) 1917-1982 109
Obituary 106
Kyemba, Henry 1939- 81-84
Kyes, Robert L(ange) 1933- 49-52
Kyger, Joanne (Elizabeth) 1934- CANR-17
Earlier sketch in CA 101
See also DLB 16
Kyle, Duncan
See Broxholme, John Franklin
Kyle, Elisabeth
See Dunlop, Agnes M. R.
Kyle, Marlaine
See Hager, Jean
Kyle, Robert
See Terrall, Robert
Kyme, Ernest Hector 1906- 103
Kynett, Harold Havelock 1889-1973
Obituary 106
Kyper, Frank 1940- 85-88
Kyprianos, Iossif
See Samarakis, Antonis
Kyre, Joan Randolph 1935- 25-28R
Kyre, Martin (Theodore, Jr.) 1928- 25-28R
Kyrle, Roger (Ernie) Money
See Money-Kyrle, Roger (Ernie)
Kysar, Robert (Dean) 1934- CANR-22
Earlier sketch in CA 69-72
Kyselka, Will 1921- 106
Kyte, Kathy S. 1946- SATA-44, 50
Kytle, Elizabeth 112
Kytle, Ray(mond) 1941- 29-32R
Kyvig, David E(dward) 1944- 101

L

La-Anyane, Seth 1922- 9-10R
Laas, William M. 1910(?)-1975 Obituary .. 61-64
LaBar, Tom 1937- 25-28R
Labaree, Benjamin Woods 1927- CANR-6
Earlier sketch in CA 9-10R
Labaree, Leonard W(oods) 1897-1980 73-76
Obituary 97-100
Labarge, Margaret Wade 1916- CANR-11
Earlier sketch in CA 25-28R
LaBarge, William Howard 1948- 116
La Barr, Creighton
See von Block, Bela W(illiam)
La Barre, Weston 1911- CANR-22
Earlier sketch in CA 2R
LaBastille, Anne 1938- CANR-8
Earlier sketch in CA 57-60
L'Abate, Luciano 1928- 111
Labatut, Jean 1899-1986 Obituary 121
Labbe, John T. CANR-17
Earlier sketch in CA 97-100
La Beau, Dennis (George) 1941- 97-100
LaBelle, Maurice Marc 1939- 113
Laber, Jeri 1931- CANR-9
Earlier sketch in CA 65-68
Laberge, Albert 1871-1960 .... DLB-68
Laberge, Marie 1950- DLB-60
LaBier, Douglas 1944- 124
Labin, Suzanne (Devoyon) 1913- CANR-14
Earlier sketch in CA 29-32R
Labor, Earle G. 1928- 21-22R
LaBorde, Rene
See Neuffer, Irene LaBorde
Labovitz, I(srael) M(ilton) 1907- 5-6R
Labrador, James
See Hamel Dobkin, Kathleen
Labrador, Judy
See Hamel Dobkin, Kathleen
LaBrecque, Claude X. 85-88
La Brie, Henry George III 1946- 57-60
Labrie, Roger P(aul) 1952- 113
Labroca, Mario 1897(?)-1973 Obituary ... 41-44R
Labus, Marta Haake 1943- 109
Labuta, Joseph A(nthony) 1931- 57-60
Labuz, Ronald M. 1953- 123
Labys, Walter C(arl) 1937- 73-76
La Camera, Anthony 1914(?)-1984
Obituary 114
Lacan, Jacques (Marie Emile) 1901-1981 ... 121
Obituary 104
LaCapra, Dominick 1939- 109
La Capria, Raffaele 1922- CANR-4
Earlier sketch in CA 9-10R
Lacarriere, Jacques 1925- Brief entry 125
La Casce, Steward 1935- 37-40R
Laccetti, (Silvio) Richard 1941- CANR-13
Earlier sketch in CA 37-40R
Lace, O(live) Jessie 1906- 17-18R
Lacerda, Carlos 1914-1977 Obituary 69-72
Lacey, A(lan) R(obert) 1926- 112
Lacey, Archie L(ouis) 1923- 9-10R
Lacey, Douglas R(aymond) 1913- 29-32R
Lacey, Jeannette F. 77-80
Lacey, John
See Alexander, Boyd
Lacey, Louise 1940- 81-84
Lacey, Paul A. 1934- 41-44R
Lacey, Peter 1929- 23-24R
Lacey, Robert 1944- CANR-16
Earlier sketch in CA 33-36R
Lacey, W(alter) K(irkpatrick) 1921- CANR-11
Earlier sketch in CA 25-28R
Lach, Donald F(rederick) 1917- 102
La Charite, Virginia Anding 1937- 29-32R
Lachenbruch, David 1921- 89-92
Lachenmeyer, Charles W(illiam) 1943- 105
Lachmann, Frank M(ichael) 1929- 103
Lachs, John 1934- 23-24R
Lack, David Lambert 1910-1973 .... CANR-4
Obituary 89-92
Earlier sketch in CA 7-8R
Lackey, Douglas Paul 1945- 103
Lackey, Mercedes R. 1950- 126
Lackmann, Ron(ald) 1934- CANR-13
Earlier sketch in CA 29-32R
Lackner, Stephan 1910- CANR-15
Earlier sketch in CA 29-32R
Lacks, Cecilia 1945- 69-72
Lacks, Cissy
See Lacks, Cecilia
Lacks, Roslyn 1933- 102
La Clair, Earl E. 1916- 21-22R
La Claustra, Vera Berneicia (Derrick)
1903- 53-56
Lacocque, Andre (Marie) 1927- 112
Lacocque, Pierre-Emmanuel 1952- 112
La Colere, Francois
See Aragon, Louis
Lacolere, Francois
See Aragon, Louis
Lacombe, Gabriel 1905(?)-1973
Obituary 37-40R
Lacoste, Paul 1923- CANR-1
Earlier sketch in CA 45-48
Lacouture, Jean Marie Gerard 1921- 101
Lacretelle, Jacques de 1888-1985 ...... DLB-65
Lacroix, Louise
See Swift, Helen C(ecilia)
LaCroix, Mary 1937- CANR-22
Earlier sketch in CA 106
Lacroix, Ramon
See McKeag, Ernest L(ionel)
LaCrosse, E. Robert 1937- 33-36R
Lacy, A(lexander) D(acre) 1894-1969 .... CAP-2
Earlier sketch in CA 25-28
Lacy, Charles
See Hippisley Coxe, Antony D(acres)
Lacy, Creighton (Boutelle) 1919- 15-16R
Lacy, Dan (Mabry) 1914- 37-40R
Lacy, Donald Charles 1933- 105
Lacy, Eric Russell 1933- 17-18R
Lacy, Gene M(elvin) 1934- 53-56
Lacy, Gerald M(orris) 1940- 77-80
Lacy, Leslie Alexander 1937- 33-36R
See also SATA 6
Lacy, Mary Lou (Pannill) 1914- 17-18R
Lacy, Norris J(oiner) 1940- CANR-23
Earlier sketches in CA 61-64, CANR-8
Ladas, Gerasimos 1937- 53-56
Ladas, Stephen P(ericles) 1898-1976 102
Ladd, Bruce 1936- 25-28R
Ladd, Edward T(aylor) 1918-1973 ...... CANR-4
Earlier sketch in CA 5-6R
Ladd, Everett Carll, Jr. 1937- CANR-11
Earlier sketch in CA 25-28R
Ladd, George E(ldon) 1911- CANR-5
Earlier sketch in CA 7-8R
Ladd, Helen F. 1945- 111
Ladd, John 1917- 81-84
Ladd, Joseph Brown 1764-1786 .... DLB-37
Ladd, Veronica
See Miner, Jane Claypool
Ladenson, Alex 1907- 17-18R
Ladenson, Robert Franklin 1943- 113
Lader, Lawrence 1919- CANR-2
Earlier sketch in CA 1R
See also SATA 6
Laderman, Carol (C.) 121
Ladner, Joyce A(nn) 1943- 124
Brief entry 122
See also BW
Ladner, Kurt
See DeMille, Nelson
Ladner, Mildred D. 1918- 97-100
Lado, Robert 1915- CANR-7
Earlier sketch in CA 11-12R
Ladurie, Emmanuel Le Roy
See Le Roy Ladurie, Emmanuel
Lady, A
See Taylor, Ann
Lady Gregory
See Gregory, Isabella Augusta (Persse)
Ladyman, Phyllis 103
Lady Mears
See Tempest, Margaret Mary
Lady of Quality, A
See Bagnold, Enid
Lael, Richard L(ee) 1946- 111
Laemmar, Jack W. 1909- 1R
Laertes, Joseph
See Saltzman, Joseph
Laestadius, Lars-Levi 1909-1982 Obituary .. 107
Laeuchli, Samuel 1924- CANR-4
Earlier sketch in CA 5-6R
Laevastu, Taivo 1923- CANR-15
Earlier sketch in CA 41-44R
LaFantasie, Glenn W(arren) 1949- 125
La Farge, Oliver (Hazard Perry)
1901-1963 81-84
See also SATA 19
See also DLB 9
La Farge, Phyllis 73-76
See also SATA 14
Lafarge, Rene 1902- CAP-2
Earlier sketch in CA 29-32
LaFauci, Horatio M(ichael) 1917- 33-36R
Lafayette, Carlos
See Boiles, Charles Lafayette (Jr.)
Lafayette, Rene
See Hubbard, L(afayette) Ron(ald)

LaFeber, Walter (Fredrick) 1933- ... CANR-5
Earlier sketch in CA 11-12R
Laffal, Julius 1920- ... 49-52
Laffan, Kevin (Barry) 1922- ... 37-40R
Lafferty, Perry (Francis) 1917- ... CANR-6
Earlier sketch in CA 9-10R
Lafferty, R(aphael) A(loysius) 1914- ... CANR-12
Earlier sketch in CA 57-60
See also DLB 8
Laffin, John (Alfred Charles) 1922- ... CANR-23
Earlier sketches in CA 53-56, CANR-7
See also SATA 31
Laffont, Jean-Pierre 1935- ... 115
LaFitte, Pat Chew 1950- ... 107
LaFleur, William R. 1936- ... 115
La Follette, Marcel (Evelyn) Chotkowski 1944- ... 114
La Follette, Suzanne 1894(?)-1983
Obituary ... 109
LaFontaine, Blanche
See Schwalberg, Carol(yn Ernestine Stein)
LaFontaine, Charles Vivian 1936- ... 57-60
La Fontaine, Jean de 1621-1695 ... SATA-18
Lafore, Laurence Davis 1917-1985 ... 13-14R
Obituary ... 118
LaForte, Robert Sherman 1933- ... 57-60
La Fountaine, George 1934- ... CANR-7
Earlier sketch in CA 57-60
Lafourcade, Bernard 1934-1986 ... 115
Obituary ... 118
Lafreniere, Gyslaine F. 1948- ... 116
Lagace, Louise Lambert
See Lambert-Lagace, Louise
LaGattuta, Margo 1942- ... 115
Lager, Marilyn 1939- ... 121
See also SATA 52
Lagercrantz, Rose (Elsa) 1947- ... 108
See also SATA 39
Lagerkvist, Paer (Fabian) 1891-1974 ... 85-88
Obituary ... 49-52
See also CLC 7, 10, 13
Lagerkvist, Par
See Lagerkvist, Paer (Fabian)
Lagerloef, Selma (Ottiliana Lovisa) 1858-1940 Brief entry ... 108
See also SATA 15
See also TCLC 4
See also CLR 7
Lagerlof, Selma (Ottiliana Lovisa)
See Lagerloef, Selma (Ottiliana Lovisa)
See also SATA 15
See also CLR 7
Lagerwall, Edna ... 45-48
Lagerwerff, Ellen Best 1919- ... 85-88
Lagevi, Bo
See Blom, Karl Arne
Lagneau-Kesteloot, Lilyan
See Kesteloot, Lilyan
Lago, Mary M(cClelland) 1919- ... CANR-15
Earlier sketch in CA 85-88
LaGrand, Louis E. 1935- ... 33-36R
La Grange, Henry Louis De
See De La Grange, Henry Louis
LaGuardia, David M(ichael) 1943- ... 118
La Guardia, Fiorello Henry 1882-1947
Brief entry ... 120
Laguerre, Andre 1915(?)-1979 ... 97-100
Obituary ... 85-88
Laguerre, Michel S(aturnin) 1945- ... 115
La Guma, (Justin) Alex(ander) 1925-1985 ... CANR-25
Obituary ... 118
Earlier sketch in CA 49-52
See also BW
See also CLC 19
La Gumina, Salvatore John 1928- ... 77-80
LaHaye, Tim 1926- ... CANR-9
Earlier sketch in CA 65-68
Lahee, Frederic Henry 1884-1968 ... CAP-2
Earlier sketch in CA 19-20
Lahey, Edwin A(loysius) 1902-1969
Obituary ... 115
LaHood, Marvin J(ohn) 1933- ... CANR-10
Earlier sketch in CA 25-28R
Lahr, John (Henry) 1941- ... CANR-21
Earlier sketch in CA 25-28R
Lahr, Raymond M(errill) 1914-1973
Obituary ... 41-44R
Lahue, Kalton C. 1934- ... CANR-7
Earlier sketch in CA 15-16R
Lai, T'ien-Ch'ang 1921- ... CANR-11
Earlier sketch in CA 69-72
Lai, Violet Lau 1916- ... 119
Laidlaw, A. K.
See Grieve, C(hristopher) M(urray)
Laidlaw, Harry Hyde, Jr. 1907- ... 7-8R
Laidlaw, Marc 1960- ... 119
Laidlaw, Ross 1931- ... 118
Laidlaw, W(illiam) A(llison) 1898-1983
Obituary ... 109
Laidler, Harry W(ellington) 1884-1970 ... CANR-5
Obituary ... 29-32R
Earlier sketch in CA 5-6R
Laiken, Deirdre S(usan) 1948- ... 104
See also SATA 40, 48
Laikin, Paul 1927- ... 7-8R
Laimgruber, Monika 1946- ... SATA-11
Laine, Barry 1951-1987 Obituary ... 123
Laine, Gloria
See Hanna, David
Lainez, Manuel Mujica
See Mujica Lainez, Manuel
Laing, Alexander (Kinnan) 1903-1976 ... CANR-4
Obituary ... 65-68
Earlier sketch in CA 5-6R
Laing, Anne C.
See Schachterle, Nancy (Lange)
Laing, Frederick ... 105
Laing, Jennifer 1948- ... 106
Laing, Lloyd (Robert) 1944- ... CANR-5
Earlier sketch in CA 53-56
Laing, Martha
See Celestino, Martha Laing
Laing, R(onald) D(avid) 1927- ... 107
Lair, Jacqueline Carey 1930- ... 119
Lair, Jess K. 1926- ... CANR-14
Earlier sketch in CA 41-44R
Lair, Robert L(eland) 1932- ... 53-56
Laird, Bailey
See Goodwin, Richard N(aradhof)
Laird, Betty A(nn) 1925- ... CANR-15
Earlier sketch in CA 33-36R
Laird, Carobeth 1895-1983 ... CANR-8
Obituary ... 110
Earlier sketch in CA 61-64
See also DLBY 82
Laird, Charlton G(rant) 1901- ... 13-14R
Laird, David
See Laird, W(ilbur) David, Jr.
Laird, Donald A(nderson) 1897-1969 ... 7-8R
Obituary ... 25-28R
Laird, Dorothy
See Carr, Dorothy Stevenson Laird
Laird, Dugan 1920- ... CANR-12
Earlier sketch in CA 73-76
Laird, Eleanor Childs 1908- ... 73-76
Laird, Helen 1933- ... 122
Laird, J(ohn) T(udor) 1921- ... 69-72
Laird, Jean E(louise) 1930- ... CANR-6
Earlier sketch in CA 11-12R
See also SATA 38
Laird, Melvin R(obert) 1922- ... 65-68
Laird, Robbin F. 1946- ... 113
Laird, Roy D(ean) 1925- ... CANR-15
Earlier sketch in CA 33-36R
Laird, W(ilbur) David, Jr. 1937- ... 113
Lait, Robert 1921- ... CANR-2
Earlier sketch in CA 4R
Laite, Gordon 1925- ... SATA-31
Laite, William Edward, Jr. 1932- ... 37-40R
Laithwaite, Eric Roberts 1921- ... 103
Laitin, Ken 1963- ... 102
Laitin, Lindy 1968- ... 108
Laitin, Steve 1965- ... 102
Lajolo, Davide 1913(?)-1984 Obituary ... 113
Lakatos, Imre 1922-1974 Obituary ... 116
Lake, Carolyn 1932- ... 25-28R
Lake, David J. 1929- ... CANR-10
Earlier sketch in CA 65-68
Lake, Frank 1914-1982 ... CANR-10
Earlier sketch in CA 21-22R
Lake, Harriet
See Taylor, Paula (Wright)
Lake, Kenneth R(obert) 1931- ... CANR-5
Earlier sketch in CA 53-56
Lakeman, Enid 1903- ... 107
Laken, Bob
See Holman, Robert
Lakey, George (Russell) 1937- ... CANR-7
Earlier sketch in CA 17-18R
Lakin, Martin 1925- ... 73-76
Laklan, Carli 1907- ... CANR-1
Earlier sketch in CA 3R
See also SATA 5
Lakoff, George 1941- ... 29-32R
Lakoff, Robin Tolmach 1942- ... 103
Lakoff, Sanford A(llan) 1931- ... CANR-1
Earlier sketch in CA 1R
Lakritz, Esther Himmelman 1928- ... 3R
Lal, Gobind Behari 1890(?)-1982 Obituary ... 106
Lal, Kishori Saran 1920- ... 23-24R
Lal, P. 1929- ... CANR-9
Earlier sketch in CA 13-14R
Laliberte, Norman 1925- ... 104
Lalicki, Barbara ... 119
Lalley, Joseph M. 1897(?)-1980 Obituary ... 102
Lalli, Judy 1949- ... 110
Lally, Michael 1942- ... CANR-14
Earlier sketch in CA 77-80
La Londe, Bernard J. 1933- ... 33-36R
Lalonde, Michele 1937- ... DLB-60
Lalonde, Robert 1947- ... 109
Lalumia, Joseph 1916- ... 23-24R
Lam, Charlotte (Dawson) 1924- ... 37-40R
Lam, Truong Buu 1933- ... 25-28R
Laman, Russell 1907- ... CAP-1
Earlier sketch in CA 9-10
LaMancusa, Katherine C.
See Koop, Katherine C.
Lamanna, Dolores B. 1930-1980 ... 11-12R
Obituary ... 97-100
Lamantia, Philip 1927- ... 117
Brief entry ... 111
See also DLB 16
Lamar, Howard R(oberts) 1923- ... 19-20R
Lamar, Lavoisier 1907- ... 7-8R
Lamar, Nedra Newkirk ... 69-72
Lamarque, Peter 1948- ... 120
LaMarre, Virgil E. 1910(?)-1985 Obituary ... 115
LaMarsh, Judy
See LaMarsh, Julia Verlyn
LaMarsh, Julia Verlyn 1924-1980 ... CANR-13
Obituary ... 105
Earlier sketch in CA 29-32R
Lamb, Antonia 1943- ... 23-24R
Lamb, Beatrice Pitney 1904- ... 5-6R
See also SATA 21
Lamb, Charles 1775-1834 ... SATA-17
Lamb, Charles Bentall 1914-1981 ... 102
Obituary ... 105
Lamb, Charles M(oody) 1945- ... 124
Lamb, Charlotte
See Holland, Sheila
Lamb, Dana S(torrs) 1900-1986 Obituary ... 120
Lamb, David 1940- ... 110
Lamb, Edward 1902-1987 ... 108
Obituary ... 122
Lamb, Eleanor 1917- ... 69-72
Lamb, Elizabeth Searle 1917- ... 33-36R
See also SATA 31
Lamb, F(rank) Bruce 1913- ... 33-36R
Lamb, G(eoffrey) F(rederick) ... CANR-19
Earlier sketches in CA 53-56, CANR-4
See also SATA 10
Lamb, H(ubert) H(orace) 1913- ... 23-24R
Lamb, Harold (Albert) 1892-1962 ... 101
Obituary ... 89-92
See also SATA 53
Lamb, Helen B.
See Lamont, Helen Lamb
Lamb, Hugh 1946- ... CANR-1
Earlier sketch in CA 49-52
Lamb, Karl A(llen) 1933- ... CANR-18
Earlier sketches in CA 7-8R, CANR-3
Lamb, Lawrence E(dward) 1926- ... 97-100
Lamb, Lynton (Harold) 1907-1977 ... CANR-4
Earlier sketch in CA 1R
See also SATA 10
Lamb, Marion M(inerva) 1905- ... 7-8R
Lamb, Mary Ann 1764-1847 ... SATA-17
Lamb, Patricia Frazer 1931- ... 126
Lamb, Robert (Boyden) 1941- ... 29-32R
See also SATA 13
Lamb, Ruth S(tanton) ... CANR-21
Earlier sketch in CA 45-48
Lamb, Sydney M(acDonald) 1929- ... 33-36R
Lamb, William
See Jameson, (Margaret) Storm
Lamb, William Kaye 1904- ... 81-84
Lambasa, Frank Slavko 1921-1987
Obituary ... 123
Lambdin, William 1936- ... 102
Lambec, Zoltan
See Kimbro, John M.
Lamberg, Robert F(elix) 1929- ... 65-68
Lamberg-Karlovsky, Clifford Charles 1937- ... 85-88
Lambert, B. Geraldine 1922- ... 41-44R
Lambert, Betty
See Lambert, Elizabeth (Minnie)
See also DLB 60
Lambert, Byron Cecil 1923- ... 97-100
Lambert, Christine
See Albrand, Martha
Lambert, Darwin (Seymour) 1916- ... CANR-2
Earlier sketch in CA 7-8R
Lambert, David (Compton) 1932- ... 122
See also SATA 49
Lambert, Derek 1929- ... CANR-17
Earlier sketch in CA 25-28R
Lambert, Eleanor ... 102
Lambert, Elisabeth
See Ortiz, Elisabeth Lambert
Lambert, Elizabeth (Minnie) 1933-1983 ... 102
Lambert, Eric 1918-1966 ... CAP-1
Earlier sketch in CA 13-14
Lambert, Gavin 1924- ... CANR-1
Earlier sketch in CA 3R
Lambert, Hazel Margaret (?)-1968 ... 2R
Lambert, Herbert H. 1929- ... 69-72
Lambert, J(ack) W(alter) 1917-1986 ... 108
Obituary ... 120
Lambert, Jacques Edward 1901- ... CAP-2
Earlier sketch in CA 23-24
Lambert, Janet 1895(?)-1973 Obituary ... 41-44R
See also SATA 25
Lambert, John (Robin) 1936- ... CANR-8
Earlier sketch in CA 5-6R
Lambert, Mark 1942- ... 73-76
Lambert, Ronald Dick 1936- ... 108
Lambert, Roy Eugene 1918- ... 37-40R
Lambert, Royston James 1932-1982
Obituary ... 108
Lambert, Saul 1928- ... 106
See also SATA 23
Lambert, Sheila 1926- ... 85-88
Lambert, William Wilson 1919- ... 11-12R
Lamberti, Marjorie 1937- ... 103
Lambert-Lagace, Louise 1941- ... 111
Lamberton, Donald McLean 1927- ... 103
Lamberts, J(acob) J. 1910- ... 37-40R
Lambeth, Edmund Barry 1932- ... 123
Lambley, Peter 1946- ... 109
Lambo, Thomas Adeoye 1923- ... 29-32R
Lamborn, LeRoy L(eslie) 1937- ... 23-24R
Lambot, Isobel 1926- ... 73-76
Lambourne, John
See Lamburn, John Battersby Crompton
Lambrick, Hugh Trevor 1904- ... CANR-6
Earlier sketch in CA 9-10R
Lambright, William Henry 1939- ... 103
Lambro, Donald (Joseph) 1940- ... CANR-25
Earlier sketches in CA 57-60, CANR-7
Lambton, Anne (Patricia St. Clair) 1918- ... 85-88
Lamburn, John Battersby Crompton 1893- ... CAP-1
Earlier sketch in CA 9-10
Lamburn, Richmal Crompton 1890-1969 ... CAP-1
Obituary ... 25-28R
Earlier sketch in CA 9-10
See also SATA 5
Lame Deer 1895(?)-1976 Obituary ... 69-72
Lamensdorf, Leonard 1930- ... 29-32R
La Meri
See Hughes, Russell Meriwether
L'Ami, Charles Ernest 1896- ... 102
Lamirande, Emilien 1926- ... CANR-8
Earlier sketch in CA 17-18R
Lamis, Alexander P. 1946- ... 125
Lamm, Joyce 1933- ... 57-60
Lamm, Maurice 1930- ... 17-18R
Lamm, Norman 1927- ... 49-52
Lamme, Linda Leonard 1942- ... 102
Lamming, George (William) 1927- ... CANR-26
Earlier sketch in CA 85-88
See also BW
See also CLC 2, 4
Lamming, R. M. 1949- ... 125
Brief entry ... 119
Lamon, Lester C(rawford) 1942- ... 89-92
Lamond, Henry George 1885-1969
Obituary ... 25-28R
Lamont, Corliss 1902- ... CANR-11
Earlier sketch in CA 15-16R
Lamont, Douglas Felix 1937- ... 41-44R
Lamont, Helen Lamb 1906(?)-1975
Obituary ... 61-64
Lamont, Lansing 1930- ... CANR-11
Earlier sketch in CA 17-18R
Lamont, Marianne
See Rundle, Anne
Lamont, N. B.
See Barnitt, Nedda Lemmon
Lamont, Nedda
See Barnitt, Nedda Lemmon
Lamont, Rosette C(lementine) ... 33-36R
Lamont, William D(awson) 1901-1982 ... CAP-1
Obituary ... 108
Earlier sketch in CA 11-12
Lamont-Brown, Raymond 1939- ... CANR-14
Earlier sketch in CA 73-76
Lamorisse, Albert (Emmanuel) 1922-1970 ... 101
See also SATA 23
Lamott, Kenneth (Church) 1923-1979 ... 25-28R
Obituary ... 89-92
Lamotte, Etienne 1904(?)-1983 Obituary ... 109
Lamour, Dorothy
See Kaumeyer, Dorothy
L'Amour, Louis (Dearborn) 1908-1988 ... CANR-25
Obituary ... 125
Earlier sketches in CA 4R, CANR-3
See also DLBY 80
See also CLC 25
See also AITN 2
Lamparski, Richard ... 21-22R
Lampe, David 1923- ... CANR-1
Earlier sketch in CA 4R
Lampedusa, Giuseppe (Tomasi) di
See Tomasi di Lampedusa, Giuseppe
See also TCLC 13
Lampell, Millard 1919- ... 11-12R
Lampert, Emily 1951- ... 121
See also SATA 49, 52
Lamphere, Louise (Anne) 1940- ... 89-92
Lampkin, William R(obert) 1932- ... 106
Lampl, Paul 1915- Brief entry ... 104
Lamplugh, Lois 1921- ... CANR-24
Earlier sketches in CA 13-14R, CANR-9
See also SATA 17
Lampman, Ben Hur 1886-1954 Brief entry ... 111
Lampman, Evelyn Sibley 1907-1980 ... CANR-11
Obituary ... 101
Earlier sketch in CA 15-16R
See also SATA 4, 23
Lampman, Robert James 1920- ... 103
Lampo, Hubert 1920- Brief entry ... 105
Lamport, Felicia 1916- ... 1R
Lamppa, William R(ussell) 1928- ... 53-56
Lamprecht, Sterling P(ower) 1890-1973 ... CAP-1
Earlier sketch in CA 17-18
Lamprey, Louise 1869-1951 Brief entry ... 117
See also YABC 2
Lampson, Robin 1900-1978 Obituary ... 77-80
Lampton, Chris
See Lampton, Christopher
Lampton, Christopher ... 125
See also SATA 47
Lamsa, George M(amishisho) 1892-1975 ... CANR-9
Earlier sketches in CA 23-24, CAP-2
Lamson, Peggy 1912- ... 25-28R
La Mure, Pierre 1909-1976 Obituary ... 104
Lan, David 1952- ... CANR-24
Earlier sketch in CA 97-100
Lana, Robert E(dward) 1932- ... 33-36R
Lancaster, Bob 1943- ... 111
Lancaster, Bruce 1896-1963 ... CAP-1
Earlier sketch in CA 9-10
See also SATA 9
See also CLC 36
Lancaster, Burt(on Stephen) 1913- ... 122
Brief entry ... 116
Lancaster, Clay 1917- ... CANR-8
Earlier sketch in CA 7-8R
Lancaster, Evelyn
See Sizemore, Chris(tine) Costner
Lancaster, F. Donald
See Fredriksson, Don
Lancaster, F(rederick) Wilfrid 1933- ... CANR-19
Earlier sketches in CA 53-56, CANR-4
Lancaster, Kelvin (John) 1924- ... 33-36R
Lancaster, Lydia
See Meaker, Eloise
Lancaster, Marie-Jaqueline 1922- ... 25-28R
Lancaster, Matthew 1973(?)-1983
Obituary ... 117
See also SATA 45
Lancaster, Osbert 1908-1986 ... 105
Obituary ... 119
Lancaster, Otis Ewing 1909- ... 103
Lancaster, Richard ... 21-22R
Lancaster, Sheila
See Holland, Sheila

Lancaster-Brown, Peter 1927- CANR-19
 Earlier sketches in CA 53-56, CANR-4
Lance, Derek (Paul) 1932- CANR-9
 Earlier sketch in CA 15-16R
Lance, H(ubert) Darrell 1935- 115
Lance, James Waldo 1926- 65-68
Lance, Kathryn 1943- 122
Lance, LaBelle D(avid) 1931- 81-84
Lance, Leslie
 See Swatridge, Charles (John)
Lancer, Jack CAP-2
Lanchester, Elsa 1902-1986 Obituary 121
Lanciano, Claude O(lwen), Jr. 1922- CANR-1
 Earlier sketch in CA 45-48
Lancour, Gene
 See Fisher, Gene L(ouis)
Lancour, (Adlore) Harold 1908-1981 23-24R
 Obituary 105
Lancy, David F(alcon) 1945- 110
Land
 See Landry, Robert John
Land, Aubrey C(hristian) 1912- 41-44R
Land, Barbara (Neblett) 1923- 81-84
 See also SATA 16
Land, (Reginald) Brian 1927- 101
Land, George T(homas) Lock 1933- 53-56
Land, Jane
 See Borland, Kathryn Kilby
 and Speicher, Helen Ross S(mith)
Land, Jane and Ross
 See Borland, Kathryn Kilby
 and Speicher, Helen Ross S(mith)
Land, Myrick (Ebben) 1922- CANR-11
 Earlier sketch in CA 13-14R
 See also SATA 15
Landar, Herbert (Jay) 1927- 33-36R
Landau, Elaine 1948- CANR-5
 Earlier sketch in CA 53-56
 See also SATA 10
Landau, Genevieve Millet 1927- 107
Landau, Jacob 1917- SATA-38
Landau, Jacob M. 1924- CANR-24
 Earlier sketches in CA 19-20R, CANR-8
Landau, Lev Davidovich 1908-1968
 Obituary 113
Landau, Mark Alexandrovich
 See Aldanov, Mark (Alexandrovich)
Landau, Martin 1921- 45-48
Landau, Rom 1899-1974 CANR-4
 Obituary 49-52
 Earlier sketch in CA 3R
Landau, Sidney I(van) 1933- CANR-7
 Earlier sketch in CA 57-60
Landau, Sol 1920- 49-52
Landau-Aldanov, Mark Alexandrovich
 See Aldanov, Mark (Alexandrovich)
Landauer, Carl 1891-1983 CANR-21
 Earlier sketch in CA 2R
Landauer, Jerry Gerd 1932-1981 109
 Obituary 103
Lande, Henry F(rank) 1920- 29-32R
Lande, Lawrence (Montague) 1906- 105
Lande, Nathaniel 1939- 104
Landeck, Beatrice 1904- 73-76
 See also SATA 15
Landecker, Manfred 1929- 29-32R
Landeen, William M. 1891-1982 Obituary 109
Landeira, Ricardo L(opez) 1917- 81-84
Landen, Robert Geran 1930- 21-22R
Lander, Ernest McPherson, Jr. 1915- CANR-4
 Earlier sketch in CA 2R
Lander, Jack Robert 1921- 101
Lander, Jeannette 1931- 33-36R
Lander, Louise 1938- 85-88
Lander, Mamie Stubbs 1891(?)-1975
 Obituary 53-56
Landers, Ann
 See Lederer, Esther Pauline
Landers, Gunnard W(illiam) 1944- 93-96
Landes, David S(aul) 1924- CANR-22
 Earlier sketch in CA 103
Landes, Ruth 1908- CAP-2
 Earlier sketch in CA 29-32
Landes, Sonia 1925- CANR-22
 Earlier sketch in CA 104
Landesman, Charles 1932- 85-88
Landesman, Fran(ces) 1927- Brief entry 120
 See also DLB 16
Landesman, Irving Ned
 See Landesman, Jay (Irving)
Landesman, Jay (Irving) 1919- Brief entry 118
 See also DLB 16
Landgren, Marchal E. 1907(?)-1983
 Obituary 109
Landi, Ferruccio Rossi
 See Rossi-Landi, Ferruccio
Landin, Les 1923- 5-6R
 See also SATA 2
Landis, Benson Y. 1897-1966 CAP-1
 Earlier sketch in CA 13-14
Landis, Dennis Channing 1947- 110
Landis, Fred S(imon) 1943- 107
Landis, J(ames) D(avid) 1942- 126
 See also SATA 52
Landis, Jessie Royce 1904-1972
 Obituary 33-36R
Landis, John 1950- 122
Landis, John (David) 1950- Brief entry 112
 See also CLC 26
Landis, Judson R(ichard) 1935- 33-36R
Landis, Lincoln 1922- 45-48
Landis, Paul H(enry) 1901- CANR-5
 Earlier sketch in CA 5-6R
Landman, David 1917- CANR-11
 Earlier sketch in CA 69-72
Lando, Barry Mitchell 1939- 77-80
Landolfi, Tommaso 1908-1979 Obituary 117
 See also CLC 11, 49
Landon, Donald D. 1930- 25-28R
Landon, H(oward) C(handler) Robbins
 1926- CANR-13
 Earlier sketch in CA 77-80
Landon, Lucinda 1950- 123
 See also SATA 51
Landon, Margaret (Dorothea Mortenson)
 1903- CAP-1
 Earlier sketch in CA 13-14
 See also SATA 50
Landon, Michael de L(aval) 1935- 29-32R
Landorf, Joyce 1932- 124
 See also AITN 1
Landow, George P(aul) 1940- CANR-19
 Earlier sketches in CA 53-56, CANR-4
Landowska, Wanda (Aleksandra)
 1879-1959 Brief entry 122
Landreth, Catherine 1899- 77-80
Landrith, Harold Fochone 1919- 103
Landrum, Phil 1939- 81-84
Landry, Hilton (James) 1924- 13-14R
Landry, Robert John 1903- 69-72
Landsberg, Hans H. 1913- CANR-10
 Earlier sketch in CA 17-18R
Landsberg, Helmut Erich 1906-1985 107
 Obituary 118
Landsberg, Michele 1939- 123
Landsbergis, Algirdas J. 1924- CANR-13
 Earlier sketch in CA 33-36R
Landsburg, Alan William 1933- 103
Landsburg, Sally (Breit) 1933- 57-60
Landshoff, Fritz Helmut 1901-1988
 Obituary 125
Landshoff, Ursula 1908- 29-32R
 See also SATA 13
Landsman, Ned C. 1951- 126
Landstrom, Bjorn O(lof) 1917- 15-16R
Landsverk, O(le) G(odfred) 1901- 61-64
Landvater, Dorothy 1927- 103
Landwehr, Arthur J. II 1934- 37-40R
Landwirth, Heinz 1927- CANR-7
 Earlier sketch in CA 11-12R
Landy, David 1917- 77-80
Landy, Eugene E(llsworth) 1934- 41-44R
Landynski, Jacob W. 1930- 21-22R
Lane, Allen 1902-1970 Obituary 29-32R
Lane, Ann J(udith) 1931- 126
 Brief entry 110
Lane, Anthony 1916- 13-14R
Lane, Arthur (Ernest) 1937- 41-44R
Lane, Carl D(aniel) 1899- 105
Lane, Carolyn 1926- CANR-12
 Earlier sketch in CA 29-32R
 See also SATA 10
Lane, Charles 1800-1870 DLB-1
Lane, Charles
 See Gatti, Arthur Gerard
Lane, David (Stuart) 1933- CANR-17
 Earlier sketch in CA 29-32R
Lane, E(ugene Numa) 1936- 37-40R
Lane, Frank Walter 1908- 9-10R
Lane, Frederic C(hapin) 1900-1984 105
 Obituary 114
Lane, Gary 1943- 37-40R
Lane, Hana Umlauf 1946- 118
Lane, Harlan (Lawson) 1936- 126
 Brief entry 111
Lane, Helen 1920- 123
Lane, Helen R(uth) CANR-2
 Earlier sketch in CA 45-48
Lane, Irving M(ark) 1944- 53-56
Lane, Jack C(onstant) 1932- CANR-4
 Earlier sketch in CA 53-56
Lane, James B(uchanan) 1942- 93-96
Lane, Jane
 See Dakers, Elaine Kidner
Lane, Jerry
 See Martin, Patricia Miles
Lane, John 1932- SATA-15
Lane, John (Richard) 1932- 106
Lane, Laura Gordon 1913- 102
Lane, M(illicent) Travis 1934- 112
 See also DLB 60
Lane, Marc J(ay) 1946- CANR-21
 Earlier sketch in CA 105
Lane, Margaret 1907- CANR-13
 Earlier sketch in CA 25-28R
 See also SATA 38
Lane, Mark 1927- CANR-21
 Earlier sketch in CA 61-64
Lane, Mary (Lois) B(eauchamp) 1911- CANR-9
 Earlier sketch in CA 15-16R
Lane, Mary D.
 See Delaney, Mary Murray
Lane, Michael (John) 1941- 85-88
Lane, Patrick 1939- 97-100
 See also DLB 53
 See also CLC 25
Lane, Pinkie Gordon 1923- CANR-25
 Earlier sketch in CA 41-44R
 See also BW
 See also DLB 41
Lane, Raymond A. 1894(?)-1974
 Obituary 53-56
Lane, Richard 1926- CANR-10
 Earlier sketch in CA 21-22R
Lane, Robert E(dwards) 1917- CANR-6
 Earlier sketch in CA 1R
Lane, Roger 1934- 105
Lane, Ronnie M(ack) 1949- 41-44R
Lane, Rose Wilder 1887-1968 102
 See also SATA 28, 29
Lane, Roumelia
 See Green, Kay
Lane, Sherry
 See Smith, Richard Rein
Lane, Sylvia 1916- CANR-8
 Earlier sketch in CA 5-6R
Lane, Thomas A(lphonsus) 1906-1975 15-16R
 Obituary 125
Lane, Thomas A. 1906- 15-16R
Lane, Wheaton J. 1902-1983 Obituary 111
Lane, William G(uerrant) 1919- 25-28R
Lane, William L(ister) 1931- 29-32R
Lane, Yoti 2R
Lanegran, David A(ndrew) 1941- CANR-16
 Earlier sketch in CA 89-92
Lanes, Selma Gordon 1929- 25-28R
 See also SATA 3
Laney, Al 1896- 108
 See also DLB 4
Laney, J(ohn) Carl 1948- 114
Laney, James Thomas 1927- 103
Lanford, H(orace) W(haley) 1919- 41-44R
Lang, Allen Kim 1928- 17-18R
Lang, Andrew 1844-1912 Brief entry 114
 See also SATA 16
 See also TCLC 16
Lang, Barbara 1935- 11-12R
Lang, Berel 1933- CANR-15
 Earlier sketch in CA 41-44R
Lang, Daniel 1915-1981 CANR-4
 Obituary 105
 Earlier sketch in CA 7-8R
Lang, David 1913- 106
Lang, David Marshall 1924- CANR-17
 Earlier sketches in CA 7-8R, CANR-2
Lang, Derek 1913- 102
Lang, Frances
 See Mantle, Winifred (Langford)
Lang, Fritz 1890-1976 77-80
 Obituary 69-72
 See also CLC 20
Lang, George 1924- 101
Lang, Gottfried O(tto) 1919- 45-48
Lang, Grace
 See Floren, Lee
Lang, Gregor
 See Birren, Faber
Lang, H. Jack 1904- 115
Lang, Jack (Frederick) 1921- 5-6R
Lang, Jovian Peter 1919- CANR-15
 Earlier sketch in CA 41-44R
Lang, King
 See Tubb, E(dwin) C(harles)
Lang, Kurt 1924- 33-36R
Lang, Mabel L(ouise) 1917- 126
 Brief entry 106
Lang, Martin
 See Birren, Faber
Lang, Martin A(ndrew) 1930- 115
Lang, Maud
 See Williams, Claerwen
Lang, Miriam (Milman) 1915- 7-8R
Lang, Nancy M.
 See Mace, Nancy L(awson)
Lang, Ned
 See Sheckley, Robert
Lang, Paul Henry 1901- 103
Lang, Robert (Peregrine) 1912- 41-44R
Lang, Ronald William 1933- 103
Lang, Rupert
 See Turner, E(rnest) S(ackville)
Lang, T. T.
 See Taylor, Theodore
Lang, William Rawson 1909- CANR-21
 Earlier sketch in CA 103
Langacker, Ronald W(ayne) 1942- 23-24R
Langan, Ruth Ryan 1937- CANR-24
 Earlier sketch in CA 107
Langan, Thomas 1929- CANR-17
 Earlier sketch in CA 3R
Langbaum, Robert (Woodrow) 1924- CANR-1
 Earlier sketch in CA 45-48
Langbein, John H(arriss) 1941- 124
Langdale, Cecily 1939- 126
Langdale, Eve
 See Craig, E(velyn) Quita
Langdon, Charles 1934- 77-80
Langdon, Frank C(orriston) 1919- 23-24R
Langdon, George D(orland), Jr. 1933- 21-22R
Langdon, Grace 1889- 2R
Langdon, John 1913- 7-8R
Langdon, Margaret Hoffmann (Storms)
 1926- Brief entry 107
Langdon, Philip 1937- 109
Langdon, Robert Adrian 1924- CANR-20
 Earlier sketch in CA 104
Lange, Dorothea 1895-1965 Obituary 107
Lange, Gerald 1946- 69-72
Lange, John
 See Crichton, (John) Michael
Lange, John Frederick, Jr. 1931- CANR-25
 Earlier sketches in CA 97-100, CANR-8
Lange, (Leo) Joseph (Jr.) 1932- CANR-8
 Earlier sketch in CA 17-18R
Lange, Kelly 89-92
Lange, Oliver (a pseudonym) 1927- CANR-23
 Earlier sketch in CA 103
Lange, Oskar (Richard) 1904-1965
 Obituary 116
Lange, Suzanne 1945- 29-32R
 See also SATA 5
Lange, (Hermann Walter) Victor 1908- 11-12R
Langendoen, D(onald) Terence 1939- 33-36R
Langer, Elinor 1939- 121
 See also CLC 34
Langer, Ellen J(ane) 1947- 49-52
Langer, Jonas 1936- 33-36R
Langer, Lawrence L(ee) 1929- CANR-11
 Earlier sketch in CA 65-68
Langer, Marshall J. 1928- 105
Langer, Susanne (Katherina) K(nauth)
 1895-1985 41-44R
 Obituary 116
Langer, Sydney 1914- 109
Langer, Thomas Edward 1929- 7-8R
Langer, Walter Charles 1899-1981 102
 Obituary 104
Langer, William L(eonard) 1896-1977 CANR-14
 Obituary 73-76
 Earlier sketch in CA 29-32R
Langevin, Andre 1927- DLB-60
Langevin, Sister Jean Marie 1917- 53-56
Langford, Alec J. 1926- 97-100
Langford, Gary R(aymond) 1947- CANR-20
 Earlier sketch in CA 103
Langford, George 1939- 53-56
Langford, Gerald 1911- 1R
Langford, James R(ouleau) 1937- 53-56
Langford, Jane
 See Mantle, Winifred (Langford)
Langford, Jerome J.
 See Langford, James R(ouleau)
Langford, Thomas Anderson 1929- 9-10R
Langford, Walter McCarty 1908- 33-36R
Langgaesser, Elisabeth (Maria) 1899-1950
 Brief entry 121
 See also DLB 69
Langgasser, Elisabeth (Maria)
 See Langgaesser, Elisabeth (Maria)
 See also DLB 69
Langguth, A(rthur) J(ohn) 1933- 61-64
Langhoff, Severin Peter, Jr. 1910-1987
 Obituary 122
Langholm, Neil
 See Bulmer, (Henry) Kenneth
Langhorne, Elizabeth 49-52
Langhorne, Richard (Tristan Bailey) 1940- 122
Langiulli, Nino 1932- 53-56
Langland, Elizabeth 1948- 112
Langland, Joseph (Thomas) 1917- CANR-8
 Earlier sketch in CA 7-8R
Langley, Adria (Locke) 1899(?)-1983
 Obituary 110
Langley, Bob 1936- 85-88
Langley, Dorothy
 See Kissling, Dorothy (Hight)
Langley, Harold D. 1925- 21-22R
Langley, Helen
 See Rowland, D(onald) S(ydney)
Langley, James Maydon 1916-1983 102
 Obituary 109
Langley, Lester D(anny) 1940- CANR-19
 Earlier sketch in CA 102
Langley, Michael (John) 1933- 97-100
Langley, Noel 1911-1980 15-16R
 Obituary 102
 See also SATA 25
Langley, Raymond J. 1935- Brief entry 108
Langley, Roger 1930- 73-76
Langley, Stephen G(ould) 1938- 41-44R
Langley, Tania
 See Armstrong, Tilly
Langley, Wright 1935- 57-60
Langlois, Walter G(ordon) 1925- CANR-9
 Earlier sketch in CA 23-24R
Langman, Ida Kaplan 1904- CAP-1
 Earlier sketch in CA 15-16
Langman, Larry 1930- 109
Langner, Lawrence 1890-1962 Obituary 116
Langner, Nola 1930- CANR-15
 Earlier sketch in CA 37-40R
 See also SATA 8
Langone, John (Michael) 1929- CANR-1
 Earlier sketch in CA 49-52
 See also SATA 38, 46
Langsam, Walter Consuelo 1906-1985 CANR-2
 Obituary 117
 Earlier sketch in CA 3R
Lang-Sims, Lois Dorothy 1917- 106
Langsley, Donald G(ene) 1925- CANR-4
 Earlier sketch in CA 53-56
Langstaff, J(ohn) Brett 1889-1985 3R
 Obituary 115
Langstaff, John Meredith 1920- CANR-4
 Earlier sketch in CA 2R
 See also SATA 6
 See also CLR 3
Langstaff, Josephine
 See Herschberger, Ruth (Margaret)
Langstaff, Launcelot
 See Irving, Washington
Langstaff, Nancy 1925- CANR-12
 Earlier sketch in CA 73-76
Langton, Clair V(an Norman) 1895- 5-6R
Langton, Daniel J(oseph) 1927- 93-96
Langton, Jane (Gillson) 1922- CANR-18
 Earlier sketches in CA 4R, CANR-1
 See also SATA 3
 See also SAAS 5
Langton, Kenneth P(atrick) 1933- 25-28R
Langwill, Lyndesay Graham 1897- 15-16R
Langworth, Richard M(ichael) 1941- 73-76
Langworthy, Harry W(ells III) 1939- 57-60
Lanham, Charles Trueman 1902-1978
 Obituary 81-84
Lanham, Edwin (Moultrie) 1904-1979 9-10R
 Obituary 89-92
 See also DLB 4
Lanham, Frank W(esley) 1914- CANR-6
 Earlier sketch in CA 4R
Lanham, Richard Alan 1936- CANR-10
 Earlier sketch in CA 25-28R
Lanham, Url(ess Norton) 1918- 25-28R
Lanier, Alison Raymond 1917- CANR-12
 Earlier sketch in CA 19-20R

Lanier, Sidney 1842-1881 ... SATA-18
See also DLB 64
Lanier, Sterling E(dmund) 1927-
Brief entry ... 118
Lanigan, Catherine 1947- ... 108
Laning, Edward 1906- ... 53-56
Lank, Edith H(andleman) 1926- ... 109
Lankevich, George J(ohn) 1939- ... CANR-13
Earlier sketch in CA 77-80
Lankford, John (Errett) 1934- ... 19-20R
Lankford, Philip Marlin 1945- ... CANR-7
Earlier sketch in CA 57-60
Lankford, T(homas) Randall 1942- ... 65-68
Lanks, Herbert C(harles) 1899-1987
Obituary ... 122
Lanne, William F.
See Leopold, Nathan F.
Lanner, Ronald Martin 1930- ... 107
Lanning, Edward P(utnam) 1930- ... 17-18R
Lanning, George (William), Jr. 1925- ... 11-12R
Lanning, John Tate 1902-1976 Obituary ... 108
Lanoil, Georgia Hope Witkin
See Witkin-Lanoil, Georgia Hope
Lanoue, Fred Richard 1908-1965 ... CAP-1
Earlier sketch in CA 13-14
La Noue, George R(ichard) 1937- ... 73-76
Lanoux, Armand 1913-1983 Obituary ... 109
Lansbury, Angela 1946- ... 81-84
Lansdale, Edward Geary 1908-1987
Obituary ... 121
Lansdale, Joe R(ichard) 1951- ... 113
Lansdale, Robert Tucker 1900-1980
Obituary ... 103
Lansdowne, J(ames) F(enwick) 1937- ... 49-52
Lanser, Susan Sniader ... 107
Lansing, Alfred 1921-1975 ... 13-14R
Obituary ... 61-64
See also SATA 35
Lansing, Elisabeth Hubbard 1911- ... 7-8R
Lansing, Gerrit (Yates) 1928- ... 73-76
Lansing, Henry
See Rowland, D(onald) S(ydney)
Lansing, John B(elcher) 1919-1970
Obituary ... 108
Lansky, Bruce 1941- ... 109
Lansky, Vicki 1942- ... CANR-26
Earlier sketch in CA 81-84
Lanson, Lucienne (Therese) 1930-
Brief entry ... 108
Lant, Harvey
See Rowland, D(onald) S(ydney)
Lant, Jeffrey Ladd 1947- ... 109
Lanterman, Ray(mond E.) 1916- ... 106
Lantis, David W(illiam) 1917- ... 13-14R
Lantis, Margaret (Lydia) 1906- ... CAP-2
Earlier sketch in CA 29-32
Lantry, Mike
See Tubb, E(dwin) C(harles)
Lantz, Fran
See Lantz, Francess L(in)
Lantz, Francess L(in) 1952- ... 115
Lantz, Herman R. 1919-1987 ... 37-40R
Obituary ... 122
Lantz, Louise K. 1930- ... 45-48
Lantz, Paul 1908- ... SATA-45
Lantz, Walter 1900- Brief entry ... 108
See also SATA 37
Lanyon, Carla 1906-1971 ... CAP-1
Earlier sketch in CA 13-14
Lanzillotti, Robert F(ranklin) 1921- ... 77-80
Lao, Kan 1907- ... 41-44R
Lao She
See Shu Ch'ing-ch'un
Lapage, Geoffrey 1888- ... CAP-1
Earlier sketch in CA 9-10
La Palombara, Joseph 1925- ... CANR-6
Earlier sketch in CA 3R
Lapaquellerie, Yvon
See Bizardel, Yvon
Lapati, Americo D. 1924- ... CANR-1
Earlier sketch in CA 3R
La Patra, Jack W(illiam) 1927- ... 93-96
Lape, Esther Everett 1881-1981 Obituary ... 108
Lape, Fred 1900- ... 102
Lapedes, Daniel N. 1913(?)-1979
Obituary ... 93-96
LaPenta, Anthony V(incent), Jr. 1943- ... 69-72
Lapeza, David (Henry) 1950- ... 73-76
Lapham, Arthur L(owell) 1922- ... 49-52
Lapham, Lewis H(enry) 1935- ... 77-80
Lapham, Maxwell E(dward) 1900(?)-1983
Obituary ... 110
Lapham, Samuel, Jr. 1892-1972 Obituary ... 106
Lapide, Phinn E.
See Lapide, Pinchas E.
Lapide, Pinchas E. 1922- ... CANR-13
Earlier sketch in CA 23-24R
Lapidus, Elaine 1939- ... 21-22R
Lapidus, Jacqueline (Anita) 1941- ... 97-100
Lapidus, Morris 1902- ... 77-80
Lapierre, Dominique 1931- ... CANR-19
Earlier sketch in CA 69-72
LaPierre, Laurier L. 1929- Brief entry ... 107
La Pietra, Mary 1929- ... 61-64
Lapin, Howard S(idney) 1922- ... 19-20R
Lapin, Jackie 1951- ... 85-88
Lapine, James (Elliot) 1949- Brief entry ... 123
See also CLC 39
Lapinski, Susan 1948- ... 115
La Place, John 1922- ... 103
LaPointe, Frank 1936- ... 93-96
Lapointe, Paul-Marie 1929- Brief entry ... 109
Laponce, Jean Antoine 1925- ... 53-56
Laporte, Jean 1924- ... 41-44R
Laporte, Maurice 1901(?)-1987 Obituary ... 123
LaPorte, Robert, Jr. 1940- ... 41-44R
Lapp, Charles (Leon) 1914- ... CANR-1
Earlier sketch in CA 45-48
Lapp, Chuck
See Lapp, Charles (Leon)
Lapp, Eleanor J. 1936- ... 69-72
Lapp, Eunice Willis Bodine 1905- ... 123
Lapp, John Allen 1933- ... 41-44R
Lapp, John Clarke 1917-1977 ... 85-88
Lapp, Ralph Eugene 1917- ... 81-84
Lapp, Rudolph M(athew) 1915- ... 113
Lappe, Frances Moore 1944- ... 37-40R
Lappe, Marc 1943- ... 126
Lappin, Ben
See Lappin, Bernard William
Lappin, Bernard William 1916- ... 9-10R
Lappin, Peter 1911- ... CANR-25
Earlier sketches in CA 57-60, CANR-7
See also SATA 32
Lapping, Brian 1937- ... 25-28R
Laprade, William Thomas 1883-1975
Obituary ... 89-92
LaPray, (Margaret) Helen 1916- ... CANR-7
Earlier sketch in CA 53-56
Lapsley, James N(orvell) 1930- ... 25-28R
Laqueur, Walter (Ze'ev) 1921- ... CANR-23
Earlier sketch in CA 7-8R
Laquian, Aprodicio A(rcilla) 1935- ... CANR-26
Earlier sketch in CA 29-32R
Lara
See Griffith-Jones, George Chetwynd
Lara, Agustin 1900-1970 Obituary ... 104
Laramore, Darryl 1928- ... 101
Larbaud, Valery (Nicolas) 1881-1957
Brief entry ... 106
See also TCLC 9
Larco, Isabel Granda 1911(?)-1983
Obituary ... 109
Lardas, Konstantinos 1927- ... 13-14R
Lardner, George, Jr. 1934- ... 73-76
Lardner, James 1948- ... 118
Lardner, John (Abbott) 1912-1960
Obituary ... 93-96
Lardner, Ring(gold Wilmer) 1885-1933
Brief entry ... 104
See also DLB 11, 25
See also TCLC 2, 14
Lardner, Ring(gold Wilmer), Jr. 1915- ... CANR-13
Earlier sketch in CA 25-28R
See also DLB 26
Lardner-Burke, Desmond William
1909-1984 Obituary ... 114
Laredo, Betty
See Codrescu, Andrei
Laredo, Johnny
See Caesar, (Eu)Gene (Lee)
La Reyniere
See Courtine, Robert
Large, Peter Somerville
See Somerville-Large, Peter
Large, R(ichard) Geddes 1901- ... 102
Large, Stephen S(toker) 1942- ... 120
Largo, Michael 1950- ... 73-76
Lariar, Lawrence 1908- ... CAP-1
Earlier sketch in CA 9-10
Larimore, Bertha B(urnham) 1915- ... 61-64
La Rivers, Ira II 1915-1977 ... 41-44R
Larkey, Patrick Darrel 1943- ... 85-88
Larkin, Amy
See Burns, Olive Ann
Larkin, Emmet 1927- ... CANR-9
Earlier sketch in CA 15-16R
Larkin, John A(lan) 1936- ... 41-44R
Larkin, John Day 1897-1986 Obituary ... 118
Larkin, Maia
See Wojciechowska, Maia (Teresa)
Larkin, Maurice (John Milner) 1932- ... 102
Larkin, Miriam Therese 1930- Brief entry ... 108
Larkin, Oliver Waterman 1896-1970 ... 4R
Obituary ... 29-32R
Larkin, Philip (Arthur) 1922-1985 ... CANR-24
Obituary ... 117
Earlier sketch in CA 7-8R
See also DLB 27
See also CLC 3, 5, 8, 9, 13, 18, 33, 39
Larkin, R. T.
See Larkin, Rochelle
Larkin, Rochelle 1935- ... CANR-13
Earlier sketch in CA 33-36R
Larkin, Sarah
See Loening, Sarah (Elizabeth) Larkin
Larlham, Hattie 1914- ... 113
Larminie, Margaret Beda 1924- ... CANR-18
Earlier sketches in CA 7-8R, CANR-2
Larmore, Lewis 1915- ... 45-48
Larn, Richard (James Vincent) 1930- ... CANR-20
Earlier sketch in CA 103
Larnach, Rupert
See Nevill, Barry St-John
Larner, Christina (Ross) ?-1983 Obituary ... 115
Larner, Jeremy 1937- ... 11-12R
Larner, John (Patrick) 1930- ... 81-84
Larneuil, Michel
See Batbedat, Jean
Laroche, Rene
See McKeag, Ernest L(ionel)
Larock, Bruce Edward 1940- ... 53-56
La Rocque, Gilbert 1943-1984 ... DLB-60
Larom, Henry V. 1903(?)-1975 Obituary ... 61-64
See also SATA 30
Laroque de Roquebrune, Robert
See Roquebrune, Robert de
La Rosa, Paul (Frank) 1953- ... 113
Larose, Paul 1947- ... 114
LaRouche, Lyndon H(ermyle), Jr. 1922-
Brief entry ... 124
Larrabee, Carroll Burton 1896-1983
Obituary ... 110
Larrabee, Eric 1922- ... CANR-1
Earlier sketch in CA 1R
Larrabee, Harold A(tkins) 1894-1979 ... CAP-1
Obituary ... 85-88
Earlier sketch in CA 11-12
Larranaga, Robert O. 1940- ... 49-52
Larrea, Jean-Jacques 1960- ... 45-48
Larrecq, John M(aurice)
1926-1980 ... SATA-25, 44
Larrick, Nancy 1910- ... CANR-1
Earlier sketch in CA 1R
See also SATA 4
See also DLB 61
Larrie, Reginald R. 1928- ... 123
Brief entry ... 118
Larrison, Earl J(unior) 1919- ... CANR-9
Earlier sketch in CA 57-60
Larrowe, Charles P(atrick) 1916- ... 41-44R
Larry
See Parkes, Terence
Larsen, Beverly (Namen) 1929- ... 17-18R
Larsen, Carl 1934- ... 77-80
Larsen, Charles E(dward) 1923- ... 33-36R
Larsen, David C(harles) 1944- ... 73-76
Larsen, E(gner) John 1926- ... CANR-16
Earlier sketch in CA 25-28R
Larsen, Egon 1904- ... CANR-3
Earlier sketch in CA 9-10R
See also SATA 14
Larsen, Elyse 1957- ... 41-44R
Larsen, Erik 1911- ... 41-44R
Larsen, Erling 1909- ... 13-14R
Larsen, Ernest 1946- ... 106
Larsen, Gaylord 1932- ... 112
Larsen, J(akob) A(all) O(tteson)
1888-1974 Obituary ... 111
Larsen, Jack Lenor 1927- ... 126
Larsen, Jens Peter 1902-1988 Obituary ... 126
Larsen, Kalee 1952- ... 41-44R
Larsen, Knud S(onderhede) 1938- ... 53-56
Larsen, Lawrence H. 1931- ... 21-22R
Larsen, Nella 1891-1964 ... 125
See also BW
See also DLB 51
See also CLC 37
Larsen, Otto N. 1922- ... CANR-2
Earlier sketch in CA 3R
Larsen, Paul E(manuel) 1933- ... 93-96
Larsen, Peter 1933- ... CANR-22
Earlier sketch in CA 29-32R
Larsen, Rebecca 1944- ... 122
Larsen, Ronald J(ames) 1948- ... 41-44R
Larsen, Roy E(dward) 1899-1979
Obituary ... 89-92
Larsen, Stephen 1941- ... 69-72
Larsen, Susan C(arol) 1946- ... 125
Larsen, Tony 1949- ... 107
Larsen, Wendy Wilder 1940- ... 120
Larsen, William E(dward) 1936- ... 17-18R
Larsgaard, Mary L(ynette) 1946- ... 122
Larson, Albert J. 1934- ... 112
Larson, Andrew Karl 1899- ... CAP-2
Earlier sketch in CA 33-36
Larson, Arthur 1910- ... CANR-1
Earlier sketch in CA 2R
Larson, Bob 1944- ... CANR-5
Earlier sketch in CA 53-56
Larson, Bruce 1925- ... CANR-13
Earlier sketch in CA 57-60
Larson, Bruce L(lewellyn) 1936- ... 85-88
Larson, Calvin J. 1933- ... 49-52
Larson, Carl M. 1916- ... 41-44R
Larson, Cedric Arthur 1908- ... 65-68
Larson, Charles 1922- ... 25-28R
Larson, Charles R(aymond) 1938- ... CANR-4
Earlier sketch in CA 53-56
See also CLC 31
Larson, Charles U(rban) 1940- ... 97-100
Larson, Clinton F(oster) 1919- ... 57-60
Larson, Donald (Norman) 1925- ... 57-60
Larson, Doran 1957- ... 124
Larson, E. Richard 1944- ... 105
Larson, Esther Elisabeth ... 17-18R
Larson, Eve
See St. John, Wylly Folk
Larson, Gary 1950- ... 118
Larson, Gary O(tto) 1949- ... 115
Larson, George C(harles) 1942- ... CANR-9
Earlier sketch in CA 65-68
Larson, Gerald James 1938- ... 93-96
Larson, Glen A. 1937(?)- Brief entry ... 115
Larson, Gustive O(lof) 1897-1978 ... 29-32R
Obituary ... 125
Larson, Gustive O. 1897- ... 29-32R
Larson, Harold J. 1934- ... 53-56
Larson, Henrietta M(elia) 1894-1983 ... CAP-2
Obituary ... 110
Earlier sketch in CA 23-24
Larson, James F(rederick) 1947- ... 115
Larson, Janet Karsten 1945- ... 104
Larson, Jean Russell 1930- ... 21-22R
Larson, Jeanne 1920- ... 57-60
Larson, Knute (G.) 1919- ... 9-10R
Larson, Kris 1953- ... 77-80
Larson, Magali Sarfatti 1936- ... 97-100
Larson, Martin Alfred 1897- ... CANR-2
Earlier sketch in CA 7-8R
Larson, Mel(vin Gunnard) 1916- ... 7-8R
Larson, Muriel 1924- ... CANR-24
Earlier sketches in CA 23-24R, CANR-9
Larson, Norita D(ittberner) 1944- ... 105
See also SATA 29
Larson, Orvin Prentiss 1910- ... 77-80
Larson, P(aul) Merville 1903- ... 41-44R
Larson, Peggy (Ann Pickering) 1931- ... 81-84
Larson, Richard Francis 1931- ... CANR-15
Earlier sketch in CA 41-44R
Larson, Robert H(erbert) 1942- ... 113
Larson, Robert W. 1927- ... 85-88
Larson, Simeon 1925- ... 61-64
Larson, T(aft) A(lfred) 1910- ... 33-36R
Larson, Thomas B(ryan) 1914- ... 25-28R
Larson, Victor E. 1898- ... 25-28R
Larson, William H. 1938- ... 23-24R
See also SATA 10
Larsson, Carl (Olof) 1853-1919
Brief entry ... 115
See also SATA 35
Larsson, Flora (Benwell) 1904- ... 93-96
Lartigue, Jacques-Henri 1894-1986 ... 33-36R
Obituary ... 120
La Rue, Daniel Wolford, Jr. 1878-1969
Obituary ... 116
Larue, Gerald A(lexander) 1916- ... 23-24R
LaRusso, Dominic A(nthony) 1924- ... 33-36R
Lary, N(ikita) M(ichael) 1940- ... 61-64
Lasagna, Louis (Cesare) 1923- Brief entry ... 106
LaSalle, Charles A.
See Ellis, Edward S(ylvester)
LaSalle, Charles E.
See Ellis, Edward S(ylvester)
La Salle, Donald (Philip) 1933- ... 29-32R
La Salle, Dorothy (Marguerite) 1895-1980 ... 5-6R
Obituary ... 126
LaSalle, Peter 1947- ... 103
La Salle, Victor
See Fanthorpe, R(obert) Lionel
Lasater, Alice E(lizabeth) 1936- ... 57-60
Lasby, Clarence G(eorge) 1933- ... 105
Lasch, Christopher 1932- ... CANR-25
Earlier sketch in CA 73-76
Lasch, Robert 1907- ... 102
Laschever, Barnett D. 1924- ... CANR-6
Earlier sketch in CA 4R
LaScola, Ray(mond) L. 1915- ... 3R
Lasdun, Susan 1929- ... 111
Lasell, Elinor H. 1929- ... CANR-7
Earlier sketch in CA 7-8R
See also SATA 19
Lasell, Fen H.
See Lasell, Elinor H.
Laser, Marvin 1914- ... 9-10R
Lash, Joseph P. 1909-1987 ... CANR-16
Obituary ... 123
Earlier sketch in CA 17-18R
See also SATA 43
Lasher, Albert C. 1928- ... 25-28R
Lasher, Faith B. 1921- ... 37-40R
See also SATA 12
Laska
See Laska, P(eter) J(erome)
Laska, P(eter) J(erome) 1938- ... CANR-15
Earlier sketch in CA 65-68
Laska, Vera
See Laska, Vera O(ravec)
Laska, Vera O(ravec) 1923- ... 119
Lasker, David 1950- ... 112
See also SATA 38
Lasker, Edward 1885-1981 ... 5-6R
Obituary ... 103
Lasker, Gabriel Ward 1912- ... 2R
Lasker, Joe 1919- ... CANR-1
Earlier sketch in CA 49-52
See also SATA 9
Lasker-Schueler, Else 1869-1945 ... DLB-66
Laski, Marghanita 1915-1988 ... 105
Obituary ... 124
Laskin, Bora 1912-1984 Obituary ... 112
Laskowski, Jerzy 1919- ... 77-80
Lasky, Betty 1927- ... 119
Lasky, Jesse Louis, Jr. 1910- ... CANR-20
Earlier sketches in CA 2R, CANR-4
See also AITN 1
Lasky, Kathryn 1944- ... CANR-11
Earlier sketch in CA 69-72
See also SATA 13
See also CLR 11
Lasky, Melvin J(onah) 1920- ... 53-56
Lasky, Victor 1918- ... CANR-10
Earlier sketch in CA 5-6R
See also AITN 1
Lasky, William R(aymond) 1921- ... 97-100
Laslett, John H(enry) M(artin) 1933- ... CANR-12
Earlier sketch in CA 29-32R
Laslett, Peter 1915- ... CANR-12
Earlier sketch in CA 73-76
Lasley, Jack
See Lasley, John Wayne III
Lasley, John Wayne III 1925- ... 19-20R
LaSor, William Sanford 1911- ... CANR-21
Earlier sketches in CA 4R, CANR-2
La Sorte, A(ntonio) Michael 1931- ... 15-16R
La Spina, (Fanny) Greye 1880- ... CAP-1
Earlier sketch in CA 13-14
Lass, Abraham H(arold) 1907- ... 11-12R
Lass, Betty (Lipschitz) 1908(?)-1976
Obituary ... 69-72
Lass, William E(dward) 1928- ... CANR-2
Earlier sketch in CA 4R
Lass, William M. 1910(?)-1975 Obituary ... 104
Lassalle, C. E.
See Ellis, Edward S(ylvester)
Lassam, Robert (Errington) 1914- ... 112
Lassen-Willems, James
See Willems, J. Rutherford
Lassers, Willard J. 1919- ... 17-18R
Lassimonne, Denise ... 25-28R
Lassiter, Adam
See Krauzer, Steven M(ark)
Lassiter, Isaac Steele 1941- ... 33-36R
Lassiter, (Albin) Perry (Jr.) 1935- ... 97-100
Lassiter, Roy L(eland), Jr. 1927- ... 21-22R
Lassner, Jacob 1935- ... CANR-20
Earlier sketch in CA 29-32R

Lasson, Kenneth (Lee) 1943- CANR-13
Earlier sketch in CA 33-36R
Lasswell, Harold D. 1902-1978 Obituary ... 104
Lasswell, Marcia 1927- 97-100
Lasswell, Thomas Ely 1919- 17-18R
Last, Jef
See Last, Josephus Carel Franciscus
Last, Joan 1908- 107
Last, Josephus Carel Franciscus
1898-1972 .... CAP-2
Earlier sketch in CA 33-36
Laster, Ann A(ppleton) 1936- 29-32R
Laszlo, Ervin 1932- 41-44R
Laszlo, Miklos 1904(?)-1973 Obituary ... 41-44R
Latane, Bibb 1937- 37-40R
Latch, William 1950(?)-1985 Obituary 117
Latchaw, Marjorie Elizabeth 1914- 5-6R
Latham, Aaron 1943- 33-36R
Latham, Barbara 1896- SATA-16
Latham, Caroline S. 1940- 125
Latham, Donald Crawford 1932- 11-12R
Latham, Earl Ganson 1907- 103
Latham, Frank B(rown) 1910- 49-52
See also SATA 6
Latham, Harold Strong 1887-1969 .... CAP-1
Earlier sketch in CA 9-10
Latham, Ian 1956- 109
Latham, Jean Lee 1902- CANR-7
Earlier sketch in CA 7-8R
See also SATA 2
See also CLC 12
See also AITN 1
Latham, John H. 1917- 5-6R
Latham, Joyce 1943- 73-76
Latham, Lenn Learner 1901-197(?) 2R
Latham, Lorraine 1948- 65-68
Latham, Marte Hooper 1924- 9-10R
Latham, Mavis
See Clark, Mavis Thorpe
Latham, Peter 1910- CAP-1
Earlier sketch in CA 11-12
Latham, Philip
See Richardson, Robert S(hirley)
Latham, Roger M. 1914(?)-1979
Obituary 85-88
Lathen, Emma
See Hennissart, Martha
and Latsis, Mary J(ane)
See also CLC 2
Lathrop, Dorothy P(ulis) 1891-1980 73-76
Obituary 102
See also SATA 14, 24
See also DLB 22
Lathrop, Francis
See Leiber, Fritz (Reuter, Jr.)
Lathrop, George Parsons 1851-1898 .... DLB-71
Lathrop, Irvin T(unis) 1927- CANR-22
Earlier sketch in CA 45-48
Lathrop, JoAnna 1931- 61-64
Lathrop, John, Jr. 1772-1820 .... DLB-37
Latimer, H(enry) C. 1893- 29-32R
Latimer, Jonathan (Wyatt) 1906-1983
Obituary 110
Latman, Alan 1930-1984 Obituary 113
Latner, Helen (Stambler) 1918- 106
Latner, Pat Wallace
See Strother, Pat Wallace
Latorre, Dolores L(aguarta Blasco) 1903- .. 65-68
Latorre, Felipe A(ugusto) 1907- 65-68
La Tour du Pin, Patrice de 1911-1975
Obituary 115
La Tourette, Aileen 1946- 119
Latourette, Kenneth Scott 1884-1967 .... CAP-2
Earlier sketch in CA 23-24
La Tourette, Jacqueline 1926- 49-52
Latow, (Muriel) Roberta 1931- 116
Latsis, Mary J(ane) 85-88
Latta, Richard 1946- CANR-19
Earlier sketches in CA 53-56, CANR-4
Latta, William (Charlton, Jr.) 1929- 115
Lattimer, John Kingsley 1914- 106
Lattimore, Eleanor Frances 1904-1986 .. CANR-6
Obituary 119
Earlier sketch in CA 9-10R
See also SATA 7, 48
Lattimore, Owen 1900- 97-100
Lattimore, Richmond (Alexander)
1906-1984 .... CANR-1
Obituary 112
Earlier sketch in CA 4R
See also CLC 3
Lattin, Ann
See Cole, Lois Dwight
Lattin, Harriet Pratt 1898- 33-36R
Latukefu, Sione 1927- 73-76
Latzer, Beth Good 1911- 65-68
Lau, Charles Richard 1933-1984 Obituary .. 112
Lau, Charley
See Lau, Charles Richard
Lau, Joseph S(hui) M(ing) 1934- 77-80
Laub, (Martin) Julian 1929- 37-40R
Laubach, Frank Charles 1884-1970 ...... CAP-1
Earlier sketch in CA 9-10
Laube, Clifford J(ames) 1891-1974
Obituary 53-56
Laubenthal, Sanders Anne 1943- 61-64
Lauber, Patricia (Grace) 1924- CANR-24
Earlier sketches in CA 9-10R, CANR-6
See also SATA 1, 33
See also CLR 16
Laubin, Gladys (Winifred) 111
Laubin, Reginald K(arl) 111
Laucanno, Christopher Sawyer
See Sawyer-Laucanno, Christopher
Lauck, Carol 1934- 93-96
Lauder, George
See Dick-Lauder, George (Andrew)
Lauder, George (Andrew) Dick
See Dick-Lauder, George (Andrew)
Lauder, Phyllis 1898- 93-96
Lauderdale, Pat 1944- 101
Laudicina, Paul A(ndrew) 1949- 93-96
Laudin, Harvey 1922- 77-80
Laue, Max Theodor Felix von 1879-1960
Obituary 113
Lauer, Evelyn G(erda) 1938- 29-32R
Lauer, Jeanette C(arol) 1935- CANR-19
Earlier sketch in CA 104
Lauer, Jean-Philippe 1902- 85-88
Lauer, Robert H(arold) 1933- CANR-19
Earlier sketches in CA 53-56, CANR-4
Lauer, Rosemary Zita 1919- 5-6R
Lauer, Theodore E. 1931- 37-40R
Lauerman, David A(nthony) 1931- 19-20R
Lauersen, Niels H(elth) 1939- CANR-15
Earlier sketch in CA 85-88
Lauf, Detlef I. Charles 1936- 103
Laufe, Abe 1906- 17-18R
Laufer, Leopold 1925- 21-22R
Lauffer, Armand A(lbert) 1933- CANR-19
Earlier sketches in CA 53-56, CANR-5
Laugesen, Mary E(akin) 1906- CAP-2
Earlier sketch in CA 29-32
See also SATA 5
Laughbaum, Steve 1945- SATA-12
Laughlin, Clarence John 1905-1985
Obituary 114
Laughlin, Florence Young 1910- 9-10R
See also SATA 3
Laughlin, Henry Prather 1916- CANR-8
Earlier sketch in CA 61-64
Laughlin, James 1914- CANR-9
Earlier sketch in CA 21-22R
See also DLB 48
See also CLC 49
Laughlin, Ledlie Irwin 1890-1977 .... 37-40R
Laughlin, Tom 1938(?)- Brief entry 116
Laughton, Tom 1904(?)-1984 Obituary 112
Laugier, Odile 1956- 108
Laugier, R.
See Cumberland, Marten
Laumann, Edward O. 1938- 33-36R
Laumer, (John) Keith 1925- CANR-7
Earlier sketch in CA 11-12R
See also DLB 8
Launay, Andre (Joseph) 1930- 25-28R
Launay, Droo
See Launay, Andre (Joseph)
Laune, Paul Sidney 1899- 19-20R
Launitz-Schurer, Leopold (Sidney), Jr.
1942- 103
Laurance, Alfred D.
See Tralins, S(andor) Robert
Laurance, Alice (a pseudonym) 1938- 101
Laure, Ettagale
See Blauer, Ettagale
Laure, Jason 1940- 104
See also SATA 44, 50
Laurel, Alicia Bay 1949- 41-44R
Lauren, Linda
See Bunce, Linda Susan (Staines)
Laurence, Dan H. 1920- CANR-13
Earlier sketch in CA 17-18R
Laurence, Ester Hauser 1935- 29-32R
See also SATA 7
Laurence, John 1939- 69-72
Laurence, (Jean) Margaret (Wemyss)
1926-1987 .... 7-8R
Obituary 121
See also SATA 50
See also DLB 53
See also CLC 3, 6, 13, 50
Laurence, Michael M(arshall) 1940- 33-36R
Laurence, Will
See Smith, Willard L(aurence)
Laurence, William Leonard 1888-1977 77-80
Obituary 69-72
Laurent, Antoine 1952- CLC-50
Laurent, Lawrence (Bell) 1925- 69-72
Laurenti, Joseph L(ucian) 1931- 49-52
Laurentin, Rene 1917- 106
Laurents, Arthur 1918- CANR-8
Earlier sketch in CA 15-16R
See also DLB 26
Lauria, Frank (Jonathan) 1935- 103
Laurie, Annie
See Black, Winifred
Laurie, Bruce 1943- 115
Laurie, Edward J(ames) 1925- CANR-8
Earlier sketch in CA 19-20R
Laurie, Harry C.
See Cahn, Zvi
Laurie, James 1947- 69-72
Laurie, Michael M. 1932- 126
Laurie, Rona CANR-15
Earlier sketch in CA 85-88
Laurin, Anne
See McLaurin, Anne
Lauritsen, John (Phillip) 1939- 57-60
Lauritzen, Elizabeth Moyes 1909- CAP-1
Earlier sketch in CA 15-16
Lauritzen, Jonreed 1902- 5-6R
See also SATA 13
Lauri-Volpi, Giacomo 1893(?)-1979
Obituary 85-88
Lauro, Shirley (Shapiro) Mezvinsky 1933- ... 126
Laury, Jean Ray 1928- 77-80
Lauscher, Hermann
See Hesse, Hermann
Lautenbach, Renee 1932- 110
Lauter
See Chamson, Andre J(ules) L(ouis)
Lauter, Geza Peter 1932- 41-44R
Lauter, Paul 1932- 15-16R
Lauterbach, Albert 1904- CANR-1
Earlier sketch in CA 3R
Lauwerys, Joseph (Albert) 1902-1981 .... 15-16R
Obituary 104
Laux, Dorothy 1920- 61-64
See also SATA 49
Laux, James M(ichael) 1927- 33-36R
Laux, P(eter) J(ohn) 1922- 25-28R
Lavagnino, Allessandra 1927- CANR-2
Earlier sketch in CA 45-48
LaValle, Irving H(oward) 1939- 33-36R
Lavan, Spencer 1937- CANR-8
Earlier sketch in CA 57-60
Lave, Lester B(ernard) 1939- CANR-15
Earlier sketch in CA 41-44R
Lavelle, Mike 1933- 65-68
Lavelle, Sheila 1939- 109
Lavender, David (Sievert) 1910- CANR-18
Earlier sketches in CA 4R, CANR-2
Lavender, William 1921- CANR-10
Earlier sketch in CA 65-68
Lavenson, James H. 1919- 103
Lavenson, Jim
See Lavenson, James H.
Laver, James 1899-1975 .... CANR-3
Obituary 57-60
Earlier sketch in CA 2R
Laver, Michael 1949- CANR-23
Earlier sketch in CA 107
Laver, Rod(ney George) 1938- Brief entry .. 112
La Verdiere, Eugene Armand 1936- CANR-19
Earlier sketch in CA 102
Lavers, Norman 1935- 104
Laverty, Carroll D(ee) 1906- 77-80
Laverty, Donald
See Blish, James (Benjamin)
and Knight, Damon (Francis)
Lavery, Emmet (Godfrey) 1902-1986
Obituary 118
Laves, Walter H(erman) C(arl) 1902-1983
Obituary 111
La Vey, Anton Szandor 1930- Brief entry ... 109
Lavin, David E(dwin) 1931- CANR-2
Earlier sketch in CA 2R
Lavin, Henry St. C. 1921-1985 Obituary 114
Lavin, J(oseph) A(nthony) 1932- 33-36R
Lavin, Marilyn Aronberg 1925- 106
Lavin, Mary 1912- 9-10R
See also DLB 15
See also CLC 4, 18
Lavine, David 1928- SATA-31
Lavine, Harold 1915-1984 .... 41-44R
Obituary 113
Lavine, Richard A. 1917- 23-24R
Lavine, Sigmund Arnold 1908- CANR-19
Earlier sketches in CA 3R, CANR-4
See also SATA 3
Lavington, H(arold) Dude 1907- 117
Lavinson, Joseph
See Kaye, Marvin (Nathan)
Laviolette, Emily A. 1923(?)-1975 ..... SATA-49
Lavond, Paul Dennis
See Kornbluth, C(yril) M.
and Lowndes, Robert A(ugustine) W(ard)
and Pohl, Frederik
Lavori, Nora 1950- 93-96
Lavrin, Janko Matthew 1887-1986 .... 9-10R
Obituary 120
Law, Carol Russell 106
Law, Howard W(illiam) 1919- 23-24R
Law, Janice
See Trecker, Janice Law
Law, Marie Hamilton 1884-1981 Obituary ... 106
Law, Richard 1901-1980 Obituary 105
Law, Virginia W.
See Shell, Virginia Law
Lawder, Douglas W(ard) 1934- CANR-1
Earlier sketch in CA 45-48
Lawford, J(ames) P(hilip) 1915- 33-36R
Lawford, Paula Jane 1960- 125
See also SATA 53
Lawhead, Victor B(ernard) 1919- 41-44R
Lawhorne, Clifton O. 1927-1983 104
Obituary 110
Lawler, Donald L(ester) 1935- 105
Lawler, James R. 1929- 57-60
Lawler, Lillian B. 1898- 15-16R
Lawler, Philip F(rederick) 1950- 110
Lawler, Raymond Evenor 1922- 103
Lawler, Ronald (David) 1926- 126
Brief entry 110
Lawless, Anthony
See MacDonald, Philip
Lawless, Bettyclare Hamilton 1915- 61-64
Lawless, Dorothy (Mae) Kennedy 1906- 7-8R
Lawless, Edward W(illiam) 1931- 114
Lawless, Elaine J. 1947- 126
Lawless, Gary 1951- CANR-13
Earlier sketch in CA 73-76
Lawlor, Florine 1925- 65-68
Lawlor, John (James) 1918- 5-6R
Lawlor, Monica (Mary) 1926- 9-10R
Lawlor, Pat
See Lawlor, Patrick Anthony
Lawlor, Patrick Anthony 1893- CAP-1
Earlier sketch in CA 9-10
Lawner, Lynne 1935- 9-10R
Lawrence, A. R.
See Foff, Arthur R(aymond)
Lawrence, Alexander Atkinson 1906-1979 ... 102
Lawrence, Ann (Margaret) 1942- 104
See also SATA 41
Lawrence, Berta 73-76
Lawrence, Bill 1930- 25-28R
Lawrence, D. Baloti 1950- 113
Lawrence, D(avid) H(erbert Richards)
1885-1930 121
Brief entry 104
See also DLB 10, 19, 36
See also TCLC 2, 9, 16
Lawrence, Daniel 1940- 57-60
Lawrence, David 1888-1973 102
Obituary 41-44R
See also DLB 29
Lawrence, David, Jr. 1942- 73-76
Lawrence, E. S.
See Bradburne, E(lizabeth) S.
Lawrence, Eddie
See Eisler, Lawrence
Lawrence, Edward
See Eisler, Lawrence
Lawrence, Elizabeth L. 1904-1985 124
Lawrence, Emeric Anthony 1908- CANR-5
Earlier sketch in CA 3R
Lawrence, Francis L(eo) 1937- 49-52
Lawrence, Gale 1941- 126
Lawrence, George H(ill Mathewson)
1910-1978 Obituary 81-84
Lawrence, H(enry) L(ionel) 1908- CAP-1
Earlier sketch in CA 9-10
Lawrence, Helen M(ary) 1925- 111
Lawrence, Isabelle (Wentworth) SATA-29
Lawrence, J. D.
See Lawrence, James Duncan
Lawrence, J. T.
See Rowland-Entwistle, (Arthur)
Theodore (Henry)
Lawrence, Jack
See Fitzgerald, Lawrence P(ennybaker)
Lawrence, James Duncan 1918- 17-18R
Lawrence, Jerome 1915- 41-44R
Lawrence, Jock
See Lawrence, Justus Baldwin
Lawrence, Jodi 1938- CANR-3
Earlier sketch in CA 45-48
Lawrence, John (Waldemar) 1907- 81-84
Lawrence, John 1933- CANR-24
Earlier sketch in CA 107
See also SATA 30
Lawrence, John
See Lawrence, Jodi
Lawrence, John A. 1908-1976 Obituary ... 65-68
Lawrence, John S(helton) 1938- 123
Brief entry 107
Lawrence, Joseph D(ouglas) 1895- 126
Lawrence, Josephine 1890(?)-1978 77-80
See also SATA 24
Lawrence, Justus Baldwin 1903-1987
Obituary 122
Lawrence, Karen 1949- 126
Lawrence, Karen 1951- 126
Lawrence, Karl
See Foff, Arthur R(aymond)
Lawrence, Kenneth G.
See Ringgold, Gene
Lawrence, Lesley
See Lewis, Lesley
Lawrence, Louise
See Holden, Elizabeth Rhoda
See also SATA 38
Lawrence, Louise de Kiriline 1894- 25-28R
See also SATA 13
Lawrence, Margaret Morgan 1914- 33-36R
Lawrence, Marjorie 1907-1979 Obituary ... 85-88
Lawrence, Martin
See Greif, Martin
and Grow, Lawrence
Lawrence, Mary
See Young, Mary Lou Daves
Lawrence, Mary Margaret 1920- 93-96
Lawrence, Merle 1915- 21-22R
Lawrence, Michael
See Lariar, Lawrence
Lawrence, Mildred Elwood 1907- CANR-5
Earlier sketch in CA 1R
See also SATA 3
Lawrence, Nathaniel (Morris)
1917-1986 .... CANR-22
Earlier sketch in CA 45-48
Lawrence, P.
See Tubb, E(dwin) C(harles)
Lawrence, Peter 1921-1988 Obituary 124
Lawrence, R(onald) D(ouglas) 1921- ... CANR-11
Earlier sketch in CA 65-68
Lawrence, Richard A.
See Leopold, Nathan F.
Lawrence, Robert 1912(?)-1981 Obituary ... 105
Lawrence, Robert
See Beum, Robert (Lawrence)
Lawrence, Robert A(llen) 1948- 118
Lawrence, Roy 1930- 45-48
Lawrence, Samuel A. 1928- 21-22R
Lawrence, Sharon 1945- 65-68
Lawrence, Steven C.
See Murphy, Lawrence A(gustus)
Lawrence, T(homas) E(dward) 1888-1935
Brief entry 115
See also TCLC 18
Lawrence, Thomas
See Roberts, Thom(as Sacra)
Lawrence, Vera Brodsky 1909- Brief entry .. 109
Lawrence, William Howard 1916-1972
Obituary 33-36R
Lawrence, William J(ohn) C(ooper)
1899(?)-1985 Obituary 118
Lawrence Of Arabia
See Lawrence, T(homas) E(dward)
Lawrenson, Helen 1907-1982 117
Obituary 106
Lawrenson, Thomas Edward 1918-1982
Obituary 106
Lawry, Jon Sherman 1924- 7-8R

INDEX

Laws, G(eorge) Malcolm, Jr. 1919- 37-40R
Laws, Priscilla W(atson) 1940- 73-76
Lawshe, C(harles) H(ubert) 1908- CAP-2
Earlier sketch in CA 23-24
Lawson, (Richard) Alan 1934- 53-56
Lawson, Annetta 1939- 116
Lawson, Carol (Antell) 1946- SATA-42
Lawson, Chet
See Tubb, E(dwin) C(harles)
Lawson, David 1927- 57-60
Lawson, Don(ald Elmer) 1917- CANR-26
Earlier sketches in CA 1R, CANR-2
See also SATA 9
Lawson, Donna Roberta 1937- 41-44R
Lawson, E(verett) LeRoy 1938- CANR-19
Earlier sketches in CA 53-56, CANR-4
Lawson, Evelyn 1917- 57-60
Lawson, F(loyd) Melvyn 1907- 53-56
Lawson, Frederick Henry 1897-1983
Obituary 109
Lawson, H(orace) L(owe) 1900- 5-6R
Lawson, H. Lowe
See Lawson, H(orace) L(owe)
Lawson, Henry (Archibald Hertzberg)
1867-1922 Brief entry 120
See also TCLC 27
Lawson, Jacob
See Burgess, M(ichael) R(oy)
Lawson, James 1938- 65-68
Lawson, Joan 1906- 103
Lawson, John 1909- CANR-3
Earlier sketch in CA 2R
Lawson, John ?-1711 .... DLB-24
Lawson, John Howard 1894-1977 .... CAP-1
Obituary 73-76
Earlier sketch in CA 15-16
Lawson, Kay 1933- 104
Lawson, Lewis A. 1931- 21-22R
Lawson, M. C.
See Lawson, H(orace) L(owe)
Lawson, Marion Tubbs 1896- CAP-1
Earlier sketch in CA 9-10
See also SATA 22
Lawson, Michael
See Ryder, M(ichael) L(awson)
Lawson, Philip J. 1908(?)-1978 Obituary ..77-80
Lawson, (Phillippe) Reed 1929- 7-8R
Lawson, Richard H(enry) 1919- CANR-8
Earlier sketch in CA 17-18R
Lawson, Robert 1892-1957 Brief entry 118
See also YABC 2
See also DLB 22
See also CLR 2
Lawson, Robert G. 1938- 118
Lawson, Ronald (Lynton) 1940- 126
Lawson, Ruth C(atherine) 1911- 9-10R
Lawson, S. Alexander 1912- 57-60
Lawson, Sarah (Anne) 1943- 120
Lawson, Steve
See Turner, Robert (Harry)
Lawson, Steven F(red) 1945- 122
Lawson, Victor F. 1850-1925 .... DLB-25
Lawson, W. B.
See Jenks, George C(harles)
Lawton, Charles
See Heckelmann, Charles N(ewman)
Lawton, Dennis
See Faust, Frederick (Shiller)
Lawton, Harry Wilson 1927- 33-36R
Lawton, Manny
See Lawton, Marion R(ussell)
Lawton, Marion R(ussell) 1918-1986 118
Lawton, Sherman P(axton) 1908- CAP-2
Earlier sketch in CA 19-20
Lawyer, Annabel Glenn 1906(?)-1974
Obituary 53-56
Law Yone, Edward Michael 1911(?)-1980
Obituary 101
Lax, Robert 1915- CANR-11
Earlier sketch in CA 25-28R
Laxalt, Robert P(eter) 1923- 13-14R
Laxness, Halldor
See Gudjonsson, Halldor Kiljan
See also CLC 25
Lay, Bennett 1910- CAP-1
Earlier sketch in CA 11-12
Lay, Bierne, Jr. 1909-1982 Obituary 107
Lay, Daniel W(ayne) 1914- 118
Lay, Nancy Duke S. 1938- CANR-21
Earlier sketch in CA 105
Lay, Norvie L(ee) 1940- 49-52
Lay, S(amuel) Houston 1912- 33-36R
Lay, Shawn 1953- 124
Laybourne, Lawrence E. 1914(?)-1976
Obituary 65-68
Laycock, Ellen (Mae) 1921- 112
Laycock, George (Edwin) 1921- CANR-19
Earlier sketches in CA 7-8R, CANR-4
See also SATA 5
Laycock, Harold R. (I. O.) 1916- 7-8R
Laye, Camara 1928-1980 .... CANR-25
Obituary 97-100
Earlier sketch in CA 85-88
See also BW
See also CLC 4, 38
Layman, Constance 1943- 111
Layman, Emma McCloy 1910- 81-84
Layman, Richard 1947- 65-68
Laymon, Charles Martin 1904- CANR-7
Earlier sketch in CA 11-12R
Layne, Bobby
See Layne, Robert Lawrence
Layne, Laura
See Knott, William C(ecil, Jr.)
Layne, Robert Lawrence 1927-1986
Obituary 121
Layton, Andrea
See Bancroft, Iris (May Nelson)
Layton, Aviva 1933- 116
Layton, Edwin T(homas), Jr. 1928- 29-32R
Layton, Felix 1910- CAP-2
Earlier sketch in CA 23-24
Layton, Irving (Peter) 1912- CANR-2
Earlier sketch in CA 3R
See also CLC 2, 15
Layton, Marilyn Smith 1941- 114
Layton, Robert 1930- 21-22R
Layton, Thomas Arthur 1910- 9-10R
Layton, Wilbur L. 1922- Brief entry 106
Layton, William (Isaac) 1913- 19-20R
Lazar, Wendy 1939- 104
Lazare, Gerald John 1927- SATA-44
Lazare, Jerry
See Lazare, Gerald John
Lazareff, Pierre 1907-1972 Obituary 33-36R
Lazareth, William Henry 1928- CANR-16
Earlier sketches in CA 3R, CANR-1
Lazarevich, Mila 1942- SATA-17
Lazaron, Hilda R(othschild) 1895- 49-52
Lazarre, Jane D(eitz) 1943- 101
Lazarsfeld, Paul F(elix) 1901-1976 73-76
Obituary 69-72
Lazarus, A(rnold) L(eslie) 1914- CANR-11
Earlier sketch in CA 25-28R
Lazarus, Arnold A(llan) 1932- CANR-14
Earlier sketch in CA 41-44R
Lazarus, Arthur 1892(?)-1978 Obituary 77-80
Lazarus, Edward H. 1959- 122
Lazarus, Felix
See Cable, George Washington
Lazarus, Harold 1927- 23-24R
Lazarus, Keo Felker 1913- 41-44R
See also SATA 21
Lazarus, Marguerite 1916- 106
Lazarus, Mell 1927- CANR-11
Earlier sketch in CA 19-20R
Lazarus, Paul N. 1913- 126
Lazarus, Richard S(tanley) 1922- CANR-5
Earlier sketch in CA 3R
Lazarus, Simon 1941- 57-60
LaZebnik, Edith 1897- 85-88
Lazell, James Draper, Jr. 1939- 65-68
Lazenby, Walter S(ylvester), Jr. 1930- 65-68
Lazer, William 1924- CANR-19
Earlier sketches in CA 3R, CANR-4
Lazere, Donald 1935- 105
Lazerowitz, Alice Ambrose 1906- CANR-17
Earlier sketches in CA 49-52, CANR-1
Lazerowitz, Morris 1907- CANR-17
Earlier sketches in CA 11-12R, CANR-3
Lazlo, Kate
See Angus, Sylvia
Lazo, Hector 1899-1965 .... CANR-3
Earlier sketch in CA 3R
Lazreg, Marnia 1941- 69-72
Lea, Alec 1907- 73-76
See also SATA 19
Lea, David A(lexander) M(aclure)
1934- CANR-10
Earlier sketch in CA 21-22R
Lea, F(rank) A(lfred) 1915-1977 .... CANR-3
Earlier sketch in CA 4R
Lea, Frederick (Measham) 1900-1984
Obituary 113
Lea, Henry Charles 1825-1909 Brief entry .. 122
See also DLB 47
Lea, Joan
See Neufeld, John (Arthur)
Lea, John Sedgwick 1910(?)-1987
Obituary 124
Lea, Kathleen M(arguerite) 1903- 119
Lea, Sydney (L. Wright, Jr.) 1942- CANR-22
Earlier sketch in CA 106
Lea, Timothy
See Wood, Christopher (Hovelle)
Lea, Tom 1907- Brief entry 115
See also DLB 6
Leab, Daniel Josef 1936- CANR-11
Earlier sketch in CA 29-32R
Leabo, Dick A. 1921- 9-10R
Leacacos, John P. 1908-1986 ....25-28R
Obituary 121
Leach, Aroline Beecher 1899- 61-64
Leach, Barry Arthur 1930- 102
Leach, Bernard Howell 1887-1979 97-100
Obituary 85-88
Leach, Douglas Edward 1920- 19-20R
Leach, Eleanor Winsor 1937- 103
Leach, Gerald Adrian 1933- CANR-21
Earlier sketch in CA 7-8R
Leach, Graham (John) 1948- 122
Leach, John Robert 1922- 23-24R
Leach, Joseph (Lee) 1921- 29-32R
Leach, Maria 1892-1977 53-56
Obituary 69-72
See also SATA 28, 39
Leach, (Richard) Max(well) 1909- 41-44R
Leach, Michael 1940- 73-76
Leach, Paul Roscoe 1890-1977 Obituary ..73-76
Leach, Penelope (Jane) 1937- CANR-21
Earlier sketch in CA 97-100
Leach, Richard H(eald) 1922- Brief entry ... 113
Leach, Robert J. 1916- 29-32R
Leach, (Carson) Wilford 1932- CANR-2
Earlier sketch in CA 45-48
Leach, (Carson) Wilford 1932(?)-1988 .. CANR-2
Obituary 125
Earlier sketch in CA 45-48
Leachman, Robert Briggs 1921- 104
Leacock, Eleanor Burke 1922-1987 .... CANR-15
Obituary 122
Earlier sketch in CA 37-40R
Leacock, John 1729-1802 .... DLB-31
Leacock, Ruth 1926- 37-40R
Leacock, Stephen (Butler) 1869-1944
Brief entry 104
See also TCLC 2
Leacroft, Helen (Mabel Beal) 1919- CANR-2
Earlier sketch in CA 5-6R
See also SATA 6
Leacroft, Richard (Vallance Becher)
1914- CANR-2
Earlier sketch in CA 5-6R
See also SATA 6
Leadbetter, Eric 1892(?)-1971 Obituary 104
Leadbitter, Mike 1942- 41-44R
Leader, (Evelyn) Barbara (Blackburn)
1898- 61-64
Leader, Charles
See Smith, Robert Charles
Leader, Mary (Bartelt) 85-88
Leader, Ninon 1933- 21-22R
Leader, Shelah Gilbert 1943- 110
Leaf, David 1952- 117
Leaf, Margaret P. 1909(?)-1988 Obituary ... 124
Leaf, (Wilbur) Munro 1905-1976 73-76
Obituary 69-72
See also SATA 20
Leaf, Murray J(ohn) 1939- CANR-1
Earlier sketch in CA 45-48
Leaf, Russell C(harles) 1935- 21-22R
Leaf, VaDonna Jean 1929- 57-60
See also SATA 26
Leagans, John Paul 1911- 103
Leahy, Syrell Rogovin 1935- CANR-12
Earlier sketch in CA 57-60
Leake, Chauncey D(epew) 1896-1978 ... CANR-3
Obituary 73-76
Earlier sketch in CA 49-52
Leake, Jane Acomb 1928- 21-22R
Leakey, Louis S(eymour) B(azett)
1903-1972 97-100
Obituary 37-40R
Leakey, Mary (Douglas Nicol) 1913- ... CANR-18
Earlier sketch in CA 97-100
Leakey, Richard E(rskine Frere) 1944- .. CANR-18
Earlier sketch in CA 93-96
See also SATA 42
Leaman, David R(ay) 1947- 115
Leamer, Edward E(mery) 1944- 29-32R
Leamer, Laurence Allen 1941- CANR-13
Earlier sketch in CA 65-68
Leaming, Barbara CANR-25
Earlier sketch in CA 107
Lean, Arthur E(dward) 1909- 73-76
Lean, David 1908- Brief entry 111
Lean, E(dward) Tangye 1911-1974
Obituary 53-56
Lean, Garth Dickinson 1912- CANR-17
Earlier sketch in CA 29-32R
Leander, Ed
See Richelson, Geraldine
Leaney, Alfred Robert Clare 1909- CANR-2
Earlier sketch in CA 7-8R
Leap, Harry P(atrick) 1908-1976 .... 3R
Obituary 103
Leapman, Michael 1938- 109
Lear, Edward 1812-1888 .... SATA-18
See also DLB 32
See also CLR 1
Lear, Floyd Seyward 1895- CAP-1
Earlier sketch in CA 17-18
Lear, John 1909- 37-40R
Lear, Martha Weinman 1930- CANR-9
Earlier sketch in CA 9-10R
Lear, Melva Gwendoline Bartlett 1917- 7-8R
Lear, Norman (Milton) 1922- 73-76
See also CLC 12
Lear, Peter
See Lovesey, Peter
Leard, G(eorge) Earl 1918- 9-10R
Leard, John E. 1916- 73-76
Learmonth, Andrew Thomas Amos
1916- 15-16R
Learned, Edmund Philip 1900- 104
Leary, David E. 1945- 124
Leary, Edward A(ndrew) 1913- CANR-12
Earlier sketch in CA 29-32R
Leary, James F. 1942- 126
Leary, John P(atrick) 1919- 11-12R
Leary, Lewis (Gaston) 1906- CANR-4
Earlier sketch in CA 1R
Leary, Paris 1931- 17-18R
Leary, Timothy (Francis) 1920- 107
See also DLB 16
Leary, William G(ordon) 1915- 49-52
Leary, William M., Jr. 1934- 93-96
Leas, Speed 1937- 49-52
Lease, Benjamin 1917- Brief entry 114
Lease, Gary 1940- 45-48
Leasher, Evelyn M(arie) 1941- 115
Leaska, Mitchell A(lexander) 1934- CANR-13
Earlier sketch in CA 77-80
Leasor, (Thomas) James 1923- CANR-2
Earlier sketch in CA 4R
Least Heat Moon, William
See Trogdon, William (Lewis)
Leasure, Robert E. 1921- 112
Leather, Edwin (Hartley Cameron) 1919- ..97-100
Leather, George
See Swallow, Norman
Leatherman, LeRoy 1922-1984 ....23-24R
Obituary 112
Leautaud, Paul 1872-1956 .... DLB-65
Leavell, Landrum P(inson) II 1926- 89-92
Leavenworth, Carol 1940- CANR-14
Earlier sketch in CA 81-84
Leavenworth, James Lynn 1915- 21-22R
Leaver, Robin Alan 1939- CANR-9
Earlier sketch in CA 61-64
Leavis, F(rank) R(aymond) 1895-1978 ...21-22R
Obituary 77-80
See also CLC 24
Leavis, Q(ueenie) D(orothy) 1906-1981 ...97-100
Obituary 108
Leavitt, David 1961- 122
Brief entry 116
See also CLC 34
Leavitt, Harold J(ack) 1922- 125
Brief entry 117
Leavitt, Hart Day 1909- 15-16R
Leavitt, Harvey R(obert) 1934- 65-68
Leavitt, Jack 1931- 97-100
Leavitt, Jerome E(dward) 1916- CANR-17
Earlier sketches in CA 4R, CANR-1
See also SATA 23
Leavitt, Judith A(nn) 1947- 110
Leavitt, Richard Freeman 1929- 89-92
Leavitt, Ruby R.
See Rohrlich, Ruby
Leavitt, William J. 1928-1984 Obituary 112
Leavy, Stanley A(rnold) 1915- 120
LeBar, Lois E. 1907- 21-22R
LeBar, Mary E(velyn) 1910-1982 ...... CANR-25
Earlier sketch in CA 107
See also SATA 35
LeBaron, Charles W. 1943- CANR-9
Earlier sketch in CA 61-64
Lebeaux, Richard 1946- CANR-12
Earlier sketch in CA 73-76
Lebedoff, David (Michael) 1938- 126
Leber, George L. 1917(?)-1976 Obituary ..61-64
Lebergott, Stanley 1918- 103
Lebert, Randy
See Brannon, William T.
Lebeson, Anita Libman 1896-1987 ......29-32R
Obituary 121
Leblanc, Maurice (Marie Emile)
1864-1941 Brief entry 110
LeBlanc, Rena Dictor 1938- 104
Leblon, Jean (Marcel Jules) 1928- 41-44R
Lebo, Dell 1922- 57-60
LeBoeuf, Michael 1942- CANR-15
Earlier sketch in CA 93-96
Le Boutillier, Cornelia Geer 1894(?)-1973
Obituary 45-48
Lebovich, William Louis 1948- 115
Lebovitz, Harold Paul 1916- 77-80
Lebow, Victor 1902- 37-40R
Lebowitz, Alan 1934- 25-28R
Lebowitz, Albert 1922- 73-76
Lebowitz, Fran(ces Ann) 1951(?)- CANR-14
Earlier sketch in CA 81-84
See also CLC 11, 36
Lebowitz, Naomi 1932- 37-40R
Leboyer, Frederick 1918- 106
Lebra, Joyce C(hapman) CANR-1
Earlier sketch in CA 45-48
Lebra, Takie Sugiyama 1930- 77-80
Lebra, William P(hilip) 1922- 33-36R
Lebrecht, Norman 1948- 117
Lebreo, Steward
See Weiner, Stewart
Lebreo, Stewart
See Weiner, Stewart
Le Breton, Auguste
See Montfort, Auguste
Le Brown, Andreas
See Brown, Andreas Le
LeBrun, Gautier
See Gibson, Walter B(rown)
LeBrun, George P. 1862-1966 ....5-6R
Lebrun, Richard Allen 1931- 41-44R
Le Cain, Errol John 1941- CANR-13
Earlier sketch in CA 33-36R
See also SATA 6
Lecale, Errol
See McNeilly, Wilfred (Glassford)
Lecar, Helene Lerner 1938- 25-28R
le Carre, John
See Cornwell, David (John Moore)
See also CLC 3, 5, 9, 15, 28
Lecavele, Roland
See Dorgeles, Roland
Le Chanois, Jean-Paul
See Drefus, Jean-Paul Etienne
Lechlitner, Ruth N. 1901- 105
See also DLB 48
Lechner, Robert F(irman) 1918- 33-36R
Lecht, Charles Philip 1933- 21-22R
Lecht, Leonard A. 1920- CANR-11
Earlier sketch in CA 25-28R
Lechtenberg, Richard 1947- 125
Lecker, Robert 1951- 111
Leckey, Dolores (Conklin) 1933- 109
Leckie, Robert (Hugh) 1920- 13-14R
Leckie, William H. 1915- 23-24R
LeClair, Thomas 1944- 113
LeClair, Tom
See LeClair, Thomas
LeClaire, Gordon 1905- 69-72
Leclerc, Felix 1914- DLB-60
Leclerc, Ivor 1915- 33-36R
Leclerc, Victor
See Parry, Albert
Le Clercq, Jacques Georges Clemenceau
1898-1972 Obituary 37-40R
Le Clezio, J(ean) M(arie) G(ustave) 1940-
Brief entry 116
See also CLC 31
Le Cocq, Rhoda P(riscilla) 1921- 73-76
Lecron, Louis 1888(?)-1971 Obituary 33-36R
Lecomber, Brian 1945- CANR-13
Earlier sketch in CA 73-76
Lecompte, Janet 1923- 122
Le Comte, Edward (Semple) 1916- CANR-5
Earlier sketch in CA 4R

Lecomte du Nouey
See Lecomte du Nouey, Pierre (-Andre-Leon)
Lecomte du Nouey, P.
See Lecomte du Nouey, Pierre (-Andre-Leon)
Lecomte du Nouey, Pierre (-Andre-Leon) 1883-1947 Brief entry ... 119
Lecomte du Nouy, Pierre (-Andre-Leon)
See Lecomte du Nouey, Pierre (-Andre-Leon)
LeCroy, Anne K(ingsbury) 1930- ... CANR-16
Earlier sketch in CA 41-44R
LeCroy, Ruth Brooks ... 45-48
Ledbetter, J(ack) T(racy) 1934- ... 73-76
Ledbetter, Jack Wallace 1930- ... 5-6R
Ledbetter, Joe O(verton) 1927- ... 45-48
Ledbetter, Ken(neth Lee) 1931- ... 117
Ledbetter, Les 1941(?)-1985 Obituary ... 116
Ledbetter, Virgil C. 1918-19(?) ... CAP-1
Earlier sketch in CA 15-16
Ledderose, Lothar 1942- ... 85-88
Leder, Jane Mersky 1945- ... 117
See also SATA 51
Leder, Lawrence H. 1927- ... 25-28R
Leder, Rudolf
See Hermlin, Stephan
Lederer, Charles 1910-1976 Obituary ... 65-68
See also DLB 26
Lederer, Chloe 1915- ... 77-80
Lederer, Edith Madelon 1943- ... 97-100
Lederer, Esther Pauline 1918- ... 89-92
Lederer, Ivo J(ohn) 1929- ... 11-12R
Lederer, Jiri 1922-1983 Obituary ... 111
Lederer, Joseph 1927- ... 73-76
Lederer, Lajos 1904-1985 Obituary ... 118
Lederer, Laura 1951- ... 121
Lederer, Muriel 1929- ... 77-80
See also SATA 48
Lederer, Paul Joseph 1944- ... 111
Lederer, Rhoda Catharine (Kitto) 1910- ... CANR-22
Earlier sketches in CA 9-10R, CANR-6
Lederer, William J(ulius) 1912- ... CANR-5
Earlier sketch in CA 4R
Lederman, Leonard L(awrence) 1931- ... 61-64
Ledermann, Erich Kurt 1908- ... 107
Ledermann, Walter 1911- ... 49-52
Ledesert, (Dorothy) Margaret 1916- ... 45-48
Ledesert, R(ene) P(ierre) L(ouis) 1913-1984 ... 45-48
Obituary ... 114
Le Duan 1908(?)-1986 Obituary ... 119
Le Duc, Don R(aymond) 1933- ... 49-52
Leduc, Violette 1907-1972 ... CAP-1
Obituary ... 33-36R
Earlier sketch in CA 13-14
See also CLC 22
Ledwidge, Francis 1887(?)-1917
Brief entry ... 123
See also DLB 20
See also TCLC 23
Ledwidge, William (Bernard) John 1915- ... 103
Ledwith, Frank 1907- ... 103
Ledyard, Gleason H(ines) 1919- ... 7-8R
Lee, A. R.
See Ash, Rene Lee
Lee, Addison E(arl) 1914- ... 9-10R
Lee, Adrian Iselin, Jr. 1920- ... 89-92
Lee, Al(fred Matthew) 1938- ... 45-48
Lee, Alfred McClung 1906- ... CANR-19
Earlier sketches in CA 1R, CANR-3
Lee, Alvin A. 1930- ... 33-36R
Lee, Amanda
See Baggett, Nancy
and Buckholtz, Eileen (Garber)
and Glick, Ruth (Burtnick)
Lee, Amber
See Baldwin, Faith
Lee, Andrea 1953- ... 125
See also BW
See also CLC 36
Lee, Andrea
See Toona, Elin(-Kai)
Lee, Andrew
See Auchincloss, Louis (Stanton)
Lee, Arthur M(atthias) 1918- ... 41-44R
Lee, Asher 1909- ... 73-76
Lee, Audrey ... 25-28R
Lee, Austin 1904-19(?) ... CAP-1
Earlier sketch in CA 15-16
Lee, Barbara 1932- ... 109
Lee, Barbara (Moore) 1934- ... CANR-9
Earlier sketch in CA 53-56
Lee, Benjamin 1921- ... 104
See also SATA 27
Lee, Betsy 1949- ... 106
See also SATA 37
Lee, Betty 1921- ... 103
Lee, Betty
See Lambert, Elizabeth (Minnie)
Lee, Bill
See Lee, William Saul
Lee, Bob
See McGrath, Robert L(ee)
Lee, Brother Basil Leo 1909-1974
Obituary ... 53-56
Lee, C(live) H(oward) 1942- ... 126
Lee, C(harles) Nicholas 1933- ... 49-52
Lee, C(larence) P(endleton) 1913- ... 49-52
Lee, Calvin B. T. 1934- ... 33-36R
Lee, Carol
See Fletcher, Helen Jill
Lee, Carolina
See Dern, Erolie Pearl Gaddis
Lee, Carvel (Bigham) 1910- ... CAP-1
Earlier sketch in CA 13-14
Lee, Charles 1913- ... 33-36R
Lee, Charles Robert, Jr. 1929- ... 7-8R
Lee, Charlotte I(rene) 1909- ... 23-24R
Lee, Chong-Sik 1931- ... CANR-15
Earlier sketch in CA 41-44R
Lee, Christine Eckstrom 1952- ... 110
Lee, Christopher Frank Carandini 1922- ... 73-76
Lee, C(hin)-Y(ana) 1917- ... 11-12R
Lee, David 1944- ... 111
Lee, David Dale 1948- ... 117
Lee, Deemer 1905-1979 ... 111
Lee, Dennis (Beynon) 1939- ... CANR-11
Earlier sketch in CA 25-28R
See also SATA 14
See also DLB 53
See also CLR 3
Lee, Derek 1937- ... 107
Lee, (Henry) Desmond (Pritchard) 1908- ... 102
Lee, Devon
See Pohle, Robert W(arren), Jr.
Lee, Don L.
See Madhubuti, Haki R.
See also CLC 2
Lee, Doris Emrick 1905-1983 Obituary ... 110
See also SATA 35, 44
Lee, Dorris M(ay Potter) 1905- ... 13-14R
Lee, Douglas A(llen) 1932- ... 53-56
Lee, Dwight E(rwin) 1898- ... 7-8R
Lee, Eddie H. 1917- ... 69-72
Lee, Edward Edson ... AITN-1
Lee, Edward N(icholls) 1935- ... 29-32R
Lee, Elizabeth Briant 1908- ... 37-40R
Lee, Elsie 1912- ... 85-88
Lee, Eric
See Lee, Fleming
and Page, Gerald W(ilburn)
Lee, Essie E. 1920- ... CANR-4
Earlier sketch in CA 49-52
Lee, Eugene (Huey) 1941- ... 49-52
Lee, Fleming 1933- ... CANR-7
Earlier sketch in CA 9-10R
Lee, Florence Henry 1910- ... CAP-1
Earlier sketch in CA 17-18
Lee, Francis Nigel 1934- ... CANR-8
Earlier sketch in CA 57-60
Lee, Frank F(reeman) 1920- ... 2R
Lee, Fred 1927- ... 109
Lee, G. Avery 1916- ... 104
Lee, George J. 1920(?)-1976 Obituary ... 65-68
Lee, George Leslie
See Lee, Brother Basil Leo
Lee, George W(ashington) 1894-1976 ... 125
See also BW
See also DLB 51
Lee, Gerard (Majella) 1951- ... 93-96
Lee, Ginffa 1900(?)-1976 Obituary ... 69-72
Lee, Gordon C(anfield) 1916- ... 13-14R
Lee, Gypsy Rose
See Hovick, Rose Louise
Lee, H. Alton 1942- ... 81-84
Lee, Hahn-Been 1921- ... CANR-11
Earlier sketch in CA 25-28R
Lee, Harold N(ewton) 1899- ... 37-40R
Lee, (Nelle) Harper 1926- ... 15-16R
See also SATA 11
See also DLB 6
See also CDALB 1941-1968
See also CLC 12
Lee, Harriet 1757-1851 ... DLB-39
Lee, Harry J., Jr. 1914-1985 Obituary ... 118
Lee, Hector (Haight) 1908- ... 97-100
Lee, Helen Clara 1919- ... 49-52
Lee, Helen Jackson 1908- ... 81-84
Lee, Henry (Walsh) 1911- ... 5-6R
Lee, Henry F(oster) 1913- ... 89-92
Lee, Herbert d'H.
See Kastle, Herbert D(avid)
Lee, Hermione 1948- ... CANR-15
Earlier sketch in CA 73-76
Lee, Howard
See Goulart, Ron(ald Joseph)
Lee, Irvin H. 1932- ... 21-22R
Lee, J(erry) W(allace) 1932- ... 93-96
Lee, James A(lvin) 1922- ... 126
Lee, James F. 1905(?)-1975 Obituary ... 61-64
Lee, James Michael 1931- ... CANR-13
Earlier sketch in CA 19-20R
Lee, James W. 1931- ... 25-28R
Lee, Janice (Jeanne) 1944- ... 33-36R
Lee, Joe Won 1921- ... 41-44R
Lee, John (Darrell) 1931- ... CANR-9
Earlier sketch in CA 25-28R
Lee, John A(lexander) 1891- ... CANR-7
Earlier sketch in CA 53-56
Lee, John Eric 1919- ... 33-36R
Lee, John Michael 1932- ... CANR-6
Earlier sketch in CA 13-14R
Lee, John R(obert) 1923-1976 ... 57-60
Obituary ... 120
See also SATA 27
Lee, Judy
See Carlson, Judith Lee
Lee, Julian
See Latham, Jean Lee
Lee, Jung Young 1935- ... 33-36R
Lee, Kay
See Kelly, Karen
Lee, L(awrence) L(ynn) 1924- ... 73-76
Lee, Lamar, Jr. 1911- ... 17-18R
Lee, Lance 1942- ... CANR-13
Earlier sketch in CA 77-80
Lee, Laurel 1945(?)- Brief entry ... 113
Lee, Laurie 1914- ... 77-80
See also DLB 27
Lee, Lawrence 1903- ... 25-28R
See also CLC 34
Lee, (Enoch) Lawrence 1912- ... 15-16R
Lee, Leo Ou-fan 1939- ... 102
Lee, Lincoln 1922- ... 9-10R
Lee, Linda 1947- ... CANR-13
Earlier sketch in CA 77-80
Lee, Loyd Ervin 1939- ... 102
Lee, Lucy
See Talbot, Charlene Joy
Lee, M(ark) Owen 1930- ... 33-36R
Lee, Mabel Barbee 1886(?)-1978
Obituary ... 85-88
Lee, Malka 1905(?)-1976 Obituary ... 65-68
Lee, Manfred B(ennington) 1905-1971 ... CANR-2
Obituary ... 29-32R
Earlier sketch in CA 1R
See also CLC 11
Lee, Manning de Villeneuve 1894-1980
Obituary ... 104
See also SATA 22, 37
Lee, Maria Berl 1924- ... CANR-9
Earlier sketch in CA 61-64
Lee, Marian
See Clish, (Lee) Marian
Lee, Marjorie 1921- ... CANR-4
Earlier sketch in CA 4R
Lee, Mark W. 1923- ... CANR-18
Earlier sketches in CA 11-12R, CANR-3
Lee, Martin A. 1954- ... 121
Lee, Mary 1949- ... 29-32R
Lee, Mary Price 1934- ... CANR-24
Earlier sketches in CA 57-60, CANR-9
See also SATA 8
Lee, Maryat ... 25-28R
Lee, Maurice (duPont), Jr. 1925- ... CANR-21
Earlier sketch in CA 45-48
Lee, Meredith 1945- ... 93-96
Lee, Mildred
See Scudder, Mildred Lee
See also SATA 6
Lee, Molly K(yung) S(ook) C(hang) 1934- ... 53-56
Lee, Muna 1895-1965 Obituary ... 25-28R
Lee, Nata
See Frackman, Nathaline
Lee, Norma E. 1924- ... 65-68
Lee, Oliver M(inseem) 1927- ... 41-44R
Lee, Parker
See Turner, Robert H(arry)
Lee, Patricia 1941- ... 115
Lee, Patrick C(ornelius) 1936- ... 65-68
Lee, Peter H(acksoo) 1929- ... CANR-3
Earlier sketch in CA 9-10R
Lee, Philip J. 1932- ... 124
Lee, Polly Jae 1929- ... CANR-13
Earlier sketch in CA 29-32R
Lee, R(oy) Alton 1931- ... 21-22R
Lee, Raymond 1910(?)-1974 Obituary ... 49-52
Lee, Raymond L(awrence) 1911- ... 41-44R
Lee, Rebecca Smith 1894- ... 5-6R
Lee, Rensselaer W(right) 1898-1984
Obituary ... 114
Lee, Richard
See Lee, Richard B(orshay)
Lee, Richard B(orshay) 1937- ... CANR-20
Earlier sketch in CA 45-48
Lee, Robert 1929- ... CANR-3
Earlier sketch in CA 5-6R
Lee, Robert
See Fairman, Paul W.
Lee, Robert C. 1931- ... CANR-10
Earlier sketch in CA 25-28R
See also SATA 20
Lee, Robert E(arl) 1906- ... 53-56
See also AITN 1
Lee, Robert E(dwin) 1918- ... CANR-2
Earlier sketch in CA 45-48
Lee, Robert E. A. 1921- ... 11-12R
Lee, Robert Edson 1921- ... 25-28R
Lee, Robert Edward 1912- ... 111
Lee, Robert Greene 1886-19(?) ... CANR-3
Earlier sketch in CA 2R
Lee, Robert J. 1921- ... SATA-10
Lee, Roberta
See McGrath, Robert L(ee)
Lee, Ronald 1934- ... 37-40R
Lee, Rowena
See Bartlett, Marie (Swan)
Lee, Roy
See Hopkins, Clark
Lee, Roy Stuart 1899- ... CAP-1
Earlier sketch in CA 9-10
Lee, Russel V(an Arsdale) 1895-1982
Obituary ... 110
Lee, Ruth (Wile) 1892- ... CAP-2
Earlier sketch in CA 23-24
Lee, S(amuel) E(dgar) 1894- ... 73-76
Lee, S(idney) G(illmore) M(cKenzie) 1920-1973 ... CAP-2
Earlier sketch in CA 33-36
Lee, Samuel J(ames) 1906- ... CAP-2
Earlier sketch in CA 29-32
Lee, Shelton Jackson 1957(?)- ... 125
See also BW
Lee, Sherman Emery 1918- ... CANR-1
Earlier sketch in CA 2R
Lee, Sophia 1750-1824 ... DLB-39
Lee, Spike
See Lee, Shelton Jackson
Lee, Stan 1922- ... 111
Brief entry ... 108
See also CLC 17
Lee, Stewart M(unro) 1925- ... 57-60
Lee, Susan 1944- ... 110
Lee, Susan Dye 1939- ... 85-88
Lee, Tanith 1947- ... 37-40R
See also SATA 8
See also CLC 46
Lee, Terence R(ichard) 1938- ... 29-32R
Lee, Tom(my L.) 1950- ... 65-68
Lee, Vernon
See Paget, Violet
See also DLB 57
See also TCLC 5
Lee, Virginia 1905(?)-1981 Obituary ... 105
Lee, Virginia (Yew) 1927- ... 9-10R
Lee, W. Storrs
See Lee, William Storrs
Lee, Walt(er William, Jr.) 1931- ... 61-64
Lee, Warren M. 1908- ... 77-80
Lee, Wayne C. 1917- ... CANR-17
Earlier sketches in CA 4R, CANR-2
Lee, William
See Burroughs, William S(eward)
Lee, William R(owland) 1911- ... CANR-19
Earlier sketches in CA 9-10R, CANR-4
Lee, William Saul 1938- ... 104
Lee, William Storrs 1906- ... CANR-1
Earlier sketch in CA 4R
Lee, Willy
See Burroughs, William S(eward)
Lee, Yur Bok 1934- ... 29-32R
Leech, Alfred B. 1918(?)-1974 Obituary ... 49-52
Leech, Bryan Jeffery 1931- ... 93-96
Leech, Clifford 1909-1977 ... CANR-4
Earlier sketch in CA 4R
Leech, Geoffrey N(eil) 1936- ... CANR-12
Earlier sketch in CA 29-32R
Leech, Kenneth 1939- ... 103
Leech, Margaret (Kernochan) 1893-1974 ... 93-96
Obituary ... 49-52
Leecing, Walden A. 1932- ... 33-36R
Leed, Eric J. 1942- ... 89-92
Leed, Jacob R. 1924- ... CANR-7
Earlier sketch in CA 17-18R
Leed, Richard L. 1929- ... 15-16R
Leed, Theodore W(illiam) 1927- ... 126
Brief entry ... 106
Leedham, Charles 1926- ... 15-16R
Leedham, John 1912- ... CANR-13
Earlier sketch in CA 23-24R
Leeds, Anthony 1925- ... 19-20R
Leeds, Barry H. 1940- ... 29-32R
Leeds, Morton (Harold) 1921- ... 15-16R
Leeds, Patricia (Miriam) 1920(?)-1985
Obituary ... 114
Leedy, Jack J. 1921- ... 23-24R
Leedy, Loreen (Janelle) 1959- ... 122
See also SATA 50
Leedy, Paul D. 1908- ... CANR-1
Earlier sketch in CA 3R
Leefeldt, Christine 1941- ... 93-96
Lee-Hamilton, Eugene (Jacob) 1845-1907
Brief entry ... 117
See also TCLC 22
Lee Howard, Leon Alexander 1914-1979(?) Obituary ... 104
Leek, Sybil 1923-1982 ... 102
Obituary ... 108
Leekley, Richard N. 1912-1976 Obituary ... 69-72
Leekley, Thomas B(riggs) 1910- ... 5-6R
See also SATA 23
Leeman, Wayne A(lvin) 1924- ... 15-16R
Leeming, David Adams 1937- ... 49-52
Leeming, Donald 1944- ... 114
Leeming, Glenda 1943- ... CANR-4
Earlier sketch in CA 53-56
Leeming, Jo Ann
See Leeming, Joseph
Leeming, John F(ishwick) 1900- ... CAP-1
Earlier sketch in CA 9-10
Leeming, Joseph 1897-1968 ... 73-76
See also SATA 26
Leeming, Owen (Alfred) 1930- ... CANR-15
Earlier sketch in CA 65-68
Leenhouts, Keith J(ames) 1925- ... 61-64
Leepa, Allen 1919- ... 45-48
Leeper, Sarah H(ammond) 1912- ... 57-60
Leepson, Marc 1945- ... 111
Leer, Norman Robert 1937- ... 19-20R
Leerburger, Benedict A., Jr. 1932- ... 11-12R
Lees, Andrew 1940- ... 122
Lees, Carlton Brown 1924- ... 103
Lees, Charles J. 1919- ... 25-28R
Lees, Dan 1927- ... CANR-13
Earlier sketch in CA 33-36R
Lees, Francis A(nthony) 1931- ... CANR-9
Earlier sketch in CA 65-68
Lees, Gene 1928- ... CANR-24
Earlier sketches in CA 23-24R, CANR-9
Lees, Hannah
See Fetter, Elizabeth Head
Lees, Hilda Frances 1900-1983 Obituary ... 111
Lees, John D(avid) 1936- ... 53-56
Lees, John G(arfield) 1931- ... 57-60
Lees, Lynn Hollen 1941- ... 113
Lees, Ray 1931- ... CANR-8
Earlier sketch in CA 61-64
Lees, Richard 1948- ... CANR-26
Earlier sketch in CA 108
Leese, Elizabeth 1937- ... 85-88
Lees-Milne, James 1908- ... CANR-13
Earlier sketch in CA 9-10R
Leeson, C(harles) Roland 1926- ... 93-96
Leeson, Howard A(lfred) 1942- ... 118
Leeson, R. A.
See Leeson, Robert (Arthur)
Leeson, Robert (Arthur) 1928- ... CANR-22
Earlier sketch in CA 105
See also SATA 42
Leet, Judith 1935- ... CLC-11
Le Fanu, Joseph Sheridan 1814-1873 ... DLB-21, 70
Lefco, Helene 1922- ... 53-56
Lefcoe, George 1938- ... 21-22R
Lefcowitz, Barbara F(reedgood) 1935- ... 104
Lefebure, Marcus 1933- ... 113

INDEX

Lefebure, Molly ... 57-60
Lefebvre, Henri 1901- ... CANR-11
Earlier sketch in CA 25-28R
Lefebvre d'Argence, Rene-Yvon 1928- .. CANR-11
Earlier sketch in CA 23-24R
Le Feuvre, Amy ?-1929 Brief entry ... 111
Lefever, D(avid) Welty 1901- ... 49-52
Lefever, Ernest W(arren) 1919- ... CANR-1
Earlier sketch in CA 1R
LeFevre, Adam 1950- ... 81-84
Lefevre, Carl A(nthony) 1913- ... CANR-7
Earlier sketch in CA 11-12R
Lefevre, Gui
See Bickers, Richard Leslie Townshend
Lefevre, Helen (Elveback) ... 19-20R
LeFevre, Perry D(eyo) 1921- ... CANR-25
Earlier sketches in CA 21-22R, CANR-10
LeFevre, Robert (Thomas) 1911-1986 ... CANR-9
Obituary ... 119
Earlier sketch in CA 57-60
Leff, Arthur A(llen) 1935-1981 Obituary ... 105
Leff, Gordon 1926- ... CANR-3
Earlier sketch in CA 11-12R
Leff, Nathaniel H. 1938- ... 25-28R
Leffelaar, Hendrik Louis 1929- ... 5-6R
Lefferts, George 1921- ... CANR-14
Earlier sketch in CA 69-72
Leffland, Ella 1931- ... 29-32R
See also DLBY 84
See also CLC 19
Leffler, Melvyn Paul 1945- ... 89-92
Lefkoe, Morty R. 1937- ... 29-32R
Lefkowitz, Annette S(ara) 1922- ... 19-20R
Lefkowitz, Bernard 1937- ... 29-32R
Lefkowitz, Joel M. 1940- ... 45-48
Lefkowitz, Mary Rosenthal 1935- ... CANR-19
Earlier sketch in CA 103
Lefkowitz, R(obert) J. 1942- ... 45-48
Leflar, Robert A(llen) 1901- ... 29-32R
Le Fleming, Christopher (Kaye) 1908-1985
Obituary ... 117
Lefler, Hugh Talmage 1901- ... 7-8R
Lefler, Irene (Whitney) 1917- ... CANR-1
Earlier sketch in CA 45-48
See also SATA 12
LeFlore, Ron(ald) 1948(?)- Brief entry ... 115
Le Fontaine, Joseph (Raymond) 1927- ... 106
le Fort, Gertrud (Petrea) von 1876-1971 ... 69-72
Obituary ... 33-36R
See also DLB 66
Lefranc, Pierre 1927- ... 41-44R
Lefrancois, Guy R(enald) 1940- ... CANR-18
Earlier sketches in CA 45-48, CANR-2
Lefton, Robert Eugene 1931- ... 49-52
Leftwich, James (Adolf) 1902- ... CANR-15
Earlier sketch in CA 41-44R
Leftwich, Joseph 1892-1983 ... 7-8R
Obituary ... 109
Leftwich, Richard Henry 1920- ... CANR-5
Earlier sketch in CA 13-14R
LeGalley, Donald P(aul) 1901- ... CAP-2
Earlier sketch in CA 17-18
Le Galliene, Eva 1899- ... 45-48
See also SATA 9
Le Gallienne, Richard 1866-1947
Brief entry ... 107
See also DLB 4
Legare, Hugh Swinton
1797-1843 ... DLB-3, 59, 73
Legare, James Mathewes 1823-1859 ... DLB-3
Legaret, Jean 1913-1976 ... CAP-2
Earlier sketch in CA 29-32
Legarreta, Dorothy 1926- ... 118
Legat, Michael (Ronald) 1923- ... 122
Legault, Albert 1938- ... 53-56
Leger, (Marie-Rene) Alexis Saint-Leger
1887-1975 ... 13-14R
Obituary ... 61-64
See also CLC 11
Leger, Fernand 1881-1955 Brief entry ... 123
Leger, Saintleger
See Leger, (Marie-Rene) Alexis
Saint-Leger
Legeza, (Ireneus) Laszlo 1934- ... 65-68
Legg, Sarah Martha Ross Bruggeman
?-1982 ... SATA-40
Legg, (Francis) Stuart 1910-1988
Obituary ... 126
Leggatt, Alexander (Maxwell) 1940- ... 97-100
Legge, Elisabeth Schwarzkopf
See Schwarzkopf-Legge, Elisabeth
Legge, J(ohn) D(avid) 1921- ... CANR-2
Earlier sketch in CA 2R
Legge, M(ary) Dominica 1905-1986
Obituary ... 121
Legge-Bourke, (Edward Alexander) Henry
1914-1973 ... CAP-1
Earlier sketch in CA 9-10
Leggett, B(obby) J(oe) 1938- ... 53-56
Leggett, Eric
See Rimel, Duane (Weldon)
Leggett, Glenn 1918- ... CANR-5
Earlier sketch in CA 13-14R
Leggett, John (Ward) 1917- ... CANR-2
Earlier sketch in CA 1R
Leggett, John C. 1930- ... 25-28R
Leggett, Linda 1941- ... 108
Leggett, Stephen 1949- ... 77-80
Leggitt, (Samuel) Hunter (Jr.) 1935- ... 65-68
Legh, Kathleen Louise Wood
See Wood-Legh, Kathleen Louise
Legler, Henry M. 1897- ... 97-100
Legler, Philip 1928- ... 9-10R
Legman, G(ershon) 1917- ... CANR-15
Earlier sketch in CA 21-22R
LeGrand
See Henderson, LeGrand
Legrand, Catherine Carlisle 1947- ... 126
Legrand, Lucien 1926- ... 7-8R
Legrand, Michel (Jean) 1932- Brief entry ... 114
Legters, Lyman H(oward) 1928- ... CANR-15
Earlier sketch in CA 33-36R
Le Guin, Ursula K(roeber) 1929- ... CANR-9
Earlier sketch in CA 21-22R
See also SATA 4, 52
See also DLB 8, 52
See also CLC 8, 13, 22, 45
See also CLR 3
See also AITN 1
Legum, Colin 1919- ... CANR-4
Earlier sketch in CA 1R
See also SATA 10
Legvold, Robert 1940- ... 85-88
Lehan, Richard (D'Aubin Daniel) 1930- ... 21-22R
Lehane, Brendan 1936- ... CANR-26
Earlier sketches in CA 23-24R, CANR-10
Lehiste, Ilse 1922- ... 37-40R
Lehman, Anita Jacobs 1920- ... 23-24R
Lehman, Celia 1928- ... CANR-1
Earlier sketch in CA 49-52
Lehman, Chester K. 1895-1980 ... CANR-1
Earlier sketch in CA 4R
Lehman, Dale 1920- ... 11-12R
Lehman, David 1948- ... CANR-24
Earlier sketches in CA 57-60, CANR-8
Lehman, Ernest Paul 1915- ... 85-88
See also DLB 44
Lehman, F(rederick) K. 1924- ... 9-10R
Lehman, Godfrey ... 25-28R
Lehman, Harold D(aniel) 1921- ... 81-84
Lehman, John F(rancis), Jr. 1942- ... 15-16R
Lehman, Milton 1917-1966 ... CAP-1
Earlier sketch in CA 13-14
Lehman, Peter 1944- ... 115
Lehman, Sam 1899- ... 49-52
Lehman, Warren (Winfred, Jr.) 1930- ... 21-22R
Lehman, Yvonne 1936- ... CANR-12
Earlier sketch in CA 29-32R
Lehmann, A(ndrew) George 1922- ... CANR-4
Earlier sketch in CA 4R
Lehmann, Arno 1901- ... CAP-2
Earlier sketch in CA 29-32
Lehmann, Geoffrey (John) 1940-
Brief entry ... 107
Lehmann, Irving J(ack) 1927- ... 53-56
Lehmann, Johannes 1929- ... CANR-14
Earlier sketch in CA 37-40R
Lehmann, (Rudolph) John (Frederick)
1907-1987 ... CANR-8
Obituary ... 122
Earlier sketch in CA 9-10R
See also DLB 27
Lehmann, Linda 1906- ... 85-88
Lehmann, Lotte 1888-1976 ... 73-76
Obituary ... 69-72
Lehmann, Martin Ernest 1915- ... 7-8R
Lehmann, Michael Boas 1941- ... 119
Lehmann, Paul Louis 1906- ... 85-88
Lehmann, Peter 1938- ... 57-60
Lehmann, Robert A(rthur) 1932- ... 57-60
Lehmann, Rosamond (Nina) 1901- ... CANR-8
Earlier sketch in CA 77-80
See also DLB 15
See also CLC 5
Lehmann, Theo 1934- ... 41-44R
Lehmann, Wilhelm 1882-1968 ... DLB-56
Lehmann, Winfred P(hilipp) 1916- ... 33-36R
Lehmann-Haupt, Christopher (Charles
Herbert) 1934- ... 109
Lehmann-Haupt, Hellmut 1903- ... 9-10R
Lehmberg, Paul 1946- ... 102
Lehmberg, Stanford Eugene 1931- ... CANR-2
Earlier sketch in CA 2R
Lehn, Cornelia 1920- ... CANR-12
Earlier sketch in CA 29-32R
See also SATA 46
Lehner, Christine (Reine) 1952- ... 109
Lehnert, Herbert (Hermann) 1925- ... 41-44R
Lehning, James R(obert) 1947- ... 105
Lehninger, Albert L(ester) 1917-1986
Obituary ... 119
Lehnus, Donald James 1934- ... CANR-9
Earlier sketch in CA 57-60
Lehnus, Opal (Hull) 1920- ... 9-10R
Lehovich, Eugenie Ouroussow
See Ouroussow, Eugenie
Lehr, Delores 1920- ... 19-20R
See also SATA 10
Lehr, Paul E(dwin) 1918- ... 65-68
Lehrer, Adrienne (Joyce) 1937- ... 29-32R
Lehrer, James (Charles) 1934- ... 114
Brief entry ... 109
Lehrer, Keith 1936- ... 17-18R
Lehrer, Robert N(athaniel) 1922- ... 61-64
Lehrer, Stanley 1929- ... CANR-2
Earlier sketch in CA 5-6R
Lehrer, Thomas Andrew 1928- ... 123
Lehrer, Tom
See Lehrer, Thomas Andrew
Lehrman, Liza
See Williams, Liza
Lehrman, Nat 1929- ... 93-96
Lehrman, Robert L(awrence) 1921- ... CANR-7
Earlier sketch in CA 5-6R
Lehrman, Simon Maurice 1900- ... CAP-1
Earlier sketch in CA 9-10
Lehrmann, Chanan
See Lehrmann, Charles C(uno)
Lehrmann, Charles C(uno) 1905-1977 ... 33-36R
Lehrmann, Cuno Chanan
See Lehrmann, Charles C(uno)
Leib, Amos Patten 1917- ... 45-48
Leibbrand, Kurt 1914- ... 45-48
Leibel, Charlotte P(ollack) 1899- ... 33-36R
Leibenguth, Charla Ann
See Banner, Charla Ann Leibenguth
Leibenstein, Harvey 1922- ... 103
Leiber, Fritz (Reuter, Jr.) 1910- ... CANR-2
Earlier sketch in CA 45-48
See also SATA 45
See also DLB 8
See also CLC 25
Leiber, Justin Fritz 1938- ... CANR-17
Earlier sketch in CA 97-100
Leibert, Julius A(mos) 1888- ... CAP-2
Earlier sketch in CA 17-18
Leibold, Jay 1957- ... 123
See also SATA 52
Leibold, (William) John 1926- ... 37-40R
Leibowitz, Herbert A. 1935- ... 25-28R
Leibowitz, Herschel W. 1925- ... CANR-8
Earlier sketch in CA 17-18R
Leibowitz, Irving 1922-1979 ... 11-12R
Obituary ... 85-88
Leibowitz, Rene 1913-1972 Obituary ... 37-40R
Leibson, Jacob J. 1883(?)-1971
Obituary ... 33-36R
Leiby, Adrian C(oulter) 1904-1976 ... CAP-1
Obituary ... 65-68
Earlier sketch in CA 9-10
Leiby, James 1924- ... 33-36R
Leichman, Seymour 1933- ... 25-28R
See also SATA 5
Leichter, Otto 1898(?)-1973 Obituary ... 41-44R
Leiden, Carl 1922- ... 7-8R
Leider, Emily Wortis 1937- ... 81-84
Leider, Frida 1888-1975 Obituary ... 57-60
Leigh, Carolyn 1926-1983 Obituary ... 111
Leigh, Egbert Giles, Jr. 1940- ... 57-60
Leigh, Eugene
See Seltzer, Leon E(ugene)
Leigh, James L(eighton) 1930- ... 9-10R
Leigh, Michael 1914- ... 13-14R
Leigh, Mike 1943- ... 109
Leigh, Palmer
See Palmer, Pamela Lynn
Leigh, Ralph Alexander 1915-1987
Obituary ... 124
Leigh, Spencer 1945- ... 102
Leigh, Susannah 1938- ... CANR-15
Earlier sketch in CA 81-84
Leigh, Tom 1947- ... SATA-46
Leigh Fermor, Patrick Michael
See Fermor, Patrick Leigh
Leigh-Pemberton, John 1911- ... 108
See also SATA 35
Leight, Robert L(ewis) 1932- ... 110
Leighton, Albert C(hester) 1919- ... 37-40R
Leighton, Alexander H(amilton) 1908- ... 41-44R
Leighton, Ann
See Smith, Isadore Leighton Luce
Leighton, Clare (Veronica Hope) 1899- ... 108
See also SATA 37
Leighton, David S(truan) R(obertson)
1928- ... CANR-2
Earlier sketch in CA 5-6R
Leighton, Frances Spatz ... 81-84
Leighton, Jack Richard 1918- ... 3R
Leighton, Lauren G(ray) 1934- ... 118
Leighton, Lee
See Overholser, Wayne D.
Leighton, Margaret (Carver) 1896-1987 ... 9-10R
Obituary ... 123
See also SATA 1, 52
Leikind, Morris C. 1906(?)-1976
Obituary ... 65-68
Leimbach, Patricia Penton 1927- ... 57-60
Leimberg, Stephan R(obert) 1943- ... 117
Leimert, Lucille 1895(?)-1983 Obituary ... 110
Leinbach, Esther V(ashti) 1924- ... 61-64
Leinfellner, Werner (Hubertus) 1921- ... CANR-5
Earlier sketch in CA 53-56
Leininger, Madeleine M. 1925- ... 33-36R
Leino, Eino
See Loennbohm, Armas Eino Leopold
See also TCLC 24
Leinsdorf, Erich 1912- ... 119
Brief entry ... 112
Leinster, Murray
See Jenkins, Will(iam) F(itzgerald)
See also DLB 8
Leinwand, Gerald 1921- ... CANR-9
Earlier sketch in CA 7-8R
Leip, Hans 1893-1983 Obituary ... 110
Leipart, Charles 1944- ... 108
Leiper, Henry Smith 1891-1975 Obituary ... 53-56
Leipold, L. Edmond 1902- ... 69-72
See also SATA 16
Leiris, Michel (Julien) 1901- Brief entry ... 119
Leiser, Burton M. 1930- ... CANR-12
Earlier sketch in CA 29-32R
Leiser, Erwin (Moritz) 1923- ... CANR-14
Earlier sketch in CA 29-32R
Leiserson, Michael 1939- ... 37-40R
Leishman, J(ames) Blair 1902-1963 ... CANR-6
Earlier sketch in CA 7-8R
Leishman, Thomas L. 1900-1978
Obituary ... 81-84
Leisk, David Johnson 1906-1975 ... 9-10R
Obituary ... 57-60
See also SATA 1, 26, 30
Leiss, William 1939- ... 41-44R
Leister, Mary 1917- ... CANR-11
Earlier sketch in CA 65-68
See also SATA 29
Leistritz, F(redrick) Larry 1945- ... 104
Leisy, James (Franklin) 1927- ... CANR-20
Earlier sketches in CA 11-12R, CANR-4
Leitch, Adelaide 1921- ... 101
Leitch, D(avid) B(ruce) 1940- ... 57-60
Leitch, Maurice 1933- ... 102
See also DLB 14
Leitch, Patricia 1933- ... CANR-9
Earlier sketch in CA 61-64
See also SATA 11
Leitch, Vincent Barry 1944- ... 113
Leitenberg, Milton 1933- ... CANR-19
Earlier sketch in CA 101
Leiter, Louis (Henry) 1921- ... 37-40R
Leiter, Marcia 1942- ... 116
Leiter, Robert D(avid) 1922-1976 ... CANR-4
Obituary ... 69-72
Earlier sketch in CA 7-8R
Leiter, Samuel Louis 1940- ... 93-96
Leiter, Sharon 1942- ... 57-60
Leites, Edmund 1939- ... 126
Leites, Nathan Constantin 1912-1987 ... 126
Obituary ... 122
Leith, (James) Andrew 1931- ... CANR-20
Earlier sketch in CA 45-48
Leith, J(ames) Clark 1937- ... 57-60
Leith, John H. 1919- ... CANR-3
Earlier sketch in CA 5-6R
Leithauser, Brad 1953- ... 107
See also CLC 27
Leithauser, Gladys Garner 1925- ... 15-16R
Leitmann, George 1925- ... 53-56
Leitner, Moses J. 1908- ... CAP-1
Earlier sketch in CA 15-16
Leivick, H.
See Halpern, Leivick
Leivick, Halper
See Halpern, Leivick
Lekachman, Robert 1920- Brief entry ... 106
Lekai, J(ulius) Louis 1916- ... 33-36R
Lekis, Lisa 1917- ... 11-12R
Lekson, Stephen H(enry) 1950- ... 122
Leland, Charles G(odfrey) 1824-1903
Brief entry ... 118
See also DLB 11
Leland, Christopher Towne 1951- ... 108
Leland, Henry 1923- ... CANR-18
Earlier sketch in CA 89-92
Leland, Jeremy (Francis David) 1932- .. CANR-13
Earlier sketch in CA 33-36R
Leland, Timothy 1937- ... 102
Lelchuk, Alan 1938- ... CANR-1
Earlier sketch in CA 45-48
See also CLC 5
Lele, Uma 1941- ... 73-76
Leliaert, Richard Maurice 1940- ... 101
Lelouch, Claude (Barruck Joseph) 1937-
Brief entry ... 113
LeLoup, Lance T. 1949- ... 110
Lelyveld, Arthur J(oseph) 1913- ... 25-28R
Lelyveld, Joseph (Salem) 1937- ... 126
Brief entry ... 117
Lem, Stanislaw 1921- ... 105
See also CAAS 1
See also CLC 8, 15, 40
LeMahieu, D(an) L(loyd) 1945- ... 69-72
LeMair, H(enriette) Willebeek
1889-1966 ... SATA-29
LeMaire, H. Paul 1933- ... 113
Lemaitre, Georges E(douard) 1898-1972 .. CAP-2
Obituary ... 37-40R
Earlier sketch in CA 25-28
Lemann, Bernard 1905- ... CANR-21
Earlier sketch in CA 41-44R
Lemann, Nancy 1956- Brief entry ... 118
See also CLC 39
Lemarchand, Elizabeth (Wharton)
1906- ... CANR-26
Earlier sketches in CA 25-28R, CANR-10
Lemarchand, Rene 1932- ... 15-16R
LeMaster, J(immie) R(ay) 1934- ... CANR-13
Earlier sketch in CA 33-36R
LeMaster, Leslie Jean 1943- ... 125
LeMay, Alan 1899-1964 Obituary ... 115
Lemay, Harding 1922- ... CANR-21
Earlier sketches in CA 45-48, CANR-1
Lemay, J(oseph) A(lberic) Leo 1935- ... CANR-24
Earlier sketches in CA 19-20R, CANR-9
le May, Reginald Stuart 1885- ... 7-8R
Lembeck, Ruth (Louise) 1919- ... 105
Lembke, Janet (Nutt) 1933- ... 45-48
Lembo, Diana L.
See Spirt, Diana L(ouise)
Lembo, John M(ario) 1937- ... 29-32R
Lembourn, Hans Joergen 1923- ... 105
Lemelle, Wilbert J. 1931- ... 45-48
Lemert, Charles C(lay) 1937- ... 111
Lemert, Edwin M(cCarty) 1912- ... 93-96
Lemert, James B(olton) 1935- ... 73-76
Lemert, Jim
See Lemert, James B(olton)
Lemesurier, Peter
See Britton, Peter Ewart
Lemieux, Joanne (Hero) 1946- ... 114
Lemieux, Lucien 1934- ... 41-44R
Lemieux, Marc 1948- ... 102
Lemir, Andre
See Rimel, Duane (Weldon)
Le Mire, Eugene D(ennis) 1929- ... 41-44R
Lemire, Robert A(rthur) 1933- ... 101
Lemish, John 1921- ... 7-8R
Lemke, Horst 1922- ... 107
See also SATA 38
Lemme, Janet E(llen) 1941- ... 29-32R
Lemmon, Kenneth 1911- ... 65-68
Lemmon, Sarah McCulloh 1914- ... 21-22R
Lemoine, Ernest
See Roy, Ewell Paul
LeMon, Cal 1945- ... 53-56
Lemon, James Thomas 1929- ... 37-40R
Lemon, Lee T(homas) 1931- ... 17-18R

LeMon, Lynn
See Wert, Lynette L(emon)
LeMond, Alan 1938- CANR-9
Earlier sketch in CA 61-64
Lemonnier, (Antoine Louis) Camille
1844-1913 Brief entry 121
See also TCLC 22
Lemons, J. Stanley 1938- 37-40R
Lemont, George 1927- 65-68
Lemos, Ramon M(arcelino) 1927- 37-40R
Lenanton, Carola Mary Anima Oman
See Oman, Carola (Mary Anima)
Lenarcic, R(aymond) J(ames) 1942- 49-52
Lenard, Alexander 1910-1972 .... CANR-4
Obituary 89-92
Earlier sketch in CA 7-8R
See also SATA 21
Lenard, Yvone 1921- CANR-7
Earlier sketch in CA 53-56
Lenardon, Robert J(oseph) 1928- 33-36R
Lenburg, Greg 1956- 105
Lenburg, Jeff 1956- CANR-20
Earlier sketch in CA 104
Lenczowski, George 1915- CANR-4
Earlier sketch in CA 3R
Lendon, Kenneth Harry 1928- 9-10R
Lendvai, Paul 1929- CANR-15
Earlier sketch in CA 85-88
Lenehan, William T. 1930- 23-24R
L'Enfant, Julie 1944- 109
Lengel, Frances
See Trocchi, Alexander
Lengle, James I(rvin) 1949- 106
L'Engle, Madeleine 1918- CANR-21
Earlier sketches in CA 3R, CANR-3
See also SATA 1, 27
See also DLB 52
See also CLC 12
See also CLR 1, 14
See also AITN 2
Lengyel, Alfonz 1921- 116
Lengyel, Cornel Adam 1915- CANR-24
Earlier sketches in CA 4R, CANR-1
See also SATA 27
Lengyel, Emil 1895-1985 .... CANR-3
Obituary 115
Earlier sketch in CA 9-10R
See also SATA 3, 42
Lengyel, Jozsef 1896-1975 85-88
Obituary 57-60
See also CLC 7
Lengyel, Melchior 1879(?)-1974 Obituary ..53-56
Lenhoff, Alan (Stuart) 1951- 73-76
Lenier, Sue 1957- 120
Lenihan, John (Howard) 1941- 105
Lenihan, Kenneth J. 1928- 97-100
Lenin 1870-1924 Brief entry 121
Lenin, N.
See Lenin
Lenin, Nikolai
See Lenin
Lenin, V. I.
See Lenin
Lenin, Vladimir I.
See Lenin
Lenin, Vladimir Ilyich
See Lenin
Lenn, Theodore I. 1914- 45-48
Lennart, Isobel 1915-1971 Obituary 29-32R
See also DLB 44
Lenneberg, Eric H. 1921-1975 .... CANR-7
Obituary 57-60
Earlier sketch in CA 53-56
Lennig, Arthur 1933- 57-60
Lennon, Florence Becker (Tanenbaum)
1895- 15-16R
Lennon, Helen M.
See Goulart, Frances Sheridan
Lennon, John (Ono) 1940-1980 102
See also CLC 12, 35
Lennon, Joseph Luke 1919- 33-36R
Lennon, Nigey 1954- 109
Lennon, Sister M. Isidore 1901- 41-44R
Lennon, Thomas M. 1942- 125
Lennox, Charlotte 1729(?)-1804 .... DLB-39
Lennox, Terry
See Harvey, John (Barton)
Lennox-Short, Alan 1913- 102
Lens, Sidney 1912-1986 .... CANR-17
Obituary 119
Earlier sketches in CA 4R, CANR-1
See also SATA 13, 48
Lensen, George Alexander 1923-1980 ... CANR-2
Earlier sketch in CA 1R
Lenski, Gerhard Emmanuel, Jr. 1924- 2R
Lenski, Lois 1893-1974 .... CAP-1
Obituary 53-56
Earlier sketch in CA 13-14
See also SATA 1, 26
See also DLB 22
Lenson, David (Rollar) 1945- 73-76
Lent, Blair CANR-11
Earlier sketch in CA 21-22R
See also SATA 2
Lent, D(ora) Geneva 1904- 5-6R
Lent, Henry Bolles 1901-1973 73-76
See also SATA 17
Lent, John A(nthony) 1936- CANR-12
Earlier sketch in CA 29-32R
Lentfoehr, Therese 1902- 97-100
Lentilhon, Robert Ward 1925- 11-12R
Lentin, Antony 1941- 103
Lentner, Howard H(enry) 1931- 106
Lenton, Henry Trevor 1924- 103
Lentricchia, Frank (Jr.) 1940- CANR-19
Earlier sketch in CA 25-28R
See also CLC 34
Lentz, Donald A. 1910- 19-20R
Lentz, Harold H(erbert) 1910- 57-60
Lentz, Perry 1943- 23-24R
Lenz, Carolyn Ruth Swift
See Swift, Carolyn Ruth
Lenz, Frederick 1950- 97-100
Lenz, Hermann 1913- DLB-69
Lenz, Siegfried 1926- 89-92
See also DLB 75
See also CLC 27
Lenz, William E(rnest) 1950- 118
Leodhas, Sorche Nic
See Alger, Leclaire (Gowans)
LeoGrande, William M(ark) 1949- 122
Leokum, Arkady 1916(?)- 116
See also SATA 45
Leon, Frances
See Swadesh, Frances Leon
Leon, Henry Cecil 1902-1976 Obituary 115
Leon, Pierre R. 1926- CANR-17
Earlier sketches in CA 45-48, CANR-1
Leonard, Calista V(erne) 1919- 21-22R
Leonard, Charlene M(arie) 1928- 33-36R
Leonard, Constance (Brink) 1923- 49-52
See also SATA 40, 42
Leonard, Edith Marian CAP-1
Earlier sketch in CA 15-16
Leonard, Elmore 1925- CANR-12
Earlier sketch in CA 81-84
See also CLC 28, 34
See also AITN 1
Leonard, Eugenie Andruss 1888-1980 .... CAP-2
Obituary 97-100
Earlier sketch in CA 17-18
Leonard, Frank G. 1935(?)-1974
Obituary 49-52
Leonard, George (Jay) 1946- 112
Leonard, George B(urr) 1923- CANR-20
Earlier sketches in CA 9-10R, CANR-3
Leonard, George E(dward) 1931- 23-24R
Leonard, George H. 1921- 65-68
Leonard, George K., Jr. 1915- 17-18R
Leonard, Gladys Osborne 1882-1968
Obituary 112
Leonard, Graham Douglas 1921- 103
Leonard, Hugh
See Byrne, John Keyes
See also DLB 13
Leonard, Irving A(lbert) 1896- CANR-5
Earlier sketch in CA 5-6R
Leonard, Jason
See Escott, Jonathan
Leonard, John 1939- CANR-12
Earlier sketch in CA 13-14R
Leonard, Jonathan N(orton) 1903-1975 ...61-64
Obituary 57-60
See also SATA 36
Leonard, Joseph T. 1916- 9-10R
Leonard, Justin W(ilkinson) 1909- CAP-1
Earlier sketch in CA 19-20
Leonard, Lawrence 121
Leonard, Leo D(onald) 1938- CANR-5
Earlier sketch in CA 53-56
Leonard, Maurice 1939- 107
Leonard, Neil 1927- 4R
Leonard, Phyllis B. 1929- 117
Leonard, Phyllis G(rubbs) 1924- CANR-12
Earlier sketch in CA 69-72
Leonard, Richard Anthony 1900(?)-1979
Obituary 85-88
Leonard, Robert 1928-1984 Obituary 112
Leonard, Robert C(arl) 1928- 45-48
Leonard, Roger Ashley 1940- 25-28R
Leonard, Ruth S(haw) 1906- CAP-2
Earlier sketch in CA 23-24
Leonard, Thomas C(harles) 1944- 77-80
Leonard, Thomas M. 1937- 122
Leonard, Tom 1944- CANR-13
Earlier sketch in CA 77-80
Leonard, V. A. 1898- CANR-15
Earlier sketch in CA 37-40R
Leonard, William Ellery 1876-1944 ..... DLB-54
Leonard, William N. 1912- 37-40R
Leonard, William Torbert 1918- 107
Leondes, Cornelius Thomas 1927- 17-18R
Leone, Bruno 1939- 110
Leone, Leonard 1914- 115
Leone, Mark P(aul) 1940- 93-96
Leone, Robert A. 1945- 122
Leone, Sergio 1929- 123
Leong, Charles L. 1911(?)-1984 Obituary ... 112
Leong, Gor Yun
See Ellison, Virginia H(owell)
Leonhard, Charles 1915- 5-6R
Leonhardt, Fritz 1909- 123
Leonhardt, Rudolf Walter 1921- CANR-3
Earlier sketch in CA 9-10R
Leoni, Edgar (Hugh) 1925- 125
Leon-Portilla, Miguel 1926- CANR-11
Earlier sketch in CA 21-22R
Leontiades, Milton 1932- 110
Leontief, Wassily 1906- CAP-1
Earlier sketch in CA 17-18
Leontyev, Lev Abramovich 1901-1974
Obituary 49-52
Leopold, A(ldo) Starker 1913-1983
Obituary 110
Leopold, Allison Kyle 1955- 112
Leopold, Carolyn Clugston 1923- 73-76
Leopold, Luna B(ergere) 1915- 49-52
Leopold, Nathan F. 1904-1971 .... CAP-1
Obituary 29-32R
Earlier sketch in CA 15-16
Leopold, Richard William 1912- CANR-2
Earlier sketch in CA 3R
Leopold, Werner F. 1896- 45-48
Leopold III 1901-1983 Obituary 110
Le Pan, Douglas (Valentine) 1914-
Brief entry 117
Le Patourel, John Herbert 1909-1981 .... CAP-1
Obituary 104
Earlier sketch in CA 9-10
Lepawsky, Albert 1908- 45-48
Le Pelley, Guernsey 1910- 81-84
Lepetit, Charles
See Sala, Charles
Lepidus, Henry 1916(?)-1983 Obituary 110
Lepko, E.
See Kopelev, Lev (Zinovievich)
Lepley, Jean Elizabeth 1934- 69-72
Lepley, Paul M(ichael) 1933- 53-56
Le Poer Trench, (William Francis) Brinsley
1911- Brief entry 116
Lepore, D(ominick) J(ames) 1911- 45-48
Le Poulain, Jean 1924-1988 Obituary 125
Lepp, Henry 1922- 53-56
Leppmann, Peter K. 1931- 25-28R
Leppmann, Wolfgang Arthur 1922- 3R
Leppzer, Robert 1958- 105
Leprohon, Pierre 1903- CANR-1
Earlier sketch in CA 45-48
Le Quesne, A(lfred) L(aurence) 1928- 116
Le Quesne, Laurence
See Le Quesne, A(lfred) L(aurence)
Le Queux, William (Tufnell) 1864-1927
Brief entry 109
See also DLB 70
Lerbinger, Otto 1925- 23-24R
Lerche, Charles O(lsen), Jr. 1918-1966 ....7-8R
Le Reveler
See Artaud, Antonin
le Riche, William Harding 1916- 107
Lerman, Eleanor 1952- 85-88
See also CLC 9
Lerman, Leo 1914- 45-48
Lerman, Paul 1926- 97-100
Lerman, Rhoda 1936- 49-52
Lerner, Aaron Bunsen 1920- 108
See also SATA 35
Lerner, Abba P(tachya) 1903-1982 ..... CANR-2
Obituary 108
Earlier sketch in CA 3R
Lerner, Alan Jay 1918-1986 77-80
Obituary 119
Lerner, Arthur 1915- 102
Lerner, Carol 1927- 102
See also SATA 33
Lerner, Daniel 1917-1980 .... CANR-6
Obituary 97-100
Earlier sketch in CA 1R
Lerner, Eugene Max 1928- 17-18R
Lerner, Gerda 1920- CANR-26
Earlier sketch in CA 25-28R
Lerner, Herbert J. 1933- 53-56
Lerner, I. Michael 1910- 41-44R
Lerner, Janet W(eiss) 1926- CANR-7
Earlier sketch in CA 57-60
Lerner, Joel J. 1936- 53-56
Lerner, Laurence (David) 1925- CANR-20
Earlier sketches in CA 7-8R, CANR-3
Lerner, Lily Gluck 1928- 117
Lerner, Linda 73-76
Lerner, Louis A. 1935-1984 Obituary 114
Lerner, Marguerite Rush 1924-1987 .....13-14R
Obituary 122
See also SATA 11, 51
Lerner, Maura 1953- 97-100
Lerner, Max(well Alan) 1902- CANR-25
Earlier sketch in CA 13-14R
See also DLB 29
See also AITN 1
Lerner, Michael G(ordon) 1943- 49-52
Lerner, Michael P(hillip) 1943- 45-48
Lerner, Richard E(dward) 1941- 73-76
Lerner, Richard M(artin) 1946- 93-96
Lerner, Robert E. 1940- CANR-8
Earlier sketch in CA 23-24R
Lerner, Sharon (Ruth) 1938-1982 ...... CANR-3
Obituary 106
Earlier sketch in CA 7-8R
See also SATA 11, 29
Lerner, Warren 1929- 29-32R
Lernet-Holenia, Alexander 1898(?)-1976
Obituary 65-68
Lernoux, Penny (Mary) 1940- 77-80
Leroe, Ellen W(hitney) 1949- 116
See also SATA 51
Le Roi, David (de Roche) 1905- CANR-3
Earlier sketch in CA 11-12R
Leroi-Gourhan, Andre (Georges Leandre)
1911-1986 Obituary 118
Leroux, Etienne
See Leroux, S(tephanus) P(etrus)
D(aniel)
Leroux, Gaston 1868-1927 Brief entry 108
See also TCLC 25
Leroux, S(tephanus) P(etrus) D(aniel)
1922- CANR-2
Earlier sketch in CA 49-52
Le Roy, Bruce Murdock 1920- Brief entry ... 106
LeRoy, Dave
See LeRoy, (Lemuel) David
LeRoy, (Lemuel) David 1920- 81-84
LeRoy, Douglas 1943- CANR-18
Earlier sketches in CA 49-52, CANR-3
LeRoy, Gaylord C. 1910- 37-40R
LeRoy, Gen Brief entry 115
See also SATA 36, 52
Leroy, Maurice (A. L.) 1909- 25-28R
LeRoy, Mervyn 1900-1987 Obituary 123
Brief entry 108
Le Roy Ladurie, Emmanuel 1929- 113
Lerrigo, Marion Olive 1898-1968 Obituary .. 109
See also SATA 29
Lerro, Anthony Joseph 1932- 33-36R
Lerski, George Jan 1917- 73-76
Lerteth, Oban
See Fanthorpe, R(obert) Lionel
Lerude, Warren (Leslie) 1937- Brief entry ... 122
Le Sage, Laurent 1913- CANR-25
Earlier sketch in CA 3R
Leschak, Peter M. 1951- 126
Lescoe, Francis J(oseph) 1916- 61-64
Lescroart, John T. 1948- 122
Lesesne, J(oab) Mauldin 1899- CAP-2
Earlier sketch in CA 33-36
LeShan, Eda J(oan) 1922- CANR-21
Earlier sketch in CA 15-16R
See also SATA 21
See also CLR 6
LeShan, Lawrence L(ee) 1920- CANR-21
Earlier sketch in CA 19-20R
Le Shana, David C(harles) 1932- 29-32R
Lesher, Phyllis A(senath Bayers)
1912- CANR-17
Earlier sketch in CA 25-28R
Lesher, Stephan 1935- 103
LeSieg, Theo.
See Geisel, Theodor Seuss
Lesieur, Henry R(ichard) 1946- 77-80
Lesikar, Raymond Vincent 1922- CANR-2
Earlier sketch in CA 1R
Lesikin, Joan 1947- 93-96
Lesins, Knuts 1909- 73-76
Lesko, George 1932- 19-20R
Lesko, Leonard Henry 1938- CANR-8
Earlier sketch in CA 61-64
Lesky, Albin (Hans) 1896- 85-88
Leslau, Wolf 1906- 104
Lesley, Blake
See Duckworth, Leslie Blakey
Lesley, Cole
See Cole, Leonard Leslie
Leslie, A. L.
See Lazarus, A(rnold) L(eslie)
Leslie, Aleen 5-6R
Leslie, Anita 1914-1985 49-52
Obituary 117
Leslie, Cecilie 1914- 17-18R
Leslie, Charles M. 1923- 7-8R
Leslie, Clare Walker 1947- 108
Leslie, Conrad 1923- 29-32R
Leslie, Desmond 1921- 9-10R
Leslie, Donald Daniel 1922- 102
Leslie, Doris
See Fergusson Hannay, Doris
Leslie, F(rederic) Andrew 1927- CANR-7
Earlier sketch in CA 17-18R
Leslie, Frank 1821-1880 .... DLB-43
Leslie, Gerald R(onnell) 1925- 17-18R
Leslie, Jane
See Coade, Jessie
Leslie, John Andrew 1940- 112
Leslie, Josephine Aimee Campbell
1898-1979 85-88
Leslie, Kenneth 1892-1974 93-96
Obituary 53-56
Leslie, Michael 1952- 118
Leslie, O. H.
See Slesar, Henry
Leslie, Phil 1909(?)-1988 Obituary 126
Leslie, Robert B.
See Wooley, John (Steven)
Leslie, Robert C(ampbell) 1917- 33-36R
Leslie, Robert Franklin 1911- 49-52
See also SATA 7
Leslie, Rochelle
See Diamond, Graham
Leslie, Roy F. 1922- 41-44R
Leslie, S(amuel) Clement 1898- 85-88
Leslie, San
See Crook, Bette (Jean)
Leslie, Sarah
See McGuire, Leslie Sarah
Leslie, Seymour 1890(?)-1979 Obituary ...89-92
Leslie, (John Randolph) Shane 1885-1971
Obituary 33-36R
Leslie, Sir Shane
See Leslie, (John Randolph) Shane
Leslie, Ward S.
See Ward, Elizabeth Honor (Shedden)
Leslie, Warren III 1927- 9-10R
Leslie-Melville, Betty 1929- 81-84
Leslie-Melville, Jock
See Leslie-Melville, John D.
Leslie-Melville, John D. 1933-1984 81-84
Obituary 112
Lesly, Philip 1918- CANR-14
Earlier sketch in CA 81-84
Lesnoff-Caravaglia, Gari 41-44R
LeSourd, Catherine
See Marshall, (Sarah) Catherine (Wood)
Lesowitz, Robert I(rwin) 1939- 57-60
L'Esperance, Wilford L(ouis) III
1930-1982 ....33-36R
Lessa, William A(rmand) 1908- 61-64
Lessac, Arthur 1910- Brief entry 110
Lessard, Michel 1942- 104
Lessel, William M. 1906- CAP-2
Earlier sketch in CA 33-36
Lesser, Alexander 1902-1982 49-52
Obituary 107
Lesser, Charles H(uber) 1944- 73-76
Lesser, Eugene (Bernard) 1936- 49-52
Lesser, Gerald S(amuel) 1926- 97-100
Lesser, Margaret 1899(?)-1979 Obituary ..93-96
See also SATA 22
Lesser, Michael 1939- 102
Lesser, Milton
See Marlowe, Stephen

Lesser, R(oger) H(arold) 1928- CANR-14
Earlier sketch in CA 73-76
Lesser, Rika 1953- 118
See also SATA 53
Lesser, Robert C. 1933- 104
Lessere, Samuel E. 1892- CAP-2
Earlier sketch in CA 21-22
Lessing, Bruno 1870-1940 .... DLB-28
Lessing, Doris (May) 1919- 9-10R
See also DLB 15
See also DLBY 85
See also CLC 1, 2, 3, 6, 10, 15, 22, 40
Lessler, Richard Sigmund 1924- 2R
Lessmann, Paul G. 1919- 17-18R
LesStrang, Jacques 1926- CANR-17
Earlier sketch in CA 65-68
Lester, Alison 1952- 125
See also SATA 50
Lester, Andrew D(ouglas) 1939- CANR-26
Earlier sketch in CA 109
Lester, Anthony 1936- 37-40R
Lester, David 1942- CANR-12
Earlier sketch in CA 33-36R
Lester, Frank
See Usher, Frank (Hugh)
Lester, Gene
See Mercer, Jean
Lester, Godfrey Allen 1943- 111
Lester, Helen 1936- 115
See also SATA 46
Lester, James
See Blake, L(eslie) J(ames)
Lester, James D. 1935- CANR-15
Earlier sketch in CA 89-92
Lester, James P(inkney) 1944- 114
Lester, John
See Werner, Vivian
Lester, Julius (Bernard) 1939- CANR-23
Earlier sketches in CA 17-18R, CANR-8
See also BW
See also SATA 12
See also CLR 2
Lester, Mark
See Russell, Martin
Lester, Reginald Mounstephens 1896- CAP-1
Earlier sketch in CA 9-10
Lester, Richard 1932- CLC-20
Lester, Richard A. 1908- 102
Lester, Robert C(arlton) 1933- 73-76
Lester, William 57-60
Lester-Rands, A.
See Judd, Frederick Charles
LeStourgeon, Diana E. 1927- 15-16R
L'Estrange, Anna
See Ellerbeck, Rosemary (Anne L'Estrange)
Le Sueur, Lucille 1908(?)-1977 Obituary 111
Le Sueur, Meridel 1900- CANR-2
Earlier sketch in CA 49-52
See also SATA 6
Lesure, Francois 1923- Brief entry 108
Lesure, Thomas B(arbour) 1923- 102
Leszlei, Marta
See Dosa, Marta Leszlei
L'Etang, Hugh J(oseph) C(harles) J(ames) 1917- 45-48
LeTarte, Clyde E(dward) 1938- 53-56
Leterman, Elmer G. 1897- 25-28R
Lethbridge, Rex
See Meyers, Roy (Lethbridge)
Lethbridge, T(homas) C(harles) 1901-1971 .... CAP-2
Earlier sketch in CA 29-32
Letiche, John M(arion) 1918- 49-52
Le Tord, Bijou 1945- 65-68
See also SATA 49
LeTourneau, Richard (Howard) 1925- CANR-23
Earlier sketches in CA 53-56, CANR-7
Letrusco
See Martini, Virgilio
Lettau, Reinhard 1929- CANR-9
Earlier sketch in CA 17-18R
See also DLB 75
Letterman, Edward John 1926- 29-32R
Lettis, Richard 1928- 7-8R
Lettvin, Maggie 1927- 73-76
Letwin, Shirley Robin 1924- 17-18R
Letwin, William L(ouis) 1922- 11-12R
Leuba, Clarence J(ames) 1899- 37-40R
Leubsdorf, Carl P(hilipp) 1938- 73-76
Leuchtenburg, William E(dward) 1922- CANR-12
Earlier sketch in CA 7-8R
Leuci, Bob
See Leuci, Robert
Leuci, Robert 1940- 125
Leukel, Francis 1922- 53-56
Leuthner, Stuart 1939- 125
Leuthold, David Allen 1932- 23-24R
Leutscher, Alfred (George) 1913- 73-76
See also SATA 23
Lev, Daniel S(aul) 1933- 41-44R
Levack, Brian P(aul) 1943- 53-56
Levai, Blaise 1919- 108
See also SATA 39
Levant, Howard 1929- 89-92
Levant, Oscar 1906-1972 Obituary 37-40R
Levant, Victor 1947- 126
Levantrosser, William F(rederick) 1925- 21-22R
Levanway, Russell W(ilford) 1919- Brief entry 107
Levarie, Siegmund 1914- 13-14R
Le Vay, David 1915- 89-92
Levell, Byrd 1911(?)-1979 Obituary 89-92
Leven, Charles L(ouis) 1928- CANR-14
Earlier sketch in CA 41-44R
Leven, Jeremy 1941- 102
Levendosky, Charles (Leonard) 1936- CANR-12
Earlier sketch in CA 29-32R
Levene, Malcolm 1937- 45-48
Levenkron, Steven 1941- 109
Levenson, Alan Ira 1935- 45-48
Levenson, Christopher 1934- 29-32R
Levenson, Dorothy (Perkins) 1927- 9-10R
Levenson, Edgar A. 1924- Brief entry 108
Levenson, J(acob) C(lavner) 1922- 25-28R
Levenson, Jordan 1936- CANR-23
Earlier sketches in CA 57-60, CANR-7
Levenson, Joseph Richmond 1920-1969 .... CANR-6
Earlier sketch in CA 1R
Levenson, Myron H(erbert) 1926-1974 53-56
Levenson, Sam(uel) 1911-1980 .... CANR-26
Obituary 101
Earlier sketch in CA 65-68
See also AITN 1
Levenson, William B. 1907- CAP-2
Earlier sketch in CA 25-28
Levenstein, Aaron 1910-1986 .... CAP-1
Obituary 119
Earlier sketch in CA 19-20
Levenstein, Harvey A(llan) 1938- 106
Levenstein, Sidney 1917- 11-12R
Leventhal, Albert Rice 1907-1976 65-68
Obituary 61-64
Leventhal, Donald B(ecker) 1930- 45-48
Leventhal, Fred Marc 1938- Brief entry 109
Leventhal, Herbert 1941- 69-72
Leventhal, Lance A. 1945- 110
Leventman, Seymour 1930- CANR-1
Earlier sketch in CA 2R
Lever, Charles 1806-1872 .... DLB-21
Lever, J(ulius) W(alter) 1913-1975 .... CAP-2
Obituary 61-64
Earlier sketch in CA 23-24
Lever, Janet 1946- 85-88
Lever, Judy 1947- 107
Lever, Katherine 1916- 17-18R
Lever, Tresham (Joseph Philip) 1900-1975 .... 13-16R
Obituary 57-60
Lever, Walter
See Lever, J(ulius) W(alter)
Leverence, William John 1946- 102
Levering, Frank (Graham) 1952- 119
Levering, Ralph (Brooks) 1947- 85-88
Leverson, Ada 1865(?)-1936(?)
Brief entry 117
See also TCLC 18
LeVert, (William) John 1946- 122
Levertov, Denise 1923- CANR-3
Earlier sketch in CA 2R
See also DLB 5
See also CLC 1, 2, 3, 5, 8, 15, 28
Levesque, Rene 1922-1987 Obituary 125
Levey, Martin 1913-1970 .... CANR-10
Earlier sketch in CA 15-16R
Levey, Michael (Vincent) 1927- CANR-25
Earlier sketches in CA 7-8R, CANR-4
Levey, Samuel 1932- CANR-2
Earlier sketch in CA 45-48
Levi, Albert William 1911- Brief entry 107
Levi, Anthony H(erbert) T(igar) 1929- CANR-24
Earlier sketches in CA 15-16R, CANR-9
Levi, Carlo 1902-1975 .... CANR-10
Obituary 53-56
Earlier sketch in CA 65-68
Levi, Edward H(irsch) 1911- CANR-2
Earlier sketch in CA 49-52
Levi, Hans 1935- 41-44R
Levi, Helen I(sabel) 1929- 117
Levi, Isaac 1930- 97-100
Levi, Julian (Edwin) 1900-1982 Obituary 106
Levi, Lennart 1930- CANR-8
Earlier sketch in CA 19-20R
Levi, Leo 1926- 114
Levi, Maurice 1945- 111
Levi, Peter (Chad Tigar) 1931- 7-8R
See also DLB 40
See also CLC 41
Levi, Primo 1919-1987 .... CANR-12
Obituary 122
Earlier sketch in CA 15-16R
See also CLC 37, 50
Levi, Vicki Gold 1941- 101
Levi, Werner 1912- CANR-16
Earlier sketch in CA 25-28R
Levi D'Ancona, Mirella
See D'Ancona, Mirella Levi
Levien, Sonya
See Hovey, Sonya
See also DLB 44
Levin, Alexandra Lee 1912- 11-12R
Levin, Alfred 1908- 15-16R
Levin, Alvin Irving 1921- CANR-1
Earlier sketch in CA 45-48
Levin, Beatrice Schwartz 1920- CANR-18
Earlier sketches in CA 11-12R, CANR-3
Levin, Benjamin H. 49-52
Levin, Betty 1927- CANR-25
Earlier sketches in CA 65-68, CANR-9
See also SATA 19
Levin, Bob
See Levin, Robert A.
Levin, Dan 1914- Brief entry 108
Levin, David 1924- CANR-8
Earlier sketch in CA 7-8R
Levin, Gail 1948- 102
Levin, Gerald H(enry) 1929- CANR-15
Earlier sketch in CA 33-36R
Levin, Harold L(eonard) 1929- 93-96
Levin, Harry (Tuchman) 1912- CANR-2
Earlier sketch in CA 2R
Levin, Harry 1925- 109
Levin, Harvey J(oshua) 1924- 11-12R
Levin, Henry M(ordecai) 1938- 122
Levin, Ira 1929- CANR-17
Earlier sketch in CA 21-22R
See also CLC 3, 6
Levin, Jack 1941- CANR-19
Earlier sketches in CA 53-56, CANR-4
Levin, James (Benesch) 1940- 111
Levin, Jane Whitbread 1914- Brief entry 106
Levin, Jenifer 1955- CANR-26
Earlier sketch in CA 108
Levin, John 1944- 107
Levin, Jonathan V(ictor) 1927- 11-12R
Levin, Kenneth 1944- Brief entry 115
Levin, Kim 73-76
Levin, Kristine Cox 1944- 65-68
Levin, Marcia Obrasky 1918- 13-14R
See also SATA 13
Levin, Marlin 1921- CANR-9
Earlier sketch in CA 65-68
Levin, Meyer 1905-1981 .... CANR-15
Obituary 104
Earlier sketch in CA 11-12R
See also SATA 21, 27
See also DLB 9, 28
See also DLBY 81
See also CLC 7
See also AITN 1
Levin, Milton 1925- 25-28R
Levin, Molly Apple 61-64
Levin, N. Gordon, Jr. 1935- 25-28R
Levin, Nora 1916- 25-28R
Levin, Richard Louis 1922- 4R
Levin, Robert A. 1942- 81-84
Levin, Robert J. 1921(?)-1976 Obituary 65-68
Levin, Saul 1921- 13-14R
Levin, William C. 1946- 105
Levine, A(aron) L(awrence) 1925- 23-24R
Levine, Abby 1943- 126
See also SATA 52
Levine, Adeline 1925- 49-52
Levine, Andrew 1944- 65-68
Levine, Arthur E(lliott) 1948- 73-76
Levine, Barry B(ernard) 1941- 101
Levine, Bernard 1934- 29-32R
Levine, Betty K(rasne) 1933- 93-96
Levine, Bob
See Levine, Robert
Levine, Caroline Anne 1942- 89-92
Levine, Charles H(oward) 1939-1988 .... CANR-15
Obituary 126
Earlier sketch in CA 89-92
Levine, Daniel 1934- 15-16R
Levine, Daniel H(arris) 1942- 73-76
Levine, Daniel Urey 1935- 57-60
Levine, David 1926- 116
Brief entry 113
See also SATA 35, 43
Levine, David 1928- 17-18R
Levine, David O(scar) 1955- 124
Levine, Donald N(athan) 1931- 53-56
Levine, Edna S(imon) 85-88
See also SATA 35
Levine, Edward M(onroe) 1924- 21-22R
Levine, Edwin Burton 1920- 25-28R
Levine, Ellen 1939- CANR-22
Earlier sketch in CA 69-72
Levine, Erwin L(eon) 1926- 11-12R
Levine, Faye (Iris) 1944- CANR-3
Earlier sketch in CA 49-52
Levine, Frederick S(pencer) 1945- 120
Levine, Gary 1938- 61-64
Levine, Gene N(orman) 1930- 7-8R
Levine, George 1931- CANR-20
Earlier sketch in CA 25-28R
Levine, George R. 1929- 23-24R
Levine, Herbert S(amuel) 1928-
Brief entry 107
Levine, I(srael) E. 1923- CANR-1
Earlier sketch in CA 3R
See also SATA 12
Levine, Irving R(askin) 1922- 15-16R
Levine, Isaac Don 1892-1981 .... CANR-11
Obituary 103
Earlier sketch in CA 13-14R
Levine, Isidore N. 1909-1972 .... 41-44R
Levine, Israel 1893(?)-1988(?) Obituary 125
Levine, Joan Goldman 61-64
See also SATA 11
Levine, Joseph 1910- 108
See also SATA 33
Levine, Laurence William 1931- 103
Levine, Lawrence 1916- 9-10R
Levine, Lawrence W(illiam) 1933-
Brief entry 115
Levine, Lois (Elaine) L. 1931- 106
Levine, Louis 1921- Brief entry 116
Levine, Mark Lee 1943- CANR-2
Earlier sketch in CA 49-52
Levine, Marvin J. 1930- CANR-21
Earlier sketch in CA 45-48
Levine, Maurice 1902-1971 85-88
Levine, Michael 1954- 89-92
Levine, Milton I(sra) 1902- 109
Levine, Miriam 1939- 116
Levine, Mortimer 1922- 19-20R
Levine, Murray 1928- 49-52
Levine, Norman 1924- CANR-14
Earlier sketch in CA 73-76
Levine, Norman D(ion) 1912- 85-88
Levine, Peter D. 1944- 126
Levine, Philip 1928- CANR-9
Earlier sketch in CA 9-10R
See also DLB 5
See also CLC 2, 4, 5, 9, 14, 33
Levine, Rhoda 73-76
See also SATA 14
Levine, Robert 1944- 121
LeVine, Robert A(lan) 1932- CANR-13
Earlier sketch in CA 21-22R
Levine, Robert M. 1910(?)-1981 Obituary 108
Levine, Robert M. 1941- CANR-11
Earlier sketch in CA 21-22R
Levine, Sarah 1970- 125
Levine, Saul V. 1938- 123
Levine, Sol 1914-1987 .... 9-10R
Obituary 124
Levine, Solomon B. 1920- 104
Levine, Stephen 1937- 45-48
Levine, Stuart (George) 1932- 19-20R
Levine, Suzanne Jill 1946- CANR-13
Earlier sketch in CA 49-52
LeVine, Victor T(heodore) 1928- 15-16R
Levine-Shneidman, Conalee 1930- 119
Levinger, George 1927- CANR-2
Earlier sketch in CA 49-52
Levins, Richard 1930- 119
Levinson, Barry (Michael) 1932-
Brief entry 112
Levinson, Boris M(ayer) 1907-1984 .... CANR-13
Obituary 112
Earlier sketch in CA 33-36R
Levinson, Charles 1920- CANR-21
Earlier sketch in CA 45-48
Levinson, Daniel Jacob 1920- 102
Levinson, Deirdre 1931- 73-76
See also CLC 49
Levinson, Harold M(yer) 1919- 21-22R
Levinson, Harry 1922- CANR-1
Earlier sketch in CA 4R
Levinson, Henry Samuel 1948- CANR-26
Earlier sketch in CA 109
Levinson, Horace C(lifford) 1895-19(?) CAP-1
Earlier sketch in CA 19-20
Levinson, Irene
See Zahava, Irene
Levinson, Leonard 1935- CANR-14
Earlier sketch in CA 77-80
Levinson, Leonard L. 1905(?)-1974
Obituary 45-48
Levinson, Nancy Smiler 1938- CANR-23
Earlier sketch in CA 107
See also SATA 33
Levinson, Olga May 103
Levinson, Richard (Leighton) 1934-1987 .... CANR-13
Obituary 121
Earlier sketch in CA 73-76
Levinson, Riki 121
See also SATA 49, 52
Levinthal, Israel Herbert 1888- 13-14R
Levis, Donald J(ames) 1936- 41-44R
Levis, Larry 1946- 77-80
Levison, Andrew 1948- 93-96
Levi-Strauss, Claude 1908- CANR-6
Earlier sketch in CA 4R
See also CLC 38
Levit, Herschel 1912- 111
Levit, Martin 1918- 45-48
Levit, Rose 1922- 73-76
Levitan, Donald 1928- 104
Levitan, Max 1921- 53-56
Levitan, Sar A. 1914- CANR-3
Earlier sketch in CA 11-12R
Levitan, Tina (Nellie) 1928- 11-12R
Levitas, Gloria B(arach) 1931- CANR-21
Earlier sketch in CA 45-48
Levitas, Maurice 1917- 77-80
Levitch, Joel A. 1942- 37-40R
Levith, Murray J(ay) 1939- 81-84
Levitin, Sonia (Wolff) 1934- CANR-14
Earlier sketch in CA 29-32R
See also SATA 4
See also SAAS 2
See also CLC 17
Levitine, George 1916- 41-44R
Levitsky, David A(aron) 1942- 116
Levitt, I(srael) M(onroe) 1908- 45-48
Levitt, Jesse 1919- 45-48
Levitt, Leonard 1941- 104
Levitt, Morris J(acob) 1938- CANR-15
Earlier sketch in CA 41-44R
Levitt, Mortimer 1907- 118
Levitt, Morton 1920- 61-64
Levitt, Morton P(aul) 1936- 111
Levitt, Saul 1911-1977 81-84
Obituary 73-76
Levitzky, Sergei A. 1909-1983 Obituary 110
Levon, Fred
See Ayvazian, L. Fred
Levoy, Myron CANR-18
Earlier sketch in CA 93-96
See also SATA 37, 49
Levtzion, Nehemia 1935- CANR-4
Earlier sketch in CA 53-56
Levy, Alan 1932- CANR-21
Earlier sketches in CA 9-10R, CANR-6
Levy, Babette May 1907-1977 81-84
Obituary 73-76
Levy, Benn W(olfe) 1900-1973 101
Obituary 45-48
See also DLB 13
See also DLBY 81
Levy, Bernard 1907- 61-64
Levy, Bernard-Henri 1949- 122
Levy, Bill
See Levy, William V.
Levy, Charles K(ingsley) 1924- 120
Levy, D(arryl) A(llen) 1942-1968 .... CAP-2
Earlier sketch in CA 19-20
Levy, Darline Gay Shapiro 1939- 102
Levy, David 1913- 13-14R
Levy, David A(rthur) 1955- 108

Levy, David M(ordecai) 1892-1977 73-76
Obituary 69-72
Levy, David N(eil) L(aurence) 1945- 119
Levy, David W(illiam) 1937- 41-44R
Levy, Elizabeth 1942- CANR-15
Earlier sketch in CA 77-80
See also SATA 31
Levy, Emanuel 1947- CANR-26
Earlier sketch in CA 108
Levy, Eugene Donald 1933- 102
Levy, Faye 1951- 125
Levy, Fred D(avid), Jr. 1937- CANR-14
Earlier sketch in CA 37-40R
Levy, G(ertrude) Rachel 1883-1966 .... 7-8R
Levy, Harold B(ernard) 1918- 73-76
Levy, Harry L(ouis) 1906-1981 .... 33-36R
Obituary 103
Levy, Herta Hess
See Kahn, Herta Hess
Levy, Howard S(eymour) 1923- CANR-25
Earlier sketches in CA 17-18R, CANR-10
Levy, Hyman 1889-1975 Obituary 57-60
Levy, Isaac Jack 1928- 41-44R
Levy, Jack Steven 1948- 115
Levy, Jonathan 1935- CANR-10
Earlier sketch in CA 61-64
Levy, Joseph V(ictor) 1928- 106
Levy, Julien 1906-1981 Obituary 103
Levy, Leonard W(illiams) 1923- CANR-20
Earlier sketches in CA 1R, CANR-1
Levy, Lester S(tern) 1896- 61-64
Levy, Lillian (Rae Berliner) 1918-1986 .... 17-18R
Obituary 120
Levy, Lorelei
See Schwalberg, Carol(yn Ernestine Stein)
Levy, Marion Joseph, Jr. 1918- 73-76
Levy, Michael E(rnst) 1929- CANR-2
Earlier sketch in CA 5-6R
Levy, Michael R(ichard) 1946- 77-80
Levy, Morton 1930- 77-80
Levy, Owen 1948- 118
Levy, Raphael 1900-1969 .... CAP-1
Earlier sketch in CA 15-16
Levy, Reynold 1945- 97-100
Levy, Richard C. 1947- 73-76
Levy, Robert 1926- 77-80
Levy, Robert Calmann
See Calmann-Levy, Robert
Levy, Robert J(oseph) 1931- 37-40R
Levy, Rosalie Marie 1889- CAP-1
Earlier sketch in CA 9-10
Levy, S Jay 1922- 108
Levy, Sidney Jay 1921- Brief entry 106
Levy, Stephen 1947- 105
Levy, Sue 1936- CANR-8
Earlier sketch in CA 57-60
Levy, Wilbert J. 1917- CANR-6
Earlier sketch in CA 57-60
Levy, William Turner 1922- 25-28R
Levy, William V. 1930- 9-10R
Levytskjy, Borys 1915- 65-68
Lewald, H(erald) Ernest 1922-1982 .... 23-24R
Obituary 114
Lewald, (Theo) Roon 1942- 93-96
Lewallen, John 1942- 69-72
Lewalski, Barbara Kiefer 1931- 104
Lewandowski, Dan 1947- 77-80
Lewandowski, Stephen 1947- 93-96
Lewanski, Richard C(asimir) 1918- 19-20R
LeWarne, Charles P(ierce) 1930- 57-60
Lewbin, Hyman J(oseph) 1894- 61-64
Lewcock, Ronald (B.) 1929- 121
Lewellen, T(ed) C(harles) 1940- CANR-6
Earlier sketch in CA 13-14R
Lewels, Francisco J(ose), Jr. 1944- 104
Lewenstein, Morris R. 1923- 13-14R
Lewes, George Henry 1817-1878 .... DLB-55
Lewes, Lettie
See Cleveland, Philip Jerome
Lewesdon, John
See Daniell, Albert Scott
Lewin, Bertram D(avid) 1896-1971 65-68
Lewin, Betsy 1937- 104
See also SATA 32
Lewin, C. L.
See Brister, Richard
Lewin, Elsa 118
Lewin, Esther 1922- 61-64
Lewin, Hugh 1939- 113
See also SATA 40
See also CLR 9
Lewin, L(eonard) 1919- 49-52
Lewin, Leonard C(ase) 1916- 19-20R
Lewin, Michael Zinn 1942- 73-76
Lewin, Nathan 1936- 101
Lewin, (George) Ronald 1914-1984 .... CANR-13
Obituary 111
Earlier sketch in CA 25-28R
Lewin, Ted 1935- CANR-25
Earlier sketch in CA 69-72
See also SATA 21
Lewine, Richard 1910- 81-84
Lewing, Anthony Charles 1933- 81-84
LeWinter, Oswald 1931- 3R
Lewis, A(rthur) J(ames) 1914- 7-8R
Lewis, A(drian) S(teven) 1945- 116
Lewis, Adele
See Corwin, Adele Beatrice Lewis
Lewis, Albert 1885(?)-1978 Obituary 77-80
Lewis, Alfred Allan 1929- CANR-15
Earlier sketch in CA 73-76
Lewis, Alfred E. 1912-1968 Obituary 111
See also SATA 32
Lewis, Alfred Henry 1857-1914
Brief entry 120
See also DLB 25
Lewis, Alice C. 1936- SATA-46
Lewis, Alice Hudson 1895(?)-1971
Obituary 109
See also SATA 29
Lewis, Allan 1905- 15-16R
Lewis, Alun 1915-1944 Brief entry 104
See also DLB 20
See also TCLC 3
Lewis, (Joseph) Anthony 1927- 11-12R
See also SATA 27
Lewis, Anthony Carey 1915-1983
Obituary 110
Lewis, Archibald Ross 1914- 81-84
Lewis, Arthur H. 1906- CANR-1
Earlier sketch in CA 1R
Lewis, Arthur O(rcutt), Jr. 1920- 9-10R
Lewis, Arthur William 1905-1970 .... CAP-1
Earlier sketch in CA 9-10
Lewis, Barbara 1928-1984 Obituary 113
Lewis, Benjamin F. 1918- 45-48
Lewis, Bernard 1916- 118
Brief entry 113
Lewis, Beth Irwin 1934- 33-36R
Lewis, Bill
See Lewis, William
Lewis, Bill H. 1927- 3R
Lewis, C. Day
See Day Lewis, C(ecil)
Lewis, C(larence) I(rving) 1883-1964 .... 7-8R
Lewis, C(live) S(taples) 1898-1963 81-84
See also SATA 13
See also DLB 15
See also CLC 1, 3, 6, 14, 27
See also CLR 3
Lewis, Charles
See Dixon, Roger
Lewis, Charles Bertrand 1842-1924
Brief entry 114
See also DLB 11
Lewis, Claude A. 1934- 11-12R
Lewis, Claudia (Louise) 1907- CANR-6
Earlier sketch in CA 7-8R
See also SATA 5
Lewis, Clay(ton Wilson) 1936- 101
Lewis, D. B.
See Bixby, Jerome Lewis
Lewis, D(ominic) B(evan) Wyndham
1894-1969 Obituary 25-28R
Lewis, Dave
See Lewis, David V.
Lewis, David 1909-1981 104
Lewis, David 1922- 41-44R
Lewis, David 1942- CANR-12
Earlier sketch in CA 69-72
Lewis, David B(enjamin) 1965- 111
Lewis, David Kellogg 1941- CANR-15
Earlier sketch in CA 81-84
Lewis, David L(anier) 1927- 69-72
Lewis, David L(evering) 1936- CANR-2
Earlier sketch in CA 45-48
Lewis, David Marshall
See Cook, Michael Lewis
Lewis, David T(revor) 1920- 45-48
Lewis, David V. 1923- 7-8R
Lewis, Donald Earle 1925- 5-6R
Lewis, Dorothy Roe 1904-1985 Obituary 115
Lewis, E. M. 69-72
See also SATA 20
Lewis, Edith 1882(?)-1972 Obituary 111
Lewis, Edward W(illiams) 1899-1986
Obituary 118
Lewis, Edwin C(lark) 1933- 25-28R
Lewis, Eils Moorhouse 1919- 106
Lewis, Elizabeth Foreman 1892-1958 .... YABC-2
Lewis, Elliott (Bruce) 1917- CANR-22
Earlier sketch in CA 104
Lewis, Eugene 1940- CANR-4
Earlier sketch in CA 53-56
Lewis, (E.) Faye (Cashatt) 1896- 25-28R
Lewis, Felice (Elizabeth) Flanery 1920- 73-76
Lewis, Finlay 1938- 101
Lewis, Flora Brief entry 119
Lewis, Francine
See Wells, Helen
Lewis, Francis Ames
See Ames-Lewis, Francis
Lewis, Freeman 1908-1976 Obituary 69-72
Lewis, Fulton, Jr. 1903-1966 Obituary 89-92
Lewis, G(ranville) Douglass 1934- 106
Lewis, Gene D. 1931- 45-48
Lewis, Geoffrey (Lewis) 1920- 13-14R
Lewis, George 1941- 29-32R
Lewis, George 1943- 77-80
Lewis, George H(allam) 1943- 53-56
Lewis, George L. 1916- CANR-3
Earlier sketch in CA 45-48
Lewis, George Q. 1916- 21-22R
Lewis, Gordon R(ussell) 1926- CANR-25
Earlier sketches in CA 21-22R, CANR-10
Lewis, Grover Virgil 1934- 106
Lewis, H(ywel) D(avid) 1910- CANR-3
Earlier sketch in CA 9-10R
Lewis, H. Warren 1924- 29-32R
Lewis, Harold M. 1891(?)-1973 Obituary 45-48
Lewis, Harry 1917- 109
Lewis, Harry 1942- CANR-3
Earlier sketch in CA 49-52
Lewis, Helen (Lillian) Block 1913-1987 110
Obituary 121
Lewis, Henry Clay 1825-1850 .... DLB-3
Lewis, Henry T(rickey) 1928- 73-76
Lewis, Herbert S(amuel) 1934- 17-18R
Lewis, Hilda (Winifred) 1896-1974 93-96
Obituary 49-52
See also SATA 20
Lewis, Horacio D(elano) 1944- 57-60
Lewis, Howard R(obert) 1934- CANR-10
Earlier sketch in CA 25-28R
Lewis, Hunter 1947- 109
Lewis, I(oan) M(yrddin) 1930- CANR-21
Earlier sketches in CA 11-12R, CANR-5
Lewis, Ian
See Bensman, Joseph
Lewis, J. R.
See Lewis, (John) Roy(ston)
Lewis, Jack P(earl) 1919- 37-40R
Lewis, James 1935- 65-68
Lewis, James, Jr. 1930- CANR-12
Earlier sketch in CA 29-32R
Lewis, Jan (Ellen) 1949- 115
Lewis, Janet
See Winters, Janet Lewis
See also DLBY 87
See also CLC 41
Lewis, Jean 1924- CANR-11
Earlier sketch in CA 23-24R
Lewis, Jerry 1926- 121
Brief entry 113
Lewis, John 1889- CANR-5
Earlier sketch in CA 5-6R
Lewis, John (Noel Claude) 1912- CANR-19
Earlier sketch in CA 102
Lewis, John D(onald) 1905-1988 65-68
Obituary 124
Lewis, John E(arl) 1931- CANR-21
Earlier sketches in CA 57-60, CANR-6
Lewis, John P(rior) 1921- 9-10R
Lewis, John Parry 1927- 107
Lewis, John W(ilson) 1930- 11-12R
Lewis, Joseph 1889-1968 .... CAP-1
Earlier sketch in CA 13-14
Lewis, Judith Mary 1921- 97-100
Lewis, June E(thelyn) 1905- CAP-2
Earlier sketch in CA 29-32
Lewis, Lange
See Brandt, Jane Lewis
Lewis, Larry L(ynn) 1935- 115
Lewis, Lawrence E(dwin) 1928- 69-72
Lewis, Leon 1904- CAP-1
Earlier sketch in CA 15-16
Lewis, Leon Ray 1883- CAP-1
Earlier sketch in CA 9-10
Lewis, Lesley 1909- 102
Lewis, Linda 1927- 93-96
Lewis, Lionel Stanley 1933- CANR-5
Earlier sketch in CA 53-56
Lewis, Lucia Z.
See Anderson, Lucia (Lewis)
Lewis, Margie M. 1923- 101
Lewis, Marianna Olmstead 1923- 9-10R
Lewis, Marjorie 1929- 108
See also SATA 35, 40
Lewis, Martha E(llen) 1941- CANR-10
Earlier sketch in CA 25-28R
Lewis, Marvin 1923-1971 .... CAP-2
Earlier sketch in CA 21-22
Lewis, Mary (Christianna Milne) 1907- CANR-13
Earlier sketch in CA 77-80
Lewis, Mary (Christianna)
1907(?)-1988 .... CANR-13
Obituary 125
Earlier sketch in CA 77-80
Lewis, Mary F. W.
See Bond, Mary Fanning Wickham
Lewis, Matthew Gregory 1775-1818 .... DLB-39
Lewis, Maynah 1919- CANR-16
Earlier sketch in CA 25-28R
Lewis, Mervyn
See Frewer, Glyn (M.)
Lewis, Mervyn K(eith) 1941- 125
Lewis, Michael 1937- CANR-1
Earlier sketch in CA 45-48
Lewis, Michael Arthur 1890-1970 .... CANR-5
Obituary 29-32R
Earlier sketch in CA 7-8R
Lewis, Mildred D. 1912- 13-14R
Lewis, Mort(imer) R(eis) 1908- 105
Lewis, Naphtali 1911- 110
Lewis, Nigel (Stephen) 1948- 116
Lewis, Nolan D(on) C(arpenter) 1889- 7-8R
Lewis, Norman Brief entry 112
Lewis, Norman 1912- CANR-3
Earlier sketch in CA 11-12R
Lewis, Oren Ritter 1902-1983 Obituary 110
Lewis, Oscar 1893- 5-6R
Lewis, Oscar 1914-1970 .... CAP-1
Obituary 29-32R
Earlier sketch in CA 19-20
Lewis, Patricia Ann 1933- 112
Lewis, Paul
See Gerson, Noel Bertram
Lewis, Paul H. 1937- 73-76
Lewis, Peirce F(ee) 1927- 41-44R
Lewis, Peter 1922- 9-10R
Lewis, Peter 1938- CANR-21
Earlier sketch in CA 45-48
Lewis, Philip 1913- 3R
Lewis, R. Duffy 1908- CAP-1
Earlier sketch in CA 11-12
Lewis, R(ichard) W(arrington) B(aldwin)
1917- 102
Lewis, Ralph F(erguson) 1918-1979 .... 29-32R
Obituary 89-92
Lewis, Ralph L(oren) 1919- 117
Lewis, Richard 1700(?)-1734 .... DLB-24
Lewis, Richard 1935- CANR-5
Earlier sketch in CA 11-12R
See also SATA 3
Lewis, Richard S. 1916- CANR-9
Earlier sketch in CA 57-60
Lewis, Robert 1932- 97-100
Lewis, Robert T(urner) 1923- 85-88
Lewis, Roger
See Zarchy, Harry
Lewis, Ronello B. 1909- CAP-1
Earlier sketch in CA 17-18
Lewis, (Ernest Michael) Roy 1913- CANR-3
Earlier sketch in CA 7-8R
Lewis, (John) Roy(ston) 1933- 105
Lewis, Samella S(anders) 1924-
Brief entry 112
Lewis, Sasha Gregory 1947- CANR-15
Earlier sketch in CA 85-88
Lewis, Saunders 1893-1985 Obituary 117
Lewis, Selma S. 1921- 123
Lewis, Shari 1934- CANR-19
Earlier sketch in CA 89-92
See also SATA 30, 35
Lewis, (Harry) Sinclair 1885-1951
Brief entry 104
See also DLB 9
See also DLBD 1
See also TCLC 4, 13, 23
Lewis, Stephen 1947(?)-1981 Obituary 103
See also AITN 1
Lewis, Stephen Richmond, Jr. 1939- 41-44R
Lewis, Sylvan R.
See Aronson, Virginia
Lewis, T(heodore) G(yle) 1941- 111
Lewis, Ted
See Lewis, Edward W(illiams)
Lewis, Theophilus 1891-1974 125
See also BW
Lewis, Therese 1912(?)-1984 Obituary 113
Lewis, Thomas P(arker) 1936- 29-32R
See also SATA 27
Lewis, Thomas S(pottswood) W(ellford)
1942- 49-52
Lewis, Tom 1940- 105
Lewis, Tony 1938- 122
Lewis, Voltaire
See Ritchie, Edwin
Lewis, W(illiam) Arthur 1915- CANR-13
Brief entry 111
Earlier sketch in CA 19-20R
Lewis, W(alter) David 1931- CANR-9
Earlier sketch in CA 15-16R
Lewis, Walker 1904- CAP-2
Earlier sketch in CA 19-20
Lewis, Warren 1940- 115
Lewis, William 1946- 120
Lewis, William Hubert 1928- 13-14R
Lewis, Willie Newbury 1891-1985 93-96
Obituary 116
Lewis, Wilmarth Sheldon 1895-1979 .... CANR-15
Obituary 89-92
Earlier sketch in CA 65-68
Lewis, (Percy) Wyndham 1884(?)-1957
Brief entry 104
See also DLB 15
See also TCLC 2, 9
Lewisohn, Ludwig 1883-1955 Brief entry 107
See also DLB 4, 9, 28
See also TCLC 19
Lewiston, Robert R(ueben) 1909- CAP-2
Earlier sketch in CA 23-24
Lewis-Williams, J(ames) David 1934- 117
Lewiton, Mina 1904-1970 .... CAP-2
Obituary 29-32R
Earlier sketch in CA 23-24
See also SATA 2
Lewitt, Shariann (N.) 1954- 119
Lewittes, Mordecai Henry
See Lewittes, Morton H(enry)
Lewittes, Morton H(enry) 1911- 25-28R
Lewontin, Richard Charles 1929- 104
Lewsen, Phyllis 1916- 109
Lewton-Brain, James 1923- 97-100
Lewty, Marjorie 1906- CAP-1
Earlier sketch in CA 9-10
Lewy, Guenter 1923- CANR-21
Earlier sketches in CA 11-12R, CANR-3
Lexau, Joan M. CANR-11
Earlier sketch in CA 19-20R
See also SATA 1, 36
Ley, Alice Chetwynd 1913- CANR-21
Earlier sketches in CA 15-16R, CANR-6
Ley, Arthur Gordon 1911-1968 Obituary 102
Ley, Charles David 1913- 9-10R
Ley, Ralph 1929- 41-44R
Ley, Robert Arthur
See Ley, Arthur Gordon
Ley, Sandra 1944- 57-60
Ley, Willy 1906-1969 .... 9-10R
Obituary 25-28R
See also SATA 2
Leyburn, Ellen Douglass 1907-1966 .... CAP-2
Earlier sketch in CA 25-28
Leyburn, James G(raham) 1902- 5-6R
Leyda, Jay 1910-1988 108
Obituary 124
Leydet, Francois G(uillaume) 1927- 9-10R
Leydon, Rita (Floden) 1949- SATA-21
Leyhart, Edward
See Edwards, Elwyn Hartley
Leyland, Eric (Arthur) 1911- SATA-37
Leyland, Mal(colm Rex) 1944- 108
Leyland, Winston 1940- 107
Leynard, Martin
See Berger, Ivan (Bennett)
Leyner, Mark 1956- 110
Leypoldt, Martha M. 1918-1975 .... CAP-2
Earlier sketch in CA 23-24
Leys, Mary Dorothy Rose 1890- 7-8R
Leys, Simon
See Ryckmans, Pierre
Leys, Wayne A(lbert) R(isser) 1905-1973 .... CAP-1
Earlier sketch in CA 17-18
Leyser, Karl Joseph 1920- 112

Leyton, Elliott (Hastings) 1939- ... 120
Leyton, Sophie
  See Walsh, Sheila
Leyva, Ricardo
  See Valdes, Nelson P.
Lezama Lima, Jose 1910-1976 ... 77-80
  See also CLC 4, 10
Lezra, Grizzella Paull 1934- ... 61-64
Lhamon, W(illiam) T(aylor), Jr. 1945- ... 65-68
L'Heureux, Bill
  See L'Heureux, W(illard) J(oseph)
L'Heureux, John (Clarke) 1934- ... CANR-23
  Earlier sketch in CA 15-16R
L'Heureux, W(illard) J(oseph) 1918- ... 7-8R
L'Hommedieu, Dorothy Keasley
  1885-1961 Obituary ... 109
  See also SATA 29
Li, C(hing) C(hun) 1912- ... 19-20R
Li, Chiang-Kwang 1915- ... 73-76
Li, Choh-Ming 1912- ... 2R
Li, David H(siang-fu) 1928- ... 15-16R
Li, Fang Kuei 1902- ... 112
Li, Hui-Lin 1911- ... CANR-15
  Earlier sketch in CA 85-88
Li, Shu Hua 1890(?)-1979 Obituary ... 89-92
Li, Tien-yi 1915- ... 37-40R
Li, Tze-chung 1927- ... CANR-14
  Earlier sketch in CA 41-44R
Li, Yao-wen 1924- ... 106
Liang, Chin-tung 1893- ... 81-84
Liang, Yen 1908- ... 5-6R
Liao, David C. E. 1925- ... 41-44R
Lias, Edward J(ohn) 1934- ... 120
Lias, Godfrey ... 7-8R
Libbey, Elizabeth 1947- ... 110
Libbey, James K(eith) 1942- ... 81-84
Libby, Anthony 1942- ... 118
Libby, Bill
  See Libby, William M.
Libby, Leona Marshall 1919-1986 ... 101
  Obituary ... 121
Libby, Violet K(elway) 1892(?)-1981
  Obituary ... 105
Libby, Willard F(rank) 1908-1980
  Obituary ... 113
Libby, William C(harles) ... 104
Libby, William M. 1927-1984 ... CANR-10
  Obituary ... 113
  Earlier sketch in CA 25-28R
  See also SATA 5, 39
Liberace
  See Liberace, Wladziu Valentino
Liberace, Wladziu Valentino
  1919-1987 ... CANR-22
  Obituary ... 121
  Earlier sketch in CA 89-92
Liberman, Alexander 1912- Brief entry ... 113
Liberman, Anatoly 1937- ... 116
Liberman, Evsei Grigorevich 1897-1983
  Obituary ... 109
Liberman, Judith 1929- ... 73-76
Liberman, M(yron) M(andell) 1921- ... 57-60
Liberman, Robert Paul 1937- ... CANR-22
  Earlier sketches in CA 61-64, CANR-7
Liberman, Yevsei Grigorievich
  See Liberman, Evsei Grigorevich
Libersat, Henry 1934- ... 53-56
Liberty, Gene 1924- ... CANR-8
  Earlier sketch in CA 7-8R
  See also SATA 3
Libin, Laurence (Elliot) 1944- ... 119
Liblit, Jerome ... 15-16R
Libman, Carol 1928- ... 113
Libo, Kenneth (Harold) 1937- Brief entry ... 109
Libo, Lester M(artin) 1923- ... 77-80
Librach, Jan 1904(?)-1973 Obituary ... 41-44R
LiBretto, Ellen V. 1947- ... 110
Lichello, Robert 1926- ... 15-16R
Lichine, Alexis 1913- ... 9-10R
Licht, Fred (Stephen) 1928- ... 101
Licht, Sidney Herman 1907-1979 Obituary ... 108
Lichtblau, Myron Ivor 1925- ... 17-18R
Lichten, Joseph L. 1906(?)-1987 Obituary ... 125
Lichtenberg, Elisabeth Jacoba 1913- ... 13-14R
Lichtenberg, Jacqueline 1942- ... 73-76
Lichtenberg, Philip 1926- ... CANR-13
  Earlier sketch in CA 37-40R
Lichtenstadter, Ilse 1907- ... CANR-13
  Earlier sketch in CA 33-36R
Lichtenstein, Aharon 1933- ... 19-20R
Lichtenstein, Grace 1941- ... CANR-22
  Earlier sketches in CA 49-52, CANR-2
Lichtheim, George 1912-1973 Obituary ... 41-44R
Lichtman, Allan J. 1947- ... 124
Lichtman, Celia S(chmukler) 1932- ... 41-44R
Lichtman, Wendy 1946- ... 114
Lichty, George M(aurice) 1905-1983 ... 104
  Obituary ... 110
Lichty, Lawrence W(ilson) 1937- ... 53-56
Lichty, Ron 1950- ... CANR-18
  Earlier sketch in CA 101
Licklider, Roy E(ilers) 1941- ... 33-36R
Lickona, Thomas Edward 1943- ... 113
Lida, Denah (Levy) 1923- ... 23-24R
Liddell, Brendan E(dwin) A(lexander)
  1927- ... 29-32R
Liddell, C. H.
  See Kuttner, Henry
Liddell, (John) Robert 1908- ... 13-14R
Liddell Hart, Basil Henry 1895-1970 ... 103
  Obituary ... 89-92
Lidderdale, Halliday Adair 1917- ... 21-22R
Liddicoat, Richard T., Jr. 1918- ... 45-48
Liddle, Peter Hammond 1934- ... CANR-18
  Earlier sketch in CA 102
Liddle, William 1925- ... 77-80
Liddy, G(eorge) Gordon (Battle) 1930- ... 114
Liddy, James (Daniel Reeves) 1934- ... CANR-20
  Earlier sketches in CA 13-14R, CANR-5
  See also AITN 2
Lidman, David 1905- ... 69-72
Lidoff, Joan (Ilene) 1944- ... 115
Lidtke, Vernon L. 1930- ... 23-24R
Lidz, Theodore 1910- ... 29-32R
Lie, Jonas (Lauritz Idemil) 1833-1908(?)
  Brief entry ... 115
  See also TCLC 5
Lie, Trygve (Halvdan) 1896-1968 Obituary ... 113
Lieb, Fred(erick George) 1888-1980 ... 69-72
  Obituary ... 97-100
Lieb, Irwin Chester 1925- Brief entry ... 105
Lieb, Michael 1940- ... 65-68
Lieb, Robert C. 1944- ... 37-40R
Lieb, Sandra ... 112
Liebenow, J. Gus 1925- ... 45-48
Lieber, Arnold L(ou) 1937- Brief entry ... 113
Lieber, Joel 1937-1971 ... 73-76
  Obituary ... 29-32R
  See also CLC 6
Lieber, Robert J(ames) 1941- ... CANR-12
  Earlier sketch in CA 29-32R
Lieber, Stanley Martin
  See Lee, Stan
Lieber, Todd M(ichael) 1944- ... 45-48
Lieberg, Owen S. 1896-1973 ... CAP-2
  Earlier sketch in CA 25-28
Lieberman, Arnold (Leo) 1903- ... CAP-1
  Earlier sketch in CA 19-20
Lieberman, Donald 1927- ... 111
Lieberman, E(dwin) James 1934- ... CANR-22
  Earlier sketch in CA 45-48
Lieberman, Elias 1883- ... 7-8R
Lieberman, Fredric 1940- ... CANR-7
  Earlier sketch in CA 53-56
Lieberman, Gerald F. 1923-1986 ... 85-88
  Obituary ... 119
Lieberman, Herbert (Henry) 1933- ... CANR-19
  Earlier sketches in CA 11-12R, CANR-5
Lieberman, J. Ben 1914-1984 Obituary ... 113
Lieberman, Jethro K(oller) 1943- ... CANR-10
  Earlier sketch in CA 21-22R
Lieberman, Joseph I. 1942- ... 19-20R
Lieberman, Laurence 1935- ... CANR-8
  Earlier sketch in CA 17-18R
  See also CLC 4, 36
Lieberman, Mark 1942- ... 29-32R
Lieberman, Mendel Halliday 1913- ... 106
Lieberman, Morton A(lexander) 1931- ... 41-44R
Lieberman, Myron 1919- ... CANR-8
  Earlier sketch in CA 5-6R
Lieberman, Philip 1934- ... 93-96
Lieberman, Robert (Howard) 1941- ... CANR-10
  Earlier sketch in CA 57-60
  See also AITN 1
Lieberman, Rosalie ... 11-12R
Lieberman, Samuel 1911- ... 17-18R
Lieberman, Saul 1898-1983 Obituary ... 109
Liebers, Arthur 1913- ... CANR-3
  Earlier sketch in CA 5-6R
  See also SATA 12
Liebers, Ruth 1910- ... CAP-1
  Earlier sketch in CA 9-10
Lieberson, Goddard 1911- ... CAP-2
  Earlier sketch in CA 25-28
Lieberson, Stanley 1933- ... CANR-17
  Earlier sketches in CA 4R, CANR-1
Lieberstein, Stanley H. 1934- ... 105
Liebert, Burt 1925- ... 33-36R
Liebert, Doris 1934- ... 105
Liebert, Robert M. 1942- ... 41-44R
Liebert, Robert S. 1930-1988 Obituary ... 125
Liebertahl, Milton M(orton) 1911- ... 117
Liebeschuetz, Hans 1893(?)-1978(?)
  Obituary ... 85-88
Liebhafsky, Herbert Hugo 1919- ... 5-6R
Liebhafsky, Herman A(lfred) 1905- ... 53-56
Lieblich, Amia 1939- ... 93-96
Lieblich, Irene 1923- ... SATA-22
Liebling, A(bbott) J(oseph) 1904-1963 ... 104
  Obituary ... 89-92
  See also DLB 4
Liebman, Arthur 1926- ... CANR-6
  Earlier sketch in CA 57-60
Liebman, Charles S(eymour) 1934- ... 61-64
Liebman, Marcel 1930(?)-1986 Obituary ... 118
Liebman, Ron(ald S.) 1943- ... 120
Liebman, Seymour B(ertrand)
  1907-1986 ... CANR-7
  Obituary ... 120
  Earlier sketch in CA 17-18R
Liebow, Averill A(braham) 1911-1978
  Obituary ... 111
Liederbach, Clarence Andrew 1910- ... 93-96
Liederman, Judith 1927- ... 85-88
Liedholm, Carl (Edward) 1940- ... 41-44R
Liedloff, Jean ... 81-84
Liedtke, Kurt E(rnst) H(einrich) 1919- ... 19-20R
Lief, N. H.
  See Bayes, Ronald H(omer)
Lief, Nina R. 1907- ... 118
Lief, Philip 1947- ... 107
Liehm, Antonin J. 1924- ... 102
Lieksman, Anders
  See Haavikko, Paavo Juhani
Liem, Nguyen Dang 1936- ... 57-60
Lien, Arnold J. 1920-1979 ... 23-24R
  Obituary ... 122
Lienhard, John H(enry IV) 1930- ... CANR-4
  Earlier sketch in CA 53-56
Lientz, Bennet Price 1942- ... CANR-8
  Earlier sketch in CA 61-64
Liepolt, Werner 1944- ... 25-28R
Liers, Emil E(rnest) 1890-1975 ... 107
  See also SATA 37
Liesner, Hans Hubertus (Karl Kurt Otto)
  1929- ... 104
Lietaer, Bernard A(rthur) 1942- ... 33-36R
Lietaert Peerbolte, Maarten 1905- ... 102
Lietz, Gerald S. 1918- ... SATA-11
Lieuwen, Edwin 1923- ... CANR-5
  Earlier sketch in CA 2R
Liew, Kit Siong 1932- ... 77-80
Lifar, Serge 1905-1986 Obituary ... 121
Lifchitz, Boris 1895-1984 Obituary ... 114
Li Fei-kan 1904- ... 105
  See also CLC 18
Liffring, Joan Louise 1929- ... 19-20R
Lifshin, Lyn (Diane) 1944- ... CANR-25
  Earlier sketches in CA 33-36R, CANR-8
Lifson, David S. 1908- ... 33-36R
Lifton, Betty Jean ... CANR-12
  Earlier sketch in CA 5-6R
  See also SATA 6
Lifton, Robert Jay 1926- ... 17-18R
Lifton, Walter M. 1918- ... CANR-16
  Earlier sketch in CA 33-36R
Liggero, John 1921- ... 25-28R
Liggett, Clayton E(ugene) 1930- ... 29-32R
Liggett, Hunter
  See Paine, Lauran (Bosworth)
Liggett, John 1923- ... 57-60
Liggett, Thomas 1918- ... 5-6R
Light, Albert 1927- ... 93-96
Light, Ivan 1941- ... 73-76
Light, James F. 1921- ... CANR-1
  Earlier sketch in CA 3R
Light, Martin 1927- ... 53-56
Light, Patricia Kahn 1939- ... 61-64
Lightbody, Charles Wayland 1904- ... 5-6R
Lightbody, Donna Mae 1920-1976
  Obituary ... 110
Lightbown, Ronald William 1932- ... 104
Lightfoot, Alfred 1936- ... CANR-4
  Earlier sketch in CA 53-56
Lightfoot, Claude M. 1910- ... 123
  See also BW
Lightfoot, David (William) 1945- ... 116
Lightfoot, Gordon 1938- Brief entry ... 109
  See also CLC 26
Lightfoot, Neil R(oland) 1929- ... 81-84
Lightfoot, Paul 1946- ... 110
Lightman, Bernard 1950- ... 116
Lightner, A. M.
  See Hopf, Alice (Martha) L(ightner)
Lightner, Alice
  See Hopf, Alice (Martha) L(ightner)
Lightner, Robert P(aul) 1931- ... CANR-16
  Earlier sketches in CA 49-52, CANR-1
Lightner, Theodore 1893(?)-1981
  Obituary ... 113
Lightwood, Martha B. 1923- ... 33-36R
Lignell, Lois 1911- ... SATA-37
Ligomenides, Panos A. 1928- ... 29-32R
Ligon, Ernest M(ayfield) 1897- ... CAP-1
  Earlier sketch in CA 9-10
Ligotti, Thomas 1953- ... 123
  See also CLC 44
Liguori, Frank E. 1917- ... 21-22R
Lihani, John 1927- ... CANR-14
  Earlier sketch in CA 37-40R
Lihn, Enrique 1929- ... 104
Lijphart, Arend 1936- ... CANR-25
  Earlier sketches in CA 21-22R, CANR-10
Likeness, George C(lark) 1927- ... 17-18R
Likert, Rensis 1903- ... 93-96
Likhovski, Eliahou 1927- ... 45-48
Liles, Bruce (Lynn) 1934- ... 53-56
Liley, Helen Margaret Irwin 1928- ... 25-28R
Liliencron, (Friedrich Adolf Axel) Detlev von
  1844-1909 Brief entry ... 117
  See also TCLC 18
Lilienfeld, Abraham M(orris) 1920-1984
  Obituary ... 113
Lilienfeld, Robert Henry 1927- ... CANR-1
  Earlier sketch in CA 3R
Lilienthal, Alfred M(orton) 1913- ... 37-40R
Lilienthal, David E(li) 1899-1981 ... CANR-3
  Obituary ... 102
  Earlier sketch in CA 7-8R
Li Ling-Ai ... 77-80
Lilje, Hanns 1899-1977 Obituary ... 69-72
Lillard, Charles (Marion) 1944- ... CANR-8
  Earlier sketch in CA 61-64
Lillard, Paula Polk 1931- ... 73-76
Lillard, Richard G(ordon) 1909- ... 21-22R
Lilley, Dorothy B(race) 1914- ... 113
Lilley, Peter 1943- ... 77-80
Lillibridge, G(eorge) D(onald) 1921- ... 13-14R
Lillich, Meredith Parsons 1932-
  Brief entry ... 105
Lillich, Richard B(onnot) 1933- ... 119
Lillie, Helen 1915- ... 65-68
Lillie, John Adam 1884-1983 Obituary ... 110
Lillie, Ralph D(ougall) 1896-1979
  Obituary ... 89-92
Lillie, William 1899- ... 5-6R
Lillington, Kenneth (James) 1916- ... CANR-3
  Earlier sketch in CA 7-8R
  See also SATA 39
Lilly, Charles ... SATA-33
Lilly, Doris 1926- ... CANR-11
  Earlier sketch in CA 29-32R
Lilly, Eli 1885-1977 Obituary ... 69-72
Lilly, John C(unningham) 1915- ... CANR-1
  Earlier sketch in CA 4R
Lilly, Ray
  See Curtis, Richard (Alan)
Lim, Genny 1946- ... 116
Lim, John 1932- ... 116
  See also SATA 43
Lim, Paul Stephen 1944- ... CANR-25
  Earlier sketch in CA 108
Lima, Carolyn W(omack) 1938- ... 118
Lima, Frank 1939- ... 73-76
Lima, Robert 1935- ... 9-10R
Lima Barreto, Afonso Henrique de
  1881-1922 Brief entry ... 117
  See also TCLC 23
Liman, Claude Gilbert 1943- ... 57-60
Liman, Ellen (Fogelson) 1936- ... CANR-13
  Earlier sketch in CA 61-64
  See also SATA 22
Limb, Sue 1946- ... 115
Limbacher, James L. 1926- ... CANR-17
  Earlier sketches in CA 5-6R, CANR-2
Limburg, James 1935- ... 112
Limburg, Peter R(ichard) 1929- ... 33-36R
  See also SATA 13
Limentani, Uberto 1913- ... 19-20R
Limerick, Jeffrey W. 1948- ... 102
Limmer, Ruth 1927- ... CANR-1
  Earlier sketch in CA 45-48
Limpert, John A. 1934- ... 77-80
Lin, Adet J(usu) 1923- ... 5-6R
Lin, Florence (Shen) ... CANR-12
  Earlier sketch in CA 61-64
Lin, Frank
  See Atherton, Gertrude (Franklin Horn)
Lin, Julia C(hang) 1928- ... 73-76
Lin, Nan 1938- ... 73-76
Lin, Robert K(wan-Hwan) 1937- ... CANR-10
  Earlier sketch in CA 65-68
Lin, San-su C(hen) 1916- ... 19-20R
Lin, Tai-yi 1926- ... 11-12R
Lin, Yu-sheng 1934- ... 89-92
Lin, Yutang 1895-1976 ... CANR-2
  Obituary ... 65-68
  Earlier sketch in CA 45-48
Linamen, Harold Frederick 1921- ... 17-18R
Linck, Orville F. 1906- ... 7-8R
Lincke, Jack 1909- ... CAP-2
  Earlier sketch in CA 29-32
Lincoff, Gary Henry 1942- ... 112
Lincoln, Alan Jay 1945- ... 123
Lincoln, Bruce 1948- ... CANR-22
  Earlier sketch in CA 105
Lincoln, C(harles) Eric 1924- ... CANR-1
  Earlier sketch in CA 2R
  See also BW
  See also SATA 5
Lincoln, Edith Maas 1891-1977 Obituary ... 73-76
Lincoln, G(eorge) Gould 1880-1974
  Obituary ... 113
  See also AITN 1
Lincoln, George Arthur 1907-1975 ... 3R
  Obituary ... 57-60
Lincoln, Harry B. 1922- ... 25-28R
Lincoln, Henry ... 110
Lincoln, James Finney 1883-1965 ... 2R
Lincoln, James H. 1916- ... 25-28R
Lincoln, Kenneth Robert 1943- ... 114
Lincoln, Murray D. 1892-1966 ... CAP-2
  Earlier sketch in CA 19-20
Lincoln, Roger J(ohn) 1942- ... 117
Lincoln, Victoria 1904-1981 ... CAP-1
  Obituary ... 104
  Earlier sketch in CA 17-18
Lincoln, W(illiam) Bruce 1938- ... 85-88
Lind, Alan R(obert) 1940- ... CANR-12
  Earlier sketch in CA 61-64
Lind, Andrew W(illiam) 1901- ... CANR-21
  Earlier sketch in CA 45-48
Lind, Jakov
  See Landwirth, Heinz
  See also CAAS 4
  See also CLC 1, 2, 4, 27
Lind, L(evi) R(obert) 1906- ... CANR-4
  Earlier sketch in CA 5-6R
Lind, Millard C. 1918- ... 115
Lind, Sidney Edmund 1914- ... 37-40R
Lind, William S(turgiss) 1947- ... 123
Lindaman, Edward B. 1920-1982 ... 77-80
  Obituary ... 107
Lindars, Barnabas 1923- ... CANR-11
  Earlier sketch in CA 25-28R
Lindauer, John Howard 1937- ... 23-24R
Lindauer, Lois Lyons 1933- ... 49-52
Lindauer, Martin 1918- ... 7-8R
Linday, Ryllis Elizabeth Paine 1919- ... 13-14R
Lindbeck, (K.) Assar (E.) 1930- ... 37-40R
Lindberg, Carter 1937- ... 112
Lindberg, David C. 1935- ... CANR-11
  Earlier sketch in CA 69-72
Lindberg, Gary H(ans) 1941- ... 65-68
Lindberg, Leon N. 1932- ... 33-36R
Lindberg, Lucile 1913- ... 37-40R
Lindberg, Paul M(artin) 1905- ... 5-6R
Lindberg, Richard 1953- ... 110
Lindberg, Stanley W(illiam) 1939- ... 112
Lindbergh, Anne
  See Sapieyevski, Anne Lindbergh
Lindbergh, Anne (Spencer) Morrow
  1906- ... CANR-16
  Earlier sketch in CA 17-18R
  See also SATA 33
Lindbergh, Charles A(ugustus, Jr.)
  1902-1974 ... CANR-16
  Obituary ... 53-56
  Earlier sketch in CA 93-96
  See also SATA 33
Lindberg-Seyersted, Brita 1923- ... 111
Lindblom, Charles E(dward) 1917- ... CANR-1
  Earlier sketch in CA 3R
Lindblom, (Christian) Johannes
  1882-1974 Obituary ... 53-56

Lindblom, Steven (Winther) 1946- CANR-23
Earlier sketch in CA 106
See also SATA 39, 42
Linde, Gunnel 1924- CANR-11
Earlier sketch in CA 21-22R
See also SATA 5
Linde, Shirley Motter 1929- CANR-18
Earlier sketches in CA 45-48, CANR-1
Lindeburg, Franklin Alfred 1918- 5-6R
Lindeman, Jack 1924- 23-24R
Lindemann, Albert S(hirk) 1938- 49-52
Lindemann, Constance 1923- 61-64
Lindemann, Herbert Fred 1909- 29-32R
Linden, Catherine 1939- 110
Linden, George William 1938- 65-68
Linden, Kathryn (Wolaver) 1925- 37-40R
Linden, Sara
See Bartlett, Marie (Swan)
Lindenau, Judith Wood 1941- 77-80
Lindenberger, Herbert (Samuel) 1929- .. CANR-3
Earlier sketch in CA 7-8R
Lindenfeld, David Frank 1944- 106
Lindenfeld, Frank 1934- 33-36R
Lindenmeyer, Otto J. 1936- 77-80
Linder, Bertram L. 1931- CANR-2
Earlier sketch in CA 49-52
Linder, Bill R. 1937- 112
Linder, Darwyn E(llsworth) 1939- 57-60
Linder, Erich 1925(?)-1983 Obituary 109
Linder, Ivan H. 1894- CAP-1
Earlier sketch in CA 9-10
Linder, Leslie ?-1973 Obituary 41-44R
Linder, Mark 1944- 120
Linder, Norma West 1928- 97-100
Linder, Robert D(ean) 1933- 41-44R
Linder, Staffan B(urenstam) 1931-
Brief entry 105
Linder, Steven 1953- 112
Linderman, Earl W. 1931- 33-36R
Linderman, Gerald F(loyd) 1934- 85-88
Linderman, Winifred B. CAP-2
Earlier sketch in CA 25-28
Lindesmith, Alfred Ray 1905- CAP-1
Earlier sketch in CA 9-10
Lindey, Christine 1947- 126
Lindfors, Judith Wells 1937- 117
Lindgren, Alvin J. 1917- CANR-8
Earlier sketch in CA 17-18R
Lindgren, Astrid 1907- 13-14R
See also SATA 2, 38
See also CLR 1
Lindgren, Barbro 1937- SATA-46
Lindgren, Ernest H. 1910-1973 ..... CAP-1
Earlier sketch in CA 13-14
Lindgren, Ethel John
See Lindgren-Utsi, E(thel) J(ohn)
Lindgren, Henry Clay 1914- CANR-1
Earlier sketch in CA 2R
Lindgren-Utsi, E(thel) J(ohn) 1905-1988
Obituary 125
Lindheim, Irma Levy 1886-1978 ..... 5-6R
Obituary 77-80
Lindholm, Richard W(adsworth) 1914- .. CANR-5
Earlier sketch in CA 4R
Lindley, Betty G(rimes) 1900(?)-1976
Obituary 65-68
Lindley, Denver 1904-1982 Obituary 106
Lindley, Erica
See Quigley, Aileen
Lindley, Ernest K(idder) 1899-1979
Obituary 89-92
Lindley, Hilda 1919(?)-1980 Obituary 102
Lindley, Kenneth (Arthur) 1928- CANR-10
Earlier sketch in CA 7-8R
Lindman, Maj (Jan) 1886-1972 ..... SATA-43
Lindner, D. Berry
See Du Breuil, (Elizabeth) L(or)inda
Lindner, Edgar T(heodore) 1911- 57-60
Lindop, Audrey (Beatrice Noel) Erskine
See Erskine-Lindop, Audrey (Beatrice Noel)
Lindop, Edmund 1925- CANR-17
Earlier sketches in CA 5-6R, CANR-2
See also SATA 5
Lindop, Grevel 1948- CANR-13
Earlier sketch in CA 61-64
Lindow, John Frederick 1946- 113
Lindow, Wesley 1910- 45-48
Lindquist, Donald 1930- 65-68
Lindquist, E(veret) F(ranklin) 1901-1978
Obituary 77-80
Lindquist, Emory Kempton 1908- 49-52
Lindquist, Jennie Dorothea 1899-1977 73-76
Obituary 69-72
See also SATA 13
Lindquist, John H(enry) 1931- 41-44R
Lindquist, Ray (Irving) 1941- 45-48
Lindquist, Willis 1908- 73-76
See also SATA 20
Lindsay, Catherine Brown 1928- 23-24R
Lindsay, Cressida 1934- 23-24R
Lindsay, David 1878-1945 Brief entry 113
See also TCLC 15
Lindsay, Dorothy 1902(?)-1983 Obituary ... 110
Lindsay, Frank Whiteman 1909- 104
Lindsay, Harold Arthur 1900- 7-8R
Lindsay, Howard 1889-1968 Obituary 25-28R
Lindsay, Ian G(ordon) 1906-1966 ..... CAP-1
Earlier sketch in CA 9-10
Lindsay, Inabel (Frances) B(urns)
1900-1983 Obituary 110
Lindsay, J(ohn) Robert 1925- 13-14R
Lindsay, Jack 1900- CANR-11
Earlier sketch in CA 9-10R
See also DLBY 84
Lindsay, James Martin 1924- 29-32R
Lindsay, Jean 1926- CANR-11
Earlier sketch in CA 25-28R
Lindsay, Jeanne Warren 1929- CANR-22
Earlier sketch in CA 106
Lindsay, John Vliet 1921- 101
Lindsay, Kenneth C(lement) 1919- 112
Lindsay, Martin Alexander 1905-1981
Obituary 103
Lindsay, Mary
See Nonhebel, Clare
Lindsay, (John) Maurice 1918- CANR-22
Earlier sketches in CA 9-10R, CANR-6
Lindsay, Merrill K(irk) 1915-1985 73-76
Obituary 115
Lindsay, Michael Francis Morris 1909- .. CANR-1
Earlier sketch in CA 45-48
Lindsay, Norman Alfred William
1879-1969 102
See also CLR 8
Lindsay, Perry
See Dern, Erolie Pearl Gaddis
Lindsay, R(obert) Bruce 1900- CANR-8
Earlier sketch in CA 15-16R
Lindsay, Rae 109
Lindsay, Robert 1924- 77-80
Lindsay, Thomas Fanshawe 1910- 23-24R
Lindsay, (Nicholas) Vachel 1879-1931
Brief entry 114
See also SATA 40
See also DLB 54
See also CDALB 1865-1917
See also TCLC 17
Lindsay, Zaidee 1923- 29-32R
Lindsell, Harold 1913- CANR-5
Earlier sketch in CA 13-14R
Lindsey, Alfred J. 1931- 41-44R
Lindsey, Almont 1906- 2R
Lindsey, David 1914- 11-12R
Lindsey, George R(oy) 1920- 65-68
Lindsey, Hal CANR-22
Earlier sketch in CA 104
Lindsey, Jim 1957- 65-68
Lindsey, (Helen) Johanna 1952- CANR-18
Earlier sketch in CA 73-76
Lindsey, Karen 1944- 73-76
Lindsey, Robert (Hughes) 1935- CANR-22
Earlier sketch in CA 97-100
Lindskoog, Kathryn (Ann) 1934- CANR-25
Earlier sketches in CA 65-68, CANR-10
Lindsley, Mary F(rances) CANR-9
Earlier sketch in CA 61-64
Lindstrom, Carl E(inar) 1896-1969 ..... 3R
Obituary 103
Lindstrom, Naomi (Eva) 1950- 112
Lindstrom, Thais (Stakhy) 1917- 23-24R
Lindt, Gillian 1932- 107
Line, Les 1935- 73-76
See also SATA 27
Line, Maurice Bernard 1928- 107
Lineaweaver, Thomas H(astings) III
1926- 73-76
Lineback, Richard H(arold) 1936- 29-32R
Linebarger, J(ames) M(orris) 1934- CANR-2
Earlier sketch in CA 49-52
Linebarger, Paul M(yron) A(nthony)
1913-1966 ..... CANR-6
Earlier sketch in CA 5-6R
Lineberry, John H(arvey) 1926- 4R
Lineberry, Robert L(eon) 1942- CANR-18
Earlier sketch in CA 73-76
Linecar, Howard (Walter Arthur) 1912- 110
Linedecker, Clifford L. 1931- 73-76
Linen, James A., III 1912-1988 Obituary ... 124
Linenthal, Edward Tabor 1947- 112
Linet, Beverly 1929- CANR-22
Earlier sketch in CA 89-92
Linett, Deena 1938- 113
Linfield, Esther 112
See also SATA 40
Ling, Arthur (William) 1901- 7-8R
Ling, Cyril Curtis 1936- 17-18R
Ling, Dwight L(eroy) 1923- CANR-11
Earlier sketch in CA 21-22R
Ling, H(sien) C(hang) 1910- 57-60
Ling, Hung-hsun 1894(?)-1981 Obituary ... 105
Ling, Jack (Chieh Sheng) 1930- 25-28R
Ling, Mona 9-10R
Ling, Roger (John) 1942- CANR-19
Earlier sketch in CA 103
Ling, Trevor 1920- CANR-11
Earlier sketch in CA 21-22R
Lingard, Joan 1932- CANR-18
Earlier sketch in CA 41-44R
See also SATA 8
See also SAAS 5
Lingeman, Richard R(oberts) 1931- CANR-11
Earlier sketch in CA 17-18R
Lingenfelter, Richard Emery 1934- CANR-5
Earlier sketch in CA 15-16R
Lingenfelter, Sherwood Galen 1941- 53-56
Lingis, Alphonso Frank 1933- CANR-15
Earlier sketch in CA 37-40R
Lings, Martin 1909- 57-60
Linington, (Barbara) Elizabeth
1921-1988 ..... CANR-20
Obituary 125
Earlier sketch in CA 2R
Linington, Elizabeth 1921- CANR-20
Earlier sketches in CA 2R, CANR-1
Link, Arthur S(tanley) 1920- CANR-3
Earlier sketch in CA 1R
See also DLB 17
Link, Edwin A(lbert) 1904-1981 Obituary ... 108
Link, Eugene P(erry) 1907- 37-40R
Link, Frederick M(artin) 1930- CANR-4
Earlier sketch in CA 53-56
Link, (S.) Gordden 1907-1986 120
Link, John R(einhardt) 1907- 19-20R
Link, Mark J(oseph) 1924- CANR-20
Earlier sketches in CA 15-16R, CANR-5
Link, Martin 1934- 106
See also SATA 28
Link, (Eugene) Perry (Jr.) 1944- 105
Link, Robert G(rant) 1918-1984 Obituary ... 113
Link, Ruth 1923- 29-32R
Link, Theodore Carl 1905(?)-1974
Obituary 104
Link, William 1933- CANR-13
Earlier sketch in CA 73-76
Linke, Maria (Zeitner) 1908- 65-68
Linke-Poot
See Doeblin, Alfred
Linker, Robert White 1905- 104
Linklater, Eric (Robert Russell)
1899-1974 ..... CAP-2
Obituary 53-56
Earlier sketch in CA 13-14
Linkletter, Art(hur Gordan) 1912- CANR-4
Earlier sketch in CA 9-10R
Linkletter, John A(ustin) 1923-1985 69-72
Obituary 115
Links, J(oseph) G(luckenstein) 1904- 81-84
Linkugel, Wil(mer) A(lbert) 1929- CANR-13
Earlier sketch in CA 17-18R
Linley, John (William) 1916- 41-44R
Lin Mao
See Shen Congwen
Linn, Allen 1955- 126
Linn, Bill
See Linn, William J(oseph)
Linn, Charles F. 1930- 85-88
Linn, Edward Allen 1922- 97-100
Linn, John Blair 1777-1804 ..... DLB-37
Linn, John Gaywood 1917- 25-28R
Linn, William J(oseph) 1943- 117
Linnell, Charles Lawrence Scruton 1915- ... 7-8R
Linnell, Robert H(artley) 1922- 53-56
Linneman, Robert E. 1928- 29-32R
Linneman, William R(ichard) 1926- 125
Brief entry 118
Linner, Birgitta 1920- CANR-10
Earlier sketch in CA 23-24R
Linney, Romulus 1930- 2R
Linowes, David F(rancis) 1917- 49-52
Lins, Osman 1924- Brief entry 105
Linsenmeyer, Helen Walker 1906- CANR-1
Earlier sketch in CA 45-48
Linsky, Leonard 1922- Brief entry 112
Linsley, William A(llan) 1933- 25-28R
Linstone, Harold A(drian) 1924- 112
Linstrum, Derek 1925- 107
Linthicum, Robert Charles 1936- 65-68
Lintner, John (Virgil) 1916-1983 104
Obituary 110
Linton, Barbara Leslie 1945- 33-36R
Linton, Calvin D(arlington) 1914- CANR-5
Earlier sketch in CA 15-16R
Linton, David (Hector) 1923- 11-12R
Linton, Eliza Lynn 1822-1898 ..... DLB-18
Linton, James M(ichael) 1946- 123
Linton, Robert R. 1909(?)-1979 Obituary .. 89-92
Linton, Ron(ald) M. 1929- 41-44R
Linton, William James 1812-1897 ..... DLB-32
Lintott, Andrew (William) 1936- 116
Lintz, Harry McCormick 3R
Linzee, David (Augustine Anthony) 1952- .. 73-76
Linzey, Donald Wayne 1939- CANR-13
Earlier sketch in CA 61-64
Lionberger, Herbert F(rederick) 1912- 73-76
Lionel, Robert
See Fanthorpe, R(obert) Lionel
Lionni, Leo 1910- 53-56
See also SATA 8
See also DLB 61
See also CLR 7
Lipe, Dewey 1933- 85-88
Lipetz, Ben-Ami 1927- 33-36R
Lipez, Richard 1938- CANR-18
Earlier sketch in CA 101
Lipham, James Maurice 1927- 81-84
Lipinsky de Orlov, Lino S. 1908- SATA-22
Lipkin, Gladys B(albus) 1925- CANR-2
Earlier sketch in CA 49-52
Lipkin, Mack, Jr. 1943- CANR-18
Earlier sketch in CA 101
Lipkina, Lawrence (Irwin) 1934- 41-44R
Lipkind, William 1904-1974 101
Obituary 53-56
See also SATA 15
Lipman, Aaron 1925- 21-22R
Lipman, Burton E(llis) 1931- 109
Lipman, David 1931- 23-24R
See also SATA 21
Lipman, Eugene Jay 1919- 9-10R
Lipman, Ira A 1940- 65-68
Lipman, Jean CANR-10
Earlier sketch in CA 21-22R
Lipman, Marilyn 1938- 69-72
Lipman, Matthew 1923- CANR-13
Earlier sketch in CA 33-36R
See also SATA 14
Lipman, Samuel 1934- 77-80
Lipman, Vivian David 1921- 9-10R
Lipmann, Fritz Albert 1899-1986 Obituary .. 119
Lipp, Frederick (John) 1916- 106
Lipp, Martin R(obert) 1940- 106
Lipp, Solomon 1913- Brief entry 111
Lippard, Lucy R. 1937- CANR-20
Earlier sketch in CA 25-28R
Lippert, Clarissa Start 1917- 77-80
Lipphard, William B(enjamin) 1886-1971 . CAP-2
Earlier sketch in CA 29-32
Lippincott, Bertram 1898(?)-1985
Obituary 115
See also SATA 42
Lippincott, David (McCord) 1925- CANR-9
Earlier sketch in CA 61-64
Lippincott, Joseph W(harton) 1887-1976 .. 73-76
Obituary 69-72
See also SATA 17
Lippincott, Sara Jane Clarke 1823-1904
Brief entry 120
See also DLB 43
Lippincott, Sarah Lee 1920- 17-18R
See also SATA 22
Lippitt, Gordon L(eslie) 1920- CANR-12
Earlier sketch in CA 29-32R
Lippitt, Ronald O. 1914- 37-40R
Lippman, Edward A. 1920- 122
Lippman, Leopold 1919- 49-52
Lippman, Peter J. 1936- CANR-26
Earlier sketch in CA 108
See also SATA 31
Lippman, Theo, Jr. 1929- 33-36R
Lippmann, Walter 1889-1974 ..... CANR-6
Obituary 53-56
Earlier sketch in CA 9-10R
See also DLB 29
See also AITN 1
Lipschutz, Ilse Hempel 1923- 41-44R
Lipscomb, Commander F. W.
See Lipscomb, F(rank) W(oodgate)
Lipscomb, David M(ilton) 1935- CANR-1
Earlier sketch in CA 49-52
Lipscomb, Elizabeth J(ohnston) 1938- 115
Lipscomb, F(rank) W(oodgate)
1903-1983 ..... 29-32R
Obituary 126
Lipscomb, James 1926- 85-88
Lipsen, Charles B. 1925- 73-76
Lipset, Seymour Martin 1922- CANR-1
Earlier sketch in CA 3R
Lipsett, Laurence Cline 1915- 11-12R
Lipsey, Richard A(llan) 1930- CANR-23
Earlier sketch in CA 107
Lipsey, Richard G(eorge) 1928- CANR-17
Earlier sketch in CA 97-100
Lipsey, Robert E(dward) 1926- CANR-18
Earlier sketches in CA 7-8R, CANR-2
Lipsitz, George R(aymond) 1947- 113
Lipsitz, Lou 1938- CANR-18
Earlier sketch in CA 101
Lipski, Alexander 1919- 49-52
Lipsky, David Bruce 1939- 103
Lipsky, Eleazar 1911- Brief entry 115
Lipsky, Michael 1940- 61-64
Lipsky, Mortimer 1915- 73-76
Lipson, Charles 1948- 123
Lipson, Goldie 1905- 33-36R
Lipson, Harry A(aron, Jr.) 1919- 61-64
Lipson, Leon Samuel 1921- 104
Lipson, Leslie (Michel) 1912- 106
Lipson, Milton 1913- 65-68
Lipson, Shelley 1948- 119
Lipstadt, Deborah E(sther) 1947- 111
Lipstein, Kurt 1909- 117
Lipstreu, Otis 1919-1970 ..... CAP-1
Earlier sketch in CA 15-16
Lipsyte, Marjorie (Rubin) 1932- 105
Lipsyte, Robert (Michael) 1938- CANR-8
Earlier sketch in CA 19-20R
See also SATA 5
See also CLC 21
Lipton, David R(obert) 1947- 97-100
Lipton, Dean 1919- 29-32R
Lipton, Lawrence 1898-1975 93-96
Obituary 57-60
See also DLB 16
Lipton, Lenny 1940- 101
Liptzin, Sol(omon) 1901- 11-12R
Liroff, Richard A(lan) 1948- CANR-11
Earlier sketch in CA 69-72
Lisagor, Peter 1915-1976 Obituary 69-72
Lisca, Peter 1925- 37-40R
Lischer, Richard 1943- 101
Lisci, Leonardo Ginori
See Ginori Lisci, Leonardo
Lish, Gordon (Jay) 1934- 117
Brief entry 113
See also CLC 45
Lishka, Gerald R 1949- 89-92
Lisi, Albert 1929- 25-28R
Lisio, Donald J(ohn) 1934- 124
Lisk, Jill 1938- 25-28R
Liska, Edward G. 1914(?)-1984 Obituary ... 113
Liska, George 1922- 104
Lisker, Sonia O. 1933- CANR-2
Earlier sketch in CA 49-52
See also SATA 44
Lisle, Janet Taylor SATA-47
Lisle, Seward D.
See Ellis, Edward S(ylvester)
Lison-Tolosana, Carmelo 1929- CANR-13
Earlier sketch in CA 21-22R
Lisowski, Gabriel 1946- 97-100
See also SATA 31, 47
Lispector, Clarice 1925-1977 Obituary 116
See also CLC 43
Liss, Howard 1922- CANR-16
Earlier sketch in CA 25-28R
See also SATA 4
Liss, Jerome 1938- 53-56
Liss, Peggy K(orn) 1927- 41-44R
Liss, Robert E. 1945(?)-1979 Obituary 115
Liss, Sheldon B. 1936- 23-24R
Lissak, Moshe (Avraham) 1928- 97-100
Lissim, Simon 1900-1981 Obituary 109
See also SATA 28
Lissitzyn, Oliver J(ames) 1912- 45-48

Lissner, Will 1908- 101
List, Ilka Katherine 1935- 37-40R
See also SATA 6
List, Jacob Samuel 1896-1967 .... CAP-1
Earlier sketch in CA 19-20
List, Robert Stuart 1903-1983 Obituary 109
Lister, Eric 1926(?)-1988(?) Obituary 125
Lister, Hal
See Lister, Harold
Lister, Harold 1922- 73-76
Lister, Laurier L. 1907-1986 Obituary 120
Lister, R(ichard) P(ercival) 1914- CANR-5
Earlier sketch in CA 9-10R
Lister, Raymond (George) 1919- CANR-24
Earlier sketches in CA 13-14R, CANR-8
Liston, Jack
See Maloney, Ralph Liston
Liston, Mary Dawn 1936- 53-56
Liston, Robert A. 1927- CANR-12
Earlier sketch in CA 19-20R
See also SATA 5
Listowel, Judith (de Marffy-Mantuano)
1904- 15-16R
Litchfield, Ada B(assett) 1916- CANR-10
Earlier sketch in CA 25-28R
See also SATA 5
Litchfield, Harry R(obert) 1898-1973
Obituary 41-44R
Litchfield, Robert O(rbin) ?-1977
Obituary 73-76
Lite, James
See Schneck, Stephen
Lithwick, Norman Harvey 1938- 61-64
Litoff, Judy Barrett 1944- 85-88
Litowinsky, Olga (Jean) 1936- 81-84
See also SATA 26
Litsey, Sarah 5-6R
Littauer, Florence 1928- 115
Littauer, Raphael (Max) 1925- Brief entry 109
Littell, Franklin H(amlin) 1917- Brief entry 112
Littell, Robert 1896-1963 Obituary 93-96
Littell, Robert 1935(?)- 112
Brief entry 109
See also CLC 42
Litterer, Joseph A(ugust) 1926- CANR-3
Earlier sketch in CA 9-10R
Littke, Lael J. 1929- CANR-15
Earlier sketch in CA 85-88
See also SATA 51
Little, A. Edward
See Klein, Aaron E.
Little, Alan M(acNaughton) G(ordon)
1901-1987 Obituary 124
Little, Bryan (Desmond Greenway)
1913- CANR-22
Earlier sketch in CA 104
Little, David 1933- 29-32R
Little, Elbert L(uther), Jr. 1907- 57-60
Little, Elbert Payson 1912(?)-1983
Obituary 110
Little, Geraldine C(linton) 109
Little, Ian M(alcolm) D(avid) 1918- CANR-15
Earlier sketch in CA 21-22R
Little, Jack
See Little, John D(utton)
Little, Jane Sneddon 1942- Brief entry 113
Little, (Flora) Jean 1932- 23-24R
See also SATA 2
See also CLR 4
Little, John D(utton) 1894- 65-68
Little, Kenneth
See Scotland, James
Little, Kenneth L(indsay) 1908- 17-18R
Little, Lawrence Calvin 1897-1976 .... CANR-3
Earlier sketch in CA 2R
Little, Lessie Jones 1906-1986 101
Obituary 121
See also SATA 50
Little, Lester Knox 1935- 103
Little, Loyd (Harry), Jr. 1940- 81-84
Little, Malcolm 1925-1965 125
Obituary 111
See also BW
Little, Mary E. 1912- 105
See also SATA 28
Little, Nina Fletcher 1903- Brief entry 106
Little, Paul E. 1928-1975 .... CAP-2
Earlier sketch in CA 21-22
Little, Paul H(ugo) 1915-1987 .... CANR-13
Obituary 122
Earlier sketch in CA 17-18R
Little, Paula
See Little, Paul H(ugo)
Little, Pippa 1958- 123
Little, Ray 1918(?)-1980 Obituary 102
Little, Richard 1944- 114
Little, Roger W(illiam) 1922- 29-32R
Little, Royal 1896- 106
Little, S. George 1903-1974 Obituary 49-52
Little, Sara (Pamela) 1919- 116
Little, Stuart W. 1921- CANR-1
Earlier sketch in CA 45-48
Little, Thomas Russell 1911- 13-14R
Little, Tom
See Little, Thomas Russell
Little, William Alfred
See Little, Wm. A.
Little, Wm. A. 1929- 57-60
Littleboy, Sheila M.
See Ary, Sheila M(ary Littleboy)
Littledale, Freya (Lota) CANR-25
Earlier sketches in CA 23-24R, CANR-10
See also SATA 2
Littledale, Harold (Aylmer) 1927- 5-6R
Littlefair, Duncan (Elliot) 1912- 45-48
Littlefield, David Joseph 1928- 41-44R
Littlefield, James Edward 1932- 53-56
Littlejohn, (Cameron) Bruce 1913- 61-64
Littlejohn, David 1937- CANR-14
Earlier sketch in CA 41-44R
Littleton, C(ovington) Scott 1933- 23-24R
Littleton, Harvey K(line) 1922- 53-56
Littlewit, Humphrey, Gent.
See Lovecraft, H(oward) P(hillips)
Littlewood, Joan (Maud) 1914- Brief entry 116
See also DLB 13
Littlewood, Robert Percy 1910- 7-8R
Littlewood, Thomas B. 1928- 29-32R
Littman, Robert J. 1943- 81-84
Litto, Fredric M. 1939- 25-28R
Litto, Gertrude 1929- 69-72
Litvag, Irving 1928- 57-60
Litvak, Isaiah A(llan) 1936- 15-16R
Litvinoff, Barnet 1917- 17-18R
Litvinoff, Emanuel 1915- Brief entry 117
Litvinoff, Saul 1925- 41-44R
Litvinov, Ivy 1890(?)-1977 Obituary 69-72
Litvinov, Pavel 1940- 89-92
Litwack, Leon F(rank) 1929- CANR-1
Earlier sketch in CA 4R
Litwak, Eugene 1925- Brief entry 114
Litwak, Leo (E.) 1924- CANR-22
Earlier sketch in CA 7-8R
Litwos
See Sienkiewicz, Henryk (Adam
Aleksander Pius)
Litz, A(rthur) Walton (Jr.) 1929- 33-36R
Litzel, Otto 1901- 57-60
Litzinger, Boyd (A., Jr.) 1929- CANR-20
Earlier sketches in CA 13-14R, CANR-5
Liu, Aimee 1953- 89-92
Liu, Alan P(ing-) L(in) 1937- 61-64
Liu, Da 1910- 85-88
Liu, James J(o) Y(u) 1926- CANR-7
Earlier sketch in CA 7-8R
Liu, James T(zu) C(hien) 1919- 21-22R
Liu, Jung-Chao 1929- 29-32R
Liu, Leo Yueh-yun 1940- 41-44R
Liu, Sarah 1943- 115
Liu, Sydney (Chieh) 1920- 103
Liu, Tzu-chien
See Liu, James T(zu) C(hien)
Liu, William T(homas) 1930- CANR-13
Earlier sketch in CA 23-24R
Liu, Wu-chi 1907- CANR-25
Earlier sketches in CA 15-16R, CANR-10
Liu, Yong
See Liu, William T(homas)
Liu E 1857-1909 Brief entry 115
See also TCLC 15
Liu Zongren 1940- 116
Livant, Rose Adleman 1899(?)-1986
Obituary 120
Lively, Penelope (Margaret) 1933- 41-44R
See also SATA 7
See also DLB 14
See also CLC 32, 50
See also CLR 7
Lively, Walter
See Elliott, Bruce (Walter Gardner Lively
Stacy)
Liverani, Giuseppe 1903- CANR-6
Earlier sketch in CA 5-6R
Liverani, Mary Rose 1939- 104
Livergood, Norman D(avid) 1933- 37-40R
Livermore, Jean
See Sanville, Jean
Livermore, Seward W. 1901(?)-1984
Obituary 112
Livermore, Shaw 1902- CAP-2
Earlier sketch in CA 19-20
Liversidge, (Henry) Douglas 1913- CAP-1
Earlier sketch in CA 9-10
See also SATA 8
Liversidge, Joan (Eileen Annie)
1915(?)-1984 103
Obituary 112
Liverton, Joan 1913- CAP-1
Earlier sketch in CA 9-10
Livesay, Dorothy 1909- 25-28R
See also DLB 68
See also CLC 4, 15
See also AITN 2
Livesey, Claire Warner 1927- 29-32R
Livgren, Kerry 1949- 114
Livia, Anna 1955- 119
Livie-Noble, Frederick Stanley 1899-1970 . CAP-1
Earlier sketch in CA 9-10
Livingood, James W(eston) 1910- CANR-8
Earlier sketch in CA 17-18R
Livings, Henry 1929- 15-16R
See also DLB 13
Livingston, A(lfred) D(elano) 1932- CANR-13
Earlier sketch in CA 17-18R
Livingston, Anne Home 1763-1841 .... DLB-37
Livingston, Bernard 1911- 81-84
Livingston, Carole 1941- 105
See also SATA 42
Livingston, Dorothy Michelson 1906- 49-52
Livingston, Elizabeth J(ane) 1952- 113
Livingston, George Herbert 1916- 53-56
Livingston, Harold 1924- 2R
Livingston, J(oseph) A(rnold) 1905- 1R
Livingston, James C(raig) 1930- CANR-21
Earlier sketch in CA 45-48
Livingston, Jane S(helton) 1944- 107
Livingston, Jon 1944- 49-52
Livingston, M. Jay
See Livingston, Myran Jabez, Jr.
Livingston, Martha 1945- 115
Livingston, Myra Cohn 1926- CANR-1
Earlier sketch in CA 3R
See also SATA 5
See also SAAS 1
See also DLB 61
See also CLR 7
Livingston, Myran Jabez, Jr. 1934- CANR-22
Earlier sketch in CA 105
Livingston, Peter Van Rensselaer
See Townsend, James B(arclay)
J(ermain)
Livingston, Richard R(oland) 1922- 45-48
See also SATA 8
Livingston, Robert B(urr) 1918- 97-100
Livingston, William 1723-1790 .... DLB-31
Livingston, William S. 1920- CANR-3
Earlier sketch in CA 11-12R
Livingstone, Angela 1934- 119
Livingstone, Bernard L. 1907(?)-1984
Obituary 112
Livingstone, Douglas (James) 1932- CANR-20
Earlier sketches in CA 15-16R, CANR-5
Livingstone, Harrison Edward 1937- 33-36R
Livingstone, J(ohn) Leslie 1932- 73-76
Livingstone, Leon 1912- 33-36R
Livingstone, Marco (Eduardo) 1952- CANR-24
Earlier sketch in CA 107
Livo, Norma J. 1929- 123
Livoni, Cathy 1956- 113
Livsey, Clara G(rabois) 1924- 107
Livson, Norman 1924- 49-52
Liyong, Taban lo 1938- 105
See also BW
Lizotte, Ken 1948- 126
Ljoka, Daniel J. 1935- 49-52
Llano, George A(lbert) 1911- 125
Lleo, Manuel Urrutia
See Urrutia Lleo, Manuel
Llerena, Mario 1913- 81-84
Llerena Aguirre, Carlos (Antonio) 1952- 77-80
See also SATA 19
Llewellyn, D(avid) W(illiam) Alun 1903- 57-60
Llewellyn, Edward
See Llewellyn-Thomas, Edward
Llewellyn, Richard
See Llewellyn Lloyd, Richard Dafydd
Vivian
See also DLB 15
See also CLC 7
Llewellyn-Jones, Derek 1923- CANR-15
Earlier sketch in CA 37-40R
Llewellyn Lloyd, Richard Dafydd Vivian
1906-1983 .... CANR-7
Obituary 111
Earlier sketch in CA 53-56
See also SATA 11, 37
Llewellyn-Thomas, Edward 1917- 104
Llewelyn, T. Harcourt
See Hamilton, Charles Harold St. John
Llewelyn-Davies, Richard 1912-1981 .... 13-14R
Obituary 105
Llorens, Vicente 1906-1979 Obituary 89-92
Lloret, Antoni 1935- 29-32R
Llosa, Ricardo Pau
See Pau-Llosa, Ricardo
Lloyd, Adrien
See Gelb, Alan Lloyd
Lloyd, Alan C(hester) 1915- CANR-1
Earlier sketch in CA 2R
Lloyd, Albert Lancaster 1908-1982
Obituary 107
Lloyd, Charles
See Birkin, Charles (Lloyd)
Lloyd, (Charles) Christopher 1906-1986
Obituary 119
Lloyd, Christopher 1921- 120
Lloyd, Craig 1940- 61-64
Lloyd, Cynthia B(rown) 1943- CANR-8
Earlier sketch in CA 61-64
Lloyd, David 1946- 89-92
Lloyd, David Demarest 1911-1962 .... CAP-1
Earlier sketch in CA 11-12
Lloyd, Dennis 1915- 13-14R
Lloyd, E. James
See James, Elizabeth
Lloyd, Errol 1943- 101
See also SATA 22
Lloyd, Francis V(ernon), Jr. 1908- CAP-2
Earlier sketch in CA 21-22
Lloyd, G(eoffrey) E(rnest) R(ichard)
1933- 57-60
Lloyd, Howell Arnold 1937- 103
Lloyd, Hugh (Pughe) 1894-1981 Obituary 108
Lloyd, J. Ivester 1905- 13-14R
Lloyd, Jack Ivester
See Lloyd, J. Ivester
Lloyd, James
See James, Elizabeth
Lloyd, James Barlow 1945- 112
Lloyd, John Ivester
See Lloyd, J. Ivester
Lloyd, John S. B. Selwyn
See Selwyn-Lloyd, John S. B.
Lloyd, Marjorie 1909- CANR-8
Earlier sketch in CA 7-8R
Lloyd, Norman 1909-1980 .... 37-40R
Obituary 101
See also SATA 23
Lloyd, (Mary) Norris 1908- CANR-1
Earlier sketch in CA 3R
See also SATA 10
Lloyd, Peter C(utt) 1927- CANR-11
Earlier sketch in CA 25-28R
Lloyd, Peter Edward 1938- 107
Lloyd, Robin 1925- 73-76
Lloyd, Ronald
See Friedland, Ronald Lloyd
Lloyd, Rosemary (Helen) 1949- 116
Lloyd, Stephanie
See Golding, Morton J(ay)
Lloyd, Trevor (Owen) 1934- 25-28R
Lloyd Evans, Barbara 1924- 93-96
Lloyd Evans, Gareth 1923-1984 Obituary 117
Lloyd George (of Dwyor), Frances (Louise
Stevenson) 1888(?)-1972 Obituary 37-40R
Lloyd-Jones, Esther McDonald 1901- 15-16R
Lloyd-Jones, (Peter) Hugh (Jefferd)
1922- CANR-21
Earlier sketches in CA 7-8R, CANR-4
Lloyd-Jones, Robin 1934- 111
Lloyd Owen, David Lanyon 1917- 117
Lloyd-Thomas, Catherine 1917- 65-68
Lloyd Webber, Andrew 1948- Brief entry 116
Llywelyn, Morgan 1937- CANR-16
Earlier sketch in CA 81-84
Llywelyn-Williams, Alun 1913- CAP-1
Earlier sketch in CA 9-10
Lo, Irving Yucheng 1922- 57-60
Lo, Ruth Earnshaw 1910- 106
Lo, Samuel E. 1931- 29-32R
Loader, William Reginald 1916- 4R
Loades, David Michael 1934- 19-20R
Loane, Marcus L(awrence) 1911- CANR-2
Earlier sketch in CA 3R
Loasby, Brian John 1930- 93-96
Lobb, Charlotte 1935- CANR-15
Earlier sketch in CA 65-68
Lobb, Ebenezer
See Upward, Allen
Lobdell, Helen 1919- 11-12R
Lobdell, Jared C(harles) 1937- 49-52
Lobel, Anita (Kempler) 1934- CANR-9
Earlier sketch in CA 53-56
See also SATA 6
Lobel, Arnold Stark 1933-1987 .... CANR-2
Obituary 124
Earlier sketch in CA 4R
See also SATA 6
See also DLB 61
See also CLR 5
See also AITN 1
Lobel, Brana 1942- 97-100
Lobel, Edgar 1889-1982 Obituary 107
Lobel, Stanley 1937- 111
Lo Bello, Nino 1921- CANR-12
Earlier sketch in CA 29-32R
Loberg, Mary Alice 1943- 29-32R
Lobkowicz, Nicholas 1931- CANR-10
Earlier sketch in CA 21-22R
Lobley, Robert (John) 1934- 29-32R
Lobo, Anthony S(avio) 1937- 49-52
Lobsenz, Amelia 13-14R
See also SATA 12
Lobsenz, Norman M(itchell) 1919- CANR-4
Earlier sketch in CA 9-10R
See also SATA 6
Loch, Joice N(anKivell) 1893-1982 .... 25-28R
Obituary 108
Lochak, Michele 1936- 106
See also SATA 39
Lochard, Metz T(ullus) P(aul) 1896-1984
Obituary 112
Lochbiler, Don 1908- 49-52
Locher, Dick
See Locher, Richard (Earl)
Locher, Frances C(arol) CANR-17
Earlier sketch in CA 97-100
Locher, Richard (Earl) 1929- CANR-16
Earlier sketch in CA 85-88
Lochhead, Douglas (Grant) 1922- CANR-16
Earlier sketches in CA 45-48, CANR-1
Lochhead, Liz 1947- 81-84
Lochhead, Marion Cleland 1902-1985 101
Obituary 115
Lochlons, Colin
See Jackson, C(aary) Paul
Lochman, Jan Milic 1922- CANR-12
Earlier sketch in CA 29-32R
Lochner, Louis P(aul) 1887-1975 65-68
Obituary 53-56
Lochridge, Betsy Hopkins
See Fancher, Betsy
Lochte, Dick
See Lochte, Richard S(amuel)
Lochte, Richard S(amuel) 1944- CANR-23
Earlier sketch in CA 105
LoCicero, Donald 1937- 25-28R
Lock, C(lara) B(eatrice) Muriel 1914- 49-52
Lock, Dennis (Laurence) 1929- CANR-14
Earlier sketch in CA 41-44R
Lock, F(rederick) P(eter) 1948- 118
Lock, Fred
See Lock, F(rederick) P(eter)
Lock, Margaret M. 1936- 126
Lockard, Craig Alan 1942- 122
Lockard, (Walter) Duane 1921- 17-18R
Lockard, Leonard
See Thomas, Theodore L.
Locke, Alain (Le Roy) 1886-1954 124
Brief entry 106
See also BW
See also DLB 51
Locke, Charles O. 1896(?)-1977 Obituary 69-72
Locke, Clinton W. CANR-26
Earlier sketches in CA 19-20, CAP-2
See also SATA 1
Locke, David M(illard) 1929- 41-44R
Locke, David Ross 1833-1888 .... DLB-11, 23
Locke, Duane CANR-1
Earlier sketch in CA 49-52
Locke, Edwin A. III 1938- 15-16R
Locke, Elsie 1912- CANR-26
Earlier sketches in CA 25-28R, CANR-11
Locke, Frederick W. 1918- 13-14R

Locke, Hubert G. 1934- 29-32R
Locke, Louis G(lenn) 1912- 33-36R
Locke, Lucie 1904- 53-56
See also SATA 10
Locke, Martin
See Duncan, W(illiam) Murdoch
Locke, Michael (Stephen) 1943- 73-76
Locke, Peter
See McCutchan, J(ohn) Wilson
Locke, R. E.
See Raffelock, David
Locke, Ralph P(aul) 1949- 124
Locke, Richard Adams 1800-1871 .... DLB-43
Locke, Wende 1945- 33-36R
Locke-Elliott, Sumner
See Elliott, Sumner Locke
Locker, Thomas 1937- CLR-14
Lockerbie, D(onald) Bruce 1935- CANR-14
Earlier sketch in CA 37-40R
Lockerbie, Jeanette W. Honeyman CANR-5
Earlier sketch in CA 11-12R
Lockerbie, Jeannie 1938- CANR-13
Earlier sketch in CA 73-76
Locker-Lampson, Frederick 1821-1895 .. DLB-35
Lockert, (Charles) Lacy (Jr.) 1888-1974 .. CAP-2
Earlier sketch in CA 25-28
Lockert, Lucia (Alicia Ungaro Fox)
1928- CANR-14
Earlier sketch in CA 73-76
Lockhart, (Jeanne) Aileene Simpson
1911- 15-16R
Lockhart, Freda Bruce 1909-1987
Obituary 124
Lockhart, Jack Herbert 1909-1985
Obituary 117
Lockhart, Robert (Hamilton) Bruce
1886-1970 Obituary 89-92
Lockhart, Russell A(rthur) 1938- CANR-21
Earlier sketch in CA 45-48
Locklair, Wriston 1924(?)-1984 Obituary ... 112
Lockley, Lawrence Campbell 1899-1969 .. CAP-1
Earlier sketch in CA 11-12
Lockley, Ronald M(athias) 1903- CANR-22
Earlier sketches in CA 9-10R, CANR-5
Locklin, Gerald (Ivan) 1941- CANR-14
Earlier sketch in CA 37-40R
Locklin, (David) Philip 1897- 2R
Lockmann, Ronald F(rederick) 1942- 117
Lockmiller, David A(lexander) 1906- 77-80
Lockridge, Ernest (Hugh) 1938- 25-28R
See also AITN 1
Lockridge, Frances Louise ?-1963
Obituary 93-96
Lockridge, Hildegarde (Dolson)
1908-1981 .... CANR-3
Obituary 102
Earlier sketch in CA 5-6R
Lockridge, Kenneth A(lan) 1940-
Brief entry 107
Lockridge, Norman
See Roth, Samuel
Lockridge, Richard 1898-1982 85-88
Obituary 107
Lockridge, Ross (Franklin), Jr. 1914-1948
Brief entry 108
See also DLBY 80
Lockspeiser, Edward 1905-1973 .... CANR-6
Earlier sketch in CA 7-8R
Lockwood, Allison 1920- 115
Lockwood, C. C. 1949- 117
Lockwood, Charles Andrews 1890-1967 .... 2R
Lockwood, Douglas (Wright) 1918- 21-22R
Lockwood, Guy C. 1943- 65-68
Lockwood, Lee 1932- 37-40R
Lockwood, Margo 1939- 117
Lockwood, Mary
See Spelman, Mary
Lockwood, Michael 1944- 122
Lockwood, Theodore Davidge 1924- CANR-1
Earlier sketch in CA 4R
Lockwood, W(illiam) B(urley) 1917- 29-32R
Lockwood, William W(irt) 1906- CAP-2
Earlier sketch in CA 23-24
Lockyer, Herbert 1888(?)-1984 Obituary 115
Lockyer, Roger 1927- CANR-12
Earlier sketch in CA 19-20R
Lodder, Christina (Anne) 1948- 125
Lode, Rex
See Goldstein, William Isaac
Loden, Barbara (Ann) 1937-1980 Obituary .. 101
Lodge, Bernard 1933- 107
See also SATA 33
Lodge, David (John) 1935- CANR-19
Earlier sketch in CA 17-18R
See also DLB 14
See also CLC 36
Lodge, George Cabot 1873-1909
Brief entry 123
See also DLB 54
Lodge, George Cabot 1927- 17-18R
Lodge, Henry Cabot 1850-1924 .... DLB-47
Lodge, Henry Cabot (Jr.) 1902-1985 53-56
Obituary 115
Lodge, Oliver (Joseph) 1851-1940
Brief entry 117
Lodge, Orlan Robert 1917-1975 Obituary ..57-60
Lodrick, Deryck O(scar) 1942- 106
Loeb, Catherine (Roberta) 1949- 89-92
Loeb, Gerald M(artin) 1899-1974 .... CAP-1
Obituary 49-52
Earlier sketch in CA 15-16
Loeb, Harold A(lbert) 1891-1974 106
Obituary 45-48
See also DLB 4
Loeb, Jeffrey 1946- 123
Loeb, Madeleine H. 1905(?)-1974
Obituary 45-48
Loeb, Marshall Robert 1929- 23-24R
Loeb, Paul Rogat 1952- 109
Loeb, Robert F(rederick) 1895-1973
Obituary 45-48
Loeb, Robert H., Jr. 1917- CANR-12
Earlier sketch in CA 29-32R
See also SATA 21
Loeb, William 1905-1981 93-96
Obituary 104
Loebl, Eugen 1907-1987 Obituary 123
Loebl, Suzanne 69-72
Loefgren, Ulf 1931- CANR-16
Earlier sketch in CA 25-28R
See also SATA 3
Loefstedt, Bengt 1931- CANR-1
Earlier sketch in CA 45-48
Loehlin, John C(linton) 1926- 23-24R
Loemker, Leroy E(arl) 1900- 41-44R
Loening, Grover C. 1889(?)-1976
Obituary 65-68
Loening, Sarah (Elizabeth) Larkin
1896-1988 .... CANR-21
Obituary 124
Earlier sketch in CA 45-48
Loennbohm, Armas Eino Leopold
1878-1926 Brief entry 123
Loeoef, Jan 1940- 81-84
Loeper, John J(oseph) 1929- CANR-12
Earlier sketch in CA 29-32R
See also SATA 10
Loertscher, David V. 1940- 126
Loesch, Juli(anne) 1951- 89-92
Loescher, Ann Dull 1942- CANR-9
Earlier sketch in CA 61-64
See also SATA 20
Loescher, Gil(burt Damian) 1945- CANR-9
Earlier sketch in CA 61-64
See also SATA 20
Loeschke, Maravene Sheppard 1947- 115
Loeser, Herta 1921- 57-60
Loeser, Katinka 1913- 17-18R
Loesser, Francis Henry 1910-1969
Obituary 112
Loesser, Frank
See Loesser, Francis Henry
Loether, Herman J(ohn) 1930- 21-22R
Loetscher, Lefferts A(ugustine) 1904- 5-6R
Loevinger, Jane 1918- 41-44R
Loevinger, Lee 1913- CANR-15
Earlier sketch in CA 81-84
Loew, Ralph William 1907- CAP-1
Earlier sketch in CA 19-20
Loew, Sebastian 1939- CANR-19
Earlier sketch in CA 103
Loewald, Hans W. 1906- 101
Loewe, Ralph E. 1923- 23-24R
Loewe, Raphael J(ames) 1919- 118
Loewen, James W. 1942- CANR-14
Earlier sketch in CA 37-40R
Loewenberg, Bert James 1905-1974 .... CANR-5
Earlier sketch in CA 11-12R
Loewenberg, Frank M(eyer) 1925- CANR-2
Earlier sketch in CA 45-48
Loewenberg, Gerhard 1928- CANR-9
Earlier sketch in CA 23-24R
Loewenberg, J(orn) Joseph 1933- 33-36R
Loewenberg, Peter J(acob) 1933- 109
Loewenberg, Robert J(ames) 1938-
Brief entry 114
Loewenfeld, Claire 1899-1974 .... CAP-2
Earlier sketch in CA 23-24
Loewenstein, Bernice SATA-40
Loewenstein, Hubertus Prinz zu
See
Loewenstein(-Wertheim-Freudenberg),
Hubertus (Friedrich Maria Johannes
Leopold Ludwig) zu
Loewenstein(-Wertheim-Freudenberg),
Hubertus (Friedrich Maria Johannes
Leopold Ludwig) zu 1906-1984 .... CANR-4
Obituary 114
Earlier sketch in CA 7-8R
Loewenstein, Joseph 1952- 124
Loewenstein, Karl 1891-1973 Obituary ...41-44R
Loewenstein, Louis Klee 1927- 37-40R
Loewenstein, Prince Hubertus (zu)
See
Loewenstein(-Wertheim-Freudenberg),
Hubertus (Friedrich Maria Johannes
Leopold Ludwig) zu
Loewenstein, Rudolph M(aurice)
1898-1976 .... CAP-2
Obituary 65-68
Earlier sketch in CA 21-22
Loewenstein-Wertheim-Freudenberg,
Hubertus Prinz zu
See
Loewenstein(-Wertheim-Freudenberg),
Hubertus (Friedrich Maria Johannes
Leopold Ludwig) zu
Loewenthal, L(eonard) J(oseph) A(lfonso) ...61-64
Loewinsohn, Ron(ald William) 1937- 25-28R
Loewith, Karl 1897-1973 Obituary 116
Loewy, Ariel G(ideon) 1925- 89-92
Loewy, Raymond Fernand 1893-1986 104
Obituary 119
Lofaro, Michael Anthony 1948- 89-92
Lofland, John (Franklin) 1936- CANR-12
Earlier sketch in CA 33-36R
Lofland, Lyn (Hebert) 1937- 61-64
Lofstedt, Bengt
See Loefstedt, Bengt
Loftas, Tony 1940- 21-22R
Lofthouse, Jessica 1916-1988 ....29-32R
Obituary 125
Lofthus, Myrna 1935- 115
Lofting, Hugh (John) 1886-1947
Brief entry 109
See also SATA 15
Loftis, Anne 1922- 45-48
Loftis, John (Clyde, Jr.) 1919- CANR-3
Earlier sketch in CA 2R
Lofton, John (Marion) 1919- CANR-6
Earlier sketch in CA 11-12R
Lofts, Norah (Robinson) 1904-1983 .... CANR-6
Obituary 110
Earlier sketch in CA 7-8R
See also SATA 8, 36
See also AITN 2
Loftus, Elizabeth F. 1944- 105
Loftus, Ernest Achey 1884-1987 Obituary ... 123
Loftus, John (Joseph) 1950- 117
Loftus, Richard J. 1929- 15-16R
Logan, Albert Boyd 1909- 53-56
Logan, Daniel 1936- 25-28R
Logan, Don
See Crawford, William (Elbert)
Logan, Elizabeth D(ulaney) 1914- 61-64
Logan, F(rancis) Donald 1930- 45-48
Logan, Ford
See Newton, D(wight) B(ennett)
Logan, Frank A(nderson) 1924- 41-44R
Logan, Gene A(dams) 1922- CANR-7
Earlier sketch in CA 11-12R
Logan, Gerald E(lton) 1924- 73-76
Logan, Jake
See Knott, William C(ecil, Jr.)
and Krepps, Robert W(ilson)
and Pearl, Jacques Bain
and Riefe, Alan
and Rifkin, Shepard
and Smith, Martin Cruz
Logan, James 1674-1751 .... DLB-24
Logan, James Phillips 1921- 37-40R
Logan, Jane
See Gardner, Virginia (Marberry)
Logan, John (Burton) 1923-1987 77-80
Obituary 124
See also DLB 5
See also CLC 5
Logan, John A(rthur), Jr. 1923- 2R
Logan, Joshua (Lockwood) 1908-1988 89-92
Obituary 126
See also AITN 1
Logan, Lillian M(ay) 1909- CANR-1
Earlier sketch in CA 2R
Logan, Rayford W(hittingham)
1897-1982 .... CANR-25
Obituary 108
Earlier sketches in CA 2R, CANR-1
See also BW
Logan, Sara
See Haydon, June
and Simpson, Judith H(olroyd)
Logan, Sister Mary Francis Louise 1928- ...7-8R
Logan, Spencer 1912(?)-1980 Obituary ...93-96
Logan, Terence P(atrick) 1936- 57-60
Logan, Virgil G(lenn) 1904- 21-22R
Loganbill, G. Bruce 1938- 37-40R
Logelin, Warren E. 1940(?)-1985
Obituary 117
Loggins, Vernon 1893-1968 ....7-8R
Loggins, William Kirk 1946- 77-80
Logsdon, John M(ortimer III) 1937-
Brief entry 115
Logsdon, Joseph 1938- 25-28R
Logsdon, Richard Henry 1912- CANR-2
Earlier sketch in CA 5-6R
Logsdon, Thomas S(tanley) 1937- CANR-21
Earlier sketches in CA 57-60, CANR-6
Logsdon, Tom
See Logsdon, Thomas S(tanley)
Logue, Cal(vin McLeod) 1935- Brief entry .. 105
Logue, Christopher 1926- CANR-3
Earlier sketch in CA 11-12R
See also SATA 23
See also DLB 27
Logue, Jeanne 1921- 89-92
Logue, John 1933- 126
Logue, William (Herbert) 1934- 45-48
Loh, Jules 1931- 33-36R
Loh, Pichon P(ei) Y(ung) 1928- 17-18R
Loh, Robert 1924- 19-20R
Lohf, Kenneth A. 1925- CANR-3
Earlier sketch in CA 9-10R
Lohman, Joseph D(ean) 1910-1968 .... CAP-2
Earlier sketch in CA 23-24
Lohnes, Walter F. W. 1925- 49-52
Lohr, Thomas F. 1926- 77-80
Lohrer, M(ary) Alice 1907- 17-18R
Lohrli, Anne 1906- 111
Lohrman, Paul
See Fairman, Paul W.
Lohse, Eduard 1924- 107
Loisy, Alfred (Firmin) 1857-1940
Brief entry 120
Lo-Johansson, (Karl) Ivar 1901- CANR-20
Earlier sketch in CA 102
Loken, Newton Clayton 1919- 3R
See also SATA 26
Loki
See Pearson, Karl
Lokken, Roy N(orman) 1917- 53-56
Lokos, Lionel 1928- 25-28R
Loll, Leo M(arius), Jr. 1923-1968 .... CAP-2
Earlier sketch in CA 25-28
Lollar, Coleman Aubrey (Jr.) 1946- 49-52
Lolli, Giorgio 1905-1979 .... CANR-2
Obituary 85-88
Earlier sketch in CA 4R
Lollis, Lorraine 1911- CAP-2
Earlier sketch in CA 29-32
Lolos, Kimon 1917- 4R
Lomas, Charles W(yatt) 1907- CAP-1
Earlier sketch in CA 13-14
Lomas, Derek 1933- 29-32R
Lomas, Geoffrey (Robert) 1950- 93-96
Lomas, Peter 1923- 23-24R
Lomas, Steve
See Brennan, Joseph Lomas
Lomask, Milton (Nachman) 1909- CANR-1
Earlier sketch in CA 3R
See also SATA 20
Lomax, Alan 1915- CANR-1
Earlier sketch in CA 4R
Lomax, Bliss
See Drago, Harry Sinclair
Lomax, John A(lbert) 1930- 61-64
Lomax, Louis E(manuel) 1922-1970 .... CAP-2
Earlier sketch in CA 25-28
See also BW
Lomax, Pearl
See Cleage, Pearl (Michelle)
Lombard, C(harles) M(orris) 1920- CANR-1
Earlier sketch in CA 49-52
Lombard, Helen
See Vischer, Helen (Cassin Lombard)
Carusi
Lombard, Lawrence Brian 1944- 124
Lombard, Nap
See Johnson, Pamela Hansford
Lombardi, John V(incent) 1942- CANR-20
Earlier sketches in CA 53-56, CANR-5
Lombardi, Mary 1940- 61-64
Lombardo, Josef Vincent 1908- 7-8R
LoMedico, Brian T.
See Monteleone, Thomas F(rancis)
Lommasson, Robert C(urtis) 1917- 41-44R
Lomosia, Andrew
See Stern, Jay B(enjamin)
Lomperis, Timothy J. 1947- 126
Lomupo, Brother Robert 1939- 15-16R
London, Artur 1915-1986 .... CANR-12
Obituary 120
Earlier sketch in CA 65-68
London, Carolyn 1918- 57-60
London, H(oyt) H(obson) 1900- 49-52
London, Hannah R. 1894- 29-32R
London, Herbert I(ra) 1939- CANR-12
Earlier sketch in CA 33-36R
London, Jack 1915-1988 .... CANR-25
Obituary 126
Earlier sketch in CA 89-92
London, Jack
See London, John Griffith
See also SATA 18
See also DLB 8, 12
See also CDALB 1865-1917
See also TCLC 9, 15
See also AITN 2
London, Jane
See Geis, Darlene Stern
London, Joan 1901-1971 .... CAP-2
Earlier sketch in CA 25-28
London, John Griffith 1876-1916 119
Brief entry 110
London, Julius 1917- 118
London, Kurt L(udwig) 1900- CANR-6
Earlier sketch in CA 3R
London, Laura
See Curtis, Sharon
and Curtis, Thomas Dale
London, Mel 1923- CANR-24
Earlier sketch in CA 107
London, Perry 1931- 45-48
London, Roy 1946- 108
Londre, Felicia Hardison 1941- CANR-21
Earlier sketch in CA 105
Lonergan, Bernard J(oseph) F(rancis)
1904-1984 .... CANR-11
Obituary 114
Earlier sketch in CA 53-56
Lonergan, (Pauline) Joy (MacLean) 1909- 3R
See also SATA 10
Lonesome Cowboy
See White, John I(rwin)
Lone Star Ranger
See White, John I(rwin)
Lonette, Reisie (Dominee) 1924- SATA-43
Loney, Glenn (Meredith) 1928- CANR-14
Earlier sketch in CA 33-36R
Loney, Martin 1944- CANR-18
Earlier sketch in CA 102
Long, A(nthony) A(rthur) 1937- CANR-13
Earlier sketch in CA 33-36R
Long, Ann Marie
See Jensen, Pauline Marie (Long)
Long, Charles 1938- 65-68
Long, Charles R(ussell) 1904- CAP-1
Earlier sketch in CA 11-12
Long, Chester, Clayton 1932- 25-28R
Long, Clayton
See Long, Chester Clayton
Long, Cynthia 1956- 126
Long, David E(dwin) 1937- 89-92
Long, David F(oster) 1917- CANR-8
Earlier sketch in CA 61-64
Long, E(verette) B(each) 1919-1981 .... CANR-1
Obituary 103
Earlier sketch in CA 3R
Long, Earlene (Roberta) 1938- 126
See also SATA 50
Long, Edward LeRoy, Jr. 1924- CANR-22
Earlier sketches in CA 5-6R, CANR-7
Long, Emmett
See Leonard, Elmore
Long, Esmond R(ay) 1890-1979
Obituary 89-92
Long, Eugene Thomas (III) 1935- 25-28R
Long, Father Valentine W. 1902- 19-20R

Long, Fern ... CAP-2
Earlier sketch in CA 23-24
Long, Frank Belknap 1903- ... CANR-16
Earlier sketch in CA 81-84
Long, Frederick Lawrence 1917- ... 11-12R
Long, Haniel (Clark) 1888-1956
Brief entry ... 122
See also DLB 45
Long, Helen Beecher ... CANR-26
Earlier sketches in CA 19-20, CAP-2
See also SATA 1
Long, Howard Rusk 1906- ... CANR-3
Earlier sketch in CA 7-8R
Long, Huey P(ierce) 1893-1935
Brief entry ... 115
Long, J(ohn) C(uthbert) 1892- ... CAP-1
Earlier sketch in CA 9-10
Long, James M. 1907-1979 Obituary ... 85-88
Long, John D(ouglas) 1920- ... 17-18R
Long, John H(enderson) 1916- ... 13-14R
Long, John L(atham) 1932- ... 111
Long, Judith Elaine 1953- ... 65-68
See also SATA 20
Long, Judy
See Long,Judith Elaine
Long, Laura Mooney 1892-1967 Obituary ... 109
See also SATA 29
Long, Lois 1901-1974 Obituary ... 104
Long, Louise ... 37-40R
Long, Lucile
See Brandt, Lucile (Long Strayer)
Long, Luman H(arrison) 1907-1971 ... 108
Obituary ... 104
Long, M(olly) 1916- ... 23-24R
Long, Naomi Cornelia
See Madgett, Naomi Long
Long, Norton E. 1910- ... 45-48
Long, Priscilla 1943- ... 29-32R
Long, Ralph B(ernard) 1906- ... 5-6R
Long, Richard A(lexander) 1927- ... CANR-24
Earlier sketch in CA 37-40R
See also BW
Long, Robert 1954- ... 110
Long, Robert Emmet 1934- ... 122
Long, Steven 1944- ... 125
Long, T(heodore) Dixon 1933- ... 121
Brief entry ... 118
Long, Theodore E(dward) 1944- ... 126
Long, Thomas (Joseph) 1938- ... 119
Long, William Stuart
See Stuart, (Violet) Vivian (Finlay)
Longacre, Edward G(eorge) 1946- ... CANR-22
Earlier sketches in CA 53-56, CANR-5
Longacre, Robert E(dmondson) 1922- ... CANR-19
Earlier sketches in CA 53-56, CANR-4
Longacre, William A(tlas) II 1937- ... CANR-12
Earlier sketch in CA 29-32R
Longaker, Richard P(ancoast) 1924- ... CANR-1
Earlier sketch in CA 3R
Longbeard, Frederick
See Longyear, Barry Brookes
Longeaux y Vasquex, Enriqueta 1930- ... 57-60
Longenecker, Justin G. 1917- ... CANR-1
Earlier sketch in CA 2R
Longenecker, Richard N(orman) 1930- ... 15-16R
Longest, George C(alvin) 1938- ... 107
Longfellow, Henry Wadsworth
1807-1882 ... SATA-19
See also DLB 1, 59
See also CDALB 1640-1865
Longfellow, Samuel 1819-1892 ... DLB-1
Longford, Elizabeth Harmon 1906- ... 7-8R
Longgood, William (Frank) 1917- ... CANR-17
Earlier sketch in CA 2R
Longhurst, Henry Carpenter 1909-1978 ... 85-88
Obituary ... 81-84
Longino, Charles F(reeman), Jr.
1938- ... CANR-24
Earlier sketches in CA 53-56, CANR-7
Longland, Jean R(ogers) 1913- ... CANR-10
Earlier sketch in CA 21-22R
Longleigh, Peter J., Jr.
See Korges, James
Longley, John Lewis, Jr. 1920- ... 7-8R
Longley, Lawrence D(ouglas) 1939- ... 41-44R
Longley, Michael 1939- ... 102
See also DLB 40
See also CLC 29
Longley, Richmond W(ilberforce) 1907- ... 73-76
Longley, W. B.
See Randisi, Robert J(oseph)
Longman, Harold S. 1919- ... 25-28R
See also SATA 5
Longman, Lester Duncan 1905-1987
Obituary ... 121
Longman, Mark Frederic Kerr 1916-1972
Obituary ... 37-40R
Longmate, Norman Richard 1925- ... CANR-6
Earlier sketch in CA 9-10R
Longmore, Laura ... 7-8R
Long-Neck Woman
See Cheatham, K(aryn) Follis
Longo, Lucas 1919- ... 25-28R
Longrigg, Jane Chichester 1929- ... 9-10R
Longrigg, Roger (Erskine) 1929- ... CANR-3
Earlier sketch in CA 4R
Longrigg, Stephen Hemsley 1893-1979
Obituary ... 89-92
Longstreet, Augustus Baldwin
1790-1870 ... DLB-3, 11, 74
Longstreet, Stephen 1907- ... CANR-7
Earlier sketch in CA 9-10R
Longstreet, Wilma S. 1935- ... 93-96
Longstreth, Edward 1894-19(?) ... CAP-1
Earlier sketch in CA 15-16
Longstreth, T(homas) Morris 1886- ... 7-8R
Longsword, John
See Long, John Frederick Lawrence
Longsworth, Polly 1933- ... 106
See also SATA 28
Longsworth, Robert M. 1937- ... 21-22R
Longtemps, Kenneth 1933- ... SATA-17
Longway, A. Hugh
See Lang, Andrew
Longworth, Alice Lee (Roosevelt)
1884-1980 Obituary ... 93-96
Longworth, I(an) H(eaps) 1935- ... 120
Longworth, Philip 1933- ... CANR-10
Earlier sketch in CA 23-24R
Longworth, Richard C(ole) 1935- ... 85-88
Longyear, Barry Brookes 1942- ... 102
Longyear, Christopher R(udston) 1929- ... 105
Longyear, Marie Marcia Bernstein 1928- ... 115
Longyear, Rey M(organ) 1930- ... CANR-22
Earlier sketch in CA 45-48
Lonnbohm, Armas Eino Leopold
See Loennbohm, Armas Eino Leopold
Lonsdale, Adrian L. 1927- ... 15-16R
Lonsdale, Frederick 1881-1954 Brief entry ... 109
See also DLB 10
Lonsdale, Gordon Arnold 1923(?)-1970
Obituary ... 104
Lonsdale, Kathleen (Yardley) 1903-1971 ... 7-8R
Obituary ... 33-36R
Lonsdale, Richard E. 1926- ... CANR-13
Earlier sketch in CA 23-24R
Lonsdale, Steven (Hancock) 1952- ... 114
Look, Al 1893- ... 57-60
Look, Dennis 1949- ... 73-76
Looker, Antonina (Hansell) ... 29-32R
Looker, (Reginald) Earle 1895-1976 ... CAP-2
Obituary ... 65-68
Earlier sketch in CA 29-32
Lookout
See Noble, John (Appelbe)
Lookstein, Haskel 1932- ... 119
Loomba, N(arendra) Paul 1927- ... 57-60
Loomes, Brian 1938- ... CANR-12
Earlier sketch in CA 69-72
Loomie, Albert Joseph 1922- ... 5-6R
Loomis, Albertine (G.) 1895-1985 ... 93-96
Obituary ... 117
Loomis, Charles P(rice) 1905- ... CANR-13
Earlier sketch in CA 21-22R
Loomis, Chauncey C(hester), Jr. 1930- ... 33-36R
Loomis, Edward 1924- ... CANR-2
Earlier sketch in CA 1R
Loomis, Noel M(iller) 1905-1969 ... 3R
Obituary ... 25-28R
Loomis, Rae
See Steger, Shelby
Loomis, Robert D. ... 19-20R
See also SATA 5
Loomis, Roger Sherman 1887-1966 ... CANR-8
Earlier sketch in CA 7-8R
Loomis, Stanley 1922-1972 ... CAP-1
Obituary ... 37-40R
Earlier sketch in CA 11-12
Loomis, Zona Kemp 1911- ... 45-48
Looney, Robert E(dward) 1941- ... 104
Loory, Stuart H. 1932- ... 25-28R
Loos, Anita 1893(?)-1981 ... CANR-26
Obituary ... 104
Earlier sketch in CA 21-22R
See also DLB 11, 26
See also DLBY 81
See also AITN 1
Loos, Mary ... AITN-1
Loose, Gerhard 1907- ... 45-48
Loose, H.
See Lourie, Dick
Loots, Barbara Kunz 1946- ... 57-60
Loovis, David (Mactavish) 1926- ... CANR-1
Earlier sketch in CA 2R
Lopata, Helena Znaniecka 1925- ... 104
Lopate, Carol
See Ascher, Carol
Lopate, Phillip 1943- ... 97-100
See also DLBY 80
See also CLC 29
Lopatin, Judy 1954- ... 124
Loper, William C. 1927- ... 15-16R
Lopes, Michael 1943- ... 57-60
Lopez, Adalberto 1943- ... 103
Lopez, Andrew 1910-1986 Obituary ... 120
Lopez, Barry Holstun 1945- ... CANR-23
Earlier sketches in CA 65-68, CANR-7
Lopez, Cecilia L(uisa) 1941- ... 53-56
Lopez, Claude-Anne 1920- ... 104
Lopez, Ella B. 1900(?)-1978 Obituary ... 81-84
Lopez, Enrique 1921(?)-1985 Obituary ... 117
Lopez, Felix Manuel, Jr. 1917- ... 15-16R
Lopez, Manuel Dennis 1934- ... CANR-22
Earlier sketch in CA 105
Lopez, Nancy (Marie) 1957- Brief entry ... 113
Lopez, Robert S(abatino) 1910-1986
Obituary ... 119
Brief entry ... 112
Lopez, Vincent (Joseph) 1895-1975
Obituary ... 61-64
Lopez-Morillas, Juan 1913- ... CANR-1
Earlier sketch in CA 2R
Lopez Portillo (y Pacheco), Jose 1920- ... CLC-46
Lopez-Rey, Jose 1905- ... 37-40R
Lopez-Rey (y Arrojo), Manuel
1902-1987 ... 29-32R
Obituary ... 124
Lopez y Fuentes, Gregorio 1897-1966 ... CLC-32
Lopez Y Rivas, Gilberto 1943- ... 97-100
LoPiccolo, Joseph 1943- ... CANR-15
Earlier sketch in CA 81-84
Lo Pinto, Maria 1900(?)-1970 Obituary ... 104
Lopreato, Joseph 1928- ... 33-36R
Lopshire, Robert M(artin) 1927- ... CANR-8
Earlier sketch in CA 5-6R
See also SATA 6
Lopukhov, Fyodor V(asilevich) 1886-1973
Obituary ... 41-44R
Lora, Josephine
See Alexander, Josephine
Lora, Ronald 1938- ... 41-44R
Lorac, E. C. R.
See Rivett, Edith Caroline
Loram, Ian Craig 1917- ... 5-6R
Loran, Martin
See Baxter, John
Lorand, (Alexander) Sandor
1893(?)-1987 ... CAP-1
Obituary ... 123
Earlier sketch in CA 9-10
Lorang, Ruth Mary
See Lorang, Sister Mary Corde
Lorang, Sister Mary Corde 1904- ... 49-52
Lorant, Stefan 1901- ... CANR-9
Earlier sketch in CA 5-6R
See also AITN 1
Lorayne, Harry 1926- ... 41-44R
Lorberg, Aileen Dorothy 1910- ... CANR-2
Earlier sketch in CA 5-6R
Lorca, Federico Garcia
See Garcia Lorca, Federico
Lorch, Robert Stuart 1925- ... 73-76
Lord, Albert Bates 1912- ... 103
Lord, Athena V. 1932- ... 109
See also SATA 39
Lord, Beman 1924- ... 33-36R
See also SATA 5
Lord, Bette Bao 1938- ... 107
See also CLC 23
Lord, Clifford L(ee) 1912-1980 ... CANR-8
Obituary ... 102
Earlier sketch in CA 15-16R
Lord, Donald Charles 1930- ... 37-40R
Lord, (Doreen Mildred) Douglas 1904- ... CAP-1
Earlier sketch in CA 13-14
See also SATA 12
Lord, Douglas
See Cooper, Douglas
Lord, Eda 1907-1976 Obituary ... 104
Lord, Edith Elizabeth 1907- ... 41-44R
Lord, Eugene Hodgdon 1894- ... 4R
Lord, Francis A. 1911- ... 19-20R
Lord, Frederic Mather 1912- ... 37-40R
Lord, Gabrielle 1946- ... 106
Lord, George deF(orest) 1919- ... CANR-25
Earlier sketches in CA 65-68, CANR-10
Lord, Graham 1943- ... CANR-4
Earlier sketch in CA 53-56
Lord, Jeffrey
See Nelson, R(adell) Faraday
Lord, Jeremy
See Redman, Ben Ray
Lord, Jess R. 1911- ... 65-68
Lord, John Vernon 1939- ... 53-56
See also SATA 21
Lord, Mary Stinson Pillsbury 1904-1978 ... 85-88
Obituary ... 81-84
Lord, Nancy
See Titus, Eve
Lord, Phillips H.
See Yolen, Will (Hyatt)
Lord, Priscilla Sawyer 1908- ... 9-10R
Lord, Robert (Needham) 1945- ... 61-64
Lord, Shirley
See Rosenthal, Shirley Lord
Lord, Vivian
See Strother, Pat Wallace
Lord, Walter 1917- ... CANR-22
Earlier sketches in CA 3R, CANR-5
See also SATA 3
Lord, William Jackson, Jr. 1926- ... 7-8R
Lord Altrincham
See Grigg, John (Edward Poynder)
Lord Astor of Hever
See Astor, Gavin
Lord Auch
See Bataille, Georges
Lord Beveridge
See Beveridge, William (Henry)
Lord Blake
See Blake, Robert (Norman William)
Lord Boyle of Handsworth
See Boyle, Edward Charles Gurney
Lord Brooke
See Greville, Fulke
Lord Butler of Saffron Walden
See Butler, Richard Austen
Lord Chalfont
See Jones, (Alun) Arthur Gwynne
Lord Crowther-Hunt
See Crowther-Hunt, Norman Crowther
Lord Denning
See Denning, Alfred Thompson
Lord Dunsany
See Dunsany, Edward John Moreton
Drax Plunkett
See also TCLC 2
Lorde, Audre (Geraldine) 1934- ... CANR-26
Earlier sketches in CA 25-28R, CANR-16
See also BW
See also DLB 41
See also CLC 18
Lord Energlyn
See Evans, William David
Lord Evans of Hungershall
See Evans, Benjamin Ifor
Lord Francis Williams
See Williams, Edward Francis
Lord George-Brown
See George-Brown, George Alfred
Lord Hailsham of St. Marylebone
See Hogg, Quintin McGarel
Lord Home
See Home, Alexander Frederick
Lord Houghton
See Milnes, Richard Monckton
Lordi, Robert J(oseph) 1923- ... 89-92
Lord Killanin
See Morris, Michael
Lord Moran
See Wilson, (Richard) John (McMoran)
Lord Rhyl
See Birch, (Evelyn) Nigel (Chetwode)
Lord Snowdon
See Armstrong-Jones, Antony (Charles Robert)
Lord Strange
See Drummond, John
Lord Thomas
See Thomas, (William) Miles (Webster)
Lord Windlesham
See Hennessy, David James George
Loree, Kate (Lambie) 1920- ... 21-22R
Lorek, Daniel N. 1958(?)-1983 Obituary ... 110
Loren, Sophia 1934- Brief entry ... 111
Lorenz, Alfred Lawrence 1937- ... 45-48
Lorenz, J(ames) D(ouglas) 1938- ... 102
Lorenz, Konrad Zacharias 1903- ... 61-64
Lorenz, Lee (Sharp) 1932- Brief entry ... 124
See also SATA 39
Lorenz, Sarah E.
See Winston, Sarah
Lorenzen, Coral Elsie 1925- ... 113
Lorenzen, David N(eal) 1940- ... 33-36R
Lorenzini, Carlo 1826-1890 ... SATA-29
Lorenzo, Carol Lee 1939- ... 53-56
Loria, Jeffrey H. 1940- ... 19-20R
Lorie, James Hirsch 1922- ... 103
Lorig, Kate R. 1942- ... 117
Lorimer, Frank 1894-1985 Obituary ... 116
Lorimer, James 1942- ... 123
Lorimer, Lawrence T(heodore) 1941- ... CANR-6
Earlier sketch in CA 57-60
Lorimer, Scat
See Fuentes, Martha Ayers
Loring, Ann 1915- ... 97-100
Loring, Emilie (Baker) 1864(?)-1951 ... SATA-51
Loring, J. M.
See Warner-Crozetti, R(uth G.)
Loring, Murray 1917- ... CANR-22
Earlier sketch in CA 45-48
Lorion, R(aymond) P(aul) 1946- ... 85-88
Loris
See Hofmannsthal, Hugo von
Loris, Joseph James 1943-1987 Obituary ... 125
Lornquest, Olaf
See Rips, Ervine M(ilton)
Lorrah, Jean ... CANR-19
Earlier sketch in CA 103
Lorraine, Walter (Henry) 1929- ... SATA-16
Lorrance, Arleen 1939- ... 85-88
Lorrimer, Claire
See Robins, Patricia (Denise)
Lorsch, Jay William 1932- ... 97-100
Lorsch, Susan E. 1950- ... 116
Lortie, Dan C(lement) 1926- ... 115
Lortz, Richard 1917-1980 ... CANR-11
Obituary ... 102
Earlier sketch in CA 57-60
Lorwin, Val Rogin 1907-1982 Obituary ... 111
Lory, Robert (Edward) 1936- ... CANR-10
Earlier sketch in CA 53-56
Los, George
See Amabile, George
Losang, Rato Khyongla Ngawang 1923- ... 81-84
Lose, M(argaret) Phyllis 1925- ... CANR-18
Earlier sketch in CA 101
Losev, S(ergei) A(ndreevich) 1927-1988
Obituary ... 126
Losey, Joseph (Walton) 1909-1984
Obituary ... 113
Loshak, David (Leslie Ivor) 1933- ... 41-44R
Losoncy, Lawrence J. 1941- ... CANR-14
Earlier sketch in CA 37-40R
Losoncy, Mary Jan 1942- ... 37-40R
los Rios, Francisco Giner de
See Giner de los Rios, Francisco
Loss, Joan 1933- ... SATA-11
Loss, Louis 1914- ... CANR-2
Earlier sketch in CA 5-6R
Loss, Richard (Archibald John) 1938- ... 65-68
Lossing, Benson J. 1813-1891 ... DLB-30
Lossky, Andrew 1917- ... 93-96
Lossy, Rella 1934- ... 81-84
Loth, Calder 1943- ... 73-76
Loth, David 1899-1988 ... CANR-1
Obituary ... 125
Earlier sketch in CA 3R
Lothian, John Maule 1896-1970 ... CAP-1
Earlier sketch in CA 9-10
Lothringen, Geza Louis Eusebius Gebhard Ralphael Albert Maria von Habsburg
See von Habsburg-Lothringen, Geza Louis Eusebius Gebhard Ralphael Albert Maria
Lothrop, Harriet Mulford Stone
1844-1924 ... SATA-20
See also DLB 42
Lothstein, Leslie Martin 1942- ... 126
Loti, Pierre
See Viaud, (Louis Marie) Julien
See also TCLC 11
Lott, Arnold S(amuel) 1912- ... 15-16R
Lott, Bret 1958- ... 126
Lott, Davis Newton 1913- ... CANR-10
Earlier sketch in CA 21-22R
Lott, Milton 1919- ... 19-20R

Lott, Monroe
See Howard, Edwin
Lott, Robert E(ugene) 1926- ... CANR-4
Earlier sketch in CA 5-6R
Lottich, Kenneth V(erne) 1904- ... 19-20R
Lottie
See Grimke, Charlotte L(ottie) Forten
Lottinville, Savoie 1906- ... 105
Lottman, Eileen 1927- ... CANR-12
Earlier sketch in CA 57-60
Lottman, Herbert R. 1927- ... 105
Lotz, David W(alter) 1937- Brief entry ... 115
Lotz, James Robert 1929- ... CANR-14
Earlier sketch in CA 37-40R
Lotz, Jim
See Lotz, James Robert
Lotz, John 1913-1973 Obituary ... 45-48
Lotz, Wolfgang 1912- ... 81-84
Louch, A(lfred) R(ichard) 1927- ... 19-20R
Louchheim, Kathleen 1903- ... 21-22R
Louchheim, Katie
See Louchheim, Kathleen
Loucks, William Negele 1899- ... 2R
Loud, Pat(ricia Russell) 1926- Brief entry ... 114
Louden, Robert Stuart 1912- ... 7-8R
Loudon, Irvine 1924- ... 126
Lougee, Robert Wayne 1919- ... 5-6R
Loughary, John W(illiam) 1930- ... 41-44R
Loughead, LaRue A(lvin) 1927- ... 61-64
Loughlin, Caroline 1940- ... 126
Loughlin, Richard L(awrence) 1907- ... CANR-21
Earlier sketch in CA 45-48
Loughmiller, Campbell 1906- ... CANR-13
Earlier sketch in CA 77-80
Loughran, Bernice B(ingham) 1919- ... 7-8R
Loughran, Peter 1938- ... 25-28R
Lougy, Robert E. 1940- ... 118
Louie, Ai-Ling 1949- ... 112
See also SATA 34, 40
Louis, Arthur M(urray) 1938- ... 106
Louis, Debbie 1945- ... 29-32R
Louis, Father M.
See Merton, Thomas
Louis, J(ack) C(harles), Jr. 1949- ... 105
Louis, Joe
See Barrow, Joseph Louis
Louis, Murray 1926- ... 126
Louis, Pat
See Francis, Dorothy Brenner
Louis, Paul P(anickavede) 1918- ... CANR-12
Earlier sketch in CA 61-64
Louis, Pierre(-Felix) 1870-1925 Brief entry ... 105
Louis, Ray Baldwin 1949- ... 65-68
Louis, Tobi 1940- ... 57-60
Louisburgh, Sheila Burnford
See Burnford, Sheila (Philip Cochrane Every)
Louisell, David William 1913-1977 ... CANR-4
Obituary ... 73-76
Earlier sketch in CA 2R
Loukes, Harold 1912- ... 17-18R
Lounsbury, Myron O. 1940- ... 37-40R
Lounsbury, Thomas R. 1838-1915 ... DLB-71
Loup, Jacques 1942- ... 120
Louria, Donald B(ruce) 1928- ... 107
Lourie, Dick 1937- ... 33-36R
Lourie, Helen
See Storr, Catherine (Cole)
Lourie, Richard 1940- Brief entry ... 125
Lousley, J(ob) E(dward) 1907-1976
Obituary ... 104
Louthan, Robert 1951- ... 109
Louviere, Vernon Ray 1920- ... 108
Louvish, Misha 1909- ... CANR-1
Earlier sketch in CA 45-48
Louvish, Simon 1947- ... 121
Louw, Nicholaas Petrus Van Wyk
1906-1970 Obituary ... 89-92
Loux, Michael Joseph 1942- ... 103
Louys, Pierre
See Louis, Pierre(-Felix)
Lovaas, O(le) Ivar 1927- ... CANR-22
Earlier sketch in CA 45-48
Lovasik, Lawrence George 1913- ... CANR-20
Earlier sketches in CA 3R, CANR-1
Lovatt, Edwin A(lbert) 1944- ... 119
Love, Alan C(arson) 1937- ... 53-56
Love, Barbara J. 1937- ... 37-40R
Love, Charles (Ross) 1932- ... 25-28R
Love, Charles K.
See Swicegood, Thomas L. P.
Love, Edmund G(eorge) 1912- ... CANR-4
Earlier sketch in CA 4R
Love, Glen A. 1932- ... 29-32R
Love, Iris Cornelia 1933- ... 29-32R
Love, Janet
See Ferrier, Janet Mackay
Love, Jean O. 1920- ... 29-32R
Love, Joseph L., (Jr.) 1938- ... 29-32R
Love, Katherine (Isabel) 1907- ... SATA-3
Love, Kennett 1924- ... 77-80
Love, Philip H(ampton) 1905-1977 ... 77-80
Obituary ... 73-76
Love, Richard S. 1923- ... 81-84
Love, Sandra (Weller) 1940- ... CANR-11
Earlier sketch in CA 69-72
See also SATA 26
Love, Sydney F(rancis) 1923- ... 81-84
Love, Thomas Teel 1931- ... 15-16R
Lovecraft, H(oward) P(hillips) 1890-1937
Brief entry ... 104
See also TCLC 4, 22
Lovegrove, Philip
See Ray, John (Philip)
Lovehill, C. B.
See Beaumont, Charles
Lovejoy, Bahija Fattuhi 1914- ... 5-6R
Lovejoy, Clarence Earle 1894-1974 ... 5-6R
Obituary ... 45-48
Lovejoy, David Sherman 1919- ... 103
Lovejoy, Elijah P(arish) 1940- ... 45-48
Lovejoy, Jack 1937- ... 114
Lovejoy, L(awrence) C(lark) 1893- ... 3R
Lovejoy, Paul E(llsworth) 1943- ... 115
Lovelace, Delos Wheeler 1894-1967 ... 7-8R
Obituary ... 25-28R
See also SATA 7
Lovelace, Earl 1935- ... 77-80
Lovelace, Linda
See Marciano, Linda Boreman
Lovelace, Marc Hoyle 1920- ... 37-40R
Lovelace, Maud Hart 1892-1980 ... 7-8R
Obituary ... 104
See also SATA 2, 23
Lovelace, Richard Franz 1930- ... 101
Loveland, Anne C(arol) 1938- ... 126
Brief entry ... 114
Loveless, E(dward) E. 1919- ... 57-60
Lovell, Ann 1933- ... CANR-19
Earlier sketch in CA 97-100
Lovell, (Alfred Charles) Bernard 1913- ... CANR-6
Earlier sketch in CA 13-14R
Lovell, Colin Rhys 1917- ... 5-6R
Lovell, Ernest J(ames), Jr. 1918-1975 ... 4R
Obituary ... 103
Lovell, Ingraham
See Bacon, Josephine Dodge (Daskam)
Lovell, John, Jr. 1907-1974 ... CAP-2
Obituary ... 49-52
Earlier sketch in CA 33-36
Lovell, John P(hilip) 1932- ... CANR-15
Earlier sketch in CA 29-32R
Lovell, Marc
See McShane, Mark
Lovell, Mark 1934- ... CANR-8
Earlier sketch in CA 61-64
Lovell, Michael Christopher 1930- ... 33-36R
Lovell, Ronald P. 1937- ... CANR-13
Earlier sketch in CA 73-76
Lovell, Stanley P(latt) 1890- ... 5-6R
Lovelock, J. E.
See Lovelock, James (Ephraim)
Lovelock, James (Ephraim) 1919- ... 123
Loveman, Brian E(lliot) 1944- ... CANR-17
Earlier sketch in CA 89-92
Loveman, Samuel 1885(?)-1976 Obituary ... 65-68
Lovenstein, Meno 1909- ... CANR-3
Earlier sketch in CA 7-8R
Lovequist, Gwendlelynn
See Stafford, Linda (Crying Wind)
Loverde, Lorin (James Bell) 1943- ... 45-48
Loveridge, Ronald O. 1938- ... 33-36R
Lovering, Joseph Paul 1921- ... 104
Lovesey, Peter (Harmer) 1936- ... 41-44R
Lovestrand, Harold 1925- ... 21-22R
Lovett, A(lbert) W(inston) 1944- ... 124
Lovett, Clara Maria 1939- ... CANR-16
Earlier sketch in CA 93-96
Lovett, Gabriel H(arry) 1921- ... 65-68
Lovett, Margaret (Rose) 1915- ... 61-64
See also SATA 22
Lovett, Robert W. 1913- ... 33-36R
Lovin, Clifford R(amsey) 1937- ... 37-40R
Lovin, Roger Robert 1941- ... CANR-6
Earlier sketch in CA 57-60
Loving, Jerome MacNeill 1941- ... 112
Lovins, Amory B(loch) 1947- ... 69-72
Lovoll, Odd Sverre 1934- ... CANR-7
Earlier sketch in CA 61-64
Lovoos, Janice
See Garbutt, Janice (D.) Lovoos
Low, Alfred D(avid) 1913- ... 33-36R
Low, Alice 1926- ... CANR-8
Earlier sketch in CA 61-64
See also SATA 11
Low, Ann Marie 1912- ... 118
Low, Anthony 1935- ... CANR-13
Earlier sketch in CA 37-40R
Low, D(onald) A(nthony) 1927- ... 73-76
Low, David (Alexander Cecil) 1891-1963
Obituary ... 89-92
Low, Dorothy Mackie
See Low, Lois Dorothea
Low, Elizabeth Hammond 1898- ... CAP-2
Earlier sketch in CA 19-20
See also SATA 5
Low, Francis 1893-1972 Obituary ... 115
Low, Gardner
See Rodda, Charles
Low, George M(ichael) 1926-1984
Obituary ... 113
Low, Ivy
See Litvinov, Ivy
Low, Joseph 1911- ... CANR-15
Earlier sketch in CA 85-88
See also SATA 14
Low, Lois Dorothea 1916- ... CANR-15
Earlier sketch in CA 37-40R
Low, Rachael 1923- ... 125
Low, Samuel 1765-? ... DLB-37
Low, Victor N. 1931- ... CANR-1
Earlier sketch in CA 49-52
Lowance, Mason I(ra), Jr. 1938- ... 57-60
Lowbury, Edward (Joseph Lister)
1913- ... CANR-12
Earlier sketch in CA 29-32R
Lowden, Desmond 1937- ... 53-56
Lowder, Jerry 1932- ... 65-68
Lowder, Paul D(aniel) 1929- ... 93-96
Lowdermilk, W(alter) C(lay) 1888-1974
Obituary ... 49-52
Lowe, Alfonso
See Loewenthal, L(eonard) J(oseph A(lfonso)
Lowe, C(arrington) Marshall 1930- ... 29-32R
Lowe, Carl 1949- ... 125
Lowe, Corke
See Pepper, Choral
Lowe, David (Garrard) 1933- ... CANR-22
Earlier sketch in CA 104
Lowe, David A(llan) 1948- ... 111
Lowe, Donald M. 1928- ... 21-22R
Lowe, Gordon R(obb) 1928- ... 49-52
Lowe, Gustav E. 1901- ... CAP-2
Earlier sketch in CA 23-24
Lowe, Henry Paget
See Lovecraft, H(oward) P(hillips)
Lowe, Jay, Jr.
See Loeper, John J(oseph)
Lowe, Jeanne R. 1924(?)-1972
Obituary ... 33-36R
Lowe, John (Evelyn) 1928- ... 123
Lowe, John W(esley) G(uinn) 1946- ... 121
Lowe, Judah
See Lyon, Christopher (Leslie)
Lowe, Marjorie G(riffiths) Lowe 1909- ... 4R
Lowe, Richard Barrett 1902-1972
Obituary ... 33-36R
Lowe, Richard G. 1942- ... 123
Lowe, Robert W. 1910- ... CAP-1
Earlier sketch in CA 13-14
Lowe, Roberta (Justine) 1940- ... CANR-24
Earlier sketches in CA 61-64, CANR-8
Lowe, Sue Davidson 1922- ... 118
Lowe, Victor (Augustus) 1907- ... 17-18R
Lowe, Victoria Lincoln
See Lincoln, Victoria
Lowe, William T(ebbs) 1929- ... 73-76
Lowell, Amy 1874-1925 Brief entry ... 104
See also DLB 54
See also TCLC 1, 8
Lowell, C. Stanley 1909- ... CANR-6
Earlier sketch in CA 5-6R
Lowell, James Russell
1819-1891 ... DLB-1, 11, 64
See also CDALB 1640-1865
Lowell, Jon 1938- ... 97-100
Lowell, Juliet 1901- ... CANR-1
Earlier sketch in CA 3R
Lowell, Mildred Hawksworth 1905-1974 ... CAP-2
Earlier sketch in CA 33-36
Lowell, Robert (Traill Spence, Jr.)
1917-1977 ... CANR-26
Obituary ... 73-76
Earlier sketch in CA 9-10R
See also CABS 2
See also DLB 5
See also CLC 1, 2, 3, 4, 5, 8, 9, 11, 15, 37
Lowell, Susan 1950- ... 126
Lowell, Tex
See Turner, George E(ugene)
Lowen, Alexander 1910- ... 19-20R
Lowenfeld, Andreas F(rank) 1930- ... CANR-8
Earlier sketch in CA 61-64
Lowenfeld, Berthold 1901- ... 17-18R
Lowenfels, Walter 1897-1976 ... CANR-3
Obituary ... 65-68
Earlier sketch in CA 1R
See also DLB 4
Lowenfish, Lee (Elihu) 1942- ... 106
Lowenkopf, Shelly A(lan) 1931- ... CANR-4
Earlier sketch in CA 49-52
Lowens, Irving 1916-1983 ... CANR-11
Obituary ... 111
Earlier sketch in CA 17-18R
Lowenstein, Dyno 1914- ... 9-10R
See also SATA 6
Lowenstein, Hubertus (Prinz) zu
See Loewenstein(-Wertheim-Freudenberg), Hubertus (Friedrich Maria Johannes Leopold Ludwig) zu
Lowenstein, Ralph Lynn 1930- ... 17-18R
Lowenstein, Sharon R. 1937- ... 122
Lowenstein, Tom 1941- ... 93-96
Lowenthal, David 1923- ... 115
Lowenthal, Leo 1900- ... CANR-20
Earlier sketches in CA 2R, CANR-5
Lowenthal, Marjorie Fiske
See Fiske, Marjorie
Lower, Arthur R(eginald) M(arsden)
1889-1988 ... CANR-4
Obituary ... 124
Earlier sketch in CA 11-12R
Lower, J(oseph) Arthur 1907- ... 23-24R
Lowery, Bruce Arlie 1931- ... CANR-1
Earlier sketch in CA 2R
Lowery, Daniel L(orne) 1929- ... 113
Lowery, James L(incoln), Jr. 1932- ... 45-48
Lowery, Lynn 1949- ... 93-96
Lowery, Thomas V(incent) 1919- ... 37-40R
Lowi, Theodore J(ay) 1931- ... 37-40R
Lowing, Anne
See Geach, Christine
Lowinsky, Edward E(lias) 1908-1985 ... CAP-1
Obituary ... 117
Earlier sketch in CA 13-14
Lowith, Karl
See Loewith, Karl
Lowitz, Anson C. 1901(?)-1978 ... 81-84
Obituary ... 73-76
See also SATA 18
Lowitz, Sadyebeth Heath 1901-1969 ... 85-88
See also SATA 17
Lowman, Charles LeRoy 1880(?)-1977
Obituary ... 69-72
Lowman, Eleanor B(arry) 1906-1983
Obituary ... 110
Lowman, Josephine (Cherry)
1899(?)-1983 Obituary ... 110
Lowndes, Betty 1929- ... 61-64
Lowndes, George Alfred Norman 1897- ... 7-8R
Lowndes, Marie Adelaide (Belloc)
1868-1947 Brief entry ... 107
See also DLB 70
See also TCLC 12
Lowndes, Robert A(ugustine) W(ard)
1916- Brief entry ... 113
Lowndes, William 1914- ... 13-14R
Lowney, Paul Benjamin 1922- ... CANR-17
Earlier sketch in CA 93-96
Lowrey, Janette Sebring 1892- ... 13-14R
See also SATA 43
Lowrey, Kathleen 1943- ... 57-60
Lowrey, P(errin) H(olmes) 1923-1965 ... CAP-1
Earlier sketch in CA 11-12
Lowrey, Sara 1897- ... 17-18R
Lowrie, Donald A(lexander) 1889-1974 ... 5-6R
Obituary ... 53-56
Lowrie, Jean E(lizabeth) 1918- ... 45-48
Lowry, Albert J(ames) 1927- Brief entry ... 118
Lowry, Bates 1923- ... CANR-1
Earlier sketch in CA 3R
Lowry, Beverly (Fey) 1938- ... 101
Lowry, Charles W(esley) 1905- ... 37-40R
Lowry, Fern 1896(?)-1983 Obituary ... 111
Lowry, Joan (Catlow) 1911- ... 13-14R
Lowry, Lois 1937- ... CANR-13
Earlier sketch in CA 69-72
See also SATA 23
See also SAAS 3
See also DLB 52
See also CLR 6
Lowry, (Clarence) Malcolm 1909-1957
Brief entry ... 105
See also DLB 15
See also TCLC 6
Lowry, Martin John Clement 1940- ... 107
Lowry, Mina Gertrude 1882-1966 ... 113
Lowry, Nan
See MacLeod, Ruth
Lowry, Peter 1953- ... 49-52
See also SATA 7
Lowry, Ritchie P(eter) 1926- ... 17-18R
Lowry, Robert (James Collas) 1919- ... 61-64
Lowry, S(tanley) Todd 1927- ... 126
Lowry, Shirley Park 1933- ... 109
Lowry, Thomas P. 1932- ... 21-22R
Lowther, George F. 1913-1975 Obituary ... 57-60
See also SATA 30
Lowther, Kevin G(eorge) 1941- ... 81-84
Lowther, Pat 1935-1975 ... DLB-53
Lowy, George 1924- ... 17-18R
Loxmith, John
See Brunner, John (Kilian Houston)
Loxton, (Charles) Howard 1934- ... CANR-11
Earlier sketch in CA 25-28R
Loy, J(ohn) Robert 1918- Brief entry ... 108
Loy, Jane M.
See Rausch, Jane M(eyer)
Loy, Mina
See Lowry, Mina Gertrude
See also DLB 4, 54
See also CLC 28
Loyd, Marianne 1955- ... 115
Loye, David (Elliot) 1925- ... 33-36R
Loyn, H(enry) R(oyston) 1922- ... 117
Loyn, Henry
See Loyn, H(enry) R(oyston)
Loyn, Henry R.
See Loyn, H(enry) R(oyston)
Loyson-Bridet
See Schwob, (Mayer Andre) Marcel
Lozano, Wendy 1941- ... 102
Lozier, Herbert 1915- ... 49-52
See also SATA 26
Lozowick, Louis 1892-1973 Obituary ... 107
Lu, David J(ohn) 1928- ... CANR-5
Earlier sketch in CA 9-10R
Lu, K'uan-yu
See Luk, Charles
Lu, Paul Hsien 1926- ... 41-44R
Luard, (David) Evan (Trant) 1926- ... CANR-1
Earlier sketch in CA 4R
Luard, Nicholas 1937- ... 85-88
Lubalin, Herb(ert Frederick) 1918-1981
Obituary ... 104
Lubans, John, Jr. 1941- ... 57-60
Lubar, Joel F. 1938- ... 37-40R
Lubar, Robert 1920- ... 73-76
Lubbe, Catherine Case ... AITN-1
Lubbock, (Mary Katherine) Adelaide
1906- ... 29-32R
Lubbock, Mark Hugh 1898-1986 Obituary ... 121
Lubbock, Percy 1879-1965 ... 85-88
Lubeck, Steven G. 1944- ... 29-32R
Lubell, Cecil 1912- ... CANR-4
Earlier sketch in CA 9-10R
See also SATA 6
Lubell, Harold 1925- ... 9-10R
Lubell, Samuel 1911-1987 ... 15-16R
Obituary ... 123
Lubell, Winifred (A. Milius) 1914- ... CANR-4
Earlier sketch in CA 49-52
See also SATA 6
Lubenow, William (Cornelius) 1939-
Brief entry ... 107
Luber, Philip 1948- ... 124
Lubetski, Edith 1940- ... 112
Lubetski, Meir 1938- ... 112
Lubin, Bernard 1923- ... CANR-9
Earlier sketch in CA 21-22R
Lubin, David M. 1950- ... 120
Lubin, Ernest 1916-1977 ... 41-44R
Lubin, Isador 1896-1978 Obituary ... 77-80
Lubin, Leonard
See Lubin, Leonard B.

Lubin, Leonard B. 1943- ... 125
Brief entry ... 115
See also SATA 37, 45
Lubis, Mochtar 1922- ... 29-32R
Lubitz, Raymond 1937-1984 Obituary ... 113
Lubove, Roy 1934- ... 23-24R
Lubow, Robert E. 1932- ... 77-80
Lubowe, Irwin I(rville) 1905- ... 53-56
Lubrano, Linda L. 1943- ... 126
Brief entry ... 108
Lucas, Alec 1913- ... 101
Lucas, Barbara
See Wall, Barbara
Lucas, Bryan Keith
See Keith-Lucas, Bryan
Lucas, C. Payne 1933- ... 85-88
Lucas, Carol 1929- ... 17-18R
Lucas, Celia 1938- ... CANR-24
Earlier sketch in CA 107
Lucas, Christopher J(ohn) 1940- ... 25-28R
Lucas, D(onald) W(illiam) 1905-1985 ... CAP-1
Obituary ... 116
Earlier sketch in CA 13-14
Lucas, Darrel B(laine) 1902- ... CAP-1
Earlier sketch in CA 9-10
Lucas, Dione (Narnona Margaris Wilson)
1909-1971 Obituary ... 104
Lucas, E(dna) Louise 1899-1970 ... CAP-2
Earlier sketch in CA 25-28
Lucas, E(dward) V(errall) 1868-1938 ... SATA-20
Lucas, F(rank) L(aurence) 1894-1967 ... CANR-4
Obituary ... 25-28R
Earlier sketch in CA 4R
Lucas, George 1944- ... 77-80
See also CLC 16
Lucas, Hans
See Godard, Jean-Luc
Lucas, Henry C(ameron), Jr. 1944- ... 109
Lucas, J. K.
See Paine, Lauran (Bosworth)
Lucas, J(ohn) R(andolph) 1929- ... CANR-11
Earlier sketch in CA 23-24R
Lucas, J(ames) R(aymond) 1950- ... 118
Lucas, Jason 1904- ... CAP-1
Earlier sketch in CA 9-10
Lucas, Jeremy 1953- ... 108
Lucas, Jerry 1940- ... 108
See also SATA 33
Lucas, Jim Griffing 1914-1970 Obituary ... 104
Lucas, John 1937- ... CANR-14
Earlier sketch in CA 37-40R
Lucas, Joseph 1928- ... 69-72
Lucas, Joyce 1927- ... 57-60
Lucas, Lawrence E(dward) 1933- ... 65-68
Lucas, Marion B(runson) 1935- ... 81-84
Lucas, Martin 1944- ... 111
Lucas, N. B. C. 1901- ... 81-84
Lucas, Noah 1927- ... 57-60
Lucas, Robert 1904-1984 ... 101
Obituary ... 111
Lucas, Robert Emerson, Jr. 1937- ... 107
Lucas, Robert Harold 1933- ... 37-40R
Lucas, Ruth (Baxendale) 1909- ... CAP-2
Earlier sketch in CA 19-20
Lucas, Scott 1937- ... 93-96
Lucas, Stephen E. 1946- ... 125
Lucas, T(homas) E(dward) 1919- ... 77-80
Lucas, Victoria
See Plath, Sylvia
Lucas, W(ilmer) F(rancis, Jr.) 1927- ... 77-80
See also BW
Lucash, Frank S. 1938- ... 120
Lucas Phillips, C(ecil) E(rnest)
1897-1984 ... CANR-3
Obituary ... 112
Earlier sketch in CA 4R
Lucchesi, Aldo
See von Block, Bela W(illiam)
Luce, Celia (Geneva Larsen) 1914- ... 61-64
See also SATA 38
Luce, Clare Boothe 1903-1987 ... 45-48
Obituary ... 123
Luce, Don 1934- ... CANR-12
Earlier sketch in CA 29-32R
Luce, Gay Gaer 1930- ... 103
Luce, Henry R(obinson) 1898-1967 ... 104
Obituary ... 89-92
Luce, J(ohn) V(ictor) 1920- ... 61-64
Luce, Willard (Ray) 1914- ... 61-64
See also SATA 38
Luce, William (Aubert) 1931- ... CANR-25
Earlier sketches in CA 65-68, CANR-11
Lucente, Gregory L. 1948- ... 120
Lucentini, Mauro 1924- ... 69-72
Lucero, Roberto
See Meredith, Robert C(hidester)
Lucey, James D(ennis) 1923- ... 25-28R
Lu-ch'iao
See Wu, Nelson I(kon)
Luchins, Abraham S(amuel) 1914- ... CANR-11
Earlier sketch in CA 69-72
Luchins, Edith H(irsch) 1921- ... CANR-11
Earlier sketch in CA 19-20R
Luchsinger, Elaine King 1902- ... CAP-2
Earlier sketch in CA 17-18
Lucia, Ellis (Joel) 1922- ... CANR-22
Earlier sketches in CA 2R, CANR-4
Lucia, Salvatore Pablo 1901-1984 ... 13-14R
Obituary ... 112
Luciani, Vincent 1906- ... 61-64
Lucid, Robert F(rancis) 1930- ... 25-28R
Lucie-Smith, (John) Edward (McKenzie)
1933- ... CANR-7
Earlier sketch in CA 15-16R
See also DLB 40
Luck, David Johnston 1912- ... CANR-4
Earlier sketch in CA 53-56
Luck, G(eorge) Coleman 1913- ... 15-16R
Luck, George Hans 1926- ... 7-8R
Luck, Thomas Jefferson 1922- ... 5-6R
Luckert, Karl W(ilhelm) 1934- ... 81-84
Luckett, Hubert Pearson 1916- ... 77-80
Luckett, Karen Beth 1944- ... 77-80
Luckey, Eleanore Braun 1915- ... 33-36R
Luckhardt, C(harles) Grant 1943- ... 93-96
Luckhardt, Mildred Corell 1898- ... 15-16R
See also SATA 5
Luckless, John
See Burkholz, Herbert
and Irving, Clifford Michael
Luckmann, Thomas 1927- ... CANR-19
Earlier sketch in CA 101
Luckock, Elizabeth 1914- ... 21-22R
Luckyj, George S(tephen) N(estor)
1919- ... CANR-21
Earlier sketch in CA 45-48
Ludden, Allen (Ellsworth) 1918(?)-1981
Obituary ... 104
See also SATA 27
Ludel, Jacqueline 1945- ... 111
Luder, William Fay 1910- ... 29-32R
Ludington, (Charles) Townsend 1936- ... CANR-25
Earlier sketches in CA 45-48, CANR-9
Ludlam, Charles 1943-1987 ... 85-88
Obituary ... 122
See also CLC 46, 50
Ludlow, Geoffrey
See Meynell, Laurence Walter
Ludlow, George
See Kay, Ernest
Ludlow, Howard T(homas) 1921- ... 23-24R
Ludlow, James Minor 1917-1974
Obituary ... 53-56
Ludlum, Mabel Cleland
See Widdemer, Mabel Cleland
Ludlum, Robert 1927- ... CANR-25
Earlier sketch in CA 33-36R
See also DLBY 82
See also CLC 22, 43
Ludlum, Robert P(hillips) 1909-1987 ... CAP-1
Obituary ... 122
Earlier sketch in CA 15-16
Ludmerer, Kenneth M. 1947- ... 45-48
Ludovici, Anthony M(ario) 1882-19(?) ... CAP-1
Earlier sketch in CA 11-12
Ludovici, L. J.
See Ludovici, Lorenz James
Ludovici, Laurence James
See Ludovici, Lorenz James
Ludovici, Lorenz James 1910- ... CANR-10
Earlier sketch in CA 23-24R
Ludowyk, E(velyn) F(rederick) C(harles)
1906-1985 ... CAP-1
Obituary ... 117
Earlier sketch in CA 11-12
Ludtke, James Buren 1924- ... 2R
Ludvigsen, Karl (Eric- 1934- ... 73-76
Ludvigson, Susan 1942- ... CANR-7
Earlier sketch in CA 57-60
Ludwig, Charles Shelton 1918- ... CANR-20
Earlier sketches in CA 9-10R, CANR-5
Ludwig, Ed(ward William) 1920- ... 97-100
Ludwig, Eric
See Grunwald, Stefan
Ludwig, Frederic
See Grunwald, Stefan
Ludwig, Helen ... SATA-33
Ludwig, Jack 1922- ... CANR-1
Earlier sketch in CA 4R
See also DLB 60
Ludwig, Jerry 1934- ... 81-84
Ludwig, Lyndell 1923- ... 115
Ludwig, Myles Eric 1942- ... 25-28R
Ludwig, Richard M(ilton) 1920- ... 19-20R
Ludwigson, Kathryn Romaine 1921- ... CANR-6
Earlier sketch in CA 53-56
Luebke, Frederick Carl 1927- ... CANR-12
Earlier sketch in CA 33-36R
Luecke, Janemarie 1924- ... CANR-21
Earlier sketch in CA 104
Lueders, Edward (George) 1923- ... CANR-5
Earlier sketch in CA 15-16R
See also SATA 14
Luedtke, Kurt (Mamre) 1939- ... 111
Brief entry ... 109
Lueker, Erwin L(ouis) 1914- ... CANR-23
Earlier sketches in CA 17-18R, CANR-8
Luening, Otto 1900- ... 102
Luenn, Nancy 1954- ... 116
See also SATA 51
Lueschen, Guenther R(udolf) 1930- ... CANR-4
Earlier sketch in CA 53-56
Luescher, Max 1923- ... 101
Luetgen, Kurt (Bodo Heinrich) 1911- ... 108
Luethi, Max 1909- ... 29-32R
Luetzelschwab, John (William) 1940- ... 121
Brief entry ... 118
Lufburrow, William 1931(?)-1986
Obituary ... 118
Luff, S(tanley) G(eorge) A(nthony) 1921- ... 9-10R
Lufkin, Raymond H. 1897- ... SATA-38
Luft, David Sheers 1944- ... 106
Lugard, Flora Louisa Shaw 1852-1929 ... SATA-21
Luger, Harriett Mandelay 1914- ... CANR-1
Earlier sketch in CA 45-48
See also SATA 23
Lugg, George Wilson 1902- ... 105
Lugo, Ariel E(milio) 1943- ... 41-44R
Lugo, James O. 1928- ... 29-32R
Lugones, Leopoldo 1874-1938 Brief entry ... 116
See also TCLC 15
Lugt, Herbert Vander
See Vander Lugt, Herbert
Luhr, William 1946- ... 106
Luhrmann, Winifred B(ruce) 1934- ... 61-64
See also SATA 11
Lu Hsun 1881-1936 ... TCLC-3
Luick, John F(rancis) 1920- ... 25-28R
Luis, Earlene W. 1929- ... 61-64
See also SATA 11
Luisada, Aldo A(ugusto) 1901-1987
Obituary ... 124
Luisi, Billie M(eisner) 1940- ... 73-76
Luk, Charles 1898- ... 9-10R
Luka, Ronald 1937- ... 61-64
Lukach, Joan M(ickelson) 1935- ... 118
Lukacher, Ned 1950- ... 120
Lukacs, Georg
See Lukacs, Gyorgy
Lukacs, George
See Lukacs, Gyorgy
See also CLC 24
Lukacs, Gyorgy 1885-1971 ... 101
Obituary ... 29-32R
Lukacs, John (Adalbert) 1923- ... CANR-17
Earlier sketches in CA 3R, CANR-1
Lukaczer, Moses 1911-1984 Obituary ... 112
Lukas, Charlotte Koplinka 1954- ... 93-96
Lukas, Ellen ... 97-100
Lukas, J(ay) Anthony 1933- ... CANR-19
Earlier sketches in CA 49-52, CANR-2
Lukas, Mary ... 101
Lukas, Richard C. 1937- ... 33-36R
Lukas, Susan 1940- ... 53-56
Lukashevich, Stephen 1931- ... 33-36R
Luke, Hugh J(ay) 1932- ... 89-92
Luke, Mary M. 1919- ... CANR-14
Earlier sketch in CA 23-24R
Luke, Peter (Ambrose Cyprian) 1919- ... 81-84
See also DLB 13
See also CLC 38
Luke, Thomas
See Masterton, Graham
Lukenbill, Willis B(ernard) 1939- ... 103
Luker, Kristin Carol 1946- ... 61-64
Lukes, Steven (Michael) 1941- ... CANR-16
Earlier sketch in CA 93-96
Lukodianov, Isai (Borisovich) 1913- ... 101
Lukonin, Mikhail K. 1920(?)-1977
Obituary ... 69-72
Lum, Peter
See Crowe, Bettina Lum
Lumian, Norman C. 1928- ... 29-32R
Lumiansky, R(obert) M(ayer) 1913-1987
Obituary ... 122
Lumley, Brian 1937- Brief entry ... 120
Lummis, Keith 1904- ... 104
Lumpkin, Angela 1950- ... 112
Lumpkin, Grace ... 69-72
Lumpkin, Henry H(ope) 1913- ... 122
Lumpkin, William Latane 1916- ... CANR-4
Earlier sketch in CA 2R
Lumsden, Charles J(ohn) 1949- ... 111
Lumsden, D(an) Barry 1939- ... CANR-21
Earlier sketch in CA 45-48
Lunan, Duncan (Alasdair) 1945- ... 107
Lunar, Dennis
See Mungo, Raymond
Lunch, Lydia (a pseudonym) 1959- ... 115
Lund, A. Morten 1926- ... 13-14R
Lund, Doris Herold 1919- ... 17-18R
See also SATA 12
Lund, Gerald N. 1939- ... CANR-13
Earlier sketch in CA 33-36R
Lund, Gilda E. 1909- ... 7-8R
Lund, Herb(ert Frederick) 1926- ... 45-48
Lund, James
See Stonehouse, John (Thomson)
Lund, Philip R(eginald) 1938- ... 57-60
Lund, Robert P. 1915- ... 2R
Lund, Robert T. 1924- ... 126
Lund, Thomas A. 1922- ... 33-36R
Lundahl, Gene 1933- ... 21-22R
Lundberg, Dan
See Lundberg, Daniel
Lundberg, Daniel 1912-1986 ... 114
Obituary ... 119
Lundberg, Donald E(mil) 1916- ... CANR-12
Earlier sketch in CA 33-36R
Lundberg, Erik F(ilip) 1907- ... CANR-17
Earlier sketch in CA 25-28R
Lundberg, (Edgar) Ferdinand 1905- ... CAP-1
Earlier sketch in CA 9-10
Lundberg, Margaret (Jessie) 1919- ... 61-64
Lundborg, Louis B(illings) 1906- ... 81-84
Lunde, Donald T(heodore) 1937- ... 101
Lunde, Karl (Roy) 1931- ... 61-64
Lunden, Walter A(lbin) 1899- ... 21-22R
Lundgren, Paul Arthur 1925-1981
Obituary ... 103
Lundgren, William R. 1918- ... 13-14R
Lundin, Robert W(illiam) 1920- ... 2R
Lundkvist, Artur (Nils) 1906- Brief entry ... 117
Lundquist, James (Carl) 1941- ... 65-68
Lundsgaarde, Henry P(eder) 1938- ... CANR-14
Earlier sketch in CA 73-76
Lundsteen, Sara W. ... 109
Lundstrom, David E. 1929- ... 126
Lundwall, Sam J(errie) 1941- ... CANR-17
Earlier sketches in CA 49-52, CANR-1
Lundy, Robert F(ranklin) 1937- ... 7-8R
Lunenfeld, Marvin C. 1934- ... 61-64
Lunin, Lois F(ranklin) ... 102
Lunn, Arnold 1888-1974 ... 81-84
Obituary ... 49-52
Lunn, Eugene 1941- ... 45-48
Lunn, Janet (Louise Swoboda) 1928- ... CANR-22
Earlier sketch in CA 33-36R
See also SATA 4
Lunn, John Edward 1930- ... 41-44R
Lunsford, Cin Forshay
See Forshay-Lunsford, Cin
Lunt, Elizabeth Graves 1922- ... 33-36R
Lunt, Horace Gray 1918- Brief entry ... 107
Lunt, James D(oiran) 1917- ... CANR-3
Earlier sketch in CA 3R
Lunt, Lois
See Metz, Lois Lunt
Lunt, Richard D(eForest) 1933- ... 15-16R
Luomala, Katharine 1907- ... 37-40R
Luongo, C. Paul 1930- ... 105
Luper, Harold L(ee) 1924- ... 17-18R
Lupo, Alan 1938- ... 41-44R
Lupoff, Dick
See Lupoff, Richard A(llen)
Lupoff, Richard A(llen) 1935- ... CANR-25
Earlier sketches in CA 23-24R, CANR-9
Lupul, Manoly Robert 1927- Brief entry ... 106
Lurgan, Lester
See Knowles, Mabel Winifred
Luria, Alexander R(omanovich)
1902-1977 ... 25-28R
Obituary ... 73-76
Luria, Maxwell Sidney 1932- ... 37-40R
Luria, S(alvador) E(dward) 1912- ... 61-64
Lurie, Alison 1926- ... CANR-17
Earlier sketches in CA 3R, CANR-2
See also SATA 46
See also DLB 2
See also CLC 4, 5, 18, 39
Lurie, Edward 1927- ... CANR-7
Earlier sketch in CA 9-10R
Lurie, Harry L. 1892(?)-1973 Obituary ... 41-44R
Lurie, Nancy Oestreich 1924- ... CANR-16
Earlier sketch in CA 2R
Lurie, Ranan R(aymond) 1932- ... 57-60
Lurie, Richard G. 1919- ... 23-24R
Lurie, Toby 1925- ... 45-48
Luriya, Aleksander Romanovich
See Luria, Alexander R(omanovich)
Luschei, Eugene C(harles) 1928- ... 37-40R
Luscher, Max
See Luescher, Max
Luscombe, David Edward 1938- ... 41-44R
Luscombe, William 1912- ... 7-8R
Lusinchi, Victor 1912-1985 Obituary ... 115
Luskin, Bernard J(ay) 1937- ... 33-36R
Luskin, John 1908- ... 45-48
Lussier, (Joseph) Ernest 1911-1979 ... CANR-9
Earlier sketch in CA 57-60
Lussu, Joyce (Salvadori) 1912- ... CANR-14
Earlier sketch in CA 29-32R
Lust, John (Benedict) 1920- ... 116
Lust, Peter 1911- ... 103
Lustbader, Eric Van 1946- ... CANR-14
Earlier sketch in CA 85-88
Lustgarten, Edgar (Marcus)
1907-1978 ... CANR-22
Earlier sketch in CA 25-28R
Lustgarten, Karen 1944- ... 85-88
Lustick, Ian Steven 1949- ... 117
Lustig, Arnost 1926- ... 69-72
Lustig, Loretta 1944- ... SATA-46
Lustig, R(ichard) Jeffrey 1943- ... 112
Lustig-Arecco, Vera 1942- ... 101
Lutes, Catherine Urell 1900(?)-1983
Obituary ... 110
Lutetius
See Stearns, Harold Edmund
Lutgen, Kurt
See Luetgen, Kurt (Bodo Heinrich)
Luthans, Fred 1939- ... 29-32R
Luther, Edward T(urner) 1928- ... 77-80
Luther, Frank 1905-1980 Obituary ... 102
See also SATA 25
Luther, James W(allace) 1940- ... 69-72
Luther, Jim
See Luther, James W(allace)
Luther, Ray
See Ley, Arthur Gordon
Luthi, Max
See Luethi, Max
Luthuli, A. J.
See Luthuli, Albert John
Luthuli, Albert John 1898(?)-1967
Obituary ... 113
Lutin, Michael 1940- ... 89-92
Luttbeg, Norman R. 1938- ... CANR-10
Earlier sketch in CA 25-28R
Luttrell, Guy L. 1938- ... 97-100
See also SATA 22
Luttrell, Ida (Alleene) 1934- ... 110
See also SATA 35, 40
Luttrell, Mark H. 1914- ... 97-100
Luttwak, Edward N(icholae) 1942- ... CANR-11
Earlier sketch in CA 25-28R
Lutwack, Leonard 1917- ... 41-44R
Lutyens, (Agnes) Elisabeth 1906-1983
Obituary ... 109
Lutyens, Mary 1908- ... 25-28R
Lutz, Alma 1890-1973 ... CAP-1
Obituary ... 45-48
Earlier sketch in CA 9-10
Lutz, Charles P(aul) 1931- ... 115
Lutz, Cora Elizabeth 1906-1985 ... 102
Obituary ... 115
Lutz, Frank W. 1928- ... 33-36R
Lutz, Gertrude May 1899- ... 33-36R
Lutz, Harley L. 1882-1975 Obituary ... 53-56
Lutz, Jerry 1939- ... 89-92
Lutz, Jessie Gregory 1925- ... 15-16R
Lutz, John (Thomas) 1939- ... CANR-24
Earlier sketches in CA 65-68, CANR-9
Lutz, Paul E(ugene) 1934- ... 61-64
Lutz, William D. 1940- ... 33-36R
Lutz, William W(alter) 1919- ... 49-52
Lutze, Karl E(rnst) 1920- ... 89-92

Lutzer, Erwin W(esley) 1941- CANR-2
Earlier sketch in CA 45-48
Lutzker, Edythe 1904- 37-40R
See also SATA 5
Luvaas, Jay 1927- 15-16R
Luvaas, William 1945- 121
Lux, Thomas 1946- 41-44R
Luxemburg, Rosa 1870(?)-1919
Brief entry 118
Luxenburg, Norman 1927- 41-44R
Luxton, Leonora Kathrine 1895- 85-88
Luxton, Richard (Neil) 1950- 110
Luyben, Helen L. 1932- 17-18R
Luytens, David (Edwin) Bulwer 1929- 13-14R
Luza, Radomir 1922- CANR-24
Earlier sketches in CA 11-12R, CANR-9
Luzbetak, Louis J(oseph) 1918- 33-36R
Luzi, Mario 1914- CANR-9
Earlier sketch in CA 61-64
See also CLC 13
Luzwick, Dierdre 1945- 65-68
Luzzati, Emanuele 1921- 29-32R
See also SATA 7
Luzzatto, Paola Caboara 1938- 112
See also SATA 38
Lyall, Gavin (Tudor) 1932- CANR-26
Earlier sketches in CA 9-10R, CANR-4
Lyall, Katharine Elizabeth 1928- CANR-7
Earlier sketch in CA 7-8R
Lyall, Leslie T(heodore) 1905- 15-16R
Lycan, Gilbert L(ester) 1909- CAP-2
Earlier sketch in CA 33-36
Lyday, Leon F(aidherbee) III 1939- 33-36R
Lydecker, Beatrice 1938- 106
Lyden, Fremont J(ames) 1926- 25-28R
Lydenberg, John 1913- 37-40R
Lydolph, Paul E. 1924- 13-14R
Lydon, James G(avin) 1927- 126
Brief entry 105
Lydon, Michael 1942- 85-88
See also SATA 11
Lyfick, Warren
See Reeves, Lawrence F.
Lyford, Joseph Philip 1918- 37-40R
Lyford-Pike, Margaret (Prudence) 1911- 109
Lygre, David G(erald) 1942- 93-96
Lykiard, Alexis (Constantine) 1940- 81-84
Lykken, David Thoreson 1928- 105
Lyle, Albert Walter 1944- 124
Brief entry 117
Lyle, David 1927- 118
Lyle, Guy R(edvers) 1907- 61-64
Lyle, Jack 1929- 13-14R
Lyle, Jerolyn R(oss) 1937- 89-92
Lyle, Katie Letcher 1938- 49-52
See also SATA 8
Lyle, Sparky
See Lyle, Albert Walter
Lyles, Vina Honish 1935- 11-12R
Lyles, William H(using) 1946- 111
Lyle-Smythe, Alan 1914- 103
Lyly, John 1554(?)-1606 .... DLB-62
Lyman, Albert Robison 1880-1973 ...... CAP-1
Earlier sketch in CA 15-16
Lyman, Helen (Lucille) Huguenor 1910- ...65-68
Lyman, Howard B(urbeck) 1920- 41-44R
Lyman, Irene (Vera) Ponting 7-8R
Lyman, Lauren D(wight) 1891-1972
Obituary 89-92
Lyman, Marilyn F(lorence) 1925- 93-96
Lyman, Mary Ely 1887-1975 Obituary 53-56
Lyman, Stanford M(orris) 1933- CANR-12
Earlier sketch in CA 29-32R
Lyman, Susan Elizabeth 1906-1976
Obituary 69-72
Lymington, John
See Chance, John Newton
Lynch, Brian
See Liddy, James (Daniel Reeves)
Lynch, David 1946- Brief entry 124
Lynch, Edith M. (Carstensen) 1912-1986 ... 105
Obituary 119
Lynch, Eric
See Bingley, David Ernest
Lynch, Etta Lee 1924- 69-72
Lynch, Frances
See Compton, D(avid) G(uy)
Lynch, Hayden Wood 1927(?)-1979
Obituary 89-92
Lynch, Henry T(homson) 1928- 89-92
Lynch, Hollis Ralph 1935- CANR-1
Earlier sketch in CA 45-48
Lynch, J(ohn) Joseph 1894-1987
Obituary 123
Lynch, James 1936- CANR-18
Earlier sketch in CA 101
Lynch, James
See Andreyev, Leonid (Nikolaevich)
Lynch, James F. 1919(?)-1985 Obituary 117
Lynch, James J(oseph) 1938- 73-76
Lynch, John 1927- 85-88
Lynch, Kathleen M(artha) 1898- 73-76
Lynch, Kevin (Andrew) 1918-1984 ...... CANR-3
Obituary 112
Earlier sketch in CA 5-6R
Lynch, Lorenzo 1932- 29-32R
See also SATA 7
Lynch, Malcolm 1922- 119
Lynch, Marietta 1947- 106
See also SATA 29
Lynch, Marilyn 1938- 89-92
Lynch, Owen M(artin) 1931- CANR-11
Earlier sketch in CA 29-32R
Lynch, Patricia (Nora) 1898-1972 .... CAP-1
Earlier sketch in CA 11-12
See also SATA 9
Lynch, Patrick B(eavis) 1927- 9-10R
Lynch, Thomas Francis 1938- 45-48
Lynch, W(illiam) E(dward) 1930- CANR-10
Earlier sketch in CA 19-20R
Lynch, William F. 1908-1987 .... CANR-3
Obituary 121
Earlier sketch in CA 1R
Lynch Davis, B.
See Bioy Casares, Adolfo
and Borges, Jorge Luis
Lynch-Fraser, Diane 1953- 111
Lynch-Watson, Janet 1936- 93-96
Lynd, Helen Merrell 1896-1982 Obituary ... 105
Lynd, Robert S. 1892-1970 Obituary 29-32R
Lynd, Staughton (Craig) 1929- Brief entry .. 112
Lynde, Stan 1931- 65-68
Lynden, Patricia 1937- 73-76
Lyndon, Amy
See Radford, Richard F(rancis), Jr.
Lyndon, Diana
See Anthony, Diana
Lynds, Dennis 1924- CANR-22
Earlier sketches in CA 3R, CANR-6
See also SATA 37, 47
Lyne, John Alexander 1909- 97-100
Lyneis, Richard George 1935- 81-84
Lynen, John Fairbanks 1924- CANR-2
Earlier sketch in CA 4R
Lynes, (Joseph) Russell (Jr.) 1910- CANR-3
Earlier sketch in CA 2R
Lyngseth, Joan
See Davies, Joan
Lyngstad, Alexandra Halina 1925- 37-40R
Lyngstad, Sverre 1922- CANR-16
Earlier sketch in CA 37-40R
Lynn
See Brown, Velma Darbo
Lynn, Arthur D(ellert), Jr. 1921- CANR-10
Earlier sketch in CA 25-28R
Lynn, Conrad J. 1908- CAP-2
Earlier sketch in CA 23-24
Lynn, David B(randon) 1925- 57-60
Lynn, Edward S(hird) 1919- 57-60
Lynn, Edwin Charles 1935- 45-48
Lynn, Elizabeth A. 1946- 81-84
Lynn, Frank
See Leisy, James (Franklin)
Lynn, Irene
See Rowland, D(onald) S(ydney)
Lynn, Janet
See Salomon, Janet Lynn (Nowicki)
Lynn, Jeannette Murphy 1905- CAP-2
Earlier sketch in CA 21-22
Lynn, (Dorcas) Joanne (Harley) 1951- 125
Lynn, Jonathan 1943- 104
Lynn, Kenneth S(chuyler) 1923- CANR-3
Earlier sketch in CA 1R
See also CLC 50
Lynn, Laurence Edwin, Jr. 1937- 105
Lynn, Loretta (Webb) 1932(?)- 81-84
Lynn, Margaret
See Battye, Gladys Starkey
Lynn, Mary
See Brokamp, Marilyn
Lynn, Naomi B. 1933- 61-64
Lynn, Patricia
See Watts, Mabel Pizzey
Lynn, Richard 1930- 37-40R
Lynn, Roa 1937- 101
Lynn, Robert A(than) 1930- 17-18R
Lynn, Robert Wood 1925- 23-24R
Lynn, Ruth Nadelman 1948- 103
Lynne, Becky
See Zawadsky, Patience
Lynne, James Broom 1920- 77-80
Lynskey, Winifred 1904- CAP-2
Earlier sketch in CA 23-24
Lynton, Ann
See Rayner, Claire (Berenice)
Lynton, Harriet Ronken 1920- 73-76
Lynx
See West, Rebecca
Lyon, Bryce Dale 1920- 126
Brief entry 106
Lyon, Buck
See Paine, Lauran (Bosworth)
Lyon, Christopher (Leslie) 1949-
Brief entry 118
Lyon, E(lijah) Wilson 1904- 97-100
Lyon, Elinor 1921- 25-28R
See also SATA 6
Lyon, Eugene 1929- 106
Lyon, George Ella 1949- 120
Lyon, Harold C(lifford), Jr. 1935- 41-44R
Lyon, James K(arl) 1934- CANR-1
Earlier sketch in CA 45-48
Lyon, Jessica
See DeLeeuw, Cateau
Lyon, John 1932- CANR-15
Earlier sketch in CA 41-44R
Lyon, Katherine
See Mix, Katherine Lyon
Lyon, Lyman R.
See de Camp, L(yon) Sprague
Lyon, Matthew 1749-1822 .... DLB-43
Lyon, Melvin (Ernest) 1927- 33-36R
Lyon, Peter 1915- CANR-5
Earlier sketch in CA 7-8R
Lyon, Peyton V(aughan) 1921- CANR-3
Earlier sketch in CA 11-12R
Lyon, Quinter M(arcellus) 1898- CAP-1
Earlier sketch in CA 19-20
Lyon, Thomas Edgar, Jr. 1939- 37-40R
Lyon, William Henry 1926- 15-16R
Lyon, Winston
See Woolfolk, William
Lyons, Albert S. 1912- 126
Lyons, Arthur (Jr.) 1946- CANR-12
Earlier sketch in CA 29-32R
Lyons, Augusta Wallace 85-88
Lyons, Barbara (Baldwin) 1912- 93-96
Lyons, Catherine 1944- 85-88
Lyons, Daniel 1920- 41-44R
Lyons, David (Barry) 1935- 33-36R
Lyons, Delphine C.
See Smith, Evelyn E.
Lyons, Dorothy M(arawee) 1907- CANR-24
Earlier sketch in CA 2R
See also SATA 3
Lyons, Elena
See Fairburn, Eleanor
Lyons, Enid (Muriel) 1897-1981 ....23-24R
Obituary 108
Lyons, Eugene 1898-1985 ....9-10R
Obituary 114
Lyons, F(rancis) S(tewart) L(eland)
1923-1983 ....29-32R
Obituary 110
Lyons, Gene 1943- 126
Lyons, Grant 1941- CANR-15
Earlier sketch in CA 41-44R
See also SATA 30
Lyons, Ivan 1934- CANR-19
Earlier sketch in CA 101
Lyons, J. B. 1922- CANR-17
Earlier sketch in CA 97-100
Lyons, James
See Loewen, James W.
Lyons, John O(rmsby) 1927- 4R
Lyons, John T. 1926- 29-32R
Lyons, Joseph 1918- 13-14R
Lyons, Len 1942- 93-96
Lyons, Leonard 1906-1976 Obituary 69-72
Lyons, Louis M. 1897-1982 Obituary 106
Lyons, Marcus
See Blish, James (Benjamin)
Lyons, Mark Joseph 1910- 7-8R
Lyons, Nan 1935- CANR-19
Earlier sketch in CA 101
Lyons, Nick 1932- CANR-4
Earlier sketch in CA 53-56
Lyons, Phyllis I. 1942- 126
Lyons, Richard D(aniel) 1928- 69-72
Lyons, Richard E(ugene) 1920- CANR-21
Earlier sketch in CA 45-48
Lyons, Sister Jeanne Marie 1904- CAP-1
Earlier sketch in CA 11-12
Lyons, Thomas Tolman 1934- CANR-3
Earlier sketch in CA 11-12R
Lyons, Timothy J(ames) 1944- 73-76
Lyons, Tom W(allace) 1943- 116
Ly-Qui, Chung 1940- 29-32R
Lyre, Pinchbeck
See Sassoon, Siegfried (Lorraine)
Lys, Daniel 1924- 23-24R
Lysaght, Averil M(argaret) 85-88
Lysaught, Jerome Paul 1930- CANR-6
Earlier sketch in CA 7-8R
Lysenko, T(rofim) D(enisovich) 1898-1976
Obituary 69-72
Lysons, Kenneth 1923- CANR-15
Earlier sketch in CA 85-88
Lystad, Mary (Hanemann) 1928- CANR-26
Earlier sketches in CA 65-68, CANR-10
See also SATA 11
Lystad, Robert A(rthur) 1920- 15-16R
Lyte, Charles 1935- 104
Lyte, Richard
See Whelpton, (George) Eric
Lytle, Andrew (Nelson) 1902- 9-10R
See also DLB 6
See also CLC 22
Lytle, Clifford M(erle) 1932- 93-96
Lytle, Guy Fitch (III) 1944- 118
Lytle, Ruby (Coker) 1917-19(?) CAP-1
Earlier sketch in CA 15-16
Lyttelton, Humphrey (Richard Adeane)
1921- Brief entry 118
Lyttle, Charles Harold 1885(?)-1980 109
Obituary 97-100
Lyttle, G(erald) R(oland) 1908- CAP-1
Earlier sketch in CA 9-10
Lyttle, Jean
See Garrett, Eileen J(eanette)
Lyttle, Richard B(ard) 1927- CANR-13
Earlier sketch in CA 33-36R
See also SATA 23
Lytton, Edward G(eorge) E(arle) L(ytton)
Bulwer-Lytton, Baron 1803-1873 .... SATA-23
Lytton, Edward Robert Bulwer
1831-1891 .... DLB-32
Lytton, Hugh 1921- 45-48
Lytton, Noel (Anthony Scawen)
1900-1985 .... CAP-1
Obituary 115
Earlier sketch in CA 9-10
Lytton-Sells, Iris (Esther) 1903- 29-32R
Lyudvinskaya, Tatyana 1885(?)-1976
Obituary 65-68

M

M
See Stone, Susan Berch
M. C.
See Cook, Mabel Collins
M. G.
See Giergielewicz, Mieczyslaw F.
Ma, John T(a-jen) 1920- 49-52
Ma, Nancy Chih 1919- CANR-10
Earlier sketch in CA 65-68
Maakestad, William J(ohn) 1951- 126
Maar, Leonard (Frank, Jr.) 1927- 106
See also SATA 30
Maas, Audrey Gellen 1936-1975 .... CAP-2
Obituary 57-60
Earlier sketch in CA 23-24
Maas, Henry 1929- 25-28R
Maas, Jeremy 1928- 29-32R
Maas, Peter 1929- 93-96
See also CLC 29
Maas, Selve 69-72
See also SATA 14
Maas, Virginia H(argrave) 1913- 105
Maas, Willard 1911-1971 .... CAP-1
Obituary 29-32R
Earlier sketch in CA 13-14
Maasarani, Aly Mohamed 1927- 49-52
Maass, Arthur 1917- Brief entry 105
Maass, Joachim 1901-1972 Obituary 37-40R
See also DLB 69
Maass, John 1918- Brief entry 108
Mabberley, D(avid) J(ohn) 1948- 122
Mabbett, I(an) W(illiam) 1939- 29-32R
Mabbott, John David 1898-1988 ....13-14R
Obituary 124
Mabee, Carleton 1914- CANR-21
Earlier sketch in CA 1R
Maberly, Allan 1922-1977 103
Maberly, Norman C(harles) 1926- 33-36R
Mabery, D. L. 1953- 121
See also SATA 53
Mabey, Richard (Thomas) 1941- CANR-26
Earlier sketches in CA 23-24R, CANR-9
Mabie, Hamilton Wright 1845-1916 ..... DLB-71
Mabie, Margot C(auldwell) J(ones) 1944- ... 125
Mabley, Edward (Howe) 1906-1984 ......29-32R
Obituary 114
Mabley, Jack 1915- 105
Mabogunje, Akin(lawon) L(adipo)
1931- CANR-16
Earlier sketch in CA 77-80
Mabon, John Scott 1910(?)-1980
Obituary 104
Mabry, Bevars Dupre 1928- 45-48
Mabry, Donald J(oseph) 1941- 49-52
Mac
See MacManus, Seumas
Mac, Carm
See Armstrong, Keith F(rancis)
W(hitfield)
MacAdam, Eve
See Leslie, Cecilie
MacAdams, Lewis (Perry, Jr.) 1944- 97-100
MacAfee, Norman 1943- 122
MacAgy, Douglas G(uernsey) 1913-1973 ... 102
Macainsh, Noel Leslie 1926- 103
MacAlan, Peter
See Ellis, Peter Berresford
MacAlpin, Rory
See Mackinnon, Charles Roy
MacAlpine, Margaret H(esketh Murray)
1907- CAP-1
Earlier sketch in CA 11-12
Macan, T(homas) T(ownley) 1910- 107
MacAndrew, Elizabeth 1924-1983(?) 126
Macao, Marshall
See Tuleja, Thaddeus F(rancis)
MacAodhagain, Eamon
See Egan, E(dward) W(elstead)
MacApp, C. C.
See Capps, Carroll M.
Macarov, David 1918- CANR-12
Earlier sketch in CA 29-32R
MacArthur, Charles 1895-1956 Brief entry .. 108
See also DLB 7, 25, 44
MacArthur, D(avid) Wilson 1903- CANR-5
Earlier sketch in CA 11-12R
MacArthur, Douglas 1880-1964 Obituary ... 113
MacArthur, John F., Jr. 1939- 81-84
MacArthur, Robert H(elmer) 1930-1972
Obituary 37-40R
MacArthur-Onslow, Annette Rosemary
1933- 102
See also SATA 26
Macartney, (Carlile) Aylmer 1895-1978 ...19-20R
Obituary 125
Macaulay, David (Alexander) 1946- CANR-5
Earlier sketch in CA 53-56
See also SATA 27, 46
See also DLB 61
See also CLR 3, 14
Macaulay, John (Ure) 1925- 107
Macaulay, Neill (Webster, Jr.) 1935- 21-22R
Macaulay, Rose 1881-1958 Brief entry 104
See also DLB 36
See also TCLC 7
Macaulay, Stewart 1931- 77-80
Macaulay, Susan Schaeffer 1941- 120
Macaulay, Thomas Babington
1800-1859 .... DLB-32, 55
Macauley, Robie Mayhew 1919- CANR-3
Earlier sketch in CA 3R
MacCauley, Stephen 19(?)- CLC-50
MacAusland, Earle R(utherford)
1893-1980 Obituary 101
MacAvoy, Paul W(ebster) 1934- 126
Brief entry 105
MacAvoy, Roberta Ann 1949- 113
MacBean, Dilla Whittemore 1895- 5-6R
MacBeth, George (Mann) 1932- 25-28R
See also SATA 4
See also DLB 40
See also CLC 2, 5, 9
Macbeth, Norman 1910- CAP-2
Earlier sketch in CA 33-36
MacBride, Robert O(liver) 1926- 19-20R
MacBride, Roger Lea 1929- 81-84
MacBride, Sean 1904-1988 Obituary 124

MacCaffrey, Isabel Gamble 1924-1978 ... 81-84
Obituary ... 77-80
MacCaffrey, Wallace T(revethic) 1920-
Brief entry ... 112
Mac Caig, Norman (Alexander) 1910- ... CANR-3
Earlier sketch in CA 9-10R
See also DLB 27
See also CLC 36
MacCall, Libby
See Machol, Libby
MacCallum Scott, John H. 1911- ... 25-28R
MacCampbell, James C(urtis) 1916- ... 9-10R
MacCann, Donnarae 1931- ... CANR-1
Earlier sketch in CA 45-48
MacCann, Richard Dyer 1920- ... CANR-5
Earlier sketch in CA 9-10R
MacCarthy, Fiona 1940- ... 105
MacCarthy, J(oseph) A(idan) 1913- ... 107
MacCauley, Sister Rose Agnes 1911- ... 37-40R
Macciocchi, Maria Antoinetta 1922- ... 73-76
MacClintock, Dorcas 1932- ... CANR-6
Earlier sketch in CA 57-60
See also SATA 8
MacCloskey, Monro 1902- ... CANR-5
Earlier sketch in CA 11-12R
Maccoby, Eleanor E(mmons) 1917-
Brief entry ... 113
Maccoby, Michael 1933- ... CANR-14
Earlier sketch in CA 33-36R
MacCollam, Joel A(llan) 1946- ... 105
MacCombie, John 1932- ... 37-40R
MacCorkle, Stuart A(lexander) 1903- ... 19-20R
MacCormac, Earl Ronald 1935- ... 85-88
MacCormack, Sabine G(abriele) 1941- ... 106
MacCormick, Austin H(arbutt) 1893-1979
Obituary ... 93-96
MacCorquodale, Patricia (Lee) 1950- ... 101
MacCracken, Calvin D(odd) 1919- ... 116
MacCracken, Henry Noble 1880-1970 ... CAP-1
Obituary ... 29-32R
Earlier sketch in CA 19-20
MacCracken, Mary 1926- ... 49-52
MacCraig, Hugh
See Ward, Craig
MacCulloch, Diarmaid 1951- ... 125
MacCurdy, Raymond R(alph, Jr.) 1916- ... 41-44R
MacDermott, Mercia 1927- ... 106
MacDiarmid, Hugh
See Grieve, C(hristopher) M(urray)
See also DLB 20
See also CLC 2, 4, 11, 19
MacDonagh, Donagh 1912-1968
Obituary ... 93-96
MacDonald, Aeneas
See Thomson, George Malcolm
MacDonald, Anne Elizabeth Campbell Bard
1908-1958 Brief entry ... 121
MacDonald, Anson
See Heinlein, Robert A(nson)
MacDonald, Bernell 1948- ... 113
MacDonald, Betty
See MacDonald, Anne Elizabeth Campbell Bard
See also YABC 1
Macdonald, Blackie
See Emrich, Duncan (Black Macdonald)
MacDonald, Bonnie 1941- ... 117
MacDonald, Charles B(rown) 1922- ... CANR-23
Earlier sketches in CA 9-10R, CANR-6
Macdonald, Coll 1924- ... 19-20R
MacDonald, Craig 1949- ... CANR-9
Earlier sketch in CA 57-60
Macdonald, Cynthia 1928- ... CANR-4
Earlier sketch in CA 49-52
See also CLC 13, 19
Macdonald, David W(hyte) 1951- ... 106
MacDonald, Dennis Ronald 1946- ... 111
Macdonald, Dwight 1906-1982 ... 29-32R
Obituary ... 108
See also SATA 29, 33
MacDonald, Edgar E(dgeworth) 1919- ... 115
MacDonald, Edwin A(nderson) 1907- ... 41-44R
Macdonald, Eleanor 1910- ... CAP-1
Earlier sketch in CA 9-10
Macdonald, Elisabeth 1926- ... 65-68
MacDonald, George 1824-1905
Brief entry ... 106
See also SATA 33
See also DLB 18
See also TCLC 9
Macdonald, Gerard 1940- ... 119
MacDonald, Golden
See Brown, Margaret Wise
Macdonald, Gordon A(ndrew)
1911-1978 ... CANR-15
Earlier sketch in CA 65-68
Macdonald, H(enry) Malcolm 1914- ... 19-20R
MacDonald, J. Fred(erick) 1941-
Brief entry ... 117
MacDonald, Jake (M.) 1949- ... 126
Macdonald, John (Barfoot) 1918- ... CANR-1
Earlier sketch in CA 49-52
Macdonald, John
See Millar, Kenneth
MacDonald, John D(ann) 1916-1986 ... CANR-19
Obituary ... 121
Earlier sketches in CA 2R, CANR-1
See also DLB 8
See also DLBY 86
See also CLC 3, 27, 44
Macdonald, John M. ... CANR-2
Earlier sketch in CA 4R
Macdonald, John Ross
See Millar, Kenneth
Macdonald, Julie 1926- ... 19-20R
Macdonald, Kenneth 1905- ... 73-76
Macdonald, Malcolm
See Ross-Macdonald, Malcolm J(ohn)
MacDonald, Malcolm John 1901-1981 ... 11-12R
Obituary ... 102
MacDonald, Malcolm M(urdoch) 1935- ... 41-44R
Macdonald, Marcia
See Hill, Grace Livingston
MacDonald, Margaret Read 1940- ... 110
Macdonald, Mary
See Gifford, Griselda
Macdonald, Nancy (Gardiner Rodman)
1910- ... 126
Macdonald, Neil (William) 1936- ... 89-92
Macdonald, Nina Hansell
See Looker, Antonina (Hansell)
MacDonald, Philip 1896(?)- ... 81-84
Macdonald, R. Ross 1923(?)-1983
Obituary ... 110
Macdonald, Robert M(unro) 1923- ... 11-12R
Macdonald, Robert S. 1925- ... 15-16R
Macdonald, Robert W. 1922- ... 19-20R
Macdonald, Ronald St. John 1928- ... 103
Macdonald, Ross
See Millar, Kenneth
See also CLC 1, 2, 3, 14, 34, 41
MacDonald, Ruby (DeAngelo Norton)
1930- ... 115
MacDonald, Sandy 1949- ... 103
Macdonald, Shelagh 1937- ... 97-100
See also SATA 25
MacDonald, Simon G(avin) G(eorge)
1923- ... 53-56
MacDonald, Suse 1940- ... 125
See also SATA 52
MacDonald, Timothy I(gnatius) 1941- ... 121
MacDonald, William L. 1921- ... 23-24R
Macdonald, Zillah K(atherine) 1885- ... CAP-1
Earlier sketch in CA 9-10
See also SATA 11
Macdonnell, James Edmond 1917- ... CANR-8
Earlier sketch in CA 7-8R
MacDonnell, Kevin 1919- ... 45-48
MacDonnell, Megan
See Stevens, Serita (Deborah)
MacDouall, Robertson
See Mair, George Brown
MacDougal, John
See Blish, James (Benjamin)
and Lowndes, Robert A(ugustine) W(ard)
MacDougall, A(llan) Kent 1931- ... 45-48
MacDougall, Curtis D(aniel) 1903-1985 ... 53-56
Obituary ... 117
MacDougall, (George) Donald (Alastair)
1912- ... 106
MacDougall, Fiona
See MacLeod, Robert F.
MacDougall, Malcolm D(ouglas) 1928-
Brief entry ... 110
MacDougall, Mary Katherine ... CANR-12
Earlier sketch in CA 29-32R
MacDougall, Ruth Doan 1939- ... CANR-8
Earlier sketch in CA 19-20R
MacDowell, Douglas M(aurice) 1931- ... CANR-6
Earlier sketch in CA 5-6R
Mace, C(ecil) Alec 1894- ... CAP-1
Earlier sketch in CA 13-14
Mace, Carroll Edward 1926- ... 41-44R
Mace, David Robert 1907- ... CANR-23
Earlier sketches in CA 57-60, CANR-7
Mace, Don 1899(?)-1983 Obituary ... 109
Mace, Elisabeth 1933- ... CANR-23
Earlier sketch in CA 77-80
See also SATA 27
Mace, Myles L(a Grange) 1911-
Brief entry ... 110
Mace, Nancy L(awson) 1941- ... 119
Mace, Varian 1938- ... SATA-49
Mace, Vera C(hapman) 1902- ... 113
MacEoin, Gary 1909- ... CANR-2
Earlier sketch in CA 4R
Macer-Story, E(ugenia) 1945- ... CANR-23
Earlier sketch in CA 107
Macesich, George 1927- ... 15-16R
MacEwan, J(ohn) W(alter) Grant 1902- ... 41-44R
MacEwan, Paul W. 1943- ... CANR-7
Earlier sketch in CA 61-64
MacEwen, Gwendolyn (Margaret)
1941-1987 ... CANR-22
Obituary ... 124
Earlier sketches in CA 9-10R, CANR-7
See also SATA 50
See also DLB 53
See also CLC 13
MacEwen, Malcolm 1911- ... 110
Macey, Samuel L(awson) 1922- ... 102
Macfadden, Bernarr 1868-1955 ... DLB-25
MacFall, Russell P(atterson) 1903-1983 ... CAP-1
Obituary ... 110
Earlier sketch in CA 11-12
Macfarlan, Allan A. 1892-1982 ... 107
See also SATA 35
Macfarlane, (Robert) Gwyn 1907-1987
Obituary ... 122
MacFarlane, Iris 1922- ... 89-92
See also SATA 11
MacFarlane, Kenneth
See Walker, Kenneth Macfarlane
Macfarlane, Leslie John 1924- ... 21-22R
MacFarlane, Louise 1917(?)-1979
Obituary ... 89-92
MacFarlane, Stephen
See Cross, John Keir
MacFarquhar, Roderick 1930- ... CANR-13
Earlier sketch in CA 21-22R
MacFee, Maxwell
See Rennie, James Alan
MacGaffey, Wyatt 1932- ... 73-76
MacGibbon, Jean 1913- ... 97-100
MacGill, Patrick 1890(?)-1963 ... 116
MacGillivray, John H(enry) 1899- ... CAP-2
Earlier sketch in CA 25-28
MacGorman, J(ohn) W(illiam) 1920- ... 102
Macgowan, Kenneth 1888-1963 Obituary ... 93-96
MacGregor, Alasdair Alpin (Douglas)
1899-1970 ... CAP-1
Obituary ... 29-32R
Earlier sketch in CA 11-12
MacGregor, Bruce (Alan) 1945- ... 77-80
MacGregor, David Roy 1925- ... 93-96
MacGregor, Ellen 1906-1954 Brief entry ... 111
See also SATA 27, 39
Macgregor, Frances Cooke ... CANR-1
Earlier sketch in CA 1R
MacGregor, (John) Geddes 1909- ... CANR-21
Earlier sketches in CA 3R, CANR-2
Macgregor, James (Murdoch) 1925- ... CANR-5
Earlier sketch in CA 13-14R
MacGregor, James G(rierson) 1905- ... CANR-10
Earlier sketch in CA 25-28R
MacGregor, Loren J. 1950- ... 126
MacGregor, Malcolm D(ouglas) 1945- ... 102
MacGregor, Robert Mercer 1911-1974
Obituary ... 104
MacGregor, T. J.
See Janeshutz, Patricia M(arie)
MacGregor-Hastie, Roy (Alasdhair Niall)
1929- ... CANR-20
Earlier sketches in CA 4R, CANR-2
See also SATA 3
Macgregor-Morris, Pamela 1925- ... CANR-25
Earlier sketch in CA 29-32R
MacGuigan, Mark R(udolph) 1931- ... 23-24R
Machado (y Ruiz), Antonio 1875-1939
Brief entry ... 104
See also TCLC 3
Machado, Manuel Anthony, Jr. 1939- ... 29-32R
Machado de Assis, Joaquim Maria
1839-1908 Brief entry ... 107
See also TCLC 10
Machan, Tibor R(ichard) 1939- ... CANR-1
Earlier sketch in CA 45-48
MacHardy, Charles 1926- ... 104
Machen, Arthur
See Jones, Arthur Llewellyn
See also DLB 36
See also TCLC 4
Machetanz, Frederick 1908- ... SATA-34
Machetanz, Sara Burleson 1918- ... 4R
Machiavelli
See McCready, Warren T(homas)
Machin, G(eorge) Ian T(hom) 1937- ... 15-16R
Machin Goodall, Daphne (Edith) ... CANR-7
Earlier sketch in CA 7-8R
See also SATA 37
Machlin, Milton Robert 1924- ... CANR-2
Earlier sketch in CA 4R
Machlis, Joseph 1906- ... CANR-22
Earlier sketches in CA 2R, CANR-2
Machlowitz, Marilyn M(arcia) 1952- ... 101
Machlup, Fritz 1902-1983 ... CANR-6
Obituary ... 109
Earlier sketch in CA 3R
Machol, Libby 1916- ... 23-24R
Machol, Robert E(ngel) 1917- ... 37-40R
Macholtz, James Donald 1926- ... 53-56
Machorton, Ian (Duncan) 1923- ... CANR-8
Earlier sketch in CA 19-20R
MacHorton, Ian
See Machorton, Ian (Duncan)
Machotka, Otakar (Richard) 1899-1970 ... CAP-1
Obituary ... 29-32R
Earlier sketch in CA 15-16
Macht, Joel 1938- ... 57-60
Macia, Rafael 1946- ... 97-100
Maciel, Judi(th Anne) 1942- ... 33-36R
MacInnes, Colin 1914-1976 ... CANR-21
Obituary ... 65-68
Earlier sketch in CA 69-72
See also DLB 14
See also CLC 4, 23
MacInnes, Helen (Clark) 1907-1985 ... CANR-1
Obituary ... 117
Earlier sketch in CA 1R
See also SATA 22, 44
See also CLC 27, 39
MacInnis, Donald E(arl) 1920- ... 41-44R
MacIntosh, J(ohn) J(ames) 1934- ... 37-40R
MacIntosh, Joan 1924- ... 107
MacIntosh, Keitha 1954- ... 112
MacIntyre, Alasdair (Chalmers) 1929-
Brief entry ... 118
Macintyre, Angus (Donald) 1935- ... 118
MacIntyre, Christine Melba 1939-1987
Obituary ... 123
Macintyre, Donald George (Frederick
Wyville) 1904- ... 7-8R
MacIntyre, Elisabeth 1916- ... CANR-5
Earlier sketch in CA 11-12R
See also SATA 17
MacIre, Esor B.
See Ambrose, Eric (Samuel)
MacIsaac, David 1935- ... CANR-14
Earlier sketch in CA 77-80
MacIsaac, Sharon ... 57-60
Maciuszko, Jerzy J. 1913- ... 25-28R
Maciuszko, Kathleen L(ynn) 1947- ... 113
MacIver, Robert M(orrison) 1882-1970 ... CAP-1
Obituary ... 25-28R
Earlier sketch in CA 11-12
Mack, Charles R. 1940- ... 126
Mack, Edward C. 1905(?)-1973 Obituary ... 45-48
Mack, Evalina
See McNamara, Lena Brooke
Mack, Gerstle 1894-1983 Obituary ... 109
Mack, J. A. 1906- ... 65-68
Mack, James D(ecker) 1916- ... 21-22R
Mack, Jerry
See Johnson, Jerry Mack
Mack, John E(dward) 1929- ... 106
Mack, Karin E(ileen) 1946- ... 97-100
Mack, Kirby
See McEvoy, Harry K(irby)
Mack, Marjorie
See Dixon, Marjorie (Mack)
Mack, Mary Peter 1927-1973 ... 4R
Obituary ... 103
Mack, Max Noble 1916- ... 61-64
Mack, Maynard 1909- ... CANR-25
Earlier sketch in CA 9-10R
Mack, Raymond (Wright) 1927- ... 13-14R
Mack, Stan(ley) ... 85-88
See also SATA 17
Mack, Walter Staunton 1895- ... 109
Mackal, Roy P(aul) 1925- ... 73-76
Mackaman, Frank H(indes) II 1950- ... 111
Mackarness, Richard 1916- ... 103
MacKay, Alfred F(arnum) 1938- ... 104
MacKay, Alistair McColl 1931- ... 81-84
Mackay, Barbara E. 1944- ... 77-80
Mackay, Claire 1930- ... CANR-22
Earlier sketch in CA 105
See also SATA 40
Mackay, Constance D'Arcy (?)-1966 ... 102
MacKay, D(onald) I(ain) 1937- ... CANR-24
Earlier sketch in CA 29-32R
MacKay, Donald M(acCrimmon)
1922-1987 ... CANR-13
Obituary ... 121
Earlier sketch in CA 29-32R
Mackay, James (Alexander) 1936- ... CANR-23
Earlier sketches in CA 53-56, CANR-7
Mackay, John Alexander 1889-1983
Obituary ... 110
MacKay, Joy 1918- ... 65-68
Mackay, Malcolm George 1919- ... 108
Mackay, Mary 1855-1924 Brief entry ... 118
Mackay, Mercedes (Isabelle) 1906- ... CAP-1
Earlier sketch in CA 11-12
MacKay, Robert A(lexander) 1894- ... 11-12R
Mackay, Ruddock F(inlay) 1922- ... 102
Mackay, Shena 1944- ... 104
MacKay, William 1943(?)- Brief entry ... 110
MacKaye, Benton 1879-1975 Obituary ... 61-64
MacKaye, Milton 1901-1979 ... 93-96
Obituary ... 85-88
MacKaye, Percy (Wallace) 1875-1956
Brief entry ... 113
See also SATA 32
See also DLB 54
MacKaye, William Ross 1934- Brief entry ... 109
MacKeever, Maggie
See Clark, Gail
MacKeith, Ronald Charles 1908-1977
Obituary ... 77-80
MacKellar, William 1914- ... CANR-13
Earlier sketch in CA 33-36R
See also SATA 4
Mackelworth, R(onald) W(alter) 1930- ... 29-32R
Macken, Walter 1915-1967 ... CAP-1
Obituary ... 25-28R
Earlier sketch in CA 13-14
See also SATA 36
See also DLB 13
Mackendrick, John 1946- ... 81-84
MacKendrick, Paul Lachlan 1914- ... CANR-1
Earlier sketch in CA 1R
Mackensen, Heinz Friedrich 1921-
Brief entry ... 107
Mackenzie, Alastair (Ian Folliott) 1933- ... 118
MacKenzie, Andrew 1911- ... 49-52
Mackenzie, Basil William Sholto
1900-1983 Obituary ... 111
MacKenzie, Christine Butchart 1917- ... 15-16R
Mackenzie, Compton (Edward Montague)
1883-1972 ... CAP-2
Obituary ... 37-40R
Earlier sketch in CA 21-22
See also DLB 34
See also CLC 18
MacKenzie, David 1927- ... 21-22R
MacKenzie, Donald 1918- ... CANR-21
Earlier sketch in CA 25-28R
MacKenzie, Fred 1905- ... CAP-2
Earlier sketch in CA 25-28
MacKenzie, Garry 1921- ... SATA-31
Mackenzie, Henry 1745-1831 ... DLB-39
MacKenzie, Jean 1928- ... 93-96
MacKenzie, (Daisy) Jeanne 1922-1986
Obituary ... 120
MacKenzie, Joan Finnigan 1925- ... CANR-13
Earlier sketch in CA 17-18R
MacKenzie, John P(ettibone) 1930- ... 65-68
Mackenzie, Kathleen Guy 1907- ... 7-8R
Mackenzie, Kenneth (Ivo) 1913-1955
Brief entry ... 122
Mackenzie, Kenneth Donald 1937- ... 37-40R
Mackenzie, Locke L. 1900(?)-1977
Obituary ... 69-72
MacKenzie, Louise (Wilks) 1920- ... 29-32R
Mackenzie, Manfred 1934- ... 65-68
MacKenzie, Norman H(ugh) 1915- ... 23-24R
MacKenzie, Ossian 1907-1980 ... 25-28R
Obituary ... 120
MacKenzie, R(oderick) A(ndrew) F(rancis)
1911- ... 7-8R
Mackenzie, R. Alec
See Mackenzie, Richard Alexander
MacKenzie, Rachel 1909-1980 ... 102
Obituary ... 97-100
Mackenzie, Richard Alexander 1923- ... 109

Mackenzie, Seaforth
See Mackenzie, Kenneth (Ivo)
Mackenzie, W(illiam) J(ames) M(illar)
1909- 104
Mackenzie-Grieve, Averil (Salmond)
1903- 9-10R
Mackerras, Colin Patrick 1939- CANR-15
Earlier sketch in CA 85-88
Mackesy, Piers G(erald) 1924- CANR-3
Earlier sketch in CA 9-10R
MacKethan, Lucinda Hardwick 1945- 102
Mackey, Ernan
See McInerny, Ralph
Mackey, Helen T. 1918- 5-6R
Mackey, J(ames) P(atrick) 1934- CANR-9
Earlier sketch in CA 65-68
Mackey, Louis H(enry) 1926- 33-36R
Mackey, Mary 1945- CANR-15
Earlier sketch in CA 77-80
Mackey, William Francis 1918- 37-40R
Mackey, William J., Jr. 1902(?)-1972
Obituary 37-40R
Mackey, William Wellington 1937- 124
Brief entry 120
See also BW
See also DLB 38
Mackie, Alastair 1925- 19-20R
Mackie, Albert D(avid) 1904- CAP-1
Earlier sketch in CA 9-10
Mackie, J(ohn) L(eslie) 1917- CANR-7
Earlier sketch in CA 57-60
Mackie, (Benjamin) James 1932- 41-44R
Mackie, John
See Levinson, Leonard
Mackie, Margaret Davidson 1914- 102
Mackie, Maron
See McNeely, Jeannette
Mackie, Philip 1918-1985 103
Obituary 118
Mackiewicz, Jozef 1902-1985 Obituary 116
MacKillop, James (John) 1939- 113
Mackin, Anita
See Donson, Cyril
Mackin, Catherine (Patricia) 1939-1982 109
Obituary 108
Mackin, Cooper R(icherson) 1933- 41-44R
Mackin, Dorothy (May Mabee) 1917- 107
Mackin, John H(oward) 1921- 33-36R
Mackin, Theodore 1922- 116
Mackinlay, Leila Antoinette Sterling
1910- CANR-24
Earlier sketches in CA 11-12, CAP-1
Mackinlock, Duncan
See Watts, Peter Christopher
Mackinnon, Charles Roy 1924- CANR-7
Earlier sketch in CA 9-10R
MacKinnon, Edward M(ichael) 1928- CANR-12
Earlier sketch in CA 61-64
MacKinnon, Frank 1919- 49-52
MacKinnon, John Ramsay 1947- 103
MacKinnon, Stephen Robert 1940- 107
MacKinstry, Elizabeth 1879-1956 .... SATA-42
Mackintosh, Athole S(palding) 1926- 7-8R
Mackintosh, Elizabeth 1896(?)-1952
Brief entry 110
MacKintosh, Ian 1940- 73-76
Mackintosh, John (Pitcairn) 1929-1978 103
Mackintosh, (John) Malcolm 1921- 7-8R
Mackintosh, N(icholas) J(ohn) 1935- 124
Mackintosh, Prudence 1944- 124
Mackle, Jeff
See McLeod, John F(reeland)
Mackler, Bernard 1934- 23-24R
Mackley, George 1900-1983 Obituary 109
Macklin, Barbara J(une) 1925- Brief entry 118
Macklin, June
See Macklin, Barbara J(une)
MacKnight, Nancy (Margaret) 1940- 118
Mackowski, Richard M(artin) 1929- 106
Macksey, (Catherine Angela) Joan 1925- 65-68
Macksey, Kenneth J. 1923- CANR-11
Earlier sketch in CA 25-28R
Macksey, Major K. J.
See Macksey, Kenneth J.
Macksey, Richard (Alan) 1930- 101
Mack Smith, Denis 1920- CANR-17
Earlier sketch in CA 23-24R
Mackworth, Cecily 57-60
Mackworth, Jane F. 1917- 37-40R
Macky, Peter W(allace) 1937- 53-56
MacLachlan, James Angell 1891-1967 .... CAP-2
Earlier sketch in CA 19-20
Maclachlan, Lewis 1894-1980 .... CANR-6
Earlier sketch in CA 7-8R
MacLachlan, Patricia 1938- Brief entry 118
See also SATA 42
See also CLR 14
Maclagan, Bridget
See Borden, Mary
Maclagan, Michael 1914- 7-8R
MacLaine, Allan H(ugh) 1924- 15-16R
MacLaine, Shirley
See Beaty, Shirley MacLean
MacLaren, A. Allan 1938- 106
Maclaren, Colin Shaw 1898-1985
Obituary 116
MacLaren, James
See Grieve, C(hristopher) M(urray)
MacLaren, Sherrill M. 1939- 124
Mac Laverty, Bernard 1942- 118
Brief entry 116
See also CLC 31
Maclay, George 1943- 45-48
Maclay, Joanna Hawkins 1938- 112
Maclean, Alasdair 1926- Brief entry 113
MacLean, Alistair (Stuart) 1922(?)-1987 57-60
Obituary 121
See also SATA 23, 50
See also CLC 3, 13, 50
Maclean, Arthur
See Tubb, E(dwin) C(harles)
MacLean, Barbara Anne Hutmacher
See Hutmacher (MacLean), Barbara Anne
Maclean, Charles 1946- 109
Maclean, Donald Duart 1913-1983
Obituary 109
Maclean, Fitzroy (Hew) 1911- CANR-14
Earlier sketch in CA 29-32R
MacLean, Jane 1935- 101
MacLean, Janet Rockwood 1917- 33-36R
MacLean, Katherine 1925- 33-36R
See also DLB 8
Maclean, Norman 1902- 102
Maclean, Una 1925- 69-72
MacLeish, Andrew 1923- 19-20R
MacLeish, Archibald 1892-1982 .... 9-10R
Obituary 106
See also DLB 4, 7, 45
See also DLBY 82
See also CLC 3, 8, 14
MacLeish, Kenneth 1917-1977 81-84
Obituary 73-76
MacLeish, Rod(erick) 1926- 41-44R
MacLeish, William H(itchcock) 1928- 120
MacLennan, David Alexander
1903-1978 .... CANR-2
Earlier sketch in CA 3R
MacLennan, (John) Hugh 1907- 7-8R
See also DLB 68
See also CLC 2, 14
MacLennan, Toby 1939- 115
Macleod, Alison 1920- 53-56
MacLeod, Alistair 1936- 123
See also DLB 60
MacLeod, Beatrice (Beach) 1910- CAP-1
Earlier sketch in CA 19-20
See also SATA 10
MacLeod, Celeste (Lipow) 1931- 105
MacLeod, Charlotte (Matilda Hughes)
1922- CANR-18
Earlier sketch in CA 23-24R
See also SATA 28
Macleod, David I(rving, Jr.) 1943- 123
Macleod, Donald 1914- 19-20R
MacLeod, Doug 1959- 112
MacLeod, Duncan J(ohn) 1939- 61-64
MacLeod, Earle Henry 1907- CAP-1
Earlier sketch in CA 9-10
MacLeod, Ellen Jane (Anderson) 1916- CANR-3
Earlier sketch in CA 7-8R
See also SATA 14
MacLeod, Jay 1961- 126
MacLeod, Jean Sutherland 1908- CANR-3
Earlier sketch in CA 11-12R
Macleod, Jennifer Selfridge 1929- 102
Macleod, Joseph (Todd Gordon)
1903-1984(?) 65-68
Obituary 112
Macleod, Norman (Wicklund) 1906-1985 73-76
Obituary 116
See also DLB 4
MacLeod, Robert
See Knox, William
MacLeod, Robert F. 1917- 77-80
MacLeod, Roderick 1892(?)-1984
Obituary 113
MacLeod, Ruth 1903- 93-96
Mac Liammhoir, Micheal
See Mac Liammoir, Micheal
Mac Liammhoir, Micheal
See Mac Liammoir, Micheal
Mac Liammoir, Micheal 1899-1978 .... CANR-3
Obituary 77-80
Earlier sketch in CA 45-48
Mac Low, Jackson 1922- 81-84
Maclure, (John) Stuart 1926- 61-64
MacLysaght, Edward Anthony
1887-1986 .... CANR-1
Obituary 118
Earlier sketch in CA 3R
Macmahon, Arthur W(hittier) 1890- 19-20R
MacMahon, Bryan (Michael) 1909- CANR-23
Earlier sketch in CA 41-44R
MacMahon, Candace W(addell) 1950- 112
Macmann, Elaine
See Willoughby, Elaine Macmann
MacManus, James
See MacManus, Seumas
MacManus, Seumas 1869-1960 102
Obituary 93-96
See also SATA 25
Macmanus, Sheila 1946- 111
MacManus, Susan A(nn) 1947- 116
MacManus, Yvonne 1931- CANR-11
Earlier sketch in CA 25-28R
MacMaster, Eve (Ruth) B(owers) 1942- 112
See also SATA 46
MacMaster, Richard Kerwin 1935- 115
Mac Master, Robert E(llsworth) 1919- 33-36R
MacMillan, Annabelle
See Quick, Annabelle
Macmillan, C(harles) J(ames) B(arr)
1935- 21-22R
MacMillan, Cecile 1898(?)-1986 Obituary 120
Macmillan, David S(tirling) 1925- 113
MacMillan, Donald L(ee) 1940- 57-60
MacMillan, Gail 1944- 97-100
Macmillan, (Maurice) Harold 1894-1986
Obituary 121
Brief entry 113
Macmillan, Maurice Victor 1921-1984
Obituary 112
Macmillan, Mona 1908- 33-36R
Macmillan, Norman 1892-1976 .... CAP-1
Obituary 69-72
Earlier sketch in CA 11-12
Macmillan, William Miller 1885-1974 .... CANR-9
Obituary 53-56
Earlier sketches in CA 11-12, CAP-1
MacMullan, Charles Walden Kirkpatrick
1889-1973 Obituary 89-92
MacMullen, Ramsay 1928- CANR-13
Earlier sketch in CA 21-22R
Macnab, Francis Auchline 1931- 25-28R
MacNab, P(eter) A(ngus) 1903- 33-36R
Macnab, Roy 1923- 65-68
MacNalty, Arthur (Salusbury)
1880-1969 .... CANR-5
Earlier sketch in CA 7-8R
MacNamara, Brinsley
See Weldon, John
See also DLB 10
Mac Namara, Donal E(oin) J(oseph)
1916- CANR-14
Earlier sketch in CA 33-36R
Macnamara, Ellen 1924- 103
Macnamara, John (Theodore) 1929- CANR-13
Earlier sketch in CA 21-22R
Macnaughton, William R(obert) 1939- 119
MacNeice, Jill 1956- 115
MacNeice, (Frederick) Louis 1907-1963 85-88
See also DLB 10, 20
See also CLC 1, 4, 10
MacNeil, Duncan
See McCutchan, Philip (Donald)
Macneil, Ian R(oderick) 1929- 33-36R
MacNeil, Neil 1891-1969 .... CAP-1
Obituary 29-32R
Earlier sketch in CA 19-20
MacNeil, Neil
See Ballard, (Willis) Todhunter
MacNeil, Robert (Breckenridge Ware)
1931- 114
Brief entry 108
MacNeill, Dand
See Fraser, George MacDonald
MacNeill, Earl S(chwom) 1893-1972
Obituary 37-40R
Macneill, Janet
See McNeely, Jeannette
Macneill, Norma 1922- 117
MacNeish, Richard S(tockton) 1918- 37-40R
Macnell, James
See Macdonnell, James Edmond
MacNelly, C(larence) L(amont)
1920(?)-1986 Obituary 118
MacNelly, Jeff(rey Kenneth) 1947- 102
MacNib
See Mackie, Albert D(avid)
MacNicholas, John (Malcolm) 1943- 123
Brief entry 118
Macnicol, Eona K(athleen) Fraser 1910- 9-10R
MacNutt, Francis S. 1925- CANR-12
Earlier sketch in CA 73-76
Macomber, Daria
See Robinson, Patricia Colbert
Macomber, William (Butts, Jr.) 1921- 61-64
Mac Orlan, Pierre
See Dumarchais, Pierre
MacPeek, Walter G. 1902-1973 .... CAP-2
Obituary 41-44R
Earlier sketch in CA 29-32
See also SATA 4, 25
Macpherson, C(rawford) Brough
1911-1987 .... CANR-2
Obituary 123
Earlier sketch in CA 7-8R
Macpherson, (Jean) Jay 1931- 5-6R
See also DLB 53
See also CLC 14
Macpherson, Jeanie 1884-1946
Brief entry 123
See also DLB 44
Macpherson, Kenneth 1903(?)-1971
Obituary 29-32R
MacPherson, Malcolm C(ook) 1943- CANR-24
Earlier sketch in CA 102
MacPherson, Margaret 1908- 49-52
See also SATA 9
See also SAAS 4
MacPherson, Thomas George
1915-1976 .... CANR-4
Earlier sketch in CA 4R
See also SATA 30
Macquarrie, Alan (Denis) 1954- 122
Macquarrie, Heath Nelson 1919- CANR-20
Earlier sketch in CA 41-44R
Macquarrie, John 1919- CANR-1
Earlier sketch in CA 3R
Macqueen, James G(alloway) 1932- 19-20R
MacQuitty, William CANR-7
Earlier sketch in CA 19-20R
MacRae, C(hristopher) Fred(erick) 1909- 45-48
MacRae, Donald E. 1907- 93-96
MacRae, Donald G. 1921- 15-16R
MacRae, Duncan (Jr.) 1921- 23-24R
MacRae, George W(insor) 1928-1985
Obituary 117
Macrae, John, Jr. 1898(?)-1983 Obituary 111
Macrae, Marjorie Knight ?-1973
Obituary 41-44R
Macrae, Norman 1923- CANR-22
Earlier sketch in CA 106
Macrae, Travis
See Feagles, Anita M(acRae)
Macridis, Roy C(onstantine) 1918- 115
Macro, Eric 1920- 29-32R
Macrorie, Ken(neth) 1918- 65-68
Macrow, Brenda G(race Joan) Barton
1916- 11-12R
MacShane, Denis 1948- 109
MacShane, Frank 1927- CANR-3
Earlier sketch in CA 11-12R
See also CLC 39
MacStiofain, Sean
See Stephenson, John Edward Drayton
MacSweeney, Barry 1948- CANR-20
Earlier sketch in CA 25-28R
MacTaggart, Morna Doris
See Brown, Morna Doris
MacThomais, Ruaraidh
See Thomson, Derick S(mith)
Macumber, Mari
See Sandoz, Mari(e Susette)
Macura, Paul 1924- CANR-8
Earlier sketch in CA 19-20R
MacVane, John (Franklin) 1912-1984 .... CANR-16
Obituary 111
Earlier sketch in CA 65-68
MacVeagh, Lincoln 1890-1972 Obituary 33-36R
Macvey, John W(ishart) 1923- CANR-7
Earlier sketch in CA 19-20R
MacVicar, Angus 1908- CANR-10
Earlier sketch in CA 13-14R
Macy, Helen 1904(?)-1978 Obituary 81-84
Macy, Joanna Rogers 1929- 125
Macy, John W(illiams), Jr. 1917-1986 .... 33-36R
Obituary 121
Macy, Mike 1951- 122
Madachy, Joseph S(teven) 1927- 5-6R
Madame Simone
See Porche, Simone (Benda)
Madan, T(riloki) N(ath) 1931- CANR-7
Earlier sketch in CA 19-20R
Madaras, Area 1969- 116
Madaras, Lynda 1947- 107
Madariaga, Isabel de
See de Madariaga, Isabel
Madariaga (Y Rojo), Salvador de
1886-1978 .... CANR-6
Obituary 81-84
Earlier sketch in CA 9-10R
Maday, Bela C(harles) 1912- 41-44R
Madden, Arthur Gerard 1911- 1R
Madden, Betty I(senbarger) 1915- 57-60
Madden, Carl H(alford) 1920-1978 .... 41-44R
Obituary 81-84
Madden, Cecil (Charles) 1902-1987
Obituary 122
Madden, Charles F(rank) 1921- 25-28R
Madden, Daniel Michael 1916- 65-68
Madden, (Jerry) David 1933- CANR-4
Earlier sketch in CA 3R
See also CAAS 3
See also DLB 6
See also CLC 5, 15
Madden, Don 1927- 25-28R
See also SATA 3
Madden, Donald L(eo) 1937- CANR-4
Earlier sketch in CA 53-56
Madden, E(dward) S(tanislaus) 1919- 11-12R
Madden, Edward H. 1925- CANR-1
Earlier sketch in CA 1R
Madden, Henry Miller 1912-1982 Obituary 108
Madden, Myron C(rowson) 1918- 115
Madden, Peter 1939- 115
Madden, Richard Raymond 1924- 5-6R
Madden, Tara Roth 1942- 126
Madden, Warren
See Cameron, Kenneth Neill
Madden, William A. 1923- 23-24R
Maddern, Al(an)
See Ellison, Harlan
Madderom, Gary 1937- 45-48
Maddex, Jack P(endleton), Jr. 1941-
Brief entry 111
Maddi, Salvatore R(ichard) 1933- 13-14R
Maddison, Angela Mary 1923- 53-56
See also SATA 10
Maddison, Angus 1926- CANR-10
Earlier sketch in CA 13-14R
Maddison, Carol Hopkins 1923- 19-20R
Maddock, Brent 1950- 81-84
Maddock, Kenneth ?-1971 Obituary 104
Maddock, Larry
See Jardine, Jack
Maddock, Mary (Denise Catharine Majdak)
1951- 116
Maddock, Reginald (Bertram) 1912- 81-84
See also SATA 15
Maddocks, Margaret (Kathleen Avern)
1906- 116
Maddocks, Morris Henry St. John 1928- 116
Maddow, Ben 1909- DLB-44
Maddox, Brenda 1932- CANR-22
Earlier sketch in CA 97-100
Maddox, Carl
See Tubb, E(dwin) C(harles)
Maddox, Conroy 1912- 101
Maddox, Gaynor 9-10R
Maddox, George L(amar), Jr. 1925- 19-20R
Maddox, James G(ray) 1907-1973 .... CAP-2
Obituary 45-48
Earlier sketch in CA 21-22
Maddox, Jerrold (Warren) 1932- 19-20R
Maddox, Lester (Garfield) 1915-
Brief entry 112
Maddox, Marion Errol 1910- 23-24R
Maddox, Robert James 1931- 33-36R
Maddox, Russell W(ebber), Jr. 1921- 3R
Maddox, Sara Higgins Sturm
See Sturm-Maddox, Sara Higgins
Maddux, Rachel 1912- CANR-5
Earlier sketch in CA 4R

Madeleva, Sister Mary
See Wolff, Mary Evaline
Madelung, A. Margaret (Arent) 1926- 15-16R
Mader, (Stanley) Chris(topher, Jr.)
1943(?)-1980 Obituary 103
Mader, Katherine 1948- 126
Madge, Charles Henry 1912- 97-100
Madge, John (Hylton) 1914-1968 .... CAP-1
Earlier sketch in CA 9-10
Madge, Violet 1916-19(?) CAP-2
Earlier sketch in CA 21-22
Madgett, Naomi Long 1923- CANR-13
Earlier sketch in CA 33-36R
See also BW
See also DLB 76
Madgwick, P(eter) J(ames) 1925- CANR-24
Earlier sketch in CA 29-32R
Madhubuti, Haki R. 1942- CANR-24
Earlier sketch in CA 73-76
See also BW
See also DLB 5, 41
See also CLC 6
Madian, Jon 1941- 61-64
See also SATA 9
Madigan, Marian East 1898- CAP-2
Earlier sketch in CA 19-20
Madigan, Mary Jean Smith 1941- 110
Madison, Arnold 1937- CANR-9
Earlier sketch in CA 21-22R
See also SATA 6
Madison, Charles A(llan) 1895- CANR-1
Earlier sketch in CA 3R
Madison, Frank
See Hutchins, Francis Gilman
Madison, Hank
See Rowland, D(onald) S(ydney)
Madison, James 1751-1836 .... DLB-37
Madison, Jane
See Horne, Hugh Robert
Madison, Joyce
See Mintz, Joyce Lois
Madison, Peter 1918- 9-10R
Madison, Russ 1929- 25-28R
Madison, Thomas A(lvin) 1926- 57-60
Madison, Tom
See Madison, Thomas A(lvin)
Madison, Winifred 37-40R
See also SATA 5
Madle, Dorothy
See Madlee, Dorothy (Haynes)
Madlee, Dorothy (Haynes) 1917-1980 .. CANR-10
Earlier sketch in CA 19-20R
Madott, Darlene (Patrice) 1952- 123
Madow, Leo 1915- CANR-13
Earlier sketch in CA 33-36R
Madow, Pauline (Reichberg) 11-12R
See also CLC 1
Madrigal, Margarita 1912(?)-1983
Obituary 110
Madruga, Lenor 1942- 102
Madsen, Axel 1930- 25-28R
Madsen, Borge Gedso 1920- 1R
Madsen, Brigham Dwaine 1914- 103
Madsen, David Lawrence 1929- 23-24R
Madsen, Richard (Paul) 1941- 123
Madsen, Roy Paul 1928- 89-92
Madsen, Truman Grant 1926- Brief entry 106
Maduell, Charles Rene, Jr. 1918- 73-76
Mae, Eydie
See Hunsberger, Edith Mae
Maedke, Wilmer O(tto) 1922- 57-60
Maehl, William H(arvey) 1915- 89-92
Maehl, William Henry, Jr. 1930- 23-24R
Maehlqvist, (Karl) Stefan 1943- CANR-24
Earlier sketch in CA 107
See also SATA 30
Maenchen, Otto John 1894-1969 Obituary .. 109
Maenchen-Helfen, Otto J.
See Maenchen, Otto John
Maend, Evald
See Mand, Ewald
Maepenn, Hugh
See Kuttner, Henry
Maepenn, K. H.
See Kuttner, Henry
Maeroff, Gene I(rving) 1939- 61-64
Maertz, Richard Charles 1935- 73-76
Maes-Jelinek, Hena 1929- 107
Maestro, Betsy C. 1944- CANR-23
Earlier sketches in CA 61-64, CANR-8
See also SATA 30
Maestro, Giulio 1942- CANR-23
Earlier sketches in CA 57-60, CANR-8
See also SATA 8
Maeterlinck, Maurice 1862-1949
Brief entry 104
See also TCLC 3
Maffei, Paolo 1926- CANR-25
Earlier sketch in CA 108
Magalaner, Marvin 1920- CANR-1
Earlier sketch in CA 1R
Magaret, Helene 1906- 4R
Magarshack, David 1899- 7-8R
Magary, Alan 1944- CANR-8
Earlier sketch in CA 61-64
Magary, James F(rederick) 1933- 25-28R
Magary, Kerstin Fraser 1947- CANR-12
Earlier sketch in CA 61-64
Magdalany, Philip 1936(?)-1985 Obituary 117
Magdol, Edward 1918- CANR-9
Earlier sketch in CA 21-22R
Magee, Bryan 1930- CANR-2
Earlier sketch in CA 7-8R
Magee, David (Bickersteth) 1905-1977 81-84
Obituary 73-76
Magee, John 1901-1987 Obituary 122
Magee, Wes 1939- CANR-23
Earlier sketch in CA 107
Mager, George C(lyde) 1937- 49-52
Mager, Nathan H. 1912-1986 .... CANR-18
Earlier sketches in CA 45-48, CANR-2
Maggal, Moshe M(orris) 1908- CAP-2
Earlier sketch in CA 23-24
Maggin, Elliot S. 1950- 102
Maggio, Joe 1938- CANR-1
Earlier sketch in CA 45-48
Maggiolo, Walter A(ndrew) 1908- 85-88
Maggs, Peter B(lount) 1936- CANR-23
Earlier sketches in CA 19-20R, CANR-8
Maggs, Will(iam) Colston 1912- 13-14R
Magidoff, Robert 1905-1970 .... CAP-1
Earlier sketch in CA 19-20
Magidson, Herbert (Adolph) 1906-1986
Obituary 118
Magill, Frank N(orthen) 1907- CANR-6
Earlier sketch in CA 7-8R
Magill, Kathleen 1948- 116
Magill, Marcus
See Hill, Brian (Merrikin)
Magill, Robert S(amuel) 1941- 89-92
Maginnis, Andrew Francis 1923- 45-48
Magister, Joseph
See Grant, Louis T(heodore)
Magloire-Saint-Aude, Clement 1912- 15-16R
Magnarella, Paul J(oseph) 93-96
Magner, James A. 1901- CAP-1
Earlier sketch in CA 13-14
Magner, James Edmund, Jr. 1928- CANR-7
Earlier sketch in CA 19-20R
Magner, Thomas F(reeman) 1918- 19-20R
Magnin, Cyril I(saac) 1899-1988 107
Obituary 125
Magnin, Cyril I. 1899- 107
Magnus, Philip
See Magnus-Allcroft, Sir Philip
(Montefiore)
Magnus, Samuel Woolf 1910- CAP-1
Earlier sketch in CA 9-10
Magnus-Allcroft, Sir Philip (Montefiore)
1906- CAP-1
Earlier sketch in CA 11-12
Magnuson, Don(ald Hammer) 1911-1979
Obituary 89-92
Magnuson, Edward F. 1926- 102
Magnuson, Keith (Arlen) 1947- 93-96
Magnuson, Paul 1939- 69-72
Magnuson, Paul Budd 1884-1968
Obituary 106
Magnuson, Warren G(rant) 1905- 85-88
Magnussen, Daniel Osar 1919- 65-68
Magnusson, Magnus 1929- CANR-23
Earlier sketch in CA 105
Magog, Paul Dowsey
See Dowsey-Magog, Paul
Magoon, Robert A(rnold) 1922- CANR-24
Earlier sketch in CA 107
Magorian, Christopher 1959- 111
Magorian, James 1942- CANR-18
Earlier sketch in CA 102
See also SATA 32
Magoun, F(rederick) Alexander 1896- CAP-2
Earlier sketch in CA 17-18
Magoun, Francis P(eabody), Jr.
1895-1979(?) 107
Magowan, Robin 1936- CANR-20
Earlier sketches in CA 9-10R, CANR-4
Magrath, C(laude) Peter 1933- 19-20R
Magrid, Henry M. 1918(?)-1979 Obituary .. 89-92
Magruder, Jeb Stuart 1934- 101
Magsam, Charles Michael 1907- CAP-1
Earlier sketch in CA 15-16
Magubane, Bernard (Makhosezwe) 1930- .. 93-96
Maguen, David
See Markish, David
Maguinness, W(illiam) Stuart 1903-1982 . CAP-1
Obituary 108
Earlier sketch in CA 15-16
Maguire, Anne
See Nearing, Penny
Maguire, Daniel Charles 1931- 49-52
Maguire, Francis T(homas) 1911-1976
Obituary 69-72
Maguire, Gregory 1954- 81-84
See also SATA 28
Maguire, Henry Pownall 1943- 111
Maguire, Jack 1920- 81-84
Maguire, John David 1932- CANR-9
Earlier sketch in CA 21-22R
Maguire, John T(homas) 1917- 2R
Maguire, Michael 1945- 104
Maguire, R(obert) A(gustine) J(oseph)
1898- 7-8R
Maguire, Robert A(lan) 1930- 73-76
Magwood, John McLean 1912- 106
Mahajan, Vidya Dhar 1913- CANR-11
Earlier sketch in CA 25-28R
Mahajani, Usha 1933- 53-56
Mahan, Alfred Thayer 1840-1914 .... DLB-47
Mahan, Bill
See Mahan, William Allen
Mahan, Pat
See Wheat, Patte
Mahan, Patte Wheat
See Wheat, Patte
Mahan, William Allen 1930- CANR-15
Earlier sketch in CA 85-88
Mahapatra, Jayanta 1928- CANR-15
Earlier sketch in CA 73-76
See also CLC 33
Mahar, J. Michael 1929- 13-14R
Mahdi, Muhsin S(ayyid) 1926- CANR-3
Earlier sketch in CA 1R
Maher, Brendan A(rnold) 1924- 25-28R
Maher, James T(homas) 1917- 65-68
Maher, John E. 1925- 19-20R
Maher, Ramona 1934- CANR-9
Earlier sketch in CA 21-22R
See also SATA 13
Maher, Robert F. 1922- 19-20R
Maher, Trafford P(atrick) 1914- 21-22R
Maheshwari, Shriram 1931- CANR-11
Earlier sketch in CA 23-24R
Maheux-Forcier, Louise 1929- DLB-60
Mahin, John Lee 1902(?)-1984 Obituary 112
See also DLB 44
Mahl, George F(ranklin) 1917- 93-96
Mahl, Mary R. 1914- 25-28R
Mahlendorf, Ursula R. 1929- 49-52
Mahler, Gregory S. 1950- 123
Mahler, Jane Gaston 1906- 37-40R
Mahler, Margaret S(choenberger)
1897-1985 103
Obituary 117
Mahlqvist, (Karl) Stefan
See Maehlqvist, (Karl) Stefan
See also SATA 30
Mahmood, Mamdani 1946- 105
Maholick, Leonard T(homas) 1921- CANR-1
Earlier sketch in CA 4R
Mahon, Derek 1941- Brief entry 113
See also DLB 40
See also CLC 27
Mahon, John K(eith) 1912- 19-20R
Mahon, Julia C(unha) 1916- 61-64
See also SATA 11
Mahon, Thomas (Cavan) 1944- 119
Mahoney, Irene 1921- 61-64
Mahoney, J. Daniel 1931- 61-64
Mahoney, John (Francis) 1929- 41-44R
Mahoney, John Leo 1928- CANR-14
Earlier sketch in CA 33-36R
Mahoney, John Thomas 1905-1981 .... CAP-1
Obituary 104
Earlier sketch in CA 11-12
Mahoney, Michael J(ohn) 1946- CANR-8
Earlier sketch in CA 53-56
Mahoney, Patrick 1927- 81-84
Mahoney, Robert F. 1914- 15-16R
Mahoney, Thomas Arthur 1928- 1R
Mahoney, Thomas H(enry) D(onald)
1913- 13-14R
Mahoney, Tim 1947- 123
Mahoney, Tom
See Mahoney, John Thomas
Mahony, Elizabeth Winthrop 1948- 41-44R
See also SATA 8
Mahony, Patrick
See O'Mahony, Patrick
Mahony, Peter (Bernard) 1931- 118
Mahood, Kenneth 1930- 103
See also SATA 24
Mahood, Ruth I. 1908- CAP-1
Earlier sketch in CA 19-20
Mahrer, Alvin R(aymond) 1927- 23-24R
Mahy, Margaret 1936- CANR-13
Earlier sketch in CA 69-72
See also SATA 14
See also CLR 7
Mai, Ludwig H(ubert) 1898- 73-76
Maibaum, Richard 1909- 102
Maiden, Cecil (Edward) 1902-1981 73-76
See also SATA 52
Maidoff, Ilka
See List, Ilka Katherine
Maier, Charles S(teven) 1939- 69-72
Maier, Ernest L(ouis) 1938- 105
Maier, Howard 1906(?)-1983 Obituary 109
Maier, Joseph (Ben) 1911- 23-24R
Maier, Norman R(aymond) F(rederick)
1900-1977 .... CANR-4
Obituary 73-76
Earlier sketch in CA 1R
Maier, Paul L(uther) 1930- CANR-2
Earlier sketch in CA 5-6R
Maier, Pauline (Rubbelke) 1938- 37-40R
Maier, (Henry) William (Jr.) 1901- 2R
Maik, Henri
See Hecht, Henri Joseph
Mailer, Norman 1923- 11-12R
See also CABS 1
See also DLB 2, 16, 28
See also DLBY 80, 83
See also DLBD 3
See also CLC 1, 2, 3, 4, 5, 8, 11, 14,
28, 39
See also AITN 2
Maillard, Keith 1942- 93-96
Maillet, Adrienne 1885-1963 .... DLB-68
Maillet, Antonine 1929- 120
Brief entry 115
See also DLB 60
Mailloux, Steven 1950- CANR-25
Earlier sketch in CA 107
Mails, Thomas E. 1920(?)- Brief entry 111
Maimon, Morton A. 1931- 33-36R
Main, Gloria (Jean) L(und) 1933- 112
Main, Jackson Turner 1917- CANR-1
Earlier sketch in CA 1R
Main, Mildred Miles 1898- CAP-1
Earlier sketch in CA 15-16
Maine, Charles Eric
See McIlwain, David
Maine, David
See Avice, Claude (Pierre Marie)
Maingot, Rodney 1893-1982 Obituary 105
Mainland, William Faulkner 1905-1988(?)
Obituary 125
Mainprize, Don 1930- CANR-7
Earlier sketch in CA 19-20R
Mains, David R(andall) 1936- 93-96
Mainstone, Rowland J(ohnson) 1923- .. CANR-23
Earlier sketch in CA 107
Mainwaring, Daniel 1902-1977 .... DLB-44
Mainwaring, Marion CANR-3
Earlier sketch in CA 4R
Maiolo, Joseph 1938- 49-52
Maiorano, Robert 1946- 116
See also SATA 43
Mair, Alistair 1924- 11-12R
Mair, (Alexander) Craig 1948- 102
Mair, George Brown 1914- CANR-12
Earlier sketch in CA 13-14R
Mair, George F(isk) 1922-1978 Obituary 111
Mair, Lucy Philip 1901-1986 Obituary 119
Mair, Margaret
See Crompton, Margaret (Norah Mair)
Mair, Victor H(enry) 1943- 113
Mairowitz, David Zane 1943- 122
Mais, Roger 1905-1955 124
Brief entry 105
See also BW
See also TCLC 8
Mais, S(tuart) P(etre) B(rodie) 1885-1975 .. 69-72
Obituary 57-60
Maisel, Herbert 1930- 53-56
Maisel, Louis Sandy 1945- 117
Maisel, Sherman J(oseph) 1918- CANR-19
Earlier sketches in CA 5-6R, CANR-4
Maisels, Maxine S. 1939- 49-52
Maisky, Ivan (Mikhailovich) 1884-1975 65-68
Obituary 61-64
Maison, Della
See Katz, Bobbi
Maison, Margaret M(ary Bowles) 1920- .. 17-18R
Maissi, Elie 1911(?)-1983 Obituary 110
Maital, Shlomo 1942- CANR-25
Earlier sketch in CA 108
Maitland, Antony Jasper 1935- 101
See also SATA 25
Maitland, David J(ohnston) 1922- 116
Maitland, Derek 1943- CANR-23
Earlier sketch in CA 29-32R
Maitland, Margaret
See Du Breuil, (Elizabeth) L(or)inda
and Wallmann, Jeffrey M(iner)
Maitland, Sara (Louise) 1950- CANR-13
Earlier sketch in CA 69-72
See also CLC 49
Maitra, Priyatosh 1930- 107
Maizel, C. L.
See Maizel, Clarice Matthews
Maizel, Clarice Matthews 1919- 11-12R
Maizel, Leah
See Maizel, Clarice Matthews
Maja-Pearce, Adewale 1953- 126
Majault, Joseph 1916- 101
Majerus, Janet 1936- 65-68
Majeski, Bill
See Majeski, William
Majeski, William 1927- CANR-18
Earlier sketch in CA 25-28R
Majka, Linda C. 1947- 124
Majonica, Ernst 1920- 29-32R
Major, Alan P(ercival) 1929- CANR-7
Earlier sketch in CA 57-60
Major, Andre 1942- DLB-60
Major, Clarence 1936- CANR-25
Earlier sketches in CA 23-24R, CANR-13
See also CAAS 6
See also BW
See also DLB 33
See also CLC 3, 19, 48
Major, Geraldyn Hodges 1894-1984 85-88
Obituary 113
Major, Gerri
See Major, Geraldyn Hodges
Major, H. M.
See Jarvis, Sharon
Major, Henriette 1933- 109
Major, J(ames) Russell 1921- CANR-2
Earlier sketch in CA 7-8R
Major, Jean-Louis 1937- CANR-18
Earlier sketches in CA 49-52, CANR-2
Major, John M(cClellan) 1918- 13-14R
Major, Kevin (Gerald) 1949- CANR-21
Earlier sketch in CA 97-100
See also SATA 32
See also DLB 60
See also CLC 26
See also CLR 11
Major, Mabel 1893- 45-48
Major, Mark Imre 1923- 65-68
Major, Ralph Hermon 1884-1970 .... CAP-1
Earlier sketch in CA 9-10
Major, Reginald W. 1926- 29-32R
Major-General of Marsland
See Duncan, Ronald
Major-Poetzl, Pamela 1943- 116
Majumdar, R(amesh) C(handra) 1888- .. 33-36R
Majumder, Sanat K(umer) 1929- 33-36R
Makanowitzky, Barbara
See Norman, Barbara
Makarova, Marina 1942- 120
Makarova, Natalia 1940- 113
Makary
See Iranek-Osmecki, Kazimierz
Makeba, (Zensi) Miriam 1932- 104
See also BW
Makely, William O(rson) 1932- 53-56
Makemie, Francis 1658(?)-1708 .... DLB-24
Makepeace, Joanna
See York, Margaret Elizabeth
Makepeace, R(oyston) W(illiam) 1950- 116
Makerney, Edna Smith 1921- 61-64
Maki, James
See Ozu, Yasujiro
Maki, John M(cGilvrey) 1909- 109

Makie, Pam 1943- SATA-37
Makin, Peter (Julian) 1946- 93-96
Makino, Seiichi 1935- 113
Makins, Roger Mellor 1904- 111
Makkai, Adam 1935- CANR-10
Earlier sketch in CA 57-60
Makkreel, Rudolf A. 1939- 122
Makow, Henry 1949- 7-8R
Makower, Addie (Gertrude Leonaura) 1906- 65-68
Makower, Joel 1952- 124
Makowsky, Veronica A(nn) 1954- 116
Maksimov, Vladimir (Yemelyanovich)
See Maximov, Vladimir (Yemelyanovich)
Maktari, Abdulla M. A. 1936- 37-40R
Maktos, John 1902-1977 Obituary 69-72
Mal
See Hancock, Malcolm
Malabaila, Damianos
See Levi, Primo
Malabre, Alfred L(eopold, Jr.) 1931- CANR-12
Earlier sketch in CA 65-68
Malamud, Bernard 1914-1986 7-8R
Obituary 118
See also CABS 1
See also DLB 2, 28
See also DLBY 80, 86
See also CDALB 1941-1968
See also CLC 1, 2, 3, 5, 8, 9, 11, 18, 27, 44
Malamud, Phyllis Carole 1938- 125
Malan, Roy Mark 1911- 41-44R
Maland, David 1929- 103
Malanga, Gerard (Joseph) 1943-
Brief entry 112
Malanos, George J(ohn) 1919-1962 3R
Obituary 103
Malarek, Victor 1948- 123
Malavie, M. J. 1920- 29-32R
Malbin, Michael J(acob) 1943- CANR-17
Earlier sketch in CA 73-76
Malcolm, Andrew (Ian) 1927- 97-100
Malcolm, Andrew H(ogarth) 1943- 53-56
Malcolm, Dan
See Silverberg, Robert
Malcolm, Donald 1932(?)-1975 Obituary 104
Malcolm, Ian
See Malcolm, Andrew (Ian)
Malcolm, Janet 123
Malcolm, John
See Andrews, John Malcolm
Malcolm, Margaret
See Kuether, Edith Lyman
Malcolm, Norman 1911- 37-40R
Malcolmson, Anne
See von Storch, Anne B.
Malcolmson, David 1899- 7-8R
See also SATA 6
Malcolmson, Robert W(illiam) 1943- CANR-19
Earlier sketch in CA 103
Malcolm X
See Little, Malcolm
Malcom, Robert E. 1933- 19-20R
Malcomson, R(osalie) M(ary) 1925- 119
Malcomson, William L. 1932- 25-28R
Malcoskey, Edna Walker 19-20R
Maldonado-Denis, Manuel 1933-
Brief entry 113
Male, David Arthur 1928- 57-60
Male, Roy R(aymond) 1919- 104
Malecki, Edward S(tanley) 1938- 41-44R
Malefakis, Edward E(manuel) 1932- 29-32R
Malefijt, Annemarie de Waal
See de Waal Malefijt, Annemarie
Malek, Frederic Vincent 1937- 81-84
Malek, James S(tanley) 1941- 57-60
Malenbaum, Wilfred 1913- CANR-1
Earlier sketch in CA 3R
Malerich, Edward P. 1940- 33-36R
Maleska, Eugene Thomas 1916- CANR-1
Earlier sketch in CA 4R
Malet, B(aldwyn) Hugh G(renville) 1928- 19-20R
Malgonkar, Manohar (Dattatray) 1913- CANR-18
Earlier sketches in CA 2R, CANR-1
Malherbe, Abraham J(ohannes) 1930- CANR-1
Earlier sketch in CA 49-52
Malherbe, Ernst Gideon 1895- CAP-1
Earlier sketch in CA 13-14
Malherbe, Janie Antonia (Nel) 1897- CAP-1
Earlier sketch in CA 15-16
Malhotra, Ashok Kumar 1940- 110
Mali, Jane Lawrence 1937- 114
See also SATA 44, 51
Mali, Paul 1926- CANR-8
Earlier sketch in CA 57-60
Malick, Terrence 1943- 101
Malick, Terry
See Malick, Terrence
Malickson, David L. 1928- 110
Malik, Charles Habib 1906-1987 CANR-7
Obituary 124
Earlier sketch in CA 45-48
Malik, Hafeez 1930- CANR-21
Earlier sketch in CA 77-80
Malik, Yogendra K(umar) 1929- 81-84
Malikin, David 1913- 77-80
Malin, David (Frederick) 1941- 118
Malin, Irving 1934- CANR-6
Earlier sketch in CA 13-14R
Malin, James Claude 1893-1979 Obituary 113
Malin, Peter
See Conner, Patrick Reardon
Malina, Bruce J(ohn) 1933- 112
Malina, Frank J(oseph) 1912-1981 93-96
Obituary 108
Malina, Judith 1926- CANR-18
Earlier sketch in CA 102
Maling, Arthur (Gordon) 1923- CANR-22
Earlier sketches in CA 49-52, CANR-3
Malinin, Theodore I 1933- 93-96
Malino, Frances 1940- 115
Malinowski, Bronislaw (Kasper) 1884-1942 Brief entry 114
Malins, Edward (Greenway) 1910- 103
Malins, Penelope 1929- 126
Malipiero, Gian Francesco 1882-1973
Obituary 45-48
Malkiel, Burton Gordon 1932- 49-52
Malkiel, Yakov 1914- 25-28R
Malkiewicz, J(an) Kris 1931- 57-60
Malkin, Lawrence 1930- 126
Malkin, Maurice L. 1900- 49-52
Malkin, Sol(omon) M. 1910-1986
Obituary 118
Malkoff, Karl 1938- 19-20R
Malkus, Alida Wright 1899- 5-6R
Mall, E. Jane 1920- CANR-13
Earlier sketch in CA 23-24R
Mall, Viktor
See Beskow, Bo
Mallaby, (Howard) George 1902-1978
Obituary 108
Mallalieu, John Percival William 1908-1980 Obituary 97-100
Mallan, Lloyd 1914- 5-6R
Malle, Louis 1932- 101
Mallea, Eduardo 1903-1982(?) Obituary 114
Mallen, Bruce E. 1937- CANR-14
Earlier sketch in CA 21-22R
Mallery, David 1923- 5-6R
Malleson, Andrew (Graeme) 1931-
Brief entry 112
Malleson, Lucy Beatrice 1899-1973 97-100
Obituary 49-52
Mallet-Joris, Francoise 1930- CANR-17
Earlier sketch in CA 65-68
See also CLC 11
Mallett, Anne 1913- 49-52
Malley, Ern
See McAuley, James Phillip
Mallin, Jay 1927- 19-20R
Mallin, Tom 1927(?)-1978 Obituary 89-92
Mallinson, George Greisen 1918- CANR-1
Earlier sketch in CA 3R
Mallinson, Jeremy (John Crosby) 1937- CANR-6
Earlier sketch in CA 57-60
Mallinson, Vernon 1910- 7-8R
Malliol, William
See McInerny, William T(homas)
Mallis, Jackie
See Mallis, Jacqueline
Mallis, Jacqueline 1922- 113
Malloch, Peter
See Duncan, W(illiam) Murdoch
Mallock, W. H. 1849-1923 DLB-18, 57
Mallon, Bill 1952- 119
Mallon, Thomas 1951- 110
Mallone, George 1944- 115
Mallone, Ronald Stephen 1916- CAP-1
Earlier sketch in CA 9-10
Mallonee, Richard C(arvel) II 1923- 109
Mallory, Bob F(ranklin) 1932- 89-92
Mallory, Enid Lorraine 1938- 105
Mallory, Kenneth 1945- 124
Mallory, Mark
See Reynolds, Dallas McCord
Mallory, Walter Hampton 1892-1980 11-12R
Obituary 101
Mallough, Don 1914- 23-24R
Mallowan, Agatha Christie
See Christie, Agatha (Mary Clarissa)
Mallowan, Max (Edgar Lucien) 1904-1978 CANR-21
Obituary 81-84
Earlier sketch in CA 69-72
Mallows, (Edward) Wilfrid (Nassau) 1905- 119
Malloy, Ruth Lor 1932- CANR-22
Earlier sketch in CA 69-72
Malloy, Terry 1950- 69-72
Mally, E(mma) Louise 1908- 33-36R
Malm, F(inn) T(heodore) 1919- 19-20R
Malm, William P(aul) 1928- 9-10R
Malmberg, Carl 1904- 33-36R
See also SATA 9
Malmgren, Harald B(ernard) 1935- 45-48
Malmo, Robert Beverley 1912- 61-64
Malmstroem, Vincent H(erschel)
See Malmstrom, Vincent H(erschel)
Malmstrom, Jean 1908- 53-56
Malmstrom, Vincent H(erschel) 1926- 112
Malo, John W. 1911- CANR-12
Earlier sketch in CA 33-36R
See also SATA 4
Malocsay, Zoltan 1946- 81-84
Malof, Joseph F(etler) 1934- 29-32R
Maloff, Saul 1922- 33-36R
See also CLC 5
Malone, Bill C(harles) 1934- 65-68
Malone, Colonel Dick
See Malone, Richard S(ankey)
Malone, Dick
See Malone, Richard S(ankey)
Malone, Dumas 1892-1986 CANR-2
Obituary 121
Earlier sketch in CA 1R
See also DLB 17
Malone, Elmer Taylor, Jr. 1943- CANR-17
Earlier sketches in CA 49-52, CANR-1
Malone, Joseph James 1924-1983
Obituary 111
Malone, Kemp 1889-1971 Obituary 89-92
Malone, Louis
See MacNeice, (Frederick) Louis
Malone, Margaret Gay 1939- 112
Malone, Mary CANR-2
Earlier sketch in CA 1R
Malone, Michael (Christopher) 1942- CANR-14
Earlier sketch in CA 77-80
See also CLC 43
Malone, Michael P. 1940- CANR-12
Earlier sketch in CA 29-32R
Malone, R. S.
See Malone, Richard S(ankey)
Malone, Richard S(ankey) 1909-1985
Obituary 116
Brief entry 107
Malone, Ruth 1918- 93-96
Malone, Ted
See Malone, Elmer Taylor, Jr.
Malone, Wex S(mathers) 1906- 11-12R
Maloney, Frank E(dward) 1918-1980 73-76
Obituary 97-100
Maloney, George A(nthony) 1924- CANR-8
Earlier sketch in CA 23-24R
Maloney, J(oseph) J(ohn) 1940- 109
Maloney, Joan M(arie) 1931- 37-40R
Maloney, Pat
See Markun, Patricia Maloney
Maloney, Ralph Liston 1927-1973 CANR-3
Obituary 45-48
Earlier sketch in CA 2R
Malony, H(enry) Newton 1931- 104
Malory, (Sir) Thomas 1410(?)-1471(?) SATA-33
Malouf, (George Joseph) David 1934- 124
Malouf, David 1934- CLC-28
Malouf, Pyrrha 1929- 117
Malpass, E(ric) L(awson) 1910- CANR-18
Earlier sketches in CA 9-10R, CANR-3
Malpass, Leslie F(rederick) 1922- CANR-8
Earlier sketch in CA 19-20R
Malpede, Karen (Sophia) 1945- CANR-26
Earlier sketch in CA 45-48
Malraux, (Georges-)Andre 1901-1976 CAP-2
Obituary 69-72
Earlier sketch in CA 21-22
See also DLB 72
See also CLC 1, 4, 9, 13, 15
Malraux, Clara (Goldschmidt) 1897(?)-1982 Obituary 108
Malraux-Goldschmidt, Clara
See Malraux, Clara (Goldschmidt)
Malta, Demetrio Aguilera
See Aguilera Malta, Demetrio
Maltby, Arthur 1935- CANR-10
Earlier sketch in CA 25-28R
Maltby, William S(aunders) 1940-
Brief entry 113
Malten, William 1902- CAP-2
Earlier sketch in CA 23-24
Maltese, Michael 1909(?)-1981 Obituary 103
See also SATA 24
Maltin, Leonard 1950- CANR-12
Earlier sketch in CA 29-32R
Maltman, Kim 1950- 112
Maltz, Albert 1908-1985 41-44R
Obituary 115
Maltz, Maxwell 1899-1975 65-68
Obituary 57-60
Maltz, Stephen 1932- 57-60
Maluf, Chafic 1905(?)-1976 Obituary 69-72
Malveaux, Julianne M(arie) 1953- CANR-23
Earlier sketch in CA 105
Malvern, Corinne 1905-1956 Brief entry 115
See also SATA 34
Malvern, Gladys ?-1962 73-76
See also SATA 23
Malville, J. McKim
See Malville, John McKim
Malville, John McKim 1934- 120
Malville, Kim
See Malville, John McKim
Maly, Eugene H. 1920-1981 CANR-14
Earlier sketch in CA 23-24R
Malz, Betty 1929- 113
Malzberg, Barry N(athaniel) 1939- CANR-16
Earlier sketch in CA 61-64
See also CAAS 4
See also DLB 8
See also CLC 7
Malzberg, Benjamin 1893-1975 CAP-1
Obituary 57-60
Earlier sketch in CA 15-16
Mama G.
See Davis, Grania
Mamalakis, Markos J(ohn) 1932- 45-48
Maman, Andre 1927- 73-76
Mamatey, Victor S(amuel) 1917- 9-10R
Mamet, David (Alan) 1947- CANR-15
Earlier sketch in CA 81-84
See also DLB 7
See also CLC 9, 15, 34, 46
Mamis, Justin E. 1929- 11-12R
Mamleev, Yury
See Mamleyev, Yuri
Mamleyev, Yuri 1931- 85-88
Mamonova, Tatyana 1943- 114
Mamoulian, Rouben (Zachary) 1897-1987 25-28R
Obituary 124
See also CLC 16
Man, Felix H.
See Baumann, Hans Felix S(iegismund)
Man, John 1941- CANR-16
Earlier sketch in CA 93-96
Manach, Jorge 1898(?)-1961 Obituary 111
Manard, Barbara Bolling 1945- 121
Manarin, Louis H(enry) 1932- 23-24R
Mana-Zucca
See Cassel, Mana-Zucca
Mancewicz, Bernice Winslow 1917- 37-40R
Manch, Joseph (Rodman) 1910- 53-56
Manchee, Fred B. 1903(?)-1981 Obituary 105
Manchel, Frank 1935- CANR-14
Earlier sketch in CA 37-40R
See also SATA 10
Manchester, Harland 1898-1977 4R
Obituary 73-76
Manchester, Paul T(homas) 1893- 61-64
Manchester, William 1922- CANR-3
Earlier sketch in CA 1R
See also AITN 1
Mancini, Anthony 1939- 73-76
Mancini, Pat McNees
See McNees, Pat
Mancke, Richard B(ell) 1943- 81-84
Mancroft, Stormont Mancroft Samuel 1914- 49-52
Mancusi-Ungaro, Harold R(aymond), Jr. 1947- 97-100
Mancuso, Joe
See Mancuso, Joseph R.
Mancuso, Joseph R. 1941- 93-96
Mand, Ewald 1906- 19-20R
Mandel, Adrienne Schizzano 1934- 37-40R
Mandel, Benjamin 1891(?)-1973 Obituary 45-48
Mandel, Bernard 1920- 4R
Mandel, Eli(as Wolf) 1922- CANR-15
Earlier sketch in CA 73-76
See also DLB 53
Mandel, Ernest 1923- CANR-15
Earlier sketch in CA 37-40R
Mandel, George 1920- 2R
Mandel, Jerome 1937- 37-40R
Mandel, Leon 1928- CANR-13
Earlier sketch in CA 77-80
Mandel, Loring 1928- 73-76
Mandel, Morris 1911- CANR-6
Earlier sketch in CA 7-8R
Mandel, Oscar 1926- CANR-21
Earlier sketches in CA 1R, CANR-2
Mandel, Ruth Blumenstock 1938- 105
Mandel, Sally Elizabeth 1944- 102
Mandel, Sheila 1930(?)-1987 Obituary 124
Mandel, Sidney Albert 1923- 93-96
Mandel, Siegfried 1922- CANR-20
Earlier sketches in CA 4R, CANR-5
Mandel, William M(arx) 1917- 11-12R
Mandela, Nelson R(olihlahla) 1918- 125
See also BW
Mandela, (Nomzamo) Winnie (Madikileza) 1936- 125
See also BW
Mandelbaum, Allen 111
Mandelbaum, David G(oodman) 1911-1987 41-44R
Obituary 122
Mandelbaum, Maurice (H.) 1908-1987
Obituary 121
Brief entry 113
Mandelbaum, Michael 1946- 101
Mandelbaum, Seymour J. 1936- 19-20R
Mandelker, Daniel Robert 1926- CANR-20
Earlier sketches in CA 3R, CANR-5
Mandelkorn, Eugenia Miller 1916- 11-12R
Mandell, Arnold Joseph 1934- 101
Mandell, Betty Reid 1924- CANR-8
Earlier sketch in CA 61-64
Mandell, Fran Gare 1939- 115
Mandell, Gail Porter 1940- 123
Mandell, Maurice I(ra) 1925- CANR-11
Earlier sketch in CA 25-28R
Mandell, Mel 1926- 41-44R
Mandell, Muriel (Hortense Levin) 1921- 9-10R
Mandell, Richard Donald 1929- CANR-10
Earlier sketch in CA 25-28R
Mandelshtam, Nadezhda
See Mandelstam, Nadezhda (Yakovlevna)
Mandelstam, Nadezhda (Yakovlevna) 1899-1980 110
Obituary 102
Mandelstam, Osip (Emilievich) 1891(?)-1938(?) Brief entry 104
See also TCLC 2, 6
Mandelstamm, Allan B(eryle) 1928- 41-44R
Mander, A(lfred) E(rnest) 1894- CAP-1
Earlier sketch in CA 11-12
Mander, Anica Vesel 1934- CANR-8
Earlier sketch in CA 61-64
Mander, Gertrud 1927- 93-96
Mander, Jerry 1936- 81-84
Mander, Raymond (Josiah Gale) 1911(?)-1983 101
Obituary 111
Mander, Rosalie Grylls 7-8R
Mandiargues, Andre Pieyre de
See Pieyre de Mandiargues, Andre
See also CLC 41
Mandino, Og 1923- 103
Mandler, George 1924- CANR-19
Earlier sketches in CA 1R, CANR-4
Mandler, Jean Matter 1929- CANR-19
Earlier sketch in CA 15-16R
Mandrake, Ethel Belle
See Thurman, Wallace (Henry)
Mandrepelias, Loizos
See Hartocollis, Peter
Mane, Robert 1926- 37-40R
Manella, Raymond L(awrence) 1917- 19-20R
Manes, Stephen 1949- 97-100
See also SATA 40, 42
Manfred, Frederick (Feikema) 1912- CANR-25
Earlier sketches in CA 9-10R, CANR-5
See also SATA 30
See also DLB 6

Manfred, Freya 1944- ... 69-72
Manfred, Robert
See Marx, Erica Elizabeth
Manfredi, John Francis 1920- ... 109
Manfredi, V.
See Musciano, Walter A.
Mang, Karl 1922- ... 101
Mangalam, J(oseph) J(oseph) 1924- ... 37-40R
Mangan, James Thomas 1896- ... CAP-2
Earlier sketch in CA 19-20
Mangan, (John Joseph) Sherry 1904-1961
Obituary ... 112
See also DLB 4
Manganiello, Dominic 1951- ... 124
Mangat, J(agjit) S(ingh) 1937- ... 73-76
Mangione, Jerre 1909- ... CANR-16
Earlier sketch in CA 15-16R
See also SATA 6
Mango, Cyril (Alexander) 1928- ... 109
Mango, Karin N. 1936- ... 123
See also SATA 52
Mangold, Tom 1934- ... 69-72
Mangum, Garth L(eroy) 1926- ... 81-84
Mangurian, David 1938- ... CANR-10
Earlier sketch in CA 57-60
See also SATA 14
Manhattan, Avro 1914- ... CANR-5
Earlier sketch in CA 11-12R
Manheim, Emanuel 1897-1988 Obituary ... 125
Manheim, Jarol B(ruce) 1946- ... CANR-21
Earlier sketches in CA 57-60, CANR-6
Manheim, Leonard (Falk) 1902- ... CAP-2
Earlier sketch in CA 21-22
Manheim, Michael 1928- ... 81-84
Manheim, Ralph 1907(?)- Brief entry ... 115
Manheim, Sylvan D. 1897-1977 Obituary ... 73-76
Manheim, Theodore 1921- Brief entry ... 108
Manheim, Werner 1915- ... 53-56
Manhire, Bill 1946- ... CANR-20
Earlier sketch in CA 103
Manhoff, Bill
See Manhoff, Wilton
Manhoff, Wilton 1919-1974 Obituary ... 49-52
Maniates, Maria Rika 1937- ... 113
Maniaty, Anthony 1949- ... 119
Maniaty, Tony
See Maniaty, Anthony
Manicas, Peter T(heodore) 1934- ... 53-56
Maniere, J.-E.
See Giraudoux, (Hippolyte) Jean
Manifold, J(ohn) S(treeter) 1915- ... CANR-24
Earlier sketch in CA 69-72
Manigault, Edward 1897(?)-1983 Obituary ... 109
Manilla, James ... 97-100
Manis, Jerome G. 1917- ... 25-28R
Manis, Melvin 1931- ... 21-22R
Maniscalco, Joseph 1926- ... CANR-8
Earlier sketch in CA 5-6R
See also SATA 10
Manjon, Maite
See Manjon-Alonso, Maria Teresa
Manjon-Alonso, Maria Teresa 1931- ... 116
Mank, Gregory William 1950- ... 89-92
Mankekar, D. R. 1910- ... CANR-13
Earlier sketch in CA 21-22R
Mankiewicz, Don M(artin) 1922- ... 13-14R
Mankiewicz, Frank (Fabian) 1924- ... 89-92
Mankiewicz, Herman (Jacob) 1897-1953
Brief entry ... 120
See also DLB 26
Mankiewicz, Joseph L(eo) 1909- ... 73-76
See also DLB 44
Mankiewicz, Thomas F. 1942- Brief entry ... 124
Mankiewicz, Tom
See Mankiewicz, Thomas F.
Mankin, Paul A. 1924- ... 37-40R
Mankoff, Allan H. 1935- ... 45-48
Mankowitz, Wolf 1924- ... CANR-5
Earlier sketch in CA 7-8R
See also DLB 15
Mankowska, Joyce Kells Batten 1919- ... CAP-1
Earlier sketch in CA 9-10
Manley, Deborah 1932- ... CANR-22
Earlier sketch in CA 105
See also SATA 28
Manley, Delariviere 1672(?)-1724 ... DLB-39
Manley, Frank 1930- ... 5-6R
Manley, John F(rederick) 1939- ... 77-80
Manley, Lawrence (Gordon) 1949- ... 109
Manley, Michael Norman 1924- ... 85-88
Manley, Ruth Rodney King 1907(?)-1973
Obituary ... 41-44R
Manley, Seon 1921- ... 85-88
See also SATA 15
See also SAAS 2
See also CLR 3
Manley-Tucker, Audrie 1924(?)-1983(?)
Obituary ... 108
Manlove, Colin Nicholas 1942- ... 113
Mann, A. Philo
See Ald, Roy A(llison)
Mann, Abby 1927- ... 109
See also DLB 44
Mann, Abel
See Creasey, John
Mann, (Francis) Anthony 1914- ... CAP-1
Earlier sketch in CA 9-10
Mann, Arthur 1922- ... 109
Mann, Avery
See Breetveld, Jim Patrick
Mann, Bob 1948- ... 61-64
Mann, Charles W., Jr. 1929- ... 41-44R
Mann, Chris(topher Michael Zithulele)
1948- ... 126
Mann, (Robert Francis) Christopher Stephen
1917- ... 89-92
Mann, D. J.
See Freeman, James Dillet
Mann, Dale 1938- ... 61-64
Mann, David Douglas 1934- ... 49-52
Mann, Dean Edson 1927- ... CANR-5
Earlier sketch in CA 11-12R
Mann, Deborah
See Bloom, Ursula
Mann, Donald Nathaniel 1920-1985
Obituary ... 114
Mann, Edward
See Fried, Emanuel
Mann, Edward Andrew 1932- ... 103
Mann, Erika 1905-1969 Obituary ... 25-28R
Mann, Esther Kingston
See Kingston-Mann, Esther
Mann, Floyd C(hristopher) 1917- ... 1R
Mann, Georg K(arl) F(riedrich) 1913- ... 1R
Mann, Golo 1909- ... 97-100
Mann, Harold W(ilson) 1925- ... 19-20R
Mann, (Luiz) Heinrich 1871-1950
Brief entry ... 106
See also DLB 66
See also TCLC 9
Mann, Horace 1796-1859 ... DLB-1
Mann, James
See Harvey, John (Barton)
Mann, Jessica ... CANR-24
Earlier sketches in CA 49-52, CANR-2
Mann, John H. 1928- ... 85-88
Mann, Josephine
See Pullein-Thompson, Josephine (Mary Wedderburn)
Mann, Julia de Lacy 1891-1985 Obituary ... 116
Mann, Katharina 1883(?)-1980 Obituary ... 97-100
Mann, Kenneth Walker 1914- ... 29-32R
Mann, Klaus 1906-1949 ... DLB-56
Mann, Lucile Q.
See Mann, Lucile Quarry
Mann, Lucile Quarry 1897(?)-1986
Obituary ... 121
Mann, Marty 1904-1980 ... 103
Obituary ... 101
Mann, Michael 1919-1977 ... CANR-3
Obituary ... 69-72
Earlier sketch in CA 49-52
Mann, Michael 1943(?)- Brief entry ... 120
Mann, Milton B(ernard) 1937- ... 45-48
Mann, Patrick,
See Waller, Leslie
Mann, Peggy ... CANR-10
Earlier sketch in CA 25-28R
See also SATA 6
Mann, Peter (Clifford) 1948- ... 93-96
Mann, Peter H. 1926- ... CANR-12
Earlier sketch in CA 25-28R
Mann, Philip A(lan) 1934- ... 73-76
Mann, Ralph 1943- ... 112
Mann, Richard G(eorge) 1949- ... 124
Mann, Thomas 1875-1955 Brief entry ... 104
See also DLB 66
See also TCLC 2, 8, 14, 21
Mann, W(illiam) Edward 1918- ... 49-52
Mann, William S(omervell) 1924- ... 109
Mann, Zane B. 1924- ... 101
Manne, Henry G. 1928- ... 33-36R
Mannello, George Jr. 1913- ... 33-36R
Mannering, Julia
See Bingham, Madeleine (Mary Ebel)
Manners, Alexandra
See Rundle, Anne
Manners, Ande Miller 1923(?)-1975
Obituary ... 57-60
Manners, David X. 1912- ... 106
Manners, Elizabeth (Maude) 1917- ... 49-52
Manners, Gerald 1932- ... 37-40R
Manners, John (Errol) 1914- ... 106
Manners, Julia
See Greenaway, Gladys
Manners, Robert A(lan) 1913- ... 33-36R
Manners, William 1907- ... 65-68
Mannes, Marya 1904- ... CANR-3
Earlier sketch in CA 2R
Mannetti, Lisa 1953- ... 125
See also SATA 51
Manngian, Peter
See Monger, (Ifor) David
Mannheim, Grete (Salomon) 1909- ... 11-12R
See also SATA 10
Manniche, Lise 1943- ... CANR-25
Earlier sketch in CA 107
See also SATA 31
Mannin, Ethel (Edith) 1900-1984 ... CANR-8
Obituary ... 114
Earlier sketch in CA 53-56
Manning, Ambrose N(uel) 1922- ... 114
Manning, Bayless Andrew 1923- ... CANR-9
Earlier sketch in CA 13-14R
Manning, Beverley J(ane) 1942- ... 109
Manning, Clarence A(ugustus) 1893-1972
Obituary ... 37-40R
Manning, David
See Faust, Frederick (Shiller)
Manning, David John 1938- ... 103
Manning, Frank E(dward) 1944- ... CANR-7
Earlier sketch in CA 53-56
Manning, Frederic 1887(?)-1935
Brief entry ... 124
See also TCLC 25
Manning, Harvey (Hawthorne) 1925- ... 112
Manning, Helen Taft 1891(?)-1987
Obituary ... 121
Manning, Jack 1920- ... 69-72
Manning, Margaret Raymond 1921-1984
Obituary ... 114
Manning, Marie 1873(?)-1945 ... DLB-29
Manning, Marsha
See Grimstead, Hettie
Manning, Martin
See Smith, R(eginald) D(onald)
Manning, Mary Louise
See Cameron, Lou
Manning, Matthew 1955- Brief entry ... 111
Manning, Michael 1940- ... 65-68
Manning, Olivia 1915-1980 ... 5-6R
Obituary ... 101
See also CLC 5, 19
Manning, Paul 1912- ... 107
Manning, Peter J. 1942- ... 125
Manning, Peter K(irby) 1940- ... CANR-14
Earlier sketch in CA 37-40R
Manning, Philip 1930(?)-1983 Obituary ... 110
Manning, Phyllis A(nne) Sergeant 1903- ... 5-6R
Manning, Reg(inald West) 1905-1986
Obituary ... 118
Manning, Robert (Joseph) 1919- ... 69-72
Manning, Rosemary (Joy) 1911-1988 ... CANR-25
Earlier sketches in CA 3R, CANR-1
See also SATA 10
Manning, Rosemary
See Cole, Margaret Alice
Manning, Stanley Arthur 1921- ... 110
Manning, Sylvia 1943- ... 81-84
Manning, Thomas Davys 1898-1972 ... CAP-1
Earlier sketch in CA 19-20
Manning-Sanders, Ruth 1895(?)-1988 ... 73-76
Obituary ... 126
See also SATA 15
Mannion, John J(oseph) 1941- ... 73-76
Mannix, Edward 1928- ... 15-16R
Mannon, James M(onroe) 1942- ... 110
Mannon, Warwick
See Hopkins, (Hector) Kenneth
Mannon, Warwick
See Hopkins, Kenneth
Mannoni, Octave 1899- ... 102
Mano, D. Keith 1942- ... CANR-26
Earlier sketch in CA 25-28R
See also CAAS 6
See also DLB 6
See also CLC 2, 10
Mano, M(oshe) Morris 1927- ... 103
Manocchia, Benito 1934- ... 69-72
Manoff, Robert Karl 1944- ... 126
Manogaran, Chelvadurai 1935- ... 124
Manolson, Frank 1925- ... 19-20R
Manoni, Mary H(allahan) 1924- ... CANR-4
Earlier sketch in CA 49-52
Manoogian, Haig P. 1916(?)-1980
Obituary ... 97-100
Manor, Jason
See Hall, Oakley (Maxwell)
Manos, Charley 1923-1985 ... 29-32R
Obituary ... 116
Manosevitz, Martin 1938- ... 29-32R
Manross, William Wilson 1905- ... 57-60
Manry, Robert 1918-1971 ... CAP-2
Obituary ... 29-32R
Earlier sketch in CA 21-22
Mansbach, Richard W(allace) 1943- ... 53-56
Mansbridge, John 1901(?)-1981 Obituary ... 105
Manschreck, Clyde Leonard 1917- ... CANR-5
Earlier sketch in CA 9-10R
Mansell, Darrel (Lee, Jr.) 1934- ... 57-60
Manser, Martin H(ugh) 1952- ... 118
Mansergh, (Philip) Nicholas (Seton) 1910- ... 105
Mansfield, Bruce Edgar 1926- ... 103
Mansfield, Comins 1896-1984 Obituary ... 112
Mansfield, Edwin 1930- ... CANR-18
Earlier sketches in CA 11-12R, CANR-3
Mansfield, Elizabeth
See Schwartz, Paula
Mansfield, Harold H. 1912- ... 19-20R
Mansfield, Harvey C(laflin) 1905-1988 ... 1R
Obituary ... 125
Mansfield, Irving 1908(?)-1988 Obituary ... 126
Mansfield, John M(aurice) 1936- ... 29-32R
Mansfield, Katherine
See Beauchamp, Kathleen Mansfield
See also TCLC 2, 8
Mansfield, Libby
See Schwartz, Paula
Mansfield, Norman
See Gladden, E(dgar) Norman
Mansfield, Peter 1928- ... 65-68
Mansfield, Roger (Ernest) 1939- ... CANR-11
Earlier sketch in CA 25-28R
Manship, David 1927- ... 25-28R
Manso, Peter 1940- ... 29-32R
See also CLC 39
Manson, Beverlie 1945- ... 113
See also SATA 44
Manson, Richard 1939- ... 29-32R
Mansoor, Menahem 1911- ... CANR-15
Earlier sketch in CA 41-44R
Mansur, Ina 1910- ... 116
Mantague, John 1929- ... 11-12R
Mantel, Hilary (Mary) 1952- ... 125
Mantel, Samuel J(oseph), Jr. 1921- ... 15-16R
Mantell, Leroy H. 1919- ... 37-40R
Mantell, Martin E(den) 1936- ... 45-48
Manternach, Janaan 1927- ... 116
Mantey, Julius Robert 1890- ... CAP-1
Earlier sketch in CA 11-12
Mantle, Mickey (Charles) 1931- ... 89-92
Mantle, Winifred (Langford) ... CANR-6
Earlier sketch in CA 13-14R
Manton, Jo
See Gittings, Jo (Grenville) Manton
Manton, Peter
See Creasey, John
Manuel, E(spiridion) Arsenio 1909- ... 118
Manuel, Frank Edward 1910- ... CANR-6
Earlier sketch in CA 11-12R
Manuel, George 1921- ... 107
Manus, Mavis 1929- ... 116
Manus, Willard 1930- ... 108
Manushkin, Fran 1942- ... CANR-1
Earlier sketch in CA 49-52
See also SATA 7
Manvell, (Arnold) Roger 1909-1987 ... CANR-23
Obituary ... 124
Earlier sketches in CA 4R, CANR-6
Manville, W(illiam) H(enry) 1930- ... 93-96
Manwell, Reginald D. 1897- ... 37-40R
Man Without a Spleen, A
See Chekhov, Anton (Pavlovich)
Many, Seth E(dward) 1939- ... 97-100
Manyan, Gladys 1911- ... 57-60
Manzalaoui, Mahmoud (Ali) 1924- ... CANR-12
Earlier sketch in CA 29-32R
Manzella, David (Bernard) 1924- ... 5-6R
Manzini, Gianna 1899-1974 Obituary ... 53-56
Manzoni, Pablo Michelangelo 1939-
Brief entry ... 106
Mao, James C. T. 1925- ... 37-40R
Mao Tse-tung 1893-1976 ... 73-76
Obituary ... 69-72
Mapel, William 1902-1984 Obituary ... 112
Mapes, Arthur Franklin 1913-1986
Obituary ... 118
Mapes, Mary A.
See Ellison, Virginia H(owell)
Maple, Eric William 1915- ... CANR-6
Earlier sketch in CA 53-56
Maple, Terry 1946- ... CANR-1
Earlier sketch in CA 49-52
Maples, Evelyn Palmer 1919- ... CANR-17
Earlier sketches in CA 7-8R, CANR-2
Mapp, Alf J(ohnson), Jr. 1925- ... CANR-1
Earlier sketch in CA 4R
Mapp, Edward C(harles) ... 33-36R
Maquet, Jacques Jerome Pierre 1919- ... CANR-8
Earlier sketch in CA 61-64
Mara, Barney
See Roth, Arthur J(oseph)
Mara, Jeanette
See Cebulash, Mel
Mara, Thalia 1911- ... 11-12R
Marable, Manning 1950- ... 110
Maraini, Dacia 1936- ... CANR-11
Earlier sketch in CA 7-8R
Maraini, Fosco 1912- Brief entry ... 116
Marais, Josef 1905-1978 Obituary ... 77-80
See also SATA 24
Maran, Rene 1887-1960 ... 125
Obituary ... 107
See also BW
Maran, Stephen P(aul) 1938- ... 57-60
Maranda, Elli Kongas 1932- Brief entry ... 107
Maranda, Pierre 1930- ... 37-40R
Maranell, Gary M. 1932- ... 37-40R
Marangell, Virginia J(ohnson) 1924- ... 93-96
Maras, Karl
See Bulmer, (Henry) Kenneth
Marasmus, Seymour
See Rivoli, Mario
Marath, Laurie
See Roberts, Suzanne
Marath, Sparrow
See Roberts, Suzanne
Maravich, Pete(r Press) 1947(?)-1988
Obituary ... 124
Marazzi, Rich(ard Thomas) 1943- ... 102
Marberry, M. M(arion) 1905-1968 ... CAP-2
Earlier sketch in CA 21-22
Marble, Harriet Clement 1903-1975 ... 73-76
Marble, Samuel D(avey) 1915- ... 106
Marbrook, Del
See Marbrook, Djelloul
Marbrook, Djelloul 1934- ... 73-76
Marbut, F(rederick) B(rowning) 1905- ... 33-36R
Marc
See Boxer, (Charles) Mark (Edward)
Marcal, Annette B.
See Callaway, Bernice (Anne)
Marcatante, John 1930- ... CANR-10
Earlier sketch in CA 25-28R
Marceau, Felicien
See Carette, Louis
Marceau, LeRoy 1907- ... CAP-1
Earlier sketch in CA 19-20
Marceau, Marcel 1923- ... 85-88
Marcel, Gabriel Honore 1889-1973 ... 102
Obituary ... 45-48
See also CLC 15
Marcelin, Pierre 1908- ... 106
Marcelino
See Agnew, Edith J(osephine)
Marcell, David Wyburn 1937- ... 41-44R
March, Andrew Lee 1932- ... 110
March, Anthony 1912-1973 Obituary ... 45-48
March, Hilary
See Adcock, Almey St. John
March, James Gardner 1928- ... 13-14R
March, Joseph 1899(?)-1977 Obituary ... 69-72
March, Josie
See Titchener, Louise
March, Robert H(erbert) 1934- ... 61-64
March, William
See Campbell, William Edward March
See also DLB 9
March, William J. 1915- ... 13-14R
Marchaj, C(zeslaw) A(ntony) 1918- ... CANR-5
Earlier sketch in CA 11-12R
Marchak, M(aureen) Patricia 1936- ... 111
Marchak, Maureen
See Marchak, M(aureen) Patricia
Marcham, Frederick George 1898- ... 13-14R

Marchand, C(harles) Roland 1933-
Brief entry ... 110
Marchand, Leslie A(lexis) 1900- ... CANR-12
Earlier sketch in CA 65-68
Marchant, Anyda 1911- ... 15-16R
Marchant, Bessie 1862-1941 ... YABC-2
Marchant, Catherine
See Cookson, Catherine (McMullen)
Marchant, Herbert S(tanley) ... 106
Marchant, John H. 1951- ... 125
Marchant, Leslie R(onald) 1924-
Brief entry ... 110
Marchant, Maurice P(eterson) 1927- ... 110
Marchant, R(ex) A(lan) 1933- ... 15-16R
Marchant, William 1923- ... 69-72
Marchbanks, Samuel
See Davies, (William) Robertson
Marchenko, Anatoly (Timofeevich)
1938-1986 ... 25-28R
Obituary ... 121
Marcher, Marion Walden 1890- ... 1R
See also SATA 10
Marchessault, Jovette 1938- ... DLB-60
Marchetti, Albert 1947- ... 89-92
Marchetti, Victor Brief entry ... 108
Marchi, Giacomo
See Bassani, Giorgio
Marchione, Margherita (Frances)
1922- ... CANR-15
Earlier sketch in CA 37-40R
Marciano, Linda Boreman 1949(?)-
Brief entry ... 114
Marciniak, Ed(ward) 1917- ... 29-32R
Marckwardt, Albert H(enry) 1903-1975 .. CANR-4
Obituary ... 61-64
Earlier sketch in CA 2R
Marco
See Mountbatten, Louis (Francis Albert Victor Nicholas)
Marco, Anton N(icholas) 1943- ... 110
Marco, Barbara (Starkey) 1934- ... 11-12R
Marco, Guy A(nthony) 1927- ... 118
Marco, Lou
See Gottfried, Theodore Mark
Marcombe, Edith Marion
See Shiffert, Edith (Marcombe)
Marcosson, Isaac Frederick 1877-1961
Obituary ... 89-92
Marcovich, Miroslav 1919- ... 115
Marcson, Simon 1910- ... 49-52
Marcum, John A(rthur) 1927- ... CANR-14
Earlier sketch in CA 25-28R
Marcus, Aaron 1943- ... 53-56
Marcus, Adrianne 1935- ... CANR-1
Earlier sketch in CA 45-48
Marcus, Alfred A(llen) 1950- ... 118
Marcus, Anne M(ulkeen) 1927- ... 73-76
Marcus, Betty Blum 1923-1984 Obituary ... 113
Marcus, David 1926- Brief entry ... 110
Marcus, Edward 1918- ... CANR-14
Earlier sketch in CA 21-22R
Marcus, Frank 1928- ... CANR-2
Earlier sketch in CA 45-48
See also DLB 13
Marcus, Fred H(arold) 1921- ... 104
Marcus, Genevieve Grafe 1932- ... 111
Marcus, George E. 1946- ... 124
Marcus, George H. 1939- ... 120
Marcus, Greil (Gerstley) 1945- ... 122
Marcus, Harold G. 1936- ... 37-40R
Marcus, Irwin M. 1919- ... 45-48
Marcus, Jacob Rader 1896- ... 23-24R
Marcus, Jerry 1924- ... 97-100
Marcus, Joanna
See Andrews, Lucilla Mathew
Marcus, Joe 1933- ... 65-68
Marcus, Maeva 1941- Brief entry ... 108
Marcus, Martin 1933- ... 25-28R
Marcus, Mildred Rendl 1928- ... CANR-2
Earlier sketch in CA 1R
Marcus, Mordecai 1925- ... CANR-17
Earlier sketch in CA 77-80
Marcus, Morton 1936- ... 105
Marcus, Phillip L. 1941- Brief entry ... 111
Marcus, Rebecca B(rian) 1907- ... CANR-1
Earlier sketch in CA 5-6R
See also SATA 9
Marcus, Robert D. 1936- Brief entry ... 110
Marcus, Ruth Barcan 1921- ... 41-44R
Marcus, Sheldon 1937- Brief entry ... 106
Marcus, Stanley 1905- ... 53-56
Marcus, Steven 1928- ... 41-44R
Marcuse, F(rederick) L(awrence) 1916- ... 11-12R
Marcuse, Herbert 1898-1979 Obituary ... 89-92
Marcuse, Ludwig 1894-1971 Obituary ... 33-36R
Marden, Charles F(rederick) 1902- ... 37-40R
Marden, William (Edward) 1947- ... 61-64
Marder, Arthur (Jacob) 1910-1980 ... 105
Obituary ... 102
Marder, Daniel 1923- ... 21-22R
Marder, Herbert 1934- ... 69-72
Marder, Louis 1915- ... 7-8R
Mardock, Robert W(inston) 1921- ... 19-20R
Mardon, Michael (Claude) 1919- ... 13-14R
Mardor, Munya Meir 1913- ... 19-20R
Mardus, Elaine Bassler 1914- ... 9-10R
Mare, W(illiam) Harold 1918- ... 105
Marei, Sayed (Ahmed) 1913- ... 73-76
Marein, Shirley 1926- ... CANR-1
Earlier sketch in CA 45-48
Marek, George R(ichard) 1902-1987 ... CANR-1
Obituary ... 121
Earlier sketch in CA 49-52
Marek, Hannelore M(arie) C(harlotte)
1926- ... 15-16R
Marek, Kurt W(illi) 1915-1972 ... CAP-2
Obituary ... 33-36R
Earlier sketch in CA 17-18
Marek, Margot L. 1934(?)-1987 Obituary ... 123
Marek, Richard (William) 1933- ... 126
Marelli, Leonard R(ussell) 1933-1973 ... CAP-1
Earlier sketch in CA 15-16
Maremaa, Thomas 1945- ... 85-88
Marenco, Ethne (Elsie) K(aplan) 1925- ... 103
Marer, Paul 1936- ... 105
Mares, F(rancis) H(ugh) 1925- ... 25-28R
Maresca, Thomas Edward 1938- ... 85-88
Mareth, Glenville
See Gilbert, Willie
Marett, Robert Hugh Kirk 1907- ... 25-28R
Marevna
See Vorobeva, Maria
Margadant, Ted W(inston) 1941- ... 93-96
Margalith, Pinhas Z(alman) 1926- ... 110
Margaret, Karla
See Andersdatter, Karla M(argaret)
Margenau, Henry 1901- ... CANR-14
Earlier sketch in CA 37-40R
Marger, Mary Ann 1934- ... 93-96
Margerson, David
See Davies, David Margerison
Margetson, Stella 1912- ... CANR-13
Earlier sketch in CA 33-36R
Marghieri, Clotilde 1901(?)-1981 Obituary ... 105
Margold, Stella ... 81-84
Margolies, Alan 1933- ... 125
Margolies, Edward 1925- ... CANR-11
Earlier sketch in CA 65-68
Margolies, Joseph A(aron) 1889-1982
Obituary ... 108
Margolies, Luise 1945- ... 102
Margolies, Marjorie 1942- ... CANR-13
Earlier sketch in CA 65-68
Margolin, Edythe ... 69-72
Margolin, Judith B(elle) 1946- ... 117
Margolin, Malcolm 1940- ... 57-60
Margolin, Victor 1941- ... 65-68
Margolis, Diane Rothbard 1933- ... 97-100
Margolis, Ellen (Edelman) 1934- ... 2R
Margolis, Gary 1945- ... 73-76
Margolis, Jack S 1934- ... 69-72
Margolis, John D(avid) 1941- Brief entry ... 113
Margolis, Joseph 1924- ... 37-40R
Margolis, Julius 1920- Brief entry ... 109
Margolis, Maxine L(uanna) 1942- ... 53-56
Margolis, Michael (Stephen) 1940- ... 93-96
Margolis, Richard J(ules) 1929- ... CANR-25
Earlier sketch in CA 29-32R
See also SATA 4
Margolis, Susan Spector 1941- ... 81-84
Margolis, Susanna 1944- ... 107
Margolis, Vivienne 1922- ... SATA-46
Margolius, Sidney (Senier) 1911-1980 . CANR-11
Obituary ... 93-96
Earlier sketch in CA 21-22R
Margon, Lester 1892- ... CAP-1
Earlier sketch in CA 15-16
Margoshes, Dave 1941- ... 111
Margulies, Harry D. 1907(?)-1980
Obituary ... 97-100
Margulies, Herbert F(elix) 1928- ... 77-80
Margulies, Leo 1900-1975 Obituary ... 61-64
Margulies, Newton 1932- ... 61-64
Margulis, Lynn 1938- ... CANR-4
Earlier sketch in CA 53-56
Margull, Hans J(ochen) 1925- ... 9-10R
Marhoefer, Barbara (McGeary) 1936- ... 61-64
Maria Del Rey, Sister 1908- ... 5-6R
Mariah, Paul 1937- ... CANR-4
Earlier sketch in CA 53-56
Mariana
See Foster, Marian Curtis
Mariani, John Francis 1945- ... 117
Mariani, Paul L(ouis) 1940- ... CANR-12
Earlier sketch in CA 29-32R
Mariano, Frank 1931(?)-1976 Obituary ... 69-72
Marias (Aguilera), Julian 1914- ... CANR-22
Earlier sketches in CA 9-10R, CANR-5
Marie, Beverly Sainte
See Sainte-Marie, Beverly
Marie, Buffy Sainte
See Sainte-Marie, Beverly
Marie, Geraldine (a pseudonym) 1949- ... 108
Marie, Jeanne
See Wilson, Marie B(eatrice)
Marie-Andre du Sacre-Coeur, Sister 1899- ... 7-8R
Marien, Michael 1938- ... CANR-16
Earlier sketches in CA 49-52, CANR-1
Marier, Captain Victor
See Griffith, D(avid Lewelyn) W(ark)
Marie Therese, Mother 1891- ... CAP-1
Earlier sketch in CA 13-14
Maril, Nadja 1954- ... CANR-17
Earlier sketch in CA 85-88
Marill, Alvin H(erbert) 1934- ... CANR-12
Earlier sketch in CA 73-76
Marilla, E(smond) L(inworth) 1900- ... CAP-2
Earlier sketch in CA 23-24
Marilue
See Johnson, Marilue Carolyn
Marimow, William K. 1947- ... 93-96
Marin, A. C.
See Coppel, Alfred
Marin, Cheech
See Marin, Richard Anthony
Marin, Diego 1914- ... 19-20R
Marin, Luis Munoz
See Munoz Marin, Luis
Marin, Richard Anthony 1946- Brief entry ... 112
Marinacci, Barbara 1933- ... CANR-9
Earlier sketch in CA 21-22R
Marinaccio, Anthony 1912- ... 53-56
Marine, David 1880(?)-1976 Obituary ... 69-72
Marine, Gene 1926- ... 65-68
Marine, Nick
See Oursler, Will(iam Charles)
Marinelli, Peter V(incent) 1933- ... 41-44R
Mariner, David
See Smith, David MacLeod
Mariner, Scott
See Pohl, Frederik
Marinetti, Filippo Tommaso 1876-1944
Brief entry ... 107
See also TCLC 10
Maring, Joel M(arvin) 1935- ... 49-52
Maring, Norman H(ill) 1914- ... 19-20R
Marini, Frank N(ick) 1935- ... 45-48
Marino, Carolyn Fitch 1942- ... 110
Marino, Dorothy Bronson 1912- ... 73-76
See also SATA 14
Marino, John J. 1948- ... 106
Marino, Joseph D. 1912(?)-1983 Obituary ... 109
Marino, Trentino J(oseph) 1917- ... 65-68
Marinoni, Rosa Zagnoni 1888-1970 ... CAP-1
Earlier sketch in CA 13-14
Marion, Frances 1886-1973 Obituary ... 41-44R
See also DLB 44
Marion, Frieda 1912- ... CANR-8
Earlier sketch in CA 61-64
Marion, Henry
See del Rey, Lester
Marion, John Francis 1922- ... CANR-3
Earlier sketch in CA 7-8R
Mariotti, (Raffaello) Marcello 1938- ... 29-32R
Marique, Joseph M(arie-) F(elix) 1899- ... 33-36R
Maris, Roger (Eugene) 1934-1985
Obituary ... 118
Maris, Ron ... SATA-45
Marisa
See Nucera, Marisa Lonette
Mariscal, Richard N(orth) 1935- ... 53-56
Maritain, Jacques 1882-1973 ... 85-88
Obituary ... 41-44R
Maritano, Nino 1919- ... 13-14R
Marius, Richard 1933- ... 25-28R
See also DLBY 85
Marjolin, Robert (Ernest) 1911-1986
Obituary ... 119
Marjoram, J.
See Mottram, R(alph) H(ale)
Mark, Charles Christopher 1927- ... CANR-1
Earlier sketch in CA 1R
Mark, David 1922- ... 2R
Mark, Edwina
See Fadiman, Edwin, Jr.
Mark, Irving 1908-1987 ... CAP-1
Obituary ... 121
Earlier sketch in CA 19-20
Mark, Jan 1943- ... CANR-17
Earlier sketch in CA 93-96
See also SATA 22
See also CLR 11
Mark, Jon
See Du Breuil, (Elizabeth) L(or)inda
Mark, Julius 1898-1977 ... 81-84
Obituary ... 73-76
Mark, Matthew
See Babcock, Frederic
Mark, Max 1910- ... 73-76
Mark, Michael L(aurence) 1936- ... 93-96
Mark, Norman (Barry) 1939- ... 113
Mark, Pauline (Dahlin) 1913- ... CANR-7
Earlier sketch in CA 19-20R
See also SATA 14
Mark, Polly
See Mark, Pauline (Dahlin)
Mark, Robert 1930- ... 110
Mark, Shelley M(uin) 1922- ... CANR-1
Earlier sketch in CA 1R
Mark, Steven Joseph 1913- ... 19-20R
Mark, Ted
See Gottfried, Theodore Mark
Mark, Theonie Diakidis 1938- ... 69-72
Mark, Yudel 1897-1975 Obituary ... 61-64
Mark-Alan, Roy
See Malan, R(enato) M(arco)
Markandaya, Kamala
See Taylor, Kamala (Purnaiya)
See also CLC 8, 38
Markbreit, Jerry 1935- ... 49-52
Marke, Julius J(ay) 1913- ... 19-20R
Markel, Geraldine (Ponte) 1939- ... 108
Markel, Lester 1894-1977 ... 37-40R
Obituary ... 73-76
Markels, Julian 1925- ... 25-28R
Marken, Jack W(alter) 1922- ... 49-52
Marker, Frederick (Joseph, Jr.) 1936- .. CANR-16
Earlier sketch in CA 41-44R
Marker, Gary 1948- ... 125
Marker, Lise-Lone (Christensen) 1934- .. CANR-8
Earlier sketch in CA 61-64
Market Man
See Lake, Kenneth R(obert)
Markevitch, Igor 1912-1983 Obituary ... 109
Markey, Gene 1895-1980 ... CAP-1
Obituary ... 97-100
Earlier sketch in CA 11-12
Markfield, Wallace 1926- ... 69-72
See also CAAS 3
See also DLB 2, 28
See also CLC 8
Markgraf, Carl 1928- ... 49-52
Markham, Beryl 1902-1986 Obituary ... 119
Markham, Clarence M(atthew), Jr. 1911- .. 69-72
Markham, Dewey 1904-1981 Obituary ... 108
Markham, Edwin 1852-1940 ... DLB-54
Markham, Felix (Maurice Hippisley)
1908- ... CAP-1
Earlier sketch in CA 11-12
Markham, James M(orris) 1943- ... 93-96
Markham, James W(alter) 1910-1972 ... CAP-2
Earlier sketch in CA 21-22
Markham, Jesse William 1916- ... 9-10R
Markham, Meeler 1914- ... CANR-12
Earlier sketch in CA 25-28R
Markham, Pigmeat
See Markham, Dewey
Markham, Reed 1957- ... 110
Markham, Robert
See Amis, Kingsley (William)
Marki, Ivan 1934- ... 97-100
Markides, Kyriacos (Costa) 1942- ... 81-84
Markie, Peter J(oseph) 1950- ... 123
Markins, W. S.
See Jenkins, Marie M(agdalen)
Markish, David 1938- ... 69-72
Markle, Fletcher 1921- ... DLB-68
Markle, Joyce B(onners) 1942- ... 69-72
Markle, Sandra L(ee) 1946- ... 111
See also SATA 41
Markley, Kenneth A(lan) 1933- ... 61-64
Markley, R(ayner) W(are) 1934- ... 111
Markman, Howard (Joel) 1950- ... 69-72
Markman, Sherwin J. 1929- ... 104
Markman, Sidney David 1911- ... CAP-2
Earlier sketch in CA 33-36
Markmann, Charles Lam 1913- ... 15-16R
Marko, Katherine D(olores) ... CANR-15
Earlier sketch in CA 29-32R
See also SATA 28
Markoe, Karen 1942- ... 81-84
Markoosie
See Patsauq, Markoosie
Markov, Georgi 1929(?)-1978 Obituary ... 104
Markov, Vladimir 1920- ... 19-20R
Markova, Alicia 1910- ... CAP-2
Earlier sketch in CA 19-20
Markovic, Miroslav
See Marcovich, Miroslav
Markovic, Vida E. 1916- ... 33-36R
Markovitz, Irving Leonard 1934- ... 33-36R
Markowitz, Norman Daniel 1943- ... 45-48
Marks, Alfred H(arding) 1920- ... CANR-23
Earlier sketch in CA 45-48
Marks, Barry A(lan) 1926- ... 19-20R
Marks, Bayly Ellen 1943- ... 115
Marks, Burton 1930- ... 107
See also SATA 43, 47
Marks, Charles 1922- ... CANR-5
Earlier sketch in CA 53-56
Marks, Claude (Mordecai) 1915- ... 61-64
Marks, Edith Bobroff 1924- ... 17-18R
Marks, Edward S(tanford) 1936- ... 45-48
Marks, Elaine 1930- ... CANR-23
Earlier sketches in CA 19-20R, CANR-7
Marks, Eli S(amplin) 1911- ... 85-88
Marks, Frederick (William III) 1940- ... 97-100
Marks, Geoffrey 1906- ... 33-36R
Marks, Hannah K.
See Trivelpiece, Laurel
Marks, Henry S(eymour) 1933- ... 73-76
Marks, J
See Highwater, Jamake (Mamake)
Marks, J(ames) M(acdonald) 1921- ... 61-64
See also SATA 13
Marks, James R(obert) 1932- ... 19-20R
Marks, Jane (A. Steinberg) 1943- ... 113
Marks, John 1943- ... 110
Marks, John David 1909-1985 Obituary ... 117
Marks, John H(enry) 1923- ... 19-20R
Marks, Johnny
See Marks, John David
Marks, Margaret L. 1911(?)-1980
Obituary ... 101
See also SATA 23
Marks, Mickey Klar ... CANR-6
Earlier sketch in CA 2R
See also SATA 12
Marks, Norton E(lliott) 1932- ... 23-24R
Marks, Pat R.
See Feinman, Jeffrey
Marks, Peter
See Smith, Robert Kimmel
Marks, Rita 1938- ... 106
See also SATA 47
Marks, Sally (Jean) 1931- ... 102
Marks, Sema 1942- ... 29-32R
Marks, Stan(ley) 1929- ... CANR-12
Earlier sketch in CA 29-32R
See also SATA 14
Marks, Stuart A. 1939- ... 69-72
Marks, Vic(tor James) 1955- ... 118
Marksberry, Mary Lee ... 15-16R
Markson, David M(errill) 1927- ... CANR-1
Earlier sketch in CA 49-52
Markstein, David L. 1920- ... 29-32R
Markstein, George 1929-1987 Obituary ... 121
Markun, Alan Fletcher 1925- ... 45-48
Markun, Patricia Maloney 1924- ... CANR-4
Earlier sketch in CA 5-6R
See also SATA 15
Markus, Julia 1939- ... 105
Markus, R(obert) A(ustin) 1924- ... CANR-16
Earlier sketch in CA 65-68
Marland, Edward Allen 1912- ... 19-20R
Marland, Michael 1934- ... 103
Marland, Sidney P(ercy, Jr.) 1914- ... 53-56
Marlatt, Daphne (Buckle) 1942- ... CANR-17
Earlier sketch in CA 25-28R
See also DLB 60
Marlborough
See Oaksey, John
Marley, Augusta Anne ?-1973 Obituary ... 41-44R
Marley, Bob
See Marley, Robert Nesta
See also CLC 17

Marley, Robert Nesta 1945-1981 ... 107
Obituary ... 103
Marlin, Alice Tepper 1944- ... 123
Marlin, Henry
See Giggal, Kenneth
Marlin, Hilda
See Van Stockum, Hilda
Marlin, Jeffrey 1940- ... 45-48
Marlin, John Tepper 1942- ... 124
Marling, William 1951- ... 123
Marling, Yvonne Rodd
See Rodd-Marling, Yvonne
Marlo, John A. 1934- ... 29-32R
Marlor, Clark Strang 1922- ... 37-40R
Marlot, Raymond
See Angremy, Jean-Pierre
Marlow, Cecilia Ann 1952- ... 121
Marlow, David 1943- ... 107
Marlow, Edwina
See Huff, T(om) E.
Marlow, Joyce
See Connor, Joyce Mary
Marlow, Louis
See Wilkinson, Louis (Umfreville)
Marlowe, Alan Stephen 1937- ... 23-24R
Marlowe, Amy Bell ... CANR-26
Earlier sketches in CA 19-20, CAP-2
See also SATA 1
Marlowe, Christopher 1564-1593 ... DLB-62
Marlowe, Dan J(ames) 1914- ... CANR-1
Earlier sketch in CA 2R
Marlowe, Derek 1938- ... CANR-11
Earlier sketch in CA 19-20R
Marlowe, Don ... 61-64
Marlowe, Hugh
See Patterson, Henry
Marlowe, Kenneth 1926- ... 13-14R
Marlowe, Stephen 1928- ... CANR-6
Earlier sketch in CA 13-14R
Marlowe, Webb
See McComas, J(esse) Francis
Marlyn, John 1912- ... 11-12R
Marmion, Harry A. 1931- ... 25-28R
Marmion, Shakerley 1603-1639 ... DLB-58
Marmon, William F., Jr. 1942- ... 77-80
Marmor, J(udd) 1910- ... CANR-12
Earlier sketch in CA 25-28R
Marmor, T(heodore) R(ichard) 1939- ... 29-32R
Marmur, Dow 1935- ... 121
Marmur, Jacland 1901- ... 9-10R
Marmur, Mildred 1930- ... 7-8R
Marnell, William H. 1907- ... 23-24R
Marney, (Leonard) Carlyle 1916- ... 57-60
Marney, Dean 1952- ... 110
Marney, John 1933- ... 69-72
Marnham, Patrick 1943- ... 102
Marokvia, Artur 1909- ... SATA-31
Marokvia, Mireille (Journet) 1918- ... 29-32R
See also SATA 5
Maron, Margaret ... 122
Marossi, Ruth
See Krefetz, Ruth
Marot, Marc
See Koch, Kurt E(mil)
Marple, Allen Clark 1901(?)-1968
Obituary ... 106
Marple, Hugo D(ixon) 1920- ... 53-56
Marples, William F(rank) 1907- ... CAP-1
Earlier sketch in CA 15-16
Marquand, John P(hillips) 1893-1960 ... 85-88
See also DLB 9
See also CLC 2, 10
Marquand, Josephine
See Gladstone, Josephine
Marquard, Leo(pold) 1897- ... 7-8R
Marquardt, Dorothy Ann 1921- ... 15-16R
Marques, Rene 1919-1979 ... 97-100
Obituary ... 85-88
Marquess, Harlan E(arl) 1931- ... 49-52
Marquess, William Henry 1954- ... 126
Marquess of Anglesey
See Paget, George Charles Henry Victor
Marquez, Gabriel Garcia
See Garcia Marquez, Gabriel (Jose)
Marquez, Robert 1942- ... 53-56
Marquis, Arnold ... 57-60
Marquis, Dave 1951- ... 113
Marquis, Don(ald Robert Perry)
1878-1937 Brief entry ... 104
See also DLB 11, 25
See also TCLC 7
Marquis, Donald G(eorge) 1908-1973
Obituary ... 45-48
Marquis, G(eorge) Welton 1916- ... 19-20R
Marr, David G. 1937- ... 33-36R
Marr, James Pratt 1898-1986 Obituary ... 121
Marr, John S(tuart) 1940- ... 81-84
See also SATA 48
Marranca, Bonnie 1947- ... CANR-9
Earlier sketch in CA 65-68
Marreco, Anne
See Wignall, Anne
Marric, J. J.
See Creasey, John
Marrin, Albert 1936- ... 49-52
See also SATA 43, 53
Marriner, Ernest (Cummings)
1891-1983 ... 37-40R
Obituary ... 109
Marrington, Pauline 1921- ... CANR-10
Earlier sketch in CA 65-68
Marriott, Alice Lee 1910- ... 57-60
See also SATA 31
Marriott, (Joyce) Anne 1913- ... CANR-18
Earlier sketch in CA 102
See also DLB 68
Marriott, Pat(ricia) 1920- ... SATA-35
Marriott, William H. 1909(?)-1986
Obituary ... 118
Marriott-Watson, Nan 1899-1982 Obituary ... 107
Marris, Peter (Horsey) 1927- ... 111
Marris, Robin Lapthorn 1924- ... CANR-8
Earlier sketch in CA 5-6R
Marris, Ruth 1948- ... 106
Marrison, L(eslie) W(illiam) 1901- ... 29-32R
Marr-Johnson, Diana (Maugham) 1908- ... 13-14R
Marrocco, W(illiam) Thomas 1909- ... 11-12R
Marrone, Robert 1941- ... 77-80
Marroquin, Patricio
See Markun, Patricia Maloney
Marrow, Alfred J. 1905-1978 ... 81-84
Obituary ... 77-80
Marrow, Bernard
See Moore, Brian
Marrow, Stanley B. 1931- ... CANR-26
Earlier sketches in CA 25-28R, CANR-10
Marrs, Edwin W(ilson), Jr. 1928- ... 25-28R
Marrus, Michael R(obert) 1941- ... CANR-12
Earlier sketch in CA 33-36R
Marryat, Frederick 1792-1848 ... DLB-21
Mars, Alastair 1915-1985 Obituary ... 116
Mars, Florence L. 1923- ... 101
Mars, Jean Price
See Price-Mars, Jean
Mars, W. T.
See Mars, Witold Tadeusz J.
Mars, Witold Tadeusz J. 1912- ... 25-28R
See also SATA 3
Marsano, Ramon
See Dinges, John (Charles)
Marsden, George (Mish) 1939- ... CANR-12
Earlier sketch in CA 73-76
Marsden, James
See Creasey, John
Marsden, Lorna R(uth) 1942- ... 85-88
Marsden, Malcolm Morse 1922- ... 7-8R
Marsden, Peter (Richard Valentine)
1940- ... CANR-14
Earlier sketch in CA 77-80
Marsden, Philip Kitson 1916-1984
Obituary ... 113
Marsden-Smedley, Hester 1901-1982
Obituary ... 107
Marsh, Analyticus
See Morrison, Marsh
Marsh, Andrew
See O'Donovan, John
Marsh, Clifton E. 1946- ... 77-80
Marsh, Dave 1950- ... CANR-17
Earlier sketch in CA 97-100
Marsh, David Charles 1917- ... 103
Marsh, Edwin
See Schorb, E(dwin) M(arsh)
Marsh, George Perkins 1801-1882 ... DLB-1, 64
Marsh, Henry
See Saklatvala, Beram
Marsh, Irving T. 1907-1982 ... 11-12R
Obituary ... 107
Marsh, J. E.
See Marshall, Evelyn
Marsh, James 1794-1842 ... DLB-1, 59
Marsh, Jean
See Marshall, Evelyn
Marsh, Jeanne C(ay) 1948- ... 111
Marsh, Jeri 1940- ... 85-88
Marsh, John 1904- ... CAP-1
Earlier sketch in CA 9-10
Marsh, John 1907- ... CAP-1
Earlier sketch in CA 15-16
Marsh, John L(eslie) 1927- ... CANR-1
Earlier sketch in CA 45-48
Marsh, Leonard (Charles) 1906- ... 37-40R
Marsh, Leonard (George) 1930- ... CANR-13
Earlier sketch in CA 73-76
Marsh, Margaret Sammartino 1945- ... 106
Marsh, Mary Val 1925- ... CANR-26
Earlier sketches in CA 69-72, CANR-11
Marsh, Meredith 1946- ... 77-80
Marsh, (Edith) Ngaio 1899-1982 ... CANR-6
Earlier sketch in CA 11-12R
See also CLC 7
Marsh, Norman Stayner 1913- ... 117
Marsh, Patrick O(tis) 1928- ... 25-28R
Marsh, Paul
See Hopkins, (Hector) Kenneth
Marsh, Paul
See Hopkins, Kenneth
Marsh, Peter T(imothy) 1935- ... 33-36R
Marsh, Philip M(errill) 1893- ... 11-12R
Marsh, Rebecca
See Neubauer, William Arthur
Marsh, Robert (Harrison) 1926- ... 19-20R
Marsh, Robert C(harles) 1924- ... 15-16R
Marsh, Robert M(ortimer) 1931- ... CANR-2
Earlier sketch in CA 1R
Marsh, Ronald (James) 1914- ... 13-14R
Marsh, Spencer 1931- ... 61-64
Marsh, Susan (Sherry Raymond) 1914- ... 9-10R
Marsh, U(lysses) Grant 1911- ... 57-60
Marsh, Willard 1922-1970 ... CAP-2
Earlier sketch in CA 25-28
Marshak, Robert Eugene 1916- ... 107
Marshak, Samuil Yakovlevich 1887-1964
Obituary ... 111
Marshall, Alan 1902- ... 85-88
Marshall, Alfred 1884-1965 ... 7-8R
Marshall, Annie Jessie 1922- ... CAP-1
Earlier sketch in CA 9-10
Marshall, Anthony D(ryden) 1924- ... 29-32R
See also SATA 18
Marshall, Bill 1937- ... CANR-17
Earlier sketch in CA 65-68
Marshall, Bruce 1899-1987 ... 5-6R
Obituary ... 123
Marshall, Burke 1922- ... 15-16R
Marshall, Byron K. 1936- ... 33-36R
Marshall, (Sarah) Catherine (Wood)
1914-1983 ... CANR-8
Obituary ... 109
Earlier sketch in CA 19-20R
See also SATA 2, 34
Marshall, Charles Burton 1908- ... 37-40R
Marshall, Charles Wheeler 1906- ... 110
Marshall, D(onald) Bruce 1931- ... 65-68
Marshall, David F(ranklin) 1938- ... 25-28R
Marshall, Don
See Marshall, Donovan
Marshall, Donald R. 1934- ... 93-96
Marshall, Donald S(tanley) 1919- ... 29-32R
Marshall, Donovan 1908- ... 117
Marshall, Dorothy 1900- ... CAP-1
Earlier sketch in CA 13-14
Marshall, Douglas
See McClintock, Marshall
Marshall, E(dmund) Jesse 1888- ... CAP-1
Earlier sketch in CA 11-12
Marshall, Edison 1894-1967 ... CAP-1
Obituary ... 29-32R
Earlier sketch in CA 9-10
Marshall, Edmund
See Hopkins, (Hector) Kenneth
Marshall, Edmund
See Hopkins, Kenneth
Marshall, Edward 1932- ... DLB-16
Marshall, Emily
See Hall, Bennie Caroline (Humble)
Marshall, Evelyn 1897- ... CANR-18
Earlier sketches in CA 7-8R, CANR-2
See also SATA 11
Marshall, F(reddie) Ray 1928- ... CANR-8
Earlier sketch in CA 19-20R
Marshall, Garry 1934- ... 111
See also CLC 17
Marshall, George (Nichols) 1920- ... 77-80
Marshall, George C(atlett), Jr. 1880-1959
Brief entry ... 115
Marshall, George O(ctavius), Jr. 1922- ... 19-20R
Marshall, H.H.
See Jahn, Joseph Michael
Marshall, Helen E(dith) 1899- ... 37-40R
Marshall, Helen Lowrie 1904-1975 ... 103
Marshall, Herbert (Percival James)
1906- ... 25-28R
Marshall, Herbert Hedley 1909(?)-1982
Obituary ... 112
Marshall, Hermine H(alprin) 1935- ... CANR-14
Earlier sketch in CA 41-44R
Marshall, Howard D(rake) 1924-1972 ... CAP-2
Obituary ... 37-40R
Earlier sketch in CA 23-24
Marshall, Howard Wight 1944- ... 107
Marshall, Hubert (Ray) 1920- ... 23-24R
Marshall, I(an) Howard 1934- ... 122
Marshall, J(ohn) D(uncan) 1919- ... 73-76
Marshall, Jack 1937- ... 97-100
Marshall, James 1896-1986 ... 41-44R
Obituary ... 120
Marshall, James 1942- ... 41-44R
See also SATA 6, 51
See also DLB 61
Marshall, James M(orse) 1924- ... 120
Marshall, James Vance 1887-1964 ... CAP-1
Earlier sketch in CA 11-12
Marshall, James Vance
See Payne, Donald Gordon
Marshall, Jeff
See Laycock, George (Edwin)
Marshall, Joanne
See Rundle, Anne
Marshall, John 1905(?)-1985(?) Obituary ... 116
Marshall, John 1922- ... CANR-15
Earlier sketch in CA 89-92
Marshall, John David 1928- ... CANR-19
Earlier sketches in CA 9-10R, CANR-3
Marshall, John Ross 1912- ... 109
Marshall, John S(edberry) 1898- ... CAP-1
Earlier sketch in CA 19-20
Marshall, Joyce 1913- ... 102
Marshall, Kathryn 1951- ... 57-60
See also AITN 1
Marshall, Kim
See Marshall, Michael (Kimbrough)
Marshall, Lenore Guinzburg 1899-1971 ... CAP-2
Obituary ... 33-36R
Earlier sketch in CA 25-28
Marshall, Lovat
See Duncan, W(illiam) Murdoch
Marshall, Margaret 1901(?)-1974
Obituary ... 104
Marshall, Margaret Wiley 1908- ... CAP-1
Earlier sketch in CA 9-10
Marshall, Martin V(ivan) 1922- ... 2R
Marshall, Max Lawrence 1922- ... 19-20R
Marshall, Max S(kidmore) 1897- ... CAP-1
Earlier sketch in CA 13-14
Marshall, Megan 1954- ... 124
Marshall, Mel(vin D.) 1911- ... CANR-12
Earlier sketch in CA 29-32R
Marshall, Michael (Kimbrough) 1948- ... CANR-3
Earlier sketch in CA 49-52
See also SATA 37
Marshall, Muriel ... 106
Marshall, Natalie J(unemann) 1929- ... 41-44R
Marshall, Norman 1901-1980 Obituary ... 108
Marshall, Paule 1929- ... CANR-25
Earlier sketch in CA 77-80
See also BW
See also DLB 33
See also CLC 27
Marshall, Percy
See Young, Percy M(arshall)
Marshall, Peter 1902-1949 Brief entry ... 112
Marshall, Ray
See Marshall, F(reddie) Ray
Marshall, Raymond
See Raymond, Rene (Brabazon)
Marshall, Richard (D.) 1947- ... 125
Marshall, Robert G. 1919- ... 37-40R
Marshall, Robert L(ewis) 1939- ... 104
Marshall, Roderick 1903-1975 Obituary ... 53-56
Marshall, Ronald 1905- ... CAP-2
Earlier sketch in CA 33-36
Marshall, Rosalind Kay 1939- ... CANR-19
Earlier sketches in CA 53-56, CANR-4
Marshall, S(amuel) L(yman) A(twood)
1900-1977 ... 81-84
Obituary ... 73-76
See also SATA 21
Marshall, Shirley E(velyn) 1925- ... 21-22R
Marshall, Sybil Mary (Edwards) 1913- ... CANR-1
Earlier sketch in CA 4R
Marshall, T(homas) H(umphrey)
1893-1981 ... 109
Obituary ... 105
Marshall, Thomas Archibald 1938- ... CANR-17
Earlier sketches in CA 49-52, CANR-1
Marshall, Thomas F(rederic) 1908- ... CAP-2
Earlier sketch in CA 23-24
Marshall, Thomas R. 1949- ... 115
Marshall, Tom
See Marshall, Thomas Archibald
See also DLB 60
Marshall, William H(arvey) 1925-1968 ... CAP-1
Earlier sketch in CA 11-12
Marshall-Cornwall, James (Handyside)
1887-1985 ... 107
Obituary ... 118
Marshburn, Joseph Hancock 1890-1975 ... 109
Obituary ... 106
Marshner, Connaught Coyne 1951- ... CANR-16
Earlier sketch in CA 93-96
Mars-Jones, Adam 1954- ... 109
Marsland, Amy 1924- ... CANR-19
Earlier sketch in CA 103
Marsoli, Lisa Ann 1958- ... 120
See also SATA 53
Marson, Philip 1892- ... 11-12R
Marsteller, Bill
See Marsteller, William A.
Marsteller, William A. 1914-1987 Obituary ... 123
Marsten, Richard
See Hunter, Evan
Marston, David W(eese) 1942- ... 125
Marston, Elsa 1933- ... 113
Marston, Hope Irvin 1935- ... 101
See also SATA 31
Marston, John 1576-1634 ... DLB-58
Marston, John E. 1911- ... 5-6R
Marston, Philip Bourke 1850-1887 ... DLB-35
Marston, Thomas Ewart 1904-1984
Obituary ... 112
Marszalek, John F(rancis, Jr.) 1939- ... CANR-14
Earlier sketch in CA 37-40R
Martchenko, Michael 1942- ... SATA-50
Marteka, Vincent (James) 1936- ... 15-16R
Martel, Jane G. 1926- ... 57-60
Martel, Leon C. 1933- ... 125
Martell, James
See Bingley, David Ernest
Martell, Paul 1921(?)-1985 Obituary ... 116
Martellaro, Joseph A. 1924- ... 19-20R
Martelli, Leonard J. 1938(?)-1988
Obituary ... 125
Martens, Kurt 1870-1945 ... DLB-66
Marter, Joan M. 1946- ... 124
Marth, Del 1925- ... 61-64
Martha, Henry
See Harris, Mark
Marti, Fritz 1894- ... 107
Martianoff, Nicholas 1893-1984 Obituary ... 112
Martignoni, Margaret E. 1908(?)-1974
Obituary ... 104
See also SATA 27
Marti-Ibanez, Felix 1912(?)-1972
Obituary ... 33-36R
Martin, Albert
See Nussbaum, Al(bert F.)
and Mehan, Joseph Albert
Martin, Albro 1921- ... 77-80
Martin, Alfred 1916- ... 117
Martin, Alfred Manuel 1928- ... 108
Martin, Allie Beth 1914-1976 Obituary ... 65-68
Martin, Anamae 1919- ... 9-10R
Martin, Andre
See Jacoby, Henry
Martin, Andrew 1906-1985 Obituary ... 115
Martin, Ann Bodenhamer 1927- ... CANR-11
Earlier sketch in CA 69-72
Martin, Ann M(atthews) 1955- ... 111
See also SATA 41, 44
Martin, April
See Sherrill, Dorothy
Martin, Arlan Stone 1932- ... 69-72
Martin, Augustine 1935- ... 93-96
Martin, Barclay (Cluck) 1923- ... 73-76
Martin, Ben(jamin S.) 1921- ... 1R
Martin, Benjamin F(ranklin, Jr.) 1947- ... 89-92
Martin, Bernard (Davis) 1897- ... CAP-1
Earlier sketch in CA 9-10
Martin, Bernard 1905- ... CAP-1
Earlier sketch in CA 11-12
Martin, Bernard 1928- ... CANR-4
Earlier sketch in CA 53-56
Martin, Betty
See Martin, Elizabeth DuVernet
Martin, Bill, Jr.
See Martin, William Ivan

Martin, Billy
 See Martin, Alfred Manuel
Martin, Boyd A(rcher) 1911- ... 37-40R
Martin, Brian P(hilip) 1947- ... 116
Martin, Bruce
 See Paine, Lauran (Bosworth)
Martin, C(arol) Dianne 1943- ... 113
Martin, C(harles) Leslie 1897- ... 5-6R
Martin, C. Lewis 1915- ... 25-28R
Martin, Calvin (L.) 1948- Brief entry ... 113
Martin, Carter W(illiams) 1933- ... 25-28R
Martin, Charles 1906- ... 3R
Martin, Charles B(asil) 1930- ... 93-96
Martin, Charles Burton 1924- ... 25-28R
Martin, Charles E.
 See Mastrangelo, Charles E.
Martin, Charles-Noel 1923- ... 29-32R
Martin, Chip
 See Martin, Stoddard (Hammond), Jr.
Martin, Christopher
 See Hoyt, Edwin P(almer), Jr.
Martin, Chryssee (MacCasler) Perry 1940- .. 126
Martin, Claire 1914- ... DLB-60
Martin, Cort
 See Sherman, Jory (Tecumseh)
Martin, Curtis 1915- ... 53-56
Martin, David 1915- ... CANR-24
 Earlier sketch in CA 103
Martin, David (Lozell) 1946- ... 89-92
Martin, David Alfred 1929- ... 107
Martin, David C(lark) 1943- ... 102
Martin, David Grant 1939- ... 65-68
Martin, David L(incoln) 1947- ... 119
Martin, David Stone 1913- ... SATA-39
Martin, Don 1931- ... 101
Martin, Don W. 1934- ... 126
Martin, Donald Franklin 1944- ... 65-68
Martin, Donald L(loyd) 1939- ... 111
Martin, Dorothy 1921- ... CANR-6
 Earlier sketch in CA 57-60
 See also SATA 47
Martin, Dwight 1921-1978 Obituary ... 77-80
Martin, E(rnest) W(alter) 1914- ... CANR-20
 Earlier sketches in CA 11-12R, CANR-5
Martin, Earl S(auder) 1944- ... 102
Martin, Edward A(lexander) 1927- ... 120
Martin, Elizabeth DuVernet 1910- ... 103
Martin, Ellis
 See Ryan, Marah Ellis
Martin, Emily 1944- ... 49-52
Martin, Esmond Bradley 1941- ... CANR-16
 Earlier sketch in CA 93-96
Martin, Eugene ... CANR-26
 Earlier sketches in CA 19-20, CAP-2
 See also SATA 1
Martin, Eva M. 1939- ... 126
Martin, F(rancis) David 1920- ... 33-36R
Martin, F(rancis) X(avier) 1922- ... CANR-13
 Earlier sketch in CA 23-24R
Martin, Frances M(cEntee) 1906- ... 61-64
 See also SATA 36
Martin, Francis
 See Reid, Charles (Stuart)
Martin, Frederick M(orris) 1923-1985
 Obituary ... 115
Martin, Fredric
 See Christopher, Matt(hew F.)
Martin, G(eoffrey H(oward) 1928- ... 5-6R
Martin, Gary M. 1936- ... 89-92
Martin, Ged
 See Martin, Gerald Warren
Martin, Geoffrey John 1934- ... CANR-14
 Earlier sketch in CA 37-40R
Martin, George (Whitney) 1926- ... CANR-21
 Earlier sketches in CA 9-10R, CANR-3
Martin, George R(aymond) R(ichard)
 1948- ... 81-84
Martin, Gerald Warren 1945- ... CANR-17
 Earlier sketches in CA 45-48, CANR-1
Martin, Graham Dunstan 1932- ... CANR-23
 Earlier sketch in CA 106
Martin, Greg
 See Miller, George Louquet
Martin, Harold Clark 1917- ... 9-10R
Martin, Harold Harber 1910- ... CANR-7
 Earlier sketch in CA 61-64
Martin, Harold S(heaffer) 1930- ... 57-60
Martin, Herbert 1913- ... 29-32R
Martin, Herbert Woodward 1933- ... 73-76
 See also BW
Martin, Hubert M., Jr. 1932- ... 103
Martin, Ian Kennedy
 See Kennedy-Martin, Ian
Martin, Ira Jay III 1911- ... 53-56
Martin, J(ohn) P(ercival) 1880(?)-1966 ... 81-84
 See also SATA 15
Martin, Jack
 See Etchison, Dennis (William)
Martin, James 1921- ... 119
Martin, James (Thomas) 1933- Brief entry .. 112
Martin, James Alfred, Jr. 1917- ... 73-76
Martin, James Gilbert 1926- ... 11-12R
Martin, James J(oseph) 1916- ... CANR-8
 Earlier sketch in CA 5-6R
Martin, James Kirby 1943- ... 125
Martin, James L. 1948- ... 81-84
Martin, James Perry 1923- ... 5-6R
Martin, Jane Roland 1929- ... 119
Martin, Janet
 See Garfinkel, Bernard Max
Martin, Jay (Herbert) 1935- ... CANR-21
 Earlier sketch in CA 5-6R
Martin, Jay
 See Golding, Morton J(ay)
Martin, Jeremy
 See Levin, Marcia Obrasky
Martin, John 1893-1985 Obituary ... 116
Martin, John Bartlow 1915-1987 ... CANR-8
 Obituary ... 121
 Earlier sketch in CA 15-16R
Martin, John Hanbury 1892-1983
 Obituary ... 109
Martin, John Henry 1915- ... 102
Martin, John Rupert 1916- ... 19-20R
Martin, John Sayre 1921- ... 103
Martin, John Stuart 1900-1977 ... 9-10R
 Obituary ... 69-72
Martin, Jose L(uis) 1921- ... CANR-12
 Earlier sketch in CA 61-64
Martin, Joseph George 1915-1981 ... 108
 Obituary ... 102
Martin, Joy 1922- ... 57-60
Martin, Judith (Sylvia) 1938- ... CANR-12
 Earlier sketch in CA 97-100
Martin, June Hall
 See McCash, June Hall
Martin, Kathryn 1908- ... 108
Martin, Ken
 See Hubbard, L(afayette) Ron(ald)
Martin, Kenneth R(obert) 1938- ... CANR-17
 Earlier sketches in CA 45-48, CANR-1
Martin, Kevin
 See Pelton, Robert W(ayne)
Martin, (Basil) Kingsley 1897-1969 ... CANR-11
 Obituary ... 25-28R
 Earlier sketch in CA 7-8R
Martin, L(eslie) John 1921- ... CANR-22
 Earlier sketches in CA 57-60, CANR-6
Martin, Laura C(oogle) 1952- ... 117
Martin, Laurence W(oodward) 1928- ... CANR-7
 Earlier sketch in CA 5-6R
Martin, Lawrence 1895- ... CAP-1
 Earlier sketch in CA 9-10
Martin, Lee
 See Wingate, (Martha) Anne (Guice)
Martin, Lee Nicholson 1916(?)-1987
 Obituary ... 124
Martin, Les
 See Schulman, L(ester) M(artin)
Martin, Lucien
 See Gabel, Joseph
Martin, Luther H(oward), Jr. 1937- ... 124
Martin, Lynne 1923- ... 65-68
 See also SATA 21
Martin, M(arilynn) Kay 1942- ... 65-68
Martin, Malachi ... 81-84
 See also AITN 1
Martin, Marcia
 See Levin, Marcia Obrasky
Martin, Margaret Joan 1928- ... 69-72
Martin, Marie-Louise 1912- ... 69-72
Martin, Mario, Jr.
 See Monteleone, Thomas F(rancis)
Martin, Marjorie 1942- ... 53-56
Martin, Marta San
 See San Martin, Marta
Martin, Mary 1913(?)- ... 113
 Brief entry ... 111
Martin, Mary Steichen
 See Calderone, Mary S(teichen)
Martin, Maurice 1946- ... 115
Martin, Michael L. 1932- ... 19-20R
Martin, Michael William 1946- ... 121
Martin, Michelle 1957- ... 119
Martin, Mike W.
 See Martin, Michael William
Martin, Milward Wyatt 1895-1974 ... CAP-1
 Earlier sketch in CA 19-20
Martin, Morgan 1921- ... 19-20R
Martin, Murray S(impson) 1928- ... 112
Martin, Nancy
 See Salmon, Annie Elizabeth
Martin, Noah S(ensenig) 1940- ... 69-72
Martin, Norma F(rances) 1936- ... 113
Martin, Oliver
 See Smith, R(eginald) D(onald)
Martin, Ovid A. 1904-1979 Obituary ... 89-92
Martin, Patricia Miles 1899-1986 ... CANR-2
 Obituary ... 119
 Earlier sketch in CA 4R
 See also SATA 1, 43, 48
Martin, Paul
 See Deale, Kenneth Edwin Lee
Martin, Paul Sidney 1899-1974 ... CANR-8
 Earlier sketch in CA 7-8R
Martin, Pete
 See Martin, William Thorton
Martin, (Roy) Peter 1931- ... 125
 Brief entry ... 120
Martin, Peter
 See Chaundler, Christine
Martin, Peter W(illiam) 1939- ... 89-92
Martin, Philip (John Talbot) 1931- ... CANR-24
 Earlier sketches in CA 61-64, CANR-9
Martin, Phyllis Cook 1908- ... 5-6R
Martin, Quinn 1922-1987 Obituary ... 123
Martin, R. Johnson
 See Mehta, Rustam Jehangir
Martin, R(ichard) M(ilton) 1916- ... CANR-15
 Earlier sketch in CA 41-44R
Martin, Ralph 1942- ... CANR-9
 Earlier sketch in CA 57-60
Martin, Ralph C. 1924- ... 9-10R
Martin, Ralph G. 1920- ... 5-6R
Martin, Ralph P(hilip) ... CANR-9
 Earlier sketch in CA 65-68
Martin, Reginald 1956- ... 126
Martin, Rene 1891-1977 ... SATA-20, 42
Martin, Renee C(ohen) 1928- ... 49-52
Martin, Rhona 1922- ... 121
 Brief entry ... 116
Martin, Richard 1946- ... 124
Martin, Richard
 See Creasey, John
Martin, Robert (Lee) 1908-1976 ... 2R
 Obituary ... 103
Martin, Robert A(llen) 1930- ... 110
Martin, Robert Bernard 1918- ... CANR-25
 Earlier sketches in CA 4R, CANR-2
Martin, Robert K(essler) 1941- ... 102
Martin, Robert Sidney 1949- ... 122
Martin, Robert W.
 See Pelton, Robert W(ayne)
Martin, Roderick 1940- ... CANR-12
 Earlier sketch in CA 29-32R
Martin, Ron 1941- ... 122
Martin, Ronald E(dward) 1933- ... 19-20R
Martin, Roscoe C(oleman) 1903-1972 ... CAP-1
 Obituary ... 33-36R
 Earlier sketch in CA 19-20
Martin, Rupert (Claude) 1905- ... SATA-31
Martin, Ruth
 See Rayner, Claire (Berenice)
Martin, Sam
 See Moskowitz, Sam
Martin, Samuel Elmo 1924- Brief entry ... 105
Martin, Stefan 1936- ... SATA-32
Martin, Stella
 See Heyer, Georgette
Martin, Steve 1945(?)- ... 97-100
 See also CLC 30
Martin, Stoddard (Hammond), Jr. 1948- ... 117
Martin, Susan Ehrlich 1940- ... 124
Martin, Sylvia (Pass) 1913- ... 19-20R
Martin, Taffy 1945- ... 125
Martin, Thom(as) Francis 1934- ... 7-8R
Martin, Thomas Lyle, Jr. 1921- ... 11-12R
Martin, Tom
 See Paine, Lauran (Bosworth)
Martin, Tony 1942- ... CANR-26
 Earlier sketches in CA 57-60, CANR-6
 See also BW
Martin, Valerie 1948- ... 85-88
Martin, Vance G(regory) 1949- ... 114
Martin, Vernon N(orthfleet) 1930- ... 45-48
Martin, Vicky
 See Storey, Victoria Carolyn
Martin, Wallace 1933- ... 122
Martin, Walter T(ilford) 1917- ... 11-12R
Martin, Warren Bryan 1925- ... CANR-20
 Earlier sketch in CA 41-44R
Martin, Webber
 See Silverberg, Robert
Martin, Wendy 1940- ... 37-40R
Martin, Wendy
 See Martini, Teri
Martin, Wilfred B(enjamin) W(eldon)
 1940- ... 116
Martin, William C. 1937- ... CANR-14
 Earlier sketch in CA 77-80
Martin, William Ivan 1916- Brief entry ... 117
 See also SATA 40
Martin, William Keble 1877-1969 Obituary .. 104
Martin, William Thorton 1901(?)-1980
 Obituary ... 102
Martinco, John P. 1917(?)-1986 Obituary .. 118
Martindale, Charles (Anthony) 1949- ... 124
Martindale, Colin (Eugene) 1943- ... 61-64
Martindale, Don (Albert) 1915- ... CANR-6
 Earlier sketch in CA 13-14R
Martin du Gard, Roger 1881-1958
 Brief entry ... 118
 See also DLB 65
 See also TCLC 24
Martine
 See Woolfolk, Joanna Martine
Martine, James J(ohn) 1937- ... 57-60
Martineau, Gilbert ... CANR-17
 Earlier sketch in CA 29-32R
Martineau, Harriet 1802-1876 ... YABC-2
 See also DLB 21, 55
Martineau, James 1805-1900 Brief entry ... 122
Martineau, Robert Arnold Schurhoff 1913- .. 106
Martine-Barnes, Adrienne 1942- ... 110
Martinelli, Ricardo
 See Brandon, Johnny
Martines, Julia
 See O'Faolain, Julia
Martines, Lauro 1927- ... CANR-12
 Earlier sketch in CA 25-28R
Martinet, Andre 1908- ... CAP-1
 Earlier sketch in CA 11-12
Martinetti, Ronald 1945- ... 57-60
Martinetz, V(ivian) L. 1927- ... 61-64
Martinez, Al 1929- ... 57-60
Martinez, Elizabeth Sutherland 1925- ... 121
Martinez, Jacinto Benavente y
 See Benavente (y Martinez), Jacinto
Martinez, Julio A(ntonio) 1931- ... CANR-18
 Earlier sketch in CA 101
Martinez, Oscar J(aquez) 1943- ... 120
Martinez, Rafael V. 1923- ... 11-12R
Martinez, Raymond J(oseph) 1889- ... 61-64
Martinez, S(ally) A. 1938- ... 81-84
Martinez Ruiz, Jose 1873-1969 ... 93-96
Martinez Sierra, Gregorio 1881-1947
 Brief entry ... 115
 See also TCLC 6
Martinez Sierra, Maria (de la O'LeJarraga)
 1874-1974 Obituary ... 115
Martinez Sierra, Maria (de la O'LeJarraga)
 1880(?)-1974 ... TCLC-6
Martini, Teri 1930- ... CANR-2
 Earlier sketch in CA 5-6R
 See also SATA 3
Martini, Therese
 See Martini, Teri
Martini, Virgilio 1903- ... 37-40R
Martino, Bill 1933- ... 57-60
Martino, Joseph P(aul) 1931- ... 61-64
Martino, Rocco L(eonard) 1929- ... 15-16R
Martins, Maria 1898(?)-1973 Obituary ... 41-44R
Martins, Maria Isabel Barreno de Faria
 1939- ... 105
Martins, Peter 1946- ... 113
Martins, Wilson 1921- ... 19-20R
Martinsen, Ella Barbara Lung 1901-1977 ... 103
Martinsen, Martin
 See Follett, Ken(neth Martin)
Martinson, David (Keith) 1946- ... CANR-1
 Earlier sketch in CA 45-48
Martinson, Floyd M(ansfield) 1916- ... 93-96
Martinson, Harry (Edmund) 1904-1978 ... 77-80
 See also CLC 14
Martinson, Robert M. 1927- ... 41-44R
Martinson, Ruth A(lice) 1915- ... CANR-17
 Earlier sketch in CA 25-28R
Martinson, Tom L. 1941- ... 77-80
Martinson, William D. 1924- ... 23-24R
Martland, Thomas R(odolphe) 1926- ... 5-6R
Marton, Beryl M(itchell) 1922- ... CANR-11
 Earlier sketch in CA 69-72
Marton, Endre 1910- ... 37-40R
Marton, George 1900- ... 29-32R
Martone, Michael 1955- ... 124
 Brief entry ... 118
Martos, Borys 1879-1977 Obituary ... 73-76
Martos, Joseph (John) 1943- ... 105
Marty, Martin E(mil) 1928- ... CANR-21
 Earlier sketch in CA 5-6R
Marty, Myron A. 1932- ... CANR-11
 Earlier sketch in CA 25-28R
Marty, Sid 1944- ... 108
Martyn, Edward 1859-1923 ... DLB-10
Martyn, Howe 1906- ... 11-12R
Martyn, J(ames) Louis 1925- ... 126
 Brief entry ... 105
Martyn, Kenneth A(lfred) 1926- ... 23-24R
Martynov, Leonid (Nikolaevich) 1905-
 Brief entry ... 116
Martz, John D(anhouse) 1934- ... CANR-1
 Earlier sketch in CA 45-48
Martz, Lawrence J. 1933- ... 69-72
Martz, Louis L(ohr) 1913- ... CANR-5
 Earlier sketch in CA 13-14R
Martz, William J. 1928- ... CANR-9
 Earlier sketch in CA 21-22R
Marut, Ret
 See Traven, B.
Marut, Robert
 See Traven, B.
Maruyama, Masao 1914- ... 13-14R
Marvel, Tom 1901-1970 Obituary ... 104
Marvick, Elizabeth Wirth 1925- ... 117
Marvin, Burton Wright 1913-1979
 Obituary ... 85-88
Marvin, David Keith 1921- ... 15-16R
Marvin, Dorothy Betts 1894(?)-1975
 Obituary ... 57-60
Marvin, Harold Myers 1893-1977 ... 7-8R
 Obituary ... 73-76
Marvin, John R(obert) 1923- ... 117
Marvin, John T. 1906- ... 19-20R
Marvin, Philip (Roger) 1916- ... CANR-13
 Earlier sketch in CA 37-40R
Marvin, Richard
 See Ellis, Julie
Marvin, Susan
 See Ellis, Julie
Marvin, W. R.
 See Cameron, Lou
Marvin X
 See El Muhajir
 See also DLB 38
Marwell, Gerald 1937- ... 41-44R
Marwick, Arthur 1936- ... CANR-13
 Earlier sketch in CA 29-32R
Marwick, Helen
 See Lillie, Helen
Marwick, Lawrence 1909-1981 Obituary ... 106
Marwick, M(axwell) G(ay) 1916- ... 37-40R
Marwil, Jonathan L(evy) 1940- ... 114
Marx, Anne ... CANR-12
 Earlier sketch in CA 29-32R
Marx, Arthur 1893-1964 Obituary ... 113
Marx, Arthur 1921- ... CANR-24
 Earlier sketch in CA 81-84
Marx, Erica Elizabeth 1909-1967 ... CAP-1
 Earlier sketch in CA 13-14
Marx, Gary T. 1938- ... CANR-14
 Earlier sketch in CA 37-40R
Marx, Groucho
 See Marx, Julius Henry
Marx, Harpo
 See Marx, Arthur
Marx, Herbert L(ewis), Jr. 1922- ... CANR-6
 Earlier sketch in CA 9-10R
Marx, Jenifer (Grant) 1940- ... 101
Marx, Jerry
 See Bernstein, Jerry Marx
Marx, Julius Henry 1890-1977 ... 81-84
 Obituary ... 73-76
Marx, Kenneth S(amuel) 1939- ... 69-72
Marx, Leo 1919- ... 126
Marx, Melvin H(erman) 1919- ... CANR-6
 Earlier sketch in CA 5-6R
Marx, Paul 1920- ... 37-40R
Marx, Robert F(rank) 1936- ... CANR-6
 Earlier sketch in CA 11-12R
 See also SATA 24
Marx, Samuel 1902- ... 103
Marx, Werner 1910- ... 81-84
Marx, Wesley 1934- ... CANR-12
 Earlier sketch in CA 23-24R
Marxhausen, Joanne G. 1935- ... 37-40R
Mary Agnes Therese, Sister 1910- ... 2R
Mary Francis, Mother
 See Aschmann, Alberta

Mary Kay
See Ash, Mary Kay (Wagner)
Mary Madeleine, Sister 1916-1974 CAP-1
Earlier sketch in CA 15-16
Marzan, Julio 1946- Brief entry 113
Marzani, Carl (Aldo) 1912- 61-64
See also SATA 12
Marzials, Theo 1850-1920 DLB-35
Marzolf, Marion Tuttle 1930- 124
Brief entry 114
Marzollo, Jean 1942- CANR-15
Earlier sketch in CA 81-84
See also SATA 29
Masani, Shakuntala 112
Masani, Zareer 1947- 97-100
Masannat, George S. 1933- 25-28R
Masao, Maruyama 1914- 107
Masaoka Shiki
See Masaoka Tsunenori
See also TCLC 18
Masaoka Tsunenori 1867-1902 Brief entry 117
Mascall, Eric L(ionel) 1905- 7-8R
Mascott, Trina 81-84
Masefield, Geoffrey Bussell 1911- 7-8R
Masefield, John (Edward) 1878-1967 CAP-2
Obituary 25-28R
Earlier sketch in CA 19-20
See also SATA 19
See also DLB 10
See also CLC 11, 47
Masefield, (John) Richard (William) 1943- 119
Maser, Edward A(ndrew) 1923-1988 45-48
Obituary 126
Maser, Jack D(avid) 1937- 57-60
Masey, Mary Lou(ise) 1932- 21-22R
Masha
See Stern, Marie
Masheck, Joseph (Daniel) 1942- 105
Masia, Seth 1948- 110
Masinton, Charles G(erald) 1938- 77-80
Maslach, Christina 1946- 111
Maslenikov, Oleg A(lexander) 1907-1972
Obituary 111
Maslin, Alice 1914(?)-1981 Obituary 104
Maslin, Bonnie L(ynn) 1947- 107
Maslow, Abraham H. 1908-1970 CANR-4
Obituary 29-32R
Earlier sketch in CA 2R
Maslow, Jonathan Evan 1948- 126
Maslowski, Peter 1944- 97-100
Maslowski, Raymond M(arion) 1931- 93-96
Maslowski, Stanley 1937- 21-22R
Masnata, Albert 1900- 93-96
Maso, Carole 19(?)- CLC-44
Mason, A. E. W. 1865-1948 DLB-70
Mason, Alpheus Thomas 1899- 1R
Mason, Betty (Oxford) 1930- 37-40R
Mason, Bobbie Ann 1940- CANR-11
Earlier sketch in CA 53-56
See also DLBY 87
See also CLC 28, 43
Mason, Bruce B(onner) 1923- 11-12R
Mason, Bruce Edward George 1921-1982
Obituary 110
Mason, Carola
See Zentner, Carola
Mason, Chuck
See Rowland, D(onald) S(ydney)
Mason, Clarence (Eugene), Jr. 1904- 57-60
Mason, David E(rnest) 1928- 21-22R
Mason, Douglas R(ankine) 1918- CANR-17
Earlier sketches in CA 49-52, CANR-1
Mason, Edmund (John) 1911- 103
Mason, Edward S(agendorph) 1899- 73-76
Mason, Edwin A. 1905-1979 CAP-2
Obituary 89-92
Earlier sketch in CA 25-28
See also SATA 32
Mason, Ellsworth (Goodwin) 1917- 126
Mason, Ernst
See Pohl, Frederik
Mason, Eudo C(olecestra) 1901-1969 CAP-1
Earlier sketch in CA 9-10
Mason, F(rancis) van Wyck 1901-1978 CANR-8
Obituary 81-84
Earlier sketch in CA 5-6R
See also SATA 3, 26
Mason, Francis K(enneth) 1928- 103
Mason, Frank Earl 1893-1979 Obituary 89-92
Mason, Frank W.
See Mason, F(rancis) van Wyck
Mason, Gabriel Richard 1884-1979
Obituary 85-88
Mason, Gene (William) 1928- 89-92
Mason, George E(van) 1932- CANR-12
Earlier sketch in CA 29-32R
Mason, George Frederick 1904- 73-76
See also SATA 14
Mason, Haydn T(revor) 1929- CANR-3
Earlier sketch in CA 11-12R
Mason, Herbert Molloy, Jr. 1927- CANR-6
Earlier sketch in CA 15-16R
Mason, Herbert Warren, Jr. 1932- CANR-16
Earlier sketch in CA 85-88
Mason, James (Neville) 1909-1984
Obituary 113
Mason, John Brown 1904- 49-52
Mason, Joseph B(igsbee) 1903- 125
Mason, Julian D(ewey) Jr. 1931- 37-40R
Mason, Lee W.
See Malzberg, Barry N(athaniel)
Mason, Lowell Blake 1893-1983 Obituary 110
Mason, Madeline 1913- 9-10R
Mason, Michael 1939- 120
Mason, Michael Henry 1900-1982
Obituary 108
Mason, Mike 1952- 126
Mason, Miriam E(vangeline)
1900-1973 CANR-15
Obituary 103
Earlier sketch in CA 2R
See also SATA 2, 26
Mason, Nicholas (Charles Sheppard)
1938- CANR-24
Earlier sketch in CA 104
Mason, Nick 1945- CLC-35
Mason, Pamela 1918- Brief entry 105
Mason, Paul T(aylor) 1937- 33-36R
Mason, Peter (Geoffrey) 1914- 114
Mason, Philip 1906- CANR-3
Earlier sketch in CA 9-10R
Mason, Philip (Parker) 1927- 19-20R
Mason, R(ichard) A(nthony) 1932- 119
Mason, R(onald) A(lison) K(ells)
1905-1971 Obituary 89-92
Mason, Raymond 1926- 9-10R
Mason, Richard (Lakin) 1919- 11-12R
Mason, Robert E(mmett) 1914- CANR-17
Earlier sketch in CA 1R
Mason, Ronald (Charles) 1912- CANR-24
Earlier sketch in CA 13-14R
Mason, Ronald M. 1949- 111
Mason, Ruth Fitch 1890-1974 Obituary 53-56
Mason, Tally
See Derleth, August (William)
Mason, Ted
See Mason, Theodore C(harles)
Mason, Theodore C(harles) 1921- 109
Mason, Thomas A(lexander) 1944- 120
Mason, Tyler
See Mason, Madeline
Mason, Van Wyck
See Mason, F(rancis) van Wyck
Mason, Will Edwin 1912- 5-6R
Masotti, Louis H(enry) 1934- 41-44R
Mass, Jeffrey P(aul) 1940- Brief entry 111
Mass, William
See Gibson, William
Massa, Ann 1940- 29-32R
Massa, Richard W(ayne) 1932- 57-60
Massanari, Jared (Dean) 1943- 65-68
Massaquoi, Hans J(urgen) 1926- 69-72
Massarik, Fred 1926- 4R
Massel, Mark S. 1910- CAP-1
Earlier sketch in CA 11-12
Masselink, Ben 1919- 19-20R
Masselman, George 1897-1971 9-10R
See also SATA 19
Massengale, John (Edward) Montague
1951- 125
Masserman, Jules H(oman) 1905- 69-72
Massey, Ellen Gray 1921- 118
Massey, Erika 1900- 61-64
Massey, Floyd, Jr. 1915- 65-68
Massey, Gerald 1828-1907 DLB-32
Massey, Gerald J. 1934- 89-92
Massey, Harrie Stewart Wilson 1908-1983
Obituary 111
Massey, Irving (Joseph) 1924- 77-80
Massey, James A(idege) 1939- 121
Massey, James Earl 1930- CANR-12
Earlier sketch in CA 29-32R
Massey, Joseph Earl 1897- 29-32R
Massey, Mary Elizabeth 1915-197(?) CAP-2
Earlier sketch in CA 23-24
Massey, Raymond (Hart) 1896-1983 104
Obituary 110
Massey, Reginald 1932- 23-24R
Massialas, Byron G. 1929- CANR-8
Earlier sketch in CA 21-22R
Massie, Diane Redfield 81-84
See also SATA 16
Massie, Joseph Logan 1921- CANR-2
Earlier sketch in CA 3R
Massie, Robert K(inloch) 1929- CANR-14
Earlier sketch in CA 77-80
Massine, Leonide
See Myassin, Leonid Fedorovich
Massing, Hede 1899-1981 Obituary 108
Massinger, Philip 1583-1640 DLB-58
Massingham, Harold William 1932- 65-68
Massis, Henri 1886-1970 Obituary 29-32R
Massman, Patti 1945- 117
Massman, Virgil Frank 1929- 37-40R
Masson, Andre (Aime Rene) 1896-1987
Obituary 124
Masson, David I. 1915- 25-28R
Masson, Georgina
See Johnson, Marion Georgina Wikeley
Masson, J. Moussaieff
See Masson, Jeffrey Moussaieff
Masson, Jeffrey M.
See Masson, Jeffrey Moussaieff
Masson, Jeffrey Moussaieff 1941- 122
Masson, Loyes 1915-1969 CAP-1
Earlier sketch in CA 13-14
Massow, Rosalind 89-92
Massy, William F(rancis) 1934- 41-44R
Mast, Gerald 1940-1988 CANR-12
Obituary 126
Earlier sketch in CA 69-72
Mast, Russell L. 1915- 13-14R
Masterman, John Cecil 1891-1977 CANR-6
Obituary 69-72
Earlier sketch in CA 9-10R
Masterman-Smith, Virginia 1937- 110
Masters, Anthony 25-28R
Masters, Anthony 1948(?)-1985 Obituary 115
Masters, Brian 1939- 118
Masters, Edgar Lee 1869(?)-1950
Brief entry 104
See also DLB 54
See also CDALB 1865-1917
See also TCLC 2, 25
Masters, Elaine 1932- 57-60
Masters, G(eorge) Mallary 1936- 25-28R
Masters, Hardin (Wallace) 1899(?)-1979
Obituary 89-92
Masters, Hilary 1928- CANR-13
Earlier sketch in CA 25-28R
See also CLC 48
Masters, John 1914-1983 110
Brief entry 108
Masters, Kelly R. 1897- 3R
See also SATA 3
Masters, Mildred 1932- 110
See also SATA 42
Masters, Nicholas A. 1929- 13-14R
Masters, Olga 1919- 121
Masters, Roger D(avis) 1933- 21-22R
Masters, William
See Cousins, Margaret
Masters, William H(owell) 1915- 21-22R
See also AITN 1
Masters, Zeke
See Bensen, Donald R.
and Goulart, Ron(ald Joseph)
Masterson, Dan 1934- 81-84
Masterson, Dave 1951- 118
Masterson, J. B.
See Edmondson, G. C.
Masterson, James F(rancis) 1925- 69-72
Masterson, Patrick 1936- 73-76
Masterson, Thomas R(obert) 1915- 25-28R
Masterson, Whit
See Miller, (H.) Bill(y)
and Wade, Robert (Allison)
Masterson, William Henry 1914-1983 123
Masterton, Elsie (Lipstein) 1914-1966 5-6R
Masterton, Graham 1946- CANR-22
Earlier sketch in CA 105
Mastny, Vojtech 1936- CANR-13
Earlier sketch in CA 33-36R
Maston, T(homas) B(ufford) 1897- CANR-18
Earlier sketches in CA 5-6R, CANR-2
Mastrangelo, Charles E. 1910- 113
Mastro, Susan (Duff) 1945- 69-72
Mastrosimone, William 19(?)- CLC-36
Masuda, Takeshi 1944- 123
Masuda, Yoneji 1909- 109
Masur, Gerhard Strassman 1901-1975 CANR-4
Earlier sketch in CA 3R
Masur, Harold Q. 1909- CANR-13
Earlier sketch in CA 77-80
Masur, Jenny 1948- 65-68
Mata, Daya 1914- 77-80
Matanzo, Jane Brady 1940- 103
Matarazzo, James M. 1941- CANR-14
Earlier sketch in CA 37-40R
Matarazzo, Joseph D(ominic) 1925- 57-60
Matcha, Jack 1919- CANR-2
Earlier sketch in CA 2R
Matchett, William H(enry) 1923- 13-14R
Matchette, Katharine E. 1941- 53-56
See also SATA 38
Matczak, Sebastian A(lexander) 1914- 9-10R
Matejic, Mateja 1924- 112
Matejka, Ladislav 1919- 73-76
Matejko, Alexander J. 1924- CANR-22
Earlier sketches in CA 57-60, CANR-6
Matek, Ord 1922- 89-92
Matenko, Percy 1901- CANR-1
Earlier sketch in CA 45-48
Mateosian, S. Richard 1941- 111
Materer, Timothy (John) 1940- 89-92
Mates, Julian 1927- 1R
Matesky, Ralph 1913- 7-8R
Math, Irwin 1940- 112
See also SATA 42
Mathabane, Mark 1960- 125
See also BW
Mathai, M. O. 1909-1981 Obituary 108
Mathay, Francis 1925- 57-60
Mathe, Albert
See Camus, Albert
Mather, Berkely
See Davies, John Evan Weston
Mather, Bertrand 1914- CAP-1
Earlier sketch in CA 9-10
Mather, Bob
See Mather, Robert E(dward)
Mather, Cotton 1663-1728 DLB-24, 30
See also CDALB 1640-1865
Mather, Eleanore Price 1910- 116
Mather, Increase 1639-1723 DLB-24
Mather, Jean 1946- 115
Mather, June 1924- 107
Mather, Kirtley F(letcher) 1888- 19-20R
Mather, Melissa
See Brown, Melissa Mather
Mather, Richard 1596-1669 DLB-24
Mather, Richard B(urroughs) 1913- 73-76
Mather, Robert E(dward) 1945- 115
Mathers, Michael 1945- 65-68
Mathers, Peter 1931- Brief entry 116
Mathes, J(ohn) C(harles) 1931- 49-52
Mathes, W(illiam) Michael 1936- CANR-26
Earlier sketches in CA 61-64, CANR-8
Matheson, Don(ald S.) 1948- 126
Matheson, Joan (Transue) 1924- 97-100
Matheson, John Ross 1917- CANR-23
Earlier sketch in CA 106
Matheson, Richard Burton 1926- 97-100
See also DLB 8, 44
See also CLC 37
Matheson, Sylvia A.
See Schofield, Sylvia Anne
Matheson, William H(oward) 1929- 23-24R
Matheus, John F(rederick) 1887-1983 124
See also BW
See also DLB 51
Mathew, David 1902-1975 CAP-2
Earlier sketch in CA 25-28
Mathew, (Anthony) Gervase 1905- 11-12R
Mathew, Ray(mond Frank) 1929- 19-20R
Mathews, Anthony Stuart 1930- 93-96
Mathews, Arthur 1903(?)-1980 Obituary 102
Mathews, Cornelius 1817(?)-1889 DLB-3, 64
Mathews, Denise
See Mathews, Patricia J.
Mathews, Donald G. 1932- 19-20R
Mathews, Donald K(enneth) 1923- 57-60
Mathews, Eleanor Muth 1923- 15-16R
Mathews, Evelyn Craw 1906- CAP-2
Earlier sketch in CA 19-20
Mathews, F(rancis) X. 1935- 25-28R
Mathews, H(arry) Lee 1939- 37-40R
Mathews, Harry 1930- CANR-18
Earlier sketch in CA 21-22R
See also CAAS 6
See also CLC 6
Mathews, J(oseph) Howard 1881-1970 9-10R
Obituary 103
Mathews, Jackson 1907(?)-1978 Obituary 104
Mathews, Jane DeHart 1936- 23-24R
Mathews, Janet 1914- 115
See also SATA 41
Mathews, John Joseph 1895- CAP-2
Earlier sketch in CA 19-20
Mathews, Louise
See Tooke, Louise Mathews
Mathews, Marcia Mayfield 9-10R
Mathews, Mitford M(cLeod) 1891-1985
Obituary 115
Mathews, Patricia J. 1929(?)-1983
Obituary 109
Mathews, Richard (Barrett) 1944- CANR-1
Earlier sketch in CA 45-48
Mathews, Russell Lloyd 1921- 109
Mathews, Thomas G(eorge) 1925- 49-52
Mathews, Virginia H(opper) 1925- 121
Mathews, Walter M(ichael) 1942- 110
Mathewson, Rufus Wellington, Jr.
1919(?)-1978 Obituary 81-84
Mathewson, William (Glen, Jr.) 1940- 106
Mathias, Frank Furlong 1925- CANR-12
Earlier sketch in CA 61-64
Mathias, Peter 1928- 19-20R
Mathias, Roland (Glyn) 1915- CANR-19
Earlier sketch in CA 97-100
See also DLB 27
See also CLC 45
Mathiesen, Egon 1907-1976 Obituary 109
See also SATA 28
Mathiesen, Thomas J(ames) 1947- 113
Mathieson, John A(ndrew) 1949- 111
Mathieson, Theodore 1913- 11-12R
Mathieu, Beatrice 1904-1976 Obituary 65-68
Mathieu, Bertrand 1936- 73-76
Mathieu, Joe
See Mathieu, Joseph P.
Mathieu, Joseph P. 1949- 125
Brief entry 117
See also SATA 36, 43
Mathieu, Noel Jean 1916-1984 Obituary 113
Mathis, (Byron) Claude 1927- 45-48
Mathis, Cleopatra 1947- 104
Mathis, (Luster) Doyle 1936- 45-48
Mathis, Edward 1927- 119
Mathis, F(erdinand) John 1941- 37-40R
Mathis, James L. 1925- 105
Mathis, June 1892-1927 DLB-44
Mathis, (Gerald) Ray 1937-1981 37-40R
Obituary 113
Mathis, Sharon Bell 1937- 41-44R
See also BW
See also SATA 7
See also SAAS 3
See also DLB 33
See also CLR 3
Mathison, Richard Randolph
1919-1980 CANR-3
Earlier sketch in CA 3R
Mathison, Stuart L. 1942- 29-32R
Mathur, Dinesh C(handra) 1918- 41-44R
Mathur, Y. B. 1930- 49-52
Matias, Waldemar 1934- 7-8R
Matilal, Bimal Krishna 1935- CANR-13
Earlier sketch in CA 23-24R
Matisoff, James A(lan) 1937- 103
Matisoff, Susan 1940- 104
Matisse, Henri (Emile Benoit) 1869-1954
Brief entry 122
Matlaw, Myron 1924- 33-36R
Matlin, Margaret White 1944- 119
Matloff, Maurice 1915- CANR-6
Earlier sketch in CA 13-14R
Matney, Bill
See Matney, William C., Jr.
Matney, William C., Jr. 1924- 69-72
Matossian, Mary Kilbourne 1930- 125
Matossian, Nouritza 1945- 124
Matrat, Jean 1915- 61-64
Matschat, Cecile H. 1895(?)-1976
Obituary 65-68
Matsen, Herbert Stanley 1926- 57-60
Matson, Albert Thomas 1915(?)-1987
Obituary 124
Matson, Emerson N(els) 1926- 45-48
See also SATA 12
Matson, Floyd W(illiam) 1921- 15-16R
Matson, Theodore E. 1906- 3R
Matson, Virginia (Mae) Freeberg 1914- 33-36R
Matson, Wallace I(rving) 1921- 13-14R
Matsuba, Moshe 1917- 37-40R
Matsui, Tadashi 1926- 41-44R
See also SATA 8
Matsumoto, Toru 1914(?)-1979 Obituary 89-92

Matsunaga, Alicia 1936- 29-32R
Matsunaga, Daigan Lee 1941- 41-44R
Matsuno, Masako
See Kobayashi, Masako Matsuno
See also SATA 6
Matsutani, Miyoko 1925- 69-72
Matt, Daniel C(hanan) 1950- 116
Matt, Paul R(obert) 1926- 33-36R
Mattam, Donald 1909- 45-48
Matte, (Encarnacion) L'Enc 1936- SATA-22
Matte, Robert G., Jr. 1948- CANR-16
Earlier sketch in CA 65-68
Matteo, P. B., Jr.
See Ringgold, Gene
Matter, Joseph Allen 1901- 29-32R
Mattersdorf, Leo 1903-1985 Obituary 117
Mattes, Merrill J(ohn) 1910- 41-44R
Matteson, Michael T(ownsend) 1943- .. CANR-16
Earlier sketch in CA 89-92
Mattessich, Richard V(ictor) 1922- CANR-9
Earlier sketch in CA 15-16R
Matthaei, Julie Ann 1951- 110
Mattheson, Rodney
See Creasey, John
Matthew, Christopher C(harles) F(orrest)
1939- Brief entry 116
Matthew, Donald J(ames) A(lexander)
1930- CANR-15
Earlier sketch in CA 7-8R
Matthew, Henry Colin Gray 1941- 53-56
Matthews, Anthony
See Barker, Dudley
Matthews, Brad
See DeMille, Nelson
Matthews, Brander 1852-1929 .... DLB-71
Matthews, C(onstance) M(ary) 1908- 25-28R
Matthews, Carola 1937- 25-28R
Matthews, Carole Smith 1943- 111
Matthews, Clayton (Hartley) 1918- CANR-25
Earlier sketches in CA 53-56, CANR-9
Matthews, Clyde 1917- 103
Matthews, (Robert) Curt(is, Jr.) 1934- 73-76
Matthews, Denis (James) 1919- 103
Matthews, Desmond S. 1922- 23-24R
Matthews, Donald Rowe 1925- CANR-2
Earlier sketch in CA 1R
Matthews, Ellen 1950- 89-92
See also SATA 28
Matthews, Elmora Messer 1925- 21-22R
Matthews, Geoffrey M. 1920-1984
Obituary 115
Matthews, Glenna C. 1938- 126
Matthews, Greg 1949- CLC-45
Matthews, Harry G(len) 1939- 73-76
Matthews, Herbert Lionel 1900-1977 .... CANR-2
Obituary 73-76
Earlier sketch in CA 1R
Matthews, Honor 1901- CAP-2
Earlier sketch in CA 23-24
Matthews, J(ohn) H(erbert) 1930- CANR-20
Earlier sketches in CA 15-16R, CANR-5
Matthews, Jack 1917- 11-12R
Matthews, Jack
See Matthews, John H(arold)
See also DLB 6
Matthews, Jacklyn Meek
See Meek, Jacklyn O'Hanlon
Matthews, Jessie 1907-1981 Obituary 108
Matthews, Joan E(thel) 1914- 21-22R
Matthews, John (Pengwerne) 1927- 118
Matthews, John H(arold) 1925- CANR-15
Earlier sketch in CA 33-36R
Matthews, Kathy 1949- 110
Matthews, Kevin
See Fox, G(ardner) F(rancis)
Matthews, L(eonard) Harrison
1901-1986 .... CANR-4
Obituary 121
Earlier sketch in CA 53-56
Matthews, Patricia (Anne) 1927- CANR-25
Earlier sketches in CA 29-32R, CANR-9
See also SATA 28
Matthews, Ralph 1904(?)-1978 85-88
Obituary 81-84
Matthews, Richard K(evin) 1952- 117
Matthews, Robert J(ames) 1926- 65-68
Matthews, Roy A(nthony) 1927- CANR-13
Earlier sketch in CA 33-36R
Matthews, Roy T(homas) 1932- 109
Matthews, Rupert O(liver) 1961- 118
Matthews, Stanley 1915- Brief entry 115
Matthews, Stanley G(oodwin) 1924- 21-22R
Matthews, T(homas) S(tanley) 1901- ... CANR-18
Earlier sketches in CA 11-12, CAP-1
Matthews, Tom
See Klewin, W(illiam) Thomas
Matthews, Victor Monroe 1921- 93-96
Matthews, Walter Robert 1881-1973 ..... CAP-1
Earlier sketch in CA 13-14
Matthews, William (Richard) 1905-1975 ...61-64
Obituary 57-60
Matthews, William 1942- CANR-12
Earlier sketch in CA 29-32R
See also DLB 5
See also CLC 40
Matthews, William Henry III 1919- 9-10R
See also SATA 28, 45
Matthias, Catherine 1945- 110
See also SATA 41
Matthias, John (Edward) 1941- 33-36R
See also CLC 9
Matthiessen, F. O. 1902-1950 .... DLB-63
Matthiessen, Peter 1927- CANR-21
Earlier sketch in CA 11-12R
See also SATA 27
See also DLB 6
See also CLC 5, 7, 11, 32
Matthis, Raimund Eugen 1928- 37-40R
Mattick, Paul 1904-1981 Obituary 115
Mattil, Edward La Marr 1918- Brief entry ... 106
Mattill, A(ndrew) J(acob), Jr. 1924- ... CANR-14
Earlier sketch in CA 37-40R
Mattingley, Christobel (Rosemary)
1931- CANR-20
Earlier sketch in CA 97-100
See also SATA 37
Mattingly, Garrett 1900-1962 Obituary 111
Mattingly, George E. 1950- 105
Mattioli, Raffaele 1895-1973 Obituary 45-48
Mattis, George 1905- CAP-2
Earlier sketch in CA 29-32
Mattison, Alice 1942- 110
Mattison, Christopher 1949- 125
Mattison, Judith 1939- CANR-24
Earlier sketches in CA 61-64, CANR-8
Mattlin, Paula Plotnick 1934(?)-1981
Obituary 104
Mattson, George E(dward) 1937- 7-8R
Mattson, Lloyd 1923- CANR-17
Earlier sketch in CA 93-96
Matulay, Laszlo 1912- SATA-43
Matulka, Jan 1890-1972 .... SATA-28
Matura, Mustapha 1939- CANR-12
Earlier sketch in CA 65-68
Matus, Greta 1938- 93-96
See also SATA 12
Matute, Ana Maria 1925- 89-92
See also CLC 11
Mau, Ernest E(ugene) 1945- 112
Mau, James A. 1935- 25-28R
Mauchline, Mary 1915- 53-56
Maud, John Redcliffe
See Redcliffe-Maud, John
Maude, George 1931- 113
Maude, H(enry) E(vans) 1906- 103
Maududi, Maulana Abdul Ala
1903(?)-1979 Obituary 89-92
Maue, Kenneth 1947- 97-100
Mauermann, Mary Anne 1927- 33-36R
Maugham, Diana
See Marr-Johnson, Diana (Maugham)
Maugham, Robert Cecil Romer
1916-1981 ....9-10R
Obituary 103
Maugham, Robin
See Maugham, Robert Cecil Romer
Maugham, W(illiam) Somerset 1874-1965 ..5-6R
Obituary 25-28R
See also DLB 10, 36
See also CLC 1, 11, 15
Maughan, A(nne) M(argery) 53-56
Mauldin, Bill
See Mauldin, William Henry
Mauldin, William Henry 1921- Brief entry ... 111
Maule, Christopher J(ohn) 1934- 37-40R
Maule, Hamilton Bee 1915- CANR-3
Earlier sketch in CA 1R
Maule, Harry E(dward) 1886-1971
Obituary 104
Maule, Tex
See Maule, Hamilton Bee
Maultsby, Maxie C(larence), Jr. 1932- 81-84
Maund, Alfred (Thomas, Jr.) 1923- 4R
Maunder, Elwood R(ondeau) 1917- 85-88
Maunder, W(illiam) J(ohn) 1932- 33-36R
Maung, Mya 1933- 37-40R
Maupassant, (Henri Rene Albert) Guy de
1850-1893 .... SSC-1
Maupin, Armistead 1944- Brief entry 125
Maura, Sister
See Eichner, Maura
Maureen, Sister Mary 1924- 23-24R
Maurer, Armand A(ugustine) 1915- 21-22R
Maurer, Charles Benes 1933- 33-36R
Maurer, David J(oseph) 1935- 102
Maurer, David W(arren) 1906-1981 ......19-20R
Obituary 104
Maurer, Joan Howard 1927- 119
Maurer, John G. 1937- 37-40R
Maurer, Otto
See Mason, Eudo C(olecestra)
Maurer, Rose
See Somerville, Rose M(aurer)
Maurhut, Richard
See Traven, B.
Mauriac, Claude 1914- 89-92
See also CLC 9
Mauriac, Francois (Charles) 1885-1970 ... CAP-2
Earlier sketch in CA 25-28
See also DLB 65
See also CLC 4, 9
Maurice, David (John Kerr) 1899- CAP-1
Earlier sketch in CA 11-12
Maurice, Frederick Denison 1805-1872 .. DLB-55
Maurice, Roger
See Asselineau, Roger (Maurice)
Mauricio, Victoria Courtney 1928- 106
Maurina, Zenta 1897-1978 Obituary 85-88
Maurois, Andre 1885-1967 .... CAP-2
Obituary 25-28R
Earlier sketch in CA 21-22
See also DLB 65
Mauron, Charles (Paul) 1899-1966 ...... CAP-1
Earlier sketch in CA 9-10
Maury, Inez 1909- 61-64
Maury, James 1718-1769 .... DLB-31
Maury, Reuben 1899-1981 Obituary 103
Mauser, Ferdinand F. 1914- CANR-2
Earlier sketch in CA 1R
Mauser, Patricia Rhoads 1943- CANR-22
Earlier sketch in CA 106
See also SATA 37
Mauskopf, Seymour Harold 1938- 104
Mauss, Armand L(ind) 1928- 111
Mautner, Franz H(einrich) 1902- CANR-12
Earlier sketch in CA 61-64
Mauzey, Merritt 1897-1975 102
Maves, Carl (Edwin) 1940- 69-72
Maves, Karl
See Maves, Carl E(dwin)
Maves, Mary Carolyn 1916- 49-52
See also SATA 10
Maves, Paul B(enjamin) 1913- CANR-17
Earlier sketches in CA 45-48, CANR-1
See also SATA 10
Mavin, John
See Rickword, (John) Edgell
Mavis, Walter Curry 1905- 5-6R
Mavor, Elizabeth (Osborne) 1927- 107
See also DLB 14
Mavor, Osborne Henry 1888-1951
Brief entry 104
Mavrodes, George I(on) 1926- 21-22R
Mavrogordato, J(ohn) G(eorge)
1905-1987 Obituary 122
Mavrogordato, Jack G.
See Mavrogordato, J(ohn) G(eorge)
Mavrogordatos, George T(hemistocles)
1945- 115
Mawby, Janet
See Garton, Janet
Mawdsley, Norman
See Hargreaves-Mawdsley, W(illiam)
Norman
Mawer, Ronald Knox
See Knox-Mawer, Ronald
Mawer, Ronnie Knox
See Knox-Mawer, Ronald
Mawicke, Tran 1911- SATA-15
Max
See Diop, Birago (Ismael)
Max, Nicholas
See Asbell, Bernard
Max, Peter 1939- 116
See also SATA 45
Maxa, Rudolph Joseph, Jr. 1949- 65-68
Maxa, Rudy
See Maxa, Rudolph Joseph, Jr.
Maxcy, Spencer J. 1939- 110
Maxey, Chester Collins 1890- CAP-1
Earlier sketch in CA 15-16
Maxey, David R(oy) 1936-1984 73-76
Obituary 112
Maxfield, Elizabeth
See Miller, Elizabeth Maxfield
Maxhim, Tristan
See Jones, (Max Him) Henri
Maxim, John R. 1937- 118
Maximov, Vladimir (Yemelyanovich) 1930- .. 104
Maxmen, Jerrold S(amuel) 1942- 106
Maxon, Anne
See Best, (Evangel) Allena Champlin
Maxon, John 1916-1977 Obituary 69-72
Maxon, Lou R(ussell) 1900-1971 Obituary .. 116
Maxtone Graham, James Anstruther
1924- 69-72
Maxtone-Graham, John 1929- 69-72
Maxwell, A(lbert) E(rnest) 1916- 7-8R
Maxwell, A. E.
See Maxwell, Ann (Elizabeth)
Maxwell, Ann (Elizabeth) 1944- 105
Maxwell, Arthur S. 1896-1970 .... CAP-1
Earlier sketch in CA 9-10
See also SATA 11
Maxwell, Cassandre 1942- 117
Maxwell, D(esmond) E(rnest) S(tewart)
1925- 33-36R
Maxwell, Edith 1923- 49-52
See also SATA 7
Maxwell, Edward
See Allan, Ted
Maxwell, Elsa 1883-1963 Obituary 89-92
Maxwell, Gavin 1914-1969 ....7-8R
Obituary 25-28R
Maxwell, Gilbert 1910-1979 .... CAP-1
Obituary 93-96
Earlier sketch in CA 9-10
Maxwell, Grant
See Richardson, Gladwell
Maxwell, Grover (Edward) 1918-1981 ... CANR-9
Earlier sketch in CA 7-8R
Maxwell, Jack
See McKeag, Ernest L(ionel)
Maxwell, James A. 1912- 13-14R
Maxwell, John
See Freemantle, Brian Harry
Maxwell, Kenneth (Robert) 1941- CANR-15
Earlier sketch in CA 85-88
Maxwell, Kenneth E(ugene) 1908- 73-76
Maxwell, Margaret F(inlayson) 1927- 109
Maxwell, Maurice 1910-1982 Obituary 107
Maxwell, Neville (George Anthony)
1926- CANR-4
Earlier sketch in CA 49-52
Maxwell, Nicole (Hughes) 3R
Maxwell, Patricia 1942- CANR-12
Earlier sketch in CA 29-32R
Maxwell, Rhonda 1950- 112
Maxwell, Richard C(allender) 1919- 41-44R
Maxwell, (Ian) Robert 1923- 11-12R
Maxwell, Robert S(idney) 1911- 57-60
Maxwell, Ronald
See Smith, Ronald Gregor
Maxwell, Sister Mary 1913- 37-40R
Maxwell, Vicky
See Worboys, Anne(tte Isobel) Eyre
Maxwell, W(illiam) David 1926- 61-64
Maxwell, William (Keepers, Jr.) 1908- 93-96
See also DLBY 80
See also CLC 19
Maxwell-Hudson, (Rachel) Clare 1946- 69-72
Maxwell-Lefroy, Cecil Anthony 1907- CAP-1
Earlier sketch in CA 15-16
May, Allan 1923- 85-88
May, Arthur James 1899-1968 .... CAP-1
Earlier sketch in CA 11-12
May, Charles E(dward) 1941- 117
May, Charles Paul 1920- CANR-5
Earlier sketch in CA 1R
See also SATA 4
May, Dean E(dward) 1944- 57-60
May, Derwent (James) 1930- CANR-11
Earlier sketch in CA 25-28R
May, Edgar 1929- 9-10R
May, Elaine 1932- Brief entry 124
See also DLB 44
See also CLC 16
May, Elaine Tyler 1947- 111
May, Elizabeth 1907- CAP-2
Earlier sketch in CA 19-20
May, Ernest R(ichard) 1928- CANR-22
Earlier sketches in CA 1R, CANR-6
May, Eugene 1906- 4R
May, Florissa
See Green, Kay
May, Francis Barns 1915- 9-10R
May, George S(mith) 1924- 65-68
May, Georges Claude 1920- CANR-6
Earlier sketch in CA 15-16R
May, Gerald G(ordon) 1940- Brief entry 112
May, Gita 1929- CANR-13
Earlier sketch in CA 29-32R
May, H(enry) J(ohn) 1903- 13-14R
May, Henry F(arnham) 1915- 11-12R
May, Herbert Gordon 1904-1977 .... CANR-6
Obituary 89-92
Earlier sketch in CA 5-6R
May, Irvin M(arion), Jr. 1939- 123
May, J. C.
See May, Julian
May, Jacques M. 1896-1975 Obituary 57-60
May, James Boyer 1904- CAP-1
Earlier sketch in CA 11-12
May, John D(ickinson) 1932- 45-48
May, John R(ichard) 1931- CANR-18
Earlier sketches in CA 45-48, CANR-2
May, Judy Gail 1943- 57-60
May, Julian 1931- CANR-6
Earlier sketch in CA 2R
See also SATA 11
May, Kenneth Ownsworth 1915-1977
Obituary 73-76
May, Lawrence Alan 1948- 106
May, Philip Radford 1928- 45-48
May, Robert E(van) 1943- 57-60
May, Robert Lewis 1905-1976 Obituary 104
See also SATA 27
May, Robert M(cCredie) 1936- 69-72
May, Robert Stephen 1929- CANR-13
Earlier sketch in CA 29-32R
See also SATA 46
May, Robin
See May, Robert Stephen
May, Rollo (Reece) 1909- 111
May, Sophie
See Clarke, Rebecca Sophia
May, Stephen 1946- 124
May, Thomas 1595(?)-1650 .... DLB-58
May, Timothy C(laude) 1940- 73-76
May, William E(ugene) 1928- CANR-14
Earlier sketch in CA 41-44R
Mayakovski, Vladimir (Vladimirovich)
1893-1930 Brief entry 104
See also TCLC 4, 18
Mayall, David 1953- 119
Mayall, R(obert) Newton 1904- CAP-1
Earlier sketch in CA 11-12
Maybaum, Ignaz 1897- CAP-1
Earlier sketch in CA 9-10
Mayberry, Florence V(irginia) Wilson 9-10R
See also SATA 10
Mayberry, Genevieve 1900- CAP-1
Earlier sketch in CA 19-20
Maybray-King, Horace 1901-1986 ....29-32R
Obituary 120
Maybury, Anne
See Buxton, Anne (Arundel)
Maybury-Lewis, David H(enry) P(eter)
1929- 19-20R
Maye, Patricia 1940- 53-56
Mayer, Adrian C(urtius) 1922- 4R
Mayer, Agatha
See Maher, Ramona
Mayer, Albert 1897-1981 73-76
Obituary 105
Mayer, Albert Ignatius, Jr. 1906-1960
Obituary 109
See also SATA 29
Mayer, Alfred 1903(?)-1984 Obituary 114
Mayer, (Henri) Andre (Van Huysen) 1946- .. 110
Mayer, Ann M(argaret) 1938- 57-60
See also SATA 14
Mayer, Arno J. 1926- 85-88
Mayer, Arthur L(oeb) 1886-1981 Obituary .. 108
Mayer, Bernadette 1945- 33-36R
Mayer, Carl J. 1959- 122
Mayer, Charles Leopold 1881- CANR-6
Earlier sketch in CA 3R
Mayer, Christa Charlotte
See Thurman, Christa C(harlotte) Mayer
Mayer, Clara Woollie 1895- CAP-2
Earlier sketch in CA 19-20
Mayer, Debby
See Mayer, Deborah Anne
Mayer, Deborah Anne 1946- 109
Mayer, Ellen Moers
See Moers, Ellen
Mayer, Fanny (Alice) Hagin 1899- 118

INDEX

Mayer, Gary (Richard) 1945- ... 53-56
Mayer, Gerda (Kamilla) 1927- ... 106
Mayer, Hannelore Valencak 1929- ... 116
Mayer, Hans (Heinrich) 1907- Brief entry ... 113
Mayer, Harold M(elvin) 1916- ... 41-44R
Mayer, Harry F(rederick) 1912- ... 101
Mayer, Henry 1941- ... 122
Mayer, Herbert Carleton 1893-1978 ... 41-44R
Mayer, Herbert T. 1922- ... 33-36R
Mayer, Jane Rothschild 1903- ... 9-10R
See also SATA 38
Mayer, Jean 1920- Brief entry ... 117
Mayer, Lawrence C(lark) 1936- ... 97-100
Mayer, Leo V. 1936- ... 73-76
Mayer, Lynne Rhodes 1926- ... 73-76
Mayer, Marianna 1945- ... 93-96
See also SATA 32
Mayer, Martin (Prager) 1928- ... 5-6R
Mayer, Mercer 1943- ... 85-88
See also SATA 16, 32
See also DLB 61
See also CLR 11
Mayer, Michael F. 1917- ... 15-16R
Mayer, Milton (Sanford) 1908-1986 ... 37-40R
Obituary ... 119
Mayer, Orlando Benedict 1818-1891 ... DLB-3
Mayer, Philip 1910- ... 49-52
Mayer, Ralph 1895-1979 ... 29-32R
Obituary ... 89-92
Mayer, Raymond Richard 1924- ... 4R
Mayer, Robert 1879-1985 Obituary ... 115
Mayer, S(ydney) L(ouis) 1937- ... 103
Mayer, Sigrid 1933- ... 121
Mayer, Thomas 1927- ... CANR-9
Earlier sketch in CA 23-24R
Mayer, Tom 1943- ... 9-10R
Mayers, Lewis 1890-1975 Obituary ... 61-64
Mayers, Marvin K(eene) 1927- ... 41-44R
Mayerson, Charlotte Leon ... 13-14R
See also SATA 36
Mayerson, Evelyn Wilde 1935- ... 101
Mayerson, Philip 1918- ... 41-44R
Mayer-Thurman, Christa C.
See Thurman, Christa C(harlotte) Mayer
Mayes, Edythe Beam 1902- ... CANR-7
Earlier sketch in CA 53-56
Mayes, Frances ... 81-84
Mayes, Herbert R(aymond) 1900-1987 ... 105
Obituary ... 124
Mayes, Stanley (Herbert) 1911- ... 1R
Mayes, Wendell 1919- ... 103
See also DLB 26
Mayeux, Peter E(dmond) 1942- ... 119
Mayfair, Bertha
See Raborg, Frederick A(shton), Jr.
Mayfair, Franklin
See Mendelsohn, Felix, Jr.
Mayfield, Chris 1951- ... 107
Mayfield, Guy 1905-1976 ... 7-8R
Obituary ... 122
Mayfield, Jack
See Cooper, Parley J(oseph)
Mayfield, James Bruce 1934- ... 69-72
Mayfield, John S. 1904-1983 Obituary ... 109
Mayfield, Julia
See Hastings, Phyllis (Dora Hodge)
Mayfield, Julian (Hudson) 1928-1984 ... CANR-26
Obituary ... 114
Earlier sketch in CA 13-14R
See also BW
See also DLB 33
See also DLBY 84
Mayfield, L(afayette) H(enry) II 1910- ... CAP-2
Earlier sketch in CA 19-20
Mayfield, Marlys 1931- ... CANR-10
Earlier sketch in CA 25-28R
Mayfield, Robert C(harles) 1928- ... 37-40R
Mayfield, Sara (Martin) 1905-1979 ... 25-28R
Obituary ... 85-88
Mayhall, Jane (Francis) 1921- ... CANR-8
Earlier sketch in CA 19-20R
Mayhall, Mildred P(ickle) 1902- ... CANR-1
Earlier sketch in CA 4R
Mayhar, Ardath 1930- ... CANR-19
Earlier sketch in CA 103
See also SATA 38
Mayhew, Christopher Paget 1915-
Brief entry ... 106
Mayhew, David R(aymond) 1937- ... 19-20R
Mayhew, Edgar deNoailles 1913- ... 37-40R
Mayhew, Elizabeth
See Bear, Joan
Mayhew, Henry 1812-1887 ... DLB-18, 55
Mayhew, Jonathan 1720-1766 ... DLB-31
Mayhew, Lenore 1924- ... 49-52
Mayhew, Lewis B. 1917- ... CANR-4
Earlier sketch in CA 2R
Mayhue, Richard L(ee) 1944- ... 116
Ma Yinchu 1882-1982 Obituary ... 110
Mayleas, William 1927- ... 120
Mayman, Martin 1924- ... 11-12R
Maynard, Alan (Keith) 1944- ... CANR-7
Earlier sketch in CA 57-60
Maynard, Chris
See Maynard, Christopher
Maynard, Christopher 1949- Brief entry ... 118
See also SATA 43
Maynard, Fredelle (Bruser) 1922- ... 85-88
Maynard, Geoffrey W(alter) 1921- ... 5-6R
Maynard, Harold Bright 1902-1975 ... 11-12R
Obituary ... 103
Maynard, John (Rogers) 1941- ... 65-68
Maynard, Joyce 1953- Brief entry ... 111
See also CLC 23
Maynard, Olga 1920- ... 114
See also SATA 40
Maynard, Richard Allen 1942- ... 33-36R
Maynard, Robert C(lyve) 1937- ... 115
Brief entry ... 110
Mayne, Richard (John) 1926- ... CANR-6
Earlier sketch in CA 13-14R
Mayne, Seymour 1944- ... CANR-18
Earlier sketch in CA 101
See also DLB 60
Mayne, William (James Carter) 1928- ... 11-12R
See also SATA 6
See also CLC 12
Maynes, E(dwin) Scott 1922- ... 45-48
Maynes, J. O. Rocky, Jr.
See Maynes, J. Oscar, Jr.
Maynes, J. Oscar, Jr. 1929- ... 115
See also SATA 38
Mayo, Bernard 1902-1979 Obituary ... 89-92
Mayo, Charles G(eorge) 1931-1985
Obituary ... 116
Mayo, E(dward) L(eslie) 1904- ... 97-100
Mayo, James
See Coulter, Stephen
Mayo, Janet 1949- ... 121
Mayo, Jim
See L'Amour, Louis (Dearborn)
Mayo, Lida (Smith) 1904-1978 Obituary ... 112
Mayo, Lucy Graves 1909-1963 ... 5-6R
Mayo, Margaret (Mary) 1935- ... 107
See also SATA 38
Mayo, Margot 1910- ... CAP-1
Earlier sketch in CA 15-16
Mayo, Mark
See Lane, Yoti
Mayo, Nick 1922-1983 ... 103
Obituary ... 110
Mayo, Patricia Elton 1915- ... 103
Mayo, William L. 1931- ... 19-20R
Mayor, A(lpheus) Hyatt 1901-1980 ... CANR-1
Obituary ... 97-100
Earlier sketch in CA 45-48
Mayor, Alfred Hyatt 1934- ... 65-68
Mayor, Beatrice ?-1971 ... CAP-1
Earlier sketch in CA 9-10
Mayor, Flora Macdonald 1872-1932 ... DLB-36
Mayor, Stephen (Harold) 1927- ... 23-24R
Mayoux, Jean-Jacques 1901(?)-1987(?)
Obituary ... 125
Mayr, Ernst 1904- ... CANR-2
Earlier sketch in CA 5-6R
Mayrant, Drayton
See Simons, Katherine Drayton Mayrant
Mays, Benjamin E(lijah) 1894-1984 ... CANR-25
Obituary ... 112
Earlier sketch in CA 45-48
See also BW
Mays, Buddy (Gene) 1943- ... CANR-12
Earlier sketch in CA 73-76
Mays, Cedric Wesley 1907- ... 29-32R
Mays, James A(rthur) 1939- ... CANR-25
Earlier sketch in CA 57-60
See also BW
Mays, John Barron 1914-1987 Obituary ... 123
Mays, Lucinda L(a Bella) 1924- ... 101
See also SATA 49
Mays, Spike
See Mays, Cedric Wesley
Mays, (Lewis) Victor (Jr.) 1927- ... 25-28R
See also SATA 5
Mays, Willie (Howard, Jr.) 1931- ... 105
Mayshark, Cyrus 1926- ... 19-20R
Maysi, Kadra
See Simons, Katherine Drayton Mayrant
Maysles, Albert 1926- ... 29-32R
See also CLC 16
Maysles, David 1932- ... CLC-16
Maytham, Thomas N(orthrup) 1931- ... 103
Maza, Regino Sainz de la
See Sainz de la Maza, Regino
Maze, Edward 1925- ... 7-8R
Mazer, Harry 1925- ... 97-100
See also SATA 31
See also CLR 16
Mazer, Milton 1911- ... 85-88
Mazer, Norma Fox 1931- ... CANR-12
Earlier sketch in CA 69-72
See also SATA 24
See also SAAS 1
See also CLC 26
Mazia, Marjorie
See Guthrie, Marjorie (Greenblatt Mazia)
Maziarz, Edward A(nthony) 1915- ... 37-40R
Mazlish, Bruce 1923- ... CANR-2
Earlier sketch in CA 7-8R
Mazmanian, Arthur B(arkev) 1931- ... 77-80
Mazmanian, Daniel (Aram) 1945- ... CANR-5
Earlier sketch in CA 53-56
Mazo, Earl 1919- ... 37-40R
Mazo, Joseph H(enry) 1938- ... 69-72
Mazonowicz, Douglas 1920- ... 57-60
Mazour, Anatole G. 1900- ... 13-14R
Mazow, Julia Wolf 1937- ... 103
Mazrui, Ali A(l'Amin) 1933- ... CANR-13
Earlier sketch in CA 21-22R
Mazumdar, Maxim 1952(?)-1988 Obituary ... 125
Mazur, Allan Carl 1939- ... 105
Mazur, Gail 1937- ... 77-80
Mazur, Paul M(yer) 1892-1979 ... 102
Obituary ... 89-92
Mazur, Ronald Michael 1934- ... 25-28R
Mazurkiewicz, Albert J. 1926- ... CANR-3
Earlier sketch in CA 11-12R
Mazursky, Paul 1930- ... CANR-24
Earlier sketch in CA 77-80
See also DLB 44
Mazza, Adriana 1928- ... CANR-4
Earlier sketch in CA 3R
See also SATA 19
Mazzaro, Jerome 1934- ... CANR-13
Earlier sketch in CA 33-36R
Mazze, Edward M(ark) 1941- ... CANR-5
Earlier sketch in CA 13-14R
Mazzei, George 1941- ... 117
Mazzeo, Guido E(ttore) 1914-1984 ... 45-48
Obituary ... 113
Mazzeo, Joseph Anthony 1923- ... 19-20R
Mazzetti, Lorenza 1933- ... 11-12R
Mazzotta, Giuseppe 1942- ... CANR-16
Earlier sketch in CA 93-96
Mazzulla, Fred 1903- ... CAP-2
Earlier sketch in CA 29-32
Mberi, Antar Sudan Katara 1949- ... 81-84
Mbiti, John S(amuel) 1931- ... CANR-11
Earlier sketch in CA 23-24R
See also BW
McAdam, Charles Vincent 1892-1985
Obituary ... 116
McAdam, Doug 1951- ... 126
Mc Adam, Robert E(verett) 1920- ... 81-84
McAdoo, Henry Robert 1916- ... 107
McAfee, (James) Thomas 1928- ... CANR-1
Earlier sketch in CA 45-48
McAfee, Ward M(erner) 1939- ... 57-60
McAleavey, David 1946- ... 65-68
McAleavy, Henry 1912-1968 ... CAP-2
Earlier sketch in CA 21-22
McAleer, John J(oseph) 1923- ... CANR-13
Earlier sketch in CA 21-22R
McAleer, Neil 1942- ... 119
McAlester, A(rcie) Lee 1933- ... 118
McAlester, Lee
See McAlester, A(rcie) Lee
McAlester, Virginia 1943- ... 120
McAlindon, Thomas 1932- ... 97-100
McAlister, Neil Harding 1952- ... 110
McAlister, W(alter) Robert 1930- ... 69-72
McAllaster, Elva 1922- ... 33-36R
McAllister, Alister 1877-1943 Brief entry ... 121
McAllister, Amanda
See Dowdell, Dorothy (Florence) Karns
and Hager, Jean
and Meaker, Eloise
McAllister, Annie Laurie
See Cassiday, Bruce (Bingham)
McAllister, Bruce (Hugh) 1946- ... 33-36R
McAllister, Harry E(dward) ... 5-6R
McAllister, Lester G(rover) 1919- ... 41-44R
McAlmon, Robert (Menzies) 1895-1956
Brief entry ... 107
See also DLB 4, 45
McAlpin, Heller 1955- ... 109
McAnally, Mary E(llen) 1939- ... CANR-21
Earlier sketch in CA 105
McAndrew, John 1904-1978 Obituary ... 77-80
McAndrews, John
See Steward, Samuel M(orris)
McAnelly, James R. 1932- ... 57-60
McArdle, Catherine
See Kelleher, Catherine McArdle
McArdle, Hugh M(c Lure) 1905- ... 107
McArdle, William D(aniel) 1939- ... 110
McArthur, Charles C(ampbell) 1920- ... 41-44R
McArthur, Edwin Douglas 1907-1987 ... 19-20R
Obituary ... 121
McArthur, Harvey K(ing) 1912- ... 25-28R
McArthur, John
See Wise, Arthur
McAulay, John D(avid) 1912- ... 15-16R
McAuley, James J(ohn) 1936- ... 77-80
McAuley, James Phillip 1917-1976 ... 97-100
See also CLC 45
McAuley, Patricia Ann Calistro
See Calistro McAuley, Patricia Ann
McAuliffe, Clarence 1903- ... CAP-2
Earlier sketch in CA 19-20
McAuliffe, Kevin Michael 1949- ... 81-84
McAuliffe, Mary Sperling 1943- ... 81-84
McAvoy, Thomas T(imothy)
1903-1969 ... CANR-15
Earlier sketch in CA 3R
McBain, Donald J(ames) 1945- ... 45-48
McBain, Ed
See Hunter, Evan
McBain, Gordon D(uncan) III 1946- ... 106
McBain, John M(aurice) 1921- ... 41-44R
McBain, Laurie 1949- ... 97-100
McBath, James Harvey 1922- ... 19-20R
McBee, Mary Louise 1924- ... 103
McBrearty, James C(onnell) 1941-
Brief entry ... 113
McBriar, Alan M(arne) 1918- ... 7-8R
McBride, Alfred 1928- ... CANR-6
Earlier sketch in CA 15-16R
McBride, (Mary) Angela Barron 1941- ... CANR-1
Earlier sketch in CA 49-52
McBride, Chris(topher James) 1941- ... 81-84
McBride, David P(aul) 1947- ... 116
McBride, Donald O(pie) 1903-1978
Obituary ... 77-80
McBride, Earl Duwain 1891- ... CAP-1
Earlier sketch in CA 13-14
McBride, James H(ubert) 1924- ... 25-28R
McBride, John Cosgrove 1911-1983
Obituary ... 110
McBride, John G. 1919- ... 9-10R
McBride, Joseph (Pierce) 1947- ... 41-44R
McBride, Katharine 1904-1976 Obituary ... 65-68
McBride, Mary Margaret 1899-1976 ... 69-72
Obituary ... 65-68
McBride, Patricia
See Bartz, Patricia McBride
McBride, Richard William 1928- ... 19-20R
McBride, Robert 1941- Brief entry ... 116
McBride, Robert H(enry) 1918-1983 ... 107
Obituary ... 111
McBride, Theresa Marie 1947- ... 112
McBride, William Leon 1938- ... CANR-6
Earlier sketch in CA 57-60
McBrien, Richard P(eter) 1936- ... CANR-10
Earlier sketch in CA 19-20R
McBrien, William Augustine 1930- ... 107
See also CLC 44
McBroom, R. Curtis 1910- ... CAP-2
Earlier sketch in CA 21-22
McBurney, James H(oward) 1905- ... 19-20R
McCabe, Bernard P(atrick), Jr. 1933- ... 53-56
McCabe, Cameron
See Borneman, Ernest
McCabe, Charles B. 1899-1970 Obituary ... 89-92
McCabe, Charles Raymond 1915-1983
Obituary ... 109
McCabe, Cynthia Jaffee 1943-1986 ... 117
Obituary ... 120
McCabe, David Aloysius 1884(?)-1974
Obituary ... 45-48
McCabe, Herbert 1926- ... 13-14R
McCabe, James P(atrick) 1937- ... 101
McCabe, John Charles III 1920- ... CANR-1
Earlier sketch in CA 1R
McCabe, Joseph E. 1912- ... 19-20R
McCabe, Sybil Anderson 1902- ... CAP-1
Earlier sketch in CA 15-16
McCabe, Victoria 1948- ... 29-32R
McCafferty, Lawrence ... 25-28R
McCaffery, Janet 1936- ... SATA-38
McCaffery, John K(erwin) M(ichael)
1914(?)-1983 Obituary ... 111
McCaffery, Larry 1946- ... 115
McCaffery, Margo (Smith) 1938- ... 37-40R
McCaffrey, Anne (Inez) 1926- ... CANR-15
Earlier sketch in CA 25-28R
See also SATA 8
See also DLB 8
See also CLC 17
See also AITN 2
McCaffrey, Donald W. 1926- Brief entry ... 114
McCaffrey, Joseph A. 1940- ... 37-40R
McCaffrey, Lawrence John 1925- ... 25-28R
McCaffrey, Mary
See Szudek, Agnes S(usan) P(hilomena)
McCaffrey, Phillip 1945- ... CANR-15
Earlier sketch in CA 77-80
McCagg, William O., Jr. 1930- ... 93-96
McCaghy, Charles H(enry) 1934- ... 25-28R
McCague, James (P.) 1909-1977 ... CANR-2
Earlier sketch in CA 2R
McCahill, Thomas 1907(?)-1975 Obituary ... 104
McCaig, Donald 1940- ... CANR-14
Earlier sketch in CA 104
McCaig, Robert Jesse 1907- ... CANR-1
Earlier sketch in CA 1R
McCaig, Snee
See McCaig, Donald
McCain, Murray (David, Jr.)
1926-1981 ... CANR-15
Obituary ... 105
Earlier sketch in CA 4R
See also SATA 7, 29
McCaleb, Robert Bruce 1950- ... 111
McCaleb, Walter Flavius 1873-1967 ... CAP-1
Earlier sketch in CA 9-10
McCall, Dan (Elliott) 1940- Brief entry ... 113
McCall, Daniel F(rancis) 1918- ... 19-20R
McCall, Dorothy Lawson 1889(?)-1982 ... 109
Obituary ... 106
McCall, Edith (Sansom) 1911- ... CANR-19
Earlier sketches in CA 1R, CANR-4
See also SATA 6
McCall, George J(ohn) 1939- ... CANR-9
Earlier sketch in CA 21-22R
McCall, Grant 1943- ... 107
McCall, John Corey
See Morland, Nigel
McCall, John R(obert) 1920- ... CANR-1
Earlier sketch in CA 45-48
McCall, Marsh H(oward), Jr. 1939- ... 29-32R
McCall, Mary C(aldwell), Jr. 1904-1986
Obituary ... 118
McCall, Robert B(ooth) 1940- ... CANR-14
Earlier sketch in CA 33-36R
McCall, Storrs 1930- ... 11-12R
McCall, Thomas (Lawson) 1913-1983
Obituary ... 108
McCall, Thomas S(creven) 1936- ... CANR-1
Earlier sketch in CA 49-52
McCall, Tom
See McCall, Thomas (Lawson)
McCall, Vincent
See Morland, Nigel
McCall, Virginia Nielsen 1909- ... CANR-17
Earlier sketches in CA 2R, CANR-1
See also SATA 13
McCall, William A(nderson) 1891- ... CAP-1
Earlier sketch in CA 19-20
McCalley, John W(allace) 1916-1983 ... 110
McCallum, George E(dward) 1931- ... 37-40R
McCallum, Ian R(obert) M(ore)
1919-1987 ... 13-14R
Obituary ... 124
McCallum, James Dow 1893-1971
Obituary ... 104
McCallum, John D(ennis) 1924- ... CANR-4
Earlier sketch in CA 53-56
McCallum, Neil 1916- ... 13-14R
McCallum, Phyllis 1911- ... CANR-4
Earlier sketch in CA 53-56
See also SATA 10
McCallum, Ronald Buchanan 1898-1973 ... 7-8R
Obituary ... 89-92
McCamant, John F. 1933- ... 25-28R
McCammon, Robert R(ick) 1952- ... 81-84
McCampbell, James M. 1924- ... 49-52

McCamy, James L(ucian) 1906- 5-6R
McCandless, Hugh (Douglas) 1907- 7-8R
McCandless, Perry 1917- CANR-1
Earlier sketch in CA 49-52
McCandlish, George E(dward) 1914-1975 .. 65-68
Obituary 61-64
McCanles, Michael (Frederick) 1936- 69-72
McCann, Arthur
See Campbell, John W(ood)
McCann, Coolidge
See Fawcett, F(rank) Dubrez
McCann, Dennis P(atrick) 1945- 115
McCann, Eamonn 1943- Brief entry 117
McCann, Edson
See del Rey, Lester
and Pohl, Frederik
McCann, Francis Daniel, Jr. 1938- 117
McCann, Frank D., Jr.
See McCann, Francis Daniel, Jr.
McCann, Gerald 1916- SATA-41
McCann, Kevin 1904-1981 Obituary 103
McCann, Sean 1929- Brief entry 115
McCann, Thomas 1934- 73-76
McCannon, Dindga 114
See also SATA 41
McCants, Olga 1901- CANR-14
Earlier sketch in CA 73-76
McCants, Sister Dorothea Olga
See McCants, Olga
McCardell, John (Malcolm, Jr.) 1949- 101
McCardle, Carl W(esley) 1904(?)-1972 ... 37-40R
McCardle, Dorothy Bartlett 1904-1978 85-88
Obituary 81-84
McCarr, Ken(neth George) 1903-1977 109
Obituary 106
McCarrick, Earlean M. 1930- 103
McCarroll, Marion C(lyde) 1893(?)-1977
Obituary 73-76
McCarroll, Tolbert (Henry) 1931- 110
McCarry, Charles 1930- 103
McCarten, John (Bernard Francis James)
1916(?)-1974 Obituary 115
McCarter, Alan 1943- 107
McCarter, Neely Dixon 1929- 109
See also SATA 47
McCarter, P(ete) Kyle (Jr.) 1945- 105
McCarthy, Agnes 1933- 19-20R
See also SATA 4
McCarthy, Barry (Wayne) 1943- 113
McCarthy, Cavan 1943- 61-64
McCarthy, Charlene B(arbara) 1929- 41-44R
McCarthy, Clarence F. 1909- 29-32R
McCarthy, Cormac 1933- CANR-10
Earlier sketch in CA 15-16R
See also DLB 6
See also CLC 4
McCarthy, Darry 1930- 7-8R
McCarthy, David (Edgar) 1925- 3R
McCarthy, David Seymour 1935- 115
McCarthy, Dennis John 1924- 23-24R
McCarthy, E(dmund) Jerome 1928-
Brief entry 112
McCarthy, Edward V., Jr. 1924- 93-96
McCarthy, Emily J(eannette) 1945- 113
McCarthy, Eugene J(oseph) 1916- CANR-2
Earlier sketch in CA 4R
McCarthy, Gary 1943- CANR-22
Earlier sketch in CA 69-72
McCarthy, James J(erome) 1927- 41-44R
McCarthy, Joe
See McCarthy, Joseph Weston
McCarthy, John 1898- 45-48
McCarthy, John P(atrick) 1938- 97-100
McCarthy, Joseph M(ichael) 1940- 97-100
McCarthy, Joseph Raymond 1909-1957
Brief entry 111
McCarthy, Joseph Weston 1915-1980 ... CANR-1
Obituary 97-100
Earlier sketch in CA 2R
McCarthy, Kevin M. 1940- 120
McCarthy, Martha M(ay) 1945- 111
McCarthy, Marvin 1902-1983 Obituary 110
McCarthy, Mary (Therese) 1912- CANR-16
Earlier sketch in CA 7-8R
See also DLB 2
See also DLBY 81
See also CLC 1, 3, 5, 14, 24, 39
McCarthy, Patrick Joseph 1922- 11-12R
McCarthy, Paul Eugene 1921- 103
McCarthy, R. Delphina (Polley) 1894- CAP-1
Earlier sketch in CA 15-16
McCarthy, Ray 1920(?)-1984 Obituary 112
McCarthy, Richard D(ean Max) 1927- 41-44R
McCarthy, Shaun (Lloyd) 1928- CANR-6
Earlier sketch in CA 9-10R
McCarthy, Teresa
See Anderson, Teresa
McCarthy, Thomas N. 1927- 37-40R
McCarthy, Thomas P. 1920- 13-14R
McCarthy, (Daniel) Todd 1950- 105
McCarthy, William E(dward) J(ohn)
1925- CANR-6
Earlier sketch in CA 11-12R
McCartney, Christine Maye 1949- 116
McCartney, James H(arold) 1925- 73-76
McCartney, Mike
See McCartney, Peter Michael
McCartney, (James) Paul 1942- CLC-12, 35
McCartney, Peter Michael 1944- 109
McCarty, Clifford 1929- 19-20R
McCarty, Doran Chester 1931- CANR-10
Earlier sketch in CA 65-68
McCarty, Maclyn 1911- 120
McCarty, Norma
See Crandall, Norma
McCarty, Rega Kramer 1904- 7-8R
See also SATA 10
McCary, James Leslie 1919-1978 85-88
McCash, June Hall 1938- 37-40R
McCasland, S(elby) Vernon 1896- 5-6R
McCaslin, Nellie 1914- 33-36R
See also SATA 12
McCaughey, Ellen
See Koshland, Ellen
McCaughey, Robert A(nthony) 1939- 77-80
McCaughrean, Geraldine 1951- 117
McCaughrean, Geraldine
See Jones, Geraldine
McCauley, Carole Spearin 1939- CANR-25
Earlier sketches in CA 57-60, CANR-8
McCauley, Elfrieda B(abnick) 1915- 9-10R
McCauley, Leon 1908(?)-1984 Obituary 112
McCauley, Martin 1934- CANR-23
Earlier sketch in CA 107
McCauley, Michael F(rederick) 1947- CANR-9
Earlier sketch in CA 61-64
McCauley, Stephen 19(?)- CLC-50
McCaull, M. E.
See Bohlman, (Mary) Edna McCaull
McCaw, Kenneth Malcolm 1907- 109
McCaw, Mabel Niedermeyer 1899- CAP-2
Earlier sketch in CA 19-20
McCay, Winsor 1871-1934 .... SATA-41
See also DLB 22
McChesney, Kathryn 1936- 115
McClain, Alva J. 1888-1968 65-68
McClain, Carl S. 1899- 37-40R
McClain, John O. 1942- 110
McClain, Leanita 1952(?)-1984 Obituary 112
McClain, Russell H(arding) 1910- CAP-2
Earlier sketch in CA 21-22
McClane, A(lbert) J(ules) 1922- 126
McClane, Albert Jules 1922- Brief entry 106
McClane, Kenneth Anderson, Jr.
1951- CANR-21
Earlier sketches in CA 57-60, CANR-6
McClary, Andrew 1927- 61-64
McClary, Ben Harris 1931- CANR-3
Earlier sketch in CA 11-12R
McClary, Jane Stevenson 1919- CANR-1
Earlier sketch in CA 2R
McClatchy, C. K. 1858-1936 .... DLB-25
McClatchy, Eleanor Grace 1895(?)-1980
Obituary 102
McClatchy, J(oseph) D(onald, Jr.) 1945- ... 105
McClaurin, Irma Pearl 1952- 57-60
McClean, Joseph Lucius 1919- CAP-1
Earlier sketch in CA 9-10
McCleary, Elliott H(arold) 1927- 57-60
McCleary, Robert A(ltwig) 1923- 19-20R
McCleary, William J(ames) 1938- 119
McCleery, William (Thomas) 1911- CANR-5
Earlier sketch in CA 1R
McClellan, A(rchibald) W(illiam) 1908- 77-80
McClellan, Albert (Alfred) 1922- 122
McClellan, Edwin 1925- Brief entry 115
McClellan, George Marion 1860-1934 125
See also BW
See also DLB 50
McClellan, Grant S(amuel) 1914-
Brief entry 114
McClellan, James (Paul) 1937- 23-24R
McClellan, James Edward, Jr. 1922- 25-28R
McClellan, Norris 1905-1984 Obituary 116
McClellan, Robert F., Jr. 1934- 33-36R
McClelland, Charles A. 1917- 85-88
McClelland, Charles E(dgar III) 1940- ... 33-36R
McClelland, David C(larence) 1917- 25-28R
McClelland, Diane Margaret 1931- 105
McClelland, Doug 1934- CANR-14
Earlier sketch in CA 41-44R
McClelland, Ivy Lilian 1908- 29-32R
McClelland, Lucille Hudlin 1920- 23-24R
McClelland, Vincent Alan 1933- 103
McClendon, James William, Jr. 1924- ... CANR-5
Earlier sketch in CA 11-12R
McClendon, Sarah 1910- 73-76
McClennen, Sandra Elaine 1942- 103
McClintock, Marshall 1906-1967 .... CAP-1
Earlier sketch in CA 9-10
See also SATA 3
McClintock, Mike
See McClintock, Marshall
McClintock, Robert (Mills) 1909- CAP-2
Earlier sketch in CA 21-22
McClintock, Theodore 1902-1971 73-76
Obituary 33-36R
See also SATA 14
McClinton, Katharine Morrison 1899- ... CANR-5
Earlier sketch in CA 4R
McClinton, Leon 1933- 65-68
See also SATA 11
McClory, Robert J(oseph) 1932- CANR-13
Earlier sketch in CA 77-80
McCloskey, Donald N(ansen) 1942- CANR-8
Earlier sketch in CA 57-60
McCloskey, Eunice (Loncoske) 1906- 11-12R
McCloskey, H(enry) J(ohn) 1925- 110
McCloskey, Mark 1938- CANR-1
Earlier sketch in CA 45-48
McCloskey, Maxine E(laine) 1927- 33-36R
McCloskey, Patrick 1948- 115
McCloskey, Paul N., Jr. 1927- 37-40R
McCloskey, (John) Robert 1914- 11-12R
See also SATA 2, 39
See also DLB 22
See also CLR 7
McCloskey, William B(ertine), Jr. 1928- 101
McCloy, Helen (Worrell Clarkson) 1904- .. 25-28R
McCloy, James F(loyd) 1941- 103
McCloy, Shelby Thomas 1898-19(?) CAP-2
Earlier sketch in CA 23-24
McClung, Floyd, Jr. 1945- 61-64
McClung, Patricia A. 1950- 119
McClung, Robert M(arshall) 1916- CANR-21
Earlier sketches in CA 13-14R, CANR-6
See also SATA 2
See also CLR 11
See also AITN 2
McClung, William Alexander 1944- 113
McClure, Arthur F(rederick) II 1936- ... CANR-10
Earlier sketch in CA 65-68
McClure, Charles R(obert) 1949- 111
McClure, Gillian Mary 1948- 103
See also SATA 31
McClure, Grace 1918- 123
McClure, Hal 1921- 81-84
McClure, James (Howe) 1939- 69-72
McClure, Joanna 1930- Brief entry 116
See also DLB 16
McClure, Larry 1941- CANR-26
Earlier sketch in CA 69-72
McClure, Michael (Thomas) 1932- CANR-17
Earlier sketch in CA 21-22R
See also DLB 16
See also CLC 6, 10
McClure, Ron 1941- 37-40R
McClure, Ruth Koonz 107
McCluskey, John (A.), Jr. 1944- CANR-24
Earlier sketches in CA 57-60, CANR-7
See also BW
See also DLB 33
McCluskey, Neil Gerard 1921- CANR-12
Earlier sketch in CA 25-28R
McCollam, James Graham 1913- CANR-4
Earlier sketch in CA 45-48
McCollam, Jim
See McCollam, James Graham
McColley, Robert (McNair) 1933- 15-16R
McCollough, Albert W. 1917- 102
McCollough, Celeste 1926- 13-14R
McCollough, Charles R(andolph) 1934- 118
McCollum, Audrey T(almage) 1924- 107
McCollum, Elmer Verner 1879-1967 ..... CAP-1
Earlier sketch in CA 13-14
McCollum, Michael A. 1946- DLBY-87
McComas, Annette Peltz 1911- 109
McComas, J(esse) Francis 1911-1978
Obituary 104
McComb, David G(lendinning) 1934- ... CANR-12
Earlier sketch in CA 29-32R
McComb, K(atherine Woods) 1895- 13-14R
McCombs, Don 1948- 115
McCombs, Judith 1939- 102
McCombs, Maxwell E(lbert) 1938- CANR-12
Earlier sketch in CA 73-76
McCombs, Philip A(lgie) 1944- 49-52
McConagha, Alan 1932- 77-80
McConahay, John B. 1938- 110
McCondach, J. P. 1912- 117
McCone, R(obert) Clyde 1915- 77-80
McConica, James Kelsey 1930- CANR-13
Earlier sketch in CA 33-36R
McConkey, Clarence 1925- 29-32R
McConkey, Dale Durant 1928- 93-96
McConkey, James (Rodney) 1921- 19-20R
McConkie, Bruce R(edd) 1915-1985
Obituary 115
McConnell, Allen 1923- 77-80
McConnell, Campbell R(obertson) 1928- 7-8R
McConnell, Frank D(eMay) 1942- 104
McConnell, Grant 1915- 65-68
McConnell, James Douglas Rutherford
1915-1988 .... CANR-22
Obituary 125
Earlier sketches in CA 11-12R, CANR-6
See also SATA 40
McConnell, James V(ernon) 1925- 5-6R
McConnell, Jean 1928- CANR-16
Earlier sketch in CA 85-88
McConnell, John Lithgow Chandos 1918- .. 53-56
McConnell, John W(ilkinson) 1907- 107
McConnell, Jon Patrick 1928- 21-22R
McConnell, Malcolm 1939- 106
McConnell, Raymond A(rnott) 1915-1979
Obituary 89-92
McConnell, Roland C(alhoun) 1910- 73-76
McConnell, T. R.
See McConnell, Thomas Raymond
McConnell, Terrance C(allihan) 1948- 110
McConnell, Thomas Raymond 1901- 118
McConnell, Virginia (McCorison) 1928- ... 13-14R
McConnell, William T(ate) 1941- 115
McConnor, Vincent CANR-23
Earlier sketch in CA 106
McCord, Anne 1942- 109
See also SATA 41
McCord, Arline F(ujii) 1934- CANR-1
Earlier sketch in CA 45-48
McCord, David (Thompson Watson)
1897- 73-76
See also SATA 18
See also DLB 61
See also CLR 9
McCord, Guy
See Reynolds, Dallas McCord
McCord, Howard 1932- CANR-18
Earlier sketches in CA 11-12R, CANR-4
McCord, James I(ley) 1919- 23-24R
McCord, James W(alter), Jr. 1918?- AITN-1
McCord, Jean 1924- 49-52
See also SATA 34
McCord, John H(arrison) 1934- CANR-17
Earlier sketch in CA 25-28R
McCord, Whip
See Norwood, Victor G(eorge) C(harles)
McCord, William Maxwell 1930- CANR-1
Earlier sketch in CA 3R
McCorduck, Pamela 1940- CANR-15
Earlier sketch in CA 81-84
McCorison, Marcus Allen 1926- 33-36R
McCorkle, Chester O(liver), Jr. 1925- 110
McCorkle, Jill (Collins) 1958- 121
See also DLBY 87
McCorkle, Samuel Eusebius 1746-1811 .. DLB-37
McCormac, John W. 1926- 41-44R
McCormack, Arthur Gerard 1911- 7-8R
McCormack, Gavan Patrick 1937- CANR-22
Earlier sketch in CA 105
McCormack, Mark H(ume) 1930- CANR-17
Earlier sketch in CA 49-52
McCormack, S(usan) Allison 1943- 111
McCormack, William A. 1932- 25-28R
McCormick, Anne (Elizabeth) O'Hare
1882(?)-1954 Brief entry 118
See also DLB 29
McCormick, Brooks
See Adams, William Taylor
McCormick, Claire
See Labus, Martha Haake
McCormick, Dell J. 1892-1949 .... SATA-19
McCormick, Diana Festa
See Festa-McCormick, Diana
McCormick, (George) Donald (King)
1911- CANR-14
Earlier sketch in CA 73-76
See also SATA 14
McCormick, E(dward) Allen 1925- 107
McCormick, E(ric) H(all) 1906- 103
McCormick, Edgar L(indsley) 1914- 5-6R
McCormick, Edith (Joan) 1934- SATA-30
McCormick, Ernest J(ames) 1911- 93-96
McCormick, Jack (Sovern) 1929-1979 ... CANR-5
Obituary 85-88
Earlier sketch in CA 9-10R
McCormick, James (Phillip) 1920- 25-28R
McCormick, James P(atton) 1911-1988
Obituary 125
McCormick, John O(wen) 1918- 19-20R
McCormick, Mary
See McCormick, Sister Rose M(atthew)
McCormick, Merla Jean 1938- 97-100
McCormick, Mona 77-80
McCormick, Peter J(oseph) 1940- 112
McCormick, Richard Arthur 1922- CANR-22
Earlier sketch in CA 105
McCormick, Richard P(atrick) 1916- 11-12R
McCormick, Robert (K.) 1911-1985 115
Obituary 117
McCormick, Robert R. 1880-1955 ...... DLB-29
McCormick, Scott, Jr. 1929- 19-20R
McCormick, Sister Rose M(atthew)
1914- 23-24R
McCormick, Wilfred 1903- CANR-1
Earlier sketch in CA 2R
McCormmach, Russell (Keith) 1933- 118
Brief entry 112
McCorquodale, Barbara
See Cartland, Barbara (Hamilton)
McCorquodale, Robin (Hunt) 121
McCourt, Edward (Alexander)
1907-1972 .... 11-12R
Obituary 103
See also SATA 28
McCourt, James 1941- 57-60
See also CLC 5
McCowen, George S(mith), Jr. 1935- 89-92
McCown, James H. 1911- 89-92
McCown, Wayne (Gordon) 1942- 111
McCoy, Alfred W. 1945- CANR-17
Earlier sketch in CA 29-32R
McCoy, Andrew 117
McCoy, Arch
See Miller, Victor (Brooke)
McCoy, Charles A(llan) 1920- CANR-16
Earlier sketch in CA 65-68
McCoy, D(onald) E(dward) 1923- 37-40R
McCoy, Donald R(ichard) 1928- CANR-2
Earlier sketch in CA 5-6R
McCoy, Elaine 1945- 119
McCoy, F(lorence) N(ina) 1925- 65-68
McCoy, Horace (Stanley) 1897-1955
Brief entry 108
See also DLB 9
See also TCLC 28
McCoy, Iola Fuller 13-14R
See also SATA 3
McCoy, J(oseph) J(erome) 1917- CANR-6
Earlier sketch in CA 13-14R
See also SATA 8
McCoy, John P(leasant) 1906(?)-1974
Obituary 49-52
McCoy, Joseph A(loysius) 1911- 4R
McCoy, Kathleen 1945- CANR-22
Earlier sketch in CA 81-84
McCoy, Kathy
See McCoy, Kathleen
McCoy, Lois (Rich) 1941- CANR-22
Earlier sketch in CA 101
See also SATA 38
McCoy, Malachy
See Caulfield, Malachy Francis
McCoy, Marjorie Casebier 1934-1985
Obituary 114
McCoy, Maureen 1949- 119
McCoy, Ralph E(dward) 1915- 37-40R
McCoy, Ronald 1947- 81-84
McCoy, Roy 1935- 29-32R
McCoy, Samuel (Duff) 1882-1964
Obituary 93-96
McCoy, Tim(othy John Fitzgerald)
1891-1978 81-84
Obituary 77-80
McCracken, (James) David 1939- 119
McCracken, Esther 1902-1971 Obituary .. 33-36R
McCracken, George E(nglert) 1904- 19-20R
McCracken, Glenn 1908- 7-8R
McCracken, Harold 1894- 107

INDEX

McCracken, J(ohn) L(eslie) 1914- 25-28R
McCracken, James (Eugene) 1926-1988
Obituary 126
McCracken, Karen Harden 1905- 122
McCracken, Kay
See McCracken, Karen Harden
McCracken, Kenneth David 1901-1983
Obituary 109
McCracken, Mary Lou 1943- 61-64
McCracken, Paul Winston 1915- CANR-6
Earlier sketch in CA 7-8R
McCracken, Samuel 111
McCrackin, Mark (Owens) 1949- 107
McCrady, Lady 1951- 93-96
See also SATA 16
McCrae, John 1872-1918 Brief entry 109
See also TCLC 12
McCrank, Lawrence J(oseph) 1945- 110
McCrary, (James) Peyton 1943- 85-88
McCraw, James Edward 1943- 101
McCraw, Louise Harrison 1893-1975 .... 2R
Obituary 103
McCraw, Thomas K(incaid) 1940- CANR-17
Earlier sketch in CA 33-36R
McCrea, James (Craig, Jr.) 1920- CANR-8
Earlier sketch in CA 7-8R
See also SATA 3
McCrea, Joan Marie Ryan 1922- 57-60
McCrea, Ruth (Pirman) 1921- CANR-8
Earlier sketch in CA 7-8R
See also SATA 3
McCrea, William Hunter 1904- 107
McCreadie, Marsha A. 1943- 111
McCready, Jack
See Powell, Talmage
McCready, Warren T(homas) 1915- 21-22R
McCreary, Alf(red) 1940- 69-72
McCreary, W. Burgess 1894- CAP-1
Earlier sketch in CA 19-20
McCreery, Charles (Anthony Selby)
1942- 25-28R
McCreigh, James
See Pohl, Frederik
McCrimmon, Barbara (Smith) 1918- 108
McCrimmon, James M(cNab) 1908- 9-10R
McCrindle, Joseph F(eder) 1923- 29-32R
McCrohan, Donna 1947- 111
McCrorey, Sanders
See Counselman, Mary Elizabeth
McCroskey, James C(layborne) 1936- .. CANR-13
Earlier sketch in CA 77-80
McCrossen, V(incent) A(loysius) 1918- 53-56
McCrosson, Doris Ross 1923- 19-20R
McCrum, Robert 1953- 101
McCuaig, Ronald 1908- 114
McCue, George R(obert) 1910- 110
McCue, Lillian Bueno 1902- CANR-2
Earlier sketch in CA 2R
McCuen, Jo Ray 1929- 85-88
McCuen, John J(oachim) 1926- 21-22R
McCullagh, Joseph B. 1842-1896 .... DLB-23
McCullagh, Sheila K(athleen) 1920- 110
McCullar, Michael 1951- 122
McCullers, (Lula) Carson (Smith)
1917-1967 .... CANR-18
Obituary 25-28R
Earlier sketch in CA 5-6R
See also CABS 1
See also SATA 27
See also DLB 2, 7
See also CDALB 1941-1968
See also CLC 1, 4, 10, 12, 48
McCulley, Johnston 1883-1958
Brief entry 115
McCullin, Donald 1935- Brief entry 106
McCulloch, Alan McLeod 1907- 104
McCulloch, Derek (Ivor Breashur)
1897-1967 Obituary 109
See also SATA 29
McCulloch, Frank E(liot) 1898- 112
McCulloch, John I(rvin) B(eggs)
1909(?)-1983 Obituary 110
McCulloch, Sarah
See Ure, Jean
McCulloch, Warren S(turgis) 1898-1969 .. CAP-2
Earlier sketch in CA 21-22
McCulloh, William Ezra 1931- 49-52
McCullough, Bonnie Runyan 1944- CANR-18
Earlier sketch in CA 102
McCullough, Colleen 1938(?)- CANR-17
Earlier sketch in CA 81-84
McCullough, Constance Mary 1912- CANR-5
Earlier sketch in CA 3R
McCullough, Dale Richard 1933- 125
McCullough, David (Gaub) 1933- CANR-2
Earlier sketch in CA 49-52
McCullough, Edo
See McCullough, Edward Joseph Tilyou
McCullough, Edward Joseph Tilyou
1901(?)-1987 Obituary 123
McCullough, Frances Monson 1938- 41-44R
See also SATA 8
McCullough, John Gerard 1917-1984
Obituary 111
McCullough, Ken(neth Douglas) 1943- . CANR-22
Earlier sketch in CA 45-48
McCullough, W(illiam) Stewart 1902- 23-24R
McCully, Emily Arnold
See Arnold, Emily
See also SATA 5
McCully, Ethel Walbridge 1896-1980
Obituary 103
McCully, Helen 1902(?)-1977 81-84
Obituary 73-76
McCully, Robert (Stephen) 1921- 53-56
McCune, Shannon 1913- CANR-13
Earlier sketch in CA 77-80
McCunn, Ruthanne Lum 1946- 119
McCurdy, Charles Robert 1926- 7-8R
McCurdy, Frances Lea 1906- 41-44R
McCurdy, Harold Grier 1909- CANR-7
Earlier sketch in CA 19-20R
McCurdy, Howard E(arl) 1941- 81-84
McCurdy, Jack 1933- 69-72
McCurdy, Michael 1942- CANR-25
Earlier sketch in CA 69-72
See also SATA 13
McCurley, Foster R., Jr. 1937- Brief entry .. 107
McCusker, John J(ames) 1939- 102
McCutchan, J(ohn) Wilson 1909- 7-8R
McCutchan, Philip (Donald) 1920- CANR-22
Earlier sketches in CA 11-12R, CANR-5
McCutchen, Samuel Proctor 1909-1966 .. CAP-1
Earlier sketch in CA 9-10
McCutcheon, Hugh Davie-Martin 1909- .. CANR-5
Earlier sketch in CA 9-10R
McCutcheon, James
See Lundgren, Paul Arthur
McCutcheon, James M(iller) 1932- 45-48
McCutcheon, John Tinney, Jr. 1917- 69-72
McCutcheon, Lynn E(llis) 1944- 57-60
McCutcheon, W(illiam) A(lan) 1934- 53-56
McCutcheon, W(illiam) J(ohn) 1928- 41-44R
McDade, Thomas M. 1907- CAP-1
Earlier sketch in CA 15-16
McDaniel, Becky Bring 1953- 117
McDaniel, C. Yates 1907(?)-1983
Obituary 109
McDaniel, David (Edward) 1939-1977 .. CANR-10
Earlier sketch in CA 23-24R
McDaniel, Elsiebeth 65-68
McDaniel, Eugene B(arker) 1931- 65-68
McDaniel, George William 1944- 116
McDaniel, Gerald G(reen) 1945- 122
McDaniel, Herman 1938- 111
McDaniel, John N(oble) 1941- 57-60
McDaniel, Joseph Milton, Jr. 1902-1980
Obituary 97-100
McDaniel, Roderick D. 1927- 37-40R
McDaniel, Ruel 1896- CAP-1
Earlier sketch in CA 13-14
McDaniel, Walton Brooks 1871-1978 77-80
Obituary 81-84
McDaniels, Carl 1930- 93-96
McDarrah, Fred W(illiam) 1926- CANR-24
Earlier sketch in CA 81-84
McDavid, John E., Jr. 1934- 37-40R
McDavid, John W(alter, Jr.) 1933- 41-44R
McDavid, Raven I(oor), Jr. 1911-1984 ...41-44R
Obituary 114
McDavid, Virginia (Glenn) 1926- 37-40R
McDearmon, Kay CANR-11
Earlier sketch in CA 69-72
See also SATA 20
McDermott, A(gnes) Charlene Senape
1937- 77-80
McDermott, Alice 1953- 109
McDermott, Beatrice Schmulling 19-20R
McDermott, Beverly Brodsky 1941- CANR-16
Earlier sketch in CA 65-68
See also SATA 11
McDermott, Catherine 1952- 125
McDermott, Charles J(ames) 1905- CAP-1
Earlier sketch in CA 15-16
McDermott, Geoffrey (Lyster) 1912- 73-76
McDermott, Gerald 1941- 85-88
See also SATA 16
See also CLR 9
See also AITN 2
McDermott, John F(rancis), Jr. 1929-
Brief entry 114
McDermott, John Francis (III)
1902-1981 .... CANR-6
Earlier sketch in CA 5-6R
McDermott, John J(oseph) 1932- 73-76
McDermott, John R(alph) 1921-1977
Obituary 69-72
McDermott, Robert
See Hawley, Donald Thomas
McDermott, Robert A(nthony) 1939- 57-60
McDermott, Sister Maria Concepta
1913- 19-20R
McDermott, Thomas J. 1915- 11-12R
McDermott, Walsh 1909-1981 Obituary 105
McDill, Edward L. 1930- 77-80
McDole, Carol
See Farley, Carol
McDonagh, Don(ald Francis) 1932- CANR-1
Earlier sketch in CA 49-52
McDonagh, Enda 1930- 101
McDonagh, John Michael 1944- 109
McDonald, Alan (Patrick) 1949- 124
McDonald, Angus W(illiam), Jr. 1941- 105
McDonald, Archie P(hilip) 1935- CANR-15
Earlier sketch in CA 81-84
McDonald, Claude C(omstock), Jr.
1925- 29-32R
McDonald, David J(ohn) 1902-1979 45-48
Obituary 125
McDonald, Dianna
See Shomaker, Dianna
McDonald, Elvin 1937- CANR-8
Earlier sketch in CA 7-8R
McDonald, Erwin L(awrence) 1907- 73-76
McDonald, Eva (Rose) CANR-6
Earlier sketch in CA 15-16R
McDonald, Forrest 1927- CANR-5
Earlier sketch in CA 11-12R
See also DLB 17
McDonald, Frank J(ames) 1941- 97-100
McDonald, Gerald D(oan) 1905-1970 .... CAP-1
Earlier sketch in CA 11-12
See also SATA 3
McDonald, Gregory 1937- CANR-3
Earlier sketch in CA 7-8R
McDonald, Hugh C(hisholm) 1913- 65-68
McDonald, Hugh Dermot 1910- CANR-3
Earlier sketch in CA 11-12R
McDonald, Ian A(rchie) 1933- CANR-26
Earlier sketch in CA 29-32R
McDonald, James Robert 1934- 41-44R
McDonald, Jamie
See Heide, Florence Parry
McDonald, Jerry N(ealon) 1944- 105
McDonald, Jill (Masefield) 1927-1982 .. CANR-12
Obituary 105
Earlier sketch in CA 65-68
See also SATA 13, 29
McDonald, John D(ennis) 1906- CAP-2
Earlier sketch in CA 19-20
McDonald, Julie 1929- CANR-12
Earlier sketch in CA 29-32R
McDonald, Kay L(aureen) 1934- 57-60
McDonald, Lee Cameron 1925- 7-8R
McDonald, Linda 1939- CANR-4
Earlier sketch in CA 49-52
McDonald, Lucile Saunders 1898- CANR-18
Earlier sketches in CA 3R, CANR-4
See also SATA 10
McDonald, (Mary) Lynn 1940- 101
McDonald, Mary Reynolds 1888- CAP-1
Earlier sketch in CA 15-16
McDonald, Nicholas 1923- 15-16R
McDonald, Paula 1939?- AITN-1
McDonald, Pauline 1907- 33-36R
McDonald, (Duncan) Peter 1962- 124
McDonald, Richard C. 1935?- AITN-1
McDonald, Robert 1943- 115
McDonald, Roger 1941- 101
McDonald, Stephen L(ee) 1924- 89-92
McDonald, Walter (Robert) 1934- CANR-12
Earlier sketch in CA 73-76
McDonald, William Andrew 1913- 41-44R
McDonald, William Francis 1898-1976 ...37-40R
McDonald, William U(lma), Jr. 1927- 19-20R
McDonnell, Christine 1949- CANR-23
Earlier sketch in CA 107
See also SATA 34
McDonnell, Helen M(argaret) 1923- CANR-13
Earlier sketch in CA 33-36R
McDonnell, Jinny
See McDonnell, Virginia B(leecker)
McDonnell, Kilian (Perry) 1921- 33-36R
McDonnell, Lois Eddy 1914- 7-8R
See also SATA 10
McDonnell, Robert F. 1928- 19-20R
McDonnell, Virginia B(leecker) 1917- CANR-8
Earlier sketch in CA 21-22R
McDonough, George Edward 1924- 41-44R
McDonough, Jack 1944- 125
McDonough, James Lee 1934- 73-76
McDonough, Jerome 1946- 109
McDonough, Jerry
See McDonough, Jerome
McDonough, Nancy 1935- 57-60
McDonough, Sheila 1928- 77-80
McDonough, Thomas E(dmund) 1929- ...21-22R
McDonough, William K. 1900- CAP-1
Earlier sketch in CA 9-10
McDormand, Thomas Bruce 1904- CAP-1
Earlier sketch in CA 19-20
McDougal, Myres Smith 1906- CANR-6
Earlier sketch in CA 5-6R
McDougal, Stan
See Diamant, Lincoln
McDougal, Stuart Y(eatman) 1942- CANR-13
Earlier sketch in CA 73-76
McDougall, Anne 1926- 104
McDougall, Colin 1917-1984 .... DLB-68
McDougall, Donald 1907- 81-84
McDougall, John Lorne 1900- 37-40R
McDougall, Joyce 1926- CANR-11
Earlier sketch in CA 25-28R
McDougall, Marina 1945- 97-100
McDougall, Walter A(llan) 1946- 126
Brief entry 121
McDow, Gerald
See Scortia, Thomas N(icholas)
McDowall, Robert William 1914-1987
Obituary 123
McDowell, (Ho)Bart (Kelliston, Jr.)
1923- 25-28R
McDowell, Charles (Rice), Jr. 1926- 2R
McDowell, Crosby
See Freeman, John Crosby
McDowell, David 1918(?)-1985 Obituary ... 115
McDowell, Dimmes 1925(?)-1976
Obituary 69-72
McDowell, Edward Allison, Jr. 1898- CAP-2
Earlier sketch in CA 21-22
McDowell, Edwin (Stewart) 1935- 11-12R
McDowell, Elizabeth Tibbals 1912- 5-6R
McDowell, Frank 1911- 53-56
McDowell, Frederick P(eter) W(oll)
1915- CANR-5
Earlier sketch in CA 3R
McDowell, John (Henry) 1942- 103
McDowell, John Holmes 1946- 97-100
McDowell, Margaret B(laine) 1923- 69-72
McDowell, Michael 1950- 93-96
McDowell, Michael P(aul) Kube
See Kube-McDowell, Michael P(aul)
McDowell, Robert Emmett 1914-1975 .... 3R
Obituary 103
McDowell, Virginia (Duncan) H(ecker)
1933- 85-88
McEachern, Theodore 1928- 23-24R
McElaney, (Joseph) Paul 1922- 11-12R
McElderry, Bruce R., Jr. 1900-1970 .... CAP-1
Earlier sketch in CA 13-14
McEldowney, (Richard) Dennis 1926- 103
McEleney, Neil Joseph 1927- 115
McElfresh, (Elizabeth) Adeline 1918- 4R
McElhaney, James W(illson) 1937- 85-88
McElhanon, K(enneth) A(ndrew) 1939- .. CANR-5
Earlier sketch in CA 53-56
McElhenney, John Galen 1934- 53-56
McElrath, Damian (Edmund) 1928-
Brief entry 111
McElrath, Dennis Cornealius 1929- 45-48
McElrath, Joseph R(ichard), Jr. 1945- 65-68
McElrath, William N. 1932- 77-80
McElroy, Bernard (Patrick, Jr.) 1938- 61-64
McElroy, Colleen J(ohnson) 1935- CANR-17
Earlier sketches in CA 49-52, CANR-2
See also BW
McElroy, Davis Dunbar 1917- 37-40R
McElroy, Elam E. 1922- 57-60
McElroy, John Alexander 1913- 19-20R
McElroy, Joseph 1930- 19-20R
See also CLC 5, 47
McElroy, Lee
See Kelton, Elmer
McElroy, Paul Simpson 1902- 5-6R
McElroy, Thomas P(arker), Jr. 1914- 73-76
McElvaine, Robert S(tuart) 1947- 114
McElwee, William (Lloyd) 1907-1979 57-60
Obituary 104
McEntee, Dorothy (Layng) 1902- SATA-37
McEvedy, Colin (Peter) 1930- 97-100
McEvoy, Dennis 1918- 73-76
McEvoy, Harry K(irby) 1910- 19-20R
McEvoy, Hubert 1899- 7-8R
McEvoy, James III 1940-1976 .... CAP-2
Earlier sketch in CA 33-36
McEvoy, Marjorie Harte CANR-18
Earlier sketches in CA 7-8R, CANR-2
McEwan, Ian (Russell) 1948- CANR-14
Earlier sketch in CA 61-64
See also DLB 14
See also CLC 13
McEwan, Jenny 1951- 124
McEwan, Keith 1926- 21-22R
McEwan, Peter J(ames) M(ichael)
1924- CANR-17
Earlier sketch in CA 25-28R
McEwen, Robert (Lindley) 1926-1980
Obituary 101
See also SATA 23
McFadden, Charles Joseph 1909- 77-80
McFadden, Cyra 1937- 77-80
McFadden, David 1940- 104
See also DLB 60
See also CLC 48
McFadden, Dorothy Loa 1902- 19-20R
McFadden, George 1916- 111
McFadden, James A., Jr. 1913- 19-20R
McFadden, Maggie
See McFadden, Margaret
McFadden, Margaret 1941- 115
McFadden, Robert D(ennis) 1937- CANR-15
Earlier sketch in CA 85-88
McFadden, Roy 1921- Brief entry 111
McFadden, Thomas M(ore) 1935- 89-92
McFague, Sallie 1933- CANR-11
Earlier sketch in CA 21-22R
McFall, Christie 1918- 7-8R
See also SATA 12
McFarlan, Donald M(aitland) 1915- CANR-10
Earlier sketch in CA 65-68
McFarlan, F. Warren 1937- 19-20R
McFarland, Andrew S(tuart) 1940- CANR-13
Earlier sketch in CA 25-28R
McFarland, C(harles) K(eith) 1934- 29-32R
McFarland, Carl 1904-1979 Obituary 85-88
McFarland, Dalton E(dward) 1919- CANR-2
Earlier sketch in CA 5-6R
McFarland, Dorothy Tuck 1938- 11-12R
McFarland, Ernest W(illiam) 1894-1984
Obituary 114
McFarland, Gerald Ward 1938- 85-88
McFarland, John 1943- 116
McFarland, Keith D(onavon) 1940- 57-60
McFarland, Kenton D(ean) 1920- 61-64
See also SATA 11
McFarland, M(alcolm) Carter 1912- 85-88
McFarland, Marvin W(ilks) 1919-1985
Obituary 115
McFarland, Philip (James) 1930- CANR-12
Earlier sketch in CA 73-76
McFarland, Ronald E(arl) 1942- 113
McFarland, Ross A(rmstrong) 1901- CAP-2
Earlier sketch in CA 21-22
McFarland, Thomas (Alfred, Jr.) 1926- ...41-44R
McFarlane, Brian 1931- 122
McFarlane, Bruce John 1936- CANR-16
Earlier sketch in CA 81-84
McFarlane, I(an) D(alrymple) 1915- 107
McFarlane, James Walter 1920- CANR-5
Earlier sketch in CA 3R
McFarlane, K. B. 1903-1966 Obituary 114
McFarlane, Leslie 1902-1977 112
See also SATA 31
McFate, Patricia Ann 1932- 103
McFather, Nelle 1936- CANR-4
Earlier sketch in CA 49-52
McFeat, Tom Farrar Scott 1919- 103
McFee, June King 1917- CANR-16
Earlier sketch in CA 81-84
McFee, Michael 1954- 112
McFee, Oonah 1922- 116
McFee, William (Morley Punshon)
1881-1966 Obituary 116
McFeely, Mary Drake 1932- 110
McFeely, William S(hield) 1930- CANR-15
Earlier sketch in CA 33-36R

McFerran, Ann
See Townsend, Doris McFerran
McFerran, Doris
See Townsend, Doris McFerran
McFerran, Douglass David 1934- 65-68
McGaa, Ed 1936- 97-100
McGaffin, William 1910-1975 .... CAP-2
Earlier sketch in CA 25-28
McGahern, John 1935- 19-20R
See also DLB 14
See also CLC 5, 9, 48
McGahey, Michael J(oseph) 1948- 116
McGann, George T(homas) 1913- 93-96
McGann, Jerome J(ohn) 1937- CANR-14
Earlier sketches in CA 45-48, CANR-1
McGann, Thomas F. 1920- 13-14R
McGannon, J(ohn) Barry 1924- 13-14R
McGarey, Gladys T(aylor) 1920- 57-60
McGarey, William A. 1919- 57-60
McGarrigle, Francis Joseph 1888- 5-6R
McGarrity, Mark 1943- CANR-17
Earlier sketches in CA 45-48, CANR-1
McGarry, Daniel D(oyle) 1907- CAP-1
Earlier sketch in CA 11-12
McGarry, Jean 1952- 126
McGarry, Kevin J(ohn) 1935- 102
McGarry, Michael B(rett) 1948- 102
McGarvey, Robert 1948- 113
McGaugh, James L(afayette) 1931- CANR-7
Earlier sketch in CA 57-60
McGaughey, (Florence) Helen 1904- 37-40R
McGavin, E(lmer) Cecil 1900- CAP-1
Earlier sketch in CA 11-12
McGavran, Donald 1897- 13-14R
McGaw, Charles James 1910-1978
Obituary 106
McGaw, Jessie Brewer 1913- 1R
See also SATA 10
McGaw, Naomi Blanche Thoburn 1920- ..11-12R
McGaw, William C(ochran) 1914- 101
McGeachy, D(aniel) P(atrick) III 1929- .. CANR-8
Earlier sketch in CA 61-64
McGear, Mike
See McCartney, Peter Michael
McGee, Barbara 1943- 25-28R
See also SATA 6
McGee, (Doctor) Frank 1921-1974 105
Obituary 89-92
McGee, Harold 1951- 118
McGee, Reece (Jerome) 1929- CANR-17
Earlier sketches in CA 5-6R, CANR-2
McGee, Robert W(illiam) 1947- 112
McGee, T. D.
See Savage, Teresa
McGee, T(erence) G(ary) 1936- CANR-10
Earlier sketch in CA 21-22R
McGee, Victor (Errol) 1935- 41-44R
McGeehan, Robert 1933- 33-36R
McGeehan, W. O. 1879-1933 .... DLB-25
McGeeney, Patrick John 1918- 7-8R
McGehee, Ralph W(alter) 1928- 112
McGeown, Patrick 1897- CAP-2
Earlier sketch in CA 23-24
McGerr, Patricia 1917-1985 .... CANR-1
Obituary 116
Earlier sketch in CA 2R
See also AITN 1
McGhan, Barry (Robert) 1939- 69-72
McGhie, Andrew 1926- 97-100
McGiffert, Michael 1928- 13-14R
McGiffert, Robert C(arnahan) 1922- 49-52
McGiffin, (Lewis) Lee (Shaffer) 1908- CAP-1
Earlier sketch in CA 15-16
See also SATA 1
McGill, Dan M(ays) 1919- Brief entry 107
McGill, Ian
See Allegro, John Marco
McGill, Leonard J(ames) 1956- 115
McGill, Ormond 1913- CANR-2
Earlier sketch in CA 49-52
McGill, Ralph (Emerson) 1898-1969 ....7-8R
Obituary 25-28R
See also DLB 29
McGill, Thomas E(merson) 1930- 19-20R
McGilligan, Patrick (Michael) 1951- CANR-10
Earlier sketch in CA 65-68
McGilvery, Laurence 1932- 33-36R
McGimsey, Charles Robert III 1925- 37-40R
McGinley, Patrick (Anthony) 1937-
Brief entry 120
See also CLC 41
McGinley, Phyllis 1905-1978 .... CANR-19
Obituary 77-80
Earlier sketch in CA 11-12R
See also SATA 2, 24, 44
See also DLB 11, 48
See also CLC 14
McGinn, Bernard John 1937- 113
McGinn, Donald Joseph 1905- CAP-2
Earlier sketch in CA 23-24
McGinn, John T. 1900(?)-1972
Obituary 33-36R
McGinn, Matt 1928-1977 106
McGinn, Maureen Ann
See Sautel, Maureen Ann
McGinn, Noel F(rancis) 1934- 73-76
McGinn, Richard 1939- 126
McGinnies, Elliott M(orse) 1921- 77-80
McGinnies, W(illiam) G(rovenor) 1899- .. CANR-7
Earlier sketch in CA 57-60
McGinnis, Bruce 1941- 97-100
McGinnis, Dorothy Jean 1920- 29-32R
McGinnis, Duane
See Niatum, Duane
McGinnis, K. K.
See Page, Grover, Jr.
McGinnis, Lila S(prague) 1924- 93-96
See also SATA 44
McGinnis, Marilyn 1939- 57-60
McGinnis, Robert 1927- 45-48
McGinnis, Thomas C(harles) 1925-1987 ...65-68
Obituary 123
McGinniss, Joe 1942- CANR-26
Earlier sketch in CA 25-28R
See also CLC 32
See also AITN 2
McGirt, James E. 1874-1930 .... DLB-50
McGivering, John H. 1923- 25-28R
McGivern, Maureen Daly 11-12R
McGivern, William P(eter) 1922-1982 ... CANR-7
Obituary 108
Earlier sketch in CA 49-52
McGlade, Francis S(tanley) 1930- 41-44R
McGlamry, Beverly 1932- 119
McGlashan, Alan (Fleming) 1898- 41-44R
McGlennon, John J(oseph) 1949- 119
McGlinchee, Claire CAP-2
Earlier sketch in CA 23-24
McGlinn, Dwight
See Brannon, William T.
McGloin, John Bernard 1912- 33-36R
McGloin, Joseph T(haddeus) 1917- CANR-18
Earlier sketches in CA 4R, CANR-1
McGlone, Edward Leon 1941- Brief entry ... 108
McGlothlin, William J(oseph) 1908- CAP-2
Earlier sketch in CA 19-20
McGlynn, Christopher
See Ginder, Richard
McGlynn, James V(incent) 1919-1973 .... 2R
Obituary 103
McGoey, John Heck 1915- CANR-21
Earlier sketches in CA 11-12R, CANR-6
McGoldrick, Desmond Francis 1919- 19-20R
McGoldrick, Edward J., Jr. 1909-1967 ... CAP-1
Earlier sketch in CA 19-20
McGoldrick, Joseph D. 1901-1978
Obituary 97-100
McGoldstein, Paddy
See Page, William
McGoon, Clifford D. 1939- 113
McGough, Elizabeth (Hemmes) 1934- 107
See also SATA 33
McGough, Roger 1937- 105
See also DLB 40
McGovern, Ann CANR-2
Earlier sketch in CA 49-52
See also SATA 8
McGovern, Arthur F(rancis) 1929- 116
McGovern, Constance M(adeline) 1938- 120
McGovern, George S(tanley) 1922- CANR-8
Earlier sketch in CA 45-48
McGovern, James 1923- CANR-7
Earlier sketch in CA 19-20R
McGovern, James R(ichard) 1928- 108
McGovern, John P(hillip) 1921- CANR-13
Earlier sketch in CA 21-22R
McGovern, Robert 1927- 49-52
McGowan, Jack 1896(?)-1977 Obituary ...69-72
McGowan, James A(lfred) 1932- 97-100
McGowan, John J. 1936(?)-1982
Obituary 106
McGowan, Margaret M(ary) 69-72
McGowen, Charles H(ammond) 1936- 69-72
McGowen, Thomas 1927- CANR-25
Earlier sketches in CA 23-24R, CANR-8
See also SATA 2
McGowen, Tom
See McGowen, Thomas
McGrade, Arthur Stephen 1934- 25-28R
McGrady, Donald Lee 1935- 25-28R
McGrady, Mike 1933- CANR-2
Earlier sketch in CA 49-52
See also SATA 6
McGrady, Patrick M(ichael), Jr. 1932- .. CANR-12
Earlier sketch in CA 29-32R
McGrady, Patrick Michael, Sr. 1908-1980 ... 103
Obituary 97-100
McGrail, Joie 1922(?)-1977 Obituary 69-72
McGrath, Alice (Greenfield) 1917- 112
McGrath, Doyle
See Schorb, E(dwin) M(arsh)
McGrath, Earl James 1902- CAP-1
Earlier sketch in CA 19-20
McGrath, Edward G(orham) 1917- 25-28R
McGrath, Francis E. 1903(?)-1976
Obituary 61-64
McGrath, J. H. 1923- 29-32R
McGrath, James Bernard, Jr. 1917- 5-6R
McGrath, Joan Rosita (Torr)
1895(?)-1967 Obituary 116
McGrath, John (Peter) 1935- Brief entry 112
McGrath, Lee Parr 1933- 29-32R
McGrath, Robert L(ee) 1920- 97-100
McGrath, Roger D. 1947- 118
McGrath, Sean
See Douglas, John (Frederick James)
McGrath, Susan 1955- 121
McGrath, Sylvia Wallace 1937- 61-64
McGrath, Thomas 1916- CANR-6
Earlier sketch in CA 9-10R
See also SATA 41
See also CLC 28
McGrath, William J(ames) 1937- 85-88
McGrath, William Thomas 1917- 103
McGratty, Arthur R. 1909-1975 Obituary ..53-56
McGraw, Eloise Jarvis 1915- CANR-19
Earlier sketches in CA 7-8R, CANR-4
See also SATA 1
See also SAAS 6
McGraw, Harold Whittlesey, Sr.
1890(?)-1970 Obituary 29-32R
McGraw, James (Paul) 1913-1977 .... 4R
McGraw, James R. 1935- 93-96
McGraw, Walter John, Jr. 1919(?)-1978
Obituary 81-84
McGraw, William Corbin 1916- 29-32R
See also SATA 3
McGreal, Elizabeth
See Yates, Elizabeth
McGreal, Ian Philip 1919- 77-80
McGreevey, William Paul 1938- CANR-11
Earlier sketch in CA 69-72
McGreevy, Susan Brown 1934- 126
McGregor
See Hurley, Doran
McGregor, Craig 1933- CANR-13
Earlier sketch in CA 23-24R
See also SATA 8
McGregor, Iona 1929- 105
See also SATA 25
McGregor, John C(harles) 1905- CAP-1
Earlier sketch in CA 19-20
McGregor, Malcolm Francis 1910- 45-48
McGregor, Rob Roy, Jr. 1929- 108
McGrew, William W. 1933- 122
McGrory, Mary 1918- 106
See also AITN 2
McGuane, Thomas (Francis III) 1939- .. CANR-24
Earlier sketches in CA 49-52, CANR-5
See also DLB 2
See also DLBY 80
See also CLC 3, 7, 18, 45
See also AITN 2
McGuckian, Medbh 1950- DLB-40
See also CLC 48
McGuffey, William Holmes 1800-1863 ... DLB-42
McGuffie, Tom H(enderson) 1902- CAP-2
Earlier sketch in CA 19-20
McGuigan, Dorothy Gies 1914-1982 ... CANR-11
Earlier sketch in CA 21-22R
McGuigan, F(rank) J(oseph) 1924- CANR-8
Earlier sketch in CA 5-6R
McGuinness, Arthur E(dward) 1936- 25-28R
McGuire, E(dward) Patrick 1932- 25-28R
McGuire, Edna 1899- CANR-2
Earlier sketch in CA 7-8R
See also SATA 13
McGuire, Frances Margaret (Cheadle) CAP-1
Earlier sketch in CA 9-10
McGuire, James Dean 1936- 21-22R
McGuire, Jerry 1934- 93-96
McGuire, Joseph William 1925- 9-10R
McGuire, Leslie Sarah 1945- 107
See also SATA 45, 52
McGuire, Martin C. 1933- 37-40R
McGuire, Martin Rawson Patrick
1897-1969 Obituary 111
McGuire, Meredith Anne (Black) 1944- 118
McGuire, Michael Terrance 1929- 41-44R
McGuire, Richard L(en) 1940- 57-60
McGuire, Robert G. (III) 1938(?)-1975
Obituary 61-64
McGuire, Thomas (Vertin) 1945- 73-76
McGuire, Thomas G. 1950- 111
McGurk, Patrick (Maurice) 1928- 118
McGurk, Slater
See Roth, Arthur J(oseph)
McGurn, Barrett 1914- CANR-1
Earlier sketch in CA 4R
McGurn, William 1958- 126
McHale, John 1922-1978 .... CANR-17
Earlier sketch in CA 61-64
McHale, Philip John 1928- 103
McHale, Tom 1942(?)-1982 77-80
Obituary 106
See also CLC 3, 5
See also AITN 1
McHale, Vincent E(dward) 1939- 112
McHam, David 1933- 73-76
McHaney, Thomas L(afayette) 1936- ... CANR-24
Earlier sketches in CA 65-68, CANR-9
McHarg, Ian L(ennox) 1920- 29-32R
McHargue, Georgess 1941- CANR-24
Earlier sketch in CA 25-28R
See also SATA 4
See also SAAS 5
See also CLR 2
McHenry, Dean E(ugene) 1910- 109
McHenry, Paul G(raham), Jr. 1924- 61-64
McHugh, Arona 1924- 7-8R
McHugh, Edna 69-72
McHugh, (Berit) Elisabet 1941- 113
See also SATA 44
McHugh, Heather 1948- CANR-11
Earlier sketch in CA 69-72
McHugh, John (Francis) 1927- 103
McHugh, Leroy 1891(?)-1975 Obituary 104
McHugh, Mary 1928- 85-88
McHugh, Maxine Davis 1899(?)-1978
Obituary 77-80
McHugh, P(atrick) J(oseph) 1922- 23-24R
McHugh, Roger Joseph 1908- 7-8R
McHugh, Roland 1945- CANR-10
Earlier sketch in CA 65-68
McHugh, Ruth Nelson
See Nelson, Ruth
McHugh, Stuart
See Rowland, D(onald) S(ydney)
McHugh, Thomas Cannell 1926- 103
McHugh, Tom
See McHugh, Thomas Cannell
McHugh, Vincent 1904-1983 Obituary 109
McIlhany, William H(erbert) II 1951- CANR-6
Earlier sketch in CA 57-60
McIlroy, Thad 1956- 122
McIlvaine, Betsy 1945- 123
McIlvaine, Jane
See McClary, Jane Stevenson
McIlvanney, William 1936- 25-28R
See also DLB 14
See also CLC 42
McIlwain, Charles Howard 1871-1968 102
McIlwain, David 1921- 109
McIlwain, William (Franklin, Jr.) 1925- .. CANR-1
Earlier sketch in CA 1R
McIlwraith, Maureen Mollie Hunter
1922- 29-32R
See also SATA 2
McInenly, William T(homas) 1932- 124
McInerney, Jay 1955- 123
Brief entry 116
See also CLC 34
McInerney, Judith W(hitelock) 1945- 118
See also SATA 46, 49
McInerny, Dennis Q(uentin) 1936- 97-100
McInerny, Ralph 1929- CANR-12
Earlier sketch in CA 21-22R
McInnes, Edward 1935- 109
McInnes, Graham (Campbell) 1912-1970 . CAP-2
Earlier sketch in CA 25-28
McInnes, Ian (Andrew Stuart Fraser)
1925- 25-28R
McInnes, Neil 1924- 77-80
McInnis, Edgar Wardwell 1899- 7-8R
McInnis, Noel F. 1936- CANR-14
Earlier sketch in CA 33-36R
McInnis, Raymond G(eorge) 1936- 110
McIntire, Roger W(arren) 1935- 53-56
McIntosh, Alexander 1947- CANR-2
Earlier sketch in CA 45-48
McIntosh, Carey 1934- 77-80
McIntosh, Christopher 1943- 33-36R
McIntosh, Donal W. 1919- 69-72
McIntosh, Douglas M. 1909- CAP-1
Earlier sketch in CA 13-14
McIntosh, E. 1894(?)-1970 Obituary 104
McIntosh, J. T.
See Macgregor, James (Murdoch)
McIntosh, James (Henry) 1934- 104
McIntosh, John 1930-1970 .... CAP-2
Earlier sketch in CA 21-22
McIntosh, Kinn Hamilton 25-28R
McIntosh, Louis
See Johnson, Christopher
McIntosh, Michael (Scott) 1945- 107
McIntosh, Peter Chisholm 1915- 102
McIntosh, Sandy
See McIntosh, Alexander
McInturff, Roy A(rthur) 1905- 53-56
McIntyre, John A(rmin) 1920- 57-60
McIntyre, Kenneth E. 1918- CANR-9
Earlier sketch in CA 21-22R
McIntyre, Michael P(erry) 1921- 41-44R
McIntyre, O. O. 1884-1938 .... DLB-25
McIntyre, Thomas (Alfred) 1952- 120
McIntyre, Thomas J(ames) 1915-
Brief entry 114
McIntyre, Vonda N(eel) 1948- CANR-17
Earlier sketch in CA 81-84
See also CLC 18
McIntyre, W(illiam) David 1932- CANR-26
Earlier sketches in CA 21-22R, CANR-10
McIntyre, William (Alexander) 1916- 37-40R
McIver, J(ohn) R(abie) 1931- 25-28R
McIver, Ray 1913- 25-28R
McIver, Stuart B(etts) 1921- 69-72
McJimsey, George T(ilden) 1936- 93-96
McJimsey, Harriet Tilden 1902- 7-8R
McKain, David W. 1937- CANR-5
Earlier sketch in CA 11-12R
McKale, Donald M(arshall) 1943- CANR-5
Earlier sketch in CA 53-56
McKane, William 1921- 117
McKay, Alexander G(ordon) 1924- 37-40R
McKay, (Herbert) Alwyn (Cochrane) 1913- .. 119
McKay, Arthur R(aymond) 1918- 5-6R
McKay, Claude
See McKay, Festus Claudius
See also DLB 4, 45, 51
See also TCLC 7
McKay, Derek 1942- 81-84
McKay, Don(ald) 1932- 33-36R
McKay, Donald 1895- SATA-45
McKay, Douglas R(ich) 1936- CANR-7
Earlier sketch in CA 57-60
McKay, Ernest A. 1918- 21-22R
McKay, Festus Claudius 1889-1948 124
Brief entry 104
See also BW
McKay, George Frederick 1899-1970
Obituary 106
McKay, Jim
See McManus, James Kenneth
McKay, John H(arvey) 1923- Brief entry 115
McKay, John P(atrick) 1938- 29-32R
McKay, Quinn G(unn) 1926- 57-60
McKay, Robert B(udge) 1919- 57-60
McKay, Robert W. 1921- CANR-10
Earlier sketch in CA 15-16R
See also SATA 15
McKay, Vernon 1912- 7-8R
McKay, William Paul 1951- 116
McKeachie, Wilbert J(ames) 1921- 21-22R
McKeag, Ernest L(ionel) 1896- CAP-1
Earlier sketch in CA 15-16
McKean, Dayton D(avid) 1904- CAP-1
Earlier sketch in CA 19-20
McKean, Gil(bert S.) 1918- 7-8R
McKean, Hugh Ferguson 1908- 102
McKean, John (Maule) 1943- 107
McKean, John Richard 1939- 33-36R
McKean, Keith F. 1915- 37-40R
McKean, Margaret A(nne) 1946- 108
McKean, Robert C(laud) 1920- 13-14R
McKean, Roland N(eely) 1917- 33-36R

INDEX

McKean, William V. 1820-1903 .... DLB-23
McKeating, Henry 1932- 37-40R
McKeay, Eileen
See McKeag, Ernest L(ionel)
McKee, Alexander (Paul Charrier)
1918- CANR-11
Earlier sketch in CA 11-12R
McKee, Barbara H(astings) 1902- 57-60
McKee, Christopher (Fulton) 1935- 77-80
McKee, Edwin D(inwiddie) 1906- 57-60
McKee, Eric
See McKee, J. E. G.
McKee, J. E. G. ?-1983 Obituary 111
McKee, John DeWitt 1919- 41-44R
McKee, Louis 1951- 110
McKee, Paul Gordon 1897- CAP-1
Earlier sketch in CA 11-12
McKeefery, William James 1918-1987
Obituary 123
McKeever, James Ross 1909(?)-1986
Obituary 120
McKeever, Marcia
See Laird, Jean E(louise)
McKelvey, Blake F. 1903- 19-20R
McKelvey, James Lee 1934- 45-48
McKelvey, John J(ay), Jr. 1917- CANR-8
Earlier sketch in CA 61-64
McKelway, Alexander J(effery) 1932- 15-16R
McKelway, Benjamin M. 1895-1976
Obituary 69-72
McKelway, St. Clair 1905-1980 ....5-6R
Obituary 93-96
McKemy, Kay 1924- 29-32R
McKendrick, (Hector) Fergus 1933- 115
McKendrick, Melveena (Christine)
1941- CANR-17
Earlier sketch in CA 93-96
McKendry, John (Joseph) 1933-1975
Obituary 61-64
McKenna, A. Daniel
See Corson-Finnerty, Adam Daniel
McKenna, Evelyn
See Joscelyn, Archie L.
McKenna, F(rancis) E(ugene) 1921-1978
Obituary 85-88
McKenna, George 1937- CANR-14
Earlier sketch in CA 81-84
McKenna, J(ane) J(essica) 1945- 93-96
McKenna, J(ohn) W(illiam) 1938- 37-40R
McKenna, Marian Cecilia 1926- CANR-22
Earlier sketch in CA 1R
McKenna, Michael C(layton) 1947- 116
McKenna, Richard (Milton) 1913-1964 . CANR-13
Earlier sketch in CA 5-6R
McKenna, Sister Margaret Mary 1930- ...23-24R
McKenna, Sister Mary Lawrence
See McKenna, Sister Margaret Mary
McKenna, Stephen 1888-1967 .... CAP-1
Earlier sketch in CA 9-10
McKenna, Terry 1949- 109
McKenney, Kenneth 1929- 69-72
McKenney, Mary 1946- 61-64
McKenney, Ruth 1911-1972 93-96
Obituary 37-40R
McKennon, Joe
See McKennon, Joseph W(esley)
McKennon, Joseph W(esley) 1907- CANR-2
Earlier sketch in CA 49-52
Mc Kenny, Margaret 73-76
McKenzie, Barbara 1934- 21-22R
McKenzie, Dorothy Clayton 1910-1981 . SATA-28
McKenzie, Doug
See Thomas, Dave
McKenzie, Garry D(onald) 1941- 41-44R
McKenzie, George W(ashington) 1939- 69-72
McKenzie, John L(awrence) 1910- 9-10R
McKenzie, Leon R(oy) 1932- 29-32R
McKenzie, Paige
See Blood, Marje
McKenzie, Robert T(relford) 1917-1981 ...19-20R
Obituary 105
McKeon, Richard P(eter) 1900-1985
Obituary 115
McKeon, Zahava Karl 1927- 126
McKeown, James E(dward) 1919- 15-16R
McKeown, Thomas 1912-1988 Obituary 125
McKeown, Tom 1937- CANR-20
Earlier sketches in CA 45-48, CANR-2
McKercher, Berneth N(oble) 1915- 53-56
McKern, Sharon S(mith) 1941- 37-40R
McKernan, John J(oseph) 1942- 110
McKersie, R. B.
See McKersie, Robert Bruce
McKersie, Robert Bruce 1929- Brief entry ... 116
McKhann, Charles Fremont 1930- 112
McKibbin, Alma E(stelle Baker)
1871-1974 .... CAP-1
Earlier sketch in CA 19-20
McKibbin, Frank L(owell) 1917- 65-68
McKibbin, Jean 1919- 65-68
McKie, Ronald (Cecil Hamlyn) 1909- CANR-6
Earlier sketch in CA 11-12R
McKillip, Patricia A(nne) 1948- CANR-18
Earlier sketches in CA 49-52, CANR-4
See also SATA 30
McKillop, Alan D(ugald) 1892-1974 ...... CAP-1
Obituary 53-56
Earlier sketch in CA 19-20
McKillop, Menzies 1929- 77-80
McKillop, Norman 1892-1974 ....7-8R
McKillop, Susan Regan 1929- CANR-8
Earlier sketch in CA 61-64
McKim, Audrey Margaret 1909- CANR-4
Earlier sketch in CA 4R
See also SATA 47
McKim, Donald K(eith) 1950- CANR-17
Earlier sketch in CA 93-96
McKimmey, James 1923- CANR-22
Earlier sketch in CA 85-88
McKinlay, Brian John 1933- CANR-19
Earlier sketch in CA 103
McKinley, Daniel (Lawson) 1924- 25-28R
McKinley, David Hopwood 1906- CAP-2
Earlier sketch in CA 33-36
McKinley, James (Courtright) 1935- 69-72
McKinley, (Jennifer Carolyn) Robin 1952- ... 107
See also SATA 32, 50
See also DLB 52
See also CLR 10
McKinnell, James 1933- CANR-12
Earlier sketch in CA 61-64
McKinnell, Robert Gilmore 1926- 102
McKinney, D. J.
See Cooper, Parley J(oseph)
McKinney, David Walter, Jr. 1920- 37-40R
McKinney, Don(ald Lee) 1923- 73-76
McKinney, Donald 1909- CANR-7
Earlier sketch in CA 57-60
McKinney, Eleanor Ruth 1918- 33-36R
McKinney, Eugene 1922- CANR-15
Earlier sketch in CA 73-76
McKinney, Fred 1908- 19-20R
McKinney, Gene
See McKinney, Eugene
McKinney, George Dallas, Jr. 1932- 7-8R
McKinney, George W(esley), Jr. 1922- 57-60
McKinney, Gordon B(artlett) 1943- 85-88
McKinney, H(enry) Lewis 1935- 41-44R
McKinney, John William 1908- 3R
McKinney, Virginia (Marie) 1940- 57-60
McKinney, William 1946- 121
McKinnon, Alastair Thomson 1925- 102
McKinnon, Robert Scott 1937- 37-40R
McKinzie, Richard D. 1936- 77-80
McKisack, May 1900-1981 107
Obituary 103
McKissack, Fredrick L(emuel) 1939- 120
See also SATA 53
McKissack, Patricia (L'Ann) C(arwell)
1944- 118
See also SATA 51
McKissick, Floyd Bixler 1922- 49-52
McKitrick, Eric Louis 1919- 23-24R
McKittrick, David 1938- 61-64
McKivigan, John R(aymond) 1949- 119
McKnight, Allan Douglas 1918- 104
McKnight, Brian Emerson 1938- 106
McKnight, C(olbert) A(ugustus)
1916-1986 Obituary 120
McKnight, C. A.
See Russell, Rosalind
McKnight, Edgar V(ernon) 1931- 21-22R
McKnight, Gerald 1919- 15-16R
McKnight, John P(roctor) 1908(?)-1987
Obituary 123
McKnight, Thomas Lee
See McKnight, Tom Lee
McKnight, Tom Lee 1928- CANR-5
Earlier sketch in CA 9-10R
McKowen, Clark 1929- 41-44R
McKown, Dave Ross 1895- 97-100
McKown, Robert 1908-1973 Obituary 104
McKown, Robin ?-1976 .... CANR-1
Earlier sketch in CA 3R
See also SATA 6
McKuen, Rod 1933- 41-44R
See also CLC 1, 3
See also AITN 1
McKusick, Marshall Bassford 1930- CANR-9
Earlier sketch in CA 13-14R
McLachlan, Ian 1938- 69-72
McLaglen, John J.
See Harvey, John (Barton)
McLanathan, Richard 1916- 81-84
McLandress, Herschel
See Galbraith, John Kenneth
McLane, Charles B(ancroft) 1919- 25-28R
McLane, Helen J. CANR-4
Earlier sketch in CA 11-12R
McLane, John R. 1935- 97-100
McLane, Paul Elliott 1907- CAP-1
Earlier sketch in CA 9-10
McLaren, Colin Andrew 1940- 106
McLaren, Floris Clark 1904-1978 .... DLB-68
McLaren, Homer D. 1887- CAP-2
Earlier sketch in CA 29-32
McLaren, Ian A. 1928- 103
McLaren, Ian Francis 1912- CANR-24
Earlier sketch in CA 106
McLaren, John (David) 1932- 29-32R
McLaren, Moray (David Shaw) 1901-1971 .. 103
McLaren, N(orman) Loyall 1892(?)-1977
Obituary 73-76
McLaren, Robert Bruce 1923- 29-32R
McLarry, Newman R(ay) 1923- 15-16R
McLaughlin, Arthur Leo 1921- 19-20R
McLaughlin, Bill
See Phillips, James W.
McLaughlin, Charles Bernard 1937- 61-64
McLaughlin, Curtis P. 1932- CANR-5
Earlier sketch in CA 53-56
McLaughlin, David J(ohn) 1936- 73-76
McLaughlin, Dean (Jr.) 1931- 9-10R
McLaughlin, Elizabeth Taylor 1923- 93-96
McLaughlin, Emma Maude 1901- 65-68
McLaughlin, Joseph 1940- CANR-20
Earlier sketches in CA 45-48, CANR-4
McLaughlin, Joseph F., Jr. 1919-1978
Obituary 77-80
McLaughlin, Lorrie (Bell) 1924-1971 .... CANR-5
Earlier sketch in CA 7-8R
McLaughlin, Mignon 11-12R
McLaughlin, Robert (Emmet) 1908-1973 ..... 3R
Obituary 45-48
McLaughlin, Robert William 1900- 1R
McLaughlin, Samuel Clarke 1924- 89-92
McLaughlin, Sister Raymond 1897- 25-28R
McLaughlin, Ted J(ohn) 1921- 15-16R
McLaughlin, Terence (Patrick) 1928- 33-36R
McLaughlin, Virginia Yans
See Yans-McLaughlin, Virginia
McLaughlin, William (DeWitt) 1918- 107
McLaughlin, William Raffian Davidson
1908- CAP-1
Earlier sketch in CA 11-12
McLaurin, Anne 1953- 106
See also SATA 27
McLaurin, Melton Alonza 1941- 81-84
McLaurin, R(onald) D(e) 1944- CANR-17
Earlier sketch in CA 65-68
McLaverty, Michael 1904- CAP-1
Earlier sketch in CA 13-14
See also DLB 15
McLean, Albert F(orbes), Jr. 1928- 19-20R
McLean, Allan Campbell 1922- CANR-4
Earlier sketch in CA 3R
McLean, Anne (Julia) 1951- 120
McLean, Beth Bailey 1892- CAP-2
Earlier sketch in CA 19-20
McLean, Don(ald George) 1932- 122
McLean, Donald 1905-1975 .... CANR-4
Earlier sketch in CA 2R
McLean, George 1905(?)-1983 Obituary 109
McLean, George F(rancis) 1929- CANR-6
Earlier sketch in CA 15-16R
McLean, Gordon R(onald) 1934- CANR-2
Earlier sketch in CA 49-52
McLean, Hugh 1925- 65-68
McLean, J. Sloan
See Gillette, Virginia M(ary)
and Wunsch, Josephine (McLean)
McLean, Janice W(alker) 1944- 119
McLean, John R. 1848-1916 .... DLB-23
McLean, Joseph E(rigina) 1915-1985
Obituary 118
McLean, Kathryn (Anderson) 1909-1966 .. CAP-2
Obituary 25-28R
Earlier sketch in CA 21-22
See also SATA 9
McLean, Malcolm Dallas 1913- CANR-16
Earlier sketch in CA 93-96
McLean, Robert 1891-1980 Obituary 103
McLean, Robert Colin 1927- 19-20R
McLean, Ruari 1917- CANR-10
Earlier sketch in CA 21-22R
McLean, Sammy Kay 1929- 37-40R
McLean, Susan 1937- 106
McLean, William L. 1852-1931 .... DLB-25
McLeave, Hugh George 1923- CANR-6
Earlier sketch in CA 7-8R
McLeavy, Gus 1951- 105
McLeish, Garen
See Stine, Whitney Ward
McLeish, John 1917- CANR-7
Earlier sketch in CA 57-60
McLeish, Kenneth 1940- CANR-13
Earlier sketch in CA 29-32R
See also SATA 35
McLellan, David 1940- CANR-15
Earlier sketch in CA 33-36R
McLellan, David S(tanley) 1924- 103
McLellan, Diana 1937- 114
McLellan, Robert 1907-1985 ....41-44R
Obituary 115
McLemore, Richard Aubrey 1903-1976 49-52
Obituary 103
McLemore, S(amuel) Dale 1928- 9-10R
McLendon, Gloria H(ouston) 1940- 112
McLendon, Gordon (Barton) 1921-1986
Obituary 120
McLendon, James (Nelson) 1942-1982 ...41-44R
Obituary 106
McLendon, Jonathon C(ollins) 1919- 19-20R
McLendon, Will L(oving) 1925- 9-10R
McLendon, Winzola Poole 93-96
McLenighan, Valjean 1947- 108
See also SATA 40, 46
McLennan, Barbara N(ancy) 1940- 85-88
McLeod, Alan L(indsey) 1928- 11-12R
McLeod, Emilie Warren 1926-1982 ....33-36R
Obituary 108
See also SATA 23, 31
McLeod, Enid Devoge 1896-1985
Obituary 116
McLeod, James R(ichard) 1942- 41-44R
McLeod, John F(reeland) 1917- 69-72
McLeod, Kirsty
See Hudson, (Margaret) Kirsty
McLeod, Malcolm Donald 1941- 110
McLeod, Margaret Vail
See Holloway, Teresa (Bragunier)
McLeod, Mary Alice 1937- 112
McLeod, Raymond, Jr. 1932- CANR-19
Earlier sketches in CA 49-52, CANR-3
McLeod, Ross
See Feldman, Herbert (H. S.)
McLeod, Wallace (Edmond) 1931- CANR-14
Earlier sketch in CA 37-40R
McLin, Jon (Blythe) 1938- 102
McLin, Ruth (Arlene) 1924- 61-64
McLoughlin, John C. 1949- 108
See also SATA 47
McLoughlin, R. B.
See Mencken, H(enry) L(ouis)
McLoughlin, William G. 1922- CANR-6
Earlier sketch in CA 13-14R
McLouth, Gary (Michael) 1944- 119
McLowery, Frank
See Keevill, Henry J(ohn)
McLuhan, (Herbert) Marshall
1911-1980 .... CANR-12
Obituary 102
Earlier sketch in CA 11-12R
See also CLC 37
McLure, Charles E., Jr. 1940- CANR-8
Earlier sketch in CA 57-60
McMahan, Ian SATA-45
McMahon, Bob 1943- 111
McMahon, Bryan T(homas) 1950- 45-48
McMahon, Charles P. 1916(?)-1983
Obituary 109
McMahon, Dorothy 1912-1984 Obituary 112
McMahon, Ed(ward Leo Peter, Jr.) 1923- ..89-92
McMahon, Edwin Mansfield 1930- 126
McMahon, Francis E(lmer) 1906-1987
Obituary 123
McMahon, Jeremiah 1919- 109
McMahon, Joseph H(enry) 1930-1987 ...11-12R
Obituary 124
McMahon, Michael 1943- 69-72
McMahon, Pat
See Hoch, Edward D(entinger)
McMahon, Robert
See Weverka, Robert
McMahon, Robert J. 1949- 109
McMahon, Thomas 1923(?)-1972
Obituary 37-40R
McMahon, Thomas (Arthur) 1943- CANR-15
Earlier sketch in CA 33-36R
McManis, Douglas R. 69-72
McManners, John 1916- CANR-14
Earlier sketch in CA 37-40R
McManus, Edgar J. 1924- 97-100
McManus, Frederick R(ichard) 1923- 2R
McManus, James 1951- 117
McManus, James Kenneth 1921- 85-88
McManus, Jason 1934- 125
McManus, Marjorie 1950- 73-76
McManus, Patrick (Francis) 1933- 105
See also SATA 46
McMaster, Beth 1935- 112
McMaster, John Bach 1852-1932 ...... DLB-47
McMaster, Juliet 1937- 37-40R
McMeekin, Clark
See McMeekin, Isabel McLennan
McMeekin, Dorothy 1932- 125
McMeekin, Isabel McLennan 1895- 5-6R
See also SATA 3
McMenemey, William Henry 1905- CAP-1
Earlier sketch in CA 11-12
McMenemy, Nickie 1925- 97-100
McMichael, George 1927- 103
McMichael, James 1939- 69-72
McMichael, Joan K(atharine) 1906- 107
McMillan, Bruce 1947- CANR-13
Earlier sketch in CA 73-76
See also SATA 22
McMillan, Colin 1923- 29-32R
McMillan, Constance (VanBrunt Johnson)
1949- 85-88
McMillan, George 1913-1987 102
Obituary 123
McMillan, James B. 1907- 85-88
McMillan, James F(rancis) 1948- 122
McMillan, Polly Miller 1920- 4R
McMillan, Priscilla Johnson 1928- 41-44R
McMillan, Roddy 1923-1979 Obituary 109
McMillan, Terry 1951- CLC-50
McMillen, Howard 1938- 57-60
McMillen, Neil R(aymond) 1939- 33-36R
McMillen, S(im) I. (Socrates) 1898- 7-8R
McMillen, Wheeler 1893- 33-36R
McMillin, (Joseph) Laurence (Jr.) 1923- ..33-36R
McMillin, (Harvey) Scott 1934- 126
McMillion, Bonner 1921- 15-16R
McMorran, Susan
See Beattie, Susan
McMorrow, Fred 1925- 57-60
McMullan, Frank (Alonzo) 1907- 7-8R
McMullan, Kate
See McMullan, Kate Hall
McMullan, Kate Hall 1947- 123
See also SATA 48, 52
McMullen, Jay L. 1921- 118
Brief entry 114
McMullen, Jeremy (John) 1948- 103
McMullen, Lorraine 1926- 117
McMullen, Mary
See Reilly, Mary
McMullen, Roy 1911-1984 ....25-28R
Obituary 113
McMullin, Ernan 1924- CANR-22
Earlier sketches in CA 13-14R, CANR-6
McMullin, Ruth R(oney) 1942- 61-64
McMurdie, Annie Laurie
See Cassiday, Bruce (Bingham)
McMurray, George R(ay) 1925- 103
McMurray, Nancy A(rmistead) 1936- 41-44R
McMurrin, Sterling M(oss) 1914- 29-32R
McMurry, James Burton 1941- 69-72
McMurry, Linda O. 1945- 106
McMurry, Robert N(oleman) 1901- 19-20R
McMurry, Sarah L. 1944- 123
McMurtrey, Martin A(loysias) 1921- 69-72
See also SATA 21
McMurtry, Jo 1937- 89-92
McMurtry, Larry (Jeff) 1936- CANR-19
Earlier sketch in CA 7-8R
See also DLB 2
See also DLBY 80, 87
See also CLC 2, 3, 7, 11, 27, 44
See also AITN 2
McMurtry, Robert Gerald 1906- CAP-1
Earlier sketch in CA 11-12
McNab, Thomas 1933- 108

McNab, Tom
See McNab, Thomas
McNail, Eddie Gathings 1905- ... CANR-6
Earlier sketch in CA 57-60
McNair, Kate ... 19-20R
See also SATA 3
McNair, Malcolm P(errine) 1894-1985 ... CAP-1
Obituary ... 117
Earlier sketch in CA 11-12
McNair, Philip Murray Jourdan 1924- ... 23-24R
McNair, Sylvia 1924- ... 121
McNair Scott, Ronald (Guthrie) 1906- ... 111
McNairy, Philip F(rederick) 1911- ... 19-20R
McNall, P(reston) E(ssex) 1888- ... 29-32R
McNall, Scott G(rant) 1941- ... CANR-11
Earlier sketch in CA 25-28R
McNally, Curtis
See Birchall, Ian H(arry)
McNally, Dennis 1949- ... 103
McNally, Gertrude Bancroft 1908(?)-1985
Obituary ... 115
McNally, John 1914- ... 19-20R
McNally, Raymond T. 1931- ... CANR-14
Earlier sketch in CA 37-40R
McNally, Robert 1946- ... 107
McNally, Robert E(dward) 1917-1978 ... CANR-11
Earlier sketch in CA 23-24R
McNally, Terrence 1939- ... CANR-2
Earlier sketch in CA 45-48
See also DLB 7
See also CLC 4, 7, 41
McNally, Tom 1923- ... 85-88
McNamara, Brooks 1937- ... 25-28R
McNamara, Eugene (Joseph) 1930- ... CANR-26
Earlier sketches in CA 21-22R, CANR-10
McNamara, Jo Ann 1931- ... CANR-15
Earlier sketch in CA 85-88
McNamara, John J(oseph), Jr.
1932-1986 ... 41-44R
Obituary ... 120
McNamara, John S. 1908(?)-1977
Obituary ... 69-72
McNamara, Kevin (John) 1926-1987 ... 25-28R
Obituary ... 122
McNamara, Lena Brooke 1891- ... CAP-1
Earlier sketch in CA 11-12
McNamara, Margaret C(raig)
1915-1981 ... SATA-24
McNamara, Michael M. 1940-1979
Obituary ... 89-92
McNamara, Robert S(trange) 1916-
Brief entry ... 112
McNamara, Sister Marie Aquinas
See Schaub, Marilyn McNamara
McNamara, William E. 1926- ... CANR-4
Earlier sketch in CA 4R
McNamee, James 1904- ... 7-8R
McNamee, Lawrence F. 1917- ... 25-28R
McNamee, Maurice B(asil) 1909- ... 5-6R
McNamee, Thomas 1947- ... 125
McNaspy, Clement James 1915- ... CANR-2
Earlier sketch in CA 7-8R
McNaught, Brian Robert 1948- ... 105
McNaught, Harry ... 106
See also SATA 32
McNaught, Kenneth (William Kirkpatrick)
1918- ... 29-32R
McNaughton, Arnold 1930- ... 57-60
McNaughton, Colin 1951- ... 112
See also SATA 39
McNaughton, Frank 1906(?)-1978
Obituary ... 81-84
McNaughton, Howard (Douglas) 1945- ... 57-60
McNaughton, Wayne L. 1902- ... 1R
McNaughton, William (Frank) 1933- ... 41-44R
McNeal, Robert H(atch) 1930- ... 11-12R
McNear, Robert 1930(?)-1985 Obituary ... 117
McNeely, Jeannette 1918- ... 41-44R
See also SATA 25
McNeely, Jerry Clark 1928- Brief entry ... 115
McNeer, May ... CANR-2
Earlier sketch in CA 7-8R
See also SATA 1
McNees, Pat 1940- ... CANR-7
Earlier sketch in CA 57-60
McNeil, Art 1944- ... 124
McNeil, Barbara L(aurie) 1951- ... 97-100
McNeil, Elton B(urbank) 1924-1974 ... CAP-2
Earlier sketch in CA 25-28
McNeil, Florence 1940- ... 116
See also DLB 60
McNeill, Anthony 1941- ... 97-100
McNeill, Donald P(aul) 1936- ... 107
McNeill, Janet
See Alexander, Janet
See also SATA 1
McNeill, John J. 1925- ... 65-68
McNeill, John Thomas 1885-1975 ... CANR-10
Obituary ... 57-60
Earlier sketches in CA 11-12, CAP-1
McNeill, Robert B(lakely) 1915- ... 19-20R
McNeill, Stuart 1942- ... 65-68
McNeill, William H(ardy) 1917- ... CANR-2
Earlier sketch in CA 7-8R
McNeilly, Wilfred (Glassford) 1921- ... 29-32R
McNeir, Waldo F(orest) 1908- ... 19-20R
McNeish, James 1931- ... CANR-12
Earlier sketch in CA 69-72
McNelly, Theodore (Hart) 1919- ... 7-8R
McNelly, Willis E(verett) 1920- ... 107
McNew, Ben(nie) B(anks) 1931- ... CANR-3
Earlier sketch in CA 11-12R
McNickle, (William) D'Arcy 1904-1977 ... CANR-5
Obituary ... 85-88
Earlier sketch in CA 9-10R
See also SATA 22
McNicoll, Alan (Wedel Ramsay)
1908-1987 Obituary ... 124
McNicoll, Robert E. 1907- ... 37-40R
McNiece, Harold Francis 1923-1972
Obituary ... 37-40R
McNierney, Mary Alice ... 11-12R
McNiff, William John 1899-1987 Obituary ... 122
McNitt, Gale 1921- ... 57-60
McNiven, Malcolm A(lbert) 1929- ... 29-32R
McNown, John S(tephenson) 1916- ... 57-60
McNulty, Edward N. 1936- ... CANR-25
Earlier sketches in CA 65-68, CANR-10
McNulty, Faith 1918- ... CANR-25
Earlier sketches in CA 49-52, CANR-1
See also SATA 12
McNulty, James Edmund, Jr. 1924-1965 ... 3R
Obituary ... 103
McNulty, James Francis 1934-1979
Obituary ... 113
McNutt, Dan James 1938- ... 61-64
McNutt, James (Allen) 1944- ... 49-52
McOwan, Rennie 1933- ... 115
McPhail, David M(ichael) 1940- ... CANR-22
Earlier sketch in CA 85-88
See also SATA 32, 47
McPharlin, Paul 1903-1948 Brief entry ... 110
See also SATA 31
McPhaul, Jack
See McPhaul, John J.
McPhaul, John J. 1904-1983 ... 9-10R
Obituary ... 110
McPhee, Arthur G(ene) 1945- Brief entry ... 116
McPhee, John (Angus) 1931- ... CANR-20
Earlier sketch in CA 65-68
See also CLC 36
McPhee, Richard B(yron) 1934- ... 111
See also SATA 41
McPhee, William N(orvell) 1921- ... 19-20R
McPherson, Anna Talbott 1904- ... CANR-19
Earlier sketches in CA 4R, CANR-4
McPherson, Gertrude H(untington) 1923- ... 45-48
McPherson, Harry Cummings, Jr. 1929- ... 104
McPherson, Holt 1907(?)-1979 Obituary ... 89-92
McPherson, Hugo (Archibald) 1921- ... 29-32R
McPherson, James Alan 1943- ... CANR-24
Earlier sketch in CA 25-28R
See also BW
See also DLB 38
See also CLC 19
McPherson, James Lowell 1921- ... 15-16R
McPherson, James M. 1936- ... 11-12R
See also SATA 16
McPherson, John 1925- ... 119
McPherson, Sandra 1943- ... CANR-12
Earlier sketch in CA 29-32R
See also DLBY 86
McPherson, Thomas Herdman 1925- ... 19-20R
McPherson, William (Alexander) 1933- ... 69-72
See also CLC 34
McPherson, William 1939- ... 57-60
McPhie, Walter E(van) 1926- ... 29-32R
McPolk, Andre (Hans) 1935- ... CANR-25
Earlier sketch in CA 93-96
McQuade, Ann Aikman 1928- ... 1R
McQuade, De Rosset Morrissey
1934(?)-1978 Obituary ... 81-84
McQuade, Donald A(nthony) 1941- ... CANR-16
Earlier sketch in CA 65-68
McQuade, Walter 1922- ... 103
McQuaid, Kim 1947- ... CANR-24
Earlier sketch in CA 107
McQuaig, Jack Hunter ... 11-12R
McQueen, Ian 1930- ... 104
McQueen, Lucinda ... SATA-48
McQueen, Mildred Hark 1908- ... CAP-1
Earlier sketch in CA 9-10
See also SATA 12
McQueen, William A. 1926- ... 23-24R
McQuigg, R. Bruce 1927- ... 19-20R
McQuilkin, Frank 1936- ... CANR-13
Earlier sketch in CA 33-36R
McQuiston, Joanne W(orth) 1922(?)-1985
Obituary ... 117
McQuown, F(rederic) R(ichard) 1907- ... 11-12R
McQuown, Judith H(ershkowitz) 1941- ... 107
McQuown, Norman A(nthony) 1914- ... 126
Brief entry ... 106
McRae, Hamish (Malcolm Donald) 1943- ... 57-60
McRae, Kenneth D(ouglas) 1925- ... CANR-17
Earlier sketch in CA 2R
McRae, Lindsay
See Sowerby, A(rthur) L(indsay) M(cRae)
McRae, Robert (Forbes) 1914- ... 77-80
McRae, William John 1933- ... 106
McReynolds, David 1929- ... 29-32R
McReynolds, Edwin C(larence)
1890-1967 ... CAP-1
Earlier sketch in CA 19-20
McReynolds, Ronald W(eldon) 1934- ... 49-52
McRoberts, Agnesann
See Meek, Pauline Palmer
McRoberts, R(obert) Lewis 1944- ... 33-36R
McShan, James 1937- ... 69-72
McShane, Mark 1930- ... CANR-22
Earlier sketches in CA 19-20R, CANR-7
McShane, Philip 1932- ... 69-72
McShean, Gordon 1936- ... 108
See also SATA 41
McSherry, Frank D(avid), Jr. 1927- ... CANR-23
Earlier sketch in CA 107
McSherry, James E(dward) 1920- ... 49-52
McShine, Kynaston (Leigh) 1935-
Brief entry ... 115
McSorley, Joseph 1874-1963 ... CAP-1
Earlier sketch in CA 15-16
McSweeney, Kerry ... CLC-34
McSweeny, Maxine 1905- ... 61-64
Mc Swigan, Marie 1907-1962 ... 73-76
See also SATA 24
McTaggart, Fred 1939- ... 65-68
McTaggart, J. McT. Ellis
See McTaggart, John McTaggart Ellis
McTaggart, John McTaggart Ellis
1866-1925 Brief entry ... 120
McTaggart, Lynne (Ann) 1951- Brief entry ... 113
McTeer, Wilson 1905- ... 41-44R
McVay, Gordon 1941- ... 73-76
McVean, James
See Luard, Nicholas
McVeigh, Malcolm J(ames) 1931- ... 61-64
McVey, Ruth T(homas) 1930- ... 109
McVickar, Elinor Guthrie 1902(?)-1982
Obituary ... 106
McVicker, Charles (Taggart) 1930- ... SATA-39
McVicker, Chuck
See McVicker, Charles (Taggart)
McVicker, Daphne Alloway 1895-1979
Obituary ... 85-88
McWaters, Barry 1937- ... 108
McWhiney, Grady 1928- ... CANR-6
Earlier sketch in CA 7-8R
McWhinney, Edward Watson 1926- ... CANR-12
Earlier sketch in CA 29-32R
McWhinnie, Donald 1920-1987 Obituary ... 123
McWhirter, A(lan) Ross 1925-1975 ... 19-20R
Obituary ... 61-64
See also SATA 31, 37
McWhirter, George 1939- ... CANR-13
Earlier sketch in CA 77-80
See also DLB 60
McWhirter, Glenna S. 1929- ... 89-92
McWhirter, Nickie
See McWhirter, Glenna S.
McWhirter, Norris Dewar 1925- ... 13-14R
See also SATA 37
McWilliams, Carey 1905-1980 ... CANR-2
Obituary ... 101
Earlier sketch in CA 45-48
McWilliams, John P(robasco), Jr. 1940- ... 49-52
McWilliams, Margaret (Ann Edgar)
1929- ... CANR-26
Earlier sketches in CA 19-20R, CANR-8
McWilliams, Peter 1949- ... 41-44R
McWilliams, Wilson Carey 1933- ... CANR-19
Earlier sketch in CA 103
Meacham, Ellis K. 1913- ... 25-28R
Meacham, Harry M(onroe) 1901-1975 ... CAP-2
Earlier sketch in CA 25-28
Meacham, Margaret 1952- ... 118
Meacham, Standish (Jr.) 1932-
Brief entry ... 110
Meacher, Michael Hugh 1939- ... 109
Mead, D(onald) Eugene 1934- ... 65-68
Mead, Edgar T(horn), Jr. 1922- ... 113
Mead, Frank Spencer 1898-1982 ... CANR-9
Obituary ... 107
Earlier sketches in CA 19-20, CAP-1
Mead, G(eorge) R(obert) S(tow)
1863-1933 Brief entry ... 122
Mead, Harold C(harles) H(ugh) 1910- ... CAP-1
Earlier sketch in CA 13-14
Mead, Jude 1919- ... 25-28R
Mead, Margaret 1901-1978 ... CANR-4
Obituary ... 81-84
Earlier sketch in CA 3R
See also SATA 20
See also CLC 37
See also AITN 1
Mead, Matthew 1924- ... 101
See also DLB 40
Mead, Peter (Willan) 1911- ... 116
Mead, Robert Douglas 1928-1983 ... 41-44R
Obituary ... 110
Mead, Russell (M., Jr.) 1935- ... 11-12R
See also SATA 10
Mead, Russell
See Koehler, Margaret Hudson
Mead, (Edward) Shepherd 1914- ... 9-10R
Mead, Sidney E(arl) 1904- ... CAP-1
Earlier sketch in CA 9-10
Mead, Sidney Moko 1927- ... CANR-23
Earlier sketch in CA 106
Mead, Stella ?-1981 Obituary ... 103
See also SATA 27
Mead, Taylor 1931(?)- ... 126
Brief entry ... 116
See also DLB 16
Mead, Walter B(ruce) 1934- ... 37-40R
Mead, William B(owmar) 1934- ... CANR-15
Earlier sketch in CA 85-88
Mead, William Richard 1915- ... 103
Meade, Bill C.
See Rogers, Paul T(aylor)
Meade, Dorothy (Joan Sampson) 1923- ... 9-10R
Meade, Elizabeth Thomasina
1854(?)-1914(?) Brief entry ... 112
Meade, Ellen
See Roddick, Ellen
See also SATA 5
Meade, Everard 1914- ... 25-28R
Meade, James Edward 1907- ... CANR-2
Earlier sketch in CA 1R
Meade, L. T.
See Meade, Elizabeth Thomasina
Meade, Marion 1934- ... CANR-1
Earlier sketch in CA 49-52
See also SATA 23
Meade, Mary
See Church, Ruth Ellen (Lovrien)
Meade, Richard
See Haas, Ben(jamin) L(eopold)
Meade, Richard A(ndrew) 1911- ... 45-48
Meade, Robert Douthat 1903-197(?) ... CAP-2
Earlier sketch in CA 25-28
Meader, Stephen W(arren) 1892- ... 5-6R
See also SATA 1
Meador, Roy 1929- ... CANR-11
Earlier sketch in CA 69-72
Meadow, Barry 1947- ... 125
Meadow, Charles T(roub) 1929- ... CANR-15
Earlier sketch in CA 29-32R
See also SATA 23
Meadow, Kathryn Pendleton 1929- ... CANR-7
Earlier sketch in CA 57-60
Meadowcroft, Enid LaMonte
See Wright, Enid Meadowcroft (LaMonte)
Meadowes, Alicia
See Burak, Linda (Gallina)
and Zieg, Joan (Gallina)
Meadows, Eddie S(pencer) 1939- ... 109
Meadows, Edward 1944- ... 101
Meadows, Paul 1913- ... 41-44R
Meadows, Peter
See Lindsay, Jack
Meagher, John C. 1935- ... CANR-11
Earlier sketch in CA 19-20R
Meagher, Paul Kevin 1907-1976 Obituary ... 69-72
Meagher, Robert E(mmett) 1943- ... CANR-10
Earlier sketch in CA 25-28R
Meagher, Robert F. 1927- ... 41-44R
Meaker, Eloise 1915- ... 105
Meaker, M. J.
See Meaker, Marijane
Meaker, Marijane 1927- ... 107
See also SATA 20
Meakin, David 1943- ... 69-72
Means, Florence Crannell 1891-1980 ... 4R
Obituary ... 103
See also SATA 1, 25
Means, Gardiner C(oit) 1896-1988
Obituary ... 124
Means, Gordon P(aul) 1927- ... 33-36R
Means, John Barkley 1939- ... 33-36R
Means, Louis Edgar 1902- ... CANR-2
Earlier sketch in CA 5-6R
Means, Marianne Hansen 1934- ... 11-12R
Means, Richard K(eith) 1929- ... CANR-17
Earlier sketches in CA 7-8R, CANR-2
Meany, George 1894-1980 Obituary ... 97-100
Meara, (Mary) Jane (Frances) Cavolina
1954- ... 120
Meara, Mary Jane Frances Cavolina
See Meara, (Mary) Jane (Frances)
Cavolina
Meares, Ainslie Dixon 1910- ... CANR-11
Earlier sketch in CA 25-28R
Mearian, Judy Frank 1936- ... 101
See also SATA 49
Mearns, David Chambers 1899-1981 ... 2R
Obituary ... 104
Mears, Brainerd, Jr. 1921- ... 53-56
Mears, Richard Chase 1935- ... 101
Mears, Walter R(obert) 1935- ... 113
Brief entry ... 111
Mearsheimer, John J(oseph) 1947- ... 117
Measday, George
See Soderberg, Percy Measday
Measham, D(onald) C. 1932- ... 21-22R
Measures, (William) Howard 1894- ... CAP-1
Earlier sketch in CA 13-14
Mebane, John (Harrison) 1909- ... 15-16R
Mebane, Mary E(lizabeth) 1933- ... 73-76
Mech, Dave
See Mech, L(ucyan) David
Mech, L(ucyan) David 1937- ... CANR-14
Earlier sketch in CA 33-36R
Mecham, John Lloyd 1893- ... 2R
Mechanic, David 1936- ... CANR-19
Earlier sketches in CA 5-6R, CANR-3
Mechanic, Sylvia (Gertrude) 1920- ... 69-72
Mechin, Jacques Benoist
See Benoist-Mechin, Jacques
Meckier, Jerome (Thomas) 1941- ... 33-36R
Meckler, Alan Marshall 1945- ... 57-60
Meckley, Richard F(rederick) 1928- ... 37-40R
Mecklin, John Martin 1918-1971
Obituary ... 33-36R
Meckstroth, Jacob A. 1887(?)-1985
Obituary ... 115
Meckstroth, Jake
See Meckstroth, Jacob A.
Medalia, Leon S. 1881- ... 85-88
Medary, Marjorie 1890- ... 73-76
See also SATA 14
Medawar, Peter Brian 1915-1987 ... 97-100
Obituary ... 123
Medd, Patrick 1919- ... 25-28R
Meddaugh, Susan 1944- ... 106
See also SATA 29
Meddis, Ray 1944- ... 77-80
Medea, Andra 1953- ... 57-60
Medearis, Mary 1915- ... 69-72
See also SATA 5
Medeiros, Earl Caton 1933- ... 89-92
Medhin, Tsegaye (Kawessa) Gabre
See Gabre-Medhin, Tsegaye (Kawessa)
Medhurst, Joan
See Liverton, Joan
Medicus II
See Philipp, Elliot Elias
Medill, Joseph 1823-1899 ... DLB-43
Medina, Jeremy T(yler) 1942- ... CANR-11
Earlier sketch in CA 69-72
Medina, William A.
See Medina, William Antonio
Medina, William Antonio 1935-1985
Obituary ... 117
Medley, Anne
See Borchard, Ruth (Berendsohn)
Medley, (Rachel) Margaret 1918- ... 15-16R
Medley, Morris L(ee) 1942- ... 57-60

Medlicott, Alexander G(uild), Jr. 1927- ... 37-40R
Medlicott, Margaret P(aget) 1913- ... 29-32R
Medlicott, William Norton 1900-1987 ... 9-10R
Obituary ... 123
Medlin, Virgil D(ewain) 1943- ... 57-60
Mednick, Murray 1939- ... 21-22R
Medoff, Mark (Howard) 1940- ... CANR-5
Earlier sketch in CA 53-56
See also DLB 7
See also CLC 6, 23
See also AITN 1
Medsger, Betty (Louise) 1942- ... 113
Medsker, Leland L. 1905- ... CANR-2
Earlier sketch in CA 3R
Medved, Harry 1961(?)- ... 93-96
Medved, Michael 1948- ... CANR-11
Earlier sketch in CA 65-68
Medvedev, Pavel
See Bakhtin, Mikhail (Mikhailovich)
Medvedev, Roy (Alexandrovich) 1925- ... 81-84
Medvedev, Zhores A(leksandrovich)
1925- ... 69-72
Mee, Charles L., Jr. 1938- ... CANR-3
Earlier sketch in CA 45-48
See also SATA 8
Mee, Fiona 1946(?)-1978 Obituary ... 104
Mee, John F(ranklin) 1908- ... CAP-1
Earlier sketch in CA 9-10
Meechan, Hugh L(awrence) 1933- ... 19-20R
Meehan, Daniel Joseph 1930-1978
Obituary ... 77-80
Meehan, Danny
See Meehan, Daniel Joseph
Meehan, Eugene J(ohn) 1923- ... CANR-14
Earlier sketch in CA 37-40R
Meehan, Francis X(avier) 1937- ... 116
Meehan, Richard Lawrence 1939- ... 107
Meehan, Thomas Edward 1932- ... 29-32R
Meehl, Paul E(verett) 1920- ... 93-96
Meek, Alexander Beaufort 1814-1865 ... DLB-3
Meek, Forrest B(urns) 1928- ... 110
Meek, Jacklyn O'Hanlon 1933- ... 77-80
See also SATA 34, 51
Meek, Jay 1937- ... CANR-25
Earlier sketch in CA 107
Meek, Lois Hayden
See Stolz, Lois Meek
Meek, Loyal George 1918- ... 73-76
Meek, Margaret
See Meek Spencer, Margaret (Diston)
Meek, Pauline Palmer 1917- ... 106
Meek, Ronald L(indley) 1917-1978 ... CANR-6
Earlier sketch in CA 9-10R
Meek, S(terner St.) P(aul) 1894-1972 ... 4R
Obituary ... 103
See also SATA 28
Meeker, Alice (MacCutcheon) 1904- ... CAP-2
Earlier sketch in CA 25-28
Meeker, Joseph W(arren) 1932- ... 49-52
Meeker, Mary Nacol 1928- ... 53-56
Meeker, Oden 1919(?)-1976 ... 73-76
Obituary ... 65-68
See also SATA 14
Meeker, Richard Kilburn 1925-19(?) ... CAP-2
Earlier sketch in CA 19-20
Meeks, Esther MacBain ... 4R
See also SATA 1
Meeks, John E. ... 33-36R
Meeks, Linda A.
See Brower, Linda A.
Meeks, M(errill) Douglas 1941- ... 93-96
Meeks, Wayne A. 1932- ... CANR-5
Earlier sketch in CA 15-16R
Meek Spencer, Margaret (Diston)
1925- ... CANR-21
Earlier sketch in CA 105
Meen, Victor Ben 1910-1971 Obituary ... 106
Meenan, James F(rancis) 1910-1987 ... 124
Meer, Fatima 1929- ... 73-76
Meerhaeghe, M(arcel) A(lfons) G(ilbert) Van
See Van Meerhaeghe, M(arcel) A(lfons)
G(ilbert)
Meerloo, Joost A(braham) M(aurits)
1903-1976 ... CANR-4
Obituary ... 69-72
Earlier sketch in CA 1R
Meeropol, Abel 1903(?)-1986 Obituary ... 121
Meese, Elizabeth Ann 1943- ... 122
Meeter, Glenn 1934- ... CANR-12
Earlier sketch in CA 33-36R
Meeth, Louis Richard 1934- ... 19-20R
Meeuse, Bastiaan (Jacob Dirk) 1916- ... 119
Meezan, William 1947- ... 117
Megargee, Edwin I(nglee) 1937- ... CANR-7
Earlier sketch in CA 19-20R
Meged, Aharon
See Megged, Aharon
Meged, Aron
See Megged, Aharon
Megged, Aharon 1920- ... CANR-1
Earlier sketch in CA 49-52
See also CLC 9
Meggendorfer, Lothar 1847-1925
Brief entry ... 115
See also SATA 36
Meggers, Betty J(ane) 1921- ... 19-20R
Meggitt, M(ervyn) J(ohn) 1924- ... 15-16R
Meggs, Brown (Moore) 1930- ... CANR-7
Earlier sketch in CA 61-64
Meggs, Philip B(axter) 1942- ... 116
Meggyesy, Dave
See Meggyesy, David M.
Meggyesy, David M. 1941- ... 33-36R
Megill, Kenneth Alden 1939- Brief entry ... 106
Meglin, Nick 1935- ... CANR-21
Earlier sketch in CA 69-72
Meglitsch, Paul A(llen) 1914- ... 53-56
Mego, Al
See Roberts, Arthur O.
Megrah, Maurice Henry 1896-1985
Obituary ... 116
Megson, Barbara 1930- ... 29-32R
Mehaffy, Robert E(ugene) 1935- ... 113
Mehan, Joseph Albert 1929- ... 101
Mehdevi, Alexander (Sinclair) 1947- ... 49-52
See also SATA 7
Mehdevi, Anne (Marie) Sinclair 1947- ... 5-6R
See also SATA 8
Mehdi, M(ohammed) T(aki) 1928- ... CANR-8
Earlier sketch in CA 19-20R
Mehegan, John (Francis) 1920(?)-1984 ... 7-8R
Obituary ... 112
Meher Baba
See Baba, Meher
Mehl, Roger 1912- ... CANR-21
Earlier sketches in CA 11-12R, CANR-6
Mehlinger, Howard D(ean) 1931- ... CANR-6
Earlier sketch in CA 11-12R
Mehlmann, Marilyn 1939- ... 119
Mehnert, Klaus 1906-1984 ... CANR-2
Obituary ... 111
Earlier sketch in CA 2R
Mehr, Joseph (John) 1941- Brief entry ... 113
Mehrabian, Albert 1939- ... 33-36R
Mehrens, William A(rthur) 1937- ... 37-40R
Mehring, Walter 1896-1981 Obituary ... 105
Mehrotra, S(ri) Ram 1931- ... CANR-8
Earlier sketch in CA 15-16R
Mehrtens, Susan E(mily) 1945- ... 53-56
Mehta, Gaganvihari L(allubhai) 1900-1974
Obituary ... 49-52
Mehta, J. L. 1912(?)-1988 Obituary ... 126
Mehta, Rustam Jehangir 1912- ... 11-12R
Mehta, Shahnaz ... 106
Mehta, Ved (Parkash) 1934- ... CANR-23
Earlier sketches in CA 3R, CANR-2
See also CLC 37
Mei, Ko-Wang 1918- ... CANR-2
Earlier sketch in CA 45-48
Meiden, Walter 1907- ... CANR-8
Earlier sketch in CA 13-14R
Meier, August 1923- ... CANR-3
Earlier sketch in CA 11-12R
Meier, Gerald M(arvin) 1923- ... 112
Meier, Heinz K(arl) 1929- ... 61-64
Meier, Joel F(rancis) 1940- ... 109
Meier, Matt S(ebastian) 1917- ... CANR-14
Earlier sketch in CA 41-44R
Meier, Richard L(ouis) 1920- ... 19-20R
Meierhenry, Wesley Carl 1915- ... 41-44R
Meiggs, Russell 1902- ... 103
Meighan, Donald Charles 1929- ... CANR-24
Earlier sketch in CA 107
See also SATA 30
Meigs, Alexander James 1921- ... 104
Meigs, Cornelia Lynde 1884-1973 ... 9-10R
Obituary ... 45-48
See also SATA 6
Meigs, Peveril 1903- ... 37-40R
Meigs, Walter B(erkeley) 1912- ... 23-24R
Meij, Jacob L(ouis) 1900- ... 7-8R
Meijer, M(arinus) J(ohan) 1912- ... 69-72
Meikle, Clive
See Brooks, Jeremy
Meikle, Jeffrey L(ee) 1949- ... 101
Meiklejohn, Alexander 1872-1964
Obituary ... 111
Meilach, Dona Z(weigoron) 1926- ... CANR-22
Earlier sketches in CA 11-12R, CANR-5
See also SATA 34
Meilach, Michael D(avid) 1932- ... CANR-2
Earlier sketch in CA 7-8R
Meilaender, Gilbert 1946- ... 109
Meilen, Bill 1932- ... 69-72
Meillassoux, Claude 1925- ... 25-28R
Mein, Margaret ... 61-64
Meine, Curt 1958- ... 126
Meiners, R(oger) K(eith) 1932- ... CANR-3
Earlier sketch in CA 7-8R
Meiners, Roger Evert 1948- ... 110
Meinig, Donald William 1924- ... 112
Meinke, Peter 1932- ... 25-28R
See also DLB 5
Meinkoth, Norman A(ugust) 1913- ... 113
Meintjes, Johannes 1923-1980 ... CANR-8
Earlier sketch in CA 19-20R
Meir, Golda 1898-1978 ... 89-92
Obituary ... 81-84
Meiring, Desmond
See Rice, Desmond Charles
Meiring, Jane (Muriel) 1920- ... CANR-20
Earlier sketch in CA 103
Meisch, Lynn A. 1945- ... 105
Meisch, Richard A(lden) 1943- ... 33-36R
Meisel, Anthony C(lark) 1943- ... 105
Meisel, Gerald Stanley 1937- ... 9-10R
Meisel, John 1923- ... 19-20R
Meisel, Martin 1931- ... CANR-15
Earlier sketch in CA 5-6R
Meisel, Perry 1949- ... 102
Meisel, Tony
See Meisel, Anthony C(lark)
Meiselas, Susan 1948- ... 106
Meiselman, David I(srael) 1924- ... 13-14R
Meisenholder, Robert 1915- ... 37-40R
Meisler, Richard 1940- ... 124
Meisler, Stanley 1931- ... 73-76
Meisner, Maurice 1931- ... 21-22R
Meiss, Millard (Lazare) 1904-1975 ... 61-64
Obituary ... 57-60
Meissner, Hans-Otto 1909- ... CANR-2
Earlier sketch in CA 49-52
Meissner, Kurt 1885-1976 ... CAP-2
Earlier sketch in CA 29-32
Meissner, W(illiam) W. 1931- ... CANR-13
Earlier sketch in CA 33-36R
Meister, Anton D(iderik) 1944- ... 118
Meister, Barbara 1932- ... 102
Meister, Richard J(ulius) 1938- ... 57-60
Meister, Robert 1926- ... CANR-9
Earlier sketch in CA 7-8R
Meixner, John A(lbert) 1925- ... 5-6R
Mejia, Arthur, Jr. 1934- ... 81-84
Mekas, Jonas 1922- Brief entry ... 113
Meketa, Jacqueline
See Meketa, Jacqueline Dorgan
Meketa, Jacqueline Dorgan 1926- ... 125
Melady, John 1938- ... 122
See also SATA 49
Melady, Thomas Patrick 1927- ... CANR-5
Earlier sketch in CA 9-10R
Melahn, Martha 1924- ... 107
Melamid, Alexander 1914- ... 45-48
Melancon, Robert 1947- ... DLB-60
Meland, Bernard Eugene 1899- ... 19-20R
Melanson, Richard A(llen) 1944- ... 113
Melanter
See Blackmore, R(ichard) D(oddridge)
Melaro, Constance L(oraine) 1929- ... 17-18R
Melas, Evi 1930- ... 65-68
Melber, Jehuda 1916- ... 29-32R
Melbin, Murray 1927- ... 45-48
Melbo, Irving Robert 1908- ... 49-52
Melby, Ernest O(scar) 1891-1987
Obituary ... 121
Melby, John Fremont 1913- Brief entry ... 106
Melcher, Daniel 1912-1985 ... 33-36R
Obituary ... 116
See also SATA 43
Melcher, Frederic Gershom 1879-1963
Obituary ... 89-92
See also SATA 22
Melcher, Marguerite Fellows 1879-1969 ... 7-8R
See also SATA 10
Melcher, Robert Augustus 1910- ... 19-20R
Melchert, Norman Paul 1933- ... 25-28R
Melchett, Sonia
See Sinclair, Sonia
Melchinger, Siegfried 1906- ... 81-84
Melchior, Ib (Jorgen) 1917- ... CANR-22
Earlier sketches in CA 45-48, CANR-2
Meldal-Johnsen, Trevor Bernard
1944- ... CANR-19
Earlier sketch in CA 101
Melden, A(braham) I(rving) 1910- ... 19-20R
Melder, Keith E(ugene) 1932- ... 81-84
Mele, Frank Michael 1935- ... 53-56
Mele, Jim 1950- ... 113
Melendy, H(oward) Brett 1924- ... CANR-23
Earlier sketches in CA 19-20R, CANR-8
Meleski, Patricia F(erguson) 1935- ... 61-64
Melezh, Ivan 1921(?)-1976 Obituary ... 69-72
Melfi, Leonard 1935- ... 73-76
Melfi, Mary 1951- ... 113
Melford, Austin (Alfred) 1884-1971
Obituary ... 115
Melhem, D(iana) H(elen) ... CANR-2
Earlier sketch in CA 49-52
Melhorn, Charles M(ason) 1918-1983 ... 57-60
Obituary ... 111
Melhuish, George (William Seymour)
1916-1985 Obituary ... 117
Melick, Arden Davis 1940- ... 106
Melikow, Loris
See Hofmannsthal, Hugo von
Melin, Grace Hathaway 1892-1973 ... CAP-2
Obituary ... 45-48
Earlier sketch in CA 21-22
See also SATA 10
Mell
See Lazarus, Mell
Mell, Donald C(harles), Jr. 1931- ... 115
Mellaart, James 1925- Brief entry ... 118
Mellan, Eleanor 1905- ... 7-8R
Mellan, Ibert 1901- ... 5-6R
Mellanby, Kenneth 1908- ... 85-88
Mellander, Gustavo Adolfo 1935- ... 33-36R
Mellard, James Milton 1938- ... 105
Mellen, Ida M(ay) 1877- ... 7-8R
Mellen, Joan 1941- ... CANR-11
Earlier sketch in CA 65-68
Mellencamp, Virginia Lynn 1917- ... 9-10R
Meller, Norman 1913- ... 25-28R
Mellers, Wilfrid (Howard) 1914- ... CANR-4
Earlier sketch in CA 7-8R
Mellersh, H(arold) E(dward) L(eslie)
1897- ... CANR-9
Earlier sketch in CA 53-56
See also SATA 10
Mellert, Robert B(oros) 1937- ... 61-64
Mellichamp, Josephine 1923- ... 93-96
Mellin, Jeanne 1929- ... CANR-24
Earlier sketch in CA 49-52
Mellini, Peter 1935- ... 93-96
Mellinkoff, David 1914- ... 13-14R
Mellinkoff, Ruth 1924- ... CANR-14
Earlier sketch in CA 37-40R
Mellins, Thomas 1957- ... 122
Mellon, Constance A. 1938- ... 123
Mellon, James R(oss) 1942- ... 69-72
Mellon, John C(raig) 1933- Brief entry ... 107
Mellon, Knox
See Mellon, William Knox, Jr.
Mellon, Matthew T(aylor) 1897- ... 29-32R
Mellon, Stanley 1927- Brief entry ... 108
Mellon, William Knox, Jr. 1925- ... 37-40R
Mellor, Anne Kostelanetz 1941- ... 45-48
Mellor, J(ohn) Leigh 1928- ... 19-20R
Mellor, John W(illiams) 1928- ... 33-36R
Mellor, William Bancroft 1906- ... 61-64
Mellors, John (Parkin) 1920- ... 65-68
Mellors, Samantha
See Lottman, Eileen
Mellow, James R(obert) 1926- ... 105
Mellown, Elgin W(endell, Jr.) 1931- ... 19-20R
Mellows, Joan ... 77-80
Melly, George 1926- ... 81-84
Melman, Seymour 1917- ... CANR-4
Earlier sketch in CA 1R
Melmoth, Sebastian
See Wilde, Oscar (Fingal O'Flahertie
Wills)
Melnick, Donald 1926-1977 Obituary ... 69-72
Melnick, Jack 1929- ... 89-92
Melnyk, Z(inowii) Lew 1928- ... 41-44R
Meloan, Taylor Wells 1919- ... 45-48
Melone, Albert P(hilip) 1942- ... 109
Melone, Joseph J(ames) 1931- ... 13-14R
Meloney, Franken
See Franken, Rose (Dorothy)
Meloney, William Brown 1905-1971
Obituary ... 104
Meloon, Marion 1921- ... 65-68
Melosi, Martin Victor 1947- ... CANR-13
Earlier sketch in CA 77-80
Melrose, Andrea La Sonde
See Anastos, Andrea La Sonde (Melrose)
Melsa, James L(ouis) 1938- ... 104
Melson, Robert 1937- ... 85-88
Melton, David 1934- ... CANR-22
Earlier sketch in CA 69-72
Melton, J(ohn) Gordon 1942- ... 110
Melton, John L. 1920- ... 11-12R
Melton, Julius W(emyss), Jr. 1933- ... 23-24R
Melton, William 1920- ... 37-40R
Meltsner, Arnold J(erry) 1931- ... 57-60
Meltsner, Michael (Charles) 1937-
Brief entry ... 108
Meltzer, Allan H. 1928- ... CANR-18
Earlier sketches in CA 5-6R, CANR-3
Meltzer, Bernard N(athan) 1916- ... 23-24R
Meltzer, David 1937- ... CANR-6
Earlier sketch in CA 9-10R
See also DLB 16
Meltzer, Jack 1921- ... 119
Meltzer, Milton 1915- ... 13-14R
See also SATA 1, 50
See also SAAS 1
See also DLB 61
See also CLC 26
See also CLR 13
Meltzer, Morton F. 1930- ... 23-24R
Meltzer, Peter D. 1951- ... 120
Meltzoff, Julian 1921- ... 23-24R
Meltzoff, Nancy 1952- ... 93-96
Meluch, R(ebecca) M. 1956- ... 109
Melvill, Harald 1895- ... 7-8R
Melville, Alan
See Caverhill, William Melville
Melville, Annabelle McConnell 1910- ... 7-8R
Melville, Anne
See Potter, Margaret (Newman)
Melville, Herman 1819-1891 ... DLB-3, 74
See also CDALB 1640-1865
See also SSC 1
Melville, J. Keith 1921- ... 53-56
Melville, James
See Martin, (Roy) Peter
Melville, Jennie
See Butler, Gwendoline Williams
Melville, Jock Leslie
See Leslie-Melville, John D.
Melville, John D. Leslie
See Leslie-Melville, John D.
Melville, Joy 1932- ... 85-88
Melville, Keith 1945- ... 41-44R
Melvin, A(rthur) Gordon 1894- ... 9-10R
Melvin, Ann (Patricia) Skene
See Skene-Melvin, Ann (Patricia)
Melvin, (Lewis) David (St. Columb) Skene
See Skene-Melvin, (Lewis) David (St.
Columb)
Melvin, Herman 1819-1891 ... DLB-3
Melwani, Murli Das 1939- ... 61-64
Melwood, Mary
See Lewis, E. M.
Melzack, Ronald 1929- ... CANR-15
Earlier sketch in CA 41-44R
See also SATA 5
Melzer, John Henry 1908-1967 ... CAP-1
Earlier sketch in CA 13-14
Melzi, Robert C. 1915- ... 37-40R
Memling, Carl 1918-1969 ... CANR-4
Earlier sketch in CA 4R
See also SATA 6
Memmi, Albert 1920- ... CANR-14
Earlier sketch in CA 81-84
Mena, Janet Gonzalez
See Gonzalez-Mena, Janet
Menacker, Julius 1933- ... 41-44R
Menaker, Daniel 1941- ... 65-68
Menard, H(enry) William 1920-1986 ... 37-40R
Obituary ... 118
Menard, Jean 1930(?)-1977 Obituary ... 69-72
Menard, Orville D. 1933- ... 23-24R
Menard, Russell 1942- ... 126
Menasco, Norman
See Guin, Wyman (Woods)
Menashe, Louis 1935- ... 21-22R
Menashe, Samuel 1925- ... 115
Brief entry ... 111
Mencher, Melvin 1927- ... 73-76
Menchin, Robert S(tanley) 1923- ... CANR-13
Earlier sketch in CA 21-22R
Mencken, H(enry) L(ouis) 1880-1956 ... 125
Brief entry ... 105
See also DLB 11, 29, 63
See also TCLC 13

Menczer, Bela 1902-1983 Obituary ... 110
Mendel, Arthur 1905-1979 ... 41-44R
Obituary ... 89-92
Mendel, Arthur P(aul) 1927-1988 ... 13-14R
Obituary ... 124
Mendel, Douglas H(eusted), Jr. 1921- ... 19-20R
Mendel, Jo
See Bond, Gladys Baker
and Gilbertson, Mildred Geiger
Mendel, Sydney 1925- Brief entry ... 109
Mendel, Werner M(ax) 1927- ... CANR-11
Earlier sketch in CA 21-22R
Mendele mocher seforim
See Abramowitz, Shalom Jacob
Mendell, Clarence W(hittlesey) 1883-1970 ... CAP-1
Earlier sketch in CA 19-20
Mendeloff, Henry 1917-1984 Obituary ... 113
Mendelowitz, Daniel M(arcus) 1905- ... 11-12R
Mendels, Joseph 1937- ... 29-32R
Mendels, Ora 1936- ... 124
Mendelsohn, Allan R(obert) 1928- ... 45-48
Mendelsohn, Everett (Irwin) 1931- ... CANR-11
Earlier sketch in CA 19-20R
Mendelsohn, Felix, Jr. 1906- ... 29-32R
Mendelsohn, Harold 1923- ... 49-52
Mendelsohn, Jack 1918- ... CANR-1
Earlier sketch in CA 4R
Mendelsohn, Martin 1935- ... CANR-13
Earlier sketch in CA 33-36R
Mendelsohn, Michael John 1931- ... 85-88
Mendelsohn, Oscar (Adolf) 1896-1978 . CANR-22
Earlier sketch in CA 9-10R
Mendelsohn, Pamela 1944- ... 101
Mendelsohn, Robert S(aul) 1926-1988
Obituary ... 125
Mendelsohn, Stefan 1930(?)-1987(?)
Obituary ... 122
Mendelson, Edward 1946- ... CANR-11
Earlier sketch in CA 65-68
Mendelson, Lee 1933- ... 33-36R
Mendelson, Mary Adelaide (Jones) 1917- .. 85-88
Mendelson, Morris 1922- ... CANR-2
Earlier sketch in CA 7-8R
Mendelson, Sara Heller 1947- ... 126
Mendelson, Wallace 1911- ... 3R
Mendelssohn, Kurt (Alfred Georg) 1906-1980 ... CANR-7
Obituary ... 105
Earlier sketch in CA 53-56
Mendenhall, George E(mery) 1916- ... 33-36R
Mendenhall, James Edgar 1903-1971
Obituary ... 33-36R
Mendenhall, John D(ale) 1911(?)-1983
Obituary ... 110
Mendenhall, Ruth Dyar 1912- ... 65-68
Mendenhall, Thomas C(orwin II) 1910- ... 115
Mendes-France, Pierre 1907-1982 ... 81-84
Obituary ... 108
Mendez, Charlotte (Walker) 1935- ... 120
Mendl, Robert William Sigismund 1892-1983 Obituary ... 111
Mendlovitz, Saul H. 1925- ... 23-24R
Mendonca, Susan
See Smith, Susan Vernon
See also SATA 45
Mendonsa, Eugene L(ouis) 1942- ... 109
Mendoza, George 1934- ... 73-76
See also SATA 39, 41
Mendoza, Manuel G. 1936- ... 53-56
Mendras, Henri 1927- ... CANR-13
Earlier sketch in CA 73-76
Mendus, Susan 1951- ... 123
Menen, (Salvator) Aubrey (Clarence) 1912- ... CANR-2
Earlier sketch in CA 2R
Menendez, Albert J(ohn) 1942- ... CANR-22
Earlier sketches in CA 53-56, CANR-7
Menendez Pidal, Ramon 1869-1968
Obituary ... 116
Meneses, Enrique 1929- ... CANR-11
Earlier sketch in CA 25-28R
Meng, Heinz (Karl) 1924- ... 69-72
See also SATA 13
Meng, John J(oseph) 1906-1988 Obituary .. 124
Menges, Karl (Heinrich) 1908- ... 37-40R
Menhennet, Alan 1933- ... 97-100
Menikoff, Barry 1939- ... 37-40R
Menkiti, Ifeanyi 1940- ... 65-68
Menkus, Belden 1931- ... 19-20R
Mennel, Robert McKisson 1938-
Brief entry ... 109
Mennell, Stephen (John) 1944- ... 107
Menning, J(ack) H(arwood) 1915- ... 23-24R
Menninger, Edwin A(rnold) 1896- ... 11-12R
Menninger, Karl A. 1893- ... 19-20R
Menninger, W(illiam) Walter 1931- ... 111
Menninger, Walt
See Menninger, W(illiam) Walter
Menninger, William C(laire) 1899-1966
Obituary ... 25-28R
Mennis, Bernard 1938- ... 41-44R
Menolascino, Frenk J(oseph) 1930- ... 73-76
Menon, K(umara) P(admanabha) S(ivasankara) 1898-1982 ... CANR-5
Obituary ... 108
Earlier sketch in CA 7-8R
Menon, R(amakrishna) Rabindranath 1927- ... CANR-11
Earlier sketch in CA 65-68
Menotti, Gian Carlo 1911- ... 104
See also SATA 29
Menshikov, Marina 1928(?)-1979
Obituary ... 93-96
Mensoian, Michael G(eorge), Jr. 1927- ... 85-88
Menton, Seymour 1927- ... 45-48
Mentor
See Lake, Kenneth R(obert)
Mentschikoff, Soia 1915-1984 Obituary ... 113
Mentzer, Michael J(ohn) 1949- ... 118
Menuhin, Hephzibah 1920-1981 Obituary ... 108
Menuhin, Yehudi 1916- ... CANR-2
Earlier sketch in CA 45-48
See also SATA 40
Menut, Albert D. 1894- ... 25-28R
Menville, Douglas 1935- ... 57-60
Menyuk, Paula 1929- ... 37-40R
Menzel, Barbara Jean 1946- ... 114
Menzel, Donald H(oward) 1901-1976 ... CAP-2
Obituary ... 69-72
Earlier sketch in CA 21-22
Menzel, Johanna
See Meskill, Johanna Menzel
Menzel, Paul T(heodore) 1942- ... 53-56
Menzel, Roderich 1907- ... 93-96
Menzies, Edna O(live) 1921- ... 116
Menzies, Elizabeth G(rant) C(ranbrook) 1915- ... 19-20R
Menzies, Robert Gordon 1894-1978 ... 81-84
Obituary ... 77-80
Menzies, William W(atson) 1931-
Brief entry ... 110
Meo, Lucy Dorothy 1920- ... 25-28R
Meras, Phyllis 1931- ... CANR-16
Earlier sketch in CA 41-44R
Merbaum, Michael 1933- ... 65-68
Mercatante, Anthony Stephen 1940- ... 41-44R
Mercer, Blaine (Eugene) 1921- ... CANR-2
Earlier sketch in CA 2R
Mercer, Cecil William 1885-1960 Obituary .. 114
Mercer, Charles (Edward) 1917- ... CANR-2
Earlier sketch in CA 1R
See also SATA 16
Mercer, Colin 1952- ... 117
Mercer, David 1928-1980 ... CANR-23
Obituary ... 102
Earlier sketch in CA 11-12R
See also DLB 13
See also CLC 5
Mercer, James L(ee) 1936- ... 112
Mercer, Jane R. ... 45-48
Mercer, Jean 1941- ... CANR-13
Earlier sketch in CA 33-36R
Mercer, Jessie ... CANR-2
Earlier sketch in CA 2R
Mercer, Joan Bodger 1923- ... 101
Mercer, John 1704-1768 ... DLB-31
Mercer, Johnny 1906-1976 Obituary ... 65-68
Mercer, Marilyn 1923- Brief entry ... 107
Mercer, Paul 1950- ... 111
Mercer, Virginia Fletcher 1916- ... 7-8R
Mercey, Arch Andrew 1906-1980 Obituary .. 102
Merchant, Carolyn 1936- ... 113
Merchant, Jane (Hess) 1919-1972 ... CANR-4
Obituary ... 33-36R
Earlier sketch in CA 3R
Merchant, Larry 1931- ... 102
Merchant, Paul
See Ellison, Harlan
Mercie, Jean-Luc Henri 1939- ... 49-52
Mercier, Jean Doyle 1916- ... 4R
Mercier, Vivian (Herbert Samuel) 1919- ... 81-84
Mercouri, Melina 1925- Brief entry ... 106
Mercury
See Allen, Cecil J(ohn)
Meredith, Anne
See Malleson, Lucy Beatrice
Meredith, Arnold
See Hopkins, (Hector) Kenneth
Meredith, Arnold
See Hopkins, Kenneth
Meredith, Char(lotte) 1921- ... 106
Meredith, Christopher (Laurence) 1954- ... 126
Meredith, David William
See Miers, Earl Schenck
Meredith, Dean
See Dean, Edith M(ae)
Meredith, Don 1938- ... 102
Meredith, George 1828-1909 Brief entry ... 117
See also DLB 18, 35, 57
See also TCLC 17
Meredith, George (Marlor) 1923- ... CANR-4
Earlier sketch in CA 11-12R
Meredith, George Patrick 1904-1978
Obituary ... 108
Meredith, James Howard 1933- ... 77-80
Meredith, Joel L(yman) 1935- ... 116
Meredith, Joseph C(harlton) 1914- ... 53-56
Meredith, Nicolete
See Stack, Nicolete
Meredith, Owen
See Lytton, Edward Robert Bulwer
Meredith, Richard C(arlton) 1937- ... 85-88
Meredith, Robert (King) 1923- ... 5-6R
Meredith, Robert C(hidester) 1921- ... 7-8R
Meredith, Roy 1914(?)-1984 Obituary ... 111
Meredith, Scott 1923- ... CANR-3
Earlier sketch in CA 11-12R
Meredith, William (Morris) 1919- ... CANR-6
Earlier sketch in CA 9-10R
See also DLB 5
See also CLC 4, 13, 22
Merewitz, Leonard (Alan) 1943- ... 69-72
Merezhkovsky, Dmitry Sergeyevich 1865-1941 ... TCLC-29
Merezhkovsky, Zinaida
See Gippius, Zinaida (Nikolayevna)
Mergen, Bernard 1937- ... 112
Merick, Wendell S. 1928(?)-1988
Obituary ... 124
Merideth, Robert 1935- ... 49-52
Merillat, Herbert C(hristian) L(aing) 1915- ... 29-32R
Merin, Peter
See Bihalji-Merin, Oto
Meringoff, Laurene Krasny
See Brown, Laurene Krasny
Meritt, Lucy Shoe 1906- ... 37-40R
Merivale, Patricia 1934- ... 29-32R
Meriwether, James B. 1928- ... 15-16R
Meriwether, Lee 1862-1966 Obituary ... 116
Meriwether, Louise 1923- ... 77-80
See also BW
See also SATA 31, 52
See also DLB 33
Merk, Frederick 1887-1977 ... 41-44R
Obituary ... 73-76
Merkel, Miles Adair 1929- ... 53-56
Merkin, Daphne 1954- ... 123
See also CLC 44
Merkin, Donald H. 1945- ... 69-72
Merkin, Robert (Bruce) 1947- ... 109
Merkl, Peter H(ans) 1932- ... CANR-24
Earlier sketches in CA 7-8R, CANR-7
Merkle, Edgar A. 1900(?)-1984 Obituary ... 113
Merkle, Judith A(stria) 1942- ... 105
Merklinghaus, Michele 1965- ... 116
Merle, Robert (Jean Georges) 1908- ... 93-96
Merleau-Ponty, Maurice 1908-1961 ... 114
Obituary ... 89-92
Merli, Frank J(ohn) 1929- Brief entry ... 113
Merlin, Arthur
See Blish, James (Benjamin)
Merlin, Christina
See Heaven, Constance
Merlin, David
See Moreau, David Merlin
Merlin, Jan 1925- ... 108
Merlin, Mark D(avid) ... 118
Merlin, Samuel 1910- ... 115
Merlis, George 1940- ... 33-36R
Merliss, Reuben 1915- ... 19-20R
Merman, Ethel
See Zimmermann, Ethel Agnes
Mermin, Samuel 1912- ... 53-56
Merne, Oscar James 1943- ... 102
Mernit, Susan 1953- ... 69-72
Meroff, Deborah 1948- ... 89-92
Merrell, James L(ee) 1930- ... 19-20R
Merrell, Jo Ann 1945- ... 113
Merrell, Karen Dixon 1936- ... CANR-6
Earlier sketch in CA 13-14R
Merrell, V(ictor) Dallas 1936- ... 11-12R
Merrens, H(arry) Roy 1931- ... 11-12R
Merrett, Robert James 1944- ... 111
Merriam, Alan P(arkhurst) 1923-1980 ... CANR-1
Earlier sketch in CA 2R
Merriam, Eve 1916- ... 5-6R
See also SATA 3, 40
See also DLB 61
See also CLR 14
Merriam, Harold G(uy) 1883-1981 ... CANR-10
Earlier sketch in CA 61-64
Merriam, Robert E(dward) 1918- ... 7-8R
Merrick, Gordon 1916-1988 ... CANR-11
Obituary ... 125
Earlier sketch in CA 13-14R
Merrick, Hugh
See Meyer, H(arold) A(lbert)
Merrick, William 1916-1969 ... CAP-1
Earlier sketch in CA 11-12
Merril, Judith 1923- ... CANR-15
Earlier sketch in CA 15-16R
Merrill, Antoinette June 1912- ... 45-48
Merrill, Arch 1895(?)-1974 Obituary ... 49-52
Merrill, Boynton, Jr. 1925- ... 69-72
Merrill, David W. 1928- ... 108
Merrill, Dean 1943- ... CANR-8
Earlier sketch in CA 61-64
Merrill, Dick
See Merrill, Henry Tindall
Merrill, Edward C(lifton), Jr. 1920- ... 23-24R
Merrill, Edward H. 1903- ... CAP-1
Earlier sketch in CA 15-16
Merrill, Francis E(llsworth) 1904-1969 ... CAP-1
Earlier sketch in CA 19-20
Merrill, Frederick Thayer 1905-1974
Obituary ... 53-56
Merrill, Harwood F(erry) 1904-1984
Obituary ... 114
Merrill, Henry Tindall 1897-1982 Obituary .. 108
Merrill, James (Ingram) 1926- ... CANR-10
Earlier sketch in CA 13-14R
See also DLB 5
See also DLBY 85
See also CLC 2, 3, 6, 8, 13, 18, 34
Merrill, James M(ercer) 1920- ... 11-12R
Merrill, Jane 1946- ... SATA-42
Merrill, Jean (Fairbanks) 1923- ... CANR-4
Earlier sketch in CA 1R
See also SATA 1
Merrill, John Calhoun 1924- ... CANR-13
Earlier sketch in CA 73-76
Merrill, John N(igel) 1943- ... CANR-22
Earlier sketch in CA 103
Merrill, M. David 1937- ... CANR-16
Earlier sketch in CA 41-44R
Merrill, P. J.
See Roth, Holly
Merrill, Phil
See Filstrup, Jane (Merrill)
Merrill, Robert 1919- ... 81-84
Merrill, Robert 1944- ... 89-92
Merrill, Thomas F. 1932- ... 29-32R
Merrill, Toni
See Merrill, Antoinette June
Merrill, Walter M. 1915- ... CANR-13
Earlier sketch in CA 23-24R
Merrill, Wilfred K. 1903- ... 11-12R
Merrill, William C. 1934- ... 29-32R
Merriman, Alex
See Silverberg, Robert
Merriman, Ann Lloyd 1934- ... 77-80
Merriman, Beth
See Taylor, Demetria
Merriman, Jerry Johnson 1939- ... 25-28R
Merriman, John 1924-1974 Obituary ... 104
Merriman, Pat
See Atkey, Philip
Merrit, Elizabeth
See Goudge, Eileen
Merritt, A.
See Merritt, Abraham (P.)
Merritt, Abraham (P.) 1884-1943
Brief entry ... 120
Merritt, Dixon Lanier 1879-1972
Obituary ... 33-36R
Merritt, Don 1945- ... CANR-22
Earlier sketch in CA 106
Merritt, E. B.
See Waddington, Miriam
Merritt, Helen Henry 1920- ... 19-20R
Merritt, James D. 1934- ... 33-36R
Merritt, LeRoy Charles 1912-1970 ... CAP-2
Earlier sketch in CA 33-36
Merritt, Miriam 1925- ... 19-20R
Merritt, Muriel 1905- ... 69-72
Merritt, Ray E(merson), Jr. 1948- ... 73-76
Merritt, Raymond H(arland) 1936- ... 85-88
Merritt, Richard L(awrence) 1933- ... 41-44R
Merry, Henry J(ohn) 1908- ... 37-40R
Mersand, Joseph 1907- ... CANR-1
Earlier sketch in CA 3R
Mersereau, John, Jr. 1925- ... CANR-2
Earlier sketch in CA 1R
Mersky, Roy M. 1925- ... 37-40R
Mersmann, James Frederick 1938- ... 61-64
Mertens, Lawrence E(dwin) 1929- ... 85-88
Mertens, Thomas R(obert) 1930- ... CANR-6
Earlier sketch in CA 57-60
Mertins, Herman, Jr. 1931- ... 41-44R
Mertins, (Marshall) Louis 1885-1973 ... 41-44R
Merton, Andrew H(arris) 1944- ... 107
Merton, Giles
See Curran, Mona (Elisa)
Merton, Robert K(ing) 1910- ... 41-44R
Merton, Stephen 1912- ... 21-22R
Merton, Thomas 1915-1968 ... CANR-22
Obituary ... 25-28R
Earlier sketch in CA 5-6R
See also DLB 48
See also DLBY 81
See also CLC 1, 3, 11, 34
Mertz, Barbara (Gross) 1927- ... CANR-11
Earlier sketch in CA 21-22R
See also SATA 49
Mertz, Richard R(olland) 1927- ... 23-24R
Merwe, A. v.d.
See Geyl, Pieter (Catharinus Arie)
Merwin, Decie 1894-1961 Obituary ... 111
See also SATA 32
Merwin, W(illiam) S(tanley) 1927- ... CANR-15
Earlier sketch in CA 15-16R
See also DLB 5
See also CLC 1, 2, 3, 5, 8, 13, 18, 45
Mery, Fernand 1897- ... 105
Merz, Charles 1893-1977 Obituary ... 73-76
Merzer, Meridee 1947- ... 102
Mesa-Lago, Carmelo 1934- ... CANR-26
Earlier sketches in CA 25-28R, CANR-10
Meserve, Walter Joseph, Jr. 1923- ... CANR-1
Earlier sketch in CA 2R
Meshack, B(illie) A(ugusta) 1922- ... 93-96
Meshenberg, Michael J(ay) 1942- ... CANR-16
Earlier sketch in CA 93-96
Meske, Eunice Boardman 1926- ... CANR-4
Earlier sketch in CA 11-12R
Meskill, Johanna Menzel 1930- ... 19-20R
Meskill, Robert 1918(?)-1970 Obituary ... 104
Mesquita, Bruce James Bueno de
See Bueno de Mesquita, Bruce James
Messager, Charles 1882-1971 Obituary ... 93-96
Messdeck Annie
See Coade, Jessie
Messegue, Maurice 1921- ... 103
Messel, Harry 1922- ... CANR-21
Earlier sketch in CA 103
Messenger, Charles (Rynd Milles) 1941- ... CANR-13
Earlier sketch in CA 73-76
Messenger, Elizabeth Margery (Esson) 1908- ... CAP-1
Earlier sketch in CA 11-12
Messent, Peter Ronald 1949- ... 106
Messer, Alfred A(mes) 1922- ... 29-32R
Messer, Ronald Keith 1942- ... 57-60
Messer, Sarah Carlin 1924(?)-1984
Obituary ... 112
Messer, Thomas M. 1920- ... 111
Brief entry ... 106
Messerer, Asaf Mikhailovich 1903- ... 104
Messerli, Douglas 1947- ... 116
Messerli, Jonathan C. 1926- ... 41-44R
Messick, Dale 1906- ... SATA-48
Messick, Hank
See Messick, Henry H(icks)
Messick, Henry H(icks) 1922- ... CANR-2
Earlier sketch in CA 45-48
Messieres, Nicole de
See de Messieres, Nicole
Messing, Shep 1949- Brief entry ... 111
Messing, Simon D(avid) 1922- ... 57-60
Messinger, C. F. 1913- ... 21-22R
Messinger, Sheldon L(eopold) 1925- ... 25-28R
Messmer, Otto 1892(?)-1983 Obituary ... 111
See also SATA 37
Messner, Fred(rick) R(ichard) 1926- ... 13-14R

Messner, Gerald 1935- 29-32R
Messner, Johannes 1891-1984 Obituary 112
Messner, Reinhold 1944- CANR-15
Earlier sketch in CA 81-84
Messner, Stephen Dale 1936- 23-24R
Mesta, Perle 1893(?)-1975 Obituary 57-60
Mesthene, Emmanuel George 1920- 77-80
Meston, John 1915(?)-1979 Obituary 85-88
Meszaros, Istvan 1930- CANR-9
Earlier sketch in CA 57-60
Meta
See Tomkiewicz, Mina
Metalious, Grace (de Repentigny)
1924-1964 .... CAP-2
Earlier sketch in CA 21-22
Metaxas, B(asil) N(icolas) 1925- 37-40R
Metcalf, E(ugene) W(esley) 1945- 65-68
Metcalf, George R. 1914- 25-28R
Metcalf, John 1938- 113
See also DLB 60
See also CLC 37
Metcalf, Kenneth N(olan) 1923-1965 ....5-6R
Metcalf, Keyes DeWitt 1889-1983 ....19-20R
Obituary 111
Metcalf, Lawrence E(ugene) 1915- 21-22R
Metcalf, Paul 1917- CANR-17
Earlier sketches in CA 45-48, CANR-1
Metcalf, Peter 116
Metcalf, Suzanne
See Baum, L(yman) Frank
Metcalf, Thomas R. 1934- 15-16R
Metcalf, Vicky 1901- 89-92
Metcalfe, John Wallace 1901-1982
Obituary 107
Metcalfe, Steve 1953- 108
Metereau, Rebecca Bell
See Bell-Metereau, Rebecca
Metesky, George
See Hoffman, Abbie
Methold, Kenneth (Walter) 1931- 13-14R
Methvin, Eugene H. 1934- 29-32R
Metos, Thomas H(arry) 1932- 93-96
See also SATA 37
Metraux, Guy S(erge) 1917- 9-10R
Metraux, Rhoda 1914- 57-60
Metress, James F(rancis)
See Metress, Seamus P.
Metress, Seamus P. 1933- CANR-21
Earlier sketches in CA 57-60, CANR-6
Metropolis, Nicholas Constantine 1915- 110
Mets, David Raymond 1928- 118
Mettler, George B(arry) 1934- 93-96
Metwally, M(okhtar) M(ohamed)
1939- CANR-15
Earlier sketch in CA 65-68
Metz, Donald L(ehman) 1935- 21-22R
Metz, Donald S(hink) 1916- 45-48
Metz, Jerred 1943- CANR-22
Earlier sketch in CA 104
Metz, Leon C(laire) 1930- CANR-16
Earlier sketches in CA 45-48, CANR-1
Metz, Lois Lunt 1906- CAP-1
Earlier sketch in CA 9-10
Metz, Mary (Seawell) 1937- 53-56
Metz, Mary Haywood 1939- CANR-15
Earlier sketch in CA 85-88
Metz, Robert (Henry) 1928- CANR-13
Earlier sketch in CA 61-64
Metz, William 1918- 77-80
Metzdorf, Robert F(rederic) 1912-1975
Obituary 57-60
Metzger, Barbara 1944- 110
Metzger, Bruce Manning 1914- CANR-4
Earlier sketch in CA 9-10R
Metzger, Charles R(eid) 1921- 25-28R
Metzger, Erika A(lma) 1933- 33-36R
Metzger, H(owell) Peter 1931- Brief entry ... 107
Metzger, Michael M(oses) 1935- 21-22R
Metzger, Norman 1924- CANR-9
Earlier sketch in CA 53-56
Metzger, Philip W. 1931- 45-48
Metzger, Robert 1950- 117
Metzger, Stanley D. 1916- 9-10R
Metzger, Thomas A(lbert) 1933- 97-100
Metzger, Walter P. 1922- CANR-17
Earlier sketch in CA 61-64
Metzker, Isaac 1901- 45-48
Metzler, Ken(neth Theodore) 1929- CANR-4
Earlier sketch in CA 53-56
Metzler, Lloyd A(ppleton) 1913- 104
Metzler, Paul 1914- CANR-6
Earlier sketch in CA 57-60
Metzner, Ralph 1936- 69-72
Metzner, Seymour 1924- 23-24R
Meudt, Edna Kritz 1906- CANR-9
Earlier sketch in CA 15-16R
Meurice, Blanca
See von Block, Bela W(illiam)
Meux, Milton O(tto) 1930- 45-48
Meves, Christa 1925- CANR-24
Earlier sketch in CA 93-96
Mew, Charlotte (Mary) 1870-1928
Brief entry 105
See also DLB 19
See also TCLC 8
Mewburn, Martin
See Hitchin, Martin Mewburn
Mewhinney, Bruce 1949- 118
Mews, Hazel 1909-1975 .... CAP-2
Earlier sketch in CA 29-32
Mews, Siegfried 1933- CANR-22
Earlier sketches in CA 57-60, CANR-7
Mewshaw, Michael 1943- CANR-7
Earlier sketch in CA 53-56
See also DLBY 80
See also CLC 9
Mey, Jacob Lovis
See Meij, Jacob Lovis
Meyen, Edward L. 1937- 33-36R
Meyendorff, John 1926- CANR-9
Earlier sketch in CA 21-22R
Meyer, Agnes E(lizabeth Ernst) 1887-1970
Obituary 29-32R
Meyer, Albert Julius 1919-1983 Obituary ... 111
Meyer, Alfred (Herman) 1893- CAP-1
Earlier sketch in CA 13-14
Meyer, Alfred George 1920- 19-20R
Meyer, Armin Henry 1914- 85-88
Meyer, Ben F. 1927- CANR-14
Earlier sketch in CA 37-40R
Meyer, Bernard C. 1910- 73-76
Meyer, Bernard F. 1891(?)-1975
Obituary 57-60
Meyer, Carl S(tamm) 1907-1972 .... CAP-1
Earlier sketch in CA 15-16
Meyer, Carol H. 1924- CANR-13
Earlier sketch in CA 73-76
Meyer, Carolyn 1935- CANR-2
Earlier sketch in CA 49-52
See also SATA 9
Meyer, Charles R. 1920- 33-36R
Meyer, Charles R(obert) 1926- 69-72
Meyer, Clarence 1903- 97-100
Meyer, D. Swing 1938- 19-20R
Meyer, David R. 1943- 65-68
Meyer, Donald (Burton) 1923- 23-24R
Meyer, Donald H(arvey) 1935- Brief entry ... 113
Meyer, Doris 1942- 89-92
Meyer, Duane Gilbert 1926- 5-6R
Meyer, E. Y. 1946- DLB-75
Meyer, Edith Patterson 1895- CANR-1
Earlier sketch in CA 2R
See also SATA 5
Meyer, Elizabeth C(ooper) 1958- 69-72
Meyer, Ellen Hope 1928- 119
Meyer, Erika 1904- 73-76
Meyer, Eugene 1875-1959 .... DLB-29
Meyer, F(ranklyn) E(dward) 1932- 4R
See also SATA 9
Meyer, Frank S(traus) 1909-1972 .... CAP-1
Obituary 33-36R
Earlier sketch in CA 9-10
Meyer, Fred(erick Robert) 1922-1985 57-60
Obituary 117
Meyer, George H(erbert) 1928- 116
Meyer, Gladys (Eleanor) 1908-1986
Obituary 118
Meyer, H(arold) A(lbert) 1898-1980 ..... CANR-4
Obituary 102
Earlier sketch in CA 7-8R
Meyer, H. K. Houston
See Meyer, Heinrich
Meyer, Harold D(iedrich) 1892-1974(?) ... CAP-2
Earlier sketch in CA 19-20
Meyer, Harold G. 1909(?)-1986 Obituary ... 118
Meyer, Heinrich 1904-1977 49-52
Obituary 85-88
Meyer, Herbert W(alter) 1892- CAP-2
Earlier sketch in CA 33-36
Meyer, Herman 1911- 23-24R
Meyer, Howard N(icholas) 1914- 13-14R
Meyer, Jean Shepherd SATA-11
Meyer, Jerome Sydney 1895-1975 ...... CANR-4
Obituary 57-60
Earlier sketch in CA 2R
See also SATA 3, 25
Meyer, Joachim-Ernst 1917- 57-60
Meyer, John Robert 1927- CANR-9
Earlier sketch in CA 13-14R
Meyer, June
See Jordan, June
Meyer, Karl E(rnest) 1928- CANR-1
Earlier sketch in CA 3R
Meyer, Kathleen Allan 1918- 123
See also SATA 46, 51
Meyer, Lawrence R(obert) 1941- 73-76
Meyer, Leonard B. 1918- 13-14R
Meyer, Lillian Nicholson 1917(?)-1983
Obituary 109
Meyer, Linda D(oreen) 1948- CANR-16
Earlier sketch in CA 93-96
Meyer, Louis A(lbert) 1942- 37-40R
See also SATA 12
Meyer, Mabel H. 1890(?)-1976 Obituary ..61-64
Meyer, Marie-Louise 1936- 97-100
Meyer, Mary Keysor 1919- 102
Meyer, Michael (Leverson) 1921- CANR-13
Earlier sketch in CA 25-28R
Meyer, Michael A. 1937- 21-22R
Meyer, Michael C. 1935- CANR-10
Earlier sketch in CA 21-22R
Meyer, Nicholas 1945- CANR-7
Earlier sketch in CA 49-52
Meyer, Philip (Edward) 1930- CANR-10
Earlier sketch in CA 65-68
Meyer, Renate 1930- 53-56
See also SATA 6
Meyer, Robert H. 1934- 37-40R
Meyer, Roy W(illard) 1925- 19-20R
Meyer, Ruth F(ritz) 1910- CAP-2
Earlier sketch in CA 23-24
Meyer, Stewart (Martin) 1947- 118
Meyer, Susan E. 1940- CANR-19
Earlier sketches in CA 45-48, CANR-2
Meyer, Thomas 1947- CANR-1
Earlier sketch in CA 49-52
Meyer, William Eugene 1923- 45-48
Meyer, William R(obert) 1949- 77-80
Meyerhoff, Arthur E(dward) 1895-1986
Obituary 120
Meyerhoff, Howard A(ugustus) 1899- CAP-2
Earlier sketch in CA 19-20
Meyering, Ralph A. 1930- 29-32R
Meyer-Meyrink, Gustav 1868-1932
Brief entry 117
Meyerowitz, Eva (Leonie) L(ewin-)
R(ichter) 11-12R
Meyerowitz, Patricia 1933- 23-24R
Meyers, Albert L. 1904(?)-1981 Obituary ... 102
Meyers, Bert(ram) 1928-1979 101
Meyers, Carlton R(oy) 1922- 57-60
Meyers, Carol L(yons) 1942- 113
Meyers, Carole Terwilliger 1945- 69-72
Meyers, Cecil H(arold) 1920- 29-32R
Meyers, David W. 1942- 29-32R
Meyers, Edward 1934- 101
Meyers, Eric M(ark) 1940- 110
Meyers, Gertrude Barlow 1902- 3R
Meyers, Jeffrey 1939- 73-76
See also CLC 39
Meyers, Joan Simpson 1927- CANR-14
Earlier sketch in CA 19-20R
Meyers, Lawrence Stanley 1943- 57-60
Meyers, Marvin 1921- Brief entry 108
Meyers, Mary Ann 1937- 116
Meyers, Michael Jay 1946- 65-68
Meyers, Robert Rex 1923- 19-20R
Meyers, Roy (Lethbridge) 1910-1974 .... CAP-2
Earlier sketch in CA 25-28
Meyers, Ruth S(chlaff) 1923- 117
Meyers, Susan 1942- CANR-13
Earlier sketch in CA 21-22R
See also SATA 19
Meyers, Susan
See Falk, Susan Meyers
Meyers, Walter E(arl) 1939- CANR-6
Earlier sketch in CA 53-56
Meyerson, Edward L(eon) 1904-1980 .. CANR-12
Earlier sketch in CA 61-64
Meyerson, Martin 1922- Brief entry 115
Meynell, Alice (Christina Gertrude
Thompson) 1847-1922 Brief entry 104
See also DLB 19
See also TCLC 6
Meynell, Francis Meredith Wilfrid
1891-1975 .... CAP-2
Obituary 57-60
Earlier sketch in CA 19-20
Meynell, Laurence Walter 1899- CANR-15
Earlier sketch in CA 81-84
Meyners, J. Robert 1922- 104
Meynier, Yvonne (Pollet) 1908- 73-76
See also SATA 14
Meyrink, Gustav
See Meyer-Meyrink, Gustav
See also TCLC 21
Meyrink, Gustav Meyer
See Meyer-Meyrink, Gustav
Meza, Pedro Thomas 1941- 37-40R
Mezerick, Avrahm G. 1901-1986 Obituary .. 119
Mezey, Michael L(loyd) 1943- 118
Mezey, Robert 1935- CANR-7
Earlier sketch in CA 57-60
See also SATA 33
Mezvinsky, Edward M. 1937- 103
Mezvinsky, Shirley
See Lauro, Shirley (Shapiro) Mezvinsky
Mezzrow, Mezz
See Mezzrow, Milton
Mezzrow, Milton 1890(?)-1972 ....37-40R
Miall, Robert
See Burke, John (Frederick)
Mian, Mary (Lawrence Shipman)
1902- SATA-47
Micale, Albert 1913- SATA-22
Micallef, Benjamin A(nthony) 1925-1980 ...53-56
Obituary 103
Micallef, John 1923- 25-28R
Micaud, Charles Antoine 1910- 5-6R
Miceli, Frank 1932- 57-60
Miceli, Vincent P(eter) 1915- Brief entry 114
Michael, David J. 1944- 29-32R
Michael, Franz H(enry) 1907- CANR-4
Earlier sketch in CA 7-8R
Michael, George 1919- 41-44R
Michael, Henry N(athaniel) 1913- 33-36R
Michael, Ian (Lockie) 1915- 104
Michael, James
See Scagnetti, Jack
Michael, Manfred
See Winterfeld, Henry
Michael, Paul Martin 1934- CANR-10
Earlier sketch in CA 19-20R
Michael, Phyllis C(allender) 1908- CANR-2
Earlier sketch in CA 7-8R
Michael, S(tanley) T(heodore) 1912- 13-14R
Michael, Thomas A. 1933- 33-36R
Michael, Tom
See Michael, Thomas A.
Michael, William B(urton) 1922- 45-48
Michael, Wolfgang F(riedrich) 1909- ... CANR-14
Earlier sketch in CA 41-44R
Michaeles, M. M.
See Golding, Morton J(ay)
Michaelides, Constantine E. 1930- 25-28R
Michaelis, David (Tead) 1957- 114
Michaelis, John U(dell) 1912- 69-72
Michaelis-Jena, Ruth
See Ratcliff, Ruth
Michaels, Barbara
See Mertz, Barbara (Gross)
Michaels, Carolyn Leopold
See Leopold, Carolyn Clugston
Michaels, Dale
See Rifkin, Shepard
Michaels, Fern
See Anderson, Roberta
and Kuczkir, Mary
Michaels, J. Ramsey 1931- 116
Michaels, Joanne 1950- CANR-23
Earlier sketch in CA 107
Michaels, Joanne Louise
See Teitelbaum, Michael
Michaels, Joe
See Saltzman, Joseph
Michaels, Kasey
See Seidick, Kathryn A(melia)
Michaels, Kristin
See Williams, Jeanne
Michaels, Leonard 1933- CANR-21
Earlier sketch in CA 61-64
See also CLC 6, 25
Michaels, Lynn
See Strongin, Lynn
Michaels, Neal
See Teitelbaum, Michael
Michaels, Norman 97-100
Michaels, Philip
See van Rjndt, Philippe
Michaels, Ralph
See Filicchia, Ralph
Michaels, Sidney R(amon) 1927- 19-20R
Michaels, Ski
See Pellowski, Michael (Joseph)
Michaels, Steve
See Avallone, Michael (Angelo), Jr.
Michaelson, L(ouis) W. 1917- CANR-14
Earlier sketch in CA 77-80
Michaely, Michael 1928- 103
Michalczyk, John Joseph 1941- 104
Michalopoulos, Andre 1897- CAP-2
Earlier sketch in CA 23-24
Michalos, Alex C. 1935- 37-40R
Michalowski, Kazimierz 1901-1981
Obituary 108
Michalski, John 1934- 25-28R
Michalson, Carl (Donald, Jr.) 1915-1965 .... 4R
Michaud, Charles Regis 1910- CAP-2
Earlier sketch in CA 19-20
Michaud, Stephen G(age) 1948- 109
Michaux, Henri 1899-1984 85-88
Obituary 114
See also CLC 8, 19
Michaux, William W(hitehead) 1919- 41-44R
Miche, Giuseppe
See Bochenski, Joseph M.
Micheaux, Oscar 1884-1951 .... DLB-50
Michel, Anna 1943- 85-88
See also SATA 40, 49
Michel, Beth
See Dubus, Elizabeth Nell
Michel, Georges 1926- 25-28R
Michel, Henri (Jules) 1907- CANR-19
Earlier sketches in CA 53-56, CANR-4
Michel, Joseph 1922- CANR-13
Earlier sketch in CA 25-28R
Michel, Michel Georges
See Georges-Michel, Michel
Michel, Pierre 1934- 57-60
Michel, Sandra (Seaton) 1935- 77-80
Michel, Sandy
See Michel, Sandra (Seaton)
Michel, (Milton) Scott 1916- 4R
Michel, Walter 1922- 81-84
Micheli, Lyle Joseph 1940- CANR-20
Earlier sketch in CA 97-100
Micheline, Jack 1929- 122
Brief entry 114
See also DLB 16
Michell, John (F.) 1933- CANR-23
Earlier sketch in CA 107
Michelman, Herbert 1913-1980 Obituary ... 102
Michelman, Irving S(imon) 1917- 69-72
Michelmore, Peter 1930- CANR-7
Earlier sketch in CA 5-6R
Michelon, L. C. 1918- CANR-1
Earlier sketch in CA 45-48
Michels, Caroll Chesy 1943- 117
Michelson, Edward J(ulias) 1915- 77-80
Michelson, Florence B. CAP-2
Earlier sketch in CA 21-22
Michelson, Peter 1937- CANR-1
Earlier sketch in CA 45-48
Michelson, Stephan 1938- 93-96
Michelson, William M. 1940- 33-36R
Michener, Charles D(uncan) 1918- 117
Michener, Charles Thomson 1940- 104
Michener, James A(lbert) 1907(?)- CANR-21
Earlier sketch in CA 5-6R
See also DLB 6
See also CLC 1, 5, 11, 29
See also AITN 1
Michie, Allan (Andrew) 1915-1973
Obituary 45-48
Michie, Donald 1923- 121
Michie, James 1927- Brief entry 116
Michman, Ronald D(avid) 1931- CANR-7
Earlier sketch in CA 57-60
Mickel, Emanuel John, Jr. 1937- 37-40R
Mickelsen, A(nton) Berkeley 1920- 9-10R
Mickelsen, Olaf 1912- 19-20R
Mickelson, Sig 1913- 111
Micken, Charles M. 1918- 13-14R
Mickey, Paul A(lbert) 1937- CANR-1
Earlier sketch in CA 49-52
Mickiewicz, Ellen Propper 1938- CANR-24
Earlier sketches in CA 23-24R, CANR-9
Micklejohn, George 1717(?)-1818 ...... DLB-31
Micklem, Nathaniel 1888-1976 103
Micklish, Rita 1931- 49-52
See also SATA 12
Mickolus, Edward F(rancis) 1950- 106
Micks, Marianne H(offman) 1923- CANR-12
Earlier sketch in CA 19-20R
Micunovic, Veljko 1916-1982 109
Obituary 107

Middeldorf, Ulrich Alexander 1901-1983
Obituary 109
Middendorf, John Harlan 1922- 104
Middlebrook, David
See Rosenus, Alan (Harvey)
Middlebrook, Diane Wood 1939- CANR-15
Earlier sketch in CA 81-84
Middlebrook, Jonathan 1940- 65-68
Middlebrook, (Norman) Martin 1932- .. CANR-14
Earlier sketch in CA 37-40R
Middlekauff, Robert (Lawrence) 1929-
Brief entry 112
Middleman, Ruth J. Rosenbloom 1923- 104
Middlemas, Keith
See Middlemas, Robert Keith
Middlemas, Robert Keith 1935- CANR-12
Earlier sketch in CA 29-32R
Middlemiss, Robert (William) 1938- ... CANR-12
Earlier sketch in CA 73-76
Middleton, Bernard C(hester) 1924- 41-44R
Middleton, Christopher 1926- 15-16R
See also DLB 40
See also CLC 13
Middleton, David L. 1940- 37-40R
Middleton, Drew 1914(?)- Brief entry 110
Middleton, George 1880-1967 Obituary .. 25-28R
Middleton, Michael (Humfrey) 1917- 124
Middleton, Nigel (Gordon) 1918- CANR-25
Earlier sketch in CA 45-48
Middleton, O(sman) E(dward) 1925- 81-84
Middleton, Richard 1945- 109
Middleton, Roger 1955- 126
Middleton, Stanley 1919- CANR-21
Earlier sketch in CA 25-28R
See also DLB 14
See also CLC 7, 38
Middleton, Thomas 1580-1627 .... DLB-58
Middleton-Murry, Colin
See Middleton-Murry, John (Jr.)
Middleton-Murry, John (Jr.) 1926- CANR-3
Earlier sketch in CA 7-8R
Middleton Murry, Mary
See Murry, Mary Middleton
Midelfort, H(ans) C(hristian) Erik
1942- CANR-26
Earlier sketch in CA 45-48
Midgett, Elwin W. 1911- CAP-2
Earlier sketch in CA 29-32
Midgett, Wink
See Midgett, Elwin W.
Midgley, David A(lan) 1898- 19-20R
Midgley, E(rnest) B(rian) F(rancis) 1927- .. 93-96
Midgley, Graham 1923- 73-76
Midgley, Louis C(asper) 1931- 41-44R
Midgley, Mary 1919- CANR-20
Earlier sketch in CA 89-92
Midlarsky, Manus I(ssacher) 1937- 57-60
Midler, Bette 1945- 106
Midtlyng, Joanna 1927- 61-64
Midwinter, E(ric) C(lare) 1932- CANR-26
Earlier sketch in CA 29-32R
Mieczkowski, Bogdan 1924- 111
Miegel, Agnes 1879-1964 .... DLB-56
Miel, Alice Marie 1906- CANR-20
Earlier sketches in CA 3R, CANR-5
Mielke, Arthur W(illard) 1912-1978 ..... CANR-4
Earlier sketch in CA 2R
Mielziner, Jo 1901-1976 45-48
Obituary 65-68
Miernyk, William Henry 1918- 19-20R
Miers, Earl Schenck 1910-1972 .... CANR-2
Obituary 37-40R
Earlier sketch in CA 3R
See also SATA 1, 26
Miers, Suzanne (Doyle) 1922- 61-64
Mierzenski, Stanislaw 1903-1964 .... 2R
Miethe, Terry Lee 1948- 105
Miewald, Robert D(ale) 1938- 117
Migdal, Joel S(amuel) 1945- CANR-6
Earlier sketch in CA 57-60
Migdalski, Edward C(harles) 1918- CANR-4
Earlier sketch in CA 9-10R
Migliore, R. Henry 1940- 110
Migliorini, Bruno 1896-1975 Obituary 116
Miglis, John 1950- CANR-20
Earlier sketch in CA 81-84
Mignani, Rigo 1921- 37-40R
Migueis, Jose Rodrigues 1901- CLC-10
Miguez-Bonino, Jose 1924- 49-52
Mihailovich, Vasa D. 1926- CANR-14
Earlier sketch in CA 41-44R
Mihajlov, Mihajlo 1934- Brief entry 105
Mihalas, Dimitri M(anuel) 1939- CANR-4
Earlier sketch in CA 53-56
Mihaly, Mary E(llen) 1950- 97-100
Mihanovich, Clement Simon 1913- 7-8R
Mikan, Baron
See Barba, Harry
Mikdashi, Zuhayr 1933- CANR-17
Earlier sketch in CA 89-92
Mikes, George 1912-1987 .... CANR-6
Obituary 123
Earlier sketch in CA 11-12R
Mikesell, Arthur M. 1932- 13-14R
Mikesell, John L(ee) 1942- 102
Mikesell, Marvin Wray 1930- CANR-4
Earlier sketch in CA 3R
Mikesell, Raymond F(rech) 1913- CANR-19
Earlier sketches in CA 4R, CANR-4
Mikesell, Rufus Merrill 1893-1972 .... CAP-2
Earlier sketch in CA 25-28
Mikesell, William H(enry) 1887-1969 ..... CAP-2
Earlier sketch in CA 19-20
Mikhail, E(dward) H(alim) 1928- CANR-14
Earlier sketch in CA 37-40R
Mikhalkov, Sergei Vladimirovich 1913-
Brief entry 116
Miki, Chihan
See Naruse, Mikio
Mikkelsen, Ejnar 1881(?)-1971 Obituary .. 29-32R
Miklowitz, Gloria D. 1927- CANR-26
Earlier sketches in CA 25-28R, CANR-10
See also SATA 4
Mikolaycak, Charles 1937- CANR-23
Earlier sketches in CA 61-64, CANR-8
See also SATA 9
See also SAAS 4
Mikulas, William Lee 1942- 53-56
Mikus, Joseph A(ugust) 1909- 61-64
Milano, Paolo 1904-1988 Obituary 125
Milberg, Warren H(oward) 1941- 109
Milbrath, Lester W(alter) 1925- CANR-4
Earlier sketch in CA 11-12R
Milburn, George 1906-1966 Obituary 109
Milburn, Josephine F(ishel) 1928- CANR-13
Earlier sketch in CA 21-22R
Milburn, Joyce 1953- 114
Milch, Robert J(effrey) 1938- 25-28R
Milcsik, Margie 1950- 110
Mild, Warren (Paul) 1922- CANR-8
Earlier sketch in CA 23-24R
See also SATA 41
Mildo, Albert 1945- CANR-21
Earlier sketch in CA 73-76
Mileck, Joseph 1922- 107
Milenkovitch, Michael M. 1932- 37-40R
Miles, Angela R(ose) 1946- 122
Miles, (Louise) Bebe 1924-1980 .... CANR-9
Earlier sketch in CA 61-64
Miles, Betty 1928- CANR-20
Earlier sketches in CA 3R, CANR-5
See also SATA 8
Miles, Beverly Parkhurst 1940- 107
Miles, Charles 1894- 5-6R
Miles, David H(olmes) 1940- 57-60
Miles, Dorien K(lein) 1915- CANR-8
Earlier sketch in CA 61-64
Miles, Edwin A(rthur) 1926- 1R
Miles, Elliot
See Ludvigsen, Karl (Eric)
Miles, Elton (Roger) 1917- 37-40R
Miles, Gary Britten 1940- 102
Miles, George C(arpenter) 1904-1975
Obituary 61-64
Miles, Herbert J(ackson) 1907- 23-24R
Miles, Ian (Douglas) 1948- 115
Miles, John
See Bickham, Jack M(iles)
Miles, Josephine 1911-1985 .... CANR-2
Obituary 116
Earlier sketch in CA 3R
See also DLB 48
See also CLC 1, 2, 14, 34, 39
Miles, Joyce C(rudgington) 1927- 105
Miles, Judith Mary (Huhta) 1937- 65-68
Miles, Keith
See Tralins, S(andor) Robert
Miles, Leland, (Weber, Jr.) 1924- 15-16R
Miles, Margaret R(uth) 1937- 117
Miles, Mary Lillian (Brown) 1908- 15-16R
Miles, Matthew B(ailey) 1926- CANR-15
Earlier sketch in CA 81-84
Miles, Michael W. 1945- 33-36R
Miles, Miska
See Martin, Patricia Miles
Miles, O. Thomas 1923- 21-22R
Miles, (Mary) Patricia 1930- CANR-11
Earlier sketch in CA 69-72
See also SATA 29
Miles, Peter
See Miles, Richard
Miles, Richard 1938- 105
Miles, Robert H. 1944- 118
Miles, Robert L(ee) 1939- 107
Miles, Russell Hancock 1895- CAP-1
Earlier sketch in CA 9-10
Miles, Stanley 1911-1987 Obituary 123
Miles, Sylva
See Miles, Dorien K(lein)
and Mularchyk, Sylva
Miles, T(homas) R(ichard) 1923- CANR-17
Earlier sketches in CA 49-52, CANR-1
Milestone, Lewis 1895-1980 Obituary 101
Miletus, Rex
See Burgess, M(ichael) R(oy)
Milford, D(avid) S(umner) 1905-1984
Obituary 113
Milford, Nancy 1938- 29-32R
Milgate, Rodney Armour 1934- 107
Milgram, Gail Gleason 1942- 29-32R
Milgram, Morris 1916- 73-76
Milgram, Stanley 1933-1984 105
Obituary 114
Milgrom, Harry 1912- CANR-3
Earlier sketch in CA 4R
See also SATA 25
Milgrom, Jacob 1923- 53-56
Milhaud, Darius 1892-1974 Obituary 49-52
Milhaven, John Giles 1927- 29-32R
Milhous, Katherine 1894-1977 Obituary 104
See also SATA 15
Milhouse, Paul W(illiam) 1910- CANR-11
Earlier sketch in CA 25-28R
Mili, Gjon 1904-1984 Obituary 112
Milic, Louis T(onko) 1922- 23-24R
Milio, Nancy 1938- CANR-13
Earlier sketch in CA 29-32R
Militant
See Sandburg, Carl (August)
Militello, Pietro
See Natali, Alfred Maxim
Milius, John 1945- 101
See also DLB 44
Milkomane, George Alexis Milkomanovich
1903- CANR-20
Earlier sketch in CA 104
Milks, Harold Keith 1908-1979 108
Obituary 93-96
Mill, C. R.
See Crnjanski, Milos
Mill, John Stuart 1806-1873 .... DLB-55
Milland, Jack
See Milland, Ray
Milland, Ray 1908(?)-1986 Obituary 118
Brief entry 113
Millar, Barbara F. 1924- 25-28R
See also SATA 12
Millar, Fergus 1935- CANR-20
Earlier sketches in CA 13-14R, CANR-5
Millar, George Reid 1910- 73-76
Millar, Gilbert John 1939- 104
Millar, J(ohn) Halket 1899- 11-12R
Millar, James Primrose Malcolm 1893- ... CAP-1
Earlier sketch in CA 9-10
Millar, James R(obert) 1936- 29-32R
Millar, Jeff(ery Lynn) 1942- CANR-11
Earlier sketch in CA 69-72
Millar, (Minna Henrietta) Joy 1914- 93-96
Millar, Kenneth 1915-1983 .... CANR-16
Obituary 110
Earlier sketch in CA 9-10R
See also DLB 2
See also DLBY 83
See also CLC 14
Millar, Margaret (Ellis Sturm) 1915- ... CANR-16
Earlier sketch in CA 13-14R
Millar, Ronald (Graeme) 1919- 73-76
Millar, T(homas) B(ruce) CANR-26
Earlier sketch in CA 29-32R
Millard, A(lan) R(alph) 1937- CANR-11
Earlier sketch in CA 25-28R
Millard, Charles W(arren III) 1932-
Brief entry 115
Millard, Gregory B. 1947(?)-1984
Obituary 114
Millard, Joe
See Millard, Joseph (John)
Millard, Joseph (John) 1908- 15-16R
Millay, Edna St. Vincent 1892-1950
Brief entry 104
See also DLB 45
See also TCLC 4
Millbank, Captain H. R.
See Ellis, Edward S(ylvester)
Millburn, Cynthia
See Brooks, Anne Tedlock
Milldyke, (John) William 1937-1983 77-80
Obituary 111
Millen, Clifford H. 1901(?)-1972 Obituary ... 104
Millender, Dharathula H(ood) 1920- 19-20R
Miller, Abraham H(irsh) 1940- 104
Miller, Al 1936- 65-68
Miller, Alan Robert 1929- 73-76
Miller, Alan W. 1926- 29-32R
Miller, Albert G(riffith) 1905-1982 ...... CANR-1
Obituary 107
Earlier sketch in CA 3R
See also SATA 12, 31
Miller, Albert Jay 1928- CANR-1
Earlier sketch in CA 45-48
Miller, Alden D(ykstra) 1940(?)-1984
Obituary 113
Miller, Alden Holmes 1906-1965 Obituary .. 109
Miller, Alfred W. 1893(?)-1983 Obituary 111
Miller, Alice P(atricia McCarthy) CANR-26
Earlier sketch in CA 29-32R
See also SATA 22
Miller, Anita 1926- 111
Miller, Ann
See Collier, Lucille Ann
Miller, Arthur 1915- CANR-2
Earlier sketch in CA 2R
See also DLB 7
See also CDALB 1941-1968
See also CLC 1, 2, 6, 10, 15, 26, 47
See also AITN 1
Miller, Arthur B(urton) 1922- 37-40R
Miller, Arthur R(aphael) 1934- Brief entry ... 114
Miller, Arthur S(elwyn) 1917-1988 ..... CANR-11
Obituary 125
Earlier sketch in CA 69-72
Miller, Barbara D(iane) 1948- CANR-23
Earlier sketch in CA 106
Miller, Barbara S(toler) 1940- CANR-11
Earlier sketch in CA 25-28R
Miller, Barry 1946- 33-36R
Miller, Benj.
See Loomis, Noel M(iller)
Miller, Benjamin F(rank) 1907-1971 ..... CANR-4
Obituary 29-32R
Earlier sketch in CA 3R
Miller, Bernard S. 1920- 106
Miller, Beulah Montgomery 1917- 61-64
Miller, (H.) Bill(y) 1920-1961 108
Miller, Bill D. 1936- 102
Miller, Brent C(arlton) 1947- 112
Miller, (Harvey) Brown 1943- 101
Miller, Byron Strongman 1912(?)-1978
Obituary 77-80
Miller, C(larence) William 1914- 53-56
Miller, Calvin 1936- CANR-13
Earlier sketch in CA 21-22R
Miller, Caroline 1903- DLB-9
Miller, Carroll H(iram) 1907-197(?) CAP-1
Earlier sketch in CA 19-20
Miller, Casey (Geddes) 1919- 69-72
Miller, Cecilia Parsons 1909- CANR-12
Earlier sketch in CA 23-24R
Miller, Cecille (Boyd) 1908- 11-12R
Miller, Char
See Miller, Frank L(ubbock) IV
Miller, Charles 1918- 77-80
Miller, Charles A. 1937- 29-32R
Miller, Charles D(avid) 1942- 69-72
Miller, Charles E. 1929- 33-36R
Miller, Charles Henderson 1905- CAP-2
Earlier sketch in CA 19-20
Miller, Charles Leslie 1908- 49-52
Miller, Christian 1920- 108
Miller, Clarence H(arvey) 1930- 102
Miller, Clarence J(ohn) 1916- CANR-13
Earlier sketch in CA 23-24R
Miller, Clement (Albin) 1915- 41-44R
Miller, Conrad
See Strung, Norman
Miller, D(ean) A(rthur) 1931- 23-24R
Miller, Daniel Adlai II 1918- 37-40R
Miller, Danny 1947- 126
Miller, Darlis A(nn) 1939- 125
Miller, David E(ugene) 1909-1978 45-48
Obituary 103
Miller, David Harry 1938- 57-60
Miller, David L(eroy) 1936- 49-52
Miller, David Lee 1951- 122
Miller, David Louis 1903-1986 .... 23-24R
Obituary 118
Miller, David Merlin 1934- 93-96
Miller, David W. 1940- 49-52
Miller, Deborah Uchill 1944- 116
Miller, Delbert C(harles) 1913- 25-28R
Miller, Don 1923- SATA-15
Miller, Donald 1893-1986 Obituary 119
Miller, Donald 1934- 97-100
Miller, Donald C(urtis) 1933- CANR-6
Earlier sketch in CA 57-60
Miller, Donald Eugene 1929- CANR-24
Earlier sketch in CA 106
Miller, Donald George 1909- CANR-4
Earlier sketch in CA 5-6R
Miller, Donald L(ane) 1918- 19-20R
Miller, Doris R.
See Mosesson, Gloria R(ubin)
Miller, Dorothy (Ryan)
See Ryan, Dorothy (Barger)
Miller, Douglas T(aylor) 1937- 21-22R
Miller, E. Ethelbert 1950- DLB-41
Miller, E. F.
See Pohle, Robert W(arren), Jr.
Miller, E(dwin) S(hepard) 1904- 45-48
Miller, E(ugene) Willard 1915- CANR-17
Earlier sketches in CA 5-6R, CANR-2
Miller, Ed(die) L(eRoy) 1937- 37-40R
Miller, Eddie
See Miller, Edward
Miller, Edna Anita 1920- 112
See also SATA 29
Miller, Edward 1905-1974 .... CAP-2
Earlier sketch in CA 25-28
See also SATA 8
Miller, Edwin Haviland 1918- 110
Miller, Elizabeth 1933- 117
See also SATA 41
Miller, Elizabeth Kubota 1932- 15-16R
Miller, Elizabeth Maxfield 1910- 45-48
Miller, Ella May 1915- CANR-11
Earlier sketch in CA 23-24R
Miller, Elwood E. 1925- 122
Miller, Ethel Prince 1893- CAP-1
Earlier sketch in CA 13-14
Miller, Eugene 1925- 101
See also SATA 33
Miller, Eugenia
See Mandelkorn, Eugenia Miller
Miller, F(rederick) W(alter) G(ascoyne)
1904- CANR-11
Earlier sketch in CA 25-28R
Miller, Florence B. 1895(?)-1976
Obituary 69-72
Miller, Floyd C. 1912- CANR-2
Earlier sketch in CA 4R
Miller, Forrest A. 1931- 25-28R
Miller, Frances A. 1937- 123
See also SATA 46, 52
Miller, Francis Pickens 1895- 69-72
Miller, Frank 1925-1983 Obituary 109
Miller, Frank
See Loomis, Noel M(iller)
Miller, Frank L(ubbock) IV 1951- 113
Miller, G. R.
See Judd, Frederick Charles
Miller, Gabriel 1948- 115
Miller, Gary M(ichael) 1941- 113
Miller, Gene Edward 1928- 97-100
Miller, Genevieve 1914- 19-20R
Miller, Geoffrey 1921-1984 Obituary 112
Miller, Geoffrey Samuel 1945- 104
Miller, George (Eric) 1943- CANR-14
Earlier sketch in CA 73-76
Miller, George A(rmitage) 1920- CANR-1
Earlier sketch in CA 4R
Miller, George H(all) 1919- 33-36R
Miller, George Louquet 1934- 89-92
Miller, Gerald 1928(?)-1970 Obituary 104
Miller, Gerald R(aymond) 1931- CANR-16
Earlier sketch in CA 93-96
Miller, Glenn T(homas) 1942- Brief entry ... 110
Miller, Gordon W(esley) 1918- 89-92
Miller, Gus
See Miller, Gustavus Hindman
Miller, Gustavus Hindman 1857-1929
Brief entry 120
Miller, Haskell M(orris) 1910- CAP-2
Earlier sketch in CA 23-24
Miller, Heather Ross 1939- CANR-5
Earlier sketch in CA 13-14R
Miller, Helen Hill 1899- 11-12R

Miller, Helen M(arkley) CANR-2
Earlier sketch in CA 2R
See also SATA 5
Miller, Helen Topping 1884-1960 Obituary .. 109
See also SATA 29
Miller, Henry (Valentine) 1891-1980 ..... 9-10R
Obituary 97-100
See also DLB 4, 9
See also DLBY 80
See also CLC 1, 2, 4, 9, 14, 43
Miller, Henry Knight 1920- CANR-2
Earlier sketch in CA 3R
Miller, Herbert E(lmer) 1914- CANR-11
Earlier sketch in CA 19-20R
Miller, Hope Ridings 25-28R
Miller, Howard S(mith) 1936- 29-32R
Miller, Hubert John 1927- 37-40R
Miller, Hugh 1897(?)-1979 Obituary 89-92
Miller, Hugh 1937- CANR-12
Earlier sketch in CA 61-64
Miller, Hugh Milton 1908- 33-36R
Miller, Isabel
See Routsong, Alma
Miller, J(ohn) D(onald) B(ruce) 1922- .. CANR-13
Earlier sketch in CA 73-76
Miller, J. Dale 1923- 105
Miller, J(oseph) Hillis 1928- 85-88
See also DLB 67
Miller, J. Innes 1892-1976 ..... CAP-2
Earlier sketch in CA 29-32
Miller, J(ames) Maxwell 1937- 110
Miller, J(ames) P. 1919- 25-28R
See also AITN 1, 2
Miller, J(ohn) Robert 1913- 45-48
Miller, Jake C. 1929- 126
Miller, James A. 1957- 126
Miller, James C(lifford) III 1942- CANR-10
Earlier sketch in CA 25-28R
Miller, James Edwin (Jr.) 1920- CANR-1
Earlier sketch in CA 3R
Miller, James G(rier) 1916- 23-24R
Miller, Jane (Judith) 1925- CANR-13
Earlier sketch in CA 77-80
See also SATA 15
Miller, Jason 1939(?)- 73-76
See also DLB 7
See also CLC 2
See also AITN 1
Miller, Jay W(ilson) 1893- CAP-1
Earlier sketch in CA 13-14
Miller, Jean Baker 1927- Brief entry 108
Miller, Jerome K. 1931- 105
Miller, Jim Wayne 1936- CANR-20
Earlier sketches in CA 49-52, CANR-1
Miller, Joan (Irene) 1944- 117
Miller, Joan M(ary) 1941- 108
Miller, John (Laurence) 1947- 93-96
Miller, John
See Samachson, Joseph
Miller, John C. 1916(?)-1979 Obituary 89-92
Miller, John Chester 1907- 73-76
Miller, John Harold 1925- 7-8R
Miller, John N. 1933- 33-36R
Miller, John P(earse, Jr.) 1943- 69-72
Miller, Johnny
See Miller, John (Laurence)
Miller, Jolonda 1945- 108
Miller, Jon (Gordon) 1921- 53-56
Miller, Jonathan (Wolfe) 1934- 115
Brief entry 110
Miller, Jordan Y(ale) 1919- CANR-2
Earlier sketch in CA 3R
Miller, Joseph C(alder) 1939- 93-96
Miller, Judi 1941- 106
Miller, Judith von Daler 1940- 69-72
Miller, Julian M. 1922-1976 Obituary 69-72
Miller, June 1923- 89-92
Miller, K(eith) Bruce 1927- 33-36R
See also AITN 1
Miller, Karl (Fergus Connor) 1931-
Brief entry 107
Miller, Kenneth Dexter 1887- CAP-1
Earlier sketch in CA 13-14
Miller, Kenneth E(ugene) 1926- 23-24R
Miller, Kent S(amuel) 1927- Brief entry 109
Miller, Lanora 1932- 61-64
Miller, Lenore 1924- 107
Miller, Leon Gordon 1917- 104
Miller, Levi 1944- 113
Miller, Lewis (Ames) 1928- 93-96
Miller, Liam 1924(?)-1987 Obituary 122
Miller, Libuse (Lukas) 1915-1973 ..... 3R
Obituary 103
Miller, Lillian B(eresnack) 1923- CANR-25
Earlier sketches in CA 21-22R, CANR-9
Miller, Lily Poritz 1938- 126
Miller, Linda B. 1937- 21-22R
Miller, Linda Lael 1949- 110
Miller, Luree 1926- 93-96
Miller, Lyle L. 1919- CANR-6
Earlier sketch in CA 13-14R
Miller, Lynn F(ieldman) 1938- 109
Miller, Lynn H(ellwarth) 1937- 37-40R
Miller, Lynne (Ellen) 1945- 89-92
Miller, Madelaine Hemingway 1904- 103
See also AITN 2
Miller, Madge 1918- 123
Brief entry 117
Miller, Mara (Jayne) 1944- 97-100
Miller, Marc S(cott) 1947- 105
Miller, Margaret J.
See Dale, Margaret J(essy) Miller
Miller, Margery
See Welles, Margery Miller
Miller, Marilyn (Jean) 1925- SATA-33
Miller, Marilyn McMeen
See Brown, Marilyn McMeen Miller
Miller, Marjorie M. 1922- 101
Miller, Marshall Lee 1942- CANR-9
Earlier sketch in CA 57-60
Miller, Martha
See Ivan, Martha Miller Pfaff
Miller, Martha Porter 1897(?)-1983
Obituary 109
Miller, Martin A. 1938- 65-68
Miller, Mary
See Northcott, (William) Cecil
Miller, Mary Agnes 1888(?)-1973
Obituary 45-48
Miller, Mary Beth 1942- 61-64
See also SATA 9
Miller, Mary Britton 1883-1975 ..... CANR-16
Obituary 57-60
Earlier sketch in CA 2R
Miller (Riis), Maurine 1910- 118
Miller, Max (Carlton) 1899-1967 ..... CANR-16
Obituary 25-28R
Earlier sketch in CA 3R
Miller, May 1899- DLB-41
Miller, Melvin H(ull) 1920- 15-16R
Miller, Merl Kem 1942- 111
Miller, Merle 1919-1986 ..... CANR-4
Obituary 119
Earlier sketch in CA 9-10R
See also AITN 1
Miller, Merton Howard 1923- Brief entry 109
Miller, Michael M. 1910(?)-1977
Obituary 73-76
Miller, Milt 1916- 117
Miller, Minnie M. 1899-1983 ..... CAP-2
Obituary 110
Earlier sketch in CA 21-22
Miller, Morris 1914- 19-20R
Miller, Muriel
See Minor, Muriel Miller
Miller, N(ewton) Edd 1920- 25-28R
Miller, Naomi 1928- 111
Miller, Natalie 1917-1976 ..... SATA-35
Miller, Nathan 1927- CANR-4
Earlier sketch in CA 53-56
Miller, Neal E(lgar) 1909- 81-84
Miller, Nicole Puleo 1944- 49-52
Miller, Nina Hull 1894-1974 ..... CAP-1
Earlier sketch in CA 9-10
Miller, Nolan 1912- 11-12R
Miller, Norman 1933- 37-40R
Miller, Norman C(harles) 1934- 37-40R
Miller, Nyle H. 1907- CAP-2
Earlier sketch in CA 23-24
Miller, Olga K(omarkova) 1908- 107
Miller, Orson K., Jr. 1930- 126
Brief entry 110
Miller, Osborn (Maitland) 1896(?)-1979
Obituary 89-92
Miller, Oscar J. 1913- 37-40R
Miller, Patrick Dwight, Jr. 1935- 112
Miller, Paul Martin 1914- CANR-10
Earlier sketch in CA 19-20R
Miller, Paul R(ichard) 1929- 21-22R
Miller, Paul William 1926- 41-44R
Miller, Perry (Gilbert Eddy) 1905-1963
Obituary 93-96
See also DLB 17, 63
Miller, (Mitchell) Peter 1934- 37-40R
Miller, Peter M(ichael) 1942- CANR-25
Earlier sketch in CA 69-72
Miller, Philip L(ieson) 1906- CAP-1
Earlier sketch in CA 11-12
Miller, R(onald) Baxter 1948- 115
Miller, R(ay Stephans) June 1923- 65-68
Miller, R. S. 1936- 45-48
Miller, Randall Martin 1945- CANR-15
Earlier sketch in CA 81-84
Miller, Randolph Crump 1910- CANR-1
Earlier sketch in CA 3R
Miller, Raymond W(iley) 1895-1988
Obituary 124
Miller, Rene Fueloep
See Fueloep-Miller, Rene
Miller, Rene Fulop
See Fueloep-Miller, Rene
Miller, Rex 1929- 110
Miller, Richard (Connelly) 1925- CANR-26
Earlier sketch in CA 19-20R
Miller, Richard
See Pietschmann, Richard John III
Miller, Richard I(rwin) 1924- 41-44R
Miller, Richard S(herwin) 1930- 23-24R
Miller, Richard Ulric 1932- CANR-17
Earlier sketch in CA 41-44R
Miller, Rob(ert) Hollis 1944- 37-40R
Miller, Robert A(llen) 1932- 33-36R
Miller, Robert H(enry) 1889- 33-36R
Miller, Robert Henry 1938- 110
Miller, Robert Keith 1949- 114
Miller, Robert L. 1928- 25-28R
Miller, Robert Moats 1924- Brief entry 105
Miller, Robert Ryal 1923- 41-44R
Miller, Roger LeRoy 1943- Brief entry 107
Miller, Ron 1947- 117
Miller, Ronald E(ugene) 1933- 5-6R
Miller, Roy Andrew 1924- CANR-18
Earlier sketches in CA 7-8R, CANR-2
Miller, Ruby 1890(?)-1976 Obituary 65-68
Miller, Russell E(lliott) 1916- Brief entry 117
Miller, Ruth 1921- Brief entry 106
Miller, Ruth
See Jacobs, Ruth Harriet
Miller, Ruth White
See White, Ruth C.
Miller, S(eymour) M(ichael) 1922- 19-20R
Miller, Sally M. 1937- CANR-26
Earlier sketch in CA 45-48
Miller, Samuel Jefferson 1919- 53-56
Miller, Sandra (Peden) 1948- 115
Miller, Sandy
See Miller, Sandra (Peden)
See also SATA 35, 41
Miller, Shane 1907- CAP-2
Earlier sketch in CA 21-22
Miller, Shirley 1920- 93-96
Miller, Sigmund Stephen 1917- CANR-4
Earlier sketch in CA 3R
Miller, Stanley 1916(?)-1977 Obituary 69-72
Miller, Stanley L(loyd) 1930- 45-48
Miller, Stanley S. 1924- 13-14R
Miller, Stephen J(ohn) 1936- 33-36R
Miller, Stuart 1937- 41-44R
Miller, Stuart Creighton 1927- 33-36R
Miller, Sue 19(?)- CLC-44
Miller, Susan 1944- 107
Miller, Teresa 1952- 105
Miller, Thomas Lloyd 1913- 25-28R
Miller, Timothy (Alan) 1944- 126
Miller, Tom 1947- CANR-14
Earlier sketch in CA 73-76
Miller, Vassar 1924- CANR-4
Earlier sketch in CA 11-12R
Miller, Victor (Brooke) 1940- 107
Miller, Wade
See Miller, (H.) Bill(y)
and Wade, Robert (Allison)
Miller, Walter James 1918- 81-84
Miller, Walter M(ichael, Jr.) 1923- 85-88
See also DLB 8
See also CLC 4, 30
Miller, Warren 1921-1966 Obituary 25-28R
Miller, Warren E. 1924- CANR-11
Earlier sketch in CA 15-16R
Miller, Wayne Charles 1939- CANR-1
Earlier sketch in CA 45-48
Miller, Webb 1892-1940 ..... DLB-29
Miller, William (Moseley) 1909- 81-84
Miller, William Alvin 1931- CANR-17
Earlier sketches in CA 49-52, CANR-1
Miller, William D. 1916- 15-16R
Miller, William Hugh 1905-1975 ..... 2R
Miller, William McElwee 1892- CANR-6
Earlier sketch in CA 57-60
Miller, William Robert 1927-1970 ..... CAP-1
Obituary 29-32R
Earlier sketch in CA 11-12
Miller, Wilma H(ildruth) 1936- CANR-12
Earlier sketch in CA 33-36R
Miller, Wright (Watts) 1903-1974 ..... 19-20R
Obituary 120
Miller, Zane L. 1934- CANR-12
Earlier sketch in CA 25-28R
Millerson, Geoffrey L. 1931- 19-20R
Millet, Stanton 1931- 25-28R
Millett, Allan R(eed) 1937- 23-24R
Millett, Fred B(enjamin) 1890-1976
Obituary 61-64
Millett, John (Antill) 1922- CANR-20
Earlier sketch in CA 103
Millett, John D(avid) 1912- 104
Millett, Kate 1934- 73-76
See also AITN 1
Millett, Richard L(eroy) 1938- 117
Millgate, Jane 1937- 57-60
Millgate, Michael (Henry) 1929- 29-32R
Millgram, Abraham E(zra) 1901- 33-36R
Millham, C(harles) B(lanchard) 1936- 37-40R
Millhauser, Milton 1910- CAP-1
Earlier sketch in CA 15-16
Millhauser, Steven 1943- 111
Brief entry 110
See also DLB 2
See also CLC 21
Millhiser, Marlys (Joy) 1938- 53-56
Millican, Arthenia Jackson Bates 1920- 105
See also BW
See also DLB 38
Millicent
See Jordan, Mildred Arlene
Millichap, Joseph R(obert) 1940- 116
Millies, Suzanne 1943- 49-52
Milligan, Edward Archibald 1903-1977 ..... 41-44R
Milligan, Spike
See Milligan, Terence Alan
Milligan, Terence Alan 1918- CANR-4
Earlier sketch in CA 9-10R
See also SATA 29
Milliken, Ernest Kenneth 1899- 7-8R
Milliken, Stephen F(rederick) 1928- 93-96
Milliken, William Mathewson 1889- CAP-2
Earlier sketch in CA 23-24
Millimaki, Robert H. 1931- 57-60
Millin, Sarah Gertrude 1889-1968 102
Obituary 93-96
See also CLC 49
Millington, Ada
See Deyneka, Anita
Millington, Barry 1951- 119
Millington, Frances Ryan 1899-1977
Obituary 69-72
Millington, Patrick 1910-1982 Obituary 107
Millington, Roger 1939- 65-68
Million, Elmer M(ayse) 1912- 41-44R
Millis, Walter 1899-1968 ..... CAP-1
Obituary 37-40R
Earlier sketch in CA 9-10
Millman, Lawrence 1946- CANR-17
Earlier sketch in CA 93-96
Millon, Henry (Armand) 1927- 97-100
Millon, Rene 1921- 116
Brief entry 113
Millon, Robert Paul 1932- 23-24R
Millon, Theodore 1929- 57-60
Mills, Alison 1951- 53-56
Mills, Barriss 1912- CANR-12
Earlier sketch in CA 25-28R
Mills, Belen Collantes 1930- 37-40R
Mills, Betty (Lidstrom) 1926- 11-12R
Mills, Brenda J. 1940- 120
Mills, C(harles) Wright 1916-1962
Obituary 107
Mills, Carley 1897-1962 ..... 2R
Obituary 103
Mills, Clarence A(lonzo) 1891-1974 ..... CAP-1
Obituary 53-56
Earlier sketch in CA 15-16
Mills, Claudia 1954- 109
See also SATA 41, 44
Mills, Constance (Quinby) 1898-1987
Obituary 122
Mills, Daniel Quinn 1941- 112
Mills, David Harlow 1932- 104
Mills, Dorothy
See Howard, Dorothy Gray
Mills, Edward D(avid) 1915- CANR-19
Earlier sketches in CA 7-8R, CANR-4
Mills, G(len) E(arl) 1908- CAP-1
Earlier sketch in CA 13-14
Mills, Gary B(ernard) 1944- 81-84
Mills, George S(torginne) 1906- 97-100
Mills, Gordon H(arrison) 1914-1978
Obituary 117
Mills, Helen 1923- CANR-16
Earlier sketch in CA 97-100
Mills, Hilary (Paterson) 1950- 115
Mills, Irving 1894-1985 Obituary 115
Mills, J(anet) M(elanie) A(ilsa) 1894- 69-72
Mills, James R(obert) 1927- 85-88
Mills, Jeannie 1939- 93-96
Mills, John 1908- 108
Mills, John 1930- 81-84
Mills, John FitzMaurice 1917- 103
Mills, John W(illiam) 1933- 69-72
Mills, Leonard Russell 1917- 45-48
Mills, Liston O. 1928- 107
Mills, (William) Mervyn 1906- CAP-1
Earlier sketch in CA 11-12
Mills, Ralph J(oseph), Jr. 1931- CANR-18
Earlier sketches in CA 9-10R, CANR-3
Mills, Richard W. 1945- Brief entry 112
Mills, Robert P(ark) 1920-1986 97-100
Obituary 118
Mills, Terry Kenneth 1949- 107
Mills, Theodore M(ason) 1920- 23-24R
Mills, Watson Early 1939- 57-60
Mills, William 1935- Brief entry 118
Mills, William Donald 1925- 33-36R
Mills, Yaroslava Surmach 1925- SATA-35
Millstead, Thomas E. 106
See also SATA 30
Millstein, Rose Silverman 1903(?)-1975
Obituary 61-64
Millum, Trevor 1945- CANR-21
Earlier sketch in CA 104
Millward, Celia M(cCullough) 1935- 53-56
Millward, Eric (Geoffrey William) 1935- 65-68
Millward, John S(candrett) 1924- 13-14R
Milman, Donald S. 1924- Brief entry 111
Milman, Miriam 1928- 112
Milne, A(lan) A(lexander) 1882-1956
Brief entry 104
See also YABC 1
See also DLB 10
See also TCLC 6
See also CLR 1
Milne, Antony 1942- 101
Milne, Christopher (Robin) 1920- CANR-11
Earlier sketch in CA 61-64
See also AITN 2
Milne, Edward James 1915-1983 Obituary .. 109
Milne, Evander Mackay 1920- 7-8R
Milne, (Charles) Ewart 1903-1987 ..... CANR-16
Obituary 121
Earlier sketch in CA 97-100
Milne, (William) Gordon 1921- 21-22R
Milne, Jean (Killgrove) 1920- 19-20R
Milne, Lorus J. CANR-14
Earlier sketch in CA 33-36R
See also SATA 5
Milne, Margery CANR-14
Earlier sketch in CA 33-36R
See also SATA 5
Milne, Roseleen 1945- CANR-13
Earlier sketch in CA 73-76
Milner, Christina 1942- 49-52
Milner, Clyde A. II 1948- CANR-26
Earlier sketch in CA 108
Milner, Esther 1918- 23-24R
Milner, Ian Frank George 1911- 104
Milner, Jay (Dunston) 1926- 4R
Milner, Lucille Bernheimer 1888(?)-1975
Obituary 61-64
Milner, Marion (Blackett) 1900- 11-12R
Milner, Michael
See Cooper, Saul
Milner, Murray, Jr. 1935- 41-44R
Milner, Neal A(lan) 1941- Brief entry 112
Milner, Richard B(ruce) 1941- 49-52
Milner, Ron(ald) 1938- CANR-24
Earlier sketch in CA 73-76
See also BW
See also DLB 38
See also AITN 1
Milnes, Eric Charles 1912-1984 Obituary ... 112
Milnes, Richard Monckton 1809-1885 ... DLB-32
Milns, R(obert) D(avid) 1938- 33-36R
Milo, Ronald D(mitri) 1935- 25-28R
Milonas, Rolf
See Myller, Rolf
Miloradovich, Milo 1901(?)-1972
Obituary 37-40R

Milosh, Joseph E(dmund) 1936- 21-22R
Miloslavsky, Nikolai Dimitrievich Tolstoy
See Tolstoy (-Miloslavsky), Nikolai (Dimitrievich)
Milosz, Czeslaw 1911- CANR-23
Earlier sketch in CA 81-84
See also CLC 5, 11, 22, 31
Milotte, Alfred G(eorge) 1904- CAP-1
Earlier sketch in CA 19-20
See also SATA 11
Milsen, Oscar
See Mendelsohn, Oscar (Adolf)
Milson, Fred(erick William) 1912- 73-76
Milstead, Jessica L(ee) 1939- CANR-14
Earlier sketch in CA 33-36R
Milstead, John 1924- 49-52
Milstein, Mike M(yron) 1937- 81-84
Milton, Arthur 1922- 109
Milton, Charles R(udolph) 1925- 53-56
Milton, David Scott 1934- CANR-13
Earlier sketch in CA 73-76
Milton, Hilary (Herbert) 1920- CANR-21
Earlier sketches in CA 57-60, CANR-6
See also SATA 23
Milton, Jack
See Kimbro, John M.
Milton, John R(onald) 1924- 33-36R
See also SATA 24
Milton, Joyce 1946- 106
See also SATA 41, 52
Milton, Mark
See Pelton, Robert W(ayne)
Milton, Oliver
See Hewitt, Cecil Rolph
Milunsky, Aubrey 1936- 103
Milverton, Charles A.
See Penzler, Otto
Milward, Alan S. 1935- 45-48
Milward, Peter 1925- 101
Mims, Forrest M(arion) III 1944- CANR-16
Earlier sketch in CA 97-100
Mims, Lambert C. 1930- 29-32R
Mims, Roddey Earl 1936(?)-1982
Obituary 108
Minadeo, Richard (William) 1929- 25-28R
Minahan, John 1933- CANR-2
Earlier sketch in CA 45-48
Minale, Marcello 1938- 108
Minar, David W(illiam) 1925-1973
Obituary 111
Minarik, Else Holmelund 1920- 73-76
See also SATA 15
Minarik, John Paul 1947- CANR-13
Earlier sketch in CA 73-76
Mincer, Jacob 1922- Brief entry 114
Minchinton, W(alter) E(dward) 1921- .. CANR-12
Earlier sketch in CA 29-32R
Mincieli, Rose Laura 1912- CANR-4
Earlier sketch in CA 5-6R
Minckler, (Sherwood) Leon 1906- 57-60
Mindel, Eugene D. 1934- 41-44R
Mindell, Earl L(awrence) 1940- 105
Mindlin, Murray 1924(?)-1987 Obituary 122
Mindszenty, Jozsef 1892-1975 65-68
Obituary 57-60
Mindt, Heinz R. 1940- Brief entry 115
Minear, Paul Sevier 1906- CANR-3
Earlier sketch in CA 4R
Minear, Richard H(offman) 1938- 33-36R
Minehaha, Cornelius
See Wedekind, (Benjamin) Frank(lin)
Mineka, Francis Edward 1907- Brief entry ... 106
Miner, Caroline Eyring 1907- CANR-11
Earlier sketch in CA 25-28R
Miner, Charles S(ydney) 1906- CAP-1
Earlier sketch in CA 19-20
Miner, Dwight Carroll 1904-1978
Obituary 81-84
Miner, Earl (Roy) 1927- CANR-1
Earlier sketch in CA 2R
Miner, H. Craig 1944- CANR-16
Earlier sketches in CA 45-48, CANR-1
Miner, (Opal) Irene Sevrey (Frazine) 1906- ..5-6R
Miner, Jane Claypool 1933- 106
See also SATA 37, 38
Miner, John B(urnham) 1926- CANR-20
Earlier sketches in CA 11-12R, CANR-5
Miner, Joshua L. 1920- 106
Miner, Lewis S. 1909- CAP-1
Earlier sketch in CA 11-12
See also SATA 11
Miner, Mary Green 1928- 69-72
Miner, Matthew
See Wallmann, Jeffrey M(iner)
Miner, Valerie 1947- 97-100
See also CLC 40
Miner, Ward L(ester) 1916- 9-10R
Mines, Jeanette (Marie) 1948- 119
Mines, Samuel 1909- CANR-1
Earlier sketch in CA 45-48
Mines, Stephanie 1944- 77-80
Minetree, Harry 1935- 93-96
Mingay, G(ordon) E(dmund) 1923- CANR-11
Earlier sketch in CA 19-20R
Minge, Ward Alan 1924- 97-100
Minghi, Julian V(incent) 1933- 29-32R
Mingus, Charles 1922-1979 93-96
Obituary 85-88
Minhinnick, Robert 1952- 126
Minichiello, Sharon 126
Minick, Michael 1945- 65-68
Minier, Nelson
See Stoutenburg, Adrien (Pearl)
Minifie, James MacDonald 1900-1974 49-52
Minihan, Janet
See Oppenheim, Janet
Minimo, Duca
See D'Annunzio, Gabriele
Minio-Paluello, Lorenzo 1907-1986
Obituary 119
Minium, Edward W(headon) 1917- 29-32R
Mink, Louis Otto, Jr. 1921-1983 104
Obituary 109
Mink, Nelson G. 1907- 123
Minkovitz, Moshe
See Shokeid, Moshe
Minnelli, Vincente 1913(?)-1986 Obituary ... 119
Brief entry 117
Minney, R(ubeigh) J(ames) 1895- CANR-5
Earlier sketch in CA 7-8R
Minnich, Helen Benton 1892- CAP-1
Earlier sketch in CA 9-10
Minnick, Wayne C. 1915- 25-28R
Minnigerode, Meade 1887-1967 Obituary ... 116
Minogue, Kenneth R(obert) 1930- 7-8R
Minor, Andrew Collier 1918- 15-16R
Minor, Anthropopagus
See Conniff, James C(lifford) G(regory)
Minor, Audax
See Ryall, George (Francis Trafford)
Minor, Edward Orville 1920- 9-10R
Minor, Marz 1928- 103
Minor, Muriel Miller 1908-1987 Obituary ... 122
Minor, Nono 1932- 103
Minot, Stephen 1927- CANR-17
Earlier sketch in CA 13-14R
Minot, Susan 1956- CLC-44
Minott, Rodney G(lisan) 1928- 11-12R
Minow, Newton N(orman) 1926- 15-16R
Minrath, William R(ichard) 1900-1971 .... CAP-1
Obituary 89-92
Earlier sketch in CA 9-10
Minshall, Merlin (Theodore) 1906-1987
Obituary 123
Minshall, Vera (Wild) 1924- 13-14R
Minshull, Evelyn 1929- 37-40R
Minshull, Roger (Michael) 1935- 21-22R
Minsky, Betty Jane (Toebe) 1932- 7-8R
Minsky, Hyman P(hilip) 1919- 85-88
Minsky, Marvin (Lee) 1927- 23-24R
Minsky, Morton 1902(?)-1987 Obituary 122
Minter, David L. 1935- CANR-12
Earlier sketch in CA 25-28R
Minter, William 1942- 124
Minters, Arthur Herman 1932- 102
Minto-Cowen, Frances
See Munthe, Frances
Minton, Lynn 107
Minton, Madge Rutherford 1920- 45-48
Minton, Paula
See Little, Paul H(ugo)
Minton, Robert 1918- 57-60
Minton, Sherman A(nthony), Jr. 1919- 45-48
Mintonye, Grace 25-28R
See also SATA 4
Minturn, Leigh 1928- 23-24R
Minty, Judith 1937- CANR-21
Earlier sketches in CA 49-52, CANR-2
Mintz, Barbara 1931- 110
Mintz, Donald E(dward) 1932- 19-20R
Mintz, Elizabeth E. 1913- 73-76
Mintz, Joyce Lois 1933- 65-68
Mintz, Lannon W. 1938-1988 126
Mintz, Leigh W(ayne) 1939- 57-60
Mintz, Max M. 1919- 33-36R
Mintz, Morton A. 1922- 15-16R
Mintz, Norman N(elson) 1934- 41-44R
Mintz, Ruth Finer 1919- 15-16R
Mintz, Samuel I(saiah) 1923- 5-6R
Mintz, Sidney W(ilfred) 1922- CANR-21
Earlier sketches in CA 3R, CANR-5
Mintz, Steven (Harry) 1953- 118
Mintz, Thomas 1931- 108
Mintzberg, Henry 1939- CANR-1
Earlier sketch in CA 45-48
Mintzer, Yvette 1947- 77-80
Minus, Ed 1938- CLC-39
Minus, Paul M(urray, Jr.) 1935- 118
Minyard, John Douglas 1943- 120
Mirabehn
See Slade, Madeleine
Mirabelli, Eugene (Jr.) 1931- 25-28R
Miracle, Gordon E. 1930- 33-36R
Miracle, Marvin P(reston) 1933- 19-20R
Miranda, Javier
See Bioy Casares, Adolfo
Mirande, Alfredo M(anuel) 1940- 115
Mireaux, Emile 1885(?)-1969 Obituary 104
Mireles, Marina 1927(?)-1986 Obituary 119
Mirenburg, Barry (Leonard Steffan) 1952- ... 101
Mirepoix, Camille 1926- 105
Miro (Ferrer), Gabriel (Francisco Victor)
1879-1930 Brief entry 104
See also TCLC 5
Miro, Joan 1893-1983 121
Obituary 111
Miron, Dan 1934- 77-80
Miron, Gaston 1928- DLB-60
Miron, Murray S(amuel) 1932- 81-84
Mirsky, Jeannette 1903-1987 .... CAP-2
Obituary 122
Earlier sketch in CA 19-20
See also SATA 8, 51
Mirsky, Mark Jay 1939- 25-28R
Mirsky, Reba Paeff 1902-1966 .... 2R
See also SATA 1
Mirsky, Stanley 1929- 110
Mirvish, Robert Franklin 1921- 2R
Miscall, Peter D(arwin) 1943- 111
Misch, Robert J(ay) 1905- 23-24R
Mische, Gerald F(rederick) 1926- 97-100
Mische, Patricia M(ary) 1939- CANR-16
Earlier sketch in CA 93-96
Mischke, Bernard Cyril 1926- 13-14R
Mischke, Fridolin 1916- 117
Mischke, Fritz
See Mischke, Fridolin
Mises, Ludwig (Edler) von 1881-1973 .. CANR-19
Obituary 45-48
Earlier sketch in CA 7-8R
Mises, Margit von 1896- CANR-19
Earlier sketch in CA 89-92
Mish, Charles C(arroll) 1913- 33-36R
Mishael, Bert
See Mishael, Herbert Stanley
Mishael, Herbert Stanley 1900(?)-1985
Obituary 117
Mishan, E(zra) J(oshua) 1917- CANR-13
Earlier sketch in CA 73-76
Misheiker, Betty Fairly 1919- 11-12R
Mishima, Yukio
See Hiraoka, Kimitake
See also CLC 2, 4, 6, 9, 27
Mishkin, Paul J. 1927- 19-20R
Mishler, William (Thomas Earle II) 1947- ... 125
Mishra, Vishwa Mohan 1937- 61-64
Misiak, Henryk 1911- CANR-5
Earlier sketch in CA 2R
Misiunas, Romuald John 1945- 109
Miskimin, Harry A(lvin, Jr.) 1932-
Brief entry 109
Miskovits, Christine 1939- 53-56
See also SATA 10
Misner, Arthur J(ack) 1921- 21-22R
Misra, Bankey Bihari 1909- 104
Miss C. L. F.
See Grimke, Charlotte L(ottie) Forten
Missen, Leslie R(obert) 1897-1983
Obituary 110
Miss Frances
See Horwich, Frances R(appaport)
Missildine, (Whitney) Hugh 1915- 77-80
Missinne, Leo E(miel) 1927- 116
Missiroli, Mario 1886-1974 Obituary 53-56
Miss Lou
See Bennett-Coverley, Louise
Miss Manners
See Martin, Judith (Sylvia)
Miss Read
See Saint, Dora Jessie
Mister Rogers
See Rogers, Fred McFeely
Mister X
See Hoch, Edward D(entinger)
Mistral, Frederic 1830-1914 Brief entry 122
Mistral, Gabriela
See Godoy Alcayaga, Lucila
See also TCLC 2
Mitcalfe, Barry 1930- 110
Mitcham, Carl 1941- CANR-16
Earlier sketch in CA 85-88
Mitcham, Gilroy
See Newton, William Simpson
Mitcham, Samuel W(ayne), Jr. 1949- 106
Mitchel, Jonathan 1624-1668 .... DLB-24
Mitchell, Adam
See Pyle, Hilary
Mitchell, Adrian 1932- 33-36R
See also DLB 40
Mitchell, Alan 1922- CANR-8
Earlier sketch in CA 57-60
Mitchell, Alexander Ross Kerr 1934- 73-76
Mitchell, Allan 1933- 102
Mitchell, Allison
See Butterworth, W(illiam) E(dmund III)
Mitchell, Andrew W. 1953- 124
Mitchell, Arthur A(ustin) 1926- 11-12R
Mitchell, Austin (Vernon) 1934- CANR-12
Earlier sketch in CA 25-28R
Mitchell, B(rian) R(edman) 1929- 49-52
Mitchell, Barbara 1941- 117
Mitchell, Barbara A. 1939- 25-28R
Mitchell, Basil George 1917- 104
Mitchell, Betty L(ou) 1947- 107
Mitchell, Bonner 1929- 25-28R
Mitchell, Breon 1942- 112
Mitchell, Broadus 1892-1988 .... CANR-5
Obituary 125
Earlier sketch in CA 4R
Mitchell, Burroughs 1914(?)-1979
Obituary 89-92
Mitchell, Carlton
See Marshall, Mel(vin D.)
Mitchell, Charles 1912- 11-12R
Mitchell, Clyde
See Ellison, Harlan
and Silverberg, Robert
Mitchell, Colin W(are) 1927- 73-76
Mitchell, Curtis Cornelius, Jr. 1927- 105
Mitchell, Cynthia 1922- 106
See also SATA 29
Mitchell, Daniel J(esse) B(rody) 1942- 123
Mitchell, David (John) 1924- CANR-12
Earlier sketch in CA 53-56
Mitchell, Don(ald Earl) 1947- CANR-14
Earlier sketch in CA 33-36R
Mitchell, Donald (Charles Peter) 1925- 103
Mitchell, Donald Grant 1822-1908 .... DLB-1
Mitchell, Edgar D(ean) 1930- 53-56
Mitchell, Edward B. 1937- 23-24R
Mitchell, Elizabeth P(ryse) 1946- 101
Mitchell, (Sibyl) Elyne (Keith) 1913- ... CANR-21
Earlier sketches in CA 53-56, CANR-5
See also SATA 10
Mitchell, Emerson Blackhorse Barney
1945- 45-48
Mitchell, Erica
See Posner, Richard
Mitchell, Ewan
See Janner, Greville Ewan
Mitchell, Fay Langellier 1884-1964 ....5-6R
Mitchell, Frank
See Mitchell, George Francis
Mitchell, Frank Vincent 1919-19(?) 9-10R
Mitchell, Franklin D. 1932- Brief entry 118
Mitchell, G(eoffrey) Duncan 1921- CANR-11
Earlier sketch in CA 29-32R
Mitchell, George Francis 1912- 77-80
Mitchell, Giles 1928- 93-96
Mitchell, Gladys (Maude Winifred)
1901-1983 .... CANR-9
Obituary 110
Earlier sketch in CA 11-12R
See also SATA 35, 46
Mitchell, Greg 1947- 73-76
Mitchell, Harold P(aton) 1900-1983 ......11-12R
Obituary 109
Mitchell, (Arthur) Harris 1916- 119
Mitchell, Helen S(wift) 1895-1984 ....25-28R
Obituary 114
Mitchell, Henry H(eywood) 1919- CANR-10
Earlier sketch in CA 57-60
Mitchell, (William) Hobart 1908- 119
Mitchell, Howard E(still) 1921- 108
Mitchell, J(ames) Clyde 1918- CANR-9
Earlier sketch in CA 13-14R
Mitchell, Jack 1925- 11-12R
Mitchell, Jackson
See Matcha, Jack
Mitchell, James 1926- CANR-12
Earlier sketch in CA 13-14R
Mitchell, James (Alexander Hugh)
1939-1985 Obituary 115
Mitchell, James Leslie 1901-1935
Brief entry 104
See also DLB 15
Mitchell, Jay
See Roberson, Jennifer
Mitchell, Jeremy 1929- 41-44R
Mitchell, Jerome 1935- 25-28R
Mitchell, Jerry 1905(?)-1972 Obituary ...33-36R
Mitchell, Joan Cattermole 1920- CAP-1
Earlier sketch in CA 9-10
Mitchell, John
See Slater, Patrick
Mitchell, John D(ietrich) 1917- 49-52
Mitchell, John D(avid) B(awden)
1917-1980 Obituary 105
Mitchell, John Howard 1921- 11-12R
Mitchell, John J(oseph) 1941- CANR-1
Earlier sketch in CA 45-48
Mitchell, Joni 1943- 112
See also CLC 12
Mitchell, Joseph (Quincy) 1908- 77-80
Mitchell, Joseph B(rady) 1915- 11-12R
Mitchell, Joyce Slayton 1933- CANR-15
Earlier sketch in CA 65-68
See also SATA 43, 46
Mitchell, Judith Paige CANR-18
Earlier sketch in CA 85-88
Mitchell, (Charles) Julian 1935- CANR-5
Earlier sketch in CA 7-8R
See also DLB 14
Mitchell, Juliet 1940- 45-48
Mitchell, K. L.
See Lamb, Elizabeth Searle
Mitchell, Ken(neth Ronald) 1940- CANR-16
Earlier sketch in CA 93-96
See also DLB 60
Mitchell, Kenneth R. 1930- 19-20R
Mitchell, Kerry
See Wilkes-Hunter, R(ichard)
Mitchell, Lane 1907- CAP-1
Earlier sketch in CA 19-20
Mitchell, Langdon (Elwyn) 1862-1935
Brief entry 120
See also DLB 7
Mitchell, Lee M(ark) 1943- CANR-1
Earlier sketch in CA 49-52
Mitchell, Leeds 1912- 89-92
Mitchell, Leonel Lake 1930- 89-92
Mitchell, Leslie 1905-1985 Obituary 118
Mitchell, Lionel H. 1942- 106
Mitchell, Loften 1919- CANR-26
Earlier sketch in CA 81-84
See also BW
See also DLB 38
Mitchell, Marcia L(ouise) 1942- 113
Mitchell, Margaret (Munnerlyn) 1900-1949 .. 125
Brief entry 109
See also DLB 9
See also TCLC 11
Mitchell, Margaretta K. 1935- CANR-14
Earlier sketch in CA 29-32R
Mitchell, Marianne Helen 1937- 85-88
Mitchell, Memory F(armer) 1924- 37-40R
Mitchell, Otis C. 1935- CANR-13
Earlier sketch in CA 37-40R
Mitchell, P(hilip) M(arshall) 1916- CANR-20
Earlier sketch in CA 104
Mitchell, Paige
See Mitchell, Judith Paige
Mitchell, Pamela Holsclaw 1940- CANR-6
Earlier sketch in CA 57-60
Mitchell, Peggy
See Mitchell, Margaret (Munnerlyn)
Mitchell, Peter M(cQuilkin) 1934- 85-88
Mitchell, Richard H(anks) 1931- 23-24R
Mitchell, Robert H(ughes) 1921- 117
Mitchell, Roger (Sherman) 1935- 25-28R
Mitchell, Ruth K. 33-36R
Mitchell, S. Valentine
See Gammell, Susanna Valentine Mitchell
Mitchell, Sally 1937- 110
Mitchell, Scott
See Godfrey, Lionel (Robert Holcombe)
Mitchell, Sidney Alexander 1895- 7-8R

INDEX

Mitchell, Stephen Arnold 1903-1974
Obituary ... 49-52
Mitchell, Stephen O. 1930- ... 15-16R
Mitchell, Thomas N(oel) 1939- ... 103
Mitchell, W.J.T. 1942- ... CANR-14
Earlier sketch in CA 81-84
Mitchell, W(illiam) O(rmond) 1914- ... CANR-15
Earlier sketch in CA 77-80
See also CLC 25
Mitchell, William E(dward) 1927- ... 81-84
Mitchell, William E. 1936- ... 93-96
Mitchell, William Hamilton 1907(?)-1982
Obituary ... 107
Mitchell, Yvonne 1925-1979 ... CANR-10
Obituary ... 85-88
Earlier sketch in CA 19-20R
See also SATA 24
Mitchelson, Marvin M. 1928- ... 104
Mitchenson, Francis Joseph Blackett ... 101
Mitchenson, Joe
See Mitchenson, Francis Joseph Blackett
Mitchison, (Sonja) Lois ... 2R
Mitchison, Naomi Margaret (Haldane)
1897- ... CANR-15
Earlier sketch in CA 77-80
See also SATA 24
Mitchison, Rosalind (Mary) 1919- ... 33-36R
Mitchner, Stuart 1938- ... 61-64
Mitchnik, Helen 1901- ... 117
See also SATA 35, 41
Mitchum, Hank
See Knott, William C(ecil, Jr.)
and Newton, D(wight) B(ennett)
and Sherman, Jory (Tecumseh)
Mitelman, Bonnie Cossman 1941- ... 111
Mitford, Jessica 1917- ... CANR-1
Earlier sketch in CA 2R
Mitford, Nancy 1904-1973 ... 9-10R
See also CLC 44
Mitgang, Herbert 1920- ... CANR-4
Earlier sketch in CA 11-12R
Mitgang, Lee D. 1949- ... 77-80
Mitrany, David 1888-1975 ... 65-68
Obituary ... 61-64
Mitscherlich, Alexander Joseph 1908-1982
Obituary ... 107
Mitson, Eileen N(ora) 1930- ... 25-28R
Mitsuhashi, Yoko ... SATA-33, 45
Mittelholzer, Edgar Austin 1909-1965 ... CAP-1
Earlier sketch in CA 13-14
See also BW
Mittelman, James H(oward) 1944- ... CANR-13
Earlier sketch in CA 73-76
Mitterling, Philip Ira 1926- ... 102
Mittermeyer, Helen (Hayton Monteith)
1930- ... 124
Mittlebeeler, Emmet V(aughn) 1915- ... 57-60
Mitton, Bruce H(arold) 1950- ... 108
Mitton, Charles Leslie 1907- ... CANR-4
Earlier sketch in CA 4R
Mitton, Jacqueline 1948- ... 97-100
Mitton, Simon 1946- ... 97-100
Mittra, S(id) 1930- ... 41-44R
Mitzman, Arthur Benjamin 1931- ... 104
Mitzman, Max E. 1908- ... 97-100
Miura, Akira 1927- ... 117
Miura, Ayako 1922- ... 73-76
Mix, C(larence) Rex 1935- ... 29-32R
Mix, Katherine Lyon ... 53-56
Mix, Paul E(merson) 1934- ... 45-48
Mix, Susan Shank 1943- ... 29-32R
Mixter, Elisabeth W.
See Morss, Elisabeth W.
Mixter, Keith Eugene 1922- ... 41-44R
Mixter, Russell Lowell 1906- ... CAP-1
Earlier sketch in CA 15-16
Miyakawa, T(etsuo) Scott 1906- ... 19-20R
Miyamoto, Kazuo 1900- ... CAP-1
Earlier sketch in CA 11-12
Miyoshi, Masao 1928- ... 29-32R
Mizener, Arthur (Moore) 1907-1988 ... CANR-5
Obituary ... 124
Earlier sketch in CA 5-6R
Mizner, Elizabeth Howard 1907- ... 13-14R
See also SATA 27
Mizruchi, Ephraim H(arold) 1926- ... 41-44R
Mizruchi, Mark S(heldon) 1953- ... 110
Mizumura, Kazue ... 85-88
See also SATA 18
Mjelde, Michael Jay 1938- ... 69-72
Mnacko, Ladislav 1919- ... 29-32R
Mo, Timothy 1953- ... 117
See also CLC 46
Moak, Lennox L. 1912- ... 23-24R
Moak, Samuel K(uhn) 1929- ... 37-40R
Moan, Terrence 1947- ... 97-100
Moat, John 1936- ... CANR-13
Earlier sketch in CA 33-36R
Moats, Alice-Leone ... CAP-1
Earlier sketch in CA 15-16
Moberg, David O(scar) 1922- ... CANR-18
Earlier sketches in CA 2R, CANR-2
Moberg, (Carl Arthur) Vilhelm
1898-1973 ... 97-100
Obituary ... 45-48
Moberly, R(obert) B(asil) 1920- ... 29-32R
Moberly, Walter (Hamilton) 1881-1974 ... CAP-2
Earlier sketch in CA 29-32
Moberly-Bell, Enid 1881- ... 7-8R
Mobley, Harris W(itsel) 1929- ... 37-40R
Mobley, Tony Allen 1938- ... 102
Mobley, Walt
See Burgess, M(ichael) R(oy)
Moche, Dinah (Rachel) L(evine) 1936- ... 89-92
See also SATA 40, 44
Mochi, Ugo (A.) 1889-1977 ... SATA-38
Mock, Edward J(oseph) 1934- ... 21-22R
Mocker, Donald W(ilbur) 1935- ... 102
Mockler, Anthony 1937- ... 69-72
Mockler, Mike 1945- ... 109
Mockler, Robert J. 1932- ... 33-36R
Mockridge, Norton 1915- Brief entry ... 110
Mocsy, Andras 1929- ... 65-68
Modak, Manorama Ramkrishna 1895- ... 97-100
Modarressi, Taghi (M.) 1931- Brief entry ... 121
See also CLC 44
Mode, Heinz (Adolf) 1913- Brief entry ... 111
Model, Lisette 1906-1983 Obituary ... 109
Modell, Frank B. 1917- ... 116
See also SATA 36, 39
Modell, John 1941- ... 93-96
Modell, Judith Schachter 1941- ... 111
Modelski, George 1926- ... CANR-2
Earlier sketch in CA 49-52
Modesitt, L(eland) E(xton), Jr. 1943- ... 109
Modgil, Celia 1937- ... 124
Modgil, Sohan (Lal) 1938- ... 124
Modiano, Patrick (Jean) 1945- ... CANR-17
Earlier sketch in CA 85-88
See also CLC 18
Modigliani, Andre 1940- ... 53-56
Modigliani, Jeanne 1918(?)-1984 Obituary ... 113
Modisane, Bloke
See Modisane, William
Modisane, William 1923-1986 Obituary ... 118
Modley, Rudolph 1906-1976 Obituary ... 69-72
Modras, Ronald E(dward) 1937- ... CANR-9
Earlier sketch in CA 23-24R
Moe, Barbara 1937- ... 69-72
See also SATA 20
Moe, Christian (Hollis) 1929- ... 41-44R
Moe, Edith Monroe 1896(?)-1987
Obituary ... 122
Moehlman, Arthur H(enry) 1907- ... 11-12R
Moehlmann, F. Herbert 1893- ... 93-96
Moelleken, Wolfgang W. 1934- ... 33-36R
Moeller, Charles 1912- ... 73-76
Moeller, Dorothy W(ilson) 1902- ... 45-48
Moeller, Helen (Elaine) 1921- ... CANR-13
Earlier sketch in CA 23-24R
Moellering, Ralph L(uther) 1923- ... 15-16R
Moenkemeyer, Heinz 1914- ... 102
Moenssens, Andre A. 1930- ... 29-32R
Moerck, Paal
See Roelvaag, O(le) E(dvart)
Moeri, Louise 1924- ... CANR-9
Earlier sketch in CA 65-68
See also SATA 24
Moerk, Ernst L(orenz) 1937- ... 126
Moerman, Daniel E(llis) 1941- ... 105
Moerman, Michael (Harris) 1934- ... 25-28R
Moers, Ellen 1928-1979 ... 9-10R
Obituary ... 89-92
Moes, Joh(a)n E(rnst) 1926- ... 3R
Moeser, John V(ictor) 1942- ... 116
Moffat, Abbot Low 1901- ... 4R
Moffat, Alexander W(hite) 1891- ... 69-72
Moffat, Anne Simon 1947- ... 107
Moffat, Frances 1912- ... 97-100
Moffat, Gwen 1924- ... CANR-10
Earlier sketch in CA 13-14R
Moffat, John Lawrence 1916- ... 103
Moffat, Mary Jane 1933- ... CANR-17
Earlier sketch in CA 97-100
Moffatt, Doris 1919- ... 105
Moffatt, (Marston) Michael 1944- ... CANR-20
Earlier sketch in CA 85-88
Moffett, Eileen Flower 1928- ... 123
Moffett, George D(inwiddie) III 1943- ... 118
Moffett, Hugh (Oliver) 1910-1985 ... 73-76
Obituary ... 115
Moffett, Judith 1942- ... CANR-14
Earlier sketch in CA 69-72
Moffett, Kenworth W(illiam) 1934-
Brief entry ... 118
Moffett, Martha (Leatherwood) 1934- ... 37-40R
See also SATA 8
Moffett, Samuel Hugh 1916- ... CANR-5
Earlier sketch in CA 9-10R
Moffett, (Anthony) Toby 1944- ... 85-88
Moffitt, Donald (Anthony) 1936-
Brief entry ... 111
Moffitt, John 1908- ... CANR-10
Earlier sketch in CA 25-28R
Moffitt, Phillip 1946- ... 114
Brief entry ... 110
Moffitt, William J. 1930- ... 57-60
Mofolo, Thomas (Mokopu) 1875(?)-1948
Brief entry ... 121
See also TCLC 22
Mofsie, Louis B. 1936- ... SATA-33
Mogal, Doris P(ick) 1918- ... 69-72
Mogan, Joseph J(ohn), Jr. 1924- ... 49-52
Mogel, Leonard Henry 1922- ... 104
Moger, Allen W(esley) 1905- ... CAP-2
Earlier sketch in CA 25-28
Moger, Art 1911- ... 120
Moggach, Deborah 1948- ... CANR-18
Earlier sketch in CA 89-92
Moggridge, D(onald) E(dward) 1943- ... 29-32R
Moglen, Helene 1936- ... 65-68
Mogulof, Melvin B(ernard) 1926- ... 105
Mohammed Riza Pahlevi
See Pahlevi, Mohammed Riza
Mohan, Beverly Moffett 1918- ... 7-8R
Mohan, Brij 1939- ... 110
Mohan, Peter John 1930- ... CANR-10
Earlier sketch in CA 61-64
Mohan, Robert Paul 1920- ... 41-44R
Mohanty, Jitendra N(ath) 1928- ... 117
Mohl, Raymond A(llen) 1939- ... CANR-13
Earlier sketch in CA 33-36R
Mohl, Ruth 1891- ... CAP-1
Earlier sketch in CA 15-16
Mohlenbrock, Robert H. 1931- ... CANR-5
Earlier sketch in CA 53-56
Mohler, Charles 1913- ... 29-32R
Mohler, James A(ylward) 1923- ... CANR-23
Earlier sketches in CA 23-24R, CANR-8
Mohn, Peter B(urnet) 1934- ... 106
See also SATA 28
Mohn, Viola Kohl 1914- ... SATA-8
Mohr, Gordon 1916- ... CANR-12
Earlier sketch in CA 25-28R
Mohr, Jack
See Mohr, Gordon
Mohr, James C(rail) 1943- ... 73-76
Mohr, Nicholasa 1935- ... CANR-1
Earlier sketch in CA 49-52
See also SATA 8
See also CLC 12
Mohrenschildt, Dimitri Sergius Von
See Von Mohrenschildt, Dimitri Sergius
Mohrhardt, Foster E(dward) 1907- ... CAP-1
Earlier sketch in CA 15-16
Mohrmann, Christine A(ndrina) E(lisabeth)
M(aria) 1903- ... CAP-1
Earlier sketch in CA 9-10
Mohrt, Michel 1914- ... 13-14R
Moir, Alfred 1924- ... CANR-24
Earlier sketches in CA 21-22R, CANR-9
Moir, Duncan Wilson 1930-1983 Obituary ... 110
Moir, John S(argent) 1926- ... 41-44R
Moir, May A(rstad) 1907- ... 111
Moir, Ronald Eugene 1928- ... 29-32R
Moise, Lotte E(lla) 1917- ... 103
Mojica, Jose 1896-1974 Obituary ... 53-56
Mojtabai, A(nn) G(race) 1938- ... 85-88
See also CLC 5, 9, 15, 29
Mok, Paul P. 1934- ... 11-12R
Mokashi-Punekar, Shankar 1925- ... 97-100
Mokgatle, (Monyadio Moreleba) Naboth
1911-1985 ... CAP-2
Obituary ... 115
Earlier sketch in CA 33-36
Mokgatle, Naboth Nyadioe
See Mokgatle, (Monyadio Moreleba)
Naboth
Mokgatle, Nyadioe Naboth
See Mokgatle, (Monyadio Moreleba)
Naboth
Mokres, James A(llen) 1945- ... 49-52
Mol, Hans
See Mol, J(ohannis) J(acob)
Mol, J(ohannis) J(acob) 1922- ... CANR-18
Earlier sketches in CA 49-52, CANR-2
Molan, Dorothy L(ennon) 1911- ... 9-10R
Molan, Pat Carlson 1941- ... 112
Molarsky, Osmond 1909- ... 25-28R
See also SATA 16
Moldafsky, Annie 1930- ... 61-64
Moldea, Dan E. 1950- ... 122
Moldenhauer, Hans 1906- ... CANR-3
Earlier sketch in CA 3R
Moldenhauer, Joseph J(ohn) 1934- ... 33-36R
Moldenhauer, Rosaleen 1926- ... 97-100
Moldon, Peter L(eonard) 1937- ... 121
See also SATA 49
Moldovsky, Joel S(amuel) 1939- ... 97-100
Mole, John 1941- ... CANR-18
Earlier sketch in CA 101
See also SATA 36
Mole, Robert L. 1923- ... 29-32R
Molen, Ronald Lowry 1929- ... 65-68
Molenaar, Dee 1918- ... 37-40R
Moler, Kenneth Lloyd 1938- ... 89-92
Molesworth, Charles 1941- ... CANR-18
Earlier sketch in CA 77-80
Molette, Barbara Jean 1940- ... CANR-26
Earlier sketch in CA 45-48
See also BW
Molette, Carlton W(oodard) II 1939- ... CANR-25
Earlier sketches in CA 45-48, CANR-1
See also BW
Moley, Raymond (Charles) 1886-1975 ... 61-64
Molho, Anthony 1939- Brief entry ... 106
Molin, Sven Eric 1929- ... 19-20R
Molinaro, Julius A(rthur) 1918- ... 41-44R
Molinaro, Ursule ... 69-72
Moline, Jon Nelson 1937- ... 111
Moline, Mary 1932- ... CANR-7
Earlier sketch in CA 57-60
Molinsky, Joan Sandra 1933- ... 123
Brief entry ... 116
Moll, Elick 1907- ... CANR-2
Earlier sketch in CA 2R
Molland, Einar 1908- ... 53-56
Mollegen, Albert Theodore 1906-1984
Obituary ... 111
Mollegen, Anne Rush
See Smith, Anne Mollegen
Mollenhoff, Clark R(aymond) 1921- ... CANR-13
Earlier sketch in CA 19-20R
Mollenkott, Virginia R(amey) 1932- ... CANR-12
Earlier sketch in CA 33-36R
Moller, Richard Jay 1952- ... 106
Mollinger, Robert N. 1945- ... 106
Mollo, Andrew 1940- ... CANR-15
Earlier sketch in CA 65-68
Mollo, Terry (Madeline) 1949- ... 102
Mollo, Victor 1909-1987 ... CANR-20
Obituary ... 123
Earlier sketches in CA 11-12R, CANR-5
Molloy, Anne Baker 1907- ... 13-14R
See also SATA 32
Molloy, John T. 1937(?)- ... 81-84
Molloy, Julia Sale 1905-1983 ... CANR-1
Obituary ... 110
Earlier sketch in CA 2R
Molloy, M(ichael) J(oseph) 1917- ... 103
Molloy, Paul (George) 1924- ... CANR-17
Earlier sketch in CA 2R
See also SATA 5
Molloy, Robert (William) 1906-1977 ... CAP-2
Obituary ... 69-72
Earlier sketch in CA 29-32
Molloy, Tom 1948- ... 107
Molnar, Ferenc 1878-1952 Brief entry ... 109
See also TCLC 20
Molnar, Imre
See Lakatos, Imre
Molnar, Maria 1910(?)-1985 Obituary ... 117
Molnar, Thomas 1921- ... CANR-19
Earlier sketches in CA 3R, CANR-3
Molody, Konan Trofimovich
See Lonsdale, Gordon Arnold
Molotch, Harvey L(uskin) 1940- ... CANR-15
Earlier sketch in CA 41-44R
Molotov, V.
See Molotov, Viacheslav Mikhailovich
Molotov, V. M.
See Molotov, Viacheslav Mikhailovich
Molotov, Viacheslav Mikhailovich
1890-1986 Obituary ... 121
Moltmann, Juergen 1926- ... 93-96
Molumby, Lawrence E. 1932- ... 23-24R
Molz, (Redmond) Kathleen 1928- ... 49-52
Momaday, N(avarre) Scott 1934- ... CANR-14
Earlier sketch in CA 25-28R
See also SATA 30, 48
See also CLC 2, 19
Momboisse, Raymond M. 1927- ... 29-32R
Momen, Moojan 1950- ... 122
Moment, David 1925- ... 11-12R
Momigliano, Arnaldo (Dante) 1908-1987
Obituary ... 123
Mommsen, Katharina 1925- ... 69-72
Mommsen, Wolfgang J(ustin) 1930- ... 101
Monaco, James 1942- ... CANR-15
Earlier sketch in CA 69-72
Monaco, Richard 1940- ... CANR-15
Earlier sketch in CA 65-68
Monad, Jacques 1910-1976 Obituary ... 65-68
Monagan, Charles A(ndrew) 1950- ... 109
Monagan, John S(tephen) 1911- ... 126
Monaghan, E(dith) Jennifer 1933- ... 115
Monaghan, (James) Jay (IV) 1891-1981 ... 41-44R
Obituary ... 103
Monaghan, (Mary) Patricia 1946- ... CANR-23
Earlier sketch in CA 107
Monaghan, Patrick C. 1903(?)-1972
Obituary ... 37-40R
Monahan, Arthur P(atrick) 1928- ... 57-60
Monahan, Brent J(effrey) 1948- ... 93-96
Monahan, James (Henry Francis)
1912-1985 Obituary ... 118
Monahan, John
See Burnett, W(illiam) R(iley)
Monahan, Kaspar ... AITN-1
Monas, Sidney 1924- ... 13-14R
Monath, Elizabeth 1907- ... 5-6R
Monbeck, Michael E(ugene) 1942- ... CANR-2
Earlier sketch in CA 49-52
Moncreiffe, (Rupert) Iain (Kay) 1919-1985
Obituary ... 115
Moncrieff, David (William Hardy) Scott
See Scott-Moncrieff, David (William
Hardy)
Moncrieff, Earnest
See Chi, Richard Hu See-Yee
Moncrieff, Martha Christian Scott
See Scott Moncrieff, Martha Christian
Moncure, Jane Belk 1926- ... CANR-6
Earlier sketch in CA 11-12R
See also SATA 23
Mondadori, Alberto 1914(?)-1976
Obituary ... 65-68
Mondadori, Arnoldo 1889-1971
Obituary ... 29-32R
Mondale, Joan Adams 1930- ... 41-44R
Mondale, Walter F(rederick) 1928- ... 65-68
Monday, James 1951- ... 61-64
Monday, Michael
See Ginder, Richard
Mondey, David (Charles) 1917- ... 93-96
Mondor, Henri 1885(?)-1962 Obituary ... 111
Monegal, Emir Rodriguez
See Rodriguez Monegal, Emir
Monelli, Paolo 1894(?)-1984 Obituary ... 114
Monet, Dorothy 1927- ... 81-84
Monet, Jacques 1930- ... CANR-11
Earlier sketch in CA 65-68
Money, David Charles 1918- ... 107
Money, John (William) 1921- ... CANR-18
Earlier sketches in CA 45-48, CANR-1
Money, Keith 1935- ... 107
Moneyhon, Carl H. 1944- ... 120
Money-Kyrle, Roger (Ernie) 1898-1980
Obituary ... 101
Monfalcone, Wesley R. 1942- ... 109
Monfolo, Rodolpho 1899(?)-1976
Obituary ... 69-72
Monger, (Ifor) David 1908- ... 7-8R
Monguio, Luis 1908- ... 5-6R
Monheim, Leonard M. 1911-1971
Obituary ... 33-36R
Monhoff, June Hildegarde Flanner
1899-1987 Obituary ... 122
Monie, Willis J. 1945- ... 112
Monier-Williams, Randall Herbert
1892(?)-1984 Obituary ... 113
Monig, Christopher
See Crossen, Kendell Foster
Monjo, F(erdinand) N. 1924-1978 ... 81-84
See also SATA 16
See also CLR 2

Monk, Alan
See Kendall, Willmoore
Monk, Galdo
See Riseley, Jerry B(urr, Jr.)
Monk, Janice J(ones) 1937- 93-96
Monk, Lorraine (Althea Constance) 101
Monk, Robert C(larence) 1930- 21-22R
Monka, Paul 1935- 29-32R
Monkhouse, Alan 1858-1936 .... DLB-10
Monkhouse, Francis John 1914-1975 .. CANR-10
Obituary 57-60
Earlier sketch in CA 13-14R
Monkkonen, Eric H(enry) 1942- 61-64
Monkman, Leslie
See Monkman, Leslie G.
Monkman, Leslie G. 1946- 125
Monmonier, Mark Stephen 1943- 109
Monnet, Jean (Omer Marie) 1888-1979 102
Monninger, Joseph 1953- 121
Monnow, Peter
See Croudace, Glynn
Monod, Jacques 1910-1976 69-72
Monod, Rene
See Koch, Kurt E(mil)
Monod, Sylvere 1921- 21-22R
Monod, (Andre) Theodore 1902- 65-68
Monongo
See Clytus, John
Monro, Gavin
See Monro-Higgs, Gertrude
Monro, Harold 1879-1932 .... DLB-19
Monro, Isabel S(tevenson) 1884- CAP-2
Earlier sketch in CA 19-20
Monro, Kate M. 1883-19(?) CAP-2
Earlier sketch in CA 19-20
Monroe, Alan D(ouglas) 1944- 57-60
Monroe, Alan Houston 1903- 5-6R
Monroe, Bill
See Monroe, William Blanc, Jr.
Monroe, Carole 1944- 105
Monroe, Charles R(exford) 1905- 73-76
Monroe, Elizabeth 1905-1986 ....13-14R
Obituary 118
Monroe, Frank
See Chapman, Frank M(onroe)
Monroe, Harriet 1860-1936 Brief entry 109
See also DLB 54
See also TCLC 12
Monroe, Jonathan B(eck) 1954- 126
Monroe, Keith 1917- CANR-2
Earlier sketch in CA 5-6R
Monroe, Lyle
See Heinlein, Robert A(nson)
Monroe, (Marilyn) Lynn Lee 1935- 53-56
Monroe, Margaret Ellen 1914- 5-6R
Monroe, Marilyn
See Baker, Norma Jean
Monroe, Marion
See Cox, Marion Monroe
See also SATA 34
Monroe, Ruskyn Y. (a pseudonym) 1958- .. 116
Monroe, William Blanc, Jr. 1920- 108
Monro-Higgs, Gertrude 1905- 105
Monsarrat, Ann Whitelaw 1937- 73-76
Monsarrat, Nicholas (John Turney)
1910-1979 .... CANR-3
Earlier sketch in CA 2R
See also DLB 15
Monsell, Helen Albee 1895-1971 .... CAP-1
Earlier sketch in CA 9-10
See also SATA 24
Monsen, R(aymond) Joseph, Jr. 1931- 9-10R
Monsey, Derek 1921-1979 .... CANR-2
Obituary 85-88
Earlier sketch in CA 4R
Monsky, Mark 1941- 65-68
Monsma, James E. 1929- 29-32R
Monsma, Stephen V(os) 1936- 33-36R
Monsman, Gerald Cornelius 1940- CANR-8
Earlier sketch in CA 21-22R
Monson, Charles H., Jr. 1924- 5-6R
Monson, Karen Ann 1945-1988 .... CANR-20
Obituary 124
Earlier sketch in CA 97-100
Monsour, Sally A. 1929- 23-24R
Montag, Thomas 1947- 103
Montag, Tom
See Montag, Thomas
Montagnes, Ian 1932- 45-48
Montagu, Ashley 1905- CANR-5
Earlier sketch in CA 5-6R
Montagu, Elizabeth 1917- 11-12R
Montagu, Ewen (Edward Samuel)
1901-1985 77-80
Obituary 116
Montagu, Ivor (Goldsmid Samuel)
1904-1984 ....15-16R
Obituary 114
Montagu, Jeremy (Peter Samuel) 1927- 93-96
Montague, Gene Bryan 1928- 93-96
Montague, Jeanne
See Yarde, Jeanne Betty Frances
Montague, Joel B(enjamin), Jr. 1912- 5-6R
Montague, John (Patrick) 1929- CANR-9
Earlier sketch in CA 11-12R
See also DLB 40
See also CLC 13, 46
Montague, Lisa
See Shulman, Sandra (Dawn)
Montague, Peter Gunn 1938- 85-88
Montague-Smith, Patrick Wykeham 1920- ... 107
Montagu of Beaulieu, Edward John
Barrington 1926- CANR-6
Earlier sketch in CA 9-10R
Montaigne, Sanford H(oward) 1935- 65-68
Montalbano, William D(aniel) 1940- CANR-22
Earlier sketch in CA 105
Montale, Eugenio 1896-1981 ....19-20R
Obituary 104
See also CLC 7, 9, 18
Montana, Bob 1920-1975 Obituary 89-92
See also SATA 21
Montana, Patrick J(oseph) 1937- CANR-10
Earlier sketch in CA 25-28R
Montanari, A(delio) J(oseph) 1917- 104
Montandon, Pat 57-60
Montapert, Alfred Armand 1906- 108
Montapert, William D(avid) 1930- 107
Montclair, Dennis
See Sladen, Norman St. Barbe
Monteilhet, Hubert 1928- Brief entry 117
Monteiro, George 1932- CANR-7
Earlier sketch in CA 19-20R
Monteiro, Luis (Infante de la Cerda) de
Sttau 1926- CANR-10
Earlier sketch in CA 15-16R
Monteith, Hayton
See Mittermeyer, Helen (Hayton
Monteith)
Monteleone, Thomas F(rancis) 1946- 113
Brief entry 109
Montell, William Lynwood 1931- CANR-11
Earlier sketch in CA 29-32R
Monter, E. William 1936- 23-24R
Montero, Darrel Martin 1946- 101
Monterosso, Carlo 1921- 29-32R
Montes, Antonio Llano 1924- CANR-14
Earlier sketch in CA 69-72
Montes de Oca, Marco Antonio 1932- 114
Montesi, Albert Joseph 1921- 37-40R
Montessori, Maria 1870-1952 Brief entry ... 115
Monteux, Doris (Hodgkins) 1894-1984 ... CAP-2
Obituary 112
Earlier sketch in CA 19-20
Montey, Vivian M(arie) 1956- 105
Montfort, Auguste 1913- CANR-18
Earlier sketch in CA 101
Montgomerie, Norah (Mary) 1913- 105
See also SATA 26
Montgomery, Albert A. 1929- 13-14R
Montgomery, Bernard Law 1887-1976 69-72
Obituary 65-68
Montgomery, Brian (Frederick) 1903- 53-56
Montgomery, (Robert) Bruce 1921-1978
Obituary 104
Montgomery, Charles F(ranklin)
1910-1978 81-84
Obituary 77-80
Montgomery, Constance
See Cappel, Constance
Montgomery, David 1927- 81-84
Montgomery, David Bruce 1938- 29-32R
Montgomery, Edward F(inley) 1918- 9-10R
Montgomery, Elizabeth
See Julesberg, Elizabeth Rider
Montgomery
Montgomery, Elizabeth Rider
See Julesberg, Elizabeth Rider
Montgomery
See also SATA 3, 34, 41
Montgomery, Elizabeth Wakefield 1891- ..41-44R
Montgomery, Helen
See Gunn, Helen Montgomery
Montgomery, Herbert J. 1933- CANR-18
Earlier sketches in CA 49-52, CANR-3
Montgomery, Horace 1906- 11-12R
Montgomery, John (McVey) 1919- 25-28R
See also DLB 16
Montgomery, John D(ickey) 1920- CANR-18
Earlier sketches in CA 7-8R, CANR-3
Montgomery, John Warwick 1931- CANR-25
Earlier sketches in CA 21-22R, CANR-10
Montgomery, L(ucy) M(aud) 1874-1942
Brief entry 108
See also YABC 1
See also CLR 8
Montgomery, Marion H., Jr. 1925- CANR-3
Earlier sketch in CA 2R
See also DLB 6
See also CLC 7
See also AITN 1
Montgomery, Max
See Davenport, Guy (Mattison, Jr.)
Montgomery, Michael B. 1950- 122
Montgomery, Nancy S(chwinn) 93-96
Montgomery, Raymond A. (Jr.) 1936- . CANR-16
Earlier sketch in CA 97-100
See also SATA 39
Montgomery, Robert 1904-1981 Obituary ... 108
Montgomery, Robert L(angford), Jr.
1927- 5-6R
Montgomery, Ruth Shick CANR-17
Earlier sketches in CA 4R, CANR-2
See also AITN 1
Montgomery, Rutherford George 1894- 9-10R
See also SATA 3
Montgomery, Thomas (Andrew) 1925- 49-52
Montgomery, Tommie Sue 1942- 112
Montgomery, Vivian 102
See also SATA 36
Monthan, Doris Born 1924- 115
Montherlant, Henry (Milon) de
1896-1972 85-88
Obituary 37-40R
See also DLB 72
See also CLC 8, 19
Monti, Laura V(irginia) 1930- 111
Montias, John Michael 1928- CANR-2
Earlier sketch in CA 3R
Monticone, Ronald Charles 1937- 73-76
Montini, Giovanni Battista (Enrico Antonio
Maria)
See Paul VI, Pope
Montresor, Beni 1926- 29-32R
See also SATA 3, 38
See also SAAS 4
Montrose, Graham
See Mackinnon, Charles Roy
Montrose, James St. David
See Appleman, John Alan
Montross, David
See Backus, Jean L(ouise)
Monty, Jeanne R(uth) 1935- 49-52
Monty Python
See Chapman, Graham
and Cleese, John (Marwood)
and Gilliam, Terry (Vance)
and Idle, Eric
and Jones, Terry
and Palin, Michael
See also CLC 21
Mood, Alexander M(cFarlane) 1913- 53-56
Mood, John J(ordan) L(indemann) 1932- ..57-60
Moodie, Graeme C(ochrane) 1924- CANR-2
Earlier sketch in CA 3R
Moodie, T(homas) Dunbar 1940- 77-80
Moody, Anne 1940- 65-68
See also BW
Moody, Dale 1915- 19-20R
Moody, Eric N(elson) 1946- 116
Moody, Ernest A(ddison) 1903-1975 ....15-16R
Obituary 61-64
Moody, G. F.
See Hamel Dobkin, Kathleen
Moody, J. Carroll 1934- 33-36R
Moody, Jess C. 1925- 23-24R
Moody, Joseph Nestor 1904- CANR-1
Earlier sketch in CA 49-52
Moody, Joshua 1633(?)-1697 .... DLB-24
Moody, Paul Amos 1903- 53-56
Moody, Paul E(lliot) 1936- 118
Moody, Peter R(ichard, Jr.) 1943-
Brief entry 107
Moody, R. Bruce 1933- 19-20R
Moody, Ralph Owen 1898- CAP-1
Earlier sketch in CA 9-10
See also SATA 1
Moody, Raymond Avery, Jr. 1944- 93-96
Moody, Richard 1911- 33-36R
Moody, Ron 1924- 108
Moody, T(heodore) W(illiam) 1907- 13-14R
Moody, William Vaughn 1869-1910
Brief entry 110
See also DLB 7, 54
Moolb, Leinad
See Bloom, Daniel Halevi
Moolson, Melusa
See Solomon, Samuel
Moomaw, Ira W. 1894- CAP-1
Earlier sketch in CA 13-14
Moon, Carl 1879-1948 Brief entry 111
See also SATA 25
Moon, Douglas Mark 1937- 19-20R
Moon, G(eoff) J. H. 1915- 105
Moon, Grace Purdie 1877(?)-1947
Brief entry 113
See also SATA 25
Moon, Harold K(ay) 1932- 53-56
Moon, Henry Lee 1901-1985 Obituary 116
Moon, Michael E(lliott) 1948- 85-88
Moon, (Edward) Penderel 1905-1987
Obituary 122
Moon, Rexford G(eorge), Jr. 1922- 41-44R
Moon, Robert 1925- 73-76
Moon, Sheila (Elizabeth) 1910- 25-28R
See also SATA 5
Moon, Warren G. 1946- 125
Moonblood, Q.
See Stallone, Sylvester (Enzio)
Mooney, Bill
See Mooney, William F.
Mooney, Booth 1912-1977 .... CANR-3
Obituary 69-72
Earlier sketch in CA 49-52
Mooney, Canice (Albert James)
1911-1963 ....7-8R
Mooney, Chase C(urran) 1913-1972 .... CAP-2
Earlier sketch in CA 19-20
Mooney, Christopher F(rancis) 1925- .. CANR-14
Earlier sketch in CA 37-40R
Mooney, Elizabeth C(omstock)
1918-1986 .... CANR-9
Obituary 119
Earlier sketch in CA 61-64
See also SATA 48
Mooney, Eugene F. 1930- 19-20R
Mooney, George A(ustin) 1911-1979
Obituary 89-92
Mooney, Harry J(ohn), Jr. 1927- 7-8R
Mooney, Michael M.
See Mooney, Michael Macdonald
Mooney, Michael Macdonald
1930-1985 .... CANR-21
Obituary 117
Earlier sketch in CA 65-68
Mooney, Patrick 1937- 115
Mooney, Ted 1951- CLC-25
Mooney, William F. 1919(?)-1985
Obituary 116
Mooneyham, W(alter) Stanley 1926- CANR-6
Earlier sketch in CA 13-14R
Moonitz, Maurice 1910- CANR-2
Earlier sketch in CA 5-6R
Moonman, Eric 1929- 103
Mooradian, Karlen 1935- 97-100
Moorcock, Michael (John) 1939- CANR-17
Earlier sketches in CA 45-48, CANR-2
See also CAAS 5
See also DLB 14
See also CLC 5, 27
Moore, Acel 1940- 69-72
Moore, Alan 1960- 123
Moore, Alice Ruth
See Nelson, Alice Ruth Moore Dunbar
Moore, Alma Chesnut 1901- CAP-1
Earlier sketch in CA 13-14
Moore, Amos
See Hubbard, George (Barron)
Moore, Andrew
See Binder, Frederick Moore
Moore, Anne Carroll 1871-1961 73-76
See also SATA 13
Moore, Archie Lee 1916- 33-36R
Moore, Arthur 1906(?)-1977 Obituary 69-72
Moore, Arthur James 1888-1974 ....7-8R
Obituary 49-52
Moore, Austin
See Muir, (Charles) Augustus
Moore, Barbara
See Lee, Barbara (Moore)
Moore, Barrington, Jr. 1913- 117
Moore, Basil John 1933- 23-24R
Moore, Bernard 1904- CANR-13
Earlier sketch in CA 69-72
Moore, Bidwell 1917- 33-36R
Moore, Bob 1948- 61-64
Moore, Brian 1921- CANR-25
Earlier sketches in CA 2R, CANR-1
See also CLC 1, 3, 5, 7, 8, 19, 32
Moore, C(atherine) L(ucile) 1911- 104
See also DLB 8
Moore, Carey Armstrong 1930- 37-40R
Moore, Carl L(eland) 1921- CANR-15
Earlier sketch in CA 5-6R
Moore, Carman L(eroy) 1936- 61-64
Moore, Charles
See Moore, Reg(inald Charles Arthur)
Moore, Charles A(lexander) 1901-1967 .. CANR-3
Earlier sketch in CA 3R
Moore, Charles Garrett Ponsonby 1910- 108
Moore, Chauncey O. 1895-1965 .... CAP-1
Earlier sketch in CA 11-12
Moore, Christopher (Hugh) 1950- 119
Moore, Clayton
See Brandner, Gary
and Henderson, M(arilyn) R(uth)
Moore, Clement Clarke 1779-1863 .... SATA-18
See also DLB 42
Moore, Clyde B. 1886-1973 .... CANR-4
Earlier sketch in CA 3R
Moore, Colleen 1902(?)-1988 Obituary 124
Moore, Cora R. 1902- CAP-2
Earlier sketch in CA 25-28
Moore, Cory
See Sturgeon, Wina
Moore, Dan Tyler 1908- 7-8R
Moore, Daniel G(eorge) 1899-1977 57-60
Obituary 126
Moore, David G. 1918- CANR-2
Earlier sketch in CA 4R
Moore, David Moresby 1933- 112
Moore, Deborah Dash 1946- 108
Moore, Dick
See Moore, John Richard, Jr.
Moore, Don W. 1905(?)-1986 Obituary 119
See also SATA 48
Moore, Donald Joseph 1929- 57-60
Moore, Doris Langley CANR-1
Earlier sketch in CA 1R
Moore, Dorothea (Mary) 1881-1933
Brief entry 121
Moore, Dorothy N(elson) 1915- CANR-21
Earlier sketch in CA 89-92
Moore, Douglas Stuart 1893-1969 .... CAP-1
Earlier sketch in CA 15-16
Moore, E(velyn) Garth 1906- CAP-1
Earlier sketch in CA 11-12
Moore, Edmund A(rthur) 1903- 5-6R
Moore, Edward
See Muir, Edwin
Moore, Edward C(arter) 1917- CANR-5
Earlier sketch in CA 2R
Moore, Edward J(ames) 1935- 65-68
Moore, Edward M(umford) 1940- 57-60
Moore, Elizabeth
See Atkins, Meg Elizabeth
Moore, Ethel Pauline Perry 1902- CAP-1
Earlier sketch in CA 11-12
Moore, Eva 1942- 45-48
See also SATA 20
Moore, Everett T(homson) 1909- CAP-1
Earlier sketch in CA 11-12
Moore, Fenworth CANR-26
Earlier sketches in CA 19-20, CAP-2
Moore, Francis D(aniels) 1913- Brief entry .. 113
Moore, Francis Edward 1898- CAP-1
Earlier sketch in CA 9-10
Moore, Frank Harper 1920- 5-6R
Moore, Frank Ledlie 1923- 7-8R
Moore, Franklin G. 1905- 2R
Moore, G(ranville) Alexander Jr. 1937- ...21-22R
Moore, Gary T(homas) 1945- CANR-15
Earlier sketch in CA 85-88
Moore, Gene D. 1919- 23-24R
Moore, Geoffrey H(oyt) 1914- CANR-19
Earlier sketch in CA 81-84
Moore, Geoffrey Herbert 1920- 109
Moore, George Augustus 1852-1933
Brief entry 104
See also DLB 10, 18, 57
See also TCLC 7
Moore, George Ellis 1916- 7-8R
Moore, Gerald 1899-1987 .... CANR-5
Obituary 122
Earlier sketch in CA 4R
Moore, Glover 1911- 107
Moore, (David) Harmon 1911- 15-16R

INDEX

Moore, Harold A. 1913- 33-36R
Moore, Harris
See Harris, Alf(red)
Moore, Harry Estill 1897- CAP-1
Earlier sketch in CA 13-14
Moore, Harry T(hornton) 1908-1981 .... CANR-3
Obituary 103
Earlier sketch in CA 7-8R
Moore, Henry (Spencer) 1898-1986 126
Obituary 121
Moore, Honor 1945- 85-88
Moore, J(ohn) Preston 1906- 65-68
Moore, J(ohn) William 1928- 5-6R
Moore, Jack (William) 1941- 112
See also SATA 32, 46
Moore, Jack B(ailey) 1933- 33-36R
Moore, Jack L(ynne) 1920- 89-92
Moore, James 1928- 97-100
Moore, James R(ichard) 1947- CANR-22
Earlier sketch in CA 105
Moore, James T. III 1939- 29-32R
Moore, James Tice 1945- 73-76
Moore, Jane Ann 1931- 37-40R
Moore, Janet Gaylord 1905- 77-80
See also SATA 18
Moore, Jenny 1923-1973 Obituary 45-48
Moore, Jerome (Aaron) 1903- 81-84
Moore, Jerrold Northrup 1934- 104
Moore, Jessie Eleanor 1886-19(?) CAP-1
Earlier sketch in CA 19-20
Moore, Jim 1946- SATA-42
Moore, Jimmy
See Moore, James T. III
Moore, John (Cecil) 1907- 7-8R
Moore, John A(lexander) 1915- CANR-26
Earlier sketch in CA 45-48
Moore, John A(ndrew) 1918-1972
Obituary 37-40R
Moore, John A.
See Moore, John Allen
Moore, John Allen 1912- 119
Moore, John C(lare) 1933- 49-52
Moore, John H. 1935- 118
Moore, John Hammond 1924- 57-60
Moore, John Hebron 1920- 21-22R
Moore, John Michael 1935- 104
Moore, John Norton 1937- CANR-14
Earlier sketch in CA 37-40R
Moore, John R(obert) 1928- CANR-3
Earlier sketch in CA 2R
Moore, John Rees 1918- 33-36R
Moore, John Richard, Jr. 1925- 19-20R
Moore, John Robert 1890-1973 .... CAP-1
Earlier sketch in CA 9-10
Moore, John Travers 1908- CANR-3
Earlier sketch in CA 5-6R
See also SATA 12
Moore, Julia A. (Davis) 1847-1920
Brief entry 116
Moore, Katharine 1898- CANR-20
Earlier sketch in CA 89-92
Moore, Katherine Davis 1915- 13-14R
Moore, Keith L(eon) 1925- 69-72
Moore, Kenneth Clark 1943- 102
Moore, Kenneth E(ugene) 1930- 73-76
Moore, Kenny
See Moore, Kenneth Clark
Moore, L(ittleton) Hugh 1935- 49-52
Moore, L. Silas (Jr.) 1936- 41-44R
Moore, Lamont 1909- SATA-29
Moore, Lander
See Fensch, Thomas
Moore, Lester L(ee) 1924- 33-36R
Moore, Lilian 1909- 103
See also SATA 52
See also CLR 15
Moore, Lillian 1917-1967 .... CANR-2
Earlier sketch in CA 2R
Moore, Linda Perigo 1946- 107
Moore, Lisa
See Chater, Elizabeth (Eileen)
Moore, Lorrie
See Moore, Marie Lorena
See also CLC 39, 45
Moore, Madeline (Roberta) 1934- 124
Moore, Marcia 1928- CANR-13
Earlier sketch in CA 61-64
Moore, Margaret R(umberger) 1903- 9-10R
See also SATA 12
Moore, Marianne (Craig) 1887-1972 .... CANR-3
Obituary 33-36R
Earlier sketch in CA 4R
See also SATA 20
See also DLB 45
See also CLC 1, 2, 4, 8, 10, 13, 19, 47
Moore, Marie Drury 1926- 33-36R
Moore, Marie Lorena 1957- 116
Moore, Marna
See Reynolds, (Marjorie) Moira Davison
Moore, (Georgina) Mary (Galbraith) 1930-
Brief entry 112
Moore, Maxine 1927- 73-76
Moore, Michael
See Harris, Herbert
Moore, Nicholas 1918- 69-72
Moore, P(eter) G(erald) 1928- CANR-26
Earlier sketch in CA 45-48
Moore, Pamela 1937-1964 .... 4R
Moore, Patrick (Alfred) 1923- CANR-8
Earlier sketch in CA 13-14R
See also SATA 39, 49
Moore, Paul, Jr. 1919- 89-92
Moore, Paul L. 1917-1976 .... 4R
Obituary 103
Moore, R(obert) Laurence 1940- 29-32R
Moore, Ray (S.) 1905(?)-1984 Obituary 111
See also SATA 37
Moore, Rayburn Sabatzky 1920- CANR-17
Earlier sketches in CA 4R, CANR-2
Moore, Raylyn 1928- 29-32R
Moore, Raymond Arthur, Jr. 1925- 5-6R
Moore, Raymond S. 1915- CANR-21
Earlier sketch in CA 29-32R
Moore, Reg(inald Charles Arthur) 1930- 104
Moore, Regina
See Dunne, Mary Collins
Moore, Richard (Thomas) 1927- CANR-20
Earlier sketch in CA 33-36R
Moore, Richard B. 1893(?)-1978
Obituary 81-84
Moore, Richard H(arlan) 1945- 121
Moore, Richard R. 1934- 105
Moore, Robert (Samuel) 1936- CANR-11
Earlier sketch in CA 25-28R
Moore, Robert
See Williams, Robert Moore
Moore, Robert E(verett) 1914- 57-60
Moore, Robert Etheridge 1919- 61-64
Moore, Robert Hamilton 1913-1984
Obituary 114
Moore, Robert L(owell), Jr. 1925- 15-16R
See also AITN 1
Moore, Robin
See Moore, Robert L(owell), Jr.
Moore, Roger George 1927- 109
Moore, Rosalie (Gertrude) 1910- CANR-3
Earlier sketch in CA 5-6R
Moore, Russell Franklin 1920- CANR-6
Earlier sketch in CA 11-12R
Moore, Ruth CANR-6
Earlier sketch in CA 4R
See also SATA 23
Moore, Ruth Nulton 1923- CANR-15
Earlier sketch in CA 81-84
See also SATA 38
Moore, S(arah) E. CANR-2
Earlier sketch in CA 49-52
See also SATA 23
Moore, Sally Falk 1924- CANR-6
Earlier sketch in CA 57-60
Moore, Samuel Taylor 1893-1974
Obituary 53-56
Moore, Sebastian 1917- 23-24R
Moore, Sonia 1902- CANR-2
Earlier sketch in CA 45-48
Moore, Steven 1951- 123
Moore, Susanna 1948- 109
Moore, T(om) Inglis 1901- 21-22R
Moore, T(homas) Sturge 1870-1944
Brief entry 118
See also DLB 19
Moore, Tara 1950- 116
Moore, Thomas Gale 1930- CANR-12
Earlier sketch in CA 29-32R
Moore, Tom 1950- CANR-18
Earlier sketch in CA 101
Moore, Trevor Wyatt 1924- CANR-12
Earlier sketch in CA 29-32R
Moore, Tui De Roy 1953- 107
Moore, Vardine (Russell) 1906- 41-44R
Moore, Virginia Dryden 1911- 19-20R
Moore, W(illiam) Glenn 1925- 49-52
Moore, Walter Lane 1905- CAP-1
Earlier sketch in CA 19-20
Moore, Ward 1903-1978 .... CAP-2
Obituary 113
Earlier sketch in CA 29-32
See also DLB 8
Moore, Warren (M., Jr.) 1923- 25-28R
Moore, Wilbert E(llis) 1914- CANR-5
Earlier sketch in CA 4R
Moore, Wilfred George 1907- CANR-4
Earlier sketch in CA 11-12R
Moore, William Howard 1942- 73-76
Moore, William L(eonard, Jr.) 1943- 93-96
Moorehead, Agnes 1906-1974 Obituary 49-52
Moorehead, Alan (McCrae) 1910-1983 .... CANR-6
Obituary 110
Earlier sketch in CA 7-8R
Moorehead, Caroline 1944- CANR-18
Earlier sketch in CA 101
Moore-Rinvolucri, Mina Josephine 1902- 107
Moores, Dick
See Moores, Richard (Arnold)
Moores, Richard (Arnold) 1909-1986 69-72
Obituary 119
See also SATA 48
Moorhead, Diana 1940- 105
Moorhead, James H(owell) 1947- 124
Moorhead, Max L(eon) 1914- 23-24R
Moorhouse, Charles Edmund 1911- 108
Moorhouse, Frank 1938- 118
Moorhouse, Geoffrey 1931- 25-28R
Moorhouse, Hilda Vansittart CAP-1
Earlier sketch in CA 11-12
Moorman, Charles (Wickliffe) 1925-
Brief entry 114
Moorman, John Richard Humpidge
1905- CANR-2
Earlier sketch in CA 4R
Moorshead, Henry
See Pine, Leslie Gilbert
Moorsom, Sasha 1931- CANR-14
Earlier sketch in CA 69-72
Moorsteen, Richard H. 1926(?)-1975
Obituary 57-60
Moos, Malcolm C(harles) 1916-1982 ....37-40R
Obituary 105
Moos, Rudolf H. 1934- CANR-1
Earlier sketch in CA 49-52
Moose, Ruth 1938- 101
Mooser, Stephen 1941- CANR-15
Earlier sketch in CA 89-92
See also SATA 28
Moote, A(lanson) Lloyd 1931- 33-36R
Moquin, Wayne-(Francis) 1930- 33-36R
Mora, Carl J(ose) 1936- 109
Mora, George 1923- CANR-1
Earlier sketch in CA 45-48
Morace, Robert A(nthony) 1947- 113
Moraes, Dom(inic F.) 1938- 25-28R
Moraes, Frank Robert 1907-1974 .... CAP-1
Obituary 49-52
Earlier sketch in CA 13-14
Moraes, (Marcus) Vinicius (Cruz) de (Mello)
1913-1980 Obituary 101
Morain, Lloyd L. 1917- 69-72
Morais, Vamberto 1921- 69-72
Morales, Angel Luis 1919- 49-52
Moramarco, Fred Stephen 1938- 57-60
Moran, Barbara B. 1944- 124
Moran, Charles McMoran Wilson
See Wilson, Charles McMoran
Moran, Emilio F(ederico) 1946- 117
Moran, Gabriel 1935- CANR-4
Earlier sketch in CA 53-56
Moran, George 1942- 115
Moran, Hugh Anderson 1881-1977
Obituary 73-76
Moran, James Sterling 1909- CANR-12
Earlier sketch in CA 9-10R
Moran, Jim
See Moran, James Sterling
Moran, John 1930- 45-48
Moran, John C(harles) 1942- 110
Moran, Mike
See Ard, William (Thomas)
Moran, Patrick Alfred Pierce 1917- 11-12R
Moran, Richard (Jerome) 1942- 121
Moran, Ronald (Wesson, Jr.) 1936- 37-40R
Moran, Tom 1943- 111
Moran, William E(dward), Jr. 1916- 13-14R
Morand, Paul 1888-1976 Obituary 69-72
See also DLB 65
See also CLC 41
Morano, Donald V(ictor) 1934- 45-48
Morante, Elsa 1918-1985 85-88
Obituary 117
See also CLC 8, 47
Morantz, Regina Markell
See Morantz-Sanchez, Regina (Ann)
Markell
Morantz-Sanchez, Regina (Ann) Markell
1943- 124
Morasky, Robert Louis 1940- 105
Moraud, Marcel I(an) 1917- 53-56
Moravia, Alberto
See Pincherle, Alberto
See also CLC 2, 7, 11, 27, 46
Morawetz, Thomas H(ubert) 1942- 101
Morawski, Stefan T(adeusz) 1921- 81-84
Moray, Helga 89-92
Moray, Neville (Peter) 1935- 29-32R
Moray Williams, Ursula 1911- CANR-26
Earlier sketch in CA 111
Morcom, John Brian 1925- 7-8R
Mordden, Ethan (Christopher) 1947- 73-76
Mordechai, Ben
See Gerber, Israel J(oshua)
Mordock, John B. 1938- 61-64
Mordvinoff, Nicolas 1911-1973 73-76
Obituary 41-44R
See also SATA 17
More, Caroline
See Cone, Molly Lamken
and Strachan, Margaret Pitcairn
More, Daphne 1929- 65-68
More, Harry W(illiam) 1929- CANR-20
Earlier sketches in CA 53-56, CANR-4
More, Jasper 1907-1987 .... CAP-1
Obituary 124
Earlier sketch in CA 9-10
More, Kenneth 1914-1982 Obituary 107
Moreas, Jean
See Papadiamantopoulos, Johannes
See also TCLC 18
Moreau, Daniel 1949- 125
Moreau, David Merlin 1927- 93-96
Moreau, John Adam 1938- 37-40R
Moreau, Jules Laurence 1917-1971 .... 3R
Obituary 103
Moreau, Reginald E(rnest) 1897-1970
Obituary 104
Morecambe, Eric 1926-1984 Obituary 112
Morehead, Albert H(odges) 1909-1966 .... CAP-1
Earlier sketch in CA 13-14
Morehead, Joe
See Morehead, Joseph H(yde), Jr.
Morehead, Joseph H(yde), Jr. 1931- CANR-6
Earlier sketch in CA 57-60
Morehouse, Clifford P(helps) 1904- 11-12R
Morehouse, Laurence E(nglemohr)
1913- CANR-4
Earlier sketch in CA 11-12R
Morehouse, Thomas A(lvin) 1937- 124
Morehouse, Ward 1899(?)-1966
Obituary 25-28R
Morel, Dighton
See Warner, Kenneth (Lewis)
Moreland, Lois B. 45-48
Morell, David 1939- 110
Morella, Joseph (James) 1949- 104
Morello, Karen Berger 1949- 126
Moremen, Grace E(llen Partin) 1930- CANR-1
Earlier sketch in CA 45-48
Moren, Sally M(oore) 1947- 97-100
Morency, Pierre 1942- DLB-60
Moreno, Antonio Elosegui 1918- 33-36R
Moreno, Francisco Jose 1934- 29-32R
Moreno, Jacob L. 1892-1974 .... CAP-2
Obituary 49-52
Earlier sketch in CA 19-20
Moreno, Jose A. 1928- 25-28R
Moreno, Martin
See Swartz, Harry (Felix)
Moreno, Pedro R. 1947- 69-72
Morentz, Ethel Irene 29-32R
Morentz, Pat
See Morentz, Ethel Irene
Morenus, Constance Gay 1895(?)-1985
Obituary 117
Moreton, John
See Cohen, Morton N(orton)
Moretti, Marino 1885(?)-1979 Obituary 89-92
Morewedge, Parviz 1934- 93-96
Morey, Charles
See Fletcher, Helen Jill
Morey, Robert A(lbert) 1946- 113
Morey, Roy D. 1937- 19-20R
Morey, Walt(er Nelson) 1907- 29-32R
See also SATA 3, 51
Morford, Mark P(ercy) O(wen) 1929-
Brief entry 111
Morgan, Al(bert Edward) 1920- CANR-1
Earlier sketch in CA 45-48
Morgan, Alfred P(owell) 1889-1972 107
See also SATA 33
Morgan, Alison Mary 1930- CANR-18
Earlier sketches in CA 49-52, CANR-1
See also SATA 30
Morgan, Alyssa
See Delatush, Edith G.
Morgan, Angela
See Paine, Lauran (Bosworth)
Morgan, Ann Lee 1941- 125
Morgan, Anne Hodges 1940- 117
Morgan, Arlene
See Paine, Lauran (Bosworth)
Morgan, Arthur Ernest 1878-1975 .... CANR-3
Obituary 61-64
Earlier sketch in CA 5-6R
Morgan, B(ayard) Q(uincy) 1883-1967 .... CAP-1
Earlier sketch in CA 11-12
Morgan, Barton 1889- CAP-1
Earlier sketch in CA 9-10
Morgan, Berry 1919- 49-52
See also DLB 6
See also CLC 6
Morgan, Bill 1949- 110
Morgan, Brian 1919- 7-8R
Morgan, Bryan S(tanford) 1923-1976 .... CANR-9
Earlier sketch in CA 7-8R
Morgan, Cary
See Cutler, Roland
Morgan, Charles 1894-1958 .... DLB-34
Morgan, Charles H(ill) 1902-1984 ....37-40R
Obituary 112
Morgan, Charles, Jr. 1930- CANR-13
Earlier sketch in CA 19-20R
Morgan, Chester A(lan) 1914- 19-20R
Morgan, Christopher 1952- 105
Morgan, Claire
See Highsmith, (Mary) Patricia
Morgan, Clifford T(homas) 1915-1976 .... CANR-4
Obituary 65-68
Earlier sketch in CA 2R
Morgan, Dale L. 1914-1971 Obituary 104
Morgan, Dan 1925- CANR-14
Earlier sketch in CA 37-40R
Morgan, Daniel C(roxton), Jr. 1931- 19-20R
Morgan, Darold H. 1924- 23-24R
Morgan, Davd (Rhys) 1937- 45-48
Morgan, David P(age) 1927- 123
Brief entry 118
Morgan, David T(aft, Jr.) 1937- 69-72
Morgan, Dewi (Lewis) 1916- CANR-1
Earlier sketch in CA 2R
Morgan, Donald G(rant) 1911- 19-20R
Morgan, Donn F(arley) 1943- 113
Morgan, Edmund S(ears) 1916- CANR-4
Earlier sketch in CA 11-12R
See also DLB 17
Morgan, Edward James Ranembe
1900-1978 Obituary 108
Morgan, Edward P. 1910- CAP-1
Earlier sketch in CA 19-20
Morgan, Edwin (George) 1920- CANR-3
Earlier sketch in CA 7-8R
See also DLB 27
See also CLC 31
Morgan, Elaine (Neville) 1920- 41-44R
Morgan, Elizabeth 1947- 108
Morgan, Ellen
See Bumstead, Kathleen Mary
Morgan, Emanuel
See Bynner, Witter
Morgan, Frank
See Paine, Lauran (Bosworth)
Morgan, Fred Bruce, Jr. 1919-1975 65-68
Obituary 61-64
Morgan, Fred Troy 1926- 89-92
Morgan, (George) Frederick 1922- CANR-21
Earlier sketch in CA 19-20R
See also CLC 23
Morgan, G. J.
See Rowland, D(onald) S(ydney)
Morgan, Geoffrey 1916- 23-24R
See also SATA 46
Morgan, Gerald 1925- 41-44R
Morgan, Glenn G(uy) 1926- 9-10R
Morgan, Gwen 101
Morgan, Gwyneth
See Beal, Gwyneth
Morgan, H(oward) Wayne 1934- CANR-18
Earlier sketches in CA 5-6R, CANR-2

Morgan, Hal
See Morgan, Henry A.
Morgan, Harriet
See Mencken, H(enry) L(ouis)
Morgan, Helen (Gertrude Louise) 1921- ...57-60
See also SATA 29
Morgan, Henry
See von Ost, Henry Lerner
Morgan, Henry A. 1954- 112
Morgan, Hilda Campbell 1892-1985
Obituary 118
Morgan, Irvonwy 1907-1982 Obituary 107
Morgan, James N(ewton) 1918- 21-22R
Morgan, Jane
See Moren, Sally M(oore)
and Cooper, James Fenimore
Morgan, Janet 1945- 65-68
See also CLC 39
Morgan, Jean (Werner) 1922- 102
Morgan, (Walter) Jefferson 1940- CANR-12
Earlier sketch in CA 73-76
Morgan, Jim 1950- 45-48
Morgan, Joan 1905- 7-8R
Morgan, Joe Warner 1912- 9-10R
Morgan, John
See Paine, Lauran (Bosworth)
Morgan, John A(ndrew), Jr. 1935- 49-52
Morgan, John S. 1921- 15-16R
Morgan, Joy Elmer 1889-1986 Obituary 119
Morgan, Judith A(dams) 1939- 49-52
Morgan, Kathryn L. 117
Morgan, Kay Summersby 1909-1975
Obituary 53-56
Morgan, Kenneth Owen 1934- CANR-23
Earlier sketches in CA 15-16R, CANR-7
Morgan, Kenneth R(emsen) 1916- 13-14R
Morgan, Lael 1936- CANR-5
Earlier sketch in CA 53-56
Morgan, Lenore H. 1908-1976 .... CAP-2
Earlier sketch in CA 33-36
See also SATA 8
Morgan, Louise 9-10R
Morgan, Lucy 1940- 108
Morgan, M(argaret) Ruth 1942(?)-1983
Obituary 109
Morgan, Marabel 1937- CANR-2
Earlier sketch in CA 49-52
See also AITN 1
Morgan, Marion (Nora Eluned) 1942- 120
Morgan, Marjorie
See Chibnall, Marjorie (McCallum)
Morgan, Mark
See Overholser, Wayne D.
Morgan, McKayla
See Basile, Gloria Vitanza
Morgan, Memo
See Avallone, Michael (Angelo), Jr.
Morgan, Michael Croke 1911- 93-96
Morgan, Michaela
See Basile, Gloria Vitanza
Morgan, Murray 1916- 107
Morgan, Neil 1924- CANR-2
Earlier sketch in CA 5-6R
Morgan, Nicholas
See Morgan, Thomas Bruce
Morgan, Patricia 1944- 89-92
Morgan, Patrick M. 1940- 37-40R
Morgan, Paul 1928- 61-64
Morgan, Peter F(rederick) 1930- 113
Morgan, Raleigh, Jr. 1916- 41-44R
Morgan, Rebecca
See Forrest, Richard (Stockton)
Morgan, Richard E(rnest) 1937- CANR-15
Earlier sketch in CA 41-44R
Morgan, Robert 1921- CANR-20
Earlier sketch in CA 103
Morgan, Robert (R.) 1944- CANR-21
Earlier sketch in CA 33-36R
Morgan, Robert
See Turner, Robert (Harry)
Morgan, Roberta 1953- CANR-15
Earlier sketch in CA 93-96
Morgan, Robin 1941- 69-72
See also CLC 2
Morgan, Roger P(earce) 1932- CANR-12
Earlier sketch in CA 19-20R
Morgan, Roy A(mos) 1916- 41-44R
Morgan, Ruth P. 1934- 37-40R
Morgan, Sarah (Williams) 1901- CAP-1
Earlier sketch in CA 9-10
Morgan, Scott
See Kuttner, Henry
Morgan, Sharon A(ntonia) 1951- 61-64
Morgan, Shirley
See Kiepper, Shirley Morgan
See also SATA 10
Morgan, Speer 1946- 97-100
Morgan, Stanley 1929- 69-72
Morgan, Steven Michael 1942- 115
Morgan, Ted 1932- CANR-3
Earlier sketch in CA 45-48
See also CAAS 4
Morgan, (Joseph) Theodore 1910- 19-20R
See also CAAS 3
Morgan, Thomas (Bruce) 1885(?)-1972
Obituary 37-40R
Morgan, Thomas Bruce 1926- 13-14R
Morgan, Tom 1942- 108
See also SATA 42
Morgan, Valerie
See Paine, Lauran (Bosworth)
Morgan, Virginia
See Mundis, Hester
Morgan, Wesley
See Bennett, Isadora
Morgan, William 1944- 109
Morgan-Grenville, Gerard (Wyndham)
1931- 57-60
Morgan Witts, Max 1931- 29-32R
Morgello, Clemente Frank 1923- 103
Morgenroth, Barbara Brief entry 117
See also SATA 36
Morgenstein, Gary 1952- 116
Morgenstern, Christian 1871-1914
Brief entry 105
See also TCLC 8
Morgenstern, Dan Michael 1929-
Brief entry 111
Morgenstern, Julian 1881-1976 .... CAP-1
Obituary 89-92
Earlier sketch in CA 19-20
Morgenstern, Oskar 1902-1977 .... CANR-5
Obituary 73-76
Earlier sketch in CA 9-10R
Morgenstern, Soma 1891(?)-1976
Obituary 65-68
Morgenthau, Hans Joachim 1904-1980 ....9-10R
Obituary 101
Morgenthau, Henry, Jr. 1891-1967
Obituary 116
Morghen, Raffaello 1896-1983 Obituary 109
Morgner, Irmtraud 1933- DLB-75
Morgulas, Jerrold 1934- CANR-13
Earlier sketch in CA 23-24R
Morhaim, Victoria Kelrich 1937- 2R
Mori, Kyozo 1907(?)-1984 Obituary 112
Mori, Toshio 1910- Brief entry 116
Moriarty, Alice Marie Ewell 1917- 23-24R
Moriarty, Christopher 1936- 81-84
Moriarty, Florence Jarman 104
Moriarty, Frederick Leo 1913- CANR-2
Earlier sketch in CA 7-8R
Moriarty, Tim 1923- 61-64
Morice, Anne
See Shaw, Felicity
Morice, Dave 1946- 109
Morich, Stanton
See Griffith-Jones, George Chetwynd
Morick, Harold 1933- 25-28R
Morin, Claire
See Dore, Claire (Morin)
Morin, Edgar 1921- 107
Morin, Relman George 1907-1973 ...... CANR-4
Obituary 41-44R
Earlier sketch in CA 3R
Morin, William J(ames) 1939- 111
Morine, Hoder
See Conroy, John Wesley
Morini, Simona 1932- 110
Mori Ogai
See Mori Rintaro
See also TCLC 14
Mori Rintaro 1862-1922 Brief entry 110
Morisey, A. Alexander 1913-1979
Obituary 89-92
Morison, David Lindsay 1920- 15-16R
Morison, Samuel Eliot 1887-1976 ...... CANR-4
Obituary 65-68
Earlier sketch in CA 2R
See also DLB 17
Morisseau, James J(oseph) 1929- 41-44R
Morita, James R. 1931- 103
Morita, Yuzo 1940- CANR-1
Earlier sketch in CA 45-48
Moritz, A(lbert) F(rank) 1947- 110
Moritz, Charles Fredric 1917- 118
Morken, Lucinda Oakland 1906- 61-64
Morkovin, Bela V.
See Morkovin, Boris V(ladimir)
Morkovin, Boris V(ladimir) 1882-1968 .... CAP-1
Earlier sketch in CA 19-20
Morlan, George K(olmer) 1904- 29-32R
Morlan, John E(dmund) 1930- 11-12R
Morlan, Robert L(oren) 1920-1985 ......19-20R
Obituary 118
Morland, Dick
See Hill, Reginald (Charles)
Morland, Howard 1942- 107
Morland, (John) Kenneth 1916- 41-44R
Morland, Nigel 1905-1986 53-56
Obituary 119
Morland, Peter Henry
See Faust, Frederick (Shiller)
Morle, Albert Henry George 1919- 7-8R
Morley, Brian
See Bradley, Marion Zimmer
Morley, Christopher (Darlington)
1890-1957 Brief entry 112
See also DLB 9
Morley, David 1923- 108
Morley, Don 1937- 108
Morley, Felix M. 1894-1982 Obituary 106
Morley, Frank V(igor) 1899-1980 105
Morley, Frank Vigor 1899-1980 Obituary ... 102
Morley, (John) Geoffrey (Nicholson)
1905-1983 Obituary 109
Morley, Hugh 1908(?)-1978 Obituary 77-80
Morley, James William 1921- 13-14R
Morley, John 1838-1923 .... DLB-57
Morley, John(athan) David 1948- 126
Morley, Patricia (Ann) 1929- 73-76
Morley, Robert 1908- Brief entry 113
Morley, S(ylvanus) Griswold 1878- 5-6R
Morley, Samuel A. 1934- 37-40R
Morley, Sheridan 1941- 29-32R
Morley, Susan
See Cross, John Keir
Morley, Wilfred Owen
See Lowndes, Robert A(gustine) W(ard)
Morman, Jean Mary 1925- 61-64
Morn, Frank T(homas) 1937- 107
Morneau, Robert Fealey 1938- 113
Morningstar, Connie 1927- 69-72
Moroney, John R. 1939- CANR-17
Earlier sketch in CA 41-44R
Morowitz, Harold Joseph 1927- 104
Morpurgo, J(ack) E(ric) 1918- CANR-4
Earlier sketch in CA 9-10R
Morra, Marion Eleanor 104
Morra, Umberto ?-1981 Obituary 105
Morrah, Dave
See Morrah, David Wardlaw, Jr.
Morrah, David Wardlaw, Jr. 1914- 4R
See also SATA 10
Morrah, Dermot (Michael Macgregor)
1896-1974 .... CAP-2
Obituary 53-56
Earlier sketch in CA 29-32
Morrall, John B. 1923- 25-28R
Morray, Joseph Parker 1916- 5-6R
Morreale, Ben 1924- 57-60
Morrell, David 1943- CANR-7
Earlier sketch in CA 57-60
Morrell, David C. 1929- 81-84
Morrell, Robert E(llis) 1930- 121
Morrell, William Parker 1899- CANR-1
Earlier sketch in CA 3R
Morren, Theophil
See Hofmannsthal, Hugo von
Morressy, John 1930- CANR-8
Earlier sketch in CA 23-24R
See also SATA 23
Morrice, J(ames) K(enneth) W(att) 1924- ... 118
Morrice, Ken
See Morrice, J(ames) K(enneth) W(att)
Morrie
See Turner, Morris
Morrill, Allen C(onrad) 1904- 101
Morrill, Claire 1900(?)-1981 Obituary 103
Morrill, Eleanor D(unlap) 1907- 101
Morrill, George Percival 1920- 33-36R
Morrill, Leslie H(olt) 1934- SATA-33, 48
Morrill, Richard
See Schreck, Everett M.
Morrill, Richard L(eland) 1934- 29-32R
Morris, A(ndrew) J(ames) A(nthony)
1936- CANR-12
Earlier sketch in CA 73-76
Morris, Adalaide K(irby) 1942- 57-60
Morris, Aldyth V. 1901- 29-32R
Morris, Alton C(hester) 1903- 15-16R
Morris, Ben(jamin Stephen) 1910- 113
Morris, Bernadine (Taub) 1925- 102
Morris, Bertram 1908- CANR-18
Earlier sketch in CA 2R
Morris, Brian 1930- CANR-18
Earlier sketch in CA 29-32R
Morris, Bruce R(obert) 1909- 5-6R
Morris, Charles (William) 1901- 13-14R
Morris, Charles Lee 1943(?)-1986
Obituary 118
Morris, Christopher 1938- 21-22R
Morris, Clyde M(cMahon) 1921- 93-96
Morris, (Edward) Craig 1939- 123
Morris, Cynthia Taft 1928- 25-28R
Morris, Dan (H.) 1912- 21-22R
Morris, David 1945- 85-88
Morris, David Brown 1942- CANR-22
Earlier sketch in CA 105
Morris, Desmond (John) 1928- CANR-18
Earlier sketches in CA 45-48, CANR-2
See also SATA 14
Morris, Donald R. 1924- 19-20R
Morris, Edgar Poe
See Kinnaird, Clark
Morris, Edita (deToll) CANR-1
Earlier sketch in CA 3R
Morris, Edmund 1940- 89-92
Morris, (Murrell) Edward 1935- CANR-14
Earlier sketch in CA 69-72
Morris, Edwin Bateman 1881-1971
Obituary 112
Morris, Eric 1940- 81-84
Morris, Everett B. 1899-1967 .... CAP-1
Earlier sketch in CA 9-10
Morris, Freda 1933- CANR-4
Earlier sketch in CA 53-56
Morris, George Pope 1802-1864 .... DLB-73
Morris, Gilbert (Leslie) 1929- 117
Morris, Grant Harold 1940- 29-32R
Morris, Gregory L(ynn) 1950- 119
Morris, Harry (Caesar) 1924- 11-12R
Morris, Helen 1909- CANR-18
Earlier sketch in CA 101
Morris, Henry M(adison, Jr.) 1918- CANR-13
Earlier sketch in CA 37-40R
Morris, Herbert 1928- CANR-1
Earlier sketch in CA 2R
Morris, Ira (Victor) 1903- 9-10R
Morris, Ivan (Ira Esme) 1925-1976 .... CANR-11
Obituary 65-68
Earlier sketch in CA 9-10R
Morris, J(ohn) H(umphrey) C(arlile) 1910- ..7-8R
Morris, J(ames) Kenneth 1896- 5-6R
Morris, J. R. 1914(?)-1977 Obituary 73-76
Morris, Jackson E(dgar) 1918- 19-20R
Morris, James (Humphrey)
See Morris, Jan
Morris, James A(lvin) 1938- 120
Morris, James E(lliot) 1942- 112
Morris, James M(atthew) 1935- 89-92
Morris, Jan 1926- CANR-1
Earlier sketch in CA 3R
Morris, Jane
See Ardmore, Jane Kesner
Morris, Janet E(llen) 1946- CANR-13
Earlier sketch in CA 73-76
Morris, (Margaret) Jean 1924- Brief entry .. 116
Morris, Jerrold 1911- CANR-11
Earlier sketch in CA 23-24R
Morris, Joan 1901- 45-48
Morris, Joe A(lex) 1904- 65-68
Morris, Joe Alex, Jr. 1927- 73-76
Morris, John 1895-1980 Obituary 102
Morris, John
See Hearne, John (Edgar Caulwell)
Morris, John D(avid) 1946- 111
Morris, John N(elson) 1931- 33-36R
Morris, John O(sgood) 1918- 41-44R
Morris, John W(esley) 1907- CANR-6
Earlier sketch in CA 15-16R
Morris, Jonas 1933- 117
Morris, Judy K. 1936- 116
Morris, Julian
See West, Morris L(anglo)
Morris, Katharine CAP-1
Earlier sketch in CA 15-16
Morris, Kenneth T(hompson) 1941- 57-60
Morris, Leon (Lamb) 1914- CANR-20
Earlier sketches in CA 9-10R, CANR-4
Morris, Lewis 1833-1907 .... DLB-35
Morris, Loverne Lawton 1896- 7-8R
Morris, M.
See Thibaudeau, Colleen
Morris, Margaret 1891-1980 Obituary 97-100
Morris, Margaret Francine 1938- 57-60
Morris, Mary (Elizabeth Davis)
1913-1986 53-56
Obituary 121
Morris, Mary Lee 120
Morris, Max 1913- 109
Morris, Mel (Merrill) 1930- 69-72
Morris, Michael 1914- CANR-5
Earlier sketch in CA 7-8R
Morris, Michael (Spence Lowdell)
1940- CANR-23
Earlier sketch in CA 107
Morris, Michelle 1941- 108
Morris, Milton D(onald) 1939- 57-60
Morris, Monica B. 1928- Brief entry 113
Morris, Nobuko
See Albery, Nobuko
Morris, Norman S. 1931- 33-36R
Morris, Norval 1923- 37-40R
Morris, Phyllis 1894-1982 Obituary 106
Morris, Phyllis Sutton 1931- 104
Morris, R(oger) J(ohn) B(owring) 1946- ...93-96
Morris, Raymond N. 1936- 25-28R
Morris, Raymond Philip 1904- 45-48
Morris, Richard (Ward) 1939- CANR-18
Earlier sketches in CA 45-48, CANR-1
Morris, Richard B(randon) 1904- CANR-2
Earlier sketch in CA 49-52
See also DLB 17
Morris, Richard J(ules) 1942- CANR-16
Earlier sketch in CA 89-92
Morris, Richard K(nowles) 1915- 21-22R
Morris, Robert 1910- CANR-16
Earlier sketch in CA 89-92
Morris, Robert (Lyle) 1942- Brief entry 116
Morris, Robert A(da) 1933- 49-52
See also SATA 7
Morris, Robert Kerwin 1933- 33-36R
Morris, Ruby Turner 1908- CANR-1
Earlier sketch in CA 2R
Morris, Ruth
See Webb, Ruth Enid Borlase Morris
Morris, Sara
See Burke, John (Frederick)
Morris, Sarah M(iller) 1906- 81-84
Morris, Scot 1942- 101
Morris, Stephen 1935- CANR-20
Earlier sketch in CA 103
Morris, Steveland Judkins 1950(?)-
Brief entry 111
Morris, Suzanne 1944- CANR-17
Earlier sketch in CA 89-92
Morris, T(homas) B(aden) 1900- CANR-2
Earlier sketch in CA 7-8R
Morris, Taylor 1923- 103
Morris, Terry Lesser 1914- 9-10R
Morris, Thomas D(ean) 1938- Brief entry ... 112
Morris, Thomas Victor 1952- 120
Morris, Tina 1941- CANR-12
Earlier sketch in CA 29-32R
Morris, W. R. 1936- 77-80
Morris, William 1834-1896 ......DLB-18, 35, 57
Morris, William 1913- CANR-12
Earlier sketch in CA 19-20R
See also SATA 29
Morris, William E(dgar) 1926- 9-10R
Morris, William O. 1922- 37-40R
Morris, William T(homas) 1928- 19-20R
Morris, Willie 1934- CANR-13
Earlier sketch in CA 19-20R
See also DLBY 80
See also AITN 2
Morris, Wright 1910- CANR-21
Earlier sketch in CA 9-10R
See also DLB 2
See also DLBY 81
See also CLC 1, 3, 7, 18, 37
Morrisey, George L(ewis) 1926- CANR-14
Earlier sketch in CA 73-76
Morris-Goodall, Vanne 1909- 29-32R
Morrish, (Ernest) Ivor (James) 1914- 33-36R
Morris-Jones, W(yndraeth) H(umphreys)
1918- CANR-11
Earlier sketch in CA 21-22R
Morrison, Arnold Telford 1928- 110
Morrison, Arthur 1863-1945 Brief entry 120
See also DLB 70
Morrison, Bill 1935- Brief entry 115
See also SATA 37
Morrison, Bruce 1904(?)-1983 Obituary 109
Morrison, Carl V(incent) 1908- 93-96

INDEX

Morrison, Charles Clayton 1874-1966
Obituary 89-92
Morrison, Cheryl 1947- 107
Morrison, Chloe Anthony Wofford
See Morrison, Toni
Morrison, Claudia C(hristopherson)
1936- 29-32R
Morrison, Clinton (Dawson, Jr.) 1924- 15-16R
Morrison, David (Douglas) 1940- 112
Morrison, Denton E(dward) 1932- CANR-6
Earlier sketch in CA 57-60
Morrison, Donald George 1938- 85-88
Morrison, Dorothy Nafus CANR-24
Earlier sketches in CA 61-64, CANR-8
See also SATA 29
Morrison, Edward
See Humphrey, Paul
Morrison, Eleanor S(helton) 1921- CANR-1
Earlier sketch in CA 49-52
Morrison, Eula Atwood 1911- 25-28R
Morrison, Frank G. 1894(?)-1983
Obituary 111
Morrison, Frank M. 1914- 37-40R
Morrison, Fred L. 1939- Brief entry 112
Morrison, G.F.
See Bernstein, Gerry
Morrison, Gertrude W. CANR-26
Earlier sketches in CA 19-20, CAP-2
Morrison, Hobe 1904- 77-80
Morrison, Howard A(lexander) 1955- 118
Morrison, Ida Edith 2R
Morrison, J. S.
See Morrison, John (Sinclair)
Morrison, Jack 1912- 105
Morrison, James (Harris) 1918- 73-76
Morrison, James (Ryan) 1924- 105
Morrison, James Douglas 1943-1971 73-76
Morrison, James F(rederic) 1937- 25-28R
Morrison, James L(unsford), Jr. 1923- 57-60
Morrison, James R(oy) 1940- 123
Brief entry 118
Morrison, Jim
See Morrison, James Douglas
See also CLC 17
Morrison, John (Sinclair) 1913- 122
Morrison, John Gordon 1904- 103
Morrison, Joseph L(ederman) 1918-1970 5-6R
Obituary 122
Morrison, Kristin (Diane) 1934- CANR-14
Earlier sketch in CA 37-40R
Morrison, Lester M. 1907- CAP-1
Earlier sketch in CA 15-16
Morrison, Lillian 1917- CANR-22
Earlier sketches in CA 11-12R, CANR-7
See also SATA 3
Morrison, Lucile Phillips 1896- SATA-17
Morrison, Margaret Mackie 19(?)-1973
Obituary 41-44R
Morrison, Marsh 1902- CANR-10
Earlier sketch in CA 61-64
Morrison, N(ancy Agnes) Brysson (Inglis)
?-1986 15-16R
Obituary 118
Morrison, Paul Fix 1902-1983 Obituary 111
Morrison, Peggy
See Morrison, Margaret Mackie
Morrison, Philip 1915- Brief entry 106
Morrison, Phylis 1927- 117
Morrison, Richard
See Lowndes, Robert A(ugustine) W(ard)
Morrison, Robert
See Lowndes, Robert A(ugustine) W(ard)
Morrison, Robert H(aywood) 1927- 5-6R
Morrison, Robert S(tanley) 1909- 65-68
Morrison, Roberta
See Webb, Jean Francis
Morrison, Susan Dudley 1949- 119
Morrison, Theodore 1901- CANR-1
Earlier sketch in CA 4R
Morrison, Toni 1931- 29-32R
See also BW
See also DLB 6, 33
See also DLBY 81
See also CLC 4, 10, 22
Morrison, Tony 1936- 81-84
Morrison, Van 1945- Brief entry 116
See also CLC 21
Morrison, Velma Ford 1909- 9-10R
See also SATA 21
Morrison, Victor
See Glut, Donald F(rank)
Morrison, Wilbur Howard 1915- CANR-1
Earlier sketch in CA 3R
Morrison, William
See Samachson, Joseph
Morrison, William R(obert) 1942- 124
Morrison-Reed, Mark D(ouglas) 1949- 116
Morriss, Frank 1923- CANR-3
Earlier sketch in CA 5-6R
Morriss, J. H.
See Ghnassia, Maurice (Jean-Henri)
Morriss, James E(dward) 1932- 57-60
See also SATA 8
Morriss, Mack 1920(?)-1976 Obituary 65-68
Morrissette, Bruce A(rcher) 1911- 19-20R
Morrissey, Charles Thomas 1933- 108
Morrissey, L(eroy) J(ohn) 1935- CANR-1
Earlier sketch in CA 49-52
Morrissey, Leonard E., Jr. 1925- 11-12R
Morrissey, Stephen 1950- 115
Morris-Suzuki, Tessa 1951- 123
Morritt, Hope 1930- CANR-16
Earlier sketch in CA 97-100
Morrow, Betty
See Bacon, Elizabeth
Morrow, Bradford 1951- 113
Morrow, Charlotte
See Kirwan, Molly (Morrow)
Morrow, E(verett) Frederic 1909- CANR-2
Earlier sketch in CA 7-8R
See also BW
Morrow, Felix 1906- 107
Morrow, Glenn R(aymond) 1895-197(?) CAP-1
Earlier sketch in CA 19-20
Morrow, James 1947- 108
Morrow, John Howard 1910- 25-28R
Morrow, John Howard, Jr. 1944- 113
Morrow, Lance 1939- Brief entry 119
Morrow, Mable 1892-1977 Obituary 106
Morrow, Mary Lou 1926- 61-64
Morrow, Patrick David 1940- CANR-8
Earlier sketch in CA 61-64
Morrow, Stephen 1939- 73-76
Morrow, William L(ockhart) 1935- 33-36R
Mors, Victor
See Roeseler, W(olfgang) G(uenter)
Mors, Wallace P. 1911- 19-20R
Morsberger, Katharine M. 1931- 105
Morsberger, Robert Eustis 1929- CANR-3
Earlier sketch in CA 5-6R
Morscher, Betsy 1939- 115
Morse, A. Reynolds 1914- CANR-7
Earlier sketch in CA 19-20R
Morse, Anne Christensen 1915- 4R
Morse, Arthur David 1920-1971
Obituary 29-32R
Morse, B. J. ?-1977 Obituary 73-76
Morse, Carol
See Yeakley, Marjory Hall
Morse, Chandler 1906- 5-6R
Morse, Charles A. 1898- CAP-1
Earlier sketch in CA 19-20
Morse, David 1940- 37-40R
Morse, Donald E. 1936- 37-40R
Morse, Donald R(oy) 1931- CANR-21
Earlier sketch in CA 105
Morse, Dorothy B(ayley) 1906-1979 SATA-24
Morse, Edward Lewis 1942- CANR-7
Earlier sketch in CA 57-60
Morse, Flo 1921- 106
See also SATA 30
Morse, Grant W(esley) 1926- 19-20R
Morse, H(enry) Clifton Iv 1924- 9-10R
Morse, Harold Marston 1892-1977
Obituary 69-72
Morse, Hermann Nelson 1887-1977
Obituary 73-76
Morse, J(osiah) Mitchell 1912- 65-68
Morse, James Herbert 1841-1923 DLB-71
Morse, Jedidiah 1761-1826 DLB-37
Morse, John D. 1906- 104
Morse, John T., Jr. 1840-1937 DLB-47
Morse, L(arry) A(lan) 1945- 107
Morse, Peter 1935- CANR-14
Earlier sketch in CA 73-76
Morse, Philip M(cCord) 1903-1985 108
Obituary 117
Morse, Richard M(cGee) 1922- CANR-10
Earlier sketch in CA 15-16R
Morse, Roger A(lfred) 1927- CANR-23
Earlier sketches in CA 57-60, CANR-8
Morse, Samuel French 1916- CANR-4
Earlier sketch in CA 9-10R
Morse, Theresa Adler 1901-1980 89-92
Obituary 97-100
Morse, Thomas S(purr) 1925- 109
Morse, Wayne (Lyman) 1900-1974
Obituary 49-52
Morse-Boycott, Desmond (Lionel)
1892-1979 107
Obituary 104
Morsey, Royal J(oseph) 1910- 73-76
Morshead, Ian 1922- 111
Morshiel, George
See Shiels, George
Morson, Gary S(aul) 1948- 121
Morss, Elisabeth W. 1918- 41-44R
Mort, Vivian
See Cromie, Alice Hamilton
Mortensen, Ben(jamin) F. 1928- 104
Mortensen, C. David 1939- 37-40R
Mortimer, Anthony 1936- 116
Mortimer, Armine Kotin 1943- 117
Mortimer, Chapman
See Chapman-Mortimer, William Charles
Mortimer, John (Clifford) 1923- CANR-21
Earlier sketch in CA 13-14R
See also DLB 13
See also CLC 28, 43
Mortimer, John L(ynn) 1908- 69-72
Mortimer, Mary H.
See Coury, Louise Andree
Mortimer, Penelope (Ruth) 1918- 57-60
See also CLC 5
Mortimer, Peter
See Roberts, Dorothy James
Mortimore, Olive 1890- 49-52
Morton, A(rthur) L(eslie) 1903-1987 11-12R
Obituary 124
Morton, A(ndrew) Q(ueen) 1919- 105
Morton, Alexander C(lark) 1936- CANR-12
Earlier sketch in CA 25-28R
Morton, Anthony
See Creasey, John
Morton, C(lement) Manly 1884-1976 CAP-2
Earlier sketch in CA 29-32
Morton, Carlos 1947- 73-76
Morton, Desmond 1937- CANR-15
Earlier sketch in CA 29-32R
Morton, Donald E(dward) 1938- 57-60
Morton, Frederic 1924- CANR-20
Earlier sketches in CA 2R, CANR-3
Morton, Gregory 1911-1986 102
Obituary 118
Morton, H(enry Canova) V(ollam)
1892-1979 103
Obituary 89-92
Morton, Harry 1925- CANR-15
Earlier sketch in CA 81-84
Morton, Henry W(alter) 1929- 13-14R
Morton, Jane 1931- 93-96
See also SATA 50
Morton, Jocelyn 1912- 73-76
Morton, John (Cameron Andrieu) Bingham
(Michael) 1893-1979 93-96
Obituary 85-88
Morton, Joseph
See Richmond, Al
Morton, Lee Jack, Jr. 1928- SATA-32
Morton, Lena Beatrice 1901- 19-20R
Morton, Leopold 1922- 110
Morton, Louis 1913-1976 CANR-21
Obituary 65-68
Earlier sketch in CA 69-72
Morton, Lucie T. 1950- 118
Morton, Lynne 1952- 106
Morton, Marcia Colman 1927- 73-76
Morton, Marian J(ohnson) 1937- 77-80
Morton, Miriam 1918(?)-1985 CANR-2
Obituary 117
Earlier sketch in CA 49-52
See also SATA 9, 46
Morton, Nathaniel 1613-1685 DLB-24
Morton, Newton 1901-1967 CAP-1
Earlier sketch in CA 19-20
Morton, Patricia
See Golding, Morton J(ay)
Morton, Phyllis Digby ?-1984 Obituary 113
Morton, R(obert) S(teel) 1917- 49-52
Morton, Richard (Everett) 1930- 37-40R
Morton, Richard Lee 1889-1974 CANR-16
Obituary 53-56
Earlier sketch in CA 2R
Morton, Robert 1934- 69-72
Morton, Robert L(ee) 1889- 45-48
Morton, Sarah Wentworth 1759-1846 DLB-37
Morton, T(homas) Ralph 1900- 29-32R
Morton, Thomas 1579(?)-1647(?) DLB-24
Morton, W(illiam) L(ewis) 1908- CAP-1
Earlier sketch in CA 19-20
Morton, W(illiam) Scott 1908- 81-84
Morton, Ward McKinnon 1907- 2R
Morton, William C(uthbert) 1875-1971 CAP-2
Earlier sketch in CA 25-28
Morwood, James 1943- 124
Moscati, Sabatino 1922- 77-80
Mosco, Vincent 1948- 114
Moscotti, Albert D(ennis) 1920- 65-68
Moscovitch, Allan 1946- 111
Moscovitz, Judy 1942- 123
Moscow, Alvin 1925- CANR-4
Earlier sketch in CA 2R
See also SATA 3
Moscow, Henry (I.) 1904(?)-1983
Obituary 108
Moscow, Warren 1908- 23-24R
Moscowitz, Raymond 1938- 111
Mosel, Arlene (Tichy) 1921- 49-52
See also SATA 7
Mosel, Tad 1922- 73-76
Moseley, David (Victor) 1939- 97-100
Moseley, Edwin M(aurice) 1916-1978 CANR-8
Earlier sketch in CA 5-6R
Moseley, George (V. H. III) 1931- 49-52
Moseley, J(oseph) Edward 1910-1973 37-40R
Moseley, James G(wyn) 1946- 116
Moseley, Ray 1932- 85-88
Moseley, Spencer A(ltemont) 1925- 93-96
Moseley, Virginia D(ouglas) 1917- 23-24R
Mosely, Philip Edward 1905-1972
Obituary 33-36R
Moser, Charles A. 1935- 29-32R
Moser, Don(ald Bruce) 1932- 106
See also SATA 31
Moser, Lawrence E. 1939- 33-36R
Moser, Mary Beck 1924- 122
Moser, Norman Calvin 1931- CANR-10
Earlier sketch in CA 57-60
Moser, Reta C(arol) 1936- 15-16R
Moser, Shia 1906- CAP-2
Earlier sketch in CA 25-28
Moser, Thomas (Colborn) 1923- 7-8R
Moses, Anna Mary Robertson 1860-1961
Obituary 93-96
Moses, Claire Goldberg 1941- 113
Moses, Elbert R(aymond), Jr. 1908- CAP-1
Earlier sketch in CA 15-16
Moses, Gerald Robert 1938- 57-60
Moses, Grandma
See Moses, Anna Mary Robertson
Moses, Joel C(harles) 1944- CANR-10
Earlier sketch in CA 65-68
Moses, Robert 1888-1981 45-48
Obituary 104
Moses, W(illiam) R(obert) 1911- 11-12R
Moses, Wilson Jeremiah 1942- 85-88
Mosesson, Gloria R(ubin) 41-44R
See also SATA 24
Mosey, Anne Cronin 1938- 49-52
Moshe, David
See Winkelman, Donald M.
Mosher, Arthur Theodore 1910- 85-88
Mosher, Frederick C(amp) 1913- 37-40R
Mosher, Ralph Lamont 1928- CANR-7
Earlier sketch in CA 19-20R
Mosher, Steven W(estley) 1948- 116
Mosher, (Christopher) Terry 1942- 93-96
Moshier, W(illiam) Franklyn 1929- 97-100
Mosiman, Billie Sue (Stahl) 1947- 119
Mosk
See Moskowitz, Gene
Moskin, J(ohn) Robert 1923- 19-20R
Moskin, Marietta D(unston) 1928- CANR-13
Earlier sketch in CA 73-76
See also SATA 23
Moskof, Martin Stephen 1930- 29-32R
See also SATA 27
Moskos, Charles C. 1934- CANR-26
Earlier sketches in CA 25-28R, CANR-10
Moskow, Michael H. 1938- CANR-14
Earlier sketch in CA 37-40R
Moskowitz, Gene 1921(?)-1982 Obituary 108
Moskowitz, Ira 1912- 102
Moskowitz, Moses 1911- Brief entry 114
Moskowitz, Robert 1946- 109
Moskowitz, Sam 1920- CANR-4
Earlier sketch in CA 7-8R
Moskvitin, Jurij 1938- 93-96
Mosley, Diana 1910- 106
Mosley, J(ohn) Brooke (Jr.) 1915-1988
Obituary 125
Mosley, Jean Bell 1913- 9-10R
Mosley, Leonard O(swald) 1913- 109
Brief entry 108
Mosley, Nicholas 1923- 69-72
See also DLB 14
See also CLC 43
Mosley, Oswald (Ernald) 1896-1980 CAP-2
Obituary 102
Earlier sketch in CA 25-28
Moss, Arthur 1889-1969 Obituary 112
See also DLB 4
Moss, Barbara 1946- 116
Moss, Bernard H(aym) 1943- Brief entry 115
Moss, Bobby Gilmer 1932- 49-52
Moss, C(laude) Scott 1924- CANR-8
Earlier sketch in CA 19-20R
Moss, Cynthia J(ane) 1940- CANR-12
Earlier sketch in CA 65-68
Moss, Don(ald) 1920- SATA-11
Moss, Elaine (Dora) 1924- Brief entry 110
See also SATA 31
Moss, Frank Edward 1911- CANR-13
Earlier sketch in CA 61-64
Moss, Gordon E(rvin) 1937- 57-60
Moss, Howard 1922-1987 CANR-1
Obituary 123
Earlier sketch in CA 2R
See also DLB 5
See also CLC 7, 14, 45, 50
Moss, J. Joel 1922- 45-48
Moss, James A(llen) 1920- 33-36R
Moss, John 1940- CANR-17
Earlier sketch in CA 97-100
Moss, Leonard (Jerome) 1931- 25-28R
Moss, Michael (Stanley) 1947- 108
Moss, Nancy
See Moss, Robert (Alfred)
Moss, Norman 1928- 49-52
Moss, (Victor) Peter (Cannings) 1921- CANR-2
Earlier sketch in CA 49-52
Moss, Ralph W(alter) 1943- 101
Moss, Robert (Alfred) 1903- CAP-1
Earlier sketch in CA 11-12
Moss, Robert (John) 1946- Brief entry 118
Moss, Robert F. 1942- CANR-20
Earlier sketch in CA 81-84
Moss, Roberta
See Moss, Robert (Alfred)
Moss, Roger 1951- 124
Moss, Rose 1937- 49-52
Moss, Sanford Alexander III 1939- 118
Moss, Sidney P(hil) 1917- 5-6R
Moss, Stanley 1925- 97-100
Moss, Stephen Joseph 1935- 103
Moss, Stirling 1929- 7-8R
Moss, Walter (Gerald) 1938- 65-68
Mosse, George L(achmann) 1918- CANR-12
Earlier sketch in CA 5-6R
Mosse, Werner E(ugen Emil) 1918- 9-10R
Mossiker, Frances (Sanger) 1906-1985 11-12R
Obituary 116
Mossman, Dow 1943- 45-48
Mossman, Frank H(omer) 1915- CANR-5
Earlier sketch in CA 3R
Mossman, Jennifer 1944- CANR-17
Earlier sketch in CA 97-100
Mossner, Ernest C(ampbell) 1907-1986 123
Obituary 120
Mossop, D(eryk) J(oseph) 1919- 3R
Mossop, Irene
See Swatridge, Irene Maude (Mossop)
Most, Bernard 1937- 104
See also SATA 40, 48
Most, Glenn W(arren) 1952- 112
Most, William G(eorge) 1914- 49-52
Mostel, Kate
See Mostel, Kathryn Harkin
Mostel, Katherine Harkin
See Mostel, Kathryn Harkin
Mostel, Kathryn Harkin 1918-1986 81-84
Obituary 118
Mostel, Samuel Joel 1915-1977 89-92
Mostel, Zero
See Mostel, Samuel Joel
Mosteller, (Charles) Frederick 1916- CANR-23
Earlier sketches in CA 19-20R, CANR-7
Mostert, Noel 1929- 105
Mostofsky, David I(saac) 1931- 19-20R
Mota, Avelino Teixeira da
See Teixeira da Mota, Avelino
Mother Mary Anthony
See Weinig, Jean Maria
Mothershead, Harmon Ross 1931- 33-36R
Mothner, Ira S(anders) 1932- CANR-13
Earlier sketch in CA 21-22R

Motion, Andrew 1952- DLB-40
See also CLC 47
Motley, Arthur H(arrison) 1900-1984
Obituary 112
See also AITN 2
Motley, John Lothrop
1814-1877 .... DLB-1, 30, 59
Motley, Mary
See De Reneville, Mary Margaret Motley Sheridan
Motley, Mary Penick 1920- 73-76
Motley, Red
See Motley, Arthur H(arrison)
Motley, Willard (Francis) 1912-1965 117
Obituary 106
See also BW
See also DLB 76
See also CLC 18
Motley, Wilma E(lizabeth) 1912- 41-44R
Motmot, Snik P.
See Tompkins, Everett Thomas
Motoyama, Hiroshi 1925- 110
Mott, Frank Luther 1886-1964 .... 4R
Mott, George Fox 1907-1987 ....13-14R
Obituary 123
Mott, Michael (Charles Alston) 1930- ... CANR-7
Earlier sketch in CA 7-8R
See also CAAS 7
See also CLC 15, 34
Mott, Paul E. 103
Mott, Stephen Charles 1940- 116
Mott, Vincent Valmon 1916- 41-44R
Motta, Dick 1931- Brief entry 111
Mottahedeh, Roy Parviz 1940- CANR-21
Earlier sketch in CA 104
Motter, Alton M(yers) 1907- CAP-1
Earlier sketch in CA 11-12
Motto, Anna Lydia 41-44R
Motto, Carmine J. 1914- 33-36R
Mottram, Anthony John 1920- 7-8R
Mottram, (Vernon) Henry 1882-19(?) CAP-1
Earlier sketch in CA 11-12
Mottram, R(alph) H(ale) 1883-1971 108
Obituary 29-32R
See also DLB 36
Mottram, Tony
See Mottram, Anthony John
Motz, Lloyd 1909- CANR-4
Earlier sketch in CA 9-10R
See also SATA 20
Mouat, Kit 1920- 113
Mould, Daphne D(esiree) C(harlotte) Pochin
1920- CANR-4
Earlier sketch in CA 9-10R
Mould, George 1894- 57-60
Moule, C(harles) F(rancis) D(igby)
1908- CANR-5
Earlier sketch in CA 4R
Moulier, (Antoine) Fernand 1913- 81-84
Moult, Edward (Walker) 1926-1986
Obituary 120
Moult, Ted
See Moult, Edward (Walker)
Moult, Thomas 1895-1974 Obituary 89-92
Moulton, Edward C. 1936- 77-80
Moulton, Eugene R(ussell) 1916-1981 .. CANR-11
Earlier sketch in CA 23-24R
Moulton, Gary E(van) 1942- 115
Moulton, Harland B. 1925- 37-40R
Moulton, J(ames) L(ouis) 1906- 23-24R
Moulton, Nancy 1946- 116
Moulton, Phillips P(rentice) 1909- 37-40R
Moulton, William G(amwell) 1914- 9-10R
Mouly, George J(oseph) 1915- CANR-17
Earlier sketch in CA 3R
Mounce, R(obert H.) 1921- CANR-2
Earlier sketch in CA 3R
Mount, Charles Merrill 1928- 13-14R
Mount, Elisabeth
See Dougherty, Betty
Mount, Ellis 1921- 116
Mount, (William Robert) Ferdinand
1939- CANR-11
Earlier sketch in CA 21-22R
Mount, Marshall Ward 1927- 73-76
Mountain, Julian
See Cowie, Donald
Mountain, Marian
See Wisberg, Marian Aline
Mountain, Robert
See Montgomery, Raymond A. (Jr.)
Mountbatten, Louis (Francis Albert Victor Nicholas) 1900-1979 Obituary 113
Mountbatten, Richard
See Wallmann, Jeffrey M(iner)
Mountfield, David
See Grant, Neil
Mountfield, Stuart 1903(?)-1984 Obituary .. 115
Mountfort, Guy 1905- 19-20R
Mountjoy, Roberta Jean
See Sohl, Jerry
Mountsier, Robert 1888(?)-1972
Obituary 37-40R
Mourant, John A(rthur) 1903- CAP-1
Earlier sketch in CA 9-10
Moure, Erin 1955- 113
See also DLB 60
Mourelatos, Alexander P(hoebus)
D(ionysiou) 1936- 29-32R
Mourier, Marguerite
See Boulton, Marjorie
Moursund, David G. 1936- CANR-12
Earlier sketch in CA 25-28R
Moursund, Janet (Peck) 1936- 45-48
Moussa, Pierre L(ouis) 1922- 13-14R
Moussard, Jacqueline 1924- CANR-8
Earlier sketch in CA 61-64
See also SATA 24
Mouton, Jane Srygley 1930- 123
Moutoux, John T. 1901(?)-1979
Obituary 89-92
Mouzelis, Nicos P. 1939- 33-36R
Mouzon, Olin T(errell) 1912- 7-8R
Mow, Anna Beahm 1893- CANR-3
Earlier sketch in CA 9-10R
Mowat, C(harles) L(och) 1911-1970 ..... CAP-1
Earlier sketch in CA 15-16
Mowat, David 1943- 77-80
Mowat, Farley (McGill) 1921- CANR-24
Earlier sketches in CA 3R, CANR-4
See also SATA 3
See also DLB 68
See also CLC 26
Mowat, R(obert) C(ase) 1913- 29-32R
Mowatt, Ian 1948- 41-44R
Mowitz, Robert J(ames) 1920- CANR-3
Earlier sketch in CA 5-6R
Mowrer, Edgar Ansel 1892-1977 .... CAP-1
Obituary 69-72
Earlier sketch in CA 15-16
See also DLB 29
Mowrer, Lilian Thomson 65-68
Mowrer, O(rval) Hobart 1907- CANR-1
Earlier sketch in CA 4R
Mowrer, Paul Scott 1887-1971 .... CANR-4
Obituary 29-32R
Earlier sketch in CA 5-6R
See also DLB 29
Mowry, George E(dwin) 1909-1984 .... CANR-17
Earlier sketch in CA 2R
Mowshowitz, Abbe 1939- 109
Moxham, Robert Morgan 1919-1978
Obituary 77-80
Moyer, Claire B. (Inch) 1905- CAP-2
Earlier sketch in CA 19-20
Moyer, Elgin Sylvester 1890- 5-6R
Moyer, Kenneth E(van) 1919- CANR-13
Earlier sketch in CA 33-36R
Moyers, Bill 1934- 61-64
See also AITN 2
Moyes, John Steward 1884- CAP-1
Earlier sketch in CA 13-14
Moyes, Norman Barr 1931- 37-40R
Moyes, Patricia
See Haszard, Patricia Moyes
Moyler, Alan (Frank Powell) 1926- SATA-36
Moyles, R(obert) Gordon 1939- CANR-17
Earlier sketch in CA 65-68
Moynahan, John F. 1912-1985 Obituary 115
Moynahan, Julian (Lane) 1925- CANR-1
Earlier sketch in CA 2R
Moyne, Ernest J(ohn) 1916-1976 .... CAP-2
Earlier sketch in CA 25-28
Moynihan, Daniel P(atrick) 1927- 7-8R
Moynihan, John Dominic 1932- 103
Moynihan, Maurice (Gerard) 1902- 107
Moynihan, Ruth B(arnes) 1933- 117
Moynihan, William T. 1927- 23-24R
Moyse-Bartlett, Hubert 1902(?)-1973(?)
Obituary 104
Mozley, Charles 1915- SATA-32, 43
Mphahlele, Es'kia
See Mphahlele, Ezekiel
Mphahlele, Ezekiel 1919- CANR-26
Earlier sketch in CA 81-84
See also BW
See also CLC 25
Mqhayi, S(amuel) E(dward) K(rune Loliwe)
1875-1945 ....TCLC-25
Mr. Cleveland
See Seltzer, Louis B(enson)
Mr. Kenneth
See Marlowe, Kenneth
Mr. Martin
See Burroughs, William (Seward)
Mr. McGillicuddy
See Abisch, Roslyn Kroop
Mr. Metropolitan Opera
See Robinson, Francis (Arthur)
Mr. Sniff
See Abisch, Roslyn Kroop
Mr. Wizard
See Herbert, Don
Mrabet, Mohammed
See el Hajjam, Mohammed ben Chaib
Mrazek, James E(dward) 1914- 33-36R
Mrozek, Donald J(ohn) 1945- 107
Mrozek, Slawomir 1930- 13-14R
See also CLC 3, 13
Mrs. Belloc-Lowndes
See Lowndes, Marie Adelaide (Belloc)
Mrs. Bishop
See Bishop, Isabella Lucy (Bird)
Mrs. Fairstar
See Horne, Richard Henry
Mrs. G.
See Griffiths, Kitty Anna
Mrs. Miggy
See Krentel, Mildred White
Mrs. R.F.D.
See Peden, Rachel (Mason)
M'Taggart, John M'Taggart Ellis
See McTaggart, John McTaggart Ellis
M'Timkulu, Donald (Guy Sidney) 1910- ... 97-100
Mtwa, Percy 19(?)- CLC-47
Mu, Yang
See Wang, C(hing) H(sien)
Mucha, Jiri 1915- CANR-26
Earlier sketches in CA 23-24R, CANR-11
Muchnic, Helen (Lenore) 1903- CANR-5
Earlier sketch in CA 2R
Mudd, Emily Hartshorne 1898- 15-16R
Mudd, Roger H(arrison) 1928- 105
Mudd, Stuart 1893-1975 ....11-12R
Obituary 57-60
Mude, O
See Gorey, Edward (St. John)
Mudge, Jean McClure 1933- CANR-6
Earlier sketch in CA 7-8R
Mudge, Lewis Seymour 1929- 89-92
Mudgeon, Apeman
See Mitchell, Adrian
Mudgett, Herman W.
See White, William A(nthony) P(arker)
Mudie, Ian (Mayelston) 1911- 25-28R
Mudrick, Marvin 1921- CANR-20
Earlier sketch in CA 25-28R
Muecke, D(ouglas) C(olin) 1919- 53-56
Muehl, Lois Baker 1920- CANR-18
Earlier sketch in CA 3R
Muehl, (Ernest) William 1919- 45-48
Muehlen, Norbert 1909-1981 69-72
Obituary 104
Muehsam, Gerd 1913(?)-1979 Obituary ...93-96
Muelder, Walter George 1907- CAP-1
Earlier sketch in CA 13-14
Mueller, Amelia 1911- 57-60
Mueller, Barbara R(uth) 1925- 11-12R
Mueller, Charles S(teinkamp) 1929- CANR-20
Earlier sketches in CA 13-14R, CANR-5
Mueller, Claus 1941- 65-68
Mueller, David L. 1929- 29-32R
Mueller, Dennis C(ary) 1940- 116
Mueller, Dorothy 1901- 102
Mueller, Erwin W. 1911-1977 Obituary 69-72
Mueller, Gerald F(rancis) 1927- 15-16R
Mueller, Gerhard G(ottlob) 1930- CANR-12
Earlier sketch in CA 25-28R
Mueller, Gerhard O. W. 1926- CANR-20
Earlier sketches in CA 2R, CANR-5
Mueller, Gerhardt
See Bickers, Richard Leslie Townshend
Mueller, Gustav Emil 1898- CANR-7
Earlier sketch in CA 19-20R
Mueller, James W(illiam) 1941- 57-60
Mueller, John E(rnest) 1937- CANR-14
Earlier sketch in CA 37-40R
Mueller, Kate Hevner 1898- 41-44R
Mueller, Klaus Andrew 1921- CANR-4
Earlier sketch in CA 49-52
Mueller, Lisel 1924- 93-96
See also CLC 13
Mueller, M(ax) G(erhard) 1925- 19-20R
Mueller, Marlies K(uhfuss) 1937- 114
Mueller, Merrill 1916-1980 Obituary 103
Mueller, Red
See Mueller, Merrill
Mueller, Reuben Herbert 1897-1982
Obituary 107
Mueller, Robert E(mmett) 1925- 4R
Mueller, Robert Kirk 1913- CANR-12
Earlier sketch in CA 73-76
Mueller, Virginia 1924- CANR-10
Earlier sketch in CA 65-68
See also SATA 28
Mueller, Willard Fritz 1925- 19-20R
Mueller, William R(andolph) 1916- CANR-2
Earlier sketch in CA 3R
Mueller-Vollmer, Kurt 1928- 126
Muenchen, Al(fred) 1917- 49-52
Muesing, Edith E(lizabeth)
See Muesing-Ellwood, Edith E(lizabeth)
Muesing-Ellwood, Edith E(lizabeth) 1947- ... 114
Muffett, D(avid) J(oseph) M(ead) 1919- ...45-48
Muggeridge, Malcolm (Thomas) 1903- 101
See also AITN 1
Muggeson, Margaret Elizabeth 1942- 103
Muhajir, Nazzam Al Fitnah
See El Muhajir
Muheim, Harry Miles 1920- 85-88
Muhlen, Norbert
See Muehlen, Norbert
Muhlenfeld, Elisabeth 1944- CANR-24
Earlier sketch in CA 108
Muhlhausen, John Prague 1940- 61-64
Muhlstein, Anka 1935- 114
Mui, Hoh-cheung 1916- 45-48
Muileman, Kathryn Saltzman 1946- 85-88
Muilenburg, Grace (Evelyn) 1913- 61-64
Muir, (Charles) Augustus 13-14R
Muir, Barbara K(enrick Gowing) 1908- ...11-12R
Muir, Dexter
See Gribble, Leonard (Reginald)
Muir, Edwin 1887-1959 Brief entry 104
See also DLB 20
See also TCLC 2
Muir, Frank 1920- 81-84
See also SATA 30
Muir, Helen AITN-2
Muir, Helen 1937- DLB-14
Muir, Jane
See Petrone, Jane Muir
Muir, Jean 1906-1973 .... CAP-2
Obituary 41-44R
Earlier sketch in CA 29-32
Muir, John 1838-1914 ....TCLC-28
Muir, Kenneth (Arthur) 1907- CANR-4
Earlier sketch in CA 2R
Muir, Lynette R(oss) 1930- 122
Muir, Malcolm 1885-1979 93-96
Obituary 85-88
Muir, Malcolm, Jr. 1915-1984 Obituary 113
Muir, Marie 1904- CANR-5
Earlier sketch in CA 4R
Muir, Percival H(orace) 1894-1979 ..... CANR-5
Obituary 97-100
Earlier sketch in CA 11-12R
Muir, Percy H.
See Muir, Percival H(orace)
Muir, Richard 1943- CANR-23
Earlier sketch in CA 106
Muir, William Ker, Jr. 1931- 53-56
Muirhead, Ian A(dair) 1913- 15-16R
Muirhead, Thorburn 1899- 7-8R
Mujica Lainez, Manuel 1910-1984 81-84
Obituary 112
See also CLC 31
Mukerji, Chandra 1945- 113
Mukerji, Dhan Gopal 1890-1936
Brief entry 119
See also SATA 40
See also CLR 10
Mukerji, Kshitimohon 1920- 19-20R
Mukherjee, Bharati 1940- 107
See also DLB 60
Mukherjee, Meenakshi 1937- 65-68
Mukherjee, Ramkrishna 1919- CANR-7
Earlier sketch in CA 57-60
Mulac, Margaret E(lizabeth) 1912- CANR-2
Earlier sketch in CA 7-8R
Mulaisho, Dominic (Chola) 1933- 97-100
Mularchyk, Sylva 93-96
Mulay, Larry L. 1904(?)-1987 Obituary 122
Mulcahy, Lucille Burnett 5-6R
See also SATA 12
Mulchrone, Vincent 1919(?)-1977
Obituary 73-76
Mulder, John M(ark) 1946- Brief entry 112
Muldoon, Paul 1951- Brief entry 113
See also DLB 40
See also CLC 32
Muldoon, Roland W. 1941- 105
Mule, Marty 1944- 108
Mulesko, Angelo
See Oglesby, Joseph
Mulford, David Campbell 1937- 11-12R
Mulford, Philippa G(reene) 1948- 116
See also SATA 43
Mulgan, Catherine 1931- CANR-11
Earlier sketch in CA 25-28R
Mulgrew, Peter David 1927- 15-16R
Mulhauser, Ruth (Elizabeth) 1913-1980 .. CANR-7
Earlier sketch in CA 7-8R
Mulhearn, John 1932- 65-68
Mulholland, Jim 1949- 61-64
Mulholland, John 1898-1970 ....7-8R
Obituary 89-92
Mulholland, John F(ield) 1903- 41-44R
Mulisch, Harry 1927- CANR-26
Earlier sketches in CA 9-10R, CANR-6
See also CLC 42
Mulkeen, Anne
See Marcus, Anne M(ulkeen)
Mulkeen, Thomas P(atrick) 1923- 85-88
Mulkerne, Donald James Dennis 1921- ...11-12R
Mull, Martin 1943- 105
See also CLC 17
Mullally, Frederic 1920- CANR-1
Earlier sketch in CA 4R
Mullaly, Edward (Joseph) 1941- 41-44R
Mullan, Bob 1947- 123
Mullan, Fitzhugh 1942- 69-72
Mullaney, Marie Marmo 1953- 112
Mullaney, Thomas E. 1922(?)-1978 93-96
Obituary 81-84
Mullard, Chris(topher Paul) 1944-
Brief entry 112
Mullarky, Taylor 1922- CANR-26
Earlier sketch in CA 103
Mullen, Barbara 1914-1979 Obituary 85-88
Mullen, C.J.J.
See Mullen, Cyril J.
Mullen, Cyril J. 1908- 61-64
Mullen, Dore
See Mullen, Dorothy
Mullen, Dorothy 1933- 104
Mullen, Edward John, Jr. 1942- CANR-17
Earlier sketches in CA 49-52, CANR-2
Mullen, Harris H. 1924- 69-72
Mullen, James H. 1924- 3R
Mullen, Michael 1937- 116
Mullen, Robert R(odolph) 1908- CAP-1
Earlier sketch in CA 19-20
Mullen, Thomas J(ames) 1934- CANR-5
Earlier sketch in CA 11-12R
Mullen, William Charles 1944- 73-76
Mullendore, William Clinton 1892-1983
Obituary 111
Müller, Alexander V(ilhelm) 1932- 45-48
Muller, Billex
See Ellis, Edward S(ylvester)
Muller, Charles G(eorge Geoffrey)
1897- CANR-2
Earlier sketch in CA 1R
Muller, Charles Geoffrey
See Muller, Charles G(eorge Geoffrey)
Muller, Dorothy
See Mueller, Dorothy
Muller, Edward John 1916- 57-60
Muller, Gilbert H(enry) 1941- CANR-14
Earlier sketch in CA 41-44R
Muller, H(erman) J(oseph) 1890-1967
Obituary 106
Muller, Herbert J(oseph) 1905- CANR-1
Earlier sketch in CA 2R
Muller, Herman J(oseph) 1909- 73-76
Muller, Hilgard 1914-1985 Obituary 117
Muller, John E.
See Fanthorpe, R(obert) Lionel
Muller, John P(aul) 1940- 103
Muller, Leo C., Jr. 1924- 7-8R
Muller, Marcia 1944- 81-84
Muller, Peter O. 1942- 110
Muller, Priscilla E(lkow) 1930- 61-64
Muller, Robert George 1923- 103
Muller, Ronald E(rnst) 1939- 107

INDEX

Muller, Siegfried H(ermann) 1902-1965 ... CAP-1
  Earlier sketch in CA 11-12
Mulligan, Hugh A. 1925- ... CANR-11
  Earlier sketch in CA 23-24R
Mulligan, James J. 1936- ... 45-48
Mulligan, John Joseph 1918- ... 33-36R
Mulligan, Raymond A(lexander) 1914- ... 37-40R
Mulligan, Robert S(mith) 1941- ... 65-68
Mulliken, Robert Sanderson 1896-1986 ... 109
  Obituary ... 120
Mullin, Michael 1944- ... 103
Mullin, Robert N(orville) 1893- ... 89-92
Mullin, Willard 1902-1978 Obituary ... 89-92
Mullings, Llewellyn M. 1932- ... 37-40R
Mullins, (George) Aloysius 1910- ... CAP-1
  Earlier sketch in CA 13-14
Mullins, Ann
  See Dally, Ann Mullins
Mullins, Carolyn J(ohns) 1940- ... CANR-10
  Earlier sketch in CA 65-68
Mullins, Claud 1887-1968 ... CAP-1
  Earlier sketch in CA 13-14
Mullins, Edward S(wift) 1922- ... 19-20R
  See also SATA 10
Mullins, Edwin (Brandt) 1933- ... CANR-22
  Earlier sketches in CA 53-56, CANR-4
Mullins, Helene 1899- ... 77-80
Mullins, June B(onner) 1927- ... 126
Mullins, Larry E(dward) 1935- ... 117
Mullins, Nicholas C(reed) 1939- ... 33-36R
Mullins, Vera (Annie) Cooper 1903- ... 61-64
Mulloy, Elizabeth D(ibert) 1945- ... 93-96
Mulock, Dinah Maria
  See Craik, Dinah Maria (Mulock)
Multhauf, Robert P(hilip) 1919- ... 93-96
Mulvaney, Robert J(oseph) 1937- ... 126
Mulvanity, George 1903(?)-1976
  Obituary ... 69-72
Mulvey, Ruth Watt
  See Harmer, Ruth Mulvey
Mulvihill, Edward Robert 1917- ... 11-12R
Mulvihill, William Patrick 1923- ... 3R
  See also SATA 8
Mulville, Frank 1924- ... 107
Mumey, Glen A(llen) 1933- ... 73-76
Mumford, Bob 1930- ... 103
Mumford, Emily (Hamilton)
  1920(?)-1987 ... 57-60
  Obituary ... 123
Mumford, Erika 1935(?)-1988 Obituary ... 126
Mumford, Lewis 1895- ... CANR-5
  Earlier sketch in CA 2R
  See also DLB 63
Mummery, David R. 1932- ... 23-32R
Mumms, Hardee
  See McLellan, Diana
Munari, Bruno 1907- ... 73-76
  See also SATA 15
  See also CLR 9
Munby, A(lan) N(oel) L(atimer) 1913-1974
  Obituary ... 53-56
Munby, Arthur Joseph 1828-1910 ... DLB-35
Munby, D(enys) L(awrence) 1919-1976 . CANR-2
  Earlier sketch in CA 4R
Munce, Ruth Hill 1898- ... CAP-1
  Earlier sketch in CA 9-10
  See also SATA 12
Munch, Peter A(ndreas) 1908-1984 ... 29-32R
  Obituary ... 111
Munch, Theodore W(illiam) 1919- ... 57-60
Muncy, Raymond Lee 1928- ... 49-52
Mund, Vernon A(rthur) 1906- ... CANR-20
  Earlier sketch in CA 2R
Munday, Anthony 1560-1633 ... DLB-62
Mundel, Marvin E(verett) 1916- ... 21-22R
Mundell, Robert A(lexander) 1932- ... CANR-2
  Earlier sketch in CA 45-48
Mundell, William Daniel 1913- ... 73-76
Mundis, Hester 1938- ... CANR-15
  Earlier sketch in CA 69-72
Mundis, Jerrold 1941- ... CANR-11
  Earlier sketch in CA 69-72
Mundlak, Max 1899- ... CAP-1
  Earlier sketch in CA 9-10
Mundy, John Hine 1917- ... 45-48
Mundy, Max
  See Schofield, Sylvia Anne
Munford, Robert 1737(?)-1783 ... DLB-31
Munford, W(illiam) A(rthur) 1911- ... 116
Mungello, David Emil 1943- ... 110
Munger, Al
  See Unger, Maurice Albert
Munger, Frank James 1929-1981 ... CANR-1
  Obituary ... 116
  Earlier sketch in CA 3R
Munger, Hortense Roberta
  See Roberts, Hortense Roberta
Munger, Robert Boyd 1910- ... 77-80
Mungo, Raymond 1946- ... CANR-2
  Earlier sketch in CA 49-52
Munholland, John K(im) 1934- ... CANR-25
  Earlier sketch in CA 29-32R
Munir, Muhammad 1895-1981 Obituary ... 108
Munitz, Milton K(arl) 1913- ... CANR-16
  Earlier sketch in CA 93-96
Munk, Arthur W. 1909- ... CANR-7
  Earlier sketch in CA 15-16R
Munk, Christian
  See Weisenborn, Guenther
Munk, Erika 1939- ... 19-20R
Munn, Geoffrey C(harles) 1953- ... 118
Munn, Glenn (Gaywaine) 1890(?)-1977
  Obituary ... 73-76
Munn, H(arold) Warner 1903-1981 ... CANR-11
  Earlier sketch in CA 21-22R
Munn, Hart
  See Hardy, C. Colburn
Munnecke, Wilbur C(heney) 1906-1984
  Obituary ... 112
Munnell, Alicia H(aydock) 1942- ... CANR-13
  Earlier sketch in CA 73-76
Munonye, John 1929- ... 103
Munowitz, Ken 1935-1977 ... SATA-14
Munoz, Braulio 1946- ... 110
Munoz, Heraldo 1948- ... 111
Munoz, William 1949- ... SATA-42
Munoz Marin, Luis 1898-1980 Obituary ... 97-100
Munro, Alice 1931- ... 33-36R
  See also SATA 29
  See also DLB 53
  See also CLC 6, 10, 19, 50
  See also AITN 2
Munro, Bertha 1887-1983 ... 45-48
Munro, C. K.
  See MacMullan, Charles Walden
  Kirkpatrick
Munro, Dana Gardner 1892- ... 3R
Munro, David
  See Devine, D(avid) M(cDonald)
Munro, Duncan H.
  See Russell, Eric Frank
Munro, Eleanor 1928- ... 4R
  See also SATA 37
Munro, Hector Hugh 1870-1916
  Brief entry ... 104
  See also DLB 34
Munro, (Macfarlane) Hugh ... 11-12R
Munro, Ian S. ... 29-32R
Munro, James
  See Cave, Roderick (George James
  Munro)
  and Mitchell, James
Munro, Jane 1943- ... 112
Munro, John (Henry Alexander) 1938- ... 41-44R
Munro, John M(urchinson) 1932- ... CANR-11
  Earlier sketch in CA 69-72
Munro, Leslie Knox 1901-1974 Obituary ... 49-52
Munro, Mary
  See Howe, Doris Kathleen
Munro, Thomas 1897-1974 ... CANR-3
  Earlier sketch in CA 5-6R
Munroe, Elizabeth L(ee) 1900- ... CANR-2
  Earlier sketch in CA 19-20R
Munroe, John A(ndrew) 1914- ... 49-52
Munroe, Kirk 1850-1930 Brief entry ... 123
  See also DLB 42
Munrow, David John 1942-1976 ... 103
  Obituary ... 106
Munsch, Robert (Norman) 1945- ... 121
  See also SATA 48, 50
Munsey, Cecil (Richard, Jr.) 1935- ... CANR-17
  Earlier sketch in CA 41-44R
Munsey, Frank A(ndrew) 1854-1925
  Brief entry ... 116
  See also DLB 25
Munshi, Kiki Skagen 1943- ... CANR-15
  Earlier sketch in CA 37-40R
Munshi, Shehnaaz
  See Munshi, Kiki Skagen
Munshower, Suzanne 1945- ... 97-100
Munsinger, Harry 1935- ... 45-48
Munsinger, Lynn 1951- ... SATA-33
Munslow, Barry 1950- ... 117
Munson, Amelia H. (?)-1972 Obituary ... 33-36R
Munson, Byron Edwin 1921- ... 41-44R
Munson, Charlie E(llis) 1877-1975 ... 57-60
Munson, Don 1908- ... 73-76
Munson, Fred C(aleb) 1928- ... 33-36R
Munson, Gorham B(ert) 1896-1969 ... CAP-1
  Earlier sketch in CA 11-12
Munson, Harold L(ewis) 1923- ... 29-32R
Munson, Henry (Lee), Jr. 1946- ... 115
Munson, James (Edward Bradbury) 1944- ... 124
Munson, Kenneth (George) 1929-
  Brief entry ... 111
Munson, Lou
  See Munson, Mary Lou (Easley)
Munson, Mary Lou (Easley) 1935- ... 11-12R
Munson, Thomas N(olan) 1924- ... CANR-20
  Earlier sketch in CA 2R
Munson, Thurman (Lee) 1947-1979 ... 108
  Obituary ... 89-92
Munson-Benson, Tunie 1946- ... 77-80
  See also SATA 15
Munsterberg, Hugo 1916- ... CANR-2
  Earlier sketch in CA 7-8R
Munsterhjelm, Erik 1905- ... 49-52
Munter, Robert (L.) 1926- ... 23-24R
Munthe, Adam John 1946- ... 107
Munthe, Frances 1915- ... 11-12R
Munthe, Malcolm Grane 1920- ... 7-8R
Munthe, Nelly 1947- ... 117
  See also SATA 53
Munton, Alan (Guy) 1945- ... CANR-24
  Earlier sketch in CA 107
Muntyan, Miodrag 1914-1985 Obituary ... 117
Muntz, (Isabelle) Hope 1907- ... 15-16R
Muntz, James
  See Crowcroft, Peter
Munves, James (Albert) 1922- ... CANR-3
  Earlier sketch in CA 5-6R
  See also SATA 30
Munz, Peter 1921- ... 15-16R
Munz, Philip Alexander 1892- ... 7-8R
Munzer, Martha E. 1899- ... CANR-4
  Earlier sketch in CA 2R
  See also SATA 4
Murad, Anatol 1904- ... 73-76
Murad, Gauhar-i
  See Sa'Idi, Ghulam Husayn
Murari, Timeri N(rupendra) 1941- ... 102
Muravin, Victor 1929- ... 85-88
Murawski, Benjamin J(oseph) 1926- ... 45-48
Murbarger, Nell Lounsberry 1909- ... CAP-1
  Earlier sketch in CA 15-16
Murch, Edward (William Lionel) 1920- ... 61-64
Murch, James DeForest 1892-1973 ... CANR-4
  Earlier sketch in CA 7-8R
Murchie, Guy 1907- ... 2R
Murchison, Thomas Moffat 1907-1984
  Obituary ... 111
Murchland, Bernard 1929- ... 112
Murden, Forrest D(ozier), Jr. 1921-1977
  Obituary ... 73-76
Murdick, Robert Gordon 1920- ... CANR-6
  Earlier sketch in CA 7-8R
Murdin, Paul 1942- ... CANR-23
  Earlier sketch in CA 106
Murdoch, (Henry) Derrick 1909-1985 ... 89-92
  Obituary ... 116
Murdoch, (Jean) Iris 1919- ... CANR-8
  Earlier sketch in CA 13-14R
  See also DLB 14
  See also CLC 1, 2, 3, 4, 6, 8, 11, 15,
  22, 31
Murdoch, Joseph S(impson) F(erguson)
  1919- ... 102
Murdoch, (Keith) Rupert 1931- Brief entry ... 111
Murdock, Eugene C(onverse) 1921- ... CANR-13
  Earlier sketch in CA 33-36R
Murdock, George Peter 1897- ... CAP-1
  Earlier sketch in CA 13-14
Murdock, Kenneth Ballard 1895-1975 ... 65-68
  Obituary ... 61-64
Murdock, Laurette P. 1900- ... 101
Murdock, M(elinda) S(eabrooke) 1947- ... 113
Murdock, Myrtle Cheney 1886(?)-1980
  Obituary ... 97-100
Murdy, Louise Baughan 1935- ... 33-36R
Mure, David William Alexander
  1912-1986(?) Obituary ... 120
Mure, G(eoffrey) R(eginald) G(ilchrist)
  1893-1979 ... 107
Murfin, James Vernon 1930(?)-1987
  Obituary ... 122
Murfin, Ross C. 1948- ... 125
Murfree, Mary Noailles 1850-1922
  Brief entry ... 122
  See also DLB 12, 74
Murie, Margaret Elizabeth 1902- ... 110
Murnau, Friedrich Wilhelm
  See Plumpe, Friedrich Wilhelm
Murnion, Philip (Joseph) 1938- ... 116
Muro, Diane Patricia 1940- ... 65-68
Muro, James J(oseph) 1934- ... 33-36R
Murphet, Howard 1906- ... 61-64
Murphey, Murray Griffin 1928- ... CANR-6
  Earlier sketch in CA 5-6R
Murphey, Rhoads 1919- ... 33-36R
Murphey, Robert W(entworth) 1916- ... 15-16R
Murphy, Agnes Louise Keating 1912- ... 3R
Murphy, Arthur Lister 1906- ... 77-80
Murphy, Arthur Richard, Jr. 1915-1987
  Obituary ... 123
Murphy, Barbara Beasley 1933- ... CANR-20
  Earlier sketch in CA 41-44R
  See also SATA 5
Murphy, Beatrice M. 1908- ... CANR-9
  Earlier sketch in CA 53-56
  See also DLB 76
Murphy, Brenda C(arol) 1950- ... 120
Murphy, Brian (Michael) 1931- ... CANR-13
  Earlier sketch in CA 21-22R
Murphy, Brian 1939- ... 108
Murphy, Buck
  See Whitcomb, Ian
Murphy, C. L.
  See Murphy, Charlotte A(lice)
  and Murphy, Lawrence A(gustus)
Murphy, Charles J(ohn) V(incent)
  1904-1987 Obituary ... 124
Murphy, Charlotte A(lice) 1924- ... 105
Murphy, Cornelius Francis, Jr. 1933- ... 89-92
Murphy, Dervla (Mary) 1931- ... CANR-21
  Earlier sketch in CA 103
Murphy, Dorothy Dey 1911(?)-1983
  Obituary ... 110
Murphy, E(mmett) Jefferson 1926- ... 25-28R
  See also SATA 4
Murphy, Earl Finbar 1928- ... 13-14R
Murphy, Ed
  See Murphy, Edward Francis
Murphy, Edward Francis 1914- ... 102
Murphy, Edward J. 1927- ... 37-40R
Murphy, Emmy Lou Osborne 1910- ... 5-6R
Murphy, Francis 1932- ... CANR-7
  Earlier sketch in CA 13-14R
Murphy, Frank Hughes 1940- ... 61-64
Murphy, Fred P. 1889-1979 Obituary ... 89-92
Murphy, Gardner 1895-1979 ... 93-96
  Obituary ... 85-88
Murphy, George E(dward), Jr. 1948- ... CANR-13
  Earlier sketch in CA 77-80
Murphy, George G(regory) S(tanislaus)
  1924- ... 21-22R
Murphy, George Lloyd 1902- ... 45-48
Murphy, Grace E. Barstow 1888-1975
  Obituary ... 57-60
Murphy, Hazel
  See Thurston, Hazel (Patricia)
Murphy, Herta A(lbrecht) 1908- ... 49-52
Murphy, Irene L(yons) 1920- ... 53-56
Murphy, J(ohn) Carter 1921- ... 15-16R
Murphy, James F(redrick) 1943- ... CANR-8
  Earlier sketch in CA 61-64
Murphy, James J(erome) 1923- ... CANR-12
  Earlier sketch in CA 33-36R
Murphy, James M(artin) 1917- ... 29-32R
Murphy, James M(aurice) 1932-1966(?) ... CAP-1
  Earlier sketch in CA 11-12
Murphy, Jane Brevoort Walden
  1902(?)-1980 Obituary ... 97-100
Murphy, Jeffrie G(uy) 1940- Brief entry ... 118
Murphy, Jill 1949- ... 105
  See also SATA 37
Murphy, Jim 1947- ... 111
  See also SATA 32, 37
Murphy, John
  See Grady, Ronan Calistus, Jr.
Murphy, John L(awrence) 1924- ... CANR-20
  Earlier sketch in CA 2R
Murphy, John W(illiam) 1948- ... 112
Murphy, Karen A(lee) 1945- ... 115
Murphy, Larry
  See Murphy, Lawrence R(ichard)
Murphy, Lawrence A(gustus) 1924- ... 104
Murphy, Lawrence R(ichard) 1942- ... 105
Murphy, Lois Barclay 1902- ... CANR-19
  Earlier sketches in CA 4R, CANR-4
Murphy, Louis J.
  See Hicks, Tyler Gregory
Murphy, Mario
  See Edmondson, G. C.
Murphy, Marion Fisher 1902- ... 53-56
Murphy, Michael 1930- ... 73-76
Murphy, N(orman) T. P. 1933- ... 125
Murphy, Nonie Carol
  See Caroll, Nonie
Murphy, Pat
  See Murphy, E(mmett) Jefferson
Murphy, Patrick T(homas) 1939- ... 108
Murphy, Patrick V(incent) 1920- ... 105
Murphy, Paul 1917(?)-1983 Obituary ... 111
Murphy, Paul J(ames) 1943- ... 112
Murphy, Paul L(loyd) 1923- ... CANR-7
  Earlier sketch in CA 19-20R
Murphy, Raymond E(dward) 1898- ... 41-44R
Murphy, Reg 1934- ... 33-36R
Murphy, Richard 1927- ... 29-32R
  See also DLB 40
  See also CLC 41
Murphy, Richard T. A. 1908- ... CANR-1
  Earlier sketch in CA 3R
Murphy, Robert (William) 1902-1971 ... CAP-1
  Obituary ... 29-32R
  Earlier sketch in CA 9-10
  See also SATA 10
Murphy, Robert Cushman 1887-1973 ... CAP-2
  Obituary ... 41-44R
  Earlier sketch in CA 23-24
Murphy, Robert D(aniel) 1894-1978 ... CAP-1
  Obituary ... 73-76
  Earlier sketch in CA 9-10
Murphy, Robert F(rancis) 1924- ... 118
Murphy, Roland Edmund 1917- ... CANR-6
  Earlier sketch in CA 5-6R
Murphy, Romaine 1941- ... 77-80
Murphy, Sharon M. 1940- ... 77-80
Murphy, Shirley Rousseau 1928- ... CANR-13
  Earlier sketch in CA 21-22R
  See also SATA 36
Murphy, Sylvia 19(?)- ... CLC-34
Murphy, Sylvia 1937- ... 121
Murphy, Terrence J. 1921- ... 7-8R
Murphy, Thomas (Bernard) 1935- ... 101
Murphy, Thomas Basil, Jr. 1935- ... CANR-11
  Earlier sketch in CA 69-72
Murphy, Thomas P(atrick) 1931- ... CANR-16
  Earlier sketch in CA 41-44R
Murphy, Tom
  See Murphy, Thomas Basil, Jr.
Murphy, Vi 1924(?)-1987 Obituary ... 124
Murphy, Walter F(rancis) 1929- ... CANR-2
  Earlier sketch in CA 2R
Murphy, Warren B. 1933- ... CANR-13
  Earlier sketch in CA 33-36R
Murphy, William Francis 1906- ... 19-20R
Murphy, William M(ichael) 1916- ... 85-88
Murphy-O'Connor, Jerome James
  1935- ... CANR-5
  Earlier sketch in CA 15-16R
Murra, John V(ictor) 1916- ... CANR-1
  Earlier sketch in CA 45-48
Murrah, David Joe 1941- ... 106
Murray, Adrian
  See Curran, Mona (Elisa)
Murray, Albert L. 1916- ... CANR-26
  Earlier sketch in CA 49-52
  See also BW
  See also DLB 38
Murray, Andrew Evans 1917- ... 25-28R
Murray, Beatrice
  See Posner, Richard
Murray, Bruce C(hurchill) 1931- ... 103
Murray, Christopher 1940- ... 117
Murray, Clara Elizabeth 1894- ... CAP-1
  Earlier sketch in CA 9-10
Murray, Cromwell
  See Morgan, Murray
Murray, D. Stark
  See Murray, David Stark
Murray, Daniel E(dward) 1925- ... 45-48
Murray, David Stark 1900-1977 Obituary ... 111
Murray, Dick 1924- ... 106
Murray, Donald M(orison) 1924- ... CANR-17
  Earlier sketch in CA 4R
Murray, Dorothy Garst 1915- ... 21-22R
Murray, Edmund P(atrick) 1930- ... 81-84
Murray, Edna
  See Rowland, D(onald) S(ydney)
Murray, Edward (James, Jr.) 1928- ... CANR-1
  Earlier sketch in CA 49-52
Murray, Edward J(ames) 1928- ... 15-16R
Murray, Elwood 1897- ... 73-76
Murray, Eugene Bernard 1927- ... 104
Murray, Frances
  See Booth, Rosemary Frances

Murray, G(erald) E(dward, Jr.) 1945- ... CANR-5
Earlier sketch in CA 53-56
Murray, George (McIntosh) 1900-1970 ... CAP-1
Earlier sketch in CA 13-14
Murray, (Jesse) George 1909- ... 19-20R
Murray, (George) Gilbert (Aime)
1866-1957 Brief entry ... 110
See also DLB 10
Murray, Hallard T(homas), Jr. 1937- ... 19-20R
Murray, Henry A(lexander) 1893-1988
Obituary ... 125
Brief entry ... 116
Murray, Irene
See Witherspoon, Irene Murray
Murray, J(ohn) Alex ... 41-44R
Murray, J. Harley 1910(?)-1977 Obituary ... 73-76
Murray, J(ohn) Joseph 1915- ... CANR-4
Earlier sketch in CA 7-8R
Murray, James 1946- ... CANR-1
Earlier sketch in CA 49-52
Murray, James Patrick 1919- ... CANR-15
Earlier sketch in CA 65-68
Murray, Jean Shaw 1927(?)-1985
Obituary ... 116
Murray, Jerome T(homas) 1928- ... 33-36R
Murray, Jim
See Murray, James Patrick
Murray, Joan 1943- ... 124
Murray, Joan 1945- ... 77-80
Murray, Joan E. 1941- ... 81-84
Murray, Jocelyn (Margaret) 1929- ... 113
Murray, John 1923- ... CANR-19
Earlier sketches in CA 7-8R, CANR-4
See also SATA 39
Murray, John Bernard 1915- ... 41-44R
Murray, John Courtney 1904-1967
Obituary ... 106
Murray, John E(dward), Jr. 1932- ... 45-48
Murray, John F(rancis) 1923-1977 ... CAP-2
Obituary ... 69-72
Earlier sketch in CA 29-32
Murray, John L(arry) 1937- ... 108
Murray, John MacDougall 1910- ... 33-36R
Murray, Judith Sargent 1751-1820 ... DLB-37
Murray, K. F.
See Carlisle, Fred
Murray, K(atherine) M(aud) Elisabeth
1909- ... 77-80
Murray, Keith A. 1910- ... CAP-2
Earlier sketch in CA 33-36
Murray, Ken 1903-1988 Obituary ... 126
Murray, Ken
See Turner, Robert H(arry)
Murray, Les(lie) A(llan) 1938- ... CANR-11
Earlier sketch in CA 23-24R
See also CLC 40
Murray, Linda Charlton 1936(?)-1986
Obituary ... 118
Murray, Lois Smith 1906- ... 37-40R
Murray, Margaret Alice 1863-1963 ... 7-8R
Murray, Marian ... 41-44R
See also SATA 5
Murray, Mary (Morrison) 1925- ... 25-28R
Murray, Maynard 1911(?)-1983 Obituary ... 110
Murray, Merrill G. 1900(?)-1976
Obituary ... 69-72
Murray, Michael
See McLaren, Moray (David Shaw)
Murray, Michael V(ivian) 1906- ... 7-8R
Murray, (Judith) Michele (Freedman)
1933-1974 ... 49-52
See also SATA 7
Murray, Ossie 1938- ... SATA-43
Murray, (Anna) Pauli(ne) 1910-1985 ... 125
Obituary ... 116
See also BW
See also DLB 41
Murray, Peter (John) 1920- ... CANR-10
Earlier sketch in CA 13-14R
Murray, Philip 1924- ... 65-68
Murray, Ralph L(a Verne) 1921- ... 15-16R
Murray, Rebecca (Jean) 1936- ... 57-60
Murray, Robert A. 1929- ... 29-32R
Murray, Robert Keith 1922- ... 53-56
Murray, Robin 1940- ... 126
Murray, Roger N(icholas) 1932- ... 23-24R
Murray, Ruth Lovell 1900- ... 103
Murray, Sister Mary Verona 1909- ... 19-20R
Murray, Sonia Bennett 1936- ... 65-68
Murray, Thomas J(oseph) 1943- ... 77-80
Murray, W(illiam) H(utchison) 1913- ... CANR-4
Earlier sketch in CA 11-12R
Murray, Walter I(saiah) 1910-1978 ... 85-88
Obituary ... 73-76
Murray, William Cotter 1929- ... 53-56
Murray, William J(oseph) III 1946- ... 110
Murray-Brown, Jeremy 1932- ... 77-80
Murray-Smith, Stephen 1922- ... 103
Murrell, Elsie Kathleen Seth-Smith 1883- . CAP-1
Earlier sketch in CA 9-10
Murrell, K(eith) F(rank) H(ywel)
1908(?)-1984 Obituary ... 112
Murrett, John Charles 1892- ... 4R
Murrow, Casey 1945- ... 97-100
Murrow, Edward R(oscoe) 1908-1965 ... 103
Obituary ... 89-92
Murry, J. Middleton
See Murry, John Middleton
Murry, John Middleton 1889-1957
Brief entry ... 118
See also TCLC 16
Murry, Mary Middleton 1897-1983
Obituary ... 110
Murstein, Bernard I(rving) 1929- ... CANR-3
Earlier sketch in CA 11-12R
Murtagh, John M(artin) 1911-1976 ... 19-20R
Obituary ... 61-64
Murtagh, William J. 1923- ... 25-28R
Murton, Jessie Wilmore ... 7-8R
Murton, Mary 1933- ... 117
Musa, Mark 1934- ... 15-16R
Musafir
See Tagore, Amitendranath
Musaphia, Joseph 1935- ... CANR-17
Earlier sketch in CA 97-100
Muscat, Robert J. 1931- ... 19-20R
Muscatine, Charles 1920- ... 21-22R
Muscatine, Doris (Corn) 1926- ... 9-10R
Muschamp, Thomas
See Lloyd-Thomas, Catherine
Muschenheim, Carl 1905-1977 Obituary ... 69-72
Muschenheim, William 1902- ... CAP-1
Earlier sketch in CA 15-16
Muschg, Adolf 1934- ... DLB-75
Musciano, Walt
See Musciano, Walter A.
Musciano, Walter A. 1922- ... 121
Muse, Beatriz de Regil 1901(?)-1983
Obituary ... 109
Muse, Benjamin 1898- ... CANR-1
Earlier sketch in CA 3R
Muse, Clarence 1889-1979 Obituary ... 104
Muse, Daphne P. 1944- ... 112
Muse, Ken 1925- ... 111
Muse, Patricia (Alice) 1923- ... 69-72
Muses, C. A.
See Muses, Charles Arthur
Muses, Charles Arthur 1919- Brief entry ... 115
Musetto, Andrew P(aul) 1945- ... 111
Musgrave, Barbara S(tewart) 1913- ... 5-6R
Musgrave, Clifford 1904-1982 Obituary ... 107
Musgrave, Florence 1902- ... CAP-1
Earlier sketch in CA 13-14
See also SATA 3
Musgrave, Richard Abel 1910- ... 113
Musgrave, Susan 1951- ... 69-72
See also CLC 13
Musgraves, Don 1935- ... 65-68
Musgrove, Frank 1922- ... CANR-6
Earlier sketch in CA 15-16R
Musgrove, Margaret Wynkoop 1943- ... 65-68
See also SATA 26
Musgrove, Philip 1940- ... CANR-11
Earlier sketch in CA 29-32R
Musgrove, Stanley (E.) 1924-1986 ... 108
Obituary ... 118
Mushabac, Jane 1944- ... 108
Mushkat, Jerome 1931- ... 81-84
Mushkat, Mari'on 1919- ... 120
Mushkin, Selma J. 1913-1979 Obituary ... 93-96
Musial, Joe 1905(?)-1977 Obituary ... 69-72
Musial, Stan(ley Frank) 1920- ... 93-96
Musicant, Elke (Alice) 1919- ... 107
Musicant, Tobias (Ted) 1921- ... 108
Musiker, Reuben 1931- ... 57-60
Musil, Robert (Edler von) 1880-1942
Brief entry ... 109
See also TCLC 12
Muske, Carol 1945- ... 65-68
Muske, Irmgard (Gertrud) 1912- ... CANR-18
Earlier sketch in CA 25-28R
Muskie, Edmund S(ixtus) 1914- ... CANR-2
Earlier sketch in CA 49-52
Musmanno, Michael A(ngelo) ?-1968 ... CAP-1
Earlier sketch in CA 9-10
Musolf, Lloyd D(aryl) 1919- ... CANR-9
Earlier sketch in CA 19-20R
Musselman, George Paul 1895-1987
Obituary ... 123
Musselman, Vernon A(rmor) 1912- ... 37-40R
Mussen, Paul Henry 1922- Brief entry ... 114
Musser, Joe
See Musser, Joseph L.
Musser, Joseph L. 1936- ... CANR-12
Earlier sketch in CA 29-32R
Mussey, Virginia Howell
See Ellison, Virginia H(owell)
Mussey, Virginia T.H.
See Ellison, Virginia H(owell)
Mussi, Mary 1907- ... CANR-6
Earlier sketch in CA 53-56
Mussoff, Lenore 1927- ... 21-22R
Mussolini, Benito (Amilcare Andrea)
1883-1945 Brief entry ... 116
Mussolini, Rachele Guidi 1890-1979
Obituary ... 111
Mussulman Joseph A(gee) 1928- ... 37-40R
Mustafa, Zaki 1934- ... 41-44R
Muste, John M(artin) 1927- ... 21-22R
Musteikis, Antanas 1914- ... 45-48
Musto, Barry 1930- ... 106
Musto, David Franklin 1936- ... 104
Musurillo, Herbert (Anthony Peter)
1917-1974 ... CAP-1
Obituary ... 49-52
Earlier sketch in CA 13-14
Mutchler, David E(dward) 1941- ... 33-36R
Muth, John F(raser) 1930- ... 13-14R
Muth, Richard F(erris) 1927- ... 13-14R
Mutharika, B(rightson) W(ebster) T(hom)
1934- ... 41-44R
Muthesius, Stefan 1939- ... 61-64
Mutke, Peter H(ans) C(hristoph) 1927- ... 93-96
Muto, Susan Annette 1942- ... 110
Mutton, Alice F. A. 1908- ... 5-6R
Mutz
See Kuenstler, Morton
Muus, Bent J(oergen) 1926- ... 103
Muus, Flemming B(ruun) 1907-1982
Obituary ... 110
Muuss, Rolf E(duard Helmut) 1924- ... 9-10R
Muzumdar, Ammu Menon 1919- ... 21-22R
Mwanga
See Stark, Claude Alan
Myassin, Leonid Fedorovich 1895-1979 ... 97-100
Obituary ... 85-88
My Brother's Brother
See Chekhov, Anton (Pavlovich)
Mycue, Edward 1937- ... CANR-4
Earlier sketch in CA 53-56
Mydans, Carl ... 97-100
Mydans, Shelley Smith 1915- Brief entry ... 105
Myddleton, Robert
See Hebblethwaite, Peter
Myer, Dillon S(eymour) 1891-1982 ... CAP-2
Obituary ... 116
Earlier sketch in CA 29-32
Myer, John Colby 1912- ... 45-48
Myer, John Randolph 1927- ... 7-8R
Myerhoff, Barbara G. 1936(?)-1985
Obituary ... 114
Myers, A(lexander) J(ohn) William 1877- . CAP-1
Earlier sketch in CA 11-12
Myers, Albert M(orris) 1917- ... 118
Myers, Alec Reginald
See Myers, Alexander Reginald
Myers, Alexander Reginald 1912-1980 . CANR-10
Earlier sketch in CA 13-14R
Myers, Alonzo F(ranklin) 1895-1970
Obituary ... 104
Myers, Andrew Breen 1920- ... 61-64
Myers, Arthur 1922- ... CANR-7
Earlier sketch in CA 19-20R
See also SATA 35
Myers, Arthur Sim 1928-1984 Obituary ... 113
Myers, Bernard S(amuel) 1908- ... 65-68
Myers, Bernice ... CANR-8
Earlier sketch in CA 61-64
See also SATA 9
Myers, Bettye (Blanche) 1926- Brief entry .. 107
Myers, C. F.
See Fairbanks, Carol
Myers, C(hauncie) Kilmer 1916-1981
Obituary ... 108
Myers, Carol Fairbanks
See Fairbanks, Carol
Myers, Caroline Elizabeth Clark
1887-1980 ... 29-32R
See also SATA 28
Myers, Charles A(ndrew) 1913- ... 85-88
Myers, Charles B(ennett) 1939- ... 57-60
Myers, David G. 1942- ... CANR-22
Earlier sketch in CA 106
Myers, (Eugene Victor) Debs 1911-1971
Obituary ... 104
Myers, Desaix B. III 1945- ... 104
Myers, Edward 1950- ... 116
Myers, Elisabeth P(erkins) 1918- ... CANR-3
Earlier sketch in CA 5-6R
See also SATA 36
Myers, Eugene A(braham) 1910- ... 45-48
Myers, Francis Milton 1917- ... 7-8R
Myers, Gail E(ldridge) 1923- ... CANR-1
Earlier sketch in CA 49-52
Myers, Garry Cleveland 1884-1971 ... CAP-2
Earlier sketch in CA 29-32
Myers, Gay Nagle 1943- ... 102
Myers, George (Francis), Jr. 1953- ... 119
Myers, Gerald E(ugene) 1923- ... 29-32R
Myers, Gustavus 1872-1942 Brief entry ... 123
See also DLB 47
Myers, Harriet Kathryn
See Whittington, Harry (Benjamin)
Myers, (Mary) Hortense (Powner)
1913-1987 ... CANR-2
Obituary ... 123
Earlier sketch in CA 4R
See also SATA 10
Myers, Irma A(shley) 1924- ... 112
Myers, J(ohn) William 1919- ... CANR-12
Earlier sketch in CA 33-36R
Myers, (Elliott) Jack 1941- ... 73-76
Myers, Jacob M(artin) 1904- ... 19-20R
Myers, John Bernard 1920(?)-1987
Obituary ... 123
Myers, John H(olmes) 1915- ... 11-12R
Myers, John Myers 1906- ... CANR-1
Earlier sketch in CA 3R
Myers, Katherine 1952- ... 110
Myers, L. H. 1881-1944 ... DLB-15
Myers, L(ouis) M(cCorry) 1901- ... 21-22R
Myers, Lonny 1922- ... 65-68
Myers, M(arvin) Scott 1922- ... 69-72
Myers, Martin 1927- ... CANR-20
Earlier sketch in CA 29-32R
Myers, Mary Ruth 1947- ... CANR-16
Earlier sketch in CA 85-88
Myers, Neil 1930- ... 105
Myers, Norma 1929- ... 61-64
Myers, Norman 1934- ... CANR-20
Earlier sketches in CA 49-52, CANR-1
Myers, Patricia 1929- ... 37-40R
Myers, Paul 1932- ... 123
Myers, R(obert) E(ugene) 1924- ... CANR-23
Earlier sketch in CA 77-80
Myers, Ramon H. 1929- ... 113
Myers, Raymond E(dward) 1902- ... CAP-1
Earlier sketch in CA 15-16
Myers, Robert J(ulius) 1912- ... CANR-6
Earlier sketch in CA 15-16R
Myers, Robert J(ohn) 1924- ... 107
Myers, Robert Manson 1921- ... 37-40R
Myers, Rollo Hugh 1892-1984(?) ... 19-20R
Obituary ... 115
Myers, Samuel 1897(?)-1983 Obituary ... 109
Myers, Walter Dean 1937- ... CANR-20
Earlier sketch in CA 33-36R
See also BW
See also SATA 27, 41
See also SAAS 2
See also DLB 33
See also CLC 35
See also CLR 4, 16
Myers, Walter M.
See Myers, Walter Dean
Myerscough-Walker, Raymond 1912-1984
Obituary ... 113
Myerson, Bess 1924- ... 108
Myerson, Joel 1945- ... CANR-19
Earlier sketch in CA 102
Myerson, Michael 1940- ... 73-76
Myhers, John 1921- ... 105
Myhill, Henry (James) 1925-1977 ... 103
Mykle, Agrar 1915- ... 15-16R
Mylander, Maureen 1937- ... CANR-5
Earlier sketch in CA 53-56
Myler, Joseph L. 1905(?)-1973
Obituary ... 41-44R
Myles, Eugenie Louise (Butler) 1905- ... CAP-1
Earlier sketch in CA 11-12
Myles, Symon
See Follett, Ken(neth Martin)
Myller, Rolf 1926- ... CANR-8
Earlier sketch in CA 7-8R
See also SATA 27
Mylonas, George Emmanuel 1898-1988
Obituary ... 125
Mynors, Roger A(ubrey) B(askerville)
1903- ... 7-8R
Myra, Harold L(awrence) 1939- ... CANR-8
Earlier sketch in CA 61-64
See also SATA 42, 46
Myrdal, Alva Reimer 1902-1986 ... 69-72
Obituary ... 118
Myrdal, (Karl) Gunnar 1898-1987 ... CANR-4
Obituary ... 122
Earlier sketch in CA 9-10R
Myrdal, Jan 1927- Brief entry ... 117
Myrer, Anton 1922- ... CANR-3
Earlier sketch in CA 2R
Myres, J(ohn) N(owell) L(inton) 1902- ... 123
Myres, Sandra Lynn 1933- ... CANR-14
Earlier sketch in CA 33-36R
Myrick, David F. ... CANR-6
Earlier sketch in CA 13-14R
Myrick, Robert D(eWayne) 1935- ... CANR-17
Earlier sketch in CA 41-44R
Myrick, William J(ennings, Jr.) 1932- ... 73-76
Myrland, Doug 1952- ... 117
Myron, Robert 1926- ... 15-16R
Myrsiades, Kostas J. 1940- ... 109
Myrus, Donald (Richard) 1927- ... CANR-4
Earlier sketch in CA 4R
See also SATA 23

N

Naamani, Israel T(arkow) 1913(?)- ... 124
Brief entry ... 106
Naar, Jon 1920- ... 102
Nabbes, Thomas 1605(?)-1641 ... DLB-58
Nabholtz, John R(obert) 1931- ... 65-68
Nabokov, Nicolas 1903-1978 ... 85-88
Obituary ... 77-80
Nabokov, Peter (Francis) 1940- ... CANR-9
Earlier sketch in CA 21-22R
Nabokov, Vladimir (Vladimirovich)
1899-1977 ... CANR-20
Obituary ... 69-72
Earlier sketch in CA 7-8R
See also DLB 2
See also DLBY 80
See also DLBD 3
See also CDALB 1941-1968
See also CLC 1, 2, 3, 6, 8, 11, 15, 23,
44, 46
Nacci, Chris (Natale) 1909- ... 41-44R
Nachbar, Herbert 1930(?)-1980
Obituary ... 97-100
Nachbar, Jack 1941- ... 53-56
Nachman, Gerald 1938- ... CANR-16
Earlier sketch in CA 65-68
Nachtigal, Paul M. 1930- ... 112
Nachtigall, Lila Ehrenstein 1934-
Brief entry ... 105
Nachtmann, Francis Weldon 1913- ... 37-40R
Nadan, Paul 1933(?)-1978 Obituary ... 104
Naddor, Eliezer 1920- ... 21-22R
Nadeau, Maurice 1911- ... 49-52
Nadeau, R(aymond) E(rnest) 1913-
Brief entry ... 107
Nadeau, Ray E.
See Nadeau, R(aymond) E(rnest)
Nadeau, Remi A(llen) 1920- ... CANR-2
Earlier sketch in CA 1R
Nadeau, Roland 1928- ... CANR-4
Earlier sketch in CA 53-56
Nadel, Frances 1905(?)-1977 Obituary ... 69-72
Nadel, Gerald H. 1944-1977 ... 81-84
Obituary ... 73-76
Nadel, Ira Bruce 1943- ... CANR-18
Earlier sketch in CA 102
Nadel, Mark V(ictor) 1943- ... 33-36R
Nadel, Norman (Sanford) 1915- ... 106
Nader, George 1921- Brief entry ... 109
Nader, George Albert 1940- ... 111
Nader, Laura 1930- ... CANR-7
Earlier sketch in CA 19-20R
Nader, Ralph 1934- ... 77-80
Nadler, Harvey 1933- ... 15-16R

INDEX

Nadler, Leonard 1922- CANR-20
Earlier sketches in CA 53-56, CANR-5
Nadler, Paul S(tephen) 1930- 25-28R
Nadler, Susan
See Gantry, Susan Nadler
Nadler, Zeace 1925- 121
Naef, Weston J(ohn) 1942- Brief entry 111
Naeslund, Erik 1948- 103
Naess, Harald Sigurd 1925- 41-44R
Naether, Carl (Albert) 1892- 25-28R
Nafziger, E(stel) Wayne 1938- 85-88
Nag
See Grauer, Neil A(lbert)
Nag, Moni 1925- 41-44R
Nagai Berthrong, Evelyn 1946- 115
Nagai Kafu
See Nagai Sokichi
Nagai Sokichi 1879-1959 Brief entry 117
Nagara, Susumu 1932- CANR-3
Earlier sketch in CA 45-48
Nagatsu, Toshiharu 1930- 107
Nagatsuka, Ryuji 1924- Brief entry 125
na gCopaleen, Myles
See O Nuallain, Brian
Nagel, Andreas Fischer
See Fischer-Nagel, Andreas
Nagel, Ernest 1901-1985 93-96
Obituary 117
Nagel, Heiderose Fischer
See Fischer-Nagel, Heiderose
Nagel, James (Edward) 1940- 29-32R
Nagel, Otto 1894-1967 Obituary 106
Nagel, Paul C(hester) 1926- CANR-22
Earlier sketches in CA 11-12R, CANR-5
Nagel, Shirley 1922- 93-96
Nagel, Stuart S(amuel) 1934- CANR-14
Earlier sketch in CA 33-36R
Nagel, Thomas 1937- CANR-4
Earlier sketch in CA 53-56
Nagel, William G(eorge) 1916- 49-52
Nagenda, Musa
See Howard, Moses L(eon)
Nagera, Humberto 1927- 57-60
Nagi, Mostafa H. 1934- 33-36R
Nagi, Saad Z. 1925- 29-32R
Nagle, James J. 1909-1978 85-88
Obituary 81-84
Naglee, David Ingersoll 1930- 53-56
Nagler, Alois Maria 1907- CANR-19
Earlier sketch in CA 103
Nagler, Barney 1912- 19-20R
Nagler, Michael N(icholas) 1937- CANR-13
Earlier sketch in CA 73-76
na Gopaleen, Myles
See O Nuallain, Brian
Nagorski, Andrew 1947- 93-96
Nagorski, Zygmunt 1885(?)-1973
Obituary 41-44R
Nagorski, Zygmunt, Jr. 1912- 73-76
Nagourney, Peter (Jon) 1940- 37-40R
Naguib, Mohammed 1902(?)-1984
Obituary 113
Nagy, Ferenc 1903-1979 Obituary 89-92
Nagy, Gil D. 1933- 25-28R
Nagy, Gregory 1942- 102
Nagy, Imre 1895(?)-1958 Brief entry 118
Nagy, Laszlo 1925-1978 Obituary 112
See also CLC 7
Nagy-Talavera, Nicholas M(anuel) 1929- 33-36R
Naha, Ed 1950- 109
Nahal, Chaman 1927- CANR-17
Earlier sketch in CA 37-40R
Nahas, Gabriel G(eorges) 1920- CANR-17
Earlier sketches in CA 49-52, CANR-1
Nahas, Rebecca 1946- 69-72
Nahem, Joseph 1917- 113
Nahm, Milton C(harles) 1903- 15-16R
Nahum, Lucien 1930(?)-1983 Obituary 111
Naidis, Mark 1918- 33-36R
Naifeh, Steven Woodward 1952- 102
Naik, Madhukar Krishna 1926- CANR-25
Earlier sketches in CA 21-22R, CANR-10
Naim, C(houdhri) M(ohammed) 1936-
Brief entry 112
Naiman, Arthur 1941- 108
Naimy, Mikhail 1889-1988 Obituary 124
Naipaul, Shiva(dhar Srinivasa) 1945-1985 112
Obituary 116
Brief entry 110
See also DLBY 85
See also CLC 32, 39
Naipaul, V(idiadhar) S(urajprasad)
1932- CANR-1
Earlier sketch in CA 4R
See also DLBY 85
See also CLC 4, 7, 9, 13, 18, 37
Nairn, Ian (Douglas) 1930-1983 Obituary 110
Nairn, Ronald C(harles) 1922- 21-22R
Naisawald, L. Van Loan 1920- CANR-6
Earlier sketch in CA 5-6R
Naisbitt, John 1929(?)- Brief entry 113
Naismith, Grace (Akin) 1904-1983 CANR-20
Obituary 111
Earlier sketch in CA 65-68
Naismith, Helen 1929- 69-72
Naismith, Horace
See Helmer, William J.
Naismith, James 1861-1939 Brief entry 118
Naismith, Marion (Overend) 1922- 29-32R
Naismith, Robert J. 1916- 121
Najafi, Najmeh 25-28R
Najarian, Nevart 1901(?)-1985 Obituary 117
Najder, Zdzislaw 1930- 19-20R
Najemy, John Michael 1943- 118
Nakadate, Neil Edward 1943- 115
Nakae, Noriko 1940- 49-52
Nakamura, Hajime 1912- CANR-10
Earlier sketch in CA 53-56
Nakamura, James I. 1919- 21-22R
Nakamura, Yasuo 1919- 45-48
Nakanishi, Don T(oshiaki) 1949- 114
Nakanishi, Marsha
See Hirano-Nakanishi, Marsha J(oyce)
Nakanishi, Marsha J(oyce) Hirano
See Hirano-Nakanishi, Marsha J(oyce)
Nakano, Hirotaka 1942- 33-36R
Nakarai, Toyozo W(ada) 1898- 41-44R
Nakashima, George Katsutoshi 1905- 106
Nakatani, Chiyoko 1930- 77-80
See also SATA 40
Nakayama, Shigeru 1928- 29-32R
Nakhleh, Emile A. 1938- 77-80
Nakhnikian, George 1920- CANR-2
Earlier sketch in CA 2R
Nakos, Lilika 1899(?)- CLC-29
Nalder, Eric C(hristopher) 1946- 89-92
Nale, Sharon Anne 1944- 108
Nall, Hiram Abiff 1950- 57-60
Nall, T(orney) Otto 1900- 19-20R
Nallin, Walter E. 1917(?)-1978 Obituary 77-80
Nalty, Bernard Charles 1931- CANR-18
Earlier sketch in CA 102
Nam, Charles B(enjamin) 1926- CANR-10
Earlier sketch in CA 65-68
Nam, Koon Woo 1928- 61-64
Namath, Joe
See Namath, Joseph William
Namath, Joseph William 1943- 89-92
Namba, Toshio 1910-1987 Obituary 124
Nambiar, O. K. 1910- 13-14R
Nameroff, Rochelle 1943- 41-44R
Namias, June 1941- 81-84
Namier, Julia 1893-1977 61-64
Obituary 120
Namier, Lewis Bernstein 1888-1960
Obituary 113
Namikawa, Banri 1931- CANR-8
Earlier sketch in CA 53-56
Namikawa, Ryo 1905- 93-96
Namioka, Lensey 1929- CANR-11
Earlier sketch in CA 69-72
See also SATA 27
Namir, Mordecai 1897-1975 Obituary 57-60
Namjoshi, Suniti 1941- 113
Namovicz, Gene Inyart 1927- 19-20R
Nanassy, Louis C(harles) 1913- CANR-19
Earlier sketches in CA 53-56, CANR-4
Nance, Guinevera Ann 1939- 106
Nance, James Clark 1893(?)-1984
Obituary 113
Nance, Joseph Milton 1913- CANR-1
Earlier sketch in CA 4R
Nanda, B(al) R(am) 1917- CANR-23
Earlier sketches in CA 13-14R, CANR-7
Nandakumar, Prema 1939- 9-10R
Nandy, Pritish 1947- CANR-12
Earlier sketch in CA 65-68
Nangia, Sudesh 1942- CANR-22
Earlier sketches in CA 53-56, CANR-4
NanKivell, Joice M.
See Loch, Joice N(anKivell)
Nannes, Caspar Harold 1906-1978 11-12R
Obituary 81-84
Nanry, Charles (Anthony) 1938- 73-76
Nanus, Burt 1936- 115
Napier, B(unyan) Davie 1915- CANR-4
Earlier sketch in CA 2R
Napier, Mark
See Laffin, John (Alfred Charles)
Napier, Mary
See Wright, (Mary) Patricia
Napier, Priscilla 1908- 23-24R
Napier, William
See Seymour, William Napier
Napjus, Alice James 1913- 21-22R
Napjus, James
See Napjus, Alice James
Napoleon, Art
See Sudhalter, Richard M(errill)
Napolitan, Joseph 1929- 37-40R
Napolitane, Catherine A(nn) Durrum
1936- 85-88
Narain, Jai Prakash
See Narayan, Jayaprakash
Narang, Gopi Chand 1931- CANR-14
Earlier sketch in CA 29-32R
Narasimha Char, K. T. 1903- CANR-5
Earlier sketch in CA 53-56
Narasimhachar, K. T.
See Narasimha Char, K. T.
Narasimhan, Chakravarthi V. 1915- 19-20R
Narayan, Jayaprakash 1902-1979 97-100
Obituary 89-92
Narayan, Ongkar 1926- 103
Narayan, R(asipuram) K(rishnaswami)
1906- 81-84
See also CLC 7, 28, 47
Narayn, Deane 1929- 1R
Nardin, Terry 1942- 41-44R
Narell, Irena 1923- CANR-1
Earlier sketch in CA 3R
Naremore, James 1941- CANR-11
Earlier sketch in CA 69-72
Naroll, Raoul 1920-1985 33-36R
Obituary 116
Narramore, Stanley Bruce 1941- 57-60
Naruse, Mikio 1905-1969 118
Narveson, Jan F(redric) 1936- CANR-24
Earlier sketches in CA 23-24R, CANR-9
Nasatir, A(braham) P(hineas) 1904- CANR-5
Earlier sketch in CA 11-12R
Nasatir, David 1934- 41-44R
Nasaw, David 1945- 116
Nasaw, Jonathan Lewis 1947- 61-64
Nasby, A(sher Gordon) 1909-1983
Obituary 109
Nasby, Petroleum Vesuvius
See Locke, David Ross
Nash, Allan N(ylin) 1932- 41-44R
Nash, Bruce M(itchell) 1947- CANR-15
Earlier sketch in CA 85-88
See also SATA 34
Nash, Daniel
See Loader, William Reginald
Nash, David T(heodore) 1929- 93-96
Nash, Eno
See Stevens, Austin N(eil)
Nash, Ethel Miller 1909- CAP-1
Earlier sketch in CA 15-16
Nash, Father Stephen
See Kavanaugh, James J(oseph)
Nash, Gary B. 1933- 37-40R
Nash, Gerald D(avid) 1928- CANR-8
Earlier sketch in CA 23-24R
Nash, Howard P(ervear), Jr. 1900- 73-76
Nash, Isabel
See Eberstadt, Isabel
Nash, J(essie) Madeleine 1943- 69-72
Nash, James E(dward) 1933- 29-32R
Nash, Jay Robert 1937- 21-22R
Nash, June (Caprice) 1927- 29-32R
Nash, Lee (Marten) 1927- 41-44R
Nash, Linell
See Smith, Linell Nash
Nash, Manning 1924- 19-20R
Nash, Mary (Hughes) 1925- 5-6R
See also SATA 41
Nash, N. Richard 1913- CANR-14
Earlier sketch in CA 85-88
Nash, Nancy 1943- 21-22R
Nash, Newlyn
See Howe, Doris Kathleen
and Howe, Muriel
Nash, (Fredric) Ogden 1902-1971 CAP-1
Obituary 29-32R
Earlier sketch in CA 13-14
See also SATA 2, 46
See also DLB 11
See also CLC 23
Nash, Padder
See Sewart, Alan
Nash, Paul 1924- 19-20R
Nash, Ralph (Lee) 1925- 19-20R
Nash, Ray 1905-1982 Obituary 106
Nash, Robert 1902- CAP-1
Earlier sketch in CA 9-10
Nash, Roderick 1939- 19-20R
Nash, Ronald H. 1936- CANR-23
Earlier sketches in CA 5-6R, CANR-8
Nash, Simon
See Chapman, Raymond
Nash, William (Wray), Jr. 1928- 85-88
Naske, Claus-M(ichael) 1935- CANR-13
Earlier sketch in CA 77-80
Naslund, Erik
See Naeslund, Erik
Nason, Alvin 1919-1978 Obituary 77-80
Nason, Donna 1944- 97-100
Nason, Leonard H(astings) 1895-1970
Obituary 114
Nason, Leslie J. 7-8R
Nasr, Seyyed Hossein 1933- CANR-10
Earlier sketch in CA 23-24R
Nass, Elyse (Linda) 1947- 111
Nass, Stanley 1940- 115
Nassaar, Christopher S(uhayl) 1944- 97-100
Nassar, Eugene Paul 1935- 33-36R
Nassau, Wilhelmina Helena Pauline Maria
1880-1962 Obituary 113
Nassauer, Rudolf 1924- 105
Nasser, Gamal Abdel 1918-1970 Obituary 113
Nassivera, John 1950- 109
Nassour, Ellis (Michael) 1941- 119
Nast, Elsa Ruth
See Watson, Jane Werner
Nast, Thomas 1840-1902 Brief entry 112
See also SATA 33, 51
Nastick, Sharon 1954- 114
See also SATA 41
Natale, Samuel M(ichael) 1943- 116
Natali, Alfred Maxim 1915- 57-60
Natanson, George 1928- 73-76
Natanson, Maurice (Alexander) 1924- CANR-12
Earlier sketch in CA 19-20R
Natchez, Gladys W. 1915- CANR-4
Earlier sketch in CA 11-12R
Natella, Arthur A(ristides), Jr. 1941- CANR-15
Earlier sketch in CA 89-92
Nathan, Adele (Gutman) 1900(?)-1986 73-76
Obituary 119
See also SATA 48
Nathan, Andrew J(ames) 1943- 65-68
Nathan, Daniel
See Dannay, Frederic
Nathan, David 1926- CANR-12
Earlier sketch in CA 29-32R
Nathan, Dorothy (Goldeen) ?-1966 81-84
See also SATA 15
Nathan, George Jean 1882-1958
Brief entry 114
See also TCLC 18
Nathan, Hans 1910- CANR-1
Earlier sketch in CA 3R
Nathan, James A. 1942- CANR-16
Earlier sketch in CA 85-88
Nathan, Joan 1943- 61-64
Nathan, Joe 1948- 115
Nathan, Leonard E(dward) 1924- CANR-7
Earlier sketch in CA 5-6R
Nathan, Norman 1915- CANR-1
Earlier sketch in CA 1R
Nathan, Otto 1893-1987 Obituary 121
Nathan, Paul S. 1913- Brief entry 116
Nathan, Peter E. 1935- 73-76
Nathan, Richard P(erle) 1935- CANR-7
Earlier sketch in CA 57-60
Nathan, Robert (Gruntal) 1894-1985 CANR-6
Obituary 116
Earlier sketch in CA 15-16R
See also SATA 6, 43
See also DLB 9
Nathan, Robert Stuart 1948- 81-84
Nathanson, Jerome 1908-1975 Obituary 57-60
Nathanson, Laura Walther 1941- 123
Nathanson, Leonard 1933- 23-24R
Nathanson, Nathaniel L(ouis) 1908-1983 89-92
Obituary 111
Nathanson, Yale S(amuel) 1895- 77-80
Nations, Opal (Louis) 1941- 112
Natow, Annette 1933- 114
Natsume, Kinnosuke 1867-1916
Brief entry 104
Natsume, Soseki
See Natsume, Kinnosuke
See also TCLC 2, 10
Natta, Giulio 1903-1979 Obituary 113
Natti, (Mary) Lee 1919- CANR-2
Earlier sketch in CA 7-8R
Natti, Susanna 1948- SATA-32
Natusch, Sheila (Ellen) 1926- CANR-20
Earlier sketch in CA 103
Natwar-Singh, K. 1931- 13-14R
Nau, Erika S(chwager) 1918- 65-68
Naude, (Aletta) Adele da Fonseca-Wollheim
1910- 11-12R
Nauer, Barbara Joan 1932- Brief entry 105
Naughton, Bill 1910- 105
See also DLB 13
Naughton, John 1933- 57-60
Naugle, Helen Harrold 1920- 53-56
Naugle, John E(arl) 1923- 65-68
Nauheim, Ferd(inand Alan) 1909- CANR-16
Earlier sketches in CA 49-52, CANR-1
Nauman, St. Elmo, Jr. 1935- 53-56
Naumann, Anthony Frank 1921-1971 21-22R
Obituary 89-92
Naumann, Marina 1938- 93-96
Naumann, Oscar E(dward) 1912- 77-80
Naumann, Rose 1919- 65-68
Naumburg, Margaret 1890-1983 Obituary 109
Nauticus
See Waltari, Mika (Toimi)
Nava, Julian 1927- 61-64
Nava, Michael 1954- 124
Nava, Roberto 1906(?)-1983 Obituary 111
Navarra, Fernand Jean 1915- 108
Navarra, John Gabriel 1927- 41-44R
See also SATA 8
Navarro, Antonio 1922- 107
Navarro (Gerassi), Marysa 1934- 106
Navarro, Peter 1949- 118
Navas, Deborah 1943- 112
Navasky, Victor S. 1932- CANR-10
Earlier sketch in CA 21-22R
Navas-Ruiz, Ricardo 1932- Brief entry 107
Navone, John J(oseph) 1930- CANR-10
Earlier sketch in CA 23-24R
Navrozov, Lev 1928- 61-64
Naydler, Merton 1920- 45-48
Naylor, Chris(topher Michael) 1947- 118
Naylor, Eric W(oodfin) 1936- 45-48
Naylor, Gloria 1950- 107
See also BW
See also CLC 28
Naylor, Harriet H. 1915- CANR-9
Earlier sketch in CA 21-22R
Naylor, James C(harles) 1932- CANR-1
Earlier sketch in CA 45-48
Naylor, John 1920- 93-96
Naylor, Margot (Ailsa) Lodge 1907- 11-12R
Naylor, Penelope 1941- 37-40R
See also SATA 10
Naylor, Phyllis (Reynolds) 1933- CANR-24
Earlier sketches in CA 21-22R, CANR-8
See also SATA 12
Nazareth, Peter 1940- 101
Nazarian, Nikki
See Nichols, Cecilia Fawn
Nazaroff, Alexander I. 1898- 33-36R
See also SATA 4
Nazzaro, Anthony M. 1927- Brief entry 106
Neagle, Anna 1904-1986 Obituary 119
Neagley, Ross Linn 1907- 106
Neagoe, Anna (Frankel) 1885(?)-1986
Obituary 120
Neagoe, Peter 1881-1960 105
See also DLB 4
Neal, Alfred C. 1912- 121
Neal, Ann Parker 1934- Brief entry 114
Neal, Arminta Pearl 1921- 85-88
Neal, Bruce W(alter) 1931- 21-22R
Neal, Charles Dempsey 1908- CANR-5
Earlier sketch in CA 5-6R
Neal, Emily Gardiner CANR-3
Earlier sketch in CA 5-6R
Neal, Ernest G(ordon) 1911- 13-14R
Neal, Fred Warner 1915- CANR-2
Earlier sketch in CA 7-8R
Neal, Harry
See Bixby, Jerome Lewis
Neal, Harry Edward 1906- CANR-2
Earlier sketch in CA 5-6R
See also SATA 5
Neal, Helen Keating 1907-1987 124
Obituary 122

Neal, Hilary
See Norton, Olive (Claydon)
Neal, James M(adison) 1925- 73-76
Neal, James T(homas) 1936- 57-60
Neal, John 1793-1876 ....DLB-1, 59
Neal, Joseph C. 1807-1847 ....DLB-11
Neal, Julia 1905- 69-72
Neal, Larry
See Neal, Lawrence (P.)
See also DLB 38
Neal, Lawrence (P.) 1937-1981 81-84
Obituary 102
See also BW
Neal, Marie Augusta 1921- 114
Neal, Michael
See Teitelbaum, Michael
Neal, Nelson 1921(?)-1983 Obituary 109
Neal, Patsy 1938- 61-64
Neal, Sister Marie Augusta 1921- 29-32R
Neale, Gay Weeks 1935- 113
Neale, John E(rnest) 1890-1975 65-68
Obituary 61-64
Neale, Robert George 1919- Brief entry 108
Neale, Walter Castle 1925- CANR-7
Earlier sketch in CA 5-6R
Neale-Silva, Eduardo 1905- Brief entry 106
Nealon, Eleanor 103
Nealon, Thomas E. 1933- 33-36R
Neaman, Judith S(ilverman) 1936- 61-64
Neame, Alan John 1924- CANR-2
Earlier sketch in CA 4R
Nearing, Guy 1890-1986 Obituary 118
Nearing, Helen K(nothe) 1904- CANR-11
Earlier sketch in CA 29-32R
Nearing, Penny 1916- 81-84
See also SATA 42, 47
Nearing, Scott 1883-1983 ....CANR-11
Obituary 110
Earlier sketch in CA 41-44R
Neary, John (Anthony, Jr.) 1937-
Brief entry 107
Neatby, H(erbert) Blair 1924- Brief entry 111
Neatby, Leslie Hamilton 1902- CANR-3
Earlier sketch in CA 7-8R
Neate, Frank Anthony 1928- 105
Neave, Airey (Middleton Sheffield)
1916-1979 85-88
Neavles, Janet Talmadge 1919- 5-6R
Nebel, Gustave E. SATA-33, 45
Nebel, Mimouca
See Nebel, Gustave E.
Nebenzahl, Kenneth 1927- 111
Brief entry 109
Nebrensky, Alex
See Cooper, Parley J(oseph)
Nebylitsyn, Vladimir Dmitrievich
1930(?)-1972 Obituary 37-40R
Necheles, Ruth F. 1936- 41-44R
Necker, Claire (Kral) 1917- 33-36R
Nederhood, Joel H(oman) 1930- 29-32R
Nee, Brett de Bary 1943- 101
Nee, Kay Bonner CANR-2
Earlier sketch in CA 49-52
See also SATA 10
Needham, David C. 1929- 118
Needham, (Noel) Joseph (Terence
Montgomery) 1900- CANR-5
Earlier sketch in CA 11-12R
Needham, Richard (John) 1912- 101
Needham, Rodney 1923- CANR-15
Earlier sketch in CA 81-84
Needham, (Amy) Violet 1876-1967
Obituary 116
Needle, Jan 1943- 106
See also SATA 30
Needleman, Jacob 1934- CANR-12
Earlier sketch in CA 29-32R
See also SATA 6
Needleman, Morriss H. 1907- 25-28R
Needler, Howard I(an) 1937- 111
Needler, Martin C(yril) 1933- CANR-18
Earlier sketches in CA 7-8R, CANR-2
Needles, Robert Johnson 1903- CAP-1
Earlier sketch in CA 11-12
Neef, Elton T.
See Fanthorpe, R(obert) Lionel
Neel, (Louis) Boyd 1905-1981 Obituary 108
Neel, Janet
See Cohen, Janet
Neel, Joanne Loewe 1920- 25-28R
Neely, Bill 1930- CANR-13
Earlier sketch in CA 33-36R
Neely, Carol Thomas 1939- Brief entry 107
Neely, James C. 1926- 109
Neely, Mark E(dward), Jr. 1944- CANR-25
Earlier sketch in CA 106
Neely, Martina 1939- 61-64
Neely, Richard (Forlani) 1941- 107
Neenan, William B(raunger) 1929- 41-44R
Neeper, Carolyn 1937- 57-60
Neeper, Cary
See Neeper, Carolyn
Neerskov, Hans Kristian 1932- 65-68
Nef, Evelyn Stefansson 1913- CANR-20
Earlier sketch in CA 49-52
Nef, John Ulric 1899- CANR-20
Earlier sketch in CA 2R
Neff, Alan (Henry) 1949- 117
Neff, Donald 1930- 77-80
Neff, Emery E. 1892-1983 ....5-6R
Obituary 109
Neff, H(arry) Richard 1933- 33-36R
Neff, Hildegard
See Knef, Hildegard
Neff, John C. 1913- 19-20R
Neff, Miriam 1945- 115
Neff, Renfreu (de St. Laurence) 1938- ...29-32R
Neff, Robert W(ilbur) 1936- 106
Neff, Walter S(cott) 1910- CAP-2
Earlier sketch in CA 25-28
Neff, William Lee 1906-1973 .... 2R
Obituary 103
Neft, David S(amuel) 1937- 41-44R
Negandhi, A(nant) R(anchoddas) 1933- ...33-36R
Neggers, Carla A(malia) 1955- 112
Negley, Glenn (Robert) 1907-1988 ......19-20R
Obituary 125
Negri, Rocco 1932- SATA-12
Negroponte, Nicholas Peter 1943- 29-32R
Negus, Arthur George 1903-1985
Obituary 116
Negus, Kenneth George 1927- 19-20R
Nehamas, Alexander 1946- 126
Neher, Andre 1914- CANR-26
Earlier sketch in CA 109
Neher, Clark D(umont) 1938- 118
Neher, Jack 1918- 118
Nehrling, Arno H. 1886-1974 ....11-12R
Obituary 53-56
Nehrling, Irene Dahlberg 1900- 11-12R
Nehrt, Lee Charles 1926- CANR-13
Earlier sketch in CA 23-24R
Nehru, Jawaharlal 1889-1964 85-88
Neiburg, Gladys Eudas 1898- 61-64
Neider, Charles 1915- CANR-24
Earlier sketch in CA 19-20R
Neiderman, Andrew 1940- CANR-13
Earlier sketch in CA 33-36R
Neidermyer, Dan 1947- CANR-24
Earlier sketch in CA 45-48
Neidhardt, W(ilfried) S(teffen) 1941- 65-68
Neidpath, James
See Charteris, James Donald
Neier, Aryeh 1937- 57-60
Neighbour, Ralph W(ebster) 1906- CANR-1
Earlier sketch in CA 2R
Neighbour, Rhona M.
See Martin, Rhona
Neighbours, Kenneth Franklin 1915- 61-64
Neigoff, Anne 41-44R
See also SATA 13
Neigoff, Mike 1920- CANR-2
Earlier sketch in CA 5-6R
See also SATA 13
Neihardt, John Gneisenau 1881-1973 .... CAP-1
Earlier sketch in CA 13-14
See also DLB 9, 54
See also CLC 32
Neikirk, William (Robert) 1938- 117
Neil, Hugh Michael 1930- Brief entry 109
Neil, J. Meredith 1937- 33-36R
Neil, Randolph L. 1941- 93-96
Neil, Randy
See Neil, Randolph L.
Neil, William 1909-1979 ....CANR-6
Obituary 93-96
Earlier sketch in CA 11-12R
Neilan, Sarah 69-72
Neilands, J(ohn) B(rian) 1921- 97-100
Neill, A(lexander) S(utherland) 1883-1973 ... 101
Obituary 45-48
Neill, Christopher Harry Douglas 1955- 117
Neill, Stephen Charles 1900-1984 ...... CANR-7
Obituary 113
Earlier sketch in CA 11-12R
Neill, Thomas Patrick 1915-1970 .... CANR-3
Earlier sketch in CA 7-8R
Neilson, Andrew 1946- 110
Neilson, Frances Fullerton (Jones) 1910- ..73-76
See also SATA 14
Neilson, James Warren 1933- 4R
Neilson, Marguerite
See Tompkins, Julia (Marguerite Hunter Manchee)
Neilson, N(eils) P. 1895- CANR-2
Earlier sketch in CA 5-6R
Neiman, David 1921- 69-72
Neiman, Fraser 1911- 25-28R
Neimark, Anne E. 1935- CANR-16
Earlier sketch in CA 29-32R
See also SATA 4
Neimark, Edith D(eborah) 1928- 41-44R
Neimark, Paul G. 1934- Brief entry 115
See also SATA 37
Neipris, Janet
See Wille, Janet Neipris
Neisser, Hans P(hilip) 1895-1975 .... CAP-1
Obituary 53-56
Earlier sketch in CA 15-16
Neisser, Ulric 1928- CANR-26
Earlier sketch in CA 108
Nekrasov, Viktor (Platonovich) 1911-1987
Obituary 123
Nekrich, Aleksandr M(oisei) 1920- 81-84
Neligan, David 1899- CAP-2
Earlier sketch in CA 29-32
Nelkin, Dorothy 1933- CANR-14
Earlier sketch in CA 41-44R
Nell, Edward John 1935- 65-68
Nelles, Henry Vivian 1942- 103
Nelli, Humbert S(teven) 1930- CANR-14
Earlier sketch in CA 41-44R
Nelligan, Emile 1879-1941 Brief entry 114
See also TCLC 14
Nellis, Muriel 102
Nellist, John B(owman) 1923- 25-28R
Nelms, C(larice) E. 1919- 25-28R
Nelms, Henning C(unningham) 1900-1986
Obituary 119
Nelsen, Anne Kusener 1942- 97-100
Nelsen, Hart M(ichael) 1938- CANR-8
Earlier sketch in CA 53-56
Nelson, A(ndrew) Thomas 1933- 7-8R
Nelson, Alan H(olm) 1938- 104
Nelson, Alice Fray 1911(?)-1983 Obituary .. 110
Nelson, Alice Ruth Moore Dunbar
1875-1935 124
Brief entry 122
See also BW
See also DLB 50
Nelson, Alvin F(redolph) 1917-1973 ..... CAP-2
Earlier sketch in CA 25-28
Nelson, Amirtharaj 1934- 57-60
Nelson, Andrew N(athaniel) 1893-1975 .. CANR-3
Earlier sketch in CA 7-8R
Nelson, Anne 1954- 123
Nelson, Benjamin N. 1911-1977 81-84
Obituary 73-76
Nelson, Benjamin N(athaniel) 1935- CANR-1
Earlier sketch in CA 2R
Nelson, Beth
See Nelson, Mary Elizabeth
Nelson, C(arl) Ellis 1916- 108
Nelson, Carl Leroy 1910- 104
Nelson, Carnot E(dward) 1941- 37-40R
Nelson, Cary (Robert) 1946- 49-52
Nelson, Charles Lamar 1917- 69-72
Nelson, Charles R(owe) 1942- 37-40R
Nelson, Cholmondeley M. 1903- 5-6R
Nelson, Clifford Ansgar 1906- CAP-1
Earlier sketch in CA 11-12
Nelson, Conny E(dwin) 1933- Brief entry ... 108
Nelson, Cordner (Bruce) 1918- 29-32R
See also SATA 29
Nelson, Dalmas H(ildor) 1925- 119
Nelson, Daniel 1941- 25-28R
Nelson, David Moir 1920- CANR-17
Earlier sketch in CA 2R
Nelson, Donald F. 1929- 37-40R
Nelson, E(ugene) Clifford 1911- 13-14R
Nelson, Edna Deu Pree 5-6R
Nelson, Elof G. 1924- 23-24R
Nelson, Eric Hilliard 1940-1985 Obituary ... 118
Nelson, Esther L. 1928- CANR-11
Earlier sketch in CA 69-72
See also SATA 13
Nelson, Ethel Florence 1913- CANR-6
Earlier sketch in CA 53-56
Nelson, Eugene 1929- 61-64
Nelson, F(rancis) William 1922- 13-14R
Nelson, Geoffrey K(enneth) 1923- CANR-24
Earlier sketch in CA 29-32R
Nelson, George (H.) 1908-1986 81-84
Obituary 118
Nelson, George (Carl) E(dward)
1900-1982 ....CANR-24
Earlier sketch in CA 45-48
Nelson, Gideon E(dmund, Jr.) 1924- 53-56
Nelson, Harold A(lfred) 1932- 114
Nelson, Harold L(ewis) 1917- 93-96
Nelson, Herbert B(enjamin) 1903- CAP-2
Earlier sketch in CA 19-20
Nelson, Indiana 1940- 97-100
Nelson, J. Bryan 1932- CANR-10
Earlier sketch in CA 25-28R
Nelson, J(oseph) Raleigh 1873-1961
Obituary 110
Nelson, J(ohn) Robert 1920- CANR-19
Earlier sketches in CA 11-12R, CANR-3
Nelson, Jack
See Nelson, John Howard
Nelson, Jack L. 1932- CANR-10
Earlier sketch in CA 25-28R
Nelson, James B(ruce) 1930- CANR-17
Earlier sketches in CA 49-52, CANR-1
Nelson, James C(ecil) 1908- CANR-13
Earlier sketch in CA 77-80
Nelson, James G(raham) 1929- 11-12R
Nelson, Jan Alan 1935- 41-44R
Nelson, Jane Armstrong 1927- Brief entry .. 105
Nelson, Janet 1930- 115
Nelson, Jean Erichsen
See Erichsen-Nelson, Jean
Nelson, John Charles 1925- 49-52
Nelson, John Howard 1929- 29-32R
Nelson, John Oliver 1909- 37-40R
Nelson, Joseph Schieser 1937- 73-76
Nelson, June Kompass 1920- 73-76
Nelson, Katherine Shaw 1926- 110
Nelson, Kay Shaw
See Nelson, Katherine Shaw
Nelson, Keith L(ebahn) 1932- Brief entry ... 113
Nelson, Kent 1943- 77-80
Nelson, L(ester) Ivar 1941- 119
Nelson, Lawrence E(rnest) 1928-1977 53-56
Obituary 103
See also SATA 28
Nelson, Lawrence Emerson 1893- 19-20R
Nelson, Lois (Ney) 1930- 61-64
Nelson, Lowry, Jr. 1926- 5-6R
Nelson, Malcolm A. 1934- 45-48
Nelson, Marg (Raibley) 1899- CANR-2
Earlier sketch in CA 2R
Nelson, Marguerite
See Floren, Lee
Nelson, Marion Harvey 1925- 11-12R
Nelson, Martha 1923- 29-32R
Nelson, Mary Carroll 1929- CANR-16
Earlier sketches in CA 49-52, CANR-1
See also SATA 23
Nelson, Mary Elizabeth 1926- 93-96
Nelson, Michael Harrington 1921- CANR-2
Earlier sketch in CA 7-8R
Nelson, Nina
See Nelson, Ethel Florence
Nelson, Oliver W(endell) 1904- 29-32R
Nelson, Oswald George 1907-1975 93-96
Obituary 57-60
Nelson, Ozzie
See Nelson, Oswald George
Nelson, Paul David 1941- 120
Nelson, Peter 1940- CANR-12
Earlier sketch in CA 61-64
Nelson, Peter
See Solow, Martin
Nelson, Philip Bradford 1951- 113
Nelson, R(adell) Faraday 1931- CANR-26
Earlier sketch in CA 69-72
Nelson, Rachel W(est) 1955- 117
Nelson, Ralph 1916-1987 49-52
Obituary 124
Nelson, Ralph C(arl) 1927- 53-56
Nelson, Randy F(ranklin) 1948- 125
Brief entry 110
Nelson, Ray
See Nelson, R(adell) Faraday
Nelson, Raymond S(tanley) 1921- CANR-16
Earlier sketches in CA 45-48, CANR-1
Nelson, Richard 1950- Brief entry 123
Nelson, Richard K(ing) 1941- CANR-12
Earlier sketch in CA 29-32R
Nelson, Richard R(obinson) 1930- CANR-16
Earlier sketch in CA 97-100
Nelson, Rick
See Nelson, Eric Hilliard
Nelson, Ricky
See Nelson, Eric Hilliard
Nelson, Robert James 1925- CANR-8
Earlier sketch in CA 5-6R
Nelson, Rosanne E(ierdanz) 1939- 49-52
Nelson, Rowland Whiteway 1902-1979
Obituary 105
Nelson, Roy Paul 1923- CANR-22
Earlier sketches in CA 19-20R, CANR-7
Nelson, Ruben F(rederick) W(erthenbach)
1939- 112
Nelson, Ruth 1914- 41-44R
Nelson, Ruth Youngdahl 1904(?)-1984
Obituary 112
Nelson, Severing E. 1896- 7-8R
Nelson, Sharon H. 1948- 113
Nelson, Stanley 1933- CANR-18
Earlier sketches in CA 49-52, CANR-1
Nelson, Thomas P. 1925(?)-1983
Obituary 110
Nelson, Truman (John Seymour)
1911-1987 .... CANR-1
Obituary 123
Earlier sketch in CA 2R
Nelson, W(esley) Dale 1927- 77-80
Nelson, Walter Henry 1928- CANR-7
Earlier sketch in CA 15-16R
Nelson, Warren L. 1940- 89-92
Nelson, William 1908-1978 49-52
Obituary 103
Nelson, William R(ichard) 1924- 25-28R
Nelson, William Rockhill 1841-1915 .... DLB-23
Nelson, Willie 1933- 107
See also CLC 17
Nelton, Sharon (Lee) 1937- 123
Nemanic, Gerald Carl 1941- 107
Nemec, David 1938- CANR-2
Earlier sketch in CA 49-52
Nemerov, Howard 1920- CANR-1
Earlier sketch in CA 3R
See also CABS 2
See also DLB 6
See also DLBY 83
See also CLC 2, 6, 9, 36
Nemeth, Laszlo 1901-1975 93-96
Obituary 57-60
Nemir, Alma 1902-1971 .... CAP-2
Earlier sketch in CA 29-32
Nemiro, Beverly Anderson 1925- CANR-5
Earlier sketch in CA 53-56
Nemiroff, Robert Brief entry 116
See also AITN 2
Nemirow, Steven 1949- 110
Nemmers, Erwin Esser 1916- 11-12R
Nemser, Cindy 1937- 61-64
Nenni, Pietro 1891-1980 Obituary 105
Nerbovig, Marcella H. 1919- 89-92
Nere, Jacques 1917- 57-60
Nerhood, Harry W(arren) 1910- 29-32R
Nerlich, Graham 73-76
Nerlove, Marc L(eon) 1933- 104
Nerlove, Miriam 1959- 121
See also SATA 49, 53
Neruda, Pablo 1904-1973 .... CAP-2
Obituary 45-48
Earlier sketch in CA 19-20
See also CLC 1, 2, 5, 7, 9, 28
Nerval, Gaston
See Diez de Medina, Raul
Nervi, Pier Luigi 1891-1979 Obituary 113
Nervo, Amado (Ruiz de) 1870-1919
Brief entry 109
See also TCLC 11
Nesbin, Esther W(inter) 1910- 41-44R
Nesbit, E(dith) 1858-1924 Brief entry 118
See also YABC 1
See also CLR 3
Nesbit, Robert C(arrington) 1917- 45-48
Nesbit, Troy
See Folsom, Franklin (Brewster)
Nesbitt, Cathleen 1888-1982 Obituary 107
Nesbitt, Elizabeth 1897(?)-1977 Obituary ..73-76
Nesbitt, George L(yman) 1903- 41-44R
Nesbitt, Paul H(omer) 1904- 77-80
Nesbitt, Ralph Beryl 1891(?)-1975
Obituary 61-64
Nesbitt, Rosemary (Sinnett) 1924- 81-84
Neshamith, Sara
See Dushnitzky-Shner, Sara
Nesmith, Robert I. 1891-1972 .... CANR-15
Obituary 103
Earlier sketch in CA 3R

INDEX

Nespojohn, Katherine V(eronica) 1912- 37-40R
See also SATA 7
Ness, Evaline (Michelow) 1911-1986 CANR-5
Obituary 120
Earlier sketch in CA 7-8R
See also SATA 1, 26, 49
See also SAAS 1
See also DLB 61
See also CLR 6
Ness, Gayl D(eForrest) 1929- 29-32R
Ness, John H., Jr. 1919- 21-22R
Nessen, (Lewis) Robert 1932- 107
Nessen, Ron(ald Harold) 1934-
Brief entry 106
Nessi, Pio Baroja y
See Baroja (y Nessi), Pio
Nestle, John Francis 1912- 89-92
Nestor, William P(rodromos) 1947- CANR-26
Earlier sketch in CA 109
See also SATA 49
Nesvadba, Josef 1926- 97-100
Netanyahu, Benzion 1910- 61-64
Netanyahu, Jonathan 1946(?)-1976
Obituary 114
Netanyahu, Yonatan
See Netanyahu, Jonathan
Netboy, Anthony 1906- CANR-7
Earlier sketch in CA 19-20R
Neter, John 1923- 53-56
Netherclift, Beryl (Constance) 1911- 93-96
Nethercot, Arthur H(obart) 1895- 2R
Netland, Dwayne 1932- 110
Neto, Antonio Agostinho 1922-1979 101
Obituary 89-92
Nettel, Reginald 1899- 13-14R
Nettelbeck, F(red) A(rthur) 1950- 118
Nettell, Richard (Geoffrey) 1907- CAP-2
Earlier sketch in CA 25-28
Nettels, Curtis Putnam 1898- CANR-1
Earlier sketch in CA 2R
Nettels, Elsa 1931- 77-80
Netter, (Jean) Patrick 1952- 119
Netting, Robert M(cCorkle) 1934- 61-64
Nettis, Joseph 1928- 11-12R
Nettl, Bruno 1930- 19-20R
Nettl, J(ohn) P(eter) 1926-1968 CAP-2
Earlier sketch in CA 23-24
Nettl, Paul 1889-1972 CAP-1
Obituary 33-36R
Earlier sketch in CA 9-10
Nettleford, Rex M. 37-40R
Nettler, Gwynn 1913- 33-36R
Nettles, Thomas Julian 1946- 117
Nettles, Tom
See Nettles, Thomas Julian
Netzer, Dick 1928- Brief entry 112
Netzer, Lanore A. 1916- 19-20R
Neu, Charles E. 1936- 21-22R
Neubauer, David William 1944- 65-68
Neubauer, John 1933- 101
Neubauer, William Arthur 1916- 9-10R
Neubeck, Gerhard 1918- 41-44R
Neuberger, Egon 1925- 25-28R
Neuberger, Richard Lewis 1912-1960
Obituary 89-92
Neubert, Christopher J. 1948- 106
Neuburg, Paul 1939- 45-48
Neuburg, Victor E. 1924- 33-36R
Neuenschwander, John A. 1941-
Brief entry 113
Neufeld, John (Arthur) 1938- CANR-11
Earlier sketch in CA 25-28R
See also SATA 6
See also SAAS 3
See also CLC 17
Neufeld, Maurice Frank 1910- 4R
Neufeld, Peter Lorenz 1931- 25-28R
Neufeld, Rose 1924- 29-32R
Neufelder, Jerome M(ichael) 1929- 115
Neufeldt, Leonard N(ick) 1937- 108
Neufer Emswiler, Sharon
See Emswiler, Sharon Neufer
Neuffer, Claude Henry 1911- 41-44R
Neuffer, Irene LaBorde 1919- 61-64
Neugeboren, Jay (Michael) 1938- CANR-21
Earlier sketch in CA 19-20R
See also DLB 28
Neuharth, Allen AITN-2
Neuhaus, Richard (John) 1936- 33-36R
Neuhaus, Ruby (Hart) 1932- 103
Neulinger, John 1924- CANR-16
Earlier sketch in CA 41-44R
Neuls-Bates, Carol 1939- 114
Neuman, Abraham A(aron) 1890-1970
Obituary 104
Neuman, Betty Mavine 1924- 33-36R
Neuman, Fredric (Jay) 1934- CANR-20
Earlier sketch in CA 97-100
Neuman, Ladd A. 1942- 97-100
Neuman, Shirley Carol 1946- 121
Neuman, William Frederick 1919-1981
Obituary 103
Neumann, Alfred 1895-1952 DLB-56
Neumann, Emanuel 1893-1980 Obituary 105
Neumann, Gareth William 1930- 61-64
Neumann, John von
See von Neumann, John
Neumann, Jonathan 1950- 85-88
Neumann, Robert 1897-1975 103
Obituary 89-92
Neumann, Robert G(erhard) 1916- 7-8R
Neumann, William Louis 1915-1971 CAP-1
Obituary 33-36R
Earlier sketch in CA 11-12
Neumeyer, Alfred 1900(?)-1973
Obituary 41-44R
Neumeyer, Ken(neth Walter) 1953- 107
Neumeyer, M(artin) Henry 1892- CAP-2
Earlier sketch in CA 19-20
Neumeyer, Peter F(lorian) 1929- 33-36R
See also SATA 13
Neurath, Marie (Reidemeister) 1898- 13-14R
See also SATA 1
Neurath, Otto 1882-1945 Brief entry 117
Neuschel, Richard F(rederick) 1915- 15-16R
Neuschuetz, Karin 1946- 116
Neuschutz, Karin
See Neuschuetz, Karin
Neuse, Erna Kritsch 1923- 105
Neusner, Jacob 1932- CANR-22
Earlier sketches in CA 15-16R, CANR-7
See also SATA 38
Neustadt, Bertha C(ummings)
1921(?)-1984 Obituary 112
Neustadt, Egon 1898(?)-1984 Obituary 112
Neustadt, Richard E(lliott) 1919- 11-12R
Neustadt, Richard M(itchells) 1948- 45-48
Neutra, Richard Joseph 1892-1970 CANR-5
Obituary 29-32R
Earlier sketch in CA 7-8R
Neutrelle, Dale 1937- 61-64
Neuville, H(enry) Richmond, Jr. 1937- 23-24R
Neve, Herbert T(heodore) 1931- 25-28R
Neve, Lloyd 1923- 53-56
Nevell, Dick
See Nevell, Richard (William Babcock)
Nevell, Richard (William Babcock) 1947- 102
Nevelson, Louise 1900- 108
Nevelson, Louise 1900(?)-1988 108
Obituary 125
Neveux, Georges 1900-1982 Obituary 108
Nevill, Barry St-John 1941- 119
Neville, Anna
See Fairburn, Eleanor
Neville, B(arbara) Alison (Boodson)
1925- CANR-11
Earlier sketch in CA 7-8R
Neville, Charles
See Bodsworth, (Charles) Fred(erick)
Neville, Emily Cheney 1919- CANR-3
Earlier sketch in CA 7-8R
See also SATA 1
See also SAAS 2
See also CLC 12
Neville, Gwen Kennedy 1938- 114
Neville, Heather Buckley
See Buckley Neville, Heather
Neville, James Edmund Henderson
1897-1982 Obituary 107
Neville, Jill 1932- 21-22R
Neville, Joyce 115
Neville, Kris (Ottman) 1925-1980 Obituary 117
Neville, Mary
See Woodrich, Mary Neville
Neville, Pauline 1924- 29-32R
Neville, Richard F. 1931- 85-88
Neville, Robert 1905-1970 Obituary 104
Neville, Robert C(ummings) 1939- CANR-11
Earlier sketch in CA 25-28R
Neville, Susan 1951- 119
Nevin, David 1927- 121
Nevin, Evelyn C. 1910- 19-20R
Nevins, Albert J. 1915- CANR-19
Earlier sketches in CA 5-6R, CANR-5
See also SATA 20
Nevins, (Joseph) Allan 1890-1971 5-6R
Obituary 29-32R
See also DLB 17
Nevins, Deborah 1947- 105
Nevins, Edward M(ichael) 1938- 29-32R
Nevins, Francis M(ichael), Jr. 1943- CANR-16
Earlier sketch in CA 41-44R
Nevinson, C(hristopher) R(ichard) W(ynne)
1889-1946 Brief entry 120
Nevitt, H(enry) J(ohn) Barrington
1908- CANR-14
Earlier sketch in CA 37-40R
Nevius, Blake (Reynolds) 1916- 19-20R
Nevo, Ruth 1924- 61-64
New, Anthony (Sherwood Brooks)
1924- CANR-23
Earlier sketch in CA 107
New, Christopher 116
New, William Herbert 1938- Brief entry 114
Newall, Venetia 1935- 37-40R
Newberry
See Vellacott, Jo
Newberry, Clare Turlay 1903-1970 CAP-2
Earlier sketch in CA 19-20
See also SATA 1, 26
Newberry, Lida 1909- 97-100
Newberry, Vellacott
See Vellacott, Jo
Newberry, Wilma (Jean) 1927- 73-76
Newbery, John 1713-1767 SATA-20
Newbigin, (James Edward) Lesslie
1909- CANR-26
Earlier sketches in CA 13-14R, CANR-10
Newbill, James Guy 1931- 61-64
Newbold, H(erbert) L(eon, Jr.) 1921- CANR-5
Earlier sketch in CA 2R
Newbold, Robert T(homas, Jr.) 1920- 89-92
Newbold, Stokes
See Adams, Richard N(ewbold)
Newbolt, Henry (John) 1862-1938
Brief entry 118
See also DLB 19
Newborn, Jud 1952- 125
Newbound, Bernard Slade 1930- 81-84
Newbury, Colin (Walter) 1929- CANR-8
Earlier sketch in CA 7-8R
Newbury, Will 1912- 45-48
Newby, Eric 1919- 7-8R
Newby, I(dus) A. 1931- 19-20R
Newby, James R(ichard) 1949- 112
Newby, Leroy Winfred 1921- 114
Newby, P(ercy) H(oward) 1918- 7-8R
See also DLB 15
See also CLC 2, 13
Newcomb, Benjamin H. 1938- 45-48
Newcomb, Charles King 1820-1894 DLB-1
Newcomb, Covelle 1908- CAP-2
Earlier sketch in CA 19-20
Newcomb, Duane G(raham) 1929- CANR-5
Earlier sketch in CA 53-56
Newcomb, Ellsworth
See Kenny, Ellsworth Newcomb
Newcomb, Franc(es Lynette) J(ohnson)
1887- 17-18R
Newcomb, John (Robert) 1937- 123
Newcomb, Kerry 1946- CANR-10
Earlier sketch in CA 65-68
Newcomb, Norma
See Neubauer, William Arthur
Newcomb, Richard F(airchild) 1913- 1R
Newcomb, Robert N(orman) 1925- 21-22R
Newcomb, Simon 1835-1909 Brief entry 108
Newcomb, Theodore Mead 1903-1984 33-36R
Obituary 114
Newcomb, Wilburn Wendell 1935- 19-20R
Newcomb, William W(ilmon), Jr. 1921- 102
Newcombe, Jack 113
See also SATA 33, 45
Newcombe, John (David) 1944- CANR-25
Earlier sketch in CA 69-72
Newcombe, Park Judson 1930- 106
Newcomer, James (William) 1912- CANR-15
Earlier sketch in CA 41-44R
Newell, Allen 1927- 104
Newell, Arlo F(rederic) 1926- 114
Newell, Barbara Warne 1929- 2R
Newell, Crosby
See Bonsall, Crosby Barbara (Newell)
Newell, D. A.
See Musciano, Walter A.
Newell, David McCheyne 1898(?)-1986
Obituary 120
Newell, Edythe W(eatherford) 1910- 65-68
See also SATA 11
Newell, Fred D(elmer) 1912- 97-100
Newell, Gordon 1913- CANR-20
Earlier sketches in CA 9-10R, CANR-4
Newell, Helen M(arie) 1909- 93-96
Newell, Homer E(dward) 1915-1983 97-100
Obituary 110
Newell, Hope Hockenberry 1896-1965 73-76
See also SATA 24
Newell, Kenneth B(ernard) 1930- 41-44R
Newell, Norman Dennis 1909- CANR-21
Earlier sketch in CA 104
Newell, Peter (Sheaf Hersey) 1862-1924
Brief entry 122
See also DLB 42
Newell, Peter F(rancis) 1915- 13-14R
Newell, Richard S. 1933- Brief entry 112
Newell, Robert Henry 1836-1901
Brief entry 111
See also DLB 11
Newell, Rosemary 1922- 49-52
Newell, William H(are) 1922- 103
Newell, William T(hrift) 1929- 37-40R
Newfeld, Frank 1928- 105
See also SATA 26
Newfield, Jack 1939- CANR-13
Earlier sketch in CA 21-22R
Newhafer, Richard L. 1922- 15-16R
Newhall, Beaumont 1908- 11-12R
Newhall, Nancy 1908-1974 Obituary 49-52
Newhall, Richard A. 1888-1973
Obituary 41-44R
Newhouse, Edward 1911- 97-100
Newhouse, Joseph P. 1942- 111
Newhouse, Neville H. 1919- 23-24R
Newhouse, Samuel I(rving) 1895-1979
Obituary 89-92
Newick, John 1919- CAP-1
Earlier sketch in CA 11-12
Newkirk, Glen A. 1931- 37-40R
Newland, Kathleen 1951- 97-100
Newland, T. Ernest 1903- 105
Newley, Anthony (George) 1931- 105
Newlin, Dika 1923- 107
Newlin, Margaret Rudd 1925- CANR-1
Earlier sketch in CA 49-52
Newlon, (Frank) Clarke 1905(?)-1982 CANR-10
Obituary 108
Earlier sketch in CA 49-52
See also SATA 6, 33
Newlove, Donald 1928- CANR-25
Earlier sketch in CA 29-32R
See also CLC 6
Newlove, John (Herbert) 1938- CANR-25
Earlier sketches in CA 23-24R, CANR-9
See also CLC 14
Newlyn, Walter T(essier) 1915- 21-22R
Newman, Adrien Ann 1941- 102
Newman, Albert H. 1913(?)-1987
Obituary 122
Newman, Alyse 1953- 107
Newman, Andrea 1938- 73-76
Newman, Arthur J. 1939- 117
Newman, Aubrey N(orris) 1927- CANR-25
Earlier sketch in CA 29-32R
Newman, Barbara
See Newman, Mona Alice Jean
Newman, Barclay M., Jr. 1931- CANR-9
Earlier sketch in CA 19-20R
Newman, Bernard (Charles) 1897-1968 97-100
Obituary 25-28R
Newman, Charles 1938- 21-22R
See also CLC 2, 8
Newman, Charles L. 1923- CANR-6
Earlier sketch in CA 13-14R
Newman, Christina McCall 1935- 112
Newman, Coleman J. 1935- 77-80
Newman, Daisy 1904- 37-40R
See also SATA 27
Newman, David 1937- 102
See also DLB 44
Newman, E. J. 1943- 61-64
Newman, Edwin (Harold) 1919- CANR-5
Earlier sketch in CA 69-72
See also CLC 14
See also AITN 1
Newman, Elmer S(imon) 1919- 106
Newman, Eric P. 1911- 7-8R
Newman, Ernest
See Roberts, William
Newman, Frances 1883(?)-1928
Brief entry 110
See also DLBY 80
Newman, Frank
See Abrams, Sam(uel)
Newman, G(ordon) F. 1942- 104
Newman, George 1936- 106
Newman, Gerald 1939- 101
See also SATA 42, 46
Newman, Greatrex 1892-1984(?) Obituary 112
Newman, Harold 1899- CANR-10
Earlier sketch in CA 65-68
Newman, Harold 1927- 53-56
Newman, Herbert Ellis 1914- 25-28R
Newman, Howard 1911-1977 57-60
Obituary 73-76
Newman, Jacob 1914- 11-12R
Newman, Jay Hartley 1951- CANR-9
Earlier sketch in CA 65-68
Newman, Jeremiah Joseph 1926- CANR-8
Earlier sketch in CA 5-6R
Newman, John Henry
1801-1890 DLB-18, 32, 55
Newman, John Kevin 1928- 123
Newman, Jon O(rmond) 1932- 23-24R
Newman, Joseph 1912- CANR-17
Earlier sketch in CA 89-92
Newman, Joseph W(illiam) 1918- 37-40R
Newman, Judie 1950- 117
Newman, Katharine D. 1911- 37-40R
Newman, Kim (James) 1959- 119
Newman, L(eonard) Hugh 1909- 11-12R
Newman, Lea Bertani Vozar 1926- 120
Newman, Lee Scott 1953- CANR-15
Earlier sketch in CA 65-68
Newman, Leslea 1955- 126
Newman, Loretta Marie 1911- 45-48
Newman, Louis Israel 1893-1972 CAP-1
Obituary 33-36R
Earlier sketch in CA 19-20
Newman, Michael 1946- 116
Newman, Mona Alice Jean 102
Newman, Oscar 1935- 102
Newman, P(aul) B(aker) 1919- 33-36R
Newman, Parley Wright 1923- Brief entry 106
Newman, Peter (Kenneth) 1928- 17-18R
Newman, Peter C(harles) 1929- CANR-3
Earlier sketch in CA 11-12R
Newman, Philip L(ee) 1931- 17-18R
Newman, Ralph Abraham 1892- CANR-6
Earlier sketch in CA 3R
Newman, Ralph G(eoffrey) 1911- CANR-25
Earlier sketch in CA 45-48
Newman, Randolph H. 1904-1975
Obituary 61-64
Newman, Richard (Alan) 1930- 110
Newman, Robert (Howard) 1909- CANR-19
Earlier sketches in CA 2R, CANR-4
See also SATA 4
Newman, Robert Chapman 1941- 115
Newman, Robert D(ouglas) 1951- 120
Newman, Robert P(reston) 1922- 2R
Newman, Robert S. 1935- 65-68
Newman, Ruth (May) G(allert) 1914- 105
Newman, Sharan 1949- CANR-25
Earlier sketch in CA 106
Newman, Shirlee Petkin 1924- 5-6R
See also SATA 10
Newman, Shirley S. 1924- 123
Newman, Stephen A(aron) 1946- 97-100
Newman, Stewart A(lbert) 1907- CAP-2
Earlier sketch in CA 23-24
Newman, Terence 1927- 7-8R
Newman, Terry
See Newman, Terence
Newman, Thelma R(ita) 1925-1978 CANR-7
Obituary 81-84
Earlier sketch in CA 15-16R
Newman, Walter (Brown) 1920-
Brief entry 110
Newman, William H(erman) 1909- CANR-19
Earlier sketches in CA 5-6R, CANR-3
Newman, William Mark 1943- 57-60
Newman, William S(tein) 1912- CANR-3
Earlier sketch in CA 4R
Newmar, Rima
See Wagman, Naomi
Newmark, Joseph 1943- 53-56
Newmark, Leonard 1929- 19-20R
Newmyer, R. Kent 1930- 77-80
Newport, John P(aul) 1917- CANR-13
Earlier sketch in CA 33-36R
Newquist, Jerreld L. 1919- 19-20R
Newquist, Roy 1925- 13-14R
Newsham, Ian (Alan) 1953- 115
Newsham, Wendy (Elizabeth) 1952- 117
Newsom, Carol 1948- SATA-40
Newsom, Carroll V(incent) 1904- CAP-2
Earlier sketch in CA 17-18
Newsom, Doug(las Ann) 1934- 73-76

Newsome, Arden J(eanne) 1932- 29-32R
Newsome, David Hay 1929- CANR-17
Earlier sketch in CA 89-92
Newsome, Effie Lee 1885-1979 .... DLB-76
Newsome, George L(ane), Jr. 1923- 29-32R
Newsome, Walter L(ee) 1941- 105
Newson, Elizabeth (Palmer) 1929- CANR-5
Earlier sketch in CA 11-12R
Newson, John 1925- 11-12R
Newson, Tony 1953- 124
Newth, Rebecca 1940- 33-36R
Newton, Brian 1928- 49-52
Newton, Byron Louis 1913- 53-56
Newton, D(wight) B(ennett) 1916- CANR-17
Earlier sketches in CA 7-8R, CANR-2
Newton, David C.
See Chance, John Newton
Newton, Derek A(rnold) 1930- 120
Newton, Douglas 1920- 104
Newton, Earle Williams 1917- 41-44R
Newton, Eric 1893-1965 .... CAP-1
Earlier sketch in CA 15-16
Newton, Ethel (de la Bete) 1921- 101
Newton, Francis
See Hobsbawm, Eric J(ohn Ernest)
Newton, Huey P(ercy) 1942- Brief entry 114
Newton, Ian 1940- 123
Newton, Ivor 1892-1981 Obituary 108
Newton, James R(obert) 1935- 101
See also SATA 23
Newton, Kenneth 1940- CANR-16
Earlier sketch in CA 29-32R
Newton, Macdonald
See Newton, William Simpson
Newton, Maxwell 1929- 126
Newton, Michael 1951- 108
Newton, Norman (Lewis) 1929- 11-12R
Newton, Norman Thomas 1898- 104
Newton, Peter 1906- CAP-1
Earlier sketch in CA 9-10
Newton, Peter A(nthony) 1935-1987
Obituary 124
Newton, Ray C(lyde) 1935- 77-80
Newton, Robert (Henry) G(erald) 1903- ... CAP-1
Earlier sketch in CA 9
Newton, Robert P(arr) 1929- 113
Newton, Roy 1904(?)-1974 Obituary 104
Newton, Stu
See Whitcomb, Ian
Newton, Suzanne 1936- CANR-14
Earlier sketch in CA 41-44R
See also SATA 5
See also CLC 35
Newton, Virgil Miller, Jr. 1904-1977 .... 3R
Obituary 103
Newton, William Simpson 1923- CANR-7
Earlier sketch in CA 53-56
Ney, James W(alter) 1932- CANR-15
Earlier sketch in CA 41-44R
Ney, John 1923- 115
See also SATA 33, 43
Ney, Patrick
See Bolitho, (Henry) Hector
Ney, Richard 1917?- AITN-1
Ney, Virgil 1905-1979 Obituary 85-88
Neyland, James (Elwyn) 1939- 103
Neyman, Jerzy 1899-1981 Obituary 108
Neyrey, Jerome H(enry) 1940- 126
Nezval, Vitezslav 1900-1958 Brief entry 123
Ng, David 1934- 115
Ng, Larry K. Y. 1940- CANR-9
Earlier sketch in CA 17-18R
Ngagoyeanes, Nicholas 1939- 49-52
Ngara, Emmanuel 1947- 109
Ngoc, Nguyen Huy
See Nguyen Ngoc Huy
Ngubane, Jordan K(hush) 1917- 121
Ngugi, James T(hiong'o)
See Ngugi wa Thiong'o
See also CLC 3, 7, 13
Ngugi wa Thiong'o 1938- 81-84
See also BW
See also CLC 36
Nguyen, Dinh Hoa 1924- CANR-10
Earlier sketch in CA 23-24R
Nguyen, Vuong Hung 1922(?)-1985
Obituary 118
Nguyen Ngoc Bich 1937- CANR-15
Earlier sketch in CA 81-84
Nguyen Ngoc Huy 1924- 126
Niall, Sean
See Mangan, (John Joseph) Sherry
Nias, D(avid) K(enneth) B(oydell) 1940- 105
Niatum, Duane 1938- CANR-21
Earlier sketch in CA 41-44R
Niblett, W(illiam) R(oy) 1906- CANR-3
Earlier sketch in CA 2R
Niccolini, Dianora 1936- 113
Nicely, Thomas S(hryock), Jr. 1939- 93-96
Nicely, Tom
See Nicely, Thomas S(hryock), Jr.
Nichelson, F(loyd) Patrick 1942- 33-36R
Nichol, B(arrie) P(hillip) 1944- 53-56
See also DLB 53
See also CLC 18
Nichol, John Thomas 1928- 19-20R
Nicholas, Anna Katherine 1917- 93-96
Nicholas, Barry 1919- 7-8R
Nicholas, David M(ansfield) 1939- 49-52
Nicholas, Donald 1909- 7-8R
Nicholas, Elizabeth 1915-1985 Obituary 117
Nicholas, Herbert George 1911- CANR-26
Earlier sketch in CA 3R
Nicholas, John (Morton) 1944- 118
Nicholas, Leslie 1913- 81-84
Nicholas, Robert L(eon) 1937- 53-56
Nicholas, Ted
See Peterson, Ted Nicholas
Nicholas, Tracy (Christine) 1952- 121
Nicholas, William
See Thimmesch, Nicholas Palen
Nicholds, Elizabeth (Beckwith) CAP-1
Earlier sketch in CA 11-12
Nicholl, Louise Townsend 1890(?)-1981 .. 97-100
Obituary 105
Nicholls, David 1948- 97-100
Nicholls, F(rederick) F(rancis) 1926- 7-8R
Nicholls, Judith (Ann) 1941- 121
Nicholls, Mark
See Frewin, Leslie Ronald
Nicholls, Peter (Douglas) 1939- 105
Nicholls, (C. G.) William 1921- 17-18R
Nichols, Albert L. 1951- 122
Nichols, (John) Beverley 1898-1983 ... CANR-17
Obituary 110
Earlier sketch in CA 93-96
Nichols, Bill
See Nichols, William James
Nichols, Cecilia Fawn 1906- CAP-1
Earlier sketch in CA 15-16
See also SATA 12
Nichols, Charles H(arold) 1919- CANR-6
Earlier sketch in CA 53-56
See also BW
Nichols, Dale (William) 1904- CAP-2
Earlier sketch in CA 17-18
Nichols, Dave
See Frost, Helen
Nichols, David A(llen) 1939- 104
Nichols, Dudley 1895-1960 Obituary 89-92
See also DLB 26
Nichols, Edward J(ay) 1900- 7-8R
Nichols, Fred Joseph 1939- 114
Nichols, Frederick Adams 1907-1983
Obituary 111
Nichols, Harold 1903- CAP-1
Earlier sketch in CA 15-16
Nichols, Irby C(oghill), Jr. 1926- 41-44R
Nichols, J(ohn) G(ordon) 1930- 33-36R
See also CAAS 2
Nichols, Jack 1938- 41-44R
Nichols, James Hastings 1915- Brief entry .. 114
Nichols, James R(ichard) 1938- 105
Nichols, Jeannette 1931- 77-80
Nichols, Jeannette Paddock 1890-1982 ...11-12R
Obituary 107
Nichols, John (Treadwell) 1940- CANR-6
Earlier sketch in CA 11-12R
See also CAAS 2
See also DLBY 82
See also CLC 38
Nichols, Joseph C. 1905(?)-1984
Obituary 114
Nichols, K(enneth) D(avid) 1907- 126
Nichols, Leigh
See Koontz, Dean R(ay)
Nichols, Lewis 1903-1982 Obituary 106
Nichols, Maggie
See Nichols, Margaret
Nichols, Margaret 1931- 81-84
Nichols, Marie Hochmuth 1908-1978 103
Nichols, Marion 1921- 102
Nichols, Mary Sargeant (Neal) Gove
1810-1884 .... DLB-1
Nichols, Nina (Marianna) da Vinci
1932- CANR-14
Earlier sketch in CA 73-76
Nichols, Paul D(yer) 1938- 109
Nichols, Peter 1927- 104
See also DLB 13
See also CLC 5, 36
Nichols, Peter
See Youd, Samuel
Nichols, R(oy) Eugene 1914- 29-32R
Nichols, Robert (Molise Bowyer) 1919- 93-96
Nichols, Roger 1939- 108
Nichols, Roger L(ouis) 1933- CANR-5
Earlier sketch in CA 15-16R
Nichols, Roy F(ranklin) 1896-1973 ..... CANR-3
Obituary 37-40R
Earlier sketch in CA 5-6R
See also DLB 17
Nichols, (Joanna) Ruth 1948- CANR-16
Earlier sketch in CA 25-28R
See also SATA 15
See also DLB 60
Nichols, Scott
See Scortia, Thomas N(icholas)
Nichols, Stephen G(eorge, Jr.) 1936- 45-48
Nichols, Sue 11-12R
Nichols, William James 1942- 93-96
Nichols, William Thomas 1927- 41-44R
Nicholsen, Margaret E(sther) 1904- 29-32R
Nicholson, Arnold 1902- CAP-2
Earlier sketch in CA 19-20
Nicholson, Ben 1894-1982 Obituary 110
Nicholson, C(harles) A. III 1922- 41-44R
Nicholson, Dorothy Nelis 1923-
Brief entry 109
Nicholson, Geoffrey (George) 1929- CANR-8
Earlier sketch in CA 7-8R
Nicholson, Gerald W(illiam) L(ingen)
1902-1980 101
Nicholson, Hubert 1908- 13-14R
Nicholson, Jack 1937(?)- Brief entry 116
Nicholson, Jane
See Steen, Marguerite
Nicholson, Joe
See Nicholson, Joseph Hugh, Jr.
Nicholson, John Greer 1929- 45-48
Nicholson, Joseph Hugh, Jr. 1943- 81-84
Nicholson, Joyce Thorpe 1919- CANR-5
Earlier sketch in CA 11-12R
See also SATA 35
Nicholson, (Edward) Max 1904-
Brief entry 106
Nicholson, Norman (Cornthwaite)
1914-1987 .... CANR-24
Obituary 122
Earlier sketches in CA 9-10R, CANR-3
See also DLB 27
Nicholson, Norman L(eon) 1919- CANR-3
Earlier sketch in CA 9-10R
Nicholson, Patrick J(ames) 1920- 120
Nicholson, Paul (Joseph), Jr. 1937- 73-76
Nicholson, Ranald (George) 1931- 37-40R
Nicholson, Robert Lawrence 1908-1985 ...53-56
Obituary 117
Nicholson, Shirley J. 1925- CANR-26
Earlier sketch in CA 29-32R
Nicholson, Simon 1934- 114
Nicholson, W(illiam) G(eorge) 1935- 93-96
Nichter, Rhoda 1926- 81-84
Nichtern, Sol 1920-1988 ....17-18R
Obituary 126
Ni Chuilleanain, Eilean 1942- 126
See also DLB 40
Nickel, Herman 1928- 73-76
Nickel, Mildred L(ucille) 1912- 108
Nickell, Joe 1944- 110
Nickell, Lesley J(acqueline) 1944- 103
Nickels, William G(eorge) 1939- 108
Nickelsburg, George W(illiam) E(lmer), Jr.
1934- CANR-19
Earlier sketches in CA 53-56, CANR-5
Nickelsburg, Janet 1893- 65-68
See also SATA 11
Nickerson, Betty 1922- 77-80
Nickerson, Clarence B(entley) 1906- 5-6R
Nickerson, Elizabeth
See Nickerson, Betty
See also SATA 14
Nickerson, Jan ?-19(?) 4R
Nickerson, Jane Soames (Bon)
1900-1988 77-80
Obituary 124
Nickerson, John Mitchell 1937- 53-56
Nickerson, Roy 1927- 114
Nickerson, Sheila B(unker) 1942- 118
Nickerson, William (Ernest) 1908- 2R
Nicklanovich, Michael David 1941- 107
Nicklaus, Carol SATA-33
Nicklaus, (Charles) Frederick 1936- 37-40R
Nicklaus, Jack (William) 1940- CANR-16
Earlier sketch in CA 89-92
Nickle, Keith Fullerton 1933- 115
Nickless, Will 1902- 81-84
Niclas, Yolla 1900- 25-28R
Nic Leodhas, Sorche
See Alger, Leclaire (Gowans)
Nicol, Abioseh
See Nicol, Davidson (Sylvester Hector
Willoughby)
Nicol, Ann
See Turnbull, Ann (Christine)
Nicol, Charles (David) 1940- 115
Nicol, D(onald) M(acGillivray) 1923- CANR-4
Earlier sketch in CA 53-56
Nicol, Davidson (Sylvester Hector
Willoughby) 1924- CANR-26
Earlier sketch in CA 61-64
See also BW
Nicol, Eric (Patrick) 1919- CANR-16
Earlier sketches in CA 49-52, CANR-1
See also DLB 68
Nicol, Jean 1919- 21-22R
Nicolaeff, Ariadne 1915- 57-60
Nicolas
See Mordvinoff, Nicolas
Nicolas, Claire
See White, Claire Nicolas
Nicolas, F. R. E.
See Freeling, Nicolas
Nicolay, Helen 1866-1954 Brief entry 121
See also YABC 1
Nicolay, John G(eorge) 1832-1901
Brief entry 122
See also DLB 47
Nicolaysen, Bruce 1934- 105
Nicole, Christopher Robin 1930- 13-14R
See also SATA 5
Nicoll, (John Ramsay) Allardyce
1894-1976 .... CANR-5
Obituary 65-68
Earlier sketch in CA 9-10R
Nicoll, Bruce H. 1913(?)-1983 Obituary 111
Nicoll, Helen 1937- 122
Nicolle, Jacques Maurice Raoul 1901- 9-10R
Nicoloff, Philip Loveless 1926- 3R
Nicolson, (Lionel) Benedict 1914-1978 .. CANR-6
Earlier sketch in CA 13-14R
Nicolson, Catherine 121
Nicolson, Harold George 1886-1968 ..... CAP-1
Earlier sketch in CA 15-16
Nicolson, I(an) F(erguson) 1921- 29-32R
Nicolson, James R(obert) 1934- CANR-9
Earlier sketch in CA 65-68
Nicolson, Marjorie Hope 1894-1981 ......9-10R
Obituary 103
Nicolson, Nigel 1917- 101
Nicolson, Victoria Mary
See Sackville-West, V(ictoria Mary)
Nicosia, Francesco M(ichael) 1933- 81-84
Nicosia, Franco M.
See Nicosia, Francesco M(ichael)
Nicosia, Gerald (Martin) 1949- 115
Nida, Eugene A(lbert) 1914- CANR-17
Earlier sketches in CA 4R, CANR-1
Nidditch, Peter (Harold) 1928-1983
Obituary 109
Niddrie, David Lawrence 1917- 25-28R
Nideffer, Robert M(orse) 1942- CANR-9
Earlier sketch in CA 65-68
Nidetch, Jean 1923- 89-92
Nie, Norman H. 1943- CANR-15
Earlier sketch in CA 65-68
Niebuhr, H(elmut) Richard 1894-1962
Obituary 116
Niebuhr, Reinhold 1892-1971 ....41-44R
Obituary 29-32R
See also DLB 17
Niebuhr, Richard R. 1926- 77-80
Niebuhr, Ursula 1907- 89-92
Nieburg, H(arold) L. 1927- 11-12R
Niedecker, Lorine 1903-1970 .... CAP-2
Earlier sketch in CA 25-28
See also DLB 48
See also CLC 10, 42
Niederauer, David J(ohn) 1924- 45-48
Niederhoffer, Arthur 1917-1981 Obituary ... 103
Niederland, William G(ugliemo) 1904- 81-84
Niedzielski, Henri 1931- 49-52
Nieh, Hualing 1925- 81-84
Niehoff, Arthur H. 1921- 21-22R
Nielander, William Ahlers 1901- 7-8R
Nielsen, Aage Rosendal 1921- 25-28R
Nielsen, Dulcimer 1943- 93-96
Nielsen, Eduard 1923- 29-32R
Nielsen, Gary (Elton) 1939- 97-100
Nielsen, Helen Berniece 1918- CANR-1
Earlier sketch in CA 2R
Nielsen, Jean Sarver 1922- 5-6R
Nielsen, Kay (Rasmus) 1886-1957 ..... SATA-16
See also CLR 16
Nielsen, Knut Schmidt
See Schmidt-Nielsen, Knut
Nielsen, Margaret A(nne) 105
Nielsen, Niels Christian, Jr. 1921- CANR-3
Earlier sketch in CA 11-12R
Nielsen, Niels Juel
See Juel-Nielsen, Niels
Nielsen, Oswald 1904- CAP-2
Earlier sketch in CA 19-20
Nielsen, Robert F. 1937- 122
Nielsen, Sven Sigurd 1901-1976 Obituary .. 104
Nielsen, Torben 1918- Brief entry 114
Nielsen, Veneta Leatham 1909- 89-92
Nielsen, Virginia
See McCall, Virginia Nielsen
Nielsen, Waldemar August 1917- 103
Nielssen, Eric
See Ludvigsen, Karl (Eric)
Nieman, Egbert William 1909- CAP-1
Earlier sketch in CA 11-12
Nieman, Lucius W. 1857-1935 .... DLB-25
Niemeier, Jean (Gilbreath) 1912- 25-28R
Niemeyer, Eberhardt Victor, Jr. 1919- 102
Niemeyer, Gerhart 1907- 2R
Niemeyer, Roy K(urt) 1922- 2R
Niemi, Albert (William), Jr. 1942- 73-76
Niemi, John A. 1932- 77-80
Niemi, Richard G(ene) 1941- 41-44R
Niemoeller, (Friedrich Gustav Emil) Martin
1892-1984 Obituary 112
Niemoller, Ara
See Llerena, Mario
Niemoller, (Friedrich Gustav Emil) Martin
See Niemoeller, (Friedrich Gustav Emil)
Martin
Nienhauser, William H., Jr. 1943- 125
Nierenberg, Gerard I. 1923- 25-28R
Nierman, M. Murray 1918- 3R
Nies, Judith 1941- 77-80
Niesewand, Peter 1944-1983 101
Obituary 109
Niess, Robert Judson 1911- CAP-2
Earlier sketch in CA 29-32
Niethammer, Carolyn 1944- 85-88
Nietz, John Alfred 1888- 4R
Nietzke, Ann 1945- 105
Nietzsche, Friedrich (Wilhelm) 1844-1900 ... 121
Brief entry 107
See also TCLC 10, 18
Nievergelt, Jurg 1938- CANR-26
Earlier sketch in CA 29-32R
Niewyk, Donald L. 1940- 33-36R
Nigg, Joe
See Nigg, Joseph E(ugene)
Nigg, Joseph E(ugene) 1938- 114
Niggli, Josefina CAP-2
Earlier sketch in CA 21-22
See also DLBY 80
Nightingale, Anne Redmon 1943- 103
Nightingale, Elena O(ttolenghi) 1932- 123
Nightingale, Sir Geoffrey (Slingsby)
1904- CAP-1
Earlier sketch in CA 13-14
Nightrate, Emil
See Spielmann, Peter James
Nigro, Felix A(nthony) 1914- CANR-14
Earlier sketch in CA 37-40R
Nihal Singh, Surendra 1929- 93-96
Nihilo, Arthur X. 1938- 105
Niizaka, Kazuo 1943- 77-80
Nijinska, Bronislava 1891-1972 117
Nijinsky, Romola Flavia 1891-1978
Obituary 81-84
Nijinsky, Vaslav (Fomitch) 1890-1950
Brief entry 115
Nik.T.O.
See Annensky, Innokenty Fyodorovich
Nikelly, Arthur G(eorge) 1927- 19-20R
Niklas, Gerald R. 1933- 118
Niklaus, Robert 1910- 9-10R
Niklaus, Thelma (Jones) 1912- 11-12R

Nikolay, Michael 1941- ... 97-100
Niland, D'Arcy Francis 1920-1967 ... CANR-3
Earlier sketch in CA 3R
Niland, Deborah 1951- ... 106
See also SATA 27
Niland, Powell 1919- ... 23-24R
Nile, Dorothea
See Avallone, Michael (Angelo), Jr.
Niles, D(aniel) T(hambyrajah) 1908-1970
Obituary ... 29-32R
Niles, Gwendolyn 1914- ... 11-12R
Niles, Hezekiah 1777-1839 ... DLB-43
Niles, John D(eWitt) 1945- ... 125
Niles, John Jacob 1892-1980 ... 41-44R
Obituary ... 97-100
Nill, Michael 1942- ... 124
Nilles, Jack M(athias) 1932- ... 108
Nilsen, Alleen Pace 1936- ... 112
Nilsen, Don L(ee) F(red) 1934- ... CANR-15
Earlier sketch in CA 41-44R
Nilsson, Usha Saksena 1930- ... 41-44R
Nimble, Jack B.
See Burgess, M(ichael) R(oy)
Nimeth, Albert J. 1918-1984 ... 25-28R
Obituary ... 114
Nimitz, Chester W(illiam) 1885-1966
Obituary ... 113
Nimmer, Melville B(ernard) 1923-1985 ... 49-52
Obituary ... 117
Nimmo, Dan D(ean) 1933- ... CANR-7
Earlier sketch in CA 15-16R
Nimmo, Derek (Robert) 1933- ... 109
Nimmo, Jenny 1942- ... 108
Nimnicht, Nona 1930- ... 73-76
Nimocks, Walter 1930- ... 41-44R
Nimoy, Leonard 1931- ... CANR-25
Earlier sketch in CA 57-60
Nims, Charles F(rancis) 1906- ... 17-18R
Nims, John Frederick 1913- ... CANR-6
Earlier sketch in CA 15-16R
See also DLB 5
Nin, Anais 1903-1977 ... CANR-22
Obituary ... 69-72
Earlier sketch in CA 13-14R
See also DLB 2, 4
See also CLC 1, 4, 8, 11, 14
See also AITN 2
Nineham, Dennis (Eric) 1921- ... 85-88
Nininger, H(arvey) H(arlow) 1887-1986 ... 23-24R
Obituary ... 118
Nioche, Brigitte ... 109
Nir, Yehuda 1930- ... 107
Nirenberg, Jesse S(tanley) 1921- ... 69-72
Nirmala-Kumara, V
See Bose, N(irmal) K(umar)
Nirodi, Hira 1930- ... 5-6R
Nisbet, Ada Blanche 1907- ... 41-44R
Nisbet, Robert A(lexander) 1913- ... CANR-17
Earlier sketch in CA 25-28R
Nisbet, Stanley (Donald) 1912- ... CAP-1
Earlier sketch in CA 13-14
Nisbett, (Thomas) Alec 1930- ... CANR-22
Earlier sketch in CA 81-84
Nisbett, Richard E. 1941- ... 37-40R
Nisetich, Frank Joseph 1942- ... 97-100
Nish, Ian Hill 1926- ... CANR-17
Earlier sketch in CA 21-22R
Nishihara, Masashi 1937- ... CANR-12
Earlier sketch in CA 69-72
Nishio, Suehiro 1891-1981 Obituary ... 108
Nishiwaki, Junzaburo 1894-1982 Obituary ... 107
Nishiyama, Chiaki 1924- Brief entry ... 110
Niskanen, William Arthur, Jr. 1933- ... 41-44R
Nissen, Lowell A(llen) 1932- ... 33-36R
Nissenbaum, Stephen 1941- ... 77-80
Nissenson, Hugh 1933- ... 17-18R
See also DLB 28
See also CLC 4, 9
Nissman, Albert 1930- ... 37-40R
Nissman, Blossom S. 1928- ... CANR-19
Earlier sketch in CA 37-40R
Nist, John (Albert) 1925-1981 ... CANR-11
Earlier sketch in CA 21-22R
Nitchie, George W(ilson) 1921- ... 11-12R
Nitske, W(illiam) Robert 1909- ... CANR-5
Earlier sketch in CA 15-16R
Nittler, Alan H(opkins) 1918- ... CANR-13
Earlier sketch in CA 61-64
Nityanandan, P(erumpilavil) M(adhava Menon) 1926- ... 11-12R
Nitzsche, Jane Chance 1945- ... CANR-8
Earlier sketch in CA 57-60
Niven, Alastair 1944- ... CANR-16
Earlier sketch in CA 81-84
Niven, Alexander Curt 1920- ... CANR-2
Earlier sketch in CA 5-6R
Niven, (James) David (Graham)
1910-1983 ... 77-80
Obituary ... 110
Niven, John 1921- ... 65-68
Niven, Larry
See Niven, Laurence Van Cott
See also DLB 8
See also CLC 8
Niven, Laurence Van Cott 1938- ... CANR-14
Earlier sketch in CA 21-22R
Niven, Marian
See Alston, Mary Niven
Niven, (Cecil) Rex 1898- ... 120
Niven, Vern
See Grier, Barbara G(ene Damon)
Nivens, Beatryce 1948- ... 114
Nivison, David Shepherd 1923- ... 103
Niwa, Tamako 1922- Brief entry ... 106
Nixon, Agnes Eckhardt 1927- ... 110
See also CLC 21
Nixon, Allan 1918- ... 17-18R
Nixon, Edna (Mary) ... 5-6R
Nixon, George 1924- ... 49-52
Nixon, Hershell Howard 1923- ... 89-92
See also SATA 42
Nixon, Howard Millar 1909-1983 Obituary ... 109
Nixon, Ivor Gray 1905- ... CAP-2
Earlier sketch in CA 29-32
Nixon, Joan Lowery 1927- ... CANR-24
Earlier sketches in CA 11-12R, CANR-7
See also SATA 8, 44
Nixon, John Erskine 1917- ... 101
Nixon, K.
See Nixon, Kathleen Irene (Blundell)
Nixon, Kathleen Irene (Blundell)
1894-1988(?) ... 73-76
Obituary ... 126
See also SATA 14
Nixon, Lucille M. 1908-1963 ... 5-6R
Nixon, Marion 1930- ... 49-52
Nixon, Richard M(ilhous) 1913- ... 73-76
Nixon, Robert E(arl, Jr.) 1918- ... 5-6R
Nixon, St. John Cousins 1885- ... 7-8R
Nixon, William R(ussell) 1918- ... 29-32R
Nixson, Frederick Ian 1943- ... CANR-20
Earlier sketch in CA 104
Nizan, Paul 1905-1940 ... DLB-72
Nizer, Louis 1902- ... 53-56
Njururi, Ngumbu 1930- ... 19-20R
Nketia, J(oseph) H(anson) Kwabena
1921- ... CANR-7
Earlier sketch in CA 11-12R
Nkosi, Lewis 1936- ... 65-68
See also BW
See also CLC 45
Nkrumah, Kwame 1909-1972 Obituary ... 113
Noad, Frederick (McNeill) 1929- ... CANR-4
Earlier sketch in CA 11-12R
Noah, Harold J(ulius) 1925- ... CANR-13
Earlier sketch in CA 33-36R
Noah, Joseph W(atson) 1928- ... 81-84
Noakes, Jeremy 1941- ... 101
Noakes, Vivien 1937- ... 65-68
Noall, Roger 1935- ... 11-12R
Nobile, Umberto 1885-1978 Obituary ... 81-84
Noble, Allen G(eorge) 1930- ... 116
Noble, Charles
See Pawley, Martin Edward
Noble, David Watson 1925- ... CANR-1
Earlier sketch in CA 49-52
Noble, Dudley (Henry) 1893(?)-1970
Obituary ... 104
Noble, Elizabeth Marian 1945- ... CANR-9
Earlier sketch in CA 65-68
Noble, G(eorge) Bernard 1892-1972 ... CAP-2
Obituary ... 37-40R
Earlier sketch in CA 33-36
Noble, Iris (Davis) 1922-1986 ... CANR-2
Obituary ... 120
Earlier sketch in CA 3R
See also SATA 5, 49
Noble, J(ames) Kendrick 1896(?)-1978
Obituary ... 104
Noble, J(ames) Kendrick, Jr. 1928- ... 19-20R
Noble, Jeanne L(aveta) 1926- Brief entry ... 112
Noble, John (Appelbe) 1914- ... CANR-1
Earlier sketch in CA 45-48
Noble, John 1923- ... 45-48
Noble, John Wesley 1913- ... 9-10R
Noble, Joseph Veach 1920- ... 61-64
Noble, June (Solveig) 1924-1984 ... CANR-18
Earlier sketch in CA 97-100
Noble, Marguerite (Buchanan) 1910- ... 105
Noble, Stanley R(odman) 1904(?)-1977
Obituary ... 104
Noble, Trinka Hakes Brief entry ... 116
See also SATA 37
Noble, William Charles 1935- ... 107
Noble, William P(arker) 1932- ... CANR-18
Earlier sketch in CA 101
Nochlin, Linda Weinberg 1931- ... CANR-6
Earlier sketch in CA 11-12R
Nock, Albert Jay 1870(?)-1945 Brief entry ... 122
Nock, Francis J. 1905-1969 ... CAP-1
Earlier sketch in CA 13-14
Nock, O(swald) S(tevens) 1905- ... CANR-16
Earlier sketch in CA 85-88
Nockolds, Harold 1907-1982 Obituary ... 108
Noddings, Nel 1929- ... 115
Noddings, Thomas C. 1933- ... CANR-2
Earlier sketch in CA 49-52
Nodel, Sol 1912-1976 Obituary ... 107
Nodset, Joan L.
See Lexau, Joan M.
Noe, Thomas R. 1947- ... 112
Noe, Tom
See Noe, Thomas R.
Noel, Daniel C(alhoun) 1936- ... 101
Noel, Hilda Bloxton, Jr.
See Schroetter, Hilda Noel
Noel, John
See Bird, Dennis L(eslie)
Noel, John V(avasour), Jr. 1912- ... CANR-15
Earlier sketch in CA 21-22R
Noel, Roden 1834-1894 ... DLB-35
Noel, Ruth (Swycaffer) 1947- ... 69-72
Noel, Sterling 1903-1984 Obituary ... 114
Noel, Thomas Jacob 1945- ... CANR-24
Earlier sketch in CA 107
Noel-Baker, Philip John 1889-1982
Obituary ... 108
Noel Hume, Ivor 1927- ... CANR-12
Earlier sketch in CA 13-14R
Noer, Thomas John 1944- ... 102
Noestlinger, Christine 1936- ... 123
Brief entry ... 115
See also SATA 37
See also CLR 12
Noether, Emiliana P. ... 101
Nofi, Albert A(urelio) 1944- ... 112
Nofziger, Margaret 1946- ... 110
Nogee, Joseph Lippman 1929- ... 17-18R
Noggle, Burl L. 1924- Brief entry ... 107
Noguere, Suzanne 1947- ... 107
See also SATA 34
Nohl, Frederick 1927- ... CANR-3
Earlier sketch in CA 7-8R
Nohrnberg, James (Carson) 1941- ... 69-72
Nojiri, Kiyohiko 1897-1973 ... 93-96
Obituary ... 41-44R
Nokes, Gerald Dacre 1899-1971 Obituary ... 104
Nolan, Alan T. 1923- ... 1R
Nolan, Albert 1934- ... 117
Nolan, Bob 1908(?)-1980 Obituary ... 101
Nolan, Brian
See O Nuallain, Brian
Nolan, Carroll A(nthony) 1906- ... 17-18R
Nolan, Christopher 1965- ... 111
Nolan, Chuck
See Edson, J(ohn) T(homas)
Nolan, Dennis 1945- ... 112
See also SATA 34, 42
Nolan, Edward Francis 1915- Brief entry ... 108
Nolan, James 1947- ... CANR-5
Earlier sketch in CA 53-56
Nolan, Jeannette Covert 1897-1974 ... CANR-4
Obituary ... 53-56
Earlier sketch in CA 7-8R
See also SATA 2, 27
Nolan, Keith W(illiam) 1964- ... 114
Nolan, Madeena Spray 1943- ... 89-92
Nolan, Michael 1940- ... 126
Nolan, Paul T(homas) 1919- ... CANR-2
Earlier sketch in CA 5-6R
See also SATA 48
Nolan, Richard Thomas 1937- ... CANR-10
Earlier sketch in CA 25-28R
Nolan, Tom 1948- ... 77-80
Nolan, William F(rancis) 1928- ... CANR-1
Earlier sketch in CA 4R
See also SATA 28
See also DLB 8
Nolan, Winefride (Bell) 1913- ... 13-14R
Noland, C. F. M. 1810(?)-1858 ... DLB-11
Noland, Ronald G(ene) 1936- ... 41-44R
Nolde, O(tto) Frederick 1899-1972 ... CAP-2
Obituary ... 37-40R
Earlier sketch in CA 29-32
Nolen, Barbara 1902- ... 104
Nolen, Claude H. 1921- ... 21-22R
Nolen, William A(nthony) 1928-1986 ... CANR-15
Obituary ... 121
Earlier sketch in CA 77-80
Nolin, Bertil 1926- ... 65-68
Noling, A(lfred) W(ells) 1899- ... CAP-2
Earlier sketch in CA 29-32
Noll, Bink
See Noll, Lou Barker
Noll, Lou Barker 1927- ... 7-8R
Noll, Mark A(llan) 1946- ... 115
Noll, Martin David
See Buxbaum, Martin
Noll, Roger G(ordon) 1940- ... CANR-8
Earlier sketch in CA 53-56
Nollau, Gunther 1911- ... 7-8R
Nollen, Stanley D(ale) 1940- ... 110
Nolte, Carl William 1933- ... 77-80
Nolte, Elleta 1919- ... 61-64
Nolte, M(ervin) Chester 1911- ... 11-12R
Nolte, William H(enry) 1928- ... 33-36R
Nolting, Orin F(rederyc) 1903- ... 29-32R
Noltingk, B(ernard) E(dward) 1918- ... 17-18R
Noma, Koremichi 1938(?)-1987 Obituary ... 122
Nomad, Max 1880(?)-1973 Obituary ... 41-44R
Noma Shoichi 1911-1984 Obituary ... 113
Nonas, Elisabeth 1949- ... 119
Nonet, Philippe 1939- ... 57-60
Nonhebel, Clare 1953- ... 119
Noon, Brian 1919- ... 49-52
Noon, William T(homas) 1912-1975 ... 65-68
Obituary ... 53-56
Noonan, John Ford 1943- ... 85-88
Noonan, John T(homas), Jr. 1926- ... CANR-13
Earlier sketch in CA 15-16R
Noonan, Julia 1946- ... 33-36R
See also SATA 4
Noonan, Lowell G(erald) 1922- ... 29-32R
Noonan, Michael John 1921- ... 21-22R
Noone, Edwina
See Avallone, Michael (Angelo), Jr.
Noone, John 1936- Brief entry ... 109
See also DLB 14
Noone, Richard 1918(?)-1973 Obituary ... 104
Noorbergen, Rene 1928- ... 77-80
Nooteboom, Cees 1933- Brief entry ... 124
Nora, James Jackson 1928- ... CANR-20
Earlier sketch in CA 104
Norback, Craig T(homas) 1943- ... 113
Norbeck, Edward 1915- ... CANR-1
Earlier sketch in CA 2R
Norberg-Schulz, Christian 1926- ... 81-84
Norbu, Thubten Jigme
See Thubten Sigme Norbu
Norcross, John
See Conroy, John Wesley
Norcross, Lisabet
See Gladstone, Arthur M.
Norcutt, Bill
See Norcutt, William E.
Norcutt, William E. 1946- Brief entry ... 118
Nord, Ole C. 1935- ... 13-14R
Nord, Paul 1900(?)-1981 Obituary ... 103
Nord, Walter R(obert) 1939- ... 37-40R
Nordan, Lewis 1939- ... 117
Nordberg, H(arold) Orville 1916- ... 2R
Nordberg, Robert B. 1921- ... 15-16R
Nordby, Vernon James 1945- ... 57-60
Nordell, (Hans) Roderick 1925- ... 104
Norden, Albert 1904-1982 Obituary ... 107
Norden, Charles
See Durrell, Lawrence (George)
Norden, Denis 1922- ... 104
Norden, Heinz 1905- ... 53-56
Norden, Helen Brown
See Lawrenson, Helen
Nordham, George Washington 1929- ... CANR-23
Earlier sketch in CA 106
Nordhaus, William D(awbney) 1941- ... 97-100
Nordhoff, Charles (Bernard) 1887-1947
Brief entry ... 108
See also SATA 23
See also DLB 9
See also TCLC 23
Nordholm, Harriet 1912- ... 29-32R
Nordicus
See Snyder, Louis L.
Nordin, D(ennis) Sven 1942- ... 61-64
Nordland, Gerald John 1927- ... 104
Nordland, Rod(ney Lee) 1949- ... 118
Nordlicht, Lillian ... 105
See also SATA 29
Nordlinger, Eric A. 1939- ... 77-80
Nordmann, Joseph (Behrens) 1922- ... 25-28R
Nordness, Lee 1924- ... 9-10R
Nordoff, Paul 1909-1977 ... 102
Nordquist, Barbara K(ay) 1940- ... 77-80
Nordskog, John Eric 1893-1974 ... 2R
Obituary ... 120
Nordstrom, Ursula 1910-1988 ... 13-14R
Obituary ... 126
See also SATA 3
Nordtvedt, Matilda 1926- ... 124
Nordyke, Eleanor C(ole) 1927- ... 107
Nordyke, James W(alter) 1930- ... 49-52
Noreen, Robert Gerald 1938- ... 77-80
Norelli, Martina R(oudabush) 1942- ... 73-76
Noren, Catherine (Hanf) 1938- ... CANR-16
Earlier sketch in CA 65-68
Noren, Paul Harold Andreas 1910- ... CAP-1
Earlier sketch in CA 11-12
Norfleet, Barbara P. 1926- Brief entry ... 107
Norfleet, Mary Crockett 1919- ... 4R
Norgate, Matthew 1901- ... 103
Norgay, Tenzing 1914-1986 Obituary ... 119
Nori, Claude 1949- ... CANR-18
Earlier sketch in CA 101
Norland, Howard Bernett 1932- ... 49-52
Norling, Bernard 1924- ... 29-32R
Norling, Jo(sephine Stearns) ... 2R
Norling, Rita ... 61-64
Norman, Adrian R(oger) D(udley)
1938- ... CANR-26
Earlier sketch in CA 29-32R
Norman, Alexander Vesey Bethune
1930- ... CANR-9
Earlier sketch in CA 21-22R
Norman, Barbara ... 33-36R
Norman, Bruce 1936- ... 61-64
Norman, C. J.
See Barrett, Norman (S.)
Norman, Cecilia 1927- ... CANR-23
Earlier sketches in CA 57-60, CANR-7
Norman, Charles 1904- ... 107
See also SATA 38
Norman, Don(ald) Cleveland 1909(?)-1979
Obituary ... 89-92
Norman, Donald A(rthur) 1935- ... CANR-1
Earlier sketch in CA 49-52
Norman, Dorothy 1905- ... 25-28R
Norman, E.D.
See Goodwin, Bennie Eugene
Norman, Edward (Robert) 1938- ... CANR-10
Earlier sketch in CA 17-18R
Norman, Frank 1930-1980 ... CANR-6
Obituary ... 102
Earlier sketch in CA 2R
Norman, Geraldine (Lucia) 1940- ... 93-96
Norman, Hilary ... 126
Norman, James
See Schmidt, James Norman
Norman, Jillian 1940- ... 25-28R
Norman, Joe
See Heard, J(oseph) Norman
Norman, John 1912- ... 19-20R
Norman, John
See Lange, John Frederick, Jr.
Norman, Joyce Ann 1937- ... 65-68
Norman, Kerry
See Le Pelley, Guernsey
Norman, Lilith 1927- ... CANR-1
Earlier sketch in CA 45-48
Norman, Lloyd (Henry) 1913-1987 ... 102
Obituary ... 124
Norman, Louis
See Whittemore, Don
Norman, Marc 1941- ... 49-52
Norman, Marsha 1947- ... 105
See also DLBY 84
See also CLC 28
Norman, Mary 1931- ... SATA-36
Norman, Maxwell H(erbert) 1917- ... 29-32R
Norman, Nicole
See Cudlipp, Edythe
Norman, Ruth 1903(?)-1977 Obituary ... 73-76
Norman, Steve
See Pashko, Stanley
Norman, Sylva 1901- ... CAP-1
Earlier sketch in CA 13-14
Norman, Theodore 1910-1987 ... 124
Obituary ... 122
Norman, Vesey
See Norman, Alexander Vesey Bethune

Norman, W. S.
See Wilson, N(orman) Scarlyn
Norman, Yvonne
See Seely, Norma
Normyx
See Douglas, (George) Norman
Norodom Sihanouk (Varman), Samdech
Preah 1922- Brief entry 106
Norquest, Carrol 1901- 41-44R
Norquist, Richard F(ranklin) 1933- 113
Norrie, Ian 1927- CANR-23
Earlier sketch in CA 106
Norris, Benjamin Franklin, Jr. 1870-1902
Brief entry 110
See also TCLC 24
Norris, Charles G(ilman Smith) 1881-1945
Brief entry 118
See also DLB 9
Norris, Christopher (Charles) 1947- 111
Norris, Christopher Neil Foxley
See Foxley-Norris, Christopher Neil
Norris, Donald F(ranklin) 1942- CANR-2
Earlier sketch in CA 49-52
Norris, Dorothy E. Koch 1907- CAP-2
Earlier sketch in CA 21-22
Norris, Edgar Poe
See Kinnaird, Clark
Norris, Francis Hubert 1909- 7-8R
Norris, Frank
See Norris, Benjamin Franklin, Jr.
See also DLB 12, 71
See also CDALB 1865-1917
Norris, Frank C(allan) 1907-1967
Obituary 25-28R
Norris, Gunilla Brodde 1939- 93-96
See also SATA 20
Norris, Harold 1918- 108
Norris, Hoke 1913-1977 ....11-12R
Obituary 73-76
Norris, J(ames) A(lfred) 1929- 25-28R
Norris, James Donald 1930- 19-20R
Norris, Joan 1943- 73-76
Norris, John 1925- 11-12R
Norris, Kathleen (Thompson) 1880-1966
Obituary 25-28R
Norris, Kathleen 1947- 33-36R
Norris, Katrin 19-20R
Norris, Ken 1951- 113
Norris, Kenneth S(tafford) 1924- 77-80
Norris, Leslie 1921- CANR-14
Earlier sketches in CA 11-12, CAP-1
See also DLB 27
See also CLC 14
Norris, Louanne 1930- CANR-20
Earlier sketch in CA 53-56
Norris, Louis William 1906- CAP-1
Earlier sketch in CA 9-10
Norris, Maureen
See Cudlipp, Edythe
Norris, Nigel (Harold) 1943- 65-68
Norris, Richard A(lfred), Jr. 1930- 19-20R
Norris, Ronald V. 1940- 116
Norris, Ruby Turner
See Morris, Ruby Turner
Norris, Russell Bradner (Jr.) 1942- 53-56
Norris, Theo L. 1926- 23-24R
Norse, Harold (George) 1916- CANR-4
Earlier sketch in CA 53-56
See also DLB 16
North, Alvin J(ohn) 1917- 49-52
North, Andrew
See Norton, Alice Mary
North, Anthony
See Koontz, Dean R(ay)
North, Captain George
See Stevenson, Robert Louis (Balfour)
North, Charles W.
See Bauer, Erwin A.
North, Christopher R(ichard) 1888-1975
Obituary 61-64
North, Colin
See Bingley, David Ernest
North, Edmund H(all) 1911- 121
North, Eleanor B(eryl) 1898- 49-52
North, Elizabeth 1932- 81-84
North, Gary 1942- CANR-16
Earlier sketch in CA 65-68
North, Gil
See Horne, Geoffrey
North, Helen Florence 1921- 104
North, Joan 1920- 13-14R
See also SATA 16
North, John (Francis Allen) 1894-1973 107
Obituary 104
North, Joseph 1904-1976 .... CANR-4
Obituary 69-72
Earlier sketch in CA 2R
North, Mark
See Miller, Wright (Watts)
North, Morgan 1915(?)-1978 Obituary 104
North, Robert
See Withers, Carl A.
North, Robert Carver 1914- CANR-4
Earlier sketch in CA 5-6R
North, Robert Grady 1916- 17-18R
North, Sara
See Bonham, Barbara Thomas
and Hager, Jean
North, Sterling 1906-1974 ....5-6R
Obituary 53-56
See also SATA 1, 26, 45
North, Wheeler James 1922- 101
Northam, Ray M(ervyn) 1929- 73-76
Northart, Leo J(oseph) 1929- 69-72
Northcote, Peter
See Cotes, Peter
Northcott, (William) Cecil 1902-1987 ......9-10R
Obituary 124
Northcott, Kenneth J(ames) 1922- 45-48
Northedge, Frederick Samuel 1918-1985 104
Obituary 115
Northen, Helen 1914- CANR-13
Earlier sketch in CA 33-36R
Northen, Henry T(heodore) 1908-1979 ...97-100
Northen, Rebecca Tyson 1910- 105
Northgrave, Anne
See Tibble, Anne
Northmore, Elizabeth Florence
1906-1974 .... CAP-2
Earlier sketch in CA 19-20
Northouse, Cameron (George) 1948- 81-84
Northrop, Filmer S(tuart) C(uckow)
1893- CANR-17
Earlier sketch in CA 4R
Northrop, J. H.
See Northrop, John H(oward)
Northrop, John H(oward) 1891-1987
Obituary 123
Northrup, B. A.
See Hubbard, L(afayette) Ron(ald)
Northrup, Herbert Roof 1918- 9-10R
North Staffs
See Hulme, T(homas) E(rnest)
Northumbrian Gentleman, The
See Tegner, Henry (Stuart)
Northway, Mary L(ouise) 1909- 45-48
Northwood, Lawrence K(ing) 1917- 15-16R
Norton, Alan (Lewis) 1926- CANR-15
Earlier sketch in CA 81-84
Norton, Alden H(olmes) 1903- 101
Norton, Alice 1926- 33-36R
Norton, Alice Mary 1912- CANR-2
Earlier sketch in CA 4R
See also SATA 1, 43
Norton, Andre
See Norton, Alice Mary
See also DLB 8, 52
See also CLC 12
Norton, Andrews 1786-1853 .... DLB-1
Norton, Augustus Richard 1946- 113
Norton, Bess
See Norton, Olive (Claydon)
Norton, Bettina A(ntonia) 1936- 93-96
Norton, Boyd 1936- 37-40R
Norton, Bram
See Bramesco, Norton J.
Norton, Browning
See Norton, Frank R. B(rowning)
Norton, Caroline 1808-1877 .... DLB-21
Norton, Charles A(lbert) 1920- 109
Norton, Charles Eliot 1827-1908 ..... DLB-1, 64
Norton, David Fate 1937- 107
Norton, David L. 1930- 37-40R
Norton, (William) Elliot 1903- Brief entry ... 109
Norton, Frank R. B(rowning) 1909- 61-64
See also SATA 10
Norton, Frederick H. 1896- 61-64
Norton, Glyn P(eter) 1941- 122
Norton, Herman A. 1921- CANR-7
Earlier sketch in CA 5-6R
Norton, Howard Melvin 1911- CANR-3
Earlier sketch in CA 4R
Norton, Hugh S(tanton) 1921- 11-12R
Norton, John 1606-1663 .... DLB-24
Norton, Joseph L(ouis) 1918- 29-32R
Norton, M. D. Herter
See Crena de Iongh, Mary (Dows Herter
Norton)
Norton, Mary 1903- 97-100
See also SATA 18
See also CLR 6
Norton, Mary Beth 1943- CANR-5
Earlier sketch in CA 49-52
Norton, Mary E(lizabeth) 1913- 41-44R
Norton, Olive (Claydon) 1913-1973 ......11-12R
Norton, Paul Foote 1917- 41-44R
Norton, Perry L. 1920- 15-16R
Norton, Peter (John) 1913- 13-14R
Norton, Roger C(ecil) 1921- 114
Norton, Thomas 1532-1584 .... DLB-62
Norton, Thomas Elliot 1942- 61-64
Norton, Victor 1906-1983 Obituary 109
Norton, Wesley 1923- 114
Norton-Smith, John 1931- 107
Norton-Taylor, Duncan 1904-1982 102
Obituary 107
Norvil, Manning
See Bulmer, (Henry) Kenneth
Norville, Warren 1923- 73-76
Norwak, Mary 1929- 109
Norway, Kate
See Norton, Olive (Claydon)
Norway, Nevil Shute 1899-1960 102
Obituary 93-96
Norwich, John Julius (Cooper) 1929- ... CANR-5
Earlier sketch in CA 49-52
Norwood, Fred W(ayland) 1920-
Brief entry 112
Norwood, Frederick Abbott 1914- CANR-20
Earlier sketches in CA 4R, CANR-5
Norwood, Gilbert 1880-1954 Brief entry 116
Norwood, John
See Stark, Raymond
Norwood, Paul
See Nettl J(ohn) P(eter)
Norwood, Victor G(eorge) C(harles)
1920- CANR-10
Earlier sketch in CA 21-22R
Norwood, Warren C. 1945- 112
Nosco, Peter 1950- 93-96
Nosille, Nabrah
See Ellison, Harlan
Noss, John Boyer 1896- 85-88
Noss, Luther (Melancthon) 1907- 5-6R
Nossack, Hans Erich 1901-1978 93-96
Obituary 85-88
See also DLB 69
See also CLC 6
Nossal, Frederick (Christian) 1927-1979 ....7-8R
Obituary 89-92
Nossal, Gustav Joseph Victor 1931- 109
Nossiter, Bernard D(aniel) 1926- 41-44R
Nostlinger, Christine
See Noestlinger, Christine
See also SATA 37
See also CLR 12
Nostrand, Howard Lee 1910- 9-10R
Nosu, Chuji
See Ozu, Yasujiro
Notar, Stephen 1926- 119
Notarius
See Martin, Andrew
Notehelfer, F(red) G(eorge) 1939- 81-84
Notestein, Frank Wallace 1902-1983
Obituary 109
Notestein, Wallace 1878-1969 .... CAP-1
Earlier sketch in CA 9-10
Noth, Martin D. 1902-1968 .... CAP-2
Earlier sketch in CA 21-22
Nothing Venture
See Finney, Humphrey S.
Notlep, Robert
See Pelton, Robert W(ayne)
Notley, Alice 1945- Brief entry 124
Nott, David 1928- 45-48
Nott, Kathleen Cecilia CANR-3
Earlier sketch in CA 4R
Notterman, Joseph M(elvin) 1923- 17-18R
Nottingham, Elizabeth K. 1900- 93-96
Nottingham, William Jesse 1927- 25-28R
Notz, Rebecca Love 1888-1974 Obituary ... 104
Nourissier, Francois 1927- 81-84
Nourse, Alan E(dward) 1928- CANR-21
Earlier sketches in CA 1R, CANR-3
See also SATA 48
See also DLB 8
Nourse, Edwin G(riswold) 1883-1974
Obituary 49-52
Nourse, Hugh O(liver) 1933- Brief entry 107
Nourse, James G(regory) 1947- 105
Nourse, Joan Thellusson 1921- 11-12R
Nourse, Mary Augusta 1880(?)-1971
Obituary 33-36R
Nourse, Robert Eric Martin 1938- 23-24R
Nouveau, Arthur
See Whitcomb, Ian
Nouwen, Henri J(osef Machiel) 1932- 73-76
Nova, Craig 1945- CANR-2
Earlier sketch in CA 45-48
See also CLC 7, 31
Novack, Evelyn Reed 1906(?)-1979
Obituary 85-88
Novack, George (Edward) 1905- 49-52
Novak, Barbara 97-100
Novak, Bogdan C(yril) 1919- 33-36R
Novak, David 1941- 93-96
Novak, Jane Dailey 1917- 105
Novak, Joe
See Novak, Joseph
Novak, Joseph 1898- CAP-1
Earlier sketch in CA 11-12
Novak, Joseph
See Kosinski, Jerzy (Nikodem)
Novak, Lorna 1927- 19-20R
Novak, Matt 1962- 125
See also SATA 52
Novak, Maximillian E(rwin) 1930- CANR-12
Earlier sketch in CA 33-36R
Novak, Michael 1933- CANR-1
Earlier sketch in CA 2R
Novak, Michael Paul 1935- 49-52
Novak, Robert
See Levinson, Leonard
Novak, Robert D(avid) 1931- CANR-12
Earlier sketch in CA 13-14R
Novak, Rose 1940- CANR-22
Earlier sketch in CA 105
Novak, Stephen R(obert) 1922- 85-88
Novak, William (Arnold) 1948- CANR-26
Earlier sketch in CA 93-96
Novarr, David 1917- 19-20R
Nove, Alec 1915- CANR-3
Earlier sketch in CA 4R
Novelli, Florence 1931- 112
Novello, Don 1943- 107
Nover, Barnet 1899-1973 Obituary 41-44R
Noverr, Douglas A(rthur) 1942- 102
Novick, David 1906- 33-36R
Novick, Julius Lerner 1939- 103
Novick, Marian 1951- 123
Novik, Mary 1945- 61-64
Novitski, Joseph (W. D.) 1940- 124
Novitz, Charles R. 1934- 69-72
Novo, Salvador 1904-1974 Obituary 110
Novoa, John David Bruce
See Bruce-Novoa, John David
Novoa, Juan Bruce
See Bruce-Novoa, John David
Novogrod, R(eevan) Joseph 1916- 29-32R
Novomesky, Ladislav 1904-1976
Obituary 69-72
Novotny, Ann M. 1936-1982 ....25-28R
Obituary 108
Novotny, Fritz 1903-19(?) CANR-18
Earlier sketch in CA 65-68
Novotny, Louise Miller 1889- CAP-2
Earlier sketch in CA 23-24
Novy, Marianne (Lucille) 1945- 118
Nowacki, Walenty 1906- 37-40R
Nowak, Mariette 1941- 102
Nowakowski, Marek 1935- 119
Nowell, Elizabeth Cameron CANR-1
Earlier sketch in CA 2R
See also SATA 12
Nowlan, Alden (Albert) 1933-1983 ...... CANR-5
Earlier sketch in CA 9-10R
See also DLB 53
See also CLC 15
Nowlan, James Dunlap 1941- Brief entry ... 105
Nowlan, Philip Francis 1888-1940
Brief entry 108
Nowlan, Robert Anthony, Jr. 1934- 113
Nowlis, Helen H(oward) 1913- Brief entry ... 111
Noxon, James Herbert 1924- 85-88
Noyce, Gaylord B. 1926- CANR-13
Earlier sketch in CA 37-40R
Noyes, Alfred 1880-1958 Brief entry 104
See also DLB 20
See also TCLC 7
Noyes, Charles Edmund 1904-1972 ......37-40R
Noyes, Crosby S. 1825-1908 .... DLB-23
Noyes, Crosby S(tuart) 1921-1988
Obituary 125
Noyes, David 1898(?)-1981 Obituary 104
Noyes, James H(oyt) 1927- 118
Noyes, Jeanice W. 1914- 25-28R
Noyes, Joan 1935- 115
Noyes, Kathryn Johnston 1930- 17-18R
Noyes, Morgan Phelps 1891-1972 .... CAP-1
Obituary 37-40R
Earlier sketch in CA 11-12
Noyes, Nell Braly 1921- 37-40R
Noyes, Nicholas 1647-1717 .... DLB-24
Noyes, Peter R. 1930- 49-52
Noyes, Russell 1901- 25-28R
Noyes, Stanley 1924- CANR-1
Earlier sketch in CA 45-48
Noyes, Theodore W. 1858-1946 .... DLB-29
Noyes-Kane, Dorothy 1906- CAP-1
Earlier sketch in CA 13-14
Noyle, Ken(neth Alfred Edward) 1922- 85-88
Nozick, Martin 1917- 37-40R
Nozick, Robert 1938- 61-64
Nsarkoh, J. K(wasi) 1931- 15-16R
Nucera, Marisa Lonette 1959- 17-18R
Nuchtern, Jean 1939- 25-28R
Nuckolls, James L(awton) 1938-1987
Obituary 123
Nudel, Adele Rice 1927- 124
Nudelman, Jerrold 1942- 33-36R
Nuechterlein, Donald Edwin 1925- CANR-1
Earlier sketch in CA 2R
Nuelle, Helen S(hearman) 1923- CANR-12
Earlier sketch in CA 61-64
Nuernberger, Phil 1942- 114
Nuessel, Frank H(enry) 1943- 111
Nuetzel, Charles (Alexander) 1934- 105
Nugent, Bruce
See Nugent, Richard Bruce
Nugent, Donald G(ene) 1930- 45-48
Nugent, Elliott (John) 1899-1980 ....5-6R
Obituary 101
Nugent, Frances Roberts 1904-1964(?) 5-6R
Nugent, Frank 1908-1965 .... DLB-44
Nugent, Jeffrey B(ishop) 1936- 93-96
Nugent, John Peer 1930- 15-16R
Nugent, Nancy 1938- CANR-16
Earlier sketch in CA 65-68
Nugent, Richard Bruce 1906(?)- 125
See also BW
See also DLB 51
Nugent, Robert 1920- 61-64
Nugent, Tom 1943- 49-52
Nugent, Vincent Joseph 1913- 41-44R
Nugent, Walter T(erry) K(ing) 1935- CANR-5
Earlier sketch in CA 7-8R
Null, Gary CANR-17
Earlier sketch in CA 65-68
Nulman, Macy 1923- 57-60
Numbers, Ronald L(eslie) 1942- CANR-18
Earlier sketch in CA 101
Numeroff, Laura Joffe 1953- 106
See also SATA 28
Nummi, Seppo (Antero Yrjoepoika)
1932-1981 Obituary 108
Nunan, Desmond J. 1927- 19-20R
Nunes, Claude 1924- Brief entry 112
Nunes, Rhoda (Gwylleth) 1938-
Brief entry 113
Nunez, Ana Rosa 1926- CANR-14
Earlier sketch in CA 69-72
Nunis, Doyce B(lackman), Jr. 1924- ... CANR-19
Earlier sketches in CA 5-6R, CANR-3
Nunley, Maggie Rennert
See Rennert, Maggie
Nunn, Frederick M. 1937- 33-36R
Nunn, G(odfrey) Raymond 1918- CANR-13
Earlier sketch in CA 33-36R
Nunn, Henry L(ightfoot) 1878-1972
Obituary 37-40R
Nunn, John 1955- 115
Nunn, Kem 19(?)- CLC-34
Nunn, Marshall E(arl) 1928- 112
Nunn, Walter (Harris) 1942- CANR-23
Earlier sketch in CA 45-48
Nunn, William Curtis 1908- CANR-1
Earlier sketch in CA 3R
Nunnerley, (Gould) David 1947- 45-48
Nuquist, Andrew E(dgerton) 1905-1975
Obituary 61-64
Nuraini
See Sim, Katharine (Thomasset)
Nurcombe, Barry 1933- 65-68
Nurenberg, Thelma
See Greenhaus, Thelma Nurenberg
Nurge, Ethel 1920- 33-36R

Nurmi, Martin Karl 1920- ... CANR-17
Earlier sketch in CA 2R
Nurnberg, Maxwell 1897-1984 ... CANR-2
Obituary ... 114
Earlier sketch in CA 7-8R
See also SATA 27, 41
Nurnberg, Walter 1907- ... 13-14R
Nurse, Malcolm Ivan Meredith 1903-1959
Brief entry ... 119
Nurse, Peter H(arold) 1926- ... 11-12R
Nusbaum, N. Richard
See Nash, N. Richard
Nusbaum, Rosemary 1907- ... 113
Nussbaum, Aaron 1910-1981 ... 49-52
Obituary ... 104
Nussbaum, Al(bert F.) 1934- ... 85-88
Nussbaumer, Paul (Edmund) 1934- ... 93-96
See also SATA 16
Nusser, J(ames) L(ivingston) 1925- ... 3R
Nutini, Hugo G(ino) 1928- Brief entry ... 109
Nutt, Grady 1934- ... 97-100
Nuttall, A(nthony) D(avid) 1937- ... CANR-11
Earlier sketch in CA 23-24R
Nuttall, Geoffrey Fillingham 1911- ... CANR-25
Earlier sketches in CA 15-16R, CANR-10
Nuttall, Jeff 1933- ... CANR-14
Earlier sketch in CA 29-32R
Nuttall, Kenneth 1907- ... 17-18R
Nuttall-Smith, Margaret Emily Noel 1919- ... 104
Nutter, G(ilbert) Warren 1923-1979 ... CANR-2
Obituary ... 85-88
Earlier sketch in CA 4R
Nutting, (Harold) Anthony 1920- ... CANR-7
Earlier sketch in CA 5-6R
Nutting, Willis D(wight) 1900-1975 ... CAP-2
Earlier sketch in CA 25-28
Nwankwo, Nkem 1936- ... 65-68
Nwoauau, Edwin Ifeanyichukwu 1933- ... 19-20R
Nyabongo, Akiki K. 1905-1975 Obituary ... 61-64
Nyad, Diana 1949- Brief entry ... 111
Nyanaponika 1901- ... CAP-1
Earlier sketch in CA 9-10
Nybakken, Elizabeth I. 1940- ... 114
Nybakken, Oscar Edward 1904- ... 93-96
Nyberg, David (Alan) 1943- ... 107
Nyberg, Kathleen Neill 1919- ... 21-22R
Nyce, (Nellie) Helene von Strecker
1885-1969 ... SATA-19
Nyce, Vera 1862-1925 ... SATA-19
Nye, Bill
See Nye, Edgar Wilson
See also DLB 11
Nye, Doug(las Charles) 1945- Brief entry ... 114
Nye, Edgar Wilson 1850-1896 ... DLB-23
Nye, F(rancis) Ivan 1918- ... CANR-21
Earlier sketches in CA 11-12R, CANR-6
Nye, Hermes 1908- ... CAP-2
Earlier sketch in CA 19-20
Nye, Joseph S(amuel), Jr. 1937- ... CANR-12
Earlier sketch in CA 25-28R
Nye, Loyal 1921- ... 106
Nye, Miriam (Maurine Hawthorn) Baker
1918- ... 85-88
Nye, Nelson C(oral) 1907- ... CANR-4
Earlier sketch in CA 7-8R
Nye, Robert 1939- ... 33-36R
See also SATA 6
See also DLB 14
See also CLC 13, 42
Nye, Robert D(onald) 1934- ... 73-76
Nye, Robert Evans 1911- ... CANR-1
Earlier sketch in CA 4R
Nye, Russel B(laine) 1913- ... CANR-4
Earlier sketch in CA 3R
Nye, Vernice Trousdale 1913- ... CANR-1
Earlier sketch in CA 4R
Nye, Wilbur S. 1898-1970 ... CANR-15
Obituary ... 103
Earlier sketch in CA 2R
Nyenhuis, Jacob E(ugene) 1935-
Brief entry ... 117
Nyerere, Julius K(ambarage) 1922- ... 125
Brief entry ... 105
See also BW
Nygaard, Anita 1934- ... 65-68
Nygaard, Norman E. 1897-1971 ... CANR-2
Earlier sketch in CA 3R
Nygard, Roald 1935- ... 103
Nygren, Anders T(heodor) S(amuel)
1890- ... 9-10R
Nykoruk, Barbara (Christine) 1949-
Brief entry ... 115
Nylander, Carl 1932- ... 33-36R
Nynych, Stephanie J.
See Caulder, Colline
Nyquist, Ewald B(erger) 1914- Brief entry ... 113
Nyquist, Thomas E. 1931- ... 41-44R
Nyren, Dorothy Elizabeth 1927- ... CANR-5
Earlier sketch in CA 2R
Nyren, Karl 1922(?)-1988 Obituary ... 126
Nyro, Laura 1947- ... CLC-17
Nystrom, Carolyn 1940- ... 114
Nzimiro, Ikenna 1927- ... CANR-2
Earlier sketch in CA 45-48

O

O(rdonez), Jaime E(dmundo) Rodriguez
See Rodriguez O(rdonez), Jaime E(dmundo)
Oak, Liston M. 1895-1970 Obituary ... 104
Oakes, James 1953- ... 107
Oakes, John Bertram 1913- ... 15-16R
Oakes, Philip (Barlow) 1928- ... CANR-4
Earlier sketch in CA 53-56
Oakes, Urian 1631(?)-1681 ... DLB-24
Oakes, Vanya 1909-1983 ... 33-36R
Obituary ... 111
See also SATA 6, 37
Oakeshott, Michael (Joseph) 1901- ... 4R
Oakeshott, Walter (Fraser) 1903-1987 ... 13-14R
Obituary ... 123
Oakie, Jack
See Offield, Lewis Delaney
Oakland, Thomas David 1939- ... 53-56
Oakley, Allen 1943- ... 126
Oakley, Ann (Rosamund) 1944- ... CANR-25
Earlier sketches in CA 57-60, CANR-6
Oakley, Barry K(ingham) 1931- ... 104
Oakley, Charles Allen 1900- ... 108
Oakley, Don(ald G.) 1927- ... 29-32R
See also SATA 8
Oakley, Eric Gilbert 1916- ... 9-10R
Oakley, Francis (Christopher) 1931- ... 15-16R
Oakley, Giles (Francis) 1946- ... 103
Oakley, Graham 1929- ... 106
See also SATA 30
See also CLR 7
Oakley, Helen (McKelvey) 1906- ... 17-18R
See also SATA 10
Oakley, J. Ronald 1941- ... 121
Oakley, Josephine 1903(?)-1978
Obituary ... 81-84
Oakley, K. P.
See Oakley, Kenneth Page
Oakley, Kenneth P.
See Oakley, Kenneth Page
Oakley, Kenneth Page 1911-1981 ... 122
Obituary ... 108
Oakley, Mary Ann B. 1940- ... 45-48
Oakley, Stewart P(hilip) 1931- ... 21-22R
Oakman, Barbara F(rances) 1931- ... 57-60
Oaks, Dallin H(arris) 1932- ... 25-28R
Oaksey, John 1929- ... 105
Oana, Katherine 1929- ... 108
See also SATA 37, 53
Oates, Jeannette 1912(?)-1984 Obituary ... 112
Oates, John (Frederick) 1944- ... 69-72
Oates, John F. 1934- ... 19-20R
Oates, Joyce Carol 1938- ... CANR-25
Earlier sketch in CA 7-8R
See also DLB 2, 5
See also DLBY 81
See also CLC 1, 2, 3, 6, 9, 11, 15, 19, 33
See also AITN 1
Oates, Stephen B. 1936- ... CANR-26
Earlier sketches in CA 11-12R, CANR-4
Oates, Wallace Eugene 1937- ... CANR-14
Earlier sketch in CA 37-40R
Oates, Wayne Edward 1917- ... 85-88
Oates, Whitney J(ennings) 1904-1973 ... CANR-3
Obituary ... 45-48
Earlier sketch in CA 5-6R
Oathout, John D(avid) 1913- ... 111
Oatley, Keith 1939- ... 45-48
Oatman, Eric F(urber) 1939- ... CANR-19
Earlier sketch in CA 103
Oatts, Balfour
See Oatts, Lewis Balfour
Oatts, Henry Augustus 1898-1980 ... 7-8R
Obituary ... 103
Oatts, Lewis Balfour 1902- ... 110
Obach, Robert 1939- ... 106
Obaldia, Rene de 1918- Brief entry ... 116
O'Ballance, Edgar 1918- ... CANR-7
Earlier sketch in CA 7-8R
O'Banion, Terry 1936- ... 33-36R
O'Barr, William M(cAlston) 1942- ... 49-52
O'Beirne, T(homas) H(ay) 1915-1982 ... 17-18R
Obituary ... 120
Obele, Norma Taylor 1933- ... 104
Obenchain, Anne DeCroes 1914(?)-1984
Obituary ... 112
Obenhaus, Victor 1903- ... CAP-1
Earlier sketch in CA 13-14
Ober, Stuart Alan 1946- ... 103
Ober, Warren U(pton) 1925- ... 15-16R
Oberdorf, Charles (Donnell) 1941- ... 126
Oberg, Arthur K. 1938-1977 Obituary ... 112
Oberg, James E(dward) 1944- ... CANR-26
Earlier sketch in CA 108
Oberhansli, Trudi
See Schlapbach-Oberhansli, Trudi
Oberhelman, Harley D(ean) 1928- ... 53-56
Oberholtzer, Ellis Paxton 1868-1936 ... DLB-47
Oberholtzer, Peter
See Brannon, William T.
Oberholtzer, W(alter) Dwight 1939- ... 101
Oberholzer, Emil, Jr. 1926(?)-1981
Obituary ... 102
Oberman, Heiko Augustinus 1930- ... CANR-25
Earlier sketches in CA 5-6R, CANR-7
Obermann, C. Esco 1904- ... 53-56
Obermayer, Herman J. 1924- ... 65-68
Obermeyer, Barrett John 1937- ... 5-6R
Obermeyer, Henry 1899- ... CAP-2
Earlier sketch in CA 29-32
Obermeyer, Marion Barrett ... 7-8R
Oberschall, Antony R. 1936- ... 97-100
Obert, John C. 1924-1987 Obituary ... 122
Oberth, Hermann Julius 1894-1979(?)
Obituary ... 113
Obey, Andre 1892-1975 ... 97-100
Obituary ... 57-60
Obichere, Boniface Ihewunwa 1932- ... 41-44R
Obiechina, Emmanuel Nwanonye
1933- ... CANR-15
Earlier sketch in CA 41-44R
Obligado, Lilian (Isabel) 1931- ... SATA-45
Oboe, Peter
See Jacobs, Walter Darnell
Obojski, Robert 1929- ... CANR-24
Earlier sketch in CA 108
Obolensky, Dimitri 1918- ... CANR-25
Earlier sketch in CA 45-48
Oboler, Arch 1909(?)-1987 Obituary ... 122
Brief entry ... 105
Oboler, Eli M(artin) 1915-1983 ... CANR-6
Obituary ... 110
Earlier sketch in CA 57-60
Obourn, Ellsworth Scott 1897- ... CAP-2
Earlier sketch in CA 17-18
O'Brady, Frederic Michel Maurice
1903- ... CANR-3
Earlier sketch in CA 9-10R
Obrant, Susan 1946- ... SATA-11
O'Brawes, Tarnel
See La Barre, Weston
Obregon, Mauricio 1921- ... CANR-1
Earlier sketch in CA 45-48
O'Brian, Frank
See Garfield, Brian (Wynne)
O'Brian, Jack 1921- ... 103
O'Brian, John Lord 1874-1973 Obituary ... 41-44R
O'Briant, Walter H(erbert) 1937- ... 25-28R
O'Brien, Andrew William 1910- ... CANR-17
Earlier sketch in CA 25-28R
O'Brien, Andy
See O'Brien, Andrew William
O'Brien, Anne Sibley 1952- ... 122
See also SATA 48, 53
O'Brien, Conor Cruise 1917- ... 65-68
O'Brien, Cyril C(ornelius) 1906- ... 53-56
O'Brien, Darcy 1939- ... CANR-8
Earlier sketch in CA 21-22R
O'Brien, David J(oseph) 1938- ... 25-28R
O'Brien, Dean D.
See Binder, Otto, O(scar)
O'Brien, Dee
See Bradley, Marion Zimmer
O'Brien, Des(mond John) 1930- ... 114
O'Brien, E. G.
See Clarke, Arthur C(harles)
O'Brien, Edna 1936- ... CANR-6
Earlier sketch in CA 3R
See also DLB 14
See also CLC 3, 5, 8, 13, 36
O'Brien, Edward C.
See Schrodt, Philip A(ndrew)
O'Brien, Elmer 1911- ... 19-20R
O'Brien, Esse Forrester 1895(?)-1975
Obituary ... 61-64
See also SATA 30
O'Brien, Fitz-James 1828-1862 ... DLB-74
O'Brien, Flann
See O Nuallain, Brian
See also CLC 1, 4, 5, 7, 10, 47
O'Brien, Frances (Kelly) 1906- ... CAP-2
Earlier sketch in CA 17-18
O'Brien, Francis J(oseph) 1903- ... 81-84
O'Brien, Geoffrey 1948- ... 106
O'Brien, George Dennis 1931- ... 103
O'Brien, Gregory (C., Jr.) 1945- ... 117
O'Brien, J(ohn) W(ilfrid) 1931- ... 15-16R
O'Brien, Jacqueline Robin 1949- ... 105
O'Brien, James A(loysius) 1936-
Brief entry ... 110
O'Brien, James J. 1929- ... CANR-9
Earlier sketch in CA 17-18R
O'Brien, John Anthony 1893-1980 ... CANR-1
Obituary ... 97-100
Earlier sketch in CA 4R
O'Brien, John J(oseph) 1937- ... 111
O'Brien, Justin (McCortney) 1906-1968 ... CANR-5
Earlier sketch in CA 5-6R
O'Brien, K.
See O'Brien, Katherine
O'Brien, Kate 1897-1974 ... 93-96
Obituary ... 53-56
See also DLB 15
O'Brien, Katherine 1915-1982 Obituary ... 118
O'Brien, Kevin P. 1922- ... 53-56
O'Brien, Lawrence Francis 1917- ... 57-60
O'Brien, Lee 1948- ... 61-64
O'Brien, Marian P(lowman) 1915- ... 53-56
O'Brien, Michael 1943- ... 126
O'Brien, Michael 1948- ... 121
O'Brien, Michael J. 1920- ... 25-28R
O'Brien, (William Joseph) Pat(rick)
1899-1983 Obituary ... 111
O'Brien, Patrick 1932- ... 23-24R
O'Brien, Richard 1934- ... 73-76
O'Brien, Richard 1942- ... 124
See also CLC 17
O'Brien, Robert C.
See Conly, Robert Leslie
See also CLR 2
O'Brien, Robert W(illiam) 1907- ... CANR-25
Earlier sketch in CA 45-48
O'Brien, Saliee
See Janas, Frankie-Lee
O'Brien, Sister Mary Celine 1922- ... 21-22R
O'Brien, Thomas C(lement) 1938- ... 106
See also SATA 29
O'Brien, Tim 1946- ... 85-88
See also DLBY 80
See also CLC 7, 19, 40
O'Brien, Vincent 1916- ... 9-10R
O'Brien, William V(incent) 1923- ... 15-16R
O'Broin, Leon 1902- ... CANR-8
Earlier sketch in CA 61-64
O'Brynt, Jon
See Barnum, W(illiam) Paul
Observer
See Velikovsky, Immanuel
Obst, Frances Melanie ... 19-20R
Obstfeld, Raymond 1952- ... 116
Obstfelder, Sigbjoern 1866-1900
Brief entry ... 123
See also TCLC 23
O'Callaghan, Denis F(rancis) 1931- ... 17-18R
O'Callaghan, Joseph F(rancis) 1928- ... 81-84
O'Callaghan, Julie 1954- ... 117
Ocampo, Victoria 1891-1979 ... 105
Obituary ... 85-88
O'Carroll, Ryan
See Markun, Patricia Maloney
O'Casey, Eileen (Reynolds) 1904(?)-
Brief entry ... 112
O'Casey, Sean 1880-1964 ... 89-92
See also DLB 10
See also CLC 1, 5, 9, 11, 15
O'Cathasaigh, Donal
See Casey, Daniel J(oseph)
O'Cathasaigh, Sean
See O'Casey, Sean
Occomy, Marita Bonner 1899-1971 ... DLB-51
Ocean, Julian
See de Mesne, Eugene (Frederick Peter Cheshire)
O Ceithearnaigh, Seumas
See Carney, James (Patrick)
Ochester, Ed(win Frank) 1939- ... CANR-25
Earlier sketch in CA 45-48
Ochiltree, Thomas H 1912- ... 77-80
Ochojski, Paul M(aximilian)
1916-1983 ... CANR-20
Earlier sketch in CA 25-28R
Ochorowicz, Julian 1850-1917 Brief entry ... 114
Ochs, Adolph S(imon) 1858-1935
Brief entry ... 118
See also DLB 25
Ochs, Carol (Rebecca) 1939- ... 114
Ochs, Donovan J(oseph) 1938- ... 45-48
Ochs, Michael 1943- ... 119
Ochs, Phil 1940-1976 Obituary ... 65-68
See also CLC 17
Ochs, Robert J. 1930- ... 29-32R
Ochse, Orpha Caroline 1925- ... 93-96
Ochsenschlager, Edward L(loyd) 1932- ... 19-20R
Ochsner, (Edward William) Alton
1896-1981 ... 17-18R
Obituary ... 105
Ochsner, Jeffrey Karl 1950- ... 111
Ockenga, Harold John 1905-1985 ... CANR-1
Obituary ... 115
Earlier sketch in CA 4R
O'Clair, Robert M. 1923- ... 77-80
O'Clery, Helen (Gallagher) 1910- ... 11-12R
O'Collins, Gerald Glynn 1931- ... CANR-15
Earlier sketch in CA 85-88
O'Connell, Brian (Vincent) J(ohn) 1923-
Brief entry ... 113
O'Connell, Daniel Patrick 1924-1979 ... CANR-25
Obituary ... 89-92
Earlier sketch in CA 29-32R
O'Connell, David 1940- ... 102
O'Connell, Frank 1892- ... 5-6R
O'Connell, Jeffrey 1928- ... CANR-11
Earlier sketch in CA 25-28R
O'Connell, Jeremiah Joseph 1932- ... CANR-7
Earlier sketch in CA 13-14R
O'Connell, John James III 1921-1982
Obituary ... 107
O'Connell, Margaret F(orster) 1935-1977 ... 73-76
See also SATA 30, 49
O'Connell, Marvin R(ichard) 1930-
Brief entry ... 111
O'Connell, Maurice R. 1922- ... 17-18R
O'Connell, Michael (William) 1943- ... 101
O'Connell, Peg
See Ahern, Margaret McCrohan
O'Connell, Richard L(eo), Jr.
1912-1975 ... 41-44R
O'Connell, Timothy E(dward) 1943- ... CANR-12
Earlier sketch in CA 73-76
O'Connell, Walter E(dward) 1925- ... 41-44R
O'Conner, R(ay) L. 1928- ... 17-18R
O'Connor, A(nthony) M(ichael) 1939- ... CANR-11
Earlier sketch in CA 21-22R
O'Connor, Anthony ?-1983(?) Obituary ... 109
O'Connor, Clint
See Paine, Lauran (Bosworth)
O'Connor, Daniel William 1925- ... 33-36R
O'Connor, David 1949- ... 110
O'Connor, Dick 1930- ... 97-100
O'Connor, Edward Dennis 1922- ... 41-44R
O'Connor, Edwin (Greene) 1918-1968 ... 93-96
Obituary ... 25-28R
See also CLC 14
O'Connor, Egan 1937- ... 119
O'Connor, Elizabeth Anita 1921- ... 25-28R
O'Connor, (Mary) Flannery 1925-1964 ... CANR-3
Earlier sketch in CA 1R
See also DLB 2
See also DLBY 80
See also CDALB 1941-1968
See also CLC 1, 2, 3, 6, 10, 13, 15, 21
See also SSC 1
O'Connor, Francine M(arie) 1930- ... 111
O'Connor, Francis V(alentine) 1937- ... CANR-13
Earlier sketch in CA 21-22R
O'Connor, Frank
See O'Donovan, Michael John
See also CLC 23
O'Connor, Garry 1938- ... CANR-20
Earlier sketch in CA 89-92
O'Connor, Harvey 1897-1987 ... 7-8R
Obituary ... 123
O'Connor, Jack
See O'Connor, John Woolf
O'Connor, James I(gnatius) 1910-1988 ... CAP-1
Obituary ... 126
Earlier sketch in CA 15-16

O'Connor, Jane 1947- 124
See also SATA 47
O'Connor, John (Morris) 1937- 29-32R
O'Connor, John E. 1943- Brief entry 109
O'Connor, John J(oseph) 1918- 73-76
O'Connor, John Joseph 1904-1978
Obituary 77-80
O'Connor, John P. 1892-1986 Obituary 119
O'Connor, John Woolf 1902-1978 CANR-3
Obituary 77-80
Earlier sketch in CA 7-8R
O'Connor, June (Elizabeth) 1941- 114
O'Connor, Karen 1938- 89-92
See also SATA 34
O'Connor, Liam
See Liddy, James (Daniel Reeves)
O'Connor, Lillian M. 1894(?)-1987
Obituary 122
O'Connor, M.
See O'Connor, Michael Patrick
O'Connor, Mark 1945- CANR-11
Earlier sketch in CA 65-68
O'Connor, Michael Patrick 1950- 113
O'Connor, Patricia Walker 1931- CANR-17
Earlier sketch in CA 37-40R
O'Connor, Patrick 77-80
O'Connor, Patrick
See Wibberley, Leonard (Patrick O'Connor)
O'Connor, Patrick J(oseph) 1947- 113
O'Connor, Patrick Joseph 1924- 53-56
O'Connor, Philip F(rancis) 1932- 33-36R
O'Connor, Philip Marie Constant Bancroft
1916- 11-12R
O'Connor, Raymond G(ish) 1915- CANR-4
Earlier sketch in CA 7-8R
O'Connor, Richard 1915-1975 61-64
Obituary 57-60
See also SATA 21
O'Connor, Rory 1951- 109
O'Connor, Sister Mary Catharine CAP-2
Earlier sketch in CA 17-18
O'Connor, Thomas Henry 1922- 33-36R
O'Connor, Ulick 1928- CANR-4
Earlier sketch in CA 11-12R
O'Connor, William E(dmund) 1922- 37-40R
O'Connor, William P., Jr. 1916- 11-12R
O'Connor, William Van 1915-1966 CANR-1
Obituary 25-28R
Earlier sketch in CA 1R
O'Connor Howe, Josephine (Mary) 1924- 119
O'Conor, John F(rancis) 1918- 33-36R
October, John
See Portway, Christopher (John)
Octopus
See Drachman, Julian M(oses)
Ocvirk, Otto G(eorge) 1922- 61-64
Odaga, Asenath (Bole) 1937- 124
See also BW
Odahl, Charles Matson 1944- 37-40R
Odajnyk, Walter 1938- 15-16R
O Danachair, Caoimhin
See Danaher, Kevin
O'Daniel, Janet 1921- 29-32R
See also SATA 24
O'Daniel, Therman B(enjamin) 1908- 45-48
See also BW
O'Day, Cathy
See Crane, Barbara (Joyce)
O'Day, Edward Francis 1925- 29-32R
O'Day, Rey 1947- 105
Odd, Gilbert E(dward) 1902- 110
Oddo, Gilbert L. 1922- CANR-1
Earlier sketch in CA 1R
Oddo, Sandra (Schmidt) 1937- 65-68
O'Dea, Agnes C. 1911- 124
O'Dea, Thomas F(rancis) 1915-1974 CAP-2
Obituary 53-56
Earlier sketch in CA 23-24
Odegaard, Charles Edwin 1911-
Brief entry 106
Odegard, Douglas Andrew 1935- 108
Odegard, Holtan Peter 1923- 61-64
O'Dell, Andrew C(harles) 1909-1966 CAP-1
Earlier sketch in CA 15-16
Odell, Gill
See Gill, Traviss
Odell, Jonathan 1737-1818 DLB-31
Odell, Ling Chung 1945- 45-48
O'Dell, M(ary) E(lise) 11-12R
Odell, Peter R(andon) 1930- 97-100
Odell, Rice 1928- 77-80
Odell, Robin 1935- CANR-12
Earlier sketch in CA 73-76
O'Dell, Scott 1903- CANR-12
Earlier sketch in CA 61-64
See also SATA 12
See also DLB 52
See also CLC 30
See also CLR 1, 16
O'Dell, William F(rancis) 1909- CANR-12
Earlier sketch in CA 25-28R
Odem, J.
See Rubin, Jacob A.
Oden, Clifford 1916- 65-68
Oden, Gloria (Catherine) 1923- CANR-25
Earlier sketch in CA 108
Oden, Marilyn Brown 1937- 33-36R
Oden, Thomas C(lark) 1931- CANR-19
Earlier sketches in CA 11-12R, CANR-5
Oden, William E(ugene) 1923- 37-40R
Odenwald, Robert P(aul) 1899-1965 2R
See also SATA 11
Odescalchi, Esther Kando 1938- 69-72
Odets, Clifford 1906-1963 85-88
See also DLB 7, 26
See also CLC 2, 28
Odgers, Merle Middleton 1900-1983
Obituary 110
Odier, Daniel 1945- 29-32R
Odiorne, George Stanley 1920- CANR-1
Earlier sketch in CA 1R
Odishaw, Hugh 1916-1984 Obituary 112
Odle, Joe T(aft) 1908-1980 33-36R
Obituary 97-100
Odling-Smee, John (Charles) 1943- 112
Odlum, Doris Maude 1890-1985 CAP-1
Obituary 118
Earlier sketch in CA 13-14
O'Doherty, Brian 1934- 105
O'Doherty, E(amonn) F(elchin) 1918- 37-40R
O'Doire, Annraoi
See Beechhold, Henry F(rank)
Odom, William E(ldridge) 1932- 73-76
O'Donnell, Bernard 1929- 41-44R
O'Donnell, Cyril 1900- CAP-1
Earlier sketch in CA 11-12
O'Donnell, Dick
See Lupoff, Richard A(llen)
and Thompson, Don(ald Arthur)
O'Donnell, Donat
See O'Brien, Conor C(ruise)
O'Donnell, Elliott 1872-1965 CAP-1
Earlier sketch in CA 15-16
O'Donnell, Francis ?-1984 Obituary 114
O'Donnell, Harry J(ames) 1914-1985
Obituary 117
O'Donnell, James H(owlett) III 1937- 45-48
O'Donnell, James J(oseph, Jr.) 1950- CANR-16
Earlier sketch in CA 89-92
O'Donnell, James Kevin 1951- CANR-6
Earlier sketch in CA 57-60
O'Donnell, Jim
See O'Donnell, James Kevin
O'Donnell, John A. 1916- 19-20R
O'Donnell, John P. 1923- 19-20R
O'Donnell, K. M.
See Malzberg, Barry N(athaniel)
O'Donnell, (Philip) Kenneth 1924-1977 81-84
Obituary 73-76
O'Donnell, Kenneth P.
See O'Donnell, (Philip) Kenneth
O'Donnell, Kevin, Jr. 1950- CANR-23
Earlier sketch in CA 106
O'Donnell, Lawrence
See Kuttner, Henry
and Moore, C(atherine) L(ucile)
O'Donnell, Lawrence F(rancis), Jr. 1951- 117
O'Donnell, Lillian Udvardy 1926- CANR-18
Earlier sketches in CA 7-8R, CANR-3
O'Donnell, Margaret Jane 1899- 7-8R
O'Donnell, Mark 1954- CANR-21
Earlier sketch in CA 104
O'Donnell, Patrick (James) 1948- 114
O'Donnell, Peadar 1893-1986 Obituary 119
O'Donnell, Peter 1920- 117
Brief entry 114
O'Donnell, Red
See O'Donnell, Francis
O'Donnell, Thomas Francis 1915- CANR-1
Earlier sketch in CA 1R
O'Donnell, Thomas J(oseph) 1918- 65-68
O'Donnevan, Finn
See Sheckley, Robert
O'Donoghue, Bryan 1921- 77-80
O'Donoghue, Gregory 1951- 114
Brief entry 109
O'Donoghue, Joseph 1931- 23-24R
O'Donovan, John 1921- CANR-11
Earlier sketch in CA 25-28R
O'Donovan, Katherine 1942- 123
O'Donovan, Michael John 1903-1966 93-96
See also CLC 14
Odor, Ruth Shannon 1926- 120
See also SATA 44
O'Dowd, Liam 1947- 116
O'Driscoll, Robert 1938- 53-56
O'Dwyer, James F. 1939- 33-36R
O'Dwyer, Paul 1907- 97-100
Odysseus
See Johnson, Donald McI(ntosh)
Oe, Kenzaburo 1935- 97-100
See also CLC 10, 36
Oechsli, Kelly 1918- CANR-16
Earlier sketch in CA 97-100
See also SATA 5
Oehmke, T(homas) H(arold) 1947- CANR-11
Earlier sketch in CA 65-68
Oehser, Paul H(enry) 1904- CANR-12
Earlier sketch in CA 29-32R
Oeksenholt, Svein 1925- Brief entry 106
Oenslager, Donald (Mitchell) 1902-1975 61-64
Obituary 57-60
Oepik, Ernst Julius 1893-1985 Obituary 118
Oerkeny, Istvan
See Orkeny, Istvan
Oerum, Poul (Erik) 1919- CANR-13
Earlier sketch in CA 65-68
Oesterle, John A(rthur) 1912- 5-6R
Oesterreicher, John M(aria) 1904- CANR-26
Earlier sketch in CA 29-32R
Oettinger, Anthony Gervin 1929- 1R
Oettinger, Elmer R(osenthal, Jr.) 1913- 29-32R
O'Faolain, Julia 1932- CANR-12
Earlier sketch in CA 81-84
See also CAAS 2
See also DLB 14
See also CLC 6, 19, 47
O'Faolain, Sean 1900- CANR-12
Earlier sketch in CA 61-64
See also DLB 15
See also CLC 1, 7, 14, 32
Ofari, Earl 1945- 41-44R
O'Farrell, Patrick (James) 1933- CANR-20
Earlier sketch in CA 103
Ofek, Uriel 1926- CANR-18
Earlier sketch in CA 101
See also SATA 36
Offen, Karen Marie Stedtfeld 1939- 113
Offen, Neil 1946- 49-52
Offen, Ron 1930- 45-48
Offer, Daniel 1930- CANR-11
Earlier sketch in CA 21-22R
Offerle, Mildred 1912- 77-80
Offield, Lewis Delaney 1903-1978
Obituary 111
Offiong, Daniel A(sukwo) 1942- 118
Offit, Avodah K(omito) 1931- CANR-13
Earlier sketch in CA 77-80
Offit, Sidney 1928- CANR-1
Earlier sketch in CA 4R
See also SATA 10
Offner, Arnold A. 1937- 25-28R
Offner, Eric D(elmonte) 1928- CANR-9
Earlier sketch in CA 19-20R
Offord, Carl Ruthven 1910- DLB-76
Offord, Lenore Glen 1905- 77-80
Offutt, Andrew J(efferson V) 1934(?)- CANR-15
Earlier sketch in CA 41-44R
O Fiaich, Tomas 1923- 103
O'Finn, Thaddeus
See McGloin, Joseph T(haddeus)
O'Flaherty, James C(arneal) 1914- 21-22R
O'Flaherty, Liam 1896-1984 101
Obituary 113
See also DLB 36
See also DLBY 84
See also CLC 5, 34
O'Flaherty, Louise 1920- CANR-6
Earlier sketch in CA 57-60
O'Flaherty, Terrence 1917- 73-76
O'Flaherty, Wendy Doniger 1940- CANR-23
Earlier sketch in CA 65-68
O'Flinn, Peter
See Fanthorpe, R(obert) Lionel
O'Flynn, Peter
See Fanthorpe, R(obert) Lionel
Ofomata, G(odfrey) E(zediaso) K(ingsley)
1936- 93-96
Ofosu-Appiah, L(awrence) H(enry)
1920- 33-36R
See also SATA 13
Ofshe, Richard 1941- 89-92
Og, Liam
See O'Neill, William
O'Gallagher, Liam 1917- 45-48
Ogan, George F. 1912- CANR-4
Earlier sketch in CA 9-10R
See also SATA 13
Ogan, M. G.
See Ogan, George F.
and Ogan, Margaret E. (Nettles)
Ogan, Margaret E. (Nettles) 1923-1979 CANR-4
Earlier sketch in CA 11-12R
See also SATA 13
O'Gara, James Vincent, Jr. 1918-1979 69-72
Obituary 85-88
Ogata, Sadako (Nakamura) 1927- CANR-9
Earlier sketch in CA 19-20R
Ogawa, Dennis Masaaki 1943- 37-40R
Ogawa, Tetsuro 1912-1978 41-44R
Ogbu, John U(zor) 1939- 93-96
Ogburn, Charlton (Jr.) 1911- CANR-3
Earlier sketch in CA 5-6R
See also SATA 3
Ogburn, W. F.
See Ogburn, William Fielding
Ogburn, William F.
See Ogburn, William Fielding
Ogburn, William Fielding 1886-1959
Brief entry 122
Ogden, Daniel M(iller), Jr. 1922- 11-12R
Ogden, Dunbar H. 53-56
Ogden, Gina 1935- 81-84
Ogden, Margaret Sinclair 1909-
Brief entry 107
Ogden, (John) Michael (Hubert) 1923- 13-14R
Ogden, Samuel R(obinson) 1896- 29-32R
Ogden, Schubert Miles 1928- CANR-21
Earlier sketch in CA 104
Ogg, Oscar (John) 1908-1971 CAP-1
Obituary 33-36R
Earlier sketch in CA 11-12
Ogilvie, Elisabeth May 1917- CANR-19
Earlier sketch in CA 103
See also SATA 29, 40
Ogilvie, Gordon (Bryant) 1934- CANR-8
Earlier sketch in CA 61-64
Ogilvie, Lloyd John 1930- 73-76
Ogilvie, Mardel 1910- 1R
Ogilvie, Robert Maxwell 1932-1981 CANR-6
Obituary 105
Earlier sketch in CA 15-16R
Ogilvy, C(harles) Stanley 1913- CANR-4
Earlier sketch in CA 5-6R
Ogilvy, David Mackenzie 1911- Brief entry 105
Ogilvy, Stewart Marks 1914-1985(?)
Obituary 118
Oglanby, Elva
See Clairmont, Elva
Ogle, James Lawrence 1911- 7-8R
Ogle, Jim
See Ogle, James Lawrence
Ogle, Robert 1926(?)-1984 Obituary 112
Oglesby, Joseph 1931- CANR-17
Earlier sketch in CA 97-100
Oglesby, Richard E(dward) 1931- CANR-6
Earlier sketch in CA 11-12R
Oglesby, William B(arr), Jr. 1916- 25-28R
Ogletree, Earl Joseph 1930- CANR-10
Earlier sketch in CA 65-68
Ogletree, Thomas W(arren) 1933- 19-20R
Ognall, Leopold Horace 1908-1979 CANR-12
Earlier sketch in CA 9-10R
Ognibene, Peter J(ohn) 1941- 110
O'Gorman, Edward Charles 1929- 81-84
O'Gorman, Frank 1940- 61-64
O'Gorman, Gerald 1916- 21-22R
O'Gorman, James F(rancis) 1933- 53-56
O'Gorman, John
See MacGill, Patrick
O'Gorman, Ned
See O'Gorman, Edward Charles
O'Gorman, Richard F. 1928- 37-40R
O'Gorman, Samuel F.
See Cusack, Michael J.
O'Grada, Sean
See O'Grady, John (Patrick)
O'Grady, Anne 53-56
O'Grady, Desmond (James Bernard)
1935- CANR-14
Earlier sketch in CA 25-28R
See also DLB 40
O'Grady, Francis Dominic 1909- CAP-1
Earlier sketch in CA 9-10
O'Grady, Frank
See O'Grady, Francis Dominic
O'Grady, John (Patrick) 1907- 104
O'Grady, John F(rancis) 1939- 93-96
O'Grady, Joseph P(atrick) 1934- 41-44R
O'Grady, Rohan
See Skinner, June O'Grady
O'Grady, Ron 1930- 114
O'Grady, Standish James 1846-1928
Brief entry 104
See also TCLC 5
Ogram, Ernest W(illiam), Jr. 1928- 57-60
O'Green, Jennifer
See Roberson, Jennifer
Ogul, Morris S(amuel) 1931- 15-16R
Oh, John Kie-chiang 1930- 29-32R
O'Hagan, Caroline 1946- 111
See also SATA 38
O'Hagan, Howard 1902-1982 3R
See also DLB 68
O'Hair, Madalyn (Mays) Murray 1919- CANR-12
Earlier sketch in CA 61-64
O'Hanlon, Daniel John 1919- 61-64
O'Hanlon, Jacklyn
See Meek, Jacklyn O'Hanlon
O'Hanlon, Redmond (Douglas) 1947- 123
O'Hanlon, Thomas J(oseph) 1933- 61-64
O'Hara, Charles E. 1912-1984 29-32R
Obituary 125
O'Hara, Dale
See Gillese, John Patrick
O'Hara, Frank 1926-1966 9-10R
Obituary 25-28R
See also DLB 5, 16
See also CLC 2, 5, 13
O'Hara, Frederic James 1917- 103
O'Hara, Georgina 1956- 126
O'Hara, John (Henry) 1905-1970 5-6R
Obituary 25-28R
See also DLB 9
See also DLBD 2
See also CLC 1, 2, 3, 6, 11, 42
O'Hara, Kenneth
See Morris, (Margaret) Jean
O'Hara, Kevin
See Cumberland, Marten
O'Hara, Mary
See Alsop, Mary O'Hara
Ohashi, Wataru 1944- 73-76
O'Hayre, John 1923-1986 Obituary 121
O'hearn, Peter J(oseph) T(homas)
1917- 17-18R
O'Heffernan, Patrick 1944- 117
O Hehir, Diana 1922- 93-96
See also CLC 41
O'Higgins, Donal Peter 1922-1984 77-80
Obituary 112
Ohira, Masayoshi 1910-1980 Obituary 105
Ohkawa, Kazushi 1908- 85-88
Ohl, (Mary) Suzanne Sickler 1923- 69-72
Ohles, John Ford 1920- 57-60
Ohlig, Karl-Heinz 1938- CANR-13
Earlier sketch in CA 69-72
Ohlin, Bertil 1899(?)-1979 Obituary 89-92
Ohlin, Lloyd E(dgar) 1918- 104
Ohlinger, Gustavus 1877-1972 Obituary 37-40R
Ohlsen, Merle M(arvel) 1914- CANR-15
Earlier sketch in CA 37-40R
Ohlsson, Ib 1935- SATA-7
Ohman, Jack 1960- 110
Brief entry 108
Ohmann, Richard (Malin) 1931- 15-16R
Ohmer, Merlin M(aurice) 1923- 57-60
Ohon
See Barba, Harry
Ohsberg, H(arry) Oliver 1926- 114
Ohtomo, Yasuo 1946- SATA-37
Oinas, Felix J(ohannes) 1911- CANR-13
Earlier sketch in CA 33-36R
Ojany, Francis Frederick 1935- 77-80
Ojo, G. J. Afolabi 1930- 25-28R
Okamoto, Shumpei 1932- 29-32R
Okara, Gabriel Imomotimi Gbaingbain
1921- 105
See also BW
Okasha, Elisabeth 1942- 45-48
Oke, Janette 1935- 111
O'Keefe, Bernard J(oseph) 1919- 120
O'Keefe, Daniel Lawrence 1928-
Brief entry 116
O'Keefe, M(aurice) Timothy 1943- 77-80

INDEX

O'Keefe, Patrick E.
See Grace, John Patrick
O'Keefe, Paul 1900(?)-1976 Obituary 65-68
O'Keefe, Richard R(obert) 1934- 57-60
O'Keefe, Sister Maureen 1917- 5-6R
O'Keeffe, Georgia 1887-1986 110
Obituary 118
O'Keeffe, Laurence 1931- 122
Okeke, Uchefuna 1933- 97-100
O'Kelley, Mattie Lou 1908- 116
See also SATA 36
O'Kelly, Charlotte G. 1946- 111
O'Kelly, Elizabeth 1915- CANR-20
Earlier sketch in CA 103
Oken, Alan C(harles) 1944- 45-48
O'Key
See Radwanski, Pierre A(rthur)
Okigbo, Christopher (Ifenayichukwu)
1932-1967 77-80
See also BW
See also CLC 25
Okigbo, P(ius) N(wabufo) C. 1924- 19-20R
Okihiro, Gary Y(ukio) 1945- 120
Okimoto, Jean Davies 1942- CANR-16
Earlier sketch in CA 97-100
See also SATA 34
Okin, Susan Moller 1946- 93-96
Oklahoma Peddler
See Gilles, Albert S(imeon), Sr.
Okner, Benjamin A. 1936- 21-22R
Okonjo, Chukuka 1928- 29-32R
Okpaku, Joseph (Ohiomogben) 1943- 29-32R
See also BW
Okpewho, Isidore 1941- CANR-3
Earlier sketch in CA 49-52
Okrent, Daniel 1948- CANR-22
Earlier sketch in CA 105
Oksenberg, Michel Charles 1938- 111
Oksenholt, Svein
See Oeksenholt, Svein
Okubo, Genji 1915- 25-28R
Okudzhava, Bulat Shalvovich 1924-
Brief entry 116
Okun, Arthur M. 1928-1980 ..... CANR-11
Obituary 97-100
Earlier sketch in CA 61-64
Okun, Lawrence E(ugene) 1929- 101
Olafson, Frederick A(rlan) 1924- 17-18R
Olan, Ben 1923- 111
Olan, Levi Arthur 1903- 109
O'Laoghaire, Liam
See O'Leary, Liam
Olbricht, Thomas H. 1929- 33-36R
Olby, Robert C(ecil) 1933- 23-24R
Olcheski, Bill 1925- CANR-8
Earlier sketch in CA 61-64
Olcott, Anthony 1950- 106
Olcott, Frances Jenkins 1872(?)-1963 .. SATA-19
Olcott, Henry Steel 1832-1907 Brief entry .. 118
Olcott, Jack 1932- 53-56
Old, Bruce S(cott) 1913- CANR-17
Earlier sketch in CA 4R
Old Boy
See Hughes, Thomas
Oldenburg, Claes (Thure) 1929- 121
Brief entry 117
Oldenburg, E(gbert) William 1936-1974 105
See also SATA 35
Older, Fremont 1856-1935 ..... DLB-25
Older, Julia 1941- CANR-14
Earlier sketch in CA 73-76
Olderman, Murray 1922- CANR-1
Earlier sketch in CA 45-48
Olderman, Raymond M. 1937- 41-44R
Old Fag
See Bell, Robert S(tanley) W(arren)
Oldfeld, Peter
See Bartlett, Vernon
Oldfield, A(rthur) Barney 1909- 105
Oldfield, James E(dmund) 1921- 89-92
Oldfield, R(ichard) C(harles) 1909-1972 .. CAP-2
Earlier sketch in CA 25-28
Oldfield, Ruth L(atzer) 1922- 15-16R
Oldham, Frank 1903- 9-10R
Oldham, Mary 1944- 109
Oldham, Perry (Donald) 1943- 107
Oldham, W(illiam) Dale 1903- 11-12R
Oldman, Oliver 1920- 33-36R
Oldroyd, Harold 1913- 77-80
Olds, Elizabeth 1896- 5-6R
See also SATA 3
Olds, Elizabeth Fagg 1913- 123
Olds, Helen Diehl 1895-1981 ..... CANR-3
Obituary 103
Earlier sketch in CA 4R
See also SATA 9, 25
Olds, Sally Wendkos 1933- CANR-18
Earlier sketches in CA 45-48, CANR-1
Olds, Sharon 1942- CANR-18
Earlier sketch in CA 101
See also CLC 32, 39
Oldsey, Bernard 1923- CANR-7
Earlier sketch in CA 7-8R
Oldson, William O(rville) 1940- 53-56
Old Stager
See Gore, John Francis
Oldstyle, Jonathan
See Irving, Washington
Olea, Maria Florencia Varas 1938- 105
O'Leary, Brian (Todd) 1940- CANR-20
Earlier sketch in CA 33-36R
See also SATA 6
O'Leary, Chester F.
See Kuehnelt-Leddihn, Erik (Maria) Ritter
von
O'Leary, Frank(lin) J. 1922- 7-8R
O'Leary, K. Daniel 1940- 41-44R
O'Leary, Liam 1910- 109
O'Leary, Thomas V(incent) 1910- 5-6R
Oleck, Howard L(eoner) 1911- CANR-4
Earlier sketch in CA 9-10R
Oleksy, Walter 1930- CANR-17
Earlier sketches in CA 45-48, CANR-1
Olen, Jeffrey 1946- 112
Olendorf, William 1924- 117
Olesha, Yuri (Karlovich) 1899-1960 85-88
See also CLC 8
Oleszek, Walter J(oseph) 1941- 120
O'Levenson, Jordan
See Levenson, Jordan
Oleyar, Rita Balkey 1922- 111
Olford, Stephen F(rederick) 1918- 17-18R
Olfson, Lewy 1937- 93-96
Olgyay, Victor 1910-1970 .....7-8R
Obituary 103
Olien, Diana Davids 1943- 113
Olien, Michael D(avid) 1937- CANR-3
Earlier sketch in CA 49-52
Olien, Roger M. 1938- 113
Olin, John C(harles) 1915- 126
Olin, Spencer C(arl), Jr. 1937- 93-96
Olin, William 1929- 106
Olins, Wally 1930- 120
Oliphant, J(ames) Orin 1894-1979
Obituary 85-88
Oliphant, Laurence 1829(?)-1888 ..... DLB-18
Oliphant, Margaret 1828-1897 ..... DLB-18
Oliphant, Patrick (Bruce) 1935- 101
Oliphant, Robert (Thompson) 1924- 102
Oliva, L(awrence) Jay 1933- 13-14R
Oliva, Leo E. 1937- CANR-24
Earlier sketches in CA 21-22R, CANR-9
Olivares, Julian (Jr.) 1940- 118
Oliveira, Antonio Ramos
See Ramos-Oliveira, Antonio
Oliveira Salazar, Antonio de
See Salazar, Antonio de Oliveira
Oliven, John F. 1915(?)-1975 Obituary 53-56
Oliver, A. Richard 1912- 15-16R
Oliver, Amy Roberta
See Ruck, Amy Roberta
Oliver, Andrew 1906-1981 109
Obituary 105
Oliver, Anthony 1923- CANR-20
Earlier sketch in CA 103
Oliver, Bernard John Jr. 1918-1966 .....7-8R
Oliver, Burton
See Burt, Olive Woolley
Oliver, Carl Russell 1941- 106
Oliver, Chad 1928- DLB-8
Oliver, Chad
See Oliver, Symmes C(hadwick)
Oliver, Covey T(homas) 1913- 111
Oliver, Dawn 1942- 123
Oliver, Douglas Llewellyn 1913- 97-100
Oliver, E(dward) J(ames) 1911- 11-12R
Oliver, Egbert S(amuel) 1902- 103
Oliver, G(uillaume) Raymond 1909- CAP-2
Earlier sketch in CA 25-28
Oliver, H(arold) J(ames) 1916-1982
Obituary 111
Oliver, Herman 1885- CAP-1
Earlier sketch in CA 11-12
Oliver, James A(rthur) 1914-1981
Obituary 106
Oliver, James Henry 1905- CANR-17
Earlier sketch in CA 1R
Oliver, Jane
See Rees, Helen Christina Easson
(Evans)
Oliver, John Edward 1933- 33-36R
See also SATA 21
Oliver, Kenneth A(rthur) 1912- 53-56
Oliver, Mark
See Tyler-Whittle, Michael Sidney
Oliver, Mary 1935- CANR-9
Earlier sketch in CA 21-22R
See also DLB 5
See also CLC 19, 34
Oliver, Mary Hempstone 1885(?)-1973
Obituary 41-44R
Oliver, Paul (Hereford) 1927- CANR-1
Earlier sketch in CA 4R
Oliver, R(ichard) A(lexander) C(avaye)
1904- CAP-1
Earlier sketch in CA 11-12
Oliver, Raymond (Davies) 1936- CANR-26
Earlier sketch in CA 109
Oliver, Revilo P(endleton) 1910- 121
Oliver, Richard (Bruce) 1942-1985 116
Oliver, Robert (Shelton) 1934- 105
Oliver, Robert T(arbell) 1909- CANR-19
Earlier sketches in CA 7-8R, CANR-4
Oliver, Roland Anthony 1923- CANR-12
Earlier sketch in CA 73-76
Oliver, Rupert
See Matthews, Rupert O(liver)
Oliver, Smith Hempstone 1912- 25-28R
Oliver, Symmes C(hadwick) 1928- 113
Oliver, W. Andrew 1941- 37-40R
Oliver, William Irvin 1926- 19-20R
Olivera, Otto 1919- 49-52
Oliveri, Mario 1944- 107
Olivier, Charles P(ollard) 1884-1975
Obituary 61-64
Olivier, Laurence (Kerr) 1907- Brief entry ... 111
See also CLC 20
Olivier, Robert L(ouis) 1903- 93-96
Olivova, Vera 1926- 81-84
Olkowski, Helga 1931- 85-88
Olkowski, William 1941- 97-100
Ollard, Richard (Laurence) 1923- CANR-20
Earlier sketch in CA 93-96
Oller, John W(illiam), Jr. 1943- CANR-5
Earlier sketch in CA 53-56
Ollerenshaw, Kathleen (Mary) 1912-
Brief entry 107
Ollestad, Norman (Tennyson) 1935- 21-22R
Olli, John B. 1893(?)-1984 Obituary 112
Ollier, Cliff(ord) David 1931- 61-64
Ollif, Lorna (Anne) 1918- 93-96
Olliff, Donathan C(arnes) 1933- 115
Ollman, Bertell 1935- CANR-16
Earlier sketch in CA 85-88
Olm, Kenneth W(illiam) 1924- 21-22R
Olmstead, Alan H. 1907(?)-1980 Obituary .. 101
Olmstead, Clifton Earl 1926-1962 ..... 2R
Olmsted, Charlotte
See Kursh, Charlotte Olmsted
Olmsted, Frederick Law 1822-1903
Brief entry 120
Olmsted, John Charles 1942- 93-96
Olmsted, Lorena Ann 1890- 29-32R
See also SATA 13
Olmsted, Robert W(alsh) 1936- 41-44R
Olmsted, Sterling P(itkin) 1915- 25-28R
Olney, James 1933- 77-80
Olney, Ross R. 1929- CANR-7
Earlier sketch in CA 15-16R
See also SATA 13
Olorunsola, Victor A. 1939- CANR-7
Earlier sketch in CA 57-60
O'Loughlin, Carleen CAP-2
Earlier sketch in CA 25-28
Olscamp, Paul James 1937- 104
Olschewski, Alfred 1920- 41-44R
See also SATA 7
Olschki, G. Cesare 1890-1971 Obituary 104
Olsen, Alfa-Betty 1947- 103
Olsen, Alfred Johannes, Jr. 1884-1956
Brief entry 113
Olsen, Bob
See Olsen, Alfred Johannes, Jr.
Olsen, Donald J(ames) 1929- 15-16R
Olsen, Edward G(ustave) 1908- CANR-11
Earlier sketches in CA 9-10, CAP-1
Olsen, Hans Christian, Jr. 1929-
Brief entry 106
Olsen, Ib Spang 1921- CANR-3
Earlier sketch in CA 49-52
See also SATA 6
Olsen, Jack
See Olsen, John Edward
Olsen, James 1933- 49-52
Olsen, John Edward 1925- CANR-9
Earlier sketch in CA 19-20R
Olsen, Larry Dean 1939- 69-72
Olsen, Marvin E(lliott) 1936- CANR-26
Earlier sketch in CA 29-32R
Olsen, Otto H(arald) 1925- 33-36R
Olsen, R(obert) Arthur 1910- CAP-2
Earlier sketch in CA 23-24
Olsen, Richard E(llison) 1941- 81-84
Olsen, T(heodore) V(ictor) 1932- CANR-18
Earlier sketches in CA 2R, CANR-3
Olsen, Tillie 1913- CANR-1
Earlier sketch in CA 4R
See also DLB 28
See also DLBY 80
See also CLC 4, 13
Olsen, V(iggo) Norskov 1916- 53-56
Olsen, Violet 1922- 113
Olshaker, Bennett 1921- Brief entry 108
Olshaker, Mark 1951- 73-76
Olshaker, Thelma 114
Olshan, Neal H(ugh) 1947- 119
Olshen, Barry N(eil) 1944- 89-92
Olshewsky, Thomas M(ack) 1934- 37-40R
Olson, Alan M(elvin) 1939- CANR-8
Earlier sketch in CA 61-64
Olson, Alison Gilbert 1931- Brief entry 109
Olson, (Elizabeth) Ann 1953- 126
Olson, Arnold O(rville) 1917- 45-48
Olson, Bernhard Emanuel 1910-1975 .. CANR-24
Obituary 61-64
Earlier sketch in CA 45-48
Olson, Carl 1941- 114
Olson, Charles (John) 1910-1970 ..... CAP-1
Obituary 25-28R
Earlier sketch in CA 15-16
See also CABS 2
See also DLB 5, 16
See also CLC 1, 2, 5, 6, 9, 11, 29
Olson, Clair C(olby) 1901-1972 .....41-44R
Olson, (Carl Bernard) David 1904- 61-64
Olson, David F. 1938- 49-52
Olson, David John 1941- 53-56
Olson, David R(ichard) 1935- 33-36R
Olson, Donald 1938- 65-68
Olson, Elder (James) 1909- CANR-6
Earlier sketch in CA 7-8R
See also DLB 48, 63
Olson, Eric 1944- 53-56
Olson, Everett C. 1910- 53-56
Olson, Gene 1922- 106
See also SATA 32
Olson, Harry E(dwin), Jr. 1932- 61-64
Olson, Harry F(erdinand) 1901- 37-40R
Olson, Harvey S(tuart) 1908-1985 ..... CANR-1
Obituary 118
Earlier sketch in CA 4R
Olson, Helen Kronberg CANR-12
Earlier sketch in CA 29-32R
See also SATA 48
Olson, Herbert Waldo 1927- 1R
Olson, James C(lifton) 1917- 37-40R
Olson, James R(obert) 1938- 49-52
Olson, Jane Virginia 1916- 89-92
Olson, Keith W(aldemar) 1931- 49-52
Olson, Ken(neth John) 1930- 97-100
Olson, Lawrence Alexander 1918-
Brief entry 110
Olson, Lois Ellen 1941- 105
Olson, Mancur, Jr. 1932- 13-14R
Olson, McKinley C(lar) 1931- 110
Olson, Merle Theodore
See Olson, Toby
Olson, Mildred Thompson 1922- 23-24R
Olson, Paul R(ichard) 1925- 21-22R
Olson, Philip G(ilbert) 1934- 11-12R
Olson, Richard G(eorge) 1940- CANR-17
Earlier sketch in CA 89-92
Olson, Richard Paul 1934- CANR-24
Earlier sketches in CA 61-64, CANR-8
Olson, Robert G(oodwin) 1924- 29-32R
Olson, Sidney 1908- CAP-1
Earlier sketch in CA 11-12
Olson, Sigurd F(erdinand) 1899-1982 ... CANR-1
Obituary 105
Earlier sketch in CA 3R
Olson, Stanley 1948- 89-92
Olson, Ted
See Olson, Theodore B.
Olson, Theodore B. 1899- 49-52
Olson, Toby 1937- CANR-9
Earlier sketch in CA 65-68
See also CLC 28
Olson, Willard Clifford 1899-1978
Obituary 111
Olsson, Axel Adolf 1889-1977 Obituary ...73-76
Olsson, Karl A(rthur) 1913- CANR-4
Earlier sketch in CA 7-8R
Olsson, Nils 1909- 73-76
Olstad, Charles (Frederick) 1932- 17-18R
Olthuis, James H(erman) 1938- 61-64
Oltmans, Willem L(eonard) 1925- 57-60
Olton, Charles S(haw) 1938- Brief entry 108
Olton, Roy 1922- 103
Olugebefola, Ademole 1941- SATA-15
Olyesha, Yuri
See Olesha, Yuri (Karlovich)
Olzendam, Roderic Marble 1892-1986
Obituary 121
O'Mahoney, Rich
See Warner-Crozetti, R(uth G.)
O'Mahony, Patrick 1911- 15-16R
O'Malley, Brian (Jack Morgan)
1918(?)-1980 Obituary 101
O'Malley, Charles Donald 1907-1970
Obituary 109
O'Malley, Frank
See O'Rourke, Frank
O'Malley, J(ohn) Steven 1942- 53-56
O'Malley, John W(illiam) 1927-
Brief entry 114
O'Malley, Joseph James 1930- 37-40R
O'Malley, Kevin
See Hossent, Harry
O'Malley, Mary Brief entry 110
O'Malley, Mary Dolling (Sanders)
1889-1974 65-68
O'Malley, Michael (Anthony) 4R
O'Malley, Patrick
See O'Rourke, Frank
O'Malley, Richard K(ilroy) 1911- 97-100
O'Malley, Suzanne 1951- 110
O'Malley, William J(ohn) 1931- CANR-12
Earlier sketch in CA 73-76
Oman, Carola (Mary Anima) 1897-1978 . CANR-4
Earlier sketch in CA 7-8R
See also SATA 35
Oman, Charles Chichele 1901-1982 103
Obituary 105
Oman, Julia Trevelyan 1930- 126
Omansky, Dorothy Linder 1905(?)-1977
Obituary 73-76
O Maolain, Ciaran 1958- 123
O'Maonaigh, Cainneach
See Mooney, Canice (Albert James)
Omari, T(hompson) Peter 1930- 29-32R
Omarr, Sydney Brief entry 116
O'Meara, John J. 1915- CANR-3
Earlier sketch in CA 4R
O'Meara, Patrick 1938- 113
O'Meara, Thomas F(ranklin) 1935- 110
O'Meara, Walter (Andrew) 1897- 13-14R
Omer, Garth St.
See St. Omer, Garth
Ommanney, F(rancis) D(ownes)
1903-1980 ..... CANR-7
Obituary 101
Earlier sketch in CA 13-14R
See also SATA 23
O'More, Peggy
See Blocklinger, Peggy O'More
O'Morrison, Kevin CANR-9
Earlier sketch in CA 53-56
O Mude
See Gorey, Edward (St. John)
Onacewicz, Wlodzimierz 1893(?)-1986
Obituary 120
Onadipe, (Nathaniel) Kola(wole) 1922- 101
O'Nair, Mairi
See Evans, Constance May
Onate, Andres David 1940- Brief entry 112
Ondaatje, Christopher 1933- 49-52
Ondaatje, Michael 1943- 77-80
See also DLB 60
See also CLC 14, 29
O'Neal, Bill
See O'Neal, John W(illiam)
O'Neal, Charles E. 1904- CAP-2
Earlier sketch in CA 19-20
O'Neal, Cothburn M(adison) 1907- 2R
Oneal, Elizabeth 1934- 106
See also SATA 30
O'Neal, Forest Hodge 1917- 7-8R

O'Neal, Glenn (Franklin) 1919- 49-52
O'Neal, John W(illiam) 1942- 89-92
O'Neal, William B(ainter) 1907- 73-76
Oneal, Zibby
See Oneal, Elizabeth
See also CLC 30
See also CLR 13
O'Neil, Daniel J. 1936- 89-92
O'Neil, Dennis 1939- 97-100
O'Neil, Eric
See Barnum, W(illiam) Paul
O'Neil, Isabel MacDonald 1908(?)-1981
Obituary 105
O'Neil, Paul E. 1909(?)-1988 Obituary 125
O'Neil, Robert M(archant) 1934- 106
O'Neil, Terry 1949- 61-64
O'Neil, W(illiam) M(atthew) 1912- 113
O'Neil, Will(iam Daniel III) 1938- 101
O'Neill, Archie
See Henaghan, Jim
O'Neill, Barbara Powell 1929- 19-20R
O'Neill, Carlota 1918- 101
O'Neill, Carlotta Monterey 1888-1970
Obituary 29-32R
O'Neill, Charles Edwards 1927- CANR-9
Earlier sketch in CA 23-24R
O'Neill, Cherry Boone 1954- 112
O'Neill, Daniel Joseph 1905- Brief entry 106
O'Neill, David P(atrick) 1918- 19-20R
O'Neill, Dennis (Bernard) 1947- 114
O'Neill, E. Bard 1941- 85-88
O'Neill, Egan
See Linington, (Barbara) Elizabeth
O'Neill, Egan
See Linington, Elizabeth
O'Neill, Eugene (Gladstone) 1888-1953
Brief entry 110
See also DLB 7
See also TCLC 1, 6, 27
See also AITN 1
O'Neill, Eugene 1922- 77-80
O'Neill, Frank (Quale) 1943- 120
O'Neill, Frank F. 1926(?)-1983 Obituary 109
O'Neill, George 1921(?)-1980 Obituary 102
See also AITN 1
O'Neill, Gerard (Michael) 1942- 69-72
O'Neill, Gerard K(itchen) 1927- CANR-21
Earlier sketch in CA 93-96
O'Neill, James E(dward) 1929-1987 117
Obituary 121
O'Neill, John 1933- 53-56
O'Neill, John Joseph 1920- 23-24R
O'Neill, Joseph Harry 1915- 13-14R
O'Neill, Judith (Beatrice) 1930- CANR-26
Earlier sketch in CA 109
See also SATA 34
O'Neill, Mary L(e Duc) 1908- CANR-4
Earlier sketch in CA 5-6R
See also SATA 2
O'Neill, Michael J. 104
O'Neill, Michael J. 1913- 15-16R
O'Neill, Michael J(ames) 1922- 112
O'Neill, Michael J. 1922- Brief entry 108
O'Neill, Nena AITN-1
O'Neill, Olivia
See Barstow, Phyllida
O'Neill, Patrick Geoffrey 1924- 21-22R
O'Neill, Paul 1928- 107
O'Neill, Reginald F. 1915- 2R
O'Neill, Richard W(inslow) 1925-
Brief entry 107
O'Neill, Robert J(ohn) 1936- 25-28R
O'Neill, Shane
See O'Neill, William
O'Neill, Terence Marne 1914- 108
O'Neill, Tim 1918- 2R
O'Neill, Timothy P. 1941- 85-88
O'Neill, William 1927- 37-40R
O'Neill, William F. 1931- 29-32R
O'Neill, William L. 1935- CANR-12
Earlier sketch in CA 21-22R
O'Neill Of The Maine, Baron of Ahoghill
See O'Neill, Terence Marne
O'Nell, Carl William 1925- 73-76
Onetti, Juan Carlos 1909- 85-88
See also CLC 7, 10
Ong, Walter J(ackson) 1912- CANR-21
Earlier sketches in CA 2R, CANR-4
Ongaro, Alberto 1925- 25-28R
O'Niell, C. M.
See Wilkes-Hunter, R(ichard)
Onions, Charles Talbut 1873-1965
Obituary 107
Onley, David C(harles) 1950- 112
Onlooker
See Grange, Cyril
Ono, Chiyo 1941- CANR-12
Earlier sketch in CA 29-32R
Onoda, Hiroo 1922(?)- Brief entry 108
O'Nolan, Brian
See O Nuallain, Brian
Onopa, Robert 1943- 112
Onorato, Richard James 1933- Brief entry .. 108
Onslow, Annette Rosemary MacArthur
See MacArthur-Onslow, Annette
Rosemary
Onslow, John 1906-1985 Obituary 118
See also SATA 47
Onstott, Kyle 1887-1966 .... 7-8R
Obituary 126
O Nuallain, Brian 1911-1966 .... CAP-2
Obituary 25-28R
Earlier sketch in CA 21-22
Onyeama, (Charles) Dillibe 1951- 125
See also BW
Ooi Jin-Bee 1931- 73-76
Ooiman, Jo Ann
See Robinson, Jo Ann Ooiman
Oost, Stewart Irvin 1921- 29-32R
Oosterman, Gordon 1927- 49-52
Oosterwal, Gottfried 1930- 93-96
Oosthuizen, G(erhardus) C(ornelis)
1922- 29-32R
Oparin, Aleksandr (Ivanovich) 1894-1980
Obituary 108
Opdahl, Keith Michael 1934- 61-64
Opdahl, Richard D(ean) 1924- 21-22R
Opgenoorth, Winfried 1939- SATA-50
Ophuls, Max 1902-1957 Brief entry 113
Opie, Iona 1923- 61-64
See also SATA 3
See also SAAS 6
Opie, John 1934- 29-32R
Opie, Peter (Mason) 1918-1982 .... CANR-2
Obituary 106
Earlier sketch in CA 7-8R
See also SATA 3, 28
Opie, Redvers 1900-1984 Obituary 112
Opik, E.
See Oepik, Ernst Julius
Opik, Ernst
See Oepik, Ernst Julius
Opik, Ernst J.
See Oepik, Ernst Julius
Opik, Ernst Julius
See Oepik, Ernst Julius
Opitz, Edmund A. 1914- 29-32R
Opland, Jeff 1943- 106
Opler, Marvin K(aufmann) 1914- 23-24R
Opler, Morris E(dward) 1907- 45-48
Opotowsky, Stan 1923- CANR-1
Earlier sketch in CA 1R
Oppen, George 1908-1984 .... CANR-8
Obituary 113
Earlier sketch in CA 15-16R
See also DLB 5
See also CLC 7, 13, 34
Oppen, Mary 1908- 119
Oppenheim, A(dolph) Leo 1904-1974
Obituary 49-52
Oppenheim, E(dward) Phillips 1866-1946
Brief entry 111
See also DLB 70
Oppenheim, Felix E(rrera) 1913- 2R
Oppenheim, Frank Mathias 1925- 116
Oppenheim, Irene 1928- 77-80
Oppenheim, James 1882-1932 .... DLB-28
Oppenheim, Janet 1948- 117
Oppenheim, Joanne 1934- CANR-25
Earlier sketches in CA 23-24R, CANR-9
See also SATA 5
Oppenheim, Paul 1885(?)-1977 Obituary .. 69-72
Oppenheim, S(aul) Chesterfield 1897-1988
Obituary 124
Oppenheim, Shulamith (Levey) 1930- 73-76
Oppenheimer, Evelyn 1907- CANR-3
Earlier sketch in CA 3R
Oppenheimer, George 1900-1977 .... 15-16R
Obituary 73-76
Oppenheimer, Harold L. 1919- 17-18R
Oppenheimer, J(ulius) Robert 1904-1967 ... 103
Oppenheimer, Joan L(etson) 1925- CANR-17
Earlier sketch in CA 37-40R
See also SATA 28
Oppenheimer, Joe A(llan) 1941- 111
Oppenheimer, Joel (Lester)
1930-1988 .... CANR-21
Obituary 126
Earlier sketches in CA 9-10R, CANR-4
See also DLB 5
Oppenheimer, Martin 1930- 29-32R
Oppenheimer, Max, Jr. 1917- 17-18R
Oppenheimer, Paul 1939- 21-22R
Oppenheimer, Samuel P(hilip) 1903- 33-36R
Opper, F.
See Opper, Frederick (Burr)
Opper, Frederick (Burr) 1857-1937
Brief entry 118
See also AITN 1
Opper, Jacob 1935- 49-52
Opperby, Preben 1924- 110
Oppitz, Rene 1905(?)-1976 Obituary 65-68
Oppong, Christine 1940- CANR-7
Earlier sketch in CA 57-60
Optic, Oliver
See Adams, William Taylor
and Stratemeyer, Edward L.
Opton, Edward M., Jr. 1936- CANR-11
Earlier sketch in CA 21-22R
Opuls, Max
See Ophuls, Max
O'Quill, Scarlett
See Mossman, Dow
O'Quinn, Garland 1935- 23-24R
O'Quinn, Hazel Hedick 37-40R
Orage, A(lfred) R(ichard) 1873-1934
Brief entry 122
Oraison, Marc 1914- 85-88
Oram, Hiawyn 1946- 106
Oram, Malcolm 1944(?)-1976 Obituary 104
O'Ramus, Seamus
See O'Neill, William
O'Rand, Angela M(etropulos) 1945- 104
Oras, Ants 1900- CAP-1
Earlier sketch in CA 15-16
Orbaan, Albert F. CANR-8
Earlier sketch in CA 5-6R
Orbach, Ruth Gary 1941- 65-68
See also SATA 21
Orbach, Susie 1946- CANR-19
Earlier sketch in CA 85-88
Orbach, William W(olf) 1946- 73-76
Orben, Robert 1927- 81-84
Orbis, Victor
See Powell-Smith, Vincent (Walter
Francis)
Orcutt, Georgia 1949- 112
Orczy, Emma Magdalena Rosalia Maria
Josefa Barbara 1865-1947 Brief entry 104
See also SATA 40
See also DLB 70
Orczy, Emmuska
See Orczy, Emma Magdalena Rosalia
Maria Josefa Barbara
See also SATA 40
Ord, John E. 1917- 81-84
Orde, Lewis 1943- 109
Ord-Hume, Arthur W. J. G. 101
Ordish, George 1908- CANR-9
Earlier sketch in CA 61-64
Ordway, Frederick I(ra) III 1927- CANR-20
Earlier sketches in CA 7-8R, CANR-5
Ordway, Roger
See Pauker, John
Ordway, Sally 1939- 57-60
O'Regan, Richard Arthur 1919- 73-76
O'Reilly, Don 1913- 111
O'Reilly, Jane 1936- 73-76
O'Reilly, John (Thomas) 1945- 29-32R
O'Reilly, Montagu
See Andrews, Wayne
O'Reilly, Robert P. 1936- 29-32R
O'Reilly, Timothy 1954- CANR-23
Earlier sketch in CA 106
Orel, Harold 1926- CANR-19
Earlier sketches in CA 7-8R, CANR-3
Orellana, Sandra L. 1941- 126
O'Relley, Z(oltan) Edward 1940- 119
Orem, R(eginald) C(alvert) 1931- 17-18R
Oren, Uri 1931- 65-68
Orengo, Charles 1913(?)-1974 Obituary 104
Orenstein, Denise Gosliner 1950- 110
Orenstein, Frank (Everett) 1919- 111
Orenstein, Gloria Feman 1938- 65-68
Orenstein, Henry 1924- 15-16R
Orent, Norman B. 1920- 17-18R
Oreshnik, A. F.
See Nussbaum, Al(bert F.)
Oresick, Peter (Michael) 1955- CANR-13
Earlier sketch in CA 73-76
Orest
See Bedrij, Orest (John)
Orewa, George Oka 1928- 7-8R
Orff, Carl 1895-1982 Obituary 106
Orfield, Olivia 1922- 103
Orga, Ates 1944- 93-96
Organ, John 1925- CANR-7
Earlier sketch in CA 7-8R
Organ, Troy Wilson 1912- 37-40R
Organski, A(bramo) F(imo) K(enneth)
1923- 103
Orgel, Doris 1929- CANR-2
Earlier sketch in CA 45-48
See also SATA 7
See also AITN 1
Orgel, Joseph Randolph 1902-1987 ...... CAP-1
Obituary 123
Earlier sketch in CA 11-12
Orgel, Stephen (Kitay) 1933- CANR-14
Earlier sketch in CA 73-76
Orgill, Douglas 1922- 81-84
Orgill, Michael (Thomas) 1946- 61-64
Orians, George H(arrison) 1900- 49-52
Orians, Gordon H(owell) 1932- 45-48
Oriard, Michael (Vincent) 1948- 110
Origo, Iris (Margaret Cutting) 1902- 105
O'Riley, Warren
See Richardson, Gladwell
Oring, Elliott 1945- 111
Oriolo, Joe
See Oriolo, Joseph D.
Oriolo, Joseph D. 1913-1985 Obituary 118
See also SATA 46
Orion
See Naylor, John
O'Riordan, Robert (Garrett) 1943- 119
Orjuela, Hector H(ugo) 1930- CANR-2
Earlier sketch in CA 45-48
Orkeny, Istvan 1912-1979 103
Obituary 89-92
Orkin, Harvey 1918(?)-1975 Obituary 61-64
Orkin, Ruth 1921-1985 119
Obituary 114
Orlando, Guido 1908(?)-1988 Obituary 126
Orlans, Harold 1921- CANR-15
Earlier sketch in CA 33-36R
Orleans, Ilo 1897-1962 .... CANR-15
Earlier sketch in CA 2R
See also SATA 10
Orleans, Leo A(nton) 1924- CANR-15
Earlier sketch in CA 41-44R
Orledge, Robert (Nicholas) 1948- 113
Orlen, Steve 1942- 101
Orlev, Uri 1931- 101
Orlich, Donald C(harles) 1931- CANR-22
Earlier sketches in CA 15-16R, CANR-7
Orlick, Terrance D(ouglas) 1945- CANR-21
Earlier sketches in CA 57-60, CANR-6
Orlick, Terry
See Orlick, Terrance D(ouglas)
Orlicky, Joseph A. 1922- 25-28R
Orlier, Blaise
See Sylvestre, (Joseph Jean) Guy
Orlinsky, Harry M(eyer) 1908- 85-88
Orlob, Helen Seaburg 1908- 7-8R
Orlock, Carol (Ellen) 1947- 122
Orloff, Ed(gar Sam) 1923-1983 69-72
Obituary 110
Orloff, Max
See Crowcroft, Peter
Orlofsky, Myron 1928(?)-1976 Obituary ... 69-72
Orloski, Richard J(ohn) 1947- 97-100
Orlova, R.
See Orlova-Kopelev, Raissa (Davydovna)
Orlova, R. D.
See Orlova-Kopelev, Raissa (Davydovna)
Orlova, Raisa
See Orlova-Kopelev, Raissa (Davydovna)
Orlova-Kopelev, Raissa (Davydovna)
1918- 123
Orlovitz, Gil 1918-1973 77-80
Obituary 45-48
See also DLB 2, 5
See also CLC 22
Orlovsky, Peter 1933- CANR-9
Earlier sketch in CA 15-16R
See also DLB 16
Orlow, Dietrich 1937- 65-68
Ormai, Stella SATA-48
Orme, Antony R(onald) 1936- 73-76
Ormerod, Jan(ette Louise) 1946- 113
See also SATA 44
Ormerod, Roger 1920- CANR-15
Earlier sketch in CA 77-80
Ormes, Jackie
See Ormes, Zelda J.
Ormes, Robert M. 1904- CAP-1
Earlier sketch in CA 11-12
Ormes, Robert Verner 1921-1984
Obituary 112
Ormes, Zelda J. 1914-1986 Obituary 118
See also SATA 47
Ormesson, Jean (Bruno Waldemar
Francois-de-Paule Lefevre) d'
See d'Ormesson, Jean (Bruno Waldemar
Francois-de-Paule Lefevre)
Ormesson, Wladimir d' 1888-1973
Obituary 45-48
Ormiston, Roberta
See Fletcher, Adele (Whitely)
Ormond, (Willard) Clyde 1906-1985 ...... 9-10R
Obituary 115
Ormond, Frederic
See Dey, Frederic (Merrill) Van
Rensselaer
Ormond, John 1923- 65-68
See also DLB 27
Ormond, Leonee (Jasper) 1940- 85-88
Ormond, Richard (Louis) 1939- CANR-15
Earlier sketch in CA 41-44R
Ormondroyd, Edward 1925- 73-76
See also SATA 14
Ormont, Louis Robert 1918- 13-14R
Ormrod, Richard (James) 1946- 119
Ormsbee, David
See Longstreet, Stephen
Ormsby, Frank 1947- CANR-23
Earlier sketch in CA 107
Ormsby, Virginia H(aire) 11-12R
See also SATA 11
Ormsby, William (George) 1921- 73-76
Orna, Mary Virginia 1934- 29-32R
Ornati, Oscar A(braham) 1922- CANR-14
Earlier sketch in CA 37-40R
Ornis
See Winchester, Clarence
Ornitz, Samuel (Badisch) 1890-1957
Brief entry 117
See also DLB 28, 44
Ornstein, Allan C(harles) 1941- CANR-4
Earlier sketch in CA 53-56
Ornstein, Dolph 1947- 77-80
Ornstein, J. L.
See Ornstein-Galicia, J(acob) L(eonard)
Ornstein, Jack H(ervey) 1938- 103
Ornstein, Norman J(ay) 1948- 93-96
Ornstein, Robert 1925- 2R
Ornstein, Robert E. 1942- 53-56
Ornstein-Galicia, J(acob) L(eonard) 1915- .. 93-96
O'Rourke, Andrew P(atrick) 1933- 126
O'Rourke, Edward William 1917- 112
O'Rourke, Frank 1916- 118
Brief entry 114
O'Rourke, John James Joseph 1926- 33-36R
O'Rourke, John T(homas) 1900-1983
Obituary 111
O'Rourke, Lawrence Michael 1938- 69-72
O'Rourke, P. J. 1947- CANR-13
Earlier sketch in CA 77-80
O'Rourke, Terrence James 1932- 41-44R
O'Rourke, Timothy G(erald) 1949- 111
O'Rourke, William (Andrew) 1945- CANR-1
Earlier sketch in CA 45-48
Orpaz, Yitzhak 1923- 101
Orpen, Eve 1926(?)-1978 Obituary 104
Orpen, Neil (Newton D'Arcy) 1913- 120
Orpen, Neil D.
See Orpen, Neil (Newton D'Arcy)
Orr, Bobby
See Orr, Robert Gordon
Orr, Daniel 1933- 29-32R
Orr, David 1929- 33-36R
Orr, Gregory 1947- CANR-22
Earlier sketch in CA 105
Orr, J(ames) Edwin 1912- CANR-4
Earlier sketch in CA 11-12R
Orr, John Boyd 1880-1971 Obituary 113
Orr, Linda 1943- 97-100
Orr, Mary
See Denham, Mary Orr
Orr, Mary E. E. McCombe 1917- 7-8R
Orr, Oliver H(amilton), Jr. 1921- 2R
Orr, Robert Gordon 1948- 112
Orr, Robert R(ichmond) 1930- 25-28R
Orr, Robert T. 1908- 33-36R
Orr, William F(ridell) 1907- 108

Orrell, John (Overton) 1934- CANR-15
Earlier sketch in CA 37-40R
Orris
See Ingelow, Jean
Orrmont, Arthur 1922- CANR-4
Earlier sketch in CA 2R
Orsborn, Carol 1948- 124
Orsini, Gian Napoleone Giordano
1903-19(?) 5-6R
Orsini, Joseph E(mmanuel) 1937- 37-40R
Orso, Kathryn Wickey 1921-1979 57-60
Obituary 85-88
Orsy, Ladislas M. 1921- 25-28R
Orszagh, Laszlo 1907-1984 Obituary 112
Ort, Ana
See Andrews, Arthur (Douglas, Jr.)
Ortega y Gasset, Jose 1883-1955
Brief entry 106
See also TCLC 9
Orth, Charles D., III 1921- 7-8R
Orth, Penelope 1938- 45-48
Orth, Ralph H(arry) 1930- 21-22R
Orth, Richard
See Gardner, Richard (M.)
Orthwine, Rudolf 1900(?)-1970 Obituary ... 104
Ortiz, Alfonso A(lex) 1939- 29-32R
Ortiz, Elisabeth Lambert 1928- 97-100
Ortiz, Simon J. 1941- CLC-45
Ortiz, Victoria 1942- 107
Ortiz y Pino, Jose III 1932- 112
Ortlund, Anne 1923- 106
Ortlund, Raymond C(arl) 1923- 114
Ortman, E(lmore) Jan 1884- CAP-2
Earlier sketch in CA 25-28
Ortman, Elmer John
See Ortman, E(lmore) Jan
Ortner, Donald John 1938- 117
Ortner-Zimmerman, Toni 1941- CANR-19
Earlier sketches in CA 53-56, CANR-5
Orton, Alvin E. 1906-1987 Obituary 122
Orton, Barry 1949- 111
Orton, Harold 1898-1975 Obituary 57-60
Orton, Joe
See Orton, John Kingsley
See also DLB 13
See also CLC 4, 13, 43
Orton, John Kingsley 1933-1967 85-88
Orton, Lawrence D(wayne) 1941-
Brief entry 118
Orton, Vrest 1897-1986 .... 33-36R
Obituary 121
Ortzen, Len
See Ortzen, Leonard Edwin
Ortzen, Leonard Edwin 1912-1979 118
Brief entry 114
Orum, Anthony M(endl) 1939- 41-44R
Orvell, Miles 1944- 41-44R
Orwell, George
See Blair, Eric Hugh
See also DLB 15
See also TCLC 2, 6, 15
Orwell, Sonia 1919(?)-1980 Obituary 102
Orwen, (Phillips) Gifford 37-40R
Ory, Edward 1886-1973 Obituary 41-44R
Ory, Kid
See Ory, Edward
Orzeck, Arthur Z(alman) 1921- CANR-1
Earlier sketch in CA 45-48
Osanka, Franklin Mark 1936- 5-6R
Osaragi, Jiro
See Nojiri, Kiyohiko
Osbeck, Kenneth W. 1924- CANR-19
Earlier sketches in CA 3R, CANR-3
Osbon, B. S. 1827-1912 .... DLB-43
Osborn, Albert D. 1896(?)-1972 Obituary ... 104
Osborn, Alex(ander) F(aickney) 1888-1966
Obituary 106
Osborn, Arthur W(alter) 1891- 23-24R
Osborn, Barbara M(onroe)
See Henkel, Barbara Osborn
Osborn, Carolyn 1934- 93-96
Osborn, Catherine B. 1914- 29-32R
Osborn, David (D.) 1923- Brief entry 109
Osborn, Eric (Francis) 1922- 65-68
Osborn, Frederic J(ames) 1885-1978 ... CANR-5
Earlier sketch in CA 7-8R
Osborn, Frederick (Henry) 1889-1981 ... 25-28R
Obituary 102
Osborn, George C(oleman) 1904-1982 . CANR-19
Earlier sketch in CA 25-28R
Osborn, James M(arshall) 1906-1976 .... CAP-2
Obituary 69-72
Earlier sketch in CA 25-28
Osborn, John Jay, Jr. 1945- CANR-6
Earlier sketch in CA 57-60
Osborn, Lois D(orothy) 1915- 116
Osborn, Mary Elizabeth 1898- 7-8R
Osborn, Merton B(idwell) 1908- 25-28R
Osborn, Paul 1901-1988 112
Obituary 125
Brief entry 108
Osborn, Percy George 1899(?)-1972
Obituary 104
Osborn, Robert (Chesley) 1904- 15-16R
Osborn, Robert T(appan) 1926- 21-22R
Osborn, Ronald E(dwin) 1917- 15-16R
Osborn, Stella Brunt
See Osborn, Stellanova
Osborn, Stellanova 1894-1988 Obituary 125
Osborn, Thomas Noel II 1940- 114
Osborne, Adam 1939- 109
Osborne, (Reginald) Arthur 1906-1970 ... 19-20R
Obituary 125
Osborne, Betsy
See Boswell, Barbara (S.)
Osborne, C(harles) H(umfrey) C(aufeild)
1891- 7-8R
Osborne, Cecil G. 1904- CANR-1
Earlier sketch in CA 45-48
Osborne, Charles 1927- CANR-13
Earlier sketch in CA 13-14R
Osborne, Chester G. 1915- CANR-9
Earlier sketch in CA 21-22R
See also SATA 11
Osborne, Dan 1948(?)-1983 Obituary 110
Osborne, David
See Silverberg, Robert
Osborne, Dorothy (Gladys) Yeo 1917- 9-10R
Osborne, Elsie L(etitia) 1924- 118
Osborne, Ernest (Glenn) 1903-1963 .... 7-8R
Osborne, G(erald) S(tanley) 1926- 23-24R
Osborne, Geoffrey 1930- 110
Osborne, George
See Silverberg, Robert
Osborne, George E(dward) 1893- CAP-2
Earlier sketch in CA 23-24
Osborne, Harold 1905-1987 .... CANR-6
Obituary 122
Earlier sketch in CA 13-14R
Osborne, Harold W(ayne) 1930- 57-60
Osborne, Helena
See Moore, (Georgina) Mary (Galbraith)
Osborne, J(ulius) K(enneth) 1941- 33-36R
Osborne, John (Franklin) 1907-1981 ... CANR-10
Obituary 108
Earlier sketch in CA 61-64
Osborne, John (James) 1929- CANR-21
Earlier sketch in CA 13-14R
See also DLB 13
See also CLC 1, 2, 5, 11, 45
Osborne, John W(alter) 1927- 33-36R
Osborne, Juanita Tyree 1916- CANR-23
Earlier sketches in CA 61-64, CANR-8
Osborne, Lawrence 1958- CLC-50
Osborne, Leone Neal 1914- 23-24R
See also SATA 2
Osborne, Linda Barrett 1949- 65-68
Osborne, Maggie
See Osborne, Margaret Ellen
Osborne, Margaret 1909- 13-14R
Osborne, Margaret Ellen 1941- CANR-18
Earlier sketch in CA 102
Osborne, Martha Lee 1928- 113
Osborne, Mary Pope 1949- 111
See also SATA 41
Osborne, Maureen 1924- 109
Osborne, Milton Edgeworth 1936- CANR-9
Earlier sketch in CA 15-16R
Osborne, Richard 1943- 123
Osborne, Richard Horsley 1925- 21-22R
Osborne, William (Terry, Jr.) 1934- 25-28R
Osborne, William A(udley) 1919- 61-64
Osborne, William S(tewart) 1923- 53-56
Osbourn, R(ichard) A(lton) 1930- 120
Osbourne, Ivor Livingstone 1951- 108
Osburn, Charles B(enjamin) 1939- CANR-13
Earlier sketch in CA 33-36R
Osceola
See Blixen, Karen (Christentze Dinesen)
Osen, Lynn M(oses) 1920- 65-68
Osenenko, John 1918-1983 Obituary 109
Oser, Jacob 1915- CANR-2
Earlier sketch in CA 5-6R
Osgood, Charles
See Wood, Charles Osgood III
Osgood, Charles E(gerton) 1916- 19-20R
Osgood, Charles Grosvenor 1871-1964 .. CANR-4
Earlier sketch in CA 7-8R
Osgood, Cornelius 1905-1985 Obituary 114
Osgood, David William 1940- 89-92
Osgood, Don(ald W.) 1930- CANR-11
Earlier sketch in CA 61-64
Osgood, Ernest S(taples) 1888- CAP-1
Earlier sketch in CA 11-12
Osgood, Herbert L(evi) 1855-1918
Brief entry 122
See also DLB 47
Osgood, Lawrence 1929- 85-88
Osgood, Robert Endicott 1921-1986 .... CANR-3
Obituary 121
Earlier sketch in CA 1R
Osgood, Samuel M(aurice) 1920-1975 ... 33-36R
Osgood, William E(dward) 1926- 33-36R
See also SATA 37
O'Shaughnessy, Arthur 1844-1881 ..... DLB-35
O'Shea, (Martin) Lester 1938- 108
O'Shea, Sean
See Tralins, S(andor) Robert
Oshima, Nagisa 1932- 121
Brief entry 116
See also CLC 20
Osiek, Betty Tyree 1931- 45-48
O Siochain, P(adraig) A(ugustine) 1905- .. CAP-2
Earlier sketch in CA 17-18
Osipow, Samuel H(erman) 1934- CANR-1
Earlier sketch in CA 49-52
Osis, Karlis 1917- 85-88
Oskam, Bob
See Oskam, Robert T(heo)
Oskam, Robert T(heo) 1945- 108
Oskamp, Stuart 1930- CANR-12
Earlier sketch in CA 29-32R
Oski, Frank A(ram) 1932- 119
Osler, Margaret Jo 1942- 126
Osler, Robert Willard 1911-1984 ...... CANR-17
Obituary 114
Earlier sketch in CA 2R
Osley, A(rthur) S(idney) 1917-1987 125
Osman, Betty B(arshad) 1929- 93-96
Osman, Jack D(ouglas) 1943- CANR-11
Earlier sketch in CA 61-64
Osman, John 1907(?)-1978 Obituary 77-80
Osmer, Margaret 93-96
Osmond, Andrew 1938- 25-28R
Osmond, Edward 1900- CAP-1
Earlier sketch in CA 13-14
See also SATA 10
Osmond, Humphrey (Fortescue) 1917- ... 23-24R
Osmond, Marie 1959- Brief entry 112
Osmond-Smith, David 1946- 120
Osmun, Mark 1952- 93-96
Osmunson, Robert Lee 1924- 11-12R
Osofsky, Gilbert 1935-1974 65-68
Obituary 53-56
Osserman, Richard A. 1930- 29-32R
Osslinger, Kurt
See Allen, Bob
Ossman, David (H.) 1936- 9-10R
Ossoli, Sarah Margaret (Fuller marchesa d')
1810-1850 .... SATA-25
Ossorgin, Mikhail
See Ilyin, Mikhail Andreyevich
Ossowska, Maria 1896- 29-32R
Ossowski, Stanislaw 1897-1963 .... CAP-1
Earlier sketch in CA 13-14
Ost, David H(arry) 1940- CANR-6
Earlier sketch in CA 53-56
Ost, John William Philip 1931- 37-40R
Osten, Gar 1923- 65-68
Ostendorf, (Arthur) Lloyd (Jr.) 1921- ... CANR-6
Earlier sketch in CA 2R
Ostenso, Martha 1900-1963 .... CAP-1
Earlier sketch in CA 15-16
Oster, Jerry 1943- 77-80
Oster, Ludwig (Friedrich) 1931- 53-56
Osterburg, James W(illiam) 1917- 45-48
Ostergaard, G(eoffrey) N(ielsen) 1926- ... 25-28R
Osterhaven, M(aurice) Eugene 1915- 49-52
Osterhoudt, Robert G(erald) 1942- 53-56
Osterlund, Steven 1943- 77-80
Osterritter, John F. 1923- 45-48
Osterweis, Rollin G(ustav)
1907-1982(?) 41-44R
Obituary 106
Ostheimer, John 1938- 41-44R
Ostle, Bernard 1921- 7-8R
Ostlere, Gordon (Stanley) 1921- 107
Ostling, Richard N(eil) 1940- 53-56
Ostow, Mortimer 1918- 49-52
Ostrander, Gilman Marston 1923- 65-68
Ostriker, Alicia 1937- CANR-10
Earlier sketch in CA 25-28R
Ostrinsky, Meir Simha 1906- CAP-2
Earlier sketch in CA 29-32
Ostroff, Anthony J(ames) 1923-1978 .... CANR-3
Obituary 77-80
Earlier sketch in CA 7-8R
Ostrom, Alan (Baer) 1925- 21-22R
Ostrom, John Ward 1903- 1R
Ostrom, Thomas M. 1936- 37-40R
Ostrom, Vincent (Alfred) 1919- Brief entry .. 113
Ostrov, Eric 1941- 113
Ostrow, Joanna 1938- 29-32R
Ostrower, Alexander 1901-1979 .... 17-18R
Obituary 120
Ostrowsky
See Holmquist, Anders
Ostry, Sylvia 1927- CANR-15
Earlier sketch in CA 41-44R
Ostwald, Martin 1922- 33-36R
Ostwald, Peter F. 1928- 17-18R
O Suilleabhain, Sean 1903- CANR-18
Earlier sketch in CA 25-28R
O'Sullivan, Joan (D'Arcy) 77-80
O'Sullivan, John J. 1939- Brief entry 114
O'Sullivan, Judith 1942- 120
O'Sullivan, P. Michael 1940- 93-96
O'Sullivan, Sean
See O Suilleabhain, Sean
O'Sullivan, Vincent (Gerard) 1937- 97-100
Osusky, Stefan 1889-1973 Obituary 45-48
Oswald, Eleazer 1755-1795 .... DLB-43
Oswald, Ian 1929- CANR-13
Earlier sketch in CA 19-20R
Oswald, J(oseph) Gregory 1922- 104
Oswald, Russell G. 1908- 45-48
Oswalt, John N(ewell) 1940- 117
Oswalt, Sabine
See MacCormack, Sabine G(abriele)
Oswalt, Wendell H(illman) 1927- CANR-12
Earlier sketch in CA 19-20R
Otake, Sadao 1913(?)-1983 Obituary 109
Otchis, Ethel (Herberg) 1920- 15-16R
Otero, Blas de 1916- 89-92
See also CLC 11
Otis, George
See Mellen, Ida M(ay)
Otis, Jack 1923- 2R
Otis, James
See Kaler, James Otis
Otis, James, Jr. 1725-1783 .... DLB-31
O'Toole, James (Joseph) 1945- 126
O'Toole, Rex
See Tralins, S(andor) Robert
O'Trigger, Sir Lucius
See Horne, Richard Henry
Ott, Attiat F(arag) 1935- CANR-10
Earlier sketch in CA 21-22R
Ott, David Jackson 1934-1975 .... CANR-8
Earlier sketch in CA 5-6R
Ott, Maggie Glen
See Ott, Virginia
Ott, Peter
See von Hildebrand, Dietrich
Ott, Thomas O(liver) III 1938- 49-52
Ott, Virginia 1917- 77-80
Ott, William Griffith 1909- CANR-1
Earlier sketch in CA 2R
Ottemiller, John H(enry) 1916-1968 ..... CAP-2
Earlier sketch in CA 17-18
Otten, Anna 21-22R
Otten, C. Michael 1934- 33-36R
Otten, Charlotte M(arie) 1915- 29-32R
Otten, Terry (Ralph) 1938- CANR-15
Earlier sketch in CA 37-40R
Ottenberg, Miriam 1914-1982 .... CANR-10
Obituary 108
Earlier sketch in CA 7-8R
Ottenberg, Simon 1923- 33-36R
Ottendorfer, Oswald 1826-1900
Brief entry 123
See also DLB 23
Otter, Anthony 1896-1986 Obituary 118
Otterbein, Keith Frederick 1936- 21-22R
Ottersen, (John) Ottar 1918- 33-36R
Ottesen, Thea Tauber 1913- 5-6R
Otteson, Schuyler Franklin 1917-
Brief entry 106
Ottley, Reginald Leslie 93-96
See also SATA 26
Ottley, Roi (Vincent) 1906-1960 Obituary .. 89-92
Ottlik, Geza 1912- 19-20R
Ottman, Robert W(illiam) 1914- CANR-3
Earlier sketch in CA 1R
Otto, Calvin P. 1930- 29-32R
Otto, Henry J. 1901- CAP-2
Earlier sketch in CA 15-16
Otto, Herbert Arthur 1922- CANR-1
Earlier sketch in CA 45-48
Otto, Margaret Glover 1909-1976
Obituary 61-64
See also SATA 30
Otto, Wayne (R.) 1931- CANR-11
Earlier sketch in CA 29-32R
Ottum, Bob
See Ottum, Robert K., Jr.
Ottum, Robert K., Jr. 1925(?)-1986
Obituary 119
Otwell, John H(erbert) 1915- 73-76
Ouellette, Fernand 1930- CANR-17
Earlier sketches in CA 49-52, CANR-2
See also DLB 60
Oughton, Frederick 1923- 2R
Ouida
See De La Ramee, (Marie) Louise
See also DLB 18
Ouimette, Victor 1944- 73-76
Oulahan, Richard 1918-1985 .... 33-36R
Obituary 117
Oulanoff, Hongor 1929- 25-28R
Ouologuem, Yambo 1940- Brief entry 111
Ouroussoff, Peter Sergeievich
1900(?)-1984 Obituary 114
Ouroussow, Eugenie 1908-1975 Obituary .. 53-56
Oursler, (Charles) Fulton 1893-1952
Brief entry 108
Oursler, Fulton, Jr. 1932- Brief entry 116
Oursler, Will(iam Charles) 1913-1985 ... CANR-2
Obituary 115
Earlier sketch in CA 7-8R
Ousby, Ian (Vaughan Kenneth) 1947- 89-92
Ousley, Odille 1896- CAP-1
Earlier sketch in CA 11-12
See also SATA 10
Ousmane, Sembene 1923- 125
Brief entry 117
See also BW
Ouston, Philip (Anfield) 1924(?)-1988(?)
Obituary 125
Outerbridge, David E(ugene) 1933- CANR-16
Earlier sketch in CA 93-96
Outhwaite, Leonard 1892- 53-56
Outka, Gene 1937- 41-44R
Outland, Charles 1910- 11-12R
Outler, Albert C(ook) 1908- CANR-1
Earlier sketch in CA 3R
Ouverson, Marlin D(ean) 1952- 111
Ovard, Glen F. 1928- 33-36R
Overacker, Louise 1891- CAP-2
Earlier sketch in CA 29-32
Overbeck, Pauletta 1915- 97-100
Overbeek, J(ohannes) 1932- 73-76
Overberg, Kenneth R(ichard) 1944- 114
Overbury, Stephen 1954- 119
Overholser, Stephen 1944- CANR-16
Earlier sketch in CA 97-100
Overholser, Wayne D. 1906- CANR-16
Earlier sketches in CA 7-8R, CANR-2
Overholt, William H. 1945- 117
Overman, Michael 1920- 108
Overstreet, Bonaro (Wilkinson) 1902-1985
Obituary 117
Overstreet, Harry Allen 1875-1970 .... CAP-1
Obituary 29-32R
Earlier sketch in CA 15-16
Overton, Jenny (Margaret Mary) 1942- 57-60
See also SATA 36, 52
Overton, Richard Cleghorn 1907- 108
Overton, Robert
See Knox-Mawer, Ronald
Overy, Paul 1940- 29-32R
Overy, R(ichard) J(ames) 1947- 119
Ovesen, Ellis
See Smith, Shirley M(ae)
Owen, Alan Robert George 1919- 11-12R
Owen, Alun Davies 1926- 7-8R
Owen, Bob
See Geis, Richard E(rwin)
Owen, Bruce M(anning) 1943- 57-60
Owen, Caroline Dale
See Snedeker, Caroline Dale (Parke)
Owen, Charles A(braham), Jr. 1914- 53-56
Owen, Clifford
See Hamilton, Charles Harold St. John
Owen, D(enis) F(rank) 1931- CANR-4
Earlier sketch in CA 53-56
Owen, David (Edward) 1898-1968 .... CAP-1
Earlier sketch in CA 15-16

Owen, David E(lystan) 1912-1987 124
Owen, David Lanyon Lloyd
See Lloyd Owen, David Lanyon
Owen, Dilys
See Gater, Dilys
Owen, Dolores B(ullock) 53-56
Owen, Douglas David Roy 1922- 89-92
Owen, Edmund
See Teller, Neville
Owen, (Benjamin) Evan 1918-1984 109
See also SATA 38
Owen, Frank 1907(?)-1979 Obituary 85-88
Owen, G(ail) L(ee) 1937- 45-48
Owen, G(eorge) Vale 1869-1931
Brief entry 119
Owen, George Earle 1908- 77-80
Owen, Guy (Jr.) 1925-1981 .... CANR-3
Obituary 104
Earlier sketch in CA 2R
See also DLB 5
Owen, Gwilym Ellis Lane 1922-1982
Obituary 107
Owen, (William) Harold 1897-1971 ...... 15-16R
Obituary 89-92
Owen, Henry 1920- Brief entry 111
Owen, Hugh
See Faust, Frederick (Shiller)
Owen, Irvin 1910- 97-100
Owen, Jack 1929- 33-36R
Owen, Jennifer 1936- 116
Owen, John E. 1919- CANR-4
Earlier sketch in CA 11-12R
Owen, Lewis 1915- 29-32R
Owen, Lewis J(ames) 1925- Brief entry 116
Owen, Marsha
See Stanford, Sally
Owen, Norman G. 1944- 126
Owen, Oliver S. 1920- 104
Owen, Philip
See Philips, Judson (Pentecost)
Owen, Reginald 1887-1972 Obituary 37-40R
Owen, Robert N.
See Geis, Richard E(rwin)
Owen, Roderic
See Fenwick-Owen, Roderic (Franklin Rawnsley)
Owen, Roderic (Franklin Rawnsley) Fenwick
See Fenwick-Owen, Roderic (Franklin Rawnsley)
Owen, Roger C(orey) 1928- 77-80
Owen, Thomas Richard 1918- CANR-10
Earlier sketch in CA 23-24R
Owen, Tobias Chant 1936- 111
Owen, Tom
See Watts, Peter Christopher
Owen, W(arwick) J(ack) B(urgoyne) 1916-
Brief entry 111
Owen, Wilfred 1893-1918 Brief entry 104
See also DLB 20
See also TCLC 5, 27
Owen, Wilfred 1912- 37-40R
Owen, William Vern 1894- CAP-2
Earlier sketch in CA 17-18
Owen, Wyn F(oster) 1923- Brief entry 115
Owendoff, Robert S(cott) 1945- 19-20R
Owens, Bill 1938- 73-76
Owens, Carole (Ehrlich) 1942- 116
Owens, Carolyn 1946- 109
Owens, Edgar (Leonard) 1924-1987
Obituary 124
Owens, Gary 1936- 97-100
Owens, Jesse 1913-1980 110
Owens, Joan (Margaret) Llewelyn 1919- .. 15-16R
Owens, John R(obert) 1926- 77-80
Owens, Joseph 1908- CANR-20
Earlier sketches in CA 7-8R, CANR-5
Owens, Pat(rick) J. 1929- 73-76
Owens, Richard Meredith 1944- 61-64
Owens, Robert Goronwy 1923- 29-32R
Owens, Rochelle 1936- 17-18R
See also CAAS 2
See also CLC 8
Owens, Thelma 1905- 69-72
Owens, Virginia Stem 1941- CANR-14
Earlier sketch in CA 81-84
Owens, William A. 1905- 11-12R
Ower, John 1942- 77-80
Owings, Loren C(lyde) 1928- 37-40R
Owings, Mark (Samuel) 1945- Brief entry ... 114
Owings, Nathaniel Alexander 1903-1984 ... 61-64
Obituary 113
Owomoyela, Oyekan 1938- 112
Owsley, Frank L(awrence) 1890-1956
Brief entry 116
See also DLB 17
Owsley, Harriet Chappell 1901- 81-84
Oxenbury, Helen 1938- 25-28R
See also SATA 3
Oxenham, Elsie J.
See Dunkerley, Elsie Jeanette
Oxenhandler, Neal 1926- CANR-6
Earlier sketch in CA 13-14R
Oxley, Dorothy (Anne) 1948- 116
Oxley, William 1939- 73-76
Oxnam, Robert B(romley) 1942- CANR-5
Earlier sketch in CA 53-56
Oxnard, Charles (Ernest) 1933- CANR-16
Earlier sketches in CA 45-48, CANR-1
Oxorn, Harry 1920- 111
Oxtoby, Willard Gurdon 1933- 49-52
Oyle, Irving 1925- CANR-6
Earlier sketch in CA 57-60
Oyler, Philip (Tom) 1879- CAP-1
Earlier sketch in CA 9-10
Oy-Vik
See Holmvik, Oyvind
Oz, Amos 1939- 53-56
See also CLC 5, 8, 11, 27, 33
Ozaki, Robert S(higeo) 1934- 49-52
Ozawa, Terutomo 1935- 85-88
Ozbudun, Ergun 1937- 126
Ozer, Jerome S. 1927- 107
Ozer, Mark N(orman) 1932- 112
Ozick, Cynthia 1928- CANR-23
Earlier sketch in CA 17-18R
See also DLB 28
See also DLBY 82
See also CLC 3, 7, 28
Ozinga, James Richard 1932- 97-100
Ozment, Robert V. 1927- 17-18R
Ozment, Steven E(dgar) 1939- 108
Ozmon, Howard A. 25-28R
Ozu, Yasujiro 1903-1963 112
See also CLC 16
Ozy
See Rosset, B(enjamin) C(harles)

P

P. L. K.
See Kirk-Greene, Anthony (Hamilton Millard)
P.Q.
See Quennell, Peter (Courtney)
P. W.
See Strasser, Bernard Paul
Paak, Carl Erich 1922- 106
Paananen, Eloise (Katherine) 1923- CANR-18
Earlier sketches in CA 2R, CANR-2
Paananen, Victor Niles 1938- 73-76
Paarlberg, Don 1911- 23-24R
Paasche, Carol L(evine) 1937- 5-6R
Paauw, Douglas Seymour 1921- 103
Pab
See Blooman, Percy A.
Paca, Lillian Grace (Baker) 1883- CAP-1
Earlier sketch in CA 11-12
Pacaut, Marcel 1920- 29-32R
Pace, C(harles) Robert 1912- 81-84
Pace, Denny F. 1925- 49-52
Pace, Donald Metcalf 1906-1982 Obituary .. 108
Pace, Eric 1936- 45-48
Pace, J. Blair 1916- 69-72
Pace, Mildred Mastin 1907- CANR-5
Earlier sketch in CA 7-8R
See also SATA 29, 46
Pace, Nathaniel 1925- 110
Pace, Peter
See Burnett, David (Benjamin Foley)
Pace, R(alph) Wayne 1931- CANR-1
Earlier sketch in CA 45-48
Pace, Robert Lee 1924- 4R
Pacernick, Gary 1941- 73-76
Pacey, (William Cyril) Desmond
1917-1975 .... CANR-4
Earlier sketch in CA 7-8R
Pachai, Bridglal 1927- CANR-17
Earlier sketch in CA 93-96
Pacheco, C.
See Pessoa, Fernando (Antonio Nogueira)
Pacheco, Ferdie 1927- 81-84
Pacheco, Henry L(uis) 1947- 49-52
Pacheco, Jose Emilio 1939- Brief entry 111
Pa Chin
See Li Fei-kan
Pachmuss, Temira 1927- CANR-20
Earlier sketches in CA 11-12R, CANR-4
Pachter, Henry M(aximillian) 1907- 9-10R
Pacifici, Sergio 1925- CANR-3
Earlier sketch in CA 3R
Pacifico, Carl 1921- 23-24R
Pack, Robert 1929- CANR-3
Earlier sketch in CA 3R
See also DLB 5
See also CLC 13
Pack, Roger A(mbrose) 1907- CAP-1
Earlier sketch in CA 15-16
Pack, S(tanley) W(alter) C(roucher)
1904-1977 .... 13-14R
Obituary 125
Packard, Andrew 1929- 2R
Packard, Cindy
See Richmond, Cindy Packard
Packard, Edward 1931- 114
See also SATA 47
Packard, Frederick Clifton, Jr. 1899-1985
Obituary 116
Packard, George R(andolph) III 1932-
Brief entry 112
Packard, Jerrold M(ichael) 1943- CANR-23
Earlier sketch in CA 106
Packard, Karl 1911(?)-1977 Obituary 69-72
Packard, Reynolds 1903-1976 73-76
Obituary 69-72
Packard, Robert G(eorge) 1933- 57-60
Packard, Rosa Covington 1935- 97-100
Packard, Rosalie 1R
Packard, Russell C. 1946- 119
Packard, Sidney R(aymond) 1893- 61-64
Packard, Vance (Oakley) 1914- CANR-7
Earlier sketch in CA 11-12R
See also AITN 1
Packard, William 1933- CANR-7
Earlier sketch in CA 13-14R
Packenham, Robert Allen 1937- 73-76
Packer, Arnold H. 1935- 37-40R
Packer, Bernard J(ules) 1934- CANR-19
Earlier sketch in CA 65-68
Packer, David W(illiam) 1937- 11-12R
Packer, Herbert L(eslie) 1925-1972 ...... 37-40R
Packer, J(ames) I(nnell) 1926- CANR-16
Earlier sketches in CA 49-52, CANR-1
Packer, Joy (Petersen) 1905-1977 ...... CANR-3
Earlier sketch in CA 4R
Packer, Lady
See Packer, Joy (Petersen)
Packer, Nancy Huddleston 1925- 65-68
Packer, Rod Earle 1931- 109
Packer, Vin
See Meaker, Marijane
Packman, David 1949- 123
Pacosz, Christina V(ivian) 1946- 77-80
Padberg, Daniel I(van) 1931- 33-36R
Padberg, John W(illiam) 1926- 25-28R
Padden, R(obert) C(harles) 1922- 21-22R
Paddison, Ronan 1945- 117
Paddleford, Clementine Haskin 1900-1967
Obituary 89-92
Paddock, John 1918- 17-18R
Paddock, Paul (Ezekiel, Jr.) 1907-1975 ... CAP-2
Obituary 61-64
Earlier sketch in CA 21-22
Paddock, William (Carson) 1921- 21-22R
Pade, Victoria 1953- 113
Paden, William D(oremus, Jr.) 1941- 124
Padfield, Harland (Irvine) 1926-
Brief entry 112
Padfield, Peter 1932- CANR-26
Earlier sketch in CA 101
Padgett, Desmond
See von Block, Bela W(illiam)
Padgett, Dora 1893(?)-1976 Obituary 61-64
Padgett, Lewis
See Kuttner, Henry
and Moore, C(atherine) L(ucile)
Padgett, Ron 1942- CANR-12
Earlier sketch in CA 25-28R
See also DLB 5
Padilla (Lorenzo), Heberto 1932-
Brief entry 123
See also CLC 38
See also AITN 1
Padilla, Victoria 1907-1986 103
Obituary 120
Padley, Walter Ernest 1916-1984 Obituary .. 112
Padmore, George
See Nurse, Malcolm Ivan Meredith
Padovano, Anthony T(homas) 1934- ... CANR-22
Earlier sketches in CA 17-18R, CANR-7
Padover, Saul K(ussiel) 1905-1981 ..... CANR-2
Obituary 103
Earlier sketch in CA 49-52
Padwick, E(ric) W(illiam) 1923- 119
Paetro, Maxine 1946- 123
Paffard, Michael Kenneth 1928- 103
Pafford, John Henry Pyle 1900- CANR-21
Earlier sketch in CA 104
Pagden, Anthony 1945- 101
Page, Benjamin I(ngrim) 1940- 112
Page, Carole Gift 1942- 117
Page, Charles H(unt) 1909- CANR-4
Earlier sketch in CA 7-8R
Page, Curtis C(arling) 1914- 21-22R
Page, Diana (Preuthun) 1946- 126
Page, Drew 1905- 105
Page, Eileen
See Heal, Edith
Page, Eleanor
See Coerr, Eleanor (Beatrice)
Page, Ellis Batten 1924- 15-16R
Page, Emma
See Tirbutt, Honoria
Page, Evelyn 1902- 7-8R
Page, G. S.
See Galbraith, Georgie Starbuck
Page, Gerald W(ilburn) 1939- 93-96
Page, Grover, Jr. 1918- 17-18R
Page, Harry Robert 1915- 11-12R
Page, Homer (Gordon) 1918-1985
Obituary 117
Page, Jake
See Page, James K(eena), Jr.
Page, James A(llen) 1918- 107
Page, James D. 1910- 73-76
Page, James K(eena), Jr. 1936- 97-100
Page, Jimmy 1944- CLC-12
Page, Joseph A(nthony) 1934- CANR-14
Earlier sketch in CA 81-84
Page, Lorna
See Rowland, D(onald) S(ydney)
Page, Lou Williams 1912- CANR-5
Earlier sketch in CA 5-6R
See also SATA 38
Page, Louise 1955- CLC-40
Page, Malcolm 1935- 45-48
Page, Marian 69-72
Page, Martin 1938- CANR-12
Earlier sketch in CA 19-20R
Page, Mary
See Heal, Edith
Page, Norman 1930- CANR-8
Earlier sketch in CA 61-64
Page, P(atricia) K(athleen) 1916- CANR-22
Earlier sketches in CA 53-56, CANR-4
See also DLB 68
See also CLC 7, 18
Page, Robert Collier 1908-1977 Obituary .. 73-76
Page, Robert J(effress) 1922- 17-18R
Page, Robert Morris 1903- CAP-2
Earlier sketch in CA 17-18
Page, Robin 1943- 103
Page, Roch 1939- 33-36R
Page, Russell 1906-1985 Obituary 114
Page, Stanton
See Fuller, Henry Blake
Page, Thomas 1942- 81-84
Page, Thomas Nelson 1853-1922
Brief entry 118
See also DLB 12
Page, Thornton (Leigh) 1913- CANR-2
Earlier sketch in CA 5-6R
Page, Vicki
See Avey, Ruby
Page, Walter Hines 1855-1918 .... DLB-71
Page, Warren (Kempton) 1910-1977
Obituary 111
Page, William 1929- 114
Page, William 1946- 115
Page, William Roberts 1904- 21-22R
Pagel, Walter T. U. 1898-1983 Obituary 109
Pagels, Elaine Hiesey 1943- CANR-24
Earlier sketches in CA 45-48, CANR-2
Pagels, Heinz R(udolf) 1939-1988 ..... CANR-23
Obituary 126
Earlier sketch in CA 107
Pages, Pedro
See Alba, Victor
Paget, George Charles Henry Victor
1922- 17-18R
Paget, John
See Aiken, John (Kempton)
Paget, Julian 1921- 23-24R
Paget, Margaret
See Medlicott, Margaret P(aget)
Paget, Violet 1856-1935 Brief entry 104
Paget-Fredericks, Joseph E. P.
Rous-Marten 1903-1963 .... SATA-30
Paget-Lowe, Henry
See Lovecraft, H(oward) P(hillips)
Paglin, Morton 1922- 97-100
Pagnol, Marcel 1895-1974 Obituary 49-52
Paher, Stanley W(illiam) 1940- 29-32R
Pahl, R(aymond) E(dward) 1935- 25-28R
Pahlavi, Mohammed Riza
See Pahlevi, Mohammed Riza
Pahlen, Kurt 1907- CANR-7
Earlier sketch in CA 15-16R
Pahlevi, Mohammed Riza 1919-1980
Obituary 106
Pahz, (Anne) Cheryl Suzanne 1949- CANR-8
Earlier sketch in CA 53-56
See also SATA 11
Pahz, James Alon 1943- CANR-8
Earlier sketch in CA 53-56
See also SATA 11
Pai, Anna C(hao) 1935- 89-92
Pai, Young 1929- 33-36R
Paice, Margaret 1920- CANR-20
Earlier sketch in CA 29-32R
See also SATA 10
Paier, Robert (David) 1943- 89-92
Paige, Glenn D(urland) 1929- 25-29R
Paige, Harry W(orthington) 1922- 113
See also SATA 35, 41
Paige, Leo
See Cochrane, William E.
Paige, Leroy Robert 1907(?)-1982
Obituary 107
Paige, Richard
See Koontz, Dean R(ay)
Paige, Richard E(aton) 1904-1988 111
Obituary 126
Paige, Satchel
See Paige, Leroy Robert
Pain, Barry (Eric Odell) 1864-1928
Brief entry 109
Pain, Philip ?-1666(?) DLB-24
Paine, Albert Bigelow 1861-1937
Brief entry 108
Paine, J. Lincoln
See Kramish, Arnold
Paine, Lauran (Bosworth) 1916- CANR-7
Earlier sketch in CA 45-48
Paine, Philbrook 1910- CAP-1
Earlier sketch in CA 11-12
Paine, R(ussell) Howard 1922- 7-8R
Paine, Robert Treat, Jr. 1773-1811 ..... DLB-37
Paine, Roberta M. 1925- 33-36R
See also SATA 13
Paine, Roger W(arde) III 1942- 65-68
Paine, Stephen William 1908- 3R
Paine, Thomas 1737-1809 ...... DLB-31, 43, 73
See also CDALB 1640-1865
Painter, Charlotte CANR-3
Earlier sketch in CA 2R
Painter, Daniel
See Burgess, M(ichael) R(oy)
Painter, George D(uncan) 1914- 101
Painter, Helen W(elch) 1913- 33-36R
Painter, Nell Irvin 1942- CANR-19
Earlier sketch in CA 65-68
See also BW
Painter, Pamela 1941- 122
Pairault, Pierre 1922- 53-56
Pais, Abraham 1918- 109
Paish, F(rank) W(alter) 1898-1988 ...... 17-18R
Obituary 125
Paisley, Tom 1932- CANR-15
Earlier sketch in CA 61-64
Paisner, Milton 1915- 113
Pak Chong-Hui
See Park Chung Hee
Pakenham, Edward Arthur Henry
1902-1961 Obituary 114
Pakenham, Francis Aungier 1905- 109
Pakenham, Frank, Seventh Earl of Longford
See Pakenham, Francis Aungier
Pakenham, Simona Vere 1916- CANR-3
Earlier sketch in CA 4R
Pakenham, Thomas (Frank Dermot) 1933- .. 109
Pakula, Alan J(ay) 1928- Brief entry 124
Pakula, Marion Broome 1926- CANR-7
Earlier sketch in CA 57-60

Pal, Pratapaditya 1935- 37-40R
Palamas, Kostes 1859-1943 Brief entry 105
See also TCLC 5
Palamountain, Joseph Cornwall, Jr.
1920-1987 45-48
Obituary 124
Palandri, Angela (Chin-ying) Jung 1926- ..37-40R
Palange, Anthony (Jr.) 1942- 37-40R
Palau, Luis (Jr.) 1934- 116
Palazzeschi, Aldo 1885-1974 89-92
Obituary 53-56
See also CLC 11
Palazzo, Anthony D.
See Palazzo, Tony
Palazzo, Tony 1905-1970 .... CANR-4
Obituary 29-32R
Earlier sketch in CA 7-8R
See also SATA 3
Palder, Edward L. 1922- SATA-5
Paleckis, Justas (Ignovich) 1899-1980
Obituary 105
Palen, J(oseph) John 1939- CANR-15
Earlier sketch in CA 41-44R
Palen, Jennie M. 7-8R
Palermo, David Stuart 1929- 19-20R
Palestrant, Simon S. 1907- CAP-1
Earlier sketch in CA 9-10
Paley, Alan L(ouis) 1943- 69-72
Paley, Grace 1922- CANR-13
Earlier sketch in CA 25-28R
See also DLB 28
See also CLC 4, 6, 37
Paley, Maggie 1939- 121
Paley, Morton D(avid) 1935- CANR-13
Earlier sketch in CA 33-36R
Paley, Nicholas M(iroslav) 1911- CANR-15
Earlier sketch in CA 41-44R
Paley, Vivian Gussin 1929- 93-96
Paley, William S(amuel) 1901- 110
Palffy-Alpar, Julius 1908- CAP-2
Earlier sketch in CA 23-24
Palfrey, John Gorham 1796-1881 .... DLB-1, 30
Palfrey, Thomas R(ossman) 1895- 61-64
Palgrave, Francis Turner 1824-1897 .... DLB-35
Palin, Michael 107
See also CLC 21
Palinchak, Robert S(tephen) 1942- 49-52
Palinurus
See Connolly, Cyril (Vernon)
Palisca, Claude V. 1921- 17-18R
Pall, Ellen Jane 1952- 93-96
Palladini, David (Mario) 1946- SATA-32, 40
Pallas, Dorothy Constance 1933-1971
Obituary 33-36R
Pallas, Norvin 1918- CANR-3
Earlier sketch in CA 2R
See also SATA 23
Pallavera, Franco
See Soldati, Mario
Palle, Albert 1916- 13-14R
Pallenberg, Corrado 1912- 15-16R
Palley, Julian I(rving) 1925- 73-76
Palley, Marian Lief 1939- CANR-8
Earlier sketch in CA 61-64
Palli, Pitsa
See Hartocollis, Peter
Pallidini, Jodi
See Robbin, (Jodi) Luna
Pallis, Alexander (Anastasius) 1883-1975
Obituary 61-64
Pallister, Janis L(ouise) 1926- CANR-14
Earlier sketch in CA 41-44R
Pallister, John C(lare) 1891-1980 ....7-8R
Obituary 103
See also SATA 26
Pallone, Nathaniel John 1935- CANR-10
Earlier sketch in CA 21-22R
Palm, Goeran 1931- 29-32R
Palm, Goran
See Palm, Goeran
Palm, John Daniel 1924- Brief entry 106
Palma, Ricardo 1833-1919 ....TCLC-29
Palmatier, Robert Allen 1926- 37-40R
Palmedo, Roland 1895-1977 53-56
Obituary 69-72
Palmer, Alan Warwick 1926- CANR-6
Earlier sketch in CA 13-14R
Palmer, Archie M(acInnes) 1896-1985 ...13-14R
Obituary 116
Palmer, Arnold (Daniel) 1929- 85-88
Palmer, B. C.
See Schmidt, Laura M(arie)
Palmer, Bernard 1914- CANR-12
Earlier sketches in CA 57-60, CANR-7
See also SATA 26
Palmer, Brooks 1900(?)-1974 Obituary 45-48
Palmer, Bruce (Hamilton) 1932- CANR-3
Earlier sketch in CA 3R
Palmer, C(yril) Everard 1930- 41-44R
See also BW
See also SATA 14
Palmer, C(edric) King 1913- 13-14R
Palmer, (Ruth) Candida 1926- 61-64
See also SATA 11
Palmer, (John) Carey (Bowden) 1943- 103
Palmer, Charles Earl 1919- 15-16R
Palmer, (Thomas) Cruise 1917- 69-72
Palmer, Dave Richard 1934- CANR-1
Earlier sketch in CA 45-48
Palmer, David 1928- 21-22R
Palmer, Donald C. 1934- 53-56
Palmer, Dorothy Ann 1935- 57-60
Palmer, E(dgar) P(oole), Jr. 1938- 116
Palmer, Earl Frank 1931- 113
Palmer, Edgar Z(avitz) 1898- 21-22R
Palmer, Edward L. 1938- 101
Palmer, Elsie Pavitt 1922- 7-8R
Palmer, Eve 1916- 23-24R
Palmer, Everett W(alter) 1906-1970 ...... CAP-2
Earlier sketch in CA 17-18
Palmer, Frank R. 1922- 17-18R
Palmer, George 1915(?)-1986 Obituary 119
Palmer, George E. 1908- 1R
Palmer, George Herbert 1842-1933
Brief entry 121
Palmer, Gerald Eustace Howell 1904-1984
Obituary 112
Palmer, (James) Gregory 1938- 121
Palmer, Heidi 1948- SATA-15
Palmer, Helen H. 1911- 21-22R
Palmer, Helen Marion
See Geisel, Helen
Palmer, Henry R(obinson), Jr. 1911- 23-24R
Palmer, (Nathaniel) Humphrey 1930- ... CANR-12
Earlier sketch in CA 29-32R
Palmer, James B. 1929- 25-28R
Palmer, Jerome Robert 1904- 45-48
Palmer, Jim
See Palmer, James B.
Palmer, John (Leslie) 1885-1944
Brief entry 121
Palmer, John A. 1926- 29-32R
Palmer, John L(ogan) 1943- 73-76
Palmer, Joseph (Mansergh) 1912- 7-8R
Palmer, Juliette 1930- 81-84
See also SATA 15
Palmer, Kenneth T. 1937- 77-80
Palmer, L(eonard) R(obert) 1906-1984 ...25-28R
Obituary 114
Palmer, Larry Garland 1938- 19-20R
Palmer, Laura
See Schmidt, Laura M(arie)
Palmer, Lilli
See Peiser, Maria Lilli
Palmer, Lynn
See Palmer, Pamela Lynn
Palmer, Madelyn 1910- 103
Palmer, Marian 1930- 53-56
Palmer, Marjorie 1919- CANR-12
Earlier sketch in CA 57-60
Palmer, Michael (Stephen) 1942- 114
Palmer, Michael D. 1933- 37-40R
Palmer, Nicholas 1950- CANR-15
Earlier sketch in CA 89-92
Palmer, Norman D(unbar) 1909- CANR-19
Earlier sketches in CA 3R, CANR-3
Palmer, Pamela Lynn 1951- CANR-4
Earlier sketch in CA 53-56
Palmer, Parker J. 1939- 115
Palmer, Pete
See Palmer, E(dgar) P(oole), Jr.
Palmer, Peter
See Palmer, Elsie Pavitt
Palmer, Peter John 1932- CANR-20
Earlier sketch in CA 103
Palmer, R(obert) R(oswell) 1909- 13-14R
Palmer, Ralph Simon 1914- 73-76
Palmer, Raymond A. 1910-1977 Obituary .. 111
Palmer, Raymond Edward 1927- 77-80
Palmer, Richard 1904- 97-100
Palmer, Richard Edward 1933- CANR-1
Earlier sketch in CA 45-48
Palmer, Richard Phillips 1921- 57-60
Palmer, Robert (Franklin, Jr.) 1945-
Brief entry 121
Palmer, Robert C(harles) 1947- 113
Palmer, Robert E(verett) A(llen) 1932-
Brief entry 114
Palmer, Robin 1911- 109
See also SATA 43
Palmer, Roy (Ernest) 1932- CANR-23
Earlier sketches in CA 61-64, CANR-8
Palmer, Spencer J(ohn) 1927- CANR-10
Earlier sketch in CA 61-64
Palmer, Stuart 1924- CANR-3
Earlier sketch in CA 1R
Palmer, Thomas 1955- 109
Palmer, Tim 1948- 121
Palmer, Tobias
See Weathers, Winston
Palmer, Tony 1941- Brief entry 111
Palmer, Winthrop Bushnell 1899-1988 65-68
Obituary 126
Palmieri, Anthony Francis 1920- 114
Palmore, Erdman B. 1930- 37-40R
Palms, Roger C(urtis) 1936- CANR-17
Earlier sketch in CA 93-96
Paloczi-Horvath, George 1908-1973 ....7-8R
Obituary 37-40R
Palombo, Stanley R(obert) 1934- 122
Palomo, G(aspar) J(esus) 1952- 61-64
Palovic, Clara Lora 1918- 25-28R
Paltenghi, Madeleine
See Anderson, Madeleine Paltenghi
Paltock, Robert 1697-1767 .... DLB-39
Paltrowitz, Donna (Milman) 1950- 119
See also SATA 50
Paltrowitz, Stuart 1946- 118
See also SATA 50
Paludan, (Stig Henning) Jacob (Puggaard)
1896-1975 Obituary 115
Paludan, Phillip S(haw) 1938- 73-76
Paluello, Lorenzo Minio
See Minio-Paluello, Lorenzo
Palumbo, Dennis J(ames) 1929- 29-32R
Palusci, Larry 1916- 29-32R
Paluszny, Maria Janina 1939- 103
Palyi, Melchior 1892(?)-1970 Obituary 104
Pan, Peter
See Bartier, Pierre
Pan, Stephen C(hao) Y(ing) 1915- 45-48
Panagopoulos, Epaminondas Peter
1915- 13-14R
Panama, Norman 1920- 104
See also DLB 26
Panassie, Hugues (Louis Marie Henri)
1912-1974 97-100
Obituary 53-56
Panati, Charles 1943- 81-84
Pancake, Breece Dexter 1952-1979 123
Obituary 109
Pancake, Breece D'J
See Pancake, Breece Dexter
See also CLC 29
Pancake, John S(ilas) 1920- 53-56
Pandey, B(ishwa) N(ath) 1929-1982 ... CANR-20
Obituary 108
Earlier sketch in CA 25-28R
Pandit, Vijaya Lakshmi 1900- 104
Panek, LeRoy Lad 1943- 113
Panella, Vincent 1939- 97-100
Panetta, George 1915-1969 81-84
See also SATA 15
Panetta, Leon Edward 1938- 101
Pang, May 1950- 118
Pangborn, Edgar 1909-1976 .... CANR-4
Earlier sketch in CA 1R
See also DLB 8
Panger, Daniel 1926- 93-96
Panglaykim, J(usuf Pangestu) 1922- ... CANR-15
Earlier sketch in CA 23-24R
Pangle, Thomas L(ee) 1944- CANR-1
Earlier sketch in CA 49-52
Pangrazzi, Arnaldo 1947- 115
Paniagua Bermudez, Domingo
1880(?)-1973 Obituary 41-44R
Panichas, George A(ndrew) 1930- CANR-25
Earlier sketches in CA 25-28R, CANR-10
Paniker, Raimundo
See Panikkar, Raimundo
Panikkar, K(avalam) Madhava 1895-1963 . CAP-1
Earlier sketch in CA 15-16
Panikkar, Raimundo 1918- CANR-25
Earlier sketch in CA 81-84
Panikkar, Raymond
See Panikkar, Raimundo
Panin, Dimitri (Mikhailovich) 1911-1987
Obituary 124
Panitch, Leo (Victor) 1945- 119
Panitt, Merrill 1917- 106
Panitz, Esther L(eah) 116
Pankey, Eric 1959- 120
Pankhurst, Emmeline (Goulden)
1858-1928 Brief entry 116
Pankhurst, Richard (Keir Pethick)
1927- CANR-21
Earlier sketches in CA 9-10R, CANR-6
Pankin, Robert M. 1935- 114
Pannabecker, Samuel Floyd 1896- 65-68
Pannell, Anne Gary 1910- CAP-2
Earlier sketch in CA 23-24
Pannenberg, Wolfhart (Ulrich) 1928- ... CANR-11
Earlier sketch in CA 25-28R
Panneton, Philippe
See Ringuet
Pannor, Reuben 1922- 61-64
Pannwitz, Rudolf 1881-1969 Obituary 89-92
Pano, Nicholas C(hristopher) 1934- 37-40R
Panofsky, Erwin 1892-1968 113
Obituary 113
Panos, Chris(tos) 1935- 65-68
Panov, Valery (Shulman) 1938- 102
Panova, Vera (Fedorovna) 1905-1973 102
Obituary 89-92
Panowski, Eileen Thompson 1920- 5-6R
See also SATA 49
Panshin, Alexei 1940- 57-60
See also DLB 8
Panshin, Cory (Seidman) 1947-
Brief entry 112
Pansy
See Alden, Isabella (Macdonald)
Pantell, Dora (Fuchs) 111
See also SATA 39
Panter, Carol 1936- 49-52
See also SATA 9
Panter, Gideon G. 1935- 77-80
Panter-Downes, Mollie Patricia 1906- 101
Panting, Phyllis
See Morton, Phyllis Digby
Panzarella, Andrew 1940- 25-28R
Panzarella, Joseph John, Jr. 1919- 85-88
Panzer, Pauline (Richman) 1911(?)-1972
Obituary 37-40R
Pao, Ping-Nie 1922- 103
Paoletti, John T(homas) 1939- 112
Paoli, Pia 1930- 25-28R
Paolini, Gilberto 1928- CANR-22
Earlier sketch in CA 45-48
Paolucci, Anne 73-76
Paolucci, Henry 1921- 102
Paone, Anthony J(oseph) 1913- 5-6R
Paor, Richard de
See Power, Richard
Papachristou, Judy 1930- 93-96
Papadiamantis, Alexandros 1851-1911 ..TCLC-29
Papadiamantopoulos, Johannes
1856-1910 Brief entry 117
Papaleo, Joseph 1925- 25-28R
Papandreou, Andreas G(eorge) 1919- 37-40R
Papandreou, Margaret C. 1923- 29-32R
Papanek, Ernst 1900-1973 .... CANR-4
Earlier sketch in CA 2R
Papanek, Gustav F(ritz) 1926- CANR-1
Earlier sketch in CA 45-48
Papas, William 1927- CANR-12
Earlier sketch in CA 25-28R
See also SATA 50
Papashvily, George 1898-1978 81-84
Obituary 77-80
See also SATA 17
Papashvily, Helen (Waite) 1906- 81-84
See also SATA 17
Papazian, Dennis R(ichard) 1931- 45-48
Papazoglou, Orania 1951- 126
Pape, D. L.
See Pape, Donna (Lugg)
Pape, Donna (Lugg) 1930- CANR-25
Earlier sketches in CA 23-24R, CANR-9
See also SATA 2
Pape, Gordon 1936- CANR-25
Earlier sketch in CA 105
Pape, Greg 1947- 113
Papenfuse, Edward C(arl), Jr. 1943- CANR-8
Earlier sketch in CA 57-60
Paper, Herbert H(arry) 1925- CANR-1
Earlier sketch in CA 45-48
Paper, Lewis J(ay) 1946- Brief entry 114
Paperny, Myra (Green) 1932- 69-72
See also SATA 33, 51
Papert, Emma N. 1926- 101
Papi, G(iuseppe) Ugo 1893- 25-28R
Papich, Stephen 1925- 69-72
Papier, Judith Barnard 1932- 21-22R
Papin, Joseph 1914- 65-68
Papini, Giovanni 1881-1956 Brief entry 121
See also TCLC 22
Papp, Charles Steven 1917- CANR-15
Earlier sketch in CA 41-44R
Pappageotes, George C(hristos)
1926-1963 .... CANR-2
Earlier sketch in CA 1R
Pappas, George 1929- 29-32R
Pappas, Lou Seibert 1930- CANR-23
Earlier sketches in CA 61-64, CANR-8
Pappworth, M(aurice) H(enry) 1910- 23-24R
Paprika
See Holmvik, Oyvind
Papus
See Encausse, Gerard (Anaclet Vincent)
Paquet, Alfons 1881-1944 .... DLB-66
Paradis, Adrian A(lexis) 1912- CANR-18
Earlier sketches in CA 4R, CANR-3
See also SATA 1
Paradis, James G(ardiner) 1942- 93-96
Paradis, Marjorie Bartholomew
1886(?)-1970 73-76
Obituary 29-32R
See also SATA 17
Paradis, Suzanne 1936- DLB-53
Paradise, Louis V(incent) 1946- 114
Parakh, Jal Sohrab 1932- Brief entry 105
Parandowski, Jan 1895- CAP-1
Earlier sketch in CA 11-12
Parasol, Peter
See Stevens, Wallace
Parasuram, T(attamangalam) V(iswanatha
Iyer) 1923- 106
Paratore, Angela 1912- 13-14R
Parchman, William E(ugene) 1936- 93-96
Pardee, Michael 1945- 113
Pardey, Larry
See Pardey, Lawrence Fred
Pardey, Lawrence Fred 1939- 93-96
Pardey, (Mary) Lin 1944- 93-96
Paredes, Americo 1915- 37-40R
Pareek, Udai (Narain) 1925- CANR-11
Earlier sketch in CA 21-22R
Parelius, Ann Parker 1943- 81-84
Parelius, Robert J. 1941- 81-84
Parens, Henri 1928- 89-92
Parent, David J(oseph) 1931- CANR-9
Earlier sketch in CA 57-60
Parent, Gail 1940- 101
Parent, Ronald 1937-1982 Obituary 107
Parente, Pascal P(rosper) 1890-1971 .... CAP-1
Obituary 33-36R
Earlier sketch in CA 17-18
Parente, Sarah (Eleanor) 1913- CANR-16
Earlier sketch in CA 41-44R
Parenteau, Shirley Laurolyn 1935- CANR-15
Earlier sketch in CA 85-88
See also SATA 40, 47
Parenti, Michael 1933- 73-76
Pares, Marion (Stapylton) 1914- CANR-12
Earlier sketch in CA 17-18R
Paret, Peter 1924- Brief entry 114
Paretsky, Sara 1947- Brief entry 125
Paretti, Sandra CANR-7
Earlier sketch in CA 53-56
Parezo, Nancy Jean 1951- 114
Parfit, Michael 1947- 119
Parfitt, George (Albert Ekins) 1939- ... CANR-26
Earlier sketch in CA 109
Parfitt, Tudor (Vernon) 1944- 123
Pargeter, Edith Mary 1913- CANR-24
Earlier sketches in CA 4R, CANR-4
Parham, Joseph Byars 1919- 65-68
Parham, Robert Randall 1943- 57-60
Parham, William 1914- 103
Parham, William Thomas 1913- CANR-20
Earlier sketch in CA 103
Parini, Jay (Lee) 1948- 97-100
Parins, James William 1939- 109
Paris, Bernard J. 1931- CANR-7
Earlier sketch in CA 17-18R
Paris, Erna 1938- 105
Paris, Ginette 1946- 123
Paris, Jeanne 1918- 1R
Parise, Goffredo 1929-1986 Obituary 120
Pariseau, Earl J(oseph) 1928- 11-12R
Parish, Charles 1927- 25-28R
Parish, David 1932- CANR-14
Earlier sketch in CA 73-76
Parish, Helen Rand 1912- Brief entry 115

Parish, James 1904-1973 Obituary 114
Parish, James Robert 1944- 33-36R
Parish, Margaret Cecile 1927- CANR-18
Earlier sketch in CA 73-76
Parish, Margaret Holt
See Holt, Margaret
Parish, Peggy
See Parish, Margaret Cecile
See also SATA 17
Parish, Peter J(oseph) 1929- 57-60
Parish, Townsend
See Pietschmann, Richard John III
Parisi, Joseph 1944- 93-96
Parizeau, Alice 1930- DLB-60
Park, Barbara 1947- 113
See also SATA 35, 40
Park, Bill
See Park, W(illiam) B(ryan)
See also SATA 22
Park, Charles F(rederick), Jr. 1903- 57-60
Park, Clara Claiborne 1923- 23-24R
Park, D. U.
See Woods, Clee
Park, David 1919- 105
Park, Ed 1930- 73-76
Park, Edwards 1917- 123
Park, Elm
See Dunbar, Charles Stuart
Park, George 1925- 77-80
Park, James (Robert) 1956- 120
Park, James William 1936- 121
Park, Joe 1913- 23-24R
Park, Jordan
See Kornbluth, C(yril) M.
and Pohl, Frederik
Park, Joseph H. 1890(?)-1979 Obituary ...89-92
Park, Maeva
See Dobner, Maeva Park
Park, O'Hyun 1940- 53-56
Park, Peter 1929- 29-32R
Park, Richard L(eonard) 1920- 77-80
Park, Robert E(zra) 1864-1944 Brief entry .. 122
Park, Robert L. 1932- 89-92
Park, (Rosina) Ruth 105
See also SATA 25
Park, Sung-Bae 1933- 115
Park, W(illiam) B(ryan) 1936- CANR-17
Earlier sketch in CA 97-100
See also SATA 22
Park, William John 1930- 49-52
Park Chung Hee 1917-1979 .... CANR-10
Obituary 97-100
Earlier sketch in CA 61-64
Parke, Herbert William 1903- 105
Parke, John 1754-1789 .... DLB-31
Parke, Margaret Bittner 1901- 89-92
Parke, Ross D(uke) 1938- CANR-16
Earlier sketches in CA 45-48, CANR-1
Parker, Adrian David 1947- 103
Parker, Alexander A(ugustine) 1908- ... CANR-16
Earlier sketch in CA 23-24R
Parker, Alfred Browning 1916- 17-18R
Parker, Ann
See Neal, Ann Parker
Parker, Arthur C(aswell) 1881-1955
Brief entry 115
Parker, Barry (Richard) 1935- 112
Parker, Beatrice
See Huff, T(om) E.
Parker, Bert
See Ellison, Harlan
Parker, Bertha Morris 1890-1980 .... CANR-5
Obituary 102
Earlier sketch in CA 7-8R
Parker, Betty June 1929- CANR-22
Earlier sketches in CA 57-60, CANR-7
Parker, Beulah 1912- 81-84
Parker, Brant Julian 1920- Brief entry 114
Parker, Clifford S(tetson) 1891- 7-8R
Parker, Clyde A. 1927- 41-44R
Parker, David L(ambert) 1935- 108
Parker, David Marshall 1929- 77-80
Parker, Dee
See Parker, David L(ambert)
Parker, (William George) Derek 1932- .. CANR-23
Earlier sketch in CA 29-32R
Parker, Don(ald) H(enry) 1912- CANR-6
Earlier sketch in CA 7-8R
Parker, Donald Dean 1899- 37-40R
Parker, Donn B(lanchard) 1929- CANR-9
Earlier sketch in CA 65-68
Parker, Dorothy (Rothschild) 1893-1967 .. CAP-2
Obituary 25-28R
Earlier sketch in CA 19-20
See also DLB 11, 45
See also CLC 15
See also SSC 2
Parker, Dorothy 1922- 93-96
Parker, Dorothy Mills CANR-11
Earlier sketch in CA 21-22R
Parker, Douglas Hugh 1926- 1R
Parker, Edna Jean 1935- 101
Parker, Edwin B(urke) 1932- 15-16R
Parker, Elinor Milnor 1906- CANR-3
Earlier sketch in CA 4R
See also SATA 3
Parker, Elliott S(evern) 1939- 103
Parker, Francis H(oward) 1920- 21-22R
Parker, Frank J(oseph) 1940- 49-52
Parker, Franklin 1921- CANR-22
Earlier sketches in CA 33-36R, CANR-7
Parker, Franklin D(allas) 1918- 13-14R
Parker, Gail Thain 1943- 104
Parker, Geoffrey 1933- 49-52
Parker, Gordon 1940- 103
Parker, H(enry) M(ichael) D(enne)
1896(?)-1971 Obituary 104
Parker, Harold T(albot) 1907- CANR-9
Earlier sketch in CA 23-24R
Parker, Hershel 1935- CANR-13
Earlier sketch in CA 33-36R
Parker, Howard J(ohn) 1948- 57-60
Parker, J(ohn) Carlyle 1931- CANR-24
Earlier sketches in CA 57-60, CANR-7
Parker, Jack Horace 1914- 113
Parker, James 1714(?)-1770 .... DLB-43
Parker, James
See Newby, Eric
Parker, James Reid 1909-1984 Obituary 111
Parker, Jean
See Sharat Chandra, G(ubbi) S(hankara Chetty)
Parker, Joan H. 1932- 85-88
Parker, (Herbert) John (Harvey)
1906-1987 ....7-8R
Obituary 124
Parker, John 1923- CANR-5
Earlier sketch in CA 5-6R
Parker, John
See Wyatt, John
Parker, John Thomas 1950- 118
Parker, Julia (Louise) 1932- CANR-23
Earlier sketch in CA 101
Parker, Kristy 1957- 126
Parker, Laura
See Castoro, Laura A(nn)
Parker, Lois M(ay) 1912- CANR-11
Earlier sketch in CA 69-72
See also SATA 30
Parker, Margot M. 1937- 122
See also SATA 52
Parker, Marsha Zurich 1952- 107
Parker, Nancy Winslow 1930- CANR-22
Earlier sketches in CA 49-52, CANR-1
See also SATA 10
Parker, Nathan Carlyle 1960- 102
Parker, Pat 1944- 57-60
Parker, Percy Spurlark 1940- 53-56
Parker, Richard 1915- 73-76
See also SATA 14
Parker, Robert 1920- CANR-13
Earlier sketch in CA 77-80
Parker, Robert
See Boyd, Waldo T.
Parker, Robert Allerton 1889(?)-1970
Obituary 29-32R
Parker, Robert B(rown) 1932- CANR-26
Earlier sketches in CA 49-52, CANR-1
See also CLC 27
Parker, Robert Miles 1939- 118
Parker, Robert Stewart 1915- 103
Parker, Rolland (Sandau) 1928- CANR-2
Earlier sketch in CA 45-48
Parker, Ron
See Parker, Ronald B(ruce)
Parker, Ronald B(ruce) 1932- 117
Parker, Ronald K(eith) 1939- 108
Parker, Rowland 1912- CANR-10
Earlier sketch in CA 65-68
Parker, Sanford S. 1919(?)-1980
Obituary 97-100
Parker, Scott 1950- 113
Parker, Stanley R(obert) 1927- CANR-19
Earlier sketch in CA 103
Parker, Stephen Jan 1939- 118
Parker, Stewart 1941- 103
Parker, T(homas) H(enry) L(ouis)
1916- CANR-6
Earlier sketch in CA 7-8R
Parker, Theodore 1810-1860 .... DLB-1
Parker, Thomas F(rancis) 1932- 73-76
Parker, Thomas Maynard 1906- CAP-2
Earlier sketch in CA 17-18
Parker, Tom
See Parker, John Thomas
Parker, W(illiam) H(enry) 1912- CANR-13
Earlier sketch in CA 33-36R
Parker, W(ilford) Oren 1911- 41-44R
Parker, Watson 1924- 106
Parker, William Riley 1906-1968 .... CAP-2
Earlier sketch in CA 17-18
Parker, Willie J. 1924- 77-80
Parker, Wyman W(est) 1912- 15-16R
Parkerson, John 1885(?)-1978 Obituary ...77-80
Parkes, Colin Murray 1928- 81-84
Parkes, Henry B. 1904-1972 Obituary 33-36R
Parkes, James William 1896-1981
Obituary 104
Parkes, Lucas
See Harris, John (Wyndham Parkes Lucas) Beynon
Parkes, (Grahem) Roger 1933- 53-56
Parkes, Terence 1927- 104
Parket, I(rwin) Robert 1931- 114
Parkhill, Forbes 1892- 4R
Parkhill, John
See Cox, William R(obert)
Parkhill, Wilson 1901- 5-6R
Parkhurst, Helen 1887-1973 Obituary 41-44R
Parkhurst, Louis Gifford, Jr. 1946- 113
Parkhurst, Winthrop 1892(?)-1983
Obituary 110
Parkin, Alan 1934- 29-32R
Parkin, David 1940- CANR-13
Earlier sketch in CA 25-28R
Parkin, Frank 1940- CLC-43
Parkin, G(eorge) Raleigh 1896-1977(?)
Obituary 106
Parkin, Molly 1932- 104
Parkin, Peter Hubert 1917-1984 Obituary ... 113
Parkinson, C(yril) Northcote 1909- CANR-5
Earlier sketch in CA 7-8R
Parkinson, (Frederick) Charles Douglas
1916- CAP-1
Earlier sketch in CA 11-12
Parkinson, Claire L(ucille) 1948- 120
Parkinson, Cornelia M. 1925- CANR-15
Earlier sketch in CA 81-84
Parkinson, Ethelyn M(inerva) 1906- CANR-1
Earlier sketch in CA 49-52
See also SATA 11
Parkinson, J(ohn) R(ichard) 1922- 102
Parkinson, Kathryn N. 1954- 120
Parkinson, Kathy
See Parkinson, Kathryn N.
Parkinson, Michael 1944- 29-32R
Parkinson, Roger 1939-1978 106
Parkinson, Thomas (Francis) 1920- CANR-3
Earlier sketch in CA 7-8R
Parkinson, Thomas P(aul) 102
Parkinson, Tom
See Parkinson, Thomas P(aul)
Parkman, Francis, Jr. 1823-1893 ..... DLB-1, 30
Parks, Aileen Wells 1901- 5-6R
Parks, Arva Moore 1939- 103
Parks, David 1944- 25-28R
Parks, Douglas R(ichard) 1942- 111
Parks, Edd Winfield 1906-1968 ....7-8R
See also SATA 10
Parks, Edmund 1911- 69-72
Parks, Edna D(orintha) 1910- 15-16R
Parks, Gordon (Alexander Buchanan)
1912- CANR-26
Earlier sketch in CA 41-44R
See also BW
See also SATA 8
See also DLB 33
See also CLC 1, 16
See also AITN 2
Parks, Joseph Howard 1903- 4R
Parks, Lloyd Clifford 1922- 57-60
Parks, Michael 1943- 126
Parks, Pat 1918- 61-64
Parks, Robert James 1940- 65-68
Parks, Stephen Robert 1940- 65-68
Parks, Tim(othy Harold) 1954- Brief entry .. 126
Parks, William 1698(?)-1750 .... DLB-43
Parksmith, George
See Bush, George S(idney)
Parlato, Salvatore J(oseph), Jr. 1936- 73-76
Parlett, David (Sidney) 1939- CANR-20
Earlier sketch in CA 103
Parley, Peter
See Goodrich, Samuel Griswold
Parlin, Bradley W(illiam) 1938- 69-72
Parlin, John
See Graves, Charles Parlin
Parma, Clemens
See Menzel, Roderich
Parman, Donald L(ee) 1932- 65-68
Parmelee, Alice 1903- CAP-2
Earlier sketch in CA 21-22
Parmenter, Ross 1912- 17-18R
Parmer, J(ess) Norman 1925- 7-8R
Parmet, Herbert S. 1929- CANR-11
Earlier sketch in CA 21-22R
Parmet, Robert D(avid) 1938- 77-80
Parmet, Simon 1897- CAP-1
Earlier sketch in CA 13-14
Parnaby, Owen Wilfred 1921- 11-12R
Parnall, Peter 1936- 81-84
See also SATA 16
Parnas, Raymond I. 1937- 33-36R
Parnes, Herbert S(aul) 1919- CANR-15
Earlier sketch in CA 41-44R
Parnes, Sidmore 1928-1984 Obituary 113
Parnes, Sidney J. 1922- CANR-10
Earlier sketch in CA 21-22R
Paroissien, David (Harry) 1939- 111
Parot, Joseph (John) 1940- 126
Parque, Richard (Anthony) 1935- 124
Parr, Charles McKew 1884- CAP-1
Earlier sketch in CA 11-12
Parr, James A(llan) 1936- 49-52
Parr, John (Lloyd) 1928- 102
Parr, Letitia (Evelyn) 1906- 103
See also SATA 37
Parr, Lucy 1924- 29-32R
See also SATA 10
Parr, Michael 1927- 17-18R
Parra, Nicanor 1914- 85-88
See also CLC 2
Parramore, Thomas C(ustis) 1932- 112
Parrinder, E(dward) Geoffrey 1910- CANR-10
Earlier sketch in CA 23-24R
Parrington, Vernon L(ouis) 1871-1929
Brief entry 113
See also DLB 17, 63
Parrini, Carl P. 1933- Brief entry 107
Parrino, John J(oseph) 1942- 101
Parrino, Michael 1915(?)-1976 Obituary ...65-68
Parriott, Sara 1953- 107
Parris, Addison W(ilson) 1923-1975 ..... CAP-2
Earlier sketch in CA 25-28
Parris, Guichard 1903- 81-84
Parris, Judith (Ann) H(eimlich) 1939- 57-60
Parrish, Anne 1888-1957 Brief entry 115
See also SATA 27
Parrish, Bernard P. 1936- 103
Parrish, Bernie
See Parrish, Bernard P.
Parrish, Carl (George) 1904-1965 ....7-8R
Parrish, Eugene
See Harding, Donald Edward
Parrish, John A(lbert) 1939- 37-40R
Parrish, Louis 1927- Brief entry 107
Parrish, Mary
See Cousins, Margaret
Parrish, Mary Frances
See Fisher, M(ary) F(rances) K(ennedy)
Parrish, (Frederick) Maxfield
1870-1966 .... SATA-14
Parrish, Michael E. 1942- 29-32R
Parrish, Patt
See Bucheister, Patt
Parrish, Robert (Reese) 1916- 81-84
Parrish, Stephen Maxfield 1921- 104
Parrish, Thomas (Douglas) 1927- 93-96
Parrish, Wayland Maxfield 1887-? CAP-2
Earlier sketch in CA 23-24
Parrish, Wendy 1950- 73-76
Parrish, William E(arl) 1931- CANR-3
Earlier sketch in CA 2R
Parrott, Cecil (Cuthbert) 1909-1984 103
Obituary 113
Parrott, Fred J(ames) 1913- 41-44R
Parrott, Ian 1916- CANR-2
Earlier sketch in CA 7-8R
Parrott, (Alonzo) Leslie 1922- 97-100
Parrott, Lindesay 1901-1987 Obituary 123
Parrott, Lora Lee 1923- 25-28R
Parry, Albert 1901- CANR-6
Earlier sketch in CA 4R
Parry, Clive 1917-1982 Obituary 107
Parry, David 1908- 113
Parry, Ellwood C(omly) III 1941- 93-96
Parry, Hugh J(ones) 1916- 13-14R
Parry, J(ohn) H(orace) 1914- CANR-6
Earlier sketch in CA 5-6R
Parry, John
See Whelpton, (George) Eric
Parry, Linda (Alberta) 1945- 111
Parry, Marian 1924- 41-44R
See also SATA 13
Parry, Michael Patrick 1947- 101
Parry, Thomas H. 1904-1985 Obituary 116
Parry-Jones, Daniel 1891- 15-16R
Parseghian, Ara (Raoul) 1923- Brief entry .. 105
Parsegian, V(ozcan) Lawrence 1908- 57-60
Parsifal
See Curl, James Stevens
Parsloe, Guy Charles 1900- CAP-1
Earlier sketch in CA 13-14
Parson, Ruben L(eRoy) 1907- 15-16R
Parson Lot
See Kingsley, Charles
Parsons, C(hristopher) J(ames) 1941- 103
Parsons, Charles (Dacre) 1933- 45-48
Parsons, Coleman O(scar) 1905- CAP-1
Earlier sketch in CA 15-16
Parsons, Cynthia 1926- CANR-21
Earlier sketch in CA 45-48
Parsons, Denys 1914- CANR-12
Earlier sketch in CA 15-16R
Parsons, Ellen
See Dragonwagon, Crescent
Parsons, Elmer E. 1919- 25-28R
Parsons, Geoffrey 1908-1981 Obituary 105
Parsons, Harriet Oettinger
1906(?)-1983(?) Obituary 108
Parsons, Howard L(ee) 1918- CANR-17
Earlier sketches in CA 49-52, CANR-1
Parsons, Ian (Macnaghten) 1906-1980 ...97-100
Obituary 102
Parsons, Jack 1920- 104
Parsons, James Bunyan 1921- 29-32R
Parsons, John (Anthony) 1938- 120
Parsons, Kermit Carlyle 1927- 29-32R
Parsons, Kitty ?-1976 ....15-16R
Obituary 120
Parsons, Louella (Oettinger) 1881-1972 ...93-96
Obituary 37-40R
Parsons, Malcolm Barningham 1919-
Brief entry 108
Parsons, Martin 1907- 53-56
Parsons, R(ichard) A(ugustus) 101
Parsons, Stanley B., Jr. 1927- CANR-21
Earlier sketch in CA 45-48
Parsons, Talcott 1902-1979 .... CANR-4
Obituary 85-88
Earlier sketch in CA 7-8R
Parsons, Thornton H(arris) 1921- 73-76
Parsons, Tom
See MacPherson, Thomas George
Parsons, William Edward, Jr. 1936- 21-22R
Parsons, William T(homas) 1923- 65-68
Partain, Floydene 1924- 114
Partch, Virgil Franklin II 1916-1984 108
Obituary 113
See also SATA 39, 45
Partington, F. H.
See Yoxall, Harry W(aldo)
Partington, Martin 1944- 124
Partington, Susan Trowbridge 1924- 11-12R
Partlow, Vern 1910(?)-1987 Obituary 121
Partner, Peter (David) 1924- 85-88
Parton, James 1822-1891 .... DLB-30
Parton, Margaret 1915- 97-100
Parton, Sara Payson Willis
1811-1872 .... DLB-43, 74
Partridge, Anthony
See Oppenheim, E(dward) Phillips
Partridge, Astley Cooper 1901- 103
Partridge, Benjamin W(aring), Jr. 1915- ..25-28R
See also SATA 28
Partridge, Edward B(ellamy) 1916- 65-68
Partridge, Elinore Hughes 1937- 115
Partridge, Eric (Honeywood)
1894-1979 .... CANR-3
Obituary 85-88
Earlier sketch in CA 4R
Partridge, Ernest 1935- 115
Partridge, Frances 1900- 29-32R

Partridge, Jenny (Lilian) 1947- CANR-26
Earlier sketch in CA 109
See also SATA 37, 52
Partridge, Larry (Harold) 1949- 114
Partridge, William L(ee) 1944- CANR-1
Earlier sketch in CA 45-48
Parulski, George R(ichard), Jr. 1954- .. CANR-17
Earlier sketch in CA 97-100
Parvin, Betty 1916- CANR-17
Earlier sketch in CA 97-100
Parx, C. C.
See Gilmore, Christopher Cook
Parzen, Herbert 1896- 25-28R
Pasachoff, Jay M(yron) 1943- 117
Pasamanik, Luisa 1930- 101
Pascal, Anthony H(enry) 1933- CANR-16
Earlier sketch in CA 29-32R
Pascal, David 1918- 11-12R
See also SATA 14
Pascal, Francine 1938- 123
Brief entry 115
See also SATA 37, 51
Pascal, Gerald Ross 1907- 37-40R
Pascal, John Robert 1932(?)-1981
Obituary 102
Pascal, Paul 1925- 23-24R
Pascal, Roy 1904-1980 .... CANR-6
Earlier sketch in CA 7-8R
Pascale, Richard Tanner 1938- CANR-25
Earlier sketch in CA 53-56
Pascarella, Perry (James) 1934- 93-96
Paschal, George H., Jr. 1925- 29-32R
Paschal, Nancy
See Trotter, Grace V(iolet)
Paschall, H. Franklin 1922- 25-28R
Pascoe, Elaine 1946- 124
Pascoe, Elizabeth Jean 69-72
Pascoe, John (Dobree) 1908-1972 ...... CAP-1
Earlier sketch in CA 13-14
Pascu, Stefan 1914- 117
Pascudniak, Pascal
See Lupoff, Richard A(llen)
Pasewark, William R(obert) 1924- CANR-15
Earlier sketch in CA 33-36R
Pashko, Stanley 1913- 97-100
See also SATA 29
Pasinetti, P(ier-) M(aria) 1913- 73-76
Pask, Gordon 1928- 111
Pask, Raymond (Frank) 1944- CANR-22
Earlier sketch in CA 105
Paskowicz, Patricia
See Molan, Pat Carlson
Pasley, Virginia Schmitz 1905-1986
Obituary 119
Pasmanik, Wolf 1924- 101
Pasolini, Pier Paolo 1922-1975 93-96
Obituary 61-64
See also CLC 20, 37
Pasquier, Marie-Claire 1933- 29-32R
Pass, Gail 1940- 65-68
Passage, Charles Edward 1913-1983 .....33-36R
Obituary 110
Passailaigue, Thomas E.
See Paisley, Tom
Passantino, Gretchen 1953- 110
Passantino, Robert Louis 1951- 108
Passel, Anne W(onders) 1918- CANR-11
Earlier sketch in CA 29-32R
Passell, Peter 1944- CANR-2
Earlier sketch in CA 45-48
Passerin D'Entreves, Alessandro 1902- 69-72
Passeron, Rene (Jean) 1920- CANR-17
Earlier sketch in CA 97-100
Passes(-Pazolski), Alan 1943- 85-88
Passin, Herbert 1916- CANR-20
Earlier sketches in CA 45-48, CANR-1
Passman, Brian 1934- 25-28R
Passmore, John (Arthur) 1914- CANR-6
Earlier sketch in CA 13-14R
Passmore, Richard E. (?)-1982 Obituary ... 107
Passonneau, Joseph Russell 1921- 19-20R
Passow, A(aron) Harry 1920- CANR-3
Earlier sketch in CA 3R
Passwater, Richard (Albert) 1937- CANR-19
Earlier sketch in CA 97-100
Past, Ray(mond Edgar) 1918- 29-32R
Pastan, Linda (Olenik) 1932- CANR-18
Earlier sketch in CA 61-64
See also DLB 5
See also CLC 27
Pasternack, Stefan Alan 1939- Brief entry ... 108
Pasternak, Boris (Leonidovich) 1890-1960
Obituary 116
See also CLC 7, 10, 18
Pasternak, Burton 1933- Brief entry 109
Pasternak, Velvel 1933- 73-76
Pastine, Maureen (Diane) 1944- CANR-8
Earlier sketch in CA 57-60
Paston, Herbert S. 1928- 49-52
Pastor, Robert (Alan) 1947- 105
Pastore, Arthur R(alph), Jr. 1922- 19-20R
Pastore, Nicholas 1916- 29-32R
Pastorius, Francis Daniel 1651-1720(?) .. DLB-24
Pastor X
See Johnson, Merle Allison
Pastos, Spero 1940- 126
Patai, Daphne 1943- 113
Patai, Raphael 1910- CANR-20
Earlier sketch in CA 29-32R
Pataky, Denes 1921- 15-16R
Patanne, Maria
See La Pietra, Mary
Patapoff, Elizabeth 1917- 29-32R
Patchen, Kenneth 1911-1972 .... CANR-3
Obituary 33-36R
Earlier sketch in CA 4R
See also DLB 16, 48
See also CLC 1, 2, 18
Patchen, Martin 1932- 57-60
Patchett, Mary (Osborne) Elwyn 1897- .. CANR-3
Earlier sketch in CA 7-8R
Pate, Billie 1932- 61-64
Pate, Martha B. Lucas 1912-1983
Obituary 110
Patel, Harshad C(hhotabhia) 1934- 53-56
Patel, I(ndraprasad) G(ordhanbhai) 1924- ... 126
Pateman, Carole 1940- 85-88
Pateman, Kim
See Levin, Kim
Pateman, Trevor 1947- 49-52
Patent, Dorothy Hinshaw 1940- CANR-24
Earlier sketches in CA 61-64, CANR-9
See also SATA 22
Pater, Walter 1839-1894 .... DLB-57
Paterson, Alistair (Ian Hughes) 1929- 107
Paterson, Allen P(eter) 1933- 93-96
Paterson, Ann 1916- 33-36R
Paterson, Barbara (Olive) 1933- 112
Paterson, Diane (R. Cole) 1946- 101
See also SATA 33
Paterson, George W(illiam) 1931- 103
Paterson, Huntley
See Ludovici, Anthony M(ario)
Paterson, John 1887- CAP-1
Earlier sketch in CA 13-14
Paterson, John Harris 1923- CANR-6
Earlier sketch in CA 7-8R
Paterson, Judith
See Jones, Judith Paterson
Paterson, Katherine (Womeldorf) 1932- ..23-24R
See also SATA 13, 53
See also DLB 52
See also CLC 12, 30
See also CLR 7
Paterson, (James Edmund) Neil 1916- ...13-14R
Paterson, R(onald) W(illiam) K(eith)
1933- 33-36R
Paterson, Thomas G(raham) 1941- CANR-16
Earlier sketches in CA 45-48, CANR-1
Paterson, William E(dgar) 1941- CANR-13
Earlier sketch in CA 61-64
Paterson-Jones, Judith
See Jones, Judith Paterson
Patinkin, Don 1922- CANR-10
Earlier sketch in CA 19-20R
Patka, Frederick 1922- 11-12R
Patman, (John William) Wright 1893-1976 .. 109
Obituary 107
Patmore, Coventry 1823-1896 .... DLB-35
Patmore, Derek Coventry 1908-1972 ....7-8R
Obituary 103
Patmore, John Allan 1931- 104
Paton, Alan (Stewart) 1903-1988 ...... CANR-22
Obituary 125
Earlier sketches in CA 15-16, CAP-1
See also SATA 11
See also CLC 4, 10, 25
Paton, David Macdonald 1913- 114
Paton, George (Whitecross) 1902- CAP-1
Earlier sketch in CA 11-12
Paton, Herbert James 1887-1969 .... CAP-1
Earlier sketch in CA 13-14
Paton, Jane (Elizabeth) 1934- SATA-35
Paton, Joseph Noel 1821-1901 .... DLB-35
Paton, Steven C. 1928(?)-1980
Obituary 97-100
Patoski, Margaret (Nancy Pearson) 1930- ..69-72
Patra, Atul Chandra 1915- 57-60
Patras, Louis 1931- CANR-15
Earlier sketch in CA 85-88
Patrice, Ann
See Galbraith, Georgie Starbuck
Patrick, Alison (Mary Houston) 1921- 49-52
Patrick, Clarence H(odges) 1907- 33-36R
Patrick, Cuthbert Melvin 1914-1985
Obituary 116
Patrick, Douglas Arthur 1905- 17-18R
Patrick, Hugh 1930- 41-44R
Patrick, J(ohn) Max 1911- CANR-5
Earlier sketch in CA 7-8R
Patrick, James (Arthur) 1933- CANR-20
Earlier sketch in CA 104
Patrick, John 1905- 89-92
See also DLB 7
Patrick, Johnstone G(illespie) 1918- CANR-2
Earlier sketch in CA 5-6R
Patrick, Leal
See Stone, Patti
Patrick, Lilian
See Keogh, Lilian Gilmore
Patrick, Martha 1956- 109
Patrick, Maxine
See Maxwell, Patricia
Patrick, Q.
See Wheeler, Hugh (Callingham)
Patrick, Rembert Wallace 1909- 7-8R
Patrick, Robert 1937- CANR-1
Earlier sketch in CA 45-48
See also AITN 2
Patrick, Vincent 1935- CANR-22
Earlier sketch in CA 104
Patrick, Walton Richard 1909- 37-40R
Patrides, C(onstantinos) A(postolos)
1930- CANR-20
Earlier sketches in CA 15-16R, CANR-5
Patrikeyev
See Healey-Kay, (Sydney Francis) Patrick
(Chippendall)
Patrouch, Joseph F(rancis), Jr. 1935- 49-52
Patsauq, Markoosie 1942- 101
Patsouras, Louis
See Patras, Louis
Pattee, Fred Lewis 1863-1950 .... DLB-71
Pattee, Howard Hunt, Jr. 1926-
Brief entry 109
Pattemore, Arnel W(ilfred) 1934- 53-56
Patten, Bebe H(arrison) 1913- 61-64
Patten, Brian 1946- 25-28R
See also SATA 29
Patten, Lewis B(yford) 1915-1981 ..... CANR-21
Obituary 103
Earlier sketch in CA 25-28R
Patten, Nigel 1940- 25-28R
Patten, Priscilla C(arla) 1950- 117
Patten, (Bebe) Rebecca 1950- 117
Patten, Robert L(owry) 1939- 109
Patten, Thomas H., Jr. 1929- 21-22R
Patterson, A(lfred) Temple 1902-1983 103
Obituary 111
Patterson, Alicia Brooks 1906-1963
Obituary 89-92
Patterson, Barbara 1944- 110
Patterson, Benton Rain 1929- 122
Patterson, C(ecil) H(olden) 1912- CANR-16
Earlier sketch in CA 23-24R
Patterson, Carolyn Bennett 1921- 106
Patterson, Charles 1935- 117
Patterson, Charles D(arold) 1928- 122
Patterson, Charles E(dwin), Jr. 1934- 41-44R
Patterson, Charles H(enry) 1896- 37-40R
Patterson, Charlotte (Buist) 1942- 29-32R
Patterson, Craig E(ugene) 1945- 93-96
Patterson, David S(ands) 1937- 65-68
Patterson, Edwin W(ilhite) 1889-1965 .... 3R
Patterson, Eleanor Medill 1881(?)-1948
Brief entry 118
See also DLB 29
Patterson, Elinor Josephine
See Patterson, Eleanor Medill
Patterson, Elizabeth C. 29-32R
Patterson, Emma L. 1904- CAP-2
Earlier sketch in CA 25-28
Patterson, Eric James 1891-1972 .... CAP-1
Earlier sketch in CA 11-12
Patterson, Evelyn Roelofs 1917- 5-6R
Patterson, Frank Harmon 1912-
Brief entry 109
Patterson, Frank M(organ) 1931- CANR-25
Earlier sketch in CA 45-48
Patterson, Franklin (Kessel) 1916- 45-48
Patterson, Gardner 1916- Brief entry 106
Patterson, Geoffrey 1943- 103
See also SATA 44
Patterson, Gerald R. 1926- 41-44R
Patterson, Harriet-Louise H(olland) 1903- . CAP-1
Earlier sketch in CA 15-16
Patterson, Harry
See Patterson, Henry
Patterson, Henry 1929- 15-16R
Patterson, James (Tyler) 1935- 21-22R
Patterson, Jane
See Britton, Mattie Lula Cooper
Patterson, Janet McFadden 1915- 89-92
Patterson, Jefferson 1891-1977 Obituary ... 115
Patterson, Jerry E(ugene) 1931-
Brief entry 107
Patterson, John McCready 1913-1983
Obituary 109
Patterson, Joseph Medill 1879-1946
Brief entry 118
See also DLB 29
Patterson, June (Marie) 1924- 126
Patterson, K(arl) David 1941- 65-68
Patterson, Kevin 1956(?)-1988 Obituary 126
Patterson, L(loyd) G(eorge), Jr. 1929- ...41-44R
Patterson, L(yman) Ray 1929- 33-36R
Patterson, Lawrence Thomas II 1937- 104
Patterson, Letha L(emon) 1913- 5-6R
Patterson, Lillie G. 73-76
See also SATA 14
Patterson, Lindsay 1942- 77-80
See also BW
Patterson, Margaret C(leveland) 1923- .. CANR-7
Earlier sketch in CA 57-60
Patterson, Mary H(agelin) 1928-1973
Obituary 37-40R
Patterson, Michael 1939- 111
Patterson, (James) Milton 1927- 53-56
Patterson, Olive
See Rowland, D(onald) S(ydney)
Patterson, (Horace) Orlando (Lloyd)
1940- 65-68
See also BW
Patterson, (Leighton) Paige 1942- CANR-10
Earlier sketch in CA 25-28R
Patterson, Paul 1909- 85-88
Patterson, Peter
See Terson, Peter
Patterson, Raymond R. 1929- 29-32R
Patterson, Rebecca Elizabeth Coy
1911-1975 103
Patterson, Richard 1908(?)-1976
Obituary 69-72
Patterson, Richard North 1947- 85-88
Patterson, Robert B(enjamin) 1934- 73-76
Patterson, Robert Leet 1893- 19-20R
Patterson, Ruth P(olk) 1930- 119
Patterson, Samuel C(harles) 1931- CANR-22
Earlier sketches in CA 19-20R, CANR-7
Patterson, Samuel White 1883-1975 ..... CAP-2
Obituary 61-64
Earlier sketch in CA 17-18
Patterson, Sheila Caffyn 1918- 9-10R
Patterson, Sylvia W(iese) 1940- 61-64
Patterson, Virginia 1931- 102
Patterson, W. M(acLean) 1912(?)-1976
Obituary 69-72
Patterson, W. Morgan 1925- 65-68
Patterson, Walter C(ram) 1936- CANR-20
Earlier sketch in CA 103
Patterson, Ward L(amont) 1933- CANR-23
Earlier sketches in CA 57-60, CANR-8
Patterson, Wayne 1946- CANR-16
Earlier sketch in CA 85-88
Patterson, Webster T. 1920- 25-28R
Patterson, William Dudley 1910-1986
Obituary 119
Patterson, William L(orenzo) 1890-1980 ..41-44R
Obituary 97-100
Patti, Archimedes L(eonida) A(ttilio) 1913- .. 106
Patti, Ercole 1904(?)-1976 Obituary 69-72
Pattie, Alice 1906- CAP-2
Earlier sketch in CA 29-32
Pattillo, Henry 1726-1801 .... DLB-37
Pattillo, James W(ilson) 1937- CANR-11
Earlier sketch in CA 19-20R
Pattillo, Manning M., Jr. 1919- 21-22R
Pattinson, Nancy Evelyn Brief entry 117
Pattison, O(live) R(uth) B(rown) 1916- ...29-32R
Pattison, Walter Thomas 1903- 81-84
Patton, Alva Rae 1908- 5-6R
Patton, Arch 1908- CAP-1
Earlier sketch in CA 15-16
Patton, Bobby R(ay) 1935- CANR-17
Earlier sketches in CA 45-48, CANR-1
Patton, Brian (Lee) 1943- 123
Patton, Frances Gray 1906- 101
Patton, Frank
See Palmer, Raymond A.
Patton, Gerald W(ilson) 1947- 112
Patton, James W(elch) 1900- CAP-1
Earlier sketch in CA 11-12
Patton, Kenneth L(eo) 1911- CANR-7
Earlier sketch in CA 19-20R
Patton, Oliver B(eirne) 1920- 81-84
Patton, Rob(ert Warren) 1943- 37-40R
Pattullo, George 1879-1967 Obituary 115
Patty, C. Robert 1925- CANR-10
Earlier sketch in CA 25-28R
Patty, Ernest N(ewton) 1894-1976 .... CAP-2
Earlier sketch in CA 25-28
Patty, James S(ingleton) 1925- 53-56
Paturi, Felix R.
See Mindt, Heinz R.
Pauck, Wilhelm 1901-1981 81-84
Obituary 104
Pauk, Walter 1914- CANR-18
Earlier sketches in CA 5-6R, CANR-2
Pauker, Guy J(ean) 1916- CANR-1
Earlier sketch in CA 45-48
Pauker, John 1920- 25-28R
Pauker, Ted
See Conquest, (George) Robert
(Acworth)
Paul, Aileen 1917- CANR-19
Earlier sketch in CA 41-44R
See also SATA 12
Paul, Anthony (Marcus) 1937- 77-80
Paul, (John) Anthony 1941- 77-80
Paul, Auren
See Uris, Auren
Paul, Charles B. 1931- 105
Paul, Charlotte 1916- CANR-7
Earlier sketch in CA 5-6R
Paul, Daniel
See Kessel, Lipmann
Paul, Danielle
See Mittermeyer, Helen (Hayton
Monteith)
Paul, David (Tyler) 1934-1988 Obituary 125
Paul, David W(arren) 1944- 107
Paul, Elizabeth
See Crow, Donna Fletcher
Paul, Elliot (Harold) 1891-1958
Brief entry 107
See also DLB 4
Paul, Emily
See Eicher, (Ethel) Elizabeth
Paul, F. W.
See Fairman, Paul W.
Paul, Florrie 1928- 61-64
Paul, Geoffrey John 1921-1983 Obituary ... 110
Paul, Gordon L. 1935- CANR-7
Earlier sketch in CA 19-20R
Paul, Grace 1908- 19-20R
Paul, Hugo
See Little, Paul H(ugo)
Paul, I(rving) H. 1928- 103
Paul, James 1936- SATA-23
Paul, Jordan 1936- 97-100
Paul, Judith Edison 1939- CANR-16
Earlier sketch in CA 29-32R
Paul, Leslie (Allen) 1905-1985 .... CANR-3
Obituary 117
Earlier sketch in CA 4R
Paul, Louis
See Placet, Leroi
Paul, Margaret 1939- 97-100
Paul, Norman L(eo) 1926- 61-64
Paul, Raymond 1940- 106
Paul, Robert
See Roberts, John G(aither)
Paul, Robert S(idney) 1918- CANR-3
Earlier sketch in CA 1R
Paul, Rodman Wilson 1912-1987 ...... CANR-3
Obituary 122
Earlier sketch in CA 2R
Paul, Roland A(rthur) 1937- 41-44R
Paul, Sheri
See Resnick, Sylvia (Safran)
Paul, Sherman 1920- CANR-3
Earlier sketch in CA 7-8R
Paul, William
See Eicher, (Ethel) Elizabeth

Paulden, Sydney (Maurice) 1932- CANR-12
Earlier sketch in CA 29-32R
Paulding, James Kirke
1778-1860 DLB-3, 59, 74
Pauley, Barbara Anne 1925- 89-92
Pauley, Bruce F. 1937- 41-44R
Pauley, (Margaret) Jane 1950- 106
Paulhan, Jean 1884-1968 Obituary 25-28R
Pauli, Hertha (Ernestine) 1909-1973 CANR-2
Obituary 41-44R
Earlier sketch in CA 2R
See also SATA 3, 26
Paulin, Thomas Neilson 1949- Brief entry 123
Paulin, Tom
See Paulin, Thomas Neilson
See also DLB 40
See also CLC 37
Pauling, Linus (Carl) 1901- 116
Brief entry 110
Paull, Grace A. 1898- SATA-24
Paull, Raymond Allan 1906-1972 CAP-1
Earlier sketch in CA 9-10
Pau-Llosa, Ricardo 1954- 111
Paulon, Flavia 1907(?)-1987 Obituary 122
Pauls, John P. 1916- 45-48
Paulsell, William Oliver 1935- 111
Paulsen, F(rank) Robert 1922- 21-22R
Paulsen, Gary 1939- 73-76
See also SATA 22, 50
Paulsen, Lois (Thompson) 1905- CAP-2
Earlier sketch in CA 19-20
Paulsen, Wolfgang 1910- CANR-11
Earlier sketch in CA 19-20R
Paulson, Belden 1927- 21-22R
Paulson, Jack
See Jackson, C(aary) Paul
Paulson, Morton C. 1923- 111
Paulson, Ronald (Howard) 1930- CANR-15
Earlier sketch in CA 19-20R
Paulsson, Bjoern 1932- 61-64
Paulsson, Thomas A(lfred) 1923- 11-12R
Paulston, Christina Bratt CANR-10
Earlier sketch in CA 65-68
Paulston, Rolland G(lenn) 1929- CANR-13
Earlier sketch in CA 33-36R
Paulu, Burton 1910- 15-16R
Paulus, John Douglas 1917- 69-72
Paul VI, Pope 1897-1978 81-84
Obituary 77-80
Pauly, Thomas H(arry) 1940- 115
Paun, Maggie
See Voysey, Margaret
Pauquet, Gina Ruck
See Ruck-Pauquet, Gina
Paustovsky, Konstantin (Georgievich)
1892-1968 93-96
Obituary 25-28R
See also CLC 40
Pautler, Albert J., Jr. 1935- 33-36R
Pauw, Berthold Adolf 1924- 9-10R
Pauwels, Louis 1920- Brief entry 111
Pavalko, Ronald M(ichael) 1934- 57-60
Pavarotti, Luciano 1935- Brief entry 112
Pavel, Frances 1907- 21-22R
See also SATA 10
Pavenstedt, Eleanor 1903- 21-22R
Pavese, Cesare 1908-1950 Brief entry 104
See also TCLC 3
Pavey, Don 1922- 107
Pavitranda, Swami 1896(?)-1977
Obituary 73-76
Pavlakis, Christopher 1928- 73-76
Pavletich, Aida 101
Pavlik, Evelyn Marie 1954- 97-100
Pavlov, Ivan Petrovich 1849-1936
Brief entry 118
Pavlowitch, Stevan K. 1933- CANR-13
Earlier sketch in CA 33-36R
Pavord, Anna 1940- 115
Pawelczynska, Anna 1922- 101
Pawle, Gerald 1913- 5-6R
Pawley, Bernard C(linton) 1911-1981 25-28R
Obituary 105
Pawley, Martin Edward 1938- 101
Pawley, Thomas Desire III 1917- 29-32R
Pawlick, Thomas F(rancis) 1941- 119
Pawlicki, T(homas) B(ert) 1930- 109
Pawlikowski, John T. 1940- CANR-24
Earlier sketches in CA 21-22R, CANR-9
Pawlowicz, Sala Kaminska 1925- 7-8R
Pawlowski, Gareth L. 1939- 29-32R
Pawson, G(eoffrey) P(hilip) H(enry) 1904- 7-8R
Pax, Clyde 1928- 49-52
Paxman, Jeremy Dickson 1950- 108
Paxson, Ethel 1885- 25-28R
Paxton, Dr. John
See Lawton, Sherman P(axton)
Paxton, Jack 1939-1985 Obituary 117
Paxton, Jack
See Lawton, Sherman P(axton)
Paxton, John 1911-1985 Obituary 114
See also DLB 44
Paxton, Lois
See Low, Lois Dorothea
Paxton, Mary Jean Wallace 1930- 109
Paxton, Robert O(wen) 1932- 73-76
Paxton, Thomas R. 1937- 105
Paxton, Tom
See Paxton, Thomas R.
Payack, Paul J. J. 1950- 69-72
Paye, Robert
See Campbell, (Gabrielle) Margaret (Vere)
Payelle, Raymond-Gerard 1898-1971
Obituary 33-36R
Payer, Cheryl Ann 1940- 61-64
Payes, Rachel C(osgrove) 1922- CANR-16
Earlier sketches in CA 49-52, CANR-1
Payn, James 1830-1898 DLB-18
Payne, A. J.
See Payne, Anthony
Payne, Alan
See Jakes, John (William)
Payne, Alma Smith
See Ralston, Alma (Smith Payne)
Payne, Anthony 1952- 125
Payne, B(en) Iden 1888-1976 73-76
Obituary 65-68
Payne, Basil 1928- 81-84
Payne, Bruce 1911- 11-12R
Payne, Charles 1909- 103
Payne, David A(llen) 1935- 25-28R
Payne, Donald Gordon 1924- CANR-24
Earlier sketches in CA 15-16R, CANR-9
See also SATA 37
Payne, Emmy
See West, Emily Govan
Payne, Eric Francis Jules 1895- 57-60
Payne, Ernest A(lexander) 1902-1980 CANR-9
Obituary 105
Earlier sketch in CA 11-12R
Payne, F(rances) Anne 1932- 73-76
Payne, J(ohn) Barton 1922- CANR-3
Earlier sketch in CA 1R
Payne, J(ames) Gregory 1949- 123
Payne, Jack 1926- 33-36R
Payne, James L. 1939- 33-36R
Payne, Joan Balfour (?)-1973 Obituary 41-44R
Payne, John 1842-1916 DLB-35
Payne, John Howard 1791-1852 DLB-37
Payne, Karen 1951- 111
Payne, Ladell 1933- Brief entry 111
Payne, Laurence 1919- 7-8R
Payne, LaVeta Maxine 1916- 37-40R
Payne, Leanne 1932- 115
Payne, Michael 1941- CANR-12
Earlier sketch in CA 29-32R
Payne, Mildred Y(ounger) 1906- 41-44R
Payne, Richard A. 1934- 97-100
Payne, (Pierre Stephen) Robert
1911-1983 25-28R
Obituary 109
Payne, Robert O. 1924- 97-100
Payne, Ronald 1926- 97-100
Payne, Stanley G(eorge) 1934- CANR-3
Earlier sketch in CA 1R
Paynter, Will(iam) 1903-1984 Obituary 115
Paynter, William Henry 1901- 15-16R
Paynton, Clifford T. 1929- 37-40R
Payson, Dale 1943- CANR-3
Earlier sketch in CA 49-52
See also SATA 9
Payson, Herb(ert III) 1927- 115
Payzant, Charles SATA-18
Paz, A.
See Pahz, James Alon
Paz, Carlos F(ernando) 1937- 109
Paz, Gil
See Lugones, Leopoldo
Paz, Octavio 1914- 73-76
See also CLC 3, 4, 6, 10, 19
Paz, Zan
See Pahz, (Anne) Cheryl Suzanne
Pazder, Lawrence Henry 1936- 107
p'Bitek, Okot 1931-1982 124
Obituary 107
See also BW
Peabody, Barbara 1933- 122
Peabody, Elizabeth Palmer 1804-1894 DLB-1
Peabody, Oliver William Bourn
1799-1848 DLB-59
Peabody, Robert Lee 1931- 11-12R
Peabody, Velton 1936- 53-56
Peace, Richard 1938- CANR-14
Earlier sketch in CA 25-28R
Peace, Roger Craft 1899-1968 Obituary 89-92
Peach, Lawrence du Garde 1890-1974 101
Peach, William Nelson 1912- 23-24R
Peacher, Georgiana M(elicent) 1919- 25-28R
Peachey, Laban 1927- 19-20R
Peacock, Alan T(urner) 1922- CANR-3
Earlier sketch in CA 4R
Peacock, Basil 1898- 103
Peacock, D(avid) P(hilip) S(pencer) 1939- 123
Peacock, Daniel J. 1919- 125
Peacock, Dick
See Peacock, Richard
Peacock, James Craig 1888(?)-1977
Obituary 73-76
Peacock, James L(owe) 1937- Brief entry 113
Peacock, L(elon) J(ames) 1928- 21-22R
Peacock, Mary (Willa) 1942- 69-72
Peacock, Mary Reynolds (Bradshaw)
1916- 57-60
Peacock, Molly 1947- 103
Peacock, Richard 1933- 107
Peacock, Ronald 1907- CANR-5
Earlier sketch in CA 53-56
Peacock, Wilbur Scott 1915(?)-1979
Obituary 89-92
Peacocke, A(rthur) R(obert) 1924- 41-44R
Peacocke, Christopher 1950- 124
Peacocke, Isabel Maud 1881-1973
Obituary 116
Pead, Deuel ?-1727 DLB-24
Peairs, Lillian Gehrke 1925- 103
Peairs, Richard Hope 1929- Brief entry 105
Peake, C(harles) H. 1920(?)-1988
Obituary 124
Peake, Lilian (Margaret) 1924- Brief entry 115
Peake, Mervyn 1911-1968 CANR-3
Obituary 25-28R
Earlier sketch in CA 7-8R
See also SATA 23
See also DLB 15
See also CLC 7
Peake, Miriam Morrison 1901- 57-60
Peaker, G(ilbert) F. 1903(?)-1983(?)
Obituary 109
Peale, Norman Vincent 1898- 81-84
See also SATA 20
See also AITN 1
Peale, Ruth Stafford 1906- 73-76
Pear, Lillian Myers 73-76
Pearce, Ann Philippa
See Christie, (Ann) Philippa
Pearce, Arthur Williams 1913(?)-1983
Obituary 111
Pearce, Brian Louis 1933- CANR-19
Earlier sketch in CA 103
Pearce, Charles A. 1906-1970 Obituary 104
Pearce, David (Robert) 1937- 126
Pearce, Dick
See Pearce, Richard Elmo
Pearce, Donald R(oss) 1917- 119
Pearce, Donn 1928- 15-16R
Pearce, Frank 1909- 109
Pearce, J(ohn) Kenneth 1898- 45-48
Pearce, J. Winston 1907- Brief entry 106
Pearce, Janice 1931- 61-64
Pearce, John Kingston 1925- 118
Pearce, Kenneth 1921- 120
Pearce, Mary E(mily) 1932- 69-72
Pearce, Moira 103
Pearce, Philippa
See Christie, (Ann) Philippa
See also SATA 1
See also CLC 21
See also CLR 9
Pearce, Richard 1932- 41-44R
Pearce, Richard Elmo 1909- 1R
Pearce, Roy Harvey 1919- CANR-3
Earlier sketch in CA 1R
Pearce, Thomas Matthews 1902- CANR-7
Earlier sketch in CA 19-20R
Pearce, William M(artin) 1913- 11-12R
Pearcy, G(eorge) Etzel 1905-1980 CANR-3
Earlier sketch in CA 1R
Peardon, Thomas Preston 1899-1985
Obituary 116
Peare, Catherine Owens 1911- 5-6R
See also SATA 9
Pearl, Arthur 1922- 13-14R
Pearl, Chaim 1919- 49-52
Pearl, Cyril (Altson) 1906-1987(?)
Obituary 122
Pearl, Eric
See Elman, Richard
Pearl, Esther Elizabeth
See Ritz, David
Pearl, Hal 1914(?)-1975 Obituary 61-64
Pearl, Jack
See Pearl, Jacques Bain
Pearl, Jacques Bain 1923- CANR-23
Earlier sketch in CA 7-8R
Pearl, Joseph L. 1886(?)-1974 Obituary 53-56
Pearl, Leon 1922- 7-8R
Pearl, Leonard 1911- CAP-2
Earlier sketch in CA 33-36
Pearl, Ralph 1910- 73-76
Pearl, Richard M(axwell) 1913- CANR-3
Earlier sketch in CA 11-12R
Pearl, Virginia L(ou) 1930- 61-64
Pearlman, Daniel (David) 1935- CANR-24
Earlier sketches in CA 61-64, CANR-9
Pearlman, Maurice 1911- CANR-6
Earlier sketch in CA 7-8R
Pearlman, Moshe
See Pearlman, Maurice
Pearlstein, Howard J. 1942- 57-60
Pearman, Jean R(ichardson) 1915- 49-52
Pears, Charles 1873-1958 Brief entry 114
See also SATA 30
Pears, David Francis 1921- 65-68
Pearsall, Derek (Albert) 1931- CANR-24
Earlier sketch in CA 107
Pearsall, (F.) Paul 126
Pearsall, Robert Brainard 1920- CANR-2
Earlier sketch in CA 45-48
Pearsall, Ronald 1927- CANR-14
Earlier sketch in CA 21-22R
Pearsall, Thomas E. 1925- 25-28R
Pearsall, William Harold 1891-1964
Obituary 106
Pearson, Andrew Russell 1897-1969 CANR-6
Obituary 25-28R
Earlier sketch in CA 5-6R
Pearson, B(enjamin) H(arold) 1893- 65-68
Pearson, Bill
See Pearson, William Harrison
Pearson, Bruce L. 1932- 73-76
Pearson, Carol 1944- 57-60
Pearson, Diane
See McClelland, Diane Margaret
Pearson, Drew
See Pearson, Andrew Russell
Pearson, Frederic S(tephen) 1944- 113
Pearson, Gayle 1947- 122
See also SATA 53
Pearson, (Edward) Hesketh (Gibbons)
1887-1964 5-6R
Pearson, James Larkin 1879-1981
Obituary 104
Pearson, Jim Berry 1924- 19-20R
Pearson, John 1934- CANR-4
Earlier sketch in CA 49-52
Pearson, Karl 1857-1936 Brief entry 119
Pearson, Lester B(owles) 1897-1972 121
Obituary 37-40R
Pearson, (Edith) Linnea 1942- 65-68
Pearson, Lionel (Ignatius Cusack)
1908-1988 1R
Obituary 126
Pearson, Lon
See Pearson, Milo Lorentz
Pearson, M(ichael) N(aylor) 1941-
Brief entry 118
Pearson, Michael 102
Pearson, Milo Lorentz 1939- 73-76
Pearson, Neville P(ershing) 1917- 45-48
Pearson, Norman Holmes 1909-1975 CAP-1
Obituary 61-64
Earlier sketch in CA 15-16
Pearson, Richard Joseph 1938- 65-68
Pearson, Robert Paul 1938- 65-68
Pearson, Ronald Hooke 1915- 13-14R
Pearson, Roy 1914- 3R
Pearson, Scott Roberts 1938- CANR-11
Earlier sketch in CA 29-32R
Pearson, Susan 1946- CANR-14
Earlier sketch in CA 65-68
See also SATA 27, 39
Pearson, T(homas) R(eid) 1956-
Brief entry 120
See also CLC 39
Pearson, William Harrison 1922- 57-60
Peary, Dannis 1949- 109
Peary, Danny
See Peary, Dannis
Peary, Marie Ahnighito
See Kuhne, Marie (Ahnighito Peary)
Peascod, Bill
See Peascod, William
Peascod, William 1920(?)-1985 Obituary 116
Pease, Dorothy Wells 1896- 7-8R
Pease, Howard 1894-1974 7-8R
Obituary 106
See also SATA 2, 25
Pease, Jane H(anna) 1929- CANR-4
Earlier sketch in CA 11-12R
Pease, Victor Philip 1938- 107
Pease, William H(enry) 1924- CANR-4
Earlier sketch in CA 11-12R
Peaston, Monroe 1914- 49-52
Peate, Iorwerth C.
See Peate, Iorwerth Cyfeiliog
Peate, Iorwerth Cyfeiliog 1901-1982 120
Obituary 108
Peate, Patricia Flynn 1911(?)-1983
Obituary 111
Peatman, John Gray 1904- 7-8R
Peattie, Donald Culross 1898-1964 102
Peattie, Lisa Redfield 1924- CANR-10
Earlier sketch in CA 25-28R
Peattie, Mark R(obert) 1930- CANR-8
Earlier sketch in CA 61-64
Peavy, Charles D(ruery) 1931- 25-28R
Peavy, John W(esley) III 1944- 119
Peavy, Linda 1943- 109
Pebworth, Ted-Larry 1936- 121
Peccei, Aurelio 1908-1984 Obituary 112
Peccorini, Francisco L(etona) 1915- CANR-25
Earlier sketch in CA 45-48
Pech, Stanley Z. 1924- 33-36R
Pechman, Joseph Aaron 1918- 85-88
Pechter, Edward 1941- 85-88
Peck, Abe 1945- 73-76
Peck, Anne Merriman 1884- 77-80
See also SATA 18
Peck, David W(arner) 1902- 1R
Peck, Ellen 1942- Brief entry 113
Peck, Frederic Taylor 1920(?)-1983
Obituary 110
Peck, George W(ilbur) 1840-1916
Brief entry 115
See also DLB 23, 42
Peck, Harry Thurston 1856-1914 DLB-71
Peck, Helen E(stelle) 1910- 7-8R
Peck, Ira 1922- 77-80
Peck, John 1941- CANR-3
Earlier sketch in CA 49-52
See also CLC 3
Peck, John B. 1918(?)-1973 Obituary 104
Peck, Kathryn Blackburn 1904-1975 CAP-2
Earlier sketch in CA 25-28
Peck, Leonard
See Hardy, C. Colburn
Peck, M(organ) Scott 1936- CANR-20
Earlier sketch in CA 89-92
Peck, Merton J(oseph) 1925- 13-14R
Peck, Paula 1927(?)-1972 Obituary 104
Peck, Ralph H(arold-Henry) 1926- CANR-22
Earlier sketch in CA 69-72
Peck, Richard 1934- CANR-19
Earlier sketch in CA 85-88
See also SATA 18
See also SAAS 2
See also CLC 21
See also CLR 15
Peck, Richard E(arl) 1936- 81-84
Peck, Robert F. 1919- 13-14R
Peck, Robert McCracken 1952- 112
Peck, Robert Newton 1928- 81-84
See also SATA 21
See also SAAS 1
See also CLC 17
Peck, Russell A(lbert) 1933- 108
Peck, Ruth L. 1915- 29-32R
Peck, Seymour 1917-1985 Obituary 114
Peck, Sidney M. 1926- 5-6R
Peck, Stacey 1925- 123
Peck, Theodore P(arker) 1924- 103
Peckenpaugh, Angela J(ohnson) 1942- 104
Peckham, Howard Henry 1910- 11-12R

INDEX

Peckham, James O. 1903(?)-1984
Obituary ... 113
Peckham, Lawton (Parker Greenman)
1904-1979 Obituary ... 89-92
Peckham, Morse 1914- ... CANR-1
Earlier sketch in CA 1R
Peckham, Richard
See Holden, Raymond (Peckham)
Peckinpah, (David) Sam(uel) 1925-1984 ... 109
Obituary ... 114
See also CLC 20
Pecsok, Mary Bodell 1919- ... 7-8R
Peden, Margaret Sayers 1927- ... CANR-14
Earlier sketch in CA 37-40R
Peden, Rachel (Mason) 1901- ... 110
Peden, William (Harwood) 1913- ... 23-24R
Pedersen, Elsa Kienitz 1915- ... CANR-2
Earlier sketch in CA 4R
Pedersen, (Thelma) Jean J(orgenson)
1934- ... CANR-21
Earlier sketches in CA 57-60, CANR-6
Pedersen, Knut 1859-1952 ... 119
Brief entry ... 104
Pedersen, Paul B(odholdt) 1936- ... 41-44R
Pederson, Kern O(wen) 1910- ... 102
Pedicord, Harry William 1912- ... 33-36R
Pedler, Christopher Magnus Howard
1927- ... 97-100
Pedler, Frederick Johnson 1908- ... 107
Pedler, Kit
See Pedler, Christopher Magnus Howard
Pedley, Robin 1914- ... 11-12R
Pedoe, Daniel 1910- ... 65-68
Pedolsky, Andrea 1951- ... 115
Pedrick, Jean 1922- ... CANR-6
Earlier sketch in CA 57-60
Peebles, Anne
See Galloway, Priscilla
Peebles, Dick 1918-1980 ... 77-80
Obituary ... 97-100
Peek, Bertrand Meigh 1891-1964 Obituary .. 111
Peek, Merle 1938- ... CANR-22
Earlier sketch in CA 105
See also SATA 39
Peek, Walter W(illiam) 1922- ... 45-48
Peel, Bruce Braden 1916- ... 19-20R
Peel, Colin D(udley) 1936- ... 119
Peel, Edwin A(rthur) 1911- ... 13-14R
Peel, H(azel) M(ary) 1930- ... CANR-4
Earlier sketch in CA 9-10R
Peel, J(ohn) D(avid) Y(eadon) 1941- ... 33-36R
Peel, John Donald 1908- ... 33-36R
Peel, Kendal J(ohn) 1940- ... 116
Peel, Malcolm Lee 1936- ... 29-32R
Peel, Norman Lemon
See Hirsch, Phil
Peel, Robert 1909- ... 77-80
Peel, Ronald Francis (Edward Waite)
1912-1985 Obituary ... 117
Peel, Wallis
See Peel, H(azel) M(ary)
Peele, David A(rnold) 1929-1985 ... 102
Obituary ... 118
Peele, George 1556-1596 ... DLB-62
Peele, Stanton 1946- ... 57-60
Peelor, Harry N. 1922- ... 19-20R
Peeples, Edwin A(ugustus, Jr.) 1915- ... 11-12R
See also SATA 6
Peer, Lyndon A. 1899(?)-1977 Obituary ... 73-76
Peerbolte, Maarten Lietaert
See Lietaert Peerbolte, Maarten
Peerce, Jan 1904-1984 ... 101
Obituary ... 114
Peerman, Dean G(ordon) 1931- ... 13-14R
Peers, William R(aymond) 1914-1984 ... 15-16R
Obituary ... 112
Peery, Paul D(enver) 1906- ... CAP-2
Earlier sketch in CA 29-32
Peeslake, Gaffer
See Durrell, Lawrence (George)
Peet, Bill
See Peet, William Bartlett
See also CLR 12
Peet, C(harles) Donald, Jr. 1927- ... 15-16R
Peet, Creighton B. 1899-1977 ... 106
Obituary ... 69-72
See also SATA 30
Peet, Louise Jenison 1885- ... 7-8R
Peet, William Bartlett 1915- ... 19-20R
See also SATA 2, 41
Peffer, Randall S(cott) 1948- ... 101
Pegge, C(ecil) Denis 1902- ... CAP-1
Earlier sketch in CA 15-16
Pegis, Anton Charles 1905- Brief entry ... 106
Pegis, Jessie Corrigan 1907- ... CAP-1
Earlier sketch in CA 13-14
Pegler, (James) Westbrook 1894-1969 ... 103
Obituary ... 89-92
Pegram, Marjorie Anne (Dykes) 1925- ... 11-12R
Pegrum, Dudley F(rank) 1898- ... 33-36R
Pegues, Franklin J(ohnson) 1924- ... 7-8R
Peguy, Charles Pierre 1873-1914
Brief entry ... 107
See also TCLC 10
Pehnt, Wolfgang 1931- ... CANR-24
Earlier sketch in CA 107
Pehrson, Justine Davis Randers
See Randers-Pehrson, Justine Davis
Pei, Mario A(ndrew) 1901-1978 ... CANR-5
Obituary ... 77-80
Earlier sketch in CA 5-6R
Peifer, Claude J(ohn) 1927- ... 19-20R
Peikoff, Leonard 1933- ... 108
Peil, Margaret 1929- ... CANR-8
Earlier sketch in CA 61-64
Peirce, J(ames) F(ranklin) 1918- ... 41-44R
Peirce, Neal R. 1932- ... CANR-21
Earlier sketch in CA 25-28R
Peirce, Waldo 1884-1970 ... SATA-28
Peiris, Denzil 1918(?)-1985 Obituary ... 116
Peiser, Maria Lilli 1914-1986 ... 116
Obituary ... 118
Brief entry ... 110
Peissel, Michel (Francois) 1937- ... CANR-12
Earlier sketch in CA 25-28R
Peitchinis, Stephen G(abriel) 1925- ... CANR-24
Earlier sketch in CA 45-48
Pejovich, Svetozar 1931- ... CANR-12
Earlier sketch in CA 19-20R
Pekarik, Andrew J(oseph) 1946- ... 112
Pekic, Borislav 1930- ... 69-72
Peladeau, Marius B(eaudoin) 1935- ... 73-76
Pelaez, Jill 1924- ... 33-36R
See also SATA 12
Pelavin, Cheryl 1946- ... 106
Pelenski, Jaroslaw 1929- Brief entry ... 111
Pelfrey, William 1947- ... 33-36R
Pelger, Lucy J. 1913-1971 ... CAP-2
Earlier sketch in CA 21-22
Pelikan, Jaroslav Jan 1923- ... CANR-1
Earlier sketch in CA 2R
Pelissier, Anthony 1912-1988 Obituary ... 125
Pelissier, Roger 1924-1972 ... CAP-2
Obituary ... 37-40R
Earlier sketch in CA 23-24
Pell, Arthur R. 1920- ... CANR-26
Earlier sketches in CA 29-32R, CANR-11
Pell, Claiborne (de Borda) 1918- ... 49-52
Pell, Derek 1947- ... 77-80
Pell, Eve 1937- ... 33-36R
Pell, John (Howland Gibbs) 1904-1987
Obituary ... 123
Pell, Olive Bigelow 1886-1980 Obituary ... 103
Pell, Robert
See Hagberg, David J(ames)
Pell, Walden II 1902-1983 Obituary ... 109
Pella, Milton O(rville) 1914- ... 19-20R
Pellegreno, Ann Holtaren ... 33-36R
Pellegrini, Angelo M. 1904- ... 19-20R
Pellegrini, Anthony D(avid) 1949- ... 117
Pellegrino, Victoria Y(urasits) 1944- ... 107
Peller, Sigismund 1890-1985 Obituary ... 116
Pelletier, Ingrid 1912- ... 29-32R
Pelletier, Kenneth R. 1946- ... CANR-11
Earlier sketch in CA 69-72
Pelletreau, John 1925(?)-1983 Obituary ... 111
Pellew, Jill (Hosford) 1942- ... 109
Pellicer, Carlos 1900(?)-1977 Obituary ... 69-72
Pelling, Henry Mathison 1920- ... 61-64
Pellow, Deborah 1945- ... CANR-13
Earlier sketch in CA 73-76
Pellowski, Anne 1933- ... CANR-9
Earlier sketch in CA 23-24R
See also SATA 20
Pellowski, Michael (Joseph) 1949- ... 110
See also SATA 48
Pells, Richard Henry 1941- ... 53-56
Pelly, David F. 1948- ... 124
Pelshe, Arvid Yanovich 1899-1983
Obituary ... 109
Pelta, Kathy 1928- ... 85-88
See also SATA 18
Peltason, J(ack) W(alter) 1923- ... CANR-4
Earlier sketch in CA 3R
Peltier, Leslie C(opus) 1900- ... 19-20R
See also SATA 13
Pelto, Bert
See Pelto, Pertti J(uho)
Pelto, Pertti J(uho) 1927- ... 97-100
Pelton, Barry C(lifton) 1935- ... 61-64
Pelton, Beverly Jo 1939- ... 49-52
Pelton, Joseph N(eal) 1943- ... 107
Pelton, Robert D(oane) 1935- ... 103
Pelton, Robert Stuart 1921- ... 7-8R
Pelton, Robert W(ayne) 1934- ... 29-32R
Peltz, Mary Ellis 1896-1981 ... 85-88
Obituary ... 105
Peluso, Joseph L(ouis) 1929- ... 97-100
Pelz, Lotte A(uguste) Hensl 1924- ... 11-12R
Pelz, Stephen Ernest 1942- ... 114
Brief entry ... 110
Pelz, Werner 1921- ... 11-12R
Peman, Jose Maria 1897-1981 Obituary ... 104
Pemberton, John E(dward) 1930- ... 33-36R
Pemberton, John Leigh
See Leigh-Pemberton, John
Pemberton, Madge 188(?)-1970
Obituary ... 29-32R
Pemberton, Margaret 1943- ... CANR-17
Earlier sketch in CA 93-96
Pemberton, Max 1863-1950 Brief entry ... 120
See also DLB 70
Pemberton, William Baring 1897- ... 7-8R
Pemberton, William E(rwin) 1940- ... 97-100
Pembrook, Linda 1942- ... 61-64
Pembrooke, Kenneth
See Page, Gerald W(ilburn)
Pembury, Bill
See Groom, Arthur William
Pempel, T. J. 1942- ... 112
Pen, Jan 1921- ... CANR-17
Earlier sketch in CA 1R
Pena, Humberto J(ose) 1928- ... 73-76
Pena, Ramon del Valle y
See Valle-Inclan, Ramon (Maria) del
Pendar, Kenneth 1906-1972 Obituary ... 37-40R
Pendell, Elmer 1894- ... CAP-1
Earlier sketch in CA 11-12
Pendennis, Arthur, Esquire
See Thackeray, William Makepeace
Pender, Lex
See Pendower, Jacques
Pender, Lydia Podger 1907- ... CANR-2
Earlier sketch in CA 5-6R
Pender, Marilyn
See Pendower, Jacques
Pendergast, Charles 1950- ... 65-68
Pendergast, Chuck
See Pendergast, Charles
Pendergast, Richard J. 1927- ... 93-96
Penderwhistle, Judith (Blair) 1952- ... CANR-22
Earlier sketch in CA 81-84
Pendery, Rosemary (Schmitz) ... 53-56
See also SATA 7
Pendle, Alexy 1943- ... SATA-29
Pendle, George 1906-1977 ... 7-8R
Obituary ... 103
See also SATA 28
Pendlebury, B(evis) J(ohn) 1898- ... CAP-2
Earlier sketch in CA 33-36
Pendleton, Conrad
See Kidd, Walter E.
Pendleton, Don(ald Eugene) 1927- ... 33-36R
Pendleton, Don
See Obstfeld, Raymond
Pendleton, James D(udley) 1930- ... 107
Pendleton, Mary ... 65-68
Pendleton, Winston K. 1910- ... CAP-1
Earlier sketch in CA 15-16
Pendo, Stephen 1947- ... 65-68
Pendower, Jacques 1899-1976 ... 9-10R
Obituary ... 89-92
Pendray, Edward
See Pendray, George Edward
Pendray, G. Edward
See Pendray, George Edward
Pendray, George Edward 1901-1987
Obituary ... 123
Penfield, Thomas 1903- ... 5-6R
Penfield, Wilder (Graves) 1891-1976 ... CANR-3
Obituary ... 65-68
Earlier sketch in CA 7-8R
Pengelley, Eric T. 1919- ... 89-92
Penick, James (Lal), Jr. 1932- ... 33-36R
Penn, Anne
See Pendower, Jacques
Penn, Arthur (Hiller) 1922- Brief entry ... 112
Penn, Asher 1908(?)-1979 Obituary ... 93-96
Penn, Audrey 1950- ... CANR-13
Earlier sketch in CA 77-80
Penn, Christopher
See Lawlor, Patrick Anthony
Penn, John
See Harcourt, Palma
Penn, Margaret ?-1981 Obituary ... 105
Penn, Ruth Bonn
See Rosenberg, Ethel (Clifford)
Penn, William 1644-1718 ... DLB-24
Pennage, E. M.
See Finkel, George (Irvine)
Pennar, Jaan 1924- Brief entry ... 115
Pennekamp, John (David) 1897-1978
Obituary ... 89-92
See also AITN 2
Penner, Jonathan 1940- ... CANR-17
Earlier sketch in CA 97-100
See also DLBY 83
Penney, Annette Culler 1916- ... 45-48
Penney, Grace Jackson 1904- ... 5-6R
See also SATA 35
Penney, J(ames) C(ash) 1875-1971
Obituary ... 29-32R
Penney, Jennifer 1946- ... 122
Pennick, Nigel Campbell 1946- ... 110
Penniman, Clara 1914- Brief entry ... 111
Penniman, Howard R(ae) 1916- ... CANR-12
Earlier sketch in CA 13-14R
Penniman, Thomas Kenneth 1896(?)-1977
Obituary ... 69-72
Penninger, F(rieda) Elaine 1927- ... 57-60
Penningroth, Paul W(illiam) 1901-1974 ... 49-52
Obituary ... 103
Pennington, Albert Joe 1950- ... 57-60
Pennington, Anne (Elizabeth) 1934-1981
Obituary ... 114
Pennington, Chester Arthur 1916- ... 104
Pennington, Donald Henshaw 1919- ... 7-8R
Pennington, Eunice 1923- ... 57-60
See also SATA 27
Pennington, Howard (George) 1923- ... 49-52
Pennington, John Selman 1924(?)-1980
Obituary ... 102
Pennington, Lee 1939- ... 69-72
See also DLBY 82
Pennington, Lillian Boyer 1904- ... SATA-45
Pennington, Lucinda 1945- ... 117
Pennington, M. (Robert John) Basil
1931- ... CANR-16
Earlier sketch in CA 93-96
Pennington, Penny
See Galbraith, Georgie Starbuck
Pennington, Robert (Roland) 1927- ... 73-76
Pennington, Stuart
See Galbraith, Georgie Starbuck
Pennington, W(eldon) J(erry) 1919-1985
Obituary ... 115
Pennink, (John Jacob) Frank 1913- ... 7-8R
Pennock, J(ames) Roland 1906- ... CANR-13
Earlier sketch in CA 33-36R
Penny, Julie 1945- ... 117
Penny, Prudence
See Goldberg, Hyman
Penny, Ruthanna (Merrick) 1914- ... 19-20R
Pennycuick, John 1943- ... 97-100
Penrod, James 1934- ... 77-80
Penrose, Boies 1902-1976 Obituary ... 65-68
Penrose, Edith Tilton 1914- ... 25-28R
Penrose, Harald ... CANR-21
Earlier sketches in CA 13-14R, CANR-6
Penrose, Margaret ... CAP-2
Earlier sketch in CA 19-20
Penrose, Roland (Algernon) 1900-1984 ... 85-88
Obituary ... 112
Pentecost, Edward C(lyde) 1917- ... 57-60
Pentecost, Hugh
See Philips, Judson (Pentecost)
Pentecost, J(ohn) Dwight 1915- ... CANR-2
Earlier sketch in CA 5-6R
Pentecost, Martin
See Hearn, John
Pentony, DeVere Edwin 1924- ... CANR-8
Earlier sketch in CA 5-6R
Pentreath, A(rthur Godolphin) Guy
C(arleton) 1902-1985 ... CAP-1
Obituary ... 118
Earlier sketch in CA 13-14
Pentz, Croft Miner ... CANR-9
Earlier sketch in CA 7-8R
Pentz, Lundy H(urd) 1951- ... 116
Penuel, Arnold M(cCoy) 1936- ... 57-60
Penuelas, Marcelino C. 1916- ... 25-28R
Penzel, Frederick 1948- ... 85-88
Penzik, Irena
See Narell, Irena
Penzl, Herbert 1910- ... CANR-24
Earlier sketch in CA 45-48
Penzler, Otto 1942- ... 81-84
See also SATA 38
Pepe, John Frank 1920- ... 11-12R
Pepe, Phil(ip) 1935- ... CANR-18
Earlier sketch in CA 25-28R
See also SATA 20
Pepelasis, Adam(antios) A. 1923- ... CANR-2
Earlier sketch in CA 2R
Peper, George Frederick 1950- ... CANR-25
Earlier sketch in CA 108
Pepin, Jacques (Georges) 1935- ... CANR-25
Earlier sketch in CA 103
Pepinsky, Harold E(ugene) 1945- ... 119
Pepitone, Albert (Davison) 1923- ... 11-12R
Pepitone, Joe 1940- Brief entry ... 109
Pepitone, Joseph Anthony
See Pepitone, Joe
Peppard, Murray B(isbee) 1917-1974 ... CAP-2
Obituary ... 53-56
Earlier sketch in CA 21-22
Peppe, Rodney 1934- ... 33-36R
See also SATA 4
Pepper, Adeline ... 41-44R
Pepper, Art(hur Edward) 1925-1982
Obituary ... 107
Pepper, Choral 1918- ... 25-28R
Pepper, Curtis Bill
See Pepper, Curtis G.
Pepper, Curtis G. 1920- ... CANR-10
Earlier sketch in CA 23-24R
Pepper, Joan
See Wetherell-Pepper, Joan Alexander
Pepper, John 1942- ... 117
Pepper, Martin
See Krich, John
Pepper, Stephen Coburn 1891-1972 ... 3R
Obituary ... 103
Pepper, Thomas 1939- ... CANR-16
Earlier sketch in CA 97-100
Pepper, William M(ullin), Jr. 1903-1975 .. 97-100
Obituary ... 57-60
Peppercorn, David 1931- ... 118
Peppiatt, Michael 1941- ... 118
Peppin, Brigid (Mary) 1941- ... 65-68
Peppler, Alice Stolper 1934- ... 53-56
Peradotto, John Joseph 1933- ... 41-44R
Perceval-Maxwell, M(ichael) 1933- ... 53-56
Percival, Alicia C(onstance) 1903- ... 11-12R
Percival, John 1927- ... 33-36R
Percival, Walter 1896- ... CAP-1
Earlier sketch in CA 11-12
Percy, Charles H(arting) 1919- ... 65-68
Percy, Charles Henry
See Smith, Dodie
Percy, Douglas Cecil 1914- ... CANR-3
Earlier sketch in CA 7-8R
Percy, Herbert R(oland) 1920- ... 7-8R
Percy, Walker 1916- ... CANR-23
Earlier sketches in CA 3R, CANR-1
See also DLB 2
See also DLBY 80
See also CLC 2, 3, 6, 8, 14, 18, 47
Percy, William A., Jr. 1933- ... 29-32R
Perdue, Theda 1949- ... CANR-16
Earlier sketch in CA 93-96
Perdurabo, Frater
See Crowley, Edward Alexander
Pereda (y Sanchez de Porrua), Jose Maria
de 1833-1906 Brief entry ... 117
See also TCLC 16
Pereda y Porrua, Jose Maria de
See Pereda (y Sanchez de Porrua), Jose
Maria de
Peregoy, George Weems
See Mencken, H(enry) L(ouis)
Peregrine
See Deutscher, Isaac
Pereira, Harold Bertram 1890- ... 9-10R
Pereira, Sam 1949- ... 111
Pereira, W(ilfred) D(ennis) 1921- ... CANR-20
Earlier sketch in CA 104
Pereira Carneiro, Maurina 1899(?)-1983
Obituary ... 111
Perel, William M. 1927- ... 33-36R
Perella, Nicholas James 1927- ... 73-76
Perelman, Chaim 1912- ... 103
Perelman, Lewis J(oel) 1946- ... 73-76
Perelman, Michael 1939- ... 111

Perelman, S(idney) J(oseph)
1904-1979 .... CANR-18
Obituary 89-92
Earlier sketch in CA 73-76
See also DLB 11, 44
See also CLC 3, 5, 9, 15, 23, 44, 49
See also AITN 1, 2
Perenyi, Eleanor (Spencer Stone) 1918-
Brief entry 113
Perera, Gretchen G(ifford) 1940- 93-96
Perera, Thomas Biddle 1938- CANR-21
Earlier sketch in CA 37-40R
See also SATA 13
Perera, Victor 1934- 29-32R
Peres, Richard 1947- 93-96
Peres, Shimon 1923- 85-88
Peret, Benjamin 1899-1959 Brief entry 117
See also TCLC 20
Peretz, Don 1922- CANR-19
Earlier sketches in CA 11-12R, CANR-4
Peretz, Isaac Loeb 1851(?)-1915
Brief entry 109
See also TCLC 16
Peretz, Yitzkhok Leibush
See Peretz, Isaac Loeb
Pereyra, Lillian A(nita) 1920- 21-22R
Perez, Joseph F(rancis) 1930- CANR-16
Earlier sketch in CA 29-32R
Perez, Louis A., Jr. 1943- 121
Perez, Louis C(elestino) 1923- 77-80
Perez de Ayala, Ramon 1881-1962
Obituary 93-96
Perez-Firmat, Gustavo (Francisco) 1949- 123
Perez Galdos, Benito 1843-1920
Brief entry 125
See also TCLC 27
Perez Lopez, Francisco 1916- 49-52
Perham, Margery (Freda) 1895-1982 .... CANR-1
Obituary 106
Earlier sketch in CA 1R
Pericoli, Ugo 1923- 97-100
Perigoe, J. Rae 1910- 61-64
Perillo, Joseph M. 1933- 19-20R
Perin, Constance 29-32R
Perinbanayagam, Robert S(idharthan)
1934- 109
Perino, Joseph 1946- 106
Perino, Sheila C. 1948- 106
Peripatus
See Whittington-Egan, Richard
Peristiany, John G(eorge) 1911-1987 .... 19-20R
Obituary 124
Peritz, Rene 1933- 45-48
Perkes, Dan 1931- CANR-21
Earlier sketch in CA 69-72
Perkin, Harold (James) 1926- CANR-14
Earlier sketch in CA 77-80
Perkin, J(ames) R(ussell) C(onway) 1928- .. 113
Perkin, Robert L(yman) 1914-1978
Obituary 77-80
Perkins, Agnes (Regan) 1926- CANR-10
Earlier sketch in CA 57-60
Perkins, Al(bert Rogers) 1904-1975 107
Obituary 57-60
See also SATA 30
Perkins, Ann (Louise) 1915- Brief entry 113
Perkins, Bradford 1925- 1R
Perkins, Carl (Lee) 1932- 102
Perkins, David 1928- 77-80
Perkins, David (Lee) 1939- CANR-13
Earlier sketch in CA 73-76
Perkins, Dexter 1889-1984 .... 7-8R
Obituary 113
Perkins, Dwight Heald 1934- CANR-22
Earlier sketches in CA 19-20R, CANR-7
Perkins, E(rnest) Benson 1881- 7-8R
Perkins, Edward A., Jr. 1928- CANR-14
Earlier sketch in CA 21-22R
Perkins, Edwin Judson 1939- 106
Perkins, Eugene 1932- DLB-41
Perkins, Faith
See Bramer, Jennie (Perkins)
Perkins, George (Burton, Jr.) 1930- 15-16R
Perkins, Hugh V(ictor) 1918-1988 93-96
Obituary 124
Perkins, James Alfred 1911- 108
Perkins, James Ashbrook 1941- 73-76
Perkins, James Oliver Newton 1924- 11-12R
Perkins, James S(cudday) 1899- 89-92
Perkins, John (William) 1935- CANR-13
Earlier sketch in CA 73-76
Perkins, John Allen 1919- 114
Perkins, John Bryan Ward
See Ward-Perkins, John Bryan
Perkins, Lawrence A. 1917(?)-1979
Obituary 89-92
Perkins, Lucy Fitch 1865-1937 Brief entry .. 122
Perkins, (Richard) Marlin 1905-1986 103
Obituary 119
See also SATA 21, 48
Perkins, Merle Lester 1919- 45-48
Perkins, Michael 1942- CANR-8
Earlier sketch in CA 19-20R
Perkins, Newton Stephens 1925- 49-52
Perkins, Ralph 1913- 15-16R
Perkins, Robert L(ee) 1930- 25-28R
Perkins, Rollin M(orris) 1889- 53-56
Perkins, Steve
See Perkins, Newton Stephens
Perkins, Van L. 1930- Brief entry 106
Perkins, Virginia Chase 1902- CAP-2
Earlier sketch in CA 33-36
Perkins, Whitney Trow 1921- 106
Perkins, William H(ughes) 1923- 53-56
Perkins, Wilma Lord 1897-1976 Obituary 104
Perkinson, Henry J(oseph) 1930- CANR-12
Earlier sketch in CA 19-20R
Perkoff, Stuart Z. 1930-1974 Obituary 113
See also DLB 16
Perkowski, Jan Louis 1936- CANR-2
Earlier sketch in CA 45-48
Perl, Arnold 1914-1971 Obituary 33-36R
Perl, Lila 33-36R
See also SATA 6
Perl, Ruth June 1929- 25-28R
Perl, Susan 1922-1983 .... CANR-11
Obituary 110
Earlier sketch in CA 19-20R
See also SATA 22, 34
Perl, Teri (Hoch) 1926- CANR-19
Earlier sketch in CA 93-96
Perl, William R. 1906- 126
Perlberg, Deborah 1948- 118
Perlberg, Mark 1929- 37-40R
Perle, George 1915- CANR-3
Earlier sketch in CA 2R
Perles, Benjamin Max 1922- 45-48
Perley, Michael 1946- 114
Perlin, Seymour 1925- 121
Perlinski, Jerome 1940- 112
Perlis, Vivian 1928- 85-88
Perlman, Bennard B(loch) 1928- 89-92
Perlman, Helen Harris 1905- CANR-3
Earlier sketch in CA 4R
Perlman, Janice E(laine) 1943- 61-64
Perlman, Jess 1891- 89-92
Perlman, John N(iels) 1946- CANR-12
Earlier sketch in CA 33-36R
Perlman, Mark 1923- CANR-19
Earlier sketches in CA 1R, CANR-3
Perlman, Samuel 1905-1975 .... CAP-2
Earlier sketch in CA 33-36
Perlmutter, Emanuel 1907(?)-1986
Obituary 118
Perlmutter, Jerome H. 1924- 19-20R
Perlmutter, Nathan 1923-1987 .... 15-16R
Obituary 123
Perlmutter, O(scar) William 1920-1975 57-60
See also SATA 8
Perlmutter, Ruth Ann 1924- 109
Perlo, Victor 1912- CANR-2
Earlier sketch in CA 5-6R
Perloff, Harvey S(tephen) 1915-1983
Obituary 110
Perloff, Marjorie G(abrielle) 1931- CANR-22
Earlier sketches in CA 57-60, CANR-7
Perlongo, Bob 1933- 112
Perls, Eugenia Soderberg 1904(?)-1973
Obituary 37-40R
Perls, Frederick S(alomon) 1893-1970 101
Perls, Frederick S(alomon) 1894(?)-1970
Obituary 29-32R
Perls, Fritz
See Perls, Frederick S(alomon)
Perls, Hugo 1886(?)-1977 Obituary 73-76
Perlstein, Gary R(obert) 1940- 57-60
Perman, Dagmar Horna 1926(?)-1978
Obituary 77-80
Perman, Michael 1942- Brief entry 113
Pernet, A(nn) 1940- 107
Perniciaro, Tony 1917- 41-44R
Pernoud, Regine 1909- 102
Peroff, Nicholas C(arl) 1944- 113
Peron, Juan (Domingo) 1895-1974
Obituary 49-52
Perosa, Sergio 1933- CAP-1
Earlier sketch in CA 15-16
Peroutka, Ferdinand 1895(?)-1978
Obituary 77-80
Perowne, Barry
See Atkey, Philip
Perowne, Stewart Henry 1901- CANR-3
Earlier sketch in CA 4R
Perrault, Charles 1628-1703 .... SATA-25
Perreard, Suzanne Louise Butler 1919- . SATA-29
Perreault, John 1937- CANR-1
Earlier sketch in CA 45-48
Perreault, William D(aniel), Jr. 1948- 110
Perrella, Robert 1917- 61-64
Perrenod, Virginia Marion (Lacy) 1928- 117
Perret, Gene 1937- 117
Brief entry 114
Perrett, Bryan 1934- CANR-20
Earlier sketch in CA 29-32R
Perrett, Geoffrey 1940- CANR-4
Earlier sketch in CA 53-56
Perrigo, Lynn I(rwin) 1904- 33-36R
Perrin, Blanche Chenery 1894-1973 .... 5-6R
Obituary 41-44R
Perrin, Noel 1927- 13-14R
Perrin, (Horace) Norman 1920-1976 .... CANR-11
Earlier sketch in CA 15-16R
Perrin, Porter Gale 1896-1962 Obituary 113
Perrin, Robert 1939- 97-100
Perrin, Robert G(eorge) 1945- 111
Perrin, Ursula 1935- 101
Perrine, Laurence 1915- CANR-3
Earlier sketch in CA 1R
Perrine, Mary 1913- 25-28R
See also SATA 2
Perrin Jassy, Marie-France 1942- 93-96
Perrins, Lesley 1953- 123
Perrottet, Philippe (Louis Gaston)
1921-1982 .... 25-28R
Obituary 122
Perroy, Edouard (Marie Joseph)
1901-1974 Obituary 53-56
Perrucci, Robert 1931- CANR-15
Earlier sketch in CA 85-88
Perruchot, Henri 1917-1967 .... CAP-1
Earlier sketch in CA 9-10
Perry, Anne 1938- CANR-22
Earlier sketch in CA 101
Perry, Barbara Fisher
See Fisher, Barbara
Perry, Ben Edwin 1892-1968 .... CAP-2
Earlier sketch in CA 23-24
Perry, Bernard (Berenson) 1910-1985
Obituary 117
Perry, Bliss 1860-1954 .... DLB-71
Perry, Brighton
See Sherwood, Robert E(mmet)
Perry, Carmen AITN-2
Perry, Charles 1941- 124
Perry, Charles Edward AITN-2
Perry, Charner M(arquis) 1902-1985
Obituary 117
Perry, Collin 1949- 108
Perry, David L. 1931- 33-36R
Perry, David Thomas 1946- 37-40R
Perry, Dick 1922- 13-14R
Perry, Edgar C(loud) 1900- 117
Perry, Eleanor (Rosenfeld Bayer)
1915(?)-1981 111
Obituary 103
See also DLB 44
Perry, Elisabeth Israels 1939- 111
Perry, Elizabeth Jean 1948- 104
Perry, Erma (Jackson McNeil) 89-92
Perry, Gaylord (Jackson) 1938-
Brief entry 113
Perry, George 1935- CANR-26
Earlier sketch in CA 103
Perry, Gordon Arthur 1914- 108
Perry, Grace 1927- CANR-20
Earlier sketch in CA 102
Perry, Henry Ten Eyck 1890-1973 .... CAP-2
Earlier sketch in CA 19-20
Perry, Huey 1936- 49-52
Perry, James M(oorhead) 1927- 15-16R
Perry, Jim (Angelo) 1942- 53-56
Perry, John 1914- CANR-6
Earlier sketch in CA 5-6R
Perry, John Curtis 1930- 104
Perry, John D(elbert), Jr. 1940- 25-28R
Perry, John Oliver 1929- 93-96
Perry, Joseph M(cGarity) 1936- 37-40R
Perry, Kenneth F(rederick) 1902-1974 .... CAP-2
Earlier sketch in CA 19-20
Perry, Kenneth I. 1929- 29-32R
Perry, Kenneth W(ilbur) 1919- 57-60
Perry, Lewis (Curtis) 1938- CANR-1
Earlier sketch in CA 45-48
Perry, Linette (Purbi) 108
Perry, Lloyd M(erle) 1916- CANR-9
Earlier sketch in CA 23-24R
Perry, Louis B(arnes) 1918- CAP-1
Earlier sketch in CA 13-14
Perry, Margaret 1933- 89-92
See also BW
Perry, Michael (Charles) 1933- 101
Perry, Milton F(reeman) 1926- 15-16R
Perry, Nicolette E. 1949- 119
Perry, Octavia Jordan 1894- CAP-1
Earlier sketch in CA 13-14
Perry, Patricia 1949- 106
See also SATA 30
Perry, Peter John 1937- 49-52
Perry, Phillip M. 1948- 29-32R
Perry, Ralph Barton 1876-1957
Brief entry 123
Perry, Regenia (Alfreda) 1941- 126
Perry, Richard 41-44R
Perry, Richard 1944- 115
See also BW
Perry, Richard S. 1924- 13-14R
Perry, Ritchie (John Allen) 1942- CANR-21
Earlier sketches in CA 45-48, CANR-1
Perry, Robin 1917- 65-68
Perry, Roger 1933- CANR-14
Earlier sketch in CA 77-80
See also SATA 27
Perry, Rosalie Sandra 1945- 53-56
Perry, Rufus
See Gibson, Walter B(rown)
Perry, Ruth 1943- 118
Perry, Shauneille 1930- 113
Perry, Stewart E(dmond) 1928- 19-20R
Perry, (Charles) Stuart 1908- 107
Perry, Susan
See Perry, Susan M.
Perry, Susan M. 1950- 124
Perry, T. Anthony 1938- 81-84
Perry, Thomas Brief entry 123
Perry, Thomas Whipple 1925- 11-12R
Perry, Troy D(eroy) 1940- Brief entry 109
Perry, Walter (Laing Macdonald) 1921- 113
Perry, Will 1933- 65-68
Perry, William E(dward) 1931- 111
Perry, Wilma I. 1912- 105
Perse, St.-John
See Leger, (Marie-Rene) Alexis
Saint-Leger
See also CLC 4, 11, 46
Pershing, Marie
See Schultz, Pearle Henriksen
Persichetti, Vincent 1915-1987 Obituary 124
Persico, Joseph E(dward) 1930- CANR-21
Earlier sketch in CA 93-96
Persinger, Michael A. 1945- 69-72
Persis
See Haime, Agnes Irvine Constance
(Adams)
Perske, Robert 1927- 106
Persky, Mordecai 1931- 81-84
Persky, Mort
See Persky, Mordecai
Persky, Stan 1941- CANR-18
Earlier sketch in CA 101
Person, Amy L. 1896- CAP-2
Earlier sketch in CA 23-24
Person, Bernard 1895(?)-1981 Obituary 103
Person, Peter P. 1889- CAP-1
Earlier sketch in CA 11-12
Persons, Robert H(odge), Jr. 1922- CANR-13
Earlier sketch in CA 19-20R
Persons, Stow Spaulding 1913- 103
Pertinax
See Geraud, (Charles Joseph) Andre
and Haws, Duncan
Pertschuk, Michael 1933- CANR-26
Earlier sketch in CA 109
Pertwee, Michael (Henry Roland) 1916-
Brief entry 124
Pertwee, Roland 1885-1963 Obituary 93-96
Perutz, Kathrin 1939- CANR-3
Earlier sketch in CA 3R
Pervin, Lawrence A. 1936- CANR-8
Earlier sketch in CA 23-24R
Peschel, Enid Rhodes 1943- 110
Pescow, Jerome K(enneth) 1929- 45-48
Pesek, Boris P(eter) 1926- 23-24R
Pesek, Ludek 1919- 29-32R
Pesetsky, Bette 1932- CLC-28
Peshkin, Alan 1931- 81-84
Peshkov, Alexei Maximovich 1868-1936
Brief entry 105
Pesin, Harry 1919- 29-32R
Peskin, Allan 1933- Brief entry 109
Pesnot, Patrick 1943- 101
Pessen, Beth 1943- 97-100
Pessen, Edward 1920- CANR-14
Earlier sketch in CA 37-40R
Pessina, Giorgio 1902(?)-1977 Obituary 73-76
Pessino, Clara Park 1899(?)-1985
Obituary 116
Pesso, Albert 1929- 73-76
Pessoa, Fernando (Antonio Nogueira)
1888-1935 Brief entry 125
See also TCLC 27
Pestelli, Giorgio 1938- 124
Pestieau, Phyllis Smith 1946- 97-100
Petacco, Arrigo 1929- CANR-21
Earlier sketch in CA 103
Petaja, Emil (Theodore) 1915- 25-28R
Peter, Armistead (III) 1896(?)-1983
Obituary 111
Peter, James (Fletcher) 1919- 19-20R
Peter, John (Desmond) 1921- CANR-3
Earlier sketch in CA 1R
Peter, Laurence J. 1919- CANR-17
Earlier sketch in CA 19-20R
See also DLB 53
Peterfreund, Sheldon P(aul) 1917- 21-22R
Peterfreund, Stuart (Samuel) 1945- CANR-13
Earlier sketch in CA 33-36R
Peterkiewicz, Jerzy 1916- CANR-5
Earlier sketch in CA 7-8R
Peterkin, Julia Mood 1880-1961 102
See also DLB 9
See also CLC 31
Peterman, Michael A(lan) 1942- 111
Peterman, Ruth 1924- 57-60
Peters, Alexander
See Hollander, Zander
Peters, Arthur Anderson 1913-1979
Obituary 93-96
Peters, Arthur King 1919- 104
Peters, Barney
See Bauer, Erwin A.
Peters, Caroline
See Betz, Eva Kelly
Peters, Charles (Given, Jr.) 1926- 122
Brief entry 116
Peters, Christina 1942- 85-88
Peters, Daniel (James) 1948- CANR-15
Earlier sketch in CA 85-88
Peters, David A(lexander) 1923- 25-28R
Peters, Donald L. 1925- 21-22R
Peters, Edward (Murray) 1936- CANR-18
Earlier sketch in CA 101
Peters, Elizabeth
See Mertz, Barbara (Gross)
Peters, Ellis
See Pargeter, Edith Mary
Peters, Eugene H(erbert) 1929- 41-44R
Peters, F(rancis) E(dward) 1927- CANR-12
Earlier sketch in CA 73-76
Peters, Frederick George 1935- 104
Peters, Fritz
See Peters, Arthur Anderson
Peters, Geoffrey
See Palmer, Madelyn
Peters, George W(illiam) 1907- CANR-24
Earlier sketch in CA 45-48
Peters, H. Frederick 1910- 73-76
Peters, J. Ross 1936- 29-32R
Peters, Jean (Rae) 1935- 116
Peters, Joan K. 1945- CLC-39
Peters, Ken(neth Walter) 1929- 19-20R
Peters, Lane
See Lapidus, Elaine
Peters, Lawrence
See Davies, L(eslie) P(urnell)
Peters, Lenrie (Wilfred Leopold) 1932- 108
See also BW
Peters, Leslie
See Peters, Donald L.
Peters, Ludovic
See Brent, Peter (Ludwig)
Peters, Marcia
See Gouled, Vivian G(loria)
Peters, Margaret Evelyn 1936- 53-56
Peters, Margot 1933- CANR-12
Earlier sketch in CA 73-76
Peters, Maureen 1935- 33-36R

Peters, Max S(tone) 1920- 57-60
Peters, Michael
See Hornsby-Smith, Michael P(eter)
Peters, Michael Bartley 1943- 110
Brief entry 108
Peters, Mike
See Peters, Michael Bartley
Peters, Natasha
See Cleaver, Anastasia N.
Peters, R(ichard) S(tanley) 1919- CANR-16
Earlier sketch in CA 23-24R
Peters, Richard Dorland 1910-1984
Obituary 114
Peters, Robert Anthony 1926- 49-52
Peters, Robert L(ouis) 1924- 15-16R
See also CLC 7
Peters, Ronald M., Jr. 1947- 85-88
Peters, Ruth Marie 1913(?)-1978
Obituary 104
Peters, S. H.
See Porter, William Sydney
Peters, S. T.
See Brannon, William T.
Peters, Steven
See Geiser, Robert L(ee)
Peters, Ted
See Peters, Theodore F(rank)
Peters, Theodore F(rank) 1941- 81-84
Peters, Thomas J. 1942- Brief entry . . . 123
Peters, Tom
See Peters, Thomas J.
Peters, Victor 1915- 19-20R
Peters, Virginia Bergman 1918- 93-96
Peters, William 1921- CANR-20
Earlier sketches in CA 11-12R, CANR-3
Petersen, Arnold 1885-1976 Obituary 65-68
Petersen, Carol Otto 1914- 57-60
Petersen, Clarence G. 1933- 77-80
Petersen, David M(uir) 1939- 41-44R
Petersen, Donald 1928- 13-14R
Petersen, E. Allen 1903(?)-1987 Obituary . . . 122
Petersen, Gwenn Boardman 1924- CANR-2
Earlier sketch in CA 45-48
Petersen, James R(eeve) 1948- 114
Petersen, Karen Daniels 1910- 73-76
Petersen, Mark E. 1900-1984 Obituary 111
Petersen, Melba F(rances) Runtz 1919- 5-6R
Petersen, P(eter) J(ames) 1941- 112
See also SATA 43, 48
Petersen, Peter (Barron) 1932- 57-60
Petersen, Sigurd Damskov 1904- 11-12R
Petersen, William 1912- CANR-3
Earlier sketch in CA 1R
Petersen, William J. 1929- CANR-9
Earlier sketch in CA 21-22R
Petersen, William John 1901- 7-8R
Petersham, Maud (Fuller) 1890-1971 73-76
Obituary 33-36R
See also SATA 17
See also DLB 22
Petersham, Miska 1888-1960 73-76
See also SATA 17
See also DLB 22
Peterson, A(lexander) D(uncan) C(ampbell)
1908-1988 108
Obituary 126
Peterson, Agnes F(ischer) 1923- 29-32R
Peterson, Arthur L(aVerne) 1926- 11-12R
Peterson, Brent D(an) 1942- 120
Peterson, Carl 1896(?)-1983 Obituary 110
Peterson, Carolyn Sue 1938- CANR-12
Earlier sketch in CA 73-76
Peterson, Carroll V(alleen) 1929- 45-48
Peterson, Charles 1900(?)-1976 Obituary . .69-72
Peterson, Charles S. 1927- 49-52
Peterson, Christmas
See Christmas, Joyce
Peterson, Dale 1944- 109
Peterson, Donald R(obert) 1923- 25-28R
Peterson, Douglas L(ee) 1924- 41-44R
Peterson, Edward N(orman) 1925- 29-32R
Peterson, Edwin (Lewis) 1904-1972
Obituary 37-40R
Peterson, Edwin Loose 1915- 7-8R
Peterson, Eldridge 1905(?)-1977
Obituary 73-76
Peterson, Eleanor M. 1912- 25-28R
Peterson, Elmer 1930- 37-40R
Peterson, Esther (Allen) 1934- CANR-16
Earlier sketch in CA 89-92
See also SATA 35
Peterson, Evan T(ye) 1925- 45-48
Peterson, F. Ross 1941- 97-100
Peterson, Forrest H(arold) 1912- CANR-25
Earlier sketch in CA 45-48
Peterson, Franklynn 1938- 110
Peterson, Frederick Alvin 1920- 49-52
Peterson, Gilbert Allan 1935- 114
Peterson, Hans 1922- CANR-1
Earlier sketch in CA 49-52
See also SATA 8
Peterson, Harold 1939- 29-32R
Peterson, Harold F(erdinand) 1900- 5-6R
Peterson, Harold L(eslie) 1922-1978 . . . .CANR-4
Obituary 73-76
Earlier sketch in CA 3R
See also SATA 8
Peterson, Helen Stone 1910- 37-40R
See also SATA 8
Peterson, Houston 1897-1981 107
Obituary 103
Peterson, James
See Zeiger, Henry A(nthony)
Peterson, James Alfred 1913- 104
Peterson, James Allan 1932- 29-32R
Peterson, Jeanne Whitehouse
See Whitehouse, Jeanne

Peterson, Jim
See Crawford, William (Elbert)
Peterson, John Eric 1933- 53-56
Peterson, John J. 1918- 53-56
Peterson, John W(illard) 1921- 97-100
Peterson, Kenneth G(erard) 1927- 33-36R
Peterson, Levi S(avage) 1933- CANR-26
Earlier sketch in CA 109
Peterson, Linda H(aenlein) 1948- 121
Peterson, Lloyd R(ichard) 1922-
Brief entry 107
Peterson, Lorraine 1940- 113
See also SATA 44
Peterson, Louis 1922- DLB-76
Peterson, M(ildred) Jeanne 1937- 103
Peterson, Marilyn Ann 1933- 57-60
Peterson, Martin Severin 1897- CANR-3
Earlier sketch in CA 2R
Peterson, Mendel (Lazear) 1918- 73-76
Peterson, Merrill D(aniel) 1921- CANR-19
Earlier sketches in CA 1R, CANR-3
Peterson, Nancy L(ee) 1939- 105
Peterson, Norma Lois 1922- 15-16R
Peterson, Ottis 1907- 23-24R
Peterson, Owen M. 1924- CANR-26
Earlier sketch in CA 108
Peterson, Paul E(lliott) 1940- CANR-24
Earlier sketch in CA 45-48
Peterson, R(odney) D(elos) 1932- 41-44R
Peterson, Reona 1941- 73-76
Peterson, Richard A(ustin) 1932- 25-28R
Peterson, Robert 1924- CANR-17
Earlier sketch in CA 25-28R
Peterson, Robert E(ugene) 1928- 15-16R
Peterson, Robert W. 1925- 33-36R
Peterson, Roger Tory 1908- CANR-1
Earlier sketch in CA 4R
Peterson, Russell Arthur 1922- 33-36R
Peterson, Simone
See Thomson, Daisy H(icks)
Peterson, Susan (Annette) H(arnly) 1925- . .57-60
Peterson, Ted Nicholas 1934- 121
Peterson, Theodore (Bernard) 1918- 11-12R
Peterson, Trudy H(uskamp) 1945- 116
Peterson, Virgilia 1904-1966 Obituary 25-28R
Peterson, Wallace Carroll 1921- 7-8R
Peterson, Walter Scott 1944- 23-24R
Peterson, Wilferd Arlan 1900- CANR-6
Earlier sketch in CA 11-12R
Peterson, Willard James 1938- 103
Peterson, William S(amuel) 1939- CANR-11
Earlier sketch in CA 29-32R
Petersson, Robert T. 1918- 45-48
Peterzell, Jay 1952- 118
Petesch, Natalie L(evin) M(aines) CANR-21
Earlier sketches in CA 57-60, CANR-6
Petgen, Dorothea 1903(?)-1985 Obituary . . . 115
Petgen, Dorothy
See Petgen, Dorothea
Pethybridge, Roger 1934- 5-6R
Petie, Haris
See Petty, Roberta
See also SATA 10
Petievich, Gerald 1944- 105
Petiot, Henri Jules Charles 1901-1965
Obituary 114
Petit, Gaston 1930- 73-76
Petitclerc, Denne Bart 1929- 93-96
Petite, Irving (Laurence) 1920- Brief entry . . 113
Petkas, Peter (James) 1945- 37-40R
Petmecky, Ben (Joe) 1922- 3R
Peto
See White, Stanley
Peto, James
See White, Stanley
Petrakis, Harry Mark 1923- CANR-4
Earlier sketch in CA 11-12R
See also CLC 3
Petras, James Frank 1937- CANR-22
Earlier sketches in CA 61-64, CANR-7
Petras, John W. 1940- 29-32R
Petratur, Joyce 1939- Brief entry 111
Petrement, Simone 1907- 77-80
Petres, Robert E(van) 1939- 104
Petrich, Patricia Barrett 1942- 61-64
Petrides, Avra 123
Petrides, George Athan 1916- Brief entry . . 106
Petrides, Heidrun 1944- SATA-19
Petrie, Alexander 1881- CAP-1
Earlier sketch in CA 15-16
Petrie, Asenath 1914- 23-24R
Petrie, Catherine 1947- 109
See also SATA 41, 52
Petrie, Charles (Alexander) 1895-1977 . . CANR-8
Obituary 89-92
Earlier sketch in CA 19-20R
Petrie, Mildred McClary 1912- 21-22R
Petrie, Paul J(ames) 1928- CANR-18
Earlier sketches in CA 9-10R, CANR-3
Petrie, Rhona
See Buchanan, Marie
Petrie, Sidney 1923- 23-24R
Petrinovich, Lewis 1930- 41-44R
Petro, Sylvester 1917- 1R
Petrocelli, Orlando R(alph) 1930- CANR-1
Earlier sketch in CA 45-48
Petrone, Jane Muir 1929- 7-8R
Petroni, Frank A. 1936- 85-88
Petropulos, John A(nthony) 1929- 25-28R
Petroski, Catherine (Ann Groom)
1939- CANR-22
Earlier sketch in CA 106
See also SATA 48
Petrou, David Michael 1949- 73-76
Petrov, Evgeny
See Kataev, Evgeny Petrovich
See also TCLC 21

Petrov, Fyodor 1877(?)-1973 Obituary . . .41-44R
Petrov, Victor P. 1907- CANR-26
Earlier sketches in CA 23-24R, CANR-10
Petrov, Vladimir 1915- 21-22R
Petrova, Olga 1884(?)-1977 Obituary 73-76
Petrovich, Michael B(oro) 1922- 108
See also SATA 40
Petrovska, Marija 1926- 107
Petrovskaya, Kyra
See Wayne, Kyra Petrovskaya
Petrovsky, N.
See Poltoratzky, N(ikolai) P(etrovich)
Petrucci, Kenneth R(occo) 1947- 57-60
Petry, Ann (Lane) 1908- CANR-4
Earlier sketch in CA 7-8R
See also CAAS 6
See also BW
See also SATA 5
See also DLB 76
See also CLC 1, 7, 18
See also CLR 12
Petry, Carl Forbes 1943- 106
Petry, R(ay) C. 1903- 5-6R
Pettas, Mary 1918- 25-28R
Petterson, Henry William 1922- 11-12R
Petterssen, Sverre 1898-1974 Obituary 53-56
Pettersson, Karl-Henrik 1937- 65-68
Pettes, Dorothy E. CANR-12
Earlier sketch in CA 25-28R
Pettigrew, Thomas Fraser 1931- CANR-13
Earlier sketch in CA 33-36R
Pettingill, Amos
See Harris, William Bliss
Pettingill, Olin Sewall, Jr. 1907- CANR-1
Earlier sketch in CA 45-48
Pettit, Arthur G. 1938- 53-56
Pettit, Clyde Edwin 1932- 65-68
Pettit, Henry (Jewett) 1906- 2R
Pettit, Lawrence K. 1937- 33-36R
Pettit, Michael (Edwin) 1950- 114
Pettit, Norman 1929- 19-20R
Pettit, Philip 1945- CANR-17
Earlier sketch in CA 97-100
Pettitt, George A(lbert) 1901-1976 . . . . . .CAP-2
Earlier sketch in CA 29-32
Pettoello, Decio (Egberto Saadi)
1886-1984 Obituary 113
Petty, Anne C(otton) 1945- 115
Petty, Mary 1899-1976 Obituary 65-68
Petty, Norman 1927(?)-1984 Obituary 113
Petty, Roberta 1915- CANR-10
Earlier sketch in CA 61-64
Petty, Walter T. 1918- CANR-9
Earlier sketch in CA 23-24R
Petty, William Henry 1921- 65-68
Petuchowski, Jakob Josef 1925- CANR-18
Earlier sketches in CA 1R, CANR-3
Petulla, Joseph M. 1932- CANR-9
Earlier sketch in CA 23-24R
Petzold, Paul 1940- CANR-9
Earlier sketch in CA 61-64
Petzoldt, Paul Kiesow 1908- 57-60
Petzoldt, Richard 1907-1974 Obituary 111
Pevsner, Nikolaus (Bernhard Leon)
1902-1983 .CANR-7
Obituary 110
Earlier sketch in CA 9-10R
Pevsner, Stella 57-60
See also SATA 8
Peyo
See Culliford, Pierre
Peyre, Henri (Maurice) 1901- CANR-3
Earlier sketch in CA 7-8R
Peyrefitte, Alain Antoine 1925- 85-88
Peyrefitte, (Pierre) Roger 1907- 65-68
Peyser, Joan 1931- Brief entry 112
Peyton, K. M.
See Peyton, Kathleen Wendy
See also CLR 3
Peyton, Karen (Hansen) 1897-196(?) CAP-1
Earlier sketch in CA 9-10
Peyton, Kathleen Wendy 1929- 69-72
See also SATA 15
Peyton, Myron A(lvin) 1909- Brief entry . . . 114
Peyton, Patrick J(oseph) 1909- CAP-2
Earlier sketch in CA 23-24
Pezzulo, Ted 1936(?)-1979 Obituary 89-92
Pezzuti, Thomas Alexander 1936- 61-64
Pfadt, Robert Edward 1915- 73-76
Pfaff, William (Wendle III) 1928- CANR-24
Earlier sketch in CA 7-8R
Pfaffenberger, Bryan 1949- 118
Pfaffenberger, Clarence J. 1889-1967 . . . .CAP-1
Earlier sketch in CA 13-14
Pfahl, John K(erch) 1927- CANR-1
Earlier sketch in CA 1R
Pfaltz, Marilyn 1933- 103
Pfaltzgraff, Robert L., Jr. 1934- CANR-24
Earlier sketches in CA 23-24R, CANR-9
Pfanner, Helmut Franz 1933- 57-60
Pfarrer, Donald 1934- 111
Pfatteicher, Philip H(enry) 1935- 114
Pfau, Hugo 1908- 29-32R
Pfau, Richard Anthony 1942- 120
Pfeffer, J(ay) Alan 1907- CANR-3
Earlier sketch in CA 4R
Pfeffer, Jeffrey 1946- 109
Pfeffer, Leo 1910- CANR-22
Earlier sketches in CA 13-14R, CANR-7
Pfeffer, Rose 1908-1985 Obituary 115
Pfeffer, Susan Beth 1948- 29-32R
See also SATA 4
See also CLR 11
Pfeffermann, Guy 1941- 25-28R
Pfeifer, Carl J(ames) 1929- 49-52
Pfeifer, Luanne 1928- CANR-16
Earlier sketch in CA 89-92

Pfeiffer, Bruce Brooks 1930- 121
Pfeiffer, C(urtis) Boyd 1937- 57-60
Pfeiffer, Carl Curt 1908- 101
Pfeiffer, Charles F. 1919-1976 . . . . .CANR-4
Obituary 65-68
Earlier sketch in CA 2R
Pfeiffer, Eric 1935- CANR-10
Earlier sketch in CA 13-14R
Pfeiffer, John E(dward) 1914- 101
Pfeiffer, Karl G(raham) 3R
Pfeiffer, Marcella
See Syracuse, Marcella Pfeiffer
Pfeilschifter, Boniface 1900- CAP-2
Earlier sketch in CA 19-20
Pferd, William (III) 1922(?)-1987 Obituary . . . 121
Pfiffner, John M(cDonald) 1893- 7-8R
Pfingston, Roger 1940- CANR-20
Earlier sketch in CA 104
Pfister, Arthur 1949- 45-48
Pflanze, Otto (Paul) 1918- 7-8R
Pflaum, Irving Peter 1906-1985 . . . . .15-16R
Obituary 115
Pflaum, Melanie L(oewenthal) 1909- CANR-6
Earlier sketch in CA 13-14R
Pflaum, Susanna Whitney 1937- 110
Brief entry 106
Pflaum-Connor, Susanna
See Pflaum, Susanna Whitney
Pflieger, Elmer F. 1908- 19-20R
Pflum, John (Edward) 1934- Brief entry . . . 107
Pfordresher, John 1943- 65-68
Pfouts, Ralph W(illiam) 1920- 41-44R
Pfoutz, Shirley Eclov 1922- 2R
Pfriem, John E. 1923(?)-1983 Obituary 110
Pfuetze, Paul E(ugene) 1904-1985 . . . . 3R
Obituary 118
Phair, Judith Turner 1946- 61-64
Phalle, Thibaut de Saint
See de Saint Phalle, Thibaut
Phan, Peter C(ho) 1943- 114
Phares, Donald 1942- 81-84
Phares, Ross (Oscar) 1908- CAP-1
Earlier sketch in CA 11-12
Phares, Timothy B. 1954- 97-100
Pharr, Emory Charles 1896(?)-1981
Obituary 104
Pharr, Robert Deane 1916- 49-52
See also BW
See also DLB 33
Pharr, Susan J(ane) 1944- 105
Phelan, Francis Joseph 1925- 7-8R
Phelan, James Pius X 1951- 114
Phelan, John Leddy 1924-1976 . . . . .CANR-12
Earlier sketch in CA 23-24R
Phelan, John Martin 1932- 73-76
Phelan, Josephine 1905- SATA-30
Phelan, Mary Kay 1914- CANR-4
Earlier sketch in CA 4R
See also SATA 3
Phelan, Mary Michenfelder 1936- 97-100
Phelan, Nancy 1913- 101
Phelan, Terry Wolfe 1941- 97-100
Phelge, Nanker
See Richards, Keith
Phelps, Arthur Warren 1909- 49-52
Phelps, Ashton 1913-1983 Obituary 109
Phelps, D(udley) Maynard 1897- CAP-2
Earlier sketch in CA 25-28
Phelps, Digger
See Phelps, Richard
Phelps, Donald (Norman) 1929- CANR-25
Earlier sketch in CA 45-48
Phelps, Elizabeth Stuart 1844-1911 . . . . .DLB-74
Phelps, Ethel Johnston 1914- 106
See also SATA 35
Phelps, Frederic
See McCulley, Johnston
Phelps, Gilbert (Henry, Jr.) 1915- CANR-26
Earlier sketches in CA 7-8R, CANR-7
Phelps, Humphrey 1927- 111
Phelps, Jack 1926- 29-32R
Phelps, O(rme) Wheelock 1906- 2R
Phelps, Phelps 1897-1981 Obituary 104
Phelps, Richard 103
Phelps, Robert 1922- CANR-19
Earlier sketch in CA 19-20R
Phelps, Roger P(aul) 1920- 49-52
Phelps, Thomas Ross 1929- 61-64
Phenix, Philip Henry 1915- 5-6R
Pheto, Molefe 1935- 118
Phialas, Peter George 1914- 25-28R
Phibbs, Brendan (Pearse) 1916- 33-36R
Phifer, Kenneth G. 1915- 19-20R
Phifer, Allen Kellogg 1914- 117
Philbrick, Charles (Horace) II
1922-1971 .CANR-4
Earlier sketch in CA 4R
Philbrick, Helen L. 1910- 103
Philbrick, Joseph Lawrence 1927- 45-48
Philbrook, Clem(ent E.) 1917- 104
See also SATA 24
Philby, Harold Adrian Russell 1912-1988
Obituary 125
Philby, Kim
See Philby, Harold Adrian Russell
Philip, Cynthia Owen 1928- 49-52
Philip, J(ames) A(llenby) 1901- CAP-2
Earlier sketch in CA 23-24
Philip, John Robert 1927- 108
Philip, Lotte Brand
See Foerster, Lotte B(rand)
Philipp, Elliot Elias 1915- CANR-3
Earlier sketch in CA 9-10R
Philippatos, George Crito 1938-
Brief entry 106
Philippe, Charles-Louis 1874-1909 . . . . . .DLB-65
Philippi, Donald L. 1930- 108

Philips, Cyril Henry 1912- 103
Philips, G(eorge) Edward 1926- 41-44R
Philips, Judson (Pentecost) 1903- CANR-14
 Earlier sketch in CA 89-92
 See also AITN 1
Philips, Michael 1942- 125
Philips, Thomas
 See Davies, L(eslie) P(urnell)
Philipson, Morris H. 1926- CANR-4
 Earlier sketch in CA 1R
Philipson, Susan Sacher 1934- 11-12R
Philliber, William W(esley) 1943- 111
Phillifent, John Thomas 1916-1976
 Obituary 102
Phillippi, Wendell Crane 1918- 77-80
Phillips, Aileen Paul
 See Paul, Aileen
Phillips, Alan
 See Stauderman, Albert P(hilip)
Phillips, Alan Meyrick Kerr 1916- 7-8R
Phillips, Alice H(erz) 1909- 114
Phillips, Allen
 See Allen, (Evelyn) Elizabeth
Phillips, Almarin 1925- CANR-1
 Earlier sketch in CA 2R
Phillips, Anne G(arvey) 1929- 73-76
Phillips, (Elizabeth Margaret Ann) Barty
 1933- CANR-24
 Earlier sketches in CA 61-64, CANR-8
Phillips, Beeman N(oal) 1927- 122
Phillips, Bernard S. 1931- CANR-12
 Earlier sketch in CA 25-28R
Phillips, Bernice Maxine 1925- 45-48
Phillips, Betty Lou
 See Phillips, Elizabeth Louise
Phillips, Billie M(cKindra) 1925- 102
Phillips, Bob 1940- 69-72
Phillips, C(ecil) E(rnest) Lucas
 See Lucas Phillips, C(ecil) E(rnest)
Phillips, Cabell (Beverly Hatchett)
 1904-1975 97-100
 Obituary 61-64
Phillips, Carole 1938- 108
Phillips, Cecil R(andolph) 1933- 15-16R
Phillips, Celeste R(ose Nagel) 1933- 110
Phillips, Charles F(ranklin, Jr.) 1910- 85-88
Phillips, Charles F(ranklin), Jr. 1934- ... CANR-2
 Earlier sketch in CA 7-8R
Phillips, Claude S., Jr. 1923- 11-12R
Phillips, Clifton J(ackson) 1919- 37-40R
Phillips, (Preswly) Craig 1922- 11-12R
Phillips, D(ennis) J(ohn Andrew)
 1924- CANR-10
 Earlier sketch in CA 15-16R
Phillips, David Atlee 1922-1988 .... CANR-12
 Obituary 126
 Earlier sketch in CA 69-72
Phillips, David Graham 1867-1911
 Brief entry 108
 See also DLB 9, 12
Phillips, Debora R(othman) 1939- 93-96
Phillips, Derek L(ee) 1934- CANR-18
 Earlier sketch in CA 33-36R
Phillips, Dewi Zephaniah 1934- CANR-25
 Earlier sketches in CA 19-20R, CANR-9
Phillips, Dorothy S(anborn) 1893-1972
 Obituary 37-40R
Phillips, Dorothy W. 1906-1977 Obituary ..73-76
Phillips, E(lmo) Bryant 1905-1975 .... CANR-6
 Earlier sketch in CA 5-6R
Phillips, E(wing) Lakin 1915- 37-40R
Phillips, E(ugene) Lee 1941- 115
Phillips, Edward O. 1931- 124
Phillips, Edwin A(llen) 1915- 53-56
Phillips, Elizabeth C(row) 1906- 41-44R
Phillips, Elizabeth Louise SATA-48
Phillips, Emma Julia 1900- CAP-1
 Earlier sketch in CA 13-14
Phillips, Frances Lucas 1896-1986
 Obituary 119
Phillips, Frank
 See Nowlan, Philip Francis
Phillips, Gene D(aniel) 1935- CANR-17
 Earlier sketches in CA 45-48, CANR-1
Phillips, George H(oward) 1907- 112
Phillips, Gerald M. 1928- CANR-13
 Earlier sketch in CA 33-36R
Phillips, Gordon Lewis 1911-1982
 Obituary 108
Phillips, Herbert P. 1929- 15-16R
Phillips, Hiram Stone 1912(?)-1979 85-88
Phillips, Irv(ing W.) 1908- 65-68
 See also SATA 11
Phillips, J(ohn) B(ertram) 1906-1982 106
 Obituary 108
Phillips, Jack
 See Sandburg, Carl (August)
Phillips, James E(merson, Jr.) 1912-1979
 Obituary 89-92
Phillips, James Emerson, Jr. 1912-1979 101
Phillips, James M(cJunkin) 1929- 106
Phillips, James W. 1922- 33-36R
Phillips, Jayne Anne 1952- CANR-24
 Earlier sketch in CA 101
 See also DLBY 80
 See also CLC 15, 33
Phillips, Jerome C.
 See Cleveland, Philip Jerome
Phillips, Jewell Cass 1900- CAP-2
 Earlier sketch in CA 33-36
Phillips, Jill (Meta) 1952- CANR-14
 Earlier sketch in CA 65-68
Phillips, John L(awrence), Jr. 1923- 33-36R
Phillips, Josephine E(lvira Frye)
 1896-1975 ....5-6R
 Obituary 61-64
Phillips, Julien L(ind) 1945- 77-80
Phillips, Kathleen C(oleman) 1920- 116
Phillips, Keith W(endall) 1946- 102
Phillips, Kevin Price 1940- 65-68
Phillips, Klaus (Peter) 1947- 116
Phillips, L(ouis) C(hristopher) 1939- 57-60
Phillips, Laughlin 1924- 102
Phillips, Leon
 See Gerson, Noel Bertram
Phillips, Leona Rasmussen 1925- CANR-14
 Earlier sketch in CA 65-68
Phillips, Lois (Elisabeth) 1926- Brief entry .. 114
Phillips, Loretta (Hosey) 1893- CAP-1
 Earlier sketch in CA 15-16
 See also SATA 10
Phillips, Louis 1942- CANR-20
 Earlier sketches in CA 49-52, CANR-3
 See also SATA 8
Phillips, Mac
 See Phillips, Maurice J(ack)
Phillips, Margaret 1892(?)-1985 Obituary ... 116
Phillips, Margaret Mann 1906-1987 ....15-16R
 Obituary 123
Phillips, Margaret McDonald
 1910(?)-1978 Obituary 77-80
Phillips, Marjorie (Fell) 7-8R
Phillips, Mark
 See Janifer, Laurence M(ark)
Phillips, Mary Geisler 1881-1964 ....5-6R
 See also SATA 10
Phillips, Mary L. 1930- 116
Phillips, Maurice J(ack) 1914-1976 ....7-8R
 Obituary 103
Phillips, Michael 1938- 108
Phillips, Michael
 See Nolan, William F(rancis)
Phillips, Michael Joseph 1937- CANR-18
 Earlier sketches in CA 49-52, CANR-3
Phillips, Michael R(ay) 1946- 114
Phillips, Mickey
 See Phillips, Alan Meyrick Kerr
Phillips, Mike
 See Phillips, Michael R(ay)
Phillips, O(wen) Hood 1907- CANR-2
 Earlier sketch in CA 7-8R
Phillips, O(wen) M(artin) 1930- 89-92
Phillips, Osborne
 See Barcynski, Leon Roger
Phillips, Patricia 1935- 103
Phillips, Paul 1938- CANR-14
 Earlier sketch in CA 73-76
Phillips, Pauline (Esther Friedman)
 1918- CANR-19
 Earlier sketch in CA 1R
Phillips, Prentice 1894- CAP-1
 Earlier sketch in CA 15-16
 See also SATA 10
Phillips, R. Hart
 See Phillips, Ruby Hart
Phillips, Rachel 1934- 49-52
Phillips, Ray C. 1922- CANR-10
 Earlier sketch in CA 25-28R
Phillips, Richard
 See Dick, Philip K(indred)
Phillips, Richard C(laybourne) 1934- 65-68
Phillips, Robert (Schaeffer) 1938- CANR-8
 Earlier sketch in CA 19-20R
 See also CLC 28
Phillips, Robert L(eRoy), Jr. 1940- 77-80
Phillips, Ruby Hart 1902-1985 Obituary 117
Phillips, Samantha
 See Gelles-Cole, Sandi
Phillips, Stella 1927- CANR-11
 Earlier sketch in CA 21-22R
Phillips, Stephen 1864-1915 Brief entry 111
 See also DLB 10
Phillips, Steve
 See Whittington, Harry (Benjamin)
Phillips, Steven 1947- 103
Phillips, Tom
 See Drotning, Phillip T(homas)
Phillips, Ulrich B. 1877-1934 .... DLB-17
Phillips, Velma 1894- CAP-2
 Earlier sketch in CA 19-20
Phillips, Ward
 See Lovecraft, H(oward) P(hillips)
Phillips, Warren (Henry) 1926- 107
Phillips, Wendell 1921-1975 .... CAP-2
 Obituary 61-64
 Earlier sketch in CA 23-24
Phillips, Willard 1784-1873 .... DLB-59
Phillips, William 29-32R
Phillips-Birt, Douglas Hextall Chedzey
 1920-1977 .... CANR-1
 Earlier sketch in CA 4R
Phillips-Jones, Linda 1943- CANR-26
 Earlier sketch in CA 109
Phillipson, David 1930- 57-60
Phillipson, David W(alter) 1942- 107
Phillpotts, (Mary) Adelaide Eden 1896- 115
Phillpotts, Eden 1862-1960 102
 Obituary 93-96
 See also SATA 24
 See also DLB 10, 70
Philmus, Robert M. 1943- 33-36R
Philomythes
 See Dewart, Leslie
Philp, Howard Littleton 1902- 7-8R
Philp, Kenneth R(oy) 1941- 65-68
Philp, (Dennis Alfred) Peter 1920- 7-8R
Philp, Richard Nilson 1943- CANR-11
 Earlier sketch in CA 69-72
Philpott, David G(oodwin) 1927- 123
Philpott, Kent 1942- 61-64
Phin
 See Thayer, Ernest Lawrence
Phipps, Christine 1945- 123
Phipps, Frances (Lucille Walker)
 1924(?)-1986 Obituary 119
Phipps, Grace May Palk 1901- CANR-4
 Earlier sketch in CA 11-12R
Phipps, Joyce 1942- 49-52
Phipps, Nicholas 1913-1980 Obituary 97-100
Phipps, William E(ugene) 1930- CANR-12
 Earlier sketch in CA 29-32R
Phipson, Joan
 See Fitzhardinge, Joan Margaret
 See also SAAS 3
 See also CLR 5
Phiz
 See Browne, Hablot Knight
Phleger, Fred B. 1909- CANR-21
 Earlier sketch in CA 2R
 See also SATA 34
Phleger, Marjorie Temple 1908(?)-1986 ..11-12R
 Obituary 118
 See also SATA 1, 47
Phoenix, John
 See Derby, George Horatio
Phoenix, Pat
 See Pilkington, Pat
Phypers, David (John) 1939- 114
Physick, John Frederick 1923- 114
Phythian, B(rian) A(rthur) 1932- CANR-10
 Earlier sketch in CA 23-24R
Piaf, Edith 1915-1963 Obituary 113
Piaget, Jean 1896-1980 ....21-22R
 Obituary 101
 See also SATA 23
Pian, Rulan Chao 1922- 23-24R
Piano, Celeste
 See Lykiard, Alexis (Constantine)
Piasecki, Bruce 1955- CANR-12
 Earlier sketch in CA 69-72
Piatigorsky, Alexander 1929- 124
Piatigorsky, Gregor 1903-1976 Obituary ...69-72
Piatti, Celestino 1922- 73-76
 See also SATA 16
Piazza, Ben 1934- 11-12R
Picano, Felice 1944- CANR-11
 Earlier sketch in CA 69-72
Picard, Barbara Leonie 1917- CANR-2
 Earlier sketch in CA 7-8R
 See also SATA 2
Picasso, Pablo (Ruiz) 1881-1973 97-100
 Obituary 41-44R
Picazo, Jose 1910- CAP-1
 Earlier sketch in CA 13-14
Piccard, Auguste 1884-1962 Obituary 113
Piccard, Betty
 See Piccard, Elizabeth J(ane)
Piccard, Elizabeth J(ane) 1925- 65-68
Piccard, Jacques 1922- 65-68
Piccard, Joan Russell 29-32R
Picchio, Riccardo 1923- CANR-24
 Earlier sketch in CA 45-48
Piccolo, Lucio 1901-1969 97-100
 See also CLC 13
Pichaske, David Richard 1943- CANR-1
 Earlier sketch in CA 45-48
Pick, J(ohn) B(arclay) 1921- CANR-5
 Earlier sketch in CA 3R
Pick, John 1911- CAP-2
 Earlier sketch in CA 33-36
Pick, (Frederick) Michael 1949- 123
Pick, Robert 1898-1978 .... CANR-8
 Obituary 77-80
 Earlier sketch in CA 19-20R
Pickard, Charles 1932- SATA-36
Pickard, Dorothea Wilgus 1902- 23-24R
Pickard, John Benedict 1928- 2R
Pickard, Tom 1946- 81-84
 See also DLB 40
Pickell, Charles N(orman) 1927- 19-20R
Pickem, Peter
 See Stearns, Harold Edmund
Picken, Mary Brooks 1886(?)-1981
 Obituary 103
Picken, Stuart D(onald) B(lair) 1942- 106
Pickens, Donald Kenneth 1934- 53-56
Pickens, Robert S. 1900(?)-1978
 Obituary 81-84
Pickens, Roy 1939- 57-60
Picker, Fred 1927- 81-84
Picker, Ingrid 1932- 25-28R
Picker, Martin 1929- CANR-7
 Earlier sketch in CA 19-20R
Pickerell, Albert G(eorge) 1912- 25-28R
Pickerill, Don 1928- 77-80
Pickering, Ernest 1893(?)-1974 Obituary ..53-56
Pickering, Frederick Pickering 1909- 105
Pickering, George (White) 1904-1980 73-76
 Obituary 105
Pickering, James H(enry) 1937- CANR-13
 Earlier sketch in CA 33-36R
Pickering, James Sayre 1897-1969 .... CANR-16
 Obituary 103
 Earlier sketch in CA 1R
 See also SATA 28, 36
Pickering, Jerry V(ane) 1931- 57-60
Pickering, Percival
 See Stirling, Anna Maria Diana
 Wilhelmina (Pickering)
Pickering, R(obert) E(aston) 1934- 21-22R
Pickering, Samuel Francis, Jr. 1941- 104
Pickering, Stephen 1947- 57-60
Pickersgill, J(ohn) W(hitney) 1905- 45-48
Pickett, Calder M. 1921- 53-56
Pickett, Carla 1944- 37-40R
Pickett, J(arrell) Waskom 1890- CAP-1
 Earlier sketch in CA 15-16
Pickett, Robert S. 1931- 33-36R
Pickford, Cedric Edward 1926-1983 107
 Obituary 109
Pickford, Mary 1893-1979 Obituary 85-88
Pickle, Hal B(rittain) 1929- CANR-21
 Earlier sketches in CA 57-60, CANR-6
Pickles, (Maud) Dorothy 1903- 77-80
Pickles, M(abel) Elizabeth 1902- CAP-1
 Earlier sketch in CA 9-10
Pickles, Wilfred 1904-1978(?) 108
Pickoff, David 1930(?)-1986 Obituary 118
Pickrel, Paul (Murphy) 1917- 9-10R
Pickthall, Marjorie L(owry) C(hristie)
 1883-1922 Brief entry 107
 See also TCLC 21
Pickthorn, Helen 1927- 25-28R
Pico, Rafael 1912- 45-48
Picon, Molly 1898- 104
Picton, Bernard
 See Knight, Bernard
Pidal, Ramon Menendez
 See Menendez Pidal, Ramon
Pidgeon, Mary E. 1890(?)-1979 Obituary ..89-92
Piechocki, Joachim von Lang
 See von Lang-Piechocki, Joachim
Piediscalzi, Nicholas 1931- 122
 Brief entry 112
Piehl, Mel (Willis) 1946- 111
Piehler, Paul 1929- Brief entry 111
Piekalkiewicz, Jaroslaw A. 1926- 81-84
Piel, Gerard 1915- 57-60
Pielmeier, John 1949- Brief entry 125
Pienkowski, Jan 1936- CANR-11
 Earlier sketch in CA 65-68
 See also SATA 6
 See also CLR 6
Pieper, Josef 1904- 119
Piepkorn, Arthur Carl 1907-1973 ....41-44R
Pier, Arthur Stanhope 1874(?)-1966
 Obituary 25-28R
Pierard, Richard Victor 1934- CANR-17
 Earlier sketch in CA 29-32R
Pieratt, Asa B. 1938- 77-80
Pierce, Arthur Dudley 1897-1967 .... 1R
 Obituary 103
Pierce, Bessie Louise 1888-1974
 Obituary 53-56
Pierce, E(ugene) 1924- 15-16R
Pierce, Edith Gray 1893-1977 61-64
 See also SATA 45
Pierce, Edward T. 1917(?)-1978 Obituary ..77-80
Pierce, George Gilbert 1923- 7-8R
Pierce, Gerald S(wetnam) 1933- 45-48
Pierce, Glenn
 See Dumke, Glenn S.
Pierce, James Smith 1930- 21-22R
Pierce, Janis V(aughn) 1934- 45-48
Pierce, Joe E. 1924- 33-36R
Pierce, John Leonard, Jr. 1921- 11-12R
Pierce, John Robinson 1910- 17-18R
Pierce, Katherine
 See St. John, Wylly Folk
Pierce, Lawrence C(olman) 1936- 85-88
Pierce, Meredith Ann 1958- CANR-26
 Earlier sketch in CA 108
 See also SATA 48
Pierce, Milton Plotz 1933- 106
Pierce, Ovid Williams 1910- CANR-4
 Earlier sketch in CA 1R
Pierce, Patricia (May) 1943- 120
Pierce, Paul 1910- 69-72
Pierce, Philip E(arly) 1912- 110
Pierce, Richard A(ustin) 1918- CANR-2
 Earlier sketch in CA 7-8R
Pierce, Robert N(ash) 1931- 104
Pierce, Roy 1923- 37-40R
Pierce, Ruth (Ireland) 1936- 29-32R
 See also SATA 5
Pierce, Tamora 1954- 118
 See also SATA 49, 51
Pierce, Willard Bob 1914- 13-14R
Piercy, Josephine Ketcham 1895- CAP-1
 Earlier sketch in CA 15-16
Piercy, Marge 1936- CANR-13
 Earlier sketch in CA 23-24R
 See also CAAS 1
 See also CLC 3, 6, 14, 18, 27
Pierik, Robert 1921- 37-40R
 See also SATA 13
Pierman, Carol J 1947- 77-80
Pierotti, John 1911-1987 Obituary 122
Pierpoint, Robert (Charles) 1925- 107
Pierre, Andrew J. 1934- CANR-1
 Earlier sketch in CA 45-48
Pierre, Clara 1939- 65-68
Pierrot, George Francis 1898-1980 ....7-8R
 Obituary 103
 See also AITN 2
Piers, Maria W(eigl) 1911- CANR-8
 Earlier sketch in CA 23-24R
Piersen, William D. 1942- 126
Pierson, Frank
 See Pierson, Frank R(omer)
Pierson, Frank R(omer) 1925- 123
 Brief entry 114
Pierson, G(eorge) W(ilson) 1904- CANR-3
 Earlier sketch in CA 9-10R
Pierson, Howard 1922- 49-52
Pierson, Jan 1937- 112
Pierson, John H(erman) G(roesbeck)
 1906- CANR-4
 Earlier sketch in CA 11-12R
Pierson, Paul Everett 1927- 108
Pierson, Peter O'Malley 1932- 97-100
Pierson, Robert H. 1911- 21-22R
Pierson, Stanley 1925- 85-88
Pierson, William H(arvey), Jr. 1911- 122
Piet, John H(enry) 1914- 29-32R
Pietri, Pedro Juan 1943- 97-100
Pietrofesa, John J(oseph) 1940- 57-60

Pietropinto, Anthony 1938- 89-92
Pietsch, Paul Andrew 1929- 104
Pietschmann, Richard John III 1940- 69-72
Pieyre de Mandiargues, Andre 1909- CANR-22
Earlier sketch in CA 103
Pifer, Ellen 1942- CANR-23
Earlier sketch in CA 106
Pig, Edward
See Gorey, Edward (St. John)
Piggott, C. M.
See Guido, (Cecily) Margaret
Piggott, (Alan) Derek 1923- 115
Pigman, William Ward 1910-1977
Obituary 73-76
Pigney, Joseph Pape 1908- 3R
Pihera, Larry 1933- CANR-1
Earlier sketch in CA 45-48
Pihl, Marshall R(alph) 1933- 49-52
Pijewski, John 1952- 111
Piji
See Williams, Ann, Jr.
Pike, Albert 1809-1891 DLB-74
Pike, Burton 1930- 2R
Pike, Charles R.
See Bulmer, (Henry) Kenneth
and Harknett, Terry
Pike, Dag 1933- 69-72
Pike, Diane Kennedy 1938- 37-40R
Pike, E(dgar) Royston 1896-1980 9-10R
Obituary 125
See also SATA 22
Pike, Eunice V(ictoria) 1913- CANR-20
Earlier sketch in CA 97-100
Pike, James A(lbert) 1913-1969 CANR-4
Obituary 25-28R
Earlier sketch in CA 4R
Pike, Kenneth Lee 1912- 120
Pike, Margaret (Prudence) Lyford
See Lyford-Pike, Margaret (Prudence)
Pike, Nelson C. 1930- Brief entry 111
Pike, Norman 1901- CAP-2
Earlier sketch in CA 25-28
Pike, Robert E(vording) 1905- 7-8R
Pike, Robert L.
See Fish, Robert L.
Pike, Ruth 1931- Brief entry 112
Pike, William H. 1943- 115
Pikelny, Philip S. 1951- 107
Pikoulis, John 1941- 115
Pikunas, Justin 1920- 25-28R
Pilapil, Vicente R. 1941- 37-40R
Pilarski, Laura 1926- 29-32R
See also SATA 13
Pilat, O. R.
See Pilat, Oliver (Ramsay)
Pilat, Oliver (Ramsay) 1903-1987 7-8R
Obituary 123
Pilbrow, Richard (Hugh) 1933- 29-32R
Pilcer, Sonia 1949- CANR-13
Earlier sketch in CA 89-92
Pilch, John J(oseph) 1936- CANR-25
Earlier sketch in CA 108
Pilch, Judah 1902- CANR-6
Earlier sketch in CA 7-8R
Pilcher, George William 1935- 105
Pilcher, Rosamunde 1924- 57-60
Pilcher, William W. 1930- 45-48
Pilditch, James (George Christopher)
1929- 11-12R
Pile, John F(rederick) 1924- CANR-16
Earlier sketch in CA 93-96
Pileggi, Nicholas 1933- 124
Pilgrim, Anne
See Allan, Mabel Esther
Pilgrim, David 1950- 120
Pilgrim, David
See Palmer, John (Leslie)
and Saunders, Hilary Aidan St. George
Pilgrim, Geneva Hanna 1914- 25-28R
Pilgrim, Walter E(dward) 1934- 113
Piliawsky, Monte 1944- 111
Pilinszky, Janos 1921-1981 Obituary 104
Pilio, Gerone
See Whitfield, John Humphreys
Pilisuk, Marc 1934- 29-32R
Pilk, Henry
See Campbell, Ken
Pilkey, Orrin H. 1934- 97-100
Pilkington, Betty 69-72
Pilkington, Cynthia
See Horne, Cynthia Miriam
Pilkington, E(dward) C(ecil) A(rnold)
1907- CAP-2
Earlier sketch in CA 25-28
Pilkington, Francis Meredyth 1907- CAP-2
Earlier sketch in CA 25-28
See also SATA 4
Pilkington, John, Jr. 1918- 19-20R
Pilkington, Pat 1923-1986 123
Obituary 120
Pilkington, Roger (Windle) 1915- CANR-5
Earlier sketch in CA 3R
See also SATA 10
Pilkington, Walter ?-1983 Obituary 109
Pilkington, William T(homas, Jr.)
1939- CANR-8
Earlier sketch in CA 61-64
Pill, Virginia 1922- 61-64
Pillai, Karnam Chengalvaroya 1901- 7-8R
Pillar, James Jerome 1928- 15-16R
Pillin, William 1910-1985 11-12R
Obituary 116
Pilling, Arnold R(emington) 1926- CANR-3
Earlier sketch in CA 1R
Pilling, Christopher Robert 1936- CANR-19
Earlier sketch in CA 101
Pillinger, Douglass 1906(?)-1983 Obituary 111
Pillon, Nancy Bach 1917- 110
Pilnyak, Boris
See Vogau, Boris Andreyevich
See also TCLC 23
Pilo, Giuseppe Maria 1929- CANR-5
Earlier sketch in CA 9-10R
Pilon, Jean-Guy 1930- DLB-60
Pilon, Juliana Geran 1947- 97-100
Pilou
See Bardot, Louis
Pilpel, Harriet F(leischl) CAP-2
Earlier sketch in CA 21-22
Pilpel, Robert H(arry) 1943- CANR-9
Earlier sketch in CA 65-68
Pimsleur, Meira Goldwater
1905(?)-1979 13-14R
Obituary 89-92
Pimsleur, Paul 1927-1976 CAP-2
Obituary 65-68
Earlier sketch in CA 33-36
Pina, Laura ?-1984 Obituary 113
Pinar, William 1947- 57-60
Pinard, (J. L.-M.) Maurice 1929- 41-44R
Pincher, H(enry) Chapman 1914- CANR-12
Earlier sketch in CA 15-16R
Pincherle, Alberto 1907- 25-28R
See also CLC 11, 18
Pincherle, Marc 1888-1974 Obituary 49-52
Pinchin, Jane Lagoudis 1942- 69-72
Pinchot, Ann (Kramer) CANR-4
Earlier sketch in CA 4R
Pinchot, David 1914(?)-1983 Obituary 109
See also SATA 34
Pinckney, Catherine L(arkum) 19-20R
Pinckney, Cathey
See Pinckney, Catherine L(arkum)
Pinckney, Edward R(obert) 1924- 19-20R
Pinckney, Josephine (Lyons Scott)
1895-1957 Brief entry 107
See also DLB 6
Pincus, Edward R. 1938- CANR-12
Earlier sketch in CA 33-36R
Pincus, Gregory Goodwin 1903-1967
Obituary 113
Pincus, Harriet 1938- 102
See also SATA 27
Pincus, Joseph 1919- 25-28R
Pincus, Lily 1898-1981 CANR-5
Obituary 105
Earlier sketch in CA 53-56
Pinder, John H(umphrey) M(urray) CANR-18
Earlier sketches in CA 9-10R, CANR-3
Pinder, Leslie Hall
See Hall, Leslie
Pindyck, Robert (Stephen) 1945- 89-92
Pine, Leslie Gilbert 1907-1987 13-14R
Obituary 122
Pine, Theodore
See Petaja, Emil (Theodore)
Pine, Tillie S(chloss) 1896- 69-72
See also SATA 13
Pine, William
See Harknett, Terry
Pineau, Roger 1916- 25-28R
Pineda, Cecile 1942- 118
See also CLC 39
Pinero, Arthur Wing 1855-1934
Brief entry 110
See also DLB 10
Pinero, Miguel (Antonio Gomez)
1946-1988 Obituary 125
Pinero, Miguel (Gomez) 1946- 61-64
See also CLC 4
Pines, Maya 15-16R
Pines, Paul (Andre) 1941- 112
Ping, Charles J. 1930- 19-20R
Pinget, Robert 1919- 85-88
See also CLC 7, 13, 37
Pinion, F(rancis) B(ertram) 1908- CANR-12
Earlier sketch in CA 25-28R
Pinka, Patricia G(arland) 1935- 126
Pinkerton, Edward C(askin) 1911- 108
Pinkerton, James R(onald) 1932- CANR-24
Earlier sketch in CA 45-48
Pinkerton, Jan 1934- Brief entry 112
Pinkerton, Joan Trego 1928- 107
Pinkerton, Kathrene Sutherland (Gedney)
1887-1967 2R
Obituary 103
See also SATA 26
Pinkerton, Marjorie Jean 1934- 45-48
Pinkerton, Robert E(ugene) 1882-1970
Obituary 29-32R
Pinkerton, Todd 1917- 69-72
Pinkerton, W. Anson
See Steele, Henry
Pinkett, Harold T(homas) 1914- 29-32R
Pink Floyd
See Barrett, (Roger) Syd
and Gilmour, David
and Mason, Nick
and Waters, Roger
and Wright, Rick
See also CLC 35
Pinkham, Mary Ellen 101
Pinkney, Alphonso 1929- 25-28R
Pinkney, David H(enry) 1914- 11-12R
Pinkney, Jerry 1939- SATA-32, 41
Pinkowski, Edward 1916- 9-10R
Pinkston, Joe M. 1931- 7-8R
Pinkus, Oscar 1927- 7-8R
Pinkus, Philip 1922- Brief entry 113
Pinkwater, Daniel Manus 1941- CANR-12
Earlier sketch in CA 29-32R
See also SATA 46
See also SAAS 3
See also CLC 35
See also CLR 4
Pinkwater, Manus
See Pinkwater, Daniel Manus
See also SATA 8
Pinna, Giovanni 1939- CANR-4
Earlier sketch in CA 49-52
Pinner, David 1940- CANR-19
Earlier sketch in CA 25-28R
Pinner, Erna 1896- CAP-1
Earlier sketch in CA 11-12
Pinner, Joma
See Werner, Herma
Pinney, Peter (Patrick) 1922- 25-28R
Pinney, Roy 1911- CANR-6
Earlier sketch in CA 7-8R
Pinney, Thomas 1932- CANR-21
Earlier sketch in CA 85-88
Pinney, Wilson G(ifford) 1929- 45-48
Pino, E.
See Wittermans, Elizabeth (Pino)
Pino, Jose Ortiz y III
See Ortiz y Pino, Jose III
Pinoak, Justin Willard
See Prosser, H(arold) L(ee)
Pinsdorf, Marion K(atheryn) 1932- 124
Pinsent, Arthur 1888- CAP-2
Earlier sketch in CA 29-32
Pinsent, Gordon (Edward) 1930- 106
Pinsker, Sanford 1941- CANR-12
Earlier sketch in CA 33-36R
Pinsky, Robert 1940- 29-32R
See also CAAS 4
See also DLBY 82
See also CLC 9, 19, 38
Pinson, William M(eredith), Jr. 1934- CANR-9
Earlier sketch in CA 19-20R
Pintauro, Joseph 1930- 81-84
Pintel, Gerald 1922- CANR-4
Earlier sketch in CA 49-52
Pinter, Harold 1930- 7-8R
See also DLB 13
See also CLC 1, 3, 6, 9, 11, 15, 27
Pinter, Walter S. 1928- 102
Pintner, Walter McKenzie 1931- 23-24R
Pinto, David 1937- 61-64
Pinto, Edward Henry 1901-1972 CAP-1
Earlier sketch in CA 13-14
Pinto, Peter
See Berne, Eric (Lennard)
Pinto, Vivian de Sola 1895-1969 CANR-10
Earlier sketch in CA 5-6R
Pintoff, Ernest 1931- 19-20R
Pintoro, John 1947- 103
Pioneer
See Yates, Raymond F(rancis)
Piontek, Heinz 1925- CANR-13
Earlier sketch in CA 25-28R
See also DLB 75
Piotrow, Phyllis Tilson 1933- 122
Piovene, Guido 1907-1974 97-100
Obituary 53-56
Piowaty, Kim Kennelly 1957- 115
See also SATA 49
Pipa, Arshi 1920- CANR-10
Earlier sketch in CA 25-28R
Piper, Anson C(onant) 1918- 41-44R
Piper, Don Courtney 1932- CANR-15
Earlier sketch in CA 41-44R
Piper, Eileen 1906- 122
Piper, H(enry) Beam 1904-1964 117
Obituary 110
See also DLB 8
Piper, H(erbert) W(alter) 1915- 7-8R
Piper, Henry Dan 1918- 19-20R
Piper, Jim 1937- 97-100
Piper, Otto A. 1891- 5-6R
Piper, Roger
See Fisher, John (Oswald Hamilton)
Piper, Watty
See Bragg, Mabel Caroline
See also DLB 22
Piper, William Bowman 1927- CANR-12
Earlier sketch in CA 61-64
Pipes, Richard (Edgar) 1923- 23-24R
Pippert, Wesley Gerald 1934- 53-56
Pippett, (Winifred) Aileen 1895- CAP-1
Earlier sketch in CA 13-14
Pippin, Frank Johnson 1906-1968 CAP-2
Earlier sketch in CA 19-20
Pipping, Ella (Geologica) 1897- 61-64
Piquet, Howard S(amuel) 1903-1983 CANR-16
Obituary 111
Earlier sketches in CA 19-20, CAP-2
Piquet-Wicks, Eric 1915- 7-8R
Pirages, Dennis (Clark) 1942- 116
Pirandello, Luigi 1867-1936 Brief entry 104
See also TCLC 4, 29
Pires, Joe
See Stout, Robert Joe
Pirie, David (Tarbat) 1946- CANR-21
Earlier sketch in CA 97-100
Pirie, N(orman) W(ingate) 1907- 29-32R
Pirie-Gordon, (Charles) Harry (Clinton)
1883(?)-1969 Obituary 104
Pirmantgen, Pat
See Pirmantgen, Patricia H.
Pirmantgen, Patricia H. 1933- 45-48
Piro, Richard 1934- 49-52
See also SATA 7
Pirogov, Peter A. 1920-1987 Obituary 121
Pirone, Pascal P(ompey) 1907- 11-12R
Pirsig, Robert M(aynard) 1928- 53-56
See also SATA 39
See also CLC 4, 6
Pirson, Sylvain J. 1905- 5-6R
Pirtle, Caleb (Jackson) III 1941- CANR-26
Earlier sketches in CA 69-72, CANR-11
Pisano, Ronald G(eorge) 1948- CANR-20
Earlier sketch in CA 102
Pisar, Samuel 1929- 29-32R
See also DLBY 83
Piserchia, Doris (Elaine) 1928- 125
Brief entry 107
Pishkin, Vladimir 1931- CANR-24
Earlier sketch in CA 45-48
Pisk, Paul A(madeus) 1893- CAP-1
Earlier sketch in CA 13-14
Pismire, Osbert
See Hivnor, Robert
Pisor, Robert (Louis) 1939- 109
Pistole, Elizabeth (Smith) 1920- CANR-8
Earlier sketch in CA 19-20R
Piston, Walter 1894-1976 Obituary 69-72
Pitavy, Francois L(ouis) 1934- 73-76
Pitcairn, Frank
See Cockburn, (Francis) Claud
Pitcairn, Leonora 1912- 23-24R
Pitcher, Evelyn G(oodenough) 1915- 19-20R
Pitcher, George (Willard) 1925- 23-24R
Pitcher, Gladys 1890- CAP-1
Earlier sketch in CA 9-10
Pitcher, Harvey (John) 1936- CANR-3
Earlier sketch in CA 45-48
Pitcher, Robert W(alter) 1918- 29-32R
Pitchford, Kenneth S(amuel) 1931- 104
Pitkin, Dorothy (Horton) 1899(?)-1972
Obituary 37-40R
Pitkin, Hanna Fenichel 1931- 122
Brief entry 111
Pitkin, Thomas M(onroe) 1901- 19-20R
Pitkin, Timothy 1766-1847 DLB-30
Pitkin, Walter, Jr. 1913- 15-16R
Pitman, (Isaac) James 1901-1985 CAP-2
Obituary 117
Earlier sketch in CA 29-32
See also SATA 46
Pitrone, Jean Maddern 1920- CANR-8
Earlier sketch in CA 19-20R
See also SATA 4
Pitseolak, Peter 1902-1973 93-96
Pitt, Barrie (William Edward) 1918- CANR-20
Earlier sketch in CA 5-6R
Pitt, David C(harles) 1938- CANR-16
Earlier sketch in CA 29-32R
Pitt, David G(eorge) 1921- 126
Pitt, Jeremy
See Wynne-Tyson, (Timothy) Jon
(Lyden)
Pitt, Peter (Clive Crawford) 1933- 33-36R
Pitt, Valerie Joan 1925- 7-8R
Pittenger, W(illiam) Norman 1905- CANR-20
Earlier sketches in CA 4R, CANR-5
Pitter, Ruth 1897- CAP-1
Earlier sketch in CA 13-14
See also DLB 20
Pittman, David J(oshua) 1927- CANR-6
Earlier sketch in CA 7-8R
Pittock, Joan (Hornby) 1930- CANR-26
Earlier sketch in CA 107
Pitt-Rivers, Julian Alfred 1919- 101
Pitts, Denis 1930- 65-68
Pitts, Robert F. 1908-1977 Obituary 69-72
Pitz, Henry C(larence) 1895-1976 CANR-9
Obituary 69-72
Earlier sketch in CA 9-10R
See also SATA 4, 24
Pitzer, Sara 1938- 107
Pivar, David J. 1933- 45-48
Piven, Frances Fox 1932- 49-52
Pixley, Jorge V. 1937- CANR-16
Earlier sketches in CA 45-48, CANR-1
Pizer, Donald 1929- 11-12R
Pizer, Harry F(rancis) 1947- 101
Pizer, Vernon 1918- CANR-4
Earlier sketch in CA 4R
See also SATA 21
Pizzat, Frank J(oseph) 1924- 49-52
Pizzey, Erin 1939- 81-84
Pizzo, Peggy 1946- 118
Pla, Josep 1897-1981 Obituary 103
Place, Irene Magdaline (Glazik) 1912- CANR-1
Earlier sketch in CA 1R
Place, Janey Ann 1946- 73-76
Place, Marian T(empleton) 1910- CANR-20
Earlier sketches in CA 1R, CANR-5
See also SATA 3
Placere, Morris N.
See Gupta, S(ushil) (Kumar)
Placet, Leroi 1901-1970 Obituary 29-32R
Placksin, Sally 1948- 111
Placzek, Adolf Kurt 1913- 112
Plagemann, Bentz 1913- CANR-4
Earlier sketch in CA 1R
Plagens, Peter (L.) 1941- Brief entry 107
Plager, Sheldon J. 1931- 25-28R
Plaidy, Jean
See Hibbert, Eleanor Burford
Plain, Belva 1919- CANR-14
Earlier sketch in CA 81-84
Plaine, Alfred R. 1898(?)-1981 Obituary 105
See also SATA 29
Plaister, Theodore H. 1923- Brief entry 113
Plaja, Guillermo Diaz
See Diaz Plaja, Guillermo
Plamenatz, John Petrov 1912-1975 CANR-5
Earlier sketch in CA 13-14R
Planck, Carolyn H(eine) 1910- 73-76

Planck, Charles Evans 1896-1987 73-76
Obituary 121
Planck, Max (Karl Ernst Ludwig)
1858-1947 Brief entry 115
Plank, Emma N(uschi) 1905- CAP-2
Earlier sketch in CA 33-36
Plank, Robert 1907-1983 .... CANR-12
Earlier sketch in CA 25-28R
Plano, Jack Charles 1921- CANR-17
Earlier sketches in CA 7-8R, CANR-2
Plant, Marcus L. 1911- 1R
Plant, Raymond 1945- CANR-21
Earlier sketch in CA 29-32R
Plant, Robert 1948- CLC-12
Plante, David 1940- CANR-12
Earlier sketch in CA 37-40R
See also DLBY 83
See also CLC 7, 23, 38
Plante, (Joseph) Jacques (Omer)
1929-1986 Obituary 118
Brief entry 108
Plante, Julian G(erard) 41-44R
Plantinga, Alvin C. 1932- CANR-11
Earlier sketch in CA 23-24R
Plantinga, Leon B(rooks) 1935- 23-24R
Planz, Allen 1937- 53-56
Plaskow, Judith (Ellen) 1947- 126
Brief entry 108
Plastaras, James C(onstantine) 1931- 21-22R
Plate, Robert 1918- 19-20R
Plate, Thomas 1944- CANR-23
Earlier sketch in CA 69-72
Plater, Alan (Frederick) 1935- 85-88
Plater, William M(armaduke) 1945- 85-88
Plath, David W(illiam) 1930- CANR-3
Earlier sketch in CA 11-12R
Plath, Sylvia 1932-1963 .... CAP-2
Earlier sketch in CA 19-20
See also DLB 5, 6
See also CDALB 1941-1968
See also CLC 1, 2, 3, 5, 9, 11, 14, 17, 50
Platig, E(mil) Raymond 1924- 37-40R
Platonov, Andrei
See Klimentov, Andrei Platonovich
See also TCLC 14
Platov, Mariquita (Villard) 1905- 7-8R
Platt, Anthony M. 1942- 25-28R
Platt, Charles 1945- CANR-24
Earlier sketch in CA 23-24R
Platt, D(esmond) C(hristopher St.) M(artin)
1934- Brief entry 109
Platt, Eugene Robert 1939- CANR-3
Earlier sketch in CA 49-52
Platt, Frederick 1946- 61-64
Platt, Gerald M. 1933- CANR-17
Earlier sketch in CA 97-100
Platt, Harlan D. 1950- 123
Platt, Harrison Gray 1902- 41-44R
Platt, Jennifer (Ann) 1937- 29-32R
Platt, John (Rader) 1918- 19-20R
Platt, Kin 1911- CANR-11
Earlier sketch in CA 19-20R
See also SATA 21
See also CLC 26
Platt, Lyman De 1943- 102
Platt, Michael 1942- 122
Platt, Rutherford 1894-1975 Obituary 61-64
Platt, Washington 1890-1965 .... 2R
Obituary 120
Platten, Thomas George 1899- CAP-1
Earlier sketch in CA 11-12
Platts, Beryl 1918- 61-64
Plauger, P(hillip) J(ames) 1944- 57-60
Plaut, Allene Talmey 1903-1986 Obituary ... 118
Plaut, Thomas F(ranz) A(lfred) 1925- 25-28R
Plaut, W(olf) Gunther 1912- CANR-17
Earlier sketches in CA 7-8R, CANR-2
Plawin, Paul 1938- 89-92
Player, Gary (Jim) 1935- 101
Player, Ian 1927- 49-52
Playfair, Guy Lyon 1935- CANR-23
Earlier sketch in CA 106
Playfellow, Robin
See Ellis, Edward S(ylvester)
Playsted, James
See Wood, James Playsted
Pleasants, Henry 1910- 107
Pleasants, Henry, Jr. 1884-1963 .... 4R
Pleasants, Samuel A(ugustus III) 1918- ...77-80
Pleck, Elizabeth Hafkin 1945- Brief entry ... 115
Pleck, Joseph H(ealy) 1946- CANR-23
Earlier sketches in CA 57-60, CANR-7
Plekker, Robert J(ohn) 1929- 69-72
Plendello, Leo
See Saint, Andrew (John)
Plender, Richard O(wen) 1945- 101
Plenzdorf, Ulrich 1934- DLB-75
Plessen, Elisabeth 1944- DLB-75
Plesset, Isabel R(osahoff) 1912- 103
Plesur, Milton 1927-1987 .... CANR-24
Earlier sketch in CA 45-48
Pletcher, Barbara A. 1946- 123
Pletcher, David M(itchell) 1920- 3R
Pleydell, Susan
See Senior, Isabel J(anet Couper Syme)
Plick et Plock
See Simenon, Georges (Jacques Christian)
Plievier, Theodor 1892-1955 .... DLB-69
Plimmer, Charlotte 1916- 104
Plimmer, Denis 1914- 104
Plimpton, George (Ames) 1927- 21-22R
See also SATA 10
See also CLC 36
See also AITN 1
Plimpton, Ruth Talbot 1916- 13-14R
Plischke, Elmer 1914- CANR-18
Earlier sketches in CA 2R, CANR-2
Plochmann, George Kimball 1914- 5-6R
Ploeg, Johannes P(etrus) M(aria) van der
See Van Der Ploeg, Johannes P(etrus) M(aria)
Plog, Fred (Thomas III) 1944- CANR-12
Earlier sketch in CA 25-28R
Plog, Stanley C. 1930- CANR-15
Earlier sketch in CA 41-44R
Ploghoft, Milton E(rnest) 1923- 104
Plomer, William Charles Franklin
1903-1973 .... CAP-2
Earlier sketch in CA 21-22
See also SATA 24
See also DLB 20
See also CLC 4, 8
Plomley, Roy 1914-1985 Obituary 116
Brief entry 107
Plommer, (William) Hugh ?-1983
Obituary 109
Plopper, Julie Jynelle 1916- 69-72
Ploscowe, Morris 1904-1975 .... CANR-2
Obituary 61-64
Earlier sketch in CA 45-48
Ploss, Sidney I. 1932- 15-16R
Plossl, George W. 1918- 21-22R
Plotnick, Alan R(alph) 1926- 19-20R
Plotnick, Charles K(eith) 1931- 114
Plotnicov, Leonard 1930- 23-24R
Plotnik, Arthur 1937- CANR-20
Earlier sketch in CA 69-72
Plotz, Helen Ratnoff 1913- CANR-8
Earlier sketch in CA 11-12R
See also SATA 38
Plowden, Alison 1931- CANR-15
Earlier sketch in CA 33-36R
Plowden, David 1932- 33-36R
See also SATA 52
Plowden, G(eoffrey) F(rank) C(hichele)
1929- 116
Plowden, Gene 1906-1985 ....21-22R
Obituary 117
Plowhead, Ruth Gipson 1877-1967 .... SATA-43
Plowman, E(dward) Grosvenor 1899- 13-14R
Plowman, Edward E(arl) 1931- 37-40R
Plowman, Piers
See Kavanagh, Patrick (Joseph)
Plowman, Stephanie 1922- CANR-5
Earlier sketch in CA 53-56
See also SATA 6
Pluckrose, Henry (Arthur) 1931- 33-36R
See also SATA 13
Pluff, Barbara Littlefield 1926- 5-6R
Plum, J.
See Wodehouse, P(elham) G(renville)
Plum, Jennifer
See Kurland, Michael (Joseph)
Plum, Lester Virgil 1906-1972 .... 1R
Obituary 37-40R
Plumb, Barbara Louise Brown 1934- ... CANR-15
Earlier sketch in CA 89-92
Plumb, Beatrice
See Hunzicker, Beatrice Plumb
Plumb, Charles P. 1900(?)-1982 Obituary .. 105
See also SATA 29
Plumb, Charlie
See Plumb, Joseph Charles, Jr.
Plumb, J(ohn) H(arold) 1911- CANR-3
Earlier sketch in CA 7-8R
Plumb, Joseph Charles, Jr. 1942- CANR-3
Earlier sketch in CA 49-52
Plume, Ilse SATA-43
Plumly, Stanley (Ross) 1939- 110
Brief entry 108
See also DLB 5
See also CLC 33
Plummer, Alfred 1896- 29-32R
Plummer, Ben
See Bingley, David Ernest
Plummer, Beverly J. 1918- 29-32R
Plummer, Catharine 1922- 23-24R
Plummer, Clare (Emsley) 1912- 25-28R
Plummer, Kenneth 1946- 73-76
Plummer, L. Gordon 1904- CAP-2
Earlier sketch in CA 33-36
Plummer, Margaret 1911- CAP-2
Earlier sketch in CA 25-28
See also SATA 2
Plummer, Mark A(llen) 1929- 37-40R
Plummer, William (Halsey Jr.) 1945- 102
Plummer, William J(oseph) 1927- 53-56
Plumpe, Friedrich Wilhelm 1888-1931
Brief entry 112
Plumpp, Sterling D(ominic) 1940- CANR-24
Earlier sketch in CA 45-48
See also BW
See also DLB 41
Plumptre, Arthur Fitzwalter Wynne
1907-1977 109
Obituary 106
Plumstead, A(rthur) William 1933- CANR-11
Earlier sketch in CA 25-28R
Plunket, Robert 1945- 115
Plunkett, James
See Kelly, James Plunkett
See also DLB 14
Plunkett, Thomas J. 1921- 33-36R
Plutchik, Robert 1927- CANR-11
Earlier sketch in CA 21-22R
Pluto, Terry 1955- 107
Plutonius
See Mehta, Rustam Jehangir
Plutschow, Herbert Eugen 1939- CANR-18
Earlier sketch in CA 102
Plutzik, Roberta Ann 1948- 110
Plymell, Charles 1935- CANR-11
Earlier sketch in CA 21-22R
See also DLB 16
Plympton, Bill
See Plympton, William M.
Plympton, William M. 1946- 110
Poag, James F(itzgerald) 1934-
Brief entry 107
Poage, Godfrey Robert 1920- 5-6R
Poage, Scott T(abor) 1931- 53-56
Poague, Leland A(llen) 1948- CANR-6
Earlier sketch in CA 57-60
Pobo, Kenneth 1954- 104
Pochmann, Henry A(ugust) 1901-1973 ...37-40R
Pochmann, Ruth Fouts 1903- CAP-2
Earlier sketch in CA 25-28
Pocock, H(ugh) R(aymond) S(pilsbury)
1904- 25-28R
Pocock, Nick 1934- 53-56
Pocock, Thomas Allcot Guy 1925- CANR-23
Earlier sketch in CA 103
Pocock, Tom
See Pocock, Thomas Allcot Guy
Podbielski, Gisele 1918- 53-56
Podell, Janet 1954- 124
Podendorf, Illa (E.) 1903(?)-1983 81-84
Obituary 110
See also SATA 18, 35
Podeschi, John B(attista) 1942- 110
Podhajsky, Alois 1898-1973 69-72
Podhoretz, Norman 1930- CANR-7
Earlier sketch in CA 9-10R
Podhradsky, Gerhard 1929- 23-24R
Podlecki, Anthony J(oseph) 1936- CANR-3
Earlier sketch in CA 49-52
Podmarsh, Rollo
See Salter, Donald P. M.
Podoliak, Boris
See Kostiuk, Hryhory
Podulka, Fran 1933- 49-52
Poduschka, Walter 1922- 107
Poe, Charlsie 1909- CAP-2
Earlier sketch in CA 23-24
Poe, Edgar Allan 1809-1849 .... SATA-23
See also DLB 3, 59, 73, 74
See also CDALB 1640-1865
See also SSC 1
Poe, James 1921-1980 113
Obituary 93-96
See also DLB 44
Poen, Monte Mac 1930- 107
Poern, Ingmar 1935- 33-36R
Poetker, Frances Jones 1912- 85-88
Poetzl, Pamela Major
See Major-Poetzl, Pamela
Poewe, Karla 1941- 124
Poganski, Donald J(ohn) 1928- 25-28R
Pogany, Andras H(enrik) 1919- 23-24R
Pogany, Hortenzia Lers 23-24R
Pogany, William Andrew 1882-1955 .... SATA-44
Pogany, Willy
See Pogany, William Andrew
See also SATA 30
Poggi, Emil J. 1928- 29-32R
Poggi, Gianfranco 1934- 85-88
Poggi, Jack
See Poggi, Emil J.
Poggie, John J(oseph), Jr. 1937-
Brief entry 107
Poggioli, Renato 1907-1963 .... CANR-2
Earlier sketch in CA 1R
Pogrebin, Letty Cottin 1939- CANR-15
Earlier sketch in CA 29-32R
Pogue, Forrest Carlisle 1912- CANR-3
Earlier sketch in CA 7-8R
Poh, Caroline (Anne) 1938- 61-64
Pohl, Frederick Julius 1889- CANR-5
Earlier sketch in CA 1R
Pohl, Frederik 1919- CANR-11
Earlier sketch in CA 61-64
See also CAAS 1
See also SATA 24
See also DLB 8
See also CLC 18
Pohle, Linda C(arol) 1947- 45-48
Pohle, Robert W(arren), Jr. 1949- 81-84
Pohlman, Edward 1933- 33-36R
Pohlmann, Lillian (Grenfell) 1902- 11-12R
See also SATA 11
Pohndorf, Richard Henry 1916-1977
Obituary 73-76
Poignant, Raymond 1917- 29-32R
Poincelot, Raymond P. 1944- 122
Poindexter, Clarence Albert 1902(?)-1984
Obituary 111
Poindexter, David 1929- 29-32R
Poindexter, Hally Beth Walker 1927-
Brief entry 110
Poindexter, Marian J(ean) 1929- 29-32R
Poinsett, Alex(ander) Ceasar 1926- 29-32R
Pointer, Larry 1940- 101
Pointer, Michael 1927- 57-60
Pointon, Marcia R(achel) 1943- 33-36R
Pointon, Robert
See Rooke, Daphne (Marie)
Poirier, Frank E(ugene) 1940- CANR-3
Earlier sketch in CA 49-52
Poirier, Louis 1910- 126
Brief entry 122
Poirier, Normand 1928(?)-1981 Obituary ... 102
Poirier, Philip P. 1920- Brief entry 113
Poirier, Richard 1925- CANR-3
Earlier sketch in CA 1R
Pois, Joseph 1905- CAP-1
Earlier sketch in CA 15-16
Poitier, Sidney 1927- 117
See also BW
See also CLC 26
Pok Chong-Hui
See Park Chung Hee
Pokrovsky, Boris Aleksandrovich 1912-
Brief entry 109
POLA
See Watson, Pauline
Polach, Jaroslav G(eorge) 1914- 9-10R
Polack, Albert Isaac 1892- CAP-1
Earlier sketch in CA 9-10
Polak, Ada Buch 1914- Brief entry 111
Polak, Jacques Jacobus 1914- 104
Polakoff, Keith Ian 1941- 49-52
Polakoff, Murray Emanuel 1922-
Brief entry 114
Polakow, Valerie (Suransky) 1950- 111
Poland, Dorothy (Elizabeth Hayward)
1937- CANR-20
Earlier sketch in CA 103
Poland, Larry 1939- 101
Polanski, Roman 1933- 77-80
See also CLC 16
Polansky, Norman A. 1918- 85-88
Polanyi, Michael 1891-1976 81-84
Obituary 65-68
Polatnick, Florence T. 1923- 29-32R
See also SATA 5
Polcher, Egon
See Anschel, Eugene
Polder, Markus
See Kruess, James
Poldervaart, Arie 1909-1969 .... 3R
Obituary 103
Pole, J(ack) R(ichon) 1922- CANR-8
Earlier sketch in CA 19-20R
Polebaum, Elliot E(dward) 1950- 107
Poleman, Thomas T(heobald) 1928- 15-16R
Polenberg, Richard 1937- 21-22R
Polese, Marcia Ann 1949- 65-68
Polette, Nancy (Jane) 1930- CANR-21
Earlier sketches in CA 57-60, CANR-6
See also SATA 42
Polevoi, Boris
See Kampov, Boris Nikolayevich
Polhamus, Jean Burt 1928- 103
See also SATA 21
Poli, Bernard 1929- 21-22R
Poliakoff, Stephen 1952- 106
See also DLB 13
See also CLC 38
Poliakov, Leon 1910- 104
Police
See Copeland, Stewart (Armstrong)
and Summers, Andrew James
and Sumner, Gordon Matthew
See also CLC 26
Polier, Justine Wise 1903-1987 104
Obituary 123
Polin, Raymond 1918- 37-40R
Poling, Daniel Alfred 1884-1968 Obituary ..93-96
Poling, David 1928- 85-88
Polinger, Elliot Hirsch 1898-1970
Obituary 104
Polis, A(lbert) Richard 1937- CANR-6
Earlier sketch in CA 57-60
Polisensky, Josef V. 1915- Brief entry 107
Polish, David 1910- 13-14R
Polishook, Irwin H. 1935- 21-22R
Polite, Carlene Hatcher 1932- CANR-25
Earlier sketch in CA 23-24R
See also BW
See also DLB 33
Polite, Frank (C.) 1936- 125
Politella, Dario 1921- 13-14R
Politella, Joseph 1910- CAP-2
Earlier sketch in CA 21-22
Politi, Leo 1908- CANR-13
Earlier sketch in CA 19-20R
See also SATA 1, 47
Politicus
See Kilski, Wladyslaw W(szebor)
Politzer, Heinrich 1910-1978 .... CANR-3
Obituary 81-84
Earlier sketch in CA 5-6R
Politzer, Heinz
See Politzer, Heinrich
Politzer, Robert L. 1921- 5-6R
Polivy, Janet 1951- 115
Poljanski, Hristo Andonov
See Andonov-Poljanski, Hristo
Polk, Cara Saylor 1945- 116
Polk, Dora (Beale) 1923- 49-52
Polk, Edwin Weiss 1916- 37-40R
Polk, James 1939- CANR-23
Earlier sketch in CA 105
Polk, James R. 1937- 69-72
Polk, Judd (Knox) 1913(?)-1975
Obituary 57-60
Polk, Kenneth 1935- CANR-1
Earlier sketch in CA 2R
Polk, Mary 1898- CAP-1
Earlier sketch in CA 11-12
Polk, Noel E(arl) 1943- 123
Polk, Ralph Lane, Jr. 1940-1985 Obituary .. 118
Polk, Ralph Weiss 1890-1978 ....37-40R
Obituary 77-80
Polk, Stella Gipson 1901- CANR-16
Earlier sketch in CA 93-96
Polk, William R(oe) 1929- 25-28R
Polking, Kirk 1925- CANR-12
Earlier sketch in CA 29-32R
See also SATA 5
Polkinghorn, Anne T(oogood) 1937- 109
Poll, Richard Douglas 1918- 101
Pollack, Cecelia 1909- 29-32R

Pollack, Ervin H(arold) 1913-1972 .... CAP-1
Earlier sketch in CA 15-16
Pollack, (Wilburt) Erwin 1935- 49-52
Pollack, Harvey 1913- 7-8R
Pollack, Herman 1907- 69-72
Pollack, Jack H(arrison) 1915(?)-1984
Obituary 113
Pollack, Merrill S. 1924-1988 .... 7-8R
Obituary 124
Pollack, Norman 1933- 13-14R
Pollack, Peter 1911-1978 81-84
Obituary 77-80
Pollack, Reginald 1924- 37-40R
Pollack, Robert H(arvey) 1927- 49-52
Pollack, Sandra (Barbara) 1937- 119
Pollack, Seymour V(ictor) 1933- 25-28R
Pollak, Felix 1909- CANR-10
Earlier sketch in CA 25-28R
Pollak, Kurt 1919- 29-32R
Pollak, Louis Heilprin 1922- 19-20R
Pollak, Michael 1918- 122
Pollak, Richard 1934- Brief entry 111
Polland, Barbara K(ay) 1939- 73-76
See also SATA 44
Polland, Madeleine A(ngela Cahill)
1918- CANR-3
Earlier sketch in CA 5-6R
See also SATA 6
Pollard, David 1942- 123
Pollard, Edward A. 1832-1872 .... DLB-30
Pollard, (Henry) Graham 1903-1976
Obituary 69-72
Pollard, Jack 1926- 29-32R
Pollard, James E(dward) 1894-1979 ..... CAP-1
Obituary 89-92
Earlier sketch in CA 15-16
Pollard, John (Richard Thornhill) 1914- 7-8R
Pollard, Percival 1869-1911 .... DLB-71
Pollard, Sidney 1925- CANR-13
Earlier sketch in CA 19-20R
Pollard, T(homas) E(van) 1921- 29-32R
Pollard, William G(rosvenor) 1911- CANR-6
Earlier sketch in CA 13-14R
Polley, Robert L. 1933- 19-20R
Pollinger, Kenneth Joseph 1933- 57-60
Pollini, Francis 1930- CANR-1
Earlier sketch in CA 2R
Pollio, Howard R. 1937- 37-40R
Pollitt, Jerome J(ordan) 1934- 21-22R
Pollitt, Katha 1949- 122
Brief entry 120
See also CLC 28
Pollitt, Ronald 1939- 122
Pollock, Bruce 1945- CANR-23
Earlier sketches in CA 57-60, CANR-7
See also SATA 46
Pollock, David H(arold) 1922- 49-52
Pollock, George 1938- 61-64
Pollock, Harry 1920- 89-92
Pollock, James K(err) 1898-1968 .... CAP-2
Obituary 29-32R
Earlier sketch in CA 21-22
Pollock, John (Charles) 1923- CANR-18
Earlier sketches in CA 5-6R, CANR-2
Pollock, John L(eslie) 1940- 37-40R
Pollock, Linda A(nne) 1955- 116
Pollock, Mary
See Blyton, Enid (Mary)
Pollock, Norman H(all), Jr. 1909- CAP-2
Earlier sketch in CA 33-36
Pollock, Penny 1935- 101
See also SATA 42, 44
Pollock, Robert 1930- 45-48
Pollock, Seton 1910- 7-8R
Pollock, Sharon 1936- DLB-60
See also CLC 50
Pollock, Ted 1929- 85-88
Pollock, Thomas Clark 1902-1988 .... CAP-2
Obituary 125
Earlier sketch in CA 21-22
Pollock, William 1899-1982 Obituary 110
Pollowitz, Melinda Kilborn 1944- CANR-13
Earlier sketch in CA 77-80
See also SATA 26
Polmar, Norman 1938- 49-52
Polnaszek, Frank P(aul) 1947- 107
Polner, Murray 1928- CANR-23
Earlier sketches in CA 13-14R, CANR-5
Poloma, Margaret Mary 1943- 111
Polome, Edgar (Ghislain) C(harles)
1920- CANR-13
Earlier sketch in CA 29-32R
Polon, Linda Beth 1943- CANR-20
Earlier sketch in CA 103
Polonsky, Abraham (Lincoln) 1910- 104
See also DLB 26
Polonsky, Antony Barry 1940- 73-76
Polonsky, Arthur 1925- SATA-34
Polony, Raymond
See Machan, Tibor R(ichard)
Polos, Nicholas C(hristopher) 1917- 19-20R
Pols, Edward 1919- 11-12R
Polsby, Nelson W(oolf) 1934- CANR-23
Earlier sketches in CA 53-56, CANR-5
Polselli, Joseph 1950- 122
Polseno, Jo 81-84
See also SATA 17
Polsky, Abe 1935- 109
Polsky, Howard W. 1928- 25-28R
Polsky, Ned 1928- 25-28R
Poltoratzky, N(ikolai) P(etrovich) 1921- 73-76
Poltroon, Milford
See Bascom, David
Polunin, Nicholas (Vladimir) 1909- 65-68
Polunin, Oleg 1914-1985 85-88
Obituary 117
Polya, George 1887-1985 Obituary 117
Polya, Gyorgy
See Polya, George
Pomada, Elizabeth 1940- CANR-8
Earlier sketch in CA 61-64
Pomerance, Bernard 1940- 101
See also CLC 13
Pomerantz, Charlotte 1930- CANR-16
Earlier sketch in CA 85-88
See also SATA 20
Pomerantz, Edward 1934- 65-68
Pomerantz, Joel 1930- 29-32R
Pomerantz, Sidney I(rving) 1909-1975
Obituary 61-64
Pomeranz, Virginia E. 1925(?)-1986
Obituary 120
Pomerleau, Cynthia S(todola) 1943- 73-76
Pomerleau, Ovide F(elix) 1940- CANR-13
Earlier sketch in CA 73-76
Pomeroy, Charles A. 1930- 25-28R
Pomeroy, Earl 1915- 19-20R
Pomeroy, Elizabeth W(right) 1938- 113
Pomeroy, Florence Mary
See Powley, Florence Mary Pomeroy
Pomeroy, Hub(bard)
See Claassen, Harold
Pomeroy, John H(oward) 1918-1985
Obituary 115
Pomeroy, Kenneth B(rownridge)
1907-1975 Obituary 61-64
Pomeroy, Pete
See Roth, Arthur J(oseph)
Pomeroy, Sarah B(erman) 1938- 65-68
Pomeroy, Wardell B. 1913- CANR-1
Earlier sketch in CA 1R
Pomeroy, William J(oseph) 1916- 85-88
Pomfret, Baron
See Dame, Lawrence
Pomfret, John Edwin 1898-1981 .... CANR-3
Obituary 105
Earlier sketch in CA 3R
Pomfret, Richard 1948- 112
Pommer, Henry F(rancis) 1918- CANR-20
Earlier sketch in CA 1R
Pommery, Jean 1932- 101
Pomorska, Krystyna 1928- 41-44R
Pompa, Leon 1933- CANR-7
Earlier sketch in CA 57-60
Pomper, Gerald M(arvin) 1935- CANR-19
Earlier sketches in CA 11-12R, CANR-5
Pomper, Philip 1936- 77-80
Pompian, Richard O(wen) 1935- CANR-11
Earlier sketch in CA 29-32R
Pompidou, Georges (Jean Raymond)
1911-1974 Obituary 49-52
Pomrenke, Norman E. 1930- 23-24R
Pomroy, Martha 1943- 101
Ponce de Leon, Jose Luis S. 1931- 49-52
Pond, Alonzo W(illiam) 1894- CANR-1
Earlier sketch in CA 4R
See also SATA 5
Pond, Grace (Isabelle) 1910- CANR-5
Earlier sketch in CA 13-14R
Pond, L. W.
See Chute, Robert M.
Ponder, Catherine 1927- CANR-17
Earlier sketches in CA 4R, CANR-1
Ponder, James A(lton) 1933- 69-72
Ponder, Patricia
See Maxwell, Patricia
Pondrom, Cyrena N(orman) 1938-
Brief entry 111
Ponge, Francis (Jean Gaston Alfred)
1899-1988 85-88
Obituary 126
See also CLC 6, 18
Poniatowska, Elena 1933- 101
Ponicsan, Darryl 1938- CANR-21
Earlier sketch in CA 29-32R
Ponnamperuma, Cyril A. 1923- 101
Pons, Maurice 1927- CANR-5
Earlier sketch in CA 53-56
Ponsonby, D(oris) A(lmon) CANR-2
Earlier sketch in CA 7-8R
Ponsonby, Frederick Edward Neuflize
1913- 13-14R
Ponsot, Marie Birmingham 11-12R
Pont, Clarice Holt 1907- 5-6R
Ponte, Lowell (Alton) 1946- 57-60
Ponte, Pierre Viansson
See Viansson-Ponte, Pierre
Pontes, Paulo 1941(?)-1976 Obituary 69-72
Pontiero, Giovanni 1932- 29-32R
Pontiflet, Ted 1932- 105
See also SATA 32
Ponting, Kenneth 1913-1983 Obituary 109
Pontney, Jack A(rthur) 1931- 23-24R
Pontoppidan, Henrik 1857-1943 .... TCLC-29
Ponty, Maurice Merleau
See Merleau-Ponty, Maurice
Pool, David de Sola 1885-1970
Obituary 29-32R
Pool, Elizabeth 1914- 114
Pool, Eugene (Hillhouse) 1943- 85-88
Pool, Ithiel de Sola 1917-1984 .... CANR-14
Obituary 112
Earlier sketch in CA 19-20R
Pool, Phoebe Dorothy 1913- 7-8R
Pool, Tamar de Sola 1891(?)-1981
Obituary 104
Poole, Ernest 1880-1950 Brief entry 109
See also DLB 9
Poole, Frederick King 1934- 25-28R
Poole, Gary Thomas 1931- 107
Poole, Gray Johnson 1906- CANR-6
Earlier sketch in CA 7-8R
See also SATA 1
Poole, Herbert (Leslie) 103
Poole, Herbert Edmund 1912-1984
Obituary 115
Poole, Josephine
See Helyar, Jane Penelope Josephine
See also SATA 5
See also SAAS 2
See also CLC 17
Poole, Lynn 1910-1969 .... 7-8R
See also SATA 1
Poole, Peggy 1925- CANR-24
Earlier sketch in CA 107
See also SATA 39
Poole, Peter A(ndrews) 113
Poole, Robert W(illiam), Jr. 1944- 112
Poole, Roger 1939- 102
Poole, Seth
See Riemer, George
Poole, Susan 1926- 114
Poole, Victoria (Simes) 1927- 102
Pooler, Victor H(erbert), Jr. 1924- 15-16R
Pooley, Beverley J(ohn) 1934- 45-48
Pooley, Robert C(ecil) 1898-1978 ...... CANR-7
Earlier sketch in CA 5-6R
Pooley, Roger 1947- 115
Poolla, Tirupati Raju
See Raju, Poolla Tirupati
Poor, Harold Lloyd 1935- 45-48
Poor, Henry Varnum 1914(?)-1972
Obituary 37-40R
Poore, Benjamin Perley 1820-1887 ..... DLB-23
Poore, Charles (Graydon) 1902-1971
Obituary 29-32R
Poorman, Paul Arthur 1930- 106
Poortvliet, Marien
See Poortvliet, Rien
Poortvliet, Rien 1933(?)- SATA-37
Poots-Booby, Edna
See Larsen, Carl
Poovey, W(illiam) A(rthur) 1913- CANR-10
Earlier sketch in CA 23-24R
Popa, Vasko 1922- Brief entry 112
See also CLC 19
Pope, Arthur Upham 1881-1969
Obituary 25-28R
Pope, Carl 1945- 113
Pope, Clifford Hillhouse 1899-1974 .... 3R
Obituary 103
Pope, Daniel 1946- 111
Pope, Dudley (Bernard Egerton) 1925- .. CANR-2
Earlier sketch in CA 7-8R
Pope, Edwin 1928- 73-76
Pope, Elizabeth Marie 1917- 49-52
See also SATA 36, 38
Pope, Generoso Paul, Jr. 1927-1988
Obituary 126
Pope, Harrison (Graham), Jr. 1947- 41-44R
Pope, James S., Sr. 1900(?)-1985
Obituary 118
Pope, John Alexander 1906-1982
Obituary 107
Pope, Joya 1943- 124
Pope, Katherine Victoria 1939- 111
Pope, Maurice (Wildon Montague) 1926- .. 69-72
Pope, Michael James 1940- 101
Pope, Phyllis Ackerman 1894(?)-1977
Obituary 69-72
Pope, Ray 1924- 29-32R
Pope, Richard Martin 1916- 19-20R
Pope, Robert G(ardner) 1936- 29-32R
Pope, Robert H. 1925- 33-36R
Pope, Thomas Harrington 1913- 73-76
Pope, Whitney 1935- 69-72
Pope-Hennessy, James 1916-1974 97-100
Obituary 45-48
Pope-Hennessy, John W(yndham)
1913- CANR-1
Earlier sketch in CA 1R
Popenoe, David 1932- CANR-12
Earlier sketch in CA 29-32R
Popenoe, Paul (Bowman) 1888- 4R
Popescu, Christine 1930- CANR-20
Earlier sketches in CA 13-14R, CANR-7
Popescu, D. R.
See Popescu, Dumitru Radu
Popescu, Dumitru Radu 1935- Brief entry .. 122
Popescu, Julian (John Hunter) 1928- .. CANR-20
Earlier sketches in CA 2R, CANR-1
Popham, Arthur Ewart 1889-1970
Obituary 111
Popham, Estelle I. 1906- CANR-5
Earlier sketch in CA 1R
Popham, Hugh 1920- CANR-6
Earlier sketch in CA 7-8R
Popham, Margaret Evelyn 1895(?)-1982
Obituary 106
Popham, Melinda 1944- 49-52
Popham, Peter (Nicholas Home) 1952- 121
Popiel, Elda S(taver) 1915- 57-60
Popkin, Debra 1944- 118
Popkin, Jeremy D(avid) 1948- 102
Popkin, John William 1909- CAP-1
Earlier sketch in CA 13-14
Popkin, Richard H(enry) 1923- 77-80
Popkin, Roy 1921- 25-28R
Popkin, Zelda F. 1898-1983 .... 25-28R
Obituary 109
Popov, Dusko 1912(?)-1981 Obituary 105
Popov, Haralan Ivanov 1907- 21-22R
Popovic, Nenad D(ushan) 1909- CAP-2
Earlier sketch in CA 29-32
Popovsky, Mark 1922- CANR-19
Earlier sketch in CA 102
Popowski, Bert (John) 1904- CANR-17
Earlier sketch in CA 4R
Poppe, Fred C(hristoph) 1923- 114
Poppe, Nicholas N. 1897- 73-76
Popper, Frank J. 1944- CANR-12
Earlier sketch in CA 29-32R
Popper, Karl R(aimund) 1902- CANR-20
Earlier sketches in CA 7-8R, CANR-3
Popperwell, Ronald ?-1983 Obituary 111
Poppino, Rollie E(dward) 1922- 15-16R
Popple, James 1927- 107
Poppleton, Marjorie 1895- CAP-1
Earlier sketch in CA 13-14
Popplewell, Jack 1911- 11-12R
Porada, Edith 1912- 103
Porath, Jonathan David 1944- 118
Porcari, Constance Kwolek 1933- 33-36R
Porch, Douglas 1944- 107
Porche, Simone (Benda) 1877(?)-1985
Obituary 118
Porcher, Mary F. Wickham
See Bond, Mary Fanning Wickham
Porcino, Jane 1923- 116
Pore, Renate (Elfriede) 1943- 113
Porell, Bruce 1947- 102
Porges, Paul Peter 1927- 124
Poriss, Martin 1948- 81-84
Poritz, Lily
See Miller, Lily Poritz
Porlock, Martin
See MacDonald, Philip
Porosky, P. H. 45-48
Porqueras-Mayo, Alberto 1930- CANR-24
Earlier sketch in CA 45-48
Porsche, Ferdinand 1909- 89-92
Porsche, Ferry
See Porsche, Ferdinand
Port, M(ichael) H. 1930- 69-72
Port, Wymar
See Judy, Will(iam Lewis)
Portal, Colette 1936- 53-56
See also SATA 6
Portal, Ellis
See Powe, Bruce
Portal, Francis Spencer 1903-1984
Obituary 114
Porte, Barbara Ann SATA-45
Porte, Joel (Miles) 1933- CANR-24
Earlier sketches in CA 19-20R, CANR-8
Porten, Bezalel 1931- CANR-11
Earlier sketch in CA 25-28R
Porteous, (Leslie) Crichton 1901- 7-8R
Porter, Alan
See Clark, Ruth C(ampbell)
Porter, Alan L(eslie) 1945- 115
Porter, Albert Wright 1923- 107
Porter, Alvin
See Rowland, D(onald) S(ydney)
Porter, Andrew 1928- CANR-23
Earlier sketches in CA 53-56, CANR-5
Porter, Arthur T(homas) 1924- 7-8R
Porter, Bern(ard Harden) 1911- CANR-24
Earlier sketches in CA 21-22R, CANR-9
Porter, Bernard (John) 1941- CANR-24
Earlier sketch in CA 107
Porter, Brian (Ernest) 1928- 25-28R
Porter, Bruce 1938- 124
Porter, Burton F(rederick) 1936- 106
Porter, C(edric) L(ambert) 1905- CAP-2
Earlier sketch in CA 23-24
Porter, Charles A(llan) 1932- 21-22R
Porter, Cole 1893-1964 Obituary 93-96
Porter, Darwin (Fred) 1937- CANR-13
Earlier sketch in CA 69-72
Porter, David L(indsey) 1941- CANR-24
Earlier sketch in CA 107
Porter, David T. 1928- 19-20R
Porter, Donald 1939- CANR-19
Earlier sketch in CA 103
Porter, Edward A. 1936- 23-24R
Porter, Eleanor H(odgman) 1868-1920
Brief entry 108
See also DLB 9
Porter, Elias H(ull) 1914- 11-12R
Porter, Eliot (Furness) 1901- 7-8R
Porter, Ernest Graham 1889- 3R
Porter, Ethel K. 1901- CAP-2
Earlier sketch in CA 21-22
Porter, Fairfield 1907-1975 Obituary 61-64
Porter, Frank W(illiam) III 1947- 97-100
Porter, Gene L. 1935- 25-28R
Porter, Gene(va Grace) Stratton
1863(?)-1924 Brief entry 112
See also TCLC 21
Porter, George 1920- 107
Porter, Glenn 1944- 73-76
Porter, H(arry) Boone 1923- CANR-8
Earlier sketch in CA 7-8R
Porter, H(arry) C(ulverwell) 1927- 33-36R
Porter, Hal 1911-1984 .... CANR-3
Obituary 114
Earlier sketch in CA 9-10R
Porter, Henry DLB-62
Porter, J(ene) M(iles) 1937- CANR-21
Earlier sketch in CA 103
Porter, J(oshua) R(oy) 1921- CANR-5
Earlier sketch in CA 53-56
Porter, Jack Nusan 1944- CANR-20
Earlier sketch in CA 41-44R
Porter, James A(rmer), Jr. 1922- 121
Porter, Joe Ashby 1942- CANR-12
Earlier sketch in CA 73-76
Porter, John 1919- 23-24R
Porter, Jonathan 1938- 77-80
Porter, Joseph C(harles) 1946- 116
Porter, Joyce 1924- CANR-8
Earlier sketch in CA 19-20R
Porter, Judith D(eborah) R(evitch) 1940- .. 81-84

Porter, Katherine Anne 1890-1980 ...... CANR-1
Obituary 101
Earlier sketch in CA 2R
See also SATA 23, 39
See also DLB 4, 9
See also DLBY 80
See also CLC 1, 3, 7, 10, 13, 15, 27
See also AITN 2
Porter, Kathryn
See Swinford, Betty (June Wells)
Porter, Kenneth Wiggins 1905- CANR-2
Earlier sketch in CA 7-8R
Porter, Laurence M(inot) 1936- CANR-23
Earlier sketch in CA 107
Porter, Lyman W(illiam) 1930- 21-22R
Porter, Margaret Eudine 1905-1975 ...... CANR-8
Earlier sketch in CA 57-60
Porter, Mark
See Leckie, Robert (Hugh)
and Cox, James Anthony
Porter, McKenzie 1911- 69-72
Porter, Michael E. 1947- CANR-22
Earlier sketch in CA 105
Porter, Michael Leroy 1947- 118
Porter, Monica 1952- 107
Porter, Peter (Neville Frederick) 1929- 85-88
See also DLB 40
See also CLC 5, 13, 33
Porter, Philip W(iley) 1900-1985 69-72
Obituary 116
Porter, R(obert) Russell 1908-1986
Obituary 120
Porter, Raymond J(ames) 1935- 85-88
Porter, Richard C(orbin) 1931- 11-12R
Porter, Robert 1946- 122
Porter, Sheena 1935- 81-84
See also SATA 24
Porter, Sue
See Limb, Sue
Porter, Sylvia F(ield) 1913- 81-84
Porter, Theodore M(ark) 1953- 123
Porter, Thomas E. 1928- 29-32R
Porter, W(alter) Thomas, Jr. 1934- 29-32R
Porter, Willard H(all) 1920- 57-60
Porter, William E. 1918- CANR-13
Earlier sketch in CA 69-72
Porter, William Sydney 1862-1910
Brief entry 104
See also YABC 2
See also DLB 12
See also CDALB 1865-1917
Porter, William Trotter 1809-1858 ...... DLB-3, 43
Porterfield, Bruce 1925- 23-24R
Porterfield, Nolan 1936- 33-36R
Portes, Alejandro 1944- CANR-16
Earlier sketch in CA 93-96
Porteus, Stanley D(avid) 1883- CANR-17
Earlier sketch in CA 4R
Portis, Charles (McColl) 1933- CANR-1
Earlier sketch in CA 45-48
See also DLB 6
Portisch, Hugo 1927- 21-22R
Portman, David N(athan) 1937- 45-48
Portnoy, Howard N. 1946- 81-84
Portoghesi, Paolo 1931- 108
Portteus, Eleanora Marie Manthei
?-1983 ...... SATA-36
Portugal, Franklin H. 1940- Brief entry 116
Portuges, Paul 1945- 77-80
Portway, Christopher (John) 1923- 57-60
Porush, David H(illel) 1952- CANR-17
Earlier sketch in CA 93-96
Porzelt, Paul 1902- 108
Posell, Elsa Z. CANR-20
Earlier sketches in CA 2R, CANR-4
See also SATA 3
Posener, Georges (Henri) 1906-1988
Obituary 125
Posey, Carl A(lfred, Jr.) 1933- 111
Posey, Sam 1944- 93-96
Posey, Walter B(rownlow) 1900- CAP-1
Earlier sketch in CA 15-16
Posin, Daniel Q. 1909- CAP-1
Earlier sketch in CA 13-14
Posin, Jack A. 1900- 15-16R
Posner, Alice
See Fins, Alice
Posner, Barry Z(ane) 1949- 111
Posner, David Louis 1938-1985 106
Obituary 117
Posner, Donald 1931- Brief entry 115
Posner, Ernst (Maximilian) 1892-1980 ...... 41-44R
Obituary 97-100
Posner, Mitchell Jay 1949- 110
Posner, Richard 1944- CANR-20
Earlier sketches in CA 53-56, CANR-5
Pospelov, Pyotr Nikolayevich 1898-1979
Obituary 85-88
Pospesel, Howard Andrew 1937- 73-76
Pospielovsky, Dimitry V. 1935- 29-32R
Pospisil, J(aroslav) Leopold 1923- 13-14R
Possony, Stefan T(homas) 1913-
Brief entry 117
Post, Austin 1922- 85-88
Post, C(harles) Gordon 1903- CAP-1
Earlier sketch in CA 11-12
Post, Elizabeth L(indley) 1920- 49-52
Post, Emily Price 1873-1960 103
Obituary 89-92
Post, Felix 1913- 21-22R
Post, Gaines 1902- CAP-1
Earlier sketch in CA 13-14
Post, Gaines, Jr. 1937- CANR-12
Earlier sketch in CA 73-76
Post, Henry 1948- 61-64
Post, Homer A(very) 1888- CAP-2
Earlier sketch in CA 25-28
Post, J(eremiah) B(enjamin) 1937- 97-100
Post, Jonathan F(rench) S(cott) 1947- 115
Post, Joyce A(rnold) 1939- CANR-8
Earlier sketch in CA 61-64
Post, Marie J. 1919- 111
Post, Melville Davisson 1869-1930
Brief entry 110
Post, Steve(n A.) 1944- 103
Postal, Bernard 1905-1981 ...... CANR-2
Obituary 103
Earlier sketch in CA 5-6R
Postan, Michael Moissey 1899-1981
Obituary 105
Posten, Margaret L(ois) 1915- 29-32R
See also SATA 10
Poster, Carol 1956- 118
Poster, Cyril D(ennis) 1924- CANR-7
Earlier sketch in CA 15-16R
Poster, John B. 1939- 29-32R
Poster, Mark 1941- 33-36R
Posteuca, Vasile 1912-1972 Obituary 37-40R
Postgate, Raymond (William)
1896-1971 ...... CANR-3
Obituary 89-92
Earlier sketch in CA 5-6R
Posthumus, Cyril 1918- 104
Postlethwait, S(amuel) N(oel) 1918- CANR-8
Earlier sketch in CA 19-20R
Postma, Lidia 1952- 101
Postma, Magdalena Jacomina 1908- 65-68
Postma, Minnie
See Postma, Magdalena Jacomina
Postman, Neil 102
Poston, Richard W(averly) 1914- 65-68
Poston, Ted
See Poston, Theodore Roosevelt
Augustus Major
See also DLB 51
Poston, Theodore Roosevelt Augustus
Major 1906-1974 125
Obituary 104
See also BW
Posvar, Wesley W(entz) 1925- 19-20R
Posy, Arnold 1894- 9-10R
Potash, Betty 1933- 122
Potash, Robert A(aron) 1921- CANR-19
Earlier sketch in CA 102
Poteet, G(eorge) Howard 1935- CANR-13
Earlier sketch in CA 33-36R
Pothan, Kap 1929- 29-32R
Potholm, Christian Peter II 1940- 29-32R
Potichnyj, Peter J(oseph) 1930- 41-44R
Potiphar
See Hern, (George) Anthony
Potok, Chaim 1929- CANR-19
Earlier sketch in CA 19-20R
See also SATA 33
See also DLB 28
See also CLC 2, 7, 14, 26
See also AITN 1, 2
Potoker, Edward M(artin) 1931- 33-36R
Pottebaum, Gerald A. 1934- CANR-5
Earlier sketch in CA 11-12R
Potter, A(lfred) Neal 1915- 15-16R
Potter, Beatrice
See Webb, (Martha) Beatrice (Potter)
Potter, (Helen) Beatrix 1866-1943
Brief entry 108
See also YABC 1
See also CLR 1
Potter, Beverly A(nn) 1944- 119
Potter, Carole A. 1940- 123
Potter, Charles E(dward) 1916- 61-64
Potter, Clare J. 1946- 122
Potter, Dan (Scott) 1932- 33-36R
Potter, David 1915- 29-32R
Potter, David Morris 1910-1971 108
See also DLB 17
Potter, Dennis (Christopher George) 1935- 107
Potter, E. B. 1908- 37-40R
Potter, Eloise Fretz 1931- CANR-21
Earlier sketch in CA 105
Potter, Faith
See Toperoff, Sam
Potter, G(eorge) W(illiam, Jr.) 1930- 3R
Potter, Gail M(ac Leod) 1914- 25-28R
Potter, George Richard 1900- 7-8R
Potter, J(im) 1922- 23-24R
Potter, Jack M(ichael) 1936- 41-44R
Potter, James Gerrard 1944- 97-100
Potter, James H(arry) 1912-1978
Obituary 77-80
Potter, James L(ane) 1922- 107
Potter, Jeremy 1922- 53-56
Potter, John Mason 1907- CAP-1
Earlier sketch in CA 11-12
Potter, Joy Hambuechen 1935- 123
Potter, Karl Harrington 1927- 5-6R
Potter, Kathleen 1929(?)-1987 Obituary 122
Potter, Kathleen Jill 1932- 104
Potter, Lois 1941- CANR-15
Earlier sketch in CA 41-44R
Potter, Loren D(avid) 1918- 121
Potter, M(aurice) David 1900- CAP-2
Earlier sketch in CA 23-24
Potter, Margaret (Newman) 1926- CANR-21
Earlier sketches in CA 13-14R, CANR-6
See also SATA 21
Potter, Marian 1915- CANR-1
Earlier sketch in CA 49-52
See also SATA 9
Potter, Miriam Clark 1886-1965 ...... 5-6R
See also SATA 3
Potter, Philip 1907-1988 Obituary 125
Potter, Robert Alonzo 1934- CANR-1
Earlier sketch in CA 45-48
Potter, Robert D(ucharme) 1905-1978
Obituary 77-80
Potter, Simeon 1898-1976 ...... CANR-4
Earlier sketch in CA 7-8R
Potter, Stephen 1900-1969 101
Obituary 25-28R
Potter, Sulamith Heins 1944- 81-84
Potter, Van Rensselaer 1911- 37-40R
Potter, Vincent G. 1928- 25-28R
Potter, William Hotchkiss 1914- 2R
Potterton, Gerald 1931- 49-52
Potterton, Homan 1946- CANR-25
Earlier sketch in CA 108
Pottker, Janice Marie 1948- 118
Pottle, Frederick A(lbert) 1897-1987 ...... CANR-3
Obituary 122
Earlier sketch in CA 7-8R
See also DLBY 87
Potts, Albert M(intz) 1914- 116
Potts, Charles 1943- 105
Potts, E(li) Daniel 1930- 25-28R
Potts, Eve 1929- 103
Potts, George Chapman 1898- CAP-1
Earlier sketch in CA 11-12
Potts, Jean 1910- CANR-2
Earlier sketch in CA 5-6R
Potts, Ralph Bushnell 1901- 57-60
Potts, Richard 1938- 103
Potts, Willard (Charles) 1929- 123
Potvin, Denis (Charles) 1953- Brief entry 113
Potvin, Georges C. 1928- 45-48
Potvin, Raymond H(erve) 1924- 21-22R
Pou, Genevieve Long 1919- Brief entry 114
Poucher, William Arthur 1891- CAP-1
Earlier sketch in CA 11-12
Pough, Frederick Harvey 1906- 81-84
Pouillon, Fernand 1912- 29-32R
Poulakidas, Andreas K. 1934- 45-48
Poulet, Georges 1902- 13-14R
Poulin, A(lfred A.), Jr. 1938- CANR-12
Earlier sketch in CA 23-24R
Poulin, Jacques 1937- DLB-60
Poullada, Leon B(aqueiro) 1913-1987
Obituary 123
Poulos, Constantine 1916(?)-1986
Obituary 119
Poulter, S(cott) L(arry) 1943- 49-52
Poulton, Edith Eleanor (Diana) Chloe
1903- 85-88
Poulton, Helen Jean 1920-1971 ...... CAP-2
Earlier sketch in CA 33-36
Poulton, Richard (Christopher) 1938- 107
Pound, Arthur 1884-1966 Obituary 89-92
Pound, Ezra (Loomis) 1885-1972 ...... 7-8R
Obituary 37-40R
See also DLB 4, 45, 63
See also CLC 1, 2, 3, 4, 5, 7, 10, 13,
18, 34, 48, 50
Pound, Merritt B(loodworth) 1898-1970 ...... CAP-2
Earlier sketch in CA 19-20
Pound, Omar S(hakespear) 1926- CANR-16
Earlier sketches in CA 49-52, CANR-1
Pound, Roscoe 1870-1964 Obituary 111
Pounds, Norman John Greville 1912- CANR-4
Earlier sketch in CA 3R
Pounds, Ralph Linnaeus 1910- 7-8R
Pournelle, Jerry (Eugene) 1933- 77-80
See also SATA 26
Poussaint, Alvin F(rancis) 1934- 53-56
Povenmire, (Edward) King(sley) 1904- 61-64
Poverman, C. E. 1944- Brief entry 115
Povey, John F. 1929- 85-88
Povod, Reinaldo 1959- CLC-44
Powdermaker, Hortense 1900-1970 ...... CAP-1
Obituary 29-32R
Earlier sketch in CA 13-14
Powe, Bruce 1925- 53-56
Powell, A. M.
See Morgan, Alfred P(owell)
Powell, Adam Clayton, Jr. 1908-1972 102
Obituary 33-36R
See also BW
Powell, Ann 1951- SATA-51
Powell, Anthony (Dymoke) 1905- CANR-1
Earlier sketch in CA 4R
See also DLB 15
See also CLC 1, 3, 7, 9, 10, 31
Powell, Barbara 1929- 119
Powell, Brian S(harples) 1934- 25-28R
Powell, Cecil Frank 1903-1969 Obituary 113
Powell, Clarence Alva 1905- CAP-1
Earlier sketch in CA 11-12
Powell, Clilan B. 1894-1977 Obituary 73-76
Powell, (John) Craig 1940- 77-80
Powell, Dawn 1897-1965 ...... 5-6R
Powell, Donald M. 1914- 13-14R
Powell, Dorothy Baden
See Baden-Powell, Dorothy
Powell, Dorothy M. 1914- 106
Powell, (Drexel) Dwane (Jr.) 1944- 89-92
Powell, Elwin H(umphreys) 1925- 81-84
Powell, Eric F(rederick) W(illiam) 1899- CANR-6
Earlier sketch in CA 7-8R
Powell, Evan Arnold 1937- CANR-21
Earlier sketch in CA 69-72
Powell, Fern 1942- 25-28R
Powell, G. Bingham, Jr. 1942- CANR-11
Earlier sketch in CA 29-32R
Powell, Geoffrey Stewart 1914- 61-64
Powell, Gordon (George) 1911- 2R
Powell, Ivor 1910- CANR-17
Earlier sketch in CA 4R
Powell, J(ohn) Enoch 1912- 97-100
Powell, James 1932- 107
Powell, James M(atthew) 1930- CANR-8
Earlier sketch in CA 7-8R
Powell, James V(irgil) 1938- 104
Powell, John Roland 1889- CAP-1
Earlier sketch in CA 13-14
Powell, L(awrence) F(itzroy) 1881-1975
Obituary 57-60
Powell, Larson Merrill 1932- 103
Powell, Lawrence Clark 1906- CANR-25
Earlier sketches in CA 21-22R, CANR-8
Powell, Lawrence N(elson) 1943- 104
Powell, Lily
See Froissard, Lily Powell
Powell, Marcia (Leonora) 108
Powell, Margaret 1907(?)-1984 ...... CANR-15
Obituary 112
Earlier sketch in CA 29-32R
Powell, Marvin 1924- CANR-8
Earlier sketch in CA 21-22R
Powell, Meredith (Ann) 1936- 37-40R
Powell, Milton Bryan 1934- 23-24R
Powell, Neil 1948- CANR-15
Earlier sketch in CA 85-88
Powell, Neil
See Innes, Brian
Powell, (Caryll) Nicolas (Peter) 1920- CANR-12
Earlier sketch in CA 61-64
Powell, Norman J(ohn) 1908-1974 ...... CAP-2
Obituary 49-52
Earlier sketch in CA 21-22
Powell, Padgett 1952- 126
See also CLC 34
Powell, Paul W. 1933- 116
Powell, Peter 1908-1985 Obituary 116
Powell, Peter John 1928- 33-36R
Powell, Philip Wayne 1913- 85-88
Powell, Ralph L. 1917-1975 Obituary 57-60
Powell, Raymond P(ark) 1922-1980
Obituary 97-100
Powell, Reed M(adsen) 1921- 29-32R
Powell, Richard (Pitts) 1908- CANR-4
Earlier sketch in CA 1R
Powell, Richard Stillman
See Barbour, Ralph Henry
Powell, Robert (Stephenson Smyth) Baden
See Baden-Powell, Robert (Stephenson
Smyth)
Powell, Robert Richard 1909- 7-8R
Powell, Ronald R(owe) 1944- 114
Powell, Shirley 1931- 106
Powell, Sidney W. 7-8R
Powell, Sumner Chilton 1924- 7-8R
Powell, Talmage 1920- CANR-2
Earlier sketch in CA 7-8R
Powell, Terry 1949- 103
Powell, Theodore 1919- 1R
Powell, Thomas F. 1933- 25-28R
Powell, Victor M(organ) 1919- 45-48
Powell, Violet Georgiana 1912- 103
Powell, William S(tevens) 1919- 69-72
Powell-Smith, Vincent (Walter Francis)
1939- 25-28R
Powelson, John Palen 1920- CANR-19
Earlier sketches in CA 1R, CANR-4
Power, Arthur
See Dudden, Arthur P(ower)
Power, Catherine
See Du Breuil, (Elizabeth) L(or)inda
Power, Edward John 1921- CANR-2
Earlier sketch in CA 7-8R
Power, Francis C. 1909(?)-1987 Obituary 124
Power, John 1927- 61-64
Power, Jonathan 1941- 107
Power, Michael 1933- CAP-1
Earlier sketch in CA 11-12
Power, Norman S(andiford) 1916- CANR-10
Earlier sketch in CA 65-68
Power, Paul F(rederick) 1925- 41-44R
Power, Rex
See Langley, John
Power, Richard 1928-1970 ...... CAP-1
Earlier sketch in CA 9-10
Power, Tyrone
See Guthrie, (William) Tyrone
Power, (Patrick) Victor 1930- CANR-13
Earlier sketch in CA 77-80
Power-Ross, Robert W. 1922- 102
Powers, Andy 1896- CANR-6
Earlier sketch in CA 57-60
Powers, Anne
See Schwartz, Anne Powers
Powers, Barbara Hudson
See Dudley, Barbara Hudson
Powers, Bill 1931- 77-80
See also SATA 31, 52
Powers, Bob
See Powers, Robert L(eroy)
and Repp, William
Powers, David Guy 1911-1967 ...... CAP-2
Earlier sketch in CA 19-20
Powers, Doris Cooper 1918- 105
Powers, Edward A(lvin) 1941- 77-80
Powers, Edward Alton 1927- 53-56
Powers, Edward D(oyle) 1900- 45-48
Powers, Edwin 1896- 73-76
Powers, Francis Gary 1929-1977 Obituary 109
Powers, George
See Infield, Glenn (Berton)
Powers, Helen 1925- 97-100
Powers, J(ames) F(arl) 1917- CANR-2
Earlier sketch in CA 3R
See also CLC 1, 4, 8
Powers, Jeffrey W(ells) 1950- 61-64
Powers, John J(ames) 1945- 69-72
Powers, John R.
See Powers, John J(ames)
Powers, Joseph M(ichael) 1926- 85-88
Powers, Lyall H(arris) 1924- Brief entry 115
Powers, M. L.
See Tubb, E(dwin) C(harles)

Powers, Margaret
See Heal, Edith
Powers, Mark James 1940- 110
Powers, Patrick W(illiam) 1924- 13-14R
Powers, Richard M. Gorman 1921- 21-22R
Powers, Robert L(eroy) 1924- 93-96
Powers, Robert M(aynard) 1942- CANR-14
Earlier sketch in CA 77-80
Powers, Ron(ald Dean) 1941- 97-100
Powers, Thomas (Moore) 1940- CANR-17
Earlier sketch in CA 37-40R
Powers, William 1930- 45-48
Powers, William Edwards 1902- CAP-2
Earlier sketch in CA 19-20
Powers, William K(eegan) 1934- 25-28R
Powers, William T(reval) 1926- 111
Power-Waters, Alma Shelley
1896-1983 .... CANR-18
Earlier sketch in CA 3R
Power-Waters, Brian 1922- CANR-18
Earlier sketch in CA 93-96
Powicke, Michael Rhys 1920- CANR-8
Earlier sketch in CA 7-8R
Powledge, Fred 1935- CANR-9
Earlier sketch in CA 23-24R
See also SATA 37
Powley, Edward Barzillai 1887-1968 .... CAP-1
Earlier sketch in CA 13-14
Powley, Florence Mary Pomeroy 1892- CAP-1
Earlier sketch in CA 15-16
Powling, Chris 1943- 121
Pownall, David 1938- 89-92
See also DLB 14
See also CLC 10
Powrie, Peter James 1927- 21-22R
Powys, John Cowper 1872-1963 85-88
See also DLB 15
See also CLC 7, 9, 15, 46
Powys, T(heodore) F(rancis) 1875-1953
Brief entry 106
See also DLB 36
See also TCLC 9
Poyer, David 1949- 111
Poyer, Joe
See Poyer, Joseph John (Jr.)
Poyer, Joseph John (Jr.) 1939- CANR-17
Earlier sketches in CA 49-52, CANR-1
Poynter, Dan(iel Frank) 1938- CANR-24
Earlier sketch in CA 89-92
Poynter, Margaret 1927- CANR-16
Earlier sketch in CA 93-96
See also SATA 27
Poynter, Nelson 1903-1978 Obituary 77-80
Pozzetta, George Enrico 1942- 111
Prabhavananda, Swami 1893-1976 .... CANR-8
Obituary 65-68
Earlier sketch in CA 19-20R
Prabhu, Pandharinath H. 1911- CANR-7
Earlier sketch in CA 13-14R
Prabhupada, A. C. Bhaktivedanta
1896-1977 .... CANR-14
Earlier sketch in CA 73-76
Prabhupada, A. C. Bhaktivedanta Swami
See Prabhupada, A. C. Bhaktivedanta
Prada Oropeza, Renato 1937- 41-44R
Prado, C(arlos) G(onzalez) 1937- 110
Prados, John 1951- 106
Prager, Arthur CANR-12
Earlier sketch in CA 29-32R
See also SATA 44
Prager, Jonas 1938- 105
Prager, Karsten 1936- 73-76
Prago, Albert 1911- 29-32R
Prain, Ronald (Lindsay) 1907- 109
Prall, Stuart E(dward) 1929- 23-24R
Prance, Claude A(nnett) 1906- CANR-20
Earlier sketch in CA 89-92
Prance, June E(lizebeth) 1929- 69-72
Prandy, K(en) 1938- 117
Prange, Erwin (Edward) 1917- 113
Prange, Gordon W(illiam) 1910-1980
Obituary 97-100
Pranger, Robert J(ohn) 1931- CANR-10
Earlier sketch in CA 25-28R
Prantera, Amanda 1942- Brief entry 126
Prasad, S(rinivas) Benjamin 1929- CANR-5
Earlier sketch in CA 53-56
Prassel, Frank Richard 1937- CANR-1
Earlier sketch in CA 49-52
Prather, Hugh 1938- CANR-2
Earlier sketch in CA 45-48
Prather, Richard S(cott) 1921- CANR-5
Earlier sketch in CA 2R
Pratley, Gerald 1923- 112
Pratney, William Alfred 1944- 124
Pratney, Winkie
See Pratney, William Alfred
Pratson, Frederick John 1935- 101
Pratt, Allan D(aniel) 1933- 112
Pratt, Charles 1926-1976 .... CANR-21
Obituary 65-68
Earlier sketch in CA 69-72
Pratt, Chris (James) 1950- 118
Pratt, (Mildred) Claire 1921- 103
Pratt, Dallas 1914- 106
Pratt, Edwin John 1883-1964 Obituary 93-96
See also CLC 19
Pratt, (Murray) Fletcher 1897-1956
Brief entry 113
Pratt, J(oseph) Gaither 1910-1979 .... CANR-6
Obituary 89-92
Earlier sketch in CA 11-12R
Pratt, James Norwood 1942- 112
Pratt, John 1931- CANR-1
Earlier sketch in CA 3R
Pratt, John Clark 1932- CANR-17
Earlier sketch in CA 13-14R
Pratt, John Lowell 1906-1968 .... CANR-3
Earlier sketch in CA 2R
Pratt, Julius W(illiam) 1888- CAP-1
Earlier sketch in CA 11-12
Pratt, Keith L(eslie) 1938- 29-32R
Pratt, Norman T(wombly), Jr. 1911- 118
Pratt, Robert Cranford 1926- 101
Pratt, Samuel Jackson 1749-1814 .... DLB-39
Pratt, Theodore 1901-1969 .... CANR-4
Earlier sketch in CA 3R
Pratt, William C(rouch, Jr.) 1927- CANR-6
Earlier sketch in CA 13-14R
Pratt, Willis Winslow 1908- Brief entry 105
Pratt-Butler, Grace Kipp 1916- 103
Pratte, Richard (Norman) 1929- 93-96
Prattis, Percival L. 1895-1980 Obituary 97-100
Prawer, Joshua 1917- 41-44R
Prawer, S(iegbert) S(alomon) 1925- 103
Pray, Lawrence M. 1947- 113
Praz, Mario 1896-1982 101
Obituary 106
Prchal, Mildred 1895-1983 Obituary 109
Prebble, John Edward Curtis 1915- CANR-3
Earlier sketch in CA 7-8R
Prebble, Marjorie Mary Curtis 1912- CANR-15
Earlier sketch in CA 19-20R
Prebish, Charles S(tuart) 1944- 57-60
Preble, Duane 1936- 61-64
Preble, Robert Curtis 1897-1983 Obituary 111
Predmore, Michael 1938- 45-48
Predmore, Richard L. 1911- 19-20R
Preece, Harold 1906- 7-8R
Preece, Rod(ney John) 1939- 113
Preedy, George
See Campbell, (Gabrielle) Margaret (Vere)
Preeg, Ernest H. 1934- 33-36R
Prefontaine, Yves 1937- DLB-53
Pregel, Boris 1893-1976 Obituary 106
Preger, Paul D(aniel), Jr. 1926- 49-52
Preheim, Marion Keeney 1934- 25-28R
Preil, Gabriel 1911- CANR-1
Earlier sketch in CA 49-52
Preiser, Wolfgang F(riedrich) E(rnst)
1941- CANR-7
Earlier sketch in CA 57-60
Preiss, Byron (Cary) CANR-14
Earlier sketch in CA 69-72
See also SATA 42, 47
Preiss, David (Lee) 1935- 69-72
Prelinger, Ernst 1926- 11-12R
Prelutsky, Jack 1940- 93-96
See also SATA 22
See also DLB 61
See also CLR 13
Prem, Dhani 1904(?)-1979 Obituary 93-96
Premacanda
See Srivastava, Dhanpat Rai
Premack, Ann J(ames) 1929- 57-60
Premack, David 1925- 126
Premchand
See Srivastava, Dhanpat Rai
See also TCLC 21
Prem Chand, Munshi
See Srivastava, Dhanpat Rai
Premchand, Munshi
See Srivastava, Dhanpat Rai
Preminger, Alex 1915- 15-16R
Preminger, Marion Mill 1913-1972
Obituary 33-36R
Preminger, Otto (Ludwig) 1906(?)-1986
Obituary 119
Brief entry 110
Premont, Brother Jeremy
See Willett, Brother Franciscus
Prendergast, Alan 1956- 124
Prendergast, Karen A(nn) 1951- 117
Prentice, Amy
See Kaler, James Otis
Prentice, Ann E(thelynd) 1933- CANR-6
Earlier sketch in CA 57-60
Prentice, Charlotte
See Platt, Charles
Prentice, George D. 1802-1870 .... DLB-43
Prenting, Theodore O(tto) 1933- 57-60
Prentis, Steve ?-1987 Obituary 122
Prentiss, Augustin M. 1890-1977
Obituary 69-72
Presberg, Miriam Goldstein 1919-1978 .. CANR-3
Earlier sketch in CA 2R
See also SATA 38
Prescott, Allen 1904(?)-1978 Obituary 73-76
Prescott, Caleb
See Bingley, David Ernest
Prescott, David M(arshall) 1926-
Brief entry 113
Prescott, J(ohn) R(obert) V(ictor)
1931- CANR-23
Earlier sketch in CA 107
Prescott, John Brewster 1919- 5-6R
Prescott, Kenneth W(ade) 1920- CANR-8
Earlier sketch in CA 57-60
Prescott, Orville 1906- 41-44R
Prescott, Peter S(herwin) 1935- CANR-14
Earlier sketch in CA 37-40R
Prescott, William Hickling
1796-1859 .... DLB-1, 30, 59
Preshing, W(illiam) A(nthony) 1929- 85-88
Preslan, Kristina 1945- 106
Presland, John
See Bendit, Gladys Williams
Presley, Delma E(ugene) 1939- 112
Presley, James (Wright) 1930- CANR-10
Earlier sketch in CA 21-22R
Presnell, Robert (Jr.) 1915(?)-1986
Obituary 119
Press, (Otto) Charles 1922- CANR-6
Earlier sketch in CA 13-14R
Press, John (Bryant) 1920- CANR-3
Earlier sketch in CA 9-10R
Press, Simone Juda 1943- 111
Press, Toni 1949- 108
Pressau, Jack Renard 1933- 77-80
Pressburger, Emeric 1902-1988 104
Obituary 124
Presseisen, Ernst L(eopold) 1928- 15-16R
Presser, (Gerrit) Jacob 1899-1970 .... CAP-2
Earlier sketch in CA 25-28
Presser, Janice 1946- CANR-24
Earlier sketch in CA 107
Pressly, Thomas J(ames) 1919- 19-20R
Pressman, David 1937- 89-92
Pressman, Jeffrey L(eonard) 1943- CANR-3
Earlier sketch in CA 45-48
Prest, Alan Richmond 1919-1985 93-96
Obituary 115
Prest, Wilfred 1907-1985 111
Obituary 117
Prest, Wilfrid R(obertson) 1940- 112
Prestbo, John A(ndrew) 1941- CANR-2
Earlier sketch in CA 49-52
Prestera, Hector A(nthony) 1932- 65-68
Presthus, Robert 1917- CANR-20
Earlier sketches in CA 1R, CANR-5
Prestidge, Pauline 1922- 103
Preston, Dickson J(oseph) 1914-1985 .... CANR-8
Obituary 114
Earlier sketch in CA 61-64
Preston, Edna Mitchell 111
See also SATA 40
Preston, Edward
See Guess, Edward Preston
Preston, Florence (Margaret) 1905- 103
Preston, Frances I(sabella) 1898- 61-64
Preston, Harry 1923- CANR-23
Earlier sketch in CA 57-60
Preston, Ivan L. 1931- 57-60
Preston, Ivy (Alice) Kinross 1914- CANR-12
Earlier sketches in CA 9-10, CAP-1
Preston, James 1913- CAP-1
Earlier sketch in CA 9-10
Preston, James
See Unett, John
Preston, James J(ohn) 1941- 109
Preston, John Hyde 1906-1980 Obituary 102
Preston, Lee E. 1930- CANR-11
Earlier sketch in CA 23-24R
Preston, Lillian Elvira 1918- 108
See also SATA 47
Preston, Michael B. 1933- 126
Preston, Nathaniel Stone 1928- 29-32R
Preston, Ralph C(lausius) 1908- CANR-6
Earlier sketch in CA 13-14R
Preston, Richard
See Lindsay, Jack
Preston, Richard Arthur 1910- CANR-18
Earlier sketches in CA 7-8R, CANR-3
Preston, Thomas 1537-1598 .... DLB-62
Preston, Thomas A(rthur) 1933- 112
Preston, Thomas R(onald) 1936-
Brief entry 109
Preston, William L(ee) 1949- 105
Prestwich, Menna 1917- 23-24R
Pretorius, Hertha
See Kouts, Hertha Pretorius
Preto-Rodas, Richard (Anthony) 1936- 49-52
Prettyman, E(lijah) Barrett, Jr. 1925- 11-12R
Preus, Anthony 1936- 49-52
Preus, Herman Amberg 1896- 85-88
Preus, Jacob A(all) O(ttesen) 1920- 33-36R
Preus, Johan Carl Keyser 1881-1983
Obituary 111
Preus, Robert 1924- 33-36R
Preussler, Otfried 1923- 77-80
See also SATA 24
See also CLC 17
Prevelakis, Pandelis 1909-1986 Obituary 118
Prevert, Jacques (Henri Marie)
1900-1977 77-80
Obituary 69-72
See also SATA 30
See also CLC 15
Previn, Andre (George) 1929- 115
Previn, Dor(oth)y (Langan) 1929(?)- 111
Prevost, Alain 1930(?)-1971 Obituary 33-36R
Prevost, Marcel 1862-1941 Brief entry 116
Prewitt, Kenneth 1936- CANR-12
Earlier sketch in CA 29-32R
Preziosi, Donald 1941- 93-96
Prezzolini, Giuseppi 1882-1982 Obituary 107
Pribam, Karl 1878(?)-1973 Obituary 41-44R
Pribichevich, Stoyan 1905(?)-1976
Obituary 65-68
Price, Alfred 1936- CANR-24
Earlier sketches in CA 23-24R, CANR-9
Price, Anthony 1928- CANR-15
Earlier sketch in CA 77-80
Price, Archibald Grenfell 1892-1977 .... 9-10R
Obituary 125
Price, Arnold H(ereward) 1912- 45-48
Price, Barbara Anne Ellvinger
1946(?)-1987 Obituary 122
Price, Barbara Pradal 103
Price, Beverley Joan 1931- CANR-24
Earlier sketch in CA 106
Price, Bruce D(eitrick) 1941- 25-28R
Price, Byron 1891-1981 Obituary 104
Price, Cecil (John Layton) 1915- 21-22R
Price, Charles 1925- 11-12R
Price, Charles C(oale) 1913- 107
Price, Charles P(hilip) 1920- 115
Price, Christine (Hilda) 1928-1980 .... CANR-4
Obituary 93-96
Earlier sketch in CA 5-6R
See also SATA 3, 23
Price, Daniel O('Haver) 1918- 21-22R
Price, David Deakins 1902-1983 Obituary 110
Price, Derek (John) de Solla
1922-1983 .... CANR-3
Obituary 110
Earlier sketch in CA 1R
Price, Don C(ravens) 1937- 81-84
Price, Don K(rasher, Jr.) 1910- 73-76
Price, E(dgar) Hoffmann 1898- CANR-10
Earlier sketch in CA 61-64
Price, E(dgar) Hoffmann (Trooper)
1898-1988 .... CANR-10
Obituary 125
Earlier sketch in CA 61-64
Price, Emerson 1902(?)-1977 Obituary 104
Price, Eugenia 1916- CANR-18
Earlier sketches in CA 7-8R, CANR-2
Price, Evadne 1896-1985 Obituary 116
Price, Frances Brown 1895- 49-52
Price, Francis Wilson 1895-1974 .... CAP-1
Earlier sketch in CA 13-14
Price, Frank James 1917- 104
Price, Frank W.
See Price, Francis Wilson
Price, Garrett 1896-1979 Obituary 85-88
See also SATA 22
Price, George 1901- 103
Price, George (Henry) 1910-19(?) CAP-1
Earlier sketch in CA 13-14
Price, George R(ennie) 1909- CANR-4
Earlier sketch in CA 1R
Price, Glenn W(arren) 1918- 23-24R
Price, Harry 1881-1948 Brief entry 119
Price, Henry Habberley 1899-1984
Obituary 114
Price, J(oseph) H(enry) 1924- 25-28R
Price, Jacob M(yron) 1925- CANR-1
Earlier sketch in CA 45-48
Price, James Ligon, Jr. 1915- 3R
Price, Jennifer
See Hoover, Helen (Drusilla Blackburn)
Price, Jimmie
See White, John I(rwin)
Price, Joan 1931- 111
Price, John A(ndrew) 1933- CANR-7
Earlier sketch in CA 57-60
Price, John Valdimir 1937- 19-20R
Price, Jonathan (Reeve) 1941- CANR-19
Earlier sketches in CA 45-48, CANR-3
See also SATA 46
Price, Kenneth M(arsden) 1954- 115
Price, Kingsley Blake 1917- 23-24R
Price, Larkin B(url) 1927- Brief entry 112
Price, Leo 1941- 77-80
Price, Lucie Locke
See Locke, Lucie
Price, Margaret (Evans) 1888-1973
Obituary 109
See also SATA 28
Price, Marion E(lizabeth) 1947- 111
Price, Marjorie 1929- 53-56
Price, Martin 1920- CANR-13
Earlier sketch in CA 19-20R
Price, Miles O(scar) 1890-1968 .... CAP-1
Earlier sketch in CA 15-16
Price, Molly 1903(?)-1984 Obituary 114
Price, Morgan Philips 1885-1973 .... CAP-1
Earlier sketch in CA 13-14
Price, (Lilian) Nancy (Bache) 1880-1970
Obituary 111
Price, Nelson Lynn 1931- CANR-24
Earlier sketches in CA 61-64, CANR-8
Price, Olive 1903- 41-44R
See also SATA 8
Price, Paul 1912(?)-1985 Obituary 116
Price, R(onald) F(rancis) 1926- CANR-26
Earlier sketch in CA 29-32R
Price, R(ichard) G(eoffrey) G(eorge)
1910- CAP-1
Earlier sketch in CA 13-14
Price, Ray(mond John) 1931- 25-28R
Price, Ray Glenn 1903- CANR-2
Earlier sketch in CA 7-8R
Price, Raymond (Kissam, Jr.) 1930- 105
Price, (Edward) Reynolds 1933- CANR-1
Earlier sketch in CA 2R
See also DLB 2
See also CLC 3, 6, 13, 43, 50
Price, Rhys
See Price, George (Henry)
Price, Richard 1941- 105
Price, Richard 1949- CANR-3
Earlier sketch in CA 49-52
See also DLBY 81
See also CLC 6, 12
Price, Robert 1900- 33-36R
Price, Robert W. 1925(?)-1979 Obituary 89-92
Price, Roger 1921- 11-12R
Price, Roger (David) 1944- 107
Price, S(eymour) Stephen 1919- 25-28R
Price, Sally 1943- 106
Price, Stanley 1931- 13-14R
Price, Steven D(avid) 1940- CANR-16
Earlier sketches in CA 49-52, CANR-1
Price, Susan 1955- 105
See also SATA 25
Price, V(incent) B(arrett) 1940- 69-72
Price, Victor 1930- 11-12R
Price, Vincent 1911- 89-92
Price, Walter K(leber) 1924- CANR-7
Earlier sketch in CA 19-20R
Price, Willadene Anton 1914- 5-6R
Price, Willard 1887-1983 .... CANR-1
Earlier sketch in CA 4R
See also SATA 38, 48
Price, William 1938- 37-40R
Price, Wilson T(itus) 1931- 37-40R

Price-Mars, Jean 1875-1969 Obituary ... 112
Prichard, Caradog 1904-1980 ... 103
Obituary ... 97-100
Prichard, Doris (Smith) 1947- ... 116
Prichard, James W(illiam) 1925- ... 15-16R
Prichard, Katharine Susannah 1883-1969 . CAP-1
Earlier sketch in CA 11-12
See also CLC 46
Prichard, Nancy S(awyer) 1924- ... 29-32R
Prichard, Robert Williams 1923- ... 89-92
Prichard, Susan Perez 1953- ... 108
Prickett, (Alexander Thomas) Stephen 1939- ... 29-32R
Priddy, Fran(ces Rosaleen) 1931- ... CANR-17
Earlier sketch in CA 3R
Pride, Cletis 1925- ... 41-44R
Pride, J(ohn) B(ernard) 1929- Brief entry ... 110
Prideaux, Tom 1908- ... 108
See also SATA 37
Pridham, Geoffrey 1942- ... CANR-17
Earlier sketch in CA 97-100
Pridham, Radost 1922- ... 23-24R
Pries, Nancy R(uth) 1944- ... 118
Priesand, Sally J(ane) 1946- ... 65-68
Priest, Alice L. 1931- ... 102
Priest, Christopher 1943- ... 33-36R
See also DLB 14
Priest, Harold Martin 1902- ... 73-76
Priest, Robert 1951- ... 118
Priestley, Barbara 1937- ... 33-36R
Priestley, F(rancis) E(thelbert) L(ouis) 1905- ... 21-22R
Priestley, Harold E(dford) 1901- ... 73-76
Priestley, J(ohn) B(oynton) 1894-1984 ... 9-10R
Obituary ... 113
See also DLB 10, 34
See also DLBY 84
See also CLC 2, 5, 9, 34
Priestley, Lee (Shore) 1904- ... CANR-2
Earlier sketch in CA 5-6R
See also SATA 27
Priestley, Mary 1925- ... 61-64
Priestley, Philip 1939- ... 123
Prieto, Mariana Beeching 1912- ... CANR-5
Earlier sketch in CA 5-6R
See also SATA 8
Prigmore, Charles S(amuel) 1919- ... CANR-25
Earlier sketch in CA 45-48
Priley, Margaret Hubbard 1909- ... 2R
Prill, Felician 1904- ... 103
Primack, Joel (Robert) 1945- ... 61-64
Primavera, Elise 1954- ... SATA-48
Prime, Benjamin Young 1733-1791 ... DLB-31
Prime, C(ecil) T(homas) 1909-1979 ... CANR-3
Earlier sketch in CA 49-52
Prime, Derek (James) 1931- ... CANR-25
Earlier sketch in CA 108
See also SATA 34
Primeau, Ronald 1946- ... 108
Primeaux, Walter J(oseph) Jr. 1928- ... 41-44R
Primm, Brother Orrin
See Willett, Brother Franciscus
Primm, James Neal 1918- ... 45-48
Primmer, Phyllis (Cora Griesbach) 1926- ... 7-8R
Primo, Albert T. 1935- ... 73-76
Primrose, William 1904-1982 ... 116
Obituary ... 106
Prince (Rogers Nelson) 1958?- ... CLC-35
Prince, Alison (Mary) 1931- ... CANR-26
Earlier sketch in CA 29-32R
See also SATA 28
Prince, Carl E. 1934- ... CANR-14
Earlier sketch in CA 21-22R
Prince, (Peter) Derek 1915- ... 113
Prince, Don 1905(?)-1983 Obituary ... 110
Prince, F(rank) T(empleton) 1912- ... 101
See also DLB 20
See also CLC 22
Prince, Gary Michael 1948- ... 89-92
Prince, Gerald (Joseph) 1942- ... 57-60
Prince, J(ack) H(arvey) 1908- ... 81-84
See also SATA 17
Prince, Melvin 1932- ... 116
Prince, Morton 1854-1929 Brief entry ... 121
Prince, Suzan D(enise) 1957- ... 111
Prince, Thomas 1687-1758 ... DLB-24
Prince, Thomas Richard 1934- ... 15-16R
Prince Ibis
See Randi, James
Prince Kropotkin
See Kropotkin, Peter (Aleksieevich)
Princess Grace
See Kelly, Grace (Patricia)
Prindl, A(ndreas) R(obert) 1939- ... 69-72
Pring, Julian Talbot 1913- ... 7-8R
Pring, Martin J(ohn) 1943- ... 111
Pringle, J(ohn) M(artin) Douglas 1912- ... 13-14R
Pringle, Laurence P. 1935- ... CANR-14
Earlier sketch in CA 29-32R
See also SATA 4
See also SAAS 6
See also CLR 4
Pringle, Mia (Lilly) Kellmer 1920(?)-1983 ... 65-68
Obituary ... 109
Pringle, Peter 1940- ... 69-72
Pring-Mill, Robert D(uguid) F(orrest) 1924- ... 9-10R
Printz, Peggy 1945- ... 73-76
Prinz, Joachim 1902- ... CAP-1
Earlier sketch in CA 11-12
Priolo, Pauline Pizzo 1907- ... 2R
Prior, A(rthur) N(orman) 1914-1969 ... CANR-3
Earlier sketch in CA 1R
Prior, Allan 1922- ... CANR-10
Earlier sketch in CA 65-68
Prior, Andrew 1940- ... 112
Prior, Ann 1949- ... 25-28R
Prior, Kenneth Francis William 1926- ... 19-20R
Prisco, Michele 1920- ... 53-56
Prisco, Salvatore III 1943- ... CANR-12
Earlier sketch in CA 61-64
Prising, Robin 1933- ... 57-60
Pritchard, Arnold 1949- ... 97-100
Pritchard, J(ohn) Harris 1923- ... 21-22R
Pritchard, James Bennett 1909- ... 5-6R
Pritchard, John Paul 1902-1976 ... 11-12R
Obituary ... 126
Pritchard, John Wallace 1912- ... 81-84
Pritchard, Leland J(ames) 1908- ... CAP-1
Earlier sketch in CA 11-12
Pritchard, Norman Henry II 1939- ... 77-80
Pritchard, R(onald) E(dward) 1936- ... 37-40R
Pritchard, R(obert) John 1945- ... 116
Pritchard, Sheila (Edwards) 1909- ... CAP-1
Earlier sketch in CA 15-16
Pritchard, William H(arrison) 1932- ... CANR-23
Earlier sketch in CA 65-68
See also CLC 34
Pritchett, C(harles) Herman 1907- ... CANR-18
Earlier sketches in CA 2R, CANR-3
Pritchett, Elaine H(illyer) 1920- ... 108
See also SATA 36
Pritchett, John Perry 1902- ... 2R
Pritchett, Price 1941- ... 123
Pritchett, V(ictor) S(awdon) 1900- ... 61-64
See also DLB 15
See also CLC 5, 13, 15, 41
Pritchett, W(illiam) Kendrick 1909- ... 97-100
Pritikin, Nathan 1915-1985 ... 89-92
Obituary ... 114
Pritikin, Robert C(harles) 1929- ... 104
Prittie, Terence Cornelius Farmer 1913-1985 ... CANR-4
Obituary ... 116
Earlier sketch in CA 2R
Private 19022
See Manning, Frederic
Priyamvada, Usha
See Nilsson, Usha Saksena
Prizzia, Ross 1942- ... 119
Probert, Walter 1925- ... 77-80
Probst, Leonard 1921-1982 ... 65-68
Obituary ... 106
Prochnau, William W. 1937- ... 33-36R
Prochnow, Herbert V. 1897- ... CANR-4
Earlier sketch in CA 2R
Prochnow, Herbert V(ictor), Jr. 1931- ... 110
Procktor, Richard (Edward Christopher) 1933- ... 53-56
Procopio, Mariellen
See Grutz, Mariellen Procopio
Procter, Adelaide Anne 1825-1864 ... DLB-32
Procter, Ben H. 1927- ... CANR-9
Earlier sketch in CA 5-6R
Procter, Maurice 1906-1973 ... 7-8R
Obituary ... 122
Proctor, Charles S(heridan) 1925- ... 29-32R
Proctor, (Philip) Dennis 1905-1983
Obituary ... 110
Proctor, Dorothea Hardy 1910- ... 61-64
Proctor, E(velyn) E(mma) S(tefanos) 1897-1980 ... 103
Obituary ... 97-100
Proctor, Elsie 1902- ... 29-32R
Proctor, Everitt
See Montgomery, Rutherford George
Proctor, Lillian Cummins 1900- ... CAP-2
Earlier sketch in CA 23-24
Proctor, Priscilla 1945- ... 65-68
Proctor, Raymond L(ambert) 1920- ... 45-48
Proctor, Samuel 1919- ... CANR-3
Earlier sketch in CA 11-12R
Proctor, Samuel D(eWitt) 1921-
Brief entry ... 118
Proctor, Thelwall 1912- ... 29-32R
Proctor, William (Gilbert, Jr.) 1941- ... CANR-16
Earlier sketch in CA 37-40R
Prodan, Mario 1911- ... 11-12R
Proface, Dom
See Sheehy, Maurice S(tephen)
Proffer, Carl R(ay) 1938-1984 ... 41-44R
Obituary ... 113
Proffer, Ellendea 1944- ... CANR-1
Earlier sketch in CA 45-48
Proffitt, Charles G. 1896-1982 Obituary ... 108
Proger, Samuel (Herschel) 1906-
Brief entry ... 106
Prohias, Antonio 1921- ... 104
Prokasy, William F(rederick) 1930- ... 49-52
Prokhovnik, Simon Jacques 1920- ... 107
Prokofiev, Aleksandr Andreyevich 1900-1971 Obituary ... 33-36R
Prokofiev, Camilla Gray 1938(?)-1971
Obituary ... 33-36R
Prokofiev, Sergei (Sergeevich) 1891-1953
Brief entry ... 112
Prokop, Phyllis Stillwell 1922- ... CANR-9
Earlier sketch in CA 21-22R
Prokopczyk, Czeslaw 1935- ... 108
Prokosch, Frederic 1908- ... 73-76
See also DLB 48
See also CLC 4, 48
Prole, Lozania
See Bloom, Ursula
Pronin, Alexander 1927- ... 49-52
Pronko, Leonard Cabell 1927- ... CANR-1
Earlier sketch in CA 1R
Pronko, N(icholas) Henry 1908- ... 11-12R
Pronzini, Bill 1943- ... CANR-14
Earlier sketches in CA 49-52, CANR-1
Proosdii, Cornelis Van
See Van Proosdy, Cornelis
Propes, Stephen Charles 1942- ... CANR-1
Earlier sketch in CA 49-52
Propes, Steve
See Propes, Stephen Charles
Propper, Dan 1937- ... 104
See also DLB 16
Prosch, Harry 1917- ... 13-14R
Prose, Francine 1947- ... 112
Brief entry ... 109
See also CLC 45
Proske, Beatrice (Irene) Gilman 1899- ... CAP-1
Earlier sketch in CA 9-10
Proskouriakoff, Tatiana (Avenivovna) 1909-1985 Obituary ... 117
Prosper, John (joint pseudonym)
See Farrar, John C(hipman)
Prosper, Lincoln
See Cannon, Helen
Prosser, Eleanor 1922- ... 3R
Prosser, H(arold) L(ee) 1944- ... CANR-15
Earlier sketch in CA 77-80
Prosser, Michael H. 1936- ... CANR-17
Earlier sketch in CA 25-28R
Prostano, Emanuel Theodore, Jr. 1931- ... 29-32R
Prostano, Joyce S. ... 126
Prosterman, Roy L. 1935- ... 57-60
Prothero, R(alph) Mansell 1924- ... 41-44R
Prothro, Edwin Terry 1919- ... 53-56
Prothro, James W(arren) 1922- ... CANR-8
Earlier sketch in CA 5-6R
Protopapas, George 1917- ... 57-60
Prou, Suzanne (Marcelle Henriette) 1920- ... CANR-20
Earlier sketch in CA 33-36R
Proud, Robert 1728-1813 ... DLB-30
Proudfoot, J(ohn) J(ames) 1918- ... 21-22R
Proudhon
See Cunha, Euclides (Rodrigues Pimenta) da
Proujan, Carl 1929- ... 81-84
Proussis, Costas M(ichael) 1911- ... CANR-15
Earlier sketch in CA 41-44R
Proust, (Valentin-Louis-George-Eugene-)Marcel 1871-1922 ... 120
Brief entry ... 104
See also DLB 65
See also TCLC 7, 13
Prout, W(illiam) Leslie 1922- ... 9-10R
Prouty, L. Fletcher 1917- ... 45-48
Prouty, Morton D(ennison), Jr. 1918- ... 3R
Prouty, Olive Higgins 1882(?)-1974 ... 11-12R
Obituary ... 49-52
Prouvost, Jean 1885-1978 Obituary ... 89-92
Provan, Jill E(llen) 1948- ... 117
Provence, Marcel
See Jouhandeau, Marcel Henri
Provensen, Alice 1918- ... CANR-5
Earlier sketch in CA 53-56
See also SATA 9
See also CLR 11
Provensen, Martin (Elias) 1916-1987 ... CANR-5
Obituary ... 122
Earlier sketch in CA 53-56
See also SATA 9, 51
See also CLR 11
Provist, d'Alain
See Diop, Birago (Ismael)
Provo, Frank 1913(?)-1975 Obituary ... 61-64
Provus, Malcolm M. 1928- Brief entry ... 108
Prowe, Diethelm (Manfred-Hartmut) 1941- ... 57-60
Prowler, Don(ald) 1950- ... 121
Prowler, Harley
See Masters, Edgar Lee
Prown, Jules David 1930- ... 29-32R
Proxmire, William 1915- ... 29-32R
Prpic, George J(ure) 1920- ... CANR-17
Earlier sketch in CA 25-28R
Prucha, Francis Paul 1921- ... CANR-17
Earlier sketches in CA 5-6R, CANR-2
Prudden, Bonnie 1914- ... CANR-14
Earlier sketch in CA 77-80
Prude, Agnes George 1905- ... 65-68
Pruden, (James) Wesley, Jr. 1935- ... 19-20R
Prueitt, Melvin L(ewis) 1932- ... 118
Pruett, John H(aywood) 1947- ... 102
Prugh, Jeff(ery Douglas) 1939- ... 41-44R
Pruitt, Evelyn L(ord) 1918- ... 5-6R
Pruitt, Ida 1888-1985 Obituary ... 116
Pruitt, William O(badiah), Jr. 1922- ... 21-22R
Pruner, Leonora 1931- ... 114
Prunty, Merle C(harles) 1917-1983 ... 37-40R
Obituary ... 109
Prunty, (Eugene) Wyatt 1947- ... 110
Prusek, Jaroslav 1906- Brief entry ... 117
Prusina, Katica 1935- ... 69-72
Pruthi, Surinder P(aul) S(ingh) 1934- ... 61-64
Pruyser, Paul W(illem) 1916- ... CANR-9
Earlier sketch in CA 23-24R
Prybyla, Jan S(tanislaw) 1927- ... 23-24R
Pryce, Roy 1928- ... 29-32R
Pryce-Jones, David 1936- ... CANR-14
Earlier sketch in CA 13-14R
Pryde, Philip Rust 1938- ... 61-64
Pryer, Pauline
See Roby, Mary Linn
Prynne, J. H. 1936- ... 97-100
See also DLB 40
Pryor, Adel
See Wasserfall, Adel
Pryor, Frederic L(eRoy) 1933- ... CANR-2
Earlier sketch in CA 7-8R
Pryor, Helen Brenton 1897-1972 ... CAP-2
Earlier sketch in CA 33-36
See also SATA 4
Pryor, Karen 1932- ... 119
Pryor, Larry
See Pryor, Lawrence A(lderdice)
Pryor, Lawrence A(lderdice) 1938- ... 85-88
Pryor, Richard (Franklin Lenox Thomas) 1940- Brief entry ... 122
See also CLC 26
Pryor, Vanessa
See Yarbro, Chelsea Quinn
Prys-Jones, Arthur Glyn 1888- ... 104
Przybyszewski, Stanislaw 1868-1927 ... DLB-66
Psathas, George 1929- ... 23-24R
Pteleon
See Grieve, C(hristopher) M(urray)
Puccetti, Roland (Peter) 1924- ... 93-96
Pucci, Albert John 1920- ... SATA-44
Pucciani, Oreste F(rancesco) 1916- ... 23-24R
Puche, Jose Luis Castillo
See Castillo Puche, Jose Luis
Puck, Wolfgang 1949- ... 124
Puck, Y. U.
See Andre, (Kenneth) Michael
Puckett, Lute
See Masters, Edgar Lee
Puckett, Robert Hugh 1935- ... 41-44R
Puckett, (William) Ronald 1936- ... 33-36R
Puckett, Ruby Parker 1932- ... 57-60
Puckey, Walter (Charles) 1899-1983 ... CAP-2
Obituary ... 111
Earlier sketch in CA 29-32
Pudaite, Rochunga 1927- ... 120
Puddepha, Derek (Noel) 1930- ... 61-64
Pudney, John (Sleigh) 1909-1977 ... CANR-5
Obituary ... 77-80
Earlier sketch in CA 9-10R
See also SATA 24
Pudovkin, V(sevolod) I(llarionovich) 1893-1953 Brief entry ... 112
Puechner, Ray 1935- ... 25-28R
Puette, William J(oseph) 1946- ... 77-80
Puffer, K(enneth) Hart 1910- ... 7-8R
Pugh, Anthony (Roy) 1931- ... 53-56
Pugh, Charles 1948- ... 81-84
Pugh, Ellen (Tiffany) 1920- ... 49-52
See also SATA 7
Pugh, Griffith T(hompson) 1908- ... 7-8R
Pugh, J(ohn) W(ilbur) 1912- ... 21-22R
Pugh, John Charles 1919- ... 110
Pugh, L(eslie) P(enrhys) 1895-1983
Obituary ... 110
Pugh, Ralph B(ernard) 1910-1982 ... 25-28R
Obituary ... 108
Pugh, Rod(erick) W(ellington) 1919- ... 45-48
Pugh, Samuel F(ranklin) 1904- ... CAP-1
Earlier sketch in CA 13-14
Pugh, Wynette 1942- Brief entry ... 111
Pugin, A. Welby 1812-1852 ... DLB-55
Pugliese, Anthony J(ulian) 1912-1985
Obituary ... 117
Pugsley, Clement H. 1908- ... CAP-1
Earlier sketch in CA 13-14
Pugsley, John A. 1934- ... CANR-19
Earlier sketch in CA 103
Puharich, Henry (Andrija) Karl 1918- ... 85-88
Puhvel, Jaan 1932- ... 29-32R
Puig, Manuel 1932- ... CANR-2
Earlier sketch in CA 45-48
See also CLC 3, 5, 10, 28
Pulaski, Mary Ann Spencer 1916- ... CANR-10
Earlier sketch in CA 25-28R
Pulay, George 1923- ... 45-48
Puleo, Nicole
See Miller, Nicole Puleo
Pulgram, Ernst 1915- ... 49-52
Puligandla, Ramakrishna 1930- ... CANR-7
Earlier sketch in CA 61-64
Pulis, Clifford A(lton) 1916- ... 116
Pulitzer, Joseph 1847-1911 Brief entry ... 114
See also DLB 23
Pulitzer, Joseph, Jr. 1885-1955 ... DLB-29
Pulkingham, Betty (Jane) 1928- ... CANR-26
Earlier sketches in CA 61-64, CANR-8
Pulkingham, W(illiam) Graham 1926- ... 53-56
Pullapilly, Cyriac K(alapura) 1932- ... 61-64
Pullar, Philippa 1935- Brief entry ... 116
Pullein-Thompson, Christine
See Popescu, Christine
See also SATA 3
Pullein-Thompson, Denis
See Cannan, Denis
Pullein-Thompson, Diana
See Farr, Diana (Pullein-Thompson)
See also SATA 3
Pullein-Thompson, Joanna Maxwell 1898-1961 ... 106
Pullein-Thompson, Josephine (Mary Wedderburn) ... CANR-20
Earlier sketches in CA 7-8R, CANR-7
See also SATA 3
Pullen, John James 1913- ... 19-20R
Pulliam, Eugene C(ollins) 1889-1975
Obituary ... 89-92
See also AITN 2
Pulliam, H(oward) Ronald 1945- ... 114
Pulliam, Myrta 1947- ... 97-100
Pullias, Earl V(ivon) 1907- ... CAP-1
Earlier sketch in CA 11-12
Pulling, Albert Van Siclen 1891- ... 53-56
Pulling, Christopher Robert Druce 1893- ... CAP-1
Earlier sketch in CA 13-14
Pulling, Pierre
See Pulling, Albert Van Siclen
Pulman, Jack 1928(?)-1979 Obituary ... 85-88
Pulman, Michael Barraclough 1933- ... 33-36R
Pulos, William L(eroy) 1920- ... 45-48
Pulsipher, Gerreld L(ewis) 1939- ... 101
Pulzer, Peter George Julius 1929- ... 15-16R
Pumphrey, H(enry) George 1912- ... 13-14R
Pumroy, Donald K(eith) 1925- ... 49-52
Punch, Maurice 1941- ... 65-68

Pundeff, Marin 1921- ... 11-12R
Pundt, Helen Marie ... 7-8R
Punekar, Shankar Mokashi
See Mokashi-Punekar, Shankar
Puner, Helen W(alker) 1915- ... CANR-2
Earlier sketch in CA 7-8R
See also SATA 37
Puner, Morton 1921- ... 73-76
Punnett, R(obert) M(alcolm) 1936- ... 25-28R
Purcal, John T(homas) 1931- ... 33-36R
Purcell, Arthur Henry 1944- ... 102
Purcell, Donald 1916- ... 122
Purcell, Gillis Philip 1904-1987 Obituary ... 124
Purcell, H(ugh) D(ominic) 1932- ... CANR-17
Earlier sketch in CA 25-28R
Purcell, Mary 1906- ... CANR-2
Earlier sketch in CA 7-8R
Purcell, Roy E(verett) 1936- ... CANR-6
Earlier sketch in CA 57-60
Purcell, Sally 1944- ... 49-52
Purcell, Susan Kaufman 1942- Brief entry ... 114
Purcell, Theodore V(incent) 1911-1984 ... 41-44R
Obituary ... 112
Purcell, Victor 1896-1965 ... 5-6R
Purdom, Charles B(enjamin) 1883-1965 ... CAP-1
Earlier sketch in CA 9-10
Purdom, P(aul) Walton 1917- ... 57-60
Purdom, Thomas E. 1936- ... 15-16R
Purdom, Tom
See Purdom, Thomas E.
Purdon, Eric (Sinclaire) 1913- ... 93-96
Purdue, A(rthur) W(illiam) 1941- ... 124
Purdue, Bill
See Purdue, A(rthur) W(illiam)
Purdy, A(lfred) W(ellington) 1918- ... 81-84
See also CLC 3, 6, 14, 50
Purdy, Al
See Purdy, A(lfred) W(ellington)
Purdy, Alexander 1890-1976 Obituary ... 65-68
Purdy, Anne S. 1902(?)-1987 Obituary ... 122
Purdy, (Charles) Anthony 1932- ... 19-20R
Purdy, Captain Jim
See Gillelan, G(eorge) Howard
Purdy, James (Amos) 1923- ... CANR-19
Earlier sketch in CA 33-36R
See also CAAS 1
See also DLB 2
See also CLC 2, 4, 10, 28
Purdy, John David 1946- ... 122
Purdy, Ken W(illiam) 1913-1972
Obituary ... 37-40R
Purdy, Susan Gold 1939- ... CANR-10
Earlier sketch in CA 15-16R
See also SATA 8
Purdy, Theodore Martindale 1903-1979
Obituary ... 89-92
Pure, Simon
See Swinnerton, Frank Arthur
Purkey, Roy (Delbert) 1905- ... CAP-2
Earlier sketch in CA 23-24
Purkey, William Watson 1929- ... 29-32R
Purkis, John 1933- ... 97-100
Purkiser, W(estlake) T(aylor) 1910- ... CAP-1
Earlier sketch in CA 15-16
Purl, Sandy M. 1953- ... 122
Purnell, Idella 1901- ... 61-64
Purpel, David E(dward) 1932- ... 49-52
Purrington, Robert Daniel 1936- ... 122
Purscell, Phyllis 1934- ... 25-28R
See also SATA 7
Pursell, Carroll W(irth), Jr. 1932- ... 77-80
Purser, John Whitley 1942- ... 103
Purser, Philip John 1925- ... CANR-21
Earlier sketch in CA 104
Purtill, Richard L. 1931- ... 37-40R
See also SATA 53
Purton, Rowland W(illiam Crisby)
1925- ... CANR-4
Earlier sketch in CA 53-56
Purves, Alan C(arroll) 1931- ... CANR-9
Earlier sketch in CA 21-22R
Purvis, Charles C. 1902(?)-1985 Obituary ... 115
Puryear, Alvin N(elson) 1937- Brief entry ... 115
Puryear, Edgar F., Jr. 1930- ... 115
Pusey, Edward Bouverie 1800-1882 ... DLB-55
Pusey, Merlo John 1902-1985 ... 11-12R
Obituary ... 117
Pusey, Nathan Marsh 1907- ... 109
Pushkarev, Boris S. 1929- ... CANR-6
Earlier sketch in CA 7-8R
Pushkarev, Sergei Germanovich 1888- ... CANR-6
Earlier sketch in CA 7-8R
Pustay, John S(tephen) 1931- ... 19-20R
Putcamp, Luise, jr. 1924- ... 29-32R
Puthoff, Harold E(dward) 1936-
Brief entry ... 113
Putnam, Alice 1916- ... 113
Putnam, Arnold Oscar 1922- ... 11-12R
Putnam, Arthur Lee
See Alger, Horatio, Jr.
Putnam, Carleton 1901- ... 65-68
Putnam, Donald F(ulton) 1903- ... CAP-2
Earlier sketch in CA 29-32
Putnam, George Palmer 1814-1872 ... DLB-3
Putnam, George Palmer 1887-1950
Brief entry ... 109
Putnam, Hilary 1926- ... 61-64
Putnam, J. Wesley
See Drago, Harry Sinclair
Putnam, Jackson K(eith) 1929- ... 29-32R
Putnam, John
See Beckwith, Burnham Putnam
Putnam, John Fay 1924(?)-1982 Obituary ... 106
Putnam, Michael Courtney Jenkins 1933- ... 105
Putnam, Peter B(rock) 1920- ... 85-88
See also SATA 30
Putnam, Robert D(avid) 1941- ... CANR-10
Earlier sketch in CA 65-68
Putnam, Robert E. 1933- ... CANR-19
Earlier sketches in CA 53-56, CANR-5
Putnam, Roy Clayton 1928- ... 69-72
Putnam, Samuel Whitehall 1892-1950
Brief entry ... 107
See also DLB 4
Putney, Gail J.
See Fullerton, Gail Jackson
Putra, Kerala
See Panikkar, K(avalam) Madhava
Putt, Robert C. 1938- ... 120
Putt, S(amuel) Gorley 1913- ... CANR-6
Earlier sketch in CA 7-8R
Putter, Irving 1917- ... 65-68
Putter, Polly
See Adomeit, Ruth E(lizabeth)
Putterman, Ron 1946- ... 108
Puttfarken, Thomas 1943- ... 122
Putz, Louis J. 1909- ... CAP-1
Earlier sketch in CA 13-14
Putzar, Edward (David) 1930- ... 41-44R
Putzel, Max 1910- ... 11-12R
Putzel, Michael 1942- ... 73-76
Puxon, Grattan 1939- ... 81-84
Puzo, Mario 1920- ... CANR-4
Earlier sketch in CA 65-68
See also DLB 6
See also CLC 1, 2, 6, 36
Pybus, Rodney 1938- ... 107
Pye, (John) David 1932- ... 25-28R
Pye, Lloyd (Anthony, Jr.) 1946- ... 77-80
Pye, Lucian W(ilmot) 1921- ... 23-24R
Pye, Norman 1913- ... 109
Pyk, Ann Phillips 1937- ... 77-80
Pyke, Helen Godfrey 1941- ... 29-32R
Pyke, Magnus 1908- ... CANR-6
Earlier sketch in CA 13-14R
Pyle, A(lbert) M(offett) 1945- ... 123
Pyle, Ernest Taylor 1900-1945 Brief entry ... 115
Pyle, Ernie
See Pyle, Ernest Taylor
See also DLB 29
Pyle, (William) Fitzroy 1907- ... CAP-2
Earlier sketch in CA 29-32
Pyle, Hilary 1936- ... 77-80
Pyle, Howard 1853-1911 Brief entry ... 109
See also SATA 16
See also DLB 42
Pyles, Aitken
See McDavid, Raven I(oor), Jr.
Pyles, Thomas 1905- ... 15-16R
Pylyshyn, Zenon W(alter) 1937- ... 29-32R
Pym, Barbara (Mary Crampton)
1913-1980 ... CANR-13
Obituary ... 97-100
Earlier sketches in CA 13-14, CAP-1
See also DLB 14
See also DLBY 87
See also CLC 13, 19, 37
Pym, Christopher 1929- ... 13-14R
Pym, Denis 1936- ... 25-28R
Pym, Dora Olive (Ivens) 1890- ... CAP-1
Earlier sketch in CA 13-14
Pym, Michael 1890(?)-1983 Obituary ... 109
Pym, Peter and Delores
See Sandlin, Tim
Pynchon, Thomas 1937- ... CANR-22
Earlier sketch in CA 19-20R
See also DLB 2
See also CLC 2, 3, 6, 9, 11, 18, 33
Pyne, Mable Mandeville 1903-1969 ... 4R
Obituary ... 103
See also SATA 9
Pyne, Stephen J(oseph) 1949- ... 106
Pynn, Ronald 1942- ... 85-88
Pyrnelle, Louise-Clarke 1850-1907 ... DLB-42
Pyros, John 1931- ... 77-80
Pytchely, R. F. St. B.
See Cowie, Donald

Q

Q
See Quiller-Couch, Arthur Thomas
Qadar, Basheer
See Alexander, C(harles) K(halil)
Qazzaz, Ayad (Sayyid Ali) Al
See Al-Qazzaz, Ayad (Sayyid Ali)
Qian Hao 1925- ... 111
Qoboza, Percy 1938-1988 Obituary ... 124
Qroll
See Dagerman, Stig (Halvard)
Quackenbush, Margery (Carlson) 1943- ... 73-76
Quackenbush, Robert M(ead) 1929- ... CANR-17
Earlier sketches in CA 45-48, CANR-2
See also SATA 7
Quad, M.
See Lewis, Charles Bertrand
Quade, E(dward) S(chaumberg)
1908-1988 Obituary ... 125
Quade, Quentin Lon 1933- Brief entry ... 106
Quaife, Milo Milton 1880-1959 Brief entry ... 114
Quain, Edwin A. 1906(?)-1975 Obituary ... 61-64
Quale, G(ladys) Robina 1931- ... 23-24R
Qualey, Carlton C(hester) 1904- ... 77-80
Qualter, Terence H(all) 1925- ... 37-40R
Quammen, David 1948- ... 29-32R
See also SATA 7
Quanbeck, Philip A. 1927- ... 25-28R
Quandt, B. Jean 1932- ... 33-36R
Quandt, Richard E(meric) 1930- ... 45-48
Quandt, William B. 1941- ... 29-32R
Quantrill, Malcolm 1931- ... 13-14R
Quarles, Benjamin 1904- ... CANR-16
Earlier sketches in CA 2R, CANR-1
See also BW
See also SATA 12
Quarles, John R(hodes), Jr. 1935- ... CANR-15
Earlier sketch in CA 65-68
Quarm, Daisy 1948- ... 122
Quarmby, Arthur 1934- ... 45-48
Quarrie, Bruce (Roy Bryant) 1947- ... 103
Quartermain, James
See Lynne, James Broom
Quartermain, Peter (Allan) 1934- ... 117
Quasimodo, Salvatore 1901-1968 ... CAP-1
Obituary ... 25-28R
Earlier sketch in CA 15-16
See also CLC 10
Quastel, J. H.
See Quastel, Juda Hirsch
Quastel, Juda Hirsch 1899-1987 Obituary ... 123
Quasten, Johannes 1900- ... 9-10R
Quay, Herbert C. 1927- ... 13-14R
Quayle, Eric 1921- ... 21-22R
Qubain, Fahim I(ssa) 1924- ... 3R
Quebedeaux, Richard (Anthony) 1944- ... CANR-12
Earlier sketch in CA 73-76
Queen, Ellery
See Dannay, Frederic
and Davidson, Avram
and Lee, Manfred B(ennington)
See also CLC 3, 11
Queen, Ellery, Jr.
See Dannay, Frederic
and Holding, James (Clark Carlisle, Jr.)
and Lee, Manfred B(ennington)
Queen, Stuart Alfred 1890- ... 23-24R
Queen Wilhelmina
See Nassau, Wilhelmina Helena Pauline
Maria
Quelch, John A(nthony) 1951- ... 112
Queller, Donald E(dward) 1925- ... CANR-4
Earlier sketch in CA 53-56
Queneau, Raymond 1903-1976 ... 77-80
Obituary ... 69-72
See also DLB 72
See also CLC 2, 5, 10, 42
Quenelle, Gilbert 1914- ... 25-28R
Quennell, Marjorie Courtney 1884-1972 ... 73-76
See also SATA 29
Quennell, Peter (Courtney) 1905- ... 115
Brief entry ... 113
Quentin, Patrick
See Wheeler, Hugh (Callingham)
Querry, Ronald B(urns) 1943- ... 117
Query, William T(heodore), Jr. 1929- ... 41-44R
Quesnell, John G(eorge) 1936- ... CANR-1
Earlier sketch in CA 45-48
Quesnell, Quentin 1927- ... 120
Quest, Linda (Gerber) 1935- ... 77-80
Quest, (Edna) Olga W(ilbourne) Hall
See Hall-Quest, (Edna) Olga W(ilbourne)
Quest, Rodney ... CAP-2
Earlier sketch in CA 29-32
Quester, George H. 1936- ... CANR-10
Earlier sketch in CA 25-28R
Quezada, Abel 1920- ... 7-8R
Quichot, Dona
See Tomkiewicz, Mina
Quick, Annabelle 1922- ... 23-24R
See also SATA 2
Quick, Armand James 1894-1978
Obituary ... 73-76
Quick, Philip
See Strage, Mark
Quick, Thomas L(ee) 1929- ... 41-44R
Quickel, Stephen (Woodside) 1936- ... 73-76
Quie, Gretchen 1927- ... 117
Quiery, William H. 1926- ... 23-24R
Quigg, Jane (Hulda) ?-1986 Obituary ... 120
See also SATA 49
Quigg, Philip W. 1920- ... 11-12R
Quigless, Helen Gordon 1944- Brief entry ... 105
Quigley, Aileen 1930- ... 124
Brief entry ... 104
Quigley, Austin E(dmund) 1942- ... 101
Quigley, Carroll 1910-1977 ... 37-40R
Obituary ... 69-72
Quigley, Eileen Elliott
See Vivers, Eileen Elliott
Quigley, Ellen 1955- ... 111
Quigley, Harold Scott 1889-1968 ... 3R
Obituary ... 103
Quigley, Joan ... 29-32R
Quigley, John 1927- ... 19-20R
Quigley, John M(ichael) 1942- ... 110
Brief entry ... 107
Quigley, Martin (Peter) 1913- ... CANR-18
Earlier sketch in CA 19-20R
Quigley, Martin, Jr. 1917- ... CANR-17
Earlier sketch in CA 4R
Quilici, Folco 1930- ... 105
Quill
See Grange, Cyril
Quill, Barnaby
See Brandner, Gary
Quill, Monica
See McInerny, Ralph
Quiller, Andrew
See Bulmer, (Henry) Kenneth
Quiller-Couch, Arthur Thomas 1863-1944
Brief entry ... 118
Quilligan, Maureen 1944- ... CANR-16
Earlier sketch in CA 89-92
Quimber, Mario
See Alexander, C(harles) K(halil)
Quimby, George Irving 1913- ... 57-60
Quimby, Myron J. ... 25-28R
Quimby, Myrtle 1891- ... CAP-2
Earlier sketch in CA 25-28
Quin, Ann (Marie) 1936-1973 ... 11-12R
Obituary ... 45-48
See also DLB 14
See also CLC 6
Quin, Mike
See Ryan, Paul William
Quinan, Jack
See Quinan, John F.
Quinan, John F. 1939- ... 125
Quince, Peter
See Day, George Harold
Quince, Peter Lum
See Ritchie, (Harry) Ward
Quincunx, Ramona J.
See Borgmann, Dmitri A(lfred)
Quincy, Samuel 1734-1789 ... DLB-31
Quinderpunte, Raoul (Cornelius)
1907- ... CANR-15
Earlier sketch in CA 85-88
Quine, Willard Van Orman 1908- ... CANR-16
Earlier sketches in CA 4R, CANR-1
Quin-Harkin, Janet 1941- ... CANR-15
Earlier sketch in CA 81-84
See also SATA 18
Quinlan, Red
See Quinlan, Sterling C(arroll)
Quinlan, Sterling C(arroll) 1916- ... CANR-8
Earlier sketch in CA 5-6R
Quinley, Harold E(arl) 1942- ... 61-64
Quinn, A(lexander) James 1932- ... 29-32R
Quinn, Anthony (Rudolph Oaxaca) 1915-
Brief entry ... 111
Quinn, Arthur 1942- ... 110
Quinn, (Mary) Bernetta 1915- ... 105
Quinn, Charles (Nicholas) 1930- ... 123
Brief entry ... 110
Quinn, David B(eers) 1909- ... CANR-15
Earlier sketch in CA 77-80
Quinn, Edward 1932- ... 77-80
Quinn, Elisabeth 1881-1962 ... SATA-22
Quinn, Esther Casier 1922- ... 7-8R
Quinn, Francis X. 1932- ... CANR-4
Earlier sketch in CA 11-12R
Quinn, Herbert F(urlong) 1910- ... CAP-1
Earlier sketch in CA 19-20
Quinn, James 1919- ... 15-16R
Quinn, James Brian 1928- ... 13-14R
Quinn, Jane Bryant 1939- ... 93-96
Quinn, John Francis 1925- Brief entry ... 115
Quinn, John M(ichael) 1922- ... 45-48
Quinn, John Paul 1943- ... 33-36R
Quinn, John R. 1938- ... 97-100
Quinn, Kenneth (Fleming) 1920- ... CANR-17
Earlier sketch in CA 25-28R
Quinn, Martin
See Smith, Martin Cruz
Quinn, Michael A(lan) 1945- ... CANR-25
Earlier sketch in CA 45-48
Quinn, Niall 1943- ... 108
Quinn, R(obert) M(acLean) 1920- ... 23-24R
Quinn, Sally 1941- ... 65-68
See also AITN 2
Quinn, Seabury (Grandin) 1889-1969 ... 108
Obituary ... 104
Quinn, Simon
See Smith, Martin Cruz
Quinn, Sister Bernetta
See Quinn, (Mary) Bernetta
Quinn, Susan 1940- ... 103
Quinn, Terry 1945- ... CANR-18
Earlier sketch in CA 101
Quinn, Vernon
See Quinn, Elisabeth
Quinn, Vincent 1926- ... 23-24R
Quinn, William Arthur 1920- ... 7-8R
Quinn, Zdenka (Hodbodova) 1942- ... 33-36R
Quinnett, Paul G(uthrie) 1939- ... 114
Quinney, Richard 1934- ... CANR-9
Earlier sketch in CA 57-60
Quinones, Ricardo J(oseph) 1935-
Brief entry ... 112
Quint, Barbara Gilder 1928- ... 103
Quint, Bert 1930- ... 69-72
Quint, Howard H. 1917- ... 97-100
Quint, Jeanne
See Benoliel, Jeanne Quint
Quintal, Claire 1930- ... 15-16R
Quintana, Bertha B(eatrice) 1924-
Brief entry ... 113
Quintana, Frances
See Swadesh, Frances Leon
Quintana, Ricardo (Beckwith) 1898- ... 25-28R
Quintanilla, Maria Aline Griffith y Dexter,
Condesa de 1921- ... 11-12R
Quinto, Leon 1926- ... 37-40R
Quinton, Anthony Meredith 1925- ... CANR-10
Earlier sketch in CA 23-24R
Quirarte, Jacinto 1931- ... 45-48
Quirin, G(eorge) David 1931- ... CANR-9
Earlier sketch in CA 21-22R
Quirin, William L(ouis) 1942- ... 93-96
Quirk, James P(atrick) 1926- ... CANR-7
Earlier sketch in CA 57-60
Quirk, John E(dward) 1920- ... 5-6R
Quirk, Lawrence J. 1923- ... CANR-12
Earlier sketch in CA 25-28R
Quirk, Paul J. 1949- ... 108
Quirk, Randolph 1920- ... CANR-2
Earlier sketch in CA 7-8R
Quirk, Robert E. 1918- ... 2R
Quirk, Thomas Vaughan 1946- ... 122
Quirk, Tom
See Quirk, Thomas Vaughan
Quiroga, Horacio 1878-1937 Brief entry ... 117
See also TCLC 20

Quispel, Gilles 1916- 89-92
Quist, Susan 1944- 57-60
Quitslund, Sonya A(ntoinette) 1935- CANR-1
Earlier sketch in CA 49-52
Quoirez, Francoise 1935- CANR-6
Earlier sketch in CA 49-52
See also CLC 9
Quoist, Michel 1921- 65-68
Quong, Rose Lanu 1879(?)-1972
Obituary 37-40R
Qureshi, Ishtiaq Husain 1903- CAP-1
Earlier sketch in CA 11-12

R

R
See Rees, (Morgan) Goronwy
R. R.
See Iyengar, K(odaganallur) R(amaswami) Srinivasa
Ra, Jong Oh 1945- 85-88
Raab, Lawrence 1946- 65-68
Raab, Menachem 1923- 114
Raab, Robert Allen 1924- 29-32R
Raab, Selwyn 1934- 73-76
Raack, R(ichard) C(harles) 1928- 41-44R
Ra'Anan, Gavriel D. 1954(?)-1983
Obituary 110
Ra'Anan, H. F. Frischwasser
See Ra'Anan, Uri
Ra'Anan, Uri 1926- CANR-25
Earlier sketch in CA 108
Raat, W(illiam) Dirk 1939- CANR-23
Earlier sketch in CA 106
Rabalais, Maria 1921- 61-64
Raban, Jonathan 1942- CANR-17
Earlier sketch in CA 61-64
Rabassa, Gregory 1922- CANR-26
Earlier sketches in CA 45-48, CANR-2
Rabasseire, Henri
See Pachter, Henry M(aximilian)
Rabb, Theodore K. 1937- CANR-10
Earlier sketch in CA 21-22R
Rabbie
See Towers, Maxwell
Rabbitt, Thomas 1943- 57-60
Rabdau, Marianne
See Bakker-Rabdau, Marianne K(atherine)
Rabe, Berniece (Louise) 1928- CANR-1
Earlier sketch in CA 49-52
See also SATA 7
Rabe, David (William) 1940- 85-88
See also DLB 7
See also CLC 4, 8, 33
Rabe, Olive H(anson) ?-1968 CAP-2
Earlier sketch in CA 19-20
See also SATA 13
Rabe, Stephen G(eorge) 1948- 108
Raben, Joseph 1924- CANR-12
Earlier sketch in CA 69-72
Rabi, I(sidor) I(saac) 1898-1988 Obituary 125
Rabie, Jan 1920- 29-32R
Rabikovitz, Dalia 1936- Brief entry 108
Rabikowitz, Dalyah
See Rabikovitz, Dalia
Rabil, Albert, Jr. 1934- CANR-10
Earlier sketch in CA 25-28R
Rabin, A(lbert) I(srael) 1912- CANR-19
Earlier sketches in CA 53-56, CANR-4
Rabin, Chaim 1915- 105
Rabin, Edward H(arold) 1937- 49-52
Rabin, Yitzhak 1922- Brief entry 111
Rabinovich, Abraham 1933- 61-64
Rabinovich, Isaiah 1904-1972 CAP-2
Earlier sketch in CA 25-28
Rabinovitch, Sholem 1859-1916
Brief entry 104
Rabinovitz, Rubin 1938- 21-22R
Rabinow, Paul 1944- CANR-13
Earlier sketch in CA 61-64
Rabinowich, Ellen 1946- 106
See also SATA 29
Rabinowicz, Mordka Harry 1919- 5-6R
Rabinowitch, Alexander 1934- 23-24R
Rabinowitch, Eugene 1901-1973 77-80
Obituary 41-44R
Rabinowitz, Alan 1927- 29-32R
Rabinowitz, Ezekiel 1892- 25-28R
Rabinowitz, Howard Neil 1942- 105
Rabinowitz, Isaac 1909-1988 Obituary 126
Rabinowitz, Louis Isaac 1906-1984
Obituary 113
Rabinowitz, Peter MacGarr 1956- 104
Rabinowitz, Sandy 1954- 103
See also SATA 39, 52
Rabinowitz, Solomon
See Rabinovitch, Sholem
Rabins, Peter V(incent) 1947- 109
Rabkin, Brenda 1945- 101
Rabkin, Eric S. 1946- CANR-4
Earlier sketch in CA 49-52
Rabkin, Gerald Edward 1930- Brief entry 105
Rabkin, Norman C. 1930- CANR-4
Earlier sketch in CA 3R
Rabkin, Richard 1932- 33-36R
Rable, George C(alvin) 1950- 116
Raboff, Ernest Lloyd SATA-37
Raborg, Frederick A(shton), Jr. 1934- CANR-20
Earlier sketch in CA 103
Rabow, Gerald 1928- 25-28R
Rabushka, Alvin 1940- Brief entry 116
Rabuzzi, Kathryn Allen 1938- 113
Raby, Derek Graham 1927- 103
Raby, William L(ouis) 1927- CANR-23
Earlier sketches in CA 19-20R, CANR-8
Race, Jeffrey 1943- 37-40R
Race, Robert Russell 1907-1984 Obituary 113
Racevskis, Karlis 1939- 117
Rachleff, Owen S(pencer) 1934- CANR-14
Earlier sketch in CA 21-22R
Rachlin, Carol K(ing) 1919- 57-60
Rachlin, Harvey (Brant) 1951- CANR-26
Earlier sketch in CA 107
See also SATA 47
Rachlin, Nahid CANR-14
Earlier sketch in CA 81-84
Rachlis, Eugene (Jacob) 1920-1986 5-6R
Obituary 121
See also SATA 50
Rachman, David Jay 1928- 57-60
Rachman, Stanley Jack 1934- 89-92
Rachow, Louis A(ugust) 1927- 57-60
Racina, Thom 1946- CANR-12
Earlier sketch in CA 73-76
Rack, Henry D(enman) 1931- 15-16R
Racker, Efraim 1913- 89-92
Rackham, Arthur 1867-1939 SATA-15
Rackham, John
See Phillifent, John Thomas
Rackham, Thomas W(illiam) 1919- 25-28R
Rackin, Phyllis 1933- 85-88
Rackman, Emanuel 1910- 29-32R
Rackowe, Alec 1897- 25-28R
Rad, Gerhard von
See von Rad, Gerhard
Radan, G. T.
See Radan, George T(ivadar)
Radan, George T(ivadar) 1923- 116
Radbill, Samuel X. 1901- 49-52
Radcliff, Alan L(awrence) 1920- 49-52
Radcliff, Peter (Edward, Jr.) 1932- 21-22R
Radcliffe, Ann 1764-1823 DLB-39
Radcliffe, George L. 1878(?)-1974
Obituary 53-56
Radcliffe, Janette
See Roberts, Janet Louise
Radcliffe, Lynn J. 1896- 2R
Radcliffe, Philip (Fitzhugh) 1905-1986
Obituary 120
Radcliffe, Virginia
See Hurst, Virginia Radcliffe
Radcliffe-Brown, A(lfred) R(eginald)
1881-1955 Brief entry 114
Radcliff-Umstead, Douglas 1944- CANR-13
Earlier sketch in CA 33-36R
Raddall, Thomas Head 1903- 2R
See also DLB 68
Raddysh, Garry
See Radison, Garry
Radel, John J(oseph) 1934- 29-32R
Radelet, Louis A(ugust) 1917- 89-92
Rader, Benjamin G(ene) 1935- 21-22R
Rader, Dotson 1942- CANR-11
Earlier sketch in CA 61-64
Rader, Melvin (Miller) 1903-1981 CANR-5
Earlier sketch in CA 13-14R
Rader, Ralph Wilson 1930- 13-14R
Rader, Randall R(ay) 1949- 121
Rader, Rosemary 1931- 112
Rader, (John) Trout (III) 1938- 37-40R
Radest, Howard B(ernard) 1928- 41-44R
Radford, Edwin Isaac 1891- 104
Radford, John 1901-1967 CAP-2
Earlier sketch in CA 21-22
Radford, Richard F(rancis), Jr. 1939- CANR-20
Earlier sketch in CA 104
Radford, Ruby L(orraine) 1891-1971 CANR-4
Earlier sketch in CA 3R
See also SATA 6
Radha, Sivananda 1911- 114
Radhakrishnan, C(hakkorayil) 1939- 57-60
Radhakrishnan, Sarvepalli 1888-1975 CAP-1
Obituary 57-60
Earlier sketch in CA 15-16
Radice, Betty 1912-1985 CANR-12
Obituary 115
Earlier sketch in CA 25-28R
Radice, Giles 1936- CANR-17
Earlier sketch in CA 25-28R
Radiguet, Raymond 1903-1923 DLB-65
See also TCLC 29
Radimsky, Ladislaw 1898-1970
Obituary 29-32R
Radin, Edward D(avid) 1909-1966
Obituary 114
Radin, George 1896-1981 Obituary 102
Radin, Paul 1883-1959 Brief entry 120
Radin, Ruth Yaffe 1938- 124
See also SATA 52
Radison, Garry 1949- 117
Radke, Don 1940- 57-60
Radl, Shirley L(ouise) 1935- CANR-12
Earlier sketch in CA 69-72
Radlauer, David 1952- 106
See also SATA 28
Radlauer, Edward 1921- CANR-13
Earlier sketch in CA 69-72
See also SATA 15
Radlauer, Ruth Shaw 1926- CANR-13
Earlier sketch in CA 81-84
See also SATA 15
Radler, D(on) H. 1926- 13-14R
Radley, Eric John 1917- 109
Radley, Gail 1951- CANR-16
Earlier sketch in CA 89-92
See also SATA 25
Radley, Paul John 1962- 121
Radley, Sheila
See Robinson, Sheila Mary
Radley, Virginia L. 1927- 25-28R
Radner, Roy 1927- 49-52
Radnoti, Miklos 1909-1944 Brief entry 118
See also TCLC 16
Rado, Alexander
See Rado, Sandor
Rado, James 1939- 105
See also CLC 17
Rado, Sandor 1900-1981 109
Obituary 105
Radoff, Morris L(eon) 1905-1978 85-88
Obituary 81-84
Radom, Matthew 1905- 57-60
Radosh, Ronald 1937- 101
Radtke, Guenter 1920- 110
Radtke, Gunter
See Radtke, Guenter
Radvanyi, Janos 1922- 41-44R
Radvanyi, Netty 1900-1983 85-88
Obituary 110
Radwanski, Pierre A(rthur) 1903- CAP-2
Earlier sketch in CA 23-24
Radwanski-Szinagel, Dr. Pierre A.
See Radwanski, Pierre A(rthur)
Radway, Ann
See Geis, Richard E(rwin)
Radway, Janice A(nne) 1949- 121
Radyr, Tomos
See Haldane-Stevenson, James Patrick
Radzinowicz, Leon 1906- CANR-26
Earlier sketch in CA 106
Rae, Daphne 1933- 109
Rae, (Margaret) Doris 1907- CANR-15
Earlier sketches in CA 11-12, CAP-1
Rae, Douglas W(hiting) 1939- 77-80
Rae, Evonne 1928-1974 Obituary 104
Rae, Gwynedd 1892-1977 65-68
See also SATA 37
Rae, Hugh C(rauford) 1935- CANR-8
Earlier sketch in CA 19-20R
Rae, John B(ell) 1911- 13-14R
Rae, John Malcolm 1931- CANR-4
Earlier sketch in CA 2R
Rae, Milford Andersen 1946- CANR-8
Earlier sketch in CA 61-64
Rae, Rusty
See Rae, Milford Andersen
Rae, Walter 1916- 57-60
Rae, Wesley D(ennis) 1932- 23-24R
Raebeck, Lois 1921- 13-14R
See also SATA 5
Raeburn, Antonia 1934- 101
Raeburn, John (Hay) 1941- 57-60
See also CLC 34
Raeburn, Michael 1940- 107
Raeburn, Michael 1943- 103
Raef, Laura (Gladys) C(auble) CANR-11
Earlier sketch in CA 29-32R
Raeff, Marc 1923- 61-64
Rael, Leyla 1948- 106
Raelin, Joseph A(lan) 1948- 125
Raeschild, Sheila 1936- CANR-22
Earlier sketch in CA 105
Rafael, Gideon 1913- Brief entry 106
Rafelson, Bob 1933(?)- Brief entry 112
Raffa, Frederick Anthony 1944- 53-56
Raffaele, Joseph A(ntonio) 1916- CANR-8
Earlier sketch in CA 7-8R
Raffel, Burton 1928- CANR-7
Earlier sketch in CA 11-12R
Raffelock, David 1897- CAP-2
Earlier sketch in CA 25-28
See also AITN 1
Rafferty, Kathleen Kelly 1915-1981
Obituary 103
Rafferty, Max L. 1917-1982 CANR-1
Obituary 107
Earlier sketch in CA 2R
Rafferty, Milton 1932- 101
Rafferty, S.S.
See Hurley, John J(erome)
Raffini, James O. 1941- 117
Raftery, Gerald (Bransfield) 1905- CAP-1
Earlier sketch in CA 13-14
See also SATA 11
Ragan, David 1925- 65-68
Ragan, Sam(uel Talmadge) 1915- 15-16R
Ragan, William Burk 1896-1973 CANR-2
Earlier sketch in CA 3R
Ragaway, Martin A(rnold) 1928- CANR-12
Earlier sketch in CA 61-64
Ragen, Joseph E(dward) 1897-1971 CAP-2
Obituary 33-36R
Earlier sketch in CA 21-22
Raghavan, Manayath D. 1892- CAP-2
Earlier sketch in CA 19-20
Ragins, Sanford 117
Raglan, Baron
See Raglan, FitzRoy
Raglan, FitzRoy 1885-1964 7-8R
Ragni, Gerome 1942- 105
See also CLC 17
Rago, Henry Anthony 1915-1969 CAP-2
Earlier sketch in CA 25-28
Rago, Louis J(oseph von) 1924- 9-10R
Ragosta, Millie J(ane) 1931- CANR-12
Earlier sketch in CA 73-76
Ragsdale, Ray W(aldo) 1909- 45-48
Ragsdale, W(arner) B(ernice) 1898-1986 73-76
Obituary 121
Raguin, Yves (Emile) 1912- 81-84
Ragusa, Olga (M.) 1922- 122
Rahill, Peter J(ames) 1910- 5-6R
Rahim, Enayetur 1938- 107
Rahl, James A(ndrew) 1917- 77-80
Rahm, David A. 1931- 57-60
Rahman, Abdul
See Wayman, Tony Russell
Rahman, F.
See Rahman, Fazlur
Rahman, Fazlur 1919-1988 Obituary 126
Rahn, Joan Elma 1929- CANR-13
Earlier sketch in CA 37-40R
See also SATA 27
Rahner, Karl 1904-1984 109
Obituary 112
Rahner, Raymond M. 101
Rahsepar
See Yar-Shater, Ehsan O(llah)
Rahtjen, Bruce D(onald) 1933- 21-22R
Rahv, Betty T(homas) 1931- 105
Rahv, Philip
See Greenberg, Ivan
See also CLC 24
Rai, Kul B(husan) 1937- 105
Rai, Navab
See Srivastava, Dhanpat Rai
Raia, Anthony P(aul) 1928- 61-64
Raible, Alton (Robert) 1918- SATA-35
Raiff, Stan 1930- 61-64
See also SATA 11
Railton, Esther P(auline) 1929- 101
Raimi, Sam(uel M.) 1959- 123
Raimond, C. E.
See Robins, Elizabeth
Raimy, Eric 1942- 93-96
Raimy, Victor 1913- 81-84
Rainbird, George (Meadus) 1905-1986
Obituary 120
Rainbow-Wind, Shandor
See Weiss, (Paul) Shandor
Raine, Craig 1944- 108
See also DLB 40
See also CLC 32
Raine, Kathleen (Jessie) 1908- 85-88
See also DLB 20
See also CLC 7, 45
Raine, Norman Reilly 1895-1971
Obituary 33-36R
Raine, Richard
See Sawkins, Raymond H(arold)
Rainer, George
See Greenburger, Ingrid Elisabeth
Rainer, Julia
See Goode, Ruth
Raines, Howell (Hiram) 1943- 73-76
Raines, John C. 1933- 73-76
Raines, Robert A(rnold) 1926- CANR-7
Earlier sketch in CA 13-14R
Raines, Shirley (Carol) 1945- 113
Rainey, Bill G. 1926- 89-92
Rainey, Buck
See Rainey, Bill G.
Rainey, Gene E(dward) 1934- 25-28R
Rainey, Homer Price 1896-1985 Obituary 118
Rainey, Patricia Ann 1937- 49-52
Rainey, W. B.
See Blassingame, Wyatt Rainey
Rainham, Thomas
See Barren, Charles (MacKinnon)
Rainis, Janis 1865-1929 TCLC-29
Rainsberger, Todd J(effrey) 1951- 106
Rainsford, George Nichols 1928- 49-52
Raintree, Lee
See Sellers, Con(nie Leslie, Jr.)
Rainwater, (Mary) Catherine 1953- 119
Rainwater, Dorothy T(hornton) 1918- CANR-1
Earlier sketch in CA 45-48
Rainwater, Lee 1928- 53-56
Raistrick, Arthur 1896- CANR-3
Earlier sketch in CA 11-12R
Raisz, Erwin J(osephus) 1893-1968 4R
Obituary 103
Raitt, A(lan) W(illiam) 1930- 29-32R
Raizis, M(arios) Byron 1931- 41-44R
Rajan, Balachandra 1920- 69-72
Rajan, M(annarswamighala) S(reeranga)
1920- CANR-13
Earlier sketch in CA 13-14R
Rajan, Tilottama 1951- 107
Rajanen, Aini 109
Rajaram
See Iyengar, K(odaganallur) R(amaswami) Srinivasa
Rajasekharaiah, T(umkur) R(udraradhya)
1926- 33-36R
Rajec, Elizabeth M(olnar) 1931- 109
Rajneesh, Acharya 1931- 93-96
Rajneesh, Bhagwan Shree
See Rajneesh, Acharya
Rajski, Raymond B. 1917- 23-24R
Raju, Poolla Tirupati 1904- 33-36R
Rakel, Robert E(dwin) 1932- CANR-26
Earlier sketch in CA 107
Raknes, Ola 1887-1975 CAP-2
Earlier sketch in CA 29-32
Rako, Susan Mandell 1939- 117
Rakoff, Alvin 1927- 102
Rakosi, Carl
See Rawley, Callman
See also CAAS 5
See also CLC 47
Rakosi, Matyas 1892-1971 Obituary 29-32R
Rakove, Jack N(orman) 1947- 93-96
Rakove, Milton L(eon) 1918-1983 CANR-15
Obituary 111
Earlier sketch in CA 65-68
Rakowski, James Peter 1945- 105
Rakowski, John 1922- 106
Rakstis, Ted J(ay) 1932- 101
Ralbovsky, Martin Paul 1942- 49-52
Rale, Nero
See Burgess, M(ichael) R(oy)
Raleigh, Donald J(oseph) 1949- 125

INDEX

Raleigh, John Henry 1920- ... CANR-3
Earlier sketch in CA 2R
Raleigh, Richard
See Lovecraft, H(oward) P(hillips)
Raley, Harold (Cecil) 1934- ... 41-44R
Raley, Patricia E(ward) 1940- ... 73-76
Raley, Rowena
See McCulley, Johnston
Rallentando, H. P.
See Sayers, Dorothy L(eigh)
Ralph, David Clinton 1922- ... CANR-2
Earlier sketch in CA 5-6R
Ralph, Elizabeth K(ennedy) 1921- ... 33-36R
Ralph, Julian 1853-1903 ... DLB-23
Ralph, Margaret Nutting 1941- ... 121
Ralphs, Sheila 1923- ... 106
Ralston, Alma (Smith Payne) ... CANR-11
Earlier sketch in CA 19-20R
Ralston, Gilbert A(lexander) 1912- ... CANR-2
Earlier sketch in CA 45-48
Ralston, James Kenneth 1896- ... 49-52
Ralston, Jan
See Dunlop, Agnes M. R.
Ralston, Leonard F. 1925- ... 45-48
Ralston, Melvin B. 1937- ... 49-52
Ram, Immanuel
See Velikovsky, Immanuel
Rama
See Gupta, Ram Chandra
Rama, Swami
See Swami Rama
Ramacharaka, Yogi
See Atkinson, William Walker
Ramage, Edwin S(tephen) 1929- ... 65-68
Ramage, James A(lfred) 1940- ... 61-64
Ramal, Walter
See de la Mare, Walter (John)
Ramamurty, K(otamraju) Bhaskara 1924- ... 53-56
Raman, Chandrasekhara Venkata
1888-1970 Obituary ... 113
Ramanujan, A(ttipat) K(rishnaswami)
1929- ... CANR-24
Earlier sketches in CA 19-20R, CANR-8
Ramanujan, Molly 1932- ... CANR-24
Earlier sketch in CA 29-32R
Ramanujan, Shouri
See Ramanujan, Molly
Rama Rau, Dhanvanthi (Handoo)
1893-1987 Obituary ... 123
Brief entry ... 106
Rama Rau, Santha
See Wattles, Santha Rama Rau
Ramaswamy, Mysore 1902- ... CAP-1
Earlier sketch in CA 13-14
Ramati, Alexander 1921- ... CANR-7
Earlier sketch in CA 13-14R
Ramati, Yohanan (Joseph) 1921- ... 111
Ramazani, Rouhollah K(aregar) 1928- ... CANR-26
Earlier sketches in CA 13-14R, CANR-10
Rambam, Cyvia
See Rambert, Marie
Rambam, Myriam
See Rambert, Marie
Rambeau, James (Morris) 1938- ... 117
Ramberg, Bennett 1946- ... 111
Rambert, Marie 1888-1982 ... 103
Obituary ... 107
Rambo, Lewis Ray 1943- ... 109
Rame, David
See Divine, Arthur Durham
Rameh, Clea 1927- ... 53-56
Ramenofsky, Ann F. 1942- ... 125
Ramey, James W(alter) 1928- ... 112
Ramey, Mary Ann 1947- ... 125
Ramge, Sebastian Victor 1930- ... 11-12R
Ramirez, Carolyn H(olmes) 1933- ... CANR-2
Earlier sketch in CA 5-6R
Ramirez de Arellano, Diana 1919- ... 45-48
Ramis, Harold (Allen) 1944- Brief entry ... 124
Ramke, Bin 1947- ... CANR-14
Earlier sketch in CA 81-84
Ramm, Bernard L(awrence) 1916-
Brief entry ... 112
Rammelkamp, Julian S(turtevant) 1917- ... 19-20R
Ramo, Simon 1913- Brief entry ... 111
Ramond, Charles K(night) 1930- ... 101
Ramos, Suzanne 1942- ... 101
Ramos-Oliveira, Antonio 1907-1973
Obituary ... 104
Ramp, Eugene A(ugust) 1942- ... 49-52
Rampa, Tuesday Lobsang
See Hoskin, Cyril Henry
Rampersad, Arnold ... CLC-44
Ramquist, Grace (Bess) Chapman
1907- ... CANR-3
Earlier sketch in CA 11-12R
Ramrus, Al 1930- ... 105
Rams, Edwin M(arion) 1922- ... 19-20R
Ramsaur, Ernest Edmondson, Jr. 1915- ... 41-44R
Ramsay, David 1749-1815 ... DLB-30
Ramsay, J(ames) A(rthur) 1909-1988
Obituary ... 124
Ramsay, Raymond (Henry) 1927- ... 77-80
Ramsay, William M(cDowell) 1922- ... CANR-12
Earlier sketch in CA 15-16R
Ramsbottom, John 1885-1974 Obituary ... 53-56
Ramsdell, Kristin (Romeis) 1940- ... 125
Ramsden, E. H. ... 102
Ramsden, Herbert 1927- ... CANR-25
Earlier sketch in CA 108
Ramsden, John Andrew 1947- ... 108
Ramsell, Donald 1926(?)-1983 Obituary ... 110
Ramsett, David E. 1942- ... 29-32R
Ramsey, Charles E(ugene) 1923- ... 15-16R
Ramsey, Dan(ny Clarence) 1945- ... 101
Ramsey, Eric
See Hagberg, David J(ames)
Ramsey, (Charles) Frederic, Jr. 1915- ... 7-8R
Ramsey, G(ordon) C(lark) 1941- ... CANR-9
Earlier sketch in CA 21-22R
Ramsey, George Wilson 1937- ... 113
Ramsey, Ian T(homas) 1915-1972 ... CANR-4
Earlier sketch in CA 7-8R
Ramsey, Jackson E. 1938- ... 122
Ramsey, Jarold 1937- ... 33-36R
Ramsey, John F(raser) 1907- ... 49-52
Ramsey, Lee C(arter) 1935- ... 120
Ramsey, (Arthur) Michael 1904-1988 ... CANR-14
Obituary ... 125
Earlier sketch in CA 77-80
Ramsey, (Robert) Paul 1913-1988 ... CANR-1
Obituary ... 124
Earlier sketch in CA 2R
Ramsey, Paul 1924- ... 41-44R
Ramsey, Paul W. 1905-1976 Obituary ... 69-72
Ramsey, Robert D. 1934- ... 25-28R
Ramsey, Roy S. 1920(?)-1976 Obituary ... 65-68
Ramsey, Russell W. 1935- ... 124
Ramseyer, John A(lvin) 1908-1968 ... CANR-4
Earlier sketch in CA 7-8R
Ramseyer, Lloyd L. 1899- ... CAP-2
Earlier sketch in CA 19-20
Ramskill, Valerie Patricia Roskams ... CAP-1
Earlier sketch in CA 9-10
Ramson, W(illiam) S(tanley) 1933- ... 45-48
Ramundo, Bernard A. 1925- ... 21-22R
Rana, J.
See Bhatia, Jamunadevi
Ranadive, Gail 1944- ... 53-56
See also SATA 10
Rand, Ann (Binkley) ... 106
See also SATA 30
Rand, Austin Loomer 1905- ... 89-92
Rand, Ayn 1905-1982 ... 15-16R
Obituary ... 105
See also CLC 3, 30, 44
Rand, Brett
See Norwood, Victor G(eorge) C(harles)
Rand, Christopher 1912-1968 ... 77-80
Rand, Clayton (Thomas) 1891-1971 ... 5-6R
Obituary ... 29-32R
Rand, Earl (James) 1933- ... 23-24R
Rand, Frank Prentice 1889- ... CAP-1
Earlier sketch in CA 11-12
Rand, J. H.
See Holland, James R.
Rand, James S.
See Attenborough, Bernard George
Rand, Paul 1914- ... 23-24R
See also SATA 6
Rand, Peter 1942- ... 77-80
Rand, Willard J., Jr. 1913- ... 11-12R
Randal, Beatrice (a pseudonym) 1916- ... 61-64
Randal, Vera 1922- ... 11-12R
Randall, Belle 1940- ... 118
Randall, Bob 1937- ... 106
Randall, Charles Edgar 1897- ... 41-44R
Randall, Clarence Belden 1891-1967 ... CAP-1
Earlier sketch in CA 13-14
Randall, Clay
See Adams, Clifton
Randall, Dale B(ertrand) J(onas) 1929- ... CANR-2
Earlier sketch in CA 5-6R
Randall, David A(nton) 1905-1975
Obituary ... 57-60
Randall, Diane
See Ross, W(illiam) E(dward) D(aniel)
Randall, Donald A. 1933- ... 61-64
Randall, Dudley (Felker) 1914- ... CANR-23
Earlier sketch in CA 25-28R
See also BW
See also DLB 41
See also CLC 1
Randall, Florence Engel 1917- ... 41-44R
See also SATA 5
Randall, Francis Ballard 1931- ... 11-12R
Randall, Henry S. 1811-1876 ... DLB-30
Randall, J. G.
See Randall, James Garfield
Randall, James G.
See Randall, James Garfield
See also DLB 17
Randall, James Garfield 1881-1953
Brief entry ... 118
Randall, Janet
See Young, Janet Randall
and Young, Robert W(illiam)
Randall, Jo Anne Yarus 1942- ... 118
Randall, John E(rnest, Jr.) 1924- ... 65-68
Randall, John Herman, Jr. 1899-1980 ... CANR-1
Obituary ... 102
Earlier sketch in CA 3R
Randall, John L(eslie) 1933- ... 107
Randall, Joseph Hungerford 1897- ... 3R
Randall, Julia (Sawyer) 1923- ... 33-36R
Randall, Laura 1935- ... 37-40R
Randall, Lillian M. C. 1931- ... 23-24R
Randall, Margaret 1936- ... 41-44R
Randall, Marta ... 107
Randall, Mary
See Colver, Alice Mary (Ross)
Randall, Mercedes M. 1895-1977 ... 15-16R
Obituary ... 69-72
Randall, Monica 1944- ... 97-100
Randall, Randolph C. 1900- ... 19-20R
Randall, Robert
See Silverberg, Robert
Randall, Ruth (Elaine) Painter 1892-1971 ... 1R
Obituary ... 103
See also SATA 3
Randall, Steven
See Andrews, Clarence A(delbert)
Randall, Willard Sterne 1942- ... 69-72
Randall-Mills, Elizabeth West 1906- ... 15-16R
Randel, William (Peirce) 1909- ... 13-14R
Randell, Beverley
See Price, Beverley Joan
Randell, John Bulmer 1918-1982 ... 109
Obituary ... 106
Randers-Pehrson, Justine Davis 1910- ... 111
Randhawa, Mohinder Singh 1909- ... 29-32R
Randi, James 1928- ... 117
Randisi, Robert J(oseph) 1951- ... 116
Randles, Anthony V(ictor), Jr. 1942- ... 65-68
Randles, Slim
See Randles, Anthony V(ictor), Jr.
Randoll, Anthony
See Blacking, John (Anthony Randoll)
Randolph, A(sa) Philip 1889-1979 ... 125
Obituary ... 85-88
See also BW
Randolph, Arthur C.
See Greene, A(lvin) C(arl)
Randolph, Boynton, M.D.
See Ellis, Edward S(ylvester)
Randolph, David James 1934- ... CANR-3
Earlier sketch in CA 49-52
Randolph, Ellen
See Ross, W(illiam) E(dward) D(aniel)
Randolph, Geoffrey
See Ellis, Edward S(ylvester)
Randolph, Georgiana Ann 1908-1957
Brief entry ... 116
Randolph, Gordon
See von Block, Bela W(illiam)
and von Block, Sylvia
Randolph, J. H.
See Ellis, Edward S(ylvester)
Randolph, John 1915- ... 45-48
Randolph, Lieutenant J. H.
See Ellis, Edward S(ylvester)
Randolph, Marion
See Rodell, Marie F(reid)
Randolph, Melanie
See Ragosta, Millie J(ane)
Randolph, Nancy
See Robb, Inez (Callaway)
Randolph, Thomas 1605-1635 ... DLB-58
Randolph, Vance 1892- ... 105
Random, Alan
See Kay, Ernest
Random, Alex
See Rowland, D(onald) S(ydney)
Rands, William Brighty 1823-1882 ... SATA-17
Ranga, N. G. 1900- ... 29-32R
Ranganathan, S(hiyali) R(amamrita)
1892-1972 ... CANR-5
Earlier sketch in CA 5-6R
Range, Willard Edgar Allen 1910- ... 2R
Rangel, Carlos 1929-1988 ... 104
Obituary ... 124
Rangell, Leo 1913- ... 105
Ranger, Ken
See Creasey, John
Ranger, Paul 1933- ... 37-40R
Ranger, T(erence) O(sborn) 1929- ... CANR-19
Earlier sketch in CA 25-28R
Ranis, Gustav 1929- ... CANR-3
Earlier sketch in CA 11-12R
Ranis, Peter 1935- ... 41-44R
Ranjee
See Shahani, Ranjee
Rank, Benjamin (Keith) 1911- ... 109
Rank, Hugh (Duke) 1932- ... CANR-12
Earlier sketch in CA 73-76
Rank, Maureen Joy 1947- ... 117
Ranki, Gyoergy 1930-1988 Obituary ... 124
Rankin, Daniel S(tanislaus) 1895-1972 ... CAP-1
Earlier sketch in CA 15-16
Rankin, David J. 1945- ... 108
Rankin, Herbert David 1931- ... 103
Rankin, Hugh F(ranklin) 1913- ... CANR-1
Earlier sketch in CA 2R
Rankin, Jeannette 1880-1973 Obituary ... 41-44R
Rankin, Judith Torluemke 1945-
Brief entry ... 107
Rankin, Judy
See Rankin, Judith Torluemke
Rankin, Karl Lott 1898- ... CAP-1
Earlier sketch in CA 15-16
Rankin, Paula C(lark) 1945- ... CANR-21
Earlier sketch in CA 104
Rankin, Robert 1915- ... 126
Brief entry ... 108
Rankin, Robert P(arks) 1912- ... 77-80
Rankin, Ruth (DeLone) I(rvine) 1924- ... 61-64
Rankine, John
See Mason, Douglas R(ankine)
Rankine, Paul Scott 1909(?)-1983
Obituary ... 109
Ranly, Ernest W. 1930- ... 37-40R
Ranney, Agnes V. 1916- ... 5-6R
See also SATA 6
Ranney, (Joseph) Austin 1920- ... 77-80
Rannit, Aleksis 1914-1985 Obituary ... 114
Brief entry ... 109
Ranous, Charles A. 1912- ... 15-16R
Ransel, David L(orimer) 1939- ... 73-76
Ransford, Oliver 1914- ... CANR-10
Earlier sketch in CA 21-22R
Ransley, Peter 1931- ... CANR-21
Earlier sketch in CA 69-72
Ransohoff, Paul M(artin) 1948- ... 103
Ransom, Bill 1945- ... CANR-19
Earlier sketch in CA 101
Ransom, Candice F. 1952- ... 121
See also SATA 49, 52
Ransom, Harry Howe 1922- ... 11-12R
Ransom, Jay Ellis 1914- ... CANR-20
Earlier sketches in CA 9-10R, CANR-3
Ransom, John Crowe 1888-1974 ... CANR-6
Obituary ... 49-52
Earlier sketch in CA 7-8R
See also DLB 45, 63
See also CLC 2, 4, 5, 11, 24
Ransom, William Michael 1945-
Brief entry ... 108
Ransom, William R. 1876-1973
Obituary ... 37-40R
Ransome, Arthur Michell 1884-1967 ... 73-76
See also SATA 22
See also CLR 8
Ransome, Eleanor 1915- ... 93-96
Ransome, Stephen
See Davis, Frederick C(lyde)
Ransome-Davies, Basil
See Colley, Iain
Ransone, Coleman B(ernard), Jr. 1920- ... 45-48
Rant, Tol E.
See Longyear, Barry Brookes
Ranum, Orest Allen 1933- ... CANR-8
Earlier sketch in CA 11-12R
Ranum, Patricia M(cGroder) 1932- ... 45-48
Ranz, James 1921- ... 11-12R
Ranz, Jim
See Ranz, James
Ranzini, Addis Durning 1909-1983
Obituary ... 110
Rao, B. Shiva 1900(?)-1975 Obituary ... 61-64
Rao, C. H. Hanumantha 1929- ... CANR-7
Earlier sketch in CA 19-20R
Rao, R(anganatha) P(admanabha)
1924- ... 13-14R
Rao, Raja 1909- ... 73-76
See also CLC 25
Raoul, Anthony
See Wilmot, Anthony
Rapaport, Herman 1947- ... 114
Rapaport, Ionel F. 1909(?)-1972
Obituary ... 37-40R
Rapaport, Stella F(read) ... 4R
Raper, Arthur F(ranklin) 1899-1979 ... CANR-12
Obituary ... 89-92
Earlier sketch in CA 61-64
Raper, J(ulius) R(owan) 1938- ... 33-36R
Raper, Jack
See Raper, J(ulius) R(owan)
Raphael, Bertram 1936- ... 97-100
Raphael, Beverley 1934- ... 117
Raphael, Chaim 1908- ... CANR-16
Earlier sketch in CA 85-88
Raphael, Dan 1952- ... 104
Raphael, Dana ... 61-64
Raphael, David D(aiches) 1916- ... CANR-20
Earlier sketches in CA 7-8R, CANR-2
Raphael, Elaine
See Bolognese, Elaine Raphael
(Chionchio)
See also SATA 23
Raphael, Frederic (Michael) 1931- ... CANR-1
Earlier sketch in CA 4R
See also DLB 14
See also CLC 2, 14
Raphael, Jay
See Josephs, Ray
Raphael, Marc Lee 1942(?)- Brief entry ... 113
Raphael, Phyllis 1940- ... 45-48
Raphael, Rick 1919- ... CANR-10
Earlier sketch in CA 21-22R
Raphael, Robert 1927- ... 45-48
Raphael, Sandra (Joan) 1939- ... 104
Raphaelson, Elliot 1937- ... 124
Raphaelson, Samson 1896-1983 ... 65-68
Obituary ... 110
See also DLB 44
Rapkin, Chester 1918- ... 19-20R
Rapoport, Amos 1929- ... 65-68
Rapoport, Anatol 1911- ... 41-44R
Rapoport, Janis 1946- ... CANR-18
Earlier sketch in CA 101
Rapoport, Louis (Harvey) 1942- ... 117
Rapoport, Rhona (Ross) 1927- ... CANR-8
Earlier sketch in CA 61-64
Rapoport, Robert Norman 1924- ... CANR-17
Earlier sketches in CA 7-8R, CANR-2
Rapoport, Roger 1946- ... 33-36R
Rapoport, Ron 1940- ... 89-92
Rapp, Doris Jean 1929- ... CANR-21
Earlier sketch in CA 37-40R
Rapp, Joel ... AITN-1
Rapp, Lynn ... AITN-1
Rappaport, Alfred 1932- Brief entry ... 110
Rappaport, Armin H. 1916- Brief entry ... 111
Rappaport, David 1907- ... CAP-2
Earlier sketch in CA 19-20
Rappaport, Eva 1924- ... 29-32R
See also SATA 6
Rappaport, Julian 1942- Brief entry ... 112
Rappaport, Roy A(braham) 1926- ... 41-44R
Rappaport, Sheldon R(aphael) 1926- ... 29-32R
Rappole, John H(ilton) 1946- ... 123
Rappoport, Ken 1935- ... CANR-20
Earlier sketches in CA 53-56, CANR-4
Rappoport, Leon 1932- ... 41-44R
Rapson, Richard L(awrence) 1937- ... CANR-10
Earlier sketch in CA 23-24R
Rarick, Carrie 1911- ... 115
See also SATA 41
Rasberry, Robert W. 1945- ... 110
Rasberry, Salli 1940- ... CANR-23
Earlier sketch in CA 107
Rasch, Sunna Cooper 1925- ... 105
Raschke, Carl A(llan) 1944- ... 104
Rascoe, Jesse Ed
See Bartholomew, Ed(ward Ellsworth)
Rascoe, Judith 1941(?)- ... 107
Rascovich, Mark 1918(?)-1976 Obituary ... 69-72

Rasey, Ruth M.
See Simpson, Ruth Mary Rasey
Rash, Dora Eileen Agnew (Wallace) 1897- ... CANR-2
Earlier sketch in CA 7-8R
Rash, J(esse) Keogh 1906- ... 93-96
Rashidof, Sharif Rashidovich
See Rashidov, Sharaf Rashidovich
Rashidov, Sharaf Rashidovich 1917(?)-1983 Obituary ... 111
Rashke, Richard L. 1936- ... CANR-24
Earlier sketch in CA 107
Raskin, A(braham) H(enry) 1911- ... 104
Raskin, Barbara 1935- Brief entry ... 126
Raskin, Edith Lefkowitz 1908- ... CANR-3
Earlier sketch in CA 11-12R
See also SATA 9
Raskin, Ellen 1928-1984 ... 23-24R
Obituary ... 113
See also SATA 2, 38
See also DLB 52
See also CLR 1, 12
Raskin, Eugene 1909- ... 33-36R
Raskin, Herbert A(lfred) 1919-1979 ... 29-32R
Obituary ... 122
Raskin, Jonah 1942- ... 81-84
Raskin, Joseph 1897-1982 ... CANR-13
Obituary ... 105
Earlier sketch in CA 33-36R
See also SATA 12, 29
Raskin, Marcus G. 1934- ... 37-40R
Rasky, Frank (John) 1923- Brief entry ... 107
Rasky, Harry 1928- ... 105
Rasmusen, Henry N(eil) 1909- ... 5-6R
Rasmussen, David (William) 1942- ... 53-56
Rasmussen, Douglas B(ruce) 1948- ... 119
Rasmussen, John Peter 1933- Brief entry ... 110
Rasmussen, Knud Johan Victor 1879-1933 Brief entry ... 113
See also SATA 34
Rasmussen, Larry L. 1939- ... 118
Rasmussen, Louis J(ames, Jr.) 1921- ... 73-76
Rasmussen, R. Kent 1943- ... 93-96
Rasmussen, Wayne D(avid) 1915- ... 33-36R
Rasof, Henry 1946- ... 113
Rasor, Eugene L(atimer) 1936- ... 89-92
Raspberry, William J(ames) 1935- ... 122
Brief entry ... 110
See also BW
Rasponi, Lanfranco 1914-1983 ... 19-20R
Obituary ... 109
Rasputin, Maria
See Bern, Maria Rasputin Soloviev
Rasputin, Valentin (Grigorevich) 1937- Brief entry ... 108
Rass, Rebecca 1936- ... 105
Rast, Walter E(mil) 1930- ... 73-76
Ratch, Jerry 1944- ... 118
Ratcliff, Carter 1941- ... CANR-13
Earlier sketch in CA 61-64
Ratcliff, John Drury 1903-1973 ... 108
Obituary ... 106
Ratcliff, Ruth 1905- ... 121
Ratcliffe, Barrie M(ichael) 1940- ... 114
Ratcliffe, F(rederick) W(illiam) 1927- ... 125
Ratcliffe, James M(axwell) 1925- ... 21-22R
Ratcliffe, James P.
See Mencken, H(enry) L(ouis)
Ratcliffe, T(om) A(rundel) 1910- ... CAP-2
Earlier sketch in CA 25-28
Ratermanis, J(anis) B(ernhards) 1904- ... 9-10R
Rath, Frederick L(ouis), Jr. 1913- ... 41-44R
Rath, Patricia M(ink) ... 19-20R
Rath, R. John 1910- ... 37-40R
Rath, Sara 1941- ... 108
Rathbone, Julian 1935- ... 101
See also CLC 41
Rathbone, Lucy 1896- ... 7-8R
Rathbone, Ouida Bergere 1886(?)-1974 Obituary ... 53-56
Rathbone, Robert Reynolds 1916- ... 21-22R
Rathe, Alex W(erner) 1912- ... 19-20R
Rathenau, Walther 1867-1922 Brief entry ... 121
Rather, Dan (Irvin) 1931- ... CANR-9
Earlier sketch in CA 53-56
See also AITN 1
Rather, L(elland) J(oseph) 1913- ... 77-80
Rathjen, Carl Henry 1909- ... CANR-2
Earlier sketch in CA 7-8R
See also SATA 11
Rathjen, Frederick W(illiam) 1929- ... 41-44R
Rathlesberger, James (H.) 1948- Brief entry ... 114
Rathmell, J(ohn) C. A. 1935- ... 11-12R
Rathmell, Neil 1947- ... 104
Ratigan, Eleanor Eldridge 1916- ... 5-6R
Ratigan, William 1910- ... 29-32R
Ratiu, Ion 1917- ... 7-8R
Ratliff, Charles Edward, Jr. 1926- ... CANR-1
Earlier sketch in CA 4R
Ratliff, Gerald Lee 1944- ... 107
Ratliff, Richard C(harles) 1922- ... 65-68
Ratliffe, Sharon A(nn) 1939- ... 61-64
Ratner, Joseph 1901(?)-1979 Obituary ... 85-88
Ratner, Leonard G(ilbert) 1916- ... 21-22R
Ratner, Lorman 1932- ... CANR-10
Earlier sketch in CA 25-28R
Ratner, Marc L. 1926- ... 45-48
Ratner, Rochelle 1948- ... CANR-12
Earlier sketch in CA 33-36R
Ratner, Sidney 1908- ... 23-24R
Ratner, Stanley C(harles) 1925- ... 15-16R
Rattenbury, Arnold (Foster) 1921- ... 29-32R
Ratti, John 1933- ... 73-76
Ratti, Oscar ... 41-44R
Rattigan, Terence (Mervyn) 1911-1977 ... 85-88
Obituary ... 73-76
See also DLB 13
See also CLC 7
Rattner, David S(amuel) 1916- ... 69-72
Rattray, Everett T(ennant) 1932-1980 ... 89-92
Obituary ... 97-100
Rattray, Simon
See Trevor, Elleston
Ratzan, Scott C. 1962- ... 124
Rau, Dhanvanthi (Handoo) Rama
See Rama Rau, Dhanvanthi (Handoo)
Rau, Margaret 1913- ... CANR-8
Earlier sketch in CA 61-64
See also SATA 9
See also CLR 8
Rauch, Basil 1908-1986 ... CAP-2
Obituary ... 119
Earlier sketch in CA 19-20
Rauch, Constance 1937- ... 57-60
Rauch, Earl Mac 1950(?)- Brief entry ... 118
Rauch, Georg Von
See Von Rauch, Georg
Rauch, Irmengard 1933- ... CANR-11
Earlier sketch in CA 21-22R
Rauch, Leo 1927- ... 110
Rauch, Mabel Thompson 1888-1972 ... 7-8R
Obituary ... 103
See also SATA 26
Rauch, Rufus William, Jr. 1929-1977 Obituary ... 113
Raucher, Alan R(ichard) 1939- ... 118
Raucher, Herman 1928- ... 29-32R
See also SATA 8
Raudive, Konstantin 1909-1974 ... 29-32R
Obituary ... 126
Rauf, Abdur 1924- ... CANR-13
Earlier sketch in CA 73-76
Rauf, Muhammad Abdul
See Abdul-Rauf, Muhammad
Raulston, J(ames) Leonard 1905- ... 89-92
Rault, Walter
See Gorham, Maurice Anthony Coneys
Rauner, Robert M(cKenzie) 1925- ... CANR-1
Earlier sketch in CA 2R
Raunikar, Robert 1931- ... 124
Raup, H(allock) F(loyd) 1901- ... 37-40R
Raup, Robert 1888(?)-1976 Obituary ... 65-68
Rausch, Edward N. 1919- ... CANR-7
Earlier sketch in CA 15-16R
Rausch, Jane M(eyer) 1940- ... 119
Rauschenberg, Roy A(nthony) 1929- ... 45-48
Rauscher, Donald J. 1921- ... 11-12R
Rauschning, Hermann 1887-1982 Obituary ... 109
Raush, Harold L(ester) 1921- Brief entry ... 110
Raushenbush, Esther (Mohr) 1898- ... CAP-1
Earlier sketch in CA 15-16
Ravel, Aviva 1928- ... 119
Raven, Frithjof Andersen 1907-1966 ... CAP-1
Earlier sketch in CA 15-16
Raven, J(ohn) E(arle) 1914-1980 ... 103
Obituary ... 97-100
Raven, Ronald William 1904- ... CANR-23
Earlier sketch in CA 107
Raven, Simon (Arthur Noel) 1927- ... 81-84
See also CLC 14
Ravenal, Earl C(edric) 1931- ... 33-36R
Ravenel, Shannon 1938- ... 108
Ravenna, Roger
See Horbach, Michael
Ravenscroft, Arthur 1924- ... 110
Ravetch, Irving 1915(?)- Brief entry ... 110
Ravetz, Alison 1930- ... 116
Ravetz, Jerome R(aymond) 1929- ... 97-100
Ravetz, Jerry
See Ravetz, Jerome R(aymond)
Ravich, Robert A(lan) 1920- Brief entry ... 113
Ravielli, Anthony 1916- ... CANR-11
Earlier sketch in CA 29-32R
See also SATA 3
Ravikovitch, Dahlia
See Rabikovitz, Dalia
Ravikovitz, Dalia
See Rabikovitz, Dalia
Ravin, Neil 1947- ... 105
Ravindra, Ravi 1939- ... 114
Ravitch, Diane 1938- ... CANR-4
Earlier sketch in CA 53-56
Ravitch, Norman 1936- ... 37-40R
Ravitz, Abe Carl 1927- ... 9-10R
Ravitz, Shlomo 1885-1980 Obituary ... 103
Raw, Isaias 1927- ... 57-60
Rawcliffe, (John) Michael 1934- ... 115
Rawford, W. C.
See Crawford, William (Elbert)
Rawick, George P(hilip) 1929- ... 61-64
Rawles, Beverly A(rcher) 1930- ... 107
Rawley, Callman 1903- ... CANR-12
Earlier sketch in CA 23-24R
Rawley, James A. 1916- ... 21-22R
Rawling, Thomas Jackson 1916- ... 114
Rawling, Tom
See Rawling, Thomas Jackson
Rawlings, Hunter Ripley III 1944- ... 103
Rawlings, John 1930(?)-1981(?) Obituary ... 102
Rawlings, Louisa
See Baumgarten, Sylvia
Rawlings, Marjorie Kinnan 1896-1953 Brief entry ... 104
See also YABC 1
See also DLB 9, 22
See also TCLC 4
Rawlings, Maurice S(kaggs) 1922- ... 108
Rawlins, Clive Leonard 1940- ... CANR-22
Earlier sketch in CA 105
Rawlins, Dennis 1937- ... 45-48
Rawlins, Eustace Robert
See Barton, Eustace Robert
Rawlins, Jack P. 1946- ... 57-60
Rawlins, Jennie Brown 1910- ... CAP-2
Earlier sketch in CA 23-24
Rawlins, Winifred 1907- ... 9-10R
Rawlinson, A(rthur) R(ichard) 1894-1984 Obituary ... 113
Rawlinson, Dick
See Rawlinson, A(rthur) R(ichard)
Rawls, Eugene S. 1927- ... 11-12R
Rawls, James J(abus) 1945- ... 112
Rawls, John Bordley 1921- Brief entry ... 114
Rawls, Philip
See Levinson, Leonard
Rawls, Walter Cecil, Jr. 1928- ... 111
Rawls, Walton (Hendry) 1933- ... 121
Rawls, Wendell L(ee), Jr. 1941- ... CANR-22
Earlier sketch in CA 73-76
Rawls, (Woodrow) Wilson 1913- ... CANR-5
Earlier sketch in CA 3R
See also SATA 22
See also AITN 1
Rawlyk, George Alexander 1935- ... CANR-26
Earlier sketch in CA 109
Raworth, Thomas Moore 1938- ... 29-32R
Raworth, Tom
See Raworth, Thomas Moore
See also DLB 40
Rawski, Conrad H(enry) 1914- ... 73-76
Rawski, Evelyn S(akakida) 1939- ... 89-92
Rawson, Beryl 1933- ... 121
Rawson, C(laude) J(ulien) 1935- ... 25-28R
Rawson, Clayton 1906-1971 ... CANR-4
Obituary ... 29-32R
Earlier sketch in CA 5-6R
Rawson, Elizabeth (Donata) 1934- Brief entry ... 115
Rawson, Margaret B(yrd) 1899- ... 25-28R
Rawson, Philip Stanley 1924- ... CANR-21
Earlier sketches in CA 5-6R, CANR-6
Rawson, Wyatt Trevelyan Rawson 1894-1980 ... 7-8R
Obituary ... 103
Ray, Ann 1937- ... 114
Ray, Cyril 1908- ... CANR-21
Earlier sketches in CA 7-8R, CANR-5
Ray, D(avid) Michael 1935- ... CANR-9
Earlier sketch in CA 19-20R
Ray, David 1932- ... CANR-5
Earlier sketch in CA 11-12R
See also CAAS 7
See also DLB 5
Ray, Deborah
See Kogan Ray, Deborah
See also SATA 8
Ray, Dorothy Jean 1919- ... CANR-12
Earlier sketch in CA 25-28R
Ray, George McNeill 1910- ... 2R
Ray, Gordon N(orton) 1915-1986 ... 57-60
Obituary ... 121
Ray, H(enrietta) Cordelia 1849(?)-1916 ... 124
Brief entry ... 122
See also BW
See also DLB 50
Ray, Irene
See Sutton, Margaret Beebe
Ray, JoAnne 1935- ... 61-64
See also SATA 9
Ray, John (Philip) 1929- ... CANR-11
Earlier sketch in CA 25-28R
Ray, John B(ernard) 1930- ... 61-64
Ray, John R(obert) 1921- ... 37-40R
Ray, Joseph M(alchus) 1907- ... 41-44R
Ray, (Suzanne) Judy 1939- ... 111
Ray, Karen 1956- ... 108
Ray, Kenneth Clark 1901- ... CAP-2
Earlier sketch in CA 19-20
Ray, Man 1890-1976 ... 77-80
Obituary ... 69-72
Ray, Mary (Eva Pedder) 1932- ... CANR-12
Earlier sketch in CA 29-32R
See also SATA 2
Ray, Michele S. 1938- ... 25-28R
Ray, N(ancy) L(ouise) 1918- ... CANR-26
Earlier sketch in CA 109
Ray, Oakley S(tern) 1931- ... 45-48
Ray, Paul C(harles) 1926- ... 104
Ray, Philip A(lexander) 1911-1970 ... CAP-2
Earlier sketch in CA 23-24
Ray, Robert J. 1935- ... 126
Ray, Russell
See Strait, Raymond
Ray, Satyajit 1921- ... 114
See also CLC 16
Ray, Sibnarayan 1921- ... CANR-15
Earlier sketch in CA 23-24R
Ray, Talton F. 1939- ... 29-32R
Ray, Trevor 1934- ... 107
Ray, Wesley
See Gaulden, Ray
Ray, Wilbert S(cott) 1901- ... CAP-2
Earlier sketch in CA 25-28
Rayback, Joseph G(eorge) 1914- ... 7-8R
Rayburn, James Chalmers III 1945- ... 121
Rayburn, Jim III
See Rayburn, James Chalmers III
Rayburn, Robert G(ibson) 1915- ... 25-28R
Raycraft, Donald R(obert) 1942- ... 41-44R
Rayfield, David 1940- ... 45-48
Rayfield, (Patrick) Donald 1942- ... 103
Rayfield, Stanley C. 1901(?)-1983(?) Obituary ... 108
Raygor, Alton Lamon 1922- ... 49-52
Rayman, Paula Marian 1947- ... 107
Raymond, Agnes G. 1916- ... 25-28R
Raymond, Alex(ander Gillespie) 1909-1956 Brief entry ... 112
Raymond, Charles
See Koch, Charlotte and Koch, Raymond
Raymond, Diana (Joan) 1916- ... 89-92
Raymond, E.V.
See Gallun, Raymond Z(inke)
Raymond, Ellsworth (Lester) 1912- ... 37-40R
Raymond, Ernest 1888-1974 Obituary ... 89-92
Raymond, Father M.
See Flanagan, Joseph David Stanislaus
Raymond, G. Alison
See Lanier, Alison Raymond
Raymond, Harold 1887-1975 Obituary ... 104
Raymond, Henry 1820-1869 ... DLB-43
Raymond, James (Charles) 1940- ... 119
Raymond, James Crossley 1917-1981 Obituary ... 105
See also SATA 29
Raymond, Janice G. 1943- ... 89-92
Raymond, Joseph H.
See Le Fontaine, Joseph (Raymond)
Raymond, Lee
See Hill, Mary Raymond
Raymond, Margaret E(lmendorf) 1912- ... 104
Raymond, Mary
See Keegan, Mary Heathcott
Raymond, P. L.
See Gibson, Walter B(rown)
Raymond, Patrick (Ernest) 1924- ... 102
Raymond, Rene (Brabazon) 1906-1985 ... 126
Obituary ... 115
Raymond, Robert
See Alter, Robert Edmond
Raymond, Steve 1940- ... 49-52
Raymond, Walter J(ohn) 1930- ... 53-56
Raymond, William O. 1880-1970 ... CAP-2
Earlier sketch in CA 19-20
Raymond de Jesus, Mother
See Dion, Sister Anita
Raynal, Paul 1885(?)-1971 Obituary ... 33-36R
Rayne, Alan
See Tobin, James Edward
Rayner, Claire (Berenice) 1931- ... CANR-13
Earlier sketch in CA 21-22R
Rayner, E(dgar) G(eoffrey) 1927- ... CANR-10
Earlier sketch in CA 23-24R
Rayner, John Desmond 1924- ... 103
Rayner, Mary 1933- ... CANR-12
Earlier sketch in CA 69-72
See also SATA 22
Rayner, Ray
See Rahner, Raymond M.
Rayner, Richard
See McIlwain, David
Rayner, William 1929- ... 77-80
See also SATA 36
Raynor, David R(alph) 1948- ... 111
Raynor, Dorka ... 106
See also SATA 28
Raynor, Henry (Broughton) 1917- ... 85-88
Rayside, Betty 1931- ... 57-60
Rayson, Paul
See Jennings, Leslie Nelson
Rayson, Steven 1932- ... 106
See also SATA 30
Rayward, W(arden) Boyd 1939- ... 102
Raywid, Mary Anne ... 7-8R
Raz, Joseph 1939- ... 125
Razaf, Andy 1895-1973 Obituary ... 41-44R
Razik, Taher A. 1924- ... CANR-19
Earlier sketch in CA 25-28R
Razor Saltboy
See Louis, Ray Baldwin
Razran, Gregory 1901-1973 ... 41-44R
Obituary ... 45-48
Razzell, Arthur (George) 1925- ... 85-88
See also SATA 11
Razzi, James 1931- ... CANR-5
Earlier sketch in CA 53-56
See also SATA 10
Re, Edward D(omenic) 1920- ... CANR-12
Earlier sketch in CA 21-22R
Rea, Frederick B(eatty) 1908- ... 9-10R
Rea, Gardner 1892-1966 Obituary ... 93-96
Rea, K(enneth) J(ohn) 1932- Brief entry ... 107
Rea, Kenneth Wesley 1944- ... 107
Rea, Robert R(ight) 1922- ... 4R
Reach, Angus 1821-1856 ... DLB-70
Reach, James 1910(?)-1970 Obituary ... 29-32R
Read, Al 1919-1987 Obituary ... 123
Read, Anthony 1935- ... 107
Read, Bill 1917- ... 13-14R
Read, Brian (Ahier) 1927- ... 108
Read, Cecil B(yron) 1901-1972 ... CAP-1
Earlier sketch in CA 15-16
Read, David Haxton Carswell 1910- ... CANR-3
Earlier sketch in CA 3R
Read, Donald 1930- ... CANR-1
Earlier sketch in CA 4R
Read, Elfreida 1920- ... CANR-25
Earlier sketches in CA 23-24R, CANR-9
See also SATA 2
Read, Forrest 1926-1980 Obituary ... 112
Read, Gardner 1913- ... CANR-6
Earlier sketch in CA 15-16R
Read, Hadley 1918- ... 81-84
Read, Helen Appleton 1887(?)-1974 Obituary ... 53-56
Read, Herbert Edward 1893-1968 ... 85-88
Obituary ... 25-28R
See also DLB 20
See also CLC 4
Read, Jan
See Read, John Hinton

Read, John Hinton 1917- ... CANR-15
Earlier sketch in CA 77-80
Read, Kenneth E(yre) 1917- ... 101
Read, Leonard Edward 1898-1983 ... CANR-11
Obituary ... 109
Earlier sketch in CA 19-20R
Read, Maureen Hay 1937- ... 113
Read, Opie 1852-1939 ... DLB-23
Read, Piers Paul 1941- ... 23-24R
See also SATA 21
See also DLB 14
See also CLC 4, 10, 25
Read, R. B. 1916-1982 ... CANR-13
Earlier sketch in CA 61-64
Read, Ritchard 1914- ... 57-60
Read, Sylvia Joan ... 103
Read, William M(erritt) 1901- ... 33-36R
Reade, B(rian) Edmund 1913- ... 23-24R
Reade, Charles 1814-1884 ... DLB-21
Reade, Hamish
See Gray, Simon
Reade, Lang
See Carter, David C(harles)
Reader, Dennis Joel 1939- ... 106
Reader, Desmond H. 1920- ... 21-22R
Reader, W(illiam) J(oseph) 1920- ... CANR-16
Earlier sketch in CA 37-40R
Reading, Peter 1946- ... 103
See also DLB 40
See also CLC 47
Ready, Kirk L(ewis) 1943- ... 114
See also SATA 39
Ready, William B(ernard) 1914-1981 ... CANR-22
Earlier sketch in CA 25-28R
Reagan, Charles E(llis) 1942- ... 53-56
Reagan, Michael D(aniel) 1927- ... 49-52
Reagan, Nancy Davis 1923- ... 110
Reagan, Ronald 1911- ... 85-88
Reagan, Sydney C(handler) 1916- ... 41-44R
Reagan, Thomas (James) B(utler)
1916- ... 37-40R
Reagen, Edward P(aul) 1924- ... 49-52
Reagen, Michael V. 1942- ... 81-84
Reagin, Ewell Kerr 1900- ... 41-44R
Reaman, George Elmore 1889-1969 ... CAP-1
Earlier sketch in CA 11-12
Reamer, Judy 1940- ... 125
Reams, Bernard D(insmore), Jr.
1943- ... CANR-16
Earlier sketch in CA 93-96
Reamy, Tom 1935-1977 ... 81-84
Reaney, James 1926- ... 41-44R
See also SATA 43
See also DLB 68
See also CLC 13
Rearden, Jim 1925- ... 65-68
Reardon, B(ernard) M(orris) G(arvin)
1914- ... CANR-2
Earlier sketch in CA 7-8R
Reardon, Dennis J(oseph) 1944- ... 113
Brief entry ... 110
Reardon, Joan 1930- ... 116
Reardon, John J(oseph) 1926- ... 61-64
Reardon, William R. 1920- ... CANR-2
Earlier sketch in CA 2R
Rearick, Charles Walter 1942- ... 102
Reaske, Christopher R(ussell) 1941- ... 23-24R
Reason, James T(ootle) 1938- ... 104
Reasoner, Harry 1923- ... 111
See also AITN 1
Reaver, J(oseph) Russell 1915- ... 33-36R
Reaves, Philip
See Kiester, Edwin, Jr.
Reaves, Wendy Wick 1950- ... 114
Reavey, George 1907-1976 Obituary ... 69-72
Reavey, Jean (Bullowa) 1917(?)-1987
Obituary ... 123
Reb, Paul 1924- ... 49-52
Rebatet, Lucien 1903-1972 Obituary ... 37-40R
Rebay, Luciano 1928- ... 45-48
Rebbot, Olivier 1951(?)-1981 Obituary ... 103
Rebelsky, Freda Gould 1931- ... 41-44R
Rebert, M. Charles 1920- ... 53-56
Rebeta-Burditt, Joyce ... 81-84
Rebholz, Ronald A(lexander) 1932- ... 111
Rebischung, James A. 1928- ... 53-56
Rebreanu, Liviu 1885-1944 ... TCLC-28
Rebuffat, Gaston (Louis Simon)
1921-1985 ... 21-22R
Obituary ... 116
Rechcigl, Miloslav, Jr. 1930- ... CANR-12
Earlier sketch in CA 19-20R
Rechy, John (Francisco) 1934- ... CANR-6
Earlier sketch in CA 7-8R
See also CAAS 4
See also DLBY 82
See also CLC 1, 7, 14, 18
Reck, Alma Kehoe 1901- ... 4R
Reck, Andrew J(oseph) 1927- ... CANR-6
Earlier sketch in CA 13-14R
Reck, David 1935- ... 73-76
Reck, Franklin Mering 1896-1965
Obituary ... 109
See also SATA 30
Reck, Rima Drell 1933- ... 21-22R
Reck, W(aldo) Emerson 1903- ... 61-64
Recker, Colane 1940- ... 113
Reckless, Walter Cade 1899- ... 37-40R
Reckord, Barry ... 77-80
Record, Cy Wilson 1916- ... 11-12R
Record, Jane Cassels 1915-1981 ... CANR-5
Earlier sketch in CA 13-14R
Rector, Frank ... 106
Reday, Ladislaw 1913- ... 112
Red Butterfly
See Lauritsen, John (Phillip)
Redcam, Tom 1870-1933 ... TCLC-25
Redcliffe-Maud, John 1906-1982 Obituary ... 108
Redd, (Newton) Lawrence 1941- ... 57-60
Reddan, Harold J. 1926- ... 15-16R
Reddaway, Peter (Brian) 1939- ... CANR-10
Earlier sketch in CA 23-24R
Reddaway, W(illiam) Brian 1913- ... 17-18R
Redden, James Erskine 1928- ... 41-44R
Redder, George
See Drummond, Jack
Reddick, DeWitt Carter 1904- ... 7-8R
Reddick, L(awrence) D(unbar) 1910- ... 61-64
Reddin, W(illiam) J(ames) 1930- ... 29-32R
Redding, Bud
See Redding, Edward C.
Redding, David A. 1923- ... CANR-3
Earlier sketch in CA 4R
Redding, Edward C. 1917-1984 Obituary ... 113
Redding, Robert Hull 1919- ... CANR-11
Earlier sketch in CA 23-24R
See also SATA 2
Redding, (Jay) Saunders 1906-1988 ... CANR-26
Obituary ... 124
Earlier sketches in CA 4R, CANR-5
See also BW
See also DLB 63, 76
Reddish, Bessie Braid 1905-1974 ... 25-28R
Reddy, John F. X. 1912(?)-1975
Obituary ... 53-56
Reddy, Michael 1933- ... 61-64
Reddy, T. J. 1945- ... 45-48
Reddy, T(hammaiahgari) Ramakrishna
1937- ... 45-48
Redekop, Calvin Wall 1925- ... CANR-26
Earlier sketches in CA 25-28R, CANR-10
Redekop, John Harold 1932- ... 21-22R
Reder, Philip 1924-1983 Obituary ... 110
Redfern, George B. 1910- ... 11-12R
Redfern, W(alter) D(avid) 1936- ... 21-22R
Redfield, Alden 1941- ... 77-80
Redfield, Alfred Clarence 1890-1983
Obituary ... 109
Redfield, Clark
See McMorrow, Fred
Redfield, Jennifer
See Hoskins, Robert
Redfield, Malissa
See Elliott, Malissa Childs
Redfield, Margaret Park 1899(?)-1977
Obituary ... 69-72
Redfield, Robert 1897-1958 Brief entry ... 121
Redfield, William 1927-1976 Obituary ... 69-72
Redford, Emmette Shelburn 1904- ... 112
Redford, Polly 1925-1972 ... CAP-2
Earlier sketch in CA 33-36
Redford, (Charles) Robert (Jr.) 1937- ... 107
Red Fox, William 1871(?)-1976 Obituary ... 65-68
Redgate, John
See Kennedy, Adam
Redgrave, Michael (Scudamore)
1908-1985 Obituary ... 115
Redgrave, Paul 1920- ... 7-8R
Redgrove, Peter (William) 1932- ... CANR-3
Earlier sketch in CA 4R
See also DLB 40
See also CLC 6, 41
Redinger, Ruby V(irginia) 1915-1981 ... 65-68
Obituary ... 120
Redish, Bessie Braid 1905-1974 ... CAP-2
Earlier sketch in CA 25-28
Redkey, Edwin S(torer) 1931- ... 29-32R
Redlich, Frederick Carl 1910- Brief entry ... 106
Redman, Ben Ray 1896-1961 Obituary ... 93-96
Redman, Eric 1948- ... 49-52
Redman, L(ister) A(ppleton) 1933- ... 108
Redmayne, John
See Wood, Herbert Fairlie
Redmayne, Paul (Brewis) 1900- ... 7-8R
Redmon, Anne
See Nightingale, Anne Redmon
See also DLBY 86
See also CLC 22
Redmond, Eugene B. 1937- ... CANR-25
Earlier sketches in CA 25-28R, CANR-12
See also BW
See also DLB 41
Redmond, Gerald 1934- ... 37-40R
Redmond, Howard A(lexander) 1925- ... 15-16R
Redmond, Juanita
See Hipps, Juanita Redmond
Redmont, Bernard Sidney 1918- ... 73-76
Redmont, Dennis Foster 1942- ... 77-80
Redner, Harry 1937- ... 110
Redpath, (Robert) Theodore (Holmes)
1913- ... 104
Redpath, William 1893(?)-1985 Obituary ... 116
Redstone, Louis G(ordon) 1903- ... CANR-2
Earlier sketch in CA 49-52
Redway, Ralph
See Hamilton, Charles Harold St. John
Redway, Ridley
See Hamilton, Charles Harold St. John
Redwood, Alec
See Milkomane, George Alexis
Milkomanovich
Redwood, John (Alan) 1951- ... CANR-19
Earlier sketch in CA 102
Ree, Jonathan 1948- ... 57-60
Reece, Benny R(amon) 1930- ... 41-44R
Reece, Jack Eugene 1941- ... 101
Reeck, Darrell (Lauren) 1939- ... 104
Reed, A(lfred) H(amish) 1875-1975 ... CANR-4
Obituary ... 57-60
Earlier sketch in CA 9-10R
Reed, A(lexander) W(yclif) 1908-1979 ... CANR-4
Earlier sketch in CA 9-10R
Reed, Alison Touster 1952- ... 105
Reed, Barry
See Reed, Barry C(lement)
Reed, Barry C(lement) 1927- ... CANR-23
Earlier sketch in CA 29-32R
Reed, Betty Jane 1921- ... 29-32R
See also SATA 4
Reed, Bobbie (Butler) 1944- ... 77-80
Reed, Carroll E(dward) 1914- ... 103
Reed, Daniel 1892(?)-1978 Obituary ... 77-80
Reed, Don C(harles) 1945- ... 106
Reed, Donald A(nthony) 1935- ... 103
Reed, Douglas 1895-1976 ... 103
Obituary ... 89-92
Reed, Edward W(ilson) 1913- ... 29-32R
Reed, Eliot
See Ambler, Eric
Reed, Elizabeth Liggett 1895- ... 77-80
Reed, Elizabeth Stewart 1914- ... 2R
Reed, Emmett X.
See King, Florence
Reed, Evelyn 1905-1979 ... 102
Reed, Graham 1923- ... CANR-24
Earlier sketch in CA 45-48
Reed, Gwendolyn E(lizabeth) 1932- ... 25-28R
See also SATA 21
Reed, H(erbert) Owen 1910- ... CANR-19
Earlier sketches in CA 53-56, CANR-4
Reed, Harold W(illiam) 1909- ... 118
Reed, Harrison Merrick, Jr. 1898-19(?) ... 4R
Reed, Henry 1808-1854 ... DLB-59
Reed, Henry 1914-1986 ... 104
Obituary ... 121
See also DLB 27
Reed, Henry Clay 1899-1972 Obituary ... 111
Reed, Howard Alexander 1920- ... 15-16R
Reed, Ishmael 1938- ... CANR-25
Earlier sketch in CA 23-24R
See also BW
See also DLB 2, 5, 33
See also CLC 2, 3, 5, 6, 13, 32
Reed, J(ames) D(onald) 1940- ... 33-36R
Reed, James 1922- ... 102
Reed, James F(red) 1909- ... CAP-1
Earlier sketch in CA 11-12
Reed, James Wesley 1944- ... 112
Reed, John (Silas) 1887-1920 Brief entry ... 106
See also TCLC 9
Reed, John 1909- ... 125
Reed, John F(ord) 1911- ... 15-16R
Reed, John L(incoln) 1938- ... 57-60
Reed, John P(lume) 1921- ... 65-68
Reed, John Q(uincy) 1918-1978 ... 45-48
Obituary ... 103
Reed, John R(obert) 1938- ... CANR-8
Earlier sketch in CA 19-20R
Reed, John Shelton (Jr.) 1942- ... CANR-5
Earlier sketch in CA 53-56
Reed, Joseph Verner 1902-1973
Obituary ... 45-48
Reed, Joseph W(ayne), Jr. 1932- ... 37-40R
Reed, Kenneth 1944- ... 57-60
Reed, Kenneth T(errence) 1937- ... 73-76
Reed, Kit 1932- ... CANR-16
Earlier sketches in CA 2R, CANR-1
See also SATA 34
Reed, Lawrence
See Reday, Ladislaw
Reed, Lou
See Firbank, Louis
See also CLC 21
Reed, Louis S(chultz) 1902-1975
Obituary ... 61-64
Reed, Luther D(otterer) 1873- ... 7-8R
Reed, M(athilda) N(ewman) 1905-19(?) ... 4R
Reed, Macon, Jr. 1911(?)-1986 Obituary ... 121
Reed, Marcia 1929- ... 120
Reed, Mark D(ouglas) Morrison
See Morrison-Reed, Mark D(ouglas)
Reed, Mark L(afayette) III 1935- ... 93-96
Reed, Mary Jane (Pobst) 1920- ... 25-28R
Reed, Michael 1930- ... 123
Reed, (Fred) Mort(on) 1912- ... 61-64
Reed, Nelson A. 1926- ... 11-12R
Reed, Paul 1956- ... 113
Reed, Peter J. 1935- ... 53-56
Reed, Philip G. 1908- ... SATA-29
Reed, Rex (Taylor) 1938- ... CANR-9
Earlier sketch in CA 53-56
See also AITN 1
Reed, Robert C(arroll) 1937- ... CANR-10
Earlier sketch in CA 65-68
Reed, Robert Rentoul, Jr. 1911- ... 33-36R
Reed, Ronald F. 1945- ... 116
Reed, S(amuel) Kyle 1922- ... 41-44R
Reed, Sampson 1800-1880 ... DLB-1
Reed, Thomas (James) 1947- ... 103
See also SATA 34
Reed, Thomas Harrison 1881-1971
Obituary ... 110
Reed, Thomas Thornton 1902- ... 107
Reed, Victor (Brenner) 1926- ... 33-36R
Reed, Walter Logan 1943- ... 102
Reed, William Maxwell 1871-1962 ... SATA-15
Reed, Willis 1942- ... 104
Reeder, Colonel Red
See Reeder, Russell P., Jr.
Reeder, John P., Jr. 1937- ... 101
Reeder, Russell P., Jr. 1902- ... CANR-5
Earlier sketch in CA 3R
See also SATA 4
Reedstrom, Ernest Lisle 1928- ... 89-92
Reedy, George E(dward) 1917- ... 29-32R
Reedy, Jerry Edward 1936- ... 119
Reedy, John Louis 1925-1983 Obituary ... 111
Reedy, William A. 1916(?)-1975
Obituary ... 61-64
Reedy, William James 1921- ... 15-16R
Reefe, Thomas Q(uentin) 1943- ... 123
Brief entry ... 116
Reel, A(dolf) Frank 1907- ... 93-96
Reeman, Douglas Edward 1924- ... CANR-3
Earlier sketch in CA 2R
See also SATA 28
Reems, Harry 1947- ... 61-64
Reens, Mary
See Singleton, Betty
Reep, Edward 1918- ... 33-36R
Rees, Alan M(axwell) 1929- ... 106
Rees, Albert (Everett) 1921- ... CANR-12
Earlier sketch in CA 29-32R
Rees, Barbara (Elizabeth) 1934- ... CANR-9
Earlier sketch in CA 53-56
Rees, Clair (Francis) 1938- ... 117
Rees, David 1928- ... CANR-11
Earlier sketch in CA 11-12R
Rees, David Bartlett 1936- ... 105
See also SATA 36
See also SAAS 5
Rees, David Morgan 1904- ... 104
Rees, Dilwyn
See Daniel, Glyn (Edmund)
Rees, Ennis (Samuel, Jr.) 1925- ... CANR-2
Earlier sketch in CA 2R
See also SATA 3
Rees, (Morgan) Goronwy 1909- ... CANR-3
Earlier sketch in CA 45-48
Rees, Helen Christina Easson (Evans)
1903-1970 ... 7-8R
Obituary ... 89-92
Rees, Henry 1916- ... 107
Rees, Ioan Bowen 1929- ... 29-32R
Rees, Jean A(nglin) 1912- ... CANR-1
Earlier sketch in CA 2R
Rees, Joan 1927- ... CANR-12
Earlier sketch in CA 25-28R
Rees, Joan Alice Gladys
See Rees, Joan
Rees, (George) Leslie (Clarence)
1905- ... CANR-26
Earlier sketch in CA 104
Rees, Lucy 1943- ... 107
Rees, Margaret A(nn) 1933- ... CANR-18
Earlier sketch in CA 101
Rees, Meriel
See Lambot, Isobel
Rees, Paul Stromberg 1900- ... 7-8R
Rees, Richard (Lodowick Edward Montagu)
1900-1970 ... CANR-4
Obituary ... 89-92
Earlier sketch in CA 7-8R
Rees, Robert A(lvin) 1935- ... 81-84
Rees, (Margaret) Una 1920- ... 124
Rees, William 1887-1978(?) ... 7-8R
Obituary ... 104
Reese, Alexander 1881-1969 ... 97-100
Reese, Algernon B(everly) 1896-1981
Obituary ... 105
Reese, Bob
See Reese, Robert A.
Reese, Carolyn Johnson 1938- ... 112
Reese, Curtis W(illiford) 1887-1961
Obituary ... 110
Reese, Edward, Jr. 1928- ... 113
Reese, Francesca Gardner 1940- ... 65-68
Reese, Gustave 1899-1977 Obituary ... 73-76
Reese, Heloise (Bowles) 1919-1977 ... 11-12R
Obituary ... 73-76
Reese, Jim E(anes) 1912- ... 15-16R
Reese, John (Henry) ... 102
Reese, Lizette Woodworth 1856-1935 ... DLB-54
Reese, Lyn
See Reese, Carolyn Johnson
Reese, M(ax) M(eredith) 1910-1987 ... CANR-3
Obituary ... 123
Earlier sketch in CA 9-10R
Reese, Mason 1966- ... 97-100
Reese, Robert A. 1938- ... 114
See also SATA 53
Reese, Sammy
See Reese, Samuel Pharr
Reese, Samuel Pharr 1930-1985 ... 49-52
Obituary ... 117
Reese, (John) Terence 1913- ... 109
Reese, Thomas 1742-1796 ... DLB-37
Reese, Thomas J(oseph) 1945- ... 106
Reese, Thomas R. 1890(?)-1974
Obituary ... 53-56
Reese, Trevor Richard 1929- ... 11-12R
Reese, William Lewis 1921- ... CANR-8
Earlier sketch in CA 19-20R
Reese, William S(herman) 1955- ... 111
Reese, Willis L(ivingston) M(esier) 1913- ... 57-60
Reesink, Maryke 1919- ... 25-28R
Reeve, Clara 1729-1807 ... DLB-39
Reeve, F(ranklin) D(olier) 1928- ... 77-80
Reeve, Frank D(river) 1899-1967 ... CAP-1
Earlier sketch in CA 11-12
Reeve, G. Joan (Price) 1901- ... 15-16R
Reeve, Joel
See Cox, William R(obert)
Reeve, Richard M(ark) 1935- ... 37-40R
Reeve, Wilfred D. 1895- ... CAP-1
Earlier sketch in CA 13-14
Reeve, William Charles 1943- ... 93-96
Reeves, Alexander Stuart Frere
See Frere-Reeves, Alexander Stuart
Reeves, Amber
See Blanco White, Amber
Reeves, (Richard) Ambrose 1899-1980
Obituary ... 105
Reeves, Bruce Douglas 1940- ... CANR-11
Earlier sketch in CA 21-22R
Reeves, Charles Everand 1889- ... 7-8R
Reeves, Donald 1952- ... 37-40R

Reeves, Dorothea D(resser) 1901- CAP-1
Earlier sketch in CA 11-12
Reeves, Earl J(ames, Jr.) 1933- 61-64
Reeves, Elton T(raver) 1912- 29-32R
Reeves, Fionnuala 1943- 112
Reeves, Floyd (Wesley) 1890-1979
Obituary 89-92
Reeves, Gareth 1947- 119
Reeves, Gene (Arthur) 1933- 61-64
Reeves, Gregory Shaw 1950- 77-80
Reeves, James 1909- 7-8R
See also SATA 15
Reeves, Joan Wynn 1910-1972 .... CAP-2
Earlier sketch in CA 21-22
Reeves, John 1926- 113
Reeves, John K(night) 1907- CAP-2
Earlier sketch in CA 25-28
Reeves, Joyce 1911- CANR-12
Earlier sketch in CA 73-76
See also SATA 17
Reeves, Lawrence F. 1926- 105
See also SATA 29
Reeves, Marjorie E(thel) 1905- CANR-20
Earlier sketches in CA 13-14R, CANR-5
Reeves, Martha Emilie 1941- 65-68
Reeves, Mavis Mann 1921- CANR-25
Earlier sketch in CA 45-48
Reeves, Nancy 1913- 33-36R
Reeves, Paschal 1917-1976 81-84
Reeves, Patricia Houts 1947- 126
Reeves, Richard 1936- 69-72
Reeves, Rosser 1910-1984 89-92
Obituary 111
Reeves, Ruth Ellen
See Ranney, Agnes V.
Reeves, Thomas C(harles) 1936- CANR-9
Earlier sketch in CA 57-60
Reeves, Thomas Carl 1939- 33-36R
Reeves, Trish
See Reeves, Patricia Houts
Reff, Theodore Franklin 1930- 89-92
Refregier, Anton 1905- 5-6R
Regalado, Nancy Freeman 1935- 19-20R
Regan, Brad
See Norwood, Victor G(eorge) C(harles)
Regan, Cronan 1925- 45-48
Regan, Donald T(homas) 1918-
Brief entry 106
Regan, Richard Joseph 1930- 7-8R
Regan, Robert (Charles) 1930- 19-20R
Regan, Thomas Howard 1938- 104
Regan, Tom
See Regan, Thomas Howard
Regardie, (Francis) Israel 1907- 85-88
Regehr, Lydia 1903- 45-48
See also SATA 37
Regelski, Thomas A(dam) 1941- 57-60
Regenstein, Lewis 1943- 57-60
Regensteiner, Else (Friedsam) 1906-
Brief entry 111
Reger, Roger 1933- 23-24R
Reggiani, Renee 1925- 85-88
See also SATA 18
Reghaby, Heydar 1932- 29-32R
Regin, Deric (Wagenvort) 37-40R
Reginald
See Burgess, M(ichael) R(oy)
Reginald, R(obert)
See Burgess, M(ichael) R(oy)
Regis, Sister Mary 1908- CAP-1
Earlier sketch in CA 13-14
Register, Cheri
See Register, Cheryl Lynn
Register, Cheryl Lynn 1945- 126
Register, Willie Raymond 1937- 45-48
Regnery, Henry 1912- 101
Regoli, Robert M. 1950- 116
Regosin, Richard L(loyd) 1937-
Brief entry 109
Regueiro, Helen 1943- 104
Rehak, Peter (Stephen) 1936- 77-80
Rehder, Helmut 1905-1977 .... CANR-4
Earlier sketch in CA 7-8R
Rehder, Jessie Clifford 1908-1967 .... CAP-1
Earlier sketch in CA 9-10
Rehfuss, John Alfred 1934- 85-88
Rehrauer, George 1923- 53-56
Reibel, Paula
See Schwartz, Paula
Reich, Ali
See Katz, Bobbi
Reich, Bernard 1941- CANR-14
Earlier sketch in CA 81-84
Reich, Charles Alan 1928- 108
Reich, Edward 1903(?)-1983 Obituary 109
Reich, Ilse Ollendorff 1909- 49-52
Reich, John Theodore 1906-1988
Obituary 124
Reich, Kenneth 1938- 69-72
Reich, Nancy B(assen) 126
Reich, Peter M(aria) 1929- 85-88
Reich, Sheldon 1931- 112
Reich, Steve 1936- CANR-8
Earlier sketch in CA 61-64
Reich, Tova Rachel 1942- 103
Reichard, Gary Warren 1943- CANR-26
Earlier sketches in CA 61-64, CANR-10
Reichard, Robert S. 1923- 23-24R
Reichardt, Jasia 1933- CANR-2
Earlier sketch in CA 7-8R
Reichart, Walter A(lbert) 1903- 5-6R
Reiche, Reimut 1941- 41-44R
Reichek, Morton A(rthur) 1924- 85-88
Reichel, Mary 1946- 125
Reichel, O. Asher 1921- 45-48
Reichenbach, Bruce R. 1943- 33-36R
Reichenberger, Arnold G(ottfried) 1903- ..19-20R
Reichert, Edwin C(lark) 1909-1988
Obituary 126
Reichert, Herbert W(illiam) 1917-1978 . CANR-24
Earlier sketch in CA 45-48
Reichert, Victor Emanuel 1897- 15-16R
Reichl, Ernst 1900-1980 Obituary 102
Reichl, Ruth 1948- 61-64
Reichler, Joseph Lawrence 1918- 103
Reichley, (Anthony) James 1929- 2R
Reichmann, Felix 1899- 104
Reicke, Bo I(var) 1914- 15-16R
Reid, Alan 1915(?)-1987 Obituary 123
Reid, Alastair 1926- CANR-3
Earlier sketch in CA 7-8R
See also SATA 46
See also DLB 27
Reid, Albert Clayton 1894- 53-56
Reid, Alfred S(andlin) 1924-1976 .... CANR-2
Earlier sketch in CA 45-48
Reid, Anthony 1916- 29-32R
Reid, B(enjamin) L(awrence) 1918- 19-20R
Reid, Barbara 1922- CANR-12
Earlier sketch in CA 25-28R
See also SATA 21
Reid, Charles (Stuart) 1900-1987 101
Obituary 121
Reid, Charles K(er) II 1912-19(?) CAP-1
Earlier sketch in CA 19-20
Reid, Charles L(loyd) 1927- 37-40R
Reid, Charles R(obert) 1926- 114
Reid, Christopher 1949- DLB-40
See also CLC 33
Reid, Clyde H. 1928- CANR-12
Earlier sketch in CA 25-28R
Reid, Daniel P. (Jr.) 1948- 125
Reid, Desmond
See McNeilly, Wilfred (Glassford)
and Moorcock, Michael (John)
Reid, Donald (Matthew) 1952- 124
Reid, Dorothy M(arion) ?-1974 Obituary 109
See also SATA 29
Reid, E. Emmet 1872-1973 Obituary 45-48
Reid, Ela 1907-1982 Obituary 107
Reid, Escott (Meredith) 1905- CANR-20
Earlier sketch in CA 101
Reid, Esmond 1945- 123
Reid, Eugenie Chazal 1924- 15-16R
See also SATA 12
Reid, Frances P(ugh) 1910- CANR-2
Earlier sketch in CA 7-8R
Reid, H. 1925- 19-20R
Reid, Helen Rogers 1882-1970 Obituary 115
See also DLB 29
Reid, Hilda (Stewart) 1898-1982 Obituary .. 106
Reid, Ian 1915-1984 Obituary 113
Reid, Inez Smith 49-52
Reid, J(ohn) C(owie) 1916-1972 ....11-12R
Obituary 103
Reid, James DLB-31
Reid, James Macarthur 1900-1970 ...... CAP-1
Earlier sketch in CA 9-10
Reid, James Malcolm 1902-1982 ....7-8R
Obituary 107
Reid, James W. 1912-197(?) CAP-2
Earlier sketch in CA 25-28
Reid, Jan 1945- 61-64
Reid, Jim 1929- 61-64
Reid, John Calvin CANR-11
Earlier sketch in CA 25-28R
See also SATA 21
Reid, John Kelman Sutherland 1910- ... CANR-3
Earlier sketch in CA 4R
Reid, John Phillip 1930- CANR-19
Earlier sketch in CA 25-28R
Reid, John T(urner) 1908-1978 81-84
Reid, Leslie Hartley 1895- CAP-1
Earlier sketch in CA 13-14
Reid, Loren (Dudley) 1905- CANR-1
Earlier sketch in CA 3R
Reid, Louis Arnaud 1895- CAP-1
Earlier sketch in CA 13-14
Reid, Malcolm 1941- 53-56
Reid, (Thomas) Mayne 1818-1883 ..... SATA-24
See also DLB 21
Reid, Meta Mayne 13-14R
See also SATA 36
Reid, Mildred I. 1908- 23-24R
Reid, Philip
See Ingrams, Richard (Reid)
and Osmond, Andrew
Reid, R(obert) W(illiam) 1933- 29-32R
Reid, Randall 1931- 25-28R
Reid, Robert G(eorge) B(urnside) 1939- 119
Reid, Seerley 1909(?)-1972 Obituary 37-40R
Reid, Sue Titus 1939- CANR-14
Earlier sketch in CA 37-40R
Reid, Tim
See Reid, Timothy E. H.
Reid, Timothy E. H. 1936- 19-20R
Reid, Vic(tor Stafford) 1913- CANR-16
Earlier sketch in CA 65-68
See also BW
Reid, W(illiam) Stanford 1913- CANR-18
Earlier sketches in CA 49-52, CANR-1
Reid, Whitelaw 1837-1912 .... DLB-23
Reid, William 1926- 85-88
Reid, William H(oward) 1945- CANR-16
Earlier sketch in CA 93-96
Reid, William J(ames) 1928- CANR-17
Earlier sketch in CA 77-80
Reida, Bernice 1915- 93-96
Reid Banks, Lynne 1929- CANR-22
Earlier sketches in CA 1R, CANR-6
See also SATA 22
Reidel, Carl Hubert 1937- 107
Reidel-Geubtner, Virginia 1921- 116
Reidenbaugh, Lowell (Henry) 1919- 121
Reidy, John Patrick 1930- 19-20R
Reidy, Joseph 1920- 53-56
Reierson, Gary B(ruce) 1948- 114
Reif, Rita 1929- 41-44R
Reifen, David 1911- 93-96
Reiff, Henry 1899-1983 Obituary 110
Reiff, Robert (Frank) 1918- 19-20R
Reiff, Stephanie Ann 1948- 93-96
See also SATA 28, 47
Reiffel, Leonard 1927- 101
Reifler, Samuel 1939- 93-96
Reifsnyder, William E(dward) 1924- 65-68
Reig, June 1933- 105
See also SATA 30
Reigelman, Milton Monroe 1942- 65-68
Reiger, George (Wesley) 1939- CANR-18
Earlier sketch in CA 101
Reiger, John F(ranklin) 1943- 57-60
Reiger, Kurt (Edward) 1956- 116
Reigle, Donald W(ayne), Jr. 1938- 61-64
Reigot, Betty Polisar 1924- 111
See also SATA 41
Reigstad, Paul (Matthew) 1921- 81-84
Reik, Theodor 1888-1969 .... CANR-5
Obituary 25-28R
Earlier sketch in CA 5-6R
Reile, Louis 1925- 29-32R
Reill, Peter Hanns 1938- 101
Reilly, Catherine W(inifred) 1925- 118
Reilly, Christopher T(homas) 1924- 101
Reilly, D(avid) Robin 1928- CANR-8
Earlier sketch in CA 7-8R
Reilly, Edward R(andolph) 1929- 93-96
Reilly, Edwin David, Jr. 1932- 111
Reilly, Esther H(untington) 1917- 33-36R
Reilly, Francis E(agan) 1922- 29-32R
Reilly, Harold J. 1895(?)-1987 Obituary 123
Reilly, John H(urford) 1934- 77-80
Reilly, John M(arsden) 1933- 104
Reilly, Judith G(ladding) 1935- 61-64
Reilly, Mary 1920- Brief entry 114
Reilly, Mary Lonan 1926- 33-36R
Reilly, Michael (Francis) 1910(?)-1973
Obituary 41-44R
Reilly, Patrick 1932- 115
Reilly, Patrick D.
See Rogers, Peter D(amien)
Reilly, Paul 1912- 125
Reilly, Robert Thomas 1922- CANR-2
Earlier sketch in CA 5-6R
Reilly, Robin 1928- CANR-5
Earlier sketch in CA 53-56
Reilly, William J(ohn) 1899- CAP-2
Earlier sketch in CA 19-20
Reilly, William K.
See Creasey, John
Reiman, Donald H(enry) 1934- CANR-14
Earlier sketch in CA 33-36R
Reiman, Jeffrey H. 1942- 93-96
Reimann, Brigitte 1933-1973 .... DLB-75
Reimann, Guenter Hans 1904- 25-28R
Reimann, Lewis C. 1890-1961 Obituary 113
Reimann, Viktor 1915- 69-72
Reimer, Bennett 1932- CANR-3
Earlier sketch in CA 45-48
Reimers, David 1931- 115
Rein, Irving J. 1937- 25-28R
Rein, Martin 1928- 93-96
Rein, Richard
See Smith, Richard Rein
Reina, Ruben E. 1924- 49-52
Reinach, Jacquelyn (Krasne) 1930- CANR-22
Earlier sketch in CA 105
See also SATA 28
Reincheld, Bill 1946- 57-60
Reindorp, George E(dmund) 1911- CANR-5
Earlier sketch in CA 7-8R
Reindorp, Reginald C(arl) 1907- 25-28R
Reinecke, Ian 1945- 117
Reinemer, Vic 1923- 21-22R
Reiner, Carl 1922- Brief entry 112
Reiner, Joseph H. 1912(?)-1983 Obituary .. 111
Reiner, Laurence E(rwin) 102
Reiner, Max
See Caldwell, (Janet Miriam) Taylor
(Holland)
Reiner, William B(uck) 1910-1976 ...... CANR-3
Obituary 61-64
Earlier sketch in CA 45-48
See also SATA 30, 46
Reinerman, Alan J(erome) 1935- 114
Reinert, Paul C(lare) 1910- 85-88
Reines, Alvin J. 1926- 53-56
Reinfeld, Fred 1910-1964 .... CAP-1
Earlier sketch in CA 9-10
See also SATA 3
Reinhard, David W(illiam) 1952- 118
Reinhard, Ernst
See Frank, Rudolf
Reinhardt, Ad(olph Frederick) 1913-1967
Obituary 111
Reinhardt, Gottfried 1913- 93-96
Reinhardt, James Melvin 1894-1974 .... CANR-4
Obituary 49-52
Earlier sketch in CA 2R
Reinhardt, Jon M(c Ewen) 1936- 41-44R
Reinhardt, Kurt F(rank) 1896- CANR-1
Earlier sketch in CA 4R
Reinhardt, Richard 1927- CANR-13
Earlier sketch in CA 25-28R
Reinhart, Bruce Aaron 1926- 5-6R
Reinhart, Charles (Franklin) 1946- 104
Reinhart, Theodore R(ussell) 1938- 125
Reinhartz, Dennis 1944- 123
Reinharz, Jehuda 1944- CANR-24
Earlier sketches in CA 65-68, CANR-9
Reinhold, Meyer 1909- CANR-26
Earlier sketches in CA 7-8R, CANR-5
Reiniger, Lotte 1899-1981 Obituary 108
See also SATA 33, 40
Reining, Conrad C(opeland) 1918-1984 ...21-22R
Obituary 114
Reinitz, Richard (Martin) 1934- 89-92
Reinke, William A(ndrew) 1928- CANR-24
Earlier sketch in CA 45-48
Reinmuth, Oscar William 1900- 37-40R
Reinsmith, Richard
See Smith, Richard Rein
Reis, Claire Raphael 1889-1978 Obituary ..77-80
Reis, Ricardo
See Pessoa, Fernando (Antonio Nogueira)
Reis, Richard H(erbert) 1930- 41-44R
Reisch, Walter 1903-1983 Obituary 109
See also DLB 44
Reischauer, August Karl 1879-1971 ...... CAP-2
Earlier sketch in CA 19-20
Reischauer, Edwin O(ldfather) 1910- 19-20R
Reiser, Martin 1927- 53-56
Reiser, Morton F(rancis) 1919- 124
Reiser, Oliver Leslie 1895-1974 .... CANR-4
Obituary 49-52
Earlier sketch in CA 3R
Reiser, William (Edward) 1943- 114
Reisfeld, Bert 1906- 112
Reising, Robert W(illiam) 1933- 89-92
Reisman, Arnold 1934- CANR-12
Earlier sketch in CA 33-36R
Reisman, George Gerald 1937- 104
Reisman, John M(ark) 1930- CANR-8
Earlier sketch in CA 21-22R
Reisner, George
See Ben-Ephraim, Gavriel
Reisner, Robert George 1921- 11-12R
Reisner, Thomas Andrew 1935- 113
Reiss, Albert J(ohn), Jr. 1922- CANR-24
Earlier sketches in CA 23-24R, CANR-9
Reiss, Alvin 1932- 61-64
Reiss, Alvin H(erbert) 1930- 81-84
Reiss, Barbara Eve 1941- CANR-15
Earlier sketch in CA 41-44R
Reiss, David S. 1953- 108
Reiss, Edmund (Allan) 1934- CANR-10
Earlier sketch in CA 23-24R
Reiss, Ira L(eonard) 1925- 15-16R
Reiss, James 1941- 33-36R
Reiss, Johanna (de Leeuw) 1929(?)- 85-88
See also SATA 18
Reiss, John J. 106
See also SATA 23
Reiss, Stephen (Charles) 1918- 57-60
Reiss, Timothy James 1942- 107
Reissig, Herman F. 1899(?)-1985
Obituary 116
Reissman, Leonard 1921-1975 .... CANR-4
Obituary 53-56
Earlier sketch in CA 5-6R
Reister, Floyd Nester 1919- 69-72
Reit, Seymour (V.) 1918- CANR-16
Earlier sketch in CA 93-96
See also SATA 21
Reit, Sy
See Reit, Seymour (V.)
Reitan, E(arl) A(aron) 1925- 19-20R
Reitci, John G(eorge) 1922-1983 Obituary .. 109
Reitci, Rita Krohne 1930- 5-6R
Reitemeyer, John Reinhart 1898-1979
Obituary 85-88
Reiter, Charles Jules 1928- 25-28R
Reiter, Robert E. 1932- 25-28R
Reiter, Seymour 1921- 101
Reiterman, Carl 1921- 49-52
Reiterman, Tim 1947- 109
Reith, Charles C. 1953- 122
Reith, J.C.W.
See Reith, John Charles Walsham
Reith, John Charles Walsham 1889-1971
Obituary 113
Reither, Joseph 1903- 109
Reitlinger, Gerald R. 1900(?)-1978
Obituary 104
Reitmeister, Louis Aaron 1903-1975 49-52
Obituary 61-64
Reitsch, Hanna 1912(?)-1979 Obituary 89-92
Reitz, Donald J(oseph) 1932- 25-28R
Reitze, Arnold W(infred), Jr. 1938- 49-52
Rejai, Mostafa 1931- CANR-13
Earlier sketch in CA 37-40R
Rejaunier, Jeanne 1934- 29-32R
Rekai, Kati 1921- 105
Rekers, George A(lan) 1948- 119
Relgis, Eugene 1895- 81-84
Relis, Harry
See Endore, (Samuel) Guy
Rella, Ettore 1907(?)-1988 Obituary 126
Relyea, Suzanne 1945- 77-80
Remak, Henry H. H. 1916- 19-20R
Remak, Joachim 1920- CANR-3
Earlier sketch in CA 1R
Remarque, Erich Maria 1898-1970 77-80
Obituary 29-32R
See also DLB 56
See also CLC 21
Rembar, Charles 1915- 25-28R
Remen, (Rachelle) Naomi 1938- 122
Brief entry 118
Remenih, Maurine 1916(?)-1985 Obituary .. 118
Remer, Theodore G. 1899- CAP-1
Earlier sketch in CA 15-16
Remi, Georges 1907-1983 69-72
Obituary 109
See also SATA 13, 32
Remington, Ella-Carrie 1914- 69-72

Remington, Frederic 1861-1909
Brief entry ... 108
See also SATA 41
See also DLB 12
Remington, Mark
See Bingley, David Ernest
Remington, Robin Alison 1938- ... CANR-12
Earlier sketch in CA 33-36R
Remini, Robert V(incent) 1921- ... CANR-20
Earlier sketches in CA 11-12R, CANR-3
Remizov, A. M.
See Remizov, Alexey (Mikhailovich)
Remizov, Alexey (Mikhailovich) 1877-1957
Brief entry ... 125
See also TCLC 27
Remley, David A. 1931- ... 45-48
Remley, Mary L(ouise) 1930- ... 102
Remmers, H(ermann) H(enry) 1892-1969 ... 2R
Obituary ... 103
Remmling, Gunter W(erner) 1929- ... 41-44R
Remoff, Heather T(rexler) 1938- ... 117
Remonda-Ruibal, Jorge Silvestre 1928- ... 108
Remsberg, Bonnie K(ohn) 1937- ... 69-72
Remsberg, Charles A(ndruss) 1936- ... CANR-7
Earlier sketch in CA 57-60
Remson, Irwin 1923- ... 53-56
Remy
See Renault, Gilbert (Leon Etienne Theodore)
Remy, Georges
See Remi, Georges
Remy, Pierre-Jean
See Angremy, Jean-Pierre
Remy, Richard C. 1942- ... 111
Rena, Sally
See Rena, Sarah Mary
Rena, Sarah Mary 1941- ... 103
Renan, Sheldon (Jackson) 1941- ... CANR-14
Earlier sketch in CA 23-24R
Renard, Alexandre Charles 1906-1983
Obituary ... 111
Renard, Jules 1864-1910 Brief entry ... 117
See also TCLC 17
Renaud, Jacques 1943- ... DLB-60
Renault, Gilbert (Leon Etienne Theodore)
1904-1984 Obituary ... 113
Renault, Mary
See Challans, Mary
See also DLBY 83
See also CLC 3, 11, 17
Renault, Rick
See Wallmann, Jeffrey M(iner)
Renay, Liz 1926- ... 33-36R
Rendall, Ted S. ... 101
Rendel, George William 1889-1979 ... 7-8R
Obituary ... 103
Rendel, John 1906(?)-1978 Obituary ... 104
Rendell, Joan ... CANR-23
Earlier sketches in CA 61-64, CANR-7
See also SATA 28
Rendell, Ruth 1930- ... 109
See also CLC 28, 48
Render, Sylvia Lyons 1913- ... CANR-15
Earlier sketch in CA 41-44R
Rendina, Laura (Jones) Cooper 1902- ... 11-12R
See also SATA 10
Rendleman, Danny L(ee) 1945- ... 65-68
Rendon, Armando B. 1939- ... 37-40R
Rene, Leon (T.) 1902-1982 Obituary ... 107
Rene, Natalia 1908(?)-1977 Obituary ... 69-72
Renehan, Robert (Francis Xavier) 1935-
Brief entry ... 108
Renetzky, Alvin 1940- ... 101
Renfield, Richard L. 1932- ... 29-32R
Renfrew, Jane Margaret 1942- ... 49-52
Renfroe, Martha Kay 1938- ... CANR-9
Earlier sketch in CA 65-68
Renich, Fred C. 1916-1979 ... 115
Renich, Jill 1916- ... 25-28R
Renick, Marion (Lewis) 1905- ... CANR-1
Earlier sketch in CA 3R
See also SATA 1
Renier, Elizabeth
See Baker, Betty D(oreen Flook)
Renken, Aleda 1907- ... CANR-12
Earlier sketch in CA 21-22R
See also SATA 27
Renkiewicz, Frank 1935- ... CANR-26
Earlier sketch in CA 45-48
Renlie, Frank H. 1936- ... SATA-11
Renn, Casey
See Crim, Keith R(enn)
Renn, Ludwig
See Vieth von Golssenau, Arnold Friedrich
Renn, Thomas E(dward) 1939- ... 29-32R
Renne, Roland Roger 1905- ... 2R
Renner, Al G. 1912- ... 89-92
Renner, Beverly Hollett 1929- ... 85-88
Renner, Bruce 1944- ... 33-36R
Renner, John Wilson 1924- ... 41-44R
Renner, K(enneth) Edward 1936- ... 101
Renner, Thomas C(hoate) 1928- ... 73-76
Renner, Tom
See Renner, Thomas C(hoate)
Rennert, Maggie 1922- ... CANR-13
Earlier sketch in CA 61-64
Rennick, Robert M(orris) 1932- ... 122
Rennie, Christopher
See Ambrose, Eric (Samuel)
Rennie, Eric 1947- ... 45-48
Rennie, James Alan 1899-1969 ... CAP-1
Earlier sketch in CA 11-12
Rennie, Ysabel Fisk 1918- ... CANR-2
Earlier sketch in CA 7-8R
Reno, Clint
See Ballard, (Willis) Todhunter
Reno, Dawn E. 1953- ... 125
Reno, Marie R(oth) ... CANR-10
Earlier sketch in CA 65-68
Reno, Ottie W(ayne) 1929- ... 41-44R
Reno, Philip 1913-1981 Obituary ... 111
Renoir, Alain 1921- ... 77-80
Renoir, Jean 1894-1979 Obituary ... 85-88
See also CLC 20
Renouf, Alan 1919- ... 108
Rensberger, Boyce 1942- ... 81-84
Rensch, Bernhard (Carl Emmanuel) 1900- ... 102
Renshaw, Domeena C(ynthia) 1929- ... 89-92
Renshaw, Patrick (Richard George)
1936- ... 21-22R
Renshaw, Samuel 1892- ... 77-80
Renshon, Stanley Allen 1943- Brief entry ... 109
Rensie, Willis
See Eisner, Will(iam Erwin)
Renton, Cam
See Armstrong, Richard
Renton, Julia
See Cole, Margaret Alice
Rentschler, Eric 1949- ... 118
Renvoize, Jean ... 41-44R
See also SATA 5
Renwick, Ethel Hulbert 1910- ... 7-8R
Renwick, Fred B(lackwell) 1930- ... 33-36R
Renzulli, L(ibero) Marx, Jr. 1934-
Brief entry ... 108
Replansky, Naomi 1918- ... 33-36R
Repp, Arthur C(hristian) 1906- ... CAP-1
Earlier sketch in CA 15-16
Repp, Ed Earl 1900(?)-1979 Obituary ... 85-88
Repp, William 1936- ... 110
Reps, John W(illiam) 1921- ... CANR-18
Earlier sketches in CA 45-48, CANR-1
Reps, (Saladin) Paul 1895- ... CANR-6
Earlier sketch in CA 7-8R
ReQua, Eloise Gallup 1902- ... CAP-1
Earlier sketch in CA 15-16
Resch, John Phillips 1940- Brief entry ... 108
Rescher, Nicholas 1928- ... CANR-12
Earlier sketch in CA 21-22R
Rescoe, A(ntoine) Stan(ley) 1910- ... 7-8R
Reshetar, John S(tephen) Jr. 1924- ... 7-8R
Reshevsky, Samuel Herman 1911- ... 65-68
Resick, Matthew C(larence) 1916- ... 57-60
Reske, Hermann 1911- ... 45-48
Reskind, John
See Wallmann, Jeffrey M(iner)
Resnais, Alain 1922- ... CLC-16
Resnick, H(arvey) L(ewis) P(aul) 1930- ... 23-24R
Resnick, Marvin D. 1933- ... 21-22R
Resnick, Michael D(iamond) 1942- ... CANR-24
Earlier sketch in CA 107
See also SATA 38
Resnick, Mike
See Resnick, Michael D(iamond)
Resnick, Nathan 1910-1977 ... CAP-2
Obituary ... 73-76
Earlier sketch in CA 19-20
Resnick, Rose ... 61-64
Resnick, Seymour 1920- ... 73-76
See also SATA 23
Resnick, Sylvia (Safran) 1927- ... 93-96
Resnik, H(arvey) L(ewis) P(aul) 1930- ... CANR-10
Earlier sketch in CA 23-24R
Resnik, Henry S. 1940- ... 29-32R
Resnik, Michael D(avid) 1938- ... 116
Resposo, Epifania R. Castro 1922-1974
Obituary ... 113
Ressler, Alice 1918- ... 53-56
Ressner, Phil(ip) 1922- ... 15-16R
Rest, Friedrich Otto 1913- ... CANR-17
Earlier sketches in CA 5-6R, CANR-2
Rest, Karl H(einrich) A(lbert) 1908- ... 7-8R
Restak, Richard M(artin) 1942- ... CANR-24
Earlier sketches in CA 61-64, CANR-8
Restivo, Sal 1940- ... 112
Restle, Frank 1927- ... 41-44R
Reston, James (Barrett) 1909- ... 65-68
See also AITN 1, 2
Reston, James B(arrett), Jr. 1941- ... 37-40R
Reston, Jody ... AITN-2
Reston, Richard ... AITN-2
Retla, Robert
See Alter, Robert Edmond
Retner, Beth A.
See Brown, Beth
Rettig, Edward B(ertram) 1940- ... 57-60
Rettig, Jack L(ouis) 1925- ... 57-60
Reuben, David 1933- ... 41-44R
See also AITN 1
Reuber, Grant L(ouis) 1927- ... CANR-3
Earlier sketch in CA 49-52
Reul, R(ose) Myrtle 1919- ... 21-22R
Reuman, Robert E(verett) 1923- ... 37-40R
Reumann, John 1927- ... CANR-5
Earlier sketch in CA 2R
Reuss, Carl F(rederick) 1915- ... 41-44R
Reuss, Frederick G(ustav) 1904- ... CAP-1
Earlier sketch in CA 11-12
Reuss, Henry S(choellkopf) 1912- ... CANR-6
Earlier sketch in CA 11-12R
Reuter, Carol (Joan) 1931- ... 23-24R
See also SATA 2
Reuter, Frank T. 1926- ... 21-22R
Reuter, Gabriele 1859-1941 ... DLB-66
Reuther, David L(ouis) 1946- ... 112
Reuther, Ruth E. 1917- ... CANR-12
Earlier sketch in CA 33-36R
Reuther, Victor G(eorge) 1912- ... 77-80
Rev, B.
See Eisner, Betty Grover
Reval, Jacques
See Laver, James
Revankar, Ratna G. 1937- ... 33-36R
Revard, Stella Purce 1933- ... 97-100
Reve, Karel van het
See van het Reve, Karel
Revel, Jean-Francois 1924- Brief entry ... 109
Reveley, Edith 1930- ... 123
Reveley, W(alter) Taylor III 1943- ... 126
Revell, Donald 1954- ... 116
Revell, J(ohn) R(obert) S(tephen)
1920- ... CANR-26
Earlier sketches in CA 25-28R, CANR-11
Revell, Jack
See Revell, J(ohn) R(obert) S(tephen)
Revell, Peter 1929-1983 ... CANR-13
Earlier sketch in CA 29-32R
ReVelle, Charles S. 1938- ... 45-48
ReVelle, Penelope 1941- ... 49-52
Revena
See Wright, Betty Ren
Reventlow, Franziska Graefin zu
1871-1918 ... DLB-66
Reverdy, Pierre 1889-1960 ... 97-100
Obituary ... 89-92
Reverend Mandju
See Su Chien
Reves, Emery 1904-1981 Obituary ... 105
Rewald, John 1912- ... CANR-5
Earlier sketch in CA 9-10R
Rewoldt, Stewart H(enry) 1922- ... 37-40R
Rex, Barbara (Clayton) 1904- ... 77-80
Rex, John A(rderne) 1925- ... CANR-24
Earlier sketches in CA 5-6R, CANR-6
Rex, Walter E(dwin) 1927- ... 45-48
Rexine, John E(fstratios) 1929- ... CANR-15
Earlier sketch in CA 37-40R
Rexroth, Kenneth 1905-1982 ... CANR-14
Obituary ... 107
Earlier sketch in CA 5-6R
See also DLB 16, 48
See also DLBY 82
See also CDALB 1941-1968
See also CLC 1, 2, 6, 11, 22, 49
Rey, H(ans) A(ugusto) 1898-1977 ... CANR-6
Obituary ... 73-76
Earlier sketch in CA 5-6R
See also SATA 1, 26
See also DLB 22
See also CLR 5
Rey, Margret (Elisabeth) 1906- ... 105
See also SATA 26
See also CLR 5
Rey, Michael Stephan 1946- ... 113
Reyam
See Mayer, Charles Leopold
Reybold, Malcolm 1911(?)-1988 Obituary ... 124
Reyburn, Wallace (Macdonald) 1913- ... CANR-1
Earlier sketch in CA 49-52
Reyes, Carlos 1935- ... CANR-3
Earlier sketch in CA 49-52
Reyes y Basoalto, Ricardo Eliecer Neftali
See Neruda, Pablo
Reyher, Becky
See Reyher, Rebecca Hourwich
Reyher, Rebecca Hourwich 1897-1987
Obituary ... 121
See also SATA 18, 50
Reymont, Wladyslaw (Stanislaw)
1868(?)-1925 Brief entry ... 104
See also TCLC 5
Reynolds, Alan 1942- ... 61-64
Reynolds, Ann
See Bly, Carol(yn)
Reynolds, Anne
See Steinke, Ann (Elizabeth)
Reynolds, Barbara 1914- ... 9-10R
Reynolds, Barbara (Ann) 1942- ... 73-76
Reynolds, Barrie (Gordon Robert)
1932- ... 13-14R
Reynolds, Bart
See Emblen, D(onald) L(ewis)
Reynolds, Bertha Capen 1885- ... CAP-2
Earlier sketch in CA 19-20
Reynolds, Charles O. 1921- ... 9-10R
Reynolds, (Alfred) Christopher 1911- ... 104
Reynolds, Clark G(ilbert) 1939- ... CANR-12
Earlier sketch in CA 25-28R
Reynolds, Clark Winton 1934- ... CANR-8
Earlier sketch in CA 23-24R
Reynolds, Dallas McCord 1917- ... CANR-9
Earlier sketch in CA 7-8R
Reynolds, David K(ent) 1940- ... CANR-25
Earlier sketches in CA 65-68, CANR-9
Reynolds, David S(pencer) 1948- ... 124
Reynolds, Dickson
See Reynolds, Helen Mary Greenwood Campbell
Reynolds, Donald E. 1931- ... 33-36R
Reynolds, Elizabeth
See Steinke, Ann (Elizabeth)
Reynolds, Ernest (Randolph) 1910- ... CANR-6
Earlier sketch in CA 3-14R
Reynolds, Frank 1923-1983 ... 114
Obituary ... 109
Reynolds, G. Scott 1925- ... 29-32R
Reynolds, G. W. M. 1814-1879 ... DLB-21
Reynolds, (Arthur) Graham 1914- ... CANR-17
Earlier sketch in CA 13-14R
Reynolds, Harry W., Jr. 1924- ... 15-16R
Reynolds, Helen Mary Greenwood Campbell
1884-1969 ... 7-8R
Obituary ... 103
See also SATA 26
Reynolds, Jack
See Jones, Jack
Reynolds, Joe
See Steward, Samuel M(orris)
Reynolds, John 1901- ... 11-12R
Reynolds, John
See Whitlock, Ralph
Reynolds, John J(oseph) 1924- ... 37-40R
Reynolds, Jonathan 1942- ... 65-68
See also CLC 6, 38
Reynolds, Julia Louise 1883(?)-1980
Obituary ... 102
Reynolds, Larry T(homas) 1938-
Brief entry ... 107
Reynolds, Lloyd George 1910- ... CANR-15
Earlier sketch in CA 23-24R
Reynolds, Louis B. 1917- ... 41-44R
Reynolds, Mack
See Reynolds, Dallas McCord
See also DLB 8
Reynolds, Madge
See Whitlock, Ralph
Reynolds, Malvina 1900-1978 ... 114
Obituary ... 105
See also SATA 24, 44
Reynolds, Marie E. 1912- ... 19-20R
Reynolds, Marjorie Harris 1903- ... 7-8R
Reynolds, Mary Trackett 1914- ... 109
Reynolds, Michael Shane 1937- ... CANR-9
Earlier sketch in CA 65-68
See also CLC 44
Reynolds, (Marjorie) Moira Davison
1915- ... CANR-21
Earlier sketch in CA 105
Reynolds, Morgan O(wen) 1942- ... 117
Reynolds, Pamela 1923- ... 103
See also SATA 34
Reynolds, Paul Davidson 1938- ... CANR-12
Earlier sketch in CA 33-36R
Reynolds, Paul R(evere) 1904-1988 ... 102
Obituary ... 125
Reynolds, Peter C(arlton) 1943- ... 105
Reynolds, Philip Alan 1920- ... CANR-3
Earlier sketch in CA 7-8R
Reynolds, Quentin (James) 1902-1965 ... 73-76
Reynolds, Robert Leonard 1902-1966 ... 2R
Obituary ... 103
Reynolds, Roger 1934- ... 53-56
Reynolds, Ruth Sutton 1890(?)-1977
Obituary ... 69-72
Reynolds, Susan (Mary Grace) 1929- ... 117
Reynolds, Terry S(cott) 1946- ... 117
Reynolds, Timothy (Robin) 1936- ... CANR-8
Earlier sketch in CA 9-10R
Reynolds, Valrae 1944- ... 93-96
Reynolds, William Howard 1922-1972
Obituary ... 107
Reynolds, William J. 1956- ... 123
Reynolds, William Jensen 1920- ... CANR-7
Earlier sketch in CA 7-8R
Rezits, Joseph 1925- ... 107
Rezler, Julius 1911- ... 25-28R
Rezmerski, John Calvin 1942- ... 29-32R
Rezneck, Samuel 1897-1983 ... CANR-24
Obituary ... 110
Earlier sketch in CA 45-48
Reznikoff, Charles 1894-1976 ... CAP-2
Obituary ... 61-64
Earlier sketch in CA 33-36
See also DLB 28, 45
See also CLC 9
Rezny, Arthur A(dolph) 1910- ... CAP-2
Earlier sketch in CA 19-20
Rezzori (d'Arezzo), Gregor von 1914-
Brief entry ... 122
See also CLC 25
Rhea, Claude H(iram), Jr. 1927- ... 103
Rhea, Nicholas
See Walker, Peter N.
Rhein, Francis Bayard 1915- ... 19-20R
Rhein, Phillip H(enry) 1923- ... 81-84
Rheinstein, Max 1899-1977 Obituary ... 73-76
Rhenisch, Harold (Arthur) 1958- ... 113
Rhett, Robert Barnwell 1800-1876 ... DLB-43
Rhie, Schi-Zhin 1936- ... 77-80
Rhine, J(oseph) B(anks) 1895-1980 ... CANR-4
Obituary ... 93-96
Earlier sketch in CA 7-8R
Rhine, Louisa (Weckesser) E. 1891- ... CANR-4
Earlier sketch in CA 3R
Rhinehart, Luke
See Cockcroft, George Powers
Rhinehart, Susan Oneacre 1938- ... 4R
Rhoades, Jonathan
See Olsen, John Edward
Rhoades, Judith G(rubman) 1935- ... 97-100
Rhoads, Dorothy M(ary) 1895- ... CAP-2
Earlier sketch in CA 19-20
Rhoads, Edward J(ohn) M(ichael) 1938- ... 33-36R
Rhoads, Jonathan E(vans) 1907- ... 104
Rhode, Austen
See Francis, Basil (Hoskins)
Rhode, Eric 1934- ... 21-22R
Rhode, Irma 1900-1982 Obituary ... 106
Rhode, Robert B(artlett) 1916- ... 19-20R
Rhode, Robert D(avid) 1911- ... 93-96
Rhode, Winslow
See Roe, F(rederic) Gordon
Rhodehamel, Josephine DeWitt 1901- ... 61-64
Rhodes, Albert 1916-1977 ... CANR-14
Earlier sketch in CA 21-22R
Rhodes, Anthony (Richard Ewart) 1916- ... 9-10R
Rhodes, Arnold Black 1913- ... 15-16R
Rhodes, Bennie (Loran) 1927- ... 108
See also SATA 35
Rhodes, Carolyn Hodgson 1925- ... 122
Rhodes, Clifford Oswald 1911-1985 ... 65-68
Obituary ... 118
Rhodes, David 1946- ... 57-60
Rhodes, Dennis Everard 1923- ... 15-16R
Rhodes, Ernest Lloyd 1915- ... 119

Rhodes, Evan H. 1929- CANR-10
Earlier sketch in CA 57-60
Rhodes, Frank Harold Trevor 1926- 107
See also SATA 37
Rhodes, Hari 1932- 19-20R
Rhodes, Irwin Seymour 1901- 73-76
Rhodes, James Allen 1909- Brief entry 105
Rhodes, James Ford 1848-1927 DLB-47
Rhodes, James M. 1940- 89-92
Rhodes, John J(acob) 1916- 103
Rhodes, Laura
See Robinson, Lisa
Rhodes, Margaret 1915- 45-48
Rhodes, Philip 1922- 107
Rhodes, Richard (Lee) 1937- CANR-20
Earlier sketches in CA 45-48, CANR-1
Rhodes, Robert E(dward) 1927- 122
Rhodes, Robert I. 1942- 69-72
Rhodes, William C(onley) 1918- 81-84
Rhodes James, Robert (Vidal) 1933- CANR-14
Earlier sketch in CA 101
Rhodin, Eric Nolan 1916- CANR-3
Earlier sketch in CA 3R
Rhone, Trevor D(ave) 1940- BW
Rhue, Morton
See Strasser, Todd
Rhydderch, Ieuan
See Jones, Evan David
Rhymer, Joseph 1927- CANR-9
Earlier sketch in CA 23-24R
Rhys, Frank
See Rees, Clair (Francis)
Rhys, Ioan
See Rees, Ioan Bowen
Rhys, J(ohn) Howard W(inslow) 1917- 19-20R
Rhys, Jean 1894-1979 25-28R
Obituary 85-88
See also DLB 36
See also CLC 2, 4, 6, 14, 19
Rhys, Kate
See Donald, Anabel
Rhys, Keidrych 1915-1987 Obituary 122
Riasanovsky, Nicholas V(alentine)
1923- CANR-3
Earlier sketch in CA 5-6R
Ribal, Joseph E(dward) 1931- 61-64
Ribalow, Harold U(riel) 1919-1982 CANR-2
Obituary 108
Earlier sketch in CA 5-6R
Ribar, Joe 1943- 77-80
Ribbons, Ian 1924- 108
See also SATA 30, 37
See also SAAS 3
Ribeiro, Aileen 1944- 124
Ribeiro, Darcy 1922- 33-36R
See also CLC 34
Ribeiro, Joao Ubaldo (Osorio Pimentel)
1941- 81-84
See also CLC 10
Ribicoff, Abraham (Alexander) 1910- 108
Ribman, Ronald (Burt) 1932- 21-22R
See also CLC 7
Ribner, Irving 1921-1972 CANR-3
Obituary 37-40R
Earlier sketch in CA 2R
Riboud, Barbara (Dewayne Tosi) Chase
See Chase-Riboud, Barbara (Dewayne
Tosi)
Ribuffo, Leo P(aul) 1945- 118
Ricardo, Harry R(alph) 1885-1974
Obituary 114
Ricardo-Campbell, Rita CANR-26
Earlier sketches in CA 57-60, CANR-8
Ricart, Josep Gudiol i
See Gudiol i Ricart, Josep
Riccards, Michael P(atrick) 1944- 61-64
Ricchiuti, Paul B(urton) 1925- 107
Ricci, Larry J. 1948- 109
Ricciardi, Lorenzo 1930- 109
Ricciuti, Edward R(aphael) 1938- 41-44R
See also SATA 10
Rice, A(lbert) Kenneth 1908- 7-8R
Rice, Albert
See Leventhal, Albert Rice
Rice, Allan Lake 1905-1984 37-40R
Rice, Anne 1941- CANR-12
Earlier sketch in CA 65-68
See also CLC 41
Rice, Arnold Sanford 1928- 113
Rice, Berkeley 1937- 21-22R
Rice, C(harles) David 1941- 118
Rice, C(harles) Duncan 1942- CANR-10
Earlier sketch in CA 57-60
Rice, Charles D(uane) 1910-1971
Obituary 104
See also SATA 27
Rice, Charles E. 1931- CANR-1
Earlier sketch in CA 4R
Rice, Charles L(ynvel) 1936- 65-68
Rice, Craig
See Randolph, Georgiana Ann
Rice, Cy 1905-1971 CAP-1
Obituary 33-36R
Earlier sketch in CA 11-12
Rice, Dale R(ichard) 1948- 116
See also SATA 42
Rice, David G(ordon) 1938- 101
Rice, David Talbot 1903-1972 CANR-5
Earlier sketch in CA 9-10R
Rice, Desmond Charles 1924- CANR-21
Earlier sketches in CA 11-12R, CANR-5
Rice, Donald L. 1938- CANR-14
Earlier sketch in CA 37-40R
Rice, Dorothy Mary 1913- 11-12R
Rice, Edmund C. 1910(?)-1982 Obituary 106
Rice, Edward E(arl) 1909- 41-44R
Rice, Edward E. 1918- CANR-1
Earlier sketch in CA 49-52
See also SATA 42, 47
Rice, Elinor
See Hays, Elinor Rice
Rice, Elizabeth 1913- 23-24R
See also SATA 2
Rice, Elmer 1892-1967 CAP-2
Obituary 25-28R
Earlier sketch in CA 21-22
See also DLB 4, 7
See also CLC 7, 49
Rice, Eugene F(ranklin), Jr. 1924- 29-32R
Rice, Eve (Hart) 1951- CANR-4
Earlier sketch in CA 53-56
See also SATA 34
Rice, Frank M(artin) 1908- 45-48
Rice, George H(all), Jr. 1923- 53-56
Rice, Grantland 1880-1954 Brief entry 114
See also DLB 29
Rice, Homer C(ranston) 1927- 73-76
Rice, Inez 1907- 29-32R
See also SATA 13
Rice, James 1934- CANR-8
Earlier sketch in CA 61-64
See also SATA 22
Rice, John R(ichard) 1895-1980 CANR-5
Earlier sketch in CA 5-6R
Rice, Joseph Peter 1930- 29-32R
Rice, Julius 1923- 41-44R
Rice, Keith A(lan) 1954- 109
Rice, Lawrence D. 1929- 33-36R
Rice, Martin P(aul) 1938- 57-60
Rice, Max M(cGee) 1928- 93-96
Rice, Otis K(ermit) 1919- 29-32R
Rice, R. B.
See Chapman, Frank M(onroe)
Rice, Ross R(ichard) 1922- 45-48
Rice, Stan 1942- 77-80
Rice, Tamara (Abelson) Talbot 1904-
Brief entry 111
Rice, Thomas Jackson 1945- CANR-18
Earlier sketch in CA 101
Rice, Tim 1944- 103
See also CLC 21
Rice, Wayne 1945- 89-92
Rice, William (Edward) 1938- 118
Rice, William C(arroll) 1911- 11-12R
Rich, Adrienne (Cecile) 1929- CANR-20
Earlier sketch in CA 11-12R
See also DLB 5, 67
See also CLC 3, 6, 7, 11, 18, 36
Rich, Alan 1924- 11-12R
Rich, Daniel Catton 1904-1976 73-76
Obituary 69-72
Rich, Edwin Ernest 1904-1979 Obituary 89-92
Rich, Elaine Sommers 1926- CANR-24
Earlier sketches in CA 19-20R, CANR-9
See also SATA 6
Rich, Elizabeth 1935- 29-32R
Rich, (Ora) Everett 1900- CAP-1
Earlier sketch in CA 11-12
Rich, Frank 1949- 73-76
Rich, Gerry
See Brandon, Johnny
Rich, (David) Gibson 1936- 57-60
Rich, Joe 1935- 57-60
Rich, John H., Jr. 1917- 81-84
Rich, John Martin 1931- 21-22R
Rich, Josephine Bouchard 1912- 5-6R
See also SATA 10
Rich, Louise Dickinson 1903- 73-76
Rich, Mark J. 1948- SATA-53
Rich, Michael B(enjamin) 1935- 29-32R
Rich, Norman 1921- 45-48
Rich, Paul B(enjamin) 1950- 124
Rich, Robert
See Trumbo, Dalton
Rich, Russell R(ogers) 1912- 101
Richard, Adrienne 1921- 29-32R
See also SATA 5
Richard, Arthur Windsor
See Windsor-Richards, Arthur
(Bedlington)
Richard, Betty Byrd 1922- 106
Richard, James Robert
See Bowen, Robert Sydney
Richard, John 1954- 106
Richard, Keith
See Richards, Keith
Richard, Lee
See Le Pelley, Guernsey
Richard, Lionel (Camille Paul) 1938- 93-96
Richard, Lucien J(oseph) 1931- 105
Richard, Marthe 1889-1982 Obituary 110
Richard, Michel Paul 1933- 45-48
Richard, Olga 1914- 103
Richard-Amato, Patricia (Abbott) 1940- 126
Richards, Alayna
See Posner, Richard
Richards, Alfred (Luther) 1939- 45-48
Richards, Allen
See Rosenthal, Richard A.
Richards, Alun 1929- CANR-17
Earlier sketch in CA 65-68
Richards, Arlene Kramer 1935- CANR-11
Earlier sketch in CA 65-68
Richards, Audrey I(sabel) 1899-1984 23-24R
Obituary 113
Richards, Blair P(atton) 1940- 69-72
Richards, Cara E(lizabeth) 1927- CANR-1
Earlier sketch in CA 49-52
Richards, Carl Edward, Jr. 1933- CANR-24
Earlier sketch in CA 45-48
Richards, Caroline 1939- 77-80
Richards, Charles
See Marvin, John T.
Richards, Clare
See Titchener, Louise
Richards, Clay
See Crossen, Kendell Foster
Richards, David
See Bickers, Richard Leslie Townshend
Richards, David Adams 1950- 93-96
See also DLB 53
Richards, Denis (George) 1910- 11-12R
Richards, Dennis L(ee) 1938- 102
Richards, Dorothy B(urney) 1894- 85-88
Richards, Duane
See Hurley, Vic
Richards, E. B.
See Bayley, Edwin Richard
Richards, Frank
See Hamilton, Charles Harold St. John
Richards, Fred
See Richards, Alfred (Luther)
Richards, George 1760(?)-1814 DLB-37
Richards, Guy 1905-1979 CANR-11
Obituary 81-84
Earlier sketch in CA 61-64
Richards, H(arold) M(arshall) S(ylvester)
1894-1985 CAP-2
Obituary 116
Earlier sketch in CA 23-24
Richards, Hilda
See Hamilton, Charles Harold St. John
Richards, Horace G(ardiner) 1906- 5-6R
Richards, I(vor) A(rmstrong)
1893-1979 41-44R
Obituary 89-92
See also DLB 27
See also CLC 14, 24
Richards, J(ohn) Howard 1916- CANR-18
Earlier sketches in CA 45-48, CANR-2
Richards, J(ames) M(aude) 1907- CANR-25
Earlier sketches in CA 5-6R, CANR-5
Richards, Jack W(esley) 1933- 33-36R
Richards, James O(lin) 1936- 37-40R
Richards, Jane 1934- 33-36R
Richards, Jeffrey (Michael) 1945- CANR-13
Earlier sketch in CA 73-76
Richards, Jock 1918- 107
Richards, Joe 1909- CAP-1
Earlier sketch in CA 9-10
Richards, John 1939- 57-60
Richards, John F(olsom) 1938- 115
Richards, John Marvin 1929- 15-16R
Richards, Kathleen
See Dale, Kathleen
Richards, Kay
See Baker, Susan (Catherine)
Richards, Keith 1943- 107
Richards, Kenny
See Broderick, Richard L(awrence)
Richards, Kent David 1938- 104
Richards, Larry
See Richards, Lawrence O.
Richards, Laura E(lizabeth Howe)
1850-1943 Brief entry 120
See also YABC 1
See also DLB 42
Richards, Lawrence O. 1931- CANR-20
Earlier sketch in CA 29-32R
Richards, Lewis A(lva) 1925- 45-48
Richards, M(ary) C(aroline) 1916- 108
Richards, Mark
See Ra'Anan, Uri
Richards, Martin P(aul) M(eredith)
1940- CANR-23
Earlier sketches in CA 61-64, CANR-8
Richards, Max D(eVoe) 1923- CANR-16
Earlier sketch in CA 23-24R
Richards, Nat
See Richardson, James Nathaniel
Richards, Norman 1932- 112
See also SATA 48
Richards, Owain Westmacott 1901-1984
Obituary 114
Richards, Pamela Spence 1941- 111
Richards, Peter
See Monger, (Ifor) David
Richards, Peter Godfrey 1923-1987 108
Obituary 123
Richards, Phyllis
See Auty, Phyllis
Richards, R(onald) C(harles) W(illiam)
1923- CANR-26
Earlier sketches in CA 21-22R, CANR-10
See also SATA 43
Richards, Stanley 1918-1980 25-28R
Obituary 101
Richards, Todd
See Sutphen, Richard Charles
Richards, Victor 1918- 57-60
Richards, Walter Alden (Jr.) 1907-1988
Obituary 125
Richards, William Carey 1818-1892 DLB-73
Richardson, Alan 1923- 29-32R
Richardson, Ann 1942- 119
Richardson, Anne
See Roiphe, Anne Richardson
Richardson, Arleta 1923- CANR-16
Earlier sketch in CA 93-96
Richardson, Beth
See Gutcheon, Beth R(ichardson)
Richardson, Betty 1935- 53-56
Richardson, Bradley M. 1928- 49-52
Richardson, C.
See Munsey, Cecil (Richard, Jr.)
Richardson, Cecil Antonio 1928- 121
Brief entry 115
Richardson, Charles E(verett) 1928- 57-60
Richardson, Charles F. 1851-1913 DLB-71
Richardson, Cyril Charles 1909-1976 37-40R
Obituary 69-72
Richardson, Don(ald MacNaughton)
1935- CANR-9
Earlier sketch in CA 65-68
Richardson, Donald P(orter) 1932- 119
Richardson, Dorothy Lee 1900-1986 106
Obituary 121
Richardson, Dorothy Miller 1873-1957
Brief entry 104
See also DLB 36
See also TCLC 3
Richardson, Dorsey 1896-1981 Obituary 105
Richardson, Edgar Preston 1902-1985 110
Obituary 115
Richardson, Elliot L(ee) 1920- Brief entry 111
Richardson, Elmo (R.) 1930- CANR-11
Earlier sketch in CA 13-14R
Richardson, Ethel Florence (Lindesay)
1870-1946 Brief entry 105
Richardson, Evelyn M(ay Fox) 1902- CAP-1
Earlier sketch in CA 13-14
Richardson, Frank Howard 1882-1970
Obituary 104
See also SATA 27
Richardson, Frank McLean 1904- CANR-20
Earlier sketch in CA 103
Richardson, Gayle E(lwin) 1911- 11-12R
Richardson, George Barclay 1924- 4R
Richardson, Gladwell 1903-1980 123
Richardson, Grace Lee
See Dickson, Naida
Richardson, H(arold) Edward 1929- CANR-15
Earlier sketch in CA 29-32R
Richardson, Harry V(an Buren) 1901- 69-72
Richardson, Harry W(ard) 1938- 29-32R
Richardson, Henrietta
See Richardson, Ethel Florence
(Lindesay)
Richardson, Henry Handel
See Richardson, Ethel Florence
(Lindesay)
See also TCLC 4
Richardson, Henry V(okes) M(ackey)
1923- 25-28R
Richardson, Howard (Dixon) 1917-1984 41-44R
Obituary 114
Richardson, Isla Paschal 1886-1971 CAP-1
Earlier sketch in CA 9-10
Richardson, Ivan L(eRoy) 1920- 101
Richardson, Ivor Lloyd Morgan 1930- 11-12R
Richardson, J. G.
See Richardson, Jacques (Gabriel)
Richardson, Jack (Carter) 1935- 7-8R
See also DLB 7
Richardson, Jacques (Gabriel) 1924- 125
Richardson, James 1950- 77-80
Richardson, James F(rancis) 1931- 29-32R
Richardson, James L(ongden) 1933- 21-22R
Richardson, James Nathaniel 1942- 53-56
Richardson, James R. 1911- 2R
Richardson, Jeremy John 1942- 29-32R
Richardson, Joanna CANR-26
Earlier sketches in CA 13-14R, CANR-10
Richardson, Joe M(artin) 1934- CANR-26
Earlier sketch in CA 45-48
Richardson, John Adkins 1929- 57-60
Richardson, John Martin, Jr. 1938- CANR-12
Earlier sketch in CA 33-36R
Richardson, Justin 1900(?)-1975
Obituary 61-64
Richardson, Kenneth Ridley 1934- 29-32R
Richardson, Laurel 1938- 111
Richardson, Laurence E(aton) 1893- CAP-1
Earlier sketch in CA 11-12
Richardson, (Stewart) Lee (Jr.) 1940- CANR-9
Earlier sketch in CA 21-22R
Richardson, Leopold John Dixon
1893-1979(?) Obituary 104
Richardson, Malcolm 1947- 120
Richardson, Midge Turk 1930- 33-36R
Richardson, Miles (Edward) 1932- 33-36R
Richardson, Mozelle Groner 1914- 33-36R
Richardson, Neil R(yan) 1944- 103
Richardson, Nola 1936- 57-60
See also BW
Richardson, (George) Peter 1935- 114
Richardson, R(alph) Daniel 1931- 109
Richardson, Richard C(olby), Jr.
1933- CANR-13
Earlier sketch in CA 77-80
Richardson, Richard Judson 1935- 29-32R
Richardson, Robert (Dale, Jr.) 1934- CANR-12
Earlier sketch in CA 29-32R
Richardson, Robert Galloway 1926- CANR-7
Earlier sketch in CA 15-16R
Richardson, Robert S(hirley) 1902- 49-52
See also SATA 8
Richardson, Rupert Norval 1891- 19-20R
Richardson, S(tanley) D(ennis) 1925- CANR-10
Earlier sketch in CA 21-22R
Richardson, Samuel 1689-1761 DLB-39
Richardson, Stephen A. 1920- 61-64
Richardson, Thomas Dow 1887- 7-8R
Richardson, Tony
See Richardson, Cecil Antonio
Richardson, Vokes
See Richardson, Henry V(okes) M(ackey)
Richardson, W(alter) C(ecil) 1902- CANR-1
Earlier sketch in CA 2R
Richardson, William John 1920- 21-22R
Richardson, Willis 1889-1977 124
See also BW
See also DLB 51
Richason, Benjamin F(ranklin, Jr.)
1922- 41-44R

Richberg, Donald R(andall) 1881-1960
Obituary ... 113
Riche, Pierre 1921- ... 123
Riche, Robert 1925- ... 108
Riche, William Harding le
See le Riche, William Harding
Richelieu, Peter
See Robinson, P. W.
Richelson, Geraldine 1922- ... 106
See also SATA 29
Richelson, Jeffrey T(albot) 1949- ... 119
Richens, Richard Hook 1919-1984
Obituary ... 114
Riches, John (Kenneth) 1939- ... 117
Riches, Pierre 1927- ... 118
Richette, Lisa Aversa 1928- ... 25-28R
Richetti, John J(oseph) 1938- ... 110
Richey, David 1939- ... CANR-10
Earlier sketch in CA 57-60
Richey, Dorothy Hilliard ... CANR-6
Earlier sketch in CA 9-10R
Richey, Elinor 1920- ... 45-48
Richey, Margaret Fitzgerald 1883(?)-1974
Obituary ... 53-56
Richey, Robert W(illiam) 1912-1978 ... CANR-17
Obituary ... 116
Earlier sketch in CA 25-28R
Richey, Russell Earle 1941- ... 69-72
Richie, Donald (Steiner) 1924- ... CANR-24
Earlier sketches in CA 19-20R, CANR-8
Richland, W(ilfred) Bernard 1909- ... 102
Richler, Mordecai 1931- ... 65-68
See also SATA 27, 44
See also DLB 53
See also CLC 3, 5, 9, 13, 18, 46
See also AITN 1
Richman, Barry M(artin) 1936-1978 ... CANR-17
Earlier sketch in CA 23-24R
Richman, Milton (Saul) 1922-1986 ... 69-72
Obituary ... 119
Richman, Phyllis C. 1939- ... 89-92
Richman, Robert (Maxwell) 1914-1987
Obituary ... 124
Richman, Saul 1917(?)-1979 Obituary ... 85-88
Rich-McCoy, Lois
See McCoy, Lois (Rich)
Richmond, Al 1913-1987 ... 41-44R
Obituary ... 124
Richmond, Anthony H(enry) 1925- ... 23-24R
Richmond, Cindy Packard 1948- ... 112
Richmond, Dick 1933- ... 61-64
Richmond, Douglas W(ertz) 1946- ... 111
Richmond, Grace
See Marsh, John
Richmond, H(ugh) M(acrae) 1932- ... CANR-3
Earlier sketch in CA 9-10R
Richmond, Ian Archibald 1902-1965
Obituary ... 111
Richmond, John C(hristopher) B(lake)
1909- Brief entry ... 106
Richmond, Julius B(enjamin) 1916- ... 29-32R
Richmond, Lee 1943- ... 49-52
Richmond, Lee J(oyce) 1934- ... 113
Richmond, Leigh (Tucker) 1911- ... 23-24R
Richmond, Roaldus Frederick 1910- ... 114
Richmond, Robert P. 1914- ... 21-22R
Richmond, Robert W(illiam) 1927- ... 53-56
Richmond, Rod
See Glut, Donald F(rank)
Richmond, Roe
See Richmond, Roaldus Frederick
Richmond, Samuel B(ernard) 1919- ... 41-44R
Richmond, Sandra 1948- ... 117
Richmond, (John) Stanley 1906- ... 45-48
Richmond, Velma E. B(ourgeois) 1931- ... 61-64
Richmond, W(illiam) Kenneth 1910- ... CANR-10
Earlier sketch in CA 25-28R
Richmond, Walt(er F.) 1922-1977 ... 23-24R
Obituary ... 117
Richoux, Pat(ricia) 1927- ... 25-28R
See also SATA 7
Richstatter, Thomas 1939- ... 112
Richter, Alice 1941- ... 105
See also SATA 30
Richter, C(harles) F(rancis) 1900-1985
Obituary ... 117
Richter, Conrad (Michael) 1890-1968 ... CANR-23
Obituary ... 25-28R
Earlier sketch in CA 7-8R
See also SATA 3
See also DLB 9
See also CLC 30
Richter, David H. 1945- ... 101
Richter, Derek 1907- ... 101
Richter, Dorothy 1906- ... 29-32R
Richter, Gerard R(ichard) 1905- ... 5-6R
Richter, Gisela M(arie) A(ugusta)
1882-1972 ... CANR-4
Earlier sketch in CA 7-8R
Richter, Hans 1888-1976 ... 73-76
Obituary ... 65-68
Richter, Hans Peter 1925- ... CANR-2
Earlier sketch in CA 45-48
See also SATA 6
Richter, Hans Werner 1908- ... 97-100
See also DLB 69
Richter, Harvena 1919- ... CANR-3
Earlier sketch in CA 7-8R
Richter, Horst-Eberhard 1923- ... CANR-20
Earlier sketches in CA 53-56, CANR-5
Richter, Irving 1911- ... 57-60
Richter, J. H(ans) 1901- ... CAP-1
Earlier sketch in CA 15-16
Richter, Joan 1930- ... 101
Richter, Lin 1936- ... 73-76
Richter, Linda K. 1942- ... 117
Richter, Maurice N(athaniel), Jr. 1930- ... 49-52
Richter, Melvin 1921- Brief entry ... 110
Richter, Valentin
See Pick, Robert
Richter, Vernon
See Hutchcroft, Vera
Richter, William L. 1942- ... 126
Rickard, Bob
See Rickard, Robert J(ohn) M(oberley)
Rickard, Robert J(ohn) M(oberley) 1945- ... 106
Rickards, Colin (William) 1937- ... 25-28R
Rickards, Maurice 1919- ... 103
Rickel, Annette U. 1941- ... 123
Rickels, Karl 1924- ... CANR-1
Earlier sketch in CA 45-48
Rickels, Milton H. 1920- ... 5-6R
Rickenbacker, Eddie
See Rickenbacker, Edward Vernon
Rickenbacker, Edward Vernon 1890-1973 ... 101
Obituary ... 41-44R
Ricker, George Marvin 1922- ... CANR-20
Earlier sketch in CA 89-92
Rickert, Corinne Holt
See Sawyer, Corinne Holt
Rickert, John E(arl) 1923- ... CANR-24
Earlier sketch in CA 45-48
Rickett, Frances 1921- ... 107
Rickett, Harold William 1896- ... 19-20R
Ricketts, C(arl) E(verett) 1906- ... 57-60
Ricketts, Ralph Robert 1902- ... 116
Ricketts, Viva Leone (Harris) 1900- ... CAP-1
Earlier sketch in CA 11-12
Rickey, Don, Jr. 1925- ... CANR-9
Earlier sketch in CA 7-8R
Rickey, George Warren 1907- ... 65-68
Rickey, Mary Ellen 1929- ... 23-24R
Rickford, John R(ussell) 1949- ... 126
Rickman, Geoffrey (Edwin) 1932- ... 29-32R
Rickman, H(ans) P(eter) 1918- ... CANR-14
Earlier sketch in CA 19-20R
Rickover, H. G.
See Rickover, Hyman George
Rickover, Hyman George 1900-1986
Obituary ... 119
Ricks, Chip
See Ricks, Nadine
Ricks, Christopher (Bruce) 1933- ... CANR-23
Earlier sketches in CA 11-12R, CANR-7
Ricks, David F(rank) 1927- ... CANR-10
Earlier sketch in CA 21-22R
Ricks, David Trulock 1936- ... 25-28R
Ricks, Don(ald) M(ax) 1936- ... 25-28R
Ricks, Nadine 1925- ... CANR-13
Earlier sketch in CA 77-80
Rickword, (John) Edgell 1898-1982 ... 101
Obituary ... 106
See also DLB 20
Rico, Don(ato) 1917-1985 ... 81-84
Obituary ... 115
See also SATA 43
Rico, Gabriele Lusser 1937- ... 110
Ricoeur, Paul 1913- ... CANR-10
Earlier sketch in CA 61-64
Ricou, Laurence (Rodger) 1944- ... CANR-25
Earlier sketches in CA 61-64, CANR-8
Riday, George E(mil) 1912- ... 15-16R
Riddel, Frank S(tephen) 1940- ... 85-88
Riddel, Joseph N(eill) 1931- ... CANR-5
Earlier sketch in CA 9-10R
Riddell, Alan 1927- ... 104
Ridder, Bernard J. 1913-1983 Obituary ... 110
Ridder, Marie 1925- ... 73-76
Ridderbos, Herman N(icolaas) 1909- ... 57-60
Riddle, Donald H(usted) 1921- ... 11-12R
Riddle, John M(arion) 1937- ... 45-48
Riddle, Kenneth Wilkinson 1920- ... 3R
Riddle, Maxwell 1907- ... CANR-3
Earlier sketch in CA 7-8R
Riddle, Thomas Wilkinson 1886-1983
Obituary ... 110
Riddleberger, Patrick Williams 1915- ... 21-22R
Ridenour, Fritz 1932- ... CANR-25
Earlier sketch in CA 108
Ridenour, George M(eyer) 1928- ... 93-96
Ridenour, Ron 1939- ... 69-72
Rider, Alice Damon 1895- ... 69-72
Rider, (Arthur) Fremont 1885-1962
Obituary ... 89-92
Rider, John R. 1923- ... 25-28R
Ridge, Antonia (Florence) ?-1981 ... 9-10R
Obituary ... 104
See also SATA 7, 27
Ridge, George Ross 1931- ... 3R
Ridge, Julie 1956- ... 120
Ridge, Lola 1873-1941 ... DLB-54
Ridge, Martin 1923- ... 121
See also SATA 43
Ridgely, Beverly S(ellman) 1920- ... CANR-17
Earlier sketch in CA 25-28R
Ridgely, Joseph Vincent 1921- ... 7-8R
Ridgeway, James Fowler 1936- ... 106
Ridgeway, Jason
See Marlowe, Stephen
Ridgeway, Marian E(lizabeth) 1913- ... 33-36R
Ridgeway, Rick 1949- ... 93-96
Ridgway, Brunilde Sismondo 1929- ... CANR-1
Earlier sketch in CA 45-48
Ridgway, John M. 1938- ... 25-28R
Ridgway, Judith 1939- ... CANR-26
Earlier sketch in CA 109
Ridgway, Judy
See Ridgway, Judith
Ridgway, Ronald S(idney) 1923- ... 45-48
Ridgway, Whitman H(awley) 1941- ... 101
Riding, Alan 1943- ... 122
Riding, Laura
See Jackson, Laura (Riding)
See also CLC 3, 7
Ridle, Julia Brown 1923- ... 4R
Ridler, Anne Barbara 1912- ... CANR-3
Earlier sketch in CA 5-6R
See also DLB 27
Ridley, Anthony 1933- ... 107
Ridley, Arnold 1896-1984 Obituary ... 112
Ridley, B(rian) K(idd) 1931- ... 104
Ridley, Charles P(rice) 1933- ... 73-76
Ridley, Jasper (Godwin) 1920- ... CANR-22
Earlier sketches in CA 13-14R, CANR-6
Ridley, Nat, Jr. ... CANR-26
Earlier sketches in CA 19-20, CAP-2
Ridlon, Marci
See Balterman, Marcia Ridlon
See also SATA 22
Ridout, Albert K(ilburn) 1905- ... CAP-2
Earlier sketch in CA 19-20
Ridout, Ronald 1916- ... CANR-20
Earlier sketch in CA 103
Ridpath, Ian (William) 1947- ... 77-80
Ridruejo, Dionisio 1913(?)-1975
Obituary ... 57-60
Rieber, Alfred J(oseph) 1931- ... 11-12R
Rieber, R(obert) W(olff) 1932- ... CANR-3
Earlier sketch in CA 45-48
Riedel, Eunice 1931(?)-1986 Obituary ... 120
Riedel, Richard Langham 1908- ... CAP-2
Earlier sketch in CA 29-32
Riedel, Walter E(rwin) 1936- ... CANR-24
Earlier sketch in CA 45-48
Riedesel, C(lark) Alan 1930- ... 25-28R
Riedl, John O(rth) 1905- ... CAP-2
Earlier sketch in CA 21-22
Riedman, Sarah R(egal) 1902- ... CANR-1
Earlier sketch in CA 4R
See also SATA 1
Riefe, Alan 1925- ... CANR-9
Earlier sketch in CA 61-64
Riefe, Barbara
See Riefe, Alan
Riefenstahl, Berta Helene Amalia 1902- ... 108
Riefenstahl, Leni
See Riefenstahl, Berta Helene Amalia
See also CLC 16
Rieff, Philip 1922- ... 49-52
Riegel, Robert Edgar 1897- ... 5-6R
Rieger, James H(enry) 1936- ... 93-96
Rieger, Shay 1929- ... 29-32R
Riegert, Eduard Richard 1932- ... 69-72
Riegert, Ray 1947- ... 105
Riely, John (Cabell) 1945- ... 113
Riemer, George 1920-1973 ... CAP-2
Obituary ... 41-44R
Earlier sketch in CA 25-28
Riemer, Neal 1922- ... 21-22R
Rienits, Rex 1909-1971 ... CAP-1
Obituary ... 29-32R
Earlier sketch in CA 13-14
Rienow, Leona Train 1903(?)-1983 ... 111
Rienow, Robert 1909- ... 21-22R
Rienstra, Ellen Walker 1940- ... 123
Riepe, Dale (Maurice) 1918- ... 37-40R
Ries, Al 1929- ... 120
Ries, Estelle H. 1896- ... 25-28R
Ries, John C(harles) 1930- ... 15-16R
Ries, Lawrence R(obert) 1940- ... 65-68
Riese, Walther 1890- ... 49-52
Rieseberg, Harry E(arl) 1892- ... 5-6R
Rieselbach, Leroy N(ewman) 1934- ... CANR-24
Earlier sketches in CA 23-24R, CANR-9
Riesenberg, Felix, Jr. 1913-1962 ... 101
See also SATA 23
Riesenberg, Saul H(erbert) 1911- ... 49-52
Rieser, Dolf 1898-1983 Obituary ... 109
Riesman, David 1909- ... 7-8R
Riesman, Evelyn Thompson 1912- ... 21-22R
Riess, Claudia 1937- ... 110
Riess, Oswald George Lorenz 1896- ... 7-8R
Riess, Steven A(llan) 1947- ... 112
Riess, Walter 1925- ... 19-20R
Riessen, Martin Clare 1941- ... 41-44R
Riessman, Frank 1924- ... CANR-6
Earlier sketch in CA 2R
Riesterer, Berthold P(hillip) 1935- ... 41-44R
Rieth, Marian
See Amft, M(arian) J(anet)
Rietz, Sandra A. 1943- ... 123
Rieu, E(mile) V(ictor) 1887-1972 ... CANR-15
Obituary ... 103
Earlier sketch in CA 4R
See also SATA 26, 46
Riewald, J(acobus) G(erhardus) 1910- ... CANR-21
Earlier sketches in CA 57-60, CANR-6
Rifaat, Alifa
See Rifaat, Fatma Abdallah
Rifaat, Fatma Abdallah 1930- ... 123
Rifbjerg, Klaus (Thorvald) 1931-
Brief entry ... 124
Rife, J(ohn) Merle 1895- ... 61-64
Rife, Joanne 1932- ... 110
Rife, Rosemary
See Nusbaum, Rosemary
Riffaterre, Michael 1924- ... DLB-67
Riffe, Ernest
See Bergman, (Ernst) Ingmar
Riffel, Herman H(arold) 1916- ... 112
Rifkin, Jeremy 1945- Brief entry ... 121
Rifkin, Shepard 1918- ... CANR-1
Earlier sketch in CA 3R
Rifkind, Carole 1935- ... 85-88
Rifkind, Simon H(irsch) 1901- ... 109
Rift, Valerie
See Bartlett, Marie (Swan)
Riga, Frank P(eter) 1936- ... 89-92
Riga, Peter J(ohn) 1933- ... 5-6R
Rigault, Andre 1922- ... 45-48
Rigby, Andrew 1944- ... 61-64
Rigby, Ida Katherine 1944- ... CANR-10
Earlier sketch in CA 65-68
Rigby, Paul H(erbert) 1924- ... 19-20R
Rigby, T(homas) H(enry Richard)
1925- ... CANR-10
Earlier sketch in CA 19-20R
Rigdon, Raymond M. 1919- ... 29-32R
Rigdon, Walter 1930- ... 15-16R
Rigelhof, T(errance) F(rederick) 1944- ... 112
Rigg, A(rthur) G(eorge) 1937- ... 37-40R
Rigg, H(enry Hemmingway) K(ilburn)
1911-1980 ... 29-32R
Obituary ... 93-96
Rigg, John Linton 1894- ... 7-8R
Rigg, Robinson P(eter) 1918- ... 33-36R
Riggan, (John) Rob(inson) 1943- ... 115
Riggan, William (Edward, Jr.) 1946- ... 103
Riggio, Thomas P(asquale) 1943- ... 109
Riggs, Dionis Coffin 1898- ... CAP-2
Earlier sketch in CA 29-32
Riggs, Fred(erick) W(arren) 1917- ... CANR-16
Earlier sketch in CA 25-28R
Riggs, James (Lear) 1929- ... 33-36R
Riggs, John R(aymond) 1945- ... 115
Riggs, Robert E. 1927- ... CANR-8
Earlier sketch in CA 15-16R
Riggs, Sidney Noyes 1892-1975 ... 2R
Obituary ... 103
See also SATA 28
Riggs, William (George) 1938- ... 61-64
Righter, Carroll 1900- ... 93-96
Righter, Carroll (Burch) 1900-1988 ... 93-96
Obituary ... 125
Righter, James H(aslam) 1916-1984
Obituary ... 113
Righter, Robert Willms 1933- ... 108
Right Honourable Lord Denning
See Denning, Alfred Thompson
Rigoni, Orlando (Joseph) 1897- ... CANR-11
Earlier sketch in CA 15-16R
Rigsby, Howard 1909- ... 11-12R
Riha, Thomas 1929- ... 11-12R
Riis, Jacob A(ugust) 1849-1914
Brief entry ... 113
See also DLB 23
Riker, John H. 1943- ... 111
Riker, Leigh 1941- ... 119
Riker, Tom L. 1936- ... 104
Riker, William H(arrison) 1920- ... CANR-24
Earlier sketch in CA 4R
Rikhoff, James C. 1931- ... 13-14R
Rikhoff, Jean 1928- ... 61-64
See also SATA 9
Rikhye, Indar Jit 1920- ... CANR-17
Earlier sketch in CA 93-96
Rikki
See Ducornet, Erica
Rikon, Irving 1931- ... 29-32R
Riley, Carroll L(averne) 1923- ... CANR-10
Earlier sketch in CA 25-28R
Riley, Clara (Mae Deatherage) 1931- ... 25-28R
Riley, Dick 1946- ... 101
Riley, E(dward) C(alverley) 1923- ... 11-12R
Riley, G. Micheal 1934- ... 45-48
Riley, Glenda 1938- ... CANR-23
Earlier sketch in CA 106
Riley, James F. 1912- ... 29-32R
Riley, James Whitcomb 1849-1916
Brief entry ... 118
See also SATA 17
Riley, Jocelyn (Carol) 1949- ... 115
See also SATA 50
Riley, John 1937-1978 ... DLB-40
Riley, Lawrence 1897(?)-1975 Obituary ... 61-64
Riley, Madeleine 1933- ... 25-28R
Riley, Matilda White 1911- Brief entry ... 114
Riley, Miles O'Brien 1937- ... CANR-21
Earlier sketch in CA 104
Riley, (Thomas) Nord 1914- ... 13-14R
Riley, R. David 1944(?)-1983 Obituary ... 111
Riley, (Hugh) Ridge(ly, Jr.) 1907-1976 ... 101
Riley, Roy, Jr. 1943(?)-1977 Obituary ... 73-76
Riley, Sandra 1938- ... 104
Riley, Tex
See Creasey, John
Riley, Thomas J. 1901(?)-1977 Obituary ... 73-76
Riley-Smith, Jonathan (Simon Christopher)
1938- ... 23-24R
Riling, Raymond L. J. 1896(?)-1974
Obituary ... 53-56
Rilke, Rainer Maria 1875-1926 Brief entry ... 104
See also TCLC 1, 6, 19
Rilla, Wolf 1925- ... 49-52
Rils
See Bohr, R(ussell) L(eRoi)
Rima, I(ngrid) H(ahne) 1925- ... 23-24R
Rimanoczy, Richard Stanton 1902- ... 73-76
Rimberg, John 1929- ... 57-60
Rimel, Duane (Weldon) 1915- ... 29-32R
Rimington, Critchell 1907-1976 Obituary ... 61-64
Rimland, Bernard 1928- ... CANR-6
Earlier sketch in CA 15-16R
Rimland, Ingrid 1936- ... 61-64
Rimlinger, Gaston V. 1926- ... 37-40R
Rimmer, C(harles) Brandon 1918- ... CANR-12
Earlier sketch in CA 61-64
Rimmer, Douglas 1927- ... 111
Rimmer, Robert H(enry) 1917- ... CANR-20
Earlier sketches in CA 11-12R, CANR-4
Rimmer, W. J.
See Rowland, D(onald) S(ydney)
Rimmington, Gerald T(horneycroft)
1930- ... 19-20R
Rinaldi, Ann 1934- ... 111
See also SATA 50, 51
Rinaldi, Nicholas M. 1934- ... CANR-22
Earlier sketch in CA 104

Rinaldini, Angiolo
See Battisti, Eugenio
Rinard, Judith E(llen) 1947- 97-100
See also SATA 44
Rinchen, Byambyn 1905(?)-1977
Obituary 69-72
Rinder, Walter (Murray) 1934- CANR-11
Earlier sketch in CA 69-72
Rindfleisch, Norval (William) 1930- 65-68
Rinehart, Frederick Roberts 1903(?)-1981
Obituary 104
Rinehart, Mary Roberts 1876-1958
Brief entry 108
Rinehart, Stanley Marshall, Jr. 1897-1969
Obituary 29-32R
Ring, Alfred A. 1905- 29-32R
Ring, Daniel F(rank) 1945- 113
Ring, Douglas
See Prather, Richard S(cott)
Ring, Elizabeth 1912- 103
Ring, Malvin E. 1919- 120
Ringdalh, Mark
See Longyear, Barry Brookes
Ringe, Donald A(rthur) 1923- 3R
Ringenbach, Paul T(homas) 1936- CANR-25
Earlier sketch in CA 45-48
Ringer, Alexander L(othar) 1921- CANR-24
Earlier sketch in CA 45-48
Ringer, Barbara Alice 1925- 11-12R
Ringer, Fritz (Franz) K(laus) 1934- 73-76
Ringer, Robert J. 81-84
Ringgold, Gene 1918- 25-28R
Ringgren, (Karl Vilhelm) Helmer 1917- .. CANR-3
Earlier sketch in CA 7-8R
Ringi, Kjell (Arne Soerensen) 1939- CANR-1
Earlier sketch in CA 45-48
See also SATA 12
Ringkamp, Jonathan 1929-1986 Obituary ... 120
Ringler, William A(ndrew), Jr.
1912-1987(?) 5-6R
Obituary 121
Ringmaster, The
See Mencken, H(enry) L(ouis)
Ringo, Johnny
See Keevill, Henry J(ohn)
Ringold, Clay
See Hogan, (Robert) Ray
Ringold, May Spencer 1914- 21-22R
Ringrose, David R. 1938- 53-56
Ringuet 1895-1960 .... DLB-68
Ringwald, Donald C(harles) 1917-1987 ...21-22R
Obituary 122
Ringwood, Gwen(dolyn Margaret) Pharis
1910-1984 Obituary 112
See also CLC 48
Rinhart, Floyd (Lincoln) 1915- CANR-10
Earlier sketch in CA 25-28R
Rinhart, Marion (Hutchinson) 1916- ... CANR-10
Earlier sketch in CA 25-28R
Rink, Oliver A(lbert) 1947- 125
Rinker, Rosalind Beatrice 1906- CANR-5
Earlier sketch in CA 7-8R
Rinkoff, Barbara Jean (Rich) 1923-1975 .. CAP-2
Obituary 57-60
Earlier sketch in CA 19-20
See also SATA 4, 27
Rinpoche
See Chogyam Trungpa
Rinser, Luise 1911- DLB-69
Rintels, David 1939- 73-76
Rinvolucri, Mario (Francesco Giuseppe)
1940- CANR-26
Earlier sketches in CA 23-24R, CANR-10
Rinvolucri, Mina Josephine Moore
See Moore-Rinvolucri, Mina Josephine
Rinzema, Jakob 1931- 102
Rinzler, Alan 1938- CANR-12
Earlier sketch in CA 21-22R
Rinzler, Carol Eisen 1941- 49-52
Rio, Michel 19(?)- CLC-43
Riols, Noreen 1926- 124
Riopelle, Arthur J. 1920- 37-40R
Riordan, James 1936- CANR-11
Earlier sketch in CA 69-72
See also SATA 28
Riordan, James 1949- 111
Riordan, Mary Marguerite 1931- 106
Riordan, Michael 1946- 106
Rios, Alberto (Alvaro) 1952- 113
Rios, Francisco Giner de los
See Giner de los Rios, Francisco
Rios, Tere
See Versace, Marie Teresa Rios
Riotte, Louise 1909- 57-60
Riotto, Guy Michael 1943- 73-76
Riou, Roger 1909- 61-64
Ripa, Karol 1895-1983 Obituary 109
Ripley, Alexandra 1934- 119
Ripley, Arthur 1895-1961 .... DLB-44
Ripley, (Sidney) Dillon 1913- 57-60
Ripley, Elizabeth Blake 1906-1969 ...... CANR-3
Earlier sketch in CA 4R
See also SATA 5
Ripley, Francis Joseph 1912- CANR-18
Earlier sketches in CA 3R, CANR-3
Ripley, George 1802-1880 ....DLB-1, 64, 73
Ripley, Jack
See Wainwright, John
Ripley, Randall B(utler) 1938- CANR-19
Earlier sketches in CA 53-56, CANR-5
Ripley, Sheldon N(ichols) 1925- 7-8R
Ripley, Stephens 1901(?)-1984 Obituary ... 111
Ripley, Theresa M(argaret) 1944- 85-88
Ripley, (William Young) Warren 1921- . CANR-15
Earlier sketch in CA 33-36R
Rippa, S(ol) Alexander 1925- 53-56
Ripper, Charles L(ewis) 1929- CANR-1
Earlier sketch in CA 4R
See also SATA 3
Ripper, Chuck
See Ripper, Charles L(ewis)
Ripperger, Helmut Lothar 1897-1974
Obituary 53-56
Ripperger, Henrietta
See Hawley, Henrietta Ripperger
Rippey, Mari 1939- 112
Rippey, Robert (Max) 1926- 45-48
Ripple, Paula 112
Ripple, Richard E. 1931- CANR-22
Earlier sketch in CA 33-36R
Rippley, La Vern J. 1935- 33-36R
Rippon, Angela 1944- 126
Rippon, Marion E(dith) 1921- CANR-1
Earlier sketch in CA 49-52
Rippy, Frances (Marguerite) Mayhew
1929- 89-92
Rips, Ervine M(ilton) 1921- 101
Rips, Geoffrey 1950- 108
Rips, Rae Elizabeth 1914-1970 Obituary 104
Riq
See Atwater, Richard Tupper
Riquelme, John Paul 1946- 119
Risatti, Howard A(nthony) 1943- 49-52
Rischin, Moses 1925- CANR-3
Earlier sketch in CA 11-12R
Riseley, Jerry B(urr, Jr.) 1920- CANR-13
Earlier sketch in CA 23-24R
Riseling, John J. W. 1888(?)-1977
Obituary 73-76
Risenhoover, Morris 1940- 65-68
Riser, Wayne H. 1909- CAP-1
Earlier sketch in CA 13-14
Risjord, Norman K. 1931- CANR-22
Earlier sketches in CA 19-20R, CANR-7
Riskin, Robert 1897-1955 .... DLB-26
Riskind, Mary 1944- CANR-26
Earlier sketch in CA 108
Riss, Richard 1952- 81-84
Risse, Heinz 1898- DLB-69
Rissi, Mathias 1920- 45-48
Rissman, Art
See Sussman, Susan
Rissman, Susan
See Sussman, Susan
Rissover, Fredric 1940- 33-36R
Rist, John M(ichael) 1936- CANR-18
Earlier sketch in CA 101
Rist, Ray C(harles) 1944- CANR-3
Earlier sketch in CA 49-52
Rist Arnold, Elisabeth 1950- 65-68
Riste, Olav 1933- CANR-12
Earlier sketch in CA 29-32R
Ristic, Dragisha N. 1909- CAP-2
Earlier sketch in CA 21-22
Ristow, Walter W(illiam) 1908- 19-20R
Ritcheson, Charles R(ay) 1925-
Brief entry 112
Ritchey, John A(rthur) 1919- 23-24R
Ritchie, (John) Andrew 1943- 85-88
Ritchie, Andrew Carnduff 1907-1978
Obituary 81-84
Ritchie, Anna Cora (Ogden) Mowatt
1819-1870 .... DLB-3
Ritchie, Anne Thackeray 1837-1919 ..... DLB-18
Ritchie, Barbara Gibbons 73-76
See also SATA 14
Ritchie, Bill
See Edgar, Frank Terrell Rhoades
Ritchie, C(icero) T(heodore) 1914- 11-12R
Ritchie, Donald A(rthur) 1945- 122
Brief entry 106
Ritchie, Donald D(irk) 1914- 112
Ritchie, Edwin 1931- 29-32R
Ritchie, Elisavietta (Yurievna Artamonoff) .. CANR-2
Earlier sketch in CA 49-52
Ritchie, G(eorge) Stephen 1914- 13-14R
Ritchie, Jack
See Reitci, John G(eorge)
Ritchie, James McPherson 1927- 25-28R
Ritchie, James T. R. 1908- CAP-2
Earlier sketch in CA 19-20
Ritchie, John C(ollins) 1927- 49-52
Ritchie, M(iller) A(lfred) F(ranklin) 1909- .. CAP-2
Earlier sketch in CA 29-32
Ritchie, Paul 1923- 23-24R
Ritchie, Rita
See Reitci, Rita Krohne
Ritchie, Ruth 1900- CANR-2
Earlier sketch in CA 4R
Ritchie, Thomas 1778-1854 .... DLB-43
Ritchie, (Harry) Ward 1905- CANR-22
Earlier sketches in CA 57-60, CANR-7
Ritchie, William A(ugustus) 1903- CANR-24
Earlier sketch in CA 45-48
Ritchie-Calder, Peter Ritchie 1906-1982 . CANR-4
Obituary 105
Earlier sketch in CA 1R
Ritner, Peter Vaughn 1927(?)-1976 77-80
Obituary 69-72
Ritschl, Dietrich 1929- CANR-24
Earlier sketches in CA 21-22R, CANR-9
Ritsos, Giannes
See Ritsos, Yannis
Ritsos, Yannis 1909- 77-80
See also CLC 6, 13, 31
Rittenhouse, Mignon 1904- 41-44R
Ritter, Alan 1937- 117
Brief entry 113
Ritter, Ed 1917- 19-20R
Ritter, Felix
See Kruess, James
Ritter, Gerhard 1888-1967 Obituary 111
Ritter, Henry, Jr. 1920- 93-96
Ritter, Jess(e P., Jr.) 1930- 37-40R
Ritter, Lawrence S(tanley) 1922- CANR-22
Earlier sketch in CA 23-24R
Ritterbush, Philip C. 1936- CANR-6
Earlier sketch in CA 11-12R
Ritts, Paul 1920(?)-1980 Obituary 102
See also SATA 25
Ritvala, M.
See Waltari, Mika (Toimi)
Ritvo, Harriet 1946- 124
Ritz, Charles 1891-1976 Obituary 65-68
Ritz, David 1943- 85-88
Ritz, Jean-Georges 1906- 7-8R
Ritz, Joseph P. 1929- 21-22R
Ritzenthaler, Pat 1914- 25-28R
Ritzer, George 1940- CANR-20
Earlier sketches in CA 53-56, CANR-5
Rivas, Gilberto Lopez y
See Lopez Y Rivas, Gilberto
Rive, Richard (Moore) 1931- 15-16R
See also BW
Rivel, Isade
See Cuevas, Clara
Rivenburgh, Viola K(leinke) 1897- 19-20R
Rivera, Feliciano (Moreno) 1932- CANR-24
Earlier sketch in CA 45-48
Rivera, Geraldo (Miguel) 1943- 108
See also SATA 28
Rivera, Tomas 1935- 49-52
Rivere, Alec
See Nuetzel, Charles (Alexander)
Rivero, Eliana Suarez 1942- 41-44R
Rivers, Caryl 1937- CANR-22
Earlier sketches in CA 49-52, CANR-4
Rivers, Clarence Joseph 1931- 77-80
Rivers, Conrad Kent 1933-1968 85-88
See also BW
See also DLB 41
See also CLC 1
Rivers, Elfrida
See Bradley, Marion Zimmer
Rivers, Elias L(ynch) 1924- 19-20R
Rivers, Joan
See Molinsky, Joan Sandra
Rivers, Julian Alfred Pitt
See Pitt-Rivers, Julian Alfred
Rivers, Larry 1923- 124
Brief entry 117
Rivers, William L. 1925- CANR-7
Earlier sketch in CA 19-20R
Rivers-Coffey, Rachel 1943- 73-76
Riverside, John
See Heinlein, Robert A(nson)
Rives, Leigh
See Seward, William W(ard), Jr.
Rives, Stanley G(ene) 1930- CANR-11
Earlier sketch in CA 23-24R
Rives, William T. 1911(?)-1983 Obituary ... 111
Rivet, A(lbert) L(ionel) F(rederick)
1915- CANR-24
Earlier sketches in CA 23-24R, CANR-9
Rivett, Carol
See Rivett, Edith Caroline
Rivett, Edith Caroline 1894-1958
Brief entry 110
Rivett, Rohan (Deakin) 1917- 25-28R
Rivett-Carnac, Charles Edward 1901- CAP-2
Earlier sketch in CA 19-20
Rivette, Marc 1916- 7-8R
Riviere, Bill
See Riviere, William Alexander
Riviere, Claude 1932- 102
Riviere, Peter Gerard 1934- 103
Riviere, William Alexander 1916- CANR-8
Earlier sketch in CA 5-6R
Rivington, James 1724(?)-1802 .... DLB-43
Rivkin, Allen (Erwin) 1903- CANR-11
Earlier sketch in CA 65-68
See also DLB 26
Rivkin, Ann 1920- 112
See also SATA 41
Rivkin, Arnold 1919-1968 .... CANR-3
Earlier sketch in CA 3R
Rivkin, Ellis 1918- 33-36R
Rivlin, Alice M(itchell) 1931- 33-36R
Rivlin, Harry N. 1904- 19-20R
Rivoire, Jean 1929- CANR-21
Earlier sketches in CA 9-10R, CANR-5
Rivoli, Mario 1943- SATA-10
Rix, Donna
See Rowland, D(onald) S(ydney)
Rizzo, Betty 1926- 111
Rizzo, Mario 1948- 124
Rizzoli, Andrea 1914-1983 Obituary 109
Rizzoli, Angelo 1889-1970 Obituary 104
Rizzuto, Anthony 1937- 106
Rizzuto, James J(oseph) 1939- 107
Rizzuto, Jim
See Rizzuto, James J(oseph)
Roa (y Garcia), Raul 1908-1982 Obituary ... 107
Roa Bastos, Augusto 1917- CLC-45
Roach, Helen P(auline) 1903- CAP-1
Earlier sketch in CA 11-12
Roach, Hildred 1937- 57-60
Roach, Jack L. 1925- Brief entry 109
Roach, James P. 1907-1978 Obituary 77-80
Roach, Joyce Gibson 1935- CANR-18
Earlier sketch in CA 101
Roach, Marilynne K(athleen) 1946- CANR-12
Earlier sketch in CA 57-60
See also SATA 9
Roach, Marion 1956- 120
Roach, Mary Ellen 1921- 19-20R
Roach, Portia
See Takajian, Portia
Roadarmel, Gordon 1932-1972 Obituary 104
Roadarmel, Paul 1942- 93-96
Roaden, Arliss L. 1930- 37-40R
Roadstrum, William H(enry) 1915- 25-28R
Roalfe, William R(obert) 1896- 93-96
Roam, Pearl (Sovern) 1920- 3R
Roark, Albert E(dward) 1933- 85-88
Roark, Dallas M(organ) 1931- 37-40R
Roark, Garland 1904-1985 .... CANR-1
Obituary 115
Earlier sketch in CA 2R
Roark, James L. 1941- CANR-19
Earlier sketch in CA 85-88
Roazen, Paul 1936- 25-28R
Roback, A(braham) A(aron) 1890-1965 .....5-6R
Robacker, Earl Francis 1904- 53-56
Robana, Abderrahman 1938- 65-68
Robard, Jackson
See Wallmann, Jeffrey M(iner)
Robards, Karen 1954- 122
Robards, Sherman M(arshall) 1939- 61-64
Robards, Terry
See Robards, Sherman M.
Robathan, Dorothy M(ae) 1898- 41-44R
Robb, Brian 1913-1979 113
Robb, David M(etheny) 1903- Brief entry ... 113
See also AITN 1
Robb, (George) Douglas 1899-1974
Obituary 114
Robb, Frank Thomson 1908- 57-60
Robb, Inez (Callaway) 1901(?)-1979 97-100
Obituary 85-88
Robb, J(ohn) Wesley 1919- 7-8R
Robb, James H(arding) 1920- 9-10R
Robb, James Willis 1918- 41-44R
Robb, Mary K(unkle) 1908- CAP-2
Earlier sketch in CA 19-20
Robb, Nesca A(deline) 1905- 9-10R
Robbe-Grillet, Alain 1922- 9-10R
See also CLC 1, 2, 4, 6, 8, 10, 14, 43
Robben, John 1930- 93-96
Robbert, Louise Buenger 1925- 41-44R
Robbin, (Jodi) Luna 1936- 103
Robbins, Anthony J. 1960- 126
Robbins, Brother Gerald 1940- 15-16R
Robbins, Caroline 1903- 107
Robbins, Ceila Dame 1943- 118
Robbins, Daniel 1933- CANR-3
Earlier sketch in CA 45-48
Robbins, Frank 1917- 109
See also SATA 32, 42
Robbins, Glaydon Donaldson 1908- 7-8R
Robbins, Harold 1916- CANR-26
Earlier sketch in CA 73-76
See also CLC 5
Robbins, Henry 1928(?)-1979 Obituary ...89-92
Robbins, Horace 1909-1982 Obituary 107
Robbins, Ira A(braham) 1954- 123
Robbins, J(ohn) Albert 1914- 19-20R
Robbins, Jane
See Robbins-Carter, Jane (Borsch)
Robbins, June 61-64
Robbins, Kay
See Hooper, Kay
Robbins, Keith (Gilbert) 1940- CANR-11
Earlier sketch in CA 25-28R
Robbins, Ken SATA-53
Robbins, Lionel (Charles) 1898-1984
Obituary 112
Robbins, Martin 1931- CANR-12
Earlier sketch in CA 29-32R
Robbins, Marty
See Robinson, Martin David
Robbins, Matthew Brief entry 110
Robbins, Mildred Brown CAP-2
Earlier sketch in CA 33-36
Robbins, Millie
See Robbins, Mildred Brown
Robbins, Paul R(ichard) 1930- 114
Robbins, Raleigh
See Hamilton, Charles Harold St. John
Robbins, Richard G., Jr. 1939- 53-56
Robbins, Rossell Hope 1912- CANR-2
Earlier sketch in CA 45-48
Robbins, Roy M(arvin) 1904- 65-68
Robbins, Ruth 1917(?)- 73-76
See also SATA 14
Robbins, S(allie) A(nn) 1940- 23-24R
Robbins, Sam
See Potter, Carole A.
Robbins, Thomas Eugene 1936- 81-84
Robbins, Tom
See Robbins, Thomas Eugene
See also DLBY 80
See also CLC 9, 32
Robbins, Tony
See Pashko, Stanley
Robbins, Trina 1938- CLC-21
Robbins, Vesta O(rdelia) 1891- 53-56
Robbins, Wayne
See Cox, William R(obert)
Robbins-Carter, Jane (Borsch) 1939- 116
Robe, Stanley L(inn) 1915- CANR-6
Earlier sketch in CA 7-8R
Robeck, Mildred C(oen) 1915- 57-60
Roberge, Earl 1918- 85-88
Roberson, (Charles) Ed(win) 1939- 77-80
Roberson, Jennifer 1953- 117
Roberson, John R(oyster) 1930- SATA-53
Roberson, Marie
See Hamm, Marie Roberson
Roberson, Ricky James 1956- 101
Roberson, William H(oward) 1952- 110
Robert, Marc 1927- 114
Robert, Marika Barna 11-12R
Robert, Paul 1911(?)-1980 Obituary 101
Robert, Paul A.
See Roubiczek, Paul (Anton)

Robertiello, Richard C. 1923- ... CANR-3
Earlier sketch in CA 9-10R
Roberto, Brother
See Mueller, Gerald F(rancis)
Roberts, (Edward) Adam 1940- ... CANR-9
Earlier sketch in CA 21-22R
Roberts, Allen 1914- ... 29-32R
Roberts, Anthony
See Watney, John B(asil)
Roberts, Archibald Edward 1915- ... CANR-6
Earlier sketch in CA 57-60
Roberts, Arthur O. 1923- ... 25-28R
Roberts, Arthur Sydney 1905(?)-1978 ... 85-88
Obituary ... 81-84
Roberts, Ben
See Eisenberg, Benjamin
Roberts, Benjamin Charles 1917- ... 102
Roberts, Bill 1914(?)-1978 Obituary ... 81-84
Roberts, Bleddyn J(ones) 1906- ... CAP-1
Earlier sketch in CA 13-14
Roberts, Brian 1930- ... CANR-12
Earlier sketch in CA 29-32R
Roberts, Bruce (Stuart) 1930- ... CANR-6
Earlier sketch in CA 9-10R
See also SATA 39, 47
Roberts, C(atherine) 1917- ... 23-24R
Roberts, Carey 1935- ... 106
Roberts, Carol A. 1933- ... 37-40R
Roberts, Cecil (Edric Mornington)
1892-1976 ... CAP-2
Obituary ... 69-72
Earlier sketch in CA 29-32
Roberts, Chalmers M(cGeagh) 1910- ... 41-44R
Roberts, Charles G(eorge) D(ouglas)
1860-1943 Brief entry ... 105
See also SATA 29
See also TCLC 8
Roberts, Charles Wesley 1916- ... 19-20R
Roberts, (Ray) Clayton 1923- ... 21-22R
Roberts, Clete 1910(?)-1984 Obituary ... 113
Roberts, Colette Jacqueline 1910-1971
Obituary ... 115
Roberts, Dan
See Ross, W(illiam) E(dward) D(aniel)
Roberts, Daniel (Frank) 1922- ... CANR-6
Earlier sketch in CA 11-12R
Roberts, David
See Cox, John Roberts
Roberts, David Arthur 1924-1987
Obituary ... 122
Roberts, David D(ion) 1943- ... 101
Roberts, David S(tuart) 1943- ... 33-36R
Roberts, Dell
See Fendell, Bob
Roberts, Dennis W(ayne) 1947- ... 109
Roberts, Denys (Tudor Emil) 1923- ... CAP-1
Earlier sketch in CA 9-10
Roberts, Denys Kilham 1904(?)-1976
Obituary ... 65-68
Roberts, Derrell C(layton) 1927- ... 29-32R
Roberts, Donald Alfred 1897-1978
Obituary ... 77-80
Roberts, Donald Frank, Jr. 1939- ... 107
Roberts, Doreen 1922- ... 108
Roberts, Dorothy James 1903- ... CAP-1
Earlier sketch in CA 13-14
Roberts, Edgar V. 1928- ... 23-24R
Roberts, Edward B(aer) 1935- ... CANR-9
Earlier sketch in CA 21-22R
Roberts, Edward Barry 1900-1972 ... CAP-2
Earlier sketch in CA 19-20
Roberts, Edwin A(lbert), Jr. 1932- ... 23-24R
Roberts, Elizabeth H. 1913- ... 61-64
Roberts, Elizabeth Madox 1886-1941
Brief entry ... 111
See also SATA 27, 33
See also DLB 9, 54
Roberts, Elizabeth (Allan) Mauchline
1936- Brief entry ... 114
Roberts, Ellen Elizabeth Mayhew
1946- ... CANR-26
Earlier sketch in CA 108
Roberts, Elliott B. 1899-1988 ... 4R
Obituary ... 126
Roberts, Eric 1914- ... 7-8R
Roberts, Estelle (Wills) 1889-1970
Obituary ... 112
Roberts, Eugene (L., Jr.) 1932- ... 97-100
Roberts, Evelyn Lutman 1917- ... 65-68
Roberts, F(rederick) David 1923- ... 5-6R
Roberts, Florence Bright 1941- ... 65-68
Roberts, Frances C(abaniss) 1916- ... 11-12R
Roberts, Francis Warren 1916- ... 13-14R
Roberts, Geoffrey R(ansford) 1924- ... 101
Roberts, Grant
See Wallmann, Jeffrey M(iner)
Roberts, Harold 1896(?)-1982 Obituary ... 108
Roberts, Harold S(elig) 1911-1970 ... CAP-2
Earlier sketch in CA 23-24
Roberts, Henry L(ithgow) 1916-1972
Obituary ... 37-40R
Roberts, Hortense Roberta ... 89-92
Roberts, Howard R(adclyffe) 1906- ... 109
Roberts, I.
See Roberts, Irene
Roberts, I(olo) F(rancis) 1925- ... 29-32R
Roberts, I. M.
See Roberts, Irene
Roberts, Irene 1925- ... CANR-21
Earlier sketches in CA 13-14R, CANR-6
Roberts, Ivor
See Roberts, Irene
Roberts, J(ohn) A(lexander) Fraser
1899-1987 Obituary ... 121
Roberts, J(ohn) Kimberley 1935- ... 117
Roberts, J. R.
See Randisi, Robert J(oseph)
Roberts, James Deotis 1927- ... CANR-15
Earlier sketch in CA 33-36R
Roberts, James Hall
See Duncan, Robert L(ipscomb)
Roberts, Jane
See Butts, Jane Roberts
Roberts, Janet Louise 1925- ... CANR-13
Earlier sketch in CA 61-64
Roberts, Jason
See Bock, Fred
Roberts, Jeanne Addison ... 89-92
Roberts, Jim
See Bates, Barbara S(nedeker)
Roberts, Joan Ila 1935- ... 29-32R
Roberts, Joe
See Saltzman, Joseph
Roberts, John
See Bingley, David Ernest
Roberts, John G(aither) 1913- ... 49-52
See also SATA 27
Roberts, John M(ilton) 1916- ... 37-40R
Roberts, John M(orris) 1928- ... CANR-16
Earlier sketch in CA 85-88
Roberts, John R. 1934- ... CANR-12
Earlier sketch in CA 33-36R
Roberts, John Storm 1936- ... CANR-12
Earlier sketch in CA 25-28R
Roberts, Joseph B(oxley), Jr. 1918- ... 41-44R
Roberts, Julian
See Bardens, Dennis (Conrad)
Roberts, K.
See Lake, Kenneth R(obert)
Roberts, Kate 1891-1985 ... 107
Obituary ... 116
See also CLC 15
Roberts, Keith (John Kingston) 1935- ... 25-28R
See also CLC 14
Roberts, Keith 1937(?)-1979 Obituary ... 85-88
Roberts, Ken
See Lake, Kenneth R(obert)
Roberts, Kenneth (Lewis) 1885-1957
Brief entry ... 109
See also DLB 9
See also TCLC 23
Roberts, Kenneth H(arris) 1930- ... 33-36R
Roberts, Kevin E(rnest) A(lbert) 1940- ... 113
Roberts, Lee
See Martin, Robert (Lee)
Roberts, Len
See Roberts, Leonard
Roberts, Leonard 1947- ... 113
Roberts, Leonard W(ard) 1912-1983 ... 33-36R
Roberts, Leslie 1896-1980 ... 103
Roberts, Lionel
See Fanthorpe, R(obert) Lionel
Roberts, Lisa
See Turner, Robert H(arry)
Roberts, MacLennan
See Terrall, Robert
Roberts, Mary D(uffy) 1925- ... 4R
Roberts, Mervin F(rancis) 1922- ... CANR-24
Earlier sketches in CA 65-68, CANR-9
Roberts, Michael 1945- ... 69-72
Roberts, Michele (B.) 1949- ... 115
See also CLC 48
Roberts, Myron 1923- ... 29-32R
Roberts, Nancy Correll 1924- ... CANR-6
Earlier sketch in CA 11-12R
See also SATA 28, 52
Roberts, Nora 1950- ... 123
Roberts, Oral 1918- ... 41-44R
Roberts, (Thomas) Patrick 1920- ... 61-64
Roberts, Paul Craig 1939- ... CANR-22
Earlier sketch in CA 33-36R
Roberts, Paul McHenry 1917-1967 ... 3R
Obituary ... 103
Roberts, Percival R(udolph) III 1935- ... 41-44R
Roberts, Philip Davies 1938- ... CANR-26
Earlier sketch in CA 109
Roberts, Phyllis Barzillay 1932- ... 41-44R
Roberts, Rachel 1927-1980 Obituary ... 115
Roberts, Rand
See Parham, Robert Randall
Roberts, Richard J(erome) 1928- ... 7-8R
Roberts, Richard W. 1935-1978 Obituary ... 73-76
Roberts, Rinalda
See Cudlipp, Edythe
Roberts, Robert B. 1911- ... 117
Roberts, Robert C(ampbell) 1942- ... CANR-14
Earlier sketch in CA 69-72
Roberts, Ron E. 1939- ... 33-36R
Roberts, Roy Allison 1887-1967 Obituary ... 89-92
Roberts, Rufus Putnam 1926- ... 2R
Roberts, Sally
See Jones, Sally Roberts
Roberts, Sheila 1942- ... 102
Roberts, Spencer Eugene 1920- ... 89-92
Roberts, Steven V(ictor) 1943- ... 61-64
Roberts, Susan F. 1919- ... 104
Roberts, Suzanne 1931- ... 106
Roberts, Sydney (Castle) 1887-1966 ... CAP-1
Earlier sketch in CA 15-16
Roberts, Terence
See Sanderson, Ivan T(erence)
Roberts, Thom(as Sacra) 1940- ... CANR-15
Earlier sketch in CA 81-84
Roberts, Thomas J(ohn) 1925- ... 41-44R
Roberts, Tom
See Thomas, R(obert) Murray
Roberts, Trev
See Trevathan, Robert E.
Roberts, Vera Mowry 1918- ... 19-20R
Roberts, Virginia
See Dean, Nell Marr
Roberts, Walter R(onald) 1916- ... CANR-1
Earlier sketch in CA 49-52
Roberts, Warren (Errol) 1933- ... 73-76
Roberts, Warren Aldrich 1901- ... CAP-1
Earlier sketch in CA 11-12
Roberts, Wayne
See Overholser, Wayne D.
Roberts, William 1868-1959 Brief entry ... 122
Roberts, William P(utnam) 1931- ... 113
Roberts, Willo Davis 1928- ... CANR-19
Earlier sketches in CA 49-52, CANR-3
See also SATA 21
Robertshaw, (James) Denis 1911- ... 65-68
Robertson, Alec
See Robertson, Alexander Thomas Parke
Anthony Cecil
Robertson, Alexander Thomas Parke
Anthony Cecil 1892-1982 ... 104
Obituary ... 105
Robertson, Andrew 1921-1986 Obituary ... 120
Robertson, Arthur Henry 1913-1984 ... 9-10R
Obituary ... 113
Robertson, Barbara (Anne) 1931- ... 25-28R
See also SATA 12
Robertson, Brian 1951- ... 101
Robertson, Carol P. 1934- ... 123
Robertson, Charles L(angner) 1927- ... 23-24R
Robertson, Charles Martin 1911- ... 104
Robertson, Colin 1906- ... 11-12R
Robertson, Constance (Pierrepont Noyes)
1896(?)-1985 ... 29-32R
Obituary ... 116
Robertson, Cordelia Biddle 1898(?)-1984
Obituary ... 114
Robertson, D(onald) J(ames)
1926-1970 ... CANR-10
Earlier sketch in CA 5-6R
Robertson, D(urant) W(aite), Jr. 1914- ... CANR-9
Earlier sketch in CA 61-64
Robertson, Dale 1923- Brief entry ... 107
Robertson, David (Allan, Jr.) 1915- ... 81-84
Robertson, Dede 1927- ... 114
Robertson, Don 1929- ... CANR-23
Earlier sketches in CA 9-10R, CANR-7
See also SATA 8
Robertson, Donald S. 1918- ... 123
Robertson, Dorothy Lewis 1912- ... 25-28R
See also SATA 12
Robertson, Dougal 1924- ... 61-64
Robertson, Durant Waite, Jr. 1914- ... 109
Robertson, E(smonde) M(anning)
1923-1987 ... 29-32R
Obituary ... 121
Robertson, Edith Anne (Stewart)
1883-19(?) ... CAP-1
Earlier sketch in CA 11-12
Robertson, Elizabeth Chant 1899- ... 49-52
Robertson, Ellis
See Ellison, Harlan
and Silverberg, Robert
Robertson, Eric Desmond 1914-1987
Obituary ... 122
Robertson, Frank C(hester) 1890-1969 ... CANR-4
Earlier sketch in CA 2R
Robertson, H(ector) M(enteith) 1905-1984
Obituary ... 113
Robertson, Heather Margaret 1942- ... CANR-17
Earlier sketch in CA 93-96
Robertson, Howard Stephen 1931- ... 41-44R
Robertson, James 1911- ... 7-8R
Robertson, James Douglas 1904- ... 7-8R
Robertson, James (Irvin), Jr. 1930- ... CANR-6
Earlier sketch in CA 11-12R
Robertson, James Louis 1907- ... CAP-2
Earlier sketch in CA 29-32
Robertson, James Oliver 1932- ... 111
Brief entry ... 106
Robertson, James Wilson 1899-1983 ... 109
Obituary ... 110
Robertson, Jennifer Sinclair 1942- ... CANR-5
Earlier sketch in CA 53-56
See also SATA 12
Robertson, Jenny
See Robertson, Jennifer Sinclair
Robertson, John (Charles) 1951- ... 124
Robertson, Keith (Carlton) ... 9-10R
See also SATA 1
Robertson, Leon S(purgeon) 1936- ... 41-44R
Robertson, M(arion) G(ordon) 1930- ... 111
Robertson, Marian 1921- ... 111
Robertson, Martin
See Robertson, Charles Martin
Robertson, Mary D(emmond) 1927- ... 102
Robertson, Mary Elsie 1937- ... CANR-15
Earlier sketch in CA 81-84
Robertson, Nan 1926- ... 121
Robertson, Olivia (Melian) 1917- ... 9-10R
Robertson, Pat
See Robertson, M(arion) G(ordon)
Robertson, Patrick 1940- ... 61-64
Robertson, Priscilla (Smith) 1910- ... CAP-2
Earlier sketch in CA 23-24
Robertson, Roland 1938- ... 29-32R
Robertson, Thomas Anthony 1897- ... CAP-1
Earlier sketch in CA 15-16
Robertson, Wally
See Robertson, Walter
Robertson, Walter 1892-1983 Obituary ... 109
Robertson, Wilfrid 1892- ... 7-8R
Roberts-Wray, Kenneth (Owen) 1899- ... CAP-2
Earlier sketch in CA 25-28
Robeson, Gerald B(yron) 1938- ... 65-68
Robeson, Kenneth
See Dent, Lester
and Goulart, Ron(ald Joseph)
Robeson, Paul (Leroy Bustill) 1898-1976 ... 124
Obituary ... 109
See also BW
Robey, Daniel 1944- ... 111
Robey, Edward George (Haydon)
1900-1983 Obituary ... 109
Robey, Harriet 1900- ... 107
Robey, Ralph W(est) 1899-1972
Obituary ... 37-40R
Robhs, Dwight
See Monaco, Richard
Robichaud, Gerald A(laric) 1912-1979
Obituary ... 85-88
Robichaud, Gerard 1908- ... CAP-2
Earlier sketch in CA 17-18
Robichon, Jacques 1920- ... 101
Robie, Edward H(odges) 1886- ... CAP-2
Earlier sketch in CA 19-20
Robilliard, Eileen Dorothy 1921- ... 23-24R
Robilliard, St. John Anthony 1953- ... 124
Robin
See Roberts, Eric
Robin, Arthur de Quetteville 1929- ... 104
Robin, Leo 1900(?)-1984 Obituary ... 114
Robin, Ralph 1914- ... 65-68
Robin, Richard S(hale) 1926- ... 23-24R
Robinet, Harriette Gillem 1931- ... 69-72
See also SATA 27
Robinett, Betty Wallace 1919- ... 41-44R
Robinett, Stephen (Allen) 1941- ... 101
Robins, Corinne 1934- ... 118
Robins, Denise (Naomi) 1897(?)-1985 ... CANR-19
Obituary ... 116
Earlier sketches in CA 65-68, CANR-10
Robins, Dorothy B.
See Robins-Mowry, Dorothy B(ernice)
Robins, Eli 1921- ... 109
Robins, Elizabeth 1862(?)-1952
Brief entry ... 116
Robins, Harry Franklin 1915- ... 5-6R
Robins, Lee N(elken) 1922- ... CANR-14
Earlier sketch in CA 23-24R
Robins, Natalie S. 1938- ... 19-20R
Robins, Patricia (Denise) 1921- ... CANR-19
Earlier sketch in CA 89-92
Robins, Robert Henry 1921- ... 7-8R
Robins, Rollo, Jr.
See Ellis, Edward S(ylvester)
Robins, Seelin
See Ellis, Edward S(ylvester)
Robins-Mowry, Dorothy B(ernice) 1921- ... 25-28R
Robinson, A(ntony) M(eredith) Lewin
1916- ... CANR-9
Earlier sketch in CA 21-22R
Robinson, A(rthur) N(apoleon) R(aymond)
1926- ... 33-36R
Robinson, Abby 1947- ... 117
Robinson, Adjai 1932- ... 45-48
See also SATA 8
Robinson, Alan R(onald) 1920- ... CAP-1
Earlier sketch in CA 11-12
Robinson, Albert J(ohn) 1926- ... 53-56
Robinson, Alice Gram 1896(?)-1984
Obituary ... 111
Robinson, Alice M(erritt) 1920-1983 ... 108
Obituary ... 109
Robinson, Anthony (Christopher) 1931- ... CANR-1
Earlier sketch in CA 3R
Robinson, Archie W. 1906(?)-1987
Obituary ... 123
Robinson, B(asil) W(illiam) 1912- ... CANR-3
Earlier sketch in CA 7-8R
Robinson, Barbara Webb 1927- ... 3R
See also SATA 8
Robinson, Barry (James) 1938- ... 25-28R
Robinson, Betsy Julia 1951- ... 109
Robinson, Bill
See Robinson, William Wheeler
Robinson, Blackwell P(ierce) 1916- ... CANR-24
Earlier sketch in CA 45-48
Robinson, Brooks (Calbert, Jr.) 1937- ... 116
Robinson, Budd
See Robinson, David
Robinson, C(harles) A(lexander), Jr.
1900-1965 ... CANR-4
Earlier sketch in CA 1R
See also SATA 36
Robinson, Casey 1903-1979 ... DLB-44
Robinson, Cecil 1921- ... 15-16R
Robinson, Cervin 1928- ... 61-64
Robinson, Chaille Howard (Payne) ... 13-14R
Robinson, Charles 1870-1937 ... SATA-17
Robinson, Charles 1931- ... CANR-2
Earlier sketch in CA 49-52
See also SATA 6
Robinson, Charles E(dward) 1941- ... CANR-13
Earlier sketch in CA 77-80
Robinson, Charles Knox (Jr.) 1909-1980 ... 103
Obituary ... 97-100
Robinson, Charles M. III 1949- ... 120
Robinson, Corinne H(ogden) 1909- ... 93-96
Robinson, Daniel N. 1937- ... 33-36R
Robinson, Daniel Sommer 1888-1977 ... 29-32R
Obituary ... 125
Robinson, David 1915- ... 81-84
Robinson, David A. 1925- ... 17-18R
Robinson, Dean (Stewart) 1946- ... 114
Robinson, Derek 1932- ... 77-80
Robinson, Donald 1913- ... 25-28R
Robinson, Donald H(oy) 1910- ... CAP-2
Earlier sketch in CA 33-36
Robinson, Donald L(eonard) 1936- ... 41-44R
Robinson, Donald W(ittmer)
1911-1980 ... CANR-12
Earlier sketch in CA 23-24R
Robinson, Douglas Hill 1918- ... CANR-8
Earlier sketch in CA 7-8R

Robinson, E(dwin) A(rlington) 1869-1935
Brief entry 104
See also DLB 54
See also CDALB 1865-1917
See also TCLC 5
Robinson, Earl (Hawley) 1910- CANR-2
Earlier sketch in CA 45-48
Robinson, Edgar Eugene 1887-1977
Obituary 73-76
Robinson, Edward G. 1893-1973
Obituary 45-48
Robinson, Edward L(ouis) 1921- 41-44R
Robinson, Elwyn B(urns) 1905- CAP-2
Earlier sketch in CA 19-20
Robinson, Eric 1924- 49-52
Robinson, Forrest G(len) 1940- 41-44R
Robinson, Francis (Arthur) 1910-1980
Obituary 97-100
Robinson, Francis (Christopher Rowland)
1944- 112
Robinson, Frank M(alcolm) 1926- CANR-19
Earlier sketches in CA 49-52, CANR-3
Robinson, Frank M(elvin), Jr. 1928- 57-60
Robinson, Frank S(teven) 1947- 97-100
Robinson, Fred Colson 1930- 37-40R
Robinson, Fred Miller 1942- 107
Robinson, Godfrey Clive 1913- 13-14R
Robinson, Gustavus H. 1881-1972
Obituary 37-40R
Robinson, Haddon W. 1931- 73-76
Robinson, Halbert B(enefiel)
1925-1981 .... CANR-9
Earlier sketch in CA 19-20R
Robinson, Helen Caister 1899- CANR-16
Earlier sketch in CA 93-96
Robinson, Helen Mansfield 1906- 13-14R
Robinson, Helene M. 15-16R
Robinson, Henry Morton 1898-1961
Obituary 116
Robinson, Herbert Spencer 93-96
Robinson, Horace W(illiam) 1909- 93-96
Robinson, Howard 1885- CAP-1
Earlier sketch in CA 13-14
Robinson, Hubbell 1905-1974 Obituary 53-56
Robinson, Ira E(dwin) 1927- 81-84
Robinson, J(ohn) Lewis 1918- 107
Robinson, J(ohn) W(illiam) 1934- 17-18R
Robinson, James A(rthur) 1932- 17-18R
Robinson, James Harvey 1863-1936 .... DLB-47
Robinson, James K(eith) 1916- 17-18R
Robinson, James M(cConkey) 1924- 15-16R
Robinson, Jan M. 1933- 61-64
See also SATA 6
Robinson, Janet O(live) 1939- 33-36R
Robinson, Janice S(tevenson) 1941- 111
Robinson, Jay (Luke) 1932- 41-44R
Robinson, Jean O. 1934- 29-32R
See also SATA 7
Robinson, Jeffrey 1945- 121
Robinson, Jerry 1922- Brief entry 112
See also SATA 34
Robinson, Jill 1936- 102
See also CLC 10
Robinson, Jo Ann Ooiman 1942- 111
Robinson, Joan (Mary) G(ale Thomas)
1910- CANR-5
Earlier sketch in CA 7-8R
See also SATA 7
Robinson, Joan Violet 1903-1983 .... CANR-6
Obituary 110
Earlier sketch in CA 9-10R
Robinson, John A(rthur) T(homas)
1919-1983 .... CANR-6
Obituary 111
Earlier sketch in CA 7-8R
Robinson, John W(esley) 1929- CANR-2
Earlier sketch in CA 49-52
Robinson, Joseph 1927- 45-48
Robinson, Joseph Frederick 1912- 13-14R
Robinson, Joseph William 1908- CAP-2
Earlier sketch in CA 25-28
Robinson, Karl Frederic 1904-1967 .... CANR-5
Earlier sketch in CA 5-6R
Robinson, Kathleen
See Robinson, Chaille Howard (Payne)
Robinson, Kenneth Ernest 1914- 7-8R
Robinson, Kim Stanley 1952- 126
See also CLC 34
Robinson, L(eonard) W(allace) 1912- 69-72
Robinson, (Esme Stuart) Lennox
1886-1958 Brief entry 120
See also DLB 10
Robinson, Leonard A. 1904(?)-1980 97-100
Robinson, Lisa 1936- 93-96
Robinson, Lloyd
See Silverberg, Robert
Robinson, Logan Gilmore 1949- 108
Robinson, Louie, Jr. 1926- 107
Robinson, Lytle W(ebb) 1913- 61-64
Robinson, Mabel Louise 1874-1962
Obituary 113
See also DLB 22
Robinson, Mairi 1945- 123
Robinson, Margaret A(twood) 1937- 107
Robinson, Marguerite S. 1935- 49-52
Robinson, Marileta 1942- 101
See also SATA 32
Robinson, Marilynne 1944- 116
See also CLC 25
Robinson, Martin David 1925-1982
Obituary 108
Robinson, Matt(hew) 1937- 45-48
Robinson, Maudie Millian Oller 1914- CANR-8
Earlier sketch in CA 61-64
See also SATA 11
Robinson, Maurice R(ichard) 1895-1982
Obituary 106
See also SATA 29
Robinson, Max (C.) 1939- 124
Brief entry 110
See also BW
Robinson, Michael J(ay) 1945- 113
Robinson, Nancy K(onheim) 1942- CANR-24
Earlier sketch in CA 106
See also SATA 31, 32
Robinson, Nancy (Lou) M(ayer) 1930- 61-64
Robinson, Norman H(amilton) G(alloway)
1912- 13-14R
Robinson, O(liver) Preston 1903- 13-14R
Robinson, (Frances) Olvis 1923- 53-56
Robinson, P. W. 1893- 103
Robinson, Patricia Colbert 1923- 77-80
Robinson, Paul 1940- 81-84
Robinson, Philip (Bedford) 1926- CANR-16
Earlier sketch in CA 21-22R
Robinson, Ras 1935- 105
Robinson, Ray(mond Kenneth) 1920- 77-80
See also SATA 23
Robinson, Ray Charles 1932- Brief entry 115
Robinson, Raymond Henry 1927- 41-44R
Robinson, Richard 1945- CANR-13
Earlier sketch in CA 57-60
Robinson, Richard Dunlop 1921- 7-8R
Robinson, Robert 1886-1975 Obituary 113
Robinson, Robert (Reginald) 1922- CANR-14
Earlier sketch in CA 41-44R
Robinson, Robert 1927- 11-12R
Robinson, Robert H(ouston) 1936- CANR-6
Earlier sketch in CA 7-8R
Robinson, Roland Inwood 1907- CANR-1
Earlier sketch in CA 4R
Robinson, Rollo S(mith) 1915- 41-44R
Robinson, Rose 77-80
Robinson, Selma 1899(?)-1977 Obituary 73-76
Robinson, Shari
See McGuire, Leslie Sarah
Robinson, Sheila Mary 1928- Brief entry 126
Robinson, Sidney K. 1943- 113
Robinson, Sister Marian Dolores 1916- 11-12R
Robinson, Smokey
See Robinson, William, Jr.
See also CLC 21
Robinson, Sondra Till 1931- CANR-7
Earlier sketch in CA 53-56
Robinson, Spider 1948- CANR-11
Earlier sketch in CA 65-68
Robinson, T(homas) H(eath)
1869-1950 .... SATA-17
Robinson, T(homas) M(ore) 1936- 29-32R
Robinson, Terry 1916- 108
Robinson, Therese 1797-1870 .... DLB-59
Robinson, Thomas W. 1935- 33-36R
Robinson, Trevor 1929- 53-56
Robinson, (Wanda) Veronica 1926- 105
See also SATA 30
Robinson, Vince
See Newton, Michael
Robinson, Virgil E. 1908- 23-24R
Robinson, W(illiam) Gordon 1903-1977 .... CANR-5
Earlier sketch in CA 7-8R
Robinson, W(illiam) Heath 1872-1944 .... SATA-17
Robinson, W(illiam) R(onald) 1927- 23-24R
Robinson, W. Stitt
See Robinson, W(alter) Stitt, Jr.
Robinson, W(alter) Stitt, Jr. 1917- 126
Brief entry 105
Robinson, Wayne 1916- 2R
Robinson, Wayne A(ustin) 1937- 73-76
Robinson, Wilhelmena S(impson) 1912- 25-28R
Robinson, Willard B(ethurem) 1935- 57-60
Robinson, William Childs 1897-1982 .... 4R
Obituary 116
Robinson, William F(rank) 1946- 118
Robinson, William H. 1912-1984 Obituary 111
Robinson, William H(enry) 1922- CANR-25
Earlier sketch in CA 37-40R
See also BW
Robinson, William, Jr. 1940- Brief entry 116
Robinson, William P(owell) 1910- 5-6R
Robinson, William Wheeler 1918- CANR-18
Earlier sketches in CA 7-8R, CANR-3
Robison, Bonnie 1924- 57-60
See also SATA 12
Robison, David V. 1911(?)-1978 93-96
Obituary 81-84
Robison, Mabel Otis 1891- CAP-1
Earlier sketch in CA 11-12
Robison, Mary 1949- 116
Brief entry 113
See also CLC 42
Robison, Nancy L(ouise) 1934- 93-96
See also SATA 32
Robison, Sophia Moses 1888-1969 .... 7-8R
Obituary 103
Robitscher, Jonas B(ondi, Jr.)
1920-1981 .... CANR-19
Obituary 103
Earlier sketch in CA 21-22R
Robles, Emmanuel 1914- 81-84
Robles, Mireya 1934- 81-84
Robley, Grace 1918- 61-64
Robley, Rob
See Robley, Wendell
Robley, Wendell 1916- 61-64
Robo, Etienne 1879- CAP-1
Earlier sketch in CA 11-12
Robock, Stefan H. 1915- 19-20R
Robottom, John 1934- CANR-16
Earlier sketch in CA 29-32R
See also SATA 7
Robsjohn-Gibbings, Terence Harold
1905-1976 Obituary 69-72
Robson, B(rian) T(urnbull) 1939- 29-32R
Robson, D(erek) I(an) 1935- 25-28R
Robson, Dirk
See Robinson, Derek
Robson, E(manuel) W(alter) 1897- 65-68
Robson, Elizabeth 1942- 101
Robson, Ernest (Mack) 1902- CANR-24
Earlier sketch in CA 45-48
Robson, James 1890- 7-8R
Robson, Jeremy 1939- CANR-4
Earlier sketch in CA 7-8R
Robson, John M(ercel) 1927- 29-32R
Robson, Lucia St. Clair 1942- 108
Robson, Marion M. 1908- 89-92
Robson, William Alexander 1895-1980 103
Obituary 97-100
Robson, William N. AITN-1
Roby, Kinley E. 1929- 77-80
Roby, Mary Linn CANR-7
Earlier sketch in CA 15-16R
Roby, Pamela A. 1942- 29-32R
Roby, Robert C(urtis) 1922- 7-8R
Robyns, Gwen 1917- 93-96
Roca-Pons, Josep 1914- 49-52
Roccapriore, Marie 1933- 115
Roch, John H(enry) 1916- 102
Rochard, Henri
See Charlier, Roger H(enri)
Rochberg-Halton, Eugene 1950- 111
Roche, A. K.
See Abisch, Roslyn Kroop
and Kaplan, Boche
Roche, Alphonse Victor 1895- 104
Roche, Douglas J. 1929- 101
Roche, George Charles III 1935- 29-32R
Roche, J. Jeffrey 1916(?)-1975 Obituary 61-64
Roche, John
See Le Roi, David (de Roche)
Roche, John P(earson) 1923- 69-72
Roche, Kennedy Francis 1911- 61-64
Roche, Orion 1948- 61-64
Roche, Owen I. A. 1911(?)-1973
Obituary 41-44R
Roche, P(atricia) K. Brief entry 112
See also SATA 34
Roche, Paul 1928- CANR-4
Earlier sketch in CA 7-8R
Roche, T(homas) W(illiam) E(dgar)
1919-197(?) CAP-2
Earlier sketch in CA 21-22
Roche, Terry
See Poole, Peggy
Roche, Thomas P(atrick), Jr. 1931- 106
Rochelle, Jay C. 1938- 53-56
Rocher, Guy 1924- CANR-24
Earlier sketch in CA 45-48
Rocher, Ludo 1926- Brief entry 106
Rochester, Devereaux 1917- 105
Rochester, Harry A(rthur) 1897(?)-1983
Obituary 109
Rochester, J. Martin 1945- 37-40R
Rochester, Jack B. 1944- 122
Rochlin, Gregory 1912- 49-52
Rochlin, Harriet 1924- 117
Rochmis, Lyda N(onne) 1912- 29-32R
Rock, David (Peter) 1945- CANR-19
Earlier sketch in CA 101
Rock, Gail Brief entry 111
See also SATA 32
Rock, Irvin 1922- CANR-10
Earlier sketch in CA 21-22R
Rock, James M(artin) 1935- 102
Rock, John 1890-1984 Obituary 114
Rock, Maxine 1940- 113
Rock, Milton L(ee) 1921- 49-52
Rock, Phillip 1927- 101
Rock, Richard
See Mainprize, Don
Rock, Stanley A(rthur) 1937- 101
Rock, William R(ay) 1930- 41-44R
Rockas, Leo 1928- 15-16R
Rockcastle, Verne N(orton) 1920- 73-76
Rocke, Russell 1945- 33-36R
Rockefeller, John D(avison, Sr.)
1839-1937 Brief entry 116
Rockefeller, John Davison III 1906-1978 81-84
Obituary 77-80
Rockefeller, John William, Jr.
1899(?)-1987 Obituary 122
Rocker, Fermin 1907- SATA-40
Rockingham, Montague
See Nye, Nelson C(oral)
Rockland, Mae Shafter 1937- 65-68
Rockland, Michael Aaron 1935- 37-40R
Rockley, L(awrence) E(dwin) 1916- 29-32R
Rocklin, Ross Louis 1913- 61-64
Rocklynne, Ross
See Rocklin, Ross Louis
Rockne, Dick 1939- 61-64
Rockowitz, Murray 1920- 25-28R
Rocks, Lawrence 1933- 85-88
Rockwell, Anne (F.) 1934- CANR-22
Earlier sketch in CA 21-22R
See also SATA 33
Rockwell, F(rederick) F(rye) 1884-1976 49-52
Obituary 103
Rockwell, Gail SATA-36
Rockwell, Harlow 1910-1988 109
Obituary 125
See also SATA 33
Rockwell, Jane 1929- 65-68
Rockwell, John (Sargent) 1940- 126
Brief entry 114
Rockwell, Kiffin Ayres 1917- 37-40R
Rockwell, Matt
See Rowland, D(onald) S(ydney)
Rockwell, Norman (Percevel) 1894-1978 89-92
Obituary 81-84
See also SATA 23
Rockwell, Thomas 1933- 29-32R
See also SATA 7
See also CLR 6
Rockwell, Wilson (Miller) 1909- CAP-2
Earlier sketch in CA 19-20
Rockwood, Joyce 1947- CANR-6
Earlier sketch in CA 57-60
See also SATA 39
Rockwood, Louis G. 1925- 45-48
Rockwood, Roy CAP-2
Earlier sketch in CA 19-20
See also SATA 1
Rodahl, Kaare 1917- 9-10R
Rodale, J(erome) I(rving) 1898-1971
Obituary 29-32R
Rodale, Robert 1930- 53-56
Rodan, Paul N. Rosenstein
See Rosenstein-Rodan, Paul N.
Rodaway, Angela 1918- 120
Rodberg, Leonard S(idney) 1932- CANR-24
Earlier sketch in CA 45-48
Rodberg, Lillian 1936- 29-32R
Rodd, Kylie Tennant 1912-1988 .... CANR-26
Obituary 124
Earlier sketches in CA 5-6R, CANR-5
Rodda, Charles 1891- 7-8R
Rodda, Peter (Gordon) 1937- 81-84
Roddenberry, Eugene Wesley 1921- 110
See also SATA 45
Roddenberry, Gene
See Roddenberry, Eugene Wesley
See also CLC 17
Roddick, Alan (Melven) 1937- CANR-15
Earlier sketch in CA 77-80
Roddick, Ellen 1936- 41-44R
Roddis, Louis Harry 1887- 7-8R
Roddis, Roland J. 1908- 7-8R
Rodd-Marling, Yvonne 1912-1982
Obituary 107
Roddy, Lee 1921- 123
Rodefer, Stephen 1940- CANR-23
Earlier sketch in CA 107
Rodell, Fred 1907-1980 Obituary 97-100
Rodell, Marie F(reid) 1912-1975 Obituary 61-64
Rodenberg, Julius 1884-1970 Obituary 104
Roder, Wolf 1932- 17-18R
Roderus, Frank 1942- CANR-17
Earlier sketch in CA 89-92
Rodes, John E(dward) 1923- 15-16R
Rodes, Robert Emmet, Jr. 1927- 112
Rodewyk, Adolf 1894- 65-68
Rodger, Alec
See Rodger, Thomas Alexander
Rodger, Anne 1910-1983 Obituary 111
Rodger, Ian (Graham) 1926- CANR-4
Earlier sketch in CA 7-8R
Rodger, Thomas Alexander 1907-1982
Obituary 106
Rodgers, Betsy (Aikin-Sneath) 1907- CAP-1
Earlier sketch in CA 13-14
Rodgers, Betty June (Flint) 1921- 11-12R
Rodgers, Brian 1910- 29-32R
Rodgers, Buck
See Rodgers, Francis G.
Rodgers, Carolyn M(arie) 1945- CANR-2
Earlier sketch in CA 45-48
See also BW
See also DLB 41
Rodgers, Daniel T(racy) 1942- 124
Rodgers, Dorothy F(einer) 1909- 89-92
Rodgers, Francis G. 1926- 123
Rodgers, Frank
See Infield, Glenn (Berton)
Rodgers, Frank P(eter) 1924- 11-12R
Rodgers, Harrell R(oss), Jr. 1939- CANR-25
Earlier sketches in CA 53-56, CANR-7
Rodgers, Joann Ellison 1941- 77-80
Rodgers, John (Charles) 1906- CAP-1
Earlier sketch in CA 11-12
Rodgers, Mary 1931- CANR-8
Earlier sketch in CA 49-52
See also SATA 8
See also CLC 12
Rodgers, Raboo 1945- 119
Rodgers, Richard (Charles) 1902-1979 89-92
Rodgers, Stanley 1928-1977 Obituary 106
Rodgers, W(illiam) R(obert) 1909-1969 85-88
See also DLB 20
See also CLC 7
Rodgers, William H. 1918- 19-20R
Rodgers, William Henry 1947- 101
Rodick, Burleigh Cushing 1889- 5-6R
Rodimer, Eva 1895- CAP-2
Earlier sketch in CA 21-22
Rodimstev, Aleksandr 1905(?)-1977
Obituary 69-72
Rodin, Alvin E(li) 1926- 119
Rodin, Arnold W. 1917- 89-92
Rodini, Robert J(oseph) 1936- 29-32R
Rodinson, Maxime 1915- CANR-4
Earlier sketch in CA 53-56
Roditi, Edouard Herbert 1910- 101
Rodli, Agnes Sylvia 1921- 11-12R
Rodman, Bella (Kashin) 1903- CAP-2
Earlier sketch in CA 19-20
Rodman, Emerson
See Ellis, Edward S(ylvester)
Rodman, Eric
See Silverberg, Robert
Rodman, F(rancis) Robert 1934- 122
Brief entry 117
Rodman, Howard 1920(?)-1985 Obituary 118
Rodman, Hyman 1931- CANR-25
Earlier sketches in CA 17-18R, CANR-8

Rodman, Maia
See Wojciechowska, Maia (Teresa)
Rodman, Selden 1909- CANR-25
Earlier sketches in CA 5-6R, CANR-5
See also SATA 9
Rodney, Bob
See Rodrigo, Robert
Rodney, Robert M(orris) 1911- 77-80
Rodney, Walter 1942-1980 125
Rodney, William 1923- 25-28R
Rodnick, David 1908- 33-36R
Rodnitzky, Jerome Leon 1936- 41-44R
Rodolph, Utto
See Ouologuem, Yambo
Rodowsky, Colby (F.) 1932- CANR-23
Earlier sketch in CA 69-72
See also SATA 21
Rodrigo, Robert 1928- 13-14R
Rodrigues, Jose Honorio 1913- CANR-13
Earlier sketch in CA 29-32R
Rodriguez, Claudio 1934- CLC-10
Rodriguez, Judith Green 1936- CANR-23
Earlier sketch in CA 107
Rodriguez, Mario 1922- 17-18R
Rodriguez, Richard 1944- 110
Rodriguez-Alcala, Hugo (Rosendo) 1917- CANR-14
Earlier sketch in CA 21-22R
Rodriguez-Alcala, Sally 1938- 23-24R
Rodriguez Cepeda, Enrique 1939- 45-48
Rodriguez Delgado, Jose M(anuel)
See Delgado, Jose Manuel R(odriguez)
Rodriguez Monegal, Emir 1921-1985
Obituary 117
Brief entry 115
Rodriguez O(rdonez), Jaime E(dmundo) 1940- 110
Rodway, Allan 1919- 13-14R
Rodwin, Lloyd 1919- CANR-19
Earlier sketches in CA 5-6R, CANR-4
Rodwin, Victor G(eorge) 1950- 120
Rodzinski, Halina 1904- 69-72
Roe, Anne 1904- 17-18R
Roe, Daphne A(nderson) 1923- 93-96
Roe, Derek A(rthur) 1937- CANR-23
Earlier sketch in CA 107
Roe, Dorothy
See Lewis, Dorothy Roe
Roe, F(rederic) Gordon 1894-1985 .... 9-10R
Obituary 115
Roe, Gerald 1940- 117
Roe, Harry Mason CANR-26
Earlier sketches in CA 19-20, CAP-2
Roe, Kathleen Robson 1910- 93-96
Roe, Richard L(ionel) 1936- CANR-15
Earlier sketch in CA 65-68
Roe, W(illiam) G(ordon) 1932- 21-22R
Roe, William Henry 1918- 5-6R
Roeber, Edward C(harles) 1913-1969 .... CANR-5
Earlier sketch in CA 5-6R
Roebuck, Carl Angus 1914- Brief entry 105
Roebuck, Derek 1935- 111
Roebuck, Janet 1943- 49-52
Roebuck, Julian B(aker) 1920- 101
Roebuck, Peter (Michael) 1956- 119
Roeburt, John 1909(?)-1972 Obituary 33-36R
Roecker, W(illiam) A. 1942- 61-64
Roeder, Bill 1922-1982 Obituary 107
Roeder, Ralph Leclerq 1890-1969
Obituary 104
Roehr, George L. 1931(?)-1983 Obituary 110
Roehrs, Walter R(obert) 1901- 103
Roeiker, Nancy Lyman 1915- 11-12R
Roelofs, H. Mark 1923- 111
Roelvaag, O(le) E(dvart) 1876-1931
Brief entry 117
See also DLB 9
See also TCLC 17
Roemer, Kenneth Morrison 1945- 112
Roemer, Michael 1937- 111
Roemer, Milton I(rwin) 1916- CANR-21
Earlier sketches in CA 57-60, CANR-6
Roemer, Norma H. 1905-1973 .... CAP-2
Earlier sketch in CA 19-20
Roeming, Robert Frederick 1911- 29-32R
Roepke, Wilhelm (Theodor) 1899-1966 .... CAP-1
Earlier sketch in CA 9-10
Roer, Berniece Marie 9-10R
Roes, Nicholas 1926- 29-32R
Roes, Nicholas A. 1952- 124
Roesch, Roberta F(leming) 1919- CANR-2
Earlier sketch in CA 5-6R
Roesch, Ronald 1947- 106
Roeseler, Robert O. 1882- CAP-2
Earlier sketch in CA 17-18
Roeseler, W(olfgang) G(uenter) 1925- 111
Roesler, Robert Harry 1927- 120
Roessel-Waugh, C. C.
See Waugh, Carol-Lynn Roessel
and Waugh, Charles G(ordon)
Roessler, Carl (Fred) 1933- 117
Roethenmund, Robert 1956- 103
Roethke, Theodore (Huebner) 1908-1963 81-84
See also CABS 2
See also DLB 5
See also CDALB 1941-1968
See also CLC 1, 3, 8, 11, 19, 46
Roett, Riordan Joseph Allenby III 1938- 57-60
Roetter, Charles Frederick 1919- 61-64
Roetzel, Calvin J. 1931- 112
Roever, J(oan) M(arilyn) 1935- 105
See also SATA 26
Rofe, (Fevzi) Husein 1922- CAP-1
Earlier sketch in CA 9-10
Rofes, Eric Edward 1954- 106
See also SATA 52
Roff, William R(obert) 1929- 57-60
Roffey, Maureen 1936- 108
See also SATA 33
Roffman, Howard 1953- 61-64
Roffman, Roger A. 1942- 110
Roffman, Sara
See Hershman, Morris
Rogal, Samuel J. 1934- CANR-17
Earlier sketch in CA 25-28R
Rogaly, (Henry) Joseph 1935- 104
Rogan, Barbara 1951- 124
Rogan, Donald L(ynn) 1930- 29-32R
Roger, Mae Durham 57-60
Rogers, A(mos) Robert 1927- CANR-8
Earlier sketch in CA 61-64
Rogers, Agnes
See Allen, Agnes Rogers
Rogers, Alan 1933- CANR-11
Earlier sketch in CA 21-22R
Rogers, (Thomas) Alan (Stinchcombe) 1937- CANR-18
Earlier sketch in CA 25-28R
See also SATA 2
Rogers, Augustus James III 1929- 33-36R
Rogers, Barbara 1945- CANR-17
Earlier sketch in CA 65-68
Rogers, Berto 1903-1974 .... CAP-2
Earlier sketch in CA 29-32
Rogers, Bruce 1870-1957 Brief entry 123
Rogers, Carl R(ansom) 1902-1987 .... CANR-18
Obituary 121
Earlier sketches in CA 3R, CANR-1
Rogers, (Grenville) Cedric (Harry) 1915- CANR-1
Earlier sketch in CA 4R
Rogers, Charles B. 1911- 89-92
Rogers, Clara Coltman
See Vyvyan, Clara C(oltman Rogers)
Rogers, Cyril A(lfred) 1923- 5-6R
Rogers, Cyril H(arold) 1907- CANR-20
Earlier sketches in CA 11-12R, CANR-5
Rogers, Dale Evans 1912- 103
Rogers, David 1930- 29-32R
Rogers, David C(harles) D(rummond) 1931- CANR-5
Earlier sketch in CA 11-12R
Rogers, Donald I(rwin) 1918-1980 57-60
Obituary 102
Rogers, Dorothy 1914-1986 .... CANR-1
Obituary 118
Earlier sketch in CA 3R
Rogers, Edith R(andam) 1924- 117
Rogers, Elizabeth F(rances) 1892-1974 .... 5-6R
Obituary 53-56
Rogers, Elyse M(acFadyen) 1932- 102
Rogers, Florence K(atherine) 1936- 101
Rogers, Floyd
See Spence, William John Duncan
Rogers, Frances 1888-1974 .... 5-6R
See also SATA 10
Rogers, Francis M(illet) 1914- CANR-1
Earlier sketch in CA 3R
Rogers, Franklin R(obert) 1921- 2R
Rogers, Fred B(aker) 1926- 109
Rogers, Fred McFeely 1928- 107
See also SATA 33
Rogers, Garet 2R
Rogers, Gayle 1923- 69-72
Rogers, George Calvin, Jr. 1922- CANR-1
Earlier sketch in CA 4R
Rogers, George W(illiam) 1917- CANR-1
Earlier sketch in CA 1R
Rogers, H(ugh) C(uthbert) Basset 1905- CANR-14
Earlier sketch in CA 73-76
Rogers, Henry C. 1914- 102
Rogers, Ingrid 1951- 116
Rogers, Jack 1934- 93-96
Rogers, James Allen 1929- 13-14R
Rogers, James T(racy) 1921- 45-48
Rogers, Jane 1952- 113
Rogers, Jean 1919- 115
See also SATA 47
Rogers, Jeanne F. 1926(?)-1984 Obituary 113
Rogers, JoAnn V. 1940- 89-92
Rogers, Joel Townsley 1896-1984
Obituary 114
Rogers, John 1906- 7-8R
Rogers, Josephine 1925- 61-64
Rogers, Kate Ellen 1920- 13-14R
Rogers, Katharine M(unzer) 1932- CANR-8
Earlier sketch in CA 21-22R
Rogers, Keith
See Harris, Marion Rose (Young)
Rogers, Kenneth Paul 1940- 53-56
Rogers, Kenneth Ray 85-88
Rogers, Kenny
See Rogers, Kenneth Ray
Rogers, Linda (Hall) 1944- 77-80
Rogers, Matilda 1894-1976 .... CAP-2
Earlier sketch in CA 29-32
See also SATA 5, 34
Rogers, Max Gray 1932- 53-56
Rogers, Michael 1950- CANR-1
Earlier sketch in CA 49-52
Rogers, Mick
See Glut, Donald F(rank)
Rogers, Millard F(oster), Jr. 1932- 101
Rogers, Neville William 1908- 108
Rogers, Pamela 1927- CANR-4
Earlier sketch in CA 49-52
See also SATA 9
Rogers, Pat 1938- 85-88
Rogers, Pattiann 1940- CANR-26
Earlier sketch in CA 109
Rogers, Paul (Patrick) 1900- 41-44R
Rogers, Paul 1950- 123
Rogers, Paul T(aylor) 1936-1984 119
Obituary 113
Rogers, Peter 1934- 101
Rogers, Peter D(amien) 1942- 116
Rogers, Raymond A(rthur) 1911- 21-22R
Rogers, Robert
See Hamilton, Charles Harold St. John
Rogers, Rolf E(rnst) 1931- 57-60
Rogers, Rosemary 1932- CANR-23
Earlier sketches in CA 49-52, CANR-3
See also AITN 1
Rogers, Roy 1912- 112
Rogers, Rutherford D(avid) 1915-
Brief entry 109
Rogers, Sarah F. 1923(?)-1976 Obituary 69-72
Rogers, Thomas Hunton 1927- 89-92
Rogers, Timothy (John Godfrey) 1927- CANR-1
Earlier sketch in CA 45-48
Rogers, (George) Truett 1931- 69-72
Rogers, Tyler Stewart 1895- 7-8R
Rogers, Vincent R(obert) 1926-
Brief entry 115
Rogers, W(illiam) G(arland) 1896-1978 .... 11-12R
Obituary 77-80
See also SATA 23
Rogers, Wade
See Madlee, Dorothy (Haynes)
Rogers, Warren (Joseph, Jr.) 1922- CANR-13
Earlier sketch in CA 77-80
Rogers, Warren
See Brucker, Roger W(arren)
Rogers, Will(iam Penn Adair) 1879-1935
Brief entry 105
See also DLB 11
See also TCLC 8
Rogers, William C(ecil) 1919- 19-20R
Rogers, William D(ill) 1927- 41-44R
Rogers, William Elford 1944- 113
Rogers, William R(aymond) 1932- 104
Rogers, William Warren 1929- Brief entry 112
Rogerson, J(ohn) W(illiam) 1935- 115
Rogerson, John
See Rogerson, J(ohn) W(illiam)
Rogg, Eleanor H(ertha) Meyer 1942- 57-60
Rogg, Sanford G. 1917- 19-20R
Rogge, Oetje John 1903-1981 .... 4R
Obituary 103
Rogin, Gilbert 1929- CANR-15
Earlier sketch in CA 65-68
See also CLC 18
Rogin, Michael Paul 1937- 101
Roginski, J(ames) W. 1945- 119
Roginski, Jim
See Roginski, J(ames) W.
Rogler, Lloyd H(enry) 1930- 17-18R
Roglieri, John Louis 1939- 105
Rogness, Alvin N. 1906- CANR-8
Earlier sketch in CA 21-22R
Rogness, Michael 1935- 101
Rogo, D. Scott 1950- CANR-13
Earlier sketch in CA 33-36R
Rogoff, Barbara 1950- 118
Rogoff, Harry 1882-1971 Obituary 33-36R
Rogosin, (William) Donn 1947- 123
Rogovin, Anne 1918- 97-100
Rogow, Arnold Austin 1924- CANR-1
Earlier sketch in CA 3R
Rogowski, Ronald (Lynn) 1944- 125
Roh, Jae Min 1927- 117
Rohan, Koda
See Koda Shigeyuki
See also TCLC 22
Rohatyn, Dennis 1949- 69-72
Rohatyn, Felix G(eorge) 1928- 118
Rohen, Edward 1931- CANR-4
Earlier sketch in CA 53-56
Rohlen, Tom 1940- 85-88
Rohmer, Eric
See Scherer, Jean-Marie Maurice
See also CLC 16
Rohmer, Richard 1924- CANR-19
Earlier sketch in CA 103
Rohmer, Sax
See Ward, Arthur Henry Sarsfield
See also DLB 70
See also TCLC 28
Rohn, Arthur H(enry, Jr.) 1929- CANR-25
Earlier sketch in CA 45-48
Rohner, Ronald P(reston) 1935- 37-40R
Rohr, John A. 1934- 33-36R
Rohrbach, Peter Thomas 1926- CANR-1
Earlier sketch in CA 2R
Rohrbaugh, Joanna Bunker 1943- 101
Rohrberger, Mary 1929- CANR-1
Earlier sketch in CA 45-48
Rohrbough, Malcolm J(ustin) 1932- 29-32R
Rohrer, Alyce Stevens 1922- 123
Rohrer, Daniel M(organ) 1941- 33-36R
Rohrer, Norman B(echtel) 1929- CANR-16
Earlier sketch in CA 93-96
Rohrer, Wayne C(urry) 1920- 21-22R
Rohrl, Vivian J. (Lober) 110
Rohrlich, Chester 1900(?)-1974 Obituary 53-56
Rohrlich, George F(riedrich) 1914- CANR-14
Earlier sketch in CA 37-40R
Rohrlich, Ruby CANR-5
Earlier sketch in CA 53-56
Rohrlich-Leavitt, Ruby
See Rohrlich, Ruby
Rohrlick, Paula 1955- 111
Rohrman, Nicholas L(eroy) 1937- 29-32R
Rohwer, Juergen 1924- 65-68
Rohwer, Jurgen
See Rohwer, Juergen
Roider, Karl A(ndrew), Jr. 1943- 111
Roiphe, Anne Richardson 1935- 89-92
See also DLBY 80
See also CLC 3, 9
Rojan
See Rojankovsky, Feodor Stephanovich
Rojankovsky, Feodor Stepanovich 1891-1970 77-80
See also SATA 21
Rojas, Carlos 1928- CANR-22
Earlier sketches in CA 19-20R, CANR-7
Rojko, Anthony J. 1918(?)-1978
Obituary 77-80
Rojo, Ricardo 1923- 25-28R
Rokeach, Milton 1918- CANR-5
Earlier sketch in CA 3R
Rokeby-Thomas, Anna E(lma) 1911- 77-80
See also SATA 15
Rokes, Willis Park 1926- 25-28R
Roland, Albert 1925- 61-64
See also SATA 11
Roland, Betty 1903- 103
Roland, Charles P(ierce) 1918- 41-44R
Roland, Mary
See Lewis, Mary (Christianna Milne)
Roland, Mary
See Lewis, Mary (Christianna)
Roland, Nicholas
See Walmsley, Arnold Robert
Roland Smith, Gordon 1931- 102
Rolant, Rene
See Fanthorpe, R(obert) Lionel
Roldos Aguilera, Jaime 1940-1981
Obituary 108
Roleder, George 1928- CANR-21
Earlier sketch in CA 105
Rolerson, Darrell A(llen) 1946- 49-52
See also SATA 8
Rolfe, Bari 1916- 113
Rolfe, Eugene (Edward Musgrave) 1914- 13-14R
Rolfe, Franklin P(rescott) 1902-1985
Obituary 117
Rolfe, Frederick (William Serafino Austin Lewis Mary) 1860-1913 Brief entry 107
See also DLB 34
See also TCLC 12
Rolfe, Lionel (Menuhin) 1942- 110
Rolfe, Sheila Constance 1935- 102
Rolfe, Sidney 1921-1976 69-72
Obituary 65-68
Rolfsrud, Erling Nicolai 1912- 65-68
Roll, Charles W(eissert), Jr. 1928- CANR-1
Earlier sketch in CA 45-48
Roll, Eric 1907- 102
Roll, Richard J(effrey) 1952- 124
Roll, Samuel 1942- 124
Roll, William George, Jr. 1926- 81-84
Roll, Winifred 1909- 49-52
See also SATA 6
Rolland, Barbara J(une) 1929- 77-80
Rolland, Romain 1866-1944 Brief entry 118
See also DLB 65
See also TCLC 23
Rolle, Andrew Frank 1922- CANR-3
Earlier sketch in CA 4R
Roller, David C(harles) 1937- 107
Roller, Duane H(enry) D(uBose) 1920- 61-64
Rolleston, James Lancelot 1939- 85-88
Rollin, Bernard Elliot 1943- 108
Rollin, Betty 1936- CANR-22
Earlier sketches in CA 15-16R, CANR-7
Rollin, Roger Best 1930- CANR-8
Earlier sketch in CA 17-18R
Rollins, Alfred Brooks, Jr. 1921- 5-6R
Rollins, Bryant 1937- 49-52
Rollins, C(alvin) D(wight) 1918- 41-44R
Rollins, Charlemae Hill 1897-1979 .... 11-12R
Obituary 104
See also BW
See also SATA 3, 26
Rollins, Judith 122
Rollins, Kelly (a pseudonym) 1924- 106
Rollins, Peter C(ushing) 1942- CANR-26
Earlier sketch in CA 108
Rollins, Richard M(eryl) 1945- 121
Rollins, Royce
See Pepper, Choral
Rollins, Steed 1916-1985 Obituary 118
Rollins, Wayne G(ilbert) 1929- CANR-3
Earlier sketch in CA 11-12R
Rollison, William D(ewey) 1897-1971 .... CAP-2
Earlier sketch in CA 19-20
Rollo, Vera Foster 1924- 81-84
Rolls, Anthony
See Vulliamy, Colwyn Edward
Rolls, Charles J(ubilee) 1887- 107
Rolls, Eric C(harles) 1923- CANR-13
Earlier sketch in CA 33-36R
Rolo, Charles J(acques) 1916-1982 101
Obituary 108
Rolo, Paul Jacques Victor 1917- 21-22R
Roloff, Leland Harold 1927- 49-52
Rolph, C. H.
See Hewitt, Cecil Rolph
Rolph, Earl R(obert) 1910- CAP-2
Earlier sketch in CA 23-24
Rolston, Holmes 1900-1977 .... CANR-3
Earlier sketch in CA 3R
Rolston, Holmes III 1932- 113
Rolt, L(ionel) T(homas) C(aswall) 1910-1974 .... CANR-1
Earlier sketch in CA 4R
Rolt-Wheeler, Francis William 1876-1960
Obituary 89-92
Rolvaag, O(le) E(dvart)
See Roelvaag, O(le) E(dvart)
Rom, M. Martin 1946- 81-84

Romagnoli, G(ian) Franco 1926- 73-76
Romagnoli, Margaret O'Neill 1922- 73-76
Romain Arnaud, Saint
See Aragon, Louis
Romaine, Lawrence B. 1900- CAP-1
Earlier sketch in CA 13-14
Romaine, Paul
See Bleamer, Burton
Romains, Jules 1885-1972 85-88
See also DLB 65
See also CLC 7
Roman, Daniel (David) 1921- 41-44R
Roman, Eric 1926- CANR-1
Earlier sketch in CA 1R
Roman, Murray 1920-1984 Obituary 112
Roman, Stephen B(oleslav) 1921-
Brief entry 112
Romanell, Patrick 1912- 23-24R
Romanelli, Charles S. 1930- 15-16R
Romano, Clare 1922- CANR-24
Earlier sketch in CA 41-44R
Romano, Deane Louis 1927- 25-28R
Romano, Don
See Turner, Robert (Harry)
Romano, Louis G. 1921- CANR-8
Earlier sketch in CA 19-20R
See also SATA 35
Romanoff, Alexis Lawrence 1892-1980 .. CANR-5
Earlier sketch in CA 11-12R
Romanoff, Harry 1892(?)-1970 Obituary 104
Romans, J(ohn) Thomas 1933- 15-16R
Romanucci-Ross, Lola 1928- CANR-18
Earlier sketch in CA 101
Romanus, Charles Franklin 1915-1983 ...23-24R
Obituary 111
Romanyshyn, Robert Donald 1942- 108
Romasco, Albert U(go) 1930- 110
Romberger, Judy 1940- 106
Rome, Anthony
See Albert, Marvin H.
Rome, Beatrice K(aufman) 1913- 13-14R
Rome, Florence 1910- 33-36R
Romein, J. M.
See Romein, Jan (Marius)
Romein, Jan (Marius) 1893-1962
Obituary 111
Romer, Alfred 1906- 37-40R
Romer, (Louis) John 1941- 110
Romer, Stephen 1957- 125
Romero, George A. 1940(?)- Brief entry 116
Romero, Gerry
See Neyland, James (Elwyn)
Romero, Jose Ruben 1890-1952
Brief entry 114
See also TCLC 14
Romero, Luis 1916- Brief entry 111
Romero, Orlando 1945- 69-72
Romero, Patricia W.
See Curtin, Patricia (W.) Romero
Romerstein, Herbert 1931- 11-12R
Romey, Bill
See Romey, William D(owden)
Romey, William D(owden) 1930- 57-60
Romig, Edna Davis 1889-1978 45-48
Obituary 103
Romig, Walter 1903-1977 Obituary 110
Romijn, Johanna Maria Kooyker
See Kooyker-Romijn, Johanna Maria
Romm, Ethel Grodzins 1925- 33-36R
Romm, Sharon 1942- 118
Rommel, (Mimi) Dayton 7-8R
Rommetveit, Ragnar 1924- 57-60
Romney, George W(ilcken) 1907-
Brief entry 106
Romney, Rodney Ross 1931- 102
Romney, Ronna 1943- 116
Romney, Steve
See Bingley, David Ernest
Romo, Ricardo 1943- 111
Romoser, George K(enneth) 1929- 41-44R
Rompkey, Ronald (George) 1943- 118
Romtvedt, David 1950- 125
Romulo, Carlos P(ena) 1899(?)-1985 .. CANR-10
Obituary 118
Earlier sketch in CA 15-16R
Romyn, Johanna Maria Kooyker
See Kooyker-Romijn Johanna Maria
Rona, Peter A(rnold) 1934- 108
Ronald, Ann 1939- 124
Ronald, David William 1937- 65-68
Ronald, Hugh 1912(?)-1983 Obituary 109
Ronalds, Mary Teresa 1946- 25-28R
Ronaldson, Agnes S. 1916- 17-18R
Ronan, Colin A(listair) 1920- CANR-6
Earlier sketch in CA 7-8R
Ronan, Georgia
See Crampton, Georgia Ronan
Ronan, Margaret 1918- 102
Ronan, Thomas Matthew 1907- CAP-1
Earlier sketch in CA 9-10
Ronan, Tom
See Ronan, Thomas Matthew
Ronan, William W. 1917- 33-36R
Ronay, Gabriel Ernest 1930- 85-88
Roncali, Angelo Giuseppe
See John XXIII, Pope
Ronck, Ronn 1946- 121
Ronda, James P(aul) 1943- Brief entry 113
Rondell, Florence 1907- 57-60
Ronder, Paul 1940(?)-1977 Obituary 73-76
Rondinelli, Dennis A(ugust) 1943- 111
Rondthaler, Edward 1905- 15-16R
Ronen, Dov 1933- CANR-10
Earlier sketch in CA 57-60
Roney, Ruth Anne
See McMullin, Ruth R(oney)
Rongen, Bjoern 1906- CAP-2
Earlier sketch in CA 29-32
See also SATA 10
Rongen, Bjorn
See Rongen, Bjoern
Rongione, Louis Anthony 1912- 57-60
Ronken, Harriet
See Lynton, Harriet Ronken
Ronne, Finn 1899-1980 .... CANR-1
Obituary 97-100
Earlier sketch in CA 3R
Ronnie, Art(hur William) 1931- 41-44R
Ronning, C. Neale 1927- 7-8R
Ronning, Chester A. 1894-1984 Obituary ... 114
Ronns, Edward
See Aarons, Edward S(idney)
Ronsheim, Sally B(ober) 57-60
Ronsin, Jean
See Rodinson, Maxime
Ronsley, Joseph 1931- CANR-10
Earlier sketch in CA 25-28R
Ronsman, M. M.
See Nowak, Mariette
Ronson, Mark
See Alexander, Marc
Rood, Allan 1894- CAP-1
Earlier sketch in CA 13-14
Rood, John (Hiram) 1902-1974 ....5-6R
Obituary 120
Rood, Karen Lane 1946- 102
Rood, Robert Thomas 1942- 107
Rood, Ronald (N.) 1920- CANR-24
Earlier sketches in CA 23-24R, CANR-9
See also SATA 12
Roodenburg, Nancy McKee 1909-1972
Obituary 104
Roof, Wade Clark 1939- 114
Rook, (William) Alan 1909- 97-100
Rook, Earnest Robert 1917- 104
Rook, Tony 1932- 69-72
Rooke, Constance 1942- 126
Rooke, Daphne (Marie) 1914- 53-56
See also SATA 12
Rooke, Leon 1934- CANR-23
Earlier sketch in CA 25-28R
See also CLC 25, 34
Rookmaaker, Hendrik Roelof
1922-1977 .... CANR-26
Earlier sketch in CA 57-60
Rooks, George (M.) 1951- CANR-22
Earlier sketch in CA 105
Room, Adrian 1933- CANR-16
Earlier sketch in CA 97-100
Roome, Katherine Ann Davis 1952- 85-88
Rooney, Andrew A(itken) 1919- CANR-9
Earlier sketch in CA 5-6R
Rooney, Andy
See Rooney, Andrew A(itken)
Rooney, David Douglas 1924- CANR-11
Earlier sketch in CA 21-22R
Rooney, Elmo
See Perry, Charles
Rooney, James 1938- 101
Rooney, James R(owell) 1927- 61-64
Rooney, Jim
See Rooney, James
Rooney, John F(rancis), Jr. 1939- 101
Rooney, Miriam Theresa 81-84
Rooney, Patrick C. 1937- 29-32R
Rooney, William Richard 1938- 102
Roop, Connie
See Roop, Constance Betzer
Roop, Constance Betzer 1951- 122
See also SATA 49
Roop, Peter (G.) 1951- 122
See also SATA 49
Roos, Audrey Kelley 1912-1982 Obituary ... 108
Roos, Charles A. 1914(?)-1974 Obituary ..53-56
Roos, Hans
See Meissner, Hans-Otto
Roos, Hans Dietrich 1919- 19-20R
Roos, Kelley
See Roos, Audrey Kelley
Roos, Leslie L(eon), Jr. 1940- 33-36R
Roos, Murphre (joint pseudonym)
See Mele, Jim
Roos, Noralou P(reston) 1942- 33-36R
Roos, Stephen (Kelley) 1945- 112
See also SATA 41, 47
Roosa, Robert V(incent) 1918- 25-28R
Roose, Ronald 1945- 81-84
Roose-Evans, James 1927- 29-32R
Roosen, William (James) 1940- 117
Roosenburg, Henriette 1920-1972
Obituary 37-40R
Roosevelt, Edith Kermit 1926- 69-72
Roosevelt, (Anna) Eleanor 1884-1962
Obituary 89-92
See also SATA 50
Roosevelt, Elliott 1910- 105
See also AITN 1
Roosevelt, Felicia Warburg 1927- 57-60
Roosevelt, Franklin Delano 1882-1945
Brief entry 116
Roosevelt, James 1907- CANR-12
Earlier sketch in CA 69-72
Roosevelt, Nicholas 1893-1982 Obituary ... 106
Roosevelt, Theodore 1858-1919
Brief entry 115
See also DLB 47
Root, Deane L(eslie) 1947- CANR-23
Earlier sketch in CA 107
Root, E(dward) Merrill 1895-1973 .... CAP-1
Earlier sketch in CA 15-16
Root, Franklin Russell 1923- 7-8R
Root, Judith C(arol) 65-68
Root, Lin (Segal) 69-72
Root, Oren 1911- 85-88
Root, Phyllis 1949- 123
See also SATA 48
Root, Shelton L., Jr. 1923-1986 .... SATA-51
Root, Waverley (Lewis) 1903-1982 ......25-28R
Obituary 108
See also DLB 4
Root, William Pitt 1941- CANR-12
Earlier sketch in CA 25-28R
Rooth, Gerhard Theodore 1898(?)-1983
Obituary 110
Rootham, Jasper (St. John) 1910- CANR-19
Earlier sketches in CA 7-8R, CANR-4
Roots, Clive (George) 1935- Brief entry 111
Roots, Ivan Alan 1921- 11-12R
Roots, John McCook 1904(?)-1988
Obituary 126
Rooze, Gene E(dward) 1934- 120
Rope, Henry Edward George 1880-1978 ....7-8R
Obituary 103
Roper, Gayle G(ordinier) 1940- 97-100
Roper, H(ugh) R(edwald) Trevor
See Trevor-Roper, H(ugh) R(edwald)
Roper, John Stephen 1924(?)-1980
Obituary 102
Roper, Lanning 1912-1983 Obituary 109
Roper, Laura Wood 1911- 57-60
See also SATA 34
Roper, Robert 1946- 73-76
Roper, Ronnalie J. 1936- 41-44R
Roper, Steve 1941- 103
Roper, Susan Bonthron 1948- 81-84
Roper, William L(eon) 1897- 33-36R
Ropke, Wilhelm (Theodor)
See Roepke, Wilhelm (Theodor)
Ropp, Theodore 1911- 5-6R
Roppolo, Joseph Patrick 1913- 15-16R
Rops, Daniel
See Petiot, Henri Jules Charles
Roquebrune, Robert de 1889-1978 ..... DLB-68
Roquemore, Kathleen (Ann) 1941- 61-64
Rorabaugh, William Joseph 1945- 101
Rorem, Ned 1923- 17-18R
Roripaugh, A(lan) Robert 1930- 13-14R
Rorke, Margaret (Curry) 1915- 110
Rorty, Amelie Oksenberg 1932- 107
Rorty, James 1891(?)-1973 Obituary 41-44R
Rorty, Richard M(cKay) 1931- CANR-9
Earlier sketch in CA 23-24R
Rorty, Winifred Raushenbush
1894(?)-1979 Obituary 93-96
Rorvik, David M(ichael) 1946- 85-88
Rosa, Alfred F(elix) 1942- 41-44R
Rosa, Joao Guimaraes 1908-1967
Obituary 89-92
See also CLC 23
Rosa, Joseph G. 1932- 15-16R
Rosa, Nicholas 1926- 110
Rosage, David E. 1913- CANR-21
Earlier sketches in CA 13-14R, CANR-6
Rosaldo, Michelle Z(imbalist) 1944-1981 ... 101
Obituary 108
Rosaldo, Renato I(gnacio), Jr. 1941- 89-92
Rosand, David 1938- 111
Rosa-Nieves, Cesareo 1901-1974 57-60
Rosbottom, Ronald C(arlisle) 1942- 61-64
Roscoe, A(drian) A(lan) 1939- 49-52
Roscoe, Charles
See Rowland, D(onald) S(ydney)
Roscoe, D(onald) T(homas) 1934- 113
See also SATA 42
Roscoe, Edwin Scott 1896-1978 ....7-8R
Obituary 103
Roscoe, George B(oggs) 1907- 65-68
Rosdail, Jesse Hart 1914(?)-1977
Obituary 73-76
Rose, A(rthur) James 1927- 19-20R
Rose, Ada Campbell 1902(?)-1976
Obituary 65-68
Rose, Al 1916- 97-100
Rose, Alan Henry 1938- 93-96
Rose, Albert H(enry) 1903- 41-44R
Rose, Alvin E(manuel) 1903-1983
Obituary 109
Rose, Anna Perrott
See Wright, Anna (Maria Louisa Perrott)
Rose
Rose, Anne CANR-2
Earlier sketch in CA 49-52
See also SATA 8
Rose, Anthony Lewis 1939- 101
Rose, Arnold 1916-1983 Obituary 109
Rose, Arnold M(arshall) 1918-1968 ....7-8R
Rose, Barbara E. 1937- Brief entry 111
Rose, Betsy
See Rose, Elizabeth
Rose, Billy 1899-1966 Obituary 116
Rose, Brian Waldron 1915- 97-100
Rose, Camille Davied 1893- CAP-2
Earlier sketch in CA 21-22
Rose, Carl 1903-1971 Obituary 29-32R
See also SATA 31
Rose, Clarkson 1890-1968 ....7-8R
Rose, Clive (Martin) 1921- 121
Rose, Constance Hubbard 1934- CANR-16
Earlier sketch in CA 29-32R
Rose, Daniel M. 1940- 33-36R
Rose, David S. 1947- 121
Rose, Elinor K(iess) 1920- 29-32R
Rose, Elizabeth 1915- 73-76
Rose, Elizabeth (Jane Pretty) 1933- CANR-9
Earlier sketch in CA 7-8R
See also SATA 28
Rose, (Edward) Elliot 1928- 65-68
Rose, Ernst A(ndreas) G(ottlieb) 1899- .. CANR-4
Earlier sketch in CA 7-8R
Rose, Florella
See Carlson, Vada F.
Rose, Frank 1949- 103
Rose, Gerald (Hembdon Seymour)
1935- CANR-9
Earlier sketch in CA 65-68
See also SATA 30
Rose, Gilbert J(acob) 1923- 103
Rose, (Arthur) Gordon 1920-1975 .... CANR-4
Earlier sketch in CA 1R
Rose, Grace B(erne) 1914- 108
Rose, Hannah T. 1909(?)-1976 Obituary ..69-72
Rose, Harold 1921-1967 ....7-8R
Obituary 103
Rose, Harold Wickliffe 1896- CAP-1
Earlier sketch in CA 9-10
Rose, Helen 1904(?)-1985 Obituary 117
Rose, Hilary
See Mackinnon, Charles Roy
Rose, Homer C. 1909-1967 .... CAP-1
Earlier sketch in CA 15-16
Rose, James M. 1941- 102
Rose, Jeanne 1940- CANR-16
Earlier sketch in CA 93-96
Rose, Jennifer
See Weber, Nancy
Rose, Jerome G. 1926- CANR-8
Earlier sketch in CA 15-16R
Rose, Jerry D. 1933- 33-36R
Rose, Kenneth (Vivian) 1924- Brief entry ... 123
Rose, Kenneth Jon 1954- 115
Rose, Leo E. 1926- 85-88
Rose, Lisle A(bbott) 1936- CANR-10
Earlier sketch in CA 65-68
Rose, Lynn Edmondson 1934- Brief entry .. 105
Rose, Marcia
See Kamien, Marcia
and Novak, Rose
Rose, Marilyn Gaddis 1930- 33-36R
Rose, Mark 1939- CANR-10
Earlier sketch in CA 25-28R
Rose, Nancy (Ann) 1934- 37-40R
Rose, Nancy A.
See Sweetland, Nancy A(nn)
Rose, Norman Anthony 1934- 104
Rose, Paul (Bernard) 1935- 103
Rose, Pete(r Edward) 1942- Brief entry 113
Rose, Peter I(saac) 1933- CANR-5
Earlier sketch in CA 13-14R
Rose, Phyllis
See Thompson, Phyllis Hoge
Rose, R(obert) B(arrie) 1929- 61-64
Rose, Ralph 1911(?)-1984 Obituary 112
Rose, Reginald 1920- 73-76
See also DLB 26
Rose, Richard 1933- CANR-10
Earlier sketch in CA 21-22R
Rose, Stuart 1899(?)-1975 Obituary 61-64
Rose, Susan (Phyllida) 1938- 111
Rose, Thomas 1938- 33-36R
Rose, Wendy 1948- CANR-5
Earlier sketch in CA 53-56
See also SATA 12
Rose, Will(iam Palen) 1889- 57-60
Rose, William 1920(?)-1987 Obituary 121
Rose, Willie Lee (Nichols) 1927- 13-14R
Rose-Ackerman, Susan 1942- 111
Roseberry, Cecil R. 1902- 21-22R
Roseboom, Eugene Holloway 1892- 5-6R
Roseboro, John 1933- 102
Rosebrock, Ellen Fletcher 1947- CANR-10
Earlier sketch in CA 57-60
Rosebury, Theodor 1904-1976 .... CAP-2
Obituary 69-72
Earlier sketch in CA 25-28
Rosecrance, Francis Chase 1897- 7-8R
Rosecrance, Richard (Newton) 1930-
Brief entry 111
Rosedale, Valerie
See Harron, Don(ald)
Rosefielde, Steven 1942- CANR-25
Earlier sketch in CA 45-48
Roseliep, Raymond 1917- CANR-6
Earlier sketch in CA 9-10R
Roselle, Daniel 1920- 13-14R
Roseller, David
See Timms, E(dward) V(ivian)
Roseman, Ellen Barbara 1947- 124
Roseman, Kenneth David 1939- 110
See also SATA 52
Rosemeyer, Nita (Mary) 1907- 119
Rosemond, John K(irk) 1947- 110
Rosemont, Henry, Jr. 1934- 41-44R
Rosen, Barbara 1929- 37-40R
Rosen, Benson 1942- 120
Rosen, Carol (Cynthia) 1950- 119
Rosen, Charles (Welles) 1927- 126
Rosen, Dorothy 1916- 119
Rosen, Edward 1906-1985 ....23-24R
Obituary 115
Rosen, Elliot A(lfred) 1928- 93-96
Rosen, Frederick 1938- 120
Rosen, George 1910-1977 81-84
Obituary 73-76
Rosen, George 1920- 57-60
Rosen, Gerald 1938- 33-36R
Rosen, Haiim B(aruch) 1922- CANR-20
Earlier sketch in CA 1R
Rosen, Hjalmar 1922- 19-20R
Rosen, Ira 1954- 114
Rosen, James Alan 1908(?)-1972
Obituary 37-40R
Rosen, Joe
See Rosen, Joseph
Rosen, Joseph 1937- CANR-9
Earlier sketch in CA 65-68
Rosen, Laura 1948- 116

INDEX

Rosen, Lawrence R(onald) 1938- ... 57-60
Rosen, Leonard 1954- ... 125
Rosen, Lillian (Diamond) 1928- ... 108
Rosen, Martin Meyer
See Rosen, Moishe (Martin)
Rosen, Marvin J(erold) 1929- ... 69-72
Rosen, Michael 1946- ... CANR-15
Earlier sketch in CA 25-28R
See also SATA 40, 48
Rosen, Moishe (Martin) 1932- ... CANR-4
Earlier sketch in CA 49-52
Rosen, Mortimer (Gilbert) 1931- ... 101
Rosen, Norma (Gangel) 1925- ... 33-36R
See also DLB 28
Rosen, Paul L(yon) 1939- ... 61-64
Rosen, R(ichard) D(ean) 1949- ... 77-80
See also CLC 39
Rosen, Robert C(harles) 1947- ... 106
Rosen, Ruth (E.) 1945- ... 125
Rosen, S. McKee 1902(?)-1978 Obituary ... 77-80
Rosen, Sam 1920- ... 7-8R
Rosen, Samuel 1897-1981 Obituary ... 108
Rosen, Seymour Michael 1924- ... 33-36R
Rosen, Sheldon 1943- ... 109
Rosen, Shirley 1933- ... 105
Rosen, Sidney 1916- ... 11-12R
See also SATA 1
Rosen, Stanley H. 1929- ... 25-28R
Rosen, Stephen 1934- ... 65-68
Rosen, Trix 1947- ... 116
Rosen, Winifred 1943- ... 29-32R
See also SATA 8
Rosenast, Eleanor S(trauss) 1929- ... 97-100
Rosenau, Helen ... 101
Rosenau, James N(athan) 1924- ... CANR-18
Earlier sketches in CA 1R, CANR-2
Rosenauer, Johnnie L(ee) 1951- ... 110
Rosenbaum, Alan S(helby) 1941- ... 124
Brief entry ... 106
Rosenbaum, Alvin 1945- ... 113
Rosenbaum, Bernard L. 1937- ... 107
Rosenbaum, Eileen 1936- ... 21-22R
Rosenbaum, Ernest H. 1929- ... 97-100
Rosenbaum, H. Jon 1941- ... 41-44R
Rosenbaum, Jean 1927- ... 19-20R
Rosenbaum, Kurt 1926- ... 15-16R
Rosenbaum, Maurice 1907- ... 17-18R
See also SATA 6
Rosenbaum, Max 1923- ... 41-44R
Rosenbaum, Nathan 1897- ... CAP-2
Earlier sketch in CA 23-24
Rosenbaum, Patricia L(eib) 1932- ... 105
Rosenbaum, Peter S. 1940- ... CANR-14
Earlier sketch in CA 23-24R
Rosenbaum, S(tanford) P(atrick) 1929- ... 15-16R
Rosenbaum, Samuel R(awlins) 1888-1972
Obituary ... 37-40R
Rosenbaum, Veryl 1936- ... CANR-1
Earlier sketch in CA 49-52
Rosenbaum, Walter A(nthony) 1937- ... 21-22R
Rosenberg, Arthur D(onald) 1939- ... 61-64
Rosenberg, Betty 1916- ... 113
Rosenberg, Bruce A(lan) 1934- ... 29-32R
Rosenberg, Charles E(rnest) 1936- ... 97-100
Rosenberg, Claude N(ewman), Jr.
1928- ... CANR-5
Earlier sketch in CA 4R
Rosenberg, David A(aron) 1940- ... 93-96
Rosenberg, Dorothy 1906- ... CANR-18
Earlier sketches in CA 45-48, CANR-2
See also SATA 40
Rosenberg, Edgar 1925- ... 13-14R
Rosenberg, Ellis Howard 1936(?)-1986
Obituary ... 121
Rosenberg, Emily S(chlaht) 1944- ... 108
Rosenberg, Ethel (Clifford) 1915- ... CANR-16
Earlier sketch in CA 29-32R
See also SATA 3
Rosenberg, George S(tanley) 1930- ... 29-32R
Rosenberg, Harold 1906-1978 ... 21-22R
Obituary ... 77-80
Rosenberg, Harry E. 1932- ... 57-60
Rosenberg, Isaac 1890-1918 Brief entry ... 107
See also DLB 20
See also TCLC 12
Rosenberg, Israel 1909- ... 49-52
Rosenberg, J(ehiol) Mitchell 1906- ... 37-40R
Rosenberg, Jakob 1893-1980 Obituary ... 97-100
Rosenberg, James L. 1921- ... 15-16R
Rosenberg, Jane 1949- ... 121
Rosenberg, Janet 1930- ... 117
Rosenberg, Jerome Roy 1926- ... 104
Rosenberg, Jerry M. 1935- ... CANR-24
Earlier sketches in CA 23-24R, CANR-9
Rosenberg, Jessie 1941- ... 23-24R
Rosenberg, Joel 1954- ... 115
Rosenberg, John D(avid) 1929- ... CANR-5
Earlier sketch in CA 3R
Rosenberg, John J.
See Ramati, Yohanan (Joseph)
Rosenberg, Joseph
See Ramati, Yohanan (Joseph)
Rosenberg, Judith K(aren) 1945- ... 57-60
Rosenberg, Kenyon Charles 1933- ... 57-60
Rosenberg, Marvin 1912- ... 1R
Rosenberg, Maurice 1919- ... 81-84
Rosenberg, Maxine B(erta) 1939- ... 117
See also SATA 47
Rosenberg, Morris 1922- ... CANR-2
Earlier sketch in CA 7-8R
Rosenberg, Nancy (Sherman) 1931- ... CANR-22
Earlier sketches in CA 1R, CANR-5
See also SATA 4
Rosenberg, Nathan 1927- Brief entry ... 113
Rosenberg, Neil V. 1939- ... 122
Rosenberg, Norman J(ack) 1930- ... 57-60
Rosenberg, Norman L(ewis) 1942- ... 122
Rosenberg, Philip 1942- ... 103
Rosenberg, Rosalind 1946- ... 108
Rosenberg, Samuel 1912- ... 53-56
Rosenberg, Sharon 1942- ... CANR-10
Earlier sketch in CA 57-60
See also SATA 8
Rosenberg, Shirley Sirota 1925- ... CANR-12
Earlier sketch in CA 21-22R
Rosenberg, Stephen N(icholas) 1941- ... 111
Rosenberg, Stuart E. 1922- ... CANR-9
Earlier sketch in CA 5-6R
Rosenberg, William Gordon 1938- ... 61-64
Rosenberg, Wolfgang 1915- ... CANR-9
Earlier sketch in CA 65-68
Rosenberger, Francis Coleman 1915- ... CANR-15
Earlier sketch in CA 41-44R
Rosenberger, Harleigh M. 1913- ... 21-22R
Rosenberger, Homer Tope 1908- ... CANR-8
Earlier sketch in CA 19-20R
Rosenblatt, Arthur S. 1938- ... SATA-45
Rosenblatt, Bernard A. 1886- ... CAP-1
Earlier sketch in CA 13-14
Rosenblatt, Fred 1914- ... 41-44R
Rosenblatt, Gary 1947- ... 77-80
Rosenblatt, Joe
See Rosenblatt, Joseph
See also CLC 15
Rosenblatt, Jon M(ichael) 1947- ... 89-92
Rosenblatt, Joseph 1933- ... 89-92
Rosenblatt, Louise M(ichelle) 1904- ... 49-52
Rosenblatt, Milton B. 1908(?)-1975
Obituary ... 53-56
Rosenblatt, Roger 1940- ... 85-88
Rosenblatt, Samuel 1902- ... 53-56
Rosenblatt, Stanley M. 1936- ... 29-32R
Rosenblatt, Suzanne Maris 1937- ... 69-72
Rosenblith, Judy F(rancis) 1921- ... 25-28R
Rosenbloom, Bert 1944- ... 109
Rosenbloom, David H(arry) 1943- ... 73-76
Rosenbloom, David L. 1944- ... 45-48
Rosenbloom, Jerry S(amuel) 1939-
Brief entry ... 110
Rosenbloom, Joseph 1928- ... CANR-21
Earlier sketches in CA 57-60, CANR-6
See also SATA 21
Rosenbloom, Joseph R. 1928- ... 29-32R
Rosenbloom, Noah H. 1915- ... CANR-14
Earlier sketch in CA 37-40R
Rosenblum, Art 1927- ... 57-60
Rosenblum, Davida 1927- ... 93-96
Rosenblum, Gershen 1924- ... 41-44R
Rosenblum, Helen Faye 1941- ... 121
Rosenblum, Joseph 1947- ... 111
Rosenblum, Leonard A. 1936- ... CANR-11
Earlier sketch in CA 57-60
Rosenblum, Marc J. 1936- ... 29-32R
Rosenblum, Martin J(ack) 1946- ... CANR-18
Earlier sketches in CA 45-48, CANR-2
Rosenblum, Mort 1943- ... 73-76
Rosenblum, Richard 1928- ... CANR-9
Earlier sketch in CA 65-68
See also SATA 11
Rosenblum, Robert H. 1927- ... CANR-5
Earlier sketch in CA 3R
Rosenbluth, Gideon 1921- ... 61-64
Rosenburg, John M. 1918- ... 23-24R
See also SATA 6
Rosenburg, Robert K(emper) 1920- ... CANR-4
Earlier sketch in CA 7-8R
Rosendall, Betty 1916- ... 49-52
Rosenfarb, Chawa 1923- ... 53-56
Rosenfeld, Albert (Hyman) 1920- ... CANR-11
Earlier sketch in CA 65-68
Rosenfeld, Alvin 1919- ... 73-76
Rosenfeld, Alvin H(irsch) 1938- ... CANR-24
Earlier sketches in CA 49-52, CANR-4
Rosenfeld, Arnold (Solomon) 1933- ... 65-68
Rosenfeld, Edward J(ulius) 1943- ... 41-44R
Rosenfeld, Harry M(orris) 1929- ... 69-72
Rosenfeld, Harvey 1939- ... 110
Rosenfeld, Isaac 1918-1956 ... DLB-28
Rosenfeld, Isadore 1926- ... 81-84
Rosenfeld, Jeffrey P(hilip) 1946- ... 115
Rosenfeld, Lulla 1914- ... 85-88
Rosenfeld, Marthe 1928- ... 45-48
Rosenfeld, Sam 1920- ... 11-12R
Rosenfeld, Samuel 1896-1963 Obituary ... 89-92
Rosenfeld, Sybil (Marion) 1903- ... 119
Rosenfield, Isadore 1893-1980 Obituary ... 97-100
Rosenfield, James A(lexander) 1943- ... 49-52
Rosenfield, John M(ax) 1924- ... CANR-14
Earlier sketch in CA 23-24R
Rosenfield, Leonora Cohen 1909-1982 ... 41-44R
Obituary ... 105
Rosengart, Oliver A. 1941- ... 49-52
Rosengarten, Frank 1927- ... 73-76
Rosengarten, Frederic (Jr.) 1916- ... 118
Rosengarten, Theodore 1944- ... 103
Rosengren, William R(udolph) 1929-
Brief entry ... 114
Rosenhaupt, Hans 1911-1985 Obituary ... 116
Rosenheim, Edward W(eil), Jr. 1918- ... 25-28R
Rosenhouse, Archie 1878- ... CAP-2
Earlier sketch in CA 21-22
Rosenkrantz, Linda 1934- ... CANR-11
Earlier sketch in CA 25-28R
Rosenkranz, Richard S. 1942- ... 37-40R
Rosenman, John B(rown) 1941- ... 106
Rosenman, Ray H(arold) 1920- ... 97-100
Rosenman, Samuel I(rving) 1896-1973
Obituary ... 41-44R
Rosenmeyer, Thomas Gustav 1920- ... 111
Rosenn, Keith S(amuel) 1938- ... 111
Rosenof, Theodore 1943- ... CANR-10
Earlier sketch in CA 65-68
Rosenow, John E(dward) 1949- ... 97-100
Rosenquist, Carl M(artin) 1895-1973 ... CAP-2
Earlier sketch in CA 29-32
Rosenrauch, Heinz Erich
See Rosen, Haiim B(aruch)
Rosensaft, Menachem Z. 1948- ... 23-24R
Rosenstein-Rodan, Paul N. 1902-1985 ... 107
Obituary ... 116
Rosenstiel, Annette 1911- ... 115
Rosenstiel, Leonie 1947- ... 85-88
Rosenstock, (Patricia) Janet (Stearns)
1933- ... 108
Rosenstock-Huessy, Eugen 1888-1973 ... CAP-1
Obituary ... 41-44R
Earlier sketch in CA 15-16
Rosenstone, Robert A(llan) 1936- ... 29-32R
Rosenstone, Steven J(ay) 1952- ... 104
Rosenthal, A(braham) M(ichael) 1922- ... 21-22R
Rosenthal, Alan 1936- ... 105
Rosenthal, Albert H(arold) 1914- ... 23-24R
Rosenthal, Andrew 1918(?)-1979
Obituary ... 89-92
Rosenthal, Bernard G(ordon) 1922- ... CANR-11
Earlier sketch in CA 29-32R
Rosenthal, Bernice (Glatzer) 1938- ... 121
Rosenthal, David 1916- ... 41-44R
Rosenthal, Donald B. 1937- ... CANR-14
Earlier sketch in CA 37-40R
Rosenthal, Douglas E(urico) 1940- ... 57-60
Rosenthal, Earl E(dgar) 1921- ... 41-44R
Rosenthal, Edwin Stanley 1914- ... 77-80
Rosenthal, Eric 1905- ... CANR-6
Earlier sketch in CA 9-10R
Rosenthal, Erwin Isak Jacob 1904- ... 102
Rosenthal, F(rank) F(ranz) 1911(?)-1979
Obituary ... 89-92
Rosenthal, Harold 1914- ... 111
See also SATA 35
Rosenthal, Harold (David) 1917-1987 ... 7-8R
Obituary ... 122
Rosenthal, Harry F(rederick) 1927- ... 65-68
Rosenthal, Harry Kenneth 1941- ... 57-60
Rosenthal, Henry Moses 1906-1977
Obituary ... 73-76
Rosenthal, Joe
See Rosenthal, Joseph J.
Rosenthal, Joel T(homas) 1934- ... 57-60
Rosenthal, Joseph J. 1911- ... 69-72
Rosenthal, Jules M. 1924- ... 19-20R
Rosenthal, M(acha) L(ouis) 1917- ... CANR-4
Earlier sketch in CA 4R
See also CAAS 6
See also DLB 5
See also CLC 28
Rosenthal, Mitchell S(tephen) 1935- ... 104
Rosenthal, Peggy 1944- ... 121
Rosenthal, Renee ?-1975 Obituary ... 57-60
Rosenthal, Richard A. 1925- ... 3R
Rosenthal, Ricky 1930(?)-1984 Obituary ... 114
Rosenthal, Robert 1933- ... CANR-16
Earlier sketch in CA 41-44R
Rosenthal, Shirley Lord 1934- ... CANR-11
Earlier sketch in CA 65-68
Rosenthal, Stuart 1934- ... 117
Rosenthal, Sylvia 1911- ... 109
Rosenus, Alan (Harvey) 1940- ... 73-76
Rosenwald, Henry M(artin) 1905- ... 33-36R
Rosenwasser, Dorothy Eckmann 1917- ... 2R
Rosenzweig, Michael L(eo) 1941- ... 101
Rosenzweig, Norman 1924- ... CANR-6
Earlier sketch in CA 57-60
Rosenzweig, Robert Myron 1931- ... 113
Rosenzweig, Roy 1950- ... 113
Rosett, Arthur (Irwin) 1934- ... 69-72
Rosette, Bennetta Jules
See Jules-Rosette, Bennetta
(Washington)
Roseveare, Helen Margaret 1925- ... 73-76
Rosewell, Paul Truman 1926- ... 17-18R
Roseyear, John 1936- ... 21-22R
Roshco, Bernard 1929- ... 7-8R
Rosher, Grace ?-1980 Obituary ... 111
Roshwalb, Irving 1924- ... 45-48
Roshwald, Mordecai Marceli 1921- ... 1R
Rosi, Eugene J(oseph) 1931- ... 61-64
Rosichan, Richard H(arry) 1941- ... 45-48
Rosie, George 1941- ... 120
Rosier, Bernard 1931- ... CANR-12
Earlier sketch in CA 29-32R
Rosier, James L(ouis) 1932- ... CANR-22
Earlier sketch in CA 2R
Rosillo-Calle, Francisco 1945- ... 121
Rositzke, Harry A(ugust) 1911- ... 45-48
Roskamp, Karl Wilhelm 1923- ... 15-16R
Roske, Ralph Joseph 1921- ... 122
Roskies, David G(regory) 1948- ... 120
Roskies, Ethel 1933- ... CANR-25
Earlier sketch in CA 45-48
Roskill, Mark W(entworth) 1933- ... CANR-6
Earlier sketch in CA 5-6R
Roskill, Stephen W(entworth)
1903-1982 ... CANR-6
Obituary ... 108
Earlier sketch in CA 15-16R
Rosko, Milt 1930- ... 41-44R
Roskolenko, Harry 1907-1980 ... CANR-17
Obituary ... 101
Earlier sketch in CA 15-16R
Roslavleva, Natalia
See Rene, Natalia
Rosman, Abraham 1930- ... 89-92
Rosmond, Babette 1921- ... CANR-6
Earlier sketch in CA 7-8R
Rosner, David K(arl) 1947- ... 112
Rosner, Fred 1935- ... 113
Rosner, Joseph 1914- ... 57-60
Rosner, Lynn 1944- ... 61-64
Rosner, Stanley 1928- ... 41-44R
Rosnow, Ralph L(eon) 1936- ... CANR-10
Earlier sketch in CA 23-24R
Rosochacki, Daniel 1942- ... 45-48
Rosoff, Sidney D. 1924- ... 1R
Rosovsky, Henry 1927- Brief entry ... 105
Rosow, Irving 1921- ... 85-88
Rosow, Jerome M(orris) 1919- ... 81-84
Rosowski, Susan J(ean) 1942- ... 111
Ross, Alan 1922- ... CANR-21
Earlier sketches in CA 11-12R, CANR-6
Ross, Alan
See Warwick, Alan R(oss)
Ross, Alan O(tto) 1921- ... 41-44R
Ross, Alan Strode Campbell 1907-1980 ... 11-12R
Obituary ... 102
Ross, Alec 1926- ... 29-32R
Ross, Alex(ander) 1909- ... SATA-29
Ross, Alf (Niels Christian Hansen) 1899- ... 53-56
Ross, Angus 1911- ... 21-22R
Ross, Angus
See Giggal, Kenneth
Ross, Barnaby
See Dannay, Frederic
and Lee, Manfred B(ennington)
Ross, Bernard H(arvey) 1934- ... 102
Ross, Bernard L.
See Follett, Ken(neth Martin)
Ross, Bette M. 1932- ... 106
Ross, Betty ... 69-72
Ross, Bill D. 1921- ... 123
Ross, Billy I(rvan) 1925- ... 57-60
Ross, Brian (Elliot) 1948- ... 126
Brief entry ... 119
Ross, Caroline
See Nicolson, Catherine
Ross, Catherine
See Beaty, Betty
Ross, Charles (Derek) 1924(?)-1986
Obituary ... 118
Ross, Charlotte (Brand) 1921- ... 117
Ross, Clare
See Romano, Clare
See also SATA 48
Ross, Clarissa
See Ross, W(illiam) E(dward) D(aniel)
Ross, Colin
See Roskolenko, Harry
Ross, Corinne Madden 1931- ... 106
Ross, Dallas
See Reynolds, Dallas McCord
Ross, Dan
See Ross, W(illiam) E(dward) D(aniel)
Ross, Dana
See Ross, W(illiam) E(dward) D(aniel)
Ross, Dave
See Ross, David
See also SATA 32
Ross, David 1896-1975 ... 65-68
Obituary ... 61-64
See also SATA 20, 49
Ross, David 1949- ... 111
Ross, David O(liver), Jr. 1936- Brief entry ... 117
Ross, David P(reston), Jr. 1908-1984
Obituary ... 112
Ross, Davis R. B. 1934- ... 33-36R
Ross, Diana
See Denney, Diana
Ross, Donald K. 1943- ... 49-52
Ross, Elizabeth Irvin 1942- ... 121
Ross, Emory 1887-1973 Obituary ... 41-44R
Ross, Eric (De Witt) 1929- ... 29-32R
Ross, Eulalie Steinmetz 1910- ... 17-18R
Ross, Eva J(eany) 1903-1969 ... CAP-2
Earlier sketch in CA 23-24
Ross, Floyd H(iatt) 1910- ... 73-76
Ross, Frances Aileen 1909- ... CAP-1
Earlier sketch in CA 9-10
Ross, Frank E. 1925- ... 19-20R
Ross, Frank (Xavier), Jr. 1914- ... CANR-16
Earlier sketch in CA 93-96
See also SATA 28
Ross, Gary 1948- ... 115
Ross, George
See Morgan-Grenville, Gerard
(Wyndham)
Ross, H(ugh) Laurence 1934- ... CANR-13
Earlier sketch in CA 77-80
Ross, Hal 1941- ... 65-68
Ross, Harold Raymond 1904- ... CAP-2
Earlier sketch in CA 19-20
Ross, Harold W(allace) 1892-1951
Brief entry ... 119
Ross, Helaine
See Daniels, Dorothy
Ross, Helen 1890(?)-1978 ... 85-88
Obituary ... 81-84
Ross, Ian
See Rossmann, John F(rancis)
Ross, Ian Simpson 1930- ... CANR-3
Earlier sketch in CA 45-48
Ross, Irwin 1919- ... 97-100
Ross, Ishbel 1897-1975 ... 93-96
Obituary ... 61-64
Ross, Ivan T.
See Rossner, Robert
Ross, J. H.
See Lawrence, T(homas) E(dward)
Ross, James Davidson 1924- ... 49-52
Ross, James F(rancis) 1931- ... CANR-11
Earlier sketch in CA 21-22R
Ross, James Frederick Stanley 1886- ... 11-12R
Ross, James S(tiven) 1892-1975
Obituary ... 57-60
Ross, Janet 1914- ... 37-40R
Ross, Joel E(lmore, Jr.) 1922- ... 29-32R
Ross, John 1921- ... 108
See also SATA 45

Ross, John A(ddison) 1919- 19-20R
Ross, John O'C(onnell) 1916- 25-28R
Ross, Jonathan
See Rossiter, John
Ross, Joseph
See Wrzos, Joseph Henry
Ross, Judith Wilson 1937- 114
Ross, K. G. M. ?-1985 Obituary 116
Ross, Katherine
See Walter, Dorothy Blake
Ross, Kenneth (Michael Andrew) 1941- 107
Ross, Kenneth Lynn 1940- 125
Ross, Kenneth N(eedham) 1908-1970 ... CANR-5
Earlier sketch in CA 7-8R
Ross, Lanson Clifford, Jr. 1936- 120
Ross, Laura
See Mincieli, Rose Laura
Ross, Leah 1938- 61-64
Ross, Leonard
See Rosten, Leo C(alvin)
Ross, Leonard M(ichael) 1945-1985 .....29-32R
Obituary 116
Ross, Leonard Q.
See Rosten, Leo C(alvin)
Ross, Lillian 1927- 11-12R
Ross, Lola Romanucci
See Romanucci- Ross, Lola
Ross, Lynne Nannen
See Ross-Robertson, Lynne Nannen
Ross, Mabel (Irene) H(ughes) 1909- 81-84
Ross, Malcolm
See Ross-Macdonald, Malcolm J(ohn)
Ross, Marc H(ansen) 1928- 114
Ross, Marilyn
See Ross, W(illiam) E(dward) D(aniel)
Ross, Marilyn (Ann) Heimberg 1939- .. CANR-14
Earlier sketch in CA 81-84
Ross, Marjorie Drake Rhoades 1901- 3R
Ross, Martha 1951- 103
Ross, Martin J. 1912- 53-56
Ross, Marvin C(hauncey) 1904-1977 ..... CAP-2
Obituary 69-72
Earlier sketch in CA 19-20
Ross, Mary Adelaide Eden
See Phillpotts, (Mary) Adelaide Eden
Ross, Michael 1905- 85-88
Ross, Michael W(allis) 1952- 118
Ross, Mitchell S(cott) 1953- 81-84
Ross, Murray George 1912- 19-20R
Ross, Nancy
See DeRoin, Nancy
Ross, Nancy Wilson 1910-1986 97-100
Obituary 118
Ross, Nathaniel 1904- 21-22R
Ross, Pat 1943- SATA-48, 53
Ross, Patricia
See Baxter, Patricia E. W.
Ross, Paul
See Crawford, William (Elbert)
Ross, Philip 1939- 69-72
Ross, Phyllis (Freedman) 1926-1970 ..... CAP-2
Earlier sketch in CA 17-18
Ross, Ralph 1911- 13-14R
Ross, Raymond S(amuel) 1925- CANR-8
Earlier sketch in CA 21-22R
Ross, Robert H(enry), Jr. 1916- 15-16R
Ross, Robert Horace 106
Ross, Robert S(amuel) 1940- 57-60
Ross, Robert W.
See Power-Ross, Robert W.
Ross, Russell M. 1921- 21-22R
Ross, Ruth 1930(?)-1986 Obituary 119
Ross, Sam 1912- 15-16R
Ross, Sheila Muriel 1925- 106
Ross, (James) Sinclair 1908- 73-76
See also CLC 13
Ross, Stanley R(obert) 1921- CANR-7
Earlier sketch in CA 17-18R
Ross, Stanley Ralph 1940- CANR-20
Earlier sketch in CA 97-100
Ross, Stephen David 1935- CANR-17
Earlier sketch in CA 41-44R
Ross, Steven Thomas 1937- 41-44R
Ross, Sutherland
See Callard, Thomas Henry
Ross, T(heodore) J(ohn) 1924- 57-60
Ross, Terrence 1947- 103
Ross, Thomas B. 1929- 29-32R
Ross, Thomas W(ynne) 1923- 41-44R
Ross, Timothy A(rrowsmith) 1936- 57-60
Ross, Tony 1938- 77-80
See also SATA 17
Ross, Veronica 1946- 113
Ross, W(illiam) E(dward) D(aniel)
1912- CANR-14
Earlier sketch in CA 81-84
Ross, W(illiam) Gordon 1900- 45-48
Ross, Wilda 1915- 85-88
See also SATA 39, 51
Ross, William
See Dewart, Leslie
Ross, William B. 1915- 25-28R
Ross, Z. H.
See Ross, Zola Helen
Ross, Zola Helen 1912- 53-56
Rossabi, Morris 1941- 102
Rossant, Murray J(oseph) 1923-1988
Obituary 125
Rossbach, Richard M. 1915(?)-1987
Obituary 123
Rossbacher, Lisa A(nn) 1952- 117
Rossberg, Robert H. 1926- 45-48
Rosse, Ian
See Straker, J(ohn) F(oster)
Rosse, Susanna
See Connolly, Vivian
Rossel, Seymour 1945- CANR-21
Earlier sketches in CA 53-56, CANR-5
See also SATA 28
Rossel, Sven H(akon) 1943- CANR-22
Earlier sketch in CA 105
Rossellini, Roberto 1906-1977 Obituary ...69-72
Rossel-Waugh, C. C.
See Waugh, Carol-Lynn Roessel
Rossen, Robert 1908-1966 Obituary 113
See also DLB 26
Rosser, Neill A(lbert) 1916-1973 .... CAP-1
Earlier sketch in CA 15-16
Rosset, B(enjamin) C(harles)
1910-1974 ....11-12R
Obituary 103
Rosset, Barnet Lee, Jr. 1922- 97-100
Rosset, Barney
See Rosset, Barnet Lee, Jr.
Rossetti, Christina (Georgina)
1830-1894 .... SATA-20
See also DLB 35
Rossetti, Dante Gabriel 1828-1882 ..... DLB-35
Rossetti, Minerva
See Rowland, D(onald) S(ydney)
Rossi, Aga
See Agarossi, Elena
Rossi, Alfred 1935- 29-32R
Rossi, Alice S(chaerr) 1922- CANR-17
Earlier sketches in CA 45-48, CANR-1
Rossi, Bruno
See Levinson, Leonard
Rossi, Ernest Lawrence 1933- CANR-14
Earlier sketch in CA 37-40R
Rossi, Ino 89-92
Rossi, Lino 1923- 104
Rossi, Mario 1916- CANR-8
Earlier sketch in CA 5-6R
Rossi, Nicholas Louis, Jr. 1924- CANR-6
Earlier sketch in CA 15-16R
Rossi, Nick
See Rossi, Nicholas Louis, Jr.
Rossi, Paul A. 1929- Brief entry 110
Rossi, Peter Henry 1921- CANR-19
Earlier sketches in CA 3R, CANR-4
Rossi, Philip Joseph 1943- 115
Rossi, Sanna Morrison Barlow 1917- 93-96
Rossi, William A(nthony) 1916- 65-68
Rossie, Jonathan Gregory 1935-
Brief entry 106
Rossi-Landi, Ferruccio 1921- 114
Rossini, Frederick A(nthony) 1939- CANR-12
Earlier sketch in CA 73-76
Rossit, Edward A. 1921- 17-18R
Rossiter, Clinton (Lawrence) 1917-1970
Obituary 25-28R
Rossiter, Frank R(aymond) 1937- 61-64
Rossiter, Ian
See Ross Williamson, Hugh
Rossiter, Jane
See Ross, W(illiam) E(dward) D(aniel)
Rossiter, John 1916- 33-36R
Rossiter, Margaret W(alsh) 1944- CANR-13
Earlier sketch in CA 77-80
Rossiter, (Percival) Stuart (Bryce) 1923- ...85-88
Rosskam, Edwin 1903(?)-1985 Obituary 115
Rosskopf, Myron Frederick 1907-1973 .. CANR-5
Obituary 41-44R
Earlier sketch in CA 5-6R
Ross-Macdonald, Malcolm J(ohn)
1932- CANR-13
Earlier sketch in CA 65-68
Rossman, Charles Raymond 1938- 113
Rossman, Evelyn
See Rothchild, Sylvia
Rossman, Jack E(ugene) 1936- 49-52
Rossman, Marlene L. 1948- 124
Rossman, Michael Dale 1939- 101
Rossman, (George) Parker 1919- 69-72
Rossmann, John F(rancis) 1942- 101
Rossner, Judith (Perelman) 1935- CANR-18
Earlier sketch in CA 19-20R
See also DLB 6
See also CLC 6, 9, 29
See also AITN 2
Rossner, Robert 1932- CANR-1
Earlier sketch in CA 2R
Rossoff, Martin 1910- 11-12R
Rossomando, Frederic William 1924- 49-52
Ross-Robertson, Lynne Nannen 1936- . CANR-25
Earlier sketch in CA 107
Ross Williamson, Hugh 1901-1978 ..... CANR-8
Earlier sketch in CA 17-18R
Rostand, Edmond (Eugene Alexis)
1868-1918 126
Brief entry 104
See also TCLC 6
Rostand, J.
See Rostand, Jean
Rostand, Jean 1894-1977 126
Brief entry 124
Rostand, Robert
See Hopkins, Robert S(ydney)
Rosten, Leo C(alvin) 1908- CANR-6
Earlier sketch in CA 7-8R
See also DLB 11
Rosten, Norman 1914- CANR-21
Earlier sketch in CA 77-80
Rostenberg, Leona 1908- CANR-5
Earlier sketch in CA 7-8R
Roston, Murray 1928- CANR-5
Earlier sketch in CA 53-56
Rostow, Eugene Victor 1913- 7-8R
Rostow, Walt W(hitman) 1916- CANR-8
Earlier sketch in CA 15-16R
Rostvold, Gerhard N(orman) 1919- CANR-10
Earlier sketch in CA 21-22R
Roszak, Betty 1933- 29-32R
Roszak, Theodore 1933- 77-80
Rota, Gian-Carlo 1932- 126
Rotarius
See Kerekes, Tibor
Rotberg, Robert I. 1935- CANR-21
Earlier sketches in CA 15-16R, CANR-6
Rotblat, Joseph 1908- CANR-26
Earlier sketch in CA 109
Rotchstein, Janice 1944- CANR-25
Earlier sketch in CA 106
Rote, Kyle 1928- 23-24R
Rotella, Guy Louis 1947- 115
Rotenstreich, Nathan 1914- CANR-23
Earlier sketches in CA 61-64, CANR-8
Roth, Alexander
See Dunner, Joseph
Roth, Andrew 1919- 53-56
Roth, Arlen 1952- 103
Roth, Arnold 1929- 21-22R
See also SATA 21
Roth, Arthur 1920- 3R
Roth, Arthur J(oseph) 1925- CANR-7
Earlier sketch in CA 53-56
See also SATA 28, 43
Roth, Audrey J. 1927- 23-24R
Roth, Cecil 1899-1970 .... CANR-13
Obituary 25-28R
Earlier sketch in CA 9-10R
Roth, Charles E(dmund) 1934- 111
Roth, Claire Jarett 1923- 7-8R
Roth, David 1940- 106
See also SATA 36
Roth, David F(rancisco) 1939- 41-44R
Roth, David M. 1874(?)-1971 Obituary 104
Roth, David M(orris) 1935- 57-60
Roth, Don A. 1927- 25-28R
Roth, Ernst 1896-1971 .... CAP-2
Earlier sketch in CA 25-28
Roth, Eugen 1895-1976 Obituary 65-68
Roth, Geneen 1951- 111
Roth, Hal 1927- 37-40R
Roth, Harold SATA-49
Roth, Harold L(eo) 1919-1982 Obituary 108
Roth, Harry 1903(?)-1976 Obituary 65-68
Roth, Henry 1906- CAP-1
Earlier sketch in CA 11-12
See also DLB 28
See also CLC 2, 6, 11
Roth, Herbert (Otto) 1917- 61-64
Roth, Herrick S. 1916- 77-80
Roth, Holly 1916-1964 .... CANR-6
Earlier sketch in CA 4R
Roth, Jack J(oseph) 1920- 23-24R
Roth, John K(ing) 1940- CANR-26
Earlier sketches in CA 25-28R, CANR-10
Roth, Julius A(lfred) 1924- 21-22R
Roth, June (Spiewak) 1926- CANR-19
Earlier sketches in CA 11-12R, CANR-5
Roth, Leland M(artin) 1943- CANR-16
Earlier sketch in CA 93-96
Roth, (Hyam) Leon 1896-1963 Obituary 106
Roth, Lillian 1910-1980 Obituary 97-100
Roth, Mark J(oseph) 1941- 77-80
Roth, Mary Jane 21-22R
Roth, Moira 1933- 121
Roth, Peggy (Meehan) ?-1973 Obituary 104
Roth, Philip (Milton) 1933- CANR-22
Earlier sketches in CA 2R, CANR-1
See also DLB 2, 28
See also DLBY 82
See also CLC 1, 2, 3, 4, 6, 9, 15, 22, 31, 47
Roth, Richard H(enry) 1949- 77-80
Roth, Robert Howard 1933- CANR-14
Earlier sketch in CA 41-44R
Roth, Robert J. 1920- 17-18R
Roth, Robert Paul 1919- 61-64
Roth, Samuel 1894-1974 Obituary 49-52
Roth, Sister Mary Augustine 1926- CANR-3
Earlier sketch in CA 9-10R
Roth, Sol 1927- 65-68
Roth, Theodore W(illiam) 1916- 57-60
Roth, William 1942- 101
Roth, Wolfgang M(ax) W(ilhelm) 1930- ...41-44R
Rotha, Paul 1907-1984 ....9-10R
Obituary 112
Rothafel, Roxy
See Rothafel, Samuel L(ionel)
Rothafel, Samuel L(ionel)
1881(?)-1936(?) Brief entry 123
Rothbard, Murray N(ewton) 1926- CANR-22
Earlier sketches in CA 7-8R, CANR-6
Rothbart, Harold A(rthur) 1917- 111
Rothbaum, Melvin 1926- 7-8R
Rothberg, Abraham 1922- 33-36R
Rothblatt, Ben 1924- 25-28R
Rothblatt, Donald N(oah) 1935- CANR-23
Earlier sketches in CA 61-64, CANR-8
Rothblatt, Henry B(arnett) 1916-1985 .. CANR-19
Obituary 117
Earlier sketch in CA 25-28R
Rothchild, Donald (Sylvester) 1928- ... CANR-14
Earlier sketch in CA 41-44R
Rothchild, Sylvia 1923- 77-80
Rothel, David 1936- CANR-10
Earlier sketch in CA 65-68
Rothenberg, Alan B(aer) 1907-1977
Obituary 73-76
Rothenberg, Albert 1930- CANR-25
Earlier sketches in CA 57-60, CANR-8
Rothenberg, B(arbara) Annye 1940- 107
Rothenberg, Diane Brodatz 1932- 115
Rothenberg, Gunther Eric 1923- CANR-8
Earlier sketch in CA 21-22R
Rothenberg, Jerome 1924- 29-32R
Rothenberg, Jerome 1931- CANR-1
Earlier sketch in CA 45-48
See also DLB 5
See also CLC 6
Rothenberg, Joshua 1911- 37-40R
Rothenberg, Lillian 1922- 11-12R
Rothenberg, Marc 1949- 115
Rothenberg, Polly 1916- 85-88
Rothenberg, Randall 1956- 118
Rothenberg, Robert E(dward) 1908- 37-40R
Rothenstein, John K(newstub) M(aurice)
1901- CANR-1
Earlier sketch in CA 1R
Rothermere, Viscount
See Harmsworth, Esmond Cecil
Rothery, Brian 1934- CANR-1
Earlier sketch in CA 49-52
Rothfork, John 1946- 110
Rothkopf, Carol Z. 1929- 25-28R
See also SATA 4
Rothman, Barbara Katz 1948- 111
Rothman, Charles Warren 1952- 120
Rothman, Chuck
See Rothman, Charles Warren
Rothman, David B. 1956- 111
Rothman, David J. 1937- 33-36R
Rothman, Esther P. 1919- 37-40R
Rothman, Joel 1938- 37-40R
See also SATA 7
Rothman, Judith
See Peters, Maureen
Rothman, Milton A. 1919- 41-44R
Rothman, Stanley 1927- 93-96
Rothman, Theodore 1907- CAP-2
Earlier sketch in CA 29-32
Rothman, Tony 1953- CANR-15
Earlier sketch in CA 85-88
Rothmuller, Aron Marko 1908- 73-76
Rothrock, George A(bel) 1932- 61-64
Rothschild, Alfred 1894(?)-1972 ....37-40R
Rothschild, Fritz A(lexander) 1919-
Brief entry 106
Rothschild, J(acquard) H(irshorn) 1907- .. CAP-2
Earlier sketch in CA 17-18
Rothschild, Joseph 1931- CANR-3
Earlier sketch in CA 11-12R
Rothschild, Kurt Wilhelm 1914- CANR-23
Earlier sketch in CA 102
Rothschild, Lincoln 1902-1983 .... CANR-12
Obituary 109
Earlier sketch in CA 45-48
Rothschild, Norman 1913- 103
Rothschild, Richard Charles 1895-1986
Obituary 118
Rothstein, Arthur 1915-1985 .... CANR-6
Obituary 117
Earlier sketch in CA 57-60
Rothstein, Eric 1936- 73-76
Rothstein, Samuel 1902(?)-1978
Obituary 77-80
Rothstein, Samuel 1921- 61-64
Rothstein, Stanley William 1929- 120
Rothstein, William G(ene) 1937- 73-76
Rothweiler, Paul Roger 1931- CANR-10
Earlier sketch in CA 65-68
Rothwell, Bruce 1923(?)-1984 Obituary 114
Rothwell, Kenneth J(ames) 1925- CANR-14
Earlier sketch in CA 23-24R
Rothwell, Kenneth S(prague) 1921- 33-36R
Rothwell, Talbot (Nelson Conn)
1916-1981 Obituary 103
Rothwell, V(ictor) H(oward) 1945- 37-40R
Rotimi, E. G. O.
See Rotimi, (Emmanuel Gladstone) Ola(wale)
Rotimi, (Emmanuel Gladstone) Ola(wale)
1938(?)- 124
See also BW
Rotimi, Olawale
See Rotimi, (Emmanuel Gladstone) Ola(wale)
Rotkin, Charles E. 1916- 7-8R
Rotmans, Elmer A. 1896- 7-8R
Rotondi, Cesar 1926- 97-100
Rotsler, William 1926- CANR-4
Earlier sketch in CA 53-56
Rotstein, Abraham 1929- 104
Rottenberg, Dan(iel) 1942- CANR-19
Earlier sketch in CA 102
Rottenberg, Isaac C. 1925- 15-16R
Rottensteiner, Franz 1942- CANR-15
Earlier sketch in CA 81-84
Rotter, Julian B(ernard) 1916- 33-36R
Rotter, Marion 1940(?)-1973 Obituary 104
Roubiczek, Paul (Anton) 1898-1972
Obituary 115
Roubinek, Darrell L(eRoy) 1935- 57-60
Roucek, Joseph S. 1902- 11-12R
Roudiez, Leon S(amuel) 1917- 37-40R
Roudybush, Alexandra (Brown) 1911- 65-68
Roueche, Berton 1911- CANR-1
Earlier sketch in CA 2R
See also SATA 28
Roueche, John E(dward) 1938- 49-52
Rougemont, Denis de
See de Rougemont, Denis
Roughsey, Dick 1921(?)- 109
See also SATA 35
Rougier, Louis (Auguste Paul)
1889-1982 .... CANR-13
Earlier sketch in CA 29-32R
Rougier, Nicole 1929- 29-32R
Rouhani, Fuad 1907- 37-40R
Roukes, Nicholas 1925- 25-28R
Roulac, Stephen E. 1945- 104
Rouleau, Raymond (Edgard Marie)
1904-1981 Obituary 108

Roulston, Marjorie Hillis 1890-1971
Obituary ... 104
Roumain, Jacques 1907-1944 Brief entry ... 117
See also TCLC 19
Roumain, Jacques (Jean Baptiste)
1907-1944 ... 125
Brief entry ... 117
See also BW
See also TCLC 19
Rounds, David 1930-1983 Obituary ... 111
Rounds, Glen (Harold) 1906- ... CANR-22
Earlier sketches in CA 53-56, CANR-7
See also SATA 8
Rouner, Arthur A(cy), Jr. 1929- ... CANR-5
Earlier sketch in CA 11-12R
Rouner, Leroy S(tephens) 1930- ... 73-76
Rountree, Owen
See Kittredge, William
and Krauzer, Steven M(ark)
Rountree, Thomas J. 1927- ... 25-28R
Rourke, Constance (Mayfield) 1885-1941
Brief entry ... 107
See also YABC 1
See also TCLC 12
Rourke, Francis E(dward) 1922- ... CANR-6
Earlier sketch in CA 2R
Rous, Stanley (Ford) 1895- ... 108
Rousculp, Charles G(ene) 1923- ... 29-32R
Rouse, (Hubert) Blair 1912- ... 4R
Rouse, (Benjamin) Irving, (Jr.) 1913- ... 11-12R
Rouse, John E(vans) 1892- ... 73-76
Rouse, John E(dward), Jr. 1942- ... 89-92
Rouse, Parke (Shepherd), Jr. 1915- ... 17-18R
Rouse, Richard H(unter) 1933- ... 29-32R
Rouse, Russell 1913(?)-1987 Obituary ... 123
Rouse Jones, Lewis 1907- ... CAP-1
Earlier sketch in CA 13-14
Roush, Barbara 1940- ... 109
Roush, John H., Jr. 1923- ... 37-40R
Rousmaniere, John 1944- ... CANR-17
Earlier sketch in CA 93-96
Rousseau, George Sebastian 1941- ... CANR-11
Earlier sketch in CA 29-32R
Rousseau, Richard W(ilfred) 1924- ... 110
Roussel, Raymond 1877-1933 Brief entry ... 117
See also TCLC 20
Roussin, Andre (Jean Paul Marie)
1911-1987 Obituary ... 124
Rout, Leslie B(rennan), Jr. 1936-1987 ... 57-60
Obituary ... 122
Routh, C(harles) R(ichard) N(airne)
1896- ... CAP-1
Earlier sketch in CA 13-14
Routh, Donald K(ent) 1937- ... 57-60
Routh, Francis John 1927- ... 13-14R
Routh, Jonathan ... 110
Routh, Porter W(roe) 1911- ... 77-80
Routley, Erik (Reginald) 1917-1982 ... CANR-5
Obituary ... 108
Earlier sketch in CA 3R
Routsong, Alma 1924- ... 49-52
Routt, Mary Patterson 1890(?)-1986
Obituary ... 119
Routtenberg, Max Jonah 1909- ... 77-80
Rouverol, Jean
See Butler, Jean Rouverol
Roux, Edward R(udolph) 1903- ... 13-14R
Roux, Georges 1914- ... 17-18R
Roux, Willan Charles 1902- ... CAP-2
Earlier sketch in CA 17-18
Rover, Constance (Mary) 1910- ... 23-24R
Rovere, Richard H(alworth) 1915-1979 ... CANR-3
Obituary ... 89-92
Earlier sketch in CA 49-52
Rovin, Ben
See Clevenger, Ernest Allen, Jr.
Rovin, Jeff 1951- ... 77-80
Rovit, Earl (Herbert) 1927- ... CANR-12
Earlier sketch in CA 7-8R
See also CLC 7
Rowan, Andrew N(icholas) 1946- ... 124
Rowan, Carl Thomas 1925- ... 89-92
See also BW
Rowan, Dan (Hale) 1922-1987 Obituary ... 125
Rowan, Deirdre
See Williams, Jeanne
Rowan, Ford 1943- ... 69-72
Rowan, Helen 1927(?)-1972 Obituary ... 37-40R
Rowan, Hester
See Robinson, Sheila Mary
Rowan, Richard Lamar 1931- ... 11-12R
Rowan, Stephen A(nthony) 1928- ... 45-48
Rowan, Steven William 1943- ... 116
Rowans, Virgina
See Tanner, Edward Everett III
Rowat, Donald C(ameron) 1921- ... CANR-20
Earlier sketches in CA 11-12R, CANR-5
Rowatt, G(eorge) Wade, Jr. 1943- ... 126
Rowbotham, David (Harold) 1924-
Brief entry ... 112
Rowbotham, Sheila 1943- ... 101
Rowdon, Maurice 1922- Brief entry ... 110
Rowe, A(lbert) W(ard) 1915- ... CANR-14
Earlier sketch in CA 23-24R
Rowe, Clarence J(ohn), Jr. 1916- ... 104
Rowe, David Knox ... 77-80
Rowe, David Nelson 1905- ... CANR-2
Earlier sketch in CA 7-8R
Rowe, Elizabeth 1674-1737 ... DLB-39
Rowe, Erna (Dirks) 1926- ... 93-96
Rowe, Frank 1921-1985 Obituary ... 115
Rowe, Frederick William 1912- ... 101
Rowe, G(ail) S(tuart) 1936- ... 112
Rowe, George E(rnest), Jr. 1947- ... 93-96
Rowe, H. Edward 1927- ... 69-72
Rowe, James L(ester), Jr. 1948- ... 69-72
Rowe, James N(icholas) 1938- ... 37-40R
Rowe, Jeanne A. 1938- ... 29-32R
Rowe, John (Seymour) 1936- ... 109
Rowe, John Carlos 1945- ... 114
Rowe, John L. 1914- ... 19-20R
Rowe, Margaret (Kevin) 1920- ... 15-16R
Rowe, Mary Budd 1925- ... 113
Rowe, Robert 1920- ... 17-18R
Rowe, Terry ... AITN-2
Rowe, Viola Carson 1903-1969 ... 2R
Obituary ... 103
See also SATA 26
Rowe, Vivian C(laud) 1902-1978 ... CANR-2
Earlier sketch in CA 3R
Rowe, William D(avid) 1930- ... 114
Rowe, William L. 1931- Brief entry ... 108
Rowell, Galen 1940- ... CANR-18
Earlier sketch in CA 65-68
Rowell, George (Rignall) 1923- ... CANR-18
Earlier sketches in CA 7-8R, CANR-2
Rowell, Henry T(hompson) 1904- ... CAP-1
Earlier sketch in CA 13-14
Rowell, John W(illiam) 1914- ... 33-36R
Rowen, Betty Jane Rose 1920- Brief entry ... 109
Rowen, Henry S(tanislaus) 1925- ... 123
Brief entry ... 118
Rowen, Herbert H(arvey) 1916- ... CANR-3
Earlier sketch in CA 11-12R
Rowen, Hobart 1918- ... 11-12R
Rowen, Lilian 1925- ... 108
Rowen, Ruth Halle 1918- ... 33-36R
Rowes, Barbara Gail ... 101
Rowland, Arthur R(ay) 1930- ... CANR-21
Earlier sketches in CA 13-14R, CANR-6
Rowland, Benjamin, Jr. 1904-1972
Obituary ... 37-40R
Rowland, Beryl ... 89-92
Rowland, Christopher (Charles) 1947- ... 116
Rowland, Claude K. 1943- ... 112
Rowland, D(onald) S(ydney) 1928- ... 21-22R
Rowland, Diana 1950- ... 122
Rowland, Florence Wightman 1900- ... CANR-5
Earlier sketch in CA 5-6R
See also SATA 8
Rowland, Iris
See Roberts, Irene
Rowland, J(ohn) R(ussell) 1925- ... 101
Rowland, Judith 1944- ... 124
Rowland, Peter (Kenneth) 1938- ... 25-28R
Rowland, Stanley J., Jr. 1928- ... 15-16R
Rowland, Virgil K(enneth) 1909- ... 5-6R
Rowland-Entwistle, (Arthur) Theodore
(Henry) 1925- ... CANR-24
Earlier sketch in CA 107
See also SATA 31
Rowlands, John Robert 1947- ... 109
Rowlands, Peter
See Lovell, Mark
Rowlandson, Mary 1635(?)-1678(?) ... DLB-24
Rowlatt, Mary 1908- ... 5-6R
Rowley, Ames Dorrance
See Lovecraft, H(oward) P(hillips)
Rowley, Anthony 1939- ... 61-64
Rowley, Brian A(lan) 1923- ... 7-8R
Rowley, Charles (Dunford) 1906-1985 ... 103
Obituary ... 117
Rowley, Peter 1934- ... 65-68
Rowley, Peter T(empleton) 1929-
Brief entry ... 112
Rowley, Thomas
See Pauker, John
Rowley, William 1585(?)-1626 ... DLB-58
Rowley, William Dean 1939- ... 112
Rowling, Marjorie A(lice Thexton) 1900- ... 7-8R
Rowlingson, Donald T(aggart) 1907- ... CANR-6
Earlier sketch in CA 2R
Rowney, Don Karl 1936- ... 108
Rowse, A(lfred) L(eslie) 1903- ... CANR-1
Earlier sketch in CA 4R
Rowsome, Frank (Howard), Jr.
1914-1983 ... 112
See also SATA 36
Rowson, Susanna Haswell
1762(?)-1824 ... DLB-37
Rowthorn, Anne W(heeler) 1939- ... 113
Roxas, Savina A. ... 37-40R
Roxborough, Henry Hall 1891- ... 7-8R
Roxon, Lillian 1933(?)-1973 Obituary ... 111
Roy, Archibald Edmiston 1924- ... 102
Roy, Archie E.
See Roy, Archibald Edmiston
Roy, David Tod 1933- ... 41-44R
Roy, Emil L. 1933- ... 25-28R
Roy, Ewell Paul 1929- ... 11-12R
Roy, G(eorge) Ross 1924- ... 77-80
Roy, Gabrielle 1909-1983 ... CANR-5
Obituary ... 110
Earlier sketch in CA 53-56
See also DLB 68
See also CLC 10, 14
Roy, Gregor 1929- ... 23-24R
Roy, Jack
See Dangerfield, Rodney
Roy, James A(lexander) 1884- ... CAP-1
Earlier sketch in CA 11-12
Roy, Jessie Hailstalk 1895-1986 Obituary ... 121
See also SATA 51
Roy, Joaquin 1943- ... 77-80
Roy, John (Flint) 1913- ... 93-96
Roy, Katherine (Morris) 1906- ... 3R
Roy, Liam
See Scarry, Patricia (Murphy)
Roy, Michael 1913-1976 ... CANR-10
Obituary ... 65-68
Earlier sketch in CA 61-64
Roy, Mike
See Roy, Michael
Roy, Reginald H(erbert) 1922- ... 49-52
Roy, Robert L(ouis) 1947- ... 106
Roy, Robin 1946- ... 114
Roy, Ron(ald) 1940- ... 114
See also SATA 35, 40
Roy, Rustum 1924- ... 113
Royal, Claudia Smith 1904- ... 7-8R
Royal, D.
See Du Breuil, (Elizabeth) L(or)inda
Royal, Denise 1935- ... 25-28R
Royal, William Robert 1905- ... 101
Royall, Anne 1769-1854 ... DLB-43
Royall, Vanessa
See Hinkemeyer, Michael T(homas)
Royce, Anya Peterson 1940- ... 101
Royce, James E(mmet) 1914- ... 3R
Royce, Kenneth
See Gandley, Kenneth Royce
Royce, Patrick M(ilan) 1922- ... 15-16R
Royce, R(ussell) Joseph 1921- ... CANR-9
Earlier sketch in CA 23-24R
Royds, Caroline 1953- ... 123
Royer, Fanchon 1902- ... 7-8R
Royko, Mike 1932- ... CANR-26
Earlier sketch in CA 89-92
Roylance, William H(erbert) 1927- ... 61-64
Royle, Edward 1944- ... 61-64
Royle, Selena 1904-1983 Obituary ... 109
Royle, Trevor 1945- ... 112
Royster, Charles 1944- ... 101
Royster, Philip M. 1943- ... CANR-13
Earlier sketch in CA 65-68
Royster, Salibelle 1895-1975 ... CAP-2
Earlier sketch in CA 25-28
Royster, Vermont (Connecticut) 1914- ... 21-22R
Royston, Olive 1904- ... 102
Rozeboom, William W(arren) 1928- ... 17-18R
Rozek, Evalyn Robillard 1941- ... 61-64
Rozental, Alek A(ron) 1920- ... 33-36R
Rozewicz, Tadeusz 1921- ... 108
See also CLC 9, 23
Rozhdestvensky, Vsevolod A.
1895(?)-1977 Obituary ... 73-76
Rozier, John W(iley) 1918- ... 107
Rozin, Skip 1941- ... 89-92
Rozman, Deborah 1949- ... 115
Rozman, Gilbert Friedell 1943- ... CANR-26
Earlier sketch in CA 109
Rozovsky, Lorne Elkin 1942- ... CANR-24
Earlier sketch in CA 108
Rozwenc, Edwin C(harles) 1915-1974 ... CAP-1
Earlier sketch in CA 13-14
Ruane, Gerald P(atrick) 1934- ... 69-72
Ruano, Argimiro 1924- ... 33-36R
Ruano, Nazario
See Ruano, Argimiro
Ruark, Gibbons 1941- ... CANR-14
Earlier sketch in CA 33-36R
See also CLC 3
Ruark, Robert (Chester) 1915-1965 ... CAP-2
Obituary ... 25-28R
Earlier sketch in CA 19-20
Ruas, Charles (Edward) 1938- ... 124
Rubadeau, Duane O. 1927- ... 29-32R
Rubashov, Schneor Zalman
See Shazar, (Schneor) Zalman
Rubashov, Zalman
See Shazar, (Schneor) Zalman
Rubbra, Edmund 1901-1986 Obituary ... 119
Rubel, Arthur J. 1924- ... CANR-15
Earlier sketch in CA 41-44R
Rubel, Marc (Reid) 1949- ... 123
Rubel, Maximilien 1905- ... CAP-1
Earlier sketch in CA 11-12
Rubel, Nicole 1953- ... 125
See also SATA 18
Rubel, Paula G(licksman) 1933- ... 89-92
Ruben, Brent David 1944- ... 41-44R
Ruben, Harvey L. 1941- ... 119
Rubens, Bernice 1923- ... 25-28R
See also DLB 14
See also CLC 19, 31
Rubens, Jeff(rey Peter) 1941- ... CANR-17
Earlier sketch in CA 25-28R
Rubenson, Sven (Abel) 1921- ... 115
Rubenstein, Boris B. 1907(?)-1974
Obituary ... 53-56
Rubenstein, Joshua 1949- ... 103
Rubenstein, Richard E(dward) 1938- ... 29-32R
Rubenstein, Richard L(owell) 1924- ... CANR-17
Earlier sketch in CA 21-22R
Rubenstein, (Clarence) Robert 1926- ... 21-22R
Rubenstein, Roberta 1944- ... 89-92
Rubenstone, Jessie 1912- ... 69-72
Rubia Barcia, Jose 1914- ... CANR-19
Earlier sketch in CA 103
Rubicam, Harry Cogswell, Jr. 1902- ... CAP-2
Earlier sketch in CA 17-18
Rubicon
See Lunn, Arnold
Rubin, Alan (Michael) 1936- ... 113
Rubin, Amy Kateman 1945- ... 106
Rubin, Arnold P(erry) 1946- ... 69-72
Rubin, Barry (M.) 1950- ... 108
Rubin, Benny 1899-1986 Obituary ... 119
Rubin, Charles J. 1950- ... 101
Rubin, Cynthia Elyce 1944- ... 97-100
Rubin, David Lee 1939- ... CANR-15
Earlier sketch in CA 41-44R
Rubin, David M. 1945- ... 77-80
Rubin, Dorothy 1932- ... CANR-19
Earlier sketch in CA 101
Rubin, Duane R(oger) 1931- ... 57-60
Rubin, Eli Z(under) 1922- ... 17-18R
Rubin, Ernest 1915-1978 Obituary ... 81-84
Rubin, Eva Johanna 1925- ... SATA-38
Rubin, Eva R(edfield) 1926- ... 113
Rubin, Frederick 1926- ... 33-36R
Rubin, Ida Ely 1923- ... 107
Rubin, Isadore 1912-1970 ... CAP-1
Obituary ... 29-32R
Earlier sketch in CA 15-16
Rubin, Israel 1923- ... 37-40R
Rubin, Jacob A. 1910-1972 ... CAP-1
Obituary ... 37-40R
Earlier sketch in CA 11-12
Rubin, James Henry 1944- ... 106
Rubin, Jerry 1938- ... 69-72
Rubin, Joan 1932- ... 102
Rubin, Julia Danielle 1944- ... 113
Rubin, Larry (Jerome) 1930- ... 5-6R
Rubin, Leona G(reenstone) 1920- ... 49-52
Rubin, Lillian Breslow 1924- ... 65-68
Rubin, Louis D(ecimus), Jr. 1923- ... CANR-21
Earlier sketches in CA 3R, CANR-6
Rubin, Mann 1927- ... 119
Rubin, Mark 1946- ... CANR-9
Earlier sketch in CA 53-56
Rubin, Michael 1935- ... CANR-1
Earlier sketch in CA 1R
Rubin, Morris H(arold) 1911-1980
Obituary ... 101
Rubin, Morton 1923- ... 41-44R
Rubin, Stanley 1928- ... 107
Rubin, Steven Jay 1951- ... 110
Rubin, Steven Joel 1943- ... 107
Rubin, Theodore Isaac 1923- ... 110
Brief entry ... 108
See also AITN 1
Rubin, Vera (Dourmashkin) 1911-1985
Obituary ... 115
Rubin, Vitalii 1923-1981 ... 69-72
Obituary ... 105
Rubin, William 1927- ... 77-80
Rubin, Zick 1944- ... CANR-1
Earlier sketch in CA 49-52
Rubinfeld, William A. 1914(?)-1984
Obituary ... 113
Rubington, Earl 1923- ... 73-76
Rubinoff, (M.) Lionel 1930- ... 25-28R
Rubinow, Sol (Isaac) 1923-1981 Obituary ... 103
Rubins, Harriett 1942- ... 120
Rubins, Jack L(awrence) 1916-1982 ... 85-88
Obituary ... 107
Rubinstein, Alvin Zachary 1927- ... CANR-18
Earlier sketches in CA 9-10R, CANR-3
Rubinstein, Amnon 1931- ... CANR-7
Earlier sketch in CA 15-16R
Rubinstein, Arthur 1887(?)-1982 ... 113
Obituary ... 108
Rubinstein, Daryl Reich 1938(?)-1981
Obituary ... 102
Rubinstein, David H(ugh) 1915- ... 109
Rubinstein, David M(ichael) 1942- ... 93-96
Rubinstein, E(lliott) 1936- ... 41-44R
Rubinstein, Erna F(erber) 1922- ... 120
Rubinstein, H(arold) F(rederick)
1891-1975 Obituary ... 115
Rubinstein, Helena 1871(?)-1965 Obituary ... 113
Rubinstein, Hilary 1926- ... 57-60
Rubinstein, Moshe F(ajwel) 1930- ... 57-60
Rubinstein, Paul (Arthur) ... CANR-7
Earlier sketch in CA 61-64
Rubinstein, Robert E(dward) 1943- ... 106
See also SATA 49
Rubinstein, S(amuel) Leonard 1922- ... 45-48
Rubinstein, Stanley (Jack) 1890-1975 ... CAP-2
Earlier sketch in CA 29-32
Rubinstein, W(illiam) D(avid) 1946- ... 114
Rublowsky, John M(artin) 1928- ... 17-18R
Rubsamen, Walter H. 1911- ... 13-14R
Rubulis, Aleksis 1922- ... 37-40R
Ruby, Kathryn 1947- ... 65-68
Ruby, Lois F. 1942- ... CANR-18
Earlier sketch in CA 97-100
See also SATA 34, 35
Ruby, Robert Holmes 1921- ... CANR-7
Earlier sketch in CA 19-20R
Ruchames, Louis 1917-1976 ... CANR-2
Obituary ... 65-68
Earlier sketch in CA 2R
Ruchelman, Leonard I. 1933- ... 29-32R
Ruchlis, Hy(man) 1913- ... CANR-2
Earlier sketch in CA 4R
See also SATA 3
Ruck, Amy Roberta 1878-1978 ... CANR-5
Earlier sketch in CA 7-8R
Ruck, Berta
See Ruck, Amy Roberta
Ruck, Carl A(nton) P(aul) 1935- ... 25-28R
Ruck, Peter F(rederick) Carter
See Carter-Ruck, Peter F(rederick)
Rucker, Bryce W(ilson) 1921- ... 11-12R
Rucker, (Egbert) Darnell 1921- ... 41-44R
Rucker, Frank Warren 1886-1975 ... 4R
Obituary ... 103
Rucker, Helen (Bornstein) ... 1R
Rucker, Rudolf v(on) B(itter) 1946- ... 124
Brief entry ... 119
Rucker, Rudy
See Rucker, Rudolf v(on) B(itter)
Rucker, W(infred) Ray 1920- ... 13-14R
Ruckman, Ivy 1931- ... 111
See also SATA 37
Ruck-Pauquet, Gina 1931- ... 122
Brief entry ... 116
See also SATA 37, 40
Rudd, Enid ... 108
Rudd, Hughes (Day) 1921- ... 73-76
Rudd, Margaret
See Newlin, Margaret Rudd
Rudd, Margaret T(homas) 1907- ... 19-20R
Rudd, Robert D(ean) 1924- ... 93-96
Rudd, Robert L. 1921- ... 117

Rudd, Steele
See Davis, Arthur Hoey
Ruddell, Robert B(yron) 1937- ... 93-96
Rudder, Robert S(ween) 1937- ... CANR-5
Earlier sketch in CA 53-56
Rudder, Virginia L. 1941- ... 65-68
Ruddick, Sara 1935- ... 77-80
Ruddock, Ralph 1913- ... 53-56
Ruddy, Frank C.
See Frank, Rudolf
Ruddy, T(homas) Michael 1946- ... 124
Rude, George F. E(lliot) 1910- ... CANR-24
Earlier sketches in CA 7-8R, CANR-5
Rudeen, Kenneth Brief entry ... 117
See also SATA 36
Rudel, Hans-Ulrich 1916-1982 Obituary ... 110
Rudelius, William 1931- ... 45-48
Rudensky, Morris "Red"
See Friedman, Max Motel
Rudenstine, Neil Leon 1935- Brief entry ... 105
Ruder, William 1921- ... 19-20R
Rudhart, Alexander 1930- ... 61-64
Rudhyar, Dane 1895-1985 ... CANR-21
Obituary ... 117
Earlier sketch in CA 29-32R
Rudin, Jacob Philip 1902-1982 Obituary ... 107
Rudin, Marcia Ruth 1940- ... 102
Rudinsky, Joseph F(rancis) 1891- ... 5-6R
Rudis, Al 1943- ... 77-80
Rudisill, D(orus) P(aul) 1902- ... 45-48
Rudkin, (James) David 1936- ... 89-92
See also DLB 13
See also CLC 14
Rudley, Stephen 1946- ... 106
See also SATA 30
Rudloe, Jack 1943- ... 97-100
Rudman, Mark 1948- ... 119
Rudman, Masha Kabakow 1933- ... 110
Rudnick, Hans H(einrich) 1935- ... 41-44R
Rudnick, Lois Palken 1944- ... 121
Rudnick, Milton Leroy 1927- ... CANR-3
Earlier sketch in CA 2R
Rudnik, Raphael 1933- ... 29-32R
See also CLC 7
Rudofsky, Bernard 1905-1988 ... 17-18R
Obituary ... 125
Rudolf, Anthony 1942- ... CANR-24
Earlier sketches in CA 61-64, CANR-9
Rudolph, Albert
See Frank, Rudolf
Rudolph, Donna Keyse 1934- ... 33-36R
Rudolph, Erwin Paul 1916- ... 33-36R
Rudolph, Frederick 1920- ... 11-12R
Rudolph, L(avere) C(hristian) 1921- ... CANR-2
Earlier sketch in CA 7-8R
Rudolph, Lee (Norman) 1948- ... CANR-7
Earlier sketch in CA 57-60
Rudolph, Lloyd I(rving) 1927- ... 57-60
Rudolph, Marguerita 1908- ... CANR-13
Earlier sketch in CA 33-36R
See also SATA 21
Rudolph, Nancy 1923- ... 57-60
Rudolph, Robert S. 1937- ... 41-44R
Rudolph, Susanne Hoeber 1930- ... 25-28R
Rudomin, Esther
See Hautzig, Esther Rudomin
Rudrum, Alan (William) 1932- ... 25-28R
Rudwick, Elliot M. 1927-1986(?) ... 104
Obituary ... 118
Rudy, Ann 1927- ... 101
Rudy, Peter 1922- ... 53-56
Rudy, Willis 1920- ... 37-40R
Rue, John E. 1924- ... 21-22R
Rue, Leonard Lee III 1926- ... CANR-1
Earlier sketch in CA 4R
See also SATA 37
Rue, Leslie W(aits) 1944- ... 110
Rue, Nancy Naylor 1951- ... 122
Ruebsaat, Helmut J(ohannes) 1920- ... 61-64
Ruechelle, Randall C(ummings) 1920- ... 41-44R
Rueckert, William H(owe) 1926- ... 23-24R
Ruedi, Norma Paul
See Ainsworth, Norma
Ruef, John S. 1927- ... 37-40R
Rueff, Jacques (Leon) 1896-1978 ... CANR-12
Obituary ... 77-80
Earlier sketch in CA 65-68
Ruege, Klaus 1934- ... CANR-11
Earlier sketch in CA 65-68
Ruehle, Juergen 1924- ... 25-28R
Ruehlmann, William 1946- ... 105
Ruell, Patrick
See Hill, Reginald (Charles)
Ruesch, Hans 1913- ... 15-16R
Ruesch, Jurgen 1909- ... 73-76
Rueschemeyer, Marilyn 1938- ... 122
Rueschhoff, Phil H. 1924- ... 29-32R
Ruether, Rosemary Radford 1936- ... 97-100
Rueveni, Uri 1933- ... 102
Ruff, Ann 1930- ... 120
Ruff, Howard J. ... 93-96
Ruffell, Ann 1941- ... CANR-23
Earlier sketch in CA 107
See also SATA 30
Ruffell, Thomas
See Laslett, Peter
Ruffian, M.
See Hasek, Jaroslav (Matej Frantisek)
Ruffin, C(aulbert) Bernard III 1947- ... 109
Ruffini, (Jacopo) Remo 1942- ... 57-60
Ruffins, Reynold 1930- ... 112
See also SATA 41
Ruffle, The
See Tegner, Henry (Stuart)
Ruffner, Budge
See Ruffner, Lester Ward
Ruffner, Lester Ward 1918- ... 89-92
Ruffo, Vinnie ... 25-28R
Ruffridge, Frank(lin James) 1931- ... CANR-12
Earlier sketch in CA 25-28R
Rugel, Miriam 1911- ... 101
Rugg, Dean S(prague) 1923- ... 41-44R
Ruggiero, Guido 1944- ... 118
Ruggiers, Paul G(eorge) 1918- ... CANR-24
Earlier sketch in CA 25-28R
Ruggles, Eleanor 1916- ... 7-8R
Ruggles, Henry Joseph 1813-1906 ... DLB-64
Ruggles, Joanne Beaule 1946- ... 73-76
Ruggles, Philip (Kent) 1944- ... 73-76
Rugh, Belle Dorman 1908- ... CAP-1
Earlier sketch in CA 15-16
Rugh, Roberts 1903-1978 ... 93-96
Obituary ... 81-84
Rugoff, Milton 1913- ... 21-22R
See also SATA 30
Ruhen, Olaf 1911- ... CANR-20
Earlier sketches in CA 4R, CANR-5
See also SATA 17
Ruhlen, Merritt 1944- ... 122
Ruibal, Jorge Silvestre Remonda
See Remonda-Ruibal, Jorge Silvestre
Ruihley, Glenn Richard ... 107
Ruitenbeek, Hendrik M(arinus)
1928-1983 ... CANR-8
Obituary ... 109
Earlier sketch in CA 7-8R
Ruiz, Jose Martinez
See Martinez Ruiz, Jose
See also CLC 11
Ruiz, Ramon Eduardo 1921- ... CANR-11
Earlier sketch in CA 25-28R
Ruiz, Ricardo Navas
See Navas-Ruiz, Ricardo
Ruiz, Roberto 1925- ... 41-44R
Ruiz-De-Conde, Justina (Malaxechevarria)
1909- ... 73-76
Ruiz-Fornells, Enrique 1925- ... 33-36R
Ruja, Harry 1912- ... 41-44R
Rukeyser, Louis 1933- ... 65-68
Rukeyser, Merryle Stanley 1897-1974 ... CAP-2
Earlier sketch in CA 23-24
Rukeyser, Muriel 1913-1980 ... CANR-26
Obituary ... 93-96
Earlier sketch in CA 7-8R
See also SATA 22
See also DLB 48
See also CLC 6, 10, 15, 27
Rukeyser, William Simon 1939- ... 69-72
Ruksenas, Algis 1942- ... 49-52
Ruland, Richard (Eugene) 1932- ... 21-22R
Ruland, Vernon Joseph 1931- ... 19-20R
Rule, Gordon Wade 1906-1982 Obituary ... 107
Rule, James B(ernard) 1943- ... 73-76
Rule, Jane (Vance) 1931- ... CANR-12
Earlier sketch in CA 25-28R
See also DLB 60
See also CLC 27
Rulfo, Juan 1918-1986 ... CANR-26
Obituary ... 118
Earlier sketch in CA 85-88
See also CLC 8
Rulon, Philip Reed 1934- ... CANR-14
Earlier sketch in CA 37-40R
Rumaker, Michael 1932- ... CANR-2
Earlier sketch in CA 3R
See also DLB 16
Rumanes, George N(icholas) 1925- ... 45-48
Rumbelow, Donald 1940- ... 49-52
Rumberger, Russell W(illiam) 1949- ... CANR-26
Earlier sketch in CA 109
Rumble, Thomas C(lark) 1919- ... 15-16R
Rumble, Wilfrid E., Jr. 1931- ... 25-28R
Rumbold-Gibbs, Henry St. John Clair
1913- ... CANR-3
Earlier sketch in CA 1R
Rumens, Carol 1944- ... DLB-40
Rummel, J(osiah) Francis 1911- ... 19-20R
Rummel, R(udolph) J(oseph) 1932- ... 65-68
Rumpleforeskin
See Krassner, Paul
Rumscheidt, H(ans) Martin 1935- ... 57-60
Rumsey, Marian (Barritt) 1928- ... 21-22R
See also SATA 16
Runcie, Robert Alexander Kennedy 1921- ... 108
Runciman, (James Cochran) Steven(son)
1903- ... CANR-3
Earlier sketch in CA 3R
Rundell, Walter, Jr. 1928- ... CANR-3
Earlier sketch in CA 11-12R
Rundle, Anne ... CANR-12
Earlier sketch in CA 57-60
Runes, Dagobert D(avid) 1902-1982 ... CANR-26
Obituary ... 108
Earlier sketch in CA 25-28R
Runge, C(arlisle) Ford 1953- ... 122
Runge, William H(arry) 1927- ... 2R
Runia, Klaas 1926- ... CANR-20
Earlier sketches in CA 7-8R, CANR-5
Runkel, Philip J(ulian) 1917- ... CANR-11
Earlier sketch in CA 29-32R
Runkle, Gerald 1924- ... CANR-14
Earlier sketch in CA 37-40R
Runnels, Curtis 1950- ... 126
Running, Leona Glidden 1916- ... 89-92
Runte, Alfred 1947- ... CANR-19
Earlier sketch in CA 102
Runyan, Harry (John) 1913-(?) ... CAP-2
Earlier sketch in CA 23-24
Runyan, John
See Palmer, Bernard
Runyan, Thora J. 1931- ... 69-72
Runyon, A(lfred) Milton 1905-1983
Obituary ... 109
Runyon, Catherine 1947- ... 61-64
Runyon, Charles W. 1928- ... 17-18R
Runyon, (Alfred) Damon 1884(?)-1946
Brief entry ... 107
See also DLB 11
See also TCLC 10
Runyon, Daniel V. 1954- ... 120
Runyon, John H(arold) 1945- ... 33-36R
Runyon, Richard P(orter) 1925- ... CANR-3
Earlier sketch in CA 45-48
Ruoff, James E. 1925- ... 41-44R
Ruotolo, Andrew K(eogh) 1926(?)-1979 ... 103
Obituary ... 89-92
Ruotolo, Lucio P(eter) 1927- ... 41-44R
Rupert, Hoover 1917- ... CANR-3
Earlier sketch in CA 2R
Rupert, Raphael Rudolph 1910- ... CAP-2
Earlier sketch in CA 19-20
Ruple, Wayne Douglas 1950- ... 53-56
Rupp, E. G.
See Rupp, E(rnest) Gordon
Rupp, E(rnest) Gordon 1910-1986 ... 124
Brief entry ... 113
Rupp, Gordon
See Rupp, E(rnest) Gordon
Rupp, Leila J(ane) 1950- ... 81-84
Rupp, Richard H(enry) 1934- ... 29-32R
Ruppenthal, Karl M. 1917- ... 19-20R
Ruppersburg, Hugh Michael 1950- ... 124
Ruppli, Michel 1934- ... 101
Ruprecht, Mary M(argaret Wyant) 1934- ... 118
Rus, Vladimir 1931- ... 17-18R
Rusalem, Herbert 1918- ... 41-44R
Rusbridger, Alan 1953- ... 125
Rusch, Hermann G. 1907- ... 61-64
Rusch, John J(ay) 1942- ... 106
Rusco, Elmer R(itter) 1928- ... 65-68
Ruscoe, (Steuart) James (Bailey) 1947- ... 116
Ruse, Gary Alan 1946- ... CANR-12
Earlier sketch in CA 61-64
Ruse, Michael E. 1940- ... 107
Rush, Alison 1951- ... 115
See also SATA 41
Rush, Anne Kent 1945- ... CANR-8
Earlier sketch in CA 61-64
Rush, Benjamin 1746-1813 ... DLB-37
Rush, Christopher 1944- ... 122
Rush, Elizabeth 1918- ... 115
Rush, James J. 1929- ... 120
Rush, Joseph H(arold) 1911- ... 5-6R
Rush, Joshua
See Pearlstein, Howard J.
Rush, Michael (David) 1937- ... 61-64
Rush, Myron 1922- ... 45-48
Rush, N(ixon) Orwin 1907- ... CANR-25
Earlier sketch in CA 45-48
Rush, Norman 1933- ... 126
Brief entry ... 121
See also CLC 44
Rush, Peter 1937- ... 111
See also SATA 32
Rush, Philip 1908- ... 104
Rush, Philip
See Lardner, Ring(gold Wilmer), Jr.
Rush, Ralph E(ugene) 1903-1965 ... 7-8R
Rush, Richard Henry 1915- ... CANR-6
Earlier sketch in CA 5-6R
Rush, Robert
See Barber, D(ulan) F(riar Whilberton)
Rush, Theressa Gunnels 1945- ... 104
Rushbrook Williams, L(aurence) F(rederic)
1890-1978 ... 97-100
Rushdie, (Ahmed) Salman 1947- ... 111
Brief entry ... 108
See also CLC 23, 31
Rushdoony, R(ousas) J(ohn) 1916- ... 93-96
Rusher, William A(llen) 1923- ... 103
Rushford, Patricia H(elen) 1943- ... 115
Rushforth, Peter (Scott) 1945- ... 101
See also CLC 19
Rushing, Francis W(illard) 1939- ... 112
Rushing, Jane Gilmore 1925- ... 49-52
Rushing, William A. 1930- ... 81-84
Rushmer, Robert F(razer) 1914-
Brief entry ... 111
Rushmore, Helen 1898- ... 25-28R
See also SATA 3
Rushmore, Robert (William) 1926-1986 ... 25-28R
Obituary ... 120
See also SATA 8, 49
Rusholm, Peter
See Powell, Eric F(rederick) W(illiam)
Rushton, J(ohn) Philippe 1943- ... 111
Rushton, William Faulkner 1947- ... CANR-22
Earlier sketch in CA 101
Rusinek, Alla 1949- ... 45-48
Rusinow, Dennison I. 1930- ... 85-88
Rusk, Howard A(rchibald) 1901- ... 103
Rusk, Ralph Leslie 1888-1962 ... 5-6R
Ruskay, Joseph A. 1910- ... CAP-2
Earlier sketch in CA 29-32
Ruskay, Sophie 1887-1980 ... 69-72
Obituary ... 97-100
Ruskin, Ariane
See Batterberry, Ariane Ruskin
Ruskin, John 1819-1900 Brief entry ... 114
See also SATA 24
See also DLB 55
See also TCLC 20
Ruskin, Ronald 1944- ... 115
Russ, Joanna 1937- ... CANR-11
Earlier sketch in CA 25-28R
See also DLB 8
See also CLC 15
Russ, Laurence 1943- ... 114
Russ, Lavinia 1904- ... 25-28R
Russ, Martin 1931- ... 106
Russ, William Adam, Jr. 1903- ... 3R
Russel, Robert R(oyal) 1890- ... 15-16R
Russell, Albert
See Bixby, Jerome Lewis
Russell, Allan Melvin 1930- ... 122
Russell, Amanda
See Feldman, Ellen (Bette)
Russell, Andy 1915- ... CANR-26
Earlier sketches in CA 21-22R, CANR-10
Russell, Annie V(est) 1880(?)-1974
Obituary ... 49-52
Russell, Arthur (Wolseley) 1908- ... CANR-16
Earlier sketches in CA 13-14, CAP-1
Russell, Benjamin 1761-1845 ... DLB-43
Russell, Bertrand (Arthur William)
1872-1970 ... CAP-1
Obituary ... 25-28R
Earlier sketch in CA 15-16
Russell, Bill
See Russell, William Felton
Russell, C(harles) Allyn 1920- ... 65-68
Russell, Carroll Mason 1898(?)-1983
Obituary ... 111
Russell, Charles 1944- ... 111
Russell, Charles Edward 1860-1941 ... DLB-25
Russell, Charlotte
See Rathjen, Carl Henry
Russell, Claude Vivian 1919- ... 17-18R
Russell, Clifford S(pringer) 1938- ... CANR-12
Earlier sketch in CA 73-76
Russell, Colin Archibald 1928- ... 45-48
Russell, Conrad 1937- ... 33-36R
Russell, D(iana) E(lizabeth) H(amilton)
1938- ... CANR-8
Earlier sketch in CA 61-64
Russell, D(avid) S(yme) 1916- ... 15-16R
Russell, Daniel 1937- ... 41-44R
Russell, Diarmuid 1902(?)-1973 Obituary ... 45-48
Russell, Don(ald Bert) 1899-1986 ... CANR-1
Obituary ... 118
Earlier sketch in CA 2R
See also SATA 47
Russell, Donald Andrew (Frank Moore)
1920- ... 110
Russell, Dora (Winifred Black) 1894-1986 ... 125
Obituary ... 119
Russell, Douglas A(ndrew) 1927- ... CANR-16
Earlier sketch in CA 41-44R
Russell, Edward (Frederick Langley)
1895-1981 ... 107
Obituary ... 103
Russell, Eric Frank 1905-1978 ... 124
Obituary ... 102
Russell, Foster Meharry 1907- ... 111
Russell, Francis 1910- ... 25-28R
Russell, Frank D. 1923- ... 126
Russell, Franklin (Alexander) 1926- ... CANR-11
Earlier sketch in CA 19-20R
See also SATA 11
Russell, Frederick Stratten 1897-1984
Obituary ... 113
Russell, George William 1867-1935
Brief entry ... 104
Russell, Gertrude Barrer
See Barrer-Russell, Gertrude
Russell, (Sydney) Gordon 1892- ... CAP-2
Earlier sketch in CA 29-32
Russell, Gordon 1930(?)-1981 Obituary ... 102
Russell, H. Diane 1936- ... 110
Russell, Helen Ross 1915- ... 33-36R
See also SATA 8
Russell, Howard S(ymmes) 1887-1980 ... 105
Russell, I(saac) Willis 1903-1985 ... 118
Russell, Ivy E(thel Southern) 1909- ... 7-8R
Russell, J.
See Bixby, Jerome Lewis
Russell, J(effrey) P(eter) 1954- ... 112
Russell, James 1933- ... SATA-53
Russell, James
See Harknett, Terry
Russell, James E. 1916-1975 Obituary ... 57-60
Russell, Jeffrey Burton 1934- ... CANR-11
Earlier sketch in CA 25-28R
Russell, Jeremy Longmore 1935- ... 110
Russell, Jim
See Russell, James
Russell, Joan Mercedes 1921- ... 102
Russell, John 1919- ... 13-14R
Russell, John David 1928- ... 11-12R
Russell, John L(eonard) 1906- ... 13-14R
Russell, John L(owry), Jr. 1921- ... 11-12R
Russell, Josiah Cox 1900- ... 41-44R
Russell, (Henry) Ken(neth Alfred) 1927- ... 105
See also CLC 16
Russell, Ken(neth Victor) 1929- ... CANR-11
Earlier sketch in CA 25-28R
Russell, Letty M(andeville) 1929- ... CANR-8
Earlier sketch in CA 57-60
Russell, Lois Ann 1931- ... 113
Russell, Mariann Barbara 1935- ... 109
Russell, Mark 1932- ... 113
Brief entry ... 108
Russell, Martin 1934- ... 73-76
Russell, Maurin
See Russell, Maurine (Fletcher)
Russell, Maurine (Fletcher) 1899- ... CAP-1
Earlier sketch in CA 9-10
Russell, Norma Hull Lewis 1902- ... 7-8R
Russell, Norman H(udson), Jr. 1921- ... 49-52
Russell, O(liver) Ruth 1897- ... 57-60
Russell, P(eggy) J(ean) 1934- ... 97-100
Russell, Pamela Redford 1950- ... 81-84
Russell, Patrick
See Sammis, John
Russell, (Irwin) Peter 1921- ... 97-100
Russell, Ray 1924- ... CANR-6
Earlier sketch in CA 3R
Russell, Robert (William) 1924- ... 2R

Russell, Ronald (Stanley) 1904-1974 . . . . . CAP-1
Earlier sketch in CA 11-12
Russell, Ronald 1924- 102
Russell, Rosalind 1911-1976 116
Obituary 111
Russell, Ross 1909- 2R
Russell, Roy 1918- CANR-26
Earlier sketch in CA 107
Russell, Sarah
See Laski, Marghanita
Russell, Shane
See Norwood, Victor G(eorge) C(harles)
Russell, Solveig Paulson 1904- CANR-5
Earlier sketch in CA 3R
See also SATA 3
Russell, Thomas 1902(?)-1984 Obituary 114
Russell, Victor L. 1948- 117
Russell, William F(rank) 1945- 126
Russell, William Felton 1934- 108
Russell, William H. 1911- 61-64
Russell Taylor, Elisabeth 1930- CANR-15
Earlier sketch in CA 81-84
Russell-Wood, A(nthony) J(ohn) R(ussell)
1939- CANR-7
Earlier sketch in CA 57-60
Russett, Bruce M(artin) 1935- CANR-2
Earlier sketch in CA 7-8R
Russett, Cynthia Eagle 1937- 21-22R
Russo, Anthony 1933- 61-64
Russo, Giuseppe Luigi 1884- CAP-1
Earlier sketch in CA 9-10
Russo, John Paul 1944- 41-44R
Russo, Joseph Louis
See Russo, Giuseppe Luigi
Russo, Sarett Rude 1918(?)-1976
Obituary 65-68
Russo, Susan 1947- 106
See also SATA 30
Russo, Vito 1946- 107
Russon, Allien R. 1905- 105
Russon, L(eslie) J(ohn) 1907- 19-20R
Rust, Brian Arthur Lovell 1922- CANR-2
Earlier sketch in CA 45-48
Rust, Claude 1916- 109
Rust, Doris (Dibblin) 13-14R
Rust, Eric C(harles) 1910- 15-16R
Rust, Richard Dilworth 1937- 29-32R
Rusticus
See Martin, Brian P(hilip)
Rustin, Bayard 1910(?)-1987 . . . . . CANR-25
Obituary 123
Earlier sketch in CA 53-56
See also BW
Rustomji, Nari Kaikhosru 1919- 101
Rustow, Dankwart A(lexander) 1924- . . . CANR-1
Earlier sketch in CA 3R
Rutberg, Sidney 1924- 69-72
Rutenber, Culbert G(erow) 1909- CAP-2
Earlier sketch in CA 17-18
Rutgers van der Loeff, An
See Rutgers van der Loeff-Basenau,
An(na) Maria Margaretha
Rutgers van der Loeff-Basenau, An(na)
Maria Margaretha 1910- CANR-7
Earlier sketch in CA 9-10R
See also SATA 22
Ruth, Babe
See Ruth, George Herman (Jr.)
Ruth, Claire (Merritt) 1900-1976
Obituary 69-72
Ruth, George Herman (Jr.) 1895-1948
Brief entry 116
Ruth, John L(andis) 1930- 73-76
Ruth, Kent Ringelman 1916- CANR-2
Earlier sketch in CA 5-6R
Ruth, Rod 1912- SATA-9
Rutherford, Andrew 1929- CANR-9
Earlier sketch in CA 5-6R
Rutherford, Douglas
See McConnell, James Douglas
Rutherford
Rutherford, Malcolm 1939- 119
Rutherford, Margaret 1882-1972
Obituary 33-36R
Rutherford, Mark
See White, William Hale
See also DLB 18
See also TCLC 25
Rutherford, Meg 1932- 29-32R
See also SATA 34
Rutherford, Michael (Andrew) 1946- . . . CANR-26
Earlier sketch in CA 45-48
Rutherford, Phillip Roland 1939- 37-40R
Rutherford, Ward 1927- CANR-14
Earlier sketch in CA 77-80
Ruthin, Margaret SATA-4
Ruthstrom, Dorotha 1936- 107
Ruthven, K(enneth) K(nowles) 1936- . . . CANR-26
Earlier sketch in CA 25-28R
Rutkoff, Peter M. 1942- 116
Rutkowski, Edwin H(enry) 1923- 37-40R
Rutland, Dodge
See Singleton, Betty
Rutland, Robert A(llen) 1922- CANR-2
Earlier sketch in CA 45-48
Rutledge, Aaron L(eslie) 1919- 45-48
Rutledge, Albert J(ohn) 1934- 33-36R
Rutledge, Archibald (Hamilton)
1883-1973 . . . . . CANR-5
Obituary 45-48
Earlier sketch in CA 5-6R
Rutledge, Brett
See Paul, Elliot (Harold)
Rutledge, Dom Denys
See Rutledge, Edward William
Rutledge, Edward William 1906- 7-8R
Rutledge, Harley Dean 1926- 107
Rutledge, Howard Elmer 1929(?)-1984
Obituary 113
Rutman, Darrett B(ruce) 1929- CANR-6
Earlier sketch in CA 15-16R
Rutman, Gilbert L(ionel) 1935- 25-28R
Rutman, Leo 1935- 45-48
Rutsala, Vern 1934- CANR-20
Earlier sketches in CA 11-12R, CANR-6
Rutstein, David D(avis) 1909-1986 . . . . . 33-36R
Obituary 118
Rutstein, Harry Sidney 1929- 108
Rutstein, Nat(han) 1930- 53-56
Rutstrum, Calvin 1895-1982 . . . . . CANR-1
Obituary 106
Earlier sketch in CA 3R
Rutt, M. E.
See Shah, Amina
Rutt, Richard 1925- CANR-6
Earlier sketch in CA 11-12R
Ruttan, Vernon W(esley) 1924- 41-44R
Ruttenberg, Joseph 1889-1983 Obituary 109
Ruttenberg, Stanley H(arvey) 1917- 33-36R
Rutter, Barbara A. 1943- 118
Rutter, Eileen Joyce 1945- CANR-10
Earlier sketch in CA 61-64
Rutter, Michael (Llewellyn) 1933- 109
Ruttkowski, Wolfgang Victor 1935- CANR-15
Earlier sketch in CA 41-44R
Ruttle, Lee 1909- 81-84
Rutz, Viola Larkin 1932- 23-24R
See also SATA 12
Rutzebeck, Hjalmar 1889- 11-12R
Ruud, Charles A(rthur) 1933- 121
Ruud, Josephine Bartow 1921- 73-76
Ruuth, Marianne 1937- CANR-21
Earlier sketches in CA 57-60, CANR-6
Ruxin, Robert H(arris) 1953- 110
Ruyerson, James Paul
See Rothweiler, Paul Roger
Ruyslinck, Ward
See Belser, Reimond Karel Maria de
Ruz, Fidel Castro
See Castro, Fidel
Ruzic, Neil P. 1930- CANR-8
Earlier sketch in CA 17-18R
Ruzicka, Rudolph 1883-1978 Obituary 81-84
See also SATA 24
Ryall, Edward W(illiam) 1902- 61-64
Ryall, George (Francis Trafford)
1887(?)-1979 103
Obituary 89-92
Ryalls, Alan 1919- 102
Ryals, Clyde de L(oache) 1928- 23-24R
Ryan, Alan 1940- 29-32R
Ryan, Allan A(ndrew), Jr. 1945- 124
Ryan, Alvan Sherman 1912- 19-20R
Ryan, Bernard, Jr. 1923- CANR-6
Earlier sketch in CA 7-8R
Ryan, Betsy
See Ryan, Elizabeth (Anne)
Ryan, Bob 1946- CANR-4
Earlier sketch in CA 49-52
Ryan, Bryce F(inley) 1911- 81-84
Ryan, Charles W(illiam) 1929- 57-60
Ryan, Charles W(illiam) 1932- 93-96
Ryan, Cheli Duran 102
See also SATA 20
Ryan, Claude 1925- Brief entry 111
Ryan, Cornelius John 1920-1974 69-72
Obituary 53-56
See also CLC 7
Ryan, Desmond 1893-1964 Obituary 113
Ryan, Dorothy (Barger) 1942- CANR-13
Earlier sketch in CA 73-76
Ryan, Edwin 1916- 5-6R
Ryan, Elizabeth (Anne) 1943- CANR-7
Earlier sketch in CA 61-64
See also SATA 30
Ryan, Herbert J(oseph) 1931- 41-44R
Ryan, James H(erbert) 1928- 53-56
Ryan, Jeanette Mines
See Mines, Jeanette (Marie)
Ryan, Jessica Cadwalader 1915(?)-1972
Obituary 33-36R
Ryan, John (Gerald Christopher)
1921- CANR-16
Earlier sketches in CA 49-52, CANR-1
See also SATA 22
Ryan, John Barry 1933- CANR-7
Earlier sketch in CA 57-60
Ryan, John Fergus 1931- 73-76
Ryan, John J. 1922(?)-1977 Obituary 69-72
Ryan, John Julian 1898- 73-76
Ryan, John K(enneth) 1897-1981 . . . . . CANR-16
Earlier sketch in CA 13-14R
Ryan, Joseph J. 1910(?)-1976 Obituary . . . 69-72
Ryan, Juanita 1949- 120
Ryan, Kathryn Morgan 1925- 102
Ryan, Kevin 1932- CANR-12
Earlier sketch in CA 29-32R
Ryan, Lawrence Vincent 1923- 5-6R
Ryan, Leonard Eames 1930- 11-12R
Ryan, Marah Ellis 1866(?)-1934
Brief entry 122
Ryan, Marleigh Grayer 1930- 19-20R
Ryan, Mary P(atricia) 1945- Brief entry 113
Ryan, Maureen Jones
See Jones-Ryan, Maureen
Ryan, Michael 1946- 49-52
See also DLBY 82
Ryan, Milo 1907- 5-6R
Ryan, Neil Joseph 1930- 13-14R
Ryan, Oscar 1904- DLB-68
Ryan, Pat M(artin) 1928- CANR-13
Earlier sketch in CA 33-36R
Ryan, Patrick J. 1902- CAP-1
Earlier sketch in CA 11-12
Ryan, Paul B(rennan) 1913- CANR-15
Earlier sketch in CA 81-84
Ryan, Paul William 1906-1947 Brief entry . . 114
Ryan, Peter (Charles) 1939- 61-64
See also SATA 15
Ryan, Peter Allen 1923- 109
Ryan, Regina (Claire) 1938- 118
Ryan, Regina S(ara) 1945- 119
Ryan, Robert Michael 1934- 29-32R
Ryan, Sister Joseph Eleanor 61-64
Ryan, T. Antoinette 1924- 41-44R
Ryan, Thomas Arthur 1911- 41-44R
Ryan, Thomas Richard 1897-1981 . . . . . 29-32R
Obituary 122
Ryan, Tim
See Dent, Lester
Ryan, Tom 1938- CANR-10
Earlier sketch in CA 57-60
Ryan, William (Howard) 1914- 104
Ryan, William (Michael) 1948- 122
Ryan, William H. 1928(?)-1986 Obituary . . . 121
Ryan, William M(artin) 1918- 33-36R
Ryans, David Garriott 1909- 7-8R
Ryans, John K(elley), Jr. 1932- 61-64
Ryback, Eric 1952- 37-40R
Rybak, Nathan 1913-1978(?) Obituary 81-84
Rybakov, Anatoli (Naumovich) 1911-
Brief entry 126
See also CLC 23
Rybalka, Michel 1933- 41-44R
Rybczynski, Witold Marian 1943- 110
Rybka, Edward F(rank) 1928- 33-36R
Rybot, Doris
See Ponsonby, D(oris) A(lmon)
Rychlak, Joseph F(rank) 1928- CANR-14
Earlier sketch in CA 37-40R
Ryckmans, Pierre 1935- CANR-16
Earlier sketch in CA 85-88
Rycroft, Charles (Frederick) 1914- CANR-11
Earlier sketch in CA 21-22R
Rydberg, Ernest E(mil) 1901- 15-16R
See also SATA 21
Rydberg, Lou(isa Hampton) 1908- 69-72
See also SATA 27
Rydel, Christine A(nn) 1944- 118
Rydell, Forbes
See Forbes, DeLoris (Florine) Stanton
Rydell, Robert W(illiam) 1952- 126
Rydell, Wendell
See Rydell, Wendy
Rydell, Wendy 33-36R
See also SATA 4
Ryden, Ernest Edwin 1886-1981 Obituary . . . 102
Ryden, Hope CANR-14
Earlier sketch in CA 33-36R
See also SATA 8
Ryder, A(rthur) J(ohn) 1913- 21-22R
Ryder, Eileen 1908- 117
Ryder, Ellen 1913- 29-32R
Ryder, Frank G(lessner) 1916- 7-8R
Ryder, Joanne Brief entry 112
See also SATA 34
Ryder, John 1917- CANR-5
Earlier sketch in CA 7-8R
Ryder, Jonathan
See Ludlum, Robert
Ryder, M(ichael) L(awson) 1927- 102
Ryder, Meyer S. 1909- 21-22R
Ryder, Norman B(urston) 1923- 37-40R
Ryder, Ron 1904- 61-64
Ryder, Rowland (Vint) 1914- 85-88
Ryder, T(homas) A(rthur) 1902- 7-8R
Ryder, Thom
See Harvey, John (Barton)
Ryding, William W. 1924- 77-80
Rye, Anthony
See Youd, Samuel
Rye, Bjoern Robinson 1942- 61-64
Ryerson, Martin 1907- CANR-8
Earlier sketch in CA 15-16R
Ryf, Robert S. 1918-1985 . . . . . 17-18R
Obituary 117
Ryga, George 1932-1987 101
Obituary 124
See also DLB 60
See also CLC 14
Ryken, Leland 1942- CANR-12
Earlier sketch in CA 29-32R
Rykwert, Joseph 1926- CANR-11
Earlier sketch in CA 69-72
Ryland, Lee
See Arlandson, Leone
Rylant, Cynthia 1954- SATA-44, 50
See also CLR 15
Ryle, Anthony 1927- 107
Ryle, Gilbert 1900-1976 73-76
Obituary 69-72
Rylski, Aleksander Scibor
See Scibor-Rylski, Aleksander
Rymer, Alta May 1925- CANR-1
Earlier sketch in CA 49-52
See also SATA 34
Rymes, Thomas Kenneth 1932- 37-40R
Rynearson, Edward H(arper) 1901-1987
Obituary 121
Rynew, Arden N. 1943- 37-40R
Ryrie, Charles C(aldwell) 1925- CANR-18
Earlier sketches in CA 11-12R, CANR-3
Ryskamp, Charles (Andrew) 1928- 104
Ryskind, Morrie 1895-1985 Obituary 117
Brief entry 109
See also DLB 26
Rystrom, Kenneth 1932- 110
Rywell, Martin 1905-1971 . . . . . CAP-2
Earlier sketch in CA 19-20
Rywkin, Michael 1925- 13-14R
Ryzl, Milan 1928- 29-32R
Rzhevsky, Leonid 1905- CANR-14
Earlier sketch in CA 41-44R
Rzhevsky, Nicholas 1943- 115

S

S. S. E.
See Sperry, (Sally) Baxter
Saab, E(velyn) Ann Pottinger 1934- 107
Saab, Edouard 1929-1976 Obituary 65-68
Saadawi, Nawal El
See El Saadawi, Nawal
Saal, Jocelyn
See Sachs, Judith
Saalman, Howard 1928- CANR-1
Earlier sketch in CA 1R
Saarinen, Aline B(ernstein Louchheim)
1914-1972 Obituary 37-40R
Saarinen, Eero 1910-1961 Obituary 113
Saatkamp, Herman J(oseph), Jr. 1942- 126
Saaty, Thomas L(orie) 1926- CANR-8
Earlier sketch in CA 57-60
Saavedra, Luis Spota
See Spota Saavedra, Luis
Sabais, Heinz Winfried 1922-1981
Obituary 114
Sabaliunas, Leonas 1934- 61-64
Sabar, Yona 1939- 112
Sabaroff, Rose Epstein 1918- 85-88
Sabatier, Robert 1923- CANR-18
Earlier sketch in CA 102
Sabato, Ernesto 1911- 97-100
See also CLC 10, 23
Sabato, Larry (J.) 1952- 108
Sabbag, Robert 1946- 101
Sabbah, Hassan i
See Butler, William Huxford
Saberhagen, Fred(erick Thomas) 1930- . . CANR-7
Earlier sketch in CA 57-60
See also SATA 37
See also DLB 8
Sabiad
See White, Stanhope
Sabin, Edwin L(egrand) 1870-1952 . . . . . YABC-2
Sabin, Francene CANR-11
Earlier sketch in CA 69-72
See also SATA 27
Sabin, Katharine Cover 1910- 57-60
Sabin, Lou
See Sabin, Louis
Sabin, Louis 1930- CANR-11
Earlier sketch in CA 69-72
See also SATA 27
Sabin, Mark
See Fox, Norman A(rnold)
Sabine, B.E.V. 1914- 97-100
Sabine, Ellen S. (Borcherding) 1908- CAP-1
Earlier sketch in CA 17-18
Sabine, Gordon Arthur 1917- 117
Sabine, Waldo
See Sabine, William H(enry) W(aldo)
Sabine, William H(enry) W(aldo) 1903- . . CANR-4
Earlier sketch in CA 53-56
Sabini, John Anthony 1921- 9-10R
Sabki, Hisham M. 1934- Brief entry 106
Sable, Martin Howard 1924- CANR-12
Earlier sketch in CA 33-36R
Sabloff, Jeremy A(rac) 1944- CANR-8
Earlier sketch in CA 61-64
Sablosky, Irving L. 1924- 124
Sabom, Michael Bruce 1944- 109
Sabourin, Anne Winifred 1910- 101
Sabourin, Justine
See Sabourin, Anne Winifred
Sabourin, Leopold 1919- CANR-11
Earlier sketch in CA 65-68
Sabre, Dirk
See Laffin, John (Alfred Charles)
Sabri-Tabrizi, Gholam-Reza 1934- 61-64
Sacastru, Martin
See Bioy Casares, Adolfo
Saccio, Peter (Churchill) 1941- 61-64
Sach, Nathan
See Zach, Nathan
Sachar, Abram Leon 1899- 97-100
Sachar, Howard Morley 1928- CANR-6
Earlier sketch in CA 7-8R
Sachar, Louis 1954- CANR-15
Earlier sketch in CA 81-84
See also SATA 50
Sacharoff, Shanta Nimbark 1945- 61-64
Sachdev, Paul 115
Sachem, E. B.
See Creel, Stephen Melville
Sacher, Jack, Jr. 1931- 57-60
Sacher-Masoch, Alexander 1902(?)-1972
Obituary 37-40R
Sachs, Albert Louis 1935- CANR-14
Earlier sketch in CA 21-22R
Sachs, Albie
See Sachs, Albert Louis
Sachs, Alexander 1893-1973 Obituary . . . 41-44R
Sachs, Elizabeth-Ann 1946- 111
See also SATA 48
Sachs, Georgia
See Adams, Georgia Sachs
Sachs, (Stewart) Harvey 1946- 85-88
Sachs, Herbert L. 1929- 25-28R
Sachs, Judith 1947- 122
See also SATA 51, 52
Sachs, Lewis Benjamen 1938- 61-64
Sachs, Margaret 1948- Brief entry 115
Sachs, Marianne 1945- 114

Sachs, Marilyn (Stickle) 1927- CANR-13
Earlier sketch in CA 19-20R
See also SATA 3, 52
See also SAAS 2
See also CLC 35
See also CLR 2
Sachs, Mary P(armly) K(oues)
1882(?)-1973 Obituary 45-48
Sachs, Mendel 1927- CANR-12
Earlier sketch in CA 29-32R
Sachs, Michael L(eo) 1951- 115
Sachs, Murray 1924- CANR-14
Earlier sketch in CA 37-40R
Sachs, Nelly 1891-1970 .... CAP-2
Obituary 25-28R
Earlier sketch in CA 17-18
See also CLC 14
Sachse, William L(ewis) 1912- 25-28R
Sack, James J(ohn) 1944- 101
Sack, John 1930- CANR-14
Earlier sketch in CA 21-22R
Sack, Saul 1912- 53-56
Sackerman, Henry
See Kahm, H(arold) S.
Sackett, L(eyland) H(ugh) 1928- 119
Sackett, S(amuel) J(ohn) 1928- CANR-6
Earlier sketch in CA 1R
See also SATA 12
Sackett, Susan 1943- CANR-22
Earlier sketch in CA 106
Sackett, Theodore Alan 1940- 89-92
Sackett, Walter W(allace), Jr. 1905-1985 ... 5-6R
Obituary 117
Sackheim, Maxwell 1890-1982 Obituary 108
Sackler, Howard (Oliver) 1929-1982 61-64
Obituary 108
See also DLB 7
See also CLC 14
Sackman, Harold 1927- CANR-12
Earlier sketch in CA 23-24R
Sackrey, Charles 1936- 77-80
Sacks, Benjamin 1903- CAP-2
Earlier sketch in CA 23-24
Sacks, Claire
See Sprague, Claire S(acks)
Sacks, Karen 1941- CANR-26
Earlier sketch in CA 109
Sacks, Norman P(aul) 1914- 45-48
Sacks, Oliver W(olf) 1933- 53-56
Sacks, Peter
See Sacks, Peter M.
Sacks, Peter M. 1950- 124
Sacks, Sheldon 1930-1979 .... 17-18R
Obituary 122
Sackson, Sid 1920- CANR-12
Earlier sketch in CA 69-72
See also SATA 16
Sackton, Alexander H(art) 1911- 37-40R
Sackville, Thomas 1536-1608 .... DLB-62
Sackville-West, V(ictoria Mary) 1892-1962 .. 104
Obituary 93-96
See also DLB 34
(el-)Sadat, Anwar 1918-1981 101
Obituary 104
Sadd, Susan 1951- 103
Saddhatissa, Hammalawa 1914- CANR-17
Earlier sketch in CA 97-100
Saddlemyer, E(leanor) Ann 1932- 17-18R
Saddler, Allen
See Richards, R(onald) C(harles) W(illiam)
Saddler, K. Allen
See Richards, R(onald) C(harles) W(illiam)
Sadecky, Petr Milos 1943- 41-44R
Sadeh, Pinhas 1929- CANR-13
Earlier sketch in CA 25-28R
Sadie, Stanley (John) 1930- CANR-9
Earlier sketch in CA 19-20R
See also SATA 14
Sadiq, Muhammad 1898-1984 .... CANR-18
Earlier sketch in CA 19-20R
Sadker, Myra Pollack 1943- CANR-22
Earlier sketches in CA 53-56, CANR-5
Sadler, Arthur Lindsay 1882- 7-8R
Sadler, Catherine Edwards SATA-45
Sadler, Christine 1908-1983 .... CAP-1
Obituary 110
Earlier sketch in CA 11-12
Sadler, Ella Jo 1942- 57-60
Sadler, Glenn Edward 1935- 97-100
Sadler, Julius Trousdale, Jr. 1923- 65-68
Sadler, Mark
See Lynds, Dennis
Sadler, William A(lan), Jr. 1931- 25-28R
Sadock, Benjamin James 1933-
Brief entry 105
Sadoff, Ira 1945- CANR-21
Earlier sketches in CA 53-56, CANR-5
See also CLC 9
Sadun, Elvio H. 1918(?)-1974 Obituary ... 49-52
Saerchinger, Cesar 1884-1971 Obituary .. 33-36R
Saetone
See Camus, Albert
Safa, Helen Icken 1930- CANR-1
Earlier sketch in CA 45-48
Safarian, Albert Edward 1924- 105
Safarik, Allan 1948- 114
Safdie, Moshe 1938- 69-72
Safer, Daniel J. 1934- CANR-11
Earlier sketch in CA 69-72
Safer, Elaine Berkman 1937- 41-44R
Safer, Morley 1931- 93-96
See also AITN 2
Saffell, David C(lyde) 1941- CANR-11
Earlier sketch in CA 61-64
Saffin, John 1626(?)-1710 .... DLB-24
Saffron, Morris Harold 1905- 45-48
Saffron, Robert 1918(?)-1985 Obituary 114
Safian, Jill
See Bharti, Ma Satya
Safilios-Rothschild, Constantina 1936- 45-48
Safir, Leonard 1921- 109
Safire, William 1929- 19-20R
See also CLC 10
Safran, Claire 1930- 101
Safran, Nadav 1925- 5-6R
Safran, William 1930- 113
Sagall, Elliot L. 1918- 29-32R
Sagan, Carl (Edward) 1934- CANR-11
Earlier sketch in CA 25-28R
See also CLC 30
Sagan, Eli 1927- 124
Sagan, Francoise
See Quoirez, Francoise
See also CLC 3, 6, 9, 17, 36
Sagan, Leonard A. 1928- 49-52
Sagan, Miriam 1954- 77-80
Sagar, Keith (Milsom) 1934- CANR-14
Earlier sketch in CA 21-22R
Sagarin, Edward 1913- CANR-4
Earlier sketch in CA 7-8R
Sagarin, Mary 1903- 81-84
Sagarra, Eda 1933- CANR-11
Earlier sketch in CA 65-68
Sage, George Harvey 1929- 61-64
Sage, Joe
See Sage, Joseph
Sage, Joseph 1921-1987 Obituary 122
Sage, Juniper
See Brown, Margaret Wise
and Hurd, Edith (Thacher)
Sage, Leland L(ivingston) 1899- 61-64
Sage, Robert 1899-1962 106
See also DLB 4
Sagendorf, Bud
See Sagendorf, Forrest C(owles)
Sagendorf, Forrest C(owles) 1915-
Brief entry 112
Sagendorph, Robb Hansell 1900-1970 .. CANR-7
Obituary 29-32R
Earlier sketch in CA 7-8R
Sager, Clifford J. 1916- CANR-12
Earlier sketch in CA 29-32R
Sager, Samuel 1923- 123
Sageser, A(delbert) Bower 1902- 29-32R
Saggs, Henry W(illiam) F(rederick) 1920- ... 7-8R
Saghir, Marcel T(awfic) 1937- 49-52
Sagnier, Thierry (Bright) 1946- 53-56
Sagsoorian, Paul 1923- SATA-12
Sagstetter, Karen 1941- 105
Sahakian, Lucille 1894- 53-56
Sahakian, Mabel Lewis 1921- 21-22R
Sahakian, William S(ahak) 1921- CANR-8
Earlier sketch in CA 17-18R
Sahgal, Nayantara (Pandit) 1927- CANR-11
Earlier sketch in CA 11-12R
See also CLC 41
Sahl, Hans 1902- DLB-69
Sahl, Mort(on Lyon) 1927- Brief entry 113
Sahlins, Marshall (David) 1930-
Brief entry 114
Sahn, Seung 1927- 113
Sahni, Balbir S. 1934- CANR-3
Earlier sketch in CA 45-48
Said, Abdul Aziz 1930- 81-84
Said, Edward W. 1935- 21-22R
See also DLB 67
Saida
See LeMair, H(enriette) Willebeek
Saidel, Rochelle G. 1942- 121
Sa'Idi, Ghulam Husayn 1936-1985
Obituary 119
Saidy, Anthony Fred 1937- 89-92
Saidy, Fareed Milhem 1907-1982 Obituary .. 106
Saidy, Fred M.
See Saidy, Fareed Milhem
Sailor, Charles 1947- 97-100
Sailor, Merlin F(orrest) 1906- CAP-1
Earlier sketch in CA 15-16
Saine, Thomas P(rice) 1941- 41-44R
Sainer, Arthur 1924- CANR-3
Earlier sketch in CA 49-52
Saini, B(alwant) S(ingh) 1930- 107
Sainsbury, Eric (Edward) 1925- CANR-13
Earlier sketch in CA 33-36R
Sainsbury, Maurice Joseph 1927- 108
Saint, Andrew (John) 1946- 65-68
Saint, Dora Jessie 1913- CANR-22
Earlier sketches in CA 13-14R, CANR-7
See also SATA 10
Saint, H(arry) F. 1941- CLC-50
Saint, Phil(ip) 1912- 61-64
St. Andre, Lucien
See Mott, Vincent Valmon
St. Angelo, Douglas 1931- 45-48
St. Antoine, Theodore J(oseph) 1929- 41-44R
St. Aubin de Teran, Lisa 1953- 126
Brief entry 118
St. Aubyn, F(rederic) C(hase) 1921- 25-28R
St. Aubyn, Fiona 1952- CANR-23
Earlier sketch in CA 106
St. Aubyn, Giles 1925- CANR-19
Earlier sketches in CA 7-8R, CANR-4
St. Bruno, Albert Francis 1909- CAP-1
Earlier sketch in CA 9-10
St. Clair, (Howard) Barry 1945- 120
St. Clair, Byrd Hooper 1905-1976 .... 3R
Obituary 103
See also SATA 28
St. Clair, Clovis
See Skarda, Patricia Lyn
St. Clair, David 1932- 33-36R
St. Clair, Elizabeth
See Cohen, Susan
St. Clair, Katherine
See Huff, T(om) E.
St. Clair, Leonard 1916-1986 101
Obituary 118
St. Clair, Margaret 1911- 49-52
St. Clair, Philip
See Howard, Munroe
St. Clair, Robert James 1925- 11-12R
St. Clair, William 77-80
St. Cyr, Cyprian
See Berne, Eric (Lennard)
St. Cyr, Margaret 1920- 29-32R
Saint-Denis, Michel Jacques 1897-1971 .. CAP-2
Obituary 33-36R
Earlier sketch in CA 19-20
Saint Dorliae
See Dorliae, Peter Gondro
Saint-Eden, Dennis
See Foster, Don(ald)
Sainte-Marie, Beverly 1941- 107
Sainte-Marie, Buffy
See Sainte-Marie, Beverly
Saint-Exupery, Antoine (Jean Baptiste Marie Roger) de 1900-1944 Brief entry 108
See also SATA 20
See also DLB 72
See also TCLC 2
See also CLR 10
Saint-Gall, Auguste Amedee de
See Strich, Christian
St. George, Arthur
See Paine, Lauran (Bosworth)
St. George, David
See Markov, Georgi
St. George, Edith
See Delatush, Edith G.
St. George, George 1904- 25-28R
St. George, Judith 1931- CANR-14
Earlier sketch in CA 69-72
See also SATA 13
St. George, Margaret
See Osborne, Margaret Ellen
St. Germain, Gregory
See Wallmann, Jeffrey M(iner)
St. Hereticus
See Brown, Robert McAfee
Saint-Jacques, Bernard 1928- CANR-16
Earlier sketch in CA 41-44R
St. James, Bernard
See Treister, Bernard W(illiam)
St. James, Blakely
See Gottfried, Theodore Mark
and Platt, Charles
St. John, Beth
See John, Elizabeth Beaman
St. John, Bob (J.) 1937- Brief entry 122
St. John, Bruce (Carlisle) 1923- 107
St. John, David
See Hunt, E(verette) Howard, Jr.
St. John, Elizabeth
See John, Elizabeth Beaman
St. John, John 1917- CANR-5
Earlier sketch in CA 7-8R
St. John, Leonie
See Bayer, William
and Jenkins, Nancy (Harmon)
St. John, Nicole
See Johnston, Norma
St. John, Patricia Mary 1919- CANR-3
Earlier sketch in CA 7-8R
St. John, Philip
See del Rey, Lester
St. John, Primus 1939- 113
See also BW
St. John, Robert 1902- CANR-5
Earlier sketch in CA 2R
St. John, Wylly Folk 1908-1985 .... 21-22R
Obituary 117
See also SATA 10, 45
St-John Nevill, Barry
See Nevill, Barry St-John
Saint-John Perse
See Leger, (Marie-Rene) Alexis Saint-Leger
St. Johns, Adela Rogers 1894-1988 108
Obituary 126
See also DLB 29
See also AITN 1
St. John-Stevas, Norman Anthony Francis
1929- CANR-4
Earlier sketch in CA 49-52
St. Max, E. S.
See Ellis, Edward S(ylvester)
St. Mox, E. A.
See Ellis, Edward S(ylvester)
St. Myer, Ned
See Stratemeyer, Edward L.
St. Omer, Garth 73-76
Saint Phalle, Thibaut de
See de Saint Phalle, Thibaut
St. Pierre, Dorothy
See Nyren, Dorothy Elizabeth
St. Pierre, Paul 1923- 113
Saintsbury, George 1845-1933 .... DLB-57
St. Tamara
See Kolba, St. Tamara
St. Vivant, M.
See Bixby, Jerome Lewis
Sainty, John Christopher 1934- 93-96
Sainz de la Maza, Regino 1896-1981
Obituary 108
Saisselin, Remy G(ilbert) 1925- 11-12R
Sait Faik
See Abasiyanik, Sait Faik
See also TCLC 23
Saito, Fred
See Saito, Hiroyuki
Saito, Hiroyuki 1917- 61-64
Saito, Michiko
See Fujiwara, Michiko
Sakamaki, Shunzo 1906-1973 .... 4R
Obituary 103
Sakell, Achilles Nicholas 1906-1987 .... 4R
Obituary 123
Sakers, George 1950- 108
Sakharov, Andrei Dimitrievich 1921-
Brief entry 105
Saki
See Munro, Hector Hugh
See also TCLC 3
Saklatvala, Beram 1911-1976 89-92
Sakoian, Frances 1912- 65-68
Sakol, Jeannie 1928- CANR-11
Earlier sketch in CA 7-8R
Sakran, Frank Charles 1895(?)-1983
Obituary 111
Saks, Elmer Eliot
See Fawcett, F(rank) Dubrez
Saks, Katia 1939- 29-32R
Sala, Charles 1924- 116
Salaam, Kalamu ya 1947- 126
See also DLB 38
Saladino, Salvatore 1922- 33-36R
Salaff, Janet W. 1940- 112
Salama, Hannu 1936- CLC-18
Salaman, Esther 1900- 61-64
Salaman, Nicholas 1936- Brief entry 116
Salamanca, J(ack) R(ichard) 1922- 25-28R
See also CLC 4, 15
Salamanca, Lucy
See del Barco, Lucy Salamanca
Salamatullah
See Ullah, Salamat
Salamon, Lester M(ilton) 1943- 89-92
Salant, Nathan N(athaniel) 1955- 106
Salant, Walter S. 1911- CANR-2
Earlier sketch in CA 7-8R
Salas, Floyd Francis 1931- 119
Salas, Rafael M(ontinola) 1928-1987
Obituary 121
Salassi, Otto R(ussell) 1939- 106
See also SATA 38
Salazar, Antonio de Oliveira 1889-1970
Obituary 113
Salazar, Fred A. 1942- 23-24R
Salazar, Rachel 1954- 123
Salazar, Ruben 1928-1970 Obituary 115
Salber, Eva J. 1916- 125
Saldutti, Denise 1953- SATA-39
Sale, J. Kirkpatrick
See Sale, Kirkpatrick
Sale, Kirkpatrick 1937- CANR-10
Earlier sketch in CA 13-14R
Sale, Larry L(owell) 1939- Brief entry 113
Sale, Richard (Bernard) 1911- 9-10R
Sale, Roger 1932- 21-22R
Sale, William (Merritt III) 1929- 45-48
Saleh, Dennis 1942- CANR-13
Earlier sketch in CA 33-36R
Salem, Elie Adib 1930- 49-52
Salem, James M. 1937- 23-24R
Salemme, Lucia (Autorino) 1919- 89-92
Salemson, Harold J(ason) 1910-1988 110
Obituary 126
Brief entry 108
See also DLB 4
Salerno, Lynn M(cCormick) 1926- 119
Sales, Grover 1919- 65-68
Sales, Jane M(agorian) 1931- 49-52
Sales, M(ary) E(ileen) 1936- 29-32R
Sales, M(illard) Vance 1929- 53-56
Saletore, Bhasker Anand 1900- 7-8R
Salgado, Gamini 1929- 102
Salgado, Maria Antonia 1933- 41-44R
Saliba, John A. 1937- 114
Saliers, Don E(arl) 1937- 119
Salih, H(alil) Ibrahim 1939- 93-96
Salin, Mary Wolff
See Wolff-Salin, Mary
Salinas (y Serrano), Pedro 1891(?)-1951
Brief entry 117
See also TCLC 17
Salinger, Herman 1905- CAP-1
Earlier sketch in CA 13-14
Salinger, J(erome) D(avid) 1919- 5-6R
See also DLB 2
See also CDALB 1941-1968
See also CLC 1, 3, 8, 12
See also SSC 2
Salinger, Margaretta 1908(?)-1985
Obituary 115
Salinger, Pierre (Emil George) 1925- ... CANR-14
Earlier sketch in CA 19-20R
Salisbury, Carola (Isobel Julien) 1943- 89-92
Salisbury, Dorothy (Kendall Cleveland)
1891(?)-1976 Obituary 69-72
Salisbury, Edward J(ames) 1886- CAP-1
Earlier sketch in CA 13-14
Salisbury, Frank 1930- 108
Salisbury, Frank B(oyer) 1926- CANR-8
Earlier sketch in CA 17-18R
Salisbury, Harrison E(vans) 1908- CANR-3
Earlier sketch in CA 2R
Salisbury, Ralph 1926- CANR-15
Earlier sketch in CA 41-44R
Salisbury, Ray(mond Eric) 1942- 110
Salisbury, Richard Frank 1926- CANR-9
Earlier sketch in CA 7-8R
Salisbury, Robert H(olt) 1930- 11-12R
Salisbury, Ruth 1921- 73-76
Salisbury-Jones, Guy 1896-1985 Obituary .. 115

Salivarova, Zdena
See Skvorecka, Zdena Salivarova
Salk, Erwin Arthur 1918- ... 81-84
Salk, Jonas Edward 1914- ... 49-52
Salk, Lee 1926- ... 104
See also AITN 1
Salkeld, Robert J. 1932- ... 29-32R
Salkever, Louis R(omov) 1914- ... 19-20R
Salkey, (Felix) Andrew (Alexander) 1928- ... CANR-13
Earlier sketch in CA 7-8R
See also BW
See also SATA 35
Sallada, Logan Henry 1942-1987 Obituary ... 123
Sallaska, Georgia 1933- ... 25-28R
Sallaway, George H(enry) 1930- ... 21-22R
Sallis, James 1944- ... 33-36R
Sallis, John C(leveland) 1938- ... 41-44R
Salls, Betty Ruth 1926- ... 49-52
Salm, Peter 1919- ... 41-44R
Salma, Abu
See Karmi, Abdul Karim
Salmon, Annie Elizabeth 1899- ... CANR-12
Earlier sketch in CA 69-72
See also SATA 13
Salmon, Charles Gerald 1930- ... 49-52
Salmon, Edward T(ogo) 1905- ... CANR-2
Earlier sketch in CA 7-8R
Salmon, H. Morrey 1892(?)-1985
Obituary ... 116
Salmon, J(ohn) B(rynmor) 1942- ... 118
Salmon, J(ohn) H(earsey) M(cMillan) 1925- ... 25-28R
Salmon, James F(rancis) 1925- ... 111
Salmon, John Tenison 1910- ... 13-14R
Salmon, Margaret Belais 1921- ... CANR-8
Earlier sketch in CA 17-18R
Salmon, Nathan Ucuzoglu 1951- ... 109
Salmon, Wesley C(harles) 1925- ... CANR-23
Earlier sketches in CA 17-18R, CANR-8
Salmond, John A(lexander) 1937- ... 114
Salmonson, Jessica Amanda 1950- ... 114
Salmonson, R(oland) F(rank) 1922- ... CANR-17
Earlier sketch in CA 25-28R
Saloma, John S. III 1935(?)-1983
Obituary ... 110
Salomon, Albert 1891-1966 ... 7-8R
Salomon, Herman Prins 1930- ... 41-44R
Salomon, I(sidore) L(awrence) 1899-1985 ... 73-76
Obituary ... 116
Salomon, Irving 1897-1979 Obituary ... 85-88
Salomon, Janet Lynn (Nowicki) 1953- ... 61-64
Salomon, Julian Harris 1896-1987
Obituary ... 123
Salomon, Roger Blaine 1928- ... 1R
Salomon, Sir Walter
See Salomon, Walter (Hans)
Salomon, Walter (Hans) 1906-1987
Obituary ... 123
Salomone, A(rcangelo) William 1915- ... 15-16R
Salop, Lynne
See Hawes, Lynne Gusikoff Salop
Salot, Lorraine 1914- ... 17-18R
Saloutos, Theodore 1910- ... 11-12R
Salper, Roberta Linda 1940- ... 105
Salpeter, Eliahu (Arnost) 1927- ... 93-96
Salsbury, Barbara G(race) 1937- ... 121
Brief entry ... 118
Salsbury, Edith Colgate 1907-1971 ... CAP-2
Earlier sketch in CA 17-18
Salsbury, Kathryn H(errick) 1924- ... 107
Salsbury, Stephen 1931- ... CANR-11
Earlier sketch in CA 23-24R
Salsini, Paul E(dward) 1935- ... 77-80
Salt, Beryl (Winifred) 1931- ... 110
Salt, Waldo 1914-1987 ... 111
Obituary ... 121
See also DLB 44
Salten, Felix
See Salzmann, Siegmund
Salter, Cedric
See Knight, Francis Edgar
Salter, Donald P. M. 1942- ... 93-96
Salter, Elizabeth 1918-1981 ... CANR-9
Obituary ... 103
Earlier sketch in CA 53-56
Salter, Elizabeth 1925-1980 ... 105
Obituary ... 97-100
Salter, James 1925- ... 73-76
See also CLC 7
Salter, Lionel (Paul) 1914- ... CANR-3
Earlier sketch in CA 7-8R
Salter, Margaret Lennox
See Donaldson, Margaret
Salter, Mary D.
See Ainsworth, Mary D(insmore) Salter
Salter, Mary Jo 1954- ... 119
Salter, Paul Sanford 1926- ... 61-64
Salter, Robbie
See Salter, Robina
Salter, Robina ... 123
Salter, Stefan 1908(?)-1985 Obituary ... 115
Salter, W(illiam) H(enry) 1880-1970
Obituary ... 112
Salter-Mathieson, Nigel Cedric Stephen 1932- ... 4R
Salthe, Stanley N(orman) 1930- ... 53-56
Saltman, Judith 1947- ... 126
Saltman, Juliet 1923- ... 101
Saltonstall, Richard, Jr. 1937-1981 ... 33-36R
Obituary ... 103
Saltus, Edgar (Everton) 1855-1921
Brief entry ... 105
See also TCLC 8
Saltz, Donald 1933- ... 102
Saltz, Eli 1926- Brief entry ... 108
Saltzgaber, Jan M. 1933- ... 115
Saltzman, Joe
See Saltzman, Joseph
Saltzman, Joseph 1939- ... 81-84
Saltzman, Marvin L(ouis) 1922- ... 85-88
Salu, Mary 1919- ... 93-96
Salusinszky, Imre 1955- ... 126
Salvadori, Joyce
See Lussu, Joyce (Salvadori)
Salvadori, Mario (George) 1907- ... 108
See also SATA 40
Salvadori, Massimo
See Salvadori-Paleotti, Massimo
Salvadori, Max (William)
See Salvadori-Paleotti, Massimo
Salvadori-Paleotti, Massimo 1908- ... CANR-7
Earlier sketch in CA 11-12R
Salvan, Jacques-Leon 1898- ... 2R
Salvato, Larry 1948- ... 118
Salvato, Sharon 1938- ... CANR-15
Earlier sketch in CA 65-68
Salvatore, Nicholas 1943- ... 109
Salvatore, Nick
See Salvatore, Nicholas
Salvendy, Gavriel 1938- ... 49-52
Salzano, F(rancisco) M(auro) 1928- ... CANR-12
Earlier sketch in CA 29-32R
Salzer, Felix 1904-1986 ... 109
Obituary ... 120
Salzer, L. E.
See Wilson, Lionel
Salzer, Linda P(arsons) 1951- ... 122
Salzinger, Kurt 1929- Brief entry ... 107
Salzman, Eric 1933- ... CANR-13
Earlier sketch in CA 25-28R
Salzman, Jack 1937- ... CANR-11
Earlier sketch in CA 25-28R
Salzman, Paul 1953- ... 125
Salzman, Yuri ... SATA-42
Salzmann, Siegmund 1869-1945
Brief entry ... 108
See also SATA 25
Salzmann, Zdenek 1925- ... CANR-16
Earlier sketch in CA 97-100
Samachson, Dorothy (Mirkin) 1914- ... 11-12R
See also SATA 3
Samachson, Joseph 1906-1980 ... 17-18R
Obituary ... 122
See also SATA 3, 52
Samarakis, Antonis 1919- ... 25-28R
See also CLC 5
Samarin, William J. 1926- ... 93-96
Samartha, S(tanley) J(edidiah) 1920- ... CAP-1
Earlier sketch in CA 11-12
Samay, Sebastian 1926- ... 37-40R
Sambrook, Arthur James 1931- ... 13-14R
Sambrot, William 1920- ... 25-28R
Samek, Hana 1953- ... 126
Samelson, William 1928- ... CANR-17
Earlier sketch in CA 25-28R
Sametz, Arnold W(illiam) 1919- ... CANR-1
Earlier sketch in CA 4R
Samford, Clarence D(ouglas) 1905- ... CAP-2
Earlier sketch in CA 19-20
Samford, Doris E. 1923- ... 21-22R
Samhaber, Ernst Marzell 1901-1974 ... 11-12R
Obituary ... 122
Samigli, E.
See Schmitz, Aron Hector
Samkange, S. J. T.
See Samkange, Stanlake (John Thompson)
Samkange, Stanlake (John Thompson) 1922-1988 ... 29-32R
Obituary ... 125
Samli, A. Coskun 1931- ... CANR-22
Earlier sketch in CA 105
Sammartino, Peter 1904- ... CANR-7
Earlier sketch in CA 57-60
Sammis, John 1942- ... 29-32R
See also SATA 4
Sammons, David 1938- ... 73-76
Sammons, Jeffrey L(eonard) 1936- ... CANR-19
Earlier sketch in CA 23-24R
Samoiloff, Louise Cripps
See Cripps, L(ouise) L(ilian)
Samolin, William 1911- ... 61-64
Samora, Julian 1920- ... 37-40R
Samore, Theodore 1924- Brief entry ... 108
Sampedro, Jose Luis 1917- ... CANR-11
Earlier sketch in CA 23-24R
Sampford, Michael 1924(?)-1983
Obituary ... 109
Sampley, Arthur M(cCullough) 1903-1975 ... 41-44R
Sampley, J(ohn) Paul 1935- ... 105
Sampson, A(ylwin) A(rthur) 1926- ... 117
Sampson, Anthony 1926- ... CANR-3
Earlier sketch in CA 1R
Sampson, Edward C(oolidge) 1920- ... 57-60
Sampson, Edward E. 1934- ... CANR-14
Earlier sketch in CA 37-40R
Sampson, Fay (Elizabeth) 1935- ... CANR-18
Earlier sketch in CA 101
See also SATA 40, 42
Sampson, Geoffrey 1944- ... 97-100
Sampson, H(erbert) Grant 1932- ... 45-48
Sampson, Henry T(homas) 1934- ... 117
Sampson, R. Neil 1938- ... 106
Sampson, R(onald) V(ictor) 1918- ... CANR-5
Earlier sketch in CA 11-12R
Sampson, Robert C. 1909- ... 21-22R
Sampson, Roy J(ohnson) 1919- ... CANR-1
Earlier sketch in CA 4R
Samra, Cal 1931- ... 37-40R
Sams, Eric 1926- ... 123
Sams, Jonathan Carter 1942- Brief entry ... 110
Samsell, R(ay) L(ane) 1925- ... 69-72
Samson, Anne S(tringer) 1933- ... 25-28R
See also SATA 2
Samson, Jack
See Samson, John Gadsden
Samson, Joan 1937-1976 ... 73-76
See also SATA 13
Samson, John Gadsden 1936- Brief entry ... 109
Samsonov, Leon
See Maximov, Vladimir (Yemelyanovich)
Samstag, Nicholas 1903-1968 ... 7-8R
Obituary ... 25-28R
Samter, Linda Bantel
See Bantel, Linda
Samtur, Susan J(oy) 1944- ... 97-100
Samuel, Alan E(douard) 1932- ... CANR-17
Earlier sketch in CA 73-76
Samuel, Athanasius Y.
See Samuel, Yeshue
Samuel, Dorothy T(ucker) 1918- ... 45-48
Samuel, Edwin Herbert 1898-1978 ... CANR-2
Earlier sketch in CA 2R
Samuel, Irene 1915- ... 17-18R
Samuel, Maurice 1895-1972 ... 102
Obituary ... 33-36R
Samuel, Yeshue 1907- ... CAP-2
Earlier sketch in CA 21-22
Samuels, Charles 1902-1982 ... CANR-5
Obituary ... 106
Earlier sketch in CA 4R
See also SATA 12
Samuels, Charles Thomas 1936-1974 ... 41-44R
Obituary ... 49-52
Samuels, E. A.
See Tiffany, E. A.
Samuels, Ernest 1903- ... CAP-1
Earlier sketch in CA 11-12
Samuels, Gertrude ... CANR-6
Earlier sketch in CA 11-12R
See also SATA 17
Samuels, Harold 1917- ... 93-96
Samuels, Harry 1893- ... 13-14R
Samuels, Lesser 1894(?)-1980 Obituary ... 102
Samuels, M(ichael) L(ouis) 1920- ... 41-44R
Samuels, Peggy 1922- ... 97-100
Samuels, Warren J. 1933- ... CANR-14
Earlier sketch in CA 23-24R
Samuelson, Arnold 1912(?)-1981
Obituary ... 116
Samuelson, Paul A(nthony) 1915- ... 5-6R
Samway, Patrick H(enry) 1939- ... CANR-21
Earlier sketch in CA 105
Sanborn, B. X.
See Ballinger, William Sanborn
Sanborn, Duane 1914- ... CANR-1
Earlier sketch in CA 4R
See also SATA 38
Sanborn, Franklin Benjamin 1831-1917 ... DLB-1
Sanborn, Margaret 1915- ... CANR-4
Earlier sketch in CA 53-56
Sanborn, Patricia F. 1937- ... 25-28R
Sanborn, Ruth Cummings 1917- ... 29-32R
Sancha, Sheila 1924- ... CANR-11
Earlier sketch in CA 69-72
See also SATA 38
Sanchez, Federico
See Semprun, Jorge
Sanchez, Jose M(ariano) 1932- ... 11-12R
Sanchez, Luis Rafael 1936- ... CLC-23
Sanchez, Ramiro Guerra y
See Guerra y Sanchez, Ramiro
Sanchez, Ricardo 1941- ... 73-76
Sanchez, Sonia 1934- ... CANR-24
Earlier sketch in CA 33-36R
See also BW
See also SATA 22
See also DLB 41
See also CLC 5
Sanchez, Thomas 1944- ... CANR-2
Earlier sketch in CA 45-48
Sanchez Albornoz (y Mediuna), Claudio 1893-1984 Obituary ... 113
Sanchez-Hidalgo, Efrain Sigisfredo 1918-1974 ... 57-60
Sanchez-Silva, Jose Maria 1911- ... 73-76
See also SATA 16
See also CLR 12
Sanctuary, Gerald 1930- ... CANR-12
Earlier sketch in CA 29-32R
Sand, George X. ... 15-16R
See also SATA 45
Sand, Margaret 1932- ... 85-88
Sand, Richard E(ugene) 1924- ... 33-36R
Sandak, Cass R(obert) 1950- ... 108
See also SATA 37, 51
Sandars, N(ancy) K(atharine) 1914- ... 61-64
Sandbach, Francis Henry 1903- ... 93-96
Sandbach, Mary (Warburton) 1901- ... 25-28R
Sandberg, (Karin) Inger 1930- ... CANR-26
Earlier sketches in CA 65-68, CANR-11
See also SATA 15
Sandberg, John H(ilmer) 1930- ... 49-52
Sandberg, Karl C. 1931- ... 49-52
See also SATA 35
Sandberg, Larry 1944- ... 77-80
Sandberg, Lars G(unnarsson) 1939- ... 53-56
Sandberg, Lasse (E. M.) 1924- ... SATA-15
Sandberg, Margaret M(ay) 1919- ... 61-64
Sandberg, Peter Lars 1934- ... CANR-24
Earlier sketches in CA 61-64, CANR-9
Sandbrook, K(eith) R(ichard) J(ames) 1943- ... CANR-16
Earlier sketch in CA 97-100
Sandburg, Carl (August) 1878-1967 ... 7-8R
Obituary ... 25-28R
See also SATA 8
See also DLB 17, 54
See also CDALB 1865-1917
See also CLC 1, 4, 10, 15, 35
Sandburg, Charles A.
See Sandburg, Carl (August)
Sandburg, Helga 1918- ... CANR-5
Earlier sketch in CA 4R
See also SATA 3
Sande, Theodore Anton 1933- ... CANR-12
Earlier sketch in CA 65-68
Sandeen, Ernest (Emanuel) 1908- ... 15-16R
Sandeen, Ernest Robert 1931- ... CANR-1
Earlier sketch in CA 45-48
Sandelowski, Margarete J. 1946- ... 116
Sander, (Jane) Ellen 1944- ... 41-44R
Sander, Joseph Lincoln 1926- Brief entry ... 108
Sander, Volkmar 1929- ... 113
Sanderlin, David 1943- ... 123
Sanderlin, George 1915- ... 13-14R
See also SATA 4
Sanderlin, Owenita (Harrah) 1916- ... CANR-7
Earlier sketch in CA 17-18R
See also SATA 11
Sanders, Albert
See Davidson, David
Sanders, Ann(a Pearl Goodman) 1935- ... 7-8R
Sanders, Buck
See Frentzen, Jeffrey
Sanders, Byrne Hope
See Sperry, Byrne Hope
Sanders, Charles 1935- ... 25-28R
Sanders, D(onald) G(len) 1899- ... 85-88
Sanders, Daphne
See Randolph, Georgiana Ann
Sanders, David (Scott, Jr.) 1926- ... 25-28R
Sanders, (Franklin) David 1934- ... 41-44R
Sanders, Dennis 1949- ... 108
Sanders, Donald 1915(?)-1979 Obituary ... 89-92
Sanders, Donald H. 1932- ... CANR-10
Earlier sketch in CA 25-28R
Sanders, Dorothy Lucie 1917- ... 33-36R
Sanders, (James) Ed(ward) 1939- ... CANR-13
Earlier sketch in CA 15-16R
See also DLB 16
Sanders, Ed Parish 1937- ... 105
Sanders, Frederick K(irkland) 1936- ... 65-68
Sanders, Gerald D(eWitt) 1895- ... CAP-1
Earlier sketch in CA 13-14
Sanders, Gladys (Shultz) 1919(?)-1988
Obituary ... 125
Sanders, Harland 1890-1980 ... 114
Obituary ... 102
Sanders, Herbert H(arvey) 1909- ... 15-16R
Sanders, Ivan 1944- ... 119
Sanders, J(ohn) Oswald 1902- ... CANR-21
Earlier sketches in CA 15-16R, CANR-6
Sanders, Jack T(homas) 1935- ... 37-40R
Sanders, Jacquin 1922- ... 3R
Sanders, James A(lvin) 1927- ... CANR-14
Earlier sketch in CA 21-22R
Sanders, James Bernard 1924- ... 41-44R
Sanders, James Edward 1911- ... 103
Sanders, Jeanne
See Rundle, Anne
Sanders, Jennings B(ryan) 1901- ... CAP-2
Earlier sketch in CA 25-28
Sanders, Joan Allred 1924- ... 11-12R
Sanders, Joseph Lee 1940- ... 105
Sanders, Kent
See Wilkes-Hunter, R(ichard)
Sanders, Lawrence 1920- ... 81-84
See also CLC 41
Sanders, Leonard 1929- ... CANR-3
Earlier sketch in CA 11-12R
Sanders, Margaret ... 7-8R
Sanders, Marion K. 1905-1977 ... 33-36R
Obituary ... 73-76
Sanders, Marlene 1931- ... 65-68
Sanders, Noah
See Blount, Roy (Alton), Jr.
Sanders, Norman (Joseph) 1929- ... 11-12R
Sanders, Peter B(asil) 1938- ... 105
Sanders, Pieter 1912- ... CANR-12
Earlier sketch in CA 29-32R
Sanders, (Charles) Richard 1904- ... 53-56
Sanders, Ronald 1932- ... CANR-20
Earlier sketch in CA 23-24R
Sanders, Scott Russell 1945- ... CANR-15
Earlier sketch in CA 85-88
Sanders, Sol (Witner) 1926- ... CANR-2
Earlier sketch in CA 49-52
Sanders, Stephen (Jesse, Jr.) 1919- ... 29-32R
Sanders, Thomas E. 1926- ... 21-22R
Sanders, Thomas Griffin 1932- ... 11-12R
Sanders, Tobi Gillian
See Hammes, Tobi Gillian Sanders
Sanders, William B(rauns) 1944- ... CANR-10
Earlier sketch in CA 65-68
Sanders, William T(imothy) 1926- ... CANR-3
Earlier sketch in CA 45-48
Sanders, Winston P.
See Anderson, Poul (William)
Sanderson, Isabel S(aunders) 1913-1987
Obituary ... 123
Sanderson, Ivan T(erence) 1911-1973 ... 37-40R
Obituary ... 41-44R
See also SATA 6
Sanderson, James L(ee) 1926- Brief entry ... 111
Sanderson, Jayne 1943- ... 23-24R
Sanderson, Milton W(illiam) 1910- ... CANR-9
Earlier sketch in CA 11-12R
Sanderson, Peter (Crawshaw) 1929- ... 33-36R
Sanderson, Ruth (L.) 1951- ... SATA-41

Sanderson, Sabina W(arren) 1931- CANR-3
Earlier sketch in CA 11-12R
Sanderson, Stewart (Forson) 1924- 108
Sanderson, Warren 1931- 105
Sandford, Cedric Thomas 1924- 113
Sandford, Christopher 1902-1983
Obituary 109
Sandford, John 1929- 101
Sandford, Nell Mary 1936- 81-84
Sandford, Paula 1931- 101
Sandford, William P(hillips) 1896-1975 ... CAP-2
Earlier sketch in CA 17-18
Sandhaus, Paul 1923- 25-28R
Sandifer, Durward Valdamir 1900-1981
Obituary 108
Sandifer, Linda P(rophet) 1951- 120
Sandin, Joan 1942- SATA-12
Sandin, Robert T(heodore) 1927- 111
Sandison, Alan 1932- 23-24R
Sandison, Janet
See Cameron, Elizabeth Jane
Sandle, Floyd Leslie 1913- Brief entry 106
Sandler, Benjamin P. 1902(?)-1979
Obituary 85-88
Sandler, Irving (Harry) 1925- 29-32R
Sandler, Lucy Freeman 1930- Brief entry ... 113
Sandler, Stanley Lawrence 1937- 113
Sandlin, Joann S(chepers) De Lora
1935- CANR-4
Earlier sketch in CA 53-56
Sandlin, John L(ewis) 1908- CANR-4
Earlier sketch in CA 3R
Sandlin, Tim 1950- 126
Sandman, Peter M(ark) 1945- 25-28R
Sandmel, Samuel 1911-1979 .... CANR-2
Earlier sketch in CA 1R
Sando, Joe S. 1923- 123
Sandon, Henry 1928- 81-84
Sandon, J. D.
See Harvey, John (Barton)
Sandor, Bela I(mre) 1935- 102
Sandor, Gyorgy 108
Sandoz, (George) Ellis (Jr.) 1931- CANR-14
Earlier sketch in CA 37-40R
Sandoz, Mari(e Susette) 1896-1966 .... CANR-17
Obituary 25-28R
Earlier sketch in CA 2R
See also SATA 5
See also DLB 9
See also CLC 28
Sandrof, Ivan 1912(?)-1979 93-96
Obituary 85-88
Sandroff, Ronni 1943- 102
Sandrow, Edward T. 1906-1975 Obituary .. 61-64
Sands, Donald B. 1920- 15-16R
Sands, Dorothy 1893-1980 Obituary 102
Sands, Edith Sylvia (Abeloff) 1912- 23-24R
Sands, John Edward 1930- 15-16R
Sands, Kathleen M.
See Sands, Kathleen Mullen
Sands, Kathleen Mullen 118
Sands, Leo G(eorge) 1912-1984 .... 19-20R
Obituary 114
Sands, Martin
See Burke, John (Frederick)
Sands, Melissa 1949- 109
Sandusky, Annie Lee 1900(?)-1976
Obituary 69-72
Sandved, Arthur O. 1931- 33-36R
Sandy, Max
See Saunders, Carl Maxon
Sandy, Stephen 1934- CANR-22
Earlier sketches in CA 49-52, CANR-5
Sandys, Elspeth (Somerville) 1940- CANR-26
Earlier sketch in CA 108
Sandys, George 1578-1644 .... DLB-24
Saner, Reg(inald Anthony) 1931- 65-68
See also CLC 9
Sanfield, Steve 1937- 124
Sanfilip, Thomas 1952- 57-60
Sanford, Agnes (White) 1897- 17-18R
Sanford, Charles B(elding) 1920- 113
Sanford, Charles Le Roy 1920- 5-6R
Sanford, David (Boyer) 1943- Brief entry 114
Sanford, Fillmore H(argrave) 1914-1967 ...... 4R
Obituary 103
Sanford, George 1943- 118
Sanford, Harry Allen 1929- 3R
Sanford, Jack D(onald) 1925- 7-8R
Sanford, John 1904- 123
Brief entry 117
Sanford, John A. 1929- CANR-10
Earlier sketch in CA 25-28R
Sanford, John B.
See Sanford, John
Sanford, Leda 1933- CANR-12
Earlier sketch in CA 65-68
Sanford, Terry 1917- 17-18R
Sanford, Thomas K(yle), Jr. 1921-1977 ... 73-76
Sanger, Andrew 1948- 123
Sanger, Clyde 1928- 114
Sanger, Margaret (Higgins) 1883-1966
Obituary 89-92
Sanger, Marjory Bartlett 1920- 37-40R
See also SATA 8
Sanger, Richard H. 1905(?)-1979
Obituary 85-88
Sangiuliano, Iris (Agatha) 1923-
Brief entry 114
Sangrey, Dawn 1942- CANR-15
Earlier sketch in CA 85-88
Sangster, Ian 1934- 61-64
Sangster, Jimmy 1927- CANR-14
Earlier sketch in CA 23-24R
Sangster, Margaret E(lizabeth) 1894-1981
Obituary 105
Sanguinetti, Elise Ayers 1926- CANR-1
Earlier sketch in CA 2R
Saniel, Josefa M. 1925- 13-14R
Sanjian, Avedis K(rikor) 1921- 33-36R
San Juan, Epifanio, Jr. 1938- CANR-10
Earlier sketch in CA 25-28R
Sankar, D(evarakonda) V(enkata) Siva
1927- 53-56
Sankey, Alice (Ann-Susan) 1910- 61-64
See also SATA 27
Sankhala, Kailash S. 1925- 101
San Martin, Marta 1942- 102
Sann, Paul 1914-1986 .... CANR-5
Obituary 120
Earlier sketch in CA 13-14R
Sannebeck, Norvelle 1909- 97-100
Sansom, Arthur B(aldwin) 1920- 112
Sansom, Clive 1910- 104
Sansom, William 1912-1976 .... 7-8R
Obituary 65-68
See also CLC 2, 6
Sansone, Sam J(ohn) 1915- 115
San Souci, Robert D. 1946- 108
See also SATA 40
Sansweet, Stephen Jay 1945- 61-64
Santa Maria
See Powell-Smith, Vincent (Walter
Francis)
Santas, Joan Foster 1930- 19-20R
Santayana, George 1863-1952 Brief entry ... 115
See also DLB 54, 71
Santee, Ross 1889(?)-1965 108
Santesson, Hans Stefan 1914(?)-1975 93-96
Obituary 57-60
See also SATA 30
Santi, Enrico Mario 1950- 116
Santiago, Danny
See James Daniel (Lewis)
See also CLC 33
Santiago, Danny
See James, Daniel (Lewis)
Santini, Rosemarie 81-84
Santmire, H(arold) Paul 1935- 53-56
Santmyer, Helen Hooven 1895-1986 ... CANR-15
Obituary 118
Earlier sketch in CA 4R
See also DLBY 84
See also CLC 33
Santoli, Al 1949- 105
Santoni, Georges V. 1938- 103
Santoni, Ronald E(rnest) 1931- 7-8R
Santos, Bienvenido N(uqui) 1911- CANR-19
Earlier sketch in CA 101
See also CLC 22
Santos, Eduardo 1888-1974 Obituary 89-92
Santostefano, Sebastiano 1929- 41-44R
Santrey, Louis
See Sabin, Louis
Sanville, Jean 1918- 89-92
Sanwal, B(hairava) D(at) 1917- 19-20R
Saperstein, Alan 103
Saphier, Michael 1911- 25-28R
Saphire, Saul 1896(?)-1974 Obituary 53-56
Sapia, Yvonne (V.) 1946- 126
Sapiets, Janis 1921-1983(?) Obituary 109
Sapieyevski, Anne Lindbergh 1940- 115
Brief entry 113
See also SATA 35
Sapinsley, Alvin 1921- CANR-21
Earlier sketch in CA 104
Sapir, Richard (Ben) 1936-1987 ...... CANR-13
Obituary 121
Earlier sketch in CA 69-72
Sapiro, Virginia 1951- 126
Sapori, Armando 1892- 33-36R
Saporta, Marc(el) 1923- 21-22R
Saporta, Sol 1925- 17-18R
Saposnik, Irving Seymour 1936- 97-100
Saposs, David Joseph 1886-1968 ..... CANR-15
Obituary 103
Earlier sketch in CA 4R
Sapp, Phyllis Woodruff 1908- CANR-1
Earlier sketch in CA 3R
Sappington, Roger E(dwin) 1929- 15-16R
Sara
See Blake, Sally Mirliss
Sara, Dorothy 1897(?)-1976 Obituary 69-72
Sarac, Roger
See Caras, Roger A(ndrew)
Saracevic, Tefko 1930- 37-40R
Sarah, Robyn 1949- 112
Sarano, Jacques 1920- 29-32R
Sarant, P(eter) C. 1933(?)-1979 Obituary .. 89-92
Sarasin, Jennifer
See Sachs, Judith
Sarason, Seymour Bernard 1919- 120
Sarasy, Phyllis Powell 1930- 13-14R
Sarat, Austin Dean 1947- 106
SarDesai, D(amodar) R. 1931- CANR-11
Earlier sketch in CA 25-28R
Sardeson, Charles T. 1921- 7-8R
Sarducci, Father Guido
See Novello, Don
Sarduy, Severo 1937- 89-92
See also CLC 6
Sarett, Alma (Johnson) 1908- CAP-2
Earlier sketch in CA 17-18
Sarett, Morton R(euben) 1916- 93-96
Sarf, Wayne M(ichael) 1957- 114
Sarg, Anthony Frederick
See Sarg, Tony
Sarg, Tony 1880-1942 .... YABC-1
Sargant, Norman 1909-1982 Obituary 107
Sargant, William (Walters) 1907- 65-68
Sargeant, Howland H(ill) 1911-1984
Obituary 112
Sargeant, Winthrop 1903-1986 .... 29-32R
Obituary 120
Sargent, Alice G(oldstein) 1939-1988 110
Obituary 125
Sargent, Alvin 121
Brief entry 111
Sargent, Ben 1948- 118
Brief entry 113
Sargent, Brian (Lawrence) 1927- 97-100
Sargent, Daniel 1890-1987 Obituary 121
Sargent, David R(utledge) 1920- 93-96
Sargent, Frederic O(berlin) 1919- 41-44R
Sargent, Jean Vieth 1918- 106
Sargent, John Richard 1925- 13-14R
Sargent, Lyman Tower 1940- CANR-15
Earlier sketch in CA 29-32R
Sargent, Pamela CANR-8
Earlier sketch in CA 61-64
See also SATA 29
See also DLB 8
Sargent, Ralph M(illard) 1904-1985 ..... 37-40R
Obituary 116
Sargent, Robert 1933- 23-24R
See also SATA 2
Sargent, Ruth (Sexton) 1920- 112
Sargent, Sarah 1937- 106
See also SATA 41, 44
Sargent, Shirley 1927- CANR-2
Earlier sketch in CA 4R
See also SATA 11
Sargent, (Francis) William (Jr.) 1946- 106
Sargent, Wyn 49-52
Sargeson, Frank 1903-1982 .... 25-28R
Obituary 106
See also CLC 31
Sarhan, Samir 1941- 103
Sari
See Fleur, Anne
Saricks, Ambrose 1915- 17-18R
Sariego, Patricia Treece
See Treece, Patricia
Sariola, Sakari 1919- 41-44R
Sarjeant, William A(ntony) S(within) 1935- .. 105
Sarkar, Asoke 1911(?)-1983 Obituary 109
Sarkar, (Anvil) Kumar 1912- 37-40R
Sarkesian, Sam C(harles) 1927- 57-60
Sarlos, Robert Karoly 1931- 109
Sarma, G. V. L. N. 1925- 19-20R
Sarmiento, Felix Ruben Garcia 1867-1916
Brief entry 104
Sarna, Jonathan D(aniel) 1955- 109
Sarna, Nahum M(attathias) 1923- 19-20R
Sarnat, Marshall 1929- CANR-26
Earlier sketches in CA 21-22R, CANR-10
Sarndal, Carl Erik 1937- 105
Sarner, Harvey 1934- 19-20R
Sarno, Arthur D. 1921(?)-1982 Obituary ... 106
Sarno, Ronald A(nthony) 1941- CANR-12
Earlier sketch in CA 29-32R
Sarnoff, David 1891-1971 Obituary 113
Sarnoff, Dorothy 1917- 33-36R
Sarnoff, Irving 1922- CANR-8
Earlier sketch in CA 19-20R
Sarnoff, Jane 1937- CANR-9
Earlier sketch in CA 53-56
See also SATA 10
Sarnoff, Paul 1918- CANR-18
Earlier sketches in CA 7-8R, CANR-2
Sarnoff, Suzanne 1928- 97-100
Saroyan, Aram 1943- 21-22R
See also CAAS 5
Saroyan, Arshalyus 1923-1974 Obituary ... 53-56
Saroyan, William 1908-1981 .... 7-8R
Obituary 103
See also SATA 23, 24
See also DLB 7, 9
See also DLBY 81
See also CLC 1, 8, 10, 29, 34
Sarrantonio, Al 1952- 120
Sarratt, Reed 1918(?)-1986 Obituary 118
Sarraute, Nathalie 1900- CANR-23
Earlier sketch in CA 9-10R
See also CLC 1, 2, 4, 8, 10, 31
Sarre, Winifred Turner 1931- 29-32R
Sarri, Rosemary C(onzemius) 1926- 111
Sarris, Andrew 1928- 21-22R
Sarsfield, C. P.
See Marshner, Connaught Coyne
Sartain, Aaron Quinn 1905- 4R
Sarti, Roland 1937- 37-40R
Sarto, Ben
See Fawcett, F(rank) Dubrez
Sarton, (Eleanor) May 1912- CANR-1
Earlier sketch in CA 4R
See also SATA 36
See also DLB 48
See also DLBY 81
See also CLC 4, 14, 49
Sartor, Margaret 1959- 125
Sartori, Giovanni 1924- CANR-17
Earlier sketches in CA 7-8R, CANR-2
Sartre, Jean-Paul 1905-1980 .... CANR-21
Obituary 97-100
Earlier sketch in CA 9-10R
See also DLB 72
See also CLC 1, 4, 7, 9, 13, 18, 24, 44,
50
Sarvepalli, Gopal 1923- 81-84
Sarver, Hannah
See Nielsen, Jean Sarver
Sasaki, Tazu 1932- CANR-10
Earlier sketch in CA 25-28R
Sasek, Lawrence A(nton) 1923- CANR-1
Earlier sketch in CA 1R
Sasek, Miroslav 1916-1980 73-76
Obituary 101
See also SATA 16, 23
See also CLR 4
Saslow, Helen 1926- 105
Sasnett, Martena T(enney) 1908- 53-56
Saso, Michael R. 1930- 112
Sass, Lorna Janet 1945- 102
Sass, Steven A(rthur) 1949- 116
Sasser, Charles W(ayne) 1942- 122
Sasson, Sarah Diane Hyde 1946- 125
Sassoon, Beverly Adams 65-68
Sassoon, Rosemary 1931- 118
Sassoon, Siegfried (Lorraine) 1886-1967 ... 104
Obituary 25-28R
See also DLB 20
See also CLC 36
Sassoon, Vidal 1928- CANR-15
Earlier sketch in CA 65-68
Sasuly, Richard 1913- 109
Satchidananda, Swami
See Dharmi, Santana
Satchwell, John SATA-49
Sater, William F(rederick) 1937- 118
Sather, Julia Coley Duncan 1940- 103
Satin, Joseph 1922- 11-12R
Satin, Mark 1946- 41-44R
Satir, Virginia (Mildred) 1916-1988
Obituary 126
Satiricus
See Roetter, Charles Frederick
Sato, Esther Masako Tateishi 1915- 108
Satprem 1923- CANR-15
Earlier sketch in CA 85-88
Satran, Pamela Redmond 1953- 110
Sattelmeyer, Robert 1946- 125
Satterfield, Archie 1933- CANR-14
Earlier sketch in CA 57-60
Satterfield, Charles
See del Rey, Lester
and Pohl, Frederik
Satterlund, Donald R(obert) 1928- 53-56
Satterly, Weston
See Sunners, William
Sattin, Anthony (Neil) 1956- 126
Sattler, Helen Roney 1921- CANR-14
Earlier sketch in CA 33-36R
See also SATA 4
Sattler, Henry V(ernon) 1917- CANR-7
Earlier sketch in CA 5-6R
Sattler, Jerome M(urray) 1931- 49-52
Sattler, Warren 1934- 65-68
Sattley, Helen R(owland) 2R
Satz, Paul 1932- 61-64
Satz, Ronald Norman 1944- CANR-8
Earlier sketch in CA 61-64
Saucy, Robert L(loyd) 1930- 123
Brief entry 118
Sauer, Carl Ortwin 1889-1975 .... CANR-9
Earlier sketch in CA 61-64
Sauer, Julia Lina 1891-1983 81-84
See also SATA 32, 36
Sauer, Muriel Stafford 13-14R
Sauer, Val John, Jr. 1938- 107
Sauerhaft, Stan 1926- 85-88
Sauerlaender, Willibald 1924- 118
Sauerlander, Willibald
See Sauerlaender, Willibald
Sauers, Richard James 1930- 53-56
Sauers, Wendy 1958- 116
Saul, George Brandon 1901-1986 ...... CANR-6
Obituary 120
Earlier sketch in CA 13-14R
Saul, John (W. III) 1942- CANR-16
Earlier sketch in CA 81-84
See also CLC 46
Saul, Leon J(oseph) 1901- CANR-10
Earlier sketch in CA 21-22R
Saul, Mary 105
Saul, Nigel Edward 1952- 117
Saul, Norman E(ugene) 1932- 53-56
Saul, Oscar
See Halpern, Oscar Saul
Saul, (Ellen) Wendy 1946- 114
See also SATA 42
Saulnier, Raymond Joseph 1908- 7-8R
Sauls, Roger 1944- 33-36R
Saunders, Allen 1899-1986 69-72
Obituary 118
Saunders, Ann Loreille 1930- 103
Saunders, Aretas (Andrews) 1884- CAP-1
Earlier sketch in CA 11-12
Saunders, B(ernard) C(harles) 1903-1983
Obituary 115
Saunders, Beatrice 49-52
Saunders, Blanche 1906- CAP-1
Earlier sketch in CA 13-14
Saunders, Caleb
See Heinlein, Robert A(nson)
Saunders, Carl Maxon 1890-1974
Obituary 89-92
Saunders, Charles B(askerville), Jr.
1928- 61-64
Saunders, Christopher T(homas) 1907- 119
Saunders, David
See Sontup, Dan(iel)
Saunders, Doris E(vans) 1921- 77-80
Saunders, E. Dale 1919- 5-6R
Saunders, Ernest 1901(?)-1983 Obituary ... 109
Saunders, Helen E(lizabeth) 1912- 25-28R
Saunders, Hilary Aidan St. George
1898-1951 Brief entry 121
Saunders, Ione
See Cole, Margaret Alice
Saunders, J(ohn) W(hiteside) 1920- 116

INDEX

Saunders, James (Arthur) 1925-
Brief entry ... 124
See also DLB 13
Saunders, Jason Lewis 1922- Brief entry ... 106
Saunders, Jean 1932- ... CANR-19
Earlier sketch in CA 102
Saunders, John Monk 1897-1940 ... DLB-26
Saunders, John Turk 1929-1974 ... CAP-2
Earlier sketch in CA 21-22
Saunders, Keith 1910- ... 57-60
See also SATA 12
Saunders, Peter 1950- ... 114
Saunders, Richard 1947- ... CANR-21
Earlier sketch in CA 105
Saunders, Roy 1911- ... CAP-1
Earlier sketch in CA 11-12
Saunders, Rubie (Agnes) 1929- ... 49-52
See also SATA 21
Saunders, Sally Love 1940- ... 125
Saunders, Susan 1945- ... 106
See also SATA 41, 46
Saunders, Thomas 1909- ... CANR-12
Earlier sketch in CA 73-76
Saura, Carlos 1932- Brief entry ... 114
See also CLC 20
Sauro, Regina Calderone 1924- ... 11-12R
Sause, George G(abriel) 1919- ... 41-44R
Sauser-Hall, Frederic 1887-1961 ... 102
Obituary ... 93-96
See also CLC 18
Saussure, Eric de
See de Saussure, Eric
Sautel, Maureen Ann 1951- ... 61-64
Sauter, Edwin Charles Scott, Jr. 1930- ... 15-16R
Sauter, Eric 1948- ... 117
Sauter, Van Gordon 1935- ... 73-76
Sauvage, Franck
See Horn, Maurice
Sauvage, Roger 1917-1977 Obituary ... 73-76
Sauvageau, Juan 1917- ... CANR-11
Earlier sketch in CA 65-68
Sauvain, Philip Arthur 1933- ... CANR-21
Earlier sketch in CA 104
Sauvant, Karl P(eter) 1944- ... 77-80
Sauvy, Jean (Maurice Paul) 1916- ... 65-68
Sauvy, Simonne 1922- ... 65-68
Sava, George
See Milkomane, George Alexis Milkomanovich
Savacool, John K(enneth) 1917- ... 45-48
Savage, Blake
See Goodwin, Harold Leland
Savage, Brian 1933- ... 41-44R
Savage, Candace (M.) 1949- ... 123
Savage, Catharine
See Brosman, Catharine Savage
Savage, Charles 1918- ... 53-56
Savage, Christina
See Newcomb, Kerry
and Schaefer, Frank
Savage, Christopher I(vor) 1924-1969 ... CANR-6
Earlier sketch in CA 7-8R
Savage, D(ouglas) J(oseph) 1950- ... 118
Savage, D(erek) S(tanley) 1917- ... 104
Savage, Elizabeth Fitzgerald 1918- ... CANR-1
Earlier sketch in CA 3R
Savage, Ernest 1918- ... 112
Savage, Frances Higginson (Fuller) 1898- . CAP-1
Earlier sketch in CA 19-20
Savage, (Leonard) George (Gimson)
1909- ... CANR-5
Earlier sketch in CA 11-12R
Savage, Helen 1915- ... 97-100
Savage, Henry, Jr. 1903- ... CAP-2
Earlier sketch in CA 25-28
Savage, James 1784-1873 ... DLB-30
Savage, James F(rancis) 1939- ... 73-76
Savage, Joseph P. 1895(?)-1977
Obituary ... 69-72
Savage, Katharine James 1905- ... 15-16R
Savage, Lee 1928- ... 101
Savage, Leonard J(immie) 1917-1971 ... CAP-2
Obituary ... 33-36R
Earlier sketch in CA 17-18
Savage, Marc 1945- ... 65-68
Savage, Marmion 1803(?)-1872 ... DLB-21
Savage, Michael D(onald) 1946- ... 101
Savage, Mildred (Spitz) 1919- ... 11-12R
Savage, Minot Judson 1841-1918
Brief entry ... 115
Savage, Robert L(ynn) 1939- ... 109
Savage, Roth
See Kehrer, Daniel M(ark)
Savage, Teresa 1950- ... 113
Savage, Thomas 1915- Brief entry ... 126
See also CLC 40
Savage, Thomas Gerard 1926- ... 49-52
Savage, W(illiam) Sherman 1890- ... 69-72
Savage, William W(oodrow) 1914- ... 37-40R
Savage, William W(oodrow), Jr. 1943- ... 57-60
Savain, Petion ?-1973 Obituary ... 41-44R
Savan, Bruce (Sheldon) 1927-1987 ... 5-6R
Obituary ... 122
Savan, Glenn 19(?)- ... CLC-50
Savard, Felix-Antoine 1896-1982 ... DLB-68
Savarese, Julia ... 37-40R
Savarin
See Courtine, Robert
Savary, Louis M(ichael) 1936- ... CANR-24
Earlier sketches in CA 23-24R, CANR-9
Savas, E(manuel) S(tephen) 1931- ... 17-18R
Saveland, Robert N(elson) 1921- ... 41-44R
Savell, Don P(atrick) 1939- ... 119
Savelle, Max(well) 1896- ... 21-22R
Savery, Constance (Winifred) 1897- ... CANR-7
Earlier sketch in CA 11-12R
See also SATA 1
Savery, Ranald 1903(?)-1974 Obituary ... 104
Saveson, John E(dward) 1923- ... 41-44R
Saveth, Edward N(orman) 1915- ... 21-22R
Saville, Eugenia (Curtis) 1913- ... 41-44R
Saville, Lloyd (Blackstone) 1913- ... 21-22R
Saville, (Leonard) Malcolm 1901-1982 ... 101
Obituary ... 107
See also SATA 23, 31
Savin, Marc 1948- ... 106
Saviozzi, Adriana
See Mazza, Adriana
Savitch, Jessica 1948-1983 ... 108
Obituary ... 110
Savitt, Ronald 1939- ... 33-36R
Savitt, Sam ... CANR-17
Earlier sketches in CA 4R, CANR-1
See also SATA 8
Savitt, Todd Lee 1943- ... 102
Savitz, Harriet May 1933- ... CANR-14
Earlier sketch in CA 41-44R
See also SATA 5
Savitz, Leonard D. 1926- ... CANR-8
Earlier sketch in CA 23-24R
Savoie, Donald J(oseph) 1947- ... 112
Savoie, Paul 1946- ... 113
Savory, Alan Forsyth 1905- ... 11-12R
Savory, Hubert Newman 1911- ... CANR-26
Earlier sketches in CA 25-28R, CANR-10
Savory, Jerold 1933- ... CANR-10
Earlier sketch in CA 25-28R
Savory, Teo ... 29-32R
Savory, Theodore Horace 1896-1980 ... CANR-6
Earlier sketch in CA 5-6R
Savours, Ann (Margaret) 1927- ... 57-60
Savoy, Mark
See Turner, Robert H(arry)
Sawai, Gloria Ostrem ... 113
Saward, Michael 1932- ... 97-100
Sawatsky, Harry Leonard 1931- ... 89-92
Sawer, Geoffrey 1910- ... 19-20R
Sawey, Orlan (Lester) 1920- ... CANR-12
Earlier sketch in CA 29-32R
Sawicki, Marianne 1950- ... 114
Sawin, Martica 1927- ... 124
Sawkins, Raymond H(arold) 1923- ... 103
Sawyer, Albert E(rnest) 1898- ... 7-8R
Sawyer, Charles 1887-1979 ... CAP-2
Obituary ... 85-88
Earlier sketch in CA 25-28
Sawyer, Corinne Holt ... 17-18R
Sawyer, Diane K. 1946(?)- ... 115
Brief entry ... 109
Sawyer, Jack 1931- ... 61-64
Sawyer, Jesse O. 1918- ... 17-18R
Sawyer, John
See Foley, (Cedric) John
Sawyer, Mark
See Greenhood, (Clarence) David
Sawyer, P(eter) H(ayes) 1928- ... CANR-6
Earlier sketch in CA 11-12R
Sawyer, R(obert) McLaran 1929- ... 45-48
Sawyer, Ralph Alanson 1895-1978
Obituary ... 81-84
Sawyer, Roger 1931- ... 123
Sawyer, Ruth 1880-1970 ... 73-76
See also SATA 17
See also DLB 22
Sawyer, W(alter) W(arwick) 1911- ... 53-56
Sawyer-Laucanno, Christopher 1951- ... 114
Sawyerr, Harry (Alphonso Ebun)
1909-1986 ... 37-40R
Obituary ... 120
Sax, Gilbert 1930- ... 23-24R
Sax, Joseph L. 1936- ... 33-36R
Sax, Karl 1892-1973 Obituary ... 45-48
Sax, Richard 1949- ... 125
Sax, Saville 1924- ... 97-100
Saxberg, Borje O(svald) 1928- ... 41-44R
Saxe, Isobel
See Rayner, Claire (Berenice)
Saxe, Richard W(arren) 1923- ... 49-52
Saxe, Thomas E., Jr. 1903-1975
Obituary ... 61-64
Saxon, A(rthur) H(artley) 1935- ... CANR-16
Earlier sketch in CA 25-28R
Saxon, Alex
See Pronzini, Bill
Saxon, Antonia
See Sachs, Judith
Saxon, Bill
See Wallmann, Jeffrey M(iner)
Saxon, Charles D(avid) 1920- Brief entry ... 118
Saxon, Gladys Relyea ... 7-8R
Saxon, John
See Rumbold-Gibbs, Henry St. John Clair
Saxon, Lyle 1891-1946 Brief entry ... 119
Saxon, Van
See Henderson, M(arilyn) R(uth)
Saxon, William
See Mayleas, William
Saxton, Alexander P(laisted) 1919- ... 105
Saxton, Josephine (Mary) 1935- ... 29-32R
Saxton, Judith 1936- ... 105
Saxton, Lloyd 1919- ... 29-32R
Saxton, Mark 1914-1988 ... 93-96
Obituary ... 124
Saxton, Martha 1945- ... 81-84
Say, Allen 1937- ... 29-32R
See also SATA 28
Saya, Peter
See Peterson, Robert E(ugene)
Sayce, Richard Anthony 1917- ... 61-64
Saydah, J. Roger 1939-1976 ... 25-28R
Obituary ... 120
Saye, Albert B(erry) 1912- ... CANR-5
Earlier sketch in CA 7-8R
Sayeed, Khalid B. 1926- ... 25-28R
Sayegh, Fayez A(bdullah) 1922-1980 ... 11-12R
Obituary ... 102
Sayer, Angela 1935- ... 89-92
Sayers, Dorothy L(eigh) 1893-1957 ... 119
Brief entry ... 104
See also DLB 10, 36
See also TCLC 2, 15
Sayers, Frances Clarke 1897- ... 19-20R
See also SATA 3
Sayers, Gale 1943- ... 73-76
Sayers, Peig 1873-1958 Brief entry ... 113
Sayers, Raymond S. 1912- ... CANR-10
Earlier sketch in CA 25-28R
Sayers, Valerie 19(?)- ... CLC-50
Sayles, E(dwin) B(ooth) 1892- ... CAP-2
Earlier sketch in CA 25-28
Sayles, George O(sborne) 1901- ... CANR-4
Earlier sketch in CA 53-56
Sayles, John Thomas 1950- ... 57-60
See also DLB 44
See also CLC 7, 10, 14
Sayles, Leonard Robert 1926- ... CANR-1
Earlier sketch in CA 3R
Sayles, Nettie Leitch Major 1903(?)-1984
Obituary ... 113
Sayles, Ted
See Sayles, E(dwin) B(ooth)
Saylor, David J(onathan) 1945- ... 89-92
Saylor, Irene 1932- ... 33-36R
Saylor, J(ohn) Galen 1902- ... CANR-9
Earlier sketch in CA 19-20R
Saylor, Neville 1922- ... 61-64
Sayre, Anne 1923- ... 61-64
Sayre, Eleanor Axson 1916- ... 25-28R
Sayre, Henry M(arshall) 1948- ... 119
Sayre, J(ohn) Woodrow 1913- ... CANR-5
Earlier sketch in CA 11-12R
Sayre, Joel 1900-1979 Obituary ... 89-92
Sayre, John L(eslie) 1924- ... 53-56
Sayre, Kenneth Malcolm 1928- ... CANR-3
Earlier sketch in CA 11-12R
Sayre, Leslie C. 1907- ... CAP-1
Earlier sketch in CA 11-12
Sayre, Nora 1932- ... 118
Sayre, Robert F(reeman) 1933- ... 11-12R
Sayre, Wallace S. 1905-1972 Obituary ... 33-36R
Sayres, Alfred Nevin 1893-19(?) ... CAP-1
Earlier sketch in CA 17-18
Sayres, William C(ortlandt) 1927- ... 17-18R
Sayrs, Henry John 1904- ... 7-8R
Saywell, John T(upper) 1929- ... 13-14R
Sazer, Nina 1949- ... 69-72
See also SATA 13
Scabrini, Janet 1953- ... SATA-13
Scacco, Anthony M., Jr. 1939- ... 109
Scaduto, Anthony ... 104
Scaduto, Tony
See Scaduto, Anthony
Scaer, David P(aul) 1936- ... CANR-12
Earlier sketch in CA 33-36R
Scaglione, Aldo D(omenico) 1925- ... CANR-21
Earlier sketches in CA 13-14R, CANR-6
Scaglione, Cecil F(rank) 1934- ... 81-84
Scagnetti, Jack 1924- ... CANR-4
Earlier sketch in CA 49-52
See also SATA 7
Scala, James 1934- ... 124
Scalapino, Leslie 1947- ... 123
Scalapino, Robert A(nthony) 1919- ... CANR-18
Earlier sketches in CA 1R, CANR-2
Scales, James Ralph 1919- ... 120
Scales, Junius Irving 1920- ... 126
Scales, Pat(sy) R. 1944- ... 122
Scali, John (Alfred) 1918- ... 65-68
Scally, M. A.
See Scally, Sister (Mary) Anthony
Scally, Robert James 1937- ... 61-64
Scally, Sister (Mary) Anthony 1905- ... 110
Scally, Sister Mary Anthony
See Scally, Sister (Mary) Anthony
Scalzo, Joe 1941- ... 49-52
Scamehorn, H(oward) Lee 1926- ... 69-72
Scammell, Michael ... CLC-34
Scammell, William McConnell 1920- ... CANR-6
Earlier sketch in CA 7-8R
Scammon, John H(umphrey) 1905- ... 53-56
Scammon, Richard M(ontgomery) 1915- ... 61-64
Scandura, Joseph M(ichael) 1931- ... CANR-5
Earlier sketch in CA 53-56
Scanlan, James P(atrick) 1927- ... 11-12R
Scanlan, Michael 1931- ... CANR-23
Earlier sketches in CA 57-60, CANR-7
Scanlan, Patrick F. 1895(?)-1983
Obituary ... 109
Scanlan, Thomas J. 1934- ... 114
Scanlon, David G. 1921- ... 15-16R
Scanlon, James Edward 1940- ... 125
Scanlon, Kathryn I(da) 1909- ... CAP-1
Earlier sketch in CA 11-12
Scanlon, Marion Stephany ... 7-8R
See also SATA 11
Scannell, Francis P. 1915-1988 Obituary ... 125
Scannell, Frank
See Scannell, Francis P.
Scannell, Vernon 1922- ... CANR-24
Earlier sketches in CA 7-8R, CANR-8
See also DLB 27
See also CLC 49
Scanzoni, John H. 1935- ... CANR-24
Earlier sketches in CA 23-24R, CANR-9
Scanzoni, Letha Dawson 1935- ... CANR-14
Earlier sketch in CA 57-60
Scarborough, Alma May C. 1913- ... 5-6R
Scarborough, Elizabeth (Ann) 1947- ... 120
Scarborough, John 1940- ... CANR-15
Earlier sketch in CA 41-44R
Scarborough, Ruth 1904- ... 115
Scarborough, William Kauffman 1933- ... 19-20R
Scarbrough, George (Addison) 1915- ... CANR-16
Earlier sketch in CA 77-80
Scardino, Albert 1948- Brief entry ... 119
Scaretti, Marjorie ?-1982 Obituary ... 107
Scarf, Maggi
See Scarf, Maggie
Scarf, Maggie 1932- ... CANR-22
Earlier sketch in CA 29-32R
See also SATA 5
Scarfe, Allan (John) 1931- ... CANR-13
Earlier sketch in CA 25-28R
Scarfe, Francis Harold 1911-1986
Obituary ... 118
Scarfe, Wendy (Elizabeth) 1933- ... CANR-13
Earlier sketch in CA 25-28R
Scargall, Jeanne Anna 1928- ... 93-96
Scargill, (David) Ian 1935- ... CANR-12
Earlier sketch in CA 61-64
Scarisbrick, J(ohn) J(oseph) 1928- ... CANR-18
Earlier sketch in CA 25-28R
Scarlett, Roger
See Page, Evelyn
Scarlett, Susan
See Streatfeild, (Mary) Noel
Scarne, John 1903-1985 Obituary ... 116
Scarpitti, Frank R(oland) 1936- ... CANR-14
Earlier sketch in CA 41-44R
Scarr, Dee 1948- ... 122
Scarr(-Salapatek), Sandra (Wood) 1936- ... 126
Scarrott, Michael
See Fisher, A(rthur) Stanley T(heodore)
Scarrow, Howard A(lbert) 1928- ... 110
Scarry, Huck
See Scarry, Richard, Jr.
Scarry, Patricia (Murphy) 1924- ... 19-20R
See also SATA 2
Scarry, Patsy
See Scarry, Patricia (Murphy)
Scarry, Richard (McClure) 1919- ... CANR-18
Earlier sketch in CA 19-20R
See also SATA 2, 35
See also DLB 61
See also CLR 3
Scarry, Richard, Jr. 1953- ... SATA-35
Scavullo, Francesco 1929- ... 102
Schaaf, C(arl) Hart 1912- ... 7-8R
Schaaf, Martha Eckert 1911- ... CANR-1
Earlier sketch in CA 4R
Schaaf, Peter 1942- ... 106
Schaafsma, Polly 1935- ... 57-60
Schaal, John H. 1908- ... 73-76
Schaap, Dick
See Schaap, Richard J(ay)
Schaap, James C(alvin) 1948- ... 118
Schaap, Richard J(ay) 1934- ... CANR-5
Earlier sketch in CA 11-12R
Schaar, John H(omer) 1928- ... 3R
Schaarwaechter, Georg 1929- ... 25-28R
Schabert, Kyrill S. 1909(?)-1983 Obituary ... 109
Schachner, Nat(han) 1895-1955
Brief entry ... 120
Schacht, Al(exander) 1894(?)-1984
Obituary ... 113
Schacht, Hjalmar (Horace Greeley)
1877-1970 Obituary ... 113
Schacht, Richard (Lawrence) 1941- ... 29-32R
Schachtel, Ernest G(eorge) 1903-1975 ... 37-40R
Schachtel, Hyman Judah 1907- ... 49-52
Schachtel, Roger (Bernard) 1949- ... 106
See also SATA 38
Schachter, Gustav 1926- ... 17-18R
Schachter, Michael 1941- ... 102
Schachter, Oscar 1915- ... 65-68
Schachter, Stanley 1922- ... 37-40R
Schachterle, Nancy (Lange) 1925- ... 101
Schachtman, Max 1903-1972 Obituary ... 37-40R
Schackne, Stewart 1905-1975 Obituary ... 61-64
Schad, Jasper G(ripper) 1932- ... 110
Schad, Wilhelm
See Reichert, Herbert W(illiam)
Schaechter, Mordkhe 1927- ... 41-44R
Schaedel, Richard P. 1920- ... 45-48
Schaef, Anne Wilson 1934- ... 118
Schaefer, Charles E. 1933- ... 37-40R
Schaefer, Claude 1913- ... 33-36R
Schaefer, Frank 1936- ... CANR-10
Earlier sketch in CA 65-68
Schaefer, Jack Warner 1907- ... CANR-15
Earlier sketches in CA 11-12, CAP-1
See also SATA 3
Schaefer, John 1958- ... 126
Schaefer, John H(arrison) 1937- ... 57-60
Schaefer, Josephine O'Brien 1929- ... 37-40R
Schaefer, Leah Cahan 1920- ... 49-52
Schaefer, Nicola Caroline 1939- ... 104
Schaefer, Ted 1939- ... 77-80
Schaefer, Vincent J(oseph) 1906- ... 120
Schaefer, Walter Erich 1901-1982(?)
Obituary ... 106
Schaeffer, Albrecht 1885-1950 ... DLB-66
Schaeffer, Claude Frederic Armand
1898-1982 Obituary ... 108
Schaeffer, Edith (Seville) 1914- ... 77-80
Schaeffer, Elizabeth 1939- ... 45-48
Schaeffer, Francis A(ugust) 1912-1984 ... 77-80
Obituary ... 112
Schaeffer, K(laus) H(eymann) 1921- ... 61-64
Schaeffer, Mead 1898- ... SATA-21
Schaeffer, Neil 1940- ... 107
Schaeffer, Norma 1924-1985 ... 119
Schaeffer, Susan Fromberg 1941- ... CANR-18
Earlier sketch in CA 49-52
See also SATA 22
See also DLB 28
See also CLC 6, 11

Schaeffer-Forrer, Claude F. A.
See Schaeffer, Claude Frederic Armand
Schaeling, Marianne
See Amft, M(arian) J(anet)
Schaeper, Thomas J(erome) 1948- ... 109
Schaeren, Beatrix 1941- ... 29-32R
Schaetzel, J(oseph) Robert 1917- ... 65-68
Schafer, Charles (Louis) 1916- ... 61-64
Schafer, Edward Hetzel 1913- ... CANR-1
Earlier sketch in CA 1R
Schafer, Grant C. 1926- ... 23-24R
Schafer, R(aymond) Murray 1933- ... 77-80
Schafer, Robert 1942- ... 108
Schafer, Stephen 1911-1976 ... 37-40R
Schafer, Violet (Christine) 1910- ... 61-64
Schafer, William J. 1937- ... 49-52
Schaff, Adam 1913- ... CANR-12
Earlier sketch in CA 25-28R
Schaff, David 1943- ... 33-36R
Schaffer, (Benjamin) Bernard 1925-1984
Obituary ... 113
Schaffer, Daniel 1950- ... 114
Schaffer, Frank 1910- ... 103
Schaffer, Jeff(rey P.) 1943- ... CANR-22
Earlier sketch in CA 105
Schaffer, Lewis A(dam) 1934- ... 101
Schaffer, Marion 1931- ... 111
Schaffer, Ulrich 1942- ... 69-72
Schaffner, Cynthia V. A. 1947- ... 121
Schaffner, Kenneth 1939- ... 45-48
Schaffner, Nicholas 1953- ... CANR-15
Earlier sketch in CA 85-88
Schaffner, Val(entine) 1951- ... 107
Schaflander, Gerald M(aurice) 1920- ... 37-40R
Schagrin, Morton L(ouis) 1930- ... 25-28R
Schaie, K(laus) Warner 1928- ... CANR-15
Earlier sketch in CA 41-44R
Schakne, Robert 1926- ... 65-68
Schakovskoy, Zinaida 1908- ... CANR-8
Earlier sketch in CA 17-18R
Schaldenbrand, Mary 1922- ... 49-52
Schaleben, Arville Orman 1907- ... CANR-1
Earlier sketch in CA 3R
Schalk, Adolph F(rancis) 1923- ... 33-36R
Schalk, David L(ouis) 1936- ... 89-92
Schall, James V(incent) 1928- ... CANR-20
Earlier sketches in CA 11-12R, CANR-6
Schaller, George B(eals) 1933- ... CANR-9
Earlier sketch in CA 7-8R
See also SATA 30
Schaller, Michael 1947- ... 126
Brief entry ... 110
Schalm, Bernard 1928-1974 ... 3R
Obituary ... 103
Scham, Alan (Myron) 1937- ... 29-32R
Schama, Simon Michael 1945- ... 105
Schanberg, Sydney H(illel) 1934- ... 69-72
Schanche, Don A. 1926- ... CANR-6
Earlier sketch in CA 5-6R
Schandler, Herbert Y(ale) 1928- ... 69-72
Schang, Frederick C. 1893- ... CANR-13
Earlier sketch in CA 33-36R
Schanz, John P(hilip) 1924- ... 107
Schanzer, George O(swald) 1914- ... 41-44R
Schaper, Edzard 1908-1984 ... DLB-69
Schapiro, J(acob) Salwyn 1879-1973 ... CANR-5
Obituary ... 45-48
Earlier sketch in CA 7-8R
Schapiro, Leonard (Bertram)
1908-1983 ... CANR-13
Obituary ... 111
Earlier sketch in CA 65-68
Schapiro, Meyer 1904- ... 97-100
Schapper, Beatrice Aronson 1906-1974 ... 11-12R
Obituary ... 45-48
Schappes, Morris U(rman) 1907- ... 49-52
Schapsmeier, Edward L(ewis) 1927- ... 29-32R
Schapsmeier, Frederick H(erman) 1927- ... 29-32R
Schara, Ron 1942- ... 69-72
Scharbach, (John) Alexander 1909- ... 114
Scharbach, J. Alexander
See Scharbach, (John) Alexander
Scharf, Bertram 1931- ... 53-56
Scharf, J. Thomas 1843-1898 ... DLB-47
Scharfenberg, Doris 1925- ... 108
Scharff, Edward E. 1946- ... 123
Scharfstein, Ben-Ami 1919- ... 101
Scharfstein, Zevi 1884-1972 Obituary ... 37-40R
Scharine, Richard (G.) 1938- Brief entry ... 118
Scharine, Richard G. 1938- ... 123
Scharlatt, Hal 1936(?)-1974 Obituary ... 104
Scharlemann, Dorothy Hoyer 1912- ... 65-68
Scharlemann, Martin H(enry) 1910- ... 15-16R
Scharlemann, Robert Paul 1929- ... 11-12R
Scharnhorst, Gary (Francis) 1950- ... 119
Scharper, Phillip (Jenkins) 1919-1985 ... 73-76
Obituary ... 116
Schary, Dore 1905-1980 ... CANR-1
Obituary ... 101
Earlier sketch in CA 3R
Schary, Jill
See Robinson, Jill
Schatell, Brian ... 124
See also SATA 47
Schatkin, Margaret 1944- ... 118
Schatkin, Sidney B. 1903- ... 25-28R
Schatt, Stanley 1943- ... CANR-26
Earlier sketch in CA 69-72
Schatten, Fritz (Max Robert) 1930- ... 15-16R
Schatten, Robert 1911-1977 Obituary ... 73-76
Schatz, Mark N(orton) 1929- ... 113
Schatz, Ronald W. 1949- ... 125
Schatz, Sayre P(erry) 1922- ... 41-44R
Schatzki, Walter 1899- ... SATA-31
Schau, Michael 1945- ... 85-88
Schaub, Marilyn McNamara 1928- ... 19-20R
Schaub, Thomas Hill 1947- ... 105
Schauer, Frederick Franklin 1946- ... 112
Schauf, George Edward 1925- ... 41-44R
Schaufele, William E., Jr. 1923- ... 111
Scheader, Catherine 1932- ... 85-88
Schealer, John M(ilton) 1920- ... 5-6R
Schechner, Richard 1934- ... CANR-17
Earlier sketches in CA 45-48, CANR-1
Schechter, Alan H(enry) 1936- ... 11-12R
Schechter, Betty (Goodstein) 1921- ... 7-8R
See also SATA 5
Schechter, Harold 1948- ... 108
Schechter, Ruth Lisa 1927- ... 33-36R
Schechter, William 1934- ... 23-24R
Schechtman, Joseph B. 1891-1970 ... CANR-3
Earlier sketch in CA 4R
Schecter, Jerrold L. 1932- ... 23-24R
Scheel, J(oergen) D(itlev) 1918- ... 11-12R
Scheele, Adele M. 1938- ... CANR-18
Earlier sketch in CA 97-100
Scheele, Carl H(arry) 1928- ... 85-88
Scheer, George F(abian) 1917- ... 15-16R
Scheer, Julian (Weisel) 1926- ... 49-52
See also SATA 8
Scheer, Robert 1936- ... 106
Scheer, Wilbert E. 1909- ... CANR-17
Earlier sketch in CA 25-28R
Scheff, Thomas Joel 1929- ... 105
Scheffer, Nathalie P. 1890(?)-1981
Obituary ... 105
Scheffer, Victor B(lanchard) 1906- ... CANR-11
Earlier sketch in CA 29-32R
See also SATA 6
Scheffler, Harold W(alter) 1932- ... 19-20R
Scheffler, Israel 1923- ... CANR-1
Earlier sketch in CA 1R
Scheflen, Albert E. 1920-1980 ... CANR-3
Obituary ... 101
Earlier sketch in CA 45-48
Schefter, Jim 1940- ... 89-92
Scheibe, Karl E(dward) 1937- ... CANR-11
Earlier sketch in CA 29-32R
Scheiber, Harry N(oel) 1935- ... CANR-1
Earlier sketch in CA 3R
Scheiber, Jane L(ang) 1937- ... 93-96
Scheibla, Shirley 1919- ... 41-44R
Scheick, William J(oseph) 1941- ... CANR-17
Earlier sketches in CA 49-52, CANR-1
Scheid, Francis J(ames) 1920- ... 17-18R
Scheidler, Joseph M. 1927- ... 122
Scheier, Ivan Henry 1926- ... CANR-7
Earlier sketch in CA 5-6R
Scheier, Michael 1943- ... 115
See also SATA 36, 40
Scheimann, Eugene 1897- ... 33-36R
Schein, Clarence J(acob) 1918- ... 65-68
Schein, James Arns 1920(?)-1983
Obituary ... 110
Schein, Jerome D(aniel) 1923- ... 118
Scheiner, Seth M(ordecai) 1933- ... 17-18R
Scheinfeld, Aaron 1899-1970 ... CAP-2
Earlier sketch in CA 29-32
Scheinfeld, Amram 1897-1979 ... 17-18R
Obituary ... 89-92
Scheingold, Stuart A(llen) 1931- ... 53-56
Scheleen, Joseph C(arl) 1904-1985
Obituary ... 116
Schell, Bunny
See Schell, Rolfe F(inch)
Schell, Edgar T(homas) 1931- ... 45-48
Schell, Herbert S(amuel) 1899- ... CANR-21
Earlier sketch in CA 2R
Schell, Jonathan 1943- ... CANR-12
Earlier sketch in CA 73-76
See also CLC 35
Schell, Maximilian 1930- Brief entry ... 116
Schell, Mildred 1922- ... 113
See also SATA 41
Schell, Orville H. 1940- ... 25-28R
See also SATA 10
Schell, Rolfe F(inch) 1916- ... CANR-7
Earlier sketch in CA 57-60
Schellenberg, Helene Chambers ... 13-14R
Schellenberg, James A. 1932- ... 37-40R
Schellenberg, Theodore R. 1903-19(?) ... CAP-1
Earlier sketch in CA 17-18
Schellie, Don 1932- ... 101
See also SATA 29
Schelling, Thomas Crombie 1921- ... 1R
Schelly, William 1951- ... 114
Schemering, (Crien) Christopher 1956- ... 123
Schemm, Mildred Walker 1905- ... CANR-1
Earlier sketch in CA 3R
See also SATA 21
Schemmer, Benjamin Franklin 1932- ... 61-64
Schemmer, Kenneth E(dwin) 1936- ... 110
Schenck, Anita A(llen) 1909- ... 89-92
Schenck, Janet Daniels 1883(?)-1976
Obituary ... 69-72
Schendler, Sylvan 1925- ... 25-28R
Schenk, H(ans) G(eorg) 1912- ... 23-24R
Schenken, Howard 1904(?)-1979 ... 93-96
Obituary ... 85-88
Schenker, Alexander M(arian) 1924- ... 33-36R
Schenker, Eric 1931- ... 37-40R
Scheper, Nancy
See Scheper-Hughes, Nancy
Scheper-Hughes, Nancy 1944- ... 89-92
Schepers, Maurice B. 1928- ... 13-14R
Scheps, Clarence 1915- ... 33-36R
Scher, Helene L(enz) 1935- ... 123
Scher, Helene Lenz 1935- Brief entry ... 118
Scher, Les 1946- ... 101
Scher, Paula 1948- ... 115
See also SATA 47
Scher, Steven Paul 1936- ... CANR-3
Earlier sketch in CA 49-52
Schere, Monroe 1913- ... 85-88
Scherer, F(rederic) M(ichael) 1932- ... CANR-12
Earlier sketch in CA 29-32R
Scherer, Frances Schlosser 1912- ... 69-72
Scherer, Jack F(ranklin) 1939- ... 69-72
Scherer, Jacqueline Rita 1931- ... 53-56
Scherer, Jean-Marie Maurice 1920- ... 110
Scherer, Joanna Cohan 1942- ... 107
Scherer, Klaus R(ainer) 1943- ... 101
Scherer, Paul (Ehrman) 1892- ... 5-6R
Scherer, Priscilla 1948- ... 119
Scherer, Raymond Lewis 1919- ... 104
Scherer, William F(rederick) 1939- ... 41-44R
Scherf, Margaret 1908-1979 ... CANR-6
Earlier sketch in CA 7-8R
See also SATA 10
Scherle, Victor 1935- ... 25-28R
Scherman, Bernadine Kielty 1890(?)-1973
Obituary ... 45-48
Scherman, David E(dward) 1916- ... 102
Scherman, Katharine 1915- ... CANR-11
Earlier sketch in CA 5-6R
Scherman, Thomas K(ielty) 1917-1979
Obituary ... 106
Schermer, Judith (Denise) 1941- ... 106
See also SATA 30
Schermerhorn, Richard A(lonzo) 1903- ... 37-40R
Scherr, George Harry 1920- ... 114
Scherr, Max 1916(?)-1981 Obituary ... 105
Schertenleib, Charles 1905-1972
Obituary ... 37-40R
Schertle, Alice 1941- ... CANR-23
Earlier sketch in CA 107
See also SATA 36
Scherzer, Carl John 1901- ... 4R
Scheub, Harold 1931- ... 61-64
Scheuer, Joseph F(rancis) 1918-1975
Obituary ... 61-64
Scheuer, Philip K(atz) 1902-1985
Obituary ... 115
Scheuerle, William H(oward) 1930- ... 33-36R
Scheuerman, Richard D(ean) 1951- ... 57-60
Scheuring, Lyn 1937- ... 73-76
Scheuring, Tom 1942- ... 73-76
Schevill, James (Erwin) 1920- ... 7-8R
See also CLC 7
Schevitz, Jeffrey M(orrie) 1941- ... 65-68
Scheyer, Ernst 1900- ... 15-16R
Schiaparelli, Elsa 1890-1973 Obituary ... 113
Schiappa, Barbara D(ublin) 1943- ... 109
Schiavone, James 1933- ... CANR-9
Earlier sketch in CA 7-8R
Schick, Alice 1946- ... CANR-15
Earlier sketch in CA 81-84
See also SATA 27
Schick, Eleanor 1942- ... CANR-19
Earlier sketches in CA 49-52, CANR-4
See also SATA 9
Schick, George B(aldwin Powell) 1903- ... 41-44R
Schick, Joel 1945- ... 107
See also SATA 30, 31
Schickel, Julia Whedon 1936- ... 49-52
Schickel, Richard (Warren) 1933- ... CANR-1
Earlier sketch in CA 3R
See also AITN 1
Schickele, Peter 1935- ... 85-88
Schickele, Rene 1883-1940 ... DLB-66
Schiddel, Edmund 1909-1982 ... 7-8R
Obituary ... 107
Schiefelbusch, Richard L. 1918- ... CANR-11
Earlier sketch in CA 25-28R
Schieffer, Bob 1937- ... 69-72
Schier, Donald (Stephen) 1914- ... 29-32R
Schier, Ernest L. 1918- ... 77-80
Schier, Flint 1954(?)-1988 Obituary ... 126
Schiff, Dorothy 1903- ... 121
Brief entry ... 114
Schiff, Harold (Irvin) 1923- ... 89-92
Schiff, Irwin A(llan) 1928- ... CANR-25
Earlier sketch in CA 65-68
Schiff, Jacqui Lee 1934- ... 37-40R
Schiff, Ken(neth Roy) 1942- ... 49-52
See also SATA 7
Schiff, Michael 1915- ... 15-16R
Schiffer, Irvine 1917- Brief entry ... 114
Schiffer, Michael 1948- ... 106
Schiffer, Michael B(rian) 1947- ... 110
Schifferes, Justus J(ulius) 1907- ... CANR-5
Earlier sketch in CA 5-6R
Schiffhorst, Gerald J. 1940- ... 19-20R
Schiffman, Jack 1921- ... 49-52
Schiffman, Joseph Harris 1914- ... 19-20R
Schiffrin, Harold Z. 1922- ... 29-32R
Schiler, Marc (Eugene) 1951- ... 106
Schillaci, Anthony
See Schillaci, Peter Paul
Schillaci, Peter Paul 1929- ... 29-32R
Schillebeeckx, Edward (Cornelis Florentius
Alfons) 1914- Brief entry ... 111
Schiller, A. Arthur 1902-1977 ... 37-40R
Obituary ... 73-76
Schiller, Andrew 1919- ... 41-44R
See also SATA 21
Schiller, Barbara (Heyman) 1928- ... 17-18R
See also SATA 21
Schiller, Bob
See Schiller, Robert Achille
Schiller, Bradley R(obert) 1943- ... 57-60
Schiller, Craig 1951- ... 81-84
Schiller, Dorothea E. 1898(?)-1987
Obituary ... 123
Schiller, Herbert I(rving) 1919- ... 29-32R
Schiller, Jerome P(aul) 1934- ... 25-28R
Schiller, Justin G. 1943- Brief entry ... 110
See also SATA 31
Schiller, Lee Virginia Chambers
See Chambers-Schiller, Lee Virginia
Schiller, Mayer
See Schiller, Craig
Schiller, Robert Achille 1918- ... 123
Brief entry ... 118
Schiller, Rose Leiman
See Goldemberg, Rose Leiman
Schilling, Betty 1925- ... 106
Schilling, S. Paul 1904- ... CANR-16
Earlier sketches in CA 2R, CANR-1
Schilling, Warner R(oller) 1925-
Brief entry ... 112
Schilpp, Madelon Golden ... 117
Schilpp, Paul A(rthur) 1897- ... CANR-19
Earlier sketches in CA 4R, CANR-4
Schilz, Thomas F. 1950- ... 125
Schimel, John L(ouis) 1916- ... 25-28R
Schimmel, Annemarie (Brigitte) 1922-
Brief entry ... 120
Schimmel, Herbert D(avid) 1927- ... 117
Schimmels, Cliff 1937- ... 115
Schinagl, Mary S(onora) 1914- ... 17-18R
Schindeler, Fred(erick) Fernand 1934- ... 41-44R
Schindelman, Joseph 1923- ... SATA-32
Schindler, Marvin Samuel 1932-
Brief entry ... 106
Schindler, S(tephen) D. ... SATA-50
Schinhan, Jan Philip 1887-1975 ... CAP-2
Obituary ... 61-64
Earlier sketch in CA 23-24
Schioetz, Aksel 1906-1975 Obituary ... 111
Schiotz, Aksel
See Schioetz, Aksel
Schipf, Robert G(eorge) 1923- ... 61-64
Schirmer, Daniel B(oone) 1915- ... 41-44R
Schirmer, Gregory A(llan) 1944- ... 117
Schirmer, Henry W. 1922- ... 107
Schirmer, Jennifer G(ay) 1947- ... 113
Schirmerhorn, Clint
See Riemer, George
Schirokauer, Conrad M(ax) 1929- ... 107
Schisgal, Murray (Joseph) 1926- ... 21-22R
See also CLC 6
Schisgall, Oscar 1901-1984 ... CANR-9
Obituary ... 112
Earlier sketch in CA 53-56
See also SATA 12, 38
Schivelbusch, Wolfgang 1941- ... 105
Schjeldahl, Peter 1942- Brief entry ... 113
Schkade, Lawrence L. 1930- ... CANR-7
Earlier sketch in CA 17-18R
Schlabach, Theron F(rederick) 1933- ... 25-28R
Schlabrendorff, Fabian von
See von Schlabrendorff, Fabian
Schlachter, Gail Ann 1943- ... CANR-14
Earlier sketch in CA 77-80
Schlachter, Susan
See Thaler, Susan
Schlafly, Phyllis 1924- ... CANR-26
Earlier sketch in CA 25-28R
See also AITN 1
Schlain, Bert H(oward) 1898- ... 19-20R
Schlamm, William S(iegmund)
1904-1978 ... 93-96
Obituary ... 81-84
Schlanger, Henry 1918(?)-1984 Obituary ... 113
Schlant, Ernestine 1935- ... 81-84
Schlapbach-Oberhansli, Trudi 1944- ... 23-24R
Schlatter, Richard 1912-1987 ... 23-24R
Obituary ... 123
Schlauch, Margaret 1898-1986 ... CAP-1
Obituary ... 119
Earlier sketch in CA 13-14
Schlebecker, John T(homas) 1923- ... 11-12R
Schleck, Charles A. 1925- ... CANR-6
Earlier sketch in CA 7-8R
Schlee, Ann 1934- ... 101
See also SATA 36, 44
See also CLC 35
Schlee, Susan 1940- ... 93-96
Schlegel, Dorothy B(adders) 1910- ... 37-40R
Schlegel, Richard 1913- ... 65-68
Schlegel, Stuart A(llen) 1932- ... 61-64
Schlegelmann, V. E.
See Hartz, Fred R.
Schleicher, Charles P. 1907- ... 11-12R
Schleier, Curt 1944- ... 89-92
Schleier, Gertrude 1933- ... 3R
Schleifer, James T(homas) 1942- ... 97-100
Schleifer, Ronald 1948- ... 118
Schlein, Miriam 1926- ... CANR-2
Earlier sketch in CA 4R
See also SATA 2
Schleiner, Winfried 1938- ... 29-32R
Schlem
See Prevost, Marcel
Schlender, William E(lmer) 1920- ... CANR-14
Earlier sketch in CA 17-18R
Schlenker, Elizabeth D. (Wallace) 1912- ... 17-18R
Schlenther, Boyd (Stanley) 1936- ... 41-44R
Schlepp, Wayne Allen 1931- ... 29-32R
Schlereth, Howard (Hewitt) 1936- ... 57-60
Schlereth, Thomas J(ohn) 1941- ... 97-100
Schlesinger, Alfred Cary 1900- ... CAP-1
Earlier sketch in CA 13-14
Schlesinger, Arthur (Meier), Jr. 1917- ... CANR-1
Earlier sketch in CA 4R
See also DLB 17
See also AITN 1
Schlesinger, Arthur Meier 1888-1965 ... CANR-5
Obituary ... 25-28R
Earlier sketch in CA 5-6R
Schlesinger, Benjamin 1928- ... CANR-22
Earlier sketches in CA 19-20R, CANR-7
Schlesinger, Bruno Walter 1876-1962 ... 116
Obituary ... 111
Schlesinger, Elizabeth Bancroft 1886-1977
Obituary ... 69-72

INDEX

Schlesinger, Hilde S(tephanie) CANR-6
Earlier sketch in CA 53-56
Schlesinger, Joseph A(braham) 1922- 61-64
Schlesinger, Lawrence E(rwin) 1921- 41-44R
Schlesinger, Leonard A. 1952- 126
Schlesinger, Marian Cannon 1912- 89-92
Schlesinger, Roger 1943- 126
Schlesinger, Stephen C(annon) 1942- 57-60
Schlesinger, Thomas O(tto) 1925- 41-44R
Schlessinger, Philip J. 1914- 7-8R
Schleunes, Karl A(lbert) 1937- 29-32R
Schley, Jim 1956- 118
Schlichting, Harold E(ugene, Jr.) 1926- 112
Schlimbach, Alice (Paula) 1898- CAP-1
Earlier sketch in CA 15-16
Schlink, Frederick John 1891- 65-68
Schlink, Klara 1904- 101
Schlink, M. Basilea
See Schlink, Klara
Schlink, Mother Basilea
See Schlink, Klara
Schlissel, Lillian 1930- CANR-13
Earlier sketch in CA 25-28R
Schlitzer, Albert Lawrence 1902- 2R
Schloat, G. Warren, Jr. 1914- 23-24R
See also SATA 4
Schlobin, Roger Clark 1944- CANR-18
Earlier sketch in CA 102
Schlosberg, H. J.
See May, H(enry) J(ohn)
Schloss, Arthur David
See Waley, Arthur (David)
Schlossberg, Dan 1948- CANR-19
Earlier sketch in CA 101
Schlossberg, Edwin (Arthur) 1945-
Brief entry 112
Schlossberg, Herbert 1935- 111
Schlossman, Beryl 1955- 124
Schlossman, Steven L(awrence)
1947- CANR-16
Earlier sketch in CA 81-84
Schlossstein, Steven 1941- 122
Schlueter, June 1942- 101
Schlueter, Paul (George) 1933- CANR-11
Earlier sketch in CA 15-16R
Schlumberger, Daniel 1904-1972
Obituary 37-40R
Schlumberger, Jean 1877-1968 Obituary 116
See also DLB 65
Schmalenbach, Werner 1917- CANR-13
Earlier sketch in CA 73-76
Schmandt, Henry J. 1918- CANR-9
Earlier sketch in CA 7-8R
Schmandt, Raymond H(enry, Jr.) 1925- 11-12R
Schmandt-Besserat, Denise 1933- CANR-20
Earlier sketch in CA 69-72
Schmeck, Harold M(arshall), Jr. 1923- 17-18R
Schmeidler, Gertrude Raffel 1912- 37-40R
Schmeiser, Douglas Albert 1934- CANR-3
Earlier sketch in CA 11-12R
Schmeling, Gareth L(on) 1940- 73-76
Schmeling, Marianne 1930- 101
Schmeltz, Susan Alton 111
Schmeltz, Susan M.
See Schmeltz, Susan Alton
Schmeltz, William Frederick 1924- 41-44R
Schmemann, Alexander 1921-1983 117
Obituary 111
Schmertz, Herb(ert) 1930- 120
Schmid, A. Allan 1935- 37-40R
Schmid, Carlo 1896-1979 Obituary 97-100
Schmid, Carol L(ouise) 1946- 105
Schmid, Claus-Peter 1942- 61-64
Schmid, Eduard 1890-1966 Obituary 113
Schmid, Elenore 1939- CANR-21
Earlier sketches in CA 53-56, CANR-5
See also SATA 12
Schmid, Mark J(oseph) 1901-19(?) CAP-1
Earlier sketch in CA 13-14
Schmiderer, Dorothy 1940- 85-88
See also SATA 19
Schmidgall, Gary 1945- 77-80
Schmidhauser, John R(ichard) 1922- CANR-1
Earlier sketch in CA 45-48
Schmidt, Albert J(ohn) 1925- 37-40R
Schmidt, Alexander 1956- 125
Schmidt, Alice M(ahany) 1925- 65-68
Schmidt, Alvin J(ohn) 1932- CANR-1
Earlier sketch in CA 45-48
Schmidt, Arno (Otto) 1914-1979 Obituary 109
See also DLB 69
Schmidt, Charles T., Jr. 1934- 25-28R
Schmidt, Claire Harman 1957- 109
Schmidt, Dana Adams 1915- 11-12R
Schmidt, Dolores Barracano 1931- 41-44R
Schmidt, Dorothea
See Wender, Dorothea
Schmidt, Elizabeth 1915- SATA-15
Schmidt, Emerson Peter 1899-1976
Obituary 111
Schmidt, Fred H(artz) 1918- 85-88
Schmidt, Frederick G. 1924- 49-52
Schmidt, Hans 1938- 61-64
Schmidt, Helmut Dan 1915- 11-12R
Schmidt, Hubert (Glasgow) 1905-1980
Obituary 112
Schmidt, J(akob) E(dward) 1906- 13-14R
Schmidt, James Norman 1912- CANR-1
Earlier sketch in CA 1R
See also SATA 21
Schmidt, James W. 1947- 121
Schmidt, Jerry A(rthur) 1945- 69-72
Schmidt, John 1905-1969 CAP-1
Earlier sketch in CA 19-20
Schmidt, Karl M. (Jr.) 1917- 13-14R
Schmidt, Laura M(arie) 1952- CANR-16
Earlier sketch in CA 65-68
Schmidt, Lyle D(arrel) 1933- 61-64
Schmidt, Margaret Fox 1925-1979 65-68
Obituary 125
Schmidt, Michael Jack 1949- 126
Schmidt, Michael Norton 1947- CANR-2
Earlier sketch in CA 49-52
See also DLB 40
Schmidt, Mike
See Schmidt, Michael Jack
Schmidt, Nancy Jeanne 1936- CANR-7
Earlier sketch in CA 57-60
Schmidt, Paul Frederic 1925- CANR-1
Earlier sketch in CA 1R
Schmidt, Peggy Jeanne 1951- 109
Schmidt, Rick
See Schmidt, William R(ichard) III
Schmidt, Robert Milton 1930- 7-8R
Schmidt, Royal Jae (Jr.) 1915- 41-44R
Schmidt, Sandra
See Oddo, Sandra Schmidt
Schmidt, Stanley (Albert) 1944- CANR-24
Earlier sketches in CA 61-64, CANR-8
Schmidt, Steven (Thomas) 1927- 33-36R
Schmidt, Warren H(arry) 1920- CANR-1
Earlier sketch in CA 45-48
Schmidt, Werner Felix 1923- 11-12R
Schmidt, William E. 1947- 73-76
Schmidt, William R(ichard) III 1949- 110
Schmidt, Wilson Emerson 1927- 103
Schmidt-Nielsen, Knut 1915- 106
Schmiechen, James A. 1940- 126
Schmier, Louis Eugene 1940- 112
Schmithals, Walter 1923- CANR-9
Earlier sketch in CA 65-68
Schmitt, Abraham 1927- CANR-17
Earlier sketch in CA 97-100
Schmitt, Albert R(ichard) 1929- 73-76
Schmitt, Bernadotte Everly 1886-1969 2R
Obituary 103
Schmitt, Charles 1934(?)-1986 Obituary 119
Schmitt, David (Edward) 1940- 53-56
Schmitt, Gladys 1909-1972 CANR-2
Obituary 37-40R
Earlier sketch in CA 2R
Schmitt, Hans A. 1921- CANR-5
Earlier sketch in CA 4R
Schmitt, Heinrich 1894-1976 Obituary 115
Schmitt, Karl Michael 1922- 41-44R
Schmitt, Marshall L. 1919- 13-14R
Schmitt, Martin (Ferdinand) 1917-1978 CANR-9
Earlier sketch in CA 53-56
Schmitt, Raymond L(ouis) 1936- 93-96
Schmitt, Richard 1927- 118
Schmitter, Dean Morgan 1917- 41-44R
Schmitter, Phillipe Charles 1936- 115
Schmitthoff, Clive M(acmillan) 1903- CANR-18
Earlier sketches in CA 7-8R, CANR-3
Schmittroth, John 1924-1988 49-52
Obituary 125
Schmittroth, John (William), Jr.
1949- CANR-19
Earlier sketch in CA 97-100
Schmitz, Aron Hector 1861-1928 122
Brief entry 104
Schmitz, Carl August 1920-1966 Obituary 116
Schmitz, Charles Henry 1904- 7-8R
Schmitz, Dennis 1937- 29-32R
Schmitz, Ettore
See Schmitz, Aron Hector
Schmitz, James H(enry) 1911- 103
See also DLB 8
Schmitz, Joseph William 1905-1966 7-8R
Schmitz, Michael J. 1934- 23-24R
Schmitz, Virginia
See Pasley, Virginia Schmitz
Schmokel, Wolfe W(illiam) 1933- 11-12R
Schmoller, Hans 1916-1985 Obituary 117
Schmuck, Richard A(llen) 1936- 15-16R
Schmucke, Anne
See Strich, Christian
Schmuller, Aaron 1910- 53-56
Schnabel, Billie H(agen) 1944(?)-1980
Obituary 101
Schnabel, Truman Gross, Jr. 1919- 105
Schnacke, Dick
See Schnacke, Richard N(ye)
Schnacke, Richard N(ye) 1919- 61-64
Schnackenberg, Gjertrud 1953-
Brief entry 116
See also CLC 40
Schnackenburg, Rudolf 1914- CANR-12
Earlier sketch in CA 29-32R
Schnall, Maxine (Swartz) 1934- 19-20R
Schnaubelt, Franz Joseph 1914- 65-68
Schneck, Jerome M. 1920- 17-18R
Schneck, Stephen 1933- CANR-10
Earlier sketch in CA 13-14R
Schneebaum, Tobias 1921- CANR-15
Earlier sketch in CA 29-32R
Schneede, Uwe M(ax) 1939- Brief entry 111
Schneewind, Elizabeth Hughes 1940- CANR-2
Earlier sketch in CA 45-48
Schneewind, J(erome) B(orges) 1930- 25-28R
Schneidau, Herbert N. 1935- 29-32R
Schneider, Anna
See Sequoia, Anna
Schneider, Ben Ross, Jr. 1920- 37-40R
Schneider, Benjamin 1938- 41-44R
Schneider, Carl D(avid) 1942- 69-72
Schneider, Clement J(oseph)
1927-1972 41-44R
Schneider, Daniel J(ohn) 1927- 61-64
Schneider, David 1918- 114
Schneider, David M(urray) 1918-
Brief entry 112
Schneider, Delwin Byron 1926- 37-40R
Schneider, Dick
See Schneider, Richard H(enry)
Schneider, Duane 1937- 103
Schneider, Elisabeth Wintersteen 1897- CAP-1
Earlier sketch in CA 11-12
Schneider, Elizabeth (Susan) 1943- CANR-16
Earlier sketch in CA 93-96
Schneider, Hans J(uergen) 1935- 73-76
Schneider, Harold K(enneth) 1925- 33-36R
Schneider, Herbert Wallace 1892-1984 13-14R
Obituary 114
Schneider, Herman 1905- CANR-16
Earlier sketch in CA 29-32R
See also SATA 7
Schneider, Howie AITN-2
Schneider, Isidor 1896-1977 CAP-1
Obituary 73-76
Earlier sketch in CA 13-14
Schneider, John C(harles) 1945- 102
Schneider, Joyce Anne 1942- 107
Schneider, Kenneth Ray 1927- 49-52
Schneider, Lambert 1900-1970 Obituary 104
Schneider, Laurence Allen 1937- 81-84
Schneider, Laurie
See Adams, Laurie
Schneider, Leo 1916- 5-6R
Schneider, Leonard Alfred 1925-1966 89-92
Schneider, Louis 1915-1979 CANR-13
Earlier sketch in CA 57-60
Schneider, Myles J(ay) 1943- 116
Schneider, Myra 1936- CANR-24
Earlier sketch in CA 107
Schneider, Nicholas A. 1930- 25-28R
Schneider, Nina 1913- CANR-15
Earlier sketch in CA 29-32R
See also SATA 2
Schneider, Rex 1937- 122
See also SATA 44
Schneider, Richard H(enry) 1922- 97-100
Schneider, Robert G. 1930- 112
Schneider, Robert T(homas) 1925- 7-8R
Schneider, Robert W. 1933- 15-16R
Schneider, Rolf 1932- Brief entry 112
Schneider, Ronald M(ilton) 1932- 53-56
Schneider, Stanley D(ale) 1921- 17-18R
Schneider, Stephen H(enry) 1945- CANR-12
Earlier sketch in CA 69-72
Schneider, Steven A. 1952- 120
Schneider, Susan Weidman 1944- 118
Schneider, William, Jr. 1941- CANR-19
Earlier sketch in CA 29-32R
Schneiderman, Beth Kline 97-100
Schneiderman, Harry 1885-1975
Obituary 61-64
Schneiderman, L(awrence) J(erome)
1932- 57-60
Schneiderman, Stuart (Alan) 1943- 114
Schneiders, Alexander A(loysius)
1909-1968 CAP-1
Earlier sketch in CA 17-18
Schneier, Edward V(incent), Jr. 1939- 29-32R
Schneir, Miriam 1933- 77-80
Schnell, George A(dam) 1931- CANR-12
Earlier sketch in CA 29-32R
Schnell, R(odolph) L(eslie) 1931- 113
Schnell, William J(acob) 7-8R
Schnelle, Kenneth E(dward) 1914- 23-24R
Schnepper, Jeff A(lan) 1947- CANR-21
Earlier sketch in CA 85-88
Schneps, Maurice 1917- 2R
Schnessel, S. Michael 1947- CANR-14
Earlier sketch in CA 73-76
Schneyder, J. F.
See Taylor, (Frank Herbert) Griffin
Schnirel, James R. 1931- 69-72
See also SATA 14
Schnitzer, Martin C(olby) 1925-
Brief entry 110
Schnitzler, Arthur 1862-1931 Brief entry 104
See also TCLC 4
Schnore, Leo F(rancis) 1927- 19-20R
Schnurre, Wolfdietrich 1920- DLB-69
Schob, David Eugene 1941- 61-64
Schochet, Gordon J(oel) 1937- 45-48
Schochet, J(acob) Immanuel 1935- CANR-1
Earlier sketch in CA 45-48
Schock, Pauline 1928- 111
See also SATA 45
Schocken, Theodore 1914-1975 Obituary 104
Schoder, Raymond V(ictor) 1916-1987 CANR-1
Obituary 122
Earlier sketch in CA 3R
Schoeck, Richard J(oseph) 1920- CANR-5
Earlier sketch in CA 4R
Schoeffler, Oscar E(dmund) 1899-1979 73-76
Obituary 85-88
Schoeman, Karel 1939- 101
Schoen, Barbara 1924- 21-22R
See also SATA 13
Schoen, Elin 1945- 101
Schoen, Juliet P. 1923- 69-72
Schoenbach, Carrie 1928- 120
Schoenbaum, S(amuel) 1927- 107
Schoenbaum, Thomas John 1939- 104
Schoenberg, Arnold 1874-1951
Brief entry 109
Schoenberg, B(ernhardt) Mark 1928- 97-100
Schoenberg, Bernard 1927-1979 CANR-2
Obituary 85-88
Earlier sketch in CA 45-48
Schoenberg, Ronald 1942- 126
Schoenberg, Wilfred Paul 1915- 11-12R
Schoenberger, Guido L. 1891-1974
Obituary 53-56
Schoenberger, Nancy 1950- 126
Schoenberger, Walter Smith 1920- 29-32R
Schoenberner, Franz 1892-1970 Obituary 104
Schoenbohm, Wilko B. 1913- 19-20R
Schoenbrun, David (Franz) 1915-1988 CANR-3
Obituary 125
Earlier sketch in CA 49-52
Schoendoerffer, Pierre 1928- Brief entry 111
Schoenfeld, Clarence Albert 1918- CANR-6
Earlier sketch in CA 1R
Schoenfeld, David 1923- CANR-12
Earlier sketch in CA 19-20R
Schoenfeld, Eugene 1935- Brief entry 118
Schoenfeld, Hanns Martin W(alter)
1928- CANR-6
Earlier sketch in CA 57-60
Schoenfeld, Maxwell Philip 1936- 33-36R
Schoenfield, Allen 1896(?)-1979 Obituary 85-88
Schoenherr, John (Carl) 1935- SATA-37
Schoenherr, Richard Anthony 1935- CANR-21
Earlier sketch in CA 29-32R
Schoenholtz, Larry 1948- 57-60
Schoenman, Ralph 1935- 25-28R
Schoenstein, Paul 1902-1974 Obituary 89-92
Schoenstein, Ralph 1933- 13-14R
Schoenwald, Richard L. 1927- 17-18R
Schoep, Arthur Paul 1920- 53-56
Schoepfer, Virginia B. 1934- 33-36R
Schoepflin, George A. 1939- 29-32R
Schoeps, Hans-Joachim 1909- Brief entry 106
Schoeps, Karl-Heinz 1935- CANR-24
Earlier sketch in CA 107
Schoer, Lowell A(ugust) 1931- 29-32R
Schoettle, Lynn 49-52
Schofer, Lawrence 1940- 77-80
Schofield, B(rian) B(etham) 1895-1984 23-24R
Obituary 114
Schofield, J(ohn) N(oel) 1899-1986
Obituary 120
Schofield, Jonathan
See Streib, Dan(iel Thomas)
Schofield, Mary Anne 1948- 124
Schofield, Michael 1919- CANR-14
Earlier sketch in CA 41-44R
Schofield, Paul
See Tubb, E(dwin) C(harles)
Schofield, Sylvia Anne 1918- CANR-13
Earlier sketch in CA 73-76
Schofield, William 1921- 11-12R
Schofield, William G(reenough) 1909- CANR-2
Earlier sketch in CA 7-8R
Scholastica, Sister Mary
See Jenkins, Marie M(agdalen)
Scholberg, Henry 1921- 77-80
Scholderer, Victor 1880-1971 Obituary 104
Scholefield, Alan 1931- 97-100
Scholefield, Edmund O.
See Butterworth, W(illiam) E(dmund III)
Scholem, Gershom (Gerhard) 1897-1982 45-48
Obituary 106
Scholer, David M(ilton) 1938- 101
Scholes, Katherine 1959- 123
Scholes, Marie V(ielmetti) 1916- 29-32R
Scholes, Robert (Edward) 1929- CANR-14
Earlier sketch in CA 11-12R
Scholes, Walter V(inton) 1916-1975 CAP-2
Earlier sketch in CA 29-32
Scholey, Arthur 1932- 93-96
See also SATA 28
Scholl, John 1922- 11-12R
Scholl, Lisette 1945- 89-92
Scholl, Sharon L. 1932- 41-44R
Scholl, William M(athias) 1882-1968
Obituary 113
Scholt, Grayce 1925- 104
Scholtz, William 1916- 7-8R
Scholz, Albert A(ugust) 1899-19(?) CAP-2
Earlier sketch in CA 29-32
Scholz, Carter 1953- 119
Scholz, Jackson Volney 1897-1986 7-8R
Obituary 120
See also SATA 49
Scholz, William 1916- 7-8R
Schomaker, Mary Zimmeth 1928- 108
Schomp, Gerald 1937- 29-32R
Schon, Donald A(lan) 1930- 19-20R
Schon, Isabel 1940- 110
Schonberg, Arnold
See Schoenberg, Arnold
Schonberg, Harold C(harles) 1915- 112
Schonberg, Rosalyn Krokover
1913(?)-1973 Obituary 41-44R
Schonberger, Richard J. 1937- 110
Schonborg, Virginia 1913- 77-80
Schone, Virginia 97-100
See also SATA 22
Schonell, Fred(erick) Joyce 1900-1969 CANR-2
Earlier sketch in CA 4R
Schonfeld, William R(ost) 1942- CANR-17
Earlier sketch in CA 37-40R
Schonfield, Hugh J(oseph) 1901-1988 9-10R
Obituary 124
Schongut, Emanuel 1936- SATA-36, 52
Schooler, Carmi 1933- 114
Schooler, (Seward) Dean, Jr. 1941- 73-76
Schoolfield, George C(larence) 1925- CANR-6
Earlier sketch in CA 1R
Schoolland, Marian M(argaret) 1902- CANR-2
Earlier sketch in CA 5-6R
Schoonhoven, Calvin R(obert) 1931- 21-22R
Schoonmaker, Alan N. 1936- 25-28R
Schoonmaker, Ann 1928- 73-76
Schoonmaker, Frank 1905-1976 Obituary 61-64
Schoonover, Frank (Earle) 1877-1972 106
See also SATA 24
Schoonover, Lawrence Lovell
1906-1980 CANR-4
Obituary 97-100
Earlier sketch in CA 1R

Schoonover, Melvin E(ugene) 1926-
Brief entry 114
Schoonover, Shirley 1936- 77-80
Schoonover, Thelma I(rene) 1907- 41-44R
Schoonover, Thomas D(avid) 1936- 120
Schoor, Gene 1921- 29-32R
See also SATA 3
Schopflin, George A.
See Schoepflin, George A.
Schor, Amy 1954- 105
Schor, Lynda 1938- 73-76
Schor, Naomi 1943- CANR-16
Earlier sketch in CA 89-92
Schorb, E(dwin) M(arsh) 1940- 61-64
Schorer, Mark 1908-1977 CANR-7
Obituary 73-76
Earlier sketch in CA 5-6R
See also CLC 9
Schorr, Alan Edward 1945- 85-88
Schorr, Alvin L. 1921- CANR-15
Earlier sketch in CA 29-32R
Schorr, Daniel (Louis) 1916- 65-68
See also AITN 2
Schorr, Jerry 1934- 29-32R
Schorr, Mark 1953- 122
Schorsch, Ismar 1935- Brief entry 115
Schorske, Carl E(mil) 1915- 85-88
Schosberg, Paul A. 1938- 13-14R
Schossberger, Emily Maria 1905-1979
Obituary 104
Schott, Jeffrey J. 1949- 126
Schott, John R(obert) 1936- CANR-7
Earlier sketch in CA 57-60
Schott, Penelope Scambly 1942- 77-80
Schott, Richard Lockwood 1939- 117
Schott, Webster 1927- 49-52
Schottland, Charles Irwin 1906- 13-14R
Schouler, James 1839-1920 DLB-47
Schowalter, John E(rwin) 1936- 109
Schoyer, B. Preston 1912(?)-1978
Obituary 77-80
Schrader, Constance 1933- CANR-18
Earlier sketch in CA 101
Schrader, George A(lfred), Jr. 1917- 23-24R
Schrader, Paul Joseph 1946- 37-40R
See also DLB 44
See also CLC 26
Schrader, Richard James 1941- 85-88
Schrader, Robert F(ay) 1931- 119
Schraff, Anne E(laine) 1939- CANR-17
Earlier sketches in CA 49-52, CANR-1
See also SATA 27
Schraff, Francis Nicholas 1937- 101
Schraffenberger, Nancy 1933- CANR-16
Earlier sketch in CA 93-96
Schrag, Adele Frisbie 1921- 105
Schrag, Calvin Orville 1928- CANR-1
Earlier sketch in CA 1R
Schrag, Oswald O. 1916- 49-52
Schrag, Peter 1931- CANR-8
Earlier sketch in CA 15-16R
Schrag, Philip G(ordon) 1943- 102
Schram, Martin 1942- CANR-13
Earlier sketch in CA 69-72
Schram, Stuart R(eynolds) 1924- 97-100
Schramm, Percy Ernst 1894-1970
Obituary 104
Schramm, Richard (Howard) 1934- 41-44R
Schramm, Sarah Slavin 1942- 93-96
Schramm, Wilbur (Lang) 1907-1987 CANR-22
Obituary 124
Earlier sketch in CA 105
Schrank, Jeffrey 1944- 29-32R
Schrank, Joseph 1900-1984 CANR-20
Obituary 112
Earlier sketch in CA 5-6R
See also SATA 38
Schreck, Alan (Edward) 1951- 124
Schreck, Everett M. 1897- CAP-2
Earlier sketch in CA 33-36
Schrecker, John (Ernest) 1937-
Brief entry 112
Schreiber, Daniel 1909-1981 CAP-1
Obituary 103
Earlier sketch in CA 13-14
Schreiber, Elizabeth Anne (Ferguson)
1947- 69-72
See also SATA 13
Schreiber, Flora Rheta 1918- CANR-11
Earlier sketch in CA 53-56
See also AITN 1
Schreiber, Georges 1904-1977 Obituary 109
See also SATA 29
Schreiber, Hermann 1920- 25-28R
Schreiber, Jan 1941- 65-68
Schreiber, Jean-Jacques Servan
See Servan-Schreiber, Jean-Jacques
Schreiber, Mark 1960- 116
Schreiber, Michael 1937- 116
Schreiber, Ralph W(alter) 1942- 69-72
See also SATA 13
Schreiber, Ron 1934- 41-44R
Schreiber, Ted
See Schreiber, V. Theodore
Schreiber, V. Theodore 1905-1986 124
Schreiber, Vernon R(oy) 1925- 61-64
Schreiber-Wicke, Edith 1943- 123
Schreider, Frank(lin David) 1924- 7-8R
Schreiner, George F(rederic) 1949- 117
Schreiner, Lee
See Schreiner, George F(rederic)
Schreiner, Olive (Emilie Albertina)
1855-1920 Brief entry 105
See also DLB 18
See also TCLC 9
Schreiner, Samuel A(gnew), Jr. 1921- CANR-26
Earlier sketches in CA 65-68, CANR-9
Schreiner-Mann, Joan 1939- 45-58
Schreiter, Rick 1936- 21-22R
Schreivogel, Paul A. 1930- 25-28R
Schrepfer, Susan R(ita) 1941- 117
Schreuder, D(eryck) M(arshall) 1942- 120
Schreyer, George M(aurice) 1913- 5-6R
Schriber, Mary Suzanne 1938- 126
Schrier, Arnold 1925- 49-52
Schrier, Nettie Vander
See Vander-Schrier, Nettie
Schrier, William 1900-1973 41-44R
Schrift, Shirley 1922(?)- 113
Brief entry 110
Schriftgiesser, Karl (John) 1903-1988 CAP-1
Obituary 126
Earlier sketch in CA 11-12
Schrire, Theodore 1906- 21-22R
Schrock, Simon 1938- 113
Schroder, Amund A. Schulze 1925- CANR-5
Earlier sketch in CA 13-14R
Schroder, John Henry Erle 1895- CAP-1
Earlier sketch in CA 13-14
Schrodinger, Erwin
See Schroedinger, Erwin
Schrodt, Philip A(ndrew) 1951- 111
Schroedel, Jean Reith 1951- 122
Schroeder, Albert H(enry) 1914- CANR-14
Earlier sketch in CA 41-44R
Schroeder, Andreas (Peter) 1946- CANR-16
Earlier sketch in CA 93-96
See also DLB 53
Schroeder, David 1924- 23-24R
Schroeder, Eric 1904- CAP-1
Earlier sketch in CA 13-14
Schroeder, Fred E(rich) H(arald) 1932- 41-44R
Schroeder, Frederick W(illiam) 1896- 3R
Schroeder, Henry A(lfred) 1906-1975 CAP-2
Earlier sketch in CA 25-28
Schroeder, John H(erman) 1943- 49-52
Schroeder, Mary 1903- 73-76
Schroeder, Oliver Charles, Jr. 1916- 110
Schroeder, Paul Walter 1927- 7-8R
Schroeder, Ted 1931(?)-1973 SATA-20
Schroeder, W(illiam) Widick 1928-
Brief entry 111
Schroedinger, Erwin 1887-1961 Obituary 113
Schroeter, James 1927- 21-22R
Schroeter, Louis C(larence) 1929- 29-32R
Schroetter, Hilda Noel 1917- 29-32R
Schroll, Herman T(heodore III) 1946- 33-36R
Schruben, Francis W(illiam) 1918- 45-48
Schruth, Peter Elliott 1917-1979
Obituary 89-92
Schubart, Mark Allen 1918- 105
Schubel, J(erry) R(obert) 1936- 126
Schubert, Delwyn George 1919- 11-12R
Schubert, Dieter 1947- 111
Schubert, Glendon 1918- CANR-21
Earlier sketches in CA 5-6R, CANR-6
Schubert, Kurt 1923- 7-8R
Schubert-Gabrys, Ingrid 1953- 111
Schuberth, Christopher J. 1933- CANR-18
Earlier sketch in CA 25-28R
Schuchman, Joan 1934- 101
Schudson, Michael 1946- CANR-19
Earlier sketch in CA 101
Schueler, Donald G(ustave) 1929- 106
Schuerer, Ernst 1933- CANR-17
Earlier sketches in CA 45-48, CANR-1
Schuessler, Hermann E. 1929(?)-1975
Obituary 61-64
Schuessler, Karl F(rederick) 1915- 105
Schuettinger, Robert Lindsay 1936- 33-36R
Schuetz, John Howard 1933- 97-100
Schuetze, Armin William 1917- 57-60
Schug, Willis E(rvin) 1924- 49-52
Schuh, Dwight R(aymond) 1945- 101
Schuh, G(eorge) Edward 1930- 29-32R
Schuker, Stephen Alan 1939- 69-72
Schul, Bill D(ean) 1928- CANR-8
Earlier sketch in CA 61-64
Schulberg, Budd (Wilson) 1914- CANR-19
Earlier sketch in CA 25-28R
See also DLB 6, 26, 28
See also DLBY 81
See also CLC 7, 48
Schulberg, Herbert C(harles) 1934- CANR-8
Earlier sketch in CA 61-64
Schulberg, Stuart 1922-1979 Obituary 89-92
Schulder, Diane Blossom 1937- 37-40R
Schuler, Carol Ann 1946- 106
Schuler, Edgar A(lbert) 1905- CAP-2
Earlier sketch in CA 23-24
Schuler, Stanley Carter 1915- CANR-5
Earlier sketch in CA 7-8R
Schulke, Flip Phelps Graeme 1930- CANR-22
Earlier sketch in CA 105
Schulkind, Eugene (Walter) 1923- 97-100
Schull, (John) Joseph 1916-1980 CANR-8
Earlier sketch in CA 53-56
Schuller, Gunther 1925- 69-72
Schuller, Robert (Harold) 1926- CANR-14
Earlier sketch in CA 11-12R
Schullery, Paul (David) 1948- 111
Schulman, Arnold 1925- 103
Schulman, Bob
See Schulman, Robert
Schulman, Grace 65-68
Schulman, J(oseph) Neil 1953- 89-92
Schulman, Janet 1933- 101
See also SATA 22
Schulman, L(ester) M(artin) 1934- CANR-12
Earlier sketch in CA 33-36R
See also SATA 13
Schulman, Robert 1916- 77-80
Schulman, Rosalind 1914- 41-44R
Schulman, Sam 1924- 45-48
Schulman, Sarah 1958- 118
Schulmerich, Alma 1902(?)-1985
Obituary 115
Schulte, Elaine L(ouise) 1934- CANR-12
Earlier sketch in CA 73-76
See also SATA 36
Schulte, Henry F(rank) 1924- 25-28R
Schulte, Paul C(larence) 1890-1984
Obituary 112
Schulte, Rainer 23-24R
Schultes, Richard Evans 1915- CANR-25
Earlier sketch in CA 108
Schultheis, Rob 1943- 111
Schulthess, Emil 1913- 65-68
Schults, Raymond L. 1926- 105
Schultz, Barbara 1923- 21-22R
Schultz, Barbara A. 117
Schultz, Dodi 1930- CANR-16
Earlier sketches in CA 45-48, CANR-1
Schultz, Donald O. 1939- CANR-17
Earlier sketch in CA 25-28R
Schultz, Duane P(hilip) 1934- 29-32R
Schultz, Ed 1933- 45-48
Schultz, Edna Moore 1912- 13-14R
Schultz, Edward W(illiam) 1936- CANR-1
Earlier sketch in CA 45-48
Schultz, George F(ranklin) 1908- CAP-2
Earlier sketch in CA 19-20
Schultz, George J(oseph) 1932-
Brief entry 109
Schultz, Gerard 1902-1974 Obituary 110
Schultz, Gladys Denny 1896(?)-1984
Obituary 113
Schultz, Gwendolyn 65-68
See also SATA 21
Schultz, Harold John 1923- 103
Schultz, Harry D. CANR-14
Earlier sketch in CA 23-24R
Schultz, James Willard 1859-1947
Brief entry 121
See also YABC 1
Schultz, John (Ludwig) 1932- CANR-15
Earlier sketch in CA 41-44R
Schultz, Joseph P(enn) 1928- 113
Schultz, Mark 1935- 116
Schultz, Mort(on) J(oel) 1930- CANR-12
Earlier sketch in CA 73-76
Schultz, Pearle Henriksen 1918- CANR-1
Earlier sketch in CA 49-52
See also SATA 21
Schultz, Philip 1945- 104
Schultz, Samuel J(acob) 1914- CANR-12
Earlier sketch in CA 25-28R
Schultz, Sigrid (Lillian) 1893-1980
Obituary 97-100
Schultz, Stanley K(enton) 1938-
Brief entry 116
Schultz, Terri 1946- CANR-10
Earlier sketch in CA 65-68
Schultz, Theodore William 1902- 85-88
Schultz, Vernon B(urdette) 1924- 11-12R
Schultze, Charles L(ouis) 1924-
Brief entry 114
Schultze, William Andrew 1937- 37-40R
Schulz, Ann Tibbitts 1938- 116
Schulz, Anne Markham 1938- 121
Schulz, Bruno 1892-1942 123
Brief entry 115
See also TCLC 5
Schulz, Charles M(onroe) 1922- CANR-6
Earlier sketch in CA 9-10R
See also SATA 10
See also CLC 12
Schulz, Clare Elmore 1924- 15-16R
Schulz, David A. 1933- 29-32R
Schulz, Ernst B(ernhard) 1896- 73-76
Schulz, Florence 1908- CAP-2
Earlier sketch in CA 21-22
Schulz, James Henry 1936- 89-92
Schulz, John E. 1939- 29-32R
Schulz, Juergen 1927- 41-44R
Schulz, Max F(rederick) 1923- 7-8R
Schulz, Phillip Stephen 1946- 123
Schulz-Behrend, George 1913- 45-48
Schulze, Franz 1927- 41-44R
Schulze, Gene 1912- 85-88
Schulze, Hertha 1935- 122
Schulzinger, Robert D(avid) 1945- 61-64
Schumacher, Alvin J. 1928- 15-16R
Schumacher, Ernst Friedrich
1911(?)-1977 81-84
Obituary 73-76
Schuman, Ben N. 1923- 17-18R
Schuman, David Feller 1942- CANR-17
Earlier sketch in CA 97-100
Schuman, Frederick Lewis 1904- 45-48
Schuman, Howard 1928- 124
Schuman, Patricia Glass 1943- CANR-14
Earlier sketch in CA 33-36R
Schumann, Elizabeth Creighton 1907- CAP-1
Earlier sketch in CA 11-12
Schumann, Paul L. 1955- 112
Schumm, Ruth Frances 1921-1988
Obituary 125
Schuon, Frithjof 1907- CANR-13
Earlier sketch in CA 73-76
Schuon, Karl Albert 1913-1984 15-16R
Obituary 114
Schur, Edwin M(ichael) 1930- CANR-7
Earlier sketch in CA 13-14R
Schur, Maxine 1948- SATA-49, 53
Schur, Norman W(arren) 1907- CANR-17
Earlier sketch in CA 41-44R
Schurer, Ernst
See Schuerer, Ernst
Schurer, Leopold (Sidney) Launitz, Jr.
See Launitz-Schurer, Leopold (Sidney),
Jr.
Schurfranz, Vivian 1925- 61-64
See also SATA 13
Schurke, Paul 1955- 126
Schurmacher, Emile C. 1903(?)-1976
Obituary 69-72
Schurman, D(onald) M. 1924- 37-40R
Schurr, Cathleen 11-12R
Schurz, Carl 1829-1906 DLB-23
Schuschnigg, Kurt von
See von Schuschnigg, Kurt
Schusky, Ernest L(ester) 1931- CANR-8
Earlier sketch in CA 17-18R
Schuster, George 1873-1972 Obituary 37-40R
Schuster, George 1881-1982 Obituary 107
Schuster, Louis A. 1916- 15-16R
Schuster, Max Lincoln 1897-1970
Obituary 29-32R
Schutte, William Metcalf 1919- 5-6R
Schutz, Anton Friedrich Joseph
1894-1977 81-84
Obituary 73-76
Schutz, Benjamin Merrill 1949- 107
Schutz, John Adolph 1919- 7-8R
Schutz, John Howard
See Schuetz, John Howard
Schutz, Susan Polis 1944- 105
Schutz, Wilhelm Wolfgang 1911- 25-28R
Schutz, William C(arl) 1925- CANR-10
Earlier sketch in CA 25-28R
Schutze, Gertrude 1917- 17-18R
Schutze, Jim 1946- 123
Schutzer, A. I. 1922- 25-28R
See also SATA 13
Schutzman, Steven 1947- 114
Schuyler, David 1950- 126
Schuyler, George Samuel 1895-1977 81-84
Obituary 73-76
See also BW
See also DLB 29, 51
Schuyler, James Marcus 1923- 101
See also DLB 5
See also CLC 5, 23
Schuyler, Jane 1943- 65-68
Schuyler, Joseph B(ernard) 1921- 3R
Schuyler, Judy
See Eshbach, Lloyd Arthur
Schuyler, Keith C. 1919- CANR-12
Earlier sketch in CA 29-32R
Schuyler, Pamela R. 1948- 106
See also SATA 30
Schuyler, Philippa Duke 1934-1967 5-6R
See also BW
Schuyler, Robert Livingston 1883-1966 CAP-1
Earlier sketch in CA 11-12
Schvaneveldt, Jay D. 1937- 103
Schwab, Arnold T. 1922- 11-12R
Schwab, George 1931- CANR-16
Earlier sketches in CA 45-48, CANR-1
Schwab, John J. 1923- 85-88
Schwab, Joseph J(ackson) 1909- CANR-5
Earlier sketch in CA 5-6R
Schwab, Paul Josiah 1894-1966 7-8R
Obituary 103
Schwab, Peter 1940- CANR-14
Earlier sketch in CA 41-44R
Schwabacher, Ethel K(remer) 1903-1984
Obituary 114
Schwabe, William
See Cassidy, William L(awrence Robert)
Schwaber, Paul 1936- 13-14R
Schwadron, Abraham A(be) 1925-1987
Obituary 123
Schwalberg, Carol(yn Ernestine Stein)
1930- 69-72
Schwaller, John Frederick 1948- 126
Schwamm, Ellen 1934- 122
Schwandt, Stephen (William) 1947- 126
Schwark, Mary Beth 1954- SATA-51
Schwartz, Al(bert) 1911(?)-1988 Obituary 125
Schwartz, Alfred 1922- 19-20R
Schwartz, Alvin 1927- CANR-24
Earlier sketches in CA 13-14R, CANR-7
See also SATA 4
See also CLR 3
Schwartz, Amy 1954- 110
See also SATA 41, 47
Schwartz, Anna J(acobson) 1915- 125
Schwartz, Anne Powers 1913- CANR-1
Earlier sketch in CA 1R
See also SATA 10
Schwartz, Arthur Nathaniel 1922- CANR-8
Earlier sketch in CA 61-64
Schwartz, Audrey James 1928- 89-92
Schwartz, Barry 1938- 77-80
Schwartz, Barry N. 1942- 33-36R
Schwartz, Benjamin I. 1916- 13-14R
Schwartz, Bernard 1923- Brief entry 117
Schwartz, Bernard (Sherman) 1945- 106
Schwartz, Bertie G. 1901(?)-1976
Obituary 69-72
Schwartz, Betty 1927- 93-96
Schwartz, Charles 73-76
Schwartz, Charles W(alsh) 1914- 13-14R
See also SATA 8
Schwartz, Daniel (Bennet) 1929- SATA-29
Schwartz, David C. 1939- 37-40R
Schwartz, David J(oseph), Jr. 1927- CANR-13
Earlier sketch in CA 19-20R
Schwartz, David M(artin) 1951- 118
Schwartz, Delmore 1913-1966 CAP-2
Obituary 25-28R
Earlier sketch in CA 17-18
See also DLB 28, 48
See also CLC 2, 4, 10, 45

Schwartz, Douglas W(right) 1929- ... CANR-17
Earlier sketch in CA 25-28R
Schwartz, Eleanor Brantley 1937- ... 57-60
Schwartz, Eli 1921- ... 4R
Schwartz, Elias 1923- ... 41-44R
Schwartz, Elizabeth Reeder 1912- ... 15-16R
See also SATA 8
Schwartz, Elkanah 1937- ... 23-24R
Schwartz, Elliott S. 1936- ... 15-16R
Schwartz, Emanual K. 1912-1973 ... 37-40R
Obituary ... 41-44R
Schwartz, Ernst
See Ozu, Yasujiro
Schwartz, Eugene M. 1927- ... 13-14R
Schwartz, Gail Garfield ... 117
Schwartz, George 1908-1974 Obituary ... 104
Schwartz, George Leopold 1891-1983
Obituary ... 109
Schwartz, George R. 1942- ... CANR-17
Earlier sketch in CA 97-100
Schwartz, Gerald 1932- ... 120
Schwartz, Harry W. 1903(?)-1984
Obituary ... 114
Schwartz, Helen 1935- ... 111
Schwartz, Helene E(nid) 1941- ... 65-68
Schwartz, Hillel 1948- ... CANR-20
Earlier sketch in CA 102
Schwartz, Howard 1945- ... CANR-22
Earlier sketches in CA 49-52, CANR-5
Schwartz, Israel J(acob) 1885-1971
Obituary ... 33-36R
Schwartz, Jerome
See Lawrence, Jerome
Schwartz, Joel L. 1940- ... 121
See also SATA 51
Schwartz, Jonathan 1938- ... 97-100
See also DLBY 82
Schwartz, Joseph 1925- ... 33-36R
Schwartz, Julius 1907- ... 109
See also SATA 45
Schwartz, K(arlene) V. 1936- ... 104
Schwartz, Kessel 1920- ... CANR-6
Earlier sketch in CA 4R
Schwartz, Larry 1922- ... 53-56
Schwartz, Leon 1922- ... 113
Schwartz, Lester J(erome) 1927- ... 113
Schwartz, Lewis M(arvin) 1935- ... 45-48
Schwartz, Lita Linzer 1930- ... 29-32R
Schwartz, Lloyd 1941- ... 112
Schwartz, Lois C. 1935- ... 33-36R
Schwartz, Loretta 1943- ... 97-100
Schwartz, Louis B. 1913- ... 23-24R
Schwartz, Lynne Sharon 1939- ... 103
See also CLC 31
Schwartz, Martin D(avid) 1945- ... 118
Schwartz, Michael 1942- ... 113
Schwartz, Mildred A(nne) 1932- ... CANR-9
Earlier sketch in CA 21-22R
Schwartz, Morris S. 1916- ... 17-18R
Schwartz, Mortimer (Donald) 1922- ... 116
Schwartz, Muriel A.
See Eliot, T(homas) S(tearns)
Schwartz, Murray M. 1942- ... 116
Schwartz, Nancy Lynn 1952-1978 ... 107
Schwartz, Ned 1948- ... 107
Schwartz, Norman B(oris) 1932- ... 111
Schwartz, Paula 1925- ... CANR-18
Earlier sketch in CA 85-88
Schwartz, Pedro 1935- ... CANR-24
Earlier sketch in CA 107
Schwartz, Pepper 1945- ... 33-36R
Schwartz, Richard B. 1941- ... CANR-15
Earlier sketch in CA 85-88
Schwartz, Richard D(erecktor) 1925- ... CANR-6
Earlier sketch in CA 1R
Schwartz, Ronald 1937- ... 65-68
Schwartz, S.
See Starr, S(tephen) Frederick
Schwartz, Selwyn S. 1907(?)-1988
Obituary ... 125
Schwartz, Sheila (Ruth) 1929- ... CANR-11
Earlier sketch in CA 25-28R
See also SATA 27
Schwartz, Shloime
See Schwartz, Selwyn S.
Schwartz, Stephen (Lawrence) 1948- ... 85-88
See also SATA 19
Schwartz, Steven 1950- ... 118
Schwartz, Stuart B. 1940- ... 126
Brief entry ... 108
Schwartz, William 1916-1982 Obituary ... 107
Schwartzberg, Julie 1943- ... 29-32R
Schwartzman, Aaron 1900(?)-1981
Obituary ... 102
Schwartzman, David 1924- ... 41-44R
Schwartzman, Edward 1927- ... 73-76
Schwartzman, Sylvan D(avid) 1913- ... CANR-21
Earlier sketch in CA 41-44R
Schwartzmann, Mischa 1919- ... 29-32R
Schwarz, Alfred 1925- Brief entry ... 118
Schwarz, Boris 1906-1983 ... 37-40R
Obituary ... 111
Schwarz, Egon 1922- ... 57-60
Schwarz, Fred(erick) Charles 1913- ... 1R
Schwarz, Hans 1939- ... 41-44R
Schwarz, Henry G(uenter) 1928- ... 37-40R
Schwarz, Jack
See Schwarz, Jacob
Schwarz, Jacob 1924- ... 103
Schwarz, Jordan A(braham) 1937- ... 105
Schwarz, Leo W(alder) 1906-1967 ... 7-8R
Schwarz, Richard W(illiam) 1925- ... CANR-12
Earlier sketch in CA 29-32R
Schwarz, Robert 1921- ... 77-80
Schwarz, Solomon M. 1882(?)-1973
Obituary ... 45-48
Schwarz, Ted
See Schwarz, Theodore R., Jr.
Schwarz, Theodore R., Jr. 1945- ... CANR-26
Earlier sketches in CA 65-68, CANR-10
Schwarz, Walter 1930- ... 13-14R
Schwarz, Wilhelm Johannes 1929- ... 65-68
Schwarz-Bart, Andre 1928- ... 89-92
See also CLC 2, 4
Schwarz-Bart, Simone 1938- ... 97-100
See also CLC 7
Schwarzenberger, Georg 1908- ... 13-14R
Schwarzenegger, Arnold 1947- ... CANR-21
Earlier sketch in CA 81-84
Schwarzkopf, LeRoy C(arl) 1920- ... 115
Schwarzkopf-Legge, Elisabeth 1915- ... 109
Schwarzschild, Bettina 1925- ... 29-32R
Schwarzschild, Stuart 1918- ... 7-8R
Schwarzweller, Harry K(arl) 1929- ... 37-40R
Schwebel, Milton 1914- ... 19-20R
Schwebel, Stephen M(yron) 1929- ... 77-80
Schwebell, Gertrude C(lorius) ... 9-10R
Schwed, Peter 1911- ... CANR-13
Earlier sketch in CA 57-60
Schweid, Eliezer 1929- ... CANR-18
Earlier sketches in CA 45-48, CANR-1
Schweid, Richard M. 1946- ... 106
Schweik, Robert C(harles) 1927- ... 45-48
Schweitzer, Albert 1875-1965 Obituary ... 93-96
Schweitzer, Arthur 1905- ... 11-12R
Schweitzer, Byrd Baylor
See Baylor, Byrd
Schweitzer, Christoph E(ugen) 1922-
Brief entry ... 107
Schweitzer, Darrell 1952- ... 116
Schweitzer, George K(eene) 1924- ... 17-18R
Schweitzer, Gertrude 1909- ... 85-88
Schweitzer, Iris Brief entry ... 117
See also SATA 36
Schweitzer, Jerome William 1908- ... 41-44R
Schweitzer, John C. 1934- ... 19-20R
Schweizer(-Hanhart), Eduard 1913- ... CANR-20
Earlier sketches in CA 13-14R, CANR-5
Schwendeman, J(oseph) R(aymond)
1897- ... 81-84
Schweninger, Ann 1951- ... 107
See also SATA 29
Schweninger, Loren (Lance) 1941- ... 101
Schwerin, Doris H(alpern) 1922- ... CANR-9
Earlier sketch in CA 65-68
Schwerin, Kurt 1902- ... 45-48
Schwerner, Armand 1927- ... 11-12R
Schwiebert, Ernest G(eorge) 1895- ... CAP-1
Earlier sketch in CA 15-16
Schwieder, Dorothy 1933- ... 89-92
Schwitzgebel, Robert L. 1934- ... 41-44R
Schwob, (Mayer Andre) Marcel
1867-1905 Brief entry ... 117
See also TCLC 20
Schwoerer, Lois G(reen) 1927- ... CANR-15
Earlier sketch in CA 77-80
Schydlowsky, Daniel M(oses) 1940- ... 45-48
Scialiano, Robert (G.) 1925- ... 11-12R
Sciascia, Leonardo 1921- ... 85-88
See also CLC 8, 9, 41
Scibor-Rylski, Aleksander 1927(?)-1983
Obituary ... 109
Scicluna, Hannibal Publius 1880-1981(?)
Obituary ... 106
Scifres, Bill(y N.) 1925- ... 103
Scipio
See Watson, (John Hugh) Adam
Scire
See Gardner, G(erald) B(rosseau)
Scism, Carol K. 1931- ... 41-44R
Scithers, George H(arry) 1929- ... 57-60
Scitovsky, Tibor 1910- ... 104
Scoales, William 1933- ... 33-36R
Scobel, Donald N. 1929- ... 122
Scobey, Joan 1927- ... CANR-7
Earlier sketch in CA 57-60
Scobey, Mary-Margaret 1915- ... CANR-1
Earlier sketch in CA 4R
Scobie, James R(alston) 1929-1981 ... CANR-6
Obituary ... 104
Earlier sketch in CA 11-12R
Scobie, Stephen 1943- ... 111
Scoby, Donald R(ay) 1931- ... 33-36R
Scofield, Jonathan
See Levinson, Leonard
and Rothweiler, Paul Roger
and Toombs, John
Scofield, Norma Margaret Cartwright
1924- ... 103
Scofield, William H. 1915- ... 19-20R
Scoggin, Margaret C(lara)
1905-1968 ... SATA-28, 47
Scoggins, James (Lawrence) 1934- ... 21-22R
Scoles, Eugene F(rancis) 1921- ... CANR-15
Earlier sketch in CA 37-40R
Scollan, E. A.
See O'Grady, Anne
Scolnick, Sylvan 1930(?)-1976 Obituary ... 69-72
Scopes, John T. 1900-1970 Obituary ... 29-32R
Scoppettone, Sandra 1936- ... 7-8R
See also SATA 9
See also CLC 26
Scorer, Richard 1919- ... 77-80
Scorsese, Martin 1942- ... 114
Brief entry ... 110
See also CLC 20
Scortia, Thomas N(icholas) 1926-1986 ... CANR-6
Obituary ... 119
Earlier sketch in CA 3R
Scorza, Manuel 1928-1983 Obituary ... 113
Scot, Chesman
See Bulmer, (Henry) Kenneth
Scotford, John Ryland 1888-1976 ... 7-8R
Obituary ... 103
Scotland, Andrew 1905- ... 7-8R
Scotland, James 1917-1983 ... 33-36R
Obituary ... 110
Scotland, Jay
See Jakes, John (William)
Scotson, John L(loyd) 1928- ... 21-22R
Scott, A(dolphe) C(larence) 1909- ... CANR-2
Earlier sketch in CA 7-8R
Scott, Alexander 1920- ... 105
Scott, Allen John 1938- ... 97-100
Scott, Amoret (Scudamore) 1930- ... CANR-10
Earlier sketch in CA 21-22R
Scott, Andrew M(acKay) 1922- ... 19-20R
Scott, Ann Herbert 1926- ... 21-22R
See also SATA 29
Scott, Anne Firor 1921- ... 33-36R
Scott, Anthony
See Dresser, Davis
Scott, Anthony Dalton 1923- ... CANR-11
Earlier sketch in CA 65-68
Scott, Arthur Finley 1907- ... CANR-18
Earlier sketches in CA 7-8R, CANR-2
Scott, Arthur L(incoln) 1914- ... 23-24R
Scott, Austin (Wakeman) 1885(?)-1981
Obituary ... 103
Scott, Bill 1920(?)-1985 Obituary ... 117
See also SATA 46
Scott, Bonnie Kime 1944- ... 119
Scott, C(atharine) A(my) Dawson
See Dawson-Scott, C(atharine) A(my)
Scott, C(ecil) Winfield 1905- ... 7-8R
Scott, Casey
See Kubis, Pat
Scott, Cecil Alexander 1902(?)-1981
Obituary ... 104
Scott, Charles R(alph), Jr. 1914- ... CANR-16
Earlier sketch in CA 89-92
Scott, Charles T. 1932- ... 21-22R
Scott, Charles W(esley) 1932- ... 116
Scott, Christopher 1930- ... 21-22R
Scott, Claudia 1948-1979 Obituary ... 114
Scott, Clinton Lee 1890- ... CAP-2
Earlier sketch in CA 19-20
Scott, Cora Annett (Pipitone) 1931- ... 17-18R
See also SATA 11
Scott, Cyril (Meir) 1879-1970 Obituary ... 111
Scott, Dan ... CAP-2
Earlier sketch in CA 19-20
Scott, Dan
See Barker, S. Omar
Scott, Dana
See Robertson, Constance (Pierrepont
Noyes)
Scott, David (Aubrey) 1919- ... 109
Scott, David W(infield) 1916- ... 109
Scott, Denise ... 114
Scott, Donald F(letcher) 1930- ... 89-92
Scott, Dorothea Hayward ... 93-96
Scott, Duncan Campbell 1862-1947
Brief entry ... 104
See also TCLC 6
Scott, Edward M. 1919- ... 33-36R
Scott, Elaine 1940- ... CANR-21
Earlier sketch in CA 105
See also SATA 36
Scott, Eleanor 1921- ... 61-64
Scott, Ellis L(averne) 1915- ... 49-52
Scott, Eve
See Rodgers, Joann Ellison
Scott, Evelyn 1893-1963 ... 104
Obituary ... 112
See also DLB 9, 48
See also CLC 43
Scott, F(rancis) R(eginald) 1899-1985 ... 101
Obituary ... 114
See also CLC 22
Scott, Frances V.
See Wing, Frances (Scott)
Scott, Frank
See Scott, F(rancis) R(eginald)
Scott, Franklin D(aniel) 1901- ... CANR-5
Earlier sketch in CA 7-8R
Scott, Gavin 1936- ... 77-80
Scott, Geoffrey 1952- ... 106
Scott, George (Edwin) 1925- ... 29-32R
Scott, George Walton 1921- ... 23-24R
Scott, Harold George 1925- ... 61-64
Scott, Harold Richard 1887- ... 7-8R
Scott, Harold W(illiam) 1906- ... 118
Scott, Harvey W. 1838-1910 ... DLB-23
Scott, Helen G. 1915(?)-1987 Obituary ... 124
Scott, Herbert 1931- ... CANR-6
Earlier sketch in CA 53-56
Scott, Hilda 1915- ... 124
Scott, Ira O(scar), Jr. 1918- ... 19-20R
Scott, J(ohn) D(ick) 1917-1980 ... 77-80
Obituary ... 97-100
Scott, J(ohn) Irving E(lias) ... 73-76
Scott, J(ames) M(aurice) 1906-1986 ... 105
Obituary ... 118
Scott, Jack B(rown) 1928- ... 77-80
Scott, Jack Denton 1915- ... 108
See also SATA 31
Scott, Jack S.
See Escott, Jonathan
Scott, James A. 1946- ... 123
Scott, James B(urton) 1926- ... 85-88
Scott, James C(ampbell) 1936- ... 29-32R
Scott, James Frazier 1934- ... CANR-22
Earlier sketch in CA 77-80
Scott, Jane
See McElfresh, (Elizabeth) Adeline
Scott, Jean
See Muir, Marie
Scott, Jeffrey
See Usher, Shaun
Scott, Jeremy
See Dick, Kay
Scott, Joanna 1960- ... 126
See also CLC 50
Scott, Jody ... 81-84
Scott, John 1912-1976 ... CANR-6
Obituary ... 69-72
Earlier sketch in CA 7-8R
See also SATA 14
Scott, John (Peter) 1949- ... 126
Scott, John Anthony 1916- ... CANR-23
Earlier sketches in CA 11-12R, CANR-6
See also SATA 23
Scott, John M(artin) 1913- ... CANR-25
Earlier sketches in CA 65-68, CANR-10
See also SATA 12
Scott, Johnie Harold 1946- ... CANR-14
Earlier sketch in CA 33-36R
Scott, (Henry) Joseph 1917- ... 57-60
Scott, Joseph Reid 1926- ... 41-44R
Scott, Judith Unger 1916- ... 5-6R
Scott, Justin ... CANR-26
Earlier sketch in CA 104
Scott, Kenneth 1900- ... CANR-26
Earlier sketches in CA 69-72, CANR-11
Scott, Kenneth J. 1933(?)-1983 Obituary ... 111
Scott, Lalla (McIntosh) 1893- ... CAP-2
Earlier sketch in CA 21-22
Scott, Latayne Colvett 1952- ... CANR-17
Earlier sketch in CA 97-100
Scott, Lauren
See Frentzen, Jeffrey
Scott, Laurence Prestwich 1909-1983
Obituary ... 110
Scott, Lloyd
See Turner, George E(ugene)
Scott, Lloyd F. 1926- ... 23-24R
Scott, Louise Binder 1910- ... CANR-4
Earlier sketch in CA 4R
Scott, Marcia (Adele Morse) 1943- ... 97-100
Scott, Margaret B(rodie) ?-1976 Obituary ... 61-64
Scott, Martin
See Gehman, Richard (Boyd)
Scott, Marvin B(ailey) 1944- Brief entry ... 118
Scott, Mel(lier Goodin) 1906- ... 29-32R
Scott, (Guthrie) Michael 1907-1983
Obituary ... 110
Scott, Natalie Anderson 1906- ... CAP-2
Earlier sketch in CA 23-24
Scott, Nathan A(lexander), Jr. 1925- ... CANR-20
Earlier sketches in CA 9-10R, CANR-5
See also BW
Scott, Nerissa
See Ring, Elizabeth
Scott, Norford
See Rowland, D(onald) S(ydney)
Scott, Otto J. 1918- ... 85-88
Scott, Owen Le Grand 1898-1985
Obituary ... 117
Scott, P. T.
See Poage, Scott T(abor)
Scott, Patrick (Greig) 1945- ... 112
Scott, Paul (Mark) 1920-1978 ... 81-84
Obituary ... 77-80
See also DLB 14
See also CLC 9
Scott, Peter (Markham) 1909- ... 101
Scott, Peter Dale 1929- ... CANR-9
Earlier sketch in CA 21-22R
Scott, Peter Graham
See Graham Scott, Peter
Scott, R(obert) B(algarnie) Y(oung)
1899-1987 Obituary ... 124
Scott, Rachel (Ann) 1947- ... 103
Scott, Ralph S(amuel) 1927- ... 41-44R
Scott, Richard A(llen) 1931- ... 25-28R
Scott, Robert A. 1936- ... 89-92
Scott, Robert Adrian 1901(?)-1972
Obituary ... 37-40R
Scott, Robert E(dwin) 1923- ... CANR-1
Earlier sketch in CA 1R
Scott, Robert F(alcon) 1868-1912
Brief entry ... 115
Scott, Robert Haney 1927- ... 17-18R
Scott, Robert Ian 1931- ... 106
Scott, Robert Lee 1928- ... CANR-3
Earlier sketch in CA 5-6R
Scott, Robert Lee, Jr. 1908- ... CAP-1
Earlier sketch in CA 11-12
Scott, Robin
See Wilson, Robin Scott
Scott, Roger (Dennis) 1939- ... 97-100
Scott, Ronald Bodley 1906-1982 ... 109
Obituary ... 106
Scott, Ronald (Guthrie) McNair
See McNair Scott, Ronald (Guthrie)
Scott, Roney
See Gault, William Campbell
Scott, Roy Vernon 1927- ... CANR-1
Earlier sketch in CA 4R
Scott, Sally 1909-1978 ... 116
See also SATA 43
Scott, Sally (Elisabeth) 1948- ... 125
See also SATA 44
Scott, Sarah 1723-1795 ... DLB-39
Scott, Sheila (Christine) 1927-1988 ... 53-56
Obituary ... 126
Scott, Sir Walter 1771-1832 ... YABC-2
Scott, Stanley
See Fagerstrom, Stan
Scott, Stephen E. 1948- ... 119
Scott, Steve
See Crawford, William (Elbert)
Scott, Stuart
See Aitken, W(illiam) R(ussell)

Scott, Tirsa Saavedra 1920- ... 13-14R
Scott, Tom 1918- ... 9-10R
See also DLB 27
Scott, Valerie
See Rowland, D(onald) S(ydney)
Scott, Virgil (Joseph) 1914- ... CANR-2
Earlier sketch in CA 7-8R
Scott, Virginia M(uhleman) 1945- ... 121
Scott, W(illiam) E(dgar), Jr. 1929- ... 49-52
Scott, W(illiam) Richard 1932- ... 19-20R
Scott, Warwick
See Trevor, Elleston
Scott, Willard H., Jr. 1934- ... 109
Scott, William Abbott 1926- ... CANR-9
Earlier sketch in CA 7-8R
Scott, William B(utler) 1945- ... 126
Scott, William Bell 1811-1890 ... DLB-32
Scott, William C(lyde) 1937- ... 119
Scott, William G(eorge) 1926- ... CANR-11
Earlier sketch in CA 23-24R
Scott, William R(eese) 1907- ... 77-80
Scott, William R(alph) 1918- ... 101
Scott, Wilson L(udlow) 1909-1983 ... 45-48
Obituary ... 111
Scott, Winfield H(arker) 1932- ... 21-22R
Scott, Winfield Townley 1910-1968 ... CANR-7
Obituary ... 25-28R
Earlier sketch in CA 7-8R
Scott-Giles, C(harles) W(ilfred)
1893-1982(?) Obituary ... 106
Scott-Heron, Gil 1949- ... CANR-24
Earlier sketch in CA 45-48
See also BW
See also DLB 41
Scotti, Paul C(arl) 1943- ... 118
Scotti, R. A. 1946- ... 122
Scott-James, Anne Eleanor 1913- ... 105
Scott-Moncrieff, David (William Hardy)
1907-1987 Obituary ... 123
Scott-Moncrieff, George (Irving) 1910- ... CAP-1
Earlier sketch in CA 11-12
Scott Moncrieff, Martha Christian 1897- ... 61-64
Scotto, Robert M(ichael) 1942- ... 57-60
Scott-Stokes, Henry J.M. Brief entry ... 117
Scott-Taggart, John 1897-1979 Obituary ... 104
Scott Thorn, Ronald
See Wilkinson, Ronald
Scout, Ted
See Brand, Kurt
Scouten, Arthur Hawley 1910- ... CANR-11
Earlier sketches in CA 13-14, CAP-1
Scovel, Myra (Scott) 1905- ... CANR-2
Earlier sketch in CA 7-8R
Scovell, Jane (Frances) 1934- ... 116
Scoville, Herbert, Jr. 1915-1985 ... 29-32R
Obituary ... 116
Scoville, James G(riffin) 1940- ... 29-32R
Scoville, Warren Candler 1913-1969 ... CANR-2
Earlier sketch in CA 4R
Scowcroft, Richard P(ingree) 1916- ... 11-12R
Scriabine, Helen (Gorstrine) 1906- ... CANR-14
Earlier sketch in CA 23-24R
Scribner, Charles III 1951- ... 126
Scribner, Charles, Jr. 1921- ... 69-72
See also SATA 13
Scribner, Joanne L. 1949- ... SATA-33
Scrimgeour, Gary J(ames) 1934- ... 108
Scrimshaw, Nevin Stewart 1918- ... 89-92
Scrimsher, Lila Gravatt 1897-1974 ... 4R
Obituary ... 103
See also SATA 28
Scripps, E(dward) W(yllis) 1854-1926
Brief entry ... 118
See also DLB 25
Scripps, James G. 1911-1986 Obituary ... 121
Scriven, Michael (John) 1928- ... CANR-14
Earlier sketch in CA 21-22R
Scriver, Bob
See Scriver, Robert MacFie
Scriver, Robert MacFie 1914- ... 115
Scrivner, Wilma Possien 1915- ... 107
Scroggins, Daniel C(oy) 1937- ... 33-36R
Scroggs, Robin (Jerome) 1930- ... 116
Scruggs, C(harles) Eugene 1937- ... 113
Scrum, R.
See Crumb, R(obert)
Scruton, Roger 1944- ... CANR-16
Earlier sketch in CA 89-92
Scudder, C(leo) W(ayne) 1915- ... CANR-3
Earlier sketch in CA 1R
Scudder, Horace E(lisha) 1838-1902
Brief entry ... 119
See also DLB 42, 71
Scudder, Kenyon J. 1890-1977 Obituary ... 73-76
Scudder, Mildred Lee 1908- ... 9-10R
Scudder, Rogers V(aughn) 1912- ... 19-20R
Scudder, Thayer 1930- ... 126
Brief entry ... 106
Scudder, Townsend (III) 1900-1988
Obituary ... 126
Scudder, Vida Dutton 1861-1954 ... DLB-71
Sculatti, (Eu)Gene 1947- ... 110
Scull, Andrew 1947- ... CANR-15
Earlier sketch in CA 81-84
Scull, Florence Doughty 1905- ... CAP-1
Earlier sketch in CA 11-12
Scullard, Howard Hayes 1903-1983 ... CANR-3
Obituary ... 109
Earlier sketch in CA 11-12R
Scully, Frank 1892-1964 ... 7-8R
Scully, Gerald William 1941- ... 65-68
Scully, James 1937- ... CANR-11
Earlier sketch in CA 25-28R
Scully, Julia S(ilverman) 1929- ... 103
Scully, Vincent (Joseph, Jr.) 1920-
Brief entry ... 113
Scum
See Crumb, R(obert)
Scumbag, Little Bobby
See Crumb, R(obert)
Scuorzo, Herbert E(rnest) 1928- ... 23-24R
Scupham, John Peter 1933- ... CANR-9
Earlier sketch in CA 65-68
See also DLB 40
Scuro, Vincent 1951- ... CANR-5
Earlier sketch in CA 53-56
See also SATA 21
Scutt, Ronald 1916- ... 97-100
Seaberg, Stanley 1929- ... 21-22R
Seaborg, Glenn T(heodore) 1912- ... CANR-2
Earlier sketch in CA 49-52
Seabough, Ed(ward Ellis) 1932- ... 29-32R
Seabrook, Jeremy 1939- ... 108
Seabrook, John
See Hubbard, L(afayette) Ron(ald)
Seabrook, William B(uehler) 1886-1945
Brief entry ... 107
See also DLB 4
Seabrooke, Brenda 1941- ... 107
See also SATA 30
Seabury, Paul 1923- Brief entry ... 115
Seabury, Samuel 1729-1796 ... DLB-31
Seagears, Clayton B. 1902(?)-1983
Obituary ... 110
Seager, Allan 1906-1968 ... 7-8R
Obituary ... 25-28R
Seager, Ralph William 1911- ... CANR-6
Earlier sketch in CA 11-12R
Seager, Robert II 1924- ... CANR-6
Earlier sketch in CA 7-8R
Seager, Walter H(arold) T(ennant) 1938- ... 120
Seagle, Janet 1924- ... 102
Seagle, William 1898-1977 ... 7-8R
Obituary ... 73-76
Seagoe, May V(iolet) 1906-1980 ... CANR-10
Earlier sketch in CA 15-16R
Seagrave, Sterling 1937- Brief entry ... 125
Seagroatt, Margaret 1920- ... CANR-13
Earlier sketch in CA 73-76
Seagull, Louis Martin 1941- ... 112
Seal, Anil 1938- ... 25-28R
Seal, Basil
See Kavanagh, Dan(iel)
Seale, Bobby
See Seale, Robert George
Seale, Patrick 1930- ... 97-100
Seale, Robert George 1936- ... 110
See also BW
Seale, William 1939- ... CANR-7
Earlier sketch in CA 19-20R
Sealey, Bruce
See Sealey, D(onald) Bruce
Sealey, D(onald) Bruce 1929- ... 121
Sealey, Danguole 1931- ... 33-36R
Sealey, Leonard (George William) 1923- ... 103
Sealey, (Bertram) Raphael (Izod) 1927- ... 65-68
Sea-Lion
See Bennett, Geoffrey (Martin)
Sealock, Richard Burl 1907- ... CAP-2
Earlier sketch in CA 23-24
Sealts, Merton M(iller), Jr. 1915- ... 13-14R
Seaman, Augusta Huiell 1879-1950
Brief entry ... 110
See also SATA 31
Seaman, Barbara 1935- ... 29-32R
Seaman, (A.) Barrett 1945- ... 73-76
Seaman, Don F(erris) 1935- ... 77-80
Seaman, Donald (Peter) 1922- Brief entry ... 114
Seaman, Elizabeth Cochrane
See Cochrane, Elizabeth
Seaman, Gerald Roberts 1934- ... 25-28R
Seaman, John E(ugene) 1932- ... 89-92
Seaman, L(ewis) C(harles) B(ernard)
1911- ... 57-60
Seaman, Sylvia S(ybil) ... CAP-2
Earlier sketch in CA 23-24
Seaman, William M(illard) 1907- ... 41-44R
Seamands, John Thompson 1916- ... 11-12R
Seamands, Ruth 1916- ... 45-48
See also SATA 9
Sear, Frank 1944- ... 121
Seara Vazquez, M(odesto) 1931- ... CANR-14
Earlier sketch in CA 17-18R
Search, Alexander
See Pessoa, Fernando (Antonio Nogueira)
Search-Light
See Frank, Waldo (David)
Searcy, Margaret Zehmer 1926- ... 81-84
See also SATA 39
Seare, Nicholas
See Whitaker, Rod
Searight, Mary W(illiams) 1918- ... 29-32R
See also SATA 17
Searing, Helen E. 1933- ... 111
Searing, Susan Ellis 1950- ... 122
Searle, Humphrey 1915-1982 ... 9-10R
Obituary ... 106
Searle, John R(ogers) 1932- ... CANR-26
Earlier sketch in CA 25-28R
Searle, Kathryn Adrienne 1942- ... 29-32R
See also SATA 10
Searle, Leroy F(rank) 1942- ... 73-76
Searle, Mark 1941- ... 114
Searle, Ronald (William Fordham)
1920- ... CANR-25
Earlier sketch in CA 9-10R
See also SATA 42
Searles, (William) Baird 1934- ... 123
Searles, Herbert L(eon) 1891- ... 45-48
Searls, Hank
See Searls, Henry Hunt, Jr.
Searls, Henry Hunt, Jr. 1922- ... 15-16R
Sears, David O'Keefe 1935- ... 29-32R
Sears, Deane
See Rywell, Martin
Sears, Donald A(lbert) 1923- ... CANR-6
Earlier sketch in CA 7-8R
Sears, Francis W. 1898-1975 Obituary ... 61-64
Sears, Hal D(on) 1942- ... 122
Sears, Paul Bigelow 1891- ... 17-18R
Sears, Paul M(cCutcheon) 1920- ... 1R
Sears, Pauline Snedden 1908- ... 29-32R
Sears, Peter 1937- ... 110
Sears, Robert R(ichardson) 1908- ... 17-18R
Sears, Sallie 1932- ... 41-44R
Sears, Stephen W. 1932- ... 33-36R
See also SATA 4
Sears, Val 1927- ... 73-76
Sears, William P(aul), Jr. 1902-1976
Obituary ... 61-64
Seary, E(dgar) R(onald) 1908- ... 41-44R
Seashore, Stanley E. 1915- ... CANR-24
Earlier sketch in CA 33-36R
Seasoltz, R(obert) Kevin 1930- ... 11-12R
Seasongood, Murray 1878-1983 Obituary ... 109
Seat, William R(obert), Jr. 1920- ... 13-14R
Seaton, Beryl
See Platts, Beryl
Seaton, Don Cash(ius) 1902- ... CAP-1
Earlier sketch in CA 9-10
Seaton, Douglas P(aul) 1947- ... 107
Seaton, Frederick Andrew 1909-1974
Obituary ... 89-92
Seaton, George 1911-1979 ... 105
Obituary ... 89-92
See also DLB 44
Seaton, Mary Ethel ?-1974 Obituary ... 53-56
Seaton, William Winston 1785-1866 ... DLB-43
Seaver, George (Fenn) 1890- ... CAP-1
Earlier sketch in CA 13-14
Seaver, Paul S(iddall) 1932- ... 29-32R
Seay, James 1939- ... 29-32R
Seay, Thomas A(ustin) 1942- ... 97-100
Sebald, Hans 1929- ... 73-76
Sebald, William J(oseph) 1901-1980 ... CAP-1
Obituary ... 101
Earlier sketch in CA 15-16
Sebastian, Jeanne
See Newsome, Arden J(eanne)
Sebastian, Lee
See Silverberg, Robert
Sebastian, Margaret
See Gladstone, Arthur M.
Sebastian Owl
See Thompson, Hunter S(tockton)
Sebenthall, R(oberta) E(lizabeth) 1917- ... 33-36R
Sebeok, Thomas A(lbert) 1920- ... 11-12R
Seberg, Jean 1938-1979 Obituary ... 89-92
Sebesta, Sam L(eaton) 1930- ... 85-88
Sebestyen, Gyorgy 1930- ... CANR-6
Earlier sketch in CA 9-10R
Sebestyen, Ouida 1924- ... 107
See also SATA 39
See also CLC 30
Seboldt, Roland H(enry) A(ugust) 1924- ... 7-8R
Sebree, Charles 1914-1985 Obituary ... 117
Sebrey, Mary Ann 1951- ... 116
Secher, Bjorn 1929- ... 33-36R
Sechrest, Lee 1929- ... 19-20R
Sechrist, Elizabeth Hough 1903- ... 7-8R
See also SATA 2
Seckel, Al 1958- ... 122
Seckler, David William 1935- ... 115
Secombe, Harry (Donald) 1921- ... 57-60
Secondari, John Hermes 1919-1975 ... 61-64
Obituary ... 57-60
Secor, Robert 1939- ... CANR-15
Earlier sketch in CA 89-92
Secrest, Meryle
See Beveridge, Meryle Secrest
Secrist, Margaret C(rystal) 1905- ... 111
Secunda, Sholom 1894-1974 Obituary ... 49-52
Sedaka, Neil 1939- ... 103
Sederberg, Arelo Charles 1930- ... 37-40R
Sederberg, Peter C(arl) 1943- ... 65-68
Sedges, John
See Buck, Pearl S(ydenstricker)
Sedgewick, Ellery 1872-1960 Obituary ... 89-92
Sedgwick, Alexander 1930- ... 19-20R
Sedgwick, Arthur George 1844-1915 ... DLB-64
Sedgwick, Catharine Maria
1789-1867 ... DLB-1, 74
Sedgwick, Jeffrey Leigh 1951- ... 116
Sedgwick, Michael Carl 1926-1983 ... 89-92
Obituary ... 111
Sedgwick, Peter 1934-1983 Obituary ... 110
Sedgwick, Walter (Bradbary) 1885- ... CAP-1
Earlier sketch in CA 13-14
Sedlacek, William E(dward) 1939- ... 69-72
Sedler, Robert Allen 1935- ... 41-44R
Seduro, Vladimir 1910- ... 41-44R
Sedwick, B(enjamin) Frank 1924- ... 9-10R
Sedych, Andrei
See Zwibak, Jacques
See, Carolyn (Penelope) 1934- ... CANR-25
Earlier sketch in CA 29-32R
See, (Nadine) Ingram 1904- ... 112
See, Lisa
See Kendall, Lisa See
See, Ruth Douglas 1910- ... CANR-1
Earlier sketch in CA 4R
Seeber, Edward Derbyshire 1904- ... 15-16R
Seeber, Gerd Christian 1941- ... 113
Seebohm, Caroline 1940- ... 102
Seebord, G. R.
See Soderberg, Percy Measday
Seed, Cecile Eugenie 1930- ... CANR-26
Earlier sketches in CA 21-22R, CANR-10
Seed, Jenny
See Seed, Cecile Eugenie
See also SATA 8
Seed, Sheila Turner 1937(?)-1979
Obituary ... 89-92
See also SATA 23
Seedman, Albert A. 1918- Brief entry ... 112
Seeger, Alan 1888-1916 ... DLB-45
Seeger, Charles Louis 1886-1979 ... 101
Obituary ... 85-88
Seeger, Elizabeth 1889-1973 Obituary ... 45-48
See also SATA 20
Seeger, Pete(r R.) 1919- ... 69-72
See also SATA 13
Seegers, Kathleen Walker 1915- ... 23-24R
Seeley, John R(onald) 1913- ... 25-28R
Seelhammer, Ruth 1917- ... 41-44R
Seelig, Sharon Cadman 1941- ... 119
Seely, Gordon M. 1930- ... 37-40R
Seely, Norma 1942- ... 113
Seely, Rebecca Z(ahm) 1935- ... 104
Seelye, H(ugh) Ned 1934- ... 102
Seelye, John 1931- ... CLC-7
Seelye, John (Douglas) 1931- ... 97-100
Seeman, Bernard 1911- ... 23-24R
Seeman, Elizabeth (Brickel) 1904- ... CAP-1
Earlier sketch in CA 19-20
Seeman, Ernest Albright 1887- ... 85-88
Seers, Dudley 1920-1983 Obituary ... 109
Seese, Ethel Gray 1903- ... 89-92
Seever, R.
See Reeves, Lawrence F.
Seferiades, Giorgos Stylianou
1900-1971 ... CANR-5
Obituary ... 33-36R
Earlier sketch in CA 5-6R
Seferis, George
See Seferiades, Giorgos Stylianou
See also CLC 5, 11
Sefler, George Francis 1945- ... 81-84
Sefton, Catherine
See Waddell, Martin
Sefton, James E(dward) 1939- ... 21-22R
Segal, Abraham 1911(?)-1977 Obituary ... 69-72
Segal, Alan F(ranklin) 1945- ... 119
Segal, Charles Paul 1936- ... CANR-16
Earlier sketch in CA 41-44R
Segal, David I. 1928(?)-1970 Obituary ... 104
Segal, David R(obert) 1941- ... 111
Segal, Elliot A(lan) 1938- ... 93-96
Segal, Erich (Wolf) 1937- ... CANR-20
Earlier sketch in CA 25-28R
See also DLBY 86
See also CLC 3, 10
Segal, Fred 1924(?)-1976 ... 69-72
Obituary ... 65-68
Segal, Gerald 1953- ... 117
Segal, Geraldine R(osenbaum) 1908- ... 113
Segal, Hanna M(aria) 1918- ... 101
Segal, Harold S. 1903- ... 29-32R
Segal, Harriet 1931- ... 123
Segal, Harvey H(irst) 1922- ... 4R
Segal, Henry 1901(?)-1985 Obituary ... 116
Segal, Jeanne (Sandra) 1939- ... 108
Segal, Joyce 1940- ... 101
See also SATA 35
Segal, Julius 1924- Brief entry ... 112
Segal, Lore (Groszmann) 1928- ... CANR-5
Earlier sketch in CA 15-16R
See also SATA 4
Segal, Marilyn 1927- ... CANR-23
Earlier sketches in CA 19-20R, CANR-8
Segal, Martin ... CANR-1
Earlier sketch in CA 4R
Segal, Melvin J(ames) 1910- ... 37-40R
Segal, Mendel 1914- ... 49-52
Segal, Muriel 1913- ... 121
Segal, Robert M. 1925- ... 29-32R
Segal, Ronald (Michael) 1932- ... CANR-14
Earlier sketch in CA 21-22R
Segal, S(tanley) S. 1919- ... 25-28R
Segalman, Ralph 1916- ... 106
Segel, Harold B(ernard) 1930- ... 23-24R
Segel, Thomas D(onald) 1931- ... 93-96
Seger, Bob 1945- ... CLC-35
Segerberg, Osborn, Jr. 1924- ... 115
Segger, Sydney Walter 1902-19(?) ... CAP-1
Earlier sketch in CA 15-16
Seghers
See Radvanyi, Netty
Seghers, Anna
See Radvanyi, Netty
See also DLB 69
See also CLC 7
Segler, Franklin Morgan 1907- ... 19-20R
Segovia, Andres 1893(?)-1987 Obituary ... 122
Brief entry ... 111
See also SATA 52
Segrave, Edmond 1904-1971 Obituary ... 29-32R
Segraves, Kelly L(ee) 1942- ... CANR-13
Earlier sketch in CA 61-64
Segre, Claudio Giuseppe 1937- ... 53-56
Segre, Dan V(ittorio) 1922- ... 104
Segre, Emilio (Gino) 1905- ... CANR-13
Earlier sketch in CA 33-36R
Segundo, Bart
See Rowland, D(onald) S(ydney)
Segy, Ladislas 1904- ... 45-48
Seib, Kenneth Allen 1938- ... 29-32R
Seibel, C(lifford) W(inslow) 1890- ... CAP-2
Earlier sketch in CA 25-28
Seibel, Hans Dieter 1941- ... CANR-11
Earlier sketch in CA 65-68
Seid, Ruth 1913- ... 5-6R
Seide, Diane 1930- ... CANR-14
Earlier sketch in CA 73-76
Seide, Michael 1911- ... 111

Seidel, Frederick (Lewis) 1936- ... CANR-8
Earlier sketch in CA 15-16R
See also DLBY 84
See also CLC 18
Seidel, George J(oseph) 1932- ... 15-16R
Seidel, Ina 1885-1974 Obituary ... 116
See also DLB 56
Seidel, Kathleen G(illes) 1951- ... 112
Seidel, Michael Alan 1943- ... 93-96
Seidelman, James Edward 1926- ... 25-28R
See also SATA 6
Seiden, Art(hur) ... SATA-42
Seiden, Martin H. 1934- ... 15-16R
Seiden, Morton Irving 1921- ... 19-20R
Seidenbaum, Art(hur) 1930- ... 29-32R
Seidenberg, Robert 1920- ... 25-28R
Seidenberg, Roderick 1890(?)-1973
Obituary ... 45-48
Seidensticker, Edward G. 1921- ... 89-92
Seidick, Kathryn A(melia) 1943- ... 108
Seidler, Ann (G.) 1925- ... 25-28R
Seidler, Grzegorz Leopold 1913- ... CANR-12
Earlier sketch in CA 29-32R
Seidler, Lee J. 1935- ... 73-76
Seidler, Murray Benjamin 1924- ... 5-6R
Seidler, Tor 1952- ... 123
See also SATA 46, 52
Seidlin, Oskar 1911- ... 41-44R
Seidman, Ann (Willcox) 1926- ... 81-84
Seidman, Harold 1911- ... 29-32R
Seidman, Hugh 1940- ... 29-32R
Seidman, Jerome M(artin) 1911- ... 45-48
Seidman, Joel 1906- ... CANR-9
Earlier sketch in CA 5-6R
Seidman, Laurence Ivan 1925- ... 77-80
See also SATA 15
Seidman, Robert J(erome) 1941- ... 73-76
Seidmann, Ginette
See Spanier, Ginette
Seidner, Diane
See Seide, Diane
Seiferheld, Alfredo M. 1950-1988
Obituary ... 125
Seifert, Anne 1943- ... 105
Seifert, Elizabeth
See Gasparotti, Elizabeth Seifert
Seifert, Harvey (J.D.) 1911- ... CANR-3
Earlier sketch in CA 11-12R
Seifert, Jaroslav 1901-1986 ... CLC-34, 44
Seifert, Shirley L(ouise) 1888-1971 ... CANR-2
Obituary ... 33-36R
Earlier sketch in CA 4R
Seifman, Eli 1936- ... 37-40R
Seigel, Jerrold (Edward) 1936- ... 85-88
Seigel, Jules 1931- ... 93-96
Seigel, Kalman 1917- ... 25-28R
See also SATA 12
Seigenthaler, John (Lawrence) 1927-
Brief entry ... 113
Seignobosc, Francoise 1897-1961 ... 73-76
See also SATA 21
Seignolle, Claude 1917- ... 23-24R
Seiler, John A(ndrew) 1927- ... 23-24R
Seiler, Robert E. 1925- ... 19-20R
Seilhamer, Frank Henry 1933- ... 85-88
Seim, Richard K(nudt) 1928- ... 102
Seimer, Stanley J(ames) 1918- ... 2R
Seinfel, Ruth
See Goode, Ruth
Seip, Terry Lee 1944- ... 113
Seitlin, Charlotte 1907(?)-1979 Obituary ... 89-92
Seitz, Georg J(osef) 1920- ... 13-14R
Seitz, Jacqueline 1931- ... SATA-50
Seitz, Nick 1939- ... 97-100
Seitz, William Chapin 1914-1974 ... CANR-2
Obituary ... 53-56
Earlier sketch in CA 3R
Seixas, Judith S. 1922- ... 85-88
See also SATA 17
Sejima, Yoshimasa 1913- ... 33-36R
See also SATA 8
Sejour, Victor 1817-1874 ... DLB-50
Sejour Marcou et Ferrand, Juan Victor
See Sejour, Victor
Sekers, Simone 1945- ... 119
Sekler, Eduard F(ranz) 1920- ... 69-72
Sekora, John 1939- Brief entry ... 106
Selavy, Rrose
See Duchamp, (Henri-Robert) Marcel
Selbourne, David 1937- ... CANR-16
Earlier sketch in CA 89-92
Selby, Bettina 1934- ... 117
Selby, Curt
See Piserchia, Doris (Elaine)
Selby, Donald Joseph 1915- ... CANR-24
Earlier sketch in CA 1R
Selby, Edward B(urford), Jr. 1938- ... 45-48
Selby, Hazel Barrington 1889-1972 ... CAP-2
Earlier sketch in CA 17-18
Selby, Henry A. 1934- ... 37-40R
Selby, Hubert, Jr. 1928- ... 15-16R
See also DLB 2
See also CLC 1, 2, 4, 8
Selby, James Winford III 1947- ... 108
Selby, John (Allen) 1897-1980 ... 1R
Obituary ... 97-100
Selby, John M(illin) 1905- ... 25-28R
Selcamm, George
See Machlis, Joseph
Selcher, Wayne A(lan) 1942- ... CANR-10
Earlier sketch in CA 65-68
Selden, George
See Thompson, George Selden
See also DLB 52
See also CLR 8
Selden, Mark 1938- ... 81-84
Selden, Neil R(oy) 1931- ... 106
Selden, Samuel 1899-1979 ... CANR-3
Earlier sketch in CA 1R
Selden, William K(irkpatrick) 1911- ... 3R
Seldes, George (Henry) 1890- ... CANR-2
Earlier sketch in CA 7-8R
Seldes, Gilbert (Vivian) 1893-1970 ... 7-8R
Obituary ... 29-32R
Seldes, Marian (Hall) 1928- ... CANR-19
Earlier sketch in CA 85-88
Seldin, Maury 1931- ... CANR-15
Earlier sketch in CA 29-32R
Seldis, Henry 1925-1978 Obituary ... 77-80
Seldon, James R(alph) 1944- ... 112
Seldon, Mary Elisabeth 1921- ... 37-40R
Seldon-Truss, Leslie 1892- ... 7-8R
Selegen, Galina V(assily) 1899- ... 41-44R
Selement, George Joseph 1946- ... 113
Self, Carolyn Shealy 1931- ... CANR-16
Earlier sketch in CA 93-96
Self, Edwin F(orbes) 1920- ... 69-72
Self, Huber 1914- ... 73-76
Self, Jerry M(arvin) 1938- ... 61-64
Self, Margaret Cabell 1902- ... CANR-3
Earlier sketch in CA 7-8R
See also SATA 24
Self, Peter J(ohn) O(tter) 1919- ... 120
Self, William L(ee) 1932- ... 122
Selg, Herbert 1935- ... 69-72
Selig, Elaine Booth 1935- ... 104
Selig, Sylvie 1942- ... SATA-13
Seligman, Barnard 1923- ... 113
Seligman, Ben B(aruch) 1912-1970 ... CANR-2
Obituary ... 29-32R
Earlier sketch in CA 4R
Seligman, Daniel 1924- Brief entry ... 113
Seligman, Edwin R. A. 1861-1939 ... DLB-47
Seligman, Eustace 1889(?)-1976
Obituary ... 69-72
Seligman, Germain 1893-1978 Obituary ... 77-80
Seligman, Lester George 1918- ... 13-14R
Seligman, Linda H(elen Goldberg) 1944- ... 114
Seligman, Susan Meilach 1950- ... 105
Seligmann, G(ustav) L(eonard) Jr. 1934- ... 45-48
Seligmann, Herbert J(acob) 1891-1984
Obituary ... 112
Seligmann, Nancy 1948- ... 57-60
Seligson, Mitchell A(llan) 1945- ... 119
Seligson, Tom 1946- ... 33-36R
Selimovic, Mehmed 1910-1982 Obituary ... 108
Selimovic, Mesa
See Selimovic, Mehmed
Selkirk, Jane
See Chapman, John Stanton Higham
Sell, Betty (Marie) H(aas) 1928- ... 102
Sell, Charles M(urray) 1933- ... 113
Sell, DeWitt E(llsworth) 1915- ... 4R
Sell, Francis Edmund 1902- ... 7-8R
Sell, Henry Blackman 1889-1974
Obituary ... 89-92
Sell, Joseph
See Haley, William (John)
Sell, Kenneth D(aniel) 1928- ... 102
Sell, Roger D(avid) 1944- ... 116
Sell, Ted 1928- ... 69-72
Sellen, Robert W(alker) 1930- ... 45-48
Seller, Maxine Schwartz 1935- ... 104
Sellers, Bettie M(ixon) 1926- ... 77-80
Sellers, Charles Coleman 1903-1980 ... CANR-11
Earlier sketch in CA 17-18R
Sellers, Con(nie Leslie, Jr.) 1922- ... 97-100
Sellers, James Earl 1926- ... 113
Sellers, Naomi
See Flack, Naomi John White
Sellers, Robert Victor 1894-1973 ... CAP-1
Obituary ... 89-92
Earlier sketch in CA 13-14
Sellers, Ronnie 1948- ... 115
Sellery, C. Morley 1894- ... CAP-2
Earlier sketch in CA 21-22
Sellew, Gladys 1887- ... CAP-1
Earlier sketch in CA 11-12
Sellin, Eric 1933- ... CANR-22
Earlier sketches in CA 17-18R, CANR-7
Sellin, Paul R(oland) 1930- ... 45-48
Sellings, Arthur
See Ley, Arthur Gordon
Sellman, Hunton Dade 1900- ... 7-8R
Sellman, Roger R(aymond) 1915- ... CANR-1
Earlier sketch in CA 4R
Sells, Arthur Lytton 1895- ... CANR-6
Earlier sketch in CA 7-8R
Sells, Iris (Esther) Lytton
See Lytton-Sells, Iris (Esther)
Sells, S(aul) B. 1913- ... CANR-19
Earlier sketches in CA 3R, CANR-4
Selltiz, Claire (Alice) 1914- ... 7-8R
Selmark, George
See Seldon-Truss, Leslie
Selness, Craig A(lan) 1955- ... 119
Selormey, Francis 1927- ... 21-22R
See also BW
Selsam, Howard 1903-1970 Obituary ... 29-32R
Selsam, Millicent Ellis 1912- ... CANR-5
Earlier sketch in CA 11-12R
See also SATA 1, 29
See also CLR 1
Seltzer, Alvin J(ay) 1939- ... 65-68
Seltzer, Daniel 1933-1980 ... 89-92
Obituary ... 97-100
Seltzer, David 1920(?)- Brief entry ... 110
Seltzer, George 1924- ... 73-76
Seltzer, Leon E(ugene) 1918-1988 ... 89-92
Obituary ... 124
Seltzer, Leon F(rancis) 1940- ... 33-36R
Seltzer, Louis B(enson) 1897-1980
Obituary ... 97-100
Seltzer, Meyer 1932- ... SATA-17
Seltzer, Richard (Warren, Jr.) 1946- ... 105
See also SATA 41
Selver, (Percy) Paul 1888-1970 ... CAP-2
Earlier sketch in CA 29-32
Selvin, David F(rank) 1913- ... 25-28R
Selvin, Hanan C(harles) 1921- ... 11-12R
Selvon, Sam
See Selvon, Samuel (Dickson)
Selvon, Samuel (Dickson) 1923-
Brief entry ... 117
Selwyn-Clarke, Selwyn 1893-1976
Obituary ... 65-68
Selwyn-Lloyd, John S. B. 1904-1978
Obituary ... 110
Selye, Hans 1907-1982 ... CANR-2
Obituary ... 108
Earlier sketch in CA 7-8R
Selz, Peter (Howard) 1919- ... 2R
Selzer, Joae Graham 1926- ... 53-56
Selzer, Michael (I.) 1940- ... CANR-9
Earlier sketch in CA 53-56
Selzer, Richard 1928- ... CANR-14
Earlier sketch in CA 65-68
Selznick, David O(liver) 1902-1965
Obituary ... 110
Semaan, Khalil I. H. 1920- ... 37-40R
Sembene, Ousmane
See Ousmane, Sembene
Semeiks, Jonna Gormely 1944- ... 109
Semenov, Julian Semenovich 1931- ... 85-88
Semkiw, Virlyana
See Bishop, Tania Kroitor
Semler, H. Eric 1965- ... 125
Semloh
See Holmes, Peggy
Semmel, Bernard 1928- ... 77-80
Semmelroth, Otto 1912-1979 ... CANR-10
Earlier sketch in CA 13-14R
Semmens, James P(ike) 1919- ... 61-64
Semmler, Clement (William) 1914- ... CANR-14
Earlier sketch in CA 23-24R
Semonche, John E(rwin) 1933- ... 45-48
Sempell, Charlotte 1909- ... 41-44R
Semple, Gordon
See Neubauer, William Arthur
Semple, Lorenzo, Jr. Brief entry ... 125
Semprun, Jorge 1920(?)- Brief entry ... 111
Sen, Ela
See Reid, Ela
Sen, Sudhir 1906- ... 33-36R
Sena, John F(rancis) 1940- ... 110
Sencourt, Robert
See George, Robert Esmonde Gordon
Sencourt, Robert Esmonde
See George, Robert Esmonde Gordon
Sendak, Jack ... 77-80
See also SATA 28
Sendak, Maurice (Bernard) 1928- ... CANR-11
Earlier sketch in CA 7-8R
See also SATA 1, 27
See also DLB 61
See also CLR 1
Sender, Ramon (Jose) 1902-1982 ... CANR-8
Obituary ... 105
Earlier sketch in CA 7-8R
See also CLC 8
Sendler, David A. 1938- ... 65-68
Sendrey, A(ladar) Alfred 1884- ... 15-16R
Sendy, Jean 1910-1978 ... CANR-12
Earlier sketch in CA 53-56
Senelick, Laurence P(hilip) 1942- ... CANR-22
Earlier sketch in CA 106
Senesh, Hannah 1921-1944 Brief entry ... 119
Senesi, Mauro 1931- ... 19-20R
Seng, Peter J. 1922- ... 19-20R
Senghor, Leopold Sedar 1906- ... 125
Brief entry ... 116
See also BW
Sengler, Johanna 1924- ... SATA-18
Sengstacke, John H(erman Henry) 1912- ... 101
See also BW
Sen Gupta, Pranati 1938- ... 102
Sen Gupta, Rajeswar 1908- ... CAP-1
Earlier sketch in CA 9-10
Senick, Gerard J(oseph) 1953- ... 97-100
Senior, Clarence (Ollson) 1903-1974 ... 65-68
Obituary ... 53-56
Senior, Donald 1940- ... CANR-13
Earlier sketch in CA 77-80
Senior, Isabel J(anet Couper Syme) ... CANR-9
Earlier sketch in CA 7-8R
Senior, Michael 1940- ... 103
Senior, Nancy 1941- ... 119
Senkevitch, Anatole, Jr. 1942- ... CANR-19
Earlier sketch in CA 101
Senn, Alfred Erich 1932- Brief entry ... 112
Senn, Frank C(olvin) 1943- ... 115
Senn, Fritz 1928- ... 41-44R
Senn, Milton J(ohn) E(dward) 1902- ... 81-84
Senn, Peter R(ichard) 1923- ... 33-36R
Senn, Steve 1950- ... 105
See also SATA 48
Senna, Carl 1944- ... CANR-19
Earlier sketches in CA 49-52, CANR-4
Sennett, Richard 1943- ... 73-76
Sennett, Ted 1928- ... 33-36R
Sennholz, Hans F. 1922- ... 120
Brief entry ... 118
Sensabaugh, George Frank 1906- ... CAP-1
Earlier sketch in CA 13-14
Senser, Robert A(nton) 1921- ... 5-6R
Senter, Florence H.
See Ellis, Florence Hawley
Senter, Sylvia 1921- ... 113
Sentner, David P. 1898-1975 Obituary ... 57-60
Sentner, Mary Steele 1900(?)-1983
Obituary ... 110
Seoane, Rhoda 1905- ... CAP-2
Earlier sketch in CA 25-28
Sepetys, Jonas 1901- ... 57-60
Sepheriades, Georgios
See Seferiades, Giorgos Stylianou
Sepia
See Holmvik, Oyvind
Sequoia, Anna ... 109
Serafian, Michael
See Martin, Malachi
Serafini, Anthony Louis 1945- ... 112
Serage, Nancy 1924- ... 65-68
See also SATA 10
Serb, Ann Toland 1937- ... 81-84
Serban, William M(ichael) 1949- ... 102
Serebryakova, Galina Iosifovna 1905-1980
Obituary ... 102
Seredy, Kate 1899-1975 ... 7-8R
Obituary ... 57-60
See also SATA 1, 24
See also DLB 22
See also CLR 10
Sereni, Vittorio 1913-1983 Obituary ... 109
Sereny, Gitta
See Serenyi, Gitta
Serenyi, Gitta 1923- ... 119
Serenyi, Peter 1931- ... 61-64
Serfaty, Simon 1940- ... CANR-26
Earlier sketches in CA 25-28R, CANR-10
Sergeant, (Herbert) Howard
1914-1987 ... CANR-20
Obituary ... 121
Earlier sketches in CA 7-8R, CANR-5
Sergievsky, Orest 1911-1984 Obituary ... 114
Sergio, Lisa 1905- ... 61-64
Seriel, Jerome
See Vallee, Jacques F.
Serif, Med 1924- ... 17-18R
Serig, Beverly J. 1934- ... 101
Serle, (Alan) Geoffrey 1922- ... 13-14R
Serling, Robert J(erome) 1918- ... CANR-1
Earlier sketch in CA 45-48
Serling, (Edward) Rod(man) 1924-1975 ... 65-68
Obituary ... 57-60
See also DLB 26
See also CLC 30
See also AITN 1
Serna-Maytorena, Manuel Antonio
1932- ... CANR-3
Earlier sketch in CA 45-48
Sernett, Milton C(harles) 1942- ... 61-64
Seroff, Victor I(ilyitch) 1902-1979 ... 25-28R
Obituary ... 85-88
See also SATA 12, 26
Seroka, James H. 1950- ... 124
Seroka, Jim
See Seroka, James H.
Serpieres
See Guillevic, (Eugene)
Serra, Diana
See Cary, Peggy-Jean Montgomery
Serraillier, Ian (Lucien) 1912- ... CANR-1
Earlier sketch in CA 1R
See also SATA 1
See also SAAS 3
See also CLR 2
Serrano, Napoleon Diestro Valeriano
See Valeriano, Napoleon D(iestro)
Serrano Plaja, Arturo 1909-1979 ... CANR-13
Earlier sketch in CA 29-32R
Serrifile, F. O. O.
See Holmes, William Kersley
Serron, Luis A(ugusto) 1930- ... 102
Sert, Josep Lluis 1902-1983 Obituary ... 109
Servadio, Gaia 1938- ... CANR-11
Earlier sketch in CA 25-28R
Servan-Schreiber, Jean-Jacques 1924- ... 102
Servello, Joe 1932- ... SATA-10
Serventy, Vincent (Noel) 1916- ... CANR-10
Earlier sketch in CA 65-68
Service, Elman Rogers 1915- ... 112
Service, John S(tewart) 1909- Brief entry ... 113
Service, Pamela F. 1945- ... 120
Service, Robert
See Service, Robert W(illiam)
Service, Robert W(illiam) 1874(?)-1958
Brief entry ... 115
See also SATA 20
See also TCLC 15
Servin, Manuel P(atrick) 1920- ... 37-40R
Serviss, Garrett P(utnam) 1851-1929
Brief entry ... 119
Serwadda, W(illiam) Moses 1931- ... 107
See also SATA 27
Serwer, Blanche L. 1910- ... 65-68
See also SATA 10
Serwicher, Kurt 1912-1979 Obituary ... 89-92
Seskin, Eugene P(aul) 1948- ... 89-92
Sesonske, Alexander 1917- ... 15-16R
Sessions, Kyle Cutler 1934- Brief entry ... 106
Sessions, Roger Huntington 1896-1985 ... 93-96
Obituary ... 115
Sessions, Will 1905- ... 1R
Sessoms, H(anson) Douglas 1931- ... 41-44R
Seth, Ronald (Sydney) 1911-1985 ... 106
Obituary ... 115
Seth, Vikram 1952- Brief entry ... 121
See also CLC 43
Sethi, Narendra Kumar 1935- ... CANR-14
Earlier sketch in CA 37-40R
Sethi, S. Prakash 1934- ... 41-44R
Sethna, Jehangir Minocher 1941- ... 37-40R
Sethna, Minocher Jehangirji 1911- ... 11-12R
Seth-Smith, Elsie K.
See Murrell, Elsie Kathleen Seth-Smith
Seth-Smith, Leslie James 1923- ... 104

Seth-Smith, Michael 1928- CANR-16
Earlier sketch in CA 29-32R
Seton, Anya 17-18R
See also SATA 3
Seton, Cynthia Propper 1926-1982 ..... CANR-7
Obituary 108
Earlier sketch in CA 5-6R
See also CLC 27
Seton, Ernest (Evan) Thompson
1860-1946 Brief entry 109
See also SATA 18
Seton, Marie 1910- 105
Seton-Thompson, Ernest
See Seton, Ernest (Evan) Thompson
Seton-Watson, Christopher 1918- CANR-11
Earlier sketch in CA 23-24R
Seton-Watson, (George) Hugh (Nicholas)
1916-1984 117
Obituary 114
Settel, Gertrude S. 17-18R
Settel, Irving 1916- 17-18R
Settel, Trudy S.
See Settel, Gertrude S.
Settle, Edith
See Andrews, (William) Linton
Settle, Mary Lee 1918- 89-92
See also CAAS 1
See also DLB 6
See also CLC 19
Setton, Kenneth M. 1914- CANR-18
Earlier sketches in CA 11-12R, CANR-3
Setzekorn, William David 1935- 65-68
Setzler, Frank M(aryl) 1902-1975
Obituary 57-60
Seufert, Karl Rolf 1923- 9-10R
Seuling, Barbara 1937- CANR-26
Earlier sketches in CA 61-64, CANR-8
See also SATA 10
Seung, Thomas Kaehao 1930- 108
Seuphor, Michel
See Arp, Jean
Seuren, Pieter A. M. 1934- 49-52
Seuss, Dr.
See Geisel, Theodor Seuss
See also CLR 9
Sevareid, (Arnold) Eric 1912- 69-72
See also AITN 1
Sevela, Efraim 1928- 69-72
Severin, Mark (Fernand) 1906- 107
Severin, (Giles) Timothy 1940- CANR-10
Earlier sketch in CA 23-24R
Severino, Alexandrino E(usebio) 1931- ... 41-44R
Severn, Bill
See Severn, William Irving
Severn, David
See Unwin, David S(torr)
Severn, Sue 1918- 5-6R
Severn, William Irving 1914- CANR-16
Earlier sketches in CA 4R, CANR-1
See also SATA 1
Severo, Richard 1932- 73-76
Severs, Jerome
See Wooley, John (Steven)
Severs, Vesta-Nadine 1935- CANR-15
Earlier sketch in CA 89-92
Severson, John H(ugh) 1933- 15-16R
Sewall, Joseph 1688-1769 .... DLB-24
Sewall, Marcia 1935- CANR-18
Earlier sketches in CA 45-48, CANR-1
See also SATA 37
Sewall, Mary Franklin 1884-19(?) CAP-2
Earlier sketch in CA 21-22
Sewall, Richard B(enson) 1908- 93-96
Sewall, Samuel 1652-1730 .... DLB-24
Seward, Desmond 1935- Brief entry 114
Seward, Jack
See Seward, John Neil
Seward, James H(odson) 1928- 65-68
Seward, John Neil 1924- CANR-8
Earlier sketch in CA 23-24R
Seward, Prudence 1926- SATA-16
Seward, William W(ard), Jr. 1913- 11-12R
Sewart, Alan 1928- CANR-25
Earlier sketch in CA 108
Sewel, John 1946- 103
Sewell, Anna 1820-1878 .... SATA-24
Sewell, Brocard 1912- 107
Sewell, (Margaret) Elizabeth 1919- 49-52
Sewell, Helen (Moore) 1896-1957
Brief entry 123
See also SATA 38
Sewell, J. Leslie 1923- 21-22R
Sewell, James Patrick 1930- 73-76
Sewell, Richard H(erbert) 1931-
Brief entry 117
Sewell, W. R. Derrick 1931- CANR-9
Earlier sketch in CA 23-24R
Sewell, William H(amilton) 1909- 45-48
Sewell, Winifred 1917- 102
Sewny, Kathryn Wiehe 1909- CAP-1
Earlier sketch in CA 15-16
Sewter, Albert Charles 1912- 89-92
Sexton, A(da) Jeanette 1924- 65-68
Sexton, Anne (Harvey) 1928-1974 ...... CANR-3
Obituary 53-56
Earlier sketch in CA 4R
See also CABS 2
See also SATA 10
See also DLB 5
See also CDALB 1941-1968
See also CLC 2, 4, 6, 8, 10, 15
Sexton, James D(ean) 1942- 113
Sexton, Linda Gray 1953- 101
Sexton, Michael J(oseph) 1939- 45-48
Sexton, Richard J(oseph) 1912- 45-48
Sexton, Virgil Wesley 1918- 33-36R
Sexton, Virginia Staudt 1916- 29-32R
Seybolt, Peter J(ordan) 53-56
Seydel, Mildred Woolley 1890(?)-1988 ... 37-40R
Obituary 124
Seydell, Mildred
See Seydel, Mildred Woolley
Seydor, Paul 1947- 97-100
Seyer, Philip C. 1941- 119
Seyersted, Brita Lindberg
See Lindberg-Seyersted, Brita
Seyersted, Per 1921- CANR-15
Earlier sketch in CA 29-32R
Seyfert, Carl K(eenan) 1938- 57-60
Seyler, Dorothy U(pton) 1938- 109
Seymour, A(rthur) J(ames) 1914- 97-100
Seymour, Alan 1927- 53-56
Seymour, Alta Halverson CAP-1
Earlier sketch in CA 11-12
See also SATA 10
Seymour, Anne
See Morton, Phyllis Digby
Seymour, Charles, Jr. 1912-1977 .... 11-12R
Obituary 69-72
Seymour, Digby G. 1923- 19-20R
Seymour, Dorothy Jane Z(ander) 1928- ... 89-92
Seymour, Emery W. 1921- 13-14R
Seymour, Forrest W. 1905-1983 Obituary .. 111
Seymour, (William Herschel Kean) Gerald
1941- 101
Seymour, Henry
See Hartmann, Helmut Henry
Seymour, John 1914- CANR-9
Earlier sketch in CA 13-14R
Seymour, Miranda
See Sinclair, Miranda
Seymour, Raymond B(enedict) 1912- .. CANR-13
Earlier sketch in CA 73-76
Seymour, Rogers James 1942- 110
Seymour, Stephan A(ndrew) 1920- 21-22R
Seymour, W(illiam) Douglas 1910- 49-52
Seymour, Whitney North, Jr. 1923- ... CANR-14
Earlier sketch in CA 81-84
Seymour, William Kean 1887-1975 ...... 9-10R
Obituary 126
Seymour, William Napier 1914- 77-80
Seymour-Smith, Martin 1928- 7-8R
Seymour-Ure, Colin K. 1938- CANR-18
Earlier sketch in CA 25-28R
Seyton, Marion
See Saxon, Gladys Relyea
Seznec, Jean J. 1905-1983 Obituary 111
Sgroi, Peter Philip 1936- 57-60
Sgroi, Suzanne M(ary) 1943- 108
Shaaber, M. A.
See Shaaber, Matthias A(dam)
Shaaber, Matthias A(dam) 1897-1979
Obituary 111
Shaara, Michael (Joseph, Jr.) 1929-1988 ... 102
Obituary 125
See also DLBY 83
See also CLC 15
See also AITN 1
Shabad, Theodore 1922-1987 .... CANR-10
Obituary 122
Earlier sketch in CA 25-28R
Shachtman, Tom 1942- 89-92
See also SATA 49
Shack, William A(lfred) 1923- 113
Shackelford, Jean 1946- 105
Shacket, Sheldon R(ubin) 1941- 102
Shackford, Martha Hale 1875-1963 .... 3R
Shackford, R(oland) H(erbert) 1908- 3R
Shackle, G(eorge) L(ennox) S(harman)
1903- CANR-2
Earlier sketch in CA 7-8R
Shackleford, Bernard L. 1889-1975 ...... CAP-2
Earlier sketch in CA 29-32
Shackleford, Ruby P(aschall) 1913- 57-60
Shackleton, C. C.
See Aldiss, Brian W(ilson)
Shackleton, Doris (Cavell) 1918- 93-96
Shackleton, Edward Arthur Alexander
1911- 13-14R
Shackleton, Ernest Henry 1874-1922
Brief entry 118
Shackleton, Keith Hope 1923- 7-8R
Shackleton, Philip 1923- 101
Shackleton, Robert 1919-1986 .... 3R
Obituary 120
Shackleton Bailey, D(avid) R(oy)
1917- CANR-19
Earlier sketches in CA 7-8R, CANR-3
Shackley, Myra (Lesley) 1949- 115
Shackley, Theodore (George, Jr.) 1927-
Brief entry 117
Shacochis, Bob
See Shacochis, Robert G.
See also CLC 39
Shacochis, Robert G. 1951- 124
Brief entry 119
Shadbolt, Maurice (Francis Richard)
1932- CANR-5
Earlier sketch in CA 13-14R
See also CAAS 3
Shade, Rose (Marian) 1927- 57-60
Shade, William G(erald) 1939- 41-44R
Shade, William L(eonard) 1945-
Brief entry 113
Shadegg, Stephen C. 1909- 13-14R
Shadi, Dorothy Clotelle Clarke 1908- 13-14R
Shadily, Hassan 1920- 105
Shadlick, Harold (Ernest) 1902- 41-44R
Shadoian, Jack 1940- 105
Shadow, Slim
See Shepard, Sam
Shadowitz, Albert 1915- 69-72
Shaearman, John 1931- 15-16R
Shaevitz, Marjorie Hansen 1943- 101
Shaevitz, Morton H(erbert) 1935- 102
Shafarevich, Igor Rostislavovich 1923- 105
Shafer, Boyd Carlisle 1907- 17-18R
Shafer, Neil 1933- 33-36R
Shafer, Robert E(ugene) 1925- CANR-10
Earlier sketch in CA 57-60
See also SATA 9
Shafer, Robert Jones 1920- 37-40R
Shafer, Ronald G. 1939- CANR-10
Earlier sketch in CA 65-68
Shafer, Thomas 1910(?)-1986 Obituary 119
Shaff, Albert L(averne) 1937- 29-32R
Shaffer, Anthony (Joshua) 1926- 116
Brief entry 110
See also DLB 13
See also CLC 19
Shaffer, Betty
See Shaffer, Elizabeth (Nickerson)
Shaffer, Dale Eugene 1929- 37-40R
Shaffer, Elizabeth (Nickerson) 1925- 113
Shaffer, Harry George 1919- CANR-6
Earlier sketch in CA 7-8R
Shaffer, Helen B. 1909(?)-1978 85-88
Obituary 81-84
Shaffer, Jerome A(rthur) 1929- 37-40R
Shaffer, K(atherine) Stevenson 1902- CAP-2
Earlier sketch in CA 17-18
Shaffer, Kenneth R(aymond) 1914- 5-6R
Shaffer, Laurance Frederic 1903-1976
Obituary 65-68
Shaffer, Peter (Levin) 1926- CANR-25
Earlier sketch in CA 25-28R
See also DLB 13
See also CLC 5, 14, 18, 37
Shaffer, Samuel 1910- 104
Shaffer, Thomas Lindsay 1934- 37-40R
Shaffer, Wilma L. 1916- 19-20R
Shafritz, Jay M(ichael) 1944- 117
Shaftel, Oscar 1912- 57-60
Shaftner, Dorothy 1918- 25-28R
Shagan, Steve 1927- CANR-6
Earlier sketch in CA 53-56
Shaginyan, Marietta Sergeyevna
1888-1982 Obituary 106
Shah, A(ruind) M(anilal) 1931- 73-76
Shah, Amina 1918- 49-52
Shah, Diane K(iver) 1945- 73-76
Shah, (Sayed) Idries 1924- CANR-22
Earlier sketches in CA 17-18R, CANR-7
Shah, Krishna B. 1933- 17-18R
Shaha, Rishikesh 1925- 69-72
Shahan, Lynn 1941- 106
Shahane, Vasant Anant 1923- CANR-12
Earlier sketch in CA 25-28R
Shahani, Ranjee 1904-1968 .... CANR-2
Earlier sketch in CA 2R
Shahar, David 1926- 65-68
Shaheen, Jack G(eorge) 1935- 124
Shaheen, Naseeb 1931- 65-68
Shahn, Ben(jamin) 1898-1969 121
Obituary 89-92
See also SATA 21
Shahn, Bernarda Bryson
See Bryson, Bernarda
Shah Of Iran
See Pahlevi, Mohammed Riza
Shain, Henry 1941- 57-60
Shain, Merle 1935- 61-64
See also AITN 1
Shainmark, Eliezer L. 1900-1976 Obituary .. 104
Shainmark, Lou
See Shainmark, Eliezer L.
Shairp, (Alexander) Mordaunt 1887-1939
Brief entry 110
See also DLB 10
Shakabpa, Tsepon W(angchuk) D(edan)
1907- CAP-2
Earlier sketch in CA 23-24
Sha'Ked, Ami 1945- 101
Shakesby, Paul S(tewart) 1946- 57-60
Shakespeare, Geoffrey (Hithersay)
1893-1980 Obituary 105
Shakespeare, William 1564-1616 .... DLB-62
Shakey, Bernard
See Young, Neil
Shakow, David 1901-1981 Obituary 108
Shalamov, Varlam (Tikhonovich)
1907(?)-1982 Obituary 105
See also CLC 18
Shale, Richard 1947- 89-92
Shales, Thomas William 1948- 112
Brief entry 110
Shales, Tom
See Shales, Thomas William
Shalett, Anita Effron 1917(?)-1984
Obituary 112
Shalhope, Robert E. 1941- 85-88
Shallcrass, John James 1922- CANR-20
Earlier sketch in CA 103
Shallow, Robert
See Atkinson, Frank
Shaloff, Stanley 1939- 29-32R
Shalom, Stephen Rosskamm 1948- 112
Shalvey, Thomas (Joseph) 1937- 105
Shamburger, (Alice) Page 9-10R
Shames, Laurence 1951- 124
Shamlu, Ahmad 1925- CLC-10
Shamon, Albert Joseph 1915- 15-16R
Shan, Yeh
See Wang, C(hing) H(sien)
Shanahan, Eileen 1924- 102
Shanahan, William J. 1935- 29-32R
Shands, Harley C. 1916-1981 Obituary 105
Shands, Harley Cecil 1916-1981 109
Shane, Alex M(ichael) 1933- 45-48
Shane, C(harles) Donald 1895-1983
Obituary 109
Shane, Don (Graves) 1933- 53-56
Shane, Harold Gray 1914- CANR-21
Earlier sketches in CA 11-12R, CANR-3
See also SATA 36
Shane, John
See Durst, Paul
Shane, Mark
See Norwood, Victor G(eorge) C(harles)
Shane, Maxwell 1905(?)-1983 Obituary 111
Shane, Rhondo
See Norwood, Victor G(eorge) C(harles)
Shaner, Madeleine 1932- 73-76
Shange, Ntozake 1948- 85-88
See also BW
See also DLB 38
See also CLC 8, 25, 38
Shank, Alan 1936- 53-56
Shank, David Arthur 1924- 29-32R
Shank, Joseph E(lmer) 1892- CAP-2
Earlier sketch in CA 25-28
Shank, Margarethe Erdahl 1910- CAP-2
Earlier sketch in CA 19-20
Shankel, George Edgar 1894- CAP-2
Earlier sketch in CA 23-24
Shankland, Peter Macfarlane 1901- CANR-16
Earlier sketches in CA 11-12, CAP-1
Shankle, Ralph O(tis) 1933- 11-12R
Shanklin, William L(eslie) 1941- 120
Shankman, Florence V(ogel) 1912- 41-44R
Shankman, Paul (Andrew) 1943- 93-96
Shanks, Ann Zane (Kushner) 53-56
See also SATA 10
Shanks, Bob 1932- 101
Shanks, Bruce AITN-1
Shanks, Hershel 1930- 126
Brief entry 106
Shanks, Michael (James) 1927-1984 .... CANR-8
Obituary 111
Earlier sketch in CA 5-6R
Shann, Renee 1907(?)-1979 Obituary 89-92
Shannon, David Allen 1920- 1R
Shannon, Dell
See Linington, (Barbara) Elizabeth
Shannon, Dell
See Linington, Elizabeth
Shannon, Doris 1924- CANR-23
Earlier sketches in CA 61-64, CANR-8
Shannon, Edgar F(inley), Jr. 1918- 11-12R
Shannon, Ellen 1927- 77-80
Shannon, Foster (Houts) 1930- 106
Shannon, Fred Albert 1893-1963 Obituary .. 111
Shannon, George (William Bones)
1952- CANR-23
Earlier sketch in CA 106
See also SATA 35
Shannon, Jasper Berry 1903-1984 .... 2R
Obituary 114
Shannon, John 1943- 57-60
Shannon, Lyle William 1920- 61-64
Shannon, M.
See Geddie, John
Shannon, Monica 1905(?)-1965 Obituary ... 109
See also SATA 28
Shannon, Richard 1945- 73-76
Shannon, Robert
See Wieder, Robert S(hannon)
Shannon, Robert C. 1930- 15-16R
Shannon, Robert L(eroy) 1926- 93-96
Shannon, Terry
See Mercer, Jessie
See also SATA 21
Shannon, Thomas A(nthony) 1940- CANR-20
Earlier sketches in CA 53-56, CANR-5
Shannon, William H(enry) 1917- 45-48
Shannon, William V(incent) 1927-1988 .. CANR-6
Obituary 126
Earlier sketch in CA 11-12R
Shanor, Donald Read 1927- CANR-12
Earlier sketch in CA 61-64
Shanwa
See Haarer, Alec Ernest
Shao, Stephen P(inyee) 1924- CANR-11
Earlier sketch in CA 23-24R
Shapard, Robert (Perry) 1942- 126
Shapcott, Thomas William 1935- 69-72
See also CLC 38
Shapell, Nathan 1922- 49-52
Shapere, Dudley 1928- 17-18R
Shapiro, Alan 1952- 125
Shapiro, Cecile 85-88
Shapiro, Charles K. 1926- 7-8R
Shapiro, David (Joel) 1947- 15-16R
Shapiro, David S(idney) 1923-1983 ..... CANR-1
Obituary 109
Earlier sketch in CA 4R
Shapiro, Deborah 1923- 106
Shapiro, Dolph
See Sharp, Dolph
Shapiro, Edward 1920- 19-20R
Shapiro, Elizabeth Klein
See Klein, Elizabeth
Shapiro, Fred(eric) C(harles) 1931- 19-20R
Shapiro, Harold I(srael) 1931- 45-48
Shapiro, Harry L(ionel) 1902- 49-52
Shapiro, Harvey 1924- CANR-15
Earlier sketch in CA 41-44R
Shapiro, Henry D(avid) 1937- CANR-3
Earlier sketch in CA 11-12R
Shapiro, Herbert 1929- 37-40R
Shapiro, Herman 1922- 15-16R
Shapiro, Howard I(ra) 1937- 73-76
Shapiro, Irving 1917- 29-32R
Shapiro, Irwin 1911- 81-84
See also SATA 32
Shapiro, James E(arnest) 1946- 108
Shapiro, Jane P.
See Zacek, Jane Shapiro

INDEX

Shapiro, Jim
See Shapiro, James E(arnest)
Shapiro, Joan Hatch 1928- 33-36R
Shapiro, Julian L.
See Sanford, John
Shapiro, Karl (Jay) 1913- CANR-1
Earlier sketch in CA 4R
See also CAAS 6
See also DLB 48
See also CLC 4, 8, 15
Shapiro, Kenneth A(llan) 1942- 118
Shapiro, Lillian L(adman) 1913- 102
Shapiro, Linda Gaye 1953- 65-68
Shapiro, Marianne (Goldner) 1940- 123
Brief entry 118
Shapiro, Martin M(athew) 1933- 102
Shapiro, Max 1912(?)-1981 Obituary 105
Shapiro, Mel 1937- 101
Shapiro, Milton J. 1926- 81-84
See also SATA 32
Shapiro, Nat(haniel M.) 1922-1983 .... CANR-15
Obituary 111
Earlier sketch in CA 29-32R
Shapiro, Norman R(ichard) 1930- 93-96
Shapiro, Robert 1935- 113
Shapiro, Samuel 1927- CANR-1
Earlier sketch in CA 3R
Shapiro, Sue A. 1947- 109
Shapiro, William E. 1934- CANR-20
Earlier sketch in CA 25-28R
Shaplen, June Herman 1924(?)-1982
Obituary 108
Shaplen, Robert (Modell) 1917-1988 ...... 9-10R
Obituary 125
Shapley, Fern Rusk 1890-1984 .... 41-44R
Obituary 114
Shapley, Harlow 1885-1972 Obituary 37-40R
Shapley, John 1890(?)-1978 Obituary 81-84
Shapo, Marshall S(chambelan) 1936- .. CANR-15
Earlier sketch in CA 41-44R
Shapp, Charles M(orris) 1906- 57-60
Shapp, Martha Glauber 1910- CANR-2
Earlier sketch in CA 1R
See also SATA 3
Shappiro, Herbert (Arthur) 1899(?)-1975 . CAP-2
Obituary 57-60
Earlier sketch in CA 21-22
Sharabi, H(isham) B(ashir) 1927- CANR-2
Earlier sketch in CA 7-8R
Sharat Chandra, G(ubbi) S(hankara Chetty)
1938- 53-56
Sharfman, Amalie 73-76
See also SATA 14
Sharif, M(ohammad) Nawaz 1942- 114
Sharif, Omar
See Chalhoub, Michael
Sharkansky, Ira 1938- 29-32R
Sharkawi, A(bdel)-R(ahman) 1920-1987
Obituary 125
Sharkey, Bernarda 1934- 33-36R
Sharkey, Jack
See Sharkey, John Michael
Sharkey, John Michael 1931- CANR-3
Earlier sketch in CA 3R
Sharkey, (Neil) Owen 1917- 61-64
Sharlet, Robert (Stewart) 1935- 37-40R
Sharlin, Harold I(ssadore) 1925- 11-12R
Sharma, Chandradhar 1920- 13-14R
Sharma, Govind Narain 1927- 45-48
Sharma, Jagdish Prasad 1934- 81-84
Sharma, Partap 1939- CANR-14
Earlier sketch in CA 77-80
See also SATA 15
Sharma, Ravindra N(ath) 1944- 110
Sharma, Shripad Rama 1879- CAP-2
Earlier sketch in CA 29-32
Sharman, Maisie
See Bolton, Maisie Sharman
Sharman, Miriam
See Bolton, Maisie Sharman
Sharmat, Marjorie Weinman 1928- CANR-12
Earlier sketch in CA 25-28R
See also SATA 4, 33
Sharmat, Mitchell 1927- 104
See also SATA 33
Sharon, Donna Haye
See Scharlemann, Dorothy Hoyer
Sharon, Rose
See Merril, Judith
Sharon, Sylvia
See Little, Paul H(ugo)
Sharot, Stephen 1943- 109
Sharp, Aaron John 1904- 11-12R
Sharp, Alan 1934- 15-16R
Sharp, Andrew 1906-1974 .... CANR-3
Earlier sketch in CA 2R
Sharp, Ann Margaret 1942- 81-84
Sharp, Ansel M(iree) 1924- 77-80
Sharp, Buchanan 1942- 105
Sharp, Clifford Henry 1922- 108
Sharp, Daniel A(sher) 1932- 49-52
Sharp, Dolph 1914- 29-32R
Sharp, Donald Bruce 1938- 29-32R
Sharp, Doreen Maud 1920- CANR-25
Earlier sketch in CA 108
Sharp, Dorothea Elizabeth 21-22R
Sharp, Edith Lambert 1917- 5-6R
Sharp, Ernest Jack
See Sharpsteen, Ernest Jack
Sharp, Francis Michael 1941- 106
Sharp, Hal
See Sharp, Harold W(ilson)
Sharp, Harold S(pencer) 1909- CANR-3
Earlier sketch in CA 11-12R
Sharp, Harold W(ilson) 1914- 93-96
Sharp, Helen
See Paine, Lauran (Bosworth)
Sharp, James
See Kinghorn, A(lexander) M(anson)
Sharp, James Roger 1936- 29-32R
Sharp, John Kean 1892-1979 Obituary 93-96
Sharp, John R. 1921- 17-18R
Sharp, Laure M(etzger) 1921- 29-32R
Sharp, Margery 1905- CANR-18
Earlier sketch in CA 21-22R
See also SATA 1, 29
Sharp, Martin 1900(?)-1987 Obituary 124
Sharp, Roger (William) 1935-1986 73-76
Obituary 119
Sharp, Ronald A(lan) 1945- 123
Sharp, Saundra 1942- 45-48
See also BW
Sharp, Shirley I. 1934- 45-48
Sharp, Sister Mary Corona 1922- 13-14R
Sharp, Zerna A. 1889-1981 Obituary 104
See also SATA 27
Sharpe, Genell J(ackson) Subak
See Subak-Sharpe, Genell J(ackson)
Sharpe, Grant W(illiam) 1925- 69-72
Sharpe, J(ames) A(nthony) 1946- 117
Sharpe, Jon
See Knott, William C(ecil, Jr.)
Sharpe, Lawrence A(lbright) 1920- 49-52
Sharpe, Lucretia
See Burgess, M(ichael) R(oy)
Sharpe, Mitchell R(aymond) 1924- 29-32R
See also SATA 12
Sharpe, Roger Carter 1948- 93-96
Sharpe, Thomas Ridley 1928- 122
Brief entry 114
Sharpe, Tom
See Sharpe, Thomas Ridley
See also DLB 14
See also CLC 36
Sharpe, William D(onald) 1927- 19-20R
Sharpes, Donald K(enneth) 1934- CANR-1
Earlier sketch in CA 45-48
Sharples, Win(ston S.), Jr. 1932- 45-48
Sharpless, F(rancis) Parvin 1929- 25-28R
Sharpsteen, Ernest Jack 1880-1976
Obituary 110
Sharpton, Robert E(arl) 1936- 104
Sharrock, Roger (Ian) 1919- CANR-2
Earlier sketch in CA 7-8R
Sharwood Smith, Bryan Evers
1899-1983 .... CAP-2
Obituary 111
Earlier sketch in CA 29-32
Shatto, Gloria M. 1931- 41-44R
Shattock, Ernest (Henry) 1904- 102
Shattuck, Charles H(arlen) 1910- CANR-2
Earlier sketch in CA 7-8R
Shattuck, Roger (Whitney) 1923- CANR-7
Earlier sketch in CA 7-8R
Shatzkin, Leonard 1919- 109
Shaughnessy, Edward J(oseph, Jr.) 1934- .. 110
Shaul, Frank
See Rowland, D(onald) S(ydney)
Shaull, (Millard) Richard 1919- CANR-11
Earlier sketch in CA 21-22R
Shave, Gordon A(shton) 1922- 101
Shavelson, Melville 1917- CANR-4
Earlier sketch in CA 53-56
Shaver, James P. 1933- CANR-7
Earlier sketch in CA 19-20R
Shaver-Crandell, Anne (Elizabeth) 1941- 113
Shaver-Crandell, Annie
See Shaver-Crandell, Anne (Elizabeth)
Shavin, Norman 1926- 81-84
Shaw, Alan George Lewers 1916- CANR-9
Earlier sketch in CA 23-24R
Shaw, Arnold 1909- CANR-1
Earlier sketch in CA 3R
See also SATA 4
Shaw, B(iswanath) N. 1923- 37-40R
Shaw, Barton C(arr) 1947- 123
Shaw, Bernard 1940- 119
Brief entry 109
See also BW
Shaw, Bob 1931- CANR-19
Earlier sketches in CA 49-52, CANR-1
Shaw, Brian
See Tubb, E(dwin) C(harles)
Shaw, Bruce 1941- 119
Shaw, Bruno 1905-1984 Obituary 114
Shaw, Bynum (Gillette) 1923- CANR-4
Earlier sketch in CA 3R
Shaw, Carleton Ford 1908- CAP-1
Earlier sketch in CA 15-16
Shaw, Carolyn Hagner 1903(?)-1977
Obituary 69-72
Shaw, Charles (Green) 1892-1974 .... CAP-1
Earlier sketch in CA 17-18
See also SATA 13
Shaw, Charles R(aymond) 1921- CANR-14
Earlier sketch in CA 21-22R
Shaw, Chester Lee 1898(?)-1985 Obituary .. 118
Shaw, David 1943- 49-52
Shaw, Dawn
See Shaw, Thelma
Shaw, Donald Lewis 1936- 61-64
Shaw, Earl Bennett 1889- CAP-1
Earlier sketch in CA 17-18
Shaw, Edward P(ease) 1911-1986 .... 21-22R
Obituary 118
Shaw, Elizabeth
See Prance, June E(lizebeth)
Shaw, Ellen Torgerson
See Torgerson Shaw, Ellen
Shaw, Evelyn S. 1927- 104
See also SATA 28
Shaw, Felicity 1918- 104
Shaw, Flora Louisa
See Lugard, Flora Louisa Shaw
Shaw, Fred ?-1972 Obituary 104
Shaw, Frederick 1912- CANR-1
Earlier sketch in CA 45-48
Shaw, Frederick W. 1916(?)-1983
Obituary 111
Shaw, Gaylord 1942- 81-84
Shaw, George
See Bickham, Jack M(iles)
Shaw, George Bernard 1856-1950
Brief entry 104
See also DLB 10, 57
See also TCLC 3, 9, 21
Shaw, Graham 1944- 118
Shaw, Harold 1916(?)-1986 Obituary 118
Shaw, Harry (Lee, Jr.) 1905- 81-84
Shaw, Harry Edmund 1946- 114
Shaw, Helen 1913-1985 .... CANR-20
Earlier sketch in CA 103
Shaw, Henry I(var), Jr. 1926- 33-36R
Shaw, Henry Wheeler 1818-1885 .... DLB-11
Shaw, Howard 1934- 106
Shaw, Irene
See Roberts, Irene
Shaw, Irwin 1913-1984 .... CANR-21
Obituary 112
Earlier sketch in CA 15-16R
See also DLB 6
See also DLBY 84
See also CDALB 1941-1968
See also CLC 7, 23, 34
See also AITN 1
Shaw, J(oseph) Thomas 1919- 17-18R
Shaw, John Bennett 1913- 21-22R
Shaw, John Mackay 1897-1984 .... CANR-13
Earlier sketch in CA 29-32R
Shaw, Lau
See Shu Ch'ing-ch'un
Shaw, Lawrence H(ugh) 1940- 69-72
Shaw, Leroy R(obert) 1923- 13-14R
Shaw, Linda 1938- CANR-23
Earlier sketch in CA 106
Shaw, Luci N(orthcote) 1928- CANR-17
Earlier sketch in CA 101
Shaw, Malcolm Edwin 1926- CANR-1
Earlier sketch in CA 1R
Shaw, Marvin E(vert) 1919- 23-24R
Shaw, Maxine 1945- 57-60
Shaw, Nancy Stoller 1942- 57-60
Shaw, Peter 1936- CANR-9
Earlier sketch in CA 65-68
Shaw, Priscilla Washburn 1930- 13-14R
Shaw, Ralph R(obert) 1907-1972
Obituary 37-40R
Shaw, Ray 33-36R
See also SATA 7
Shaw, Richard 1923- 37-40R
See also SATA 12
Shaw, Robert 1927-1978 .... CANR-4
Obituary 81-84
Earlier sketch in CA 1R
See also DLB 13, 14
See also CLC 5
See also AITN 1
Shaw, Robert Byers 1916- 37-40R
Shaw, Ronald D. M. 1883- CAP-1
Earlier sketch in CA 13-14
Shaw, Ronald E. 1923- 19-20R
Shaw, Russell B(urnham) 1935- CANR-3
Earlier sketch in CA 3R
Shaw, Stanford Jay 1930- CANR-6
Earlier sketch in CA 7-8R
Shaw, Steven John 1918- 19-20R
Shaw, T. D. W.
See Shaw, Thelma
Shaw, T. E.
See Lawrence, T(homas) E(dward)
Shaw, Thelma 25-28R
Shaw, Thurstan 1914- 103
Shaw, Timothy Milton 1945- 112
Shaw, Vivian
See Seldes, Gilbert (Vivian)
Shaw, W. David 1937- 29-32R
Shaw, (Harold) Watkins 1911- 4R
Shaw, Wayne E(ugene) 1932- 53-56
Shaw, William Harlan 1922- CANR-15
Earlier sketch in CA 41-44R
Shawchuck, Norman 1935- 126
Shawcross, John T. 1924- 15-16R
Shawcross, William 1946- 105
Shawn, Edwin Meyers 1891-1972
Obituary 33-36R
Shawn, Frank S.
See Goulart, Ron(ald Joseph)
Shawn, Ted
See Shawn, Edwin Meyers
Shawn, Wallace 1943- 112
See also CLC 41
Shawn, William 1907- 108
Shay, Arthur 1922- 33-36R
See also SATA 4
Shay, Lacey
See Shebar, Sharon Sigmond
Shayne, Gordon
See Winter, Bevis (Peter)
Shayon, Robert Lewis 49-52
Shayon, Samuel 1904(?)-1984 Obituary 112
Shazar, Rachel
See Katznelson-Shazar, Rachel
Shazar, (Schneor) Zalman 1889-1974 101
Obituary 53-56
Shea, Donald F(rancis) 1925- 73-76
Shea, George 1940- 108
See also SATA 42
Shea, George E., Jr. 1902-1980
Obituary 97-100
Shea, James J. 1890(?)-1977 Obituary 69-72
Shea, John 1941- 73-76
Shea, John Gerald 1906- 11-12R
Shea, John Gilmary 1824-1892 .... DLB-30
Shea, John S. 1933- 21-22R
Shea, Michael 1946- 112
Shea, Robert (Joseph) 1933- 101
Shea, Shirley 1924- 121
Sheaffer, Louis
See Slung, Louis Sheaffer
Sheaffer, Robert M(errill) 1949- 106
Sheagren, Thomas G(eorge) 1949- 118
Sheahan, John 1923- 19-20R
Sheahan, Richard T(homas) 1942- CANR-15
Earlier sketch in CA 65-68
Shealy, C(lyde) Norman 1932- CANR-7
Earlier sketch in CA 57-60
Shean, Glenn (Daniel) 1939- 53-56
Sheard, Kevin 1916- 41-44R
Shearer, John 1947- 125
See also SATA 27, 43
Shearer, Ronald A(lexander) 1932- 77-80
Shearer, Ted 1919- SATA-43
Shearing, Joseph
See Campbell, (Gabrielle) Margaret (Vere)
See also DLB 70
Shearman, Hugh (Francis) 1915- 13-14R
Shearman, John 1931- 15-16R
Shears, Billie
See Watson, O(scar) Michael
Sheats, Mary Boney 1918- 15-16R
Sheats, Paul Douglas 1932- 101
Shebar, Sharon Sigmond 1945- CANR-19
Earlier sketch in CA 103
See also SATA 36
Shebbeare, John 1709-1788 .... DLB-39
Shebl, James M(ichael) 1942- CANR-23
Earlier sketches in CA 61-64, CANR-8
Shechner, Mark E. 1940- 124
Sheckley, Robert 1928- CANR-2
Earlier sketch in CA 3R
See also DLB 8
Shecter, Ben 1935- 81-84
See also SATA 16
Shecter, Leonard 1926-1974 Obituary 45-48
Shedd, Charlie W. 1915- 19-20R
Shedd, Clarence Prouty 1887-1973
Obituary 45-48
Shedd, Margaret Cochran 1900-1986
Obituary 118
Shedd, William G. T. 1820-1894 .... DLB-64
Shedley, Ethan I.
See Beizer, Boris
Sheean, Diana 1915(?)-1987 Obituary 124
Sheean, (James) Vincent 1899-1975 61-64
Sheed, Francis Joseph 1897-1981
Obituary 105
Sheed, Frank
See Sheed, Francis Joseph
Sheed, Wilfrid (John Joseph) 1930- 65-68
See also DLB 6
See also CLC 2, 4, 10
Sheedy, Alexandra Elizabeth 1962- 85-88
See also SATA 19, 39
Sheehan, Arthur 1910(?)-1975 Obituary ... 61-64
Sheehan, Bernard W(illiam) 1934- 41-44R
Sheehan, Donald Henry 1917-1974 ..... CANR-2
Earlier sketch in CA 4R
Sheehan, Ethna 1908- 61-64
See also SATA 9
Sheehan, George (Augustine) 1918- ... CANR-13
Earlier sketch in CA 73-76
Sheehan, James J(ohn) 1937- CANR-11
Earlier sketch in CA 19-20R
Sheehan, John F(rancis) X(avier) 1933- 122
Brief entry 118
Sheehan, Joseph Green 1918-1983
Obituary 111
Sheehan, Margaret A(nne) 1956- 111
Sheehan, Neil 1936- 29-32R
Sheehan, Patrick Augustine
See O Siochain, P(adraig) A(ugustine)
Sheehan, Paul V(incent) 1904- 33-36R
Sheehan, Sister Helen 1904- CAP-1
Earlier sketch in CA 17-18
Sheehan, Susan 1937- CANR-12
Earlier sketch in CA 21-22R
Sheehan, Thomas 1941- 122
Sheehan, Valerie Harms
See Harms, Valerie
Sheehy, Eugene P(aul) 1922- 9-10R
Sheehy, Gail CANR-1
Earlier sketch in CA 49-52
Sheehy, Jeanne 1939- 110
Sheehy, Maurice S(tephen) 1898-1972
Obituary 111
Sheekman, Arthur 1901-1978 81-84
Obituary 73-76
Sheen, Fulton J(ohn) 1895-1979 .... CANR-5
Obituary 89-92
Earlier sketch in CA 5-6R
Sheeran, James Jennings 1932- 65-68
Sheerin, John Basil 1906- CANR-4
Earlier sketch in CA 2R
Sheets, Elva (Darah) 1898- 57-60
Sheets, John R(ichard) 1922- 25-28R
Sheetz, Ann Kindig 1934- 101
Shefelman, Janice Jordan 1930- 120
Sheffer, H. R.
See Abels, Harriette S(heffer)
Sheffer, Isaiah 1935- 17-18R
Sheffield, James Rockwell 1936-
Brief entry 106
Sheffield, Janet N. 1926- 65-68
See also SATA 26
Sheffy, Lester Fields 1887- CAP-1
Earlier sketch in CA 13-14
Shefter, Harry 1910- 11-12R
Shefts, Joelle SATA-49

Shehan, Lawrence Joseph 1898-1984 117
Shein, Brian 1947- 110
Shein, Louis J(ulius) 1914- 25-28R
Sheiness, (Lee) Marsha 1940- CANR-15
Earlier sketch in CA 89-92
Sheinwold, Alfred 1912- 61-64
Sheinwold, Patricia
See Fox-Sheinwold, Patricia
Shek, Ben-Zion 1927- 110
Shekerjian, Regina Tor SATA-16
Shelbourne, Cecily
See Goodwin, Suzanne
Shelby, Brit
See Grady, James (Thomas)
Shelby, Carroll Hall 1923- 19-20R
Shelby, Graham 1940- 102
Shelby, Susan
See Kinnicutt, Susan Sibley
Sheldon, Alan 1933- 114
Sheldon, Alice Hastings Bradley
1915(?)-1987 108
Obituary 122
Sheldon, Ann CAP-2
Earlier sketch in CA 19-20
See also SATA 1
Sheldon, Aure 1917-1976 61-64
See also SATA 12
Sheldon, Charles Harvey 1929- 107
Sheldon, Charles S(tuart) II 1917-1981
Obituary 105
Sheldon, Deyan 53-56
Sheldon, Edward 1886-1946 .... DLB-7
Sheldon, Eleanor Bernert 1920- 85-88
Sheldon, Esther K. 1906- 37-40R
Sheldon, George E.
See Stahl, Le Roy
Sheldon, John
See Bloch, Robert (Albert)
Sheldon, Lee
See Lee, Wayne C.
Sheldon, Michael 1918- 19-20R
Sheldon, Muriel 1926- CANR-18
Earlier sketch in CA 101
See also SATA 39, 45
Sheldon, Peter 1922- 25-28R
Sheldon, Raccoona
See Sheldon, Alice Hastings Bradley
Sheldon, Richard (Robert) 1932- 33-36R
Sheldon, Roy AITN-1
Sheldon, Roy
See Tubb, E(dwin) C(harles)
Sheldon, Scott
See Wallmann, Jeffrey M(iner)
Sheldon, Sidney 1917- 29-32R
See also AITN 1
Sheldon, Suzanne Eaton 1928(?)-1985
Obituary 117
Sheldon, Walt
See Sheldon, Walter J.
Sheldon, Walter J. 1917- CANR-10
Earlier sketch in CA 25-28R
See also AITN 1
Sheldon, William (Herbert) 1898-1977 ...25-28R
Obituary 116
Sheldon, William Denley 1915- 17-18R
Sheldrick, Daphne 1934- CANR-3
Earlier sketch in CA 49-52
Shell, Virginia Law 1923- 21-22R
Shelley, Bruce L(eon) 1927- CANR-9
Earlier sketch in CA 23-24R
Shelley, Dolores 1937- 122
Shelley, Florence D(ubroff) 1921- 65-68
Shelley, Frances
See Wees, Frances Shelley
Shelley, Lillian
See Koppel, Lillian
and Koppel, Shelley R(uth)
Shelley, Louise I(sabel) 1952- 108
Shelley, Mack Clayton II 1950- 126
Shelley, Mary Wollstonecraft (Godwin)
1797-1851 .... SATA-29
Shelley, Noreen 1920- 104
Shelley, Rebecca 1887(?)-1984 Obituary ... 111
Shelly, (Michael) Bruce 1929- 57-60
Shelly, Judith A(llen) 1944- 115
Shelly, Maynard W(olfe) 1928- CANR-7
Earlier sketch in CA 15-16R
Shelly, Peter
See Dresser, Davis
Shelmerdine, Cynthia Wright 1949- 117
Shelp, Earl E(dward) 1947- 116
Shelton, Barrett C(linton) 1903(?)-1984
Obituary 112
Shelton, (Austin) Jess(e), Jr. 1926- ... CANR-25
Earlier sketch in CA 3R
Shelton, Lola
See Klaue, Lola Shelton
Shelton, Regina Maria 1927- 112
Shelton, Richard 1933- CANR-13
Earlier sketch in CA 33-36R
Shelton, Suzanne
See Buckley, Suzanne Shelton
Shelton, William Roy 1919- CANR-11
Earlier sketch in CA 5-6R
See also SATA 5
See also AITN 1
Shemin, Margaretha (Hoeneveld) 1928- ..13-14R
See also SATA 4
Shen, James C. H. 1909- 126
Shen, Peter 110
Shen Congwen 1902-1988 Obituary 125
Shenk, David W(itmer) 1937- 106
Shenk, Lois (Landis) 1944- 114
Shenk, Marcia Ann 1953- 73-76
Shenk, Wilbert R. 1935- 23-24R
Shenkin, Elizabeth Shoemaker ?-1975
Obituary 61-64
Shennan, Joseph Hugh 1933- 103
Shenoy, B(ellikoth) R(aghunath) 1905- 77-80
Shenton, Edward 1895-1977 .... SATA-45
Shenton, Edward H(eriot) 1932- CANR-17
Earlier sketch in CA 25-28R
Shenton, James P(atrick) 1925- CANR-2
Earlier sketch in CA 5-6R
Shepard, David W. 1922- 93-96
Shepard, Elaine (Elizabeth) 1923- 21-22R
Shepard, Ernest Howard 1879-1976 ... CANR-23
Obituary 65-68
Earlier sketch in CA 9-10R
See also SATA 3, 24, 33
Shepard, Francis P(arker) 1897- 13-14R
Shepard, Gary 1939- 97-100
Shepard, Jean H(eck) 1930- 49-52
Shepard, Jim 19??- CLC-36
Shepard, Jon M(ax) 1939- CANR-7
Earlier sketch in CA 57-60
Shepard, Leslie (Alan) 1917- CANR-8
Earlier sketch in CA 19-20R
Shepard, Leslie Albert 1929- 29-32R
Shepard, Lucius 19(?)- CLC-34
Shepard, Martin 1934- 33-36R
Shepard, Mary
See Knox, (Mary) Eleanor Jessie
Shepard, Odell 1884-1967 .... CANR-3
Obituary 25-28R
Earlier sketch in CA 5-6R
Shepard, Paul (Howe) 1925- CANR-10
Earlier sketch in CA 23-24R
Shepard, Richard F. 1922- 115
Shepard, Richmond 1929- 29-32R
Shepard, Sam 1943- CANR-22
Earlier sketch in CA 69-72
See also DLB 7
See also CLC 4, 6, 17, 34, 41, 44
Shepard, Thomas I 1604(?)-1649 ...... DLB-24
Shepard, Thomas II 1635-1677 .... DLB-24
Shepard, Thomas Rockwell, Jr. 1918- 105
Shepardson, Mary (Thygeson) 1906- 29-32R
Shephard, Esther 1891-1975 .... CAP-2
Obituary 57-60
Earlier sketch in CA 25-28
See also SATA 5, 26
Shephard, John (Brownlow) 1900- CAP-1
Earlier sketch in CA 13-14
Shephard, Roy J(esse) 1929- CANR-11
Earlier sketch in CA 29-32R
Shepherd, (Richard) David 1931- 65-68
Shepherd, David Gwynne 1924- 5-6R
Shepherd, Donald (Lee) 1932- 61-64
Shepherd, Elizabeth 33-36R
See also SATA 4
Shepherd, Geoffrey (Seddon) 1898- ... CANR-20
Earlier sketch in CA 4R
Shepherd, George W., Jr. 1926- CANR-6
Earlier sketch in CA 4R
Shepherd, Gordon
See Brook-Shepherd, (Fred) Gordon
Shepherd, J(ohn) Barrie 1935- 111
Shepherd, Jack 1937- 57-60
Shepherd, James L(eftwich) III 1921- 21-22R
Shepherd, Jean (Parker) 1929- 77-80
See also AITN 2
Shepherd, Joan
See Buchanan, Betty (Joan)
Shepherd, John
See Ballard, (Willis) Todhunter
Shepherd, L. P. 53-56
Shepherd, Massey H., Jr.
See Shepherd, Massey Hamilton, Jr.
Shepherd, Massey Hamilton
See Shepherd, Massey Hamilton, Jr.
Shepherd, Massey Hamilton, Jr. 1913- 122
Shepherd, Michael
See Ludlum, Robert
Shepherd, Nan 1893- 105
Shepherd, Neal
See Morland, Nigel
Shepherd, Robert Henry Wishart
1888-1971 .... CAP-1
Earlier sketch in CA 13-14
Shepherd, Simon 1951- 120
Shepherd, Walter Bradley 1904- 105
Shepherd, William C(hauncey) 1942- ... CANR-18
Earlier sketch in CA 25-28R
Shepley, James R(obinson) 1917-
Brief entry 112
Sheppard, Barry 1937- 61-64
Sheppard, Cynthia A(nne) 1955- 108
Sheppard, David Stuart 1929- 103
Sheppard, Eugenia (Benbow)
1900(?)-1984 103
Obituary 114
Sheppard, Francis Henry Wollaston
1921- 21-22R
Sheppard, Harold L(loyd) 1922- CANR-1
Earlier sketch in CA 45-48
Sheppard, Joseph 1930- CANR-23
Earlier sketches in CA 61-64, CANR-8
Sheppard, Lancelot C(apel) 1906- CANR-5
Earlier sketch in CA 7-8R
Sheppard, Lila (Brooks) 1906- CAP-1
Earlier sketch in CA 13-14
Sheppard, Mary 29-32R
Sheppard, Roger 1939- 77-80
Sheppard, Sally 1917- 69-72
Sheppard, Stephen 1945- 105
Sheppard, Thomas F(rederick) 1935- 73-76
Sheppard, Walter Lee, Jr. 1911- 69-72
Sheppard-Jones, Elisabeth 1920- 13-14R
Shepperson, Wilbur Stanley 1919- CANR-6
Earlier sketch in CA 1R
Sheps, Cecil G(eorge) 1913- 11-12R
Sheps, Mindel (Cherniack) 1913-1973
Obituary 37-40R
Sher, Eva CAP-2
Earlier sketch in CA 23-24
Sher, Gerson S(amuel) 1947- 81-84
Sher, Jack 1913-1988 Obituary 126
Sher, Zelig 1888-1971 Obituary 104
Shera, Jesse Hauk 1903-1982 .... CANR-2
Obituary 106
Earlier sketch in CA 7-8R
Sherar, Mariam G(hose) 1924- 45-48
Sherashevski, Boris
See Brown, John J.
Sheraton, Mimi 1926- 126
Sheraton, Neil
See Smith, Norman Edward Mace
Sheratsky, Rodney E(arl) 1933- 25-28R
Sherbo, Arthur 1918- Brief entry 113
Sherburne, Donald W(ynne) 1929- 1R
Sherburne, James (Robert) 1925- 33-36R
Sherburne, Zoa (Morin) 1912- CANR-3
Earlier sketch in CA 3R
See also SATA 3
See also CLC 30
Sherby, Linda B(arbara) 1946- 108
Shercliff, Jose 1902(?)-1985 Obituary 115
Sherdeman, Ted 1910(?)-1987 Obituary 123
Shere, Dennis 1940- 77-80
Sherek, Henry 1900-1967 .... CAP-1
Earlier sketch in CA 15-16
Sherer, Mary Louise 1901- 101
Sherer, Robert G(lenn, Jr.) 1940- 69-72
Sheret, Rene (Dundee) 1933- 29-32R
Sherfey, Mary Jane 1933-1983 Obituary 109
Shergold, N(orman) D(avid) 1925- 25-28R
Sheridan, Adora
See Hong, Jane Fay
and Pavlik, Evelyn Marie
Sheridan, Anne-Marie 1948- 85-88
Sheridan, Dorothy Elizabeth 1948- 116
Sheridan, Eugene Robert 1945- CANR-23
Earlier sketch in CA 107
Sheridan, Frances 1724-1766 .... DLB-39
Sheridan, James E(dward) 1922- 23-24R
Sheridan, James F(rancis), Jr. 1927- 29-32R
Sheridan, Jane
See Winslow, Pauline Glen
Sheridan, John V. 1915- CANR-3
Earlier sketch in CA 9-10R
Sheridan, L(ionel) A(stor) 1927- CANR-9
Earlier sketch in CA 21-22R
Sheridan, Lane
See Winslow, Pauline Glen
Sheridan, Lee
See Lee, Elsie
Sheridan, Marion Campbell 17-18R
Sheridan, Martin 1914- 104
Sheridan, Polly
See Oates, Jeannette
Sheridan, Richard B. 1918- 45-48
Sheridan, Thomas 1938- 61-64
Sheridan, Thomas L. 1926- 37-40R
Sherif, Carolyn W(ood) 1922- 17-18R
Sherif, Muzafer 1906-1988 .... CAP-1
Obituary 126
Earlier sketch in CA 13-14
Sheriff, John K(eith) 1944- 120
Sherlock, John 1932- CANR-3
Earlier sketch in CA 11-12R
Sherlock, Philip Manderson 1902- CANR-6
Earlier sketch in CA 5-6R
Sherlock, Richard 1947- 126
Sherman, A(lan) Robert 1942- 57-60
Sherman, Allan 1924-1973 101
Obituary 45-48
Sherman, Arnold 1932- CANR-14
Earlier sketch in CA 33-36R
Sherman, Arthur W(esley), Jr. 1917- .. CANR-21
Earlier sketch in CA 3R
Sherman, Barbara H(ayes) 1942- 25-28R
Sherman, Bernard 1929- 29-32R
Sherman, Cecil E(dwin) 1927- Brief entry ... 110
Sherman, Charles Bezalel 1896-1971 .... 2R
Obituary 103
Sherman, Charlotte A.
See Sherman, Jory (Tecumseh)
Sherman, Claire Richter 1930- 106
Sherman, Constance D(enise) 1909- 45-48
Sherman, D(enis) R(onald) 1934- CANR-8
Earlier sketch in CA 15-16R
See also SATA 29, 48
Sherman, Dan(iel Michael) 1950- 77-80
Sherman, Diane (Finn) 1928- CANR-5
Earlier sketch in CA 11-12R
See also SATA 12
Sherman, Eileen Bluestone 1951- 119
Sherman, Eleanor Rae 1929- 15-16R
Sherman, Elizabeth
See Friskey, Margaret (Richards)
Sherman, Eric 1947- 69-72
Sherman, Franklin (Eugene) 1928- 57-60
Sherman, G(eorge) W(itters) 1903- 117
Sherman, Harold (Morrow) 1898- 77-80
See also SATA 37
Sherman, (Marcus) Harvey 1917-1985 ...21-22R
Obituary 114
Sherman, Howard J. 1931- CANR-10
Earlier sketch in CA 15-16R
Sherman, Ingrid 1919- 103
Sherman, James E(dward) 1939- 25-28R
Sherman, Jane 1908- CANR-12
Earlier sketch in CA 73-76
Sherman, Jerry 1924- 97-100
Sherman, Joan
See Dern, Erolie Pearl Gaddis
Sherman, Jory (Tecumseh) 1932- CANR-11
Earlier sketch in CA 69-72
Sherman, Julia A(nn) 1934- 37-40R
Sherman, Kenneth 1950- 117
Sherman, L. L.
See Armentrout, Fred S(herman)
Sherman, Lawrence W(illiam) 1949- CANR-7
Earlier sketch in CA 57-60
Sherman, Martin Brief entry 116
See also CLC 19
Sherman, Martin 1941(?)- 123
Sherman, Michael
See Lowndes, Robert A(ugustine) W(ard)
Sherman, Michele 1945- 114
Sherman, Murray H(erbert) 1922- 19-20R
Sherman, Nancy
See Rosenberg, Nancy (Sherman)
Sherman, Patrick 1928- 103
Sherman, Peter Michael
See Lowndes, Robert A(ugustine) W(ard)
Sherman, Philip M(artin) 1930- 29-32R
Sherman, Ray W(esley) 1884-1971
Obituary 33-36R
Sherman, Richard B. 1929- 29-32R
Sherman, Richard M(orton) 1928-
Brief entry 107
Sherman, Robert B(ernard) 1925-
Brief entry 108
Sherman, Roger 1930- 37-40R
Sherman, Spencer E. 1936- 112
Sherman, Steve (Barry) 1938- 37-40R
Sherman, Susan Jean 1939- 1R
Sherman, T. P. 1917-1976 .... CAP-2
Earlier sketch in CA 29-32
Sherman, Theodore A(llison) 1901- 17-18R
Sherman, William David 1940- CANR-21
Earlier sketch in CA 105
Sherman, William Lewis 1927- 105
Shero, Fred (Alexander) 1925- 105
Sherover, Charles M. 25-28R
Sherr, Lynn Beth 1942- Brief entry 109
Sherr, Paul C(linton) 1920- 77-80
Sherrard, Philip (Owen Arnould) 1922- .. CANR-7
Earlier sketch in CA 13-14R
Sherriff, R(obert) C(edric) 1896-1975 85-88
Obituary 61-64
See also DLB 10
Sherriffs, Ronald E(verett) 1934-
Brief entry 112
Sherrill, Dorothy 1901- 69-72
Sherrill, Elizabeth 1928- 110
Sherrill, Henry Knox 1890-1980
Obituary 97-100
Sherrill, John L. 1923- 110
Sherrill, Robert G(lenn) 1925- CANR-15
Earlier sketch in CA 21-22R
Sherrill, Suzanne
See Woods, Sherryl
Sherrin, Edward George 1931- CANR-15
Earlier sketch in CA 23-24R
Sherrin, Ned
See Sherrin, Edward George
Sherrington, Richard (Wallace) 1940-1977 .. 108
Sherrod, Blackie AITN-2
Sherrod, Drury 1943- 109
Sherrod, Jane
See Singer, Jane Sherrod
Sherrod, Robert (Lee) 1909- 77-80
Sherry, James 1946- 112
Sherry, John (Olden) 1923- 119
Sherry, John E(rnest) H(orwath)
1932- CANR-16
Earlier sketch in CA 89-92
Sherry, Michael S(tephen) 1945- 73-76
Sherry, Norman 1925- 49-52
Sherry, Pearl Andelson 1899- 109
Sherry, (Dulcie) Sylvia 49-52
See also SATA 8
Sherry, Vincent B(ernard), Jr. 1948- 116
Shershow, Scott Cutler 1953- 123
Shertzer, Bruce E(ldon) 1928- CANR-3
Earlier sketch in CA 11-12R
Sherwan, Earl 1917- 7-8R
See also SATA 3
Sherwin, Byron L(ee) 1946- 123
Sherwin, Judith Johnson 1936- 25-28R
See also CLC 7, 15
Sherwin, Martin J(ay) 1937- Brief entry 110
Sherwin, Oscar 1902-1976 .... 3R
Obituary 65-68
Sherwin, Richard E(lliott) 1933- 69-72
Sherwin, Sidney 1920- 65-68
Sherwin, Sterling
See Hagen, John Milton
Sherwin-White, A(drian) N(icholas) 1911- ... 119
Sherwood, Debbie
See Sherwood, Deborah
Sherwood, Deborah 25-28R
Sherwood, Frank Persons 1920- CANR-9
Earlier sketch in CA 7-8R
Sherwood, Hugh C. 1928- 29-32R
Sherwood, John (Herman Mulso)
1913- CANR-21
Earlier sketches in CA 7-8R, CANR-6
Sherwood, John C(ollingwood) 1918- 13-14R
Sherwood, John J(oseph) 1933- 29-32R
Sherwood, Martin (Anthony) 1942- CANR-19
Earlier sketch in CA 102
Sherwood, Michael 1938-1976 .... CAP-2
Earlier sketch in CA 29-32
Sherwood, Morgan B(ronson) 1929- CANR-6
Earlier sketch in CA 15-16R
Sherwood, Nelson
See Bulmer, (Henry) Kenneth
Sherwood, Robert D(an) 1949- 118
Sherwood, Robert E(mmet) 1896-1955
Brief entry 104
See also DLB 7, 26
See also TCLC 3
Sherwood, William Robert 1929- 21-22R
Shesgreen, Sean N(icholas) 1939- 45-48

Shestack, Alan 1938- ... 33-36R
Shestack, Jerome J(oseph) 1925- ... 118
Shestack, Melvin (Bernard) 1931- ... 120
Sheth, Jagdish N(anchand) 1938- ... CANR-11
Earlier sketch in CA 61-64
Shetter, William Z(eiders, Jr.) 1927- ... 81-84
Shetterly, Will(iam Howard) 1955- ... 119
Shettles, Landrum Brewer 1909- ... CANR-13
Earlier sketch in CA 77-80
Shetty, C(handrashekar) M(ajur)
1927- ... CANR-10
Earlier sketch in CA 13-14R
Shetty, Sharat 1940- ... 73-76
Shev, Edward E(lmer) 1919- ... 93-96
Shevchuk, Tetiana
See Bishop, Tania Kroitor
Shevelove, Burt 1915-1982 Obituary ... 106
Shevin, David (Avram) 1951- ... 77-80
Shew, E(dward) Spencer 1908-1977 ... CANR-3
Obituary ... 69-72
Earlier sketch in CA 1R
Shewbridge, Edythe A(nne) 1943- ... 41-44R
Shewell-Cooper, W(ilfred) E(dward)
1900- ... CANR-7
Earlier sketch in CA 9-10R
Shewmaker, Kenneth E. 1936- ... 33-36R
Shi, David Emory 1951- ... 106
Shiarella, Robert 1936- ... 57-60
Shibles, Warren 1933- ... CANR-12
Earlier sketch in CA 29-32R
Shibutani, Tamotsu 1920- ... 17-18R
Shideler, John C(lement) 1949- ... 118
Shideler, Mary McDermott 1917- ... 25-28R
Shidle, Norman G(lass) 1895- ... 17-18R
Shiefman, Vicky 1942- ... 57-60
See also SATA 22
Shieh, Francis S(hih-hoa) 1926- ... 37-40R
Shiel, M(atthew) P(hipps) 1865-1947
Brief entry ... 106
See also TCLC 8
Shield, Renee Rose 1948- ... 115
Shields, Allan (Edwin) 1919- ... 65-68
Shields, Brenda Desmond (Armstrong)
1914- ... 7-8R
See also SATA 37
Shields, Carol 1935- ... 81-84
Shields, Charles 1944- ... SATA-10
Shields, Currin Vance 1918- ... 3R
Shields, David 1956- ... 124
Shields, Donald J(ames) 1937- ... 53-56
Shields, Gerald R. 1925- ... 110
Shields, Joyce Farley 1930- Brief entry ... 109
Shiels, Frederick L(ambert) 1949- ... 118
Shiels, George 1886-1949 Brief entry ... 111
See also DLB 10
Shiels, W(illiam) Eugene 1897- ... CAP-1
Earlier sketch in CA 9-10
Shiers, George 1908- ... 73-76
Shiff, Nathan A. 1914- ... 25-28R
Shiffert, Edith (Marcombe) 1916- ... CANR-6
Earlier sketch in CA 13-14R
Shiffrin, Nancy 1944- ... 81-84
Shiflet, Kenneth E(lwood) 1918-1978 ... CANR-2
Obituary ... 81-84
Earlier sketch in CA 2R
Shiflett, Lee
See Shiflett, Orvin Lee
Shiflett, Orvin Lee 1947- ... 115
Shiga, Naoya 1883-1971 ... 101
Obituary ... 33-36R
See also CLC 33
Shigley, Forrest Dwight 1930- ... 4R
Shih, Chung-wen ... 81-84
Shih, Vincent Y(u) C(hung) 1903- ... 77-80
Shih Hsio-Yen 1933- ... 119
Shikes, Ralph E. 1912- ... CANR-12
Earlier sketch in CA 29-32R
Shillaber, Benjamin Penhallow
1814-1890 ... DLB-1, 11
Shiller, Jack G(erald) 1928- ... 73-76
Shilling, Dana 1953- ... 109
Shilling, N(ed) 1924- ... 29-32R
Shillinglaw, Gordon 1925- ... CANR-7
Earlier sketch in CA 17-18R
Shillony, Ben-Ami 1937- ... 73-76
Shiloh, Ailon 1924- ... 33-36R
Shils, Edward B. 1915- ... CANR-6
Earlier sketch in CA 7-8R
Shilton, Lance(lot) R(upert) 1921- ... 7-8R
Shilts, Randy 1952(?)- Brief entry ... 115
Shimazaki, Haruki 1872-1943 Brief entry ... 105
Shimazaki, Toson
See Shimazaki, Haruki
See also TCLC 5
Shimberg, Benjamin 1918- ... 45-48
Shimberg, Elaine Fantle 1937- ... 112
Shimer, Dorothy Blair 1911- ... 45-48
Shimin, Symeon 1902- ... 81-84
See also SATA 13
Shimoniak, Wasyl 1923- Brief entry ... 108
Shimota, Helen
See Gross, Helen Shimota
Shinagel, Michael 1934- ... 25-28R
Shindell, Sidney 1923- ... 15-16R
Shine, Deborah 1932- ... 110
Shine, Frances L(ouise) 1927- ... 25-28R
Shine, Ted 1931- ... CANR-24
Earlier sketches in CA 77-80, CANR-13
See also BW
See also DLB 38
Shiner, Larry (Ernest) 1934- ... 21-22R
Shiner, Roger A(lfred) 1940- Brief entry ... 109
Shingleton, John D. ... 115
Shingleton, Royce (Gordon, Sr.)
1935- ... CANR-12
Earlier sketch in CA 29-32R
Shinkle, James D. 1897(?)-1973 Obituary ... 104
Shinkle, Tex
See Shinkle, James D.
Shinn, Everett 1876-1953 ... SATA-21
Shinn, Larry Dwight 1942- ... 107
Shinn, Roger L(incoln) 1917- ... CANR-18
Earlier sketch in CA 4R
Shinnie, Peter Lewis 1915- ... 103
Shinoda, Minoru 1915- ... 7-8R
Shinwell, Emanuel 1884-1986 Obituary ... 119
Shipler, David K(arr) 1942- ... CANR-21
Earlier sketch in CA 103
Shiplett, June Lund 1930- ... CANR-16
Earlier sketch in CA 81-84
Shipley, David
See Holden, David (Shipley)
Shipley, David O. 1925- ... 37-40R
Shipley, Joseph T(wadell) 1893-1988 ... CANR-9
Obituary ... 125
Earlier sketch in CA 15-16R
Shipley, Nan (Sommerville) ... 11-12R
Shipley, Peter (Samuel) 1946- ... CANR-20
Earlier sketch in CA 103
Shipley, (Howard) Thorne 1927- ... 7-8R
Shipman, David 1932- ... CANR-12
Earlier sketch in CA 29-32R
Shipman, Harry L(ongfellow) 1948- ... CANR-10
Earlier sketch in CA 65-68
Shipp, Nelson 1892- ... 57-60
Shipp, Thomas J. 1918- ... 13-14R
Shippen, Katherine B(inney) 1892-1980 ... 7-8R
Obituary ... 93-96
See also SATA 1, 23
Shipper, Frank M(artin) 1945- ... 119
Shippey, Frederick Alexander 1908- ... CAP-1
Earlier sketch in CA 13-14
Shippey, (Henry) Lee 1884-1969
Obituary ... 89-92
Shippey, Thomas Alan 1943- ... 108
Shippy, Richard W. 1927- ... 81-84
Shipton, Clifford K(enyon) 1902-1973 ... CAP-2
Earlier sketch in CA 17-18
Shipton, Eric Earle 1907-1977 ... 65-68
Obituary ... 69-72
See also SATA 10
Shipway, George 1908- ... 25-28R
Shirakawa, Yoshikazu 1935- ... CANR-14
Earlier sketch in CA 73-76
Shire, Helena (Mary) Mennie 1912- ... 29-32R
Shirer, William L(awrence) 1904- ... CANR-7
Earlier sketch in CA 9-10R
See also SATA 45
See also DLB 4
Shires, Henry M(illis) 1913- ... 19-20R
Shires, Linda M(arguerite) 1950- ... 118
Shirk, Evelyn Urban 1918- ... 17-18R
Shirk, George H(enry) 1913- ... 17-18R
Shirk, Susan L(ee) 1945- ... 108
Shirkey, Albert P(atterson) 1904- ... CAP-2
Earlier sketch in CA 17-18
Shirley, Frances A(nn) 1931- ... CANR-2
Earlier sketch in CA 7-8R
Shirley, Glenn 1916- ... 89-92
Shirley, Hardy L(omax) 1900- ... 37-40R
Shirley, James 1596-1666 ... DLB-58
Shirley, John 1953- ... 126
Shirley, John William 1908- ... 126
Brief entry ... 114
Shirley, Ralph 1865-1946 Brief entry ... 117
Shirley-Smith, Hubert 1901-1981 Obituary ... 113
Shirreffs, Gordon D(onald) 1914- ... CANR-21
Earlier sketches in CA 15-16R, CANR-6
See also SATA 11
Shirts, Morris A(lpine) 1922- ... 73-76
Shissler, Barbara J(ohnson) 1931- ... 29-32R
Shivanandan, Mary 1932- ... CANR-12
Earlier sketch in CA 73-76
Shively, Donald H(oward) 1921-
Brief entry ... 115
Shively, George Jenks 1893(?)-1980
Obituary ... 97-100
Shivers, Alfred Samuel 1929- ... 41-44R
Shivers, Jay S(anford) 1930- ... CANR-12
Earlier sketch in CA 33-36R
Shivers, Samuel A.
See Shivers, Alfred Samuel
Shivpuri, Gopi Krishna 1903-1984 ... 101
Obituary ... 113
Shklovsky, Iosif Samuilovitch 1916-1985
Obituary ... 115
Shklovsky, Viktor Borisovich 1893-1984
Obituary ... 114
Shlemon, Barbara Leahy 1936- ... 112
Shlonsky, Abraham 1898(?)-1973
Obituary ... 41-44R
Shmueli, Adi 1941- ... CANR-1
Earlier sketch in CA 45-48
Shneerson, Grigory Mikhailovich
1901-1982 Obituary ... 106
Shneiderman, Ben A. 1947- ... 115
Shneiderman, Samuel L(oeb) 1906- ... 97-100
Shneidman, Conalee Levine
See Levine-Shneidman, Conalee
Shneidman, Edwin S. 1918- ... 29-32R
Shneidman, J(erome) Lee 1929- ... 37-40R
Shneour, Elie A(lexis) 1925- ... 37-40R
Shoaf, Richard Allen 1948- ... 119
Shoben, Edward Joseph, Jr. 1918- ... 21-22R
Shober, Joyce Lee 1932- ... 4R
Shoberg, Lore 1949- ... 33-36R
Shobin, David 1945- ... CANR-20
Earlier sketch in CA 104
Shoblad, Richard H(anson) 1937- ... 41-44R
Shock, Julian
See Williamson, Gerald Neal
Shock, Nathan W(etherill) 1906- ... 7-8R
Shockley, Ann Allen 1927- ... CANR-1
Earlier sketch in CA 49-52
See also BW
See also DLB 33
Shockley, Donald G(rady) 1937- ... 103
Shockley, William (Bradford) 1910-
Brief entry ... 113
Shoe, Lucy T.
See Meritt, Lucy Shoe
Shoemaker, Don(ald) C(leavenger)
1912- ... 97-100
Shoemaker, Donald J(ay) 1927- ... 37-40R
Shoemaker, Leonard Calvin 1881- ... CAP-1
Earlier sketch in CA 15-16
Shoemaker, Lynn Henry 1939- ... CANR-9
Earlier sketch in CA 65-68
Shoemaker, Richard H(eston) 1907-1970 ... CAP-1
Earlier sketch in CA 11-12
Shoemaker, Robert John 1919- ... 15-16R
Shoemaker, Robin 1949- ... 108
Shoemaker, William H(utchinson) 1902- ... 15-16R
Shoemaker, William Lee 1931- Brief entry ... 115
Shoemaker, Willie
See Shoemaker, William Lee
Shoenight, Aloise 1914- ... 77-80
Shoesmith, Kathleen A(nne) 1938- ... CANR-17
Earlier sketches in CA 49-52, CANR-1
Shofner, Jerrell H(arris) 1929- ... 57-60
Shofner, Robert D(ancey) 1933- ... 57-60
Shokeid, Moshe 1936- ... CANR-16
Earlier sketch in CA 41-44R
Sholinsky, Jane 1943- ... 89-92
Sholokhov, Mikhail (Aleksandrovich)
1905-1984 ... 101
Obituary ... 112
See also SATA 36
See also CLC 7, 15
Shomaker, Dianna 1934- ... 109
Shomon, Joseph James 1914- ... 73-76
Shomroni, Reuven
See von Block, Bela W(illiam)
Shone, Patric
See Hanley, James
Shone, Robert 1906- ... 109
Shone, Ronald 1946- ... CANR-20
Earlier sketch in CA 103
Shonfield, Andrew (Akiba) 1917-1981 ... 105
Obituary ... 102
Shontz, Franklin C(urtis) 1926- ... 19-20R
Shook, Karel 1920-1985 Obituary ... 117
Shook, Laurence K(ennedy) 1909- ... 73-76
Shook, Robert L. 1938- ... CANR-23
Earlier sketches in CA 61-64, CANR-8
Shoolbred, C(laude) F(rederick) 1901- ... CAP-2
Earlier sketch in CA 25-28
Shor, Elizabeth N(oble) 1930- ... 110
Shor, Franc(is Marion Luther) 1914-1974
Obituary ... 111
Shor, Ira 1945- ... 126
Shor, Joel 1919- ... 89-92
Shor, Pekay 1923- ... 45-48
Shor, Ronald (Edwin) 1930- ... 61-64
Shorb, Wil(bert Hanson, Jr.) 1938- ... 45-48
Shore, Bernard (Alexander Royle)
1896-1985 Obituary ... 116
Shore, Jane 1947- ... 77-80
Shore, June Lewis ... 105
See also SATA 30
See also AITN 1
Shore, Norman
See Smith, Norman Edward Mace
Shore, Paul J(ohn) 1956- ... 118
Shore, Philippa
See Holbeche, Philippa Jack
Shore, Robert 1924- ... SATA-39
Shore, Sidney 1921-1981 Obituary ... 103
Shore, William B(urton) 1925- ... 53-56
Shore, Wilma 1913- ... 15-16R
Shores, David L(ee) 1933- ... 123
Brief entry ... 118
Shores, Louis 1904-1981 ... CANR-8
Obituary ... 104
Earlier sketch in CA 15-16R
Shorris, Earl 1936- ... CANR-10
Earlier sketch in CA 65-68
Shorrock, William I(rwin) 1941- ... 65-68
Short, Alan Lennox
See Lennox-Short, Alan
Short, Alison 1920- ... 61-64
Short, Bobby
See Short, Robert Waltrip
Short, (Charles) Christopher (Dudley)
(?)-1978 ... CANR-2
Earlier sketch in CA 4R
Short, Clarice 1910-1977 ... 45-48
Obituary ... 103
Short, Edmund C(oen) 1931- ... 25-28R
Short, Howard E(lmo) 1907- ... 61-64
Short, Jackson ... 53-56
Short, James F(ranklin, Jr.) 1924- ... CANR-25
Earlier sketches in CA 5-6R, CANR-8
Short, James R. 1922(?)-1980 Obituary ... 103
Short, Luke
See Glidden, Frederick D(illey)
Short, Michael 1937- ... 117
Short, Philip 1945- ... 105
Short, Robert L(ester) 1932- ... 77-80
Short, Robert Stuart 1938- ... 29-32R
Short, Robert Waltrip 1924(?)- Brief entry ... 107
Short, Roger
See Arkin, Alan (Wolf)
Short, Roger, Jr.
See Eyen, Tom
Short, Roy Hunter 1902- ... 120
Short, Ruth Gordon ... CANR-6
Earlier sketch in CA 3R
Short, Thayne R(edford) 1929- ... 108
Short, Wayne 1926- ... 11-12R
Shortall, Leonard W. ... 81-84
See also SATA 19
Shorter, Aylward 1932- ... 81-84
Shorter, Carl
See Schwalberg, Carol(yn Ernestine
Stein)
Shorter, Edward 1941- ... 73-76
Shorthouse, Joseph Henry 1834-1903
Brief entry ... 121
See also DLB 18
Shorto, Harry L(eonard) 1919- ... 7-8R
Shortt, Terence Michael 1911- ... 77-80
Shostak, Arthur B. 1937- ... 108
Shostak, Jerome 1913- ... CANR-7
Earlier sketch in CA 19-20R
Shostak, Stanley 1938- ... 117
Shostakovich, Dmitri 1906-1975 Obituary ... 113
Shosteck, Robert 1910-1979 ... CANR-11
Obituary ... 85-88
Earlier sketch in CA 61-64
Shotwell, Louisa Rossiter 1902- ... CANR-4
Earlier sketch in CA 3R
See also SATA 3
Shouksmith, George A. 1931- ... 49-52
Shoumatoff, Alex(ander) 1946- ... CANR-9
Earlier sketch in CA 53-56
Shoup, Carl S(umner) 1902- ... 49-52
Shoup, Laurence H(enry) 1943- ... 102
Shoup, Paul Snedden 1929- ... 106
Shover, John L. 1927- ... 21-22R
Showalter, Dennis 1942- ... 89-92
Showalter, Elaine 1941- ... 57-60
See also DLB 67
Showalter, English, Jr. 1935- ... 53-56
Showalter, Jean B(reckinridge) ... 21-22R
See also SATA 12
Showalter, Ronda Kerr 1942- ... 37-40R
Showell, Ellen Harvey 1934- ... 85-88
See also SATA 33
Showers, Paul C. 1910- ... CANR-4
Earlier sketch in CA 1R
See also SATA 21
See also CLR 6
Showers, Renald E(dward) 1935- ... CANR-13
Earlier sketch in CA 77-80
Showers, Victor 1910- ... 53-56
Shoy, Lee Ang
See Sheridan, L(ionel) A(stor)
Shrady, Maria 1924- ... 49-52
Shragin, Boris 1926- ... 102
Shrake, Bud
See Shrake, Edwin
Shrake, Edwin 1931- Brief entry ... 116
Shreve, L(evin) G(ale) 1910- ... 101
Shreve, Susan Richards 1939- ... CANR-5
Earlier sketch in CA 49-52
See also CAAS 5
See also SATA 41, 46
See also CLC 23
Shriber, Ione Sandberg 1911-1987
Obituary ... 121
Shrimpton, Gordon Spencer 1941- ... 115
Shrimsley, Anthony 1934-1984 Obituary ... 114
Shrimsley, Bernard 1931- ... 103
Shriver, Donald W(oods), Jr. 1927- ... CANR-1
Earlier sketch in CA 45-48
Shriver, George H(ite), Jr. 1931- ... 21-22R
Shriver, Harry C(lair) 1904- ... CANR-10
Earlier sketch in CA 65-68
Shriver, Peggy (Ann) L(eu) 1931- ... 107
Shriver, Phillip Raymond 1922- ... 15-16R
Shriver, Rosalia (Oliver) 1927- ... 115
Shroder, Maurice Z(orensky) 1933- ... 1R
Shrodes, Caroline 1908- ... CANR-4
Earlier sketch in CA 4R
Shropshire, W(alter), Jr. 1932- ... 118
Shrout, Thomas R(euben) 1919- ... 41-44R
Shroyer, Frederick B(enjamin)
1916-1983 ... CANR-13
Earlier sketch in CA 13-14R
Shryock, (Edwin) Harold 1906- ... CANR-8
Earlier sketch in CA 23-24R
Shryock, Richard Harrison 1893-1972 ... CAP-2
Obituary ... 33-36R
Earlier sketch in CA 17-18
Shtainmets, Leon ... 105
See also SATA 32
Shtemenko, Sergei Matveyevich
1907-1976 ... 103
Shternfeld, Ari A(bramovich) 1905-1980
Obituary ... 105
Shu, Austin Chi-wei 1915- ... 29-32R
Shub, Beth
See Pessen, Beth
Shub, David 1887-1973 Obituary ... 41-44R
Shub, Elizabeth ... CANR-15
Earlier sketch in CA 41-44R
See also SATA 5
Shubik, Martin 1926- ... CANR-2
Earlier sketch in CA 7-8R
Shubin, Seymour 1921- ... 3R
Shucard, Alan R(obert) 1935- ... CANR-26
Earlier sketch in CA 61-64
Shu Ch'ing-ch'un 1899-1966 Obituary ... 109
Shuchman, Abraham 1919-1978
Obituary ... 77-80
Shue, Larry 1946-1985 Obituary ... 117
Shuffelton, Frank 1940- ... 115
Shuford, Cecil Eugene 1907- ... 13-14R
See also AITN 1
Shuford, Gene
See Shuford, Cecil Eugene
Shugrue, Michael F(rancis) 1934- ... 21-22R
Shu-Jen, Chou 1881-1936 Brief entry ... 104
Shukman, Harold 1931- ... 53-56
Shula, Don(ald Francis) 1930- Brief entry ... 106

Shulberg, Alan
See Wilkes-Hunter, R(ichard)
Shulevitz, Uri 1935- CANR-3
Earlier sketch in CA 11-12R
See also SATA 3, 50
See also DLB 61
See also CLR 5
Shull, Fremont Adam, Jr. 1924- CANR-1
Earlier sketch in CA 3R
Shull, Margaret Anne Wyse 1940- 77-80
Shull, Peg
See Shull, Margaret Anne Wyse
Shulman, Albert M(aimon) 1902- 49-52
Shulman, Alix Kates 1932- 29-32R
See also SATA 7
See also CLC 2, 10
Shulman, Arnold 1914- 29-32R
Shulman, Bernard H. 1922- 108
Shulman, Charles E. 1904-1968 CAP-1
Earlier sketch in CA 13-14
Shulman, David Dean 1949- 102
Shulman, Frank Joseph 1943- CANR-12
Earlier sketch in CA 29-32R
Shulman, Harry 1903-1955 Brief entry 112
Shulman, Harry Manuel 1899- 4R
Shulman, Irving 1913- CANR-6
Earlier sketch in CA 4R
See also SATA 13
Shulman, Marshall Darrow 1916- 3R
Shulman, Max 1919-1988 89-92
Obituary 126
See also DLB 11
Shulman, Milton 1913- 103
Shulman, Morton 1925- CANR-14
Earlier sketch in CA 23-24R
See also AITN 1
Shulman, Neil B(arnett) 1945- CANR-26
Earlier sketches in CA 65-68, CANR-9
Shulman, Sandra (Dawn) 1944- CANR-9
Earlier sketch in CA 21-22R
Shultz, George P(ratt) 1920- 104
Shultz, Gladys Denny 1895- 49-52
Shultz, William J(ohn) 1902-1970 CANR-16
Obituary 103
Earlier sketch in CA 2R
Shulvass, Moses A. 1909- 15-16R
Shumaker, Wayne 1910- 7-8R
Shuman, Bruce A(lan) 1941- 110
Shuman, James B(urrow) 1932- 61-64
Shuman, Nicholas R(oman) 1921- 109
Shuman, R(obert) Baird 1929- CANR-4
Earlier sketch in CA 4R
Shuman, Samuel I(rving) 1925- CANR-3
Earlier sketch in CA 11-12R
Shumsky, Zena
See Hampson, Zena
Shumway, Floyd M(allory, Jr.) 1917- 29-32R
Shumway, George (Alfred, Jr.) 1928- 9-10R
Shumway, Mary L. 1926- CANR-7
Earlier sketch in CA 17-18R
Shupp, Mike 1946- 121
Shura, Mary Francis
See Craig, Mary (Francis) S(hura)
Shurden, Walter B(yron) 1937- CANR-21
Earlier sketch in CA 69-72
Shurkin, Joel N. 1938- CANR-14
Earlier sketch in CA 69-72
Shurr, William H(oward) 1932- CANR-18
Earlier sketch in CA 41-44R
Shurter, Robert L(e Fevre) 1907-1974 CANR-2
Earlier sketch in CA 1R
Shurtleff, Malcolm C., Jr. 1922- 7-8R
Shurtleff, Michael 1930- 41-44R
Shurtleff, William 1941- CANR-16
Earlier sketch in CA 93-96
Shuseki, Hayashi
See Hubbell, Lindley Williams
Shuster, Albert H., Jr. 1917- 19-20R
Shuster, Alvin 1930- Brief entry 113
Shuster, George Nauman 1894-1977 77-80
Obituary 69-72
Shuster, Joe 1914- CLC-21
Shuster, Ronald L(owell) 1927- 45-48
Shusterman, David 1912- 25-28R
Shute, Alberta V(an Horn) 1906- CANR-7
Earlier sketch in CA 57-60
Shute, Gary Brana
See Brana-Shute, Gary
Shute, Henry A. 1856-1943 DLB-9
Shute, Nerina 101
Shute, Nevil
See Norway, Nevil Shute
See also CLC 30
Shute, R(eginald) Wayne 1933- 29-32R
Shute, Wallace B. 1911- 29-32R
Shute, Wilfred Eugene 1907- 105
Shuttle, Penelope (Diane) 1947- 93-96
See also DLB 14, 40
See also CLC 7
Shuttlesworth, Dorothy Edwards CANR-4
Earlier sketch in CA 1R
See also SATA 3
Shuttleworth, John 1937- AITN-1
Shuval, Judith T(annenbaum) 1925- CANR-25
Earlier sketch in CA 45-48
Shuy, Roger W(ellington) 1931- CANR-13
Earlier sketch in CA 61-64
Shwadran, Benjamin 1907- CANR-20
Earlier sketches in CA 13-14R, CANR-5
Shwartz, Susan Martha 1949- 109
Shwayder, David S(amuel) 1926- 106
Shy, John W(illard) 1931- CANR-3
Earlier sketch in CA 5-6R
Shyer, Marlene Fanta CANR-11
Earlier sketch in CA 69-72
See also SATA 13
Shyne, Ann W(entworth) 1914- 115
Shyre, Paul 1929- 103
Siano, Mary M(artha) 1924- 77-80
Siberell, Anne 104
See also SATA 29
Siberry, (Jane) Elizabeth 1957- 122
Sibley, Agnes M(arie) 1914- 61-64
Sibley, Celestine 1917- 85-88
Sibley, Don 1922- SATA-12
Sibley, Elbridge 1903- CAP-1
Earlier sketch in CA 13-14
Sibley, Marilyn McAdams 1923- 21-22R
Sibley, Mulford Quickert 1912- CANR-6
Earlier sketch in CA 7-8R
Sibley, Patricia (Hayles) 1928- 97-100
Sibley, Susan
See Kinnicutt, Susan Sibley
Sibly, John 1920- 2R
Sices, David 1933- 25-28R
Sichel, Peter M(ax) F(erdinand) 1922- 65-68
Sichel, Pierre (Laugier) 1915- 1R
Sichel, Werner 1934- CANR-23
Earlier sketches in CA 23-24R, CANR-8
Sichov, Vladimir 1945- 108
Sicignano, Robert 1946- 116
Siciliano, Vincent Paul 1911- CAP-2
Earlier sketch in CA 29-32
Sicinski, Andrzej 1924- 115
Sickels, Robert J(udd) 1931- 41-44R
Sicker, Philip 1951- 103
Sickles, William Russell 1913- 57-60
Sickman, Laurence C(halfant) S(tevens)
1906-1988 CAP-1
Obituary 125
Earlier sketch in CA 11-12
Siculan, Daniel 1922- SATA-12
Siddall, William R(ichard) 1928- 41-44R
Siddiqi, Akhtar Husain 1925- 61-64
Siddiqui, Ashraf (Hossain) 1927- CANR-2
Earlier sketch in CA 7-8R
Siddons, Anne Rivers 101
Siddons, Robert 1952- 119
Sidel, Victor W(illiam) 1931- CANR-9
Earlier sketch in CA 65-68
Sider, Don 1933- 77-80
Sider, Robert Dick 1932- CANR-16
Earlier sketch in CA 37-40R
Sider, Ronald J(ames) 1939- CANR-17
Earlier sketch in CA 93-96
Siders, Ellis L(eroy) 1920- 17-18R
Sidetracked Home Executives
See Jones, Peggy
and Young, Pam
Sidey, Hugh (Swanson) 1927- 124
Brief entry 111
Sidgwick, Henry 1838-1900 Brief entry 120
Sidhwa, Bapsy (N.) 1938- CANR-25
Earlier sketch in CA 108
Sidhwa, Keki R(attanshah) 1926- 69-72
Sidjakov, Nicolas 1924- SATA-18
Sidley, Nathan T(heodore) 1929- 113
Sidnell, Michael John 1935- 113
Sidney, Frank
See Warwick, Alan R(oss)
Sidney, Jonathan
See Cooper, Emmanuel
Sidney, Kathleen M(arion) 1944- 103
Sidney, Margaret
See Lothrop, Harriet Mulford Stone
Sidney, Neilma
See Gantner, Neilma
Sidney-Fryer, Donald 1934- 45-48
Sidowski, Joseph B(oleslaus) 1925- 21-22R
Sidran, Ben H. 1943- 102
Siebel, Fritz (Frederick) 1913- SATA-44
Siebenheller, Norma 1937- 107
Siebenschuh, William R(obert) 1942- 89-92
Sieber, Joan E. 1937- 114
Sieber, Roy 1923- 102
Sieber, Sam Dixon 1931- 13-14R
Siebert, Fred(rick) Seaton 1901- 21-22R
Siedel, Frank 1914- 25-28R
Siedel, James M. 1937- 25-28R
Siegal, Aranka 1930- 112
See also SATA 37
Siegal, Mordecai 1934- 102
Siegal, Sanford (Sherwin) 1928- 105
Siegan, Bernard H(erbert) 1924- 65-68
Siegel, Adrienne 1936- CANR-12
Earlier sketch in CA 61-64
Siegel, Beatrice CANR-18
Earlier sketch in CA 101
See also SATA 36
Siegel, Ben 1925- 77-80
Siegel, Benjamin 1914- CANR-4
Earlier sketch in CA 3R
Siegel, Bernie S(hepard) 1932- 123
Siegel, Bertram M. 1936- 25-28R
Siegel, Dorothy (Schainman) 1932- 11-12R
Siegel, Eli 1902-1978 CANR-9
Obituary 81-84
Earlier sketch in CA 19-20R
Siegel, Ernest 1922- 73-76
Siegel, Esther 1949- 102
Siegel, Gonnie McClung 1928- 110
Siegel, Helen
See Siegl, Helen
Siegel, Irving H(erbert) 1914-1988 CANR-9
Obituary 125
Earlier sketch in CA 21-22R
Siegel, Jack
See Siegel, Jacob
Siegel, Jacob 1913- 17-18R
Siegel, James T. 1937- Brief entry 113
Siegel, Jerome 1914- Brief entry 116
See also CLC 21
Siegel, Jerry
See Siegel, Jerome
Siegel, June 1929- 77-80
Siegel, Lee 1945- 126
Siegel, Marcia B. 1932- 69-72
Siegel, Mark Richard 1949- 110
Siegel, Martin 1933- 33-36R
Siegel, Mary-Ellen
See Siegel, Mary-Ellen Kulkin
Siegel, Mary-Ellen Kulkin 1932- 116
Siegel, Max 1904-1972 Obituary 104
Siegel, Maxwell E(dward) 1933- 101
Siegel, Paul N. 1916- 37-40R
Siegel, Richard L(ewis) 1940- 73-76
Siegel, Robert (Harold) 1939- CANR-21
Earlier sketches in CA 53-56, CANR-5
See also SATA 39
Siegel, Seymour 1927-1988 Obituary 124
Siegel, Stanley E(lliott) 1928- 41-44R
Siegel-Gorelick, Bryna 1954- 115
Siegelman, James Howard 1951- 81-84
Siegelman, Jim
See Siegelman, James Howard
Siegener, Ray 1931- Brief entry 118
Siegener, Ray(mond) 1931- 123
Siegl, Helen 1924- SATA-34
Siegle, Bernard A(ndrew) 1914- 89-92
Siegler, Frederick Adrian 1932- 49-52
Siegler, Ilene C. 1946- 114
Siegman, Gita 1939- 112
Siegmeister, Elie 1909- CANR-1
Earlier sketch in CA 3R
Siegner, C(larence) Vernon, Jr. 1920- 4R
Sielaff, Theodore J. 1920- 13-14R
Sieller, William Vincent 1917- 29-32R
Siemanowski, Richard F. 1922(?)-1981
Obituary 104
Siemens, Reynold Gerrard 1932- 41-44R
Siemon, James Ralph 1948- 121
Siemon, Jeff 1950- 103
Sienkiewicz, Henryk (Adam Aleksander
Pius) 1846-1916 Brief entry 104
See also TCLC 3
Sienko, Michell J. 1923-1983 Obituary 111
Siepmann, Charles Arthur 1899-1985 1R
Obituary 115
Sierra, Gregorio Martinez
See Martinez Sierra, Gregorio
Sierra, Maria (de la O'LeJarraga) Martinez
See Martinez Sierra, Maria (de la
O'LeJarraga)
Sies, Luther F(rank) 1927- 111
Siev, Asher 1913- 57-60
Sievers, Allen M. 1918- 89-92
Sievers, Harry J(oseph) 1920-1977 25-28R
Obituary 73-76
Sievers, W(ieder) David 1919-1966 1R
Obituary 103
Siewert, Frances E. (Cornelius) 1881- CAP-1
Earlier sketch in CA 11-12
Sifakis, G(regory) M(ichael) 1935- 25-28R
Siffert, Robert S(pencer) 1918- 109
Sifford, (Charles) Darrell 1931- CANR-15
Earlier sketch in CA 77-80
Sifton, Claire 1897(?)-1980 Obituary 93-96
Sifton, Paul F. 1893(?)-1972 Obituary 33-36R
Sigal, Clancy 1926- 3R
See also CLC 7
Sigal, Leon V(ictor) 1942- Brief entry 114
Sigband, Norman Bruce 1920- CANR-17
Earlier sketches in CA 7-8R, CANR-2
Sigel, Efrem 1943- 121
Sigelschiffer, Saul 1902- 81-84
Sigler, Jay A(drian) 1933- 25-28R
Sigmund, Paul E(ugene) 1929- CANR-18
Earlier sketches in CA 7-8R, CANR-2
Signoret, Simone 1921-1985 Obituary 117
Sigourney, Lydia Howard (Huntley)
1791-1865 DLB-1, 42, 73
Sigurjonsson, Johann 1880-1919 TCLC-27
Sigworth, Oliver F(rederic) 1921- 15-16R
Sihanouk, Norodom
See Norodom Sihanouk (Varman),
Samdech Preah
Siirala, Aarne 1919- 13-14R
Sik, Endre 1891-1978 Obituary 77-80
Sikes, Herschel Moreland 1928- 17-18R
Sikes, Walter W(allace) 1925- 57-60
Sikora, Frank J(oseph) 1936- 115
Sikora, Joseph (John) 1932-1967 CAP-2
Earlier sketch in CA 17-18
Sikora, Stefan
See Rey, Michael Stephan
Sikorsky, Igor (Ivan) 1889-1972 Obituary 113
Siks, Geraldine Brain 1912- 25-28R
Sikula, Andrew F(rank) 1944- CANR-2
Earlier sketch in CA 49-52
Silangan, Manuel
See Yabes, Leopoldo Y(abes)
Silbajoris, Frank
See Silbajoris, Rimvydas
Silbajoris, Rimvydas 1926- 25-28R
Silber, Evelyn (Ann) 1949- 124
Silber, Irwin 1925- 11-12R
Silber, Joan 1945- CANR-20
Earlier sketch in CA 104
Silber, Kate 1902- 77-80
Silber, Mark 1946- 45-48
Silber, Norman I. 1951- 114
Silber, William L. 1942- 29-32R
Silberg, Moshe 1900-1975 Obituary 61-64
Silberg, Richard 1942- 23-24R
Silberger, Julius 1929- CANR-21
Earlier sketch in CA 105
Silberkleit, Louis Horace 1905-1986
Obituary 118
Silberman, Charles E(liot) 1925- CANR-7
Earlier sketch in CA 9-10R
Silberman, Jerome 1935(?)- Brief entry 116
Silberman, Neil Asher 1950- 108
Silbermann, Eileen Z(ieget) 1925- 114
Silbersack, John (Walter) 1954- 107
Silberschlag, Eisig 1903- CANR-17
Earlier sketches in CA 4R, CANR-1
Silberschmidt, Max 1899- 65-68
Silberstang, Edwin 1930- CANR-3
Earlier sketch in CA 49-52
Silberstein, Gerard Edward 1926- 37-40R
Silberstein, Howard E. 1907(?)-1984
Obituary 112
Silberstein, Warren P(aul) 1948- 110
Silberstein-Storfer, Muriel (Rosoff) 111
Silbey, Joel H. 1933- 21-22R
Silcock, Sara Lesley 1947- SATA-12
Silcock, Thomas H(enry) 1910- 11-12R
Silcox, David Phillips 1937- 109
Silen, Juan Angel 1938- 33-36R
Silet, Charles L(oring) P(rovine) 1942- CANR-17
Earlier sketch in CA 93-96
Silitch, Clarissa MacVeagh 1930- 112
Silk, Andrew 1953(?)-1981 Obituary 106
Silk, Leonard S(olomon) 1918- CANR-4
Earlier sketch in CA 2R
Silkin, Jon 1930- 7-8R
See also CAAS 5
See also DLB 27
See also CLC 2, 6, 43
Silko, Leslie Marmon 1948- 122
Brief entry 115
See also CLC 23
Sill, Geoffrey M(ichael) 1944- 111
Sill, Gertrude Grace 69-72
Sill, Sterling Welling 1903- CANR-6
Earlier sketch in CA 57-60
Sillanpaa, Frans Eemil 1888-1964
Obituary 93-96
See also CLC 19
Sillem, Edward 1916-1964 5-6R
Sillen, Samuel 1911(?)-1973 Obituary 41-44R
Sillery, Anthony 1903-1976 CANR-5
Obituary 65-68
Earlier sketch in CA 7-8R
Silliman, Ron(ald Glenn) 1946- 45-48
Silliphant, Stirling (Dale) 1918- CANR-14
Earlier sketch in CA 73-76
See also DLB 26
Sillitoe, Alan 1928- CANR-26
Earlier sketches in CA 11-12R, CANR-8
See also CAAS 2
See also DLB 14
See also CLC 1, 3, 6, 10, 19
See also AITN 1
Sillman, Leonard (Dexter) 1908-1982
Obituary 105
Sills, Beverly 1929- 89-92
Sills, David Lawrence 1920- 33-36R
Sills, Frank D(reyer) 1914- 4R
Sills, Jennifer
See Lewis, Stephen
Sills, Ruth C(urtis) 29-32R
Silman, Roberta 1934- 101
See also DLB 28
Silone, Ignazio 1900-1978 CAP-2
Obituary 81-84
Earlier sketch in CA 25-28
See also CLC 4
Siluriensis, Leolinus
See Jones, Arthur Llewellyn
Silva, Eduardo Neale
See Neale-Silva, Eduardo
Silva, Joseph
See Goulart, Ron(ald Joseph)
Silva, Julian 1927- 115
Silva, Julio A(lberto) 1933- 17-18R
Silva, Ruth C. 13-14R
Silvanus
See Strasser, Bernard Paul
Silvaroli, Nicholas J. 1930- CANR-12
Earlier sketch in CA 29-32R
Silver, A(aron) David 1941- 124
Silver, A(aron) Henry 1891-1986 Obituary 121
Silver, Abba Hillel 1893-1963 2R
Silver, Alain (Joel) 1947- CANR-10
Earlier sketch in CA 57-60
Silver, Alfred 1951- CANR-15
Earlier sketch in CA 85-88
Silver, Daniel Jeremy 1928- CANR-3
Earlier sketch in CA 7-8R
Silver, Gary (Thomas) 1944- 89-92
Silver, Gerald A(lbert) 1932- CANR-13
Earlier sketch in CA 33-36R
Silver, Harold 1928- CANR-10
Earlier sketch in CA 23-24R
Silver, Isidore 1934- 53-56
Silver, James W(esley) 1907-1988 9-10R
Obituary 126
Silver, Joan Micklin 1935- 121
Brief entry 114
See also CLC 20
Silver, Jody 1942- 109
Silver, Marjorie A. 1948- 93-96
Silver, Nathan 1936- CANR-11
Earlier sketch in CA 21-22R
Silver, Nicholas
See Faust, Frederick (Shiller)
Silver, Philip Warnock 1932- 106
Silver, Richard
See Bulmer, (Henry) Kenneth
Silver, Rollo G(abriel) 1909- CAP-1
Earlier sketch in CA 19-20
Silver, Roy R. 1918-1979 Obituary 89-92
Silver, Ruth
See Chew, Ruth
Silver, Samuel 1915(?)-1976 Obituary 69-72
Silver, Samuel M. 1912- CANR-11
Earlier sketch in CA 23-24R

Silver, Warren A. 1914- ... 65-68
Silvera, Alain 1930- ... 23-24R
Silverberg, Robert 1935- ... CANR-20
 Earlier sketches in CA 3R, CANR-1
 See also CAAS 3
 See also SATA 13
 See also DLB 8
 See also CLC 7
Silverlock, Anne
 See Titchener, Louise
Silverman, Al 1926- ... 11-12R
Silverman, Alvin Michaels 1912- ... 11-12R
Silverman, Burt(on Philip) 1928- ... 103
Silverman, Corinne 1930- ... 7-8R
Silverman, David 1907- ... CAP-2
 Earlier sketch in CA 21-22
Silverman, Harold M(artin) 1945- ... 112
Silverman, Hillel E. 1924- ... CANR-11
 Earlier sketch in CA 21-22R
Silverman, Hirsch Lazaar 1915- ... 45-48
Silverman, Hugh J(erald) 1945- ... 118
Silverman, Jason H(oward) 1952- ... 110
Silverman, Jerry 1931- ... CANR-7
 Earlier sketch in CA 15-16R
Silverman, Joseph H(erman) 1924- ... 104
Silverman, Judith 1933- ... 103
Silverman, Kenneth 1936- ... CANR-17
 Earlier sketch in CA 57-60
Silverman, Mel(vin Frank) 1931-1966 ... 5-6R
 See also SATA 9
Silverman, Milton J. 1944- ... 108
Silverman, Morris 1894-1972 Obituary ... 33-36R
Silverman, Oscar Ansell 1903-1977
 Obituary ... 69-72
Silverman, Robert A(llan) 1943- ... 57-60
Silverman, Robert E(ugene) 1924- ... 41-44R
Silverman, Robert J(ay) 1940- ... 101
Silverman, Rose
 See Millstein, Rose Silverman
Silverman, S(ol) Richard 1911- ... 107
Silverman, Samuel ... AITN-1
Silverman, Sydel 1933- ... 77-80
Silverman, William B. 1913- ... 49-52
Silvern, Leonard C. 1919- ... CANR-7
 Earlier sketch in CA 17-18R
Silvers, Phil
 See Silversmith, Philip
Silvers, Vicki 1941- ... 93-96
Silversmith, Philip 1912-1985 Obituary ... 117
 Brief entry ... 111
Silverstein, Alvin 1933- ... CANR-2
 Earlier sketch in CA 49-52
 See also SATA 8
 See also CLC 17
Silverstein, Charles 1935- ... 73-76
Silverstein, Josef 1922- ... CANR-14
 Earlier sketch in CA 37-40R
Silverstein, Mel(vin Jerome) 1940- ... 101
Silverstein, Norman 1922-1974 ... 37-40R
 Obituary ... 49-52
Silverstein, Shel(by) 1932- ... 107
 See also SATA 27, 33
 See also CLR 5
Silverstein, Theodore 1904- ... 106
Silverstein, Virginia B(arbara Opshelor)
 1937- ... CANR-2
 Earlier sketch in CA 49-52
 See also SATA 8
 See also CLC 17
Silverstone, Lou 1928- ... 108
Silverstone, Paul H. 1931- ... 21-22R
Silvert, Kalman H(irsch) 1921-1976 ... CANR-6
 Obituary ... 65-68
 Earlier sketch in CA 13-14R
Silverthorn, J(ames) E(dwin) 1906- ... CAP-1
 Earlier sketch in CA 15-16
Silverthorne, Elizabeth 1930- ... 89-92
 See also SATA 35
Silverton, Michael 1935- ... 65-68
Silverwood, Jane
 See Titchener, Louise
Silvester, Frank
 See Bingley, David Ernest
Silvester, Victor ... CAP-1
 Earlier sketch in CA 13-14
Silvestri, Richard 1944- ... 81-84
Silving, Helen 1906- ... 41-44R
Silvius, G(eorge) Harold 1908-1981 ... CANR-3
 Obituary ... 104
 Earlier sketch in CA 7-8R
Sim, Georges
 See Simenon, Georges
Sim, John Cameron 1911- ... 25-28R
Sim, Katharine (Thomasset) 1913- ... 13-14R
Sim, Myre 1915- ... 61-64
Sim, Yawsoon 1937- ... 108
Simak, Clifford D(onald) 1904-1988 ... CANR-1
 Obituary ... 125
 Earlier sketch in CA 4R
 See also DLB 8
 See also CLC 1
Simbari, Nicola 1927- ... CANR-1
 Earlier sketch in CA 4R
Simckes, L(azarre) S(eymour) 1937- ... 9-10R
Simcox, George Augustus 1841-1905 ... DLB-35
Sime, Mary 1911- ... 53-56
Simenon, Georges (Jacques Christian)
 1903- ... 85-88
 See also DLB 72
 See also CLC 1, 2, 3, 8, 18, 47
Simeon, Mother Mary 1888- ... CAP-1
 Earlier sketch in CA 13-14
Simeon, Richard 1943- ... CANR-9
 Earlier sketch in CA 61-64
Simeone, Diane A. 1953(?)-1983 Obituary .. 109
Simic, Andrei 1930- ... 93-96
Simic, Charles 1938- ... CANR-12
 Earlier sketch in CA 29-32R
 See also CAAS 4
 See also CLC 6, 9, 22, 49
Simini, Joseph Peter 1921- ... CANR-8
 Earlier sketch in CA 17-18R
Simirenko, Alex 1931- ... 15-16R
Simister, Florence Parker 1913- ... CANR-2
 Earlier sketch in CA 7-8R
Simkin, C(olin) G(eorge) F(rederick)
 1915- ... 29-32R
Simkin, Penny 1938- ... 116
Simkin, William E(dward) 1907- ... 45-48
Simkins, Lawrence D(avid) 1933- ... 41-44R
Simley, Anne 1891- ... 5-6R
Simmel, Edward C(lemens) 1932- ... 45-48
Simmel, Johannes M(ario) 1924- ... 81-84
 See also DLB 69
Simmel, Marianne L(enore) 1923- ... 21-22R
Simmie, James Martin 1941- ... 115
Simmonds, A(ndrew) J(effrey) 1943- ... 81-84
Simmonds, George W. 1929- ... 21-22R
Simmonds, James D(udley) 1933- ... 104
Simmonds, Walter H(enry) C(live) 1917- ... 118
Simmons, A(lan) John 1950- ... 106
Simmons, Anthony 1922- ... 103
Simmons, Billy E. 1931- ... CANR-10
 Earlier sketch in CA 23-24R
Simmons, Blake
 See Wallmann, Jeffrey M(iner)
Simmons, Charles (Paul) 1924- ... 89-92
Simmons, D(avid) R(oy) 1930- ... 110
Simmons, Dan ... CLC-44
Simmons, David
 See Gold, Alan R(obert)
Simmons, Dawn Langley ... 29-32R
Simmons, Edwin Howard 1921- ... 89-92
Simmons, Ernest J(oseph) 1903-1972 .. CANR-3
 Earlier sketch in CA 2R
Simmons, Geoffrey 1943- ... 104
Simmons, Gloria Mitchell 1932- ... 37-40R
Simmons, Henry T. 1927(?)-1986
 Obituary ... 120
Simmons, Herbert A(lfred) 1930- ... 3R
 See also BW
 See also DLB 33
Simmons, Ian 1937- ... 106
Simmons, J(oseph) Edgar (Jr.) 1921- ... 21-22R
Simmons, J(erry) L(aird) 1933- ... 29-32R
Simmons, Jack 1915- ... CANR-2
 Earlier sketch in CA 7-8R
Simmons, James (Stewart Alexander)
 1933- ... 105
 See also DLB 40
 See also CLC 43
Simmons, James E(dwin) 1923- ... 41-44R
Simmons, James W(illiam) 1936- ... CANR-12
 Earlier sketch in CA 17-18R
Simmons, John Edwards 1918-1986
 Obituary ... 121
Simmons, Joseph Larry 1935- ... 65-68
Simmons, Judy Dothard 1944- ... 77-80
Simmons, Mabel Clark 1899-1988
 Obituary ... 124
Simmons, Marc 1937- ... CANR-26
 Earlier sketches in CA 25-28R, CANR-10
Simmons, Mary Kay 1933- ... 81-84
Simmons, Matty 1926- ... 29-32R
Simmons, Merle Edwin 1918- ... CANR-2
 Earlier sketch in CA 7-8R
Simmons, Otis D(avis) 1928- ... 57-60
Simmons, Ozzie Gordon 1919- ... 11-12R
Simmons, Patricia A. 1930- ... 93-96
Simmons, Paul D(ewayne) 1936- ... 45-48
Simmons, Robert R. 1940- ... 97-100
Simmons, S. H.
 See Simmons, Sylvia
Simmons, Sylvia ... 49-52
Simmons, William S(cranton) 1938- ... 121
Simms, D(enton) Harper 1912- ... 29-32R
Simms, Eric Arthur 1921- ... 101
Simms, George (Otto) 1910- ... CANR-25
 Earlier sketch in CA 108
Simms, Peter (F. J.) 1925- ... 21-22R
Simms, Ruth P. 1937- ... 17-18R
Simms, Willard S. 1943- ... 29-32R
Simms, William Gilmore
 1806-1870 ... DLB-3, 30, 59, 73
Simon, Alfred 1907- ... 41-44R
Simon, Andre (Louis) 1877-1970
 Obituary ... 29-32R
Simon, Anne W(ertheim) 1914- ... 105
Simon, Arthur 1930- ... 33-36R
Simon, Bennett 1933- ... 101
Simon, Boris-Jean 1913(?)-1972
 Obituary ... 33-36R
Simon, Carl P(aul) 1945- ... 107
Simon, Carly 1945- ... 105
 See also CLC 26
Simon, Charlie May
 See Fletcher, Charlie May Hogue
Simon, Christopher Fitz
 See Fitz-Simon, Christopher
Simon, Claude 1913- ... 89-92
 See also CLC 4, 9, 15, 39
Simon, Disney 1927- ... 23-24R
Simon, Eckehard 1939- ... 61-64
Simon, Edith 1917- ... 13-14R
Simon, George T(homas) 1912- ... CANR-17
 Earlier sketch in CA 25-28R
Simon, Henry W(illiam) 1901-1970 ... CANR-4
 Obituary ... 29-32R
 Earlier sketch in CA 5-6R
Simon, Herbert 1898(?)-1974 Obituary ... 53-56
Simon, Herbert A(lexander) 1916- ... CANR-9
 Earlier sketch in CA 13-14R
Simon, Hilda Rita 1921- ... 77-80
 See also SATA 28
Simon, Howard 1903-1979 ... 33-36R
 Obituary ... 89-92
 See also SATA 21, 32
Simon, Hubert K. 1917- ... 15-16R
Simon, James E(dward) 1954- ... 119
Simon, Jo Ann 1946- ... 106
Simon, Joan L. 1921- ... 15-16R
Simon, Joe
 See Simon, Joseph H.
Simon, John (Ivan) 1925- ... 21-22R
Simon, John G. 1928- ... 37-40R
Simon, John Y. 1933- ... CANR-12
 Earlier sketch in CA 25-28R
Simon, Joseph H. 1913- ... 29-32R
 See also SATA 7
Simon, Julian L. 1932- ... 33-36R
Simon, Kate (Grobsmith) 1912-
 Brief entry ... 115
Simon, Leonard 1922- ... 11-12R
Simon, Linda 1946- ... CANR-13
 Earlier sketch in CA 73-76
Simon, Lorena Cotts 1897- ... 5-6R
Simon, Louis M(ortimer) 1906- ... 77-80
Simon, Marcia L. 1939- ... 93-96
Simon, Martin P(aul William) 1903-1969 . CAP-1
 Earlier sketch in CA 11-12
 See also SATA 12
Simon, Mary of the Angels 1897(?)-1985
 Obituary ... 116
Simon, Matila 1908- ... 17-18R
Simon, Michael A(rthur) 1936- ... CANR-13
 Earlier sketch in CA 33-36R
Simon, Mina Lewiton
 See Lewiton, Mina
Simon, Morton J. 1913- ... 19-20R
Simon, (Marvin) Neil 1927- ... CANR-26
 Earlier sketch in CA 21-22R
 See also DLB 7
 See also CLC 6, 11, 31, 39
 See also AITN 1
Simon, Norma (Feldstein) 1927- ... CANR-21
 Earlier sketches in CA 7-8R, CANR-6
 See also SATA 3
Simon, Paul 1928- ... 81-84
Simon, Paul 1942(?)- Brief entry ... 116
 See also CLC 17
Simon, Pierre-Henri 1903-1972
 Obituary ... 37-40R
Simon, Rita James 1931- ... CANR-8
 Earlier sketch in CA 21-22R
Simon, Robert
 See Musto, Barry
Simon, Robert A. 1897(?)-1981 Obituary ... 103
Simon, Roger David 1943- ... 109
Simon, Samuel A(lan) 1945- ... 117
Simon, Seymour 1931- ... CANR-11
 Earlier sketch in CA 25-28R
 See also SATA 4
 See also CLR 9
Simon, Sheldon W(eiss) 1937- ... CANR-26
 Earlier sketches in CA 25-28R, CANR-10
Simon, Shirley (Schwartz) 1921- ... CANR-16
 Earlier sketches in CA 4R, CANR-1
 See also SATA 11
Simon, Sidney B(lair) 1927- ... 101
Simon, Solomon 1895-1970 Obituary ... 104
 See also SATA 40
Simon, (Edward) Ted 1931- ... 105
Simon, Tony 1921- ... 5-6R
Simon, Ulrich E(rnst) 1913- ... 29-32R
Simon, Walter G(old) 1924- ... 19-20R
Simon, William 1927- ... 11-12R
Simon, William E(dward) 1927- ... 81-84
Simonds, John Ormsbee 1913- ... 77-80
Simonds, Roger (Tyrrell) 1929- ... 93-96
Simonds, Rollin Head 1910- ... 1R
Simonds, William Adams 1887-19(?) ... CAP-1
 Earlier sketch in CA 11-12
Simone
 See Porche, Simone (Benda)
Simone, Albert Joseph 1935- ... 17-18R
Simone, Charles B(rian) 1949- ... 116
Simonelli, Maria Picchio 1921- ... 49-52
Simonet, Thomas Solon 1942- ... 116
Simonetta, Linda 1948- ... 77-80
 See also SATA 14
Simonetta, Sam 1936- ... 77-80
 See also SATA 14
Simonhoff, Harry 1891- ... 7-8R
Simoni, John Peter 1911- Brief entry ... 106
Simonin, Albert (Charles) 1905-1980
 Obituary ... 104
Simonini, R(inaldo) C(harles), Jr.
 1922-1967 ... CAP-1
 Earlier sketch in CA 11-12
Simonon, Paul 1956(?)- ... CLC-30
Simonov, Konstantin (Kirill) Mikhailovich
 1915-1979 Obituary ... 89-92
Simons, Barbara B(rooks) 1934- ... 108
 See also SATA 41
Simons, Beverley 1938- ... 104
Simons, David G(oodman) 1922- ... 19-20R
Simons, Elwyn LaVerne 1930- ... CANR-22
 Earlier sketch in CA 105
Simons, Eric N(orman) 1896- ... 15-16R
Simons, Hans 1893-1972 Obituary ... 33-36R
Simons, Harry 1912- ... 3R
Simons, Howard, 1929- ... 65-68
Simons, James Marcus 1939- ... 106
Simons, Jim
 See Simons, James Marcus
Simons, John D(onald) 1935- ... 41-44R
Simons, Joseph 1933- ... 81-84
Simons, Katherine Drayton Mayrant
 1892(?)-1969 ... 9-10R
 Obituary ... 112
 See also DLBY 83
Simons, Lewis M(artin) 1939- Brief entry ... 123
Simons, Myron (Bud) 1920- ... 113
Simons, Robin 1951- ... 65-68
Simons, Thomas G(erald) 1950- ... 111
Simons, William Edward 1927- ... 17-18R
Simonson, Conrad 1931- ... 49-52
Simonson, Harold P(eter) 1926- ... 33-36R
Simonson, Lee 1888-1967 ... 9-10R
Simonson, Mary Jane
 See Wheeler, Mary Jane
Simonson, Solomon S. 1914- ... 23-24R
Simont, Marc 1915- ... 61-64
 See also SATA 9
Simonton, Dean Keith 1948- ... 119
Simoons, Frederick J. 1922- ... CANR-23
 Earlier sketch in CA 1R
Simos, Miriam 1951- ... 104
Simper, Robert 1937- ... CANR-23
 Earlier sketches in CA 61-64, CANR-8
Simpich, Frederick, Jr. 1911-1975 ... 61-64
 Obituary ... 57-60
Simpkin, Richard E(velyn) 1921-1986 ... 124
Simpson, A(lfred) W. Brian 1931- ... 5-6R
Simpson, Alan 1912- ... 3R
Simpson, Cedric Keith 1907-1985 ... 111
 Obituary ... 117
Simpson, Claude M(itchell), Jr.
 1910-1976 ... 5-6R
 Obituary ... 65-68
Simpson, Colin 1908- ... CANR-5
 Earlier sketch in CA 53-56
 See also SATA 14
Simpson, Craig M(ichael) 1942- ... 119
Simpson, D(avid) P(enistan) 1917- ... 11-12R
Simpson, Dick 1940- ... CANR-13
 Earlier sketch in CA 33-36R
Simpson, Dorothy 1933- ... 107
Simpson, E(rvin) P(eter) Y(oung) 1911- .. 19-20R
Simpson, Elizabeth Leonie ... 33-36R
Simpson, Ethel 1937- ... 117
Simpson, (John) Evan 1940- ... 97-100
Simpson, George E(dward) 1944- ... 101
Simpson, George Eaton 1904- ... 77-80
Simpson, George Gaylord 1902-1984 .. CANR-16
 Obituary ... 114
 Earlier sketches in CA 19-20, CAP-1
Simpson, Harold Brown 1917- ... CANR-4
 Earlier sketch in CA 11-12R
Simpson, Harriette
 See Arnow, Harriette (Louisa) Simpson
Simpson, Hassell A(lgernon) 1930- ... 41-44R
Simpson, Helen (De Guerry) 1897-1940
 Brief entry ... 109
Simpson, Howard Russell 1925- ... CANR-1
 Earlier sketch in CA 1R
Simpson, Ian J(ames) 1895- ... CAP-1
 Earlier sketch in CA 13-14
Simpson, Ida Harper 1928- ... 19-20R
Simpson, Jacqueline (Mary) 1930- ... CANR-5
 Earlier sketch in CA 15-16R
Simpson, Jacynth Hope
 See Hope Simpson, Jacynth
Simpson, James B(easley) 1926- ... CANR-9
 Earlier sketch in CA 7-8R
Simpson, Jean I(rwin) 1896- ... 7-8R
Simpson, Joan Murray 1918-1977
 Obituary ... 89-92
Simpson, John (Andrew) 1953- ... 122
Simpson, John L(iddle) ... 11-12R
Simpson, Judith H(olroyd) 1941- ... 110
Simpson, Kemper 1893- ... CAP-1
 Earlier sketch in CA 11-12
Simpson, Kirke L(arue) 1882(?)-1972
 Obituary ... 37-40R
Simpson, Leo 1934- ... 101
 See also AITN 2
Simpson, Lewis P(earson) 1916- ... CANR-8
 Earlier sketch in CA 19-20R
Simpson, Louis (Aston Marantz) 1923- .. CANR-1
 Earlier sketch in CA 4R
 See also CAAS 4
 See also DLB 5
 See also CLC 4, 7, 9, 32
Simpson, Michael Andrew 1944- ... 89-92
Simpson, Mona (Elizabeth) 1957-
 Brief entry ... 122
 See also CLC 44
Simpson, Myrtle L(illias) 1931- ... CANR-11
 Earlier sketch in CA 23-24R
 See also SATA 14
Simpson, N(orman) F(rederick) 1919- ... 13-14R
 See also DLB 13
 See also CLC 29
Simpson, Norman T. 1919(?)-1988
 Obituary ... 125
Simpson, O(renthal) J(ames) 1947- ... 103
Simpson, R(onald) A(lbert) 1929- ... CANR-14
 Earlier sketch in CA 77-80
Simpson, Ray H. 1907- ... 4R
Simpson, Richard L(ee) 1929- ... 11-12R
Simpson, Robert (Wilfred Levick) 1921- ... 103
Simpson, Robert 1924- ... 49-52
Simpson, Robert H. 1912- ... 108
Simpson, Ruth 1926- ... 73-76
Simpson, Ruth Mary Rasey 1902- ... CANR-1
 Earlier sketch in CA 4R
Simpson, (Robert) Smith 1906- ... CAP-2
 Earlier sketch in CA 21-22
Simpson, Stanhope Rowton 1903- ... 73-76
Simpson, W. W.
 See Simpson, William Wynn
Simpson, William Hays 1903- ... 41-44R
Simpson, William Kelly 1928- ... 105

Simpson, William Wynn 1907-1987
Obituary 123
Sims, Bernard John 1915- 13-14R
Sims, Bobbi 1931- 117
Sims, Charles A(gustus) 1901-1983
Obituary 111
Sims, Edward H. 1923- CANR-6
Earlier sketch in CA 1R
Sims, Edward J(ames) 1927- 41-44R
Sims, George (Frederick Robert)
1923- CANR-12
Earlier sketch in CA 25-28R
Sims, George R. 1847-1922 .... DLB-35, 70
Sims, Harold D(ana) 1935- 41-44R
Sims, James H(ylbert) 1924- 1R
Sims, Janet L.
See Sims-Wood, Janet L(ouise)
Sims, Lois Dorothy Lang
See Lang-Sims, Lois Dorothy
Sims, Mary Sophia Stephens 1886-1976
Obituary 65-68
Sims, Naomi (Ruth) 1949- CANR-26
Earlier sketch in CA 69-72
Sims, Patsy 1938- Brief entry 110
Sims, Patterson 1947- 124
Sims, Phillip L(eon) 1940- 105
Simson, Eve 1937- 73-76
Simsova, Sylva 1931- CANR-12
Earlier sketch in CA 29-32R
Sims-Wood, Janet L(ouise) 1945- 108
Sinai, I(saac) Robert 1924- CANR-10
Earlier sketch in CA 23-24R
Sinclair, Andrew (Annandale) 1935- CANR-14
Earlier sketch in CA 9-10R
See also CAAS 5
See also DLB 14
See also CLC 2, 14
Sinclair, Bennie Lee 1939- CANR-1
Earlier sketch in CA 49-52
Sinclair, Bruce A. 1929- 126
Brief entry 106
Sinclair, Clover
See Gater, Dilys
Sinclair, Donna 1943- CANR-23
Earlier sketch in CA 106
Sinclair, Emil
See Hesse, Hermann
Sinclair, (Allan) Gordon 1900-1984 102
Obituary 112
See also AITN 1
Sinclair, Grace
See Wallmann, Jeffrey M(iner)
Sinclair, Grant
See Drago, Harry Sinclair
Sinclair, Harold (Augustus) 1907-1966 .... 7-8R
Sinclair, Heather
See Johnston, William
Sinclair, Ian
See Foley, (Cedric) John
Sinclair, Irene
See Griffith, D(avid Lewelyn) W(ark)
Sinclair, James
See Staples, Reginald Thomas
Sinclair, Jo
See Seid, Ruth
See also DLB 28
Sinclair, John L(eslie) 1902- 105
Sinclair, Julian
See Sinclair, Mary Amelia St. Clair
Sinclair, Keith 1922- 17-18R
Sinclair, Lister (Shedden) 1921- 105
Sinclair, Mary Amelia St. Clair
1865(?)-1946 Brief entry 104
Sinclair, Max 1945- 113
Sinclair, May
See Sinclair, Mary Amelia St. Clair
See also DLB 36
See also TCLC 3, 11
Sinclair, Miranda 1948- 77-80
Sinclair, Murray 1950- 108
Sinclair, Olga 1923- CANR-26
Earlier sketches in CA 61-64, CANR-11
Sinclair, Rose
See Smith, Susan Vernon
Sinclair, Roy
See Griffith, D(avid Lewelyn) W(ark)
Sinclair, Sandra 1940- 120
Sinclair, Sonia 1928- 126
Sinclair, Upton (Beall) 1878-1968 .... CANR-7
Obituary 25-28R
Earlier sketch in CA 5-6R
See also SATA 9
See also DLB 9
See also CLC 1, 11, 15
Sinclair-Stevenson, Christopher 1939- 102
Sincoff, Michael Z(olman) 1943- 85-88
Sindler, Allan Paul 1928- 97-100
Sinel, Allen 1936- 45-48
Siner, Howard W(alter) 1946- 117
Sinfield, Alan 1941- 113
Singer, Adam
See Karp, David
Singer, Amanda
See Brooks, Janice Young
Singer, Armand Edwards 1914- CANR-14
Earlier sketch in CA 41-44R
Singer, Benjamin D. 1931- 37-40R
Singer, Beth J(udith) 1927- 113
Singer, Burns
See Singer, James Hyman
Singer, C(harles) Gregg 1910- CANR-12
Earlier sketch in CA 73-76
Singer, David L(in) 1937- 73-76
Singer, Fred J. 1931- 23-24R
Singer, Irving 1925- 23-24R
Singer, Isaac
See Singer, Isaac Bashevis
Singer, Isaac Bashevis 1904- CANR-1
Earlier sketch in CA 1R
See also SATA 3, 27
See also DLB 6, 28, 52
See also CDALB 1941-1968
See also CLC 1, 3, 6, 9, 11, 15, 23, 38
See also CLR 1
See also AITN 1, 2
Singer, J(oel) David 1925- CANR-6
Earlier sketch in CA 4R
Singer, Jack W(olfe) 1942- 104
Singer, James Hyman 1928-1964 102
Obituary 89-92
Singer, Jane Sherrod 1917-1985 .... CANR-17
Obituary 115
Earlier sketch in CA 25-28R
See also SATA 4, 42
Singer, Joe
See Singer, Joseph
Singer, Joseph 1923-19? CANR-2
Earlier sketch in CA 45-48
Singer, Joseph I.
See Singer, Joseph
Singer, Joy Daniels 1928- 29-32R
Singer, Judith 1926- 61-64
Singer, Julia 1917- 65-68
See also SATA 28
Singer, June (Kurlander) 1918- CANR-10
Earlier sketch in CA 41-44R
Singer, June Flaum 1933- 106
Singer, Kurt D(eutsch) 1911- CANR-2
Earlier sketch in CA 49-52
See also SATA 38
Singer, Marcus George 1926- CANR-3
Earlier sketch in CA 2R
Singer, Marilyn 1948- CANR-9
Earlier sketch in CA 65-68
See also SATA 38, 48
Singer, Marshall R. 1932- 41-44R
Singer, Michael A(lan) 1947- 57-60
Singer, Milton Borah 1912- CANR-23
Earlier sketch in CA 105
Singer, Neil M(ichael) 1939- 93-96
Singer, Norman 1925- 41-44R
Singer, Peter (Albert David) 1946- CANR-8
Earlier sketch in CA 57-60
Singer, Phylis
See Morrison, Phylis
Singer, Ray 1916- 105
Singer, Richard G. 1943- 89-92
Singer, (Dennis) Robert 1931- 49-52
Singer, Robert N. CANR-25
Earlier sketches in CA 53-56, CANR-5
Singer, Rochelle 1939- CANR-20
Earlier sketch in CA 104
Singer, S(iegfried) Fred 1924- Brief entry 118
Singer, Samuel L(oewenberg) 1911- 65-68
Singer, Sarah 1915- 81-84
Singer, Shelley
See Singer, Rochelle
Singer, Sholom A. 1924-1987 Obituary 123
Singer, Susan (Mahler) 1941- 61-64
See also SATA 9
Singerman, Robert 1942- 110
Singh, Ajit 1940- 109
Singh, Amritjit 1945- 102
Singh, Arjan 1917- 49-52
Singh, Avtar 1929- 65-68
Singh, Baliit 1929- 41-44R
Singh, Bawa Satinder 1932- 101
Singh, G(han Shyam) 1926- CANR-20
Earlier sketches in CA 11-12R, CANR-5
Singh, Harbans 1921- 19-20R
Singh, Karan 1931- 15-16R
Singh, Khushwant 1915- CANR-6
Earlier sketch in CA 9-10R
See also CLC 11
Singh, Lalita Prasad 1936- 23-24R
Singh, Madanjeet 1924- 19-20R
Singh, Nagendra 1914- CANR-7
Earlier sketch in CA 19-20R
Singh, R. K. Janmeja 1932- 37-40R
Singh, St. Nihal 1884- 105
Singh, Surender 1932- 49-52
Singh, Surendra Nihal
See Nihal Singh, Surendra
Singh, Vijai Pratap 1939- Brief entry 106
Singhal, D(amodar) P(rasad) 1925- 49-52
Singing Nun, The
See Deckers, Jeanine
Singletary, Otis Arnold, Jr. 1921- 45-48
Singleton, Betty 1910- CAP-2
Earlier sketch in CA 25-28
Singleton, Charles S(outhward)
1909-1985 Obituary 117
Brief entry 113
Singleton, Frederick Bernard 1926- 89-92
Singleton, Ira C(uster) 1920- 7-8R
Singleton, Jack 1911- 13-14R
Singleton, John 1930- 23-24R
Singleton, M(arvin) K(enneth) 1933- 3R
Singleton, Mary Ann 1934- 57-60
Singleton, Ralph Herbert 1900- 15-16R
Singleton, Rebecca (Jane) 1948- 121
Singleton, V(ernon) L(eRoy) 1923- 25-28R
Singmaster, Elsie 1879-1958 Brief entry 110
See also DLB 9
Sinha, Krishna N(andan) 1924- 15-16R
Sinha, Sasadhar 1901- 17-18R
Sinibaldi, Fosco
See Kacew, Romain
Sinick, Daniel 1913- 45-48
Sinicropi, Giovanni Andrea 1924- 45-48
Sinisgalli, Leonardo 1908-1981 Obituary 103
Sinjohn, John
See Galsworthy, John
Sinjun
See John, Elizabeth Beaman
Sinkankas, John 1915- CANR-6
Earlier sketch in CA 4R
Sinkler, George 1927- 85-88
Sinnema, John R(alph) 1911- 41-44R
Sinnen, Jeanne 1926-1976 Obituary 104
Sinnigen, William G. 1928- 15-16R
Sinning, Wayne E. 1931- 77-80
Sinofsky, Esther R. 1951- 126
Sinor, Denis 1916- CANR-6
Earlier sketch in CA 3R
Sinor, John 1930- CANR-11
Earlier sketch in CA 69-72
Sinyavsky, Andrei (Donatevich) 1925- 85-88
See also CLC 8
Siodmak, Curt 1902- 113
Brief entry 111
See also DLB 44
Sionil Jose, F(rancisco) 1924- CANR-10
Earlier sketch in CA 23-24R
Sions, Harry 1906-1974 Obituary 104
Siotis, Jean 1931- 25-28R
Sippl, Charles J. 1924- CANR-18
Earlier sketch in CA 21-22R
Siracusa, Joseph 1929- CANR-1
Earlier sketch in CA 45-48
Siracusa, Joseph M(arcus) 1944- CANR-12
Earlier sketch in CA 73-76
Sirageldin, Ismail A(bdel-Hamid)
1930- CANR-16
Earlier sketch in CA 29-32R
Sirc, Ljubo 1920- 103
Sire, James W(alter) 1933- CANR-11
Earlier sketch in CA 29-32R
Sirica, John J(oseph) 1904- 110
Sirin, V.
See Nabokov, Vladimir (Vladimirovich)
Siris, Peter 1944- 117
Sirjamaki, John 1911- 15-16R
Sirkin, Gerald 1920- 25-28R
Sirkis, Nancy 1936- 102
Sirluck, Ernest 1918- 25-28R
Sirof, Harriet 1930- CANR-20
Earlier sketch in CA 104
See also SATA 37
Sirrom, Wes
See Weiss, Morris S(amuel)
Sisco, John I(sodore) 1931- 41-44R
Sisk, Dorothy Poole 1897-1983 Obituary 111
Sisk, Frank A., Jr. 1915-1985 Obituary 115
Sisk, Henry L(ybran) 1914- 49-52
Sisk, John P(aul) 1914- 29-32R
Siskel, Eugene Kal 1946- 113
Brief entry 110
Siskel, Gene
See Siskel, Eugene Kal
Sisler, Harry Hall 1917- 109
Sisler, Rebecca 1932- 104
Sisley, Emily L(ucretia) 1930- Brief entry 113
Sissle, Noble 1889-1975 Obituary 112
Sissman, L(ouis) E(dward) 1928-1976 .... CANR-13
Obituary 65-68
Earlier sketch in CA 21-22R
See also DLB 5
See also CLC 9, 18
Sisson, A(lbert) F(ranklin) 1901- 5-6R
Sisson, C(harles) H(ubert) 1914- CANR-3
Earlier sketch in CA 2R
See also CAAS 3
See also DLB 27
See also CLC 8
Sisson, Rosemary Anne 1923- CANR-12
Earlier sketch in CA 13-14R
See also SATA 11
Sister Luc-Gabrielle
See Deckers, Jeanine
Sister M. Victoria
See Maria Del Rey, Sister
Sister Mary Annette
See Buttimer, Anne
Sister Mary Terese
See Donze, Mary Terese
Sister Maura
See Eichner, Maura
Sister Smile
See Deckers, Jeanine
Sister Teresa Margaret
See Rowe, Margaret (Kevin)
Sisyphus
See Barthelmes, (Albert) Wes(ley, Jr.)
Sitaram, K(ondavagil) S(urya) 1935- 69-72
Sitarz, Paula (Gaj) 1955- 122
Sitchin, Zecharia 1920- CANR-22
Earlier sketch in CA 69-72
Sites, James N(eil) 1924- 4R
Sites, Paul 1926- 53-56
Sithole, Ndabaningi 1920- Brief entry 110
Sitomer, Harry 1903- 101
See also SATA 31
Sitomer, Mindel 1903- 101
See also SATA 31
Sitter, John E(dward) 1944- Brief entry 114
Sittler, Joseph 1904-1987 Obituary 124
Sitton, Claude (Fox) 1925- Brief entry 122
Sitwell, Dame Edith 1887-1964 .... 11-12R
See also DLB 20
See also CLC 2, 9
Sitwell, (Francis) Osbert (Sacheverell)
1892-1969 .... CAP-2
Obituary 25-28R
Earlier sketch in CA 21-22
Sitwell, Sacheverell 1897-1988 .... 21-22R
Obituary 126
Sitzfleisch, Vladimir
See Spirer, Herbert F(rederick)
Siu, Helen 1950- 114
Siu, R(alph) G(un) H(oy) 1917- CANR-10
Earlier sketch in CA 25-28R
Sive, Helen R(obinson) 1951- 107
See also SATA 30
Sive, Mary Robinson 1928- CANR-10
Earlier sketch in CA 65-68
Siviero, Rodolpho 1912(?)-1983 Obituary 111
Sivulich, Sandra (Jeanne) Stroner 1941- 61-64
See also SATA 9
Siwek, Manuel 1908-1976 Obituary 65-68
Siwundhla, Alice Msumba 1928- 45-48
Sixsmith, Eric Keir Gilborne 1904-1986 .... 33-36R
Obituary 118
Siy, Robert Y(oung), Jr. 1955- 119
Sizemore, Burlan A. 1933- 45-48
Sizemore, Chris(tine) Costner 1927- 81-84
Sizemore, Margaret D(avidson) CAP-2
Earlier sketch in CA 19-20
Sizer, John 1938- CANR-12
Earlier sketch in CA 29-32R
Sizer, Nancy F(aust) 1935- 45-48
Sizer, Theodore R(yland) 1932- CANR-13
Earlier sketch in CA 33-36R
Sjoeberg, Leif 1925- 65-68
Sjoewall, Maj 1935- 65-68
See also CLC 7
Sjowall, Maj
See Sjoewall, Maj
Skaar, Grace Brown 1903- 69-72
Skaer, Peter M(acKall) 1953- 103
Skagen, Kiki
See Munshi, Kiki Skagen
Skaggs, David Curtis (Jr.) 1937- 41-44R
Skaggs, Jimmy M(arion) 1940- CANR-1
Earlier sketch in CA 45-48
Skaggs, Merrill Maguire 1937- 45-48
Skala, John J. 1923- 19-20R
Skaldaspillir, Sigfridur
See Broxon, Mildred Downey
Skallerup, Harry R(obert) 1927- 73-76
Skard, Sigmund 1903- CANR-22
Earlier sketches in CA 19-20R, CANR-7
Skarda, Patricia Lyn 1946- 106
Skardal, Dorothy Burton 1922- 61-64
Skardon, Alvin W(ilson, Jr.) 1912- 53-56
Skarsten, Malvin O. 1892- CAP-1
Earlier sketch in CA 15-16
Skartvedt, Dan (L.) 1945- 77-80
Skates, John R(ay) 1934- 97-100
Skeaping, John Rattenbury 1901-1980 108
Obituary 97-100
Skeaping, Mary 1902-1984 Obituary 112
Skedgell, Marian Jay 1921- CANR-14
Earlier sketch in CA 17-18R
Skeel, Dorothy J(une) CANR-8
Earlier sketch in CA 61-64
Skeen, Carl Edward 1937- 113
Skehan, James W(illiam) 1923- 57-60
Skei, Allen B(ennet) 1935- 108
Skellings, Edmund 1932- 77-80
Skelly, James R(ichard) 1927- 85-88
See also SATA 17
Skelly, Madge 1903- 41-44R
Skelton, Eugene (Lamar) 1914- CANR-1
Earlier sketch in CA 45-48
Skelton, Geoffrey (David) 1916- CANR-18
Earlier sketches in CA 49-52, CANR-1
Skelton, John E. 1934- 37-40R
Skelton, Peter 1928- 13-14R
Skelton, Red 1913- 104
Skelton, Robin 1925- 7-8R
See also CAAS 5
See also DLB 27, 53
See also CLC 13
See also AITN 2
Skelton, Roger
See Horn, Peter (Rudolf Gisela)
Skemp, Joseph Bright 1910- 106
Skemp, Richard R(owland) 1919- 107
Skendi, Stavro 1906- 25-28R
Skene-Melvin, Ann (Patricia) 1936- 108
Skene-Melvin, (Lewis) David (St. Columb)
1936- 108
Skibbe, Eugene M(oritz) 1930- 23-24R
Skidelsky, Robert 1939- CANR-11
Earlier sketch in CA 25-28R
Skidmore, Ian 1929- CANR-10
Earlier sketch in CA 61-64
Skidmore, Max J(oseph, Sr.) 1933- CANR-12
Earlier sketch in CA 29-32R
Skidmore, Rex A(ustin) 1914- 15-16R
Skidmore, Thomas E. 1932- 21-22R
Skiles, Jacqueline D(ean) 1937- 108
Skilken, Patricia S(tout) 1943- 119
Skilling, H(arold) Gordon 1912- CANR-7
Earlier sketch in CA 15-16R
Skillings, R(oger) D(eering) 1937- 61-64
Skilliter, S(usan) A. 1931(?)-1985
Obituary 117
Skilton, John H. 1906- 37-40R
Skimin, Robert (Elwayne) 1929- 108
Skinner, Ainslie
See Gosling, Paula
Skinner, B(urrhus) F(rederic) 1904- CANR-18
Earlier sketch in CA 11-12R
Skinner, Charles Edward 1891- CAP-1
Earlier sketch in CA 17-18
Skinner, Constance Lindsay 1882-1939 .... YABC-1
Skinner, Cornelia Otis 1901-1979 .... 19-20R
Obituary 89-92
See also SATA 2
Skinner, Elliott P(ercival) 1924- 13-14R
Skinner, G(eorge) William 1925- CANR-2
Earlier sketch in CA 49-52
Skinner, Gordon S(weetland) 1924- 13-14R
Skinner, Jeffrey 1949- 126
Skinner, John Emory 1925- 7-8R

Skinner, John Stuart 1788-1851 ... DLB-73
Skinner, June O'Grady 1922- ... 5-6R
Skinner, Knute (Rumsey) 1929- ... CANR-24
Earlier sketches in CA 17-18R, CANR-9
Skinner, Rulon Dean 1931- ... 61-64
Skinner, Thomas Edward 1909- ... 109
Skinner, Tom 1942- ... 25-28R
Skiold, Birgit ?-1982 Obituary ... 107
Skipp, Victor (Henry Thomas) 1925- ... 123
Brief entry ... 118
Skipper, Betty
See Barr, Betty
Skipper, G. C. 1939- ... CANR-14
Earlier sketch in CA 77-80
See also SATA 38, 46
Skipper, James K(inley), Jr. 1934- ... CANR-12
Earlier sketch in CA 17-20R
Skipsey, Joseph 1832-1903 ... DLB-35
Skipwith, Sofka 1907- ... 29-32R
Skira, Albert 1904-1973 Obituary ... 104
Skirpa, Kazys 1895(?)-1979 Obituary ... 89-92
Skjei, Eric William 1947- ... 97-100
Sklansky, Morris Aaron 1919- ... 17-18R
Sklar, Dusty 1928- ... 65-68
Sklar, George 1908-1988 ... 1R
Obituary ... 125
Sklar, Kathryn Kish 1939- ... CANR-18
Earlier sketches in CA 45-48, CANR-3
Sklar, Lawrence 1938- ... 105
Sklar, Michael Joel 1945(?)-1984
Obituary ... 112
Sklar, Morty 1935- ... CANR-13
Earlier sketch in CA 77-80
Sklar, Richard L(awrence) 1930- ... 9-10R
Sklar, Robert 1936- ... CANR-8
Earlier sketch in CA 21-22R
Sklare, Arnold B(eryl) 1924- ... 17-18R
Sklare, Marshall 1921- ... CANR-12
Earlier sketch in CA 23-24R
Sklarew, Myra 1934- ... 109
Sklarewitz, Norman 1924- ... 69-72
Skocpol, Theda Ruth 1947- Brief entry ... 105
Skofield, James ... SATA-44
Skoglund, Elizabeth 1937- ... CANR-15
Earlier sketch in CA 41-44R
Skoglund, Goesta 1904- ... 65-68
Skoglund, John Egnar 1912- ... 11-12R
Skold, Betty Westrom 1923- ... 112
See also SATA 41
Skolimowski, Jerzy 1938- ... CLC-20
Skolnick, Jerome H(erbert) 1931-
Brief entry ... 114
Skolnik, Alfred 1920(?)-1977 Obituary ... 69-72
Skolnik, Peter L(aurence) 1944- ... 57-60
Skolnikoff, Eugene B. 1928- ... 21-22R
Skolsky, Sidney 1905-1983 ... 103
Obituary ... 109
Skornia, Harry J(ay) 1910- ... CAP-2
Earlier sketch in CA 17-18
Skorpen, Liesel Moak 1935- ... 25-28R
See also SATA 3
Skotheim, Robert Allen 1933- ... 21-22R
Skou-Hansen, Tage 1925- ... CANR-6
Earlier sketch in CA 13-14R
Skousen, Mark ... 104
Skousen, W(illard) Cleon 1913- ... CANR-5
Earlier sketch in CA 7-8R
Skowronski, JoAnn ... 108
Skoyles, John 1949- ... 104
Skrade, Carl 1935- ... 65-68
Skram, Amalie (Bertha) 1847-1905 ... TCLC-25
Skrivanek, John M(arion) 1913- ... 49-52
Skulicz, Matthew V. 1944- ... 37-40R
Skulsky, Harold Lawrence 1935- ... 107
Skura, Meredith Anne 1944- ... 117
Skurdenis, Juliann V.
See Skurdenis-Smircich, Juliann V(eronica)
Skurdenis-Smircich, Juliann V(eronica) 1942- ... 77-80
Skurnik, W. A. E. 1926- ... 41-44R
Skurzynski, Gloria (Joan) 1930- ... CANR-13
Earlier sketch in CA 33-36R
See also SATA 8
Skutch, Alexander F(rank) 1904- ... CANR-21
Earlier sketch in CA 33-36R
Skutch, Margaret F. 1932- ... 105
Skutsch, Otto 1906- ... 126
Skvorecka, Zdena Salivarova 1933- ... 41-44R
Skvorecky, Josef (Vaclav) 1924- ... CANR-10
Earlier sketch in CA 61-64
See also CAAS 1
See also CLC 15, 39
Sky, Kathleen
See Goldin, Kathleen Mckinney
Skyrms, Brian 1938- ... CANR-26
Earlier sketch in CA 108
Slaatte, Howard A(lexander) 1919- ... CANR-14
Earlier sketch in CA 41-44R
Slaby, Andrew Edmund 1942- ... CANR-7
Earlier sketch in CA 57-60
Slack, Adrian (Charles) ... 104
Slack, Charles W(illiam) 1929- ... 61-64
Slack, Kenneth 1917-1987 Obituary ... 123
Slack, Robert C(harles) 1914- ... 81-84
Slack, Walter H. 1932- ... 23-24R
Slackman, Charles B. 1934- ... SATA-12
Slade, Afton 1919- ... 89-92
Slade, Bernard
See Newbound, Bernard Slade
See also DLB 53
See also CLC 11, 46
Slade, Caroline (Beach) 1886-1975
Obituary ... 61-64
Slade, Jack
See Ballard, (Willis) Todhunter and Germano, Peter B.
Slade, Joseph W(arren) 1941- ... 89-92
Slade, Madeleine 1892-1982 Obituary ... 115
Slade, Peter 1912- ... 13-14R
Slade, Richard 1910-1971 ... CAP-2
Earlier sketch in CA 23-24
See also SATA 9
Slade, Tony 1936- ... 33-36R
Sladek, John 1937- ... 25-28R
Sladen, Kathleen 1904- ... 69-72
Sladen, Norman St. Barbe ?-1969 ... CAP-1
Earlier sketch in CA 13-14
Slaght, Lawrence T(ownsend) 1912- ... 73-76
Slakter, Malcolm J(ulian) 1929- ... 41-44R
Slamecka, Vladimir 1928- ... 7-8R
Slaney, George Wilson 1884- ... CAP-1
Earlier sketch in CA 13-14
Slappey, Sterling G(reene) 1917- ... 65-68
Slate, Joseph 1927- ... 45-48
Slate, Joseph (Frank) 1928- ... 110
See also SATA 38
Slate, Sam J(ordan) 1909- ... 49-52
Slaten, Yeffe Kimball 1914(?)-1978
Obituary ... 77-80
Slater, Charlotte (Wolpers) 1944- ... 65-68
Slater, Eliot (Trevor Oakeshott) 1904- ... 53-56
Slater, Ian 1941- ... 85-88
Slater, Jerome N(orman) 1935- ... 17-18R
Slater, Jim 1929- Brief entry ... 112
See also SATA 34
Slater, Layton Ernest Alfred 1916-1984
Obituary ... 114
Slater, Leonard 1920- ... 15-16R
Slater, Mariam K(reiselman) 1922- ... 123
Brief entry ... 118
Slater, Mary Louise 1923- ... 29-32R
Slater, Maya 1941- ... 119
Slater, Miriam 1931- ... 120
Slater, Niall W. 1954- ... 126
Slater, Nigel 1944- ... CANR-18
Earlier sketch in CA 102
Slater, Patrick 1880-1951 ... DLB-68
Slater, Peter Gregg 1940- ... 81-84
Slater, Philip E(lliot) 1927- ... 23-24R
Slater, Ralph P(hipps) 1915- ... 23-24R
Slater, Ray
See Lansdale, Joe R(ichard)
Slater, Robert 1943- ... 119
Slater, Robert (Henry) Lawson 1896- ... CAP-1
Earlier sketch in CA 13-14
Slater, Veronica
See Sullivan, Victoria
Slatin, John M. 1952- ... 126
Slatkin, Charles Eli 1907-1977 Obituary ... 73-76
Slatoff, Walter J(acob) 1922- ... 11-12R
Slattery, Timothy Patrick 1911- ... 25-28R
Slattery, William J(ames) 1930- ... 101
Slatzer, Robert F(ranklin) 1927-
Brief entry ... 113
Slaughter, Carolyn 1946- ... 85-88
Slaughter, Eugene Edward 1909- ... 37-40R
Slaughter, Frank G(ill) 1908- ... CANR-5
Earlier sketch in CA 7-8R
See also CLC 29
See also AITN 2
Slaughter, Howard K(ey) 1927- ... 45-48
Slaughter, Jane M(undy) 1908- ... 73-76
Slaughter, Jean
See Doty, Jean Slaughter
Slaughter, Jim
See Paine, Lauran (Bosworth)
Slavens, Thomas P(aul) 1928- ... CANR-22
Earlier sketch in CA 104
Slavet, Joseph S. 1920- ... 61-64
Slavic, Rosalind Welcher
See Welcher, Rosalind
Slavick, William H(enry) 1927- ... 104
Slavin, Arthur Joseph 1933- ... CANR-3
Earlier sketch in CA 11-12R
Slavin, Morris 1913- ... 118
Slavin, Stephen L(oren) 1939- ... 111
Slavitt, David R. 1935- ... 21-22R
See also CAAS 3
See also DLB 5, 6
See also CLC 5, 14
Slavson, Samuel R(ichard) 1891- ... 17-18R
Slavutych, Yar 1918- ... CANR-17
Earlier sketches in CA 45-48, CANR-2
Slawson, William David 1931- ... 110
Slaymaker, R(edsecker) Samuel II 1923- ... 65-68
Slayton, Mariette (Elizabeth) Paine 1908- ... 65-68
Sleator, William (Warner III) 1945- ... 29-32R
See also SATA 3
Sledd, James Hinton 1914- ... 19-20R
Sledge, Linda Ching 1944- ... 108
Sleigh, Barbara 1906-1982 ... CANR-6
Obituary ... 106
Earlier sketch in CA 13-14R
See also SATA 3, 30
Sleigh, (Brocas) Linwood 1902- ... 7-8R
Sleigh, Robert Collins, Jr. 1932- ... 37-40R
Sleight, Robert B(enton) 1922- ... 41-44R
Slepian, Jan(ice B.) 1921- ... SATA-45, 51
Slesar, Henry 1927- ... CANR-1
Earlier sketch in CA 2R
Slesin, Suzanne 1944- ... 123
Slesinger, Doris P(eyser) 1927- ... 113
Slesinger, Reuben E. 1916- ... 5-6R
Slesinger, Tess 1905-1945 Brief entry ... 107
See also TCLC 10
Slesinger, Warren 1933- ... 33-36R
Slesser, Malcolm 1926- ... 19-20R
Slessor, Kenneth 1901-1971 ... 102
Obituary ... 89-92
See also CLC 14
Sletholt, Erik 1919- ... 77-80
Slezak, Walter 1902-1983 Obituary ... 109
Slicer, Margaret O. 1920- ... 25-28R
See also SATA 4
Slide, Anthony 1944- ... CANR-12
Earlier sketch in CA 33-36R
Slim, William Joseph 1891-1970 Obituary ... 107
Slimming, John 1927-1979 ... 25-28R
Obituary ... 89-92
Slitor, Richard Eaton 1911- ... 45-48
Slive, Seymour 1920- ... 103
Sliwa, Curtis 1954- ... 111
Sljivic-Simsic, Biljana 1933- ... 41-44R
Sloan, Alfred P(ritchard), Jr. 1875-1966
Obituary ... 113
Sloan, Allan 1944- ... 118
Sloan, Edward William III 1931- ... 37-40R
Sloan, Harold Stephenson 1887- ... CAP-1
Earlier sketch in CA 17-18
Sloan, Irving J. 1924- ... CANR-7
Earlier sketch in CA 17-18R
Sloan, James Park (Jr.) 1944- ... 29-32R
Sloan, Kay 1951- ... 108
Sloan, Pat(rick Alan) 1908- ... 65-68
Sloan, Phillip R(eid) 1938- ... 109
Sloan, Raymond Paton 1893-1983 ... CAP-1
Obituary ... 109
Earlier sketch in CA 19-20
Sloan, Ruth Catherine 1898(?)-1976
Obituary ... 65-68
Sloan, Stephen 1936- ... 33-36R
Sloan, Thomas 1928- ... 93-96
Sloan, William Wilson 1901- ... 1R
Sloane, Arthur A(llan) 1931- ... 33-36R
Sloane, Eric 1910(?)-1985 ... 108
Obituary ... 115
See also SATA 42, 52
Sloane, Eugene A(nthony) 1926- ... 65-68
Sloane, Howard N(orman) 1932- ... 81-84
Sloane, Joseph C(urtis) 1909- ... CAP-1
Earlier sketch in CA 11-12
Sloane, Leonard 1932- ... 21-22R
Sloane, Peter J(ames) 1942- ... 108
Sloane, R(obert) Bruce 1923- ... 53-56
Sloane, Sara
See Bloom, Ursula
Sloane, Thomas O. 1929- ... 37-40R
Sloane, William M. 1906-1974 Obituary ... 53-56
Sloate, Daniel 1931- ... 113
Slobin, Dan Isaac 1939- ... CANR-11
Earlier sketch in CA 65-68
Slobin, Mark 1943- ... 93-96
Slobodin, Richard 1915- ... 102
Slobodkin, Florence Gersh 1905- ... 4R
See also SATA 5
Slobodkin, Louis 1903-1975 ... 13-14R
Obituary ... 57-60
See also SATA 1, 26
Slobodkina, Esphyr 1908- ... CANR-1
Earlier sketch in CA 1R
See also SATA 1
Slochower, Harry 1900- ... CANR-2
Earlier sketch in CA 49-52
Slocum, Bill
See Slocum, William J(oseph Michael), Jr.
Slocum, Donald Barclay 1911-1983
Obituary ... 110
Slocum, John W(esley), Jr. 1940- ... 112
Slocum, Michael
See Slocum, William J(oseph Michael), Jr.
Slocum, Milton Jonathan 1905- ... 126
Slocum, Robert Bigney 1922- ... 11-12R
Slocum, Walter L(ucius) 1910- ... 21-22R
Slocum, William J(oseph Michael), Jr. 1912(?)-1974 Obituary ... 53-56
Sloggatt, Arthur H(astings) 1917(?)-1975
Obituary ... 61-64
Sloggett, Nellie 1851-1923 ... SATA-44
Sloma, Richard Stanley 1929- ... CANR-19
Earlier sketch in CA 103
Sloman, Albert Edward 1921- ... 7-8R
Sloman, Larry 1948- ... CANR-20
Earlier sketch in CA 81-84
Slomovitz, Philip 1896- ... 81-84
Slone, Dennis 1930-1982 Obituary ... 106
Slone, Verna Mae 1914- ... 89-92
Slonim, Marc 1894-1976 Obituary ... 65-68
Slonim, Morris J(ames) 1909- ... 3R
Slonim, Reuben 1914- ... 97-100
Slonim, Ruth 1918- ... 19-20R
Slonimski, Antoni 1895-1976 Obituary ... 65-68
Slonimsky, Nicolas 1894- ... 17-18R
Slonimsky, Yuri 1902-1978 Obituary ... 77-80
Slosberg, Mike 1934- ... 69-72
Slosberg, Myron
See Slosberg, Mike
Slosser, Bob G(ene) 1929- ... CANR-10
Earlier sketch in CA 65-68
Slosson, Preston (William) 1892- ... CANR-8
Earlier sketch in CA 61-64
Slote, Alfred 1926- ... SATA-8
See also CLR 4
Slote, Bernice D. 1915(?)-1983 Obituary ... 109
Slote, Michael A(nthony) 1941- ... 61-64
Slote, Stanley J(ames) 1917- ... 61-64
Slotkin, Richard S. 1942- ... 102
Slotnick, Daniel L(eonid) 1931-1985
Obituary ... 117
Slovenko, Ralph 1926- ... 19-20R
Sloyan, Gerard Stephen 1919- ... CANR-18
Earlier sketches in CA 5-6R, CANR-2
Sluckin, W(ladyslaw) 1919-1985 ... 21-22R
Obituary ... 116
Slung, Louis Sheaffer 1912- ... 53-56
Slung, Michele (Beth) 1947- ... 102
Slusher, Howard S. 1937- ... 25-28R
Slusser, Dorothy M. 1922- ... 33-36R
Slusser, George Edgar 1939- ... CANR-13
Earlier sketch in CA 69-72
Slusser, Gerald H(erbert) 1920- ... 15-16R
Slusser, Robert M(elville) 1916- ... CANR-3
Earlier sketch in CA 3R
Slye, Leonard
See Rogers, Roy
Small, Bertrice 1937- ... CANR-13
Earlier sketch in CA 77-80
Small, David 1937- ... 108
Small, David 1945- ... SATA-46, 50
Small, Dwight Hervey 1919- ... CANR-8
Earlier sketch in CA 61-64
Small, Ernest
See Lent, Blair
Small, George L(eroy) 1924- ... 85-88
Small, George Raphael 1918- ... 57-60
Small, Kenneth A(lan) 1945- ... 112
Small, Melvin 1939- ... CANR-12
Earlier sketch in CA 29-32R
Small, Miriam Rossiter 1899- ... 4R
Small, Norman M. 1944- ... 41-44R
Small, William
See Eversley, D(avid) E(dward) C(harles)
Smallenburg, Harry W. 1907- ... CAP-1
Earlier sketch in CA 13-14
Smalley, Barbara Martin 1926- ... 105
Smalley, Beryl 1905-1984 ... 103
Obituary ... 112
Smalley, Donald (Arthur) 1907- ... 17-18R
Smalley, Ruth E(lizabeth) 1903- ... CAP-2
Earlier sketch in CA 21-22
Smalley, Stephen Stewart 1931- ... 103
Smalley, William A. 1923- ... CANR-1
Earlier sketch in CA 45-48
Smallwood, Carol 1939- ... 122
Smallwood, Frank(lin) 1927- ... 123
Brief entry ... 118
Smallwood, James (Milton) 1944- ... 115
Smallwood, Joseph R(oberts) 1900- ... 105
Smallwood, Norah (Evelyn) 1910(?)-1984
Obituary ... 114
See also SATA 41
Smaridge, Norah (Antoinette) 1903- ... 37-40R
See also SATA 6
Smart, (Peter) Alastair (Marshall) 1922- ... 37-40R
Smart, Barry 1946- ... 117
Smart, Carol 1948- ... CANR-16
Earlier sketch in CA 73-76
Smart, Carolyn (Alexandra) 1952- ... 116
Smart, Charles Allen 1904-1967 ... CAP-1
Earlier sketch in CA 11-12
Smart, Elizabeth 1913-1986 ... 81-84
Obituary ... 118
Smart, Graydon F. 1906(?)-1984 Obituary ... 111
Smart, Harold R(obert) 1892- ... CAP-1
Earlier sketch in CA 9-10
Smart, J(ohn) J(amieson) C(arswell) 1920- ... CANR-7
Earlier sketch in CA 13-14R
Smart, James D(ick) 1906-1982 ... CANR-8
Obituary ... 105
Earlier sketch in CA 57-60
Smart, Mollie S(tevens) 1916- ... 61-64
Smart, (Roderick) Ninian 1927- ... CANR-12
Earlier sketch in CA 29-32R
Smart, William (Edward, Jr.) 1933- ... CANR-7
Earlier sketch in CA 15-16R
Smead, (Edwin) Howard 1953- ... 124
Smedes, Lewis B. 1921- ... CANR-11
Earlier sketch in CA 69-72
Smedley, Hester Marsden
See Marsden-Smedley, Hester
Smeds, Dave 1955- ... 118
Smee, John (Charles) Odling
See Odling-Smee, John (Charles)
Smeeton, Miles (Richard) 1906-1988 ... 13-14R
Obituary ... 126
Smellie, K.
See Smellie, Kingsley Bryce (Speakman)
Smellie, K. B.
See Smellie, Kingsley Bryce (Speakman)
Smellie, Kingsley Bryce (Speakman) 1897-1987 ... 5-6R
Obituary ... 124
Smelser, Marshall 1912- ... 17-18R
Smelser, Neil J(oseph) 1930- ... CANR-8
Earlier sketch in CA 19-20R
Smelser, William T. 1924- ... 29-32R
Smeltzer, C(larence) H(arry) 1900-19(?) ... CANR-15
Earlier sketch in CA 4R
Smelyakov, Yaroslav 1913(?)-1972
Obituary ... 37-40R
Smerk, George M(artin) 1933- ... 107
Smertenko, Johan J. 1897(?)-1983
Obituary ... 109
Smerud, Warren D(ouglas) 1928- ... 49-52
Smetana, Josette 1928- ... 93-96
Smethurst, William (Knowles) 1945- ... 117
Smidt, Kristian 1916- ... 17-18R
Smigel, Erwin O. 1917-1973 ... 41-44R
Obituary ... 45-48
Smil, Vaclav 1943- ... 112
Smiles, Samuel 1812-1904 ... DLB-55
Smiley, Charles W(esley) 1940- ... 113
Smiley, David L(eslie) 1921- ... 5-6R
Smiley, Jane (Graves) 1949- ... 104
Smiley, Sam Max 1931- ... 105
Smiley, Virginia Kester 1923- ... CANR-12
Earlier sketch in CA 29-32R
See also SATA 2
Smirnov, Sergei Sergeevich 1915-1976
Obituary ... 65-68
Smith, A(nthony) C(harles) H(ockley) 1935- ... 119
Brief entry ... 116

Smith, A(lexander) G(raham) Cairns
See Cairns-Smith, A(lexander) G(raham)
Smith, A(lbert) H(ugh) 1903- 7-8R
Smith, A(lbert) J(ames) 1924- 65-68
Smith, A(rthur) J(ames) M(arshall) 1902-1980 .... CANR-4
Obituary 102
Earlier sketch in CA 2R
See also CLC 15
Smith, A. Robert 1925- 73-76
Smith, A. Weston 1900(?)-1975 Obituary ..57-60
Smith, Abbot E(merson) 1906-1983
Obituary 109
Smith, Ada Beatrice Queen Victoria Louisa Virginia 1894-1984 Obituary 111
Smith, Adam
See Goodman, George J(erome) W(aldo)
Smith, Alan M(cKinley) 1937- 41-44R
Smith, Alexander 1829-1867 .... DLB-32, 55
Smith, Alfred Edward 1895-1969 .... CAP-1
Earlier sketch in CA 11-12
Smith, Alfred G(oud) 1921- CANR-4
Earlier sketch in CA 11-12R
Smith, Alice Upham 1908- 45-48
Smith, Allen William 1938- 61-64
Smith, Alson Jesse 1908-1965 .... 4R
Obituary 103
Smith, Alton E. 1917- 19-20R
Smith, Angel
See Masterton, Graham
Smith, Anna H(ester) 1912- CANR-6
Earlier sketch in CA 57-60
Smith, Anna Piszczan-Czaja 1920- 110
Smith, Anne Mollegen 1940- 81-84
Smith, Anne Warren 1938- 111
See also SATA 34, 41
Smith, Anthony (John Francis) 1926- ... CANR-3
Earlier sketch in CA 11-12R
Smith, Anthony 1938- CANR-10
Earlier sketch in CA 53-56
Smith, Anthony D(avid) 1939- 101
Smith, Anthony Peter 1912-1980 Obituary .. 105
Smith, Arnold Cantwell 1915- 109
Smith, Arthur 1948- 120
Smith, Arthur C. 1916- 21-22R
Smith, Arthur L(ee)
See Asante, Molefi K(ete)
Smith, Arthur L(ee), Jr. 1927- 37-40R
Smith, Arthur M(umford) 1903- CAP-2
Earlier sketch in CA 17-18
Smith, Audrey D(owling) 1930- 119
Smith, Barbara Clark 1951- 124
Smith, Barbara Herrnstein 1932- 13-14R
Smith, Bardwell L(eith) 1925- 41-44R
Smith, Barry D(ecker) 1940- 29-32R
Smith, Beatrice S(chillinger) CANR-10
Earlier sketch in CA 57-60
See also SATA 12
Smith, Ben A(rwood) 1916- 4R
Smith, Benjamin Franklin 1902- 41-44R
Smith, Bernard (William) 1916- CANR-17
Earlier sketches in CA 1R, CANR-1
Smith, Bert Kruger 1915- CANR-11
Earlier sketch in CA 15-16R
Smith, Betsy Covington 1937- 111
See also SATA 43
Smith, Betty (Wehner) 1896-1972 ....5-6R
Obituary 33-36R
See also SATA 6
See also DLBY 82
See also CLC 19
Smith, Beulah Fenderson 1915- 15-16R
Smith, Bonnie G(ene) 1940- CANR-25
Earlier sketch in CA 108
Smith, Boyd M. 1888(?)-1973 Obituary ..41-44R
Smith, Bradford 1909-1964 .... CANR-16
Earlier sketch in CA 2R
See also SATA 5
Smith, Bradley 1910- CANR-19
Earlier sketches in CA 5-6R, CANR-2
Smith, Bradley F. 1931- 108
Smith, Brian (Clive) 1938- 110
Smith, Bromley K(eables) 1911-1987
Obituary 121
Smith, Bruce 1949- 108
Smith, Bryan Evers Sharwood
See Sharwood Smith, Bryan Evers
Smith, C. Busby
See Smith, John (Charles)
Smith, C. Pritchard
See Hoyt, Edwin P(almer), Jr.
Smith, C. Ray 1929-1988 109
Obituary 126
Smith, C(lifford) T(horpe) 1924- 23-24R
Smith, C. U. 1901- 41-44R
Smith, C(hristopher) U(pham) M(urray) 1930- 33-36R
Smith, C(harles) W(illiam) 1940- 61-64
Smith, C. Willard 1899(?)-1979 Obituary ..89-92
Smith, Caesar
See Trevor, Elleston
Smith, Carleton 1910-1984 Obituary 112
Smith, Carlton
See Rocklin, Ross Louis
Smith, Carmichael
See Linebarger, Paul M(yron) A(nthony)
Smith, Carol H(ertzig) 1929- 7-8R
Smith, Carol Sturm 1938- CANR-25
Earlier sketch in CA 25-28R
See also DLBY 81
Smith, Carole 1935- 101
Smith, (Charles) Carter (Jr.) 1930- 107
Smith, Catherine C. 1929- 29-32R
Smith, Cecil (Howard III) 1917- 69-72
Smith, Celina Janson
See Janson-Smith, Celina
Smith, Chard Powers 1894-1977 ....7-8R
Obituary 73-76
Smith, Charles E(dward) 1904-1970
Obituary 29-32R
Smith, Charles Harvard Gibbs
See Gibbs-Smith, Charles Harvard
Smith, Charles Henry 1826-1903
Brief entry 119
See also DLB 11
Smith, Charles Merrill ?-1985 Obituary 115
Smith, Charles W(illiam) (Frederick) 1905- 13-14R
Smith, Charlotte 1749-1806 .... DLB-39
Smith, Cherry 1931- 120
Smith, Clagett G. 1930- 37-40R
Smith, Clark Ashton 1893-1961 ....CLC-43
Smith, Clifford Neal 1923- 41-44R
Smith, Clodus R(ay) 1928- CANR-8
Earlier sketch in CA 21-22R
Smith, (Christopher) Colin 1927- 102
Smith, Cordelia Titcomb 1902- CAP-1
Earlier sketch in CA 11-12
Smith, Cordwainer
See Linebarger, Paul M(yron) A(nthony)
See also DLB 8
Smith, Cornelius C(ole, Jr.) 1913- CANR-22
Earlier sketch in CA 23-24R
Smith, Courtland L(ester) 1939- 81-84
Smith, Craig R(alph) 1944- 81-84
Smith, Curt 1951- 81-84
Smith, Cynthia S. 1924- 106
Smith, Cyril 1928- 109
Smith, Cyril James 1909-1974 Obituary ...53-56
Smith, D(avid) Howard 1900-1987 ....25-28R
Obituary 123
Smith, D. MacLeod
See Smith, David MacLeod
Smith, D(wight) Moody, Jr. 1931- CANR-20
Earlier sketch in CA 41-44R
Smith, D(onald) V(incent) 1933-1978 ....25-28R
Obituary 117
Smith, D(avid) W(arner) 1932- CANR-12
Earlier sketch in CA 19-20R
Smith, Dale O(rville) 1911- 73-76
Smith, Dan Throop 1908-1982 Obituary 106
Smith, Dana Prom 1927- 49-52
Smith, Daniel M(alloy) 1922-1976 .... CANR-8
Earlier sketch in CA 19-20R
Smith, Darren L. 1958- 124
Smith, Datus C(lifford), Jr. 1907- CANR-11
Earlier sketches in CA 11-12, CAP-1
See also SATA 13
Smith, Dave
See Smith, David (Jeddie)
See also CAAS 7
See also DLB 5
See also CLC 22, 42
Smith, David 1906-1965 Obituary 113
Smith, David (Jeddie) 1942- CANR-1
Earlier sketch in CA 49-52
Smith, David C(layton) 1929- 49-52
Smith, David C. 1931- 69-72
Smith, David C. 1952- 120
Smith, David Elvin 1939- 29-32R
Smith, David Fay 1939- 112
Smith, David H. 1939- 93-96
Smith, David Horton 1939- CANR-7
Earlier sketch in CA 57-60
Smith, David M(arshall) 1936- CANR-12
Earlier sketch in CA 29-32R
Smith, David MacLeod 1920- CANR-5
Earlier sketch in CA 53-56
Smith, David Osmond
See Osmond-Smith, David
Smith, David Shiverick 1918- 108
Smith, David T. 1935- 53-56
Smith, David W. 1921-1981 110
Obituary 108
Smith, Dean E(llis) 1923- CANR-4
Earlier sketch in CA 9-10R
Smith, Delos Owen 1905-1973 Obituary ..41-44R
Smith, Denison Langley 1924- 15-16R
Smith, Dennis 1940- CANR-10
Earlier sketch in CA 61-64
Smith, Desmond 1927- 103
Smith, Dian G. 1946- 120
Smith, Diana Kappel
See Kappel-Smith, Diana
Smith, Dick 1908-1974 .... CAP-1
Earlier sketch in CA 19-20
Smith, Dick King
See King-Smith, Dick
Smith, Dodie 33-36R
See also SATA 4
See also DLB 10
Smith, Don(ald Taylor) 1909- 49-52
Smith, Don Ian 1918- 45-48
Smith, Donal Ian Bryce 1934- 41-44R
Smith, Donald Eugene 1927- 9-10R
Smith, Donald G. 1927- 13-14R
Smith, Doris Buchanan 1934- CANR-11
Earlier sketch in CA 69-72
See also SATA 28
See also DLB 52
Smith, Doris E(dna Elliott) 1919- CANR-18
Earlier sketch in CA 25-28R
Smith, Dorothy Stafford 1905- 23-24R
See also SATA 6
Smith, Dorothy Valentine 1908- 29-32R
Smith, Douglas 1918- 73-76
Smith, Douglas 1949- 113
Smith, Duane A(llan) 1937- CANR-23
Earlier sketches in CA 23-24R, CANR-8
Smith, Dwight C(hichester), Jr. 1930- 77-80
Smith, Dwight L. 1918- CANR-24
Earlier sketch in CA 33-36R
Smith, Dwight R. 1921- 106
Smith, E(lmer) Boyd 1860-1943 .... YABC-1
Smith, E(dric) Brooks 1917- 5-6R
See also SATA 40
Smith, E(ric) D(avid) 1923- 118
Smith, E. E.
See Smith, Edward Elmer
Smith, E. E. "Doc"
See Smith, Edward Elmer
Smith, Edgar H(erbert) 1934- 25-28R
Smith, Edna Hopkins 1932(?)-1979
Obituary 89-92
Smith, Edward Conrad 1891- 45-48
Smith, Edward E.
See Smith, Edward Elmer
Smith, Edward E. "Doc"
See Smith, Edward Elmer
Smith, Edward Ellis 1921- 25-28R
Smith, Edward Elmer 1890-1965 118
Obituary 102
See also DLB 8
Smith, Edward W(illiam) 1920-1975
Obituary 57-60
Smith, Edwin H. 1920- 15-16R
Smith, Elbert B(enjamin) 1920- 23-24R
Smith, Eleanor Touhey 1910- 25-28R
Smith, Elihu Hubbard 1771-1798 .... DLB-37
Smith, Elinor Goulding 1917- CANR-3
Earlier sketch in CA 2R
Smith, Eliot Fremont
See Fremont-Smith, Eliot
Smith, Elizabeth Oakes (Prince) 1806-1893 .... DLB-1
Smith, Elliott Dunlap 1890(?)-1976
Obituary 61-64
Smith, Elsdon C(oles) 1903- CANR-6
Earlier sketch in CA 2R
Smith, Elske v(an)P(anhuys) 1929- 77-80
Smith, Elton E(dward) 1915- CANR-14
Earlier sketch in CA 15-16R
Smith, Elva Sophronia 1871-1965
Obituary 107
See also SATA 31
Smith, Elwyn Allen 1919- CANR-9
Earlier sketch in CA 5-6R
Smith, Emma 1923- 73-76
See also SATA 36, 52
Smith, Ernest A(llyn) 1911-1977 .... 3R
Obituary 103
Smith, Ethel Sabin 1887- CAP-1
Earlier sketch in CA 15-16
Smith, Eugene L(ewis) 1912-1986 ....23-24R
Obituary 118
Smith, Eugene Waldo 1905- CAP-1
Earlier sketch in CA 9-10
Smith, (Katherine) Eunice (Young) 1902- CANR-2
Earlier sketch in CA 7-8R
See also SATA 5
Smith, Evelyn E. 1927- Brief entry 113
Smith, F(rederick) G(eorge) Walton 1909- ..45-48
Smith, F. Joseph 1925- CANR-2
Earlier sketch in CA 45-48
Smith, Fay Jackson 1912- 25-28R
Smith, Florence Margaret 1902-1971 .... CAP-2
Obituary 29-32R
Earlier sketch in CA 17-18
See also CLC 8
Smith, Frances C(hristine) 1904- CANR-1
Earlier sketch in CA 2R
See also SATA 3
Smith, Frances Scott Fitzgerald Lanahan 1921-1986 Obituary 119
Smith, Frank (Arthur) 1917- 69-72
Smith, Frank E(llis) 1918- 17-18R
Smith, Frank E. 1919-1984 Obituary 114
Smith, Frank Kingston 1919- CANR-18
Earlier sketch in CA 102
Smith, Frank O. M. ?-1983 Obituary 109
Smith, Frank Seymour 1898-1972 ....9-10R
Obituary 89-92
Smith, (David) Fred(erick) 1898(?)-1976
Obituary 69-72
Smith, Frederick E(screet) 1922- CANR-19
Earlier sketches in CA 7-8R, CANR-3
Smith, Frederick W(illiam) 1920- 73-76
Smith, Frederick William Robin 1936-1985
Obituary 115
Smith, Frederick Winston Furneaux 1907-1975 65-68
Obituary 57-60
Smith, Fredrika Shumway 1877-1968
Obituary 109
See also SATA 30
Smith, G(eorge) E(verard) Kidder 1913- ..11-12R
Smith, Gaddis 1932- 23-24R
Smith, Garry (Van Dorn) 1933- 5-6R
Smith, Gary (Milton) 1943- 97-100
Smith, Gary R. 1932- 69-72
See also SATA 14
Smith, Gary V(incent) 1943- 101
Smith, Gene 1924- 77-80
Smith, Gene 1929- 81-84
Smith, Genevieve Love 1917- 21-22R
Smith, Geoffrey (John) 1943- 120
Smith, Geoffrey (Francis) Hattersley
See Hattersley-Smith, Geoffrey (Francis)
Smith, Geoffrey Sutton 1941- 49-52
Smith, George (Henry) 1922- 103
Smith, George E. 1938- 37-40R
Smith, George Harmon 1920- 49-52
See also SATA 5
Smith, George Ivan 1915- 121
Smith, George O(liver) 1911-1981 97-100
Obituary 103
See also DLB 8
Smith, Gerald A(lfred) 1921- 37-40R
Smith, Gerald B. 1909- CAP-2
Earlier sketch in CA 25-28
Smith, Gerald L(yman) K(enneth) 1898-1976 Obituary 65-68
Smith, Gerald Stanton 1938- 123
Smith, Glenn C. 1924- 123
Smith, Godfrey 1926- 9-10R
Smith, Goldwin (Albert) 1912- 41-44R
Smith, Gordon Roland
See Roland Smith, Gordon
Smith, Gordon Ross 1917- 7-8R
Smith, Grahame 1933- 25-28R
Smith, Gretchen L. ?-1972 Obituary 104
Smith, Grover C(leveland) 1923- 33-36R
Smith, Gudmund J(ohn) W(ilhelm) 1920- ... 102
Smith, Guy-Harold 1895- CAP-2
Earlier sketch in CA 19-20
Smith, H(arry) Allen 1907-1976 .... CANR-5
Obituary 65-68
Earlier sketch in CA 7-8R
See also SATA 20
See also DLB 11, 29
See also AITN 2
Smith, H(arold) Wendell 1923- 111
Smith, Hale G(illiam) 1918- 61-64
Smith, Hallett (Darius) 1907- 23-24R
Smith, Harmon L. 1930- 29-32R
Smith, Harold Ivan 1947- 121
Smith, Harold L(ester) 1942- 125
Smith, Harris (Gordon) 1921- 49-52
Smith, (Oliver) Harrison 1888-1971
Obituary 29-32R
Smith, Harry 1936- CANR-13
Earlier sketch in CA 77-80
Smith, Harry E(dmund) 1928- 25-28R
Smith, Harry W(illiam) 1937- 112
Smith, Harvey K(ennedy) 1904-1968 .... CAP-1
Earlier sketch in CA 13-14
Smith, Hedrick (Laurence) 1933- CANR-11
Earlier sketch in CA 65-68
Smith, Helen Zenna
See Price, Evadne
Smith, Henry 1905-1988 Obituary 124
Smith, Henry
See Smith, Henry DeWitt II
Smith, Henry Clay 1913- 2R
Smith, Henry DeWitt II 1940- 119
Smith, Henry Lee, Jr. 1913-1972
Obituary 37-40R
Smith, Henry Nash 1906-1986 .... CANR-2
Obituary 119
Earlier sketch in CA 4R
Smith, Henry Peter 1910-1968 .... 4R
Obituary 103
Smith, Herbert F(rancis) 1922- CANR-13
Earlier sketch in CA 77-80
Smith, Herbert F. A. 1915-1969 .... CAP-1
Earlier sketch in CA 15-16
Smith, Hermon Dunlap 1900-1983
Obituary 109
Smith, Hilda Worthington 1889(?)-1984
Obituary 112
Smith, Hobart M(uir) 1912- CANR-9
Earlier sketch in CA 65-68
Smith, Hope M(ayhew) 1916- 2R
Smith, Howard E(verett), Jr. 1927- CANR-21
Earlier sketch in CA 25-28R
See also SATA 12
Smith, Howard K(ingsbury) 1914- CANR-2
Earlier sketch in CA 45-48
Smith, Howard R(oss) 1917- 4R
Smith, Howard Van 1910(?)-1986 ....5-6R
Obituary 120
Smith, Hubert Shirley
See Shirley-Smith, Hubert
Smith, Hugh L(etcher) 1921-1968 .... CAP-2
Earlier sketch in CA 25-28
See also SATA 5
Smith, Huston (Cummings) 1919- 61-64
Smith, I(rving) Norman 1909- 107
Smith, Iain Crichton 1928- 23-24R
See also DLB 40
Smith, Imogene Henderson 1922- 7-8R
See also SATA 12
Smith, Irene 1903- 73-76
Smith, Irving H(arold) 1932- 49-52
Smith, Irwin 1892-1977 ....7-8R
Obituary 73-76
Smith, Isadore Leighton Luce 1901-1985 ... 101
Obituary 118
Smith, J. Allen 1860-1924 .... DLB-47
Smith, J.C.S.
See Smith, Jane S.
Smith, J(ohn) Holland 1932- 17-18R
Smith, J(ames) L(eonard) B(rierley) 1897-1968 .... CAP-1
Earlier sketch in CA 13-14
Smith, J(ohn) Malcolm 1921- 49-52
Smith, J(oseph) Russell 1874-1966 .... CAP-1
Earlier sketch in CA 13-14
Smith, J(oe) W(illiam) Ashley 1914- 7-8R
Smith, Jack (Clifford) 1916- CANR-12
Earlier sketch in CA 69-72
Smith, Jackie M. 1930- 93-96
Smith, Jackson Algernon 1917-
Brief entry 105
Smith, Jacqueline B. 1937- SATA-39
Smith, James 1904-1972 85-88
Smith, James A. 1914- 23-24R
Smith, James D(ale) 1940- 121
Smith, James L(eslie Clarke) 1936- 25-28R
Smith, James Morton 1919- 103
Smith, James R. 1941- 101
Smith, James Roy 1920- 23-24R
Smith, Jane F(rances) 1916- 123
Brief entry 117
Smith, Jane I(dleman) 1937- 107

Smith, Jane S. 1947- ... 118
Smith, Janet (Buchanan) Adam
See Adam Smith, Janet (Buchanan)
Smith, Jean
See Smith, Frances C(hristine)
Smith, Jean DeMouthe 1949- ... 65-68
Smith, Jean Edward 1932- ... 37-40R
Smith, Jean Pajot 1945- ... 53-56
See also SATA 10
Smith, Jerome F(ranken) 1928- ... 107
Smith, Jessica 1895- ... CANR-2
Earlier sketch in CA 49-52
Smith, Jessie Carney 1930- ... CANR-17
Earlier sketch in CA 89-92
Smith, Jessie Willcox 1863-1935 ... SATA-21
Smith, Jim 1920- Brief entry ... 115
See also SATA 36
Smith, Joan 1933- ... SATA-46
Smith, Joan 1935- ... 61-64
Smith, Joan K(aren) 1939- ... 93-96
Smith, Joanmarie 1932- ... CANR-16
Earlier sketch in CA 85-88
Smith, Jody Brant 1943- ... 113
Smith, John 1580(?)-1631 ... DLB-24, 30
Smith, John (Charles) 1924- ... 103
Smith, John
See Herrick, Marvin Theodore
Smith, John Chabot 1915- ... 69-72
Smith, John Coventry 1903-1984 ... 115
Smith, John David 1949- ... 111
Smith, John Edwin 1921- ... 103
Smith, John F(erris) 1934- ... 81-84
Smith, John H(azel) 1928- ... 11-12R
Smith, John Norton
See Norton-Smith, John
Smith, Johnston
See Crane, Stephen (Townley)
Smith, Jon R(ichard) 1946- ... 77-80
Smith, Jordan 1954- ... 110
Smith, Joseph B(urkholder) 1921- ... 65-68
Smith, Joseph Fielding 1876-1972
Obituary ... 37-40R
Smith, Joseph H(enry) 1913-1981
Obituary ... 105
Smith, Josiah 1704-1781 ... DLB-24
Smith, Julia Floyd 1914- ... 85-88
Smith, Julian 1937- ... 61-64
Smith, Julian W. 1901- ... 13-14R
Smith, Julie 1944- ... 112
Smith, K(ermit) Wayne 1938- ... 29-32R
Smith, Karl U(lrich) 1907- ... CANR-9
Earlier sketch in CA 61-64
Smith, Kate
See Smith, Kathryn Elizabeth
Smith, Kathleen J(oan) 1929- ... 103
Smith, Kathryn Elizabeth 1907(?)-1986
Obituary ... 119
Smith, Kay
See Smith, Catherine C.
Smith, Kay Nolte 1932- ... CANR-18
Earlier sketch in CA 101
Smith, Keith V(an) 1937- ... 112
Smith, Ken(neth Danforth) 1902- ... CANR-1
Earlier sketch in CA 45-48
Smith, Ken(neth John) 1938- ... 33-36R
See also DLB 40
Smith, Kenneth Lee 1925- ... 77-80
Smith, Kenneth M(anley) 1892-1981
Obituary ... 108
Smith, L(eonard) Glenn 1939- ... 93-96
Smith, Lacey Baldwin 1922- ... CANR-6
Earlier sketch in CA 5-6R
Smith, Lafayette
See Higdon, Hal
Smith, Larry 1940- ... 49-52
Smith, Laura I(vory) 1902- ... 19-20R
Smith, Laurence D. 1950- ... 123
Smith, Lavon B(enson) 1921- ... 23-24R
Smith, Lawrence Berk 1939- ... CANR-13
Earlier sketch in CA 73-76
Smith, Lawrence R(ichard) 1945- ... 117
Smith, Lee 1937- ... 73-76
Smith, Lee 1944- ... 119
Brief entry ... 114
See also DLBY 83
See also CLC 25
Smith, Lee
See Albion, Lee Smith
Smith, Lee L. 1930- ... 29-32R
Smith, Lena (Kennedy) 1914- ... 93-96
Smith, Lendon H(oward) 1921- ... 81-84
Smith, LeRoi Tex 1934- ... 29-32R
Smith, Leslie F(rancis) 1901- ... CAP-1
Earlier sketch in CA 19-20
Smith, Leslie James Seth
See Seth-Smith, Leslie James
Smith, Leslie R(aymond) 1904- ... 4R
Smith, Lew
See Floren, Lee
Smith, Lillian (Eugenia) 1897-1966 ... CAP-2
Obituary ... 25-28R
Earlier sketch in CA 17-18
Smith, Lillian H(elena) 1887-1983
Obituary ... 111
See also SATA 32
Smith, Linell Nash 1932- ... 5-6R
See also SATA 2
Smith, Liz 1923- ... 65-68
Smith, Lou 1918- ... 73-76
Smith, Louis
See Barzini, Luigi (Giorgio, Jr.)
Smith, Louis M(ilde) 1929- ... 19-20R
Smith, Lucia B. 1943- ... 108
See also SATA 30
Smith, Lynnette 1951- ... 116
Smith, M(ahlon) Brewster 1919- ... 61-64
Smith, M. Estellie 1935- ... CANR-8
Earlier sketch in CA 61-64
Smith, M. Weston
See Weston-Smith, M.
Smith, Malcolm 1938- ... 97-100
Smith, Malcom N(orman) 1919(?)-1985
Obituary ... 116
Smith, Manuel (Juan) 1934- ... 105
Smith, Marcus J(oel) 1918- ... 73-76
Smith, Margaret Chase 1897- ... 73-76
Smith, Margaret Emily Noel Nuttall
See Nuttall-Smith, Margaret Emily Noel
Smith, Margaret F(oltz) 1915- ... 102
Smith, Margaret Mary 1916- ... 108
Smith, Margaret Ruth 1902- ... CAP-1
Earlier sketch in CA 19-20
Smith, Margarita G. 1923(?)-1983
Obituary ... 109
Smith, Marie D. ... 13-14R
Smith, Marilyn Cochran
See Cochran-Smith, Marilyn
Smith, Marion Hagens 1913- ... 17-18R
See also SATA 12
Smith, Marion Jaques 1899- ... CANR-11
Earlier sketch in CA 69-72
See also SATA 13
Smith, Mark (Richard) 1935- ... CANR-10
Earlier sketch in CA 15-16R
See also DLBY 82
Smith, Marny 1932- ... 108
Smith, Martin
See Smith, Martin Cruz
Smith, Martin Cruz 1942- ... CANR-23
Earlier sketches in CA 85-88, CANR-6
See also CLC 25
Smith, Mary Ann 1934- ... 126
Smith, Mary Benton 1903- ... CAP-2
Earlier sketch in CA 17-18
Smith, Mary Elizabeth 1932- ... 41-44R
Smith, Mary Ellen ... 69-72
See also SATA 10
Smith, Mary-Ann Tirone 1944- Brief entry ... 118
See also CLC 39
Smith, Mason McCann 1952- ... 108
Smith, Maxwell A(ustin) 1894- ... 37-40R
Smith, (Albert) Merriman 1913-1970 ... CANR-2
Obituary ... 29-32R
Earlier sketch in CA 2R
Smith, Merritt Roe 1940- ... 77-80
Smith, Michael 1698-1771(?) ... DLB-31
Smith, Michael (Townsend) 1935- ... CANR-11
Earlier sketch in CA 21-22R
Smith, Michael A(nthony) 1942- ... 102
Smith, Michael P(eter) 1942- ... 65-68
Smith, Michael Stephen 1944- ... 103
Smith, Mike
See Smith, Mary Ellen
Smith, Mildred C(atharine) 1891-1973 ... 101
Obituary ... 45-48
Smith, Mildred Nelson 1918- ... 69-72
Smith, Mortimer B(rewster) 1906-1981 ... 107
Obituary ... 104
Smith, Morton 1915- ... CANR-6
Earlier sketch in CA 5-6R
Smith, Morton Howison 1923- ... 45-48
Smith, Murphy D(ewitt) 1920- ... CANR-13
Earlier sketch in CA 37-40R
Smith, Murray G(ordon) 1952- ... 120
Smith, Myron J(ohn), Jr. 1944- ... CANR-16
Earlier sketches in CA 45-48, CANR-1
Smith, N(orman) J(ames) 1930- ... CANR-20
Earlier sketch in CA 103
Smith, Nancy Covert 1935- ... CANR-10
Earlier sketch in CA 57-60
See also SATA 12
Smith, Nancy Taylor ... 57-60
Smith, Neil Homer 1909(?)-1972
Obituary ... 37-40R
Smith, Nigel J(ohn) H(arwood) 1949- ... 109
Smith, Nila Banton 1890-1976 ... 21-22R
Obituary ... 120
Smith, Nina Slingsby 1928- ... 119
Smith, Norman Edward Mace 1914- ... 103
Smith, Norman F. 1920- ... 29-32R
See also SATA 5
Smith, Norman Lewis 1941- ... 77-80
Smith, Norris Kelly 1917- ... 21-22R
Smith, Ophia D(elilah) Smith 1891- ... 5-6R
Smith, Oswald J(effrey) 1889-1986
Obituary ... 119
Smith, P(eter) J(ohn) 1931- ... 41-44R
Smith, (Charles) Page 1917- ... CANR-2
Earlier sketch in CA 4R
Smith, Patricia Jean Adam
See Adam-Smith, Patricia Jean
Smith, Patrick 1936- ... 77-80
Smith, Patrick D(avis) 1927- ... 77-80
Smith, Patrick J(ohn) 1932- ... 41-44R
Smith, Patrick Wykeham Montague
See Montague-Smith, Patrick Wykeham
Smith, Patti 1946- ... 93-96
See also CLC 12
Smith, Pattie Sherwood 1909(?)-1974
Obituary ... 53-56
Smith, Paul ... CANR-2
Earlier sketch in CA 2R
Smith, Paul B(rainerd) 1921- ... CANR-10
Earlier sketch in CA 13-14R
Smith, Paul C. 1908-1976 Obituary ... 65-68
Smith, Paul F. 1919- ... 57-60
Smith, Paul H(ubert) 1931- ... 89-92
Smith, Paul Jordan
See Jordan-Smith, Paul
Smith, Pauline (Urmson) 1882-1959 ... TCLC-25
Smith, Pauline C(oggeshall) 1908- ... 29-32R
See also SATA 27
Smith, Percival Gardner
See Gardner-Smith, Percival
Smith, Perry McCoy 1934- ... 29-32R
Smith, Peter 1897-1982 Obituary ... 107
Smith, Peter C(harles Horstead) 1940- ... CANR-7
Earlier sketch in CA 57-60
Smith, Peter H(opkinson) 1940- ... 41-44R
Smith, Peter J(ohn) 1931- ... 114
Smith, Philip Chadwick Foster 1939- ... 77-80
Smith, Philip E(dward II) 1943- ... 25-28R
Smith, Philip L. 1943- ... 108
Smith, Philip Warren 1936- ... SATA-46
Smith, R(ichard) A(lbert) N(ewton) 1908- ... 9-10R
Smith, R(eginald) C(harles) 1907- ... 65-68
Smith, R(eginald) D(onald) 1914- ... 117
Smith, R(obert) Philip 1907- ... 81-84
Smith, R(ichard) Selby 1914- ... 108
Smith, Ralph (Bernard) 1939- ... 33-36R
Smith, Ralph Alexander 1929- ... 77-80
Smith, Ralph B. 1894(?)-1985 Obituary ... 115
Smith, Ralph Carlisle 1910- ... 124
Smith, Ralph Lee 1927- ... CANR-1
Earlier sketch in CA 4R
Smith, Ray 1915- ... CANR-11
Earlier sketch in CA 15-16R
Smith, Ray 1941- ... CANR-18
Earlier sketch in CA 101
Smith, Ray Winfield 1897-1982 Obituary ... 110
Smith, Red
See Smith, Walter W(ellesley)
See also DLB 29
Smith, Rex Alan 1921- ... 61-64
Smith, Rhea Marsh 1907- ... CAP-1
Earlier sketch in CA 17-18
Smith, Richard 1941- ... 81-84
Smith, Richard A(ustin) 1911- ... 19-20R
Smith, Richard C(hristopher) 1948- ... 81-84
Smith, Richard Harris 1946- ... 41-44R
Smith, Richard Joseph 1944- ... CANR-20
Earlier sketch in CA 97-100
Smith, Richard K(ent) 1936- ... 41-44R
Smith, Richard M(ills) 1946- ... 73-76
Smith, Richard N. 1937- ... 23-24R
Smith, Richard P(aul) 1949- ... 111
Smith, Richard Rein 1930- ... 97-100
Smith, Robert A(rthur) 1944- ... 69-72
Smith, Robert Allan 1909-1980 Obituary ... 105
Smith, Robert C(hester) 1912-1975
Obituary ... 114
Smith, Robert C(harles) 1947- ... 111
Smith, Robert Charles 1938- ... 65-68
Smith, Robert D. 1937- ... 37-40R
Smith, Robert Dickie 1928- ... 9-10R
Smith, Robert Eliot 1899- ... 37-40R
Smith, Robert Ellis 1940- ... CANR-16
Earlier sketch in CA 89-92
Smith, Robert Freeman 1930- ... CANR-1
Earlier sketch in CA 3R
Smith, Robert G(illen) 1913- ... 45-48
Smith, Robert G(ordon) 1947- ... 102
Smith, Robert Griffin, Jr. 1920- ... 41-44R
Smith, Robert Houston 1931- ... 105
Smith, Robert J(ohn) 1927- ... 53-56
Smith, Robert Kimmel 1930- ... CANR-8
Earlier sketch in CA 61-64
See also SATA 12
Smith, Robert Lee 1928- ... 111
Smith, Robert Paul 1915-1977 ... 73-76
Obituary ... 69-72
See also SATA 30, 52
Smith, Robert S(idney) 1904-1969 ... CAP-1
Earlier sketch in CA 15-16
Smith, Robert W(ayne) 1926- ... 45-48
Smith, Robert W(illiam) 1926- ... 15-16R
Smith, Robin Baird
See Baird-Smith, Robin
Smith, Rockwell Carter 1908- ... 53-56
Smith, Rodney P(ennell), Jr. 1930- ... 29-32R
Smith, Roger H(askell) 1932-1980 ... 69-72
Obituary ... 101
Smith, Roger Montgomery 1915(?)-1975
Obituary ... 57-60
Smith, Rogers M(ood) 1953- ... 120
Smith, Roland B(eatcher) 1909- ... 2R
Smith, Ronald Gregor 1913-1968 ... CAP-1
Earlier sketch in CA 9-10
Smith, Ronald L(ande) 1952- ... 110
Smith, Rosamond
See Oates, Joyce Carol
Smith, Rowland (James) 1938- ... 45-48
Smith, Roy C(yrus) 1896- ... 124
Smith, Roy H(armon) III 1936- ... 25-28R
Smith, Russell E. 1932- ... 77-80
Smith, Russell F. W. 1915(?)-1975
Obituary ... 61-64
Smith, Ruth Leslie 1902- ... CAP-2
Earlier sketch in CA 29-32
See also SATA 2
Smith, Ruth Schluchter 1917- ... CANR-26
Earlier sketches in CA 69-72, CANR-11
Smith, S(idney) G(erald) Denis 1932- ... 103
Smith, Sally Liberman 1929- ... CANR-11
Earlier sketch in CA 21-22R
Smith, Sam(uel Frederic Houston) 1937- ... 73-76
Smith, Samantha 1972-1985 Obituary ... 117
See also SATA 45
Smith, Samuel 1904- ... CANR-11
Earlier sketch in CA 29-32R
Smith, Samuel Harrison 1772-1845 ... DLB-43
Smith, Samuel Stanhope 1751-1819 ... DLB-37
Smith, Sandra 1940- ... 122
Smith, Sarah 1832-1911 Brief entry ... 112
Smith, Sarah Stafford
See Smith, Dorothy Stafford
Smith, Scottie
See Smith, Frances Scott Fitzgerald Lanahan
Smith, Scottie Fitzgerald
See Smith, Frances Scott Fitzgerald Lanahan
Smith, Seba 1792-1868 ... DLB-1, 11
Smith, Sharon 1947- ... 77-80
Smith, Sheila Kaye
See Kaye-Smith, Sheila
Smith, Shelley
See Bodington, Nancy H(ermione)
and Shelley, Dolores
and Smith, Sandra
Smith, Sherwin 1924(?)-1985 Obituary ... 116
Smith, Shirley M(ae) 1923- ... CANR-4
Earlier sketch in CA 53-56
Smith, Stan(ley William) 1943- ... 120
Smith, Stan(ley Roger) 1946- ... 85-88
Smith, Stephen Murray
See Murray-Smith, Stephen
Smith, Steve(n R.) 1947- ... 118
Smith, Steven A(lbert) 1939- ... 57-60
Smith, Steven Phillip 1943- ... CANR-10
Earlier sketch in CA 57-60
Smith, Stevie
See Smith, Florence Margaret
See also DLB 20
See also CLC 3, 8, 25, 44
Smith, Susan Carlton 1923- ... SATA-12
Smith, Susan Mathias 1950- ... 114
See also SATA 35, 43
Smith, Susan Vernon 1950- ... CANR-19
Earlier sketch in CA 102
See also SATA 48
Smith, Susy 1911- ... CANR-6
Earlier sketch in CA 5-6R
Smith, Sydney Goodsir 1915-1975 ... 101
Obituary ... 57-60
See also DLB 27
Smith, T(ed) C. 1915- ... 49-52
Smith, T(homas) E(dward) 1916- ... 15-16R
Smith, T(homas) Lynn 1903- ... 7-8R
Smith, Talbot 1899- ... CAP-1
Earlier sketch in CA 11-12
Smith, Terence (Fitzgerald) 1938- ... 73-76
Smith, Thomas B(ell) 1923- ... 122
Smith, Thomas G. 1945- ... 123
Smith, Thomas Malcolm 1921- Brief entry ... 106
Smith, Tilman R(ay) 1903- ... 113
Smith, Timothy Dudley
See Dudley-Smith, Timothy
Smith, Timothy L(awrence) 1924- ... 116
Smith, Toby 1946- ... 119
Smith, Tony ... 93-96
Smith, Tony
See Smith, Anthony Peter
Smith, V(incent) Kerry 1945- ... 111
Smith, Varrel Lavere 1925- ... 29-32R
Smith, Verla Lee 1927(?)-1982 Obituary ... 106
Smith, Vernon Lomax 1927- ... CANR-6
Earlier sketch in CA 4R
Smith, Vesta (Henderson) 1933- ... 5-6R
Smith, Vian (Crocker) 1920-1969 ... CANR-3
Earlier sketch in CA 4R
See also SATA 11
Smith, Victor C(lyde) 1902- ... 7-8R
Smith, Vincent E(dward) 1915-1972
Obituary ... 33-36R
Smith, Virginia Carlson 1944- ... 49-52
Smith, Virginia Masterman
See Masterman-Smith, Virginia
Smith, Vivian (Brian) 1933- ... CANR-23
Earlier sketches in CA 61-64, CANR-8
Smith, W(illiam) David 1928- ... 77-80
Smith, W. Eugene 1918(?)-1978
Obituary ... 81-84
Smith, Walter W(ellesley) 1905-1982 ... 77-80
Obituary ... 105
Smith, Ward
See Goldsmith, Howard
Smith, Warren L(ounsbury) 1914-1972 ... CAP-2
Earlier sketch in CA 21-22
Smith, Warren Sylvester 1912- ... 21-22R
Smith, Warren T(homas) 1923-1986 ... 117
Obituary ... 119
Smith, Webster
See Coleman, Clayton W(ebster)
Smith, Wendell 1914-1972 Obituary ... 104
Smith, Wendell I(rving) 1921- ... 13-14R
Smith, Wesley D(ale) 1930- Brief entry ... 111
Smith, Wesley E. 1938- ... 29-32R
Smith, Whitney, Jr. 1940- ... 97-100
Smith, Wilbur A(ddison) 1933- ... CANR-7
Earlier sketch in CA 13-14R
See also CLC 33
Smith, Wilbur M(oorehead) ... 17-18R
Smith, Wilford E(mery) 1916- ... 49-52
Smith, Wilfred Cantwell 1916- ... CANR-7
Earlier sketch in CA 13-14R
Smith, Wilfred R(obert) 1915- ... 13-14R
Smith, Willard L(aurence) 1927- ... 7-8R
Smith, William 1727-1803 ... DLB-31
Smith, William 1728-1793 ... DLB-30
Smith, William A. 1918- ... SATA-10
Smith, William A. 1929- ... 45-48
Smith, William Allen 1904- ... 45-48
Smith, William C(harles) 1881-1972
Obituary ... 111
Smith, William Dale 1929- ... 49-52
Smith, William E(rnest) 1892- ... 5-6R
Smith, William Frank 1925- ... 103
Smith, William Gardner 1926-1974 ... 65-68
Obituary ... 53-56
See also BW
See also DLB 76
Smith, William I. 1932- ... 29-32R
Smith, William J. 1907(?)-1986 Obituary ... 118

Smith, William Jay 1918- 7-8R
See also SATA 2
See also DLB 5
See also CLC 6
Smith, William Martin 1911- 105
Smith, William S. 1917- 15-16R
Smith, William Scott 1926- 117
Smith, William Stevenson 1907-1969 CAP-2
Earlier sketch in CA 21-22
Smith, (Francis) Wilson 1922- 81-84
Smith, Winsome 1935- 115
See also SATA 45
Smith, Woodrow Wilson
See Kuttner, Henry
Smith, Woodruff D(onald) 1946- 85-88
Smith, Z. Z.
See Westheimer, David
Smith Brindle, Reginald 1917- 89-92
Smithdas, Robert Joseph 1925- 17-18R
Smithells, Roger (William) 1905- CAP-1
Earlier sketch in CA 13-14
Smither, Elizabeth 1941- 107
Smitherman, P(hilip) H(enry) 1910- 21-22R
Smithers, Don LeRoy 1933- 45-48
Smithers, Peter Henry Berry Otway
1913- 29-32R
Smithgall, Elizabeth
See Watts, Elizabeth (Bailey) Smithgall
Smithies, Arthur 1907-1981 Obituary 104
Smithies, Richard H(ugo) R(ipman)
1936- 23-24R
Smithson, Alison (Margaret) 1928- CANR-5
Earlier sketch in CA 25-28R
Smithson, Norman 1931- 33-36R
Smithson, Peter (Denham) 1923- CANR-5
Earlier sketch in CA 53-56
Smithson, Rulon N(ephi) 1927- 45-48
Smithyman, (William) Kendrick 1922- 101
Smits, Teo
See Smits, Theodore R(ichard)
Smits, Theodore R(ichard) 1905- 77-80
See also SATA 28, 45
Smitten, Jeffrey Roger 1941- 105
Smoke, Jim 109
Smoke, Richard 1944- CANR-10
Earlier sketch in CA 65-68
Smolansky, Oles M. 1930- CANR-1
Earlier sketch in CA 45-48
Smolar, Boris (Ber) 1897-1986 41-44R
Obituary 118
Smolich, Yurik K. 1899(?)-1976 Obituary 69-72
Smolin, C. Roger 1948- 110
Smoll, Frank L(ouis) 1941- 115
Smolla, Rodney A(lan) 1953- 121
Smoller, Bruce M. 1944- 113
Smoller, Sanford J(erome) 1937- 57-60
Smollett, Tobias 1721-1771 DLB-39
Smoluchowski, Louise 1922- 126
Smooha, Sammy 1941- 101
Smoot, Dan 1913- CANR-1
Earlier sketch in CA 4R
Smothers, Frank A(lbert) 1901-1981
Obituary 104
Smout, T(homas) C(hristopher) 1933- CANR-9
Earlier sketch in CA 21-22R
Smucker, Barbara (Claassen) 1915- CANR-23
Earlier sketch in CA 106
See also SATA 29
See also CLR 10
Smucker, Leonard 1928- 23-24R
Smullyan, Arthur Francis 1912- 4R
Smullyan, Raymond
See Smullyan, Raymond M(errill)
Smullyan, Raymond M(errill) 1919- 125
Brief entry 120
Smurl, James F(redrick) 1934- 45-48
Smurr, John Welling 1922- 3R
Smurthwaite, Ronald 1918-1975 CAP-2
Earlier sketch in CA 21-22
Smyer, Richard 1935- 102
Smykay, Edward W(alter) 1924- CANR-12
Earlier sketch in CA 19-20R
Smylie, James H(utchinson) 1925- CANR-14
Earlier sketch in CA 37-40R
Smylie, Mark A. 1954- 111
Smyrl, Frank H(erbert) 1938- 113
Smyser, Adam A(lbert) 1920- 77-80
Smyser, H(amilton) M(artin) 1901- CAP-1
Earlier sketch in CA 15-16
Smyser, Jane Worthington 1914-1975 65-68
Obituary 61-64
Smyth, Alice M.
See Hadfield, Alice M(ary)
Smyth, David 1929- CANR-12
Earlier sketch in CA 61-64
Smyth, H. D.
See Smyth, Henry DeWolf
Smyth, H(arriet) Rucker (Crowell) 1926- 2R
Smyth, Henry DeWolf 1898-1986
Obituary 120
Smyth, Howard McGaw 1901-1975
Obituary 61-64
Smyth, Jacqui (Marie) 1960- 124
Smyth, John (George) 1893-1983 CANR-11
Obituary 109
Earlier sketch in CA 61-64
Smyth, Paul 1944- CANR-8
Earlier sketch in CA 61-64
Smyth, R(obert) L(eslie) 1922- CANR-10
Earlier sketch in CA 9-10R
Smythe, Colin 1942- CANR-16
Earlier sketch in CA 97-100
Smythe, Daniel Webster 1908- 15-16R
Smythe, David Mynders 1915- 3R
Smythe, Donald 1927- 41-44R
Smythe, Hugh H(eyne) 1913-1977 11-12R
Obituary 69-72
Smythe, Mabel M(urphy) 1918- 37-40R
Smythe, Reginald 1918?- AITN-1
Smythe, Ted Curtis 1932- 101
Smythies, J(ohn) R(aymond) 1922- 37-40R
Snadowsky, Alvin M. 1938- 61-64
Snailham, (George) Richard 1930- 37-40R
Snaith, Norman Henry 1898-1982
Obituary 106
Snaith, William Theodore 1908-1974 110
Obituary 106
Snape, H(enry) Currie 1902- 9-10R
Snape, R(ichard) H(al) 1936- 29-32R
Snapes, Joan 1925- 107
Snavely, Adam A. 1930- 25-28R
Snavely, Ellen Bartow 1910- CAP-2
Earlier sketch in CA 21-22
Snavely, Guy Everett 1881-1974 5-6R
Obituary 49-52
Snavely, Tipton Ray 1890- 19-20R
Snavely, William P(ennington) 1920- 17-18R
Snead, Rodman Eldredge 1931- 73-76
Snead, Sam(uel Jackson) 1912-
Brief entry 114
Snedeker, Bonnie 1947- 119
Snedeker, Caroline Dale (Parke)
1871-1956 YABC-2
Sneed, Joseph Donald 1938- 49-52
Sneed, Joseph Tyree 1920- 23-24R
Sneider, Vern(on) John 1916-1981 CANR-13
Obituary 103
Earlier sketch in CA 7-8R
Snell, Bruno 1896- CAP-1
Earlier sketch in CA 15-16
Snell, David 1936- 77-80
Snell, Foster Dee 1898-1980 Obituary 108
Snell, Frank 1920- 1R
Snell, George Davis 1903- 106
Snell, John Leslie, Jr. 1923-1972 CANR-3
Obituary 33-36R
Earlier sketch in CA 7-8R
Snell, John Nicholas Blashford
See Blashford-Snell, John Nicholas
Snell, Nigel (Edward Creagh) 1936- 111
See also SATA 40
Snell, Tee Loftin 1922- 105
Sneller, Delwyn Lee 1945- 111
Snellgrove, David L(lewellyn) 1920-
Brief entry 115
Snellgrove, L(aurence) E(rnest) 1928- CANR-23
Earlier sketches in CA 9-10R, CANR-3
See also SATA 53
Snellgrove, Louis 1928- 45-48
Snelling, Lois 7-8R
Snelling, O(swald) F(rederick) 1916- 17-18R
Snelling, W(illiam) Rodman 1931- 93-96
Snellings, Rolland
See Toure, Askia Muhammad Abu Bakr el
Snepp, Frank (Warren III) 1943- 105
Snetsinger, John (Goodall) 1941- 73-76
Snetsinger, Robert 1928- 107
Sneve, Virginia Driving Hawk 1933- CANR-3
Earlier sketch in CA 49-52
See also SATA 8
See also CLR 2
Snider, Delbert A(rthur) 1914- 2R
Snider, Lewis W. 119
Sniderman, Florence (Lama) 1915- 33-36R
Snipes, Wilson Currin 1924- 29-32R
Snively, Susan 1945- 117
Snively, W(illiam) D(aniel), Jr. 1911- 29-32R
Snodgrass, A(nthony) M(cElrea)
1934- CANR-10
Earlier sketch in CA 21-22R
Snodgrass, Donald R(ay) 1935- 112
Snodgrass, Joan Gay 1934- 77-80
Snodgrass, Jon 1941- 113
Snodgrass, Milton M(oore) 1931- 29-32R
Snodgrass, Thomas Jefferson
See Clemens, Samuel Langhorne
Snodgrass, W(illiam) D(e Witt) 1926- CANR-6
Earlier sketch in CA 2R
See also DLB 5
See also CLC 2, 6, 10, 18
Snoek, J(aap) Diedrick 1931- 49-52
Snoke, Albert W(aldo) 1907- 125
Snook, Barbara (Lillian) 1913-1976 109
See also SATA 34
Snook, I(van) A(ugustine) 1933- CANR-14
Earlier sketch in CA 77-80
Snook, John B. 1927- 106
Snortum, Niel K(lendenon) 1928- 23-24R
Snow, C(harles) P(ercy) 1905-1980 7-8R
Obituary 101
See also DLB 15
See also CLC 1, 4, 6, 9, 13, 19
Snow, Charles Ernest 1910-1967 Obituary 116
Snow, D(avid) W(illiam) 1924- 65-68
Snow, Davis W. 1913(?)-1975 Obituary 61-64
Snow, Donald Clifford 1917- 85-88
See also SATA 16
Snow, Donald M(erritt) 1943- 106
Snow, Dorothea J(ohnston) 1909- CANR-3
Earlier sketch in CA 4R
See also SATA 9
Snow, Dorothy Mary Barter 1897- CAP-1
Earlier sketch in CA 13-14
Snow, Edgar Parks 1905-1972 81-84
Obituary 33-36R
Snow, Edward Rowe 1902-1982 CANR-6
Obituary 106
Earlier sketch in CA 9-10R
Snow, Frances Compton
See Adams, Henry (Brooks)
Snow, George (D'Oyly) 1903- 7-8R
Snow, Helen Foster 1907- 57-60
Snow, John Hall 1924- 37-40R
Snow, Karen (a pseudonym) 1923- 120
Snow, Kathleen 1944- 81-84
Snow, Keith Ronald 1943- 110
Snow, Lois Wheeler 1920- 57-60
Snow, Lucy
See Aubert, Rosemary
Snow, Peter G(ordon) 1933- 23-24R
Snow, Philip (Albert) 1915- 9-10R
Snow, Richard F(olger) 1947- 106
See also SATA 37, 52
Snow, Roslyn 1936- CANR-9
Earlier sketch in CA 23-24R
Snow, Russell E(lwin) 1938- 65-68
Snow, Sinclair 1909-1972 CAP-2
Earlier sketch in CA 25-28
Snow, Vernon F. 1924- 37-40R
Snow, (Charles) Wilbert 1884-1977 9-10R
Obituary 73-76
Snow, William George Sinclair 1908- 7-8R
Snowden, Frank M(artin), Jr. 1911- 41-44R
Snowdon
See Armstrong-Jones, Antony (Charles Robert)
Snowman, Daniel 1938- CANR-4
Earlier sketch in CA 53-56
Snukal, Robert (Martin) 1942- 45-48
Snyder, Anne 1922- CANR-14
Earlier sketch in CA 37-40R
See also SATA 4
Snyder, Bernadette McCarver 1930- 115
Snyder, Carl Dean 1921- Brief entry 113
Snyder, Carol 1941- 85-88
See also SATA 35
Snyder, Cecil K., Jr. 1927- 29-32R
Snyder, Charles M. 1909- 49-52
Snyder, Charles Royce 1924- 105
Snyder, Chuck 1933- 122
Snyder, Don J. 1950- 126
Snyder, E(ugene) V(incent) 1943- 41-44R
Snyder, Eldon E. 1930- 49-52
Snyder, Eloise C(olleen) 1928- 29-32R
Snyder, Francis Gregory 1942- CANR-22
Earlier sketches in CA 19-20R, CANR-7
Snyder, Fred A. 1931- 37-40R
Snyder, Gary 1930- 17-18R
See also DLB 5, 16
See also CLC 1, 2, 5, 9, 32
Snyder, George Sergeant 1952- 122
Snyder, Gerald S(eymour) 1933- CANR-12
Earlier sketch in CA 61-64
See also SATA 34, 48
Snyder, Glenn Herald 1924- CANR-18
Earlier sketch in CA 3R
Snyder, Graydon F. 1930- 15-16R
Snyder, Guy (Eugene, Jr.) 1951- 57-60
Snyder, Henry Leonard 1929- 41-44R
Snyder, Howard A(lbert) 1940- 113
Snyder, James E(dward) 1928- 123
Brief entry 117
Snyder, Jerome 1916-1976 Obituary 65-68
See also SATA 20
Snyder, Joan 1943- 41-44R
Snyder, John P(arr) 1926- 41-44R
Snyder, John William 1924- 2R
Snyder, Laura (Lillie) 1940- 120
Snyder, Leslie 1945- 114
Snyder, Louis L. 1907- CANR-2
Earlier sketch in CA 3R
Snyder, Marilyn 1936- 120
Snyder, (Donald) Paul 1933- CANR-1
Earlier sketch in CA 45-48
Snyder, Rachel 1924- 9-10R
Snyder, Richard C(arlton) 1916- 61-64
Snyder, Robert Edward 1943- 120
Snyder, Robert L. 1928- 25-28R
Snyder, Solomon H(albert) 1938- CANR-14
Earlier sketch in CA 37-40R
Snyder, Susan 1934- 93-96
Snyder, Tom 1936- 121
Brief entry 109
Snyder, William 1951- 104
Snyder, William P(aul) 1928- 15-16R
Snyder, William S(tover) 1927- 123
Brief entry 118
Snyder, Zilpha Keatley 1927- 11-12R
See also SATA 1, 28
See also SAAS 2
See also CLC 17
Snyderman, Reuven K. 1922- 29-32R
See also SATA 5
Soames, Mary 1922- 111
Soares, Anthony T(homas) 1923- 45-48
Soares, Bernardo
See Pessoa, Fernando (Antonio Nogueira)
Sobel, B. Z. 1933- 77-80
Sobel, Bernard 1887-1964 5-6R
Sobel, Brian M. 1954- 107
Sobel, Harold W(illiam) 1933- 61-64
Sobel, Irwin Philip 1901- 45-48
Sobel, Lester A(lbert) 1919- CANR-9
Earlier sketch in CA 21-22R
Sobel, Robert 1931- CANR-8
Earlier sketch in CA 7-8R
Sobell, Morton 1917- 53-56
Soberman, Richard M. 1937- CANR-10
Earlier sketch in CA 25-28R
Sobh, A.
See Shamlu, Ahmad
Sobieski, Carol 1939- Brief entry 124
Sobiloff, Hy(man J.) 1912-1970
Obituary 29-32R
See also DLB 48
Sobin, A. G.
See Sobin, Anthony
Sobin, Anthony 1944- 116
Sobin, Gustaf 1935- 115
Soble, Alan 1947- 122
Soble, Jennie
See Cavin, Ruth (Brodie)
Sobol, Donald J. 1924- CANR-18
Earlier sketches in CA 1R, CANR-1
See also SATA 1, 31
See also CLR 4
Sobol, Harriet Langsam 1936- CANR-8
Earlier sketch in CA 61-64
See also SATA 34, 47
Sobol, Louis 1896-1986 CAP-2
Obituary 118
Earlier sketch in CA 29-32
Sobol, Rose 1931- 101
Sobolev, Leonid (Sergeevich) 1898-1971
Obituary 29-32R
Sobosan, Jeffrey G. 1946- 126
Soboul, Albert Marius 1914-1982
Obituary 107
Sobrino, Josephine 1915- 45-48
Soby, James Thrall 1906-1979 103
Socarides, Charles W(illiam) 1922-
Brief entry 118
Sochen, June 1937- CANR-14
Earlier sketch in CA 41-44R
Sockman, Ralph W(ashington) 1889-1970 5-6R
Obituary 89-92
Socolofsky, Homer E(dward) 1922- CANR-1
Earlier sketch in CA 4R
Socolow, Robert H(arry) 1937- 37-40R
Sodaro, Craig 1948- CANR-18
Earlier sketch in CA 101
Soderberg, Paul Stephen 1949- CANR-19
Earlier sketch in CA 103
Soderberg, Percy Measday 1901-1969 CAP-1
Earlier sketch in CA 9-10
Soderholm, Marjorie Elaine 1923- 13-14R
Soderlind, Arthur E(dwin) 1920- 69-72
See also SATA 14
Soderstrom, Edward Jonathan 1954- 111
Soekarno
See Sukarno, (Ahmed)
Soelle, Dorothee 1929- CANR-11
Earlier sketch in CA 69-72
Soeur Sourire
See Deckers, Jeanine
Sofen, Edward 1919- 9-10R
Sofer, Cyril 1921- 5-6R
Soffer, Reba N(usbaum) 1934- 85-88
Softly, Barbara Frewin 1924- CANR-2
Earlier sketch in CA 5-6R
See also SATA 12
Softly, Edgar
See Lovecraft, H(oward) P(hillips)
Softly, Edward
See Lovecraft, H(oward) P(hillips)
Soglow, Otto 1900-1975 93-96
Obituary 57-60
See also SATA 30
Sohl, Frederic J(ohn) 1916- 21-22R
See also SATA 10
Sohl, Jerry 1913- CANR-15
Earlier sketch in CA 81-84
Sohl, Robert (Allen) 1941- 103
Sohn, David A. 1929- CANR-6
Earlier sketch in CA 11-12R
Sohn, Louis B(runo) 1914- 101
Sokel, Walter H(erbert) 1917- CANR-6
Earlier sketch in CA 7-8R
Sokol, Anthony E. 1897- 37-40R
Sokol, Bill
See Sokol, William
Sokol, David M(artin) 1942- CANR-16
Earlier sketches in CA 49-52, CANR-1
Sokol, William 1923- SATA-37
Sokoloff, Alice Hunt 1912- 25-28R
Sokoloff, Boris Theodore 1889- 89-92
Sokoloff, Kiril 1947- 108
Sokoloff, Natalie B.
See Scott, Natalie Anderson
Sokoloff, Natalie J(ean) 1944- 113
Sokolov, Alexander V(sevolodovich)
1943- 73-76
Sokolov, Kirill 1930- SATA-34
Sokolov, Raymond 1941- 85-88
See also CLC 7
Sokolov, Sasha
See Sokolov, Alexander V(sevolodovich)
Sokolov, Valentin 1925(?)-1984 Obituary 114
Sokolow, Jayme Aaron 1946- 113
Sokolowski, Robert (Stanley) 1934- 89-92
Sokolski, Alan 1931- 15-16R
Sokolsky, George Ephraim 1893-1962
Obituary 89-92
Solano, Solita 1888-1975 117
Obituary 61-64
See also DLB 4
Solaun, Mauricio 1935- Brief entry 106
Solberg, Carl 1915- CANR-12
Earlier sketch in CA 73-76
Solberg, Carl Edward 1940- 61-64
Solberg, Gunard 1932- 29-32R
Solberg, Richard W. 1917- CANR-3
Earlier sketch in CA 11-12R
Solberg, S(ammy) E(dward) 1930- 21-22R
Solberg, Winton U(dell) 1922- 41-44R
Solbert, Romaine G. 1925- 29-32R
See also SATA 2
Solbert, Ronni
See Solbert, Romaine G.
Solbrig, Otto T(homas) 1930- CANR-9
Earlier sketch in CA 21-22R
Soldati, Mario 1906- 108
Soldo, John J(oseph) 1945- CANR-14
Earlier sketch in CA 77-80
Soldofsky, Robert Melvin 1920- CANR-1
Earlier sketch in CA 2R
Sole, Carlos A(lberto) 1938- 53-56

Solecki, Ralph S(tefan) 1917- Brief entry ... 109
Solem, (George) Alan 1931- ... 57-60
Solensten, John M(artin) 1929- ... 110
Soleri, Paolo 1919- ... 106
Soliday, Gerald Lyman 1939- ... CANR-12
Earlier sketch in CA 61-64
Solinger, Dorothy J(ane) 1945- ... 113
Soll, Ivan 1938- ... 29-32R
Solle, Dorothee
See Soelle, Dorothee
Solley, Charles Marion, Jr. 1925- ... 2R
Sollors, Werner 1943- ... 119
Solman, Paul 1944- Brief entry ... 119
Solmon, Lewis C(alvin) 1942- ... 41-44R
Solmsen, Friedrich (Rudolf Heinrich)
1904- ... 53-56
Solnick, Bruce B. 1933- ... 29-32R
Solnit, Albert J. 1919- ... 103
Solo, Jay
See Ellison, Harlan
Solo, Robert A(lexander) 1916- ... CANR-17
Earlier sketches in CA 45-48, CANR-1
Sologub, Fyodor
See Teternikov, Fyodor Kuzmich
See also TCLC 9
Solomon, Barbara H. 1936- ... CANR-13
Earlier sketch in CA 73-76
Solomon, Barbara Probst 1928- ... 5-6R
Solomon, Bernard S(imon) 1924- ... 61-64
Solomon, (Neal) Brad(ley) 1945- ... 103
Solomon, Brad 1945- ... 101
Solomon, Carl 1928- ... 21-22R
See also DLB 16
Solomon, Charles J. 1906(?)-1975
Obituary ... 61-64
Solomon, Daniel 1933- ... 11-12R
Solomon, David J. 1925- ... 19-20R
Solomon, Dorothy Allred 1949- ... 119
Solomon, Esther Riva 1921- ... 7-8R
Solomon, Ezra 1920- ... CANR-17
Earlier sketch in CA 85-88
Solomon, Flora 1895(?)-1984 Obituary ... 114
Solomon, George 1940- ... 45-48
Solomon, Goody L(ove) ... 57-60
Solomon, Henry A. 1937- ... 123
Solomon, Irving I. 1922- ... CANR-16
Earlier sketch in CA 21-22R
Solomon, Janis Little 1938- ... CANR-15
Earlier sketch in CA 41-44R
Solomon, Joan 1930- ... 109
See also SATA 40, 51
Solomon, Kenneth Ira 1942- ... 49-52
Solomon, Leonard 1930- ... 45-48
Solomon, Margaret C(laire) 1918- ... 29-32R
Solomon, Maynard (Elliott) 1930- ... 41-44R
Solomon, Michael M(aurice) 1909- ... 97-100
Solomon, Morris J. 1919- ... 13-14R
Solomon, Neil 1932- ... 65-68
Solomon, Norman 1951- ... CANR-9
Earlier sketch in CA 57-60
Solomon, Richard H(arvey) 1937- ... 103
Solomon, Robert 1921- ... 108
Solomon, Robert C(harles) 1942- ... CANR-15
Earlier sketch in CA 41-44R
Solomon, Ruth (Freeman) 1908- ... 23-24R
Solomon, Samuel 1904-1988 ... 53-56
Obituary ... 126
Solomon, Shirl 1928- ... 93-96
Solomon, Stanley J. 1937- ... 41-44R
Solomon, Stephen D(avid) 1950- ... 69-72
Solomon, Steve 1942- ... 117
Solomons, David 1912- ... 13-14R
Solomons, Ikey, Esquire, Jr.
See Thackeray, William Makepeace
Solon, Gregory Kent 1923(?)-1985
Obituary ... 117
Solonevich, George 1915- ... SATA-15
Solot, Mary Lynn 1939- ... 49-52
See also SATA 12
Solotaroff, Robert David 1937- ... 57-60
Solotaroff, Ted
See Solotaroff, Theodore
See also CAAS 2
Solotaroff, Theodore 1928- ... CANR-8
Earlier sketch in CA 11-12R
Soloukhin, Vladimir (Alekseevich) 1924-
Brief entry ... 111
Solow, Martin 1920- ... 81-84
Soloway, Richard Allen 1934- ... 118
Solt, Mary Ellen (Bottom) 1920- ... 17-18R
Soltau, T(heodore) Stanley 1890- ... 7-8R
Soltis, Andrew (Eden, Jr.) 1947- ... CANR-4
Earlier sketch in CA 49-52
Soltis, Andy
See Soltis, Andrew (Eden, Jr.)
Soltis, Jonas F(rancis) 1931- ... CANR-14
Earlier sketch in CA 37-40R
Soltow, James H(arold) 1924- ... 109
Soltow, Lee 1923- ... 108
Soltow, Martha-Jane 1924- ... 110
Solway, David 1941- ... 112
See also DLB 53
Solwoska, Mara
See French, Marilyn
Solyn, Paul 1951- ... 77-80
Solzhenitsyn, Aleksandr I(sayevich) 1918- ... 69-72
See also CLC 1, 2, 4, 7, 9, 10, 18, 26, 34
See also AITN 1
Soman, Alfred 1934- ... 45-48
Soman, Jean Powers 1949- ... 122
Soman, Shirley Camper ... CANR-3
Earlier sketch in CA 9-10R
Somekh, Emile 1915- ... 53-56
Somer, John (Laddie) 1936- ... 37-40R
Somerlott, Robert 1928- ... 105
Somers, Albert B(ingham) 1939- ... 115
Somers, Gerald G(eorge) 1922-1977 ... CANR-5
Earlier sketch in CA 13-14R
Somers, Herman Miles 1911- ... CANR-1
Earlier sketch in CA 3R
Somers, Paul
See Winterton, Paul
Somers, Robert H(ough) 1929- ... 45-48
Somers, Suzanne
See Daniels, Dorothy
Somerset, FitzRoy Richard
See Raglan, FitzRoy
Somerset, Henry Hugh Arthur FitzRoy
1900-1984 Obituary ... 112
Somerset Fry, (Peter George Robin)
Plantagenet 1931- ... 104
Somerville, (James) Hugh (Miller) 1922- ... 9-10R
Somerville, John 1905- ... 45-48
Somerville, (Henry) Lee 1915- ... 69-72
Somerville, Mollie ... CANR-12
Earlier sketch in CA 29-32R
Somerville, Rose M(aurer) 1908- ... 45-48
Somerville-Large, Peter 1928- ... CANR-20
Earlier sketch in CA 97-100
Somes, Jethro
See Pauker, John
Somit, Albert 1919- ... 81-84
Somkin, Fred 1924- ... 25-28R
Sommer, Elyse 1929- ... CANR-2
Earlier sketch in CA 49-52
See also SATA 7
Sommer, Joellen 1957- ... 45-48
Sommer, John 1941- ... 29-32R
Sommer, Richard J(erome) 1934- ... CANR-1
Earlier sketch in CA 45-48
Sommer, Robert 1929- ... CANR-18
Earlier sketches in CA 11-12R, CANR-3
See also SATA 12
Sommer, Scott 1951- ... 106
See also CLC 25
Sommerfeld, Ray(nard) M(atthias) 1933- ... 105
Sommerfeld, Richard Edwin 1928- ... 15-16R
Sommerfeldt, John R(obert) 1933- ... CANR-3
Earlier sketch in CA 49-52
Sommerfelt, Aimee 1892- ... 37-40R
See also SATA 5
Sommerness, Martin David 1954- ... 116
Sommers, David
See Smith, Howard Van
Sommers, Fred(eric Tamler) 1923- ... 113
Sommers, Jay 1917(?)-1985 Obituary ... 117
Sommers, Joseph 1924- ... 25-28R
Sommers, Lawrence M(elvin) 1919- ... 126
Sommers, Tish 1914(?)-1985 Obituary ... 117
Somorjai, Gabor Arpad 1935- ... 105
Somtow, S. P.
See Sucharitkul, Somtow
Sondak, Norman E(dward) 1931- ... 112
Sondermann, Fred A. 1923- ... 49-52
Sondheim, Stephen (Joshua) 1930- ... 103
See also CLC 30, 39
Sondrup, Steven P(reece) 1944- ... 103
Sonenblick, Jerry 1931- ... 104
Sonenblum, Sidney 1924- ... 29-32R
Sonenscher, Michael 1947- ... 118
Sonero, Devi
See Pelton, Robert W(ayne)
Song, Ben (Chunho) 1937- ... 37-40R
Song, C(hoan-)S(eng) 1929- ... 115
Songe, Alice Heloise 1914- ... 102
Sonkin, Robert 1911(?)-1980 Obituary ... 97-100
Sonneborn, Harry L(ee) 1919- ... 77-80
Sonneborn, Ruth (Cantor) 1899-1974 ... CAP-2
Obituary ... 49-52
Earlier sketch in CA 21-22
See also SATA 4, 27
Sonneborn, Tracy Morton 1905-1981
Obituary ... 108
Sonnenfeld, Marion (Wilma) 1928- ... 37-40R
Sonnichsen, C. L. 1901- ... CANR-17
Earlier sketches in CA 2R, CANR-2
Sonntag, Jacob 1905-1984 Obituary ... 113
Son Of The Soil
See Fletcher, J(oseph) S(mith)
Sonstegard, Manford Aldrich 1911- ... CANR-2
Earlier sketch in CA 49-52
Sonstroem, David 1936- ... 29-32R
Sontag, Alan 1946- ... 85-88
Sontag, Frederick (Earl) 1924- ... CANR-1
Earlier sketch in CA 2R
Sontag, Frederick H(erman) 1924- ... 81-84
Sontag, Raymond J(ames) 1897-1972
Obituary ... 37-40R
Sontag, Susan 1933- ... CANR-25
Earlier sketch in CA 19-20R
See also DLB 2, 67
See also CLC 1, 2, 10, 13, 31
Sontheimer, Morton ... 101
Sontup, Dan(iel) 1922- ... 4R
Soong Ching-ling 1890-1981 Obituary ... 108
Soper, Alexander Coburn 1904- ... 105
Soper, Donald Oliver 1903- ... 109
Soper, Eileen A(lice) 1905- ... 9-10R
Soper, Eileen Louise 1900- ... 103
Soper, Fred L. 1894(?)-1977 Obituary ... 69-72
Soper, Paul L(eon) 1906- ... 7-8R
Soper, Tony 1939- ... CANR-22
Earlier sketch in CA 105
Sopher, Sharon Isabel 1945- ... 101
Sorauf, Francis Joseph 1928- ... 11-12R
Sorauf, Frank J.
See Sorauf, Francis Joseph
Sorden, L(eland) G(eorge) 1898- ... CANR-1
Earlier sketch in CA 1R
Sorel, Byron
See Yatron, Michael
Sorel, Edward 1929- ... 9-10R
See also SATA 37
Sorel, Georges 1847-1922 Brief entry ... 118
Sorel, Julia
See Drexler, Rosalyn
Sorel, Nancy Caldwell 1934- ... 37-40R
Sorell, Walter 1905- ... 21-22R
Sorensen, Andrew Aaron 1938- ... 65-68
Sorensen, Chris 1942- ... 107
Sorensen, Jacki 1942- ... 110
Sorensen, Robert C(haikin) 1923- ... 45-48
Sorensen, Theodore C(haikin) 1928- ... CANR-2
Earlier sketch in CA 45-48
Sorensen, Thomas C. 1926- ... 23-24R
Sorensen, Virginia 1912- ... CANR-22
Earlier sketch in CA 15-16R
See also SATA 2
Sorenson, Herbert 1898- ... 23-24R
Sorenson, Marian 1925-1968 ... CAP-1
Earlier sketch in CA 11-12
Sorestad, Glen 1937- ... 112
Sorgman, Mayo 1912- ... 15-16R
Soria, Regina 1911- ... 126
Sorin, Gerald 1940- ... 77-80
Sorine, Stephanie Riva 1954- ... 105
Sorkin, Alan Lowell 1941- ... CANR-14
Earlier sketch in CA 41-44R
Sorley, Lewis 1934- ... 117
Sorley Walker, Kathrine ... CANR-6
Earlier sketch in CA 7-8R
See also SATA 41
Sorokin, Boris 1922- ... 116
Sorokin, Elena 1894(?)-1975 Obituary ... 61-64
Sorokin, Pitirim A(lexandrovitch)
1889-1968 ... CANR-5
Obituary ... 25-28R
Earlier sketch in CA 7-8R
Sorrell, Alan 1904-1974 ... 93-96
Sorrells, Dorothy C. ... 9-10R
Sorrells, Helen 1908- ... 37-40R
Sorrentino, Gilbert 1929- ... CANR-14
Earlier sketch in CA 77-80
See also DLB 5
See also DLBY 80
See also CLC 3, 7, 14, 22, 40
Sorrentino, Joseph N. 1937- ... CANR-3
Earlier sketch in CA 49-52
See also SATA 6
Sorsby, Arnold 1900- ... 85-88
Sortor, June Elizabeth 1939- ... 61-64
See also SATA 12
Sortor, Toni
See Sortor, June Elizabeth
Sorum, Paul Clay 1943- ... 103
Sosa, Ernest 1940- ... 53-56
Sosa de Quesada, Aristides V. 1908- ... 53-56
Soskice, Janet Martin 1951- ... 124
Soskin, V.H.
See Ellison, Virginia H(owell)
Sosna, Morton 1945- ... 102
Sosnick, Stephen H(oward) 1930- ... 45-48
Sosnow, Eric 1910-1987 Obituary ... 121
Sossaman, Stephen 1944- ... 77-80
Soth, Lauren (Kephart) 1910- ... CAP-1
Earlier sketch in CA 17-18
Soto, Gary 1952- ... 125
Brief entry ... 119
See also CLC 32
Soto, Pedro Juan 1928- Brief entry ... 114
Sotomayor, Antonio 1902- ... 73-76
See also SATA 11
Sotter, Fred
See Lake, Kenneth R(obert)
Souci, Robert D. San
See San Souci, Robert D.
Soucy, Robert J(oseph) 1933- ... 45-48
Soudley, Henry
See Wood, James Playsted
Souerwine, Andrew H(arry) 1924- ... CANR-19
Earlier sketch in CA 81-84
Soukup, James R(udolph) 1928- ... 11-12R
Soule, Gardner (Bosworth) 1913- ... CANR-2
Earlier sketch in CA 5-6R
See also SATA 14
Soule, George (Henry, Jr.) 1887-1970 ... CAP-2
Obituary ... 29-32R
Earlier sketch in CA 21-22
Soule, George (Alan) 1930- ... 57-60
Soule, Isabel Walker 1898(?)-1972
Obituary ... 37-40R
Soule, Jean Conder 1919- ... 7-8R
See also SATA 10
Soupault, Philippe 1897- Brief entry ... 116
Soupcoff, Murray 1943- ... 101
Souper, Patrick Charles 1928- ... 110
Sour, Robert B(andler) 1905-1985
Obituary ... 115
Sourian, Peter 1933- ... 1R
Sourkes, Theodore L(ionel) 1919- ... 17-18R
Sours, John Appling 1931-1983 ... CANR-9
Obituary ... 110
Earlier sketch in CA 21-22R
Sousa, Marion 1941- ... 65-68
Souster, (Holmes) Raymond 1921- ... CANR-13
Earlier sketch in CA 13-14R
See also CLC 5, 14
South, Clark
See Swain, Dwight V(reeland)
South, Cris 1950- ... 118
South, Grace
See Clark, Gail
South, Malcolm Hudson 1937- ... 107
Southall, Aidan (William) 1920- ... 77-80
Southall, Ivan (Francis) 1921- ... CANR-7
Earlier sketch in CA 9-10R
See also SATA 3
See also SAAS 3
See also CLR 2
Southam, B(rian) C(harles) 1931- ... CANR-26
Earlier sketches in CA 15-16R, CANR-10
Southard, Frank Allan, Jr. 1907- ... 107
Southard, Helen Fairbairn 1906- ... 5-6R
Southard, Samuel 1925- ... CANR-3
Earlier sketch in CA 4R
Southerington, F(rank) R(odney) 1938- ... 57-60
Southerland, Ellease 1943- ... 107
See also BW
See also DLB 33
Southern, David W. 1938- ... 25-28R
Southern, Eileen 1920- ... CANR-14
Earlier sketch in CA 37-40R
Southern, Richard William 1912- ... 9-10R
Southern, Terry 1926- ... CANR-1
Earlier sketch in CA 1R
See also DLB 2
See also CLC 7
Southgate, Vera ... 109
Southgate, W(yndham) M(ason) 1910- ... CAP-2
Earlier sketch in CA 23-24
Southwell, Eugene A. 1928- ... 17-18R
Southwell, Samuel B(eall) 1922- ... 19-20R
Southwick, Charles H(enry) 1928- ... 65-68
Southworth, Herbert Rutledge 1908- ... 85-88
Southworth, Horton C. 1926- ... 17-18R
Southworth, James G(ranville) 1896- ... CAP-2
Earlier sketch in CA 33-36
Southworth, John Van Duyn
1904-1986 ... CANR-6
Obituary ... 118
Earlier sketch in CA 7-8R
Southworth, Louis
See Grealey, Thomas Louis
Southworth, Warren H(ilbourne) 1912- ... 37-40R
Soutter, Fred
See Lake, Kenneth R(obert)
Souvarine, Boris
See Lifchitz, Boris
Souza, Ernest
See Scott, Evelyn
Souza, Raymond D(ale) 1936- ... CANR-13
Earlier sketch in CA 69-72
Souza, Steven M. 1953- ... 49-52
Souza Filho, Henrique de 1945(?)-1988
Obituary ... 124
Sovik, E(dward) A(nders) 1918-
Brief entry ... 112
Sowards, J(esse) K(elley) 1924- ... 73-76
Sowden, Lewis 1905-1974 ... CAP-1
Earlier sketch in CA 9-10
Sowell, Thomas 1930- ... CANR-26
Earlier sketch in CA 41-44R
See also BW
Sowerby, A(rthur) L(indsay) M(cRae)
1899- ... CAP-1
Earlier sketch in CA 9-10
Sowerby, E(mily) Millicent 1883-1977 ... CAP-2
Obituary ... 73-76
Earlier sketch in CA 25-28
Sowers, Miriam R. 1922- ... 89-92
Sowers, Robert (Watson) 1923- ... 17-18R
Sowers, Sidney Gerald, Jr. 1935- ... 17-18R
Sox, (Harold) David 1936- ... 124
Soyer, Raphael 1899-1987 ... 81-84
Obituary ... 124
Soyinka, Wole 1934- ... 15-16R
See also BW
See also CLC 3, 5, 14, 36, 44
Spaak, Paul-Henri 1899-1972 Obituary ... 37-40R
Spaatz, Carl A(ndrew) 1891-1974
Obituary ... 49-52
Spach, John Thom 1928- ... 29-32R
Spache, Evelyn B(ispham) 1929- ... 29-32R
Spache, George D(aniel) 1909- ... CANR-6
Earlier sketch in CA 7-8R
Spackman, Doc
See Spackman, Robert R., Jr.
Spackman, Robert R., Jr. 1917-1984 ... 15-16R
Obituary ... 111
Spackman, W(illiam) M(ode) 1905- ... 81-84
See also CLC 46
Spacks, Barry 1931- ... 29-32R
See also CLC 14
Spacks, Patricia Meyer 1929- ... CANR-1
Earlier sketch in CA 3R
Spada, James 1950- ... CANR-7
Earlier sketch in CA 57-60
Spade, Mark
See Balchin, Nigel (Marlin)
Spade, Rupert
See Pawley, Martin Edward
Spaeth, David A(nthony) 1941- ... 119
Spaeth, Eloise O'Mara 1904- ... 104
Spaeth, Gerold 1939- ... CANR-24
Earlier sketches in CA 65-68, CANR-9
See also DLB 75
Spaeth, Harold J(oseph) 1930- ... 45-48
Spaeth, Robert L(ouis) 1935- ... 119
Spaeth, Sigmund 1885-1965 ... 5-6R
Spahn, Mary Attea 1929- ... CANR-7
Earlier sketch in CA 57-60
Spain, Daphne 1949- ... 111
Spain, David H. 1939- ... 57-60
Spain, James W(illiam) 1926- ... 7-8R
Spain, John
See Adams, Cleve F(ranklin)
Spain, Rufus B(uin) 1923- ... 21-22R
Spake, Amanda 1947- ... 77-80
Spalatin, Christopher 1909- ... 49-52
Spalding, Frances 1950- ... CANR-26
Earlier sketch in CA 104
Spalding, Graydon (Edward) 1911- ... 89-92
Spalding, Henry D(aniel) 1915- ... CANR-11
Earlier sketch in CA 25-28R
Spalding, Jack 1913- ... 69-72

Spalding, Lucile
See Spalding, Ruth
Spalding, P(hilip) A(nthony) 1911- 7-8R
Spalding, (Billups) Phinizy 1930- CANR-16
Earlier sketch in CA 41-44R
Spalding, R(onald) W(olcott) 1904- 81-84
Spalding, Ruth 104
Spalek, John M. 1928- 104
Spalter, Max 1929- 21-22R
Spanfeller, James J(ohn) 1930- SATA-19
Spangenberg, Judith Dunn 1942- CANR-12
Earlier sketch in CA 29-32R
See also SATA 5
Spangler, Earl 1920- CANR-5
Earlier sketch in CA 7-8R
Spanidou, Irini 1946- CLC-44
Spanier, David 1932- CANR-18
Earlier sketch in CA 101
Spanier, Ginette 1904-1987 Obituary 125
Spanier, John W(inston) 1930- CANR-2
Earlier sketch in CA 4R
Spann, Edward K(enneth) 1931- 45-48
Spann, Gloria Carter 1926- 77-80
Spann, Meno 1903- CANR-21
Earlier sketch in CA 1R
Spann, Weldon O(ma) 1924- 17-18R
Spano, Charles 1948- 93-96
Spanos, William V(aios) 1925- CANR-11
Earlier sketch in CA 21-22R
Spar, Jerome 1918- 25-28R
See also SATA 10
Sparano, Vin(cent) T(homas) 1934- CANR-22
Earlier sketch in CA 45-48
Spargo, John 1876-1966 Obituary 89-92
Spark, Debra (Alison) 1962- 122
Spark, Muriel (Sarah) 1918- CANR-12
Earlier sketch in CA 7-8R
See also DLB 15
See also CLC 2, 3, 5, 8, 13, 18, 40
Sparke, (George) Archibald 1871-1970 ... CAP-2
Earlier sketch in CA 21-22
Sparkes, Ivan G(eorge) 1930- 115
Sparkia, Roy (Bernard) 1924- 77-80
Sparkman, Brandon B(uster) 1929- CANR-13
Earlier sketch in CA 61-64
Sparkman, G(rady) Temp 1932- CANR-15
Earlier sketch in CA 89-92
Sparkman, William
See Roger, William L(eon)
Sparks, Asa H(oward) 1937- CANR-19
Earlier sketch in CA 97-100
Sparks, Beatrice Mathews 1918- 97-100
See also SATA 28, 44
Sparks, Bertel M(ilas) 1918- 21-22R
Sparks, Donald B. 1931- 124
Sparks, Edgar H(erndon) 1908- 13-14R
Sparks, Fred 1916(?)-1981 Obituary 103
Sparks, Jack Norman 1928- 102
Sparks, James Allen 1933- 109
Sparks, Jared 1789-1866 .... DLB-1, 30
Sparks, John 1939- 103
Sparks, Mary W. 1920- SATA-15
Sparks, Merla Jean
See McCormick, Merla Jean
Sparks, Merrill 1922- 23-24R
Sparks, Will (R.) 1924-1987 ....37-40R
Obituary 124
Sparrow, (John Walter) Gerald 1903- 49-52
Sparrow, John (Hanbury Angus) 1906- 103
Sparrow, Phil
See Steward, Samuel M(orris)
Sparrow, Philip
See Steward, Samuel M(orris)
Sparse Grey Hackle
See Miller, Alfred W.
Sparshott, F. E.
See Sparshott, Francis (Edward)
Sparshott, Francis (Edward) 1926- CANR-26
Earlier sketches in CA 25-28R, CANR-10
See also DLB 60
Spartacus, Deutero
See Fanthorpe, R(obert) Lionel
Spartacus, Tertius
See Burgess, M(ichael) R(oy)
Spate, O(skar) H(ermann) K(hristian)
1911- CANR-10
Earlier sketch in CA 25-28R
Spater, George (Alexander) 1909-1984
Obituary 113
Spath, Gerold
See Spaeth, Gerold
See also DLB 75
Spatz, (Kenneth) Chris(topher, Jr.)
1940- 37-40R
Spatz, Jonas 1935- 29-32R
Spaulding, Dayton M(athewson) 1922- 61-64
Spaulding, Douglas
See Bradbury, Ray (Douglas)
Spaulding, Leonard
See Bradbury, Ray Douglas
Spaulding, Robert K(ilburn) 1898- 7-8R
Spaulding, William E(llsworth) 1898-1979
Obituary 93-96
Spaull, Hebe (Fanny Lily) 1893- 9-10R
Speaight, George Victor 1914- CANR-12
Earlier sketch in CA 29-32R
Speaight, Robert (William) 1904-1976 .. CANR-12
Earlier sketch in CA 13-14R
Spear, Allan Henry 1937- 21-22R
Spear, Benjamin
See Henisch, Heinz K.
Spear, George E(lliott) 1925- 102
Spear, Hilda D(oris) 1926- CANR-23
Earlier sketch in CA 107
Spear, (Thomas George) Percival
1901-1982 106
Obituary 108
Spear, Richard E(dmund) 1940- 45-48
Spear, Roberta 1948- 113
Speare, Elizabeth George 1908- 2R
See also SATA 5
See also CLR 8
Spearing, Judith (Mary Harlow) 1922- ... CANR-3
Earlier sketch in CA 49-52
See also SATA 9
Spearman, Arthur Dunning 1899- CAP-2
Earlier sketch in CA 21-22
Spearman, Walter (Smith) 1908- CAP-2
Earlier sketch in CA 29-32
Spears, Betty (Mary) 1918- CANR-6
Earlier sketch in CA 2R
Spears, Dorothea (Johnson) 1901- CAP-1
Earlier sketch in CA 13-14
Spears, Edward (Louis) 1886-1974 ...... CAP-2
Obituary 45-48
Earlier sketch in CA 23-24
Spears, Jack 1919- 29-32R
Spears, Monroe K(irk) 1916- CANR-2
Earlier sketch in CA 5-6R
Spears, Richard A(lan) 1939- CANR-21
Earlier sketch in CA 104
Spears, Ross 1947- 122
Spears, Woodridge 1913- 13-14R
Specht, Ernst Konrad 1926- 29-32R
Specht, Harry 1929- CANR-8
Earlier sketch in CA 53-56
Specht, Robert 1928- 103
Specht, Walter F(rederick) 1912- 97-100
Speck, Gordon 1898- CAP-2
Earlier sketch in CA 17-18
Speck, Ross V(ictor) 1927- 125
Brief entry 107
Specking, Inez 1890-196? 7-8R
See also SATA 11
Spectator
See Popovic, Nenad D(ushan)
Spector, Debra 1953- 109
Spector, Irwin 1916- 45-48
Spector, Ivar 1898- 3R
Spector, Jack J. 1925- 29-32R
Spector, Leonard S. 1945- 122
Spector, Marshall 1936- 45-48
Spector, Robert Donald 1922- 15-16R
Spector, Ronald (Harvey) 1943- 57-60
Spector, Samuel I(ra) 1924- 77-80
Spector, Sherman David 1927- CANR-22
Earlier sketch in CA 1R
Spector, Shushannah 1903- 11-12R
Spector, Stanley 1924- 9-10R
Spectorsky, A(uguste) C(omte)
1910-1972 .... CAP-2
Obituary 33-36R
Earlier sketch in CA 17-18
Spedding, C(olin) R(aymond) W(illiam)
1925- 53-56
Speed, Eric CAP-2
Earlier sketch in CA 19-20
Speed, F(rederick) Maurice 1912- 107
Speed, Frank Warren 104
Speed, (Herbert) Keith 1934- 115
Speelman, Arlene 1916- 41-44R
Speer, Albert 1905-1981 65-68
Obituary 104
Speer, David G(ordon) 1913- 45-48
Speer, Michael L. 1934- 93-96
Speeth, Kathleen Riordan 1937- 89-92
Spehar, Betty M. 1924- 45-48
Speicher, Helen Ross S(mith) 1915- CANR-4
Earlier sketch in CA 5-6R
See also SATA 8
Speicher, John 1934(?)-1986 Obituary 119
Speidel, Hans 1897-1984 Obituary 114
Speidel, Michael P(aul) 1937- 108
Speier, Hans 1905- CANR-9
Earlier sketch in CA 23-24R
Speight, Harold 1916- 7-8R
Speight, Johnny 1921(?)- Brief entry 117
Speirs, John (Hastie) 1906- 61-64
Speirs, Logan 1938- 37-40R
Speirs, Russell 1901-1975 .... CANR-4
Obituary 61-64
Earlier sketch in CA 45-48
Speiser, Jean 69-72
Speiser, Stuart Marshall 1923- Brief entry .. 106
Speitel, H. H.
See Speitel, Hans(-Henning)
Speitel, Hans(-Henning) 1937- 123
Speizman, Morris 1905- 77-80
Spekke, Arnolds 1887-1972 Obituary 37-40R
Spelios, Thomas 1930- 25-28R
Spellman, Alfred B. 1935- 97-100
See also BW
See also DLB 41
Spellman, Cathy Cash 1941- 121
Spellman, Francis (Joseph) 1889-1967
Obituary 113
Spellman, Francis Cardinal
See Spellman, Francis (Joseph)
Spellman, John W(illard) 1934- 13-14R
See also SATA 14
Spellman, Roger G.
See Cox, William R(obert)
Spelman, Mary 1934- CANR-13
Earlier sketch in CA 77-80
See also SATA 28
Spelvin, George
See Phillips, David Atlee
Spence, Bill
See Spence, William John Duncan
Spence, Clark C(hristian) 1923- CANR-6
Earlier sketch in CA 1R
Spence, Donald P(ond) 1926- Brief entry ... 109
Spence, Duncan
See Spence, William John Duncan
Spence, Eleanor (Rachel) 1928- CANR-3
Earlier sketch in CA 49-52
See also SATA 21
Spence, Gerald Leonard 1929- 118
Spence, Geraldine 1931- SATA-47
Spence, Gerry
See Spence, Gerald Leonard
Spence, Gordon William 1936- 25-28R
Spence, Hartzell 1908- 7-8R
Spence, J. A. D.
See Eliot, T(homas) S(tearns)
Spence, J(ohn) E(dward) 1931- 25-28R
Spence, James R(obert) 1927- 25-28R
Spence, Jonathan D(ermot) 1936- CANR-23
Earlier sketch in CA 21-22R
Spence, (James) Lewis (Thomas Chalmers)
1874-1955 Brief entry 115
Spence, Mary Lee 1927- 45-48
Spence, Vernon Gladden 1924- 37-40R
Spence, William John Duncan 1923- ... CANR-20
Earlier sketch in CA 103
Spencer
See Herz, Jerome Spencer
Spencer, Ann 1918- 29-32R
See also SATA 10
Spencer, Anne 1882-1975 .... DLB-51, 54
Spencer, Benjamin T(ownley) 1904- 124
Spencer, (Charles) Bernard 1909-1963
Obituary 115
Spencer, Bonnell 1909- 106
Spencer, Charles 1920- 49-52
Spencer, Christopher 1930- 13-14R
Spencer, Colin 1933- CANR-12
Earlier sketch in CA 21-22R
Spencer, Cornelia
See Yaukey, Grace S(ydenstricker)
Spencer, Dale R(ay) 1925- 57-60
Spencer, Donald D(ean) 1931- 108
See also SATA 41
Spencer, Edgar Winston 1931- 41-44R
Spencer, Elizabeth 1921- 13-14R
See also SATA 14
See also DLB 6
See also CLC 22
Spencer, Harold (Edwin) 1920- CANR-23
Earlier sketch in CA 45-48
Spencer, Herbert 1820-1903 .... DLB-57
Spencer, J(oseph) E(arle) 1907-1984 .. CANR-22
Earlier sketch in CA 45-48
Spencer, James 1932- 109
Spencer, Jean E(lizabeth) 1933- 19-20R
Spencer, Jeffry Withers B(urress) 1927- ... 45-48
Spencer, John (Walter) 1922- 9-10R
Spencer, John Hall 1928- 7-8R
Spencer, John Hathaway 1907- 112
Spencer, LaVyrle 1943- 102
Spencer, Leonard G.
See Silverberg, Robert
Spencer, Lloyd Neville 1955- 121
Spencer, Margaret 1916- 21-22R
Spencer, Metta Wells 1931- 69-72
Spencer, Michael (Clifford) 1936- 57-60
Spencer, Milton Harry 1926- CANR-6
Earlier sketch in CA 1R
Spencer, Robert Allan 1920- 7-8R
Spencer, Robert F(rancis) 1917-
Brief entry 108
Spencer, Ross (Harrison) 1921- 101
Spencer, Scott 1945- 113
See also DLBY 86
See also CLC 30
Spencer, Sharon Dougherty 1933- CANR-13
Earlier sketch in CA 7-8R
Spencer, Sidney 7-8R
Spencer, Steven M. 1905- CAP-1
Earlier sketch in CA 13-14
Spencer, Stewart 1949- 121
Spencer, Terence (John Bew) 1915-1978
Obituary 77-80
Spencer, Warren F(rank) 1923- 29-32R
Spencer, William 1922- CANR-23
Earlier sketches in CA 19-20R, CANR-8
See also SATA 9
Spencer, Zane A(nn) 1935- 89-92
See also SATA 35
Spender, Dale 1943- 125
Brief entry 120
Spender, Lynne 1946- 119
Spender, Stephen (Harold) 1909- 11-12R
See also DLB 20
See also CLC 1, 2, 5, 10, 41
Spengemann, William Charles 1932- 102
Spengler, Edwin H(arold) 1906-1981
Obituary 104
Spengler, Oswald (Arnold Gottfried)
1880-1936 Brief entry 118
See also TCLC 25
Sperber, A(nn) M. 126
Sperber, Al E(lias) 1916- 65-68
Sperber, Manes 1905-1984 124
Obituary 112
Sperber, Murray A(rnold) 1940- CANR-12
Earlier sketch in CA 61-64
Sperber, Perry Arthur 1907- 37-40R
Sperber, Philip 1944- CANR-26
Earlier sketch in CA 109
Spergel, Irving A. 1924- CANR-11
Earlier sketch in CA 23-24R
Sperka, Joshua S. 1905- 49-52
Sperlich, Peter W. 1934- 37-40R
Sperling, Dan(iel Lee) 1949- 112
Sperling, John G(len) 1921- 49-52
Sperling, Milton M. 1912-1988 Obituary 126
Spero, Sterling D. 1896-1976 65-68
Obituary 61-64
Speroni, Charles 1911-1984 93-96
Obituary 113
Sperry, Armstrong W. 1897-1976 .... CAP-1
Obituary 107
Earlier sketch in CA 9-10
See also SATA 1, 27
Sperry, (Sally) Baxter 1914- CANR-16
Earlier sketches in CA 49-52, CANR-1
Sperry, Byrne Hope 1902- 69-72
Sperry, J. E.
See Eisenstat, Jane Sperry
Sperry, Kip 1940- CANR-19
Earlier sketch in CA 101
Sperry, Len 1943- CANR-12
Earlier sketch in CA 61-64
Sperry, Margaret 1905- 37-40R
Sperry, Ralph A(ddison) 1944- 106
Sperry, Raymond, Jr. CANR-26
Earlier sketches in CA 19-20, CAP-2
See also SATA 1
Sperry, Stuart M(ajor) 1929- 49-52
Speshock, Phyllis (Nieboer) 1925- 19-20R
Spewack, Samuel 1899-1971 Obituary ...33-36R
Spice, Marjorie Davis 1924- 11-12R
Spicehandler, Daniel 1923- 2R
Spicer, Bart 1918- 103
Spicer, Dorothy Gladys CANR-4
Earlier sketch in CA 4R
See also SATA 32
Spicer, Jack 1925-1965 85-88
See also DLB 5, 16
See also CLC 8, 18
Spicer, James 1928(?)-1979 Obituary 85-88
Spicker, Stuart Francis 1937- 65-68
Spiegel, Don(ald Elwin) 1926- 41-44R
Spiegel, Henry William 1911- 3R
Spiegel, John P(aul) 1911- 103
Spiegel, Joseph 1928- 9-10R
Spiegel, Richard Alan 1947- 104
Spiegel, Robert H. 1922- 81-84
Spiegel, Shalom 1899-1984 Obituary 112
Spiegel, Steven L(ee) 1941- 77-80
Spiegel, Ted 1934- Brief entry 105
Spiegelberg, Herbert 1904- 9-10R
Spiegelman, Art 1948- 125
Spiegelman, J(oseph) Mavvin 1926- 57-60
Spiegelman, Judith 1942- 101
Spiegelman, Judith M. 23-24R
See also SATA 5
Spiegler, Charles G. 1911- CANR-3
Earlier sketch in CA 9-10R
Spiegler, Michael D(avid) 1943- 61-64
Spiel, Hilde (Maria) 1911- CANR-14
Earlier sketches in CA 9-10, CAP-1
Spielberg, Peter 1929- CANR-4
Earlier sketch in CA 5-6R
See also DLBY 81
See also CLC 6
Spielberg, Steven 1947- 77-80
See also SATA 32
See also CLC 20
Spielberger, Charles D(onald) 1927- 102
Spielberger, Walter Jakob 1925- CANR-16
Earlier sketch in CA 21-22R
Spielman, Patrick E. 1936- CANR-22
Earlier sketches in CA 15-16R, CANR-7
Spielmann, Peter James 1952- 97-100
Spier, Peter (Edward) 1927- 7-8R
See also SATA 4
See also DLB 61
See also CLR 5
Spier, Robert F(orest) G(ayton) 1922- 41-44R
Spier, William H. 1907(?)-1973
Obituary 41-44R
Spiering, Frank 1938- CANR-10
Earlier sketch in CA 25-28R
Spiers, Edward M(ichael) 1947- 119
Spies, Werner 1937- 37-40R
Spigel, Irwin M(yron) 1926- 17-18R
Spigelgass, Leonard 1908-1985 103
Obituary 115
Spike, Paul 1947- 120
Spikes, Brian S. J. 101
Spilhaus, Athelstan (Frederick) 1911- 17-18R
See also SATA 13
Spilka, Arnold 1917- 49-52
See also SATA 6
Spilka, Mark 1925- 81-84
Spilke, Francine S. 101
Spillane, Frank Morrison 1918- 25-28R
Spillane, John D(avid) 1909(?)-1985
Obituary 117
Spillane, Mickey
See Spillane, Frank Morrison
See also CLC 3, 13
Spiller, Burton L(owell) 1886- 7-8R
Spiller, Earl A(lexander), Jr. 1934- 21-22R
Spiller, Robert E. 1896- CANR-4
Earlier sketch in CA 7-8R
Spillmann, Betty Evelyn 1920- 53-56
Spilsbury, Richard J(oy) 1919-1984 104
Obituary 113
Spina, Tony 1914- 69-72
Spinage, Clive A(lfred) 1933- 15-16R
Spindler, Arthur 1918- 104
Spindler, George Dearborn 1920- 21-22R
Spindler, Louise Schaubel 1917- 49-52
Spindler, Michael (James) 1948- 116
Spinelli, Altiero 1907-1986 .... CANR-16
Obituary 119
Earlier sketch in CA 23-24R
Spinelli, Eileen 1942- 107
See also SATA 38
Spinelli, Jerry 1941- 111
See also SATA 39
Spinelli, Marcos 1904-1970 Obituary 29-32R
Sping, Dan
See Spalding, Henry D(aniel)

INDEX

Spingarn, Lawrence P(erreira) 1917- ... CANR-23
Earlier sketches in CA 3R, CANR-6
Spingarn, Natalie Davis 1922- ... 85-88
Spinifex
See Martin, David
Spink, Ian 1932- Brief entry ... 113
Spink, John Stephenson 1909-1985
Obituary ... 116
Spink, Reginald (William) 1905- ... CANR-19
Earlier sketches in CA 53-56, CANR-4
See also SATA 11
Spink, Walter M. 1928- ... 61-64
Spinka, Matthew 1890-1972 ... CANR-2
Obituary ... 37-40R
Earlier sketch in CA 1R
Spinks, G(eorge) Stephens 1903- ... CAP-2
Earlier sketch in CA 23-24
Spinks, John William Tranter 1908- ... 109
Spinner, Stephanie 1943- ... 45-48
See also SATA 38
Spinner, Thomas J(ohn), Jr. 1929- ... 45-48
Spinney, David
See Spinney, J(ohn) D(avid)
Spinney, J(ohn) D(avid) 1912- ... 29-32R
Spinossimus
See White, William, Jr.
Spinrad, Norman (Richard) 1940- ... CANR-20
Earlier sketch in CA 37-40R
See also DLB 8
See also CLC 46
Spinrad, William 1917- ... 29-32R
Spira, Ruth Rodale 1928- ... 61-64
Spirer, Herbert F(rederick) 1925- ... CANR-16
Earlier sketch in CA 93-96
Spires, Elizabeth 1952- ... 106
Spires, Robert C(ecil) 1936- ... 125
Spiro, Edward 1908- ... 25-28R
Spiro, Herbert J(ohn) 1924- ... CANR-6
Earlier sketch in CA 2R
Spiro, Herzl Robert 1935- ... 104
Spiro, Howard M(arget) 1924- ... 125
Spiro, Jack D. 1933- ... CANR-6
Earlier sketch in CA 11-12R
Spiro, Melford E(lliot) 1920- ... CANR-1
Earlier sketch in CA 45-48
Spirt, Diana L(ouise) 1925- ... 19-20R
Spisak, James W(illiam) 1951- ... 117
Spit, Sam
See Schneck, Stephen
Spittel, Richard Lionel 1881-1969 ... CAP-1
Earlier sketch in CA 13-14
Spitteler, Carl (Friedrich Georg)
1845-1924 Brief entry ... 109
See also TCLC 12
Spitz, A. Edward 1923- ... 73-76
Spitz, Allan A(ugust) 1928- ... 13-14R
Spitz, David 1916-1979 ... 41-44R
Obituary ... 85-88
Spitz, Lewis W(illiam) 1922- ... CANR-6
Earlier sketch in CA 4R
Spitz, Mark (Andrew) 1950- Brief entry ... 115
Spitzer, Abe 1912(?)-1984 Obituary ... 112
Spitzer, E(rwin) E(dwin) 1910- ... CAP-2
Earlier sketch in CA 21-22
Spitzer, Herbert Frederick 1906- ... CAP-1
Earlier sketch in CA 13-14
Spitzer, John 1956- ... CANR-18
Earlier sketch in CA 102
Spitzer, Leo 1939- ... 61-64
Spitzer, Lyman (Jr.) 1914- ... 116
Spitzer, Morton Edward ... 41-44R
Spitzer, Robert J(ames) 1953- ... 112
Spitzer, Robert S(idney) 1926- ... 61-64
Spivack, Charlotte K(esler) 1926- ... 23-24R
Spivack, Ellen Sue 1937- ... 106
Spivack, George 1927- Brief entry ... 109
Spivack, Kathleen (Romola Drucker)
1938- ... 49-52
See also CLC 6
Spivack, Robert (Gerald) 1915-1970
Obituary ... 104
Spivak, Gayatri Chakravorty 1942-
Brief entry ... 110
Spivak, John L(ouis) 1897-1981 Obituary ... 105
Spivak, Mel 1937- ... 57-60
Spivak, Talbot 1937- ... 77-80
Spivakovsky, Erika 1909- ... 49-52
Spivey, Richard L. 1937- ... 115
Spivey, Robert Atwood 1931- Brief entry ... 106
Spivey, Ted R(ay) 1927- ... 105
Splane, Richard B. 1916- ... 17-18R
Splaver, Sarah ... 85-88
See also SATA 28
Spletter, Mary 1946- ... 111
Spock, Benjamin (McLane) 1903- ... 21-22R
See also AITN 1
Spodek, Bernard 1931- ... CANR-22
Earlier sketches in CA 17-18R, CANR-7
Spoehr, Alexander 1913- ... 109
Spoelstra, Nyle (Ray) 1939- ... 29-32R
Spofford, Harriet Prescott 1835-1921 ... DLB-74
Spofford, Walter O(smon), Jr. 1936- ... 107
Spollen, Christopher 1952- ... SATA-12
Spolsky, Bernard 1932- ... CANR-1
Earlier sketch in CA 45-48
Spolsky, Ellen 1943- ... 119
Spong, John Shelby 1931- ... 104
Spooner, Frank (Clyffurde) 1924- ... 85-88
Spooner, Frederick Percy 1898- ... CAP-1
Earlier sketch in CA 13-14
Spooner, Jane R(oss) 1922- ... 5-6R
Spooner, John D. 1937- ... 23-24R
Spooner, (Glenda) Victoria Maude (Graham)
1897- ... CAP-1
Earlier sketch in CA 9-10
Spores, Ronald 1931- ... 21-22R
Spot, Ryhen
See Post, Henry
Spota, Luis
See Spota Saavedra, Luis
Spota Saavedra, Luis 1925-1985 Obituary ... 114
Spotnitz, Hyman 1908- ... CANR-6
Earlier sketch in CA 4R
Spoto, Donald 1941- ... CANR-11
Earlier sketch in CA 65-68
See also CLC 39
Spotte, Stephen 1942- ... CANR-1
Earlier sketch in CA 45-48
Spottiswoode, Raymond J. 1913-1970
Obituary ... 104
Spotts, Charles D(ewey) 1899-1974(?) ... CAP-2
Earlier sketch in CA 19-20
Spotts, Frederic 1930- ... 101
Spradley, James P(hillip) 1933-1982 ... CANR-13
Earlier sketch in CA 29-32R
Spradling, Mary Elizabeth Mace 1911- ... 104
Spragens, Thomas A(rthur), Jr. 1942- ... 85-88
Spragens, William C(lark) 1925- ... 41-44R
Spraggett, Allen (Frederick) 1932- ... CANR-18
Earlier sketch in CA 25-28R
Sprague, Arthur Colby 1895- ... 89-92
Sprague, Charles Arthur 1887-1969
Obituary ... 89-92
Sprague, Claire S(acks) 1926- ... 25-28R
Sprague, Gretchen (Burnham) 1926- ... 15-16R
See also SATA 27
Sprague, Howard B(ennet) 1898- ... 41-44R
Sprague, Irvine H(enry, Jr.) 1921- ... 123
Sprague, Ken 1945- ... 108
Sprague, Marshall 1909- ... CANR-1
Earlier sketch in CA 4R
Sprague, Richard E. 1921- ... 29-32R
Sprague, Rosamond Kent 1922- ... CANR-2
Earlier sketch in CA 5-6R
Sprague, Rosemary ... 19-20R
Sprague, W. D.
See von Block, Bela W(illiam)
and von Block, Sylvia
Spraos, John 1926- ... 5-6R
Spratt, Hereward Philip 1902- ... 7-8R
Spray, Pauline 1920- ... CANR-10
Earlier sketch in CA 25-28R
Spray, Sherrad L(ee) 1935- ... 104
Spreiregen, Paul D. 1931- ... 21-22R
Sprengel, Donald P(hilip) 1938- ... 53-56
Spriegel, William R(obert) 1893- ... 7-8R
Sprigel, Olivier
See Avice, Claude (Pierre Marie)
Sprigg, C(hristopher) St. John 1907-1937
Brief entry ... 120
Sprigg, June 1953- ... 65-68
Sprigge, Elizabeth (Miriam Squire)
1900-1974 ... 13-14R
See also SATA 10
Sprigge, Timothy L(auro) S(quire) 1932- ... 57-60
Sprinchorn, Evert Manfred 1923- ... 107
Spring, Bob
See Spring, Robert W(alton)
Spring, David 1918- ... 81-84
Spring, Gerald M(ax) 1897- ... 61-64
Spring, (Robert) Howard 1889-1965 ... CAP-1
Earlier sketch in CA 9-10
See also SATA 28
Spring, Ira L. 1918- ... CANR-7
Earlier sketch in CA 57-60
Spring, Joel Henry 1940- ... CANR-3
Earlier sketch in CA 49-52
Spring, Norma 1917- ... 61-64
Spring, Robert W(alton) 1918- ... CANR-7
Earlier sketch in CA 57-60
Springborg, Robert 1944- ... 119
Springer, Axel 1912-1985 Obituary ... 117
Springer, Bernhard J. 1907(?)-1970
Obituary ... 29-32R
Springer, E(ustace) Laurence 1903- ... 21-22R
Springer, Haskell S(aul) 1939- ... 111
Springer, John 1916- ... 53-56
Springer, John L(awrence) 1915- ... CANR-25
Earlier sketch in CA 2R
Springer, L(ois) Elsinore 1911- ... 69-72
Springer, Marilyn Harris 1931- ... CANR-9
Earlier sketch in CA 21-22R
See also SATA 47
Springer, Marlene Ann 1937- ... 107
Springer, Mary Doyle 1918- ... 116
Springer, Nancy 1948- ... CANR-18
Earlier sketch in CA 101
Springer, Nelson P(aul) 1915- ... 115
Springer, Nesha Bass 1930- ... 81-84
Springer, Otto 1905- ... CAP-1
Earlier sketch in CA 13-14
Springer, Sally P(earl) 1947- ... 108
Springfield
See Kelly, Maurice Anthony
Springfield, David
See Lewis, (John) Roy(ston)
Springsted, Eric Osmon 1951- ... 113
Springsteen, Bruce (F.) 1949- ... 111
See also CLC 17
Springstubb, Tricia 1950- ... CANR-21
Earlier sketch in CA 105
See also SATA 40, 46
Sprinkel, Beryl W(ayne) 1923- ... 11-12R
Sprinthall, Richard C(lark) 1930- ... 45-48
Sproat, John G(erald) 1921- ... 25-28R
Sproston, John
See Scott, Peter Dale
Sprott, W(alter) John Herbert
1897-1971 ... CANR-16
Obituary ... 103
Earlier sketch in CA 4R
Sproul, Barbara Chamberlain 1945- ... 105
Sproul, Dorothy Noyes
See Noyes-Kane, Dorothy
Sproul, R(obert) C(harles) 1939- ... 111
Sprouse, Mary L. 1948- ... 108
Sprout, Harold 1901-1980 ... CANR-6
Obituary ... 102
Earlier sketch in CA 3R
Spruch, Grace Marmor 1926- ... 57-60
Spruch, Larry 1923- ... 102
Sprug, Joseph W(illiam) 1922- ... 23-24R
Spruill, Charles R(ay) 1946- ... 117
Spruill, Steven G(regory) 1946- ... 73-76
Sprunger, Keith L(a Verne) 1935- ... 41-44R
Sprunt, Alexander, Jr. 1898-1973
Obituary ... 37-40R
Spuhler, J(ames) N(orman) 1917- ... CANR-3
Earlier sketch in CA 1R
Spulber, Nicolas 1915- ... CANR-3
Earlier sketch in CA 11-12R
Spuler, Bertold 1911- ... 81-84
Spungen, Deborah 1937- ... 119
Spurling, Hilary 1940- ... CANR-25
Earlier sketch in CA 104
See also CLC 34
Spurling, John 1936- ... CANR-25
Earlier sketches in CA 45-48, CANR-1
Spurr, Clinton
See Rowland, D(onald) S(ydney)
Spurr, David Anton 1949- ... 118
Spurr, Stephen Hopkins 1918- ... 81-84
Spurr, William A(lfred) 1905- ... 7-8R
Spurrier, William A(twell) 1916- ... 53-56
Spyers-Duran, Peter 1932- ... CANR-23
Earlier sketches in CA 19-20R, CANR-8
Spyker, John Howland 1918- ... 101
Spykman, E(lizabeth) C(hoate) 1896-1965 ... 101
See also SATA 10
Spyri, Johanna (Heusser) 1827-1901 ... SATA-19
See also CLR 13
Spyridakis, Stylianos 1937- ... 89-92
Squibob
See Derby, George Horatio
Squier, Charles L(a Barge) 1931- ... 17-18R
Squier, Susan Merrill 1950- ... 120
Squire, Elizabeth 1919- ... 13-14R
Squire, Jason E(dward) 1948- ... CANR-23
Earlier sketch in CA 45-48
Squire, Norman 1907- ... CANR-3
Earlier sketch in CA 9-10R
Squire, Robin 1937- ... 105
Squire, Russel Nelson 1908- ... 3R
Squire, Susan 1950- ... 112
Squires, Eric
See Ball, Sylvia Patricia
Squires, James (David) 1943- ... 119
Squires, James Duane 1904- ... 7-8R
Squires, Michael (George) 1941- ... 61-64
Squires, Patricia
See Ball, Sylvia Patricia
Squires, Phil
See Barker, S. Omar
Squires, Radcliffe 1917- ... CANR-21
Earlier sketches in CA 1R, CANR-6
Sraffa, Piero 1898-1983 ... 45-48
Obituary ... 110
Srere, Benson M. 1928- ... 77-80
S-Ringi, Kjell
See Ringi, Kjell (Arne Soerensen)
Srivastava, Dhanpat Rai 1880(?)-1936
Brief entry ... 118
Srivastava, Jane Jonas 1941- ... 119
See also SATA 37
Srole, Leo 1908- ... 125
Brief entry ... 107
Staaf, Robert J(ames) 1939- ... 93-96
Staal, Cyril 1912- Brief entry ... 113
Staal, J(ohan) F(rederik) 1930- ... 45-48
Staal, Julius D(irk) W(illem) 1917-1986
Obituary ... 120
Staar, Richard F(elix) 1923- ... CANR-16
Earlier sketches in CA 4R, CANR-1
Staats, Arthur (Wilbur) 1924- ... 15-16R
Stabb, Martin S(anford) 1928- ... 23-24R
Stabile, Toni ... 85-88
Stableford, Brian M. 1948- ... 57-60
Stablein, Marilyn 1946- ... 120
Stabler, Arthur P(hillips) 1919- ... CANR-14
Earlier sketch in CA 41-44R
Stabley, Fred(erick) W(illiam) 1915- ... 112
Stace, Christopher 1942- ... 97-100
Stace, Walter Terence 1886-1967 ... CANR-2
Earlier sketch in CA 1R
Stacey, C(harles) P(erry) 1906- ... CANR-19
Earlier sketch in CA 101
Stacey, Frank Arthur 1923- ... 57-60
Stacey, Judith 1943- ... 125
Stacey, Margaret 1922- ... CANR-17
Earlier sketch in CA 29-32R
Stacey, Nicholas Anthony Howard 1920- ... 7-8R
Stacey, Roy 1919- ... 9-10R
Stacey, Thomas Charles Gerard 1930- ... CANR-21
Earlier sketch in CA 9-10R
Stacey, Tom
See Stacey, Thomas Charles Gerard
Stachow, Hasso G(ert) 1924- ... 109
Stachys, Dimitris
See Constantelos, Demetrios J.
Stack, Edward MacGregor 1919- ... 1R
Stack, Frank H(untington) 1937- ... CANR-9
Earlier sketch in CA 61-64
Stack, George J. 1931- ... 37-40R
Stack, Herbert James 1893-1967 ... CANR-3
Earlier sketch in CA 2R
Stack, Nicolete Meredith 1896- ... 13-14R
Stackhouse, Max L. 1935- ... 23-24R
Stackhouse, Reginald 1925- ... 21-22R
Stackpole, Edouard Alexander 1903- ... CANR-16
Earlier sketches in CA 4R, CANR-1
Stackpole, Edward J(ames) 1894-1967 ... 4R
Obituary ... 103
Stacks, John F(ultz) 1942- ... 113
Stacton, David (Derek) 1925-1968 ... CANR-6
Obituary ... 25-28R
Earlier sketch in CA 7-8R
Stacy, Bruce
See Elliott, Bruce (Walter Gardner Lively Stacy)
Stacy, Donald L. 1925- ... 29-32R
Stacy, Pat(ricia A.) 1941- ... 118
Stacy, R(obert) H(arold) 1919- ... 73-76
Stacy, Walter
See Elliott, Bruce (Walter Gardner Lively Stacy)
Stade, George 1933- ... 29-32R
Stadelman, S(ara) L(ee) 1917- ... 81-84
Stadler, Karl R(udolph) 1913- ... 23-24R
Stadley, Pat (Anna May Gough) 1918-
Brief entry ... 114
Stadt, Ronald W(ilmer) 1935- ... CANR-16
Earlier sketch in CA 93-96
Stadter, Philip A(ustin) 1936- ... 104
Stadtfeld, Curtis K(arl) 1935- ... 49-52
Stadtler, Bea 1921- ... 65-68
See also SATA 17
Stadtman, Verne A. 1926- ... 29-32R
Staebler, Edna ... 101
Staebler, Neil 1905- ... 77-80
Staebler, Warren 1912- ... 45-48
Staehle, Albert 1899-1974 ... AITN-1
Staender, Gilbert F(rank) 1930- ... 104
Staender, Vivian 1923- ... 97-100
Staff, Adrienne 1947- ... 123
Staff, Frank 1908- ... 25-28R
Stafford, Caroline
See Watjen, Carolyn L. T.
Stafford, David (Christopher) 1943- ... 103
Stafford, David Alexander Tetlow
1942- ... CANR-21
Earlier sketch in CA 104
Stafford, Gilbert Wayne 1938- ... 112
Stafford, Irvin G. 1936- ... 114
Stafford, Jean 1915-1979 ... CANR-3
Obituary ... 85-88
Earlier sketch in CA 4R
See also SATA 22
See also DLB 2
See also CLC 4, 7, 19
Stafford, Kenneth R(ay) 1922- ... 17-18R
Stafford, Kim R(obert) 1949- ... CANR-22
Earlier sketch in CA 69-72
Stafford, Linda (Crying Wind) 1943- ... 108
Stafford, Muriel
See Sauer, Muriel Stafford
Stafford, Peter
See Tabori, Paul
Stafford, William (Edgar) 1914- ... CANR-22
Earlier sketches in CA 7-8R, CANR-5
See also CAAS 3
See also DLB 5
See also CLC 4, 7, 29
Stafford, William B(utler) 1931- ... 53-56
Stafford, William T(almadge) 1924- ... CANR-25
Earlier sketch in CA 1R
Stafford-Clark, David 1916- ... 21-22R
Staffordshire Knot
See Wrottesley, A(rthur) J(ohn) F(rancis)
Stageberg, Norman C(lifford) 1905- ... CAP-1
Earlier sketch in CA 11-12
Stagg, Albert 1903- ... 85-88
Stagg, Evelyn 1914- ... 85-88
Stagg, Frank 1911- ... CANR-18
Earlier sketches in CA 4R, CANR-1
Stagg, James Martin 1900-1975 Obituary ... 61-64
Stagg, Paul L. 1914- ... 23-24R
Stagge, Jonathan
See Wheeler, Hugh (Callingham)
Stagner, Lloyd Ernest 1923- ... 101
Stagner, Ross 1909- ... CANR-5
Earlier sketch in CA 5-6R
Stahl, Ben(jamin) 1910-1987 ... 29-32R
Obituary ... 123
See also SATA 5
Stahl, Donald 1935- ... 25-28R
Stahl, Fred Alan 1944- ... 45-48
Stahl, Gustav Richard 1888(?)-1978
Obituary ... 81-84
Stahl, Hilda 1938- ... 116
See also SATA 48
Stahl, Le Roy 1908- ... CAP-1
Earlier sketch in CA 11-12
Stahl, Lesley R(ene) 1941- ... 107
See also AITN 2
Stahl, Nancy 1937- ... 104
Stahl, Norman 1931- ... 85-88
Stahl, O(scar) Glenn 1910- ... CANR-14
Earlier sketch in CA 41-44R
Stahl, William Harris 1908-1969 Obituary ... 111
Stahlecker, Lotar V(ictor) 1915- ... 23-24R
Stahlman, James Geddes 1893-1976
Obituary ... 89-92
Stahnke, Arthur A(llan) 1935- ... 65-68
Stahnke, Astrida B. 1935- ... 123
Stahr, John W. 1904-1981 Obituary ... 104
Staib, Bjorn O. 1938- ... 17-18R
Staicar, Thomas Edward 1946- ... 108
Staicar, Tom
See Staicar, Thomas Edward
Staiger, Janet 1946- ... 123
Stainback, Susan Bray 1947- ... CANR-14
Earlier sketches in CA 57-60, CANR-7
Stainback, William (Clarence) 1943- ... CANR-14
Earlier sketch in CA 77-80
Staines, David 1946- ... 125

Staines, Trevor
See Brunner, John (Kilian Houston)
Stainsby, Charles 1925-1985 Obituary ... 118
Stair, Gobin (John) 1912- ... SATA-35
Stairs, Denis (Winfield) 1939- Brief entry ... 114
Stairs, Gordon
See Austin, Mary (Hunter)
Stalder, Valerie ... 41-44R
See also SATA 27
Staley, Allen 1935- Brief entry ... 115
Staley, Charles E(arl) 1927- ... 45-48
Staley, (Alvah) Eugene 1906- ... 77-80
Staley, Thomas F(abian) 1935- ... CANR-13
Earlier sketch in CA 77-80
Stallard, John (Richard) 1935-1985 ... 49-52
Obituary ... 116
Stalley, Rodney E(dward) 1930- ... 116
Stalley, Roger 1945- ... 101
Stallibrass, (Helen) Alison 1916- ... 104
Stallings, Constance L(ee) 1932- ... CANR-17
Earlier sketch in CA 97-100
Stallings, James O. 1938- ... CANR-19
Earlier sketch in CA 103
Stallings, Laurence 1894-1968 Obituary ... 89-92
See also DLB 7, 44
Stallman, Robert Wooster 1911- ... CANR-3
Earlier sketch in CA 4R
Stallone, Sylvester (Enzio) 1946- ... 77-80
Stallworth, Anne Nall 1935- ... 85-88
Stallworthy, Jon (Howie) 1935- ... CANR-8
Earlier sketch in CA 11-12R
See also DLB 40
Stallybrass, Oliver (George Weatherhead)
1925-1978 ... CANR-24
Earlier sketch in CA 29-32R
Stalvey, Lois Mark 1925- ... CANR-14
Earlier sketch in CA 29-32R
Stam, James H(enry) 1937- ... 49-52
Stam, Robert 1941- ... 115
Stamaty, Mark Alan 1947- ... CANR-15
Earlier sketch in CA 61-64
See also SATA 12
Stambaugh, Joan 1932- ... 89-92
Stambaugh, Sara 1936- ... 119
Stamberg, Susan 1938- ... 103
Stambler, Helen
See Latner, Helen (Stambler)
Stambler, Irwin 1924- ... CANR-2
Earlier sketch in CA 5-6R
See also SATA 5
Stambolian, George 1938- ... 41-44R
Stambuk, George 1927- ... 7-8R
Stames, Ward
See Steward, Samuel M(orris)
Stamey, Sara (Lucinda) 1953- ... 126
Stamm, Keith R(oman) 1941- ... 116
Stamm, Martin L. 1917- ... CANR-19
Earlier sketch in CA 37-40R
Stammers, Neil 1950- ... 119
Stamp, L(aurence) Dudley 1898-1966 ... CAP-1
Earlier sketch in CA 13-14
Stamp, Robert M(iles) 1937- ... 126
Stamper, Alexander
See Kent, Arthur William Charles
Stampfer, Judah (Leon) 1923- ... 25-28R
Stampfle, Felice 1912- ... 105
Stampp, Kenneth M. 1912- ... 13-14R
See also DLB 17
Stanbury, David 1933- ... 104
Stanbury, Walter A. 1910-1976 Obituary ... 65-68
Stancliffe, Michael (Staffurth) 1916-1987 ... 124
Stancu, Zaharia 1902-1974 ... 97-100
Obituary ... 53-56
Standard, William L. 1900(?)-1978
Obituary ... 77-80
Stander, Siegfried 1935- ... CANR-19
Earlier sketches in CA 9-10R, CANR-4
Standiford, Lester A(lan) 1945- ... 77-80
Standing, Edwin (Mortimer) 1887- ... CAP-1
Earlier sketch in CA 9-10
Standing, Sue 1952- ... 119
Standing Bear, Luther 1868(?)-1939(?)
Brief entry ... 113
Standish, Buck
See Paine, Lauran (Bosworth)
Standish, Robert 1898(?)-1981 Obituary ... 105
Standley, Fred L(loyd) 1932- ... 41-44R
Standon, Anna (Slater) 1929- ... 17-18R
Standring, Gillian 1935- ... 69-72
Stanek, Carolyn 1951- ... 107
Stanek, Muriel (Novella) 1915- Brief entry ... 112
See also SATA 34
Stanev, Emilian
See Stanev, Nikola (Stoyanov)
Stanev, Nikola (Stoyanov) 1907-1979 ... 108
Stanfield, Nancy Fisher Clay 1905- ... CAP-1
Earlier sketch in CA 9-10
Stanfield, Vernon Latrelle 1920- ... 97-100
Stanford, Alfred (Boller) 1900-1985 ... CAP-1
Obituary ... 115
Earlier sketch in CA 17-18
Stanford, Ann 1916-1987 ... CANR-4
Obituary ... 123
Earlier sketch in CA 9-10R
See also DLB 5
Stanford, Barbara Dodds 1943- ... 37-40R
Stanford, Derek 1918- ... 9-10R
Stanford, Don(ald Kent) 1918- ... 53-56
Stanford, Don
See Stanford, Donald E(lwin)
Stanford, Donald E(lwin) 1913- ... CANR-5
Earlier sketch in CA 13-14R
Stanford, Edward V(alentine) 1897-1966 ... 7-8R
Stanford, Gene 1944- ... 37-40R
Stanford, J(ohn) K(eith) 1892- ... 7-8R
Stanford, Melvin Joseph 1932- ... CANR-16
Earlier sketch in CA 89-92
Stanford, Miles J(oseph) 1914- ... 65-68
Stanford, Quentin Hunt 1935- ... 45-48
Stanford, Sally 1903-1982 Obituary ... 105
Stanford, William Bedell 1910-1984 ... 85-88
Obituary ... 115
Stanforth, Deirdre 1924- ... 102
Stang, Judit 1921-1977 ... CANR-8
Earlier sketch in CA 5-6R
See also SATA 29
Stang, Judy
See Stang, Judit
Stange, G(eorge) Robert 1919- ... 23-24R
Stanger, Frank Bateman 1914- ... 109
Stanger, Ila (Ann) 1940- ... 65-68
Stanhope, Eric
See Hamilton, Charles Harold St. John
Stanier, Maida Euphemia Kerr 1909- ... 101
Staniforth, (John Hamilton) Maxwell
1893- ... CAP-2
Earlier sketch in CA 25-28
Stanislavsky, Constantin (Sergeivich)
1863(?)-1938 Brief entry ... 118
Stanislawski, Dan 1903- ... CANR-3
Earlier sketch in CA 7-8R
Stanislawski, Michael 1952- ... 119
Stanke, Alain 1934- ... 81-84
Stanke, Don E(dward) 1929- ... 61-64
Stankevich, Boris 1928- ... 23-24R
See also SATA 2
Stankiewicz, Edward 1920- ... 45-48
Stankiewicz, Marketa Goetz
See Goetz-Stankiewicz, Marketa
Stankiewicz, W(ladyslaw) J(ozef) 1922- ... CANR-1
Earlier sketch in CA 45-48
Stanko, Elizabeth Anne 1950- ... 116
Stanley, Alexander O. 1910- ... 7-8R
Stanley, Bennett
See Hough, S(tanley) B(ennett)
Stanley, C(laude) Maxwell 1904-1984 ... 114
Stanley, Carol
See White, Carol
Stanley, Dave
See Dachs, David
Stanley, David 1944- ... 115
Stanley, David T(aylor) 1916- Brief entry ... 107
Stanley, Diana 1909- ... SATA-30
Stanley, Diane 1943- ... 112
See also SATA 32, 37
Stanley, Fay Grissom (Shulman) 1925- ... 101
Stanley, George 1934- Brief entry ... 114
Stanley, George Edward 1942- ... CANR-17
Earlier sketch in CA 97-100
See also SATA 53
Stanley, George F(rancis) G(ilman)
1907- ... CANR-15
Earlier sketch in CA 41-44R
Stanley, John 1940- ... 21-22R
Stanley, John L(angley) 1937- ... 45-48
Stanley, Julian C(ecil), Jr. 1918- ... CANR-8
Earlier sketch in CA 21-22R
Stanley, Leo Leonidas 1886- ... 69-72
Stanley, Liz 1947- ... 119
Stanley, Marge
See Weinbaum, Stanley Grauman
Stanley, Nora Kathleen Begbie Strange
1885- ... CAP-1
Earlier sketch in CA 11-12
Stanley, Peter (Alan) 1956- ... 118
Stanley, Phil
See Ind, Allison
Stanley, Robert
See Hamilton, Charles Harold St. John
Stanley, Robert Henry 1940- ... 101
Stanley, Roy M. II 1936- ... 114
Stanley, Steven M(itchell) 1941- ... 109
Stanley, Timothy Wadsworth 1927- ... 77-80
Stanley, Warwick
See Hilton, John Buxton
Stanley, William O(liver), Jr. 1902- ... CANR-1
Earlier sketch in CA 1R
Stanley-Brown, Katherine (Oliver)
1893(?)-1972 Obituary ... 33-36R
Stanley-Jones, D(ouglas) 1905- ... 9-10R
Stanley-Wrench, Margaret 1916- ... 11-12R
Stanli, Sue
See Meilach, Dona Z(weigoron)
Stanlis, Peter J(ames) 1919- ... 101
Stanmeyer, William A(nthony) 1934- ... 118
Stann, Francis E. 1912(?)-1987 Obituary ... 124
Stannard, David E(dward) 1941- ... 65-68
Stannard, Martin ... CLC-44
Stannard, Neville (George) 1949- ... 118
Stannard, Una 1927- ... 73-76
Stanner, W(illiam) E(dward) H(anley)
1905-1981 Obituary ... 108
Stannus, (James) Gordon (Dawson)
1902- ... 65-68
Stanovich, Betty Jo 1954- ... 118
See also SATA 51
Stans, Maurice H(ubert) 1908- Brief entry ... 113
Stansberger, Richard 1950- ... CANR-18
Earlier sketch in CA 101
Stansbury, Donald L. 1929- ... 37-40R
Stansfield, Richard Habberton 1921- ... 107
Stansgate, Caroline DeCamp Wedgwood
Benn
See Benn, Caroline DeCamp Wedgwood
Stansky, Peter (David Lyman) 1932- ... CANR-12
Earlier sketch in CA 17-18R
Stanstead, John
See Groom, Arthur William
Stanton, Dorothy
See Kaumeyer, Dorothy
Stanton, Edward F(eagler) 1942- ... 89-92
Stanton, Frank L. 1857-1927 ... DLB-25
Stanton, Gerald B(arry) 1918- ... 9-10R
Stanton, Graham N(orman) 1940- ... 61-64
Stanton, Jessie Earl 1887-1976 Obituary ... 65-68
Stanton, Maura 1946- ... CANR-15
Earlier sketch in CA 89-92
See also CLC 9
Stanton, Paul
See Beaty, (Arthur) David
Stanton, Peggy Smeeton 1939- ... 61-64
Stanton, Phoebe B(aroody) 1914- ... 37-40R
Stanton, Royal (Waltz) 1916- ... 37-40R
Stanton, Schuyler
See Baum, L(yman) Frank
Stanton, Vance
See Avallone, Michael (Angelo), Jr.
Stanton, Will 1918- ... 85-88
Stanton, William 1925- ... 3R
Stanton, William J(ohn, Jr.) 1919-
Brief entry ... 115
Stanwood, Brooks
See Kaminsky, Howard
and Kaminsky, Susan Stanwood
Stanwood, Brooks
See Kaminsky, Susan Stanwood
Stanwood, P(aul) G(rant) 1933- ... 49-52
Stanyer, Jeffrey 1936- ... 61-64
Stapledon, (William) Olaf 1886-1950
Brief entry ... 111
See also DLB 15
See also TCLC 22
Stapler, Harry (Bascom) 1919- ... CANR-13
Earlier sketch in CA 61-64
Staples, Reginald Thomas 1911- ... CANR-14
Earlier sketch in CA 69-72
Staples, Robert (Eugene) 1942- ... CANR-2
Earlier sketch in CA 49-52
Stapleton, Constance 1930- ... 104
Stapleton, G(eorge) Brian 1922- ... 25-28R
Stapleton, Jean 1942- ... 69-72
Stapleton, (Katharine) Laurence 1911- ... 17-18R
Stapleton, Margaret (Lucy) 1903- ... 57-60
Stapleton, Marjorie (Winifred) 1932- ... 106
See also SATA 28
Stapleton, Richard John 1940- ... 89-92
Stapleton, Ruth Carter 1929-1983 ... 81-84
Obituary ... 110
Stapp, Arthur D(onald) 1906-1972 ... CANR-2
Obituary ... 33-36R
Earlier sketch in CA 4R
See also SATA 4
Stapp, William B. 1929- ... CANR-22
Earlier sketches in CA 45-48, CANR-2
Stappenbeck, Herb(ert) Louis (Jr.) 1935- ... 65-68
Star, Angel
See Quigley, Joan
Star, Cima 1939- ... 110
Star, Jack 1920- ... 73-76
Star, Max 1890(?)-1986 Obituary ... 121
Star, Shirley A(nn) 1918-1976 ... 41-44R
Obituary ... 65-68
Starbird, Kaye ... 17-18R
See also SATA 6
Starbuck, George (Edwin) 1931- ... CANR-23
Earlier sketch in CA 21-22R
Starbuck, William H(aynes) 1934- ... CANR-7
Earlier sketch in CA 57-60
Starch, Daniel 1883- ... 37-40R
Starchild, Adam (Aristotle) 1946- ... 123
Starchuk, Orest 1915- ... 5-6R
Stardust, Alvin 1942- ... 123
Starenko, Ronald C(harles) 1930- ... 93-96
Starer, Robert 1924- ... 125
Stargell, Willie
See Stargell, Wilver Dornel
Stargell, Wilver Dornel 1941- Brief entry ... 118
Starhawk
See Simos, Miriam
Stark, Bradford 1948-1979 ... CANR-3
Earlier sketch in CA 49-52
Stark, Claude Alan 1935- ... 57-60
Stark, Freya (Madeline) 1893- ... CANR-5
Earlier sketch in CA 5-6R
Stark, Gary Duane 1948- ... CANR-21
Earlier sketch in CA 105
Stark, George Washington 1884-1966
Obituary ... 89-92
Stark, Harry 1895- ... 2R
Stark, Irwin 1912- ... 9-10R
Stark, Jack
See Stark, John H.
Stark, James
See Goldston, Robert (Conroy)
Stark, John
See Godwin, John
Stark, John H. 1914- ... 49-52
Stark, John Olsen 1939- ... CANR-5
Earlier sketch in CA 53-56
Stark, Joshua
See Olsen, T(heodore) V(ictor)
Stark, Michael
See Lariar, Lawrence
Stark, Paul C. 1891(?)-1974 Obituary ... 53-56
Stark, R. J.
See Kikel, Rudy (John)
Stark, Raymond 1919- ... 73-76
Stark, Richard
See Westlake, Donald E(dwin)
Stark, Werner 1909- ... CANR-10
Earlier sketch in CA 21-22R
Starke, Aubrey (Harrison) 1905(?)-1972
Obituary ... 37-40R
Starke, Catherine Juanita 1913- ... 37-40R
Starke, J(oseph) G(abriel) 1911- ... 115
Starke, Roland ... 53-56
Starkey, Lycurgus M(onroe), Jr. 1928- ... 5-6R
Starkey, Marion L(ena) 1901- ... CANR-1
Earlier sketch in CA 2R
See also SATA 13
Starkie, Enid 1903(?)-1970 ... CANR-2
Obituary ... 29-32R
Earlier sketch in CA 3R
Starkie, Walter F(itzwilliam) 1894-1976 ... 77-80
Obituary ... 69-72
Starkins, Edward 1946- ... 120
Starkloff, Carl F. 1933- ... 53-56
Starkman, Miriam K(osh) 1916- ... 65-68
Starkman, Moshe 1906-1975 Obituary ... 57-60
Starks, Richard 1947- ... 113
Starkweather, David 1935- ... 97-100
See also DLB 7
Starling, Thomas
See Hayton, Richard Neil
Star-Man's Padre
See Patrick, Johnstone G(illespie)
Starn, Randolph 1939- ... 45-48
Starnes, Richard 1922- Brief entry ... 114
Starobin, Joseph R(obert) 1913-1976 ... 45-48
Obituary ... 69-72
Starobin, Rosalind Gould 1912(?)-1983
Obituary ... 111
Starr, Cecile 1921- ... 65-68
Starr, Chauncey 1912- ... 109
Starr, Chester G. 1914- ... CANR-16
Earlier sketches in CA 2R, CANR-1
Starr, Edward Caryl 1911- ... 13-14R
Starr, Frank 1938- ... 69-72
Starr, Henry
See Bingley, David Ernest
Starr, Herbert F(rederick) 1932- ... 116
Starr, Isidore 1911- ... CANR-7
Earlier sketch in CA 15-16R
Starr, Jerold M. 1941- ... 77-80
Starr, John 1914(?)-1980 Obituary ... 101
Starr, John
See Counselman, Mary Elizabeth
Starr, John A.
See Gillese, John Patrick
Starr, John Bryan 1939- ... 77-80
Starr, Judy
See Gelfman, Judith S(chlein)
Starr, Kevin 1940- ... 120
Starr, Louis M(orris) 1917-1980 ... 53-56
Obituary ... 97-100
Starr, Mark 1894-1985 Obituary ... 116
See also AITN 1
Starr, Martin Kenneth 1927- ... CANR-8
Earlier sketch in CA 17-18R
Starr, Paul 1949- Brief entry ... 123
Starr, Penelope
See Gelles-Cole, Sandi
Starr, Raymond 1937- ... 65-68
Starr, Roger 1918- ... CANR-11
Earlier sketch in CA 21-22R
Starr, Roland
See Rowland, D(onald) S(ydney)
Starr, S(tephen) Frederick 1940- ... CANR-17
Earlier sketch in CA 85-88
Starr, Stephen Z. 1909-1985 ... CANR-17
Earlier sketch in CA 37-40R
Starr, William Thomas 1910- ... 41-44R
Starr, Wilmarth Holt 1913- ... 17-18R
Starratt, Alfred B(yron) 1914- ... 17-18R
Starret, William
See McClintock, Marshall
Starrett, (Charles) Vincent (Emerson)
1886-1974 ... 73-76
Obituary ... 45-48
Starrs, James E(dward) 1930- ... 118
Starry, Donn Albert 1925- ... 109
Start, Clarissa
See Lippert, Clarissa Start
Stasch, Stanley F. 1931- ... 41-44R
Stasheff, Christopher 1944- ... CANR-26
Earlier sketches in CA 65-68, CANR-10
Stasheff, (Adolph) Edward 1909- ... 7-8R
Stasiak, Krystyna ... SATA-49
Stasio, Marilyn L(ouise) 1940- ... 33-36R
Stassinopoulos, Arianna 1950- Brief entry ... 114
Stasz, Clarice ... CANR-7
Earlier sketch in CA 61-64
Staten, Patricia S. 1945- ... 53-56
Statera, Gianni 1943- ... CANR-8
Earlier sketch in CA 57-60
States, Bert O(len) 1929- ... 73-76
Statham, Frances P(atton) 1931- ... 101
Statham, Jane 1917- ... 15-16R
Statler, Oliver Hadley 1915- ... 7-8R
Staton, Knofel L. 1934- ... 114
Staton, Thomas Felix 1917- ... 7-8R
Staub, August W(illiam) 1931- ... CANR-2
Earlier sketch in CA 45-48
Staubach, Charles N(eff) 1906- ... CANR-4
Earlier sketch in CA 5-6R
Staubach, Roger (Thomas) 1942- ... 104
Staudacher, Joseph M. 1914- ... 25-28R
Staudacher, Rosemarian V(alentiner)
1918- ... 5-6R
Staudenraus, P(hilip) J(ohn) 1928-1971 ... 2R
Obituary ... 103
Stauder, Jack 1939- ... 37-40R
Stauderman, Albert P(hilip) 1910- ... CANR-18
Earlier sketch in CA 77-80
Staudinger, Hermann 1881-1965 Obituary ... 113
Staudt, Virginia
See Sexton, Virginia Staudt
Stauffer, Don
See Berkebile, Fred D(onovan)
Stauffer, Donald Barlow 1930- ... 57-60
Stauffer, Helen Winter 1922- ... 109
Staum, Martin Sheldon 1943- ... 103
Staunton, Schuyler
See Baum, L(yman) Frank
Stauter, (Justin) Jay 1907-1986 Obituary ... 118
Stave, Bruce M(artin) 1937- ... CANR-12
Earlier sketch in CA 29-32R

Staveley, Gaylord L(ee) 1931- ... 37-40R
Stavenhagen, Lee 1933- ... 104
Stavenhagen, Rodolfo 1932- ... CANR-12
Earlier sketch in CA 29-32R
Stavis, Barrie 1906- ... 49-52
Stavis, Ben(edict) 1941- ... 29-32R
Stavrianos, Leften Stavros 1913- ... CANR-6
Earlier sketch in CA 7-8R
Stavros, Niko
See King, Florence
Stavrou, Theofanis G. 1934- ... 45-48
Stayer, James M(entzer) 1935- ... CANR-26
Earlier sketch in CA 45-48
Stead, Christian Karlson 1932- ... CANR-6
Earlier sketch in CA 57-60
Stead, Christina (Ellen) 1902-1983 ... 15-16R
Obituary ... 109
See also CLC 2, 5, 8, 32
Stead, Philip John 1916- ... 108
Stead, Thistle Yolette 1902- ... 107
Steadman, David (Wilton) 1936- ... 107
Steadman, John M(arcellus III) 1918- ... 25-28R
Steadman, Mark 1930- ... 37-40R
See also DLB 6
Steadman, Ralph (Idris) 1936- ... 107
See also SATA 32
Steahly, Vivian Eugenia Emrick 1915- ... 61-64
Steakley, John 1951- ... 120
Stealingworth, Slim
See Wesselmann, Tom
Steamer
See Nason, Leonard H(astings)
Steamer, Robert J(ulius) 1920- ... 41-44R
Steane, J(ohn) B(arry) 1928- ... 11-12R
Steanson, Karen E(lizabeth) 1942- ... 116
Stearn, Gerald E. 1934(?)-1982 Obituary ... 108
Stearn, Jess ... 97-100
Stearns, Harold Edmund 1891-1943
Brief entry ... 107
See also DLB 4
Stearns, Marshall Winslow 1908-1966
Obituary ... 110
Stearns, Martha Genung 1886- ... 11-12R
Stearns, Monroe (Mather) 1913-1987 ... CANR-2
Obituary ... 124
Earlier sketch in CA 5-6R
See also SATA 5
Stearns, Pamela Fujimoto 1935- ... 65-68
Stearns, Peter N. 1936- ... CANR-10
Earlier sketch in CA 21-22R
Stearns, Raymond Phineas 1904-1970 ... CAP-1
Earlier sketch in CA 11-12
Stebbins, G(eorge) Ledyard 1906- ... 45-48
Stebbins, Richard P(oate) 1913- ... CANR-2
Earlier sketch in CA 5-6R
Stebbins, Robert A(lan) 1938- ... CANR-12
Earlier sketch in CA 29-32R
Stebbins, Robert C(yril) 1915- ... 49-52
Stebbins, Theodore Ellis, Jr. 1938- ... 89-92
Stebel, S(idney) L(eo) 1924- ... 29-32R
Steber, A. R.
See Palmer, Raymond A.
Stecher, Miriam B(rodie) 1917- ... 106
Stechow, Wolfgang 1896-1974 ... CANR-9
Obituary ... 53-56
Earlier sketch in CA 65-68
Steck, James S(perow) 1911- ... 41-44R
Steckel, William Reed 1915- ... 17-18R
Steckler, Arthur 1921- ... 108
Steckler, Doug(las) 1948- ... 107
Steckler, Phyllis B. (Schwartzbard)
1933- ... 11-12R
Stedman, Edmund Clarence 1833-1908 ... DLB-64
Stedman, James Murphy 1938- ... 77-80
Stedman, Jane W(inifred) 1920- ... 37-40R
Stedman, Murray S(alisbury), Jr. 1917- ... 17-18R
Stedman, R(aymond) William 1930- ... 29-32R
Stedman, Ray C. 1917- ... 104
Stedman Jones, Gareth 1942- ... 45-48
Stedmond, John Mitchell 1916- ... 103
Stedwell, Paki 1945- ... 103
Steed, Gitel P. 1914-1977 ... 41-44R
Steed, Thomas Jefferson 1904-1983
Obituary ... 110
Steed, Tom
See Steed, Thomas Jefferson
Steedman, Marguerite Couturier 1908- ... CANR-1
Earlier sketch in CA 4R
Steefel, Lawrence D. 1894- ... CAP-2
Earlier sketch in CA 21-22
Steeger, Henry 1903- ... 41-44R
Steeger, Henry 1929(?)-1978 Obituary ... 77-80
Steegmuller, Francis 1906- ... CANR-2
Earlier sketch in CA 49-52
Steel, Anthony Bedford 1900-1973 ... 7-8R
Obituary ... 89-92
Steel, Byron
See Steegmuller, Francis
Steel, Danielle ... CANR-19
Earlier sketch in CA 81-84
Steel, Edward M(arvin), Jr. 1918- ... 11-12R
Steel, Eric M. 1904- ... 89-92
Steel, Flora Annie (Webster) 1847-1929
Brief entry ... 116
Steel, Ronald (Lewis) 1931- ... CANR-7
Earlier sketch in CA 11-12R
Steel, Tex
See Ross, W(illiam) E(dward) D(aniel)
Steele, A(rchibald) T(rojan) 1903- ... CAP-2
Earlier sketch in CA 19-20
Steele, Addison II
See Lupoff, Richard A(llen)
Steele, Alan 1905-1985 Obituary ... 115
Steele, Arthur R(obert) 1916- ... 9-10R
Steele, Chester K. ... CANR-26
Earlier sketches in CA 19-20, CAP-2
Steele, Colin Robert 1944- ... 104
Steele, Curtis
See Davis, Frederick C(lyde)
Steele, Dale
See Glut, Donald F(rank)
Steele, Dirk
See Plawin, Paul
Steele, Elizabeth 1921- ... 45-48
Steele, Erskine
See Henderson, Archibald
Steele, Fletcher 1885-1971 ... CAP-1
Earlier sketch in CA 13-14
Steele, Frank 1935- ... 37-40R
Steele, Fred I(rving) 1938- ... CANR-17
Earlier sketches in CA 45-48, CANR-2
Steele, Fritz
See Steele, Fred I(rving)
Steele, George P(eabody II) 1924- ... 2R
Steele, Gordon (Charles) 1892-1981 ... 105
Obituary ... 102
Steele, Harwood R(obert) E(lmes) 1897- ... CAP-1
Earlier sketch in CA 15-16
Steele, Henry 1931- ... 41-44R
Steele, I(an) K(enneth) 1937- ... 45-48
Steele, Jack 1914-1980 ... 109
Obituary ... 102
Steele, James B(ruce, Jr.) 1943- ... 115
Brief entry ... 110
Steele, Mary Q(uintard Govan) 1922- ... CANR-22
Earlier sketches in CA 4R, CANR-6
See also SATA 3, 51
Steele, (Henry) Max(well) 1922- ... 25-28R
See also SATA 10
See also DLBY 80
Steele, Michael Rhoads 1945- ... 111
Steele, Peter (R.) 1935- ... 108
Steele, Phillip W(ayne) 1934- ... 61-64
Steele, Richard W(illiam) 1934-
Brief entry ... 107
Steele, Robert (Scott) 1917- ... 49-52
Steele, Thomas J(oseph) 1933- ... 61-64
Steele, Timothy (Reid) 1948- ... CANR-16
Earlier sketch in CA 93-96
See also CLC 45
Steele, Wilbur Daniel 1886-1970 ... 109
Obituary ... 29-32R
Steele, William O(wen) 1917-1979 ... CANR-2
Earlier sketch in CA 2R
See also SATA 1, 27, 51
Steelman, Robert J(ames) 1914- ... CANR-11
Earlier sketch in CA 69-72
Steely, John E(dward) 1922- ... 37-40R
Steen, Edwin B. 1901- ... 101
Steen, Frank
See Felstein, Ivor
Steen, John Warren, Jr. 1925- ... 15-16R
Steen, Malcolm Harold 1928- ... 29-32R
Steen, Marguerite 1894-1975 ... 97-100
Obituary ... 61-64
Steen, Mike
See Steen, Malcolm Harold
Steen, Sara Jayne 1949- ... 106
Steenberg, Sven 1905- ... 37-40R
Steene, Birgitta 1928- ... 85-88
Steensma, Robert Charles 1930- ... 41-44R
Steenson, Gary P(aul) 1944- ... 107
Steer, Alfred G(ilbert), Jr. 1913- ... 45-48
Steer, Charlotte
See Hunter, Maud L(ily)
Steere, Daniel C(onrad) 1938- ... 93-96
Steere, Douglas V(an) 1901- ... 13-14R
Steere, Richard 1643(?)-1721 ... DLB-24
Steers, J(ames) A(lfred) 1899-1987 ... 124
Steese, Edward 1902-1981 Obituary ... 105
Steese, Peter B(echler) 1933- ... 17-18R
Steeves, Frank Leslie 1921- ... 15-16R
Steeves, Harrison R(oss) 1881-1981
Obituary ... 104
Stefanelli, Vladimir Clain
See Clain-Stefanelli, Vladimir
Stefanics, Charlotte L(ouise) 1927- ... 116
Stefanile, Felix 1920- ... CANR-1
Earlier sketch in CA 45-48
Stefansson, Evelyn
See Nef, Evelyn Stefansson
Stefansson, Thorsteinn 1912- ... 77-80
Steffan, Alice Kennedy 1907- ... 5-6R
Steffan, Jack
See Steffan, Alice Kennedy
Steffan, Siobhan R.
See Goulart, Frances Sheridan
Steffan, Truman Guy 1910- ... 29-32R
Steffanson, Con
See Cassiday, Bruce (Bingham)
and Goulart, Ron(ald Joseph)
Steffek, Edwin F(rancis) 1912-1985 ... 89-92
Obituary ... 118
Steffen, Albert 1884-1963 Obituary ... 93-96
Steffen, Jerome O(rville) 1942- ... 112
Steffens, (Joseph) Lincoln 1866-1936
Brief entry ... 117
See also TCLC 20
Steffensmeier, Darrell J. 1942- ... 123
Stefferud, Alfred (Daniel) 1903- ... CAP-1
Earlier sketch in CA 15-16
Steffler, John 1947- ... 110
Stefflre, Buford 1916- ... 5-6R
Stegall, Carrie Coffey 1908- ... CAP-2
Earlier sketch in CA 25-28
Stegeman, Janet Allais 1923- ... SATA-49, 53
Stegeman, John F(oster) 1918- ... 19-20R
Stegenga, James A. 1937- ... 25-28R
Steger, Shelby 1906- ... 49-52
Steglich, W(infred) G(eorge) 1921- ... 45-48
Stegman, Michael A(llen) 1940- ... 41-44R
Stegner, Page 1937- ... CANR-10
Earlier sketch in CA 21-22R
Stegner, Wallace (Earle) 1909- ... CANR-21
Earlier sketches in CA 3R, CANR-1
See also DLB 9
See also CLC 9, 49
See also AITN 1
Stehling, Kurt R(ichard) 1919- Brief entry ... 110
Stehr, Hermann 1864-1940 ... DLB-66
Steible, Daniel J(oseph) 1912-1976 ... 45-48
Obituary ... 103
Steichen, Edward 1879-1973 Obituary ... 41-44R
Steichen, Paula 1943- ... 25-28R
Steig, Irwin 1901-1977 Obituary ... 73-76
Steig, William 1907- ... CANR-21
Earlier sketch in CA 77-80
See also SATA 18
See also DLB 61
See also CLR 2, 15
See also AITN 1
Steiger, Andrew Jacob 1900- ... 5-6R
Steiger, Brad (E.) 1936- ... CANR-21
Earlier sketch in CA 33-36R
Steiger, Paul E(rnest) 1942- ... 77-80
Steigman, Benjamin 1889(?)-1974
Obituary ... 53-56
Steiman, Sidney 1922- ... 7-8R
Steimle, Edmund A(ugustus) 1907- ... 121
Stein, Aaron Marc 1906-1985 ... CANR-6
Obituary ... 117
Earlier sketch in CA 9-10R
Stein, Arnold (Sidney) 1915- Brief entry ... 114
Stein, Arthur (Benjamin) 1937- ... 29-32R
Stein, Ben
See Stein, Benjamin
Stein, Benjamin 1944- ... 106
Stein, Bob 1920- ... 37-40R
Stein, Bruno 1930- ... 37-40R
Stein, Calvert 1903-1982 ... 29-32R
Obituary ... 125
Stein, Charles
See Schwalberg, Carol(yn Ernestine
Stein)
Stein, Charles S. 1940- ... 21-22R
Stein, Charles W(arner) 1918- ... 116
Stein, Dona ... 77-80
Stein, Edward V(incent) 1920- ... 15-16R
Stein, Emanuel 1908-1985 Obituary ... 114
Stein, George P(hilip) 1917- ... 65-68
Stein, Gertrude 1874-1946 Brief entry ... 104
See also DLB 4, 54
See also TCLC 1, 6, 28
Stein, Harry 1938- ... 61-64
Stein, Harry 1948- Brief entry ... 120
Stein, Harve 1904- ... SATA-30
Stein, Herb 1928- ... 65-68
Stein, Herbert 1916- ... 106
Stein, Herman D(avid) 1917- ... 2R
Stein, Jack M(adison) 1914-1976 ... CANR-15
Obituary ... 103
Earlier sketch in CA 2R
Stein, Jan
See Hegeler, Sten
Stein, Jane Jacobson 1937- ... 97-100
Stein, Jerome L(eon) 1928- ... 81-84
Stein, Jess 1914-1984 Obituary ... 113
Stein, Joseph ... 15-16R
Stein, Leo Daniel 1872-1947 Brief entry ... 107
See also DLB 4
Stein, Leon 1910- ... 17-18R
Stein, Leon 1912- ... CANR-7
Earlier sketch in CA 19-20R
Stein, M(eyer) L(ewis) 1920- ... CANR-13
Earlier sketch in CA 17-18R
See also SATA 6
Stein, Mark (Avrum) 1951- ... 118
Stein, Martha L(inda) 1942- ... 53-56
Stein, Maurice Robert 1926- ... 49-52
Stein, Michael B. 1940- ... 45-48
Stein, Mini ... 29-32R
See also SATA 2
Stein, Morris I(saac) 1921- ... CANR-1
Earlier sketch in CA 3R
Stein, Peter (Gonville) 1926- ... 21-22R
Stein, Philip L(awrence) 1939- ... 61-64
Stein, R(ichard) Conrad 1937- ... CANR-22
Earlier sketch in CA 41-44R
See also SATA 31
Stein, Rita F. 1922- Brief entry ... 106
Stein, Robert 1924- ... 49-52
Stein, Robert H(arry) 1935- ... 101
Stein, Roger B(reed) 1932- ... CANR-2
Earlier sketch in CA 45-48
Stein, Sandra Kovacs 1939- ... 106
Stein, Sara Bonnett ... SATA-34
Stein, Sol 1926- ... CANR-2
Earlier sketch in CA 49-52
See also AITN 1
Stein, Stanley J. 1920- Brief entry ... 108
Stein, Susan M. 1942- ... CANR-14
Earlier sketch in CA 37-40R
Stein, Thomas A. 1924- ... 45-48
Stein, Toby 1935- ... 7-8R
Stein, Walter 1924- ... 25-28R
Stein, William B. 1915- ... 104
Stein, William W(arner) 1921- ... 2R
Steinbach, Alexander Alan 1894-1978 ... 85-88
Obituary ... 81-84
Steinbach, Meredith 1949- ... 107
Steinbeck, John (Ernst) 1902-1968 ... CANR-1
Obituary ... 25-28R
Earlier sketch in CA 2R
See also SATA 9
See also DLB 7, 9
See also DLBD 2
See also CLC 1, 5, 9, 13, 21, 34, 45
Steinberg, Aaron Zacharovich 1891-1975
Obituary ... 61-64
Steinberg, Alfred 1917- ... CANR-9
Earlier sketch in CA 5-6R
See also SATA 9
Steinberg, Charles S(ide) 1913-1978 ... CANR-4
Earlier sketch in CA 49-52
Steinberg, Danny D(avid Charles)
1931- ... CANR-14
Earlier sketch in CA 37-40R
Steinberg, David Joel 1937- ... 25-28R
Steinberg, Eleanor B(usick) 1936- ... 65-68
Steinberg, Erwin R(ay) 1920- ... CANR-12
Earlier sketch in CA 29-32R
Steinberg, Fannie 1899- ... 115
See also SATA 43
Steinberg, Fred J. 1933- ... 37-40R
See also SATA 4
Steinberg, Israel 1903(?)-1983 Obituary ... 109
Steinberg, J(ay) Leonard 1930- ... 57-60
Steinberg, Jeffrey 1947(?)-1981 Obituary ... 104
Steinberg, Jonathan 1934- ... 21-22R
Steinberg, Joseph L(awrence) 1928- ... 25-28R
Steinberg, Judah 1861-1908 Brief entry ... 106
Steinberg, Leo 1920- ... CANR-17
Earlier sketches in CA 45-48, CANR-1
Steinberg, Phillip Orso 1921- ... CANR-2
Earlier sketch in CA 5-6R
See also SATA 34
Steinberg, Rafael (Mark) 1927- ... CANR-9
Earlier sketch in CA 61-64
See also SATA 45
Steinberg, S(igrid) H(enry) 1899-1969 ... CAP-1
Earlier sketch in CA 9-10
Steinberg, Saul 1914- ... 89-92
Steinbergh, Judith W(olinsky) 1943- ... CANR-1
Earlier sketch in CA 45-48
Steinbicker, Paul G(eorge) 1906- ... CAP-2
Earlier sketch in CA 19-20
Steinbreder, Harry John, Jr. 1930-1985
Obituary ... 117
Steinbreder, Sandy
See Steinbreder, Harry John, Jr.
Steinbrueck, Victor 1911- ... 13-14R
Steinbruner, John David 1941- ... 77-80
Steinbrunner, (Peter) Chris(tian) 1933- ... CANR-1
Earlier sketch in CA 45-48
Steincrohn, Peter J(oseph) 1899-1986
Obituary ... 118
Brief entry ... 112
Steinem, Gloria 1934- ... 53-56
Steiner, Barbara A(nnette) 1934- ... CANR-13
Earlier sketch in CA 73-76
See also SATA 13
Steiner, Barry R(aymond) ... 115
Steiner, Charlotte 1900-1981 ... SATA-45
Steiner, Claude 1935- ... 97-100
Steiner, Frederick 1949- ... 116
Steiner, Gary A(lbert) 1931-1966 ... 11-12R
Obituary ... 103
Steiner, George 1929- ... 73-76
See also DLB 67
See also CLC 24
Steiner, George A(lbert) 1912- ... CANR-7
Earlier sketch in CA 13-14R
Steiner, Gerolf 1908- ... 29-32R
Steiner, Gilbert Y(ale) 1924- Brief entry ... 115
Steiner, H. Arthur 1905- ... 5-6R
Steiner, Irene Hunter 1920- ... 97-100
Steiner, Joerg 1930- ... 108
See also SATA 35
Steiner, Jorg
See Steiner, Joerg
Steiner, Kurt 1912- ... CANR-7
Earlier sketch in CA 17-18R
Steiner, Lee R. 1901- ... CAP-1
Earlier sketch in CA 13-14
Steiner, Paul ... CANR-4
Earlier sketch in CA 9-10R
Steiner, Peter O(tto) 1922- ... CANR-14
Earlier sketch in CA 37-40R
Steiner, Ralph 1899-1986 Obituary ... 119
Brief entry ... 113
Steiner, Roger J(acob) 1924- ... 45-48
Steiner, Rudolf 1861-1925 Brief entry ... 107
See also TCLC 13
Steiner, Shari 1941- ... 73-76
Steiner, Stan(ley) 1925-1987 ... CANR-16
Obituary ... 121
Earlier sketches in CA 45-48, CANR-1
See also SATA 14, 50
Steiner, Susan Clemmer 1947- ... 115
Steiner, Thomas R(obert) 1934- ... 45-48
Steiner, Vera P(olgar) John
See John-Steiner, Vera P(olgar)
Steiner, Wendy 1949- ... CANR-14
Earlier sketch in CA 81-84
Steiner-Prag, Hugo 1880-1945 ... SATA-32
Steinert, Marlis G(ertrud) ... 81-84
Steinfels, Peter (Francis) 1941- Brief entry ... 116
Steingold, Fred S(aul) 1936- ... 109
Steinhardt, Anne Elizabeth 1941- ... 104
Steinhardt, Herschel S. 1910- ... CAP-2
Earlier sketch in CA 23-24
Steinhardt, Milton 1909- ... 77-80
Steinhart, Carol E(lder) 1935- ... 57-60
Steinhauer, Harry 1905- ... CANR-1
Earlier sketch in CA 1R
Steinhaus, Arthur H. 1897-1970 ... CAP-1
Earlier sketch in CA 19-20
Steinheimer, Richard (V.) 1929- ... 123
Steinhoff, Dan 1911- ... 77-80
Steinhoff, William (Richard) 1914- ... 85-88
Steinitz, Kate T(rauman) 1889-1975 ... CAP-2
Earlier sketch in CA 23-24
Steinitz, Paul 1909- ... 104
Steinke, Ann (Elizabeth) 1948- ... 113
Steinke, Peter L(ouis) 1938- ... 29-32R
Steinkraus, Warren E(dward) 1922- ... 21-22R

Steinle, John G. 1916- ... 9-10R
Steinle, Paul (Michael) 1939- ... 77-80
Steinman, Lisa Malinowski 1950- ... 69-72
Steinmann, Anne G. 1906(?)-1987
Obituary ... 121
Steinmann, Martin, Jr. 1915- ... CANR-26
Earlier sketch in CA 3R
Steinmetz, Eulalie
See Ross, Eulalie Steinmetz
Steinmetz, Lawrence L(eo) 1938- ... CANR-11
Earlier sketch in CA 23-24R
Steinmetz, Rollin C. 1912(?)-1986
Obituary ... 121
Steinmetz, Urban G. 1920- ... CANR-10
Earlier sketch in CA 25-28R
Steintrager, James A(lvin) 1936- ... 93-96
Steinwedel, Louis William 1943- ... 37-40R
Steirman, Hy 1921- ... 29-32R
Steiss, Alan Walter 1937- ... CANR-12
Earlier sketch in CA 29-32R
Steitz, Edward S. 1920- ... 69-72
Stekert, Ellen J(ane) 1935- ... 33-36R
Stekler, Herman O. 1932- ... 19-20R
Stell, Aaron 1911- ... 57-60
Stell, Geoffrey (Percival) 1944- ... 124
Stellman, Jeanne M(ager) 1947- ... 102
Stellman, Steven D(ale) 1945- ... 85-88
Steltenkamp, Michael F(rancis) 1950- ... 112
Stelter, Gilbert Arthur 1933- ... CANR-15
Earlier sketch in CA 41-44R
Steltzer, Ulli 1923- ... 104
Stelzer, Dick 1950- ... 107
Stelzig, Eugene Louis 1943- ... 81-84
Stem, Thad(deus Garland), Jr.
1916-1980 ... 97-100
Obituary ... 101
Stember, Charles Herbert 1916- ... 21-22R
Stemp, Isay 1922- ... 29-32R
Stemp, Robin (Jenniver Pamela) 1944- ... 107
Stempel, Guido H(ermann) III 1928- ... 77-80
Stempel, John Dallas 1938- ... 110
Stempel, Thomas Ritter 1941- ... 110
Stempel, Tom
See Stempel, Thomas Ritter
Stenberger, Marten 1898- ... CANR-5
Earlier sketch in CA 7-8R
Stendahl, Krister 1921- ... CANR-12
Earlier sketch in CA 17-18R
Stene, Edwin O(tto) 1900- ... CAP-2
Earlier sketch in CA 21-22
Steneck, Nicholas H. 1940- ... 106
Steneman, Shep 1945- ... 107
Stenerson, Douglas C. 1920- ... 37-40R
Stenhouse, David 1932- ... 89-92
Stenius, George
See Seaton, George
Stensboel, Ottar 1930- ... 69-72
Stenson, Frederick 1951- ... 113
Stent, Gunther S(iegmund) 1924- ... 29-32R
Stenton, Doris Mary (Parsons) 1894-1971
Obituary ... 104
Stenus
See Huxley, Herbert H(enry)
Stenzel, Anne K(atherine) 1911- ... 57-60
Stenzel, George 1910- ... 45-48
Stepanchev, Stephen 1915- ... CANR-7
Earlier sketch in CA 17-18R
Stepanian, Michael 1939- ... 45-48
Stephan, John J(ason) 1941- ... 41-44R
Stephan, Leslie (Bates) 1933- ... CANR-24
Earlier sketches in CA 21-22R, CANR-9
Stephan, Ruth 1910- ... 5-6R
Stephen, David 1910- ... 106
Stephen, George 1926- ... 102
Stephen, Jan 1933- ... 3R
Stephen, Leslie 1832-1904 Brief entry ... 123
See also DLB 57
See also TCLC 23
Stephen, Parel Lukose 1898- ... CAP-1
Earlier sketch in CA 9-10
Stephen, R. J.
See Barrett, Norman (S.)
Stephen, Sid 1942- ... 105
Stephen, Sir Leslie
See Stephen, Leslie
Stephens, A. Ray 1932- ... CANR-13
Earlier sketch in CA 77-80
Stephens, Alan 1925- ... 19-20R
Stephens, Alexander H. 1812-1883 ... DLB-47
Stephens, Ann Sophia 1810-1886 ... DLB-73
Stephens, Ann Sophia (Winterbotham)
1813-1886 ... DLB-3
Stephens, C(harles) Ralph 1943- ... 122
Stephens, Casey
See Wagner, Sharon B.
Stephens, Charles
See Goldin, Stephen
Stephens, Charles Asbury 1844(?)-1931 . DLB-42
Stephens, Donald G. 1931- ... 21-22R
Stephens, Edna Buell 1903- ... CANR-14
Earlier sketch in CA 37-40R
Stephens, Edward Carl 1924- ... 23-24R
Stephens, Eve
See Ward-Thomas, Evelyn Bridget
Patricia Stephens
Stephens, Frances
See Bentley, Margaret
Stephens, Henrietta Henkle 1909-1983 .. CANR-6
Obituary ... 109
Earlier sketch in CA 9-10R
Stephens, Ian Melville 1903-1984
Obituary ... 112
Stephens, J(ohn) M(ortimer) 1901- ... 13-14R
Stephens, James 1882(?)-1950
Brief entry ... 104
See also DLB 19
See also TCLC 4
Stephens, James Charles 1915- ... CANR-3
Earlier sketch in CA 7-8R
Stephens, Jeanne
See Hager, Jean
Stephens, Joyce 1941- ... 69-72
Stephens, Lester D(ow) 1933- ... 45-48
Stephens, M(ichael) G(regory) 1946- ... CANR-3
Earlier sketch in CA 49-52
Stephens, Martha (Thomas) 1937- ... 77-80
Stephens, Mary Jo 1935- ... 37-40R
See also SATA 8
Stephens, Meic 1938- ... 65-68
Stephens, Michael D(awson) 1936- ... CANR-22
Earlier sketches in CA 57-60, CANR-7
Stephens, Otis H(ammond), Jr. 1936- ... 65-68
Stephens, Reed
See Donaldson, Stephen R.
Stephens, Robert O(ren) 1928- ... 25-28R
Stephens, Rockwell R(ittenhouse) 1900- ... 53-56
Stephens, Rosemary 1924- ... 77-80
Stephens, Thomas M. 1931- ... 29-32R
Stephens, W(illiam) P(eter) 1934- ... CANR-12
Earlier sketch in CA 29-32R
Stephens, W(illiam) Richard 1932- ... 29-32R
Stephens, Wade C. 1932- ... 23-24R
Stephens, Will Beth 1918- ... 37-40R
Stephens, William M(cLain) 1925- ... 57-60
See also SATA 21
Stephens, William N(ewton) 1927- ... CANR-1
Earlier sketch in CA 2R
Stephenson, Alan M. G. ?-1984 Obituary ... 113
Stephenson, Andrew M(ichael) 1946- ... 124
Brief entry ... 118
Stephenson, David 1947- ... 118
Stephenson, Gilbert T(homas)
1884-1972 ... CAP-1
Obituary ... 37-40R
Earlier sketch in CA 17-18
Stephenson, Howard 1893-1978 ... 37-40R
Stephenson, Jean 1892-1979 Obituary ... 85-88
Stephenson, John B(ell) 1937- ... 61-64
Stephenson, John Edward Drayton 1928-
Brief entry ... 112
Stephenson, Matthew A(rnold) 1935- ... 45-48
Stephenson, Maureen 1927- ... CANR-16
Earlier sketch in CA 85-88
Stephenson, Neal 1959- ... 122
Stephenson, (William) Ralph (Ewing)
1910- ... 17-18R
Stephenson, Richard M(anning) 1918- ... 109
Stephenson, Wendell Holmes
1899-1970 ... CANR-3
Earlier sketch in CA 3R
Stepka, Milan
See Benes, Jan
Stepp, Ann 1935- ... 106
See also SATA 29
Stepto, Robert B(urns) 1945- ... 101
See also BW
Steptoe, John (Lewis) 1950- ... CANR-26
Earlier sketches in CA 49-52, CANR-3
See also BW
See also SATA 8
See also CLR 2, 12
Steptoe, Lydia
See Barnes, Djuna
Steptoe, Patrick C(hristopher) 1913-1988
Obituary ... 125
Sterba, Gunther Hans Wenzel 1922- ... 7-8R
Sterba, Richard F(rancis) 1898- ... 124
Stercho, Peter George 1919- ... 49-52
Sterland, E(rnest) G(eorge) 1919- ... 65-68
Sterling, Anthony
See Caesar, (Eu)Gene (Lee)
Sterling, Brett
See Hamilton, Edmond
and Samachson, Joseph
Sterling, Bruce 1954- ... 119
Sterling, Chandler W(infield) 1911- ... 23-24R
Sterling, Claire 1919(?)- ... 123
Sterling, Donald J(ustus), Jr. 1927- ... 77-80
Sterling, Dorothy 1913- ... CANR-5
Earlier sketch in CA 9-10R
See also SATA 1
See also SAAS 2
See also CLR 1
Sterling, George 1869-1926 Brief entry ... 117
See also DLB 54
See also TCLC 20
Sterling, Helen
See Hoke, Helen L.
Sterling, James 1701-1763 ... DLB-24
Sterling, Maria Sandra
See Floren, Lee
Sterling, Philip 1907- ... 49-52
See also SATA 8
Sterling, Richard W(hitney) 1922- ... 45-48
Sterling, Robert R. 1931- ... 29-32R
Sterling, Sandra
See Floren, Lee
Sterling, Theodor D(avid) 1923- ... 25-28R
Stermer, Bill 1947- ... 110
Stern, Alfred 1899- ... 53-56
Stern, Barbara L.
See Lang, Barbara
Stern, Bill 1907-1971 Obituary ... 89-92
Stern, Boris 1892-1984 ... CAP-2
Obituary ... 113
Earlier sketch in CA 17-18
Stern, Carl 1937- ... 97-100
Stern, Catherine B(rieger) 1894-1973
Obituary ... 37-40R
Stern, Clarence A. 1913- ... 19-20R
Stern, Curt 1902-1981 Obituary ... 105
Stern, Daniel 1928- ... CANR-5
Earlier sketch in CA 5-6R
Stern, Donald A. 1928(?)-1975 Obituary ... 57-60
Stern, E. Mark 1929- ... 37-40R
Stern, Edith Mendel 1901-1975 Obituary ... 57-60
Stern, Edward Severin 1924- ... 53-56
Stern, Elizabeth
See Uhr, Elizabeth
Stern, Ellen Norman 1927- ... CANR-14
Earlier sketch in CA 37-40R
See also SATA 26
Stern, Frances Meritt 1938- ... 112
Stern, Frederick Curtis 1929- ... 108
Stern, Frederick M. 1890(?)-1977
Obituary ... 69-72
Stern, Fritz 1926- ... CANR-1
Earlier sketch in CA 2R
Stern, G(ladys) B(ertha) 1890-1973
Obituary ... 45-48
Stern, George G(ordon) 1923-1974 ... CAP-2
Earlier sketch in CA 29-32
Stern, Gerald 1925- ... 81-84
See also CLC 40
Stern, Gerald M(ann) 1937- ... 69-72
Stern, Geraldine 1907- ... 101
Stern, Gerd Jacob 1928- Brief entry ... 106
Stern, Guy 1922- ... 41-44R
Stern, Harold P. 1922-1977 Obituary ... 69-72
Stern, Harold S. 1923(?)-1976 Obituary ... 65-68
Stern, Harry Joshua 1897- ... 69-72
Stern, Henry L. 1899- ... 97-100
Stern, J(ulius) David 1886-1971 Obituary ... 104
Stern, J(oseph) P(eter Maria) 1920- ... CANR-10
Earlier sketch in CA 23-24R
Stern, James 1904- ... 23-24R
Stern, Jane 1946- ... CANR-10
Earlier sketch in CA 61-64
Stern, Jay B(enjamin) 1929- ... CANR-18
Earlier sketch in CA 25-28R
Stern, Jean Gordon 1904(?)-1985
Obituary ... 117
Stern, Karl 1906-1975 ... CANR-12
Obituary ... 61-64
Earlier sketch in CA 11-12R
Stern, Laurence (Marcus) 1929-1979 ... 85-88
Obituary ... 89-92
Stern, Louis William 1935- ... CANR-18
Earlier sketch in CA 25-28R
Stern, Madeleine B(ettina) 1912- ... CANR-22
Earlier sketches in CA 17-18R, CANR-7
See also SATA 14
Stern, Malcolm H(enry) 1915- ... 73-76
Stern, Marie 1909- ... 45-48
Stern, Michael 1910- ... CAP-2
Earlier sketch in CA 23-24
Stern, Milton R(alph) 1928- ... CANR-15
Earlier sketch in CA 41-44R
Stern, Nancy B. 1944- ... 110
Stern, Paula 1945- ... 102
Stern, Philip M(aurice) 1926- ... 104
Stern, Philip Van Doren 1900-1984 ... CANR-6
Obituary ... 113
Earlier sketch in CA 7-8R
See also SATA 13, 39
Stern, Richard (Gustave) 1928- ... CANR-25
Earlier sketches in CA 1R, CANR-1
See also DLBY 87
See also CLC 4, 39
Stern, Richard Martin 1915- ... CANR-18
Earlier sketches in CA 3R, CANR-2
Stern, Robert A. M. 1939- ... CANR-25
Earlier sketch in CA 29-32R
Stern, Robert M. 1927- ... CANR-10
Earlier sketch in CA 23-24R
Stern, Rudi 1936- Brief entry ... 115
Stern, S. M.
See Stern, Samuel Miklos
Stern, Samuel Miklos 1920-1969 Obituary ... 111
Stern, Simon 1943- ... 89-92
See also SATA 15
Stern, Steve 1947- Brief entry ... 126
Stern, Stewart 1922- Brief entry ... 113
See also DLB 26
Stern, Stuart
See Rae, Hugh C(rauford)
Stern, Susan (Tanenbaum) 1943-1976
Obituary ... 65-68
Stern, William B(ernhard) 1910-1972 ... CAP-1
Earlier sketch in CA 15-16
Stern, Zelda 1949- ... 116
Sternberg, Cecilia 1908-1983 ... 73-76
Obituary ... 111
Sternberg, Jacques 1923- Brief entry ... 111
Sternberg, Josef von 1894-1969 ... 81-84
See also CLC 20
Sternberg, Martin L(eo) A(ltar) 1925- ... 107
Sternberg, Patricia 1930- ... 118
Sternberg, Robert J(effrey) 1949- ... 126
Brief entry ... 119
Sternberg, Vernon (Arthur) 1915-1979
Obituary ... 104
Sternberger, Dolf 1907- ... 104
Sterne, Emma Gelders 1894- ... CANR-5
Earlier sketch in CA 7-8R
See also SATA 6
Sterne, Laurence 1713-1768 ... DLB-39
Sterne, Richard S(tephen) 1921- ... 15-16R
Sterner, Lewis George 1894- ... 7-8R
Sterner, R. Eugene 1912- ... CANR-3
Earlier sketch in CA 11-12R
Sternfeld, Robert 1917- ... 81-84
Sternfield, Allen 1930- ... 53-56
Sternheim, (William Adolf) Carl
1878-1942 Brief entry ... 105
See also DLB 56
See also TCLC 8
Sternlicht, Sanford 1931- ... CANR-26
Earlier sketches in CA 25-28R, CANR-10
Sternlieb, George 1928- ... CANR-25
Earlier sketches in CA 23-24R, CANR-8
Sternsher, Bernard 1925- ... 11-12R
Sterry, Rick 1938- ... 25-28R
Stertz, Eda 1921- ... 104
Stessin, Lawrence 1911- ... 9-10R
Stetler, Charles E(dward) 1927- ... 65-68
Stetler, Russell (Dearnley, Jr.) 1945- ... 41-44R
Stetson, Damon 1915- ... 85-88
Stetson, Erlene ... 108
Stettler, Howard Frederic 1919- ... 5-6R
Stettner, Irving 1922- ... CANR-16
Earlier sketch in CA 77-80
Steurt, Marjorie Rankin 1888- ... 15-16R
See also SATA 10
Steven, Hugh 1931- ... CANR-14
Earlier sketch in CA 41-44R
Stevens, Anita 1911- Brief entry ... 110
Stevens, Anthony (George) 1933- ... 110
Stevens, Ardis 1921- ... 45-48
Stevens, Art 1935- ... 124
Stevens, (John) Austin ... 53-56
Stevens, Austin N(eil) 1930- ... 104
Stevens, Bernice A. ... 37-40R
Stevens, Blaine
See Whittington, Harry (Benjamin)
Stevens, Bryna
See Donaldson, Bryna Stevens
Stevens, Carl
See Obstfeld, Raymond
Stevens, Carla M(cBride) 1928- ... CANR-12
Earlier sketch in CA 69-72
See also SATA 13
Stevens, Cat
See Georgiou, Steven Demetre
Stevens, Christopher 1948- ... 119
Stevens, Christopher
See Tabori, Paul
Stevens, Clifford 1926- ... CANR-6
Earlier sketch in CA 11-12R
Stevens, Clysle
See Wade, John Stevens
Stevens, Dan J.
See Overholser, Wayne D.
Stevens, David Harrison 1884-1980 ... 77-80
Obituary ... 93-96
Stevens, Denis William 1922- ... CANR-3
Earlier sketch in CA 9-10R
Stevens, Diane 1944- ... 65-68
Stevens, E. S.
See Drower, E(thel) S(tefana May)
Stevens, Edmund William 1910- ... 109
Stevens, Edward 1928- ... CANR-11
Earlier sketch in CA 29-32R
Stevens, Edwin L(ockwood) 1913-1987 ... 23-24R
Obituary ... 122
Stevens, Eleanour V(irginia) 1926- ... 29-32R
Stevens, Elisabeth (Goss) 1929- ... 110
Stevens, Fae Hewston
See Stevens, Frances Isted
Stevens, Frances Isted 1907- ... CAP-1
Earlier sketch in CA 9-10
Stevens, Franklin 1933- ... 29-32R
See also SATA 6
Stevens, George 1904(?)-1985 Obituary ... 116
Stevens, George (Cooper), Jr. 1932- ... 125
Brief entry ... 118
Stevens, George Putnam 1918- ... 45-48
Stevens, Georgiana G(erlinger) 1904- ... CAP-1
Earlier sketch in CA 17-18
Stevens, Gerald 1909- ... 7-8R
Stevens, Graeme R(oy) 1932- ... 118
Stevens, Gwendolyn 1944- ... 104
See also SATA 33
Stevens, Halsey 1908- ... 25-28R
Stevens, Harold 1917- ... 89-92
Stevens, Harvey A(lonzo) 1913- ... 89-92
Stevens, Holly 1924- ... 25-28R
Stevens, J. D.
See Rowland, D(onald) S(ydney)
Stevens, James (Richard) 1940- ... CANR-16
Earlier sketch in CA 93-96
Stevens, James F. 1892-1971 Obituary ... 33-36R
Stevens, Jane Greengold 1945- ... 108
Stevens, Joan 1908- ... CANR-2
Earlier sketch in CA 7-8R
Stevens, John
See Tubb, E(dwin) C(harles)
Stevens, Joseph C(harles) 1929- ... 17-18R
Stevens, Kathleen 1936- ... 116
See also SATA 49
Stevens, L(ewell) Robert 1932- ... 111
Stevens, Lauren R(ogers) 1938- ... 5-6R
Stevens, Leonard A. 1920- ... CANR-12
Earlier sketch in CA 19-20R
Stevens, Lucile Vernon 1899- ... 61-64
Stevens, Mark 19(?)- ... CLC-34
Stevens, Mark 1951- ... 122
Stevens, Martin 1927- ... 13-14R
Stevens, Michael 1919- ... 53-56
Stevens, Norma Young 1927- ... 21-22R
Stevens, Pam
See Gilbert, George
Stevens, Patricia Bunning 1931- ... 53-56
See also SATA 27
Stevens, Paul 1946- ... 123
Stevens, Peter 1927- ... 93-96
Stevens, Peter
See Geis, Darlene Stern
Stevens, Peter S(mith) 1936- ... 53-56
Stevens, R(obert) B(ocking) 1933- ... CANR-9
Earlier sketch in CA 21-22R
Stevens, R. L.
See Hoch, Edward D(entinger)
Stevens, Richard P. 1931- ... CANR-10
Earlier sketch in CA 21-22R
Stevens, Robert D(avid) 1921- ... 112
Stevens, Robert Tyler
See Staples, Reginald Thomas

Stevens, Robert Warren 1918-1987 ... CANR-1
Obituary ... 122
Earlier sketch in CA 45-48
Stevens, Roger (Bentham) 1906-1980
Obituary ... 105
Stevens, Rolland E(lwell) 1915- ... 81-84
Stevens, Rosemary (Anne) 1935- ... 85-88
Stevens, S. P.
See Palestrant, Simon S.
Stevens, S(tanley) S(mith) 1906-1973
Obituary ... 116
Stevens, Serita (Deborah) 1949- ... 119
Stevens, Shane 1941- ... 21-22R
Stevens, Sharon 1949- ... 77-80
Stevens, Sylvester K(irby) 1904-1974 ... CAP-1
Obituary ... 45-48
Earlier sketch in CA 15-16
Stevens, Tricia
See Pearl, Jacques Bain
Stevens, Trisha
See Pearl, Jacques Bain
Stevens, Wallace 1879-1955 ... 124
Brief entry ... 104
See also DLB 54
See also TCLC 3, 12
Stevens, William 1925- ... 21-22R
Stevens, William W(ilson) 1914- ... 37-40R
Stevens-Arroyo, Antonio M. 1941- ... 120
Stevenson, Adlai E(wing) 1900-1965 ... CAP-1
Earlier sketch in CA 15-16
Stevenson, Anna (M.) 1905- ... SATA-12
Stevenson, Anne (Katharine) 1933- ... CANR-9
Earlier sketch in CA 17-18R
See also DLB 40
See also CLC 7, 33
Stevenson, Augusta 1869(?)-1976 ... 2R
Obituary ... 65-68
See also SATA 2, 26
Stevenson, (William) Bruce 1906- ... 49-52
Stevenson, Burton Egbert 1872-1962 ... 102
Obituary ... 89-92
See also SATA 25
Stevenson, Carol Dornfeld 1931- ... 7-8R
Stevenson, Charles 1908(?)-1979
Obituary ... 85-88
Stevenson, Christopher Sinclair
See Sinclair-Stevenson, Christopher
Stevenson, David 1942- ... 109
Stevenson, David Lloyd 1910-1975 ... CAP-2
Obituary ... 57-60
Earlier sketch in CA 23-24
Stevenson, Dorothy E(mily) 1892-1973 ... CAP-1
Obituary ... 49-52
Earlier sketch in CA 15-16
Stevenson, Dwight E(shelman) 1906- ... CANR-1
Earlier sketch in CA 2R
Stevenson, Elizabeth 1919- ... CANR-26
Earlier sketch in CA 1R
Stevenson, Florence ... CANR-16
Earlier sketch in CA 97-100
Stevenson, George J(ames) 1924- ... 9-10R
Stevenson, Gloria 1945- ... 61-64
Stevenson, Grace Thomas 1900- ... 37-40R
Stevenson, Harold W(illiam) 1921- ... 25-28R
Stevenson, Henry M(iller) 1914- ... 77-80
Stevenson, Herbert Frederick 1906- ... CANR-2
Earlier sketch in CA 7-8R
Stevenson, Hugh A(lexander) 1935- ... 112
Stevenson, Ian (Pretyman) 1918-
Brief entry ... 115
Stevenson, Ian Ralph 1943- ... 102
Stevenson, J. P.
See Haldane-Stevenson, James Patrick
Stevenson, James 1929- ... 115
See also SATA 34, 42
Stevenson, James Patrick
See Haldane-Stevenson, James Patrick
Stevenson, Janet 1913- ... 13-14R
See also SATA 8
Stevenson, John Albert 1890(?)-1979
Obituary ... 89-92
Stevenson, John P.
See Grierson, Edward
Stevenson, L(eland) W(ells) 1916- ... 107
Stevenson, Laura Caroline 1946- ... 120
Stevenson, Leslie (Forster) 1943- ... 65-68
Stevenson, (Arthur) Lionel 1902-1973 ... 103
Obituary ... 45-48
Stevenson, Michael Ian 1953- ... 103
Stevenson, Richard
See Lipez, Richard
Stevenson, Robert 1905-1986 Obituary ... 120
Stevenson, Robert (Murrell) 1916- ... CANR-1
Earlier sketch in CA 3R
Stevenson, Robert Louis (Balfour)
1850-1894 ... YABC-2
See also DLB 18, 57
See also CLR 10, 11
Stevenson, Suzanne Silvercruys
1898(?)-1973 Obituary ... 41-44R
Stevenson, T(homas) H(ulbert) 1919- ... 61-64
Stevenson, Tom 1899(?)-1982 Obituary ... 106
Stevenson, Vera Kemp 1920- ... 57-60
Stevenson, Victoria F. 1878(?)-1973
Obituary ... 41-44R
Stevenson, W(illiam) Taylor 1928- ... CANR-18
Earlier sketch in CA 25-28R
Stevenson, (Stanley) Warren 1933- ... 41-44R
Stevenson, William 1925- ... 13-14R
Steward, F(rederick) C(ampion) 1904- ... 41-44R
Steward, Hal D(avid) 1922- ... 69-72
Steward, Julian H. 1902-1972 Obituary ... 33-36R
Steward, Samuel M(orris) 1909- ... 112
Stewart, A(gnes) C(harlotte) ... 77-80
See also SATA 15
Stewart, A(nthony) T(erence) Q(uincey)
1929- ... 25-28R
Stewart, (John) Allan 1939- ... 4R
Stewart, Allegra 1899- ... 45-48
Stewart, Angus (J. M.) 1936- ... 106
Stewart, Bertie Ann Gardner 1912- ... 5-6R
Stewart, Bill 1942(?)-1979 Obituary ... 89-92
Stewart, Charles
See Zurhorst, Charles (Stewart, Jr.)
Stewart, Charles J(oseph) 1936- ... 41-44R
Stewart, Charles T(odd), Jr. 1922- ... 101
Stewart, Christina Duff 1926- ... 65-68
Stewart, Cochrane
See Stewart, Kenneth
Stewart, D(avid) H(ugh) 1926- ... 21-22R
Stewart, Daniel K(enneth) 1925- ... 29-32R
Stewart, David
See Politella, Dario
Stewart, Desmond (Stirling) 1924-1981 ... 37-40R
Obituary ... 104
Stewart, Donald Charles 1930- ... 37-40R
Stewart, Donald H(enderson) 1911- ... 29-32R
Stewart, Donald Ogden 1894-1980 ... 81-84
Obituary ... 101
See also DLB 4, 11, 26
Stewart, Dorothy Mary 1917-1965
Obituary ... 104
Stewart, Douglas (Alexander) 1913- ... 81-84
Stewart, Edgar I(rving) 1900- ... 7-8R
Stewart, Edith Hamilton 1883- ... CAP-1
Earlier sketch in CA 11-12
Stewart, Elbert Wilton 1916- ... 37-40R
Stewart, Eleanor
See Porter, Eleanor H(odgman)
Stewart, Elizabeth Grey
See Reed, Elizabeth Stewart
Stewart, Elizabeth Laing 1907- ... 49-52
See also SATA 6
Stewart, Ella Winter 1898-1980 Obituary ... 101
Stewart, Eve
See Napier, Priscilla
Stewart, Frank 1946- ... CANR-20
Earlier sketch in CA 104
Stewart, Fred Mustard 1936- ... 37-40R
Stewart, Garrett (Fitzgerald) 1945- ... 93-96
Stewart, George 1892-1972 Obituary ... 33-36R
Stewart, George Rippey 1895-1980 ... CANR-3
Obituary ... 101
Earlier sketch in CA 1R
See also SATA 3, 23
See also DLB 8
Stewart, Hal D(ouglas) 1899- ... CAP-1
Earlier sketch in CA 15-16
Stewart, Harold C. 1891(?)-1976
Obituary ... 69-72
Stewart, Harold Frederick 1916- ... 69-72
Stewart, Harris B(ates) Jr. 1922- ... 45-48
Stewart, Hilary 1924- ... CANR-16
Earlier sketch in CA 93-96
Stewart, Horace Floyd, Jr. 1928- ... 49-52
Stewart, J(ohn) I(nnes) M(ackintosh)
1906- ... 85-88
See also CAAS 3
See also CLC 7, 14, 32
Stewart, James Alexander 1948- ... 113
Stewart, James Brewer 1940- ... 29-32R
Stewart, James S(tuart) 1896- ... 9-10R
Stewart, Jean
See Newman, Mona Alice Jean
Stewart, Jim
See Stewart, James Alexander
Stewart, John 1904(?)-1985 Obituary ... 116
Stewart, John (William) 1920- ... 33-36R
See also SATA 14
Stewart, John 1933- ... CANR-16
Earlier sketch in CA 97-100
Stewart, John 1941- ... 97-100
Stewart, John B(enjamin) 1924- ... 9-10R
Stewart, John G(ilman) 1935- Brief entry ... 112
Stewart, Judith Anne
See Maciel, Jud(ith Anne)
Stewart, K(athleen) Alison Clarke
See Clarke-Stewart, K(athleen) Alison
Stewart, Katharine Jeanne (Dark) 1914- ... 9-10R
Stewart, Kaye
See Howe, Doris Kathleen
Stewart, Kenneth 1918-1985 Obituary ... 118
Stewart, Kenneth N. 1901-1978 Obituary ... 77-80
Stewart, Kerry
See Stewart, Linda
Stewart, Lawrence D(elbert) 1926- ... 89-92
Stewart, Lawrence H(oyle) 1922- ... 17-18R
Stewart, Linda ... 101
Stewart, Margaret 1912- ... CANR-18
Earlier sketch in CA 25-28R
Stewart, Marie M(cCaffery) 1899- ... 7-8R
Stewart, Mark Armstrong 1929- ... 89-92
Stewart, Mary (Florence Elinor) 1916- ... CANR-1
Earlier sketch in CA 2R
See also SATA 12
See also CLC 7, 35
Stewart, Mary Rainbow
See Stewart, Mary (Florence Elinor)
Stewart, (Robert) Michael (Maitland)
1906- ... CANR-22
Earlier sketch in CA 106
Stewart, Michael 1924(?)-1987 Obituary ... 123
Stewart, Michael 1933- ... 116
Stewart, Natacha
See Ullman, Natacha
Stewart, Oliver 1895-1980 ... CANR-5
Earlier sketch in CA 7-8R
Stewart, Pat(ricia) 1944- ... 97-100
Stewart, Paul D(ekker) 1918- ... 1R
Stewart, Philip Robert 1940- ... 29-32R
Stewart, Phyllis Langton 1933- Brief entry ... 106
Stewart, Ramona 1922- ... CANR-6
Earlier sketch in CA 1R
Stewart, Randall 1896-1964 ... CANR-1
Earlier sketch in CA 1R
Stewart, Rex William 1907-1967 Obituary ... 110
Stewart, Rhea Talley 1915- ... 41-44R
Stewart, Robert G(ordon) 1931- ... 65-68
Stewart, Robert Neil 1891- ... 11-12R
See also SATA 7
Stewart, Robert T. 1920(?)-1977
Obituary ... 73-76
Stewart, Robert Wilson 1935- ... 49-52
Stewart, Rosemary (Gordon) ... CANR-15
Earlier sketch in CA 37-40R
Stewart, Sam
See Stewart, Linda
Stewart, Scott
See Zaffo, George J.
Stewart, Seumas 1919- ... 61-64
Stewart, Shelia 1928- ... 21-22R
Stewart, Stanley N(ordahl) 1931- ... 17-18R
Stewart, Suzanne ... 61-64
Stewart, Vincent (Astor, Jr.) 1939- ... 29-32R
Stewart, W(illiam) A(lexander) Campbell
1915- ... 13-14R
Stewart, W(alter) P. 1924- ... SATA-53
Stewart, Walter Bingham 1913- ... CANR-16
Earlier sketch in CA 85-88
Stewart, Will
See Williamson, John Stewart
Stewart, William Stanley 1938- ... 89-92
Stewart, Wynn 1934-1985 Obituary ... 116
Stewart, Zeph 1921- ... 41-44R
Stewig, John Warren 1937- ... CANR-14
Earlier sketch in CA 81-84
See also SATA 26
Steyaert, Thomas A(dolph) 1930- ... 37-40R
Steyer, Wesley W. 1923- ... 29-32R
Steyermark, Julian A(lfred) 1909-1988 ... CANR-17
Obituary ... 126
Earlier sketches in CA 13-14, CAP-1
Stibbs, Alan M(arshall) 1901- ... CANR-2
Earlier sketch in CA 4R
Stich, Stephen P(eter) 1943- ... 41-44R
Stick, David 1919- ... CANR-17
Earlier sketch in CA 97-100
Stickells, Austin T. 1914- ... 41-44R
Stickgold, Bob 1945- ... 104
Stickney, Trumbull 1874-1904 ... DLB-54
Stieber, Jack 1919- ... CANR-6
Earlier sketch in CA 2R
Stiehm, Judith 1935- ... 61-64
Stierlin, Helm 1926- ... 29-32R
Stierwell, Jay
See Swicegood, Thomas L. P.
Stiffel, Frank 1916- ... 117
Stigger, Judith A. 1949- ... 111
Stigler, George Joseph 1911- ... 41-44R
Stigler, Stephen M(ack) 1941- ... 125
Stigum, Marcia (Lee) 1934- ... CANR-8
Earlier sketch in CA 61-64
Stigwood, Robert C. 1934- ... 102
Stiles, Ezra 1727-1795 ... DLB-31
Stiles, John R. 1916(?)-1976 Obituary ... 65-68
Stiles, Joseph 1903- ... CAP-2
Earlier sketch in CA 17-18
Stiles, Lindley Joseph 1913- ... CANR-3
Earlier sketch in CA 7-8R
Stiles, Martha Bennett ... 37-40R
See also SATA 6
Stiles, Merritt N. 1899-1975 Obituary ... 57-60
Stiles, Ned B. 1932- ... 17-18R
Stiles, Norman B. 1942- ... 114
See also SATA 36
Stilgoe, John R. ... 109
Still, C. Henry 1920- ... 11-12R
Still, James 1906- ... CANR-26
Earlier sketches in CA 65-68, CANR-10
See also SATA 29
See also DLB 9
See also CLC 49
Still, Richard R(alph) 1921- ... CANR-1
Earlier sketch in CA 1R
Still, William N(orwood), Jr. 1932- ... CANR-18
Earlier sketch in CA 25-28R
Stiller, Brian C(arl) 1942- ... 117
Stillerman, Robbie 1947- ... SATA-12
Stilley, Frank 1918- ... 61-64
See also SATA 29
Stillinger, Jack 1931- ... CANR-1
Earlier sketch in CA 1R
Stillman, Damie 1933- ... 45-48
Stillman, Edmund O. 1924-1983 Obituary ... 111
Stillman, Frances (Jennings) 1910-1975 ... CAP-1
Obituary ... 57-60
Earlier sketch in CA 15-16
Stillman, Irwin M(axwell) 1895-1975 ... 49-52
Obituary ... 61-64
Stillman, Myra Stephens 1915- ... CANR-6
Earlier sketch in CA 5-6R
Stillman, Nathan 1914- ... 5-6R
Stillman, Richard J. 1917- ... CANR-14
Earlier sketch in CA 37-40R
Stillwell, Margaret Bingham 1887-1984 ... 41-44R
Obituary ... 112
Stillwell, Norma Jamieson 1894- ... CAP-1
Earlier sketch in CA 15-16
Stillwell, Paul (Lewis) 1944- ... 126
Stillwell, Richard 1899-1982 Obituary ... 111
Stilson, Max 1919- ... 11-12R
Stilwell, William E(arle) III 1936- ... 107
Stimmel, Barry 1939- ... CANR-11
Earlier sketch in CA 69-72
Stimpson, Catherine R(oslyn) 1936- ... 41-44R
Stimson, Dorothy 1890-1988 Obituary ... 126
Stimson, William 1946- ... 122
Stinchcombe, Arthur L. 1933- ... CANR-23
Earlier sketches in CA 15-16R, CANR-8
Stinchcombe, William 1937- ... 105
Stine, G(eorge) Harry 1928- ... CANR-9
Earlier sketch in CA 65-68
See also SATA 10
Stine, Jovial Bob
See Stine, R(obert) L(awrence)
Stine, R(obert) L(awrence) 1943- ... CANR-22
Earlier sketch in CA 105
See also SATA 31
Stine, Whitney Ward 1930- ... CANR-7
Earlier sketch in CA 57-60
See also AITN 1
Stineman, Esther F. 1947- ... CANR-17
Earlier sketch in CA 97-100
Stinetorf, Louise (Allender) 1900- ... 11-12R
See also SATA 10
Sting
See Sumner, Gordon Matthew
Stinger, Charles L(ewis) 1944- ... 77-80
Stini, William A(rthur) 1930- Brief entry ... 107
Stinnett, Caskie 1911- ... 7-8R
Stinnett, Nick 1942- ... 110
Stinnett, Ronald F. 1929- ... 23-24R
Stinnett, Tim Moore 1901-1985 ... CANR-13
Obituary ... 115
Earlier sketch in CA 17-18R
Stinnette, Charles R(oy), Jr. 1914- ... 77-80
Stinson, James Emerson, Jr. 1937- ... 119
Stinson, Jim
See Stinson, James Emerson, Jr.
Stinson, Kathy 1952- ... 113
Stinson, Robert William 1941- ... 111
Stinton, T(homas) C(harles) W(arren)
1925-1985 Obituary ... 117
Stipe, Robert Edwin 1928- ... 49-52
Stirling, Alfred (Thorpe) 1902-1981 ... 110
Obituary ... 108
Stirling, Anna Maria Diana Wilhelmina
(Pickering) 1865-1965 ... CAP-1
Earlier sketch in CA 9-10
Stirling, Arthur
See Sinclair, Upton (Beall)
Stirling, Betty Rutledge 1923- ... 9-10R
Stirling, (Thomas) Brents 1904- ... CAP-2
Earlier sketch in CA 25-28
Stirling, Jessica
See Coghlan, Margaret M.
Stirling, Lilla (May Elderkin) 1902- ... 107
Stirling, Matthew Williams 1896-1975
Obituary ... 53-56
Stirling, Monica 1916-1983 ... 81-84
Obituary ... 111
Stirling, Nora B(romley) 1900- ... CANR-3
Earlier sketch in CA 7-8R
See also SATA 3
Stirnweis, Shannon 1931- ... SATA-10
Stitelman, Leonard (Arnold) 1932- ... 41-44R
Stites, Francis N(oel) 1938- ... 41-44R
Stites, Raymond S(omers) 1899-1974 ... 65-68
Obituary ... 53-56
Stith, John E(dward) 1947- ... 117
Stith, William 1707-1755 ... DLB-31
Stitskin, Leon D. 1910-1978 ... CANR-1
Earlier sketch in CA 3R
Stitt, Milan 1941- ... 69-72
See also CLC 29
Stitt, Peter 1940- ... 123
Stitzel, Thomas E(dward) 1936- ... 93-96
Stivens, Dal(las George) 1911- ... CANR-14
Earlier sketch in CA 69-72
Stiver, Mary Weeden 1909- ... CAP-1
Earlier sketch in CA 13-14
Stivers, Robert L(loyd) 1940- ... 69-72
Stjernberg, Lloyd A(rmand) 1937- ... 25-28R
Stoan, Stephen K(uzman) 1942- ... 111
Stob, Ralph 1894-1965 ... 1R
Obituary ... 103
Stobart, Thomas Ralph 1914- ... 13-14R
Stobaugh, Robert B. (Jr.) 1927- ... 101
Stobbs, John L(ouis) N(ewcombe)
1921- ... 15-16R
Stobbs, William 1914- ... 81-84
See also SATA 17
Stock, A(my) G(eraldine) 1902-1988
Obituary ... 126
Stock, Barbara R(uth) 1942- ... CANR-19
Earlier sketch in CA 112
Stock, Brian 1939- ... 41-44R
Stock, Catherine 1952- ... 119
Stock, Claudette 1934- ... 65-68
Stock, Ernest 1924- ... 23-24R
Stock, Guy 1933- ... 124
Stock, Irvin 1920- ... 25-28R
Stock, Phyllis H(artman) 1930- ... 85-88
Stock, R(obert) D(ouglas) 1941- ... CANR-14
Earlier sketch in CA 41-44R
Stockanes, Anthony E(dward) 1935- ... 109
Stockard, James Wright, Jr. 1935- ... 15-16R
Stockard, Jimmy
See Stockard, James Wright, Jr.
Stockdale, Eric 1929- ... 25-28R
Stocker, Margarita 1955- ... 121
Stockhammer, Morris 1904- ... 13-14R
Stocking, David M(ackenzie) 1919- ... 25-28R
Stocking, George W(ard), Jr. 1928- ... 73-76
Stocking, George Ward 1892-1975
Obituary ... 61-64
Stocking, Hobart E(bey) 1906- ... 101
Stocking, Marion Kingston 1922- ... 25-28R
Stocking, S(usan) Holly 1945- ... 117
Stockman, David A(llen) 1946- ... 123
Stocks, Mary (Danvers Brinton)
1891-1975 ... 13-14R
Obituary ... 118
Stockton, Adrian James 1935- ... 29-32R
Stockton, Francis Richard 1834-1902
Brief entry ... 108
See also SATA 44

Stockton, Frank R.
See Stockton, Francis Richard
See also SATA 32
See also DLB 42, 74
Stockton, J. Roy 1893(?)-1972
Obituary ... 37-40R
Stockton, Jim
See Stockton, Adrian James
Stockton, John R(obert) 1903- ... 13-14R
Stockton, Ronald R. 1940- ... 118
Stockwell, Edward G(rant) 1933- ... 23-24R
Stockwell, John R(obert) 1937- ... 104
Stockwell, Robert P(aul) 1925- ... 17-18R
Stockwin, (James) Arthur (Ainscow)
1935- ... 103
Stockwood, (Arthur) Mervyn 1913-
Brief entry ... 117
Stoddard, Charles
See Kuttner, Henry
Stoddard, Edward G. 1923- ... 11-12R
See also SATA 10
Stoddard, Ellwyn R(eed) 1927- ... CANR-17
Earlier sketches in CA 45-48, CANR-1
Stoddard, George Dinsmore 1897-1981
Obituary ... 106
Stoddard, Hope 1900- ... 49-52
See also SATA 6
Stoddard, Richard 1942- ... 102
Stoddard, Richard Henry 1825-1903
Brief entry ... 114
See also DLB 3, 64
Stoddard, Sandol 1927- ... CANR-8
Earlier sketch in CA 7-8R
Stoddard, Solomon 1643-1729 ... DLB-24
Stoddard, Tom 1933- ... 37-40R
Stoddard, Whitney Snow 1913- ... 109
Stoddart, Jack Elliott 1916-1988 Obituary ... 124
Stodelle, Ernestine 1912- ... 117
Stoehr, C(arl) Eric 1945- ... 65-68
Stoessinger, John G. 1927- ... CANR-9
Earlier sketch in CA 13-14R
Stoetzer, O(tto) Carlos (Enrique) 1921- ... 109
Stoff, Sheldon (Ptaschevitch) 1930- ... 23-24R
Stoffel, Albert Law 1909- ... 65-68
Stoffel, Betty W. 1922- ... 19-20R
Stoffel, Ernest Lee 1923- ... 114
Stoffel, Lester L(enneth, Jr.) 1920- ... 45-48
Stoffle, Carla J(oy) 1943- ... CANR-7
Earlier sketch in CA 61-64
Stogdill, Ralph M(elvin) 1904- ... CANR-1
Earlier sketch in CA 1R
Stohl, Michael (Steven) 1947- ... CANR-25
Earlier sketch in CA 107
Stohlman, Martha Lou Lemmon 1913- ... 65-68
Stoianovich, Trajan 1921- ... 21-22R
Stoiber, Rudolph M(aria) 1925- ... 1R
Stoiko, Michael 1919- ... 11-12R
See also SATA 14
Stoil, Michael Jon 1950- ... 53-56
Stojanovic, Svetozar 1931- Brief entry ... 112
Stokely, James R(orex), Jr. 1913-1977 ... 9-10R
Obituary ... 69-72
Stoker, Abraham 1847-1912 Brief entry ... 105
See also SATA 29
Stoker, Alan 1930- ... CANR-24
Earlier sketches in CA 23-24R, CANR-9
Stoker, Bram
See Stoker, Abraham
See also DLB 36, 70
See also TCLC 8
Stoker, H(oward) Stephen 1939- ... CANR-8
Earlier sketch in CA 61-64
Stokes, Adrian Durham 1902-1972 ... CANR-5
Obituary ... 89-92
Earlier sketch in CA 13-14R
Stokes, Bob
See Wilkening, Howard (Everett)
Stokes, Carl B(urton) 1927- ... 69-72
Stokes, Cedric
See Beardmore, George
Stokes, Charles (Herbert) 1932- ... 103
Stokes, Charles J(unius) 1922- ... CANR-10
Earlier sketch in CA 25-28R
Stokes, Daniel M. J. 1950- ... 57-60
Stokes, Donald (Hubert) 1913-1986
Obituary ... 119
Stokes, Donald Elkinton 1927- ... CANR-1
Earlier sketch in CA 1R
Stokes, Doris 1919-1987 Obituary ... 122
Brief entry ... 115
Stokes, Eric (Thomas) 1924-1981 ... 107
Obituary ... 103
Stokes, Geoffrey 1940- ... 69-72
Stokes, Henry J.M. Scott
See Scott-Stokes, Henry J.M.
Stokes, Jack (Tilden) 1923- ... 29-32R
See also SATA 13
Stokes, Olivia Pearl 1916- ... 37-40R
See also SATA 32
Stokes, Peg (Lee Ewing) ... 3R
Stokes, Robert
See Wilkening, Howard (Everett)
Stokes, Roy 1915- ... 19-20R
Stokes, Roy Eliot ... CANR-26
Earlier sketches in CA 19-20, CAP-2
Stokes, Simpson
See Fawcett, F(rank) Dubrez
Stokes, Thomas L. 1898-1958 ... DLB-29
Stokes, William Lee 1915- ... CANR-20
Earlier sketch in CA 41-44R
Stokesbury, James L(awton) 1934- ... CANR-17
Earlier sketch in CA 93-96
Stokesbury, Leon 1945- ... CANR-21
Earlier sketch in CA 69-72
Stokke, Baard Richard 1937- ... 25-28R
Stokoe, William C(larence), Jr. 1919- ... 41-44R
Stokstad, Marilyn 1929- ... CANR-15
Earlier sketch in CA 37-40R
Stoler, Ann Laura 1949- ... 119
Stoler, Peter (Robert) 1935- ... 97-100
Stoll, Clarice Stasz
See Stasz, Clarice
Stoll, Dennis G(ray) 1912-1987 ... 13-14R
Obituary ... 124
Stoll, John E(dward) 1933- ... 49-52
Stoller, Robert J(esse) 1924- Brief entry ... 117
Stollnitz, Fred 1939- ... 45-48
Stoloff, Carolyn 1927- ... CANR-9
Earlier sketch in CA 65-68
Stolorow, Robert D(avid) 1942- ... 102
Stolper, Wolfgang F(riedrich) 1912- ... 23-24R
Stolten, Jane (Henry) ... 97-100
Stoltenberg, Donald Hugo 1927- ... 89-92
Stoltzfus, Ben Franklin 1927- ... 103
Stolz, Lois Meek 1891- ... CAP-2
Earlier sketch in CA 21-22
Stolz, Mary (Slattery) 1920- ... CANR-13
Earlier sketch in CA 5-6R
See also SATA 10
See also SAAS 3
See also CLC 12
See also AITN 1
Stolzenbach, Norma Frizzell 1904- ... 41-44R
Stolzenberg, Mark 1950- ... 102
Stonberg, Selma F(ranks) ... 69-72
Stone, Alan
See Svenson, Andrew E(dward)
See also SATA 1
Stone, Alan A(braham) 1929- ... 17-18R
Stone, Albert E(dward) 1924- ... CANR-8
Earlier sketch in CA 19-20R
Stone, Albert E., Jr.
See Stone, Albert E(dward)
Stone, Alfred R. 1926- ... 17-18R
Stone, Alma 1908- ... 77-80
Stone, Barbara Haskins 1924(?)-1979
Obituary ... 89-92
Stone, Betty E. 1926- ... 9-10R
Stone, Brian 1919- ... 15-16R
Stone, Charles Sumner, Jr. 1924- ... 77-80
Stone, Christopher D(avid) 1937- ... 53-56
Stone, Chuck
See Stone, Charles Sumner, Jr.
Stone, Clarence N. 1935- ... 112
Stone, Clifford A. 1951-1986 Obituary ... 118
Stone, David (Anthony) 1929- ... 5-6R
Stone, David K(arl) 1922- ... 85-88
See also SATA 9
Stone, David U. 1927- ... CANR-7
Earlier sketch in CA 19-20R
Stone, Deborah
See Navas, Deborah
Stone, Donald D(avid) 1942- ... 81-84
Stone, Donald (Adelbert), Jr. 1937- ... 29-32R
Stone, Doris (Zemurray) 1909- ... 105
Stone, Doris (Mary) 1918- ... 117
Stone, Edward 1913- ... 37-40R
Stone, Elaine Murray 1922- ... CANR-17
Earlier sketch in CA 89-92
Stone, Elizabeth W(enger) 1918- ... CANR-25
Earlier sketch in CA 107
Stone, Ellery W(heeler) 1894-1981
Obituary ... 105
Stone, Elna ... CANR-5
Earlier sketch in CA 15-16R
Stone, Eugenia 1879-1971 ... 9-10R
See also SATA 7
Stone, Frank A(ndrews) 1929- ... CANR-8
Earlier sketch in CA 61-64
Stone, Gene
See Stone, Eugenia
Stone, George Winchester, Jr. 1907- ... CANR-6
Earlier sketch in CA 7-8R
Stone, Gerald (Charles) 1932- ... 104
Stone, Grace Zaring 1891- ... CAP-2
Earlier sketch in CA 25-28
Stone, Gregory P(rentice) 1921-1981 ... CANR-1
Obituary ... 116
Earlier sketch in CA 49-52
Stone, Hampton
See Stein, Aaron Marc
Stone, Harris B. 1934- ... 57-60
Stone, Harry 1928- ... 13-14R
Stone, Helen V(irginia) ... 25-28R
See also SATA 6
Stone, Howard W. 1942- ... 124
Stone, Hoyt E(dward) 1935- ... 101
Stone, I(sidor) F(einstein) 1907- ... 61-64
Stone, Idella Purnell
See Purnell, Idella
Stone, Ikey
See Purnell, Idella
Stone, Irving 1903- ... CANR-23
Earlier sketches in CA 1R, CANR-1
See also CAAS 3
See also SATA 3
See also CLC 7
See also AITN 1
Stone, James Champion 1916- ... 17-18R
Stone, James H(erbert) 1918- ... 41-44R
Stone, Jerry 1942(?)-1987 Obituary ... 124
Stone, Joan 1930- ... CANR-13
Earlier sketch in CA 77-80
Stone, John (Timothy, Jr.) 1933- ... 102
Stone, John H(enry) 1936- ... 89-92
Stone, Jon 1931- ... 107
See also SATA 39
Stone, Josephine Rector
See Dixon, Jeanne
Stone, Julius 1907-1985 ... CANR-5
Obituary ... 117
Earlier sketch in CA 53-56
Stone, Justin (Federman) 1916- ... 116
Stone, L(awrence) Joseph 1912-1975
Obituary ... 61-64
Stone, Lawrence 1919- ... 15-16R
Stone, Louis 1910(?)-1985 Obituary ... 115
Stone, Marvin Lawrence 1924- ... 69-72
Stone, Melville 1848-1929 ... DLB-25
Stone, Merlin 1931- ... CANR-17
Earlier sketch in CA 101
Stone, Mildred Fairbanks 1902- ... CAP-1
Earlier sketch in CA 11-12
Stone, Nancy (Young) 1925- ... 49-52
Stone, Natalie
See Goldenbaum, Sally
and Staff, Adrienne
Stone, Oliver 1946- ... 110
Stone, Patti 1926- ... 5-6R
Stone, Peter 1930- ... CANR-7
Earlier sketch in CA 11-12R
Stone, Philip James III 1936- ... 23-24R
Stone, Ralph A. 1934- ... 37-40R
Stone, Raymond ... CANR-26
Earlier sketches in CA 19-20, CAP-2
See also SATA 1
Stone, Reynolds 1909-1979 Obituary ... 89-92
Stone, Richard
See Delaney, Jack J(ames)
Stone, Richard H. ... CANR-26
Earlier sketches in CA 19-20, CAP-2
Stone, Robert (Anthony) 1937- ... CANR-23
Earlier sketch in CA 85-88
See also CLC 5, 23, 42
Stone, Robert B. 1916- ... 29-32R
Stone, Roger D. 1934- ... 119
Stone, Ronald H. 1939- ... CANR-16
Earlier sketch in CA 77-80
Stone, Rosetta
See Geisel, Theodor Seuss
Stone, Rufus
See Cowie, Donald
Stone, Ruth 1915- ... CANR-2
Earlier sketch in CA 45-48
Stone, Samuel 1602-1663 ... DLB-24
Stone, Scott C(linton) S(tuart) 1932- ... CANR-18
Earlier sketch in CA 25-28R
Stone, Shelley C(lyde, Jr.) 1928- ... 61-64
Stone, Susan Berch 1944- ... 61-64
Stone, Thomas H.
See Harknett, Terry
Stone, Vernon A(lfred) 1929- ... 65-68
Stone, Wilfred (Healey) 1917- ... 21-22R
Stone, William F(rank) 1931- ... 41-44R
Stone, William Sidney 1928- ... 13-14R
Stone, Zachary
See Follett, Ken(neth Martin)
Stoneburner, (Charles Joseph) Tony
1926- ... 41-44R
Stonehouse, Bernard 1926- ... CANR-19
Earlier sketches in CA 49-52, CANR-2
See also SATA 13
Stonehouse, John (Thomson) 1925- ... 112
Stonehouse, Merlin 1911- ... 15-16R
Stoneman, Elvyn Arthur 1919- ... 17-18R
Stoneman, Paul 1947- ... 115
Stoneman, William H(arlan) 1904-1987
Obituary ... 122
Stonequist, Everett Verner 1901-1979
Obituary ... 85-88
Stoner, Carol Hupping 1949- ... 53-56
Stones, E(dgar) 1922- ... CANR-15
Earlier sketch in CA 37-40R
Stones, E(dward) L(ionel) G(regory)
1914-1987 Obituary ... 121
Stonesifer, Richard James 1922- ... 15-16R
Stong, Clair L. 1902(?)-1975 Obituary ... 61-64
Stong, Phil(ip Duffield) 1899-1957 ... SATA-32
Stong, Red
See Stong, Clair L.
Stonier, Tom (Ted) 1927- ... 7-8R
Stonor, Oliver 1903- ... CAP-1
Earlier sketch in CA 15-16
Stonum, Gary Lee 1947- ... 89-92
Stoodley, Bartlett Hicks 1907-1978 ... 1R
Obituary ... 103
Stookey, Richard 1938- ... 93-96
Stookey, Robert W(ilson) 1917- ... CANR-14
Earlier sketch in CA 81-84
Stoop, David 1937- ... 119
Stoop, Norma McLain ... 65-68
Stoops, Emery 1902- ... CANR-17
Earlier sketches in CA 1R, CANR-1
Stoops, John A(lbert) 1925- ... 29-32R
Stopelman, Francis
See Stoppelman, Frans
Stopes, M. C.
See Stopes, Marie (Charlotte) Carmichael
Stopes, Marie C.
See Stopes, Marie (Charlotte) Carmichael
Stopes, Marie (Charlotte) Carmichael
1880-1958 Brief entry ... 115
Stopford, Robert Wright 1901- ... CAP-1
Earlier sketch in CA 13-14
Stopp, Elisabeth (Charlotte Vellar-Etscheit)
1911- ... 7-8R
Stoppard, Miriam 1937- ... 120
Stoppard, Tom 1937- ... 81-84
See also DLB 13
See also DLBY 85
See also CLC 1, 3, 4, 5, 8, 15, 29, 34
Stoppelman, Francis
See Stoppelman, Frans
Stoppelman, Frans 1921- ... CAP-1
Earlier sketch in CA 9-10
Storer, Doug(las) 1899-1985 ... 57-60
Obituary ... 118
Storer, J(ames) D(onald) 1928- ... CANR-23
Earlier sketch in CA 107
Storer, Norman W(illiam) 1930- ... 41-44R
Storer, Tracy I(rwin) 1889-1973 ... 13-14R
Obituary ... 126
Storey, Anthony 1928- ... CANR-2
Earlier sketch in CA 49-52
See also DLB 14
Storey, Arthur 1915- ... 45-48
Storey, David (Malcolm) 1933- ... 81-84
See also DLB 13, 14
See also CLC 2, 4, 5, 8
Storey, Edward 1930- ... 97-100
Storey, Edward J. 1901- ... 89-92
Storey, John W(oodrow) 1938- ... 121
Storey, Margaret 1926- ... CANR-1
Earlier sketch in CA 49-52
See also SATA 9
Storey, R(obin) L(indsay) 1927- ... CANR-11
Earlier sketch in CA 21-22R
Storey, Robert F(ranklin) 1945- ... 85-88
Storey, Victoria Carolyn 1945- ... 33-36R
See also SATA 16
Storey, W(illiam) George 1923- ... CANR-6
Earlier sketch in CA 7-8R
Storfer, Muriel (Rosoff) Silberstein
See Silberstein-Storfer, Muriel (Rosoff)
Storing, Herbert James 1928-1977
Obituary ... 73-76
Storke, Thomas More 1876-1971
Obituary ... 89-92
Storm, Christopher
See Olsen, T(heodore) V(ictor)
Storm, Hester G(lory) 1903- ... 11-12R
Storm, Hyemeyohsts 1935- ... 81-84
See also CLC 3
Storm, Lesley
See Clark, Mabel Margaret (Cowie)
Storm, Mallory
See Fairman, Paul W.
Storm, Marian 1892(?)-1975 Obituary ... 61-64
Storm, Russell
See Williams, Robert Moore
Storm, Virginia
See Swatridge, Irene Maude (Mossop)
Storme, Peter
See Stern, Philip Van Doren
Stormer, John A. 1928- ... 25-28R
Storni, Alfonsina 1892-1938 Brief entry ... 104
See also TCLC 5
Storr, Anthony 1920- ... CANR-17
Earlier sketch in CA 97-100
Storr, Catherine (Cole) 1913- ... CANR-23
Earlier sketch in CA 13-14R
See also SATA 9
Storrer, Carol Marchal 1949- ... 112
Storrow, H(ugh) A(lan) 1926- ... 21-22R
Storrow, James J., Jr. 1917-1984
Obituary ... 111
Storry, Richard 1914(?)-1982 Obituary ... 106
Storsve, LaVaughn (Ernestine Kipena)
1921- ... 3R
Story, E(ugenia) Macer
See Macer-Story, E(ugenia)
Story, Edward M. 1921- ... 29-32R
Story, G(eorge) M(orley) 1927- ... CANR-9
Earlier sketch in CA 23-24R
Story, Jack Trevor 1917- ... 29-32R
Story, Josephine
See Loring, Emilie (Baker)
Story, Ronald (D.) 1946- ... CANR-11
Earlier sketch in CA 65-68
Story, Thomas 1670(?)-1742 ... DLB-31
Story, William Wetmore 1819-1895 ... DLB-1
Stotland, Ezra 1924- ... 17-18R
Stott, D(enis) H(erbert) 1909-1988 ... CANR-8
Obituary ... 124
Earlier sketch in CA 13-14R
Stott, Douglas W(ayne) 1948- ... 109
Stott, Jane 1940- ... 85-88
Stott, John R. W. 1921- ... CANR-18
Earlier sketches in CA 5-6R, CANR-2
Stott, Leland H. 1897- ... 25-28R
Stott, Mary 1907- ... 104
Stott, Mike 1944- ... 104
Stott, Raymond Toole
See Toole Stott, Raymond
Stott, William (Merrell) 1940- ... 61-64
Stotts, Herbert Edward 1916- ... CANR-1
Earlier sketch in CA 1R
Stotts, Jack L. 1932- ... 49-52
Stotz, Charles Morse 1898-1985 Obituary ... 115
Stouck, David (Hamilton) 1940- ... 61-64
Stoudemire, Sterling A(ubrey) 1902- ... 37-40R
Stoudt, John Joseph 1911- ... 49-52
Stough, Furman C(harles) 1928-
Brief entry ... 107
Stoughton, Clarence Charles 1895-1975
Obituary ... 61-64
Stoughton, Gertrude K. 1901- ... CAP-2
Earlier sketch in CA 25-28
Stoughton, William 1631-1701 ... DLB-24
Stout, Alan Ker 1900-1983 Obituary ... 110
Stout, Gardner Dominick 1903-1984
Obituary ... 111
Stout, George L(eslie) 1897-1978 ... 81-84
Obituary ... 77-80
Stout, Irving Wright 1903-1972 ... CANR-3
Earlier sketch in CA 1R
Stout, James (Harvey) 1954- ... 119
Stout, Jeffrey Lee 1950- ... 106
Stout, Joseph A(llen), Jr. 1939- ... CANR-2
Earlier sketch in CA 45-48
Stout, Neil Ralph 1932- ... 97-100
Stout, Rex (Todhunter) 1886-1975 ... 61-64
See also CLC 3
See also AITN 2
Stout, Robert Joe 1936- ... 65-68
Stout, Russell, Jr. 1932- ... CANR-18
Earlier sketch in CA 101

Stout, Ruth 1884-1980 ... 33-36R
Obituary ... 120
Stout, Wesley Winans 1889-1971
Obituary ... 89-92
Stout, William 1949- ... 126
Stoutamire, Albert 1921- ... 41-44R
Stoutenburg, Adrien (Pearl) 1916- ... 7-8R
See also SATA 3
Stovall, Floyd 1896- ... 9-10R
Stover, Allan C(arl) 1938- ... CANR-12
Earlier sketch in CA 69-72
See also SATA 14
Stover, Bill
See Stover, W.H.M.
Stover, Jo Ann 1931- ... 37-40R
Stover, John F(ord) 1912- ... CANR-1
Earlier sketch in CA 2R
Stover, Leon E(ugene) 1929- ... CANR-2
Earlier sketch in CA 49-52
Stover, Marjorie Filley 1914- ... 45-48
See also SATA 9
Stover, W(illiam) H(arrison) M(owbray)
1898-1980 ... 103
Obituary ... 97-100
Stover, Webster 1902- ... 53-56
Stow, (Julian) Randolph 1935- ... 13-14R
See also CLC 23, 48
Stowe, Charles E(dwin) Hambrick
See Hambrick-Stowe, Charles E(dwin)
Stowe, David M. 1919- ... 11-12R
Stowe, Harriet (Elizabeth) Beecher
1811-1896 ... YABC-1
See also DLB 1, 12, 42, 74
See also CDALB 1865-1917
Stowe, James L(ewis) 1950- ... 89-92
Stowe, Leland 1899- ... 77-80
See also DLB 29
Stowe, Noel James 1942- ... 106
Stowe, Richard S(cribner) 1925- ... 73-76
Stowe, Rosetta
See Ogan, George F.
and Ogan, Margaret E. (Nettles)
Stowe, William McFerrin 1913- ... 7-8R
Stowell, Joseph M(ishael) 1944- ... 119
Stowers, Carlton 1942- ... CANR-14
Earlier sketch in CA 81-84
Stoy, R(ichard) H(ugh) 1910- ... 57-60
Strabolgi, Bartolomeo
See Tucci, Niccolo
Strachan, Hew (Francis Anthony) 1949- ... 61-64
Strachan, J(ohn) George 1910- ... 107
Strachan, Margaret Pitcairn 1908- ... 7-8R
See also SATA 14
Strachan, T(ony) S(impson) 1920- ... 13-14R
Strachan, W. J.
See Strachan, Walter John
Strachan, Walter John 1903- ... 120
Strachan, Winona Peacock 1918- ... 5-6R
Strachey, Barbara
See Halpern, Barbara Strachey
Strachey, Isobel 1907-1987 Obituary ... 122
Strachey, James 1889(?)-1967 Brief entry ... 124
Strachey, (Evelyn) John (St. Loe)
1901-1963 Obituary ... 93-96
Strachey, (Giles) Lytton 1880-1932
Brief entry ... 110
See also TCLC 12
Strackbein, O(scar) R(obert) 1900- ... 21-22R
Straczynski, J(oseph) Michael 1954- ... 109
Strader, June (Sellers) 1925- ... 97-100
Stradley, Mark
See Smith, Richard Rein
Stradling, Leslie Edward 1908- ... 104
Strage, Mark 1927- ... 81-84
Strahl, Leonard E. 1926- ... 29-32R
Strahlem, Richard E(arl) 1909- ... 37-40R
Straight, Michael Whitney 1916- ... CANR-7
Earlier sketch in CA 5-6R
Strain, Dudley 1909- ... CAP-1
Earlier sketch in CA 11-12
Strain, Frances Bruce ?-1975 ... CAP-2
Earlier sketch in CA 29-32
Strain, Lucille Brewton ... 69-72
Strainchamps, Ethel (Reed) 1912- ... 53-56
Strait, Raymond 1924- ... CANR-4
Earlier sketch in CA 53-56
Strait, Treva Adams 1909- ... 97-100
See also SATA 35
Straiton, E(dward) C(ornock) 1917- ... CANR-19
Earlier sketches in CA 45-48, CANR-3
Straiton, Eddie
See Straiton, E(dward) C(ornock)
Straka, Gerald Milton 1931- ... CANR-2
Earlier sketch in CA 7-8R
Straker, J(ohn) F(oster) 1904- ... CANR-11
Earlier sketch in CA 13-14R
Strakosch, Avery
See Denham, Avery Strakosch
Straley, John A(lonzo) 1894-1966 ... 1R
Obituary ... 103
Strand, Kenneth A(lbert) 1927- ... CANR-3
Earlier sketch in CA 11-12R
Strand, Mark 1934- ... 21-22R
See also SATA 41
See also DLB 5
See also CLC 6, 18, 41
Strand, Paul 1890-1976 Obituary ... 65-68
Strand, Paul E.
See Palestrant, Simon S.
Strand, Thomas 1944- ... 65-68
Strand, William K. 1931- ... 29-32R
Strandberg, Victor H(ugo) 1935- ... CANR-16
Earlier sketch in CA 89-92
Strang, Barbara M(ary) H(ope)
1925-1982 ... 37-40R
Obituary ... 106
Strang, Gerald 1908- ... CAP-2
Earlier sketch in CA 25-28
Strang, Ruth May 1895-1971 ... CANR-2
Earlier sketch in CA 3R
Strange, Dillon
See Norwood, Victor G(eorge) C(harles)
Strange, Jack Roy 1921- ... 19-20R
Strange, James F(rancis) 1938- ... 117
Strange, K(athleen) H(aidee) 1904- ... 113
Strange, Maureen 1948- ... 89-92
Strange, N. Blair
See Sargent, Brian (Lawrence)
Strange, Nora K.
See Stanley, Nora Kathleen Begbie
Strange
Strange, Philippa
See Coury, Louise Andree
Strange, Susan 1923- ... 49-52
Stranger, Joyce
See Wilson, Joyce M(uriel Judson)
Strankay, Sam J(ames) 1905- ... 57-60
Strasberg, Lee 1901-1982 ... 15-16R
Obituary ... 106
Strasberg, Susan (Elizabeth) 1938-
Brief entry ... 120
Strasburger, Victor C. 1949- ... 112
Strassels, Paul N. ... 109
Strasser, Bernard Paul 1895- ... CAP-1
Earlier sketch in CA 9-10
Strasser, Marland K(eith) 1915- ... CANR-6
Earlier sketch in CA 5-6R
Strasser, Otto (Johann Maximilian)
1897-1974 Obituary ... 53-56
Strasser, Susan 1948- ... CANR-24
Earlier sketch in CA 107
Strasser, Todd 1950- ... 123
Brief entry ... 117
See also SATA 41, 45
See also CLR 11
Strassfeld, Michael J. 1950- ... 120
Strassfeld, Sharon M(arcia) 1950- ... 107
Strassmann, W(olfgang) Paul 1926- ... 41-44R
Strassova, Helena 1924- ... 49-52
Stratemeyer, Edward L. 1862-1930 ... CAP-2
Earlier sketch in CA 19-20
See also SATA 1
See also DLB 42
Stratford, H. Philip
See Bulmer, (Henry) Kenneth
Stratford, Philip 1927- ... CANR-5
Earlier sketch in CA 9-10R
See also SATA 47
Strathern, Andrew (Jamieson) 1939- ... CANR-19
Earlier sketches in CA 49-52, CANR-2
Strathern, Ann Marilyn 1941- ... CANR-3
Earlier sketch in CA 49-52
Strati, Saverio 1924- ... CANR-23
Earlier sketches in CA 19-20R, CANR-7
Stratman, Carl J(oseph) 1917-1972 ... CAP-2
Earlier sketch in CA 19-20
Straton, Hillyer H(awthorne) 1905- ... CAP-1
Earlier sketch in CA 9-10
Stratton, Arthur M. 1910(?)-1975
Obituary ... 61-64
Stratton, George Malcolm 1865-1957
Brief entry ... 112
Stratton, Henry
See Nelson, Michael Harrington
Stratton, J(ohn) T(hedore) ... 61-64
Stratton, John R(ay) 1935- ... 45-48
Stratton, Porter Andrew 1918- ... 37-40R
Stratton, Rebecca Brief entry ... 115
Stratton, Roy (Olin) ... CAP-2
Earlier sketch in CA 21-22
Stratton, Ted
See Stratton, J(ohn) T(heodore)
Stratton, Thomas
See Coulson, Robert S(tratton)
and DeWeese, Thomas Eugene
Stratton, William David 1896- ... CAP-1
Earlier sketch in CA 9-10
Stratton-Porter, Gene 1863-1924 ... SATA-15
Stratyner, Barbara Naomi Cohen
See Cohen-Stratyner, Barbara Naomi
Straub, Gerard Thomas 1947- ... 126
Straub, Peter (Francis) 1943- ... 85-88
See also DLBY 84
See also CLC 28
Straubing, Harold (Elk) 1918- ... 126
Strauch, Carl F(erdinand) 1908- ... 41-44R
Strauch, Judith V(ivian) 1942- ... 107
Strauch, Katina (Parthemos) 1946- ... 105
Straughan, Robert P(aul) L(ouis) 1924- ... 49-52
Straughn, Charles (Thomas II) 1933- ... 117
Straumann, Heinrich 1902- ... 13-14R
Straus, Dennis ... CANR-23
Earlier sketch in CA 105
Straus, Dorothea 1916- ... 37-40R
Straus, Murray A(rnold) 1926- ... CANR-10
Earlier sketch in CA 23-24R
Straus, Nathan 1889-1961 Obituary ... 89-92
Straus, Richard 1925-1986 ... CANR-22
Earlier sketch in CA 4R
Straus, Robert 1923- ... CANR-6
Earlier sketch in CA 57-60
Straus, Roger A(ustin) 1948- ... 109
Strauss, Albrecht B(enno) 1921- ... 37-40R
Strauss, Anselm L(eonard) 1916-
Brief entry ... 114
Strauss, Bert(ram) Wiley 1901- ... 15-16R
Strauss, Botho 1944- ... CLC-22
Strauss, David 1937- ... 89-92
Strauss, Elaine Mandle 1916(?)-1982
Obituary ... 107
Strauss, Erich 1911- ... 13-14R
Strauss, Frances 1904- ... CAP-2
Earlier sketch in CA 29-32
Strauss, Gerald 1922- ... 9-10R
Strauss, Hans 1898(?)-1977 Obituary ... 69-72
Strauss, Harold 1907-1975 Obituary ... 104
Strauss, Helen M(arion) 1904(?)-1987
Obituary ... 122
Strauss, Herbert A(rthur) 1918-
Brief entry ... 121
Strauss, Joyce 1936- ... 93-96
See also SATA 53
Strauss, Leo 1899-1973 ... 101
Obituary ... 45-48
Strauss, Lewis Lichtenstein 1896-1974
Obituary ... 45-48
Strauss, (Mary) Lucille Jackson 1908- ... CAP-1
Earlier sketch in CA 11-12
Strauss, Maurice B(enjamin) 1904-1974 ... CAP-2
Earlier sketch in CA 25-28
Strauss, Patricia (Frances O'Flynn)
1909-1987 Obituary ... 123
Strauss, Richard (Georg) 1864-1949
Brief entry ... 118
Strauss, Richard L(ehman) 1933- ... CANR-16
Earlier sketches in CA 49-52, CANR-1
Strauss, Victor 1907(?)-1979 Obituary ... 89-92
Strauss, W(allace) Patrick 1923- ... 41-44R
Strauss, Walter A(dolf) 1923- ... 81-84
Strauss, Walter L(eopold) 1928-1988 ... 81-84
Obituary ... 124
Strauss, Werner 1930- ... 29-32R
Strauss, William Louis 1914- ... 61-64
Strausz-Hupe, Robert 1903- ... 9-10R
Stravinski, Igor Fedorovich
See Stravinsky, Igor Fedorovich
Stravinsky, Igor Fedorovich 1882-1971 ... 107
Obituary ... 29-32R
Stravinsky, Vera 1888-1982 ... 106
Obituary ... 107
Strawinsky, Igor Fedorovich
See Stravinsky, Igor Fedorovich
Strawson, Galen 1952- ... 126
Strawson, John 1921- ... CANR-12
Earlier sketch in CA 29-32R
Strawson, P(eter) F(rederick) 1919- ... 25-28R
Strax, Philip 1909- ... 61-64
Strayer, Barry L. 1932- ... 29-32R
Strayer, E. Ward
See Stratemeyer, Edward L.
Strayer, Joseph Reese 1904-1987 ... 103
Obituary ... 123
Strayer, Sara Barker 1896(?)-1986
Obituary ... 118
Strean, Herbert S(amuel) 1931- ... CANR-19
Earlier sketch in CA 103
Streano, Vince(nt Catello) 1945- ... 53-56
See also SATA 20
Streatfeild, (Mary) Noel 1895(?)-1986 ... 81-84
Obituary ... 120
See also SATA 20, 48
See also CLC 21
Streebeck, Nancy 1934- ... 118
Street, Alicia (Kumpula) 1911- ... 7-8R
Street, Arthur George 1892-1966 ... CAP-1
Earlier sketch in CA 13-14
Street, Harry 1919-1984 Obituary ... 112
Street, James H(arry) 1915-1988 ... CANR-4
Obituary ... 125
Earlier sketch in CA 53-56
Street, Jay
See Slesar, Henry
Street, Julia Montgomery 1898- ... CANR-2
Earlier sketch in CA 5-6R
See also SATA 11
Street, Lee
See Hampton, Kathleen
Street, Leslie
See Freemantle, Brian Harry
Street, Lucie ... 13-14R
Street, Margaret M(ary) 1907- ... 65-68
Street, Mattie (Waters) 1896- ... CAP-1
Earlier sketch in CA 15-16
Street, Pamela 1921- ... 45-48
Street, Robert
See Thomas, Gordon
Streeten, Paul Patrick 1917- ... CANR-11
Earlier sketch in CA 25-28R
Streeter, Edward 1891-1976 ... CANR-2
Obituary ... 65-68
Earlier sketch in CA 4R
See also DLB 11
Streeter, Herbert Andrus 1918- ... 5-6R
Streeter, James (Jr.) ... 61-64
Strehlow, Theodor (George Heinrich)
1908- Brief entry ... 106
Strehlow, Theodor George Henry
See Strehlow, Theodor (George Heinrich)
Streib, Dan(iel Thomas) 1928- ... 106
Streib, Gordon F(ranklin) 1918- ... 112
Streiker, Lowell D(ean) 1939- ... 49-52
Streit, Clarence Kirshman 1896-1986 ... 2R
Obituary ... 119
Streithorst, Tom 1932(?)-1981 Obituary ... 103
Strelka, Joseph P(eter) 1927- ... CANR-26
Earlier sketches in CA 61-64, CANR-8
Strelsky, Katharine (Anderson) ... 108
Strempek, Carol Campbell ... 37-40R
Stren, Patti 1949- ... 124
Brief entry ... 117
See also SATA 41
See also CLR 5
Streng, Frederick J(ohn) 1933- ... 21-22R
Streng, William D(ietrich) 1909- ... CANR-1
Earlier sketch in CA 1R
Streng, William Paul 1937- Brief entry ... 108
Streshinsky, Shirley G. 1934- ... CANR-20
Earlier sketch in CA 85-88
Strete, Craig Kee 1950- ... 114
See also SATA 44
Stretton, Barbara (Humphrey) 1936- ... 116
See also SATA 35, 43
Stretton, Charles
See Dyer, Charles (Raymond)
Stretton, Hesba
See Smith, Sarah
Stretton, Hugh 1924- ... 104
Stretton, Renshaw
See Dyer, Charles (Raymond)
Stribling, T(homas) S(igismund)
1881-1965 Obituary ... 107
See also DLB 9
See also CLC 23
Strich, Christian 1930- ... 109
Strick, Ivy 1952- ... 85-88
Strick, Philip 1939- Brief entry ... 109
Stricker, George 1936- ... CANR-14
Earlier sketch in CA 37-40R
Strickland, Arvarh E(unice) 1930- ... 21-22R
Strickland, Charles E(verett) 1930- ... 77-80
Strickland, Cowles 1903(?)-1971
Obituary ... 33-36R
Strickland, D. A.
See Strickland, Donald A(llen)
Strickland, Donald A(llen) 1934-
Brief entry ... 109
Strickland, Dorothy S(alley) 1933- ... 108
Strickland, Glenn G. 1917- ... 97-100
Strickland, Joshua 1896- ... 81-84
Strickland, Margaret 1930- ... 116
Strickland, Margot 1927- ... CANR-10
Earlier sketch in CA 65-68
Strickland, Phil D. 1941- ... 29-32R
Strickland, Rennard (James) 1940- ... 21-22R
Strickland, Rex W(allace) 1897- ... 45-48
Strickland, Ron(ald Gibson) 1943- ... 122
Strickland, Ruth Gertrude 1898- ... CANR-5
Earlier sketch in CA 5-6R
Strickland, Stephen P(arks) 1933- ... CANR-3
Earlier sketch in CA 45-48
Strickler, Susan (Elizabeth) 1952- ... 124
Strickon, Arnold 1930- Brief entry ... 108
Strieber, Whitley 1945- ... CANR-12
Earlier sketch in CA 81-84
Strieby, Irene Macy 1894- ... CAP-1
Earlier sketch in CA 11-12
Strietelmeier, John (Henry) 1920- ... 25-28R
Stright, Hayden Leroy 1898-1975 ... 37-40R
Strike, Jeremy
See Renn, Thomas E(dward)
Striker, Cecil Leopold 1932- ... 109
Strimple, Earl O. 1938- ... 97-100
Strindberg, (Johan) August 1849-1912
Brief entry ... 104
See also TCLC 1, 8, 21
Stringer, David
See Roberts, Keith (John Kingston)
Stringer, Lorene A(dair) 1908- ... 37-40R
Stringer, Ruth M(arjorie) Pearson 1905- ... 7-8R
Stringer, William Henry 1908-1976
Obituary ... 65-68
Stringfellow, (Frank) William
1928-1985 ... CANR-9
Obituary ... 115
Earlier sketch in CA 5-6R
Stringfield, Leonard H(arry) 1920- ... 85-88
Strittmatter, Erwin 1912- ... DLB-69
Strobel, Margaret 1946- ... 124
Strober, Gerald S. 1935- ... 85-88
Strobos, Robert Julius 1921- ... 102
Strobridge, Truman R(ussell) 1927- ... 41-44R
Strodach, George Kleppinger 1905- ... 5-6R
Strode, Hudson 1892-1976 ... CANR-8
Obituary ... 69-72
Earlier sketch in CA 15-16R
Strodtbeck, Fred L(ouis) 1919- ... 5-6R
Stroeyer, Poul 1923- ... CANR-14
Earlier sketch in CA 77-80
See also SATA 13
Stroh, Guy W(eston) 1931- ... 49-52
Stroh, Thomas F. 1924- ... CANR-11
Earlier sketch in CA 21-22R
Strohm, John
See Strohm, John L(ouis)
Strohm, John L(ouis) 1912-1987 Obituary ... 124
Strohmeyer, John 1924- Brief entry ... 125
Strom, Deborah 1947- ... 123
Strom, Ingrid Mathilda 1912- ... 13-14R
Strom, Leslie Winter
See Winter, Leslie
Strom, Robert D(uane) 1935- ... CANR-10
Earlier sketch in CA 25-28R
Stroman, Duane F(rederick) 1934- ... 104
Stromberg, Gustaf (Benjamin) 1882-1962
Obituary ... 112
Stromberg, Roland N(elson) 1916- ... CANR-21
Earlier sketches in CA 5-6R, CANR-6
Strommen, Merton P. 1919- ... CANR-5
Earlier sketch in CA 11-12R
Strong, Anna Louise 1885-1970
Obituary ... 29-32R
Strong, Charles
See Epstein, Beryl (M. Williams)
and Epstein, Samuel
Strong, Charles Olen 1925- ... 7-8R
Strong, David
See McGuire, Leslie Sarah
Strong, Donald Stuart 1912- ... 41-44R
Strong, Douglas H(illman) 1935- ... 117
Strong, Douglas Hillman 1935- Brief entry ... 111
Strong, Eithne 1923- ... 97-100
Strong, Harrington
See McCulley, Johnston
Strong, J. J.
See Strong, Jeremy
Strong, Jeremy 1949- ... 108
See also SATA 36

Strong, John W. 1930- ... 37-40R
Strong, John William 1935- ... 37-40R
Strong, Jonathan 1944- ... 37-40R
Strong, June 1928- ... 126
Strong, Kenneth William Dobson
1900-1982 ... 104
Obituary ... 105
Strong, Leah A(udrey) 1922- ... 23-24R
Strong, Lennox
See Grier, Barbara G(ene Damon)
Strong, Pat
See Hough, Richard (Alexander)
Strong, Philip Nigel Warrington
1899-1983 ... 109
Obituary ... 110
Strong, Roy (Colin) 1935- ... CANR-21
Earlier sketches in CA 49-52, CANR-1
Strong, Rupert 1911- ... 15-16R
Strong, Solange
See Hertz, Solange (Strong)
Strong, Susan
See Rees, Joan
Strong, Tracy B(urr) 1943- ... 93-96
Strong, William S. 1951- ... 124
Strongblood, Casper
See Webster, David Endicott
Strongin, Lynn 1939- ... CANR-1
Earlier sketch in CA 49-52
Strongman, K(enneth) T(homas)
1940- ... CANR-10
Earlier sketch in CA 61-64
Stroop, Helen E.
See Witty, Helen E. S(troop)
Strother, David B(oyd) 1928- ... 25-28R
Strother, David Hunter 1816-1888 ... DLB-3
Strother, Elsie (Frances Warmoth Weitzel)
1912- ... CANR-11
Earlier sketch in CA 65-68
Strother, Horatio Theodore 1930- ... 5-6R
Strother, Pat Wallace 1929- ... CANR-9
Earlier sketch in CA 65-68
Stroube, Hal 1921(?)-1983 Obituary ... 110
Stroud, Joe H(inton) 1936- ... 103
Stroud, Kandy (Andrea) ... 108
Stroup, Herbert H(ewitt) 1916- ... 15-16R
Stroup, Thomas B(radley) 1903- ... 25-28R
Strouse, Jean 1945- ... 103
Strousse, Flora G. 1897(?)-1974
Obituary ... 49-52
Strout, (Sewall) Cushing (Jr.) 1923- ... 15-16R
Strout, Richard L(ee) 1898- ... 69-72
Strover, Dorothea ... 9-10R
Stroyen, William Basil 1925- ... 25-28R
Stroyer, Poul
See Stroeyer, Poul
Strozier, Charles B(urnett) 1944- ... CANR-24
Earlier sketch in CA 107
Struble, Mitch 1945- ... 93-96
Struble, Virginia
See Burlingame, Virginia (Struble)
Struever, Stuart McKee 1931- ... 104
Strugatskii, Arkadii (Natanovich) 1925- ... 106
See also CLC 27
Strugatskii, Boris (Natanovich) 1933- ... 106
See also CLC 27
Struglia, Erasmus Joseph 1915- ... 15-16R
Struik, Dirk Jan 1894- ... CANR-6
Earlier sketch in CA 7-8R
Struk, Danylo 1940- ... 57-60
Strum, Philippa 1938- ... 61-64
Strummer, Joe 1953(?)- ... CLC-30
Strumpen-Darrie, Robert L. 1912- ... 13-14R
Strung, Norman 1941- ... CANR-14
Earlier sketch in CA 41-44R
Strunk, (William) Oliver 1901-1980 ... 105
Strunk, Oliver 1901-1980 Obituary ... 97-100
Strunk, Orlo, Jr. 1925- ... CANR-1
Earlier sketch in CA 1R
Strunk, William, Jr. 1869-1946
Brief entry ... 118
Strupp, Hans H(ermann) 1921- ... CANR-2
Earlier sketch in CA 1R
Strutt, Malcolm 1936- ... 115
Strutton, William Harold 1918- ... 77-80
Strutz, Henry 1932- ... CANR-24
Earlier sketches in CA 7-8R, CANR-7
Struve, Walter 1935- ... 49-52
Struyk, Raymond J(ay) 1944- Brief entry ... 107
Stryjkowski, Julian 1905- ... CANR-3
Earlier sketch in CA 49-52
Stryk, Dan 1951- ... 120
Stryk, Lucien 1924- ... CANR-10
Earlier sketch in CA 15-16R
Stryker, (Philip) David 1916- ... 45-48
Stryker, Perrin 1908- ... 7-8R
Stryker, Sheldon 1924- ... 9-10R
Stryker-Rodda, Harriet 1905- ... 81-84
Stryker-Rodda, Kenn 1903- ... 73-76
Stuart, Aimee 1886(?)-1981 Obituary ... 103
Stuart, Alex
See Stuart, (Violet) Vivian (Finlay)
Stuart, Alice V(andockum) 1899- ... 13-14R
Stuart, Anthony
See Hale, Julian A(nthony) S(tuart)
Stuart, Charles
See Mackinnon, Charles Roy
and Reid, Charles (Stuart)
Stuart, Clay
See Whittington, Harry (Benjamin)
Stuart, Colin 1910- ... 104
Stuart, Dabney 1937- ... CANR-8
Earlier sketch in CA 17-18R
Stuart, David
See Hoyt, Edwin P(almer), Jr.
Stuart, Don A.
See Campbell, John W(ood)
Stuart, Douglas (Keith) 1943- ... 115
Stuart, Forbes 1924- ... 69-72
See also SATA 13
Stuart, Francis 1902- ... 13-14R
Stuart, Graham H. 1887- ... CAP-1
Earlier sketch in CA 13-14
Stuart, Ian 1927- ... CANR-13
Earlier sketch in CA 73-76
Stuart, Ian
See MacLean, Alistair (Stuart)
Stuart, Irving R. 1916- ... CANR-14
Earlier sketch in CA 41-44R
Stuart, Jane 1942- ... 41-44R
Stuart, Jay Allison
See Tait, Dorothy
Stuart, Jesse (Hilton) 1907-1984 ... 7-8R
Obituary ... 112
See also SATA 2, 36
See also DLB 9, 48
See also DLBY 84
See also CLC 1, 8, 11, 14, 34
Stuart, Kenneth
See Cox, P(atrick) Brian
See also DLB 9
Stuart, Leslie
See Marlowe, Kenneth
Stuart, Lyle 1922- ... 81-84
Stuart, Margaret
See Paine, Lauran (Bosworth)
Stuart, Monroe
See Shapiro, Max
Stuart, Reginald (Charles) 1943- ... 116
Stuart, Richard Bernard 1933- ... 41-44R
Stuart, Sheila
See Baker, Mary Gladys Steel
Stuart, Sidney
See Avallone, Michael (Angelo), Jr.
Stuart, Simon (Walter Erskine) 1930- ... 29-32R
Stuart, V. A.
See Stuart, (Violet) Vivian (Finlay)
Stuart, (Violet) Vivian (Finlay) 1914- ... CANR-12
Earlier sketch in CA 13-14R
Stuart, W. J.
See MacDonald, Philip
Stuart, Warren
See MacDonald, Philip
Stuart-Clark, Christopher (Anthony)
1940- ... CANR-24
Earlier sketch in CA 107
See also SATA 32
Stuart-Jones, Edwyn Henry 1895-19(?) ... CAP-1
Earlier sketch in CA 15-16
Stub, Holger R(ichard) 1922- ... 41-44R
Stubbings, Hilda Uren
See U'Ren-Stubbings, Hilda
Stubblebine, James H(arvey) 1920-1987 ... 97-100
Obituary ... 121
Stubblefield, Harold W. 1934- ... 17-18R
Stubbs, Harry C(lement) 1922- ... CANR-26
Earlier sketches in CA 15-16R, CANR-7
Stubbs, Jean 1926- ... 7-8R
Stubbs, Joanna 1940- ... SATA-53
Stubbs, John C(aldwell) 1936- ... 29-32R
Stubbs, P(eter) C(harles) 1937- ... 117
Stuber, Florian (Cy) 1947- ... CANR-24
Earlier sketch in CA 106
Stuber, Stanley I(rving) 1903-1985 ... CAP-1
Obituary ... 116
Earlier sketch in CA 13-14
Stubis, Talivaldis 1926- ... SATA-5
Stubley, Trevor (Hugh) 1932- ... SATA-22
Stuckenschmidt, H(ans) H(einz)
1901-1988 ... CANR-18
Obituary ... 126
Earlier sketch in CA 25-28R
Stuckey, Elma 1907(?)-1988 Obituary ... 126
Stuckey, Gilbert B. 1912- ... 65-68
Stuckey, Sterling 1932- ... 101
Stuckey, William Joseph 1923- ... 41-44R
Stucki, Curtis W(illiam) 1928- ... 15-16R
Stucky, Solomon 1923- ... 117
Stucky, Steven 1949- ... 109
Stucley, Elizabeth
See Northmore, Elizabeth Florence
Studd, Stephen (Allen) 1946- ... 116
Studer, Gerald C. 1927- ... 65-68
Studlar, Donley T(rent) 1947- ... 120
Stueart, Robert D. 1935- ... 105
Stuebing, (Arthur) Douglas 1913- ... 25-28R
Stueck, William Whitney, Jr. 1945- ... 105
Stuempke, Harald
See Steiner, Gerolf
Stuermann, Walter E(arl) 1919-1965 ... 5-6R
Stuermer, Nina Roberta 1933- ... 104
Stuerup, Georg Kristoffer 1905- ... 25-28R
Stuhlmann, Gunther 1927- ... 25-28R
Stuhlmueller, Carroll 1923- ... CANR-24
Earlier sketches in CA 15-16R, CANR-9
Stulman, Julius 1906- ... 118
Stultifer, Morton
See Curtis, Richard (Alan)
Stultz, Newell M(aynard) 1933- ... 29-32R
Stumpf, Samuel Enoch 1918- ... 41-44R
Stumpf, Stephen A(lan) 1949- ... 111
Stumpke, Harald
See Steiner, Gerolf
Stunkard, Albert J(ames) 1922- ... 117
Stuntz, Albert Edward 1902-1976
Obituary ... 65-68
Stuntz, Laurance F(itzhugh) 1908- ... 61-64
Stupak, Ronald J(oseph) 1934- ... 29-32R
Sturdivant, Frederick D(avid) 1937- ... 41-44R
Sturgeon, Foolbert
See Stack, Frank H(untington)
Sturgeon, Theodore Hamilton 1918-1985 ... 81-84
Obituary ... 116
See also DLB 8
See also DLBY 85
See also CLC 22, 39
Sturgeon, Wina ... 85-88
Sturges, Patricia P(atterson) 1930- ... 69-72
Sturges, Preston 1898-1959 Brief entry ... 114
See also DLB 26
Sturgill, Claude C(arol) 1933- ... CANR-9
Earlier sketch in CA 15-16R
Sturgis, James L(averne) 1936- ... 37-40R
Sturm, Ernest 1932- ... 65-68
Sturm, John E. 1927- ... 37-40R
Sturm, Rudolf 1912- Brief entry ... 109
Sturm, Sara
See Sturm-Maddox, Sara Higgins
Sturmey, S(tanley) G(eorge) 1924- ... 9-10R
Sturm-Maddox, Sara Higgins 1938-
Brief entry ... 108
Sturmthal, Adolf F(ox) 1903-1986 ... 11-12R
Obituary ... 119
Sturrock, Jeremy
See Healey, Ben (James)
Stursberg, Peter 1913- ... 101
Sturt, Mary 1896- ... CAP-2
Earlier sketch in CA 23-24
Sturtevant, Catherine ?-1970 Obituary ... 104
Sturtevant, David Reeves 1926- ... 104
Sturtevant, Peter M(ann), Jr. 1943- ... 69-72
Sturton, Hugh
See Johnston, H(ugh) A(nthony)
S(tephen)
Sturtzel, Howard A(llison) 1894- ... CANR-6
Earlier sketch in CA 2R
See also SATA 1
Sturtzel, Jane Levington 1903- ... CANR-6
Earlier sketch in CA 2R
See also SATA 1
Sturup, Georg Kristoffer
See Stuerup, Georg Kristoffer
Stutler, Boyd B. 1889-1970 ... CAP-2
Earlier sketch in CA 23-24
Stutz, Robert Michael 1941- Brief entry ... 110
Stutzman, Esther M. Friesner
See Friesner-Stutzman, Esther M.
Styan, J(ohn) L(ouis) 1923- ... CANR-6
Earlier sketch in CA 5-6R
Stycos, J(oseph) Mayone 1927- ... 13-14R
Styles, Jimmie C(arter) 1931- ... 41-44R
Styles, (Frank) Showell 1908- ... CANR-21
Earlier sketches in CA 4R, CANR-6
See also SATA 10
Stylla, Joanne
See Branden, Victoria (Fremlin)
Styron, Rose (Burgunder) 1928- ... 17-18R
Styron, William 1925- ... CANR-6
Earlier sketch in CA 5-6R
See also DLB 2
See also DLBY 80
See also CLC 1, 3, 5, 11, 15
Styx, Marguerite (Salzer) 1908(?)-1975
Obituary ... 53-56
Suares, Guy 1932- ... 103
Suarez Lynch, B.
See Bioy Casares, Adolfo
and Borges, Jorge Luis
Suba, Susanne ... 29-32R
See also SATA 4
Subak-Sharpe, Genell J(ackson) 1936- ... 112
Subbiah, B(ommireddi) V(enkata)
1917-1975 ... 41-44R
Subilia, Vittorio 1911- ... CANR-4
Earlier sketch in CA 9-10R
Sublette, Edith Blanche 1909- ... 17-18R
Sublette, Walter (Edwards) 1940- ... 124
Brief entry ... 117
Subond, Valerie
See Grayland, Valerie (Merle Spanner)
Such, Peter 1939- ... DLB-60
Sucharitkul, Somtow 1952- ... 118
Sucher, Harry V(ictor) 1915- ... 89-92
Su Chien 1884-1918 Brief entry ... 123
Suchlicki, Jaime 1939- ... 29-32R
Suchman, Edward A(llen) 1915-197(?) ... CAP-1
Earlier sketch in CA 13-14
Suchocki, Marjorie Hewitt 1933- ... 109
Suchoff, Benjamin 1918- ... CANR-11
Earlier sketch in CA 69-72
Suckling, John 1609-1642 ... DLB-58
Suckow, Ruth 1892-1960 Obituary ... 113
See also DLB 9
Suda, Zdenek 1920- ... 29-32R
Sudbery, Rodie 1943- ... 104
See also SATA 42
Sudermann, Hermann 1857-1928
Brief entry ... 107
See also TCLC 15
Sudhalter, Richard M(errill) 1938- ... 101
Sudman, Seymour 1928- ... CANR-15
Earlier sketch in CA 41-44R
Sue, Judy
See Epstein, Judith Sue
Suedfeld, Peter 1935- ... 41-44R
Suelflow, August R(obert) 1922- ... 11-12R
Sueltz, Arthur Fay 1928- ... CANR-2
Earlier sketch in CA 49-52
Suenens, Leon Joseph 1904- ... 61-64
Sueskind, Patrick 1949- ... CLC-44
Suffling, Mark
See Rowland, D(onald) S(ydney)
Sufrin, Sidney Charles 1910- ... CANR-17
Earlier sketches in CA 5-6R, CANR-2
Sugano, Takuo 1931- ... 123
Sugar, Bert Randolph 1937- ... CANR-9
Earlier sketch in CA 65-68
Sugarman, Daniel A(rthur) 1931- ... 21-22R
Sugarman, Tracy 1921- ... 21-22R
See also SATA 37
Sugden, John 1947- ... 120
Sugden, Mark 1902- ... CAP-1
Earlier sketch in CA 13-14
Sugerman, Shirley 1919- ... 65-68
Sugg, Redding S(tancill), Jr. 1922- ... CANR-2
Earlier sketch in CA 45-48
Suggs, George G(raham), Jr. 1929- ... 41-44R
Suggs, M(arion) Jack 1924- ... CANR-3
Earlier sketch in CA 1R
Suggs, Robert Carl 1932- ... 9-10R
Suggs, Willie Kathryn 1950- ... 77-80
Sugita, Yutaka 1930- ... 115
See also SATA 36
Sugnet, Charles (Joseph) 1944- ... 109
Suh, Dae-Sook 1931- ... 21-22R
Suhl, Benjamin ... 49-52
Suhl, Yuri 1908-1986 ... CANR-2
Obituary ... 121
Earlier sketch in CA 45-48
See also SATA 8, 50
See also SAAS 1
See also CLR 2
Suhor, Charles 1935- ... CANR-10
Earlier sketch in CA 25-28R
Suhr, Elmer George 1902-1976 ... 11-12R
Obituary ... 65-68
Su Hsuan-ying
See Su Chien
Su Hsuean-ying
See Su Chien
Suid, Lawrence Howard 1938- ... 101
Suid, Murray 1942- ... 97-100
See also SATA 27
Suinn, Richard M(ichael) 1933- ... 29-32R
Suits, Daniel B(urbidge) 1918- ... 29-32R
Sujata, Anagarika 1948- ... 65-68
Suk, Julie ... 115
Sukarno, (Ahmed) 1901-1970 Obituary ... 113
Sukenick, Ronald 1932- ... 25-28R
See also DLBY 81
See also CLC 3, 4, 6, 48
Sukhotin-Tolstoy, Tatyana
See Tolstoy, Tatyana (Sukhotin)
Sukhwal, Bheru Lal 1929- ... 57-60
Sukiennik, Adelaide Weir 1938- ... 126
Suknaski, Andrew 1942- ... 101
See also DLB 53
See also CLC 19
Suleiman, Ezra N. 1941- ... 85-88
Suleiman, Michael W(adie) 1934- ... CANR-9
Earlier sketch in CA 21-22R
Suleiman, Susan Rubin ... 109
Sulimirski, Tadeusz Joseph 1898-1983
Obituary ... 110
Sulitzer, Paul-Loup 1946- ... 126
Brief entry ... 122
Sulkin, Sidney 1918- ... CANR-17
Earlier sketches in CA 5-6R, CANR-2
Sullens, Idelle 1921- ... 23-24R
Sullivan, A(loysius) M(ichael) 1896-1980 ... CAP-2
Obituary ... 97-100
Earlier sketch in CA 29-32
Sullivan, Alvin 1942- ... 29-32R
Sullivan, Anita T. 1942- ... 123
Sullivan, C(harles) Gardner 1886(?)-1965
Obituary ... 113
See also DLB 26
Sullivan, Chester L(amar) 1939- ... 53-56
Sullivan, Clara K(atherine) 1915- ... 23-24R
Sullivan, Colleen ... 117
Sullivan, D(ale) H(owill) 1936- ... 61-64
Sullivan, Denis G(artland) 1929- ... 103
Sullivan, Dulcie Turner 1895-1969 ... CAP-2
Earlier sketch in CA 25-28
Sullivan, Earl L. 1942- ... 124
Sullivan, Ed(ward Vincent) 1902(?)-1974
Obituary ... 89-92
Sullivan, Edmund V(incent) 1938- ... 61-64
Sullivan, Edward A(nthony) 1936- ... 115
Sullivan, Edward Daniel 1913- ... 7-8R
Sullivan, Eleanor (Regis) 1928- Brief entry ... 112
Sullivan, Elizabeth L. 1904(?)-1985
Obituary ... 115
Sullivan, Francis (Patrick) 1929- ... CANR-7
Earlier sketch in CA 57-60
Sullivan, Francis John 1892-1976 ... CAP-2
Obituary ... 65-68
Earlier sketch in CA 25-28
Sullivan, Frank 1912-1975 ... 65-68
Obituary ... 61-64
Sullivan, Frank
See Sullivan, Francis John
See also DLB 11
Sullivan, George Edward 1927- ... 13-14R
See also SATA 4
Sullivan, J(ohn) P(atrick) 1930- ... CANR-26
Earlier sketches in CA 25-28R, CANR-10
Sullivan, Jack 1946- ... 119
Sullivan, James L(enox) 1910- ... 29-32R
Sullivan, Jerry 1938- ... 115
Sullivan, John L. 1908- ... 21-22R
Sullivan, Judy 1936- ... 53-56
See also AITN 1
Sullivan, Kevin 1918(?)-1987 ... 1R
Obituary ... 122
Sullivan, Marion F. 1899- ... 37-40R
Sullivan, Mark W(ilbur) 1927- ... 25-28R
Sullivan, Martin (Gloster) 1910-1980 ... 107
Obituary ... 104
Sullivan, Martin (Richard Preece) 1934- ... 29-32R
Sullivan, Mary Ann 1954- ... 125
Sullivan, Mary B(arrett) 1918- ... 15-16R
Sullivan, Mary W(ilson) 1907- ... CANR-12
Earlier sketch in CA 73-76
See also SATA 13

Sullivan, Maurice William 1925- CANR-2
Earlier sketch in CA 7-8R
Sullivan, (Donovan) Michael 1916- CANR-3
Earlier sketch in CA 5-6R
Sullivan, Michael B. 1938- 77-80
Sullivan, Nancy 1929- 17-18R
Sullivan, Navin 1929- 5-6R
Sullivan, Pat
See Messmer, Otto
Sullivan, Peggy (Anne) 1929- CANR-12
Earlier sketch in CA 29-32R
Sullivan, Prescott 1904(?)-1985 Obituary ... 116
Sullivan, Richard 1908-1981 77-80
Obituary 104
Sullivan, Richard E(ugene) 1921-
Brief entry 115
Sullivan, Rosemary 1947- 97-100
Sullivan, Ruth Christ 1924- 57-60
Sullivan, Sean Mei
See Sohl, Jerry
Sullivan, Sheila 1927- CANR-14
Earlier sketch in CA 77-80
Sullivan, Sister Bede 1915- 25-28R
Sullivan, Thomas Joseph, Jr. 1947- 81-84
See also SATA 16
Sullivan, Tom
See Sullivan, Thomas Joseph, Jr.
Sullivan, Vernon
See Vian, Boris
Sullivan, Victoria 1943- 65-68
Sullivan, Vincent F. 1899- CAP-2
Earlier sketch in CA 29-32
Sullivan, Walter 1906- 15-16R
Sullivan, Walter (Laurence) 1924- 41-44R
Sullivan, Walter Seager 1918- CANR-2
Earlier sketch in CA 3R
Sullivan, William M. 1945- 109
Sullivant, Robert S(cott) 1925- 1R
Sulloway, Alison G. 1917- Brief entry 111
Sulloway, Frank J(ones) 1947- 124
Brief entry 118
Sully, (Lionel Henry) Francois 1927-1971 . CAP-2
Obituary 29-32R
Earlier sketch in CA 25-28
Sully, Kathleen M. 1910- 15-16R
Sully, Nina (Rosemary) 1948- 110
Sultan, Arne 1925-1986 Obituary 118
Sultan, Stanley 1928- CANR-26
Earlier sketches in CA 15-16R, CANR-10
Sultana, Donald Edward 1924- 103
Sulzberger, Arthur Hays 1891-1968
Obituary 89-92
Sulzberger, C(yrus) L(eo II) 1912- CANR-23
Earlier sketches in CA 53-56, CANR-7
Sulzberger, Marina Tatiana 1919(?)-1976
Obituary 111
Su Man-shu
See Su Chien
See also TCLC 24
Sumichrast, Jozef 1948- SATA-29
Sumichrast, Michael M. 1921- CANR-21
Earlier sketch in CA 104
Sumida, Jon Tetsuro 1949- 124
Sumiko
See Davies, Sumiko
Summer, Brian
See Du Breuil, (Elizabeth) L(or)inda
Summer, Charles Edgar 1923- 81-84
Summerfield, Harry L. 1940- 37-40R
Summerfield, Jack
See Summerfield, John D(udley)
Summerfield, Joanne 1940- 117
Summerfield, John D(udley) 1927- 23-24R
Summerfield, Margie 1949- 89-92
Summerfield, Penny 1951- 119
Summerforest, Ivy B.
See Kirkup, James
Summerhayes, Victor Samuel
1897(?)-1974 Obituary 53-56
Summerhill, J. K.
See Schere, Monroe
Summerlin, Sam(uel A.) 1928- 45-48
Summers, Andrew James 1942- CLC-26
Summers, Andy
See Summers, Andrew James
Summers, Anthony (Bruce) 1942- CANR-23
Earlier sketch in CA 69-72
Summers, Clyde Wilson 1918- 109
Summers, Essie
See Summers, Ethel Snelson
Summers, Ethel Snelson 1912- Brief entry .. 116
Summers, Festus P(aul) 1895- CAP-1
Earlier sketch in CA 11-12
Summers, Gene F(ranklin) 1936- CANR-12
Earlier sketch in CA 29-32R
Summers, Gordon
See Hornby, John (Wilkinson)
Summers, Hal
See Summers, Henry Forbes
Summers, Harrison B(oyd) 1894- 13-14R
Summers, Harry G(lenn), Jr. 1932- 123
Summers, Henry Forbes 1911- 109
Summers, Hollis (Spurgeon, Jr.) 1916- . CANR-3
Earlier sketch in CA 5-6R
See also DLB 6
See also CLC 10
Summers, Ian 1939- 105
Summers, James L(evingston) 1910- 15-16R
See also SATA 28
Summers, JoAn 1943- 106
Summers, John A.
See Lawson, H(orace) L(owe)
Summers, Joseph H(olmes) 1920- 41-44R
Summers, Lionel M(organ) 1905-1975 45-48
Obituary 103
Summers, (Alphonsus Joseph-Mary Augustus) Montague 1880-1948
Brief entry 118
See also TCLC 16
Summers, Ray 1910- 13-14R
Summers, Robert 1922- 77-80
Summers, Robert E. 1918- 25-28R
Summers, Robert S(amuel) 1933- CANR-11
Earlier sketch in CA 69-72
Summers, Rowena
See Saunders, Jean
Summerscales, William 1921- 29-32R
Summersell, Charles Grayson 1908- ... CANR-19
Earlier sketches in CA 2R, CANR-3
Summerskill, Edith 1901-1980 Obituary ...93-96
Summerson, John (Newenham) 1904-
Brief entry 117
Summerson, Rachel (Elizabeth) 1944- 107
Summerville, James 1947- 119
Sumner, Cid Ricketts 1890-1970 ....5-6R
Obituary 29-32R
Sumner, Colin 1949- 111
Sumner, David (W. K.) 1937- 57-60
Sumner, Eldon
See Bruno, James Edward
Sumner, Gordon Matthew 1951- CLC-26
Sumner, Lloyd Quinton 1943- 103
Sumner, Richard (William) 1949- 69-72
Sumwalt, Martha Murray 1924- 69-72
Sun, Ruth Q(uinlan) 1907- 57-60
Sunagel, Lois A(nn) 1926- 93-96
Sund, Robert B(ruce) 1926- 29-32R
Sundarananda
See Nakashima, George Katsutoshi
Sunday, Billy
See Sunday, William Ashley
Sunday, William Ashley 1862(?)-1935
Brief entry 120
Sundberg, Trudy James 1925- 17-18R
Sundell, Roger H(enry) 1936- 23-24R
Sunder, Shyam 1944- 118
Sunderland, Eric 1930- CANR-21
Earlier sketch in CA 103
Sunderland, Glenn W. 1925- 25-28R
Sunderland, Lane V(on) 1945- 97-100
Sunderlin, Sylvia 1911- 73-76
See also SATA 28
Sunderman, James F. 1919- 19-20R
Sunderman, Lloyd Frederick 1905-1983
Obituary 109
Sundgaard, Arnold (Olaf) 1909- CANR-2
Earlier sketch in CA 45-48
Sundman, Per Olof 1922- Brief entry 111
Sundquist, James L(loyd) 1915- 29-32R
Sundquist, Ralph Roger, Jr. 1922-
Brief entry 106
Sung, Betty Lee CANR-10
Earlier sketch in CA 25-28R
See also SATA 26
Sung, P. M.
See Chun, Jinsie K(yung) S(hein)
Sungolowsky, Joseph 1931- 41-44R
Sunners, William 1903-1988 .... CAP-1
Obituary 125
Earlier sketch in CA 9-10
Sunoo, Harold Hak-Won 1918- 41-44R
Sunseri, Alvin R(aymond) 1925- 93-96
Sunshine, John 1897(?)-1987 Obituary 123
Sunstein, Emily W(eisberg) 1924- 53-56
Suny, Ronald Grigor 1940- 111
Sun Yat-sen, Madame
See Soong Ching-ling
Sun Yefang 1908-1983 Obituary 109
Super, Donald E(dwin) 1910- CANR-3
Earlier sketch in CA 3R
Super, R(obert) H(enry) 1914- 15-16R
Super Santa
See Berman, Ed
Supervielle, Jules 1884-1960 Obituary 114
Suponev, Michael 1923- 65-68
Suppe, Frederick (Roy) 1940- 41-44R
Suppes, Patrick (Colonel) 1922- CANR-20
Earlier sketches in CA 2R, CANR-4
Supraner, Robyn 1930- CANR-26
Earlier sketch in CA 69-72
See also SATA 20
Supree, Burt(on) 1941- 65-68
Surace, Samuel J. 1919- 21-22R
Suran, Bernard G(regory) 1939- 81-84
Suransky, Valerie Polakow
See Polakow, Valerie (Suransky)
Suret-Canale, Jean 1921- CANR-1
Earlier sketch in CA 49-52
Surette, (Philip) Leon 1938- 110
Surface, Bill
See Surface, William E.
Surface, William E. 1935-1980(?) CANR-13
Earlier sketch in CA 7-8R
Surge, Frank 1931- 69-72
See also SATA 13
Surkin, Marvin 1938- 61-64
Surkov, Alexei Aleksandrovich 1899-1983
Obituary 110
Surles, Lynn 1917- 13-14R
Surman, Charles Edward 1901- 7-8R
Surmelian, Leon (Zaven) 1907- CAP-2
Earlier sketch in CA 25-28
Surplus, Robert W. 1923- 7-8R
Surrey, (Arthur) John 1933- 117
Surrey, Peter J. 1928- 106
Surrey, Stanley Sterling 1910-1984
Obituary 113
Surtees, Robert Smith 1803-1864 .... DLB-21
Surtz, Edward 1910(?)-1973 Obituary 41-44R
Susac, Andrew 1929- 49-52
See also SATA 5
Susan
See Graham, (Maude Fitzgerald) Susan
Susann, Jacqueline 1921-1974 65-68
Obituary 53-56
See also CLC 3
See also AITN 1
Suskind, Patrick
See Sueskind, Patrick
Suskind, Richard 1925- CANR-9
Earlier sketch in CA 15-16R
Suslov, Alexander 1950- 105
Suslov, Mikhail Andreyevich 1902-1982
Obituary 105
Susman, Warren (Irving) 1927-1985
Obituary 116
Suss, Elaine 102
Susser, Mervyn (Wilfred) 1921- CANR-1
Earlier sketch in CA 45-48
Susser, Samuel S. 1910- 97-100
Susskind, Charles 1921- CANR-15
Earlier sketch in CA 85-88
Sussman, Aaron 1903- Brief entry 116
Sussman, Barry 1934- 53-56
Sussman, Cornelia Silver 1914- CANR-13
Earlier sketch in CA 7-8R
Sussman, Henry 1947- 111
Sussman, Herbert L. 1937- 25-28R
Sussman, Irving 1908- CANR-13
Earlier sketch in CA 77-80
Sussman, Leonard R(ichard) 1920- CANR-4
Earlier sketch in CA 53-56
Sussman, Marvin B(ernard) 1918- CANR-19
Earlier sketches in CA 11-12R, CANR-4
Sussman, Susan 1942- 111
See also SATA 48
Sutch, Richard C(harles) 1942- 107
Sutcliff, Rosemary 1920- 5-6R
See also SATA 6, 44
See also CLC 26
See also CLR 1
Sutcliffe, Anthony (Richard) 1942- 106
Suter, Ronald 1930- 41-44R
Sutermeister, Robert Arnold 1913- 5-6R
Suther, Marshall E(dward), Jr. 1918- 1R
Sutherland, Arthur Eugene, Jr.
1902-1973 .... CAP-1
Obituary 41-44R
Earlier sketch in CA 19-20
Sutherland, C(arol) Humphrey V(ivian)
1908- 13-14R
Sutherland, Daniel E(llyson) 1946- CANR-26
Earlier sketch in CA 109
Sutherland, Donald 1915- 37-40R
Sutherland, Donald W(ayne) 1931- 9-10R
Sutherland, Douglas 1919- 23-24R
Sutherland, Earl Wilbur 1915-1974
Obituary 49-52
Sutherland, Efua (Theodora Morgue)
1924- 105
See also BW
See also SATA 25
Sutherland, Elizabeth 1926- 85-88
Sutherland, Elizabeth
See Martinez, Elizabeth Sutherland
Sutherland, Fraser 1946- 102
Sutherland, Gordon (Brims Black McIvor)
1907-1980 Obituary 108
Sutherland, H(erbert) W(arren) 1917- 13-14R
Sutherland, James (Edward) 1948- CANR-2
Earlier sketch in CA 49-52
Sutherland, John 1919-1956 .... DLB-68
Sutherland, John (Patrick) 1920-1988 ....21-22R
Obituary 125
Sutherland, John (Anthony) 1933- CANR-16
Earlier sketch in CA 93-96
Sutherland, Jon Nicholas 1941- 41-44R
Sutherland, Lucy Stuart 1903-1980 ...... CAP-1
Obituary 105
Earlier sketch in CA 13-14
Sutherland, Margaret 1941- CANR-14
Earlier sketch in CA 77-80
See also SATA 15
Sutherland, N(icola) M(ary) 1925- 49-52
Sutherland, R(ussell) Galbraith 1924- CAP-1
Earlier sketch in CA 9-10
Sutherland, Robert D(onald) 1937- 37-40R
Sutherland, Roger
See Hicks, Roger W(illiam)
Sutherland, Ronald 1933- 25-28R
Sutherland, (Norman) Stuart 1927- 65-68
Sutherland, (William) Temple (Gairdner)
1906- CAP-1
Earlier sketch in CA 9-10
Sutherland, Zena Bailey 1915- 102
See also SATA 37
Suthinee
See Ambhanwong, Suthilak
Suthren, Victor (James Henry) 1942- .. CANR-23
Earlier sketch in CA 107
Sutnar, Ladislav 1897-1976 Obituary 104
Sutphen, Dick
See Sutphen, Richard Charles
Sutphen, Richard Charles 1937- CANR-11
Earlier sketch in CA 25-28R
Sutro, Alfred 1863-1933 Brief entry 105
See also DLB 10
See also TCLC 6
Sutro, John 1903(?)-1985 Obituary 117
Sutryn, Barbara M(ay) 1927- 120
Sutter, Franz
See Strich, Christian
Sutter, Frederic Koehler 1938- 107
Sutter, Ruth E(laine) 1935- 45-48
Suttles, Gerald 1932- 85-88
Suttles, Shirley (Smith) 1922- 15-16R
See also SATA 21
Suttmeier, Richard Peter 1942- CANR-6
Earlier sketch in CA 57-60
Sutton, Ann (Livesay) 1923- CANR-10
Earlier sketch in CA 5-6R
See also SATA 31
Sutton, Antony C. 1925- 97-100
Sutton, Barry 1919-1988 Obituary 125
Sutton, Carol 1933-1985 Obituary 115
Sutton, Caroline 1953- 106
Sutton, Christine 1950- 120
Sutton, David (John) 1944- 116
Sutton, David 1947- 101
Sutton, Denys 1917- CANR-20
Earlier sketches in CA 53-56, CANR-5
Sutton, Eve(lyn Mary) 1906- CANR-10
Earlier sketch in CA 65-68
See also SATA 26
Sutton, Felix 1910(?)- 77-80
See also SATA 31
Sutton, George Miksch 1898-1982 107
Obituary 109
Sutton, Gordon 1910- 23-24R
Sutton, Henry
See Slavitt, David R.
Sutton, Horace (Ashley) 1919- CANR-10
Earlier sketch in CA 13-14R
Sutton, Howard 1930- 65-68
Sutton, Jane 1950- 89-92
See also SATA 43, 52
Sutton, Jeff
See Sutton, Jefferson (Howard)
Sutton, Jefferson (Howard)
1913-1979 .... CANR-10
Earlier sketch in CA 23-24R
Sutton, John L(awrence) 1917- 105
Sutton, L(aurence) P(aul) Elwell
See Elwell-Sutton, L(aurence) P(aul)
Sutton, Larry M(atthew) 1931- CANR-14
Earlier sketch in CA 37-40R
See also SATA 29
Sutton, Margaret Beebe 1903- 1R
See also SATA 1
Sutton, Maurice Lewis 1927- 13-14R
Sutton, Max Keith 1937- 93-96
Sutton, Myron Daniel 1925- 107
See also SATA 31
Sutton, Penny
See Wood, Christopher (Hovelle)
Sutton, Remar 1941- 126
Sutton, Robert M(ize) 1915- 77-80
Sutton, Roberta Briggs 1899- 7-8R
Sutton, S(tephanne) B(arry) 1940- 29-32R
Sutton, Stack
See Sutton, Maurice Lewis
Sutton, Tony C.
See Sutton, Antony C.
Sutton, Walter 1916- 85-88
Sutton, William A(lfred) 1915- 61-64
Sutton-Smith, Brian 1924- CANR-17
Earlier sketch in CA 29-32R
Sutton-Vane, Vane Hunt
See Vane, (Vane Hunt) Sutton
Suttor, T(imothy) L(achlan) 1926- 21-22R
Suvin, Darko (Ronald) 1930- CANR-16
Earlier sketch in CA 89-92
Suvorov, Viktor (a pseudonym) 116
Suyin, Han
See Han, Suyin
Su Yuan-ying
See Su Chien
Su Yuean-ying
See Su Chien
Suzuki, D. T.
See Suzuki, Daisetz Teitaro
Suzuki, Daisetz T.
See Suzuki, Daisetz Teitaro
Suzuki, Daisetz Teitaro 1870-1966 121
Obituary 111
Suzuki, Teitaro
See Suzuki, Daisetz Teitaro
Suzuki, Tessa Morris
See Morris-Suzuki, Tessa
Svajian, Stephen G. 1906(?)-1977
Obituary 73-76
Svareff, Count Vladimir
See Crowley, Edward Alexander
Svarlien, Oscar 1906- CAP-1
Earlier sketch in CA 15-16
Svartvik, Jan 1931- 23-24R
Svejda, George J. 1927- 41-44R
Svenson, Andrew E(dward) 1910-1975 .....5-6R
Obituary 61-64
See also SATA 2, 26
Svensson, Arne 1929- 49-52
Svestka, Oldrich 1922-1983 Obituary 110
Svevo, Italo
See Schmitz, Aron Hector
See also TCLC 2
Svirsky, Grigori 1921- 69-72
Svoboda, Frederic Joseph 1949- 116
Swaan, Wim 1927- CANR-18
Earlier sketch in CA 25-28R
Swabey, Marie Collins 1890-1966 ..... CANR-16
Earlier sketch in CA 1R
Swadesh, Frances Leon 1917- 120
Swadley, Elizabeth 1929- 21-22R
Swados, Elizabeth 1951- 97-100
See also CLC 12
Swados, Harvey 1920-1972 .... CANR-6
Obituary 37-40R
Earlier sketch in CA 7-8R
See also DLB 2
See also CLC 5
Swaffer, Hannen 1879-1962 Obituary 112
Swaim, Alice Mackenzie 1911- CANR-6
Earlier sketch in CA 9-10R
Swaim, Lawrence 1942- 69-72

Swain, Bruce M(cArthur) 1943- 101
Swain, Charles 1801-1874 .... DLB-32
Swain, Donald C(hristie) 1931- 29-32R
Swain, Dwight V(reeland) 1915- CANR-7
Earlier sketch in CA 17-18R
Swain, Frank G. 1893(?)-1975 Obituary ...53-56
Swain, James E(dgar) 1897-1975 .... CAP-2
Earlier sketch in CA 25-28
Swain, Joseph Ward 1891-1971 .... CAP-2
Earlier sketch in CA 21-22
Swain, Margaret (Helen) 1909- 53-56
Swain, Marshall (William) 1940- 124
Brief entry 117
Swain, Martha H(elen) 1929- 85-88
Swain, Olive 1896- 7-8R
Swain, Raymond Charles 1912- 9-10R
Swain, Roger (Bartlett) 1949- 102
Swain, Su Zan (Noguchi) 1916- CANR-6
Earlier sketch in CA 7-8R
See also SATA 21
Swainson, Donald 1938- 109
Swainson, Eleanor Frances 111
Swale, Rose 1947- Brief entry 116
Swale, Rosie
See Swale, Rose
Swales, Martin 1940- 81-84
Swallow, Alan 1915-1966 .... CANR-16
Obituary 25-28R
Earlier sketch in CA 1R
Swallow, Norman 1921- 21-22R
Swami Rama 1925- 119
Swami Sivananda Radha
See Radha, Sivananda
Swamy, Subramanian 1939- 49-52
Swan, Berta W(aterhouse) 1928- 29-32R
Swan, Bradford Fuller 1908(?)-1976
Obituary 65-68
Swan, Carroll J. 1914-1984 Obituary 112
Swan, Christopher C(ushing) 1946- 103
Swan, Gladys 1934- CANR-17
Earlier sketch in CA 101
Swan, Jon 1929- 89-92
Swan, Marie
See Bartlett, Marie (Swan)
Swan, Susan 1944- SATA-22
Swanberg, W(illiam) A(ndrew) 1907- CANR-8
Earlier sketch in CA 7-8R
Swander, Mary 1950- 122
Swanger, David 1940- 49-52
Swann, Brian 1940- 37-40R
Swann, Donald (Ibrahim) 1923- CANR-16
Earlier sketch in CA 23-24R
Swann, Francis 1913- CANR-4
Earlier sketch in CA 11-12R
Swann, Ingo 1933- 57-60
Swann, Lois 1944- CANR-12
Earlier sketch in CA 65-68
Swann, Peggy
See Geis, Richard E(rwin)
Swann, Peter C(harles) 1921- 7-8R
Swann, Thomas Burnett, Jr.
1928-1976 .... CANR-4
Earlier sketch in CA 5-6R
Swansea, Charleen 1932- CANR-16
Earlier sketch in CA 103
Swansen, Vern 1916- 49-52
Swanson, Arlene Collyer 1913- 5-6R
Swanson, Austin D. 1930- 25-28R
Swanson, Bert E(lmer) 1924- 29-32R
Swanson, Carl P(ontius) 1911- 45-48
Swanson, Don R(ichard) 1924- 15-16R
Swanson, Donald Roland 1927- 41-44R
Swanson, Edward I. 1923- 29-32R
Swanson, Gloria 1899(?)-1983 Obituary 109
Swanson, Gloria Borseth 1927- 77-80
Swanson, Gustav A(dolph) 1910- CANR-14
Earlier sketch in CA 77-80
Swanson, Harold B(urdette) 1917- 37-40R
Swanson, Neil H(armon) 1896-1983
Obituary 109
Swanson, Roy Arthur 1925- 17-18R
Swanson, (Karl) Thor (Waldemar)
1922- CANR-22
Earlier sketch in CA 45-48
Swanson, Walter S. J. 1917- 29-32R
Swanton, Ernest William 1907- CANR-18
Earlier sketches in CA 7-8R, CANR-2
Swanwick, Michael 1950- 119
Swarbrick, Andrew 1955- 120
Sward, Robert (Stuart) 1933- CANR-23
Earlier sketches in CA 7-8R, CANR-5
Swardson, Harold Roland, Jr. 1925- 4R
Swarthout, Doris L(ouise) 1931- 77-80
Swarthout, Glendon (Fred) 1918- CANR-1
Earlier sketch in CA 3R
See also SATA 26
See also CLC 35
Swarthout, Kathryn 1919- 41-44R
See also SATA 7
Swartley, David Warren 1950- 102
Swartley, Willard M(yers) 1936- 117
Swartz, Harry (Felix) 1911- CANR-6
Earlier sketch in CA 57-60
Swartz, Jon D(avid) 1934- 69-72
Swartz, Marc J(erome) 1931- 21-22R
Swartz, Marvin 1941- 101
Swartz, Mary I(sabelle) 1942- 97-100
Swartz, Melvin Jay 1930- 97-100
Swartz, Paul 1927- 7-8R
Swartz, Robert D(avid) 1937- 41-44R
Swartz, Robert J(ason) 1936- 17-18R
Swartz, Willis George 1902-1965 .... 1R
Swartzlow, Ruby Johnson 1903- CAP-1
Earlier sketch in CA 15-16
Swarzenski, Hanns (Peter Theophil)
1903-1985 Obituary 116
Swatridge, Charles (John) CANR-7
Earlier sketch in CA 15-16R
Swatridge, Irene Maude (Mossop) CANR-7
Earlier sketch in CA 29-32R
Swaybill, Roger E(lliot) 1943- 105
Swayne, Geoffrey
See Campion, Sidney R(onald)
Swayne, Sam(uel F.) 1907- SATA-53
Swayne, Zoa (Lourana) 1905- SATA-53
Swayze, (Sarah) Beulah G(arland) 1907- 7-8R
Swayze, E(rnest) Harold 1930- 1R
Swayze, John Cameron 1906- 102
Swearengen, Thomas F. 1924- 19-20R
Swearer, Donald K(eeney) 1934- 37-40R
Swearingen, Arthur Rodger 1923- CANR-10
Earlier sketch in CA 5-6R
Sweazey, George E. 1905- CANR-4
Earlier sketch in CA 1R
Swedburg, Wilma Adeline 7-8R
Swede, George 1940- 113
Sweeney, Amin 1938- 105
Sweeney, Barry
See Hand, G(eoffrey) J(oseph Philip
Macaulay)
Sweeney, (Roderick) Charles (Hinton)
1922- CANR-16
Earlier sketch in CA 23-24R
Sweeney, Earl M. 1937- 112
Sweeney, Francis 1916- 7-8R
Sweeney, Henry Whitcomb 1898-1967 ... CAP-2
Earlier sketch in CA 17-18
Sweeney, James B(artholomew)
1910- CANR-12
Earlier sketch in CA 29-32R
See also SATA 21
Sweeney, James Johnson 1900-1986 ... CANR-6
Obituary 119
Earlier sketch in CA 7-8R
Sweeney, Joyce (Kay) 1955- 116
Sweeney, Karen O'Connor
See O'Connor, Karen
Sweeney, (Charles) Leo 1918- CANR-15
Earlier sketch in CA 37-40R
Sweeney, R. C. H.
See Sweeney, (Roderick) Charles
(Hinton)
Sweeney, Robert Dale 1939- 45-48
Sweeney, Thomas J(ohn) 1936- 41-44R
Sweeney, William J(oseph), III 1922- 45-48
Sweeny, Mary K. 1923- 126
Sweet, Donald H(erbert) 1925- 112
Sweet, Franklyn Haley 1916- 9-10R
Sweet, Frederick A(rnold) 1903- CAP-2
Earlier sketch in CA 17-18
Sweet, George Elliott 1904- 45-48
Sweet, J(ohn) P(hilip) M(cMurdo) 1927- 119
Sweet, James Stouder 1918- 41-44R
Sweet, Jeffrey 1950- 81-84
Sweet, Leonard Ira 1947- 97-100
Sweet, Muriel W. 1888-1977 106
Sweet, Paul R(obinson) 1907- 77-80
Sweet, Robert Burdette 1930- 85-88
Sweet, Waldo Earle 1912- 1R
Sweeting, George 1924- CANR-11
Earlier sketch in CA 65-68
Sweetkind, Morris 1898- 13-14R
Sweetland, Nancy A(nn) 1934- SATA-48
Sweetland, Richard C. 1931- 119
Sweetman, Jack 1940- CANR-26
Earlier sketches in CA 25-28R, CANR-10
Sweetman, Rosita (Anne) 1948- 124
Brief entry 118
Sweets, John Frank 1945- 89-92
Sweetser, Mary (Chisholm) 1894- 41-44R
Sweetser, Ted
See Sweetser, Mary (Chisholm)
Sweetser, Thomas P(atrick) 1939- 112
Sweetser, Wesley D(uaine) 1919- 37-40R
Sweezy, Alan Richardson 1907- 41-44R
Sweezy, Paul M(arlor) 1910- CANR-5
Earlier sketch in CA 1R
Sweigard, Lulu E. ?-1974 Obituary 53-56
Swell, Lila 97-100
Sweney, Fredric 1912- 1R
Swenson, Allan A(rmstrong) 1933- 77-80
See also SATA 21
Swenson, Clifford H(enrik) Jr. 1926- 45-48
Swenson, Judy Harris 1947- 120
Swenson, Karen 1936- 53-56
Swenson, Loyd S(ylvan), Jr. 1932- CANR-15
Earlier sketch in CA 41-44R
Swenson, May 1919- 7-8R
See also SATA 15
See also DLB 5
See also CLC 4, 14
Swenson, Peggy
See Geis, Richard E(rwin)
Swenson, Peggye 1933- 73-76
Swensson, Paul S. 1907- 77-80
Swerdlow, Amy (Miriam) G(alstuck) 1923- .. 105
Swerling, Jo 1897- DLB-44
Swetman, Glenn R(obert) 1936- CANR-4
Earlier sketch in CA 53-56
Swetnam, Evelyn (Frances) 1919- 93-96
Swets, John A(rthur) 1928- CANR-9
Earlier sketch in CA 21-22R
Swezey, Kenneth M. 1905(?)-1972
Obituary 33-36R
Swicegood, Thomas L. P. 1930- 53-56
Swick, Clarence 1883(?)-1979 Obituary ...89-92
Swick, Kevin J(ames) 1943- 111
Swidler, Arlene (Anderson) 1929- CANR-12
Earlier sketch in CA 61-64
Swidler, Leonard 1929- CANR-7
Earlier sketch in CA 17-18R
Swierenga, Robert P. 1935- 25-28R
Swift, Augustus
See Lovecraft, H(oward) P(hillips)
Swift, Benjamin
See McKimmey, James
Swift, Bryan
See Knott, William C(ecil, Jr.)
Swift, Carolyn Ruth 1928- 107
Swift, David
See Kaufmann, John
Swift, E(dward) M(cKelvy) 1951- 107
Swift, Edd
See Swift, Edward
Swift, Edward 1943- 37-40R
Swift, George B. 1902(?)-1983 Obituary 110
Swift, Graham 1949- 122
Brief entry 117
See also CLC 41
Swift, Helen C(ecilia) 1920- 117
Swift, Helen Miller 1914- 2R
Swift, Hildegarde Hoyt 1890(?)-1977
Obituary 69-72
See also SATA 20
Swift, Howard W. 1908- CAP-1
Earlier sketch in CA 9-10
Swift, Joan 1926- 115
Swift, Jonathan 1667-1745 .... SATA-19
See also DLB 39
Swift, Kate 1923- 69-72
Swift, Marshall S(tefan) 1936- 53-56
Swift, Mary Grace 1927- 29-32R
Swift, Merlin
See Leeming, Joseph
Swift, Patrick 1927-1983 Obituary 110
Swift, Richard N(ewton) 1924- 2R
Swift, W. Porter 1914- 29-32R
Swigart, Rob 1941- CANR-11
Earlier sketch in CA 69-72
Swiger, Elinor Porter 1927- 37-40R
See also SATA 8
Swigg, Richard 1938- 103
Swihart, Altman K 1903- 1R
Swihart, Thomas L(ee) 1929- 107
Swinburne, Algernon Charles 1837-1909
Brief entry 105
See also DLB 35, 57
See also TCLC 8
Swinburne, Laurence (Joseph) 1924- .. CANR-15
Earlier sketch in CA 61-64
See also SATA 9
Swinburne, Richard 1934- CANR-10
Earlier sketch in CA 25-28R
Swindell, Larry (Nolan) 1929- 25-28R
Swindells, Robert (Edward) 1939- CANR-21
Earlier sketch in CA 97-100
See also SATA 34, 50
Swinden, Patrick 1941- 49-52
Swindler, William F(inley) 1913-1984 ....13-14R
Obituary 112
Swindoll, Luci 1932- 112
Swineford, Ada 1917- 61-64
Swinfen, Ann CLC-34
Swinfen, D(avid) B(erridge) 1936- 37-40R
Swinford, Betty (June Wells) 1927- CANR-7
Earlier sketch in CA 7-8R
Swinford, Bob
See Swinford, Betty (June Wells)
Swing, Raymond Gram 1887-1968
Obituary 89-92
Swing, Thomas Kaehao 1930- 9-10R
Swingle, Paul G(eorge) 1937- 41-44R
Swinglehurst, Edmund 1917- CANR-8
Earlier sketch in CA 57-60
Swinnerton, A(rnold) R(eber) 1912- 106
Swinnerton, Frank Arthur 1884-1982
Obituary 108
See also DLB 34
See also CLC 31
Swinnerton, James Guilford 1875-1974
Obituary 93-96
Swinson, Arthur 1915-1970 .... CAP-2
Earlier sketch in CA 17-18
Swint, Henry L(ee) 1909- 37-40R
Swinton, George 1917- 85-88
Swinton, John 1939- 111
Swinton, Stanley M(itchell) 1919-1982
Obituary 107
Swinton, William E(lgin) 1900- 13-14R
Swinyard, Alfred W(ilbur) 1915- 11-12R
Swire, Otta F(lora Macdonald Lois)
1898-1973 .... CAP-1
Earlier sketch in CA 13-14
Swisher, Carl Brent 1897-1968 .... CANR-16
Obituary 103
Earlier sketch in CA 1R
Swisher, (Frank) Earl 1902- CAP-2
Earlier sketch in CA 29-32
Swisher, Robert K., Jr. 1947- 61-64
Swisshelm, Jane Grey 1815-1884 ...... DLB-43
Switzer, David Karl 1925- 57-60
Switzer, Ellen 1923- CANR-2
Earlier sketch in CA 45-48
See also SATA 48
Switzer, (Perry) Richard 1925- CANR-18
Earlier sketch in CA 25-28R
Swivett, R. G. O.
See Trippett, Frank
Swomley, John M., Jr. 1915- 9-10R
Swope, George S(teel) 1915- 29-32R
Swope, Herbert Bayard 1882-1958 ...... DLB-25
Swor, Chester E(ugene) 1907- 11-12R
Sword, Randall S(tanford) 1942- 114
Sword, Wiley 1937- 85-88
Swords, James ?-1844 .... DLB-73
Swords, Thomas 1763-1843 .... DLB-73
Swortzell, Lowell (Stanley) 1930- CANR-1
Earlier sketch in CA 49-52
Swycaffer, Jefferson P(utnam) 1956- 119
Swyhart, Barbara Ann DeMartino 1942- ...61-64
Syberberg, Hans-Juergen 1935- 93-96
Syburg, Jane 1927- 29-32R
Sydenham, Michael J(ohn) 1923- 19-20R
Sydney, C.
See Tralins, S(andor) Robert
Sydney, Frank
See Warwick, Alan R(oss)
Sydnor, Charles W(right), Jr. 1943- 77-80
Sydnor, James Rawlings 1911- 5-6R
Sydnor, (Charles) William 1911- 112
Syed, Anwar H(ussain) 1926- 102
Syers, Ed
See Syers, William Edward
Syers, William Edward 1914- CANR-4
Earlier sketch in CA 1R
Sykes, (Richard) Adam 1940- 29-32R
Sykes, Alrene 77-80
Sykes, Christopher (Hugh) 1907-1986 ....29-32R
Obituary 121
Sykes, Gerald 1903-1984 Obituary 113
Sykes, Jay G(ilbert) 1922- 45-48
Sykes, John 1918- 17-18R
Sykes, Roosevelt 1906-1983 Obituary 110
Sylva, Carmen
See Elisabeth (Ottilie Luise), Queen
(Pauline)
Sylvander, Carolyn W(edin) 1939- 117
Sylvester, A(lbert) J(ames) 1889- 101
Sylvester, Arline 1914- 65-68
Sylvester, Bob
See Sylvester, Robert (McPherson)
Sylvester, Dorothy 1906- 29-32R
Sylvester, Edward J(oseph) 1942- 118
Sylvester, Janet Hart 1917-1987 Obituary ... 123
Sylvester, Kathryn F. 1901(?)-1983
Obituary 111
Sylvester, Natalie G(abry) 1922- 97-100
See also SATA 22
Sylvester, Richard Standish 1926-1978 .. CANR-2
Obituary 77-80
Earlier sketch in CA 1R
Sylvester, Robert (McPherson)
1907-1975 61-64
Obituary 57-60
Sylvester, William 1918- 45-48
Sylvestre, (Joseph Jean) Guy 1918- 61-64
Sylvia
See Ashton-Warner, Sylvia (Constance)
Sylvin, Francis
See Seaman, Sylvia S.
Symanski, Richard 1941- 111
Symcox, Geoffrey Walter 1938- 112
Syme, (Neville) Ronald 1913- CANR-6
Earlier sketch in CA 9-10R
See also SATA 2
Symeonoglou, Sarantis 1937- 126
Symington, David 1904-1984 .... CAP-2
Obituary 113
Earlier sketch in CA 29-32
Symmes, Robert Edward
See Duncan, Robert (Edward)
Symmons-Symonolewicz, Konstantin
1909- 37-40R
Symonds, Craig L. 1946- 126
Symonds, Helen Sanford 1899- 5-6R
Symonds, John 105
Symonds, John Addington 1840-1893 .. DLB-57
Symonds, (John) Richard (Charters)
1918- 21-22R
Symons, Allene 1944- 110
Symons, Arthur 1865-1945 Brief entry 107
See also DLB 19, 57
See also TCLC 11
Symons, (Dorothy) Geraldine 1909- 85-88
See also SATA 33
Symons, Julian (Gustave) 1912- CANR-3
Earlier sketch in CA 49-52
See also CAAS 3
See also CLC 2, 14, 32
Symons, Leslie John 1926- CANR-26
Earlier sketch in CA 109
Symons, R(obert) D(avid) 1898-1973 ....41-44R
Symons, (H. B.) Scott 1933- 77-80
See also DLB 53
Symser, H(amilton) M(artin) 1901- 15-16R
Synan, Edward A(loysius) 1918- 19-20R
Synan, (Harold) Vinson 1934- CANR-14
Earlier sketch in CA 37-40R
Synge, (Edmund) J(ohn) M(illington)
1871-1909 Brief entry 104
See also DLB 10, 19
See also TCLC 6
Synge, (Phyllis) Ursula 1930- CANR-1
Earlier sketch in CA 49-52
See also SATA 9
Synnestvedt, Sig(fried T.) 1924-1977 ...37-40R
Syntax, John
See Dennett, Herbert Victor
Sypher, Francis Jacques, Jr. 1941- CANR-10
Earlier sketch in CA 57-60
Sypher, Lucy Johnston 1907- CANR-2
Earlier sketch in CA 45-48
See also SATA 7
Sypher, Wylie 1905- CANR-3
Earlier sketch in CA 2R
Syracuse, Marcella Pfeiffer 1930- 23-24R
Syrdal, Rolf A(rthur) 1902- 25-28R
Syred, Celia 1911- CANR-12
Earlier sketch in CA 29-32R
Syrett, David 1939- Brief entry 106
Syrett, Harold Coffin 1913-1984 Obituary ... 113
Syrkin, Marie 1899- CANR-6
Earlier sketch in CA 9-10R
Syrop, Konrad 1914- CANR-5
Earlier sketch in CA 9-10R

Syruc, J.
See Milosz, Czeslaw
Sysyn, Frank E. 1946- ... 126
Syvertsen, Edythe 1921- ... 73-76
Syverud, Genevieve Wold 1914- ... 21-22R
Szabo, Denis 1929- ... CANR-20
Earlier sketch in CA 89-92
Szabolcsi, Bence 1899-1973 Obituary ... 116
Szajkowski, Zosa
See Frydman, Szajko
Szancer, Henryk ?-1976 Obituary ... 61-64
Szaniawski, Jerzy 1886-1970 Obituary ... 29-32R
Szanto, George H. 1940- ... 41-44R
Szanton, Peter L(oeb) 1930- ... CANR-11
Earlier sketch in CA 69-72
Szasz, Ferenc Morton 1940- ... 125
Szasz, Kathleen 1912- ... 25-28R
Szasz, Margaret Connell 1935- ... 97-100
Szasz, Suzanne (Shorr) 1915- ... CANR-18
Earlier sketches in CA 5-6R, CANR-3
See also SATA 13
Szasz, Thomas (Stephen) 1920- ... CANR-9
Earlier sketch in CA 17-18R
Szathmary, Louis (Istvan) II 1919- ... 81-84
Szaz, Zoltan Michael 1930- ... CANR-3
Earlier sketch in CA 3R
Szczesniak, Boleslaw (B.) 1908- ... 11-12R
Szechter, Szymon 1920(?)-1983 Obituary ... 110
Szekely, Endre 1922- ... 17-18R
Szekeres, Cyndy 1933- ... SATA-5
Szent-Gyoergyi, Albert (von Nagyrapolt)
1893-1986 Obituary ... 120
Brief entry ... 112
Szent-Gyorgyi, Albert (von Nagyrapolt)
See Szent-Gyoergyi, Albert (von Nagyrapolt)
Szep, Paul Michael 1941- Brief entry ... 110
Szeplaki, Joseph 1932- ... 73-76
Szerlip, Barbara 1949- ... CANR-3
Earlier sketch in CA 49-52
Szigeti, Joseph 1892-1973 ... CAP-1
Earlier sketch in CA 9-10
Szilard, Leo 1898-1964 Obituary ... 113
Szirtes, George 1948- ... 109
See also CLC 46
Szittya, Ruth Outland 1910- ... 112
Szoeverffy, Joseph 1920- ... CANR-17
Earlier sketch in CA 65-68
Szogyi, Alex 1929- ... 45-48
Szporluk, Roman 1933- ... CANR-1
Earlier sketch in CA 45-48
Szudek, Agnes S(usan) P(hilomena) ... SATA-49
Szulc, Tad 1926- ... CANR-23
Earlier sketches in CA 11-12R, CANR-4
See also SATA 26
Szumigalski, Anne 1922- ... CANR-16
Earlier sketches in CA 49-52, CANR-1
Szumski, Bonnie 1958- ... 122
Szwarc, Josef 1947- ... 118
Szydlow, Jarl
See Szydlowski, Mary Vigliante
Szydlowski, Mary Vigliante 1946- ... 104
Szydlowski, Roman 1918(?)-1983
Obituary ... 111
Szyliowicz, Joseph S. 1931- ... 41-44R
Szymanski, Albert (John) 1942(?)-1985
Obituary ... 115
Szymanski, Richard
See Symanski, Richard

T

T. B. D.
See James, William Milbourne
T. N. T.
See Thomas, Cornelius Dickinson
T.R.B.
See Strout, Richard L(ee)
T. V. Vet
See Straiton, E(dward) C(ornock)
Taaffe, Edward James 1921- ... 85-88
Taaffe, James G. 1932- ... 17-18R
Taaffe, Michael
See Maguire, R(obert) A(ugustine) J(oseph)
Taagepera, Rein 1933- ... 109
Tabachnik, Abraham B(er) 1902-1970
Obituary ... 29-32R
Taback, Simms 1932- Brief entry ... 115
See also SATA 36, 40
Tabak, Israel 1904- Brief entry ... 105
Tabard, Geoffrey
See McNelly, Willis E(verett)
Tabard, Peter
See Blake, L(eslie) J(ames)
Tabb, Jay Yanai 1907-1976 ... CAP-2
Earlier sketch in CA 29-32
Taber, Anthony Scott 1944- ... 105
Taber, George M(cCaffrey) 1942- ... 65-68
Taber, Gladys (Bagg) 1899-1980 ... CANR-4
Obituary ... 97-100
Earlier sketch in CA 5-6R
See also SATA 22
Taber, Julian Ingersoll 1929- Brief entry ... 106
Taber, Robert ... 17-18R
Taber, Robert W(illiam) 1921- ... 73-76
Tabler, Edward C. 1916- ... 7-8R
Tablet, Hilda
See Swann, Donald (Ibrahim)
Tabor, Paul
See Tabori, Paul
Tabori, George 1914- ... CANR-4
Earlier sketch in CA 49-52
See also CLC 19
Tabori, Paul 1908-1974 ... CANR-5
Obituary ... 53-56
Earlier sketch in CA 5-6R
Taborsky, Edward (Joseph) 1910- ... CANR-3
Earlier sketch in CA 1R
Tabouis, Genevieve 1892-1985 Obituary ... 117
Tabrah, Ruth Milander 1921- ... CANR-10
Earlier sketch in CA 15-16R
See also SATA 14
Tacey, William S(anford) 1904- ... 37-40R
Tachau, Frank 1929- Brief entry ... 111
Tachau, Mary K(atherine) Bonsteel 1926- ... 85-88
Tacheron, Donald Glen 1928- ... 21-22R
Tack, Alfred 1906- ... 104
Tadlock, Max R. 1919- ... 19-20R
Tadrack, Moss
See Caryl, Warren
Taegel, William S(tephens) 1940- ... 45-48
Taetzsch, Lyn 1941- ... CANR-8
Earlier sketch in CA 57-60
Taeuber, Alma Ficks 1933- ... 17-18R
Taeuber, Conrad 1906- ... 45-48
Taeuber, Irene Barnes 1906-1974
Obituary ... 106
Taeuber, Karl E(rnst) 1936- ... 17-18R
Tae-yong, Ro
See Rutt, Richard
Tafel, Edgar Allen 1912- ... 89-92
Taffy
See Llewellyn, D(avid) W(illiam) Alun
Taft, Charles P(helps II) 1897-1983
Obituary ... 110
Brief entry ... 105
Taft, Pauline Dakin 1891- ... CAP-1
Earlier sketch in CA 15-16
Taft, Philip 1902-1976 Obituary ... 69-72
Taft, Ronald 1920- ... 21-22R
Taft, William H(oward) 1915- ... 15-16R
Tafti, H. B. Dehqani
See Dehqani-Tafti, H. B.
Tafuri, Manfredo 1935- ... CANR-26
Earlier sketch in CA 69-72
Tafuri, Nancy 1946- ... 118
See also SATA 39
Tager, Jack 1936- ... 118
Tageson, Carroll W(illiam) 1925- ... 53-56
Taggard, Genevieve 1894-1948 ... DLB-45
Taggart, Dorothy T(rekell) 1917- ... 102
Taggart, (Paul) John 1942- ... CANR-1
Earlier sketch in CA 45-48
Taggart, John Scott
See Scott-Taggart, John
Taggart, Joseph Herman 1902-1984
Obituary ... 112
Taggart, Robert (III) 1945- Brief entry ... 111
Tagiuri, Renato 1919- ... 77-80
Tagliabue, John 1923- ... 21-22R
Tagliaferri, Aldo 1931- ... 77-80
Tagliavia, Sheila 1936- ... 104
Tagore, Amitendranath 1922- ... 61-64
Tagore, Rabindranath 1861-1941 ... 120
Brief entry ... 104
See also TCLC 3
Taha, Hamdy A(bdelaziz) 1937- ... 37-40R
Taha, Karen T(erry) 1942- ... 120
Tahara, Mildred Machiko 1941- ... 104
Tahir, Abe M(ahmoud), Jr. 1931- ... 69-72
Tahir, Kemal 1910(?)-1973 Obituary ... 45-48
Tahlaquah, David
See LeMond, Alan
Tahtinen, Dale R(udolph) 1945- ... 65-68
Tai, Hung-chao 1929- ... 73-76
Taichert, Louise C(ecile) 1925- ... 89-92
Taikeff, Stanley 1940- ... 109
Taines, Beatrice (Green) 1923- ... CANR-14
Earlier sketch in CA 73-76
Taira, Koji 1926- ... 41-44R
Taishoff, Sol J(oseph) 1904-1982 ... 73-76
Obituary ... 107
Tait, Alan A(nderson) 1934- ... CANR-10
Earlier sketch in CA 23-24R
Tait, Dorothy 1902(?)-1972 Obituary ... 33-36R
Tait, Douglas 1944- ... SATA-12
Tait, George E(dward) 1910- ... 7-8R
Tait, Katharine 1923- ... 65-68
Tait, L(eslie) Gordon 1926- ... 45-48
Taitz, Emily 1937- ... 85-88
Takacs, Carol Addison 1926- ... 124
Takagi, Akimitsu 1920- Brief entry ... 108
Takahashi, Akira 1932- ... 29-32R
Takahashi, Yasundo 1912- ... CANR-14
Earlier sketch in CA 41-44R
Takaki, Ronald T(oshiyuki) 1939- ... 37-40R
Takakjian, Portia 1930- ... SATA-15
Takashima, Shizuye 1928- ... 45-48
See also SATA 13
Takayama, Akira 1932- ... CANR-2
Earlier sketch in CA 49-52
Takeshita, Thomas Kohachiro
1891(?)-1973 Obituary ... 45-48
Taktsis, Costas 1927-1988 ... 23-24R
Obituary ... 126
Talafous, Don (Francis) 1926- ... 113
Talamantes, Florence Williams 1931- ... CANR-6
Earlier sketch in CA 57-60
Talamini, John T(homas) 1940- ... 126
Brief entry ... 113
Talarico, Ross 1945- ... 73-76
Talbert, Ansel Edward (McLaurine)
1912-1987 Obituary ... 124
Talbert, Charles Gano 1912- ... 5-6R
Talbert, Charles H(arold) 1934- ... CANR-14
Earlier sketch in CA 41-44R
Talbot, Alice-Mary 1939- ... 112
Talbot, Allan R. 1934- ... CANR-10
Earlier sketch in CA 21-22R
Talbot, Carol Terry 1913- ... 15-16R
Talbot, Charlene Joy 1928- ... CANR-8
Earlier sketch in CA 19-20R
See also SATA 10
Talbot, Edward Hugh Frederick Chetwynd
See Chetwynd-Talbot, Edward Hugh Frederick
Talbot, Godfrey (Walker) 1908- ... 107
Talbot, Gordon (Gray) 1928- ... CANR-14
Earlier sketch in CA 69-72
Talbot, Hugh
See Chetwynd-Talbot, Edward Hugh Frederick
Talbot, Kay
See Rowland, D(onald) S(ydney)
Talbot, Lawrence
See Bryant, Edward (Winslow, Jr.)
Talbot, Michael 1953- ... 119
Talbot, Nathan B(ill) 1909- ... 104
Talbot, Norman (Clare) 1936- ... CANR-9
Earlier sketch in CA 21-22R
Talbot, Ross B. 1919- ... 17-18R
Talbot, Toby 1928- ... 21-22R
See also SATA 14
Talbot Rice, David
See Rice, David Talbot
Talbot Rice, Tamara (Abelson)
See Rice, Tamara (Abelson) Talbot
Talbott, Basil 1899-1985 Obituary ... 117
Talbott, John E(dwin) 1940- ... 25-28R
Talbott, Robert D(ean) 1928- ... 57-60
Talbott, Strobe 1946- ... 93-96
See also AITN 1
Talcott, Dudley Vaill 1899-1986 Obituary ... 119
Talese, Gay 1932- ... CANR-9
Earlier sketch in CA 4R
See also CLC 37
See also AITN 1
Talker, T.
See Rands, William Brighty
Talkin, Gil
See Rosenthal, Alan
Talkington, Virginia Savage
See McAlester, Virginia
Tall, Deborah 1951- ... CANR-22
Earlier sketch in CA 105
Tall, Stephen
See Crook, Compton Newby
Talland, George A(lexander) 1917-19(?) ... CAP-2
Earlier sketch in CA 25-28
Tallcott, Emogene ... 29-32R
See also SATA 10
Tallent, Elizabeth (Ann) 1954- ... 117
See also CLC 45
Tallent, Norman 1921- ... 17-18R
Talleur, Richard W(iley) 1931- ... 97-100
Talley-Morris, Neva B(ennett) 1909- ... 57-60
Tallman, Albert 1902- ... 53-56
Tallon, Robert 1939- ... CANR-8
Earlier sketch in CA 11-12R
See also SATA 28, 43
Tally, Ted 1952- ... 124
Brief entry ... 120
See also CLC 42
Talmadge, Marian ... SATA-14
Talmage, Anne
See Powell, Talmage
Talmage, Frank (Ephraim) 1938- ... 97-100
Talmey, Allene
See Plaut, Allene Talmey
Talmon, Jacob L(aib) 1916-1980 ... 13-14R
Obituary ... 101
Talmon, Shemaryahu 1920- ... CANR-12
Earlier sketch in CA 29-32R
Talpalar, Morris 1900- ... 73-76
Talvi
See Robinson, Therese
Talvj
See Robinson, Therese
Tamarin, Alfred H. 1913-1980 ... CANR-4
Obituary ... 102
Earlier sketch in CA 29-32R
See also SATA 13
Tamasi, Aron 1897-1966 Obituary ... 114
Tambasco, Anthony J(oseph) 1939- ... 117
Tambi
See Tambimuttu, Thurairajah
Tambiah, S. J.
See Tambiah, Stanley Jeyaraja
Tambiah, Stanley Jeyaraja 1929- ... 123
Tambimuttu, Thurairajah 1915(?)-1983
Obituary ... 110
Tambs, Lewis Arthur 1927- ... CANR-4
Earlier sketch in CA 53-56
Tamburine, Jean 1930- ... 9-10R
See also SATA 12
Tamedly, Elisabeth L. 1931- ... 29-32R
Tames, Richard (Lawrence) 1946- ... 103
Tamir, Max Mordecai 1912- ... 29-32R
Tamir, Vicki 1924- ... 29-32R
Tammaro, Thom(as Michael) 1951- ... 109
Tammsaare, A(nton) H(ansen)
1878-1940 ... TCLC-27
Tammuz, Benjamin 1919- ... 85-88
Tamny, Martin 1941- ... 37-40R
Tampion, John 1937- ... 73-76
Tam'Si, Tchicaya U
See Tchicaya, Gerald Felix
Tamsin
See Summers, Ethel Snelson
Tamulaitis, Vytas 1913- ... 19-20R
Tamuno, Tekena N. 1932- ... 23-24R
Tana, Tomoe (Hayashima) 1913- ... 21-22R
Tanahashi, Kazuaki 1933- ... 122
Tanaka, Beatrice 1932- ... 115
Tanaquil, Paul
See Le Clercq, Jacques Georges Clemenceau
Tanay, Emanuel 1928- ... 93-96
Tanchuck, Nathaniel 1912- ... 15-16R
Tancock, John (Leon) 1942- ... 105
Tancredi, Laurence R(ichard) 1940- ... 116
Tandem, Felix
See Spitteler, Carl
Tandon, Prakash 1911- ... 93-96
Tandy, Clifford Ronald Vivien
1919(?)-1981 Obituary ... 104
Tanenbaum, Jan Karl 1936- ... 61-64
Tanenbaum, Robert Brief entry ... 116
Tang, Peter Shen-Hao 1919- ... 3R
Tang, You-Shan 1946- ... SATA-53
Tangerman, Elmer John 1907- ... CANR-23
Earlier sketch in CA 106
Tangri, Shanti S. 1928- ... 25-28R
Tangye, Nigel (Trevithick) 1909-1988
Obituary ... 125
Brief entry ... 117
Tanham, George K(ilpatrick) 1922- ... CANR-1
Earlier sketch in CA 1R
Tania B.
See Blixen, Karen (Christentze Dinesen)
Taniguchi, Kazuko 1946- ... 93-96
Taniguchi, Masaharu 1893-1985 Obituary ... 116
Tanikawa, Shuntaro 1931- ... 121
Tanis, James (Robert) 1928- ... 118
Tanis, Norman Earl 1929- ... 110
Tanizaki, Jun'ichiro 1886-1965 ... 93-96
Obituary ... 25-28R
See also CLC 8, 14, 28
Tank, Herbert 1922(?)-1982 Obituary ... 108
Tank, Ronald W(arren) 1929- ... 49-52
Tankard, Alice (Doumanian) 1926- ... 117
Tankard, James William, Jr. 1941- ... 73-76
Tanksley, Perry 1928- ... 37-40R
Tann, Jennifer 1939- ... 103
Tannahill, Reay 1929- ... CANR-2
Earlier sketch in CA 49-52
Tannehill, Robert C(ooper) 1934- ... CANR-26
Earlier sketch in CA 45-48
Tannen, Deborah F(rances) 1945- ... 118
Tannen, Jack 1907- ... 114
Tannen, Mary 1943- ... 105
See also SATA 37
Tannenbaum, Arnold S(herwood) 1925- ... 17-18R
Tannenbaum, Arthur C. 1941- ... 123
Tannenbaum, Beulah Goldstein 1916- ... CANR-7
Earlier sketch in CA 5-6R
See also SATA 3
Tannenbaum, D(onald) Leb 1948- ... 115
See also SATA 42
Tannenbaum, Edward R(obert) 1921- ... 19-20R
Tannenbaum, Frank 1893-1969 ... 9-10R
Tannenbaum, Harold E. 1914- ... 5-6R
Tannenbaum, Percy Hyman 1927-
Brief entry ... 106
Tannenbaum, Robert 1915- ... 23-24R
Tanner, C(harles) Kenneth 1938- ... 53-56
Tanner, Clara L(ee) 1905- ... 41-44R
Tanner, Daniel 1926- ... 17-18R
Tanner, Edward Everett III 1921-1976 ... 73-76
Obituary ... 69-72
Tanner, Helen Hornbeck 1916- ... 61-64
Tanner, Henry 1918- ... 73-76
Tanner, James M(ourilyan) 1920- ... CANR-5
Earlier sketch in CA 13-14R
Tanner, James T(homas) F(ontenot)
1937- ... 41-44R
Tanner, John (Ian) 1927- ... 103
Tanner, John
See Matcha, Jack
Tanner, Louise S(tickney) 1922- ... 69-72
See also SATA 9
Tanner, Paul O(ra) W(arren) 1917- ... 61-64
Tanner, Roy L(ynn) 1947- ... 118
Tanner, Stephen L. 1938- ... 123
Tanner, Tony 1935- ... 85-88
Tanner-Rutherford, C.
See Winchester, Clarence
Tanobe, Miyuki 1937- ... 69-72
See also SATA 23
Tanous, Peter (Joseph) 1938- ... CANR-7
Earlier sketch in CA 61-64
Tanselle, G(eorge) Thomas 1934- ... CANR-11
Earlier sketch in CA 21-22R
Tansill, Charles Callan 1890-1964 ... 1R
Tanter, Raymond 1938- ... CANR-25
Earlier sketch in CA 45-48
Tantrist
See Cox, P(atrick) Brian
Tanyzer, Harold Joseph 1929- ... 11-12R
Tanzer, Lester 1929- ... 19-20R
Tanzer, Michael David 1935- ... 57-60
Tanzi, Vito 1935- ... CANR-5
Earlier sketch in CA 53-56
Tao Mulian
See Totten, George Oakley III
Tapia, Ralph J(ohn) 1925- ... 41-44R
Tapio, Pat Decker
See Kines, Pat Decker
Tapley, Caroline 1934- ... 97-100
Taplin, Glen W(illiam) 1917- ... 107
Taplin, Oliver 1943- ... 102
Taplin, Walter 1910- ... CAP-1
Earlier sketch in CA 9-10
Taplinger, Cecily Lent 1943-1983 Obituary ... 110
Taplinger, Richard Jacques 1911-1973
Obituary ... 41-44R
Taplinger, Terry
See Taplinger, Cecily Lent
Tapp, Jack Thomas 1934- ... 49-52
Tapp, June Louin 1929- ... 41-44R
Tapp, Kathy Kennedy 1949- ... 116
See also SATA 50
Tapp, Robert B(erg) 1925- ... 41-44R
Tappan, Paul Wilbur 1911-1964 ... 5-6R

Tappert, Theodore G(erhardt) 1904-1973 CANR-2
Earlier sketch in CA 2R
Tapply, William G(eorge) 1940- 118
Tapply H(orace) G(ardner) 1910- 15-16R
Tapscott, Stephen (J.) 1948- CANR-17
Earlier sketch in CA 89-92
Tapsell, R(obert) F(rederick) 1936- 21-22R
Taradash, Daniel 1913- 101
See also DLB 44
Taranovsky, Kiril 1911- 114
Taranow, Gerda 37-40R
Tarascio, Vincent J(oseph) 1930- 45-48
Tarassoff, Lev
See Troyat, Henri
Tarazaga, Santiago Genoves
See Genoves Tarazaga, Santiago
Tarbell, Ida M(inerva) 1857-1944
Brief entry 122
See also DLB 47
Tarbert, Gary C(harles) 1937- 101
Tarcher, Martin 1921- 19-20R
Tardieu, Jean 1903- Brief entry 116
Tardiff, Olive 1916- 73-76
Tardy, Gaye 1929(?)-1982 Obituary 108
Targ, Harry R. 1940- 118
Targ, Russell 1934- 104
Targ, William 1907- 61-64
Targan, Barry 1932- CANR-17
Earlier sketch in CA 73-76
Target, G(eorge) W(illiam) 1924- CANR-7
Earlier sketch in CA 7-8R
Tarica, Ralph 1932- 113
Tarkenton, Fran(cis Asbury) 1940- 103
Tarkington, (Newton) Booth 1869-1946
Brief entry 110
See also SATA 17
See also DLB 9
See also TCLC 9
Tarling, (Peter) Nicholas 1931- 21-22R
Tarlock, A(nthony) Dan 1940- CANR-16
Earlier sketch in CA 97-100
Tarlov, I. M. 1905(?)-1977 Obituary 69-72
Tarlton, Gillian Leigh 1953- 119
Tarn, John Nelson 1934- 41-44R
Tarn, Nathaniel 1928- CANR-5
Earlier sketch in CA 11-12R
Tarnawski, Wit(old) 1894-1988 Obituary 126
Tarnawsky, Ostap 1917- 73-76
Tarnopol, Lester 1913- 77-80
Tarnower, Herman 1910-1980 89-92
Obituary 97-100
Tarpey, Elizabeth (Pinscher) 1880-1979 CANR-4
Earlier sketch in CA 7-8R
Tarpey, Lawrence Xavier 1928- 23-24R
Tarpley, Fred 1932- 41-44R
Tarpy, Roger M(aynard) 1941- 93-96
Tarr, Herbert 1929- 13-14R
Tarr, Joel A(rthur) 1934- CANR-14
Earlier sketch in CA 37-40R
Tarr, Judith 1955- 120
Tarr, Rodger L(eRoy) 1941- 110
Tarr, Yvonne Young 1929- CANR-8
Earlier sketch in CA 61-64
Tarrance, V(ernon) Lance, Jr. 1940- 37-40R
Tarrant, Desmond 1924- 23-24R
Tarrant, John
See Egleton, Clive (Frederick)
Tarrant, John J(oseph) 1924- CANR-19
Earlier sketches in CA 53-56, CANR-4
Tarrant, Wilma
See Sherman, Jory (Tecumseh)
Tarrok, Peer
See Zwerenz, Gerhard
Tarry, Ellen 1906- 73-76
See also BW
See also SATA 16
Tarsaidze, Alexandre 1901-1978 37-40R
Obituary 77-80
Tarshis, Jerome 1936- 61-64
See also SATA 9
Tarsis, Valery Yakovlevich 1906-1983
Obituary 109
Tarski, Alfred 1901(?)-1983 Obituary 111
Tarsky, Sue 112
See also SATA 41
Tart, Charles T(heodore) 1937- 29-32R
Tarter, Donald E(dward) 1938- 112
Tartre, Raymond S. 1901-1975 CAP-2
Earlier sketch in CA 21-22
Tarver, Ben 1927- 113
Tasca, Henry J. 1912-1979 Obituary 89-92
Tasca, Jules 1938- CANR-26
Earlier sketch in CA 109
See also AITN 1
Tasch, Peter A(nthony) 1933- 73-76
Taschdjian, Claire L(ouise) 1914- 73-76
Tashjian, Dickran (Levon) 1940- 61-64
Tashjian, Virginia A. 1921- 29-32R
See also SATA 3
Tashlin, Frank 1913-1972 113
Obituary 110
See also DLB 44
Tasker, James 1908- 49-52
See also SATA 9
Tasker, Joe 1948-1982 Obituary 108
Tassin, Myron Jude 1933- 61-64
Tassin, Ray(mond Jean) 1926- 53-56
Tatar, Maria M. 1945- 85-88
Tatarkiewicz, Wladyslaw 1886-1980 103
Obituary 97-100
Tatchell, Peter 1952- 125
Tate, (John Orley) Allen 1899-1979 5-6R
Obituary 85-88
See also DLB 4, 45, 63
See also CLC 2, 4, 6, 9, 11, 14, 24
Tate, B. H.
See Boyer, Bruce Hatton
Tate, Claudia C. 1946- 121
Tate, Edward
See Dransfield, Michael (John Pender)
Tate, Eleanora E(laine) 1948- CANR-25
Earlier sketch in CA 105
See also SATA 38
Tate, Ellalice
See Hibbert, Eleanor Burford
Tate, Gary 1930- 23-24R
Tate, George T(homas) 1931- 21-22R
Tate, Jackson R. 1899(?)-1978 Obituary 81-84
Tate, James (Vincent) 1943- 21-22R
See also DLB 5
See also CLC 2, 6, 25
Tate, Joan 1922- CANR-1
Earlier sketch in CA 49-52
See also SATA 9
Tate, Marilyn Freeman 1921- 13-14R
Tate, Mary Anne
See Hale, Arlene
Tate, Merle W(esley) 1903- CAP-1
Earlier sketch in CA 17-18
Tate, Merze 17-18R
Tate, Richard
See Masters, Anthony
Tate, Robin
See Fanthorpe, R(obert) Lionel
Tate, Velma 1913- 23-24R
Tatelbaum, Judith Ann 1938- 104
Tatelbaum, Judy
See Tatelbaum, Judith Ann
Tatford, Brian F(rederick) B(arrington) 1927- CAP-1
Earlier sketch in CA 9-10
Tatford, Frederick Albert 1901- CANR-10
Earlier sketch in CA 15-16R
Tatgenhorst, John 1938- 65-68
Tatham, Andrew Francis 1949- 125
Tatham, C. Ernest 1905- CAP-1
Earlier sketch in CA 9-10
Tatham, Campbell
See Elting, Mary
Tatham, Laura (Esther) 1919- 13-14R
Tati, Jacques
See Tatischeff, Jacques
Tatischeff, Jacques 1908-1982 Obituary 108
Tatlow, Antony 1935- 122
Taton, Rene 1915- 9-10R
Tatray, Istvan
See Rupert, Raphael Rudolph
Tattersall, Ian (Michael) 1945- 115
Tattersall, (Honor) Jill 1931- CANR-10
Earlier sketch in CA 25-28R
Tattersall, Lawrence H(olmes) 1933- 29-32R
Tattersall, M(uriel Joyce) 1931- CAP-1
Earlier sketch in CA 9-10
Tatu, Michel 1933- 25-28R
Tatum, Arlo 1923- 25-28R
Tatum, Billy Joe 1933- 61-64
Tatum, Charles M(ichael) 1943- 111
Tatum, Edward Lawrie 1909-1975
Obituary 113
Tatum, Jack
See Tatum, John David
Tatum, John David 1948- 104
Taub, Harald (Jay) 1918- 110
Taube, Evert 1890-1976 Obituary 61-64
Taube, Lester S. 1920- 69-72
Taubenfeld, Howard J(ack) 1924- 13-14R
Tauber, Abraham 1915(?)-1977 Obituary 69-72
Tauber, Edward S(anford) 1908-1988
Obituary 124
Tauber, Gerald E(rich) 1922- 89-92
Tauber, Gilbert 1935- CANR-9
Earlier sketch in CA 21-22R
Tauber, Kurt P(hilip) 1922- 21-22R
Tauber, Maurice F(alcolm) 1908-1980 105
Obituary 102
Tauber, Peter 1947- 37-40R
Taubert, Sigfred 1914- 120
Taubert, William H(owland) 1934- 103
Taubes, Frederic 1900-1981 CANR-9
Obituary 104
Earlier sketch in CA 17-18R
Taubes, Susan
See Feldmann, Susan Judith
Taubman, William 1941- 23-24R
Taubr, Paul Raymond 1937- 29-32R
Taunton, Eric
See Westcott-Jones, K(enneth)
Tauranac, John 1939- 124
Tavard, George H(enry) 1922- CANR-16
Earlier sketches in CA 1R, CANR-1
Tave, Stuart M(alcolm) 1923- 104
Tavel, Ronald 1940- 21-22R
See also CLC 6
Taverne, Dick 1928- 85-88
Tavernier, Bertrand 1941- 123
Taves, Ernest H(enry) 1916- 93-96
Taves, Isabella 1915- CANR-8
Earlier sketch in CA 23-24R
See also SATA 27
Taviss, Irene
See Thomson, Irene Taviss
Tavo, Gus
See Ivan, Martha Miller Pfaff
Tavuchis, Nicholas 1934- 57-60
Tavy, Peter
See Hemery, Eric
Tawney, R(ichard) H(enry) 1880-1962
Obituary 93-96
Tax, Sol 1907- 7-8R
Taydo
See McDonald, Erwin L(awrence)
Taylor, A(lan) J(ohn) P(ercivale) 1906- 7-8R
Taylor, Alan Carey 1905-1975 Obituary 114
Taylor, Alan R(os) 1926- 109
Taylor, Alastair M(acDonald) 1915- 17-18R
Taylor, Albert E(dward) 1908- 89-92
Taylor, Alec Clifton
See Clifton-Taylor, Alec
Taylor, Alfred 1896-1973 105
Taylor, Alice J. 1909-1969 CAP-2
Earlier sketch in CA 25-28
Taylor, Alice L(ouise) 1911-1985 61-64
Obituary 116
Taylor, Alison 1927- 21-22R
Taylor, Alix 1921- 5-6R
Taylor, Andrew (McDonald) 1940- CANR-11
Earlier sketch in CA 69-72
Taylor, Andrew 1944-1988 126
Taylor, Andrew (John Robert) 1951- 110
Taylor, Anique 1946- 109
Taylor, Ann 1782-1866 SATA-35, 41
Taylor, Ann
See Smith, Richard Rein
Taylor, Anna 1944- 25-28R
Taylor, Anne (Gary) Pannell 1910-1984
Obituary 112
Taylor, Archer 1890-1973 Obituary 107
Taylor, Arnold H. 1929- 33-36R
Taylor, Art
See Taylor, Arthur (Stephen)
Taylor, Arthur (Stephen) 1929- 122
Taylor, Arthur Samuel 1894-1963 2R
Obituary 103
Taylor, Barbara G. 1942- 25-28R
Taylor, Barbara J. 1927- 53-56
See also SATA 10
Taylor, Bayard 1825-1878 DLB-3
Taylor, Benjamin J. 1934- 21-22R
Taylor, Bernard 1934- CANR-24
Earlier sketch in CA 69-72
Taylor, Bert Leston 1866-1921 Brief entry 117
See also DLB 25
Taylor, Betty Jo 1933- 15-16R
Taylor, Bob L(eslie) 1923- 33-36R
Taylor, Brad
See Smith, Richard Rein
Taylor, Carl 1937- 69-72
See also SATA 14
Taylor, Cecil Philip 1929-1981 25-28R
Obituary 105
See also CLC 27
Taylor, Charlene M(ae) 1938- 33-36R
Taylor, Charles 1931- CANR-11
Earlier sketch in CA 15-16R
Taylor, Charles Alfred 1922- 109
Taylor, Charles D(oonan) 1938- CANR-17
Earlier sketch in CA 101
Taylor, Charles H. 1846-1921 DLB-25
Taylor, Charles Lewis 1935- CANR-13
Earlier sketch in CA 77-80
Taylor, Clyde R(ussell) 1931- 45-48
Taylor, Clyde Willis 1904-1988 Obituary 125
Taylor, Constance Lindsay 1907- 106
Taylor, Cora (Lorraine) 1936- 124
Taylor, Cora Sibal 1941(?)-1987 Obituary 123
Taylor, D. J. 1960- 122
Taylor, Dalmas A(rnold) 1933- 57-60
Taylor, David 1900-1965 3R
See also SATA 10
Taylor, David (Conrad) 1934- 105
Taylor, David Alan 1943- 108
Taylor, Dawson 1916- CANR-25
Earlier sketch in CA 13-14R
Taylor, Day
See Parkinson, Cornelia M.
and Salvato, Sharon
Taylor, Dayna
See Parkinson, Cornelia M.
Taylor, (Joseph) Deems 1885-1966
Obituary 89-92
Taylor, Demetria 1903-1977 Obituary 73-76
Taylor, (Edmund) Dennis 1940- 119
Taylor, Desmond 1930- 37-40R
Taylor, Don(ald) 1910- 13-14R
Taylor, Donald L(avor) 1916- 19-20R
Taylor, Donald Stewart 1924- Brief entry 106
Taylor, Donna June 1949- 37-40R
Taylor, Duncan (Burnett) 1912- 25-28R
Taylor, Duncan Norton
See Norton-Taylor, Duncan
Taylor, Dwight 1902-1986(?) Obituary 121
Taylor, Earl Aulick 1904-1965 CAP-1
Earlier sketch in CA 13-14
Taylor, Edith 1913- 45-48
Taylor, Edward 1642(?)-1729 DLB-24
Taylor, Eleanor Ross 1920- 81-84
See also CLC 5
Taylor, Elisabeth Russell
See Russell Taylor, Elisabeth
Taylor, Elizabeth 1912-1975 CANR-9
Earlier sketch in CA 13-14R
See also SATA 13
See also CLC 2, 4, 29
Taylor, Elizabeth Tebbetts 101
Taylor, Ethel Stoddard 1895(?)-1975
Obituary 57-60
Taylor, Eugene Jackson 1913-1978
Obituary 81-84
Taylor, Florance Walton 37-40R
See also SATA 9
Taylor, Florence M(arian Tompkins) 1892- 15-16R
See also SATA 9
Taylor, Frank J. 1894-1972 CAP-1
Obituary 37-40R
Earlier sketch in CA 13-14
Taylor, Fred James 1919- 107
Taylor, (George) Frederick 1928- 77-80
Taylor, G(eorge) Jeffrey 1944- 116
Taylor, George
See Parulski, George R(ichard), Jr.
Taylor, George A(lbert) 1942- 102
Taylor, George E(dward) 1905- CANR-22
Earlier sketch in CA 2R
Taylor, Gordon O(verton) 1938- 25-28R
Taylor, Gordon Rattray 1911-1981 85-88
Obituary 105
Taylor, (Frank Herbert) Griffin 1917- 65-68
Taylor, H. Baldwin
See Waugh, Hillary Baldwin
Taylor, H. Kerr 1891(?)-1977 Obituary 73-76
Taylor, Harold 1914- 25-28R
Taylor, Harold L(awrence) 1934- 110
Taylor, Harold McCarter 1907- 109
Taylor, Harold S. 1901(?)-1985 Obituary 116
Taylor, Harry
See Granick, Harry
Taylor, Harry H. 1926- 57-60
Taylor, Henry 1800-1886 DLB-32
Taylor, Henry (Splawn) 1942- 33-36R
See also CAAS 7
See also DLB 5
See also CLC 44
Taylor, Henry J(unior) 1902-1984 CAP-2
Obituary 112
Earlier sketch in CA 23-24
Taylor, Herb(ert Norman, Jr.) 1942-1987 97-100
Obituary 123
See also SATA 22
Taylor, Howard F(rancis) 1939- 110
Taylor, Hugh 1917(?)-1987 Obituary 123
Taylor, Hugh A(lexander) 1920- 115
Taylor, Ian 1944- 77-80
Taylor, Ina (Margaret Kathleen) 1949- 119
Taylor, Irving A. 1925- 61-64
Taylor, J. Thomas 1930- 107
Taylor, Jack W(ilson) 1915- 11-12R
Taylor, James B(entley) 1930- 37-40R
Taylor, James C(hapman) 1937- 77-80
Taylor, James R(owe) 1907- CAP-2
Earlier sketch in CA 17-18
Taylor, James Spear 1897(?)-1979
Obituary 85-88
Taylor, James Stephen 1935- 121
Taylor, Jane 1783-1824 SATA-35, 41
Taylor, Janelle (Diane Williams) 1944- 124
Brief entry 118
Taylor, (Samuel) Jared 1951- 122
Taylor, Jed H(arbottle) 1902- CAP-1
Earlier sketch in CA 15-16
Taylor, Jenny 1910- 105
Taylor, Jerome 1918- CANR-1
Earlier sketch in CA 3R
Taylor, Jerry D(uncan) 1938- 115
See also SATA 47
Taylor, Jesse
See Amidon, Bill (Vincent)
Taylor, Jim 1937- 119
Taylor, Joan du Plat ?-1983 Obituary 109
Taylor, Joe Gray 1920- CANR-6
Earlier sketch in CA 57-60
Taylor, John 1916- 93-96
Taylor, John 1921- CANR-16
Earlier sketch in CA 23-24R
Taylor, John 1925- 81-84
Taylor, John (Alfred) 1931- 61-64
Taylor, John 1955- 124
Taylor, John F(rank) A(dams) 1915- 19-20R
Taylor, John G(erald) 1931- 29-32R
Taylor, John Laverack 1937- CANR-1
Earlier sketch in CA 45-48
Taylor, John M(axwell) 1930- 25-28R
Taylor, John Randolph 1929- 1R
Taylor, John Russell 1935- 5-6R
Taylor, John Vernon 1914- CANR-21
Earlier sketches in CA 9-10R, CANR-5
Taylor, John W(illiam) R(ansom) 1922- 49-52
Taylor, Joshua Charles 1917-1981 104
Taylor, Judy
See Hough, Judy Taylor
Taylor, Kamala (Purnaiya) 1924- 77-80
Taylor, Karen
See Malpede, Karen (Sophia)
Taylor, Karl K. 1938- 41-44R
Taylor, Katharine Whiteside 1897- CAP-2
Earlier sketch in CA 25-28
Taylor, Keith Weller 1946- 111
Taylor, Ken 1922- 108
Taylor, Kenneth N(athaniel) 1917- CANR-8
Earlier sketch in CA 19-20R
See also SATA 26
See also AITN 2
Taylor, (Paul) Kent 1940- CANR-9
Earlier sketch in CA 17-18R
Taylor, L(aurie) A(ylma) 1939- 111
Taylor, L(ester) B(arbour), Jr. 1932- CANR-26
Earlier sketches in CA 57-60, CANR-11
See also SATA 27
Taylor, Laurie
See Taylor, L(aurie) A(ylma)
Taylor, Lawrence 1942- 105
Taylor, (M.) Lee 1930- 41-44R
Taylor, Lester D(ean) 1938- 17-18R
Taylor, Lloyd A(ndrew) 1921- 41-44R
Taylor, Lloyd C(hamberlain), Jr. 1923- 57-60
Taylor, Lois Dwight Cole
See Cole, Lois Dwight
Taylor, Lord
See Taylor, Stephen James Lake
Taylor, Louis 1900- CANR-2
Earlier sketch in CA 7-8R
Taylor, Louise Todd 1939- 115
See also SATA 47
Taylor, Malcolm Gordon 1915- 109

Taylor, Margaret
See Burroughs, Margaret Taylor (Goss)
Taylor, Margaret Stewart ... 89-92
Taylor, Marion Ansel 1904- ... 13-14R
Taylor, Mark 1927- ... 108
See also SATA 28, 32
Taylor, Mark C. 1945- ... 125
Taylor, Mary Ann 1912- ... 97-100
Taylor, Maxwell D(avenport) 1901-1987
Obituary ... 122
Brief entry ... 111
Taylor, Michael J. 1924- ... CANR-7
Earlier sketch in CA 19-20R
Taylor, Michael J. H. 1949- ... CANR-14
Earlier sketch in CA 77-80
Taylor, Michael M. 1944- ... 97-100
Taylor, Mildred D. ... CANR-25
Earlier sketch in CA 85-88
See also BW
See also SATA 15
See also SAAS 5
See also DLB 52
See also CLC 21
See also CLR 9
Taylor, Morris F. 1915- ... 37-40R
Taylor, Norman 1883-1967 ... CAP-2
Earlier sketch in CA 23-24
Taylor, Owen Reece 1912(?)-1983
Obituary ... 111
Taylor, Pat Ellis 1941- ... 111
Taylor, Paul 1948- ... 121
Taylor, Paul B(eekman) 1930- ... 81-84
Taylor, Paul S(chuster) 1895-1984 ... 81-84
Obituary ... 112
Taylor, Paul W(arren) 1923- ... CANR-21
Earlier sketch in CA 4R
Taylor, Paula (Wright) 1942- ... 122
Brief entry ... 111
See also SATA 33, 48
Taylor, Peggy 1946- ... 120
Taylor, Peter (Hillsman) 1917- ... CANR-9
Earlier sketch in CA 15-16R
See also DLBY 81
See also CLC 1, 4, 18, 37, 44, 50
Taylor, Philip Elbert 1908-1975 Obituary ... 61-64
Taylor, Phoebe Atwood 1909-1976
Obituary ... 61-64
Taylor, Phoebe Jean 1921(?)-1979
Obituary ... 89-92
Taylor, Ransom Theodore 1913- ... 45-48
Taylor, Ray J. 1918(?)-1977 Obituary ... 69-72
Taylor, Ray Ward 1908- ... CAP-2
Earlier sketch in CA 19-20
Taylor, Rebe Prestwich 1911- ... 13-14R
Taylor, Rex 1921- ... 13-14R
Taylor, Richard 1919- ... 17-18R
Taylor, Richard K(night) 1933- ... CANR-18
Earlier sketch in CA 101
Taylor, Richard S(helley) 1912- ... 115
Taylor, Richard W(arren) 1924- ... CANR-19
Earlier sketches in CA 7-8R, CANR-3
Taylor, Robert 1925- ... 81-84
Taylor, Robert B(artley) 1926- ... 81-84
Taylor, Robert Brown 1936- ... CANR-12
Earlier sketch in CA 61-64
Taylor, Robert, Jr. 1941- ... 118
Taylor, Robert Lewis 1912- ... CANR-3
Earlier sketch in CA 3R
See also SATA 10
See also CLC 14
Taylor, Robert Martin 1909- ... CAP-2
Earlier sketch in CA 25-28
Taylor, Robert R(atcliffe) 1939- ... 53-56
Taylor, Roland 1907- ... CAP-1
Earlier sketch in CA 13-14
Taylor, Ron(ald) W(illiam) 1922- ... CAP-1
Earlier sketch in CA 11-12
Taylor, Ronald (Jack) 1924- ... CANR-26
Earlier sketch in CA 93-96
Taylor, Ronald L(ee) 1938- ... 77-80
Taylor, Ross McLaury 1909(?)-1977
Obituary ... 69-72
Taylor, Rupert (Maurice) 1946- ... 45-48
Taylor, Ruth Mattson 1922- ... 101
Taylor, Samuel (Wooley) 1907- ... 73-76
Taylor, Samuel (Albert) 1912- ... 25-28R
Taylor, Sandra C. 1936- ... 123
Taylor, Stephen
See Taylor, Stephen James Lake
Taylor, Stephen James Lake 1910-1988
Obituary ... 124
Taylor, Sybil (Renee) 1933- ... 122
Taylor, Sydney (Brenner) 1904(?)-1978 ... CANR-4
Obituary ... 77-80
Earlier sketch in CA 5-6R
See also SATA 1, 26, 28
Taylor, T. G.
See Taylor, T(homas) Geoffrey
Taylor, T(homas) Geoffrey 1918-1987
Obituary ... 123
Taylor, Telford 1908- ... CANR-16
Earlier sketch in CA 25-28R
Taylor, Theodore 1921- ... CANR-25
Earlier sketches in CA 21-22R, CANR-9
See also SATA 5
See also SAAS 4
Taylor, Theodore Brewster 1925- ... 102
Taylor, Theodore W(alter) 1913- ... 119
Taylor, Thomas 1934- ... 23-24R
Taylor, Tim 1920-1974 ... 45-48
Obituary ... 53-56
Taylor, Tom
See Taylor, J. Thomas
Taylor, Valerie
See Tate, Velma
Taylor, Vernon L. 1922- ... 33-36R
Taylor, Verta 1948- ... 114
Taylor, W(illiam) H(odge) 1904-1984
Obituary ... 113
Taylor, Walter Fuller 1900-1966 ... 1R
Taylor, Walter W(illard) 1913- ... 61-64
Taylor, Warren 1903- ... 23-24R
Taylor, Weldon J. 1908- ... 4R
Taylor, Welford Dunaway 1938- ... 37-40R
Taylor, Wendell H(ertig) 1905- ... 102
Taylor, William 1930- ... CANR-15
Earlier sketch in CA 81-84
Taylor, William David, Jr. 1902-1975
Obituary ... 107
Taylor, William E(dwards) 1920- ... CANR-10
Earlier sketch in CA 25-28R
Taylor, William Ewart, Jr. 1927- ... 126
Taylor, William L. 1937- ... 29-32R
Taylor, Zack 1927- ... 65-68
Taylor-Gooby, Peter 1947- ... 118
Taylor-Olson, Clara Mae 1899(?)-1988
Obituary ... 124
Tazewell, Charles 1900-1972 Obituary ... 37-40R
Tazieff, Haroun 1914- Brief entry ... 113
Tchaadaieff
See Sorokin, Pitirim A(lexandrovitch)
Tchekhov, Anton
See Chekhov, Anton (Pavlovich)
Tchernichovski, Saul (Gutmanovich)
1875-1943 Brief entry ... 116
Tchicaya, Gerald Felix 1931-1988
Obituary ... 125
Tchicaya U Tam'si
See Tchicaya, Gerald Felix
Tchividjian, Gigi Graham 1945- ... 108
Tchobanoglous, George 1935- ... 102
Tchudi, Stephen N. 1942- ... CANR-22
Earlier sketch in CA 89-92
Tead, Ordway 1891-1973 Obituary ... 45-48
Teaford, Jon C(hristian) 1946- ... CANR-10
Earlier sketch in CA 65-68
Teague, Bob
See Teague, Robert
Teague, Kathleen 1937- ... 97-100
Teague, Michael 1932- ... 109
Teague, Robert 1929- ... 106
See also SATA 31, 32
Teal, G. Donn 1932- ... 33-36R
Teal, John J(erome), Jr. 1921-1982
Obituary ... 110
Teal, Val(entine M.) 1903- ... 61-64
See also SATA 10
Teale, Edwin Way 1899-1980 ... CANR-2
Obituary ... 102
Earlier sketch in CA 2R
See also SATA 7, 25
Teasdale, Sara 1884-1933 Brief entry ... 104
See also SATA 32
See also DLB 45
See also TCLC 4
Tebbel, John (William) 1912- ... 85-88
See also SATA 26
Tebbel, Robert E(verett) 1924- ... 7-8R
Tebbetts-Taylor, Elizabeth
See Taylor, Elizabeth Tebbetts
Tebeau, Charlton Watson 1904- ... 110
Tebelak, John-Michael 1949(?)-1985
Obituary ... 115
Tec, Leon 1919- ... 97-100
Tec, Nechama 1931- ... CANR-23
Earlier sketch in CA 11-12R
Teck, Alan 1934- ... 25-28R
Tedder, Arthur William 1890-1967 ... CAP-2
Earlier sketch in CA 23-24
Tedder, Lord
See Tedder, Arthur William
Teddy, Paul
See Aldrich, Jonathan
Tedeschi, (Theodore) James, Jr. 1928- ... 41-44R
Tedlock, E(rnest) W(arnock), Jr. 1910- ... CAP-2
Earlier sketch in CA 17-18
Tedrow, R. L.
See Tedrow, Richard L(ove)
Tedrow, Richard L(ove) 1913(?)-1987
Obituary ... 121
Teegen, Otto John 1899-1983 Obituary ... 109
Teer, Frank 1934- ... 53-56
Teeter, Don E(l) 1934- ... 73-76
Teeter, Karl V(an Duyn) 1929- ... 19-20R
Teeters, Negley K(ing) 1896-1971 ... CAP-2
Obituary ... 33-36R
Earlier sketch in CA 23-24
Teetor, Paul R(aymond) 1919- ... 113
Teets, Bruce E. 1914- ... 37-40R
Tee-Van, Helen Damrosch 1893-1976 ... 49-52
Obituary ... 65-68
See also SATA 10, 27
Teevan, Richard C(ollier) 1919- ... CANR-4
Earlier sketch in CA 1R
Teffeteller, Gordon Lamar 1931- ... 115
Tefft, Bess H(agaman) 1915(?)-1977
Obituary ... 110
Tega, Vasile 1921- ... CANR-18
Earlier sketch in CA 102
Tegenfeldt, Herman G(ustaf) 1913- ... 73-76
Tegner, Bruce 1928- ... CANR-8
Earlier sketch in CA 61-64
Tegner, Henry (Stuart) 1901- ... CANR-12
Earlier sketch in CA 13-14R
Teich, Albert H(arris) 1942- ... CANR-25
Earlier sketch in CA 45-48
Teicher, Morton I(rving) 1920- ... CANR-11
Earlier sketch in CA 69-72
Teichgraeber, Richard F. III 1950- ... 125
Teichmann, Howard (Miles)
1916-1987 ... CANR-17
Obituary ... 123
Earlier sketch in CA 69-72
Teikmanis, Arthur L. 1914- ... 15-16R
Teilhard de Chardin, (Marie Joseph) Pierre
1881-1955 Brief entry ... 105
See also TCLC 9
Teiser, Ruth 1915- ... 109
Teissier du Cros, Janet 1906- ... CAP-2
Earlier sketch in CA 17-18
Teitelbaum, Harry 1930- ... 23-24R
Teitelbaum, Michael 1953- ... 121
Teitelbaum, Myron 1929- ... 15-16R
Teixeira, Bernardo 1926- ... 108
Teixeira da Mota, Avelino ?-1982 Obituary ... 106
Tekeyan, Charles 1927- ... 29-32R
Telander, Richard F(orster) 1948- ... 65-68
Teleki, Geza 1943- ... CANR-19
Earlier sketches in CA 49-52, CANR-3
See also SATA 45
Telemaque, Eleanor Wong 1934- ... 104
See also SATA 43
Telescope, Tom
See Newbery, John
Telfer, Dariel (Doris) 1905-1987 ... CAP-2
Obituary ... 122
Earlier sketch in CA 25-28
Telfer, R(oss) 1937- ... 106
Telfer, William 1886-1968 ... CAP-1
Earlier sketch in CA 13-14
Telford, Charles W(itt) 1903- ... 65-68
Tell, Jack 1909(?)-1979 Obituary ... 89-92
Teller, Edward 1908- ... CAP-1
Earlier sketch in CA 13-14
Teller, James D(avid) 1906- ... 41-44R
Teller, Judd L. 1912-1972 Obituary ... 33-36R
Teller, Neville 1931- ... CANR-23
Earlier sketch in CA 103
Teller, Walter (Magnes) 1910- ... CANR-2
Earlier sketch in CA 5-6R
Tello, Carlos 1938- ... 112
Telser, Lester G(reenspan) 1931- ... 33-36R
Temianka, Henri 1906- ... 45-48
Temin, Peter 1937- ... 15-16R
Temkin, Pauline B. 1919- ... 25-28R
Temkin, Sara Anne Schlossberg 1913- ... 3R
See also SATA 26
Temko, Florence ... CANR-17
Earlier sketches in CA 49-52, CANR-1
See also SATA 13
Temmer, Mark J. 1922- Brief entry ... 107
Temp, George (Edward) 1929- ... 45-48
Temperley, Howard 1932- ... 85-88
Temperley, Nicholas 1932- ... 107
Tempest, Jan
See Swatridge, Irene Maude (Mossop)
Tempest, Margaret Mary 1892-1982
Obituary ... 108
See also SATA 33
Tempest, Sarah
See Ponsonby, D(oris) A(lmon)
Tempest, Theresa
See Kent, Louise Andrews
Tempest, Victor
See Philipp, Elliot Elias
Templar, Maurice
See Groom, Arthur William
Temple, Ann
See Mortimer, Penelope (Ruth)
Temple, Arthur
See Northcott, (William) Cecil
Temple, Cliff 1947- ... 111
Temple, Dan
See Newton, D(wight) B(ennett)
Temple, Herbert 1919- ... SATA-45
Temple, Joe 1917- ... 97-100
Temple, Nigel (Hal Longdale) 1926- ... 29-32R
Temple, Paul
See Durbridge, Francis (Henry)
and McConnell, James Douglas
Rutherford
Temple, Paul
See McConnell, James Douglas
Rutherford
Temple, Philip (Robert) 1939- ... CANR-22
Earlier sketch in CA 104
Temple, Robert (Kyle Grenville) 1945- ... CANR-16
Earlier sketch in CA 89-92
Temple, Robert M(ickler), Jr. 1935-
Brief entry ... 107
Temple, Ruth Z(abriskie) 1908- ... 61-64
Temple, Wayne C(alhoun) 1924- ... CANR-17
Earlier sketches in CA 1R, CANR-1
Temple, Willard H. 1912- ... 1R
Temple, William 1881-1944 Brief entry ... 120
Templeton, Charles B. 1915- ... 101
Templeton, Edith 1916- ... 53-56
Templeton, Janet
See Hershman, Morris
Templeton, John J(oseph), Jr. 1928- ... 25-28R
Tenax
See Lean, Garth Dickinson
ten Boom, Corrie 1892-1983 ... 111
Obituary ... 109
Tendryakov, Vladimir Fyodorovich
1923-1984(?) ... 104
Obituary ... 113
Tenenbaum, Frances 1919- ... CANR-12
Earlier sketch in CA 73-76
Tenenbaum, Shea 1910- ... CANR-1
Earlier sketch in CA 49-52
Tener, Robert L(awrence) 1924- ... 110
Teng, S(su)-Y(u) 1906- ... CANR-22
Earlier sketch in CA 13-14R
Tengbom, Mildred 1921- ... CANR-17
Earlier sketch in CA 97-100
Tenggren, Gustaf 1896-1970 ... SATA-18, 26
Ten Harmsel, Henrietta 1921- ... 106
Ten Hoor, Elvie (Marie Mortensen)
1900-1984 ... 11-12R
Obituary ... 112
TenHouten, Warren David 1939-
Brief entry ... 108
Tenison, Marika Hanbury
See Hanbury-Tenison, Marika
Tenison, Robin Hanbury
See Hanbury-Tenison, (Airling) Robin
Tenn, Ada N(ina) 1915- ... CANR-11
Earlier sketch in CA 25-28R
Tenn, William 1919- ... DLB-8
Tennant, Alan 1943- ... 108
Tennant, Emma 1937- ... CANR-10
Earlier sketch in CA 65-68
See also DLB 14
See also CLC 13
Tennant, Kylie
See Rodd, Kylie Tennant
See also SATA 6
Tennant, Nora Jackson 1915- ... CANR-4
Earlier sketch in CA 9-10R
Tennant, (Charles) Roger 1919- ... 106
Tennant, Stephen (James Napier)
1906-1987 Obituary ... 122
Tennant, Veronica 1947- ... 103
See also SATA 36
Tennenbaum, Silvia 1928- ... CANR-21
Earlier sketch in CA 77-80
Tenneshaw, S. M.
See Beaumont, Charles
and Silverberg, Robert
Tenness, George
See Delk, Robert Carlton
Tenney, H(orace) Kent 1892-1982
Obituary ... 107
Tenney, Merrill C(hapin) 1904-1985 ... CANR-4
Obituary ... 115
Earlier sketch in CA 1R
Tenney, Tabitha Gilman 1762-1837 ... DLB-37
Tenniel, John 1820-1914 Brief entry ... 111
See also SATA 27
Tennien, Mark A. 1900(?)-1983 Obituary ... 108
Tennies, Arthur C(ornelius) 1931- ... 53-56
Tennison, Patrick Joseph 1928- ... CANR-23
Earlier sketch in CA 106
Tennissen, Anthony C(ornelius)
1920-1982 ... 114
Tennov, Dorothy 1928- ... 41-44R
Tennyson, Alfred 1809-1892 ... DLB-32
Tennyson, Charles (Bruce Locker)
1879-1977 ... 81-84
Obituary ... 73-76
Tennyson, Frederick 1807-1898 ... DLB-32
Tennyson, G(eorg) B(ernhard) 1930- ... CANR-9
Earlier sketch in CA 21-22R
Tenpas, Margaret (Susan Lyon) 1923- ... 85-88
Tensen, Ruth M(arjorie) ... 7-8R
Tent, Ned
See Dennett, Herbert Victor
TePaske, John J(ay) 1929- ... 117
Teplitz, Paul V(ictor) 1940- ... 111
Tepper, Albert 1928- ... 25-28R
Tepper, Michael 1941- ... CANR-12
Earlier sketch in CA 73-76
Tepper, Terri P(atricia) 1942- ... 107
Teran, Lisa St. Aubin de
See St. Aubin de Teran, Lisa
See also CLC 36
Terayama, Shuji 1936-1983 Obituary ... 109
Terban, Marvin ... SATA-45
Terborgh, George (Willard) 1897- ... CAP-2
Earlier sketch in CA 23-24
Terbovich, John B. 1933-1969 ... CAP-2
Earlier sketch in CA 21-22
Terchek, Ronald John 1936- ... 49-52
Terdiman, Richard 1941- ... 73-76
Terenzio, Stephanie 1932- ... 118
Teresi, Judith M.
See Goldberger, Judith M.
ter Haar, Jaap 1922- ... 37-40R
See also SATA 6
terHorst, J(erald) F(ranklin) 1922- ... 107
See also AITN 1
ter Horst, Robert 1929- ... 116
Terhune, Albert Payson 1872-1942
Brief entry ... 111
See also SATA 15
See also DLB 9
Terhune, William B(arclay) 1893-1987 ... 61-64
Obituary ... 122
Terich, Thomas A. 1943- ... 125
Terkel, Louis 1912- ... CANR-18
Earlier sketch in CA 57-60
Terkel, Studs
See Terkel, Louis
See also CLC 38
See also AITN 1
Terkel, Susan N(eiburg) 1948- ... 115
Terlouw, Jan (Cornelis) 1931- ... 108
See also SATA 30
Terman, Douglas 1933- Brief entry ... 112
Terman, Sibyl 1902(?)-1975 Obituary ... 57-60
Terme, Hilary
See Hay, Jacob
Terner, Janet 1938- ... 102
Terni-Cialente, Fausta 1900- ... CANR-5
Earlier sketch in CA 7-8R
Terpstra, Vern 1927- ... CANR-11
Earlier sketch in CA 21-22R
Terr, Leonard B(rian) 1946- ... 73-76
Terrace, Edward L. B. 1936(?)-1973
Obituary ... 45-48
Terrace, Herbert S(ydney) 1936- ... 102
Terrace, Vincent 1948- ... CANR-25
Earlier sketches in CA 65-68, CANR-9
Terraine, John (Alfred) 1921- ... CANR-13
Earlier sketch in CA 5-6R
Terrall, Robert 1914- ... 102
Terras, Victor 1921- Brief entry ... 113

Terrell, Carroll F(ranklin) 1917- CANR-20
Earlier sketch in CA 102
Terrell, Donna McManus 1908- 57-60
Terrell, John Upton 1900- 29-32R
Terrell, Robert L(ouis) 1943- CANR-17
Earlier sketch in CA 41-44R
Terres, John K(enneth) 1905- CANR-5
Earlier sketch in CA 5-6R
Terrien, Samuel Lucien 1911- 81-84
Terrill, Ross 1938- 25-28R
Terrill, Tom E(dward) 1935- 41-44R
Terris, Susan 1937- CANR-12
Earlier sketch in CA 29-32R
See also SATA 3
Terris, Virginia R(inaldy) 1917- 65-68
Terry, Arthur 1927- 85-88
Terry, Bill 1931- 118
Terry, C. V.
See Slaughter, Frank G(ill)
Terry, Carol
See Talbot, Carol Terry
Terry, Charles S. 1926(?)-1982 Obituary ... 107
Terry, Doug(las) 1950- 120
Terry, Edith (Buchanan) 1952- 120
Terry, Edward D(avis) 1927- 29-32R
Terry, Luther L(eonidas) 1911-1985 ..... CAP-2
Obituary 115
Earlier sketch in CA 33-36
See also SATA 11, 42
Terry, Margaret
See Dunnahoo, Terry
Terry, Mark 1947- 37-40R
Terry, Marshall 1931- 2R
Terry, Megan 1932- 77-80
See also DLB 7
See also CLC 19
Terry, Michael 1899-1981 104
Terry, Robert H(arold) 1935- 29-32R
Terry, Robert Meredith 1939- 41-44R
Terry, Robert W(illiam) 1937- 37-40R
Terry, Sarah Meiklejohn 1937- 111
Terry, Saralee
See Kaye, Marvin (Nathan)
Terry, Walter 1913-1982 .... CANR-10
Obituary 107
Earlier sketch in CA 23-24R
See also SATA 14
Terry, William
See Harknett, Terry
Terson, Peter 1932- 104
See also DLB 13
Terstegge, Mabel Alice 1905- 93-96
Tertis, Lionel 1876-1975 93-96
Obituary 57-60
Tertz, Abram
See Sinyavsky, Andrei (Donatevich)
Terwilliger, Robert E(lwin) 1917- 65-68
Terzani, Tiziano 1938- CANR-14
Earlier sketch in CA 77-80
Terzian, James P. 1915- 15-16R
See also SATA 14
Terzian, Kathryn
See Cramer, Kathryn
Terzian, Yervant 1939- 125
TeSelle, Eugene (Arthur, Jr.) 1931- 37-40R
TeSelle, Sallie McFague
See McFague, Sallie
Tesich, Steve 1943(?)- 105
See also DLBY 83
See also CLC 40
Teslik, Kennan Lee 1952- 113
Tessier, (Ernst) M(aurice) 1885-1973 ... CANR-3
Earlier sketch in CA 7-8R
Tessler, Mark A(rnold) 1941- CANR-16
Earlier sketches in CA 45-48, CANR-1
Tessler, Stephanie Gordon 1940- 124
Tester, Sylvia Root 1939- CANR-8
Earlier sketch in CA 11-12R
See also SATA 37
Teta, Jon (Anthony) 1933- 25-28R
Tetel, Julie 1950- 118
Tetel, Marcel 1932- 23-24R
Tetens, Tete Harens 1899(?)-1976
Obituary 65-68
Teternikov, Fyodor Kuzmich 1863-1927
Brief entry 104
Tether, (Cynthia) Graham 1950- CANR-6
Earlier sketch in CA 57-60
See also SATA 36, 46
Tetlow, Edwin 1905- 17-18R
Tetreault, Wilfred F. 1927- 106
Teune, Henry 1936- CANR-3
Earlier sketch in CA 49-52
Teunissen, John James 1933- 112
Teuscher, Robert H(erman) 1934- 77-80
Teveth, Shabtai (Amotz) 1926(?)-
Brief entry 117
Tevis, Walter 1928-1984 113
See also CLC 42
Tewkesbury, Joan 1936- 101
Texon, Meyer 1909- 124
Tey, Josephine
See Mackintosh, Elizabeth
See also TCLC 14
Teynac, Francoise (Dolores Dupuis) 123
Teyte, Maggie 1888-1976 Obituary 65-68
Tezla, Albert 1915- CANR-14
Earlier sketch in CA 37-40R
Thacher, Alida McKay 1951- CANR-11
Earlier sketch in CA 69-72
Thacher, James 1754-1844 .... DLB-37
Thacher, Mary McGrath 1933- SATA-9
Thacker, Eric (Lee) 1923- Brief entry 107
Thacker, Ernest W(ichman) 1914- 13-14R
Thacker, Thomas William 1911-1984
Obituary 113
Thackeray, Milton G. 1914- 15-16R
Thackeray, William Makepeace
1811-1863 .... SATA-23
See also DLB 21, 55
Thackray, Arnold 1939- 49-52
Thackray, Derek V(incent) 1926- 103
Thackrey, Russell I. 1904- 37-40R
Thaddeus, Janice Farrar 1933- 13-14R
Thaden, Edward Carl 1922- 19-20R
Thain, Donald H(ammond) 1928- CANR-25
Earlier sketch in CA 3R
Thakur, Shivesh Chandra 1936- 29-32R
Thakura, Ravindranatha
See Tagore, Rabindranath
Thalacker, Donald William 1939-
Brief entry 108
Thalberg, Irving (Grant, Jr.) 1930-1987 ..41-44R
Obituary 123
Thale, Jerome 1927- 15-16R
Thaler, Alwin 1891- CAP-1
Earlier sketch in CA 11-12
Thaler, M. N.
See Kerner, Fred
Thaler, Michael C. 1936- 124
See also SATA 47
Thaler, Mike
See Thaler, Michael C.
Thaler, Susan 1939- 21-22R
Thalheimer, Ross 1905-1977 ....41-44R
Thalia
See Bokum, Fanny Butcher
Thalmann, Rita Renee Line 1926- CANR-19
Earlier sketches in CA 53-56, CANR-4
Thamer, Katie 1955- SATA-42
Thames, C. H.
See Marlowe, Stephen
Thames, Jack
See Ryan, John Fergus
Thamm, Robert 1933- 89-92
Thampi, Parvathi (Menon) 1925- 5-6R
Thane, (Lillian) Adele 1904- 25-28R
Thane, Elswyth 1900- 5-6R
See also SATA 32
Thanet, Neil
See Fanthorpe, R(obert) Lionel
Thant, U 1909-1974 Obituary 108
Tharaud, Lucien Rostaing, Jr. 1953- 69-72
Tharaud, Ross
See Tharaud, Lucien Rostaing, Jr.
Tharp, Louise (Marshall) Hall 1898- 4R
See also SATA 3
Tharpe, Jac Lyndon 1928-1985 .... CANR-7
Obituary 117
Earlier sketch in CA 57-60
Thass-Thienemann, Theodore 1900- 25-28R
Thatcher, David 1922- 77-80
Thatcher, Dora (Fickling) 1912- 13-14R
Thatcher, Dorothy Southwell 1903- CAP-1
Earlier sketch in CA 13-14
Thatcher, Floyd W(ilson) 1917- 102
Thatcher, Joan (Claire) 1934- 106
Thatcher, Julia
See Bensen, Donald R.
Thaxton, Ralph 1944- 114
Thayer, Charles Wheeler 1910-1969 ... CANR-26
Obituary 103
Earlier sketch in CA 2R
Thayer, Emma R(edington) Lee
1874-1973 .... CAP-1
Obituary 45-48
Earlier sketch in CA 9-10
Thayer, Ernest Lawrence 1863-1940
Brief entry 119
Thayer, Frederick C(lifton), Jr. 1924- ... CANR-12
Earlier sketch in CA 73-76
Thayer, George (Chapman, Jr.)
1933-1973 .... CAP-2
Obituary 45-48
Earlier sketch in CA 25-28
Thayer, Geraldine
See Daniels, Dorothy
Thayer, H(orace) S(tandish) 1923- 45-48
Thayer, James Stewart 1949- 73-76
Thayer, Jane
See Woolley, Catherine
Thayer, Lee (Osborne) 1927- CANR-18
Earlier sketches in CA 49-52, CANR-3
Thayer, Lee
See Thayer, Emma R(edington) Lee
Thayer, Marjorie Brief entry 116
See also SATA 37
Thayer, Mary Van Rensselaer
1903(?)-1983 97-100
Obituary 111
Thayer, Molly
See Thayer, Mary Van Rensselaer
Thayer, Nathaniel B(owman) 1929- 45-48
Thayer, Peter
See Wyler, Rose
Thayer, Theodore 1904-1981 Obituary 103
Thayer, V(ivian) T(row) 1886-1979 ...... CAP-2
Obituary 89-92
Earlier sketch in CA 17-18
Thayler, Carl 1933- 37-40R
Thayne, Emma Lou 1924- 65-68
Thayne, Miria Greenwood 1907- 21-22R
Theall, Donald Francis 1928- 105
Thebaud, Jo 1914- 49-52
Theberge, James D.
See Theberge, James Daniel
Theberge, James Daniel 1930-1988 ......25-28R
Obituary 124
Thede, Marion Draughon 1903- CAP-2
Earlier sketch in CA 25-28
Thee, Marek 1918- 101
The Ear
See McLellan, Diana
Theen, Rolf H(einz) W(ilhelm) 1937- 41-44R
The Fourth Brother
See Aung, (Maung) Htin
The Gallerite
See Bason, Frederick (Thomas)
The Great Comte
See Hawkesworth, Eric
The Great Merlini
See Rawson, Clayton
Theil, Henri 1924- CANR-22
Earlier sketches in CA 17-18R, CANR-7
Theiner, George (Fredric) 1927-1988 .....29-32R
Theis, John William 1911- Brief entry 109
Theis, Paul A(nthony) 1923- 41-44R
Theisen, Jerome Paul 1930- 113
Theissen, Gerd 1943- 117
Thekaekara, Matthew P(othen)
1914-1976 77-80
Obituary 69-72
Thelen, David Paul 1939- Brief entry 110
Thelen, Gil 1938- 73-76
Thelen, Herbert Arnold 1913- 108
Thelin, John R(obert) 1947- CANR-11
Earlier sketch in CA 69-72
Thelle, Notto R(eidar) 1941- 125
Thelwell, Michael Miles 1939- 101
See also CLC 22
Thelwell, Norman 1923- CANR-4
Earlier sketch in CA 7-8R
See also SATA 14
Themerson, Stefan 1910-1988 .... CANR-9
Obituary 126
Earlier sketch in CA 65-68
Theo, Ion
See Theodorescu, Ion N.
Theobald, Lewis, Jr.
See Lovecraft, H(oward) P(hillips)
Theobald, Robert 1929- 37-40R
Theocharis, Reghinos D(emetrios)
1929- CANR-11
Earlier sketch in CA 13-14R
Theodorakis, Michalis 1925- Brief entry 105
Theodorakis, Mikis
See Theodorakis, Michalis
Theodorakopoulos, Ioannis 1900-1981
Obituary 108
Theodoratus, Robert J(ames) 1928- 41-44R
Theodore, Athena 1919- 41-44R
Theodore, Chris A(thanasios) 1920- 15-16R
Theodore, Sister Mary 1907- 7-8R
Theodorescu, Ion N. 1880-1967 Obituary ... 116
Theodorson, George A. 1924- 29-32R
Theoharis, Athan G(eorge) 1936- CANR-12
Earlier sketch in CA 29-32R
The Old Settler
See Lyman, Albert Robison
Theriault, Albert A(ugustine), Jr. 1928- 53-56
Theriault, Yves 1915- 102
Therio, Adrien 1925- DLB-53
Thernstrom, Stephan (Albert) 1934- 15-16R
Theroux, Alexander (Louis) 1939- CANR-20
Earlier sketch in CA 85-88
See also CLC 2, 25
Theroux, Paul 1941- CANR-20
Earlier sketch in CA 33-36R
See also SATA 44
See also DLB 2
See also CLC 5, 8, 11, 15, 28, 46
Theroux, Phyllis 1939- 110
Thersites
See Bram, Christopher
Thesen, Hjalmar Peter 1925- 107
Thesiger, Wilfred (Patrick) 1910- CAP-2
Earlier sketch in CA 17-18
Thesing, William B(arney) 1947- 113
Thevenin, Denis
See Duhamel, Georges
Thibaudeau, Colleen 1925- 113
Thibault, Jacques Anatole Francois
1844-1924 Brief entry 106
Thibault, John C(rowell) 1922- 77-80
Thiebaud, Wayne 1920- 45-48
Thiebaux, Marcelle 1931- 122
Brief entry 110
Thieda, Shirley Ann 1943- 69-72
See also SATA 13
Thiele, Colin (Milton) 1920- CANR-12
Earlier sketch in CA 29-32R
See also SATA 14
See also SAAS 2
See also CLC 17
Thiele, Edwin R(ichard) 1895- CAP-1
Earlier sketch in CA 19-20
Thiele, Margaret Rossiter 1901- 21-22R
Thielen, Thoraf Theodore 1921- 7-8R
Thielens, Wagner P., Jr. 1925- 1R
Thielicke, Helmut 1908-1986 .... CANR-11
Obituary 118
Earlier sketch in CA 69-72
Thiem, (Ezra) George 1897-1987 Obituary .. 123
Thien-An, Thich 1926- 57-60
Thier, Herbert D(avid) 1932- 29-32R
Thierauf, Robert J(ames) 1933- CANR-12
Earlier sketch in CA 29-32R
Thiesenhusen, William C. 1936- 21-22R
Thiessen, John (Jack) 1931- CANR-15
Earlier sketch in CA 41-44R
Thiessen, John C(aldwell) 1890- 7-8R
Thiher, Allen 1941- CANR-14
Earlier sketch in CA 41-44R
Thiman, Eric Harding 1900- CAP-1
Earlier sketch in CA 13-14
Thimblethorpe, June Sylvia 1926-
Brief entry 117
Thimm, Alfred L. 1923- CANR-8
Earlier sketch in CA 61-64
Thimmesch, Nicholas Palen 1927-1985 ...15-16R
Obituary 116
Thimmesch, Nick
See Thimmesch, Nicholas Palen
Thirion, Andre 1907- 101
Thirkell, Angela (Margaret) 1890-1961
Obituary 93-96
Thirkell, John Henry 1913- CANR-10
Earlier sketch in CA 13-14R
Thirlwall, John C(onnop, Jr.) 1904- 69-72
Thirsk, (Irene) Joan 1922- 25-28R
Thiry, Joan (Marie) 1926- 121
See also SATA 45
Thisby
See Turner, Dona M.
Thistle, Mel(ville William) 1914- 53-56
Thistlethwaite, Miles 1945- SATA-12
Thoby-Marcelin, (Emile) Philippe
1904-1975 125
Obituary 61-64
See also BW
Thody, Philip 1928- CANR-9
Earlier sketch in CA 7-8R
Thoene, Alma E(vans) 1903- 49-52
Thoene, Peter
See Bihalji-Merin, Oto
Thoger, Marie 1923- CANR-11
Earlier sketch in CA 25-28R
Tholfsen, Trygve R(ainone) 1924-
Brief entry 108
Thollander, Earl 1922- CANR-18
Earlier sketch in CA 101
See also SATA 22
Thom, James Alexander 1933- CANR-15
Earlier sketch in CA 77-80
Thom, Robert 1929-1979 ....21-22R
Obituary 85-88
Thom, Robert Anderson 1915- 61-64
Thom, Valerie M(acLaren) 1929- 124
Thoma, Henry F. 1909(?)-1983 Obituary 110
Thoma, Ludwig 1867-1921 .... DLB-66
Thoma, Richard 1902- DLB-4
Thomae, Betty Kennedy 1920- 61-64
Thoman, Richard S(amuel) 1919- 65-68
Thomas, A(rthur) J(oshua), Jr.
1918-1982 .... CANR-10
Earlier sketch in CA 5-6R
Thomas, A(ndrew) R(owland) B(enedick)
1904- 65-68
Thomas, Abraham V(azhayil) 1934- 61-64
Thomas, Alan (Cedric) 1933- 81-84
Thomas, Alan G. 1911- 25-28R
Thomas, Alexander 1914- 103
Thomas, Andrea
See Hill, Margaret (Ohler)
Thomas, Ann Van Wynen 1919- CANR-10
Earlier sketch in CA 5-6R
Thomas, Anna (Irena) 1948- CANR-24
Earlier sketch in CA 41-44R
Thomas, Annabel 1929- 106
Thomas, Arline 1913- 49-52
Thomas, Armstrong 1909(?)-1975
Obituary 57-60
Thomas, Art(hur Lawrence) 1952- 105
See also SATA 38, 48
Thomas, Audrey (Callahan) 1935- 23-24R
See also DLB 60
See also CLC 7, 13, 37
See also AITN 2
Thomas, Ben Bowen 1899-1977 Obituary ... 108
Thomas, Bill 1934- CANR-8
Earlier sketch in CA 61-64
Thomas, Bob
See Thomas, Robert J(oseph)
Thomas, Carl H.
See Doerffler, Alfred
Thomas, (Antony) Charles 1928- 119
Thomas, Charles W. 1903-1973
Obituary 41-44R
Thomas, Charles W(ellington) 1943- 65-68
Thomas, Claire Sherman 1923- 108
Thomas, Clara (McCandless) 1919- 25-28R
Thomas, Conrad Ward 1914- 37-40R
Thomas, Cornelius Dickinson 1920-1972 . CAP-1
Earlier sketch in CA 19-20
Thomas, Craig (David) 1942- 112
Brief entry 108
Thomas, Cullen
See Kimes, Beverly Rae
Thomas, D(onald) M(ichael) 1935- CANR-17
Earlier sketch in CA 61-64
See also DLB 40
See also CLC 13, 22, 31
Thomas, D(avid) O(swald) 1924- 117
Thomas, Dan
See Sanders, Leonard
Thomas, Daniel B.
See Bluestein, Daniel Thomas
Thomas, Daniel H(arrison) 1904- 15-16R
Thomas, Dante 1922- 53-56
Thomas, Dave 1949(?)- Brief entry 115
Thomas, David 1931- 103
Thomas, David A(rthur) 1925- 13-14R
Thomas, David H(urst) 1945- 108
Thomas, David St. John 1929- 112
Thomas, David Winton 1901-1970 .... CAP-1
Earlier sketch in CA 9-10
Thomas, Denis 1922- CANR-15
Earlier sketch in CA 77-80
Thomas, Dian 1945- CANR-10
Earlier sketch in CA 65-68
Thomas, Diane Renee 1946(?)-1985
Obituary 117
Thomas, Donald 1926- 49-52
Thomas, Donald F. 1913- 29-32R
Thomas, Donald Roff 1924-1979 Obituary .. 111
Thomas, Dorothy Swaine 1899-1977 ..... CAP-2
Obituary 69-72
Earlier sketch in CA 17-18

INDEX

Thomas, Dylan (Marlais) 1914-1953 ... 120
Brief entry ... 104
See also DLB 13, 20
See also TCLC 1, 8
Thomas, E(ric) H(ubert) Gwynne
See Gwynne-Thomas, E(ric) H(ubert)
Thomas, Earl W(esley) 1915- ... 53-56
Thomas, Edison H(ugh) 1912- ... 85-88
Thomas, (Philip) Edward 1878-1917
Brief entry ... 106
See also DLB 19
See also TCLC 10
Thomas, Edward Llewellyn
See Llewellyn-Thomas, Edward
Thomas, Edwin J(ohn) 1927- ... 21-22R
Thomas, Egbert S.
See Ellis, Edward S(ylvester)
Thomas, Elizabeth Ann 1952- ... 85-88
Thomas, Elizabeth Marshall 1931- ... 19-20R
Thomas, Emory M. 1939- ... 97-100
Thomas, Ernest Lewys 1904- ... CANR-1
Earlier sketch in CA 2R
Thomas, Estelle Webb 1899- ... 23-24R
See also SATA 26
Thomas, Evangeline 1904- ... 117
Thomas, F(ranklin) Richard 1940- ... CANR-13
Earlier sketch in CA 77-80
Thomas, Frank P(atrick) 1916- ... 119
Thomas, G. K.
See Davies, L(eslie) P(urnell)
Thomas, (Thomas) George 1909- ... 126
Thomas, George Finger 1899-1977
Obituary ... 73-76
Thomas, George I. 1915- ... 25-28R
Thomas, George Leicester, Jr. 1907- ... CAP-1
Earlier sketch in CA 11-12
Thomas, Gilbert (Oliver) 1891- ... 7-8R
Thomas, Gordon 1933- ... 9-10R
Thomas, Gordon L. 1914- ... 37-40R
Thomas, Graham Stuart 1909- ... CANR-19
Earlier sketches in CA 9-10R, CANR-4
Thomas, Gwyn 1913-1981 ... CANR-9
Obituary ... 103
Earlier sketch in CA 65-68
See also DLB 15
Thomas, H. C.
See Keating, Lawrence A.
Thomas, Harold Becken 1888-1971
Obituary ... 104
Thomas, Heather Smith 1944- ... CANR-6
Earlier sketch in CA 57-60
Thomas, Helen A. 1920- ... 101
Thomas, Helen Shirley 1931-1968 ... 7-8R
Obituary ... 103
Thomas, Henri (Joseph Marie) 1912- ... CAP-1
Earlier sketch in CA 9-10
Thomas, Henry 1886-1970 Obituary ... 29-32R
Thomas, Hugh Swynnerton 1931- ... CANR-5
Earlier sketch in CA 9-10R
Thomas, I(saac) D(avid) E(llis) 1921- ... 65-68
Thomas, Ianthe 1951- ... SATA-42
See also CLR 8
Thomas, Isaiah 1750-1831 ... DLB-43, 73
Thomas, Ivo Herbert Christopher 1912- ... 5-6R
Thomas, J(eremy) A(mbler) 1947- ... 118
Thomas, J. C. ... 57-60
Thomas, J(ames) D(avid) 1910- ... CANR-6
Earlier sketch in CA 57-60
Thomas, J. James 1933- ... 53-56
Thomas, J. W. 1917- ... 101
Thomas, Jack Ray 1931- ... 41-44R
Thomas, Jack W(illiam) 1930- ... CANR-16
Earlier sketches in CA 49-52, CANR-1
Thomas, James H(arold) 1943- ... 119
Thomas, Jane Resh 1936- ... CANR-24
Earlier sketch in CA 106
See also SATA 38
Thomas, Jeannette Grise 1935- ... 101
Thomas, Jim
See Reagan, Thomas (James) B(utler)
Thomas, Joan Gale
See Robinson, Joan (Mary) G(ale Thomas)
Thomas, John 1890- ... 49-52
Thomas, John Allen Miner 1900-1932
Brief entry ... 107
See also DLB 4
Thomas, John Hunter 1928- ... 57-60
Thomas, John Lawrence 1910- ... 5-6R
Thomas, Joyce Carol 1938- ... 116
Brief entry ... 113
See also BW
See also SATA 40
See also DLB 33
See also CLC 35
Thomas, K. H.
See Kirk, T(homas) H(obson)
Thomas, Keith (Vivian) 1933- ... CANR-15
Earlier sketch in CA 37-40R
Thomas, Kenneth Bryn ?-1978 Obituary ... 81-84
Thomas, Kurt 1956- Brief entry ... 114
Thomas, Latta R(oosevelt) 1927- ... 65-68
Thomas, Lawrence L(eslie) 1924- ... 45-48
Thomas, Lee 1918- ... CANR-1
Earlier sketch in CA 1R
Thomas, Lee
See Floren, Lee
Thomas, Leslie (John) 1931- ... CANR-22
Earlier sketch in CA 15-16R
Thomas, Lewis 1913- ... 85-88
See also CLC 35
Thomas, Lewis H(erbert) 1917-1983 ... CANR-13
Earlier sketch in CA 73-76
Thomas, Lionel H(ugh) C(hristopher) 1922(?)-1978 Obituary ... 104
Thomas, Liz
See Thomas, Elizabeth Ann
Thomas, Lorenzo 1944- ... CANR-25
Earlier sketch in CA 73-76
See also BW
See also DLB 41
Thomas, Lowell (Jackson) 1892-1981 ... CANR-3
Obituary ... 104
Earlier sketch in CA 45-48
See also AITN 1, 2
Thomas, Lowell Jackson, Jr. 1923- ... 85-88
See also SATA 15
Thomas, M(ilton) Halsey 1903-1977 ... 25-28R
Obituary ... 73-76
Thomas, Mack 1928- ... 11-12R
Thomas, Mary Martha Hosford 1927- ... 53-56
Thomas, Mason P(age), Jr. 1928- ... CANR-22
Earlier sketch in CA 25-28R
Thomas, Mervyn
See Curran, Mona (Elisa)
Thomas, Michael
See Wilks, Michael Thomas
Thomas, (William) Miles (Webster) 1897-1980 Obituary ... 105
Thomas, Neal
See Thomas, Cornelius Dickinson
Thomas, Norman (Mattoon) 1884-1968 ... 101
Obituary ... 25-28R
Thomas, Norman C(arl) 1932- ... 19-20R
Thomas, Norman L(ee) 1925- ... 41-44R
Thomas, Owen Clark 1922- ... 9-10R
Thomas, Patricia J. 1934- ... 37-40R
See also SATA 51
Thomas, Paul 1908- ... CANR-22
Earlier sketches in CA 9-10, CAP-1
Thomas, Peter 1928- ... 37-40R
Thomas, Peter Wynne
See Wynne-Thomas, Peter
Thomas, Phillip Drennon 1938- ... 124
Thomas, Phyllis 1935- ... 119
Thomas, Piri 1928- ... 73-76
See also CLC 17
Thomas, R(ichard) Hinton 1912-1983 ... CANR-5
Obituary ... 110
Earlier sketch in CA 7-8R
Thomas, R(obert) Murray 1921- ... CANR-22
Earlier sketches in CA 19-20R, CANR-7
Thomas, R(onald) S(tuart) 1913- ... 89-92
See also CAAS 4
See also DLB 27
See also CLC 6, 13, 48
Thomas, Richard (Earl) 1951- ... 107
Thomas, Robert 1930- ... 25-28R
Thomas, Robert C(harles) 1925- ... 101
Thomas, Robert J(oseph) 1922- ... CANR-13
Earlier sketch in CA 77-80
Thomas, Rollin G. 1896-19(?) ... CAP-1
Earlier sketch in CA 15-16
Thomas, Rosie Brief entry ... 126
Thomas, Ross (Elmore) 1926- ... CANR-22
Earlier sketch in CA 33-36R
See also CLC 39
Thomas, S(idney) Claudewell 1932- ... 19-20R
Thomas, Sara (Sally) 1911(?)-1982
Obituary ... 106
Thomas, Sewell 1884- ... CAP-1
Earlier sketch in CA 9-10
Thomas, Sherilyn 1948- ... CANR-13
Earlier sketch in CA 73-76
Thomas, Sherry
See Thomas, Sherilyn
Thomas, Shirley ... 7-8R
Thomas, Stanley 1933- ... 21-22R
Thomas, Stephen N(aylor) 1942- ... 89-92
Thomas, T. M(athai) 1933- ... 53-56
Thomas, Ted
See Thomas, Theodore L.
Thomas, Theodore L. 1920- ... 29-32R
Thomas, Thom 1940- ... 108
Thomas, Tony 1947- ... 61-64
Thomas, Vaughan 1934- ... 81-84
Thomas, Victoria
See DeWeese, Thomas Eugene and Kugi, Constance Todd
Thomas, Virginia Castleton
See Castleton, Virginia
Thomas, W(alter) Ian 1914- ... 19-20R
Thomas, William 1906- ... 73-76
Thomas, William E(dward) 1942- ... 111
Thomas, William F. 1924- ... 69-72
Thomas, William G(ordan) 1931- ... 93-96
Thomas, William L(eRoy, Jr.) 1920- ... 41-44R
Thomasma, David Charles 1939- ... CANR-21
Earlier sketch in CA 104
Thomason, A(lan) Mims 1910-1985
Obituary ... 117
Thomason, Burke C(urtis) 1943- ... 113
Thomason, Tommy 1949- ... 73-76
Thometz, Carol Estes 1938- ... 11-12R
Thomey, Tedd 1920- ... CANR-2
Earlier sketch in CA 5-6R
Thomis, Malcolm I(an) 1936- Brief entry ... 118
Thomis, Wayne 1907-1988 Obituary ... 126
Thomison, Dennis 1937- ... 53-56
Thomlinson, Ralph 1925- ... 41-44R
Thommen, George S. 1896- ... CAP-1
Earlier sketch in CA 15-16
Thompson, A(lbert) Gray 1928- ... 41-44R
Thompson, A(rthur) L(eonard) B(ell) 1917-1975 ... CANR-5
Obituary ... 61-64
Earlier sketch in CA 53-56
Thompson, Alan Eric 1924- ... 109
Thompson, Anne Armstrong 1939- ... 85-88
Thompson, Anne Hall Whitt 1930- ... 119
Thompson, Arthur A., Jr. 1940- ... 85-88
Thompson, Arthur W(illiam) 1920-1966 ... 1R
Thompson, Bard 1925-1987 ... CANR-1
Obituary ... 123
Earlier sketch in CA 3R
Thompson, Betty A(nne) 1926- ... 111
Thompson, Blanche Jennings ... 5-6R
Thompson, Brenda 1935- ... 106
See also SATA 34
Thompson, Brian 1935- ... 109
Thompson, Buck
See Paine, Lauran (Bosworth)
Thompson, C(lara) Mildred 1881-1975
Obituary ... 57-60
Thompson, Caroline 1956- ... 110
Thompson, Charles Lowell 1937- ... CANR-3
Earlier sketch in CA 49-52
Thompson, Charles Waters, Jr.
See Thompson, Toby
Thompson, China
See Lewis, Mary (Christianna Milne)
Thompson, China
See Lewis, Mary (Christianna)
Thompson, Claude Holmes 1908- ... CAP-1
Earlier sketch in CA 11-12
Thompson, Corrie 1887- ... 61-64
Thompson, Craig 1907-1986 Obituary ... 121
Thompson, Daniel (Calbert) 1916- ... 15-16R
Thompson, David (Bradford) 1938- ... 57-60
Thompson, David H(ugh) 1941- ... 81-84
See also SATA 17
Thompson, Dennis F(rank) 1940- ... 53-56
Thompson, Dennis L. 1935- ... 41-44R
Thompson, (Arthur) Denys (Halstead) 1907-1988 ... CANR-4
Obituary ... 124
Earlier sketch in CA 9-10R
Thompson, Don(ald Arthur) 1935- ... 53-56
Thompson, Donald Eugene 1913- ... 109
Thompson, Donald L(ambert) 1930- ... 49-52
Thompson, Donald Neil 1939- ... 37-40R
Thompson, Donnis Stark 1928- ... 21-22R
Thompson, Dorothy 1894-1961 Obituary ... 89-92
See also DLB 29
Thompson, Duane G(len) 1933- ... 73-76
Thompson, Earl 1931(?)-1978 ... 85-88
Obituary ... 81-84
Thompson, Edgar T(ristram) 1900- ... 17-18R
Thompson, Edward Thorwald 1928- ... CANR-21
Earlier sketch in CA 105
Thompson, Eileen
See Panowski, Eileen Thompson
Thompson, Elizabeth Allen 1914-1984 ... 119
Thompson, Era Bell 1905-1986 ... 89-92
Obituary ... 121
Thompson, Eric
See Thompson, J(ohn) Eric S(idney)
Thompson, (Richard) Ernest 1949- ... 123
Brief entry ... 115
Thompson, Ernest Trice 1894-1985 ... 3R
Obituary ... 115
Thompson, Eugene Allen 1924- ... CANR-26
Earlier sketch in CA 104
Thompson, Evelyn Wingo 1921- ... 21-22R
Thompson, Ewa M(ajewska) 1937- ... 49-52
Thompson, Flora (Jane Timms) 1877(?)-1947 Brief entry ... 123
Thompson, Frances C(lements) 1906- ... CAP-1
Earlier sketch in CA 9-10
Thompson, Francis Clegg
See Mencken, H(enry) L(ouis)
Thompson, Francis George 1931- ... CANR-23
Earlier sketch in CA 106
Thompson, Francis Joseph 1859-1907
Brief entry ... 104
See also DLB 19
See also TCLC 4
Thompson, Frank H., Jr. 1926- ... 25-28R
Thompson, Fred 1900-1987 Obituary ... 121
Thompson, Fred Dalton 1942- ... 69-72
Thompson, Fred P(riestly), Jr. 1917- ... 89-92
Thompson, G(ary) R(ichard) 1937- ... CANR-2
Earlier sketch in CA 45-48
Thompson, Gene
See Thompson, Eugene Allen
Thompson, George Clifford 1920- ... 104
Thompson, George G(reene) 1914- ... 21-22R
Thompson, George H(yman) 1923- ... 125
Brief entry ... 117
Thompson, George Selden 1929- ... CANR-21
Earlier sketch in CA 5-6R
See also SATA 4
Thompson, Gerald E(verett) 1924- ... 53-56
Thompson, Gertrude Caton
See Caton-Thompson, Gertrude
Thompson, Grant P(helps) 1940- ... 111
Thompson, Harlan (Howard) 1894-1987 ... CAP-1
Obituary ... 123
Earlier sketch in CA 9-10
See also SATA 10, 53
Thompson, Harry C. 1921(?)-1980
Obituary ... 97-100
Thompson, (Harry) Harwood 1894- ... 65-68
Thompson, Helen M. (Smith) 1903- ... CAP-1
Earlier sketch in CA 13-14
Thompson, Henry O(rrin) 1931- ... CANR-25
Earlier sketch in CA 45-48
Thompson, Hilary 1943- ... SATA-49
Thompson, Hildegard (Steerstedter) 1901- ... 19-20R
Thompson, Hunter S(tockton) 1939- ... CANR-23
Earlier sketch in CA 19-20R
See also CLC 9, 17, 40
Thompson, Ian B(entley) 1936- ... 37-40R
Thompson, Irene 1919- ... 110
Thompson, Isabel
See Kelsay, Isabel Thompson
Thompson, J(ohn) Eric S(idney) 1898-1975 ... 65-68
Obituary ... 61-64
Thompson, J(esse) J(ackson) 1919- ... 7-8R
Thompson, Jack Maynard 1924- ... 41-44R
Thompson, Jacqueline 1945- ... CANR-17
Earlier sketch in CA 97-100
Thompson, James 1902-1983 Obituary ... 109
Thompson, James 1932- ... 73-76
Thompson, James D(avid) 1920-1973 ... CAP-2
Earlier sketch in CA 21-22
Thompson, James H.
See Freeman, G(raydon) L(a Verne)
Thompson, James W. 1935- ... 105
Thompson, Joan 1943- ... 97-100
Thompson, Joan Berengild 1915- ... 17-18R
Thompson, Joanna Maxwell Pullein
See Pullein-Thompson, Joanna Maxwell
Thompson, Joe Allen 1936- ... 37-40R
Thompson, John (Anderson) 1918- ... 5-6R
Thompson, John 1938-1976 ... DLB-60
Thompson, John Leslie 1917- ... 7-8R
Thompson, John Reuben 1823-1873 ... DLB-3, 73
Thompson, Josiah 1935- ... 41-44R
Thompson, Judith ... CLC-39
Thompson, Julian F(rancis) 1927- ... 111
See also SATA 40
Thompson, Julius Eric 1946- ... 49-52
Thompson, Karl F. 1917- ... 37-40R
Thompson, Kay 1912(?)- ... 85-88
See also SATA 16
Thompson, Ken D(avid) 1926- ... 65-68
Thompson, Kenneth W(infred) 1921- ... CANR-5
Earlier sketch in CA 11-12R
Thompson, Kent 1936- ... 49-52
Thompson, Kristin 1950- ... CANR-25
Earlier sketch in CA 108
Thompson, Laura (Maud) 1905- ... 53-56
Thompson, Laurence C(assius) 1926- ... CANR-7
Earlier sketch in CA 5-6R
Thompson, Laurence G(raham) 1920- ... 37-40R
Thompson, Lawrance (Roger) 1906-1973 ... CANR-10
Obituary ... 41-44R
Earlier sketch in CA 5-6R
Thompson, Lawrence Sidney 1916-1986 ... CANR-5
Obituary ... 121
Earlier sketch in CA 9-10R
Thompson, Leonard Monteath 1916- ... CANR-16
Earlier sketches in CA 2R, CANR-1
Thompson, Lewis 1915(?)-1972
Obituary ... 37-40R
Thompson, Loring M(oore) 1918- ... 45-48
Thompson, Luther Joe 1918- ... 21-22R
Thompson, Marian Spitzer 1899(?)-1983
Obituary ... 110
Thompson, Mary Wolfe 1886- ... 107
Thompson, Maurice 1844-1901 ... DLB-71, 74
Thompson, Mel(vin R.) 1929- ... 73-76
Thompson, Morris Mordecai 1912- ... 109
Thompson, Neil 1929- ... 108
Thompson, Neville 1938- ... 37-40R
Thompson, Noel W. 1951- ... 123
Thompson, Paul (Richard) 1935- ... CANR-16
Earlier sketch in CA 21-22R
Thompson, Paul 1943- ... CANR-14
Earlier sketch in CA 77-80
Thompson, Phyllis Hoge 1926- ... CANR-13
Earlier sketch in CA 29-32R
Thompson, Ralph 1904-1979 Obituary ... 89-92
Thompson, (William) Ralph 1910- ... 53-56
Thompson, Randall 1899-1984 Obituary ... 113
Thompson, Richard 1924- ... 9-10R
Thompson, Richard A(rlen) 1930- ... 61-64
Thompson, Robert (Grainger Ker) 1916- ... 49-52
Thompson, Robert Elliott 1921- ... 77-80
See also AITN 2
Thompson, Robert Farris 1932- ... 103
Thompson, Robert Norman 1914- ... 106
Thompson, Robert Sidney 1918- ... 111
Thompson, Roger Francis 1933- ... CANR-13
Earlier sketch in CA 73-76
Thompson, Roy Anton 1897- ... CAP-2
Earlier sketch in CA 29-32
Thompson, Russ
See Paine, Lauran (Bosworth)
Thompson, Ruth Plumly 1891(?)-1976
Obituary ... 113
See also DLB 22
Thompson, Samuel M(artin) 1902-1983
Obituary ... 110
Thompson, Sandra (Jean) 1943- ... 121
Thompson, Stanbury Dugard 1905- ... CAP-1
Earlier sketch in CA 11-12
Thompson, Steven L(ynn) 1948- ... 114
Thompson, Stith 1885-1976 ... CANR-5
Obituary ... 61-64
Earlier sketch in CA 7-8R
See also SATA 20
Thompson, Susan L. 1945- ... 114
Thompson, Susan O(tis) 1931- ... 85-88
Thompson, Sylvia
See Thompson, Sylvia Vaughn (Sheekman)
Thompson, Sylvia Vaughn (Sheekman) 1935- ... CANR-26
Earlier sketch in CA 7-8R
Thompson, Thomas 1933-1982 ... CANR-14
Obituary ... 108
Earlier sketch in CA 65-68
Thompson, Thomas Kirkland 1914- ... 15-16R
Thompson, Toby 1944- ... 65-68
Thompson, Travis I. 1937- ... 37-40R
Thompson, Victor A(lexander) 1912- ... 25-28R
Thompson, Virginia 1937- ... 108

Thompson, Vivian L(aubach) 1911- CANR-1
Earlier sketch in CA 1R
See also SATA 3
Thompson, W(illard) Scott 1942- CANR-12
Earlier sketch in CA 25-28R
Thompson, Wayne C(urtis) 1943- 109
Thompson, Wayne N. 1914- 21-22R
Thompson, Wilbur R(ichard) 1923- 15-16R
Thompson, Willa 1916- 9-10R
Thompson, Willard Mead 1913- 5-6R
Thompson, William A(ncker) 1931- 77-80
Thompson, William Bernard 1914- CAP-1
Earlier sketch in CA 9-10
Thompson, William C. L.
See Edwards, William B(ennett)
Thompson, William D. 1929- 19-20R
Thompson, William E(llison), Jr. 1923- ...13-14R
Thompson, William Fletcher, Jr. 1929- 1R
Thompson, William Irwin 1938- CANR-9
Earlier sketch in CA 23-24R
Thompson, William Tappan
1812-1882 .... DLB-3, 11
Thompson, Wolfe
See Thompson, Mary Wolfe
Thoms, Herbert 1885-1972 Obituary 110
Thomsen, Harry 1928- 7-8R
Thomsen, Moritz 1915- 29-32R
Thomsen, Robert 1915(?)-1983 Obituary ... 117
Thomsen, Russel J(ohn) 1941- 37-40R
Thomsett, Michael C. 1948- 119
Thomson, Arthur Alexander (Malcolm)
1894-1969 .... CAP-1
Earlier sketch in CA 11-12
Thomson, Basil (Home) 1861-1939
Brief entry 110
Thomson, Beatrix 1900-1986 Obituary 120
Thomson, Betty Flanders 1913- 9-10R
Thomson, C(harles) Leslie 1914- 9-10R
Thomson, Daisy H(icks) 1918- CANR-20
Earlier sketch in CA 103
Thomson, Dale C(airns) 1923- 25-28R
Thomson, David 1912-1970 .... CANR-2
Obituary 29-32R
Earlier sketch in CA 1R
Thomson, David (Robert Alexander)
1914-1988 .... CANR-24
Obituary 124
Earlier sketch in CA 107
See also SATA 40
Thomson, Derick S(mith) 1921- CANR-12
Earlier sketch in CA 25-28R
Thomson, Douglas Ferguson Scott
1919- 41-44R
Thomson, Edward
See Tubb, E(dwin) C(harles)
Thomson, F(rancis) P(aul) 1914- 23-24R
Thomson, Frank S(elee) 1881-1975 57-60
Thomson, Garry 1925- 109
Thomson, George Derwent 1903-1987
Obituary 121
Thomson, George H(enry) 1924- 23-24R
Thomson, George Malcolm 1899- 9-10R
Thomson, George Paget 1892-1975 .... CANR-4
Obituary 61-64
Earlier sketch in CA 7-8R
Thomson, (George) Ian F(alconer)
1912-1987 ....9-10R
Obituary 122
Thomson, Irene Taviss 1941- 29-32R
Thomson, James 1834-1882 .... DLB-35
Thomson, James C(utting) 1909- 61-64
Thomson, James C(laude), Jr. 1931- 29-32R
Thomson, James Miln 1921- 109
Thomson, Joan
See Charnock, Joan
Thomson, John (Edward Palmer) 1936- 109
Thomson, John W(illiam) 1940- 125
Thomson, Jonathan H.
See Thomson, Daisy H(icks)
Thomson, June (Valerie) 1930- CANR-21
Earlier sketch in CA 81-84
Thomson, Keith 1912- 29-32R
Thomson, Mortimer 1831-1875 .... DLB-11
Thomson, Peggy 1922- 85-88
See also SATA 31
Thomson, Peter 1913- 7-8R
Thomson, Peter (William) 1938- 108
Thomson, Randall J(oseph) 1946- 109
Thomson, Robert 1921- 25-28R
Thomson, Robert 1943- 122
Thomson, Robert W(illiam) 1934- CANR-21
Earlier sketch in CA 104
Thomson, Ronald William 1908- 25-28R
Thomson, Roy Herbert 1894-1976
Obituary 69-72
Thomson, S(amuel) Harrison
1895-1975 ....41-44R
Obituary 61-64
Thomson, Virgil (Garnett) 1896- 41-44R
Thomson, William A. 1879-1971
Obituary 33-36R
Thomson, William A(rchibald) R(obson)
1906-1983 103
Obituary 111
Thomy, Al(fred Marshall) 69-72
Thonssen, Lester 1904- 5-6R
Thorat, Sudhakar S. 1935- 45-48
Thorburn, David 1940- CANR-7
Earlier sketch in CA 53-56
Thorburn, Hugh G(arnet) 1924- 13-14R
Thorburn, John
See Goldsmith, John Herman Thorburn
Thoreau, Henry David 1817-1862 .... DLB-1
See also CDALB 1640-1865
Thorelli, Hans B(irger) 1921- CANR-6
Earlier sketch in CA 15-16R
Thoren, Arne 1927- 69-72
Thorer, Konrad
See Greve, Felix Paul (Berthold Friedrich)
Thoresen, Carl E. 1933- 57-60
Thorez, Maurice 1900-1964 Obituary 113
Thorlby, Anthony K. 1928- 25-28R
Thorman, Donald J. 1924-1977 ....17-18R
Obituary 73-76
Thorman, Richard 1924- 105
Thorn, Barbara
See Paine, Lauran (Bosworth)
Thorn, John 1947- CANR-17
Earlier sketch in CA 97-100
Thorn, Richard S(emour) 1929- 19-20R
Thorn, Ronald Scott
See Wilkinson, Ronald
Thorn, William E. 1923- 9-10R
Thornber, Jean H(ewitt) 1919- 61-64
Thornbrough, Emma Lou 25-28R
Thornburg, Hershel D(ean) 1936-1987 . CANR-14
Obituary 121
Earlier sketch in CA 37-40R
Thornburg, Newton K(endall) 1930- CANR-9
Earlier sketch in CA 23-24R
Thorndike, A.
See Thorndike, A(nthony) E(dward)
Thorndike, A(nthony) E(dward) 1941- 117
Thorndike, E. L.
See Thorndike, Edward L(ee)
Thorndike, Edward L(ee) 1874-1949
Brief entry 121
Thorndike, Joseph J(acobs), Jr. 1913-
Brief entry 117
Thorndike, (Everett) Lynn 1882-1965
Obituary 111
Thorndike, Robert Ladd 1910- CANR-1
Earlier sketch in CA 1R
Thorndike, (Arthur) Russell 1885-1972
Obituary 37-40R
Thorndike, Susan 1944- 41-44R
Thorndike, Tony
See Thorndike, A(nthony) E(dward)
Thorndyke, Helen Louise CAP-2
Earlier sketch in CA 19-20
See also SATA 1
Thorne, Alice Dunn 1910-1973 Obituary ...45-48
Thorne, Bliss K(irby) 1916- 17-18R
Thorne, Bradley D.
See Glut, Donald F(rank)
Thorne, Christopher 1934- CANR-11
Earlier sketch in CA 21-22R
Thorne, Edouard
See Greve, Felix Paul (Berthold Friedrich)
Thorne, Florence Calvert 1878(?)-1973
Obituary 41-44R
Thorne, Hart
See Carhart, Arthur Hawthorne
Thorne, Ian
See May, Julian
Thorne, Jean Wright
See May, Julian
Thorne, Jim 1922- CANR-1
Earlier sketch in CA 3R
Thorne, Nicola
See Ellerbeck, Rosemary (Anne
L'Estrange)
Thorne, Ramsay
See Cameron, Lou
Thorne, Sabina 1927- 106
Thorne, Sterling
See Fuller, Dorothy Mason
Thorne, William James 1898- 5-6R
Thorning, Joseph F(rancis) 1896-1985 ... CAP-1
Obituary 115
Earlier sketch in CA 9-10
Thornley, Richard 1950- 117
Thornton, Big Mama
See Thornton, Willie Mae
Thornton, Emma Shore 1908- 114
Thornton, Francis John 1938- 85-88
Thornton, Gene 93-96
Thornton, Hall
See Silverberg, Robert
Thornton, J(onathan) Mills III 1943- 77-80
Thornton, James W., Jr. 1908- CANR-1
Earlier sketch in CA 1R
Thornton, Jerry
See Thornton, Emma Shore
Thornton, John Leonard 1913- CANR-4
Earlier sketch in CA 9-10R
Thornton, John W(illiam) 1922- 106
Thornton, John W(illiam), Jr. 1948- 106
Thornton, Lee 1944- 73-76
Thornton, Martin (Stuart Farrin) 1915- 9-10R
Thornton, Michael 1941- 105
Thornton, Peter Kai 1925- CANR-20
Earlier sketch in CA 102
Thornton, R(obert) K(elsey) R(ought)
1938- 119
Thornton, Richard C. 1936- 81-84
Thornton, Thomas Perry 1931- 11-12R
Thornton, W. B.
See Burgess, Thornton Waldo
Thornton, Weldon 1934- 25-28R
Thornton, Willie Mae 1926-1984 Obituary .. 113
Thornton, Willis 1900- CAP-1
Earlier sketch in CA 15-16
Thorp, Duncan Roy 1914- 13-14R
Thorp, Edward O. 1932- 23-24R
Thorp, Margaret Farrand 1891-1970
Obituary 104
Thorp, Roderick Mayne, Jr. 1936- CANR-6
Earlier sketch in CA 2R
Thorp, Willard 1899- CANR-3
Earlier sketch in CA 7-8R
Thorp, Willard Long 1899- 1R
Thorpe, Donald W(illiam) 1928- 29-32R
Thorpe, E(ustace) G(eorge) 1916- 9-10R
See also SATA 21
Thorpe, Earl(ie) E(ndris) 1924- 61-64
Thorpe, Elliott R(aymond) 1897- 65-68
Thorpe, George P. 1913(?)-1983 Obituary .. 110
Thorpe, J. K.
See Nathanson, Laura Walther
Thorpe, James 1915- CANR-17
Earlier sketches in CA 5-6R, CANR-2
Thorpe, Lewis (Guy Melville)
1913-1977 .... CANR-10
Earlier sketch in CA 9-10R
Thorpe, Louis P(eter) 1893- CANR-20
Earlier sketch in CA 2R
Thorpe, Michael 1932- CANR-8
Earlier sketch in CA 23-24R
Thorpe, Peter 1932- 57-60
Thorpe, Sylvia
See Thimblethorpe, June Sylvia
Thorpe, Thomas Bangs 1815-1878 ... DLB-3, 11
Thorpe, Trebor
See Fanthorpe, R(obert) Lionel
Thorpe, Trevor
See Fanthorpe, R(obert) Lionel
Thorpe, William Homan 1902-1986 ..... CANR-2
Obituary 119
Earlier sketch in CA 7-8R
Thorsell, Richard Lawrence 1938- 89-92
Thorsley, Peter L(arsen), Jr. 1929- 5-6R
Thorson, Thomas Landon 1934- 17-18R
Thorstad, David 1941- 57-60
Thorstein, Eric
See Merril, Judith
Thorup, Kirsten 1942- Brief entry 125
Thorvall, Kerstin 1925- CANR-13
Earlier sketch in CA 17-18R
See also SATA 13
Thorvall-Falk, Kerstin
See Thorvall, Kerstin
Thorwald, Juergen 1916- CANR-21
Earlier sketches in CA 49-52, CANR-1
Thouless, Robert H(enry) 1894-1984 77-80
Obituary 114
Thrapp, Dan Lincoln 1913- CANR-4
Earlier sketch in CA 11-12R
Thrasher, Crystal (Faye) 1921- CANR-8
Earlier sketch in CA 61-64
See also SATA 27
Threlkeld, Richard 1937- 65-68
Thresher, B(rainard) Alden 1896-1984
Obituary 111
Throckmorton, Burton Hamilton, Jr.
1921- 5-6R
Throckmorton, Peter 1928- 19-20R
Throneberry, Jimmy B. 1933- 89-92
Throneburg, James 5-6R
Thrower, Norman J(oseph) W(illiam)
1919- 41-44R
Thrower, Percy John 1913-1988 .... CANR-4
Obituary 125
Earlier sketch in CA 9-10R
Thubron, Colin (Gerald Dryden) 1939- .. CANR-12
Earlier sketch in CA 25-28R
Thubten Sigme Norbu 1922- Brief entry 109
Thuesen, Gerald J(organ) 1938- 37-40R
Thuillier, Jacques 1928- CANR-7
Earlier sketch in CA 11-12R
Thulstrup, Niels 1924- CANR-26
Earlier sketches in CA 21-22R, CANR-10
Thum, Gladys 1920- 41-44R
See also SATA 26
Thum, Marcella CANR-21
Earlier sketches in CA 11-12R, CANR-6
See also SATA 3, 28
Thumm, Garold W(esley) 1915- 15-16R
Thuna, Lee
See Thuna, Leonora
Thuna, Leonora 1929- CANR-16
Earlier sketch in CA 23-24R
Thundercloud, Katherine
See Witt, Shirley Hill
Thundy, Zacharias Pontian 1936- 102
Thundyil, Zacharias Pontian
See Thundy, Zacharias Pontian
Thurber, Helen (Wismer) 1902(?)-1986
Obituary 121
Thurber, James (Grover) 1894-1961 ... CANR-17
Earlier sketch in CA 73-76
See also SATA 13
See also DLB 4, 11, 22
See also CLC 5, 11, 25
See also SSC 1
Thurber, Walter A(rthur) 1908- CANR-12
Earlier sketch in CA 21-22R
Thurkettle, James 1929- 69-72
Thurley, Geoffrey John 1936- CANR-13
Earlier sketch in CA 61-64
Thurley, Jon (Mark) 118
Thurman, Christa C(harlotte) Mayer
1934- CANR-2
Earlier sketch in CA 49-52
Thurman, Howard 1900-1981 .... CANR-25
Obituary 103
Earlier sketch in CA 97-100
See also BW
Thurman, Judith 1946- CANR-1
Earlier sketch in CA 49-52
See also SATA 33
Thurman, Kelly 1914- 57-60
Thurman, Wallace (Henry) 1902-1934 124
Brief entry 104
See also BW
See also DLB 51
See also TCLC 6
Thurman, Wayne L(averne) 1923- 49-52
Thurmond, Nancy Moore 1946-
Brief entry 114
Thurmond, (J.) Strom 1902- 89-92
Thurow, Lester C(arl) 1938- 81-84
Thursby, Vincent Victor 1918- 41-44R
Thurstan, Violetta CAP-1
Earlier sketch in CA 15-16
Thurston, Carol (M.) 126
Thurston, David B. 1918- CANR-6
Earlier sketch in CA 7-8R
Thurston, Elliott Ladd 1895-1975
Obituary 89-92
Thurston, Harry 1950- 113
Thurston, Hazel (Patricia) 1906- 57-60
Thurston, Jarvis 1914- 15-16R
Thurston, Lorrin P. 1900(?)-1984
Obituary 114
Thurston, Robert (Donald) 1936- CANR-15
Earlier sketch in CA 85-88
Thut, I(saac) N(oah) CAP-1
Earlier sketch in CA 15-16
Thwaite, Ann (Barbara Harrop) 1932- 5-6R
See also SATA 14
Thwaite, Anthony (Simon) 1930- 7-8R
See also DLB 40
Thwaite, M(ary) F. (Austin) 21-22R
Thwaites, Michael 1915- 77-80
Thwaites, Reuben Gold 1853-1913 ..... DLB-47
Thwing, Leroy (L.) 1879- 7-8R
Thygerson, Alton L(uie) 1940- CANR-18
Earlier sketches in CA 45-48, CANR-1
Tiant, Luis 1940- 73-76
(al-)Tibawi, A(bdul-)L(atif) 1910-1981 .. CANR-24
Obituary 105
Earlier sketch in CA 25-28R
Tibber, Robert
See Friedman, (Eve) Rosemary (Tibber)
Tibber, Rosemary
See Friedman, (Eve) Rosemary (Tibber)
Tibbets, Albert B. 1888- 7-8R
Tibbetts, Arnold M(acLean) 1927- CANR-16
Earlier sketch in CA 93-96
Tibbetts, Charlene 1921- 93-96
Tibbetts, John C(arter) 1946- 89-92
Tibbetts, John W(esley) 1928- 25-28R
Tibbetts, Norris L. 1892(?)-1983 Obituary .. 108
Tibbetts, Orlando L(ailer), Jr. 1919- ... CANR-11
Earlier sketch in CA 29-32R
Tibbetts, William
See Brannon, William T.
Tibble, Anne 1912-1980 .... CANR-10
Obituary 102
Earlier sketch in CA 9-10R
Tibbs, Ben 1907- 61-64
Tibbs, Virginia M.
See Scott, Virginia M(uhleman)
Tice, George A(ndrew) 1938- CANR-12
Earlier sketch in CA 61-64
Ticheburn, Cheviot
See Ainsworth, William Harrison
Tichenor, Tom 1923- 29-32R
See also SATA 14
Tichi, Cecelia 1942- 104
Tichy, H(enrietta) J. 1912- 21-22R
Tichy, Susan (Elizabeth) 1952- 123
Tichy, William 1924- 107
See also SATA 31
Tickle, P(hyllis) A(lexander) 1934- CANR-24
Earlier sketches in CA 65-68, CANR-9
Tickner, Fred(erick James) 1902- CAP-1
Earlier sketch in CA 9-10
Ticknor, George 1791-1871 .... DLB-1, 59
Tidball, Derek J(ohn) 1948- 120
Tidy, Michael 1943- 113
Tidyman, Ernest 1928-1984 73-76
Obituary 113
Tiede, Tom (Robert) 1937- 25-28R
Tiedt, Iris M(cClellan) 1928- CANR-24
Earlier sketches in CA 13-14R, CANR-7
Tiedt, Sidney W(illis) 1927- CANR-24
Earlier sketch in CA 13-14R
Tiegreen, Alan F. 1935- SATA-36
Tiempo, Edith (Lopez) 1919- 104
Tien, H. Yuan 1926- 49-52
Tien, Hung-Mao 1938- 73-76
Tierney, Brian 1922- 103
Tierney, Gene 1920- Brief entry 116
Tierney, John Lawrence 1892-1972 ...... CAP-2
Earlier sketch in CA 21-22
Tierney, Kevin (Hugh) 1942- CANR-26
Earlier sketch in CA 29-32R
Tierney, M. Leo 1932(?)-1986 Obituary 118
Tierney, Michael 1894-1975 Obituary 114
Tierney, Paul Ambrose 1895(?)-1979
Obituary 85-88
Tierney, Richard L(ouis) 1936- 111
Tierney, Tom 1928- CANR-23
Earlier sketches in CA 57-60, CANR-8
Tiersky, Ronald S. 1944- 118
Tietjens, Eunice 1884-1944 .... DLB-54
Tietze, Andreas 1914- 49-52
Tietze, Christopher 1908-1984 Obituary 112
Tiffany, Donald Wayne 1930- Brief entry ... 108
Tiffany, E. A. 1911- 103
Tiffany, Phyllis G. 1932- 37-40R
Tiffany, William R(obert) 1920- 5-6R
Tiffin, Joseph 1905- 17-18R
Tifft, Ellen CANR-1
Earlier sketch in CA 49-52
Tifton, Leo
See Page, Gerald W(ilburn)
Tigar, Michael E(dward) 1941- 77-80
Tigay, Alan M(errill) 1947- 124
Tiger, Derry
See Ellison, Harlan
Tiger, Jack
See Puechner, Ray
Tiger, John
See Wager, Walter H(erman)

Tiger, Lionel 1937- CANR-14
Earlier sketch in CA 25-28R
Tiger, Virginia Marie 1940- Brief entry 106
Tigerman, Stanley 1930- 114
Tiger Of The Snows
See Norgay, Tenzing
Tighe, Donald J. 1928- 29-32R
Tighe, Thomas B. 1907(?)-1983 Obituary 109
Tignor, Robert L. 1933- Brief entry 109
Tigue, Ethel Erkkila 1918- 21-22R
Tikhonov, Nikolai Semyonovich
1896-1979 Obituary 85-88
Tikhonov, Valentin
See Payne, (Pierre Stephen) Robert
Tikku, Girdhari L(al) 1925- 45-48
Tiktin, Carl 1930- CANR-13
Earlier sketch in CA 73-76
Tilden, Freeman 1884(?)-1980 97-100
Tilghman, Benjamin R(oss) 1927-
Brief entry 107
Till, Barry 1923- 49-52
Tillard, Jean-M(arie) Roger 1927- 45-48
Tillema, Herbert K(endall) 1942- 45-48
Tilleman, William Arthur 1932- 53-56
Tiller, Carl W(illiam) 1915- 108
Tiller, Ted
See Tiller, Theodore II
Tiller, Terence (Rogers) 1916-1987 101
Obituary 124
Tiller, Theodore II 1913(?)-1988 Obituary 126
Tilles, Solomon 1932- Brief entry 108
Tillett, Bill G(lenn) 1942- 118
Tillett, Gregory J. 1950- 110
Tilley, Ethel 1894- CAP-1
Earlier sketch in CA 9-10
Tilley, Patrick 1928- 106
Tilley, (William) Roger (Montgomerie)
1905-1971 .... CAP-2
Earlier sketch in CA 25-28
Tillich, Hannah 1896- 73-76
Tillich, Paul (Johannes) 1886-1965 .... 7-8R
Obituary 25-28R
Tillinghast, B(urette) S(tinson), Jr. 1930- 65-68
Tillinghast, Pardon E(lisha) 1920- 11-12R
Tillinghast, Richard (Williford) 1940- CANR-26
Earlier sketch in CA 29-32R
See also CLC 29
Tillion, Diana (Rutzebeck) 1928-
Brief entry 110
Tillion, Germaine Marie Rosine 1907- 104
Tillman, Rollie, Jr. 1933- 23-24R
Tillman, Seth Phillip 1930- 3R
Tillman, Stephen Frederick 1900(?)-1977
Obituary 69-72
Tillotson, G(iles) H(enry) R(upert) 1960- 126
Tillotson, Geoffrey 1905-1969 .... CAP-1
Earlier sketch in CA 13-14
Tilly, Charles 1929- CANR-20
Earlier sketch in CA 103
Tilly, Louise A(udino) 1930- 120
Tilly, Nancy 1935- 120
Tilly, Richard H(ugh) 1932- 17-18R
Tillyard, E(ustace) M(andeville) W(etenhall)
1889-1962 Obituary 93-96
Tilman, Harold William 1898-1978 103
Tilman, Robert O(liver) 1929- CANR-1
Earlier sketch in CA 45-48
Tilson, Everett 1923- 41-44R
Tiltman, Hessell 1897(?)-1976 Obituary 69-72
Tiltman, Ronald Frank 1901- CAP-1
Earlier sketch in CA 9-10
Tilton, Alice
See Taylor, Phoebe Atwood
Tilton, Eleanor M(arguerite) 1913-
Brief entry 110
Tilton, John W(ightman) 1928-1983 122
Brief entry 118
Tilton, Madonna Elaine 1929- 114
See also SATA 41
Tilton, Rafael
See Tilton, Madonna Elaine
Tilton, Timothy Alan 1942- 61-64
Timasheff, Nicholas S. 1886-1970 .... 2R
Obituary 29-32R
Timberlake, Carolyn
See Dresang, Eliza
Timberlake, Charles E(dward) 1935- 41-44R
Timberlake, Richard Henry, Jr. 1922- 21-22R
Timerman, Jacobo 1923- 120
Brief entry 109
Timko, Michael 1925- 19-20R
Timlett, Peter Valentine 1933- Brief entry 111
Timmen, Fritz 1918- 53-56
Timmerman, Joan 1938- 118
Timmerman, John H(ager) 1945- 111
Timmerman, John Johnson 1908- 111
Timmermans, Claire 1938- 104
Timmers, J(an) Joseph M(arie) 1907- CAP-1
Earlier sketch in CA 13-14
Timmins, Lois Fahs 1914- 45-48
Timmins, William F(rederick) SATA-10
Timmis, John Henry III 1934- 104
Timmons, Bascom N(olly) 1890-1987 104
Obituary 122
Timmons, Bonnie 1951- 120
Timmons, Jeffry A. 1941- 108
Timms, Arthur W(arren) 1940- 120
Timms, David 1946- 109
Timms, E(dward) V(ivian) 1895-1960
Brief entry 112
Timms, Kathleen 1943- 122
Timms, Noel 1927- CANR-16
Earlier sketch in CA 15-16R
Timoney, Francis 1938- 61-64
Timoshenko, Stephen P. 1878-1972
Obituary 33-36R
Timothy, Hamilton B(aird) 1913- 102
Timothy, Peter 1725(?)-1782 .... DLB-43
Timpe, Eugene Frank 1926- 77-80
Timperley, Rosemary Kenyon 1920- CANR-17
Earlier sketch in CA 97-100
Timrod, Henry 1828-1867 .... DLB-3
Tinbergen, Jan 1903- CANR-2
Earlier sketch in CA 5-6R
Tinbergen, Niko(laas) 1907- 108
Tindall, George Brown 1921- 85-88
Tindall, Gillian 1938- CANR-11
Earlier sketch in CA 23-24R
See also CLC 7
Tindall, Kenneth (Thomas) 1937- 29-32R
Tindall, P(eggy) E(leanor) N(ancy)
1927- 29-32R
Tindall, William York 1903-1981 .... CANR-16
Obituary 104
Earlier sketch in CA 3R
Tiner, John Hudson 1944- CANR-18
Earlier sketch in CA 101
See also SATA 32
Tiner, Ralph W., Jr. 1948- 124
Ting, Jan C(hing-an) 1948- 37-40R
Ting, Walasse 1929- 21-22R
Tingay, Lance 1915- 101
Tingle, Dolli 1920- CANR-10
Earlier sketch in CA 25-28R
Tingley, Donald F(red) 1922- CANR-10
Earlier sketch in CA 25-28R
Tingley, Elizabeth 1955- 114
Tingsten, Herbert 1896-1973 Obituary 45-48
Tinic, Seha M(ehmet) 1941- 37-40R
Tinkelman, Murray 1933- SATA-12
Tinker, Beamish
See Jesse, F(ryniwyd) Tennyson
Tinker, Ben (Hill) 1903- 102
Tinker, Edward Larocque 1881-1968 .... CAP-1
Earlier sketch in CA 13-14
Tinker, Hugh (Russell) 1921- CANR-3
Earlier sketch in CA 5-6R
Tinker, Miles Albert 1893-1977 .... CANR-4
Earlier sketch in CA 7-8R
Tinker, Spencer Wilkie 1909- 41-44R
Tinkle, (Julien) Lon 1906-1980 104
See also SATA 36
Tinne, Dorothea
See Strover, Dorothea
Tinne, E. D.
See Strover, Dorothea
Tinnin, David B(ruce) 1930- 49-52
Tinniswood, Peter 1936- 25-28R
Tinsley, Ernest John 1919- 5-6R
Tinsley, James Robert 1921- 15-16R
Tinsley, Jim Bob
See Tinsley, James Robert
Tinsley, (John) Russell 1932- 17-18R
Tinterow, Gary 1953- 109
Tintner, Adeline R. 1912- 123
Tiomkin, Dimitri 1899-1979 Obituary 93-96
Tippett, Michael (Kemp) 1905- 109
Tippette, Giles 1934- CANR-17
Earlier sketch in CA 65-68
Tipping, Marjorie Jean 1917- 122
Tippit, Sammy 1947- 104
Tipple, John Ord 1916- 11-12R
Tipton, Charles Leon 1932- 41-44R
Tipton, David 1934- Brief entry 111
Tipton, James 1942- CANR-8
Earlier sketch in CA 57-60
Tiptree, James, Jr.
See Sheldon, Alice Hastings Bradley
See also DLB 8
See also CLC 48, 50
Tirbutt, Honoria CANR-22
Earlier sketch in CA 106
Tirro, Frank (Pascale) 1935- 81-84
Tiryakian, Edward A(shod) 1929- CANR-19
Earlier sketches in CA 5-6R, CANR-2
Tischler, Barbara L. 1949- 123
Tischler, Hans 1915- CANR-6
Earlier sketch in CA 3R
Tischler, Nancy Marie (Patterson) 1931- 5-6R
Tischner, Rudolf (E.) 1879-1961 Obituary 112
Tisdale, Celes 1941- 57-60
Tisdell, Clement Allan 1939- CANR-15
Earlier sketch in CA 25-28R
Tise, Larry Edward 1942- 102
Tish-Tash
See Tashlin, Frank
Tisserand, Jacques
See Barnes, Jim
Titchener, James Lampton 1922- 45-48
Titchener, Louise 1941- 122
Titcomb, Margaret 1891- CANR-5
Earlier sketch in CA 5-6R
Titler, Dale M(ilton) 1926- 81-84
See also SATA 28, 35
Titley, David Paul 1929- 110
Titley, Norah M(ary) 1920- 118
Titmarsh, Michael Angelo
See Thackeray, William Makepeace
Titmuss, Richard M(orris) 1907-1973 109
Obituary 107
Tito, Josip Broz 1892-1980 Obituary 97-100
Tito, Marshal
See Tito, Josip Broz
Titon, Jeff Todd 1943- CANR-16
Earlier sketch in CA 89-92
Titra, Stephen Andrew 1945- 97-100
Titterton, Ernest William 1916- 109
Tittle, Charles R(ay) 1939- CANR-15
Earlier sketch in CA 41-44R
Tittler, Jonathan (Paul) 1945- 119
Tittler, Robert 1942- CANR-15
Earlier sketch in CA 81-84
Tittmann, George Fabian 1915-1978 .... 7-8R
Obituary 81-84
Titunik, Irwin R(obert) 1929- 126
Titus, Barry J(oseph) 1938- 1R
Titus, Charles 1942- 45-48
Titus, David Anson 1934- 97-100
Titus, Edward William 1870-1952 .... DLB-4
Titus, Eve 1922- 29-32R
See also SATA 2
Titus, Harold H(opper) 1896- 5-6R
Titus, Warren Irving 1921- 17-18R
Tiusanen, Timo 1936-1985 85-88
Obituary 117
Tjader, Marguerite 1901- 17-18R
Tjepkema, Sandra L(ynn) 1953- 114
Tjernagel, Neelak S(erawlook) 1906- 17-18R
Tkacik, Arnold J(ohn) 1919- 81-84
Toan, Arthur B(enjamin), Jr. 1915- 25-28R
Tobach, Ethel 1921- 81-84
Toback, James 1944- 41-44R
Tobe, John Harold 1907-1979 .... CANR-1
Earlier sketch in CA 3R
Tobey, George B., Jr. 1917- 49-52
Tobey, Kathrene McLandress 1908- CAP-2
Earlier sketch in CA 29-32
Tobey, Mark 1890-1976 Obituary 65-68
Tobey, Ronald C(harles) 1942- 73-76
Tobias, Andrew P. 1947- CANR-14
Earlier sketch in CA 37-40R
Tobias, Henry J(ack) 1925- 41-44R
Tobias, J(ohn) J(acob) 1925- 53-56
Tobias, Katherine
See Gottfried, Theodore Mark
Tobias, Phillip V. 1925- CANR-15
Earlier sketch in CA 37-40R
Tobias, Richard C(lark) 1925- 29-32R
Tobias, Ronald B(enjamin) 1948- 111
Tobias, Sheila 1935- 93-96
Tobias, Tobi 1938- CANR-16
Earlier sketch in CA 29-32R
See also SATA 5
See also CLR 4
Tobin, James 1918- CANR-5
Earlier sketch in CA 53-56
Tobin, James Edward 1905-1968 .... CAP-2
Earlier sketch in CA 23-24
Tobin, Kay 1930- 37-40R
Tobin, Richard Lardner 1910- CANR-1
Earlier sketch in CA 2R
Tobin, Sheldon S(idney) 1931- Brief entry 110
Tobin, Terence 1938- 53-56
Toby, Liz
See Minsky, Betty Jane (Toebe)
Toby, Mark 1913(?)-1972 Obituary 37-40R
Toch, Hans (Herbert) 1930- CANR-23
Earlier sketches in CA 19-20R, CANR-7
Toch, Henry 1923- CANR-21
Earlier sketches in CA 9-10R, CANR-6
Toczek, Nick 1950- 106
Tod, Ian J. 1945- 103
Tod, Osma Gallinger 1898-1982(?) CAP-1
Obituary 108
Earlier sketch in CA 9-10
Todd, Alden 1918- CANR-6
Earlier sketch in CA 3R
Todd, Anne Ophelia
See Dowden, Anne Ophelia
Todd, Barbara Euphan 1890-1976 104
Todd, Barbara K(eith) 1917- 61-64
See also SATA 10
Todd, Burbank L. CANR-26
Earlier sketches in CA 19-20, CAP-2
Todd, Clark 1945(?)-1983 Obituary 110
Todd, Edgeley W(oodman) 1914-
Brief entry 109
Todd, Edward N. 1931- 53-56
Todd, Frances 1910- 13-14R
Todd, Frederick Porter 1903-1977
Obituary 73-76
Todd, Galbraith Hall 1914- 3R
Todd, Herbert Eatton 1908- CANR-12
Earlier sketches in CA 9-10, CAP-1
See also SATA 11
Todd, Hollis N(elson) 1914- 57-60
Todd, Ian A(lexander) 1941- 112
Todd, Ian Menzies 1923- 69-72
Todd, Janet M(argaret) 1942- CANR-1
Earlier sketch in CA 49-52
Todd, Jerry D(ale) 1941- 53-56
Todd, John M(urray) 1918- 9-10R
Todd, Karen (Iris) Rohne (Pritchett) 1936-
Brief entry 111
Todd, Leonard 1940- 65-68
Todd, Loreto 1942- 107
See also SATA 30
Todd, Malcolm 1939- 101
Todd, Paul
See Posner, Richard
Todd, Richard (Killingworth) 1949- 125
Todd, Ruth Van Dorn 1889(?)-1976
Obituary 65-68
Todd, Ruthven 1914- 81-84
Todd, Virgil H. 1921- Brief entry 106
Todd, Vivian Edmiston 1912- 17-18R
Todd, William Burton 1919- 41-44R
Todd, William Mills III 1944- 65-68
Todman, Bill
See Todman, William S.
Todman, William S. 1916-1979 Obituary 89-92
Todorov, Tzvetan 1939- 73-76
Todrank, Gustave H(erman) 1924- 41-44R
Todrin, Boris 1915- 61-64
Todsicher, J(ohn) Edgar 1926- CANR-14
Earlier sketch in CA 29-32R
Toekes, Rudolf L(eslie) 1935- 23-24R
Toepfer, Ray Grant 1923- 21-22R
Toeplitz, Jerzy 1909- 65-68
Toernqvist, (Per) Egil 1932- 29-32R
Tofani, Loretta 1953- 116
Brief entry 113
Toffler, Alvin 1928- CANR-15
Earlier sketch in CA 15-16R
Toft, (Eric) John 1933- 103
Tofte, Arthur 1902-1980 73-76
Obituary 103
Togliatti, Palmiro 1893(?)-1964 Obituary 113
Tohata, Seiichi 1899-1983 Obituary 110
Toka, Salchak Kalbakkhoreviich
1901-1973 Obituary 41-44R
Tokayer, Marvin 1936- 102
Toker, Franklin K(arl) B(enedict) S(erchuk)
1944- CANR-15
Earlier sketch in CA 81-84
Tokes, Rudolf L(eslie) 1935- Brief entry 114
Toklas, Alice B(abette) 1877-1967 81-84
Obituary 25-28R
See also DLB 4
Tokmakoff, George 1928- 123
Tolan, Stephanie S. 1942- CANR-15
Earlier sketch in CA 77-80
See also SATA 38
Toland, John (Willard) 1912- CANR-23
Earlier sketches in CA 2R, CANR-6
See also SATA 38
Tolbert, E(lias) L(ake) 1915- CANR-3
Earlier sketch in CA 3R
Tolbert, Francis Xavier 1912-1984 .... CANR-16
Obituary 111
Earlier sketch in CA 3R
Tolbert, Frank X.
See Tolbert, Francis Xavier
Tolbert, Malcolm O(liver) 1924- 65-68
Tolbert, Mary Ann 1947- 116
Tolby, Arthur
See Infield, Glenn (Berton)
Tolchin, Martin 1928- 120
Toldson, Ivory L. 1943- 114
Toledano, Ralph de 1916- 11-12R
See also AITN 1
Toledano, Roulhac (Bunkley) 1938- 101
Tolegian, Aram 1909- CANR-6
Earlier sketch in CA 2R
Toles, Thomas G. 1951- 126
Toles, Tom
See Toles, Thomas G.
Tolf, Robert W(alter) 1929- 73-76
Tolischus, Otto D(avid) 1890-1967
Obituary 93-96
Toliver, George
See Masselink, Ben
Toliver, Harold E(arl) 1932- 23-24R
Toliver, Raymond F. 1914- 17-18R
Tolkien, J(ohn) R(onald) R(euel)
1892-1973 .... CAP-2
Obituary 45-48
Earlier sketch in CA 17-18
See also SATA 2, 24, 32
See also DLB 15
See also CLC 1, 2, 3, 8, 12, 38
See also AITN 1
Toll, Robert C(harles) 1938- 53-56
Toll, Seymour I. 1925- 29-32R
Toll, William 1941- 114
Toller, Ernst 1893-1939 Brief entry 107
See also TCLC 10
Toller, Kate Caffrey
See Caffrey, Kate
Tollers, Vincent L(ouis) 1939- 57-60
Tolles, Frederick B(arnes) 1915-1975 .... 5-6R
Obituary 103
Tolles, Martha 1921- 49-52
See also SATA 8
Tolley, A(rnold) T(revor) 1927- 123
Tolley, Howard B(oyd), Jr. 1943- 53-56
Tolley, Kemp 1908- 45-48
Tolley, William Pearson 1900- 93-96
Tolliver, Ruby C(hangos) 1922- 111
See also SATA 41
Tolman, Newton F. 1908-1986 .... 1R
Obituary 120
Tolmie, Kenneth Donald 1941- 69-72
See also SATA 15
Tolnai, Karoly
See De Tolnay, Charles Erich
Tolnai, Vagujhelyi Karoly
See De Tolnay, Charles Erich
Tolson, M. B.
See Tolson, Melvin B(eaunorus)
Tolson, Melvin B(eaunorus) 1898(?)-1966 124
Obituary 89-92
See also BW
See also DLB 48, 76
See also CLC 36
Tolstoi, Aleksei Nikolaevich
See Tolstoy, Alexey Nikolaevich
Tolstoy, Alexandra L(vovna) 1884-1979 65-68
Obituary 89-92
Tolstoy, Alexey Nikolaevich 1882-1945
Brief entry 107
See also TCLC 18
Tolstoy, Count Leo
See Tolstoy, Leo (Nikolaevich)
Tolstoy, Dimitry 1912- 29-32R
Tolstoy, Leo (Nikolaevich) 1828-1910 123
Brief entry 104
See also SATA 26
See also TCLC 4, 11, 17, 28
Tolstoy, Mary Koutouzov 1884(?)-1976
Obituary 69-72
Tolstoy(-Miloslavsky), Nikolai (Dimitrievich)
1935- 81-84
Tolstoy, Tatyana (Sukhotin) 1864-1950
Brief entry 117
Tolzmann, Don Heinrich 1945- CANR-17
Earlier sketches in CA 49-52, CANR-2

Toma, Dave
See Toma, David
Toma, David 1933- 118
Tomalin, Claire 1933- 89-92
Tomalin, Nicholas 1931-1973 Obituary 45-48
Tomalin, Ruth CANR-13
Earlier sketch in CA 15-16R
See also SATA 29
Toman, Walter 1920- 5-6R
Tomas, Andrew Paul 73-76
Tomasek, Robert D(ennis) 1928- 17-18R
Tomasevic, Nebojsa 1929- 81-84
Tomasi, Silvano M(ario) 1940- 115
Tomasic, D(inko) A(nthony) 1902- CAP-1
Earlier sketch in CA 19-20
Tomasi di Lampedusa, Giuseppe
1896-1957 Brief entry 111
Tomasson, Katherine 1895- CAP-1
Earlier sketch in CA 9-10
Tomasson, Richard F(inn) 1928- CANR-1
Earlier sketch in CA 45-48
Tomb, David A(lan) 1944- 117
Tomek, Ivan 1939- 120
Tomes, Margot (Ladd) 1917- SATA-27, 36
Tomeski, Edward Alexander 1930- 37-40R
Tomfool
See Farjeon, Eleanor
Tomikel, John 1928- CANR-4
Earlier sketch in CA 53-56
Tomin, Zdena 1941- 123
Tomkiewicz, Mina 1917-1975 CAP-2
Earlier sketch in CA 29-32
Tomkins, Calvin 1925- CANR-8
Earlier sketch in CA 15-16R
Tomkins, Jasper
See Batey, Tom
Tomkins, Mary E(ileen) 1914- 61-64
Tomkinson, Constance
See Weeks, Constance Tomkinson
Tomkinson, Michael 1940- CANR-22
Earlier sketch in CA 93-96
Tomlin, E(ric) W(alter) F(rederick)
1913-1988(?) CANR-3
Obituary 124
Earlier sketch in CA 5-6R
Tomlin, Lily
See Tomlin, Mary Jean
See also CLC 17
Tomlin, Mary Jean 1939(?)- Brief entry 117
Tomlins, Jack E(dward) 1929- 25-28R
Tomlinson, (Alfred) Charles 1927- 5-6R
See also DLB 40
See also CLC 2, 4, 6, 13, 45
Tomlinson, Edward 1891(?)-1973
Obituary 45-48
Tomlinson, Gerald (Arthur) 1933- 85-88
Tomlinson, H(enry) M(ajor) 1873-1958
Brief entry 118
See also DLB 36
Tomlinson, Jill 1931-1976 CAP-2
Earlier sketch in CA 29-32
See also SATA 3, 24
Tomlinson, Kenneth Y(oung) 1944- 65-68
Tomlinson, Reginald R(obert)
1885-1979(?) Obituary 104
See also SATA 27
Tomlinson, T(homas) B(rian) 1925- 11-12R
Tomlinson-Keasey, Carol 1942- 101
Tommeraasen, Miles 1923- 21-22R
Tompert, Ann 1918- CANR-11
Earlier sketch in CA 69-72
See also SATA 14
Tompkins, C(linton) David 1937- 41-44R
Tompkins, Dorothy (Campbell) 1908- 17-18R
Tompkins, E(dwin) Berkeley 1935- 29-32R
Tompkins, Everett Thomas 1931- 107
Tompkins, J(oyce) M(arjorie) S(anxter)
1897-1986 Obituary 121
Tompkins, Jane P(arry) 1940- CANR-17
Earlier sketch in CA 29-32R
Tompkins, Jerry R(obert) 1931- 17-18R
Tompkins, Julia (Marguerite Hunter
Manchee) 1909- 29-32R
Tompkins, Kathleen Burns 1934- 93-96
Tompkins, Peter 1919- CANR-12
Earlier sketch in CA 11-12R
Tompkins, Richard A. 1896(?)-1977
Obituary 73-76
Tompkins, Stuart R(amsay) 1886-1977 37-40R
Tompkins, Tom
See Tompkins, Everett Thomas
Tompkins, Walker A. 1909- 7-8R
Tompson, Benjamin 1642-1714 DLB-24
Toms, Bernard 1931- 17-18R
Tomson, Bernard 1909-1978 Obituary 77-80
Ton, Mary Ellen 1933- 112
Tonashi
See Harrington, Mark Raymond
Tone, Teona 1944- 112
Toner, Raymond John 1908- 5-6R
See also SATA 10
Toney, Albert (Livingston, Jr.) 1933- 120
Toney, Anthony 1913- CANR-9
Earlier sketch in CA 17-18R
Tong, Raymond 1922- CANR-2
Earlier sketch in CA 7-8R
Tong, Te-kong 1920- CANR-8
Earlier sketch in CA 11-12R
Tongren, Sally S(tetson) 1926- 118
Tonkin, Humphrey 1939- CANR-16
Earlier sketch in CA 41-44R
Tonkin, Peter (Francis) 1950- 101
Tonkinson, Robert 1928- 77-80
Tonks, A. Ronald 1934- 125
Tonks, Rosemary (D. Boswell) 89-92
See also DLB 14
Tonn, Martin H. 1921- 7-8R
Tonquedec, Joseph de 1868-1962
Obituary 112
Tonson, Jacob
See Bennett, (Enoch) Arnold
Tonsor, Stephen (John) 1923- Brief entry 114
Toobin, Jerome 1920(?)-1984 Obituary 111
Toohey, Catherine 1949- 109
Toohey, Robert E(ugene) 1935- 89-92
Took, Belladonna
See Chapman, Vera
Tooke, Ann (Mary Margaret) Hales
See Hales-Tooke, Ann (Mary Margaret)
Tooke, Louise Mathews 1950- 105
See also SATA 38
Tooke, Thomas (Renshaw) 1947- 73-76
Tooker, Elisabeth (Jane) 1927- 49-52
Toole, John Kennedy 1937-1969 104
See also DLBY 81
See also CLC 19
Toole, K(enneth) Ross 1920- Brief entry 112
Toole, Rex
See Tralins, S(andor) Robert
Toole, William Bell III 1930- 21-22R
Toole Stott, Raymond 1910-1982
Obituary 105
Tooley, M. J.
See Tooley, Michael J(ohn)
Tooley, Michael J(ohn) 1942- CANR-24
Earlier sketch in CA 106
Tooley, R(onald) Vere 1898-1986 9-10R
Obituary 120
Toomay, Patrick J(ay) 1948- 65-68
Toombs, John 1927- 106
Toombs, Lawrence Edmund 1919- CANR-8
Earlier sketch in CA 5-6R
Toomer, Derek 1946- 65-68
Toomer, Jean 1894-1967 85-88
See also BW
See also DLB 45, 51
See also CLC 1, 4, 13, 22
See also SSC 1
Toon, Peter 1939- 112
Toona, Elin(-Kai) 1937- CANR-15
Earlier sketch in CA 81-84
Toonder, Martin
See Groom, Arthur William
Toothaker, Roy Eugene 1928- 65-68
See also SATA 18
Tooze, Ruth (Anderson) 1892- 5-6R
See also SATA 4
Topel, L(ouis) John 1934- 118
Toperoff, Sam 1933- 45-48
Topkins, Katharine 1927- 49-52
Topkins, Richard 1925- 25-28R
Toplin, Robert Brent 1940- CANR-15
Earlier sketch in CA 77-80
Topol, Allan 1941- 93-96
Topolski, Daniel 1945- 110
Topolski, Feliks 1907- Brief entry 112
Topor, Tom 1938- 105
Toppin, Edgar A(llan) 1928- 21-22R
Topping, Anne Marie 25-28R
Topping, Audrey R(onning) 1928- 41-44R
See also SATA 14
Topping, C(oral) W(esley) 1889- 41-44R
Topping, Donald M(edley) 1929- 53-56
Topping, Seymour 1921- 49-52
Topping, Wesley
See Topping, C(oral) W(esley)
Topsfield, L(eslie) T(homas) 1920-1981 CANR-9
Obituary 105
Earlier sketch in CA 61-64
Tor, Regina
See Shekerjian, Regina Tor
Torack, Richard M(aurice) 1927- 106
Torberg, Friedrich
See Kantor-Berg, Friedrich
Torbert, Floyd James 1922- 105
See also SATA 22
Torbert, William Rockwell 1944- 41-44R
Torbet, Laura 1942- CANR-16
Earlier sketch in CA 69-72
Torbet, Robert G(eorge) 1912- 11-12R
Torbett, Harvey Douglas Louis 1921- 9-10R
Torchiana, Donald T(hornhill) 1923- 19-20R
Torchio, Menico 1932- 61-64
Torday, Ursula 97-100
Tordoff, William 1925- 120
Toren, Heller 77-80
Torgersen, Don Arthur 1934- 111
See also SATA 41
Torgersen, Eric 1943- 37-40R
Torgersen, Paul Ernest 1931- 81-84
Torgerson, Dial 1928- 53-56
Torgerson Shaw, Ellen 1929(?)-1983
Obituary 109
Torgoff, Martin 1952- 109
Torgovnick, Marianna 1949- 115
Torley, Luke
See Blish, James (Benjamin)
Torme, Mel(vin Howard) 1925- Brief entry 118
Tormey, John Connolly 1942- 61-64
Tornabene, Lyn 1930- 69-72
Torney, Judith V.
See Torney-Purta, Judith V(ollmar)
Torney-Purta, Judith V(ollmar) 1937- CANR-10
Earlier sketch in CA 65-68
Torok, Lou 1927- 49-52
Torr, Iain
See Mackinnon, Charles Roy
Torrance, E. Paul 1915- CANR-18
Earlier sketches in CA 3R, CANR-3
Torrance, Thomas F(orsyth) 1913- CANR-5
Earlier sketch in CA 9-10R
Torre, Jose de la
See de la Torre, Jose
Torre, Raoul della
See Mencken, H(enry) L(ouis)
Torre-Bueno, Lillian de la
See McCue, Lillian Bueno
Torregian, Sotere 1941- CANR-3
Earlier sketch in CA 45-48
Torrence, Ridgely 1874-1950 DLB-54
Torrens, Robert George ?-1981 Obituary 105
Torres, Andres Segovia
See Segovia, Andres
Torres, Edwin 111
Torres, Emmanuel 1932- 97-100
Torres, Jose Acosta 1925- 57-60
Torres, Sergio
See Torres Gonzalez, Sergio A(ntonio)
Torres, Tereska
See Torres-Levin, Tereska (Szwarc)
Torres Bodet, Jaime 1902-1974 101
Obituary 49-52
Torres Gonzalez, Sergio A(ntonio) 1929- 117
Torres-Levin, Tereska (Szwarc) CANR-15
Earlier sketch in CA 7-8R
Torres-Rioseco, Arturo 1897-1971 CAP-1
Earlier sketch in CA 9-10
Torrey, E(dwin) Fuller 1937- 119
See also CLC 34
Torrey, Gordon H(oward) 1919- 11-12R
Torrey, Norman Lewis 1894-1980 3R
Obituary 102
Torrey, Therese von Hohoff 1898(?)-1974
Obituary 45-48
Torrey, Volta (Wray) 1905- 69-72
Torrie, James H(iram) 1908- 73-76
Torrie, Malcolm
See Mitchell, Gladys (Maude Winifred)
Torro, Pel
See Fanthorpe, R(obert) Lionel
Tors, Ivan (Lawrence) 1916-1983 103
Obituary 110
Torsvan, Ben Traven
See Traven, B.
Torsvan, Benno Traven
See Traven, B.
Torsvan, Berick Traven
See Traven, B.
Torsvan, Berwick Traven
See Traven, B.
Torsvan, Bruno Traven
See Traven, B.
Torsvan, Traven
See Traven, B.
Tortolano, William 1930- 77-80
Tortora, Daniel F(rancis) 1947- CANR-13
Earlier sketch in CA 73-76
Toscano, Peter Ralph 1920- 45-48
Tosches, Nick 1949- 81-84
Tosi, Henry L(ouis), Jr. 1936- 125
Toson, Shimazaki
See Shimazaki, Haruki
Tosti, Donald Thomas 1935- 49-52
Toth, Charles W(illiam) 1919- CANR-10
Earlier sketch in CA 65-68
Toth, Emily 1944- 101
Toth, Lazlo
See Novello, Don
Toth, Robert Charles 1928- 102
Toth, Stephen, Jr. 1950- 69-72
Toth, Susan Erickson Allen 1940- 105
See also DLBY 86
Totham, Mary
See Breinburg, Petronella
Totman, Conrad 1934- CANR-17
Earlier sketch in CA 101
Totten, George Oakley III 1922- CANR-21
Earlier sketches in CA 11-12R, CANR-5
Totten, Martha Wescoat 1957- 118
Totten, Sam(uel) 1949- 118
Totten, W. Fred 1905- 37-40R
Tough, Allen (MacNeill) 1936- 108
Touliatos, John 1944- 93-96
Toulmin, Stephen Edelston 1922- CANR-20
Earlier sketches in CA 9-10R, CANR-5
Toulouse-Lautrec, Marie-Pierre (Mapie) de
1901-1972 Obituary 37-40R
Toulson, Shirley 1924- CANR-17
Earlier sketch in CA 101
Touraine, Alain 1925- 85-88
Toure, Askia Muhammad
See Toure, Askia Muhammad Abu Bakr el
See also DLB 41
Toure, Askia Muhammad Abu Bakr el
1938- 124
See also BW
Tourneur, Cyril 1580(?)-1626 DLB-58
Tourneur, Dina-Kathelijn 1934- 108
Tourney, Garfield 1927- 57-60
Tournier, Michel 1924- CANR-3
Earlier sketch in CA 49-52
See also SATA 23
See also CLC 6, 23, 36
Tournier, Paul 1898-1986 81-84
Obituary 120
Tournimparte, Alessandra
See Ginzburg, Natalia
Tours, Hugh Berthold 1910- CAP-1
Earlier sketch in CA 9-10
Tourtellot, Arthur Bernon 1913-1977 CANR-4
Obituary 73-76
Earlier sketch in CA 5-6R
Tourtellot, Jonathan B. 1946- 111
Tourville, Elsie A(lma) 1926- 57-60
Tousley, Clare M. 1889(?)-1985 Obituary 114
Toussaint, Stanley D. 1928- 115
Touster, Alison
See Reed, Alison Touster
Touval, Saadia E. 1932- 45-48
Touw, Kathleen 1949- 109
Tovey, Doreen Evelyn 1918- 104
Tovo, Jerome 1936- 45-48
Towber, Chaim 1902(?)-1972 Obituary 33-36R
Towell, Julie E. 1953- 122
Tower, Ann
See Straubing, Harold (Elk)
Tower, Diana
See Smith, Richard Rein
Tower, Don
See Bower, Donald E(dward)
Tower, John G(oodwin) 1925- Brief entry 106
Tower, Margene 1939- 37-40R
Towers, Ivar
See Kornbluth, C(yril) M.
Towers, Maxwell 1909- 57-60
Towey, Cyprian 1912- 21-22R
Towle, Joseph W(alter) 1909- CAP-1
Earlier sketch in CA 13-14
Towle, Philip 1945- 117
Towle, Tony 1939- 37-40R
Towler, Juby Earl 1913- 13-14R
Town, Glenn P(atrick) 1949- 118
Town, Harold (Barling) 1924- CANR-15
Earlier sketch in CA 41-44R
Towne, Anthony 1928-1980 25-28R
Obituary 117
Towne, Benjamin 1740(?)-1793 DLB-43
Towne, Mary
See Spelman, Mary
Towne, Peter
See Nabokov, Peter (Francis)
Towne, Robert (Burton) 1936(?)- 108
See also DLB 44
Towne, Stuart
See Rawson, Clayton
Towner, Donald (Chisholm) 1903-1985 CAP-1
Obituary 117
Earlier sketch in CA 19-20
Towner, Jason
See Smith, Harold Ivan
Towner, W. Sibley
See Towner, Wayne Sibley
Towner, Wayne Sibley 1933- Brief entry 118
Townley, Ralph 1923- 23-24R
Townley, Rod 1942- CANR-12
Earlier sketch in CA 57-60
Towns, Elmer L(eon) 1932- CANR-2
Earlier sketch in CA 45-48
Towns, James E(dward) 1942- CANR-23
Earlier sketches in CA 61-64, CANR-8,
21
Towns, Jim
See Towns, James E(dward)
Townsend, Charles Bud 1929- 53-56
Townsend, Charles E(dward) 1932- 41-44R
Townsend, Charles R(ay) 1929- 69-72
Townsend, Doris McFerran 1914- CANR-19
Earlier sketch in CA 103
Townsend, Elsie Doig 1908- 29-32R
Townsend, Harry 1925- 25-28R
Townsend, Irving 1920- 101
Townsend, J(ames) Benjamin 1918- 23-24R
Townsend, J(acob) David 1888- 5-6R
Townsend, James B(arclay) J(ermain)
1910- 49-52
Townsend, Janet (Elizabeth) 1925- 107
Townsend, John Rowe 1922- 37-40R
See also SATA 4
See also SAAS 2
See also CLR 2
Townsend, Mark
See Wallmann, Jeffrey M(iner)
Townsend, Peter (Wooldridge) 1914- 29-32R
Townsend, Ralph M. 1901(?)-1976
Obituary 65-68
Townsend, Reginald T. 1890-1977
Obituary 73-76
Townsend, Richard E. 1897(?)-1975
Obituary 61-64
Townsend, Robert 1920- 45-48
Townsend, Sue 1946- Brief entry 119
See also SATA 48
Townsend, William Cameron 1896-1982
Obituary 106
Townsend, William H(enry) 1890-1964
Obituary 111
Townshend, Peter (Dennis Blandford)
1945- 107
See also CLC 17, 42
Townshend, Richard
See Bickers, Richard Leslie Townshend
Towson, Hazel CANR-18
Earlier sketch in CA 97-100
Toy, Henry, Jr. 1915- 37-40R
Toye, Clive 1933(?)- SATA-30
Toye, John Francis 1883-1964 CAP-1
Earlier sketch in CA 9-10
Toye, William Eldred 1926- CANR-4
Earlier sketch in CA 4R
See also SATA 8
Toynbee, Arnold J(oseph) 1889-1975 5-6R
Obituary 61-64
See also AITN 2
Toynbee, Jocelyn M(ary) C(atherine)
1897-1985 37-40R
Obituary 118
Toynbee, (Theodore) Philip 1916-1981 CANR-4
Obituary 104
Earlier sketch in CA 4R
Toynbee, Polly (Mary Louisa) 1946- CANR-9
Earlier sketch in CA 21-22R
Tozer, Mary (Christine) 1947- 101
Trabasso, Tom 1935- CANR-11
Earlier sketch in CA 23-24R
Trace, Arther Storrey, Jr. 1922- CANR-20
Earlier sketch in CA 3R

Tracey, Hugh (Travers) 1903-1977 ...... CAP-2
Obituary 77-80
Earlier sketch in CA 29-32
Tracey, Patricia Cleland 1932- 7-8R
Trachman, Muriel Karlin CANR-15
Earlier sketch in CA 85-88
Trachte, Don(ald) 1915- 89-92
Trachtenberg, Inge 1923- 77-80
Trachtenberg, Marvin (Lawrence) 1939- ... 65-68
Trachtenberg, Paul 1948- 112
Trachtenberg, Stanley 119
Traci, Philip (Joseph) 1934- 41-44R
Tracy, Aloise
See Shoenight, Aloise
Tracy, Ann B(laisdell) 1941- 107
Tracy, Clarence 1908- 11-12R
Tracy, David W. 1939- 101
Tracy, Don(ald Fiske) 1905-197(?) CANR-2
Earlier sketch in CA 4R
Tracy, Doris 1925- 61-64
Tracy, Honor (Lilbush Wingfield)
1913- CANR-24
Earlier sketches in CA 61-64, CANR-8
See also DLB 15
Tracy, Jack W. 1945- 105
Tracy, James D. 1938- 102
Tracy, John A(lvin) 1934- 53-56
Tracy, L(ee) Jack 1926- 9-10R
Tracy, Leland
See Tralins, S(andor) Robert
Tracy, Louise Treadwell 1896-1983
Obituary 114
Tracy, Michael 1932- 15-16R
Tracy, Powers
See Ward, Don(ald G.)
Tracy, Robert E. 1928- 89-92
Tracy, Susan
See Marino, Carolyn Fitch
Tracy, Theodore J(ames) 1916- 29-32R
Tracy, Thomas Henry 1900- CAP-2
Earlier sketch in CA 17-18
Tracz, Richard Francis 1944- CANR-17
Earlier sketch in CA 29-32R
Trader Vic
See Bergeron, Victor (Jules, Jr.)
Traer, James Frederick 1938- 102
Trafzer, Clifford Earl 1949- CANR-26
Earlier sketch in CA 109
Trager, Frank N(ewton) 1905-1984 ..... CANR-9
Obituary 113
Earlier sketch in CA 19-20R
Trager, George L(eonard) 1906- 41-44R
Trager, Helen G. 1910- 69-72
Trager, James 1925- CANR-15
Earlier sketch in CA 37-40R
Tragle, Henry Irving 1914- 37-40R
Trahan, Ronald 1950- 106
Traherne, Michael
See Watkins-Pitchford, Denys James
Trahey, Jane 1923- CANR-17
Earlier sketch in CA 17-18R
See also SATA 36
Train, Arthur (Cheney) 1875-1945
Brief entry 112
Train, Arthur K(issam) 1902(?)-1981
Obituary 104
Train, John 1928- 106
Traina, Richard P(aul) 1937- 25-28R
Trainer, David 1947- CANR-20
Earlier sketch in CA 25-28R
Trainer, Jennifer 1956- 108
Trainer, Orvel 1925- 45-48
Trainor, Richard
See Tralins, S(andor) Robert
Traister, Aaron 1904(?)-1976 Obituary 65-68
Trakas, Pedro N(icholas) 1923- 104
Trakl, Georg 1887-1914 Brief entry 104
See also TCLC 5
Tralbaut, Mark-Edo 1902-1976 .... CAP-2
Earlier sketch in CA 29-32
Tralins, Bob
See Tralins, S(andor) Robert
Tralins, Robert S.
See Tralins, S(andor) Robert
Tralins, S(andor) Robert 1926- CANR-14
Earlier sketch in CA 21-22R
Trambley, Estela Portillo 1936- 77-80
Trani, Eugene Paul 1939- 25-28R
Transtroemer, Tomas Goesta 1931-
Brief entry 117
Transtromer, Tomas Gosta
See Transtroemer, Tomas Goesta
Transue, Jacob
See Matheson, Joan (Transue)
Transue, Joan
See Matheson, Joan (Transue)
Tranter, John Ernest 1943- 110
Tranter, Nigel (Godwin) 1909- CANR-20
Earlier sketches in CA 11-12R, CANR-5
Trantino, Tommy 1938- 65-68
Trapido, Barbara 1941- 123
Trapier, Elizabeth du Gue 1893(?)-1974
Obituary 53-56
Trapp, E(dward) Philip 1923- 45-48
Trapp, Frank Anderson 1922- 57-60
Trapp, Maria Augusta von
See von Trapp, Maria Augusta
See also SATA 16
Traschen, Isadore 1915- 25-28R
Trask, David F(rederic) 1929- CANR-17
Earlier sketches in CA 3R, CANR-1
Trask, John Jacquelin 1904(?)-1977
Obituary 69-72
Trask, Jonathan
See Levinson, Leonard
Trask, Margaret Pope 1907- 3R
Trask, Roger R(eed) 1930- 41-44R
Trask, Willard (Ropes) 1900(?)-1980
Obituary 101
Trasler, Gordon (Blair) 1929- CANR-3
Earlier sketch in CA 3R
Trattner, Walter I(rwin) 1936- CANR-13
Earlier sketch in CA 37-40R
Traube, Ruy
See Tralins, S(andor) Robert
Traube, Shepard 1907-1983 Obituary 111
Traubel, Horace
See Traubel, Horace L(ogo)
Traubel, Horace L(ogo) 1858-1919
Brief entry 123
Traudl
See Flaxman, Traudl
Trauger, Wilmer K(ohl) 1898- CAP-1
Earlier sketch in CA 9-10
Traugott, Elizabeth Closs 1939- 41-44R
Traupman, John C. 1923- 41-44R
Traut, Dennis 1953- 111
Trautman, Donald T. 1924- 37-40R
Trautman, Ray 1907- 45-48
Travell, Janet (Graeme) 1901- CAP-2
Earlier sketch in CA 29-32
Traven, B. ?-1969 .... CAP-2
Obituary 25-28R
Earlier sketch in CA 19-20
See also DLB 9, 56
See also CLC 8, 11
Traven, Beatrice
See Goldemberg, Rose Leiman
Traver, Robert
See Voelker, John D(onaldson)
Travers, Ben 1886-1980 Obituary 102
See also DLB 10
Travers, Kenneth
See Hutchin, Kenneth Charles
Travers, Louise Allderdice 1891- CAP-1
Earlier sketch in CA 9-10
Travers, P(amela) L(yndon) 1906- 33-36R
See also SATA 4
See also SAAS 2
See also CLR 2
Travers, Robert J. 1911(?)-1974
Obituary 49-52
Travers, Robert M(orris) W(illiam)
1913- CANR-2
Earlier sketch in CA 7-8R
Travers, Scott A(ndrew) 1961- 125
Travers, Virginia
See Coigney, Virginia
Travers, Will
See Rowland, D(onald) S(ydney)
Traversi, Derek A(ntona) 1912- 77-80
Travis, Charles S. 1943- 37-40R
Travis, Dempsey J. 1920- CANR-15
Earlier sketch in CA 85-88
Travis, Gerry
See Trimble, Louis P(reston)
Travis, Gretchen A. 103
Travis, John T. 1935- 25-28R
Travis, Neal 1939(?)- 103
Travis, Stephen H(enry) 1944- 106
Travis, Walter Earl 1926- 23-24R
Travis, William 1924- 25-28R
Travlos, John 1908(?)-1985 Obituary 118
Trawick, Buckner Beasley 1914- 7-8R
Traxler, Arthur E(dwin) 1900- CAP-2
Earlier sketch in CA 21-22
Traylor, Ellen Gunderson 1946- 122
Traylor, W. L. 1929- 37-40R
Traynor, Alex
See Lagerwall, Edna
Treacy, William 1919- 61-64
Treadgold, Donald W(arren) 1922- 11-12R
Treadgold, Mary 1910- 13-14R
See also SATA 49
Treadway, Terry
See Treadway, Theresa
Treadway, Theresa 1941- 107
Treadwell, Sandy 1946- 124
Treahearne, Elizabeth
See Maxwell, Patricia
Treanor, John Holland 1903(?)-1978
Obituary 77-80
Trease, (Robert) Geoffrey 1909- CANR-22
Earlier sketches in CA 7-8R, CANR-7
See also SATA 2
See also SAAS 6
Treasure, G(eoffrey) R(ussell) R(ichards)
1929- 77-80
Treat, Ida
See Bergeret, Ida Treat
Treat, Lawrence 1903- 49-52
Treat, Payson J(ackson) 1879-1972
Obituary 37-40R
Trebach, Arnold S. 1928- CANR-12
Earlier sketch in CA 11-12R
Trebing, Harry M(artin) 1926- 29-32R
Trecker, Harleigh B(radley) 1911- CANR-5
Earlier sketch in CA 5-6R
Trecker, Janice Law 1941- CANR-9
Earlier sketch in CA 65-68
Tredennick, (George) Hugh (Percival Phair)
1899-1981 109
Obituary 105
Tredez, Alain 1926- 85-88
See also SATA 17
Tredez, Denise 1930- CANR-8
Earlier sketch in CA 5-6R
See also SATA 50
Tredgold, Nye
See Tranter, Nigel (Godwin)
Tredgold, Roger F(rancis) 1911-1975 ... CANR-5
Earlier sketch in CA 7-8R
Tree, Christina 1944- CANR-12
Earlier sketch in CA 73-76
Tree, Cornelia
See Nichols, Nina (Marianna) da Vinci
Tree, Gregory
See Bardin, John Franklin
Tree, Michael (John) 1926- 9-10R
Tree, Ronald 1897-1976 69-72
Obituary 65-68
Treece, Henry 1912-1966 .... CANR-6
Obituary 25-28R
Earlier sketch in CA 1R
See also SATA 2
See also CLR 2
Treece, Patricia 1938- 110
Trefethen, Florence 1921- 29-32R
Trefethen, James B(yron, Jr.)
1916-1976 .... CANR-11
Obituary 69-72
Earlier sketch in CA 21-22R
Trefflich, Henry (Herbert Frederick)
1908-1978 .... CAP-2
Obituary 77-80
Earlier sketch in CA 23-24
Trefftzs, Kenneth Lewis 1911- 13-14R
Trefil, James S. 1938- 101
Trefor, Eirlys
See Williams, Eirlys O(lwen)
Trefousse, Hans Louis 1921- CANR-14
Earlier sketch in CA 37-40R
Tregarthen, Enys
See Sloggett, Nellie
Tregaskis, Hugh 1905(?)-1983 Obituary 110
Tregaskis, Richard 1916-1973 .... CANR-2
Obituary 45-48
Earlier sketch in CA 3R
See also SATA 3, 26
Tregear, Thomas R(efoy) 1897- 21-22R
Treger, Harvey 1924- 61-64
Treggiari, Susan (Mary) 1940- 61-64
Tregidgo, Philip Sillince 1926- 105
Treglown, Jeremy (Dickinson) 1946- 114
Brief entry 111
Tregoe, Benjamin B., Jr. 1927- 125
Tregonning, Kennedy Gordon 1923- 9-10R
Trehey, Harold F. 1902(?)-1978 Obituary .. 77-80
Treichler, Jessie C(ambron) 1906(?)-1972
Obituary 37-40R
Treister, Bernard W(illiam) 1932- 101
Trejo, Arnulfo D(uenes) 1922- 57-60
Trejos, Carlota 1920- 49-52
Trekell, Harold E(verett) 1910- 49-52
Trelease, Allen William 1928- 108
Trelease, James J(oseph) 1941- 112
Trelease, Jim
See Trelease, James J(oseph)
Trelford, Donald Gilchrist 1937- 111
Trell, Bluma L(ee) 1903- 77-80
Trell, Max 1900- 41-44R
See also SATA 14
Treloar, Dorothy 1920(?)-1983 Obituary 111
Treloar, James A(rthur) 1933- 45-48
Trelos, Tony
See Crechales, Anthony George
Tremain, Rose 1943- 97-100
See also DLB 14
See also CLC 42
Tremain, Ruthven 1922- 85-88
See also SATA 17
Tremaine, Jennie
See Chesney, Marion
Tremayne, Jonathan
See Forrest-Webb, Robert
Tremayne, Ken(neth Eugene, Jr.) 1933- .. 17-18R
Tremayne, Peter
See Ellis, Peter Berresford
Tremayne, Sydney (Durward) 1912- CANR-5
Earlier sketch in CA 7-8R
Tremblay, Bill
See Tremblay, William Andrew
Tremblay, Marc-Adelard 1922- 41-44R
Tremblay, Michel 1942- Brief entry 116
See also DLB 60
See also CLC 29
Tremblay, William Andrew 1940- 89-92
Tremble, Freda B. 1894- 73-76
Treml, Vladimir G(uy) 1929- 25-28R
Tremmel, William Calloley 1918- 97-100
Trench, (William Francis) Brinsley Le Poer
See Le Poer Trench, (William Francis)
Brinsley
Trendall, Arthur Dale 1909- CANR-22
Earlier sketches in CA 53-56, CANR-5
Treneer, Anne 1891- CAP-1
Earlier sketch in CA 9-10
Trengove, Alan Thomas 1929- 108
Trenhaile, John (Stevens) 1949- 110
Trenholm, Virginia Cole 1902- 15-16R
Trennert, Robert A., Jr. 1937- 57-60
Trensky, Paul I. 1929- 93-96
Trent, James W(illiam) 1933- 23-24R
Trent, Jimmie Douglas 1933- 49-52
Trent, May Wong 1939- 57-60
Trent, Olaf
See Fanthorpe, R(obert) Lionel
Trent, Robbie 1894- CAP-1
Earlier sketch in CA 9-10
See also SATA 26
Trent, Timothy
See Malmberg, Carl
Trent, William 1919- CANR-3
Earlier sketch in CA 3R
Trent, William P(eterfield) 1862-1939
Brief entry 122
See also DLB 47, 71
Trento, Joseph John 1947- 45-48
Trento, Salvatore Michael 1952- 101
Trepp, Leo 1913- CANR-18
Earlier sketches in CA 7-8R, CANR-2
Trepper, Leopold Leib 1904-1982(?)
Obituary 105
Tresch, John William, Jr. 1937-
Brief entry 106
Trescot, William Henry 1822-1898 ...... DLB-30
Trescott, Paul B(arton) 1925- CANR-2
Earlier sketch in CA 3R
Trese, Leo J(ohn) 1902- 5-6R
Tresemer, David 1948- 108
Treshow, Michael 1926- 57-60
Tresidder, Argus John 1907- CANR-5
Earlier sketch in CA 7-8R
Tresilian, Liz 1940- 25-28R
Tresilian, (Cecil) Stuart 1891-19(?) SATA-40
Tress, Arthur 1940- 101
Tresselt, Alvin 1916- CANR-1
Earlier sketch in CA 49-52
See also SATA 7
Tressidy, Jim
See Norwood, Victor G(eorge) C(harles)
Tressilian, Charles
See Atcheson, Richard
Tressler, Donald K(iteley) 1894-1981 .... CANR-4
Obituary 103
Earlier sketch in CA 45-48
Trethowan, K(enneth) Illtyd 1907- CANR-3
Earlier sketch in CA 1R
Tretick, Stanley 1921- 103
Trettel, (Mario) Efrem 1921- 69-72
Treuenfels, Peter 1926- 37-40R
Treuer, Robert 1926- 69-72
Trevanian (a pseudonym) 1930(?)- 108
See also CLC 29
Trevaskis, John 1911-1968 .... CAP-1
Obituary 33-36R
Earlier sketch in CA 9-10
Trevathan, Robert E. 1925- CANR-6
Earlier sketch in CA 2R
Trevelyan, George Macaulay 1876-1962 ... 89-92
Trevelyan, Humphrey 1905-1985 .... 37-40R
Obituary 115
Trevelyan, Julian O(tto) 1910-1988 ...... 11-12R
Obituary 126
Trevelyan, Katharine 1908- CAP-1
Earlier sketch in CA 11-12
Trevelyan, Raleigh 1923- CANR-22
Earlier sketches in CA 13-14R, CANR-6
Trevelyan, Robert
See Forrest-Webb, Robert
Trever, John C(ecil) 1915- 17-18R
Treverton, Gregory F(rye) 1947- 118
Treves, Ralph 1906- 13-14R
Trevino, Elizabeth B(orton) de 1904- CANR-9
Earlier sketch in CA 17-18R
See also SATA 1, 29
See also SAAS 5
Trevino, Lee (Buck) 1939- 113
Trevor, Elleston 1920- 5-6R
See also SATA 28
Trevor, Glen
See Hilton, James
Trevor, (Lucy) Meriol 1919- CANR-16
Earlier sketches in CA 3R, CANR-1
See also SATA 10
Trevor, William
See Cox, William Trevor
See also DLB 14
See also CLC 7, 9, 14, 25
Trevor-Roper, H(ugh) R(edwald) 1914- 101
Trew, Antony (Francis) 1906- CANR-2
Earlier sketch in CA 45-48
Trewin, Ion (Courtenay Gill) 1943- 69-72
Trewin, J(ohn) C(ourtenay) 1908-
Brief entry 112
Trez, Alain
See Tredez, Alain
Trez, Denise
See Tredez, Denise
Trezise, Philip Harold 1912- 109
Trezza, Alphonse F(iore) 1920- 118
Triandis, Harry C(haralambos) 1926- 41-44R
Tribbe, Frank C(alvert) 1914- 117
Tribble, Edwin 1907-1986 Obituary 119
Tribble, Harold Wayland 1899-1986
Obituary 121
Tribe, David (Harold) 1931- 25-28R
Tribe, Ivan M(athews) 1940- 122
Tribich, Susan 1945(?)-1985 Obituary 115
Tribune
See Armstrong, Douglas Albert
Trice, Borough
See Allen, A(rthur) B(ruce)
Trice, Harrison M. 1920- 23-24R
Tricker, B(rian) J(ohn) K(ingsbury)
1937- 25-28R
Trickett, Joyce 1915- 105
Trickett, Mabel Rachel 1923- 101
Triegel, Linda (Jeanette) 1942- 117
Triem, Eve 1902- CANR-9
Earlier sketch in CA 19-20R
Triere, Lynette 1941- 108
Trieschman, Albert E(well) 1931-1984 .... 29-32R
Obituary 113
Triffin, Robert 1911- CANR-3
Earlier sketch in CA 2R
Trifonov, Yuri (Valentinovich) 1925-1981 ... 126
Obituary 103
See also CLC 45
Trigg, Harry Davis 1927- 61-64
Trigg, Joseph Wilson 1949- 118
Trigg, Roger (Hugh) 1941- 49-52
Trigg, Yolanda Lillian 1926- 61-64
Trigger, Bruce G(raham) 1937- CANR-9
Earlier sketch in CA 23-24R
Trigoboff, Joseph 1947- 81-84

Trillin, Calvin 1935- CANR-20
Earlier sketch in CA 85-88
See also AITN 1
Trilling, Diana (Rubin) 1905- CANR-10
Earlier sketch in CA 7-8R
Trilling, Lionel 1905-1975 CANR-10
Obituary 61-64
Earlier sketch in CA 11-12R
See also DLB 28, 63
See also CLC 9, 11, 24
Trimball, W. H.
See Mencken, H(enry) L(ouis)
Trimble, Jacquelyn W(hitney) 1927- 15-16R
Trimble, John F(elix) 1925- 97-100
Trimble, Louis P(reston) 1917- CANR-6
Earlier sketch in CA 15-16R
Trimble, Marshall I(ra) 1939- 77-80
Trimble, Martha Scott 1914- 29-32R
Trimble, Vance H(enry) 1913- 49-52
Trimble, William Raleigh 1913- 9-10R
Trimby, Elisa 1948- 122
See also SATA 40, 47
Trimingham, J(ohn) Spencer 1904- CANR-3
Earlier sketch in CA 3R
Trimmer, Ellen McKay 1915- 9-10R
Trimmer, Eric J. 1923- 9-10R
Trimmer, Joseph F(rancis) 1941- CANR-13
Earlier sketch in CA 77-80
Tring, A. Stephen
See Meynell, Laurence Walter
Trinidad, Corky
See Trinidad, Francisco D., Jr.
Trinidad, Francisco D., Jr. 1939- 69-72
Trinkaus, Charles (Edward) 1911- 29-32R
Trinklein, Frederick E(rnst) 1924- 41-44R
Trinkner, Charles L. 1920- 29-32R
Trinquier, Roger Paul 1908- CANR-5
Earlier sketch in CA 9-10R
Triola, Mario F(rank) 1944- 57-60
Triolet, Elsa 1896-1970 Obituary 25-28R
See also DLB 72
Triplett, Kenneth E(arl) 1926- 57-60
Triplett, Raymond (Francis) 1921- 117
Tripodi, Tony 1932- CANR-12
Earlier sketch in CA 29-32R
Tripp, C(larence) A(rthur) 1919- 73-76
Tripp, Eleanor B(aldwin) 1936- 29-32R
See also SATA 4
Tripp, John 1927- 97-100
See also DLB 40
Tripp, John
See Moore, John Travers
Tripp, Karen 1923- 53-56
Tripp, L(ouis) Reed 1913- 5-6R
Tripp, Miles (Barton) 1923- CANR-12
Earlier sketch in CA 13-14R
Tripp, Paul 1916- 21-22R
See also SATA 8
Tripp, Wallace (Whitney) 1940- CANR-23
Earlier sketch in CA 106
See also SATA 31
Tripp, Wendell, Jr. 1928- 114
Trippett, Frank 1926- 21-22R
Trisco, Robert Frederick 1929- 41-44R
Triska, Jan Francis 1922- CANR-7
Earlier sketch in CA 5-6R
Trisler, Hank 1937- 121
Tristram
See Housman, A(lfred) E(dward)
Triton, A. N.
See Barclay, Oliver R(ainsford)
Tritt, Robert E(arl) 1921- 23-24R
Trittschuh, Travis Edward 1920- 5-6R
Trivas, A(lexander) Victor 1894-1970 CAP-1
Obituary 29-32R
Earlier sketch in CA 19-20
Trivelpiece, Laurel 1926- 123
See also SATA 46
Trivers, Howard 1909-1987 73-76
Obituary 122
Trivett, Daphne Harwood 1940- 97-100
See also SATA 22
Trnka, Jiri 1912-1969 Obituary 111
See also SATA 32, 43
Trobian, Helen R(eed) 1918- 5-6R
Trobisch, Ingrid 1926- 97-100
Trocchi, Alexander 1925-1984 11-12R
Obituary 112
See also DLB 15
Trocme, Etienne 1924- 49-52
Troeger, Thomas H(enry) 1945- CANR-15
Earlier sketch in CA 89-92
Troelstrup, Arch William 1901- 17-18R
Troen, Selwyn K. 1940- 104
Trofimenkoff, Susan Mann 1941- 73-76
Trogdon, William (Lewis) 1939- 119
Brief entry 115
Trohan, Walter (Joseph) 1903- 81-84
Troiden, Richard (Russell) 1946- 89-92
Troise, Joe 1942- 103
Troisgros, Jean (Georges) 1926-1983
Obituary 110
Trojanowicz, John M.
See Troyanovich, John M(ichael)
Trojanowicz, Robert (Chester) 1941- 45-48
Trojanski, John 1943- 45-48
Trolander, Judith Ann 1942- 61-64
Trollope, Anthony 1815-1882 SATA-22
See also DLB 21, 57
Trollope, Frances 1779-1863 DLB-21
Trollope, Joanna 1943- 101
Troman, Morley 1918- 13-14R
Tromanhauser, Edward (Downer) 1932- 41-44R
Trombley, Charles C(yprian) 1928- 65-68
Tromp, S. W.
See Tromp, Solco Walle
Tromp, Solco W.
See Tromp, Solco Walle
Tromp, Solco Walle 1909-1983 Obituary 116
Tronchin-James, (Robert) Nevil 1916- CAP-1
Earlier sketch in CA 9-10
Trooboff, Peter D(ennis) 1942- 65-68
Troop, Elizabeth 1931- Brief entry 116
See also DLB 14
Troop, Miriam 1917- 15-16R
Tropp, Martin 1945- 65-68
Trost, Cathy 1951- 125
Trost, Lucille W(ood) 1938- CANR-9
Earlier sketch in CA 61-64
See also SATA 12
Trotsky, Leon 1879-1940 Brief entry 118
See also TCLC 22
Trott, Susan 1937- 97-100
Trotta, John 1936- 45-48
Trotta, Maurice S. 1907-1976 Obituary 111
Trotter, Grace V(iolet) 1900- CANR-1
Earlier sketch in CA 1R
See also SATA 10
Trotter, Jesse McLane ?-1983 Obituary 110
Trotter, Patrick C. 1935- 126
Trotter, Robert J(oseph) 1943- 120
Trotter, Sallie (W. B.) 1915- 29-32R
Trotti, John H. 1936- 118
Trotti, Lamar 1898-1952 DLB-44
Trottier, Pierre 1925- DLB-60
Troughton, Joanna (Margaret) 1947- CANR-26
Earlier sketch in CA 109
See also SATA 37
Trouncer, Margaret (Lahey)
1903-1982 CANR-10
Obituary 108
Earlier sketch in CA 5-6R
Troup, Cornelius V. 1902- CAP-1
Earlier sketch in CA 9-10
Troupe, Quincy (Thomas, Jr.) 1943- 124
Brief entry 113
See also BW
See also DLB 41
Trout, Charles Hathaway 1935- 113
Trout, Kilgore
See Farmer, Philip Jose
Troutman, Charles (Henry) 1914- 69-72
Trouve, Roger 1882(?)-1984 Obituary 112
Trow, George W. S. 1943- 126
Trow, M(eirion) J(ames) 1949- 120
Trow, Martin A. 1926- 112
Trow, W(illiam) Clark 1894- CANR-6
Earlier sketch in CA 5-6R
Trowbridge, Clinton W(hiting) 1928- CANR-10
Earlier sketch in CA 65-68
Trowbridge, Keith W(ayne) 1937- 108
Trowbridge, Leslie Walter 1920- CANR-13
Earlier sketch in CA 77-80
Trowell, Kathleen Margaret 1904- 65-68
Troxell, Eugene A(nthony) 1937- 73-76
Troxell, Mary D(earborn) 1907- 37-40R
Troy, George F(rancis), Jr. 1909-1969 2R
Obituary 103
Troy, Katherine
See Buxton, Anne (Arundel)
Troy, Lawrence M. 1928- 23-24R
Troy, Nancy J. 1952- 115
Troy, Una 1913- CANR-3
Earlier sketch in CA 1R
Troy, William 1903-1961 Obituary 89-92
Troyanovich, John M(ichael) 1936- 49-52
Troyat, Henri 1911- CANR-2
Earlier sketch in CA 45-48
See also CLC 23
Troyer, Byron L(eRoy) 1909- 65-68
Troyer, Johannes 1902-1969 SATA-40
Troyer, Warner 1932- 101
Troyka, Lynn Quitman 1938- 37-40R
Troyna, Barry 1951- 117
Truax, Carol 1900- CANR-5
Earlier sketch in CA 7-8R
Truax, Charles B. 1933-197(?) CANR-13
Earlier sketches in CA 21-22, CAP-2
Truax, R. Hawley 1889(?)-1978 Obituary 81-84
Trubitt, Allen R(oy) 1931- 77-80
Trubo, Richard 1946- CANR-11
Earlier sketch in CA 61-64
Trubowitz, Sidney 1926- 23-24R
Truby, J(ohn) David 1938- CANR-24
Earlier sketches in CA 53-56, CANR-4
Truch, Stephen 1947- 115
Trudeau, G(arretson) B(eekman) 1948- 81-84
See also SATA 35
Trudeau, Garry B.
See Trudeau, G(arretson) B(eekman)
See also CLC 12
See also AITN 2
Trudeau, Margaret (Joan) 1948- 93-96
Trudeau, (Joseph Philippe) Pierre (Yves)
Elliott 1919- CANR-3
Earlier sketch in CA 45-48
Trudel, Marcel 1917- 104
Trudix, Marty
See Truman, Ruth
True, Dan 1924- 117
True, Michael 1933- CANR-17
Earlier sketch in CA 41-44R
Trueblood, Alan Stubbs 1917- 103
Trueblood, D(avid) Elton 1900- 41-44R
Trueblood, Paul Graham 1905- CANR-12
Earlier sketches in CA 17-18, CAP-1
Trueblood, Ted Whitaker 1913-1982
Obituary 111
Trueheart, Charles 1951- 45-48
Truemper, David G(eorge) 1939- 112
Truesdale, C(alvin) W(illiam) 1929- 29-32R
Truesdell, Leon E. 1881(?)-1979
Obituary 85-88
Truesdell, Sue
See Truesdell, Susan G.
Truesdell, Susan G. SATA-45
Truett, Fred M(oore) 1899- CAP-2
Earlier sketch in CA 21-22
Truett, Joe C(lyde) 1941- 118
Truffaut, Francois 1932-1984 81-84
Obituary 113
See also CLC 20
Truitt, Deborah H(unsberger) 1945- 45-48
Truitt, Evelyn Mack 1931- 57-60
Truitt, Gloria A(nn) 1939- 111
Truitt, John O(liver) 1934- 117
Truitt, Willis H(arrison) 1936- 57-60
Truman, Harry S 1884-1972 106
Obituary 37-40R
Truman, (Mary) Margaret 1924- 105
Truman, Ruth 1931- 53-56
Trumbo, Dalton 1905-1976 CANR-10
Obituary 69-72
Earlier sketch in CA 21-22R
See also DLB 26
See also CLC 19
Trumbull, Benjamin 1735-1820 DLB-30
Trumbull, John 1750-1831 DLB-31
Trumbull, Robert 1912- CANR-5
Earlier sketch in CA 11-12R
Trump, Fred(erick Leonard) 1924- 15-16R
Trump, Richard F. 1912- 126
Trumpener, Ulrich 1930- 25-28R
Trumper, Hubert Bagster 1902- CAP-1
Earlier sketch in CA 9-10
Trundlett, Helen B.
See Eliot, T(homas) S(tearns)
Trungpa, Chogyam
See Chogyam Trungpa
Trunk, Isaiah Elezer 1905-1981 89-92
Obituary 108
Trupin, James E. 1940- 37-40R
Trupp, Beverly Ann 1937- 105
Truscott, Alan (Fraser) 1925- 25-28R
Truscott, Lucian K(ing) IV 1947- 89-92
Truscott, Robert Blake 1944- 77-80
Truse, Kenneth (Philip) 1946- 105
Truss, Jan 1925- 102
See also SATA 35
Truss, Seldon
See Seldon-Truss, Leslie
Trussell, C(harles) P(rescott) 1892-1968
Obituary 89-92
Trussler, Simon 1942- CANR-12
Earlier sketch in CA 25-28R
Trustman, Alan Robert 1930- Brief entry 111
Truumaa, Aare 1926- 49-52
Truzzi, Marcello 1935- 41-44R
Tryon, Darrell Trevor 1942- 111
Tryon, Georgiana Shick 1945- 116
Tryon, Ruth Wilson 1892(?)-1987
Obituary 123
Tryon, Thomas 1926- 29-32R
See also CLC 3, 11
See also AITN 1
Tryon, Tom
See Tryon, Thomas
Tryon, W(arren) S(tenson) 1901- CAP-1
Earlier sketch in CA 11-12
Trypanis, C(onstantine) A(thanasius)
1909- CANR-24
Earlier sketches in CA 7-8R, CANR-7
Trythall, Anthony John 1927- 77-80
Trythall, J(ohn) W(illiam) D(onald)
1944- 29-32R
Tsadick, Marta Gabre
See Gabre-Tsadick, Marta
Tsai, Shih-shan Henry 1940- 125
Tsambassis, Alexander N(icholas) 1919- 23-24R
Tsatsos, Jeanne 1909- CANR-13
Earlier sketch in CA 29-32R
Tschacbasov, Nahum 1899-1984 Obituary 112
Tschebotarioff, Gregory P. 1899- 15-16R
Tschichold, Jan 1902(?)-1974 Obituary 53-56
Tschudy, James Jay 1925- 13-14R
Tschumi, Raymond Robert 1924- CANR-3
Earlier sketch in CA 7-8R
Tse, K. K. 1948- 125
Tsegaye, Gabre-Medhin (Kawessa)
See Gabre-Medhin, Tsegaye (Kawessa)
Tseng Wen-Shing 1935- 114
Tshiamala, Kabasele ?-1983(?) Obituary 109
Tsien, Tsuen-hsuin 1909- CANR-23
Earlier sketches in CA 17-18R, CANR-7
Tsiolkovsky, Konstantin Eduardovich
1857-1935 Brief entry 119
Tsipis, Kosta 1934- 110
Tsongas, Paul Efthemios 1941- 108
Tsou, Tang 1918- CANR-8
Earlier sketch in CA 5-6R
Tso Yiu-kam 1918(?)-1983 Obituary 110
Tsukahira, Toshio George 1915- 21-22R
Tsukinabe, Isao
See Vermeule, Cornelius Clarkson III
Tsuneishi, Warren M(ichio) 1921- 19-20R
Tsurutani, Taketsugu 1935- 104
Tsushima, Shuji 1909-1948 Brief entry 107
Tsuzuki, Chushichi 1926- CANR-3
Earlier sketch in CA 3R
Tsvetaeva (Efron), Marina Ivanovna
1892-1941 Brief entry 104
See also TCLC 7
Tu, Wei-ming 1940- 65-68
Tuan, Yi-Fu 1930- CANR-16
Earlier sketch in CA 93-96
Tuann, Lucy H(siu-mei) C(hen) 1938- 85-88
Tubb, E(dwin) C(harles) 1919- CANR-21
Earlier sketch in CA 101
Tubb, Ernest (Dale) 1914-1984 Obituary 114
Tubbs, Stewart L(ee) 1943- CANR-6
Earlier sketch in CA 57-60
Tucci, Giuseppe 1894-1984 Obituary 112
Tucci, Niccolo 1908- 81-84
Tuccille, Jerome 1937- CANR-12
Earlier sketch in CA 29-32R
Tuchinsky, Joseph S. 1937- CANR-10
Earlier sketch in CA 25-28R
Tuchman, Barbara (Wertheim) 1912- CANR-24
Earlier sketches in CA 1R, CANR-3
Tuchman, Gaye 1943- 85-88
Tuchman, Maurice 1936- CANR-4
Earlier sketch in CA 49-52
Tuchman, Phyllis 1947- 114
Tuchock, Wanda 1898(?)-1985 Obituary 115
Tucholsky, Kurt 1890-1935 DLB-56
Tuck, (John) Anthony 1940- 124
Tuck, Dorothy
See McFarland, Dorothy Tuck
Tuck, James A(lexander) 1940- 37-40R
Tuck, Lon 1938(?)-1987 Obituary 122
Tuck, Susan H. 1947- 118
Tucker, Ann
See Giudici, Ann Couper
Tucker, Anne 1945- CANR-19
Earlier sketch in CA 102
Tucker, Anthony 1924- 104
Tucker, Archibald Norman 1904(?)-1980
Obituary 101
Tucker, Audrie Manley
See Manley-Tucker, Audrie
Tucker, Bob
See Tucker, (Arthur) Wilson
Tucker, Caroline
See Nolan, Jeannette Covert
Tucker, David M(ilton) 1937- 101
Tucker, Edward L(lewellyn) 1921- 19-20R
Tucker, Ernest E(dward) 1916-1969 61-64
Tucker, Eva 1929- 17-18R
Tucker, Frank H(ammond) 1923- CANR-10
Earlier sketch in CA 25-28R
Tucker, Gabe
See Tucker, Gaylord B(ob)
Tucker, Gaylord B(ob) 1915- 110
Tucker, Gene M(ilton) 1935- CANR-15
Earlier sketch in CA 37-40R
Tucker, George 1775-1861 DLB-3, 30
Tucker, Georgina P. 1911- 97-100
Tucker, Gina
See Tucker, Georgina P.
Tucker, Glenn (Irving) 1892-1976 5-6R
Obituary 69-72
Tucker, Graham Harold 1925- 113
Tucker, Harry, Jr. 1921- 41-44R
Tucker, Helen 1926- CANR-11
Earlier sketch in CA 29-32R
Tucker, Irwin St. John 1886-1982
Obituary 105
Tucker, James 1929- CANR-9
Earlier sketch in CA 21-22R
Tucker, Jonathan B(rin) 1954- 109
Tucker, Lael
See Wertenbaker, Lael (Tucker)
Tucker, Link
See Bingley, David Ernest
Tucker, Marcia 1940- 65-68
Tucker, Martin 1928- 17-18R
Tucker, Melvin J(ay) 1931- 113
Tucker, Michael R(ay) 1941- CANR-12
Earlier sketch in CA 61-64
Tucker, Nathaniel Beverley 1784-1851 DLB-3
Tucker, Nicholas 1936- CANR-11
Earlier sketch in CA 65-68
Tucker, Patricia 1912- 65-68
Tucker, Paul Hayes 1950- 110
Tucker, Robert C(harles) 1918- CANR-3
Earlier sketch in CA 3R
Tucker, Robin 1950- 53-56
Tucker, Ruth A(nne) 1945- 117
Tucker, St. George 1752-1827 DLB-37
Tucker, Wallace H. 1939- 121
Tucker, William E(dward) 1932- CANR-3
Earlier sketch in CA 11-12R
Tucker, William R(ayburn) 1923- 61-64
Tucker, (Arthur) Wilson 1914- 17-18R
Tucker-Fettner, Ann
See Giudici, Ann Couper
Tuckerman, Henry Theodore 1813-1871 DLB-64
Tuckey, John S(utton) 1921- CANR-7
Earlier sketch in CA 7-8R
Tuckman, Bruce W(ayne) 1938- CANR-11
Earlier sketch in CA 25-28R
Tuckman, Howard P(aul) 1941- CANR-10
Earlier sketch in CA 57-60
Tuckner, Howard 1932(?)-1980 Obituary 101
Tudhope, Richard
See Rodda, Peter (Gordon)
Tudor, Andrew Frank 1942- 107
Tudor, Dean 1943- CANR-8
Earlier sketch in CA 61-64
Tudor, Nancy (Patricia Rice) 1943-
Brief entry 109
Tudor, Tasha 1915- 81-84
See also SATA 20
See also CLR 13
Tudor-Craig, Pamela 1928- 124
Tudyman, Al 1914- 21-22R
Tuell, Jack Marvin 1923- 29-32R
Tueni, Nadia (Hamade) 1935-1983
Obituary 110
Tuerck, David G(eorge) 1941- CANR-14
Earlier sketch in CA 21-22R
Tuerk, Hanne 1951- 118
Tufail, Muhammad 1921(?)-1984 Obituary 113
Tuffnell, Everett S(pencer) 1917- CANR-7
Earlier sketch in CA 5-6R
Tuffs, J(ack) Elsden 1922- 7-8R

Tufte, Edward R(olf) 1942- ... CANR-1
Earlier sketch in CA 49-52
Tufte, Virginia J(ames) 1918- ... 125
Brief entry ... 106
Tufts, Eleanor ... 77-80
Tufty, Barbara 1923- ... 37-40R
Tufty, Esther Van Wagoner 1896-1986
Obituary ... 119
Tugay, Emine Foat
See Foat Tugay, Emine
Tugendhat, Christopher Samuel 1937- ... 89-92
Tuggle, Ann Montgomery 1942- ... 125
Tuggy, Joy Turner 1922- ... 21-22R
Tugwell, Franklin 1942- ... 57-60
Tugwell, Rexford Guy 1891-1979 ... 85-88
Obituary ... 89-92
Tulasiewicz, J(an) B(runo) 1913- ... 41-44R
Tulchin, Joseph S(amuel) 1939- ... 37-40R
Tulchin, Lewis 1905-1971 ... CAP-1
Earlier sketch in CA 19-20
Tuleja, Tad
See Tuleja, Thaddeus F(rancis)
Tuleja, Thaddeus F(rancis) 1944- ... 108
Tulis, Jeffrey 1950- ... 111
Tull, Charles Joseph 1931- ... 17-18R
Tull, Delena 1950- ... 125
Tull, Donald S(tanley) 1924- ... 81-84
Tull, James E. 1913- ... CANR-13
Earlier sketch in CA 77-80
Tullett, James Stuart 1912- ... 106
Tullis, F. LaMond 1935- ... 81-84
Tulloch, G(ertrude) Janet 1924- ... 65-68
Tullock, Gordon 1922- ... CANR-3
Earlier sketch in CA 3R
Tully, Andrew (Frederick, Jr.) 1914- ... 19-20R
Tully, Gordon F(rederick) 1935- ... 106
Tully, Grace George 1900-1984 Obituary ... 113
Tully, John (Kimberley) 1923- ... CANR-12
Earlier sketch in CA 69-72
See also SATA 14
Tully, Mary Jo 1937- ... CANR-22
Earlier sketch in CA 105
Tuma, Elias H. 1928- Brief entry ... 115
Tumelty, James J. 1921(?)-1979(?)
Obituary ... 104
Tumin, Melvin M(arvin) 1919- ... 45-48
Tumpson, Helen ... AITN-1
Tung, Ling
See Tung, William L(ing)
Tung, Shih-tsin (Shih-chin) 1900- ... 5-6R
Tung, William L(ing) 1907- ... 85-88
Tunick, Irve 1912-1987 Obituary ... 123
Tunick, Stanley B(loch) 1900- ... CAP-1
Earlier sketch in CA 17-18
Tunink, Wilfrid Bernard 1920- ... 5-6R
Tunis, Edwin (Burdett) 1897-1973 ... CANR-7
Obituary ... 45-48
Earlier sketch in CA 7-8R
See also SATA 1, 24, 28
See also CLR 2
Tunis, John R(oberts) 1889-1975 ... 61-64
See also SATA 30, 37
See also DLB 22
See also CLC 12
Tunley, Roul 1912- ... 13-14R
Tunnard, Christopher 1910-1979 ... CANR-6
Obituary ... 85-88
Earlier sketch in CA 7-8R
Tunnell, Doug(las Alan) 1949- ... 97-100
Tunner, William H(enry) 1906-1983 ... CAP-1
Obituary ... 109
Earlier sketch in CA 15-16
Tunney, Gene
See Tunney, James Joseph
Tunney, James Joseph 1898(?)-1978
Obituary ... 111
Tunney, John V(arick) 1934- ... 61-64
Tunney, Kieran 1922- ... 117
Tunnicliffe, C(harles) F(rederick) 1901- ... 104
Tunstall, (Cuthbert) Jeremy 1934- ... CANR-20
Earlier sketches in CA 7-8R, CANR-4
Tunstall, Shana Barrett
See Tunstall, Velma
Tunstall, Velma 1914- ... 53-56
Tunyogi, Andrew C(sapo) 1907- ... CAP-2
Earlier sketch in CA 29-32
Tuohy, Frank
See Tuohy, John Francis
See also DLB 14
See also CLC 37
Tuohy, John Francis 1925- ... CANR-3
Earlier sketch in CA 5-6R
Tuohy, William 1941- ... 37-40R
Tuohy, William Klaus 1926- ... 104
Tuohy, William S. 1938- ... 41-44R
Tuplin, W(illiam) A(lfred) 1902-1975
Obituary ... 111
Tupper, Margo (Browne) 1919- ... 19-20R
Tupper, Martin F. 1810-1889 ... DLB-32
Turabian, Kate L(arimore) 1893-1987
Obituary ... 123
Turbayne, Colin Murray 1916- ... CANR-24
Earlier sketch in CA 3R
Turbyfill, Mark 1896- ... 108
See also DLB 45
Turchin, Valentin F(yodorovich) 1931- ... 101
Turco, Lewis (Putnam) 1934- ... CANR-24
Earlier sketch in CA 13-14R
See also DLBY 84
See also CLC 11
Turell, Saul J. 1921-1986 Obituary ... 120
Turetzky, Bertram Jay 1933- ... 57-60
Turgeon, Charlotte Snyder 1912- ... CANR-3
Earlier sketch in CA 7-8R
Turgeon, Lynn 1920- ... 7-8R
Turiel, Isaac 1941- ... 122
Turing, John (Ferrier) 1908- ... CAP-2
Earlier sketch in CA 25-28
Turk, Frances (Mary) 1915- ... CAP-1
Earlier sketch in CA 9-10
Turk, Hanne
See Tuerk, Hanne
Turk, Herman 1929- ... 45-48
Turk, Laurel H(erbert) 1903- ... 21-22R
Turk, Midge
See Richardson, Midge Turk
Turk, Rudy H(enry) 1927- ... 97-100
Turkel, Christopher 1955(?)-1983
Obituary ... 110
Turkel, Pauline
See K-Turkel, Judi
Turkel, Robin R. 1929(?)-1984 Obituary ... 113
Turkevich, Ludmilla Buketoff 1909- ... 5-6R
Turki, Fawaz 1940- ... 41-44R
Turkle, Brinton 1915- ... 25-28R
See also SATA 2
Turkle, Sherry 1948- ... 102
Turkus, Burton B. 1902-1982 Obituary ... 108
Turley, William S(tephen) 1943- ... CANR-21
Earlier sketch in CA 105
Turlington, Bayly 1919-1977 ... 29-32R
Obituary ... 122
See also SATA 5, 52
Turlington, Catherine (Isabel) Hackett
1900(?)-1978 Obituary ... 77-80
Turlington, Henry E. 1918- ... 21-22R
Turnage, Anne Shaw 1927- ... 77-80
Turnage, Mac(lyn) N(eil) 1927- ... 77-80
Turnbaugh, William A(rthur) 1948- ... 112
Turnbull, Agnes Sligh 1888-1982 ... CANR-2
Obituary ... 105
Earlier sketch in CA 3R
See also SATA 14
Turnbull, Andrew Winchester
1921-1970 ... CANR-3
Obituary ... 25-28R
Earlier sketch in CA 3R
Turnbull, Ann (Christine) 1943- ... 65-68
See also SATA 18
Turnbull, Bob 1936- ... CANR-14
Earlier sketch in CA 37-40R
Turnbull, Colin M(acmillan) 1924- ... CANR-3
Earlier sketch in CA 2R
See also AITN 1
Turnbull, Gael Lundin 1928- ... CANR-10
Earlier sketch in CA 65-68
See also DLB 40
Turnbull, John G. 1913- ... 3R
Turnbull, Patrick Edward Xenophon
1908- ... CANR-6
Earlier sketch in CA 7-8R
Turnbull, Stephen (Richard) 1948- ... CANR-20
Earlier sketch in CA 104
Turnell, (George) Martin 1908-1979 ... 45-48
Obituary ... 103
Turner, A(lmon) Richard 1932- ... 19-20R
Turner, Alberta Tucker 1919- ... CANR-17
Earlier sketches in CA 49-52, CANR-1
Turner, Alice K. 1940- ... 53-56
See also SATA 10
Turner, Amedee E. 1929- ... 9-10R
Turner, Ann W(arren) 1945- ... CANR-14
Earlier sketch in CA 69-72
See also SATA 14
Turner, (Henry) Arlin 1909-1980 ... CANR-6
Obituary ... 97-100
Earlier sketch in CA 7-8R
Turner, Arthur C(ampbell) 1918- ... 17-18R
Turner, Bessye Tobias 1917- ... 53-56
Turner, Bill
See Turner, W(illiam) Price
Turner, Bryan S(tanley) 1945- ... 115
Turner, Charles (Tennyson) 1808-1879 ... DLB-32
Turner, Charles W(ilson) 1916- ... CANR-13
Earlier sketch in CA 37-40R
Turner, Clair (Elsmere) 1890- ... CAP-1
Earlier sketch in CA 9-10
Turner, Clay
See Ballard, (Willis) Todhunter
Turner, D(avid) Harold 1912- ... 117
Turner, Daniel F(rank) 1947- ... 97-100
Turner, Darwin T(heodore) 1931- ... CANR-11
Earlier sketch in CA 21-22R
See also BW
Turner, David R(euben) 1915- ... 57-60
Turner, Dean (Edson) 1927- ... 29-32R
Turner, Dennis C(lair) 1948- ... 61-64
Turner, Dona M. 1951- ... 103
Turner, E(rnest) S(ackville) 1909- ... 113
Turner, Edward R(euben) A(rthur) 1924- ... 81-84
Turner, Elizabeth 1774-1846 ... YABC-2
Turner, Eloise Fain 1906- ... 5-6R
Turner, Eric Gardner 1911-1983 Obituary ... 109
Turner, Ethel (Sybil) 1872-1958
Brief entry ... 111
Turner, Francis Joseph (Michael)
1929- ... CANR-22
Earlier sketch in CA 69-72
Turner, Frederick (William III) 1937- ... CANR-15
Earlier sketch in CA 37-40R
Turner, Frederick 1943- ... CANR-12
Earlier sketch in CA 73-76
See also DLB 40
See also CLC 48
Turner, Frederick C(lair) 1938- ... 25-28R
Turner, Frederick Jackson 1861-1932
Brief entry ... 113
See also DLB 17
Turner, George (Reginald) 1916- ... CANR-21
Earlier sketch in CA 103
Turner, George Allen 1908- ... CANR-10
Earlier sketch in CA 13-14R
Turner, George E(ugene) 1925- ... CANR-5
Earlier sketch in CA 53-56
Turner, George W(illiam) 1921- ... CANR-24
Earlier sketch in CA 104
Turner, Gladys T(ressia) 1935- ... CANR-13
Earlier sketch in CA 77-80
Turner, Graham 1932- ... CANR-14
Earlier sketch in CA 23-24R
Turner, Gwenda 1947- ... 118
Turner, H(arold) W(alter) 1911- ... CANR-10
Earlier sketch in CA 23-24R
Turner, Henry Andrew, Jr. 1919- ... 11-12R
Turner, Henry Ashby, Jr. 1932- ... 49-52
Turner, Henry Dicken 1919- ... 61-64
Turner, Henry Ernest William 1907- ... CAP-1
Earlier sketch in CA 9-10
Turner, Herbert Snipes 1891-1976 ... 41-44R
Turner, Howard M(oore), Jr. 1918- ... 15-16R
Turner, John Elliot 1917- ... CANR-3
Earlier sketch in CA 5-6R
Turner, John F(reeland) 1942- ... 97-100
Turner, John Frayn 1923- ... CANR-3
Earlier sketch in CA 9-10R
Turner, John H(enry) 1938- ... 77-80
Turner, Jonathan H. 1942- ... CANR-14
Earlier sketch in CA 37-40R
Turner, Josie
See Crawford, Phyllis
Turner, Judy
See Saxton, Judith
Turner, Justin George 1898-1976 ... 41-44R
Turner, Katharine Charlotte 1910- ... CAP-2
Earlier sketch in CA 23-24
Turner, Kay 1932- ... 69-72
Turner, Kermit 1936- ... 104
Turner, L(eonard) C(harles) F(rederick)
1914- ... 29-32R
Turner, Len
See Floren, Lee
Turner, Lloyd 1924- ... 103
Turner, Louis (Mark) 1942- ... CANR-15
Earlier sketch in CA 37-40R
Turner, Lynn Warren 1906- ... 7-8R
Turner, Martha Anne (Bonner) 1904-1985
Obituary ... 117
Turner, Mary
See Lambot, Isobel
Turner, Mason 1914- ... 123
Turner, Merfyn (Lloyd) 1915- ... 104
Turner, Morrie
See Turner, Morris
Turner, Morris 1923- ... CANR-15
Earlier sketch in CA 29-32R
Turner, Myron 1935- ... 112
Turner, Paul Digby Lowry 1917- ... 105
Turner, Paul R(aymond) 1929- ... 45-48
Turner, Peter Paul
See Jeffery, Grant
Turner, Philip (William) 1925- ... CANR-11
Earlier sketch in CA 25-28R
See also SATA 11
See also SAAS 6
Turner, Ralph 1936- Brief entry ... 107
Turner, Ralph H(erbert) 1919- ... 37-40R
Turner, Ralph Lilley 1888-1983 ... 7-8R
Obituary ... 109
Turner, Ralph V(ernon) 1939- ... 77-80
Turner, Richard E(ugene) 1920- ... 29-32R
Turner, Robert (Harry) 1915- ... CANR-1
Earlier sketch in CA 45-48
Turner, Robert C(lemens) 1908- ... 77-80
Turner, Robert Edward III 1938(?)- ... 120
Turner, Robert F(oster) 1944- ... CANR-13
Earlier sketch in CA 77-80
Turner, Robert Kean, Jr. 1926- ... 17-18R
Turner, Robert Y(ongue) 1927-
Brief entry ... 110
Turner, Roger (Humphrey George) 1943- ... 123
Turner, Roland 1943- ... 106
Turner, Ronald Cordell 1939- ... 41-44R
Turner, Sheila 1906- ... CAP-1
Earlier sketch in CA 13-14
Turner, Sheila
See Rowbotham, Sheila
Turner, Sheila R.
See Seed, Sheila Turner
Turner, Silvie 1946- ... 117
Turner, Stansfield 1923- ... 124
Brief entry ... 118
Turner, Stephen P. 1951- ... 122
Turner, Steve
See Turner, Stephen P.
Turner, (Clarence) Steven 1923- ... 29-32R
Turner, Susan 1952- ... 106
Turner, T. H. D. 1946- ... 122
Turner, Ted
See Turner, Robert Edward III
Turner, Thomas B(ourne) 1902- ... 41-44R
Turner, Thomas Coleman 1927- ... 7-8R
Turner, Thomas N(oel) 1940- ... 113
Turner, Tom
See Turner, T. H. D.
Turner, Victor Witter 1920-1983 ... CANR-3
Obituary ... 111
Earlier sketch in CA 7-8R
Turner, W(illiam) Price 1927- ... CANR-16
Earlier sketch in CA 23-24R
Turner, Wallace 1921- ... 19-20R
Turner, William O(liver) 1914- ... CANR-3
Earlier sketch in CA 2R
See also AITN 1
Turner, William W. 1927- ... CANR-12
Earlier sketch in CA 25-28R
Turney, Alfred (Walter) 1916- ... 73-76
Turney, Catherine 1906- ... 101
Turngren, Annette 1902(?)-1980 ... 11-12R
Obituary ... 101
See also SATA 23
Turngren, Ellen ?-1964 ... 7-8R
See also SATA 3
Turnill, Reginald 1915- ... CANR-15
Earlier sketch in CA 37-40R
Turnock, David 1938- ... 109
Turock, Betty J(ane) ... 110
Turow, Joseph G(regory) 1950- ... 111
Turow, Rita P(astron) 1919- ... 101
Turow, Scott 1949- ... 73-76
Turpin, James W(esley) 1927- ... 23-24R
Turpin, Lorna 1950- ... 107
Turpin, Waters Edward 1910-1968 ... 125
See also BW
See also DLB 51
Turska, Krystyna (Zofia) 1933- ... 106
See also SATA 27, 31
Tursun-Zade, Mirzo 1911-1977 Obituary ... 104
Turton, Godfrey (Edmund) 1901- ... 21-22R
Turton-Jones, Edith Constance (Bradshaw)
1904-1968 ... CAP-1
Earlier sketch in CA 9-10
Turville-Petre, Edward Oswald Gabriel
1908-1978 ... 9-10R
Obituary ... 77-80
Turyn, Alexander 1900-1981 Obituary ... 104
Tusan, Stan 1936- ... 105
See also CLC 22
Tushingham, A(rlotte) Douglas 1914- ... 41-44R
Tushnet, Leonard 1908-1973 ... CAP-1
Obituary ... 45-48
Earlier sketch in CA 15-16
Tushnet, Mark V. 1945- ... 126
Tusiani, Joseph 1924- ... CANR-20
Earlier sketches in CA 9-10R, CANR-5
See also SATA 45
Tuska, Jon 1942- ... CANR-13
Earlier sketch in CA 73-76
Tussing, A(ubrey) Dale 1935- ... 17-18R
Tutaev, David 1916- ... 23-24R
Tute, Warren (Stanley) 1914- ... CANR-1
Earlier sketch in CA 1R
Tuten, Frederic 1936- ... 37-40R
Tuthill, John Wills 1910- ... 108
Tutin, Thomas Gaskell 1908-1987
Obituary ... 123
Tutko, Thomas A(rthur) 1931- ... 69-72
Tutorow, Norman E. 1934- ... 25-28R
Tuttle, Alva M(aurice) 1900- ... 7-8R
Tuttle, Day
See Tuttle, (Frank) Day, Jr.
Tuttle, (Frank) Day, Jr. 1902- ... 116
Tuttle, Frank W(aldo) 1896- ... 61-64
Tuttle, Howard Nelson 1935- ... 41-44R
Tuttle, Lisa 1952- ... 126
Tuttle, Russell (Howard) 1939- ... 77-80
Tuttle, W(ilbur) C(oleman) 1883-19(?) ... CAP-2
Earlier sketch in CA 21-22
Tuttle, William M., Jr. 1937- ... CANR-11
Earlier sketch in CA 29-32R
Tuttleton, James Welsey 1934- ... 41-44R
Tutu, Desmond M(pilo) 1931- ... 125
See also BW
Tutuola, Amos 1920- ... 9-10R
See also BW
See also CLC 5, 14, 29
Tuve, Merle Antony 1901-1982 Obituary ... 106
Tuve, Rosemond 1903-1964 ... CAP-1
Earlier sketch in CA 9-10
Tuveson, Ernest (Lee) 1915- ... 19-20R
Tuwhare, Hone 1922- ... 103
Tuzin, Donald F(rancis) 1945- ... 106
Tvardovsky, Alexandr Trifonovich
1910-1971 ... 102
Obituary ... 33-36R
Twaddell, W(illiam) F(reeman) 1906- ... 81-84
Twaddle, Andrew C. 1938- ... 120
Twain, Mark
See Clemens, Samuel Langhorne
See also DLB 11, 12, 23, 64, 74
See also TCLC 6, 12, 19
Twark, Allan J(oseph) 1931- ... 49-52
Twedt, Dik Warren 1920-1985 ... CANR-14
Obituary ... 115
Earlier sketch in CA 37-40R
Tweedale, J.
See Bickle, Judith Brundrett
Tweedale, Violet (Chambers) 1862-1936
Brief entry ... 116
Tweedie, Donald F(erguson), Jr. 1926- ... 13-14R
Tweeten, Luther 1931- ... 89-92
Twelveponies, Mary
See Cleveland, Mary
20/1631
See Upward, Allen
Twersky, Isadore 1930- ... 120
Twersky, Jacob 1920- ... 49-52
Tweton, D. Jerome 1933- ... SATA-48
Twigg, Alan (Robert) 1952- ... 125
Twiggy
See Hornby, Leslie
Twin, Stephanie L. 1948- ... 101
Twiname, Eric 1942(?)-1980 Obituary ... 102
Twining, Nathan F(arragut) 1897-1982
Obituary ... 106
Twining, William (Lawrence) 1934- ... 123
Twisleton-Wykeham-Fiennes, Richard
Nathaniel 1909- ... CANR-11
Earlier sketch in CA 23-24R
Twiss, Sumner B(arnes), Jr. 1944-
Brief entry ... 114
Twist, Ananias
See Nunn, William Curtis
Twitchell, James B(uell) 1943- ... 118
Twitchell, Paul 1908(?)-1971 Obituary ... 111

Twitchett, Carol Cosgrove 1943- CANR-26
Earlier sketch in CA 29-32R
Twitchett, Denis Crispin 1925- Brief entry .. 106
Twombly, Robert C(harles) 1940- 85-88
Twombly, Wells A. 1935-1977 ....41-44R
Obituary 69-72
Tworkov, Jack 1900-1982 Obituary 107
See also SATA 31, 47
Twyman, Gib
See Twyman, Gilbert Oscar III
Twyman, Gilbert Oscar III 1943- 109
Ty-Casper, Linda 1931- CANR-24
Earlier sketch in CA 107
Tydeman, William (Marcus) 1935- 119
Tydings, Joseph D(avies) 1928- 29-32R
Tyerman, Hugo 1880-1977 Obituary 77-80
Tyl, Noel 1936- 93-96
Tylden-Wright, David 1923- 25-28R
Tylecote, Mabel (Phythian) 1896-1987 ... CAP-1
Obituary 121
Earlier sketch in CA 13-14
Tyler, A. E.
See Armstrong, (Annette) Elizabeth
Tyler, Anne 1941- CANR-11
Earlier sketch in CA 9-10R
See also SATA 7
See also DLB 6
See also DLBY 82
See also CLC 7, 11, 18, 28, 44
Tyler, Converse 1903(?)-1978 Obituary ...81-84
Tyler, David B(udlong) 1899- 77-80
Tyler, Elias S. 1904(?)-1977 Obituary 73-76
Tyler, Hamilton A(lden) 1917- CANR-5
Earlier sketch in CA 11-12R
Tyler, J. Allen 1924- 101
Tyler, John Ecclesfield (?)-1966 .... CAP-1
Earlier sketch in CA 9-10
Tyler, Leona E(lizabeth) 1906- 17-18R
Tyler, Moses Coit 1835-1900 .... DLB-47, 64
Tyler, Parker 1907-1974 .... CANR-5
Obituary 49-52
Earlier sketch in CA 5-6R
Tyler, Patrick (Edward) 1951- 125
Tyler, (John) Poyntz 1907-1971 .... 3R
Obituary 103
Tyler, Ralph Winfred 1902- 109
Tyler, Richard W(illis) 1917- CANR-24
Earlier sketch in CA 41-44R
Tyler, Robert L(awrence) 1922- 15-16R
Tyler, Ron(nie) C(urtis) 1941- CANR-12
Earlier sketch in CA 29-32R
Tyler, Royall 1757-1826 .... DLB-37
Tyler, S(amuel) Lyman 1920- 77-80
Tyler, Stephen A(lbert) 1932- 29-32R
Tyler, Varro Eugene 1926- 110
Tyler, Vicki 1952- 121
Tyler, W. T.
See Hamrick, Samuel J., Jr.
Tyler, William R(oyall) 1910- 37-40R
Tyler, Zeke
See Marshall, Mel(vin D.)
Tyler-Whittle, Michael Sidney 1927- CANR-4
Earlier sketch in CA 5-6R
Tylor, Edward Burnett 1832-1917
Brief entry 123
See also DLB 57
Tymchuk, Alexander J(ames) 1942- 57-60
Tymeson, Mildred McClary
See Petrie, Mildred McClary
Tymieniecka, Anna-Teresa CANR-9
Earlier sketch in CA 61-64
Tymms, Ralph Vincent 1913-1987
Obituary 123
Tymn, Marshall (Benton) 1937- 107
Tymon, Dorothy 85-88
Tynan, Katharine 1861-1931 Brief entry 104
See also TCLC 3
Tynan, Kathleen 97-100
Tynan, Kenneth (Peacock) 1927-1980 .. CANR-22
Obituary 101
Earlier sketch in CA 15-16R
Tyre, Nedra 104
Tyrell, Donald J(ohn) 1929- Brief entry 110
Tyrmand, Leopold 1920-1985 .... CANR-5
Obituary 115
Earlier sketch in CA 49-52
Tyrone, Paul
See Norwood, Victor G(eorge) C(harles)
Tyrrell, Bernard (James) 1933- 57-60
Tyrrell, Francis M(artin) 1916- Brief entry 107
Tyrrell, Joseph M(orten) 1927- 41-44R
Tyrrell, R(obert) Emmett, Jr. 1943- CANR-25
Earlier sketch in CA 85-88
Tyrrell, Robert 1929- 41-44R
Tyrrell, William Blake 1940- 125
Tyrwhitt, (Mary) Jacqueline 1905-1983(?)
Obituary 109
Tyrwhitt, Janice 1928- 97-100
Tysdahl, B(joern) J(ohan) 1933- 25-28R
Tysliava, Valerie 1914(?)-1984 Obituary 112
Tyson, Joseph B(lake) 1928- CANR-14
Earlier sketch in CA 37-40R
Tyson, Nancy Jane 1949- 117
Tyson, Richard 1944- 69-72
Tysse, Agnes N. 1904- 101
Tytell, John 1939- 29-32R
See also CLC 50
Tytler, Graeme (Douglas Colville) 1934- 117
Tzannes, Nicolaos S(tamatios) 1937- 57-60
Tzara, Tristan
See Codrescu, Andrei
and Rosenfeld, Samuel
See also CLC 47
Tzitsikas, Helene 1926- 45-48
Tzonis, Alexander 1937- 101

U

Ubbelohde, Carl (William, Jr.) 1924- CANR-6
Earlier sketch in CA 3R
Ubell, Earl 1926- 37-40R
See also SATA 4
Uble, T(homas) R(alph) O(bermeyer)
1931- CANR-13
Earlier sketch in CA 29-32R
Ucelay, Margarita 1916- 21-22R
Uchida, Tadao 1939- 65-68
Uchida, Yoshiko 1921- CANR-22
Earlier sketches in CA 13-14R, CANR-6
See also SATA 1, 53
See also SAAS 1
See also CLR 6
Udall, Jan Beaney 1938- 65-68
See also SATA 10
Udall, Morris K(ing) 1922- CANR-1
Earlier sketch in CA 45-48
Udall, Nicholas 1504-1556 .... DLB-62
Udall, Stewart L(ee) 1920- 69-72
Ude, Wayne 1946- CANR-13
Earlier sketch in CA 77-80
Udell, Jon G(erald) 1935- CANR-16
Earlier sketches in CA 45-48, CANR-1
Udelson, Joseph H. 1943- 125
Uden, (Bernard Gilbert) Grant 1910- 102
See also SATA 26
Udo, Reuben Kenrick 1935- 77-80
Udoff, Yale M(aurice) 1935- CANR-12
Earlier sketch in CA 57-60
Udolf, Roy 1926- CANR-4
Earlier sketch in CA 53-56
Udovitch, Abraham Labe 1933-
Brief entry 105
Udry, J(oe) Richard 1928- 33-36R
Udry, Janice May 1928- CANR-6
Earlier sketch in CA 5-6R
See also SATA 4
Udy, Stanley Hart, Jr. 1928- Brief entry 106
Ueda, Makoto 1931- 21-22R
Uehling, Carl Theodore 1927- 29-32R
Uehling, Theodore Edward, Jr. 1935- .. CANR-20
Earlier sketch in CA 104
Ueno, Noriko
See Nakae, Noriko
Uffelman, F. C.
See Gehman, Richard (Boyd)
Uffenbeck, Lorin A(rthur) 1924- 61-64
Ugama, LeRoi
See Smith, LeRoi Tex
Ugarte, Francisco 1910-1969 .... CAP-1
Earlier sketch in CA 9-10
Ugarte, Michael 1949- 114
Ugboajah, (Francis) Okwu 1945- 93-96
Uhalley, Stephen, Jr. 1930- Brief entry 106
Uhl, Alexander H. 1899(?)-1976 Obituary ..69-72
Uhl, Melvin John 1915- 7-8R
Uhlfelder, Myra L. 1923- Brief entry 109
Uhlin, Donald M(acbeth) 1930- 49-52
Uhlinger, Susan J. 1942-1980 57-60
Obituary 120
Uhlman, Fred 1901-1985(?) 105
Obituary 116
Uhnak, Dorothy 1933- 81-84
See also AITN 1
Uhr, Carl George 1911- 81-84
Uhr, Elizabeth 1929- 25-28R
Uhr, Leonard (Merrick) 1927- CANR-7
Earlier sketch in CA 5-6R
Uhse, Bodo 1904-1963 .... DLB-69
Uitti, Karl David 1933- CANR-10
Earlier sketch in CA 17-18R
Ujfalussy, Jozsef 1920- Brief entry 114
Ulam, Adam B(runo) 1922- CANR-26
Earlier sketches in CA 13-14R, CANR-7
Ulam, S(tanislaw) M(arcin) 1909-1984 61-64
Obituary 112
See also SATA 51
Ulanoff, Stanley M(elvin) 1922- CANR-23
Earlier sketches in CA 17-18R, CANR-7
Ulanov, Ann Belford 1938- CANR-16
Earlier sketch in CA 49-52
Ulanov, Barry 1918- CANR-16
Earlier sketch in CA 4R
Ulbricht, Walter 1893-1973 Obituary 113
Ulc, Otto 1930- CANR-13
Earlier sketch in CA 77-80
Ulene, Art(hur Lawrence) 1936- 103
Ulett, George A(ndrew) 1918- 21-22R
Ulevich, Neal Hirsch 1946- 108
Ulibarri, Sabine Reyes 1919- Brief entry 105
Ulich, Robert 1890(?)-1977 Obituary 69-72
Ullah, Najib 1914- 13-14R
Ullah, Salamat 1913- 13-14R
Ulle, Robert F. 1948- 117
Ullendorff, Edward 1920- CANR-18
Earlier sketches in CA 3R, CANR-2
Ullian, Joseph S(ilbert) 1930- 41-44R
Ullman, Allan 1909(?)-1982 Obituary 106
Ullman, Barbara
See Schwalberg, Carol(yn Ernestine Stein)
Ullman, Edward L(ouis) 1912-1976 45-48
Obituary 125
Ullman, Elwood 1903(?)-1985 Obituary 117
Ullman, James Ramsey 1907-1971 ...... CANR-3
Obituary 29-32R
Earlier sketch in CA 3R
See also SATA 7
Ullman, Leslie 1947- 104
Ullman, Michael (Alan) 1945- 103
Ullman, Montague 1916- 41-44R
Ullman, Natacha 1929(?)-1986 Obituary 119
Ullman, Pierre L(ioni) 1929- 33-36R
Ullman, Richard Henry 1933- CANR-3
Earlier sketch in CA 3R
Ullmann, John E(manuel) 1923- 17-18R
Ullmann, Leonard P(aul) 1930- 17-18R
Ullmann, Liv 1939- 102
Ullmann, Stephen 1914-1976 .... CANR-4
Obituary 65-68
Earlier sketch in CA 7-8R
Ullmann, Walter 1910-1983 .... CANR-10
Obituary 108
Earlier sketch in CA 21-22R
Ullrich, Helen D(enning) 1922- 109
Ullstein, Hermann 1875(?)-1943
Brief entry 116
Ullyot, Joan 1940- 73-76
Ulm, Robert 1934-1977 .... SATA-17
Ulman, William A. 1908(?)-1979 103
Obituary 89-92
Ulmer, (Roland) Curtis 1923- 103
Ulmer, Diane K. 1943- 122
Ulmer, Louise 1943- 113
See also SATA 53
Ulmer, Melville J(ack) 1911- 21-22R
Ulmer, S(hirley) Sidney 1923- 41-44R
Ulrich, Betty Garton 1919- 29-32R
Ulrich, Carolyn F. 1881(?)-1970 Obituary ... 104
Ulrich, Heinz 1927(?)-1980 Obituary 97-100
Ulrich, (John) Homer 1906-1987 .... CANR-2
Obituary 124
Earlier sketch in CA 7-8R
Ulrich, Louis E., Jr. 1918- 13-14R
Ulrich, Roger E(lwood) 1931- 41-44R
Ultan, Lloyd 1929- 117
Ultee, (J.) Maarten 1949- 109
Ulyanov, V. I.
See Lenin
Ulyanov-Lenin
See Lenin
Ulyatt, Kenneth 1920- CANR-8
Earlier sketch in CA 61-64
See also SATA 14
Umland, Craig (Owen) 1947- 61-64
Umphlett, Wiley Lee 1931- CANR-1
Earlier sketch in CA 49-52
Umstead, William Lee 1921- 81-84
Unada
See Gliewe, Unada (Grace)
Unamuno (y Jugo), Miguel de 1864-1936
Brief entry 104
See also TCLC 2, 9
Unbegaun, Boris Ottokar 1898-1973
Obituary 41-44R
Uncle Gordon
See Roe, F(rederic) Gordon
Uncle Gus
See Rey, H(ans) A(ugusto)
Uncle Mac
See McCulloch, Derek (Ivor Breashur)
Uncle Ray
See Coffman, Ramon Peyton
Uncle Shelby
See Silverstein, Shel(by)
Undercliffe, Errol
See Campbell, (John) Ramsey
Underdown, David (Edward) 1925- CANR-26
Earlier sketches in CA 7-8R, CANR-11
Underhill, Alice Mertie (Waterman)
1900-1971 .... 3R
Obituary 103
See also SATA 10
Underhill, Charles
See Hill, Reginald (Charles)
Underhill, Hal
See Underhill, Harold
Underhill, Harold 1926-1972 .... CAP-2
Earlier sketch in CA 25-28
Underhill, Liz 1948- 121
See also SATA 49, 53
Underhill, Miriam E. 1898(?)-1976
Obituary 61-64
Underhill, Peter
See Soderberg, Percy Measday
Underhill, Ruth Murray 1884-1984 ..... CANR-3
Obituary 114
Earlier sketch in CA 3R
Underwood, Aggie
See Underwood, Agness May Wilson
Underwood, Agness May Wilson
1902-1984 Obituary 113
Underwood, Barbara 1952- 101
Underwood, Benton J. 1915- 101
Underwood, (Mary) Betty 1921- 37-40R
Underwood, Gary Neal 1940- Brief entry ... 113
Underwood, Jane H(ammons) 1931- 61-64
Underwood, John Weeden 1932- 19-20R
Underwood, Lewis Graham
See Wagner, C(harles) Peter
Underwood, Mavis Eileen 1916-
Brief entry 108
Underwood, Michael
See Evelyn, (John) Michael
Underwood, Miles
See Glassco, John
Underwood, Norman 1878(?)-1974
Obituary 53-56
Underwood, Paul S(taats) 1915-1985 77-80
Obituary 118
Underwood, Peter 1923- CANR-21
Earlier sketch in CA 104
Underwood, Sam J(esse) 1922- CANR-2
Earlier sketch in CA 45-48
Underwood, Ted Leroy 1935- 115
Underwood, Tim (Edward) 1948- CANR-24
Earlier sketch in CA 105
Undine, P. F.
See Paine, Lauran (Bosworth)
Undset, Sigrid 1882-1949 Brief entry 104
See also TCLC 3
Undy, R(oger) 1938- 115
Unett, John 13-14R
Ungar, Sanford J. 1945- CANR-13
Earlier sketch in CA 37-40R
Ungar, Steven (Ronald) 1945- 126
Ungaretti, Giuseppe 1888-1970 .... CAP-2
Obituary 25-28R
Earlier sketch in CA 19-20
See also CLC 7, 11, 15
Ungaro, Harold R(aymond) Mancusi, Jr.
See Mancusi-Ungaro, Harold R(aymond), Jr.
Ungaro, Susan Kelliher 1953- 103
Unger, Arthur 1924- 2R
Unger, Barbara 1932- CANR-13
Earlier sketch in CA 77-80
Unger, Douglas 1952- CLC-34
Unger, Hans 1915- 17-18R
Unger, Henry F. 1912- 13-14R
Unger, Irwin 1927- CANR-7
Earlier sketch in CA 11-12R
Unger, J(ames) Marshall 1947- 126
Unger, Jim 1937- CANR-13
Earlier sketch in CA 61-64
Unger, Len
See Unger, Leonard
Unger, Leonard 1916- 5-6R
Unger, Leonard 1934- 69-72
Unger, Marion
See Thede, Marion Draughon
Unger, Marvin H. 1936- 29-32R
Unger, Maurice Albert 1917- CANR-3
Earlier sketch in CA 9-10R
Unger, Merrill F. 1909- CANR-6
Earlier sketch in CA 2R
Unger, Peter K(enneth) 1942- Brief entry ... 109
Unger, Richard (Lawrence) 1939- CANR-15
Earlier sketch in CA 65-68
Unger, Richard W. 1942- 121
Unger, Walter P(eter) 1939- Brief entry 115
Ungerer, Jean Thomas 1931- 41-44R
See also SATA 5, 33
Ungerer, Miriam 1929- 117
Ungerer, Tomi
See Ungerer, Jean Thomas
See also CLR 3
Unger-Hamilton, Clive (Wolfgang)
1942- CANR-19
Earlier sketch in CA 101
Ungermann, Kenneth Armistead 1916- 9-10R
Ungs, Thomas D(ale) 1928- 81-84
Unkelbach, Kurt 1913- CANR-8
Earlier sketch in CA 23-24R
See also SATA 4
Unkovic, Charles M. 1922- 45-48
Unnerstad, Edith Totterman 1900- CANR-6
Earlier sketch in CA 5-6R
See also SATA 3
Unrau, Ruth 1922- 61-64
See also SATA 9
Unrau, William E. 1929- 37-40R
Unruh, Adolph 1908- 49-52
Unruh, Fritz von
See Von Unruh, Fritz
Unruh, Glenys Grace (Green) 1910- 29-32R
Unruh, John D., Jr. 1938(?)-1976
Obituary 105
Unser, Bobby
See Unser, Robert William
Unser, Robert William 1934- 97-100
Unstead, R(obert) J(ohn) 1915-1988 ... CANR-23
Obituary 125
Earlier sketches in CA 9-10R, CANR-7
See also SATA 12
Unsworth, Barry (Forster) 1930- 25-28R
Unsworth, Mair 1909- CANR-10
Earlier sketch in CA 25-28R
Unsworth, Walt(er) 1928- CANR-17
Earlier sketch in CA 29-32R
See also SATA 4
Unterberger, Betty Miller 1923- 25-28R
Unterbrink, Mary 1937- 113
Unterecker, John 1922- 17-18R
Untereiner, Raymond Edward 1898-1983
Obituary 110
Unterman, Alan 1942- 97-100
Unterman, Issar Y(ehuda) 1886-1976
Obituary 61-64
Untermeyer, Bryna Ivens 1909- CANR-3
Earlier sketch in CA 7-8R
Untermeyer, Jean Starr 1886-1970
Obituary 29-32R
Untermeyer, Louis 1885-1977 ....5-6R
Obituary 73-76
See also SATA 2, 26, 37
Unthank, Luisa-Teresa 33-36R
Unthank, Tessa Brown
See Unthank, Luisa-Teresa
Unwalla, Darab B. 1928- 25-28R
Unwin, David S(torr) 1918- CANR-6
Earlier sketch in CA 9-10R
See also SATA 14
Unwin, Derick (James) 1931- 23-24R
Unwin, Nora S(picer) 1907-1982 ....21-22R
Obituary 120
See also SATA 3, 49
Unwin, Rayner S(tephens) 1925- 1R
Unwin, Stanley 1884-1968 ....7-8R
Upchurch, Boyd (Bradfield) 1919- 25-28R

Updike, John (Hoyer) 1932- ... CANR-4
Earlier sketch in CA 4R
See also CABS 1
See also DLB 2, 5
See also DLBY 80, 82
See also DLBD 3
See also CLC 1, 2, 3, 5, 7, 9, 13, 15, 23, 34, 43
Updike, L(eRoy) Wayne 1916- ... 49-52
Updyke, James
See Burnett, W(illiam) R(iley)
Upfield, Arthur W(illiam) 1888-1964
Obituary ... 114
Upgren, Arthur P. 1897-1986 Obituary ... 120
Uphaus, Robert W(alter) 1942- ... 57-60
Uphaus, Willard Edwin 1890-1983 ... CAP-1
Obituary ... 111
Earlier sketch in CA 19-20
Uphoff, Norman T(homas) 1940- ... CANR-11
Earlier sketch in CA 29-32R
Uphoff, Walter H. 1913- ... CANR-14
Earlier sketch in CA 25-28R
Upits, Andrejs 1877-1970 Obituary ... 104
Upjohn, Everard M(iller) 1903-1978 ... CAP-1
Obituary ... 81-84
Earlier sketch in CA 13-14
Uppal, Jogindar S. 1927- ... CANR-1
Earlier sketch in CA 45-48
Upright, Diane W(arner) 1947- ... 120
Upshaw, Margaret Mitchell
See Mitchell, Margaret (Munnerlyn)
Upson, Norma 1919- ... CANR-8
Earlier sketch in CA 61-64
Upson, William Hazlett 1891-1975 ... 5-6R
Obituary ... 57-60
Upton, Albert 1897- ... CAP-2
Earlier sketch in CA 23-24
Upton, Anthony F. 1929- ... 17-18R
Upton, Arvin 1914- ... 81-84
Upton, Bertha (Hudson) 1849-1912
Brief entry ... 121
Upton, Charles 1948- Brief entry ... 116
See also DLB 16
Upton, Dell 1949- ... 123
Upton, Joseph C(heshire) N(ash) 1946- ... 81-84
Upton, L(eslie) F(rancis) S(tokes) 1931-1980 ... 61-64
Obituary ... 125
Upton, Lee 1953- ... 123
Upton, Monroe 1898- ... CAP-2
Earlier sketch in CA 17-18
Upton, Robert ... CANR-13
Earlier sketch in CA 73-76
Upward, Allen 1863-1926 Brief entry ... 117
See also DLB 36
Upward, Edward (Falaise) 1903- ... 77-80
Urbach, Reinhard 1939- Brief entry ... 113
Urban, Michael E(dward) 1947- ... 111
Urban, Wilbur Marshall 1873-1952
Brief entry ... 119
Urban, William L(awrence) 1939- ... CANR-18
Earlier sketches in CA 45-48, CANR-2
Urbanek, Mae 1903- ... 77-80
Urbano, Victoria (Eugenia) 1926- ... CANR-2
Earlier sketch in CA 45-48
Urbanska, Wanda (Marie) 1956- ... 124
Urbanski, Edmund Stefan
See Urbanski, Edmund Stephen
Urbanski, Edmund Stephen 1909- ... CANR-23
Earlier sketch in CA 45-48
Urbanski, Marie M. Olesen 1922- ... 102
Urch, Elizabeth 1921- ... 103
Urda, Nicholas 1922- ... 21-22R
Urdang, Constance (Henriette) 1922- ... CANR-24
Earlier sketches in CA 21-22R, CANR-9
See also CLC 47
Urdang, Laurence 1927- ... CANR-17
Earlier sketch in CA 89-92
Ure, Jean ... 125
See also SATA 48
Ure, Peter 1919-1969 ... CAP-1
Earlier sketch in CA 11-12
U'Ren, Hilda
See U'Ren-Stubbings, Hilda
Uren, Hilda
See U'Ren-Stubbings, Hilda
U'Ren-Stubbings, Hilda 1914- ... 29-32R
Uretsky, Myron 1940- ... 53-56
Urey, Harold C(layton) 1893-1981
Obituary ... 102
Uri, Pierre Emmanuel 1911- ... 97-100
Uriel, Henry
See Faust, Frederick (Shiller)
Uris, Auren 1913- ... CANR-22
Earlier sketch in CA 17-18R
Uris, Dorothy ... CANR-9
Earlier sketch in CA 61-64
Uris, Leon (Marcus) 1924- ... CANR-1
Earlier sketch in CA 1R
See also SATA 49
See also CLC 7, 32
See also AITN 1, 2
Urista, Alberto H. 1947- ... CANR-2
Earlier sketch in CA 45-48
Urkowitz, Steven 1941- ... 111
Urmson, J(ames) O(pie) 1915- ... 25-28R
Urmuz
See Codrescu, Andrei
Urness, Carol 1936- Brief entry ... 111
Uroff, Margaret Dickie 1935- ... 93-96
Urofsky, Melvin I. 1939- ... CANR-14
Earlier sketch in CA 37-40R
Urquhart, Alvin W. 1931- ... 13-14R
Urquhart, Brian (Edward) 1919- ... CANR-26
Earlier sketch in CA 105
Urquhart, Caroline 1940- ... 118
Urquhart, Colin 1940- ... 115
Urquhart, Fred(erick Burrows) 1912- ... CANR-21
Earlier sketches in CA 11-12R, CANR-6
Urquhart, Guy
See McAlmon, Robert (Menzies)
Urquhart, Jane 1949- ... 113
Urquhart, Judy 1942- ... 123
Urrutia Lleo, Manuel 1901-1981 Obituary ... 104
Urry, David (Laurence) 1931- ... 85-88
Urry, John 1946- ... 122
Urry, W(illiam) G(eorge) 1913-1981
Obituary ... 103
Ursini, James 1947- ... 61-64
Urvater, Michele 1946- ... 102
Urwick, Lyndall Fownes 1891-1983 ... CAP-1
Obituary ... 111
Earlier sketch in CA 13-14
Urwin, Gregory J(ohn) W(illiam) 1955- ... 114
Ury, William (Lauger) 1953- ... 109
Ury, Zalman F. 1924- ... CANR-17
Earlier sketch in CA 65-68
Urzidil, Johannes 1896-1970 Obituary ... 29-32R
Us
See Deal, Borden
Usborne, Richard Alexander 1910- ... 104
Usco
See Stern, Gerd Jacob
Usdin, Gene (Leonard) 1922- ... 37-40R
Useem, Michael 1942- ... 61-64
Usher, Dan 1934- ... CANR-12
Earlier sketch in CA 29-32R
Usher, Frank (Hugh) 1909-1976 ... CANR-5
Earlier sketch in CA 7-8R
Usher, George 1930- ... 109
Usher, Margo Scegge
See McHargue, Georgess
Usher, Shaun 1937- ... 77-80
Usher, Stephen 1931- ... 29-32R
Usher-Wilson, Rodney N. 1908(?)-1983
Obituary ... 109
Usherwood, Elizabeth (Ada) 1923- ... 123
Usherwood, Stephen Dean 1907- ... CANR-19
Earlier sketches in CA 5-6R, CANR-3
Usikota
See Brinitzer, Carl
Uslaner, Eric M(ichael) 1947- ... 111
Usmiani, Renate 1931- ... 113
Usry, Milton F. 1931- ... 19-20R
Ussher, (Percival) Arland 1899-1980 ... CANR-10
Obituary ... 102
Earlier sketches in CA 13-14, CAP-1
Ussher, Percy Arland
See Ussher, (Percival) Arland
Ustinov, D(mitri) F(edorovich) 1908-1984
Obituary ... 114
Ustinov, Peter (Alexander) 1921- ... CANR-25
Earlier sketch in CA 13-14R
See also DLB 13
See also CLC 1
See also AITN 1
Uston, Ken(neth Senzo) 1935-1987 ... 108
Obituary ... 123
U Tam'Si, Gerald Felix Tchicaya
See Tchicaya, Gerald Felix
U Tam'Si, Tchicaya
See Tchicaya, Gerald Felix
Utechin, S(ergei) V(asilievich) 1921- ... 11-12R
Utgard, Russell O(liver) 1933- ... 49-52
Utke, Allen R(ay) 1936- ... 81-84
Utley, Francis Lee 1907-1974 ... CANR-2
Obituary ... 49-52
Earlier sketch in CA 3R
Utley, Freda 1898-1978 ... 81-84
Obituary ... 77-80
Utley, (Clifton) Garrick 1939- ... 69-72
Utley, Ralph
See Cairns, Huntington
Utley, Robert M(arshall) 1929- ... CANR-2
Earlier sketch in CA 5-6R
Utley, T(homas) E(dwin) 1921-1988
Obituary ... 125
Utt, Richard H. 1923- ... CANR-7
Earlier sketch in CA 9-10R
Utt, Walter C(harles) 1921- ... 21-22R
Uttley, Alice Jane (Taylor) 1884-1976 ... CANR-7
Obituary ... 65-68
Earlier sketch in CA 53-56
See also SATA 3, 26
Uttley, Alison
See Uttley, Alice Jane (Taylor)
Uttley, John 1914- ... 23-24R
Utton, Albert Edgar 1931- ... CANR-1
Earlier sketch in CA 45-48
Utz, Lois (Marie) 1932-1986 ... 25-28R
Obituary ... 121
See also SATA 5, 50
Utz, Robert T(homas) 1934- ... 53-56
Uu, David
See Harris, David W.
Uveges, Joseph A(ndrew), Jr. 1938- ... 41-44R
Uvezian, Sonia ... CANR-9
Earlier sketch in CA 57-60
Uyl, Douglas J(ohn) Den
See Den Uyl, Douglas J(ohn)
Uzgiris, Ina Cepenas 1937- Brief entry ... 108
Uzzell, J(ohn) Douglas 1937- ... 93-96

V

v
See Chekhov, Anton (Pavlovich)
V., Nina
See Vickers, Antoinette L.
Vacca, Roberto 1927- ... CANR-1
Earlier sketch in CA 49-52
Vaccaro, Ernest B. 1905(?)-1979
Obituary ... 89-92
Vaccaro, Joseph P(ascal) 1935- ... 104
Vaccaro, Louis C(harles) 1930- ... CANR-1
Earlier sketch in CA 45-48
Vaccaro, Tony
See Vaccaro, Ernest B.
Vachell, Horace Annesley 1861-1955
Brief entry ... 120
Vachon, Brian 1941- ... 41-44R
Vachss, Andrew H(enry) 1942- ... 118
Vaculik, Ludvik 1926- ... 53-56
See also CLC 7
Vaczek, Louis 1913-1983 ... CANR-21
Obituary ... 111
Earlier sketch in CA 11-12R
Vadakin, James C(harles) 1924- ... 29-32R
Vadney, Thomas E(ugene) 1939- ... 45-48
Vaeth, J(oseph) Gordon 1921- ... 5-6R
See also SATA 17
Vago, Bela Adalbert 1922- ... 93-96
Vagts, Alfred (Hermann Friedrich) 1892- ... 5-6R
Vagts, Detlev F(rederick) 1929- ... 25-28R
Vagts, Miriam Beard 1901-1983 Obituary ... 110
Vahanian, Gabriel (Antoine) 1927- ... CANR-22
Earlier sketches in CA 3R, CANR-6
Vaid, Krishna Baldev 1927- ... CANR-8
Earlier sketch in CA 61-64
Vaidon, Lawdom
See Woolman, David S.
Vaihinger, Hans 1852-1933 Brief entry ... 116
Vail, (Marilyn) Elaine 1948- ... 109
Vail, Laurence 1891-1968 Obituary ... 112
See also DLB 4
Vail, Priscilla L. 1931- ... 101
Vail, Robert William 1921- ... CANR-12
Earlier sketch in CA 17-18R
Vaill, George D. 1911(?)-1986 Obituary ... 119
Vaillancourt, Jean-Guy 1937- ... CANR-21
Earlier sketch in CA 105
Vaillancourt, Pauline M(ariette) ... 104
Vailland, Roger (Francois) 1907-1965 ... 103
Obituary ... 89-92
Vaillant, George E. 1934- ... CANR-13
Earlier sketch in CA 77-80
Vairo, Philip Dominic 1933- ... 102
Vaizey, John 1929-1984 ... CANR-4
Obituary ... 113
Earlier sketch in CA 7-8R
Vaizey, Marina 1938- ... 116
Vajda, Ernest 1887-1954 Brief entry ... 122
See also DLB 44
Vajda, Stephan 1926-1987 ... 29-32R
Vajk, J(oseph) Peter 1942- ... 117
Vakar, N(icholas) P(latonovich) 1897-1970 ... CANR-20
Obituary ... 103
Earlier sketch in CA 3R
Valaskakis, Kimon Plato 1941- ... 89-92
Valbonne, Jean
See Leprohon, Pierre
Valbuena-Briones, Angel (Julian) 1928- ... CANR-3
Earlier sketch in CA 45-48
Valcoe, H. Felix
See Swartz, Harry (Felix)
Valdemi, Maria L. 1947- ... 114
Valdes, Donald M(anuel) 1922- ... 21-22R
Valdes, Ivy 1921- ... 105
Valdes, Joan 1931- ... 49-52
Valdes, Mario J. 1934- ... CANR-21
Earlier sketches in CA 13-14R, CANR-6
Valdes, Nelson P. 1945- ... 33-36R
Valdez, Luis 1940- ... 101
Valdez, Paul
See Yates, A(lan) G(eoffrey)
Valdman, Albert 1931- ... 103
Vale, C(orwyn) P(hilip) 1921- ... 49-52
Vale, (Henry) Edmund (Theodoric) 1888-1969 ... CAP-1
Earlier sketch in CA 9-10
Vale, Eugene 1916- ... CANR-12
Earlier sketch in CA 57-60
Vale, Lewis
See Oglesby, Joseph
Vale, Malcolm Graham Allan 1942-
Brief entry ... 109
Valen, Nanine 1950- ... 65-68
See also SATA 21
Valencak, Hannelore
See Mayer, Hannelore Valencak
See also SATA 42
Valency, Maurice 1903- ... CANR-26
Earlier sketches in CA 25-28R, CANR-10
Valens, E(vans) G., Jr. 1920- ... CANR-3
Earlier sketch in CA 5-6R
See also SATA 1
Valens, Evans G. ... CANR-14
Earlier sketch in CA 81-84
Valenstein, Suzanne G(ebhart) 1928- ... 77-80
Valente, Michael F(eeney) ... 57-60
Valenti, Jack 1921- ... 73-76
Valentin, Thomas 1922-1981 Obituary ... 103
Valentine, Alan (Chester) 1901-1980 ... CANR-2
Obituary ... 101
Earlier sketch in CA 5-6R
Valentine, Charles A. 1929- ... 25-28R
Valentine, Charles Wilfrid 1879-1964
Obituary ... 107
Valentine, D(onald) G(raham) 1929- ... 7-8R
Valentine, David
See Ludovici, Anthony M(ario)
Valentine, Douglas
See Williams, (George) Valentine
Valentine, Foy (Dan) 1923- ... CANR-10
Earlier sketch in CA 19-20R
Valentine, Helen (Lachman) 1893-1986
Obituary ... 121
Valentine, Helen
See Valentine, Sister Mary Hester
Valentine, James W(illiam) 1926- ... 126
Valentine, Jean 1934- ... 65-68
Valentine, Jo
See Armstrong, Charlotte
Valentine, Lloyd Magnus 1922-
Brief entry ... 110
Valentine, Roger
See Duke, Donald Norman
Valentine, Sister Mary Hester 1909- ... CAP-2
Earlier sketch in CA 23-24
Valentine, Steven Richards 1956- ... 113
Valentine, Tom 1935- ... CANR-22
Earlier sketch in CA 45-48
Valentine, William Alexander 1905- ... 57-60
Valenzuela, Arturo A. 1944- ... 101
Valenzuela, Luisa 1938- ... 101
See also CLC 31
Valeo, Francis Ralph 1916- Brief entry ... 108
Valeran, A. B.
See Starr, S(tephen) Frederick
Valera y Alcala-Galiano, Juan 1824-1905
Brief entry ... 106
See also TCLC 10
Valeriani, Richard (Gerard) 1932- ... CANR-12
Earlier sketch in CA 65-68
Valeriano, Napoleon D(iestro) 1917(?)-1975 Obituary ... 53-56
Valery, Bernard 1913(?)-1984 Obituary ... 113
Valery, (Ambroise) Paul (Toussaint Jules) 1871-1945 ... 122
Brief entry ... 104
See also TCLC 4, 15
Vales, Robert L(ee) 1933- ... 53-56
Valett, Robert E. 1927- ... CANR-22
Earlier sketches in CA 19-20R, CANR-7
Valette, Rebecca M(arianne Loose) 1938- ... CANR-8
Earlier sketch in CA 23-24R
Valgardson, W(illiam) D(empsey) 1939- ... 41-44R
See also DLB 60
Valgemae, Mardi 1935- ... 41-44R
Vali, Ferenc Albert 1905-1984 ... CANR-3
Obituary ... 114
Earlier sketch in CA 1R
Valiani, Leo 1909- ... CANR-18
Earlier sketch in CA 101
Valin, Jonathan Louis 1948- ... 101
Valin, Martial (Henry) 1898-1980 Obituary ... 105
Valis, Noel M(aureen Ritter) 1945- ... 110
Valkenier, Elizabeth Kridl 1926- ... 119
Vall, Seymour 1925(?)-1987 Obituary ... 124
Vallance, Elizabeth (Mary) 1945- ... 102
Valleau, Emily 1925- ... SATA-51
Vallee, Hubert P(rior) 1901-1986 ... CANR-2
Obituary ... 119
Earlier sketch in CA 3R
Vallee, Jacques F. 1939- ... CANR-10
Earlier sketch in CA 17-18R
Vallee, Rudy
See Vallee, Hubert P(rior)
Valle-Inclan, Ramon (Maria) del 1866-1936 Brief entry ... 106
See also TCLC 5
Vallejo, Antonio Buero
See Buero Vallejo, Antonio
Vallejo, Cesar (Abraham) 1892-1938
Brief entry ... 105
See also TCLC 3
Vallen, Jerome J(ay) 1928- ... 93-96
Vallentine, John F(ranklin) 1931- ... CANR-19
Earlier sketches in CA 53-56, CANR-4
Valle Y Pena, Ramon del
See Valle-Inclan, Ramon (Maria) del
Valmaggia, Juan S. 1895-1980 Obituary ... 97-100
Valsan, E. H. 1933- ... 29-32R
Valtz, Robert C. K. 1936- ... 13-14R
Value, Barbara Ann 1932-1986 Obituary ... 120
Vambe, Lawrence (Chinyani) 1917- ... 110
Vamos, Mara (Miriam) 1927- Brief entry ... 114
Vamplew, Wray 1943- ... CANR-20
Earlier sketch in CA 103
Van Abbe, Derek Maurice 1916- ... 57-60
Van Abbe, Salaman 1883-1955 ... SATA-18
Van Allsburg, Chris 1949- ... 117
Brief entry ... 113
See also SATA 37, 53
See also DLB 61
See also CLR 5, 13
Van Alstyne, Richard W(arner) 1900- ... 11-12R
Van Anda, Carr 1864-1945 ... DLB-25
Van Anrooy, Francine 1924- ... 23-24R
See also SATA 2
Van Anrooy, Frans
See Van Anrooy, Francine
van Appledorn, Mary Jeanne 1927- ... CANR-26
Earlier sketches in CA 25-28R, CANR-10
Vanardy, Varick
See Dey, Frederic (Merrill) Van Rensselaer
Van Arsdel, Rosemary T(horstenson) 1926- ... 108
Van Ash, Cay 1918- ... CLC-34
Van Atta, Winfred 1910- ... CANR-1
Earlier sketch in CA 3R
Vanauken, Sheldon ... CANR-15
Earlier sketch in CA 85-88
van Beeck, Frans Jozef 1930- ... 115
Vanberg, Bent J(arl) 1915- ... 118
VanBibber, Max A(rnold) 1913(?)-1981
Obituary ... 103
Van Briggle, Margaret F(rances) Jessup 1917- ... 11-12R
Van Brocklin, Norm(an Mack) 1926-1983
Obituary ... 109
Van Brunt, H(owell) L(loyd) 1936- ... 49-52

Van Buitenen, J(ohannes) A(drian)
B(ernard) 1928(?)-1979 ... 103
Obituary ... 89-92
Van Buren, Abigail
See Phillips, Pauline (Esther Friedman)
Van Buren, James G(eil) 1914- ... 57-60
van Buren, Paul (Matthews) 1924- ... CANR-11
Earlier sketch in CA 61-64
Van Buren, Raeburn 1891- ... 103
Van Caenegem, R(aoul) C(harles)
1927- ... CANR-23
Earlier sketch in CA 45-48
Van Campen, Karl
See Campbell, John W(ood)
Van Caspel, Venita 1922- ... 104
Vance, A. D.
See Vane-Wright, R(ichard) I(rwin)
Vance, Adrian 1936- ... 77-80
Vance, Barbara Jane 1934- ... 57-60
Vance, Bruce 1931- ... 33-36R
Vance, Cyrus R(oberts) 1917- ... 121
Vance, Edgar
See Ambrose, Eric (Samuel)
Vance, Eleanor Graham 1908- ... 9-10R
See also SATA 11
Vance, Ethel
See Stone, Grace Zaring
Vance, Eugene 1934- ... 126
Vance, Gerald
See Silverberg, Robert
Vance, Jack
See Vance, John Holbrook
See also DLB 8
See also CLC 35
Vance, John Holbrook 1916- ... CANR-17
Earlier sketch in CA 29-32R
Vance, Lawrence L(ee) 1911- ... 49-52
Vance, Louis Joseph 1879-1933
Brief entry ... 112
Vance, Marguerite 1889-1965 Obituary ... 109
See also SATA 29
Vance, (Robert) Norman (Colbert) 1950- ... 122
Vance, Rupert B(ayless) 1899-1975
Obituary ... 61-64
Vance, Samuel 1939- ... 29-32R
Vance, Stanley 1915- ... CANR-3
Earlier sketch in CA 3R
Vance, William E. 1911-1986 ... 105
Obituary ... 119
Vancil, Richard F(ranklin) 1931- ... CANR-8
Earlier sketch in CA 5-6R
Van Cise, Jerrold G(ordon) 1910- ... 114
Van Cleef, Eugene 1887-1973 Obituary ... 107
Van Cleve, John Walter 1950- ... 122
Van Cleve, Thomas Curtis 1888-1976 ... 41-44R
Obituary ... 65-68
Van Coevering, Jack
See Van Coevering, Jan Adrian
Van Coevering, Jan Adrian 1900- ... CAP-1
Earlier sketch in CA 9-10
van Corstanje, Auspicius
See van Corstanje, Charles
van Corstanje, Charles 1913- ... 107
van Croonenburg, Engelbert J(ohannes)
1909- ... 37-40R
Van Dahm, Thomas E(dward) 1924- ... 65-68
Van Dalen, Deobold B(ertrude) 1911- ... CANR-20
Earlier sketch in CA 3R
Van Dam, Ine 1947- ... 109
van Dam, J.
See Presser, (Gerrit) Jacob
Vande Kieft, Ruth Marguerite 1925- ... 17-18R
Van D'Elden, Karl H. 1923- ... 45-48
Vandeman, George E(dward) 1916-
Brief entry ... 114
Vandenberg, Arthur Hendrick 1884-1951
Brief entry ... 120
Vandenberg, Donald 1931- ... 29-32R
Vandenberg, Philipp 1941- ... CANR-23
Earlier sketches in CA 61-64, CANR-8
Vandenberg, T. F. 1941- ... 25-28R
van den Berghe, Pierre L. 1933- ... CANR-5
Earlier sketch in CA 11-12R
Van Den Bogarde, Derek Jules Gaspard
Ulric Niven 1921- ... 77-80
Vandenbosch, Amry 1894- ... 61-64
Vandenbosch, Robert 1922-1978 Obituary ... 107
Vandenburg, Mary Lou 1943- ... 73-76
See also SATA 17
Vandenburgh, Mildred 1898- ... 97-100
Vandenbusche, Duane (Lee) 1937- ... CANR-24
Earlier sketch in CA 45-48
van den Bussche, Henri O(mer) A(ntoine)
See Bussche, Henri O(mer) A(ntoine) van den
van den Haag, Ernest 1914- ... CANR-26
Earlier sketches in CA 7-8R, CANR-6
van den Heuvel, Albert H(endrik) 1932- ... 19-20R
van den Heuvel, Cornelisz A. 1931- ... 13-14R
Van De Pitte, Frederick P. 1932- ... 45-48
Vander, Harry J(oseph) III 1913-19(?) ... CAP-2
Earlier sketch in CA 25-28
VanDerBeets, Richard 1932- ... 29-32R
Vanderbilt, Amy 1908-1974 ... CANR-3
Obituary ... 53-56
Earlier sketch in CA 4R
Vanderbilt, Arthur T. II 1950- ... 122
Vanderbilt, Cornelius, Jr. 1898-1974 ... CAP-1
Obituary ... 49-52
Earlier sketch in CA 9-10
See also AITN 1
Vanderbilt, Gloria (Laura Morgan)
1924- ... CANR-22
Earlier sketch in CA 89-92
Vander Boom, Mae M. ... SATA-14
Vanderburgh, R(osamond) M(oate) 1926- ... 105
Vander Goot, Mary 1947- ... 112
Vandergriff, (Lola) Aola 1920- ... CANR-18
Earlier sketch in CA 89-92
Vanderhaar, Gerard A(nthony) 1931- ... 125
Vanderhaeghe, Guy 1951- ... 113
See also CLC 41
van der Heyden, A(ntonius) A(lphonsus)
M(aria) 1922- ... CANR-7
Earlier sketch in CA 57-60
Vander Hill, C(harles) Warren 1937- ... 33-36R
VanDerhoof, Jack W(arner) 1921- ... 53-56
Van der Horst, Brian 1944- ... 41-44R
Vander Kooi, Ronald C(harles) ... CANR-2
Earlier sketch in CA 45-48
van der Kroef, Justus M(aria) 1925- ... CANR-14
Earlier sketch in CA 41-44R
Vanderlip, D(odava) George 1926- ... CANR-15
Earlier sketch in CA 77-80
Vander Lugt, Herbert 1920- ... CANR-18
Earlier sketch in CA 101
van der Marck, Jan 1929- ... 119
van der Merwe, Nikolaas J(ohannes)
1940- ... 41-44R
van der Meulen, Daniel 1894- ... 117
VanderMolen, Robert 1947- ... 57-60
van der Ploeg, Johannes P(etrus) M(aria)
1909- ... CANR-15
Earlier sketches in CA 9-10, CAP-1
van der Poel, Cornelius J(ohannes)
1921- ... CANR-4
Earlier sketch in CA 53-56
Vanderpool, Harold Y(oung) 1936- ... 53-56
Vanderpool, James A(lbert) 1916-1983
Obituary ... 109
Van der Post, Laurens (Jan) 1906- ... 5-6R
See also CLC 5
Van Dersal, William R(ichard) 1907- ... 77-80
Vander-Schrier, Nettie 1922- ... 114
Vandersee, Charles (Andrew) 1938- ... 41-44R
Van Der Slik, Jack R(onald) 1936- ... 29-32R
van der Smissen, Betty
See van der Smissen, Margaret Elisabeth
van der Smissen, Margaret Elisabeth
1927- ... CANR-9
Earlier sketch in CA 19-20R
Van der Spiel, Luigi 1920- ... 102
van der Vat, Dan(iel Francis Jeroen) 1939- ... 109
Vanderveen, Bareld Harmannus 1932- ... 103
Vanderveen, Bart H.
See Vanderveen, Bareld Harmannus
Van der Veer, Judy 1912-1982 ... 33-36R
Obituary ... 108
See also SATA 4, 33
Vandervelde, Marjorie (Mills) 1908- ... CANR-10
Earlier sketch in CA 21-22R
Van der Veldt, James 1893(?)-1977
Obituary ... 73-76
Van der Veur, Paul W. 1921- ... 21-22R
Van Der Voort, Richard Lee 1936- ... 37-40R
Vanderwall, Francis W(illiam) 1946- ... CANR-26
Earlier sketch in CA 108
Vanderwerken, David L(eon) 1945- ... 119
Vanderwerth, W(illiam) C(onnor) 1904- ... 73-76
Vanderwood, Paul J. ... 29-32R
Vander Zanden, James Wilfrid 1930- ... CANR-19
Earlier sketches in CA 15-16R, CANR-5
van der Zee, Henri (Antony) 1934-
Brief entry ... 114
Van Der Zee, James (Augustus Joseph)
1886-1983 ... 104
Obituary ... 109
van der Zee, John 1936- ... CANR-15
Earlier sketch in CA 21-22R
Vanderzell, John H. 1924- ... 45-48
VanderZwaag, Harold J. 1929- ... CANR-23
Earlier sketch in CA 45-48
van Deurs, George 1901- ... 25-28R
Van Deusen, Dayton G(roff) 1914- ... 11-12R
Van Deusen, Glyndon Garlock 1897- ... CANR-1
Earlier sketch in CA 1R
Van Deusen, L. Marshall 1922- ... 61-64
Van Deusen, Ruth B(rown) 1907- ... 5-6R
Van De Vall, Mark 1923- ... CANR-12
Earlier sketch in CA 29-32R
Van Devander, Charles W(ood) 1902-1986
Obituary ... 121
Van Devanter, Lynda (Margaret) 1947- ... 117
Van de Vate, Dwight, Jr. 1928- ... 61-64
Van Deventer, David E(arl) 1937-
Brief entry ... 115
Van Deventer, Fred 1903-1971 ... CAP-1
Earlier sketch in CA 15-16
VanDeventer, Robert ... 105
Van de Water, Frederic F(ranklyn)
1890-1968 Obituary ... 110
van de Wetering, Janwillem 1931- ... CANR-4
Earlier sketch in CA 49-52
See also CLC 47
Van Dine, S. S.
See Wright, Willard Huntington
See also TCLC 23
Vandiver, Edward P(inckney), Jr. 1902- ... CAP-1
Earlier sketch in CA 13-14
Vandiver, Frank E(verson) 1925- ... CANR-7
Earlier sketch in CA 7-8R
Vandivert, Rita (Andre) 1905- ... CANR-6
Earlier sketch in CA 5-6R
See also SATA 21
Van Dommelen, David B. 1929- ... 5-6R
van Dooren, Ingrid 1949- ... 114
Van Dooren, L(eonard) A(lfred) T(heophile)
1912- ... CANR-19
Earlier sketches in CA 7-8R, CANR-3
Van Doren, Carl (Clinton) 1885-1950
Brief entry ... 111
See also TCLC 18
Van Doren, Charles L. 1926- ... CANR-4
Earlier sketch in CA 5-6R
Van Doren, Dorothy Graffe 1896- ... 4R
Van Doren, Irita 1891-1966 Obituary ... 89-92
Van Doren, Mark 1894-1972 ... CANR-3
Obituary ... 37-40R
Earlier sketch in CA 3R
See also DLB 45
See also CLC 6, 10
Van Dorne, R.
See Wallmann, Jeffrey M(iner)
Vandour, Cyril
See Surmelian, Leon (Zaven)
Van Druten, John (William) 1901-1957
Brief entry ... 104
See also DLB 10
See also TCLC 2
Van Dusen, Albert E(dward) 1916- ... CANR-3
Earlier sketch in CA 5-6R
Van Dusen, Clarence Raymond 1907- ... 5-6R
Van Dusen, Henry P(itney) 1897-1975 ... CANR-3
Obituary ... 57-60
Earlier sketch in CA 3R
Van Dusen, Robert LaBranche 1929- ... 41-44R
Van Duyn, Janet 1910- ... 69-72
See also SATA 18
Van Duyn, Mona 1921- ... CANR-7
Earlier sketch in CA 9-10R
See also DLB 5
See also CLC 3, 7
Van Duzee, Mabel 1895- ... 7-8R
Van Dyke, Carolynn 1947- ... 116
Van Dyke, Dick 1925- Brief entry ... 112
Van Dyke, Henry 1852-1933 ... DLB-71
Van Dyke, Henry 1928- ... CANR-25
Earlier sketch in CA 49-52
See also BW
See also DLB 33
Van Dyke, Jon M. 1943- ... 29-32R
Van Dyke, Lauren A. 1906- ... 29-32R
Van Dyke, Vernon Brumbaugh 1912- ... CANR-23
Earlier sketch in CA 3R
Van Dyne, Edith
See Baum, L(yman) Frank
Vane, Brett
See Kent, Arthur William Charles
Vane, Michael
See Humphries, Sydney Vernon
Vane, Roland
See McKeag, Ernest L(ionel)
Vane, (Vane Hunt) Sutton 1888-1963
Obituary ... 113
See also DLB 10
Van Eerde, Katherine S(ommerlatte)
1920- ... 61-64
Van Egmond, Peter (George) 1937- ... 61-64
Vanek, Jaroslav 1930- ... 103
Van Engen, John H. 1947- ... 117
Van Ermengem, Frederic 1881-1972
Obituary ... 33-36R
Van Ess, Dorothy 1885(?)-1975 Obituary ... 61-64
Van Ettinger, Jan 1902- ... CANR-21
Earlier sketch in CA 2R
Van Every, Dale 1896-1976 ... CANR-3
Earlier sketch in CA 3R
Vane-Wright, R(ichard) I(rwin) 1942- ... 121
Van Fossen, Richard W(aight) 1927- ... CANR-6
Earlier sketch in CA 7-8R
van Fraassen, Bastiaan Cornelis ... CANR-14
Earlier sketch in CA 37-40R
Van Geil, Mercury E. C. L.
See McGilvery, Laurence
van Gelder, Dora 1904- Brief entry ... 116
Van Gelder, Lindsy 1944- ... 97-100
Van Gelder, Richard George 1928- ... 73-76
Vangelisti, Paul 1945- ... CANR-14
Earlier sketch in CA 77-80
Vangen, Roland Dean 1935- ... 105
Vanger, Milton Isadore 1925- ... 15-16R
Van Goethem, Larry 1934- ... 101
van Gulik, Robert Hans 1910-1967 ... CANR-3
Obituary ... 25-28R
Earlier sketch in CA 4R
VanGundy, Arthur B(oice), Jr. 1946- ... 110
Van Haaften, Julia 1946- ... 109
Van Hassen, Amy
See Wiles, Domini
Van Hattum, Rolland J(ames) 1924- ... CANR-21
Earlier sketch in CA 105
Van Hecke, B(resee) C(oleman) 1926- ... 29-32R
Van Heijenoort, Jean 1912-1986 Obituary ... 120
Van Helden, Albert 1940- ... 125
Van Herik, Judith 1947- ... 108
van Herk, Aritha 1954- ... 101
van het Reve, Karel 1921- ... 49-52
van Heyningen, Christina 1900- ... 19-20R
van Heyningen, William Edward 1911- ... 112
Van Hise, Della 1955- ... 121
Van Hoesen, Walter H. 1898(?)-1977
Obituary ... 69-72
Van Hook, Roger Eugene 1943- ... 29-32R
Van Hoose, William H. 1927- ... 89-92
Van Horn, Richard L. 1932- ... 53-56
Van Horn, William 1939- ... 115
See also SATA 43
Van Horne, Harriet 1920- Brief entry ... 113
Van Houten, Lois 1918- ... 77-80
Van Huss, Wayne D(aniel) 1917- ... 61-64
van Inwagen, Peter (Jan) 1942- ... 116
van Itallie, Jean-Claude 1936- ... CANR-1
Earlier sketch in CA 45-48
See also CAAS 2
See also DLB 7
See also CLC 3
Van Itallie, Philip H. 1899- ... CAP-1
Earlier sketch in CA 9-10
Van Iterson, S(iny) R(ose) ... 102
See also SATA 26
van Jaarsveld, Floris Albertus 1922- ... CANR-7
Earlier sketch in CA 5-6R
van Kaam, Adrian (L.) 1920- ... CANR-26
Earlier sketches in CA 19-20R, CANR-10
Van Kleek, Peter Eric 1929- ... 53-56
Van Krevelen, Alice 1914- ... 45-48
van Lawick, Hugo 1937- ... 85-88
van Lawick-Goodall, Jane
See Goodall, Jane
Van Leeuwen, Jean 1937- ... CANR-11
Earlier sketch in CA 25-28R
See also SATA 6
Van Lente, Charles R(obert) 1941- ... 65-68
van Lhin, Erik
See del Rey, Lester
Van Lierde, John 1907- ... CAP-1
Earlier sketch in CA 9-10
Van Lierde, Peter Canisius
See Van Lierde, John
van Lint, June 1928- ... 65-68
van Loon, Gerard Willem 1911- ... 45-48
Van Loon, Hendrik Willem 1882-1944
Brief entry ... 117
See also SATA 18
Van Meerhaeghe, M(arcel) A(lfons) G(ilbert)
1921- ... CANR-13
Earlier sketch in CA 77-80
Van Melsen, Andreas G(erardus) M(aria)
1912- ... CANR-4
Earlier sketch in CA 3R
Vann, J(erry) Don 1938- ... 29-32R
Vann, James Allen 1939- ... 110
Vann, Richard T(ilman) 1931- ... 21-22R
Vann, Robert L. 1879-1940 ... DLB-29
Van Ness, Peter 1933- ... 29-32R
Van Niel, Cornelius B(ernardus)
1897-1985 Obituary ... 115
Vannier, Maryhelen 1915- ... CANR-22
Earlier sketches in CA 3R, CANR-6
van Nieuwenhuijze, C(hristoffel) A(nthonie)
O(livier) 1920- ... 25-28R
Van Nimmen, (Carol) Jane 1937- ... 125
Van Nooten, Barend A(drian) 1932- ... 45-48
Van Noppen, Ina (Faye) W(oestemeyer)
1906-1980 ... 5-6R
Obituary ... 103
Vannorsdall, John Warren 1924- ... 113
Van Nostrand, A(lbert) D(ouglass)
1922- ... CANR-16
Earlier sketch in CA 41-44R
Vannoy, Russell (Columbus) 1933- ... 119
Vano, Gerard S. 1943- ... 112
Vanocur, Edith C. 1924(?)-1975 Obituary ... 57-60
Vanocur, Sander 1928- ... 120
Brief entry ... 109
van Oort, Jan 1921- ... 29-32R
Van Orden, M(erton) D(ick) 1921- ... 37-40R
See also SATA 4
Van Orman, Bonny 1939(?)-1987
Obituary ... 122
Van Orman, Richard A(lbert) 1936- ... 21-22R
Van Osdol, William R(ay) 1927- ... 53-56
Van Over, Raymond 1934- Brief entry ... 112
van Overbeek, Johannes 1908- ... CAP-1
Earlier sketch in CA 13-14
Van Peebles, Melvin 1932- ... 85-88
See also BW
See also CLC 2, 20
van Peursen, Cornelis Anthonie 1920- ... 53-56
Van Praagh, Margaret 1910- ... CAP-2
Earlier sketch in CA 17-18
Van Praagh, Peggy
See Van Praagh, Margaret
Van Proosdy, Cornelis 1919- ... CANR-5
Earlier sketch in CA 11-12R
van Ravenswaay, Charles 1911- ... 119
Van Rensselaer, Alexander (Taylor Mason)
1892-1962 ... 73-76
See also SATA 14
Van Rensselaer, Mariana Griswold
1851-1934 ... DLB-47
Van Rensselaer, Mrs. Schulyer
See Van Rensselaer, Mariana Griswold
Van Rheenen, Gailyn 1946- ... 69-72
van Rijn, Ignatius
See Ingram, Forrest L(eo)
Van Riper, Francis A(lbert) 1946- ... CANR-11
Earlier sketch in CA 69-72
Van Riper, Frank
See Van Riper, Francis A(lbert)
Van Riper, Guernsey, Jr. 1909- ... CANR-6
Earlier sketch in CA 7-8R
See also SATA 3
Van Riper, Paul P(ritchard) 1916- ... 4R
Van Riper, Robert 1921- ... 37-40R
van Rjndt, Philippe 1950- ... CANR-14
Earlier sketch in CA 65-68
van Rooy, C(harles) A(ugust) 1923- ... 19-20R
Van Saher, Lilla 1912-1968 ... CAP-1
Earlier sketch in CA 11-12
Vansant, Carl 1938- ... 37-40R
Van Schaick, Frances L. 1912(?)-1979
Obituary ... 89-92
Van Scyoc, Sydney J(oyce) 1939- ... CANR-15
Earlier sketch in CA 89-92
Van Sertima, Ivan 1935- ... 104
Van Seters, John 1935- ... 115
Van Sickle, John V(alentine) 1892- ... 5-6R
Van Sickle, Neil D(avid) 1915- ... 41-44R
VanSickle, V. A.
See Carhart, Arthur Hawthorne
Vansina, Jan 1929- ... CANR-10
Earlier sketch in CA 65-68
Vansittart, Jane
See Moorhouse, Hilda Vansittart

INDEX

Vansittart, Peter 1920- ... CANR-3
Earlier sketch in CA 1R
See also CLC 42
Van Slingerland, Peter 1929- ... 21-22R
Van Slooten, Henry 1916- ... 3R
Van Slyck, Philip 1920- ... 13-14R
Van Slyke, Donald Dexter 1883-1971
Obituary ... 104
Van Slyke, Helen (Lenore) 1919-1979 ... 37-40R
Obituary ... 89-92
Van Slyke, Lyman P(age) 1929- ... 23-24R
Van Smith, Howard
See Smith, Howard Van
van Someren, Liesje
See Lichtenberg, Elisabeth Jacoba
Van Steenwyk, Elizabeth (Ann) 1928- ... CANR-18
Earlier sketch in CA 101
See also SATA 34
Van Stockum, Hilda 1908- ... CANR-5
Earlier sketch in CA 11-12R
See also SATA 5
van Straten, Florence W(ilhelmina)
1913- ... 19-20R
Van Tassel, Alfred J. 1910- ... 41-44R
Van Tassel, David Dirck 1928- ... 103
Van Tassel, Dennie L(ee) 1939- ... CANR-8
Earlier sketch in CA 57-60
Van Tassel, George W. 1910-1978
Obituary ... 112
Van Tassel, Roger (Carleton) 1924- ... 45-48
van Thal, Herbert (Maurice) 1904-1983 ... 65-68
Obituary ... 111
Van Til, Cornelius 1895- ... CANR-3
Earlier sketch in CA 3R
Van Til, William 1911- ... CANR-10
Earlier sketch in CA 25-28R
Van Tine, Warren R(ussell) 1942- ... 53-56
Van Trump, James D(enholm) 1908- ... 41-44R
Van Tuyl, Barbara 1940- ... 53-56
See also SATA 11
Van Valkenburg, Samuel 1891-1976 ... 5-6R
Obituary ... 103
Van Valkenburgh, Paul 1941- ... 89-92
Van Vechten, Benjamin D(avenport) 1935- ... 110
Van Vechten, Carl 1880-1964 Obituary ... 89-92
See also DLB 4, 9, 51
See also CLC 33
Van Vleck, David B. 1929- ... 101
Van Vleck, John Hasbrouck 1899-1980
Obituary ... 102
Van Vleck, L(loyd) Dale 1933- ... 53-56
Van Vleck, Sarita 1933- ... 13-14R
Van Vlissingen, Arthur 1894-1986
Obituary ... 120
Van Vogt, A(lfred) E(lton) 1912- ... 23-24R
See also SATA 14
See also DLB 8
See also CLC 1
Van Vooren, Monique 1933- ... 107
Van Voris, Jacqueline 1922- ... 57-60
van Vuuren, Nancy 1938- ... 49-52
Van Wagenen, Gertrude 1893-1978
Obituary ... 77-80
van Wageningen, J.
See Presser, (Gerrit) Jacob
Van Waters, Miriam 1887-1974 Obituary ... 45-48
Van Weddingen, Marthe 1924- ... CANR-14
Earlier sketch in CA 81-84
Van Wert, William F(rancis) 1945- ... 105
van Witsen, Leo 1912- ... 106
Van Woeart, Alpheus
See Halloway, Vance
Van Woerkom, Dorothy (O'Brien)
1924- ... CANR-26
Earlier sketches in CA 57-60, CANR-11
See also SATA 21
Van Wormer, Joe
See Van Wormer, Joseph Edward
Van Wormer, Joseph Edward 1913- ... CANR-5
Earlier sketch in CA 9-10R
See also SATA 35
Van Young, Eric (Julian) 1946- ... 122
Van Zandt, E. F.
See Cudlipp, Edythe
Van Zandt, Roland 1918- ... 19-20R
Van Zante, Helen Johnson 1906- ... 13-14R
Van Zanten, John W(illiam) 1913- ... 101
van Zeller, Claud 1905-1984 ... CANR-6
Obituary ... 113
Earlier sketch in CA 4R
van Zeller, Hubert
See van Zeller, Claud
Vanzi, Max (Bruno) 1934- ... 123
Van Zwienen, Ilse Charlotte Koehn 1929- ... 85-88
See also SATA 28, 34
van Zwoll, James A. 1909- ... CAP-1
Earlier sketch in CA 13-14
Vaqar, Nasrollah 1920- ... 41-44R
Vara, Albert C. 1931- ... 33-36R
Varah, Chad 1911- ... 57-60
Varandyan, Emmanuel P(aul) 1904- ... 65-68
Varas, Florencia
See Olea, Maria Florencia Varas
Varda, Agnes 1928- ... 122
Brief entry ... 116
See also CLC 16
Vardaman, E. Jerry 1927- ... 17-18R
Vardaman, George T(ruett) 1920- ... CANR-4
Earlier sketch in CA 3R
Vardaman, James M(oney) 1921- ... 104
Vardaman, Patricia B(lack) 1931- ... 37-40R
Vardamis, Alex A. 1934- ... 77-80
Vardre, Leslie
See Davies, L(eslie) P(urnell)
Vardy, Steven Bela 1936- ... CANR-19
Earlier sketches in CA 53-56, CANR-4
Vardys, V(ytautas) Stanley 1924- ... CANR-5
Earlier sketch in CA 15-16R
Vare, Daniele 1880-1956 Brief entry ... 119
Vare, Robert 1945- ... 103
Varenhorst, Barbara B(raden) 1928- ... 116
Varese, Louise 1890- ... 41-44R
Varg, Paul A(lbert) 1912- ... 118
Brief entry ... 113
Varga, Andrew Charles 1917- ... 113
Varga, Judy
See Stang, Judit
Vargas, Julie S. 1938- ... 57-60
Vargas Llosa, (Jorge) Mario (Pedro)
1936- ... CANR-18
Earlier sketch in CA 73-76
See also CLC 3, 6, 9, 10, 15, 31, 42
Vargish, Thomas 1939- ... CANR-14
Earlier sketch in CA 37-40R
Varlay, Rene G. 1927- ... 4R
Varley, Dimitry V. 1906- ... CAP-1
Earlier sketch in CA 17-18
See also SATA 10
Varley, Gloria 1932- ... 101
Varley, H(erbert) Paul 1931- ... 77-80
Varley, John (Herbert) 1947- ... CANR-25
Earlier sketch in CA 69-72
See also DLBY 81
Varley, John Philip
See Mitchell, Langdon (Elwyn)
Varma, Baidya Nath 1921- ... 41-44R
Varma, Devendra P. 1923- Brief entry ... 113
Varma, Monika 1916- ... 77-80
Varnac, d'Hugues
See Prevost, Alain
Varnado, Jewel Goodgame 1915- ... 9-10R
Varnalis, Costas 1884-1974 Obituary ... 53-56
Varner, John Grier 1905-1978 ... 25-28R
Obituary ... 120
Varner, Velma V. 1916-1972 Obituary ... 37-40R
Varney, Carleton B(ates) 1937- ... CANR-16
Earlier sketch in CA 89-92
Varney, Philip 1943- ... 125
Vars, Gordon F(orrest) 1923- ... 23-24R
Vartan, Vartanig G(arabed) 1923-1988 ... 61-64
Obituary ... 125
Vartan, Vartanig Garabed 1923- ... 61-64
Vartanian, Aram 1922- ... CANR-3
Earlier sketch in CA 3R
Vasconcelos (Calderon), Jose 1882-1959
Brief entry ... 118
Vas Dias, Robert (Leonard Michael)
1931- ... CANR-7
Earlier sketch in CA 19-20R
Vasey, Lloyd Roland ... 113
Vash, Carolyn L(ee) 1934- ... 121
Vash, Carolyn Lee 1934- Brief entry ... 116
Vasil, R(aj) K(umar) 1931- ... CANR-14
Earlier sketch in CA 37-40R
Vasiliu, Gheorghe 1881-1957 Brief entry ... 123
Vasiliu, Mircea 1920- ... 23-24R
See also SATA 2
Vaske, Martin O. 1915- ... CANR-2
Earlier sketch in CA 7-8R
Vasquez, John A(nthony) 1945- ... 108
Vass, George 1927- ... 37-40R
See also SATA 31
Vass, Winifred Kellersberger 1917- ... 57-60
Vassa, Gustavus
See Equiano, Olaudah
Vassi, Marco 1937- ... CANR-13
Earlier sketch in CA 61-64
Vassilikos, Vassilis 1933- ... 81-84
See also CLC 4, 8
Vassiliou, Yannis 1949- ... 117
Vasta, Edward 1928- ... 17-18R
Vasu, Nirmala-Kumara
See Bose, N(irmal) K(umar)
Vasvary, Edmund 1888-1977 Obituary ... 73-76
Vatikiotis, P(anayiotis) J(erasimos)
1928- ... CANR-6
Earlier sketch in CA 13-14R
Vatter, Harold Goodhue 1910- ... 5-6R
Vaudrin, Bill
See Vaudrin, William
Vaudrin, William 1943-1976 ... CAP-2
Earlier sketch in CA 29-32
Vaughan, Adrian 1941- ... 120
Vaughan, Agnes Carr 1887- ... CAP-1
Earlier sketch in CA 9-10
Vaughan, Alan 1936- ... 81-84
Vaughan, Alden T. 1929- ... CANR-7
Earlier sketch in CA 17-18R
Vaughan, Beatrice 1909(?)-1972
Obituary ... 37-40R
Vaughan, Bill
See Vaughan, William E(dward)
Vaughan, Carter A.
See Gerson, Noel Bertram
Vaughan, Clark (Alvord) 1924- ... 108
Vaughan, David 1924- ... 77-80
Vaughan, Denis 1920- ... 61-64
Vaughan, Donald S(hores) 1921- ... CANR-10
Earlier sketch in CA 17-18R
Vaughan, Frances E. 1935- ... 125
Brief entry ... 107
Vaughan, Frederick 1935- ... 120
Vaughan, Harold Cecil 1923- ... 29-32R
See also SATA 14
Vaughan, Hilda
See Morgan, Hilda Campbell
Vaughan, James A(gnew) 1936- ... 49-52
Vaughan, John Edmund 1935- ... 61-64
Vaughan, Leo
See Lendon, Kenneth Harry
Vaughan, Paul 1925- ... 29-32R
Vaughan, Richard
See Thomas, Ernest Lewys
Vaughan, Richard Patrick 1919- ... 15-16R
Vaughan, Robert (Richard) 1937- ... 103
Vaughan, Roger 1937- ... 85-88
Vaughan, Sam(uel) 1928- ... 13-14R
See also SATA 14
Vaughan, Sheila Marie 1930- ... 23-24R
Vaughan, Virginia M(ason) 1947- ... 110
Vaughan, William E(dward) 1915-1977 ... 5-6R
Obituary ... 69-72
Vaughan Williams, Ralph 1872-1958
Brief entry ... 115
Vaughan Williams, Ursula Wood
1911- ... CANR-24
Earlier sketches in CA 9-10R, CANR-6
Vaughn, Charles L(e Claire) 1911- ... 41-44R
Vaughn, Donald E(arl) 1932- ... 21-22R
Vaughn, Jack A(lfred) 1935- ... 85-88
Vaughn, Jesse Wendell 1903-1968 ... 3R
Obituary ... 103
Vaughn, Lewis 1950- ... 111
Vaughn, Michael J(effery) 1943- ... 37-40R
Vaughn, Richard C(lements) 1925- ... CANR-9
Earlier sketch in CA 21-22R
Vaughn, Robert (Francis) 1932- ... 61-64
Vaughn, Ruth 1935- ... CANR-15
Earlier sketch in CA 41-44R
See also SATA 14
Vaughn, Sally N(orthrop) 1939- ... 126
Vaughn, Sister Ann Carol 1922- ... 11-12R
Vaughn, Stephen L. 1947- ... 101
Vaughn, Toni
See Du Breuil, (Elizabeth) L(or)inda
Vaughn, William Preston 1933- ... 73-76
Vaught, Jacque
See Brogan, Jacqueline Vaught
Vaupel, James W(alton) 1945- ... 111
Vaurie, Charles 1906-1975 ... CANR-4
Earlier sketch in CA 7-8R
Vaussard, Maurice (Rene Jean Arthur
Andre) 1888- ... 9-10R
Vautier, Ghislaine 1932- ... 112
See also SATA 53
Vavra, Robert James 1935- ... CANR-25
Earlier sketch in CA 25-28R
See also SATA 8
Vawter, F(rancis) Bruce 1921- ... CANR-4
Earlier sketch in CA 3R
Vayda, Andrew P. 1931- ... 19-20R
Vayhinger, John Monroe 1916- ... 73-76
Vayle, Valerie
See Brooks, Janice Young
Vaz, Edmund (Winston) 1924- ... 108
Vazakas, Byron 1905- ... CAP-2
Earlier sketch in CA 25-28
Vazov, Ivan (Minchov) 1850-1921
Brief entry ... 121
See also TCLC 25
Veach, William B. Templeton 1896- ... CAP-1
Earlier sketch in CA 9-10
Veaner, Allen B(arnet) 1929- ... 41-44R
Veatch, Henry Babcock 1911- ... CANR-6
Earlier sketch in CA 5-6R
Veatch, Robert M(arlin) 1939- ... CANR-11
Earlier sketch in CA 69-72
Veblen, Thorstein (Bunde) 1857-1929
Brief entry ... 115
Vecoli, Rudolph J(ohn) 1927- ... CANR-26
Earlier sketches in CA 19-20R, CANR-10
Vecsey, George S. 1909(?)-1984 Obituary ... 114
Vecsey, George Spencer 1939- ... CANR-10
Earlier sketch in CA 61-64
See also SATA 9
Vedder, James S(herman) 1912- ... 117
Vedder, John K.
See Gruber, Frank
Vedder, Richard K(ent) 1940- ... 115
Vedeler, Harold C. 1903- ... 122
Veder, Bob 1940- ... 104
Vedral, Joyce L(auretta) 1943- ... 117
Veeck, Bill
See Veeck, William Louis, Jr.
Veeck, William Louis, Jr. 1914-1986
Obituary ... 118
Veedam, Voldemar 1912-1983 Obituary ... 109
Veenendaal, Cornelia 1924- ... 117
Vega, Janine Pommy 1942- ... CANR-2
Earlier sketch in CA 49-52
See also DLB 16
Veglahn, Nancy (Crary) 1937- ... CANR-7
Earlier sketch in CA 19-20R
See also SATA 5
Vehr, Bill 1940(?)-1988 Obituary ... 126
Veiga, Jose J(acinto da) 1915- ... CANR-15
Earlier sketch in CA 37-40R
Veiller, Anthony 1903-1965 ... DLB-44
Veillon, Lee 1942- ... 49-52
Veit, Fritz 1907- ... 111
Veit, Lawrence A. 1938- Brief entry ... 115
Veit, Stan(ley Stanford) 1929- ... 110
Vekemans, Roger 1921- ... 37-40R
Velasquez, Manuel G(onzales) 1942- ... 113
Veler, Richard P(aul) 1936- ... 49-52
Velez-Ibanez, Carlos G(uillermo) 1936- ... 118
Velie, Alan R. 1937- ... CANR-1
Earlier sketch in CA 45-48
Velie, Lester 1908- ... CAP-2
Earlier sketch in CA 17-18
Velikovsky, Immanuel 1895-1979 ... CANR-15
Obituary ... 89-92
Earlier sketch in CA 69-72
Veliz, Claudio 1930- ... 25-28R
Vella, Walter F(rancis) 1924- ... CANR-24
Earlier sketch in CA 45-48
Vellacott, Jo 1922- ... 126
Vellela, Tony 1945- ... 65-68
Velleman, Ruth A(nn) 1921- ... 110
Velthuijs, Max 1923- ... 89-92
See also SATA 53
Veltman, Vera
See Panova, Vera (Fedorovna)
Velvel, Lawrence R. 1939- ... 29-32R
Venable, Alan (Hudson) 1944- ... 45-48
See also SATA 8
Venable, Tom C(alvin) 1921- ... 29-32R
Venable, Vernon 1906- ... CAP-2
Earlier sketch in CA 21-22
Venafro, Mark
See Pizzat, Frank J(oseph)
Vendler, Helen (Hennessy) 1933- ... CANR-25
Earlier sketch in CA 41-44R
Vendler, Zeno 1921- ... 126
Brief entry ... 105
Vendrovskii, David Efimovich 1879-1971
Obituary ... 33-36R
Vendrovsky, David
See Vendrovskii, David Efimovich
Veness, Molly 1900(?)-1985 Obituary ... 118
Veness, (Winifred) Thelma 1919-1971 ... 5-6R
Obituary ... 122
Vengroff, Richard 1945- ... CANR-10
Earlier sketch in CA 65-68
Venison, Alfred
See Pound, Ezra (Loomis)
Veniste, Richard Ben
See Ben-Veniste, Richard
Venn, Grant 1919-1979 ... 15-16R
Obituary ... 122
Vennard, Edwin 1902- ... CAP-2
Earlier sketch in CA 25-28
Vennema, Alje 1932- ... 101
Venner, J. G.
See Lewis, John (Noel Claude)
Venning, Corey 1924- ... 49-52
Venning, Hugh
See van Zeller, Claud
Venning, Michael
See Randolph, Georgiana Ann
Venter, Al(bertus) J(ohannes) 1938- ... 117
Venton, W. B. 1898-1976 ... CAP-2
Earlier sketch in CA 25-28
Ventura, Jeffrey
See Feinman, Jeffrey
Ventura, Piero Luigi 1937- ... 103
See also SATA 43
See also CLR 16
Venturi, Denise Scott Brown
See Brown, Denise Scott
Venturi, Marcello 1925- ... CANR-13
Earlier sketch in CA 29-32R
Venturi, Robert 1925- ... 61-64
Venuti, Lawrence (Michael) 1953- ... 120
Vequin, Capini
See Quinn, Elisabeth
Verba, Sidney 1932- ... CANR-3
Earlier sketch in CA 3R
Vercors
See Bruller, Jean (Marcel)
Vercors, J. Bruller
See Bruller, Jean (Marcel)
Verdenius, W(illem) J(acob) 1913- ... 25-28R
Verdery, John D(uane) 1917- ... 11-12R
Verdi, Marie de
See Mencken, H(enry) L(ouis)
Verdick, Mary (Peyton) 1923- ... CANR-4
Earlier sketch in CA 3R
Verdon, Dorothy
See Tralins, S(andor) Robert
Verdu, Matilde
See Cela, Camilo Jose
Verduin, John R(ichard), Jr. 1931- ... CANR-24
Earlier sketches in CA 23-24R, CANR-9
Verduin, Leonard 1897- ... 61-64
Verene, Donald Phillip 1937- ... CANR-15
Earlier sketch in CA 41-44R
Verey, David (Cecil Wynter)
1913-1984 ... CANR-15
Obituary ... 113
Earlier sketch in CA 65-68
Verga, Giovanni (Carmelo) 1840-1922 ... 123
Brief entry ... 104
See also TCLC 3
Vergani, Luisa 1931- ... 23-24R
Vergara, Jose Manuel 1929- ... 97-100
Vergara, Joseph R. 1915- ... 29-32R
Vergara, Lisa 1948- ... 120
Vergara, William C(harles) 1923- ... 3R
Verghese, T. Paul
See Gregorios, Paulos Mar
Verhaeren, Emile (Adolphe Gustave)
1855-1916 Brief entry ... 109
See also TCLC 12
Verhalen, Philip A(ndrew) 1934- ... 69-72
Verhoeven, Cornelis 1928- ... CANR-23
Earlier sketches in CA 61-64, CANR-8
Verhoeven, Paul 1901-1975 Obituary ... 115
Verhonick, Phillis J. 1922(?)-1977
Obituary ... 73-76
Verhoogen, John 1912- ... 109
Verin, Velko
See Inkiow, (Janakiev) Dimiter
Verissimo, Erico (Lopes) 1905-1975
Obituary ... 115
Vermes, Geza 1924- ... 57-60
Vermes, Jean C(ampbell Pattison) 1907- ... 106
Vermes, Pamela 1918- ... 118
Vermeule, Cornelius Clarkson III 1925- ... 41-44R
Vermeule, E(mily) D. T. 1928- ... 17-18R
Vermillion, Robert 1915(?)-1987 Obituary ... 122
Vernadsky, George 1887-1973 Obituary ... 41-44R
Vernam, Glenn R. 1896-1980 ... CANR-10
Earlier sketch in CA 19-20R
Vernant, Jean-Pierre 1914- ... 109

Vernazza, Marcelle Wynn 1909- CANR-10
Earlier sketch in CA 19-20R
Verne, Jules 1828-1905 Brief entry 110
See also SATA 21
See also TCLC 6
Verner, Coolie 1917-1979 CANR-7
Earlier sketch in CA 53-56
Verner, Gerald 1897(?)-1980 Obituary 102
See also SATA 25
Verney, Douglas Vernon 1924- 13-14R
Verney, John 1913- 65-68
See also SATA 14
Verney, Michael P(almer) 1923- CANR-6
Earlier sketch in CA 13-14R
Verney, Peter (Vivian Lloyd) 1930- CANR-19
Earlier sketch in CA 81-84
Verney, Sarah
See Holloway, Brenda W(ilmar)
Verney, Stephen Edmund 1919- 104
Vernon, Eddie
See Stone, Hoyt E(dward)
Vernon, Edward
See Coleman, Vernon
Vernon, Frances 1963- 110
Vernon, Glenn M(orley) 1920- 49-52
Vernon, John 1943- 41-44R
Vernon, Judy 1945- 119
Vernon, Lee M.
See von Block, Bela W(illiam)
Vernon, Lorraine 1921- 113
Vernon, (Elda) Louise A(nderson) 1914- 53-56
See also SATA 14
Vernon, McCay 1928- 41-44R
Vernon, Philip Ewart 1905- CANR-12
Earlier sketch in CA 5-6R
Vernon, Raymond 1913- CANR-18
Earlier sketches in CA 5-6R, CANR-2
Vernon, Rosemary
See Smith, Susan Vernon
Vernon, Thomas Bowater 1939- 118
Vernon, Thomas S. 1914- 25-28R
Vernon, Tom
See Vernon, Thomas Bowater
Vernon, Walter N(ewton), Jr. 1907- CANR-12
Earlier sketch in CA 17-18R
Vernon-Jackson, Hugh (Owen Hardinge)
1925- 21-22R
Vernor, D.
See Casewit, Curtis W(erner)
Verny, Tom 1936- 73-76
Veronica, Sister Mary 1924- 19-20R
Verplanck, Gulian C. 1786-1870 DLB-59
Verral, Charles Spain 1904- CANR-16
Earlier sketches in CA 9-10, CAP-1
See also SATA 11
Verrette, Joyce
See Petratur, Joyce
Verrill, A(lpheus) Hyatt 1871-1954
Brief entry 111
Verrone, Robert J. 1935(?)-1984 Obituary 113
See also SATA 39
Versace, Marie Teresa Rios 1917- 19-20R
See also SATA 2
Ver Steeg, Clarence L(ester) 1922- 15-16R
Versteeg, Robert John 1930- 3R
Verval, Alain
See Lande, Lawrence (Montague)
Verwilghen, A(lbert-) Felix 1916- 25-28R
Verwoerdt, Adriaan 1927- 19-20R
Very, Alice (N.) 1894-1977 21-22R
Obituary 120
Very, Jones 1813-1880 DLB-1
Veryan, Patricia
See Bannister, Patricia V.
Vesaas, Tarjei 1897-1970 Obituary 29-32R
See also CLC 48
Vesely, Erik 1905(?)-1970 Obituary 57-60
Vesenyi, Paul E. 1911- 53-56
Vesey, Godfrey (Norman Agmondisham)
1923- 89-92
Vesey, Paul
See Allen, Samuel W(ashington)
Vesey-FitzGerald, Brian Seymour
1900-1981 104
Obituary 105
Vesper, Karl H(ampton) 1932- 115
Vess, David M(arshall) 1925- 89-92
Vessel, Matthew F. 1912- Brief entry 108
Vesselo, I(saac) Reginald 1903- CAP-2
Earlier sketch in CA 17-18
Vestal, David 1924- 89-92
Vestal, Edith Ballard 1884-1970 CAP-2
Earlier sketch in CA 25-28
Vestdijk, Simon 1898-1971 Obituary 89-92
Vester, Frederic 1925- 120
Vester, Horatio 1906-1985 CAP-1
Obituary 117
Earlier sketch in CA 13-14
Vesterman, William 1942- 89-92
Vestly, Anne-Cath(arina) 1920- CANR-18
Earlier sketch in CA 85-88
See also SATA 14
Vet, T. V.
See Straiton, E(dward) C(ornock)
Vetere, Richard 1952- 104
Vetoe, Miklos 1936- 49-52
Vetter, Carole 1939- 25-28R
Vetter, Harold J. 1926- 29-32R
Vetterling-Braggin, Mary (Katherine) 1947- 124
Veverka, Frank B. 1923(?)-1985 Obituary 117
Vevers, (Henry) Gwynne 1916-1988 113
Obituary 126
See also SATA 45
Vexillum
See Banner, Hubert Stewart
Veysey, Laurence R(uss) 1932- 21-22R
Vezhinov, Pavel
See Gouaov, Nikola Delchev
Vial, Fernand (Louis) 1905- CANR-21
Earlier sketch in CA 3R
Vialis, Gaston
See Simenon, Georges (Jacques
Christian)
Vian, Boris 1920-1959 Brief entry 106
See also DLB 72
See also TCLC 9
Viano, Emilio C. 1942- 107
Viansson-Ponte, Pierre 1920-1979 101
Obituary 85-88
Viator, Vacuus
See Hughes, Thomas
Viaud, (Louis Marie) Julien 1850-1923
Brief entry 107
Vicar, Henry
See Felsen, Henry Gregor
Vicarion, Count Palmiro
See Logue, Christopher
Vicary, Dorothy
See Rice, Dorothy Mary
Vichas, Robert P. 1933- CANR-14
Earlier sketch in CA 29-32R
Vicker, Angus
See Felsen, Henry Gregor
Vicker, Ray 1917- 61-64
Vickers
See Kaufman, Wallace
Vickers, Antoinette L. 1942- 103
Vickers, Douglas 1924- CANR-11
Earlier sketch in CA 13-14R
Vickers, (Charles) Geoffrey 1894-1982 41-44R
Obituary 106
Vickers, Hugo (Ralph) 1951- Brief entry 124
Vickers, John 1916- 9-10R
Vickery, Donald M(ichael) 1944- 101
Vickery, Florence E. 1906- 37-40R
Vickery, John B. 1925- 57-60
Vickery, Kate
See Kennedy, T(eresa) A.
Vickery, Olga W(estland) 1925-1970 CANR-3
Earlier sketch in CA 1R
Vickery, Robert L. (Jr.) 1932- 49-52
Vickery, Tom Rusk 1935- 53-56
Vickrey, William (Spencer) 1914- 41-44R
Victor, Charles B.
See Puechner, Ray
Victor, Edward 1914- CANR-3
Earlier sketch in CA 4R
See also SATA 3
Victor, Joan Berg 1942- 105
See also SATA 30
Victor, Sam
See Hershman, Morris
Victoria 1819-1901 DLB-55
Vida, Nina 1933- 117
Vidal, Gore 1925- CANR-13
Earlier sketch in CA 7-8R
See also DLB 6
See also CLC 2, 4, 6, 8, 10, 22, 33
See also AITN 1
Vidal, Nicole 1928- 25-28R
Vidaver, Doris 108
Vidger, Leonard P(erry) 1920- CANR-5
Earlier sketch in CA 9-10R
Vidich, Arthur J. 1922- 115
Vidler, Alec R.
See Vidler, Alexander Roper
Vidler, Alexander Roper 1899- CANR-5
Earlier sketch in CA 5-6R
Vidler, Virginia (Ellen) 1928-1986 69-72
Obituary 121
Vidor, King (Wallis) 1894(?)-1982
Obituary 108
Viebig, Clara 1860-1952 DLB-66
Vieg, John A.
See Vieg, John Albert
Vieg, John Albert 1904-1988 3R
Obituary 124
Vier, Gene 1926- 105
Viereck, Ellen K. 1928- 53-56
See also SATA 14
Viereck, George Sylvester 1884-1962
Obituary 116
See also DLB 54
Viereck, Peter (Robert Edwin) 1916- CANR-1
Earlier sketch in CA 3R
See also DLB 5
See also CLC 4
Viereck, Phillip 1925- CANR-8
Earlier sketch in CA 7-8R
See also SATA 3
Viertel, Janet 1915- 53-56
See also SATA 10
Viertel, Joseph 1915- 15-16R
Viertel, Peter 1920- 15-16R
Viessman, Warren, Jr. 1930- 53-56
Vieth, David M(uench) 1925- 5-6R
Vieth von Golssenau, Arnold Friedrich
1889-1979 89-92
Vietor, John A(dolf) 1914-1982 Obituary 108
Viets, Wallace T(rowbridge) 1919- 17-18R
Vig, Norman Joseph 1939- 25-28R
Vigeland, Carl A. 1947- 122
Vigeveno, H(enk) S. 1925- 108
Vigfusson, Robin 1949- 106
Viggiani
See Viggiani, Guy
Viggiani, Guy 1932- 123
Vigil, Lawrence
See Finnin, (Olive) Mary
Vigliante, Mary
See Szydlowski, Mary Vigliante
Viglini, Janelle (Therese) 1933- 57-60
Vigna, Judith 1936- CANR-13
Earlier sketch in CA 77-80
See also SATA 15
Vigneault, Gilles 1928- DLB-60
Vigneras, Louis-Andre 1903- 65-68
Vigness, David M(artell) 1922- 15-16R
Vigness, Paul G. 1894- 41-44R
Vignone, Joseph A. 1939- 37-40R
Viguers, Ruth Hill 1903-1971 CAP-1
Obituary 29-32R
Earlier sketch in CA 15-16
See also SATA 6
Vikis-Freibergs, Vaira 1937- 53-56
Viksnins, George J(uris) 1937- 105
Viktoria Luise 1892-1980 Obituary 102
Vila, Bob
See Vila, Robert
Vila, Robert 1946- 106
Vilar, Esther 1935- CANR-8
Earlier sketch in CA 49-52
Vildrac, Charles
See Messager, Charles
Viljoen, Helen Gill 1899-1974 45-48
Obituary 103
Vilkitis, James R(ichard) 1941- 61-64
Villa, Jose Garcia 1914- CANR-12
Earlier sketch in CA 25-28R
Villa, Susie Hoogasian
See Hoogasian-Villa, Susie
Villada, Gene Harold Bell
See Bell-Villada, Gene Harold
Villa-Gilbert, Mariana 1937- 29-32R
Villanueva, Tino 1941- CANR-1
Earlier sketch in CA 45-48
Villard, Henry 1835-1900 DLB-23
Villard, Henry Hilgard 1911-1983 Obituary 111
Villard, Henry S(errano) 1900- 17-18R
Villard, Oswald Garrison 1872-1949
Brief entry 113
See also DLB 25
Villarejo, Mary (Holan) 1915- 11-12R
Villarejo, Oscar M(ilton) 1909- 19-20R
Villars, Elizabeth
See Feldman, Ellen (Bette)
Villas Boas, Claudio 1916- Brief entry 117
Villas Boas, Orlando 1914- Brief entry 117
Villasenor, David V. 1913- 13-14R
Villasenor, Victor Edmund 1940- 45-48
Villegas, Daniel Cosio 1898-1976
Obituary 65-68
Villemaire, Yolande 1949- DLB-60
Villere, Sidney Louis 1900- 69-72
Villers, Raymond 1911- CAP-2
Earlier sketch in CA 25-28
Villers, Robert 1921-1980 Obituary 93-96
Villet, Barbara 1931- 85-88
Villiard, Paul 1910-1974 CANR-10
Obituary 53-56
Earlier sketches in CA 25-28, CAP-2
See also SATA 20, 51
Villiers, Alan (John) 1903- CANR-1
Earlier sketch in CA 4R
See also SATA 10
Villiers, Guy
See Goulding, Peter Geoffrey
Villiers, Marjorie 1903-1982 Obituary 107
Villoldo, Alberto Pedro 1949- 108
Vilmorin, Louise Leveque de 1902-1969
Obituary 104
Vilnay, Zev 1900-1988 Obituary 124
Vinacke, W(illiam) Edgar 1917- 5-6R
Vinal, Harold 1891-1965 Obituary 89-92
Vinaver, Eugene 1899- 13-14R
Vincent, Adrian 1917- 2R
Vincent, Charles 1945- 65-68
Vincent, Claire
See Allen, Charlotte Vale
Vincent, Clark E(dward) 1923- CANR-2
Earlier sketch in CA 4R
Vincent, E. Lee
See Vincent, Elizabeth Lee
Vincent, Elizabeth Lee 1897- CAP-2
Earlier sketch in CA 19-20
Vincent, Eric Douglas 1953- SATA-40
Vincent, Felix 1946- 118
See also SATA 41
Vincent, Gabrielle (a pseudonym) 126
See also CLR 13
Vincent, Howard Paton 1904- 65-68
Vincent, Jack 1904- 29-32R
Vincent, Jack E(rnest) 1932- CANR-19
Earlier sketch in CA 102
Vincent, Joan 1920- 21-22R
Vincent, John Carter 1900-1972
Obituary 37-40R
Vincent, John J(ames) 1929- CANR-26
Earlier sketches in CA 57-60, CANR-10
Vincent, John R(ussell) 1937- 120
Vincent, Leona
See Vincent, Elizabeth Lee
Vincent, Mary Keith
See St. John, Wylly Folk
Vincent, Peter 1944- 37-40R
Vincent, R(aymond) J(ohn) 1943- 77-80
Vincent, Theodore G. 1936- CANR-13
Earlier sketch in CA 77-80
Vincent, William R.
See Heitzmann, William Ray
Vincent, William S(hafer) 1907- 41-44R
Vinciguerra, Mario 1887-1973 Obituary 104
Vincitorio, Gaetano L(eonard) 1921- 89-92
Vine, Barbara 1930- CLC-50
Vine, Louis L(loyd) 1922- CANR-3
Earlier sketch in CA 3R
Vine, Paul Ashley Laurence 1927- 23-24R
Vine, Sarah
See Rowland, D(onald) S(ydney)
Vineberg, Arthur 1903- 104
Vineberg, Arthur (Martin) 1903-1988 104
Obituary 125
Vineberg, Ethel (Shane) 1902- 85-88
Vinegar, Tom
See Gregg, Andrew K.
Viner, George 1913(?)-1983 Obituary 109
Viner, Jacob 1892-1970 Obituary 104
Vines, Alice Gilmore 1923- 81-84
Vines, (Henry) Ellsworth (Jr.) 1911-
Brief entry 109
Vinest, Shaw
See Longyear, Barry Brookes
Viney, Wayne 1932- 103
Vineyard, Edwin Earle 1926- 5-6R
Vinge, Joan D(ennison) 1948- 93-96
See also SATA 36
See also CLC 30
Vinge, Vernor (Steffen) 1944- 101
Vining, Elizabeth Gray 1902- CANR-7
Earlier sketch in CA 7-8R
See also SATA 6
Vinogradov, Ivan M(atveyevich)
1891-1983 Obituary 109
Vinokur, Grigory
See Weinrauch, Herschel
Vinokurov, Yevgeny Mikhailovich 1925-
Brief entry 116
Vinson, Elaine
See Rowland, D(onald) S(ydney)
Vinson, J(ohn) Chal(mers) 1919- 11-12R
Vinson, J(ohn) William 1916-1979
Obituary 89-92
Vinson, James (Albert) 1933- 120
Brief entry 118
Vinson, Jane 1927- 77-80
Vinson, Kathryn 1911- 5-6R
See also SATA 21
Vinson, Rex Thomas 1935- 101
Vinton, Bobby
See Vinton, Stanley Robert, Jr.
Vinton, Eleanor W(inthrop) 1899-1977 61-64
Obituary 73-76
Vinton, Iris 1906(?)-1988 77-80
Obituary 124
See also SATA 24
Vinton, John 1937- 73-76
Vinton, Stanley Robert, Jr. 1935(?)-
Brief entry 120
Vinyard, C. Dale 1932- 25-28R
Vinz, Mark 1942- 93-96
Viola, Herman J(oseph) 1938- CANR-23
Earlier sketches in CA 61-64, CANR-8
Violett, Ellen 1925- 73-76
Violi, Paul 1944- CANR-24
Earlier sketch in CA 45-48
Violis, G.
See Simenon, Georges (Jacques
Christian)
Viorst, Judith 1931- CANR-26
Earlier sketches in CA 49-52, CANR-2
See also SATA 7
See also DLB 52
See also CLR 3
Viorst, Milton 1930- CANR-26
Earlier sketch in CA 9-10R
Vip
See Partch, Virgil Franklin II
Vipond, Don (Harry) 1932- 65-68
Vipont, Charles
See Foulds, Elfrida Vipont
Vipont, Elfrida
See Foulds, Elfrida Vipont
Virga, Vincent 1942- 107
Virgines, George E. 1920- CANR-12
Earlier sketch in CA 25-28R
Virginius
See Connett, Eugene Virginius III
Virtanen, Reino 1910- CANR-4
Earlier sketch in CA 3R
Vis, William Ryerson 1886-1969 Obituary 110
Viscardi, Henry, Jr. 1912- CANR-5
Earlier sketch in CA 5-6R
Vischer, Helen (Cassin Lombard) Carusi
1905(?)-1986 Obituary 119
Visconti, Luchino 1906-1976 81-84
Obituary 65-68
See also CLC 16
Viscott, David S(teven) 1938- CANR-26
Earlier sketch in CA 29-32R
See also AITN 1
Visher, Emily B. 1918- 109
Visher, Halene Hatcher 1909- 45-48
Visher, John Sargent 1921- 109
Vishniak, Mark 1883-1976 Obituary 69-72
Vishny, Michele 1932- 69-72
Visocchi, Mark 1938- CANR-16
Earlier sketch in CA 93-96
Visscher, Maurice B(olks) 1901- 77-80
Visser, Margaret 1940- 123
Visser, W(illem) F(rederik) H(endrik)
1900-1968 CAP-2
Earlier sketch in CA 25-28
See also SATA 10
Visser 't Hooft, Willem Adolf 1900-1985 9-10R
Obituary 116
Visson, Vladimir 1905(?)-1976 Obituary 69-72
Vita-Finzi, Claudio 1936- 89-92
Vital, David 1927- CANR-12
Earlier sketch in CA 29-32R
Vitale, Joseph T(homas) 1951- 107
Vitale, Philip H. 1913- 17-18R
Vitek, John D(ennis) 1942- 124
Vitelli, James R(obert) 1920- 29-32R
Vitezovic, Tomislav
See Kuehnelt-Leddihn, Erik (Maria) Ritter
von

Vittengl, Morgan John 1928- 7-8R
Vittorini, Elio 1908-1966 Obituary 25-28R
See also CLC 6, 9, 14
Vitzthum, Richard Carleton 1936- 103
Vivante, Arturo 1923- CANR-10
Earlier sketch in CA 17-18R
Vivante, Paolo 1921- 29-32R
Vivas, Eliseo 1901- CANR-5
Earlier sketch in CA 7-8R
Viveash, Cherry Jacqueline Lee 1929- CAP-1
Earlier sketch in CA 9-10
Vivers, Eileen Elliott 1905- 41-44R
Vivian, Cordy Tindell 1924- 49-52
Vivian, Francis
See Ashley, (Arthur) Ernest
Viviano, Benedict T(homas) 1940- CANR-10
Earlier sketch in CA 23-24R
Vivienne
See Entwistle, Florence Vivienne
Vizard, Stephen
See James, (David) Burnett (Stephen)
Vizedom, Monika B(asch) 1929- 69-72
Vizenor, Gerald Robert 1934- CANR-21
Earlier sketches in CA 13-14R, CANR-5
Vizinczey, Stephen 1933- CLC-40
Vizzard, Jack
See Vizzard, John Anthony
Vizzard, John Anthony 1914- 29-32R
Vizzini, Salvatore 1926- 103
Vlach, John Michael 1948- 123
Vladeck, Bruce C. 1949- 101
Vladimirov, Leonid
See Finkelstein, Leonid Vladimirovitch
Vladimov, G.
See Vladimov, Georgii Nikolaevich
Vladimov, Georgii
See Vladimov, Georgii Nikolaevich
Vladimov, Georgii Nikolaevich 1931- 123
Vlahos, Olivia 1924- 21-22R
See also SATA 31
Vlasic, Bob
See Hirsch, Phil
Vlasic, Ivan Albert 1926- 9-10R
Vliet, R(ussell) G(ordon) 1929-1984 CANR-18
Obituary 112
Earlier sketch in CA 37-40R
See also CLC 22
Vlock, Laurel F(ox) 37-40R
Vloyantes, John P. 1918- 61-64
Voaden, Herman Arthur 1903- 103
Vo-Dinh, Mai 1933- CANR-13
Earlier sketch in CA 77-80
See also SATA 16
Vodola, Thomas M(ichael) 1925- CANR-19
Earlier sketches in CA 49-52, CANR-3
Voegeli, V(ictor) Jacque 1934- 21-22R
Voegelin, Eric 1901-1985 Obituary 114
Voehringer, Erich F(rederick)
1905-1973 CANR-2
Obituary 41-44R
Earlier sketch in CA 3R
Voeks, Virginia (Wilna) 1921- 15-16R
Voelcker, Hunce 1940- 77-80
Voelkel, Robert T(ownsend) 1933- 25-28R
Voelker, John D(onaldson) 1903- 4R
Voellner, Louada McCaughen
1888(?)-1986 Obituary 119
Vogau, Boris Andreyevich 1894-1937(?)
Brief entry 123
Vogel, Alfred T(ennyson) 1906- 104
Vogel, Arthur A(nton) 1924- CANR-10
Earlier sketch in CA 25-28R
Vogel, Dan 1927- 120
Vogel, David 1947- CANR-11
Earlier sketch in CA 65-68
Vogel, Ezra F. 1930- 13-14R
Vogel, Helen Wolff 1918- 19-20R
Vogel, Ilse-Margret 1918- CANR-7
Earlier sketch in CA 15-16R
See also SATA 14
Vogel, Irving L. 1918- 122
Vogel, Jerry 1896(?)-1980 Obituary 101
Vogel, John H., Jr. 1950- 77-80
See also SATA 18
Vogel, Linda Jane 1940- 61-64
Vogel, Lucy E(laine) 49-52
Vogel, Paula A(nne) 1951- 108
Vogel, Speed
See Vogel, Irving L.
Vogel, Stanley M(orton) 1921- 77-80
Vogel, Steven 1940- 53-56
Vogel, Victor H(ugh) 1905-1978 CANR-3
Earlier sketch in CA 4R
Vogel, Virgil (Howard) J(oseph) 1918- CANR-10
Earlier sketch in CA 25-28R
Vogeler, Ingolf 1944- 107
Vogelgesang, Sandra Louise 1942- 57-60
Vogelgesang, Sandy
See Vogelgesang, Sandra Louise
Vogelman, Joyce 1936- 106
Vogelsang, Arthur 1942- 49-52
Vogelsinger, Hubert 1938- 25-28R
Vogenitz, David George 1930- 41-44R
Vogt, Fred W. 1913- 61-64
Vogler, Roger E. 1938- 126
Vogt, Bill
See Vogt, William McKinley
Vogt, Esther Loewen 1915- CANR-7
Earlier sketch in CA 17-18R
See also SATA 14
Vogt, Evon Zartman, Jr. 1918- 69-72
Vogt, Gregory SATA-45
Vogt, Joseph 1895- Brief entry 112
Vogt, Marie Bollinger 1921- 57-60
See also SATA 45
Vogt, William McKinley 1935- 89-92
Voight, Virginia Frances 1909- CANR-18
Earlier sketches in CA 7-8R, CANR-2
See also SATA 8
Voigt, Cynthia 1942- CANR-18
Earlier sketch in CA 106
See also SATA 33, 48
See also CLC 30
See also CLR 13
Voigt, David Quentin 1926- CANR-14
Earlier sketch in CA 41-44R
Voigt, Ellen Bryant 1943- CANR-11
Earlier sketch in CA 69-72
Voigt, Erna 1925- SATA-35
Voigt, Karsten D. 1941- 113
Voigt, Lieselotte E. Kurth
See Kurth-Voigt, Lieselotte E.
Voigt, Melvin J(ohn) 1911- CANR-5
Earlier sketch in CA 15-16R
Voigt, Milton 1924- 11-12R
Voigt, Robert J(oseph) 1916- 93-96
Voigt, William, Jr. 1902- 73-76
Voigt-Rother, Erna
See Voigt, Erna
Voils, Jessie Wiley CAP-2
Earlier sketch in CA 29-32
Voinovich, Vladimir (Nikolaevich) 1932- 81-84
See also CLC 10, 49
Voitle, Robert (Brown, Jr.) 1919- 2R
Vojtech, Anna 1946- SATA-42
Volbach, Walther R(ichard) 1897- 29-32R
Volcker, Paul A(dolph) 1927- Brief entry 114
Volgyes, Ivan 1936- CANR-20
Earlier sketch in CA 104
Volin, Michael 1911- 101
Volk, Hannah Marie
See Wormington, H(annah) M(arie)
Volkan, Vamik D(jemal) 1932- CANR-19
Earlier sketch in CA 102
Volkart, Edmund H(owell) 1919- 21-22R
Volkening, Henry T. 1902-1972
Obituary 37-40R
Volker, Roger 1934- 53-56
Volker, Roy 1924- 57-60
Volkoff, Vladimir 1932- 73-76
Volkov, Leon 1920(?)-1974 Obituary 45-48
Vollert, Cyril (Oscar) 1901- 61-64
Vollmer, Howard M. 1928- CANR-13
Earlier sketch in CA 19-20R
Voloshinov, Vladimir
See Bakhtin, Mikhail (Mikhailovich)
Volpe, E(rminio) Peter 1927- CANR-15
Earlier sketch in CA 37-40R
Volpe, Edmond L(oris) 1922- CANR-1
Earlier sketch in CA 3R
Voltz, Jeanne Appleton 1920- CANR-21
Earlier sketch in CA 104
Volz, Carl (Andrew) 1933- 29-32R
Volz, Marlin M(ilton) 1917- 37-40R
von Abele, Rudolph (Radama) 1922- 104
von Baeyer, Hans C(hristian) 1938- 117
von Balthasar, Hans Urs 1905-1988
Obituary 125
Brief entry 106
von Berg, J(ohan) F(riedrich) ?-1983(?)
Obituary 108
von Bertalanffy, Ludwig 1901-1972 CAP-2
Earlier sketch in CA 25-28
von Block, Bela W(illiam) 1922- 104
von Block, Sylvia 1931- CANR-7
Earlier sketch in CA 53-56
von Bothmer, Dietrich Felix 1918- 106
von Brand, Theodor C. 1900(?)-1978
Obituary 81-84
Von Braun, Wernher 1912-1977 CANR-9
Obituary 69-72
Earlier sketch in CA 7-8R
von Castlehun, Friedl
See Marion, Frieda
von Cube, Irmgard 1900(?)-1977
Obituary 73-76
von Daeniken, Erich 1935- CANR-17
Earlier sketch in CA 37-40R
See also CLC 30
See also AITN 1
von Daniken, Erich
See von Daeniken, Erich
See also CLC 30
von der Gruen, Max 1926- DLB-75
von der Mehden, Fred R. 1927- 11-12R
von Doderer, Heimito 1896-1966
Obituary 25-28R
Vondra, Josef Gert 1941- 104
von Dreele, W(illiam) H(enry) 1924- 93-96
von Eckardt, Ursula M(aria) 1925- 13-14R
Von Eckardt, Wolf 1918- 7-8R
Von Elsner, Don Byron 1909- 3R
von Ende, Richard Chaffey 1907- 103
von Euler, Ulf (Svante) 1905-1983
Obituary 109
von Frank, Albert J(ames) 1945- 120
von Franz, Marie-Louise 1915- 85-88
von Frisch, Karl (Ritter)
See Frisch, Karl (Ritter) von
von Frisch, Otto 1929- 101
von Furstenberg, Egon (Edvard) 1946- 102
von Furstenberg, George Michael
1941- CANR-10
Earlier sketch in CA 65-68
von Glahn, Gerhard E(rnst) 1911- 15-16R
von Gronicka, Andre 1912- 25-28R
von Grunebaum, G(ustave) E(dmund)
1909-1972 CANR-3
Earlier sketch in CA 2R
Von Gunden, Heidi Cecilia 1940- 125
Vo Nguyen Giap 1912(?)- Brief entry 115
von Habsburg-Lothringen, Geza Louis
Eusebius Gebhard Ralphael Albert Maria
1940- 105
Von Hagen, Victor Wolfgang 1908- 105
See also SATA 29
von Hayek, Friedrich A.
See Hayek, Friedrich August von
von Heidenstam, (Carl Gustaf) Verner
See Heidenstam, (Carl Gustaf) Verner
von
von Heller, Marcus
See Zachary, Hugh
von Hertzen, Heikki 1913- 37-40R
von Heyse, Paul (Johann Ludwig)
See Heyse, Paul (Johann Ludwig von)
von Hildebrand, Alice 1923- 21-22R
von Hildebrand, Dietrich 1889-1977 CANR-10
Obituary 69-72
Earlier sketch in CA 17-18R
Von Hilsheimer, George E(dwin III)
1934- 29-32R
von Hippel, Frank 1937- 93-96
von Hirsch, Andrew 1934- CANR-14
Earlier sketch in CA 81-84
von Hofe, Harold 1912- CANR-4
Earlier sketch in CA 3R
von Hoffman, Nicholas 1929- 81-84
von Hofmannsthal, Hugo
See Hofmannsthal, Hugo von
von Horn, Carl 1903- CAP-2
Earlier sketch in CA 21-22
von Horvath, Odon
See Horvath, Oedoen von
von Horvath, Oedoen
See Horvath, Oedoen von
von Kaschnitz-Weinberg, Marie Luise
1901-1974 Obituary 93-96
Von Klemperer, Klemens 1916- 23-24R
von Klopp, Vahrah
See Malvern, Gladys
von Koenigswald, (Gustav Heinrich) Ralph
1902-1982 Obituary 110
von Koerber, Hans Nordewin 1886- 41-44R
von Lang, Jochen
See von Lang-Piechocki, Joachim
von Lang-Piechocki, Joachim 1925- 101
von Laue, Max Theodor Felix
See Laue, Max Theodor Felix von
Von Laue, Theodore Herman 1916- 11-12R
von le Fort, Gertrud (Petrea)
See le Fort, Gertrud (Petrea) von
Von Leyden, Wolfgang Marius 1911- CANR-3
Earlier sketch in CA 5-6R
von Liliencron, (Friedrich Adolf Axel) Detlev
See Liliencron, (Friedrich Adolf Axel)
Detlev von
von Maltitz, Horst 1905- 77-80
Von Manstein, Erich 1887-1973 Obituary 45-48
von Meck, Galina 1891-1985 Obituary 116
von Mehren, Arthur T(aylor) 1922- 17-18R
von Mendelssohn, Felix 1918- 15-16R
Von Mering, Otto Oswald, Jr. 1922- 1R
von Miklos, Josephine Bogdan 1900-1972
Obituary 37-40R
von Mises, Ludwig (Edler)
See Mises, Ludwig (Edler) von
von Mises, Margit
See Mises, Margit von
Von Mohrenschildt, Dimitri Sergius 1902-
Brief entry 106
Von Molnar, Geza (Walter Elemer)
1932- 29-32R
von Moltke, Konrad 1941- CANR-19
Earlier sketch in CA 101
Von Moschzisker, Michael 1918- 37-40R
Vonnegut, Kurt, Jr. 1922- CANR-25
Earlier sketches in CA 3R, CANR-1
See also DLB 2, 8
See also DLBY 80
See also DLBD 3
See also CLC 1, 2, 3, 4, 5, 8, 12, 22,
40
See also AITN 1
Vonnegut, Mark 1947- 65-68
See also AITN 2
von Neumann, John 1903-1957
Brief entry 117
von Ost, Henry Lerner 1915- 101
Von Rachen, Kurt
See Hubbard, L(afayette) Ron(ald)
von Rad, Gerhard 1901-1971 Obituary 104
von Rago, Louis J(oseph)
See Rago, Louis J(oseph von)
Von Rauch, Georg 1904- 73-76
von Rezzori (d'Arezzo), Gregor
See Rezzori (d'Arezzo), Gregor von
von Rhein, John (Richard) 1945- 120
von Riekhoff, Harald 1937- 89-92
Von Rosenstiel, Helene 1944- 105
Von Salis, Jean-R. 1901- 21-22R
von Salomon, Ernst 1902-1972
Obituary 37-40R
von Schilcher, Florian 1944- 118
von Schlabrendorff, Fabian 1907-1980
Obituary 105
von Schmidt, Eric 1931- CANR-13
Earlier sketch in CA 17-18R
See also SATA 36, 50
Von Schmidt, Harold 1896(?)-1982
Obituary 107
von Schoenhoff, Ulrike
See Frank, Rudolf
von Schuschnigg, Kurt 1897-1977 103
von Schwarzenfeld, Gertrude
See Cochrane de Alencar, Gertrude E. L.
von Staden, Heinrich 1939- 37-40R
von Staden, Wendelgard 1925- 110
von Sternberg, Josef
See Sternberg, Josef von
von Storch, Anne B. 1910- CAP-2
Earlier sketch in CA 29-32
See also SATA 1
von Trapp, Maria Augusta 1905-1987 81-84
Obituary 122
von Trotta, Margarethe 1942- 126
Von Unruh, Fritz 1885-1970 Obituary 29-32R
See also DLB 56
von Wangenheim, Chris 1942-1981
Obituary 103
von Weizsaecker, Carl Friedrich 1912- 105
von Wiegand, Charmion 1898(?)-1983
Obituary 110
Von Wiren-Garczynski, Vera 1931- 41-44R
von Wodtke, Charlotte Buel Johnson
1918-1982 112
von Wohl-Musciny, Ludwig
See de Wohl, Louis
von Wright, G(eorg) H(enrik)
See Wright, G(eorg) H(enrik) von
von Wuthenau, Alexander 1900- 65-68
von Zuehlsdorff, Volkmar J(ohannes)
1912- CANR-20
Earlier sketch in CA 7-8R
Vooren, Monique Van
See Van Vooren, Monique
Voorhees, Richard J(oseph) 1916- 5-6R
Voorhies, Barbara 1939- 104
Voorhis, Horace Jeremiah 1901-1984 CANR-6
Obituary 113
Earlier sketch in CA 3R
Voorhis, Jerry
See Voorhis, Horace Jeremiah
Voos, Henry 1928- 25-28R
Vorhees, Melvin B. 1904(?)-1977
Obituary 69-72
Vorobeva, Maria 1892-1984 Obituary 113
Vorpahl, Ben Merchant 1937- 41-44R
Vorspan, Albert 1924- CANR-13
Earlier sketch in CA 23-24R
Vorster, Gordon 1924- CLC-34
Vorzimmer, Peter J. 1937- 93-96
Vos, Clarence J(ohn) 1920- 45-48
Vos, Nelvin (LeRoy) 1932- 19-20R
Vosburgh, Leonard (W.) 1912- SATA-15
Vose, Clement E(llery) 1923-1985 41-44R
Obituary 115
Vose, Ruth Hurst 1944- CANR-26
Earlier sketch in CA 109
Voskovec, George 1905-1981 Obituary 104
Voskuil, Dennis N(eal) 1944- 112
Voss, Carl Hermann 1910- CANR-10
Earlier sketch in CA 21-22R
Voss, E(rnst) Theodore 1928- 37-40R
Voss, Earl H. 1922- 9-10R
Voss, George L. 1922- 57-60
Voss, James F(rederick) 1930- 41-44R
Voss, Thomas M(ichael) 1945- 105
Votaw, Dow 1920- 19-20R
Voureka, Amalia
See Fleming, Amalia
Vournakis, John N(icholas) 1939- 57-60
Voute, J. Peter 1906- 125
Vowles, Richard B(eckman) 1917- 25-28R
Voyageur
See Allen, Cecil J(ohn)
Voyce, Arthur 1889- CAP-1
Earlier sketch in CA 13-14
Voyle, Mary
See Manning, Rosemary (Joy)
Voynich, Ethel Lillian (Boole) 1864-1960
Obituary 104
Voysey, Margaret 1945- 108
Voysey, Michael 1920-1987 Obituary 123
Voznesensky, Andrei 1933- 89-92
See also CLC 1, 15
Vrba, Rudolf 1924- 21-22R
Vrbovska, Anca 1905- 81-84
Vredenburg, Harvey L. 1921- 25-28R
Vreeland, Diana Dalziel 1903(?)- 111
Vreeland, Jane D. 1915- 21-22R
Vrettos, Theodore 1919- 15-16R
Vreuls, Diane 57-60
Vries, Anne de
See de Vries, Anne
Vries, Leonard de 1919- 113
Vroman, Leo 1915- 49-52
Vroman, Mary Elizabeth (Gibson)
1923-1967 125
Obituary 109
See also BW
See also DLB 33
Vroom, Victor H(arold) 1932- 11-12R
Vrooman, Jack Rochford 1929- 45-48
Vryonis, Speros (P.), Jr. 1928- 85-88
Vucinich, Alexander S. 1914- Brief entry 109
Vucinich, Wayne S. 1913- 13-14R
Vugteveen, Verna Aardema 1911- CANR-18
Earlier sketches in CA 7-8R, CANR-3
Vuilleumier, Marion 1918- 81-84
Vujica, Stanko M(irko) 1909-1976 41-44R
Vulliamy, Colwyn Edward 1886-1971
Obituary 89-92
Vuong, Lynette Dyer 1938- 117
Vuong g(ia) Thuy 1938- 69-72
Vyn, Kathleen 1949- 89-92
Vyverberg, Henry (Sabin) 1921- 109
Vyvyan, C(lara) C(oltman Rogers) 1885- CAP-1
Earlier sketch in CA 9-10
Vyvyan, Nigel
See Nevill, Barry St-John

W

Waage, Frederick 1943- 104
Waagenaar, Sam 1908- 57-60

Waber, Bernard 1924- CANR-2
Earlier sketch in CA 3R
See also SATA 40, 47
Wabun
See James, Marlise Ann
Wacher, J(ohn) S(tewart) 1927- 125
Brief entry 105
Wachhorst, Wyn 1938- 106
Wachs, Mark Marshall 1933- 25-28R
Wachs, Saul P(hilip) 1931- 112
Wachsmann, Klaus Philipp 1907-
Brief entry 106
Wachtel, Albert 1939- 123
Wachtel, Howard M(artin) 1938- 49-52
Wachtel, Isidore H. 1909(?)-1979
Obituary 89-92
Wachtel, Paul L(awrence) 1940- 115
Wachter, Oralee (Roberts) 1935- 122
See also SATA 51
Wachter, Susan M. 1943- 120
Waciuma, Wanjohi 1938- 77-80
Wacker, Charles H(enry), Jr. 1925- 73-76
Wackerbarth, Marjorie CAP-1
Earlier sketch in CA 13-14
Wadbrook, William P. 1933- 45-48
Waddams, Herbert Montague 1911-1972
Obituary 107
Waddell, D(avid) A(lan) G(ilmour)
1927- CANR-23
Earlier sketch in CA 2R
Waddell, Eric (Wilson) 1939- 45-48
Waddell, Evelyn Margaret 1918- 53-56
See also SATA 10
Waddell, Helen (Jane) 1889-1965 102
Waddell, Jack O('Brien) 1933- 33-36R
Waddell, Martin 1941- 113
See also SATA 43
Waddington, C(onrad) H(al) 1905-1975 CANR-6
Obituary 61-64
Earlier sketch in CA 13-14R
Waddington, Miriam 1917- CANR-12
Earlier sketch in CA 21-22R
See also DLB 68
See also CLC 28
Waddington, Raymond B(ruce) 1935- 53-56
Waddy, Charis 1909- 69-72
Waddy, Lawrence H(eber) 1914- CANR-7
Earlier sketch in CA 13-14R
Wade, Alan
See Vance, John Holbrook
Wade, Bob
See Wade, Robert (Allison)
Wade, Carlson 1928- 29-32R
Wade, David 1929- 103
Wade, E(ileen) K(irkpatrick) 1892(?)-1985
Obituary 117
Wade, Edwin L. 1940- 126
Wade, Francis C(larence) 1907- CAP-1
Earlier sketch in CA 13-14
Wade, Graham 1940- CANR-25
Earlier sketch in CA 107
Wade, Harry Vincent 1894-1973 Obituary 89-92
Wade, Henry
See Aubrey-Fletcher, Henry Lancelot
Wade, Henry William Rawson 1918- 109
Wade, Herbert
See Wales, Hugh Gregory
Wade, Hugh Mason 1913-1986 Obituary 118
Wade, Ira Owen 1896-1983 73-76
Obituary 109
Wade, Jennifer
See Wehen, Joy DeWeese
Wade, Jerry L(ee) 1941- 53-56
Wade, Jewel Millsap 1937- Brief entry 107
Wade, Joanna
See Berckman, Evelyn Domenica
Wade, John Stevens 1927- CANR-6
Earlier sketch in CA 13-14R
Wade, Kit
See Carson, Xanthus
Wade, L(arry) L(ee) 1935- 33-36R
Wade, Mason 1913- 11-12R
Wade, Nicholas (Michael Landon)
1942- CANR-16
Earlier sketch in CA 77-80
Wade, Rex A(rvin) 1936- 61-64
Wade, Richard Clement 1922- 17-18R
Wade, Robert (Allison) 1920- 108
Wade, Robert
See McIlwain, David
Wade, Rosalind Herschel 1909- CAP-1
Earlier sketch in CA 9-10
Wade, Theodore E., Jr. 1936- SATA-37
Wade, (Henry) William (Rawson) 1918- CANR-4
Earlier sketch in CA 4R
Wade, Wyn Craig 1944- 103
Wadekin, Karl-Eugen
See Waedekin, Karl-Eugen
Wadepuhl, Walter 1895- 61-64
Wadia, Maneck S(orabji) 1931- CANR-13
Earlier sketch in CA 19-20R
Wadinasi, Sedeka
See Nall, Hiram Abiff
Wadley, Susan S(now) 1943- 77-80
Wadlington, Walter 1931- 33-36R
Wadlington, Warwick 1938- 73-76
Wadsworth, Barry James 1935- 37-40R
Wadsworth, Frank W(hittemore) 1919- 11-12R
Wadsworth, James J(eremiah)
1905-1984 CAP-2
Obituary 112
Earlier sketch in CA 19-20
Wadsworth, Jerry
See Wadsworth, James J(eremiah)
Wadsworth, M(arshall) D. 1936- 45-48
Wadsworth, Michael E(dwin) J(ohn)
1942- 93-96
Wadsworth, Nelson B(ingham) 1930- 65-68
Waedekin, Karl-Eugen 1921- 73-76
Waehrer, Helen (Youngelson) 1938- 53-56
Waelder, Robert 1900-1967 CAP-1
Earlier sketch in CA 13-14
Waengler, Hans-Heinrich B. 1921- CANR-20
Earlier sketch in CA 41-44R
Waffle, Harvey W(illiam) 1904- 7-8R
Wagar, W(alter) Warren 1932- CANR-3
Earlier sketch in CA 5-6R
Wagatsuma, Hiroshi 1927- 21-22R
Wagemaker, Herbert, Jr. 1929- 93-96
Wagenaar, Theodore C(larence) 1948- 111
Wagener, Hans 1940- CANR-1
Earlier sketch in CA 45-48
Wagenheim, Kal 1935- CANR-26
Earlier sketch in CA 29-32R
See also SATA 21
Wagenknecht, Edward (Charles) 1900- CANR-22
Earlier sketches in CA 2R, CANR-6
Wagenvoord, James 1937- 41-44R
Wager, Walter H(erman) 1924- CANR-8
Earlier sketch in CA 5-6R
Wager, Willis Joseph 1911- 37-40R
Waggaman, William Henry 1884(?)-1978
Obituary 77-80
Waggner, George 1894-1984 Obituary 114
Waggoner, Glen 1940- 121
Waggoner, Hyatt H(owe) 1913-1988 CANR-9
Obituary 126
Earlier sketch in CA 23-24R
Wagley, Charles (Walter) 1913- CANR-10
Earlier sketch in CA 13-14R
Waglow, Irving Frederick 1915- 4R
Wagman, Fredrica 1937- 97-100
See also CLC 7
Wagman, Naomi 1937- 57-60
Wagman, Robert John 1942- 93-96
Wagner, Anthony Richard 1908- CANR-20
Earlier sketches in CA 4R, CANR-5
Wagner, C(harles) Peter 1930- CANR-24
Earlier sketches in CA 21-22R, CANR-9
Wagner, Charles Abraham 1901- 7-8R
Wagner, David G(eorge) 1949- 114
Wagner, Denson
See Iannelli, Richard
Wagner, Doc
See Wagner, Edward J., Sr.
Wagner, Edward J., Sr. 1908(?)-1986
Obituary 118
Wagner, Edwin E(ric) 1930- 45-48
Wagner, Elaine 1939- 45-48
Wagner, Eliot 1917- 105
Wagner, Francis S(tephen) 1911- CANR-8
Earlier sketch in CA 61-64
Wagner, Frederick (Reese, Jr.) 1928- 7-8R
Wagner, Geoffrey (Atheling) 1927- CANR-2
Earlier sketch in CA 1R
Wagner, Gordon Parsons 1915-1987
Obituary 124
Wagner, Harvey M. 1931- CANR-6
Earlier sketch in CA 13-14R
Wagner, Helmut R(udolf) 1904- CANR-19
Earlier sketches in CA 53-56, CANR-4
Wagner, Jack Russell 1916- 49-52
Wagner, Jane 109
Wagner, Jean Pierre 1919- 23-24R
Wagner, Jon G(regory) 1944- 109
Wagner, Joseph Frederick 1900(?)-1974
Obituary 53-56
Wagner, Karl Edward 1945- CANR-3
Earlier sketch in CA 49-52
Wagner, Ken(neth) 1911- 37-40R
Wagner, Kenneth A. 1919- 53-56
Wagner, Lilya 1940- 112
Wagner, Linda Welshimer 1936- CANR-3
Earlier sketch in CA 11-12R
Wagner, Margaret D. 1949- 7-8R
Wagner, (Griegg) Marsden 1930- 69-72
Wagner, Nathaniel N(ed) 1930- 57-60
Wagner, Peggy
See Wagner, Margaret D.
Wagner, Philip L(aurence) 1921- 41-44R
Wagner, Philip Marshall 1904- 102
Wagner, Ray(mond) David 1924- CANR-19
Earlier sketches in CA 5-6R, CANR-3
Wagner, Ray Jay 1931- 77-80
Wagner, Richard Vansant 1935-
Brief entry 105
Wagner, Roy 1938- 41-44R
Wagner, Rudolph F(red) 1921- 37-40R
Wagner, Ruth H(ortense) 1909- 29-32R
Wagner, Sharon B. 1936- CANR-10
Earlier sketch in CA 25-28R
See also SATA 4
Wagner, Stanley P(aul) 1923- 29-32R
Wagner, Walter 1927(?)-1983(?) Obituary 109
Wagner, Walter F(rederick), Jr.
1926-1985 CANR-26
Obituary 116
Earlier sketch in CA 69-72
Wagner, Wenceslas Joseph 1917- 37-40R
Wagner-Martin, Linda 1936- CLC-50
Wagoner, David (Russell) 1926- CANR-2
Earlier sketch in CA 2R
See also CAAS 3
See also SATA 14
See also DLB 5
See also CLC 3, 5, 15
Wagoner, Harless D. 1918- 29-32R
Wagoner, Jay J. 1923- 25-28R
Wagoner, John L(eonard) 1927-1984 69-72
Obituary 112
Wagoner, Walter D. 1918- 21-22R
Wagonseller, Bill R(oss) 1933- 107
Wagschal, Harry 1939- 108
Wagschal, Peter H(enry) 1944- CANR-19
Earlier sketch in CA 102
Wagstaff, (John) Malcolm 1940- 109
Wah, Fred(erick James) 1939- Brief entry 107
See also DLB 60
See also CLC 44
Wahking, Harold L(eroy) 1931- 29-32R
Wahl, Jan 1933- CANR-12
Earlier sketch in CA 25-28R
See also SATA 2, 34
See also SAAS 3
Wahl, Jean 1888-1974 Obituary 49-52
Wahl, Paul 1922- 11-12R
Wahl, Robert (Charles) 1948- CANR-1
Earlier sketch in CA 49-52
Wahl, Thomas (Peter) 1931- 9-10R
Wahlberg, Rachel Conrad 1922- 93-96
Wahler, Robert G(ordon) 1936-
Brief entry 109
Wahlke, John C(harles) 1917- CANR-11
Earlier sketch in CA 21-22R
Wahloo, Per 1926-1975 61-64
See also CLC 7
Wahloo, Peter
See Wahloo, Per
Wahlroos, Sven 1931- 57-60
Wahtera, John (Edward) 1929-1985 61-64
Obituary 117
Waide, Jan 1952- 105
See also SATA 29
Waidson, H(erbert) Morgan 1916- 7-8R
Waife, Marie
See Waife-Goldberg, Marie
Waife-Goldberg, Marie 1892-1985 CAP-2
Obituary 118
Earlier sketch in CA 25-28
Wailey, Anthony Paul 1947- 126
Wailey, Tony
See Wailey, Anthony Paul
Wain, Barry 1944- 122
Wain, John (Barrington) 1925- CANR-23
Earlier sketch in CA 7-8R
See also CAAS 4
See also DLB 15, 27
See also CLC 2, 11, 15, 46
Waine, Anthony 1946- 113
Wainer, Cord
See Dewey, Thomas B(lanchard)
Wainhouse, David Walter 1900-1976 17-18R
Obituary 65-68
Wainscott, John Milton 1910-1981 SATA-53
Wainwright, Arthur William 1925- 114
Wainwright, Charles Anthony 1933- 37-40R
Wainwright, David
See Stansfield, Richard Habberton
Wainwright, Geoffrey 1939- CANR-15
Earlier sketch in CA 37-40R
Wainwright, Gordon Ray 1937- 113
Wainwright, J(oseph) Allan 1921- 13-14R
Wainwright, Jeffrey 1944- Brief entry 122
See also DLB 40
Wainwright, John 1921- 110
Brief entry 108
Wainwright, Nicholas Biddle 1914- 65-68
Wainwright, William J(udson) 1935- 120
Waisanen, F(rederick) B(rynolf) 1923- 45-48
Waite, A. E.
See Waite, Arthur Edward
Waite, Arthur Edward 1857-1942
Brief entry 121
Waite, Helen Elmira 1903- 3R
Waite, P(eter) B(usby) 1922- 11-12R
Waite, Robert G(eorge) L(eeson) 1919- 11-12R
Waite, William W(iley) 1903- CAP-1
Earlier sketch in CA 15-16
Waith, Eugene M(ersereau) 1912- CANR-5
Earlier sketch in CA 5-6R
Waitley, Douglas 1927- CANR-9
Earlier sketch in CA 21-22R
See also SATA 30
Waitzmann, Dorothea 1915- 15-16R
Wajda, Andrzej 1926- 102
See also CLC 16
Wakefield, Connie LaVon 1948- 65-68
Wakefield, Dan 1932- 21-22R
See also CAAS 7
See also CLC 7
Wakefield, Donam Hahn 1927- 37-40R
Wakefield, Herbert Russell 1888-1965 5-6R
Wakefield, Hubert George 1915-1984
Obituary 112
Wakefield, Hugh
See Wakefield, Hubert George
Wakefield, Jean L.
See Laird, Jean E(louise)
Wakefield, R. I.
See White, Gertrude M(ason)
Wakefield, Robert A. 1916- 15-16R
Wakefield, Sherman Day 1894-1971
Obituary 29-32R
Wakefield, Tom 1935- 101
Wakefield, Walter Leggett 1911- 81-84
Wakeford, John 1936- Brief entry 112
Wakeham, Irene 1912- 29-32R
Wakeley, John H(albert) 1932- 41-44R
Wakelin, Martyn Francis 1935- 65-68
Wakelyn, Jon L(ouis) 1938- CANR-1
Earlier sketch in CA 45-48
Wakeman, Carolyn 1943- 126
Wakeman, Frederic (Evans), Jr. 1937- CANR-1
Earlier sketch in CA 49-52
Wakeman, Geoffrey 1926- CANR-15
Earlier sketch in CA 37-40R
Wakeman, John 1928- 124
Wakeman, Robert Parker 1914(?)-1981
Obituary 104
Wakil, S(heikh) P(arvez) 1935- 85-88
Wakin, Edward 1927- CANR-17
Earlier sketches in CA 5-6R, CANR-2
See also SATA 37
Wako, Mdogo
See Nazareth, Peter
Wakoski, Diane 1937- CANR-9
Earlier sketch in CA 15-16R
See also CAAS 1
See also DLB 5
See also CLC 2, 4, 7, 9, 11, 40
Wakoski-Sherbell, Diane
See Wakoski, Diane
Waksman, Selman A(braham) 1888-1973 CAP-1
Obituary 45-48
Earlier sketch in CA 15-16
Wakstein, Allen M. 1931- 29-32R
Walbank, F. W.
See Walbank, Frank William
Walbank, Frank William 1909- Brief entry 111
Walberg, Herbert J(ohn) 1937- 61-64
Walch, Timothy (George) 1947- CANR-21
Earlier sketch in CA 105
Walchars, John 1912- 81-84
Walck, Henry Z. 1908(?)-1984 Obituary 114
See also SATA 40
Walcott, Derek (Alton) 1930- CANR-26
Earlier sketch in CA 89-92
See also BW
See also DLBY 81
See also CLC 2, 4, 9, 14, 25, 42
Walcott, Fred G. 1894- 37-40R
Walcott, John 1949- 126
Walcott, Robert 1910- CAP-1
Earlier sketch in CA 13-14
Walcutt, Charles Child 1908- CANR-3
Earlier sketch in CA 2R
Wald, Carol 1935- 65-68
Wald, Malvin (Daniel) 1917- CANR-1
Earlier sketch in CA 45-48
Wald, Richard C(harles) 108
Walde, Ralph E(ldon) 1943- 53-56
Waldeck, Peter Bruce 1940- 41-44R
Walden, Amelia Elizabeth CANR-2
Earlier sketch in CA 1R
See also SATA 3
Walden, Daniel 1922- 25-28R
Walden, Howard T(albot) II 1897-1981 45-48
Obituary 103
Walden, John C(layton) 1928- 53-56
Walder, (Alan) David 1928-1978 CANR-17
Obituary 81-84
Earlier sketch in CA 65-68
Walder, Dennis 1943- 117
Walders, Joe 1948- 85-88
Waldheim, Kurt 1918- 89-92
Waldhorn, Arthur 1918- CANR-3
Earlier sketch in CA 2R
Waldinger, Ernst 1896-1970 Obituary 104
Waldman, Anne 1945- 37-40R
See also DLB 16
See also CLC 7
Waldman, Bruce 1949- SATA-15
Waldman, Diane 1936- CANR-26
Earlier sketch in CA 33-36R
Waldman, Eric 1914- 19-20R
Waldman, Max 1919-1981 105
Obituary 103
Waldman, Milton 1895-1976 69-72
Obituary 65-68
Waldman, Neil 1947- SATA-51
Waldmeir, Joseph John 1923- 11-12R
Waldo, Anna Lee 1925- 85-88
Waldo, Dave
See Clarke, D(avid) Waldo
Waldo, E. Hunter
See Sturgeon, Theodore Hamilton
Waldo, Edward Hamilton
See Sturgeon, Theodore Hamilton
Waldo, Kay Cronkite 1938- 107
Waldo, Myra 93-96
Waldo, Ralph Emerson III 1944- 102
Waldo, Terry
See Waldo, Ralph Emerson III
Waldo, Willis H. 1920- 13-14R
Waldock, (Claud) Humphrey (Meredith)
1904-1981 Obituary 108
Waldorf, Paul D(ouglass) 1908- CAP-1
Earlier sketch in CA 15-16
Waldrip, Louise B. 1912- 37-40R
Waldron, Ann Wood 1924- CANR-7
Earlier sketch in CA 15-16R
See also SATA 16
Waldron, D'Lynn
See Waldron-Shah, Diane Lynn
Waldron, Eli 1916(?)-1980 Obituary 101
Waldron, Ingrid 1939- 53-56
Waldron, Martin O. 1925-1981 Obituary 103
Waldron-Shah, Diane Lynn 1936- 9-10R
Waldrop, Howard 1946- 118
Waldrop, Keith 1932- 117
Waldrop, Rosemarie 1935- CANR-18
Earlier sketch in CA 101
Waldrop, W. Earl 1910- 5-6R
Wale, Michael 81-84
Walen, Harry L(eonard) 1915- 41-44R
Wales, Hugh Gregory 1910- CANR-2
Earlier sketch in CA 5-6R
Wales, Nym
See Snow, Helen Foster
Wales, Robert 1923- 93-96
Wales, William
See Ambrose, David (Edwin)
Waley, Arthur (David) 1889-1966 85-88
Obituary 25-28R
Walford, Christian
See Dilcock, Noreen

Walford, Lionel Albert 1905-1979
 Obituary ... 85-88
Walford, Roy L(ee, Jr.) 1924- ... 111
Walgenbach, Paul H(enry) 1923- ... 53-56
Walhout, Donald 1927- ... CANR-2
 Earlier sketch in CA 5-6R
Walicki, Andrzej 1930- ... 101
Walinsky, Louis J(oseph) 1908- ... CAP-2
 Earlier sketch in CA 17-18
Walinsky, Ossip J. 1887(?)-1973
 Obituary ... 41-44R
Waliullah, Syed 1922- ... 23-24R
Walkden, (George) Brian 1923- ... CANR-10
 Earlier sketch in CA 13-14R
Walkenstein, Eileen 1923- ... CANR-14
 Earlier sketch in CA 69-72
Walker, Alan 1911- ... CANR-26
 Earlier sketches in CA 13-14R, CANR-7
Walker, Albert L(yell) 1907- ... 41-44R
Walker, Alexander 1930- Brief entry ... 116
Walker, Alice 1944- ... CANR-9
 Earlier sketch in CA 37-40R
 See also BW
 See also SATA 31
 See also DLB 6, 33
 See also CLC 5, 6, 9, 19, 27, 46
Walker, Ardis Manly 1901- ... CANR-22
 Earlier sketch in CA 37-40R
Walker, Augusta 1914- ... 21-22R
Walker, Barbara G(oodwin) 1930- ... 73-76
Walker, Barbara (Jeanne) K(erlin)
 1921- ... CANR-16
 Earlier sketch in CA 33-36R
 See also SATA 4
Walker, Benjamin 1923- ... CANR-10
 Earlier sketch in CA 25-28R
Walker, Bessie
 See Henry, Bessie Walker
Walker, (James) Braz(elton) 1934-1983 ... 69-72
 See also SATA 45
Walker, Brooks R. 1935- ... 11-12R
Walker, Bruce (James) 1944- ... 85-88
Walker, Bryce S(tewart) 1934- ... 117
Walker, C(larence) Eugene 1939- ... CANR-10
 Earlier sketch in CA 61-64
Walker, Charles 1911- ... 19-20R
Walker, Charles
 See Gettings, Fred
Walker, Charles R(umford) 1893-1974 ... CAP-2
 Obituary ... 53-56
 Earlier sketch in CA 17-18
Walker, Cheryl 1947- ... 111
Walker, Claxton 1924- ... 101
Walker, Clive (Phillip) 1954- ... 124
Walker, D(aniel) P(ickering) 1914-1985 ... 85-88
 Obituary ... 116
Walker, Dale L(ee) 1935- ... CANR-24
 Earlier sketches in CA 57-60, CANR-8
Walker, Daniel Downing 1915- ... CANR-2
 Earlier sketch in CA 2R
Walker, Danton (MacIntyre) 1899-1960
 Obituary ... 93-96
Walker, David 1950- ... 104
Walker, David Clifton 1942- ... 69-72
Walker, David G(ordon) 1926- ... 110
Walker, David Harry 1911- ... CANR-1
 Earlier sketch in CA 4R
 See also SATA 8
 See also CLC 14
Walker, David M(axwell) 1920- ... CANR-22
 Earlier sketches in CA 11-12R, CANR-5
Walker, Deward E(dgar), Jr. 1935- ... CANR-19
 Earlier sketch in CA 25-28R
Walker, Diana 1925- ... CANR-4
 Earlier sketch in CA 49-52
 See also SATA 9
Walker, Donald Smith 1918- ... 11-12R
Walker, Earl Thomas 1891- ... 105
Walker, Edward Joseph 1934- ... CANR-12
 Earlier sketch in CA 21-22R
Walker, Edward L(ewis) 1914- ... CANR-11
 Earlier sketch in CA 25-28R
Walker, Elinor 1911- ... 15-16R
Walker, Eric Anderson 1886-1976 ... CAP-2
 Obituary ... 65-68
 Earlier sketch in CA 13-14
Walker, Ethel Valerie 1944- ... 53-56
Walker, Evan 1933(?)-1982 Obituary ... 107
Walker, Everett 1906-1983 Obituary ... 109
Walker, Frank 1930- ... 69-72
 See also SATA 36
Walker, Frank B. 1916(?)-1985 Obituary ... 117
Walker, Franklin (Dickerson) 1900-1979 ... 21-22R
 Obituary ... 85-88
Walker, Geoffrey James 1936- ... 93-96
Walker, George F. 1947- ... CANR-21
 Earlier sketch in CA 103
 See also DLB 60
 See also CLC 44
Walker, Gerald 1928- ... 11-12R
Walker, Gilbert James 1907-1982
 Obituary ... 107
Walker, Glen 1937- ... 108
Walker, Graham S. 1956- ... 122
Walker, Gregory P(iers) M(ountford)
 1942- ... 73-76
Walker, Greta 1927- ... 77-80
Walker, Harold Blake 1904- ... 17-18R
Walker, Harry
 See Waugh, Hillary Baldwin
Walker, Helen M(ary) 1891-1983 Obituary ... 109
Walker, Hill M(ontague) 1939- ... 93-96
Walker, Holly Beth
 See Bond, Gladys Baker
Walker, Ira
 See Walker, Irma Ruth (Roden)
Walker, Irma Ruth (Roden) 1921- ... CANR-21
 Earlier sketches in CA 7-8R, CANR-6
Walker, J.
 See Crawford, John Richard
Walker, J(ohn) Ingram 1944- ... 112
Walker, Jack
 See Thayer, Frederick C(lifton), Jr.
Walker, James Lynwood 1940- ... 37-40R
Walker, Janet A(nderson) 1942- ... 119
Walker, Jeanne 1924- ... 61-64
Walker, Jeanne Murray 1944- ... 111
Walker, Jeremy D(esmond) B(romhead)
 1936- ... 21-22R
Walker, Joan ... 7-8R
Walker, John 1906- ... CANR-6
 Earlier sketch in CA 7-8R
Walker, John 1933- ... 113
Walker, John (Bruce) 1938- ... 120
Walker, Joseph 1892-1985 Obituary ... 117
Walker, Joseph A. 1935- ... CANR-26
 Earlier sketch in CA 89-92
 See also BW
 See also DLB 38
 See also CLC 19
Walker, Joseph E(rdman) 1911- ... 37-40R
Walker, Kathrine Sorley
 See Sorley Walker, Kathrine
Walker, Keith 1934- ... 121
Walker, Kenneth Francis 1924- ... 33-36R
Walker, Kenneth Macfarlane 1882-1966 ... 7-8R
Walker, Kenneth R(oland) 1928- ... 37-40R
Walker, Kenneth Richard 1931- ... 17-18R
Walker, Laurence C(olton) 1924- ... 53-56
Walker, Lawrence David 1931- ... 53-56
Walker, Lenore E(lizabeth) 1942- ... 97-100
Walker, Leo ... 15-16R
Walker, Lou Ann 1952- ... 126
 See also SATA 53
Walker, Louise Jean 1891-1976 Obituary ... 110
 See also SATA 35
Walker, Lucy
 See Sanders, Dorothy Lucie
Walker, Mack 1929- ... 11-12R
Walker, Margaret Abigail 1915- ... CANR-26
 Earlier sketch in CA 73-76
 See also BW
 See also DLB 76
 See also CLC 1, 6
Walker, Margaret Pope 1901(?)-1980
 Obituary ... 101
Walker, Mark 1953- ... 117
Walker, Marshall (John) 1912- ... 17-18R
Walker, Martin 1947- ... 101
Walker, Mary Alexander 1927- ... 104
Walker, Matthew
 See Mewhinney, Bruce
Walker, Mickey 1901-1981 Obituary ... 108
Walker, Mildred
 See Schemm, Mildred Walker
Walker, (Addison) Mort 1923- ... CANR-25
 Earlier sketches in CA 49-52, CANR-3
 See also SATA 8
Walker, Morton 1929- ... CANR-22
 Earlier sketch in CA 85-88
Walker, Nicolette (Daisy) Milnes 1943- ... 41-44R
Walker, Nigel (David) 1917- ... 61-64
Walker, Pamela 1948- ... 69-72
 See also SATA 24
Walker, Peter F(ranklin) 1931- ... 13-14R
Walker, Peter N. 1936- ... CANR-14
 Earlier sketch in CA 77-80
Walker, Philip Mitchell 1943- ... 29-32R
Walker, Raymond Myerscough
 See Myerscough-Walker, Raymond
Walker, Richard L(ouis) 1922- ... CANR-7
 Earlier sketch in CA 11-12R
Walker, Robert H(arris) 1924- ... CANR-23
 Earlier sketches in CA 15-16R, CANR-7
Walker, Robert Newton 1911- ... 53-56
Walker, Robert W(ayne) 1948- ... CANR-23
 Earlier sketch in CA 93-96
Walker, Roger W(illiams) 1931- ... 45-48
Walker, Ronald G(ary) 1945- ... CANR-16
 Earlier sketch in CA 93-96
Walker, Ruth
 See Walker, Irma Ruth (Roden)
Walker, Samuel 1942- ... 85-88
Walker, Scott 1950- ... 120
Walker, Shel
 See Sheldon, Walter J.
Walker, Stanley 1898-1962 Obituary ... 93-96
Walker, Stella Archer 1907- ... 61-64
Walker, Stephen J. 1951- ... SATA-12
Walker, Stuart (Armstrong) 1880(?)-1941
 Brief entry ... 120
Walker, Stuart H(odge) 1923- ... CANR-24
 Earlier sketch in CA 45-48
Walker, Sydney III 1931- ... 23-24R
Walker, T. Michael 1937- ... 77-80
Walker, Ted
 See Walker, Edward Joseph
 See also DLB 40
 See also CLC 13
Walker, Theodore J. 1922- ... 102
Walker, Walter (Colyear) 1912- ... 117
Walker, Walter (Herbert III) 1949- ... 117
Walker, Warren S(tanley) 1921- ... CANR-16
 Earlier sketches in CA 11-12R, CANR-3
Walker, Willard (Brewer) 1926- ... CANR-23
 Earlier sketch in CA 45-48
Walker, William Edward 1925- ... 11-12R
Walker, William G(eorge) 1928- ... 77-80
Walker, William H. 1913- ... 19-20R
Walker, William Otis 1896-1981 Obituary ... 105
Walkerley, Rodney Lewis (de Burgh)
 1905- ... CAP-1
 Earlier sketch in CA 9-10
Walkinshaw, Colin
 See Reid, James Macarthur
Walkinshaw, Lawrence H(arvey) 1904- ... 45-48
Walkowitz, Daniel J(ay) 1942- ... 81-84
Wall, A(rthur) E(dward) P(atrick) 1925- ... 119
Wall, Barbara 1911- ... 97-100
Wall, Bennett H(arrison) 1914- ... 77-80
Wall, C. Edward 1942- ... 37-40R
Wall, Elizabeth S(pooner) 1924- ... 93-96
Wall, James M(cKendree) 1928-
 Brief entry ... 113
Wall, John Nelson, Jr. 1945- ... 114
Wall, Joseph Barrye 1899(?)-1985
 Obituary ... 117
Wall, Joseph Frazier 1920- ... CANR-13
 Earlier sketch in CA 29-32R
Wall, Maggie 1937- ... 65-68
Wall, Margaret
 See Wall, Maggie
Wall, Martha 1910- ... CAP-2
 Earlier sketch in CA 25-28
Wall, Michael Morris 1942- ... 53-56
Wall, Mike
 See Wall, Michael Morris
Wall, Patrick (Henry Bligh) 1916- ... 104
Wall, Patrick D(avid) 1925- ... 17-18R
Wall, Richard 1944- ... 41-44R
Wall, Robert Emmet, Jr. 1937- ... CANR-23
 Earlier sketch in CA 45-48
Wall, T. D.
 See Wall, Toby (Douglas)
Wall, Toby (Douglas) 1946- ... 119
Wall, Toby D.
 See Wall, Toby (Douglas)
Wall, Wendy Somerville 1942- ... 49-52
Wallace, Alexander Fielding 1918- ... 33-36R
Wallace, Alexander Ross 1891-1982
 Obituary ... 107
Wallace, Alfred Russel 1823-1913
 Brief entry ... 123
Wallace, Amy 1955- ... 81-84
Wallace, Andrew 1930- ... 37-40R
Wallace, Anthony F(rancis) C(larke)
 1923- ... CANR-13
 Earlier sketch in CA 61-64
Wallace, Barbara Brooks ... CANR-11
 Earlier sketch in CA 29-32R
 See also SATA 4
Wallace, Ben J. 1937- ... 45-48
Wallace, Beverly Dobrin 1921- ... 101
 See also SATA 19
Wallace, Bill
 See Wallace, William Keith
 and Wallace, William N.
 See also SATA 47
Wallace, Bronwen 1945- ... 112
Wallace, Bruce 1920- ... CANR-15
 Earlier sketch in CA 85-88
Wallace, Daisy
 See Cuyler, Margery S(tuyvesant)
Wallace, David Foster 1962- ... CLC-50
Wallace, David H(arold) 1926- ... 25-28R
Wallace, David J. 1954- ... 124
Wallace, David Rains 1945- ... CANR-14
 Earlier sketch in CA 81-84
Wallace, DeWitt 1889-1981 Obituary ... 103
Wallace, Dexter
 See Masters, Edgar Lee
Wallace, Doreen
 See Rash, Dora Eileen Agnew (Wallace)
Wallace, Ed(ward Tatum) 1906-1976
 Obituary ... 69-72
Wallace, (Richard Horatio) Edgar
 1875-1932 Brief entry ... 115
 See also DLB 70
Wallace, Ernest 1906-1985 ... CANR-25
 Earlier sketch in CA 13-14R
Wallace, Francis 1894(?)-1977 Obituary ... 73-76
Wallace, G(erald) L. 1938- ... 97-100
Wallace, George C(orley) 1919-
 Brief entry ... 114
Wallace, Helen Kingsbury 1897- ... CAP-2
 Earlier sketch in CA 25-28
Wallace, Helen M(argaret) 1913- ... CANR-12
 Earlier sketch in CA 61-64
Wallace, Henry A(gard) 1888-1965 ... 105
 Obituary ... 89-92
Wallace, Ian 1950- ... CANR-25
 Earlier sketch in CA 107
 See also SATA 53
Wallace, Ian
 See Pritchard, John Wallace
Wallace, Irving 1916- ... CANR-1
 Earlier sketch in CA 1R
 See also CAAS 1
 See also CLC 7, 13
 See also AITN 1
Wallace, James Donald 1937- ... 108
Wallace, Joanne (M.) 1938- ... 117
Wallace, John A(dam) 1915- ... 5-6R
 See also SATA 3
Wallace, John Malcolm 1928- ... 25-28R
Wallace, K(ay) K. 1949- ... 111
Wallace, Karl R(ichards) 1906-1973 ... 101
Wallace, Lew(is) 1827(?)-1905 Brief entry ... 120
Wallace, Lewis Grant 1910- ... CAP-2
 Earlier sketch in CA 23-24
Wallace, Lila Bell Acheson 1889-1984
 Obituary ... 112
 Brief entry ... 105
Wallace, Lillian Parker 1890-1971 ... 2R
 Obituary ... 103
Wallace, Luther T(ompkins) 1928- ... 15-16R
Wallace, Marc J., Jr. 1944- ... 114
Wallace, Marjorie ... 101
Wallace, Michael David 1943- ... 77-80
Wallace, Michele Faith 1952- ... 108
Wallace, Mike 1918- ... 65-68
Wallace, Myron Leon
 See Wallace, Mike
Wallace, Nigel
 See Hamilton, Charles Harold St. John
Wallace, Pamela 1949- ... 105
Wallace, Pat
 See Strother, Pat Wallace
Wallace, Paul 1931- ... 61-64
Wallace, Paul A(nthony) W(ilson) 1891- ... CAP-1
 Earlier sketch in CA 15-16
Wallace, Philip (Adrian) Hope
 See Hope-Wallace, Philip (Adrian)
Wallace, Phyllis Ann ... 105
Wallace, Richard
 See Ind, Allison
Wallace, Robert 1932- ... CANR-10
 Earlier sketch in CA 15-16R
 See also SATA 37, 47
Wallace, Robert Ash 1921- ... 2R
Wallace, Robert Kimball 1944- ... 69-72
Wallace, Ronald (William) 1945- ... CANR-20
 Earlier sketches in CA 57-60, CANR-6
Wallace, Ronald S(tewart) 1911- ... CANR-5
 Earlier sketch in CA 11-12R
Wallace, Ruby Ann 1923(?)- ... CANR-26
 Earlier sketch in CA 112
 See also BW
Wallace, Samuel E(ugene) 1935- ... 41-44R
Wallace, Sarah Leslie 1914- ... 11-12R
Wallace, Sister M. Jean
 See Paxton, Mary Jean Wallace
Wallace, Sylvia ... 73-76
Wallace, Tom 1874-1961 Obituary ... 93-96
Wallace, Walter L. 1927- ... 81-84
Wallace, Willard M(osher) 1911- ... 13-14R
Wallace, William A(ugustine) 1918- ... 41-44R
Wallace, William A(lan) 1935- ... 49-52
Wallace, William Keith 1947- ... 124
 See also SATA 53
Wallace, William N. 1924- ... 15-16R
Wallace, William Stewart 1884-1970
 Obituary ... 116
Wallace-Brodeur, Ruth 1941- ... 107
 See also SATA 41, 51
Wallace-Clarke, George 1916- ... 117
Wallace-Crabbe, Chris(topher Keith)
 1934- ... CANR-14
 Earlier sketch in CA 77-80
Wallace-Hadrill, Andrew (Frederic) 1951- ... 117
Wallace-Hadrill, D(avid) S(utherland)
 1920- ... 29-32R
Wallace-Hadrill, John Michael 1916-1985 ... 7-8R
 Obituary ... 118
Wallach, Erica 1922- ... 21-22R
Wallach, Ira 1913- ... 11-12R
Wallach, Janet 1942- ... 106
Wallach, Mark I(rwin) 1949- ... 69-72
Wallach, Michael A(rthur) 1933- ... CANR-26
 Earlier sketches in CA 15-16R, CANR-11
Wallach, Paul I. 1927- ... CANR-8
 Earlier sketch in CA 17-18R
Wallach, Robert Charles 1935- ... 107
Wallach, Sidney 1905-1979 ... 103
 Obituary ... 89-92
Wallance, Gregory Joseph 1948- ... 109
Wallant, Edward Lewis 1926-1962 ... CANR-22
 Earlier sketch in CA 4R
 See also DLB 2, 28
 See also CLC 5, 10
Wallechinsky, David 1948- ... 61-64
Wallek, Lee
 See Johnson, Curt(is Lee)
Wallen, Carl J(oseph) 1931- ... 93-96
Wallenstein, Barry J(ay) 1940- ... CANR-11
 Earlier sketch in CA 45-48
Wallenstein, Meir 1903- ... CAP-1
 Earlier sketch in CA 15-16
Waller, Altina L(aura) 1940- ... 112
Waller, Brown
 See Fraser, W(aller) B(rown)
Waller, Charles T(homas) 1934- ... 61-64
Waller, G(ary) F(redric) 1944- ... 112
Waller, Gary
 See Waller, G(ary) F(redric)
Waller, George Macgregor 1919- ... 11-12R
Waller, Irene Ellen 1928- ... 109
Waller, J(ames) Irvin 1944- ... CANR-14
 Earlier sketch in CA 61-64
Waller, John Stanier 1917- ... 45-48
Waller, Leslie 1923- ... CANR-2
 Earlier sketch in CA 4R
 See also SATA 20
Waller, Peter Louis 1935- ... 106
Waller, Robert J(ames) 1955- ... 117
Wallerstein, Immanuel 1930- ... CANR-24
 Earlier sketches in CA 23-24R, CANR-9
Wallerstein, Judith (Hannah) S(aretsky)
 1921- ... 124
 Brief entry ... 105
Wallerstein, Mitchel B(ruce) 1949- ... 105
Wallerstein, Robert S(olomon) 1921- ... CANR-12
 Earlier sketch in CA 33-36R
Walley, David 1945- ... 41-44R
Wallhauser, Henry T. 1930- ... 29-32R
Wallich, Henry C(hristopher)
 1914-1988 ... CANR-6
 Obituary ... 126
 Earlier sketch in CA 2R
Wallich-Clifford, Anton 1923- ... 61-64
Wallig, Gaird (Elizabeth) 1942- ... 106
Walling, William (Herbert) 1926- ... 103
Wallis, Charles L(angworthy) ... CANR-8
 Earlier sketch in CA 7-8R
Wallis, G. McDonald
 See Campbell, Hope
Wallis, George A. 1892- ... 17-18R

Wallis, Hal B.
See Wallis, Harold Brent
Wallis, Harold Brent 1898(?)-1986
Obituary ... 120
Wallis, Jim 1948- ... 102
Wallis, Keith 1930- ... 25-28R
Wallis, Kenneth F(rank) 1938- ... CANR-24
Earlier sketch in CA 45-48
Wallis, R(ichard) T(yrrell) 1941- ... 45-48
Wallis, Redmond Frankton 1933- ... 7-8R
Wallis, Robert 1900- ... CAP-2
Earlier sketch in CA 29-32
Wallis, Roy 1945- ... CANR-17
Earlier sketch in CA 97-100
Wallis, Ruth O(tis) S(awtell) 1895-1978
Obituary ... 73-76
Wallis, W(ilson) Allen 1912- ... 41-44R
Wallmann, Jeffrey M(iner) 1941- ... CANR-14
Earlier sketch in CA 77-80
Wallner, Alexandra 1946- ... CANR-13
Earlier sketch in CA 73-76
See also SATA 41, 51
Wallner, John C. 1945- ... SATA-10, 51
Wallop, (John) Douglass III
1920-1985 ... CANR-13
Obituary ... 115
Earlier sketch in CA 73-76
Wallop, Lucille Fletcher 1912- ... 13-14R
Wallower, Lucille ... CANR-9
Earlier sketch in CA 21-22R
See also SATA 11
Wallraff, Charles Fredric 1909- ... 2R
Walls, David Stuart 1941- ... CANR-14
Earlier sketch in CA 37-40R
Walls, Dwayne E(stes) 1932- ... CANR-14
Earlier sketch in CA 41-44R
Walls, H(enry) J(ames) 1907-1988 ... 11-12R
Obituary ... 126
Walls, Ian G(ascoigne) 1922- ... 104
Walls, Ronald 1920- ... 103
Walls, William J(acob) 1885-1975 ... 81-84
Wallsten, Robert 1912- ... 101
Wallwork, Ernest (Edward) 1937- ... 41-44R
Walman, Jerome 1937- ... 125
Walmsley, Arnold Robert 1912- ... 41-44R
Walmsley, Buck
See Walmsley, Haines
Walmsley, (Ronald) Charles 1910-1983
Obituary ... 110
Walmsley, Haines 1930(?)-1983 Obituary ... 111
Walmsley, Leo 1892-1966 ... CAP-1
Earlier sketch in CA 11-12
Walmsley, Lewis C(alvin) 1897- ... 61-64
Walmsley, Robert 1905-1976 ... CAP-2
Earlier sketch in CA 29-32
Walmsley, Tom 1948- ... 126
Waln, Nora 1895-1964 Obituary ... 89-92
Walpole, Horace 1717-1797 ... DLB-39
Walpole, Hugh (Seymour) 1884-1941
Brief entry ... 104
See also DLB 34
See also TCLC 5
Walpole, Ronald Noel 1903- ... 106
Walrath, Douglas Alan 1933- ... 120
Walrath, Jane Dwyer 1939- ... 97-100
Walrond, Eric (Derwent) 1898-1966 ... 125
See also BW
See also DLB 51
Walschap, Gerard 1898- ... 103
Walsdorf, John J(oseph) 1941- ... 115
Walser, Martin 1927- ... CANR-8
Earlier sketch in CA 57-60
See also DLB 75
See also CLC 27
Walser, Richard (Gaither) 1908- ... CANR-2
Earlier sketch in CA 5-6R
Walser, Robert 1878-1956 Brief entry ... 118
See also DLB 66
See also TCLC 18
Walsh, Annmarie Hauck 1938- ... 25-28R
Walsh, Bren(dan) 1921- ... 121
Walsh, Chad 1914- ... CANR-6
Earlier sketch in CA 3R
Walsh, Clune J(oseph), Jr. 1928- ... 114
Walsh, Des 1954- ... 116
Walsh, Donald Devenish 1903-1980 ... CANR-3
Obituary ... 97-100
Earlier sketch in CA 49-52
Walsh, Edward J(oseph) 1937- ... 37-40R
Walsh, Edward Warren 1930(?)-1986
Obituary ... 118
Walsh, Elizabeth M(iller) 1937- ... 120
Walsh, Ellen Stoll 1942- ... 104
See also SATA 49
Walsh, Ernest 1895-1926 Brief entry ... 109
See also DLB 4, 45
Walsh, George (Vincent) 1923- ... 109
Walsh, George (William) 1931- ... 118
Brief entry ... 114
Walsh, George Johnston 1889-1981 ... SATA-53
Walsh, Gillian Paton 1939- ... 37-40R
See also SATA 4
Walsh, Jack 1919(?)-1984 Obituary ... 114
Walsh, James 1920-1986(?) Obituary ... 119
Walsh, James
See Robinson, Frank M(alcolm)
Walsh, James Edward 1891-1981
Obituary ... 104
Walsh, James J(erome) 1924- ... 11-12R
Walsh, James P(atrick) 1937- ... 111
Walsh, Jill Paton
See Walsh, Gillian Paton
See also SAAS 3
See also CLC 35
See also CLR 2
Walsh, John (Dixon) 1927- ... 17-18R
Walsh, John Evangelist 1927- ... 85-88
Walsh, Justin E(arl) 1933- ... CANR-10
Earlier sketch in CA 25-28R
Walsh, M.M.B. ... 101
Walsh, Marcus 1947- ... 118
Walsh, Marnie
See Walsh, M.M.B.
Walsh, Maurice 1879-1964 Brief entry ... 124
Walsh, Michael J. 1937- ... 106
Walsh, Myles E(ugene) 1937- ... 109
Walsh, P(atrick) G(erard) 1923- ... 25-28R
Walsh, Patricia L(ouise) 1942- ... 109
Walsh, Raoul 1887-1980 Obituary ... 102
Walsh, (Walter) Richard 1923- ... 25-28R
Walsh, Richard 1941- ... 120
Walsh, Robert 1784-1859 ... DLB-59
Walsh, Sheila 1928- ... 115
Walsh, (Michael) Stephen 1942- ... 37-40R
Walsh, (Richard) Taylor 1947- ... 73-76
Walsh, Thomas (Francis Morgan)
1908-1984 Obituary ... 114
Walsh, Timothy J(ames) 1927- ... 41-44R
Walsh, W(alter) Bruce 1936- ... 93-96
Walsh, Warren Bartlett 1909- ... CAP-2
Earlier sketch in CA 15-16
Walsh, William 1916- ... CANR-11
Earlier sketch in CA 65-68
Walsh, William B(ertalan) 1920- ... CANR-4
Earlier sketch in CA 49-52
Walsh, William Henry 1913-1986 Obituary ... 119
Walshe, M(aurice) O'C(onnell) 1911- ... 7-8R
Walshe, R(obert) D(aniel) 1923- ... CANR-21
Earlier sketch in CA 104
Walster, Elaine
See Hatfield, Elaine (Catherine)
Walster, Elaine Hatfield
See Hatfield, Elaine (Catherine)
Walster, G. William 1941- ... 85-88
Walston, Joseph
See Walston, Marie
Walston, Marie 1925- ... 41-44R
Walt, Lewis W(illiam) 1913- ... 33-36R
Waltari, Mika (Toimi) 1908-1979 ... 11-12R
Obituary ... 89-92
Walter, Bruno
See Schlesinger, Bruno Walter
Walter, Claire 1943- ... 81-84
Walter, Dorothy Blake 1908- ... CAP-1
Earlier sketch in CA 11-12
Walter, Elizabeth ... CANR-17
Earlier sketch in CA 97-100
Walter, Eugene 1927- ... 11-12R
Walter, Eugene Victor 1925- ... 25-28R
Walter, Gladys Mae 1901-1973 ... 41-44R
Walter, Hartmut 1940- ... 89-92
Walter, Ingo 1940- ... CANR-22
Earlier sketches in CA 17-18R, CANR-7
Walter, J(ulian) A(nthony) 1948- ... 120
Walter, Mildred Pitts 1922- ... SATA-45
See also CLR 15
Walter, Nancy
See Holmgren, Norah
Walter, Nina Willis 1900- ... 7-8R
Walter, Otis M. 1921- ... 5-6R
Walter, Robert H(enry) K(eamer, Jr.)
1922- ... 7-8R
Walter, Samuel 1916- ... 5-6R
Walter, Tony
See Walter, J(ulian) A(nthony)
Walter, Villiam Christian
See Andersen, Hans Christian
Walter, William Grey 1910-1977 ... 103
Walters, A(lan) A(rthur) 1926- ... CANR-26
Earlier sketch in CA 29-32R
Walters, Anna L. 1946- ... 73-76
Walters, Audrey 1929- ... SATA-18
Walters, Barbara 1931- ... 65-68
See also AITN 2
Walters, Basil L(eon) 1896-1975
Obituary ... 89-92
Walters, C(harles) Glenn 1929- ... 81-84
Walters, Chad
See Smith, Richard Rein
Walters, Dorothy 1928- ... 65-68
Walters, Dorothy Mae Wells 1924- ... CANR-2
Earlier sketch in CA 7-8R
Walters, Dottie
See Walters, Dorothy Mae Wells
Walters, Eleanor 1955- ... 108
Walters, Helen B. ?-1987 Obituary ... 121
See also SATA 50
Walters, Hugh
See Hughes, Walter (Llewellyn)
Walters, Jack Edward 1896- ... 5-6R
Walters, Janet Lane 1936- ... 49-52
Walters, John Beauchamp 1906- ... CANR-6
Earlier sketch in CA 7-8R
Walters, John Bennett, Jr. 1912- ... 105
Walters, LeRoy (B., Jr.) 1940- ... 108
Walters, Nell
See Muse, Patricia (Alice)
Walters, Richard P(aul) 1935- ... 107
Walters, Rick
See Rowland, D(onald) S(ydney)
Walters, Robert Mark 1938- ... 69-72
Walters, Robert S(tephen) 1941- ... 29-32R
Walters, Ronald G(ordon) 1942- ... 85-88
Walters, Roy W(ashington) 1918- ... 93-96
Walters, Shelly
See Sheldon, Walter J.
Walters, Sister Annette 1910- ... 37-40R
Walters, Stanley D(avid) 1931- ... 53-56
Walters, Thomas N(oble) 1935- ... 65-68
Walters, Vernon A(nthony) 1917- ... 122
Waltham, Antony Clive 1942- ... CANR-26
Earlier sketches in CA 65-68, CANR-10
Walther, R(ichard) E(rnest) 1921- ... 41-44R
Walther, Regis (Hills) 1917-1983 ... CANR-8
Obituary ... 111
Earlier sketch in CA 19-20R
Walther, Thomas A. 1950- ... 107
See also SATA 31
Walther, Tom
See Walther, Thomas A.
Waltman, Jerold (Lloyd) 1945- ... 117
Waltman, John L. 1946- ... 120
Waltner, Elma 1912- ... 17-18R
See also SATA 40
Waltner, Willard H. 1909- ... SATA-40
Walton, Alfred Grant 1887-1970 ... CAP-1
Earlier sketch in CA 13-14
Walton, Bryce 1918- ... 21-22R
Walton, Clarence C. 1915- ... CANR-3
Earlier sketch in CA 1-4R
Walton, Clyde C(ameron) 1925- ... 29-32R
Walton, Craig 1934- ... 41-44R
Walton, Donald William 1917- ... 112
Walton, Douglas N(eil) 1942- ... 117
Walton, Ed(ward Hazen) 1931- ... CANR-22
Earlier sketch in CA 105
Walton, Elizabeth Cheatham ... 5-6R
Walton, Evangeline
See Ensley, Evangeline
Walton, George (H.) 1904- ... 19-20R
Walton, H(enry) J(ohn) 1924- ... 53-56
Walton, Hanes, Jr. 1942- ... 41-44R
Walton, J(ohn) Michael 1939- ... 117
Walton, John 1910- ... CANR-5
Earlier sketch in CA 2R
Walton, John 1937- ... 89-92
Walton, John K(immons) 1948- ... 124
Walton, Luke
See Henderson, Bill
Walton, Ortiz Montaigne 1933- ... CANR-26
Earlier sketch in CA 45-48
Walton, Richard Eugene 1931- ... 81-84
Walton, Richard J. 1928- ... 25-28R
See also SATA 4
Walton, Robert Cutler 1932- ... 73-76
Walton, Ronald (Gordon) 1936- ... 65-68
Walton, Su 1944- ... 25-28R
Walton, Vicki (Elizabeth) 1949- ... 65-68
Walton, W. Robert 1902- ... 69-72
Walton, William 1909- ... 125
Waltrip, Lela (Kingston) 1904- ... 5-6R
See also SATA 9
Waltrip, Mildred 1911- ... SATA-37
Waltrip, Robert
See Short, Robert Waltrip
Waltrip, Rufus (Charles) 1898- ... 5-6R
See also SATA 9
Waltz, Jon R(ichard) 1929- ... 17-18R
Waltz, Kenneth N(eal) 1924- ... 37-40R
Waltzer, Herbert 1930- ... 41-44R
Walvin, James 1942- ... CANR-17
Earlier sketches in CA 49-52, CANR-1
Walvoord, John F(lipse) 1910- ... CANR-6
Earlier sketch in CA 11-12R
Walwik, Theodore J. 1937- ... 25-28R
Walworth, Alice
See Graham, Alice Walworth
Walworth, Arthur 1903- ... 23-24R
Walworth, Nancy Zinsser 1917- ... CANR-3
Earlier sketch in CA 5-6R
See also SATA 14
Walz, Audrey Boyers 1907(?)-1983
Obituary ... 109
Walz, Edgar 1914- ... 29-32R
Walz, Jay 1907- ... 49-52
Walzer, Michael 1935- ... CANR-15
Earlier sketch in CA 37-40R
Walzer, Norman 1943- ... 111
Wambaugh, Joseph (Aloysius, Jr.)
1937- ... 33-36R
See also DLB 6
See also DLBY 83
See also CLC 3, 18
See also AITN 1
Wamble, Gaston Hugh 1923- ... 7-8R
Wamble, Thelma 1916- Brief entry ... 106
Wamsley, Gary L(ee) 1935- ... CANR-3
Earlier sketch in CA 49-52
Wanamaker, A(llison) Temple 1918- ... 17-18R
Wand, (John) William (Charles) 1885-? ... 103
Wandel, Joseph 1918- ... 93-96
Wanderer, Zev W(illiam) 1932- ... 105
Wandesforde-Smith, Geoffrey Albert
1943- ... 29-32R
Wandro, Mark 1948- ... 106
Wandycz, Piotr Stefan 1923- ... CANR-2
Earlier sketch in CA 2R
Wang, C(hing) H(sien) 1940- ... CANR-8
Earlier sketch in CA 61-64
Wang, (Fred) Fang Yu 1913- ... 37-40R
Wang, Hao 1921- ... 65-68
Wang, Hui-Ming 1922- ... 33-36R
Wang, J(en) Y(u) 1918- ... CANR-25
Earlier sketch in CA 45-48
Wang, John Ching-yu 1934- ... 41-44R
Wang, Julie C(aroline) 1947- ... 114
Wang, Leonard J(udah) 1926- ... 33-36R
Wang, Sabine E(isenberg) 1925- ... 37-40R
Wang, Yi Chu 1916- ... 61-64
Wangenheim, Chris von
See von Wangenheim, Chris
Wangensteen, Owen Harding 1898-1981 ... 103
Wangensteen, Sarah (Anne) D(avidson)
1908- ... 120
Wangerin, Theodora Scharffenberg 1888- ... 5-6R
Wangerin, Walter, Jr. 1944- ... 108
See also SATA 37, 45
Wangermann, Ernst 1925- ... 103
Wang Gungwu 1930- ... CANR-10
Earlier sketch in CA 65-68
Wangyal, Geshe 1901(?)-1983 Obituary ... 108
Wang Zhongshu 1925- ... 117
Waniek, Marilyn Nelson 1946- ... CANR-15
Earlier sketch in CA 89-92
Wankowicz, Melchoir 1892(?)-1974
Obituary ... 53-56
Wanlass, Stanley G(len) 1941- ... 61-64
Wann, Kenneth D(ouglass) 1915- ... 7-8R
Wannamaker, Bruce
See Moncure, Jane Belk
Wannan, Bill
See Wannan, William Fielding
Wannan, William Fielding 1915- ... CANR-10
Earlier sketch in CA 21-22R
Wanrooy, Willem F(rederik) 1925- ... 118
Wanshel, Jeff(rey Mark) 1947- ... CANR-13
Earlier sketch in CA 57-60
Wantland, William C(harles) 1934- ... 111
Wantling, William 1933-1974 ... 105
Obituary ... 89-92
Waples, Douglas 1893-1978 Obituary ... 77-80
Warbler, J. M.
See Cocagnac, Augustin Maurice(-Jean)
Warbridge, C. W.
See Woods, Clee
Warburg, Fredric (John) 1898-1981 ... 105
Warburg, James Paul 1896-1969 ... CAP-2
Obituary ... 25-28R
Earlier sketch in CA 21-22
Warburg, Sandol Stoddard
See Stoddard, Sandol
See also SATA 14
Warburton, Amber Arthun 1898(?)-1976
Obituary ... 61-64
Warburton, Clark (Abram) 1896-1979 ... 73-76
Obituary ... 89-92
Warburton, Minnie 1949- ... 101
Warch, Richard 1939- ... 105
Warcollier, Rene 1881-1962 Obituary ... 112
Ward, Aileen 1919- ... 7-8R
Ward, Alan Joseph 1936- ... 73-76
Ward, Allen M(ason) 1942- ... 89-92
Ward, Andrew (Spencer) 1946- ... 81-84
Ward, Anne G. 1932- ... 77-80
Ward, Artemus
See Browne, Charles Farrar
Ward, Arthur Henry Sarsfield 1883-1959
Brief entry ... 108
Ward, Barbara
See Jackson, Barbara (Ward)
Ward, Benedicta 1933- ... CANR-12
Earlier sketch in CA 65-68
Ward, Charles D(uane) 1935- ... 33-36R
Ward, Charles Dexter
See Taylor, John (Alfred)
Ward, Charlotte
See Chesney, Marion
Ward, Chester 1907-1977 Obituary ... 69-72
Ward, Colin 1924- ... 57-60
Ward, Craig 1892-1979 Obituary ... 85-88
Ward, David 1938- ... 29-32R
Ward, Dennis 1924- ... 13-14R
Ward, Don(ald G.) 1911- ... 19-20R
Ward, Donald 1909- ... 109
Ward, Donald 1930- ... 37-40R
Ward, Douglas Turner 1930- ... 81-84
See also BW
See also DLB 7, 38
See also CLC 19
Ward, Ed(mund O.) 1948- ... 114
Ward, Elizabeth 1952- ... 110
Ward, Elizabeth Campbell 1936- ... 45-48
Ward, Elizabeth Honor (Shedden) 1926- ... 9-10R
Ward, Eric
See Ebon, Martin
Ward, Evelyn
See Everett-Green, Evelyn
Ward, Fred 1935- ... 85-88
Ward, Harry Merrill 1929- ... CANR-2
Earlier sketch in CA 2R
Ward, Herman Matthew 1914- ... CANR-18
Earlier sketches in CA 7-8R, CANR-2
Ward, Hiley Henry 1929- ... CANR-2
Earlier sketch in CA 2R
Ward, J. Alan 1937- ... 114
Ward, J(oseph) Neville 1915- ... 77-80
Ward, J(ohn) P(owell) 1937- ... 109
Ward, J(ohn) T(owers) 1930- ... CANR-7
Earlier sketch in CA 7-8R
Ward, James A(rthur) 1941- ... 49-52
Ward, James Myron 1919-1984 Obituary ... 112
Ward, John (Stanton) 1917- ... SATA-42
Ward, John M(anning) 1919- ... 23-24R
Ward, John Owen 1919- ... 13-14R
Ward, John Stephen Keith 1938- ... 109
Ward, John Towers 1930-1987 ... 109
Obituary ... 122
Ward, John William 1922-1985 ... 5-6R
Obituary ... 116
Ward, Jonas
See Ard, William (Thomas)
and Cox, William R(obert)
and Garfield, Brian (Wynne)
Ward, Jonathon
See Stine, Whitney Ward
Ward, Joseph A(nthony, Jr.) 1931- ... 2R
Ward, Justine Bayard Cutting 1879-1975
Obituary ... 61-64
Ward, (John Stephen) Keith 1938- ... CANR-16
Earlier sketch in CA 29-32R
Ward, Lynd (Kendall) 1905-1985 ... 17-18R
Obituary ... 116
See also SATA 2, 36, 42
See also DLB 22
Ward, Maisie 1889-1975 ... 69-72
Obituary ... 53-56

Ward, Martha (Eads) ... 17-18R
See also SATA 5
Ward, Mary Josephine
See Ward, Maisie
Ward, Melanie
See Curtis, Richard (Alan)
and Lynch, Marilyn
Ward, Michael 1939- ... 37-40R
Ward, Mrs. Humphry 1851-1920 ... DLB-18
Ward, Nathaniel 1578(?)-1652 ... DLB-24
Ward, Norman 1918- ... 41-44R
Ward, Olivia Tucker 1927- ... 57-60
Ward, Patricia A(nn) 1940- ... 57-60
Ward, Paul W. 1905-1976 Obituary ... 69-72
Ward, Pearl L(ewis) 1920- ... 107
Ward, Peter
See Faust, Frederick (Shiller)
Ward, Philip 1938- ... CANR-12
Earlier sketch in CA 25-28R
Ward, Philip C. 1932- ... 21-22R
Ward, R(ichard) H(eron) 1910-1969 ... CAP-1
Earlier sketch in CA 11-12
Ward, R. Patrick
See Holzapfel, Rudolf Patrick
Ward, Ralph Gerard 1933- ... 107
Ward, Ralph T(homas) 1927- ... 49-52
Ward, Richard J(oseph) 1921- ... 41-44R
Ward, Ritchie R(unyan) 1906- ... 29-32R
Ward, Robert 1943- ... 104
Ward, Robert E(rnest) 1927- ... 49-52
Ward, Robert Elmer 1937- ... 49-52
Ward, Ronald A(rthur) 1908- ... 53-56
Ward, Russel (Braddock) 1914- ... CANR-22
Earlier sketch in CA 103
Ward, Russell A(very) 1947- ... 110
Ward, Stephen R(alph) 1938- ... 65-68
Ward, Ted (Warren) 1930- ... CANR-16
Earlier sketch in CA 97-100
Ward, Theodora 1890-1974 ... CAP-2
Obituary ... 53-56
Earlier sketch in CA 33-36
Ward, Theodore (James) 1902-1983 ... 125
Obituary ... 109
See also BW
See also DLB 76
Ward, Virgil S(cott) 1916- ... 2R
Ward, Waylon O. 1942- ... 114
Ward, William Alan Heaton
See Heaton-Ward, William Alan
Ward, William Arthur 1921- ... 29-32R
Ward, William B(ethea) 1912- ... 5-6R
Ward, William Ernest Frank 1900- ... CANR-19
Earlier sketches in CA 11-12R, CANR-4
Ward, William G. 1929- ... 21-22R
Ward, William R(eed) 1918- ... 61-64
Ward, Winfred O('Neil) 1933- ... 106
Warddel, Nora Helen
See Heron-Allen, Edward
Warde, Alan 1949- ... 112
Warde, William F.
See Novack, George (Edward)
Wardell, Dean
See Prince, J(ack) H(arvey)
Wardell, Phyl(lis Robinson) 1909- ... CAP-1
Earlier sketch in CA 11-12
Warden, G(erard) B(ryce) 1939- ... 29-32R
Warden, John 1936- ... 41-44R
Warden, Lewis (Christopher) 1913- ... 15-16R
Wardhaugh, Ronald 1932- ... 37-40R
Wardle, David 1930- ... 69-72
Wardle, (John) Irving 1929- ... 77-80
Wardle, Lynn D(ennis) 1947- ... 109
Wardle, Ralph Martin 1909- ... CANR-5
Earlier sketch in CA 2R
Wardman, Alan (Edgar) 1926-1986 ... 77-80
Obituary ... 120
Ward-Perkins, John Bryan 1912-1981 ... 93-96
Obituary ... 108
Wardroper, John (Edmund) 1923- ... 29-32R
Wardropper, Bruce W(ear) 1919- ... 15-16R
Ward-Thomas, Evelyn Bridget Patricia
Stephens 1928- ... CANR-26
Earlier sketches in CA 9-10R, CANR-5
Ware, Ciji 1942- ... 103
Ware, Clyde 1932- ... 33-36R
Ware, Emma 1896(?)-1975 Obituary ... 57-60
Ware, George W(hitaker) 1902- ... 13-14R
Ware, Gilbert 1933- ... 65-68
Ware, Jean (Jones) 1914- ... CAP-1
Earlier sketch in CA 11-12
Ware, John
See Mabley, Edward (Howe)
Ware, Kallistos (Timothy Richard)
1934- ... CANR-24
Earlier sketches in CA 11-12R, CANR-7
Ware, Leon (Vernon) 1909-1976 ... CANR-2
Earlier sketch in CA 2R
See also SATA 4
Ware, Leonard 1900(?)-1976 Obituary ... 69-72
Ware, Runa Erwin ... CAP-2
Earlier sketch in CA 29-32
Ware, Timothy
See Ware, Kallistos (Timothy Richard)
Ware, W. Porter 1904- ... 105
Ware, Wallace
See Karp, David
Ware, William 1797-1852 ... DLB-1
Wareham, John 1940- ... 101
Warenski, Marilyn L(iston) 1931- ... 117
Warfel, Harry R(edcay) 1899-1971 ... CAP-1
Earlier sketch in CA 13-14
Warfield, Gerald (Alexander) 1940- ... 117
Warford, Jeremy J(ames) 1938- ... 37-40R
Wargo, Dan M. 1920- ... 21-22R
Warhaft, Sidney 1921- ... 61-64
Warhol, Andy 1927(?)-1987 ... 89-92
Obituary ... 121
See also CLC 20
Wark, David M(ayer) 1934- ... 33-36R
Wark, Ian W(illiam) 1899- ... CAP-2
Earlier sketch in CA 29-32
Wark, Robert R(odger) 1924- ... CANR-8
Earlier sketch in CA 61-64
Wark, Wesley K. 1952- ... 123
Warkentin, Germaine (Therese) 1933- ... 109
Warkentin, John 1928- ... 11-12R
Warland, John
See Buchanan-Brown, John
Warlimont, Walter 1894- ... CAP-1
Earlier sketch in CA 15-16
Warlum, Michael Frank 1940- ... 37-40R
Warman, (William) Eric 1904- ... CAP-1
Earlier sketch in CA 13-14
Warman, Henry J(ohn) 1907- ... 41-44R
Warmbrand, Max 1896(?)-1976 Obituary ... 65-68
Warmbrunn, Werner 1920- ... 23-24R
Warmington, Brian Herbert 1924- ... 65-68
Warmington, E(ric) H(erbert) 1898-1987 ... 124
Warmington, William Allan 1922- ... 7-8R
Warmke, Roman F. 1929- ... CANR-9
Earlier sketch in CA 19-20R
Warnath, Charles F. 1925- ... 37-40R
Warne, Clinton L. 1921- ... 13-14R
Warne, Colston Estey 1900-1987 Obituary ... 122
Warne, William E(lmo) 1905- ... 41-44R
Warner, Alan 1912- ... 104
Warner, B. F.
See Bowers, Warner Fremont
Warner, Bob
See Warner, Robert
Warner, Charles Dudley 1829-1900 ... DLB-64
Warner, Daniel S(umner) 1906-1983 ... CANR-16
Earlier sketch in CA 3R
Warner, Deborah Jean 1941- ... 108
Warner, Denis Ashton 1917- ... CANR-3
Earlier sketch in CA 5-6R
Warner, Edythe Records 1916- ... 5-6R
Warner, Emily S(mith) 1902(?)-1980
Obituary ... 97-100
Warner, Esther S.
See Dendel, Esther (Sietmann Warner)
Warner, Francis (Robert le Plastrier)
1937- ... CANR-11
Earlier sketch in CA 53-56
See also CLC 14
Warner, Frank
See Richardson, Gladwell
Warner, Frank A. ... CANR-26
Earlier sketches in CA 19-20, CAP-2
See also SATA 1
Warner, Gary 1936- ... 23-24R
Warner, (George) Geoffrey John 1923- ... 3R
Warner, Gertrude Chandler 1890-1979 ... CANR-3
Earlier sketch in CA 4R
See also SATA 9
Warner, Glen 1947- ... 121
Warner, H(oyt) Landon 1911- ... 15-16R
Warner, Harry, Jr. 1922- ... 29-32R
Warner, Jack 1896-1981 Obituary ... 108
Warner, Jack L(eonard) 1892-1978
Obituary ... 108
Warner, James A(loysius) 1918- ... CANR-24
Earlier sketch in CA 45-48
Warner, Ken(neth Wilson, Jr.) 1928- ... CANR-10
Earlier sketch in CA 65-68
Warner, Kenneth (Lewis) 1915- ... CAP-1
Earlier sketch in CA 9-10
Warner, Langdon 1881-1955 Brief entry ... 112
Warner, Lucien (Hynes) 1900-1963
Obituary ... 112
Warner, Lucille Schulberg ... CANR-11
Earlier sketch in CA 69-72
See also SATA 30
Warner, Marina 1946- ... CANR-21
Earlier sketch in CA 65-68
Warner, Matt
See Fichter, George S.
Warner, Oliver (Martin Wilson)
1903-1976 ... CANR-3
Obituary ... 69-72
Earlier sketch in CA 3R
See also SATA 29
Warner, Philip 1914- ... CANR-18
Earlier sketch in CA 101
Warner, Rex (Ernest) 1905-1986 ... 89-92
Obituary ... 119
See also DLB 15
See also CLC 45
Warner, Richard 1943- ... 120
Warner, Robert 1905- ... 53-56
Warner, Robert M(ark) 1927- ... CANR-7
Earlier sketch in CA 11-12R
Warner, Sam Bass, Jr. 1928- ... CANR-17
Earlier sketches in CA 5-6R, CANR-2
Warner, Seth 1927- ... 53-56
Warner, Susan (Bogert) 1819-1885 ... DLB-3, 42
Warner, Sylvia (Constance) Ashton
See Ashton-Warner, Sylvia (Constance)
Warner, Sylvia Townsend 1893-1978 ... CANR-16
Obituary ... 77-80
Earlier sketch in CA 61-64
See also DLB 34
See also CLC 7, 19
Warner, Val 1946- ... CANR-23
Earlier sketch in CA 49-52
Warner, Virginia
See Brodine, Virginia Warner
Warner, W(illiam) Lloyd 1898-1970 ... CANR-2
Obituary ... 29-32R
Earlier sketch in CA 2R
Warner, Wayne E(arl) 1933- ... CANR-3
Earlier sketch in CA 49-52
Warner, William W(hitesides) 1920-
Brief entry ... 114
Warner-Crozetti, R(uth G.) 1913- ... 101
Warnick, Barbara 1946- ... 120
Warnock, G(eoffrey) J(ames) 1923- ... 21-22R
Warnock, Mary (Wilson) 1924- ... CANR-8
Earlier sketch in CA 5-6R
Warr, Peter B(ryan) 1937- ... 25-28R
Warrack, Graeme Matthew 1913-1985
Obituary ... 115
Warrack, John 1928- ... CANR-5
Earlier sketch in CA 15-16R
Warre, Michael 1922-1987 Obituary ... 121
Warren, Andrew
See Tute, Warren (Stanley)
Warren, Austin 1899-1986 ... 19-20R
Obituary ... 120
Warren, Betsy
See Warren, Elizabeth Avery
Warren, Bill 1943- ... 118
Warren, Billy
See Warren, William Stephen
Warren, Cathy ... SATA-46
Warren, Dave
See Wiersbe, Warren W(endell)
Warren, David 1943- ... 77-80
Warren, Donald Irwin 1935- ... CANR-1
Earlier sketch in CA 45-48
Warren, Donald R. 1933- ... 111
Warren, Doug(las) 1935- ... 61-64
Warren, E(ugene) H(oward), Jr. 1943- ... 111
Warren, Earl 1891-1974 ... 123
Obituary ... 49-52
Warren, Elizabeth
See Supraner, Robyn
Warren, Elizabeth Avery 1916- ... CANR-8
Earlier sketch in CA 7-8R
See also SATA 38, 46
Warren, (Francis) Eugene 1941- ... CANR-1
Earlier sketch in CA 49-52
Warren, Frank A. III 1933- Brief entry ... 115
Warren, Gordon Harris 1944- ... 114
Warren, Harold Ostrander, Jr. 1910-1985
Obituary ... 116
Warren, Harris G(aylord) 1906- ... CANR-5
Earlier sketch in CA 2R
Warren, Harry
See Guaragna, Salvatore
Warren, James E(dward), Jr. 1908- ... CANR-24
Earlier sketch in CA 23-24R
Warren, James Hugo, Jr. 1928(?)-1983
Obituary ... 110
Warren, Jefferson T(rowbridge) 1912- ... 41-44R
Warren, John Byrne Leicester
See De Tabley, Lord
Warren, Joyce W(illiams) 1935- ... 77-80
See also SATA 18
Warren, Kenneth 1931- ... 109
Warren, Lansing 1894-1987 Obituary ... 124
Warren, Lella 1899-1982 Obituary ... 113
See also DLBY 83
Warren, Louis Austin 1885-1983 ... CANR-21
Obituary ... 110
Earlier sketch in CA 5-6R
Warren, Louise 1909(?)-1981 Obituary ... 104
Warren, Lucian (Crissey) 1913-1988 ... 101
Obituary ... 126
Warren, Mary Bondurant 1930- ... CANR-12
Earlier sketch in CA 73-76
Warren, Mary Douglas
See Greig, Maysie
Warren, Mary Phraner 1929- ... CANR-5
Earlier sketch in CA 53-56
See also SATA 10
Warren, Matthew Madison 1907-1986
Obituary ... 119
Warren, Mercy Otis 1728-1814 ... DLB-31
Warren, Michael 1935- ... 112
Warren, Patricia Nell 1936- ... CANR-1
Earlier sketch in CA 45-48
Warren, Peter Whitson 1941- ... CANR-5
Earlier sketch in CA 53-56
Warren, Richard M. 1925- ... 112
Warren, Robert Penn 1905- ... CANR-10
Earlier sketch in CA 13-14R
See also SATA 46
See also DLB 2, 48
See also DLBY 80
See also CLC 1, 4, 6, 8, 10, 13, 18, 39
See also AITN 1
Warren, Roland L(eslie) 1915- ... CANR-26
Earlier sketches in CA 57-60, CANR-10
Warren, Sidney 1916- ... 25-28R
Warren, Thomas (Bratton) 1920- ... 103
Warren, Thomas L(eo) 1937- ... 111
Warren, Vernon
See Chapman, G(eorge) W(arren) Vernon
Warren, Virginia Burgess 1913- ... 15-16R
Warren, W(ilfred) Lewis 1929- ... CANR-21
Earlier sketch in CA 3R
Warren, W(illiam) Preston 1901- ... 37-40R
Warren, William Stephen 1882-1968 ... CAP-2
Earlier sketch in CA 21-22
See also SATA 9
Warrender, James Howard 1922-1985
Obituary ... 116
Warrick, Patricia Scott 1925- ... CANR-25
Earlier sketches in CA 61-64, CANR-8
See also SATA 35
Warriner, Charles K(ing) 1920- ... 41-44R
Warriner, John 1907(?)-1987 Obituary ... 123
See also SATA 53
Warrner, Thomas W(endell) 1955- ... 118
Warry, J(ohn) G(ibson) 1916- ... 7-8R
Warsaw, Irene ... CAP-1
Earlier sketch in CA 15-16
Warsh
See Warshaw, Jerry
Warsh, David (Lewis) 1944- ... 118
Warsh, Lewis 1944- ... CANR-24
Earlier sketches in CA 61-64, CANR-9
Warshaw, Jerry 1929- ... CANR-14
Earlier sketch in CA 37-40R
See also SATA 30
Warshaw, Leon J(oseph) 1917- ... 107
Warshofsky, Fred 1931- ... 11-12R
See also SATA 24
Warshofsky, Isaac
See Singer, Isaac Bashevis
Warth, Robert D(ouglas) 1921- ... 11-12R
Wartofsky, Marx W(illiam) 1928- ... 41-44R
Wartofsky, (William) Victor 1931- ... 29-32R
Wartski, Maureen (Ann Crane) 1940- ... 89-92
See also SATA 37, 50
Warwick, Alan R(oss) 1900-1973 ... 112
See also SATA 42
Warwick, Christopher 1949- ... 110
Warwick, Dennis 1930- ... 73-76
Warwick, Dolores
See Frese, Dolores Warwick
Warwick, Donald P(hillip) 1934- ... 118
Warwick, Jack 1930- ... 29-32R
Warwick, James 1894(?)-1983 Obituary ... 110
Warwick, Jarvis
See Garner, Hugh
Warwick, Ray 1911(?)-1983 Obituary ... 109
Warwick, Roger 1912- ... 109
Warzeski, Walter C. 1929- ... 37-40R
Wa-Sha-Quon-Asin
See Belaney, Archibald Stansfeld
Wa-sha-quon-asin
See Belaney, Archibald Stansfeld
Washburn, (Henry) Bradford (Jr.)
1910- ... CANR-3
Earlier sketch in CA 49-52
See also SATA 38
Washburn, Charles 1890(?)-1972
Obituary ... 104
Washburn, Dorothy K(oster) 1945- ... CANR-24
Earlier sketch in CA 106
Washburn, Jan(ice) 1926- ... 93-96
Washburn, Mark 1948- ... 77-80
Washburn, O(swell) A(aron) 1914- ... 57-60
Washburn, Sherwood L(arned) 1911-
Brief entry ... 105
Washburn, Wilcomb Edward 1925- ... 41-44R
Washburne, Carleton W(olsey) 1889- ... CAP-1
Earlier sketch in CA 15-16
Washburne, Heluiz Chandler 1892-1970 ... CAP-1
Obituary ... 104
Earlier sketch in CA 11-12
See also SATA 10, 26
Washington, Alex
See Harris, Mark
Washington, Booker T(aliaferro)
1856-1915 ... 125
Brief entry ... 114
See also BW
See also SATA 28
See also TCLC 10
Washington, Chester Lloyd 1902-1983
Obituary ... 110
Washington, George 1732-1799 ... DLB-31
Washington, Gladys J(oseph) 1931- ... 29-32R
Washington, Harold R(obert) 1935- ... 112
Washington, Ida Harrison 1924- ... 107
Washington, Joseph R(eed), Jr. 1930- ... 11-12R
Washington, (Catherine) Marguerite
Beauchamp 1892-1972 ... CAP-1
Earlier sketch in CA 9-10
Washington, Mary Helen 1941- ... CANR-26
Earlier sketch in CA 65-68
See also BW
Washington, Pat Beauchamp
See Washington, (Catherine) Marguerite
Beauchamp
Washton, Nathan S(eymour) 1916- ... 53-56
Wasiolek, Edward 1924- ... CANR-6
Earlier sketch in CA 2R
Waskin, Yvonne 1923- ... 23-24R
Waskow, Arthur I(rwin) 1933- ... CANR-4
Earlier sketch in CA 7-8R
Wasley, Robert S(echrist) 1918- ... 17-18R
Wasmuth, William J. 1925- ... CANR-24
Earlier sketch in CA 45-48
Wason, Betty
See Wason, Elizabeth
Wason, Elizabeth 1912- ... CANR-2
Earlier sketch in CA 4R
Wason, P(eter) C(athcart) 1924- ... 45-48
Wasow, Mona 1933- ... 110
Wassenbergh, Henri Abraham 1924- ... 21-22R
Wasser, Henry H. 1919- ... CANR-8
Earlier sketch in CA 21-22R
Wasserfall, Adel 1918- ... CANR-6
Earlier sketch in CA 3R
Wasserman, Aaron O(sias) 1927- ... 53-56
Wasserman, Burton 1929- ... 53-56
Wasserman, Dale 1917- ... 49-52
Wasserman, Earl R(eeves) 1913-1973 ... CAP-2
Earlier sketch in CA 17-18
Wasserman, Gary 1944- ... 69-72
Wasserman, Harvey 1945- ... 45-48
Wasserman, Jack 1921- ... 61-64
Wasserman, John L. 1938- ... 77-80
Wasserman, Mark 1946- ... 125
Wasserman, Max Judd 1895-1977 ... CANR-4
Earlier sketch in CA 5-6R
Wasserman, Paul 1924- ... CANR-25
Earlier sketches in CA 1R, CANR-1
Wasserman, Pauline 1943- ... CANR-24
Earlier sketch in CA 110
Wasserman, Selma (Ginsberg) 1929- ... 5-6R

Wasserman, Sheldon 1940- ... CANR-24
Earlier sketches in CA 65-68, CANR-9
Wassermann, (Karl) Jakob 1873-1934
Brief entry ... 104
See also DLB 66
See also TCLC 6
Wasserstein, Abraham 1921- ... 109
Wasserstein, Bruce 1947- ... 37-40R
Wasserstein, Susan 1952- ... 107
Wasserstein, Wendy 1950- Brief entry ... 121
See also CLC 32
Wasserstrom, Richard Alan 1936- ... CANR-6
Earlier sketch in CA 3R
Wasserstrom, (Jacob) William
1922-1985 ... 11-12R
Obituary ... 115
Wassersug, Joseph D. 1912- ... 19-20R
Wassil, Aly 1930- ... 19-20R
Wassmer, Arthur C(harles) 1947- ... 103
Wassner, Selig O. 1923- ... 25-28R
Wasson, Ben 1899(?)-1982 Obituary ... 114
Wasson, Chester R(eynolds) 1906- ... CANR-10
Earlier sketch in CA 15-16R
Wasson, David Atwood 1823-1887 ... DLB-1
Wasson, Donald 1914(?)-1976 Obituary ... 69-72
Wasson, John M. 1928- ... 45-48
Wasson, R(obert) Gordon 1898-
Brief entry ... 116
Wasti, Syed R(azi) 1929- ... CANR-7
Earlier sketch in CA 15-16R
Waswo, Richard 1939- ... 53-56
Watanabe, Hitoshi 1919- ... 73-76
Watanabe, Ruth T(aiko) 1916- ... 37-40R
Watanabe, Shigeo 1928- ... 112
See also SATA 32, 39
See also CLR 8
Waten, Judah Leon 1911- ... 101
Water, Silas
See Loomis, Noel (Miller)
Waterfield, Gordon 1903-1987 ... 61-64
Obituary ... 124
Waterfield, Robin (Everard) 1914- ... 49-52
Waterford, Van
See Wanrooy, Willem F(rederik)
Waterhouse, Charles 1924- ... 29-32R
Waterhouse, Ellis K(irkham) 1905-1985 ... 65-68
Obituary ... 117
Waterhouse, Keith (Spencer) 1929- ... 7-8R
See also DLB 13, 15
See also CLC 47
Waterhouse, Larry G(ene) 1944- ... 37-40R
Waterlow, Charlotte 1915- ... 25-28R
Waterman, Andrew (John) 1940- ... 109
See also DLB 40
Waterman, Arthur E. 1926- ... 17-18R
Waterman, Bic
See Joseph, Stephen M.
Waterman, Cary (Martha) 1942- ... 103
Waterman, Charles F(rederick) 1913- ... 49-52
Waterman, Guy 1932- ... 97-100
Waterman, John Thomas 1918- ... CANR-8
Earlier sketch in CA 5-6R
Waterman, Laura 1939- ... 97-100
Waterman, Leroy 1875-1972 ... CAP-1
Obituary ... 33-36R
Earlier sketch in CA 19-20
Waterman, Margaret 1909- ... 37-40R
Waterman, Richard Alan 1914-1971
Obituary ... 111
Watermeier, Daniel J(ude) 1940- ... 73-76
Water Rat
See Jones, Stephen (Phillip)
Waters, Bob 1921(?)-1987 Obituary ... 122
Waters, Brian Power
See Power-Waters, Brian
Waters, Chocolate 1949- ... 77-80
Waters, Chris
See Waters, Harold A(rthur)
Waters, D(avid) W(atkin) 1911- ... 25-28R
Waters, Enoch P. 1910(?)-1987 Obituary ... 122
Waters, Ethel 1896-1977 ... 81-84
Obituary ... 73-76
Waters, Frank (Joseph) 1902- ... CANR-18
Earlier sketches in CA 5-6R, CANR-3
See also DLBY 86
Waters, Harold A(rthur) 1926- ... 53-56
Waters, John (M.) 1946(?)- Brief entry ... 126
Waters, John F(rederick) 1930- ... CANR-23
Earlier sketch in CA 37-40R
See also SATA 4
Waters, K(enneth) H(ugh) 1912- ... 120
Waters, Marianne
See Waters, Chocolate
Waters, Mary-Alice 1942- ... CANR-9
Earlier sketch in CA 61-64
Waters, Michael 1949- ... CANR-10
Earlier sketch in CA 65-68
Waters, Roger 1944- ... CLC-35
Waters, Thomas F(rank) 1926- ... 81-84
Waters, William R(oland) 1920- ... 49-52
Waterston, Albert 1907- ... CAP-1
Earlier sketch in CA 13-14
Waterston, Barbara Johns 1940- ... 25-28R
Waterston, (Margaret) Elizabeth (Hillman)
1922- ... 69-72
Waterton, Betty (Marie) 1923- ... 111
See also SATA 34, 37
Wathen, Richard B. 1917- ... 37-40R
Wathern, Peter 1947- ... 105
Watjen, Carolyn L. T. ... 85-88
Watkin, David (John) 1941- ... CANR-26
Earlier sketch in CA 29-32R
Watkin, Edward Ingram 1888-1981
Obituary ... 103
Watkin, Lawrence Edward 1901- ... 81-84
Watkins, A(rthur) M(artin) 1924- ... CANR-7
Earlier sketch in CA 11-12R
Watkins, Alan (Rhun) 1933- ... 104
Watkins, Arthur Rich 1916- ... 41-44R
Watkins, Arthur Thomas Levi 1907-1965 ... 7-8R
Watkins, Arthur V(ivian) 1886-1973
Obituary ... 111
Watkins, Evan Paul 1946- ... 104
Watkins, Floyd C. 1920- ... CANR-18
Earlier sketches in CA 2R, CANR-2
Watkins, Frances Ellen
See Harper, Frances Ellen Watkins
Watkins, Gerrold
See Malzberg, Barry N(athaniel)
Watkins, Glenn (Elson) 1927- Brief entry ... 117
Watkins, Gordon R(onald) 1930- ... 37-40R
Watkins, Grace F. 1927- ... 23-24R
Watkins, Gwen(doline Mary) 1923- ... 116
Watkins, J(ohn) W(illiam) N(evill) 1924- ... 21-22R
Watkins, Jane 1929- ... 77-80
Watkins, Joan C.
See Casale, Joan T(herese)
Watkins, John C(umming), Jr. 1935- ... 113
Watkins, John G(oodrich) 1913- ... CANR-17
Earlier sketches in CA 2R, CANR-1
Watkins, Keith 1931- ... 106
Watkins, Mark Hanna 1903-1976
Obituary ... 65-68
Watkins, Mary M. 1950- ... CANR-20
Earlier sketch in CA 104
Watkins, Mel 1940- ... 89-92
Watkins, Peter 1934- ... 109
Watkins, Ralph J(ames) 1896-1984 ... 45-48
Obituary ... 113
Watkins, (Arthur) Ronald (Dare) 1904- ... 53-56
Watkins, T(homas) H(enry) 1936- ... CANR-14
Earlier sketch in CA 37-40R
Watkins, Tobias 1780-1855 ... DLB-73
Watkins, Vernon Phillips 1906-1967 ... CAP-1
Obituary ... 25-28R
Earlier sketch in CA 9-10
See also DLB 20
See also CLC 43
Watkins, William Jon 1942- ... 41-44R
Watkinson, Valerie
See Elliston, Valerie Mae (Watkinson)
Watkins-Pitchford, Denys James 1905- ... CANR-4
Earlier sketch in CA 9-10R
See also SATA 6
See also SAAS 4
Watkyn, Arthur
See Watkins, Arthur Thomas Levi
Watland, Charles D(unton) 1913-1972 ... CAP-2
Earlier sketch in CA 25-28
Watlington, Patricia (Sue) 1933- ... 37-40R
Watmough, David 1926- ... CANR-15
Earlier sketch in CA 85-88
See also DLB 53
Watney, John B(asil) 1915- ... CANR-5
Earlier sketch in CA 9-10R
Watney, Sanders ?-1983 Obituary ... 109
Watson, (John Hugh) Adam 1914- ... CANR-17
Earlier sketch in CA 25-28R
Watson, Alan
See Watson, William Alexander Jardine
Watson, Alan D(ouglas) 1942- ... CANR-6
Earlier sketch in CA 57-60
Watson, Aldren A(uld) 1917- ... CANR-4
Earlier sketch in CA 81-84
See also SATA 36, 42
Watson, Andrew Samuel 1920- ... 45-48
Watson, B. S.
See Teitelbaum, Michael
Watson, Barbara Bellow ... 77-80
Watson, Bernard B(ennett) 1911-1977
Obituary ... 69-72
Watson, Billy 1938- ... 77-80
Watson, Burton (DeWitt) 1925- ... CANR-18
Earlier sketches in CA 7-8R, CANR-3
Watson, Charles N(elles, Jr.) 1939- ... 113
Watson, Charles S(t. Denis), Jr. 1934- ... 61-64
Watson, Clarissa ... 69-72
Watson, Clyde 1947- ... CANR-4
Earlier sketch in CA 49-52
See also SATA 5
See also CLR 3
Watson, Colin 1920-1983 ... CANR-2
Obituary ... 108
Earlier sketch in CA 3R
Watson, David 1934- ... CANR-24
Earlier sketch in CA 45-48
Watson, David Christopher Knight
1934(?)-1984 Obituary ... 112
Watson, David Robin 1935- ... 109
Watson, Donald Stevenson 1909- ... CAP-1
Earlier sketch in CA 13-14
Watson, E(lliot) L(ovegood) Grant
1885-1970 ... CAP-1
Earlier sketch in CA 11-12
Watson, Elaine 1921- ... 115
Watson, Ernest W(illiam) 1884- ... 7-8R
Watson, Eunice L. 1932- ... 65-68
Watson, F. J. B.
See Watson, Francis John Bagott
Watson, Fletcher Guard (Jr.) 1912- ... 5-6R
Watson, Francis John Bagott 1907-
Brief entry ... 116
Watson, Francis M(arion) 1921- ... 105
Watson, Frank
See Ames, Francis H.
Watson, Gayle Hudgens
See Hudgens, A(lice) Gayle
Watson, George (Grimes) 1927- ... CANR-20
Earlier sketches in CA 13-14R, CANR-5
Watson, George (Henry) 1936- ... 77-80
Watson, Goodwin 1899(?)-1976 Obituary ... 69-72
Watson, Graham (Angus) 1913- ... 104
Watson, Harold M. 1924- ... 37-40R
Watson, Harry Legare 1949- ... 111
Watson, Helen Orr 1892-1978 ... 7-8R
Obituary ... 77-80
See also SATA 24
Watson, (George) Hugh (Nicholas) Seton
See Seton-Watson, (George) Hugh
(Nicholas)
Watson, Ian 1943- ... CANR-24
Earlier sketch in CA 61-64
Watson, Irving S.
See Mencken, H(enry) L(ouis)
Watson, J. R. 1934- ... CANR-18
Earlier sketch in CA 97-100
Watson, J(ohn) Steven 1916- ... 5-6R
Watson, J(ames) Wreford 1915- ... CANR-19
Earlier sketch in CA 25-28R
Watson, Jack Brierley 1927- ... 104
Watson, James 1936- ... CANR-4
Earlier sketch in CA 53-56
See also SATA 10
Watson, James B(ennett) 1918- ... 41-44R
Watson, James D(ewey) 1928- ... 25-28R
Watson, James Gray 1939- ... 29-32R
Watson, Jane Werner 1915- ... CANR-8
Earlier sketch in CA 7-8R
See also SATA 3
Watson, Janet Lynch
See Lynch-Watson, Janet
Watson, Jean 1936- ... CANR-16
Earlier sketch in CA 89-92
Watson, John A(rthur) F(ergus) 1903- ... 65-68
Watson, John H.
See Farmer, Philip Jose
Watson, Julia 1943- ... CANR-15
Earlier sketch in CA 41-44R
Watson, Ken 1925(?)-1984 Obituary ... 114
Watson, Lyall 1939- ... CANR-24
Earlier sketches in CA 57-60, CANR-8
Watson, Margaret Goodrich 1913- ... 15-16R
Watson, Mark Skinner 1887-1966
Obituary ... 89-92
Watson, Mary Gordon
See Gordon-Watson, Mary
Watson, Nan Marriott
See Marriott-Watson, Nan
Watson, Nancy Dingman ... CANR-4
Earlier sketch in CA 49-52
See also SATA 32
Watson, O(scar) Michael 1936- ... 33-36R
Watson, Patricia Seets 1930- ... 121
Watson, Patrick 1929- ... 97-100
Watson, Patty Jo (Andersen) 1932- ... CANR-13
Earlier sketch in CA 77-80
Watson, Pauline 1925- ... CANR-11
Earlier sketch in CA 69-72
See also SATA 14
Watson, Peter L(eslie) 1944- ... 53-56
Watson, Philip S(aville) 1909- ... 104
Watson, Richard A(bernethy) 1923- ... CANR-25
Earlier sketch in CA 45-48
Watson, Richard A(llan) 1931- ... 77-80
Watson, Richard F.
See Silverberg, Robert
Watson, Richard L(yness), Jr. 1914- ... 17-18R
Watson, Robert (Winthrop) 1925- ... CANR-4
Earlier sketch in CA 2R
Watson, Robert I(rving) 1909-1980
Obituary ... 111
Watson, Robert N(athaniel) 1953- ... 118
Watson, Roderick (Bruce) 1943- ... 102
Watson, Russell 1939- ... 77-80
Watson, Sally (Lou) 1924- ... CANR-3
Earlier sketch in CA 5-6R
See also SATA 3
Watson, Sara Ruth 1907- ... 37-40R
Watson, Sheila 1909- ... DLB-60
See also AITN 2
Watson, Thomas J(oel) 1948- ... 109
Watson, Tom, Jr. 1918- ... 21-22R
Watson, Wendy (McLeod) 1942- ... CANR-4
Earlier sketch in CA 49-52
See also SATA 5
Watson, Wilfred 1911- ... DLB-60
Watson, Will
See Floren, Lee
Watson, William 1917- ... 11-12R
Watson, William Alexander Jardine
1933- ... CANR-12
Earlier sketch in CA 13-14R
Watson Taylor, Elizabeth 1915- ... SATA-41
Watson-Watt, Robert A(lexander)
1892-1973 ... CAP-1
Obituary ... 45-48
Earlier sketch in CA 13-14
Watstein, Esther 1928- ... 57-60
Watt, (John) David (Henry) 1932-1987
Obituary ... 122
Watt, Donald 1938- ... 41-44R
Watt, Donald Beates 1893-1977 Obituary ... 73-76
Watt, Donald Cameron
See Cameron Watt, Donald
Watt, Douglas (Benjamin) 1914- ... 69-72
Watt, Frank Hedden 1889-1981 Obituary ... 105
Watt, George Steven Harvie
See Harvie-Watt, George Steven
Watt, (Raymond Egerton) Harry
1906-1987 Obituary ... 122
Watt, Ian 1917- ... 13-14R
Watt, John Robertson 1934- ... 37-40R
Watt, Kenneth E(dmund) F(erguson)
1929- ... 61-64
Watt, Richard M(artin) 1930- ... 5-6R
Watt, Ruth M. 1919- ... CANR-10
Earlier sketch in CA 57-60
Watt, Thomas 1935- ... 37-40R
See also SATA 4
Watt, W(illiam) Montgomery 1909- ... CANR-21
Earlier sketches in CA 2R, CANR-6
Wattel, Harold Louis 1921- ... 126
Wattenbarger, James L(orenzo) 1922- ... 106
Wattenberg, Ben J. 1933- ... 57-60
Wattenberg, William W(olff) 1911- ... 23-24R
Wattenmaker, Richard J. 1941- ... 104
Watters, Barbara H(unt) 1907-1984 ... CANR-3
Obituary ... 111
Earlier sketch in CA 7-8R
Watters, (Walter) Pat(terson) 1927- ... CANR-8
Earlier sketch in CA 23-24R
Watters, R(eginald) E(yre) 1912- ... 25-28R
Watterson, Henry 1840-1921 ... DLB-25
Watterson, Joseph 1900-1972 ... CAP-2
Obituary ... 33-36R
Earlier sketch in CA 25-28
Watt-Evans, Lawrence
See Evans, Lawrence Watt
Wattie, Margaret
See 'Espinasse, Margaret
Wattles, Santha Rama Rau 1923- ... CANR-1
Earlier sketch in CA 1R
Watts, A. J.
See Watts, Anthony J(ohn)
Watts, Al(bert) L. 1934- ... 85-88
Watts, Alan (James) 1925- ... 108
Watts, Alan Wilson 1915-1973 ... 41-44R
Obituary ... 45-48
See also DLB 16
Watts, Ann Chalmers 1938- ... 53-56
Watts, Anthony J(ohn) 1942- ... CANR-11
Earlier sketch in CA 25-28R
Watts, (Anna) Bernadette 1942- ... 29-32R
See also SATA 4
Watts, Charles Edwin 1929- ... CANR-2
Earlier sketch in CA 5-6R
Watts, David 1935- ... 53-56
Watts, Elizabeth (Bailey) Smithgall
1941- ... CANR-12
Earlier sketch in CA 73-76
Watts, Emily Stipes 1936- ... 81-84
Watts, Ephraim
See Horne, Richard Henry
Watts, Franklin (Mowry) 1904-1978 ... CANR-9
Obituary ... 89-92
Earlier sketches in CA 25-28, CAP-2
See also SATA 21, 46
Watts, Harold H(olliday) 1906- ... CAP-2
Earlier sketch in CA 13-14
Watts, Harriet M(ayor) 1933- ... 45-48
Watts, Isaac 1674-1748 ... SATA-52
Watts, J(ames) Wash(ington)
1896-197(?) ... CANR-20
Earlier sketch in CA 2R
Watts, John (Francis) 1926- ... CANR-21
Earlier sketch in CA 25-28R
Watts, John D. W. 1921- ... 21-22R
Watts, Lew 1922- ... 41-44R
Watts, Mabel Pizzey 1906- ... CANR-3
Earlier sketch in CA 4R
See also SATA 11
Watts, May Theilgaard 1893-1975 ... 41-44R
Watts, Meredith W(ayne, Jr.) 1941- ... CANR-24
Earlier sketch in CA 45-48
Watts, Michael J(ohn) 1951- ... 122
Watts, Peter Christopher 1919- ... CANR-12
Earlier sketch in CA 69-72
Watts, Reginald John 1931- ... 29-32R
Watts, Richard (Jr.) 1898-1981 Obituary ... 102
Watts, Ronald L(ampman) 1929- ... 23-24R
Watts, Sarah Miles 1934- ... 65-68
Watts, Stephen 1910- ... 7-8R
Watts, Thomas D(ale) 1941- ... 117
Watts, William 1930- ... CANR-1
Earlier sketch in CA 45-48
Watzlawick, Paul 1921- ... CANR-4
Earlier sketch in CA 11-12R
Waud, Elizabeth
See Tattersall, M(uriel Joyce)
Waugh, Albert E(dmund) 1902-1985 ... 37-40R
Obituary ... 115
Waugh, Alec
See Waugh, Alexander Raban
Waugh, Alexander Raban 1898-1981 ... CANR-22
Obituary ... 104
Earlier sketch in CA 17-18R
Waugh, Auberon (Alexander) 1939- ... CANR-22
Earlier sketches in CA 45-48, CANR-6
See also DLB 14
See also CLC 7
Waugh, C. C. Roessel
See Waugh, Carol-Lynn Roessel
and Waugh, Charles G(ordon)
Waugh, Carol-Lynn Roessel 1947- ... 107
See also SATA 41
Waugh, Charles
See Waugh, Charles G(ordon)
Waugh, Charles G(ordon) 1943- ... 123
Brief entry ... 118
Waugh, Coulton 1896(?)-1973 Obituary ... 41-44R
Waugh, Dorothy ... CANR-1
Earlier sketch in CA 2R
See also SATA 11
Waugh, Evelyn (Arthur St. John)
1903-1966 ... CANR-22
Obituary ... 25-28R
Earlier sketch in CA 85-88
See also DLB 15
See also CLC 1, 3, 8, 13, 19, 27, 44
Waugh, Harriet 1944- ... CANR-22
Earlier sketch in CA 85-88
See also CLC 6
Waugh, Harry 1904- ... 21-22R
Waugh, Hillary Baldwin 1920- ... CANR-2
Earlier sketch in CA 1R
Waugh, Linda R(uth) 1942- ... CANR-16
Earlier sketch in CA 89-92
Waugh, Nancy Collier 1930- ... 45-48

Waugh, Virginia
  See Sorenson, Virginia
Waughburton, Richard
  See Sykes, Christopher (Hugh)
Wauthier, Claude Rene 1923- 73-76
Wavell, Stewart Brooke 1921- 13-14R
Wax, Emmanuel 1911-1983 Obituary 109
Wax, Jimmy
  See Wax, Emmanuel
Wax, Judith 1932(?)-1979 101
  Obituary 85-88
Wax, Murray L(ionel) 1922- 37-40R
Wax, Rosalie (Amelia) H. 1911- 45-48
Wax, Sheldon 1928(?)-1979 Obituary ... 85-88
Waxberg, Joseph David 1922- 108
Waxman, Chaim I(saac) 1941- CANR-19
  Earlier sketch in CA 103
Waxman, Ruth B(ilgray) 1916- 93-96
Way, Irene 1924- 93-96
Way, Peter (Howard) 1936- Brief entry ... 115
Way, Robert E(dward) 1912- 57-60
Way, Walter L. 1931- 57-60
Way, Wayne
  See Humphries, Adelaide M.
Wayburn, Peggy 1921- CANR-24
  Earlier sketch in CA 45-48
Waylan, Mildred
  See Harrell, Irene B(urk)
Wayland, Patrick
  See O'Connor, Richard
Waymack, W(illiam) W(esley) 1888-1960
  Obituary 93-96
Wayman, Alex 1921- 104
Wayman, Dorothy G. 1893-1975 65-68
  Obituary 61-64
Wayman, Norbury Lansing 1912- 41-44R
Wayman, Thomas Ethan 1945- 101
Wayman, Tom
  See Wayman, Thomas Ethan
  See also DLB 53
Wayman, Tony Russell 1929- 25-28R
Wayne, Alice
  See Ressler, Alice
Wayne, Anderson
  See Dresser, Davis
Wayne, David
  See Balsiger, David (Wayne)
Wayne, Donald
  See Dodd, Wayne (Donald)
Wayne, Doreen 29-32R
Wayne, Frances
  See Wedge, Florence
Wayne, Jane Ellen 1936- CANR-20
  Earlier sketches in CA 49-52, CANR-4
Wayne, (Anne) Jenifer 1917-1982 105
  Obituary 108
  See also SATA 32
Wayne, Jerry 1919- 29-32R
Wayne, John 1907-1979 85-88
Wayne, Joseph
  See Overholser, Wayne D.
Wayne, Kyra Petrovskaya 1918- CANR-4
  Earlier sketch in CA 4R
  See also SATA 8
Wayne, Mary Collier 1913- 57-60
Wayne, Michael 1947- 112
Wayne, Philip
  See Powell, Philip Wayne
Wayne, Richard
  See Decker, Duane
Wayne, Stephen J(ay) 1939- CANR-20
  Earlier sketches in CA 53-56, CANR-5
Wayre, Philip 1921- 89-92
Ways, C. R.
  See Blount, Roy (Alton), Jr.
Ways, Max 1905-1985 Obituary 116
Waystaff, Simon
  See Swift, Jonathan
Wazyk, Adam 1905-1982 Obituary 114
Wead, R(oy) Douglas 1946- CANR-20
  Earlier sketch in CA 69-72
Weal, Michele 1936- 61-64
Weales, Gerald (Clifford) 1925- CANR-3
  Earlier sketch in CA 5-6R
  See also SATA 11
Wear, Ted Graham
  See Wear, Theodore G(raham)
Wear, Theodore G(raham) 1902- CAP-1
  Earlier sketch in CA 9-10
Weare, Ralston B.
  See La Barre, Weston
Weare, Walter B(urdette) 1938- 73-76
Wearin, Otha Donner 1903- CANR-5
  Earlier sketch in CA 15-16R
Wearing, J. P. CANR-19
  Earlier sketch in CA 102
Wearne, Alan (Richard) 1948- 126
Weart, Edith L. 1898(?)-1977 Obituary ...69-72
Weart, Spencer R(ichard) 1942- 25-28R
Weary, Ogdred
  See Gorey, Edward (St. John)
Weatherall, Norman Leigh 1902- CAP-1
  Earlier sketch in CA 11-12
Weatherby, Harold L(erow), Jr. 1934- 45-48
Weatherby, W(illiam) J(ohn) CANR-12
  Earlier sketch in CA 19-20R
Weathercock, The
  See Romaine, Lawrence B.
Weatherford, J(ack) McIver 1946- 111
Weatherford, Richard M(orris) 1939- 53-56
Weatherford, Willis Duke, Jr. 1916- 5-6R
Weatherhead, A(ndrew) Kingsley 1923- .. CANR-3
  Earlier sketch in CA 5-6R
Weatherhead, Leslie D(ixon) 1893-1976 . CANR-4
  Obituary 61-64
  Earlier sketch in CA 5-6R
Weatherly, Edward H(owell) 1905- 7-8R

Weatherly, (John) Max 1921- 15-16R
Weatherly, Owen M. 1915- 5-6R
Weatherly, Tom 1942- CANR-25
  Earlier sketch in CA 45-48
  See also BW
  See also DLB 41
Weathers, Wesley Wayne 1942- 111
Weathers, Winston 1926- CANR-8
  Earlier sketch in CA 23-24R
Weatherwax, Rudd (B.) 1908(?)-1985
  Obituary 115
Weatherwise, Abe
  See Sagendorph, Robb Hansell
Weaver, Anthony Frederick 1913- 15-16R
Weaver, Bertrand 1908-1973 .... CAP-1
  Obituary 45-48
  Earlier sketch in CA 15-16
Weaver, Carl H(arold) 1910- 73-76
Weaver, Charley
  See Arquette, Cliff(ord)
Weaver, David H(ugh) 1946- 111
Weaver, Denis 1906-1984 Obituary 114
Weaver, Earl S(idney) 1930- 116
Weaver, Earle
  See Willets, Walter E.
Weaver, Frank Parks 1904- 104
Weaver, Gordon (Allison) 1937- CANR-26
  Earlier sketches in CA 25-28R, CANR-10
Weaver, Harriett E. 1908- CANR-20
  Earlier sketches in CA 7-8R, CANR-5
Weaver, Herbert 1905- 61-64
Weaver, Horace R. 1915- 15-16R
Weaver, James H. 1933- 19-20R
Weaver, Jerry L(ee) 1939- 69-72
Weaver, John D(owning) 1912- CANR-4
  Earlier sketch in CA 11-12R
Weaver, John L. 1949- 112
  See also SATA 42
Weaver, Katherine Grey Dunlap 1910- ...37-40R
Weaver, Kitty
  See Weaver, Katherine Grey Dunlap
Weaver, Leon Hiram 1913- 7-8R
Weaver, Mateman
  See Greene, A(lvin) C(arl)
Weaver, Michael D. 1961- 126
Weaver, Peter 1925- CANR-15
  Earlier sketch in CA 85-88
Weaver, Peter Malcolm 1927- 15-16R
Weaver, Richard L. II 1941- CANR-23
  Earlier sketch in CA 106
Weaver, Robert C(lifton) 1907- 11-12R
Weaver, Thomas 1929- CANR-13
  Earlier sketch in CA 61-64
Weaver, Ward
  See Mason, F(rancis) van Wyck
Weaver, Warren 1894-1978 89-92
  Obituary 81-84
Weaver, Warren, Jr. 1923- 41-44R
Weaver, William 1923- 116
  Brief entry 112
Weaver, William Woys 1947- 123
Webb, Anthony
  See Wilson, N(orman) Scarlyn
Webb, Barbara (Helen) 1929- 103
Webb, (Martha) Beatrice (Potter)
  1858-1943 Brief entry 117
  See also TCLC 22
Webb, Bernice Larson CANR-15
  Earlier sketch in CA 37-40R
Webb, Bob
  See Forrest-Webb, Robert
Webb, C(harles) R(ichard), Jr. 1919- 5-6R
Webb, Charles (Richard) 1939- 25-28R
  See also CLC 7
Webb, Christopher
  See Wibberley, Leonard (Patrick
  O'Connor)
Webb, Clifford (Cyril) 1895-1972 105
Webb, Eugene 1938- 29-32R
Webb, Forrest
  See Forrest-Webb, Robert
Webb, Francis Charles 1925-1973 101
Webb, Frank J. DLB-50
Webb, George Ernest 1952- 113
Webb, Harri 1920- 104
Webb, Harry 1887-1984 Obituary 113
Webb, Henry J(ameson) 1915- 17-18R
Webb, Herschel (F.) 1924-1983 ....7-8R
  Obituary 109
Webb, Holmes 1904- CAP-2
  Earlier sketch in CA 25-28
Webb, Igor 1941- 109
Webb, Jack (Randolph) 1920-1982
  Obituary 108
  Brief entry 106
Webb, James (C. N.) 1946-1980 103
Webb, James H(enry), Jr. 1946- 81-84
  See also CLC 22
Webb, James Watson 1802-1884 .... DLB-43
Webb, Jean Francis 1910- CANR-21
  Earlier sketches in CA 5-6R, CANR-6
  See also SATA 35
Webb, Jon (Edgar) 1905(?)-1971
  Obituary 104
Webb, Karl (Eugene) 1938- 105
Webb, Kempton E. 1931- 13-14R
Webb, Kenneth B(eals) 1902- 97-100
Webb, Lance 1909- CANR-10
  Earlier sketch in CA 15-16R
Webb, Lionel
  See Hershman, Morris
Webb, Lucas
  See Burgess, M(ichael) R(oy)
Webb, Margot S. 1914- 77-80
Webb, Martha G.
  See Wingate, (Martha) Anne (Guice)

Webb, Mary (Gladys Meredith) 1881-1927
  Brief entry 123
  See also DLB 34
  See also TCLC 24
Webb, Mary Haydn
  See Ross, Leah
Webb, Melody Rae 1946- 126
Webb, Michael (Dennis Puzey) 1937- 124
Webb, Michael Gordon 1940- 109
Webb, Mrs. Sidney
  See Webb, (Martha) Beatrice (Potter)
Webb, Muriel S(chlosberg) 1913- 17-18R
Webb, Nancy (Bukeley) 1915- CANR-21
  Earlier sketch in CA 4R
Webb, Neil
  See Rowland, D(onald) S(ydney)
Webb, Pauline M(ary) 1927- CANR-24
  Earlier sketches in CA 61-64, CANR-8
Webb, Peggy (Elaine Hussey) 1942- 123
Webb, Peter B(randram) 1941- CANR-24
  Earlier sketch in CA 106
Webb, Phyllis 1927- CANR-23
  Earlier sketch in CA 104
  See also DLB 53
  See also CLC 18
Webb, R(obert) K(iefer) 1922- 25-28R
Webb, Richard 37-40R
Webb, Robert 1947- 118
Webb, Robert Forrest
  See Forrest-Webb, Robert
Webb, Rodman B. 1941- 110
Webb, Ross A. 1923- 37-40R
Webb, Rozana 1908- 29-32R
Webb, Ruth Enid Borlase Morris 1926- ...9-10R
Webb, Samuel C(lement) 1934- 69-72
Webb, Sharon 1936- 113
  See also SATA 41
Webb, Sidney (James) 1859-1947
  Brief entry 117
  See also TCLC 22
Webb, Spider
  See Gohman, Fred Joseph
Webb, Stephen S(aunders) 1937- 104
Webb, Walter Prescott 1888-1963
  Obituary 113
  See also DLB 17
Webb, Willard 1903-1978 Obituary 77-80
Webb, William (Griffin) 1919- 25-28R
Webb, Wilse B(ernard) 1920- CANR-3
  Earlier sketch in CA 3R
Webbe, Gale D(udley) 1909- 5-6R
Webber, Andrew Lloyd
  See Lloyd Webber, Andrew
  See also CLC 21
Webber, Bert
  See Webber, Ebbert T(rue)
Webber, Ebbert T(rue) 1921- CANR-17
  Earlier sketches in CA 45-48, CANR-2
Webber, George J(ulius) 1899-1982(?)
  Obituary 108
Webber, Gordon 1912-1986 89-92
  Obituary 120
Webber, Irma E(leanor Schmidt) 1904- ...69-72
  See also SATA 14
Webber, Joan Malory 1930-1978 ...... CANR-7
  Earlier sketch in CA 5-6R
Webber, Robert (Eugene) 1933- CANR-16
  Earlier sketch in CA 89-92
Webber, (Edwin) Ronald 1915- CANR-4
  Earlier sketch in CA 53-56
Webber, Ross A. 1934- 29-32R
Webber, Thomas L(ane) 1947- 85-88
Weber, Alfons 1921- 29-32R
  See also SATA 8
Weber, Brom 1917- 15-16R
Weber, Bruce 1942- CANR-21
  Earlier sketch in CA 97-100
Weber, Burton Jasper 1934- 103
Weber, Carl J(efferson) 1894-1966 .... CANR-3
  Earlier sketch in CA 7-8R
Weber, Clarence A. 1903- CANR-13
  Earlier sketch in CA 37-40R
Weber, David J. 1940- CANR-14
  Earlier sketch in CA 37-40R
Weber, David R(yder) 1943- 89-92
Weber, Eric 1942- CANR-15
  Earlier sketch in CA 101
Weber, Eugen 1925- CANR-2
  Earlier sketch in CA 5-6R
Weber, Eugene 1939- 41-44R
Weber, Francis J. 1933- CANR-4
  Earlier sketch in CA 11-12R
Weber, Frank George 1932- 45-48
Weber, Gerard Peter 1918- 11-12R
Weber, Hans H. 1935- 61-64
Weber, Hans-Ruedi 1923- CANR-2
  Earlier sketch in CA 7-8R
Weber, J(ohn) Sherwood 1918-1978 .....37-40R
  Obituary 77-80
Weber, James A(mbrose) 1932- 102
Weber, Janice 121
Weber, Jean-Paul 1917- 45-48
Weber, Jerome C(harles) 1938- 73-76
Weber, Ken(neth J.) 1940- 116
Weber, Lenora Mattingly 1895-1971 .... CAP-1
  Obituary 29-32R
  Earlier sketch in CA 19-20
  See also SATA 2, 26
  See also CLC 12
Weber, Marc 1950- CANR-1
  Earlier sketch in CA 49-52
Weber, Max 1864-1920 Brief entry 109
Weber, Nancy 1942- 101
Weber, Nathan 1942- 111
Weber, Nicholas F(ox) 1947- 120
Weber, Ralph Edward 1926- CANR-2
  Earlier sketch in CA 5-6R

Weber, Robert L(emmerman) 1913- 53-56
Weber, Ronald 1934- 115
Weber, Rubin
  See Rubinstein, S(amuel) Leonard
Weber, Sarah Appleton
  See Appleton, Sarah
Weber, Simon 1910(?)-1987 Obituary 124
Weber, William A(lfred) 1918- 77-80
Weber, William J(ohn) 1927- CANR-25
  Earlier sketch in CA 69-72
  See also SATA 14
Weberman, Ben(jamin) 1923- 77-80
Webster, Alice Jane Chandler 1876-1916
  Brief entry 116
  See also SATA 17
Webster, Anthony 1923(?)-1987 Obituary ... 123
Webster, Augusta 1837-1894 .... DLB-35
Webster, Brenda S. 1936- 53-56
Webster, C(onstance) Muriel 1906- 49-52
Webster, Cyril Charles 1909- CAP-2
  Earlier sketch in CA 25-28
Webster, David 1930- 29-32R
  See also SATA 11
Webster, David Endicott 1929- 25-28R
Webster, Donald 1926- 118
Webster, Donald Blake, Jr. 1933- 37-40R
Webster, Douglas 1920-1986 ....13-14R
  Obituary 118
Webster, Edna Robb 1896- 69-72
Webster, Elizabeth 1918- 117
Webster, Frank V. CAP-2
  Earlier sketch in CA 19-20
  See also SATA 1
Webster, Frederick E., Jr. 1937- CANR-14
  Earlier sketch in CA 37-40R
Webster, Gary
  See Garrison, Webb B(lack)
Webster, Graham 1915- 49-52
Webster, Grant T. 1933- 104
Webster, Harvey (Curtis) 1906- 41-44R
Webster, J(ames) Carson 1905- 45-48
Webster, James 1925-1981 73-76
  Obituary 104
  See also SATA 17, 27
Webster, Jan 1924- CANR-14
  Earlier sketch in CA 77-80
Webster, Jean
  See Webster, Alice Jane Chandler
Webster, John 1579(?)-1634(?) DLB-58
Webster, Josh (Lew) 1949- 113
Webster, Margaret 1905-1972 Obituary ...37-40R
Webster, Noah
  1758-1843 .... DLB-1, 37, 42, 43, 73
Webster, Noah
  See Knox, William
Webster, Norman William 1920- 104
Webster, Paul 1916- 41-44R
Webster, Paul Francis 1907-1984
  Obituary 112
Webster, Randolph Wyatt 1900- CAP-1
  Earlier sketch in CA 19-20
Webster, Richard A. 1928- 21-22R
Webster, S(tanley) Eric 1919-1971 ..... CAP-1
  Earlier sketch in CA 17-18
Webster, Staten Wentford 1928- 23-24R
Webster, Thomas Bertram Lonsdale
  1905-1974 105
  Obituary 107
Webster, Tony
  See Webster, Anthony
Wechman, Robert Joseph 1939- CANR-24
  Earlier sketch in CA 45-48
Wechsberg, Joseph 1907-1983 105
  Obituary 109
Wechsler, David 1896-1981 Obituary 103
Wechsler, Harold S(tuart) 1946- 110
Wechsler, Henry 1932- CANR-7
  Earlier sketch in CA 17-18R
Wechsler, Herbert 1909- CANR-24
  Earlier sketch in CA 2R
Wechsler, Herman J. 1904-1976 65-68
  Obituary 61-64
  See also SATA 20
Wechsler, James A(rthur) 1915-1983 101
  Obituary 110
Wechsler, Judith Glatzer 1940- CANR-8
  Earlier sketch in CA 57-60
Wechsler, Louis K. 1905- 65-68
Wechter, Nell Wise 1913- 57-60
Weckstein, Richard (Selig) 1924- 49-52
Wedberg, Anders 1913-1978 Obituary ...77-80
Wedda, John A. 1911- 17-18R
Wedde, Ian 1946- 104
Wedderburn, Dorothy (Enid Cole) 1925-
  Brief entry 113
Wedderburn, K(enneth) W(illiam) 1927- ..77-80
Wedding, Dan 1949- 93-96
Wedding, Donald Keith 1934- 41-44R
Weddle, Ethel Harshbarger 1897- CANR-4
  Earlier sketch in CA 11-12R
  See also SATA 11
Weddle, Ferris 1922- 17-18R
Weddle, Robert S(amuel) 1921- 11-12R
Wedeck, Harry E(zekiel) 1894- CANR-4
  Earlier sketch in CA 3R
Wedeen, Shirley Ullman 1926- 19-20R
Wedekind, (Benjamin) Frank(lin)
  1864-1918 Brief entry 104
  See also TCLC 7
Wedel, Alfred R(aphael) 1934- 117
Wedel, Alton F. 21-22R
Wedel, Cynthia Clark 1908-1986 Obituary ... 120
Wedel, Leonard E. 1909- 21-22R
Wedel, Theodore Otto 1892-1970 .... CANR-4
  Earlier sketch in CA 5-6R
Wedel, Waldo R(udolph) 1908- 126
  Brief entry 105

Wedell, Eberhard (Arthur Otto) George 1927- 104
Wedge, Bryant (Miner) 1921- CANR-10
Earlier sketch in CA 15-16R
Wedge, Florence 1919- 5-6R
Wedgwood, C(icely) V(eronica) 1910- CANR-21
Earlier sketch in CA 105
Wedgwood, Pamela
See Tudor-Craig, Pamela
Weed, Florence C(ollins) 1897(?)-1983
Obituary 109
Weed, Joseph J(ohn) 1901- 25-28R
Weeden, Robert B(arton) 1933- 85-88
Weedon, Chris 1952- 121
Weekes, Mark Kinkead
See Kinkead-Weekes, Mark
Weekes, Richard V. 1924- 15-16R
Weekley, Ian George 1933- 113
Weekly, William G(eorge) 1890(?)-1983
Obituary 111
Weeks, Albert L. 1923- 13-14R
Weeks, Christopher 1930- 23-24R
Weeks, Constance Tomkinson 1915- 17-18R
Weeks, (Norman) Donald CANR-25
Earlier sketch in CA 45-48
Weeks, Edward (Augustus) 1898- 85-88
Weeks, Edward J(oseph) 1902- CAP-1
Earlier sketch in CA 13-14
Weeks, Francis W(illiam) 1916-
Brief entry 111
Weeks, Grace E(zell) 1923- 49-52
Weeks, H(erbert) Ashley 1903- 45-48
Weeks, Jeffrey 1945- 108
Weeks, John (Stafford) 1928- 77-80
Weeks, Kent M(cCuskey) 1937-
Brief entry 112
Weeks, Lewis G(eorge) 1893-1977
Obituary 69-72
Weeks, Philip 1949- 110
Weeks, Robert Lewis 1924- 13-14R
Weeks, Robert P(ercy) 1915- 15-16R
Weeks, Sheldon G. 1931- CANR-13
Earlier sketch in CA 23-24R
Weeks, Thelma E(vans) 1921- 57-60
Weems, J. Eddie, Jr.
See Weems, John Edward
Weems, John Edward 1924- CANR-19
Earlier sketches in CA 3R, CANR-4
Weems, Mason Locke
1759-1825 DLB-30, 37, 42
Weenolsen, Hebe 111
Weer, William
See Kaufman, I(sadore)
Weerts, Richard Kenneth 1928- 49-52
Wees, Frances Shelley 1902- CANR-3
Earlier sketch in CA 5-6R
Wees, W(ilfred) R(usk) 1899- 61-64
Weesner, Theodore 105
Wegelin, Christof 1911- 45-48
Wegen, Ron(ald) SATA-44
Weglyn, Michi(ko Nishiura) 1926- 85-88
Wegner, Fritz 1924- SATA-20
Wegner, Robert E. 1929- 17-18R
Wehen, Joy DeWeese CANR-3
Earlier sketch in CA 5-6R
Wehlitz, (Annie) Lou(ise) Rogers 1906- 5-6R
Wehmeyer, Lillian (Mabel) Biermann
1933- CANR-8
Earlier sketch in CA 61-64
Wehringer, Cameron K(ingsley) 1924- 25-28R
Wehrle, Edmund S(heridan) 1930- 65-68
Wehrli, Eugene S(tanley) 1923- 45-48
Wehrwein, Austin C(arl) 1916- 77-80
Wei, Yung 1937- 49-52
Weichel, Kim 1951- 107
Weideger, Paula 1939- 65-68
Weidenbaum, Murray L(ew) 1927- CANR-14
Earlier sketch in CA 37-40R
Weidenfeld, Sheila Rabb 1943- 89-92
Weider, Ben 1923- 108
Weidhorn, Manfred 1931- 53-56
Weidlein, Edward R(ay) 1887-1983
Obituary 110
Weidman, Jerome 1913- CANR-1
Earlier sketch in CA 1R
See also DLB 28
See also CLC 7
See also AITN 2
Weidman, John 1946- 109
Weidman, Judith L(ynne) 1941- CANR-25
Earlier sketch in CA 107
Weidner, Edward William 1921- 15-16R
Weiers, Ronald M. 1941- CANR-19
Earlier sketch in CA 25-28R
Weigand, George R(obert) J(oseph)
1917- 15-16R
Weigand, Hermann J(ohn) 1892-1985 CAP-1
Obituary 117
Earlier sketch in CA 13-14
Weigel, George 1951- 125
Weigel, Gustave 1906-1964 Obituary 107
Weigel, John A(rthur) 1912- 57-60
Weiger, John George 1933- CANR-20
Earlier sketch in CA 104
Weigert, Andrew J(oseph) 1934- 109
Weigert, Edith 1894- CAP-2
Earlier sketch in CA 29-32
Weigert, Hans Werner 1902(?)-1983
Obituary 111
Weightman, Gavin 1945- 120
Weightman, J(ohn) G(eorge) 1915- CANR-5
Earlier sketch in CA 9-10R
Weigl, Bruce 1949- 110
Weigle, Luther Allan 1880-1976 77-80
Obituary 69-72
Weigle, Marta 1944- CANR-26
Earlier sketches in CA 69-72, CANR-11
Weigley, Russell F(rank) 1930- CANR-19
Earlier sketches in CA 5-6R, CANR-2
Weihofen, Henry 1904- 37-40R
Weihs, Erika 1917- 93-96
See also SATA 15
Weik, Mary Hays 1898(?)-1979 23-24R
Obituary 93-96
See also SATA 3, 23
Weil, Andrew (Thomas) 1942- CANR-20
Earlier sketch in CA 73-76
Weil, Ann Yezner 1908-1969 7-8R
Obituary 103
See also SATA 9
Weil, Dorothy 1929- 93-96
Weil, Gordon L(ee) 1937- CANR-12
Earlier sketch in CA 73-76
Weil, Herbert S., Jr. 1933- 21-22R
Weil, Irwin 1928- 21-22R
Weil, James L(ehman) 1929- CANR-16
Earlier sketch in CA 93-96
Weil, Jerry 1928- 3R
Weil, Joseph 1875-1976 Obituary 65-68
Weil, Lisl 1910- CANR-2
Earlier sketch in CA 49-52
See also SATA 7
Weil, Mildred 45-48
Weil, Robert 1955- 125
Weil, Roman L(ee) 1940- CANR-14
Earlier sketch in CA 37-40R
Weil, Simone (Adolphine) 1909-1943
Brief entry 117
See also TCLC 23
Weil, Ulric Henry 113
Weilbacher, William Manning 1928- 108
Weilerstein, Sadie Rose 1894- 5-6R
See also SATA 3
Weill, Gus 1933- CANR-7
Earlier sketch in CA 53-56
Weiman, Eiveen 1925- 108
Weimann, Jeanne Madeline 1943- 108
Weimar, Karl S(iegfried) 1916- 5-6R
Weimer, Arthur M(artin) 1909-1987 2R
Obituary 122
Wein, Jacqueline 1938- 93-96
Weinbaum, Stanley Grauman
1902(?)-1935 Brief entry 110
See also DLB 8
Weinberg, Arthur 1915- CANR-15
Earlier sketch in CA 25-28R
Weinberg, Bernard 1909-1973 Obituary 106
Weinberg, Daniel H. 1949- 120
Weinberg, Daniela 1936- 104
Weinberg, David Henry 1945- 89-92
Weinberg, Edgar 1917-1985 Obituary 117
Weinberg, Florence M(ay) 1933- 37-40R
Weinberg, Gerald M(arvin) 1933- CANR-18
Earlier sketch in CA 89-92
Weinberg, Gerhard L(udwig) 1928- CANR-3
Earlier sketch in CA 11-12R
Weinberg, Helen A(rnstein) 1927- 73-76
Weinberg, Herman G(ershon) 1908-1983 45-48
Obituary 111
Weinberg, Ian 1938-1969 CAP-2
Earlier sketch in CA 21-22
Weinberg, Janet Hopson
See Hopson, Janet L(ouise)
Weinberg, Julius 1922- 37-40R
Weinberg, Julius R(udolph) 1908-1971 CAP-1
Earlier sketch in CA 17-18
Weinberg, Kenneth G. 1920- 41-44R
Weinberg, Kerry 29-32R
Weinberg, Kurt 1912- 41-44R
Weinberg, Larry
See Weinberg, Lawrence (E.)
Weinberg, Lawrence (E.) SATA-48
Weinberg, Lila (Shaffer) 25-28R
Weinberg, Martin S(tephen) 1939- CANR-15
Earlier sketch in CA 41-44R
Weinberg, Meyer 1920- CANR-4
Earlier sketch in CA 3R
Weinberg, Nathan Gerald 1945- 104
Weinberg, Robert Charles 1901-1974
Obituary 45-48
Weinberg, Robert E(dward) 1946- 97-100
Weinberg, Samuel Kirson 1912- CANR-1
Earlier sketch in CA 2R
Weinberg, Sanford Bruce 1950- 109
Weinberg, Steven 1933- CANR-5
Earlier sketch in CA 53-56
Weinberg, Werner 1915- CANR-16
Earlier sketch in CA 41-44R
Weinberger, Betty Kiralfy 1932- 65-68
Weinberger, Eliot 1949- 117
Weinberger, Leon J. 1926- 77-80
Weinberger, Marvin I(rvin) 1954- 113
Weinberger, Paul E. 1931- 29-32R
Weinbrot, Howard D. 1936- Brief entry 107
Weiner, Andrew D(avid) 1943- Brief entry 111
Weiner, Annette B. 1933- 93-96
Weiner, Bernard 1935- 57-60
Weiner, Charles 1931- Brief entry 109
Weiner, Dora B(ierer) 1924- 25-28R
Weiner, Egon 1906-1987 97-100
Obituary 123
Weiner, Elliot 1943- 122
Weiner, Florence 1931- 25-28R
Weiner, Henri
See Longstreet, Stephen
Weiner, Herbert 7-8R
Weiner, Hyman J(oseph) 1926- 49-52
Weiner, Irving B(ernard) 1933- 29-32R
Weiner, J(oseph) S(idney) 1915-1982 114
Weiner, Jonathan (David) 1953- 123
Weiner, Leonard 1927- 23-24R
Weiner, Linda 1943- 114
Weiner, Marcella Bakur 1925- Brief entry 105
Weiner, Myron 1931- CANR-4
Earlier sketch in CA 2R
Weiner, Neal (Orlove) 1942- 118
Weiner, Neil S(herman) 1936- 119
Weiner, Richard 1927- 89-92
Weiner, Sandra 1922- 49-52
See also SATA 14
Weiner, Skip
See Weiner, Stewart
Weiner, Stewart 1945- CANR-16
Earlier sketch in CA 89-92
Weinfield, Henry 1949- 37-40R
Weingand, Darlene E. 1937- 115
Weingart, L(aurence) O. 1931- 19-20R
Weingarten, Henry 57-60
Weingarten, Roger 1945- CANR-10
Earlier sketch in CA 61-64
Weingarten, Violet (Brown) 1915-1976 CANR-7
Obituary 65-68
Earlier sketch in CA 11-12R
See also SATA 3, 27
Weingartner, Charles 1922- 49-52
See also SATA 5
Weingartner, James J(oseph) 1940- 93-96
Weingartner, Rudolph H(erbert) 1927- 15-16R
Weingast, David E(lliott) 1912- 5-6R
Weinig, Jean Maria 1920- CANR-12
Earlier sketch in CA 29-32R
Weinig, Sister Mary Anthony
See Weinig, Jean Maria
Weininger, Benjamin Isaac 1905-1988
Obituary 126
Weininger, Richard 1887(?)-1979
Obituary 89-92
Weinland, James D(avid) 1894- 57-60
Weinman, Benzion 1897-1987 Obituary 121
Weinman, Irving 1937- 122
Weinman, Paul 1940- CANR-13
Earlier sketch in CA 77-80
Weinrauch, Herschel 1905- CAP-1
Earlier sketch in CA 15-16
Weinreb, Lloyd L(obell) 1936- 69-72
Weinrich, A(nna) K(atharina) H(ildegard)
1933- CANR-16
Earlier sketch in CA 37-40R
Weinryb, Bernard D(ov) 1905- CANR-25
Earlier sketch in CA 45-48
Weinstein, Allen 1937- CANR-26
Earlier sketch in CA 41-44R
Weinstein, Arnold 1927- 9-10R
Weinstein, Bernard L(ee) 1942- 111
Weinstein, Bob 1941- 120
Weinstein, Brian 1937- 21-22R
Weinstein, Donald 1926- 15-16R
Weinstein, Fred 1931- 65-68
Weinstein, Gerald 1930- 25-28R
Weinstein, Grace W(ohlner) 1935- CANR-26
Earlier sketches in CA 61-64, CANR-10
Weinstein, Howard 1954- CANR-23
Earlier sketch in CA 107
Weinstein, Jacob Joseph 1902-1974 110
Obituary 108
Weinstein, James 1926- 23-24R
Weinstein, Leo 1921- Brief entry 110
Weinstein, Mark A. 1937- 25-28R
Weinstein, Marlene 1946- 45-48
Weinstein, Martin E. 1934- 85-88
Weinstein, Michael 1898- CAP-1
Earlier sketch in CA 13-14
Weinstein, Nathan
See West, Nathanael
Weinstein, Nathan von Wallenstein
See West, Nathanael
Weinstein, Norman Charles 1948- 37-40R
Weinstein, Robert A. 1914- 29-32R
Weinstein, Sol 1928- 15-16R
Weinstein, Warren 1941- 93-96
Weinstock, Herbert 1905-1971 CANR-2
Obituary 33-36R
Earlier sketch in CA 4R
Weinstock, John M(artin) 1936- 81-84
Weinstone, William W. 1898(?)-1985
Obituary 117
Weinswig, Melvin H. 1935- Brief entry 107
Weintal, Edward 1901-1973 Obituary 41-44R
Weintraub, Dov 1926- 109
Weintraub, Karl Joachim 1924- 25-28R
Weintraub, Robert E. 1925-1983 Obituary 110
Weintraub, Rodelle (Selma) 1933- 97-100
Weintraub, Sidney 1914-1983 CANR-6
Obituary 110
Earlier sketch in CA 2R
Weintraub, Sidney 1922- CANR-26
Earlier sketch in CA 108
Weintraub, Stanley 1929- CANR-22
Earlier sketches in CA 1R, CANR-2
Weintraub, Wiktor 1908-1988 CANR-3
Obituary 126
Earlier sketch in CA 7-8R
Weintraub, William 1926- 2R
Weinwurm, George F(elix) 1935- 33-36R
Weinzweig, Helen 1915- 106
Weir, Alice M.
See McLaughlin, Emma Maude
Weir, Carol S. 1924- 125
Weir, J(ohn) E(dward) 1935- 118
Weir, Joan 1928- 112
Weir, John
See Cross, Colin (John)
Weir, LaVada CANR-9
Earlier sketch in CA 23-24R
See also SATA 2
Weir, Molly 1920- CANR-12
Earlier sketch in CA 29-32R
Weir, Nancie MacCullough 1933- 65-68
Weir, Peter (Lindsay) 1944- 123
Brief entry 113
See also CLC 20
Weir, Robert M(cColloch) 1933- 93-96
Weir, Rosemary (Green) 1905- CANR-10
Earlier sketch in CA 13-14R
See also SATA 21
Weir, Thomas R(obert) 1912- 41-44R
Weir, Walter 1909- 5-6R
Weis, Elisabeth 1944- 112
Weis, Jack 1932- 105
Weis, Margaret (Edith) 1948- 111
See also SATA 38
Weis, Norman D(wight) 1923- 61-64
Weisberg, Barry 33-36R
Weisberg, Gabriel P(aul) 1942- 73-76
Weisberg, Harold 1913- 41-44R
Weisberg, Joseph Gotland 1911-1984
Obituary 112
Weisberg, Joseph S(impson) 1937- 107
Weisberger, Bernard A(llen) 1922- CANR-7
Earlier sketch in CA 5-6R
See also SATA 21
Weisberger, Eleanor (Burt) 1920- 97-100
Weisbord, Albert 1900(?)-1977 Obituary 69-72
Weisbord, Marvin R(oss) 1931- CANR-9
Earlier sketch in CA 65-68
Weisbord, Robert G. 1933- Brief entry 109
Weisbord, Vera Buch 1895-1987 73-76
Obituary 123
Weisbrod, Burton Allen 1931- CANR-21
Earlier sketches in CA 45-48, CANR-1
Weisbuch, Robert 1946- 104
Weisburd, Martin Harold 1940(?)-1978
Obituary 77-80
Weise, R. Eric 1933- 41-44R
Weisenborn, Guenther 1902-1969
Obituary 114
See also DLB 69
Weisenborn, Gunther
See Weisenborn, Guenther
See also DLB 69
Weisenburger, Francis Phelps 1900- CAP-1
Earlier sketch in CA 17-18
Weisenfeld, Murray 1923- 104
Weiser, Eric 1907- 17-18R
Weiser, Marjorie P(hillis) K(atz) 1934- 103
See also SATA 33
Weisgal, Meyer W(olf) 1894-1977
Obituary 89-92
Weisgard, Leonard Joseph 1916- 11-12R
See also SATA 2, 30
Weisgerber, Charles A(ugust)
1912-1977 41-44R
Weisgerber, Jean 1924- 65-68
Weisgerber, Robert A(rthur) 1929- 49-52
Weisheipl, James A(thanasius) 1923- CANR-15
Earlier sketch in CA 41-44R
Weisheit, Eldon 1933- CANR-14
Earlier sketch in CA 29-32R
Weisinger, Mort 1915- 11-12R
Weiskopf, Bob
See Weiskopf, Robert J.
Weiskopf, Robert J. 1914- 123
Obituary 118
Weisman, Herman M. 1916- 11-12R
Weisman, John 1942- CANR-1
Earlier sketch in CA 45-48
Weisman, Marilee 1939- 65-68
Weisman, Mary-Lou 1937- 109
Weismann, Donald L(eroy) 1914- 33-36R
Weismiller, Edward Ronald 1915- CANR-1
Earlier sketch in CA 3R
Weiss, Abraham 1895-1971 Obituary 104
Weiss, Adelle 1920- 81-84
See also SATA 18
Weiss, Allen 1918- 109
Weiss, Ann E(dwards) 1943- CANR-11
Earlier sketches in CA 45-48, CANR-1
See also SATA 30
Weiss, Arthur 1912- 25-28R
Weiss, Bennet A., Jr. 1926(?)-1983
Obituary 109
Weiss, Beno 1933- 123
Weiss, Bernard J(acob) 1936- 109
Weiss, Dale Eugene 1947- 114
Weiss, David 1909- CANR-12
Earlier sketch in CA 15-16R
Weiss, David 1928- 121
Weiss, Edna
See Barth, Edna
Weiss, Edna Smith 1916- 5-6R
Weiss, Elizabeth S(chwartz) 1944- CANR-11
Earlier sketch in CA 61-64
Weiss, Ellen 1953- 113
See also SATA 44
Weiss, Francis Joseph 1899(?)-1975
Obituary 53-56
Weiss, G(ustav) A(dolf) M(ichael) 1922- 41-44R
Weiss, Gaea (Laughingbird) 1941- 119
Weiss, Harry B(ischoff) 1883-1972 45-48
Weiss, Harvey 1922- CANR-6
Earlier sketch in CA 5-6R
See also SATA 1, 27
See also CLR 4
Weiss, Herbert F. 1930- 21-22R
Weiss, Irving J. 1921- CANR-10
Earlier sketch in CA 19-20R
Weiss, Jaqueline Shachter 1926- 119
Weiss, Jess E(dward) 1926- 49-52
Weiss, Joan Talmage 1928- CANR-2
Earlier sketch in CA 7-8R
Weiss, John 1818-1879 DLB-1
Weiss, John 1927- 19-20R
Weiss, Jonathan A(rthur) 1939- 93-96
Weiss, Kenneth M(onrad) 1941- 101

INDEX

Weiss, Leatie 1928- ... 65-68
See also SATA 50
Weiss, Leonard W(inchell) 1925- ... CANR-6
Earlier sketch in CA 7-8R
Weiss, Lillian ?-1972 Obituary ... 104
Weiss, Louise 1893-1983 Obituary ... 109
Weiss, M(orton) Jerome 1926- ... CANR-9
Earlier sketch in CA 19-20R
Weiss, M. Jerry
See Weiss, M(orton) Jerome
Weiss, Malcolm E. 1928- ... CANR-11
Earlier sketch in CA 25-28R
See also SATA 3
Weiss, Margaret R. ... 57-60
Weiss, Melford Stephen 1937- ... 53-56
Weiss, Miriam (Strauss) 1905- ... CAP-2
Earlier sketch in CA 29-32
Weiss, Miriam
See Schlein, Miriam
Weiss, Morris S(amuel) 1915- ... 89-92
Weiss, Nancy J(oan) 1944- ... CANR-13
Earlier sketch in CA 77-80
Weiss, Nicki 1954- ... CANR-26
Earlier sketch in CA 108
See also SATA 33
Weiss, Paul 1901- ... CANR-3
Earlier sketch in CA 7-8R
Weiss, Peg ... 125
Weiss, Peter (Ulrich) 1916-1982 ... CANR-3
Obituary ... 106
Earlier sketch in CA 45-48
See also DLB 69
See also CLC 3, 15
Weiss, Renee Karol 1923- ... 41-44R
See also SATA 5
Weiss, Robert M. 1929- ... 37-40R
Weiss, Robert S(tuart) 1925- ... 25-28R
Weiss, Roger W(illiam) 1930- ... 45-48
weiss, ruth 1928- ... 122
Weiss, Samuel A(bba) 1922- ... 41-44R
Weiss, Sanford 1927- ... 25-28R
Weiss, (Paul) Shandor 1954- ... 120
Weiss, Theodore (Russell) 1916- ... 9-10R
See also CAAS 2
See also DLB 5
See also CLC 3, 8, 14
Weiss, Thomas J(oseph) 1942- ... 105
Weiss, Winfried (Ferdinand) 1937- ... 117
Weissberg, Michael P. 1942- ... 126
Weissberger, L. Arnold 1907-1981
Obituary ... 103
Weissbort, Daniel 1935- ... CANR-2
Earlier sketch in CA 45-48
Weissenborn, Hellmuth 1898-1982
Obituary ... 107
See also SATA 31
Weisskopf, Kurt 1907- ... 25-28R
Weisskopf, Victor Frederick 1908- ... 107
Weisskopf, Walter A(lbert) 1904- ... 37-40R
Weissman, Benjamin M(urry) 1917- ... 73-76
Weissman, Dick
See Weissman, Richard
Weissman, Jack 1921- ... 13-14R
Weissman, Paul 1932- ... 45-48
Weissman, Philip 1911(?)-1972
Obituary ... 33-36R
Weissman, Richard 1935- ... 81-84
Weissman, Rozanne 1942- ... 101
Weissman, Stephen R(ichard) 1941- ... CANR-11
Earlier sketch in CA 57-60
Weissman, Steve
See Weissman, Stephen R(ichard)
Weissmann, Gerald 1930- ... 126
Weissmuller, Johnny
See Weissmuller, Peter John
Weissmuller, Peter John 1904-1984
Obituary ... 111
Weisstein, Ulrich W(erner) 1925- ... 21-22R
Weisstub, D(avid) N(orman) 1944- ... 29-32R
Weith, Warren 1926- ... 114
Weithorn, Stanley S(tephen) 1924- ... 15-16R
Weitz, Henry 1911- ... 41-44R
Weitz, John 1923- ... 29-32R
Weitz, Martin Mishli 1909- ... CANR-13
Earlier sketches in CA 17-18, CAP-2
Weitz, Morris 1916-1981 ... CANR-7
Obituary ... 102
Earlier sketch in CA 5-6R
Weitz, Raanan 1913- ... CANR-1
Earlier sketch in CA 45-48
Weitzel, Eugene Joseph 1927- ... 5-6R
Weitzenhoffer, Andre M(uller) 1921- ... 7-8R
Weitzman, Alan 1933- ... 29-32R
Weitzman, Arthur J(oshua) 1933- ... 53-56
Weitzman, Elliot D. 1929-1983 Obituary ... 110
Weitzman, Martin L(awrence) 1942- ... 117
Weitzmann, Kurt 1904- ... 41-44R
Weixlmann, Joe
See Weixlmann, Joseph Norman
Weixlmann, Joseph Norman 1946- ... 109
Weizenbaum, Joseph 1923- Brief entry ... 113
Weizman, Ezer 1924- ... 111
Weizsaecker, Carl Friedrich von
See von Weizsaecker, Carl Friedrich
Welber, Robert ... 104
See also SATA 26
Welbourn, F(rederick) B(urkewood)
1912- ... 21-22R
Welburn, Ron(ald Garfield) 1944- ... CANR-17
Earlier sketches in CA 45-48, CANR-1
See also BW
Welch, Ann Courtenay (Edmonds)
1917- ... CANR-18
Earlier sketches in CA 11-12R, CANR-3
Welch, Bob
See Welch, Robert Lynn
Welch, Charles Scott
See Smith, LeRoi Tex
Welch, Claude E(merson), Jr. 1939- ... CANR-14
Earlier sketch in CA 41-44R
Welch, Cyril 1939- ... 118
Welch, D'Alte Aldridge 1907-1970
Obituary ... 104
See also SATA 27
Welch, (Maurice) Denton 1915-1948
Brief entry ... 121
See also TCLC 22
Welch, Don(ovan LeRoy) 1932- ... CANR-20
Earlier sketch in CA 104
Welch, Finis R. 1938- ... 118
Welch, George Patrick 1901-1976 ... CAP-1
Obituary ... 65-68
Earlier sketch in CA 13-14
Welch, Herbert 1862-1969 ... CAP-1
Earlier sketch in CA 15-16
Welch, Holmes (Hinkley) 1921- ... 23-24R
Welch, J(oseph) Edmund 1922- ... 57-60
Welch, James 1940- ... 85-88
See also CLC 6, 14
Welch, Jean-Louise
See Kempton, Jean Welch
Welch, Jerome A. 1933- ... 65-68
Welch, June Rayfield 1927- ... 41-44R
Welch, Kenneth Frederick 1917- ... 105
Welch, Lew(is Barrett, Jr.) 1926-1971(?)
Obituary ... 113
See also DLB 16
Welch, Liliane 1937- ... 110
Welch, Martha McKeen 1914- Brief entry ... 114
See also SATA 45
Welch, Mary Ross 1918- ... 53-56
Welch, Mary-Scott (Stewart) 1914- ... 104
Welch, Michael Irene 1940- ... 97-100
Welch, Patrick
See Welch, George Patrick
Welch, Pauline
See Bodenham, Hilda Morris
Welch, Richard Edwin, Jr. 1924- ... 85-88
Welch, Robert H(enry) W(inborne), Jr.
1899-1985 Obituary ... 114
Welch, Robert Lynn 1956- ... 112
Welch, Ronald
See Felton, Ronald Oliver
Welch, Rowland
See Davies, L(eslie) P(urnell)
Welch, Stuart Cary 1928- ... 103
Welch, Timothy L. 1935- ... 85-88
Welch, William 1917- Brief entry ... 115
Welch, William A. 1915(?)-1976
Obituary ... 65-68
Welcher, Jeanne K. 1922- Brief entry ... 116
Welcher, Rosalind 1922- ... CANR-25
Earlier sketch in CA 45-48
Welchman, Gordon 1906(?)-1985
Obituary ... 117
Welcome, John
See Brennan, John N(eedham) H(uggard)
Weld, Philip S(altonstall, Sr.) 1914-1984
Obituary ... 114
Welding, Patsy Ruth 1924- ... 61-64
Weldon, Fay 1933- ... CANR-16
Earlier sketch in CA 23-24R
See also DLB 14
See also CLC 6, 9, 11, 19, 36
Weldon, John 1890(?)-1963 Obituary ... 115
Weldon, John F(rederick Stover) 1948- ... 113
Weldon, Lynn Leroy 1930- ... 97-100
Weldon, Michael J(ames) 1952- ... 117
Weldon, Rex
See Rimel, Duane (Weldon)
Weldon, (Nathaniel) Warren (Jr.) 1919- ... 29-32R
Welfare, Humphrey 1950- ... 124
Welfle, Richard A. 1901- ... CAP-1
Earlier sketch in CA 13-14
Welfling, Weldon 1912-1978 Obituary ... 111
Welford, A(lan) T(raviss) 1914- ... CANR-5
Earlier sketch in CA 13-14R
Welk, Lawrence 1903- Brief entry ... 105
Welke, Elton 1941- ... 65-68
Welker, David 1917- ... 57-60
Welker, Robert Henry 1917- ... 89-92
Welker, Robert L(ouis) 1924- ... 11-12R
Welkowitz, Joan 1929- ... 53-56
Well, Alan Stewart
See Sewart, Alan
Welland, Colin
See Williams, Colin
Welland, Dennis (Sydney Reginald)
1919- ... CANR-2
Earlier sketch in CA 5-6R
Wellard, James (Howard) 1909-1987 ... CANR-3
Obituary ... 122
Earlier sketch in CA 5-6R
Wellborn, Charles 1923- ... 29-32R
Wellborn, Fred W(ilmot) 1894- ... 11-12R
Wellborn, Grace Pleasant 1906-19(?) ... CAP-2
Earlier sketch in CA 17-18
Wellek, Rene 1903- ... CANR-8
Earlier sketch in CA 7-8R
See also CAAS 7
See also DLB 63
See also CLC 28
Wellen, Edward (Paul) 1919- ... 85-88
Weller, Allen Stuart 1907- ... CANR-24
Earlier sketch in CA 3R
Weller, Charles 1911- ... 21-22R
Weller, George (Anthony) 1907- ... 65-68
See also SATA 31
Weller, Michael 1942- ... 85-88
See also CLC 10
Weller, Paul 1958- ... CLC-26
Weller, Robert P(aul) 1953- ... 118
Weller, Sheila 1945- ... 77-80
Wellershoff, Dieter 1925- ... CANR-16
Earlier sketch in CA 89-92
See also CLC 46
Welles, Margery Miller 1923-1985
Obituary ... 115
Welles, (George) Orson 1915-1985 ... 93-96
Obituary ... 117
See also CLC 20
Welles, Samuel Gardner 1913(?)-1981
Obituary ... 105
Welles, Winifred 1893-1939 Brief entry ... 112
See also SATA 27
Wellesbourne, Peter
See Williams, P(eter) F(airney)
Wellesley, Gerald 1885-1972 Obituary ... 104
Wellesley, Kenneth 1911- ... 106
Wellesz, Egon Joseph 1885-1974
Obituary ... 53-56
Wellford, Harrison 1940- Brief entry ... 111
Welling, William 1924- ... 81-84
Wellington, C(harles) Burleigh 1920- ... 2R
Wellington, Harry H(illel) 1926- ... 25-28R
Wellington, Jean Willett 1922- ... 2R
Wellington, John H. 1892- ... CAP-2
Earlier sketch in CA 25-28
Wellington, Kate
See Schulze, Hertha
Wellington, R(ichard) A(nthony) 1919- ... 61-64
Wellisch, Hans H(anan) 1920- ... 102
Wellisz, Leopold T. 1882-1972
Obituary ... 37-40R
Wellman, Alice 1900-1984 ... 89-92
See also SATA 36, 51
Wellman, Carl (Pierce) 1926- ... 37-40R
Wellman, Frederick L(ovejoy) 1897- ... 77-80
Wellman, Henry Q. 1945- ... 37-40R
Wellman, Manly Wade 1903-1986 ... CANR-16
Obituary ... 118
Earlier sketches in CA 3R, CANR-6
See also SATA 6, 47
See also CLC 49
Wellman, Paul I(selin) 1898-1966 ... CANR-16
Obituary ... 25-28R
Earlier sketch in CA 2R
See also SATA 3
Wellman, William A(ugustus) 1896-1975
Obituary ... 61-64
Wells, Allen 1951- ... 125
Wells, Anna Mary 1906- ... CANR-2
Earlier sketch in CA 5-6R
Wells, Arvin Robert 1927- ... 2R
Wells, Bella Fromm 1901(?)-1972
Obituary ... 104
Wells, C(olin) M(ichael) 1933- ... 41-44R
Wells, Carolyn 1869(?)-1942 Brief entry ... 113
See also DLB 11
Wells, Charles Jeremiah 1800-1879 ... DLB-32
Wells, David Franklin 1928- Brief entry ... 108
Wells, Dee (Alberta) 1925- ... 85-88
See also AITN 1
Wells, (William) Dicky 1910- ... 61-64
Wells, Donald A(rthur) 1917- ... 23-24R
Wells, Edward
See Wellsted, W. Raife
Wells, Ellen B(aker) 1934- ... 103
Wells, Evelyn ... 53-56
Wells, George A(lbert) 1926- ... CANR-15
Earlier sketch in CA 81-84
Wells, George Philip 1901-1985 Obituary ... 117
Wells, H(erbert) G(eorge) 1866-1946 ... 121
Brief entry ... 110
See also SATA 20
See also DLB 34, 70
See also TCLC 6, 12, 19
Wells, Harold P(hilmore) 1925- ... CANR-10
Earlier sketch in CA 65-68
Wells, Harry Kohlsaat 1911-1976 ... 5-6R
Obituary ... 65-68
Wells, Helen 1910-1986 ... 29-32R
See also SATA 2, 49
Wells, Helen
See Campbell, Hope
Wells, Henry W(illis) 1895-1978 ... 81-84
Obituary ... 77-80
Wells, Hondo
See Whittington, Harry (Benjamin)
Wells, J. Wellington
See de Camp, L(yon) Sprague
Wells, James B(uchanan) 1909- ... 45-48
Wells, James M. 1917- ... 19-20R
Wells, Jerome C(ovell) 1936- ... 41-44R
Wells, Jessica
See Buckland, Raymond
Wells, Joel F(reeman) 1930- ... CANR-23
Earlier sketch in CA 15-16R
Wells, John Campbell 1936- ... 104
Wells, John Jay
See Coulson, Juanita (Ruth)
Wells, John Warren 1938- ... CANR-4
Earlier sketch in CA 49-52
Wells, June
See Swinford, Betty (June Wells)
Wells, Kenneth McNeill 1905- ... CAP-1
Earlier sketch in CA 13-14
Wells, Lawrence 1941- ... 120
Wells, Leon W. 1925- ... 17-18R
Wells, Linton 1893-1976 ... 97-100
Obituary ... 61-64
Wells, Lisa
See Racina, Thom
Wells, Louis T(ruitt), Jr. 1937- ... 65-68
Wells, M. Gawain 1942- ... 101
Wells, Marian (Louise Bradfield) 1931- ... 113
Wells, Merle William 1918- ... CANR-16
Earlier sketch in CA 85-88
Wells, Nigel 1944- ... 118
Wells, Peter D. 1936- ... 25-28R
Wells, (Frank Charles) Robert 1929- ... 97-100
Wells, Robert 1947- ... DLB-40
Wells, Robert
See Welsch, Roger L(ee)
Wells, Robert Vale 1943- ... CANR-12
Earlier sketch in CA 73-76
Wells, Robert W(ayne) 1918- ... CANR-2
Earlier sketch in CA 49-52
Wells, Ronald Vale 1913- ... CANR-14
Earlier sketch in CA 37-40R
Wells, Rosemary 1943- ... 85-88
See also SATA 18
See also SAAS 1
See also CLC 12
See also CLR 16
Wells, Samuel F(ogle, Jr.) 1935- ... 104
Wells, Samuel J(ames III) 1936- ... 123
Wells, Stanley W(illiam) 1930- ... CANR-10
Earlier sketch in CA 23-24R
Wells, Theodora (Westmont) 1926-
Brief entry ... 113
Wells, Tobias
See Forbes, DeLoris (Florine) Stanton
Wells, Tom H. 1917- ... 23-24R
Wells, Walter 1937- ... 25-28R
Wells, William D(eWitt) 1926- ... CANR-13
Earlier sketch in CA 61-64
Wells-Barnett, Ida B. 1862-1931 ... DLB-23
Wellsted, W. Raife 1929- ... 125
Wellstone, Paul David 1944- ... 107
Wellwarth, George E(manuel) 1932- ... CANR-3
Earlier sketch in CA 11-12R
Welmers, William Evert 1916- ... 104
Wels, Alena 1938(?)-1985 Obituary ... 115
Wels, Byron G(erald) 1924- ... CANR-8
Earlier sketch in CA 61-64
See also SATA 9
Welsch, Erwin Kurt 1935- ... 17-18R
Welsch, Glenn Albert 1915- ... CANR-10
Earlier sketch in CA 13-14R
Welsch, Roger L(ee) 1936- ... CANR-9
Earlier sketch in CA 21-22R
Welsh, Alexander 1933- ... CANR-6
Earlier sketch in CA 7-8R
Welsh, Andrew 1937- ... 110
Welsh, Anne 1922- ... 101
Welsh, David
See Hills, C(harles) A(lbert) R(eis)
Welsh, David J(ohn) 1920- ... 17-18R
Welsh, George Schlager 1918- ... 19-20R
Welsh, James Michael 1938- ... CANR-20
Earlier sketches in CA 53-56, CANR-4
Welsh, John R(ushing) 1916-1974 ... 37-40R
Welsh, Ken 1941- ... CANR-13
Earlier sketch in CA 77-80
Welsh, Marion E. 1910- ... 118
Welsh, Mary
See Hemingway, Mary Welsh
Welsh, Mary Flynn 1910(?)-1984 Obituary ... 112
See also SATA 38
Welsh, Paul 1911- ... 104
Welsh, Peter C(orbett) 1926- ... 25-28R
Welsh, Stanley L. 1928- ... 103
Welsh, Susan
See Collins, Margaret (Brandon James)
Welsh, William A(llen) 1940- ... CANR-25
Earlier sketch in CA 45-48
Welsman, Ernest 1912- ... 7-8R
Welt, Louis G(ordon) 1913-1974
Obituary ... 45-48
Welter, Erich 1900-1982 Obituary ... 107
Welter, Paul (R.) 1928- ... 121
Welter, Rush (Eastman) 1923- ... CANR-2
Earlier sketch in CA 5-6R
Weltge, Ralph (William) 1930- ... 23-24R
Welthy, Soni Halstead 1933- ... 15-16R
Weltmann, Lutz 1901- ... CAP-1
Earlier sketch in CA 11-12
Weltner, Linda R(iverly) 1938- ... 105
See also SATA 38
Weltsch, Robert 1891-1982 Obituary ... 108
Welty, Eudora 1909- ... 11-12R
See also CABS 1
See also DLB 2
See also DLBY 87
See also CDALB 1941-1968
See also CLC 1, 2, 5, 14, 22, 33
See also SSC 1
Welty, Joel Carl 1901- ... CANR-2
Earlier sketch in CA 5-6R
Welty, S. F.
See Welty, Susan F.
Welty, Susan F. 1905- ... CAP-2
Earlier sketch in CA 17-18
See also SATA 9
Welwood, John 1943- ... 120
Welzenbach, Lanora F.
See Miller, Lanora
Wemple, Suzanne Fonay 1927- ... 106
Wenar, Charles 1922- ... 93-96
Wende, Philip 1939- ... 29-32R
Wendel, Francois Jean 1905-19(?) ... CAP-1
Earlier sketch in CA 13-14
Wendel, Natalja Rose 1900- ... 61-64
Wendel, Thomas H(arold) 1924- ... 53-56
Wendel, Tim 1956- ... 105
Wendelin, Rudolph 1910- ... SATA-23
Wendell, Barrett 1855-1921 ... DLB-71
Wender, Dorothea 1934- ... CANR-24
Earlier sketch in CA 45-48
Wender, Paul H. 1934- ... CANR-26
Earlier sketch in CA 109
Wenders, Wim 1945- ... 93-96
Wendland, Michael F(letcher) 1946- ... CANR-9
Earlier sketch in CA 65-68
Wendland, Mike
See Wendland, Michael F(letcher)

Wendorf, Patricia 1928- 113
Wendorf, Richard (Harold) 1948- 114
Wendroff, Zalman
See Vendrovskii, David Efimovich
Wendrowsky, Zalman
See Vendrovskii, David Efimovich
Wendt, Albert 1939- 57-60
Wendt, Gerald L(ouis) 1891-1973
Obituary 45-48
Wendt, Ingrid 1944- 117
Wendt, Jo Ann 1935- 109
Wendt, Lloyd 1908- CANR-25
Earlier sketch in CA 102
Wendt, Viola (Sophia) 1907- 104
Wendzel, Robert L. 1938- 112
Weng, Byron S. J. 1934- CANR-16
Earlier sketch in CA 41-44R
Weng, Hsing Ching
See Weng, Wan-go
Weng, Wan-go 1918- 97-100
Wengenroth, Edith Flack Ackley
1887-1970 Obituary 104
Wengenroth, Stow 1906-1978 Obituary 104
Wenger, (Anna) Grace 1919- 13-14R
Wenger, J(ohn) C(hristian) 1910- CANR-21
Earlier sketches in CA 3R, CANR-6
Wengert, Norman Irving 1916- 85-88
Wengrov, Charles 1925- CANR-7
Earlier sketch in CA 5-6R
Wenham, John W(illiam) 1913- 57-60
Wenhe, Mary B. 1910- 65-68
Wen I-to 1899-1946 TCLC-28
Wenk, Edward, Jr. 1920- 53-56
Wenkam, Robert 1920- CANR-4
Earlier sketch in CA 53-56
Wenkart, Heni
See Wenkart, Henny
Wenkart, Henny 1928- 11-12R
Wennblom, Ralph D. 1922(?)-1986
Obituary 121
Wenner, Jann S(imon) 1946- 101
Wenner, Kate 1947- 77-80
Wenner, Lettie McSpadden 1937- 65-68
Wenner, Manfred W. 1936- 29-32R
Wenner, Sim 1922- 2R
Wennerstrom, Mary H(annah) 1939-
Brief entry 110
Wensing, Michael G. 1950- 118
Wensinger, Arthur S(tevens) 1926- CANR-15
Earlier sketch in CA 37-40R
Wentink, Andrew Mark 1948- 105
Wentworth, Barbara
See Pitcher, Gladys
Wentworth, Elise H(ughes) 1931- 77-80
Wentworth, Harold 1904- CAP-1
Earlier sketch in CA 13-14
Wentworth, Michael J(ustin) 1938- 118
Wentworth, Robert
See Hamilton, Edmond
Wentz, Frederick K(uhlman) 1921- 11-12R
Wentz, Walter B. 1929- CANR-10
Earlier sketch in CA 25-28R
Wenzel, Siegfried 1928- 21-22R
Wepman, Dennis 1933- 120
Wepman, Joseph M. 1907- 45-48
Weppner, Robert S. 1936- 121
Werblow, Dorothy N. 1908-1972
Obituary 37-40R
Were, Gideon S(aulo) 1934- CANR-11
Earlier sketch in CA 65-68
Werfel, Franz (V.) 1890-1945 Brief entry 104
See also TCLC 8
Werich, Jan 1905(?)-1980 Obituary 102
Werking, Richard Hume 1943- Brief entry 113
Werkley, Caroline E(Isea) 29-32R
Werkman, Sidney L(ee) 1927- 49-52
Werkmeister, Lucyle (Thomas) 1908- 5-6R
Werkmeister, W(illiam) H(enry) 1901- 23-24R
Werlich, David P(atrick) 1941- 81-84
Werlich, Robert 1924- 11-12R
Werlin, Herbert Holland 1932- 61-64
Wermuth, Paul C(harles Joseph) 1925- 13-14R
Werne, Benjamin 1904-1978 Obituary 77-80
Wernecke, Herbert Henry 1895- 5-6R
Werner, Alfred 1911-1979 Obituary 89-92
Werner, D. Michael 1950- 120
Werner, Elsa Jane
See Watson, Jane Werner
Werner, Emmy Elizabeth 1929- 57-60
Werner, Eric 1901-1988 15-16R
Obituary 126
Werner, Hazen G. 1895- 17-18R
Werner, Herma 1926- CANR-15
Earlier sketch in CA 85-88
See also SATA 41, 47
Werner, Jane
See Watson, Jane Werner
Werner, Jayne S(usan) 1944- 112
Werner, John R(oland) 1930- 41-44R
Werner, K.
See Casewit, Curtis W(erner)
Werner, M(orris) R(obert) 1897-1981 107
Obituary 104
Werner, Peter Howard 1944- CANR-4
Earlier sketch in CA 53-56
Werner, Victor (Emile) 1894-1980 29-32R
Obituary 93-96
Werner, Vivian 1921- 105
Wernette, J(ohn) Philip 1903- 5-6R
Wernick, Robert 1918- 97-100
Wernick, Saul 1921- 81-84
Werning, Waldo J. 1921- CANR-10
Earlier sketch in CA 13-14R
Wernstedt, Frederick L(age) 1921- 23-24R
Werr, Donald F. 1920- 21-22R
Werry, Richard R. 1916- 9-10R
Wersba, Barbara 1932- CANR-16
Earlier sketch in CA 29-32R
See also SATA 1
See also SAAS 2
See also DLB 52
See also CLC 30
See also CLR 3
Wershoven, Carol Jean 1947- 112
Werstein, Irving 1914(?)-1971 73-76
Obituary 29-32R
See also SATA 14
Wert, Lynette L(emon) 1938- 106
Wertenbaker, Lael (Tucker) 1909- CANR-18
Earlier sketches in CA 5-6R, CANR-3
Wertenbaker, Thomas Jefferson
1879-1966 7-8R
Wertenbaker, William 1938- 97-100
Werth, Alexander 1901-1969 CAP-1
Obituary 25-28R
Earlier sketch in CA 15-16
Werth, Kurt 1896- 81-84
See also SATA 20
Wertham, Fredric 1895-1981 7-8R
Obituary 105
Wertheim, Arthur Frank 1935- 97-100
Wertheim, Bill 1944- 37-40R
Wertheim, Stanley 1930- 41-44R
Wertheimer, Barbara M(ayer)
1926(?)-1983 Obituary 110
Wertheimer, Leonard 1914- 116
Wertheimer, Linda Brief entry 123
Wertheimer, Marilyn L(ou) 1928- 102
Wertheimer, Max 1880-1943 Brief entry 123
Wertheimer, Michael (Matthew) 1927- CANR-2
Earlier sketch in CA 2R
Wertheimer, Richard F(rederick) II
1943- 29-32R
Wertheimer, Roger 1942- 37-40R
Werther, William B(lanchfield), Jr.
1947- CANR-21
Earlier sketch in CA 105
Werthman, Michael S(cott) 1939- 89-92
Wertime, Theodore A(llen) 1919-1982 109
Obituary 106
Wertmuller, Lina 1928- 97-100
See also CLC 16
Werts, Margaret F. 1915- 102
Wertsman, Vladimir (F.) 1929- CANR-20
Earlier sketches in CA 61-64, CANR-8
Wertz, Richard W(ayne) 1933- 45-48
Wertz, S. K.
See Wertz, Spencer K.
Wertz, Spencer K. 1941- 125
Wesander, Bioern Kenneth
See Cox, P(atrick) Brian
Wesberry, James Pickett 1906- 85-88
Weschcke, Carl L(ouis) 1930- 61-64
Wesche, L(ilburn) E(dgar) 1929- 93-96
Wesche, Percival A. 1912- 49-52
Weschler, Louis F(redrick) 1933- 41-44R
Wescott, Glenway 1901-1987 CANR-23
Obituary 121
Earlier sketch in CA 13-14R
See also DLB 4, 9
See also CLC 13
Wescott, Roger W. 1925- 25-28R
Wesencraft, Charles Frederick 1928- 61-64
Wesker, Arnold 1932- CANR-1
Earlier sketch in CA 4R
See also CAAS 7
See also DLB 13
See also CLC 3, 5, 42
Weslager, C(linton) A(lfred) 1909- CANR-24
Earlier sketches in CA 21-22R, CANR-9
Wesley, Charles H(arris) 1891-1987 101
Obituary 123
Wesley, Elizabeth
See McElfresh, (Elizabeth) Adeline
Wesley, George R(andolph) 1931- 41-44R
Wesley, James
See Rigoni, Orlando (Joseph)
Wesley, Mary 1912- 49-52
Wesley, Richard (Errol) 1945- 57-60
See also BW
See also DLB 38
See also CLC 7
Wesling, Donald 1939- 101
Wesner, Maralene 1935- 112
Wesner, Miles 1933- 112
Wess, Martin 1906(?)-1975 Obituary 104
Wessel, Andrew E(rnest) 1925- 73-76
Wessel, Carl John 1911-1984 Obituary 113
Wessel, Helen (Strain) 1924- CANR-11
Earlier sketch in CA 13-14R
Wessel, Milton R(alph) 1923- 89-92
Wessel, Robert H. 1921- 2R
Wesselmann, Tom 1931- 108
Wessels, William L. 1889- 7-8R
Wesser, Robert F. 1933- 23-24R
Wessler, Ruth Ann 1938- 29-32R
Wessman, Alden E(benhart) 1930- 23-24R
Wesson, Joan
See Pittock, Joan (Hornby)
Wesson, Robert G(ale) 1920- CANR-18
Earlier sketches in CA 11-12R, CANR-3
West, Allan M(orrell) 1910- 109
West, Anna 1938- 106
See also SATA 40
West, Anthony (Panther) 1914-1987 CANR-19
Obituary 124
Earlier sketches in CA 45-48, CANR-3
See also DLB 15
See also CLC 50
West, Anthony C. 1910- 69-72
West, Barbara
See Price, Olive
West, Betty 1921- CANR-7
Earlier sketch in CA 7-8R
See also SATA 11
West, Beverly Henderson 1939- 119
West, Bill
See West, William G.
West, Bonnie 1946- 114
West, C. P.
See Wodehouse, P(elham) G(renville)
West, Charles Converse 1921- 81-84
West, D(onald) J(ames) 1924- CANR-20
Earlier sketches in CA 13-14R, CANR-5
West, David (Alexander) 1926- 23-24R
West, Delno C(loyde), Jr. 1936- 57-60
West, Don 1928- 57-60
West, Dorothy 1907- DLB-76
West, E(dwin) G(eorge) 25-28R
West, Earle H(uddleston) 1925- 53-56
West, Edward Nason 1909- CAP-2
Earlier sketch in CA 19-20
West, Elliot 1924- 19-20R
West, Elmer D. 1907- CAP-1
Earlier sketch in CA 13-14
West, Emily Govan 1919- 109
See also SATA 38
West, Emmy
See West, Emily Govan
West, Eugenia Lovett 85-88
West, Francis (James) 1927- CANR-3
Earlier sketch in CA 7-8R
West, Francis Horner 1909- 118
West, Frank H.
See West, Francis Horner
West, Fred 1918- 7-8R
West, G(eorge) Allen, Jr. 1915- 19-20R
West, George Algernon 1893-1980
Obituary 97-100
West, Gertrude 110
West, Gordon 1896- CAP-1
Earlier sketch in CA 13-14
West, Henry Woolliscroft 1925- 41-44R
West, Herbert B(uell) 1916- 53-56
West, Herbert Faulkner 1898-1974 CAP-2
Obituary 53-56
Earlier sketch in CA 19-20
West, J. B.
See West, J. Bernard
West, J. Bernard 1913(?)-1983 120
Obituary 110
West, James
See Withers, Carl A.
West, James King 1930- 45-48
West, (Mary) Jane 1939(?)-1981 Obituary 104
West, Jerry
See Svenson, Andrew E(dward)
West, (Mary) Jessamyn 1902-1984 11-12R
Obituary 112
See also SATA 37
See also DLB 6
See also DLBY 84
See also CLC 7, 17
West, John Anthony 1932- 81-84
West, John Foster 1918- 15-16R
West, John Frederick 1929- 103
West, Joyce (Tarlton) 106
West, Kirkpatrick
See Harris, F(rank) Brayton
West, Leonard J(ordan) 1921- 41-44R
West, Lindsay
See Weber, Nancy
West, Mae 1893-1980 89-92
Obituary 102
See also DLB 44
West, Marion B(ond) 1936- 101
West, Mark
See Runyon, Charles W.
West, Morris L(anglo) 1916- CANR-24
Earlier sketch in CA 5-6R
See also CLC 6, 33
West, Muriel (Leitzell) 1903-19(?) CAP-1
Earlier sketch in CA 15-16
West, Nancy Richard
See Westphal, Wilma Ross
West, Nathanael 1903-1940 125
Brief entry 104
See also DLB 4, 9, 28
See also TCLC 1, 14
West, Owen
See Koontz, Dean R(ay)
West, Paul 1930- CANR-22
Earlier sketch in CA 15-16R
See also CAAS 7
See also DLB 14
See also CLC 7, 14
West, Ray B(enedict), Jr. 1908- CANR-3
Earlier sketch in CA 2R
West, Rebecca 1892-1983 CANR-19
Obituary 109
Earlier sketch in CA 7-8R
See also DLB 36
See also DLBY 83
See also CLC 7, 9, 31, 50
West, Richard S(edgewick), Jr.
1902-1968 CAP-1
Earlier sketch in CA 15-16
West, Robert C(raig) 1947- 89-92
West, Robert Frederick 1916- 5-6R
West, Robert H(unter) 1907- 37-40R
West, Thomas R(eed) 1936- 124
Brief entry 118
West, Token
See Humphries, Adelaide M.
West, Trudy
See West, Gertrude
West, Uta 1928- 85-88
West, V(ictoria Mary) Sackville
See Sackville-West, V(ictoria Mary)
West, Ward
See Borland, Harold Glen
West, William G. 1930- CANR-14
Earlier sketch in CA 37-40R
Westall, Robert (Atkinson) 1929- CANR-18
Earlier sketch in CA 69-72
See also SATA 23
See also SAAS 2
See also CLC 17
See also CLR 13
Westberg, Granger E(llsworth) 1913- CANR-6
Earlier sketch in CA 2R
Westbie, Constance 1910- 85-88
Westbrook, Adele 41-44R
Westbrook, Max (Roger) 1927- 37-40R
Westbrook, Perry D(ickie) 1916- CANR-21
Earlier sketches in CA 2R, CANR-6
Westbrook, Robert 1945- 25-28R
Westbrook, Wayne W(illiam) 1939- 97-100
Westbury, Ian Douglas 1939- Brief entry 106
Westby, David L. 1929- 45-48
Westby-Gibson, Dorothy Pauline 1920- 17-18R
Westcott, Cynthia 1898-1983 7-8R
Obituary 109
Westcott, Jan Vlachos 1912- CANR-2
Earlier sketch in CA 4R
Westcott, Kathleen
See Abrahamsen, Christine Elizabeth
Westcott, W(illiam) F(ranklin) 1949- 113
Westcott-Jones, K(enneth) 1921- CANR-4
Earlier sketch in CA 53-56
Westebbe, Richard (Manning) 1925- 45-48
Westell, Anthony 1926- 101
Westerberg, Christine 1950- 61-64
See also SATA 29
Westergaard, John (Harald) 1927- CANR-11
Earlier sketch in CA 69-72
Westerhoff, John H(enry) III 1933- CANR-17
Earlier sketches in CA 45-48, CANR-1
Westerink, Leendert Gerrit 1913- 93-96
Westerman, Percy F(rancis) 1876-1959
Brief entry 110
Westermann, Claus 1909- CANR-15
Earlier sketch in CA 81-84
Westermeier, Clifford P(eter) 1910- 45-48
Westermeyer, Joseph John 1937- 109
Western, J(ohn) R(andle) 1928-1971 CAP-2
Earlier sketch in CA 21-22
Western, John (Charles) 1947- 105
Western, Mark
See Crisp, Anthony Thomas
(The) Western Spy
See Dillon, John M(yles)
Westervelt, Virginia Veeder 1914- CANR-10
Earlier sketch in CA 61-64
See also SATA 10
Westfall, David 1927- 117
Westfall, Don C. 1928-1973 CAP-2
Earlier sketch in CA 17-18
Westfall, Ralph (Libby) 1917- 5-6R
Westfall, Richard S(amuel) 1924- 23-24R
Westfeldt, Lulie 1896- CAP-1
Earlier sketch in CA 13-14
Westheimer, David 1917- CANR-2
Earlier sketch in CA 4R
See also SATA 14
Westhues, Kenneth 1944- CANR-11
Earlier sketch in CA 25-28R
Westin, Alan F(urman) 1929- CANR-10
Earlier sketch in CA 15-16R
Westin, Av(ram) 1929- 77-80
Westin, Jeane Eddy 1931- 85-88
Westin, Richard A(xel) 1945- 115
Westing, Arthur H(erbert) 1928- CANR-17
Earlier sketch in CA 41-44R
Westing, John Howard 1911- 11-12R
Westlake, Aubrey Thomas 1893-1985
Obituary 119
Westlake, Donald E(dwin) 1933- CANR-16
Earlier sketch in CA 19-20R
See also CLC 7, 33
Westlake, Helen Gum 1927- 41-44R
Westland, Lynn
See Joscelyn, Archie L.
Westley, Bruce H(utchinson) 1915- CANR-2
Earlier sketch in CA 2R
Westley, Dick
See Westley, Richard John
Westley, Richard John 1928- 112
Westley, William A. 1920- 37-40R
Westlund, Joseph 1936- 118
Westmacott, Mary
See Christie, Agatha (Mary Clarissa)
Westman, Barbara 105
Westman, Jack C(onrad) 1927- 93-96
Westman, Paul (Wendell) 1956- 106
See also SATA 39
Westman, Wesley C(harles) 1936- 29-32R
Westminster, Aynn
See Mundis, Hester
Westmore, Ann 1953- 109
Westmore, Frank 1923(?)-1985 Obituary 116
Westmoreland, Reg(inald Conway)
1926- 29-32R
Westmoreland, William C(hilds) 1914- 101
Westoff, Charles Francis 1927- 81-84
Westoff, Leslie Aldridge 1928- 77-80
Weston, Alan J(ay) 1940- 73-76
Weston, Allen
See Hogarth, Grace (Weston Allen)
and Norton, Alice Mary
Weston, Ann
See Pitcher, Gladys
Weston, Burns H. 1933- 29-32R
Weston, Carolyn 1921- 107
Weston, Corinne Comstock 1919- CANR-21
Earlier sketch in CA 2R

Weston, Glen E(arl) 1922- ... 49-52
Weston, Helen Gray
See Daniels, Dorothy
Weston, J(ohn) Fred(erick) 1916- ... CANR-1
Earlier sketch in CA 2R
Weston, John (Harrison) 1932- ... 17-18R
See also SATA 21
Weston, John
See Davies, John Evan Weston
Weston, Joseph H(arry) 1911(?)-1983
Obituary ... 111
Weston, Martha 1947- ... SATA-53
Weston, Paul B(rendan) 1910- ... 15-16R
Weston, Rubin Francis 1921- ... 104
Weston, Susan B(rown) 1943- ... 81-84
Weston-Smith, M. 1956- ... 93-96
Westphal, Barbara Osborne 1907- ... CAP-1
Earlier sketch in CA 11-12
Westphal, Clarence 1904- ... CAP-2
Earlier sketch in CA 17-18
Westphal, Siegfried 1902-1982 Obituary ... 107
Westphal, Wilma Ross 1907- ... 21-22R
Westphall, Victor 1913- ... 119
Westrup, J(ack) A(llan) 1904-1975
Obituary ... 115
Westsmith, Kim 1945- ... 57-60
Westwater, Sister Agnes Martha 1929- ... 21-22R
Westwood, Gordon
See Schofield, Michael
Westwood, Gwen 1915- ... CANR-19
Earlier sketch in CA 25-28R
Westwood, J(ohn) N(orton) 1931- ... CANR-20
Earlier sketches in CA 13-14R, CANR-5
Westwood, Jennifer
See Chandler, Jennifer (Westwood)
See also SATA 10
Wetcheek, J. L.
See Feuchtwanger, Lion
Wetering, Janwillem van de
See van de Wetering, Janwillem
Wetherbee, Winthrop (III) 1938- ... CANR-12
Earlier sketch in CA 73-76
Wetherby, Terry (Lynne) 1943- ... 102
Wetherell, Elizabeth
See Warner, Susan (Bogert)
Wetherell-Pepper, Joan Alexander 1920- ... 9-10R
Wetherill, Peter Michael 1932- ... CANR-12
Earlier sketch in CA 61-64
Wethey, Harold E(dwin) 1902-1984 ... CANR-2
Obituary ... 113
Earlier sketch in CA 4R
Wetmore, Alexander 1886-1978 ... 85-88
Obituary ... 81-84
Wetmore, Ruth Y. 1934- ... 57-60
Wetmore, Thomas Hall 1915- ... 25-28R
Wetmore, William T. 1930- ... 9-10R
Wettenhall, Roger (Llewellyn) 1931- ... CANR-26
Earlier sketch in CA 109
Wetter, Gustav A(ndreas) 1911- ... 11-12R
Wettlaufer, George 1935- ... 57-60
Wettlaufer, Nancy 1939- ... 57-60
Wettstein, Howard K(enneth) 1943- ... 105
Wetzel, (Earl) Donald 1921- ... 25-28R
Wetzel, Elizabeth 1930- ... 114
Wetzel, Richard D(ean) 1935- ... 85-88
Weverka, Robert 1926- ... CANR-2
Earlier sketch in CA 49-52
Wevers, Richard Franklin 1933-
Brief entry ... 106
Wevill, David 1937- ... 13-14R
Wexler, Jean Stewart 1921- ... 65-68
Wexler, Jerome (LeRoy) 1923- ... 73-76
See also SATA 14
Wexler, Joyce Piell 1947- ... 97-100
Wexler, Norman 1926- Brief entry ... 116
Wexley, John 1907-1985 Obituary ... 115
Wexley, Kenneth N. ... 93-96
Weyand, Alexander Mathias 1892- ... 5-6R
Weybright, Victor 1903-1978 Obituary ... 89-92
Weygant, Noemi ... CANR-2
Earlier sketch in CA 45-48
Weyl, Joachim 1915-1977 Obituary ... 73-76
Weyl, Nathaniel 1910- ... CANR-5
Earlier sketch in CA 11-12R
Weyl, Woldemar A. 1901(?)-1975
Obituary ... 61-64
Weyler, Rex 1947- ... 110
Weyrauch, Walter O(tto) 1919- ... CANR-10
Earlier sketch in CA 13-14R
Weyrich, Paul M(ichael) 1942- ... 118
Wezeman, Frederick Hartog 1915-1981 ... CANR-6
Obituary ... 106
Earlier sketch in CA 11-12R
Whale, John (Hilary) 1931- ... 101
Whalen, Barbara G. 1928- ... 120
Whalen, Charles William, Jr. 1920- ... 105
Whalen, George J. 1939- ... CANR-16
Earlier sketch in CA 89-92
Whalen, Philip 1923- ... CANR-5
Earlier sketch in CA 9-10R
See also DLB 16
See also CLC 6, 29
Whalen, Richard J(ames) 1935- ... 15-16R
Whalen, William Joseph 1926- ... CANR-4
Earlier sketch in CA 2R
Whaley, Barton Stewart 1928- ... 41-44R
Whaley, Donald L. 1934- ... 33-36R
Whaley, Russell Francis 1934- ... 57-60
Whaling, Frank 1934- ... 113
Whalley, Dorothy 1911- ... CAP-1
Earlier sketch in CA 9-10
Whalley, George 1915- ... 101
Whalley, Janet 1945- ... 117
Whalley, Joyce Irene ... 103
Whalon, Marion K(elley) 1913- ... 119
Wharf, Michael
See Weller, George (Anthony)
Wharmby, Margot ... CANR-24
Earlier sketches in CA 17-18R, CANR-8
Wharton, Annabel Jane ... 123
Wharton, Anthony
See McAllister, Alister
Wharton, Anthony P.
See McAllister, Alister
Wharton, Clifton R(eginald), Jr. 1926- ... 41-44R
Wharton, David B(ailey) 1914- ... 73-76
Wharton, Edith (Newbold Jones)
1862-1937 Brief entry ... 104
See also DLB 4, 9, 12
See also CDALB 1865-1917
See also TCLC 3, 9, 27
Wharton, Elizabeth Austin 1920-1985
Obituary ... 116
Wharton, Gary C(harles) 1940- ... 45-48
Wharton, George Frederick III 1952- ... 109
Wharton, James
See Mencken, H(enry) L(ouis)
Wharton, John Franklin 1894-1977 ... 81-84
Obituary ... 73-76
Wharton, William (a pseudonym) ... 93-96
See also DLBY 80
See also CLC 18, 37
Whateley, Leslie Violet Lucy Evelyn Mary
1899-1987 Obituary ... 123
Whatmore, Leonard Elliott 1912- ... 13-14R
Whatmough, Joshua 1897- ... 5-6R
Wheat, Cathleen Hayhurst 1904- ... CAP-1
Earlier sketch in CA 17-18
Wheat, (Marcus) Ed(ward, Jr.) 1926- ... 118
Wheat, Gilbert Collins, Jr. 1927- ... 4R
Wheat, Joe Ben 1916- ... 41-44R
Wheat, Leonard F. 1931- ... 29-32R
Wheat, Patte 1935- ... CANR-19
Earlier sketch in CA 101
Wheatcroft, Andrew (Jonathan Maclean)
1944- ... 110
Wheatcroft, Geoffrey 1945- ... 124
Wheatcroft, John 1925- ... CANR-14
Earlier sketch in CA 37-40R
Wheatcroft, Stephen F(rederick) 1921- ... 7-8R
Wheatley, Arabelle 1921- ... SATA-16
Wheatley, Dennis (Yeats) 1897-1977 ... CANR-9
Obituary ... 73-76
Earlier sketch in CA 7-8R
Wheatley, Jon 1931- ... 29-32R
Wheatley, Phillis 1754(?)-1784 ... DLB-31, 50
See also CDALB 1640-1865
Wheatley, Richard C(harles) 1904- ... CAP-1
Earlier sketch in CA 11-12
Wheatley, Ronald 1923(?)-1985 Obituary ... 115
Wheatley, Vera (Semple) ... CAP-1
Earlier sketch in CA 15-16
Wheat-Lieber, Patte
See Wheat, Patte
Wheaton, Anne (Williams) 1892-1977
Obituary ... 69-72
Wheaton, Bruce R. 1944- ... CANR-22
Earlier sketch in CA 104
Wheaton, Philip D(amon) 1916- ... 104
Wheaton, William L. C. 1913-1978 ... CANR-3
Earlier sketch in CA 3R
Whedon, Julia
See Schickel, Julia Whedon
Whedon, Margaret B(runssen) 1926- ... 105
Whedon, Peggy
See Whedon, Margaret B(runssen)
Wheeler, Allen 1903-1984 Obituary ... 111
Wheeler, Bayard O. 1905- ... 41-44R
Wheeler, Bonnie G(rant) 1943- ... 109
Wheeler, Burton K(endall) 1882-1975
Obituary ... 53-56
Wheeler, Charles (Thomas) 1892-1974 ... CAP-2
Obituary ... 53-56
Earlier sketch in CA 29-32
Wheeler, Charles Stearns 1816-1843 ... DLB-1
Wheeler, Cindy 1955- ... 110
See also SATA 40, 49
Wheeler, David L. 1934- ... 37-40R
Wheeler, David Raymond 1942- ... 73-76
Wheeler, Douglas L. 1937- ... 29-32R
Wheeler, (Charles) Gidley 1938- ... CANR-24
Earlier sketch in CA 107
Wheeler, (John) Harvey 1918- ... CANR-17
Earlier sketches in CA 45-48, CANR-1
Wheeler, Helen Rippier ... CANR-14
Earlier sketch in CA 17-18R
Wheeler, Hugh (Callingham) 1912-1987 ... 89-92
Obituary ... 123
Wheeler, J(oseph) Clyde 1910- ... 2R
Wheeler, Janet D. ... CANR-26
Earlier sketches in CA 19-20, CAP-2
See also SATA 1
Wheeler, Jesse H(arrison), Jr. 1918- ... 45-48
Wheeler, John Archibald 1911- ... 57-60
Wheeler, Keith 1911- ... CANR-7
Earlier sketch in CA 7-8R
Wheeler, Leslie A. 1945- ... CANR-11
Earlier sketch in CA 65-68
Wheeler, Lora Jeanne 1923- ... 33-36R
Wheeler, Margaret 1916- ... CAP-2
Earlier sketch in CA 25-28
Wheeler, Mary Jane ... 29-32R
Wheeler, Michael 1943- ... CANR-9
Earlier sketch in CA 65-68
Wheeler, Molly 1920- ... 29-32R
Wheeler, Monroe 1900-1988 Obituary ... 126
See also DLB 4
Wheeler, (Robert Eric) Mortimer
1890-1976 ... 77-80
Obituary ... 65-68
Wheeler, Opal 1898- ... SATA-23
Wheeler, Paul 1934- ... 25-28R
Wheeler, Penny Estes 1943- ... 33-36R
Wheeler, Raymond Milner 1919-1982
Obituary ... 106
Wheeler, Richard 1922- ... CANR-25
Earlier sketches in CA 17-18R, CANR-8
Wheeler, Richard Paul 1943- ... 108
Wheeler, Richard S(eabrook) 1928- ... 45-48
Wheeler, Robert C(ordell) 1913- ... 61-64
Wheeler, Ruth Carr 1899- ... 5-6R
Wheeler, Sessions S(amuel) 1911- ... CANR-25
Earlier sketch in CA 17-18R
Wheeler, Thomas C. 1927- ... 104
Wheeler, Thomas H(utchin) 1947- ... 93-96
Wheeler, Tom
See Wheeler, Thomas H(utchin)
Wheeler, W(illiam) Lawrence 1925- ... 13-14R
Wheeler-Bennett, John 1902-1975 ... 65-68
Obituary ... 61-64
Wheelis, Allen B. 1915- ... 17-18R
Wheelock, Arthur Kingsland, Jr. 1943- ... 107
Wheelock, (Kinch) Carter 1924- ... 61-64
Wheelock, Frederic M(elvin) 1902-1987 ... 97-100
Obituary ... 124
Wheelock, John Hall 1886-1978 ... CANR-14
Obituary ... 77-80
Earlier sketch in CA 15-16R
See also DLB 45
See also CLC 14
Wheelock, Martha E. 1941- ... 25-28R
Wheelwright, Edward Lawrence 1921- ... CANR-21
Earlier sketch in CA 103
Wheelwright, John 1592(?)-1679 ... DLB-24
Wheelwright, John 1897-1940 ... DLB-45
Wheelwright, Philip (Ellis) 1901-1970 ... CAP-2
Earlier sketch in CA 23-24
Wheelwright, Richard 1936- ... 33-36R
Wheelwright, Steven C. 1943- ... 119
Whelan, Elizabeth M(urphy) 1943- ... CANR-24
Earlier sketches in CA 57-60, CANR-8
See also SATA 14
Whelan, Gloria (Ann) 1923- ... 101
Whelan, James Robert 1933- ... 102
Whelan, Joseph P(aul) 1932- ... 41-44R
Wheldon, Huw (Pyrs) 1916-1986 ... 107
Obituary ... 118
Whelpton, (George) Eric 1894-1981 ... CANR-5
Obituary ... 103
Earlier sketch in CA 9-10R
Whelpton, Pascal K(idder) 1893-1964 ... CANR-16
Earlier sketch in CA 2R
Whelton, Clark 1937- ... 69-72
Whetstone, Colonel Pete
See Noland, C. F. M.
Whetten, Lawrence L. 1932- ... CANR-11
Earlier sketch in CA 61-64
Whetten, Nathan Laselle 1900- ... 2R
Whicher, John F. 1919- ... 17-18R
Whidden, Mary Bess 1936- ... 126
Whiffen, Marcus 1916- ... CANR-12
Earlier sketch in CA 61-64
Whigham, Peter (George) 1925-1987 ... 25-28R
Obituary ... 123
Whinney, Margaret Dickens 1897-1975
Obituary ... 61-64
Whinnom, Keith 1927-1986 Obituary ... 118
Whipkey, Kenneth Lee 1932- ... CANR-4
Earlier sketch in CA 53-56
Whipple, A(ddison) B(eecher) C(olvin)
1918- ... 125
Whipple, Beverly 1941- ... 109
Whipple, Chandler (Henry) 1905- ... 25-28R
Whipple, Dorothy 1893- ... CAP-1
Earlier sketch in CA 13-14
Whipple, Edwin Percy 1819-1886 ... DLB-1, 64
Whipple, Fred Lawrence 1906- ... CAP-1
Earlier sketch in CA 11-12
Whipple, George 1927- ... 119
Whipple, James B. 1913- ... 29-32R
Whipple, Maurine 1910- ... 7-8R
Whisenand, Paul M. 1935- ... CANR-22
Earlier sketch in CA 69-72
Whisenhunt, Donald W(ayne) 1938- ... CANR-9
Earlier sketch in CA 57-60
Whisler, John A(lbert) 1951- ... 109
Whisler, Thomas Lee 1920- Brief entry ... 115
Whisnant, Charleen
See Swansea, Charleen
Whisnant, David E(ugene) 1938- ... 41-44R
Whistler, Laurence 1912- ... CANR-19
Earlier sketches in CA 9-10R, CANR-3
Whistler, Reginald John 1905-1944 ... SATA-30
Whistler, Rex
See Whistler, Reginald John
Whiston, Lionel (Abney) 1895- ... 69-72
Whitacre, Donald (DuMont) 1920- ... 69-72
Whitaker, Alexander 1585-1617 ... DLB-24
Whitaker, Arthur Preston 1895-1979
Obituary ... 112
Whitaker, Ben(jamin Charles George)
1934- ... 53-56
Whitaker, C(leophaus) S(ylvester), Jr.
1935- ... 29-32R
Whitaker, Carl A. 1912- Brief entry ... 114
Whitaker, Daniel K. 1801-1881 ... DLB-73
Whitaker, David 1930- ... 21-22R
Whitaker, Dorothy Stock 1925- ... 13-14R
Whitaker, Frederic 1891-1980 ... CANR-4
Obituary ... 97-100
Earlier sketch in CA 7-8R
Whitaker, Gilbert R(iley), Jr. 1931- ... 11-12R
Whitaker, Haddon 1908(?)-1982 Obituary ... 105
Whitaker, James W. 1936- ... 102
Whitaker, John O(gden), Jr. 1935- ... 105
Whitaker, Malachi Taylor 1895-1976
Obituary ... 104
Whitaker, Mary 1896(?)-1976 Obituary ... 65-68
Whitaker, Peter 1952- ... 124
Whitaker, Rod 1931- ... 29-32R
Whitaker, Rogers E(rnest) M(alcolm)
1899-1981 Obituary ... 103
Whitaker, Shelagh (Dunwoody) 1930- ... 125
Whitaker, T(ommy) J(ames) 1949- ... 53-56
Whitaker, Thomas R(ussell) 1925- ... 25-28R
Whitaker, Urban George, Jr. 1924- ... 11-12R
Whitbeck, George W(alter) 1932- ... 73-76
Whitbread, Jane
See Levin, Jane Whitbread
Whitbread, Leslie George 1917- ... 37-40R
Whitbread, Thomas (Bacon) 1931- ... 13-14R
Whitburn, Joel Carver 1939- ... CANR-15
Earlier sketch in CA 33-36R
Whitby, Henry Augustus Morton
1898-1969 ... CAP-1
Earlier sketch in CA 11-12
Whitby, Sharon
See Peters, Maureen
Whitby, Thomas J. 1919- ... 126
Whitcher, Frances Miriam 1814-1852 ... DLB-11
Whitcomb, Edgar D(oud) 1918- ... 23-24R
Whitcomb, Hale C(hristy) 1907- ... CAP-2
Earlier sketch in CA 29-32
Whitcomb, Helen Hafemann ... CANR-6
Earlier sketch in CA 13-14R
Whitcomb, Ian 1941- ... CANR-8
Earlier sketch in CA 57-60
Whitcomb, John C(lement) 1924- ... CANR-4
Earlier sketch in CA 2R
Whitcomb, Jon 1906-1988 ... CAP-1
Obituary ... 125
Earlier sketch in CA 15-16
See also SATA 10
Whitcomb, Meg W. 1930- ... 123
Whitcomb, Philip W(right) 1891- ... 73-76
White, A(drian) N(icholas) Sherwin
See Sherwin-White, A(drian) N(icholas)
White, Alan ... CANR-3
Earlier sketch in CA 45-48
White, Alan R(ichard) 1922- ... 25-28R
White, Alex Sandri 1916(?)-1983(?)
Obituary ... 108
White, Alice Violet 1922- ... CANR-13
Earlier sketch in CA 61-64
White, Alicen ... 77-80
White, Amber Blanco
See Blanco White, Amber
White, Andrew 1579-1656 ... DLB-24
White, Andrew Dickson 1832-1918 ... DLB-47
White, Anne Hitchcock 1902-1970
Obituary ... 108
See also SATA 33
White, Anne S(hanklin) ... 93-96
White, Anne Terry 1896- ... 9-10R
See also SATA 2
White, Anthony Gene 1946- ... CANR-12
Earlier sketch in CA 73-76
White, Antonia 1899-1980 ... 104
Obituary ... 97-100
White, Babington
See Braddon, Mary Elizabeth
White, Barbara A(nne) 1942- ... 109
White, Beatrice (Mary Irene) 1902-1986
Obituary ... 119
White, Benjamin V(room) 1908- ... 101
White, Benton R. 1949- ... 124
White, Bessie (Felstiner) 1892(?)-1986
Obituary ... 121
See also SATA 50
White, Betty 1917- ... 7-8R
White, Brian Terence 1927- ... 105
White, Burton L(eonard) 1929- ... CANR-4
Earlier sketch in CA 45-48
White, Carl M(ilton) 1903-1983 ... 13-14R
Obituary ... 111
White, Carol 1946- ... 111
White, Carol Hellings 1939- ... 81-84
White, (Edwin) Chappell 1920- ... 25-28R
White, Claire Nicolas 1925- ... CANR-25
Earlier sketch in CA 108
White, Curtis 1951- ... 110
White, Cynthia L(eslie) 1940- ... 37-40R
White, Dale
See Place, Marian T(empleton)
White, Dan S(eligsberger) 1939- ... 97-100
White, David Manning 1917- ... CANR-4
Earlier sketch in CA 3R
White, David Omar 1927- ... 17-18R
White, Dori 1919- ... 37-40R
See also SATA 10
White, Dorothy Shipley ... CAP-1
Earlier sketch in CA 13-14
White, Douglas M(alcolm) 1909- ... CANR-4
Earlier sketch in CA 2R
White, E(lwyn) B(rooks) 1899-1985 ... CANR-16
Obituary ... 116
Earlier sketch in CA 13-14R
See also SATA 2, 29, 44
See also DLB 11, 22
See also CLC 10, 34, 39
See also CLR 1
See also AITN 2
White, Edgar (B.) 1947- ... 61-64
See also BW
See also DLB 38
White, Edmund (Valentine III) 1940- ... CANR-19
Earlier sketches in CA 45-48, CANR-3
See also CLC 27
White, Edward M. 1933- ... 37-40R
White, Elijah (Brockenborough III) 1938- ... 69-72
White, Eliza Orne 1856-1947 ... YABC-2
White, Elizabeth H(erzog) 1901(?)-1972
Obituary ... 37-40R
White, Elizabeth Wade 1906- ... 97-100
White, Elmer G. 1926- ... 23-24R
White, Emmons E(aton) 1891- ... 73-76

White, Eric Walter 1905-1985 .... CAP-1
Obituary 117
Earlier sketch in CA 11-12
White, Ethel Lina 1887-1944 Brief entry 108
White, Eugene E. 1919- 13-14R
White, F(rederick) Clifton 1918- 113
White, Florence M(eiman) 1910- 41-44R
See also SATA 14
White, Frank 1944- 126
White, G(eorge) Edward 1941- CANR-12
Earlier sketch in CA 69-72
White, Gerald Taylor 1913- CANR-2
Earlier sketch in CA 5-6R
White, Gertrude M(ason) 1915- 81-84
White, Gillian Mary 1936- 19-20R
White, Glenn M. 1918(?)-1978 93-96
Obituary 81-84
White, Gordon Eliot 1933- 101
White, H. T.
See Engh, Rohn
White, Harrison C(olyar) 1930- 45-48
White, Harry
See Whittington, Harry (Benjamin)
White, Helen Constance 1896- 7-8R
White, Hilda Crystal 1917- 5-6R
White, Horace 1834-1916 Brief entry 119
See also DLB 23
White, Howard Ashley 1913- 29-32R
White, Howard B. 1912(?)-1974 Obituary ..53-56
White, Hugh Clayton 1936- 45-48
White, Hugh Vernon 1889- 7-8R
White, Irvin L(inwood) 1932- CANR-8
Earlier sketch in CA 57-60
White, James 1913- 109
White, James 1928- CANR-4
Earlier sketch in CA 53-56
White, James Boyd 1938- 111
White, James Dillon
See White, Stanley
White, James F(loyd) 1932- CANR-24
Earlier sketch in CA 107
White, James L. ?-1981 Obituary 115
White, James P(atrick) 1940- CANR-11
Earlier sketch in CA 69-72
White, Jane
See Brady, Jane
White, Jane Neal 1918- 110
White, John 1924- CANR-20
White, John Albert 1910- CAP-2
Earlier sketch in CA 23-24
White, John Baker
See Baker White, John
White, John H(enry) 1945- 124
Brief entry 117
White, John Hoxland, Jr. 1933- 25-28R
White, John K(enneth) 1952- 116
White, John W. 1939- CANR-13
Earlier sketch in CA 37-40R
White, John Wesley 1928- 29-32R
White, Jon (Ewbank) Manchip 1924- ... CANR-15
Earlier sketch in CA 13-14R
See also CAAS 4
White, Joyce C(arol) 1952- 112
White, Jude Gilliam 1947- CANR-23
Earlier sketch in CA 106
White, K(enneth) D(ouglas) 1908- CANR-12
Earlier sketch in CA 69-72
White, K(enneth) Owen 1902- CAP-2
Earlier sketch in CA 17-18
White, Karol Koenigsberg 1938- 5-6R
White, Katharine Sergeant 1892-1977
Obituary 104
White, Kenneth 1936- 25-28R
White, Kenneth Steele 1922- 93-96
White, Laurence B(arton), Jr. 1935- ... CANR-24
Earlier sketches in CA 65-68, CANR-9
See also SATA 10
White, Lawrence 1942- 115
White, Lawrence H(enry) 1954- 118
White, Lawrence J. 1943- CANR-14
Earlier sketch in CA 37-40R
White, Lee A. 1886-1971 Obituary 115
White, Leslie A(lvin) 1900-1975 .... CANR-3
Obituary 57-60
Earlier sketch in CA 2R
White, Leslie Turner 1903-19(?) CAP-1
Earlier sketch in CA 13-14
White, Lionel 1905- 103
White, Lonnie J(oe) 1931- 15-16R
White, Lucia 123
White, Lynn (Townsend), Jr.
1907-1987 .... CANR-2
Obituary 122
Earlier sketch in CA 5-6R
White, M(ary) E(llen) 1938- 21-22R
White, Margaret B(lackburn) 1936- 115
White, Martin 1943- SATA-51
White, Mary Alice 1920- 11-12R
White, Maurine
See Miller (Riis), Maurine
White, Maury 1919- 77-80
White, Melvin R(obert) 1911- CANR-18
Earlier sketch in CA 23-24R
White, Minor (Martin) 1908-1976 ..... CANR-10
Obituary 65-68
Earlier sketch in CA 19-20R
White, Morton Gabriel 1917- CANR-7
Earlier sketch in CA 5-6R
White, Nancy Bean 1922- 15-16R
White, Nicholas P. 1942- 73-76
White, Norval (Crawford) 1926- 77-80
White, Orion F(orrest) 1938- 53-56
White, Osmar Egmont Dorkin 1909-
Brief entry 105
White, Owen R(oberts) 1945- 41-44R
White, Patricia (Ann) 1937- 117
White, Patrick (Victor Martindale) 1912- ...81-84
See also CLC 3, 4, 5, 7, 9, 18
White, Patrick C. T. 1924- 85-88
White, Paul Dudley 1886-1973 Obituary ...45-48
White, Paul Hamilton Hume 1910- CANR-23
Earlier sketches in CA 5-6R, CANR-7
White, Paulette Childress 1948- 111
White, Percival 1887-1970 .... CANR-2
Earlier sketch in CA 1R
White, Philip L(loyd) 1923- 81-84
White, Phyllis Dorothy James 1920- ... CANR-17
Earlier sketch in CA 21-22R
White, Poppy Cannon 1906(?)-1975 65-68
Obituary 57-60
White, Ramy Allison CANR-26
Earlier sketches in CA 19-20, CAP-2
See also SATA 1
White, Randall 1945- 121
White, Ray Lewis 1941- CANR-9
Earlier sketch in CA 21-22R
White, Reginald E(rnest) O(scar)
1914- CANR-21
Earlier sketches in CA 5-6R, CANR-5
White, Reginald James 1905-1971 108
Obituary 104
White, Rhea A(melia) 1931- 77-80
White, Richard 1931- 110
White, Richard Alan 1944- 97-100
White, Richard C(lark) 1926- 45-48
White, Richard Grant 1821-1885 .... DLB-64
White, Robb 1909- CANR-1
Earlier sketch in CA 2R
See also SATA 1
See also SAAS 1
See also CLR 3
White, Robert B(enjamin), Jr. 1930-
Brief entry 118
White, Robert I. 1908- 3R
White, Robert Lee 1928- 19-20R
White, Robert Mitchell II 1915- 73-76
White, Robert R(ankin) 1942- 123
White, (William) Robin(son) 1928- CANR-20
Earlier sketches in CA 11-12R, CANR-4
White, Ronald C(edric), Jr. 1939- 93-96
White, Ruth C. 1942- 111
See also SATA 39
White, Ruth M(argaret) 1914- 17-18R
White, Ruth Morris 1902(?)-1978
Obituary 81-84
White, Sarah Harriman 1929- 11-12R
White, Sheldon Harold 1928- 105
White, Stanhope 1913- 23-24R
White, Stanley 1913- CANR-6
Earlier sketch in CA 9-10R
White, Stephanie F(rances) T(hirkell)
1942- 19-20R
White, Stephen D(aniel) 1945- 93-96
White, Steve
See McGarvey, Robert
White, Steven F(orsythe) 1955- 112
White, Susan J. 1949- 126
White, Suzanne 1938- 77-80
White, T(erence) H(anbury) 1906-1964 73-76
See also SATA 12
See also CLC 30
White, Ted
See White, Theodore Edwin
White, Terence de Vere 1912- CANR-3
Earlier sketch in CA 49-52
See also CLC 49
White, Theo Ballou 1903-1978 Obituary 111
White, Theodore Edwin 1938- CANR-12
Earlier sketch in CA 21-22R
White, Theodore H(arold) 1915-1986 ... CANR-3
Obituary 118
Earlier sketch in CA 2R
White, Thomas Justin, Jr. 1919-1987
Obituary 122
White, W. D. 1926- 37-40R
White, W(illiam) J(ohn) 1920-1980 ......13-14R
Obituary 97-100
White, Walter
See White, Walter F(rancis)
White, Walter F(rancis) 1893-1955 124
Brief entry 115
See also BW
See also DLB 51
See also TCLC 15
White, William 1910- 23-24R
White, William A(nthony) P(arker)
1911-1968 .... CAP-1
Obituary 25-28R
Earlier sketch in CA 11-12
White, William Allen 1868-1944
Brief entry 108
See also DLB 9, 25
White, William F(rancis) 1928- CANR-1
Earlier sketch in CA 45-48
White, William Hale 1831-1913
Brief entry 121
White, William J(oseph) 1926- 97-100
White, William, Jr. 1934- CANR-14
Earlier sketch in CA 37-40R
See also SATA 16
White, William L(indsay) 1900-1973 101
Obituary 41-44R
White, William L. 1937-1985 Obituary 114
White, William Luther 1931- 29-32R
White, William S(mith) 1907- 5-6R
White, Zita
See Denholm, Theresa Mary Zita White
Whitebird, J(oanie) 1951- CANR-25
Earlier sketch in CA 69-72
White-Bowden, Susan 1939- 120
Whitechurch, Victor L(orenzo) 1868-1933
Brief entry 116
See also DLB 70
White Elk, Michael
See Walker, T. Michael
Whitefield, Ann
See Stone, Susan Berch
Whiteford, Andrew H(unter) 1913- CANR-26
Earlier sketch in CA 45-48
Whitefriar
See Hiscock, Eric
Whitehall, Harold 1905-1986 .... CAP-2
Obituary 118
Earlier sketch in CA 21-22
Whitehead, Alfred North 1861-1947
Brief entry 117
Whitehead, Barbara (Maude) 1930- 97-100
Whitehead, Don(ald) F. 1908-1981 ......11-12R
Obituary 102
See also SATA 4
Whitehead, E(dward) A(nthony) 1933- 65-68
See also CLC 5
Whitehead, (Walter) Edward 1908-1978 ...81-84
Obituary 77-80
Whitehead, Evelyn Annette Eaton 1938- 104
Whitehead, Frank S. 1916- 37-40R
Whitehead, G(eorge) Kenneth 1913- CANR-8
Earlier sketch in CA 61-64
Whitehead, James 1936- 77-80
See also DLBY 81
Whitehead, James D(ouglas) 1939- 105
Whitehead, John (Randolph) 1924- 120
Whitehead, John W. 1946- 117
Whitehead, Raymond Leslie 1933- 77-80
Whitehead, Robert J(ohn) 1928- CANR-13
Earlier sketch in CA 37-40R
Whitehead, William Grant 1943-1987
Obituary 124
Whitehill, Arthur M(urray, Jr.) 1919- ... CANR-13
Earlier sketch in CA 77-80
Whitehill, Walter Muir 1905-1978 ...... CANR-6
Obituary 77-80
Earlier sketch in CA 15-16R
Whitehorn, Katharine
See Lyall, Katharine Elizabeth
Whitehouse, Arch
See Whitehouse, Arthur George Joseph
Whitehouse, Arthur George Joseph
1895-1979 .... CANR-4
Obituary 89-92
Earlier sketch in CA 5-6R
See also SATA 14, 23
Whitehouse, Elizabeth S(cott) 1893-1968 . CAP-1
Earlier sketch in CA 13-14
See also SATA 35
Whitehouse, Franklin S., Jr. 1934-1985
Obituary 117
Whitehouse, Jack E(dward) 1933- 111
Whitehouse, Jeanne 1939- 103
See also SATA 29
Whitehouse, Roger 1939- 57-60
Whitehouse, Ruth D(elamain) 1942- 118
Whitehouse, W(alter) A(lexander)
1915- CANR-3
Earlier sketch in CA 2R
Whitelaw, William Menzies 1890(?)-1974
Obituary 45-48
Whiteley, Denys Edward Hugh 1914-1987
Obituary 123
Whitelock, Dorothy 1901-1982 Obituary 107
Whiteman, Maxwell 1914- CANR-10
Earlier sketch in CA 23-24R
Whiteman, Paul 1890(?)-1967 Obituary 113
Whitemore, Hugh 1936- CLC-37
Whitesell, (James) Edwin 1909- 41-44R
Whitesell, Faris Daniel 1895- 7-8R
Whiteside, Lynn W. 1908- 25-28R
Whiteside, Robert L(eo) 1907- 53-56
Whiteside, Thomas 1918(?)- Brief entry 109
Whiteson, Leon 1930- CANR-16
Earlier sketch in CA 23-24R
Whitfield, George J(oshua) N(ewbold)
1909- CAP-1
Earlier sketch in CA 11-12
Whitfield, James Monroe 1822-1871 .... DLB-50
Whitfield, John Humphreys 1906- 9-10R
Whitfield, Phil(ip John) 1944- 97-100
Whitfield, Raoul 1897(?)-1945 Brief entry .. 109
Whitfield, Shelby 1935- 49-52
Whitfield, Stephen J(ack) 1942- 61-64
Whitford, Bessie 1885(?)-1977 Obituary ...69-72
Whitford, Frank 1941- 97-100
Whitin, Thomson McLintock 1923- CANR-3
Earlier sketch in CA 2R
Whiting, Allen S(uess) 1926- 125
Whiting, Allen S. 1926- Brief entry 105
Whiting, Beatrice Blyth 1914- 7-8R
Whiting, Charles E. 1914(?)-1980
Obituary 97-100
Whiting, Frank M. 1907- 101
Whiting, John (Robert) 1917-1963 102
Obituary 89-92
See also DLB 13
Whiting, Kenneth R. 1913- CANR-5
Earlier sketch in CA 5-6R
Whiting, Nathan 1946- 41-44R
Whiting, Percy H(ollister) 1880- CAP-1
Earlier sketch in CA 15-16
Whiting, Robert 1942- 102
Whiting, Robert L(ouis) 1918- 17-18R
Whiting, Samuel 1597-1679 .... DLB-24
Whiting, Thomas A. 1917- CANR-3
Earlier sketch in CA 2R
Whitinger, R. D.
See Place, Marian T(empleton)
Whitington, R(ichard) S. 1912- 77-80
Whitlam, (Edward) Gough 1916- 109
Whitley, George
See Chandler, A(rthur) Bertram
Whitley, Mary Ann
See Sebrey, Mary Ann
Whitley, Oliver R. 1918- 77-80
Whitlock, Baird W(oodruff) 1924- 112
Whitlock, Brand 1869-1934 Brief entry 110
See also DLB 12
Whitlock, Glenn E(verett) 1917- 23-24R
Whitlock, Pamela 1921(?)-1982 Obituary ... 107
See also SATA 31
Whitlock, Quentin A(rthur) 1937- 109
Whitlock, Ralph 1914- CANR-20
Earlier sketch in CA 101
See also SATA 35
Whitlock, Virginia Bennett ?-1972
Obituary 37-40R
Whitlow, Roger 1940- 41-44R
Whitman, Albery Allson 1851-1901 ..... DLB-50
Whitman, Alden 1913- 17-18R
Whitman, (Evelyn) Ardis 11-12R
Whitman, Bertha Yerex 1892-1984
Obituary 114
Whitman, Cedric H(ubbell) 1916-1979 ....19-20R
Obituary 120
Whitman, David (deFreudiger) 1955- 113
Whitman, Edmund Spurr 1900- 17-18R
Whitman, Howard 1915(?)-1975
Obituary 53-56
Whitman, John 1944- CANR-11
Earlier sketch in CA 61-64
Whitman, Marina von Neumann 1935- ...17-18R
Whitman, Martin J. 1924- 104
Whitman, Robert Freeman 1925- 81-84
Whitman, Ruth (Bashein) 1922- CANR-12
Earlier sketch in CA 23-24R
Whitman, Sarah Helen (Power)
1803-1878 .... DLB-1
Whitman, Virginia Bruner 1901- CANR-4
Earlier sketch in CA 7-8R
Whitman, W(illiam) Tate 1909- CAP-1
Earlier sketch in CA 11-12
Whitman, Walt(er) 1819-1892 .... SATA-20
See also DLB 3, 64
See also CDALB 1640-1865
Whitman, Wanda ?-1976 Obituary 65-68
Whitmarsh, Anne (Mary Gordon) 1933- 106
Whitmont, Edward C. 1912- 115
Whitmore, Charles (Stanleigh) 1949- 117
Whitmore, Cilla
See Gladstone, Arthur M.
Whitmore, Eugene 1895- 7-8R
Whitmore, George 1945- 102
Whitnah, Donald R(obert) 1925- 11-12R
Whitnah, Dorothy L. 1926- CANR-16
Earlier sketch in CA 93-96
Whitnell, Barbara
See Hutton, Ann
Whitney, Alec
See White, Alan
Whitney, Alex(andra) 1922- 53-56
See also SATA 14
Whitney, Byrl A(lbert) 1901- CAP-1
Earlier sketch in CA 13-14
Whitney, Charles Allen 1929- 81-84
Whitney, Cornelius Vanderbilt 1899- 85-88
Whitney, Dallas (Cole) 1952- 117
Whitney, David
See Malick, Terrence
Whitney, David C(harles) 1921- CANR-5
Earlier sketch in CA 11-12R
See also SATA 29, 48
Whitney, Eleanor Noss 1938- CANR-6
Earlier sketch in CA 15-16R
Whitney, Elizabeth Dalton 1906- 21-22R
Whitney, George D(ana) 1918- 93-96
Whitney, Hallam
See Whittington, Harry (Benjamin)
Whitney, J(ohn) D(enison) 1940- CANR-3
Earlier sketch in CA 49-52
Whitney, J. L. H.
See Trimble, Jacquelyn W(hitney)
Whitney, John Hay 1904-1982 Obituary 106
Whitney, John Raymond 1920- 105
Whitney, Leon F(radley) 1894-1973 ..... CANR-5
Earlier sketch in CA 7-8R
Whitney, Marie Louise (Schroeder) Hosford
1925(?)- Brief entry 113
Whitney, Marylou
See Whitney, Marie Louise (Schroeder)
Hosford
Whitney, Peter Dwight 1915- 11-12R
Whitney, Phyllis A(yame) 1903- CANR-25
Earlier sketches in CA 4R, CANR-3
See also SATA 1, 30
See also CLC 42
See also AITN 2
Whitney, Robert Frost 1906(?)-1986
Obituary 119
Whitney, Steve(n) 1946- 81-84
Whitney, Thomas P(orter) 1917- 104
See also SATA 25
Whiton, James Nelson 1932- 13-14R
Whitridge, Arnold 1891- 11-12R
Whitrow, Gerald James 1912- CANR-3
Earlier sketch in CA 5-6R
Whitson
See Warren, Peter Whitson
Whitson, Skip 1944- 118
Whitt, Anne Hall
See Thompson, Anne Hall Whitt
Whitt, Richard 1944- 81-84
Whittaker, Kathryn Putnam 1931- 13-14R
Whittaker, Otto (Jr.) 1916- 25-28R
Whittaker, Robert Harding 1920- 105
Whittemore, Charles P(ark) 1921- 11-12R
Whittemore, Don 69-72
Whittemore, L(ouis) H(enry) 1941- 45-48
Whittemore, Mildred 1946- 11-12R

Whittemore, (Edward) Reed (Jr.) 1919- . CANR-4
Earlier sketch in CA 9-10R
See also DLB 5
See also CLC 4
Whittemore, Robert Clifton 1921- ... 11-12R
Whitten, Jamie L(loyd) 1910- ... CAP-2
Earlier sketch in CA 23-24
Whitten, Leslie H(unter) 1928- ... 17-18R
Whitten, Mary Evelyn 1922- ... 17-18R
Whitten, Norman E(arl), Jr. 1937- ... 17-18R
Whittet, G(eorge) S(orley) 1918- ... 23-24R
Whittet, T. D.
See Whittet, Thomas Douglas
Whittet, Thomas Douglas 1915-1987
Obituary ... 122
Whittick, Arnold 1898- ... CAP-1
Earlier sketch in CA 11-12
Whittier, John Greenleaf 1807-1892 ... DLB-1
See also CDALB 1640-1865
Whitting, Philip (David) 1903- ... 97-100
Whittingham, Harry E(dward), Jr. 1918- ... 7-8R
Whittingham, Jack 1910-1972 Obituary .. 37-40R
Whittingham, Richard 1939- ... 37-40R
Whittington, Geoffrey 1938- ... CANR-20
Earlier sketch in CA 104
Whittington, H(orace) G(reeley) 1929- ... 21-22R
Whittington, Harry (Benjamin) 1915- ... CANR-5
Earlier sketch in CA 23-24R
Whittington, Peter
See Mackay, James (Alexander)
Whittington-Egan, Richard 1924- ... CANR-20
Earlier sketches in CA 11-12R, CANR-5
Whittle, Amberys R(ayvon) 1935- ... 45-48
Whittle, Tyler
See Tyler-Whittle, Michael Sidney
Whittlebot, Hernia
See Coward, Noel (Pierce)
Whittlesey, E(unice) S. 1907- ... 93-96
Whittlesey, Susan 1938- ... 29-32R
Whitton, Charlotte (Elizabeth) 1896-1975
Obituary ... 89-92
Whitton, John Boardman 1892- ... CAP-2
Earlier sketch in CA 23-24
Whittow, J. B.
See Whittow, John B(yron)
Whittow, John B(yron) 1929- ... 120
Whitworth, John McKelvie 1942- ... 77-80
Whitworth, Reginald Henry 1910- ... 109
Whitworth, William 1937- ... 37-40R
Whiz, Walter
See Johnson, Curt(is Lee)
Whone, Herbert 1925- ... CANR-24
Earlier sketch in CA 108
Whorton, James C(lifton) 1942- ... 77-80
Whorton, M. Donald 1946- ... 117
Whritner, John Alden 1935- ... 45-48
Whyatt, Frances
See Boyd, Shylah
Whybray, Roger Norman 1923- ... 89-92
Whyte, Fredrica (Harriman) 1905- ... CAP-1
Earlier sketch in CA 11-12
Whyte, Henry Malcolm 1920- ... CANR-3
Earlier sketch in CA 7-8R
Whyte, James Huntington 1909- ... 7-8R
Whyte, Lancelot Law 1896-1972 ... CAP-1
Earlier sketch in CA 15-16
Whyte, Lewis (Gilmour) 1906-1986
Obituary ... 121
Whyte, Mal(colm Kenneth, Jr.) 1933- ... 106
Whyte, Martin King 1942- ... 81-84
Whyte, (Harry Archibald) Maxwell 1908- ... 105
Whyte, Robert Orr 1903- Brief entry ... 106
Whyte, William Foote 1914- ... CANR-18
Earlier sketches in CA 4R, CANR-3
Whyte, William H(ollingsworth) 1917- ... 9-10R
Wiarda, Howard J(ohn) 1939- ... CANR-21
Earlier sketches in CA 53-56, CANR-4
Wiat, Philippa
See Ferridge, Philippa
Wibberley, Leonard (Patrick O'Connor)
1915-1983 ... CANR-3
Obituary ... 111
Earlier sketch in CA 7-8R
See also SATA 2, 36, 45
See also CLR 3
Wiberg, Harald (Albin) 1908- ... SATA-40
Wice, Aubrey (Agnew) 1913(?)-1985
Obituary ... 119
Wice, Paul B(ernard) 1942- ... 57-60
Wick, Carter
See Wilcox, Collin
Wick, John W(illiam) 1935- ... CANR-15
Earlier sketch in CA 41-44R
Wick, Stuart Mary
See Freeman, Kathleen
Wick, Wendy
See Reaves, Wendy Wick
Wicke, Charles R(obinson) 1928- ... 37-40R
Wicke, Edith Schreiber
See Schreiber-Wicke, Edith
Wickenden, Elizabeth 1909- ... 2R
Wickens, Delos D(onald) 1909- ... CAP-1
Earlier sketch in CA 15-16
Wickens, James F. 1933- ... 57-60
Wicker, Brian 1929- ... 17-18R
Wicker, Ireene 1905(?)-1987 ... 69-72
Obituary ... 124
Wicker, Randolfe Hayden 1938- ... 45-48
Wicker, Thomas Grey 1926- ... CANR-21
Earlier sketch in CA 65-68
Wicker, Tom
See Wicker, Thomas Grey
See also CLC 7
Wickers, David 1944- ... 77-80
Wickersham, Edward Dean 1927-1966 ... 5-6R
Wickersham, Joan Barrett 1957- ... 105
Wickert, Frederic R(obinson) 1912- ... 23-24R
Wickes, George 1923- ... 9-10R
Wickes, Kim 1947- ... 109
Wickett, Ann 1942- ... 122
Wickett, William Harold, Jr. 1919- ... 108
Wickey, Gould 1891- ... 25-28R
Wickham, Edward Ralph 1911- ... 7-8R
Wickham, Glynne (William Gladstone)
1922- ... CANR-7
Earlier sketch in CA 7-8R
Wickham, Jean 1903- ... 69-72
Wickham, Mary Fanning
See Bond, Mary Fanning Wickham
Wickham, Thomas Frederick 1926- ... 13-14R
Wicklein, John (Frederick) 1924- ... 106
Wickremasinghe, Esmond 1920(?)-1985
Obituary ... 117
Wickremasinghe, S(ugiswara)
A(beywardena) 1901-1981 Obituary ... 108
Wicks, Ben 1926- ... 73-76
Wicks, Harold Vernon, Jr. 1931- ... 102
Wicks, Harry
See Wicks, Harold Vernon, Jr.
Wicks, Jared 1929- ... CANR-21
Earlier sketch in CA 25-28R
Wicks, John H. 1936- ... 17-18R
Wicks, Robert J(ohn) 1946- ... 113
Wicks, Robert Stewart 1923- ... 17-18R
Wickstrom, Lois 1948- ... 106
Wickwar, (William) Hardy 1903- ... 57-60
Wickwire, Franklin B(acon) 1931- ... 23-24R
Wickwire, Mary Botts 1935- ... 104
Widdemer, Mabel Cleland 1902-1964 ... 5-6R
See also SATA 5
Widdemer, Margaret 18(?)-1978 ... CANR-4
Obituary ... 77-80
Earlier sketch in CA 5-6R
Widder, (John) Arthur, (Jr.) 1928- ... 5-6R
Widder, Milton 1907(?)-1985 Obituary ... 118
Widell, Helene 1912- ... 37-40R
Wideman, John Edgar 1941- ... CANR-14
Earlier sketch in CA 85-88
See also BW
See also DLB 33
See also CLC 5, 34, 36
Widener, Alice 1905(?)-1985 Obituary ... 114
Widener, Don(ald) 1930- ... 37-40R
Widenor, William C(ramer) 1937- ... 102
Widerberg, Siv 1931- ... 53-56
See also SATA 10
Widgery, Alban G(regory) 1887- ... 5-6R
Widgery, David 1947- ... 69-72
Widgery, Jan 1920- ... 19-20R
Widick, B. J. 1910- ... 9-10R
Widicus, Wilbur W(ilson), Jr. 1932- ... 53-56
Widman, F. Lisle 1919(?)-1983 Obituary ... 111
Widmer, Eleanor (Rackow) 1925- ... 17-18R
Widmer, Emmy Louise 1925- ... 29-32R
Widmer, Kingsley 1925- ... CANR-3
Earlier sketch in CA 2R
Wiebe, M(elvin) G(eorge) 1939- ... 114
Wiebe, Robert H(uddleston) 1930- ... 5-6R
Wiebe, Rudy (H.) 1934- ... 37-40R
See also DLB 60
See also CLC 6, 11, 14
Wiebenson, Dora (Louise) 1926- ... 37-40R
Wiecek, William Michael 1938- ... 37-40R
Wiechert, Ernst 1887-1950 ... DLB-56
Wieck, Fred D(ernburg) 1910-1973
Obituary ... 104
Wieckert, Jeanne E. (Lentz) 1939- ... 89-92
Wiecking, Anna M. 1887-1973 ... CAP-1
Earlier sketch in CA 13-14
Wieczynski, Joseph L. 1934- ... 37-40R
Wieder, Laurance 1946- ... CANR-8
Earlier sketch in CA 57-60
Wieder, Robert S(hannon) 1944- ... 85-88
Wiederumb, Trotzhard
See Steiner, Gerolf
Wiedner, Donald L(awrence) 1930- ... 15-16R
Wiegand, Charmion von
See von Wiegand, Charmion
Wiegand, G(uenther) Carl 1906- ... 23-24R
Wiegand, William G(eorge) 1928- ... 11-12R
Wieghart, James G. 1933- ... 77-80
Wiegner, Kathleen K(napp) 1938- ... 93-96
Wiehl, Andrew (M.) 1904- ... 89-92
Wieland, George F(red) 1936- ... 89-92
Wieman, Harold F(rancis) 1917- ... 61-64
Wieman, Henry N(elson) 1884-1975 ... 61-64
Obituary ... 57-60
Wiemer, Rudolf Otto 1905- ... CANR-25
Earlier sketches in CA 23-24R, CANR-9
Wienandt, Elwyn A(rthur) 1917- ... 41-44R
Wiener, Allen J. 1943- ... 125
Wiener, Daniel N(orman) 1921- ... 37-40R
Wiener, Harvey Shelby 1940- ... 102
Wiener, Joan
See Bordow, Joan (Wiener)
Wiener, Joel H. 1937- ... CANR-14
Earlier sketch in CA 37-40R
Wiener, Jon
See Wiener, Jonathan M.
Wiener, Jonathan M. 1944- ... 115
Wiener, Leigh Auston 1929- ... 108
Wiener, M. Jean 1896-1982 Obituary ... 107
Wiener, Martin J. 1941- ... 85-88
Wiener, Norbert 1894-1964 Obituary ... 107
Wiener, Philip P(aul) 1905- ... CAP-1
Earlier sketch in CA 9-10
Wiener, Sally Dixon 1926- ... 101
Wiener, Sam
See Dolgoff, Sam
Wiener, Solomon 1915- ... CANR-7
Earlier sketch in CA 19-20R
Wieners, John 1934- ... 15-16R
See also DLB 16
See also CLC 7
Wieniewska, Celina
See Janson-Smith, Celina
Wienpahl, Paul D(e Velin) 1916- ... 11-12R
Wier, Allen 1946- ... 77-80
Wier, Dara 1949- ... 77-80
Wier, Ester (Alberti) 1910- ... 11-12R
See also SATA 3
See also DLB 52
Wiersbe, Warren W(endell) 1929- ... CANR-23
Earlier sketches in CA 5-6R, CANR-7
Wiersma, Stanley M(arvin) 1930- ... CANR-11
Earlier sketch in CA 29-32R
Wiersma, William, Jr. 1931- ... CANR-1
Earlier sketch in CA 45-48
Wierwille, Victor Paul 1916-1985 ... CANR-2
Obituary ... 116
Earlier sketch in CA 7-8R
Wierzynski, Gregory H(ieronim) 1939- ... 73-76
Wierzynski, Kazimierz 1894-1969 Obituary .. 115
Wiese, Arthur E(dward) 1946- ... 73-76
Wiese, Kurt 1887-1974 ... 11-12R
Obituary ... 49-52
See also SATA 3, 24, 36
Wiesel, Elie(zer) 1928- ... CANR-8
Earlier sketch in CA 7-8R
See also CAAS 4
See also DLBY 87
See also CLC 3, 5, 11, 37
See also AITN 1
Wiesen, Allen E. 1939- ... 29-32R
Wiesenfarth, Joseph (John) 1933- ... CANR-8
Earlier sketch in CA 5-6R
Wiesenthal, Simon 1908- ... CANR-13
Earlier sketch in CA 23-24R
Wiesner, Jerome B(ert) 1915- ... 15-16R
Wiesner, Portia
See Takakjian, Portia
Wiesner, William 1899- ... 41-44R
See also SATA 5
Wiest, Claire (Johnson) 1930- ... 113
Wigal, Donald 1933- ... CANR-14
Earlier sketch in CA 81-84
Wigan, Anthony ?-1983 Obituary ... 110
Wigan, Bernard (John) 1918- ... 15-16R
Wigan, Christopher
See Bingley, David Ernest
Wigan, Tony
See Wigan, Anthony
Wigforss, Ernst 1882(?)-1977 Obituary ... 69-72
Wigg, George (Edward Cecil) 1900-1983
Obituary ... 115
Wiggin, Kate Douglas 1856-1923
Brief entry ... 111
See also YABC 1
See also DLB 42
Wiggin, Maurice (Samuel) 1912- ... CANR-5
Earlier sketch in CA 11-12R
Wiggin, Paul 1934- ... 25-28R
Wiggins, Arthur W. 1938- ... 53-56
Wiggins, Charles W(illiam) 1937- ... 41-44R
Wiggins, David 1933- ... 118
Wiggins, Jack G(illmore) 1926- ... 41-44R
Wiggins, James B(ryan) 1935- ... 37-40R
Wiggins, James Russell ... AITN-2
Wiggins, James Wilhelm 1914- ... 17-18R
Wiggins, Robert A. 1921- ... 15-16R
Wiggins, Sam P. 1919- ... 21-22R
Wigginton, Eliot 1942- ... 101
See also AITN 1
Wigglesworth, Michael 1631-1705 ... DLB-24
Wigham, Eric Leonard 1904- ... 109
Wight, Frederick S.
See Wight, Frederick Stallknecht
Wight, Frederick Stallknecht (Van Buren)
1902-1986 Obituary ... 120
Wight, James Alfred 1916- ... 77-80
See also SATA 44
Wight, (Robert James) Martin
1913-1972 ... CAP-2
Earlier sketch in CA 21-22
Wightman, Edith Mary 1939(?)-1983(?)
Obituary ... 111
Wightman, George Brian Hamilton 1933- ... 107
Wighton, Charles Ernest 1913- ... 7-8R
Wighton, Rosemary Neville 1925- ... 11-12R
Wigmore
See Fabricius, Johan (Johannes)
Wignall, Anne 1912- ... 97-100
Wigner, Eugene Paul 1902- ... CAP-2
Earlier sketch in CA 25-28
Wigoder, Geoffrey Bernard 1922- ... 105
Wihl, Gary ... 120
Wiig, Howard (Calvert) 1940- ... 61-64
Wijasuriya, D(onald) E(arlian) K(ingsley)
1934- ... 81-84
Wik, Reynold M. 1910- ... CANR-14
Earlier sketch in CA 81-84
Wikander, Matthew H. 1950- ... 125
Wike, Edward L. 1922- ... 37-40R
Wikland, Ilon 1930- Brief entry ... 111
See also SATA 32
Wikler, Madeline 1943- ... 117
Wikramanayake, Marina 1938- ... 45-48
Wiksell, Milton J. 1910- ... 7-8R
Wiksell, Wesley 1906- ... CAP-1
Earlier sketch in CA 17-18
Wilber, Charles G(rady) 1916- ... CANR-21
Earlier sketch in CA 41-44R
Wilber, Charles K. 1935- Brief entry ... 113
Wilber, Donald N(ewton) 1907- ... CANR-2
Earlier sketch in CA 5-6R
See also SATA 35
Wilbers, Stephen 1949- ... 106
Wilbert, Johannes 1927- ... 124
Brief entry ... 118
Wilbourn, Carole C(ecile) 1940- ... CANR-14
Earlier sketch in CA 81-84
Wilbur, C. Keith 1923- ... CANR-11
Earlier sketch in CA 25-28R
See also SATA 27
Wilbur, C(larence) Martin 1908- ... 85-88
Wilbur, Crane 1887(?)-1973 Obituary ... 45-48
Wilbur, James B(enjamin) III 1924- ... CANR-14
Earlier sketch in CA 37-40R
Wilbur, Marguerite Eyer 1889- ... CAP-1
Earlier sketch in CA 11-12
Wilbur, Richard (Purdy) 1921- ... CANR-2
Earlier sketch in CA 2R
See also CABS 2
See also SATA 9
See also DLB 5
See also CLC 3, 6, 9, 14
Wilbur, William H(ale) 1888- ... CAP-1
Earlier sketch in CA 13-14
Wilburn, Jean Alexander 1915- ... 21-22R
Wilburn, Ralph G(lenn) 1909- ... CAP-1
Earlier sketch in CA 17-18
Wilby, Basil Leslie 1930- ... CANR-19
Earlier sketch in CA 103
Wilcher, Robert 1942- ... 121
Wilckens, Ulrich 1928- Brief entry ... 114
Wilcock, John 1927- ... CANR-2
Earlier sketch in CA 2R
Wilcocks, Julie 1943- ... 110
Wilcox, Clair 1898-1970 ... CANR-4
Earlier sketch in CA 5-6R
Wilcox, Collin 1924- ... CANR-14
Earlier sketch in CA 21-22R
Wilcox, Daniel 1941- ... 53-56
Wilcox, Dennis L. 1941- ... CANR-14
Earlier sketch in CA 37-40R
Wilcox, Desmond (John) 1931- ... CANR-21
Earlier sketch in CA 69-72
Wilcox, Donald J(ames) 1938- ... 109
Wilcox, Earl J(unior) 1933- ... 111
Wilcox, Francis (Orlando) 1908-1985 ... 37-40R
Obituary ... 115
Wilcox, Herbert 1891-1977 ... 57-60
Obituary ... 118
Wilcox, Howard 1913(?)-1987 Obituary ... 122
Wilcox, James 1949- Brief entry ... 125
Wilcox, Jess
See Hershman, Morris
Wilcox, John T(homas) 1933- ... 45-48
Wilcox, Michael (Denys) 1943- ... 77-80
Wilcox, Paul L(orentus) 1899- ... 69-72
Wilcox, R(uth) Turner 1888-1970 ... 7-8R
Obituary ... 29-32R
See also SATA 36
Wilcox, Richard L. 1918-1978 Obituary ... 77-80
Wilcox, Robert K(alleen) 1943- ... CANR-24
Earlier sketch in CA 77-80
Wilcox, Roger P. 1916- ... 21-22R
Wilcox, Tamara 1940- ... CANR-19
Earlier sketch in CA 97-100
Wilcox, Virginia Lee 1911- ... 37-40R
Wilcox, Walter 1920-1983 Obituary ... 110
Wilcox, Wayne Ayres 1932-1974 ... CANR-4
Obituary ... 49-52
Earlier sketch in CA 7-8R
Wilcoxon, George Dent, Jr. 1913- ... 93-96
Wild, Jocelyn 1941- ... 116
See also SATA 46
Wild, John D(aniel) 1902-1972
Obituary ... 37-40R
Wild, Peter 1940- ... 37-40R
See also DLB 5
See also CLC 14
Wild, Robert A(nthony) 1940- ... 111
Wild, Robin (Evans) 1936- ... 116
See also SATA 46
Wild, Rolf H(einrich) 1927- ... 81-84
Wildavsky, Aaron 1930- ... CANR-2
Earlier sketch in CA 2R
Wilde, Alan 1929- ... 110
Wilde, D. Gunther
See Hurwood, Bernhardt J.
Wilde, Daniel U(nderwood) 1937- ... 57-60
Wilde, Jean T(oeplitz) 1898-1973
Obituary ... 45-48
Wilde, Jennifer
See Huff, T(om) E.
Wilde, Jocelyn
See Toombs, John
Wilde, Kathey
See King, Patricia
Wilde, Larry 1928- ... CANR-26
Earlier sketches in CA 25-28R, CANR-10
Wilde, Meta Carpenter (Doherty) 1907- ... 81-84
Wilde, Oscar (Fingal O'Flahertie Wills)
1854(?)-1900 ... 119
Brief entry ... 104
See also SATA 24
See also DLB 10, 19, 34, 57
See also TCLC 1, 8, 23
Wilde, Richard Henry 1789-1847 ... DLB-3, 59
Wilde, W(illiam) H(enry) 1923- ... CANR-11
Earlier sketch in CA 69-72
Wildeblood, Peter 1923- ... 65-68
Wilden, Anthony 1935- ... 37-40R
Wildenhain, Marguerite 1896- ... 77-80
Wilder, Alec
See Wilder, Alexander Lafayette Chew
Wilder, Alexander Lafayette Chew
1907-1980 ... 104
Obituary ... 102
Wilder, Amos Niven 1895- ... 81-84
Wilder, Billy
See Wilder, Samuel
See also DLB 26
See also CLC 20
Wilder, Charlotte Elizabeth 1898(?)-1980
Obituary ... 97-100

Wilder, Cherry
See Grimm, Cherry Barbara
Wilder, Gene
See Silberman, Jerome
Wilder, John Bunyan 1914- ... 5-6R
Wilder, Joseph 1895-1976 Obituary ... 116
Wilder, Laura Ingalls 1867-1957
Brief entry ... 111
See also SATA 15, 29
See also DLB 22
See also CLR 2
Wilder, Robert (Ingersoll) 1901-1974 ... CAP-2
Obituary ... 53-56
Earlier sketch in CA 13-14
Wilder, Robert D. 1916- ... 41-44R
Wilder, Roy (E.), Jr. 1914- ... 121
Wilder, Samuel 1906- ... 89-92
Wilder, Stephen
See Marlowe, Stephen
Wilder, Thornton (Niven) 1897-1975 ... 15-16R
Obituary ... 61-64
See also DLB 4, 7, 9
See also CLC 1, 5, 6, 10, 15, 35
See also AITN 2
Wilders, John (Simpson) 1927- ... 23-24R
Wilder-Smith, A(rthur) E(rnest) 1915- ... CANR-11
Earlier sketch in CA 57-60
Wildes, Harry Emerson 1890- ... 57-60
Wild Horse Annie
See Johnston, Velma B.
Wilding, Ann
See Budd, Mavis
Wilding, Michael 1942- ... CANR-24
Earlier sketch in CA 104
Wildman, Allan K. 1927- ... 105
Wildman, Eugene 1938- ... 25-28R
Wildman, John Hazard 1911- ... 37-40R
Wildman, Louis Robert 1941- ... CANR-5
Earlier sketch in CA 15-16R
Wildmon, Donald E(llis) 1938- ... CANR-13
Earlier sketch in CA 61-64
Wildrick, Stanley B. 1894-1984 Obituary ... 112
Wilds, Nancy Alexander 1926- ... 15-16R
Wildsmith, Alan 1937- ... 97-100
Wildsmith, Brian 1930- ... 85-88
See also SATA 16
See also SAAS 5
See also CLR 2
Wilenski, Peter Stephen 1939- ... 109
Wilenski, R(eginald) H(oward) 1887-1975 ... 61-64
Obituary ... 57-60
Wilensky, Harold L. 1923- ... CANR-15
Earlier sketch in CA 41-44R
Wilentz, Joan Steen 1930- ... 25-28R
Wilentz, Ted
See Wilentz, Theodore
Wilentz, Theodore 1915- ... 29-32R
Wiles, David K(imball) 1942- ... CANR-7
Earlier sketch in CA 53-56
Wiles, Domini 1942- ... 102
Wiles, Gordon Pitts 1909- ... 108
Wiles, John 1924- ... 11-12R
Wiles, Kimball 1913-1969 ... CANR-4
Earlier sketch in CA 5-6R
Wiles, Maurice Frank 1923- ... 108
Wiles, Peter John de la Fosse 1919- ... 5-6R
Wiles, Roy McKeen 1903-19(?) ... CAP-1
Earlier sketch in CA 19-20
Wiley, Bell
See Strauss, Frances
Wiley, Bell I(rvin) 1906-1980 ... CANR-4
Obituary ... 97-100
Earlier sketch in CA 7-8R
See also DLB 17
Wiley, David Sherman 1935- ... CANR-12
Earlier sketch in CA 61-64
Wiley, Farida A(nna) 1887(?)-1986
Obituary ... 121
Wiley, Jack 1936- ... CANR-8
Earlier sketch in CA 61-64
Wiley, Jay Wilson 1913- ... 5-6R
Wiley, John P., Jr. 1936- ... 89-92
Wiley, Karla H(ummel) 1918- ... 61-64
Wiley, Margaret L.
See Marshall, Margaret Wiley
Wiley, Paul L(uzon) 1914-1979 ... CANR-10
Earlier sketch in CA 5-6R
Wiley, Raymond A(loysius) 1923- ... 37-40R
Wiley, Richard 1944- Brief entry ... 121
See also CLC 44
Wiley, Stan
See Hill, John S(tanley)
Wiley, Tom 1906- ... 25-28R
Wiley, William Leon 1903- ... 111
Wilf, Alexander 1905(?)-1981 Obituary ... 103
Wilford, John Noble 1933- ... CANR-15
Earlier sketch in CA 29-32R
Wilford, Walton T. 1937- ... 49-52
Wilgus, A(lva) Curtis 1897- ... CANR-3
Earlier sketch in CA 7-8R
Wilgus, D. K. 1918- ... 37-40R
Wilhelm, Hans 1945- ... 119
Wilhelm, Hellmut 1905- ... 7-8R
Wilhelm, James Jerome 1932- ... 19-20R
Wilhelm, John R(emsen) 1916- ... 7-8R
Wilhelm, Kate
See Wilhelm, Katie Gertrude
See also CAAS 5
See also DLB 8
See also CLC 7
Wilhelm, Kathryn Stephenson 1915- ... 13-14R
Wilhelm, Katie Gertrude 1928- ... CANR-17
Earlier sketch in CA 37-40R
Wilhelm, Paul A. 1916- ... 61-64
Wilhelm, Walt 1893- ... 29-32R
Wilhelm II
See Hohenzollern, Friedrich Wilhelm (Victor Albert)
Wilhelmina
See Cooper, Wilhelmina (Behmenburg)
Wilhelmsen, Frederick D(aniel) 1923- ... CANR-3
Earlier sketch in CA 2R
Wilhoit, Francis M(arion) 1920- ... 126
Brief entry ... 109
Wilk, David 1951- ... CANR-4
Earlier sketch in CA 53-56
Wilk, Gerard H(ermann) 1902- ... 69-72
Wilk, Max 1920- ... CANR-16
Earlier sketches in CA 3R, CANR-1
Wilk, Richard R(alph) 1953- ... 120
Wilke, Ekkehard-Teja 1941- ... 65-68
Wilke, Ulfert (Stephan) 1907- ... CAP-1
Earlier sketch in CA 15-16
Wilken, Robert L(ouis) 1936- ... CANR-16
Earlier sketch in CA 29-32R
Wilkening, Howard (Everett) 1909- ... 89-92
Wilkens, Emily 1917- ... 103
Wilkerson, Cynthia
See Levinson, Leonard
Wilkerson, David R(ay) 1931- ... 41-44R
Wilkerson, Hugh 1939- ... 104
Wilkerson, Loree A. R(andleman) 1923- ... 17-18R
Wilkerson, Rich(ard Preston) 1952- ... 123
Wilkes, Edward T. 1889-1983 Obituary ... 111
Wilkes, Glenn Newton 1928- ... CANR-17
Earlier sketch in CA 2R
Wilkes, Ian (Henry) 1932- ... 41-44R
Wilkes, John W(illiam) 1924- ... 25-28R
Wilkes, Paul 1938- ... CANR-15
Earlier sketch in CA 81-84
Wilkes, Peter 1937- ... 125
Wilkes, William Alfred 1910- ... 45-48
Wilkes-Hunter, R(ichard) ... 15-16R
Wilkie, Brian 1929- ... 15-16R
Wilkie, James W. 1936- ... 21-22R
Wilkie, Jane 1917- ... 102
Wilkie, Katharine E(lliott) 1904-1980 ... 21-22R
Obituary ... 125
See also SATA 31
Wilkie, Kenneth 1942- ... 85-88
Wilkin, Eloise (Burns) 1904-1987 ... 124
See also SATA 49
Wilkins, Beatrice (Brunson) 1928- ... 61-64
Wilkins, Burleigh Taylor 1932- ... 105
Wilkins, Ernest J. 1918- ... 53-56
Wilkins, Frances 1923- ... 73-76
See also SATA 14
Wilkins, H. Ford 1901(?)-1983 Obituary ... 111
Wilkins, Kathleen Sonia 1941- ... 104
Wilkins, Kay S.
See Wilkins, Kathleen Sonia
Wilkins, Leslie T. 1915- ... CANR-22
Earlier sketches in CA 19-20R, CANR-7
Wilkins, Marilyn (Ruth) 1926- ... 105
See also SATA 30
Wilkins, Marne
See Wilkins, Marilyn (Ruth)
Wilkins, Mary
See Freeman, Mary Eleanor Wilkins
Wilkins, Mary Huiskamp 1926- ... CANR-18
Earlier sketches in CA 5-6R, CANR-2
Wilkins, Mesannie 1891- ... CAP-2
Earlier sketch in CA 25-28
Wilkins, Mira 1931- Brief entry ... 112
Wilkins, Roger (Wood) 1932- ... 117
Brief entry ... 109
See also BW
Wilkins, Ronald J(ohn) 1916- ... CANR-16
Earlier sketch in CA 93-96
Wilkins, Roy 1901-1981 ... 104
See also BW
Wilkins, Thurman 1915- ... 7-8R
Wilkins, William R(ichard) 1933- ... 61-64
Wilkinson, Alec 1952- ... 109
Wilkinson, (Thomas) Barry 1923- ... SATA-32, 50
Wilkinson, Bertie 1898- ... 11-12R
Wilkinson, Bonaro
See Overstreet, Bonaro (Wilkinson)
Wilkinson, Brenda 1946- ... CANR-26
Earlier sketch in CA 69-72
See also BW
See also SATA 14
Wilkinson, Bud
See Wilkinson, Charles B(urnham)
Wilkinson, (John) Burke 1913- ... 11-12R
See also SATA 4
Wilkinson, C. E. 1948- ... 109
Wilkinson, Charles B(urnham) 1916- ... 105
Wilkinson, Charlotte Jefferson ... 69-72
Wilkinson, Clyde Winfield 1910- ... 2R
Wilkinson, David ... 93-96
Wilkinson, Doris Yvonne 1936- ... 29-32R
Wilkinson, Elizabeth C. 1926- ... 123
Wilkinson, Ernest Leroy 1899-1978 ... CANR-3
Earlier sketch in CA 49-52
Wilkinson, G(eoffrey) K(edington) 1907- ... 3R
Wilkinson, J(oseph) F. 1925- ... 105
Wilkinson, James Hardy 1919-1986
Obituary ... 120
Wilkinson, James Harvie III 1944- ... 101
Wilkinson, John (Donald) 1929- ... 9-10R
Wilkinson, John Thomas 1893-1980 ... 107
Obituary ... 104
Wilkinson, L(ancelot) P(atrick)
1907-1985 ... CANR-20
Obituary ... 116
Earlier sketches in CA 5-6R, CANR-3
Wilkinson, Lorna Hilda Kathleen 1909- ... CAP-1
Earlier sketch in CA 13-14
Wilkinson, Louis (Umfreville) 1881-1966
Obituary ... 116
Wilkinson, Maxwell Penrose 1905(?)-1985
Obituary ... 116
Wilkinson, Norman Beaumont
1910-1983 ... 37-40R
Obituary ... 126
Wilkinson, Patrick
See Wilkinson, L(ancelot) P(atrick)
Wilkinson, Paul 1937- ... CANR-14
Earlier sketch in CA 77-80
Wilkinson, Richard Gerald 1943- ... 45-48
Wilkinson, (William) Roderick 1917- ... 13-14R
Wilkinson, Ronald 1920- ... 7-8R
Wilkinson, Rosemary C(halloner)
1924- ... CANR-17
Earlier sketches in CA 49-52, CANR-1
Wilkinson, Rupert Hugh 1936- ... 11-12R
Wilkinson, Sylvia 1940- ... 17-18R
See also SATA 39
See also DLBY 86
See also AITN 1
Wilkinson, Walter 1888-1970 Obituary ... 104
Wilkinson, William Cleaver 1833-1920 ... DLB-71
Wilkinson, Winifred
See Hausmann, Winifred
Wilkon, Jozef 1930- ... 107
See also SATA 31
Wilks, Brian 1933- ... 69-72
Wilks, Ed 1928(?)-1984 Obituary ... 114
Wilks, John 1922- ... 73-76
Wilks, Michael Thomas 1947- ... 110
See also SATA 44
Wilks, Mike
See Wilks, Michael Thomas
Wilks, Yorick 1939- ... 73-76
Will
See Lipkind, William
Will, Frederic 1928- ... CANR-16
Earlier sketches in CA 49-52, CANR-1
Will, Frederick L(udwig) 1909- ... 13-14R
Will, George F. 1941- ... 77-80
Will, Lawrence Elmer 1893- ... CAP-2
Earlier sketch in CA 17-18
Will, Lester J. 1908(?)-1984 Obituary ... 111
Will, Robert E(rwin) 1928- ... 17-18R
Will, W(ilbur) Marvin 1937- ... 118
Willan, Anne 1938- ... CANR-6
Earlier sketch in CA 57-60
Willan, Thomas Stuart 1910- ... 11-12R
Willans, Jean Stone 1924- ... 65-68
Willard, Barbara (Mary) 1909- ... CANR-15
Earlier sketch in CA 81-84
See also SATA 17
See also SAAS 5
See also CLR 2
Willard, Beatrice E(lizabeth) 1925- ... 41-44R
Willard, Charles
See Armstrong, John Byron
Willard, Charlotte 1914-1977 ... 81-84
Obituary ... 73-76
Willard, Dallas (Albert) 1935- ... 116
Willard, Mildred Wilds 1911- ... 23-24R
See also SATA 14
Willard, Nancy 1936- ... CANR-10
Earlier sketch in CA 89-92
See also SATA 30, 37
See also DLB 5, 52
See also CLC 7, 37
See also CLR 5
Willard, Portman
See Norwood, Victor G(eorge) C(harles)
Willard, Samuel 1640-1707 ... DLB-24
Willcock, M(alcolm) M(aurice) 1925- ... 65-68
Willcox, A(lexander) R(obert) 1911- ... 118
Willcox, Donald J. 1933- ... 49-52
Willcox, Isobel 1907- ... 111
See also SATA 42
Willcox, Sheila 1936- ... 73-76
Willcox, William Bradford 1907-1985 ... CANR-3
Obituary ... 117
Earlier sketch in CA 5-6R
Wille, Janet Neipris 1936- ... 109
Willee, Albert William 1916-1982 ... 109
Willeford, Charles (Ray III) 1919-1988 ... CANR-15
Obituary ... 125
Earlier sketch in CA 33-36R
Willeford, William 1929- ... 25-28R
Willem, John M. 1909-1979 ... CAP-1
Obituary ... 93-96
Earlier sketch in CA 17-18
Willems, Emilio 1905- ... 105
Willems, J. Rutherford 1944- ... CANR-23
Earlier sketch in CA 45-48
Willen, Diane 1943- ... 117
Willensky, Elliot 1933- ... 29-32R
Willenson, Kim Jeremy 1937- ... 103
Willenz, June A. 1924- ... 121
Willerding, Margaret F(rances) 1919- ... 57-60
Willes, Mary (Janette) 1927- ... 120
Willets, F(rederick) W(illiam) 1930- ... 23-24R
Willets, Walter E. 1924- ... 25-28R
Willett, Brother Franciscus 1922- ... 15-16R
Willett, Edward R(ice) 1923- ... CANR-21
Earlier sketches in CA 5-6R, CANR-2
Willett, Frank 1925- ... 25-28R
Willett, John (William Mills) 1917- ... CANR-4
Earlier sketch in CA 9-10R
Willett, T(erence) C(harles) 1918- ... 37-40R
Willett, Thomas D(unaway) 1942- ... 108
Willetts, R(onald) F(rederick) 1915- ... CANR-2
Earlier sketch in CA 7-8R
Willey, Basil 1897- ... 9-10R
Willey, Darrell S. 1925- ... 41-44R
Willey, F. T.
See Willey, Frederick Thomas
Willey, Fred
See Willey, Frederick Thomas
Willey, Frederick Thomas 1910-1987
Obituary ... 124
Willey, Gordon R(andolph) 1913- ... CANR-2
Earlier sketch in CA 7-8R
Willey, Keith (Greville) 1930- ... CANR-9
Earlier sketch in CA 21-22R
Willey, Margaret 1950- ... 117
Willey, Peter (Robert Everard) 1922- ... 13-14R
Willey, R(oy) DeVerl 1910-197(?) ... CAP-2
Earlier sketch in CA 19-20
Willey, Richard J(ames) 1934- ... 41-44R
Willey, Robert
See Ley, Willy
Willgoose, Carl E(dward) 1916- ... CANR-6
Earlier sketch in CA 13-14R
Willhelm, Sidney M(clarty) 1934- ... 11-12R
William, Maurice 1882(?)-1973 Obituary ... 45-48
William II
See Hohenzollern, Friedrich Wilhelm (Victor Albert)
Williams, Alan F. 1933- ... 49-52
Williams, (Timothy) Alden 1932- ... 41-44R
Williams, Alice Cary 1892-1983 ... 65-68
Obituary ... 111
Williams, Alice Davis 1901- ... 113
Williams, Ann, Jr. 1951-1985 Obituary ... 117
Williams, Anne
See Steinke, Ann (Elizabeth)
Williams, Aston R. 1912- ... 21-22R
Williams, Aubrey L(ake) 1922- ... CANR-6
Earlier sketch in CA 2R
Williams, Barbara 1925- ... CANR-17
Earlier sketches in CA 49-52, CANR-1
See also SATA 11
Williams, Barry 1932- ... 29-32R
Williams, Ben A(mes), Jr. 1915- ... 116
Williams, Benjamin Buford 1923- ... 113
Williams, Benjamin H(arrison)
1889-1974 ... 37-40R
Williams, Bernard (Arthur Owen) 1929-
Brief entry ... 112
Williams, Bert Nolan 1930- ... 103
Williams, Beryl
See Epstein, Beryl (M. Williams)
Williams, Bill
See Crawford, William (Elbert)
Williams, Brad 1918- ... CANR-1
Earlier sketch in CA 2R
Williams, Bruce R(odda) 1919- ... 13-14R
Williams, Burton John 1927- ... 41-44R
Williams, Byron (Leigh) 1934- ... 29-32R
Williams, C(hester) Arthur, Jr. 1924- ... CANR-2
Earlier sketch in CA 2R
Williams, C(lifford) Glyn 1928- ... 29-32R
Williams, C(hristopher) J(ohn) F(ardo)
1930- ... 103
Williams, C(harles) K(enneth) 1936- ... 37-40R
See also DLB 5
See also CLC 33
Williams, Carl C(arnelius) 1903- ... 45-48
Williams, Carol M. 1917- ... 65-68
Williams, Carol T(raynor) 1935- ... 112
Williams, Catharine M(elissa) 1903- ... 37-40R
Williams, Cecil B(rown) 1901-1966 ... CAP-1
Earlier sketch in CA 11-12
Williams, Chancellor 1905- ... DLB-76
Williams, Charles (Walter Stansby)
1886-1945 Brief entry ... 104
See also TCLC 1, 11
Williams, Charles
See Collier, James L(incoln)
Williams, Chester
See Schechter, William
Williams, Cicely 1907-1985 ... 57-60
Obituary ... 117
Williams, Claerwen 1938- ... 102
Williams, Clayton (Wheat) 1895-1983 ... 125
Williams, Clyde C. 1881-1974 ... CAP-2
Earlier sketch in CA 23-24
See also SATA 8, 27
Williams, Coe
See Harrison, C. William
Williams, Colin 1934- ... 109
Williams, Colin W(ilbur) 1921- ... CANR-19
Earlier sketch in CA 25-28R
Williams, Cris
See De Cristoforo, R. J.
Williams, Cyril Glyndwr 1921- ... CANR-15
Earlier sketch in CA 37-40R
Williams, D.
See Ronald, David William
Williams, (Walter) Dakin 1919- Brief entry ... 116
Williams, Daniel Day 1910-1973 ... CANR-1
Obituary ... 45-48
Earlier sketch in CA 4R
Williams, David (Frank) 1909-1983
Obituary ... 109
Williams, David 1926- ... 122
Williams, David 1939- ... 73-76
Williams, David (Eliot) 1939- ... 123
Williams, David 1945- ... 97-100
Williams, David A. 1922- ... 29-32R
Williams, David Glenwood 1918- ... 7-8R
Williams, David L. 1940- ... CANR-10
Earlier sketch in CA 25-28R
Williams, David Rhys 1890- ... 7-8R
Williams, David Ricardo 1923- ... CANR-26
Earlier sketch in CA 101
Williams, Denis (Joseph Ivan) 1923- ... CANR-17
Earlier sketch in CA 93-96
Williams, Dorian 1914- ... CANR-3
Earlier sketch in CA 11-12R
Williams, Duncan 1927- ... 41-44R
Williams, E(ric) C(yril) 1918- ... 97-100
Williams, E(rnest) N(eville) 1917- ... 11-12R
Williams, Edward Ainsworth 1907-1976
Obituary ... 65-68

INDEX

Williams, Edward Bennett 1920-1988 3R
Obituary 126
Williams, Edward Francis 1903-1970
Obituary 29-32R
Williams, Edward G. 1929- 29-32R
Williams, Edward J(erome) 1935- CANR-10
Earlier sketch in CA 21-22R
Williams, Edward K. 1923-1966 CAP-1
Earlier sketch in CA 15-16
Williams, Edward V(inson) 1935- 121
Williams, Edwin B(ucher) 1891-1975 7-8R
Obituary 57-60
Williams, Edwin E(veritt) 1913- 45-48
Williams, Edwina Dakin 1885(?)-1980
Obituary 97-100
Williams, Eirlys O(lwen) CAP-1
Earlier sketch in CA 9-10
Williams, Elizabeth
See Dohen, Dorothy M.
Williams, (George) Emlyn 1905-1987 104
Obituary 123
See also DLB 10
See also CLC 15
Williams, Emmett 1925- CANR-2
Earlier sketch in CA 45-48
Williams, Eric (Ernest) 1911-1983 11-12R
Obituary 111
See also SATA 14, 38
Williams, Eric (Eustace) 1911-1981 125
Obituary 103
See also BW
Williams, Ernest Wells 1896(?)-1980
Obituary 97-100
Williams, Estelle S. 1908- 123
Williams, Ethel L. 37-40R
Williams, F(rederick) Winston 1935- 103
Williams, Ferelith Eccles
See Eccles Williams, Ferelith
See also SATA 22
Williams, Frances 1935- 25-28R
Williams, Frances B.
See Browin, Frances Williams
Williams, Frances Leigh 1909- 13-14R
Williams, Frances Marion 1919- 57-60
Williams, Francis 1903-1970 Obituary 104
Williams, Francis Stewart 1921-1974 37-40R
Williams, Frank B(royles), Jr. 1913- 118
Williams, Frederick D(eForrest) 1918- 65-68
Williams, G(erhard) Mennen 1911-1988
Obituary 124
Williams, G. Robert 1948- 108
Williams, Garth (Montgomery) 1912- SATA-18
See also DLB 22
Williams, Geoffrey (John) 1943- 29-32R
Williams, Geoffrey J(ames) 1936- 118
Williams, George (Guion) 1902- 15-16R
Williams, George C(hristopher) 1926- 73-76
Williams, George Huntston 1914- CANR-16
Earlier sketches in CA 2R, CANR-1
Williams, George (Joseph) III 1949- 125
Williams, George M(ason, Jr.) 1940- 61-64
Williams, George W(alton) 1922- 9-10R
Williams, George Washington
1849-1891 DLB-47
Williams, Geraint 1942- 124
Williams, Gertrude 1897-1983 Obituary 109
Williams, Gilbert M. 1917- 61-64
Williams, Glanmor 1920- 7-8R
Williams, Glanville Llewelyn 1911- 106
Williams, Gluyas 1888-1982 Obituary 108
See also AITN 2
Williams, Gordon (Maclean) 1934(?)-
Brief entry 116
Williams, Gordon Leslie 1933- 110
Williams, Greer 1909- CANR-10
Earlier sketch in CA 13-14R
Williams, Gregory 1952- 109
Williams, Griffith Wynne 1897-1972 CAP-2
Earlier sketch in CA 25-28
Williams, Gurney III 1941- 69-72
Williams, Guy Neal 1953- 77-80
Williams, Guy R. 1920- 13-14R
See also SATA 11
Williams, (David) Gwyn 1904- 103
Williams, Hank, Jr. 1949- Brief entry 117
Williams, Harold A(nthony) 1916- 37-40R
Williams, Harold R(oger) 1935- 53-56
Williams, Harold S(tannett) 1898- CANR-20
Earlier sketches in CA 11-12R, CANR-5
Williams, Harold Workman
See Wilson, Halsey William
Williams, Hawley
See Heyliger, William
Williams, Hazel Pearson 1914- 57-60
Williams, Heathcote 1941- 21-22R
See also DLB 13
Williams, Henry
See Manville, W(illiam) H(enry)
Williams, Henry Lionel 1895-1974
Obituary 45-48
Williams, Herbert (Lloyd) 1932- CANR-12
Earlier sketch in CA 29-32R
Williams, Herbert Lee 1918- 2R
Williams, Hermann Warner, Jr.
1908-1974 7-8R
Obituary 53-56
Williams, Hiram D. 1917- 13-14R
Williams, Hosea L(orenzo) 1926- 49-52
Williams, Howard L(loyd) 1950- 117
Williams, Howard Russell 1915- 15-16R
Williams, Hugh (Anthony Glanmor)
1904-1969 CAP-2
Earlier sketch in CA 25-28
Williams, Hugo 1942- 19-20R
See also DLB 40
See also CLC 42
Williams, Ioan Miles 1941- CANR-11
Earlier sketch in CA 25-28R
Williams, Ira E., Jr. 1926- 53-56
Williams, Irving G(regory) 1915- 41-44R
Williams, Isaac 1802-1865 DLB-32
Williams, J(ames) David Lewis
See Lewis-Williams, J(ames) David
Williams, J(ames) Earl 1922- 41-44R
Williams, J(ohn) H(argreaves) Harley 11-12R
Williams, J. R.
See Williams, Jeanne
Williams, J(ohn) Rodman 1918- 81-84
Williams, J. Walker
See Wodehouse, P(elham) G(renville)
Williams, J. X.
See Ludwig, Myles Eric
and Offutt, Andrew J(efferson V)
Williams, Jay 1914-1978 CANR-2
Obituary 81-84
Earlier sketch in CA 2R
See also SATA 3, 24, 41
See also CLR 8
Williams, Jay G(omer) 1932- 41-44R
Williams, Jeanne 1930- 25-28R
See also SATA 5
Williams, Jenny 1939- 112
Williams, Jeremy (Napier) Howard
See Howard-Williams, Jeremy (Napier)
Williams, Jerome 1926- CANR-1
Earlier sketch in CA 49-52
Williams, Joan 1928- 2R
See also DLB 6
Williams, Joel
See Jennings, John (Edward, Jr.)
Williams, John (Herbert) 1908-1976 CANR-10
Earlier sketch in CA 15-16R
Williams, John (Edward) 1922- CANR-2
Earlier sketch in CA 2R
See also DLB 6
Williams, John A(lfred) 1925- CANR-26
Earlier sketches in CA 53-56, CANR-6
See also CAAS 3
See also BW
See also DLB 2, 33
See also CLC 5, 13
Williams, John Alden 1928- CANR-2
Earlier sketch in CA 3R
Williams, John B. 1919- 93-96
Williams, John D(elane) 1938- 57-60
Williams, John Edwin 1928- 93-96
Williams, John G(ordon) 1906- CAP-2
Earlier sketch in CA 23-24
Williams, John G. 1915- 120
Williams, John Henry 1887-1980 Obituary 105
Williams, John R(yan) 1919- 37-40R
Williams, John Stanley 1925- CAP-1
Earlier sketch in CA 9-10
Williams, John Stuart 1920- 65-68
Williams, Jonathan (Chamberlain)
1929- CANR-8
Earlier sketch in CA 9-10R
See also DLB 5
See also CLC 13
Williams, Joy 1944- CANR-22
Earlier sketch in CA 41-44R
See also CLC 31
Williams, Joyce E(layne) 1937- 104
Williams, Juan 1954- 125
Williams, Juanita da Lomba Jones
1925- 37-40R
Williams, Justin, Sr. 1906- 101
Williams, Kate
See Flynn, Donald R(obert)
Williams, Kenneth 1926-1988 Obituary 125
Williams, Kim 1924(?)-1986 Obituary 120
Williams, Kit 1946(?)- 107
See also SATA 44
See also CLR 4
Williams, L(aurence) F(rederic) Rushbrook
See Rushbrook Williams, L(aurence)
F(rederic)
Williams, L(eslie) Pearce 1927- 65-68
Williams, Lady
See Williams, Gertrude
Williams, Lawrence 1916(?)-1983
Obituary 108
Williams, Lawrence K(enneth) 1930- 29-32R
Williams, Lee E(rskine) II 1946- 41-44R
Williams, LeRoy T. 1944- 120
Williams, Leslie 1941- 107
See also SATA 42
Williams, Linda 1946- 110
Williams, Liza 1928- 102
Williams, Loring G. 1924-1974 CAP-2
Earlier sketch in CA 29-32
Williams, Louise Bonino 1904(?)-1984
Obituary 114
See also SATA 39
Williams, Lovett E(dward), Jr. 1935- 109
Williams, Lynn
See Hale, Arlene
Williams, Marcia 1932- 123
Williams, Margaret (Anne) 1902- 23-24R
Williams, Margaret (Vyner) 1914- 25-28R
Williams, Martha E(thelyn) 1934- 125
Williams, Martin 1924- 49-52
Williams, Mary Alice 1949- Brief entry 123
Williams, Mary C(ameron) 1923- 57-60
Williams, Mary Elizabeth 1909-1976
Obituary 65-68
Williams, Mary McGee 1925- 25-28R
Williams, Mary Pat 1946- 112
Williams, Mason 1938- 25-28R
Williams, Maureen 1951- 85-88
See also SATA 12
Williams, Melvin D(onald) 1933- 73-76
Williams, Merryn 1944- CANR-15
Earlier sketch in CA 41-44R
Williams, Michael
See St. John, Wylly Folk
Williams, Miller 1930- 15-16R
Williams, Mona (Goodwyn) 1916- 81-84
Williams, Nancy M(argaret) 1929- 122
Williams, Ned 1909- 13-14R
Williams, Neville (John) 1924-1977
Obituary 111
Williams, Noel Trevor St. John 1918- 41-44R
Williams, Norman 1952- 118
See also CLC 39
Williams, Oliver F(ranklin) 1939- 114
Williams, Oliver P(erry) 1925- 37-40R
Williams, Ora (Ruby) 1926- 73-76
Williams, Oscar 1900-1964 CANR-6
Earlier sketch in CA 1R
Williams, P(eter) F(airney) 1931- 121
Williams, Patrick J.
See Butterworth, W(illiam) E(dmund III)
Williams, Patti 1936- 73-76
Williams, Paul (Revere) 1894-1980
Obituary 93-96
Williams, Paul (Hamilton) 1940- 121
Williams, Paul (Steven) 1948- 81-84
Williams, Paul O(sborne) 1935- CANR-24
Earlier sketch in CA 106
Williams, Pete
See Faulknor, Cliff(ord Vernon)
Williams, Peter W(illiam) 1944- 112
Williams, Philip Maynard 1920-1984
Obituary 114
Williams, Philip W(alter) 1941- CANR-11
Earlier sketch in CA 69-72
Williams, Phyllis S(awyer) 1931- 65-68
Williams, Ralph Mehlin 1911- 7-8R
Williams, Ralph Vaughan
See Vaughan Williams, Ralph
Williams, Randall Herbert Monier
See Monier-Williams, Randall Herbert
Williams, Raymond (Henry) 1921-1988 21-22R
Obituary 124
See also DLB 14
Williams, Rebecca (Yancy) 1899-1976
Obituary 65-68
Williams, Richard Hays 1912- CANR-2
Earlier sketch in CA 2R
Williams, Richard Lippincott 1910- 101
Williams, Robert C. 1938- CANR-14
Earlier sketch in CA 37-40R
Williams, Robert Coleman 1940- 23-24R
Williams, Robert Deryck 1917-1986 103
Obituary 120
Williams, Robert G. 1948- 125
Williams, Robert Hugh 1907(?)-1983
Obituary 109
Williams, Robert L(ewis) 1903- CANR-10
Earlier sketch in CA 15-16R
Williams, Robert Moore 1907-1977
Obituary 102
Williams, Robert P. 1906(?)-1977
Obituary 69-72
Williams, Robin M(urphy), Jr. 1914- 13-14R
Williams, Roger 1603(?)-1683 DLB-24
Williams, Roger J(ohn) 1893-1988 CANR-7
Obituary 124
Earlier sketch in CA 17-18R
Williams, Roger L(awrence) 1923-
Brief entry 112
Williams, Roger M(iller) 1934- 37-40R
Williams, Roger Neville 1943- 37-40R
Williams, Ronald Ralph 1906-1979 CANR-7
Earlier sketch in CA 15-16R
Williams, Rosalind
See Fergusson, Rosalind (Joyce)
Williams, Rosalind H. 1944- 109
Williams, Rose
See Ross, W(illiam) E(dward) D(aniel)
Williams, Russell J(ohn) 1944- 104
Williams, Samm-Art
See Williams, Samuel Arthur
See also DLB 38
Williams, Samuel Arthur 1946- 123
Brief entry 117
See also BW
Williams, Selma R(uth) 1925- CANR-1
Earlier sketch in CA 49-52
See also SATA 14
Williams, Sherley Anne 1944- CANR-25
Earlier sketch in CA 73-76
See also BW
See also DLB 41
Williams, Shirley
See Williams, Sherley Anne
Williams, Slim
See Williams, Clyde C.
Williams, Stanley W. 1917- 17-18R
Williams, Stephen 1926- Brief entry 114
Williams, Stirling B(acot), Jr. 1943- 29-32R
Williams, Strephon Kaplan 1934- CANR-20
Earlier sketch in CA 102
Williams, T(erence) C(harles) 1925- 29-32R
Williams, T(homas) David 1929- 123
Williams, T(homas) Harry 1909-1979 CANR-3
Earlier sketch in CA 4R
See also DLB 17
Williams, Tennessee 1911(?)-1983 7-8R
Obituary 108
See also DLB 7
See also DLBY 83
See also DLBD 4
See also CDALB 1941-1968
See also CLC 1, 2, 5, 7, 8, 11, 15, 19,
30, 39, 45
See also AITN 1, 2
Williams, Theodore C(urtis) 1930- 69-72
Williams, Thomas (Alonzo) 1926- CANR-2
Earlier sketch in CA 2R
See also CLC 14
Williams, Thomas (Andrew) 1931- 49-52
Williams, Thomas Howard 1935- 15-16R
Williams, Tina
See Wiles, Domini
Williams, Trevor Illtyd 1921- 109
Williams, Ursula Moray
See Moray Williams, Ursula
See also SATA 3
Williams, (George) Valentine 1883-1946
Brief entry 111
Williams, Vera B. 1927- 123
See also SATA 33, 53
See also CLR 9
Williams, Vergil L(ewis) 1935- CANR-9
Earlier sketch in CA 57-60
Williams, Wallace Edward 1926-
Brief entry 105
Williams, Walter
See Williams, Walter E(dward)
Williams, Walter E(dward) 1936-
Brief entry 123
Williams, Walter G(eorge) 1903- CAP-1
Earlier sketch in CA 15-16
Williams, (Margaret) Wetherby CANR-3
Earlier sketch in CA 45-48
Williams, Willard F(orest) 1921- 15-16R
Williams, William Appleman 1921- CANR-3
Earlier sketch in CA 3R
See also DLB 17
Williams, William Carlos 1883-1963 89-92
See also DLB 4, 16, 54
See also CLC 1, 2, 5, 9, 13, 22, 42
Williams, William David 1917- 7-8R
Williams, William H(enry) 1936- 69-72
Williams, William P(roctor) 1939- CANR-23
Earlier sketch in CA 45-48
Williams, Wirt (Alfred, Jr.) 1921-1986 9-10R
Obituary 119
See also DLB 6
Williams-Ellis, (Mary) Amabel (Nassau
Strachey) 1894-1984 105
Obituary 114
See also SATA 29, 41
Williams-Ellis, Clough 1883- 13-14R
Williamson, Alan (Bacher) 1944- 57-60
Williamson, Anthony George 1932- 101
Williamson, Audrey (May)
1913-1986(?) CANR-3
Obituary 118
Earlier sketch in CA 49-52
Williamson, Bruce 1893-1984 Obituary 111
Williamson, Bruce 1930- 101
Williamson, Chilton 1916- 15-16R
Williamson, Chilton, Jr. 1947- 102
Williamson, Claude C(harles) H. 1891-? CAP-1
Earlier sketch in CA 17-18
Williamson, Craig (Burke) 1943- CANR-16
Earlier sketch in CA 29-32R
Williamson, David Keith 1942- 103
Williamson, David L(ouis) 1937- 111
Williamson, Duncan 1928- 123
Williamson, Edward 1908-1984 Obituary 113
Williamson, Ellen Douglas 1905-1984 17-18R
Obituary 114
Williamson, Eugene L. (Jr.) 1930- 11-12R
Williamson, Geoffrey 1897- 9-10R
Williamson, Gerald Neal 1932- 112
Williamson, Glen 1909- CANR-9
Earlier sketch in CA 57-60
Williamson, H(enry) D(arvall) 1907- 65-68
Williamson, Harold Francis 1901- 7-8R
Williamson, Henry 1895-1977 81-84
Obituary 73-76
See also SATA 30, 37
Williamson, J. N.
See Williamson, Gerald Neal
Williamson, J. Peter 1929- CANR-6
Earlier sketch in CA 1R
Williamson, Jack
See Williamson, John Stewart
See also DLB 8
See also CLC 29
Williamson, Jeffrey G(ale) 1935- CANR-18
Earlier sketch in CA 85-88
Williamson, Joanne Small 1926- 13-14R
See also SATA 3
Williamson, John Butler 1943- 89-92
Williamson, John G(rant) 1933- 45-48
Williamson, John Stewart 1908- CANR-23
Earlier sketch in CA 17-18R
Williamson, Joseph 1895-1988 CAP-1
Obituary 125
Earlier sketch in CA 11-12
Williamson, Juanita V. 1917- 37-40R
Williamson, Lamar, Jr. 1926- 89-92
Williamson, Moncrieff 1915- 102
Williamson, Norma (Goff) 1934- 65-68
Williamson, Oliver E(aton) 1932- 81-84
Williamson, Porter B(eyers) 1916- 110
Williamson, Rene de Visme 1908- CANR-13
Earlier sketches in CA 17-18, CAP-1
Williamson, Richard 1930- 37-40R
Williamson, Richard 1935- 109
Williamson, Robert C(lifford) 1916- 23-24R
Williamson, Robin (Martin Eyre) 1938- 29-32R
Williamson, Robin (Duncan Harry) 1943- 102
Williamson, Stanford Winfield 1916- 7-8R
Williamson, Tony
See Williamson, Anthony George
Williamson, William Bedford 1918- CANR-6
Earlier sketch in CA 3R
Williamson, William Landram 1920- 11-12R
Willie, Charles V(ert) 1927- CANR-14
Earlier sketch in CA 41-44R

Willie, Frederick
See Lovecraft, H(oward) P(hillips)
Willig, George 1949- ... 102
Willig, John M. 1913-1982 Obituary ... 107
Willig, Rosette F. 1950- ... 114
Willimon, William H(enry) 1946- ... 106
Willing, Jules Z. 1914-1981 ... 108
Willing, Martha Kent 1920- ... 37-40R
Willingham, Calder (Baynard, Jr.)
1922- ... CANR-3
Earlier sketch in CA 5-6R
See also DLB 2, 44
See also CLC 5
Willingham, John J. 1935- ... 37-40R
Willingham, John R(obert) 1919- ... 17-18R
Willings, David 1932- ... 111
Willis, (George) Anthony Armstrong
1897-1976 ... 69-72
Willis, Arthur J(ames) 1895-1983 ... CANR-5
Obituary ... 111
Earlier sketch in CA 7-8R
Willis, Charles
See Clarke, Arthur C(harles)
Willis, Cleve E(dward) 1942- ... 123
Brief entry ... 118
Willis, Connie 1945- ... 114
Willis, Corinne Denneny ... 21-22R
Willis, Donald C(halmers) 1947- ... CANR-15
Earlier sketch in CA 41-44R
Willis, E(dward) David 1932- ... 37-40R
Willis, Edgar E(rnest) 1913- ... 5-6R
Willis, Edward Henry
See Willis, Ted
Willis, Ellen Jane 1941- ... 106
Willis, F(rank) Roy 1930- ... 15-16R
Willis, Irene 1929- ... CANR-10
Earlier sketch in CA 65-68
Willis, James 1928- ... 109
Willis, Jerry W. 1943- ... 85-88
Willis, John A(lvin) 1916- ... 19-20R
Willis, John H(oward), Jr. 1929- ... 37-40R
Willis, John Ralph 1938- ... 121
Willis, Margaret 1899- ... CANR-19
Earlier sketches in CA 5-6R, CANR-3
Willis, Maud
See Lottman, Eileen
Willis, Meredith Sue 1946- ... CANR-16
Earlier sketch in CA 85-88
Willis, Nathaniel Parker
1806-1867 ... DLB-3, 59, 73, 74
Willis, Roy (Geoffrey) 1927- ... CANR-17
Earlier sketch in CA 77-80
Willis, Samuel
See Parker, Hershel
Willis, Sharon O(zell) 1938- ... 37-40R
Willis, Stanley E. II 1923- ... 23-24R
Willis, Ted 1918- ... CANR-23
Earlier sketches in CA 11-12R, CANR-7
Willis, Wayne 1942- ... 29-32R
Willison, George F(indlay) 1896-1972 ... CAP-1
Obituary ... 37-40R
Earlier sketch in CA 13-14
Willison, Marilyn Murray 1948- ... 105
Willke, John Charles 1925- ... CANR-24
Earlier sketches in CA 65-68, CANR-9
Willkens, William H(enry) R(obert)
1919- ... 23-24R
Willmington, Harold L. 1932- ... 49-52
Willmott, Peter 1923- ... 23-24R
Willmott, Phyllis ... 117
Willner, Ann Ruth 1924- ... 23-24R
Willner, Dorothy 1927- ... 53-56
Willnow, Ronald D. 1933- ... 77-80
Willock, Colin 1919- ... CANR-10
Earlier sketch in CA 13-14R
Willock, Ruth ... 15-16R
Willoughby, Cass
See Olsen, T(heodore) V(ictor)
Willoughby, Charles Andrew 1892-1972
Obituary ... 104
Willoughby, David P(atrick) 1901- ... 37-40R
Willoughby, Elaine Macmann 1926- ... 101
Willoughby, Glynn
See Allentuck, Andrew
Willoughby, Hugh
See Harvey, Nigel
Willoughby, Lee Davis
See Brandner, Gary
and DeAndrea, William L(ouis)
and Toombs, John
and Webb, Jean Francis
Willoughby, William Reid 1910- ... 2R
Willrich, Mason 1933- ... 77-80
Willrich, Ted L. 1924- ... 29-32R
Wills, A(lfred) J(ohn) 1927- ... 21-22R
Wills, David Hilary 1904-1985 Obituary ... 117
Wills, Garry 1934- ... CANR-1
Earlier sketch in CA 3R
Wills, Geoffrey
See Staal, Cyril
Wills, Jean 1929- ... CANR-22
Earlier sketch in CA 105
Wills, John E(lliot), Jr. 1936- ... 45-48
Wills, Jonathan 1947- ... 69-72
Wills, Maurice Morning 1932- Brief entry ... 105
Wills, Maury
See Wills, Maurice Morning
Wills, Millicent A(gatha) 1901(?)-1988
Obituary ... 125
Wills, Philip Aubrey 1907-1978 ... 81-84
Wills, Thomas
See Ard, William (Thomas)
Willson, A(mos) Leslie, Jr. 1923- ... 11-12R
Willson, Meredith 1902-1984 ... 49-52
Obituary ... 113
Willson, Robina Beckles
See Beckles Willson, Robina (Elizabeth)
See also SATA 27
Willwerth, James 1943- ... 57-60
Willy
See Colette, (Sidonie-Gabrielle)
Willy, Colette
See Colette, (Sidonie-Gabrielle)
Willy, Margaret (Elizabeth) 1919- ... 9-10R
Wilma, Dana
See Faralla, Dana
Wilmer, Clive 1945- Brief entry ... 122
See also DLB 40
Wilmer, Dale
See Miller, (H.) Bill(y)
and Wade, Robert (Allison)
Wilmer, Valerie (Sybil) 1941- ... 85-88
Wilmerding, John 1938- ... 111
Wilmeth, Don B(urton) 1939- ... CANR-19
Earlier sketch in CA 102
Wilmore, Gayraud S(tephen, Jr.) 1921-
Brief entry ... 114
Wilmore, Sylvia (Joan) Bruce 1914- ... 89-92
Wilmot, Anthony 1933- ... 77-80
Wilmot, William (Wallace) 1943- ... CANR-7
Earlier sketch in CA 57-60
Wilms, Barbara 1941- ... 57-60
Wilmut, Roger (Francis) 1942- ... CANR-19
Earlier sketch in CA 102
Wilner, Eleanor 1937- ... CANR-16
Earlier sketch in CA 93-96
Wilner, Herbert 1925-1977 ... CANR-3
Earlier sketch in CA 45-48
Wilroy, Mary Edith (Farr) 1910-1987
Obituary ... 122
Wilshire, Bruce W(ithington) 1932- ... 77-80
Wilson, A(lfred) Jeyaratnam 1928- ... CANR-12
Earlier sketch in CA 61-64
Wilson, A(ndrew) N(orman) 1950- ... 122
Brief entry ... 112
See also DLB 14
See also CLC 33
Wilson, Abraham 1899(?)-1983 Obituary ... 110
Wilson, Adrian 1923-1988 Obituary ... 125
Wilson, Alison M. 1932- ... 120
Wilson, Alton H(orace) 1925- ... 61-64
Wilson, Andrew 1923- ... 29-32R
Wilson, Angus (Frank Johnstone)
1913- ... CANR-21
Earlier sketch in CA 7-8R
See also DLB 15
See also CLC 2, 3, 5, 25, 34
Wilson, Arthur 1595-1652 ... DLB-58
Wilson, Arthur M(cCandless) 1902-1979 ... 61-64
Obituary ... 89-92
Wilson, August 1945- ... 122
Brief entry ... 115
See also BW
See also CLC 39, 50
Wilson, Augusta Jane Evans 1835-1909 . DLB-42
Wilson, Barbara
See Janifer, Laurence M(ark)
Wilson, Barbara Ker
See Ker Wilson, Barbara
Wilson, Beth P(ierre) ... CANR-1
Earlier sketch in CA 49-52
See also SATA 8
Wilson, Betty 1923- ... 97-100
Wilson, Brian 1942- ... CLC-12
Wilson, Bryan R(onald) 1926- ... CANR-19
Earlier sketches in CA 5-6R, CANR-3
Wilson, Budge 1927- ... 121
Wilson, Callie C(oe) 1917- ... 124
Wilson, Camilla Jeanne 1945- ... 61-64
Wilson, Cammy
See Wilson, Camilla Jeanne
Wilson, Carlos 1941- ... 61-64
Wilson, Carole
See Wallmann, Jeffrey M(iner)
Wilson, Carolyn 1938- ... 21-22R
Wilson, Carroll L(ouis) 1910-1983 ... 89-92
Obituary ... 109
Wilson, Carter 1941- ... 17-18R
See also SATA 6
Wilson, (Lindsay) Charles 1932- ... 65-68
Wilson, Charles McMoran 1882-1977 ... CAP-2
Obituary ... 69-72
Earlier sketch in CA 21-22
Wilson, Charles Morrow 1905-1977 ... CANR-4
Earlier sketch in CA 5-6R
See also SATA 30
Wilson, Charles Reagan 1948- ... 105
Wilson, Chris(topher Paul) 1949- ... 125
Wilson, Christine
See Geach, Christine
Wilson, Christopher B. 1910(?)-1985
Obituary ... 117
See also SATA 46
Wilson, Clifford (Allan) 1923- ... 93-96
Wilson, Clifton E. 1919- ... 23-24R
Wilson, Clyde N(orman, Jr.) 1941- ... 116
Wilson, Colin 1931- ... CANR-22
Earlier sketches in CA 2R, CANR-1
See also CAAS 5
See also DLB 14
See also CLC 3, 14
Wilson, Craig R. 1947- ... 57-60
Wilson, Crane
See O'Brien, Cyril C(ornelius)
Wilson, D. A.
See Wilson, Derek (Alan)
Wilson, D(udley) B(utler) 1923- ... 23-24R
Wilson, Dagmar 1916- ... SATA-31
Wilson, Dale 1894-1987 ... CAP-1
Obituary ... 121
Earlier sketch in CA 13-14
Wilson, Daniel J(oseph) 1949- ... 117
Wilson, Dave
See Floren, Lee
Wilson, (Anthony) David 1927- ... 97-100
Wilson, David 1942- ... CANR-16
Earlier sketch in CA 93-96
Wilson, David
See MacArthur, D(avid) Wilson
Wilson, David Allen 1926- ... CANR-7
Earlier sketch in CA 5-6R
Wilson, David Henry 1937- ... 113
Wilson, David L(ee) 1943- ... 112
Wilson, David Scofield 1931- ... 106
Wilson, Deirdre (Susan Moir) 1941- ... 97-100
Wilson, Derek (Alan) 1935- ... 123
Brief entry ... 115
Wilson, Derek A.
See Wilson, Derek (Alan)
Wilson, Dick
See Wilson, Richard Garratt
Wilson, Dirk
See Pohl, Frederik
Wilson, Don(ald) 1932- ... 81-84
Wilson, Don W(hitman) 1942- ... 61-64
Wilson, Dorothy Clarke 1904- ... CANR-6
Earlier sketch in CA 4R
See also SATA 16
Wilson, Douglas L. 1935- ... 37-40R
Wilson, (Archibald) Duncan 1911- ... 103
Wilson, E(dward) Raymond 1896-1987 ... 61-64
Obituary ... 122
Wilson, (Harvey) Earl 1907-1987 ... 69-72
Obituary ... 121
Wilson, Earl (Dean) 1939- ... 118
Wilson, Edmund 1895-1972 ... CANR-1
Obituary ... 37-40R
Earlier sketch in CA 3R
See also DLB 63
See also CLC 1, 2, 3, 8, 24
Wilson, Edward A(rthur) 1886-1970
Obituary ... 116
See also SATA 38
Wilson, Edward M(eryon) 1906-1977
Obituary ... 114
Wilson, Edward O(sborne) 1929- ... CANR-16
Earlier sketch in CA 61-64
Wilson, Elena 1907(?)-1979 Obituary ... 89-92
Wilson, Elizabeth Z. 1951- ... 123
Wilson, Ellen (Janet Cameron) ?-1976 ... 49-52
Obituary ... 103
See also SATA 9, 26
Wilson, Eric (H.) 1940- ... CANR-20
Earlier sketch in CA 101
See also SATA 32, 34
Wilson, Erica ... CANR-23
Earlier sketches in CA 53-56, CANR-7
See also SATA 51
Wilson, Erle (Alexander Mann) 1898- ... 7-8R
Wilson, Ernest Charles 1896- ... 29-32R
Wilson, Ethel Davis (Bryant) 1888-1980 ... 102
See also DLB 68
See also CLC 13
Wilson, Eugene E. 1887(?)-1974
Obituary ... 49-52
Wilson, Eugene Smith 1905-1981
Obituary ... 103
Wilson, Evan M(orris) 1910-1984
Obituary ... 112
Wilson, Everett K(eith) 1913- ... 93-96
Wilson, F(rank) P(ercy) 1889-1963 ... CANR-1
Earlier sketch in CA 4R
Wilson, Forbes (Kingsbury) 1910- ... 126
Brief entry ... 112
Wilson, Forrest 1918- ... CANR-7
Earlier sketch in CA 53-56
See also SATA 27
Wilson, Francesca Mary 1888-1981
Obituary ... 103
Wilson, Francis Graham 1901-1976
Obituary ... 65-68
Wilson, Frank (Avray) 1914- ... CAP-1
Earlier sketch in CA 11-12
Wilson, Frank J. 1887-1970 ... CAP-1
Earlier sketch in CA 15-16
Wilson, Frank L(eondus) 1941- ... 57-60
Wilson, Fred 1937- ... 37-40R
Wilson, G(eorge) B(ulkeley) L(aird)
1908-1984 ... 111
Obituary ... 114
Wilson, Gahan 1930- ... CANR-19
Earlier sketch in CA 25-28R
See also SATA 27, 35
Wilson, Garff B(ell) 1909- ... 45-48
Wilson, George C. 1927- ... 124
Wilson, George M(acklin) 1937- ... 25-28R
Wilson, George W(ilton) 1928- ... CANR-7
Earlier sketch in CA 19-20R
Wilson, Gina 1943- ... 106
See also SATA 34, 36
Wilson, Glenn Daniel 1942- ... CANR-21
Earlier sketch in CA 104
Wilson, (Leslie) Granville 1912- ... CANR-11
Earlier sketch in CA 69-72
See also SATA 14
Wilson, Gregory
See DeLamotte, Roy Carroll
Wilson, H. W.
See Wilson, Halsey William
Wilson, Halsey William 1868-1954
Brief entry ... 118
Wilson, (James) Harold 1916- ... CANR-16
Earlier sketch in CA 53-56
Wilson, Harold Stacy 1935- ... 41-44R
Wilson, Harriet E. Adams
1828(?)-1863(?) ... DLB-50
Wilson, Harriett (Charlotte) 1916- ... CANR-16
Earlier sketch in CA 2R
Wilson, Harris W(ard) 1919- ... 23-24R
Wilson, Harry Leon 1867-1939 Brief entry ... 108
See also DLB 9
Wilson, Hazel (Hutchins) 1898- ... CANR-6
Earlier sketch in CA 4R
See also SATA 3
Wilson, Helen Helga (Mayne) ... CANR-4
Earlier sketch in CA 11-12R
Wilson, Helen Van Pelt 1901- ... 105
Wilson, Howard Allan 1927- Brief entry ... 106
Wilson, Howard Hazen 1908-1978
Obituary ... 77-80
Wilson, Ian (William) 1941- ... 85-88
Wilson, Iris Higbie
See Engstrand, Iris (H.) Wilson
Wilson, Ivor (Arthur) 1924- ... CAP-1
Earlier sketch in CA 11-12
Wilson, J(anice) J. 1936- ... 97-100
Wilson, J(ohn) Tuzo 1908- ... 45-48
Wilson, Jack 1937- ... 23-24R
Wilson, Jacqueline 1945- ... CANR-17
Earlier sketches in CA 45-48, CANR-1
See also SATA 52
Wilson, Jacques M(arcel) P(atrick) 1920- ... 49-52
Wilson, James C(lyde) 1948- ... 111
Wilson, James Orville 1895- ... CAP-1
Earlier sketch in CA 11-12
Wilson, James Q(uinn) 1931- Brief entry ... 116
Wilson, James Robert 1917- ... 2R
Wilson, James Vernon 1881- ... CAP-1
Earlier sketch in CA 9-10
Wilson, Jaye 1938- ... 104
Wilson, Jeanne (Patricia Pauline)
1920- ... CANR-12
Earlier sketch in CA 69-72
Wilson, Jerry V(ernon) 1928- ... CANR-7
Earlier sketch in CA 57-60
Wilson, Jim
See Wilson, James Vernon
Wilson, Joan Hoff 1937- Brief entry ... 105
Wilson, Joe
See Wilson, Joseph T(homas)
Wilson, John 1588-1667 ... DLB-24
Wilson, John 1922- ... SATA-22
Wilson, (Richard) John (McMoran) 1924- ... 117
Wilson, John A. 1900(?)-1976 Obituary ... 69-72
Wilson, John A(braham) R(oss) 1911- ... 41-44R
Wilson, John Boyd 1928- ... CANR-5
Earlier sketch in CA 11-12R
Wilson, John (Anthony) Burgess 1917- ... CANR-2
Earlier sketch in CA 3R
See also CLC 8, 10, 13
Wilson, John C.
See Morrow, Felix
Wilson, John Dover 1881-1969 ... 102
Obituary ... 93-96
Wilson, John F(rederick) 1933- Brief entry ... 117
Wilson, John Foster 1919- ... 109
Wilson, John Harold 1900-1982 Obituary ... 107
Wilson, John R. M. 1944- ... 69-72
Wilson, John Stuart Gladstone 1916- ... CANR-11
Earlier sketch in CA 13-14R
Wilson, Joseph T(homas) 1936- ... 117
Wilson, Joyce M(uriel Judson) ... CANR-12
Earlier sketch in CA 19-20R
See also SATA 21
Wilson, Julia 1927- ... 21-22R
Wilson, Jussem
See Wilson, Nelly
Wilson, Justin ... 116
Wilson, Katharine M(argaret) 1895- ... 89-92
Wilson, Keith 1927- ... CANR-9
Earlier sketch in CA 23-24R
See also CAAS 5
Wilson, Keith 1929- ... 121
Wilson, Kenneth G(eorge) 1923- ... 7-8R
Wilson, Kenneth L. 1897(?)-1979
Obituary ... 85-88
Wilson, Kenneth L(ee) 1916- ... 29-32R
Wilson, L(eland) Craig 1925- ... 37-40R
Wilson, Lanford 1937- ... 19-20R
See also DLB 7
See also CLC 7, 14, 36
Wilson, Larman C. 1930- ... CANR-14
Earlier sketch in CA 37-40R
Wilson, Leigh Allison 1957- ... 117
Wilson, Leonard G(ilchrist) 1928- ... CANR-7
Earlier sketch in CA 57-60
Wilson, Libby
See Wilson, Elizabeth Z.
Wilson, Lionel 1924- ... 105
See also SATA 31, 33
Wilson, Logan 1907- ... 45-48
Wilson, Louis D(oull) 1917- ... 93-96
Wilson, Louis Round 1876-1980
Obituary ... 93-96
Wilson, M(orris) Emett 1894- ... 5-6R
Wilson, Major L(oyce) 1926- ... 57-60
Wilson, Margaret (Wilhemina) 1882-1973
Obituary ... 113
See also DLB 9
Wilson, Margaret Gibbons 1943- ... 101
Wilson, Margery
See Strayer, Sara Barker
Wilson, Margo 1942- ... 110
Wilson, Marie B(eatrice) 1922- ... 53-56
Wilson, Marjorie
See Wilson, Budge
See also SATA 51
Wilson, Mary
See Roby, Mary Linn
Wilson, Maurice (Charles John) 1914- . SATA-46
Wilson, (Daphne) Merna 1930- ... 109
Wilson, Michael 1914-1978 ... 85-88
Obituary ... 77-80
See also DLB 44

Wilson, Mitchell 1913-1973 ... CANR-3
Obituary ... 41-44R
Earlier sketch in CA 3R
Wilson, Monica Hunter 1908-1982 ... CANR-6
Obituary ... 108
Earlier sketch in CA 2R
Wilson, N(orman) Scarlyn 1901- ... CANR-5
Earlier sketch in CA 7-8R
Wilson, Neill C(ompton) 1889- ... 7-8R
Wilson, Nelly 1930- ... 106
Wilson, Nick
See Ellis, Edward S(ylvester)
Wilson, Noel Avon 1914- ... 73-76
Wilson, Pat 1910- ... CANR-12
Earlier sketch in CA 29-32R
Wilson, Paul C(arroll) 1944- ... 77-80
Wilson, Paul R(ichard) 1942- Brief entry ... 109
Wilson, Penelope Coker
See Hall, Penelope C(oker)
Wilson, Peter (Cecil) 1913-1984 Obituary ... 113
Wilson, Peter N. 1928- ... 25-28R
Wilson, Phillip (John) 1922- ... 57-60
Wilson, Phoebe Rous 1924(?)-1980
Obituary ... 101
Wilson, Phyllis Starr 1928- ... 69-72
Wilson, R(oger) H(arris) L(ebus) 1920- ... 13-14R
Wilson, Raymond 1925- ... CANR-17
Earlier sketch in CA 97-100
Wilson, Richard Garratt 1928- ... 106
Wilson, Richard Guy 1940- ... CANR-21
Earlier sketch in CA 93-96
Wilson, Richard Lawson 1905-1981
Obituary ... 102
Wilson, Richard Trevor 1938- ... 118
Wilson, Richard W(hittingham) 1933- ... 73-76
Wilson, Robert (Edward) 1951- ... 124
Wilson, Robert Anton 1932- ... CANR-18
Earlier sketch in CA 65-68
Wilson, Robert L. 1925- ... CANR-9
Earlier sketch in CA 57-60
Wilson, Robert M(ills) 1929- ... CANR-25
Earlier sketches in CA 23-24R, CANR-9
Wilson, Robert M. 1944- ... CANR-2
Earlier sketch in CA 49-52
See also CLC 7, 9
Wilson, Robert McLachlan 1916- ... 109
Wilson, Robert N(eal) 1924- ... 17-18R
Wilson, Robert Renbert 1898-1975 ... CANR-23
Earlier sketch in CA 45-48
Wilson, Robin Scott 1928- ... 101
Wilson, Robley (Conant), Jr. 1930- ... CANR-14
Earlier sketch in CA 77-80
Wilson, Rodney N. Usher
See Usher-Wilson, Rodney N.
Wilson, Roger Burdett 1919- ... 45-48
Wilson, Ron(ald William) 1941- ... 112
See also SATA 38
Wilson, Ronald E(merson) 1932- ... 105
Wilson, (Edward) Ross (Armitage) 1914- ... 7-8R
Wilson, Samuel, Jr. 1911- ... CANR-6
Earlier sketch in CA 53-56
Wilson, Sandra 1944- ... 102
Wilson, Sarah 1934- ... SATA-50
Wilson, Sloan 1920- ... CANR-1
Earlier sketch in CA 1R
See also CLC 32
Wilson, Snoo 1948- ... 69-72
See also CLC 33
Wilson, Steve 1943- ... 73-76
Wilson, Theodore A(llen) 1940- ... 37-40R
Wilson, Thomas C(ave) 1907-1984
Obituary ... 112
Wilson, Thomas Williams, Jr. 1912- ... CANR-3
Earlier sketch in CA 7-8R
Wilson, Tom 1931- ... 106
See also SATA 30, 33
Wilson, Trevor (Gordon) 1928- ... 53-56
Wilson, W(illiam) Harmon 1905- ... 37-40R
Wilson, Walt(er N.) 1939- ... 69-72
See also SATA 14
Wilson, Wesley M. 1927- ... 11-12R
Wilson, Wilfrid George 1910- ... CAP-2
Earlier sketch in CA 21-22
Wilson, William A(lbert) 1933- ... 105
Wilson, William E(dward) 1906-1988 ... CANR-2
Obituary ... 125
Earlier sketch in CA 5-6R
Wilson, William H(enry) 1935- ... 15-16R
Wilson, William J. 1935- ... CANR-1
Earlier sketch in CA 45-48
Wilson, William P. 1922- ... 124
Wilson, William Ritchie 1911- ... 41-44R
Wilson, William S(mith) 1932- ... 81-84
See also CLC 49
Wilson, Woodrow 1856-1924 ... DLB-47
Wilson, Z. Vance 1950- ... 120
Wilson-Kastner, Patricia 1944- ... 126
Wilt, Fred(erick Loren) 1920- ... CANR-9
Earlier sketch in CA 57-60
Wilt, Judith 1941- ... CANR-12
Earlier sketch in CA 57-60
Wiltgen, Ralph M(ichael) 1921- ... CANR-11
Earlier sketch in CA 25-28R
Wilton, (James) Andrew (Rutley) 1942- ... 97-100
Wilton, Elizabeth 1937- ... 69-72
See also SATA 14
Wiltse, Charles M(aurice) 1907- ... CANR-3
Earlier sketch in CA 3R
Wiltse, David 1940- ... CANR-22
Earlier sketch in CA 105
Wiltsee, Joseph L. 1920- ... 110
Wiltz, Chris(tine) 1948- ... CANR-24
Earlier sketch in CA 106
Wiltz, John Edward 1930- ... 11-12R
Wilwerding, Walter Joseph 1891-1966 ... CAP-1
Earlier sketch in CA 15-16
See also SATA 9
Wimmer, Larry T(urley) 1935- ... 101
Wimsatt, James I(rving) 1927- ... CANR-13
Earlier sketch in CA 61-64
Wimsatt, W(illiam) K(urtz), Jr.
1907-1975 ... CANR-3
Obituary ... 61-64
Earlier sketch in CA 1R
See also DLB 63
Winans, A(llan) D(avis, Jr.) 1936- ... CANR-12
Earlier sketch in CA 57-60
Winans, Edgar Vincent 1930- ... 5-6R
Winant, Fran 1943- ... 53-56
Winawer, Bonnie P. (Josephs) 1938- ... 17-18R
Wincelberg, Shimon 1924- ... 45-48
Winch, D(avid) M(onk) 1933- ... 45-48
Winch, Donald N. 1935- ... 123
Winch, John
See Campbell, (Gabrielle) Margaret (Vere)
Winch, Michael Bluett 1907- ... CAP-1
Earlier sketch in CA 11-12
Winch, Peter G(uy) 1926- ... 29-32R
Winch, Robert F(rancis) 1911-1977 ... CANR-24
Earlier sketch in CA 25-28R
Winch, Terence 1945- ... 93-96
Winchell, Carol Ann 1936- ... CANR-7
Earlier sketch in CA 61-64
Winchell, Constance M(abel) 1896-1983 ... CAP-1
Obituary ... 109
Earlier sketch in CA 9-10
Winchell, Wallace 1914- ... 53-56
Winchell, Walter 1897-1972 ... 101
Obituary ... 33-36R
See also DLB 29
Winchester, A(lbert) M(cCombs) 1908- ... 41-44R
Winchester, Clarence 1895-1981 Obituary ... 104
Winchester, James H(ugh) 1917-1985 ... 17-18R
Obituary ... 117
See also SATA 30, 45
Winchester, Otis 1933- ... 21-22R
Winchester, Simon 1944- ... 107
Winckler, Paul A(lbert) 1926- ... 102
Wind, Edgar 1900-1971 Obituary ... 104
Wind, Herbert Warren 1916- ... CANR-6
Earlier sketch in CA 2R
Windal, Floyd, W(esley) 1930- ... 11-12R
Windchy, Eugene G. 1930- ... 41-44R
Windeler, Robert 1944- ... 102
Winder, Alvin E. 1923- ... 93-96
Winder, George Herbert 1895- ... CAP-1
Earlier sketch in CA 11-12
Winder, Mavis Areta 1907- ... 21-22R
Winder, R(ichard) Bayly 1920-1988 ... 17-18R
Obituary ... 126
Winders, Gertrude Hecker ... CANR-6
Earlier sketch in CA 4R
See also SATA 3
Windham, Basil
See Wodehouse, P(elham) G(renville)
Windham, Donald 1920- ... CANR-6
Earlier sketch in CA 2R
See also DLB 6
Windham, Douglas M(acArthur) 1943- ... 29-32R
Windham, Joan 1904- ... 21-22R
Windham, Kathryn T(ucker) 1918- ... CANR-11
Earlier sketch in CA 69-72
See also SATA 14
Windle, William Frederick 1898-1985 ... 108
Obituary ... 115
Windley, Charles Ellis 1942- ... 65-68
Windmiller, Marshall 1924- ... 21-22R
Windmuller, John P. 1923- ... CANR-10
Earlier sketch in CA 25-28R
Windolph, F(rancis) Lyman 1889-1978 ... 41-44R
Windrow, Martin (Clive) 1944- Brief entry ... 110
Windsor, Annie
See Shull, Margaret Anne Wyse
Windsor, Claire
See Hamerstrom, Frances
Windsor, Duane 1947- ... 111
Windsor, Duke of
See Edward VIII
Windsor, Gerard (Charles) 1944- ... 124
Windsor, Merrill C(ranston, Jr.) 1924- ... 113
Windsor, Patricia (Frances) 1938- ... CANR-19
Earlier sketches in CA 49-52, CANR-4
See also SATA 30
Windsor, Philip 1935- ... CANR-8
Earlier sketch in CA 5-6R
Windsor, Rex
See Armstrong, Douglas Albert
Windsor, Rudolph R. 1935- Brief entry ... 107
Windsor, (Bessie) Wallis Warfield (Spencer)
Simpson 1896-1986 Obituary ... 119
Windsor-Richards, Arthur (Bedlington)
1904- ... CAP-1
Earlier sketch in CA 11-12
Wine, Dick
See Posner, Richard
Wine, Sherwin T. 1928- ... 93-96
Winearls, Jane 1908- ... 103
Wineberg, Henry J. 1905(?)-1983
Obituary ... 109
Winebrenner, D(aniel) Kenneth 1908- ... CAP-1
Earlier sketch in CA 9-10
Winegarten, Renee 1922- ... 65-68
Winehouse, Irwin 1922- ... 11-12R
Winek, Charles L(eone) 1936- ... 65-68
Winer, Elihu 1914- Brief entry ... 111
Winer, Richard 1929- ... CANR-12
Earlier sketch in CA 73-76
Wines, Roger (Andrew) 1933- ... 23-24R
Winetrout, Kenneth 1912- ... 23-24R
Winfield, Arthur M.
See Stratemeyer, Edward L.
Winfield, Edna
See Stratemeyer, Edward L.
Winfield, Fairlee E(lizabeth) 1929- ... 118
Winfield, Gerald Freeman 1908-1984
Obituary ... 113
Winfield, Leigh
See Youngberg, Norma Ione (Rhoads)
Winfrey, Dorman H(ayward) 1924- ... 17-18R
Winfrey, John Crawford 1935- ... 57-60
Winfrey, Lee 1932- ... 69-72
Wing, Cliff W(aldron), Jr. 1922- ... 49-52
Wing, Donald G(oddard) 1904-1972
Obituary ... 37-40R
Wing, Frances (Scott) 1907- ... CAP-1
Earlier sketch in CA 17-18
Wing, George Douglas 1921- ... 17-18R
Wing, J. K. 1923- ... 29-32R
Wing, Jennifer Patai 1942- ... 57-60
Wing, R. L.
See Aero, Rita
Wing, Willis Kingsley 1899-1985 Obituary ... 116
Wingate, (Martha) Anne (Guice) 1943- ... 116
Wingate, Gifford W(endel) 1925- ... 65-68
Wingate, Isabel B(arnum) 1901-1987 ... 23-24R
Obituary ... 122
Wingate, John (Allan) 1920- ... CANR-24
Earlier sketch in CA 77-80
Wingate, John Williams 1899- ... 11-12R
Wingenbach, Charles E.
See Wingenbach, Gregory C(harles)
Wingenbach, Gregory C(harles) 1938- ... 13-14R
Winger, Fred E. 1912- ... 15-16R
Winger, Howard W(oodrow) 1914- ... CANR-7
Earlier sketch in CA 19-20R
Wingert, Paul S. 1900(?)-1974 Obituary ... 53-56
Wingfield, Sheila Claude 1906- Brief entry ... 108
Wingfield Digby, George Frederick 1911- ... CAP-1
Earlier sketch in CA 11-12
Wingler, Hans M(aria) 1920- ... CANR-14
Earlier sketch in CA 29-32R
Wingo, E(lvis) Otha 1934- ... 37-40R
Wingo, Glenn Max 1913- ... 5-6R
Wingo, T(ullius) Lowdon, Jr. 1923- ... 23-24R
Wingo, Walter (Scott) 1931- ... 81-84
Wingren, Gustaf F(redrik) 1910- ... 15-16R
Winick, Charles 1922- Brief entry ... 109
Winick, Myron 1929- ... 107
Winick, Steven 1944- ... 61-64
Wink, Richard L(ee) 1930- ... 93-96
Wink, Walter Philip 1935- ... CANR-15
Earlier sketch in CA 37-40R
Winkelman, Donald M. 1934- ... 41-44R
Winkler, Allan M(ichael) 1945- ... 81-84
Winkler, Anthony C. 1942- ... 123
Winkler, Bee (Finkelberg) 1919- ... 15-16R
Winkler, Erhard M(ario) 1921- ... 89-92
Winkler, Franz E. 1907- ... 7-8R
Winkler, Henry R(alph) 1916- ... CANR-10
Earlier sketch in CA 17-18R
Winkler, Paul 1898-1982 Obituary ... 107
Winkler, Win Ann 1935- ... 73-76
Winkless, Nels(on Brock) III 1934- ... 57-60
Winks, Donald 1928- ... 25-28R
Winks, Robin William 1930- ... CANR-3
Earlier sketch in CA 5-6R
Winn, Albert Curry 1921- ... 106
Winn, Alison
See Wharmby, Margot
Winn, Charles S. 1932- ... CANR-23
Earlier sketch in CA 69-72
Winn, Chris 1952- ... 117
See also SATA 42
Winn, Ira Jay 1929- ... 57-60
Winn, James Anderson 1947- ... 120
Winn, Janet Bruce 1928- ... 105
See also SATA 43
Winn, Laura Rocke 1902- ... CAP-1
Earlier sketch in CA 13-14
Winn, Marie 1936(?)- ... 111
See also SATA 38
Winn, Ralph Bubrich 1895- ... 5-6R
Winn, Rowland (Denys Guy) 1916-1984
Obituary ... 114
Winn, Wilkins B(owdre) 1928- ... 49-52
Winnegrad, Mark Harris 1948- ... 77-80
Winner, Anna K(ennedy) 1900- ... 29-32R
Winner, Irene P(ortis) 1923- ... CANR-14
Earlier sketch in CA 41-44R
Winner, Percy 1899-1974 Obituary ... 45-48
Winner, Thomas G(ustav) 1917- ... CANR-15
Earlier sketch in CA 37-40R
Winner, Viola Hopkins 1928- ... CANR-4
Earlier sketch in CA 53-56
Winnett, Fred Victor 1903- ... 37-40R
Winnett, Thomas 1921- ... CANR-22
Earlier sketches in CA 61-64, CANR-7
Winnick, Karen B(eth) B(inkoff) 1946- ... 73-76
See also SATA 51
Winnicott, Donald (Woods) 1896-1971 ... CAP-1
Earlier sketch in CA 13-14
Winnifrith, Thomas John 1938- ... CANR-25
Earlier sketch in CA 108
Winnikoff, Albert 1930- ... 29-32R
Winnington, Alan 1910(?)-1983 Obituary ... 111
Winokur, Joan Gelman 1935- ... 41-44R
Winokur, Stephen 1941- ... 89-92
Winold, Allen 1929- ... 17-18R
Winsberg, Morton D. 1930- ... 15-16R
Winsborough, Hal (Liman) H. 1932- ... 11-12R
Winsett, Marvin Davis 1902- ... 3R
Winship, Elizabeth 1921- ... 41-44R
Winship, Laurence Leathe 1890-1975
Obituary ... 104
Winslade, William J(oseph) 1941- ... 118
Winslow, Dean Hendricks, Jr.
1934-1972 ... 37-40R
Obituary ... 41-44R
Winslow, Donald
See Zoll, Donald Atwell
Winslow, Gerald A. ... 109
Winslow, John Hathaway 1932- ... 37-40R
Winslow, Martha
See Rickett, Frances
Winslow, Ola Elizabeth 1885(?)-1977 ... CANR-3
Obituary ... 73-76
Earlier sketch in CA 2R
Winslow, Pauline Glen ... CANR-18
Earlier sketch in CA 101
Winslow, Pete
See Winslow, Dean Hendricks, Jr.
Winslow, Robert W(allace) 1940-
Brief entry ... 108
Winslow, Ron(ald A.) 1949- ... 103
Winslow, Thyra Samter 1893-1961
Obituary ... 89-92
Winslowe, John
See Richardson, Gladwell
Winslowe, John R.
See Richardson, Gladwell
Winsor, Justin 1831-1897 ... DLB-47
Winsor, Kathleen 1919- ... 97-100
Winsor, Mary P(ickard) 1943- ... 69-72
Winsor, Roy (William) 1912-1987 ... 65-68
Obituary ... 122
Winspear, Alban Dewes 1899- ... 45-48
Winspear, Violet 1928- ... 122
Winston, Alexander 1909- ... CAP-2
Earlier sketch in CA 25-28
Winston, Carl H. ... 2R
Winston, Clara 1921-1983 ... 25-28R
Obituary ... 113
See also SATA 39
Winston, Daoma 1922- ... CANR-1
Earlier sketch in CA 45-48
Winston, Douglas Garrett ... 41-44R
Winston, Eric V(on) A(rthur) 1942- ... 29-32R
Winston, Henry 1911-1986 Obituary ... 121
Winston, Kenneth I(rwin) 1940- ... 117
Winston, Krishna 1944- ... 104
Winston, Martin Bradley 1948- ... 118
Winston, Michael R(ussell) 1941- ... 113
Winston, Mike
See King, Florence
Winston, R(obert) A(lexander)
1907-1974 ... CAP-2
Obituary ... 49-52
Earlier sketch in CA 25-28
Winston, Richard 1917-1979 ... 25-28R
Obituary ... 93-96
Winston, Sarah 1912- ... 29-32R
Winstone, H(arry) V(ictor) F(rederick)
1926- ... CANR-21
Earlier sketch in CA 104
Wint, Guy 1910-1969 ... CANR-3
Earlier sketch in CA 2R
Winter, Abigail
See Schere, Monroe
Winter, Alice 1919- ... 15-16R
Winter, Bevis (Peter) 1918- ... CANR-8
Earlier sketch in CA 7-8R
Winter, Caryl 1944- ... 117
Winter, Colin O'Brien 1928-1981 Obituary ... 105
Winter, David Brian 1929- ... CANR-20
Earlier sketch in CA 103
Winter, David G(arrett) 1939- ... 57-60
Winter, Denis 1940- ... 118
Winter, Douglas E. 1950- ... 118
Winter, Edward H(enry) 1923- ... 1R
Winter, Elmer L(ouis) 1912- ... 13-14R
Winter, Gibson 1916- ... 49-52
Winter, Ginny Linville 1925- ... CANR-1
Earlier sketch in CA 4R
Winter, Gordon 1912- ... CANR-14
Earlier sketch in CA 77-80
Winter, Herbert R(einhold) 1928- ... 45-48
Winter, J(erry) Alan 1937- ... 41-44R
Winter, J. M. 1945- ... 73-76
Winter, John F. 1913- ... 104
Winter, Keith 1906-1983 Obituary ... 109
Winter, Klaus 1928- ... 29-32R
Winter, Leslie 1940- ... CANR-6
Earlier sketch in CA 1R
Winter, Michael Morgan 1930- ... CAP-1
Earlier sketch in CA 11-12
Winter, Milo (Kendall) 1888-1956 ... SATA-21
Winter, Nathan H. 1926- ... 21-22R
Winter, Paula Cecelia 1929- ... 107
See also SATA 48
Winter, R. R.
See Winterbotham, R(ussell) R(obert)
Winter, Ralph K(arl, Jr.) 1935- ... 122
Brief entry ... 118
Winter, Roger 1931- ... 37-40R
Winter, Ruth (Nancy G.) 1930- ... 37-40R
Winter, William D(avid) 1927- ... 25-28R
Winter, William O(rville) 1918- ... 49-52
Winterbotham, F(rederick) W(illiam)
1897- ... 57-60
Winterbotham, R(ussell) R(obert)
1904-1971 ... 3R
Obituary ... 103
See also SATA 10
Winterbotham, Russ
See Winterbotham, R(ussell) R(obert)
Winterfeld, Henry 1901- ... 77-80
Wintergreen, John P.
See Ryskind, Morrie
Wintergreen, Warren
See Adamson, Joseph III
Winterich, John 1891-1970 Obituary ... 29-32R
Winternitz, Emanuel 1898-1983 ... CANR-20
Obituary ... 110
Earlier sketch in CA 25-28R
Winterowd, W. Ross 1930- ... 17-18R
Winters, Anne 1939- ... 122
Winters, Bayla 1921- ... 21-22R

Winters, Bernice
See Winters, Bayla
Winters, Catherine (Mary) 1951- 118
Winters, Donald L(ee) 1935- 29-32R
Winters, Francis Xavier 1933- 61-64
Winters, Janet Lewis 1899- CAP-1
Earlier sketch in CA 9-10
Winters, John D(avid) 1917- 11-12R
Winters, Jon
See Cross, Gilbert B.
Winters, Marian 1924-1978 101
Obituary 81-84
Winters, Marjorie
See Henri, Florette
Winters, Mike 1930- 119
Winters, Rosemary
See Breckler, Rosemary
Winters, Shelley
See Schrift, Shirley
Winters, (Arthur) Yvor 1900-1968 CAP-1
Obituary 25-28R
Earlier sketch in CA 11-12
See also DLB 48
See also CLC 4, 8, 32
Winterton, Gayle
See Adams, William Taylor
Winterton, Paul 1908- CANR-6
Earlier sketch in CA 5-6R
Winther, Barbara 1926- CANR-17
Earlier sketch in CA 97-100
Winther, Oscar Osburn 1903-1970 CANR-2
Earlier sketch in CA 3R
Winther, Sophus Keith 1893- 5-6R
Winthrop, Elizabeth
See Mahony, Elizabeth Winthrop
Winthrop, Henry 1910- 73-76
Winthrop, John 1588-1649 DLB-24, 30
Winthrop, John, Jr. 1606-1676 DLB-24
Wintle, Anne 29-32R
Wintle, Justin (Beecham) 1949- CANR-13
Earlier sketch in CA 77-80
Winton, Calhoun 1927- 11-12R
Winton, Chester Allen 1941- 89-92
Winton, Harry N(athaniel) M(cQuillian)
1907- 41-44R
Winton, John
See Pratt, John
Winton, Kate Barber 1882(?)-1974
Obituary 53-56
Wintrobe, Maxwell M(yer) 1901-1986
Obituary 121
Wintterle, John F(rancis) 1927- 29-32R
Wintz, Jack 1936- 109
Winwar, Frances 1900- 89-92
Winward, Stephen Frederick 1911- 11-12R
Winward, (Richard) Walter 1938- 105
Wippel, John Francis 1933- 114
Wippler, Migene Gonzalez
See Gonzalez-Wippler, Migene
Wirkus, Tom E(dward) 1933- 37-40R
Wirsing, Marie E(milia) 1931- 45-48
Wirt, Frederick Marshall 1924- 112
Wirt, Sherwood Eliot 1911- CANR-15
Earlier sketch in CA 41-44R
Wirt, William 1772-1834 DLB-37
Wirt, Winola Wells 1905(?)-1986 93-96
Obituary 120
Wirtenberg, Patricia Z(arrella) 1932- 61-64
See also SATA 10
Wirth, Arthur G. 1919- CANR-10
Earlier sketch in CA 21-22R
Wirth, Beverly 1938- 118
Wirth, John D(avis) 1936- CANR-26
Earlier sketch in CA 29-32R
Wirth, Niklaus 1934- CANR-21
Earlier sketch in CA 105
Wirth, Thomas 1941- 117
Wirths, Claudine (Turner) G(ibson) 1926- 126
Wirtz, (William) Willard 1912- 101
Wisberg, Aubrey 97-100
Wisberg, Marian Aline 1923- 109
Wisbeski, Dorothy (Gross) 1929- 11-12R
Wisbey, Herbert Andrew, Jr. 1919- 13-14R
Wisdom, (Arthur) John (Terence Dibben)
1904- 25-28R
Wisdom, Kenny
See Grogan, Emmett
Wisdome, Thomas
See Dunbar, Charles Stuart
Wise, Arthur 1923- 9-10R
Wise, Charles C(onrad), Jr. 1913- CANR-9
Earlier sketch in CA 21-22R
Wise, David 1930- CANR-2
Earlier sketch in CA 2R
Wise, Gene 1936- 93-96
Wise, Helen Dickerson 1928- Brief entry 106
Wise, Herbert H(erschel) 1928- 108
Wise, James Waterman 1901-1983
Obituary 111
Wise, John 1652-1725 DLB-24
Wise, John E(dward) 1905-1974 CAP-1
Obituary 49-52
Earlier sketch in CA 15-16
Wise, Leonard 77-80
Wise, Raymond L. 1895- 21-22R
Wise, S(ydney) F(rancis) 1924- CANR-16
Earlier sketch in CA 21-22R
Wise, Stephen S(amuel) 1874-1949
Brief entry 117
Wise, Terence 1935- 89-92
Wise, William 1923- CANR-6
Earlier sketch in CA 15-16R
See also SATA 4
Wise, Winifred E. 25-28R
See also SATA 2
Wisely, Rae 1938- 106
Wiseman, Adele 1928- 77-80
Wiseman, Ann (Sayre) 1926- CANR-9
Earlier sketch in CA 65-68
See also SATA 31
Wiseman, Anne Marie (Murray) 1932- 5-6R
Wiseman, B(ernard) 1922- CANR-24
Earlier sketches in CA 5-6R, CANR-8
See also SATA 4
Wiseman, Christopher S(tephen) 1936- 113
Wiseman, David 1916- 109
See also SATA 40, 43
Wiseman, Donald John 1918- 89-92
Wiseman, Francis Jowett 1905- CAP-1
Earlier sketch in CA 13-14
Wiseman, Frederick 1930- CLC-20
Wiseman, James R(ichard) 1934- CANR-1
Earlier sketch in CA 45-48
Wiseman, Robert F(rederick) 1935- 77-80
Wiseman, T(imothy) P(eter) 1940- CANR-18
Earlier sketches in CA 45-48, CANR-1
Wiseman, Thomas 1931- 25-28R
Wisenthal, J. L. 1940- 126
Wiser, William 37-40R
Wish, Harvey 1909-1968 CANR-3
Earlier sketch in CA 2R
Wishard, Armin 1941- 37-40R
Wishart, David J(ohn) 1946- 124
Brief entry 118
Wishart, E(rnest) E(dward) 1902-1987
Obituary 123
Wishart, Henry
See Shepherd, Robert Henry Wishart
Wiskemann, Elizabeth ?-1971 Obituary 111
Wisler, G(ary) Clifton 1950- SATA-46
Wisler, Gene C(harles) 1920- 11-12R
Wisloff, Carl Johan Fredrik 1908- CAP-1
Earlier sketch in CA 13-14
Wismer, Donald (Richard) 1946- 109
Wisner, Bill
See Wisner, William L.
Wisner, George 1812-1849 DLB-43
Wisner, William L. 1914(?)-1983 111
Obituary 110
See also SATA 42
Wisneski, Henry 1940- 57-60
Wisse, Ruth R(oskies) 1936- 37-40R
Wissmann, Ruth Leslie CANR-2
Earlier sketch in CA 7-8R
Wister, John C(aspar) 1887-1982
Obituary 109
Wister, Owen 1860-1938 Brief entry 108
See also DLB 9
See also TCLC 21
Wistrich, Robert Solomon 1945- 107
Wiswall, F(rank) L(awrence), Jr. 1939- 29-32R
Wiswell, Ella Lury 1909- 111
Wiswell, Thomas George 1910- CANR-2
Earlier sketch in CA 7-8R
Wiswell, Tom
See Wiswell, Thomas George
Witchel, Dinah B(rown) 1936- 105
Witcover, Jules 1927- 25-28R
Witcutt, William Purcell 1907- CAP-1
Earlier sketch in CA 11-12
Witemeyer, Hugh 1939- 25-28R
Witham, (Phillip) Ross 1917- 105
See also SATA 37
Witham, W(illiam) Tasker 1914- 15-16R
Witheford, Hubert 1921- 102
Witheridge, Elizabeth P(lumb) 1907- 97-100
Withers, Carl A. 1900-1970 73-76
See also SATA 14
Withers, E. L.
See Potter, G(eorge) W(illiam) (Jr.)
Withers, Josephine 1938- 101
Withers, Sara Cook 1924- 17-18R
Withers, William 1905-1987 13-14R
Obituary 121
Witherspoon, Frances 1887(?)-1973
Obituary 45-48
Witherspoon, Irene Murray 1913- CANR-1
Earlier sketch in CA 4R
Witherspoon, John 1723-1794 DLB-31
Witherspoon, Mary Elizabeth 1919- 77-80
Witherspoon, Naomi Long
See Madgett, Naomi Long
Witherspoon, Thomas E. 1934- 81-84
Withey, J(oseph) A(nthony) 1918- 25-28R
Withim, Gloria 1929- 112
Withington, William Adriance 1924- CANR-14
Earlier sketch in CA 41-44R
Withorn, Ann 1947- 125
Withrow, Dorothy E. 1910- 21-22R
Witkacy
See Witkiewicz, Stanislaw Ignacy
Witke, Roxane 1938- 69-72
Witker, Kristi 77-80
Witkiewicz, Stanislaw Ignacy 1885-1939
Brief entry 105
See also TCLC 8
Witkin, Erwin 1926- 37-40R
Witkin, Herman A. 1916-1979 CANR-1
Earlier sketch in CA 2R
Witkin, Lee D(aniel) 1935-1984 Obituary 114
Witkin-Lanoil, Georgia Hope 1943- 120
Witmer, Helen L(eland) 1898-1979 CAP-2
Obituary 89-92
Earlier sketch in CA 25-28
Witt, Harold (Vernon) 1923- CANR-17
Earlier sketches in CA 3R, CANR-1
Witt, Howell Arthur John 1920- 109
Witt, Hubert 1935- CANR-12
Earlier sketch in CA 65-68
Witt, James F. 1937- 89-92
Witt, John (Clermont) 1907-1982
Obituary 106
Witt, Reginald Eldred 1907-1980 37-40R
Obituary 97-100
Witt, Ronald Gene 1932- 126
Witt, Shirley Hill 1934- CANR-5
Earlier sketch in CA 53-56
See also SATA 17
Witte, Ann Dryden 1942- CANR-26
Earlier sketch in CA 107
Witte, Glenna Finley 1925- CANR-26
Earlier sketches in CA 15-16R, CANR-10
See also AITN 1
Witte, John 1948- 93-96
Wittels, Harriet Joan 1938- 107
See also SATA 31
Witten, Herbert F. 1920- 5-6R
Witten, Ian H(ugh) 1947- 111
Wittenberg, Judith Bryant 1938- 102
Wittenberg, Philip 1895-1987 CAP-2
Obituary 122
Earlier sketch in CA 23-24
Wittenberg, Rudolph M. 1906-1986 CANR-22
Earlier sketch in CA 69-72
Wittermans, Elizabeth (Pino) 17-18R
Witters, Weldon L. 1929- 93-96
Wittfogel, Karl A(ugust) 1896-1988
Obituary 125
Wittgenstein, Ludwig (Josef Johann)
1889-1951 Brief entry 113
Wittich, Claus 1932- 113
Wittich, Walter A(rno) 1910- 49-52
Wittig, Alice J(osephine) 1929- 101
Wittig, Monique 1935- Brief entry 116
See also CLC 22
Witting, Clifford 1907- 4R
Wittke, Carl (Frederick) 1892-1971
Obituary 29-32R
Wittkofski, Joseph Nicholas 1912- 9-10R
Wittkower, Rudolf 1901-1971 Obituary 33-36R
Wittkowski, Wolfgang 1925- CANR-24
Earlier sketches in CA 61-64, CANR-8
Wittliff, William D. 1940- 123
Wittlin, Alma S(tephanie) 45-48
Wittlin, Jozef 1896-1976 CANR-3
Obituary 65-68
Earlier sketch in CA 49-52
See also CLC 25
Wittlin, Thaddeus (Andrew) 1909- CANR-2
Earlier sketch in CA 45-48
Wittman, Sally (Anne Christensen) 1941- 107
See also SATA 30
Wittmer, Joe 1937- 45-48
Wittner, Lawrence S(tephen) 1941- 25-28R
Witton, Dorothy 73-76
Witton-Davies, Carl(yle) 1913- 9-10R
Wittreich, Joseph Anthony, Jr. 1939- CANR-12
Earlier sketch in CA 29-32R
Wittrock, M(erlin) C(arl) 1931- CANR-2
Earlier sketch in CA 49-52
Wittwer, Sylvan Harold 1917- 114
Witty, Helen E. S(troop) 1921- 105
Witty, Paul 1898-1976 73-76
Obituary 65-68
See also SATA 30, 50
Witty, Robert G(ee) 1906- CAP-2
Earlier sketch in CA 23-24
Witucke, Virginia 1937- 37-40R
Witze, Claude 1909(?)-1977 Obituary 73-76
Wixman, Ronald 1947- 122
Wixom, Hartt 1933- 120
Wizard, Mariann G(arner) 1946- 37-40R
Wobbe, R(oland) A(rthur) 1938- 102
Woddis, Hillel Chayim Keith 1914-
Brief entry 114
Woddis, Jack
See Woddis, Hillel Chayim Keith
Wodehouse, Lawrence 1934- CANR-19
Earlier sketches in CA 53-56, CANR-4
Wodehouse, P(elham) G(renville)
1881-1975 CANR-3
Obituary 57-60
Earlier sketch in CA 45-48
See also SATA 22
See also DLB 34
See also CLC 1, 2, 5, 10, 22
See also SSC 2
See also AITN 2
Woden, George
See Slaney, George Wilson
Wodge, Dreary
See Gorey, Edward (St. John)
Wodhams, (Herbert) Jack 1931- 115
Woebcke, Mary-Jane 1933- 25-28R
Woehr, Richard (Arthur) 1942- 57-60
Woehrlin, William F(rederick) 1928- 45-48
Woelfel, James W(arren) 1937- 41-44R
Woelfl, Paul A(loysius) 1913- 17-18R
Woerner, Karl Heinrich 1910-1969
Obituary 110
Woessner, Nina C. 1933- 29-32R
Woessner, Warren (Dexter) 1944- CANR-14
Earlier sketch in CA 37-40R
Woestemeyer, Ina Faye
See Van Noppen, Ina (Faye)
W(oestemeyer)
Woetzel, Robert K(urt) 1930- CANR-6
Earlier sketch in CA 5-6R
Wofford, Azile (May) 1896- 5-6R
Wofsey, Marvin M(ilton) 1913- 105
Wogaman, J(ohn) Philip 1932- CANR-20
Earlier sketch in CA 25-28R
Wogaman, Philip
See Wogaman, J(ohn) Philip
Wohl, Gerald 1934- 19-20R
Wohl, James P(aul) 1937- 77-80
Wohl, Paul 1901(?)-1985 Obituary 115
Wohl, Robert 1936- 104
Wohlberg, Meg 1905- SATA-41
Wohlgelernter, Maurice 1921- CANR-6
Earlier sketch in CA 15-16R
Wohl-Musciny, Ludwig von
See de Wohl, Louis
Wohlmuth, Ed 1935- 124
Wohlrabe, Raymond A. 1900-1977 CANR-3
Earlier sketch in CA 4R
See also SATA 4
Wohmann, Gabriele 1932- DLB-75
Woititz, Janet G. CANR-19
Earlier sketch in CA 101
Woito, Robert (Severin) 1937- 120
Woiwode, L.
See Woiwode, Larry (Alfred)
Woiwode, Larry (Alfred) 1941- CANR-16
Earlier sketch in CA 73-76
See also DLB 6
See also CLC 6, 10
Wojciechowska, Maia (Teresa) 1927- CANR-4
Earlier sketch in CA 11-12R
See also SATA 1, 28
See also SAAS 1
See also CLC 26
See also CLR 1
Wojtyla, Karol
See John Paul II, Pope
Wolberg, Lewis Robert 1905-1988 CANR-19
Obituary 124
Earlier sketches in CA 45-48, CANR-2
Wolcott, Harry F(letcher) 1929- 65-68
Wolcott, Leonard Thompson CANR-11
Earlier sketch in CA 13-14R
Wolcott, Patty 1929- 57-60
See also SATA 14
Wolcott, Roger 1679-1767 DLB-24
Wold, Allen L. 1943- CANR-22
Earlier sketch in CA 105
Wold, Jo Anne 1938- 61-64
See also SATA 30
Wold, Marguerite Hurrey 1914- 53-56
Wold, Ruth 1923- 37-40R
Woldendorp, R(ichard) 1927- CANR-12
Earlier sketch in CA 29-32R
Woldin, Beth Weiner 1955- 102
See also SATA 34
Woldin, Judd 1925- Brief entry 122
Wolf, Adolf Hungry
See Hungry Wolf, Adolf
Wolf, Arnold Jacob 1924- 29-32R
Wolf, Arnold Veryl 1916-1975 Obituary 104
Wolf, Barbara Herrman 1932- 57-60
Wolf, Bernard 1930- Brief entry 115
See also SATA 37
Wolf, Charlotte (Elizabeth) 1926- 29-32R
Wolf, Christa 1929- 85-88
See also DLB 75
See also CLC 14, 29
Wolf, Deborah Goleman 1938- 97-100
Wolf, Donald J(oseph) 1929- 13-14R
Wolf, Edwin II 1911- CANR-4
Earlier sketch in CA 2R
Wolf, Eric R(obert) 1923- 19-20R
Wolf, Frank 1940- 57-60
Wolf, Frank L(ouis) 1924- 57-60
Wolf, Fred Alan 1934- 115
Wolf, Frederick
See Dempewolff, Richard F(rederic)
Wolf, George 1890(?)-1980 Obituary 97-100
Wolf, George D(ugan) 1923- 29-32R
Wolf, Harold A. 1923- 15-16R
Wolf, Harvey 1935- 57-60
Wolf, Hazel Catharine 1907- 7-8R
Wolf, Herbert C(hristian) 1923- 15-16R
Wolf, Jack C(lifford) 1922- 57-60
Wolf, Jacqueline 1928- 109
Wolf, John B(aptist) 1907- 11-12R
Wolf, Karl E(verett) 1921- 17-18R
Wolf, Leonard 1923- CANR-3
Earlier sketch in CA 49-52
Wolf, Marguerite Hurrey 1914- 53-56
Wolf, Marvin J(ules) 1941- 117
Wolf, Michael D(avid) 1953- 121
Wolf, Miriam Bredow 1895- CAP-1
Earlier sketch in CA 9-10
Wolf, Peter (Michael) 1935- 53-56
Wolf, Ray 1948- 107
Wolf, Robert Charles 1955- 109
Wolf, Thomas H(oward) 1916- 69-72
Wolf, William 103
Wolf, William B. 1920- CANR-26
Earlier sketches in CA 19-20R, CANR-10
Wolf, William C(harles), Jr. 1933- 41-44R
Wolf, William J(ohn) 1918- 111
Wolfbein, Seymour L(ouis) 1915- CANR-6
Earlier sketch in CA 13-14R
Wolfe, Alan 1942- 108
Wolfe, Alvin William 1928- 2R
Wolfe, Bernard 1915-1985 CANR-3
Obituary 117
Earlier sketch in CA 3R
Wolfe, Bertram D(avid) 1896-1977 7-8R
Obituary 69-72
Wolfe, Burton H. 1932- 25-28R
See also SATA 5
Wolfe, Charles Keith 1943- CANR-15
Earlier sketch in CA 77-80
Wolfe, Christopher (F.) 1949- 123
Wolfe, Don Marion 1902-1976 Obituary 65-68
Wolfe, (George) Edgar 1906- CAP-2
Earlier sketch in CA 25-28
Wolfe, Elizabeth
See Lederer, Paul Joseph
Wolfe, Gene (Rodman) 1931- CANR-6
Earlier sketch in CA 57-60
See also DLB 8
See also CLC 25
Wolfe, George C. 1954- CLC-49
Wolfe, George Willoughby (Hooper)
1894(?)-1983 Obituary 111

Wolfe, Gerard R(aymond) 1926- CANR-11
Earlier sketch in CA 69-72
Wolfe, Harry Deane 1901-1975 .... 41-44R
Wolfe, Harvey 1938- 45-48
Wolfe, Henry C. 1898(?)-1976 Obituary ... 69-72
Wolfe, Herbert S(now) 1898- CAP-1
Earlier sketch in CA 15-16
Wolfe, J(ames) N(athan) 1927-1988
Obituary 124
Wolfe, James H(astings) 1934- 93-96
Wolfe, John N. 1910(?)-1974 Obituary 53-56
Wolfe, Josephine Brace 1917- 7-8R
Wolfe, Louis 1905- CANR-3
Earlier sketch in CA 5-6R
See also SATA 8
Wolfe, Martin 1920- 37-40R
Wolfe, Michael 1945- 123
Wolfe, Michael
See Williams, Gilbert M.
Wolfe, Peter (Bernard) 1929-1986
Obituary 121
Wolfe, Peter 1933- CANR-8
Earlier sketch in CA 21-22R
Wolfe, Randolph 1946- CANR-20
Earlier sketch in CA 104
Wolfe, Richard J(ames) 1928- 110
Wolfe, Rinna (Evelyn) 1925- 105
See also SATA 38
Wolfe, Ron 1945- 109
Wolfe, Roy I. 1917- 13-14R
Wolfe, Thomas (Clayton) 1900-1938
Brief entry 104
See also DLB 9
See also DLBY 85
See also DLBD 2
See also TCLC 4, 13, 29
Wolfe, Thomas Kennerly, Jr. 1931- CANR-9
Earlier sketch in CA 15-16R
Wolfe, Thomas W. 1914- 93-96
Wolfe, Tom
See Wolfe, Thomas Kennerly, Jr.
See also CLC 1, 2, 9, 15, 35
See also AITN 2
Wolfe, (William) Willard 1936- 93-96
Wolfe, Winifred 1929-1981 .... CANR-10
Obituary 105
Earlier sketch in CA 17-18R
Wolfenden, George
See Beardmore, George
Wolfenden, John Frederick 1906-1985 106
Obituary 114
Wolfenstein, E. Victor 1940- 21-22R
Wolfenstein, Martha 1911(?)-1976
Obituary 69-72
Wolfert, Helen 1904- CAP-2
Earlier sketch in CA 17-18
Wolff, Anthony 1938- 49-52
Wolff, (Jenifer) Ashley 1956- 118
See also SATA 50
Wolff, Charlotte 1904-1986 .... CANR-15
Obituary 120
Earlier sketch in CA 37-40R
Wolff, Cynthia Griffin 1936- 49-52
Wolff, David
See Maddow, Ben
Wolff, Diane 1945- 77-80
See also SATA 27
Wolff, Ernst, 1910- 73-76
Wolff, Geoffrey (Ansell) 1937- 29-32R
See also CLC 41
Wolff, Helen 1906- 117
Brief entry 113
Wolff, Janet 1943- 77-80
Wolff, Janet L(oeb) 1924- 5-6R
Wolff, John U(lrich) 1932- CANR-18
Earlier sketch in CA 102
Wolff, Jurgen M(ichael) 1948- 57-60
Wolff, Konrad (Martin) 1907- 37-40R
Wolff, Kurt H(einrich) 1912- CANR-17
Earlier sketches in CA 49-52, CANR-1
Wolff, Maritta 1918- 17-18R
Wolff, Mary Evaline 1887-1964 Obituary 116
Wolff, Michael 1930- CANR-19
Earlier sketch in CA 25-28R
Wolff, Miles 1945- CANR-14
Earlier sketch in CA 73-76
Wolff, Richard D(avid) 1942- 73-76
Wolff, Robert Jay 1905-1977 .... 25-28R
Obituary 73-76
See also SATA 10
Wolff, Robert Lee 1915-1980 Obituary 102
Wolff, Robert Paul 1933- 103
Wolff, Ruth 1909(?)-1972 Obituary 37-40R
Wolff, Sonia
See Levitin, Sonia (Wolff)
Wolff, Tobias (Jonathan Ansell) 1945- 117
Brief entry 114
See also CLC 39
Wolff, Victoria 1910- 111
Wolff, Virginia Euwer 1937- 107
Wolffe, B. P.
See Wolffe, Bertram (Percy)
Wolffe, Bertram (Percy) 1923(?)-1988
Obituary 124
Wolff-Salin, Mary 1932- 122
Wolfgang, Marvin E(ugene) 1924- 7-8R
Wolfinger, Raymond E(dwin) 1931-
Brief entry 112
Wolfle, Dael (Lee) 1906- 49-52
Wolfman, Augustus 1908(?)-1974
Obituary 53-56
Wolfman, Bernard 1924- 41-44R
Wolf-Phillips, Leslie 1929- 23-24R
Wolfram, Walter A. 1941- 29-32R
Wolfskill, George 1921- CANR-1
Earlier sketch in CA 2R
Wolfson, Harry Austryn 1887-1974 ...... CAP-2
Obituary 53-56
Earlier sketch in CA 19-20
Wolfson, Murray 1927- 17-18R
Wolfson, P(incus) J. 1903- 7-8R
Wolfson, Randy M(eyers) 1952- 120
Wolfson, Robert J(oseph) 1925- 93-96
Wolfson, Susan 1947- 120
Wolfson, Victor 1910- 33-36R
Wolgast, Elizabeth H(ankins) 1929- 113
Wolgensinger, Bernard 1935- 37-40R
Wolins, Leroy 1927- 107
Wolitzer, Hilma 1930- CANR-18
Earlier sketch in CA 65-68
See also SATA 31
See also CLC 17
Wolitzer, Meg 1959- CANR-18
Earlier sketch in CA 107
Wolk, Allan 1936- 77-80
Wolkers, Jan (Hendrik) 1925- Brief entry ... 116
Wolkoff, Judie (Edwards) Brief entry 115
See also SATA 37
Wolkstein, Diane 1942- CANR-14
Earlier sketch in CA 37-40R
See also SATA 7
Woll, Peter 1933- 15-16R
Wollaston, Nicholas 1926- 25-28R
Wolle, Muriel Sibell 1898- CAP-1
Earlier sketch in CA 13-14
Wollheim, Donald A(llen) 1914- CANR-19
Earlier sketches in CA 4R, CANR-1
Wollheim, Richard Arthur 1923- 101
Wollman, Nathaniel 1915- Brief entry 106
Wollstonecraft, Mary 1759-1797 .... DLB-39
Wolman, Benjamin B. 1908- CANR-11
Earlier sketch in CA 15-16R
Wolman, Harold L. 1942- 37-40R
Wolman, William 1927- 2R
Wolny, P.
See Janeczko, Paul B(ryan)
Woloch, Isser 1937- CANR-12
Earlier sketch in CA 29-32R
Woloszynowski, Julian 1898-1978
Obituary 85-88
Wolozin, Harold 1920- 37-40R
Wolpe, Joseph 1915- 17-18R
Wolpert, Stanley A(lbert) 1927- CANR-15
Earlier sketch in CA 23-24R
Wolrige Gordon, Anne 1936- 103
Wolsch, Robert Allen 1925- 57-60
Wolseley, Roland E. 1904- CANR-17
Earlier sketches in CA 2R, CANR-1
Wolsk, David 1930- 23-24R
Wolstein, Benjamin 1922- 11-12R
Wolter, Allan B(ernard) 1913- 106
Wolters, O(liver) W(illiam) 1915- 21-22R
Wolters, Raymond 1938- 29-32R
Wolters, Richard A. 1920- CANR-18
Earlier sketches in CA 7-8R, CANR-3
See also SATA 35
Wolterstorff, Nicholas Paul 1932- 69-72
Woltman, Frederick (Enos) 1905-1970
Obituary 89-92
Wolverton, Robert E(arl) 1925- 37-40R
Wolz, Henry G(eorge) 1905- 106
Womack, Brantly 1947- 114
Womack, David A(lfred) 1933- CANR-7
Earlier sketch in CA 53-56
Womack, Don (L.) 1922- 25-28R
Womack, John, Jr. 1937- 45-48
Womble, Vernon G. 1942(?)-1979
Obituary 89-92
Womer, Frank B(urton) 1921- 45-48
Womersley, Peter (John Walter) 1941- 118
Won, Ko
See Ko, Won
Wonder, Alvin
See Lourie, Dick
Wonder, Stevie
See Morris, Steveland Judkins
See also CLC 12
Wonders, Anne
See Passel, Anne W(onders)
Wonders, William C(lare) 1924- 41-44R
Wondratschek, Wolf 1943- DLB-75
Wondriska, William 1931- CANR-4
Earlier sketch in CA 4R
See also SATA 6
Wong, Bing W. 1922- 73-76
Wong, J(ohn) Y(ue-Wo) 1946- 126
Wong, Jade Snow 1922- 109
See also CLC 17
Wong, Lin Ken 1931- 13-14R
Wong, May 1944- 25-28R
Wong, Molly 1920- 93-96
Wong, Roderick 1932- 65-68
Wonnacott, Paul 1933- 21-22R
Wonnacott, Ronald J(ohnston) 1930- .. CANR-14
Earlier sketch in CA 29-32R
Wonnacott, Thomas H(erbert) 1935- ... CANR-14
Earlier sketch in CA 45-48
Wood, A(rthur) Skevington 1916- CANR-18
Earlier sketches in CA 11-12R, CANR-3
Wood, Abigail
See Marks, Jane (A. Steinberg)
Wood, Allen Tate 1947- 97-100
Wood, Allen W(illiam) 1942- CANR-17
Earlier sketch in CA 29-32R
Wood, Audrey SATA-44, 50
Wood, Audrey 1905-1985 Obituary 118
Wood, Barbara 1947- CANR-15
Earlier sketch in CA 85-88
Wood, Bari 1936- CANR-13
Earlier sketch in CA 81-84
Wood, Barry 1940- 29-32R
Wood, Benjamin 1820-1900 Brief entry 120
See also DLB 23
Wood, Bruce 1943- 57-60
Wood, Bryce 1909-1985(?) CANR-19
Earlier sketch in CA 2R
Wood, Catherine
See Etchison, Birdie L(ee)
Wood, Charles Gerald 1932- 106
See also DLB 13
Wood, Charles Monroe 1944- 125
Wood, Charles Osgood III 1933- 109
Wood, Charles T(uttle) 1933- 17-18R
Wood, Chauncey 1935- 37-40R
Wood, Christopher (Hovelle) 1935- 29-32R
Wood, Christopher 1941- 103
Wood, Clement Biddle 1925- 21-22R
Wood, David 1944- 97-100
Wood, David (Bowne) 1945- 93-96
Wood, David G. 1919- 126
Wood, David M(ichael) 1934- Brief entry ... 109
Wood, Derek Harold 1930- CANR-16
Earlier sketch in CA 93-96
Wood, Don 1945- SATA-44, 50
Wood, Donald 1926- 45-48
Wood, Donna (Marie) 1949- CANR-18
Earlier sketch in CA 97-100
Wood, Dorothy Adkins 1912-1975 ...... CANR-6
Earlier sketch in CA 13-14R
Wood, E(dward) Rudolf 1907- CANR-3
Earlier sketch in CA 11-12R
Wood, Edgar A(llardyce) 1907- 77-80
See also SATA 14
Wood, Elizabeth A(rmstrong) 1912- 25-28R
Wood, Esther
See Brady, Esther Wood
Wood, Forrest G(len) 1931- 25-28R
Wood, Frances Elizabeth 107
See also SATA 34
Wood, Fred M. 1921- CANR-26
Earlier sketches in CA 15-16R, CANR-10
Wood, Frederic C(onger), Jr. 1932-1970 . CAP-2
Earlier sketch in CA 25-28
Wood, Frederick Thomas 1905- CANR-5
Earlier sketch in CA 7-8R
Wood, G(eorge) R(obert) Harding
1878-1968 .... CAP-1
Earlier sketch in CA 9-10
Wood, Gordon R(eid) 1913- 77-80
Wood, Gordon S(tewart) 1933- 25-28R
Wood, Harley Weston 1911- 109
Wood, Harold A(rthur) 1921- 19-20R
Wood, (Elizabeth) Harriet Harvey
See Harvey Wood, (Elizabeth) Harriet
Wood, Herbert Fairlie 1914-1967 110
Obituary 108
Wood, James 1889(?)-1975 Obituary 57-60
Wood, James (Alexander Fraser)
1918-1984 .... CANR-16
Earlier sketches in CA 2R, CANR-1
Wood, James E(dward), Jr. 1922- CANR-12
Earlier sketch in CA 29-32R
Wood, James L(eslie) 1941- CANR-8
Earlier sketch in CA 57-60
Wood, James Playsted 1905- CANR-3
Earlier sketch in CA 9-10R
See also SATA 1
Wood, Janet L(ouise) Sims
See Sims-Wood, Janet L(ouise)
Wood, John A(rmstead, Jr.) 1932- 125
Brief entry 108
Wood, John Thomas 1939- 77-80
Wood, Joyce 1928- 25-28R
Wood, June S(mallwood) 1931- 61-64
Wood, Kenneth 1922- CANR-26
Earlier sketches in CA 69-72, CANR-11
Wood, Kerry
See Wood, Edgar A(llardyce)
Wood, Kirk
See Stahl, Le Roy
Wood, Larry
See Wood, Marylaird
Wood, Laura N.
See Roper, Laura Wood
Wood, Lee Blair 1893-1982 Obituary 106
Wood, Leland Foster 1885- 2R
Wood, Leon J(ames) 1918-1976 ...... CANR-26
Earlier sketch in CA 29-32R
Wood, Leonard C(lair) 1923- 37-40R
Wood, Leslie A(lfred) 1930- 29-32R
Wood, (James) Lew(is) 1928- 65-68
Wood, Linda C(arol) 1945- 110
Wood, Lorna 1913- 69-72
Wood, Margaret (L. E.) 1910- 13-14R
Wood, Margaret I(sabel) 1926- 97-100
Wood, Marion N(ewman) 1909- 61-64
Wood, Mary 1915- 23-24R
Wood, Marylaird CANR-21
Earlier sketch in CA 81-84
Wood, Maurice Arthur Ponsonby 1916- 109
Wood, Michael 1936- 37-40R
Wood, Mrs. Henry 1814-1887 .... DLB-18
Wood, Nancy 1936- CANR-9
Earlier sketch in CA 21-22R
See also SATA 6
Wood, Neal (Norman) 1922- 2R
Wood, Pat
See Baxter, Patricia E. W.
Wood, Paul W(inthrop) 1922- 61-64
Wood, Peggy 1892-1978 Obituary 77-80
Wood, Peter 1930- 93-96
Wood, Peter Weston 1953- 125
Wood, Phyllis Anderson 1923- CANR-14
Earlier sketch in CA 37-40R
See also SATA 30, 33
Wood, R(ichard) Coke 1905-1979 ...... CANR-7
Earlier sketch in CA 53-56
Wood, Ramsay 1943- 103
Wood, Raymund F(rancis) 1911- 61-64
Wood, Robert Coldwell 1923- 3R
Wood, Robert L. 1925- 23-24R
Wood, Robert Paul 1931- CANR-5
Earlier sketch in CA 53-56
Wood, Robert S(tephen) 1938- CANR-7
Earlier sketch in CA 57-60
Wood, Robin
See Wood, Robert Paul
Wood, Ruth C. 37-40R
Wood, Sara
See Bowen-Judd, Sara (Hutton)
Wood, Serry
See Freeman, G(raydon) L(a Verne)
Wood, Susan 1946- 108
Wood, Sydney (Herbert) 1935- 112
Wood, Thomas W(esley), Jr. 1920- 81-84
Wood, Ursula
See Vaughan Williams, Ursula Wood
Wood, Wallace 1927-1981 Obituary 108
See also SATA 33
Wood, Walter Hunt, Sr. 1916(?)-1987
Obituary 124
Wood, William DLB-24
Wood, William P(reston) 1951- 118
Woodall, Corbet 1929(?)-1982 Obituary 106
Woodall, Mary 1901-1988 Obituary 125
Woodall, Ronald 1935- 73-76
Woodard, Bronte 1941(?)-1980 Obituary ... 101
Woodard, Carol 1929- 73-76
See also SATA 14
Woodard, Christopher R. 1913- 13-14R
Woodard, Gloria (Jean) H(iner) 1937- 45-48
Woodberry, George Edward 1855-1930 .. DLB-71
Woodberry, Joan (Merle) 1921- CANR-6
Earlier sketch in CA 11-12R
Woodbridge, Benjamin 1622-1684 ...... DLB-24
Woodbridge, Hensley Charles 1923- CANR-3
Earlier sketch in CA 9-10R
Woodbridge, Linda 1945- 118
Woodburn, Arthur 1890-1978 Obituary 108
Woodburn, John Henry 1914- CANR-4
Earlier sketch in CA 4R
See also SATA 11
Woodbury, Frank
See Chapman, Frank M(onroe)
Woodbury, Lael J(ay) 1927- 81-84
Woodbury, Marda 1925- CANR-17
Earlier sketch in CA 97-100
Woodbury, Mildred Fairchild 1894-1975
Obituary 57-60
Woodbury, Richard B(enjamin) 1917-
Brief entry 109
Woodcock, Bruce 1948- 119
Woodcock, George 1912- CANR-1
Earlier sketch in CA 3R
See also CAAS 6
Woodcott, Keith
See Brunner, John (Kilian Houston)
Wooden, Kenneth 1935- 81-84
Wooden, Wayne S(tanley) 1943- 109
Woodfield, William Read 1928- 9-10R
Woodford, Arthur M(acKinnon) 1940- ... CANR-7
Earlier sketch in CA 53-56
Woodford, Bruce P(owers) 1919- 57-60
Woodford, Frank B(ury) 1903-1967 ...... CAP-1
Earlier sketch in CA 15-16
Woodford, Jack
See Woolfolk, Josiah Pitts
Woodford, Peggy 1937- 104
See also SATA 25
Woodforde, John 1925- CANR-10
Earlier sketch in CA 25-28R
Woodgate, Mildred Violet 11-12R
Woodham-Smith, Cecil (Blanche Fitzgerald)
1896-1977 77-80
Obituary 69-72
Woodhead, Peter 1944- 124
Woodhouse, Barbara (Blackburn)
1910-1988 .... CANR-13
Obituary 126
Earlier sketch in CA 7-8R
Woodhouse, C(hristopher) M(ontague)
1917- Brief entry 108
Woodhouse, Charles Platten 1915- 105
Woodhouse, Edward J(ames) 1946- 117
Woodhouse, Martin (Charlton) 1932- .. CANR-16
Earlier sketch in CA 21-22R
Woodin, Ann Snow 1926- 13-14R
Woodin, Noel 1929- 4R
Wooding, Dan 1940- 102
Woodiwiss, Kathleen E(rin) 1939- CANR-23
Earlier sketch in CA 89-92
Wood-Legh, Kathleen Louise 1901-1981
Obituary 105
Woodley, Winifred
See Hedden, Worth Tuttle
Woodman, Anthony John 1945- CANR-23
Earlier sketches in CA 61-64, CANR-8
Woodman, Bill
See Woodman, William
Woodman, Harold D. 1928- CANR-9
Earlier sketch in CA 23-24R
Woodman, James Monroe 1931- 17-18R
Woodman, Jim
See Woodman, James Monroe
Woodman, John E. 1932(?)-1983
Obituary 109
Woodman, Loring 1942- 45-48
Woodman, William 1936- 125
Woodmason, Charles 1720(?)-? DLB-31
Woodrell, Daniel 1953- 121
Woodress, James (Leslie, Jr.) 1916- CANR-3
Earlier sketch in CA 5-6R
Woodrew, Greta 1930- 106
Woodrich, Mary Neville 1915- 25-28R
See also SATA 2
Woodring, Carl (Ray) 1919- 5-6R
Woodring, Paul (Dean) 1907- 17-18R

Woodrock, R. A.
See Cowlishaw, Ranson
Woodroffe, John
See Woodroffe, John George
Woodroffe, John George 1865-1936
Brief entry ... 121
Woodroof, Horace M(alcolm) 1906- ... CAP-2
Earlier sketch in CA 29-32
Woodruff, Archibald Mulford, Jr.
1912-1984 ... 105
Obituary ... 113
Woodruff, Asahel D(avis) 1904- ... 2R
Woodruff, J(ohn) Douglas 1897-1978 ... 107
Woodruff, John Douglas 1897-1978
Obituary ... 104
Woodruff, Judy (Carline) 1946- ... CANR-13
Earlier sketch in CA 73-76
Woodruff, Marian
See Goudge, Eileen
Woodruff, Philip
See Mason, Philip
Woodruff, Robert W.
See Mencken, H(enry) L(ouis)
Woodruff, Sue (Carolyn) 1943- ... 117
Woodruff, William 1916- ... 101
Woodrum, Lon 1901- ... 104
Woods, B(obby) W(illiam) 1930- ... CANR-19
Earlier sketch in CA 25-28R
Woods, Clee 1893- ... 108
Woods, Constance
See McComb, K(atherine Woods)
Woods, Donald 1933- ... 121
Brief entry ... 114
Woods, Donald H. 1933- ... 25-28R
Woods, Elizabeth 1940- ... 101
Woods, Frederick 1932- ... CANR-7
Earlier sketch in CA 17-18R
Woods, George A(llan) 1926-1988 ... 29-32R
Obituary ... 126
See also SATA 30
Woods, Geraldine 1948- ... 97-100
See also SATA 42
Woods, Harold 1945- ... 97-100
See also SATA 42
Woods, James M. 1952- ... 125
Woods, Joan (LeSueur) 1932- ... 11-12R
Woods, John 1926- ... CANR-23
Earlier sketch in CA 13-14R
Woods, John (Hayden) 1937- ... CANR-11
Earlier sketch in CA 57-60
Woods, John A(ubin) 1927- ... 13-14R
Woods, John B(arrie) 1933- Brief entry ... 107
Woods, John David 1939- ... 37-40R
Woods, John E(dmund) 1938- ... 104
Woods, Kenneth F. 1930- ... 15-16R
Woods, L. B. 1938- ... 112
Woods, Lawrence
See Lowndes, Robert A(ugustine) W(ard)
Woods, Margaret 1921- ... 23-24R
See also SATA 2
Woods, Margaret S(taeger) 1911- ... 81-84
Woods, Nat
See Stratemeyer, Edward L.
Woods, Oliver (Frederick John Bradley)
1911-1972 Obituary ... 114
Woods, P. F.
See Bayley, Barrington J(ohn)
Woods, Pamela 1938- ... 106
Woods, Ralph L(ouis) 1904- ... CANR-2
Earlier sketch in CA 7-8R
Woods, Randall Bennett 1944- Brief entry ... 106
Woods, Richard (John) 1941- ... CANR-4
Earlier sketch in CA 53-56
Woods, Richard G(lenn) 1933- ... 109
Woods, Samuel H(ubert), Jr. 1926- ... 25-28R
Woods, Sara
See Bowen-Judd, Sara (Hutton)
Woods, Shadrach 1923-1973 Obituary ... 45-48
Woods, Sharon 1949- ... 125
Woods, Sherryl 1944- ... 120
Woods, Shirley E(dwards), Jr. 1934- ... 119
Woods, Sister Frances Jerome 1913- ... 21-22R
Woods, Stockton
See Forrest, Richard (Stockton)
Woods, Stuart 1938- ... 93-96
Woods, William ... 77-80
Woods, William Crawford 1944- ... 29-32R
Woodside, Alexander Barton 1938- ... 123
Woodson, Carter G. 1875-1950 ... DLB-17
Woodson, Jack
See Woodson, John Waddie Jr.
Woodson, Jeff
See Oglesby, Joseph
Woodson, John Waddie Jr. 1913- ... SATA-10
Woodson, Leslie H(arold) 1929- ... 41-44R
Woodson, Meg
See Baker, Elsie
Woodson, Thomas (Miller) 1931- ... 104
Woodson, Wesley E(dward) 1918- ... 37-40R
Woodstone, Arthur ... 69-72
Woodward, Bob
See Woodward, Robert Upshur
Woodward, C(omer) Vann 1908- ... CANR-17
Earlier sketches in CA 5-6R, CANR-2
See also DLB 17
Woodward, Carl Raymond 1890-1974 ... 41-44R
Woodward, (Landon) Cleveland
1900-1986 ... SATA-10, 48
Woodward, Daniel Holt 1931- ... 37-40R
Woodward, David 1909-1986 Obituary ... 120
Woodward, David B(rainerd) 1918- ... 65-68
Woodward, David Reid 1939- ... 114
Woodward, E. L.
See Woodward, Ernest Llewellyn
Woodward, Ernest Llewellyn 1890-1971
Obituary ... 111
Woodward, G(eorge) W(illiam) O(tway)
1924- ... CANR-3
Earlier sketch in CA 7-8R
Woodward, Grace Steele 1899- ... CAP-1
Earlier sketch in CA 9-10
Woodward, Helen Beal 1914(?)-1982
Obituary ... 108
Woodward, Helen Rosen 1882- ... 7-8R
Woodward, Herbert N(orton) 1911- ... 65-68
Woodward, Hildegard 1898- ... 5-6R
Woodward, James B(rian) 1935- ... CANR-2
Earlier sketch in CA 49-52
Woodward, John (William) 1920- ... 21-22R
Woodward, John (O.) 1922(?)-1988
Obituary ... 125
Woodward, John 1945- ... 113
Woodward, Lilian
See Marsh, John
Woodward, Llewellyn
See Woodward, Ernest Llewellyn
Woodward, Ralph Lee, Jr. 1934- ... 23-24R
Woodward, Robert H(anson) 1925- ... 17-18R
Woodward, Robert Upshur 1943- ... 69-72
Woodward, Stanley (Wingate) 1890- ... 5-6R
Woodward, Thomas B. 1937- ... 114
Woodward, W. Mary 1921- ... 45-48
Woodworth, Constance 1911-1983
Obituary ... 109
Woodworth, David (Perrin) 1932- ... 37-40R
Woodworth, G(eorge) Wallace
1902-1969 ... CAP-1
Earlier sketch in CA 15-16
Woodworth, G(eorge) Walter 1903- ... CAP-1
Earlier sketch in CA 19-20
Woodworth, Hugh (MacCallum)
1906-1978 Obituary ... 107
Woody, Regina Jones 1894- ... CANR-3
Earlier sketch in CA 5-6R
See also SATA 3
Woody, Robert H(enley) 1936- ... 93-96
Woody, Russell O(wen), Jr. 1934- ... 17-18R
Woodyard, David O. 1932- ... 23-24R
Woodyard, George 1934- ... 81-84
Woolard, Edgar 1899(?)-1978 Obituary ... 77-80
Wooldridge, Rhoda 1906- ... 77-80
See also SATA 22
Wooldridge, William C(harles) 1943- ... CANR-25
Earlier sketch in CA 45-48
Woolery, George W(illiam) 1931- ... 122
Wooley, John (Steven) 1949- ... 109
Woolf, Daniel J(ames) 1916- ... 7-8R
Woolf, Douglas 1922- ... CANR-2
Earlier sketch in CA 4R
Woolf, Harry 1923- ... CANR-1
Earlier sketch in CA 2R
Woolf, James Dudley 1914- ... 37-40R
Woolf, Leonard S(idney) 1880-1969 ... 7-8R
Obituary ... 25-28R
Woolf, Robert G(ary) 1928- ... 73-76
Woolf, S. J.
See Woolf, Stuart (Joseph)
Woolf, Stuart (Joseph) 1936- Brief entry ... 118
Woolf, (Adeline) Virginia 1882-1941
Brief entry ... 104
See also DLB 36
See also TCLC 1, 5, 20
Woolfe, H(arold) Geoffrey 1902- ... CAP-1
Earlier sketch in CA 11-12
Woolfenden, John R(ichards) 1904- ... 113
Woolfolk, Joanna Martine 1940- ... 110
Woolfolk, Josiah Pitts 1894-1971
Obituary ... 29-32R
Woolfolk, Robert L(ee IV) 1947-
Brief entry ... 112
Woolfolk, William 1917- ... 113
Woolgar, (George) Jack 1894- ... 17-18R
Woollam, William Gifford 1921- ... 11-12R
Woollcott, Alexander (Humphreys)
1887-1943 Brief entry ... 105
See also DLB 29
See also TCLC 5
Woolley, A(lban) E(dward, Jr.) 1926- ... CANR-14
Earlier sketch in CA 41-44R
Woolley, (Lowell) Bryan 1937- ... CANR-4
Earlier sketch in CA 49-52
Woolley, Catherine 1904- ... CANR-6
Earlier sketch in CA 2R
See also SATA 3
Woolley, Davis Collier 1908-1971
Obituary ... 116
Woolley, Geoffrey Harold 1892-1968 ... CAP-1
Earlier sketch in CA 11-12
Woolley, Herbert B(allantyne) 1917-1978
Obituary ... 81-84
Woolley, Richard van der Riet 1906-1986
Obituary ... 121
Woolley, (Alfred) Russell 1899- ... 7-8R
Woolls, (Esther) Blanche 1935- ... 126
Woolman, David S. 1916- ... 29-32R
Woolman, John 1720-1772 ... DLB-31
Woolner, Frank 1916- ... 53-56
Woolner, Thomas 1825-1892 ... DLB-35
Woolrich, Cornell
See Hopley-Woolrich, Cornell George
Woolrych, Austin (Herbert) 1918- ... 2R
Woolsey, Arthur (Wallace) 1906- ... 45-48
Woolsey, Janette 1904- ... CANR-2
Earlier sketch in CA 4R
See also SATA 3
Woolsey, Sarah Chauncy 1835(?)-1905
Brief entry ... 115
See also DLB 42
Woolson, Constance Fenimore
1840-1894 ... DLB-12, 74
Woolson, Roland S., Jr. 1930(?)-1977
Obituary ... 104
Woon, Basil 1894(?)-1974 Obituary ... 49-52
Wooster, Claire 1942- ... 101
Wooster, Ralph A(ncil) 1928- ... CANR-2
Earlier sketch in CA 5-6R
Wooster, Robert 1956- ... 124
Wooten, James (Terrell) 1937- Brief entry ... 112
Wootten, Morgan 1931- ... 101
Wootters, John (Henry, Jr.) 1928- ... 113
Wootton, Barbara (Frances Adam)
1897-1988 Obituary ... 126
Wootton, (Devere) Gareth 1937- ... 117
Wootton, (John) Graham (George)
1917- ... CANR-10
Earlier sketch in CA 7-8R
Worblefister, Petunia
See Gribbin, Lenore S.
Worboys, Anne(tte Isobel) Eyre ... CANR-9
Earlier sketch in CA 65-68
Worcester, Dean A(mory), Jr. 1918- ... 23-24R
Worcester, Donald E(mmet) 1915- ... CANR-19
Earlier sketches in CA 2R, CANR-4
See also SATA 18
Worcester, Gurdon Saltonstall 1897- ... CAP-1
Earlier sketch in CA 11-12
Worcester, Joseph Emerson 1784-1865 ... DLB-1
Worchel, Stephen 1946- ... CANR-16
Earlier sketch in CA 89-92
Worden, Alfred M(errill) 1932- ... 101
Worden, William L. 1910- ... CAP-1
Earlier sketch in CA 15-16
Wordsworth, Jonathan 1932- ... CANR-20
Earlier sketch in CA 29-32R
Worell, Judith 1928- ... CANR-7
Earlier sketch in CA 57-60
Work, Robert E. 1928(?)-1986 Obituary ... 121
Work, Virginia 1946- ... 113
See also SATA 45
Working, Russell (Craig) 1959- ... 124
Workman, Samuel K(linger) 1907- ... CAP-2
Earlier sketch in CA 23-24
Workman, William D(ouglas), Jr. 1914- ... 5-6R
Works, John 1949- ... 123
Worland, Stephen T. 1923- ... 23-24R
Worley, Robert Cromwell 1929-
Brief entry ... 108
Worline, Bonnie Bess 1914- ... 69-72
See also SATA 14
Worlock, Derek John Harford 1920- ... 103
Worm, Piet 1909- ... 81-84
Wormald, Francis 1904(?)-1972 Obituary ... 104
Wormald, Jenny 1942- ... 112
Worman, Charles G(ordon) 1933- ... 119
Worman, Eli
See Weil, Roman L(ee)
Wormell, Deborah 1946-1979 Obituary ... 114
Wormington, H(annah) M(arie) 1914- ... CANR-3
Earlier sketch in CA 45-48
Wormley, Cinda
See Kornblum, Cinda
Wormley, Stanton Lawrence 1909- ... CANR-12
Earlier sketch in CA 73-76
Wormser, Baron Chesley 1948- ... 110
Wormser, Rene A(lbert) 1896-1981 ... CANR-11
Obituary ... 104
Earlier sketch in CA 15-16R
Wormser, Sophie 1897- ... 65-68
See also SATA 22
Worner, Karl Heinrich
See Woerner, Karl Heinrich
Woroniak, Alexander 1920- ... 41-44R
Woronoff, Jon 1938- ... CANR-11
Earlier sketch in CA 29-32R
Worrall, Ambrose A(lexander) 1899-1972 ... CAP-2
Earlier sketch in CA 29-32
Worrall, Olga (Nathalie) 1906- ... 29-32R
Worrell, Albert C(adwallader) 1913- ... 37-40R
Worrell, Eric 1924-1987 Obituary ... 123
Worsley, Dale 1948- ... 104
Worsley, Gump
See Worsley, Lorne (John)
Worsley, Lorne (John) 1929- Brief entry ... 111
Worster, Donald E(ugene) 1941- ... CANR-12
Earlier sketch in CA 57-60
Worsthorne, Peregrine 1923- ... 45-48
Worswick, Clark 1940- ... 104
Worth, C. Brooke 1908- ... 101
Worth, Dean S(toddard) 1927- Brief entry ... 112
Worth, Douglas 1940- ... CANR-9
Earlier sketch in CA 65-68
Worth, Fred L. 1943- ... 97-100
Worth, Helen 1913- ... 15-16R
Worth, Margaret
See Strickland, Margot
Worth, Richard ... SATA-46
Worth, Sol 1922(?)-1977 ... 81-84
Obituary ... 73-76
Worth, Valerie
See Bahlke, Valerie Worth
See also SATA 8
Wortham, John David 1941- ... 37-40R
Worthen, Blaine Richard 1936- ... CANR-15
Earlier sketch in CA 85-88
Worthington, Edgar Barton 1905- ... 109
Worthington, Janet Evans 1942- ... 115
Worthington, Marjorie (Muir)
1898(?)-1976 ... CANR-2
Obituary ... 65-68
Earlier sketch in CA 1R
Worthington, Phoebe 1910- ... SATA-52
Worthington, Robin (Ann) 1932- ... 114
Worthley, Jean Reese 1925- ... 77-80
Worthy, James C(arson) 1910- ... 117
Worthy, Morgan 1936- ... 65-68
Worthylake, Mary Moore 1904- ... CANR-4
Earlier sketch in CA 3R
Wortis, Avi 1937- ... CANR-12
Earlier sketch in CA 69-72
See also SATA 14
Wortley, Ben Atkinson 1907- ... 57-60
Wortman, Marlene Stein 1937- ... 112
Wortman, Max S(idones), Jr. 1932- ... CANR-16
Earlier sketch in CA 23-24R
Wortman, Richard 1938- ... CANR-9
Earlier sketch in CA 23-24R
Wortman, (Leo) Sterling 1923-1981
Obituary ... 108
Worton, Stanley N(elson) 1923- ... 57-60
Woshinsky, Oliver Hanson 1939-
Brief entry ... 109
Wosmek, Frances 1917- ... CANR-26
Earlier sketches in CA 29-32R, CANR-11
See also SATA 29
Woudenberg, Paul Richard 1927- ... 69-72
Woudhuysen, Jan Frank 1942- ... 107
Woudstra, Marten H. 1922- ... CANR-19
Earlier sketch in CA 25-28R
Wouil, George
See Slaney, George Wilson
Wouk, Herman 1915- ... CANR-6
Earlier sketch in CA 5-6R
See also DLBY 82
See also CLC 1, 9, 38
Woy, James Bayly 1927- ... 15-16R
Woychuk, N(icholas) A(rthur) 1915- ... 13-14R
Woytinsky, Emma S(hadkhan)
1893-1969 ... CAP-1
Earlier sketch in CA 17-18
Woznicki, Andrew N(icholas) 1931- ... CANR-24
Earlier sketch in CA 45-48
Wrage, Ernest J. 1911-1965 ... 2R
Wragg, David William 1946- ... CANR-4
Earlier sketch in CA 53-56
Wragg, E(dward) C(onrad) 1938- ... CANR-23
Earlier sketches in CA 57-60, CANR-8
Wraight, A(aron) Joseph 1913- ... 21-22R
Wreen, Michael 1950- ... 117
Wreford, James
See Watson, J(ames) Wreford
Wren, Chris ?-1982 Obituary ... 108
Wren, Christopher S. 1936- ... 21-22R
Wren, Daniel Alan 1932- ... 41-44R
Wren, Ellaruth
See Elkins, Ella Ruth
Wren, M. K.
See Renfroe, Martha Kay
Wren, Melvin C(larence) 1910- ... 37-40R
Wren, Percival Christopher 1885-1941
Brief entry ... 123
Wren, Robert Meriwether 1928- ... 106
Wren, Thomas Edward 1938- ... 77-80
Wren, Wilfrid John 1930- ... 109
Wrench, David F(razer) 1932- ... 41-44R
Wrench, (John) Evelyn (Leslie) 1882-1966 ... 7-8R
Wrenn, John H(aughton) 1920- ... 2R
Wrenn, Robert L. 1933- ... 29-32R
Wrenn, Tony P(entecost) 1938- ... 89-92
Wrenn, Winnie Holden 1886(?)-1979
Obituary ... 89-92
Wriggins, Sally Hovey 1922- ... 97-100
See also SATA 17
Wriggins, W(illiam) Howard 1918- ... 61-64
Wright, A(nthony) Colin 1938- ... 120
Wright, A(mos) J(asper) 1952- ... 93-96
Wright, Alice E(dwards) 1905-1980 ... 104
Wright, Andrew (Howell) 1923- ... 17-18R
Wright, Anna (Maria Louisa Perrott) Rose
1890-1968 Obituary ... 109
See also SATA 35
Wright, Arthur Frederick 1913-1976 ... 77-80
Obituary ... 69-72
Wright, Austin 1904- ... 61-64
Wright, Austin McGiffert 1922- ... CANR-4
Earlier sketch in CA 3R
Wright, Barton A(llen) 1920- ... CANR-8
Earlier sketch in CA 61-64
Wright, Basil Charles 1907-1987 ... 105
Obituary ... 123
Wright, Beatrice A(nn) 1917- ... CANR-12
Earlier sketch in CA 21-22R
Wright, Benjamin Fletcher 1900-1976 ... 77-80
Obituary ... 69-72
Wright, Betty Ren ... SATA-48
Wright, Brooks 1922- ... 25-28R
Wright, Bruce S(tanley) 1912-1975 ... CAP-2
Earlier sketch in CA 19-20
Wright, Burton 1917- ... 81-84
Wright, Carolyne L(ee) 1949- ... 111
Wright, (Julia) Celeste Turner 1906- ... CAP-1
Earlier sketch in CA 9-10
Wright, Charles (Penzel, Jr.) 1935- ... CANR-23
Earlier sketch in CA 29-32R
See also CAAS 7
See also DLBY 82
See also CLC 6, 13, 28
Wright, Charles Alan 1927- ... CANR-16
Earlier sketches in CA 45-48, CANR-1
Wright, Charles David 1932-1978 ... 104
Wright, Charles H(oward) 1918- ... 61-64
Wright, Charles R(obert) 1927- ... CANR-1
Earlier sketch in CA 45-48
Wright, Charles Stevenson 1932- ... CANR-26
Earlier sketch in CA 11-12R
See also BW
See also DLB 33
See also CLC 49
Wright, Christopher 1926- ... 11-12R
Wright, Cobina ?-1970 Obituary ... 115
Wright, (Charles) Conrad 1917- ... 21-22R
Wright, Constance Choate 1897-1987 ... 15-16R
Obituary ... 121
Wright, Cynthia Challed 1953- ... 77-80
Wright, D(avid) G(ordon) 1937- ... 65-68
Wright, D(onald) I(an) 1934- ... CANR-3
Earlier sketch in CA 49-52

INDEX

Wright, Dare 1926(?)- ... 93-96
See also SATA 21
Wright, David (John Murray) 1920- ... CANR-3
Earlier sketch in CA 9-10R
See also CAAS 5
Wright, David McCord 1909-1968 ... CAP-2
Earlier sketch in CA 17-18
Wright, Deil S(pencer) 1930- ... 13-14R
Wright, Denis (Arthur Hepworth) 1911- ... 81-84
Wright, Don(ald Conway) 1934- ... CANR-20
Earlier sketch in CA 104
Wright, Dorothy 1910- ... 13-14R
Wright, Edward A(rlington) 1906- ... 29-32R
Wright, Elizabeth Atwell 1919-1976
Obituary ... 65-68
Wright, Enid Meadowcroft (LaMonte)
1898-1966 ... CAP-2
Earlier sketch in CA 17-18
See also SATA 3
Wright, Esmond 1915- ... CANR-6
Earlier sketch in CA 2R
See also SATA 10
Wright, F(rank) J(oseph) 1905- ... 11-12R
Wright, Frances 1795-1852 ... DLB-73
Wright, Frances Fitzpatrick 1897- ... CAP-1
Earlier sketch in CA 13-14
See also SATA 10
Wright, Frances J.
See Crothers, J(essie) Frances
Wright, Francesca
See Robins, Denise (Naomi)
Wright, Frank Cookman, Jr. 1904-1982
Obituary ... 107
Wright, G(eorge) Ernest 1909-1974 ... CANR-2
Obituary ... 53-56
Earlier sketch in CA 2R
Wright, G(eorg) H(enrik) von 1916-
Brief entry ... 112
Wright, Gavin Peter 1943- ... CANR-15
Earlier sketch in CA 89-92
Wright, George B(urton) 1912- ... 23-24R
Wright, George Nelson 1921- ... CANR-1
Earlier sketch in CA 45-48
Wright, George T(haddeus, Jr.) 1925- ... 7-8R
Wright, Gordon 1912- ... 11-12R
Wright, Grahame 1947-1977 ... 103
Wright, H(arold) Bunker 1907- ... 5-6R
Wright, H(ugh) Elliott 1937- ... CANR-14
Earlier sketch in CA 37-40R
Wright, H(arry) Norman 1937- ... CANR-8
Earlier sketch in CA 57-60
Wright, Harold Bell 1872-1944 Brief entry ... 110
See also DLB 9
Wright, Harrison M(orris) 1928- ... 41-44R
Wright, Helen 1914- ... 11-12R
Wright, Helen L(ouise) 1932- ... 116
Wright, Helena (Rosa Lowenfeld)
1887-1982 Obituary ... 110
Wright, Herbert Curtis 1928- ... 105
Wright, Howard Wilson 1915- ... CANR-3
Earlier sketch in CA 5-6R
Wright, Ione Stuessy 1905- ... CAP-1
Earlier sketch in CA 13-14
Wright, Irene Aloha 1879-1972
Obituary ... 33-36R
Wright, J(ames) Leitch, Jr. 1929- ... 23-24R
Wright, J(oseph) Patrick (Jr.) 1941- ... 103
Wright, J(ohn) Robert 1936- ... 111
Wright, J(ohn) Stafford 1905- ... CANR-11
Earlier sketch in CA 57-60
Wright, Jack R.
See Harris, Mark
Wright, James (Arlington) 1927-1980 ... CANR-4
Obituary ... 97-100
Earlier sketch in CA 49-52
See also DLB 5
See also CLC 3, 5, 10, 28
See also AITN 2
Wright, James C(laud), Jr. 1922- ... 49-52
Wright, Jay 1935- ... 73-76
See also DLB 41
Wright, Jim
See Wright, James C(laud), Jr.
Wright, John D(ean), Jr. 1920- ... 117
Wright, John Eugene, Jr. 1931- ... 112
Wright, John J(oseph) 1909-1979 ... CANR-2
Earlier sketch in CA 4R
Wright, John S(hup) 1910- ... 37-40R
Wright, John S(herman) 1920- ... CANR-6
Earlier sketch in CA 5-6R
Wright, Judith 1915- ... 15-16R
See also SATA 14
See also CLC 11
Wright, Katrina
See Gater, Dilys
Wright, Kenneth
See del Rey, Lester
Wright, L(aurali) R. ... CLC-44
Wright, Lafayette Hart 1917-1983 ... 41-44R
Obituary ... 109
Wright, Larry 1940- Brief entry ... 122
Wright, Lawrence 1947- ... 93-96
Wright, Leigh Richard 1925- ... 93-96
Wright, Leonard M(arshall), Jr. 1923- ... CANR-13
Earlier sketch in CA 61-64
Wright, Linda Raney 1945- ... CANR-11
Earlier sketch in CA 69-72
Wright, Louis Booker 1899-1984 ... CANR-1
Obituary ... 112
Earlier sketch in CA 4R
See also DLB 17
Wright, Mary Clabaugh 1917-1970
Obituary ... 109
Wright, Mary Pamela Godwin 1917- ... CAP-1
Earlier sketch in CA 9-10
Wright, Michael R(obert) 1901- ... CAP-1
Earlier sketch in CA 15-16
Wright, Monte Duane 1930- ... 41-44R
Wright, Muriel H(azel) 1889-1975
Obituary ... 57-60
Wright, Nancy Means ... 104
See also SATA 38
Wright, Nathalia 1913- ... 120
Wright, Nathan, Jr. 1923- ... 37-40R
Wright, Nathaniel, Jr.
See Wright, Nathan, Jr.
Wright, Norman Edgar 1927- ... 101
Wright, Olgivanna Lloyd 1900(?)-1985
Obituary ... 115
Wright, (Mary) Patricia 1932- ... CANR-26
Earlier sketches in CA 65-68, CANR-10
Wright, Philip Arthur 1908- ... CAP-1
Earlier sketch in CA 11-12
Wright, (Philip) Quincy 1890-1970 ... CANR-5
Obituary ... 29-32R
Earlier sketch in CA 5-6R
Wright, R(obert) Glenn 1932- ... 111
Wright, R(obert) H(amilton) 1906- ... CANR-7
Earlier sketch in CA 19-20R
See also SATA 6
Wright, R(ichard) I(rwin) Vane
See Vane-Wright, R(ichard) I(rwin)
Wright, Rebecca 1942- ... 105
Wright, Richard (Nathaniel) 1908-1960 ... 108
See also BW
See also DLB 76
See also DLBD 2
See also CLC 1, 3, 4, 9, 14, 21, 48
See also SSC 2
Wright, Richard B(ruce) 1937- ... 85-88
See also DLB 53
See also CLC 6
Wright, Richard J. 1935- ... 89-92
Wright, Rick 1945- ... CLC-35
Wright, Robert Lee 1920- ... CANR-13
Earlier sketch in CA 17-18R
Wright, Robert Roy 1917- ... 11-12R
Wright, Robin (B.) 1948- Brief entry ... 119
Wright, Ronald (William Vernon) Selby
1908- ... CANR-6
Earlier sketch in CA 2R
Wright, Rosalie Muller 1942- ... 77-80
Wright, Rosalind 1952- ... 61-64
Wright, Rowland
See Wells, Carolyn
Wright, Russel 1904-1976 Obituary ... 69-72
Wright, Sarah E. ... 37-40R
See also BW
See also DLB 33
Wright, Sewall 1889-1988 Obituary ... 125
Wright, Stephen 1922- ... CANR-1
Earlier sketch in CA 49-52
Wright, Stephen 1946- ... CLC-33
Wright, Sylvia 1917-1981 ... 29-32R
Obituary ... 104
Wright, T. M. 1947- ... 120
Wright, T(erence) R(oy) 1951- ... 125
Wright, Theodore P(aul), Jr. 1926- ... CANR-9
Earlier sketch in CA 15-16R
Wright, Theon 1904- Brief entry ... 109
Wright, Walter Francis 1912- ... 5-6R
Wright, Willard Hull 1894-1982 Obituary ... 107
Wright, Willard Huntington 1888-1939
Brief entry ... 115
Wright, William 1930- ... CANR-23
Earlier sketches in CA 53-56, CANR-7
See also CLC 44
Wright, William C(ook) 1939- ... 41-44R
Wright, William E(dward) 1926- ... 23-24R
Wrightsman, Lawrence S(amuel), Jr.
1931- ... CANR-11
Earlier sketch in CA 23-24R
Wrightson, Patricia 1921- ... CANR-19
Earlier sketches in CA 45-48, CANR-3
See also SATA 8
See also SAAS 4
See also CLR 4, 14
Wrigley, Elizabeth S(pringer) 1915- ... 41-44R
Wriston, Henry M(erritt) 1889-1978 ... CAP-1
Obituary ... 77-80
Earlier sketch in CA 11-12
Wrobel, Sylvia (Burroughs) 1941- ... 65-68
Wroblewski, Sergius C(harles) 1918- ... CANR-8
Earlier sketch in CA 7-8R
Wrone, David R(ogers) 1933- ... CANR-6
Earlier sketch in CA 57-60
Wrong, Dennis H(ume) 1923- ... 81-84
Wronker, Lili
See Wronker, Lili Cassel
Wronker, Lili Cassel 1924- ... SATA-10
Wronski, Stanley P(aul) 1919- ... 15-16R
Wroth, Lawrence Counselman 1884-1970
Obituary ... 29-32R
Wrottesley, A(rthur) J(ohn) F(rancis)
1908- ... 45-48
Wryde, Dogear
See Gorey, Edward (St. John)
Wrzos, Joseph Henry 1929- ... 49-52
Wu, Hsiu-Kwang 1935- ... 17-18R
Wu, John C(hing) H(siung) 1899-1986 ... 104
Obituary ... 118
Wu, Joseph S. 1934- ... 97-100
Wu, K(uo) C(heng) 1903-1984 ... 3R
Obituary ... 113
Wu, Nelson I(kon) 1919- ... 11-12R
Wu, Silas H. L. 1929- ... 37-40R
Wu, William F(ranking) 1951- ... 109
Wu, Yuan-li ... CANR-12
Earlier sketch in CA 17-18R
Wubben, Hubert H(ollensteiner) 1928- ... 102
Wubben, John 1938- ... 65-68
Wucherer, Ruth Marie 1948- ... CANR-8
Earlier sketch in CA 61-64
Wu Ching-hsiung
See Wu, John C(hing) H(siung)
Wuellner, Flora Slosson 1928- ... 53-56
Wuerpel, Charles E(dward) 1906- ... 105
Wul, Stefan
See Pairault, Pierre
Wulf, Helen Harlan 1913- ... 53-56
Wulfekoetter, Gertrude 1895- ... 2R
Wulff, Lee 1905- ... 61-64
Wulff, Robert M. 1926- ... 49-52
Wulffson, Don L. 1943- ... CANR-19
Earlier sketch in CA 102
See also SATA 32
Wulforst, Harry David 1923- ... 125
Wuliger, Betty 1921- ... 65-68
Wullstein, L(eroy) H(ughes) 1931- ... 29-32R
Wunder, John Remley 1945- ... 107
Wunderlich, Ray C., Jr. 1929- ... 37-40R
Wundt, Wilhelm (Max) 1832-1920
Brief entry ... 121
Wundt, Wilhelm
See de Mille, Richard
Wunnakyawhtin U Ohn Ghine
See Maurice, David (John Kerr)
Wunsch, Josephine (McLean) 1914- ... CANR-15
Earlier sketch in CA 3R
Wuorinen, John H(enry) 1897-1969
Obituary ... 111
Wuorio, Eva-Lis 1918- ... 77-80
See also SATA 28, 34
Wurdemann, Audrey
See Auslander, Audrey (May)
Wurdemann
Wurfel, Seymour W(alter) 1907- ... 73-76
Wurlitzer, Rudolph 1938(?)- ... 85-88
See also CLC 2, 4, 15
Wurmbrand, Richard Heinrich 1909- ... 61-64
Wurmser, Leon 1931- ... 106
Wurtman, Judith J(oy) 1937- ... 113
Wuthnow, Robert 1946- ... CANR-15
Earlier sketch in CA 65-68
Wu Tien-wei 1922- ... 118
Wyandotte, Steve
See Thomas, Stanley
Wyant, William K(eblinger) 1913- ... 108
Wyatt, Arthur R(amer) 1927- ... 2R
Wyatt, B. D.
See Robinson, Spider
Wyatt, David K(ent) 1937- ... 29-32R
Wyatt, Dorothea E(dith) 1909- ... CAP-2
Earlier sketch in CA 23-24
Wyatt, James
See Robinson, Louie, Jr.
Wyatt, Joan 1934- ... 97-100
Wyatt, John 1925- ... CANR-22
Earlier sketch in CA 105
Wyatt, Rachel 1929- ... 101
Wyatt, Richard Jed 1939- ... 115
Wyatt, Robert John 1931- ... 73-76
Wyatt, Stanley P(orter, Jr.) 1921-1980 ... 11-12R
Obituary ... 120
Wyatt, Stephen (John) 1948- ... CANR-15
Earlier sketch in CA 81-84
Wyatt, Wesley Butler
See Torme, Mel(vin Howard)
Wyatt, (Alan) Will 1942- ... 101
Wyatt, William F., Jr. 1932- ... 37-40R
Wyatt, Woodrow Lyle 1918- ... 103
Wyatt-Brown, Bertram 1932- ... CANR-21
Earlier sketch in CA 25-28R
Wycherley, R(ichard) E(rnest) 1909- ... 77-80
Wyckoff, Charlotte Chandler 1893-1966 ... CAP-2
Earlier sketch in CA 17-18
Wyckoff, D(onald) Daryl 1936-1985 ... CANR-7
Obituary ... 114
Earlier sketch in CA 57-60
Wyckoff, Edith Hay 1916- ... 107
Wyckoff, James M. 1918- ... 19-20R
Wyckoff, (Gregory) Jerome 1911- ... 11-12R
Wyckoff, Peter (Gerritsen) 1914- ... 41-44R
Wyckoff, Ralph W(alter) G(raystone)
1897- ... 73-76
Wyckoff, Russell L. 1916(?)-1984
Obituary ... 112
Wycoff, Mary Elizabeth Jordon 1932- ... 15-16R
Wyden, Peter H. 1923- ... 105
Wyeth, Betsy James 1921- ... 89-92
See also SATA 41
Wyeth, N(ewell) C(onvers) 1882-1945 ... SATA-17
Wyeth, Paul James Logan 1920-1982
Obituary ... 107
Wykes, Alan 1914- ... CANR-2
Earlier sketch in CA 1R
Wykstra, Ronald A. 1935- Brief entry ... 106
Wyld, Lionel D(arcy) 1925- ... CANR-4
Earlier sketch in CA 3R
Wylder, Delbert E(ugene) 1923- ... CANR-12
Earlier sketch in CA 29-32R
Wylder, Edith (Perry) 1925- ... 29-32R
Wylder, Robert C. 1921- ... 11-12R
Wyler, Brenda (Florence) 1951- ... CANR-19
Earlier sketch in CA 89-92
Wyler, Rose 1909- ... 93-96
See also SATA 18
Wyler, William 1902-1981 Obituary ... 108
Wylie, Betty Jane ... CANR-21
Earlier sketch in CA 105
See also SATA 48
Wylie, C(larence) R(aymond), Jr. 1911- ... 45-48
Wylie, Craig 1908-1976 Obituary ... 69-72
Wylie, Elinor (Morton Hoyt) 1885-1928
Brief entry ... 105
See also DLB 9, 45
See also TCLC 8
Wylie, Francis E(rnest) 1905- ... 73-76
Wylie, Jeff
See Wylie, Francis E(rnest)
Wylie, Joanne 1928- ... 118
Wylie, John Anthony Hamilton 1919-1987
Obituary ... 123
Wylie, Jonathan 1945- ... 120
Wylie, Laura
See Matthews, Patricia (Anne)
Wylie, Laurence William 1909- ... 21-22R
Wylie, Laurie
See Matthews, Patricia (Anne)
Wylie, Max (Melville) 1904-1975 ... 97-100
Obituary ... 61-64
Wylie, Philip (Gordon) 1902-1971 ... CAP-2
Obituary ... 33-36R
Earlier sketch in CA 21-22
See also DLB 9
See also CLC 43
Wylie, Ruth C(arol) 1920- ... 89-92
Wylie, Turrell V(erl) 1927- ... 41-44R
Wylie, William P(ercy) 1898- ... 7-8R
Wyllie, Eugene D(onald) 1929- ... 123
Brief entry ... 118
Wyllie, John (Vectis Carew) 1914- ... CANR-5
Earlier sketch in CA 11-12R
Wyllie, Peter J(ohn) 1930- ... CANR-5
Earlier sketch in CA 53-56
Wyly, Rachel Lumpkin 1892- ... CAP-2
Earlier sketch in CA 25-28
Wyman, David S. 1929- ... 25-28R
Wyman, Donald 1903- ... CANR-2
Earlier sketch in CA 5-6R
Wyman, Leland C(lifton) 1897-1988
Obituary ... 124
Wyman, Marc
See Howitt, Harry
Wyman, Mark 1938- ... 101
Wyman, Mary Alice 1889(?)-1976
Obituary ... 61-64
Wyman, Oliver
See Holmes, Olive
Wyman, Walker D(eMarquis) 1907- ... 17-18R
Wymark, Olwen Margaret 1932- ... 104
Wymer, Norman (George) 1911- ... 104
See also SATA 25
Wymer, Thomas L(ee) 1938- ... 105
Wynand, Derk 1944- ... CANR-17
Earlier sketch in CA 77-80
Wynants, Miche 1934- ... SATA-31
Wynar, Bohdan S(tephen) 1926- ... CANR-10
Earlier sketch in CA 19-20R
Wynar, Christine L(oraine) 1933- ... 73-76
Wynar, Lubomyr R(oman) 1932- ... CANR-14
Earlier sketch in CA 73-76
Wynd, Oswald Morris 1913- ... CANR-1
Earlier sketch in CA 2R
Wynder, Mavis Areta
See Winder, Mavis Areta
Wyndham, Esther
See Lutyens, Mary
Wyndham, Everard Humphrey 1888- ... CAP-1
Earlier sketch in CA 13-14
Wyndham, Francis (Guy Percy) 1924-
Brief entry ... 126
Wyndham, John
See Harris, John (Wyndham Parkes
Lucas) Beynon
Wyndham, Lee
See Hyndman, Jane Andrews Lee
Wyndham, Robert
See Hyndman, Robert Utley
Wynes, Charles E. 1929- ... 11-12R
Wyness, (James) Fenton 1903- ... CAP-1
Earlier sketch in CA 11-12
Wynette, Tammy
See Pugh, Wynette
Wynkoop, Mildred Bangs 1905- ... 57-60
Wynkoop, Sally 1944- ... 41-44R
Wynkoop, William M. 1916- ... 21-22R
Wynn, Alfred
See Brewer, Fredric (Aldwyn)
Wynn, Allan 1920-1987 Obituary ... 123
Wynn, D(ale) Richard 1918- ... CANR-4
Earlier sketch in CA 2R
Wynn, Daniel Webster 1919- ... 25-28R
Wynn, John Charles 1920- ... CANR-2
Earlier sketch in CA 3R
Wynn, (Francis Xavier Aloysius James
Jeremiah) Keenan 1916-1986 Obituary ... 120
Wynn, Neil A(lan) 1947- ... 113
Wynne, Brian
See Garfield, Brian (Wynne)
Wynne, Frank
See Garfield, Brian (Wynne)
Wynne, May
See Knowles, Mabel Winifred
Wynne, Nancy Blue 1931- ... 85-88
Wynne, Ronald D(avid) 1934- ... 102
Wynne, Thorne D. 1908- ... 7-8R
Wynne-Jones, Tim(othy) 1948- ... 105
Wynne-Thomas, Peter 1934- ... 118
Wynne-Tyson, Esme 1898- ... 23-24R
Wynne-Tyson, (Timothy) Jon (Lyden)
1924- ... 19-20R
Wynn-Jones, Michael 1941- ... CANR-14
Earlier sketch in CA 69-72
Wynot, Edward D(avis), Jr. 1943- ... 105
Wynter, Edward (John) 1914- ... 69-72
See also SATA 14
Wynyard, Talbot
See Hamilton, Charles Harold St. John
Wyon, Olive 1890-19(?) ... CAP-1
Earlier sketch in CA 11-12
Wyrick, V(ictor) Neil, Jr. 1928- ... 15-16R
Wyschogrod, Edith 1930- Brief entry ... 111
Wyschogrod, Michael 1928- ... 89-92
Wyse, Lois (Helene) 1926- ... 108
Wyse, Marion 1952- ... 123

Wysor, Bettie 1928- CANR-13
Earlier sketch in CA 77-80
Wyss, Johann David Von
1743-1818 .... SATA-27, 29
Wyss, Max Albert 1908-1977 106
Wyss, Thelma Hatch 1934- 29-32R
See also SATA 10
Wyss, Wallace A(lfred) 1944- 124
Brief entry 107
Wyszynski, Stefan 1901-1981 Obituary 108
Wyvis, Ben
See Munro, (Macfarlane) Hugh
Wyzanski, Charles E(dward), Jr.
1906-1986 .... CAP-1
Obituary 120
Earlier sketch in CA 17-18

X

Xaveria, M. Barton
See Barton, M. Xaveria
Xaveria, Sister
See Barton, M. Xaveria
Xavier I
See Horne, Frank (Smith)
Xeno
See Lake, Kenneth R(obert)
Ximenes, Ben Cuellar, Jr. 1911- 5-6R
Xixx, Jezebel Q.
See Borgmann, Dmitri A(lfred)

Y

Yaari, Ehud 1945- 37-40R
Yabes, Leopoldo Y(abes) 1912- 101
Yablokoff, Herman 1903-1981 Obituary 108
Yablonsky, Lewis 1924- 23-24R
Yabsley, Suzanne 1949- 124
Yacine, Kateb 1929- 11-12R
Yacorzynski, George Kassimer 1907- 2R
Yacowar, Maurice 1942- 41-44R
Yadin, (Rav-Aloof) Yigael 1917-1984 .... CANR-6
Obituary 113
Earlier sketch in CA 11-12R
Yaeger, Bart
See Strung, Norman
Yafa, Stephen H. 1941- 23-24R
Yaffe, Alan
See Yorinks, Arthur
Yaffe, Barbara 1953- 85-88
Yaffe, James 1927- CANR-12
Earlier sketch in CA 7-8R
Yaffe, Richard 1903- 69-72
Yager, Rosemary 1909- 3R
Yaggy, Duncan 1938- 116
Yaggy, Elinor 1907- 89-92
Yahil, Leni 29-32R
Yahraes, Herbert 1905- 81-84
Yahuda, Joseph 1900- CAP-1
Earlier sketch in CA 11-12
Yaker, Henri (Marc) 1922- Brief entry 109
Yakobson, Helen B(ates) 1913- 19-20R
Yakobson, Sergius O. 1901-1979
Obituary 89-92
Yakovenko, L.
See Kopelev, Lev (Zinovievich)
Yakumo Koizumi
See Hearn, (Patricio) Lafcadio (Tessima
Carlos)
Yalden, Derek William 1940- 69-72
Yale, Wesley W(oodworth) 1900- CAP-2
Earlier sketch in CA 29-32
Yale, William 1888(?)-1975 Obituary 57-60
Yalem, Ronald J(oseph) 1926- 19-20R
Yalman, Ahmet Emin 1888-1972
Obituary 37-40R
Yalom, Marilyn K. 1932- 117
Yamada, Mitsuye (May) 1923- 77-80
Yamaguchi, J(ohn) Tohr 1932- 19-20R
Yamaguchi, Marianne (Illenberger)
1936- 29-32R
See also SATA 7
Yamamoto, J(erry) Isamu 1947- 77-80
Yamamoto, Kaoru 1932- CANR-12
Earlier sketch in CA 25-28R
Yamanouchi, Hisaaki 1934- 93-96
Yamasaki, Minoru 1912-1986 Obituary 118
Yamauchi, Edwin M(asao) 1937- CANR-19
Earlier sketches in CA 45-48, CANR-3
Yan, Chiou-Shuang Jou 1934- Brief entry ... 105
Yanaga, Chitoshi 1903- CAP-2
Earlier sketch in CA 25-28
Yanagimura, Shimpu
See Verwilghen, A(lbert-) Felix
Yancey, Philip D(avid) 1949- CANR-18
Earlier sketch in CA 101
Yancey, William L(ayton) 1938- 21-22R
Yancy, Robert J(ames) 1944- 57-60
Yandell, Keith E. 1938- 37-40R
Yanev, Peter (Ivanov) 1946- 77-80
Yaney, George L(evings) 1930- 104
Yaney, Joseph P(aul) 1939- CANR-9
Earlier sketch in CA 65-68
Yang, C(hing) K(un) 1911- 7-8R
Yang, Jay 1941- SATA-12
Yang, Linda (Gureasko) 1937- 57-60
Yang, Richard F. S. 1918- CANR-10
Earlier sketch in CA 25-28R
Yang, Sung Chul 1939- 117
Yang-Jen
See Shu, Austin Chi-wei
Yanikian, Gourgen Migirdic 1895-1984
Obituary 112
Yaniv, Avner 1942- 126
Yankelovich, Daniel 1924- 105
Yanker, Gary 1947- 37-40R
Yankowitz, Susan 1941- CANR-17
Earlier sketches in CA 45-48, CANR-1
Yannarella, Philip A(nthony) 1942- 73-76
Yannatos, James 1929- 102
Yannella, Donald 1934- CANR-25
Earlier sketches in CA 57-60, CANR-8
Yanoff, Morris 1907- 108
Yanouzas, John N(icholas) 1928- 41-44R
Yanovsky, Basile S.
See Yanovsky, V(assily) S(emenovich)
Yanovsky, V(assily) S(emenovich) 1906- ..97-100
See also CLC 2, 18
Yans-McLaughlin, Virginia 1943- 89-92
Yao, Esther Lee 1944- 111
Yarber, Robert Earl 1929- 49-52
Yarborough, Betty Hathaway 1927- 45-48
Yarbro, Chelsea Quinn 1942- CANR-25
Earlier sketches in CA 65-68, CANR-9
Yarbrough, Camille 1938- 125
Brief entry 105
See also BW
Yarbrough, Ira 1910(?)-1983 Obituary 110
See also SATA 35
Yarbrough, Tinsley E(ugene) 1941- 109
Yarde, Jeanne Betty Frances 1925- CANR-23
Earlier sketch in CA 105
Yardley, Alice 1913- Brief entry 106
Yardley, Herbert O(sborn) 1889-1958
Brief entry 121
Yardley, Jonathan 1939- 73-76
Yardley, Richard Q(uincy) 1903-1979
Obituary 89-92
Yaremko, Michael 1914-1970 .... CAP-2
Earlier sketch in CA 25-28
Yarmey, A(lexander) Daniel 1938- CANR-17
Earlier sketch in CA 101
Yarmolinsky, Adam 1922- 37-40R
Yarmolinsky, Avrahm (Abraham)
1890-1975 .... CANR-7
Obituary 61-64
Earlier sketch in CA 5-6R
Yarmon, Morton 1916- 11-12R
Yarn, David H(omer), Jr. 1920- 19-20R
Yarnall, Sophia
See Jacobs, Sophia Yarnall
Yarnell, Allen 1942- 101
Yaroslava
See Mills, Yaroslava Surmach
Yarrow, Arnold 1920- 106
Yarrow, Marian J(eanette Radke) 1918-
Brief entry 105
Yarrow, P(hilip) J(ohn) 1917- 13-14R
Yarry, Mark Robert 1940- 110
Yar-Shater, Ehsan O(llah) 1920- 37-40R
Yartz, Frank Joseph 65-68
Yarwood, Doreen 1918- CANR-18
Earlier sketch in CA 101
Yashima, Taro
See Iwamatsu, Jun Atsushi
See also CLR 4
Yastrzemski, Carl (Michael, Jr.) 1939- 104
Yates, A(lan) G(eoffrey) 1923-1985 ..... CANR-3
Obituary 116
Earlier sketch in CA 4R
Yates, Alan
See Yates, A(lan) G(eoffrey)
Yates, Alayne 1929- 81-84
Yates, Alfred 1917- 21-22R
Yates, Aubrey J(ames) 1925- 11-12R
Yates, Brock W(endel) 1933- 11-12R
Yates, David O.
See Womack, David A(lfred)
Yates, Donald A(lfred) 1930- 41-44R
Yates, Dornford
See Mercer, Cecil William
Yates, Elizabeth 1905- CANR-21
Earlier sketches in CA 2R, CANR-6
See also SATA 4
See also SAAS 6
Yates, Frances A(melia) 1899-1981 57-60
Obituary 105
Yates, Gerard Francis 1907-1979
Obituary 89-92
Yates, J. Michael 1938- 21-22R
See also DLB 60
Yates, Madeleine 1937- 109
Yates, Norris W(ilson) 1923- 11-12R
Yates, Paul 1954- Brief entry 117
Yates, Peter Bertram 1909-1976 Obituary ..65-68
Yates, Raymond F(rancis) 1895-1966
Obituary 110
See also SATA 31
Yates, Richard 1926- CANR-10
Earlier sketch in CA 7-8R
See also DLB 2
See also DLBY 81
See also CLC 7, 8, 23
Yates, W(illiam) E(dgar) 1938- 49-52
Yatron, Michael 1921- 37-40R
Yauch, Wilbur Alden 1904-1982 Obituary ... 106
Yaukey, David (William) 1927- 61-64
Yaukey, Grace S(ydenstricker) 1899- CANR-1
Earlier sketch in CA 3R
See also SATA 5
Yavetz, Zvi 1925- CANR-16
Earlier sketch in CA 29-32R
Yavitz, Boris 1923- 114
Yaw, Yvonne 1936- 65-68
Yawetz, Zwy
See Yavetz, Zvi
Yazijian, Harvey Z. 1948- 107
Yeadon, David 1942- 104
Yeager, Allan Edward 1943- 101
Yeager, Leland B(ennett) 1924- 125
Yeager, Robert Cushing 1942- 102
Yeager, W(illard) Hayes 1897- CAP-2
Earlier sketch in CA 19-20
Yeakley, Marjory Hall 1908- CANR-2
Earlier sketch in CA 3R
See also SATA 21
Yearley, Clifton K(rebs), Jr. 1925- 15-16R
Yearwood, Richard M(eek) 1934- 37-40R
Yeates, Mabel
See Pereira, Harold Bertram
Yeates, Maurice 1938- CANR-14
Earlier sketch in CA 41-44R
Yeatman, Linda 1938- 117
See also SATA 42
Yeats, William Butler 1865-1939
Brief entry 104
See also DLB 10, 19
See also TCLC 1, 11, 18
Yeats-Brown, F(rancis Charles Claypon)
1886-1944 Brief entry 119
Yeazell, Ruth Bernard 1947- 102
Yeck, John D(avid) 1912- 15-16R
Yee, Albert H(oy) 1929- CANR-1
Earlier sketch in CA 49-52
Yee, Chiang
See Chiang, Yee
Yee, Min S. 1938- 101
Yeganeh, Mohammed 1923- 5-6R
Yeh, George K(ung)-C(hao) 1904-1981
Obituary 108
Yeh, Wei-lien
See Yip, Wai-lim
Yehiya, Eliezer Don
See Don-Yehiya, Eleizer
Yehoshua, Abraham B. 1936- 33-36R
See also CLC 13, 31
Yelin, Shulamis S. 121
Yellen, Samuel 1906- 1R
Yellen, Sherman 1932- 29-32R
Yellin, Carol Lynn (Gilmer) 1920- 19-20R
Yellin, David G(ilmer) 1916- Brief entry 115
Yellin, Jean Fagan 1930- 41-44R
Yellowitz, Irwin 1933- CANR-4
Earlier sketch in CA 45-48
Yelton, Donald Charles 1915- 106
Yelverton, Eric Esskildsen 1888-1964 .... CAP-1
Earlier sketch in CA 9-10
Yen-Ping, Shen 1896(?)-1981 Obituary 103
Yenser, Stephen 1941- 114
Yensid, Retlaw
See Disney, Walt(er Elias)
Yeo, Cedric Arnold 1905- CAP-1
Earlier sketch in CA 17-18
Yeo, Wilma (Lethem) 1918- 25-28R
See also SATA 24
Yeoman, John 1934- 106
See also SATA 28
Yeomans, Patricia Henry 1917- 97-100
Yep, Laurence Michael 1948- CANR-1
Earlier sketch in CA 49-52
See also SATA 7
See also DLB 52
See also CLC 35
See also CLR 3
Yepsen, Roger B(ennet), Jr. 1947- 114
Yerbury, Grace D. 1899- 37-40R
Yerby, Frank G(arvin) 1916- CANR-16
Earlier sketch in CA 11-12R
See also BW
See also DLB 76
See also CLC 1, 7, 22
Yergin, Daniel H. 103
Yerian, Cameron John 73-76
See also SATA 21
Yerian, Margaret A. 73-76
See also SATA 21
Yermakov, Nicholas 1951- 118
Yerushalmi, Yosef Hayim 1932-
Brief entry 112
Yeselson, Abraham 1921-1978 Obituary ...77-80
Yesenin, Sergei Alexandrovich
See Esenin, Sergei (Alexandrovich)
Yeshayahu, Yisrael 1910-1979 Obituary ...89-92
Yessian, Mark R(obert) 1942- CANR-10
Earlier sketch in CA 25-28R
Yetman, Norman R(oger) 1938- 29-32R
Yette, Samuel F(rederick) 1929- 102
Yeung Yue-man 1938- 110
Yevtushenko, Yevgeny (Alexandrovich)
1933- 81-84
See also CLC 1, 3, 13, 26
Yezierska, Anzia 1885(?)-1970 126
Obituary 89-92
See also DLB 28
See also CLC 46
Yezzo, Dominick 1947- 53-56
Yglesias, Helen 1915- CANR-15
Earlier sketch in CA 37-40R
See also CLC 7, 22
Yglesias, Jose 1919- 41-44R
Yglesias, Rafael 1954- 37-40R
Yiannopoulos, A(thanassios) N(ikolaos)
1928- 2R
Yim, Kwan Ha 1929- 101
Yin, Robert K(uo-zuir) 1941- CANR-1
Earlier sketch in CA 49-52
Yinger, J(ohn) Milton 1916- 89-92
Yip, Wai-lim 1937- 33-36R
Yllo, Kersti 1953- 119
Ylvisaker, Paul 1921- CANR-16
Earlier sketches in CA 3R, CANR-1
Yngve, Victor H(use) 1920- 57-60
Yntema, Theodore O(tte) 1900-1985
Obituary 117
Yoakum, Robert 1922- 77-80
Yochelson, Samuel 1906(?)-1976
Obituary 69-72
Yochim, Louise Dunn 1909- 37-40R
Yocom, Charles Frederick 1914- CANR-7
Earlier sketch in CA 17-18R
Yoder, Dale 1901- CANR-2
Earlier sketch in CA 2R
Yoder, Don 1921- 85-88
Yoder, Glee 1916- CANR-9
Earlier sketch in CA 21-22R
Yoder, J(ames) Willard 1902- 37-40R
Yoder, Janice D(ana) 1952- 114
Yoder, Jess 1922- 45-48
Yoder, John H(oward) 1927- 15-16R
Yoder, Marie Angeline 1914- 7-8R
Yoder, Norman M. 1915- 21-22R
Yoder, Paton 1912- 93-96
Yoder, Sanford Calvin 1879- CAP-1
Earlier sketch in CA 15-16
Yoffe, Elkhonon (Hona) 1928- 126
Yogiji, Harbhajan Singh Khalsa 1929- 93-96
Yogman, Michael W. 1947- 126
Yohe, W(illiam) Frederick 1943- 49-52
Yohn, David Waite 1933- 41-44R
Yohn, Rick 1937- CANR-8
Earlier sketch in CA 61-64
Yoingco, Angel Q. 1921- CANR-11
Earlier sketch in CA 25-28R
Yoken, Melvin B(arton) 1939- 65-68
Yola, Yerima
See Kirk-Greene, Anthony (Hamilton
Millard)
Yolen, Jane (Hyatt) 1939- CANR-11
Earlier sketch in CA 15-16R
See also SATA 4, 40
See also SAAS 1
See also DLB 52
See also CLR 4
Yolen, Steven H. 1942- 73-76
Yolen, Will (Hyatt) 1908-1985 .... CANR-5
Obituary 118
Earlier sketch in CA 5-6R
Yolton, John W(illiam) 1921- CANR-14
Earlier sketch in CA 37-40R
Yone, Edward Michael Law
See Law Yone, Edward Michael
Yonemura, Margaret V. S. 1928- 29-32R
Yonge, Charlotte (Mary) 1823-1901
Brief entry 109
See also SATA 17
See also DLB 18
Yonge, (Charles) Maurice 1899-1986
Obituary 118
Yonker, Nicholas J(unior) 1927- 117
Yoo, Grace S.
See Yoo, Young H(yun)
Yoo, Young H(yun) 1927- 41-44R
Yoo, Yushin 1940- CANR-2
Earlier sketch in CA 45-48
Yooll, Andrew M(ichael) Graham
See Graham-Yooll, Andrew M(ichael)
Yoors, Jan 1922(?)-1977 81-84
Obituary 73-76
Yora, Shandrin M(arion) 1937- 120
Yorburg, Betty 1926- CANR-16
Earlier sketch in CA 29-32R
Yorck, Ruth (Landshoff) 1909-1966
Obituary 25-28R
Yordan, Philip 1913(?)- Brief entry 116
Yorick, A. P.
See Tindall, William York
Yorinks, Arthur 1953- 106
See also SATA 33, 49
York, Amanda
See Dial, Joan
York, Andrew
See Nicole, Christopher Robin
York, Carol Beach 1928- CANR-6
Earlier sketch in CA 3R
See also SATA 6
York, Elizabeth
See York, Margaret Elizabeth
York, Georgia
See Hoffman, Lee
York, Helen 1918- CANR-4
Earlier sketch in CA 53-56
York, Herbert (Frank) 1921- 29-32R
York, Jeremy
See Creasey, John
York, Margaret Elizabeth 1927- 103
York, Pauline
See Howl, Marcia (Yvonne Hurt)
York, Rebecca
See Buckholtz, Eileen (Garber)
and Glick, Ruth (Burtnick)
York, Reginald O(scar) 1942- 117
York, Simon
See Heinlein, Robert A(nson)
York, Thomas (Lee) 1940- 73-76
York, William 1950- 107
Yorke, Henry Vincent 1905-1974 85-88
Obituary 49-52
See also CLC 13
Yorke, Katherine
See Ellerbeck, Rosemary (Anne
L'Estrange)
Yorke, Margaret
See Larminie, Margaret Beda
Yorke, Ritchie 1944- 77-80
Yorke, Roger
See Bingley, David Ernest
Yorke, Susan 1915- CANR-1
Earlier sketch in CA 3R
Yorkist
See Morrah, Dermot (Michael Macgregor)
Yoseloff, Martin 1919- 45-48
Yoseloff, Thomas 1913- 77-80
Yoshida, (Katsumi) Jim 1921- 41-44R
Yoshida, Shigeru 1878-1967 Obituary 113

Yoshimasu Gozo 1939- ... 126
Yoskowitz, Irving
See Younger, Irving
Yost, Charles W(oodruff) 1907-1981 ... CANR-3
Obituary ... 104
Earlier sketch in CA 11-12R
Yost, Edna 1889-1971 ... 2R
Obituary ... 103
See also SATA 26
Yost, Elwy McMurran 1925- ... 126
Yost, F(rank) Donald 1927- ... 29-32R
Yost, Nellie Snyder 1905- ... CANR-16
Earlier sketch in CA 29-32R
Yost, Stanley K. 1924- ... 11-12R
Youcha, Geraldine 1925- ... 93-96
Youd, C. S.
See Youd, Samuel
See also SAAS 6
Youd, Samuel 1922- ... 77-80
See also SATA 30, 47
Youdale, Peter J. 1928- ... 45-48
Youman, Roger J(acob) 1932- ... 65-68
Youmans, E(lmer) Grant 1907- ... CAP-2
Earlier sketch in CA 23-24
Youmans, Marlene 1953- ... 77-80
Young, Agatha
See Young, Agnes Brooks
Young, Agnes Brooks 1898-1974
Obituary ... 109
Young, Ahdele Carrine 1923- ... 107
Young, Al(bert James) 1939- ... CANR-26
Earlier sketch in CA 29-32R
See also BW
See also DLB 33
See also CLC 19
Young, Alan 1930- ... CANR-6
Earlier sketch in CA 57-60
Young, Alan R(oger) 1941- ... 89-92
Young, Alison 1922- ... 53-56
Young, Allan Edward 1939- ... 125
Young, Allen 1941- ... CANR-18
Earlier sketch in CA 101
Young, Andrew 1885-1971 ... CANR-7
Earlier sketch in CA 7-8R
See also CLC 5
Young, Angela
See Yardley, Alice
Young, Anne P(atricia) 1921- ... 65-68
Young, Arthur C(lements) 1923- ... 25-28R
Young, Arthur N(ichols) 1890-1984 ... 11-12R
Obituary ... 113
Young, Bernice Elizabeth 1931- ... 37-40R
Young, Bertram Alfred 1912- ... 105
Young, Billie 1936- ... 53-56
Young, Bob
See Young, James Robert
and Young, Robert W(illiam)
Young, Brittany
See Young, Sandra
Young, Carrie
See Young, Ahdele Carrine
Young, Carter Travis
See Charbonneau, Louis (Henry)
Young, Catherine
See Olds, Helen Diehl
Young, Charles M(atthew) 1951- ... 93-96
Young, Charles R(obert) 1927- ... 15-16R
Young, Chesley Virginia 1919- ... 33-36R
Young, Chic
See Young, Murat Bernard (Chic)
Young, Clarence ... CAP-2
Earlier sketch in CA 19-20
See also SATA 1
Young, Collier 1908(?)-1980 Obituary ... 103
Young, Collier
See Bloch, Robert (Albert)
Young, Dallas M. 1914- ... 19-20R
Young, David C(harles) 1937- ... 41-44R
Young, David P(ollock) 1936- ... CANR-24
Earlier sketches in CA 21-22R, CANR-9
Young, David S(amuel D'arcy) 1946- ... 113
Young, Delbert Alton 1907-1975 ... 105
Young, Dennis R(alph) 1943- Brief entry ... 107
Young, Dick 1918(?)-1987 Obituary ... 123
Young, Donald (Richard) 1933- ... CANR-12
Earlier sketch in CA 15-16R
Young, Donald Ramsey 1898-1977
Obituary ... 69-72
Young, Dorothea Bennett 1924- ... CANR-13
Earlier sketch in CA 13-14R
See also SATA 31
Young, Douglas (Cuthbert Colquhoun)
1913-1973 ... CAP-1
Obituary ... 45-48
Earlier sketch in CA 17-18
Young, Ed 1931- ... SATA-10
Young, Ed (Tse-chun) 1931- Brief entry ... 116
Young, Edgar Berryhill 1908- ... 104
Young, Edith ... 49-52
Young, Edward
See Reinfeld, Fred
Young, Edward J(oseph) 1907-1968 ... CAP-1
Earlier sketch in CA 11-12
Young, (Cecil) Edwyn 1913-1988 Obituary ... 124
Young, Elaine L.
See Schulte, Elaine L(ouise)
Young, Eleanor R. 1918- ... 37-40R
Young, Elisabeth Larsh 1910- ... 81-84
Young, Elizabeth ... 108
Young, Ellin Dodge 1932- ... 106
Young, Everett
See Cosby, Yvonne Shepard
Young, Ezra P(orter) 1902- ... 113
Young, Francis Brett 1884-1954
Brief entry ... 122
Young, Frank Carl 1907- ... CAP-1
Earlier sketch in CA 13-14
Young, Frank Wilbur 1928- Brief entry ... 108
Young, Fred(erick) L(ee) 1922- ... 25-28R
Young, G(eorge) M(alcolm) 1882-1959
Brief entry ... 120
Young, Gary 1951- ... 117
Young, George Berkeley 1913-1988
Obituary ... 124
Young, George F(rederick) W(illiam)
1937- ... 57-60
Young, Gregory G. 1929- Brief entry ... 110
Young, Harold Chester 1932- Brief entry ... 109
Young, Harold H(erbert) 1903- ... CAP-2
Earlier sketch in CA 19-20
Young, Howard Thomas 1926- ... 11-12R
Young, Hugo 1938- ... 25-28R
Young, I(sador) S. 1902- ... 102
Young, Ian (George) 1945- ... CANR-11
Earlier sketch in CA 29-32R
Young, J(ames) Harvey 1915- ... CANR-6
Earlier sketch in CA 2R
Young, J(ohn) Z(achary) 1907- ... CANR-19
Earlier sketch in CA 101
Young, James Allan 1934- ... 116
Young, James D(ean) 1925- Brief entry ... 111
Young, James Douglas 1921- ... 25-28R
Young, James J(oseph) 1940- ... CANR-16
Earlier sketch in CA 93-96
Young, James O(wen) 1943- ... 49-52
Young, James Robert 1921- ... 93-96
Young, James V(an) 1936- ... 69-72
Young, Jan
See Young, Janet Randall
Young, Janet Randall 1919- ... CANR-5
Earlier sketch in CA 5-6R
See also SATA 3
Young, Jessica (Hankinson) Brett
See Brett-Young, Jessica (Hankinson)
Young, Jim 1930- ... 109
Young, Jock 1942- ... 104
Young, John 1920- ... CANR-1
Earlier sketch in CA 45-48
Young, John Orr 1886-1976 Obituary ... 65-68
Young, John Parke 1895- ... 7-8R
Young, John V. 1909- ... 121
Young, John Wray 1907- ... 45-48
Young, Jordan Marten 1920- ... 21-22R
Young, Kenneth 1916-1985 ... CANR-3
Obituary ... 118
Earlier sketch in CA 9-10R
Young, Kenneth T(odd) 1916-1972
Obituary ... 37-40R
Young, Leontine R(uth) 1910-1988 ... CAP-1
Obituary ... 126
Earlier sketch in CA 11-12
Young, Lesley 1949- ... 110
Young, Lois Horton 1911-1981 ... 11-12R
See also SATA 26
Young, Louise B. 1919- ... CANR-10
Earlier sketch in CA 25-28R
Young, Louise Merwin 1903- ... CAP-1
Earlier sketch in CA 11-12
Young, M(erwin) Crawford 1931- ... 15-16R
Young, Mahonri 1911- ... 81-84
Young, Margaret B(uckner) 1922- ... 23-24R
See also SATA 2
Young, Margaret Labash 1926-
Brief entry ... 110
Young, Marguerite ... CAP-1
Earlier sketch in CA 15-16
Young, Marjorie W(illis) ... 85-88
Young, Mary Elizabeth 1929- ... 37-40R
Young, Mary Elizabeth Reardon
1901(?)-1981 Obituary ... 105
Young, Mary Lou Daves 1918- ... 126
Young, Michael (Dunlop) 1915- ... 101
Young, Miriam 1913-1974 ... 37-40R
Obituary ... 53-56
See also SATA 7
Young, Morris N. 1909- ... 33-36R
Young, Murat Bernard (Chic) 1901-1973
Obituary ... 41-44R
Young, Nacella
See Tate, Velma
Young, Neil 1945- ... 110
See also CLC 17
Young, Noel 1922- ... 57-60
Young, Norman J(ames) 1930- ... 77-80
Young, Oran R(eed) 1941- ... 112
Brief entry ... 109
Young, Otis E., Jr. 1925- ... 53-56
Young, Pam 1943- ... 109
Young, (Rodney Lee) Patrick (Jr.) 1937- ... 69-72
See also SATA 22
Young, Paul Thomas 1892-1978 ... CANR-3
Earlier sketch in CA 2R
Young, Pauline Vislick 1896- ... 7-8R
Young, Percy M(arshall) 1912- ... 15-16R
See also SATA 31
Young, Perry Deane 1941- ... 57-60
Young, Peter 1915- ... 13-14R
Young, Peter Alan 1934- ... 107
Young, Philip 1918- ... CANR-6
Earlier sketch in CA 11-12R
Young, Philip
See Steward, Samuel M(orris)
Young, Ralph Aubrey 1902(?)-1980
Obituary ... 97-100
Young, Richard E(merson) 1932- ... 29-32R
Young, Richard Knox 1913- ... 13-14R
Young, Richard Phillip 1940- ... 29-32R
Young, Robert 1944- ... 123
Young, Robert
See Payne, (Pierre Stephen) Robert
Young, Robert Doran 1928- ... CANR-17
Earlier sketch in CA 29-32R
Young, Robert J(ohn) 1942- ... 101
Young, Robert W(illiam) 1916-1969 ... CANR-5
Earlier sketch in CA 5-6R
See also SATA 3
Young, Rose
See Harris, Marion Rose (Young)
Young, Ruth 1884-1983 Obituary ... 111
Young, Sandra 1952- ... 124
Young, Scott A(lexander) 1918- ... CANR-20
Earlier sketches in CA 11-12R, CANR-5
See also SATA 5
Young, Seymour Dilworth 1897- ... CAP-2
Earlier sketch in CA 29-32
Young, Stanley (Preston) 1906-1975
Obituary ... 57-60
Young, Stark 1881-1963 ... 105
Obituary ... 89-92
See also DLB 9
Young, Stephen M(arvin) 1889(?)-1984
Obituary ... 114
Young, Thomas
See Yoseloff, Thomas
Young, Thomas Daniel 1919- ... CANR-14
Earlier sketch in CA 37-40R
Young, Vernon 1912-1986 ... 45-48
Obituary ... 120
Young, Virginia Brady 1921- ... 61-64
Young, Virginia G(arton) 1919- ... 15-16R
Young, Vivien
See Gater, Dilys
Young, Waldemar 1880-1938 ... DLB-26
Young, Warren C(ameron) 1913- ... 13-14R
Young, Warren R(ichard) 1926- ... 21-22R
Young, Wayland 1923- ... 13-14R
Young, Whitney M(oore), Jr.
1921-1971 ... CANR-25
Earlier sketches in CA 13-14, CAP-1
See also BW
Young, William 1918- ... 45-48
Young, William C(urtis) 1928- ... 45-48
Young, William H(enry) 1912- ... 23-24R
Young, William J. 1938- ... 109
Youngberg, Norma Ione (Rhoads)
1896- ... 11-12R
Youngberg, Ruth Tanis 1915- ... 107
Youngblood, Ila Dell 1926- ... 125
Youngblood, Ronald F. 1931- ... CANR-14
Earlier sketch in CA 37-40R
Youngdahl, Benjamin E(manuel)
1897-1970 ... CAP-2
Earlier sketch in CA 21-22
Youngdahl, Reuben K(enneth Nathaniel)
1911-1968 ... 5-6R
Obituary ... 103
Younge, Sheila 1945(?)-1977 Obituary ... 73-76
Younger, Edward Eugene 1909-1979
Obituary ... 89-92
Younger, Irving 1932-1988 Obituary ... 125
Younger, Paul 1935- ... 101
Younger, R(onald) M(ichel) 1917- ... CANR-10
Earlier sketch in CA 17-18R
Younger, Richard D(avis) 1921- ... 11-12R
Younghusband, Eileen (Louise)
1902-1981 Obituary ... 108
Younghusband, Francis (Edward)
1863-1942 Brief entry ... 113
Youngman, Henny Brief entry ... 107
Youngquist, Walter 1921- ... 61-64
Youngren, J(ohn) Alan 1937- ... 108
Youngs, Betty 1934-1985 ... 117
See also SATA 42, 53
Youngs, Betty F(errell) 1928- ... 33-36R
Youngs, Frederic A., Jr. 1936- Brief entry ... 112
Youngs, J. William T., Jr. 1941- ... CANR-10
Earlier sketch in CA 65-68
Youngs, Robert W(ells) 1913- ... 15-16R
Younie, William John 1932- ... 21-22R
Younin, Wolf 1908(?)-1984 Obituary ... 112
Younker, Lucas 1942- ... 65-68
Yount, John A(lonzo) 1935- ... CANR-5
Earlier sketch in CA 45-48
Yourcenar, Marguerite 1903-1987 ... CANR-23
Earlier sketch in CA 69-72
See also DLB 72
See also CLC 19, 38, 50
Youree, Gary 1931- ... CANR-2
Earlier sketch in CA 49-52
Yousuf, Ahmed
See Essop, Ahmed
Youtie, Herbert Chayyim 1904-1980
Obituary ... 97-100
Yowa
See McMurray, Nancy A(rmistead)
Yoxall, Harry W(aldo) 1896-1984 ... 13-14R
Obituary ... 113
Yoxen, Edward (John) 1950- ... 123
Yu, Anthony C. 1938- Brief entry ... 110
Yu, Beongcheon 1925- Brief entry ... 108
Yu, Charles
See Targ, William
Yu, David C. 1918- ... 37-40R
Yu, Elena S. H. 1947- ... 125
Brief entry ... 109
Yu, Frederick T. C. 1921- ... 11-12R
Yu, George T(zuchiao) 1931- ... 19-20R
Yu, Pauline (Ruth) 1949- ... 122
Brief entry ... 118
Yu, Ying-shih 1930- ... 25-28R
Yuan, Lei Chen
See De Jaegher, Raymond-Joseph
Yuan, T'ung-li 1895-1965 ... CAP-1
Earlier sketch in CA 9-10
Yudell, Lynn D. 1943- ... 29-32R
Yudewitz, Hyman 1906- ... 93-96
Yudkin, John 1910- ... 13-14R
Yudkin, Leon Israel 1939- ... CANR-12
Earlier sketch in CA 29-32R
Yudkin, Michael D(avid) 1938- ... 29-32R
Yudof, Mark G(eorge) 1944- ... 109
Yu-ho, Tseng
See Ecke, Betty Tseng Yu-ho
Yuill, P. B.
See Williams, Gordon (Maclean)
Yuill, Phyllis Jean (Marquart) 1941- ... 65-68
Yuill, William Edward 1921- ... CANR-2
Earlier sketch in CA 3R
Yukawa, Hideki 1907-1981 Obituary ... 108
Yuki
See Inoue, Yukitoshi
Yuma, Dan
See Dunham, Robert
Yun, Tan
See Lin, Adet J(usu)
Yunck, John A(dam) III 1917- ... 11-12R
Yungblut, John R(ichard) 1913- ... 41-44R
Yunkel, Ramar
See Martin, Jose L(uis)
Yurchenco, Henrietta 1916- ... 37-40R
Yurick, Sol 1925- ... CANR-25
Earlier sketch in CA 15-16R
See also CLC 6
Yurieff, Zoya I(osifovna) 1922- Brief entry ... 109
Yurka, Blanche 1887-1974 ... 11-12R
Obituary ... 120
Yusko, A(aron) A(llen) 1935- ... 65-68
Yuzyk, Paul 1913- ... CANR-18
Earlier sketch in CA 101
Yzermans, Vincent Arthur 1925- ... 15-16R

Z

Zabaneh, Natalia (Shefka) 1946- ... 105
Zabeeh, Farhana 1919- ... 41-44R
Zabih, Sepehr 1925- ... CANR-9
Earlier sketch in CA 23-24R
Zabilka, Gladys M. 1917- ... 7-8R
Zablocki, Benjamin 1941- ... 37-40R
Zablocki, Clement J(ohn) 1912-1983
Obituary ... 111
Zabolotskii, Nikolai Alekseevich 1903-1958
Brief entry ... 116
Zacek, Jane Shapiro 1938- ... 109
Zacek, Joseph Frederick 1930- ... 37-40R
Zach, Cheryl (Byrd) 1947- ... 124
See also SATA 51
Zach, Nathan 1930- Brief entry ... 105
Zacharias, Lee
See Zacharias, Lela Ann
Zacharias, Lela Ann 1944- ... 85-88
Zacharis, John C. 1936- ... 73-76
Zachary, Elizabeth 1928- ... 109
Zachary, Hugh 1928- ... CANR-13
Earlier sketch in CA 23-24R
Zacher, Christian Keeler 1941- ... 105
Zacher, Mark W. 1938- ... 85-88
Zacher, Robert Vincent 1917- ... 2R
Zack, Arnold M(arshall) 1931- ... CANR-19
Earlier sketches in CA 11-12R, CANR-3
Zade, Mirzo Tursun
See Tursun-Zade, Mirzo
Zadeh, Norman 1950- ... 61-64
Zaehner, Robert Charles 1913-1974
Obituary ... 109
Zaffo, George J. (?)-1984 ... SATA-42
Zaffuto, Anthony A(ngelo) 1926- ... 101
Zafren, Herbert C(ecil) 1925- ... CANR-25
Earlier sketch in CA 45-48
Zagar, J. Janko 1921- ... 121
Zagarell, Sandra A(belson) 1943- ... 118
Zagat, Arthur Leo 1895(?)-1949
Brief entry ... 110
Zagona, Salvatore Vincent 1920-
Brief entry ... 108
Zagoren, Ruby 1922-1974 ... CAP-1
Earlier sketch in CA 17-18
Zagoria, Donald S. 1928- ... CANR-16
Earlier sketch in CA 23-24R
Zagorin, Perez 1920- ... 53-56
Zagst, Michael (Sidney) 1950- ... 121
Zaharias, Babe Didrikson
See Zaharias, Mildred Ella Didrikson
Zaharias, Mildred Ella Didrikson
1914(?)-1956 Brief entry ... 117
Zaharopoulos, George K. 1933- ... 41-44R
Zahava, Irene 1951- ... 57-60
Zahl, Paul Arthur 1910-1985 Obituary ... 117
Zahler, Helene S. 1911-1981 Obituary ... 104
Zahn, Curtis 1912- ... CANR-5
Earlier sketch in CA 7-8R
Zahn, Frank 1936- ... 97-100
Zahn, Gordon C(harles) 1918- ... 11-12R
Zahn, Muriel 1894- ... 5-6R
Zahn, Timothy 1951- ... 123
Zahniser, Marvin R(alph) 1934- ... 21-22R
Zahorchak, Michael G(eorge) 1929- ... CANR-15
Earlier sketch in CA 41-44R
Zahorski, Kenneth J. 1939- ... 123
Zaid, Barry 1938- ... SATA-51
Zaidenberg, Arthur 1908(?)- ... 108
See also SATA 34
Zaidi, S(yed) M(ohammad) Hafeez
1929- ... CANR-25
Earlier sketch in CA 45-48
Zainu'ddin, Ailsa
See Zainu'ddin, Ailsa G(wennyth)
Thomson
Zainu'ddin, Ailsa G(wennyth) Thomson
1927- ... CANR-12
Earlier sketch in CA 29-32R
Zajonc, Robert Boleslaw 1923- Brief entry ... 106
Zakarian, Richard H(achadoor) 1925- ... 41-44R
Zakia, Richard D(onald) 1925- ... CANR-9
Earlier sketch in CA 65-68

Zakon, Alan J. 1935- 17-18R
Zakuta, Leo 1925- 17-18R
Zalamea, Luis 1921- 19-20R
Zalan, Magda 1936- 112
Zalben, Jane Breskin 1950- CANR-4
Earlier sketch in CA 49-52
See also SATA 7
Zald, Mayer N(athan) 1931- CANR-8
Earlier sketch in CA 19-20R
Zaldivar, Fulgencio Batista y
See Batista y Zaldivar, Fulgencio
Zaleski, Eugene 1918- 77-80
Zaleznik, Abraham 1924- 73-76
Zali, Paul M. 1922- Brief entry 108
Zalkind, Sheldon S(tanley) 1922- 65-68
Zall, Paul M. 1922- CANR-20
Earlier sketches in CA 2R, CANR-6
Zaller, Angelika Bita CANR-13
Earlier sketch in CA 77-80
Zaller, Robert 1940- CANR-13
Earlier sketch in CA 77-80
Zallinger, Jean (Day) 1918- SATA-14
Zallinger, Peter Franz 1943- 108
See also SATA 49
Zalon, Jean E(ugenia) 1919- 102
Zaltkovich, Charles T(heodore) 1917- 7-8R
Zaltman, Gerald 1938- CANR-7
Earlier sketch in CA 17-18R
Zalzanick, Sheldon 1928- 77-80
Zamble, Edward 1942- Brief entry 108
Zamiatin, Yevgenii
See Zamyatin, Evgeny Ivanovich
Zamonski, Stanley W. 1919- 11-12R
Zamoyski, Adam (Stefan Jan Maria Sariusz) 1949- 103
Zamoyta, Vincent C. 1921- 23-24R
Zampaglione, Gerardo 1917- CANR-14
Earlier sketch in CA 77-80
Zamyatin, Evgeny Ivanovich 1884-1937
Brief entry 105
See also TCLC 8
Zand, Dale Ezra 1926- 111
Zander, Alvin Frederick 1913- CANR-19
Earlier sketch in CA 2R
Zanderbergen, George
See May, Julian
Zaner, Richard M(orris) 1933- CANR-16
Earlier sketch in CA 29-32R
Zanetti, J(oaquin) Enrique 1885-1974
Obituary 45-48
Zangrando, Robert L. 1932- 25-28R
Zangwill, Israel 1864-1926 Brief entry 109
See also DLB 10
See also TCLC 16
Zangwill, Oliver Louis 1913- 109
Zanjani, Sally Springmeyer 120
Zants, Emily 1937- 37-40R
Zanuck, Daryl F(rancis) 1902-1979
Obituary 93-96
Zappa, Francis Vincent, Jr. 1940- 108
Zappa, Frank
See Zappa, Francis Vincent, Jr.
See also CLC 17
Zappler, Lisbeth 1930- CANR-4
Earlier sketch in CA 49-52
See also SATA 10
Zar, Rose 1923- 117
Zara, Louis 1910- CAP-2
Earlier sketch in CA 13-14
Zarchy, Harry 1912- CANR-2
Earlier sketch in CA 4R
See also SATA 34
Zarcone, Vincent P(eter), Jr. 1937- 61-64
Zarefsky, David (Harris) 1946- Brief entry 109
Zaremba, Joseph 1923- Brief entry 112
Zaretsky, Eli 1940- 85-88
Zaring, Jane (Thomas) 1936- 108
See also SATA 40, 51
Zariski, Raphael 1925- 49-52
Zarnecki, George 1915- CANR-10
Earlier sketch in CA 57-60
Zarnecki, Jerzy
See Zarnecki, George
Zarnowitz, Victor 1919- 21-22R
Zarro, Richard A(llen) 1946- 33-36R
Zartman, I(ra) William 1932- CANR-5
Earlier sketch in CA 11-12R
Zaslavsky, Claudia 1917- CANR-1
Earlier sketch in CA 49-52
See also SATA 36
Zasloff, Joseph J(ermiah) 1925-
Brief entry 116
Zaslow, Morris 1918- CANR-24
Earlier sketch in CA 45-48
Zassenhaus, Hiltgunt 1916- 49-52
See also AITN 1
Zastrow, Erika
See Massey, Erika
Zatlin, Phyllis 1938- CANR-15
Earlier sketch in CA 41-44R
Zatlin Boring, Phyllis
See Zatlin, Phyllis
Zatlin-Boring, Phyllis
See Zatlin, Phyllis
Zatuchni, Gerald I. 1935- 37-40R
Zaturenska, Marya 1902-1982 CANR-22
Obituary 105
Earlier sketch in CA 13-14R
See also CLC 6, 11
Zauberman, Alfred 1903-1984 Obituary 112
Zavala, Albert 1930- Brief entry 117
Zavala, Iris M(ilagros) 1936- CANR-1
Earlier sketch in CA 45-48
Zavarzadeh, Mas'ud 1938- 106
Zavatsky, Bill
See Zavatsky, William Alexander
Zavatsky, William Alexander 1943- CANR-1
Earlier sketch in CA 49-52
Zavin, Benjamin B. 1920(?)-1981
Obituary 103
Zavin, Theodora 1922- 53-56
Zavrian, Suzanne (Ostro) 1928- 113
Zawadsky, Patience 1927- CANR-24
Earlier sketches in CA 23-24R, CANR-9
Zawadzki, Edward S. 1914-1967 CAP-2
Earlier sketch in CA 17-18
Zawodny, J(anusz) K(azimierz) 1921- CANR-11
Earlier sketch in CA 15-16R
Zax, Melvin 1928- 37-40R
Zayas-Bazan, Eduardo 1935- 53-56
Zdenek, Marilee 1934- 102
Zea, Leopoldo 1912- CANR-16
Earlier sketch in CA 29-32R
Zebel, Sydney H. 1914- 2R
Zebouni, Selma A(ssir) 1930- 17-18R
Zebrowski, George 1945- 41-44R
See also DLB 8
Zec, Philip 1910(?)-1983 Obituary 110
Zech, Paul 1881-1946 DLB-56
Zeck, Gerald Anthony 1939- 114
See also SATA 40
Zeck, Gerry
See Zeck, Gerald Anthony
Zeckendorf, William 1905- 73-76
Zeckhauser, Richard Jay 1940- 126
Zedler, Beatrice H(ope) 1916- 41-44R
Zedler, Empress Young 1908- 41-44R
Zeeveld, W(illiam) Gordon 1902-1975 41-44R
Zeff, Stephen A(ddam) 1933- CANR-19
Earlier sketches in CA 11-12R, CANR-3
Zegger, Robert Elie 1932- 41-44R
Zehna, Peter W(illiam) 1925- CANR-1
Earlier sketch in CA 2R
Zehnle, Richard F(rederick) 1933- 29-32R
Zehnpfennig, Gladys Burandt 1910- CANR-5
Earlier sketch in CA 7-8R
Zehring, John William 1947- 117
Zei, Alki 77-80
See also SATA 24
See also CLR 6
Zeidenstein, Harvey 1932- 57-60
Zeidman, Irving 1908- CAP-2
Earlier sketch in CA 21-22
Zeidner, Lisa 1955- 110
Zeiger, Henry A(nthony) 1930- 11-12R
Zeiger, Larry
See King, Larry
Zeigerman, Gerald 1939- 21-22R
Zeigfreid, Karl
See Fanthorpe, R(obert) Lionel
Zeigler, L(uther) Harmon 1936- CANR-10
Earlier sketch in CA 15-16R
Zeilik, Michael 1946- 65-68
Zeisel, Hans 1905- CANR-6
Earlier sketch in CA 2R
Zeit, Calvin
See Barasch, Marc Ian
Zeitlin, Irving M. 1928- 21-22R
Zeitlin, Jonathan (Hart) 1955- 121
Zeitlin, Joseph 1906- 49-52
Zeitlin, Maurice 1935- CANR-26
Earlier sketches in CA 13-14R, CANR-10
Zeitlin, Patty 1936- CANR-12
Earlier sketch in CA 25-28R
Zeitlin, Solomon 1888(?)-1976 77-80
Obituary 69-72
Zeitz, James (Victor) 1940- 110
Zeka, Valentin
See Sokolov, Valentin
Zekman, Pamela (Lois) 1944- 106
Zekowski, Arlene 1922- CANR-1
Earlier sketch in CA 45-48
Zelazny, Roger (Joseph) 1937- CANR-26
Earlier sketch in CA 23-24R
See also SATA 39
See also DLB 8
See also CLC 21
Zeldin, Jesse 1923- 49-52
Zeldis, Chayym 1927- CANR-6
Earlier sketch in CA 3R
Zelditch, Morris, Jr. 1928- 53-56
Zeldner, Max 1907- CAP-1
Earlier sketch in CA 13-14
Zeldovich, Ia(kov) B(orisovich) 1914-1987
Obituary 124
Zeleny, Lawrence 1904- 61-64
Zeleny, Leslie D(ay) 1898- 45-48
Zelermyer, William 1914- 2R
Zeligs, Meyer A(aron) 1909-1978 CAP-2
Obituary 77-80
Earlier sketch in CA 23-24
Zeligs, Rose 57-60
Zelinka, Sydney 1906(?)-1981 Obituary 102
Zelinsky, Paul O. 1953- 121
See also SATA 33, 49
Zelinsky, Wilbur 1921- 15-16R
Zelizer, Viviana A. 1946- 125
Zelk, Zoltan 1906-1981 Obituary 103
Zelko, Harold Philip 1908- CANR-1
Earlier sketch in CA 2R
Zell, Hans M(artin) 1940- 113
Zellan, Audrey Penn
See Penn, Audrey
See also SATA 22
Zeller, Belle 1903- 57-60
Zeller, Frederick A. 1931- 21-22R
Zellerbach, Merla 1930- 3R
Zellers, Parker 1927- 37-40R
Zellmann-Finkbeiner, Peter 1942- 49-52
Zellner, Arnold 1927- 41-44R
Zelman, Aaron S(hepard) 1946- 101
Zelman, Anita 1924- 101
Zelmer, A(dam) C(harles) Lynn 1943- CANR-16
Earlier sketch in CA 89-92
Zelomek, A. Wilbert 1900-1980
Obituary 97-100
Zelver, Patricia (Farrell) 1923- 29-32R
Zemach, Harve
See Fischtrom, Harvey
See also SATA 3
Zemach, Kaethe 1958- CANR-8
Earlier sketch in CA 57-60
See also SATA 39, 49
Zemach, Margot 1931- 97-100
See also SATA 21
Zeman, Jarold Knox 1926- 101
Zeman, Zbynek Anthony Bohuslav 1928- 69-72
Zemansky, Mark W(aldo) 1900-1981
Obituary 105
Zend, Robert 1929- 115
Zender, Karl F(rancis) 1937- 110
Zenger, John Peter 1697-1746 DLB-24, 43
Zenkovsky, Serge A. 1907- CANR-2
Earlier sketch in CA 2R
Zens, Patricia Martin 1926-1972 7-8R
Obituary 120
See also SATA 50
Zentner, Carola 1927- 65-68
Zentner, Peter 1932- 29-32R
Zepeda, Ofelia 1954- 114
Zephir, Jacques J(oseph) 1925- 45-48
Zepke, Brent Eric 1943- CANR-13
Earlier sketch in CA 69-72
Zepp, Ira G(ilbert), Jr. 1929- Brief entry 114
Zerafa, Judy 1941- 113
Zerbe, Jerome (B.) 1904-1988 17-18R
Obituary 126
Zerby, Lewis Kenneth 1916- 49-52
Zerden, Sheldon 1924- CANR-10
Earlier sketch in CA 25-28R
Zerin, Edward 1920- 7-8R
Zerman, Melvyn Bernard 1930- CANR-14
Earlier sketch in CA 77-80
See also SATA 46
Zernov, Nicolas (Michael) 1898-1980 CANR-6
Earlier sketch in CA 11-12R
Zerof, Herbert G. 1934- 85-88
Zesmer, David M(ordecai) 1924- 65-68
Zeta
See Cope, (Vincent) Zachary
Zetford, Tully
See Bulmer, (Henry) Kenneth
Zetler, Robert L. 1908- 2R
Zetterling, Mai (Elisabeth) 1925- 126
Brief entry 111
Zettl, Herbert (Lorenz) 1929- 41-44R
Zettler, Howard G. 1926- Brief entry 113
Zeuner, Frederick E(verard) 1905-1963 7-8R
Zevi, Bruno 1918- CANR-18
Earlier sketch in CA 101
Zevin, Ben David 1896(?)-1984 Obituary 114
Zevin, Jack 1940- 93-96
Zevin, Robert B(rooke) 1936- 117
Zeydel, Edwin H(ermann) 1893-1973 7-8R
Obituary 103
Zeyher, Lewis R. 1906- 25-28R
Zgusta, Ladislav 1924- 41-44R
Zhdanov, Andrei A(lexandrovich)
1896-1948 Brief entry 117
See also TCLC 18
Zheludkov, Sergei 1909(?)-1984 Obituary 111
Zhivkova, Lyudmila (Todorova) 1942-1981
Obituary 108
Zhukov, Georgi K(onstantinovich)
1896(?)-1974 Obituary 110
Ziadeh, Farhat Jacob 1917- CANR-14
Earlier sketch in CA 25-28R
Ziadeh, Nicola A(bdo) 1907- 29-32R
Ziavras, Charles E.
See Jarvis, Charles E(fthemios)
Zibart, Carl F. 1907- 73-76
Zidek, Anthony 1936- 17-18R
Zidek, Tony
See Zidek, Anthony
Ziedonis, Arvids, Jr. 1931- 57-60
Zieg, Joan (Gallina) 116
Ziegel, Vic 1938(?)- Brief entry 122
Ziegelmueller, George (William) 1930- 45-48
Ziegenhagen, Eduard A(rthur) 1935- CANR-25
Earlier sketch in CA 45-48
Zieger, Robert H. 1938- 29-32R
Ziegfeld, Edwin Henry 1905-1987
Obituary 123
Ziegfeld, Richard E(van) 1948- 109
Ziegler, Alan 1947- CANR-3
Earlier sketch in CA 49-52
Ziegler, Arthur P(aul), Jr. 1937- 57-60
Ziegler, Bette 1940- 81-84
Ziegler, Charles E. 1953- 126
Ziegler, Donald J(enks) 1924- 25-28R
Ziegler, Edward K(rusen) 1903- 57-60
Ziegler, Elsie Reif 1910- 3R
Ziegler, Isabelle 1904- 25-28R
Ziegler, Jack (Denmore) 1942- 109
Ziegler, Jean 1934- 97-100
Ziegler, Jesse H(unsberger) 1913- CANR-19
Earlier sketch in CA 25-28R
Ziegler, Philip (Sandeman) 1929- 49-52
Ziegler, Raymond J. 1922- 15-16R
Ziegler, Richard S. 1931- 101
Ziegler, Ronald M(elvin) 1935- 102
Ziegler, (Karl Reinhart Ludwig) Theobald
1846-1918 Brief entry 119
Ziel, Ron 1939- 23-24R
Ziemer, Gregor (Athalwin)
1899-198(?) CANR-26
Earlier sketches in CA 13-14, CAP-1
Ziemer, Paul 1921(?)-1985 Obituary 117
Ziemian, Joseph 1922-1971 65-68
Ziemienski, Dennis (Theodore) 1947- SATA-10
Ziemke, Donald C(harles) 1929- 7-8R
Ziemke, Earl F(rederick) 1922- 37-40R
Zierold, Norman (John) 1927- 19-20R
Zieroth, Dale 1946- 117
See also DLB 60
Ziesler, J(ohn) A(nthony) 1930- CANR-1
Earlier sketch in CA 45-48
Zietlow, E(dward) R. 1932- CANR-7
Earlier sketch in CA 19-20R
Zietlow, Paul Nathan 1935- 93-96
Ziewacz, Lawrence E. 1942- 125
Zif, Jay Jehiel 1936- 37-40R
Ziff, Gil 1938- 106
Ziff, Larzer 1927- CANR-25
Earlier sketches in CA 15-16R, CANR-7
Zigler, Edward F(rank) 1930- CANR-15
Earlier sketch in CA 41-44R
Zigrosser, Carl 1891-1975 Obituary 111
Zijderveld, Anton C(ornelis) 1937- CANR-12
Earlier sketch in CA 29-32R
Zikmund, Barbara Brown 1939- 117
Zikmund, Joseph II 1937- CANR-15
Earlier sketch in CA 65-68
Zilahy, Lajos 1891(?)-1974 Obituary 53-56
Zilbergeld, Bernie 1939- 112
Zilbert, Edward R(udolph) 1925- 118
Zilg, Gerard Colby 1945- 57-60
Ziliox, Marc
See Fichter, George S.
Zillah
See Macdonald, Zillah K(atherine)
Zilmer, Bertram G. 1899(?)-1976
Obituary 65-68
Zilversmit, Arthur 1932- 25-28R
Zim, Herbert S(pencer) 1909- CANR-17
Earlier sketch in CA 15-16R
See also SATA 1, 30
See also SAAS 2
See also CLR 2
Zim, Sonia Bleeker 1909-1971 CANR-3
Obituary 33-36R
Earlier sketch in CA 4R
Ziman, H(erbert) D(avid) 1902-1983
Obituary 110
Ziman, J(ohn) M(ichael) 1925- 25-28R
Zimbardo, Philip G(eorge) 1933- 85-88
Zimbardo, Rose (Abdelnour) 1932- 17-18R
Zimelman, Nathan SATA-37
Zimet, Melvin 1913- 73-76
Zimet, Sara (Florence) Goodman 1929- 25-28R
Zimiles, Martha Rogers 1946- 41-44R
Zimiles, Murray 1941- 41-44R
Zimin, Alexander 1920-1980 Obituary 97-100
Zimmer, A(rno) B. 1945- 105
Zimmer, Anne Y(oung) 1920- 85-88
Zimmer, Basil G(eorge) 1920- 13-14R
Zimmer, Eric 1932- 61-64
Zimmer, Herbert 1924- 2R
Zimmer, Jill Schary
See Robinson, Jill
Zimmer, Maude Files 1905- 25-28R
Zimmer, Paul J. 1934- 21-22R
See also DLB 5
Zimmer, Timothy W. L. 1947- 29-32R
Zimmerli, Walther Theodor 1907-1983
Obituary 111
Zimmerman, Bill 1940- 69-72
Zimmerman, Bill
See Zimmerman, William
Zimmerman, Carle C(lark) 1897-1983 CANR-21
Earlier sketch in CA 25-28R
Zimmerman, Dale A. 1928- 124
Zimmerman, David R(adoff) 1934- 57-60
Zimmerman, Deirdre A. 1959- 120
Zimmerman, Ed 1933(?)-1972 Obituary 37-40R
Zimmerman, Eleanor (Goedeke) 1916- 61-64
Zimmerman, Everett (Lee) 1936- 110
Zimmerman, Franklin B(ershir) 1923- CANR-12
Earlier sketch in CA 13-14R
Zimmerman, Fred W(esley) 1921- CANR-2
Earlier sketch in CA 2R
Zimmerman, Gary 1951- 107
Zimmerman, Gordon G(lenn) 1922- 15-16R
Zimmerman, Irene 1907- 37-40R
Zimmerman, Irla Lee 1923- 57-60
Zimmerman, Isidore 1917(?)-1983
Obituary 111
Zimmerman, Joseph Francis 1928- CANR-17
Earlier sketches in CA 7-8R, CANR-2
Zimmerman, Mary K. 1945- 81-84
Zimmerman, Michael E(dward) 1946- 108
Zimmerman, Naoma 1914- 3R
See also SATA 10
Zimmerman, Paul A(lbert) 1918-
Brief entry 109
Zimmerman, Paul D. 115
Zimmerman, Paul Lionel 1932- CANR-10
Earlier sketch in CA 25-28R
Zimmerman, Robert
See Dylan, Bob
Zimmerman, Toni
See Ortner-Zimmerman, Toni
Zimmerman, Velma E. 1902- 29-32R
Zimmerman, William 1936- 53-56
Zimmerman, William 1940- 69-72
Zimmermann, Arnold E. 1909- 101
Zimmermann, Caroline A(nna) 1944- 102
Zimmermann, Ethel Agnes 1909-1984
Obituary 112
Zimmermann, Jon E(mil) 1933- 101
Zimmeth, Mary
See Schomaker, Mary Zimmeth
Zimnik, Reiner 1930- 77-80
See also SATA 36
See also CLR 3
Zimpel, Lloyd 1929- 37-40R

INDEX

Zimring, Franklin E(ster) 1942- 93-96
Zimroth, Evan 1943- 93-96
Zimroth, Peter L. 1943- 93-96
Zinbarg, Edward D(onald) 1934- 21-22R
Zinberg, Norman E(arl) 1921- CANR-16
 Earlier sketch in CA 85-88
Zindel, Bonnie 1943- 105
 See also SATA 34
Zindel, Paul 1936- 73-76
 See also SATA 16
 See also DLB 7, 52
 See also CLC 6, 26
 See also CLR 3
Ziner, Feenie
 See Ziner, Florence
Ziner, Florence 1921- CANR-1
 Earlier sketch in CA 3R
 See also SATA 5
Zingara, Professor
 See Leeming, Joseph
Zink, David D(aniel) 1927- CANR-3
 Earlier sketch in CA 45-48
Zink, Lubor Jan 1920- CANR-9
 Earlier sketch in CA 65-68
Zinke, George William 1904- 7-8R
Zinkin, Taya (Nathalie) Ettinger 1918- ..CANR-2
 Earlier sketch in CA 4R
Zinn, Howard 1922- CANR-2
 Earlier sketch in CA 2R
Zinner, Paul E(rnest) 1922- 2R
Zinner, Stephen H. 1939- 119
Zinnes, Harriet CANR-21
 Earlier sketches in CA 45-48, CANR-1
Zinoviev, Alexander 1922- Brief entry 116
 See also CLC 19
Zinsser, William (Knowlton) 1922- CANR-12
 Earlier sketch in CA 19-20R
Zintz, Miles V(ernon) 1918- 29-32R
Ziolkowski, Theodore (Joseph) 1932- ..CANR-12
 Earlier sketch in CA 15-16R
Ziomek, Henryk 1922- CANR-1
 Earlier sketch in CA 45-48
Zion, Eugene 1913-1975 81-84
 Obituary 61-64
 See also SATA 18
Zion, Gene
 See Zion, Eugene
Zionts, Stanley 1937- 49-52
Zipes, Jack (David) 1937- CANR-7
 Earlier sketch in CA 65-68
Zipser, Arthur 1909- 113
Ziring, Lawrence 1928- CANR-13
 Earlier sketch in CA 73-76
Zisfein, Melvin Bernard 1926- 108
Zisk, Betty H(ershberger) 1930- CANR-25
 Earlier sketch in CA 45-48
Ziskind, Sylvia 1906- 29-32R
Zistel, Era CANR-19
 Earlier sketch in CA 25-28R
Zito, George V(incent) 1923- 115
Zitta, Victor 1926- 21-22R
Zivkovic, Peter D(ragi) 1929- 53-56
Zjawin, Dorothy 1945- 111
Zmijewsky, Boris 1946- CANR-20
 Earlier sketch in CA 69-72

Zneimer, John (Nicolas) 1925- 29-32R
Zobel, Hiller B(ellin) 1932- 23-24R
Zobel, Louise Purwin 1922- 110
Zober, Martin 1918- 37-40R
Zochert, Donald (Paul, Jr.) 1938- 81-84
Zodhiates, Spiros 1922- CANR-10
 Earlier sketch in CA 21-22R
Zodikoff, David H(yman) 1933- 37-40R
Zodrow, John 1944- 77-80
Zoellner, Robert 1926- 57-60
Zoffer, Gerald R. 1926(?)-1982 Obituary ...107
Zohar, Danah 1944- 124
 Brief entry 118
Zohn, Arnold 1924-1985 Obituary 116
Zohn, Harry 1923- CANR-25
 Earlier sketches in CA 25-28R, CANR-10
Zoilus
 See Lovecraft, H(oward) P(hillips)
Zola, Emile 1840-1902 Brief entry 104
 See also TCLC 1, 6, 21
Zola, Irving Kenneth 1935- 107
Zola, Marion (Joy) 1945- 108
Zolar
 See King, Bruce
Zolberg, Aristide R(odolphe) 1931- 21-22R
Zolbrod, Leon M(ax) 1930- 57-60
Zolbrod, Paul G(eyer) 1932- CANR-10
 Earlier sketch in CA 21-22R
Zolf, Larry 1934- 101
Zoll, Donald Atwell 1927- 5-6R
Zolla, Elemire 1926- CANR-6
 Earlier sketch in CA 11-12R
Zollinger, Gulielma 1856-1917 Brief entry ...109
 See also SATA 27
Zollinger, Norman 1921- 81-84
Zollitsch, Herbert G(eorge) 1916- 13-14R
Zollschan, George K(arl) 1930- 15-16R
Zolotow, Charlotte S. 1915- CANR-18
 Earlier sketches in CA 5-6R, CANR-3
 See also SATA 1, 35
 See also DLB 52
 See also CLR 2
Zolotow, Maurice 1913- CANR-1
 Earlier sketch in CA 3R
Zolynas, Al(girdas Richard) 1945- 105
Zonia, Dhimitri 1921- SATA-20
Zonik, Eleanor Dorothy 1918- 15-16R
Zonis, Marvin 1936- 37-40R
Zonker, Patricia 85-88
Zook, David H(artzler), Jr. 1930-? 2R
 Obituary 103
Zook, Deborah
 See Green, Deborah
Zook, Paul D(avid) 1912- 7-8R
Zopf, Paul E(dward), Jr. 1931- 37-40R
Zophy, Jonathan Walter 1945- 104
Zorach, William 1887-1966 ....CAP-1
 Earlier sketch in CA 15-16
Zorn, Robert L. 1938- 115
Zornes, Jeanne Doering 1947- 113
Zornow, William Frank 1920- 41-44R
Zoshchenko, Mikhail (Mikhailovich)
 1895-1958 Brief entry 115
 See also TCLC 15
Zosky, Brenda 1942- 89-92

Zotos, Stephanos 23-24R
Zsoldos, Laszlo 1925- 37-40R
Zubek, John P(eter) 1925- 37-40R
Zubin, Joseph 1900- 17-18R
Zubly, John Joachim 1724-1781 ....DLB-31
Zu-Bolton, Ahmos II 1935- DLB-41
Zubrow, Ezra B. W. 1945- CANR-10
 Earlier sketch in CA 65-68
Zubrowski, Bernard 1939- 104
 See also SATA 35
Zubrzycki, Jerzy (George) 1920- CANR-10
 Earlier sketch in CA 21-22R
Zuck, Lowell H(ubert) 1926- 65-68
Zucker, Adolf Eduard 1890-1971 Obituary ..116
Zucker, David Hard 1938- 37-40R
Zucker, Dolores Mae Bolton CANR-7
 Earlier sketch in CA 17-18R
Zucker, Jack 1935- 29-32R
Zucker, Martin 1937- 112
Zucker, Moses 1902-1987 Obituary 123
Zucker, Norman L(ivingston) 1933- 19-20R
Zucker, Paul 1888-1971 ....CAP-2
 Obituary 29-32R
 Earlier sketch in CA 23-24
Zuckerman, Alan S(aul) 1945- CANR-22
 Earlier sketch in CA 105
Zuckerman, Arthur J(acob) 1907- 41-44R
Zuckerman, Edward (Ben) 1948- 123
Zuckerman, Michael 1939- 37-40R
Zuckerman, Seth (Abram) 1961- 124
Zuckerman, Solly 1904- 65-68
Zuckerman, Yitzhak 1917-1981 Obituary 108
Zuckermann, George 1916- 53-56
Zuckmayer, Carl 1896-1977 69-72
 See also DLB 56
 See also CLC 18
Zuelke, Ruth E. 1924- 15-16R
Zuelzer, Wolf(gang) W(illiam) 1909-1987 ...110
 Obituary 122
Zuesse, Evan M. 1940- 105
Zug, Margaret Philbrook 1945(?)-1976 ...69-72
Zugsmith, Leane 1903-1969 Obituary 115
Zukerman, Eugenia 1944- 110
Zukofsky, Louis 1904-1978 ....9-10R
 Obituary 77-80
 See also DLB 5
 See also CLC 1, 2, 4, 7, 11, 18
Zulauf, Sander W(illiam) 1946- 101
Zulawski, Marek 1908-1985 Obituary 116
Zulli, Floyd (Jr.) 1922-1980 ....37-40R
 Obituary 108
Zumbo, Jim 1940- 109
Zumwalt, Elmo Russell III 1946(?)-1988
 Obituary 126
Zumwalt, Elmo Russell, Jr. 1920- 85-88
 Earlier sketch in CA 65-68
Zumwalt, Eva 1936- CANR-9
Zundel, Veronica (Elsa) 1953- 120
Zunder, William (Limbery) 1938- 117
Zunkel, Charles Edward 1905- 57-60
Zunkel, Cleda 1903- 57-60
Zunser, Jesse 1898-1985 Obituary 118
Zunz, Olivier J. 1946- 110
Zupa, G. Anthony
 See Zeck, Gerald Anthony

Zupko, Ronald Edward 1938- CANR-13
 Earlier sketch in CA 37-40R
Zupnick, I(rving) L(awrence) 1920- 45-48
Zurcher, Arnold John 1903(?)-1974
49-52
Zurcher, Louis A(nthony) 1936- CANR-15
 Earlier sketch in CA 41-44R
Zurhorst, Charles (Stewart, Jr.) 1913- ..CANR-1
 Earlier sketch in CA 45-48
Zuriff, G(erald) E(ugene) 1943- 123
zur Muehlen, Hermynia 1883-1951 .....DLB-56
zur Muhlen, Hermynia
 See zur Muehlen, Hermynia
 See also DLB 56
Zuromskis, Diane
 See Stanley, Diane
Zuromskis, Diane Stanley
 See Stanley, Diane
Zusne, Leonard 1924- 81-84
Zuwaylif, Fadil H. 1932- CANR-25
 Earlier sketch in CA 45-48
Zuwiyya, Jalal (Zakariya) 1932- 77-80
Zwaanstra, Henry 1936- Brief entry 105
Zwar, Desmond L(aurence) G(audin)
 1931- 107
Zwarensteyn, Hendrik 1913-1976 ....7-8R
 Obituary 103
Zwart, Pieter (Hendrik) 1938- 53-56
Zweifel, Frances W. 1931- CANR-12
 Earlier sketch in CA 73-76
 See also SATA 14
Zweig, Arnold 1887-1968 Obituary 115
 See also DLB 66
Zweig, Ferdynand 1896-1988 Obituary 125
Zweig, Friderike M(aria Burger Winternitz)
 1882-1971 Obituary 114
Zweig, Paul 1935-1984 85-88
 Obituary 113
 See also CLC 34, 42
Zweig, Ronald W. 1949- 124
Zweig, Stefan 1881-1942 Brief entry 112
 See also TCLC 17
Zwerdling, Alex 1932- 57-60
Zwerenz, Gerhard 1925- 33-36R
Zwerling, L. Steven 1938- 61-64
Zwibak, Jacques 1902- 77-80
Zwick, Peter Ronald 1942- 116
Zwicky, Fritz 1898-1974 Obituary 49-52
Zwiebach, Burton 1933- 57-60
Zwinger, Ann 1925- CANR-13
 Earlier sketch in CA 33-36R
 See also SATA 46
Zwirn, Jerrold 1943- 109
Zworykin, Vladimir Kosma 1889-1982
 Obituary 107
Zyla, Wolodymyr T(aras) 1919- CANR-2
 Earlier sketch in CA 45-48
Zylberberg, Michael 1907-1971 ....CAP-2
 Earlier sketch in CA 29-32
Zylbercweig, Zalman 1894-1972
 Obituary 37-40R
Zyskind, Harold 1917- 57-60
Zytaruk, George John 1927- 110
Zytowski, Donald G(lenn) 1929- 29-32R

Contemporary Authors and *Contemporary Authors New Revision Series* Encompass Authors in Every Field—From Established Writers to Individuals Best Known for Their Non-literary Activities:

Novelists

(continued from front endsheets)

Hermann Hesse
Bohumil Hrabel
Aldous Leonard Huxley
LeRoi Jones
Yasunari Kawabata
Yashar Kemal
Thomas Keneally
Jack Kerouac
Jerzy Kosinski
Milan Kundera
Oliver La Farge
Margaret Wemyss
  Laurence
Doris Lessing
Jack London
Alison Lurie
Norman Mailer
Bernard Malamud
Andre Malraux
Vladimir Maximov
Mary McCarthy
Carson McCullers
N. Scott Momaday
Brian Moore
Iris Murdoch
Vladimir Nabokov
Shiva Naipaul
V. S. Naipaul
Anais Nin
Joyce Carol Oates
Flannery O'Connor
Juan Carlos Onetti
Walker Percy
Katherine Anne Porter
Chaim Potok
Marcel Proust
Barbara Pym
Thomas Pynchon
Ayn Rand
Erich Maria Remarque
Jean Rhys
Alain Robbe-Grillet
Philip Roth
Gabrielle Roy
Juan Rulfo
Salman Rushdie
Ernesto Sabato
V. Sackville-West
J. D. Salinger

Irwin Shaw
Naoya Shiga
Mikhail Sholokhov
Claude Simon
Upton Sinclair
Isaac Bashevis Singer
Josef Skvorecky
Aleksandr I.
  Solzhenitsyn
Muriel Spark
John Steinbeck
William Styron
Jean Toomer
Anne Tyler
John Updike
Mario Vargas Llosa
Gore Vidal
Kurt Vonnegut, Jr.
Alice Walker
Evelyn Waugh
Fay Weldon
Eudora Welty
Elie Wiesel
P. G. Wodehouse
Herman Wouk
Richard Wright
Marguerite Yourcenar
. . . and more

Philosophers

Mortimer J. Adler
Theodor W. Adorno
William Barrett
Ernst Bloch
C. D. Broad
Albert Camus
Etienne Henry Gilson
Martin Heidegger
Sidney Hook
Claude Levi-Strauss
Gyorgy Lucas
Gabriel Honore Marcel
Karl R. Popper
Jean-Paul Sartre
. . . and more

Photographers

Berenice Abbott
Ansel Adams

Antony Armstrong-
  Jones
Eve Arnold
David Bailey
Margaret Bourke-White
Howard Dearstyn
Alfred Eisenstaedt
Ron Galella
Peter Jenkins
David Hume Kennerly
Francesco Scavullo
. . . and more

Physicians

Virginia Apgar
Christiaan Barnard
Beatrice Bishop Berle
T. Berry Brazelton
Mary S. Calderone
Michael E. DeBakey
Nawal El Saadawi
Henry Jay Heimlich
Milton Helpern
John H. Knowles
Frederick Leboyer
Robert B. Livingston
Elizabeth Miller
Jonathan Miller
William A. Nolen
Ray H. Rosenman
Richard Selzer
Andrew Weil
. . . and more

Playwrights

Marcel Achard
Edward Albee
Jean Anouilh
Samuel Beckett
Brendan Behan
Andre Brink
Abe Burrows
Paddy Chayefsky
Marc Connelly
Noel Coward
Friedrich Duerrenmatt
Christopher Durang

Lonne Elder III
Max Frisch
Athol Fugard
Charles Fuller
Tsegaye Gabre-Medhin
Frank D. Gilroy
John Guare
Wilson John Haire
Lorraine Hansberry
Moss Hart
Vaclav Havel
Lillian Hellman
Beth Henley
William Motler Inge
Eugene Ionesco
George S. Kaufman
Raymond Evenor
  Lawler
David Mamet
Mark Medoff
Arthur Miller
Jason Miller
Thomas Murphy
Sean O'Casey
Clifford Odets
Harold Pinter
David Rabe
Elmer Rice
Ntozake Shange
Sam Shepard
Neil Simon
Tom Stoppard
John Whiting
Oscar Wilde
Tennessee Williams
. . . and more

Poets

Ai
Anna Akhmatova
Rafael Alberti
Yehuda Amichai
Jean Arp
John Ashbery
W. H. Auden
John Berryman
Elizabeth Bishop
Paul Blackburn
Robert Bly
Gwendolyn Brooks
Paul Celan

Rene Char
John Ciardi
Cid Corman
e.e. cummings
James Dickey
Diane di Prima
Hilda Doolittle
Alan Dugan
Henry L. Dumas
Robert Duncan
Guenter Eich
T. S. Eliot
Odysseus Elytis
Hans Magnus
  Enzensberger
Lawrence Ferlinghetti
Carolyn Forche
Robert Frost
Allen Ginsberg
Nikki Giovanni
Louise Gluck
Robert Graves
Seamus Heaney
Ralph Hodgson
David Holbrook
Langston Hughes
Ted Hughes
Gyula Illyes
Robinson Jeffers
Galway Kinnell
Thomas Kinsella
Carolyn Kizer
Maxine Kumin
Stanley Kunitz
Philip Lamantia
Philip Larkin
Denise Levertov
Philip Levine
Audre Lorde
Robert Lowell
Hugh MacDiarmid
Archibald MacLeish
Louis MacNeice
Rod McKuen
Samuel Menashe
W. S. Merwin
Czeslaw Milosz
Marco Antonio Montes
  De Oca
Marianne Moore
Pablo Neruda
Christopher Okigbo
Nicanor Parra

Poets
(continued)

Octavio Paz
Lucio Piccolo
Sylvia Plath
Ezra Pound
Pierre Reverdy
Kenneth Rexroth
Adrienne Rich
Theodore Roethke
Muriel Rukeyser
Carl Sandburg
Delmore Schwartz
Giorgos Stylianou
  Seferiades
Anne Sexton
Dame Edith Sitwell
Sydney Goodsir Smith
Gary Snyder
Stephen Spender
Rabindranath Tagore
Dylan Thomas
Mona Van Duyn
Diane Wakoski
Derek Walcott
Robert Penn Warren
Richard Wilbur
William Carlos Williams
Yevgeny Yevtushenko
  . . . and more

Political and Social Activists

Jane Alpert
Daniel Berrigan
Philip Berrigan
Romulo Betancourt
Stokely Carmichael
Eldridge Cleaver
William Sloan Coffin
Angela Davis
Vine Deloria, Jr.
Bernadette Devlin
W. E. B. DuBois
Dick Gregory
Thomas E. Hayden
Julius W. Hobson
Abbie Hoffman
Martin Luther King, Jr.
Adam Clayton Powell,
  Jr.
Charles Alan Reich
Jerry Rubin
Bobby Seale
Roy Wilkins
  . . . and more

Politicians and World Leaders

David Ben-Gurion
Willy Brandt
Zbigniew K. Brzezinski
Jimmy Carter
Winston Churchill
Anthony Eden
Millicent Hammond
  Fenwick
Gerald R. Ford
Dag Hammarskjoeld
Jack Kemp
Edward Moore
  Kennedy
Ruhollah Khomeini
Nikita Sergeyevich
  Khrushchev
Henry A. Kissinger
Edward I. Koch
Mao Tse-tung
George S. McGovern
Golda Meir
Jawaharlal Nehru
Richard M. Nixon
Shimon Peres
Ronald Reagan
Anwar Sadat
Margaret Chase Smith
Strom Thurmond
Kurt Waldheim
Harold Wilson
  . . . and more

Print Journalists

Jack Anderson
Russell Baker
Carl Bernstein
Jimmy Breslin
William F. Buckley, Jr.
Herb Caen
Maxine Cheshire
Oriana Fallaci
Sheilah Graham
Bob Greene
Seymour M. Hersh
Haynes Bonner Johnson
Anthony Lewis
A. J. Liebling
Walter Lippmann
Sylvia F. Porter
Mike Royko
William Safire
Susan Sheehan
Hedrick Smith
George Will

Gary Wills
Bob Woodward
  . . . and more

Psychologists

Ernest Becker
Bruno Bettelheim
Joyce Brothers
Erik H. Erikson
Anna Freud
Erich Fromm
Howard E. Gruber
Joan Halifax
Thomas A. Harris
Arthur Janov
Carl Jung
Irene Chamie Kassorla
R. D. Laing
Timothy Leary
John E. Mack
Abraham H. Maslow
Rollo May
Stanley Milgram
Fritz Perls
Jean Piaget
Theodore Isaac Rubin
Lee Salk
Anne Seifert
June Singer
B. F. Skinner
  . . . and more

Publishers

Sylvia Beach
William Maxwell
  Aitken Beaverbrook
Barry Bingham, Jr.
Hedley Donovan
Robert Giroux
Katharine Graham
Richard L. Grossman
William Jovanovich
Howard Kaminsky
Stefan Kanfer
Alfred A. Knopf
James Laughlin
Joseph W. Lippincott
William Loeb
Henry R. Luce
Scott Meredith
Henry Regnery
Barney Rosset
Maisie Ward
Helen Wolff
  . . . and more

Radio Personalities

Bob Edwards
Garrison Keillor
Larry King
Gary Owens
Susan Stamberg
Studs Terkel
Lowell Thomas
  . . . and more

Religious Figures

William Barclay
Harvey Cox
Henry Dumery
Mircea Eliade
Jerry Falwell
Billy Graham
Andrew M. Greeley
Pope John Paul I
Hans Kueng
Harold S. Kushner
Bernard J. F. Lonergan
Jacques Maritain
Malcolm Muggeridge
William J. Murray III
Reinhold Niebuhr
Norman Vincent Peale
Karl Rahner
Oral Roberts
Robert Schuller
Fulton J. Sheen
Lawrence Joseph
  Shehan
Ruth Carter Stapleton
Paul Tillich
  . . . and more

Romance and Gothic Writers

Iris Bancroft
Barbara Cartland
Barbara P. Conklin
Janet Dailey
Daphne du Maurier
Anne Eliot
Anne Hampson
Constance Heaven
Georgette Heyer
Victoria Holt
Fannie Hurst
Johanna Lindsey
Norah Lofts

Laurie McBain
Natasha Peters
Paula Schwartz
Kathleen Winsor
Kathleen E. Woodiwiss
  . . . and more

Scholars

Hannah Arendt
Jacob Bronowski
Norman O. Brown
Michel Foucault
Ivan Illich
R. W. B. Lewis
Lewis Mumford
Robert A. Nisbet
Susan Sontag
  . . . and more

Science Fiction Writers

Poul Anderson
Isaac Asimov
Alfred Bester
James Blish
Ben Bova
Ray Bradbury
C. J. Cherryh
Arthur C. Clarke
Philip K. Dick
Gordon R. Dickson
Harlan Ellison
Joe Haldeman
Robert A. Heinlein
Frank Herbert
Ursula K. Le Guin
Fritz Leiber
Stanislaw Lem
Frank Belknap Long
Anne McCaffrey
Vonda N. McIntyre
Patricia A. McKillip
Michael Moorcock
C. L. Moore
Larry Niven
Andre Norton
Frederik Pohl
Jerry Pournelle
Joanna Russ
Robert Silverberg
Theodore Hamilton
  Sturgeon